For criminal and litigation resources
on, your one-stop source is

BALDWIN'S OHIO PRACTICE, CRIMINAL LAW, 2D

by Lewis R. Katz, Paul C. Giannelli, Beverly J. Blair and Judith P. Lipton

The second edition features expanded sentencing coverage, search and seizure topics related to electronic communication, and discussion of the U.S. Supreme Court's 2003 decision on "three-strike" statutes in *Ewing v. California*. The set now includes a softbound volume, *Statutory Charges*, for preparing criminal charges and indictments.

OHIO ARREST, SEARCH AND SEIZURE

by Lewis R. Katz

Professor Katz is a national expert on the Fourth Amendment. In clear, direct language he analyzes how the courts interpret the balance of an individual's rights with legitimate law enforcement procedures.

OHIO JUVENILE LAW

by Paul C. Giannelli and Patricia McCloud Yeomans

Both a treatise and a portable reference, this popular handbook covers all major aspects of juvenile law—abuse, neglect, dependency, unruliness and traffic offenses—and guides you through all steps in the court process.

OHIO DRIVING UNDER THE INFLUENCE LAW

by Judge Mark P. Painter

An Ohio judge answers the most frequently asked questions on D.U.I. with practical guidance on the simplest to the most complex issues. Expanded coverage and analysis of recent legislation overhauling many of Ohio's "drunk driving" statutes includes the more extensive look-back period for repeat offenders and the numbering of OVI offenses.

Get all your Ohio criminal and litigation resources by calling this number!

1-800-344-5009

Or complete and mail the attached card.

Yes, I need ___ additional copy(ies) of the *Baldwin's Ohio Practice, Ohio Criminal Justice, 2005 Edition.*

Please call me immediately.

I am also interested in the following:

___ *Baldwin's Ohio Practice, Criminal Law*
___ *Ohio Arrest, Search and Seizure*
___ *Ohio Driving Under the Influence Law*
___ *Ohio Juvenile Law*
___ *Baldwin's Ohio Practice, Evidence*
___ *Ohio Rules of Evidence Handbook*
___ *Ohio Domestic Violence Law*
___ *Ohio Felony Sentencing Law*
___ *Baldwin's Ohio Practice, Statutory Charges*

For more information about West products and services, go to:
west.thomson.com

Name (please print) ______________________

Business Phone (________) ______________________

Firm (please print) ______________________

Address ______________________

____

City ______________ State _____ Zip _______

West Account # ______________________

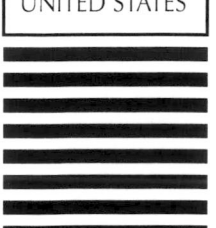

Baldwin's

OHIO PRACTICE

Katz & Giannelli
Ohio Criminal Justice

2005

Ohio Revised Code complete to February 2, 2005
Ohio Administrative Code complete to January 31, 2005

Case Western Reserve University
School of Law

Edited by
Lewis R. Katz & Paul C. Giannelli

Mat #40314821

Reprinted from
BALDWIN'S™ OHIO REVISED CODE ANNOTATED and
BALDWIN'S™ OHIO ADMINISTRATIVE CODE, Approved Edition

Ohio Criminal Justice ISBN 0-8322-1112-5

Preface

The 2005 Edition of *Ohio Criminal Justice* marks the eighteenth year of publication under the cooperative agreement between the Case Western Reserve University School of Law and West, a Thomson business (formerly Banks–Baldwin Law Publishing Company). Designed specifically for law enforcement officers, prosecutors, defense attorneys, judges, and students, it meets the need for an easy-to-use, current, and comprehensive guide to Ohio criminal law.

This 2005 Edition will bring you up-to-date on all Ohio statutes, rules, and other materials on criminal law, including:

- Elements of Crimes with Table of Definitions
- The U.S. Constitution and pertinent provisions of the Ohio Constitution
- Ohio Revised Code Title 29, "Crimes—Procedure," in its entirety
- Selected statutes from related Revised Code titles, including provisions on townships, local and common pleas courts, habeas corpus, domestic violence, schools, motor vehicles, and financial responsibility
- Rules of Criminal Procedure
- Rules of Appellate Procedure
- Rules of Juvenile Procedure
- Ohio Rules of Evidence
- Ohio Traffic Rules
- Victims of Crime Compensation
- Rules of Superintendence for the Courts of Ohio
- Ohio Administrative Rules
- Sentences and Fines—Tables and Checklists, and
- Procedure Outline in Chronological Order.

We, the CWRU Law School, and West, a Thomson business are committed to maintaining *Ohio Criminal Justice* as the most authoritative, useful, and timely publication of its kind. Your comments and suggestions for future improvements will help us to achieve our goal.

We would like to acknowledge the contribution of Daniel T. Clancy, who expertly edited this text for many years.

Lewis R. Katz
Paul C. Giannelli

Cleveland, Ohio
March 2005

Foreword

The 2005 edition of *Ohio Criminal Justice* is a compilation of the laws and rules needed for researching and practicing Ohio criminal law, with editorial enhancements and research aids. Edited by Lewis R. Katz and Paul C. Giannelli of the Case Western Reserve University School of Law, it offers attorneys, judges, and law enforcement officials an authoritative and up-to-date reference to the sources of law they refer to most often, in a compact and convenient format.

THE 1996 EDITION AND SUPPLEMENT SHOULD STILL BE RETAINED FOR PRE–SB 2 LAW AND RESEARCH AID PAGES.

This 2005 Edition contains all relevant laws passed by the Ohio General Assembly through February 2, 2005, and includes the following areas of change and expanded coverage:

- New add–on penalty for drunk driving offenses (RC 2941.1413 to RC 2941.1416)

- Misrepresentation and nondisclosure by childcare providers (RC 2919.223 to RC 2919.227)

- Abortion offense—provision or use of RU-486 (RC 2919.123)

The Elements of Crimes with Table of Definitions, Sentences and Fines—Tables and Checklists, and the Procedure Outline in Chronological Order have been updated to reflect these and all other relevant amendments.

Ohio Criminal Justice continues to be the most useful publication of its kind in Ohio. It contains the full text of all criminal and most motor vehicle statutes; laws setting forth the powers, duties, and regulations of public agencies, political subdivisions, public officeholders, and law enforcement authorities; and miscellaneous provisions governing:

- Watercraft and waterways (RC Chapters 1547 and 1548);
- Township and joint township police (RC Chapter 504, and RC 505.48 to 505.55);
- Liquor control (RC Chapters 4301, 4303, and 4399);
- Mayor's courts, county courts, and juvenile courts (RC Chapters 1905, 1907, and 2151, respectively);
- Special proceedings, including habeas corpus (RC Chapter 2725);
- Pharmacists and dangerous drugs (RC Chapter 4729);
- Court of claims and victims of crimes (RC Chapter 2743)
- Public defenders, state and county (RC Chapter 120);
- Jails and reformatories (RC Chapters 341 and 753); and
- Fireworks (RC Chapter 3743).

FOREWORD

We are committed to continually improving *Ohio Criminal Justice*. Recompiled and republished annually, it remains the most comprehensive and timely publication of its kind on the market. We would greatly appreciate your comments for future editions.

We acknowledge with appreciation the contributions of our editorial and production staffs—especially Lori Lalak Lee, Esq., Mark Knaus, Suzanne Meleney, and Diona Shaw—in preparing the 2005 Edition for publication.

The Publisher
6111 Oak Tree Boulevard
P.O. Box 318063
Cleveland, OH 44131

March 2005

About the Editors

Lewis R. Katz is the John C. Hutchins Professor of Law and Director of Foreign Graduate Legal Studies at Case Western Reserve University School of Law. He attended Queens College (A.B., 1959), the University of Hawaii, and Indiana University (J.D., 1963), where he was a Note Editor of the *Indiana Law Journal*.

His writing career, like his academic career, spans more than three decades. His credits include Baldwin's Ohio Practice, *Criminal Law* (West, a Thomson business, 2d ed. 2003), a criminal law treatise; *Know Your Rights* (West Group, 1993), a practical guide for ordinary citizens to constitutional rights and other concerns; *Ohio Arrest, Search and Seizure* (West Group, 2004), a thorough and practical guide to the law of search and seizure, interrogation and confession, and pretrial identification; *Ohio Felony Sentencing Law* (West Group, 2004), a complete guide to Ohio's sentencing guidelines; an undergraduate text book; law review articles; and treatises for practicing lawyers in Ohio and New York. Several of his publications have been cited in opinions of the United States Supreme Court and in hundreds of Ohio cases. He wrote a series of features published in the *Washington Post* and op-ed pieces in the *Christian Science Monitor, The Cleveland Plain Dealer*, and other newspapers.

Professor Katz was co-author, along with Judge Burt W. Griffin, of the original draft of 1995 Senate Bill 2, the felony sentencing reform act.

Paul C. Giannelli is the Albert J. Weatherhead III and Richard W. Weatherhead Professor of Law at Case Western Reserve University. He received his J.D. in 1970 from the University of Virginia, where he served as Articles Editor of the *Virginia Law Review*. His other degrees include an LL.M. from the University of Virginia and an M.S. in Forensic Science from George Washington University.

Professor Giannelli has written extensively in the field of evidence and criminal procedure, especially on the topic of scientific evidence. He has published articles in the Columbia, Virginia, Vanderbilt, Ohio State, Wisconsin, Hastings, Cardozo, Capital, Cleveland State, and Case Western Reserve law reviews, as well as in the *Journal of Criminal Law & Criminology* (Northwestern University), *Criminal Law Bulletin*, and the *American Criminal Law Review* (Georgetown University). He has also published in interdisciplinary journals, such as the *International Journal of Clinical & Experimental Hypnosis*, the *New Biologist, Profiles in DNA*, and the *Journal of Forensic Science*.

He has written or co-authored six books: *Scientific Evidence* (Lexis Co. 3d ed., 1999); *Courtroom Criminal Evidence* (Lexis Co. 3d ed., 1998); *Ohio Juvenile Law* (West Group, 2001); Baldwin's Ohio Practice, *Evidence* (West, a Thomson business, 2d ed. 2001); Baldwin's Ohio Practice, *Rules of Evidence Handbook* (West Group, 2001); and Baldwin's Ohio Practice, *Criminal Law* (West, a Thomson business, 2d ed. 2003), a criminal law treatise.

Professor Giannelli's works have been cited hundreds of times in court opinions and the legal literature, including decisions by the U.S. Supreme Court. The *New York Times* referred to him as an "expert on scientific evidence." He has authored an op-ed piece for the *Times: "When the Evidence Is a Matter of Life and Death," New York Times, Week in Review Op–Ed*, Aug. 21, 1994, p. E15.

Professor Giannelli has also served as: Special Counsel, Joint Select Evidence Committee, Ohio General Assembly (1978–79); Member, Ohio Supreme Court Rules Advisory Committee (1985–88); and Counsel for Rules of Evidence, Ohio Supreme Court Rules Advisory Committee (1990–2000).

About Case Western Reserve University School of Law

The School of Law of Case Western Reserve University was founded in 1892 with a faculty of three and an enrollment of twenty-four.

One of the first schools approved by the American Bar Association and a charter member of the Association of American Law Schools, Case Western Reserve today enrolls more than 700 students annually and has a faculty of 40 full-time professors.

Alumni numbering more than 7,700 are engaged throughout the United States and abroad in all aspects of law practice, including the judiciary, education, commerce and industry, government, and private firms.

Affirming the dedication to excellence in legal education, the School is housed today in Gund Hall, a facility which is among the country's finest and most modern law buildings. Opened in 1971, this architectural award-winning building provides a comfortable and dignified environment for classes, study, and research. An addition to the building and major renovations to the library and legal clinic were completed in 1994.

As one of seven graduate and professional schools on the University Circle campus of Case Western Reserve University, the School of Law enjoys a particularly advantageous association with a fine, private, independent center of learning whose heritage dates to 1826.

Related Products

STATUTES, CONSTITUTIONS, AND COURT RULES

- Baldwin's Ohio Revised Code Annotated
- Baldwin's Ohio Legislative Service Annotated
- Ohio Constitution Handbook
- Ohio Rules of Court, State and Federal
- United States Code Annotated

CASE LAW, REPORTERS, DIGESTS, ATTORNEY GENERAL OPINIONS

- Ohio Official Reports
- Ohio Digest
- Ohio Attorney General Opinions
- SERB Official Reporter
- Federal Reporter
- Federal Supplement
- West's Supreme Court Reporter

ADMINISTRATIVE LAW

- Baldwin's Ohio Administrative Code
- Ohio Administrative Law Handbook and Agency Directory
- Ohio Monthly Record
- Administrative Law and Practice 2d
- Administrative Law: Practice and Procedure

GENERAL LEGAL REFERENCES

- Ohio Jurisprudence 3d
- American Jurisprudence 2d
- American Law Reports
- Corpus Juris Secundum

OHIO DATABASES ON WESTLAW

- Cases, General & Topical

RELATED PRODUCTS

- Statutes & Court Rules
- Legislative Service, Bills & Bill Tracking
- Administrative & Executive Materials
- Public Information, Records & Filings
- Baldwin's Ohio Practice Series
- Ohio Jurisprudence 3d
- Ohio Forms, Legal & Business
- Law Reviews, Bar Journals & Legal Periodicals
- Newspapers & Periodicals
- Miscellany

CD–ROM

- Baldwin's Ohio Revised Code Annotated with Ohio Administrative Code and SERB Official Reporter
- Ohio Reports
- Ohio Unreported Appellate Decisions
- Baldwin's Ohio Practice Library
- Ohio Digest
- Ohio Jurisprudence 3d
- United States Code Annotated
- West's Sixth Circuit Reporter
- West's Federal District Court Reporter—Sixth Circuit
- West's Supreme Court Reporter
- Federal Reporter, 1st, 2d, and 3d Series
- Federal Supplement
- Federal Rules Decisions
- Wright & Miller, Federal Practice and Procedure
- Topical CD–ROM Libraries
- Ohio Jurisprudence Pleading and Practice Forms
- Ohio Criminal Defense Motions

CIVIL PRACTICE AND PROCEDURE

- Baldwin's Ohio Practice, Civil Practice   Klein, Darling, and Terez
- Baldwin's Ohio Practice, Civil Practice Laws & Rules Annotated
- Ohio Personal Injury Practice
- Trial Handbook for Ohio Lawyers Markus

CRIMINAL LAW AND PRACTICE

RELATED PRODUCTS

- Baldwin's Ohio Practice, Criminal Law 2d Katz, Giannelli, Blair, and Lipton
- Baldwin's Ohio Practice, Ohio Statutory Charges Blair
- Ohio Arrest, Search and Seizure
- Baldwin's Ohio Practice, Ohio Criminal Justice Katz and Giannelli (Eds.) (published in cooperation with the Case Western Reserve University School of Law)
- Ohio Domestic Violence Law
- Ohio Driving Under the Influence Law
- Ohio Felony Sentencing Law
- Trial Handbook for Ohio Lawyers Markus

TRIAL AND APPELLATE PRACTICE

- Baldwin's Ohio Practice, Evidence 2d Giannelli and Snyder
- Baldwin's Ohio Practice, Rules of Evidence Handbook Giannelli and Snyder
- Ohio Appellate Practice
- Trial Handbook for Ohio Lawyers Markus

DOMESTIC RELATIONS AND FAMILY LAW

- Baldwin's Ohio Practice, Domestic Relations Law 4th Sowald and Morganstern
- Baldwin's Ohio Practice, Domestic Relations Laws and Rules Annotated
- Ohio Domestic Violence Law
- Domestic Relations Journal of Ohio

PROBATE AND JUVENILE LAW

- Baldwin's Ohio Practice, Merrick–Rippner Probate Law 6th Carlin
- Ohio Probate Code Annotated
- Probate Law Journal of Ohio
- Ohio Juvenile Law

REAL ESTATE

- Ohio Landlord Tenant Law
- Baldwin's Ohio Practice, Ohio Real Estate Law 3d

BUSINESS AND LEGAL

- Baldwin's Ohio Practice, Business Organizations Blackford

RELATED PRODUCTS

- Baldwin's Ohio Practice, Business Organizations Laws & Rules Ekonomon and Heinle (Eds.)
- Ohio Consumer Law

LEGAL FORMS

- Ohio Forms Legal and Business
- Ohio Forms and Transactions
- Ohio Jurisprudence Pleading and Practice Forms
- West's Legal Forms 2d

TAX LAW

- Baldwin's Ohio Tax Law and Rules

LABOR LAW

- Ohio Civil Service & Collective Bargaining Laws & Rules Annotated
- Ohio Employment Practices Law
- Ohio Workers' Compensation Law Practice Guide
- Workers' Compensation Journal of Ohio

GOVERNMENT

- Baldwin's Ohio Township Law
- Gotherman and Babbit, Ohio Municipal Law
- Ohio Municipal Service
- Ohio Election Laws Annotated
- Ohio Planning and Zoning Law

SCHOOL LAW

- Baldwin's Ohio School Law
- Ohio School Law Handbook
- Baldwin's Ohio School Law Journal
- United States School Laws and Rules

BUILDING CONSTRUCTION AND CODE ENFORCEMENT

- Ohio Building Code and Related Codes
- Know Your Code: A Guide to the OBC

RELATED PRODUCTS

- Code News

If you would like to inquire about these West publications or place an order, please call 1–800–344–5009.

West

610 Opperman Drive

Eagan, MN 55123

Visit West on the Internet:
http://west.thomson.com

Table of Contents

TABLE OF CONTENTS

TABLE OF CONTENTS

ELEMENTS OF CRIMES
with
TABLE OF DEFINITIONS

Introduction

This unit contains the Elements of Crimes, with a Table of Definitions. In the Elements of Crimes are set forth the statutory elements, penalties, and where applicable, defenses, proofs, and exceptions, for each crime in Revised Code Title 29 and major crimes from other titles of the Revised Code. The Table of Definitions contains a list of words and phrases used in the Elements and, for each, a reference to the Revised Code sections where the full text of the definition is set forth.

In the Elements of Crimes, crimes are arranged in alphabetical order; however, certain related crimes are grouped together under a descriptive main heading, and cross references are inserted to guide users to the correct heading. For example, "Medicaid Fraud" contains a cross reference to "Theft-related Offenses—Medicaid Fraud" where it is found in alphabetical order under "Theft-related Offenses." See the Tables of Contents (in both alphabetical and Revised Code order) for a complete list of main headings and statutes, with page references.

Several subheadings are used to organize the information. Under the subheading, "Elements of the Crime," each and every element which must be present to establish the crime is set forth in summary form, in the same order as they are found in the statute. Where different statutory elements may establish the same crime, each group of elements is categorized into a "division," paralleling the organization of the statute. For example, RC 2921.44, Dereliction of Duty, is comprised of five divisions. A violation of Division (A) is established by a showing that a law enforcement officer negligently failed to serve a lawful warrant without delay or failed to prevent or halt commission of an offense or to apprehend the offender when it was in his power to do so. A violation of Division (B) is established by a showing that a law enforcement officer, ministerial, or judicial officer negligently failed to perform the officer's lawful duty in a criminal case or proceeding. Divisions (C), (D), and (E) deal with duties of an officer in charge of a detention facility, reckless spending by a public official, and reckless conduct by a public official in the performance of the official's duties.

The category—whether felony or misdemeanor—and degree of the offense are set forth under the "Penalty" subheading. For example, all of the activities covered in the five divisions of RC 2921.44, Dereliction of Duty, are second degree misdemeanors, covered by RC 2929.21 to RC 2929.28 and 2929.31. Note that sentences and fines for all categories and degrees of offenses are summarized in a separate SENTENCES AND FINES unit.

The subheadings "Defense," "Proof," and "Exceptions," are used only with crimes for which the statute provides defenses, special requirements of proof, or exceptions. For example, RC 2923.01, Conspiracy, spells out requirements for proof (overt act; belief of presence of another) and lays out affirmative defenses.

To locate the definition of a key word or phrase, look it up in the Table of Definitions, then find and read the statute cited. For example, "Drug paraphernalia" is defined in 2925.14(A).

Table of Contents in Alphabetical Order

Table of Contents In Revised Code Order

Elements of Crimes

Abduction—2905.02

See also Juveniles—Child Stealing; Kidnapping; Unlawful Restraint

ELEMENTS OF THE CRIME

(1) Without privilege

(2) Knowingly

(3)(a) By force or threat, remove another from the place where the other person is found, or

(b) By force or threat, restrain the liberty of another person, under circumstances which create a risk of physical harm to the victim, or place the other person in fear, or

(c) Hold another in a condition of involuntary servitude.

PENALTY

Felony, 3rd degree (2929.11 to 2929.18, 2929.31)

Abortion—Abortion Manslaughter—2919.13

ELEMENTS OF THE CRIME

Division (A):

(1) Purposely

(2) Take the life of a child

(3) Born by attempted abortion

(4) Who is alive when removed from the uterus of the pregnant woman

Division (B):

(1) When performing an abortion

(2) Fail to take the measures required by the exercise of medical judgment in light of the attending circumstances to preserve the life of a child

(3) Who is alive when removed from the uterus of the pregnant woman

PENALTY

Felony, 1st degree (2929.11, 2929.31)

Abortion—Abortion Trafficking—2919.14

See also Offenses Against Human Corpse

ELEMENTS OF THE CRIME

(1)(a) Experiment upon, or

(b) Sell

(2) The product of human conception

(3) Which is aborted

PENALTY

Misdemeanor, 1st degree (2929.21 to 2929.28, 2929.31)

EXCEPTION

Experiment does not include autopsies pursuant to 313.13 and 2108.50.

Abortion—Abortion Without Informed Consent—2919.12

ELEMENTS OF THE CRIME

Division (A):

(1) Perform or induce

(2) Abortion

(3) Without informed consent of the pregnant woman

Division (B):

(1) Knowingly

(2) Perform or induce

(3) Abortion

(4) On a pregnant, unmarried, unemancipated woman who is under eighteen years of age unless:

(a) At least twenty-four hours actual notice, in person or by telephone, is given to one of the woman's parents, her guardian, or her custodian, or

(b) If the woman has filed an affidavit with juvenile court, under 2919.12(B)(1)(b), stating that she is in fear of physical, sexual, or severe emotional abuse from the parent, guardian, or custodian, at least twenty-four hours actual notice, in person or by telephone, is given to specified brother or sister twenty-one years of age or older, or to specified stepparent or grandparent, or

(c) One of the woman's parents, her guardian, or her custodian has consented in writing, or

(d) Juvenile court issues order, pursuant to 2151.85, authorizing woman to consent without notification of one of her parents, her guardian, or her custodian, or

(e) Juvenile court or court of appeals, by its inaction, constructively authorizes woman to consent without notification of one of her parents, her guardian, or her custodian, pursuant to 2151.85(B)(1) or 2505.073(A)

Note: RC 2929.121 operates in lieu of this provision whenever its operation is not enjoined.

Division (C):

(1) Perform or induce

(2) Abortion

(3) On a pregnant, unmarried, unemancipated woman who is under eighteen years of age when:

(a) Division (B)(4)(c), (d), or (e) does not apply, and

(b) No parent, guardian, or custodian can be reached after a reasonable effort, pursuant to Division (B)(4)(a), or, if Division (B)(4)(b) applies, no specified brother, sister, stepparent, or grandparent can be reached after a reasonable effort

(4) Unless forty-eight hours constructive notice is given by both certified and ordinary mail to a parent, guardian, or custodian, or, if Division (B)(4)(b) applies, to specified brother, sister, stepparent, or grandparent, at person's last known address

Note: RC 2929.121 operates in lieu of this provision whenever its operation is not enjoined.

Note: Forty-eight-hour period under Division (C) begins when certified mail notice mailed. If person to be notified is not reached within forty-eight-hour period, abortion may proceed even if certified mail notice is not received.

Note: If person to be notified under Division (B) or (C) has been properly notified and clearly and unequivocally expresses that he or she does not wish to consult with pregnant woman prior to abortion, abortion may proceed without any further waiting period.

PROOF

It shall be a rebuttable presumption that a woman who is unmarried and under eighteen years of age is unemancipated.

DEFENSES

It is an affirmative defense to a charge under Division (B) or (C) that the pregnant woman provided the person who performed or induced the abortion with false, misleading, or incorrect information about her age, marital status, or emancipation, about the age of a brother or sister to whom she requested notice be given as a specified relative instead of to one of her parents, her guardian, or her custodian, or about the last known address of either of her parents, her guardian, her custodian, or a specified brother, sister, stepparent, or grandparent to whom she requested notice be given and the person who performed or induced the abortion did not otherwise have reasonable cause to believe the pregnant woman was under eighteen years of age, unmarried, or unemancipated, to believe that the age of a brother or sister to whom she requested notice be given as a specified relative instead of to one of her parents, her guardian, or her custodian was not twenty-one years of age, or to believe that the last known address of either of her parents, her guardian, her custodian, or a specified brother, sister, stepparent, or grandparent to whom she requested notice be given was incorrect.

It is an affirmative defense to a charge under Division (A), (B), or (C) that compliance with the requirements of this section was not possible because an immediate threat of serious risk to the life or physical health of the pregnant woman from the continuation of her pregnancy created an emergency necessitating the immediate performance or inducement of an abortion.

PENALTY

Division (A):

First offense—Misdemeanor, 1st degree (2929.21 to 2929.28, 2929.31)

Each subsequent offense—Felony, 4th degree (2929.11 to 2929.18, 2929.31)

Divisions (B) and (C):

First offense Misdemeanor, 1st degree (2929.21 to 2929.28, 2929.31)

Each subsequent offense—Felony, 5th degree (2929.11 to 2929.18, 2929.31)

Civil Liability: Whoever violates divisions (A), (B), or (C) of this section is liable to the pregnant woman and her parents, guardian, or custodian for civil compensatory and exemplary damages.

Abortion—Failure to Perform Viability Testing—2919.18

ELEMENTS OF THE CRIME

Division (A):

(1) Physician

(2) Perform or induce or attempt to perform or induce

(3) Abortion

(4) On a pregnant woman

(5) After the beginning of her twenty-second week of pregnancy unless:

(a) Prior to the performance or inducement of or attempt to perform or induce an abortion, the physician determines, in good faith and in the exercise of reasonable medical judgment, that the unborn human is not viable, and the physician makes that determination after performing a medical examination of the pregnant woman and after performing or causing the performing of gestational age, weight, lung maturity, or other tests of the unborn human that a reasonable physician making a determination as to whether an unborn human is or is not viable would perform or cause to be performed.

Division (B):

(1) Physician

(2) Perform or induce or attempt to perform or induce

(3) Abortion

(4) On a pregnant woman

(5) After the beginning of her twenty-second week of pregnancy unless:

(a) Prior to the performance or inducement of or attempt to perform or induce an abortion, the physician determines, in good faith and in the exercise of reasonable medical judgment, that the unborn human is not viable, and the physician makes that determination after performing a medical examination of the pregnant woman and after performing or causing the performing of gestational age, weight, lung maturity, or other tests of the unborn human that a reasonable physician making a determination as to whether an unborn human is or is not viable would perform or cause to be performed, and

(6) Fails to enter the determination and associated findings of the medical examination and tests in the medical records of the pregnant woman.

DEFENSE

These sections do not prohibit a physician from performing or inducing or attempting to perform or induce an abortion upon a pregnant woman after the beginning of her twenty-second week of pregnancy without making the determination or without making an entry if a medical emergency exists.

PENALTY

Misdemeanor, 4th degree (2929.21 to 2929.28, 2929.31)

Abortion—Partial Birth Feticide—2919.151

ELEMENTS OF THE CRIME

Division (B):

(1) Knowingly

(2) Perform

(3) A partial birth procedure

(4) On a pregnant woman if the fetus is viable

(5) Not necessary, in reasonable medical judgment, to preserve the life or health of the mother

(6) As a result of the mother's life or health being endangered by serious risk

(7) Of substantial and irreversible impairment of a major bodily function

Division (C):

(1) Knowingly

(2) Perform

(3) A partial birth procedure

(4) On a pregnant woman if the fetus is not viable

(5) Not necessary, in reasonable medical judgment, to preserve the life or health of the mother

(6) As a result of the mother's life or health being endangered by serious risk

(7) Of substantial and irreversible impairment of a major bodily function

EXCEPTIONS

Does not include the "dilation and evacuation" procedure.

A pregnant woman who is the subject of the partial birth procedure is not subject to prosecution under the statute, or for complicity, or for conspiracy.

Not applicable to provider who performs or attempts to perform a legal abortion if the act that causes the death of the fetus is performed prior to the being partially born, even though death occurs after it is partially born.

PENALTY

Felony, 2nd Degree (2929.11 to 2929.18, 2929.31)

Abortion—Performing an Unlawful Abortion Procedure—2919.15

Repealed. See Abortion—partial birth feticide at ORC 2919.151.

Abortion—Terminating or Attempting to Terminate a Human Pregnancy After Viability—2919.17

ELEMENTS OF THE CRIME

Division (A):

(1) Purposely

(2) Perform or induce or attempt to perform or induce

(3) Abortion

(4) On a pregnant woman if the unborn human is viable unless:

(a) The abortion is performed or induced or attempted to be performed or induced by a physician, and that physician determines, in good faith and in the exercise of reasonable medical judgment, that the abortion is necessary to prevent the death of the pregnant woman or a serious risk of the substantial and irreversible impairment of a major bodily function of the pregnant woman, or

(b) The abortion is performed or induced or attempted to be performed or induced by a physician, and that physician determines, in good faith and in the exercise of reasonable medical judgment, after making a determination relative to the viability of the unborn human in conformity with division (A) of section 2919.18 of the Revised Code, that the unborn human is not viable.

Division (B):

(1) Physician

(2) Purposely

(3) Perform or induce or attempt to perform or induce

(4) Abortion

(5) On a pregnant woman if the unborn human is viable and

(6) When the physician determines, in good faith and in the exercise of reasonable medical judgment, that the abortion is necessary to prevent the death of the pregnant woman or a serious risk of the substantial and irreversible impairment of a major bodily function of the pregnant woman unless:

(a) The physician who performs or induces or attempts to perform or induce the abortion certifies in writing that the physician has determined, in good faith and in the exercise of reasonable medical judgment, that the abortion is necessary to prevent the death of the pregnant woman or a serious risk of the substantial and irreversible impairment of a major bodily function of the pregnant woman, and

(b) The physician who performs or induces or attempts to perform or induce the abortion is concurred in by at least one other physician who certifies in writing that the concurring physician has determined, in good faith, in the exercise of reasonable medical judgment, and following a review of the available medical records or and any available tests results pertaining to the pregnant woman, that the abortion is necessary to prevent the death of the pregnant woman or a serious risk of the substantial and irreversible impairment of a major bodily function of the pregnant woman, and

(c) The abortion is performed or induced or attempted to be performed or induced in a health care facility that has or has access to appropriate neonatal services for premature infants, and

(d) The physician who performs or induces or attempts to perform or induce the abortion terminates or attempts to terminate the pregnancy in the manner that provides the best opportunity for the unborn human to survive, unless that physician determines, in good faith and in the exercise of reasonable medical judgment, that the termination of the pregnancy in that manner poses a significantly greater risk of death of the pregnant woman or a serious risk of substantial and irreversible impairment of a major bodily function of the pregnant woman than would other available methods of abortion, and

(e) The physician who performs or induces or attempts to perform or induce the abortion has arranged for the attendance in the same room in which the abortion is to be performed or induced or attempted to be performed or induced of at least one other physician who is to take control of, provide immediate medical care for, and take all reasonable steps necessary to preserve the life and health of the unborn human immediately upon the unborn human's complete expulsion or extraction from the pregnant woman.

DEFENSE

This section does not prohibit that performance or inducement or attempted performance or inducement of an abortion without prior satisfaction of each of the conditions of this section if the physician who performs or induces or attempts to perform or induce the abortion determines, in good faith and in the exercise of reasonable medical judgment, that a medical emergency exists that prevents compliance with one or more of those conditions.

PROOF

It shall be a rebuttable presumption that an unborn child of at least twenty–four weeks of gestational age is viable.

EXCEPTION

A pregnant woman upon whom an abortion is performed or attempted to be performed in violation of these sections is not guilty of an attempt to commit, complicity in the commission of, or conspiracy in the commission of a violation of these sections.

PENALTY

Felony, 4th Degree (2929.11 to 2929.18, 2929.31)

Abortion—Unlawful—2929.121

ELEMENTS OF THE CRIME

(1) Knowingly

(2) Perform or induce an abortion

(3) Upon a pregnant minor

EXCEPTIONS

(1) Where the attending physician has secured the informed consent of the minor and one parent, guardian or custodian.

(2) The minor is emancipated and the physician has received the written informed consent of the minor.

(3) The minor has been authorized to consent to the abortion by a court order issued under the provisions of this section, and the physician has received the written informed consent of the minor.

(4) The court has given its consent under the provisions of this section, and the minor is having the abortion willingly.

DEFENSE

It is an affirmative defense to any criminal, civil or professional disciplinary claim that compliance with the requirements of the statute were not possible because an immediate threat of serious risk to the life or physical health of the minor from the continuation of her pregnancy created an emergency necessitating the immediate performance or inducement of an abortion.

PENALTY

Violation of this section is a Misdemeanor, 1st degree (2929.21 to 2929.28, 2929.31); if the offender previously has been convicted or pleaded guilty to a violation of this section, violation is a Felony of the 4th degree (2929.11 to 2929.18, 2929.31).

Abortion—Use of RU–486—2919.123

ELEMENTS OF THE CRIME

Division (A):

(1) Knowingly

(2) Give, sell, dispense, administer, otherwise provide or prescribe

(3) RU–486

(4) To another person

(5) For the purpose of inducing an abortion

Division (B):

(1) Physician, who provides RU–486 to another to induce an abortion,

(2) Knowingly

(3) Fail to comply with federal law pertaining to follow–up and after care

Division (C):

(1) Physician, who provides RU–486 to another to induce an abortion, and

(2) Knows that the person using RU–486 for the purpose of inducing an abortion,after or during the use of RU–486 experienced any of the following:

(a) An incomplete abortion

(b) Severe bleeding,

(c) An adverse reaction,

(d) Is hospitalized,

(e) Receives a transfusion, or

(f) Experiences any other serious event

(3) Knowingly fail to provide to the medical board a written report of the of the above reactions

Note: The Medical Board shall retain all reports it receives under this division. Such records and reports are public documents subject to inspection under RC 149.43. The Board may not release the name or other personal identifying information of the person who used RU–486 to induce an abortion.

EXCEPTIONS:

Division (A) does not apply to (1) a pregnant woman who obtains or possesses RU–486 for purposes of inducing an abortion; (2) the legal transport or delivery of RU–486; (3) distribution, provision, or sale of RU–486 by any legal manufacturer or distributor who made a good faith effort to comply applicable federal requirements.

PENALTY:

Felony, Fourth degree. If offender has previously been convicted of a violation of this section or 2929.12, 2929.121, 2929.13, 2929.14, 2929.151, 2929.17, or 2929.18, Felony, Third degree. (2929.11 to 2929.19, 2929.31)

Note: If the offender is professionally licensed person, offender is subject to sanctioning as provided by law.

Abuse of a Corpse

See Offenses Against Human Corpse; Abortion—Abortion Trafficking

Abusing Harmful Intoxicants

See Drug Offenses—Abusing Harmful Intoxicants

Acquired Immune Deficiency Syndrome

See AIDS

Adulterated Food—3716.11

ELEMENTS OF THE CRIME

(1) Knowing, or having reasonable cause to believe, any person may suffer physical harm or be seriously inconvenienced or annoyed

(2)(a) Place a pin, needle, razor blade, glass, laxative, drug of abuse, or other harmful or hazardous object or substance in food or confection, or

(b) Furnish any person with food or confection adulterated in violation of (2)(a)

PENALTY

Misdemeanor, 1st degree (2929.21 to 2929.28, 2929.31)

Aggravated Offenses

See particular offense by name

AIDS—Sale or Donation of Blood by AIDS Carrier—2927.13

ELEMENTS OF THE CRIME

(1) Knowing he is a carrier of a virus that causes Acquired Immune Deficiency Syndrome

(2) Sell or donate

(3) His blood, plasma, or a product of his blood

(4) Knowing or should know the blood, plasma, or product of his blood is being accepted for the purpose of transfusion to another individual

PENALTY

Felony, 4th degree (2929.11 to 2929.18, 2929.31)

Aircraft, Endangering

See Weapons—Endangering Aircraft or Airport Operations

Alcohol Offenses—Drunk Driving

See Drunk Driving—Driving While Intoxicated or Drugged

Amphetamines

See Drug Offenses, generally

Anabolic Steroids

See Drug Offenses—Illegal Administration or Distribution of Anabolic Steroids

Animals—Assault on Police Dog or Horse

See Assault—Police Dog or Horse

Animals—Failure to Report Escape of Exotic or Dangerous Animal

See Failure to Report Escape of Exotic or Dangerous Animal

Anti–Stalking Protection Order, Violating

See Protection Order—Violating Anti–Stalking Protection Order

Arrest, Resisting

See Resisting Arrest

Arson—Aggravated Arson—2909.02

ELEMENTS OF THE CRIME

(1) By means of fire or explosion

(2) Knowingly

(3)(a) Create substantial risk of serious physical harm to any person other than the offender, or

(b) Cause physical harm to any occupied structure, or

(4)(a) Create through offer or acceptance of agreement for hire or other consideration, a substantial risk of physical harm to any occupied structure

PENALTY

If (3)(a) or (4)(a) violated

Felony, 1st degree (2929.11 to 2929.18, 2929.28, 2929.31)

If (3)(b) violated

Felony, 2nd degree (2929.11 to 2929.18, 2929.28, 2929.31)

A defendant who is convicted of or pleads guilty to committing, attempting to commit, or complicity in committing a felony violation of 2909.02, shall be required to reimburse agencies for their investigation or prosecution costs in accordance with 2929.28.

Arson—Arson—2909.03

ELEMENTS OF THE CRIME

(1) By means of fire or explosion

(2) Knowingly

(3)(a) Cause or create substantial risk of physical harm to any property of another without the other person's consent, or

(b) Cause or create substantial risk of physical harm to any property of the offender or another, with purpose to defraud, or

(c) Cause or create substantial risk of physical harm to statehouse, courthouse, school building, or other building or structure owned or controlled by state or any political subdivisions, or any department, agency, instrumentality of either, and used for public purpose, or

(d) Cause or create substantial risk of physical harm, by offer or acceptance of agreement for hire or other consideration, to another's property without the other person's consent, or to the offender's or another's property with purpose to defraud, or

(e) Cause or create substantial risk of physical harm to park, preserve, wildlands, brush–covered land, cut-over land, forest, timberland, greenlands, woods, or similar real property owned or controlled by another person, the state, or a political subdivision without the consent of that person or entity, or

(f) With purpose to defraud, cause or create substantial risk of physical harm to any park, preserve, wildlands, brush-covered land, cut–over land, forest, timberland, greenlands, woods, or similar real property owned or controlled by the offender, another person, the state, or a political subdivision

PENALTY

If (3)(a) violated and value of property or amount of physical harm is:

(1) Less than $500, Misdemeanor, 1st degree (2909.11, 2929.21 to 2929.28, 2929.31)

(2) $500 or more, Felony, 4th degree (2909.11, 2929.11 to 2929.18, 2929.28, 2929.31)

If (3)(b), (c), (e), or (f) violated Felony, 4th degree (2909.11, 2929.11 to 2929.18, 2929.28, 2929.31)

If (3)(d) violated, Felony, 3rd degree (2909.11, 2929.11 to 2929.18, 2929.28, 2929.31)

Note: Any person convicted under this section shall be required to reimburse agencies for their investigation or prosecution costs in accordance with 2929.28.

Assault—Aggravated Assault—2903.12

ELEMENTS OF THE CRIME

(1) While under the influence of sudden passion or in a sudden fit of rage

(2) Either of which is brought on by serious provocation occasioned by the victim that is reasonably sufficient to incite the person into using deadly force

(3) Knowingly

(4)(a) Cause serious physical harm to another or to another's unborn, or

(b) Cause or attempt to cause physical harm to another or to another's unborn by means of deadly weapon or dangerous ordnance.

PENALTY

Felony, 4th degree (2929.11 to 2929.18, 2929.31)

If victim is peace officer, as defined in 2935.01, and the victim suffered serious physical harm, Felony, 3rd degree with a mandatory prison sentence (2929.11 to 2929.18, 2929.31)

Assault—Assault—2903.13

See also Sex Offenses—Sexual Battery; Hazing

ELEMENTS OF THE CRIME

Division (A):

(1) Knowingly

(2) Cause or attempt to cause

(3) Physical harm to another or to another's unborn

Division (B):

(1) Recklessly

(2) Cause serious physical harm to another or to another's unborn

PENALTY

Misdemeanor, 1st degree (2929.21 to 2929.28, 2929.31)

If the offense is committed by a caretaker against a functionally impaired person under the caretaker's care, Felony, 4th degree (2929.11 to 2929.18, 2929.31)

If the offense is committed by a caretaker against a functionally impaired person under the caretaker's care and if the offender has previously been convicted or pleaded guilty to a violation of 2903.13,2903.11, or 2903.16 and in relation to that conviction the caretaker/functionally impaired person relationship existed, Felony, 3rd degree (2929.11 to 2929.18, 2929.31)

If offense occurs:

(1) In or on the grounds of a state correctional institution, or an institution of the department of youth services, and the victim is an employee of the department of rehabilitation and correction, the department of youth services, or a probation department or is on premises for business or as a visitor, and offender is incarcerated in the state correctional institution, a person institutionalized pursuant to a commitment to the department of youth services, or is a probationer, parolee or an offender under transitional control, a community control sanction, or an escorted visit, post-release control, or any other type of supervision by a government agency; or

(2) In or on the grounds of a local correctional facility, and the victim is an employee of the local correctional facility or a probation department or is on the premises of the facility for business purposes or as a visitor, and the offender is under custody in the facility subsequent to the person's arrest for any crime or delinquent act, subsequent to the person's being charged with or convicted of any crime, or subsequent to the person's being alleged to be or adjudicated a delinquent child; or

(3) Off the grounds of a state correctional institution, or department of youth services institution, and victim is employee of the department of rehabilitation and correction, the department of youth services or a probation department, offense occurs during employee's official work hours while the employee is engaged in official work responsibilities, and offender is incarcerated or institutionalized in an institution but temporarily off premises for any purpose or is probationer, parolee or an offender under transitional control, a community control sanction, or an escorted visit, post-release control, or any other type of supervision by a government agency; or

(4) Off the grounds of a local correctional facility, and the victim is an employee of the local correctional facility or a probation department, the offense occurs during employee's official work hours while the employee is engaged in official work responsibilities, and offender is under custody in the facility subsequent to the person's arrest for any crime or delinquent act, subsequent to the person being alleged to be or adjudicated a delinquent child and who is temporarily outside of the facility for any purpose or is probationer, parolee or an offender under transitional control, a community control sanction, or an escorted visit, post-release control, or any other type of supervision by a government agency; or

(5)(1) The victim is a school teacher, administrator, or bus driver *and* (2) the offense occurs in a school building or school bus *or* out of school building or school bus but while victim is engaged in duties associated with school employment.

Felony, 5th degree (2929.11 to 2929.18)

If the victim is a peace officer as defined in 2935.01,Felony, 4th degree with a mandatory prison sentence of at least 12 months (2929.11 to 2929.18, 2929.31)

If the victim is an officer or employee of a Public Children's Service Agency or a Private Child Placing Agency, and the offense relates to victim's performance or anticipated performance of responsibilities or duties, Felony, 5th degree; subsequent offenses, Felony, 4th degree (2929.11 to 2918, 2929.31)

Assault—Felonious Assault—2903.11

ELEMENTS OF THE CRIME

Division (A):

(1) Knowingly

(2)(a) Cause serious physical harm to another or to another's unborn, or

(b) Cause or attempt to cause physical harm to another or to another's unborn by means of deadly weapon or dangerous ordnance

Division (B):

(1) With knowledge that offender has tested positive as an AIDS virus carrier

(2) Knowingly

(3)(a) Engages in sexual conduct with another without prior disclosure of such knowledge

(b) Engages in sexual conduct with another whom offender knows or has reasonable cause to believe lacks mental capacity to appreciate significance of such knowledge

(c) Engages in sexual conduct with another under 18 years who is not offender's spouse.

PENALTY

Felony, 2nd degree (2929.11 to 2929.18, 2929.31)

If, under Division (A), victim is peace officer, as defined in 2935.01, and the victim suffered serious physical harm, Felony, 1st degree with a mandatory prison sentence (2929.11 to 2929.18, 2929.31)

Assault—Negligent Assault—2903.14

ELEMENTS OF THE CRIME

(1) Negligently

(2) By means of deadly weapon or dangerous ordnance

(3) Cause physical harm to another or to another's unborn

PENALTY

Misdemeanor, 3rd degree (2929.21 to 2929.28, 2929.31)

Assault—Police Dog or Horse or Service Dog—2921.321

ELEMENTS OF THE CRIME

Division (A):

(1) Knowingly

(2) Cause or attempt to cause

(3) Physical harm

(4) To a police dog or horse

(5)(a) When the police dog or horse is assisting a law enforcement officer in the performance of the officer's duties, or

(b) When the police dog or horse is not assisting a law enforcement officer in the performance of the officer's duties, but the offender has actual knowledge that the dog or horse is a police dog or horse.

Division (B):

(1) Recklessly

(2) Do any of the following

(a) Taunt, torment or strike a police dog or horse

(b) Throw any object or substance at a police dog or horse

(c) Interfere or obstruct a police dog or horse, or interfere with or obstruct a law enforcement officer's control of a police dog or horse that

(1) Inhibits or restricts the law enforcement officer's control of the dog or horse

(2) Deprives the law enforcement officer of control of the dog or horse

(3) Releases the dog or horse from its area of control

(4) Enters the area of control without the consent of the law enforcement officer, including placing food, object or substance into that area

(5) Inhibits or restricts ability of police dog or horse to assist a law enforcement officer

(d) Engage in conduct likely to cause serious physical injury or death to a police dog or horse

(e) Fail to reasonably restrain a dog from taunting, tormenting, chasing, approaching in a menacing manner, or attempting to bite or otherwise endanger a police dog or horse that is assisting a law enforcement officer or that the person knows this is a police dog or horse

Division (C):

(1) Knowingly

(2) Cause or attempt to cause physical harm to a service dog

(a) If the dog is assisting or serving a blind, deaf or mobility impaired person at the time the harm is caused or attempted

(b) If the dog is not assisting or serving a blind, deaf or mobility impaired person at the time of the offense if the offender knows that the dog is a handicapped assistance dog

Division (D):

(1) Recklessly

(2)(a) Taunt, torment or strike a service dog

(b) Throw an object or substance at a service dog.

(c) Interfere with or obstruct a service dog or an impaired person's control of a service dog by

(i) Inhibit or restrict the impaired person's control

(ii) Deprive the impaired person of control

(iii) Release service dog from its area of control

(iv) Enter the area of control without permission of the impaired person, including placing food, object or substance in the area

(v) Inhibit or restrict the ability of the service dog to assist or serve person

(d) Engage in any conduct likely to cause serious physical injury or death to a service dog

(c) Fail to reasonably restrain a dog from taunting, tormenting, chasing, approaching in a menacing manner, or attempting to bite or otherwise a service dog that is assisting an impaired person or that the person knows is a service dog.

PENALTY

Misdemeanor, 2nd degree (2929.21 to 2929.28, 2929.31)

If the violation results in the death of the police dog or horse or service dog, Felony, 3rd degree (2929.11 to 2929.18, 2929.31)

If the violation results in serious physical harm to the police dog or horse or service dog other than its death, Felony, 4th degree (2929.11 to 2929.18, 2929.31)

If the violation results in physical harm to the police dog or horse or service dog other than death or serious physical harm, Misdemeanor, 1st degree (2929.21 to 2929.28, 2929.31)

Note: This section does not apply to a licensed veterinarian whose conduct is in accordance with Chapter 4741.

Attempt—2923.02

ELEMENTS OF THE CRIME

(1) Purposely or knowingly

(2) When purpose or knowledge is sufficient culpability for commission of offense

(3) Engage in conduct that, if successful, would constitute or result in offense

DEFENSES

(1) No defense that, in retrospect, commission of offense that was object of attempt was either factually or legally impossible under attendant circumstances, if that offense could have been committed had attendant circumstances been as actor believed them to be.

(2) If convicted of offense or complicity or conspiracy of offense, no conviction for attempt of same offense.

(3) Actor abandoned effort to commit offense or prevented its commission by manifesting complete and voluntary renunciation of criminal purpose.

(4) Attempt to commit minor misdemeanor or to engage in conspiracy is no offense under 2923.02.

PENALTY

Attempt to commit aggravated murder, murder, or an offense for which the maximum penalty is imprisonment for life, Felony, 1st degree (2929.11 to 2929.18, 2929.31)

Attempt to commit drug abuse offense for which the penalty is determined by amount or number of unit doses is an offense of the next lower range based on amount or number of units.

Attempt to commit any other offense is an offense of the next lesser degree than offense attempted.

Attempt to commit offense other than violation of Chapter 3734., not specifically classified, when offense attempted is a felony, Misdemeanor, 1st degree (2929.21 to 2929.28, 2929.31)

Attempt to commit offenses other than violation of Chapter 3734., not specifically classified, when it is misdemeanor, Misdemeanor, 4th degree (2929.21 to 2929.28, 2929.31)

Attempt to commit a violation of Chapter 3734., except 3734.18, that relates to hazardous wastes, Felony:
Imprisonment: Not more than 18 months, and/or
Fine: Not more than $25,000

Barbiturates or Amphetamines

See Drug Offenses, generally

Bigamy

See Domestic Offenses—Bigamy

Bingo—Bingo Records—2915.10

ELEMENTS OF THE CRIME

Division (A): (RC 2915.10(A))

(1) Charitable organization conducting bingo session or game of chance under 2915.02(D) shall:

(2) Maintain for 3 years records of

(3)(a) Itemized list of gross receipts, and

(b) All expenses with names to whom paid and receipt, and

(c) All prizes with names and addresses of recipients of $100 or more in value, and

(d) Itemized list of charitable recipients of proceeds with names and addresses, and

(e) Number of persons participating in any bingo session or game of chance, and

(f) List of receipts from sale of food and beverages if receipts were excluded from definition of gross receipts, and

(g) Itemized list of all expenses incurred at each bingo session conducted by the charitable organization in the sale of food and beverages, name of each person to whom expenses are paid and a receipt for all the expenses

Division (B):

Charitable organization conducting bingo session or game of chance shall:

(1) Keep records at its principal place of business or headquarters within the state and notify the Attorney General of the records' location.

(2) Deposit profits from each bingo session or game into a checking account devoted exclusively to the bingo session or game. (RC 2915.10(C))

(3) Draw payments for expenses and recipients of net profits by checks drawn only on this account.

(4) Conduct and record its inventory of bingo supplies on November 1 of each year. (RC 2915.10(D))

Division (C): Distributor shall maintain for 3 years: (RC 2915.10(F))

(1) After date of sale or distribution a record of each transaction.

(2) Name of manufacturer from whom the distributor purchased bingo supplies and the date of the purchase.

(3) The name and address of the charitable organization or other distributor to whom bingo supplies were sold or provided.

(4) Invoices including nonrepeating serial numbers of all paper bingo cards and sheets and all instant bingo deals sold or provided to each charitable organization.

Division (D): Manufacturer shall maintain for 3 years: (RC 2915.10(G))

(1) After date of sale or distribution a record of each transaction.

(2) The name and address of the distributor to whom the bingo supplies were sold or provided.

(3) A description of the bingo supplies sold or provided including serial numbers.

(4) Invoices including nonrepeating serial numbers of all paper bingo cards and sheets and all instant bingo deals sold or provided to each charitable organization.

Division (E): No person shall: (RC 2915.10(I))

(1) Destroy, alter, conceal, withhold or deny access to any accounts or records of a charitable organization that have been requested for examination, or

(2) Obstruct, impede, or interfere with any inspection, audit, or observation of a bingo game or game of chance on premises where conducted, or

(3) Refuse to comply with any request of, or obstruct, impede, or interfere with any other reasonable action of the Attorney General or local law enforcement agency.

PENALTY

Violation of (A) or (I), Misdemeanor, 1st degree (2929.21 to 2929.28, 2929.31)

Bingo—Cheating

See Cheating

Bingo—Conducting Illegal Amusement Bingo Game—2915.12

Decriminalized effective 7–1–96

Bingo—Conducting Illegal Bingo Game—2915.07

ELEMENTS OF THE CRIME

Conduct or advertise bingo

DEFENSE

Charitable organization that has bingo license under 2915.08.

EXCEPTION

Raffle conducted or advertised by a charitable organization.

PENALTY

Felony, 4th degree (2929.11 to 2929.18, 2929.31)

Bingo—Felon Not to Work Bingo Session—2915.11(B)

ELEMENTS OF THE CRIME

(1) Be a bingo game operator

(2) Convicted of felony or gambling offense in any jurisdiction

PENALTY

Misdemeanor, 1st degree (2929.21 to 2929.28, 2929.31)

Bingo—Instant Bingo—Prohibitions Where Game is Conducted—2915.091

ELEMENTS OF THE CRIME

Division (A):

(1) No Charitable organization conducting instant bingo shall:

(2) Fail to comply with requirements of 2915.09(A)(1), (2) and (3)

(3) Conduct instant bingo unless the organization

(a) has received a determination letter from the I.R.S. that is currently in effect that the organization is exempt from federal incomc taxation under 501(a) of Internal Revenue Code, described in 501(c)(3) of Internal Revenue Code, is a charitable organization as defined in 2915.01, is in good standing in the state under 2915.08, and is in compliance with Chapter 1716, or

(b) has received a determination letter from the I.R.S. that is currently in effect that the organization is exempt from federal income taxation 501(a) and is described in 501(c)(8), (10), or (19) of the Internal Revenue Code, and conducts instant bingo pursuant to 2915.13.

(4) Conduct instant bingo on a day, time or place except as specified in the organization's license under 2915.08.

(5) Permit any person whom the organization knows or should have known has been convicted of a felony or gambling offense in any jurisdiction to be an operator of instant bingo.

(6) Purchase or lease supplies for instant bingo or punch board games from any person except a distributor licensed under 2915.081.

(7) Sell or provide an instant bingo ticket or card for a price different from the price printed on the ticket or card by the manufacturer.

(8) Sell instant bingo tickets or cards to a person under 18.

(9) Fail to keep unsold bingo tickets or cards for less than 3 years.

(10) Pay any compensation to a bingo game operator for

(a) conducting instant bingo,

(b) preparing, selling or serving food or beverages at site of instant bingo game, or

(c) permit any auxiliary unit of the organization to do the same.

(11) Pay fees to any person for services performed in relation to an instant bingo game or for providing refreshments to participants in instant bingo game.

(12) Allow instant bingo tickets to be sold to

(a) workers at the premises where the organization sells instant bingo tickets,

(b) employees of a D permit holder who are working at the premises at which instant bingo tickets or cards are sold on behalf of the organization.

(13) Fail to conspicuously display at each premises where it sells instant bingo tickets or cards:

(a) the organization's bingo license, and

(b) the serial numbers of the deal of instant bingo tickets or cards to be sold.

(14) Possess a deal of instant bingo tickets or cards not purchased from a distributor licensed under 2915.081 as reflected in an invoice required under 2915.10(E).

(15) Fails to continue to sell tickets or cards, once it opens a deal or instant bingo tickets or cards, until the tickets or cards with the top two highest tiers of prizes are sold.

(16) Purchase, lease, or use instant bingo tickets dispensers to sell instant bingo tickets or cards.

(17) Possess bingo supplies not obtained in accordance with 2915.01 to 2915.13.

Division (B):

(1) A charitable organization may conduct instant bingo

(2) At a bingo session, and

(3) At not more than 5 separate locations other than at a bingo session.

EXCEPTION

Division (B) is not applicable to a charitable organization created by veterans organization or a fraternal organization exempt from federal taxation under 501(a) and 501(c)(3).

PENALTY

Misdemeanor, 1st degree (2929.21 to 2929.28, 2929.31)

If prior conviction of this section, Felony, 5th degree (2929.11 to 2929.18, 2929.31)

Bingo—Instant Bingo—Restrictions on Owner or Lessor of Location—2915.094

ELEMENTS OF THE CRIME

Division (A): No owner or lessor of a location who enters into a written contract, pursuant to 2915.093(C), to assist a charitable instant bingo organization in the conduct of an instant bingo session

(1) Shall permit, aid or abet any other person to violate any provision of Chapter 2915, or

(2) Shall violate the terms of the written contract.

PENALTY

Misdemeanor, 1st degree (2929.21 to 2929.28, 2929.31)

If prior conviction of this section, Felony, 5th degree (2929.11 to 2929.18, 2929.31)

Bingo—Instant Bingo—Veteran's or Fraternal Organization May Conduct—2915.13

ELEMENTS OF THE CRIME

Division (A):

(1) Veteran's or fraternal organization authorized to conduct bingo sessions under 2915.01 to 2915.12,

(2) May conduct instant bingo, if

(a) limits the sale of instant bingo to twelve hours per day between 10 a.m. and 2 a.m.

(b) limits the sale of instant bingo to its own premises and its own members and invited guests, and

(c) is raising money for a charitable organization pursuant to a written contract with the charitable organization as required by this section.

Division (B):

(1) Veteran's or fraternal organization entering into written contract under this section

(2) Shall not violate any provision of 2929.15, or

(3) Shall not permit, aid or abet any other person in violating any provision of 2929.15.

Division (C):

(1) Veteran's or fraternal organization entering into written contract under this section

(2) Shall give all required proceeds from instant bingo to the charitable organization with which it contracted.

PENALTY

Misdemeanor, 1st degree (2929.21 to 2929.28, 2929.31)

If prior conviction of this section, Felony, 5th degree (2929.11 to 2929.18, 2929.31)

Bingo—Methods of Conducting Licensed Bingo Game—Prohibitions— 2915.09

ELEMENTS OF THE CRIME

Division (A): Charitable organization that conducts bingo shall:

(1) Fail to own all equipment used to conduct bingo or lease such equipment from charitable organization licensed to conduct bingo for rental rate not more than customary and reasonable

(2)(a) Fail to use all gross receipts from a bingo session for:

(i) Paying prizes, or

(ii) Renting premises in which to conduct bingo or for reimbursement for, or

(iii) Purchasing or leasing bingo supplies used in conducting bingo or for reimbursement for, or

(iv) Hiring security personnel for bingo or for reimbursement for, or

(v) Advertising bingo, or

(vi) Charitable purposes listed in bingo license application.

(b) Amount of receipts so spent is not to be more than is customary and reasonable for similar purchase, lease, hiring, or advertising.

(c) If building in which game is conducted is owned by the charitable organization conducting bingo, organization may deduct from total amount of gross receipts from each session lesser amount of $600 or 45% of gross receipts from session, as consideration for use of premises.

(3)(a) Fail to use, give, donate, or otherwise transfer

(b) All of the net profit from bingo

(c) Other than instant bingo

(d) For charitable purpose listed in its license application

(e) Or fail to distribute all of the net profit from instant bingo

(i) as in its license application

(ii) and in accord with 2915.101.

Division (B): Charitable organization that conducts bingo shall:

(1)(a) Fail to conduct bingo on:

(i) Premises owned by the charitable organization, or

(ii) Premises owned by another charitable organization for not more than the lesser of $600 or 45% of gross receipts per session, or

(iii) Premises leased from person other than charitable organization for rental rate not more than is customary and reasonable for premises similar in size, location, and quality, but not to exceed $450 per session, or

(iv) Premises owned by person other than charitable organization, leased from that person by another charitable organization, and subleased from that charitable organization for rental rate not to exceed $450 per session.

(b) If charitable organization leases premises from person other than charitable organization, lessor of premises shall provide only premises and not:

(i) Bingo game operators, or

(ii) Security personnel, or

(iii) Concessions or concessions operators, or

(iv) Bingo supplies, or

(v) Any other type of service or equipment.

(c) Charitable organization shall not lease or sublease premises it owns or leases to more than one other charitable organization per calendar week for purpose of conducting bingo sessions.

(d) Person who is not charitable organization shall not lease premises that he owns, leases, or is otherwise empowered to lease to more than one charitable organization per calendar week for conducting bingo sessions.

(e) No more than two bingo sessions may be conducted on any premises in any calendar week, in any case.

(2) Fail to display its license conspicuously at premises where bingo is conducted.

(3) Fail to conduct session in accordance with definition of bingo in 2915.01(S)(1).

Division (C): Charitable organization that conducts bingo shall not:

(1)(a) Pay any compensation to bingo game operator for:

(i) Operating session, or

(ii) Preparing, selling, or serving food or beverages at session site.

(b) Permit any auxiliary unit or society of the charitable organization to pay compensation to bingo game operator who prepares, sells, or serves food or beverages at bingo session conducted by the charitable organization.

(c) Permit any auxiliary unit or society of the charitable organization to prepare, sell, or serve food or beverages at bingo session conducted by the organization, if auxiliary unit or society pays any compensation to operators who prepare, sell, or serve the food or beverages.

(2) Pay consulting fees to any person for any services performed in relation to bingo session.

(3) Pay concession fees to any person who provides refreshments to participants in bingo session.

(4) Conduct more than two bingo sessions in any 7–day period.

(5) Pay out more than $3,500 in prizes during any bingo session.

(6)(a) Conduct a bingo session:

(i) Between midnight and 10 a.m., or

(ii) At any time during, or within 10 hours of, bingo game conducted for amusement only pursuant to 2915.12, or

(iii) At any location not specified on its license, or

(iv) On any day of the week or during any time period not specified on its license.

(b) Charitable organization may apply in writing for amended license under 2915.08(F) to:

(i) Conduct session at or on time or day of the week other than that specified on its bingo license, but may apply only twice in each calendar year, or

(ii) Conduct session at location other than that specified on license, if circumstances beyond control of organization make it impossible to hold session at location specified.

(7)(a) Permit any person

(b) Whom charitable organization knows or should know

(c) Is under 18

(d) To work as bingo game operator.

(8)(a) Permit any person

(b) Whom charitable organization knows or should know

(c) Has been convicted of felony or gambling offense in any jurisdiction

(d) To be a bingo game operator.

(9) Permit lessor of premises on which bingo is conducted, if lessor is not charitable organization, to provide charitable organization with:

(a) Bingo game operators, or

(b) Security personnel, or

(c) Concessions, or

(d) Bingo supplies, or

(e) Any other type of service or equipment.

(10) Purchase or lease bingo supplies from any person except a distributor licensed under 2915.081.

(11) Use or permit use of electronic bingo aids except as provided in(C)(11)(a)(i) through (vi) or in accordance with rules adopted by the Attorney General.

(12)(a) Permit any person

(b) Whom charitable organization knows or should have known

(c) Is under 18

(d) To play bingo.

Division (D): Bingo game operator shall not receive or accept, directly or indirectly:

(1) Any commission, wage, salary, reward, tip, donation, gratuity, or other form of compensation, regardless of source

(2) For conducting bingo session or providing other work or labor at site of session.

EXCEPTION

Provision (C)(4) does not apply to volunteer fire or rescue organization that conducts not more than five bingo sessions in calendar year; such organization may conduct two bingo sessions in 7 day period after notifying attorney general.

PENALTY

If Division (A)(2) violated, Felony, 4th degree (2929.11 to 2929.18, 2929.31)

If Division (A)(1) or (3), Division (B)(1), (2), or (3), Division (C)(1) to (12), or Division (D), Minor misdemeanor (2929.21 to 2929.28, 2929.31)

If prior conviction of Division (A)(1) or (3), Division (B)(1), (2), or (3), Division (C)(1) to (11), or Division (D), Misdemeanor, 1st degree (2929.21 to 2929.28, 2929.31)

If Division (C)(12), Misdemeanor, 1st degree (2929.21 to 2929.28, 2929.31)

If prior conviction of (C)(12), subsequent violation of (C)(12), Felony, 4th degree (2929.11 to 2929.18, 2929.31)

Bingo—Minor Not to Work Bingo Session—2915.11(A)

ELEMENTS OF THE CRIME

(1) Be a bingo game operator

(2) Under 18 years of age

PENALTY

Misdemeanor, 3rd degree (2929.21 to 2929.28, 2929.31)

Block Parent Symbol—Misuse—2917.46

ELEMENTS OF THE CRIME

(1) With intent to identify a building as a block parent home or building

(2) Display

(a) Block parent symbol adopted by the state board of education pursuant to 3301.076, or

(b) A symbol that falsely gives the appearance of the block parent symbol

(3) Without authorization in accordance with 3301.076 or 3313.206

PENALTY

Minor misdemeanor (2929.21 to 2929.28, 2929.31)

Blood

See AIDS

Body Cavity Searches

See Searches—Body Cavity and Strip Searches

Breaking and Entering—2911.13

ELEMENTS OF THE CRIME

Division (A):

(1) By force, stealth, or deception

(2) Trespass in unoccupied structure

(3) With purpose to commit any theft therein as defined in 2913.01 or any felony

Division (B):

(1) Trespass on land or premises of another

(2) With purpose to commit felony

PENALTY

Felony, 5th degree (2929.11 to 2929.18, 2929.31)

Bribery

See Public Officials—Bribery

Burglary—Aggravated Burglary—2911.11

ELEMENTS OF THE CRIME

(1) By force, stealth, or deception

(2) Trespass in

(a) Occupied structure, or

(b) A separately secured or separately occupied portion of an occupied structure when another person is present, other than an accomplice of the offender

(3) With purpose to commit any criminal offense in the structure

(4)(a) When offender inflicts, attempts or threatens to inflict physical harm on another, or

(b) When offender has deadly weapon or dangerous ordnance, on or about the offender's person or under the offender's control

PENALTY

Felony, 1st degree (2929.11 to 2929.18, 2929.31)

Burglary—Burglary—2911.12

See also Criminal Tools—Possessing

ELEMENTS OF THE CRIME

Division (A):

(1) By force, stealth, or deception

(2) Trespass in

(a) Occupied structure, or

(b) Separately secured or separately occupied portion of an occupied structure when another person other than an accomplice of the offender is present

(3) With purpose to commit therein any criminal offense

Division (B):

(1) By force, stealth, or deception

(2) Trespass in

(a) Occupied structure, or

(b) Separately secured or separately occupied portion of an occupied structure that is a permanent or temporary habitation of any person

(3) When any person other than an accomplice of the offender present or likely to be present

(4) With purpose to commit in the habitation any criminal offense

Division (C):

(1) By force, stealth, or deception

(2) Trespass in

(a) Occupied structure, or

(b) Separately secured or separately occupied portion of an occupied structure

(3) With purpose to commit therein any criminal offense

Division (D):

(1) By force, stealth, or deception

(2) Trespass in permanent or temporary habitation of any person

(3) When any person other than an accomplice of the offender present or likely to be present

PENALTY

If Division (A) violated, Felony, 2nd degree (2929.11 to 2929.18, 2929.31)

If Division (B) violated, Felony, 2nd degree (2929.11 to 2929.18, 2929.31)

If Division (C) violated, Felony, 3rd degree (2929.11 to 2929.18, 2929.31)

If Division (D) violated, Felony, 4th degree (2929.11 to 2929.18, 2929.31)

Cable Television—Possession of an Unauthorized Device—2913.041(A)

ELEMENTS OF THE CRIME

(1) Knowingly

(2) Possess

(3) Any device specially adapted, modified or remanufactured for gaining access to cable television service

(4) Without authorization from or payment to the owner or operator of the cable television service

PENALTY

Felony, 5th degree (2929.11 to 2929.18, 2929.31)

Cable Television—Sale of an Unauthorized Device—2913.041(B)

ELEMENTS OF THE CRIME

(1) Knowingly

(2) Sell, distribute or manufacture

(3) Any device specially adapted, modified or remanufactured for gaining access to cable television service

(4) Without authorization from or payment to the owner or operator of the cable television service

PENALTY

Felony, 4th degree (2929.11 to 2929.18, 2929.31)

Care of Functionally Impaired Person—2903.16

ELEMENTS OF THE CRIME

Division (A):

(1) Caretaker

(2) Knowingly

(3) Fails to provide functionally impaired person with any treatment, care, goods, or service necessary to maintain health or safety of the functionally impaired person

(4) Such failure results in physical harm or serious physical harm to the functionally impaired person

Division (B):

(1) Caretaker

(2) Recklessly

(3) Fails to provide functionally impaired person with any treatment, care, goods, or service necessary to maintain health or safety of the functionally impaired person

(4) Such failure results in serious physical harm to the functionally impaired person

PENALTY

If Division (A) violated, Misdemeanor, 1st degree (2929.21 to 2929.28,2929.31)

If Division (B) violated, Misdemeanor, 2nd degree (2929.21 to 2929.28, 2929.31)

If victim suffers serious physical harm while under the offender's care, Felony, 4th degree (2929.11 to 2929.18, 2929.31)

Carrying Concealed Weapon

See Weapons—Carrying Concealed Weapon

Cemetery, Desecration of Monument

See Desecration; Vandalism

Cheating—2915.05

See also Gambling

ELEMENTS OF THE CRIME

Division (A):

(1) Purpose to defraud or knowing that the person is facilitating fraud

(2) Engage in conduct designed to corrupt outcome of

(3)(a) Subject of bet, or

(b) Contest of knowledge, skill, or endurance that is not an athletic or sporting event, or

(c) Scheme or game of chance, or

(d) Bingo

Division (B):

(1) Knowingly

(2)(a) Offer, give, solicit, or accept anything of value, or

(b) Engage in conduct designed to

(3) Corrupt the outcome of an athletic or sporting event

PENALTY

If Division (A) violated, Misdemeanor, 1st degree (2929.21 to 2929.28, 2929.31)

If potential gain is $500 or more, or

If prior conviction of gambling offense, or

Of any theft offense defined in 2913.01, Felony, 5th degree (2929.11 to 2929.18, 2929.31)

If Division (B) violated, Felony, 5th degree (2929.11 to 2929.18, 2929.31)

Each subsequent offense under Division (B), Felony, 4th degree (2929.11 to 2929.18, 2929.31)

Checks, Bad, Passing

See Theft-related Offenses—Passing Bad Checks

Children, Crimes Affecting

See Juveniles

Civil Rights—Housing Discrimination

See Housing—Injuring, Intimidating, or Interfering With

Civil Rights—Interfering With—2921.45

See also Coercion

ELEMENTS OF THE CRIME

(1) Public servant

(2) Under color of his office, employment, authority

(3) Knowingly deprive or conspire or attempt to deprive

(4) Any person

(5) Of a constitutional or statutory right

PENALTY

Misdemeanor, 1st degree (2929.21 to 2929.28, 2929.31)

Coercion—2905.12

ELEMENTS OF THE CRIME

(1) With a purpose to coerce another into

(2) Taking or refraining from action concerning which he has a legal freedom of choice

(3)(a) Threaten to commit any offense, or

(b) Utter or threaten any calumny against any person, or

(c) Expose or threaten to expose any matter tending

(i) To subject any person to hatred, contempt, or ridicule, or

(ii) To damage his personal or business repute, or

(iii) To impair his credit, or

(d) Institute or threaten criminal proceedings against any person, or

(e) Take or withhold, or threaten to take or to withhold official action, or cause or threaten to cause official action to be taken or withheld

DEFENSES

To (3)(c), (3)(d), (3)(e):

(1) Actor's conduct was reasonable response to circumstances which occasioned it, and his purpose was limited to:

(a) Compelling another to refrain from misconduct or to desist from further misconduct, or

(b) Prevent or redress a wrong or injustice, or

(c) Prevent another person from taking action for which the actor reasonably believed the other person was disqualified, or

(d) Compel another to take action which the actor reasonably believed the other person was under a duty to take.

(2) (3)(d) and (3)(e) not construed to prohibit prosecutor or court in good faith and in interests of justice from:

(a) Offering, agreeing to grant, or granting immunity from prosecution pursuant to 2945.44, or

(b) In return for guilty plea to one or more offenses charged, or to one or more lesser offenses, or in return for accused's testimony in case in which he is not party, offering, agreeing to dismiss or dismissing one or more pending charges, or offering or agreeing to impose, or imposing certain sentence or sentence modification, or

(c) Imposing probation on certain conditions without limitation requiring offender to make restitution or redress to victim of offense.

PENALTY

Misdemeanor, 2nd degree (2929.21 to 2929.28, 2929.31)

Coin Machines

See Theft-related Offenses—Making or Using Slugs; Theft-related Offenses—Tampering With Coin Machines

Communications, Disrupting

See Disrupting Public Services; Interception of Communications; Telephone Harassment

Compelling Prostitution

See Prostitution—Compelling

Complicity—2923.03

See also Conspiracy

ELEMENTS OF THE CRIME

(1) Acting with kind of culpability required to commit offense

(2)(a) Solicit or procure another to commit offense, or

(b) Aid or abet another to commit offense, or

(c) Conspire with another to commit offense violating 2923.01, or

(d) Cause innocent or irresponsible person to commit offense

DEFENSES

(1) No defense that no person with whom accused was in complicity has been convicted as principal offender.

(2) No conviction unless offense actually committed; but conviction for complicity in an attempt to commit an offense under 2923.02 is permissible.

(3) Prior to commission of or attempt to commit offense, actor ended complicity, under circumstances manifesting complete and voluntary renunciation of criminal purpose.

PENALTY

Same penalty as if one were principal offender. Complicity may be stated in terms of this section or in terms of principal offense.

Note: Person can be convicted of complicity on testimony of accomplice. 2923.03 sets forth specific instructions to be given to jury.

Compounding a Crime—2921.21

ELEMENTS OF THE CRIME

(1) Knowingly demand, accept, agree to accept anything of value

(2) In consideration of abandoning or agreeing to abandon pending criminal prosecution

DEFENSES

(1)(a) No crime if pending prosecution is for violation of 2913.02, 2913.11, 2913.21(B)(2), or 2913.47 of which actor under this section is victim, and

(b) Thing of value involved did not exceed amount which actor reasonably believed due him as restitution for loss caused by offense.

(2) When prosecuting witness abandons or agrees to abandon, state is not bound to abandon prosecution.

PENALTY

Misdemeanor, 1st degree (2929.21 to 2929.28, 2929.31)

Computer Systems, Unauthorized Access to

See Theft-related Offenses—Unauthorized Use of Property, Unauthorized Access to Computer Systems

Concealed Weapon, Carrying

See Weapons—Carrying Concealed Weapon

Conduct, Disorderly

See Disorderly Conduct Offenses, generally

Conducting Illegal Bingo Game

See Bingo—Conducting Illegal Bingo Game

Confidential Information—Confidentiality of Investigatory Work Product—2953.321

ELEMENTS OF THE CRIME

Division (A):

(1) Law enforcement officer or other person employed by a law enforcement agency

(2) Knowingly

(3) Release, disseminate, or otherwise make available or discuss

(4) Investigatory work product or any information contained in that work product

(5) To any person not employed by the employing law enforcement agency

Division (B):

(1) Law enforcement agency or person employed by the law enforcement agency which receives investigatory work product from another law enforcement agency under 2953.321(B)(3)

(2) Use work product for any purpose other than the investigation of the offense for which it was obtained from the other law enforcement agency

Division (C):

(1) Law enforcement agency or person employed by the law enforcement agency which receives investigatory work product from another law enforcement agency under 2953.321(B)(3)

(2) Disclose the name of the person who is the subject of the work product

EXCEPTION

Division (C) is not applicable to the disclosure when it is necessary for the conduct of the investigation of the offense, or the prosecution of the person for committing the offense, for which the work product was obtained from the other law enforcement agency.

PENALTY

Misdemeanor, 4th degree (2929.21 to 2929.28, 2929.31)

Confidential Information—Disclosure of Confidential Information—2921.24

ELEMENTS OF THE CRIME

(1) Officer or employee of a law enforcement agency or court, or of the office of the clerk of any court

(2) During the pendency of any criminal case

(3) Disclose the home address of any peace officer as defined in 2935.01 who is a witness or arresting officer in the case

Note: The court in which any criminal case is pending may order the disclosure of the home address of any peace officer who is a witness or arresting officer in the case if the court determines after a written request for the disclosure that good cause exists.

PENALTY

Misdemeanor, 4th degree (2929.21 to 2929.28, 2929.31)

Confidential Information—Unlawful Disclosure of DNA Database Information

See DNA—Unlawful Disclosure of DNA Database Information

Consent Agreement, Violating

See Protection Order—Violating Protection Order or Consent Agreement

Conspiracy—2923.01

See also Complicity; Corrupt Activity—Engaging in a Pattern of

ELEMENTS OF THE CRIME

(1) With purpose

(2) To commit, promote, facilitate commission of aggravated murder or murder, kidnapping, compelling or promoting prostitution, aggravated arson or arson, aggravated robbery or robbery, aggravated burglary or burglary, engaging in a pattern of corrupt activity, corrupting another with drugs, a felony drug trafficking, manufacturing, processing or possession offense, theft of drugs, or illegal processing of drug documents, commission of a felony offense of unauthorized use of vehicle or trafficking in marihuana, or commission of violation of any provision of Chapter 3734., except 3734.18, that relates to hazardous waste

(3)(a) With another person or persons, plan or aid in planning commission of the specified offenses, or

(b) Agree with another person or persons that one or more will engage in conduct facilitating commission of the specified offenses

PROOF

(1) No conviction unless substantial overt act in furtherance of conspiracy alleged and proved to have been done by the accused or person with whom the accused conspired, subsequent to accused's entrance into conspiracy; overt act is substantial when it manifests a purpose on part of actor that object of conspiracy should be completed.

(2) Offender knows or has reasonable cause to believe person the offender is conspiring with, has or is conspiring with another to commit same offense, offender guilty of conspiring with other person, even if identity of other person unknown to offender.

DEFENSES

(1) No defense that, in retrospect, commission of offense which was object of conspiracy impossible under circumstances.

(2) Conspiracy ends when offenses which are its objects are committed, or abandoned by all conspirators.

(3) No defense, in absence of abandonment, that no offense which was object of conspiracy was committed.

(4) Only one conspiracy when conspiring to commit more than one offense, if all the offenses are the object of same agreement or a continuous conspiratorial relationship.

(5) Conviction of committing or attempting to commit specific offense, or of complicity in commission or attempt to commit such offense, bars conviction of conspiracy to commit same offense; however, offender may be convicted of engaging in pattern of corrupt activity in violation of 2923.32 and also of conspiracy to violate that section (2923.32(B)(1)).

(6)(a) No conviction on uncorroborated testimony of person with whom the defendant conspired.

(b) If testimony of person with whom one conspired is corroborated, specific instructions to jury are outlined in section.

(7) After conspiring to commit offense, actor thwarted success of conspiracy under circumstances manifesting complete and voluntary renunciation of his criminal purpose.

(8) After conspiring to commit offense, actor abandoned conspiracy prior to commission or attempt to commit any offense which was object of conspiracy:

(a) By advising all other conspirators of his abandonment, or

(b) By informing any law enforcement authority of existence of conspiracy and of his participation therein.

PENALTY

If object is aggravated murder, murder, or an offense for which the maximum penalty is imprisonment for life, Felony, 1st degree (2929.11 to 2929.18, 2929.31)

If the most serious offense that is object of the conspiracy is a felony of 1st, 2nd, 3rd or 4th degree, then conspiracy is a felony of next lesser degree than the most serious offense that is the object of the conspiracy.

If the most serious offense that is object of the conspiracy is 5th degree felony, Misdemeanor, 1st degree (2929.21 to 2929.28, 2929.31)

If offense that is object of the conspiracy is violation of Chapter 3734., except 3734.18, that relates to hazardous waste:

Imprisonment: not more than 18 months, and/or

Fine: not more than $25,000

If offense that is object of the conspiracy is engaging in a pattern of corrupt activity, offender is subject to fine, forfeiture provisions of 2923.32(B)(2), (3), (4), and (5) in addition to penalties imposed by 2929.11 to 2929.18.

Contaminating Substances for Human Consumption or Use—2927.24(B)

ELEMENTS OF THE CRIME

Division (A):

(1) Knowingly

(2) Mingle a poison, hazardous chemical, biological, or radioactive substance, or other harmful substance

(3) With a food, drink, nonprescription drug, prescription drug, or pharmaceutical product

(4) Knowing or having reason to know that the food, drink, drug or product may be ingested or used by another

Division (B):

(1) Knowingly

(2) Place a poison, hazardous chemical, biological, or radioactive substance, or other harmful substance

(3) In a spring, well, reservoir, or public water supply

(4) Knowing or having reason to know that the water may be ingested or used by another

Division (C):

(1) Knowingly

(2) (a) Release into the air

(b) Leave in any public place

(c) Expose one or more persons to

(3) Any hazardous chemical, biological, or radioactive substance

(4) With intent to cause or create a risk of death or serious physical harm to any person

DEFENSES

(1) Person does not know or have reason to know water may be ingested or used by another if it is disposed of as waste into a household drain, including the drain of a toilet, sink, tub, or floor.

(2) Person may place poison or harmful substance into spring, well, reservoir or public water supply if necessary to treat water to make it safe for human consumption and use.

(3) Person may mingle drug with food or drink to allow drug to be ingested in quantity described by its labeling or prescription.

(4) Provisions not to be applied so as to conflict with state or federal law or rule related to substances permitted to be applied to or present in any food or beverage.

PENALTY

Felony, 1st Degree (2929.11 to 2929.18, 2929.31)

Note: If the amount of poison, hazardous chemical, biological, or radioactive substance, or other harmful substance is sufficient to cause death to persons who are exposed to it, or if the offense resulted in serious physical harm to another person, mandatory imprisonment for life with parole eligibility after 15 years imprisonment.

Contamination—Spreading False Report of

See Poisons—Spreading False Report of Contamination

Contraband—Possession or Conveyance of Contraband; When Watercraft,Motor Vehicle, or Aircraft Considered Contraband— 2933.42

ELEMENTS OF THE CRIME

(1)(a) Possess

(b) Conceal

(c) Transport

(d) Receive

(e) Purchase

(f) Sell

(g) Lease

(h) Rent

(i) Otherwise transfer

(2) Contraband

PROOF

Illegal possession is proved by showing that the actor knowingly procured or received the thing possessed or was aware of his control for a sufficient time to end his possession. 2901.21(c)(1).

Rebuttably presumed that watercraft, motor vehicle, aircraft, or other personal property in or on which contraband is found at time of seizure has been, is being, or is intended to be used in violation of this section.

PENALTY

If the underlying offense involved in the violation of division (A) of this section is a felony, seizure and forfeiture pursuant to 2933.43

Note: This section to be liberally construed to effectuate intent of General Assembly that the contraband and forfeiture provisions apply to property possessed, or possessed and owned, by persons under 18 years of age in the same manner as they apply to the property of adults. The terms "offense," "criminal violation," "criminal case," "felony," and similar terms shall thus be construed to include acts performed by juveniles that, if committed by an adult, would be within the meaning of those terms.

Contract, Public, Unlawful Interest in

See Public Officials—Having Unlawful Interest in a Public Contract

Conveyance or Possession of Deadly Weapons or Dangerous Ordnance on School Premises

See Weapons—Conveyance or Possession of Deadly Weapons or Dangerous Ordnance on School Premises

Corpse, Abuse of

See Abortion—Abortion Trafficking; Offenses Against Human Corpse

Corrupt Activity—Criminal Gang Activity—2923.42

ELEMENTS OF THE CRIME

(1) Active participation in a criminal gang

(2) Knowing that the criminal gang engages in or has engaged in a pattern of criminal gang activity

(3) With the purpose to

(a) promote criminal conduct

(b) further criminal conduct, or

(c) assist criminal conduct

PENALTY

Violation is a Felony, 2nd degree (2929.11 to 2929.18, 2929.31).

Note: For purposes of this section, criminal conduct is defined in 2923.41(C).

Note: Prosecution under this section does not preclude a prosecution under any other section of the code.

Corrupt Activity—Engaging in a Pattern of—2923.32

ELEMENTS OF THE CRIME

Division (A)(1):

(1) While employed by or associated with any enterprise

(2) Conduct or participate in, directly, or indirectly, the affairs of an enterprise through

(a) a pattern of corrupt activity, or

(b) the collection of an unlawful debt

Division (A)(2):

(1) Through

(a) a pattern of corrupt activity, or

(b) the collection of an unlawful debt

(2) Acquire or maintain, directly or indirectly

(a) any interest in any enterprise or real property, or

(b) control of any enterprise or real property

Division (A)(3):

(1) Having knowingly received any proceeds derived, directly or indirectly, from

(a) a pattern of corrupt activity, or

(b) the collection of any unlawful debt

(2) Use or invest, directly or indirectly, any part of those proceeds, or any proceeds derived from the use or investment of any of those proceeds, in

(a) the acquisition of any title to, or any right, interest, or equity in, real property, or

(b) the establishment or operation of any enterprise

EXCEPTION

A purchase of securities on the open market with intent to make an investment, without intent to control or participate in the control of the issuer, and without intent to assist another to do so is not a violation of (3) above, if the securities of the issuer held after the purchase by the purchaser, the members of the purchaser's immediate family, and the purchaser's or the immediate family members' accomplices in any pattern of corrupt activity or the collection of an unlawful debt do not aggregate one per cent of the outstanding securities of any one class of the issuer and do not confer, in law or in fact, the power to elect one or more directors of the issuer.

PENALTY

Felony, 2nd degree (2929.11 to 2929.18, 2929.31)

If one of the incidents of corrupt activity is a 1st, 2nd, or 3rd degree felony, aggravated murder, or murder committed prior to 7–1–96 and that would constitute a 1st, 2nd, or 3rd degree felony, aggravated murder or murder following the effective date or if one of the incidents is a felony under the law of the United States or any other state, that would constitute a 1st, 2nd, or 3rd degree felony, aggravated murder or murder, in Ohio, Felony, 1st degree (2929.11 to 2929.18, 2929.31)

Penalty in addition to that imposed by 2929.11 to 2929.18 where a person derives pecuniary value or causes property damage, personal injury other than pain and suffering, or other loss through or by engaging in a pattern of corrupt activity:

(1) Fine not exceeding the greater of three times the gross value gained or three times the gross loss caused;

(2) Payment of court costs;

(3) Payment to the state, municipal, or county law enforcement agencies that handled the investigation and prosecution of the reasonable costs of investigation and prosecution.

Criminal forfeiture:

(1) Upon conviction of engaging in a pattern of corrupt activity

(2) Where

(a) The indictment or information alleges the extent of the property subject to forfeiture, or

(b) The sentence requires the forfeiture of property that was not reasonably foreseen to be subject to forfeiture at the time of the indictment or information, provided that the prosecuting attorney gave prompt notice to the defendant of such property not reasonably foreseen to be subject to forfeiture when it is discovered to be forfeitable.

(3) A person must criminally forfeit to the state, under court order, any personal or real property in which the person has an interest and that was used in the course of, intended for use in the course of, derived from, or realized through, conduct in violation of 2923.32, including any property constituting an interest in, means of control over, or influence over the enterprise involved in the violation and any property constituting proceeds derived from the violation, including all of the following:

(a) Any position, office, appointment, tenure, commission, or employment contract of any kind acquired or maintained by the person in violation of 2923.32, through which the person, in violation of 2923.32, conducted or participated in the conduct of an enterprise, or that afforded the person a source of influence or control over an enterprise that he exercised in violation of 2923.32;

(b) Any compensation, right, or benefit derived from a position, office, appointment, tenure, commission, or employment contract described in (3)(a) above that accrued to the person in violation of 2923.32 during the period of the pattern of corrupt activity;

(c) Any interest in, security of, claim against, or property or contractual right affording the person a source of influence or control over, the affairs of an enterprise that the person exercised in violation of 2923.32;

(d) Any amount payable or paid under any contract for goods or services that was awarded or performed in violation of 2923.32.

Note: A person may be convicted of violating the provisions of this section as well as of a conspiracy to violate one or more of the provisions of this section under 2923.01.

Note: The forfeiture provisions of this section also apply to juveniles who are adjudicated delinquent by reason of a violation of this section. A disposition of criminal forfeiture ordered in relation to such a delinquent child does not preclude the application of any other order or disposition under 2151.35, or any other civil remedy.

Corrupting Another With Drugs

See Drug Offenses—Corrupting Another With Drugs

Corrupting Sports

See Sports—Corrupting

Corruption of a Minor

See Juveniles—Corruption of a Minor

Court Clerks—Disclosure of Confidential Information

See Confidential Information—Disclosure of Confidential Information

Credit Card—Misuse

See Theft-related Offenses—Misuse of Credit Card; also Theft-related Offenses—Defrauding Creditors

Creditors, Defrauding

See Theft-related Offenses—Defrauding Creditors

Crime, Compounding

See Compounding a Crime

Crime, Failure to Report

See Failure to Report Felony or Certain Suspicious Circumstances

Criminal Abortion

See Abortion—Abortion Manslaughter

Criminal Damaging or Endangering—2909.06

ELEMENTS OF THE CRIME

(1) Cause or create substantial risk of physical harm to any property of another without the other person's consent

(2)(a) Knowingly, by any means, or

(b) Recklessly, by fire, explosion, flood, poison gas, poison, radioactive material, caustic or corrosive material, other inherently dangerous agency or substance.

PENALTY

If Division (A)(1), (2), (3), (4), or (5), Misdemeanor, 2nd degree (2929.21 to 2929.28, 2929.31)

If violation creates risk of physical harm to any person, Misdemeanor, 1st degree (2929.21 to 2929.28, 2929.31)

If property involved in violation is an aircraft, aircraft engine, propeller, appliance, spare part, or any other equipment or implement used or intended to be used in the operation of an aircraft and if the violation creates a risk of physical harm to any person or if the property involved is occupied aircraft, Felony, 5th degree (2929.11 to 2929.18, 2929.31)

If property involved in violation is an aircraft, aircraft engine, propeller, appliance, spare part, or any other equipment or implement used or intended to be used in the operation of an aircraft and if the violation creates a substantial risk of physical harm to any person or if the property involved is occupied aircraft, Felony, 4th degree (2929.11 to 2929.18, 2929.31)

A defendant who is convicted of or pleads guilty to committing, attempting to commit, or complicity in committing a violation of 2909.06 when the means used are fire or explosion shall be required to reimburse agencies for their investigation or prosecution costs in accordance with 2929.28. (2929.21(A))

Criminally Usurious Transaction—2905.22

ELEMENTS OF THE CRIME

Division (A):

(1) Knowingly

(2) Make or participate in extortionate extension of credit

Division (B):

(1) Knowingly

(2) Engage in criminal usury

Division (C):

(1) Possess any writing, paper, instrument or article used to record criminally usurious transaction

(2) Knowing contents record a criminally usurious transaction

PENALTY

If Divisions (A) and (B) violated, Felony, 4th degree (2929.11 to 2929.18, 2929.31)

If Division (C) violated, Misdemeanor, 1st degree (2929.21 to 2929.28,2929.31)

Criminal Mischief—2909.07

ELEMENTS OF THE CRIME

Division (A)(1):

(1) Without privilege to do so

(2) Knowingly

(3) Move, deface, damage, destroy, or otherwise improperly tamper with property of another

Division (A)(2):

(1) With purpose to interfere with use or enjoyment of property of another

(2) Employ tear gas device, stink bomb, smoke generator, other device releasing a substance harmful or offensive to persons exposed, or that tends to cause public alarm

Division (A)(3):

(1) Without privilege to do so

(2) Knowingly

(3) Move, deface, damage, destroy, or otherwise improperly tamper with bench mark, triangulation station, boundary marker, other survey station, monument, marker

Division (A)(4):

(1) Without privilege to do so

(2) Knowingly

(3) Move, deface, damage, destroy, or otherwise improperly tamper with any safety device, property of another or the offender, when required or placed for safety of others

(4) So as to destroy or diminish its effectiveness or availability for intended purpose

Division (A)(5):

(1) With purpose to interfere with the use or enjoyment of the property of another

(2)(a) Set a fire on the land of another, or

(b) Place personal property that had been set on fire on the land of another

(3) Fire or personal property is outside and apart from any building, other structure, or personal property that is on that land

Division (A)(6):

(1) Without privilege to do so

(2) With purpose to impair functioning of any computer, computer system, computer network, computer network, computer software, or computer program

(3) Knowingly

(4)(a) In any manner or by any means alter, damage, destroy, or modify

(b) Introduce a computer containment

(5) Into a computer, computer system, computer network, computer software, or computer program

PENALTY

Misdemeanor, 3rd degree (2929.21 to 2929.28, 2929.31)

If violation creates risk of physical harm to any person, Misdemeanor, 1st degree (2929.21 to 2929.28, 2929.31)

If the property involved in violation is aircraft, aircraft engine, propeller, appliance, spare part, fuel, lubricant, hydraulic fluid, any other equipment, implement or material used or intended to be used in the operation of an aircraft, or any cargo carried or intended to be carried in an aircraft and if the violation creates a risk of physical harm to any person or if the property involved is an occupied aircraft, Felony, 5th degree (2929.11 to 2929.18, 2929.31)

If the property involved in violation is aircraft, aircraft engine, propeller, appliance, spare part, fuel, lubricant, hydraulic fluid, any other equipment, implement or material used or intended to be used in the operation of an aircraft, or any cargo carried or intended to be carried in an aircraft and if the violation creates a substantial risk of physical harm to any person or if the property involved is an occupied aircraft, Felony, 4th degree (2929.11 to 2929.18, 2929.31)

If Division (A)(6), Misdemeanor, 1st degree. (2929.21 to 2929.28, 2929.31) Felony, 5th degree, if (1) value of computer, computer system, computer network, computer software, computer program or data, or loss to victim is more than $1,000 and less than $10,000, or (2) if computer, . . . is used or intended to be used in the operation of aircraft an the violation creates risk of physical harm to any person. Felony, 4th degree, if (1) value of computer is $10,000 or more, or (2) if computer is used or intended to be used in the operation of an aircraft and the violation creates substantial harm to any person, or if the aircraft is occupied.

Criminal Simulation

See Theft-related Offenses—Criminal Simulation

Criminal Tools—Possessing—2923.24

See also Burglary—Burglary

ELEMENTS OF THE CRIME

(1) Possess or have under control

(2) Any substance, device, instrument, or article

(3) With purpose to use criminally

PROOF

Prima facie evidence of criminal purpose:

(1) Possession or control of any dangerous ordnance, or materials or parts for making same, in absence of circumstances indicating intent for legitimate use.

(2) Possession or control of any substance, device, instrument, article designed or specially adapted for criminal use, or commonly used for criminal purposes, under circumstances indicating intent to use criminally.

PENALTY

Misdemeanor, 1st degree (2929.21 to 2929.28, 2929.31)

If the circumstances indicate that the substance, device, instrument or article involved in the offense was intended for use in the commission of a felony, Felony, 5th degree (2929.11 to 2929.18, 2929.31)

Criminal Trespass

See Trespass—Criminal Trespass

Crowd Control

See Disorderly Conduct Offenses—Crowd Control

Custody, Interference With

See Domestic Offenses—Interference with Custody

Damaging, Criminal

See Criminal Damaging or Endangering

Dangerous Drugs

See Drug Offenses, generally

Dangerous Ordnance

See Weapons, generally

Denying Access to a Computer

See Computers—Denying Access to

Dependents, Nonsupport

See Domestic Offenses—Nonsupport of Dependents

Dereliction of Duty—2921.44

ELEMENTS OF THE CRIME

Division (A):

(1) Law enforcement officer

(2) Negligently

(3)(a) Fails to serve lawful warrant without delay, or

(b) Fails to prevent or halt commission of offense or apprehend offender, when in his power to do so alone or with available assistance

Division (B):

(1) Law enforcement, ministerial, judicial officer

(2) Negligently

(3) Fails to perform lawful duty in criminal case or proceeding

Division (C):

(1) Officer in charge of detention facility

(2) Negligently

(3)(a) Allows facility to become littered or unsanitary, or

(b) Fails to provide confined persons with adequate food, clothing, bedding, shelter, medical attention, or

(c) Fails to control unruly prisoner, or prevent intimidation or physical harm to prisoner by another, or

(d) Allows prisoner to escape, or

(e) Fails to observe any lawful and reasonable regulation for management of facility

Division (D):

(1) Public official of state

(2) Recklessly

(3) Creates deficiency, incurs liability, expends greater sum than is appropriated by General Assembly for use in any one year of department, agency or institution of the state with which public official connected

Division (E):

(1) Public servant

(2) Recklessly

(3)(a) Fails to perform duty expressly imposed by law with respect to his office, or

(b) Does any act expressly forbidden by law with respect to his office.

PENALTY

Misdemeanor, 2nd degree (2929.21 to 2929.28, 2929.31)

Desecration—2927.11

See also Vandalism

ELEMENTS OF THE CRIME

(1) Without privilege to do so

(2) Purposely deface, damage, pollute, physically mistreat

(3)(a) United States or Ohio flag, or

(b) Public monument, or

(c) Historical or commemorative marker, any structure, Indian mound or earthwork, cemetery thing, or site of great historical or archaeological interest, or

(d) Place of worship, its furnishings or religious artifacts, or sacred texts within the place of worship or its grounds, or

(e) Work of art or museum piece, or

(f) Any object of reverence or sacred devotion

PENALTY

If violation includes elements (3)(a), (b), (c), (e), (f), Misdemeanor, 2nd degree (2929.21 to 2929.28, 2929.31)

If violation includes element (d), Felony, 5th degree, and punishable in addition to penalties for fifth degree felonies, fine of $2500 if physical harm is less than $5,000; if physical harm is $5,000 or more but less than $100,000, Felony, 4th degree; if physical harm to property is more than $100,000, Felony, 3rd degree (2929.11 to 2929.18, 2929.21 to 2929.28, 2929.31)

Detention Facilities, Illegal Conveyance of Certain Items Onto Detention/Mental Health Facility Grounds

See Illegal Conveyance of Certain Items Onto Detention/Mental Health Facility Grounds

Disability—Having Weapon

See Weapons—Having While Under Disability

Discrimination—Housing

See Housing—Injuring, Intimidating, or Interfering With

Disorderly Conduct Offenses—Crowd Control—2917.40

ELEMENTS OF THE CRIME

Division (A):

(1) Sell, offer to sell, or offer in return for a donation

(2) Any ticket that is not numbered and that does not correspond to a specific seat for admission to either of the following:

(a) A live entertainment performance that is not exempted under Division (D) of section 2917.40, that is held in a restricted entertainment area, and for which more than 8,000 tickets are offered to the public.

(b) A concert that is not exempted under division (D) of section 2917.40 and for which more than 3,000 tickets are offered to the public.

Division (B):

(1) Advertise

(2) Any live entertainment performance as described in (A)(2)(a) or any concert as described in (A)(2)(b) of this section

(3) Unless the advertisement contains the words,"Reserved Seats Only."

Division (C):

(1) Owner or operator of any restricted entertainment area

(2) Fail to open, maintain, and properly staff

(3) At least the number of entrances designated under 2917.40(E) of the Revised Code

(4) For a minimum of 90 minutes prior to the scheduled start of any live entertainment performance

(5) Held in a restricted entertainment area

(6) For which more than 3,000 tickets are sold, offered for sale, or offered in return for a donation

Division (D):

(1) Enter into contract

(2) For a live entertainment performance

(3) That does not permit or require compliance with section 2917.40

EXCEPTION

A live entertainment performance, other than a concert, is exempted from the provisions of Divisions (A), (B), and (C) of this section if both of the following apply:

(a) The restricted entertainment area in which the performance is held has at least eight entrances or, if both entrances and separate admission turnstyles or similar devices are used, has at least eight turnstyles or similar devices, and

(b) The eight entrances or, if applicable, the eight turnstyles or similar devices are opened, maintained, and properly staffed at least one hour prior to the scheduled start of the performance.

DEFENSES

(1) This section does not apply to a live entertainment performance held in a restricted entertainment area if one admission ticket entitles the holder to view or participate in three or more different games, rides, activities, or live entertainment performances occurring simultaneously at different sites within the restricted entertainment area and if the initial admittance entrance to the restricted entertainment area, for which the ticket is required, is separate from the entrance to any specific live entertainment performance and an additional ticket is not required for admission to the particular live entertainment performance.

(2) This section does not apply to a symphony orchestra performance, a ballet performance, horse races, dances, or fairs.

PENALTY

Misdemeanor, 1st degree (2929.21 to 2929.28, 2929.31)

If any individual suffers physical harm to their person as a result of a violation of this section, the sentencing court shall consider this factor in favor of imposing a term of imprisonment upon the offender.

Disorderly Conduct Offenses—Disorderly Conduct—2917.11

ELEMENTS OF THE CRIME

Division (A):

(1) Recklessly cause

(2) Inconvenience, annoyance or alarm to another by

(3)(a) Fighting, threatening harm to persons or property, violent or turbulent behavior, or

(b) Making unreasonable noise or offensively coarse utterance, gesture, display; or communicating unwarranted and grossly abusive language to anyone, or

(c) Insulting, taunting, challenging another, under circumstances in which conduct likely to provoke violent response, or

(d) Hindering or preventing movement of persons on public street, road, highway, or right-of-way, or to, from, within, or on public or private property, so as to interfere with rights of others, by any act which serves no lawful and reasonable purpose of offender, or

(e) Creating condition physically offensive or which presents risk of physical harm to persons or property, by act serving no lawful and reasonable purpose of offender

Division (B):

(1) While voluntarily intoxicated

(2)(a)(i) In public place or in presence of 2 or more persons

(ii) Engage in conduct likely to be offensive or cause inconvenience, alarm, or annoyance to persons of ordinary sensibilities, which conduct, if offender were not intoxicated, should know is likely to have that effect, or

(b) Engage in conduct or create condition of risk of physical harm to himself or another, or to property of another

EXCEPTION

Violation of any statute or ordinance of which an element is operating motor vehicle, locomotive, watercraft, aircraft, or other vehicle while under influence of alcohol or drug of abuse, is not violation of Division (B).

PENALTY

Minor Misdemeanor (2929.21 to 2929.28, 2929.31)

Misdemeanor, 4th degree (2929.21 to 2929.28, 2929.31) if (a) offender persists in disorderly conduct after reasonable warning or request to desist; (b) offense committed in vicinity of a school or in a school safety zone; (c) offense committed in presence of any law enforcement officer, firefighter, rescuer, medical person, EMS person, or other authorized person engaged in duties at scene of a fire, accident, disaster, riot, or emergency of any kind; or (d) offense committed in presence of any emergency facility person engaged in duties in an emergency facility.

Disorderly Conduct Offenses—Disturbing a Lawful Meeting— 2917.12

ELEMENTS OF THE CRIME

(1) Purpose to prevent or disrupt

(2) Lawful meeting, procession, gathering

(3)(a) Do any act which obstructs or interferes with due conduct of such meeting, procession, or gathering, or

(b) Make any utterance, gesture, display which outrages sensibilities of the group

PENALTY

Misdemeanor, 4th degree (2929.21 to 2929.28, 2929.31)

Disorderly Conduct Offenses—Failure to Disperse—2917.04

ELEMENTS OF THE CRIME

(1) Where 5 or more persons participating

(2) In disorderly conduct violating 2917.11

(3) Other persons in vicinity whose presence creates likelihood of:

(a) Physical harm to persons or property, or

(b) Serious public inconvenience, annoyance, or alarm

(4) Law enforcement officer or other public official orders participants and others to disperse

(5) Knowingly fail to obey such order

EXCEPTION

Persons peaceably assembled for lawful purpose need not disperse

PENALTY

Minor Misdemeanor (2929.21 to 2929.28, 2929.31)

If offense creates the likelihood of physical harm to persons or is committed at the scene of a fire, accident, disaster, riot, or emergency of any kind, Misdemeanor, 4th degree (2929.21 to 2929.28, 2929.31)

Disorderly Conduct Offenses—Inciting to Violence—2917.01

ELEMENTS OF THE CRIME

(1) Knowingly engage in conduct

(2) Designed to urge or incite another

(3) To commit any offense of violence, when it takes place under circumstances that:

(a) The conduct creates a clear and present danger that any offense of violence will be committed, or

(b) The conduct proximately results in commission of offense of violence

PENALTY

If the offense of violence that the other person is being urged or incited to commit is a misdemeanor, Misdemeanor, 1st degree (2929.21 to 2929.28, 2929.31)

If the offense of violence that the other person is being urged or incited to commit is a felony, Felony, 3rd degree (2929.11 to 2929.18,2929.31)

Disorderly Conduct Offenses—Inducing Panic—2917.31

ELEMENTS OF THE CRIME

(1)(a) Cause evacuation of public place, by, or

(b) Cause serious public inconvenience or alarm, by

(2)(a) Initiating or circulating report or warning of alleged or impending fire, explosion, crime, other catastrophe, knowing it to be false, or

(b) Threatening to commit any offense of violence, or

(c) Committing offense with reckless disregard of likelihood that commission will cause serious public inconvenience or alarm

EXCEPTION

Inapplicable to any person conducting authorized fire or emergency drill.

PROSECUTION NOTES

It is *not* a defense to a charge involving purported or threatened use of a weapon of mass destruction that the offender did not possess or have the ability to use a weapon of mass destruction or that which was represented to be a weapon of mass destruction was not such a weapon.

Any act which is a violation of this section and any other section may be prosecuted under this section, the other section or both.

PENALTY

Misdemeanor, 1st degree (2929.21 to 2929.28, 2929.31)

If violation results in physical harm to anyone, Felony, 4th degree (2929.11 to 2929.18, 2929.31)

If violation results in economic harm of $500 but less than $5,000, Felony, 4th degree; if economic harm is $5,000 but less than $100,000, Felony, 3rd degree; if economic harm is $100,000 or more, Felony, 2nd degree (2929.11 to 2929.18, 2929.31)

If the public place in 1(a) is a school, Felony, 4th degree (2929.11 to 2929.18, 2929.31)

If the public place in 1(a) is a school and the offense results in physical harm to any person, Felony 3rd degree (2929.11 to 2929.18, 2929.31)

If the public place in 1(a) is a school, and the violation pertains to a purported, threatened, or actual use of a weapon of mass destruction, and if the violation results in physical harm to any person, Felony, 2nd degree (2929.11 to 2929.18, 2929.31)

If the public place in 1(a) is a school, and the violation pertains to a purported, threatened, or actual use of a weapon of mass destruction, and the violation results in economic harm of $5,000 or more but less than $100,000, Felony, 3rd degree (2929.11 to 2929.18, 2929.31)

If the public place in 1(a) is a school, and the violation pertains to a purported, threatened, or actual use of a weapon of mass destruction, and the violation results in economic harm of $100,000 or more, Felony, 2nd degree (2929.11 to 2929.18, 2929.31)

If the violation pertains to a purported, threatened, or actual use of a weapon of mass destruction, Felony, 4th degree (2929.11 to 2929.18, 2929.31)

If the violation pertains to a purported, threatened, or actual use of a weapon of mass destruction and the violation results in physical harm to any person, Felony, 3rd degree (2929.11 to 2929.18, 2929.31)

If the violation pertains to a purported, threatened, or actual use of a weapon of mass destruction and the violation results in economic harm of $100,000 or more, Felony, 3rd degree (2929.11 to 2929.18, 2929.31)

Note: For calculation of economic harm see 2917.31(E)(1).

Disorderly Conduct Offenses—Making False Alarms—2917.32

ELEMENTS OF THE CRIME

Division (A):

(1) Initiate or circulate report or warning of alleged or impending fire, explosion, crime, or other catastrophe

(2) Knowing it to be false and likely to cause public inconvenience or alarm

Division (B):

(1) Knowingly cause

(2) False alarm of fire or other emergency

(3) To be transmitted to or within any public or private organization

(4) For dealing with emergencies involving risk of physical harm to persons or property

Division (C):

(1) Report to any law enforcement agency

(2) Alleged offense or other incident within its concern

(3) Knowing such offense did not occur

EXCEPTION

Inapplicable to anyone conducting authorized fire or emergency drill.

PROSECUTION NOTES

It is *not* a defense to a charge involving purported or threatened use of a weapon of mass destruction that the offender did not possess or have the ability to use a weapon of mass destruction or that which was represented to be a weapon of mass destruction was not such a weapon.

Any act which is a violation of this section and any other section may be prosecuted under this section, the other section or both.

PENALTY

Misdemeanor, 1st degree (2929.21 to 2929.28, 2929.31)

If violation results in economic harm of $500 but less than $5,000, Felony, 5th degree; if economic harm is $5,000 but less than $100,000, Felony, 4th degree; if economic harm is $100,000 or more, Felony, 3rd degree. (2929.11 to 2929.18, 2929.31)

If violation pertains to a purported, threatened, or actual use of a weapon of mass destruction, Felony, 3rd degree. (2929.11 to 2929.18,2929.31)

Note: For calculation of economic harm see 2917.31(E)(1).

Disorderly Conduct Offenses—Misconduct at an Emergency—2917.13

ELEMENTS OF THE CRIME

(1) Knowingly

(2)(a) Hamper lawful operations of any law enforcement officer, firefighter, rescuer, medical person, EMS person, or other authorized person engaged in duties at fire, accident, disaster, riot, or emergency of any kind, or

(b) Hamper lawful activities of any emergency facility person engaged in duties in an emergency facility.

(c) Fail to obey lawful order of any law enforcement officer engaged in duties at scene or in connection with fire, accident, disaster, riot, or emergency of any kind

EXCEPTION

Not to limit access or deny information to any news media representative in the lawful exercise of his duties.

PENALTY

Misdemeanor, 4th degree (2929.21 to 2929.28, 2929.31)

If violation creates risk of physical harm to persons or property, Misdemeanor, 1st degree (2929.21 to 2929.28, 2929.31)

Disorderly Conduct Offenses—Misconduct Involving a Public Transportation System—2917.41

ELEMENTS OF THE CRIME

Division (A):

(1) Evade payment

(2) Of the known fares

(3) Of a public transportation system

Division (B):

(1) Alter

(2)(a) Transfer

(b) Pass

(c) Ticket

(d) Token

(3) Of a public transportation system

(4) With purpose to

(5)(a) Evade payment of fares, or

(b) Defraud the system

Division (C):

(1) While in any facility or on any vehicle of a public transportation system

(2)(a) Play sound equipment without the proper use of a private earphone

(b) Smoke, eat, or drink in any area where the activity is clearly marked as prohibited

(c) Expectorate upon a person, facility or vehicle

Division (D):

(1)(a) Write on

(b) Deface

(c) Draw on

(d) Otherwise mark

(2) Any facility or vehicle of a public transportation system

Division (E):

(1) Fail to comply

(2) With a lawful order of a public transportation system police officer;

or,

(3)(a) Resist

(b) Obstruct

(c) Abuse

(4) A public transportation police officer in the performance of the officer's duties

PENALTY

If Divisions (A), (B), or (E) violated, Misdemeanor, 4th degree (2929.21 to 2929.28, 2929.31)

If Division (C) violated, Minor Misdemeanor. If previously convicted of any division or substantially similar municipal ordinance, Misdemeanor, 4th degree.

If Division (D) violated, Misdemeanor, 3rd degree (2929.21 to 2929.28, 2929.31)

Disrupting Public Services—2909.04

See also Interception of Communications

ELEMENTS OF THE CRIME

Division (A):

(1)(a) Purposely, by any means, or

(b) Knowingly by damaging or tampering with any property

(2)(a) Interrupt or impair:

(i) TV, radio, telephone, telegraph, or other mass communications service, or

(ii) Police, fire, other public service communications, or

(iii) Radar, loran, radio, other electronic aids to air or marine navigation or communications, or

(iv) Amateur or citizens band radio communications being used for public service or emergency communications, or

(b) Interrupt or impair public transportation, including school bus transportation, water supply, gas, power, other utility service to public, or

(c) Substantially impair ability of law enforcement officers, firefighters, rescue personnel, EMS personnel, or emergency facility personnel to respond to emergency or to protect and preserve any person or property from serious physical harm

Division (B):

(1) Knowingly

(2) Use

(3)(a) Computer

(b) Computer system

(c) Compute network

(d) Telecommunications device or system

(e) Internet

(4) Thereby

(a) Disrupting

(b) Interrupting

(c) Impairing

(5) Any police, fire, educational, commercial, or governmental operations.

PENALTY

Felony, 4th degree (2929.11 to 2929.18, 2929.31)

DNA—Unlawful Disclosure of DNA Database Information—109.573(G)(1)

ELEMENTS OF THE CRIME

(1) Knowingly

(2) Because of the person's employment or official position

(3)(a) Disclose a DNA specimen, record, or other information contained in the DNA database, or to any person or agency not entitled to receive it, or

(b) Otherwise misuse the specimen, record, or information

PENALTY

Misdemeanor, 1st degree (2929.21 to 2929.28, 2929.31)

DNA—Unlawful Possession of DNA Database Information—109.573(G)(2)

ELEMENTS OF THE CRIME

(1) Purposely

(2) Obtain information contained in the DNA database that identifies an individual person

(3) Without proper authorization or privilege

PENALTY

Misdemeanor, 1st degree (2929.21 to 2929.28, 2929.31)

Domestic Offenses

See also Juveniles, generally

Domestic Offenses—Bigamy—2919.01

ELEMENTS OF THE CRIME

(1) Married person

(2) Marry another or continue to cohabit with such person in this state

DEFENSE

Actor's spouse continuously absent for 5 years immediately preceding purported subsequent marriage, and not known by actor to be alive within that time.

PENALTY

Misdemeanor, 1st degree (2929.21 to 2929.28, 2929.31)

Domestic Offenses—Domestic Violence—2919.25

ELEMENTS OF THE CRIME

Division (A):

(1) Knowingly

(2) Cause or attempt to cause physical harm

(3) To family or household member

Division (B):

(1) Recklessly

(2) Cause serious physical harm

(3) To family or household member

Division (C):

(1) By threat of force

(2) Knowingly

(3) Cause a family or household member to believe that the offender will cause imminent physical harm to the family or household member

PENALTY

If Divisions (A) or (B) violated, Misdemeanor, 1st degree (2929.21 to 2929.28, 2929.31)

If Divisions (A) or (B) violated and prior conviction of domestic violence or of 2903.14, 2909.06, 2909.07, 2911.12, 2911.211 or 2919.22 (or a former or existing municipal ordinance, or a law of the United States, or of any state, or of a municipal ordinance of any state that is substantially similar) involving person who is family or household member at time of violation, Felony, 4th degree. If 2 or more of above, Felony, 3rd degree (2929.11 to 2929.18, 2929.31)

If Division (C) violated, Misdemeanor, 4th degree (2929.11)

If Division (C) violated and prior conviction of domestic violence or of 2903.14, 2909.06, 2909.07, 2911.12, 2911.211 or 2919.22, Misdemeanor, 2nd degree. If 2 or more of above, Misdemeanor, 1st degree (2929.21 to 2929.28, 2929.31)

Note: Written statement by complainant alleging that alleged offender committed domestic violence offense against complainant or complainant's child constitutes reasonable cause such that police officer may make warrantless arrest of alleged offender under 2935.03(B).

Domestic Offenses—Endangering Children

See Juveniles—Endangering Children

Domestic Offenses—Interference with Custody—2919.23

ELEMENTS OF THE CRIME

Division (A):

(1) Knowingly without privilege to do so or reckless in that regard

(2) Entice, take, keep, harbor from parent, guardian or custodian

(3)(a) Child under 18 or mentally or physically handicapped child under 21, or

(b) Person committed by law to institution for delinquent, unruly, neglected, abused, or dependent children, or

(c) Person committed by law to institution for mentally ill or mentally retarded.

Division (B):

(1) Aid, abet, induce, cause, or encourage

(2) A child or ward of the juvenile court who has been committed to the custody of a person, department, or public or private institution

(3) To leave the custody of that person, department, or institution

(4) Without legal consent.

DEFENSES

(1) In Division (A)(3)(a) above, actor reasonably believed conduct necessary to preserve child's health or safety.

(2) To charge of keeping or harboring under this section, actor in good faith notified law enforcement or judicial authorities within reasonable time after child or committed person came under the actor's shelter, protection, or influence.

PENALTY

Except as otherwise provided in this section, if Division (A)(3)(a) violated, Misdemeanor, 1st degree (2929.21 to 2929.28, 2929.31)

If Division (A)(3)(a) violated, and victim is removed from the state or if the offender previously has been convicted of an offense under this section, Felony, 5th degree (2929.11 to 2929.18, 2929.31). If the child suffers physical harm as a result of this violation, Felony, 4th degree (2929.11 to 2929.18, 2929.31)

If Division (A)(3)(b) or (c) violated, Misdemeanor, 3rd degree (2929.21 to 2929.28, 2929.31)

If Division (B) violated, Misdemeanor, 1st degree (2929.21 to 2929.28, 2929.31); each day of violation is a separate offense

Domestic Offenses—Interfering With Action to Issue or Modify Support Order—2919.231

ELEMENTS OF THE CRIME

(1) Use of physical harassment or threats of violence against another

(2) To interfere with or attempt to prevent

(3) Other person's initiating or continuing

(4) Of action to issue or modify support order

(5) Under Ch 3115, 2151.23, 2151.231, 2151.232, 2151.33, 2151.36, 2151.361, 2151.49, 3105.18, 3105.21, 3109.05, 3109.19, 3111.13, 3113.04, 3113.07, or 3113.31

PENALTY

Misdemeanor, 1st degree (2929.21 to 2929.28, 2929.31)

If prior conviction of this section or of 3111.19 (interference with establishment of paternity), Felony, 5th degree (2929.11 to 2929.18, 2929.31)

Domestic Offenses—Nonsupport of Dependents—2919.21

ELEMENTS OF THE CRIME

(1)(a) Abandon, or

(b) Fail to support adequately

(2)(a) Spouse, as required by law, or

(b) Child under 18 or mentally or physically handicapped child, under 21, or

(c) Aged or infirm parent or adoptive parent who is unable to provide adequately for the parent's own support because of lack of ability and means,

(3) Abandon or fail to support another person as established by court order, or

(4) Aid, abet, induce, cause, encourage, or contribute to a child or a ward of the juvenile court becoming a dependent or neglected child.

DEFENSES

(1) Legally responsible person unable to provide adequate support, and provided such support as was within the accused's ability and means.

(2) Under (2)(c) parent abandoned, or failed to support actor as required by law, when actor under 18 or was mentally and physically handicapped and under 21.

PENALTY

Misdemeanor, 1st degree (2929.21 to 2929.28, 2929.31)

Additional Fine: If the offender is guilty of nonsupport of dependents by reason of failing to provide support to the offender's child as required by a child support order issued on or after April 15, 1985, pursuant to section 2151.23, 2151.33, 3105.21, 3109.05, 3111.13, 3113.04, 3113.31, or 3115.22 of the Revised Code, the court, in addition to any other sentence imposed, shall assess all court costs arising out of the charge against the person and require the person to pay any reasonable attorney's fees of any adverse party other than the state, as determined by the court, that arose in relation to the charge

If prior conviction under (2)(b) or there has been finding that offender has failed to provide support for 26 weeks out of 104 consecutive weeks whether or not the 26 weeks were consecutive, then violation of (2)(b) is Felony, 5th degree (2929.11 to 2929.18, 2929.31).

If violation of (4), each day of violation is a separate offense.

Domestic Offenses—Violating Protection Order or Consent Agreement

See Protection Order—Violating Protection Order or Consent Agreement

Driving While Intoxicated or Drugged

See Drunk Driving—Driving While Intoxicated or Drugged

Driving While Intoxicated or Drugged—Commercial Motor Vehicles

See Motor Vehicles—Commercial Motor Vehicles—Criminal Offenses

Drug Offenses—Abusing Harmful Intoxicants—2925.31

ELEMENTS OF THE CRIME

(1) Except for lawful research, clinical, medical, dental, or veterinary purposes

(2) Purpose to induce intoxication or similar physiological effects

(3) Obtain, possess or use harmful intoxicant

PENALTY

Misdemeanor, 1st degree (2929.21 to 2929.28, 2929.31)

Mandatory Fine: $250

If prior conviction of drug abuse offense, Felony, 5th degree (2929.11 to 2929.19, 2929.31)

Note: In addition to other sanctions, court shall suspend, for 6 months to 5 years, the driver's or commercial driver's license or permit of the offender.

Note: If offender is professionally licensed person, court must notify immediately regulatory or licensing board or agency, or the commission on grievances and discipline of the Supreme Court, of conviction pursuant to 2925.38.

Drug Offenses—Controlled Substances and Schedules—3719.01(C)

A drug, compound, mixture, preparation or substance set forth in Schedules I, II, III, IV, and V in 3719.41 with Schedule I drugs being most dangerous and Schedule V drugs being least dangerous. These schedules subject to change automatically to conform to similar schedules in Federal Drug Abuse Control Law and when the State Board of Pharmacy adds, transfers or removes a drug from a schedule.

Note: Anabolic steroids are now included in Schedule III, as defined and listed in 3719.41, Schedule III(E).

Drug Offenses—Corrupting Another With Drugs—2925.02

ELEMENTS OF THE CRIME

Division (A):

(1) Knowingly

(2) By force, threat, or deception

(3) Administer, induce or cause another to use

(4) A controlled substance

Division (B):

(1) Knowingly

(2) By any means administer, furnish, induce, or cause another

(3) To use a controlled substance

(a) With purpose to cause serious physical harm to person, or

(b) With purpose to cause person to become drug dependent

Division (C):

(1) Knowingly

(2) By any means administer, furnish, induce or cause another

(3) To use a controlled substance and

(4)(a) Thereby cause serious physical harm to such person, or

(b) Thereby cause person to become drug dependent.

Division (D):

(1) Knowingly

(2) By any means

(a) Furnish or administer a controlled substance to a juvenile who is at least 2 years the offender's junior, or

(b) Induce or cause a juvenile who is at least 2 years the offender's junior to use a controlled substance, or

(c) Induce or cause a juvenile who is at least 2 years the offender's junior to commit a felony drug abuse offense

(3) Where offender knows the age of such person or is reckless in that regard.

Division (E):

(1) Knowingly

(2) By any means

(3) Use a juvenile

(4) To perform any surveillance activity that is intended

(a) To prevent the detection of the offender or any other person in the commission of a felony drug abuse offense, or

(b) To prevent the arrest of the offender or any other person for the commission of a felony drug abuse offense

(5) Whether or not the offender knows the juvenile's age

Note: Anabolic steroids are now Schedule III controlled substances, as defined and listed in 3719.41, Schedule III(E).

EXCEPTION

Division (A), (C), or (D) not applicable to manufacturers, wholesalers, licensed health professionals authorized to prescribe drugs, pharmacists, owners of pharmacies or others whose conduct is in accordance with Chapters 3719., 4715., 4723., 4729., 4731., and 4741.

PENALTY

If drug is Schedule I or II substance except marihuana, Felony, 2nd degree (2929.11 to 2929.18, 2929.31), and a mandatory prison term prescribed for a Felony, 2nd degree.

If drug is Schedule I or II substance except marihuana, and if the offense is committed in the vicinity of a school, Felony, 1st degree (2929.11 to 2929.18, 2929.31), and a mandatory prison term prescribed for a Felony, 1st degree.

If drug is Schedule III, IV or V substance, Felony, 2nd degree (2929.11 to 2929.18, 2929.31), and a presumption for a prison term prescribed for a Felony, 2nd degree.

If drug is Schedule III, IV or V substance, and if the offense is committed in the vicinity of a school, Felony, 2nd degree (2929.11 to 2929.18, 2929.31), and a mandatory prison term prescribed for a Felony, 2nd degree.

If drug is marihuana, Felony, 4th degree (2929.11 to 2929.18, 2929.31), and Division (C) of section 2929.13 applies in determining whether to impose a prison term on the offender.

If drug is marihuana, and if the offense is committed in the vicinity of a school, Felony, 3rd degree (2929.11 to 2929.18, 2929.31), and Division (C) of section 2929.13 applies in determining whether to impose a prison term on the offender.

Note: In addition to other penalties, if the violation is a felony of the 1st, 2nd, or 3rd degree, the court shall impose upon the offender the mandatory fine specified for the offense under Division (B)(1) of section 2929.18 unless, as specified in that division, the court determines that the offender is indigent.

Note: If a person is charged with any violation of this section that is a felony of the 1st, 2nd, or 3rd degree, posts bail and forfeits the bail, the forfeited bail shall be paid by the clerk of the court as if it were a fine imposed for a violation of this section.

Note: In addition to other penalties, court shall suspend the offender's driver's license, commercial driver's license or permit for a definite period of 6 months to 5 years.

Note: If offender is professionally licensed person, court must notify immediately regulatory or licensing board or agency, or the commission on grievances and discipline of the Supreme Court, of conviction pursuant to 2925.38.

Note: Notwithstanding the prison term otherwise authorized or required for the offense under this section and 2929.13 and 2929.14, if the violation of this section involves the sale, offer to sell, or possession of a schedule I or II controlled substance, with the exception of marihuana, and if the offender, as a result of the violation, is a major drug offender and is guilty of a 2941.1410 specification, the court, in lieu of the prison term that otherwise is authorized or required, shall impose upon the offender the mandatory prison term specified in division (D)(3)(a) of section 2929.14 and may impose an additional prison term under division (D)(3)(b) of that section.

Drug Offenses—Counterfeit Controlled Substances—2925.37

ELEMENTS OF THE CRIME

Division (A): (Possession of Counterfeit Controlled Substances)

(1) Knowingly

(2) Possess

(3) Counterfeit controlled substance

Division (B): (Trafficking in Counterfeit Controlled Substances)

(1) Knowingly

(2)(a) Make

(b) Sell

(c) Offer to sell

(d) Deliver

(3) Substance violator knows is counterfeit controlled substance

Division (C): (Trafficking in Counterfeit Controlled Substances)

(1)(a) Make

(b) Possess

(c) Sell

(d) Offer to sell

(e) Deliver

(2) Any
(a) Punch
(b) Die
(c) Plate
(d) Stone
(e) Other device

(3) Knowing or having reason to know

(4) It will be used to print or reproduce upon a counterfeit controlled substance a
(a) Trademark
(b) Trade name
(c) Other identifying mark

Division (D): (Aggravated Trafficking in Counterfeit Controlled Substances)

(1)(a) Sell
(b) Offer to sell
(c) Give
(d) Deliver

(2) To a person under the age of eighteen

(3) Counterfeit controlled substance

Division (E): (Promoting and Encouraging Drug Abuse)

(1) Directly or indirectly

(2) Represent a counterfeit controlled substance as a controlled substance

(3) By describing its effects as the physical or psychological effects associated with use of a controlled substance

Division (F): (Fraudulent Drug Advertising)

(1) Directly or indirectly

(2) Falsely represent or advertise (as defined in 3715.01(A)(12))

(3) Counterfeit controlled substance as a controlled substance

Note: Anabolic steroids are now Schedule III controlled substances, as defined and listed in 3719.41, Schedule III(E).

PENALTY

If Division (A) violated, Misdemeanor, 1st degree (2929.21 to 2929.28, 2929.31)

If Divisions (B), (C), (E) or (F) violated, Felony, 5th degree(2929.11 to 2929.18, 2929.31) and division (C) of section 2929.13 of the Revised Code applies in determining whether to impose a prison term on the offender.

If Divisions (B), (C), (E) or (F) violated and if the offense is committed in the vicinity of a school or in the vicinity of a juvenile, Felony, 4th degree (2929.11 to 2929.18, 2929.31) and division (C) of section 2929.13 of the Revised Code applies in determining whether to impose a prison term on the offender.

If Division (D) violated, Felony, 4th degree (2929.11 to 2929.18, 2929.31) and division (C) of section 2929.13 of the Revised Code applies in determining whether to impose a prison term on the offender.

Note: In addition to other penalties, court shall suspend, for 6 months to 5 years, the driver's or commercial driver's license or permit of the offender.

Note: If offender is professionally licensed person, court must notify immediately regulatory or licensing board or agency, or the commission on grievances and discipline of the Supreme Court, of conviction pursuant to 2925.38.

Note: Notwithstanding any contrary provision of section 3719.21 of the Revised Code, the clerk of the court shall pay a fine imposed for a violation of this section pursuant to division (A) of section 2929.18 of the Revised Code in accordance with and subject to the requirements of division (F) of section 2925.03. The agency that receives the fine shall use the fine as specified in division (F) of section 2925.03.

Drug Offenses—Deception to Obtain a Dangerous Drug—2925.22

ELEMENTS OF THE CRIME

(1) By deception as defined in 2913.01

(2) Procure administration of, prescription for, or the dispensing of, a dangerous drug, or possess an uncompleted preprinted prescription blank used for writing a prescription for a dangerous drug.

Note: Dangerous drugs are defined in 4729.02(D).

Note: Anabolic steroids are now controlled substances, as defined and listed in 3719.41, Schedule III(E).

PENALTY

If drug is a compound, mixture, preparation or substance in Schedule I or II except marihuana, Felony, 4th degree (2929.11 to 2929.18, 2929.31) and division (C) of section 2929.13 applies in determining whether to impose a prison term on the offender.

If drug is a compound, mixture, preparation or substance in Schedule III, IV or V or is marihuana, Felony, 5th degree (2929.11 to 2929.18, 2929.31) and division (C) of section 2929.13 applies in determining whether to impose a prison term on the offender.

Note: In addition to other penalties, court shall suspend, for 6 months to 5 years, the driver's or commercial driver's license or permit of the offender.

Note: If offender is professionally licensed person, court must notify immediately regulatory or licensing board or agency, or the commission on grievances and discipline of the Supreme Court, of conviction pursuant to 2925.38.

Note: Notwithstanding any contrary provision of section 3719.21 of the Revised Code, the clerk of the court shall pay a fine imposed for a violation of this section pursuant to division (A) of section 2929.18 of the Revised Code in accordance with and subject to the requirements of division (F) of section 2925.03. The agency that receives the fine shall use the fine as specified in division (F) of section 2925.03.

Drug Offenses—Driving While Intoxicated or Drugged

See Drunk Driving—Driving While Intoxicated or Drugged

Drug Offenses—Hypodermics—Possession, Sale, and Disposal—3719.172

See also Drug Offenses—Possession—Drug Abuse Instruments

ELEMENTS OF THE CRIME

Division (A):

(1) Manufacturer, distributor of, or dealer in hypodermics or medication packaged in hypodermics, authorized agent or employee of same or terminal distributor of dangerous drugs

(2) Display any hypodermic for sale

Division (B):

(1) Person authorized to possess a hypodermic pursuant to 3719.172(A) of the Revised Code

(2) Negligently

(3) Fail to take reasonable precautions to prevent any hypodermic in his possession from theft or acquisition by any unauthorized person

Division (C):

(1) Person other than: manufacturer, distributor, or dealer of hypodermics or medication packaged in them, or agents or employees, or hospital, pharmacist, or health practitioner in regular course of business as permitted by law

(2) Sell or furnish

(3) A hypodermic

(4) To another

Division (D):

(1) Sell or furnish

(2) A hypodermic

(3) To another that offender knows or has reasonable cause to believe is not authorized by 3719.172(A) to possess a hypodermic

PENALTY

If Divisions (C) or (D) violated, Felony, 5th degree (2929.11 to 2929.18, 2929.31)

If previous conviction under Divisions (C) or (D) or of drug abuse offense, Felony, 4th degree (2929.11 to 2929.18, 2929.31)

If Division (A) violated, Misdemeanor, 3rd degree (2929.21 to 2929.28, 2929.31)

If previous conviction under Divisions (A) or a drug abuse offense, Misdemeanor, 1st degree (2929.21 to 2929.28, 2929.31)

Drug Offenses—Illegal Administration or Distribution of Anabolic Steroids—2925.06

ELEMENTS OF THE CRIME

(1) Knowingly

(2)(a) Administer to a human being, or

(b) Prescribe or dispense for administration to a human being

(3) Anabolic steroid

(4) Not approved by the United States food and drug administration for administration to human beings

EXCEPTIONS

***This section does not apply to any of the following*:**

(1) Manufacturers, practitioners, pharmacists, owners of pharmacies, and other persons whose conduct is in accordance with Chapter 3719., 4715., 4729., 4731., or 4741. or section 4723.56 of the Revised Code.

(2) If the offense involves an anabolic steroid, any person who is conducting or participating in a research project involving the use of an anabolic steroid if the project has been approved by the United States food and drug administration.

(3) Any person who sells, offers for sale, prescribes, dispenses, or administers for livestock or other nonhuman species an anabolic steroid that is expressly intended for administration through implants to livestock or other nonhuman species and approved for that purpose under the "Federal Food, Drug, and Cosmetic Act", 52 Stat. 1040 (1938), 21 U.S.C.A. 301, as amended, and is sold, offered for sale, prescribed, dispensed, or administered for that purpose in accordance with that act.

PENALTY

Felony, 4th degree (2929.11 to 2929.18, 2929.31)

Note: Division (C) of section 2929.13 applies in determining whether to impose a prison term on the offender.

Note: In addition to other penalties, court shall suspend the offender's driver's license, commercial driver's license or permit for a definite period of not less than 6 months or more than 5 years.

Note: If offender is professionally licensed person, court must notify immediately regulatory or licensing board or agency, or the commission on grievances and discipline of the Supreme Court, of conviction pursuant to 2925.38.

Note: If a person commits an act that constitutes a violation of this section and that also constitutes a violation of any other provision of the Revised Code, the prosecutor, using customary prosecutorial discretion, may prosecute the person for a violation of the appropriate provision of the Revised Code.

Drug Offenses—Illegal Assembly or Possession of Chemicals Used to Manufacture Drugs—2925.041

ELEMENTS OF THE CRIME

(1) Knowingly

(2) Assemble or possess

(3) One or more chemicals that may be used to manufacture a controlled substance included in schedule I or II

(4) With intent to manufacture a controlled substance included in schedule I or II in violation of 2925.04

PROOF

As provided in division (B): It is not necessary to allege or prove that offender assembled or possessed all chemicals necessary to manufacture the controlled substance. Assembly or possession of a single chemical, with intent to manufacture, is sufficient.

PENALTY

Felony, 3rd degree

If violation occurs in vicinity of school or juvenile, Felony 2nd degree

Note: 2929.13(C) applies in determining whether to impose a prison term.

Note: In addition to other penalties, court shall revoke or suspend driving privileges.

Note: If offender is professionally licensed person or admitted to bar, court must notify regulatory board or licensing board or agency of conviction pursuant to 2925.38.

Note: Court shall impose a mandatory fine pursuant to 2929.18(B)(1) unless offender indigent. Clerk of court shall pay a fine imposed for a violation of this section under 2929.18(A) in accordance with and subject to requirements of 2950.03(F). If offender forfeits bail, the clerk shall pay forfeited bail as if it were a fine.

Drug Offenses—Illegal Cultivation of Marihuana—2925.04

ELEMENTS OF THE CRIME

(1) Knowingly

(2) Cultivate

(3) Marihuana

EXCEPTION

This section does not apply to manufacturers, practitioners, pharmacists, owners of pharmacies, and other persons whose conduct is in accordance with Chapter 3719., 4715., 4729., 4731., or 4741. or section 4723.56 of the Revised Code.

DEFENSE

It is an affirmative defense, as provided in section 2901.05 of the Revised Code, to a charge under this section that the marihuana that gave rise to the charge is in an amount, is in a form, is prepared, compounded, or mixed with substances that are not controlled substances in a manner, or is possessed or cultivated under any other circumstances that indicate that the marihuana was solely for personal use.

PENALTY

Less than 100 grams of marihuana

Minor Misdemeanor. If violation occurs in vicinity of school or juvenile, Misdemeanor, 4th degree (2929.21 to 2929.28, 2929.31)

Note: Arrest or conviction for a minor misdemeanor violation of this section does not constitute a criminal record and need not be reported by the person so arrested or convicted in response to any inquiries about the person's criminal record, including any inquiries contained in an application for employment, a license, or any other right or privilege or made in connection with the person's appearance as a witness.

100 grams to 199 grams of marihuana

Misdemeanor, 4th Degree. If violation occurs in vicinity of school or juvenile, Misdemeanor, 3rd degree (2929.21 to 2929.28, 2929.31)

200 grams to 999 grams of marihuana

Felony, 5th degree. It is a partial affirmative defense to the 5th degree cultivation offense that the marihuana was solely for personal use. If the defendant sustains the burdens of going forward and of proof, the defendant may be convicted of a misdemeanor cultivation of marihuana offense. If violation occurs in vicinity of juvenile or school, Felony, 4th degree. (2929.11 to 2929.18, 2929.31)

Note: Division (B) of 2929.13 applies in determining whether to impose a prison term on the offenders.

1000 grams to 4,999 grams of marihuana

Felony, 3rd degree. If violation occurs in vicinity of school or juvenile, Felony, 2nd degree. (2929.14, 2929.31)

Note: Division (C) of section 2929.13 applies in determining whether to impose a prison term on the offender.

5,000 grams to 19,999 grams of marihuana

Felony, 3rd degree. If violation occurs in vicinity of school or juvenile, Felony, 2nd degree. (2929.14, 2929.31)

Note: There is a presumption for a prison term for the offense.

20,000 grams or over of marihuana

Felony, 2nd degree. If violation occurs in vicinity of school or juvenile, Felony, 1st degree. (2929.14, 2929.31)

Note: The court shall impose as a mandatory prison term the maximum prison term prescribed for the felony.

Note: If a violation of this section is a felony of the second or third degree, the court shall impose upon the offender the mandatory fine specified for the offense under division (B)(1) of section 2929.18 of the Revised Code unless, as specified in that division, the court determines that the offender is indigent. If a person is charged with a violation of this section that is a felony of the second or third degree, posts bail, and forfeits the bail, the clerk shall pay the forfeited bail as if the forfeited bail were a fine imposed for a violation of this section.

Note: In addition to other penalties, court shall suspend the offender's driver's license, commercial driver's license or permit for a definite period of not less than 6 months or more than 5 years.

Note: If offender is professionally licensed person, court must notify immediately regulatory or licensing board or agency, or the commission on grievances and discipline of the Supreme Court, of conviction pursuant to 2925.38.

Drug Offenses—Illegal Dispensing of Drug Samples—2925.36

ELEMENTS OF THE CRIME

(1) Knowingly

(2) Furnish another a sample drug

Note: Anabolic steroids are now Schedule III controlled substances, as defined and listed in 3719.41, Schedule III(E).

EXCEPTION

Not applicable to manufacturers, wholesalers, pharmacists, owners of pharmacies, licensed health professionals authorized to prescribe drugs, and others whose conduct is in accordance with Chapters 3719., 4715., 4723., 4725., 4729., 4731. and 4741.

PENALTY

(1) If the drug involved in the offense is a compound, mixture, preparation, or substance included in schedule I or II, with the exception of marihuana, the penalty shall be determined as follows:

(a) Except as otherwise provided in division (C)(2)(b) of this section, Felony, 5th degree (2929.11 to 2929.18, 2929.31) and division (C) of section 2929.13 applies in determining whether to impose a prison term on the offender.

(b) If the offense was committed in the vicinity of a school or in the vicinity of a juvenile, Felony, 4th degree (2929.11 to 2929.18, 2929.31) and division (C) of section 2929.13 applies in determining whether to impose a prison term on the offender.

(c) If a violation of this section involves the sale, offer to sell, or possession of a schedule I or II controlled substance, with the exception of marihuana, and if the offender, as a result of the violation, is a major drug offender and is guilty of a 2941.1410 specification, the court, in lieu of the prison term otherwise authorized or required, shall impose upon the offender the mandatory prison term specified in division (D)(3)(a) of section 2929.14 and may impose an additional prison term under division (D)(3)(b) of that section.

(2) If the drug involved in the offense is a dangerous drug or a compound, mixture, preparation, or substance included in schedule III, IV or V, or is marihuana, the penalty shall be determined as follows:

(a) Except as otherwise provided in division (C)(3)(b) of this section, Misdemeanor, 2nd degree (2929.21 to 2929.28, 2929.31)

(b) If the offense was committed in the vicinity of a school or in the vicinity of a juvenile, Misdemeanor, 1st degree (2929.21 to 2929.28, 2929.31)

Note: In addition to other penalties, court shall suspend, for 6 months to 5 years, the driver's or commercial driver's license or permit of the offender.

Note: If offender is professionally licensed person, court must notify immediately regulatory or licensing board or agency, or the commission on grievances and discipline of the Supreme Court, of conviction pursuant to 2925.38.

Note: Notwithstanding any contrary provision of section 3719.21 of the Revised Code, the clerk of court shall pay a fine imposed for a violation of this section pursuant to division (A) of section 2929.18 of the Revised Code in accordance with and subject to the requirements of division (F) of section 2925.03. The agency that receives the fine shall use the fine as specified in division (F) of section 2925.03.

Drug Offenses—Illegal Manufacture of Drugs—2925.04

ELEMENTS OF THE CRIME

(1) Knowingly

(2) Manufacture or engage in any part of the production of

(3) A controlled substance

EXCEPTIONS

This section does not apply to any of the following:

(1) Manufacturers, practitioners, pharmacists, owners of pharmacies, and other persons whose conduct is in accordance with Chapter 3719., 4715., 4729., 4731., or 4741. or section 4723.56 of the Revised Code.

(2) If the offense involves an anabolic steroid, any person who is conducting or participating in a research project involving the use of an anabolic steroid if the project has been approved by the United States food and drug administration.

(3) Any person who sells, offers for sale, prescribes, dispenses, or administers for livestock or other nonhuman species an anabolic steroid that is expressly intended for administration through implants to livestock or other nonhuman species and approved for that purpose under the "Federal Food, Drug, and Cosmetic Act", 52 Stat. 1040 (1938), 21 U.S.C.A. 301, as amended, and is sold, offered for sale, prescribed, dispensed, or administered for that purpose in accordance with that act.

PENALTY

If the drug involved is any compound, mixture, preparation, or substance included in Schedule I or II, with the exception of marihuana

Felony, 2nd degree (2929.14, 2929.31). If violation occurs in the vicinity of a juvenile or school, Felony, 1st degree, mandatory prison term.

Note: The court shall impose as a mandatory prison term one of the prison terms prescribed for a felony of the second degree.

If drug involved is any compound, mixture, preparation, or substance included in Schedule III, IV, or V

Felony, 3rd degree (2929.14, 2929.31). If violation occurs in vicinity of juvenile or school, Felony, 2nd degree, presumption in favor of a prison term

Note: If a violation of this section is a felony of the second or third degree, the court shall impose upon the offender the mandatory fine specified for the offense under division (B)(1) of section 2929.18 of the Revised Code unless, as specified in that division, the court determines that the offender is indigent. If a person is charged with a violation of this section that is a felony of the second or third degree, posts bail, and forfeits the bail, the clerk shall pay the forfeited bail as if the forfeited bail were a fine imposed for a violation of this section.

Note: The court shall revoke or suspend the offender's driver's or commercial driver's license or permit in accordance with division (G) of section 2925.03 of the Revised Code. If an offender's driver's or commercial driver's license or permit is revoked in accordance with that division, the offender may request termination of, and the court may terminate, the revocation in accordance with that division.

Note: In addition to other penalties, court shall suspend the offender's driver's license, commercial driver's license or permit for a definite period of not less than 6 months or more than 5 years.

Note: If offender is professionally licensed person, court must notify immediately regulatory or licensing board or agency, or the commission on grievances and discipline of the Supreme Court, of conviction pursuant to 2925.38.

Drug Offenses—Illegal Processing of Drug Documents—2925.23

ELEMENTS OF THE CRIME

Division (A):

(1) Knowingly

(2) Make a false statement in any prescription order, report or record required by Chapter 3719. or 4729.

Division (B):

(1)(a) Intentionally make, utter, sell, or

(b) Knowingly possess

(2) False or forged

(3)(a) Prescription, or

(b) Uncompleted preprinted prescription blank used for writing a prescription, or

(c) Official written order, or

(d) License for terminal distributor of dangerous drugs as required in 4729.60, or

(e) Registration certificate for a wholesale distributor of dangerous drugs as required in 4729.60

Division (C):

(1) By theft as defined in 2913.02

(2) Acquire

(3)(a) A prescription, or

(b) An uncompleted preprinted prescription blank used for writing a prescription, or

(c) An official written order, or

(d) A blank official written order, or

(e) A license or blank license for a terminal distributor of dangerous drugs as required in 4729.60, or

(f) A registration certificate or blank registration certificate for a wholesale distributor of dangerous drugs as required in 4729.60

Division (D):

(1) Knowingly

(2) Make or affix

(3) Any false or forged label to a package or receptacle containing any dangerous drugs

Note: Anabolic steroids are now Schedule III controlled substances, as defined and listed in 3719.41, Schedule III(E).

EXCEPTION

Divisions (A) and (D) do not apply to licensed health professionals authorized to prescribe drugs, pharmacists, owners of pharmacies and others whose conduct is in accordance with Chapters 3719., 4715., 4723., 4725., 4729., 4731. and 4741.

PENALTY

Division (B)(2), (4), or (5); and Division (C)(2)(4), (5), or (6), Felony, 5th degree (2929.11 to 2929.18, 2929.31).

Division A; Division (B)(1) or (3); Division (C)(1) or (3); Division (D), penalty determined as follows:

(1) If the drug involved in the offense is a compound, mixture, preparation, or substance included in schedule I or II, with the exception of marihuana, Felony, 4th degree (2929.11 to 2929.18, 2929.31) and division (C) of section 2929.13 applies in determining whether to impose a prison term on the offender.

(2) If the drug involved in the offense is a dangerous drug or a compound, mixture, preparation, or substance included in schedule III, IV or V, or is marihuana, Felony, 5th degree (2929.11 to 2929.18, 2929.31) and division (C) of section 2929.13 applies in determining whether to impose a prison term on the offender.

Note: In addition to other penalties, court shall suspend, for 6 months to 5 years, the driver's or commercial driver's license or permit of the offender.

Note: If offender is professionally licensed person, court must notify immediately regulatory or licensing board or agency, or the commission on grievances and discipline of the Supreme Court, of conviction pursuant to 2925.38.

Note: Notwithstanding any contrary provision of section 3719.21 of the Revised Code, the clerk of court shall pay a fine imposed for a violation of this section pursuant to 2929.18(A) in accordance with and subject to the requirements of 2925.03(F). The agency that receives the fine shall use the fine as specified in 2925.03(F).

Drug Offenses—Paraphernalia—Illegal Use, Possession, Sale, Manufacture, or Advertisement of Drug Paraphernalia—2925.14

ELEMENTS OF THE CRIME

Division (A):

(1) Knowingly

(2) Use, or possess with purpose to use

(3) Drug paraphernalia as defined in 2925.14(A)

Division (B):

(1) Knowingly

(2) Sell, or possess or manufacture with purpose to sell

(3) Drug paraphernalia as defined in 2925.14(A)

(4) If offender knows or reasonably should know that equipment, product, or material will be used as drug paraphernalia

Division (C):

(1) Knowingly

(2) Place an advertisement

(3) In any newspaper, magazine, handbill, or other publication that is published and printed and circulated primarily within the State of Ohio

(4) For the purpose of promoting the illegal sale in the state of Ohio of the equipment, product, or material intended or designed for use as drug paraphernalia

Note: Anabolic steroids are now Schedule III controlled substances, as defined and listed in 3719.41, Schedule III(E).

EXCEPTIONS

Divisions (A) to (C) do not apply to manufacturers, licensed health professionals authorized to prescribe drugs, pharmacists, owners of pharmacies, and other persons whose conduct is in accordance with Chapters 3719., 4715., 4723., 4729., 4731., 4741.

Divisions (A) to (C) shall not be construed as prohibiting the possession or use of a hypodermic as authorized by 3719.172.

PENALTY

If Division (A) violated, Misdemeanor, 4th degree (2929.21 to 2929.28, 2929.31)

If Division (B) violated, Misdemeanor, 2nd degree (2929.21 to 2929.28, 2929.31)

If Division (B) violated by selling drug paraphernalia and the buyer is a juvenile, Misdemeanor, 1st degree (2929.21 to 2929.28, 2929.31)

If Division (C) violated, Misdemeanor, 2nd degree (2929.21 to 2929.28, 2929.31)

Note: In addition to other penalties, court shall suspend, for 6 months to 5 years, the driver's or commercial driver's license or permit of the offender.

Note: If offender is professionally licensed person, court must notify immediately regulatory or licensing board or agency, or the commission on grievances and discipline of the Supreme Court, of conviction pursuant to 2925.38.

Drug Offenses—Permitting Drug Abuse—2925.13

See also Drug Offenses—Drug Abuse

ELEMENTS OF THE CRIME

Division (A):

(1) Owner, operator or person in charge of locomotive, watercraft, aircraft or other vehicles as defined in 4501.01(A)

(2) Knowingly

(3) Permit vehicle to be used for commission of felony drug abuse offense

Division (B):

(1) Owner, lessee, or occupant, or having custody, control, or supervision of premises or real estate, including vacant land

(2) Knowingly

(3) Permit premises, or real estate, including vacant land, to be used for commission of felony drug abuse offense by another

Note: Anabolic steroids are now Schedule III controlled substances, as defined and listed in 3719.41, Schedule III(E).

PENALTY

Misdemeanor, 1st degree (2929.21 to 2929.28, 2929.31)

If offense is a violation of 2925.02 or 2925.03, Felony, 5th degree (2929.11 to 2929.18, 2929.31)

Note: In addition to other penalties, court shall suspend, for 6 months to 5 years, the driver's or commercial driver's license or permit of the offender.

Note: If offender is professionally licensed person, court must notify immediately regulatory or licensing board or agency, or the commission on grievances and discipline of the Supreme Court, of conviction pursuant to 2925.38.

Note: Notwithstanding any contrary provision of section 3719.21 of the Revised Code, the clerk of court shall pay a fine imposed for a violation of this section pursuant to division (A) of section 2929.18 of the Revised Code in accordance with and subject to the requirements of division (F) of section 2925.03. The agency that receives the fine shall use the fine as specified in division (F) of section 2925.03.

Note: Any premises or real estate under Division (B) is a nuisance subject to abatement under Chapter 3767.

Drug Offenses—Persons Who May Sell, Deliver, Distribute and Possess Dangerous Drugs—4729.51

ELEMENTS OF THE CRIME

Division (A):

(1) Person not a registered wholesale distributor of dangerous drugs

(2) Possess for sale, sell, distribute, or deliver

(3) At wholesale

(4) Dangerous drugs

(5) Except as follows:

(a) A pharmacist who is a licensed terminal distributor of dangerous drugs or who is employed by a licensed terminal distributor of dangerous drugs may make occasional sales of dangerous drugs at wholesale;

(b) A licensed terminal distributor of dangerous drugs having more than one establishment or place may transfer or deliver dangerous drugs from one establishment or place for which a license has been issued to the terminal distributor to another establishment or place for which a license has been issued to the terminal distributor if the license issued for each establishment or place is in effect at the time of the transfer or delivery.

Division (B)(1):

(1) Registered wholesale distributor of dangerous drugs

(2) Possess for sale or sell

(3) At wholesale

(4) Dangerous drugs

(5) To any person other than the following:

(a) A licensed health practitioner;

(b) A registered wholesale distributor of dangerous drugs

(c) A manufacturer of dangerous drugs

(d) A licensed terminal distributor of dangerous drugs, subject to division (B)(2) of this section;

(e) Carriers or warehousemen for the purpose of carriage or storage;

(f) Terminal or wholesale distributors of dangerous drugs who are not engaged in the sale of dangerous drugs within this state;

(g) An optometrist licensed under Chapter 4725. who is certified to administer topical ocular pharmaceutical agents under that chapter for the purposes authorized by that chapter.

(h) Person licensed under Chapter 4725. to conduct diabetes education

Division (B)(2):

(1) Registered wholesale distributor of dangerous drugs

(2) Possess for sale or sell

(3) At wholesale

(4) Dangerous drugs

(5) To a licensed terminal distributor of dangerous drugs

(6) Except to:

(a) A terminal distributor who has a category I license, only dangerous drugs described in category I, as defined in division (A)(1) of section 4729.54;

(b) A terminal distributor who has a category II license, only dangerous drugs described in category I and category II, as defined in divisions (A)(1) and (2) of section 4729.54;

(c) A terminal distributor who has a category III license, dangerous drugs described in category I, category II, and category III, as defined in divisions (A)(1),(2), and (3) of section 4729.54;

(d) A terminal distributor who has a limited category I, II, or III license, only the dangerous drugs specified in the certificate furnished by the terminal distributor in accordance with section 4729.60.

Division (C):

(1) Person or practitioner

(2) Except a licensed terminal distributor of dangerous drugs

(3) Purchase for the purpose of resale, possess for sale, or sell

(4) At retail

(5) Dangerous drugs

Division (D):

(1) Licensed terminal distributor of dangerous drugs

(2) Purchase for the purpose of resale

(3) Dangerous drugs

(4) From any person other than a registered wholesale distributor of dangerous drugs

(5) Except as follows:

(a) A licensed terminal distributor of dangerous drugs may make occasional purchases of dangerous drugs for resale from a pharmacist who is a licensed terminal distributor of dangerous drugs or who is employed by a licensed terminal distributor of dangerous drugs;

(b) A licensed terminal distributor of dangerous drugs having more than one establishment or place may transfer or receive dangerous drugs from one establishment or place for which a license has been issued to the terminal distributor to another establishment or place for which a licensed has been issued to the terminal distributor if the license issued for each establishment or place is in effect at the time of the transfer or receipt.

Division (E)(1):

(a) Licensed terminal distributor of dangerous drugs

(b) Engage

(c) In the sale or other distribution of

(d) Dangerous drugs

(e) At retail

(f) At any establishment or place other than that or those described in the license issued by the board of pharmacy to such terminal distributor, or

Division (E)(2):

(a) Licensed terminal distributor of dangerous drugs

(b) Maintain in his possession, custody, or control

(c) Dangerous drugs

(d) For any purpose other than his own use or consumption

(e) At any establishment or place other than that or those described in the license issued by the board of pharmacy to such terminal distributor.

Note: Dangerous drugs are defined in 4729.02(D).

Note: Anabolic steroids are now Schedule III controlled substances, as defined and listed in 3719.41, Schedule III(E).

PROOF

As provided in division (C) of this section: The possession by any person, other than a practitioner, registered wholesale distributor of dangerous drugs, or a licensed terminal distributor of dangerous drugs, of any dangerous drugs other than insulin or drugs obtained lawfully for medical purposes from or upon the prescription of a practitioner, shall constitute presumptive evidence that such person is in violation of this division, except that a person may lawfully possess or use dangerous drugs as provided in this section or otherwise as specifically provided by law.

EXCEPTIONS

Nothing in this section shall do either of the following:

(a) Require a person engaged solely in the sale or other distribution, at wholesale, of drugs and supplies for veterinary use only, to be registered under sections 4729.50 to 4729.66 of the Revised Code;

(b) Prohibit the purchase or sale, at wholesale, of drugs and supplies for veterinary use only by a person engaged solely in the distribution of drugs and supplies for veterinary use only.

Nothing in this section shall be construed to interfere with any law enforcement official authorized by municipal, county, state, or federal law to collect samples of any drug, regardless of its nature or in whose possession it may be, in the performance of his official duties.

PENALTY

If Division (A), (B), (D), or (E) violated, Misdemeanor 1st degree (2929.21 to 2929.28, 2929.31)

If Division (C) violated Felony, 4th degree (2929.11 to 2929.18, 2929.31)

If prior conviction of a violation of this chapter, or a violation of Chapter 2925. or 3719. of the Revised Code, Felony, 3rd degree (2929.11 to 2929.18, 2929.31)

Drug Offenses—Possessing Nitrous Oxide in a Motor Vehicle—2925.33

ELEMENTS OF THE CRIME

(1) Possess

(2) Open cartridge of nitrous oxide

(3) While operating or a passenger in or on a moving or stationary motor vehicle

(4) On a street, highway or other private public or private property open to the public

PENALTY

Misdemeanor, 4th degree (2929.21 to 2929.28, 2929.31)

Drug Offenses—Possession—Aggravated Possession of Drugs—2925.11(C)(1)

See also Drug Offenses—Permitting Drug Abuse

ELEMENTS OF THE CRIME

(1) Knowingly

(2) Obtain, possess, or use

(3) A controlled substance as set forth in 3719.41

EXCEPTIONS

(1) Does not apply to manufacturers, licensed health professionals authorized to prescribe drugs, pharmacists, owners of pharmacies, or others whose conduct is in accordance with Chapters 3719., 4715., 4723., 4729., 4731., 4741.

(2) Does not apply to persons who obtained controlled substances pursuant to prescription issued by licensed health professionals authorized to prescribe drugs where drug is in original container in which it was dispensed.

PENALTY

If drug is Schedule I or II controlled substance except marihuana, cocaine, L.S.D., heroin, and hashish, the penalty shall be determined as follows:

(a) Except as otherwise provided in this section, Felony, 5th degree (2929.11 to 2929.18, 2929.31) and division (B) of section 2929.13 applies in determining whether to impose a prison term on the offender.

(b) If the amount of the drug involved equals or exceeds the bulk amount but is less than five times the bulk amount, Felony, 3rd degree (2929.11 to 2929.18, 2929.31) and there is a presumption for a prison term for the offense.

(c) If the amount of the drug involved equals or exceeds five times the bulk amount but is less than fifty times the bulk amount, Felony, 2nd degree (2929.11 to 2929.18, 2929.31) and the court shall impose as a mandatory prison term one of the prison terms prescribed for a felony of the 2nd degree.

(d) If the amount of the drug involved equals or exceeds fifty times the bulk amount but is less than one hundred times the bulk amount, Felony, 1st degree (2929.11 to 2929.18, 2929.31) and the court shall impose as a mandatory prison term one of the prison terms prescribed for a felony of the 1st degree.

(e) If the amount of the drug involved equals or exceeds one hundred times the bulk amount, Felony, 1st degree (2929.11 to 2929.18, 2929.31) and the court shall impose as a mandatory prison term the maximum prison term prescribed for a felony of the 1st degree and may impose an additional mandatory prison term prescribed for a major drug offender under division (D)(3)(b) of section 2929.14.

Note: In addition to other penalties, if the violation is a felony of the 1st, 2nd, or 3rd degree, the court shall impose upon the offender the mandatory fine specified for the offense under Division (B)(1) of section 2929.18 unless, as specified in that division, the court determines that the offender is indigent.

Note: If a person is charged with any violation of this section that is a felony of the 1st, 2nd, or 3rd degree, posts bail and forfeits the bail, the forfeited bail shall be paid by the clerk of the court as if it were a fine imposed for a violation of this section.

Note: In addition to other penalties, court shall suspend, for 6 months to 5 years, the driver's or commercial driver's license or permit of the offender.

Note: If offender is professionally licensed person, court must notify immediately regulatory or licensing board or agency, or the commission on grievances and discipline of the Supreme Court, of conviction pursuant to 2925.38.

Note: When a person is charged with possessing a bulk amount or multiple of a bulk amount, division (E) of section 2925.03 applies regarding the determination of the amount of the controlled substance involved at the time of the offense.

Drug Offenses—Possession—Drug Abuse Instruments—2925.12

See also Drug Offenses—Hypodermics—Possession, Sale, and Disposal

ELEMENTS OF THE CRIME

(1) Knowingly

(2) Make, obtain, possess or use any instrument, article or thing

(3) Whose customary and primary purpose is for the administration or use of a dangerous drug other than marihuana

(4) When the instrument involved is a hypodermic or syringe, whether or not of crude or extemporized manufacture or assembly

(5) And the instrument, article or thing involved has been used by the offender to unlawfully administer or use a dangerous drug, other than marihuana, or to prepare a dangerous drug, other than marihuana, for unlawful administration or use

Note: Anabolic steroids are now Schedule III controlled substances, as defined and listed in 3719.41, Schedule III(E).

EXCEPTION

Does not apply to manufacturers, licensed health professionals authorized to prescribe drugs, pharmacists, owners of pharmacies and others whose conduct is in accordance with Chapters 3719., 4715., 4723., 4729., 4731. and 4741.

PENALTY

Misdemeanor, 2nd degree (2929.21 to 2929.28, 2929.31)

If prior conviction of drug abuse offense, Misdemeanor, 1st degree (2929.21 to 2929.28, 2929.31)

Note: In addition to other penalties, court shall suspend, for 6 months to 5 years, the driver's or commercial driver's license or permit of the offender.

Note: If offender is professionally licensed person, court must notify immediately regulatory or licensing board or agency, or the commission on grievances and discipline of the Supreme Court, of conviction pursuant to 2925.38.

Drug Offenses—Possession—Possession of Cocaine—2925.11(C)(4)

See also Drug Offenses—Permitting Drug Abuse

ELEMENTS OF THE CRIME

(1) Knowingly

(2) Obtain, possess, or use

(3) Cocaine

EXCEPTIONS

(1) Does not apply to manufacturers, licensed health professionals authorized to prescribe drugs, pharmacists, owners of pharmacies, or others whose conduct is in accordance with Chapters 3719., 4715., 4723., 4729., 4731., 4741.

(2) Does not apply to persons who obtained controlled substances pursuant to prescription issued by licensed health professionals authorized to prescribe drugs where drug is in original container in which it was dispensed.

DEFENSE

It is an affirmative defense to a 4th degree felony charge under this section that the substance that gave rise to the charge is in an amount, is in a form, is prepared, compounded, or mixed with substances that are not controlled substances in a manner, or is possessed or cultivated under any other circumstances, that indicate that the substance was possessed solely for personal use. If defendant sustains the burdens for this defense, s/he may be convicted of a 5th degree felony violation of RC 2925.11(C)(4).

PENALTY

If drug is cocaine or a compound, mixture, preparation, or substance containing cocaine, the penalty shall be determined as follows:

(a) Except as otherwise provided in division (C)(4)(b), (c), (d), (e), or (f) of this section, Felony, 5th degree (2929.11 to 2929.18, 2929.31) and division (D) of section 2929.13 applies in determining whether to impose a prison term on the offender.

(b) If the amount of the drug involved equals or exceeds 5 grams but is less than 25 grams of cocaine that is not crack cocaine form or exceeds 1 gram but does not exceed 5 grams of crack cocaine, Felony, 4th degree (2929.11 to 2929.18, 2929.31) and there is a presumption for a prison term for the offense.

(c) If the amount of the drug involved equals or exceeds 25 grams but is less than 100 grams of cocaine that is not crack cocaine form or exceeds 5 grams but is less than 10 grams of crack cocaine, Felony, 3rd degree (2929.11 to 2929.18, 2929.31) and the court shall impose as a mandatory prison term one of the prison terms prescribed for a felony of the 3rd degree.

(d) If the amount of the drug involved equals or exceeds 100 grams but is less than 500 grams of cocaine that is not crack cocaine form or exceeds 10 grams but does not exceed 25 grams of crack cocaine, Felony, 2nd degree (2929.11 to 2929.18, 2929.31) and the court shall impose as a mandatory prison term one of the prison terms prescribed for a felony of the 2nd degree.

(e) If the amount of the drug involved equals or exceeds 500 grams but is less than 1000 grams of cocaine that is not crack cocaine or exceeds 25 grams but does not exceed 100 grams of crack cocaine, Felony, 1st degree (2929.11 to 2929.18, 2929.31) and the court shall impose as a mandatory prison term one of the prison terms prescribed for a felony of the 1st degree.

(f) If the amount of the drug involved equals or exceeds 1000 grams that is not crack cocaine or exceeds 100 grams of crack cocaine, Felony, 1st degree (2929.11 to 2929.18, 2929.31) and the court shall impose as a mandatory prison term the maximum prison term prescribed for a felony of the 1st degree and may impose an additional mandatory prison term prescribed for a major drug offender under division (D)(3)(b) of section 2929.14.

Note: In addition to other penalties, if the violation is a felony of the 1st, 2nd, or 3rd degree, the court shall impose upon the offender the mandatory fine specified for the offense under Division (B)(1) of section 2929.18 unless, as specified in that division, the court determines that the offender is indigent.

Note: If a person is charged with any violation of this section that is a felony of the 1st, 2nd, or 3rd degree, posts bail and forfeits the bail, the forfeited bail shall be paid by the clerk of the court as if it were a fine imposed for a violation of this section.

Note: In addition to other penalties, court shall suspend, for 6 months to 5 years, the driver's or commercial driver's license or permit of the offender.

Note: If offender is professionally licensed person, court must notify immediately regulatory or licensing board or agency, or the commission on grievances and discipline of the Supreme Court, of conviction pursuant to 2925.38.

Drug Offenses—Possession—Possession of Drugs—2925.11(C)(2)

See also Drug Offenses—Permitting Drug Abuse

ELEMENTS OF THE CRIME

(1) Knowingly

(2) Obtain, possess, or use

(3) A controlled substance as set forth in 3719.41

Note: Anabolic steroids are now Schedule III controlled substances, as defined and listed in 3719.41, Schedule III(E).

EXCEPTIONS

(1) Does not apply to manufacturers, licensed health professionals authorized to prescribe drugs, pharmacists, owners of pharmacies, or others whose conduct is in accordance with Chapters 3719., 4715., 4723., 4729., 4731., 4741.

(2) If offense involves anabolic steroid, does not apply to person conducting or participating in research project involving use of anabolic steroids if project has been approved by US Food and Drug Administration.

(3) Does not apply to person who sells, offers for sale, prescribes, dispenses, or administers, for livestock or other nonhuman species, an anabolic steroid expressly intended for administration through implants to livestock or other nonhuman species and approved for that purpose under Federal Food, Drug, and Cosmetic Act, 52 Stat. 1040 (1938), 21 U.S.C.A. 301, as amended, and are sold, offered for sale, prescribed, dispensed, or administered for that purpose in accordance with that Act.

(4) Does not apply to persons who obtained controlled substances pursuant to prescription issued by licensed health professionals authorized to prescribe drugs where drug is in original container in which it was dispensed.

DEFENSE

It is an affirmative defense to a 4th degree felony charge under this section that the substance that gave rise to the charge is in an amount, is in a form, is prepared, compounded, or mixed with substances that are not controlled substances in a manner, or is possessed or cultivated under any other circumstances, that indicate that the substance was possessed solely for personal use. If defendant sustains the burdens for this defense, s/he may be convicted of a misdemeanor violation of RC 2925.11(C)(2).

PENALTY

If drug is Schedule III, IV or V controlled substance, the penalty shall be determined as follows:

(a) Except as otherwise provided in this section, Misdemeanor, 3rd degree (2929.21 to 2929.28, 2929.31)

(b) If prior conviction of drug abuse offense, Misdemeanor, 2nd degree (2929.21 to 2929.28, 2929.31)

(c) If the drug involved in the violation is an anabolic steroid included in schedule III and if the offense is a misdemeanor of the 3rd degree under this division, in lieu of sentencing the offender to a term of imprisonment in a detention facility, the court may place the offender on conditional probation pursuant to division (B) of section 2951.02.

(d) If the amount of the drug involved equals or exceeds the bulk amount but is less than five times the bulk amount, Felony, 4th degree (2929.11 to 2929.18, 2929.31) and division (C) of section 2929.13 applies in determining whether to impose a prison term on the offender.

(e) If the amount of the drug involved equals or exceeds five times the bulk amount but is less than fifty times the bulk amount, Felony, 3rd degree (2929.11 to 2929.18, 2929.31) and there is a presumption for a prison term for the offense.

(f) If the amount of the drug involved equals or exceeds fifty times the bulk amount, Felony, 2nd degree (2929.11 to 2929.18, 2929.31) and the court shall impose as a mandatory prison term one of the prison terms prescribed for a felony of the 2nd degree.

Note: In addition to other penalties, if the violation is a felony of the 1st, 2nd, or 3rd degree, the court shall impose upon the offender the mandatory fine specified for the offense under Division (B)(1) of section 2929.18 unless, as specified in that division, the court determines that the offender is indigent.

Note: If a person is charged with any violation of this section that is a felony of the 1st, 2nd, or 3rd degree, posts bail and forfeits the bail, the forfeited bail shall be paid by the clerk of the court as if it were a fine imposed for a violation of this section.

Note: In addition to other penalties, court shall suspend, for 6 months to 5 years, the driver's or commercial driver's license or permit of the offender.

Note: If offender is professionally licensed person, court must notify immediately regulatory or licensing board or agency, or the commission on grievances and discipline of the Supreme Court, of conviction pursuant to 2925.38.

Note: When a person is charged with possessing a bulk amount or multiple of a bulk amount, division (E) of section 2925.03 applies regarding the determination of the amount of the controlled substance involved at the time of the offense.

Drug Offenses—Possession—Possession of Hashish—2925.11(C)(7)

See also Drug Offenses—Permitting Drug Abuse

ELEMENTS OF THE CRIME

(1) Knowingly

(2) Obtain, possess, or use

(3) Hashish

EXCEPTIONS

(1) Does not apply to manufacturers, licensed health professionals authorized to prescribe drugs, pharmacists, owners of pharmacies, or others whose conduct is in accordance with Chapters 3719., 4715., 4723., 4729., 4731., 4741.

(2) Does not apply to persons who obtained controlled substances pursuant to prescription issued by licensed health professionals authorized to prescribe drugs where drug is in original container in which it was dispensed.

PENALTY

If drug is hashish or a substance containing hashish the penalty shall be determined as follows:

(a) Except as otherwise provided in division (C)(7)(b), (c), (d), (e), or (f) of this section, Minor misdemeanor (2929.21 to 2929.28, 2929.31)

(b) If the amount of hashish involved equals or exceeds 5 grams but is less than 10 grams of hashish in a solid form or equals or exceeds 1 gram but is less than 2 grams of hashish in a liquid concentrate, liquid extract, or liquid distillate form, Misdemeanor, 4th degree (2929.21 to 2929.28, 2929.31)

(c) If the amount of hashish involved equals or exceeds 10 grams but is less than 50 grams of hashish in a solid form or equals or exceeds 2 grams but is less than 10 grams of hashish in a liquid concentrate, liquid extract, or liquid distillate form, Felony, 5th degree (2929.11 to 2929.18, 2929.31) and division (B) of section 2929.13 applies in determining whether to impose a prison term on the offender.

(d) If the amount of hashish involved equals or exceeds 50 grams but is less than 250 grams of hashish in a solid form or equals or exceeds 10 grams but is less than 50 grams of hashish in a liquid concentrate, liquid extract, or liquid distillate form, Felony, 3rd degree (2929.11 to 2929.18,2929.31) and division (C) of section 2929.13 applies in determining whether to impose a prison term on the offender.

(e) If the amount of hashish involved equals or exceeds 250 grams but is less than 1000 grams of hashish in a solid form or equals or exceeds 50 grams but is less than 200 grams of hashish in a liquid concentrate, liquid extract, or liquid distillate form, Felony, 3rd degree (2929.11 to 2929.18,2929.31) and there is a presumption for a prison term for the offense.

(f) If the amount of hashish involved equals or exceeds 1000 grams in a solid form or exceeds 200 grams of hashish in a liquid concentrate, liquid extract, or liquid distillate form, Felony, 2nd degree (2929.11 to 2929.18,2929.31) and the court shall impose as a mandatory prison term one of the prison terms prescribed for a felony of the 2nd degree.

Note: In addition to other penalties, if the violation is a felony of the 1st, 2nd, or 3rd degree, the court shall impose upon the offender the mandatory fine specified for the offense under Division (B)(1) of section 2929.18 unless, as specified in that division, the court determines that the offender is indigent.

Note: If a person is charged with any violation of this section that is a felony of the 1st, 2nd, or 3rd degree, posts bail and forfeits the bail, the forfeited bail shall be paid by the clerk of the court as if it were a fine imposed for a violation of this section.

Note: In addition to other penalties, court shall suspend, for 6 months to 5 years, the driver's or commercial driver's license or permit of the offender.

Note: If offender is professionally licensed person, court must notify immediately regulatory or licensing board or agency, or the commission on grievances and discipline of the Supreme Court, of conviction pursuant to 2925.38.

Drug Offenses—Possession—Possession of Heroin—2925.11(C)(6)

See also Drug Offenses—Permitting Drug Abuse

ELEMENTS OF THE CRIME

(1) Knowingly

(2) Obtain, possess, or use

(3) Heroin or a compound, mixture, preparation, or substance containing heroin

EXCEPTIONS

(1) Does not apply to manufacturers, licensed health professionals authorized to prescribe drugs, pharmacists, owners of pharmacies, or others whose conduct is in accordance with Chapters 3719., 4715., 4723., 4729., 4731., 4741.

(2) Does not apply to persons who obtained controlled substances pursuant to prescription issued by licensed health professionals authorized to prescribe drugs where drug is in original container in which it was dispensed.

DEFENSE

It is an affirmative defense to a 4th degree felony charge under this section that the substance that gave rise to the charge is in an amount, is in a form, is prepared, compounded, or mixed with substances that are not controlled substances in a manner, or is possessed or cultivated under any other circumstances, that indicate that the substance was possessed solely for personal use. If defendant sustains the burdens may be convicted of a 5th degree felony violation of RC 2925.11(C)(6).

PENALTY

If drug is heroin the penalty shall be determined as follows:

(a) Except as otherwise provided in division (C)(6)(b), (c), (d), (e), or (f) of this section, Felony, 5th degree (2929.11 to 2929.18, 2929.31) and division (B) of section 2929.13 applies in determining whether to impose a prison term on the offender.

(b) If the amount of heroin involved equals or exceeds 10 unit doses but is less than 50 unit doses or equals or exceeds 1 gram but is less than 5 grams, Felony, 4th degree (2929.11 to 2929.18, 2929.31) and division (C) of section 2929.13 applies in determining whether to impose a prison term on the offender.

(c) If the amount of heroin involved equals or exceeds 50 unit doses but is less than 100 unit doses or equals or exceeds 5 grams but is less than 10 grams, Felony, 3rd degree (2929.11 to 2929.18, 2929.31) and there is a presumption for a prison term for the offense.

(d) If the amount of heroin involved equals or exceeds 100 unit doses but is less than 500 unit doses or equals or exceeds 10 grams but is less than 50 grams, Felony, 2nd degree (2929.11 to 2929.18, 2929.31) and the court shall impose as a mandatory prison term one of the prison terms prescribed for a felony of the 2nd degree.

(e) If the amount of heroin involved equals or exceeds 500 unit doses but is less than 2,500 unit doses or equals or exceeds 50 grams but is less than 250 grams, Felony, 1st degree (2929.11 to 2929.18, 2929.31) and the court shall impose as a mandatory prison term one of the prison terms prescribed for a felony of the 1st degree.

(f) If the amount of heroin involved equals or exceeds 2,500 unit doses or equals or exceeds 250 grams, Felony, 1st degree (2929.11 to 2929.18, 2929.31) and the court shall impose as a mandatory prison term the maximum prison term prescribed for a felony of the 1st degree and may impose an additional mandatory prison term prescribed for a major drug offender under division (D)(3)(b) of section 2929.14.

Note: In addition to other penalties, if the violation is a felony of the 1st, 2nd, or 3rd degree, the court shall impose upon the offender the mandatory fine specified for the offense under Division (B)(1) of section 2929.18 unless, as specified in that division, the court determines that the offender is indigent.

Note: If a person is charged with any violation of this section that is a felony of the 1st, 2nd, or 3rd degree, posts bail and forfeits the bail, the forfeited bail shall be paid by the clerk of the court as if it were a fine imposed for a violation of this section.

Note: In addition to other penalties, court shall suspend, for 6 months to 5 years, the driver's or commercial driver's license or permit of the offender.

Note: If offender is professionally licensed person, court must notify immediately regulatory or licensing board or agency, or the commission on grievances and discipline of the Supreme Court, of conviction pursuant to 2925.38.

Drug Offenses—Possession—Possession of L.S.D.—2925.11(C)(5)

See also Drug Offenses—Permitting Drug Abuse

ELEMENTS OF THE CRIME

(1) Knowingly

(2) Obtain, possess, or use

(3) L.S.D. in solid form or liquid concentrate, extract, or distillate form

EXCEPTIONS

(1) Does not apply to manufacturers, licensed health professionals authorized to prescribe drugs, pharmacists, owners of pharmacies, or others whose conduct is in accordance with Chapters 3719., 4715., 4723., 4729., 4731., 4741.

(2) Does not apply to persons who obtained controlled substances pursuant to prescription issued by licensed health professionals authorized to prescribe drugs where drug is in original container in which it was dispensed.

DEFENSE

It is an affirmative defense to a 4th degree felony charge under this section that the substance that gave rise to the charge is in an amount, is in a form, is prepared, compounded, or mixed with substances that are not controlled substances in a manner, or is possessed or cultivated under any other circumstances, that indicate that the substance was possessed solely for personal use. If defendant sustains the burdens for this defense, s/he may be convicted of a 5th degree felony violation of RC 2925.11(C)(5).

PENALTY

If drug is L.S.D. the penalty shall be determined as follows:

(a) Except as otherwise provided in division (C)(5)(b), (c), (d), (e), or (f) of this section, Felony, 5th degree (2929.11 to 2929.18, 2929.31) and division (B) of section 2929.13 applies in determining whether to impose a prison term on the offender.

(b) If the amount of L.S.D. involved equals or exceeds 10 unit doses but is less than 50 unit doses in solid form or equals or exceeds 1 gram but is less than 5 grams of LSD in one of its liquid forms, Felony, 4th degree (2929.11 to 2929.18, 2929.31) and division (C) of section 2929.13 applies in determining whether to impose a prison term on the offender.

(c) If the amount of L.S.D. involved equals or exceeds 50 unit doses but is less than 250 unit doses in solid form or equals or exceeds 5 grams but is less than 25 grams of LSD in one of its liquid forms, Felony, 3rd degree (2929.11 to 2929.18, 2929.31) and there is a presumption for a prison term for the offense.

(d) If the amount of L.S.D. involved equals or exceeds 250 unit doses but is less than 1000 unit doses in solid form or equals or exceeds 25 grams but is less than 100 grams of LSD in one of its liquid forms, Felony, 2nd degree (2929.11 to 2929.18, 2929.31) and the court shall impose as a mandatory prison term one of the prison terms prescribed for a felony of the 2nd degree.

(e) If the amount of L.S.D. involved equals or exceeds 1000 unit doses but is less than 5,000 unit doses in solid form or equals or exceeds 100 grams but is less than 500 grams of LSD in one of its liquid forms, Felony, 1st degree (2929.11 to 2929.18, 2929.31) and the court shall impose as a mandatory prison term one of the prison terms prescribed for a felony of the 1st degree.

(f) If the amount of L.S.D. involved equals or exceeds 5,000 unit doses or equals or exceeds 500 grams of LSD in one of its liquid forms, Felony, 1st degree (2929.11 to 2929.18, 2929.31) and the court shall impose as a mandatory prison term the maximum prison term prescribed for a felony of the 1st degree and may impose an additional mandatory prison term prescribed for a major drug offender under division (D)(3)(b) of section 2929.14.

Note: In addition to other penalties, if the violation is a felony of the 1st, 2nd, or 3rd degree, the court shall impose upon the offender the mandatory fine specified for the offense under Division (B)(1) of section 2929.18 unless, as specified in that division, the court determines that the offender is indigent.

Note: If a person is charged with any violation of this section that is a felony of the 1st, 2nd, or 3rd degree, posts bail and forfeits the bail, the forfeited bail shall be paid by the clerk of the court as if it were a fine imposed for a violation of this section.

Note: In addition to other penalties, court shall suspend, for 6 months to 5 years, the driver's or commercial driver's license or permit of the offender.

Note: If offender is professionally licensed person, court must notify immediately regulatory or licensing board or agency, or the commission on grievances and discipline of the Supreme Court, of conviction pursuant to 2925.38.

Drug Offenses—Possession—Possession of Marihuana—2925.11(C)(3)

See also Drug Offenses—Permitting Drug Abuse

ELEMENTS OF THE CRIME

(1) Knowingly

(2) Obtain, possess, or use

(3) Marihuana or a compound mixture, preparation or substance containing marihuana other than hashish

Note: Anabolic steroids are now Schedule III controlled substances, as defined and listed in 3719.41, Schedule III(E).

EXCEPTIONS

(1) Does not apply to manufacturers, licensed health professionals authorized to prescribe drugs, pharmacists, owners of pharmacies, or others whose conduct is in accordance with Chapters 3719., 4715., 4723., 4729., 4731., 4741.

(2) Does not apply to persons who obtained controlled substances pursuant to prescription issued by licensed health professionals authorized to prescribe drugs where drug is in original container in which it was dispensed.

PENALTY

If drug is marihuana the penalty shall be determined as follows:

(a) Except as otherwise provided in division (C)(3)(b), (c), (d), (e), or (f) of this section, Minor misdemeanor (2929.21 to 2929.28, 2929.31)

(b) If the amount of the drug involved equals or exceeds 100 grams but is less than 200 grams, Misdemeanor, 4th degree (2929.21 to 2929.28, 2929.31)

(c) If the amount of the drug involved equals or exceeds 200 grams but is less than 1000 grams, Felony, 5th degree (2929.11 to 2929.18, 2929.31) and division (B) of section 2929.13 applies in determining whether to impose a prison term on the offender.

(d) If the amount of the drug involved equals or exceeds 1000 grams but is less than 5,000 grams, Felony, 3rd degree (2929.11 to 2929.18, 2929.31) and division (C) of section 2929.13 applies in determining whether to impose a prison term on the offender.

(e) If the amount of the drug involved equals or exceeds 5,000 grams but is less than 20,000 grams, Felony, 3rd degree (2929.11 to 2929.18, 2929.31) and there is a presumption for a prison term for the offense.

(f) If the amount of the drug involved equals or exceeds 20,000 grams, Felony, 2nd degree (2929.11 to 2929.18, 2929.31) the court shall impose as a mandatory prison term the maximum prison term prescribed for a felony of the 2nd degree.

Note: In addition to other penalties, if the violation is a felony of the 1st, 2nd, or 3rd degree, the court shall impose upon the offender the mandatory fine specified for the offense under Division (B)(1) of section 2929.18 unless, as specified in that division, the court determines that the offender is indigent.

Note: If a person is charged with any violation of this section that is a felony of the 1st, 2nd, or 3rd degree, posts bail and forfeits the bail, the forfeited bail shall be paid by the clerk of the court as if it were a fine imposed for a violation of this section.

Note: In addition to other penalties, court shall suspend, for 6 months to 5 years, the driver's or commercial driver's license or permit of the offender.

Note: If offender is professionally licensed person, court must notify immediately regulatory or licensing board or agency, or the commission on grievances and discipline of the Supreme Court, of conviction pursuant to 2925.38.

Drug Offenses—Preparation of Drugs for Sale—Aggravated Preparation—2925.07(C)(1)

ELEMENTS OF THE CRIME

(1)(a) Knowingly

(b) Prepare for shipment, ship, transport, deliver, prepare for distribution, or distribute a controlled substance

(2)(a) With intent to sell or resell the controlled substance, or

(b) With knowledge or reasonable cause to believe that another intends to sell or resell the controlled substance.

EXCEPTION

Does not apply to manufacturers, licensed health professionals authorized to prescribe drugs, pharmacists, owners of pharmacies or others whose conduct is in accordance with Chapters 3719., 4715., 4729., 4731., and 4741. or 4723.56.

PENALTY

If the drug involved in the violation is any compound, mixture, preparation, or substance included in schedule I or II, with the exception of marijuana, cocaine, LSD, heroin, and hashish, the penalty for the offense shall be determined as follows:

(a) Except as otherwise provided in this section, Felony, 4th degree (2929.11 to 2929.18, 2929.31) and division C of RC 2929.13 applies in determining whether to impose a prison term on the offender.

(b) If the offense was committed in the vicinity of a school or in the vicinity of a juvenile, Felony, 3rd degree (2929.11 to 2929.18, 2929.31), and division C of RC 2929.13 applies in determining whether to impose a prison term on the offender.

Note: If a violation of this section is a Felony of the 3rd degree, the court shall impose upon the offender the mandatory fine specified for the offense under division (B)(1) of 2929.18, and may impose an additional fine under 2929.18, unless as specified in the division, the offender is indigent. If a person charged with violation of this section that is a Felony of the 3rd degree, posts bail, and forfeits the bail, the clerk of court shall pay the forfeited bail as if the forfeited bail was a fine imposed for violation of this section.

Note: The court shall suspend the driver's or commercial driver's license or permit of an offender for violation of this section for 6 months to 5 years.

Note: If offender is professionally licensed or admitted to the bar, the court must notify regulatory or licensing board or agency of conviction pursuant to 2925.38.

Drug Offenses—Preparation of Drugs (Cocaine) for Sale—2925.07(C)(4)

ELEMENTS OF THE CRIME

(1)(a) Knowingly

(b) Prepare for shipment, ship, transport, deliver, prepare for distribution, or distribute a controlled substance

(2)(a) With intent to sell or resell the controlled substance, or

(b) With knowledge or reasonable cause to believe that another intends to sell or resell the controlled substance.

EXCEPTION

Does not apply to manufacturers, licensed health professionals authorized to prescribe drugs, pharmacists, owners of pharmacies or others whose conduct is in accordance with Chapters 3719., 4715., 4729., 4731., and 4741. or 4723.56.

PENALTY

If the drug involved in the violation is cocaine, or a substance containing cocaine, the penalty for the offense shall be determined as follows:

(a) Except as otherwise provided in this section, Felony, 5th degree (2929.11 to 2929.18, 2929.31) and division C of RC 2929.13 applies in determining whether to impose a prison term on the offender.

(b) If the offense was committed in the vicinity of a school or in the vicinity of a juvenile, Felony, 4th degree (2929.11 to 2929.18, 2929.31) and division C of RC 2929.13 applies in determining whether to impose a prison term on the offender.

(c) If the amount of the drug involved exceeds five grams of cocaine (not crack cocaine) or exceeds one gram of crack cocaine, Felony, 4th degree (2929.11 to 2929.18, 2929.31) and there is a presumption in favor of a prison term. If the amount of the drug involved exceeds five grams of cocaine (not crack cocaine) or exceeds one gram of crack cocaine, and was committed in the vicinity of a school or the vicinity of a juvenile, Felony, 3rd degree (2929.11 to 2929.18, 2929.31) and there is a presumption in favor of a prison term.

Note: If a violation of this section is a Felony of the 3rd degree, the court shall impose upon the offender the mandatory fine specified for the offense under division (B)(1) of 2929.18, and may impose an additional fine under 2929.18, unless as specified in the division, the offender is indigent. If a person charged with violation of this section that is a Felony of the 3rd degree, posts bail, and forfeits the bail, the clerk of court shall pay the forfeited bail as if the forfeited bail was a fine imposed for violation of this section.

Note: The court shall suspend the driver's or commercial driver's license or permit of an offender for violation of this section for 6 months to 5 years.

Note: If offender is professionally licensed or admitted to the bar, the court must notify regulatory or licensing board or agency of conviction pursuant to 2925.38.

Drug Offenses—Preparation of Drugs (Hashish) for Sale—2925.07(C)(7)

ELEMENTS OF THE CRIME

(1)(a) Knowingly

(b) Prepare for shipment, ship, transport, deliver, prepare for distribution, or distribute a controlled substance

(2)(a) With intent to sell or resell the controlled substance, or

(b) With knowledge or reasonable cause to believe that another intends to sell or resell the controlled substance.

EXCEPTION

Does not apply to manufacturers, licensed health professionals authorized to prescribe drugs, pharmacists, owners of pharmacies or others whose conduct is in accordance with Chapters 3719., 4715., 4729., 4731., and 4741. or 4723.56.

PENALTY

If the drug involved in the violation is hashish, or a compound, mixture, preparation or substance containing hashish, the penalty for the offense shall be determined as follows:

(a) Except as otherwise provided in this section, Felony, 5th degree (2929.11 to 2929.18, 2929.31) and division C of RC 2929.13 applies in determining whether to impose a prison term on the offender.

(b) If the offense was committed in the vicinity of a school or in the vicinity of a juvenile, Felony, 4th degree (2929.11 to 2929.18, 2929.31) and division C of RC 2929.13 applies in determining whether to impose a prison term on the offender.

(c) If the amount of the drug involved exceeds ten grams of hashish in solid form or exceeds two grams in liquid concentrate, liquid extract, or liquid distillate form, Felony, 4th degree (2929.11 to 2929.18, 2929.31) and division C of RC 2929.13 applies in determining whether to impose a prison term on the offender. If the amount of the drug involved exceeds ten grams of hashish in solid form or exceeds two grams in liquid concentrate, liquid extract, or liquid distillate of more than one gram, and if the offense was committed in the vicinity of a school or in the vicinity of a juvenile, Felony, 3rd degree (2929.11 to 2929.18, 2929.31) and division C of RC 2929.13 applies in determining whether to impose a prison term on the offender.

Note: If a violation of this section is a Felony of the 3rd degree, the court shall impose upon the offender the mandatory fine specified for the offense under division (B)(1) of 2929.18, and may impose an additional fine under 2929.18, unless as specified in the division, the offender is indigent. If a person charged with violation of this section that is a Felony of the 3rd degree, posts bail, and forfeits the bail, the clerk of court shall pay the forfeited bail as if the forfeited bail was a fine imposed for violation of this section.

Note: The court shall suspend the driver's or commercial driver's license or permit of an offender for violation of this section for 6 months to 5 years.

Note: If offender is professionally licensed or admitted to the bar, the court must notify regulatory or licensing board or agency of conviction pursuant to 2925.38.

Drug Offenses—Preparation of Drugs (Heroin) for Sale—2925.07(C)(6)

ELEMENTS OF THE CRIME

(1)(a) Knowingly

(b) Prepare for shipment, ship, transport, deliver, prepare for distribution, or distribute a controlled substance

(2)(a) With intent to sell or resell the controlled substance, or

(b) With knowledge or reasonable cause to believe that another intends to sell or resell the controlled substance.

EXCEPTION

Does not apply to manufacturers, licensed health professionals authorized to prescribe drugs, pharmacists, owners of pharmacies or others whose conduct is in accordance with Chapters 3719., 4715., 4729., 4731., and 4741. or 4723.56.

PENALTY

If the drug involved in the violation is heroin, or a compound, mixture, preparation or substance containing heroin, the penalty for the offense shall be determined as follows:

(a) Except as otherwise provided in this section, Felony, 5th degree (2929.11 to 2929.18, 2929.31) and division C of RC 2929.13 applies in determining whether to impose a prison term on the offender.

(b) If the offense was committed in the vicinity of a school or in the vicinity of a juvenile, Felony, 4th degree (2929.11 to 2929.18, 2929.31) and division C of RC 2929.13 applies in determining whether to impose a prison term on the offender.

(c) If the amount of the drug involved exceeds one gram, Felony, 4th degree (2929.11 to 2929.18, 2929.31) and there is a presumption in favor of a prison term. If the amount of the drug involved exceeds one gram, and if the offense was committed in the vicinity of a school or in the vicinity of a juvenile, Felony, 3rd degree (2929.11 to 2929.18, 2929.31) and there is a presumption in favor of a prison term.

Note: If a violation of this section is a Felony of the 3rd degree, the court shall impose upon the offender the mandatory fine specified for the offense under division (B)(1) of 2929.18, and may impose an additional fine under 2929.18, unless as specified in the division, the offender is indigent. If a person charged with violation of this section that is a Felony of the 3rd degree, posts bail, and forfeits the bail, the clerk of court shall pay the forfeited bail as if the forfeited bail was a fine imposed for violation of this section.

Note: The court shall suspend the driver's or commercial driver's license or permit of an offender for violation of this section for 6 months to 5 years.

Note: If offender is professionally licensed or admitted to the bar, the court must notify regulatory or licensing board or agency of conviction pursuant to 2925.38.

Drug Offenses—Preparation of Drugs (LSD) for Sale—2925.07(C)(5)

ELEMENTS OF THE CRIME

(1)(a) Knowingly

(b) Prepare for shipment, ship, transport, deliver, prepare for distribution, or distribute a controlled substance

(2)(a) With intent to sell or resell the controlled substance, or

(b) With knowledge or reasonable cause to believe that another intends to sell or resell the controlled substance.

EXCEPTION

Does not apply to manufacturers, licensed health professionals authorized to prescribe drugs, pharmacists, owners of pharmacies or others whose conduct is in accordance with Chapters 3719., 4715., 4729., 4731., and 4741. or 4723.56.

PENALTY

If the drug involved in the violation is LSD, or a compound, mixture, preparation or substance containing LSD, the penalty for the offense shall be determined as follows:

(a) Except as otherwise provided in this section, Felony, 5th degree (2929.11 to 2929.18, 2929.31) and division C of RC 2929.13 applies in determining whether to impose a prison term on the offender.

(b) If the offense was committed in the vicinity of a school or in the vicinity of a juvenile, Felony, 4th degree (2929.11 to 2929.18, 2929.31) and division C of RC 2929.13 applies in determining whether to impose a prison term on the offender.

(c) If the amount of the drug involved exceed ten unit doses of LSD in a solid form or one gram of LSD in liquid concentrate, liquid extract, or liquid distillate form, Felony, 4th degree (2929.11 to 2929.18, 2929.31) and there is a presumption in favor of a prison term. If the amount of the drug involved exceeds one of those amounts, and if the offense was committed in the vicinity of a school or in the vicinity of a juvenile, Felony, 3rd degree (2929.11 to 2929.18, 2929.31) and there is a presumption in favor of a prison term.

Note: If a violation of this section is a Felony of the 3rd degree, the court shall impose upon the offender the mandatory fine specified for the offense under division (B)(1) of 2929.18, and may impose an additional fine under 2929.18, unless as specified in the division, the offender is indigent. If a person charged with violation of this section that is a Felony of the 3rd degree, posts bail, and forfeits the bail, the clerk of court shall pay the forfeited bail as if the forfeited bail was a fine imposed for violation of this section.

Note: The court shall suspend the driver's or commercial driver's license or permit of an offender for violation of this section for 6 months to 5 years.

Note: If offender is professionally licensed or admitted to the bar, the court must notify regulatory or licensing board or agency of conviction pursuant to 2925.38.

Drug Offenses—Preparation of Drugs (Marihuana) for Sale—2925.07(C)(3)

ELEMENTS OF THE CRIME

(1)(a) Knowingly

(b) Prepare for shipment, ship, transport, deliver, prepare for distribution, or distribute a controlled substance

(2)(a) With intent to sell or resell the controlled substance, or

(b) With knowledge or reasonable cause to believe that another intends to sell or resell the controlled substance.

EXCEPTION

Does not apply to manufacturers, licensed health professionals authorized to prescribe drugs, pharmacists, owners of pharmacies or others whose conduct is in accordance with Chapters 3719., 4715., 4729., 4731., and 4741. or 4723.56.

PENALTY

If the drug involved in the violation is marihuana or any compound, mixture, preparation, or substance containing marihuana, other than hashish, the penalty for the offense shall be determined as follows:

(a) Except as otherwise provided in this section, Felony, 5th degree (2929.11 to 2929.18, 2929.31) and division C of RC 2929.13 applies in determining whether to impose a prison term on the offender.

(b) If the offense was committed in the vicinity of a school or in the vicinity of a juvenile, Felony, 4th degree (2929.11 to 2929.18, 2929.31), and division C of RC 2929.13 applies in determining whether to impose a prison term on the offender.

(c) If the amount of the drug involved exceeds 200 grams, Felony, 4th degree (2929.11 to 2929.18, 2929.31) and division C of RC 2929.13 applies in determining whether to impose a prison term on the offender. If the amount of the drug exceeds 200 grams and if the offense was committed in the vicinity of a school or in the vicinity of a juvenile, Felony, 3rd degree (2929.11 to 2929.18, 2929.31) and division C of RC 2929.13 applies in determining whether to impose a prison term on the offender.

Note: If a violation of this section is a Felony of the 3rd degree, the court shall impose upon the offender the mandatory fine specified for the offense under division (B)(1) of 2929.18, and may impose an additional fine under 2929.18, unless as specified in the division, the offender is indigent. If a person charged with violation of this section that is a Felony of the 3rd degree, posts bail, and forfeits the bail, the clerk of court shall pay the forfeited bail as if the forfeited bail was a fine imposed for violation of this section.

Note: The court shall suspend the driver's or commercial driver's license or permit of an offender for violation of this section for 6 months to 5 years.

Note: If offender is professionally licensed or admitted to the bar, the court must notify regulatory or licensing board or agency of conviction pursuant to 2925.38.

Drug Offenses—Preparation of Drugs (Schedule III, IV or V) for Sale—2925.07(C)(2)

ELEMENTS OF THE CRIME

(1)(a) Knowingly

(b) Prepare for shipment, ship, transport, deliver, prepare for distribution, or distribute a controlled substance

(2)(a) With intent to sell or resell the controlled substance, or

(b) With knowledge or reasonable cause to believe that another intends to sell or resell the controlled substance.

EXCEPTION

Does not apply to manufacturers, licensed health professionals authorized to prescribe drugs, pharmacists, owners of pharmacies or others whose conduct is in accordance with Chapters 3719., 4715., 4729., 4731., and 4741. or 4723.56.

PENALTY

If the drug involved in the violation is any compound, mixture, preparation, or substance included in schedule III, IV or V the penalty for the offense shall be determined as follows:

(a) Except as otherwise provided in this section, Felony, 5th degree (2929.11 to 2929.18, 2929.31) and division C of RC 2929.13 applies in determining whether to impose a prison term on the offender.

(b) If the offense was committed in the vicinity of a school or in the vicinity of a juvenile, Felony, 4th degree (2929.11 to 2929.18, 2929.31), and division C of RC 2929.13 applies in determining whether to impose a prison term on the offender.

(c) If the amount of the drug involved exceeds the bulk amount, Felony, 4th degree (2929.11 to 2929.18, 2929.31) and there is a presumption in favor of a prison term. If the amount of the drug exceeds the bulk amount and if the offense was committed in the vicinity of a school or in the vicinity of a juvenile, Felony, 3rd degree (2929.11 to 2929.18, 2929.31) and there is a presumption in favor of a prison term.

Note: If a violation of this section is a Felony of the 3rd degree, the court shall impose upon the offender the mandatory fine specified for the offense under division (B)(1) of 2929.18, and may impose an additional fine under 2929.18, unless as specified in the division, the offender is indigent. If a person charged with violation of this section that is a Felony of the 3rd degree, posts bail, and forfeits the bail, the clerk of court shall pay the forfeited bail as if the forfeited bail was a fine imposed for violation of this section.

Note: The court shall suspend the driver's or commercial driver's license or permit of an offender for violation of this section for 6 months to 5 years.

Note: If offender is professionally licensed or admitted to the bar, the court must notify regulatory or licensing board or agency of conviction pursuant to 2925.38.

Drug Offenses—Sale or Use of Drugs Not Approved by Food and Drug Administration—2925.09

ELEMENTS OF THE CRIME

Division (A):

(1) Administer, dispense, distribute, manufacture, possess, sell, or use

(2) Any drug, other than a controlled substance

(3) Not approved by the United States Food and Drug Administration or the United States Department of Agriculture, unless

(4)(a) The United States Food and Drug Administration has approved an application for investigational use in accordance with the Federal Food, Drug, and Cosmetic Act, 52 Stat. 1040 (1938), 21 U.S.C.A. 301, as amended, and the drug is used only for the approved investigational use, or

(b) The United States Department of Agriculture has approved an application for investigational use in accordance with the Federal Virus–Serum–Toxin Act, 37 Stat. 832 (1913), 21 U.S.C.A. 151, as amended, and the drug is used only for the approved investigational use, or

(c) A licensed health professionals authorized to prescribe drugs, other than a veterinarian, prescribes or combines two or more drugs as a single product for medical purposes, or

(d) A pharmacist, pursuant to a prescription, compounds and dispenses two or more drugs as a single product for medical purposes.

Division (B):

(1) Administer, dispense, distribute, manufacture, possess, sell, or use

(2) Any dangerous drug

(3) To or for livestock or any animal that is generally used for food or in the production of food

(4) Unless the drug is prescribed by a licensed veterinarian by prescription or other written order, and

(5) the drug is used in accordance with the veterinarian's order or direction

EXCEPTION

Division (B) does not apply to a registered wholesale distributor of dangerous drugs, a licensed terminal distributor of dangerous drugs, or a person who possesses, possesses for sale, or sells, at retail, a drug in accordance with Chapters 3719., 4729., or 4741.

PENALTY

Felony, 5th degree (2929.11 to 2929.18, 2929.31)

Each subsequent offense, Felony, 4th degree (2929.11 to 2929.18, 2929.31)

Drugs—Tampering With—2925.24

ELEMENTS OF THE CRIME

Division (A):

(1) Knowingly

(2) (a) Adulterate or alter any dangerous drug, or

(b) Substitute any dangerous drug with another substance

Division (B):

(1) Knowingly

(2) (a) Adulterate or alter any package or receptacle containing any dangerous drug, or

(b) Substitute any package or receptacle containing any dangerous drug with another package or receptacle

EXCEPTION

Does not apply to manufacturers, practitioners, pharmacists, owners of pharmacies, nurses, and other persons, when the conduct is in accordance with Chapters 3719., 4715., 4723., 4729., 4731., and 4741.

DEFENSE

Drug lawfully prescribed for personal use and did not sell or transfer or intend to sell or transfer drug to another person.

PENALTY

Felony, 3rd degree (2929.11 to 2929.18, 2929.31)

If physical harm to any person results, Felony, 2nd degree (2929.11 to 2929.18, 2929.31)

Drug Offenses—Theft of Drugs—2925.21

Repealed. Theft of drugs is now included within the theft section, 2913.02.

Drug Offenses—Trafficking—Aggravated Trafficking in Drugs—2925.03(C)(1)

ELEMENTS OF THE CRIME

(1)(a) Knowingly

(b) Sell or offer to sell controlled substance

Note: Anabolic steroids are now Schedule III controlled substances, as defined and listed in 3719.41, Schedule III(E), and may thus be subject of offense under Division (A)(1) to (10), as well as under Division (A)(11).

PROOF

When a person is charged with the sale or offer to sell a bulk amount or a multiple of a bulk amount of a controlled substance, the jury, or the court trying the accused, shall determine the amount of the controlled substance involved at the time of the offense and, if a guilty verdict is returned, shall return the findings as part of the verdict. In any such case, it is unnecessary to find and return the exact amount of the controlled substance involved, and it is sufficient if the finding and return is to the effect that the amount of the controlled substance involved is the requisite amount, or that the amount of the controlled substance involved is less than the requisite amount.

EXCEPTIONS

(1) Does not apply to manufacturers, licensed health professionals authorized to prescribe drugs, pharmacists, owners of pharmacies or others whose conduct is in accordance with Chapters 3719., 4715., 4723., 4729., 4731., and 4741.

(2) If offense involves anabolic steroid, does not apply to any person conducting or participating in research project involving use of anabolic steroids, if project has been approved by US Food and Drug Administration.

(3) Does not apply to person who sells, offers for sale, prescribes, dispenses, or administers, for livestock or other nonhuman species, anabolic steroids expressly intended for administration through implants to livestock or other nonhuman species and approved for that purpose under Federal Food, Drug, and Cosmetic Act, 52 Stat. 1040 (1938), 21 USCA 301, as amended, and are sold, offered for sale, prescribed, dispensed, or administered for that purpose in accordance with that Act.

PENALTY

If the drug involved in the violation is any compound, mixture, preparation, or substance included in schedule I or II, with the exception of marihuana, cocaine, L.S.D., heroin, and hashish, the penalty for the offense shall be determined as follows:

(a) Except as otherwise provided in this section, Felony, 4th degree (2929.11 to 2929.18, 2929.31) and division (C) of section 2929.13 of the Revised Code applies in determining whether to impose a prison term on the offender.

(b) If the offense was committed in the vicinity of a school or in the vicinity of a juvenile, Felony, 3rd degree (2929.11 to 2929.18, 2929.31) and division (C) of section 2929.13 applies in determining whether to impose a prison term on the offender.

(c) If the amount of the drug involved equals or exceeds the bulk amount but is less than 5 times the bulk amount, Felony, 3rd degree (2929.11 to 2929.18, 2929.31) and the court shall impose as a mandatory prison term one of the prison terms prescribed for a felony of the 3rd degree. If the amount of drug involved is within that range and if the offense was committed in the vicinity of a school or in the vicinity of a juvenile, Felony, 2nd degree (2929.11 to 2929.18, 2929.31) and the court shall impose as a mandatory prison term one of the prison terms prescribed for a felony of the 2nd degree.

(d) If the amount of the drug involved equals or exceeds 5 times the bulk amount but is less than 50 times the bulk amount, Felony, 2nd degree (2929.11 to 2929.18, 2929.31) and the court shall impose as a mandatory prison term one of the prison terms prescribed for a felony of the 2nd degree. If the amount of drug involved is within that range and if the offense was committed in the vicinity of a school or in the vicinity of a juvenile, Felony, 1st degree (2929.11 to 2929.18, 2929.31) and the court shall impose as a mandatory prison term one of the prison terms prescribed for a felony of the 1st degree.

(e) If the amount of the drug involved equals or exceeds 50 times the bulk amount but is less than 100 times the bulk amount, Felony, 1st degree (2929.11 to 2929.18, 2929.31) and the court shall impose as a mandatory prison term one of the prison terms prescribed for a felony of the 1st degree.

(f) If the amount of the drug involved equals or exceeds 100 times the bulk amount, Felony, 1st degree (2929.11 to 2929.18, 2929.31), the offender is a major drug offender and the court shall impose as a mandatory prison term the maximum prison term prescribed for a felony of the 1st degree and may impose an additional prison term prescribed for a major drug offender under division (D)(3)(b) of section 2929.14.

Note: If a violation of this section is a felony of the 1st, 2nd, or 3rd degree, the court shall impose upon the offender the mandatory fine specified for the offense under division (B)(1) of section 2929.18 and may impose an additional fine under 2929.18(B)(4), unless, as specified in that division, the court determines that the offender is indigent. If a person is charged with a violation of this section that is a felony of the 1st, 2nd, or 3rd degree, posts bail, and forfeits the bail, the clerk of court shall pay the forfeited bail as if the forfeited bail was a fine imposed for a violation of this section.

Note: In addition to other penalties, court shall suspend the offender's driver's license, commercial driver's license or permit for a definite period of not less than 6 months or more than 5 years.

Note: If offender is professionally licensed person, court must notify immediately regulatory or licensing board or agency, or the commission on grievances and discipline of the Supreme Court, of conviction pursuant to 2925.38.

Drug Offenses—Trafficking—Funding of Drug Trafficking—2925.05

ELEMENTS OF THE CRIME

(1) Knowingly

(2) Provide money or other items of value

(3) To another person

(4) With the purpose that the recipient use them to obtain

(5) Any controlled substance

(6)(a) For the purpose of violating 2925.04, or

(b) For the purpose of selling or offering to sell the controlled substance in the following amounts:

(1) Schedule I or II (except marihuana, cocaine, L.S.D., heroin, or hashish), Schedule III, IV, or V: equals or exceeds the bulk amount.

(2) Marihuana or hashish: equals or exceeds 200 grams.

(3) Cocaine: equals or exceeds 5 grams, or equals or exceeds 1 gram of crack cocaine.

(4) L.S.D.: equals or exceeds 10 unit doses solid form, or equal, or exceeds 1 gram liquid form.

(5) Heroin: equals or exceeds 10 unit doses, or equals or exceeds 1 gram.

(6) Hashish: equals or exceeds 10 grams solid form, or equals or exceeds 2 grams liquid form.

EXCEPTIONS

This section does not apply to any of the following:

(1) Manufacturers, licensed health professionals authorized to prescribe drugs, pharmacists, owners of pharmacies, and other persons whose conduct is in accordance with Chapter 3719., 4715., 4729., 4731., or 4741. or section 4723.56 of the Revised Code.

(2) If the offense involves an anabolic steroid, any person who is conducting or participating in a research project involving the use of an anabolic steroid if the project has been approved by the United States food and drug administration.

(3) Any person who sells, offers for sale, prescribes, dispenses, or administers for livestock or other nonhuman species an anabolic steroid that is expressly intended for administration through implants to livestock or other nonhuman species and approved for that purpose under the "Federal Food, Drug, and Cosmetic Act", 52 Stat. 1040 (1938), 21 U.S.C.A. 301, as amended, and is sold, offered for sale, prescribed, dispensed, or administered for that purpose in accordance with that act.

PENALTY

Division (A)—Aggravated funding of drug trafficking

Felony, 1st degree (2929.11 to 2929.18, 2929.31) and the court shall impose as a mandatory prison term one of the prison terms prescribed for a felony of the first degree.

Division (B)—Funding of drug trafficking

Felony, 2nd degree (2929.11 to 2929.18, 2929.31) and the court shall impose as a mandatory prison term one of the prison terms prescribed for a felony of the second degree.

Division (C)—Funding of marihuana trafficking

Felony, 3rd degree (2929.11 to 2929.18, 2929.31) and the court shall impose as a mandatory prison term one of the prison terms prescribed for a felony of the third degree.

Note: The court shall impose upon the offender the mandatory fine specified for the offense under division (B)(1) of section 2929.18 of the Revised Code unless, as specified in that division, the court determines that the offender is indigent. If a person is charged with a violation of this section that is a felony of the second or third degree, posts bail, and forfeits the bail, the clerk shall pay the forfeited bail as if the forfeited bail were a fine imposed for a violation of this section.

Note: In addition to other penalties, court shall suspend the offender's driver's license, commercial driver's license or permit for a definite period of not less than 6 months or more than 5 years.

Note: If offender is professionally licensed person, court must notify immediately regulatory or licensing board or agency, or the commission on grievances and discipline of the Supreme Court, of conviction pursuant to 2925.38.

Note: Notwithstanding the prison term otherwise authorized or required for the offense under this section and sections 2929.13 and 2929.14 of the Revised Code, if the violation of this section involves the sale, offer to sell, or possession of a schedule I or II controlled substance, with the exception of marihuana, and if the offender, as a result of the violation, is a major drug offender and is guilty of a 2941.1410 specification, the court, in lieu of the prison term otherwise authorized or required, shall impose upon the offender the mandatory prison term specified in division (D)(3)(a) of section 2929.14 of the Revised Code and may impose an additional prison term under division (D)(3)(b) of that section.

Drug Offenses—Trafficking—Trafficking in Cocaine—2925.03(C)(4)

ELEMENTS OF THE CRIME

(1)(a) Knowingly

(b) Sell or offer to sell cocaine

EXCEPTION

Does not apply to manufacturers, licensed health professionals authorized to prescribe drugs, pharmacists, owners of pharmacies or others whose conduct is in accordance with Chapters 3719., 4715., 4723., 4729., 4731., and 4741.

PENALTY

If the drug involved in the violation is cocaine or a compound, mixture, preparation, or substance containing cocaine, the penalty for the offense shall be determined as follows:

(a) Except as otherwise provided in this section, Felony, 5th degree (2929.11 to 2929.18, 2929.31) and division (C) of section 2929.13 of the Revised Code applies in determining whether to impose a prison term on the offender.

(b) If the offense was committed in the vicinity of a school or in the vicinity of a juvenile, Felony, 4th degree (2929.11 to 2929.18, 2929.31) and division (C) of section 2929.13 applies in determining whether to impose a prison term on the offender.

(c) If the amount of cocaine involved equals or exceeds 5 grams but is less than 10 grams of cocaine that is not crack cocaine or equals or exceeds 1 gram but is less than 5 grams of crack cocaine, Felony, 4th degree (2929.11 to 2929.18, 2929.31) and there is a presumption for a prison term for the offense. If the amount of cocaine involved is within one of those ranges and if the offense was committed in the vicinity of a school or in the vicinity of a juvenile, Felony, 3rd degree (2929.11 to 2929.18, 2929.31) and there is a presumption for a prison term for the offense.

(d) If the amount of cocaine involved equals or exceeds 10 grams but is less than 100 grams of cocaine that is not crack cocaine or equals or exceeds 5 grams but is less than 10 grams of crack cocaine, Felony, 3rd degree (2929.11 to 2929.18, 2929.31) and the court shall impose as a mandatory prison term one of the prison terms prescribed for a felony of the 3rd degree. If the amount of cocaine involved is within one of those ranges and if the offense was committed in the vicinity of a school or in the vicinity of a juvenile, Felony, 2nd degree (2929.11 to 2929.18, 2929.31) and the court shall impose as a mandatory prison term one of the prison terms prescribed for a felony of the 2nd degree.

(e) If the amount of cocaine involved equals or exceeds 100 grams but is less than 500 grams of cocaine that is not crack cocaine or equals or exceeds 10 grams but is less than 25 grams of crack cocaine, Felony, 2nd degree (2929.11 to 2929.18, 2929.31) and the court shall impose as a mandatory prison term one of the prison terms prescribed for a felony of the 2nd degree. If the amount of cocaine involved is within one of those ranges and if the offense was committed in the vicinity of a school or in the vicinity of a juvenile, Felony, 1st degree (2929.11 to 2929.18, 2929.31) and the court shall impose as a mandatory prison term one of the prison terms prescribed for a felony of the 1st degree.

(f) If the amount of cocaine involved equals or exceeds 500 grams but is less than 1000 grams of cocaine that is not crack cocaine or equals or exceeds 25 grams but is less than 100 grams of crack cocaine, Felony, 1st degree (2929.11 to 2929.18, 2929.31) and the court shall impose as a mandatory prison term one of the prison terms prescribed for a felony of the 1st degree.

(g) If the amount of cocaine involved equals or exceeds 1000 grams of cocaine that is not crack cocaine or equals or exceeds 100 grams of crack cocaine, Felony, 1st degree (2929.11 to 2929.18, 2929.31) and the offender is a major drug offender the court shall impose as a mandatory prison term the maximum prison term prescribed for a felony of the 1st degree and may impose an additional mandatory prison term prescribed for a major drug offender under division (D)(3)(b) of section 2929.14.

Note: If a violation of this section is a felony of the 1st, 2nd, or 3rd degree, the court shall impose upon the offender the mandatory fine specified for the offense under division (B)(1) of section 2929.18 and may impose an additional fine under 2929.18(B)(4), unless, as specified in that division, the court determines that the offender is indigent. If a person is charged with a violation of this section that is a felony of the 1st, 2nd, or 3rd degree, posts bail, and forfeits the bail, the clerk of court shall pay the forfeited bail as if the forfeited bail was a fine impose for a violation of this section.

Note: In addition to other penalties, court shall suspend the offender's driver's license, commercial driver's license or permit for a definite period of not less than 6 months or more than 5 years.

Note: If offender is professionally licensed person, court must notify immediately regulatory or licensing board or agency, or the commission on grievances and discipline of the Supreme Court, of conviction pursuant to 2925.38.

Drug Offenses—Trafficking—Trafficking in Drugs—2925.03(C)(2)

ELEMENTS OF THE CRIME

(1)(a) Knowingly

(b) Sell or offer to sell controlled substance

Note: Anabolic steroids are now Schedule III controlled substances, as defined and listed in 3719.41, Schedule III(E), and may thus be subject of offense under Division (A)(1) to (10), as well as under Division (A)(11).

PROOF

When a person is charged with the sale or offer to sell a bulk amount or a multiple of a bulk amount of a controlled substance, the jury, or the court trying the accused, shall determine the amount of the controlled substance involved at the time of the offense and, if a guilty verdict is returned, shall return the findings as part of the verdict. In any such case, it is unnecessary to find and return the exact amount of the controlled substance involved, and it is sufficient if the finding and return is to the effect that the amount of the controlled substance involved is the requisite amount, or that the amount of the controlled substance involved is less than the requisite amount.

EXCEPTIONS

(1) Does not apply to manufacturers, licensed health professionals authorized to prescribe drugs, pharmacists, owners of pharmacies or others whose conduct is in accordance with Chapters 3719., 4715., 4723., 4729., 4731., and 4741.

(2) If offense involves anabolic steroid, does not apply to any person conducting or participating in research project involving use of anabolic steroids, if project has been approved by US Food and Drug Administration.

(3) Does not apply to person who sells, offers for sale, prescribes, dispenses, or administers, for livestock or other nonhuman species, anabolic steroids expressly intended for administration through implants to livestock or other nonhuman species and approved for that purpose under Federal Food, Drug, and Cosmetic Act, 52 Stat. 1040 (1938), 21 USCA 301, as amended, and are sold, offered for sale, prescribed, dispensed, or administered for that purpose in accordance with that Act.

PENALTY

If the drug involved in the violation is any compound, mixture, preparation, or substance included in schedule III, IV or V, the penalty for the offense shall be determined as follows:

(a) Except as otherwise provided in this section, Felony, 5th degree (2929.11 to 2929.18, 2929.31) and division (C) of section 2929.13 of the Revised Code applies in determining whether to impose a prison term on the offender.

(b) If the offense was committed in the vicinity of a school or in the vicinity of a juvenile, Felony, 4th degree (2929.11 to 2929.18, 2929.31) and division (C) of section 2929.13 applies in determining whether to impose a prison term on the offender.

(c) If the amount of the drug involved equals or exceeds the bulk amount but is less than 5 times the bulk amount, Felony, 4th degree (2929.11 to 2929.18, 2929.31) and there is a presumption for a prison term for the offense. If the amount of drug involved is within that range and if the offense was committed in the vicinity of a school or in the vicinity of a juvenile, Felony, 3rd degree (2929.11 to 2929.18, 2929.31) and there is a presumption for a prison term for the offense.

(d) If the amount of the drug involved equals or exceeds 5 times the bulk amount but is less than 50 times the bulk amount, Felony, 3rd degree (2929.11 to 2929.18, 2929.31) and there is a presumption of a prison term for the offense. If the amount of drug involved is within that range and if the offense was committed in the vicinity of a school or in the vicinity of a juvenile, Felony, 2nd degree (2929.11 to 2929.18, 2929.31) and there is a presumption for a prison term for the offense.

(e) If the amount of the drug involved equals or exceeds 50 times the bulk amount, Felony, 2nd degree (2929.11 to 2929.18, 2929.31) and the court shall impose as a mandatory prison term one of the prison terms prescribed for a felony of the 2nd degree. If the amount of drug involved equals or exceeds 50 times the bulk amount and if the offense was committed in the vicinity of a school or in the vicinity of a juvenile, Felony, 1st degree (2929.11 to 2929.18, 2929.31) and the court shall impose as a mandatory prison term one of the prison terms prescribed for a felony of the 1st degree.

Note: If a violation of this section is a felony of the 1st, 2nd, or 3rd degree, the court shall impose upon the offender the mandatory fine specified for the offense under division (B)(1) of section 2929.18 and may impose an additional fine under 2929.18(B)(4), unless, as specified in that division, the court determines that the offender is indigent. If a person is charged with a violation of this section that is a felony of the 1st, 2nd, or 3rd degree, posts bail, and forfeits the bail, the clerk of court shall pay the forfeited bail as if the forfeited bail was a fine impose for a violation of this section.

Note: In addition to other penalties, court shall suspend the offender's driver's license, commercial driver's license or permit for a definite period of not less than 6 months or more than 5 years.

Note: If offender is professionally licensed person, court must notify immediately regulatory or licensing board or agency, or the commission on grievances and discipline of the Supreme Court, of conviction pursuant to 2925.38.

Drug Offenses—Trafficking—Trafficking in Harmful Intoxicants—2925.32

ELEMENTS OF THE CRIME

Division (A)(1):

(1) Knowingly

(2) Dispense or distribute

(3) Harmful intoxicant

(4) To person 18 years of age or older

(5) With knowledge or reason to believe

(6) Harmful intoxicant will be used in violation of 2925.31 (Abusing Harmful Intoxicants)

Division (A)(2):

(1) Knowingly

(2) Dispense or distribute

(3) Harmful intoxicant

(4) To person under 18 years of age

(5) With knowledge or reason to believe

(6) Harmful intoxicant will be used in violation of 2925.31 (Abusing Harmful Intoxicants)

Division (B)(1):

(1) Knowingly

(2) Dispense or distribute nitrous oxide

(3) To person 21 years of age or older

(4) With knowledge or reason to believe

(5) Nitrous oxide will be used in violation of 2925.31

Division (B)(2):

(1) Knowingly

(2) Dispense or distribute nitrous oxide

(3) To person under 21 years of age

(4) Except for lawful medical, dental or clinical purposes

Division (B)(3):

(1) Sell a cartridge of nitrous oxide

(2) Sell a device which

(a) allows the purchaser to inhale nitrous oxide from cartridges, or

(b) hold nitrous oxide released from cartridges for purposes of inhalation

Division (B)(4):

(1) Dispense or distribute nitrous oxide in cartridges

(2) Without

(a) complying with the recordkeeping requirements of 2925.32(F), or

(b) complying with the labeling and transaction identification requirements of 2925.32(G)

EXCEPTIONS

Section inapplicable to products used in making, fabricating, assembling, transporting or constructing a product or structure for sale or lease, or to mining, refining or processing natural deposits.

Divisions (A)(1) and (2) do not apply to nitrous oxide.

DEFENSES

Division (A)(1) does not apply if the dispenser or distributor does not know or have reason to believe that the harmful intoxicant will be used in violation of 2925.31.

Division (A)(2) does not apply if there is a written order from juvenile's parent or guardian given to dispenser or distributor, or if the dispenser or distributor does not know or have reason to believe that the harmful intoxicant will be used in violation of 2925.31.

(A)(1) and (A)(2) do not apply if the person does not know or have reason to believe that substance dispensed to a juvenile will be used in violation of 2925.31.

It is an affirmative defense to a charge under (A)(2) or (B)(2) that the person displayed a driver's license or identification issued by the state purporting to establish the age of the person, and that the document appeared to be genuine and unaltered, and that defendant or defendant's agent did not have reasonable cause to believe that the person was under the age represented.

PRESUMPTION

The sale of any device, along with the sale of a nitrous oxide cartridge, that allows the purchaser to inhale nitrous oxide from the cartridge or allows the purchaser to hold nitrous oxide released from the cartridge for inhalation creates a "rebuttable presumption" (inference) that the person knew or had reason to believe that the purchaser intended to abuse nitrous oxide.

PENALTY

Felony, 5th degree if violation of (A)(1), (A)(2), (B)(1), (B)(2), or (B)(3); Felony, 4th degree if offender has a prior drug abuse offense conviction (2929.11 to 2929.18, 2929.31)

Misdemeanor, 4th degree, if violation of (B)(4) (2929.21 to 2929.28, 2929.31)

Note: In addition to other penalties, court shall suspend, for 6 months to 5 years, the driver's or commercial driver's license or permit of the offender.

Note: If offender is professionally licensed person, court must notify immediately regulatory or licensing board or agency, or the commission on grievances and discipline of the Supreme Court, of conviction pursuant to 2925.38.

Drug Offenses—Trafficking—Trafficking in Hashish—2925.03(C)(7)

ELEMENTS OF THE CRIME

(1)(a) Knowingly

(b) Sell or offer to sell hashish or a compound, mixture, preparation or substance containing hashish

EXCEPTION

Does not apply to manufacturers, licensed health professionals authorized to prescribe drugs, pharmacists, owners of pharmacies or others whose conduct is in accordance with Chapters 3719., 4715., 4723., 4729., 4731., and 4741.

PENALTY

If the drug involved in the violation is hashish, the penalty for the offense shall be determined as follows:

(a) Except as otherwise provided in this section, Felony, 5th degree (2929.11 to 2929.18, 2929.31) and division (C) of section 2929.13 of the Revised Code applies in determining whether to impose a prison term on the offender.

(b) If the offense was committed in the vicinity of a school or in the vicinity of a juvenile, Felony, 4th degree (2929.11 to 2929.18, 2929.31) and division (C) of section 2929.13 applies in determining whether to impose a prison term on the offender.

(c) If the amount of hashish involved equals or exceeds 10 grams but is less than 50 grams of hashish in a solid form or equals or exceeds 2 grams but is less than 10 grams of hashish in a liquid concentrate, liquid extract, or liquid distillate form, Felony, 4th degree (2929.11 to 2929.18, 2929.31) and division (C) of section 2929.13 applies in determining whether to impose a prison term on the offender. If the amount of hashish involved is within that range and if the offense was committed in the vicinity of a school or in the vicinity of a juvenile, Felony, 3rd degree (2929.11 to 2929.18, 2929.31) and division (C) of section 2929.13 applies in determining whether to impose a prison term on the offender.

(d) If the amount of hashish involved equals or exceeds 50 grams but is less than 250 grams of hashish in a solid form or equals or exceeds 10 grams but is less than 50 grams of hashish in a liquid concentrate, liquid extract, or liquid distillate form, Felony, 3rd degree (2929.11 to 2929.18, 2929.31) and division (C) of section 2929.13 applies in determining whether to impose a prison term on the offender. If the amount of hashish involved is within that range and if the offense was committed in the vicinity of a school or in the vicinity of a juvenile, Felony, 2nd degree (2929.11 to2929.18, 2929.31) and there is a presumption for a prison term for the offense.

(e) If the amount of hashish involved equals or exceeds 250 grams but is less than 1000 grams of hashish in a solid form or equals or exceeds 50 grams but is less than 250 grams of hashish in a liquid concentrate, liquid extract, or liquid distillate form, Felony, 3rd degree (2929.11 to 2929.18, 2929.31) there is a presumption for a prison term for the offense. If the amount of hashish involved is within that range and if the offense was committed in the vicinity of a school or in the vicinity of a juvenile, Felony, 2nd degree (2929.11 to 2929.18, 2929.31) and there is a presumption for a prison term for the offense.

(f) If the amount of hashish involved equals or exceeds 1000 grams of hashish in a solid form or equals or exceeds 250 grams of hashish in a liquid concentrate, liquid extract, or liquid distillate form, Felony, 2nd degree (2929.11 to 2929.18, 2929.31) and the court shall impose as a mandatory prison term the maximum prison term prescribed for a felony of the 2nd degree. If the amount of drug is within that range and if the offense was committed in the vicinity of a school or in the vicinity of a juvenile, Felony, 1st degree (2929.11 to 2929.18, 2929.31) and the court shall impose as a mandatory prison term the maximum prison term prescribed for a felony of the 1st degree.

Note: If a violation of this section is a felony of the 1st, 2nd, or 3rd degree, the court shall impose upon the offender the mandatory fine specified for the offense under division (B)(1) of section 2929.18 and may impose an additional fine under 2929.18(B)(4), unless, as specified in that division, the court determines that the offender is indigent. If a person is charged with a violation of this section that is a felony of the 1st, 2nd, or 3rd degree, posts bail, and forfeits the bail, the clerk of court shall pay the forfeited bail as if the forfeited bail was a fine impose for a violation of this section.

Note: In addition to other penalties, court shall suspend the offender's driver's license, commercial driver's license or permit for a definite period of not less than 6 months or more than 5 years.

Note: If offender is professionally licensed person, court must notify immediately regulatory or licensing board or agency, or the commission on grievances and discipline of the Supreme Court, of conviction pursuant to 2925.38.

Drug Offenses—Trafficking—Trafficking in Heroin—2925.03(C)(6)

ELEMENTS OF THE CRIME

(1)(a) Knowingly

(b) Sell or offer to sell heroin or a compound, mixture, preparation or substance containing heroin

EXCEPTION

Does not apply to manufacturers, licensed health professionals authorized to prescribe drugs, pharmacists, owners of pharmacies or others whose conduct is in accordance with Chapters 3719., 4715., 4723., 4729., 4731., and 4741.

PENALTY

If the drug involved in the violation is heroin, the penalty for the offense shall be determined as follows:

(a) Except as otherwise provided in this section, Felony, 5th degree (2929.11 to 2929.18, 2929.31) and division (C) of section 2929.13 of the Revised Code applies in determining whether to impose a prison term on the offender.

(b) If the offense was committed in the vicinity of a school or in the vicinity of a juvenile, Felony, 4th degree (2929.11 to 2929.18, 2929.31) and division (C) of section 2929.13 applies in determining whether to impose a prison term on the offender.

(c) If the amount of heroin involved equals or exceeds 10 unit doses but is less than 50 unit doses or equals or exceeds 1 gram but is less than 5 grams, Felony, 4th degree (2929.11 to 2929.18, 2929.31) and there is a presumption for a prison term for the offense. If the amount of heroin involved is within that range and if the offense was committed in the vicinity of a school or in the vicinity of a juvenile, Felony, 3rd degree (2929.11 to 2929.18, 2929.31) and there is a presumption for a prison term for the offense.

(d) If the amount of heroin involved equals or exceeds 50 unit doses but is less than 100 unit doses or equals or exceeds 5 grams but is less than 10 grams, Felony, 3rd degree (2929.11 to 2929.18, 2929.31) and there is a presumption for a prison term for the offense. If the amount of heroin involved is within that range and if the offense was committed in the vicinity of a school or in the vicinity of a juvenile, Felony, 2nd degree (2929.11 to 2929.18, 2929.31) and there is a presumption for a prison term for the offense.

(e) If the amount of heroin involved equals or exceeds 100 unit doses but is less than 500 unit doses or equals or exceeds 10 grams but is less than 50 grams, Felony, 2nd degree (2929.11 to 2929.18, 2929.31) and the court shall impose as a mandatory prison term one of the prison terms prescribed for a felony of the 2nd degree. If the amount of heroin involved is within that range and if the offense was committed in the vicinity of a school or in the vicinity of a juvenile, Felony, 1st degree (2929.11 to 2929.18, 2929.31) and the court shall impose as a mandatory prison term one of the prison terms prescribed for a felony of the 1st degree.

(f) If the amount of heroin involved equals or exceeds 500 unit doses but is less than 2500 unit doses or equals or exceeds 50 grams but is less than 250 grams, Felony, 1st degree (2929.11 to 2929.18, 2929.31) and the court shall impose as a mandatory prison term one of the prison terms prescribed for a felony of the 1st degree.

(g) If the amount of heroin involved equals or exceeds 2500 unit doses or equals or exceeds 250 grams, Felony, 1st degree (2929.11 to 2929.18, 2929.31) and the offender is a major drug offender the court shall impose as a mandatory prison term the maximum prison term prescribed for a felony of the 1st degree and may impose an additional mandatory prison term prescribed for a major drug offender under division (D)(3)(b) of section 2929.14.

Note: If a violation of this section is a felony of the 1st, 2nd, or 3rd degree, the court shall impose upon the offender the mandatory fine specified for the offense under division (B)(1) of section 2929.18 and may impose an additional fine under 2929.18(B)(4), unless, as specified in that division, the court determines that the offender is indigent. If a person is charged with a violation of this section that is a felony of the 1st, 2nd, or 3rd degree, posts bail, and forfeits the bail, the clerk of court shall pay the forfeited bail as if the forfeited bail was a fine impose for a violation of this section.

Note: In addition to other penalties, court shall suspend the offender's driver's license, commercial driver's license or permit for a definite period of not less than 6 months or more than 5 years.

Note: If offender is professionally licensed person, court must notify immediately regulatory or licensing board or agency, or the commission on grievances and discipline of the Supreme Court, of conviction pursuant to 2925.38.

Drug Offenses—Trafficking—Trafficking in L.S.D.—2925.03(C)(5)

ELEMENTS OF THE CRIME

(1)(a) Knowingly

(b) Sell or offer to sell L.S.D. in a solid or liquid form

EXCEPTION

Does not apply to manufacturers, licensed health professionals authorized to prescribe drugs, pharmacists, owners of pharmacies or others whose conduct is in accordance with Chapters 3719., 4715., 4723., 4729., 4731., and 4741.

PENALTY

If the drug involved in the violation is L.S.D., the penalty for the offense shall be determined as follows:

(a) Except as otherwise provided in this section, Felony, 5th degree (2929.11 to 2929.18, 2929.31) and division (C) of section 2929.13 of the Revised Code applies in determining whether to impose a prison term on the offender.

(b) If the offense was committed in the vicinity of a school or in the vicinity of a juvenile, Felony, 4th degree (2929.11 to 2929.18, 2929.31) and division (C) of section 2929.13 applies in determining whether to impose a prison term on the offender.

(c) If the amount of L.S.D. involved equals or exceeds 10 unit doses but is less than 50 unit doses in a solid form or equals or exceeds 1 gram but is less than 5 grams of L.S.D. in a liquid concentrate, liquid extract, or liquid distillate form, Felony, 4th degree (2929.11 to 2929.18, 2929.31) and there is a presumption for a prison term for the offense. If the amount of L.S.D. involved is within that range and if the offense was committed in the vicinity of a school or in the vicinity of a juvenile, Felony, 3rd degree (2929.11 to 2929.18, 2929.31) and there is a presumption for a prison term for the offense.

(d) If the amount of L.S.D. involved equals or exceeds 50 unit doses but is less than 250 unit doses in a solid form or equals or exceeds 5 grams but is less than 25 grams of L.S.D. in a liquid concentrate, liquid extract, or liquid distillate form, Felony, 3rd degree (2929.11 to 2929.18, 2929.31) and the court shall impose as a mandatory prison term one of the prison terms prescribed for a felony of the 3rd degree. If the amount of L.S.D. involved is within that range and if the offense was committed in the vicinity of a school or in the vicinity of a juvenile, Felony, 2nd degree (2929.11 to 2929.18, 2929.31) and the court shall impose as a mandatory prison term one of the prison terms prescribed for a felony of the 2nd degree.

(e) If the amount of L.S.D. involved equals or exceeds 250 unit doses but is less than 1000 unit doses in a solid form or equals or exceeds 25 grams but is less than 100 grams of L.S.D. in a liquid concentrate, liquid extract, or liquid distillate form, Felony, 2nd degree (2929.11 to 2929.18, 2929.31) and the court shall impose as a mandatory prison term one of the prison terms prescribed for a felony of the 2nd degree. If the amount of L.S.D. involved is within that range and if the offense was committed in the vicinity of a school or in the vicinity of a juvenile, Felony, 1st degree (2929.11 to 2929.18, 2929.31) and the court shall impose as a mandatory prison term one of the prison terms prescribed for a felony of the 1st degree.

(f) If the amount of L.S.D. involved equals or exceeds 1000 unit doses but is less than 5,000 unit doses in a solid form or equals or exceeds 100 grams but is less than 500 grams of L.S.D. in a liquid concentrate, liquid extract, or liquid distillate form, Felony, 1st degree (2929.11 to 2929.18, 2929.31) and the court shall impose as a mandatory prison term one of the prison terms prescribed for a felony of the 1st degree.

(g) If the amount of L.S.D. involved equals or exceeds 5,000 unit doses in a solid form or equals or exceeds 500 grams in a liquid form, Felony, 1st degree (2929.11 to 2929.18, 2929.31) and the offender is a major drug offender the court shall impose as a mandatory prison term the maximum prison term prescribed for a felony of the 1st degree and may impose an additional mandatory prison term prescribed for a major drug offender under division (D)(3)(b) of section 2929.14.

Note: If a violation of this section is a felony of the 1st, 2nd, or 3rd degree, the court shall impose upon the offender the mandatory fine specified for the offense under division (B)(1) of section 2929.18 and may impose an additional fine under 2929.18(B)(4), unless, as specified in that division, the court determines that the offender is indigent. If a person is charged with a violation of this section that is a felony of the 1st, 2nd, or 3rd degree, posts bail, and forfeits the bail, the clerk of court shall pay the forfeited bail as if the forfeited bail was a fine impose for a violation of this section.

Note: In addition to other penalties, court shall suspend the offender's driver's license, commercial driver's license or permit for a definite period of not less than 6 months or more than 5 years.

Note: If offender is professionally licensed person, court must notify immediately regulatory or licensing board or agency, or the commission on grievances and discipline of the Supreme Court, of conviction pursuant to 2925.38.

Drug Offenses—Trafficking—Trafficking in Marihuana—2925.03(C)(3)

ELEMENTS OF THE CRIME

(1)(a) Knowingly

(b) Sell or offer to sell marihuana or a compound, mixture, preparation or substance containing marihuana (other than hashish)

EXCEPTION

Does not apply to manufacturers, licensed health professionals authorized to prescribe drugs, pharmacists, owners of pharmacies or others whose conduct is in accordance with Chapters 3719., 4715., 4723., 4729., 4731., and 4741.

PENALTY

If the drug involved in the violation is marihuana, the penalty for the offense shall be determined as follows:

(a) Except as otherwise provided in this section, Felony, 5th degree (2929.11 to 2929.18, 2929.31) and division (C) of section 2929.13 of the Revised Code applies in determining whether to impose a prison term on the offender.

(b) If the offense was committed in the vicinity of a school or in the vicinity of a juvenile, Felony, 4th degree (2929.11 to 2929.18, 2929.31) and division (C) of section 2929.13 applies in determining whether to impose a prison term on the offender.

(c) If the amount of marihuana involved equals or exceeds 200 grams but is less than 1000 grams, Felony, 4th degree (2929.11 to 2929.18, 2929.31) and division (C) of section 2929.13 applies in determining whether to impose a prison term on the offender. If the amount of marihuana involved is within that range and if the offense was committed in the vicinity of a school or in the vicinity of a juvenile, Felony, 3rd degree (2929.11 to 2929.18, 2929.31) and division (C) of section 2929.13 applies in determining whether to impose a prison term on the offender.

(d) If the amount of marihuana involved equals or exceeds 1000 grams but is less than 5,000 grams, Felony, 3rd degree (2929.11 to 2929.18, 2929.31) and division (C) of section 2929.13 applies in determining whether to impose a prison term on the offender. If the amount of marihuana involved is within that range and if the offense was committed in the vicinity of a school or in the vicinity of a juvenile, Felony, 2nd degree (2929.11 to 2929.18, 2929.31) and there is a presumption for a prison term for the offense.

(e) If the amount of the marihuana involved equals or exceeds 5,000 grams but is less than 20,000 grams, Felony, 3rd degree (2929.11 to 2929.18, 2929.31) and there is a presumption that a prison term shall be imposed for the offense. If the amount of marihuana involved is within that range and if the offense was committed in the vicinity of a school or in the vicinity of a juvenile, Felony, 2nd degree (2929.11 to 2929.18, 2929.31) and there is a presumption that for a prison term for the offense.

(f) If the amount of the marihuana involved equals or exceeds 20,000 grams, Felony, 2nd degree (2929.11 to 2929.18, 2929.31) and the court shall impose as a mandatory prison term the maximum prison term prescribed for a felony of the 2nd degree. If the amount of the marihuana involved equals or exceeds 20,000 grams and if the offense was committed in the vicinity of a school or in the vicinity of a juvenile, Felony, 1st degree (2929.11 to 2929.18, 2929.31) and the court shall impose as a mandatory prison term the maximum prison term prescribed for a felony of the 1st degree.

(g) If the offense involves a gift of 20 grams or less of marihuana, Minor misdemeanor (2929.21 to 2929.28, 2929.31) for a first offense. Each subsequent offense, Misdemeanor, 3rd degree (2929.21 to 2929.28, 2929.31). If the offense involves a gift of 20 grams or less and if the offense was committed in the vicinity of a school or in the vicinity of a juvenile, Misdemeanor, 3rd degree (2929.21 to 2929.28, 2929.31)

Note: If a violation of this section is a felony of the 1st, 2nd, or 3rd degree, the court shall impose upon the offender the mandatory fine specified for the offense under division (B)(1) of section 2929.18 and may impose an additional fine under 2929.18(B)(4), unless, as specified in that division, the court determines that the offender is indigent. If a person is charged with a violation of this section that is a felony of the 1st, 2nd, or 3rd degree, posts bail, and forfeits the bail, the clerk of court shall pay the forfeited bail as if the forfeited bail was a fine impose for a violation of this section.

Note: In addition to other penalties, court shall suspend the offender's driver's license, commercial driver's license or permit for a definite period of not less than 6 months or more than 5 years.

Note: If offender is professionally licensed person, court must notify immediately regulatory or licensing board or agency, or the commission on grievances and discipline of the Supreme Court, of conviction pursuant to 2925.38.

Drunk Driving—Commercial Motor Vehicles

See Motor Vehicles—Commercial Motor Vehicles—Criminal Offenses

Drunk Driving—Driving While Intoxicated or Drugged—4511.19

See also Motor Vehicles—Resisting or Fleeing Traffic Officers; Motor Vehicles—Willful or Wanton Disregard of Safety on Highways

ELEMENTS OF THE CRIME

Division (A):

(1) Operate any vehicle, streetcar, or trackless trolley when any of the following exist:

(2)(a) Under the influence of alcohol, or drug of abuse, or combined influences of alcohol and drug of abuse, or

(b) Concentration of .10 of 1 percent or more by weight of alcohol in blood (but less than .17), or

(c) Concentration of .10 of 1 gram or more by weight of alcohol per 210 liters of breath (but less than .17), or

(d) Concentration of .14 of 1 gram or more by weight of alcohol per 100 milliliters of urine (but less than .238)

(e) Concentration of .17 of 1 percent or more by weight of alcohol in blood, or

(f) Concentration of .17 of 1 gram or more by weight of alcohol per 210 liters of breath, or

(g) Concentration of .238 of 1 gram or more by weight of alcohol per 100 milliliters of urine.

Division (B):

(1) Person under 21 years of age

(2) Operation of any vehicle, streetcar, or trackless trolley when any of the following exist:

(a) Concentration of .02 of 1 percent but less than .10 of 1 percent by weight of alcohol in blood, or

(b) Concentration of .02 of 1 gram but less than .10 of 1 gram by weight of alcohol per 210 liters of breath, or

(c) Concentration of .028 of 1 gram but less than .14 of 1 gram by weight of alcohol per 100 milliliters of urine

PENALTY

Division (A)(1), (2), (3) or (4):

Misdemeanor, 1st degree (4511.99, 2929.21 to 2929.28, 2929.31)

Imprisonment: not less than 3 days (mandatory) nor more than 6 months and

Fine: (mandatory) $250 to $1000

If prior conviction within 6 years of this section, a comparable municipal ordinance, 2903.04 (involuntary manslaughter), 2903.06 (aggravated vehicular homicide or vehicular homicide), or 2903.08 (vehicular assault) in which offender was found under influence of alcohol and/or drugs:

Imprisonment: not less than 10 days (mandatory) nor more than 6 months, or 5 consecutive days and by not less than 18 consecutive days of electronically monitored house arrest as defined in 2929.23(A)(3), the total period of imprisonment and electronically monitored house arrest not to exceed 6 months, and

Fine: (mandatory) $350 to $1500

Mandatory immobilization of vehicle used and impoundment of license plates for 90 days.

If 2 prior convictions within 6 years of this section, a comparable municipal ordinance, 2903.04 (involuntary manslaughter), 2903.06

(aggravated vehicular homicide or vehicular homicide), or 2903.08 (vehicular assault) in which offender was found under influence of alcohol and/or drugs:

Imprisonment: not less than 30 days (mandatory) nor more than 1 year, or 15 consecutive days and by not less than 55 consecutive days of electronically monitored house arrest as defined in 2929.23(A)(3), the total period of imprisonment and electronically monitored house arrest not to exceed 1 year, and

Fine: (mandatory) $550 to $2500 and

Mandatory attendance of an alcohol and drug addiction program authorized by 3793.02

Mandatory immobilization of vehicle used and impoundment of license plates for 180 days.

If 3 or more prior convictions within 6 years of this section, a comparable municipal ordinance, 2903.04 (involuntary manslaughter), 2903.06 (aggravated vehicular homicide or vehicular homicide), or 2903.08 (vehicular assault) in which offender was found under influence of alcohol and/or drugs:

Imprisonment: not less than 60 days (mandatory) nor more than 1 year, and

Fine: (mandatory) $800 to $10,000 and

Mandatory attendance of an alcohol and drug addiction program authorized by 3793.02

Mandatory criminal forfeiture of vehicle used

Division (A)(5), (6) or (7):

Misdemeanor, 1st degree (4511.99, 2929.21 to 2929.28, 2929.31)

Imprisonment: not less than 3 consecutive days (mandatory) and mandatory attendance for 3 days at drivers' intervention program (3793.10); 6 consecutive days if offender not conducive to program, offender refuses to attend, or if place of imprisonment can provide program.

Fine: (mandatory) $250 to $1,000

If prior conviction within 6 years of this section, comparable municipal ordinance, 2903.04 (involuntary manslaughter), 2903.06 (aggravated vehicular homicide and vehicular homicide), or 2903.08 (vehicular assault) in which offender under influence of alcohol and/or drugs, or substantially similar federal, state, municipal ordinance:

Imprisonment: not less than 21 consecutive days (mandatory) or longer under 2929.21; or 10 consecutive days and by not less than 36 consecutive days of electronically monitored house arrest as defined in 2929.23 (imprisonment does not have to be served either prior to or consecutively with house arrest).

Fine: (mandatory) $350 to $2,500

Attendance at drivers' intervention program under 3793.10 may be required; if program officials determine offender is alcohol dependent, mandatory attendance of an alcohol and drug addiction program authorized by 3793.02.

Mandatory immobilization of vehicle used and impoundment license plates for 90 days.

If 2 prior convictions within 6 years of this section, comparable municipal ordinance, 2903.04 (involuntary manslaughter), 2903.06 (aggravated vehicular homicide and vehicular homicide), 2903.08 (vehicular assault) in which offender under influence of alcohol and/or drugs, or substantially similar federal, state, municipal ordinance:

Imprisonment: not less than 60 consecutive days (mandatory) or longer term of not more than 1 year; or 30 consecutive days and by not less than 110 consecutive days of electronically monitored house arrest as defined in 2929.23 (imprisonment does not have to be served either prior to or consecutively with house arrest), total period of imprisonment and electronically monitored house arrest not to exceed 1 year.

Fine: (mandatory) $550 to $2,500

Mandatory attendance of an alcohol and drug addiction program authorized by 3793.02.

Mandatory immobilization of vehicle used and impoundment license plates for 180 days.

If 3 or more prior convictions within 6 years of this section, comparable municipal ordinance, 2903.04 (involuntary manslaughter), 2903.06 (aggravated vehicular homicide and vehicular homicide), or 2903.08 (vehicular assault) in which offender under influence of alcohol and/or drugs, or substantially similar federal, state, municipal ordinance:

Imprisonment: Felony, 4th degree, not less than 6 nor more than 30 months (definite) (discretionary) (notwithstanding 2929.24(A)(4)), mandatory term of 60 consecutive days of either local incarceration (2929.13(G)(1)) or prison (2929.13(G)(2)). If local incarceration, may impose electronically monitored house arrest as defined in 2929.23 (2929.17) (electronically monitored house arrest not to commence until after incarceration). Felony, 3rd degree (2929.11 to 2929.19), if previously convicted of 4511.19 felony, regardless of when, mandatory 60 consecutive days prison (2929.13(G)(2)). The court has discretion to impose a prison sentence of 1 to 5 years, less credit for the mandatory prison term.

The court, in addition to the prison sentence may impose community control sanction. (2929.16 and 2929.17)

If offender sentenced to imprisonment, and if the offender pleads guilty or convicted of 2941.1413 specification charging that offender within the previous 20 years has committed 5 or more equivalent offenses, a mandatory additional sentence f 1, 2, 3, 4, or 5 years shall be imposed to be served consecutively to the underlying offense. (2929.13(G)(2))

Fine: (mandatory) $800 to $10,000

Mandatory attendance of an alcohol and drug addiction program authorized by 3793.02.

Mandatory criminal forfeiture of vehicle used

Division (B):

Misdemeanor, 4th degree (2929.21 to 2929.28, 2929.31).

Misdemeanor, 3rd degree (2929.21 to 2929.28, 2929.31) if prior conviction within 1 year of this section, comparable municipal ordinance, 2903.04 (involuntary manslaughter), 2903.06 (aggravated vehicular homicide and vehicular homicide), or 2903.08 (vehicular assault) in which offender under influence of alcohol and/or drugs, or substantially similar federal, state, municipal ordinance.

Mandatory suspension of drivers' license, commercial driver's license, permit, or nonresident driving privileges under 4507.16(E).

PROOF

This statute also provides for admission of results of blood, breath and urine tests.

Note: 4511.191 provides for chemical tests to determine alcohol content of blood and the effect of refusal to submit to a test; procedures for seizure of operator's license.

Note: A person under 18 years of age who violates Division (2) of this section is an "unruly child" pursuant to 2151.022(G).

Note: In any proceeding arising out of one incident, a person may be charged with a violation of Division (1)(a) and a violation of Division (2)(b)(i), (2)(b)(ii), or (2)(b)(iii) of this section, but he may not be convicted of more than one violation of these Divisions.

Duty, Dereliction of

See Dereliction of Duty

Electronic Surveillance

See Interception of Communications

Emergency, Misconduct at

See Disorderly Conduct Offenses—Misconduct at an Emergency

Endangering Children

See Juveniles—Endangering Children

Endangering, Criminal

See Criminal Damaging or Endangering

Engaging in Organized Crime

See Corrupt Activity—Engaging in a Pattern of

Entering and Breaking

See Breaking and Entering

Entertainment Performance

See Disorderly Conduct Offenses, generally

Escape—Aiding Escape or Resistance to Authority—2921.35

See also Resisting Arrest

ELEMENTS OF THE CRIME

Division (A):

(1) Purpose to promote or facilitate escape or resistance to lawful authority

(2)(a) Convey into detention facility, or

(b) Provide anyone confined therein

(3) With instrument or thing which may be used for such purposes

Division (B):

(1) Person confined in detention facility

(2) Purpose to promote or facilitate escape or resistance to lawful authority

(3) Make, procure, conceal, unlawfully possess, give to another inmate

(4) Any instrument or thing which may be used for such purposes

PENALTY

Felony, 4th degree (2929.11 to 2929.18, 2929.31)

Escape—Escape—2921.34

See also Escape—Aiding Escape or Resistance to Authority

ELEMENTS OF THE CRIME

(1) Knowing the person is under detention or reckless in that regard

(2)(a) Purposely break or attempt to break such detention, or

(b) Purposely fail to return to detention

(i) Following temporary leave granted for specific purpose or limited period, or

(ii) At time required when serving a sentence in intermittent confinement

(c) Purposely leave, or fail to return to, geographic area to which person is restricted,

(i) if person was sentenced to prison as a sexually violent predator, pursuant to 2971.03(A)(3), and

(ii) prison sentence was modified restricting person to designated geographic area.

DEFENSES

Irregularity in bringing or maintaining detention or lack of jurisdiction of committing or detaining authority, no defense if detention pursuant to judicial order or in detention facility.

In case of any other detention, irregularity or lack of jurisdiction is defense if:

(1) Escape involved no substantial risk of harm to person or property of another, or

(2) Detaining authority knew or should have known there was no legal basis for detention.

PENALTY

If most serious offense for which offender was under detention or adjudicated a sexually violent predator is aggravated murder, murder, or a felony of the 1st or 2nd degree or if offender was under detention as alleged or adjudicated delinquent child and most serious offense involved would be aggravated murder, murder, or a felony of the 1st or 2nd degree if committed by an adult, Felony, 2nd degree (2929.11 to 2929.18, 2929.13)

If most serious offense for which offender was under detention or adjudicated a sexually violent predator is felony of 3rd, 4th or 5th degree or an unclassified felony, or if offender was under detention as alleged or adjudicated delinquent child and most serious offense involved would be felony of 3rd, 4th or 5th degree or an unclassified felony if committed by an adult, Felony, 3rd degree (2929.11 to 2929.18, 2929.13)

If most serious offense for which offender was under detention is a misdemeanor or following a verdict of not guilty by reason of insanity, Felony, 5th degree (2929.11 to 2929.18, 2929.13)

If the offender at the time of the commission of the offense, was under detention as an alleged or adjudicated delinquent child or an unruly child and if the act for which the offender was under detention would not be a felony if committed by an adult, Misdemeanor, 1st degree (2929.13, 2929.21 to 2929.28, 2929.31)

If offender's detention consisted of hospitalization, institutionalization, or confinement in a facility pursuant to order issued after offender found not guilty by reason of insanity under2945.40, Felony, 5th degree (2929.11 to 2929.18, 2929.13)

If the most serious offense for which the offender was under detention is a misdemeanor and when the person fails to return to detention at a specified time following temporary leave granted for a specific purpose or limited period or at the time required when serving a sentence of intermittent confinement, Misdemeanor, 1st degree (2929.13, 2929.21 to 2929.28, 2929.31)

Note: Written statement by administrator of mental health facility that an individual hospitalized or confined there pursuant to court order relating to the individual's competence to stand trial or being not guilty by reason of insanity has escaped constitutes reasonable cause for officer to make warrantless arrest of individual under 2935.03(B)(2)(c).

Ethnic Intimidation

See Intimidation—Ethnic Intimidation

Evidence, Tampering With

See Tampering—Tampering With Evidence

Extortion—2905.11

ELEMENTS OF THE CRIME

(1) With a purpose to

(a) Obtain anything of value or valuable benefit, or

(b) To induce another to do an unlawful act

(2)(a) Threaten to commit any felony, or

(b) Threaten to commit any offense of violence, or

(c) Violate 2903.21 (aggravated menacing) or 2903.22 (menacing), or

(d) Utter or threaten any calumny against any person, or

(e) Expose or threaten to expose any matter that tends:

(i) To subject any person to hatred, contempt, or ridicule, or

(ii) To damage any person's personal or business repute, or

(iii) To impair any person's credit

PENALTY

Felony, 3rd degree (2929.11 to 2929.18, 2929.31)

Failure to Aid Law Enforcement Officer

See Law Enforcement Officers—Failure to Aid

Failure to Report Escape of Exotic or Dangerous Animal—2927.21

ELEMENTS OF THE CRIME

(1) Failure of animal owner or keeper to report

(2) Escape from his custody or control of

(3) Any member of a species of the animal kingdom

(a) Not indigenous to Ohio, or

(b) Presenting a risk of serious physical harm to persons or property, or both

(4)(a) To a law enforcement officer of the municipal corporation or township and the sheriff of the county where the escape occurred, and

(b) To the clerk of the municipal legislative authority or the township clerk of the township where the escape occurred

(5) Within one hour after the discovery of the escape is, or reasonably should have been made, or within one hour after the clerk's office is next open to the public, if the office is closed to the public at the time a report is required

PENALTY

Misdemeanor, 1st degree (2929.21 to 2929.28, 2929.31)

Failure to Report Felony or Certain Suspicious Circumstances—2921.22

ELEMENTS OF THE CRIME

Division (A):

(1) Knowing

(2) Felony

(3) Has been or is being committed

(4) Knowingly fail to report same to law enforcement authorities.

Division (B):

(1) Physician, limited practitioner, nurse, person giving aid to sick or injured

(2) Negligently fail to report to law enforcement authorities

(3) Any gunshot or stab wound seen or treated, or any serious physical harm to persons he knows or has reasonable cause to believe resulted from offense of violence

Division (C):

(1) Discover body or acquire first knowledge of death of person

(2) Fail to report such death immediately

(3) To physician treating deceased for condition from which death at such time would not be unexpected, or to law enforcement officer, ambulance service, emergency squad, or coroner in political subdivision where body discovered, death is believed to have occurred, or knowledge concerning it is obtained.

Division (D):

(1) Fail to provide upon request of person to whom report made as required by Division (C) or to any law enforcement officer who has reasonable cause to assert authority to investigate the circumstances surrounding such death

(2) Any facts within knowledge that may have bearing on investigation of such death.

Division (E)(2):

(a) Physician, nurse, or limited practitioner

(b) Outside a hospital, sanitarium, or other medical facility

(c) Attends or treats a person who has sustained a burn injury

(d)(i) Inflicted by an explosion or other incendiary device, or

(ii) Shows evidence of having been inflicted in a violent, malicious, or criminal manner

(e)(i) Fails to report the burn injury immediately to the local arson bureau, if there is such a bureau in the jurisdiction in which the person is attended or treated, or

(ii) To local law enforcement authorities

Division (E)(3):

(a) Manager, superintendent, or other person in charge

(b) Of a hospital, sanitarium, or other medical facility in which a person is attended or treated

(c) For any burn inflicted by an explosion or other incendiary device, or that shows evidence of having been inflicted in a violent malicious, or criminal manner

(d)(i) Failed to report the burn injury immediately to the local arson bureau, if there is such a bureau in the jurisdiction in which the person is attended or treated, or

(ii) To local law enforcement authorities

Division (E)(4):

(a) Person who is required to report any burn injury under division (E)(2) or (3) of this section

(b) Failed to file

(c) Within three working days after attending or treating the victim

(d) Written report of the burn injury with the office of the state fire marshal

Note: Burn injury means 2nd or 3rd degree burns, any burns to upper respiratory tract or laryngeal edema due to inhalation of superheated air, or any burn injury or wound that may result in death.

EXCEPTIONS

Divisions (A) or (D) do not require disclosure of information when any of following apply:

(1) Information privileged by reason of relationship between attorney-client, doctor-patient, licensed psychologist-client, clergyman-person communicating information confidentially for religious counseling purpose in professional character, husband-wife, or communications assistant-person who is a party to a telecommunications relay service call.

(2) Information would tend to incriminate member of actor's immediate family.

(3) Disclosure of information would amount to revealing news source privileged under 2739.04 or 2739.12.

(4) Disclosure of information would amount to disclosure by ordained clergyman of organized religious body of confidential communication by person seeking aid or counsel.

(5) Disclosure would amount to revealing information acquired by actor in course of duties in connection with bona fide program of treatment or services for drug dependent people or people in danger of drug dependence, which program is maintained or conducted by hospital, clinic, person, agency, or organization certified under 3793.06.

(6) Disclosure would amount to revealing information acquired by actor in course of duties in connection with bona fide program for providing counseling services to victims of crimes that are violations of 2907.02, 2907.05, or 2907.12.

PENALTY

If Divisions (A), (C), or (D) violated, Misdemeanor, 4th degree (2929.21 to 2929.28, 2929.31)

If Division (B) violated, Misdemeanor, 2nd degree (2929.21 to 2929.28, 2929.31)

If Division (E) negligently violated, Minor misdemeanor (2929.21 to2929.28, 2929.31)

If Division (E) knowingly violated, Misdemeanor, 2nd degree (2929.21 to 2929.28, 2929.31)

False Alarm

See Disorderly Conduct Offenses—Making False Alarms

False Insurance Claim for Motor Vehicle Theft

See Falsification—Falsification

False Name or Information, Presenting to Law Enforcement Officer

See Motor Vehicles—Presenting False Name or Information to Law Enforcement Officer

False Report of Child Abuse or Neglect

See Falsification—Making or Causing a False Report of Child Abuse or Child Neglect

False Statements

See Falsification—Falsification; Patient Abuse or Neglect—False Statements

False Written Statement of Motor Vehicle Theft

See Falsification—Falsification; Theft

Falsification—Falsification—2921.13

ELEMENTS OF THE CRIME

(1)(a) Knowingly make false statement, or

(b) Knowingly swear or affirm truth of a false statement previously made

(2)(a) Statement made in official proceeding, or

(b) Statement made with purpose to incriminate another, or

(c) Statement made with purpose to mislead public official in performing public official's official function, or

(d) Statement made with purpose to secure payment of unemployment compensation, Ohio Works First, prevention, retention and contingency benefits and services, disability financial assistance retirement benefits, economic development assistance, or other benefits administered by governmental agency or paid out of public treasury, or

(e) Statement made with purpose to secure issuance by governmental agency of license, permit, authorization, certificate, registration, release, or provider agreement, or

(f) Statement sworn or affirmed before notary public or another person empowered to administer oath, or

(g) Statement in writing on or in connection with report or return required or authorized by law, or

(h) Statement in writing, and made with purpose to induce another to extend credit, employ offender; confer any degree, diploma, certificate of attainment, award of excellence, honor on offender; extend or bestow on offender any other valuable benefit or distinction, when person to whom statement directed relies upon it to that person's detriment, or

(i) Statement made with purpose to commit or facilitate the commission of a theft offense, or

(j) Statement knowingly made to a probate court in connection with any action, proceeding, or other matter within its jurisdiction, either orally or in a written document, including, but not limited to, an application, petition, complaint, or other pleading, or an inventory, account, or report, or

(k) Statement made on an account, form, record, stamp, or other writing that is required by law, or

(*l*) Statement made in connection with the purchase of a firearm and in conjunction with the furnishing to the seller of the firearm of a fictitious or altered driver's or commercial driver's license or permit, a fictitious or altered identification card, or any other document that contains false information about the purchaser's identity, or

(m) Statement made in writing purported to be a judgment, lien, or claim of indebtedness filed or recorded, or

(n) Statement made with purpose to obtain "Ohio's best Rx" program enrollment or payment from Department of Job and Family Services.

Division (B):

(1) In connection with the purchase of firearm

(2) Knowingly furnish to seller of firearm

(3)(a) A fictitious or altered driver's or commercial driver's license or permit, or

(b) A fictitious or altered identification card, or

(c) Any other document that contains false information about the purchaser's identity.

DEFENSE

No defense under (2)(d) above that oath or affirmation done in irregular manner.

PROOF

Contradictory statements relating to same fact by offender within period of statute of limitations for falsification, prosecution need not prove which statement was false, only that one or the other was.

PENALTY

Misdemeanor, 1st degree (2929.21 to 2929.28, 2929.31)

If (2)(i) violated and claim is less than $500, Misdemeanor, 1st degree (2929.21 to 2929.28, 2929.31)

If (2)(i) violated and claim is $500 or more and less than $5,000, Felony, 5th degree (2929.11 and 2929.18, 2929.31)

If (2)(i) violated and claim is $5,000 or more, and less than $100,000, Felony, 4th degree (2929.11 to 2929.18, 2929.31)

If (2)(i) violated and claim is $100,000 or more, Felony, 3rd degree (2929.11 to 2929.18, 2929.31)

If (2)(*l*) or Division (B) violated, Felony, 5th degree (2929.11 to 2929.18, 2929.31)

Falsification—Making or Causing a False Report of Child Abuse or Child Neglect—2921.14

ELEMENTS OF THE CRIME

(1) Knowingly

(2) Make or cause another person to make

(3) False report

(4) Under 2151.421(B) to children services board, county department of human services, or municipal or county peace officer

(5) Alleging that any person has committed an act or omission that resulted in.

(a) A child being an abused child as defined in 2151.031, or

(b) A child being a neglected child as defined in 2151.03.

PENALTY

Misdemeanor, 1st degree (2929.21 to 2929.28, 2929.31)

Firearms

See Weapons, generally

Food, Adulterated

See Adulterated Food

Food Stamps, Trafficking In or Illegal Use

See Theft-related Offenses—Trafficking In or Illegal Use of Food Stamps

Forgery—2913.31

ELEMENTS OF THE CRIME

Division (A):

(1) With purpose to defraud or knowing the person is facilitating fraud

(2)(a) Forge any writing of another without the other person's authority, or

(b) Forge any writing to purport it to be:

(i) Genuine when it is spurious, or

(ii) Act of another who did not authorize that act, or

(iii) Executed at time or place or with terms different from what was in fact the case, or

(iv) Copy of original when no such original existed, or

(c) Utter, or possess with purpose to utter, any writing known to have been forged

Division (B):

(1) Knowingly

(2) Forge an identification card, or

(3)(a) Sell or otherwise distribute

(b) Card that purports to be an identification card

(c) Knowing it to have been forged

Note: Identification card means card that includes personal information or characteristics of an individual, a purpose of which is to establish identity of bearer described on card, whether words "identity," "identification," "identification card," or other similar words appear on card.

PENALTY

Except as otherwise provided, Felony, 5th degree (2929.11 to 2929.18, 2929.31)

If property or services are involved in the offense or the victim suffers a loss and if the value of the property or services or the loss to the victim is $5,000 or more and is less than $100,000, Felony, 4th degree (2929.11 to 2929.18, 2929.31)

If property or services are involved in the offense or the victim suffers a loss and if the value of the property or services or the loss to the victim is $100,000 or more, Felony, 3rd degree (2929.11 to 2929.18, 2929.31)

If Division (B) violated, Misdemeanor, 1st degree (2929.21 to 2929.28, 2929.31)

If Division (B) violated and prior conviction under Division (B), Misdemeanor, 1st degree (2929.21 to 2929.28, 2929.31), and mandatory fine of not less than $250

If victim is an elderly person, Felony, 5th degree. If value of property or services, or loss to the victim is $500 or more and less than $5,000, Felony, 4th degree, $5,000 or more and less than $25,000, Felony, 3rd degree; $25,000 or more, Felony, 2nd degree (2929.11 to 2929.18, 2929.31)

Fraud, Crimes Involving

See Cheating; Falsification—Falsification; Forgery; Law Enforcement Officers—Impersonation of Certain Officers; Law Enforcement Officers—Personating an Officer; Tampering—Tampering With Records; Theft-related Offenses, generally

Fraud, Workers' Compensation

See Theft-related Offenses—Workers' Compensation Fraud

Gambling—Gambling—2915.02

See also Cheating

ELEMENTS OF THE CRIME

(1) Engage in bookmaking or knowingly engage in conduct facilitating it, including placing bet with person engaged in or facilitating illegal bookmaking, or

(2) Establish, promote, operate or knowingly engage in conduct facilitating game of chance for profit or any scheme of chance, including knowingly aiding in the conduct or operation of any game or scheme, or playing any such scheme or game, or

(3) Knowingly procure, transmit, exchange or engage in conduct facilitating procurement, transmission, exchange of, information to use in establishing odds or determining winners for bookmaking or with any game of chance for profit or scheme of chance, or

(4) Betting or playing scheme or game of chance, as substantial source of income or livelihood, or

(5) With purpose to violate (1), (2), (3) or (4) above, acquire, possess, control or operate gambling device

EXCEPTIONS

(A) Not applicable to gambling expressly permitted by law

(B) Not applicable to games of chance if all of following apply:

(1) Games are not craps, roulette or slot machines for money, and

(2) Conducted by charitable organization tax exempt under 501(C)(3) Internal Revenue Code, and

(3)(i) Games conducted at festivals of the charitable organization either for period of four consecutive days or less and not more than twice a year or for period of five consecutive days not more than once a year, and on premises owned by organization for no less than one year prior to the conducting of the games, or

(ii) Games conducted on premises leased from a governmental unit, or

(iii) Games conducted on premises leased from veteran's or fraternal organization, premises owned by organization for no less than one year prior to the conducting of the games, veteran's or fraternal organization has not already leased premises twice during preceding year to charitable organizations for conducting games, and charitable organization does not pay rental rate in excess of amount a charitable organization may pay for bingo session under 2915.09(B)(1), and

(4) All money or assets received from games, after deduction of prizes paid out, are used by, given, donated or otherwise transferred to the organization, and

(5) Games not conducted during or within 10 hours of a bingo game conducted pursuant to 2915.12, and

(6) No person receives any commission, wage, salary, reward, tip, donation, gratuity, or other form of compensation, for operating or directly assisting in operation of games.

Not applicable to any tag fishing tournament operated under a permit issued under 1533.92.

Not applicable to Bingo licensed under 2915.08.

PENALTY

Misdemeanor, 1st degree (2929.21 to 2929.28, 2929.31)

If prior conviction of any gambling offense, Felony, 5th degree (2929.11 to 2929.18, 2929.31)

Gambling—Operating Gambling House—2915.03

ELEMENTS OF THE CRIME

(1) Owner, lessee, or having custody, control, supervision of premises

(2)(a) Use or occupy premises for gambling in violation of 2915.02 or

(b) Recklessly permit said premises to be used or occupied for gambling in violation of 2915.02

PENALTY

Misdemeanor, 1st degree (2929.21 to 2929.28, 2929.31)

If prior gambling offense conviction, Felony, 5th degree (2929.11 to 2929.18, 2929.31)

Note: Premises used or occupied in violation of this section constitute nuisance subject to abatement under 3767.01 to 3767.99, inclusive.

Gambling—Public Gaming—2915.04

ELEMENTS OF THE CRIME

Division (A):

(1) Make a bet or play game or scheme of chance

(2) While at hotel, restaurant, tavern, store, arena, hall, or other place of public accommodation, business, or amusement, or resort

Division (B):

(1) Owner, lessee, person having custody, control, supervision of such places

(2) Recklessly permits such premises to be used or occupied in violation of Division (A)

EXCEPTION

Conduct in connection with gambling expressly permitted by law.

PENALTY

Minor Misdemeanor (2929.21 to 2929.28, 2929.31)

If prior gambling offense conviction, Misdemeanor, 4th degree (2929.21 to 2929.28, 2929.31)

Note: Premises used in violation of Division (B) of this section constitute nuisance subject to abatement under Chapter 3767.

Gang Activity, Criminal

See Corrupt Activity—Criminal Gang Activity

Glue Sniffing

See Drug Offenses—Abusing Harmful Intoxicants

Hallucinogens

See Drug Offenses, generally

Harassment

See Telephone Harassment

Harassment by Inmate—2921.38

ELEMENTS OF THE CRIME

Division (A): No person

(1) confined in a detention facility

(2) with intent to harass, annoy, threaten or alarm another

(3) shall cause or attempt to cause that person

(4) to come into contact with a bodily substance

(5)(a) by throwing the substance at the other person

(b) by expelling the substance upon the other person, or

(c) in any other manner

Division (B): No person

(1) confined in a detention facility

(2) knowing that the person

(a) carries the AIDs virus

(b) carries the hepatitus virus, or

(c) is infected with tuberculosis

(3) with intent to harass, annoy, threaten or alarm another

(4) shall cause or attempt to cause that person

(5) to come into contact with a bodily substance

(6)(a) by throwing the substance at the other person

(b) by expelling the substance upon the other person

(c) or, in any other manner

EXEMPTION

Section is inapplicable to a person who is hospitalized, institutionalized, or confined in a facility operated by the Departments of Mental Health, Retardation, and Developmental Disabilities.

PENALTY

Violation of Division (A) is a felony, 5th degree; violation of Division (B) is a Felony, 3rd degree (2929.11 to 2929.18, 2929.31)

Note: The court must upon request of the prosecutor or the law enforcement agency investigating the offense order a person committing the offense to submit to appropriate tests to determine if the person carries an enumerated virus.

Harmful Intoxicants

See Drug Offenses, generally; Drunk Driving—Driving While Intoxicated or Drugged

Hazing—2903.31

ELEMENTS OF THE CRIME

Division (A):

(1) Recklessly

(2) Participate in hazing of another

Division (B):

(1) Administrator, employee, or faculty member of any primary, secondary, or post-secondary school or any other educational institution, public or private

(2) Recklessly

(3) Permit hazing of another

PENALTY

Misdemeanor, 4th degree (2929.21 to 2929.28, 2929.31)

Note: Hazing means doing any act or coercing another, including victim, to do any act of initiation into any student or other organization that causes or creates substantial risk of causing mental or physical harm to any person.

Homicide

See also Manslaughter—Involuntary Manslaughter; Manslaughter—Voluntary Manslaughter; Murder—Aggravated Murder; Vehicular Homicide—Aggravated Vehicular Homicide

Homicide—Negligent—2903.05

ELEMENTS OF THE CRIME

(1) Negligently cause death of another or unlawful termination of another's pregnancy

(2) By means of deadly weapon or dangerous ordnance

PENALTY

Misdemeanor, 1st degree (2929.21 to 2929.28, 2929.31)

Homicide—Reckless—2903.041

ELEMENTS OF THE CRIME

Recklessly cause death of another or the unlawful termination of another's pregnancy.

PENALTY

Felony, 3rd degree (2929.11 to 2929.18, 2929.31)

Hostelry, Defrauding

See Theft-related Offenses—Defrauding Livery or Hostelry

Housing—Injuring, Intimidating, or Interfering With—2927.03

ELEMENTS OF THE CRIME

(1) Willfully

(2) By force or threat of force

(3) Whether or not acting under color of law

(4) Injure, intimidate, or interfere, or attempt to do so, with

(5) Any person because:

(a)(i) Of race, color, religion, sex, familial status or disability as defined in 4112.01, national origin, or ancestry, and

(ii) That person is or has been selling, purchasing, renting, financing, occupying, contracting, or negotiating for sale, purchase, rental, financing, or occupation of housing accommodations, or

(iii) That person is or has been applying for or participating in any service, organization, or facility relating to the business of selling or renting housing accommodations, or

(b) That person is or has been, or in order to intimidate that person or any other person or class of persons from:

(i) Participating in any of the activities, services, organizations, or facilities described in 5(a)(ii) or (iii)

(ii) Without discrimination on account of race, color, religion, sex, familial status or disability as defined in 4112.01, national origin, or ancestry, or

(iii) Affording another person or class of persons opportunity or protection to so participate, or

(c) That person is or has been, or to discourage that person from:

(i) Lawfully aiding or encouraging others to participate in any of the activities, services, organizations, or facilities described in 5(a)(ii) or (iii)

(ii) Without discrimination on account of race, color, religion, sex, familial status or disability as defined in 4112.01, national origin or ancestry, or

(iii) Lawfully participating in speech or peaceful assembly opposing any denial of the opportunity to so participate

PENALTY

Misdemeanor, 1st degree (2929.21 to 2929.28, 2929.31)

Hypodermics— Possession, Sale, and Disposal

See Drug Offenses—Hypodermics—Possession, Sale, and Disposal

Illegal Conveyance of Certain Items Onto Detention/Mental Health Facility Grounds—2921.36

ELEMENTS OF THE CRIME

Division (A):

(1) Knowingly

(2) Convey or attempt to convey Onto grounds of detention facility or institution under control of Department of Mental

Health or Department of Retardation and Developmental Disabilities

(3)(a) Deadly weapon or dangerous ordnance as defined in 2923.11 or any part of or ammunition for use in same, or

(b) Drug of abuse as defined in 3719.011, or

(c) Intoxicating liquor as defined in 4301.01

Division (C):

(1) Knowingly

(2) Deliver or attempt to deliver to any person confined in detention facility or to any patient in an institution under control of Department of Mental Health or Department of Retardation and Developmental Disabilities

(3) Any item listed in Division (A)(3)(a)(b) or (c)

Division (D):

(1) Knowingly

(2) Deliver or attempt to deliver

(3) Cash

(4) To any person who is confined to a detention facility

EXCEPTION

Division (A) not applicable if person conveying or attempting to convey has written authorization of person in charge of facility and authorization is in accordance with written rules of facility

DEFENSES

It is an affirmative defense to Division A(1) that weapon or dangerous ordnance was transported in a motor vehicle for a lawful purpose, not on the actor's person, or if a firearm, it was unloaded and carried in a closed package, box, or case, or in a compartment reachable only by leaving the vehicle.

It is an affirmative defense to Division C that actor otherwise not prohibited by law from delivering item to confined person or patient if any of following apply:

(a) Actor permitted by written rules of facility to deliver item to confined person or patient, or

(b) Actor given written authorization by person in charge of facility to deliver item to confined person or patient

PENALTY

If violation in Divisions (A) or (C) involving an element under Division (A)(3)(a), Felony, 4th degree (2929.11 to 2929.18, 2929.31), if offender is officer or employee of Department of Rehabilitation & Correction, mandatory prison term.

If violation in Divisions (A) or (C) involved element under Division (A)(3)(b), and if offender is officer or employee of facility or institution, Felony, 4th degree (2929.11 to 2929.18, 2929.31) if offender is not officer or employee, Felony, 5th degree (2929.11 to 2929.18, 2929.31), if offender is officer or employee of Department of Rehabilitation & Correction, mandatory prison term.

If violation in Divisions (A) or (C) involved element under Division (A)(3)(c), Misdemeanor, 2nd degree (2929.21 to 2929.28, 2929.31)

Violator of Division (D) is guilty of illegal conveyance of cash onto grounds of detention facility, Misdemeanor, 1st degree (2929.21 to 2929.28, 2929.31).

If previous conviction or guilty plea to violation of Division (D), Felony, 5th degree (2929.11 to 2929.18, 2929.31).

Impersonation of Law Enforcement Officers

See Law Enforcement Officers—Impersonation of Certain Officers; Law Enforcement Officers—Personating an Officer

Importuning—2907.07

See also Juveniles, generally

ELEMENTS OF THE CRIME

Division (A):

(1) Solicit a person under age 13

(2) To engage in sexual activity with offender

(3) Whether or not offender knows age of such person

Division (B):

(1) Solicit another, not the spouse of offender

(2) To engage in sexual conduct with offender

(3) When offender is 18 years or older and 4 or more years older than other person, and the other person is 13 years of age or older but less than 16 years of age

Division (C):

(1) Solicit another

(2) By means of a telecommunication device originating or received in this state

(3) To engage in sexual activity with the offender

(4) Where offender is 18 or older, and

(5) The person solicited is

(a) less than 13 years and the offender knows that or is reckless in that regard

(b) a law enforcement officer posing as a person less than 13 years and the offender believes that the person is less than 13 years or is reckless in that regard

Division (D):

(1) Solicit another

(2) By means of a telecommunication device originating or received in this state

(3) To engage in sexual activity with the offender

(4) Where offender is 18 years old and 4 or more years older than other person

(5) The person solicited is

(a) the other person is 13 years of age or older but less than 16 years of age, and the offender knows that the other person is 13 years of age or older but less than 16 years of age, or the offender is reckless in that regard

(b) a law enforcement officer posing as a person 13 years of age or older but less than 16 years, and the offender believes that the other person is 13 years of age or older but less than 16 years of age, or the offender is reckless in that regard

PENALTY

If Division (A) or (C) violated, Felony, 4th degree first offense, Felony, 3rd degree each subsequent offense (2929.11 to 2929.18, 2929.31)

If Division (B) or (D) violated, Felony, 5th degree first offense, Felony, 4th degree each subsequent offense

Improperly Handling Infectious Agents—2917.47

ELEMENTS OF THE CRIME

(1) Knowingly

(2) Possess, send or receive, or cause to be possessed, sent or received

(3) An isolate of an infectious agent, or a derivative thereof

(4) Except as permitted by state or federal law

PENALTY

Felony, 2nd degree (2929.11 to 2929.18, 2929.31)

Indecency, Public

See Public Indecency

Information, Confidential, Disclosure

See Confidential Information—Disclosure of Confidential Information

Injuring, Intimidating, or Interfering With Housing

See Housing—Injuring, Intimidating, or Interfering With

Interception of Communications—2933.52

ELEMENTS OF THE CRIME

Division (A):

(1) Purposely

(2) Intercept, attempt to intercept, or procure any other person to intercept or attempt to intercept

(3) Any wire or oral communication

Division (B):

(1) Purposely

(2) Use, attempt to use, or procure any other person to use or attempt to use

(3) Any interception device to intercept

(4) Any wire or oral communication

(5) If either of the following apply:

(a) The interception device is fixed to, or otherwise transmits a signal through, a wire, cable, satellite, microwave, or other similar method of connection used in wire communications

(b) The interception device transmits communications by radio, or interferes with the transmission of communications by radio

Division (C):

(1) Purposely

(2) Disclose or attempt to disclose

(3) To any other person

(4) The contents or any evidence derived from the contents

(5) Of any wire or oral communication

(6) Knowing or having reason to know

(7) The contents or the evidence derived from the contents

(8) Obtained through the interception of wire or oral communication in violation of sections 2933.51 to 2933.66 of the Revised Code

EXCEPTIONS

This section not applicable to:

(1) The interception, disclosure, or use of the contents, or any evidence derived from the contents, of any oral or wire communication that is obtained through the use of an interception warrant.

(2) An operator of a switchboard, or an officer or an agent of a communications common carrier, whose facilities are used in the transmission of a wire communication to intercept, disclose, or use that communication in the normal course of employment while engaged in any activity that is necessary to the rendition of service or the protection of the rights or property of the communications common carrier, provided that the communications common carrier shall not utilize service observing or random monitoring except for mechanical or service quality control checks.

(3) A law enforcement officer who intercepts a wire or oral communication, if the officer is a party to the communication or if one of the parties to the communication has given prior consent to the interception by the officer.

(4) A person who is not a law enforcement officer and who intercepts a wire or oral communication, if the person is a party to the communication or if one of the parties to the communication has given the person prior consent to the interception, and if the communication is not intercepted for the purpose of committing any criminal offense, tortious act, or any other injurious act.

(5) An officer, employee, or agent of any communications common carrier providing information, facilities, or technical assistance to an investigative officer who is authorized to intercept a wire or oral communication.

(6) A pen register, which means a device that records or decodes electronic impulses that identify the numbers dialed, pulsed, or otherwise transmitted on telephone lines to which the device is attached.

(7) A trap, which means any device or apparatus that connects to any telephone or telegraph instrument, equipment, or facility and determines the origin of a wire communication to a telephone or telegraph instrument, equipment or facility, but does not intercept the contents of any wire communications.

(8) Any police, fire, or emergency communications system to intercept wire communications coming into or going out of the communications system of a police department, fire department, or emergency center, if both of the following apply:

(a) The telephone, instrument, equipment, or facility is limited to the exclusive use of the communication system for administrative purposes

(b) At least one telephone, instrument, equipment, or facility that is not subject to interception is made available for public use at each police department, fire department, or emergency center.

PENALTY

Felony, 4th degree (2929.11 to 2929.18, 2929.31)

Interference with Custody

See Domestic Offenses—Interference with Custody

Interference With Establishment of Paternity

See Paternity, Interference With Establishment of

Interfering With Action to Issue or Modify Support Order

See Domestic Offenses—Interfering With Action to Issue or Modify Support Order

Interfering with Civil Rights

See Civil Rights—Interfering With

Intimidation—Ethnic Intimidation—2927.12

See also Menacing, generally

ELEMENTS OF THE CRIME

Division (A)(1) (Aggravated menacing):

(1) Knowingly

(2) By reason of race, color, religion or national origin

(3) Caused another to believe that the offender would cause serious physical harm to the person or property of such other person or member of his or her immediate family

Division (A)(2) (Menacing):

(1) Knowingly

(2) By reason of race, color, religion or national origin

(3) Caused another to believe that the offender would cause physical harm to the person or property of such other person or member of his or her immediate family

Division (A)(3) (Criminal damaging or endangering—knowingly committed):

(1) Knowingly

(2) By any means

(3) By reason of race, color, religion or national origin

(4) Caused, or created a substantial risk of causing, physical harm to the property of another without his or her consent

Division (A)(4) (Criminal damaging or endangering—recklessly committed by means of an inherently dangerous agency):

(1) Recklessly

(2) By reason of race, color, religion or national origin

(3) By means of fire or explosion or flood or poison gas or poison or radioactive material or caustic or corrosive material or other inherently dangerous agency or substance

(4) Caused, or created a substantial risk of causing, physical harm to the property of another without his or her consent

Division (A)(5) (Criminal mischief—tampering):

(1) Knowingly

(2) Without privilege to do so

(3) By reason of race, color, religion or national origin

(4) Moved or defaced or damaged or destroyed or otherwise improperly tampered with the property of another

Division (A)(6) (Criminal mischief—using a tear gas device, stink bomb, or smoke generator):

(1) With purpose to interfere with the use or enjoyment of another's property

(2) By reason of race, color, religion or national origin

(3) Employ a tear gas device or stink bomb or smoke generator or other device releasing a substance which is harmful or offensive to persons exposed or which tends to cause public alarm

Division (A)(7) (Criminal mischief—disturbing a survey mark):

(1) Knowingly

(2) Without privilege to do so

(3) By reason of race, color, religion or national origin

(4) Moved or damaged or defaced or destroyed or improperly tampered with

(5) Bench mark or triangulation station or boundary marker or any other survey station or monument or marker

Division (A)(8) (Criminal mischief—tampering with a safety device):

(1) Knowingly

(2) Without privilege to do so

(3) By reason of race, color, religion or national origin

(4) Moved or defaced or damaged or destroyed or otherwise improperly tampered with

(5) Safety device

(6)(a) Which was property of another, or

(b) Which was property of offender when required or placed for the safety of others

(7) So as to destroy or diminish effectiveness of safety device or availability of device for its intended purpose

Division (A)(9) (Criminal mischief—fire):

(1) With purpose to interfere with the use or enjoyment of the property of another

(2) By reason of race, color, religion or national origin

(3)(a) Set a fire on the land of another, or

(b) Place personal property that had been set on fire on the land of another

(4) Fire or personal property is outside and apart from any building, other structure, or personal property that is on that land

Division (A)(10) (Telephone harassment):

(1) Knowingly

(2) By reason of race, color, religion or national origin

(3) Made or caused to be made or permitted a telephone call

(4) From a telephone under offender's control

(5)(a) Violated 2903.21, aggravated menacing, during the call, or

(b) Knowingly stated to the recipient that he or she intended to cause damage to or to destroy public or private property and the recipient, member of recipient's family, or person residing at the premises to which the call was made owned or leased or resided at or worked in or would be near or in the property at the time of the damage or destruction or had responsibility for protecting or insuring the property that would be damaged or destroyed, or

(c) Knowingly made the call when the recipient or person at the premises had previously told the caller not to call any persons at the premises

PENALTY

If Division (A)(1) violated, Felony, 4th degree (2929.11 to 2929.18, 2929.31)

If Division (A)(2) violated, Misdemeanor, 3rd degree (2929.21 to 2929.28, 2929.31)

If Divisions (A)(3) or (4) violated, Misdemeanor, 1st degree (2929.21 to 2929.28, 2929.31)

If violation of Divisions (A)(3) or (4) created a risk of physical harm to any person, Felony, 4th degree (2929.11 to 2929.18, 2929.31)

If property involved in violation of Divisions (A)(3) or (4) was an aircraft, aircraft engine, propeller, appliance, spare part, or any other equipment or implement used or intended to be used in the operation of an aircraft and this violation created a risk of physical harm to any person, Felony, 3rd degree (2929.11, 2929.31)

If the property involved in the violation was an occupied aircraft, Felony, 3rd degree (2929.11 to 2929.18, 2929.31)

If Divisions (A)(5), (6), (7), (8), or (9) violated, Misdemeanor, 2nd degree (2929.21 to 2929.28, 2929.31)

If violation of Divisions (A)(5), (6), (7), (8), or (9) created a risk of physical harm to any person, Felony, 4th degree (2929.11 to 2929.18, 2929.31)

If property involved in violation of Divisions (A)(5), (6), (7), (8), or (9) was an aircraft, aircraft engine, propeller, appliance, spare part, fuel, lubricant, hydraulic fluid, any other equipment, implement, or material used or intended to be used in the operation of an aircraft or any cargo carried or intended to be carried in an aircraft and this violation created a risk of physical harm to any person, Felony, 3rd degree (2929.11 to 2929.18, 2929.31)

If the property involved in the violation was an occupied aircraft, Felony, 3rd degree (2929.11, 2929.31)

If Division (A)(10) violated, Felony, 4th degree (2929.11 to 2929.18, 2929.31)

If Division (A)(10) violated and prior conviction of telephone harassment under 2917.21, Felony, 3rd degree (2929.11 to 2929.18, 2929.31)

Intimidation—Intimidation—2921.03

See also Menacing, generally

ELEMENTS OF THE CRIME

(1) Knowingly

(2) By force or unlawful threat of harm to any person or property

(3) Or by filing, recording or using a false or fraudulent writing with malicious purpose, in bad faith, or in a reckless manner

(4) Attempt to influence, intimidate, hinder a public servant, party official, or witness

(5) In discharge of his duty

PENALTY

Felony, 3rd degree (2929.11 to 2929.18, 2929.31)

Intimidation—Intimidation of Crime Victim or Witness—2921.04

ELEMENTS OF THE CRIME

Division (A):

(1) Knowingly

(2) Attempt to intimidate or hinder

(a) Victim of a crime in filing or prosecution of criminal charges, or

(b) Witness in a criminal case in discharge of his duty

Division (B):

(1) Knowingly

(2)(a) By force, or

(b) By unlawful threat of harm to any person or property

(3) Attempt to

(a) Influence

(b) Intimidate, or

(c) Hinder

(4)(a) Victim of a crime in the filing or prosecution of criminal charges, or

(b) Witness in a criminal case in discharge of his duty

(c) An attorney involved in criminal case or proceeding in discharge of his duty

EXCEPTIONS

Division (A) does not apply to any person

(1) Attempting to resolve a dispute pertaining to the alleged commission of a criminal offense, prior or subsequent to the filing of a complaint, or

(2) Who is attempting to arbitrate or assist in the conciliation of any such dispute, prior or subsequent to the filing of a complaint

PENALTY

If Division (A) violated, Misdemeanor, 1st degree (2929.21 to 2929.28, 2929.31)

If Division (B) violated, Felony, 3rd degree (2929.11 to 2929.18, 2929.31)

Intimidation—Retaliation—2921.05

ELEMENTS OF THE CRIME

Division (A):

(1) Purposely

(2) By force or threat of harm to any person or property

(3) Retaliate

(4) Against a public servant, a party official, or an attorney or witness involved in a civil or criminal action or proceeding

(5) Because that person discharged his duties

Division (B):

(1) Purposely

(2) By force or threat of harm to any person or property

(3) Retaliate

(4) Against a victim of crime for filing charges or prosecuting

PENALTY

Retaliation is a 3rd degree felony (2929.11 to 2929.18, 2929.31)

Intoxicants, Harmful

See Drug Offenses, generally

Investigatory Work Product, Confidentiality

See Confidential Information—Confidentiality of Investigatory Work Product

Involuntary Manslaughter

See Manslaughter—Involuntary Manslaughter

Juveniles

See also Bingo—Minor Not To Work Bingo Session; Domestic Offenses, generally; Kidnapping

Juveniles—Child Stealing—2905.04

Repealed effective 7–1–96.

Juveniles—Contributing to Unruliness or Delinquency of a Child—2919.24

ELEMENTS OF THE CRIME

(1) Aid, abet, induce, cause, encourage, contribute to, or act in a way tending to cause a child or ward of the juvenile court to become

(a) An unruly child, as defined in 2151.022,

(b) A delinquent child, as defined in 2152.02, or

(2) Fail to ensure that a custodial child registers address, periodically verifies address, or sends notice of intent to reside under Chapters 2152 and 2950, if the custodian of the child.

PENALTY

Misdemeanor, 1st degree (2929.21 to 2929.28, 2929.31)

Each day of violation is separate offense

Juveniles—Criminal Child Enticement—2905.05

ELEMENTS OF THE CRIME

(1) By any means

(2) Without privilege to do so

(3) Knowingly

(4) Solicit, coax, entice, lure to accompany defendant in any manner including into any vehicle as defined in 4501.01

(5) Child under age 14, whether or not actor knows age of child

(6) Has no express or implied permission of parent, guardian or other legal custodian of the child in undertaking activity

(7) Is not law enforcement officer, medic, firefighter, other person who regularly provides emergency services, employee or agent of (or volunteer acting under direction of) any board of education or actor is one of the aforementioned persons but is not acting within the scope of the actor's lawful duties

DEFENSES

(1) Affirmative defense that actor undertook activity in response to a bona fide emergency situation.

(2) Affirmative defense that actor undertook activity in a reasonable belief that it was necessary to preserve health, safety or welfare of child.

PENALTY

Misdemeanor, 1st degree (2929.21 to 2929.28, 2929.31)

If prior conviction of an offense under 2905.05, 2907.02, 2907.03, 2907.12, or section 2905.01 or 2907.05 when the victim of that prior offense was under seventeen years of age at the time of the offense, Felony, 5th degree (2929.11 to 2929.18, 2929.31)

Juveniles—Deception to Obtain Matter Harmful to Juveniles—2907.33

ELEMENTS OF THE CRIME

Division (A):

(1) For purpose of enabling a juvenile to obtain any material or gain admission to any performance which is harmful to juveniles

(2)(a) Falsely representing he is juvenile's parent, guardian, or spouse, or

(b) Furnishing the juvenile with any identification or document purporting to show that the juvenile is 18 years old or over, or married

Division (B):

(1) Any juvenile

(2) For purpose of obtaining any material or gaining admission to any performance which is harmful to juveniles

(3)(a) Falsely represent he is 18 years old or over or married, or

(b) Exhibit any identification or document purporting to show that he is 18 years old or over or married

PENALTY

Misdemeanor, 2nd degree (2929.21 to 2929.28, 2929.31)

Note: If offender is a juvenile he is to be judged an unruly child, with disposition of case as appropriate under Chapter 2151.

Juveniles—Displaying Matter Harmful to Juveniles—2907.311

ELEMENTS OF THE CRIME

(1) Having custody, control, or supervision of a commercial establishment

(2) With knowledge of the character or content of the material involved

(3)(a) Displays at such establishment any material that is harmful to juveniles

(b) And is open to view by juveniles as part of the invited general public

EXCEPTIONS

It is not a violation if:

(1) The material is displayed behind "blinder racks" or similar devices that cover at least the lower two-thirds of the material, or

(2) The material is wrapped or placed behind the counter, or

(3) The material is otherwise covered or located so that the portion that is harmful to juveniles is not open to the view of juveniles.

PENALTY

Misdemeanor, 1st degree (2929.21 to 2929.28, 2929.31)

Each day during which the offender is in violation constitutes a separate violation

Juveniles—Disseminating Matter Harmful to Juveniles—2907.31

ELEMENTS OF THE CRIME

(1) With knowledge of its character or content

(2)(a) Recklessly directly sell, deliver, furnish, disseminate, provide, exhibit, rent, or present

(b) To a juvenile or group of juveniles, or a law enforcement officer or group of officers posing as juveniles

(c) Any material or performance which is obscene or harmful to juveniles

(3)(a) Recklessly directly offer or agree to sell, deliver, furnish, disseminate, provide, exhibit, rent, or present

(b) To a juvenile or group of juveniles, or a law enforcement officer or group of officers posing as juveniles

(c) Any material or performance which is obscene or harmful to juveniles

(4)(a) While in physical proximity of a juvenile or a law enforcement officer posing as a juvenile recklessly allow any juvenile or law enforcement officer posing as a juvenile to review or peruse

(b) Any material or live performance which is harmful to juveniles

DEFENSES

(1) When the charge involves material or a performance which is harmful to juveniles, but not obscene:

(a) Defendant is the parent, guardian, or spouse of the juvenile, or

(b) At the time of the conduct in question:

(i) Juvenile was accompanied by the juvenile's parent or guardian

(ii) Who, with knowledge of its character, consented to the material or performance being furnished or presented to the juvenile, or

(c) Juvenile exhibited to defendant or defendant's agent or employee:

(i) Draft card, driver's license, birth record, marriage license, or other official or apparently official document, purporting to show that juvenile was at least 18 years old or married

(ii) Person to whom document was shown otherwise had no reasonable cause to believe that juvenile was under 18 years old or was not married.

(2) When the material or performance presented was either harmful to juveniles or obscene:

(a) Material or performance was furnished or presented

(b) For a bona fide medical, scientific, educational, governmental, judicial or other proper purpose

(c) By a physician, psychologist, sociologist, scientist, teacher, librarian, clergyman, prosecutor, judge, or other proper person

(3) Except as provided above, mistake of age is not a defense to a charge under this section.

PENALTY

If material or performance presented is harmful to juveniles, Misdemeanor, 1st degree (2929.21 to 2929.28, 2929.31)

If material or performance presented is obscene, Felony, 5th degree (2929.11 to 2929.18, 2929.31)

If material or performance presented is obscene and the juvenile is under 13 years of age, Felony, 4th degree (2929.11 to 2929.18, 2929.31)

Juveniles—Endangering Children—2919.22

ELEMENTS OF THE CRIME

Division (A):

(1) Parent, guardian, custodian, person with custody or control, person in loco parentis

(2) Child under 18, mentally or physically handicapped child under 21

(3) Create substantial risk to health or safety of such child

(4) By violating duty of care, protection, or support.

Division (B):

(1) To child under 18 or physically or mentally handicapped child under 21

(2)(a) Abuse the child, or

(b) Torture or cruelly abuse the child, or

(c) Administer corporal punishment or other physical disciplinary measure, or physically restrain child in cruel manner or for prolonged period, which punishment, discipline, or restraint is excessive under circumstances and creates substantial risk of serious physical harm to child, or

(d) Repeatedly administer unwarranted disciplinary measures to child when substantial risk that such conduct, if continued, will seriously impair or retard child's mental health or development, or

(e) Entice, coerce, permit, encourage, compel, hire, employ, use, or allow child to act, model or in any other way participate in or be photographed for production, presentation, dissemination or advertisement of any material or performance that the offender knows or reasonably should know is obscene or is a sexually-oriented matter or nudity-oriented matter.

(f) Allow a child to be on same parcel of property and within 100 feet, or in a multi–unit property within the same housing unit and within 100 feet, of any act in violation of 2925.04 (manufacture of drugs or cultivation of marijuana) or 2925.041 (assembly of chemicals for purpose of manufacturing illegal drugs), when the person knows that the act is occurring, whether or not there is a prosecution under 2925.04 or 2925.041.

In a prosecution under Division (B)(2)(e), the trier of fact may infer that an actor, model, or participant in the material or performance involved is a juvenile if the material or performance, through its title, text, visual representation, or otherwise, represents or depicts the actor, model, or participant as a juvenile.

Division (C):

(1) Operates

(2)(a) Vehicle

(b) Streetcar

(c) Trackless trolley

(3) In violation of Division (A) of 4511.19 when one or more children under age of 18 are in vehicle, streetcar or trackless trolley.

Person may be convicted at same trial or proceeding of violation of Division (C) and of 4511.19(A) that constitutes the basis of charge of violation of Division (C). A person arrested for violation of Division (C) shall be considered to be under arrest for either

(1) operating a vehicle while under the influence of alcohol, a drug of abuse, or alcohol and a drug of abuse, or

(2) operating a vehicle with a prohibited concentration of alcohol in the blood, breath or urine.

EXCEPTIONS

Division (A) is not violated when actor treats child's physical or mental illness or defect by spiritual means through prayer alone, in accordance with tenets of recognized religious body.

Division (B)(2)(e) is not applicable to any material or performance produced, presented or disseminated for a bona fide medical, scientific, educational, religious, governmental, judicial or other proper purpose, by or to a physician, psychologist, sociologist, scientist, teacher, person pursuing bona fide studies or research, librarian, member of clergy, prosecutor, judge or other person having a proper interest in the material or performance.

DEFENSE

Mistake of age is not a defense under Division (B)(2)(e) (2919.22(B)(5)).

PENALTY

If Division (A) or (B)(2)(a) violated, Misdemeanor, 1st degree (2929.21 to 2929.28, 2929.31)

If Division (A) violated and if offender previously convicted of offense under this section or any offense involving neglect, abandonment, contributing to delinquency of, or physical abuse of child, Felony, 4th degree. If Division (B)(2)(a) violated, and if the violation results in serious physical harm, Felony, 2nd degree. (2929.11 to 2929.18, 2929.31)

If Division (A) or (B)(2)(a) violated and if the violation results is serious physical harm to the child involved, Felony, 3rd degree (2929.11 to 2929.18, 2929.31)

If Division (B)(2)(b), (c), (d), or (f) violated, Felony, 3rd degree. If Division (B)(2)(e) violated, Felony, 2nd degree. (2929.11 to 2929.18, 2929.31)

If Division (B)(2)(b), (c), (d), or(f) violated and if result is serious physical harm to child or if offender previously convicted of offense under this section or any offense involving neglect, abandonment, contributing to the delinquency of or physical abuse of a child, Felony, 2nd degree (2929.11 to 2929.18, 2929.31)

For violations of Division (C):

(1) Except as otherwise provided, Misdemeanor, 1st degree (2929.21 to 2929.28, 2929.31)

(2) If violation results in serious physical harm to child involved, and if offender previously has been convicted of RC 2903.06, 2903.08, or of RC 2903.07 prior to March 23, 2000 amendment, or of RC 2903.04 where offender was subject to sanctions in 2903.04(D), Felony, 4th degree (2929.11 to 2929.18, 2929.31)

(3) If violation of Division (C) results in serious physical harm to the child involved, or offender was previously convicted of offense under 2919.22 or any offense involving neglect, abandonment, contributing to delinquency of, or physical abuse of a child, Felony, 5th degree (2929.11 to 2929.18, 2929.31)

(4) In addition to any term of imprisonment, fine, other sentence, penalty or sanction imposed pursuant to (1), (2) or (3) above as relating to violation of Division (C), court may impose the following:

(a) The court may require offender to perform not more than 200 hours supervised community service work under authority of any agency, political subdivision, or charitable organization as described in 2951.02(F)(1), provided the court is not to require offender to perform such work unless offender agrees to perform such work.

(1) The court may require offender to pay the court a reasonable fee to cover cost of participating in the work, including, but not limited to, costs of procuring policy(ies) of liability insurance to cover period during which offender will perform work.

(2) If court requires offender to perform such work as part of his sentence, court to do so in accordance with following criteria:

(a) Work to be performed after completion of term of imprisonment for violation of 2919.22(C)

(b) Work to be subject to limitations set forth in 2951.02(F)(1)(a) to 2951.02(F)(1)(c)

(c) Work to be supervised in manner described in 2951.02(F)(1)(d) by an official or person with qualifications described in 2951.02(F). Official or person to report in writing to court regarding conduct of offender in performing such work.

(d) Court to inform the offender in writing that inadequate performance of such work may result in the court ordering that the offender be committed to a jail or workhouse for a time period not exceeding the term of imprisonment that the court could have imposed for violation of 2919.22(C), reduced by the total time that the offender was actually imprisoned under the sentence or term that was imposed for that violation and by the total time offender was confined for any reason arising out of the offense for which the offender was convicted and sentenced as described in 2949.08 and 2967.191. If the court orders such commitment, the court is authorized, but not required, to grant the offender credit for community service adequately performed.

(3) If the court does order commitment of offender who does not adequately perform such community service, then

(a) the court may order that the offender be committed to a jail or workhouse for a period of time that does not exceed the term of imprisonment the court could have imposed upon the offender for violation of 2929.11(C), reduced by (1) the total amount of time that the offender was imprisoned under the sentence or term that was imposed upon the offender for that violation, and (2) by the total amount of time the offender was confined for any reason arising out of the offense for which the offender was convicted and sentenced as described in 2949.08 and 2967.191, and

(b) the court may order that the committed person shall receive hour-for-hour credit upon the period of commitment for the community service work adequately performed.

(4) No commitment pursuant to the performance of community service work shall exceed the period of the term of imprisonment the court could have imposed upon the offender for violation of 2929.11(C), reduced by (1) the total amount of time that the offender was imprisoned under the sentence or term that was imposed upon the offender for that violation, and (2) by the total amount of time the offender was confined for any reason arising out of the offense for which he was convicted and sentenced as described in 2949.08 and 2967.191, and

(5) Authorization for the court to impose community service does not limit or affect the court's authority to (1) suspend the sentence imposed upon a misdemeanor offender and place the offender on probation, or (2) to suspend the sentence pursuant to 2929.51 and 2951.02, or (3) to require offender, as condition of probation or suspension of sentence, to perform supervised community service work in accordance with 2951.02(F), or (4) to place a felony offender under a community control sanction.

(b) The court may suspend offender's driver's or commercial driver's license or permit or non-resident operating privilege up to one year. Such suspension is in addition to any suspension or revocation of such licenses, permit or privileges under Chapter 4506., 4507., 4509., or 4511. or under any other provision of law.

(1) The period of suspension shall be consecutive to, and commence after, the suspension or revocation of such licenses, permit or privileges under Chapter 4506., 4507., 4509., or 4511. or under any other provision of law in relation to violation of 2919.22(C) that is the basis for the suspension under (b) immediately above or in relation to violation of 4511.19(A) that is the basis for that violation of 2919.22(C).

(2) When offender is not entitled to request, and when court shall not grant to offender, occupational driving privileges:

If offender's license, permit or privilege has been suspended under 2919.22(E)(5)(d)(ii), and

(b) The offender, within seven years, has been convicted of, or pleaded guilty to three or more violations of:

(1) 2919.22(C), or

(2) 4511.19(A) or 4511.19(B) or a statute of any other state or a municipal ordinance of a municipal corporation located in any other state that is substantially similar to 4511.19(A) or (B), or

(3) A municipal ordinance relating to operating a vehicle while under the influence of alcohol, a drug of abuse, or alcohol and a drug of abuse, or

(4) A municipal ordinance relating to operating a vehicle with a prohibited concentration of alcohol in the blood, breath, or urine, or

(5) 2903.04 in a case in which the offender was subject to the sanctions described in 2903.04(D), or

(6) 2903.06, 2903.07, 2903.08, or a municipal ordinance that is substantially similar to 2903.07 in a case where the jury or judge found that the offender was under the influence of alcohol, a drug of abuse, or alcohol and a drug of abuse

(3) Any other offender whose license, permit or nonresident operating privilege has been suspended under 2919.22(E)(5)(d)(ii) may file with the court that sentenced him a petition alleging that the suspension would seriously affect his ability to continue his employment. Court may grant occupational driving privileges during the period the suspension would otherwise be imposed upon satisfactory proof there is reasonable cause to believe suspension would seriously affect offender's ability to continue his

employment. The court shall not grant occupational driving privileges for employment as a driver of commercial motor vehicles to any person disqualified from operating a commercial motor vehicle under 4506.16.

(5) If, as part of the same trial or proceeding, the offender is convicted of or pleads guilty to a separate charge for violating RC 4511.19(A), then the offender is subject to all of the sanctions required or permitted for a violation of 4511.19(A). These sanctions are in addition to any of the penalties imposed upon the offender in (1) to (4) above for violations of Division (C).

(6) If, at time of violation, two or more children under age 18 were in the motor vehicle involved in the violation, offender may be convicted of a violation of 2919.22(C) for each of the children, but the court may sentence the offender for only one of the violations.

(7) Both of the following apply, if person is convicted of or pleads guilty to a violation of 2919.22(C), but the person is neither convicted of nor had pleaded guilty to a separate charge of violating 4511.19(A) that was the basis of the charge of the violation of 2919.22(C):

(a) Conviction of or guilty plea to violation of (c) shall not constitute a violation of 4511.19(A) for the purposes of the provisions of 4511.19 that set forth the penalties and sanctions for a violation of 4511.19(A).

(b) Conviction of or guilty plea to violation of 2919.22(C) shall constitute a conviction or guilty plea to a violation of 4511.19(A) for purposes of any provision of law that refers to a conviction or guilty plea to a violation of 4511.19(A) and that is not described in (6)(b) immediately above.

(8) A person who is convicted of or pleads guilty to a violation of 2919.22(C) and who is also convicted or pleads guilty to a separate charge of violating 4511.19(A) that was the basis of the charge of the violation of 2919.22(C), then the conviction or guilty plea to the violation of 2919.22(C) shall not constitute a conviction of guilty plea to a violation of 4511.19(A) for purposes of any provision of law that refers to a conviction or guilty plea to 4511.19(A).

Juveniles—Illegal Use in Nudity-oriented Material or Performance—2907.323

ELEMENTS OF THE CRIME

Division (A)(1):

(1) Any minor not the person's child or ward

(2)(a) Photograph in a state of nudity, or

(b) Create, direct, produce or transfer any material or performance that shows the minor in a state of nudity, or

Division (A)(2):

(1) Parent or guardian

(2)(a) Consent to the photographing or photographing in a state of nudity of a minor child or ward, or

(b) Consent to the use of the person's minor child or ward in a state of nudity in any material or performance or use or transfer such material or performance

Division (A)(3):

(1) Possess or view any material or performance that shows a minor who is not the person's child or ward in a state of nudity

EXCEPTIONS

(1) None of the above are applicable to any material or performance presented for a bona fide medical, scientific, educational, religious, governmental, judicial, or other proper purpose by or to a physician, psychologist, sociologist, scientist, teacher, person pursuing bona fide studies or research, librarian, clergyman, prosecutor, judge, or other person having a proper interest in the material or performance.

(2) Division (A)(1) not applicable if minor's parent, guardian or custodian consents in writing to the photographing of the minor, to use of the minor in material or performance or to transfer of the material and the specific manner in which material or performance is to be used.

(3) Division (A)(3) not applicable if person knows parent, guardian, or custodian has consented in writing to the photographing or use of the minor in a state of nudity and to the manner in which material or performance is used or transferred.

PENALTY

If Division (A)(1) or (2) violated, Felony, 2nd degree (2929.11 to2929.18, 2929.31)

If Division (A)(3) violated, Felony, 5th degree (2929.11 to 2929.18, 2929.31)

If Division (A)(3) violated and if prior conviction or guilty plea to this section, 2907.321 or 2907.322, Felony, 5th degree (2929.11 to 2929.18, 2929.31)

Juveniles—Importuning

See Importuning

Juveniles—Improperly Furnishing Firearms to Minor—2923.21

ELEMENTS OF THE CRIME

(1) Sell any firearm to person under 18 years of age, or

(2) Sell any handgun to person under 21 years of age, or

(3) Furnish firearm to any person under 18 years of age or any handgun hunting, sporting or educational purposes, including, but not limited to, instruction in firearms or handgun safety, care, handling, marksmanship under supervision or control of responsible adult.

(4)(a) Sell or furnish a firearm to person 18 years of age or older

(b) If seller or furnisher knows, or has reason to know that the person is purchasing or receiving the firearm for the purpose of

(i) Selling the firearm to a person under 18 years of age, or

(ii) Furnishing the firearm to a person under 18 years of age.

(5)(a) Sell or furnish a handgun to person 21 years of age or older

(b) If seller or furnisher knows, or has reason to know that the person is purchasing or receiving the handgun for the purpose of

(i) Selling the handgun to a person under 21 years of age, or

(ii) Furnishing the handgun to a person under 21 years of age.

(6)(a) Purchase or attempt to purchase any firearm

(b) With the intent to

(i) Sell the firearm to a person under 18 years of age, or

(ii) Furnish the firearm to a person under 18 years of age.

(7)(a) Purchase or attempt to purchase any handgun

(b) With the intent to

(i) Sell the handgun to a person under 21 years of age, or

(ii) Furnish the handgun to a person under 21 years of age.

EXCEPTIONS

(1) and (2) are not applicable when furnishing to a law enforcement officer.

PENALTY

Felony, 5th degree (2929.11 to 2929.18, 2929.31)

Juveniles—Improper Solicitation of Contributions for Missing Children—2901.32

ELEMENTS OF THE CRIME

Division (A):

(1) Solicits contributions for the purpose of distributing materials containing information relating to missing children

(2)(a) Organization not incorporated under Chapter 1702. or the nonprofit corporation law of another state for 2 years prior to solicitation, or

(b) Organization not exempt from federal income taxation as specified in 2901.32(2) for 2 years prior to solicitation, or

(c) Organization uses fund-raising counsel, professional solicitors, commercial co-venturers, or other charitable organizations, as defined in 1716.01 to solicit

Division (B):

(1) Solicits contributions for the purpose of distributing materials containing information relating to missing children

(2) Expressly states or implies affiliation with, or solicitation on behalf of, organization established to assist in location of missing children without written consent to do so

PENALTY

Misdemeanor, 3rd degree (2929.21 to 2929.28, 2929.31)

Juveniles—Pandering Obscenity Involving a Minor—2907.321

ELEMENTS OF THE CRIME

(1) With knowledge of the character of the material or performance involved

(2) (a) Create, reproduce, or publish any obscene material that has a minor as one of its participants or portrayed observers, or

(b) Promote or advertise for sale or dissemination; sell, deliver, disseminate, display, exhibit, present, rent, or provide; or offer or agree to sell, deliver, disseminate, display, exhibit, present, rent, or provide, any obscene material that has a minor as one of its participants, or portrayed observers, or

(c) Create, direct or produce an obscene performance that has a minor as one of its participants, or

(d) Advertise or promote for presentation, present, or participate in presenting an obscene performance, that has a minor as one of its participants, or

(e) Buy, procure, possess or control any obscene material that has a minor as one of its participants, or

(f) Bring or cause to be brought into Ohio any obscene material that has a minor as one of its participants or portrayed observers

The trier of fact may infer that a person in the material or performance involved is a minor if the material or performance involved, through its title, text, visual representation, or otherwise, represents or depicts the person as a minor.

EXCEPTION

Not applicable to any material or performance that is sold, disseminated, displayed, possessed, controlled, brought or caused to be brought into Ohio, or presented for a bona fide medical, scientific, educational, religious, governmental, judicial or other proper purpose, by or to a physician, psychologist, sociologist, scientist, teacher, person pursuing bona fide studies or research, librarian, clergyman, prosecutor, judge, or other person having a proper interest in the material or performance.

DEFENSE

Mistake of age is not a defense.

PENALTY

If (2)(a), (b), (c), (d), or (f) violated, Felony, 2nd degree (2929.11 to 2929.18, 2929.21, 2929.31)

If (2)(e) violated, Felony, 4th degree (2929.11 to 2929.18, 2929.31)

If (2)(e) violated and if previous conviction or guilty plea to this section, 2907.322, or 2907.323, Felony, 3rd degree (2929.11 to 2929.18, 2929.31)

Juveniles—Pandering Sexually-oriented Matter Involving a Minor—2907.322

ELEMENTS OF THE CRIME

(1) With knowledge of the character of the material or performance involved

(2)(a) Create, record, photograph, film, develop, reproduce, or publish any material that shows a minor participating or engaging in sexual activity, masturbation, or bestiality, or

(b) Advertise for sale or dissemination, sell, distribute, transport, disseminate, exhibit, or display any matter that shows a minor participating or engaging in sexual activity, masturbation, or bestiality, or

(c) Create, direct or produce a performance that shows a minor participating or engaging in sexual activity, masturbation, or bestiality, or

(d) Advertise for presentation, present, or participate in presenting a performance that shows a minor participating or engaging in sexual activity, masturbation, or bestiality, or

(e) Knowingly solicit, receive, purchase, exchange, possess, or control any material that shows a minor participating or engaging in sexual activity, masturbation, or bestiality, or

(f) Bring or cause to be brought into this state any material that shows a minor participating or engaging in sexual activity, masturbation, or bestiality, or

(g) Bring, cause to be brought, or finance the bringing of any minor into or across the state with the intent that the minor engage in sexual activity, masturbation, or bestiality in a performance or for the purpose of producing material containing a visual representation depicting the minor engaged in sexual activity, masturbation, or bestiality

The trier of fact may infer that a person in the material or performance involved is a minor if the material or performance, through its title, text, visual representation, or otherwise, represents or depicts the person as a minor.

EXCEPTION

Not applicable to any material or performance presented for a bona fide medical, scientific, educational, religious, governmental, judicial, or other proper purpose by or to a physician, psychologist, sociologist, scientist, teacher, person pursuing bona fide studies or research, librarian, clergyman, prosecutor, judge, or other person having a proper interest in the material or performance.

DEFENSE

Mistake of age is not a defense.

PENALTY

If (2)(a), (b), (c), (d), (f), or (g) violated, Felony, 2nd degree (2929.11 to 2929.18, 2929.31)

If (2)(e) violated, Felony, 4th degree (2929.11 to 2929.18, 2929.31)

If (2)(e) violated and if previous conviction or guilty plea to this section, 2907.321, or 2907.323, Felony, 3rd degree (2929.11 to 2929.18,2929.31)

Juveniles—Permitting Child Abuse—2903.15

ELEMENTS OF THE CRIME

(1) Parent, guardian, custodian, person with custody

(2) Child under 18, mentally or physically handicapped child under 21

(3) cause serious physical harm or death

(4) as a proximate result of permitting

(a) abuse

(b) torture

(c) administration of corporal punishment

(d) other physical discipline, or

(e) to be physically restrained

(5) in a cruel manner or for a prolonged period

DEFENSE

It is an affirmative defense that defendant did not have means to prevent harm or death readily available *and* that defendant took timely and reasonable steps to summon aid.

PENALTY

Felony, 3rd degree (2929.11 to 2929.18, 2929.31)

Felony, 1st degree, if death results (2929.11 to 2929.18, 2929.31)

Juveniles—Selling Drug Paraphernalia to Juveniles

See Drug Offenses—Paraphernalia—Illegal Use, Possession, Sale, Manufacture, or Advertisement of Drug Paraphernalia

Juveniles—Underage Purchase of Firearm—2923.211(A)

See also Weapons—Underage Purchase of Handgun

ELEMENTS OF THE CRIME

(1) Person under age 18

(2) Purchase or attempt to purchase

(3) Firearm

PENALTY

Delinquent child subject to an order of disposition as provided in section 2151.355 of the Revised Code.

Juveniles—Unlawful Sexual Conduct With a Minor—2907.04

ELEMENTS OF THE CRIME

Division (A)(1):

(1) No person, including a parent, guardian or other custodian

(2) Aid, abet, induce, cause, encourage, contribute to, or act in a way tending to cause

(3) A child or ward of the juvenile court to become

(a) an unruly child, as defined in 2151.022, or

(b) a delinquent child, as defined in 2152.02

Division (A)(2):

(1) No person, including a parent, guardian or other custodian

(2) Act in a way tending to cause

(3) A child or ward of the juvenile court to become

(a) an unruly child, as defined in 2151.022, or

(b) a delinquent child, as defined in 2152.02

PENALTY

Felony, 2nd degree if offender previously convicted of 2907.02, 2907.03, 2907.04 or 2907.12 (2929.11 to 2929.18, 2929.31)

Felony, 3rd degree if offender is ten or more years older than minor (2929.11 to 2929.18, 2929.31)

Felony, 4th degree (2929.11 to 2929.18, 2929.31)

If offender is less than 4 years older than other person, Misdemeanor, 1st degree (2929.21 to 2929.28, 2929.31)

Kidnapping—2905.01

See also Abduction; Juveniles—Child Stealing; Unlawful Restraint

ELEMENTS OF THE CRIME

Division (A):

(1)(a) By force, threat, or deception, or

(b) By any means in a case where the victim is under 13 years or mentally incompetent

(2)(a) Remove another person from the place where the other person is found, or

(b) Restrain the liberty of the other person

(3) For any of the following purposes:

(a) To hold for ransom, or as shield or hostage, or

(b) To facilitate commission of any felony or flight thereafter, or

(c) To terrorize or inflict serious physical harm on the victim or on another, or

(d) To engage in sexual activity, as defined in 2907.01, with the victim against the victim's will, or

(e) To hinder, impede, or obstruct a function of government, or to force any action or concession on the part of governmental authority

Division (B):

(1)(a) By force, threat, or deception, or

(b) By any means in a case where the victim is under 13 years or mentally incompetent

(2) Knowingly

(3)(a) Under circumstances that create a substantial risk of serious physical harm to the victim, or

(b) if the victim is a minor, under circumstances that either create a substantial risk of serious physical harm to the victim or cause physical harm to the victim:

(4)(a) Remove another from the place where he is found, or

(b) Restrain another of his liberty, or

(c) Hold another in a condition of involuntary servitude

PENALTY

Felony, 1st degree (2929.11 to 2929.18, 2929.31)

If victim released in safe place unharmed, Felony, 2nd degree (2929.11 to 2929.18, 2929.31)

Law Enforcement Emblem—Unlawful Display—2913.441

ELEMENTS OF THE CRIME

(1) Knowingly

(2) Display on motor vehicle law enforcement emblem

(3) When not entitled to do so

PENALTY

Minor Misdemeanor (2929.21 to 2929.28, 2929.31)

Law Enforcement Officers—Arrest, Resisting

See Motor Vehicles—Resisting or Fleeing Traffic Officer

Law Enforcement Officers—Body Cavity and Strip Searches

See Searches—Body Cavity and Strip Searches

Law Enforcement Officers—Dereliction of Duty

See Dereliction of Duty

Law Enforcement Officers—Disclosure of Confidential Information

See Confidential Information—Disclosure of Confidential Information

Law Enforcement Officers—Failure to Aid—2921.23

ELEMENTS OF THE CRIME

(1) Negligently fail or refuse to aid

(2) Law enforcement officer

(3) When called upon to assist in preventing or halting commission of offense, or in apprehension or detention of an offender

(4) When such aid can be given without substantial risk of physical harm to person giving it

PENALTY

Minor Misdemeanor (2929.21 to 2929.28, 2929.31)

Law Enforcement Officers—Impersonation of Certain Officers—2921.51

ELEMENTS OF THE CRIME

Division (A):

This division sets forth the definitions applicable to Divisions (B), (C), (D) and (E) of this section

Division (B):

(1) Impersonate

(2) Peace officer or private police officer

Division (C):

(1) By impersonating

(2) Peace officer or private police officer

(3) Arrest, detain, search any person or search any property

Division (D):

(1) Purpose to commit or facilitate commission of offense

(2) Impersonate

(3) Peace officer, private police officer, or officer, agent or employee of state

Division (E):

(1) Commit felony

(2) While impersonating

(3) Peace officer, private police officer, or officer, agent or employee of state

DEFENSE

It is an affirmative defense under division (B) that impersonation of peace officer was for a lawful purpose

PENALTY

If Division (B) violated, Misdemeanor, 4th degree (2929.21 to 2929.28, 2929.31)

If Divisions (C) or (D) violated, Misdemeanor, 1st degree (2929.21 to 2929.28, 2929.31)

If in Division (D) purpose is to commit or facilitate felony, Felony, 4th degree (2929.11 to 2929.18, 2929.31)

If Division (E) violated, Felony, 3rd degree (2929.11 to 2929.18,-2929.31)

Law Enforcement Officers—Personating an Officer—2913.44

ELEMENTS OF THE CRIME

(1)(a) With purpose to defraud or knowing he is facilitating fraud, or

(b) With purpose to induce another to purchase property or services

(2) Personate law enforcement officer, inspector, investigator, agent of any governmental agency.

PENALTY

Misdemeanor, 1st degree (2929.21 to 2929.28, 2929.31)

Law Enforcement Officers—Police Dogs or Horses

See Assault—Police Dog or Horse

Liquor Permit Premises—Firearm

See Weapons—Possessing Firearm in Liquor Permit Premises

Livery, Defrauding

See Theft-related Offenses—Defrauding Livery or Hostelry

Loitering to Engage in Solicitation; Loitering to Engage in Solicitation After Positive HIV Test—2907.241

ELEMENTS OF THE CRIME

Division (A):

(1)(a) Beckon to, stop or attempt to stop another

(b) Engage or attempt to engage another in conversation

(c) Stop or attempt to stop a vehicle or approach a stationary vehicle

(d) Stop, attempt to stop, beckon or entice another to enter a vehicle the offender is operating

(e) Interfere with another's free passage

(2) Purposely to solicit another to engage in sex for hire

(3) In or near a public place

Division (B):

(1) Engage in the conduct described in Division (A)

(2) Purposely to solicit another to engage in sex for hire

(3) In or near a public place

(4) Knowing that s/he has tested positive as a carrier of a virus that causes AIDS

PENALTY

If Division (A), Misdemeanor, 3rd degree (2929.21 to 2929.28, 2929.31, 2907.25)

If Division (B), Felony, 5th degree (2929.11 to 2929.18, 2929.31, 2907.25)

Making False Alarms

See Disorderly Conduct Offenses—Making False Alarms

Making False Allegation of Peace Officer Misconduct—2921.15

ELEMENTS OF THE CRIME

(1) Knowingly

(2) File a false complaint

(3) Against a peace officer

(4) Alleging misconduct of the officer's duties

PENALTY

Misdemeanor, 1st degree (2929.21 to 2929.28, 2929.31)

Making or Using Slugs

See Theft-related Offenses—Making or Using Slugs

Manslaughter—Abortion

See Abortion—Abortion Manslaughter

Manslaughter—Involuntary Manslaughter—2903.04

See also Homicide—Negligent

ELEMENTS OF THE CRIME

Division (A):

(1) Cause death of another or the unlawful termination of another's pregnancy

(2) As proximate result of committing or attempting to commit a felony

Division (B):

(1) Cause death of another or the unlawful termination of another's pregnancy

(2) As proximate result of committing or attempting to commit a misdemeanor of any degree, a regulatory offense, or a minor misdemeanor other than a Title 45 minor misdemeanor and other than a municipal ordinance, regardless of penalty, that is substantially equivalent to any Title 45 minor misdemeanor.

PENALTY

If Division (A) violated, Felony, 1st degree (2929.11 to 2929.18, 2929.31)

If Division (B) violated, Felony, 3rd degree (2929.11 to 2929.18, 2929.31)

Note: If either division violated and underlying offense is a violation of 4511.19(A) or (B) or a substantially equivalent municipal ordinance or includes as an element the operation or participation of a snowmobile, locomotive, watercraft, or aircraft while under the influence of alcohol and/or a drug of abuse:

(1) Offender's driver's or commercial driver's license shall be suspended for life (4510.02(A)(1)).

(2) Mandatory prison term imposed (2929.14).

Manslaughter—Voluntary Manslaughter—2903.03

See also Murder—Aggravated Murder

ELEMENTS OF THE CRIME

(1) While under influence of sudden passion or in sudden fit of rage

(2) Brought on by serious provocation occasioned by victim

(3) Reasonably sufficient to incite the person

(4) To use deadly force

(5) Knowingly cause death of another or the unlawful termination of another's pregnancy

PENALTY

Felony, 1st degree (2929.11 to 2929.18, 2929.31)

Marihuana

See Drug Offenses, generally

Medicaid Fraud

See Theft-related Offenses—Medicaid Fraud

Meeting, Disturbing

See Disorderly Conduct Offenses—Disturbing a Lawful Meeting

Menacing—Aggravated Menacing—2903.21

ELEMENTS OF THE CRIME

(1) Knowingly

(2) Cause another to believe

(3) Offender will cause serious physical harm to person, to person's unborn, or property of such other person or his immediate family member

PENALTY

Misdemeanor, 1st degree (2929.21 to 2929.28, 2929.31)

Felony, 5th degree, if victim is an officer or employee of a Public Children's Service Agency or a Private Child Placing Agency, and the offense relates to victim's performance or anticipated performance of responsibilities or duties; subsequent offenses, Felony, 4th degree (2929.11 to 2929.18, 2929.31)

Menacing—Menacing—2903.22

See also Intimidation, generally

ELEMENTS OF THE CRIME

(1) Knowingly

(2) Cause another to believe

(3) Offender will cause physical harm to person, to person's unborn, or property of such other person or his immediate family member

PENALTY

Misdemeanor, 4th degree (2929.21 to 2929.28, 2929.31)

Felony, 5th degree, if victim is an officer or employee of a Public Children's Service Agency or a Private Child Placing Agency, and the offense relates to victim's performance or anticipated performance of responsibilities or duties; subsequent offenses, Felony, 4th degree (2929.11 to 2929.18, 2929.31)

Menacing—Menacing by Stalking—2903.211

ELEMENTS OF THE CRIME

Division (A)(1):

(1) Knowingly

(2) By engaging in pattern of conduct

(3) Cause another to believe

(4) That offender will cause other person

(a) Physical harm, or

(b) Mental distress

Division (A)(2):

(1) Through use of any electronic method of remotely transferring information (not limited to computer system)

(2) Post a message

(3) With purpose to urge or incite another to commit a violation of Division (A)(1)

PROOF

Pattern of conduct is two or more acts or incidents closely related in time, regardless of whether there has been prior conviction. Actions or incidents that prevent, obstruct, or delay performance by a public official, firefighter, rescuer, emergency medical services persons or emergency facility persons of authorized activity within their official capacity may constitute a "pattern of conduct." 2903.211(C)(1). Mental distress is any mental illness or condition that involves some temporary substantial incapacity or that would normally require psychiatric treatment. 2903.211(C)(2).

PENALTY

Misdemeanor, 1st degree (2929.21 to 2929.28, 2929.31)

Felony, 4th degree (2929.11 to 2929.18, 2929.31), if (a) offender previously convicted of this section or 2911.211; (b) in committing the offense, offender made a threat of physical harm against the victim or as result of division (A)(2) violation, third person induced to make a threat of physical harm to or against victim; (c) in committing the offense, offender trespassed on land or premises where victim lives, is employed, or attends school or as result of division (A)(2) violation, third person induced to trespass on land or premises where victim lives, is employed, or attends school; (d) victim is a minor; (e) offender has a history of violence toward the victim or any other person or a history of other violent acts toward the victim or any other person; (f) while committing the offense under Division (A)(1), offender had a deadly weapon on or about offender's person or under offender's control; (g) at time of offense, offender was subject to a protection order issued under 2903.213 or 2903.214, regardless of whether protected person under the order was the victim or another person; (h) in committing offense, offender caused serious physical harm to the premises at which victim resides, to real property on which premises is located, or to any personal property located on that premises; or (i) prior to offense, offender had been determined to represent a substantial risk of physical harm to others as manifested by evidence of then-recent homicidal or other violent behavior, evidence of then-recent threats that placed another in reasonable fear of violent behavior and serious physical harm, or other evidence of then-present dangerousness.

Felony, 5th degree, if victim is an officer or employee of a Public Children's Service Agency or a Private Child Placing Agency, and the offense relates to victim's performance or anticipated performance of responsibilities or duties; subsequent offenses, Felony, 4th degree (2929.11 to 2929.18, 2929.31)

Note: Written statement by complainant alleging that alleged offender has committed offense of menacing by stalking constitutes reasonable cause for officer to make warrantless arrest under 2935.03(B)(2)(b).

Note: Following allegation of violation of this section, court may issue a protective order, *see* 2903.214. Violation of protective order may result in prosecution under 2919.27 and/or punishment for contempt of court.

Note: 2919.271 (mental evaluations) applies to a person charged with this section.

Mental Health Facilities—Illegal Conveyance of Certain Items on to Detention/Mental Health Facility Grounds—2921.36

See Illegal Conveyance of Certain Items on to Detention/Mental Health Facility Grounds

Minor, Crimes Affecting

See Bingo—Minor Not To Work Bingo Session; Domestic Offenses, generally; Juveniles, generally; Kidnapping

Mischief, Criminal

See Criminal Mischief

Misconduct at an Emergency

See Disorderly Conduct Offenses—Misconduct at an Emergency

Misuse of Block Parent Symbol

See Block Parent Symbol—Misuse

Misuse of Credit Card

See Theft-related Offenses—Misuse of Credit Card

Monument, Desecration

See Desecration

Motion Picture Privacy—2913.07

ELEMENTS OF THE CRIME

(1) Without written consent of owner or lessee of facility and licensor of motion picture

(2) Knowingly

(3) Operate an audiovisual recording device in a facility in which a motion picture is being shown

EXCEPTIONS

Lawfully authorized governmental agent when acting in an official capacity

PENALTY

Misdemeanor, 4th degree (2929.21 to 2929.28, 2929.31)

Each subsequent offense, Felony, 5th degree (2929.11 to 2929.18, 2929.31)

Note: An act that violates this section and any other RC section may be prosecuted under this section, the other section, or both.

Motor Vehicles—Altering Vehicle Identification Numbers—4549.62

ELEMENTS OF THE CRIME

Division (A):

(1) With purpose to conceal or destroy identity of a vehicle or part

(2) Remove, deface, cover, alter, destroy

(3) Vehicle identification number or derivative on a vehicle or vehicle part

Division (B):

(1) With purpose to conceal or destroy identity of a vehicle or part

(2) Remove, deface, cover, alter, destroy

(3) Identifying number that has been lawfully placed on vehicle or vehicle part by an owner thereof, other than manufacturer, for the purpose of deterring its theft and facilitating its recovery if stolen, or

Division (C):

(1) With purpose to conceal or destroy identity of a vehicle or part

(2) Place a counterfeit vehicle identification number or derivative thereof upon a vehicle or part, or

Division (D):

(1) With knowledge that vehicle identification number or derivative thereof has been removed, defaced, covered, altered or destroyed in such manner

(2) So that the identity of the vehicle or part cannot be determined by visual examination of the number site where the manufacturer placed the number

(3) Buy, offer to buy, sell, offer to sell, receive, dispose of, conceal

(4) Any vehicle or part

EXCEPTIONS

Does not apply to good faith acquisition and disposition of vehicle or parts as junk or scrap in ordinary course of business by scrap metal processing facility under 4737.05(E) or motor vehicle salvage dealer licensed under Ch 4738.

Division (D) does not apply to possession by owner or owner's insurer who provides satisfactory evidence: that tampering with vehicle identification number occurred after owner acquired possession without owner's consent, by accident, or by ordinary wear and tear; that person is valid owner with valid title; and that vehicle's original identity can be established in way excluding any reasonable probability that vehicle stolen.

PENALTY

Felony, 4th degree (2929.11 to 2929.18, 2929.31, 4549.99)

Second and subsequent offenses, Felony, 3rd degree (2929.11 to 2929.18, 2929.31)

Vehicle subject to forfeiture under 2933.41; lawful owner of parts on seized vehicle may reclaim under 4549.62(D)(2)(b)

Motor Vehicles—Commercial Motor Vehicles—Criminal Offenses—4506.15

ELEMENTS OF THE CRIME

(1) Drive a commercial motor vehicle when any of the following exist:

(a) Driver has measurable or detectable amount of alcohol or a controlled substance in blood, breath, or urine, or

(b) Driver has alcohol concentration, as defined in 4506.01(A), of .04 of 1 percent or more, or

(c) Driver is under the influence of a controlled substance

(2)(a) Drive a commercial motor vehicle

(b) Knowingly

(c) Leave the scene of an accident involving the commercial motor vehicle being driven

(3)(a) Use a commercial motor vehicle

(b) In the commission of a felony

(4)(a) Refuse to submit

(b) To alcohol and controlled substance test under 4506.17

(5)(a) Violate an out-of-service order

(b) Issued under Chapter 4506.

(6)(a) Violate any provision described in Divisions (1) to (5)

(b) While transporting hazardous materials

PENALTY

Misdemeanor, 1st degree (2929.21 to 2929.28, 2929.31, 4506.99)

If Division (1)(a) violated, or similar law of another state or foreign jurisdiction, driver shall immediately be placed out-of-service for 24 hours, in addition to any disqualification required by this section and other penalty imposed by Revised Code

Note: Registrar of motor vehicles, in addition to any other penalty imposed by Revised Code, shall disqualify offender from operating a commercial motor vehicle as follows:

On first offense for violation of Division (1)(b) or (c), or Divisions (2) to (5), or similar law of another state or foreign jurisdiction, for 1 year

On second offense for violation of Division (1)(b) or (c), or Divisions (2) to (5), or similar law of another state or foreign jurisdiction, or any combination of such violations arising from two or more separate incidents, for life, or for any other period of time determined by United States secretary of transportation and designated by director of highway safety by rule

On violation of Division (6), or similar law of another state or foreign jurisdiction, for 3 years

On violation of Division (3), or similar law of another state or foreign jurisdiction, in connection with manufacture, distribution, or dispensing of controlled substance or possession with intent to manufacture, distribute, or dispense controlled substance, for life

Note: Any driver disqualified under this section may apply to registrar for driver's license to operate non-commercial motor vehicle, provided offender's commercial driver's license not otherwise revoked or suspended.

Motor Vehicles—Handling Weapon

See Weapons—Improperly Handling Firearms in Motor Vehicle

Motor Vehicles—Master Car Keys—4549.042

ELEMENTS OF THE CRIME

Division (A):

(1) Sell or dispose of

(2) Master key designed to fit more than one motor vehicle

(3) Knowing or having reasonable cause to believe key will be used to commit a crime

Division (B):

(1) Buy, receive or possess

(2) Master key designed to fit more than one motor vehicle

(3) For purpose of using key to commit a crime

PENALTY

Felony, 4th degree (2929.11 to 2929.18, 2929.31, 4549.99)

Subsequent offenses, Felony, 3rd degree (2929.11 to 2929.18, 2929.31, 4549.99)

Motor Vehicles—Operating While Intoxicated

See Drunk Driving—Driving While Intoxicated or Drugged

Motor Vehicles—Presenting False Name or Information to Law Enforcement Officer—4513.361

ELEMENTS OF THE CRIME

(1) Knowingly

(2) Present, display, or orally communicate

(3) False name, social security number, or date of birth

(4) To law enforcement officer in process of issuing actor a traffic ticket or complaint

PENALTY

Misdemeanor, 1st degree (2929.21 to 2929.28, 2929.31, 4513.99)

Motor Vehicles—Reckless Driving

See Motor Vehicles—Willful or Wanton Disregard of Safety on Highways

Motor Vehicles—Resisting or Fleeing Traffic Officer—2921.331

ELEMENTS OF THE CRIME

Division (A):

(1) Fail to comply

(2) With lawful order or direction

(3) Of police officer

(4) Who has authority to direct, control or regulate traffic

Division (B):

(1) While operating a motor vehicle

(2) Willfully elude or flee a police officer

(3) After receiving a visible or audible signal from a police officer to stop

PENALTY

If Division (A) violated, Misdemeanor, 1st degree (2929.21 to 2929.28, 2929.31)

If Division (B) violated, Misdemeanor, 1st degree (2929.21 to 2929.28, 2929.31)

If Division (B) violated, and any one of the following factors is proved beyond a reasonable doubt, Felony, 4th degree:

(1) Offender fleeing immediately after commission of a felony; or

(2) Operation of the motor vehicle by the offender was the proximate cause of serious physical harm to persons or property; or

(3) Operation of the motor vehicle by the offender caused a substantial risk of serious physical harm to persons or property. (2929.11 to 2929.18, 2929.31)

If Division (B) violated, and any one of the following factors is proved beyond a reasonable doubt, Felony, 3rd degree:

(1) Operation of the motor vehicle by the offender resulted in serious physical harm to persons or property.

(2) Operation of the motor vehicle by the offender caused a substantial risk of serious physical harm to persons or property. (2929.11 to 2929.18, 2929.31)

Note: In addition to any other penalty, driver's license shall be suspended for a definite period of 3 years to life; if offender has a prior conviction under this section, suspension is for life. The court may not grant limited driving privileges to the offender.

Motor Vehicles—Speeding—4511.21

See also Motor Vehicles—Resisting or Fleeing Traffic Officer

ELEMENTS OF THE CRIME

(1) Operating a motor vehicle or trackless trolley or streetcar

(2) Upon the streets and highways

(3)(a) Faster or slower than reasonable or proper with due regard to traffic, surface, width of the road and other conditions, or

(b) Faster than will permit the vehicle to be stopped within the assured clear distance ahead

PENALTY

Minor Misdemeanor (2929.21 to 2929.28, 2929.31, 4511.99)

If speed exceeds 35 mph passing school at recess or when children are going to or leaving school during opening and closing hours, or in a business district of a municipality; or, is faster than 50 mph in other portions of municipality, Misdemeanor, 4th degree (2929.21 to 2929.28, 2929.31, 4511.99)

Second offense within 1 year of first, Misdemeanor, 4th degree (2929.21 to 2929.28, 2929.31, 4511.99)

Subsequent offenses within 1 year of first, Misdemeanor, 3rd degree (2929.21 to 2929.28, 2929.31, 4511.99)

Motor Vehicles—Speeding—Private Roads and Driveways—4511.211

ELEMENTS OF THE CRIME

(1) Operating a vehicle

(2) On private road or driveway in private residential area containing 20 or more dwelling units

(3) In excess of posted limit of not less than 25 mph

PENALTY

Minor Misdemeanor (2929.21 to 2929.28, 2929.31, 4511.99)

Second offense within 1 year of first, Misdemeanor, 4th degree (2929.21 to 2929.28, 2929.31, 4511.99)

Subsequent offenses within 1 year of first, Misdemeanor, 3rd degree (2929.21 to 2929.28, 2929.31, 4511.99)

Motor Vehicles—Unauthorized Use of Vehicle—2913.03

ELEMENTS OF THE CRIME

Division (A):

(1) Knowingly use or operate

(2) Aircraft, motor vehicle, motorcycle, motorboat, other motor-propelled vehicle

(3) Without consent of owner or person authorized to give consent

Division (B):

(1) Knowingly use or operate

(2) Aircraft, motor vehicle, motorcycle, motorboat, other motor-propelled vehicle

(3) Without consent of owner or person authorized to give consent

(4) Remove from Ohio, or keep possession more than 48 hours

DEFENSES

(1) At time of alleged offense, actor, though mistaken, reasonably believed the actor was authorized to use or operate property.

(2) At time of alleged offense, actor reasonably believed owner or person empowered to give consent would authorize actor to use or operate property.

PENALTY

If Division (A) violated, Misdemeanor, 1st degree (2929.21 to 2929.28, 2929.31)

If Division (B) violated, Felony, 5th degree (2929.11 to 2929.18, 2929.31)

If Division (A) or (B) violated and victim is elderly person who incurs loss, Felony, 5th degree. Felony, 4th degree, if loss is $500 or more and less than $5,000. Felony, 3rd degree, if loss is $5,000 or more and less than $25,000. Felony, 2nd degree, if loss is more than $25,000 (2929.11 to 2929.18, 2929.31)

Motor Vehicles—Vehicular Assault

See Vehicular Assault—Aggravated Vehicular Assault

Motor Vehicles—Vehicular Homicide

See Vehicular Homicide, generally

Motor Vehicles—Willful or Wanton Disregard of Safety on Highways—4511.20, 4511.201

See also Drunk Driving—Driving While Intoxicated or Drugged; Weapons—Improperly Handling Firearms in Motor Vehicle

ELEMENTS OF THE CRIME

Division (A):

(1) Operation of a vehicle, trackless trolley, or streetcar on any street or highway

(2) In willful or wanton disregard of the safety of persons or property, or

Division (B):

(1) Operation of a vehicle, trackless trolley, or streetcar on any public or private property, other than a street or highway

(2) In willful or wanton disregard of the safety of persons or property

PENALTY

Minor Misdemeanor (2929.21 to 2929.28, 2929.31, 4511.99)

Second offense within 1 year of first, Misdemeanor 4th degree, (2929.21 to 2929.28, 2929.31, 4511.99)

Each subsequent offense within one year of first offense, Misdemeanor, 3rd degree (2929.21 to 2929.28, 2929.31, 4511.99)

Murder—Aggravated Murder—2903.01

ELEMENTS OF THE CRIME

Division (A):

(1) Purposely

(2) With prior calculation and design

(3) Cause death of another or the unlawful termination of another's pregnancy

Division (B):

(1) Purposely cause death of another or the unlawful termination of another's pregnancy

(2) While committing, attempting to commit, fleeing immediately after committing or attempting to commit

(3) Kidnapping, rape, aggravated arson, arson, aggravated robbery, robbery, aggravated burglary, burglary, terrorism, or escape[1]

1 Adding terrorism as a predicate felony for felony murder.

Division (C):

(1) Purposely cause death

(2) Where victim is under 13 years of age

Division (D):

(1) Purposely cause death

(2) While under detention or breaking detention, as defined in 2921.01, as a result of having been found guilty or having plead guilty to a felony

Division (E):

(1) Purposely cause death of a law enforcement officer as defined in 2911.01

(2) With knowledge or reasonable cause to know that victim is a law enforcement officer

(3) If victim is engaged in duties at time of offense, or if offender's specific purpose is to kill a law enforcement officer.

PENALTY

Provided in 2929.02, 2929.03, 2929.31

Imprisonment for life: If no specification of aggravating circumstances or if specification of aggravating circumstances charged, but found not guilty of any specification, parole eligibility after 20 years' imprisonment.

Death: When found guilty of aggravated murder and one or more specifications of aggravating circumstances, death, or life imprisonment with parole eligibility after serving 25 years' imprisonment or 30 years' imprisonment.

No death penalty if defendant raised issue of being less than 18 years of age and was not found to be 18 years of age or older at the time of the commission of the offense.

Where a defendant is charged with aggravated murder containing a specification of the aggravated circumstance of a prior conviction, the defendant may elect to have the existence of the aggravating circumstance determined at trial or at a separate sentencing hearing following a conviction of aggravated murder.

If the trial jury unanimously finds beyond a reasonable doubt that the aggravating circumstances outweigh the mitigating factors, the jury shall recommend death. Absent such a finding, the jury shall recommend life imprisonment with parole eligibility after 25 years' imprisonment or life imprisonment with parole eligibility after 30 years' imprisonment. If the jury recommends life imprisonment, the judge shall impose it. If the jury recommends death, the judge shall impose death if the court finds beyond a reasonable doubt that aggravating circumstances the defender was found guilty of outweigh the mitigating factors.

The amount of the fine should not exceed an amount which the offender is or will be able to pay without undue hardship to himself or his dependents or which would prevent him from making reparation for the victim's wrongful death.

Murder—Murder—2903.02

See also Homicide—Negligent; Vehicular Homicide—Aggravated Vehicular Homicide

ELEMENTS OF THE CRIME

(1) Purposely

(2) Cause death of another or the unlawful termination of another's pregnancy

PENALTY

Provided in 2929.02, 2929.31

Narcotic Drugs

See Drug Offenses

Negligent Assault

See Assault—Negligent Assault

Negligent Homicide

See Homicide—Negligent

Nonsupport of Dependents

See Domestic Offenses—Nonsupport of Dependents

Obscenity

See also Juveniles, generally

Obscenity—Compelling Acceptance of Objectionable Materials—2907.34

ELEMENTS OF THE CRIME

Division (A):

(1) As a condition to the sale, allocation, consignment, or delivery of any material or goods of any kind

(2) Require purchaser or consignee

(3) To accept any other material reasonably believed to be obscene, or which, if furnished or presented to a juvenile would be in violation of 2907.31

Division (B):

(1) Deny or threaten to deny any franchise or impose or threaten to impose

(2) Any financial or other penalty upon

(3) Any purchaser or consignee

(4) Because the purchaser or consignee failed or refused to accept any material reasonably believed to be obscene as a condition to the sale, allocation, consignment, or delivery of any other material or goods or because the purchaser or consignee returned any material believed to be obscene that the purchaser or consignee initially accepted

PENALTY

Felony, 5th degree (2929.11 to 2929.18, 2929.31)

Obscenity—Pandering Obscenity—2907.32

ELEMENTS OF THE CRIME

(1) With knowledge of the character of the material or performance involved

(2)(a)(i) Create, reproduce or publish any obscene material

(ii) When offender knows that such material is to be used for commercial exploitation or will be publicly disseminated or displayed, or when offender is reckless in that regard, or

(b)(i) Promote or advertise for sale, delivery or dissemination; sell, deliver, publicly disseminate, publicly display, exhibit, present, rent, or provide; or offer or agree to sell, deliver, publicly disseminate, publicly display, exhibit, present, rent or provide

(ii) Obscene material, or

(c)(i) Create, direct, or produce

(ii) An obscene performance

(iii) When offender knows that it is to be used for commercial exploitation or will be publicly presented, or when offender is reckless in that regard, or

(d)(i) Advertise or promote an obscene performance for presentation, or present or participate in an obscene performance

(ii) When the performance is presented publicly, or when admission is charged, or

(e)(i) Buy, procure, possess or control any obscene material

(ii) With purpose to violate (2)(b) or (2)(d) above

DEFENSE

Material or performance was disseminated or presented for a bona fide medical, scientific, educational, religious, governmental, judicial, or other proper purpose by or to a physician, psychologist, sociologist, scientist, teacher, person pursuing bona fide studies or research, librarian, clergyman, prosecutor, judge, or other person having a proper interest in the material or performance.

PENALTY

Felony, 5th degree (2929.11 to 2929.18, 2929.31)

If prior conviction of violation of this section or of 2907.31, Felony, 4th degree (2929.11 to 2929.18, 2929.31)

Obstructing Justice—Altering Recordings or Resumes—2933.59

ELEMENTS OF THE CRIME

Division (A):

(1) With intent to present the altered recording or resume in any judicial proceeding or proceeding under oath or affirmation

(2) Purposely

(3) Edit, alter, tamper, or attempt to edit, alter, or tamper with

(4) Any recording or resume of

(5) Any intercepted wire or oral communication

Division (B):

(1) With intent to present the altered recording or resume in any judicial proceeding or proceeding under oath or affirmation

(2) Purposely

(3) Present or permit the presentation of

(4) Any altered recording or resume

(5) Without fully indicating the nature of the changes made in the original state of the recording or resume

PENALTY

Felony, 3rd degree (2929.11 to 2929.18, 2929.31)

Obstructing Justice—Obstructing Justice—2921.32

ELEMENTS OF THE CRIME

(1)(a) With purpose to hinder discovery, apprehension, prosecution, conviction, or punishment of another for crime, or

(b) Assist another to benefit from commission of crime

(2)(a) Harbor or conceal the other person, or

(b) Provide the other person with money, transportation, weapon, disguise, other means of avoiding discovery or apprehension, or

(c) Warn the other person of impending discovery or apprehension, or

(d) Destroy or conceal physical evidence of crime, or induce anyone to withhold testimony or information, or elude legal process summoning person to testify or supply evidence, or

(e) Communicate false information to anyone, or

(f) prevent or obstruct any person, by means of force, intimidation, or deception from performing any act to aid in discovery, apprehension, or prosecution of the other person or child

PROSECUTION NOTES

Person may be prosecuted irrespective of the resolution of the case involving the person sought.

PENALTY

If crime committed by person aided is a misdemeanor, obstructing justice is a misdemeanor of the same degree as the crime committed by the person aided.

Except as otherwise provided, if crime committed by person aided is a felony, Felony, 5th degree (2929.11 to 2929.18, 2929.31)

If crime committed by person aided is aggravated murder, murder, or a felony of the 1st or 2nd degree and if the offender knows or has reason to believe that the crime committed by the person aided is one of those offenses, Felony, 3rd degree (2929.11 to 2929.18, 2929.31)

Obstructing Justice—Tampering With Evidence

See Tampering—Tampering With Evidence

Obstructing Justice—Tampering With Records

See Tampering—Tampering With Records

Obstructing Justice—Obstructing Official Business—2921.31

ELEMENTS OF THE CRIME

(1) Without privilege to do so

(2) With purpose to prevent, obstruct, or delay performance by public official of any authorized act within official capacity

(3) Do any act that hampers or impedes public official in performance of lawful duties

PENALTY

Misdemeanor, 2nd degree (2929.21 to 2929.28, 2929.31)

Felony, 5th degree, if violation creates a risk of physical harm to any person.

Offenses Against Human Corpse—2927.01

See also Abortion—Abortion Trafficking

ELEMENTS OF THE CRIME

(1) Except as authorized by law

(a) Treat a human corpse in a way that person knows would outrage reasonable family sensibilities, or

(b) Treat a human corpse in a way that would outrage reasonable community sensibilities

PENALTY

If (a) is element of violation, Misdemeanor, 2nd degree (2929.21 to 2929.28, 2929.31)

If (b) is element of violation, Felony, 5th degree (2929.11 to 2929.18, 2929.31)

Officers, Law Enforcement

See Law Enforcement Officers, generally

Ordnance, Dangerous

See Weapons—Failure to Secure Dangerous Ordnance; Weapons—Unlawful Possession of Dangerous Ordnance

Organized Crime, Engaging in

See Corrupt Activity—Engaging in a Pattern of

Panic, Inducing

See Disorderly Conduct Offenses—Inducing Panic

Passing Bad Checks

See Theft-related Offenses—Passing Bad Checks

Paternity, Interference With Establishment of—3111.29

ELEMENTS OF THE CRIME

(1) Use of physical harassment or threats of violence against another

(2) To interfere with or attempt to prevent

(3) Other person's initiating or continuing

(4) Action to determine paternity under 3111.01 to 3111.19

PENALTY

Misdemeanor, 1st degree (2929.21 to 2929.28, 2929.31, 3111.99)

If prior conviction of this section or of 2919.231 (interfering with action to issue or modify support order), Felony, 4th degree (2929.11 to 2929.18, 2929.31, 3111.99)

Patient Abuse or Neglect—False Statements—2903.35

ELEMENTS OF THE CRIME

(1) Knowingly

(2)(a) Make a false statement, or

(b) Swear or affirm the truth of a prior false statement

(3) Alleging a violation of 2903.34

(4) To purposely incriminate another

PENALTY

Misdemeanor, 1st degree (2929.21 to 2929.28, 2929.31)

Patient Abuse or Neglect—Patient Abuse or Neglect—2903.34

ELEMENTS OF THE CRIME

(1)(a) Owner, operator, or administrator of care facility

(b) Agent or employee of care facility

(2) Against

(a) Resident, or

(b) Patient of facility

(3) Commit

(a) Division (A)(1): Abuse

(b) Division (A)(2): Gross neglect

(c) Division (A)(3): Neglect

Note: A person is not neglected who relies upon treatment by spiritual means through prayer alone, under recognized religious denomination, and is treated in that manner.

DEFENSE

Under (A)(2) or (3), actor's conduct committed in good faith and was ordered to commit conduct by person in supervisory position over actor.

PENALTY

If Division (A)(1) violated, Felony, 4th degree (2929.11 to 2929.18, 2929.31)

If Division (A)(1) violated and if previously convicted of, or pleaded guilty to, violation under this section, Felony, 3rd degree (2929.11 to 2929.18, 2929.31)

If Division (A)(2) violated, Misdemeanor, 1st degree (2929.21 to 2929.28, 2929.31)

If Division (A)(2) violated and if previously convicted of, or pleaded guilty to, violation of this section, Felony, 5th degree (2929.11 to 2929.18, 2929.31)

If Division (A)(3) violated, Misdemeanor, 2nd degree (2929.21 to 2929.28, 2929.31)

If Division (A)(4) violated and if previously convicted of, or pleaded guilty to, violation of this section, Felony, 5th degree (2929.11 to 2929.18, 2929.31)

Note: Any licensed owner, operator, administrator, agent or employee of care facility who is convicted of a felony violation of this section shall have his license revoked in accordance with Ch 119.

Patient Abuse or Neglect—Retaliation Against Person Reporting—2903.36

ELEMENTS OF THE CRIME

(1) Care facility

(2)(a) Discharge, or

(b) Retaliate or discriminate against any person

(3) For a good faith filing of

(a) Complaint

(b) Affidavit, or

(c) Other document alleging violation of 2903.34

Note: No penalty stated.

Peace Officers

See Law Enforcement Officers, generally

Perjury— 2921.11

ELEMENTS OF THE CRIME

(1) In any official proceeding

(2)(a) Knowingly make false statement under oath or affirmation, or

(b) Knowingly swear or affirm truth of false statement previously made

(3) When either statement is material

PROOF

(1) Contradictory statements relating to same material fact made by offender under oath or affirmation within statute of limitations for perjury, prosecution need not prove which statement was false, only that one or the other was.

(2) No conviction hereunder where proof of falsity rests solely upon contradictory testimony of one person other than defendant.

(3) Falsification is material, regardless of its admissibility in evidence, if it can affect course or outcome of proceeding; no defense that offender mistakenly believed falsification to be immaterial.

PENALTY

Felony, 3rd degree (2929.11 to 2929.18, 2929.31)

Poisons—Regulating the Sale of—3719.32

ELEMENTS OF THE CRIME

(1) Knowingly

(2) Sell or deliver

(3)(a) To any person otherwise than in a manner prescribed by laws, or

(b) To a minor under sixteen years of age in the manner prescribed by law but without the written order of an adult

(4) Any of the following substances or any poisonous compounds, combinations, or preparations thereof:

(a) The compounds and salts of antimony, arsenic, chromium, copper, lead, mercury, and zinc

(b) The concentrated mineral acids

(c) Oxalic and hydrocyanic acids and their salts, and carbolic acid

(d) Yellow phosphorus

(e) The essential oils of almonds, pennyroyal, tansy, and savin, crotin oil, creosote, chloroform, chloral hydrate, and cantharides

(f) Aconite, belladonna, bitter almonds, colchicum, cotton root, cocculus indicus, conium, digitalis, hyoscyamus, ignatia, lobelia, nux vomica, opium, physostigma, phytolacca, strophanthus, stramonium, veratum viride, or any of the poisonous alkaloids or alkaloidal salts or other poisonous principles derived from such alkaloids, or other poisonous alkaloids or their salts

(g) Other virulent poison

PENALTY

Minor misdemeanor (2929.21 to 2929.28, 2929.31, 3719.99)

Poisons—Spreading False Report of Contamination—2927.24(C)

ELEMENTS OF THE CRIME

Division (A):

(1) Inform another that a poison, hazardous chemical, biological, or radioactive substance, or other harmful substance

(2) Has been or will be placed in food, drink, nonprescription drug, prescription drug, or other pharmaceutical product, spring, well, reservoir, or public water supply

(3) If placement of the poison or substance would constitute contamination of a substance for human consumption or use in violation of 2927.24(B)

(4) Offender knows that the information is false *and* will likely be disseminated to the public

Division (B):

(1) Inform another that a hazardous chemical, biological, or radioactive substance

(2)(a) Has been or will be released into the air or left in a public place, or

(b) That one or more persons has been or will be exposed

(3) If the release would be a violation of 2927.24(B)(2)

(4) Offender knows that the information is false *and* will likely be disseminated to the public

PENALTY

Felony, 4th degree (2929.11 to 2929.18, 2929.31)

Note: Any act which is a violation of Division (A) or (B) and of 2917.31 or 2917.32 may be prosecuted under this section, or both this section and 2917.31 or 2917.32.

Possessing Criminal Tools

See Criminal Tools—Possessing

Possessing Drug Abuse Instruments

See Drug Offenses—Possession—Drug Abuse Instruments; also Drug Offenses—Hypodermics—Possession, Sale, and Disposal

Presenting False Name or Information to Law Enforcement Officer

See Motor Vehicles—Presenting False Name or Information to Law Enforcement Officer

Procuring

See Prostitution—Procuring

Promoting Prostitution

See Prostitution—Promoting

Property, Unauthorized Use

See Theft-related Offenses—Unauthorized Use of Property; Theft-related Offenses—Unauthorized Access to Computer Systems

Prostitution—Compelling Prostitution—2907.21

ELEMENTS OF THE CRIME

(1) Knowingly

(2)(a) Compel another to engage in sexual activity for hire, or

(b) Induce, procure, encourage, solicit, request, or otherwise facilitate a minor to engage in sexual activity for hire, whether or not offender knows the age of the minor

(c) Pay or agree to pay a minor directly or through minor's agent so that the minor will engage in sexual activity, whether or not offender knows the age of the minor

(d) Pay a minor directly or through minor's agent for the minor having engaged in sexual activity pursuant to prior agreement, whether or not offender knows the age of the minor

(e) Allow a minor to engage in sexual activity for hire if the person allowing the child to engage in the sexual activity for hire is the parent, guardian, custodian, person having custody or control, or person in loco parentis of the minor.

PENALTY

Except as otherwise provided in this section, Felony, 3rd degree (2929.11 to 2929.18, 2929.31)

If the offender commits a violation of (2)(b) of this section and the person compelled to engage in sexual activity for hire is less than 16 years of age, Felony, 2nd degree (2929.11 to 2929.18, 2929.31)

Prostitution—Procuring—2907.23

ELEMENTS OF THE CRIME

Division (A):

(1) Knowingly

(2) For gain

(3)(a) Entice or solicit another person to patronize a prostitute or brothel, or

(b) Procure a prostitute for another person to patronize, or take or direct another person at his own request to any place for the purpose of patronizing a prostitute

Division (B):

(1) Having authority or responsibility over use of premises

(2) Knowingly

(3) Permit the premises to be used

(4) For the purpose of engaging in sexual activity for hire

PENALTY

Misdemeanor, 1st degree (2929.21 to 2929.28, 2929.31)

Prostitution—Promoting—2907.22

ELEMENTS OF THE CRIME

(1) Knowingly

(2)(a) Establish, maintain, operate, manage, supervise, control, or have an interest in a brothel, or

(b) Supervise, manage or control the activities of a prostitute in engaging in sexual activity for hire, or

(c)(i) Transport another, or cause another to be transported

(ii) Across the boundary of Ohio or of any county in Ohio

(iii) In order to facilitate the other person's engaging in sexual activity for hire, or

(d)(i) Induce or procure another person to engage in sexual activity for hire

(ii) For the purpose of violating or facilitating a violation of this section.

PENALTY

Felony, 4th degree (2929.11 to 2929.18, 2929.31)

If any prostitute in brothel involved in offense, or the prostitute whose activities are supervised, managed, or controlled by offender, or the person transported, induced, or procured by offender to engage in sexual activity for hire, is a minor, regardless of whether offender knows age of minor, Felony, 3rd degree (2929.11 to 2929.18, 2929.31)

Prostitution—Prostitution—2907.25

ELEMENTS OF THE CRIME

Division (A):

(1) Engage in sexual activity

(2) For hire

Division (B):

(1) Engage in sexual activity

(2) For hire

(3) Knowing that s/he has tested positive for HIV

PENALTY

Misdemeanor, 3rd degree for violation of Division (A) (2929.21 to 2929.28, 2929.31)

Felony, 3rd degree for violation of Division (B) (2929.11 to 2929.18, 2907.27, 2929.31)

Prostitution—Soliciting

See Sex Offenses—Soliciting

Protection Order—Violating Protection Order or Consent Agreement, or Anti-stalking Protection Order—2919.27

ELEMENTS OF THE CRIME

(1) Recklessly

(2) Violate any terms of

(a) Protection order issued under 2919.26 or 3113.31, or

(b) Consent agreement approved under 2919.26 or 3113.31

(c) Protection order issued under 2903.213 or 2903.214

(d) Protection order issued by another state

DEFENSE

It is an affirmative defense that a protection order issued by another state does not comply with requirements of 18 USC 2265(b) and (c).

PENALTY

Misdemeanor, 1st degree (2929.21 to 2929.28, 2929.31)

If previously convicted of violating protection order under 2903.213 or 2903.214, 2 or more prior convictions of 2903.21, 2903.211, 2903.22 or 2911.211, involving same victim or previously convicted of 2919.27, Felony, 5th degree (2929.11 to 2929.18, 2929.31)

If violation of protection order or consent agreement while committing a felony, Felony, 3rd degree

Note: If a defendant is charged with a violation of section 2919.27 or of a municipal ordinance that is substantially similar to that section, the court may order an evaluation of the mental condition of the defendant based on the criteria set forth in section 2919.271.

Public Contract, Unlawful Interest In

See Public Officials—Having Unlawful Interest in a Public Contract

Public Indecency—2907.09

ELEMENTS OF THE CRIME

(1) Recklessly

(2) Under circumstances in which offender's conduct is likely to be viewed by and to affront others, not members of his household

(3)(a) Expose one's private parts, or masturbate, or

(b) Engage in sexual conduct, or

(c) Engage in conduct that to an ordinary observer would appear to be sexual conduct or masturbation

PENALTY

Misdemeanor, 4th degree (2929.21 to 2929.28, 2929.31)

If prior conviction, Misdemeanor, 3rd degree (2929.21 to 2929.28, 2929.31)

If two prior convictions, Misdemeanor, 2nd degree (2929.21 to 2929.28, 2929.31)

If three or more prior convictions, Misdemeanor, 1st degree (2929.21 to 2929.28, 2929.31)

Public Officials—Bribery—2921.02

ELEMENTS OF THE CRIME

Division (A):

(1) Purpose to corrupt or improperly influence in discharge of duty

(2) Public servant or party official, whether before or after elected, appointed, qualified, employed, summoned, sworn

(3) Promise, offer, give any valuable thing or benefit

Division (B):

(1) Knowingly

(2) Solicit or accept any valuable thing or benefit for himself or another

(3) Before or after elected, appointed, qualified, employed, summoned, sworn as public servant or party official

(4) To corrupt or improperly influence him or another public servant or party official with respect to discharge of his or the other public servant's or party official's duty

Division (C):

(1) Purpose to corrupt witness or to influence him in respect to testimony in official proceeding

(2) Before or after subpoenaed or sworn

(3) Promise, offer, give him or another person any valuable thing or benefit

Division (D):

(1) Before or after subpoenaed or sworn as witness

(2) Knowingly solicit or accept for himself or another person valuable thing or benefit

(3) To corrupt or improperly influence with respect to his testimony in official proceeding

PENALTY

Felony, 3rd degree (2929.11 to 2929.18, 2929.31)

Note: If public servant or party official convicted, forever disqualified from holding public office, employment, or position of trust in state.

Public Officials—Dereliction Of Duty

See Dereliction of Duty

Public Officials—Having Unlawful Interest in a Public Contract—2921.42

ELEMENTS OF THE CRIME

(1) Public official

(2) Knowingly

(3)(a) Authorize, employ authority or influence of his office:

(i) To secure authorization of public contract in which he, his family, or any business associate has interest, or

(ii) To secure investment of public funds in any share, bond, mortgage, other security which he, family member, or business associate has interest, is underwriter or receives any brokerage, origination or servicing fees, or

(b) During term of office or within one year thereafter occupy position of profit in prosecution of public contract authorized by him, or by legislative body, commission, board of which he was member at time of authorization, unless contract let by competitive bidding to the lowest and best bidder, or

(c) Have interest in profits or benefits of public contract:

(i) Entered into by or for use of political subdivision or governmental agency or instrumentality with which he is connected, or

(ii) Not let by competitive bidding when required by law and which involves more than $150

DEFENSES

(1) If no bribery or purpose to defraud, public official, family member or business associate has no interest in public contract or investment of public funds if all the following apply:

(a) Interest limited to owning or controlling corporation shares, or being creditor of corporation or other organization that is contractor involved on public contract or issuer of securities in which public funds invested;

(b) Shares owned or controlled do not exceed 5% outstanding shares and amount due person as creditor does not exceed 5% total indebtedness of corporation or other organization;

(c) That person before public contract entered into, files with political subdivision, governmental agency or instrumentality involved, affidavit giving exact status in connection with corporation or other organization.

(2) Does not apply to public contract in which public official, family member, or business associate has interest, when all the following apply:

(a) Subject of public contract is necessary supplies or services;

(b) Supplies or services unobtainable elsewhere for same or lower cost, or are being furnished political subdivision, governmental agency or instrumentality as part of continuing course of dealing established prior to public official's becoming associated with political subdivision, governmental agency or instrumentality;

(c) Treatment accorded political subdivision, governmental agency or instrumentality is either preferential to or same as that accorded other customers or clients in similar transactions;

(d) Entire transaction conducted at arm's length, with full knowledge by political subdivision, governmental agency or instrumentality involved, of interest of public official's, family member, or business associate, and public official takes no part in deliberations or decisions of political subdivision, governmental agency or instrumentality with respect to public contract.

(3) Does not apply to a public contract in which a township trustee in a township having population of 5,000 or less in its unincorporated area, member of township trustee's family, or business associate has interest, if all of following apply:

(a) Subject of public contract is necessary supplies and services for township and contract amount is less than $5,000 per year;

(b) Supplies and services furnished were part of continuing course of dealing established before trustee held that office within the township;

(c) Treatment accorded to township is either preferential to or same as that accorded other customers or clients in similar transactions; and,

(d) Entire transaction is conducted with full knowledge of township of interest of township trustee, member of his family, or business associate.

(4) Section (3)(c)(i) does not prohibit public employee participation in any housing program funded by public moneys if

(a) public employee otherwise qualifies for program and does not use authority or influence of his office or employment to secure benefits from program, and if

(b) the moneys are to be used on the primary residence of the public employee.

(5) Not a violation for a prosecuting attorney to appoint assistants and employees in accordance with 309.06 and 2921.421, for a municipal corporation's chief legal officer, or an official designated as prosecutor in municipal corporation, to appoint assistants and employees in accordance with 733.621 and 2921.421, or for a township law director appointed under 504.15 to appoint assistants and employees in accordance with 504.151 and 2921.421.

PENALTY

Misdemeanor, 1st degree (2929.21 to 2929.28, 2929.31)

If (3)(a)(i) or (ii) is element of violation, Felony, 4th degree (2929.11, 2929.31)

Public Officials—Soliciting or Receiving Improper Compensation—2921.43

ELEMENTS OF THE CRIME

Division (A):

(1)(a) Public servant solicit or accept, or

(b) Person promise or give to public servant

(2) Knowingly

(3) Any compensation, other than as allowed by divisions (G), (H), and (I) of 102.03 or other provisions of law

(4)(a) To perform his official duties, or

(b) To perform any other act or service in the public servant's public capacity, or

(c) For the general performance of the duties of the public servant's public office or public employment, or

(d) As a supplement to the public servant's public compensation

(5) Additional or greater fees or costs than are allowed by law to perform his official duties

Division (B):

(1)(a) Public servant solicit or accept, or

(b) Person solicit or accept

(2) For one's own personal or business use or for the personal or business use of a public servant or party official

(3) Anything of value

(4)(a) In consideration of appointing or securing, maintaining, or renewing the appointment of any person to any public office, employment, or agency, or

(b) In consideration of preferring, or maintaining the status of, any public employee with respect to his compensation, duties, placement, location, promotion, or other material aspects of his employment

Division (C):

(1) Person coerce

(2) For the benefit of a political party, campaign committee, legislative campaign fund or political action committee, or political contributing entity

(3) Any contribution

(4)(a) In consideration of appointing or securing, maintaining, or renewing the appointment of any person to any public office, employment, or agency, or

(b) In consideration of preferring, or maintaining the status of, any public employee with respect to his compensation, duties, placement, location, promotion, or other material aspects of his employment

PENALTY

Misdemeanor, 1st degree (2929.21 to 2929.28, 2929.31)

Note: Nothing in Divisions (A), (B), or (C) prohibits any person from making voluntary contributions to a political party, campaign committee, legislative campaign fund, political action committee, or political contributing entity, or prohibits a political party, campaign committee, legislative campaign fund, political action committee or political contributing entity from accepting voluntary contributions.

Note: If convicted, public servant disqualified from holding any public office, employment, position of trust in Ohio for period of 7 years from date of conviction.

Public Officials—Theft in Office—2921.41

ELEMENTS OF THE CRIME

(1) Public official or party official

(2) Commit any theft offense

(3)(a) When using the offender's office in aid of committing the offense, or permits, or assents to its use in aid of committing theft offense, or

(b) Property or service involved is owned by this or any other state, United States, county, municipal corporation, township, any political subdivision, department, or agency of any of them, or is owned by a political party, or is part of a political campaign fund.

VALUATION

Two or more offenses may be tried as single offense; value is the aggregate value of all property in the series of offenses.

PENALTY

Except as otherwise provided in this section, Felony, 5th degree (2929.11 to 2929.18, 2929.31)

If the value of property or services stolen is $500 or more and is less than $5,000, Felony, 4th degree (2929.11 to 2929.18, 2929.31)

If the value of property or services stolen is $5,000 or more, Felony, 3rd degree (2929.11 to 2929.18, 2929.31)

If convicted or pleads guilty, forever disqualified from holding any public office, employment, or position of trust in Ohio. Sentencing court shall order restitution in addition to penalty imposed. Officials of public pension funds or public deferred compensation programs may be ordered to withhold amount required for restitution.

Public Services, Disrupting

See Disrupting Public Services

Raffle Drawings—2915.092

ELEMENTS OF THE CRIME

Division (A):

(1) No charitable organization shall conduct a raffle

(2) Unless the organization is and has been notified by the I.R.S. that it is exempt from federal taxation under 501(a),

(3) More than 36 times during a calendar year, and

(4) Compensate any person directly or indirectly for assisting in the raffle.

Division (B):

(1) Chamber of Commerce may not conduct

(2) More than one raffle per year

(3) To raise money for Chamber of Commerce

Division (C):

(1) No person may conduct

(2)(a) a raffle that is for profit, or

(b) a raffle drawing that is not for profit

PENALTY

Misdemeanor, 1st degree (2929.21 to 2929.28, 2929.31)

If prior conviction of Division (C), Felony, 5th degree (2929.11 to 2929.18, 2929.31)

Rape—2907.02

ELEMENTS OF THE CRIME

Division (A)(1):

(1) Engaging in sexual conduct

(2) With another person who is not the spouse of the offender, or who is the spouse of the offender but is living separate and apart from the offender, when

(3)(a) Offender, for purpose of preventing resistance,

(i) Substantially impairs the other person's judgment or control

(ii) By administering a drug, intoxicant, or controlled substance to the other person, surreptitiously, by force, by threat of force, or deception, or

(b) The other person is less than 13 years old whether or not the offender knows the age of the other person, or

(c) The other person's ability to resist or consent is substantially impaired because of a mental or physical condition or advanced age, and offender knows or has reasonable cause to believe other person's ability to resist or consent is substantially impaired because of a mental or physical condition or advanced age.

Division (A)(2):

(1) Engaging in sexual conduct

(2) With another person

(3) When the offender purposely compels the other person to submit by force or threat of force

DEFENSE

It is not a defense to a charge under Division (A)(2) above that the offender and the victim were married or cohabiting at the time of the commission of the offense.

PROOF

Victim need not prove physical resistance to offender. Evidence of specific instances of victim's sexual activity and defendant's sexual activity admissible only under restricted conditions subject to specific court ruling after hearing in chambers.

PENALTY

Felony, 1st degree (2929.11 to 2929.18, 2929.31)

If Division (A)(1)(a) with controlled substance, Felony, 1st degree, not less than 5 years

If offender purposely compels victim 13 years old or younger by force or threat of force, Life imprisonment

If victim is less than ten years old, life imprisonment

If defendant previously convicted of violating (A)(1)(b) or if the defendant caused serious physical harm to the victim, life imprisonment without parole

Receiving Stolen Property

See Theft-related Offenses—Receiving Stolen Property

Records, Tampering With

See Tampering—Tampering With Records

Report of Felony or Certain Suspicious Circumstances, Failure to Make

See Failure to Report Felony or Certain Suspicious Circumstances

Resistance to Authority, Aiding

See Escape—Aiding Escape or Resistance to Authority

Resisting Arrest—2921.33

ELEMENTS OF THE CRIME

Division (A):

(1) Recklessly or by force

(2) Resist or interfere with lawful arrest

(3) Of the person or another

Division (B):

(1) Recklessly or by force

(2) Resist or interfere with lawful arrest

(3) Of the person or another

(4) During the course of or as a result of cause physical harm to a law enforcement officer

Division (C):

(1) Recklessly or by force

(2) Resist or interfere with lawful arrest

(3) Of the person or another

(4)(a) Cause physical harm to a law enforcement officer by means of a deadly weapon, or

(b) The offender, during the course of the resistance or interference, brandishes a deadly weapon

PENALTY

Violation of Division (A): Misdemeanor, 2nd degree (2929.21 to 2929.28, 2929.31)

Violation of Division (B): Misdemeanor, 1st degree (2929.21 to 2929.28, 2929.31)

Violation of Division (C): Felony, 4th degree (2929.11 to 2929.18, 2929.31)

Resisting or Fleeing Traffic Officer

See Motor Vehicles—Resisting or Fleeing Traffic Officer

Restraint, Unlawful

See Unlawful Restraint

Retaliation

See Intimidation—Retaliation

Rights, Civil

See Civil Rights—Interfering With

Riot—Aggravated Riot—2917.02

ELEMENTS OF THE CRIME

Division (A):

(1) Participate with 4 or more others

(2) In course of disorderly conduct violating 2917.11

(3)(a) With purpose to commit or facilitate commission of felony, or

(b) With purpose to commit or facilitate commission of any offense of violence, or

(c) Offender or any participant to knowledge of offender has on or about offender's or participant's person or under offender's or participant's control, uses, or intends to use, deadly weapon or dangerous ordnance as defined in 2923.11

Division (B):

An inmate of detention facility defined in 2921.01 violating Division (A) above or 2917.03

PROOF

State not required to allege or prove that offender expressly agreed with four or more others. 2917.031

PENALTY

If Division (A)(1) or (3) violated, Felony, 5th degree (2929.11 to 2929.18, 2929.31)

If Division (A)(2) or (B) violated, Felony, 4th degree (2929.11 to 2929.18, 2929.31)

Riot—Riot—2917.03

ELEMENTS OF THE CRIME

Division (A):

(1) Participate with 4 or more others

(2) In a course of disorderly conduct

(3) In violation of 2917.11

(4)(a) Purpose to commit or facilitate commission of misdemeanor, other than disorderly conduct, or

(b) Purpose to intimidate public official or employee into taking or refrain from taking official action, or

(c) Purpose to hinder, impede, obstruct function of government, or

(d) Purpose to hinder, impede, obstruct orderly process of administration or instruction at educational institution, or interfere with or disrupt its lawful activities

Division (B):

(1) Participate with 4 or more others

(2) Purpose to do act with unlawful force or violence

(3) Even though such act otherwise lawful

PROOF

State not required to allege or prove that offender expressly agreed with four or more others. 2917.031

PENALTY

Misdemeanor, 1st degree (2929.21 to 2929.28, 2929.31)

Robbery—Aggravated Robbery—2911.01

ELEMENTS OF THE CRIME

Division (A):

(1)(a) In attempting or committing a theft offense as defined in 2913.01, or

(b) In fleeing immediately after the attempt or theft

(2)(a) Have deadly weapon on or about the offender's person or under the offender's control, and either display the weapon, brandish it, indicate that the offender possesses it, or use it, or

(b) Have dangerous ordnance on or about the offender's person or under the offender's control, or

(c) Inflict or attempt to inflict serious physical harm on another

Division (B):

(1) Without privilege

(a) remove or attempt to remove

(b) deprive or attempt to deprive

(2) a deadly weapon

(3) from a law enforcement officer

(4)(a) having reasonable cause to believe that it is a law enforcement officer, and

(b) in the course and scope of the officer's duty

PENALTY

Felony, 1st degree (2929.11 to 2929.18, 2929.31). Prison term imposed for violation of Division (B) to be served consecutively to any other prison term.

Robbery—Robbery—2911.02

See also Theft-related Offenses, generally

ELEMENTS OF THE CRIME

(1)(a) In attempting or committing a theft offense or

(b) In fleeing immediately after the attempt or theft

(2)(a) Have a deadly weapon on or about the offender's person or under the offender's control, or

(b) Inflict, attempt to inflict, or threaten to inflict physical harm to another, or

(c) Use or threaten immediate use of force against another

PENALTY

A violation of division (2)(a) or (b), Felony, 2nd degree (2929.11 to 2929.18, 2929.31)

A violation of division (2)(c), Felony, 3rd degree (2929.11 to 2929.18, 2929.31)

Safecracking—2911.31

ELEMENTS OF THE CRIME

(1) With purpose to commit offense

(2) Knowingly enter, force entrance into, tamper with any vault, safe, strongbox.

PENALTY

Felony, 4th degree (2929.11 to 2929.18, 2929.31)

School, Improperly Discharging Firearm at or Into School, Improperly Discharging Firearm at or Into

See Weapons—Improperly Discharging Firearm at or Into Habitation or School

School Premises, Conveyance or Possession of Deadly Weapons or Dangerous Ordnance on

See Weapons—Conveyance or Possession of Deadly Weapons or Dangerous Ordnance on School Premises

Searches—Body Cavity and Strip Searches—2933.32

ELEMENTS OF THE CRIME

Division (B):

(1) Law enforcement officer, other employee of a law enforcement agency, physician, registered nurse, or licensed practical nurse shall

(2) Conducted or cause to be conducted

(3)(a) An unauthorized body cavity search

(b) An unauthorized strip search

Division (C):

(1) Upon completion of a body cavity search or strip search pursuant to division (A)

(2) The person(s) conducting the search

(3) Failed to prepare a written report including all of the following:

(a) Written authorization for the search obtained from the person in command of the law enforcement agency or his designee

(b) The name of the person who was searched

(c) The name of the person(s) who conducted the search, the time and date of the search, and the place at which the search was conducted

(d) A list of items, if any, recovered during the search

(e) The facts upon which the law enforcement officer or employee of the law enforcement agency based their probable cause for the search, including, but not limited to, the officer or employee's review of the nature of the offense with which the searched person is charged, the circumstances of his arrest, and, if known, his prior conviction record

(f) If the body cavity search was conducted before or without the issuance of a search warrant pursuant to division (B)(4) of 2933.32 of the Revised Code, or if the body cavity or strip search was conducted before or without the granting of written authorization pursuant to division (B)(5) of 2933.32 of the Revised Code, the legitimate medical reason or medical emergency that justified the warrantless search or made obtaining written authorization impracticable.

EXCEPTION

Does not apply to body cavity searches or strip searches of persons who have been sentenced to serve a term of imprisonment and who are serving that term in a detention facility as defined in 2921.01.

DEFENSES

Violations of division (B):

(1) A body cavity search or strip search may be conducted if a law enforcement officer or an employee of a law enforcement agency has probable cause to believe the person is concealing evidence of the commission of a criminal offense, including fruits or tools of a crime, contraband, or a deadly weapon, as defined in section 2923.11 of the Revised Code, that could not otherwise be discovered. In determining probable cause for purposes of this section, a law enforcement officer or employee of a law enforcement agency shall consider the nature of the offense with which the person to be searched is charged, the circumstances of the persons arrest, and, if known, the prior conviction record of the person.

(2) A body cavity search or strip search may be conducted for any legitimate medical or hygienic reason.

(3) Unless there is a legitimate medical reason or medical emergency justifying a warrantless search, a body cavity search shall be conducted only after a search warrant is issued that authorizes the search.

(4) A body cavity search shall be conducted under sanitary conditions and only by a physician, registered nurse, or licensed practical nurse.

(5) Written authorization from the law enforcement agency for the search must be obtained prior to the search.

(6) The person(s) who conduct the search must be the same sex as the person being searched; the search shall be conducted in a manner and in a location that permits only the person(s) conducting the search and the person being searched to observe the search.

Note: This section does not limit, and shall not be construed to limit, any statutory or common law rights of a person to obtain injunctive relief or to recover damages in a civil action.

Note: If a person is subjected to a body cavity search or strip search in violation of this section, any person may commence a civil action to recover compensatory damages for any injury, death, or loss to person or property or any indignity arising from the violation. In the civil action, the court may award punitive damages to the plaintiffs if they prevail in the action, and it may award reasonable attorney's fees to the parties who prevail in the action.

PENALTY

If violation of division (B), Misdemeanor, 1st degree (2929.21 to 2929.28, 2929.31)

If violation of division (C), Misdemeanor, 4th degree (2929.21 to 2929.28, 2929.31)

Securing Writings by Deception

See Theft-related Offenses—Securing Writings by Deception

Sex Offenses

See also Importuning; Juveniles—Corruption of a Minor; Juveniles—Illegal Use in Nudity-oriented Material or Performance; Juveniles—Pandering Sexually-oriented Matter Involving a Minor

Sex Offenses—Felonious Sexual Penetration—2907.12

Repealed.

Sex Offenses—Gross Sexual Imposition—2907.05

See also Rape; Sex Offenses—Sexual Imposition

ELEMENTS OF THE CRIME

(1)(a) Have with another, or cause another to have with offender, not the spouse of the offender, or

(b) Cause two or more others to have

(2) Sexual contact when:

(a) Offender purposely compels the other person, or one of the other persons, to submit by force or threat of force, or

(b) For purpose of preventing resistance, offender substantially impairs the other person's, or one of the other persons', judgment or control:

(i) By administering any drug, intoxicant or controlled substance to the other person

(ii) Surreptitiously, by force, by threat of force, or by deception, or

(c) Offender knows that other person's, or one of the other persons', judgment or control substantially impaired by drug or intoxicant administered with person's consent for purpose of medical or dental examination, treatment or surgery, or

(d) Other person, or one of the other persons, is less than 13 years old, regardless of whether offender knows the other person's age, or

(e) Ability of other person or one of the other persons to resist or consent is substantially impaired because of a mental or physical condition or advanced age, and offender knows or has reasonable cause to believe ability to resist or consent of the other person or one of the other persons is substantially impaired because of mental or physical condition or advanced age.

PROOF

Victim need not prove physical resistance to offender. Evidence of specific instances of victim's sexual activity and defendant's sexual activity admissible only under restricted conditions subject to specific court ruling after hearing in chambers.

PENALTY

If (2)(a), (b), or (c) violated, Felony, 4th degree (2929.11 to 2929.18, 2929.31) except

If (2)(b) with controlled substance, Felony, 3rd degree

If (2)(d) violated, Felony, 3rd degree (2929.11 to 2929.18, 2929.31)

Sex Offenses—Importuning

See Importuning

Sex Offenses—Prostitution

See Prostitution, generally

Sex Offenses—Public Indecency

See Public Indecency

Sex Offenses—Rape

See Rape

Sex Offenses—Sexual Battery—2907.03

ELEMENTS OF THE CRIME

(1) Engaging in sexual conduct

(2) With another person not the spouse of the offender when:

(a) Offender knowingly coerces the other person to submit by any means that would prevent resistance by a person of ordinary resolution, or

(b) Offender knows that the other person's ability to appraise the nature of or control his or her conduct is substantially impaired, or

(c) Offender knows that the other person submits because he or she is unaware that the act is being committed, or

(d) Offender knows that the other person submits because the other person mistakenly identifies the offender as his or her spouse, or

(e) Offender is other person's natural or adoptive parent, stepparent, guardian, custodian, or person in loco parentis of the other person, or

(f) Other person is in custody of law or patient in a hospital or other institution, and offender has supervisory or disciplinary authority over the other person,

(g) Other person is in a detention facility, and defendant is an employee of facility, or

(h) Offender is

(1) a teacher, administrator, coach, or other person in authority, and

(2) employed by or serving in a school for which the state board of education prescribes minimum standards pursuant to 3301.07(D)(i)(2)(c)

(3) the other person is enrolled in or attends that school, and

(4) the offender is not enrolled in and does not attend that school.

(i)(1) Other person is a minor, and

(2) Offender is

(a) teacher, administrator, coach, or other person in authority and

(b) employed by or serving an institution of higher education

(3) the other person is enrolled or attends that institution.

(j)(1) Other person is a mental health client or patient of the offender

(2) Offender is

(a) mental health professional

(b) induces the other person to submit

(c) by falsely representing to the other person

(d) that sexual conduct is necessary for mental health treatment purposes.

PENALTY

Felony, 3rd degree (2929.11 to 2929.18, 2929.31)

Note: If mental health professional is charged under (j)(1), prosecuting attorney shall provide written notice of the charge to the licensing board or agency; if mental health professional is convicted or pleads guilty to charge under (j)(1), the court shall submit a certified copy of the judgment entry to the licensing board or agency. (2907.17, 2907.18)

Sex Offenses—Sexual Imposition—2907.06

See also Sex Offenses—Gross Sexual Imposition

ELEMENTS OF THE CRIME

(1)(a) Have with another, or cause another to have with offender, not the spouse of the offender, or

(b) Cause two or more others to have

(2) Sexual contact when:

(a) Offender knows that the sexual contact is offensive to the other person, or one of the other persons, or is reckless in this regard, or

(b) Offender knows that the other person's, or one of the other persons', ability to appraise the nature of his conduct or to control his conduct is substantially impaired, or

(c) Offender knows that the other person, or one of the other persons, submits because of being unaware of the sexual contact, or

(d) The other person, or one of the other persons, is 13 years of age or older but less than 16 years of age, regardless of whether offender knows such age, and offender is at least 18 years old and 4 or more years older then the other person, or

(e) Offender is a mental health professional and induces the other person, a mental health client or patient of the offender, to submit to sexual contact by falsely representing that sexual contact is necessary for mental health treatment purposes.

PROOF

No conviction solely on victim's testimony unsupported by other evidence.

PENALTY

Misdemeanor, 3rd degree (2929.21 to 2929.28, 2929.31)

If the offender has been convicted of a violation of this section or sections 2907.02, 2907.03, 2907.04, 2907.05, or 2907.12, Misdemeanor, 1st degree (2929.21 to 2929.28, 2929.31)

Note: If mental health professional is charged under (2)(e), prosecuting attorney shall provide written notice of the charge to the licensing board or agency; if mental health professional is convicted or pleads guilty to charge under (2)(e), the court shall submit a certified copy of the judgment entry to the licensing board or agency. (2907.17, 2907.18)

Sex Offenses—Solicitation—2907.24

(A)(1) Solicit another

(2) To engage with such other person in sexual activity for hire

(B)(1) Knowing that he/she has tested positive for the AIDS virus

(2) Solicit another

(3) To engage with such other person in sexual activity for hire

PENALTY

Violation of Division (A) is a misdemeanor, 3rd degree (2929.21 to 2929.28, 2929.31)

Violation of Division (B) is a felony of the 3rd degree; if committed prior to July 1, 1996, a felony of the 2nd degree (2929.11 to 2929.18)

Note: Conviction of violation or attempt to violate 2907.24 or of a comparable municipal ordinance, while using, in, or on a motor vehicle, driver's license or commercial driver's license shall be suspended for a definite period of 3 months to 2 years.

Sham Legal Process

See Using Sham Legal Process

Simulation, Criminal

See Theft-related Offenses—Criminal Simulation

Slot Machine

See Theft-related Offenses—Making or Using Slugs; Theft-related Offenses—Tampering With Coin Machines

Slugs, Making or Using

See Theft-related Offenses—Making or Using Slugs

Soliciting

See Sex Offenses—Soliciting

Soliciting Improper Contributions or Compensation

See Public Officials—Soliciting or Receiving Improper Compensation

Sports—Corrupting—2915.06

ELEMENTS OF THE CRIME

Division (A):

(1) Knowingly

(2) Offer, give, solicit, accept anything of value

(3) To corrupt outcome of athletic or sporting event

Division (B):

(1) Knowingly

(2) Engage in conduct

(3) Designed to corrupt athletic or sporting event

PENALTY

Felony, 4th degree (2929.11, 2929.31)

Prior conviction of gambling offense, or theft as defined by 2913.01, Felony, 3rd degree (2929.11, 2929.31)

Sports—Corrupting—2915.06

Repealed effective 7–1–96.

Stalking, Menacing by

See Menacing—Menacing by Stalking

Stalking—Violating Anti–Stalking Protection Order

See Protection Order—Violating Anti–Stalking Protection Order

Steroids

See Drug Offenses—Illegal Administration or Distribution of Anabolic Steroids

Stolen Property, Receiving

See Theft-related Offenses—Receiving Stolen Property

Strip Searches

See Searches—Body Cavity and Strip Searches

Support Order, Interfering With Action to Issue or Modify

See Domestic Offenses—Interfering With Action to Issue or Modify Support Order

Tampering With Coin Machines

See Theft-related Offenses—Tampering With Coin Machines

Tampering—Tampering With Evidence—2921.12

ELEMENTS OF THE CRIME

(1) Knowing official proceeding or investigation in progress, or about to be or is likely to be instituted.

(2)(a)(i) Alter, destroy, conceal, remove any record, document, or thing

(ii) With purpose to impair value or availability as evidence in such proceeding or investigation, or

(b)(i) Make, present, use any record, document, thing

(ii) Knowing it to be false

(iii) With purpose to mislead public official who is or may be engaged in such proceeding or investigation, or with purpose to corrupt outcome of any such proceeding or investigation

PENALTY

Felony, 3rd degree (2929.11 to 2929.18, 2929.31)

Tampering—Tampering With Records—2913.42

ELEMENTS OF THE CRIME

Division (A):

(1) Knowing the person has no privilege to do so

(2) Purpose to defraud or knowing the person is facilitating fraud

(3)(a) Falsify, destroy, remove, conceal, alter, deface, mutilate any writing, computer software, data, or record, or

(b) Utter any writing or record knowing it has been tampered with as provided in (3)(a) above

PENALTY

If the offense does not involve data or computer software, Misdemeanor, 1st degree (2929.21 to 2929.28, 2929.31)

If the offense does not involve data or computer software and if the writing or record is a will unrevoked at the time of the offense, Felony, 5th degree (2929.11 to 2929.18, 2929.31)

If the offense involves data or computer software, Misdemeanor, 1st degree (2929.21 to 2929.28, 2929.31)

If the value of data or computer software involved in the offense or the loss to the victim is $500 or more and is less than $5,000, Felony, 5th degree (2929.11 to 2929.18, 2929.31)

If the value of data or computer software involved in the offense or the loss to the victim is $5,000 or more and is less than $100,000, Felony, 4th degree (2929.11 to 2929.18, 2929.31)

If the value of data or computer software involved in the offense or the loss to the victim is $100,000 or more or if the offense is committed for the purpose of devising or executing a scheme to defraud or to obtain property or services and the value of the property or services or the loss to the victim is $5,000 or more, Felony, 3rd degree (2929.11 to 2929.18, 2929.31)

If the writing, data, computer software, or record is kept by or belongs to a local, state, or federal governmental entity, Felony, 3rd degree

Telecommunications Harassment—2917.21

See also Disrupting Public Services and Interception of Communications

ELEMENTS OF THE CRIME

Division (A):

(1) Knowingly

(2) Make, cause to be made, a telecommunication or knowingly permit a telecommunication to be made from a telecommunications device under the person's control

(3) If the caller does any of the following:

(a) Fails to identify the caller to the recipient of the telecommunication and makes the telecommunication to harass, or abuse any person at the premises to which the telecommunication is made whether or not actual communication takes place between the caller and recipient.

(b) Describes, suggests, requests, or proposes that the caller, recipient or any other person engage in sexual activity, and the recipient or other person at premises has requested in a previous telecommunication, or in the immediate telecommunication, that the caller not make the telecommunication to the recipient or to the premises.

(c) During the telecommunication, violates 2903.21, aggravated menacing.

(d) Knowingly states to the recipient that the caller intends to cause damage to or destroy public or private property and the recipient, member of recipient's family, or persons residing at the premises to which telecommunication is made owns, leases, resides, or works in, will at the time of destruction or damaging be near or in the property or has the responsibility of protecting, or insures the property that will be destroyed or damaged.

(e) Knowingly makes the telecommunication when the recipient or person at the premises has previously told the caller not to make a telecommunication to any persons at the premises

Division (B):

(1) Make, cause to be made, or permit a telecommunication to be made from a telecommunications device under the person's control,

(2) With a purpose to abuse, threaten, or harass another person.

EXCEPTIONS

Civil and criminal immunity if acting pursuant to a court order to investigate or prosecute for alleged violation of this provision or 4931.31.

Section inapplicable to telecommunication to debtors that comply with 15 USC 1692 and 47 USC 227.

PENALTY

Violation of Division (A)(3)(a), (b), (c), and (e) [above] and Division (B), First offense, Misdemeanor, 1st degree (2929.21 to 2929.28, 2929.31)

Each subsequent offense Felony, 5th degree (2929.11 to 2929.18, 2929.31)

Violation of Division A(3)(d) [above] is a Misdemeanor of the 1st degree; each subsequent violation is a felony of the 5th degree. (2929.11 to 2929.18, 2929.31)

If a violation of (A)(3)(d) [above] results in economic harm of $500 but less than $5,000, Felony of the 5th degree; if economic harm is $5,000 but less than $100,000, Felony of the 4th degree; if economic harm is $100,000 or more, Felony of the 3rd degree

Terrorism—Hoax Weapon of Mass Destruction—2917.33

ELEMENTS OF THE OFFENSE

(1) Without privilege

(2) Manufacture, possess, sell, deliver, display, use, threaten to use, attempt to use, conspire to use, or make readily accessible to others

(3) A hoax weapon of mass destruction

(4) With intent to deceive or otherwise mislead

(5) One or more persons into believing that the hoax weapon of mass destruction will cause terror, bodily harm, or property damage

EXCEPTIONS

Inapplicable to a member or employee of U.S. armed forces, a governmental employee of the United States or any governmental agency of any state, or of a private entity, if all of the following apply:

(1) Person is engaged in lawful activity within scope of duty or employment;

(2) Person is duly authorized or licensed to manufacture, possess, sell, deliver, display, or engage in conduct described in elements of the offense; and

(3) The person is in compliance with applicable federal and state law.

PROSECUTION NOTES

Any act which is a violation of this section and any other section may be prosecuted under this section, the other section or both.

PENALTY

Felony, 4th degree (2929.11 to 2929.18, 2929.31)

Terrorism—Support of Terrorism—2909.22

ELEMENTS OF THE CRIME

(1) Raise, solicit, collect, donate, or provide

(2) Material support or resources

(3) With purpose

(a) That the material support or resources

(b) Be used in whole or in part

(c) To plan, prepare, carry out, or aid

(d) An act of terrorism or the concealment of or escape from an act of terrorism

PENALTY

Felony, 3rd degree (2929.11 to 2929.18)

In addition to financial sanctions, offender may be ordered to pay costs of investigation and prosecution (2909.25(A))

Terrorism—Terrorism—2909.24

ELEMENTS OF THE CRIME

(1) Commit

(a) Felony offense of violence,

(b) Disrupting public services,

(c) Contaminating substance for human consumption, or spreading false report of same, or

(d) A felony of the first degree that is not a drug felony

(2) With purpose to

(a) Intimidate or coerce a civilian population

(b) Influence policy of any government by intimidation or coercion, or

(c) Affect the policy of any government by the specified offense

PENALTY

Terrorism is an offense one degree higher than the most serious underlying offense the defendant committed; if the most serious underlying offense is a felony of the first degree or murder, life imprisonment without parole; if the most serious offense is aggravated murder, life imprisonment without parole or death.

In addition to financial sanctions, offender may be ordered to pay costs of investigation and prosecution (2909.25(A)) and response cost incurred as a result of the threat (2909.25(B)).

Terrorism—Terroristic Threats—2909.23

ELEMENTS OF THE CRIME

(1) Threaten to commit or threaten to cause to be committed

(2)(a) Felony offense of violence,

(b) Disrupting public services,

(c) Contaminating substance for human consumption, or spreading false report of same, or

(d) A felony of the first degree that is not a drug felony

(3) With purpose to

(a) Intimidate or coerce civilian population,

(b) Influence policy of any government by intimidation or coercion, or

(c) Effect the policy of any government by the threat or by the specified offense

(4) As a result of the threat, causes a reasonable expectation or fear of the imminent of the specific offense

DEFENSE

It is *no* defense that the offender did not have intent or capability to commit the threatened specified offense, or that the threat was not made to the person who was the subject of the threatened specified offense.

PENALTY

Felony, 3rd degree (2929.11 to 2929.18)

In addition to financial sanctions, offender may be ordered to pay costs of investigation and prosecution (2909.25(A)) and response cost incurred as a result of the threat (2909.25(B)).

Theft—2913.02

ELEMENTS OF THE CRIME

(1) Purpose to deprive owner of property or services

(2) Knowingly obtain or exert control over either

(3)(a) Without consent of owner or person authorized to give consent, or

(b) Beyond scope of express or implied consent of owner or person authorized to give consent, or

(c) By deception, or

(d) By threat

PROOF

In a prosecution of a person for a theft offense that alleges that the person, with purpose to defraud or knowing the the person was facilitating a fraud by hiring an aircraft, motor vehicle, motorcycle, motorboat, sailboat, camper, trailer, horse, or buggy, or keeping or operating any of these that has been hired, or engaging accommodations at a hotel, motel, inn, campground, or other hostelry, it is prima-facie evidence of the purpose to defraud if the person does any of the following:(a) Using deception to induce the rental agency to furnish the person with the aircraft, motor vehicle, motorcycle, motorboat, sailboat, camper, trailer, horse, or buggy, or using deception to induce the hostelry to furnish the person with accommodations, or (b) hiring any aircraft, motor vehicle, motorcycle, motorboat, sailboat, camper, trailer, horse, or buggy, or engaging accommodations knowing the person is without sufficient means to pay the hire or rental, or (c) absconding without paying the hire or rental, or (d) knowingly failing to pay the hire or rental as required by the contract of hire or rental, without reasonable excuse for such failure, or (e) knowingly failing to return hired property as required by the contract of hire, without reasonable excuse for the failure.

PENALTY

Petty theft—If value of property or services stolen is less than $500, Misdemeanor, 1st degree (2929.21 to 2929.28, 2929.31)

Theft—If value $500 or more and less than $5,000, or is a credit card; or printed form for check or negotiable instrument, which on face identifies maker or drawer for whose use designed or identifies accounts on which to be drawn, and which has not been executed or amount is blank; motor vehicle identification license plate as prescribed by 4503.22, or law of another state or United States; a temporary license placard or windshield sticker as prescribed by 4503.182, or law of another state or United States; or blank certificate of title or manufacturer's or importer's certificate to motor vehicle, prescribed by 4505.07; blank form for any license listed in 4507.01(A), Felony, 5th degree (2929.11 to 2929.18, 2929.31)

Grand theft—If value $5,000 or over and is less than $100,000, Felony, 4th degree (2929.11 to 2929.18, 2929.31)

Grand theft of a motor vehicle—If property stolen is a motor vehicle as defined in 4501.01, Felony, 4th degree (2929.11 to 2929.18, 2929.31)

Aggravated theft—If the property stolen is $100,000 and less than $500,000, Felony, 3rd degree. Felony, 2nd degree if value $500,000 and less than $1,000,000. Felony, 1st degree if value $1,000,000 or more (2929.11 to 2929.18, 2929.31)

Theft from an elderly person or disabled adult, Felony, 5th degree. Felony, 4th degree if value $500 or more and less than $5,000. Felony, 3rd degree if $5,000 or more and less than $25,000. Felony, 2nd degree if $25,000 and less than $100,000. Felony, 1st degree if value $100,000 or more (2929.11 to 2929.18, 2929.31)

Theft of a firearm or dangerous ordnance, Felony, 3rd degree; presumption in favor of imprisonment (2929.11 to 2929.18, 2929.31)

Theft of drugs—If the property stolen is any dangerous drug, as defined in section 4729.01, Felony, 4th degree (2929.11 to 2929.18, 2929.31) or if the offender previously has been convicted of a felony drug abuse offense, as defined in section 2925.01, Felony, 3rd degree (2929.11 to 2929.18, 2929.31)

Theft of police dog or horse or service dog, and offender knows or should know the animal is a police dog or horse or a service dog, Felony, 3rd degree (2929.11 to 2929.18, 2929.31)

Note: In addition to other penalties, an offender convicted of causing a motor vehicle to leave a retail gasoline establishment without full payment is subject to (1) suspension of driving privileges for not more than six months; or (2) if driving privileges previously suspended under this section, imposition of class seven suspension under 4510.02(A)(7) for at least six months. The court may grant limited driving privileges during this time under Chapter 4510.

Theft in Office

See Public Officials—Theft in Office

Theft-related Offenses—Counterfeit Goods—2913.34

ELEMENTS OF THE CRIME

(1) Knowingly

(2)(a) Attach, affix or use a counterfeit mark in the manufacture of goods or services, whether or not intended for sale or resale

(b) Possess, sell or offer for sale any property, knowing that it is designed for the production or reproduction of counterfeit marks

(c) Purchase or possess goods, knowing that a counterfeit mark is attached, affixed or otherwise used in connection with the goods, with the intent to sell or otherwise dispose of the goods

(d) Sell, offer to sell or otherwise dispose of goods, knowing that a counterfeit mark is attached, affixed or otherwise used in connection with the goods

(e) Sell, offer to sell or otherwise provide services, knowing that a counterfeit mark is used in connection with that sale, offer to sell or provision of the services

AFFIRMATIVE DEFENSE

Defendants may assert as affirmative defenses any defense that would be available in any criminal, civil or administrative action brought under 15 USC 1051—1127 and 18 USC 2320.

PENALTY

Violation of (2)(a) Felony, 5th degree; value of the goods or services or number of units sold may raise offense to Felony, 3rd or 4th degree (2929.11 to 2929.18, 2929.31)

Violation of (2)(b) Misdemeanor, 1st degree; if property involved is intended for use in commission of a felony, violation is a Felony, 5th degree (2929.11 to 2929.18, 2929.31)

Violation of (2)(c), (d) and (f) Misdemeanor, 1st degree; if cumulative sales price of the goods or services is at least $500 but less than $5,000, violation is a Felony, 5th degree; if cumulative sales price of the goods or services is at least $5,000 but less than $100,000 or if the number of units involved is more than 100 but less than 1,000, violation is a Felony, 4th degree; if the cumulative sales price of the goods or services is more than $100,000 or the number of units involved is at least 1,000, violation is a Felony, 3rd degree (2929.11 to 2929.18, 2929.31)

Theft-related Offenses—Credit Card Misuse

See Theft-related Offenses—Misuse of Credit Card; Theft-related Offenses—Defrauding Creditors

Theft-related Offenses—Criminal Simulation—2913.32

ELEMENTS OF THE CRIME

(1) With purpose to defraud, or knowing that the person is facilitating fraud

(2)(a) Make or alter any object to appear to have value because of antiquity, rarity, curiosity, source, authorship, which it does not in fact possess, or

(b) Practice deception in making, retouching, editing, reproducing any photograph, movie film, video tape, phonograph record, recording tape, or

(c) Falsely or fraudulently

(i) Make, simulate, forge, alter, or counterfeit, or

(ii) Cause to be made, simulated, forged, altered, or counterfeited, or

(iii) Use more than once

Any wrapper, label, stamp, cork, or cap prescribed by the liquor control commission under Chapters 4301. and 4303.

(d) Utter, or possess with purpose to utter, any object known to have been simulated as provided in (2)(a), (b) or (c) above

PENALTY

Misdemeanor. 1st degree (2929.21 to 2929.28, 2929.31)

If the loss to the victim is $500 or more and is less than $5,000, Felony, 5th degree (2929.11 to 2929.18, 2929.31)

If the loss to the victim is $5,000 or more and is less than $100,000, Felony, 4th degree (2929.11 to 2929.18, 2929.31)

If the loss to the victim is $100,000 or more, Felony, 3rd degree (2929.11 to 2929.18, 2929.31)

Theft-related Offenses—Defrauding Creditors—2913.45

ELEMENTS OF THE CRIME

(1) Purpose to defraud one or more creditors

(2)(a) Remove, conceal, destroy, encumber, convey, or otherwise deal with any of the person's property, or

(b) Misrepresent or refuse to disclose to fiduciary appointed to administer or manage the person's affairs or estate, the existence, amount, location of any of the person's property, or any other information regarding such property that the person is legally required to furnish fiduciary

PENALTY

Misdemeanor, 1st degree (2929.21 to 2929.28, 2929.31)

If the value of the property involved is $500 or more and is less than $5,000, Felony, 5th degree (2929.11 to 2929.18, 2929.31)

If the value of the property involved is $5,000 or more and is less than $100,000, Felony, 4th degree (2929.11 to 2929.18, 2929.31)

If the value of the property involved is $100,000 or more, Felony, 3rd degree (2929.11 to 2929.18, 2929.31)

Theft-related Offenses—Drugs, Theft of

See Drug Offenses—Theft of Drugs

Theft-related Offenses—Extortion

See Extortion

Theft-related Offenses—Identity—2913.49

ELEMENTS OF THE CRIME

Division (B):

(1) Use, obtain or possess

(2) Personal identifying information of another person

(3) Without express or implied consent

(4) With intent to

(a) Hold the person out to be the other person, or

(b) Represent the other person's personal identifying information as the person's own personal identifying information

Division (C):

(1) Create, obtain, possess, or use

(2) Personal identifying information of any person

(3) With intent to aid or abet another person in violating Division (B)

Division (D):

(1) With intent to defraud

(2) Permit another person to use the offender's own personal identifying information

Division (E):

(1) Permitted to use another person's personal identifying information as described in Division (D)

(2) Use, obtain or possess the other person's personal identifying information

(3) With intent to

(a) Hold himself to be the other person, or

(b) Represent the other person's personal identifying information as his own

AFFIRMATIVE DEFENSES

It is an affirmative defense to a charge under Division (B) that the person using the personal identifying information is acting in accord with legally recognized guardianship or conservatorship or as a trustee or fiduciary.

It is an affirmative defense to a charge under Division (B), (D) or (E) that the person using the personal identifying information is a law enforcement agency, authorized fraud personnel, or a representative of or attorney for a law enforcement agency or authorized fraud personnel and is using the personal identifying information in a bona fide investigation, an information security evaluation, a pretext calling evaluation, or in a similar matter.

It is an affirmative defense to a charge under Division (B), (D) or (E) that the personal identifying information was obtained, possessed or used for a lawful purpose.

It is *not* a defense to a charge under this section that the person whose personal identifying information was obtained, possessed or used was dead at the time of the offense.

PENALTY

Misdemeanor, 1st degree (2929.21 to 2929.28, 2929.31)

If the value of the credit, property, services, debt, or other legal obligation is $500 or more and less than $5,000, Felony, 4th degree (2929.11 to 2929.18, 2929.31)

If the value of the credit, property, services, debt, or other legal obligation is $5,000 or more and less than $100,000, Felony, 3rd degree (2929.11 to 2929.18, 2929.31)

If the value of the credit, property, services, debt, or other legal obligation is $100,000 or more, Felony, 2nd degree (2929.11 to 2929.18, 2929.31)

Note: See 2913.49(H) for determining value of credit, property, services, debt or other legal obligation.

Theft-related Offenses—Illegal Use of Food Stamps—2913.46

Note: For versions in effect until 7–1–96, see Theft-related Offenses—Trafficking In or Illegal Use of Food Stamps.

ELEMENTS OF THE CRIME

Division (A):

(1) Knowingly

(2) Possess, buy, sell, use, alter, accept or transfer food stamp coupons or WIC program benefits

(3) In any manner not authorized by Food Stamps Act of 1977, 91 Stat. 958, 7 U.S.C.A. 2011, as amended or Child Nutrition Act, 42 USCA 1786, as amended

Division (B):

(1) Organization as defined in 2901.23(D)

(2) Knowingly allows employee

(3) To sell, transfer, exchange items or services

(4) Purchase of which is prohibited by Food Stamp Act of 1977, 91 Stat. 958, 7 USCA 2011, as amended or Child Nutrition Act, 42 USCA 1786, as amended

(5) In exchange for food stamp coupons or WIC program benefits

Division (C):

(1) Organization as defined in 2901.23(D)

(2) Negligently allows employee

(3) To sell, transfer, or exchange food stamp coupons

(4) For anything of value

PENALTY

Felony, 5th degree (2929.11 to 2929.18, 2929.31)

If food stamp coupons value is $500 or more and is less than $5,000, Felony, 4th degree (2929.11 to 2929.18, 2929.31)

If food stamp coupons value is $5,000 or more and is less than $100,000, Felony, 3rd degree (2929.11 to 2929.18, 2929.31)

If food stamp coupons value is $100,000 or more, Felony, 2nd degree (2929.11 to 2929.18, 2929.31)

Theft-related Offenses—Insurance Fraud—2913.47

ELEMENTS OF THE CRIME

Division (A):

This division sets forth the definitions applicable to Division (B) of this section

Division (B):

(1)(a)(i) Purpose to defraud, or

(ii) Knowingly facilitate a fraud

(b) Present, or cause to be presented, to insurer

(c) Written or oral statement

(d) Knowing statement, or any part of statement, is false or deceptive

(e) Statement is part of, or in support of:

(i) Application for insurance, or

(ii) Claim for payment pursuant to a policy, or

(iii) Claim for any other benefit pursuant to a policy

(2)(a) Assist, aid, abet, solicit, procure, or conspire with another

(b) In preparing or making written or oral statement

(c) Intended to be presented to an insurer

(d) Statement is part of, or in support of:

(i) Application for insurance, or

(ii) Claim for payment pursuant to a policy, or

(iii) Claim for any other benefit pursuant to a policy

PENALTY

Misdemeanor, 1st degree (2929.21 to 2929.28, 2929.31)

If amount of false or deceptive claim is $500 or more and less than $5,000, Felony, 5th degree (2929.11 to 2929.18, 2929.31)

If amount of false or deceptive claim is $5,000 or more and less than $100,000, Felony, 4th degree (2929.11 to 2929.18, 2929.31)

If amount of false or deceptive claim is $100,000 or more, Felony, 3rd degree (2929.11 to 2929.18, 2929.31)

Theft-related Offenses—Making or Using Slugs—2913.33

ELEMENTS OF THE CRIME

Division (A):

(1) Insert or deposit a slug in a coin machine

(2) With purpose to defraud

Division (B):

(1) Make, possess, dispose of a slug

(2) With purpose of enabling another to defraud by inserting or depositing in a coin machine

PENALTY

Misdemeanor, 2nd degree (2929.21 to 2929.28, 2929.31)

Theft-related Offenses—Medicaid Fraud—2913.40

ELEMENTS OF THE CRIME

Division (A):

(1) Knowingly

(2) Make or cause to be made

(3) False or misleading

(4) Statement or representation

(5) For use in obtaining reimbursement from the medical assistance program

Division (B):

(1)(a)(i) Purpose to commit fraud, or

(ii) Knowingly facilitate a fraud

(b) Contrary to terms of provider agreement

(c) Charge or solicit or accept or receive

(d) For goods or services

(e) Provided under the medical assistance program

(f) Any property, money or other consideration in addition to the amount of reimbursement under the medical assistance program and provider agreement

(2)(a)(i) Purpose to commit fraud, or

(ii) Knowingly facilitate a fraud

(b) Solicit, offer or receive

(c) In cash or kind

(d) Kickback or rebate or otherwise

(e) In connection with the furnishing of goods or services

(f) When whole or partial reimbursement is or may be made under medical assistance program

Division (C):

(1)(a)(i) Submitted a claim for, or

(ii) Provided

(b) Goods or services under medical assistance program

(c) Six years or more after reimbursement of claim or goods and services

(d) Knowingly

(e) Alter, falsify, destroy, conceal or remove

(f) Necessary records

(g) (i) Nature of all goods or services, or

(ii) Reimbursement received

(2)(a)(i) Submitted a claim for, or

(ii) Provided

(b) Goods or services under medical assistance program

(c) Six years or more after reimbursement of claim or goods and services

(d) Knowingly

(e) Alter or falsify or destroy or conceal or remove

(f) Necessary records

(g) Income and expenditures

PENALTY

Misdemeanor, 1st degree (2929.21 to 2929.28, 2929.31)

If the value of the property, services, or funds obtained is $500 or more and is less than $5,000, Felony, 5th degree (2929.11 to 2929.18, 2929.31)

If the value of the property, services, or funds obtained is $5,000 or more and is less than $100,000, Felony, 4th degree (2929.11 to 2929.18, 2929.31)

If the value of the property, services, or funds obtained is $100,000 or more, Felony, 3rd degree (2929.11 to 2929.18, 2929.31)

Note: Upon application of the governmental agency, office, or other entity that conducted the investigation and prosecution, the court shall order any person who is convicted under this section to pay the applicant its cost of investigating and prosecuting the case. The costs of investigation and prosecution that a defendant is ordered to pay shall be in addition to any other penalties.

Theft-related Offenses—Misuse of Credit Card—2913.21

ELEMENTS OF THE CRIME

Division (A):

(1) Practice deception to procure issuance of credit card when credit card is issued in actual reliance thereon, or

(2) Knowingly buy or sell credit card from or to a person other than issuer.

Division (B):

(1) Purpose to defraud

(2)(a) Obtain control of credit card as security for debt, or

(b) Obtain property or services by use of credit card in one or more transactions knowing or having reasonable cause to believe card expired, revoked, obtained, retained or being used in violation of law, or

(c) Furnish property or services on presentation of credit card knowing the card is being used in violation of law, or

(d) Represent or cause to be represented to issuer of credit card that property or services have been furnished, knowing such representation is false

Division (C):

(1) Purpose to violate this section

(2) Receive, possess, control, dispose of credit card

PENALTY

If violation of Divisions (A), (B)(2)(a) or (C), Misdemeanor, 1st degree (2929.21 to 2929.28, 2929.31)

If cumulative retail of property and services in one or more violations under Division (B)(2)(b), (c) or (d) above, which violations involve one or more credit card accounts and occur within ninety consecutive days commencing on date of first violation and amount is less than $500, Misdemeanor, 1st degree (2929.21 to 2929.28, 2929.31)

If cumulative retail value of property and services in one or more violations under Division (B)(2)(b), (c) or (d) above, which violations involve one or more credit card accounts and occur within ninety consecutive days commencing on date of first violation and amount is $500 or more and is less than $5,000, Felony, 5th degree (2929.11 to 2929.18, 2929.31)

If cumulative retail value of property and services in one or more violations under Division (B)(2)(b), (c) or (d) above, which violations involve one or more credit card accounts and occur within ninety consecutive days commencing on date of first violation and amount is between $5,000 and $100,000, Felony, 4th degree (2929.11 to 2929.18, 2929.31)

If the cumulative retail value of the property and services in one or more violations under Divisions (B)(2)(b), (c) or (d) which violations involve one or more credit card accounts and occur within ninety consecutive days commencing on date of first violation and amount is $100,000 or more, Felony, 3rd degree (2929.11 to 2929.18, 2929.31)

If Division (B) violated and victim is elderly person, Felony, 5th degree. Felony, 4th degree, if debt is $500 or more and less than $5,000. Felony, 3rd degree, if debt is $5,000 or more and less than $25,000. Felony, 2nd degree, if debt is more than $25,000 (2929.11 to 2929.18, 2929.31)

Theft-related Offenses—Passing Bad Checks—2913.11

ELEMENTS OF THE CRIME

(1) Purpose to defraud

(2) Issue, transfer, cause to be issued or transferred

(3) Check or other negotiable instrument

(4) Knowing it will be dishonored

PROOF

Person issuing or transferring presumed to know it will be dishonored if:

(1) Drawer had no account with drawee at time of issue or date stated, whichever is later, or

(2) Check or instrument properly refused payment for insufficient funds on presentment within 30 days after issue or date stated, whichever is later, and liability of any party liable thereon not discharged by payment or satisfaction within 10 days after receiving dishonor notice.

Person issuing or transferring presumed to have purpose to defraud if drawer fails to comply with 1349.16, when opening checking account intended for personal, family, or household purposes at financial institution, by doing any of the following:

(1) Falsely stating the drawer has not been issued valid driver's or commercial driver's license or identification card issued under 4507.50, or

(2) Furnishing such license or card, or other identification document, containing false information, or

(3) Making false statement with respect to current address or any other relevant information reasonably required by financial institution.

PENALTY

Misdemeanor, 1st degree (2929.21 to 2929.28, 2929.31)

If instrument is for payment of $500 or more and for less than $5,000, Felony, 5th degree (2929.11 to 2929.18, 2929.31)

If instrument is for payment of $5,000 or more and for less than $100,000, Felony, 4th degree (2929.11 to 2929.18, 2929.31)

If instrument is for payment of $100,000 or more, Felony, 3rd degree (2929.11 to 2929.18, 2929.31)

Theft-related Offenses—Public Official Receiving Improper Compensation

See Public Officials—Soliciting or Receiving Improper Compensation

Theft-related Offenses—Receiving Stolen Property—2913.51

ELEMENTS OF THE CRIME

(1) Receive, retain or dispose of property of another

(2) Knowing or having reasonable cause to believe it has been obtained through commission of theft offense

PENALTY

Misdemeanor, 1st degree (2929.21 to 2929.28, 2929.31)

If value is $500 or more and is less than $5,000, or it is a credit card; printed form for check or negotiable instrument which on face identifies maker or drawer for whose use designed, or identifies account on which to be drawn, and which has not been executed or amount is blank; or motor vehicle identification license plate as prescribed by 4503.22, or law of another state or United States; or temporary license placard or windshield sticker as prescribed by 4503.182, or law of another state or United States; or blank certificate of title or manufacturer's or importer's certificate to motor vehicle, as prescribed by 4505.07; or blank form for any license listed in 4507.01(A), Felony, 5th degree (2929.11 to 2929.18, 2929.31)

If property involved is a motor vehicle as defined in 4501.01, or a dangerous drug, as defined in 4729.01, or the value of property is $5,000 or more and less than $100,000, or if the property involved is a firearm or dangerous ordnance, as defined in section 2923.11, Felony, 4th degree (2929.11 to 2929.18, 2929.31)

It is not a defense to this section that property was received other than by theft if the property was "explicitly represented" to be obtained through a theft offense

If value of property involved is $100,000 or more, Felony, 3rd degree (2929.11 to 2929.18, 2929.31)

Theft-related Offenses—Robbery

See Robbery, generally

Theft-related Offenses—Safecracking

See Safecracking

Theft-related Offenses—Securing Writings by Deception—2913.43

ELEMENTS OF THE CRIME

(1) By deception

(2) Cause another to execute any writing disposing of or encumbering property, or by which pecuniary obligation is incurred.

PENALTY

Misdemeanor, 1st degree (2929.21 to 2929.28, 2929.31)

If property or obligation is valued at $500 or more and is less than $5,000, Felony, 5th degree (2929.11 to 2929.18, 2929.31)

If property or obligation is $5,000 or more and is less than $100,000, Felony, 4th degree (2929.11 to 2929.18, 2929.31)

If property or obligation is valued at $100,000 or more, Felony, 3rd degree (2929.11 to 2929.18, 2929.31)

If victim is elderly person, Felony, 5th degree. If the value of the property or obligation is $500 or more and less than $5,000, Felony, 4th degree; if $5,000 or more and less than $25,000, Felony, 3rd degree; if $25,000 or more, Felony, 2nd degree

Theft-related Offenses—Tampering With Coin Machines—2911.32

ELEMENTS OF THE CRIME

(1) With purpose to commit theft or defraud

(2) Knowingly enter, force entrance into, tamper with, insert any part of instrument into

(3) Any coin machine.

PENALTY

Misdemeanor, 1st degree (2929.21 to 2929.28, 2929.31)

If prior conviction of this section or of theft offense defined in 2913.01, Felony, 5th degree (2929.11 to 2929.18, 2929.31)

Theft-related Offenses—Telecommunications Fraud—2913.05

ELEMENTS OF THE CRIME

(1) Devise a scheme to defraud

(2) Knowingly disseminate or transmit by wire, radio, satellite, telecommunication device or service

(3) Any writing, data, sign, signal, picture, sound, or image

(4) With the purpose to execute or otherwise further the scheme to defraud

PENALTY

Felony, 5th degree (2929.11 to 2929.18, 2929.31)

If value of benefit obtained by offender or value of detriment to victim is $5,000 or more but less than $100,000, Felony, 4th degree (2929.11 to 2929.18, 2929.31)

If value of benefit obtained by offender or value of detriment to victim is $100,000 or more, Felony, 3rd degree (2929.11 to 2929.18, 2929.31)

Theft-related Offenses—Theft in Office

See Public Officials—Theft in Office

Theft-related Offenses—Unauthorized Use of Services—2913.04

ELEMENTS OF THE CRIME

Division (A):

(1) Knowingly

(2) Use or operate

(3) Property of another

(4) Without consent of

(5) Owner or otherwise authorized person

Division (B):

(1) Knowingly

(2) Gain access or attempt to gain access or cause to gain access

(3) By any means

(4) Computer, computer system, computer network, cable service, cable system, telecommunications device or service, or information service

(5) Without or beyond scope of consent of

(6) Owner or otherwise authorized person

Division (C):

(1) Knowingly

(2) Gain access, attempt to gain access, cause access to be granted to, or disseminate information gained from

(3) Law enforcement data based system

(4) Without or beyond scope of express or implied consent of

(5) Chair of the law enforcement automated data system steering committee

DEFENSES

(1) Actor, though mistaken, reasonably believed the actor was authorized to use or operate the property

(2) Actor reasonably believed owner or otherwise authorized person would consent to actor's use or operation of property

PENALTY

Division (A):

Misdemeanor, 4th degree (2929.21 to 2929.28, 2929.31)

If the offense is committed for the purpose of devising and executing a scheme to defraud or to obtain property and services, Misdemeanor, 1st degree (2929.21 to 2929.28, 2929.31)

If the offense is committed for the purpose of devising and executing a scheme to defraud or to obtain property and services and if the value of the property or services or the loss to the victim is $500 or more and is less than $5,000, Felony, 5th degree (2929.11 to 2929.18, 2929.31)

If the offense is committed for the purpose of devising and executing a scheme to defraud or to obtain property and services and if the value of the property or services or the loss to the victim is $5,000 or more and is less than $100,000, Felony, 4th degree (2929.11 to 2929.18, 2929.31)

If the offense is committed for the purpose of devising and executing a scheme to defraud or to obtain property and services and if the value of the property or services or the loss to the victim is $100,000 or more, Felony, 3rd degree (2929.11 to 2929.18, 2929.31)

Division (B):

Felony, 5th degree (2929.11 to 2929.18, 2929.31)

If Division (A) or (B) violated and victim is elderly person who incurs loss, Felony, 5th degree. Felony, 4th degree, if loss is $500 or more and less than $5,000. Felony, 3rd degree, if loss is $5,000 or more and less than $25,000. Felony, 2nd degree, if loss is more than $25,000 (2929.11 to 2929.18, 2929.31)

Division (C):

Felony, 5th degree (2919.11 to 2929.18, 2929.31)

Theft-related Offenses—Unlawful Use of Telecommunications Device—2913.06

ELEMENTS OF THE CRIME

Division (A):

(1) Knowingly

(2) Manufacture, possess, deliver, offer to deliver, or advertise

(3) Counterfeit telecommunications device

(4) With purpose to use device criminally

Division (B):

(1) Knowingly

(2) Manufacture, possess, deliver, offer to deliver, or advertise

(3) Counterfeit telecommunications device

(4) With purpose to use device or allow it to be used, or with knowledge or reason to know that another may use the device to:

(a) Obtain or attempt to obtain telecommunications service or information service with purpose to avoid lawful charge for service, or aid or cause another to obtain or attempt to obtain service with purpose to avoid lawful charge for service

(b) Conceal existence, place of origin, or destination of a telecommunications service or information service

EXCEPTION

Section does not prohibit or restrict person with amateur service license issued by FCC from possessing a radio receiver or transreceiver intended primarily or exclusively for use in amateur radio service and issued for lawful purposes. Section also does not preclude a person from disputing charges imposed for telecommunications service or information service by provider of service

PENALTY

Felony, 5th degree (2929.11 to 2929.18, 2929.31)

Theft-related Offenses—Workers' Compensation Fraud—2913.48

ELEMENTS OF THE CRIME

(1) With purpose to defraud or knowing the person is facilitating fraud

(a) Receive workers' compensation benefits to which the person is not entitled, or

(b) Make, present, or cause to be made or presented a false or misleading statement with purpose to secure payment for goods or services rendered under Chapters 4121., 4123., 4127., or 4131., or to secure workers' compensation benefits; or

(c) Alter, falsify, destroy, conceal, or remove any record or document that is necessary to fully establish the validity of any claim filed with bureau of workers' compensation or a self-insuring employer under Chapters 4121., 4123., 4127., or 4131.; or

(d) Alter, falsify, destroy, conceal, or remove any record or document that is necessary to establish the nature and validity of all goods and services for which reimbursement or payment was received or is requested from bureau of workers' compensation or a self-insuring employer under Chapters 4121., 4123., 4127., or 4131.; or

(e) Enter into an agreement or conspiracy to defraud bureau of workers' compensation or self-insuring employer by making, presenting, or causing to be made or presented a false claim for workers' compensation benefits.

(f) Make, present or cause to be made or presented a false or misleading statement or other misrepresentation concerning manual codes, classification of employees, payroll or number of personnel, when that information is necessary to determine actual workers' compensation premium or assessment owned by an employer.

(g) Solicit, or receive any remuneration in connection with a referral for the furnishing of goods or services for which reimbursement may be made under Chapters 4121., 4123., 4127., or 4131. (not applicable to contract to provide services under the Bureau's Health Plan or a qualified health plan entered into with a managed care organization).

(h) Fail to secure or maintain workers' compensation coverage required under Chapter 4123.

PENALTY

Misdemeanor, 1st degree (2929.21 to 2929.28, 2929.31)

If value of premiums and assessments unpaid or goods, services, property, or money stolen is $500 or more but less than $5,000, Felony, 5th degree (2929.11 to 2929.18, 2929.31)

If value of premiums and assessments unpaid or goods, services, property, or money stolen is $5,000 or more but less than $100,000, Felony, 4th degree (2929.11 to 2929.18, 2929.31)

If value of premiums and assessments unpaid or goods, services, property, or money stolen is $100,000 or more, Felony, 3rd degree (2929.11 to 2929.18, 2929.31)

Note: In addition to other costs or penalties, and on application of governmental body that conducted investigation and prosecution, court shall order offender to pay costs of investigation and prosecution.

Note: Remedies and penalties under this section not exclusive and do not preclude use of other criminal or civil remedies or penalties.

Tobacco—Illegal Distribution of Cigarettes or Other Tobacco Products—2927.02

ELEMENTS OF THE CRIME

Division (B):

(1) Manufacturer, producer, distributor, wholesaler or retailer of cigarettes or other tobacco products; agent, employee or representative of manufacturer, producer, distributor, wholesaler or retailer of cigarettes, rolling papers or other tobacco products

(2)(a) Give, sell or distribute cigarettes, rolling papers or other tobacco products to person under age 18, or

(b) Give away, sell, distribute cigarettes, rolling papers or other tobacco products in place that does not have sign posted conspicuously stating that giving, selling or otherwise distributing cigarettes or other tobacco products to a person under age 18 is prohibited by law

(c) Knowingly provide false information regarding name, age, or other identification of any child purposely to obtain cigarettes, tobacco products or rolling papers

(d) Manufacture, sell or distribute

(i) pack or other container containing fewer than 20 cigarettes

(ii) package of roll-your-own tobacco containing less than 6/10 of one ounce of tobacco

(e) Sell cigarettes in a smaller quantity than that placed in the pack or container by the manufacturer

Division (C):

(1) Sell or offer to sell cigarettes, rolling papers or other tobacco products

(2) By or from vending machine

(3) Except in following locations:

(a) Area within factory, business, office, or other place not open to general public, or

(b) Area to which persons under age 18 are not generally permitted access, or

(c) Any other place on all of the following conditions:

(i) Vending machine located within immediate vicinity, plain view, and control of place's owner or operator, or employee of such person, so that purchases of cigarettes or tobacco products from vending machine will be readily observed by owner, operator, or employee (vending machine located in unmonitored area, including unmonitored coatroom, restroom, hallway, or outer waiting area, does not meet this requirement) and

(ii) Vending machine inaccessible to public when place closed

Note: Vending machine has same meaning as coin machine as defined in 2913.01(I).

EXCEPTIONS

Division (2)(a) and (b) do not apply when the child is participating in a research protocol when all of the following apply: (1) parent, guardian or legal custodian has consented in writing to the child's participation; (2) an institutional human subjects protection review board or equivalent has approved the research protocol; and (3) the child is participating at the facility or location specified in the research protocol.

AFFIRMATIVE DEFENSES

(1) The child was accompanied by a parent, spouse 18 or over, or legal guardian of the child.

(2) The person who gave, sold or distributed the product to a child is a parent, spouse 18 or over, or legal guardian of the child.

PENALTY

Misdemeanor, 4th degree (2929.21 to 2929.28, 2929.31)

If prior conviction, Misdemeanor, 3rd degree (2929.21 to 2929.28, 2929.31)

Tools, Criminal—Possessing

See Criminal Tools—Possessing

Trafficking in Harmful Intoxicants

See Drug Offenses—Trafficking—Trafficking in Harmful Intoxicants

Trafficking in Marihuana

See Drug Offenses—Trafficking—Trafficking in Controlled Substances or Drugs

Transportation, Disrupting Public

See Disrupting Public Services

Trespass—Aggravated Trespass—2911.211

ELEMENTS OF THE CRIME

(1) Enter or remain

(2) On the land or premises of another

(3) With purpose to commit on land or premises

(4) Misdemeanor, the elements of which involve:

(a) Causing physical harm to another, or

(b) Causing another to believe that offender will cause physical harm

PENALTY

Misdemeanor, 1st degree (2929.21 to 2929.28, 2929.31)

Note: Written statement by complainant alleging that alleged offender has committed offense of aggravated trespass constitutes reasonable cause for officer to make warrantless arrest under 2935.03(B)(2)(b).

Trespass—Criminal Trespass—2911.21

ELEMENTS OF THE CRIME

(1) Without privilege to do so

(2)(a) Knowingly enter or remain on land or premises of another, or

(b) Knowingly enter or remain on land or premises of another, use of which is lawfully restricted to certain persons, purposes, modes, or hours, when offender knows he is violating such restriction or is reckless in that regard, or

(c) Recklessly enter or remain on land or premises of another, where notice against unauthorized access or presence is actually communicated to offender, or in manner prescribed by law, or by posting in manner reasonably calculated to come to attention of potential intruders, or by fencing or other enclosure manifesting restricted access, or

(d) Being on land or premises of another, negligently fail or refuse to leave upon being notified to do so by owner or occupant, agent or servant of either, or by signage posted in a conspicuous place

DEFENSES

(1) No defense that land or premises owned, controlled, or in custody of public agency.

(2) No defense that offender authorized to enter or remain, when authorization secured by deception.

PENALTY

Misdemeanor, 4th degree (2929.21 to 2929.28, 2929.31)

Unauthorized Use of Vehicle

See Motor Vehicles—Unauthorized Use of Vehicle

Unlawful Display of Law Enforcement Emblem

See Law Enforcement Emblem—Unlawful Display

Unlawful Restraint—2905.03

See also Abduction; Juveniles—Child Stealing; Kidnapping

ELEMENTS OF THE CRIME

(1) Without privilege

(2) Knowingly

(3) Restrain another person of his liberty

PENALTY

Misdemeanor, 3rd degree (2929.21 to 2929.28, 2929.31)

Using Sham Legal Process—2921.52

ELEMENTS OF THE CRIME

(1) Knowing the sham legal process to be a sham

(2) Knowingly

(3)(a) Issue, display, distribute, or otherwise use sham legal process

(b) Use sham legal process to arrest, detain, search or seize any person or the property of another person

(c) Commit or facilitate the commission of an offense using sham legal process

(d) Commit a felony by using sham legal process

DEFENSE

It is an affirmative defense to (3)(a) and (3)(b) that the use of sham legal process was for a lawful purpose.

PENALTY

Misdemeanor, 4th degree if violation of (3)(a) (2929.21 to 2929.28, 2929.31)

Misdemeanor, 1st degree, if violation of (3)(b) (2929.21 to 2929.28, 2929.31)

Misdemeanor, 1st degree, if violation of (3)(c), except it is a Felony, 4th degree if offense committed is a felony

Felony, 3rd degree, if violation of (3)(d) (2929.11 to 2929.18, 2929.31)

Note: A civil action may be brought under this statute for any loss suffered as a result of the commission of the offense, and for reasonable attorney's fees, court costs and other expenses incurred as a result of prosecuting the civil action.

Note: Sham legal process is any instrument that (a) is not lawfully issued, and (b) purports (i) to be an order of a court, legislature, executive or administrative body, (ii) to assert jurisdiction over or determine the legal status, rights, duties, powers, or privileges of any person or property, or (iii) to require or authorize arrest, search, seizure, indictment, trial or sentencing of any person or property, and (c) is designed to make another believe that it is lawfully issued.

Usury

See Criminally Usurious Transaction

Utilities, Public, Disrupting

See Disrupting Public Services

Uttering

See Forgery

Vandalism—Railroad—2909.10

ELEMENTS OF THE CRIME

Division (A):

1. Knowingly
2. By any means
3. Drop or throw any object at, onto, or in the path of
4. Any
   (a) railroad rail,
   (b) railroad track,
   (c) locomotive engine,
   (d) railroad car, or
   (e) other vehicle of a railroad company while vehicle is on a railroad track

Division (B):

1. Without privilege to do so
2. Climb upon or into
3. Any
   (a) locomotive,
   (b) engine,
   (c) railroad car, or
   (d) other vehicle of a railroad company while vehicle is on a railroad track

Division (C):

1. Without privilege to do so
2. Disrupt, delay, or prevent the operation of
3. Any train or other vehicle of a railroad company while vehicle is on a railroad track

Division (D):

1. Without privilege to do so
2. Knowingly
3. Enter or remain on
4. Land or premises of a railroad company

PENALTY

Violation of Division (A), (B), or (C), Misdemeanor, 1st degree (2929.21 to 2929.28, 2929.31)

If violation of Division (A), (B), or (C) causes physical harm to property or creates a substantial risk of physical harm to any person, violation, Felony, 4th degree (2929.11 to 2929.18, 2929.31)

If violation of Division (A), (B), or (C) causes physical harm to any person, Felony, 3rd degree (2929.11 to 2929.18, 2929.31)

If violation of Division (A), (B), or (C) causes serious physical harm to any person, Felony, 2nd degree (2929.11 to 2929.18, 2929.31)

Violation of Division (D), Misdemeanor, 4th degree (2929.21 to 2929.28, 2929.31)

Vandalism—Railroad Grade Crossing Device—2909.101

ELEMENTS OF THE CRIME

1. Knowingly
2. Deface, damage, obstruct, remove, or otherwise impair the operation of any railroad crossing warning signal or other protective device (including any gate, bell, light, crossbuck, stop sign, yield sign, advance warning sign, or advance pavement marking)

PENALTY

Misdemeanor, 1st degree (2929.21 to 2929.28, 2929.31)

If violation causes serious physical harm to property or creates a substantial risk of physical harm to any person, violation, Felony, 4th degree (2929.11 to 2929.18, 2929.31)

If violation causes physical harm to any person, Felony, 3rd degree (2929.11 to 2929.18, 2929.31)

If violation causes serious physical harm to any person, Felony, 2nd degree (2929.11 to 2929.18, 2929.31)

Vandalism—Vandalism—2909.05

ELEMENTS OF THE CRIME

Division (A):

(1) Knowingly

(2) Cause serious physical harm to

(3) Occupied structure or any of its contents

Division (B):

(1)(a) Knowingly

(b) Cause physical harm to

(c) Property owned or possessed by another, either:

(i) Used in profession, business, trade, occupation, and value of property or amount of physical harm is $500 or more, or

(ii) Regardless of value or amount of damage done, such property or equivalent necessary to engage in profession, business, trade, occupation, or

(2)(a) Knowingly

(b) Cause physical harm to

(c) Property owned, leased or controlled by a governmental entity

Division (C):

(1) Knowingly

(2) Without privilege to do so

(3) Cause serious physical harm to

(a) Tomb, monument, gravestone, similar structure used as memorial for dead

(b) Fence, railing, curb, other property, used to protect, enclose, ornament any cemetery

(c) Place of burial

Division (D):

(1) Knowingly

(2) Without privilege to do so

(3) Cause physical harm to place of burial

(4) By breaking and entering a tomb, crypt, casket or other structure used as memorial for dead or enclosure for dead

PENALTY

Felony, 5th degree (2929.11 to 2929.18, 2929.31)

Additional Fine: not more than $2,500

If value of property or amount of physical harm is $5,000 or more but less than $100,000, Felony, 4th degree (2929.11 to 2929.18, 2929.31)

If value of property or amount of physical harm is $100,000 or more, Felony, 3rd degree (2929.11 to 2929.18, 2929.31)

Note: See 2909.11 for procedure, criteria used in determining value of property or amount of physical harm.

Vandalism—Vehicular—2909.09

ELEMENTS OF THE CRIME

1. Knowingly
2. by any means
3. drop or throw
4. any object into the path or onto
5. (a) vehicle, streetcar, or trackless trolley on the highway

   (b) boat or vessel on any water in the state

PENALTY

Misdemeanor, 1st degree (2929.21 to 2929.28, 2929.31)

If violation creates a substantial risk of physical harm to a person, or causes serious physical harm to property, Felony, 4th degree (2929.11 to 2929.18, 2929.31)

If violation causes physical harm to any person, Felony, 3rd degree (2929.11 to 2929.18, 2929.31)

If violation causes serious physical harm to any person, Felony, 2nd degree (2929.11 to 2929.18, 2929.31)

Vehicular Assault—Aggravated Vehicular Assault—2903.08

ELEMENTS OF THE CRIME

Division (A)(1):

(1)(a) Operating or

(b) Participating in operation of

(2)(a) Motor vehicle

(b) Motorcycle

(c) Snowmobile

(d) Locomotive

(e) Watercraft

(f) Aircraft

(3) As proximate result of violating 1547.11 (operating watercraft while intoxicated), 4511.19 (operating a motor vehicle while intoxicated), 4516.15 (operating aircraft while intoxicated), or a substantially equivalent municipal ordinance

(4) Cause serious physical harm to another or another's unborn

Division (A)(2):

(1)(a) Operating or

(b) Participating in operation of

(2)(a) Motor vehicle

(b) Motorcycle

(c) Snowmobile

(d) Locomotive

(e) Watercraft

(f) Aircraft

(3)(a) Recklessly in a construction zone, or

(b) Recklessly

(4) Cause serious physical harm to another or another's unborn

Division (A)(3):

(1)(a) Operating or

(b) Participating in operating

(2)(a) Motor vehicle, or

(b) Motorcycle

(3) Speeding in a construction zone

(4) Causing serious physical harm to a person in the construction zone

PENALTY

Division (A)(1), Felony, 3rd degree (2929.11 to 2929.18, 2929.31), mandatory prison term. Felony, 2nd degree if, at time of offense, offender driving under suspension imposed under Chapter 4510. or any other section; or if offender previously convicted of this section, any traffic-related homicide, manslaughter, or assault offense; if previously convicted three times or more of 1547.11, 4511.19, 4561.15, or a combination of these statutes or a substantially equivalent municipal ordinance within previous six years; or previously convicted of a second or subsequent felony violation of 4511.19(A).

Note: Offender's driver's or commercial driver's license shall be suspended for a definite period of two to ten years (4510.02(A)(2) and (3)).

Division (A)(2), Felony, 4th degree (2929.11 to 2929.18, 2929.31). Felony, 3rd degree if, at time of offense, driving under suspension imposed under Chapter 4510. or any other provision; or if offender previously convicted of this section or any traffic-related homicide, manslaughter, or assault offense. Mandatory prison term if previously convicted of this section or 2903.06; or at time of offense, offender driving under suspension imposed under Chapter 4510. or any other section.

Note: Offender's driver's or commercial driver's license shall be suspended for a definite period of one to five years (4510.02(A)(4)).

Division (A)(3) Misdemeanor, 1st degree (2929.21 to 2929.28, 2929.31). Mandatory jail sentence of at least 7 days for misdemeanor violation. Felony, 4th degree if, at time of offense, offender driving under suspension imposed under Chapter 4510. or any other section, or if offender previously convicted of this section, or any traffic related homicide, manslaughter or assault offense. Mandatory prison term if previously convicted of 2903.06; or at time of offense, offender driving under suspension imposed under Chapter 4510., in any other section.

Note: Offender's driver's or commercial drivers license shall be suspended for a definite period of 6 months to one year (4510.02 (B)(3) and (4)).

Note: Division (A)(3) applies only where signs required by 2903.081 denotion construction zone are erected.

Vehicular Homicide—Aggravated Vehicular Homicide—2903.06

ELEMENTS OF THE CRIME

Division (A)(1):

(1)(a) Operating or

(b) Participating in operation of

(2)(a) Motor vehicle

(b) Motorcycle

(c) Snowmobile

(d) Locomotive

(e) Watercraft

(f) Aircraft

(3) As proximate result of violating 1547.11 (operating watercraft while intoxicated), 4511.19 (operating a motor vehicle while intoxicated), 4561.15 (operating aircraft while intoxicated) or a substantially equivalent municipal ordinance.

(4) Cause death of another or the unlawful termination of another's pregnancy

Division (A)(2):

(1)(a) Operating or

(b) Participating in operation of

(2)(a) Motor vehicle

(b) Motorcycle

(c) Snowmobile

(d) Locomotive

(e) Watercraft

(f) Aircraft

(3)(a) Recklessly

(b) Recklessly in a construction zone

(4) Cause death of another or the unlawful termination of another's pregnancy

Division (A)(3):

(1)(a) Operating or

(b) Participating in operation of

(2)(a) Motor vehicle

(b) Motorcycle

(c) Snowmobile

(d) Locomotive

(e) Watercraft

(f) Aircraft

(3)(a) Negligently

(b) Negligently in a construction zone

(4) Cause death of another or the unlawful termination of another's pregnancy

Division (A)(4):

(1)(a) Operating or

(b) Participating in operation of

(2)(a) Motor vehicle

(b) Motorcycle

(c) Snowmobile

(d) Locomotive

(e) Watercraft

(f) Aircraft

(3) As proximate result of violating any Title 45 section that is a minor misdemeanor or a municipal ordinance, regardless of penalty, if substantially equivalent

(4) Cause death of another or the unlawful termination of another's pregnancy

PENALTY

Division (A)(1), Felony, 2nd degree (2929.11 to 2929.18, 2929.31). Mandatory prison term (Division (C)). Felony, 1st degree if, at time of offense, driving under suspension imposed under Chapter 4507 or any other section; if previously convicted of this section or any traffic-related homicide, manslaughter, or assault offense; if previously convicted 3 times or more of 1547.11(A), 4511.19, 4561.15, or a combination of these statutes or a substantially equivalent municipal ordinance within the previous 6 years; or if previously convicted of a second or subsequent felony violation of 4511.19(A).

Note: Offender's driver's or commercial driver's license shall be suspended for life (4510.02(A)(1)).

Division (A)(2), Felony, 3rd degree (2929.11 to 2929.18, 2929.31). Felony, 2nd degree if, at time of offense, driving under suspension imposed under Chapter 4507. or any other section; or if previously convicted of this section or any traffic-related homicide, manslaughter, or assault offense. Mandatory prison term if previously convicted of this section or 2903.08; or, if at time of offense, driving under suspension imposed under Chapter 4510.

Note: Offender's driver's or commercial driver's license shall be suspended for a definite period of three years to life (4510.02(A)(2)).

Note: Division (A)(2)(b) applies only where signs required by 2903.081 denoting construction zone

Division (A)(3), Misdemeanor, 1st degree (2929.21 to 2929.28, 2929.31). Mandatory jail sentence of at least 15 days for misdemeanor violation of (A)(3)(b). Felony, 4th degree if, at time of offense, driving under suspension or revocation imposed under Chapter 4507. or any other section; or if previously convicted of this section or any traffic-related homicide, manslaughter, or assault offense. Mandatory prison term if previously convicted of this section or 2903.08; or if at time of offense, driving under suspension imposed under Chapter 4510.

Note: Offender's driver's or commercial driver's license shall be suspended for a definite period of one to five years (4510.02(A)(4)); definite period of suspension from two to ten years if previously convicted of traffic-related homicide, manslaughter or assault (4510.02(A)(3)).

Note: Division (A)(3)(b) applies only where signs required by 2903.081 denoting construction zone are erected.

Division (A)(4), Misdemeanor, 2nd degree (2929.21 to 2929.28, 2929.31). Misdemeanor, 1st degree if, at time of offense, driving under suspension imposed under Chapter 4507.; or if previously convicted of this section or any traffic-related homicide, manslaughter, or assault offense.

Note: Offender's driver's or commercial driver's license shall be suspended for a definite period of three months to two years (4510.02(A)(6)); definite period of suspension from one to five years if previously convicted of traffic-related homicide, manslaughter or assault (4510.02(A)(4)).

Vehicular Vandalism

See Vandalism—Vehicular

Violating Anti–Stalking Protection Order

See Protection Order—Violating Anti–Stalking Protection Order

Violating Protection Order or Consent Agreement

See Protection Order—Violating Protection Order or Consent Agreement

Violence, Domestic

See Domestic Offenses—Domestic Violence

Violence, Inciting to

See Disorderly Conduct Offenses—Inciting to Violence

Voluntary Manslaughter

See Manslaughter—Voluntary Manslaughter

Voyeurism—2907.08

ELEMENTS OF THE CRIME

Division (A):

(1) With the purpose of the offender sexually arousing or gratifying himself or herself

(2) Commit trespass or otherwise surreptitiously invade the privacy of another person

(3) In order to spy or to eavesdrop on another person

Division (B):

(1) With the purpose of the offender sexually arousing or gratifying himself or herself

(2) Commit trespass or otherwise surreptitiously invade the privacy of another person

(3) In order to photograph the other person in a state of nudity

Division (C):

(1) With the purpose of the offender sexually arousing or gratifying himself or herself

(2) Commit trespass or otherwise surreptitiously invade the privacy of another person

(3) In order to photograph the other person in a state of nudity

(4) If the other person is a minor

Division (D):

(1) With the purpose of the offender sexually arousing or gratifying himself or herself

(2) Commit trespass or otherwise surreptitiously invade the privacy of another person

(3) In order to photograph the other person in a state of nudity

(4) If the other person is a minor

(5) and

(a) the offender is parent, stepparent, guardian or custodian of the minor, or stands in loco parentis to the minor

(b) the offender has supervisory or disciplinary authority over the minor in a hospital or other institution where the minor is a patient

(c) the offender is a teacher, administrator, coach or other person in authority in a school which the minor attends (and the offender is not enrolled and does not attend that school)

(d) the offender is a teacher, administrator, coach or other person in authority in an institution of higher learning which the minor attends

(e) the offender is a caregiver, administrator or other person in authority in a child day care center or family day-care home which the minor attends

(f) or, the offender is the minor's athletic or other coach, is the minor's instructor, is the leader of a scouting troop of which the minor is a member, is a babysitter for the minor or otherwise has temporary or occasional disciplinary control over the minor

Division (E):

(1) With the purpose of viewing the body or the undergarments of another person,

(2) Secretly or surreptitiously videotape, film or photograph another person,

(3) Under or through the clothing being worn by another person

PENALTY

Violation of Division (A), Misdemeanor, 3rd degree (2929.21 to 2929.28, 2929.31)

Violation of Division (B), Misdemeanor, 2nd degree (2929.21 to 2929.28, 2929.31)

Violation of Division (C), (E), Misdemeanor, 1st degree (2929.21 to 2929.28, 2929.31)

Violation of Division (D), Felony, 5th degree (2929.11 to 2929.18, 2929.31)

Weapons—Carrying Concealed Weapon—2923.12

ELEMENTS OF THE CRIME

(1) Knowingly carry or have concealed

(2) On his or her person or concealed ready at hand

(3) Any deadly weapon or dangerous ordnance

EXCEPTION

Not applicable to officers, agents, or employees of this or any other state or United States, or law enforcement officers authorized to carry concealed weapon or dangerous ordnance, and acting within scope of duties.

DEFENSE

Carrying or controlling weapon other than dangerous ordnance, actor not otherwise prohibited by law from having weapon:

(a) Carried or kept ready at hand for defense while engaged in or going to and from lawful business occupation of such character or necessarily carried on in such manner or at such time and place to render actor particularly susceptible to criminal attack, as would justify a prudent person in going armed, or

(b) Carried or kept ready at hand for defense while engaged in lawful activity and had reasonable cause to fear criminal attack on self or family member, or home, as would justify a prudent person in going armed, or

(c) Carried or kept ready at hand for any lawful purpose in own home, or

(d) Weapon being transported in motor vehicle for lawful purpose and not on actor's person, and if weapon a firearm, was carried in compliance with 2923.16(C).

PENALTY

Misdemeanor, 1st degree (2929.21 to 2929.28, 2929.31)

Previous conviction of violation of this section, or of any offense of violence, if weapon is loaded firearm or firearm for which ammunition is ready at hand, or if weapon is dangerous ordnance, Felony, 4th degree (2929.11 to 2929.18, 2929.31)

If the weapon involved is a firearm and the violation of this section is committed at premises for which a D permit has been issued under Chapter 4303., or if offense committed aboard aircraft or with purpose to carry concealed weapon aboard regardless of weapon involved, Felony, 3rd degree (2929.11 to 2929.18, 2929.31)

Weapons—Conveyance of Items Onto Detention or Mental Health Facilities—2921.36

ELEMENTS OF THE CRIME

Division (A):

(1) Knowingly

(2) Convey or attempt to convey

(3)(a) deadly weapon or dangerous ordnance

(b) drug of abuse

(c) intoxicating liquor

(4) on to the grounds of a detention facility or an institution under the control of the department of mental health or the department of mental retardation and developmental disabilities

Division (C):

(1) Knowingly

(2) Deliver or attempt to deliver

(3)(a) deadly weapon or dangerous ordnance

(b) drug of abuse

(c) intoxicating liquor

(4) to any person confined in a detention facility or to any patient in an institution under the control of the department of mental health or the department of mental retardation and developmental disabilities

Division (D):

(1) Knowingly

(2) Deliver or attempt to deliver

(3) Cash

(4) to any person confined in a detention facility

EXCEPTION

Division (A) is not applicable if the conveyor has written authorization from the person in charge of the facility.

DEFENSES

It is an affirmative defense to Division (A) that the weapon or dangerous ordnance was being transported in a motor vehicle for any lawful purpose, that it was not on the person, and if it was a firearm that it was unloaded and being carried in a closed package or in a closed compartment reached only by leaving the vehicle.

It is an affirmative defense to Division (C) that the actor was not otherwise prohibited from delivering the item *and* the written rules of the facility authorized delivery of the item to a confined person or patient, or the actor had written authorization from the director of the facility to deliver the item to a confined person or patient.

PENALTY

Violation of Division (A) or (C) involving a drug of abuse, Felony, 3rd degree. If the defendant is an employee, prison is mandatory. (2929.11 to 2929.18, 2929.31)

Violation of Division (A) or (C) involving an intoxicating liquor, Misdemeanor, 2nd degree. (2929.21 to 2929.28, 2929.31)

Violation of Division (D), Felony, 5th degree. (2929.11 to 2929.18, 2929.31)

Weapons—Conveyance or Possession of Deadly Weapons or Dangerous Ordnance on School Premises—2923.122

ELEMENTS OF THE CRIME

(1) Knowingly

(2) Convey, attempt to convey, or possess

(3) Deadly weapon or dangerous ordnance

(4) An object that is indistinguishable from a firearm, whether or not it is capable of being fired, indicating that it is a firearm

(5) Onto school premises, into a school safety zone

EXCEPTIONS

This section does not apply to:

(1) Officers, agents, or employees of this or any other state, or of the United States, or

(2) Law enforcement officers authorized to carry deadly weapons or dangerous ordnance and acting within scope of duties, or

(3) Security officer employed by board of education or school's governing body and on duty, or

(4) Any other person with written authorization from board of education or school's governing body to convey or possess deadly weapons or dangerous ordnance onto or on school property and who is acting in accordance with authorization

(5) An item that is indistinguishable from a firearm where possessed for a legitimate purpose

A charge under Element (4) above is not applicable to

(1) premises used for home schooling or

(2) administrator, teacher or

(3) employee in the legitimate course of employment, or

(4) student using such object under direction of administrator, teacher, or employee with prior approval

PENALTY

Violation of (3) above, Felony, 5th degree (2929.11 to 2929.18, 2929.31); if prior conviction, Felony, 4th degree (2929.11 to 2929.18, 2929.31)

If offender is under 19, court shall revoke learner's permit or driver's license for a definite period of 1 to 5 years. If offender is a non-resident, court shall suspend non-resident operating privileges. (For good cause shown, court may not impose these penalties.)

Violation of (4) above (possession of an object indistinguishable from a firearm), Misdemeanor, 1st degree; if prior conviction under this section, violation is a Felony, 5th degree (2929.11 to 2929.18, 2929.31)

Weapons—Conveying, Possessing, Control of a Deadly Weapon or Dangerous Ordnance in a Courthouse—2923.123

ELEMENTS OF THE CRIME

Division (A):

(1) Knowingly

(2) Convey or attempt to convey

(3) Deadly weapon or dangerous ordnance

(4) Into a courthouse or any building in which a courtroom is located

Division (B):

(1) Knowingly

(2) Possess or have under the person's control

(3) Deadly weapon or dangerous ordnance

(4) In a courthouse or any building in which a courtroom is located

EXCEPTIONS

Section is inapplicable to a judge or magistrate unless prohibited by law from conveying into or possessing a deadly weapon or dangerous ordnance in a courthouse or building in which a courtroom is located.

Section is inapplicable to peace officer or law enforcement officer of another subdivision, state or the United States, who is authorized to carry, or required to carry as a requirement of that person's duties, or is acting within the scope of that persons official duties by carrying, a deadly weapon or dangerous ordnance in a courthouse or building in which a courtroom is located.

Section is inapplicable to one who conveys, possesses or has under control a deadly weapon or dangerous ordnance that is to be used as evidence in a pending civil or criminal action or proceeding.

Section is inapplicable to bailiff unless prohibited by law who has firearm as a requirement of his/her duties and is acting within the scope of that individual's duties.

Section is inapplicable to a prosecutor or Secret Service officer appointed by a county prosecutor who is authorized to carry deadly weapon or dangerous ordnance, who is required to carry it as part of the individual's duties, and who is acting within the scope of the duties unless the Supreme Court prohibits such conduct through the Rules of Superintendence or other rule.

PENALTY

If Division (A), Felony, 5th degree; if previously convicted under Division (A) or (B) of this section, Felony, 4th degree (2929.11 to 2929.18, 2929.31)

If Division (B), except as otherwise exempted, Felony, 5th degree; if previously convicted under Division (A) or (B) of this section, Felony, 4th degree (2929.11 to 2929.18, 2929.31)

Weapons—Discharging Firearms on or Near Prohibited Premises—2923.162

ELEMENTS OF THE CRIME

(1) Discharge of firearm

(2) (a) Upon, over, or within 100 yards of a cemetery without official permission, excepting a person who discharges a firearm while on that person's own land.

(b) On a lawn, park, pleasure ground, orchard, or other ground appurtenant to a schoolhouse, church, or inhabited dwelling, the property of another, or a charitable institution, excepting a person who discharges a firearm while on that person's own enclosure.

(c) Upon or over a public road or highway

PENALTY

Division (A)(1) or (2), Misdemeanor, 4th degree (2929.21 to 2929.28, 2929.31)

Division (A)(3), Misdemeanor, 1st degree (2929.21 to 2929.28, 2929.31). If violation created substantial risk of physical harm to person or caused serious physical harm to property, Felony, 3rd degree. If violation caused physical harm to person, Felony, 2nd degree. If violation caused serious physical harm to person, Felony, 1st degree. (2929.11 to 2929.19, 2929.31)

Weapons—Endangering Aircraft or Airport Operations—2909.08

ELEMENTS OF THE CRIME

Division (A):

(1) Knowingly

(a) Throw object at or drop object upon moving aircraft, or

(b) Shoot with bow and arrow or discharge firearm, air gun or spring-operated gun at or toward any aircraft

Division (B):

(1) Knowingly or recklessly

(2) Shoot with bow and arrow or discharge a firearm, air gun or spring-operated gun upon or over any airport operational surface

EXCEPTIONS

Division (B) does not apply to an officer, agent or employee of this or any other state or the United States or a law enforcement officer, authorized to discharge firearms and acting within the scope of the officer's, agent's, or employee's duties.

Division (B) does not apply to a person who, with the consent of the owner or operator of the airport operational surface or the authorized agent of either, is lawfully engaged in any hunting or sporting activity or is otherwise lawfully discharging a firearm.

PENALTY

If Division (A) violated, Misdemeanor, 1st degree (2929.21 to 2929.28, 2929.31)

If violation of Division (A) creates a risk of physical harm to any person, Felony, 5th degree (2929.11 to 2929.18, 2929.31)

If violation of Division (A) creates a substantial risk of physical harm to any person or if the aircraft that is the subject of the violation is occupied, Felony, 4th degree (2929.11 to 2929.18, 2929.31)

If Division (B) violated, Misdemeanor, 2nd degree (2929.21 to 2929.28, 2929.31)

If violation of Division (B) creates a risk of physical harm to any person, Felony, 5th degree (2929.11 to 2929.18, 2929.31)

If violation of Division (B) creates a substantial risk of physical harm to any person, Felony, 4th degree (2929.11 to 2929.18, 2929.31)

If violation of Division (B) occurs while hunting, violator shall additionally have hunting license or permit suspended or revoked pursuant to 1533.68.

Any bow and arrow, air gun, spring-oriented gun or firearm used in felony violation of this section shall be seized and forfeited.

Weapons—Failure to Secure Dangerous Ordnance—2923.19

ELEMENTS OF THE CRIME

(1) In acquiring, possessing, carrying, using

(2) Dangerous ordnance

(3) Negligently fail to take proper precautions

(4)(a) To secure against theft, or acquisition or use by unauthorized or incompetent person, or

(b) To insure safety of persons and property

PENALTY

Misdemeanor, 2nd degree (2929.21 to 2929.28, 2929.31)

Weapons—Having While Under Disability—2923.13

ELEMENTS OF THE CRIME

(1) Unless relieved of disability under 2923.14

(2) Knowingly acquire, have, carry, use

(3) Firearm or dangerous ordnance

(4)(a) Being fugitive from justice, or

(b) Under indictment or convicted of any felony offense of violence or adjudicated juvenile delinquent for commission of an offense that, if committed by an adult, would have been a felony offense of violence, or

(c) Under indictment for or convicted of or previously convicted of offense involving illegal possession, use, sale, administration, distribution, trafficking in drug of abuse or adjudicated juvenile delinquent for commission of an offense that, if committed by an adult, would have been an offense involving the illegal possession, use, sale, administration, distribution, or trafficking in any drug of abuse, or

(d) Drug dependent person or in danger of drug dependence or chronic alcoholic, or

(e) Adjudicated mentally incompetent

PENALTY

Felony, 5th degree (2929.11 to 2929.18, 2929.31)

If a person who has been convicted of a felony of the 1st or 2nd degree violates this section within 5 years of the date of the person's release from imprisonment or from post-release control that is imposed for the commission of a felony of the 1st or 2nd degree, Felony, 3rd degree (2929.11 to 2929.18, 2929.31)

Weapons—Illegal Manufacturing or Processing Explosives—2923.17(B)

ELEMENTS OF THE CRIME

(1) Manufacture or process at any location within Ohio

(2) An explosive

DEFENSE

This section does not apply if the person has been issued a license, certificate of registration, or permit to manufacture or process explosives from a fire official of a political subdivision of this state or from the office of the fire marshal.

PENALTY

Felony, 2nd degree (2929.11 to 2929.18, 2929.31)

Weapons—Improperly Discharging Firearm at or Into Habitation or School—2923.161

ELEMENTS OF THE CRIME

(1) Knowingly

(2) Without privilege

(3) Discharge firearm at or into:

(a) Occupied structure, as defined in 2909.01, that is permanent or temporary habitation of any individual, or

(b) A school safety zone, or

(c) Discharge a firearm within 1,000 feet of school building or premises with intent to

(1) Cause physical harm to any person in the school, school building, or at a function or activity associated with the school, or

(2) Cause panic or fear of physical harm to any person in the school, school building, or at a function or activity associated with the school; or

(3) Cause the evacuation of the school, school building, or a function or activity associated with the school

EXCEPTION

This section does not apply to any officer, agent, or employee of this or any state or United States, or to law enforcement officer who discharges firearm while acting within scope of the officer's, agent's, or employee's duties.

PENALTY

Felony, 2nd degree (2929.11 to 2929.18, 2929.31)

Weapons—Improperly Furnishing Firearms to Minor

See Juveniles—Improperly Furnishing Firearms to Minor

Weapons—Improperly Handling Firearms in Motor Vehicle—2923.16

ELEMENTS OF THE CRIME

Division (A):

(1) Knowingly discharge a firearm

(2) While in or on a motor vehicle

Division (B):

(1) Knowingly transport or have a loaded firearm in a motor vehicle

(2) In such manner that firearm is accessible to operator or any passenger without leaving the vehicle

Division (C):

(1) Knowingly transport or have firearm in motor vehicle

(2) Unless unloaded and carried:

(a) In closed package, box, or case, or

(b) In compartment only reached by leaving vehicle, or

(c) In plain sight and secured in rack or holder made for that purpose, or

(d) In plain sight with action open, or weapon stripped, or, if firearm is type on which action will not stay open or which cannot be easily stripped, in plain sight

EXCEPTIONS

This section does not apply to officers, agents, or employees of this or any state or United States or law enforcement officers authorized to carry or have loaded firearms in motor vehicles and acting within scope of duties.

See 2923.16(D)(2) and (3) for other limited exemptions pertaining to acts on the offenders' own property.

DEFENSE

Defenses (2)(a) and (b) under **Weapons—Carrying Concealed Weapon, 2923.12**, are defenses to Divisions (B) or (C) of this section.

PENALTY

If Divisions (A) or (B) violated, Misdemeanor, 1st degree (2929.21 to 2929.28, 2929.31)

If Division (C) violated, Misdemeanor, 4th degree (2929.21 to 2929.28, 2929.31)

Weapons—Possessing Deadly Weapon While Under Detention—2923.131

ELEMENTS OF THE CRIME

(1) Possession of

(2) Deadly weapon

(3) While under detention

(4) At a detention facility

PENALTY

Misdemeanor, 1st degree, if the offender was under detention as an alleged or adjudicated offender if the act for which the offender was detained would not have been a felony if committed by an adult. (2929.11 to 2929.18, 2929.31)

Felony, 1st degree, if the offense for which the person was under detention is aggravated murder or murder, regardless of whether the person under detention is held as an adult or juvenile. (2929.11 to 2929.18, 2929.31)

Felony, 2nd degree, if the most serious offense for which the person was under detention is a felony of the first degree if committed on or after 7–1–96, or an aggravated felony of the first degree if committed prior to 7–1–96. Felony, 2nd degree, if the person was under detention as an alleged or adjudicated delinquent, and the most serious act for which the offender was detained is one of those listed above in this paragraph if committed by an adult. (2929.11 to 2929.18, 2929.31)

Felony, 3rd degree, if the most serious offense for which the person was under detention is a felony of the second degree if committed on or after 7–1–96, or an aggravated felony of the second degree or a felony of the first degree if committed prior to 7–1–96. Felony, 3rd degree, if the person was under detention as an alleged or adjudicated delinquent, and the most serious act for which the offender was detained is one of those listed above in this paragraph if committed by an adult. (2929.11 to 2929.18, 2929.31)

Felony, 4th degree, if the most serious offense for which the person was under detention is a felony of the third degree committed on or after 7–1–96, or an aggravated felony of the third degree or a felony of the second degree if committed prior to 7–1–96, or a felony of the third degree if committed prior to 7–1–96 but would also be a felony of the third degree if committed on or after 7–1–96. Felony, 4th degree, if the person was under detention as an alleged or adjudicated delinquent, and the most serious act for which the offender was detained is one of those listed above in this paragraph if committed by an adult. (2929.11 to 2929.18, 2929.31)

Felony, 5th degree, if the most serious offense for which the person was under detention is a felony of the fourth or fifth degree if committed on or after 7–1–96, or is a felony of the third degree if committed prior to 7–1–96 that would be a felony of the fourth degree if committed on or after 7–1–96, or a misdemeanor or unclassified felony regardless of when the misdemeanor or unclassified felony is committed. Felony, 5th degree, if the person was under detention as an alleged or adjudicated delinquent, and the most serious act for which the offender was detained is one of those listed above in this paragraph if committed by an adult. (2929.11 to 2929.18, 2929.31)

Weapons—Possessing Firearm in Liquor Permit Premises—2923.121

ELEMENTS OF THE CRIME

(1) Possessing firearm

(2) In room in which liquor is being dispensed

(3) Premises for which a D permit has been issued under Chapter 4303.

EXCEPTIONS

(1) This section does not apply to officers, agents, or employees of this or any other state or the United States, or to law enforcement officers, authorized to carry firearms, and acting within the scope of their duties.

(2) This section does not apply to any room used for the accommodation of guests of a hotel, as defined in section 4301.01 of the Revised Code.

(3) This section does not prohibit any person who is a member of veteran's organization, as defined in 2915.01, from possessing a rifle in any room in any premises owned, leased or otherwise controlled by veteran's organization, if the rifle is not loaded with live ammunition and if person otherwise is not prohibited by law from having the rifle

(4) This section does not apply to any person possessing or displaying firearms in any room used to exhibit unloaded firearms for sale or trade in a solder's memorial established pursuant to Chapter 345., in a convention center, or in any other public meeting place, if the person is an exhibitor, trader, purchaser, or seller of firearms and is not otherwise prohibited by law from possessing, trading, purchasing, or selling firearms

DEFENSES

It is an affirmative defense to a charge under this section of illegal possession of a firearm in liquor permit premises, that the actor was not otherwise prohibited by law from having the firearm, and that any of the following apply:

The firearm was carried or kept ready at hand by the actor for defensive purposes, while the actor was engaged in or was going to or from his lawful business or occupation, which business or occupation was of such character or was necessarily carried on in such manner or at such a time or place as to render the actor particularly susceptible to criminal attack, such as would justify a prudent person in going armed.

The firearm was carried or kept ready at hand by the actor for defensive purposes, while the actor was engaged in a lawful activity, and had reasonable cause to fear a criminal attack upon the actor or a member of the actor's family, or upon the actor's home, such as would justify a prudent person in going armed.

PENALTY

Felony, 5th degree (2929.11 to 2929.18, 2929.31)

Weapons—Underage Purchase of Firearm

See Juveniles—Underage Purchase of Firearm

Weapons—Underage Purchase of Handgun—2923.211(B)

ELEMENTS OF THE CRIME

Division (A):

(1) Person under age 18

(2) Purchase or attempt to purchase

(3) Firearm

Division (B):*

(1) Person under age 21

(2) Purchase or attempt to purchase

(3) Handgun

* Note: Division B inapplicable to law enforcement officer.

PENALTY

Division (A), delinquent child

Division (B), Misdemeanor, 2nd degree (2929.21 to 2929.28, 2929.31)

Weapons—Unlawful Possession of Dangerous Ordnance—2923.17(A)

ELEMENTS OF THE CRIME

(1) Knowingly

(2) Acquire, have, carry, use

(3) Any dangerous ordnance

DEFENSES

This section does not apply to:

(1) Offender is officer, agent, employee of this or any state or United States, is member of armed forces of United States or organized militia of any state, or is a law enforcement officer, to the extent that any such person authorized to acquire, have, carry, use dangerous ordnance, and acting within scope of the person's duties.

(2)(a) Importers, manufacturers, dealers, users of explosives, destructive devices, or ammunition with license or user permit issued and in effect under federal "Organized Crime Control Act of 1970," 84 Stat. 952, 18 U.S.C. 843 or "Gun Control Act of 1968," 82 Stat. 1213, 18 U.S.C. 923, and any additions or amendments to these acts, with respect to explosives and explosive devices under 1970 Act or dangerous ordnances under 1968 Act which are lawfully acquired, possessed, carried, used under laws of Ohio and applicable federal law.

(b) Persons obtaining surplus ordnance from Secretary of Army under 70A Stat. 262 and 263, 10 U.S.C. 4684 to 4686 and any amendments, additions, or reenactments, with respect to dangerous ordnance when lawfully possessed and used for purposes specified in such sections.

(3) Owners of dangerous ordnance registered under National Firearms Registration and Transfer Record under act of October 22, 1968, 82 Stat. 1229, 26 U.S.C. 5841, and any amendments and additions or reenactments and regulations issued thereunder.

(4) Carriers, warehousemen, and others engaged in business of transporting or storing goods for hire, with respect to dangerous ordnance lawfully transported or stored in usual course of business and in compliance with Ohio, federal law.

(5) Holders of license or temporary permit issued and in effect under 2923.18 with respect to dangerous ordnance lawfully acquired, possessed, carried, or used for purposes and in manner specified in license or permit.

PENALTY

Felony, 5th degree (2929.11 to 2929.18, 2929.31)

Weapons—Unlawful Transaction in Weapons—2923.20

ELEMENTS OF THE CRIME

Division (A):

(1)(a) Recklessly

(b) Sell, lend, give, furnish firearm or dangerous ordnance to anyone prohibited by 2923.13, 2923.15, or 2923.17 from acquiring or using firearm or dangerous ordnance

(2)(a) Possess

(b) Any firearm or dangerous ordnance

(c) With purpose to dispose of it in violation of Division (A)

(3)(a) Manufacture, possess for sale, sell, furnish to anyone other than law enforcement agency for authorized use in police work

(b) Brass knuckles, cestus, billy, blackjack, sandbag, switchblade knife, springblade knife, gravity knife, or similar weapon

(4)(a) When transferring dangerous ordnance to another

(b) Negligently

(i) Fail to require transferee to exhibit such identification, license, permit showing him to be authorized to acquire dangerous ordnance pursuant to 2923.17, or

(ii) Fail to make complete record of transaction and forthwith forward a copy of record to sheriff of county or safety director or chief of police of municipality where transaction occurs

(5)(a) Knowingly

(b) Fail to report to law enforcement authorities forthwith the loss or theft of any firearm or dangerous ordnance in the person's possession or under the person's control

PENALTY

Division (A) (1) or (2), Felony, 4th degree (2929.11 to 2929.18, 2929.31)

Division (A)(3) or (4), Misdemeanor, 2nd degree (2929.21 to 2929.28, 2929.31)

Division (A)(5), Misdemeanor, 4th degree (2929.21 to 2929.28, 2929.31)

Weapons—Using Weapons While Intoxicated—2923.15

ELEMENTS OF THE CRIME

(1) While under influence of alcohol or drug of abuse

(2) Use or carry

(3) Any firearm, or dangerous ordnance.

PENALTY

Misdemeanor, 1st degree (2929.21 to 2929.28, 2929.31)

Will, Securing by Deception

See Theft-related Offenses—Securing Writing by Deception

Wiretapping

See Interception of Communications

Witness, Intimidation

See Intimidation—Intimidation of Crime Victim or Witness

Workers' Compensation Fraud

See Theft-related Offenses—Workers' Compensation Fraud

Table of Definitions

Word/Phrase	Defined in
A	
Abandoned junk motor vehicle	4513.63
Abate	3767.41(A)(3)
Abatement	3767.41(A)(3)
Abortion	2919.11
Abortion trafficking	2919.14(A)
Abuse	2903.33(B)
Abused child	2151.031
Access device	2913.46(A)(1)
Act charged	2151.26(A)(4)
Acute alcohol intoxication	2935.33(D)(2)
Adequate parental care	2151.011(B)
Adjudicated being a sexual predator	2950.01
Administer	2925.01 3719.01
Administrative release	2967.01
Administrator of a child day-care center	2151.011(B)
Admitted	5120.17(A)(5)
Adult	2151.011(B)
Adult cabaret	503.51(A)
Adulterate	2925.01(HH)
Affirmative defense	2901.05(C)
Agency	2929.28(A)(1)
Aggravated vehicular homicide	2903.06(A)
Aggravating circumstances	2929.04(A)
Aggregate value of the food stamp coupons, WIC program benefits, and electronically transferred benefits involved in the violation	2913.46(A)(1)
Aggrieved person	2933.51
Agreement for temporary custody	2151.011
Agricultural tractor	4511.01(J)
Aircraft, endangering with firearm	2909.08(A)
Air gun	2909.08(A)
Airport operational surface	2909.08(A)
Alcohol	4301.01(B)(1)
Alcohol concentration	4506.01(A)
Alleged juvenile offender	2930.01
Alley	4511.01
Alternative residential facility	2929.01
Amateur athletic organization	2915.01(DD)
Ambulance	3937.41(A)(1)
Ambulatory health facility	5101.61(A)(2)
Amidone	3719.01(P)(3)
Amusement bingo game	2915.12
Ancillary services	5120.56(A)(1)
And	Gen Prov 1.02(F)
Animal shelter	3719.01(DD) 4729.01(V)
Another	Gen Prov 1.02(B) 2941.09
Another's unborn	2903.09(B)
Anything of value	Gen Prov 1.03
Appellate court	2953.07(B)
Applicant	2151.86(G)(1) 3301.32(G)(1) 3301.541(G)(1) 3701.881(A)(1) 5126.28(A)(1) 5153.111(G)(1)
Appropriate court	2963.31
Archival institution	2935.041(F)(1)
Arterial street	4511.01
Assets	2929.28(A)(2)
At retail	4301.01(B)(15)
Aural transfer	2933.51
Authority	5149.01(A)
Authorized provider	2151.011(B)
Automatic firearm	2923.11(E)
Automobile	4513.263(A)(1)
B	
Babysitting care	2151.011(B) 2907.08(D)(3)
Bad time	2929.01
Bail	2743.70(D)(2) 2919.271(G)(1)
Bail forfeiture	2953.31(C)
Bail forfeiture, agreed	2953.31(C)
Ballistic knife	2923.11
Basic probation supervision	2929.01
Beer	4301.01(B)(2)

Word/Phrase	Defined in
Beneficial interest	2923.31(A) 2933.71(C)
Bet	2915.01
Bicycle	4511.01
Bicycle, motorized	4511.01
Bingo	2915.01
Bingo, charitable	2915.01
Bingo game, amusement	2915.12
Bingo game operator	2915.01
Bingo session	2915.01
Biological agent	2917.31(E)(4) 2917.33
Blind	955.011(B)(2)
Blind pedestrian	4511.47
Blind person	4511.47
Body cavity search	2933.32(A)(1) 5120.421(A)(1)
Bond	Gen Prov 1.02(D)
Booby trap	3743.01(B)
Bookmaking	2915.01
Bookmaking, facilitate	2915.02(B)
Building	341.34(A) 753.21(A) 3767.41(A)(1)
Bulk amount	2925.01
Burn injury	2921.22(E)(1)
Bus	4511.01 4511.78(A)(2)
Bus, commercial	4511.21(C)(2) 4511.21(N)(2)
Business district	4511.01
Business of private investigation	4749.01
Business of security services	4749.01
Bus, noncommercial	4511.21(N)(3)
Bus, school	4511.01
C	
Cabaret, adult	503.51(A)
Cable operator	2913.04(F)(1)
Cable service	2913.04(F)(2)
Cable television service	2913.01
Caller	2917.21(E)(2)
Care facility	2903.33(A)
Caretaker	2903.10(B)
Case	2930.01
Category I	4729.54(A)(1)
Category II	4729.54(A)(2)
Category III	4729.54(A)(3)
Category I, II, and III licenses of terminal distributors of dangerous drugs	4729.54(A)
Category III license	3719.01(FF)
Category one offense	2151.26(A)(1)
Category two offense	2151.26(A)(2)
Cemetery	2909.05(F)(1) 2927.11(C)
Certified electronic monitoring device	2929.23(A)(2)
Certified electronic monitoring system	2929.23(A)(6)
Certified family foster home	2151.011(B)(5)
Certified grievance committee	2925.01
Certified mail	Gen Prov 1.02(G)
Certified type B family day-care home	2151.011(B)(7)
Charitable bingo game	2915.01
Charitable organization	2915.01
Chautauqua assembly	4511.90
Chemical dependency	2151.3514(A)(2)
Chief legal officer	2921.42(G)(2)
Child	Gen Prov 1.59(A) 2151.011(B)(6)(a)
Child, abused	2151.031
Child day camp	2151.011
Child day-care	2151.011
Child day-care center	2151.011
Child day-care provider	2151.011
Child, delinquent	2151.02
Child, dependent	2151.04
Child, missing	2901.30(A)(3)
Child, neglected	2151.03
Children, missing	2901.30(A)(3)
Children's hospital	2151.86(G)(3)
Child support order	3113.99(A)
Child, unruly	2151.022
Child-victim oriented offense	2950.01
Child-victim predator	2950.01
Chiropractor	4503.44(A)(4)
Cider	4301.01(B)(21)
Cigarette load	3743.01(C)
Citation	4511.95 Art II(B)(1)
Citizens reward program	Gen Prov 9.92(A)
Claim, workers' compensation fraud	2913.48(E)(4)
Class A license	4749.01
Class B license	4749.01

Word/Phrase	Defined in
Crack cocaine	2925.01
Create a substantial risk of physical harm to any person	2909.01
Credit card	2913.01
Credit, collect extension of	2905.21
Credit, extortionate extension of	2905.21
Creditor	2905.21
Credit, to extend	2905.21
Crime	2930.01(A)
Crime victims recovery fund	2969.11(A)
Criminal conduct	2923.41(C)
Criminal gang	2923.41(A)
Criminal records check	109.572(E)(1)
Criminal usury	2905.21(H)
Crisis intervention training	109.71(C)
Crosswalk	4511.01 4511.21(B)(1)(d)
Culpability	2901.22
Cultivate	2925.01
Cumulative sales price	2913.34(F)(2)
Curfew	2929.01
Custodial agency	2930.01
Custodian	2151.011(B)

D

Word/Phrase	Defined in
Dangerous drug	2925.01 3719.01(D) 4729.01(F)
Dangerous offender	2935.36(E)(2)
Dangerous ordnance	2923.11
Data	2913.01 2913.47(A)(1)
Day reporting	2929.01
Deadly force	2901.01(A)(2)
Deadly weapon	2923.11(A) 2935.03(G)(3)
Dealer engaged in the business of leasing motor vehicles	4503.20(A)(1)
Debtor	2905.21(C)
Deception	2913.01
Deceptive	2913.47(A)(2)
Defendant	2919.26(I)(1) 2930.01
Defense	2930.01
Defense, affirmative	2901.05(C)
Deferred compensation program participant	2907.15(A)(3)
Defraud	2913.01(B)
Delinquency proceeding	2930.01(K)
Delinquent act specified	2930.01
Delinquent child	2152.02
Department of mental health special police officer	2935.03(G)(1)
Department of mental retardation and developmental disabilities special police officer	2935.03(G)(2)
Dependent child	2151.04
Deprive	2913.01(C)
Designated amount	3517.20(A)(1)(j)
Designated homicide, assault, or kidnapping offense	2971.01(B)
Designated offense	2933.51(I)
Detention	2151.011(B)(12) 2921.01
Detention facility	2921.01 5120.56(A)(3)
Developmental disability	2151.011(B)(13) 5123.01
Dilation and evacuation procedure	2919.151(A)
Directional signals	4513.261
Disabled adult	2913.01
Discharge	2305.39(A)(2)
Disciplinary counsel	2925.01(T)
Dispense	2925.01(A) 3719.01(E)
Disqualification	4506.01(H)
Distribute	2925.01 3719.01(F)
Distributor	4301.01(B)(10) 4503.312(C)
DNA	109.573(A)
DNA analysis	109.573(A)
DNA database	109.573(A)
DNA record	109.573(A)
DNA specimen	109.573(A)
Dog, handicapped assistance	2921.321(E)(4)
Dog, police	2921.321(E)(2)
Domestic violence	3113.31(A)(1)
Domestic violence shelter for victims of	2151.011(B)(45)
Drive	4506.01
Driver	4506.01
Driver or operator	4511.01
Driver's license	4506.01 4507.01

Word/Phrase	Defined in
	4511.95
	Art II(B)(4)
Driveway	4511.01
Drug	4729.01(E)
Drug abuse offense	2925.01
Drug abuse offense felony	2925.01
Drug and alcohol use monitoring	2929.01
Drug, dangerous	2925.01
	3719.01(D)
	4729.01(F)
Drug dependent person	2925.01
	3719.011(B)
Drug enforcement administration	3719.01(B)
Drug of abuse	2925.01
	3719.011(A)
	4506.01(L)
Drug paraphernalia	2925.14(A)
Drug-related offense	309.08(C)
Drug, sample	3719.31
Drug treatment program	2929.01
E	
Economic harm	2917.21(E)(1)
	2917.31(E)(1)
	2917.32(D)
Economic loss	2929.01
Educational organization	2915.01
Education or training	2929.01
Elderly person	2913.01
Electronically monitored house arrest	2929.23(A)(4)
Electronically monitored house detention	2151.355(J)(1)(b)
	2929.23(A)(7)
Electronically transferred benefit	2913.46(A)(1)
Electronic communication	2933.51
Electronic communication service	2933.51
Electronic communications system	2933.51
Electronic fund transfer	2913.01
Electronic monitoring device	2929.23(A)(1)
Electronic monitoring system	2929.23(A)(5)
Electronic storage	2933.51
Eligible alcohol and drug addiction program	2925.03(H)(5)(b)
Eligible offender	2929.20(A)
	2929.23(A)(3)
Emancipated	2919.121(A)
Emergency medical services person	2903.211(D)(3)
Emergency facility	2909.04(C)(3)
Emergency facility personnel	2909.04(C)(2)
Emergency personnel	2909.01
Emergency vehicle	3937.41(A)(2)
	4511.01
Employee	4749.01(I)
Employee of a local correctional facility	2903.13(C)(5)(e)
Employer	4506.01
Employer, workers' compensation fraud	2913.48(E)(6)
Employment workers' compensation fraud	2913.48(E)(5)
Enclosed shopping center	4301.01(B)(17)
Endorsement	4506.01(N)
Enterprise	2923.31(C)
Entertainment area, restricted	2917.40(A)(2)
Entertainment performance, live	2917.40(A)(1)
Examiner	2919.271(G)(2)
	2945.37(A)(2)
Executive authority	2963.01
Explosive device	2923.11
Explosives	2923.11
	4511.01
Expressway	4511.01
Extortionate extension of credit	2905.21
Extortionate means	2905.21
F	
Facilitate bookmaking	2915.02(B)
Facilitate scheme or game of chance	2915.02(B)
Facility	2917.40(A)(4)
Fair market value	2913.61(D)(3)
False, workers' compensation fraud	2913.48(E)(1)
Falsification; material	2921.11
Family foster home	2151.011(B)
Family, immediate	2905.21(I)
Family or household member	2903.214(A)(3)
	2919.25(E)(1)
	2919.271(G)(3)

Word/Phrase	Defined in
Health care provider	2317.02(B)(4)(b)
Health care worker	2929.04(C)(5)
Highway	2935.03(G)(5) 3743.01(H) 4511.01(BB)
Highway, controlled-access	4511.01
Highway, laned	4511.01
Highway, state	4511.01
Highway, through	4511.01
Highway, unimproved	4511.21(K)(1)
Hoax weapon of mass destruction	2917.33(E)(1)
Home health agency	5101.61(A)(5)
Home health service	5101.61(A)(6)
Home jurisdiction	4511.95 Art II(B)(5)
Horse, police	2921.321(E)(2)
Hospital	2108.01(D) 3719.01(J) 3727.01
Hotel	4301.01(B)(11)
House arrest	2929.01
Hypodermic	2925.01 3719.01(K)

I

Word/Phrase	Defined in
Identification card	2913.31(B)(2) 4507.01(A)
Ignition interlock device	4511.83(A)(1)
Immediate family	2905.21(I)
Impersonate	2921.51(A)(3)
Imprisoned	Gen Prov 1.05
Inappropriate use of a physical or chemical restraint, medication or isolation	2903.33(D)
Incendiary device	2923.11(I)
Indigent	120.51(B)
Infectious agent	2917.47
Information	2901.30(A)(1)
Information service	2913.01
In-home aide	2151.011(B)
Inmate	5120.50(B)(4)
Inmate patient	5120.17(A)(4)
Innocent person	2923.31(D) 2933.71(E)
Insane	2949.28(A)
Insanity	2945.391
Institution	5120.50(B)(5)
Institution of higher education	2907.03(C) 2907.08(F)(1)
Insurer	2913.47(A)(3)
Intellectual property record	149.43(A)(5)
Intensive probation supervision	2929.01
Intercept	2933.51
Interception device	2933.51
Interception warrant	2933.51
Interested party	3767.41(A)(4) 4511.195(A)(4)
Internal Revenue Code	2915.01
Intersection	4511.01
Intersection, stop	4511.01
Interstate system	2935.03(G)(6) 4511.21(N)(1)
Intoxicating liquor	4301.01(A)(1)
Intoxication, voluntary	2917.11(D)
Investigative officer	2933.51(E)
Investigatory stop	311.31(F)(1) 505.67(F)(1) 737.40(F)(1)
Investigatory work product	2953.321(A)
In writing	Gen Prov 1.59(J)
Isoamidone	3719.01(P)(4)
Isomer	3719.01(L)
Isonipecaine	3719.01(P)(2)
Issuing jurisdiction	4511.95 Art II(B)(6)
Itemized statement	2929.28(A)(3)

J

Word/Phrase	Defined in
Jail	2929.01
Journalist	2933.51(M)
Judge	2931.01
Judge of a common pleas court	2933.51(W)
Junk motor vehicle	4513.65
Jurisdiction	4511.95 Art II(B)(7)
Juvenile	2907.01 2923.41(D) 2925.01
Juvenile court	2151.011(A)(1)
Juvenile, harmful to	2907.01(E)
Juvenile judge	2151.011(A)(2)
Juvenile offender, alleged	2930.01(P)
Juvenile-related forfeiture order	2933.44(A)

Word/Phrase	Defined in
Juvenile traffic offender	2151.021
K	
Ketobemidone	3719.01(P)(5)
Kinship caregiver	5101.85
Knowingly	2901.22(B)
L	
Laboratory	3719.01(M)
Laboratory services	5120.135(A)
Lacks the capacity to consent	2913.73
Land	2911.21(E)
Land use infraction	765.01(A)
Laned highway	4511.01(GG)
Law enforcement agency	109.573(A)(8) 2923.32(G) 2923.34(N) 2923.35(E) 2923.41(E) 2925.03(F)(3)(a) 2925.42(B)(5)(c)(i) 2933.41(I)
Law enforcement officer	109.79(B)(1) 311.31(F)(2) 505.67(F)(2) 737.40(F)(2) 765.01(B) 2901.01(A) 2933.231(A)(1) 3937.41(A)(4)
Lawfully issued	2921.52(A)(1)
Legal aid society	120.51(A)
Legal custody	2151.011(B)
Legislative candidate	3517.20(A)(1)(e)
Licensed building	3743.01(CC)
Licensed exhibitor of fireworks	3743.01(I)
Licensed health professional authorized to prescribe drugs	2925.01 4729.01(I)
Licensed manufacturer of fireworks	3743.01(J)
Licensed premises	3743.01(BB)
Licensed wholesaler of fireworks	3743.01(K)
License plates, special handicapped	4511.69(J)(3)
License violation report	2929.01
Lien	4505.01(A)(1)
Limited political action committee	3517.20(A)(1)(h)
Limited political contributing entity	3517.20(A)(1)(i)
Liquor	4301.01(A)(1)
List of licensed exhibitors	3743.01
List of licensed manufacturers	3743.01
List of licensed wholesalers	3743.01
Live entertainment performance	2917.40(A)(1)
Local authorities	4511.01
Local candidate	3517.20(A)(1)(f)
Local correctional facility	2903.13(C)(5)(d)
Low-alcohol beverage	4301.01(B)(20)
L.S.D.	2925.01
M	
Magistrate	2931.01(A) 2935.01(A)
Mail delivery, rural	4511.01
Major drug offender	2929.01
Major part	2913.82
Malt beverages	4301.01(B)(2)
Malt liquor	4301.01(B)(2)
Manage	5120.102(H)
Management	5120.102(H)
Mandatory prison term	2929.01
Mandatory term of local incarceration	2929.01
Manufacture	2925.01 4301.01(B)(8)
Manufacturer	2925.01(A) 3719.01(N) 4301.01(B)(9)
Manufacturer of dangerous drugs	4729.01(P)
Manufacturing fireworks	3743.01(O)
Marihuana	2925.01 3719.01(O)
Mass transit system	4511.78(A)(1)
Material	2907.01 2919.22(D)(4)(a) 5120.425(B)
Material (Pandering)	2907.01
Material support or resources (terrorism)	2909.21(B)
Medicaid fraud offense	2933.71(A)
Medical assistance program	2913.40(A)(2)
Medical emergency	2919.16(F)

Word/Phrase	Defined in
Medical record	149.43(A)(3)
Member of the family of an offender	2969.01
Member of the victim's family	2930.01(D)
Mental distress menacing by stalking	2903.211(D)(2)
Mental health client or patient	2907.01 2305.51
Mental health professional	2907.01(O) 2305.115
Mental illness	2151.011(B) 5120.17(A)(1)
Mental injury	2151.011(B)
Mentally ill person subject to hospitalization	5120.17(A)(2)
Mentally ill person subject to hospitalization by court order	2151.011(B)
Mentally retarded person	2151.011(B) 5123.01
Minor	2901.30(A)(2) 2907.01
Minor drug possession offense	2923.01(M)(2) 2925.01
Missing child	2901.30(A)(3)
Missing children	109.71(D) 2901.30(A)(3)
Mitigating circumstances	2929.04(B)
Mixed beverages	4301.01(B)(4)
Mobility impaired person	955.011(B)(1)
Monitored time	2929.01 2967.28(A)(1)
Motorcycle	4511.01
Motorist	4511.95 Art II(B)(8)
Motorized bicycle	4511.01
Motorized bicycle license	4507.01
Motorized wheelchair	4511.01
Motor vehicle	4501.01 4505.01(A)(2) 4506.01(S) 4511.01(B)
Motor vehicle accident	3937.41(A)(5)
Motor vehicle, aggravated vehicular homicide	2903.06(A)
Motor vehicle, emergency vehicle	4511.01
Motor vehicle, moving violation	2743.70(D)(1)
Motor vehicle, prima-facie lawful speed	4511.21(B)
Motor vehicle, public safety vehicle	4511.01
Multicounty department of probation	321.44(D)(2) 2951.021(A)(1)
Municipal OMVI offense	4511.195(A)(3)
Museum	2935.041(F)(2)
Multi-unit building	2950.01
Mutual aid group	2305.232(D)(2)
N	
Narcotic drugs	3719.01(P)
Navigable waters	3743.01(P)
Neglect	2903.33(C)(2)
Neglected child	2151.03
Negligently	2901.22(D)
Neighbor	3767.41(A)(5)
Newly elected sheriff	311.01(H)(2)
Night club	4301.01(B)(14)
No bill	2953.51(A)
No contest	2937.07
Noncommercial bus	4511.21(N)(3)
Nonconsensual entry, statutory precondition for	2933.231(A)(3)
Nonprofit medical organization	2915.01
Nonprofit organization	4303.201(A)(2)
Nonsecure care, supervision, or training	2151.011(B)
Nonsecured status	2945.37(A)(3)
Not guilty by reason of insanity	2901.01(A) 2945.391
Novelties and trick noisemakers	3743.01(Q)
Nudity	503.51(B) 2907.01
Nudity oriented matter	2919.22(D)(4)(b)
Nuisance	3767.01(C)
O	
1.3G fireworks	3743.01(D)(1)
1.4G fireworks	3743.01(D)(2)
Oath	Gen Prov 1.59(B)
Object that is indistinguishable from a firearm	2923.122(G)
Obligor	3113.99(B)

Word/Phrase	Defined in
Obscene	2907.01
Occupant restraining device	4513.263(A)(2)
Occupied structure	2909.01
Offender	2929.01 2929.28(A)(4) 5120.56(A)(4)
Offender, recovery of profits	2969.01(A)
Offender with restricted driving privileges	4511.83(A)(2)
Offense	2935.01(D)
Offense of violence	2901.01
Official proceeding	2921.01(D)
Official records	2953.51(D)
Official written order	2925.01(A) 3719.01(Q)
Of unsound mind	Gen Prov 1.02(C)
Oil	2305.39(A)(5)
Operate	5120.102(H)
Operator	4511.01
Opiate	3719.01
Opium poppy	3719.01
Or	Gen Prov 1.02(F)
Oral communication	2933.51(B)
Organization	2151.011(B)(22) 2901.23(D) 4503.44(A)(2)
Others	2941.09
Out-of-home care	2151.011(B)
Out-of-home care child abuse	2151.011(B)
Out-of-home care child neglect	2151.011(B)
Out-of-service order	4506.01(T) 4506.25(A)(2)
Owner	2913.01(D) 4509.101(I) 4511.211(E)(1)

P

Word/Phrase	Defined in
Paraphernalia drug	2925.14(A)
Pardon	2967.01(B)
Pardon, unconditional	2967.04(B)
Parent	3109.09(A)
Parole	2967.01
Parolee	2967.01
Parole violator	2967.01
Partial birth procedure	2919.151(A)(3)
Participant	2915.01
Part-time child day-care center	2151.011(B)
Party official	2921.01
Party poppers	3743.01(R)
Passenger	4513.263(A)(3)
Pattern of conduct, menacing by stalking	2903.211(D)(1)
Pattern of corrupt activity	2923.31(E)
Pattern of criminal gang activity	2923.41(B)
Payment instrument (terrorism)	2909.21(C)
Peace officer	109.71(A) 2921.51(A)(1) 2935.01(B) 3719.141(H)
Peace officer of department of natural resources	2935.03(G)(7)
Peace officer residential and familial information	149.43(A)(7)
Pecuniary value	2923.31(F)
Pedestrian	4511.01
Pen register	2933.51
Performance	2907.01
Permanent custody	2151.011(B)
Permanent surrender	2151.011(B)
Person	Gen Prov 1.59(C) 2901.01 2917.40(A)(5) 2923.31(G) 2925.01 2933.51(K) 3719.01(T) 3767.01(B) 4301.01(B)(7) 4511.01(W) 4729.01(S) 4729.54(A)(5)
Personal identifying information	2913.49(A)
Personal property	2923.31(H) 2933.71(F)
Personal recognizance	4511.95 Art II(B)(9)
Person, elderly	2913.01
Person in danger of becoming a drug dependent person	3719.011(C)
Person living as a spouse	2919.25(E)(2) 3113.31(A)(4)
Person responsible for a child's care in out-of-home care	2151.011(B)(29) 2151.86(G)(2)

Word/Phrase	Defined in
Person with a disability that limits or impairs the ability to walk	4503.44(A)(1)
Pharmacist	2925.01
	3719.01(U)
Pharmacist's care	4729.01(B)
Pharmacy	2925.01
	4301.01(B)(16)
	4729.01(A)
Pharmacy practice of	4729.01(B)
Physical harm	2921.321(E)(1)
Physical harm to persons	2901.01(A)
Physical harm to property	2901.01(A)
Physically impaired	2151.011(B)
Physician	2305.11(D)(2)
	4503.44(A)(3)
Place	3767.01(A)
Placement for adoption	2151.011(B)
Placement in foster care	2151.011(B)
Planned permanent living arrangement	2151.011(B)
Poison	3719.01
Pole trailer	4511.01
Police dog	2921.321(E)(2)
Police horse	2921.321(E)(2)
Policeman, private	2921.51(A)(2)
Police officer	4511.01
	4511.95
	Art II(B)(10)
Policy	2913.47(A)(4)
Political publication for or against a candidate	3517.20(A)(1)(a)
Political publication for or against an issue	3517.20(A)(1)(b)
Political subdivision	2909.01(D)
	2921.421(A)(2)
	2921.52(A)(3)
Poppy straw	3719.01(X)
Population	Gen Prov 1.59(D)
Possess	2925.01
Possession	2925.01
Post-release control	2967.01
Post-release control sanction	2967.01
Pregnant	2919.16
Premature infant	2919.16
Premises	2911.21(E)
Prescriber	4729.01(I)
Prescription	2925.01
	4729.01(H)
Presumption for a prison term	2925.01
Presumptive registration—exempt sexually oriented offense	2950.01
Price information	4729.01(N)
Prima-facie evidence of value	2913.61(E)
Prima-facie lawful speeds	4511.21
Prison	2929.01
Prisoner	2967.01
Prison term	2929.01
Private child placing agency	2151.011(A)
Private investigator	4749.01(A)
Private noncustodial agency	2151.011(A)
Private, nonprofit organization	5120.102(A)
Private policeman	2921.51(A)(2)
Private residential area containing twenty or more dwelling units	4511.211(E)(2)
Private residential property	4513.60(A)(3)
Private road or driveway	4511.01
Privilege	2901.01(A)
Probation	2151.011(B)
Probation agency	2951.021(A)(2)
Probationary license	4507.01(A)
Probationary motorized bicycle license	4507.01(A)
Processing of fireworks	3743.01(S)
Professional license	2925.01
Professionally licensed person	2925.01
Prohibited inflammatory material	5120.425(C)
Promote to the public	4729.01(R)
Proof beyond reasonable doubt	2901.05(D)
Property	Gen Prov 1.59(E)
	2901.01(A)
	2923.41(H)
	2925.41(B)
Prosecuting attorney	2971.01(E)
Prosecution	2930.01(N)
Prosecutor	2919.271(G)(4)
	2925.42(B)(5)(c)(ii)
	2930.01(E)
	2933.231(A)(2)
	2935.01(C)
	2945.37(A)(1)
	2953.31(B)
Prostitute	2907.01
Protection order issued by court of another state	2919.27(D)

Word/Phrase	Defined in
Protective supervision	2151.011(B)
Provider	2913.40(A)(3)
Provider agreement	2913.40(A)(4)
Psychiatric hospital	5120.17(A)(3)
Psychiatrist	2151.011(B) 2919.271(G)(5)
Psychologist	2151.011(B)
Public agency	2930.01(F)
Publication review committee	5120.425(D)
Public contract	2921.42(G)(1)
Public nuisance	3767.41(A)(2)
Public official	2921.01 2930.01
Public political advertising	3517.20(A)(1)(c)
Public premises	2925.01(II)
Public record	149.43(A)(1)
Public retirement system	2907.15(A)(1)
Public safety vehicle	4511.01
Public servant	2921.01
Public transportation system	2917.41(H)
Purposely	2901.22(A)

Q

Word/Phrase	Defined in
Qualification date	311.01(H)(1)

R

Word/Phrase	Defined in
Railroad	3743.01(T) 4511.01(P)
Railroad sign or signal	4511.01
Railroad train	4511.01
Readily accessible to the general public	2933.51(R)
Real property	2923.31(J) 2933.71(G)
Reasonable doubt	2901.05(D)
Receiving state	5120.50(B)(3)
Recipient	2913.40(A)(5)
Reciprocal fire protection agreement	2305.233(B)
Recklessly	2901.22(C)
Reckless operation	2903.06
Records	2913.40(A)(6)
Records, workers' compensation fraud	2913.48(E)(9)
Registered mail	Gen Prov 1.02(G)
Registered trademark or service mark	2913.34(F)(3)
Registration—exempt sexually oriented offense	2950.01
Registry number	3719.01
Relatives of missing persons database	109.573(A)(7)
Releasee	2967.01
Religious organization	2915.01
Removable windshield placard	4511.69(J)(3)
Remuneration, workers' compensation fraud	2913.48(E)(7)
Rented property	2913.01
Repayment	2905.21(D)
Repeat offender	2935.36(E)(1)
Repeat violent offender	2929.01
Representation	2913.40(A)(1)
Reprieve	2967.01
Residence	4506.01(U)
Residence district	4511.01
Resident	4507.01(A)
Residential camp	2151.011(B)
Residential care facility	2151.011(B)
Residential facility	2151.011(B)
Residential premises	2950.01
Residential property private	4513.60(A)(3)
Residential subdivision	4511.21(K)(5)(b)
Residential unit	2950.01
Residual parental rights, privileges, and responsibilities	2151.011(B)
Resort area	4303.183
Response costs (terrorism)	2909.21(D)
Restaurant	4301.01(B)(12)
Restricted entertainment area	2917.40(A)(2)
Restricted license	4507.01(A)
Retail sale	3743.01(U) 4729.01
Retail seller	4729.01
Revocation	4507.012
Ridesharing arrangement	4511.01
Right of way	4511.01
Right to trial by jury	2945.17
Risk	2901.01(A)
Risk, substantial	2901.01(A)
Roadway	4511.01
Route, state	4511.01
Rule	Gen Prov 1.59(F)
Rural mail delivery vehicle	4511.01

Word/Phrase	Defined in
S	
Safety device	2909.07(B)
Safety glass	4513.26
Safety zone	4511.01
Sale	2925.01(A) 3719.01 4301.01(A)(2) 4729.01
Sale at retail	4729.01
Sale at wholesale	4729.01
Sample drug	2925.01
Sanction	2929.01
Sawed-off firearm	2923.11
Schedule I to V	2925.01(A) 3719.01(BB) 4729.54(A)(6)
Scheme of chance	2915.01
Scheme or game of chance conducted for profit	2915.01
School	2901.01(C)(2) 2917.31(D)(2) 2925.01 4511.21(B)(1)(b)
School activity	2901.01(C)(3)
School building	2901.01(C)(2) 2925.01
School bus	2901.01(C)(4) 4511.01 4511.75(F)(2)
School premises	2901.01(C)(2) 2925.01
School safety zone	2901.01(C)(1)
School teacher or administrator	2903.13(C)(5)(f)
School zone	4511.21(B)(1)(c)
Seal a record	2151.358(A)
Sealed container	4301.01(B)(6)
Search of body cavity	2933.32(A)(1)
Search, strip	2933.32(A)(2)
Seat safety belt	4513.262
Secure correctional facility	2151.011(B)(42)
Security guard provider	4749.01(C)
Security personnel	2915.01
Self-insuring employer workers' compensation fraud	2913.48(E)(6)
Sell	4301.01(A)(2) 4729.01(J)
Semi-automatic firearm	2923.11(D)
Semitrailer	4511.01
Sending state	5120.50(B)(2)
Senior citizen's organization	2915.01(Q)
Senior service provider	5101.61(A)(1)
Sentence	2929.01
Serious physical harm	2909.05(F)(2) 2921.321(E)(3)
Serious physical harm to persons	2901.01
Serious physical harm to property	2901.01
Serious risk of the substantial and irreversible impairment of a major bodily function	2919.16(J)
Serious traffic violation	4506.01(W)
Service organization	2915.01(O)
Services	2913.01(E)
Services, workers' compensation fraud	2913.48(E)(3)
Sex offender, habitual	2950.01
Sex offense, nudity	2907.01
Sex offense, nudity oriented matter	2919.22(D)(4)(b)
Sex offense, performance	2907.01 2919.22(D)(4)(a)
Sexual activity	2151.011(B) 2907.01(C) 2919.22(D)(4)(a)
Sexual conduct	2907.01
Sexual contact	2907.01
Sexual excitement	2907.01(G)
Sexually oriented matter	2919.22(D)(4)(c)
Sexually oriented offense	2950.01
Sexually violent offense	2971.01
Sexually violent predator	2971.01
Sexually violent predator specification	2971.01
Sexual motivation	2971.01
Sexual motivation specification	2971.01
Sexual predator	2950.01
Sham legal process	2921.52(A)(4)
Shelter	2151.011(B)
Shelter for victims of domestic violence	2151.011(B)
Sidewalk	4511.01
Signals, directional	4513.261
Slug	2913.01
Smoke device	3743.01
Snake or glow worm	3743.01
Snapper	3743.01
Special handicapped license plates	4511.69(J)(3)
Special need	2933.51(L)

Word/Phrase	Defined in
Specified delinquent act	2930.01(O)
Specified geographical notification area	2950.11(A)
Specified offense (terrorism)	2909.21(E)
Speeding	2903.06
Spirituous liquor	4301.01(B)(5)
Spouse	2907.01
Spring-operated gun	2909.08(A)(3)
Stalking, pattern of conduct	2903.211(D)(1)
Standard pharmaceutical reference manual	2925.01
Standard time	Gen Prov 1.04
State	Gen Prov 1.59(G)
	2909.01(D)
	2921.52(A)(2)
	2935.29(B)
	2939.25(B)
	2963.01(C)
	4506.01(X)
	5120.50(B)(1)
State agency	5120.102(C)
State correctional institution	2967.01(A)
Stated prison term	2929.01
State highway	4511.01
Statement	2913.47(A)(5)
Statement or representation	2913.40(A)(1)
Statement, workers' compensation fraud	2913.48(E)(8)
State route	4511.01
Statutory precondition for nonconsensual entry	2933.231(A)(3)
Stop intersection	4511.01
Stop, investigatory	311.31(F)(1)
	505.67(F)(1)
	737.40(F)(1)
Street	2935.03(G)(5)
	4511.01
Street, arterial	4511.01
Streetcar	4511.01
Strip search	2933.32(A)(2)
	5120.421(A)(1)
Structure	341.34(A)
	753.21(A)
Subdivision, commercial	4511.21(K)(5)(a)
Subdivision, residential	4511.21(K)(5)(b)
Substantial risk	2901.01(A)
Such other person's unborn	2903.09(B)
Summons	2939.25(C)
Supervised release	2950.01
Supervision fees	2949.111(A)(2)
Suspension	4507.012
Swear	Gen Prov 1.59(B)
T	
Tamper	4933.18(B)(2)
Tank vehicle	4506.01(Y)
Telecommunication	2913.01
Telecommunications device	2913.01
Telecommunications device, counterfeit	2913.01
Telecommunications service	2913.01
Temporary custody	2151.011(B)
Temporary residence	4506.01(V)
Temporary resident	4507.01(A)
Tenant	3767.41(A)(6)
Terminal distributor of dangerous drugs	3719.01
	4729.01(Q)
Terms of the citation	4511.95
	Art II(B)(11)
Terrorism	2909.21
Theft offense	2913.01
Threat	2905.11
	2905.12(E)
Through highway	4511.01
Thruway	4511.01
To extend credit	2905.21(A)
To issue	3517.20(A)(1)(k)
Tort action	4513.263(A)(7)
Total value of any electronically transferred benefit or other access device	2913.46(A)(1)
To use gross receipts for a charitable purpose	2915.01
Township law enforcement agencies	2933.41(I)
Toxin	2917.33(E)(3)
	2927.24(A)(5)
Trackless trolley	4511.01
Tractor, agricultural	4511.01
Tractor, commercial	4511.01
Traffic	4511.01
Traffic control device	4511.18
Traffic control devices	4511.01
Traffic control signal	4511.01
Traffic offender, juvenile	2151.021
Traffic-related homicide, manslaughter, or assault offense	2903.06(D)(1)(b)
Trailer	4511.01
Trailer, pole	4511.01
Trailer, semitrailer	4511.01

Word/Phrase	Defined in
Wire communication	2933.51(A)
Wire sparkler	3743.01(Z)
Witness	2939.25(A)
Workers' compensation benefits	2913.48(E)(10)
Writing	2913.01
Written	Gen Prov 1.59(J)

Y

Word/Phrase	Defined in
Youth athletic organization	2915.01
Youth athletic park organization	2915.01

Z

Word/Phrase	Defined in
Zip-gun	2923.11

THE CONSTITUTION OF THE UNITED STATES

Effective March 4, 1789
With All Amendments to December 31, 2004

PREAMBLE

WE THE PEOPLE of the United States, in Order to form a more perfect Union, establish Justice, insure domestic Tranquility, provide for the common defence, promote the general Welfare, and secure the Blessings of Liberty to ourselves and our Posterity, do ordain and establish this CONSTITUTION for the United States of America.

ARTICLE I

Section. 1. All legislative Powers herein granted shall be vested in a Congress of the United States, which shall consist of a Senate and House of Representatives.

Section. 2. The House of Representatives shall be composed of Members chosen every second Year by the People of the several States, and the Electors in each State shall have the Qualifications requisite for Electors of the most numerous Branch of the State Legislature.

No Person shall be a Representative who shall not have attained to the Age of twenty five Years, and been seven Years a Citizen of the United States, and who shall not, when elected, be an Inhabitant of that State in which he shall be chosen.

[Representatives and direct Taxes shall be apportioned among the several States which may be included within this Union, according to their respective Numbers, which shall be determined by adding to the whole Number of free Persons, including those bound to Service for a Term of Years, and excluding Indians not taxed, three fifths of all other Persons.] [1] The actual Enumeration shall be made within three Years after the first Meeting of the Congress of the United States, and within every subsequent Term of ten Years, in such Manner as they shall by Law direct. The Number of Representatives shall not exceed one for every thirty Thousand, but each State shall have at Least one Representative; and until such enumeration shall be made, the State of New Hampshire shall be entitled to chuse three, Massachusetts eight, Rhode-Island and Providence Plantations one, Connecticut five, New-York six, New Jersey four, Pennsylvania eight, Delaware one, Maryland six, Virginia ten, North Carolina five, South Carolina five, and Georgia three.

When vacancies happen in the Representation from any State, the Executive Authority thereof shall issue Writs of Election to fill such Vacancies.

The House of Representatives shall chuse their Speaker and other Officers; and shall have the sole Power of Impeachment.

1 The clause of this paragraph inclosed in brackets was amended, as to the mode of apportionment of representatives among the several states, by the Fourteenth Amendment, § 2, and as to taxes on incomes without apportionment, by the Sixteenth Amendment.

Section. 3. [The Senate of the United States shall be composed of two Senators from each State, chosen by the Legislature thereof, for six Years; and each Senator shall have one Vote.] [1]

Immediately after they shall be assembled in Consequence of the first Election, they shall be divided as equally as may be into three Classes. The Seats of the Senators of the first Class shall be vacated at the Expiration of the second Year, of the second Class at the Expiration of the fourth Year, and of the third Class at the Expiration of the sixth Year, so that one third may be chosen every second Year; [and if Vacancies happen by Resignation, or otherwise, during the Recess of the Legislature of any State, the Executive thereof may make temporary Appointments until the next Meeting of the Legislature, which shall then fill such Vacancies.] [2]

No Person shall be a Senator who shall not have attained to the Age of thirty Years, and been nine Years a Citizen of the United States, and who shall not, when elected, be an Inhabitant of that State for which he shall be chosen.

The Vice President of the United States shall be President of the Senate, but shall have no Vote, unless they be equally divided.

The Senate shall chuse their other Officers, and also a President pro tempore, in the Absence of the Vice President, or when he shall exercise the Office of President of the United States.

The Senate shall have the sole Power to try all Impeachments. When sitting for that Purpose, they shall be on Oath or Affirmation. When the President of the United States is tried, the Chief Justice shall preside: And no Person shall be convicted without the Concurrence of two thirds of the Members present.

Judgment in Cases of Impeachment shall not extend further than to removal from Office, and disqualification to hold and enjoy any Office of honor, Trust or Profit under the United States: but the Party convicted shall nevertheless be liable and subject to Indictment, Trial, Judgment and Punishment, according to Law.

1 This paragraph, inclosed in brackets, was superseded by the Seventeenth Amendment.

2 The clause of this paragraph inclosed in brackets was superseded by the Seventeenth Amendment.

Section. 4. The Times, Places and Manner of holding Elections for Senators and Representatives, shall be prescribed in each State by the Legislature thereof; but the Congress may at any time by Law make or alter such Regulations, except as to the Places of chusing Senators.

The Congress shall assemble at least once in every Year, and such Meeting shall be on the [first Monday in December],[1] unless they shall by Law appoint a different Day.

1 The clause of this paragraph inclosed in brackets was superseded by the Twentieth Amendment.

Section. 5. Each House shall be the Judge of the Elections, Returns and Qualifications of its own Members, and a Majority of each shall constitute a Quorum to do Business; but a smaller Number may adjourn from day to day, and may be authorized to compel the Attendance of absent Members, in such Manner, and under such Penalties as each House may provide.

Each House may determine the Rules of its Proceedings, punish its Members for disorderly Behaviour, and, with the Concurrence of two thirds, expel a Member.

Each House shall keep a Journal of its Proceedings, and from time to time publish the same, excepting such Parts as may in their Judgment require Secrecy; and the Yeas and Nays of the Members of either House on any question shall, at the Desire of one fifth of those Present, be entered on the Journal.

Neither House, during the Session of Congress, shall, without the Consent of the other, adjourn for more than three days, nor to any other Place than that in which the two Houses shall be sitting.

Section. 6. The Senators and Representatives shall receive a Compensation for their Services, to be ascertained by Law, and paid out of the Treasury of the United States. They shall in all Cases, except Treason, Felony and Breach of the Peace, be privileged from Arrest during their Attendance at the Session of their respective Houses, and in going to and returning from the same; and for any Speech or Debate in either House, they shall not be questioned in any other Place.

No Senator or Representative shall, during the Time for which he was elected, be appointed to any civil Office under the Authority of the United States, which shall have been created, or the Emoluments whereof shall have been encreased during such time; and no Person holding any Office under the United States, shall be a Member of either House during his Continuance in Office.

Section. 7. All Bills for raising Revenue shall originate in the House of Representatives; but the Senate may propose or concur with Amendments as on other Bills.

Every Bill which shall have passed the House of Representatives and the Senate, shall, before it becomes a Law, be presented to the President of the United States; If he approve he shall sign it, but if not he shall return it, with his Objections to that House in which it shall have originated, who shall enter the Objections at large on their Journal, and proceed to reconsider it. If after such Reconsideration two thirds of that House shall agree to pass the Bill, it shall be sent, together with the Objections, to the other House, by which it shall likewise be reconsidered, and if approved by two thirds of that House, it shall become a Law. But in all such Cases the Votes of both Houses shall be determined by Yeas and Nays, and the Names of the Persons voting for and against the Bill shall be entered on the Journal of each House respectively. If any Bill shall not be returned by the President within ten Days (Sundays excepted) after it shall have been presented to him, the Same shall be a Law, in like Manner as if he had signed it, unless the Congress by their Adjournment prevent its Return, in which Case it shall not be a Law.

Every Order, Resolution, or Vote to which the Concurrence of the Senate and House of Representatives may be necessary (except on a question of Adjournment) shall be presented to the President of the United States; and before the Same shall take Effect, shall be approved by him, or being disapproved by him, shall be repassed by two thirds of the Senate and House of Representatives, according to the Rules and Limitations prescribed in the Case of a Bill.

Section. 8. The Congress shall have Power To lay and collect Taxes, Duties, Imposts and Excises, to pay the Debts and provide for the common Defence and general Welfare of the United States; but all Duties, Imposts and Excises shall be uniform throughout the United States;

To borrow Money on the credit of the United States;

To regulate Commerce with foreign Nations, and among the several States, and with the Indian Tribes;

To establish an uniform Rule of Naturalization, and uniform Laws on the subject of Bankruptcies throughout the United States;

To coin Money, regulate the Value thereof, and of foreign Coin, and fix the Standard of Weights and Measures;

To provide for the Punishment of counterfeiting the Securities and current Coin of the United States;

To establish Post Offices and post Roads;

To promote the Progress of Science and useful Arts, by securing for limited Times to Authors and Inventors the exclusive Right to their respective Writings and Discoveries;

To constitute Tribunals inferior to the supreme Court;

To define and punish Piracies and Felonies committed on the high Seas, and Offences against the Law of Nations;

To declare War, grant Letters of Marque and Reprisal, and make Rules concerning Captures on Land and Water;

To raise and support Armies, but no Appropriation of Money to that Use shall be for a longer Term than two Years;

To provide and maintain a Navy;

To make Rules for the Government and Regulation of the land and naval Forces;

To provide for calling forth the Militia to execute the Laws of the Union, suppress Insurrections and repel Invasions;

To provide for organizing, arming, and disciplining, the Militia, and for governing such Part of them as may be employed in the Service of the United States, reserving to the States respectively, the Appointment of the Officers, and the Authority of training the Militia according to the discipline prescribed by Congress;

To exercise exclusive Legislation in all Cases whatsoever, over such District (not exceeding ten Miles square) as may, by Cession of particular States, and the Acceptance of Congress, become the Seat of the Government of the United States, and to exercise like Authority over all Places purchased by the Consent of the Legislature of the State in which the Same shall be, for the Erection of Forts, Magazines, Arsenals, dock-Yards, and other needful Buildings;—And

To make all Laws which shall be necessary and proper for carrying into Execution the foregoing Powers, and all other Powers vested by this Constitution in the Government of the United States, or in any Department or Officer thereof.

Section. 9. The Migration or Importation of such Persons as any of the States now existing shall think proper to admit, shall not be prohibited by the Congress prior to the Year one thousand eight hundred and eight, but a Tax or duty may be imposed on such Importation, not exceeding ten dollars for each Person.

The Privilege of the Writ of Habeas Corpus shall not be suspended, unless when in Cases of Rebellion or Invasion the public Safety may require it.

No Bill of Attainder or ex post facto Law shall be passed.

No Capitation, or other direct, Tax shall be laid, unless in Proportion to the Census or Enumeration herein before directed to be taken.[1]

No Tax or Duty shall be laid on Articles exported from any State.

No Preference shall be given by any Regulation of Commerce or Revenue to the Ports of one State over those of another; nor shall Vessels bound to, or from, one State, be obliged to enter, clear, or pay Duties in another.

No Money shall be drawn from the Treasury, but in Consequence of Appropriations made by Law; and a regular Statement and Account of the Receipts and Expenditures of all public Money shall be published from time to time.

No Title of Nobility shall be granted by the United States: And no Person holding any Office of Profit or Trust under them, shall, without the Consent of the Congress, accept of any present, Emolument, Office, or Title, of any kind whatever, from any King, Prince, or foreign State.

1 This paragraph has been affected by the Sixteenth Amendment.

Section. 10. No State shall enter into any Treaty, Alliance, or Confederation; grant Letters of Marque and Reprisal; coin Money; emit Bills of Credit; make any Thing but gold and silver Coin a Tender in Payment of Debts; pass any Bill of Attainder, ex post facto Law, or Law impairing the Obligation of Contracts, or grant any Title of Nobility.

No State shall, without the Consent of the Congress, lay any Imposts or Duties on Imports or Exports, except what may be absolutely necessary for executing it's inspection Laws: and the net Produce of all Duties and Imposts, laid by any State on Imports or Exports, shall be for the Use of the Treasury of the United States; and all such Laws shall be subject to the Revision and Controul of the Congress.

No State shall, without the Consent of Congress, lay any Duty of Tonnage, keep Troops, or Ships of War in time of Peace, enter into any Agreement or Compact with another State, or with a foreign Power, or engage in War, unless actually invaded, or in such imminent Danger as will not admit of delay.

ARTICLE II

Section. 1. The executive Power shall be vested in a President of the United States of America. He shall hold his Office during the Term of four Years, and, together with the Vice President, chosen for the same Term, be elected, as follows:

Each State shall appoint, in such Manner as the Legislature thereof may direct, a Number of Electors, equal to the whole Number of Senators and Representatives to which the State may be entitled in the Congress: but no Senator or Representative, or Person holding an Office of Trust or Profit under the United States, shall be appointed an Elector.

[The Electors shall meet in their respective States, and vote by Ballot for two Persons, of whom one at least shall not be an Inhabitant of the same State with themselves. And they shall make a List of all the Persons voted for, and of the Number of Votes for each; which List they shall sign and certify, and transmit sealed to the Seat of the Government of the United States, directed to the President of the Senate. The President of the Senate shall, in the Presence of the Senate and House of Representatives, open all the Certificates, and the Votes shall then be counted. The Person having the greatest Number of Votes shall be the President, if such Number be a Majority of the whole Number of Electors appointed; and if there be more than one who have such Majority, and have an equal Number of Votes, then the House of Representatives shall immediately chuse by Ballot one of them for President; and if no Person have a Majority, then from the five highest on the List the said House shall in like Manner chuse the President. But in chusing the President, the Votes shall be taken by States, the Representation from each State having one Vote; A quorum for this Purpose shall consist of a Member or Members from two thirds of the States, and a Majority of all the States shall be necessary to a Choice. In every Case, after the Choice of the President, the Person having the greatest Number of Votes of the Electors shall be the Vice President. But if there should remain two or more who have equal Votes, the Senate shall chuse from them by Ballot the Vice President.] [1]

The Congress may determine the Time of chusing the Electors, and the Day on which they shall give their Votes; which Day shall be the same throughout the United States.

No Person except a natural born Citizen, or a Citizen of the United States, at the time of the Adoption of this Constitution, shall be eligible to the Office of President; neither shall any Person be eligible to that Office who shall not have attained to the Age of thirty five Years, and been fourteen Years a Resident within the United States.

In Case of the Removal of the President from Office, or of his Death, Resignation, or Inability to discharge the Powers and Duties of the said Office, the Same shall devolve on the Vice President, and the Congress may by Law provide for the Case of Removal, Death, Resignation or Inability, both of the President and Vice President, declaring what Officer shall then act as President, and such Officer shall act accordingly, until the Disability be removed, or a President shall be elected.

The President shall, at stated Times, receive for his Services, a Compensation, which shall neither be encreased nor diminished during the Period for which he shall have been elected, and he shall not receive within that Period any other Emolument from the United States, or any of them.

Before he enter on the Execution of his Office, he shall take the following Oath or Affirmation:—"I do solemnly swear (or affirm) that I will faithfully execute the Office of President of the United States, and will to the best of my Ability, preserve, protect and defend the Constitution of the United States."

1 This paragraph, inclosed in brackets, was superseded by the Twelfth Amendment, post.

Section. 2. The President shall be Commander in Chief of the Army and Navy of the United States, and of the Militia of the several States, when called into the actual Service of the United States; he may require the Opinion, in writing, of the principal Officer in each of the executive Departments, upon any Subject relating to the Duties of their respective Offices, and he shall have Power to grant Reprieves and Pardons for Offences against the United States, except in Cases of Impeachment.

He shall have Power, by and with the Advice and Consent of the Senate, to make Treaties, provided two thirds of the Senators present concur; and he shall nominate, and by and with the Advice and Consent of the Senate, shall appoint Ambassadors, other public Ministers and Consuls, Judges of the supreme Court, and all other Officers of the United States, whose Appointments are not herein otherwise provided for, and which shall be established by Law: but the Congress may by Law vest the Appointment of such inferior Officers, as they think proper, in the President alone, in the Courts of Law, or in the Heads of Departments.

The President shall have Power to fill up all Vacancies that may happen during the Recess of the Senate, by granting Commissions which shall expire at the End of their next Session.

Section. 3. He shall from time to time give to the Congress Information of the State of the Union, and recommend to their

Consideration such Measures as he shall judge necessary and expedient; he may, on extraordinary Occasions, convene both Houses, or either of them, and in Case of Disagreement between them, with Respect to the Time of Adjournment, he may adjourn them to such Time as he shall think proper; he shall receive Ambassadors and other public Ministers; he shall take Care that the Laws be faithfully executed, and shall Commission all the Officers of the United States.

Section. 4. The President, Vice President and all civil Officers of the United States, shall be removed from Office on Impeachment for, and Conviction of, Treason, Bribery, or other high Crimes and Misdemeanors.

ARTICLE III

Section. 1. The judicial Power of the United States, shall be vested in one supreme Court, and in such inferior Courts as the Congress may from time to time ordain and establish. The Judges, both of the supreme and inferior Courts, shall hold their Offices during good Behaviour, and shall, at stated Times, receive for their Services, a Compensation, which shall not be diminished during their Continuance in Office.

Section. 2. The judicial Power shall extend to all Cases, in Law and Equity, arising under this Constitution, the Laws of the United States, and Treaties made, or which shall be made, under their Authority;—to all Cases affecting Ambassadors, other public Ministers and Consuls;—to all Cases of admiralty and maritime Jurisdiction;—to Controversies to which the United States shall be a Party;—to Controversies between two or more States;—between a State and Citizens of another State;—between citizens of different States;—between Citizens of the same State claiming Lands under Grants of different States, and between a State, or the Citizens thereof, and foreign States, Citizens or Subjects.[1]

In all Cases affecting Ambassadors, other public Ministers and Consuls, and those in which a State shall be Party, the supreme Court shall have original Jurisdiction. In all the other Cases before mentioned, the supreme Court shall have appellate Jurisdiction, both as to Law and Fact, with such Exceptions, and under such Regulations as the Congress shall make.

The Trial of all Crimes, except in Cases of Impeachment, shall be by Jury; and such Trial shall be held in the State where the said Crimes shall have been committed; but when not committed within any State, the Trial shall be at such Place or Places as the Congress may by Law have directed.

1 This section has been affected by the Eleventh Amendment.

Section. 3. Treason against the United States, shall consist only in levying War against them, or in adhering to their Enemies, giving them Aid and Comfort. No Person shall be convicted of Treason unless on the Testimony of two Witnesses to the same overt Act, or on Confession in open Court.

The Congress shall have Power to declare the Punishment of Treason, but no Attainder of Treason shall work Corruption of Blood, or Forfeiture except during the Life of the Person attainted.

ARTICLE IV

Section. 1. Full Faith and Credit shall be given in each State to the public Acts, Records, and judicial Proceedings of every other State. And the Congress may by general Laws prescribe the Manner in which such Acts, Records and Proceedings shall be proved, and the Effect thereof.

Section. 2. The Citizens of each State shall be entitled to all Privileges and Immunities of Citizens in the several States.

A Person charged in any State with Treason, Felony, or other Crime, who shall flee from Justice, and be found in another State, shall on Demand of the executive Authority of the State from which he fled, be delivered up, to be removed to the State having Jurisdiction of the Crime.

No Person held to Service or Labour in one State, under the Laws thereof, escaping into another, shall, in Consequence of any Law or Regulation therein, be discharged from such Service or Labour, but shall be delivered up on Claim of the Party to whom such Service or Labour may be due.[1]

1 This clause was affected by the Thirteenth Amendment.

Section. 3. New States may be admitted by the Congress into this Union; but no new State shall be formed or erected within the Jurisdiction of any other State; nor any State be formed by the Junction of two or more States, or Parts of States, without the Consent of the Legislatures of the States concerned as well as of the Congress.

The Congress shall have Power to dispose of and make all needful Rules and Regulations respecting the Territory or other Property belonging to the United States; and nothing in this Constitution shall be so construed as to Prejudice any Claims of the United States, or of any particular State.

Section. 4. The United States shall guarantee to every State in this Union a Republican Form of Government, and shall protect each of them against Invasion; and on Application of the Legislature, or of the Executive (when the Legislature cannot be convened) against domestic Violence.

ARTICLE V

The Congress, whenever two thirds of both Houses shall deem it necessary, shall propose Amendments to this Constitution, or, on the Application of the Legislatures of two thirds of the several States, shall call a Convention for proposing Amendments, which, in either Case, shall be valid to all Intents and Purposes, as Part of this Constitution, when ratified by the Legislatures of three fourths of the several States, or by Conventions in three fourths thereof, as the one or the other Mode of Ratification may be proposed by the Congress; Provided that no Amendment which may be made prior to the Year One thousand eight hundred and eight shall in any Manner affect the first and fourth Clauses in the Ninth Section of the first Article; and that no State, without its Consent, shall be deprived of its equal Suffrage in the Senate.

ARTICLE VI

All Debts contracted and Engagements entered into, before the Adoption of this Constitution, shall be as valid against the United States under this Constitution, as under the Confederation.

This Constitution, and the Laws of the United States which shall be made in Pursuance thereof; and all Treaties made, or which shall be made, under the Authority of the United States, shall be the supreme Law of the Land; and the Judges in every State shall be bound thereby, any Thing in the Constitution or Laws of any State to the Contrary notwithstanding.

The Senators and Representatives before mentioned, and the Members of the several State Legislatures, and all executive and judicial Officers, both of the United States and of the several States, shall be bound by Oath or Affirmation, to support this Constitution; but no religious Test shall ever be required as a Qualification to any Office or public Trust under the United States.

ARTICLE VII

The Ratification of the Conventions of nine States, shall be sufficient for the Establishment of this Constitution between the States so ratifying the Same.

DONE in Convention by the Unanimous Consent of the States present the Seventeenth Day of September in the Year of Our Lord one thousand seven hundred and Eighty seven and of the Independence of the United States of America the Twelfth. IN WITNESS whereof We have hereunto subscribed our Names.

Go. WASHINGTON—*Presidt.*
and deputy from Virginia

Attest WILLIAM JACKSON *Secretary*

New Hampshire

JOHN LANGDON NICHOLAS GILMAN

Massachusetts

NATHANIEL GORHAM RUFUS KING

Connecticut

WM. SAML. JOHNSON ROGER SHERMAN

New York

ALEXANDER HAMILTON

New Jersey

WIL: LIVINGSTON WM. PATERSON.
DAVID BREARLEY. JONA: DAYTON

Pennsylvania

B FRANKLIN THOS. FITZSIMONS
THOMAS MIFFLIN JARED INGERSOLL
ROBT MORRIS JAMES WILSON
GEO. CLYMER GOUV MORRIS

Delaware

GEO: READ RICHARD BASSETT
GUNNING BEDFORD jun JACO: BROOM
JOHN DICKINSON

Maryland

JAMES MCHENRY DANL CARROLL
DAN OF ST THOS. JENIFER

Virginia

JOHN BLAIR— JAMES MADISON JR.

North Carolina

WM. BLOUNT HU WILLIAMSON
RICHD. DOBBS SPAIGHT

South Carolina

J. RUTLEDGE CHARLES PINCKNEY
CHARLES COTESWORTH PINCKNEY PIERCE BUTLER

Georgia

WILLIAM FEW ABR BALDWIN

Amendments to the Constitution
Amendments I–X
Bill of Rights

AMENDMENT I

Congress shall make no law respecting an establishment of religion, or prohibiting the free exercise thereof; or abridging the freedom of speech, or of the press; or the right of the people peaceably to assemble, and to petition the Government for a redress of grievances.

AMENDMENT II

A well regulated Militia, being necessary to the security of a free State, the right of the people to keep and bear Arms, shall not be infringed.

AMENDMENT III

No Soldier shall, in time of peace be quartered in any house, without the consent of the Owner, nor in time of war, but in a manner to be prescribed by law.

AMENDMENT IV

The right of the people to be secure in their persons, houses, papers, and effects, against unreasonable searches and seizures, shall not be violated, and no Warrants shall issue, but upon probable cause, supported by Oath or affirmation, and particularly describing the place to be searched, and the persons or things to be seized.

AMENDMENT V

No person shall be held to answer for a capital, or otherwise infamous crime, unless on a presentment or indictment of a Grand Jury, except in cases arising in the land or naval forces, or in the Militia, when in actual service in time of War or public danger; nor shall any person be subject for the same offence to be twice put in jeopardy of life or limb; nor shall be compelled in any criminal case to be a witness against himself, nor be deprived of life, liberty, or property, without due process of law; nor shall private property be taken for public use, without just compensation.

AMENDMENT VI

In all criminal prosecutions, the accused shall enjoy the right to a speedy and public trial, by an impartial jury of the State and district wherein the crime shall have been committed, which district shall have been previously ascertained by law, and to be informed of the nature and cause of the accusation; to be confronted with the witnesses against him; to have compulsory process for obtaining witnesses in his favor, and to have the Assistance of Counsel for his defence.

AMENDMENT VII

In Suits at common law, where the value in controversy shall exceed twenty dollars, the right of trial by jury shall be preserved, and no fact tried by a jury, shall be otherwise reexamined in any Court of the United States, than according to the rules of the common law.

AMENDMENT VIII

Excessive bail shall not be required, nor excessive fines imposed, nor cruel and unusual punishments inflicted.

AMENDMENT IX

The enumeration in the Constitution, of certain rights, shall not be construed to deny or disparage others retained by the people.

AMENDMENT X

The powers not delegated to the United States by the Constitution, nor prohibited by it to the States, are reserved to the States respectively, or to the people.

Amendments XI–XXVII.

AMENDMENT XI

The Judicial power of the United States shall not be construed to extend to any suit in law or equity, commenced or prosecuted against one of the United States by Citizens of another State, or by Citizens or Subjects of any Foreign State.

AMENDMENT XII

The Electors shall meet in their respective states, and vote by ballot for President and Vice-President, one of whom, at least, shall not be an inhabitant of the same state with themselves; they shall name in their ballots the person voted for as President, and in distinct ballots the person voted for as Vice-President, and they shall make distinct lists of all persons voted for as President, and of all persons voted for as Vice-President, and of the number of votes for each, which lists they shall sign and certify, and transmit sealed to the seat of the government of the United States, directed to the President of the Senate; The President of the Senate shall, in the presence of the Senate and House of Representatives, open all the certificates and the votes shall then be counted;—The person having the greatest number of votes for President, shall be the President, if such number be a majority of the whole number of Electors appointed; and if no person have such majority, then from the persons having the highest numbers not exceeding three on the list of those voted for as President, the House of Representatives shall choose immediately, by ballot, the President. But in choosing the President, the votes shall be taken by states, the representation from each state having one vote; a quorum for this purpose shall consist of a member or members from two-thirds of the states, and a majority of all the states shall be necessary to a choice. And if the House of Representatives shall not choose a President whenever the right of choice shall devolve upon them, before the fourth day of March next following, then the Vice-President shall act as President, as in the case of the death or other constitutional disability of the President.—The person having the greatest number of votes as Vice-President, shall be the Vice-President, if such number be a majority of the whole number of Electors appointed, and if no person have a majority, then from the two highest numbers on the list, the Senate shall choose the Vice-President; a quorum for the purpose shall consist of two-thirds of the whole number of Senators, and a majority of the whole number shall be necessary to a choice. But no person constitutionally ineligible to the office of President shall be eligible to that of Vice-President of the United States.[1]

[1] This Amendment was affected by the Twentieth Amendment.

AMENDMENT XIII

Section 1. Neither slavery nor involuntary servitude, except as a punishment for crime whereof the party shall have been duly convicted, shall exist within the United States, or any place subject to their jurisdiction.

Section 2. Congress shall have power to enforce this article by appropriate legislation.

AMENDMENT XIV

Section 1. All persons born or naturalized in the United States, and subject to the jurisdiction thereof, are citizens of the United States and of the State wherein they reside. No State shall make or enforce any law which shall abridge the privileges or immunities of citizens of the United States; nor shall any State deprive any person of life, liberty, or property, without due process of law; nor deny to any person within its jurisdiction the equal protection of the laws.

Section 2. Representatives shall be apportioned among the several States according to their respective numbers, counting the whole number of persons in each State, excluding Indians not

But when the right to vote at any election for the choice of electors for President and Vice President of the United States, Representatives in Congress, the Executive and Judicial officers of a State, or the members of the Legislature thereof, is denied to any of the male inhabitants of such State, being twenty-one years of age, and citizens of the United States, or in any way abridged, except for participation in rebellion, or other crime, the basis of representation therein shall be reduced in the proportion which the number of such male citizens shall bear to the whole number of male citizens twenty-one years of age in such State.

Section 3. No person shall be a Senator or Representative in Congress, or elector of President and Vice President, or hold any office, civil or military, under the United States, or under any State, who, having previously taken an oath, as a member of Congress, or as an officer of the United States, or as a member of any State legislature, or as an executive or judicial officer of any State, to support the Constitution of the United States, shall have engaged in insurrection or rebellion against the same, or given aid or comfort to the enemies thereof. But Congress may by a vote of two-thirds of each House, remove such disability.

Section 4. The validity of the public debt of the United States, authorized by law, including debts incurred for payment of pensions and bounties for services in suppressing insurrection or rebellion, shall not be questioned. But neither the United States nor any State shall assume or pay any debt or obligation incurred in aid of insurrection or rebellion against the United States, or any claim for the loss or emancipation of any slave; but all such debts, obligations and claims shall be held illegal and void.

Section 5. The Congress shall have power to enforce, by appropriate legislation, the provisions of this article.

AMENDMENT XV

Section 1. The right of citizens of the United States to vote shall not be denied or abridged by the United States or by any State on account of race, color, or previous condition of servi-

Section 2. The Congress shall have power to enforce this article by appropriate legislation.

AMENDMENT XVI

The Congress shall have power to lay and collect taxes on incomes, from whatever source derived, without apportionment among the several States, and without regard to any census or enumeration.

AMENDMENT [XVII]

The Senate of the United States shall be composed of two Senators from each state, elected by the people thereof, for six

and each Senator shall have one vote. The electors in each State shall have the qualifications requisite for electors of the most numerous branch of the State legislatures.

When vacancies happen in the representation of any State in the Senate, the executive authority of such State shall issue writs of election to fill such vacancies: *Provided,* That the legislature of any State may empower the executive thereof to make temporary appointments until the people fill the vacancies by election as the legislature may direct.

This amendment shall not be so construed as to affect the election or term of any Senator chosen before it becomes valid as part of the Constitution.

AMENDMENT [XVIII] [Repealed. See Article XXI]

Section 1. After one year from the ratification of this article the manufacture, sale, or transportation of intoxicating liquors within, the importation thereof into, or the exportation thereof from the United States and all territory subject to the jurisdiction thereof for beverage purposes is hereby prohibited.

Section 2. The Congress and the several States shall have concurrent power to enforce this article by appropriate legisla-

Section 3. This article shall be inoperative unless it shall have been ratified as an amendment to the Constitution by the legislatures of the several States, as provided in the Constitution, within seven years from the date of the submission hereof to the States by the Congress.

AMENDMENT [XIX]

The right of citizens of the United States to vote shall not be denied or abridged by the United States or by any State on account of sex.

Congress shall have power to enforce this article by appropriate legislation.

AMENDMENT [XX]

Section 1. The terms of the President and Vice President shall end at noon on the 20th day of January, and the terms of Senators and Representatives at noon on the 3d day of January, of the years in which such terms would have ended if this article had not been ratified; and the terms of their successors shall then begin.

Sec. 2. The Congress shall assemble at least once in every year, and such meeting shall begin at noon on the 3d day of January, unless they shall by law appoint a different day.

Sec. 3. If, at the time fixed for the beginning of the term of the President, the President elect shall have died, the Vice President elect shall become President. If a President shall not have been chosen before the time fixed for the beginning of his term, or if the President elect shall have failed to qualify, then the Vice President elect shall act as President until a President shall have qualified; and the Congress may by law provide for the case wherein neither a President elect nor a Vice President elect shall have qualified, declaring who shall then act as President, or the manner in which one who is to act shall be selected, and such person shall act accordingly until a President or Vice President shall have qualified.

Sec. 4. The Congress may by law provide for the case of the death of any of the persons from whom the House of Representatives may choose a President whenever the right of choice shall have devolved upon them, and for the case of the death of any of the persons from whom the Senate may choose a Vice President whenever the right of choice shall have devolved upon them.

Sec. 5. Sections 1 and 2 shall take effect on the 15th day of October following the ratification of this article.

Sec. 6. This article shall be inoperative unless it shall have been ratified as an amendment to the Constitution by the legislatures of three-fourths of the several States within seven years from the date of its submission.

AMENDMENT [XXI]

Section 1. The eighteenth article of amendment to the Constitution of the United States is hereby repealed.

Sec. 2. The transportation or importation into any State, Territory, or possession of the United States for delivery or use therein of intoxicating liquors, in violation of the laws thereof, is hereby prohibited.

Sec. 3. This article shall be inoperative unless it shall have been ratified as an amendment to the Constitution by conventions in the several States, as provided in the Constitution, within seven years from the date of the submission hereof to the States by the Congress.

AMENDMENT [XXII]

Section 1. No person shall be elected to the office of the President more than twice, and no person who has held the office of President, or acted as President, for more than two years of a term to which some other person was elected President shall be elected to the office of the President more than once. But this Article shall not apply to any person holding the office of President when this Article was proposed by the Congress, and shall not prevent any person who may be holding the office of President, or acting as President, during the term within which this Article becomes operative from holding the office of President or acting as President during the remainder of such term.

Sec. 2. This Article shall be inoperative unless it shall have been ratified as an amendment to the Constitution by the legislatures of three-fourths of the several States within seven years from the date of its submission to the States by the Congress.

AMENDMENT [XXIII]

Section 1. The District constituting the seat of Government of the United States shall appoint in such manner as the Congress may direct:

A number of electors of President and Vice President equal to the whole number of Senators and Representatives in Congress to which the District would be entitled if it were a State, but in no event more than the least populous State; they shall be in addition to those appointed by the States, but they shall be considered, for the purposes of the election of President and Vice President, to be electors appointed by a State; and they shall meet in the District and perform such duties as provided by the twelfth article of amendment.

Sec. 2. The Congress shall have power to enforce this article by appropriate legislation.

AMENDMENT [XXIV]

Section 1. The right of citizens of the United States to vote in any primary or other election for President or Vice President, for electors for President or Vice President, or for Senator or Representative in Congress, shall not be denied or abridged by the United States or any State by reason of failure to pay any poll tax or other tax.

Sec. 2. The Congress shall have power to enforce this article by appropriate legislation.

AMENDMENT [XXV]

Section 1. In case of the removal of the President from office or of his death or resignation, the Vice President shall become President.

Sec. 2. Whenever there is a vacancy in the office of the Vice President, the President shall nominate a Vice President who shall take office upon confirmation by a majority vote of both Houses of Congress.

Sec. 3. Whenever the President transmits to the President pro tempore of the Senate and the Speaker of the House of Representatives his written declaration that he is unable to discharge the powers and duties of his office, and until he transmits to them a written declaration to the contrary, such powers and duties shall be discharged by the Vice President as Acting President.

Sec. 4. Whenever the Vice President and a majority of either the principal officers of the executive departments or of such other body as Congress may by law provide, transmit to the President pro tempore of the Senate and the Speaker of the House of Representatives their written declaration that the President is unable to discharge the powers and duties of his office, the Vice President shall immediately assume the powers and duties of the office as Acting President.

Thereafter, when the President transmits to the President pro tempore of the Senate and the Speaker of the House of Representatives his written declaration that no inability exists, he shall resume the powers and duties of his office unless the Vice President and a majority of either the principal officers of the executive department or of such other body as Congress may by law provide, transmit within four days to the President pro tempore of the Senate and the Speaker of the House of Representatives their written declaration that the President is unable to discharge the powers and duties of his office. Thereupon Congress shall decide the issue, assembling within forty-eight hours for that purpose if not in session. If the Congress, within twenty-one days after receipt of the latter written declaration, or, if Congress is not in session, within twenty-one days after Congress is required to assemble, determines by two-thirds vote of both Houses that the President is unable to discharge the powers and duties of his office, the Vice President shall continue to discharge the same as Acting President; otherwise, the President shall resume the powers and duties of his office.

AMENDMENT [XXVI]

Section 1. The right of citizens of the United States, who are eighteen years of age or older, to vote shall not be denied or abridged by the United States or by any State on account of age.

Sec. 2. The Congress shall have power to enforce this article by appropriate legislation.

AMENDMENT [XXVII][1]

1 "Article [XXVII]" editorially added. Originally read "Article the second".

No law, varying the compensation for the services of the Senators and Representatives, shall take effect, until an election of Representatives shall have intervened.

CONSTITUTION OF THE STATE OF OHIO
(Selected Provisions)

Complete to February 2, 2005

ARTICLE I
BILL OF RIGHTS

O Const I Sec. 1 Inalienable rights

All men are, by nature, free and independent, and have certain inalienable rights, among which are those of enjoying and defending life and liberty, acquiring, possessing, and protecting property, and seeking and obtaining happiness and safety.

(1851 constitutional convention, adopted eff. 9–1–1851)

O Const I Sec. 2 Equal protection and benefit

All political power is inherent in the people. Government is instituted for their equal protection and benefit, and they have the right to alter, reform, or abolish the same, whenever they may deem it necessary; and no special privileges or immunities shall ever be granted, that may not be altered, revoked, or repealed by the General Assembly.

(1851 constitutional convention, adopted eff. 9–1–1851)

O Const I Sec. 3 Rights of assembly and petition

The people have the right to assemble together, in a peaceable manner, to consult for their common good; to instruct their Representatives; and to petition the general assembly for the redress of grievances.

(1851 constitutional convention, adopted eff. 9–1–1851)

O Const I Sec. 4 Right to bear arms

The people have the right to bear arms for their defense and security; but standing armies, in time of peace, are dangerous to liberty, and shall not be kept up; and the military shall be in strict subordination to the civil power.

(1851 constitutional convention, adopted eff. 9–1–1851)

O Const I Sec. 5 Right of trial by jury

The right of trial by jury shall be inviolate, except that, in civil cases, laws may be passed to authorize the rendering of a verdict by the concurrence of not less than three-fourths of the jury.

(1912 constitutional convention, am. eff. 1–1–13; 1851 constitutional convention, adopted eff. 9–1–1851)

O Const I Sec. 6 Slavery and involuntary servitude

There shall be no slavery in this state; nor involuntary servitude, unless for the punishment of crime.

(1851 constitutional convention, adopted eff. 9–1–1851)

O Const I Sec. 7 Religious freedom; encouraging education

All men have a natural and indefeasible right to worship Almighty God according to the dictates of their own conscience. No person shall be compelled to attend, erect, or support any place of worship, or maintain any form of worship, against his consent; and no preference shall be given, by law, to any religious society; nor shall any interference with the rights of conscience be permitted. No religious test shall be required, as a qualification for office, nor shall any person be incompetent to be a witness on account of his religious belief; but nothing herein shall be construed to dispense with oaths and affirmations. Religion, morality, and knowledge, however, being essential to good government, it shall be the duty of the General Assembly to pass suitable laws, to protect every religious denomination in the peaceable enjoyment of its own mode of public worship, and to encourage schools and the means of instruction.

(1851 constitutional convention, adopted eff. 9–1–1851)

O Const I Sec. 8 Habeas corpus

The privilege of the writ of habeas corpus shall not be suspended, unless, in cases of rebellion or invasion, the public safety require it.

(1851 constitutional convention, adopted eff. 9–1–1851)

O Const I Sec. 9 Bail; cruel and unusual punishments

All persons shall be bailable by sufficient sureties, except for a person who is charged with a capital offense where the proof is evident or the presumption great, and except for a person who is charged with a felony where the proof is evident or the presumption great and where the person poses a substantial risk of serious physical harm to any person or to the community. Where a person is charged with any offense for which the person may be incarcerated, the court may determine at any time the type, amount, and conditions of bail. Excessive bail shall not be required; nor excessive fines imposed; nor cruel and unusual punishments inflicted.

The general assembly shall fix by law standards to determine whether a person who is charged with a felony where the proof is evident or the presumption great poses a substantial risk of serious physical harm to any person or to the community. Procedures for establishing the amount and conditions of bail shall be established pursuant to Article IV, Section 5(B) of the Constitution of the state of Ohio.

(1997 HJR 5, am. eff. 1–1–98; 1851 constitutional convention, adopted eff. 9–1–1851)

O Const I Sec. 10 Rights of criminal defendants

Except in cases of impeachment, cases arising in the army and navy, or in the militia when in actual service in time of war or public danger, and cases involving offenses for which the penalty provided is less than imprisonment in the penitentiary, no person shall be held to answer for a capital, or otherwise infamous, crime, unless on presentment or indictment of a grand jury; and the number of persons necessary to constitute such grand jury and the number thereof necessary to concur in finding such indictment shall be determined by law. In any trial, in any court, the party accused shall be allowed to appear and defend in person and with counsel; to demand the nature and cause of the accusation against him, and to have a copy thereof; to meet the witnesses face to face, and to have compulsory process to procure the attendance of witnesses in his behalf, and a speedy public trial by an impartial jury of the county in which the offense is alleged to have been committed; but provision may be made by law for the taking of the deposition by the accused or by the state, to be used for or against the accused, of any witness whose attendance can not be had at the trial, always securing to the accused means and the opportunity to be present in person and with counsel at the taking of such deposition, and to examine the witness face to face as fully and in the same manner as if in court. No person shall be compelled, in any criminal case, to be a witness against himself; but his failure to testify may be considered by the court and jury and may be the subject of comment by counsel. No person shall be twice put in jeopardy for the same offense.

(1912 constitutional convention, am. eff. 1–1–13; 1851 constitutional convention, adopted eff. 9–1–1851)

O Const I Sec. 11 Freedom of speech

Every citizen may freely speak, write, and publish his sentiments on all subjects, being responsible for the abuse of the right; and no law shall be passed to restrain or abridge the liberty of speech, or of the press. In all criminal prosecutions for libel, the truth may be given in evidence to the jury, and if it shall appear to the jury, that the matter charged as libelous is true, and was published with good motives, and for justifiable ends, the party shall be acquitted.

(1851 constitutional convention, adopted eff. 9–1–1851)

O Const I Sec. 12 No transportation or forfeiture for crime

No person shall be transported out of the State, for any offense committed within the same; and no conviction shall work corruption of blood, or forfeiture of estate.

(1851 constitutional convention, adopted eff. 9–1–1851)

O Const I Sec. 13 Quartering troops

No soldier shall, in time of peace, be quartered in any house, without the consent of the owner; nor, in time of war, except in the manner prescribed by law.

(1851 constitutional convention, adopted eff. 9–1–1851)

O Const I Sec. 14 Search and seizure

The right of the people to be secure in their persons, houses, papers, and possessions, against unreasonable searches and seizures shall not be violated; and no warrant shall issue, but upon probable cause, supported by oath or affirmation, particularly describing the place to be searched, and the person and things to be seized.

(1851 constitutional convention, adopted eff. 9–1–1851)

O Const I Sec. 15 No imprisonment for debt

No person shall be imprisoned for debt in any civil action, on mesne or final process, unless in cases of fraud.

(1851 constitutional convention, adopted eff. 9–1–1851)

O Const I Sec. 16 Redress for injury; due process

All courts shall be open, and every person, for an injury done him in his land, goods, person, or reputation, shall have remedy by due course of law, and shall have justice administered without denial or delay. Suits may be brought against the state, in such courts and in such manner, as may be provided by law.

(1912 constitutional convention, am. eff. 1–1–13; 1851 constitutional convention, adopted eff. 9–1–1851)

O Const I Sec. 17 No hereditary privileges

No hereditary emoluments, honors, or privileges, shall ever be granted or conferred by this state.

(1851 constitutional convention, adopted eff. 9–1–1851)

O Const I Sec. 18 Only general assembly may suspend laws

No power of suspending laws shall ever be exercised, except by the general assembly.

(1851 constitutional convention, adopted eff. 9–1–1851)

O Const I Sec. 19 Eminent domain

Private property shall ever be held inviolate, but subservient to the public welfare. When taken in time of war or other public exigency, imperatively requiring its immediate seizure, or for the purpose of making or repairing roads, which shall be open to the public, without charge, a compensation shall be made to the owner, in money, and in all other cases, where private property shall be taken for public use, a compensation therefor shall first be made in money, or first secured by a deposit of money, and such compensation shall be assessed by a jury, without deduction for benefits to any property of the owner.

(1851 constitutional convention, adopted eff. 9–1–1851)

O Const I Sec. 19a **Wrongful death**

The amount of damages recoverable by civil action in the courts for death caused by the wrongful act, neglect, or default of another, shall not be limited by law.

(1912 constitutional convention, adopted eff. 1–1–13)

O Const I Sec. 20 **Powers not enumerated retained by people**

This enumeration of rights shall not be construed to impair or deny others retained by the people; and all powers, not herein delegated, remain with the people.

(1851 constitutional convention, adopted eff. 9–1–1851)

ARTICLE II

LEGISLATIVE

Section

O Const II Sec. 5 **Persons barred from seat in General Assembly; embezzlement or failure to account for public funds**

No person hereafter convicted of an embezzlement of the public funds, shall hold any office in this State; nor shall any person, holding public money for disbursement, or otherwise, have a seat in the General Assembly, until he shall have accounted for, and paid such money into the treasury.

(1851 constitutional convention, adopted eff. 9–1–1851)

O Const II Sec. 6 **Powers of each house**

Each House shall be judge of the election, returns, and qualifications of its own members. A majority of all the members elected to each House shall be a quorum to do business; but, a less number may adjourn from day to day, and compel the attendance of absent members, in such manner, and under such penalties, as shall be prescribed by law.

Each House may punish its members for disorderly conduct and, with the concurrence of two-thirds of the members elected thereto, expel a member, but not the second time for the same cause.

Each House has all powers necessary to provide for its safety and the undisturbed transaction of its business, and to obtain, through committees or otherwise, information affecting legislative action under consideration or in contemplation, or with reference to any alleged breach of its privileges or misconduct of its members, and to that end to enforce the attendance and testimony of witnesses, and the production of books and papers.

(1973 HJR 5, am. eff. 5–8–73; 1851 constitutional convention, adopted eff. 9–1–1851)

O Const II Sec. 12 **Legislative privilege from arrest; right of free debate**

Senators and Representatives, during the session of the General Assembly, and in going to, and returning from the same, shall be privileged from arrest, in all cases, except treason, felony, or breach of the peace; and for any speech, or debate, in either House, they shall not be questioned elsewhere.

(1851 constitutional convention, adopted eff. 9–1–1851)

O Const II Sec. 28 **Retroactive laws; laws impairing obligation of contracts**

The general assembly shall have no power to pass retroactive laws, or laws impairing the obligation of contracts; but may, by general laws, authorize courts to carry into effect, upon such terms as shall be just and equitable, the manifest intention of parties, and officers, by curing omissions, defects, and errors, in instruments and proceedings, arising out of their want of conformity with the laws of this state.

(1851 constitutional convention, adopted eff. 9–1–1851)

O Const II Sec. 39 **Expert testimony in criminal cases**

Laws may be passed for the regulation of the use of expert witnesses and expert testimony in criminal trials and proceedings.

(1912 constitutional convention, adopted eff. 1–1–13)

O Const II Sec. 41 **Laws on employment of prisoners**

Laws may be passed providing for and regulating the occupation and employment of prisoners sentenced to the several penal institutions and reformatories in the state.

(1978 SJR 23, am. eff. 11–7–78; 1912 constitutional convention, adopted eff. 1–1–13)

ARTICLE III

EXECUTIVE

O Const III Sec. 5 Executive power vested in governor

The supreme executive power of this State shall be vested in the governor.

(1851 constitutional convention, adopted eff. 9–1–1851)

O Const III Sec. 10 Governor is commander-in-chief of militia

He shall be commander-in-chief of the military and naval forces of the state, except when they shall be called into the service of the United States.

(1851 constitutional convention, adopted eff. 9–1–1851)

O Const III Sec. 11 Governor has power of executive clemency; limitations

The governor shall have power, after conviction, to grant reprieves, commutations, and pardons, for all crimes and offenses, except treason and cases of impeachment, upon such conditions as the governor may think proper; subject, however, to such regulations, as to the manner of applying for commutations and pardons, as may be prescribed by law. Upon conviction for treason, the governor may suspend the execution of the sentence, and report the case to the General Assembly, at its next meeting, when the General Assembly shall either pardon, commute the sentence, direct its execution, or grant a further reprieve. The governor shall communicate to the General Assembly, at every regular session, each case of reprieve, commutation, or pardon granted, stating the name and crime of the convict, the sentence, its date, and the date of the commutation, pardon, or reprieve, with the governor's reasons therefor.

(1995 HJR 2, eff. 1–1–96; 1851 constitutional convention, adopted eff. 9–1–1851)

ARTICLE IV

JUDICIAL

O Const IV Sec. 1 Judicial power vested in courts

The judicial power of the state is vested in a supreme court, courts of appeals, courts of common pleas and divisions thereof, and such other courts inferior to the supreme court as may from time to time be established by law.

(1973 SJR 30, am. eff. 11–6–73; 132 v HJR 42, am. eff. 5–7–68; 1912 constitutional convention, am. eff. 1–1–13; 80 v 382, am. eff. 10–9–1883; 1851 constitutional convention, adopted eff. 9–1–1851)

O Const IV Sec. 2 Organization and jurisdiction of supreme court

(A) The supreme court shall, until otherwise provided by law, consist of seven judges, who shall be known as the chief justice and justices. In case of the absence or disability of the chief justice, the judge having the period of longest total service upon the court shall be the acting chief justice. If any member of the court shall be unable, by reason of illness, disability or disqualification, to hear, consider and decide a cause or causes, the chief justice or the acting chief justice may direct any judge of any court of appeals to sit with the judges of the supreme court in the place and stead of the absent judge. A majority of the supreme court shall be necessary to constitute a quorum or to render a judgment.

(B) (1) The supreme court shall have original jurisdiction in the following:

(a) Quo warranto;

(b) Mandamus;

(c) Habeas corpus;

(d) Prohibition;

(e) Procedendo;

(f) In any cause on review as may be necessary to its complete determination;

(g) Admission to the practice of law, the discipline of persons so admitted, and all other matters relating to the practice of law.

(2) The supreme court shall have appellate jurisdiction as follows:

(a) In appeals from the courts of appeals as a matter of right in the following:

(i) Cases originating in the courts of appeals;

(ii) Cases involving questions arising under the constitution of the United States or of this state.

(b) In appeals from the courts of appeals in cases of felony on leave first obtained,

(c) In direct appeals from the courts of common pleas or other courts of record inferior to the court of appeals as a matter of right in cases in which the death penalty has been imposed;

(d) Such revisory jurisdiction of the proceedings of administrative officers or agencies as may be conferred by law;

(e) In cases of public or great general interest, the supreme court may direct any court of appeals to certify its record to the supreme court, and may review and affirm, modify, or reverse the judgment of the court of appeals;

(f) The supreme court shall review and affirm, modify, or reverse the judgment in any case certified by any court of appeals pursuant to section 3 (B)(4) of this article.

(3) No law shall be passed or rule made whereby any person shall be prevented from invoking the original jurisdiction of the supreme court.

(C) The decisions in all cases in the supreme court shall be reported, together with the reasons therefor.

(1994 HJR 15, am. eff. 1–1–95; 132 v HJR 42, am. eff. 5–7–68; 120 v 743, am. eff. 11–7–44; 1912 constitutional convention, am. eff. 1–1–13; 80 v 382, am. eff. 10–9–1883; 1851 constitutional convention, adopted eff. 9–1–1851)

O Const IV Sec. 3 Organization and jurisdiction of courts of appeals

(A) The state shall be divided by law into compact appellate districts in each of which there shall be a court of appeals consisting of three judges. Laws may be passed increasing the number of judges in any district wherein the volume of business may require such additional judge or judges. In districts having additional judges, three judges shall participate in the hearing and disposition of each case. The court shall hold sessions in each county of the district as the necessity arises. The county commissioners of each county shall provide a proper and convenient place for the court of appeals to hold court.

(B) (1) The courts of appeals shall have original jurisdiction in the following:

(a) Quo warranto;

(b) Mandamus;

(c) Habeas corpus;

(d) Prohibition;

(e) Procedendo;

(f) In any cause on review as may be necessary to its complete determination.

(2) Courts of appeals shall have such jurisdiction as may be provided by law to review and affirm, modify, or reverse judgments or final orders of the courts of record inferior to the court of appeals within the district, except that courts of appeals shall not have jurisdiction to review on direct appeal a judgment that imposes a sentence of death. Courts of appeals shall have such appellate jurisdiction as may be provided by law to review and affirm, modify, or reverse final orders or actions of administrative officers or agencies.

(3) A majority of the judges hearing the cause shall be necessary to render a judgment. Judgments of the courts of appeals are final except as provided in section 2 (B) (2) of this article. No judgment resulting from a trial by jury shall be reversed on the weight of the evidence except by the concurrence of all three judges hearing the cause.

(4) Whenever the judges of a court of appeals find that a judgment upon which they have agreed is in conflict with a judgment pronounced upon the same question by any other court of appeals of the state, the judges shall certify the record of the case to the supreme court for review and final determination.

(C) Laws may be passed providing for the reporting of cases in the courts of appeals.

(1994 HJR 15, am. eff. 1–1–95; 132 v HJR 42, adopted eff. 5–7–68)

O Const IV Sec. 4 Organization and jurisdiction of common pleas courts

(A) There shall be a court of common pleas and such divisions thereof as may be established by law serving each county of the state. Any judge of a court of common pleas or a division thereof may temporarily hold court in any county. In the interests of the fair, impartial, speedy, and sure administration of justice, each county shall have one or more resident judges, or two or more counties may be combined into districts having one or more judges resident in the district and serving the common pleas courts of all counties in the district, as may be provided by law. Judges serving a district shall sit in each county in the district as the business of the court requires. In counties or districts having more than one judge of the court of common pleas, the judges shall select one of their number to act as presiding judge, to serve at their pleasure. If the judges are unable because of equal division of the vote to make such selection, the judge having the longest total service on the court of common pleas shall serve as presiding judge until selection is made by vote. The presiding judge shall have such duties and exercise such powers as are prescribed by rule of the supreme court.

(B) The courts of common pleas and divisions thereof shall have such original jurisdiction over all justiciable matters and such powers of review of proceedings of administrative officers and agencies as may be provided by law.

(C) Unless otherwise provided by law, there shall be a probate division and such other divisions of the courts of common pleas as may be provided by law. Judges shall be elected specifically to such probate division and to such other divisions. The judges of the probate division shall be empowered to employ and control the clerks, employees, deputies, and referees of such probate division of the common pleas courts.

(1973 SJR 30, am. eff. 11–6–73; 132 v HJR 42, adopted eff. 5–7–68)

O Const IV Sec. 5 Powers and duties of supreme court; superintendence of courts; rules

(A) (1) In addition to all other powers vested by this article in the supreme court, the supreme court shall have general superintendence over all courts in the state. Such general superintending power shall be exercised by the chief justice in accordance with rules promulgated by the supreme court.

(2) The supreme court shall appoint an administrative director who shall assist the chief justice and who shall serve at the pleasure of the court. The compensation and duties of the administrative director shall be determined by the court.

(3) The chief justice or acting chief justice, as necessity arises, shall assign any judge of a court of common pleas or a division thereof temporarily to sit or hold court on any other court of common pleas or division thereof or any court of appeals or shall assign any judge of a court of appeals temporarily to sit or hold court on any other court of appeals or any court of common pleas or division thereof and upon such assignment said judge shall serve in such assigned capacity until the termination of the assignment. Rules may be adopted to provide for the temporary

assignment of judges to sit and hold court in any court established by law.

(B) The supreme court shall prescribe rules governing practice and procedure in all courts of the state, which rules shall not abridge, enlarge, or modify any substantive right. Proposed rules shall be filed by the court, not later than the fifteenth day of January, with the clerk of each house of the general assembly during a regular session thereof, and amendments to any such proposed rules may be so filed not later than the first day of May in that session. Such rules shall take effect on the following first day of July, unless prior to such day the general assembly adopts a concurrent resolution of disapproval. All laws in conflict with such rules shall be of no further force or effect after such rules have taken effect.

Courts may adopt additional rules concerning local practice in their respective courts which are not inconsistent with the rules promulgated by the supreme court. The supreme court may make rules to require uniform record keeping for all courts of the state, and shall make rules governing the admission to the practice of law and discipline of persons so admitted.

(C) The chief justice of the supreme court or any judge of that court designated by him shall pass upon the disqualification of any judge of the courts of appeals or courts of common pleas or division thereof. Rules may be adopted to provide for the hearing of disqualification matters involving judges of courts established by law.

(1973 SJR 30, am. eff. 11–6–73; 132 v HJR 42, adopted eff. 5–7–68)

O Const IV Sec. 6 Election and compensation of judges; mandatory retirement; assignment of retired judges

(A) (1) The chief justice and the justices of the supreme court shall be elected by the electors of the state at large, for terms of not less than six years.

(2) The judges of the courts of appeals shall be elected by the electors of their respective appellate districts, for terms of not less than six years.

(3) The judges of the courts of common pleas and the divisions thereof shall be elected by the electors of the counties, districts, or, as may be provided by law, other subdivisions, in which their respective courts are located, for terms of not less than six years, and each judge of a court of common pleas or division thereof shall reside during his term of office in the county, district, or subdivision in which his court is located.

(4) Terms of office of all judges shall begin on the days fixed by law, and laws shall be enacted to prescribe the times and mode of their election.

(B) The judges of the supreme court, courts of appeals, courts of common pleas, and divisions thereof, and of all courts of record established by law, shall, at stated times, receive, for their services such compensation as may be provided by law, which shall not be diminished during their term of office. The compensation of all judges of the supreme court, except that of the chief justice, shall be the same. The compensation of all judges of the courts of appeals shall be the same. Common pleas judges and judges of divisions thereof, and judges of all courts of record established by law shall receive such compensation as may be provided by law. Judges shall receive no fees or perquisites, nor hold any other office of profit or trust, under the authority of this state, or of the United States. All votes for any judge, for any elective office, except a judicial office, under the authority of this state, given by the general assembly, or the people shall be void.

(C) No person shall be elected or appointed to any judicial office if on or before the day when he shall assume the office and enter upon the discharge of its duties he shall have attained the age of seventy years. Any voluntarily retired judge, or any judge who is retired under this section, may be assigned with his consent, by the chief justice or acting chief justice of the supreme court to active duty as a judge and while so serving shall receive the established compensation for such office, computed upon a per diem basis, in addition to any retirement benefits to which he may be entitled. Laws may be passed providing retirement benefits for judges.

(1973 SJR 30, am. eff. 11–6–73; 132 v HJR 42, adopted eff. 5–7–68)

O Const IV Sec. 13 Filling vacancy in judicial office

In case the office of any judge shall become vacant, before the expiration of the regular term for which he was elected, the vacancy shall be filled by appointment by the governor, until a successor is elected and has qualified; and such successor shall be elected for the unexpired term, at the first general election for the office which is vacant that occurs more than forty days after the vacancy shall have occurred; provided, however, that when the unexpired term ends within one year immediately following the date of such general election, an election to fill such unexpired term shall not be held and the appointment shall be for such unexpired term.

(119 v 863, am. eff. 11–3–42; 1851 constitutional convention, adopted eff. 9–1–1851)

O Const IV Sec. 15 Changing number of judges; establishing other courts

Laws may be passed to increase or diminish the number of judges of the supreme court, to increase beyond one or diminish to one the number of judges of the court of common pleas in any county, and to establish other courts, whenever two-thirds of the members elected to each house shall concur therein; but no such change, addition or diminution shall vacate the office of any judge; and any existing court heretofore created by law shall continue in existence until otherwise provided.

(1912 constitutional convention, am. eff. 1–1–13; 1851 constitutional convention, adopted eff. 9–1–1851)

O Const IV Sec. 17 Judges may be removed by legislature; procedure

Judges may be removed from office, by concurrent resolution of both Houses of the General Assembly, if two-thirds of the members, elected to each House, concur therein; but, no such removal shall be made, except upon complaint, the substance of which, shall be entered on the journal, nor, until the party charged shall have had notice thereof, and an opportunity to be heard.

(1851 constitutional convention, adopted eff. 9–1–1851)

O Const IV Sec. 18 Powers and jurisdiction of judges

The several judges of the supreme court, of the common pleas, and of such other courts as may be created, shall, respectively, have and exercise such power and jurisdiction, at chambers, or otherwise, as may be directed by law.

(1851 constitutional convention, adopted eff. 9–1–1851)

O Const IV Sec. 19 Courts of conciliation

The general assembly may establish courts of Conciliation, and prescribe their powers and duties; but such courts shall not render final judgment in any case, except upon submission, by the parties, of the matter in dispute, and their agreement to abide such judgment.

(1851 constitutional convention, adopted eff. 9–1–1851)

O Const IV Sec. 20 Style of process, prosecution, and indictment

The style of all process shall be, "The State of Ohio;" all prosecutions shall be carried on, in the name, and by the authority, of the state of Ohio; and all indictments shall conclude, "against the peace and dignity of the state of Ohio."

(1851 constitutional convention, adopted eff. 9–1–1851)

O Const IV Sec. 22 Supreme court commission

A commission, which shall consist of five members, shall be appointed by the Governor, with the advice and consent of the Senate, the members of which shall hold office for the term of three years from and after the first day of February, 1876, to dispose of such part of the business then on the dockets of the Supreme Court, as shall, by arrangement between said commission and said court, be transferred to such commission; and said commission shall have like jurisdiction and power in respect to such business as are or may be vested in said court; and the members of said commission shall receive a like compensation for the time being with the judges of said court. A majority of the members of said commission shall be necessary to form a quorum or pronounce a decision, and its decision shall be certified, entered and enforced as the judgments of the Supreme Court, and at the expiration of the term of said commission, all business undisposed of, shall by it be certified to the Supreme Court and disposed of as if said commission had never existed. The clerk and reporter of said court shall be the clerk and reporter of said commission, and the commission shall have such other attendants not exceeding in number those provided by law for said court, which attendants said commission may appoint and remove at its pleasure. Any vacancy occurring in said commission, shall be filled by appointment of the Governor, with the advice and consent of the Senate, if the Senate be in session, and if the Senate be not in session, by the Governor, but in such last case, such appointments shall expire at the end of the next session of the General Assembly. The General Assembly may, on application of the supreme court duly entered on the journal of the court and certified, provide by law, whenever two-thirds of such [1] house shall concur therein, from time to time, for the appointment, in like manner, of a like commission with like powers, jurisdiction and duties; provided, that the term of any such commission shall not exceed two years, nor shall it be created oftener than once in ten years.

(72 v 269, adopted eff. 10–12–1875)

[1] So in the original on file in the office of the Secretary of State. Should it read "each"?

O Const IV Sec. 23 When judge may serve multiple courts; referendum

Laws may be passed to provide that in any county having less than forty thousand population, as determined by the next preceding federal census, the board of county commissioners of such county, by a unanimous vote or ten per cent of the number of electors of such county voting for governor at the next preceding election, by petition, may submit to the electors of such county the question of providing that in such county the same person shall serve as judge of the court of common pleas, judge of the probate court, judge of the juvenile court, judge of the municipal court, and judge of the county court, or of two or more of such courts. If a majority of the electors of such county vote in favor of such proposition, one person shall thereafter be elected to serve in such capacities, but this shall not affect the right of any judge then in office from continuing in office until the end of the term for which he was elected.

Elections may be had in the same manner to discontinue or change the practice of having one person serve in the capacity of judge of more than one court when once adopted.

(131 v SJR 21, adopted eff. 11–2–65)

ARTICLE V

ELECTIVE FRANCHISE

O Const V Sec. 4 Exclusion from franchise

The General Assembly shall have power to exclude from the privilege of voting, or of being eligible to office, any person convicted of a felony.

(1976 SJR 16, am. eff. 6–8–76; 1851 constitutional convention, adopted eff. 9–1–1851)

ARTICLE VII

PUBLIC INSTITUTIONS

O Const VII Sec. 2 Appointment of directors of penal, benevolent, and other state institutions

The directors of the penitentiary shall be appointed or elected in such manner as the general assembly may direct; and the trustees of the benevolent, and other state institutions, now elected by the general assembly, and of such other state institutions as may be hereafter created, shall be appointed by the governor, by and with the advice and consent of the senate; and upon all nominations made by the governor, the question shall be taken by yeas and nays, and entered upon the journals of the senate.

(1851 constitutional convention, adopted eff. 9–1–1851)

ARTICLE IX

MILITIA

O Const IX Sec. 1 Resident citizens liable for state military duty

All citizens, residents of this state, being seventeen years of age, and under the age of sixty-seven years, shall be subject to enrollment in the militia and the performance of military duty, in such manner, not incompatible with the Constitution and laws of the United States, as may be prescribed by law.

(129 v 1848, am. eff. 1–1–62; 125 v 1091, am. eff. 11–3–53; 1851 constitutional convention, adopted eff. 9–1–1851)

O Const IX Sec. 3 Appointment of militia officers

The governor shall appoint the adjutant general, and such other officers and warrant officers, as my [sic.] be provided for by law.

(129 v 1848, am. eff. 1–1–62; 1851 constitutional convention, adopted eff. 9–1–1851)

O Const IX Sec. 4 Governor empowered to call militia for defense or to aid in disaster

The governor shall have power to call forth the militia, to execute the laws of the state, to suppress insurrection, to repel invasion, and to act in the event of a disaster within the state.

(129 v 1848, am. eff. 1–1–62; 1851 constitutional convention, adopted eff. 9–1–1851)

O Const IX Sec. 5 Arsenals

The general assembly shall provide, by law, for the protection and safekeeping of the public arms.

(1851 constitutional convention, adopted eff. 9–1–1851)

ARTICLE XV

MISCELLANEOUS

O Const XV Sec. 6 Lotteries prohibited, except state lottery; regulation of charitable bingo

Except as otherwise provided in this section, lotteries, and the sale of lottery tickets, for any purpose whatever, shall forever be prohibited in this State.

The General Assembly may authorize an agency of the state to conduct lotteries, to sell rights to participate therein, and to award prizes by chance to participants, provided that the entire net proceeds of any such lottery are paid into a fund of the state treasury that shall consist solely of such proceeds and shall be used solely for the support of elementary, secondary, vocational, and special education programs as determined in appropriations made by the General Assembly.

The General Assembly may authorize and regulate the operation of bingo to be conducted by charitable organizations for charitable purposes.

(1987 HJR 9, am. eff. 1–1–88; 1975 HJR 16, am. eff. 11–4–75; 1972 SJR 28, am. eff. 7–1–73; 1851 constitutional convention, adopted eff. 9–1–1851)

O Const XV Sec. 7 Oath of officers

Every person chosen or appointed to any office under this state, before entering upon the discharge of its duties, shall take an oath or affirmation, to support the constitution of the United States, and of this state, and also an oath of office.

(1851 constitutional convention, adopted eff. 9–1–1851)

ARTICLE XVIII

MUNICIPAL CORPORATIONS

O Const XVIII Sec. 3 Municipal powers of local self-government

Municipalities shall have authority to exercise all powers of local self-government and to adopt and enforce within their limits such local police, sanitary and other similar regulations, as are not in conflict with general laws.

(1912 constitutional convention, adopted eff. 11–15–12)

O Const XVIII Sec. 7 Municipal charter

Any municipality may frame and adopt or amend a charter for its government and may, subject to the provisions of section 3 of this article, exercise thereunder all powers of local self-government.

(1912 constitutional convention, adopted eff. 11–15–12)

OHIO REVISED CODE
GENERAL PROVISIONS TO TITLE 27
(Selected Provisions)

CHAPTER 1

DEFINITIONS; RULES OF CONSTRUCTION

DEFINITIONS

1.01 "Revised Code"

All statutes of a permanent and general nature of the state as revised and consolidated into general provisions, titles, chapters, and sections shall be known and designated as the "Revised Code," for which designation "R. C." may be substituted. Title, Chapter, and section headings and marginal General Code section numbers do not constitute any part of the law as contained in the "Revised Code."

The enactment of the Revised Code shall not be construed to affect a right or liability accrued or incurred under any section of the General Code prior to the effective date of such enactment, or an action or proceeding for the enforcement of such right or liability. Such enactment shall not be construed to relieve any person from punishment for an act committed in violation of any section of the General Code, nor to affect an indictment or prosecution therefor. For such purposes, any such section of the General Code shall continue in full force notwithstanding its repeal for the purpose of revision.

(1953 H 1, eff. 10–1–53)

1.02 General definitions

As used in the Revised Code, unless the context otherwise requires:

(A) "Whoever" includes all persons, natural and artificial; partners; principals, agents, and employees; and all officials, public or private.

(B) "Another," when used to designate the owner of property which is the subject of an offense, includes not only natural persons but also every other owner of property.

(C) "Of unsound mind" includes all forms of mental retardation or derangement.

(D) "Bond" includes an undertaking.

(E) "Undertaking" includes a bond.

(F) "And" may be read "or," and "or" may be read "and" if the sense requires it.

(G) "Registered mail" includes certified mail and "certified mail" includes registered mail.

(1971 H 607, eff. 1–3–72; 1969 H 688; 129 v 582; 126 v 1164; 1953 H 1; Source—GC 27, 10213, 12368, 12371)

1.03 Definition of "anything of value"

As used in any section of the Revised Code for the violation of which there is provided a penalty or forfeiture, unless the context otherwise requires, "anything of value" includes:

(A) Money, bank bills or notes, United States treasury notes, and other bills, bonds, or notes issued by lawful authority and intended to pass and circulate as money;

(B) Goods and chattels;

(C) Promissory notes, bills of exchange, orders, drafts, warrants, checks, or bonds given for the payment of money;

(D) Receipts given for the payment of money or other property;

(E) Rights in action;

(F) Things which savor of the realty and are, at the time they are taken, a part of the freehold, whether they are of the substance or produce thereof or affixed thereto, although there may be no interval between the severing and taking away;

(G) Any interest in realty, including fee simple and partial interests, present and future, contingent or vested interests, beneficial interests, leasehold interests, and any other interest in realty;

(H) Any promise of future employment;

(I) Every other thing of value.

(1976 H 1040, eff. 8–27–76; 1953 H 1; GC 12369)

1.04 Definition of standard time for Ohio

The standard time throughout this state shall be the mean astronomical time of the seventy-fifth degree of longitude west from Greenwich. Courts, public offices, and official legal proceedings subject to the laws of this state shall be regulated thereby. Whenever the time of performance of any act, or the time of accrual or determination of any rights, is fixed or governed by the statutes of this state or by any resolutions, rules, regulations, or orders in effect under authority of such statutes, such time shall be the standard time provided in this section.

All clocks maintained in or upon public buildings, existing as such under the laws of this state, shall be set and run according to this section.

(1953 H 1, eff. 10–1–53; GC 5979)

1.05 Definitions

(A) As used in the Revised Code, unless the context otherwise requires, "imprisoned" or "imprisonment" means being imprisoned under a sentence imposed for an offense or serving a term of imprisonment, prison term, jail term, term of local incarceration, or other term under a sentence imposed for an offense in an institution under the control of the department of rehabilitation and correction, a county, multicounty, municipal, municipal-county, or multicounty-municipal jail or workhouse, a minimum security jail, a community-based correctional facility, a halfway house, an alternative residential facility, or another facility described or referred to in section 2929.34 of the Revised Code for the type of criminal offense and under the circumstances specified or referred to in that section.

(B) As used in division (A) of this section, "community–based correctional facility," "halfway house," and "alternative residential facility" have the same meanings as in section 2929.01 of the Revised Code.

(2002 H 490, eff. 1–1–04; 1996 S 166, eff. 10–17–96; 1996 S 269, eff. 7–1–96; 1995 S 2, eff. 7–1–96; 1994 H 571, eff. 10–6–94; 1990 S 258, eff. 11–20–90; 1987 H 455; 1983 S 210; 1982 H 269, § 4, S 199; 1972 H 511; 1953 H 1; GC 12370)

GENERAL PROVISIONS

1.07 Value of written instrument or evidence of debt

Except as provided in sections 2909.11 and 2913.61 of the Revised Code, when an evidence of debt or a written instrument is the subject of a criminal act, the amount of money due on the evidence of debt or the written instrument or secured thereby, or the amount of money or the value of property affected thereby, shall be deemed the value of the evidence of debt or the written instrument.

(1972 H 511, eff. 1–1–74; 1953 H 1; GC 12373)

1.11 Liberal construction of remedial laws

Remedial laws and all proceedings under them shall be liberally construed in order to promote their object and assist the parties in obtaining justice. The rule of the common law that statutes in derogation of the common law must be strictly construed has no application to remedial laws; but this section does not require a liberal construction of laws affecting personal liberty, relating to amercement, or of a penal nature.

(1953 H 1, eff. 10–1–53; GC 10214)

1.12 Special provision covers unless cumulative

When a special provision is made in a remedial law as to service, pleadings, competency of witnesses, or in any other respect inconsistent with the general provisions of sections of the Revised Code relating to procedure in the court of common pleas and procedure on appeal, the special provision shall govern, unless it appears that the provisions are cumulative.

(1953 H 1, eff. 10–1–53; GC 10222)

1.14 First day excluded and last day included in computing time; exceptions; legal holiday defined

The time within which an act is required by law to be done shall be computed by excluding the first and including the last day; except that, when the last day falls on Sunday or a legal holiday, the act may be done on the next succeeding day that is not Sunday or a legal holiday.

When a public office in which an act, required by law, is to be performed is closed to the public for the entire day that constitutes the last day for doing the act or before its usual closing time on that day, the act may be performed on the next succeeding day that is not a Sunday or a legal holiday as defined in this section.

"Legal holiday" as used in this section means the following days:

(A) The first day of January, known as New Year's day;

(B) The third Monday in January, known as Martin Luther King day;

(C) The third Monday in February, known as Washington–Lincoln day;

(D) The day designated in the "Act of June 28, 1968," 82 Stat. 250, 5 U.S.C. 6103, as amended, for the commemoration of Memorial day;

(E) The fourth day of July, known as Independence day;

(F) The first Monday in September, known as Labor day;

(G) The second Monday in October, known as Columbus day;

(H) The eleventh day of November, known as Veterans' day;

(I) The fourth Thursday in November, known as Thanksgiving day;

(J) The twenty-fifth day of December, known as Christmas day;

(K) Any day appointed and recommended by the governor of this state or the president of the United States as a holiday.

If any day designated in this section as a legal holiday falls on Sunday, the next succeeding day is a legal holiday.

(2000 H 738, eff. 4–10–01; 1984 H 364, eff. 3–14–85; 1981 S 68, § 1; 1980 S 93; 1975 S 18; 1974 H 460; 1969 H 5; 129 v 1073; 1953 H 1; GC 10216)

1.15 Effective date; priority of legal rights

When an act is to take effect or become operative from and after a day named, no part of that day shall be included. If priority of legal rights depends upon the order of events on the same day, such priority shall be determined by the times in the day at which they respectively occurred.

(1953 H 1, eff. 10–1–53; GC 10217)

1.22 Change in judicial construction does not affect prior valid obligations

When an officer or board of a county, township, or municipal corporation by ordinance, resolution, order, or other proceeding, in pursuance of a statute of the state, has authorized or caused the issue and delivery of any bonds, obligations, or instruments of such county, township, or municipal corporation, or has caused any county, township, or municipal contracts, grants, franchises, rights, or privileges to be made or given, which were valid according to judicial construction and adjudication at the date of such action or proceeding, and loans or other things of value have been effected or acquired or expenditures have been made by other persons in reliance upon such construction or adjudication, such bonds, obligations, contracts, grants, franchises, rights, and privileges shall be valid and binding, notwithstanding subsequent change of such rule of judicial construction and adjudication with respect to other similar legislation.

(1953 H 1, eff. 10–1–53; GC 22)

1.23 Construction of references to code sections

(A) Wherever in a penalty section reference is made to a violation of a series of sections, or of divisions or subdivisions of a section, such reference shall be construed to mean a violation of any section, division, or subdivision included in such reference.

(B) References in the Revised Code to action taken or authorized under designated sections of the Revised Code include, in every case, action taken or authorized under the applicable section of the General Code which is superseded by the Revised Code.

(1977 H 1, eff. 8–26–77; 1976 H 837; 1971 H 607; 1953 H 1)

1.30 Intent of Code revision acts is nonsubstantive

(A) In enacting any legislation with the stated purpose of correcting nonsubstantive errors in the Revised Code, it is the intent of the general assembly not to make substantive changes in the law in effect on the date of such enactment. A section of the Revised Code affected by any such act shall be construed as a restatement and correction of, and substituted in a continuing way for, the corresponding statutory provision existing on its date of enactment.

(B) Acts of the general assembly with the purpose described in division (A) of this section include:

(1) House Bill No. 1 of the 100th general assembly;

(2) House Bill No. 1 of the 104th general assembly;

(3) House Bill No. 1 of the 105th general assembly;

(4) House Bill No. 5 of the 105th general assembly special session;

(5) House Bill No. 1 of the 107th general assembly;

(6) House Bill No. 1 of the 108th general assembly;

(7) House Bill No. 1 of the 109th general assembly;

(8) House Bill No. 1 of the 110th general assembly;

(9) House Bill No. 1 of the 111th general assembly;

(10) House Bill No. 1 of the 112th general assembly;

(11) House Bill No. 1 of the 113th general assembly;

(12) House Bill No. 1 of the 114th general assembly;

(13) House Bill No. 37 of the 115th general assembly;

(14) House Bill No. 428 of the 116th general assembly;

(15) House Bill No. 708 of the 117th general assembly.

(1988 H 708, eff. 4–19–88; 1986 H 428; 1984 H 37; 1981 H 1; 1979 H 1; 1977 H 1; 1975 H 1; 1973 H 1; 1971 H 1)

STATUTORY PROVISIONS

1.41 Statutory construction, applicability

Sections 1.41 to 1.59, inclusive, of the Revised Code apply to all statutes, subject to the conditions stated in section 1.51 of the Revised Code, and to rules adopted under them.

(1971 H 607, eff. 1–3–72)

1.42 Common and technical usage

Words and phrases shall be read in context and construed according to the rules of grammar and common usage. Words and phrases that have acquired a technical or particular meaning, whether by legislative definition or otherwise, shall be construed accordingly.

(1971 H 607, eff. 1–3–72)

1.43 Singular and plural; gender; tense

(A) The singular includes the plural, and the plural includes the singular.

(B) Words of one gender include the other genders.

(C) Words in the present tense include the future.

(1971 H 607, eff. 1–3–72)

1.44 Week; year

(A) "Week" means seven consecutive days.

(B) "Year" means twelve consecutive months.

(1971 H 607, eff. 1–3–72)

1.45 Computation of time

If a number of months is to be computed by counting the months from a particular day, the period ends on the same numerical day in the concluding month as the day of the month from which the computation is begun, unless there are not that many days in the concluding month, in which case the period ends on the last day of that month.

(1971 H 607, eff. 1–3–72)

1.46 Conflict in the expression of numbers

If there is a conflict between figures and words in expressing a number, the words govern.

(1971 H 607, eff. 1–3–72)

1.47 Intentions in the enactment of statutes

In enacting a statute, it is presumed that:

(A) Compliance with the constitutions of the state and of the United States is intended;

(B) The entire statute is intended to be effective;

(C) A just and reasonable result is intended;

(D) A result feasible of execution is intended.

(1971 H 607, eff. 1–3–72)

1.471 Effective dates of appropriation and nonappropriation provisions

As used in this section, "appropriation for current expenses" means an appropriation of money for the current expenses of the state government and state institutions as contemplated by Ohio Constitution, Article II, Section 1d.

This section expresses the general assembly's interpretation of State, ex rel. Ohio AFL–CIO, v. Voinovich (1994), 69 Ohio St. 3d 225, 234 to 237, insofar as the case holds with respect to the effective date of sections of law contained in acts that contain an appropriation for current expenses.

A codified or uncodified section of law contained in an act that contains an appropriation for current expenses is not subject to the referendum and goes into immediate effect if any of the following apply:

(A) The section is an appropriation for current expenses;

(B) The section is an earmarking of the whole or part of an appropriation for current expenses; or

(C) Implementation of the section depends upon an appropriation for current expenses that is contained in the act.

The general assembly shall determine which sections go into immediate effect.

A codified or uncodified section of law contained in an act that contains an appropriation for current expenses that does not go into immediate effect as contemplated by this section is subject to the referendum and goes into effect as provided in Ohio Constitution, Article II, Section 1c.

(1994 H 790, eff. 9–12–94)

1.48 Statutes presumed prospective

A statute is presumed to be prospective in its operation unless expressly made retrospective.

(1971 H 607, eff. 1–3–72)

1.49 Aids in construction of ambiguous statutes

If a statute is ambiguous, the court, in determining the intention of the legislature, may consider among other matters:

(A) The object sought to be attained;

(B) The circumstances under which the statute was enacted;

(C) The legislative history;

(D) The common law or former statutory provisions, including laws upon the same or similar subjects;

(E) The consequences of a particular construction;

(F) The administrative construction of the statute.

(1971 H 607, eff. 1–3–72)

1.50 Severability of statutory provisions

If any provision of a section of the Revised Code or the application thereof to any person or circumstance is held invalid, the invalidity does not affect other provisions or applications of the section or related sections which can be given effect without the invalid provision or application, and to this end the provisions are severable.

(1971 H 607, eff. 1–3–72)

1.51 Special or local provision prevails over general; exception

If a general provision conflicts with a special or local provision, they shall be construed, if possible, so that effect is given to both. If the conflict between the provisions is irreconcilable, the special or local provision prevails as an exception to the general provision, unless the general provision is the later adoption and the manifest intent is that the general provision prevail.

(1971 H 607, eff. 1–3–72)

1.52 Irreconcilable statutes; amendments to same statute, one without reference to the other; amendments to be harmonized

(A) If statutes enacted at the same or different sessions of the legislature are irreconcilable, the statute latest in date of enactment prevails.

(B) If amendments to the same statute are enacted at the same or different sessions of the legislature, one amendment without reference to another, the amendments are to be harmonized, if possible, so that effect may be given to each. If the amendments are substantively irreconcilable, the latest in date of enactment prevails. The fact that a later amendment restates language deleted by an earlier amendment, or fails to include language inserted by an earlier amendment, does not of itself make the amendments irreconcilable. Amendments are irreconcilable only when changes made by each cannot reasonably be put into simultaneous operation.

(1971 H 607, eff. 1–3–72)

1.53 Enrolled act prevails; section numbers designated by Legislative Service Commission

If the language of the enrolled act deposited with the secretary of state, including any code section number designated pursuant to section 103.131 of the Revised Code, conflicts with the language of any subsequent printing or reprinting of the statute, the language and any such designated section number of the enrolled act prevails.

(1971 H 607, eff. 1–3–72)

1.54 Continuation of prior statute

A statute which is reenacted or amended is intended to be a continuation of the prior statute and not a new enactment, so far as it is the same as the prior statute.

(1971 H 607, eff. 1–3–72)

1.55 Statutory references

A reference to any portion of a statute of this state applies to all reenactments or amendments thereof.

(1971 H 607, eff. 1–3–72)

1.56 Reference to a series

If a statute refers to a series of numbers or letters, the first and the last numbers or letters are included.

(1971 H 607, eff. 1–3–72)

1.57 Repeal of a repealing statute

The repeal of a repealing statute does not revive the statute originally repealed nor impair the effect of any saving clause therein.

(1971 H 607, eff. 1–3–72)

1.58 Effect of reenactment, amendment, or repeal of statute on existing conditions

(A) The reenactment, amendment, or repeal of a statute does not, except as provided in division (B) of this section:

(1) Affect the prior operation of the statute or any prior action taken thereunder;

(2) Affect any validation, cure, right, privilege, obligation, or liability previously acquired, accrued, accorded, or incurred thereunder;

(3) Affect any violation thereof or penalty, forfeiture, or punishment incurred in respect thereto, prior to the amendment or repeal;

(4) Affect any investigation, proceeding, or remedy in respect of any such privilege, obligation, liability, penalty, forfeiture, or punishment; and the investigation, proceeding, or remedy may be instituted, continued, or enforced, and the penalty, forfeiture, or punishment imposed, as if the statute had not been repealed or amended.

(B) If the penalty, forfeiture, or punishment for any offense is reduced by a reenactment or amendment of a statute, the penalty, forfeiture, or punishment, if not already imposed, shall be imposed according to the statute as amended.

(1971 H 607, eff. 1–3–72)

1.59 Definitions of specific terms

As used in any statute, unless another definition is provided in that statute or a related statute:

(A) "Child" includes child by adoption.

(B) "Oath" includes affirmation, and "swear" includes affirm.

(C) "Person" includes an individual, corporation, business trust, estate, trust, partnership, and association.

(D) "Population" means that shown by the most recent regular federal census.

(E) "Property" means real and personal property.

(F) "Rule" includes regulation.

(G) "State," when applied to a part of the United States, includes any state, district, commonwealth, territory, insular possession thereof, and any area subject to the legislative authority of the United States of America. "This state" or "the state" means the state of Ohio.

(H) "United States" includes all the states.

(I) "Will" includes codicil.

(J) "Written" or "in writing" includes any representation of words, letters, symbols, or figures; this provision does not affect any law relating to signatures.

(K) "Internet" means the international computer network of both federal and nonfederal interoperable packet switched data networks, including the graphical subnetwork known as the world wide web.

(2004 H 204, eff. 11–5–04; 1971 H 607, eff. 1–3–72)

1.60 Definition of "state agency"

As used in Title I of the Revised Code, "state agency," except as otherwise provided in the title, means every organized body, office, or agency established by the laws of the state for the exercise of any function of state government.

(1985 H 201, eff. 7–1–85)

1.61 Agriculture defined

As used in any statute except section 303.01 or 519.01 of the Revised Code, "agriculture" includes farming; ranching; aquaculture; apiculture and related apicultural activities, production of honey, beeswax, honeycomb, and other related products; horticulture; viticulture, winemaking, and related activities; animal husbandry, including, but not limited to, the care and raising of livestock, equine, and fur-bearing animals; poultry husbandry and the production of poultry and poultry products; dairy production; the production of field crops, tobacco, fruits, vegetables, nursery stock, ornamental shrubs, ornamental trees, flowers, sod, or mushrooms; timber; pasturage; any combination of the foregoing; the processing, drying, storage, and marketing of agricultural products when those activities are conducted in conjunction with, but are secondary to, such husbandry or production; and any additions or modifications to the foregoing made by the director of agriculture by rule adopted in accordance with Chapter 119. of the Revised Code.

(1994 S 134, eff. 6–20–94)

1.62 References to county officers, boards, commissions, authorities, and resolutions

As used in the Revised Code, unless the context of a section does not permit the following or unless expressly provided otherwise in a section:

(A) References to particular county officers, boards, commissions, and authorities mean, in the case of a county that has adopted a charter under Article X, Ohio Constitution, the officer, board, commission, or authority of that county designated by or pursuant to the charter to exercise the same powers or perform the same acts, duties, or functions that are to be exercised or performed under the applicable section of the Revised Code by officers, boards, commissions, or authorities of counties that have not adopted a charter.

(B) References to resolutions mean, in the case of a county that has adopted a charter under Article X, Ohio Constitution, the appropriate form of legislation permitted by or pursuant to the charter.

(2000 H 549, eff. 3–12–01)

CHAPTER 9

PUBLIC CONTRACTS

9.06 Contract for private operation of correctional facility

(A)(1) The department of rehabilitation and correction shall contract for the private operation and management pursuant to this section of the initial intensive program prison established pursuant to section 5120.033 of the Revised Code and may contract for the private operation and management of any other facility under this section. Counties and municipal corporations to the extent authorized in sections 307.93, 341.35, 753.03, and 753.15 of the Revised Code, may contract for the private operation and management of a facility under this section. A contract entered into under this section shall be for an initial term of not more than two years, with an option to renew for additional periods of two years.

(2) The department of rehabilitation and correction, by rule, shall adopt minimum criteria and specifications that a person or entity, other than a person or entity that satisfies the criteria set forth in division (A)(3)(a) of this section and subject to division (I) of this section, must satisfy in order to apply to operate and manage as a contractor pursuant to this section the initial intensive program prison established pursuant to section 5120.033 of the Revised Code.

(3) Subject to division (I) of this section, any person or entity that applies to operate and manage a facility as a contractor pursuant to this section shall satisfy one or more of the following criteria:

(a) The person or entity is accredited by the American correctional association and, at the time of the application, operates and manages one or more facilities accredited by the American correctional association.

(b) The person or entity satisfies all of the minimum criteria and specifications adopted by the department of rehabilitation and correction pursuant to division (A)(2) of this section, provided that this alternative shall be available only in relation to the initial intensive program prison established pursuant to section 5120.033 of the Revised Code.

(4) Subject to division (I) of this section, before a public entity may enter into a contract under this section, the contractor shall convincingly demonstrate to the public entity that it can operate the facility with the inmate capacity required by the public entity and provide the services required in this section and realize at least a five per cent savings over the projected cost to the public entity of providing these same services to operate the facility that is the subject of the contract. No out-of-state prisoners may be housed in any facility that is the subject of a contract entered into under this section.

(B) Subject to division (I) of this section, any contract entered into under this section shall include all of the following:

(1) A requirement that the contractor retain the contractor's accreditation from the American correctional association throughout the contract term or, if the contractor applied pursuant to division (A)(3)(b) of this section, continue complying with the applicable criteria and specifications adopted by the department of rehabilitation and correction pursuant to division (A)(2) of this section;

(2) A requirement that all of the following conditions be met:

(a) The contractor begins the process of accrediting the facility with the American correctional association no later than sixty days after the facility receives its first inmate.

(b) The contractor receives accreditation of the facility within twelve months after the date the contractor applies to the American correctional association for accreditation.

(c) Once the accreditation is received, the contractor maintains it for the duration of the contract term.

(d) If the contractor does not comply with divisions (B)(2)(a) to (c) of this section, the contractor is in violation of the contract, and the public entity may revoke the contract at its discretion.

(3) A requirement that the contractor comply with all rules promulgated by the department of rehabilitation and correction that apply to the operation and management of correctional facilities, including the minimum standards for jails in Ohio and policies regarding the use of force and the use of deadly force, although the public entity may require more stringent standards, and comply with any applicable laws, rules, or regulations of the federal, state, and local governments, including, but not limited to, sanitation, food service, safety, and health regulations. The contractor shall be required to send copies of reports of inspections completed by the appropriate authorities regarding compliance with rules and regulations to the director of rehabilitation and correction or the director's designee and, if contracting with a local public entity, to the governing authority of that entity.

(4) A requirement that the contractor report for investigation all crimes in connection with the facility to the public entity, to all local law enforcement agencies with jurisdiction over the place at which the facility is located, and, for a crime committed at a state correctional institution, to the state highway patrol;

(5) A requirement that the contractor immediately report all escapes from the facility, and the apprehension of all escapees, by telephone and in writing to all local law enforcement agencies with jurisdiction over the place at which the facility is located, to the prosecuting attorney of the county in which the facility is located, to the state highway patrol, to a daily newspaper having general circulation in the county in which the facility is located, and, if the facility is a state correctional institution, to the department of rehabilitation and correction. The written notice may be by either facsimile transmission or mail. A failure to comply with this requirement regarding an escape is a violation of section 2921.22 of the Revised Code.

(6) A requirement that, if the facility is a state correctional institution, the contractor provide a written report within specified time limits to the director of rehabilitation and correction or the director's designee of all unusual incidents at the facility as defined in rules promulgated by the department of rehabilitation and correction or, if the facility is a local correctional institution, that the contractor provide a written report of all unusual incidents at the facility to the governing authority of the local public entity;

(7) A requirement that the contractor maintain proper control of inmates' personal funds pursuant to rules promulgated by the department of rehabilitation and correction, for state correctional institutions, or pursuant to the minimum standards for jails along with any additional standards established by the local public entity, for local correctional institutions, and that records pertaining to these funds be made available to representatives of the public entity for review or audit;

(8) A requirement that the contractor prepare and distribute to the director of rehabilitation and correction or, if contracting with a local public entity, to the governing authority of the local entity, annual budget income and expenditure statements and funding source financial reports;

(9) A requirement that the public entity appoint and supervise a full-time contract monitor, that the contractor provide suitable office space for the contract monitor at the facility, and that the contractor allow the contract monitor unrestricted access to all parts of the facility and all records of the facility except the contractor's financial records;

(10) A requirement that if the facility is a state correctional institution, designated department of rehabilitation and correction staff members be allowed access to the facility in accordance with rules promulgated by the department;

(11) A requirement that the contractor provide internal and perimeter security as agreed upon in the contract;

(12) If the facility is a state correctional institution, a requirement that the contractor impose discipline on inmates housed in a state correctional institution, only in accordance with rules promulgated by the department of rehabilitation and correction;

(13) A requirement that the facility be staffed at all times with a staffing pattern approved by the public entity and adequate both to ensure supervision of inmates and maintenance of security within the facility, and to provide for programs, transportation, security, and other operational needs. In determining security needs, the contractor shall be required to consider, among other things, the proximity of the facility to neighborhoods and schools.

(14) If the contract is with a local public entity, a requirement that the contractor provide services and programs, consistent with the minimum standards for jails promulgated by the department of rehabilitation and correction under section 5120.10 of the Revised Code;

(15) A clear statement that no immunity from liability granted to the state, and no immunity from liability granted to political subdivisions under Chapter 2744. of the Revised Code, shall extend to the contractor or any of the contractor's employees;

(16) A statement that all documents and records relevant to the facility shall be maintained in the same manner required for, and subject to the same laws, rules, and regulations as apply to, the records of the public entity;

(17) Authorization for the public entity to impose a fine on the contractor from a schedule of fines included in the contract for the contractor's failure to perform its contractual duties, or to cancel the contract, as the public entity considers appropriate. If a fine is imposed, the public entity may reduce the payment owed

to the contractor pursuant to any invoice in the amount of the imposed fine.

(18) A statement that all services provided or goods produced at the facility shall be subject to the same regulations, and the same distribution limitations, as apply to goods and services produced at other correctional institutions;

(19) Authorization for the department to establish one or more prison industries at a facility operated and managed by a contractor for the department;

(20) A requirement that, if the facility is an intensive program prison established pursuant to section 5120.033 of the Revised Code, the facility shall comply with all criteria for intensive program prisons of that type that are set forth in that section;

(21) If the institution is a state correctional institution, a requirement that the contractor provide clothing for all inmates housed in the facility that is conspicuous in its color, style, or color and style, that conspicuously identifies its wearer as an inmate, and that is readily distinguishable from clothing of a nature that normally is worn outside the facility by non-inmates, that the contractor require all inmates housed in the facility to wear the clothing so provided, and that the contractor not permit any inmate, while inside or on the premises of the facility or while being transported to or from the facility, to wear any clothing of a nature that does not conspicuously identify its wearer as an inmate and that normally is worn outside the facility by non-inmates.

(C) No contract entered into under this section may require, authorize, or imply a delegation of the authority or responsibility of the public entity to a contractor for any of the following:

(1) Developing or implementing procedures for calculating inmate release and parole eligibility dates and recommending the granting or denying of parole, although the contractor may submit written reports that have been prepared in the ordinary course of business;

(2) Developing or implementing procedures for calculating and awarding earned credits, approving the type of work inmates may perform and the wage or earned credits, if any, that may be awarded to inmates engaging in that work, and granting, denying, or revoking earned credits;

(3) For inmates serving a term imposed for a felony offense committed prior to July 1, 1996, or for a misdemeanor offense, developing or implementing procedures for calculating and awarding good time, approving the good time, if any, that may be awarded to inmates engaging in work, and granting, denying, or revoking good time;

(4) For inmates serving a term imposed for a felony offense committed on or after July 1, 1996, extending an inmate's term pursuant to the provisions of law governing bad time;

(5) Classifying an inmate or placing an inmate in a more or a less restrictive custody than the custody ordered by the public entity;

(6) Approving inmates for work release;

(7) Contracting for local or long distance telephone services for inmates or receiving commissions from those services at a facility that is owned by or operated under a contract with the department.

(D) A contractor that has been approved to operate a facility under this section, and a person or entity that enters into a contract for specialized services, as described in division (I) of this section, relative to an intensive program prison established pursuant to section 5120.033 of the Revised Code to be operated by a contractor that has been approved to operate the prison under this section, shall provide an adequate policy of insurance specifically including, but not limited to, insurance for civil rights claims as determined by a risk management or actuarial firm with demonstrated experience in public liability for state governments. The insurance policy shall provide that the state, including all state agencies, and all political subdivisions of the state with jurisdiction over the facility or in which a facility is located are named as insured, and that the state and its political subdivisions shall be sent any notice of cancellation. The contractor may not self-insure.

A contractor that has been approved to operate a facility under this section, and a person or entity that enters into a contract for specialized services, as described in division (I) of this section, relative to an intensive program prison established pursuant to section 5120.033 of the Revised Code to be operated by a contractor that has been approved to operate the prison under this section, shall indemnify and hold harmless the state, its officers, agents, and employees, and any local government entity in the state having jurisdiction over the facility or ownership of the facility, shall reimburse the state for its costs in defending the state or any of its officers, agents, or employees, and shall reimburse any local government entity of that nature for its costs in defending the local government entity, from all of the following:

(1) Any claims or losses for services rendered by the contractor, person, or entity performing or supplying services in connection with the performance of the contract;

(2) Any failure of the contractor, person, or entity or its officers or employees to adhere to the laws, rules, regulations, or terms agreed to in the contract;

(3) Any constitutional, federal, state, or civil rights claim brought against the state related to the facility operated and managed by the contractor;

(4) Any claims, losses, demands, or causes of action arising out of the contractor's, person's, or entity's activities in this state;

(5) Any attorney's fees or court costs arising from any habeas corpus actions or other inmate suits that may arise from any event that occurred at the facility or was a result of such an event, or arise over the conditions, management, or operation of the facility, which fees and costs shall include, but not be limited to, attorney's fees for the state's representation and for any court-appointed representation of any inmate, and the costs of any special judge who may be appointed to hear those actions or suits.

(E) Private correctional officers of a contractor operating and managing a facility pursuant to a contract entered into under this section may carry and use firearms in the course of their employment only after being certified as satisfactorily completing an approved training program as described in division (A) of section 109.78 of the Revised Code.

(F) Upon notification by the contractor of an escape from, or of a disturbance at, the facility that is the subject of a contract entered into under this section, the department of rehabilitation and correction and state and local law enforcement agencies shall use all reasonable means to recapture escapees or quell any disturbance. Any cost incurred by the state or its political subdivisions relating to the apprehension of an escapee or the quelling of a disturbance at the facility shall be chargeable to and borne by the contractor. The contractor shall also reimburse the state or its political subdivisions for all reasonable costs incurred relating to the temporary detention of the escapee following recapture.

(G) Any offense that would be a crime if committed at a state correctional institution or jail, workhouse, prison, or other correctional facility shall be a crime if committed by or with regard to inmates at facilities operated pursuant to a contract entered into under this section.

(H) A contractor operating and managing a facility pursuant to a contract entered into under this section shall pay any inmate workers at the facility at the rate approved by the public entity. Inmates working at the facility shall not be considered employees of the contractor.

(I) In contracting for the private operation and management pursuant to division (A) of this section of the initial intensive program prison established pursuant to section 5120.033 of the Revised Code or of any other intensive program prison established pursuant to that section, the department of rehabilitation and correction may enter into a contract with a contractor for the general operation and management of the prison and may enter into one or more separate contracts with other persons or entities for the provision of specialized services for persons confined in the prison, including, but not limited to, security or training services or medical, counseling, educational, or similar treatment programs. If, pursuant to this division, the department enters into a contract with a contractor for the general operation and management of the prison and also enters into one or more specialized service contracts with other persons or entities, all of the following apply:

(1) The contract for the general operation and management shall comply with all requirements and criteria set forth in this section, and all provisions of this section apply in relation to the prison operated and managed pursuant to the contract.

(2) Divisions (A)(2), (B), and (C) of this section do not apply in relation to any specialized services contract, except to the extent that the provisions of those divisions clearly are relevant to the specialized services to be provided under the specialized services contract. Division (D) of this section applies in relation to each specialized services contract.

(J) As used in this section:

(1) "Public entity" means the department of rehabilitation and correction, or a county or municipal corporation or a combination of counties and municipal corporations, that has jurisdiction over a facility that is the subject of a contract entered into under this section.

(2) "Local public entity" means a county or municipal corporation, or a combination of counties and municipal corporations, that has jurisdiction over a jail, workhouse, or other correctional facility used only for misdemeanants that is the subject of a contract entered into under this section.

(3) "Governing authority of a local public entity" means, for a county, the board of county commissioners; for a municipal corporation, the legislative authority; for a combination of counties and municipal corporation, all the boards of county commissioners and municipal legislative authorities that joined to create the facility.

(4) "Contractor" means a person or entity that enters into a contract under this section to operate and manage a jail, workhouse, or other correctional facility.

(5) "Facility" means the specific county, multicounty, municipal, municipal-county, or multicounty-municipal jail, workhouse, prison, or other type of correctional institution or facility used only for misdemeanants, or a state correctional institution, that is the subject of a contract entered into under this section.

(6) "Person or entity" in the case of a contract for the private operation and management of a state correctional institution, includes an employee organization, as defined in section 4117.01 of the Revised Code, that represents employees at state correctional institutions.

(2001 H 94, eff. 9–5–01; 1999 H 283, eff. 6–30–99; 1998 H 293, eff. 3–17–98; 1997 H 215, eff. 9–29–97; 1995 H 117, eff. 9–29–95)

9.07 Correctional facilities operated by local public entities or private contractors; requirements

(A) As used in this section:

(1) Deadly weapon has the same meaning as in section 2923.11 of the Revised Code.

(2) Governing authority of a local public entity means whichever of the following is applicable:

(a) For a county, the board of county commissioners of the county;

(b) For a municipal corporation, the legislative authority of the municipal corporation;

(c) For a combination of counties, a combination of municipal corporations, or a combination of one or more counties and one or more municipal corporations, all boards of county commissioners and legislative authorities of all of the counties and municipal corporations that combined to form a local public entity for purposes of this section.

(3) Local public entity means a county, a municipal corporation, a combination of counties, a combination of municipal corporations, or a combination of one or more counties and one or more municipal corporations.

(4) Non–contracting political subdivision means any political subdivision to which all of the following apply:

(a) A correctional facility for the housing of out-of-state prisoners in this state is or will be located in the political subdivision.

(b) The correctional facility described in division (A)(4)(a) of this section is being operated and managed, or will be operated and managed, by a local public entity or a private contractor pursuant to a contract entered into prior to March 17, 1998, or a contract entered into on or after March 17, 1998, under this section.

(c) The political subdivision is not a party to the contract described in division (A)(4)(b) of this section for the management and operation of the correctional facility.

(5) Out of state jurisdiction means the United States, any state other than this state, and any political subdivision or other jurisdiction located in a state other than this state.

(6) Out–of–state prisoner means a person who is convicted of a crime in another state or under the laws of the United States or who is found under the laws of another state or of the United States to be a delinquent child or the substantially equivalent designation.

(7) Private contractor means either of the following:

(a) A person who, on or after March 17, 1998, enters into a contract under this section with a local public entity to operate and manage a correctional facility in this state for out-of-state prisoners.

(b) A person who, pursuant to a contract with a local public entity entered into prior to March 17, 1998, operates and manages on March 17, 1998, a correctional facility in this state for housing out-of-state prisoners.

(B) Subject to division (I) of this section, the only entities other than this state that are authorized to operate a correctional facility to house out-of-state prisoners in this state are a local public entity that operates a correctional facility pursuant to this section or a private contractor that operates a correctional facility pursuant to this section under a contract with a local public entity.

Subject to division (I) of this section, a private entity may operate a correctional facility in this state for the housing of out-of-state prisoners only if the private entity is a private contractor that enters into a contract that comports with division (D) of this section with a local public entity for the management and operation of the correctional facility.

(C)(1) Except as provided in this division, on and after March 17, 1998, a local public entity shall not enter into a contract with an out-of-state jurisdiction to house out-of-state prisoners in a correctional facility in this state. On and after March 17, 1998, a local public entity may enter into a contract with an out-of-state jurisdiction to house out-of-state prisoners in a correctional facility in this state only if the local public entity and the out-of-state jurisdiction with which the local public entity intends to contract jointly submit to the department of rehabilitation and correction a statement that certifies the correctional facility's intended use, intended prisoner population, and custody level, and the department reviews and comments upon the plans for the design or renovation of the correctional facility regarding their suitability for the intended prisoner population specified in the submitted statement.

(2) If a local public entity and an out-of-state jurisdiction enter into a contract to house out-of-state prisoners in a correctional facility in this state as authorized under division (C)(1) of this section, in addition to any other provisions it contains, the contract shall include whichever of the following provisions is applicable:

(a) If a private contractor will operate the facility in question pursuant to a contract entered into in accordance with division (D) of this section, a requirement that, if the facility is closed or ceases to operate for any reason and if the conversion plan described in division (D)(16) of this section is not complied with, the out-of-state jurisdiction will be responsible for housing and transporting the prisoners who are in the facility at the time it is closed or ceases to operate and for the cost of so housing and transporting those prisoners;

(b) If a private contractor will not operate the facility in question pursuant to a contract entered into in accordance with division (D) of this section, a conversion plan that will be followed if, for any reason, the facility is closed or ceases to operate. The conversion plan shall include, but is not limited to, provisions that specify whether the local public entity or the out-of-state jurisdiction will be responsible for housing and transporting the prisoners who are in the facility at the time it is closed or ceases to operate and for the cost of so housing and transporting those prisoners.

(3) If a local public entity and an out-of-state jurisdiction intend to enter into a contract to house out-of-state prisoners in a correctional facility in this state as authorized under division (C)(1) of this section, or if a local public entity and a private contractor intend to enter into a contract pursuant to division (D) of this section for the private contractor's management and operation of a correctional facility in this state to house out-of-state prisoners, prior to entering into the contract the local public entity and the out-of-state jurisdiction, or the local public entity and the private contractor, whichever is applicable, shall conduct a public hearing in accordance with this division, and, prior to entering into the contract, the governing authority of the local public entity in which the facility is or will be located shall authorize the location and operation of the facility. The hearing shall be conducted at a location within the municipal corporation or township in which the facility is or will be located. At least one week prior to conducting the hearing, the local public entity and the out-of-state jurisdiction or private contractor with the duty to conduct the hearing shall cause notice of the date, time, and place of the hearing to be made by publication in the newspaper with the largest general circulation in the county in which the municipal corporation or township is located. The notice shall be of a sufficient size that it covers at least one-quarter of a page of the newspaper in which it is published. This division applies to a private contractor that, pursuant to the requirement set forth in division (I) of this section, is required to enter into a contract under division (D) of this section.

(D) Subject to division (I) of this section, on and after March 17, 1998, if a local public entity enters into a contract with a private contractor for the management and operation of a correctional facility in this state to house out-of-state prisoners, the contract, at a minimum, shall include all of the following provisions:

(1) A requirement that the private contractor seek and obtain accreditation from the American correctional association for the correctional facility within two years after accepting the first out-of-state prisoner at the correctional facility under the contract and that it maintain that accreditation for the term of the contract;

(2) A requirement that the private contractor comply with all applicable laws, rules, or regulations of the government of this state, political subdivisions of this state, and the United States, including, but not limited to, all sanitation, food service, safety, and health regulations;

(3) A requirement that the private contractor send copies of reports of inspections completed by appropriate authorities regarding compliance with laws, rules, and regulations of the type described in division (D)(2) of this section to the director of rehabilitation and correction or the director's designee and to the governing authority of the local public entity in which the correctional facility is located;

(4) A requirement that the private contractor report to the local law enforcement agencies with jurisdiction over the place at which the correctional facility is located, for investigation, all criminal offenses or delinquent acts that are committed in or on the grounds of, or otherwise in connection with, the correctional facility and report to the department of rehabilitation and correction all disturbances at the facility;

(5) A requirement that the private contractor immediately report all escapes from the facility, and the apprehension of all escapees, by telephone and in writing to the department of rehabilitation and correction, to all local law enforcement agencies with jurisdiction over the place at which the facility is located, to the state highway patrol, to the prosecuting attorney of the county in which the facility is located, and to a daily newspaper having general circulation in the county in which the facility is located. The written notice may be by either facsimile transmission or mail. A failure to comply with this requirement is a violation of section 2921.22 of the Revised Code.

(6) A requirement that the private contractor provide a written report to the director of rehabilitation and correction or the director's designee and to the governing authority of the local public entity in which the correctional facility is located of all unusual incidents occurring at the correctional facility. The private contractor shall report the incidents in accordance with the incident reporting rules that, at the time of the incident, are applicable to state correctional facilities for similar incidents occurring at state correctional facilities.

(7) A requirement that the private contractor provide internal and perimeter security to protect the public, staff members of the correctional facility, and prisoners in the correctional facility;

(8) A requirement that the correctional facility be staffed at all times with a staffing pattern that is adequate to ensure supervision of inmates and maintenance of security within the correctional facility and to provide for appropriate programs, transportation, security, and other operational needs. In determining security needs for the correctional facility, the private contractor and the contract requirements shall fully take into account all relevant factors, including, but not limited to, the proximity of the facility to neighborhoods and schools.

(9) A requirement that the private contractor provide an adequate policy of insurance that satisfies the requirements set forth in division (D) of section 9.06 of the Revised Code regarding contractors who operate and manage a facility under that section, and that the private contractor indemnify and hold harmless the state, its officers, agents, and employees, and any local public entity in the state with jurisdiction over the place at which the correctional facility is located or that owns the correctional facility, reimburse the state for its costs in defending the state or any of its officers, agents, or employees, and reimburse any local government entity of that nature for its costs in defending the local government entity, in the manner described in division (D) of that section regarding contractors who operate and manage a facility under that section;

(10) A requirement that the private contractor adopt for prisoners housed in the correctional facility the security classification system and schedule adopted by the department of rehabilitation and correction under section 5145.03 of the Revised Code, classify in accordance with the system and schedule each prisoner housed in the facility, and house all prisoners in the facility in accordance with their classification under this division;

(11) A requirement that the private contractor will not accept for housing, and will not house, in the correctional facility any out-of-state prisoner in relation to whom any of the following applies:

(a) The private entity has not obtained from the out-of-state jurisdiction that imposed the sentence or sanction under which the prisoner will be confined in this state a copy of the institutional record of the prisoner while previously confined in that out-of-state jurisdiction or a statement that the prisoner previously has not been confined in that out-of-state jurisdiction and a copy of all medical records pertaining to that prisoner that are in the possession of the out-of-state jurisdiction.

(b) The prisoner, while confined in any out-of-state jurisdiction, has a record of institutional violence involving the use of a deadly weapon or a pattern of committing acts of an assaultive nature against employees of, or visitors to, the place of confinement or has a record of escape or attempted escape from secure custody.

(c) Under the security classification system and schedule adopted by the department of rehabilitation and correction under section 5145.03 of the Revised Code and adopted by the private contractor under division (B)(10) of this section, the out-of-state prisoner would be classified as being at a security level higher than medium security.

(12) A requirement that the private contractor, prior to housing any out-of-state prisoner in the correctional facility under the contract, enter into a written agreement with the department of rehabilitation and correction that sets forth a plan and procedure that will be used to coordinate law enforcement activities of state law enforcement agencies and of local law enforcement agencies with jurisdiction over the place at which the facility is located in response to any riot, rebellion, escape, insurrection, or other emergency occurring inside or outside the facility;

(13) A requirement that the private contractor cooperate with the correctional institution inspection committee in the committee's performance of its duties under section 103.73 of the Revised Code and provide the committee, its subcommittees, and its staff members, in performing those duties, with access to the correctional facility as described in that section;

(14) A requirement that the private contractor permit any peace officer who serves a law enforcement agency with jurisdiction over the place at which the correctional facility is located to enter into the facility to investigate any criminal offense or delinquent act that allegedly has been committed in or on the grounds of, or otherwise in connection with, the facility;

(15) A requirement that the private contractor will not employ any person at the correctional facility until after the private contractor has submitted to the bureau of criminal identification and investigation, on a form prescribed by the superintendent of the bureau, a request that the bureau conduct a criminal records check of the person and a requirement that the private contractor will not employ any person at the facility if the records check or other information possessed by the contractor indicates that the person previously has engaged in malfeasance;

(16) A requirement that the private contractor will not accept for housing, and will not house, in the correctional facility any out-of-state prisoner unless the private contractor and the out-of-state jurisdiction that imposed the sentence for which the prisoner is to be confined agree that, if the out-of-state prisoner is confined in the facility in this state, commits a criminal offense while confined in the facility, is convicted of or pleads guilty to that offense, and is sentenced to a term of confinement for that offense but is not sentenced to death for that offense, the private contractor and the out-of-state jurisdiction will do all of the following:

(a) Unless section 5120.50 of the Revised Code does not apply in relation to the offense the prisoner committed while confined in this state and the term of confinement imposed for that offense, the out-of-state jurisdiction will accept the prisoner pursuant to that section for service of that term of confinement and for any period of time remaining under the sentence for which the prisoner was confined in the facility in this state, the out-of-state jurisdiction will confine the prisoner pursuant to that section for that term and that remaining period of time, and the private contractor will transport the prisoner to the out-of-state jurisdiction for service of that term and that remaining period of time.

(b) If section 5120.50 of the Revised Code does not apply in relation to the offense the prisoner committed while confined in this state and the term of confinement imposed for that offense, the prisoner shall be returned to the out-of-state jurisdiction or its private contractor for completion of the period of time remaining under the out-of-state sentence for which the prisoner was confined in the facility in this state before starting service of the term of confinement imposed for the offense committed while confined in this state, the out-of-state jurisdiction or its private contractor will confine the prisoner for that remaining period of time and will transport the prisoner outside of this state for service of that remaining period of time, and, if the prisoner is confined in this state in a facility operated by the department of rehabilitation and correction, the private contractor will be financially responsible for reimbursing the department at the per diem cost of confinement for the duration of that incarceration, with the amount of the reimbursement so paid to be deposited in the department's prisoner programs fund.

(17) A requirement that the private contractor, prior to housing any out-of-state prisoner in the correctional facility under the contract, enter into an agreement with the local public entity that sets forth a conversion plan that will be followed if, for any reason, the facility is closed or ceases to operate. The conversion plan shall include, but is not limited to, provisions that specify whether the private contractor, the local public entity, or the out-of-state jurisdictions that imposed the sentences for which the out-of-state prisoners are confined in the facility will be responsible for housing and transporting the prisoners who are in the facility at the time it is closed or ceases to operate and for the cost of so housing and transporting those prisoners.

(18) A schedule of fines that the local public entity shall impose upon the private contractor if the private contractor fails to perform its contractual duties, and a requirement that, if the private contractor fails to perform its contractual duties, the local public entity shall impose a fine on the private contractor from the schedule of fines and, in addition to the fine, may exercise any other rights it has under the contract. Division (F)(2) of this section applies regarding a fine described in this division.

(19) A requirement that the private contractor adopt and use in the correctional facility the drug testing and treatment program that the department of rehabilitation and correction uses for inmates in state correctional institutions;

(20) A requirement that the private contractor provide clothing for all out-of-state prisoners housed in the correctional facility that is conspicuous in its color, style, or color and style, that conspicuously identifies its wearer as a prisoner, and that is readily distinguishable from clothing of a nature that normally is worn outside the facility by non-prisoners, that the private contractor require all out-of-state prisoners housed in the facility to wear the clothing so provided, and that the private contractor not permit any out-of-state prisoner, while inside or on the premises of the facility or while being transported to or from the facility, to wear any clothing of a nature that does not conspicuously identify

its wearer as a prisoner and that normally is worn outside the facility by non-prisoners;

(21) A requirement that, at the time the contract is made, the private contractor provide to all parties to the contract adequate proof that it has complied with the requirement described in division (D)(9) of this section, and a requirement that, at any time during the term of the contract, the private contractor upon request provide to any party to the contract adequate proof that it continues to be in compliance with the requirement described in division (D)(9) of this section.

(E) A private correctional officer or other designated employee of a private contractor that operates a correctional facility that houses out-of-state prisoners in this state under a contract entered into prior to, on, or after March 17, 1998, may carry and use firearms in the course of the officer's or employee's employment only if the officer or employee is certified as having satisfactorily completed an approved training program designed to qualify persons for positions as special police officers, security guards, or persons otherwise privately employed in a police capacity, as described in division (A) of section 109.78 of the Revised Code.

(F)(1) Upon notification by the private contractor of an escape from, or of a disturbance at, a correctional facility that is operated by a private contractor under a contract entered into prior to, on, or after March 17, 1998, and that houses out-of-state prisoners in this state, the department of rehabilitation and correction and state and local law enforcement agencies shall use all reasonable means to recapture persons who escaped from the facility or quell any disturbance at the facility, in accordance with the plan and procedure included in the written agreement entered into under division (D)(12) of this section in relation to contracts entered into on or after March 17, 1998, and in accordance with their normal procedures in relation to contracts entered into prior to March 17, 1998. Any cost incurred by this state or a political subdivision of this state relating to the apprehension of a person who escaped from the facility, to the quelling of a disturbance at the facility, or to the investigation or prosecution as described in division (G)(2) of this section of any offense relating to the escape or disturbance shall be chargeable to and borne by the private contractor. The contractor also shall reimburse the state or its political subdivisions for all reasonable costs incurred relating to the temporary detention of a person who escaped from the facility, following the person's recapture.

(2) If a private contractor that, on or after March 17, 1998, enters into a contract under this section with a local public entity for the operation of a correctional facility that houses out-of-state prisoners fails to perform its contractual duties, the local public entity shall impose upon the private contractor a fine from the schedule of fines included in the contract and may exercise any other rights it has under the contract. A fine imposed under this division shall be paid to the local public entity that enters into the contract, and the local public entity shall deposit the money so paid into its treasury to the credit of the fund used to pay for community policing. If a fine is imposed under this division, the local public entity may reduce the payment owed to the private contractor pursuant to any invoice in the amount of the fine.

(3) If a private contractor, on or after March 17, 1998, enters into a contract under this section with a local public entity for the operation of a correctional facility that houses out-of-state prisoners in this state, the private contractor shall comply with the insurance, indemnification, hold harmless, and cost reimbursement provisions described in division (D)(9) of this section.

(G)(1) Any act or omission that would be a criminal offense or a delinquent act if committed at a state correctional institution or at a jail, workhouse, prison, or other correctional facility operated by this state or by any political subdivision or group of political subdivisions of this state shall be a criminal offense or delinquent act if committed by or with regard to any out-of-state prisoner who is housed at any correctional facility operated by a private contractor in this state pursuant to a contract entered into prior to, on, or after March 17, 1998.

(2) If any political subdivision of this state experiences any cost in the investigation or prosecution of an offense committed by an out-of-state prisoner housed in a correctional facility operated by a private contractor in this state pursuant to a contract entered into prior to, on, or after March 17, 1998, the private contractor shall reimburse the political subdivision for the costs so experienced.

(3)(a) Except as otherwise provided in this division, the state, and any officer or employee, as defined in section 109.36 of the Revised Code, of the state is not liable in damages in a civil action for any injury, death, or loss to person or property that allegedly arises from, or is related to, the establishment, management, or operation of a correctional facility to house out-of-state prisoners in this state pursuant to a contract between a local public entity and an out-of-state jurisdiction, a local public entity and a private contractor, or a private contractor and an out-of-state jurisdiction that was entered into prior to March 17, 1998, or that is entered into on or after March 17, 1998, in accordance with its provisions. The immunity provided in this division does not apply regarding an act or omission of an officer or employee, as defined in section 109.36 of the Revised Code, of the state that is manifestly outside the scope of the officer's or employee's official responsibilities or regarding an act or omission of the state, or of an officer or employee, as so defined, of the state that is undertaken with malicious purpose, in bad faith, or in a wanton or reckless manner.

(b) Except as otherwise provided in this division, a non-contracting political subdivision, and any employee, as defined in section 2744.01 of the Revised Code, of a non-contracting political subdivision is not liable in damages in a civil action for any injury, death, or loss to person or property that allegedly arises from, or is related to, the establishment, management, or operation of a correctional facility to house out-of-state prisoners in this state pursuant to a contract between a local public entity other than the non-contracting political subdivision and an out-of-state jurisdiction, a local public entity other than the non-contracting political subdivision and a private contractor, or a private contractor and an out of state jurisdiction that was entered into prior to March 17, 1998, or that is entered into on or after March 17, 1998, in accordance with its provisions. The immunity provided in this division does not apply regarding an act or omission of an employee, as defined in section 2744.01 of the Revised Code, of a non-contracting political subdivision that is manifestly outside the scope of the employee's employment or official responsibilities or regarding an act or omission of a non-contracting political subdivision or an employee, as so defined, of a non-contracting political subdivision that is undertaken with malicious purpose, in bad faith, or in a wanton or reckless manner.

(c) Divisions (G)(3)(a) and (b) of this section do not affect any immunity or defense that the state and its officers and employees or a non-contracting political subdivision and its employees may be entitled to under another section of the Revised Code or the common law of this state, including, but not limited to, section 9.86 or Chapter 2744. of the Revised Code.

(H)(1) Upon the completion of an out-of-state prisoner's term of detention at a correctional facility operated by a private contractor in this state pursuant to a contract entered into prior to, on, or after March 17, 1998, the operator of the correctional facility shall transport the prisoner to the out-of-state jurisdiction that imposed the sentence for which the prisoner was confined before it releases the prisoner from its custody.

(2) No private contractor that operates and manages a correctional facility housing out-of-state prisoners in this state pursuant to a contract entered into prior to, on, or after March 17, 1998, shall fail to comply with division (H)(1) of this section.

(3) Whoever violates division (H)(2) of this section is guilty of a misdemeanor of the first degree.

(I) Except as otherwise provided in this division, the provisions of divisions (A) to (H) of this section apply in relation to any correctional facility operated by a private contractor in this state to house out-of-state prisoners, regardless of whether the facility is operated pursuant to a contract entered into prior to, on, or after March 17, 1998. Division (C)(1) of this section shall not apply in relation to any correctional facility for housing out-of-state prisoners in this state that is operated by a private contractor under a contract entered into with a local public entity prior to March 17, 1998. If a private contractor operates a correctional facility in this state for the housing of out-of-state prisoners under a contract entered into with a local public entity prior to March 17, 1998, no later than thirty days after the effective date of this amendment, the private contractor shall enter into a contract with the local public entity that comports to the requirements and criteria of division (D) of this section.

(1999 H 283, eff. 6–30–99; 1998 H 293, eff. 3–17–98)

9.08 Internet access for prisoners; improper internet access

(A) As used in this section:

(1) "Computer," "computer network," "computer system," "computer services," "telecommunications service," and "information service" have the same meanings as in section 2913.01 of the Revised Code.

(2) "Contractor" means either of the following:

(a) A person who enters into a contract under section 9.06 of the Revised Code.

(b) A person who enters into a contract under section 9.07 of the Revised Code to operate and manage a correctional facility in this state for out-of-state prisoners.

(3) "Private correctional facility" means a correctional facility that is operated by a contractor under a contract pursuant to section 9.06 or 9.07 of the Revised Code.

(B) No officer or employee of a contractor who is operating and managing a private correctional facility shall provide a prisoner in the private correctional facility access to or permit a prisoner in the private correctional facility to have access to the internet through the use of a computer, computer network, computer system, computer services, telecommunications service, or information service unless both of the following apply:

(1) The prisoner is participating in an approved educational program with direct supervision that requires the use of the internet for training or research purposes.

(2) The provision of and access to the internet is in accordance with rules promulgated by the department of rehabilitation and correction pursuant to section 5120.62 of the Revised Code.

(C)(1) No prisoner in a private correctional facility shall access the internet through the use of a computer, computer network, computer system, computer services, telecommunications service, or information service unless both of the following apply:

(a) The prisoner is participating in an approved educational program with direct supervision that requires the use of the internet for training or research purposes.

(b) The provision of and access to the internet is in accordance with rules promulgated by the department of rehabilitation and correction pursuant to section 5120.62 of the Revised Code.

(2) Whoever violates division (C)(1) of this section is guilty of improper internet access, a misdemeanor of the first degree.

(2004 H 204, eff. 11–5–04; 2000 S 12, eff. 6–8–00)

9.62 Purchase of police dogs or horses by law enforcement officers

(A) As used in this section:

(1) "Police dog or horse" means a dog or horse that has been trained, and may be used, to assist law enforcement officers in the performance of their official duties.

(2) "Law enforcement agency" means an organization or unit made up of law enforcement officers as defined in section 2901.01 of the Revised Code.

(B) Upon the disbanding of the canine or equine unit of a law enforcement agency, the agency shall give the law enforcement officer to whom a police dog or horse is assigned the first chance to purchase the animal, for one dollar. An officer who purchases an animal under this section shall assume all responsibility for the animal thereafter.

(C) If a police dog or horse is injured in the line of duty, becomes disabled and is unfit for duty, or grows too old to be fit for duty, the law enforcement officer to whom the animal is assigned may purchase the animal, for one dollar. If an officer chooses not to purchase an animal as authorized by this division or division (B) of this section, the disposition of the animal shall be as otherwise provided by law.

(D) A law enforcement officer who leaves an equine or canine unit of a law enforcement agency while the police dog or horse assigned to the officer is still fit for duty forfeits the right to purchase the animal under this section.

(1998 H 219, eff. 6–1–98)

CHAPTER 103

LEGISLATIVE SERVICES

Section

103.71 Correctional institution inspection committee

There is hereby created a correctional institution inspection committee as a subcommittee of the legislative service commission. The committee shall consist of eight persons, four of whom shall be members of the senate appointed by the president of the senate, not more than two of whom shall be members of the same political party, and four of whom shall be members of the house of representatives appointed by the speaker of the house of representatives, not more than two of whom shall be members of the same political party. Initial appointments to the committee shall be made within fifteen days after the effective date of this section and in the manner prescribed in this section. Thereafter, appointments to the committee shall be made within fifteen days after the commencement of the first regular session of the general assembly and in the manner prescribed in this section. A vacancy on the committee shall be filled for the unexpired term in the same manner as the original appointment. Members of the committee shall serve on the committee until the appointments are made in the first regular session of the following general assembly, unless they cease to be members of the general assembly. The committee, subject to the oversight and direction of the legislative service commission, shall direct the work of the director and staff of the committee.

(1999 H 283, eff. 9–29–99; 1993 H 152, eff. 7–1–93)

103.72 Officers and expenses

The correctional institution inspection committee, by a vote of at least five members, shall select from its membership a chairman, vice-chairman, and a secretary. The members of the committee shall serve without compensation but shall be reimbursed for their actual and necessary expenses incurred in the discharge of their official duties.

(1993 H 152, eff. 7–1–93)

103.73 Duties of committee

Note: See also following version of this section, eff. 4–29–05.

(A) The correctional institution inspection committee shall do all of the following:

(1) Subject to division (C) of this section, establish and maintain a continuing program of inspection of each state correctional institution used for the custody, control, training, and rehabilitation of persons convicted of crime and of each private correctional facility. Subject to division (C) of this section, the committee may inspect any local correctional institution used for the same purposes. Subject to division (C) of this section, the committee, and each member of the committee, for the purpose of making an inspection pursuant to this section, shall have access to any state or local correctional institution, to any private correctional facility, or to any part of the institution or facility and shall not be required to give advance notice of, or to make prior arrangements before conducting, an inspection.

(2) Evaluate and assist in the development of programs to improve the condition or operation of correctional institutions;

(3) Prepare a report for submission to the succeeding general assembly of the findings the committee makes in its inspections and of any programs that have been proposed or developed to improve the condition or operation of the correctional institutions in the state. The report shall contain a separate evaluation of the inmate grievance procedure at each state correctional institution. The committee shall submit the report to the succeeding general assembly within fifteen days after commencement of that general assembly's first regular session.

(B) Subject to division (C) of this section, the committee shall make an inspection of each state correctional institution each biennium and of each private correctional facility each biennium. The inspection shall include attendance at one general meal period and one rehabilitative or educational program.

(C) An inspection of a state correctional institution, a private correctional facility, or a local correctional institution under division (A) or (B) of this section or under section 103.74 of the Revised Code is subject to and shall be conducted in accordance with all of the following:

(1) The inspection shall not be conducted unless the chairperson of the committee grants prior approval for the inspection. The grant of prior approval shall specify whether the inspection is to be conducted by a subcommittee appointed under section 103.74 of the Revised Code or is to be conducted other than by a subcommittee appointed under that section.

(2) The inspection shall not be conducted unless one of the following applies:

(a) If the inspection is to be conducted by a subcommittee appointed under section 103.74 of the Revised Code, at least two members appointed to the committee are present for the inspection;

(b) If division (C)(2)(a) of this section does not apply, at least one member appointed to the committee and at least one staff member of the committee are present for the inspection.

(3) Unless the chairperson of the committee determines that the inspection must be conducted outside of normal business hours for any reason, including emergency circumstances or a justifiable cause that perpetuates the mission of the committee, and the chairperson specifies in the grant of prior approval for the inspection that the chairperson has so determined, the inspection shall be conducted only during normal business hours. If the chairperson determines that the inspection must be conducted outside of normal business hours and the chairperson specifies in the grant of prior approval for the inspection that the chairperson has so determined, the inspection may be conducted outside of normal business hours.

(4) If the inspection is to be conducted by a subcommittee appointed under section 103.74 of the Revised Code, no staff member of the committee may be present on the inspection unless the chairperson of the committee, in the grant of prior approval for the inspection, specifically authorizes staff members to be present on the inspection. If the inspection is to be conducted other than by a subcommittee appointed under that section, staff members may be present on the inspection regardless of whether the grant of prior approval contains a specific authorization for staff members to be present on the inspection.

(D) As used in this section:

(1) "Local public entity," "out–of–state prisoner," and "private contractor" have the same meanings as in section 9.07 of the Revised Code.

(2) "Private correctional facility" means a correctional facility in this state that houses out-of-state prisoners and that is operated by a private contractor under a contract with a local public entity pursuant to section 9.07 of the Revised Code.

(1998 H 293, eff. 3–17–98; 1996 S 310, eff. 6–20–96; 1994 S 226, eff. 1–1–95; 1994 H 715, eff. 7–22–94; 1993 H 152, eff. 7–1–93)

Note: See also following version of this section, eff. 4–29–05.

103.73 Duties of committee (later effective date)

Note: See also preceding version of this section, in effect until 4–29–05.

(A) The correctional institution inspection committee shall do all of the following:

(1) Subject to division (C) of this section, establish and maintain a continuing program of inspection of each state correctional institution used for the custody, control, training, and rehabilitation of persons convicted of crime and of each private correctional facility. Subject to division (C) of this section, the committee may inspect any local correctional institution used for the same purposes. Subject to division (C) of this section, the committee, and each member of the committee, for the purpose of making an inspection pursuant to this section, shall have access to any state or local correctional institution, to any private correctional facility, or to any part of the institution or facility and shall not be required to give advance notice of, or to make prior arrangements before conducting, an inspection.

(2) Evaluate and assist in the development of programs to improve the condition or operation of correctional institutions;

(3) Prepare a report for submission to the succeeding general assembly of the findings the committee makes in its inspections and of any programs that have been proposed or developed to improve the condition or operation of the correctional institutions in the state. The report shall contain a separate evaluation of the inmate grievance procedure at each state correctional institution. The committee shall submit the report to the succeeding general assembly within fifteen days after commencement of that general assembly's first regular session.

(B) Subject to division (C) of this section, the committee shall make an inspection of each state correctional institution each biennium and of each private correctional facility each biennium. The inspection shall include attendance at one general meal period and one rehabilitative or educational program.

(C) An inspection of a state correctional institution, a private correctional facility, or a local correctional institution under division (A) or (B) of this section or under section 103.74 of the Revised Code, or an inspection under section 103.76 of the Revised Code, is subject to and shall be conducted in accordance with all of the following:

(1) The inspection shall not be conducted unless the chairperson of the committee grants prior approval for the inspection. The grant of prior approval shall specify whether the inspection is to be conducted by a subcommittee appointed under section 103.74 of the Revised Code or is to be conducted other than by a subcommittee appointed under that section.

(2) The inspection shall not be conducted unless one of the following applies:

(a) If the inspection is to be conducted by a subcommittee appointed under section 103.74 of the Revised Code, at least two members appointed to the committee are present for the inspection;

(b) If division (C)(2)(a) of this section does not apply, at least one member appointed to the committee and at least one staff member of the committee are present for the inspection.

(3) Unless the chairperson of the committee determines that the inspection must be conducted outside of normal business hours for any reason, including emergency circumstances or a justifiable cause that perpetuates the mission of the committee, and the chairperson specifies in the grant of prior approval for the inspection that the chairperson has so determined, the inspection shall be conducted only during normal business hours. If the chairperson determines that the inspection must be conducted outside of normal business hours and the chairperson specifies in the grant of prior approval for the inspection that the chairperson has so determined, the inspection may be conducted outside of normal business hours.

(4) If the inspection is to be conducted by a subcommittee appointed under section 103.74 of the Revised Code, no staff member of the committee may be present on the inspection unless the chairperson of the committee, in the grant of prior approval for the inspection, specifically authorizes staff members to be present on the inspection. If the inspection is to be conducted other than by a subcommittee appointed under that section, staff members may be present on the inspection regardless of whether the grant of prior approval contains a specific authorization for staff members to be present on the inspection.

(D) As used in this section:

(1) "Local public entity," "out-of-state prisoner," and "private contractor" have the same meanings as in section 9.07 of the Revised Code.

(2) "Private correctional facility" means a correctional facility in this state that houses out-of-state prisoners and that is operated by a private contractor under a contract with a local public entity pursuant to section 9.07 of the Revised Code.

(2004 H 375, eff. 4–29–05; 1998 H 293, eff. 3–17–98; 1996 S 310, eff. 6–20–96; 1994 S 226, eff. 1–1–95; 1994 H 715, eff. 7–22–94; 1993 H 152, eff. 7–1–93)

Note: See also preceding version of this section, in effect until 4–29–05.

103.74 Subcommittees; director; appropriations

Note: See also following version of this section, eff. 4–29–05.

Subject to division (C) of section 103.73 of the Revised Code, the chairperson of the correctional institution inspection committee may appoint subcommittees, each to consist of at least two members, for the purpose of conducting inspections pursuant to section 103.73 of the Revised Code.

The committee may employ a director and any other nonlegal staff, who shall be in the unclassified service of the state, that are necessary for the committee to carry out its duties and may contract for the services of whatever nonlegal technical advisors are necessary for the committee to carry out its duties. The attorney general shall act as legal counsel to the committee.

The chairperson and vice-chairperson of the legislative service commission shall fix the compensation of the director. The director, with the approval of the director of the legislative service commission, shall fix the compensation of other staff of the committee in accordance with a salary schedule established by the director of the legislative service commission. Contracts for the services of necessary technical advisors shall be approved by the director of the legislative service commission.

The general assembly shall biennially appropriate to the correctional institution inspection committee an amount sufficient to enable the committee to perform its duties. Salaries and expenses incurred by the committee shall be paid from that appropriation upon vouchers approved by the chairperson of the committee.

(1996 S 310, eff. 6–20–96; 1993 H 152, eff. 7–1–93)

Note: See also following version of this section, eff. 4–29–05.

103.74 Subcommittees; director; appropriations (later effective date)

Note: See also preceding version of this section, in effect until 4–29–05.

Subject to division (C) of section 103.73 of the Revised Code, the chairperson of the correctional institution inspection committee may appoint subcommittees, each to consist of at least two members, for the purpose of conducting inspections pursuant to section 103.73 or 103.76 of the Revised Code.

The committee may employ a director and any other nonlegal staff, who shall be in the unclassified service of the state, that are necessary for the committee to carry out its duties and may contract for the services of whatever nonlegal technical advisors are necessary for the committee to carry out its duties. The attorney general shall act as legal counsel to the committee.

The chairperson and vice-chairperson of the legislative service commission shall fix the compensation of the director. The director, with the approval of the director of the legislative service commission, shall fix the compensation of other staff of the committee in accordance with a salary schedule established by the director of the legislative service commission. Contracts for the services of necessary technical advisors shall be approved by the director of the legislative service commission.

The general assembly shall biennially appropriate to the correctional institution inspection committee an amount sufficient to enable the committee to perform its duties. Salaries and expenses incurred by the committee shall be paid from that appropriation upon vouchers approved by the chairperson of the committee.

(2004 H 375, eff. 4–29–05; 1996 S 310, eff. 6–20–96; 1993 H 152, eff. 7–1–93)

Note: See also preceding version of this section, in effect until 4–29–05.

103.75 Definitions

As used in sections 103.76 to 103.79 of the Revised Code, "youth services facility" means a facility operated, or contracted for, by the department of youth services that is used for the care, protection, treatment, or secure confinement of any child committed to the department's custody.

(2004 H 375, eff. 4–29–05)

103.76 Inspection of youth services facility

Subject to division (C) of section 103.73 of the Revised Code, the correctional institution inspection committee may make an inspection of any youth services facility at such times as it determines.

(2004 H 375, eff. 4–29–05)

103.77 Access to inspect youth services facility

Subject to division (C) of section 103.73 of the Revised Code, the correctional institution inspection committee, and each member of the committee, for the purpose of making inspections of youth services facilities shall have access to any youth services facility, or to any part of that facility and shall not be required to give advance notice of, or to make prior arrangements before conducting, an inspection.

(2004 H 375, eff. 4–29–05)

103.78 Powers of commission relating to youth services facility inspections

The correctional institution inspection committee may do the following:

(A) Subject to division (C) of section 103.73 of the Revised Code, establish and maintain a continuing program of inspection of youth services facilities;

(B) Evaluate and assist in the development of programs to improve the condition or operation of youth services facilities;

(2004 H 375, eff. 4–29–05)

103.79 Inspection report to be submitted to succeeding general assembly

If the correctional institution inspection committee conducts inspections of youth services facilities during a biennium, the committee shall prepare a report for submission to the succeeding general assembly of the findings the committee makes in its inspections and of any programs that have been proposed or developed to improve the condition or operation of youth services facilities. The committee shall submit the report to the succeeding general assembly within fifteen days after commencement of that general assembly's first regular session.

(2004 H 375, eff. 4–29–05)

CHAPTER 109

ATTORNEY GENERAL

ORGANIZATION, POWERS, AND DUTIES

109.01 Election; term

The attorney general shall be elected quadrennially, and shall hold his office for a term of four years. The term of office of the attorney general shall commence on the second Monday of January next after his election.

(129 v 582, eff. 1–10–61; 1953 H 1; GC 331)

109.02 Duties

The attorney general is the chief law officer for the state and all its departments and shall be provided with adequate office space in Columbus. Except as provided in division (E) of section 120.06 and in sections 3517.152 to 3517.157 of the Revised Code, no state officer or board, or head of a department or institution of the state shall employ, or be represented by, other counsel or attorneys at law. The attorney general shall appear for the state in the trial and argument of all civil and criminal causes in the supreme court in which the state is directly or indirectly interested. When required by the governor or the general assembly, the attorney general shall appear for the state in any court or tribunal in a cause in which the state is a party, or in which the state is directly interested. Upon the written request of the governor, the attorney general shall prosecute any person indicted for a crime.

(1995 S 9, eff. 8–24–95; 1992 H 210, eff. 5–1–92; 1969 S 438; 1953 H 1; GC 333)

109.03 Appointment of assistant attorney general and chief counsel; duties

The attorney general may appoint a first assistant attorney general, a chief counsel, and assistant attorneys general, each of whom shall be an attorney at law, to serve for the term for which the attorney general is elected, unless sooner discharged by him, and each shall perform such duties, not otherwise provided by law, as are assigned him by the attorney general.

(1953 H 1, eff. 10–1–53; GC 334)

109.04 Powers and duties of first assistant attorney general

During the absence or disability of the attorney general, or when so directed by the attorney general, including all the rights, privileges, and powers conferred upon the attorney general by sections 2939.10, 2939.11, and 2939.17 of the Revised Code, the first assistant attorney general shall perform the duties of the attorney general.

(1953 H 1, eff. 10–1–53; GC 335)

109.05 Employees

The attorney general may appoint such employees as are necessary.

(1953 H 1, eff. 10–1–53; GC 337)

109.06 Bond

Before entering upon the discharge of the duties of his office, the attorney general shall give a bond to the state in the sum of five thousand dollars, with two or more sureties approved by the governor, conditioned for the faithful discharge of the duties of his office. Such bond, with the approval of the governor and the oath of office indorsed thereon, shall be deposited with the secretary of state and kept in his office.

The first assistant attorney general shall give a bond to the state in the sum of five thousand dollars, and such other employees as are designated by the attorney general shall give a bond to the state in such amounts as the attorney general determines. Such bonds shall be approved by the attorney general, conditioned for the faithful discharge of the duties of their offices, and shall be deposited with the secretary of state and kept in his office.

(1953 H 1, eff. 10–1–53; GC 332, 335; Source—GC 335)

109.07 Special counsel

Except under the circumstances described in division (E) of section 120.06 of the Revised Code, the attorney general may appoint special counsel to represent the state in civil actions, criminal prosecutions, or other proceedings in which the state is a party or directly interested. The special counsel shall be paid for their services from funds appropriated by the general assembly for that purpose.

(1992 H 210, eff. 5–1–92; 1953 H 1; GC 336)

109.08 Special counsel to collect claims; letterhead stationery

The attorney general may appoint special counsel to represent the state in connection with all claims of whatsoever nature which are certified to the attorney general for collection under any law or which the attorney general is authorized to collect.

Such special counsel shall be paid for their services from funds collected by them in an amount approved by the attorney general.

The attorney general shall provide to the special counsel appointed to represent the state in connection with claims arising out of Chapters 5733., 5739., 5741., and 5747. of the Revised Code the official letterhead stationery of the attorney general. The special counsel shall use the letterhead stationery, but only in connection with the collection of such claims arising out of those taxes.

(1989 S 147, eff. 1–1–90; 1953 H 1; GC 336–1)

109.081 Attorney general claims fund

Up to eleven per cent of all amounts collected by the attorney general, whether by employees or agents of the attorney general or by special counsel pursuant to section 109.08 of the Revised Code, on claims due the state shall be paid into the state treasury to the credit of the attorney general claims fund, which is hereby created. The attorney general, after consultation with the director of budget and management, shall determine the exact percentage of those collected amounts that shall be paid into the state treasury to the credit of the fund. The fund shall be used for the payment of expenses incurred by the office of the attorney general.

(1999 H 283, eff. 6–30–99; 1991 H 298, eff. 7–26–91; 1985 H 201; 1983 H 291)

109.082 Problem resolution officers

The attorney general shall appoint one or more problem resolution officers from among the employees of the office of the attorney general. These officers shall receive and review inquiries and complaints concerning collections made pursuant to Chapters 5733., 5739., 5741., and 5747. of the Revised Code regarding which the taxpayer has been unable to obtain satisfactory information after several attempts to communicate with the employee of the office assigned to the taxpayer's collection case or the employee's immediate supervisor, or the special counsel assigned to the case.

(1989 S 147, eff. 1–1–90)

109.09 Action on official bonds

When so directed, the attorney general shall bring an action on the official bond of a delinquent officer, and shall also prosecute any officer for an offense against the revenue laws of the state that come to his knowledge. Such action may be brought by him in the court of common pleas of Franklin county, or of any county in which one or more of the defendants reside, or can be summoned.

(1953 H 1, eff. 10–1–53; GC 338)

109.10 Proceedings in quo warranto

The attorney general may prosecute a proceeding in quo warranto in the supreme court of the state, the court of appeals of Franklin county, or the court of appeals of any county wherein a defendant company has a place of business, or the officers or persons made defendants reside or may be found.

(1953 H 1, eff. 10–1–53; GC 339)

109.111 Attorney general court order fund

There is hereby created the attorney general court order fund, which shall be in the custody of the treasurer of state but shall not be part of the state treasury. The fund shall consist of all money collected or received as a result of an order of any court to be received or secured by, or delivered to, the attorney general for transfer, distribution, disbursement, or allocation pursuant to court order. All money in the fund, including investment earnings thereon, shall be used solely to make payment as directed pursuant to court order.

(1996 S 310, eff. 9–19–96)

109.12 Legal advice to state officers and board

The attorney general, when so requested, shall give legal advice to a state officer, board, commission, the warden of a state correctional institution, the superintendent, trustees, or directors of a benevolent institution of the state, and the trustees of the Ohio state university, in all matters relating to their official duties.

(1994 H 571, eff. 10–6–94; 1953 H 1, eff. 10–1–53; GC 341)

109.121 Land title review and opinion

Prior to the acquisition by the state of any right, title, or interest in real property, except highway rights-of-way, evidence of such right, title, or interest shall be submitted to the attorney general for his review and opinion. Such evidence shall be that customarily and generally used in the community in which the real property is situated and may consist of, but not be limited to, attorneys' opinions of title, abstracts of title, title guarantees, or title insurance.

(1969 S 205, eff. 11–12–69)

109.13 General assembly may require written opinions

When so required by resolution, the attorney general shall give his written opinion on questions of law to either house of the general assembly.

(1953 H 1, eff. 10–1–53; GC 342)

109.14 Attorney general shall advise prosecuting attorneys and township law directors

When requested by them, the attorney general shall advise the prosecuting attorneys of the several counties respecting their duties in all complaints, suits, and controversies in which the state is, or may be a party, and shall advise the township law director of a township that has adopted a limited home rule government under Chapter 504. of the Revised Code.

(1999 H 187, eff. 9–20–99; 1996 H 501, eff. 11–6–96; 1953 H 1, eff. 10–1–53; GC 343)

109.15 Forms of contracts

The attorney general shall prepare suitable forms of contracts, obligations, and other like instruments of writing for the use of state officers, when requested by the governor, secretary of state, auditor of state, or treasurer of state.

(1953 H 1, eff. 10–1–53; GC 344)

109.16 Suits may be brought in Franklin county

The attorney general may prosecute an action, information, or other proceeding in behalf of the state, or in which the state is interested, except prosecutions by indictment, in the proper court of Franklin county, or of any other county in which one or more of the defendants reside or may be found. No civil action, unless elsewhere specially provided, shall be commenced in Franklin county, if one or more of the defendants do not reside or cannot be found therein, unless the attorney general certifies on the writ that he believes the amount in controversy exceeds five hundred dollars.

(1953 H 1, eff. 10–1–53; GC 345)

109.17 Writs in other counties

In all cases instituted by the attorney general under sections 109.01 to 109.22, inclusive, of the Revised Code, the writ may be sent by mail to the sheriff of any county, and returned by him in like manner. For such service, the sheriff shall be allowed the same mileage and fees as if the writ had been issued from the court of common pleas or the court of appeals of his county, and made returnable thereto.

(1953 H 1, eff. 10–1–53; GC 346)

109.18 Service by publication

If a writ or mesne process in proceedings in quo warranto is returned "not found" by the sheriff of the county in which the company is authorized by law to have its place of business, the clerk of the court in which the information or other proceeding is filed shall issue a notice of the filing and substance thereof, and cause it to be published once a week for six consecutive weeks in a newspaper published in and of general circulation in the county wherein such company is authorized to have its place of business. An affidavit of the publication together with a copy of the notice shall be filed in the office of the clerk. If the defendant company fails to answer or plead to such information or proceeding within thirty days from the filing of the affidavit and copy, judgment shall be given upon the default as if the writ or mesne process had been served and returned.

(1977 H 42, eff. 10–7–77; 1953 H 1; GC 347)

109.19 Security for costs and verification of pleadings

No undertaking or security is required on behalf of the state or an officer thereof, in the prosecution or defense of any action, writ, or proceeding. In an action, writ, or proceeding it is not necessary to verify the pleadings on the part of the state or any officer thereof.

(1953 H 1, eff. 10–1–53; GC 348)

109.20 Actions to be taken out of their order

Upon motion of the attorney general, embodying a statement that the public interests require it, a civil action, brought or prosecuted by him on behalf of the state, or an officer, board, or commission thereof, or an action in which the state is a party, shall be taken out of its order upon the docket and assigned for trial at as early a day as practicable.

(1953 H 1, eff. 10–1–53; GC 349)

109.21 Deposit of moneys to credit of general revenue fund

The attorney general shall pay all moneys collected or received by the attorney general on behalf of the state into the state treasury to the credit of the general revenue fund.

(1998 S 164, eff. 1–15–98; 1953 H 1, eff. 10–1–53; GC 350)

109.22 Registers shall be kept

The attorney general shall keep a register of all actions, demands, complaints, writs, informations, and other proceedings, prosecuted or defended by him, noting therein the proceedings under each, and a register of all official opinions in writing given by him. He shall deliver to his successor the registers, papers, documents, books, and other property belonging to his office.

(1953 H 1, eff. 10–1–53; GC 351)

OBSCENITY LAWS

109.40 Compilation and distribution of statutes relative to obscenity laws

The attorney general shall compile all statutes relative to obscenity in a convenient pamphlet or paper and may distribute this compilation, without charge, to such sheriffs, police chiefs, county prosecutors, city prosecutors, mayors, constables, judges of the courts of common pleas, county court judges, municipal judges, and other interested parties, as may request such distribution, and make available a reasonable number of such compilations to fill such requests.

The attorney general shall, from time to time, supplement and keep the compilation current and he may, upon request, distribute such supplemental material in the manner provided in this section.

(128 v 554, eff. 11–5–59)

VICTIMS' RIGHTS PAMPHLET

109.42 Victims' rights pamphlet; publication and distribution; costs

Note: See also following version of this section, eff. 4–29–05.

(A) The attorney general shall prepare and have printed a pamphlet that contains a compilation of all statutes relative to victim's rights in which the attorney general lists and explains the statutes in the form of a victim's bill of rights. The attorney general shall distribute the pamphlet to all sheriffs, marshals, municipal corporation and township police departments, constables, and other law enforcement agencies, to all prosecuting attorneys, city directors of law, village solicitors, and other similar chief legal officers of municipal corporations, and to organizations that represent or provide services for victims of crime. The victim's bill of rights set forth in the pamphlet shall contain a description of all of the rights of victims that are provided for in Chapter 2930. or in any other section of the Revised Code and shall include, but not be limited to, all of the following:

(1) The right of a victim or a victim's representative to attend a proceeding before a grand jury, in a juvenile case, or in a criminal case pursuant to a subpoena without being discharged from the victim's or representative's employment, having the victim's or representative's employment terminated, having the victim's or representative's pay decreased or withheld, or otherwise being punished, penalized, or threatened as a result of time lost from regular employment because of the victim's or representative's attendance at the proceeding pursuant to the subpoena, as set forth in section 2151.211, 2930.18, 2939.121, or 2945.451 of the Revised Code;

(2) The potential availability pursuant to section 2151.359 or 2152.61 of the Revised Code of a forfeited recognizance to pay damages caused by a child when the delinquency of the child or child's violation of probation or community control is found to be proximately caused by the failure of the child's parent or guardian to subject the child to reasonable parental authority or to faithfully discharge the conditions of probation or community control;

(3) The availability of awards of reparations pursuant to sections 2743.51 to 2743.72 of the Revised Code for injuries caused by criminal offenses;

(4) The right of the victim in certain criminal or juvenile cases or a victim's representative to receive, pursuant to section 2930.06 of the Revised Code, notice of the date, time, and place of the trial or delinquency proceeding in the case or, if there will not be a trial or delinquency proceeding, information from the prosecutor, as defined in section 2930.01 of the Revised Code, regarding the disposition of the case;

(5) The right of the victim in certain criminal or juvenile cases or a victim's representative to receive, pursuant to section 2930.04, 2930.05, or 2930.06 of the Revised Code, notice of the name of the person charged with the violation, the case or docket number assigned to the charge, and a telephone number or numbers that can be called to obtain information about the disposition of the case;

(6) The right of the victim in certain criminal or juvenile cases or of the victim's representative pursuant to section 2930.13 or 2930.14 of the Revised Code, subject to any reasonable terms set by the court as authorized under section 2930.14 of the Revised Code, to make a statement about the victimization and, if applicable, a statement relative to the sentencing or disposition of the offender;

(7) The opportunity to obtain a court order, pursuant to section 2945.04 of the Revised Code, to prevent or stop the commission of the offense of intimidation of a crime victim or witness or an offense against the person or property of the complainant, or of the complainant's ward or child;

(8) The right of the victim in certain criminal or juvenile cases or a victim's representative pursuant to sections 2151.38, 2929.20, 2930.10, 2930. 16, and 2930.17 of the Revised Code to receive notice of a pending motion for judicial release or early release of the person who committed the offense against the victim, to make an oral or written statement at the court hearing on the motion, and to be notified of the court's decision on the motion;

(9) The right of the victim in certain criminal or juvenile cases or a victim's representative pursuant to section 2930.16, 2967.12, 2967.26, or 5139.56 of the Revised Code to receive notice of any pending commutation, pardon, parole, transitional control, discharge, other form of authorized release, post-release control, or supervised release for the person who committed the offense against the victim or any application for release of that person and to send a written statement relative to the victimization and the pending action to the adult parole authority or the release authority of the department of youth services;

(10) The right of the victim to bring a civil action pursuant to sections 2969.01 to 2969.06 of the Revised Code to obtain money from the offender's profit fund;

(11) The right, pursuant to section 3109.09 of the Revised Code, to maintain a civil action to recover compensatory damages not exceeding ten thousand dollars and costs from the parent of a minor who willfully damages property through the commission of an act that would be a theft offense, as defined in section 2913.01 of the Revised Code, if committed by an adult;

(12) The right, pursuant to section 3109.10 of the Revised Code, to maintain a civil action to recover compensatory damages not exceeding ten thousand dollars and costs from the parent of a minor who willfully and maliciously assaults a person;

(13) The possibility of receiving restitution from an offender or a delinquent child pursuant to section 2152.20, 2929.18, or 2929.28 of the Revised Code;

(14) The right of the victim in certain criminal or juvenile cases or a victim's representative, pursuant to section 2930.16 of the Revised Code, to receive notice of the escape from confinement or custody of the person who committed the offense, to receive that notice from the custodial agency of the person at the victim's last address or telephone number provided to the custodial agency, and to receive notice that, if either the victim's address or telephone number changes, it is in the victim's interest

to provide the new address or telephone number to the custodial agency;

(15) The right of a victim of domestic violence to seek the issuance of a civil protection order pursuant to section 3113.31 of the Revised Code, the right of a victim of a violation of section 2903.14, 2909.06, 2909.07, 2911.12, 2911.211, or 2919.22 of the Revised Code, a violation of a substantially similar municipal ordinance, or an offense of violence who is a family or household member of the offender at the time of the offense to seek the issuance of a temporary protection order pursuant to section 2919.26 of the Revised Code, and the right of both types of victims to be accompanied by a victim advocate during court proceedings;

(16) The right of a victim of a sexually oriented offense that is not a registration-exempt sexually oriented offense or of a child-victim oriented offense that is committed by a person who is convicted of or pleads guilty to an aggravated sexually oriented offense, by a person who is adjudicated a sexual predator or child-victim predator, or, in certain cases, by a person who is determined to be a habitual sex offender or habitual child-victim offender to receive, pursuant to section 2950.10 of the Revised Code, notice that the person has registered with a sheriff under section 2950.04, 2950.041, or 2950.05 of the Revised Code and notice of the person's name, the person's residence that is registered, and the offender's school, institution of higher education, or place of employment address or addresses that are registered, and a summary of the manner in which the victim must make a request to receive the notice. As used in this division, "sexually oriented offense," "adjudicated a sexual predator,' ' "habitual sex offender," "registration-exempt sexually oriented offense," "aggravated sexually oriented offense," "child-victim oriented offense," " adjudicated a child-victim predator," and "habitual child- victim offender" have the same meanings as in section 2950.01 of the Revised Code.

(17) The right of a victim of certain sexually violent offenses committed by a sexually violent predator who is sentenced to a prison term pursuant to division (A)(3) of section 2971.03 of the Revised Code to receive, pursuant to section 2930.16 of the Revised Code, notice of a hearing to determine whether to modify the requirement that the offender serve the entire prison term in a state correctional facility, whether to continue, revise, or revoke any existing modification of that requirement, or whether to terminate the prison term. As used in this division, "sexually violent offense" and "sexually violent predator" have the same meanings as in section 2971.01 of the Revised Code.

(B)(1)(a) Subject to division (B)(1)(c) of this section, a prosecuting attorney, assistant prosecuting attorney, city director of law, assistant city director of law, village solicitor, assistant village solicitor, or similar chief legal officer of a municipal corporation or an assistant of any of those officers who prosecutes an offense committed in this state, upon first contact with the victim of the offense, the victim's family, or the victim's dependents, shall give the victim, the victim's family, or the victim's dependents a copy of the pamphlet prepared pursuant to division (A) of this section and explain, upon request, the information in the pamphlet to the victim, the victim's family, or the victim's dependents.

(b) Subject to division (B)(1)(c) of this section, a law enforcement agency that investigates an offense or delinquent act committed in this state shall give the victim of the offense or delinquent act, the victim's family, or the victim's dependents a copy of the pamphlet prepared pursuant to division (A) of this section at one of the following times:

(i) Upon first contact with the victim, the victim's family, or the victim's dependents;

(ii) If the offense or delinquent act is an offense of violence, if the circumstances of the offense or delinquent act and the condition of the victim, the victim's family, or the victim's dependents indicate that the victim, the victim's family, or the victim's dependents will not be able to understand the significance of the pamphlet upon first contact with the agency, and if the agency anticipates that it will have an additional contact with the victim, the victim's family, or the victim's dependents, upon the agency's second contact with the victim, the victim's family, or the victim's dependents.

If the agency does not give the victim, the victim's family, or the victim's dependents a copy of the pamphlet upon first contact with them and does not have a second contact with the victim, the victim's family, or the victim's dependents, the agency shall mail a copy of the pamphlet to the victim, the victim's family, or the victim's dependents at their last known address.

(c) In complying on and after December 9, 1994, with the duties imposed by division (B)(1)(a) or (b) of this section, an official or a law enforcement agency shall use copies of the pamphlet that are in the official's or agency's possession on December 9, 1994, until the official or agency has distributed all of those copies. After the official or agency has distributed all of those copies, the official or agency shall use only copies of the pamphlet that contain at least the information described in divisions (A)(1) to (17) of this section.

(2) The failure of a law enforcement agency or of a prosecuting attorney, assistant prosecuting attorney, city director of law, assistant city director of law, village solicitor, assistant village solicitor, or similar chief legal officer of a municipal corporation or an assistant to any of those officers to give, as required by division (B)(1) of this section, the victim of an offense or delinquent act, the victim's family, or the victim's dependents a copy of the pamphlet prepared pursuant to division (A) of this section does not give the victim, the victim's family, the victim's dependents, or a victim's representative any rights under section 2743.51 to 2743.72, 2945.04, 2967.12, 2969.01 to 2969.06, 3109.09, or 3109.10 of the Revised Code or under any other provision of the Revised Code and does not affect any right under those sections.

(3) A law enforcement agency, a prosecuting attorney or assistant prosecuting attorney, or a city director of law, assistant city director of law, village solicitor, assistant village solicitor, or similar chief legal officer of a municipal corporation that distributes a copy of the pamphlet prepared pursuant to division (A) of this section shall not be required to distribute a copy of an information card or other printed material provided by the clerk of the court of claims pursuant to section 2743.71 of the Revised Code.

(C) The cost of printing and distributing the pamphlet prepared pursuant to division (A) of this section shall be paid out of the reparations fund, created pursuant to section 2743.191 of the Revised Code, in accordance with division (D) of that section.

(D) As used in this section:

(1) "Victim's representative" has the same meaning as in section 2930.01 of the Revised Code;

(2) "Victim advocate" has the same meaning as in section 2919.26 of the Revised Code.

(2004 H 427, eff. 6–9–04; 2003 S 50, eff. 1–8–04; 2003 S 5, § 3, eff. 1–1–04; 2003 S 5, § 1, eff. 7–31–03; 2002 H 490, eff. 1–1–04; 2000 S 179, § 3, eff. 1–1–02; 1999 H 3, eff. 11–22–99; 1997 S 111, eff. 3–17–98; 1996 H 180, eff. 1–1–97; 1996 H 601, eff. 10–29–96; 1995 S 2, eff. 7–1–96; 1995 H 18, eff. 11–24–95; 1994 H 335, eff. 12–9–94; 1994 S 186, eff. 10–12–94; 1993 H 152, eff. 7–1–93; 1990 S 3; 1988 H 708; 1987 H 207; 1986 H 657)

Note: See also following version of this section, eff. 4–29–05.

109.42 Victims' rights pamphlet; publication and distribution; costs (later effective date)

Note: See also preceding version of this section, in effect until 4–29–04.

(A) The attorney general shall prepare and have printed a pamphlet that contains a compilation of all statutes relative to victim's rights in which the attorney general lists and explains the statutes in the form of a victim's bill of rights. The attorney general shall distribute the pamphlet to all sheriffs, marshals, municipal corporation and township police departments, constables, and other law enforcement agencies, to all prosecuting attorneys, city directors of law, village solicitors, and other similar chief legal officers of municipal corporations, and to organizations that represent or provide services for victims of crime. The victim's bill of rights set forth in the pamphlet shall contain a description of all of the rights of victims that are provided for in Chapter 2930. or in any other section of the Revised Code and shall include, but not be limited to, all of the following:

(1) The right of a victim or a victim's representative to attend a proceeding before a grand jury, in a juvenile case, or in a criminal case pursuant to a subpoena without being discharged from the victim's or representative's employment, having the victim's or representative's employment terminated, having the victim's or representative's pay decreased or withheld, or otherwise being punished, penalized, or threatened as a result of time lost from regular employment because of the victim's or representative's attendance at the proceeding pursuant to the subpoena, as set forth in section 2151.211, 2930.18, 2939.121, or 2945.451 of the Revised Code;

(2) The potential availability pursuant to section 2151.359 or 2152.61 of the Revised Code of a forfeited recognizance to pay damages caused by a child when the delinquency of the child or child's violation of probation or community control is found to be proximately caused by the failure of the child's parent or guardian to subject the child to reasonable parental authority or to faithfully discharge the conditions of probation or community control;

(3) The availability of awards of reparations pursuant to sections 2743.51 to 2743.72 of the Revised Code for injuries caused by criminal offenses;

(4) The right of the victim in certain criminal or juvenile cases or a victim's representative to receive, pursuant to section 2930.06 of the Revised Code, notice of the date, time, and place of the trial or delinquency proceeding in the case or, if there will not be a trial or delinquency proceeding, information from the prosecutor, as defined in section 2930.01 of the Revised Code, regarding the disposition of the case;

(5) The right of the victim in certain criminal or juvenile cases or a victim's representative to receive, pursuant to section 2930.04, 2930.05, or 2930.06 of the Revised Code, notice of the name of the person charged with the violation, the case or docket number assigned to the charge, and a telephone number or numbers that can be called to obtain information about the disposition of the case;

(6) The right of the victim in certain criminal or juvenile cases or of the victim's representative pursuant to section 2930.13 or 2930.14 of the Revised Code, subject to any reasonable terms set by the court as authorized under section 2930.14 of the Revised Code, to make a statement about the victimization and, if applicable, a statement relative to the sentencing or disposition of the offender;

(7) The opportunity to obtain a court order, pursuant to section 2945.04 of the Revised Code, to prevent or stop the commission of the offense of intimidation of a crime victim or witness or an offense against the person or property of the complainant, or of the complainant's ward or child;

(8) The right of the victim in certain criminal or juvenile cases or a victim's representative pursuant to sections 2151.38, 2929.20, 2930.10, 2930. 16, and 2930.17 of the Revised Code to receive notice of a pending motion for judicial release or early release of the person who committed the offense against the victim, to make an oral or written statement at the court hearing on the motion, and to be notified of the court's decision on the motion;

(9) The right of the victim in certain criminal or juvenile cases or a victim's representative pursuant to section 2930.16, 2967.12, 2967.26, or 5139.56 of the Revised Code to receive notice of any pending commutation, pardon, parole, transitional control, discharge, other form of authorized release, post-release control, or supervised release for the person who committed the offense against the victim or any application for release of that person and to send a written statement relative to the victimization and the pending action to the adult parole authority or the release authority of the department of youth services;

(10) The right of the victim to bring a civil action pursuant to sections 2969.01 to 2969.06 of the Revised Code to obtain money from the offender's profit fund;

(11) The right, pursuant to section 3109.09 of the Revised Code, to maintain a civil action to recover compensatory damages not exceeding ten thousand dollars and costs from the parent of a minor who willfully damages property through the commission of an act that would be a theft offense, as defined in section 2913.01 of the Revised Code, if committed by an adult;

(12) The right, pursuant to section 3109.10 of the Revised Code, to maintain a civil action to recover compensatory damages not exceeding ten thousand dollars and costs from the parent of a minor who willfully and maliciously assaults a person;

(13) The possibility of receiving restitution from an offender or a delinquent child pursuant to section 2152.20, 2929.18, or 2929.28 of the Revised Code;

(14) The right of the victim in certain criminal or juvenile cases or a victim's representative, pursuant to section 2930.16 of the Revised Code, to receive notice of the escape from confinement or custody of the person who committed the offense, to receive that notice from the custodial agency of the person at the victim's last address or telephone number provided to the custodial agency, and to receive notice that, if either the victim's address or telephone number changes, it is in the victim's interest to provide the new address or telephone number to the custodial agency;

(15) The right of a victim of domestic violence to seek the issuance of a civil protection order pursuant to section 3113.31 of the Revised Code, the right of a victim of a violation of section 2903.14, 2909.06, 2909.07, 2911.12, 2911.211, or 2919.22 of the Revised Code, a violation of a substantially similar municipal ordinance, or an offense of violence who is a family or household member of the offender at the time of the offense to seek the issuance of a temporary protection order pursuant to section 2919.26 of the Revised Code, and the right of both types of victims to be accompanied by a victim advocate during court proceedings;

(16) The right of a victim of a sexually oriented offense that is not a registration-exempt sexually oriented offense or of a child-victim oriented offense that is committed by a person who is convicted of or pleads guilty to an aggravated sexually oriented offense, by a person who is adjudicated a sexual predator or child-victim predator, or, in certain cases, by a person who is determined to be a habitual sex offender or habitual child-victim offender to receive, pursuant to section 2950.10 of the Revised Code, notice that the person has registered with a sheriff under section 2950.04, 2950.041, or 2950.05 of the Revised Code and notice of the person's name, the person's residence that is registered, and the offender's school, institution of higher education, or place of employment address or addresses that are registered, and a summary of the manner in which the victim must make a request to receive the notice. As used in this

division, "sexually oriented offense," "adjudicated a sexual predator," "habitual sex offender," "registration-exempt sexually oriented offense," "aggravated sexually oriented offense," "child-victim oriented offense," "adjudicated a child-victim predator," and "habitual child-victim offender" have the same meanings as in section 2950.01 of the Revised Code.

(17) The right of a victim of certain sexually violent offenses committed by an offender who also is convicted of or pleads guilty to a sexually violent predator specification and who is sentenced to a prison term pursuant to division (A)(3) of section 2971.03 of the Revised Code to receive, pursuant to section 2930.16 of the Revised Code, notice of a hearing to determine whether to modify the requirement that the offender serve the entire prison term in a state correctional facility, whether to continue, revise, or revoke any existing modification of that requirement, or whether to terminate the prison term. As used in this division, "sexually violent offense" and "sexually violent predator specification" have the same meanings as in section 2971.01 of the Revised Code.

(B)(1)(a) Subject to division (B)(1)(c) of this section, a prosecuting attorney, assistant prosecuting attorney, city director of law, assistant city director of law, village solicitor, assistant village solicitor, or similar chief legal officer of a municipal corporation or an assistant of any of those officers who prosecutes an offense committed in this state, upon first contact with the victim of the offense, the victim's family, or the victim's dependents, shall give the victim, the victim's family, or the victim's dependents a copy of the pamphlet prepared pursuant to division (A) of this section and explain, upon request, the information in the pamphlet to the victim, the victim's family, or the victim's dependents.

(b) Subject to division (B)(1)(c) of this section, a law enforcement agency that investigates an offense or delinquent act committed in this state shall give the victim of the offense or delinquent act, the victim's family, or the victim's dependents a copy of the pamphlet prepared pursuant to division (A) of this section at one of the following times:

(i) Upon first contact with the victim, the victim's family, or the victim's dependents;

(ii) If the offense or delinquent act is an offense of violence, if the circumstances of the offense or delinquent act and the condition of the victim, the victim's family, or the victim's dependents indicate that the victim, the victim's family, or the victim's dependents will not be able to understand the significance of the pamphlet upon first contact with the agency, and if the agency anticipates that it will have an additional contact with the victim, the victim's family, or the victim's dependents, upon the agency's second contact with the victim, the victim's family, or the victim's dependents.

If the agency does not give the victim, the victim's family, or the victim's dependents a copy of the pamphlet upon first contact with them and does not have a second contact with the victim, the victim's family, or the victim's dependents, the agency shall mail a copy of the pamphlet to the victim, the victim's family, or the victim's dependents at their last known address.

(c) In complying on and after December 9, 1994, with the duties imposed by division (B)(1)(a) or (b) of this section, an official or a law enforcement agency shall use copies of the pamphlet that are in the official's or agency's possession on December 9, 1994, until the official or agency has distributed all of those copies. After the official or agency has distributed all of those copies, the official or agency shall use only copies of the pamphlet that contain at least the information described in divisions (A)(1) to (17) of this section.

(2) The failure of a law enforcement agency or of a prosecuting attorney, assistant prosecuting attorney, city director of law, assistant city director of law, village solicitor, assistant village solicitor, or similar chief legal officer of a municipal corporation or an assistant to any of those officers to give, as required by division (B)(1) of this section, the victim of an offense or delinquent act, the victim's family, or the victim's dependents a copy of the pamphlet prepared pursuant to division (A) of this section does not give the victim, the victim's family, the victim's dependents, or a victim's representative any rights under section 2743.51 to 2743.72, 2945.04, 2967.12, 2969.01 to 2969.06, 3109.09, or 3109.10 of the Revised Code or under any other provision of the Revised Code and does not affect any right under those sections.

(3) A law enforcement agency, a prosecuting attorney or assistant prosecuting attorney, or a city director of law, assistant city director of law, village solicitor, assistant village solicitor, or similar chief legal officer of a municipal corporation that distributes a copy of the pamphlet prepared pursuant to division (A) of this section shall not be required to distribute a copy of an information card or other printed material provided by the clerk of the court of claims pursuant to section 2743.71 of the Revised Code.

(C) The cost of printing and distributing the pamphlet prepared pursuant to division (A) of this section shall be paid out of the reparations fund, created pursuant to section 2743.191 of the Revised Code, in accordance with division (D) of that section.

(D) As used in this section:

(1) "Victim's representative" has the same meaning as in section 2930.01 of the Revised Code;

(2) "Victim advocate" has the same meaning as in section 2919.26 of the Revised Code.

(2004 H 473, eff. 4–29–05; 2004 H 427, eff. 6–9–04; 2003 S 50, eff. 1–8–04; 2003 S 5, § 3, eff. 1–1–04; 2003 S 5, § 1, eff. 7–31–03; 2002 H 490, eff. 1–1–04; 2000 S 179, § 3, eff. 1–1–02; 1999 H 3, eff. 11–22–99; 1997 S 111, eff. 3–17–98; 1996 H 180, eff. 1–1–97; 1996 H 601, eff. 10–29–96; 1995 S 2, eff. 7–1–96; 1995 H 18, eff. 11–24–95; 1994 H 335, eff. 12–9–94; 1994 S 186, eff. 10–12–94; 1993 H 152, eff. 7–1–93; 1990 S 3; 1988 H 708; 1987 H 207; 1986 H 657)

Note: See also preceding version of this section, in effect until 4–29–05.

BUREAU OF CRIMINAL IDENTIFICATION AND INVESTIGATION

109.51 Creation of bureau of criminal identification and investigation

There is hereby created in the office of the attorney general, a bureau of criminal identification and investigation to be located at the site of the London correctional institution. The attorney general shall appoint a superintendent of said bureau. The superintendent shall appoint, with the approval of the attorney general, such assistants as are necessary to carry out the functions and duties of the bureau as contained in sections 109.51 to 109.63, inclusive, of the Revised Code.

(130 v H 263, eff. 9–24–63)

109.511 Offenses affecting employment eligibility of investigators and special agents

(A) As used in this section, "felony" means any of the following:

(1) An offense committed in this state that is a felony under the law of this state;

(2) An offense committed in a state other than this state, or under the law of the United States, that, if committed in this state, would be a felony under the law of this state.

(B) The superintendent of the bureau of criminal identification and investigation shall not appoint or employ any person as an investigator or a special agent on a permanent basis, on a temporary basis, for a probationary term, or on other than a permanent basis if the person previously has been convicted of or has pleaded guilty to a felony.

(C)(1) The superintendent shall terminate the employment of an investigator or a special agent who does either of the following:

(a) Pleads guilty to a felony;

(b) Pleads guilty to a misdemeanor pursuant to a negotiated plea agreement as provided in division (D) of section 2929.43 of the Revised Code in which the investigator or special agent agrees to surrender the certificate awarded to the investigator or special agent under section 109.77 of the Revised Code.

(2) The superintendent shall suspend from employment an investigator or a special agent who is convicted, after trial, of a felony. If the investigator or special agent files an appeal from that conviction and the conviction is upheld by the highest court to which the appeal is taken or if the investigator or special agent does not file a timely appeal, the superintendent shall terminate the employment of that investigator or special agent. If the investigator or special agent files an appeal that results in that investigator's or special agent's acquittal of the felony or conviction of a misdemeanor, or in the dismissal of the felony charge against the investigator or special agent, the superintendent shall reinstate that investigator or special agent. An investigator or a special agent who is reinstated under this division shall not receive any back pay unless that investigator's or special agent's conviction of the felony was reversed on appeal, or the felony charge was dismissed, because the court found insufficient evidence to convict the investigator or special agent of the felony.

(D) This section does not apply regarding an offense that was committed prior to January 1, 1997.

(E) The suspension from employment or the termination of the employment of an investigator or a special agent under division (C) of this section shall be in accordance with Chapter 119. of the Revised Code.

(2002 H 490, eff. 1–1–04; 1996 H 566, eff. 10–16–96)

109.52 Criminal analysis laboratory; investigators and technicians

The bureau of criminal identification and investigation may operate and maintain a criminal analysis laboratory and mobile units thereof, create a staff of investigators and technicians skilled in the solution and control of crimes and criminal activity, keep statistics and other necessary data, assist in the prevention of crime, and engage in such other activities as will aid law enforcement officers in solving crimes and controlling criminal activity.

(130 v H 263, eff. 9–24–63)

109.53 Equipment and furnishings of the bureau

The bureau of criminal identification and investigation shall be supplied with furniture, fixtures, apparatus, vehicles, and materials necessary to carry out the functions and duties of the bureau as contained in sections 109.51 to 109.63, inclusive, of the Revised Code.

(130 v H 263, eff. 9–24–63)

109.54 Intergovernmental cooperation; drug investigations; recording and televising equipment for child sex offense victims; list of persons to question sex offense victims

(A) The bureau of criminal identification and investigation may investigate any criminal activity in this state that is of statewide or intercounty concern when requested by local authorities and may aid federal authorities, when requested, in their investigation of any criminal activity in this state. The bureau may investigate any criminal activity in this state involving drug abuse or illegal drug distribution prohibited under Chapter 3719. or 4729. of the Revised Code. The superintendent and any agent of the bureau may participate, as the director of an organized crime task force established under section 177.02 of the Revised Code or as a member of the investigatory staff of a task force established under that section, in an investigation of organized criminal activity anywhere within this state under sections 177.01 to 177.03 of the Revised Code.

(B) The bureau may provide any trained investigative personnel and specialized equipment that are requested by any sheriff or chief of police, by the authorized designee of any sheriff or chief of police, or by any other authorized law enforcement officer to aid and assist the officer in the investigation and solution of any crime or the control of any criminal activity occurring within the officer's jurisdiction. This assistance shall be furnished by the bureau without disturbing or impairing any of the existing law enforcement authority or the prerogatives of local law enforcement authorities or officers. Investigators provided pursuant to this section, or engaged in an investigation pursuant to section 109.83 of the Revised Code, may go armed in the same manner as sheriffs and regularly appointed police officers under section 2923.12 of the Revised Code.

(C)(1) The bureau shall obtain recording equipment that can be used to record depositions of the type described in division (A) of section 2152.81 and division (A) of section 2945.481 of the Revised Code, or testimony of the type described in division (D) of section 2152.81 and division (D) of section 2945.481 or in division (C) of section 2937.11 of the Revised Code, shall obtain closed circuit equipment that can be used to televise testimony of the type described in division (C) of section 2152.81 and division (C) of section 2945.481 or in division (B) of section 2937.11 of the Revised Code, and shall provide the equipment, upon request, to any court for use in recording any deposition or testimony of one of those types or in televising the testimony in accordance with the applicable division.

(2) The bureau shall obtain the names, addresses, and telephone numbers of persons who are experienced in questioning children in relation to an investigation of a violation of section 2905.03, 2905.05, 2907.02, 2907.03, 2907.04, 2907.05, 2907.06, 2907.07, 2907.09, 2907.21, 2907.23, 2907.24, 2907.31, 2907.32, 2907.321, 2907.322, 2907.323, or 2919.22 of the Revised Code or an offense of violence and shall maintain a list of those names, addresses, and telephone numbers. The list shall include a classification of the names, addresses, and telephone numbers by appellate district. Upon request, the bureau shall provide any county sheriff, chief of police, prosecuting attorney, village solicitor, city director of law, or similar chief legal officer with the name, address, and telephone number of any person contained in the list.

(2000 S 179, § 3, eff. 1–1–02; 1997 S 53, eff. 10–14–97; 1996 H 480, eff. 10–16–96; 1996 H 445, eff. 9–3–96; 1986 H 108, eff. 10–14–86; 1986 S 74; 1970 H 956; 130 v H 263)

109.541 Investigators

(A) As used in this section:

(1) "Investigator" means an officer or employee of the bureau of criminal identification and investigation described in section 109.54 of the Revised Code.

(2) "Peace officer" has the same meaning as in section 2935.01 of the Revised Code.

(B) An investigator, while providing assistance to a law enforcement officer pursuant to division (B) of section 109.54 of the Revised Code, has the same arrest authority as a peace officer of the law enforcement agency served by the law enforcement officer requesting the assistance. The investigator may exercise this arrest authority only in connection with the investigation or activities for which the investigator's assistance was requested.

(C)(1) No state official shall command, order, or direct an investigator to perform any duty or service that is not authorized by law. The power and duties conferred by this section on the bureau of criminal identification and investigation are supplementary to, and in no way a limitation on, the power and duties of sheriffs or other peace officers of the state or a political subdivision of the state.

(2) An investigator, pursuant to the policy established by the superintendent of the bureau of criminal identification and investigation under division (D)(1) of this section, may render emergency assistance to any peace officer who has arrest authority under section 2935.03 of the Revised Code if both of the following apply:

(a) There is a threat of imminent physical harm to the peace officer, a threat of physical harm to another person, or any serious emergency situation.

(b) The peace officer requests emergency assistance, or it appears to the investigator that the peace officer is unable to request emergency assistance and that the circumstances reasonably indicate that emergency assistance is appropriate.

(D)(1) The superintendent of the bureau of criminal identification and investigation, not later than sixty days after the effective date of this section, shall establish a policy specifying the manner and procedures by which an investigator may render emergency assistance to a peace officer pursuant to division (C)(2) of this section.

(2) An investigator who renders assistance to a law enforcement officer pursuant to division (B) of section 109.54 of the Revised Code or renders emergency assistance to any peace officer pursuant to division (C)(2) of this section and under the policy established under division (D)(1) of this section shall be considered to be engaged in the investigator's regular employment for the purpose of compensation, retirement benefits, indemnification rights, workers' compensation, and any other rights or benefits to which the investigator may be entitled incident to the investigator's regular employment.

(3) An investigator who renders emergency assistance to a peace officer pursuant to division (C)(2) of this section and under the policy established under division (D)(1) of this section has the same authority as the peace officer to whom the assistance is rendered.

(4) An investigator who renders emergency assistance to a peace officer pursuant to division (C)(2) of this section and under the policy established under division (D)(1) of this section retains personal immunity from liability as described in sections 9.85 to 9.87 of the Revised Code, the right to defense under sections 109.36 to 109.366 of the Revised Code, and the right to indemnification under section 9.87 of the Revised Code. This section does not affect the provisions of section 2743.02 of the Revised Code that pertain to the commencement of a civil action against a state officer or employee.

(1996 H 480, eff. 10–16–96)

109.55 Coordination of law enforcement activities

The superintendent of the bureau of criminal identification and investigation shall recommend cooperative policies for the coordination of the law enforcement work and crime prevention activities of all state and local agencies and officials having law enforcement duties to promote cooperation between such agencies and officials, to secure effective and efficient law enforcement, to eliminate duplication of work, and to promote economy of operation in such agencies.

In formulating and recommending cooperative policies, the superintendent shall emphasize the provisions of section 2901.30 of the Revised Code.

The superintendent shall develop procedures and forms to implement section 2901.30 of the Revised Code.

(1984 S 321, eff. 4–9–85; 130 v H 263)

109.56 Training local law enforcement authorities

The bureau of criminal identification and investigation shall, where practicable, assist in training local law enforcement officers in crime prevention, detection, and solution when requested by local authorities, and, where practicable, furnish instruction to sheriffs, chiefs of police, and other law officers in the establishment of efficient local bureaus of identification in their districts.

(130 v H 263, eff. 9–24–63)

109.57 Duties of superintendent of bureau

(A)(1) The superintendent of the bureau of criminal identification and investigation shall procure from wherever procurable and file for record photographs, pictures, descriptions, fingerprints, measurements, and other information that may be pertinent of all persons who have been convicted of committing within this state a felony, any crime constituting a misdemeanor on the first offense and a felony on subsequent offenses, or any misdemeanor described in division (A)(1)(a) of section 109.572 of the Revised Code, of all children under eighteen years of age who have been adjudicated delinquent children for committing within this state an act that would be a felony or an offense of violence if committed by an adult or who have been convicted of or pleaded guilty to committing within this state a felony or an offense of violence, and of all well-known and habitual criminals. The person in charge of any county, multicounty, municipal, municipal-county, or multicounty-municipal jail or workhouse, community-based correctional facility, halfway house, alternative residential facility, or state correctional institution and the person in charge of any state institution having custody of a person suspected of having committed a felony, any crime constituting a misdemeanor on the first offense and a felony on subsequent offenses, or any misdemeanor described in division (A)(1)(a) of section 109.572 of the Revised Code or having custody of a child under eighteen years of age with respect to whom there is probable cause to believe that the child may have committed an act that would be a felony or an offense of violence if committed by an adult shall furnish such material to the superintendent of the bureau. Fingerprints, photographs, or other descriptive information of a child who is under eighteen years of age, has not been arrested or otherwise taken into custody for committing an act that would be a felony or an offense of violence if committed by an adult, has not been adjudicated a delinquent child for committing an act that would be a felony or an offense of violence if committed by an adult, has not been convicted of or pleaded guilty to committing a felony or an offense of violence, and is not a child with respect to whom there is probable cause to believe that the child may have committed an act that would be a felony or an offense of violence if committed by an adult shall not be procured by the superintendent or furnished by any person in charge of any county, multicounty, municipal, municipal-county, or multicounty-municipal jail or workhouse, community-based correctional facility, halfway house, alternative residential facility, or state correctional institution, except as authorized in section 2151.313 of the Revised Code.

(2) Every clerk of a court of record in this state, other than the supreme court or a court of appeals, shall send to the superinten-

dent of the bureau a weekly report containing a summary of each case involving a felony, involving any crime constituting a misdemeanor on the first offense and a felony on subsequent offenses, involving a misdemeanor described in division (A)(1)(a) of section 109.572 of the Revised Code, or involving an adjudication in a case in which a child under eighteen years of age was alleged to be a delinquent child for committing an act that would be a felony or an offense of violence if committed by an adult. The clerk of the court of common pleas shall include in the report and summary the clerk sends under this division all information described in divisions (A)(2)(a) to (f) of this section regarding a case before the court of appeals that is served by that clerk. The summary shall be written on the standard forms furnished by the superintendent pursuant to division (B) of this section and shall include the following information:

(a) The incident tracking number contained on the standard forms furnished by the superintendent pursuant to division (B) of this section;

(b) The style and number of the case;

(c) The date of arrest;

(d) The date that the person was convicted of or pleaded guilty to the offense, adjudicated a delinquent child for committing the act that would be a felony or an offense of violence if committed by an adult, found not guilty of the offense, or found not to be a delinquent child for committing an act that would be a felony or an offense of violence if committed by an adult, the date of an entry dismissing the charge, an entry declaring a mistrial of the offense in which the person is discharged, an entry finding that the person or child is not competent to stand trial, or an entry of a nolle prosequi, or the date of any other determination that constitutes final resolution of the case;

(e) A statement of the original charge with the section of the Revised Code that was alleged to be violated;

(f) If the person or child was convicted, pleaded guilty, or was adjudicated a delinquent child, the sentence or terms of probation imposed or any other disposition of the offender or the delinquent child.

If the offense involved the disarming of a law enforcement officer or an attempt to disarm a law enforcement officer, the clerk shall clearly state that fact in the summary, and the superintendent shall ensure that a clear statement of that fact is placed in the bureau's records.

(3) The superintendent shall cooperate with and assist sheriffs, chiefs of police, and other law enforcement officers in the establishment of a complete system of criminal identification and in obtaining fingerprints and other means of identification of all persons arrested on a charge of a felony, any crime constituting a misdemeanor on the first offense and a felony on subsequent offenses, or a misdemeanor described in division (A)(1)(a) of section 109.572 of the Revised Code and of all children under eighteen years of age arrested or otherwise taken into custody for committing an act that would be a felony or an offense of violence if committed by an adult. The superintendent also shall file for record the fingerprint impressions of all persons confined in a county, multicounty, municipal, municipal-county, or multicounty-municipal jail or workhouse, community-based correctional facility, halfway house, alternative residential facility, or state correctional institution for the violation of state laws and of all children under eighteen years of age who are confined in a county, multicounty, municipal, municipal-county, or multicounty-municipal jail or workhouse, community-based correctional facility, halfway house, alternative residential facility, or state correctional institution or in any facility for delinquent children for committing an act that would be a felony or an offense of violence if committed by an adult, and any other information that the superintendent may receive from law enforcement officials of the state and its political subdivisions.

(4) The superintendent shall carry out Chapter 2950. of the Revised Code with respect to the registration of persons who are convicted of or plead guilty to either a sexually oriented offense that is not a registration-exempt sexually oriented offense or a child-victim oriented offense and with respect to all other duties imposed on the bureau under that chapter.

(5) The bureau shall perform centralized recordkeeping functions for criminal history records and services in this state for purposes of the national crime prevention and privacy compact set forth in section 109.571 of the Revised Code and is the criminal history record repository as defined in that section for purposes of that compact. The superintendent or the superintendent's designee is the compact officer for purposes of that compact and shall carry out the responsibilities of the compact officer specified in that compact.

(B) The superintendent shall prepare and furnish to every county, multicounty, municipal, municipal-county, or multicounty-municipal jail or workhouse, community-based correctional facility, halfway house, alternative residential facility, or state correctional institution and to every clerk of a court in this state specified in division (A)(2) of this section standard forms for reporting the information required under division (A) of this section. The standard forms that the superintendent prepares pursuant to this division may be in a tangible format, in an electronic format, or in both tangible formats and electronic formats.

(C) The superintendent may operate a center for electronic, automated, or other data processing for the storage and retrieval of information, data, and statistics pertaining to criminals and to children under eighteen years of age who are adjudicated delinquent children for committing an act that would be a felony or an offense of violence if committed by an adult, criminal activity, crime prevention, law enforcement, and criminal justice, and may establish and operate a statewide communications network to gather and disseminate information, data, and statistics for the use of law enforcement agencies. The superintendent may gather, store, retrieve, and disseminate information, data, and statistics that pertain to children who are under eighteen years of age and that are gathered pursuant to sections 109.57 to 109.61 of the Revised Code together with information, data, and statistics that pertain to adults and that are gathered pursuant to those sections. In addition to any other authorized use of information, data, and statistics of that nature, the superintendent or the superintendent's designee may provide and exchange the information, data, and statistics pursuant to the national crime prevention and privacy compact as described in division (A)(5) of this section.

(D) The information and materials furnished to the superintendent pursuant to division (A) of this section and information and materials furnished to any board or person under division (F) or (G) of this section are not public records under section 149.43 of the Revised Code.

(E) The attorney general shall adopt rules, in accordance with Chapter 119. of the Revised Code, setting forth the procedure by which a person may receive or release information gathered by the superintendent pursuant to division (A) of this section. A reasonable fee may be charged for this service. If a temporary employment service submits a request for a determination of whether a person the service plans to refer to an employment position has been convicted of or pleaded guilty to an offense listed in division (A)(1), (3), (4), (5), or (6) of section 109.572 of the Revised Code, the request shall be treated as a single request and only one fee shall be charged.

(F)(1) As used in division (F)(2) of this section, "head start agency" means an entity in this state that has been approved to be an agency for purposes of subchapter II of the "Community Economic Development Act," 95 Stat. 489 (1981), 42 U.S.C.A. 9831, as amended.

(2)(a) In addition to or in conjunction with any request that is required to be made under section 109.572, 2151.86, 3301.32,

3301.541, 3319.39, 3701.881, 5104.012, 5104.013, 5123.081, 5126.28, 5126.281, or 5153.111 of the Revised Code, the board of education of any school district; the director of mental retardation and developmental disabilities; any county board of mental retardation and developmental disabilities; any entity under contract with a county board of mental retardation and developmental disabilities; the chief administrator of any chartered nonpublic school; the chief administrator of any home health agency; the chief administrator of or person operating any child day-care center, type A family day-care home, or type B family day-care home licensed or certified under Chapter 5104. of the Revised Code; the administrator of any type C family day-care home certified pursuant to Section 1 of Sub. H.B. 62 of the 121st general assembly or Section 5 of Am. Sub. S.B. 160 of the 121st general assembly; the chief administrator of any head start agency; or the executive director of a public children services agency may request that the superintendent of the bureau investigate and determine, with respect to any individual who has applied for employment in any position after October 2, 1989, or any individual wishing to apply for employment with a board of education may request, with regard to the individual, whether the bureau has any information gathered under division (A) of this section that pertains to that individual. On receipt of the request, the superintendent shall determine whether that information exists and, upon request of the person, board, or entity requesting information, also shall request from the federal bureau of investigation any criminal records it has pertaining to that individual. The superintendent or the superintendent's designee also may request criminal history records from other states or the federal government pursuant to the national crime prevention and privacy compact set forth in section 109.571 of the Revised Code. Within thirty days of the date that the superintendent receives a request, the superintendent shall send to the board, entity, or person a report of any information that the superintendent determines exists, including information contained in records that have been sealed under section 2953.32 of the Revised Code, and, within thirty days of its receipt, shall send the board, entity, or person a report of any information received from the federal bureau of investigation, other than information the dissemination of which is prohibited by federal law.

(b) When a board of education is required to receive information under this section as a prerequisite to employment of an individual pursuant to section 3319.39 of the Revised Code, it may accept a certified copy of records that were issued by the bureau of criminal identification and investigation and that are presented by an individual applying for employment with the district in lieu of requesting that information itself. In such a case, the board shall accept the certified copy issued by the bureau in order to make a photocopy of it for that individual's employment application documents and shall return the certified copy to the individual. In a case of that nature, a district only shall accept a certified copy of records of that nature within one year after the date of their issuance by the bureau.

(3) The state board of education may request, with respect to any individual who has applied for employment after October 2, 1989, in any position with the state board or the department of education, any information that a school district board of education is authorized to request under division (F)(2) of this section, and the superintendent of the bureau shall proceed as if the request has been received from a school district board of education under division (F)(2) of this section.

(4) When the superintendent of the bureau receives a request for information under section 3319.291 of the Revised Code, the superintendent shall proceed as if the request has been received from a school district board of education under division (F)(2) of this section.

(5) When a recipient of an OhioReads classroom or community reading grant paid under section 3301.86 or 3301.87 of the Revised Code or an entity approved by the OhioReads council requests, with respect to any individual who applies to participate in providing any program or service through an entity approved by the OhioReads council or funded in whole or in part by the grant, the information that a school district board of education is authorized to request under division (F)(2)(a) of this section, the superintendent of the bureau shall proceed as if the request has been received from a school district board of education under division (F)(2)(a) of this section.

(G) In addition to or in conjunction with any request that is required to be made under section 173.41, 3701.881, 3712.09, 3721.121, or 3722.151 of the Revised Code with respect to an individual who has applied for employment in a position that involves providing direct care to an older adult, the chief administrator of a PASSPORT agency that provides services through the PASSPORT program created under section 173.40 of the Revised Code, home health agency, hospice care program, home licensed under Chapter 3721. of the Revised Code, adult day-care program operated pursuant to rules adopted under section 3721.04 of the Revised Code, or adult care facility may request that the superintendent of the bureau investigate and determine, with respect to any individual who has applied after January 27, 1997, for employment in a position that does not involve providing direct care to an older adult, whether the bureau has any information gathered under division (A) of this section that pertains to that individual. On receipt of the request, the superintendent shall determine whether that information exists and, on request of the administrator requesting information, shall also request from the federal bureau of investigation any criminal records it has pertaining to that individual. The superintendent or the superintendent's designee also may request criminal history records from other states or the federal government pursuant to the national crime prevention and privacy compact set forth in section 109.571 of the Revised Code. Within thirty days of the date a request is received, the superintendent shall send to the administrator a report of any information determined to exist, including information contained in records that have been sealed under section 2953.32 of the Revised Code, and, within thirty days of its receipt, shall send the administrator a report of any information received from the federal bureau of investigation, other than information the dissemination of which is prohibited by federal law.

(H) Information obtained by a board, administrator, or other person under this section is confidential and shall not be released or disseminated.

(I) The superintendent may charge a reasonable fee for providing information or criminal records under division (F)(2) or (G) of this section.

(2004 H 106, eff. 9–16–04; 2003 S 53, eff. 4–7–04; 2003 S 5, eff. 7–31–03; 2003 H 95, eff. 9–26–03; 2000 H 538, eff. 9–22–00; 1999 H 3, eff. 11–22–99; 1999 H 282, eff. 9–28–99; 1999 H 1, eff. 3–30–99; 1998 H 2, eff. 1–1–99; 1997 H 342, eff. 12–31–97; 1997 H 151, eff. 9–16–97; 1996 H 124, § 4, eff. 7–1–97; 1996 H 124, § 1, eff. 3–31–97; 1996 H 180, eff. 7–1–97; 1996 S 160, eff. 1–27–97; 1995 H 1, eff. 1–1–96; 1995 H 223, eff. 11–15–95; 1994 H 694, eff. 11–11–94; 1994 H 571, eff. 10–6–94; 1993 S 38, eff. 10–29–93; 1993 H 152, eff. 7–1–93; 1993 H 162, eff. 10–1–93; 1989 S 140; 1984 H 235; 1980 H 736; 1977 H 1; 1970 H 956; 130 v S 160, H 263)

109.571 National crime prevention and privacy compact

The "national crime prevention and privacy compact" is hereby ratified, enacted into law, and entered into by the state of Ohio as a party to the compact with any other state that has legally joined in the compact as follows:

NATIONAL CRIME PREVENTION AND PRIVACY COMPACT

The contracting states agree to the following:

Overview

(a) This compact organizes an electronic information sharing system among the federal government and the states to exchange criminal history records for noncriminal justice purposes authorized by federal or state law, such as background checks for governmental licensing and employment.

(b) Under this compact, the FBI and the party states agree to maintain detailed databases of their respective criminal history records, including arrests and dispositions, and to make them available to the federal government and to party states for authorized purposes. The FBI shall also manage the federal data facilities that provide a significant part of the infrastructure for the system.

Article I

As used in this compact:

(1) "Attorney general" means the attorney general of the United States.

(2) "Compact officer" means:

(A) With respect to the federal government, an official so designated by the director of the FBI; and

(B) With respect to a party state, the chief administrator of the state's criminal history record repository or a designee of the chief administrator who is a regular full-time employee of the repository.

(3) "Council" means the compact council established under Article VI of the compact.

(4)(A) "Criminal history records" means information collected by criminal justice agencies on individuals consisting of identifiable descriptions and notations of arrests, detentions, indictments, or other formal criminal charges, and any disposition arising therefrom, including acquittal, sentencing, correctional supervision, or release.

(B) "Criminal history records" does not include identification information such as fingerprint records if the information does not indicate involvement of the individual with the criminal justice system.

(5) "Criminal history record repository" means the state agency designated by the governor or other appropriate executive official or the legislature of a state to perform centralized recordkeeping functions for criminal history records and services in the state.

(6) "Criminal justice" includes activities relating to the detection, apprehension, detention, pretrial release, post-trial release, prosecution, adjudication, correctional supervision, or rehabilitation of accused persons or criminal offenders. The administration of criminal justice includes criminal identification activities and the collection, storage, and dissemination of criminal history records.

(7) "Criminal justice agency" means courts and a governmental agency or any subunit of a governmental agency that performs the administration of criminal justice pursuant to a statute or executive order and allocates a substantial part of its annual budget to the administration of criminal justice. "Criminal justice agency" also includes federal and state inspectors general offices.

(8) "Criminal justice services" means services provided by the FBI to criminal justice agencies in response to a request for information about a particular individual or as an update to information previously provided for criminal justice purposes.

(9) "Criterion offense" means any felony or misdemeanor offense not included on the list of nonserious offenses published periodically by the FBI.

(10) "Direct access" means access to the national identification index by computer terminal or other automated means not requiring the assistance of or intervention by any other party or agency.

(11) "Executive order" means an order of the president of the United States or the chief executive officer of a state that has the force of law and that is promulgated in accordance with applicable law.

(12) "FBI" means the federal bureau of investigation.

(13) "Interstate identification system" or "III system" means the cooperative federal-state system for the exchange of criminal history records and includes the national identification index, the national fingerprint file, and, to the extent of their participation in that system, the criminal history record repositories of the states and the FBI.

(14) "National fingerprint file" means a database of fingerprints, or other uniquely personal identifying information, relating to an arrested or charged individual maintained by the FBI to provide positive identification of record subjects indexed in the III system.

(15) "National identification index" means an index maintained by the FBI consisting of names, identifying numbers, and other descriptive information relating to record subjects about whom there are criminal history records in the III system.

(16) "National indices" means the national identification index and the national fingerprint file.

(17) "Nonparty state" means a state that has not ratified this compact.

(18) "Noncriminal justice purposes" means uses of criminal history records for purposes authorized by federal or state law other than purposes relating to criminal justice activities, including employment suitability, licensing determinations, immigration and naturalization matters, and national security clearances.

(19) "Party state" means a state that has ratified this compact.

(20) "Positive identification" means a determination, based upon a comparison of fingerprints or other equally reliable biometric identification techniques, that the subject of a record search is the same person as the subject of a criminal history record or records indexed in the III system. Identifications based solely upon a comparison of subject's names or other nonunique identification characteristics or numbers, or combinations thereof, shall not constitute positive identification.

(21) "Sealed record information" means both of the following:

(A) With respect to adults, that portion of a record that is not available for criminal justice uses, not supported by fingerprints or other accepted means of positive identification, or subject to restrictions on dissemination for noncriminal justice purposes pursuant to a court order related to a particular subject or pursuant to a federal or state statute that requires action on a sealing petition filed by a particular record subject;

(B) With respect to juveniles, whatever each state determines is a sealed record under its own law and procedure.

(22) "State" means any state, territory, or possession of the United States, the District of Columbia, and the Commonwealth of Puerto Rico.

Article II

The purposes of this compact are to do all of the following:

(1) Provide a legal framework for the establishment of a cooperative federal-state system for the interstate and federal-

state exchange of criminal history records for noncriminal justice uses;

(2) Require the FBI to permit use of the national identification index and the national fingerprint file by each party state, and to provide, in a timely fashion, federal and state criminal history records to requesting states, in accordance with the terms of this compact and with rules, procedures, and standards established by the council under Article VI;

(3) Require party states to provide information and records for the national identification index and the national fingerprint file and to provide criminal history records, in a timely fashion, to criminal history record repositories of other states and the federal government for noncriminal justice purposes, in accordance with the terms of this compact and with rules, procedures, and standards established by the council under Article VI;

(4) Provide for the establishment of a council to monitor III system operations and to prescribe system rules and procedures for the effective and proper operation of the III system for noncriminal justice purposes;

(5) Require the FBI and each party state to adhere to III system standards concerning record dissemination and use, response times, system security, data quality, and other duly established standards, including those that enhance the accuracy and privacy of such records.

Article III

(a) The director of the FBI shall do all of the following:

(1) Appoint an FBI compact officer who shall do all of the following:

(A) Administer this compact within the department of justice and among federal agencies and other agencies and organizations that submit search requests to the FBI pursuant to Article V(c);

(B) Ensure that compact provisions and rules, procedures, and standards prescribed by the council under Article VI are complied with by the department of justice and the federal agencies and other agencies and organizations referred to in Article III(1)(A);

(C) Regulate the use of records received by means of the III system from party states when those records are supplied by the FBI directly to other federal agencies;

(2) Provide to federal agencies and to state criminal history record repositories criminal history records maintained in its database for the noncriminal justice purposes described in Article IV, including both of the following:

(A) Information from nonparty states;

(B) Information from party states that is available from the FBI through the III system, but is not available from the party state through the III system;

(3) Provide a telecommunications network and maintain centralized facilities for the exchange of criminal history records for both criminal justice purposes and the noncriminal justice purposes described in Article IV, and ensure that the exchange of criminal history records for criminal justice purposes has priority over exchange for noncriminal justice purposes;

(4) Modify or enter into user agreements with nonparty state criminal history record repositories to require them to establish record request procedures conforming to those prescribed in Article V.

(b) Each party state shall do all of the following:

(1) Appoint a compact officer who shall do all of the following:

(A) Administer this compact within that state;

(B) Ensure that the compact provisions and rules, procedures, and standards established by the council under Article VI are complied with in the state;

(C) Regulate the in-state use of records received by means of the III system from the FBI or from other party states;

(2) Establish and maintain a criminal history record repository, which shall provide both of the following:

(A) Information and records for the national identification index and the national fingerprint file;

(B) The state's III system-indexed criminal history records for noncriminal justice purposes described in Article IV;

(3) Participate in the national fingerprint file;

(4) Provide and maintain telecommunications links and related equipment necessary to support the services set forth in this compact.

(c) In carrying out their responsibilities under this compact, the FBI and each party state shall comply with the III system rules, procedures, and standards duly established by the council concerning record dissemination and use, response times, data quality, system security, accuracy, privacy protection, and other aspects of III system operation.

(d)(1) Use of the III system for noncriminal justice purposes authorized in this compact shall be managed so as not to diminish the level of services provided in support of criminal justice purposes.

(2) Administration of compact provisions shall not reduce the level of service available to authorized noncriminal justice users on the effective date of this compact.

Article IV

(a) To the extent authorized by section 552a of title 5, United States Code (commonly known as the 'Privacy Act of 1974'), the FBI shall provide on request criminal history records (excluding sealed records) to state criminal history record repositories for noncriminal justice purposes allowed by federal statute, federal executive order, or a state statute that has been approved by the attorney general and that authorizes national indices checks.

(b) The FBI, to the extent authorized by section 552a of title 5, United States Code (commonly known as the 'Privacy Act of 1974') and state criminal history record repositories, shall provide criminal history records (excluding sealed records) to criminal justice agencies and other governmental or nongovernmental agencies for noncriminal justice purposes allowed by federal statute, federal executive order, or a state statute that has been approved by the attorney general, that authorizes national indices checks.

(c) Any record obtained under this compact may be used only for the official purposes for which the record was requested. Each compact officer shall establish procedures, consistent with this compact, and with rules, procedures, and standards established by the council under Article VI, which procedures shall protect the accuracy and privacy of the records, and shall do all of the following:

(1) Ensure that records obtained under this compact are used only by authorized officials for authorized purposes;

(2) Require that subsequent record checks are requested to obtain current information whenever a new need arises;

(3) Ensure that record entries that may not legally be used for a particular noncriminal justice purpose are deleted from the response and, if no information authorized for release remains, an appropriate 'no record' response is communicated to the requesting official.

Article V

(a) Subject fingerprints or other approved forms of positive identification shall be submitted with all requests for criminal history record checks for noncriminal justice purposes.

(b) Each request for a criminal history record check utilizing the national indices made under any approved state statute shall be submitted through that state's criminal history record repository. A state criminal history record repository shall process an interstate request for noncriminal justice purposes through the national indices only if the request is transmitted through another state criminal history record repository or the FBI.

(c) Each request for criminal history record checks utilizing the national indices made under federal authority shall be submitted through the FBI or, if the state criminal history record repository consents to process fingerprint submissions, through the criminal history record repository in the state in which the request originated. Direct access to the national identification index by entities other than the FBI or state criminal history record repositories shall not be permitted for noncriminal justice purposes.

(d) A state criminal history record repository for the FBI may charge a fee, in accordance with applicable law, for handling a request involving fingerprint processing for noncriminal justice purposes and may not charge a fee for providing criminal history records in response to an electric request for a record that does not involve a request to process fingerprints.

(e)(1) If a state criminal history record repository cannot positively identify the subject of a record request made for noncriminal justice purposes, the request, together with fingerprints or other approved identifying information, shall be forwarded to the FBI for a search of the national indices.

(2) If, with respect to a request forwarded by a state criminal history record repository under paragraph (1), the FBI positively identifies the subject as having a III system-indexed record or records, the FBI shall so advise the state criminal history repository; and the state criminal history record repository shall be entitled to obtain the additional criminal history record information from the FBI or other state criminal history record repositories.

Article VI

(a)(1) There is established a council to be known as the 'compact council,' which shall have the authority to promulgate rules and procedures governing the use of the III system for noncriminal justice purposes, not to conflict with the FBI administration of the III system for criminal justice purposes.

(2) The council shall do all of the following:

(A) Continue in existence as long as this compact remains in effect;

(B) Be located, for administrative purposes, within the FBI;

(C) Be organized and hold its first meeting as soon as practicable after the effective date of this compact.

(b) The council shall be composed of fifteen members, each of whom shall be appointed by the attorney general as follows:

(1) Nine members, each of whom shall serve a two-year term, who shall be selected from among the compact officers of party states based on the recommendation of the compact officers of all party states, except that, in the absence of the requisite number of compact officers available to serve, the chief administrators of the criminal history record repositories of nonparty states shall be eligible to serve on an interim basis;

(2) Two at-large members, nominated by the director of the FBI, each of whom shall serve a three-year term, of whom one shall be a representative of the criminal justice agencies of the federal government and may not be employed by the FBI; and one shall be a representative of the noncriminal justice agencies of the federal government;

(3) Two at-large members, nominated by the chairman of the council, once the chairman is elected pursuant to Article VI(c), each of whom shall serve a three-year term, of whom one shall be a representative of state or local criminal justice agencies; and one shall be a representative of state or local noncriminal justice agencies;

(4) One member, who shall serve a three-year term, and who shall simultaneously be a member of the FBI's advisory policy board on criminal justice information services, nominated by the membership of that policy board;

(5) One member, nominated by the director of the FBI, who shall serve a three-year term, and who shall be an employee of the FBI.

(c)(1) From its membership, the council shall elect a chairman and a vice chairman of the council, respectively. Both the chairman and the vice chairman shall be a compact officer, unless there is no compact officer on the council who is willing to serve, in which case the chairman may be an at-large member; and shall serve a two-year term and may be reelected to only one additional two-year term.

(2) The vice chairman of the council shall serve as the chairman of the council in the absence of the chairman.

(d)(1) The council shall meet at least once each year at the call of the chairman. Each meeting of the council shall be open to the public. The council shall provide prior public notice in the federal register of each meeting of the council, including the matters to be addressed at the meeting.

(2) A majority of the council or any committee of the council shall constitute a quorum of the council or of such committee, respectively, for the conduct of business. A lesser number may meet to hold hearings, take testimony, or conduct any business not requiring a vote.

(e) The council shall make available for public inspection and copying at the council office with the FBI, and shall publish in the federal register, any rules, procedures, or standards established by the council.

(f) The council may request from the FBI any reports, studies, statistics, or other information or materials that the council determines to be necessary to enable the council to perform its duties under this compact. The FBI, to the extent authorized by law, may provide such assistance or information upon such a request.

(g) The chairman may establish committees as necessary to carry out this compact and may prescribe their membership, responsibilities, and duration.

Article VII

This compact shall take effect upon being entered into by two or more states as between those states and the federal government. Upon subsequent entering into this compact by additional states, it shall become effective among those states and the federal government and each party state that has previously ratified it. When ratified, this compact shall have the full force and effect of law within the ratifying jurisdictions. The form of ratification shall be in accordance with the laws of the executing state.

Article VIII

(a) Administration of this compact shall not interfere with the management and control of the director of the FBI over the FBI's collection and dissemination of criminal history records and the advisory function of the FBI's advisory policy board chartered under the Federal Advisory Committee Act (5 U.S.C. App.) for all purposes other than noncriminal justice.

(b) Nothing in this compact shall require the FBI to obligate or expend funds beyond those appropriated to the FBI.

(c) Nothing in this compact shall diminish or lessen the obligations, responsibilities, and authorities of any state, whether a party state or a nonparty state, or of any criminal history record repository or other subdivision or component thereof, under the Departments of State, Justice, and Commerce, the Judiciary, and Related Agencies Appropriation Act, 1973 (Public Law 92–544), or regulations and guidelines promulgated thereunder, including the rules and procedures promulgated by the council under Article VI(a), regarding the use and dissemination of criminal history records and information.

Article IX

(a) This compact shall bind each party state until renounced by the party state.

(b) Any renunciation of this compact by a party state shall be effected in the same manner by which the party state ratified this compact and shall become effective one hundred and eighty days after written notice of renunciation is provided by the party state to each other party state and to the federal government.

Article X

The provisions of this compact shall be severable, and if any phrase, clause, sentence, or provision of this compact is declared to be contrary to the constitution of any participating state, or to the Constitution of the United States, or the applicability of any phrase, clause, sentence, or provision of this compact to any government, agency, person, or circumstance is held invalid, the validity of the remainder of this compact and the applicability of the remainder of this compact to any government, agency, person, or circumstance shall not be affected thereby. If a portion of this compact is held contrary to the constitution of any party state, all other portions of this compact shall remain in full force and effect as to the remaining party states and in full force and effect as to the party states affected, as to all other provisions.

Article XI

(a) The council shall do both of the following:

(1) Have initial authority to make determinations with respect to any dispute regarding all of the following:

(A) Interpretation of this compact;

(B) Any rule or standard established by the council pursuant to Article V;

(C) Any dispute or controversy between any parties to this compact;

(2) Hold a hearing concerning any dispute described in paragraph (1) at a regularly scheduled meeting of the council and only render a decision based upon a majority vote of the members of the council. The decision shall be published pursuant to the requirements of Article VI(e).

(b) The FBI shall exercise immediate and necessary action to preserve the integrity of the III system, maintain system policy and standards, protect the accuracy and privacy of records, and to prevent abuses, until the council holds a hearing on such matters.

(c) The FBI or a party state may appeal any decision of the council to the attorney general, and thereafter may file suit in the appropriate district court of the United States, which shall have original jurisdiction of all cases or controversies arising under this compact. Any suit arising under this compact and initiated in a state court shall be removed to the appropriate district court of the United States in the manner provided by section 1446 of title 28, United States Code, or other statutory authority.

(2003 S 53, eff. 4–7–04)

109.572 Criminal records check

Note: See also following version of this section, eff. 5–18–05.

(A)(1) Upon receipt of a request pursuant to section 121.08, 3301.32, 3301.541, 3319.39, 5104.012, 5104.013, or 5153.111 of the Revised Code, a completed form prescribed pursuant to division (C)(1) of this section, and a set of fingerprint impressions obtained in the manner described in division (C)(2) of this section, the superintendent of the bureau of criminal identification and investigation shall conduct a criminal records check in the manner described in division (B) of this section to determine whether any information exists that indicates that the person who is the subject of the request previously has been convicted of or pleaded guilty to any of the following:

(a) A violation of section 2903.01, 2903.02, 2903.03, 2903.04, 2903.11, 2903.12, 2903.13, 2903.16, 2903.21, 2903.34, 2905.01, 2905.02, 2905.05, 2907. 02, 2907.03, 2907.04, 2907.05, 2907.06, 2907.07, 2907.08, 2907.09, 2907.21, 2907.22, 2907.23, 2907.25, 2907.31, 2907.32, 2907.321, 2907.322, 2907.323, 2911.01, 2911.02, 2911.11, 2911.12, 2919.12, 2919.22, 2919.24, 2919.25, 2923. 12, 2923.13, 2923.161, 2925.02, 2925.03, 2925.04, 2925.05, 2925.06, or 3716.11 of the Revised Code, felonious sexual penetration in violation of former section 2907.12 of the Revised Code, a violation of section 2905.04 of the Revised Code as it existed prior to July 1, 1996, a violation of section 2919.23 of the Revised Code that would have been a violation of section 2905.04 of the Revised Code as it existed prior to July 1, 1996, had the violation been committed prior to that date, or a violation of section 2925.11 of the Revised Code that is not a minor drug possession offense;

(b) A violation of an existing or former law of this state, any other state, or the United States that is substantially equivalent to any of the offenses listed in division (A)(1)(a) of this section.

(2) On receipt of a request pursuant to section 5123.081 of the Revised Code with respect to an applicant for employment in any position with the department of mental retardation and developmental disabilities, pursuant to section 5126.28 of the Revised Code with respect to an applicant for employment in any position with a county board of mental retardation and developmental disabilities, or pursuant to section 5126.281 of the Revised Code with respect to an applicant for employment in a direct services position with an entity contracting with a county board for employment, a completed form prescribed pursuant to division (C)(1) of this section, and a set of fingerprint impressions obtained in the manner described in division (C)(2) of this section, the superintendent of the bureau of criminal identification and investigation shall conduct a criminal records check. The superintendent shall conduct the criminal records check in the manner described in division (B) of this section to determine whether any information exists that indicates that the person who is the subject of the request has been convicted of or pleaded guilty to any of the following:

(a) A violation of section 2903.01, 2903.02, 2903.03, 2903.04, 2903.11, 2903.12, 2903.13, 2903.16, 2903.21, 2903.34, 2903.341, 2905.01, 2905.02, 2905.04, 2905. 05, 2907.02, 2907.03, 2907.04, 2907.05, 2907.06, 2907.07, 2907.08, 2907.09, 2907.12, 2907.21, 2907.22, 2907.23, 2907.25, 2907.31, 2907.32, 2907.321, 2907.322, 2907.323, 2911.01, 2911.02, 2911.11, 2911.12, 2919.12, 2919.22, 2919.24, 2919.25, 2923.12, 2923.13, 2923.161, 2925.02, 2925.03, or 3716.11 of the Revised Code;

(b) An existing or former municipal ordinance or law of this state, any other state, or the United States that is substantially equivalent to any of the offenses listed in division (A)(2)(a) of this section.

(3) On receipt of a request pursuant to section 173.41, 3712.09, 3721.121, or 3722.151 of the Revised Code, a completed form prescribed pursuant to division (C)(1) of this section, and a set of fingerprint impressions obtained in the manner described in division (C)(2) of this section, the superintendent of the bureau of criminal identification and investigation shall conduct a criminal records check with respect to any person who has applied for employment in a position that involves providing direct care to an older adult. The superintendent shall conduct the criminal records check in the manner described in division (B) of this section to determine whether any information exists that indicates that the person who is the subject of the request previously has been convicted of or pleaded guilty to any of the following:

(a) A violation of section 2903.01, 2903.02, 2903.03, 2903.04, 2903.11, 2903.12, 2903.13, 2903.16, 2903.21, 2903.34, 2905.01, 2905.02, 2905.11, 2905. 12, 2907.02, 2907.03, 2907.05, 2907.06, 2907.07, 2907.08, 2907.09, 2907.12, 2907.25, 2907.31, 2907.32, 2907.321, 2907.322, 2907.323, 2911.01, 2911.02, 2911.11, 2911.12, 2911.13, 2913.02, 2913.03, 2913.04, 2913.11, 2913.21, 2913. 31, 2913.40, 2913.43, 2913.47, 2913.51, 2919.25, 2921.36, 2923.12, 2923.13, 2923.161, 2925.02, 2925.03, 2925.11, 2925.13, 2925.22, 2925.23, or 3716.11 of the Revised Code;

(b) An existing or former law of this state, any other state, or the United States that is substantially equivalent to any of the offenses listed in division (A)(3)(a) of this section.

(4) On receipt of a request pursuant to section 3701.881 of the Revised Code with respect to an applicant for employment with a home health agency as a person responsible for the care, custody, or control of a child, a completed form prescribed pursuant to division (C)(1) of this section, and a set of fingerprint impressions obtained in the manner described in division (C)(2) of this section, the superintendent of the bureau of criminal identification and investigation shall conduct a criminal records check. The superintendent shall conduct the criminal records check in the manner described in division (B) of this section to determine whether any information exists that indicates that the person who is the subject of the request previously has been convicted of or pleaded guilty to any of the following:

(a) A violation of section 2903.01, 2903.02, 2903.03, 2903.04, 2903.11, 2903.12, 2903.13, 2903.16, 2903.21, 2903.34, 2905.01, 2905.02, 2905.04, 2905. 05, 2907.02, 2907.03, 2907.04, 2907.05, 2907.06, 2907.07, 2907.08, 2907.09, 2907.12, 2907.21, 2907.22, 2907.23, 2907.25, 2907.31, 2907.32, 2907.321, 2907.322, 2907.323, 2911.01, 2911.02, 2911.11, 2911.12, 2919.12, 2919.22, 2919.24, 2919.25, 2923.12, 2923.13, 2923.161, 2925.02, 2925.03, 2925.04, 2925.05, 2925.06, or 3716.11 of the Revised Code or a violation of section 2925.11 of the Revised Code that is not a minor drug possession offense;

(b) An existing or former law of this state, any other state, or the United States that is substantially equivalent to any of the offenses listed in division (A)(4)(a) of this section.

(5) On receipt of a request pursuant to section 5111.95 or 5111.96 of the Revised Code with respect to an applicant for employment with a waiver agency participating in a department of job and family services administered home and community-based waiver program or an independent provider participating in a department administered home and community-based waiver program in a position that involves providing home and community-based waiver services to consumers with disabilities, a completed form prescribed pursuant to division (C)(1) of this section, and a set of fingerprint impressions obtained in the manner described in division (C)(2) of this section, the superintendent of the bureau of criminal identification and investigation shall conduct a criminal records check. The superintendent shall conduct the criminal records check in the manner described in division (B) of this section to determine whether any information exists that indicates that the person who is the subject of the request previously has been convicted of or pleaded guilty to any of the following:

(a) A violation of section 2903.01, 2903.02, 2903.03, 2903.04, 2903.041, 2903.11, 2903.12, 2903.13, 2903.16, 2903.21, 2903.34, 2905.01, 2905.02, 2905. 05, 2905.11, 2905.12, 2907.02, 2907.03, 2907.04, 2907.05, 2907.06, 2907.07, 2907.08, 2907.09, 2907.21, 2907.22, 2907.23, 2907.25, 2907.31, 2907.32, 2907. 321, 2907.322, 2907.323, 2911.01, 2911.02, 2911.11, 2911.12, 2911.13, 2913.02, 2913.03, 2913.04, 2913.11, 2913.21, 2913.31, 2913.40, 2913.43, 2913. 47, 2913.51, 2919.12, 2919.24, 2919.25, 2921.36, 2923.12, 2923.13, 2923.161, 2925.02, 2925.03, 2925.04, 2925.05, 2925.06, 2925.11, 2925.13, 2925.22, 2925. 23, or 3716.11 of the Revised Code, felonious sexual penetration in violation of former section 2907.12 of the Revised Code, a violation of section 2905.04 of the Revised Code as it existed prior to July 1, 1996, a violation of section 2919.23 of the Revised Code that would have been a violation of section 2905.04 of the Revised Code as it existed prior to July 1, 1996, had the violation been committed prior to that date;

(b) An existing or former law of this state, any other state, or the United States that is substantially equivalent to any of the offenses listed in division (A)(5)(a) of this section.

(6) On receipt of a request pursuant to section 3701.881 of the Revised Code with respect to an applicant for employment with a home health agency in a position that involves providing direct care to an older adult, a completed form prescribed pursuant to division (C)(1) of this section, and a set of fingerprint impressions obtained in the manner described in division (C)(2) of this section, the superintendent of the bureau of criminal identification and investigation shall conduct a criminal records check. The superintendent shall conduct the criminal records check in the manner described in division (B) of this section to determine whether any information exists that indicates that the person who is the subject of the request previously has been convicted of or pleaded guilty to any of the following:

(a) A violation of section 2903.01, 2903.02, 2903.03, 2903.04, 2903.11, 2903.12, 2903.13, 2903.16, 2903.21, 2903.34, 2905.01, 2905.02, 2905.11, 2905. 12, 2907.02, 2907.03, 2907.05, 2907.06, 2907.07, 2907.08, 2907.09, 2907.12, 2907.25, 2907.31, 2907.32, 2907.321, 2907.322, 2907.323, 2911.01, 2911.02, 2911.11, 2911.12, 2911.13, 2913.02, 2913.03, 2913.04, 2913.11, 2913.21, 2913. 31, 2913.40, 2913.43, 2913.47, 2913.51, 2919.25, 2921.36, 2923.12, 2923.13, 2923.161, 2925.02, 2925.03, 2925.11, 2925.13, 2925.22, 2925.23, or 3716.11 of the Revised Code;

(b) An existing or former law of this state, any other state, or the United States that is substantially equivalent to any of the offenses listed in division (A)(6)(a) of this section.

(7) When conducting a criminal records check upon a request pursuant to section 3319.39 of the Revised Code for an applicant who is a teacher, in addition to the determination made under division (A)(1) of this section, the superintendent shall determine whether any information exists that indicates that the person who is the subject of the request previously has been convicted of or pleaded guilty to any offense specified in section 3319. 31 of the Revised Code.

(8) On a request pursuant to section 2151.86 of the Revised Code, a completed form prescribed pursuant to division (C)(1) of this section, and a set of fingerprint impressions obtained in the manner described in division (C)(2) of this section, the superintendent of the bureau of criminal identification and investigation shall conduct a criminal records check in the manner described in division (B) of this section to determine whether any information exists that indicates that the person who is the subject of the request previously has been convicted of or pleaded guilty to any of any of[1] the following:

(a) A violation of section 2903.01, 2903.02, 2903.03, 2903.04, 2903.11, 2903.12, 2903.13, 2903.16, 2903.21, 2903.34, 2905.01, 2905. 02, 2905.05, 2907.02, 2907.03, 2907.04, 2907.05, 2907.06, 2907.07, 2907.08, 2907.09, 2907.21, 2907.22, 2907.23, 2907.25,

2907.31, 2907.32, 2907.321, 2907.322, 2907.323, 2909.02, 2909.03, 2911.01, 2911.02, 2911. 11, 2911.12, 2919.12, 2919.22, 2919.24, 2919.25, 2923.12, 2923.13, 2923.161, 2925.02, 2925.03, 2925.04, 2925.05, 2925.06, or 3716.11 of the Revised Code, a violation of section 2905.04 of the Revised Code as it existed prior to July 1, 1996, a violation of section 2919.23 of the Revised Code that would have been a violation of section 2905.04 of the Revised Code as it existed prior to July 1, 1996, had the violation been committed prior to that date, a violation of section 2925.11 of the Revised Code that is not a minor drug possession offense, or felonious sexual penetration in violation of former section 2907.12 of the Revised Code;

(b) A violation of an existing or former law of this state, any other state, or the United States that is substantially equivalent to any of the offenses listed in division (A)(8)(a) of this section.

(9) Not later than thirty days after the date the superintendent receives the request, completed form, and fingerprint impressions, the superintendent shall send the person, board, or entity that made the request any information, other than information the dissemination of which is prohibited by federal law, the superintendent determines exists with respect to the person who is the subject of the request that indicates that the person previously has been convicted of or pleaded guilty to any offense listed or described in division (A)(1), (2), (3), (4), (5), (6), (7), or (8) of this section, as appropriate. The superintendent shall send the person, board, or entity that made the request a copy of the list of offenses specified in division (A)(1), (2), (3), (4), (5), (6), (7), or (8) of this section, as appropriate. If the request was made under section 3701.881 of the Revised Code with regard to an applicant who may be both responsible for the care, custody, or control of a child and involved in providing direct care to an older adult, the superintendent shall provide a list of the offenses specified in divisions (A)(1) and (6) of this section.

(B) The superintendent shall conduct any criminal records check requested under section 121.08, 173.41, 2151.86, 3301.32, 3301.541, 3319.39, 3701.881, 3712.09, 3721.121, 3722.151, 5104.012, 5104.013, 5111.95, 5111.96, 5123.081, 5126.28, 5126.281, or 5153.111 of the Revised Code as follows:

(1) The superintendent shall review or cause to be reviewed any relevant information gathered and compiled by the bureau under division (A) of section 109.57 of the Revised Code that relates to the person who is the subject of the request, including any relevant information contained in records that have been sealed under section 2953.32 of the Revised Code;

(2) If the request received by the superintendent asks for information from the federal bureau of investigation, the superintendent shall request from the federal bureau of investigation any information it has with respect to the person who is the subject of the request and shall review or cause to be reviewed any information the superintendent receives from that bureau;

(3) The superintendent or the superintendent's designee may request criminal history records from other states or the federal government pursuant to the national crime prevention and privacy compact set forth in section 109.571 of the Revised Code.

(C)(1) The superintendent shall prescribe a form to obtain the information necessary to conduct a criminal records check from any person for whom a criminal records check is required by section 121.08, 173.41, 2151.86, 3301.32, 3301.541, 3319.39, 3701.881, 3712.09, 3721.121, 3722.151, 5104.012, 5104.013, 5111.95, 5111.96, 5123.081, 5126.28, 5126.281, or 5153.111 of the Revised Code. The form that the superintendent prescribes pursuant to this division may be in a tangible format, in an electronic format, or in both tangible and electronic formats.

(2) The superintendent shall prescribe standard impression sheets to obtain the fingerprint impressions of any person for whom a criminal records check is required by section 121.08, 173.41, 2151.86, 3301.32, 3301.541, 3319.39, 3701.881, 3712.09, 3721.121, 3722.151, 5104.012, 5104.013, 5111.95, 5111.96, 5123.081, 5126.28, 5126.281, or 5153.111 of the Revised Code. Any person for whom a records check is required by any of those sections shall obtain the fingerprint impressions at a county sheriff's office, municipal police department, or any other entity with the ability to make fingerprint impressions on the standard impression sheets prescribed by the superintendent. The office, department, or entity may charge the person a reasonable fee for making the impressions. The standard impression sheets the superintendent prescribes pursuant to this division may be in a tangible format, in an electronic format, or in both tangible and electronic formats.

(3) Subject to division (D) of this section, the superintendent shall prescribe and charge a reasonable fee for providing a criminal records check requested under section 121.08, 173.41, 2151.86, 3301.32, 3301.541, 3319.39, 3701.881, 3712.09, 3721.121, 3722.151, 5104.012, 5104.013, 5111.95, 5111.96, 5123.081, 5126.28, 5126.281, or 5153.111 of the Revised Code. The person making a criminal records request under section 121.08, 173.41, 2151.86, 3301.32, 3301.541, 3319.39, 3701.881, 3712.09, 3721.121, 3722.151, 5104.012, 5104.013, 5111.95, 5111.96, 5123.081, 5126.28, 5126.281, or 5153.111 of the Revised Code shall pay the fee prescribed pursuant to this division. A person making a request under section 3701.881 of the Revised Code for a criminal records check for an applicant who may be both responsible for the care, custody, or control of a child and involved in providing direct care to an older adult shall pay one fee for the request.

(4) The superintendent of the bureau of criminal identification and investigation may prescribe methods of forwarding fingerprint impressions and information necessary to conduct a criminal records check, which methods shall include, but not be limited to, an electronic method.

(D) A determination whether any information exists that indicates that a person previously has been convicted of or pleaded guilty to any offense listed or described in division (A)(1)(a) or (b), (A)(2)(a) or (b), (A)(3)(a) or (b), (A)(4)(a) or (b), (A)(5)(a) or (b), (A)(6), (A)(7)(a) or (b), or (A)(8)(a) or (b) of this section that is made by the superintendent with respect to information considered in a criminal records check in accordance with this section is valid for the person who is the subject of the criminal records check for a period of one year from the date upon which the superintendent makes the determination. During the period in which the determination in regard to a person is valid, if another request under this section is made for a criminal records check for that person, the superintendent shall provide the information that is the basis for the superintendent's initial determination at a lower fee than the fee prescribed for the initial criminal records check.

(E) As used in this section:

(1) "Criminal records check" means any criminal records check conducted by the superintendent of the bureau of criminal identification and investigation in accordance with division (B) of this section.

(2) "Home and community-based waiver services" and " waiver agency" have the same meanings as in section 5111.95 of the Revised Code.

(3) "Independent provider" has the same meaning as in section 5111.96 of the Revised Code.

(4) "Minor drug possession offense" has the same meaning as in section 2925.01 of the Revised Code.

(5) "Older adult" means a person age sixty or older.

(2004 H 117, eff. 9–3–04; 2004 H 306, eff. 7–23–04; 2004 S 178, eff. 1–30–04; 2003 S 53, eff. 4–7–04; 2003 H 95, eff. 9–26–03; 2000 H 448, eff. 10–5–00; 2000 H 538, eff. 9–22–00; 1997 S 96, eff. 6–11–97; 1996 S 160, eff. 1–27–97; 1996 S 269, eff. 7–1–96; 1996 H 445, eff. 9–3–96; 1995 S 2, eff. 7–1–96; 1994 H 694, eff. 11–11–94; 1993 S 38, eff. 10–29–93)

1 So in original; language appears as the result of the harmonization of 2004 H 117 and H 306.

Note: See also following version of this section, eff. 5–18–05.

109.572 Criminal records check (later effective date)

Note: See also preceding version of this section, in effect until 5–18–05.

(A)(1) Upon receipt of a request pursuant to section 121.08, 2151.86, 3301.32, 3301.541, 3319.39, 5104.012, 5104.013, or 5153.111 of the Revised Code, a completed form prescribed pursuant to division (C)(1) of this section, and a set of fingerprint impressions obtained in the manner described in division (C)(2) of this section, the superintendent of the bureau of criminal identification and investigation shall conduct a criminal records check in the manner described in division (B) of this section to determine whether any information exists that indicates that the person who is the subject of the request previously has been convicted of or pleaded guilty to any of the following:

(a) A violation of section 2903.01, 2903.02, 2903.03, 2903.04, 2903.11, 2903.12, 2903.13, 2903.16, 2903.21, 2903.34, 2905.01, 2905.02, 2905.05, 2907. 02, 2907.03, 2907.04, 2907.05, 2907.06, 2907.07, 2907.08, 2907.09, 2907.21, 2907.22, 2907.23, 2907.25, 2907.31, 2907.32, 2907.321, 2907.322, 2907.323, 2911.01, 2911.02, 2911.11, 2911.12, 2919.12, 2919.22, 2919.24, 2919.25, 2923. 12, 2923.13, 2923.161, 2925.02, 2925.03, 2925.04, 2925.05, 2925.06, or 3716.11 of the Revised Code, felonious sexual penetration in violation of former section 2907.12 of the Revised Code, a violation of section 2905.04 of the Revised Code as it existed prior to July 1, 1996, a violation of section 2919.23 of the Revised Code that would have been a violation of section 2905.04 of the Revised Code as it existed prior to July 1, 1996, had the violation been committed prior to that date, or a violation of section 2925.11 of the Revised Code that is not a minor drug possession offense;

(b) A violation of an existing or former law of this state, any other state, or the United States that is substantially equivalent to any of the offenses listed in division (A)(1)(a) of this section.

(2) On receipt of a request pursuant to section 5123.081 of the Revised Code with respect to an applicant for employment in any position with the department of mental retardation and developmental disabilities, pursuant to section 5126.28 of the Revised Code with respect to an applicant for employment in any position with a county board of mental retardation and developmental disabilities, or pursuant to section 5126.281 of the Revised Code with respect to an applicant for employment in a direct services position with an entity contracting with a county board for employment, a completed form prescribed pursuant to division (C)(1) of this section, and a set of fingerprint impressions obtained in the manner described in division (C)(2) of this section, the superintendent of the bureau of criminal identification and investigation shall conduct a criminal records check. The superintendent shall conduct the criminal records check in the manner described in division (B) of this section to determine whether any information exists that indicates that the person who is the subject of the request has been convicted of or pleaded guilty to any of the following:

(a) A violation of section 2903.01, 2903.02, 2903.03, 2903.04, 2903.11, 2903.12, 2903.13, 2903.16, 2903.21, 2903.34, 2903.341, 2905.01, 2905.02, 2905.04, 2905.05, 2907.02, 2907.03, 2907.04, 2907.05, 2907.06, 2907.07, 2907. 08, 2907.09, 2907.12, 2907.21, 2907.22, 2907.23, 2907.25, 2907.31, 2907.32, 2907.321, 2907.322, 2907.323, 2911.01, 2911.02, 2911.11, 2911.12, 2919.12, 2919.22, 2919.24, 2919.25, 2923.12, 2923.13, 2923.161, 2925.02, 2925.03, or 3716.11 of the Revised Code;

(b) An existing or former municipal ordinance or law of this state, any other state, or the United States that is substantially equivalent to any of the offenses listed in division (A)(2)(a) of this section.

(3) On receipt of a request pursuant to section 173.41, 3712.09, 3721.121, or 3722.151 of the Revised Code, a completed form prescribed pursuant to division (C)(1) of this section, and a set of fingerprint impressions obtained in the manner described in division (C)(2) of this section, the superintendent of the bureau of criminal identification and investigation shall conduct a criminal records check with respect to any person who has applied for employment in a position that involves providing direct care to an older adult. The superintendent shall conduct the criminal records check in the manner described in division (B) of this section to determine whether any information exists that indicates that the person who is the subject of the request previously has been convicted of or pleaded guilty to any of the following:

(a) A violation of section 2903.01, 2903.02, 2903.03, 2903.04, 2903.11, 2903.12, 2903.13, 2903.16, 2903.21, 2903.34, 2905.01, 2905.02, 2905.11, 2905. 12, 2907.02, 2907.03, 2907.05, 2907.06, 2907.07, 2907.08, 2907.09, 2907.12, 2907.25, 2907.31, 2907.32, 2907.321, 2907.322, 2907.323, 2911.01, 2911.02, 2911.11, 2911.12, 2911.13, 2913.02, 2913.03, 2913.04, 2913.11, 2913.21, 2913. 31, 2913.40, 2913.43, 2913.47, 2913.51, 2919.25, 2921.36, 2923.12, 2923.13, 2923.161, 2925.02, 2925.03, 2925.11, 2925.13, 2925.22, 2925.23, or 3716.11 of the Revised Code;

(b) An existing or former law of this state, any other state, or the United States that is substantially equivalent to any of the offenses listed in division (A)(3)(a) of this section.

(4) On receipt of a request pursuant to section 3701.881 of the Revised Code with respect to an applicant for employment with a home health agency as a person responsible for the care, custody, or control of a child, a completed form prescribed pursuant to division (C)(1) of this section, and a set of fingerprint impressions obtained in the manner described in division (C)(2) of this section, the superintendent of the bureau of criminal identification and investigation shall conduct a criminal records check. The superintendent shall conduct the criminal records check in the manner described in division (B) of this section to determine whether any information exists that indicates that the person who is the subject of the request previously has been convicted of or pleaded guilty to any of the following:

(a) A violation of section 2903.01, 2903.02, 2903.03, 2903.04, 2903.11, 2903.12, 2903.13, 2903.16, 2903.21, 2903.34, 2905.01, 2905.02, 2905.04, 2905. 05, 2907.02, 2907.03, 2907.04, 2907.05, 2907.06, 2907.07, 2907.08, 2907.09, 2907.12, 2907.21, 2907.22, 2907.23, 2907.25, 2907.31, 2907.32, 2907.321, 2907.322, 2907.323, 2911.01, 2911.02, 2911.11, 2911.12, 2919.12, 2919.22, 2919.24, 2919.25, 2923.12, 2923.13, 2923.161, 2925.02, 2925.03, 2925.04, 2925.05, 2925.06, or 3716.11 of the Revised Code or a violation of section 2925.11 of the Revised Code that is not a minor drug possession offense;

(b) An existing or former law of this state, any other state, or the United States that is substantially equivalent to any of the offenses listed in division (A)(4)(a) of this section.

(5) On receipt of a request pursuant to section 5111.95 or 5111.96 of the Revised Code with respect to an applicant for employment with a waiver agency participating in a department of job and family services administered home and community-based waiver program or an independent provider participating in a department administered home and community-based waiver program in a position that involves providing home and community-based waiver services to consumers with disabilities, a completed form prescribed pursuant to division (C)(1) of this section, and a set of fingerprint impressions obtained in the manner described in division (C)(2) of this section, the superintendent of the bureau of criminal identification and investigation shall conduct a criminal records check. The superintendent shall conduct the criminal records check in the manner described in division

(B) of this section to determine whether any information exists that indicates that the person who is the subject of the request previously has been convicted of or pleaded guilty to any of the following:

(a) A violation of section 2903.01, 2903.02, 2903.03, 2903.04, 2903.041, 2903.11, 2903.12, 2903.13, 2903.16, 2903.21, 2903.34, 2905.01, 2905.02, 2905. 05, 2905.11, 2905.12, 2907.02, 2907.03, 2907.04, 2907.05, 2907.06, 2907.07, 2907.08, 2907.09, 2907.21, 2907.22, 2907.23, 2907.25, 2907.31, 2907.32, 2907. 321, 2907.322, 2907.323, 2911.01, 2911.02, 2911.11, 2911.12, 2911.13, 2913.02, 2913.03, 2913.04, 2913.11, 2913.21, 2913.31, 2913.40, 2913.43, 2913. 47, 2913.51, 2919.12, 2919.24, 2919.25, 2921.36, 2923.12, 2923.13, 2923.161, 2925.02, 2925.03, 2925.04, 2925.05, 2925.06, 2925.11, 2925.13, 2925.22, 2925. 23, or 3716.11 of the Revised Code, felonious sexual penetration in violation of former section 2907.12 of the Revised Code, a violation of section 2905.04 of the Revised Code as it existed prior to July 1, 1996, a violation of section 2919.23 of the Revised Code that would have been a violation of section 2905.04 of the Revised Code as it existed prior to July 1, 1996, had the violation been committed prior to that date;

(b) An existing or former law of this state, any other state, or the United States that is substantially equivalent to any of the offenses listed in division (A)(5)(a) of this section.

(6) On receipt of a request pursuant to section 3701.881 of the Revised Code with respect to an applicant for employment with a home health agency in a position that involves providing direct care to an older adult, a completed form prescribed pursuant to division (C)(1) of this section, and a set of fingerprint impressions obtained in the manner described in division (C)(2) of this section, the superintendent of the bureau of criminal identification and investigation shall conduct a criminal records check. The superintendent shall conduct the criminal records check in the manner described in division (B) of this section to determine whether any information exists that indicates that the person who is the subject of the request previously has been convicted of or pleaded guilty to any of the following:

(a) A violation of section 2903.01, 2903.02, 2903.03, 2903.04, 2903.11, 2903.12, 2903.13, 2903.16, 2903.21, 2903.34, 2905.01, 2905.02, 2905.11, 2905. 12, 2907.02, 2907.03, 2907.05, 2907.06, 2907.07, 2907.08, 2907.09, 2907.12, 2907.25, 2907.31, 2907.32, 2907.321, 2907.322, 2907.323, 2911.01, 2911.02, 2911.11, 2911.12, 2911.13, 2913.02, 2913.03, 2913.04, 2913.11, 2913.21, 2913. 31, 2913.40, 2913.43, 2913.47, 2913.51, 2919.25, 2921.36, 2923.12, 2923.13, 2923.161, 2925.02, 2925.03, 2925.11, 2925.13, 2925.22, 2925.23, or 3716.11 of the Revised Code;

(b) An existing or former law of this state, any other state, or the United States that is substantially equivalent to any of the offenses listed in division (A)(6)(a) of this section.

(7) When conducting a criminal records check upon a request pursuant to section 3319.39 of the Revised Code for an applicant who is a teacher, in addition to the determination made under division (A)(1) of this section, the superintendent shall determine whether any information exists that indicates that the person who is the subject of the request previously has been convicted of or pleaded guilty to any offense specified in section 3319. 31 of the Revised Code.

(8) On a request pursuant to section 2151.86 of the Revised Code, a completed form prescribed pursuant to division (C)(1) of this section, and a set of fingerprint impressions obtained in the manner described in division (C)(2) of this section, the superintendent of the bureau of criminal identification and investigation shall conduct a criminal records check in the manner described in division (B) of this section to determine whether any information exists that indicates that the person who is the subject of the request previously has been convicted of or pleaded guilty to any of the following:

(a) A violation of section 2903.01, 2903.02, 2903.03, 2903.04, 2903.11, 2903.12, 2903.13, 2903.16, 2903.21, 2903.34, 2905.01, 2905.02, 2905.05, 2907. 02, 2907.03, 2907.04, 2907.05, 2907.06, 2907.07, 2907.08, 2907.09, 2907.21, 2907.22, 2907.23, 2907.25, 2907.31, 2907.32, 2907.321, 2907.322, 2907.323, 2909.02, 2909.03, 2911.01, 2911.02, 2911.11, 2911.12, 2919.12, 2919.22, 2919. 24, 2919.25, 2923.12, 2923.13, 2923.161, 2925.02, 2925.03, 2925.04, 2925.05, 2925.06, or 3716.11 of the Revised Code, a violation of section 2905.04 of the Revised Code as it existed prior to July 1, 1996, a violation of section 2919.23 of the Revised Code that would have been a violation of section 2905. 04 of the Revised Code as it existed prior to July 1, 1996, had the violation been committed prior to that date, a violation of section 2925.11 of the Revised Code that is not a minor drug possession offense, or felonious sexual penetration in violation of former section 2907.12 of the Revised Code;

(b) A violation of an existing or former law of this state, any other state, or the United States that is substantially equivalent to any of the offenses listed in division (A)(8)(a) of this section.

(9) When conducting a criminal records check on a request pursuant to section 5104.013 of the Revised Code for a person who is an owner, licensee, or administrator of a child day-care center or type A family day-care home or an authorized provider of a certified type B family day-care home, the superintendent, in addition to the determination made under division (A)(1) of this section, shall determine whether any information exists that indicates that the person has been convicted of or pleaded guilty to any of the following:

(a) A violation of section 2913.02, 2913.03, 2913.04, 2913.041, 2913.05, 2913.06, 2913.11, 2913.21, 2913.31, 2913.32, 2913.33, 2913.34, 2913. 40, 2913.41, 2913.42, 2913.43, 2913.44, 2913.441, 2913.45, 2913.46, 2913.47, 2913.48, 2913.49, 2921.11, 2921.13, or 2923.01 of the Revised Code, a violation of section 2923.02 or 2923.03 of the Revised Code that relates to a crime specified in this division or division (A)(1)(a) of this section, or a second violation of section 4511.19 of the Revised Code within five years of the date of application for licensure or certification.

(b) A violation of an existing or former law of this state, any other state, or the United States that is substantially equivalent to any of the offenses or violations described in division (A)(9)(a) of this section.

(10) Not later than thirty days after the date the superintendent receives the request, completed form, and fingerprint impressions, the superintendent shall send the person, board, or entity that made the request any information, other than information the dissemination of which is prohibited by federal law, the superintendent determines exists with respect to the person who is the subject of the request that indicates that the person previously has been convicted of or pleaded guilty to any offense listed or described in division (A)(1), (2), (3), (4), (5), (6), (7), (8), or (9) of this section, as appropriate. The superintendent shall send the person, board, or entity that made the request a copy of the list of offenses specified in division (A)(1), (2), (3), (4), (5), (6), (7), (8), or (9) of this section, as appropriate. If the request was made under section 3701.881 of the Revised Code with regard to an applicant who may be both responsible for the care, custody, or control of a child and involved in providing direct care to an older adult, the superintendent shall provide a list of the offenses specified in divisions (A)(4) and (6) of this section.

(B) The superintendent shall conduct any criminal records check requested under section 121.08, 173.41, 2151.86, 3301.32, 3301.541, 3319.39, 3701.881, 3712.09, 3721.121, 3722.151, 5104.012, 5104.013, 5111.95, 5111.96, 5123.081, 5126.28, 5126.281, or 5153.111 of the Revised Code as follows:

(1) The superintendent shall review or cause to be reviewed any relevant information gathered and compiled by the bureau under division (A) of section 109.57 of the Revised Code that relates to the person who is the subject of the request, including any relevant information contained in records that have been sealed under section 2953.32 of the Revised Code;

(2) If the request received by the superintendent asks for information from the federal bureau of investigation, the superintendent shall request from the federal bureau of investigation any information it has with respect to the person who is the subject of the request and shall review or cause to be reviewed any information the superintendent receives from that bureau.

(3) The superintendent or the superintendent's designee may request criminal history records from other states or the federal government pursuant to the national crime prevention and privacy compact set forth in section 109.571 of the Revised Code.

(C)(1) The superintendent shall prescribe a form to obtain the information necessary to conduct a criminal records check from any person for whom a criminal records check is required by section 121.08, 173.41, 2151.86, 3301.32, 3301.541, 3319.39, 3701.881, 3712.09, 3721.121, 3722.151, 5104.012, 5104.013, 5111.95, 5111.96, 5123.081, 5126.28, 5126.281, or 5153.111 of the Revised Code. The form that the superintendent prescribes pursuant to this division may be in a tangible format, in an electronic format, or in both tangible and electronic formats.

(2) The superintendent shall prescribe standard impression sheets to obtain the fingerprint impressions of any person for whom a criminal records check is required by section 121.08, 173.41, 2151.86, 3301.32, 3301.541, 3319.39, 3701.881, 3712.09, 3721.121, 3722.151, 5104.012, 5104.013, 5111.95, 5111.96, 5123.081, 5126.28, 5126.281, or 5153.111 of the Revised Code. Any person for whom a records check is required by any of those sections shall obtain the fingerprint impressions at a county sheriff's office, municipal police department, or any other entity with the ability to make fingerprint impressions on the standard impression sheets prescribed by the superintendent. The office, department, or entity may charge the person a reasonable fee for making the impressions. The standard impression sheets the superintendent prescribes pursuant to this division may be in a tangible format, in an electronic format, or in both tangible and electronic formats.

(3) Subject to division (D) of this section, the superintendent shall prescribe and charge a reasonable fee for providing a criminal records check requested under section 121.08, 173.41, 2151.86, 3301.32, 3301.541, 3319.39, 3701.881, 3712.09, 3721.121, 3722.151, 5104.012, 5104.013, 5111.95, 5111.96, 5123.081, 5126.28, 5126.281, or 5153.111 of the Revised Code. The person making a criminal records request under section 121.08, 173.41, 2151.86, 3301.32, 3301.541, 3319.39, 3701.881, 3712.09, 3721.121, 3722.151, 5104.012, 5104.013, 5111.95, 5111.96, 5123.081, 5126.28, 5126.281, or 5153.111 of the Revised Code shall pay the fee prescribed pursuant to this division. A person making a request under section 3701.881 of the Revised Code for a criminal records check for an applicant who may be both responsible for the care, custody, or control of a child and involved in providing direct care to an older adult shall pay one fee for the request.

(4) The superintendent of the bureau of criminal identification and investigation may prescribe methods of forwarding fingerprint impressions and information necessary to conduct a criminal records check, which methods shall include, but not be limited to, an electronic method.

(D) A determination whether any information exists that indicates that a person previously has been convicted of or pleaded guilty to any offense listed or described in division (A)(1)(a) or (b), (A)(2)(a) or (b), (A)(3)(a) or (b), (A)(4)(a) or (b), (A)(5)(a) or (b), (A)(6), (A)(7)(a) or (b), (A)(8)(a) or (b), or (A)(9)(a) or (b) of this section that is made by the superintendent with respect to information considered in a criminal records check in accordance with this section is valid for the person who is the subject of the criminal records check for a period of one year from the date upon which the superintendent makes the determination. During the period in which the determination in regard to a person is valid, if another request under this section is made for a criminal records check for that person, the superintendent shall provide the information that is the basis for the superintendent's initial determination at a lower fee than the fee prescribed for the initial criminal records check.

(E) As used in this section:

(1) "Criminal records check" means any criminal records check conducted by the superintendent of the bureau of criminal identification and investigation in accordance with division (B) of this section.

(2) "Home and community-based waiver services" and " waiver agency" have the same meanings as in section 5111.95 of the Revised Code.

(3) "Independent provider" has the same meaning as in section 5111.96 of the Revised Code.

(4) "Minor drug possession offense" has the same meaning as in section 2925.01 of the Revised Code.

(5) "Older adult" means a person age sixty or older.

(2004 H 11, eff. 5–18–05; 2004 H 117, eff. 9–3–04; 2004 H 306, eff. 7–23–04; 2004 S 178, eff. 1–30–04; 2003 S 53, eff. 4–7–04; 2003 H 95, eff. 9–26–03; 2000 H 448, eff. 10–5–00; 2000 H 538, eff. 9–22–00; 1997 S 96, eff. 6–11–97; 1996 S 160, eff. 1–27–97; 1996 S 269, eff. 7–1–96; 1996 H 445, eff. 9–3–96; 1995 S 2, eff. 7–1–96; 1994 H 694, eff. 11–11–94; 1993 S 38, eff. 10–29–93)

Note: See also preceding version of this section, in effect until 5–18–05.

109.573 DNA laboratory and DNA database; relatives of missing persons database

Note: See also following version of this section, eff. 5–18–05.

(A) As used in this section:

(1) "DNA" means human deoxyribonucleic acid.

(2) "DNA analysis" means a laboratory analysis of a DNA specimen to identify DNA characteristics and to create a DNA record.

(3) "DNA database" means a collection of DNA records from forensic casework or from crime scenes, specimens from anonymous and unidentified sources, and records collected pursuant to sections 2152.74 and 2901.07 of the Revised Code and a population statistics database for determining the frequency of occurrence of characteristics in DNA records.

(4) "DNA record" means the objective result of a DNA analysis of a DNA specimen, including representations of DNA fragment lengths, digital images of autoradiographs, discrete allele assignment numbers, and other DNA specimen characteristics that aid in establishing the identity of an individual.

(5) "DNA specimen" includes human blood cells or physiological tissues or body fluids.

(6) "Unidentified person database" means a collection of DNA records, and, on and after May 21, 1998, of fingerprint and photograph records, of unidentified human corpses, human remains, or living individuals.

(7) "Relatives of missing persons database" means a collection of DNA records of persons related by consanguinity of the first degree to a missing person.

(8) "Law enforcement agency" means a police department, the office of a sheriff, the state highway patrol, a county prosecuting attorney, or a federal, state, or local governmental body that enforces criminal laws and that has employees who have a statutory power of arrest.

(B)(1) The superintendent of the bureau of criminal identification and investigation may do all of the following:

(a) Establish and maintain a state DNA laboratory to perform DNA analyses of DNA specimens;

(b) Establish and maintain a DNA database;

(c) Establish and maintain an unidentified person database to aid in the establishment of the identity of unknown human corpses, human remains, or living individuals;

(d) Establish and maintain a relatives of missing persons database for comparison with the unidentified person database to aid in the establishment of the identity of unknown human corpses, human remains, and living individuals.

(2) If the bureau of criminal identification and investigation establishes and maintains a DNA laboratory and a DNA database, the bureau may use or disclose information regarding DNA records for the following purposes:

(a) The bureau may disclose information to a law enforcement agency for purposes of identification.

(b) The bureau shall disclose pursuant to a court order issued under section 3111.09 of the Revised Code any information necessary to determine the existence of a parent and child relationship in an action brought under sections 3111.01 to 3111.18 of the Revised Code.

(c) The bureau may use or disclose information from the population statistics database, for identification research and protocol development, or for quality control purposes.

(3) If the bureau of criminal identification and investigation establishes and maintains a relatives of missing persons database, all of the following apply:

(a) If a person has disappeared and has been continuously absent from the person's place of last domicile for a thirty-day or longer period of time without being heard from during the period, persons related by consanguinity of the first degree to the missing person may submit to the bureau a DNA specimen, the bureau may include the DNA record of the specimen in the relatives of missing persons database, and, if the bureau does not include the DNA record of the specimen in the relatives of missing persons database, the bureau shall retain the DNA record for future reference and inclusion as appropriate in that database.

(b) The bureau shall not charge a fee for the submission of a DNA specimen pursuant to division (B)(3)(a) of this section.

(c) If the DNA specimen submitted pursuant to division (B)(3)(a) of this section is collected by withdrawing blood from the person or a similarly invasive procedure, a physician, registered nurse, licensed practical nurse, duly licensed clinical laboratory technician, or other qualified medical practitioner shall conduct the collection procedure for the DNA specimen submitted pursuant to division (B)(3)(a) of this section and shall collect the DNA specimen in a medically approved manner. If the DNA specimen is collected by swabbing for buccal cells or a similarly noninvasive procedure, division (B)(3)(c) of this section does not require that the DNA specimen be collected by a qualified medical practitioner of that nature. No later than fifteen days after the date of the collection of the DNA specimen, the person conducting the DNA specimen collection procedure shall cause the DNA specimen to be forwarded to the bureau of criminal identification and investigation in accordance with procedures established by the superintendent of the bureau under division (H) of this section. The bureau may provide the specimen vials, mailing tubes, labels, postage, and instruction needed for the collection and forwarding of the DNA specimen to the bureau.

(d) The superintendent, in the superintendent's discretion, may compare DNA records in the relatives of missing persons database with the DNA records in the unidentified person database.

(4) If the bureau of criminal identification and investigation establishes and maintains an unidentified person database and if the superintendent of the bureau identifies a matching DNA record for the DNA record of a person or deceased person whose DNA record is contained in the unidentified person database, the superintendent shall inform the coroner who submitted or the law enforcement agency that submitted the DNA specimen to the bureau of the match and, if possible, of the identity of the unidentified person.

(5) The bureau of criminal identification and investigation may enter into a contract with a qualified public or private laboratory to perform DNA analyses, DNA specimen maintenance, preservation, and storage, DNA record keeping, and other duties required of the bureau under this section. A public or private laboratory under contract with the bureau shall follow quality assurance and privacy requirements established by the superintendent of the bureau.

(C) The superintendent of the bureau of criminal identification and investigation shall establish procedures for entering into the DNA database the DNA records submitted pursuant to sections 2152.74 and 2901.07 of the Revised Code and for determining an order of priority for entry of the DNA records based on the types of offenses committed by the persons whose records are submitted and the available resources of the bureau.

(D) When a DNA record is derived from a DNA specimen provided pursuant to section 2152.74 or 2901.07 of the Revised Code, the bureau of criminal identification and investigation shall attach to the DNA record personal identification information that identifies the person from whom the DNA specimen was taken. The personal identification information may include the subject person's fingerprints and any other information the bureau determines necessary. The DNA record and personal identification information attached to it shall be used only for the purpose of personal identification or for a purpose specified in this section.

(E) DNA records, DNA specimens, fingerprints, and photographs that the bureau of criminal identification and investigation receives pursuant to this section and sections 313.08, 2152.74, and 2901.07 of the Revised Code and personal identification information attached to a DNA record are not public records under section 149.43 of the Revised Code.

(F) The bureau of criminal identification and investigation may charge a reasonable fee for providing information pursuant to this section to any law enforcement agency located in another state.

(G)(1) No person who because of the person's employment or official position has access to a DNA specimen, a DNA record, or other information contained in the DNA database that identifies an individual shall knowingly disclose that specimen, record, or information to any person or agency not entitled to receive it or otherwise shall misuse that specimen, record, or information.

(2) No person without authorization or privilege to obtain information contained in the DNA database that identifies an individual person shall purposely obtain that information.

(H) The superintendent of the bureau of criminal identification and investigation shall establish procedures for all of the following:

(1) The forwarding to the bureau of DNA specimens collected pursuant to division (H) of this section and sections 313.08, 2152.74, and 2901.07 of the Revised Code and of fingerprints and photographs collected pursuant to section 313.08 of the Revised Code;

(2) The collection, maintenance, preservation, and analysis of DNA specimens;

(3) The creation, maintenance, and operation of the DNA database;

(4) The use and dissemination of information from the DNA database;

(5) The creation, maintenance, and operation of the unidentified person database;

(6) The use and dissemination of information from the unidentified person database;

(7) The creation, maintenance, and operation of the relatives of missing persons database;

(8) The use and dissemination of information from the relatives of missing persons database;

(9) The verification of entities requesting DNA records and other DNA information from the bureau and the authority of the entity to receive the information;

(10) The operation of the bureau and responsibilities of employees of the bureau with respect to the activities described in this section.

(I) In conducting DNA analyses of DNA specimens, the state DNA laboratory and any laboratory with which the bureau has entered into a contract pursuant to division (B)(5) of this section shall give DNA analyses of DNA specimens that relate to ongoing criminal investigations or prosecutions priority over DNA analyses of DNA specimens that relate to applications made pursuant to section 2953.73 or 2953.82 of the Revised Code.

(2003 S 11, eff. 10–29–03; 2002 H 427, eff. 8–29–02; 2000 S 179, § 3, eff. 1–1–02; 2000 S 180, eff. 3–22–01; 1998 S 140, eff. 5–21–98; 1996 H 124, eff. 3–31–97; 1995 H 5, eff. 8–30–95)

Note: See also following version of this section, eff. 5–18–05.

109.573 DNA laboratory and DNA database; relatives of missing persons database (later effective date)

Note: See also preceding version of this section, in effect until 5–18–05.

(A) As used in this section:

(1) "DNA" means human deoxyribonucleic acid.

(2) "DNA analysis" means a laboratory analysis of a DNA specimen to identify DNA characteristics and to create a DNA record.

(3) "DNA database" means a collection of DNA records from forensic casework or from crime scenes, specimens from anonymous and unidentified sources, and records collected pursuant to sections 2152.74 and 2901.07 of the Revised Code and a population statistics database for determining the frequency of occurrence of characteristics in DNA records.

(4) "DNA record" means the objective result of a DNA analysis of a DNA specimen, including representations of DNA fragment lengths, digital images of autoradiographs, discrete allele assignment numbers, and other DNA specimen characteristics that aid in establishing the identity of an individual.

(5) "DNA specimen" includes human blood cells or physiological tissues or body fluids.

(6) "Unidentified person database" means a collection of DNA records, and, on and after May 21, 1998, of fingerprint and photograph records, of unidentified human corpses, human remains, or living individuals.

(7) "Relatives of missing persons database" means a collection of DNA records of persons related by consanguinity to a missing person.

(8) "Law enforcement agency" means a police department, the office of a sheriff, the state highway patrol, a county prosecuting attorney, or a federal, state, or local governmental body that enforces criminal laws and that has employees who have a statutory power of arrest.

(9) "Administration of criminal justice" means the performance of detection, apprehension, detention, pretrial release, post-trial release, prosecution, adjudication, correctional supervision, or rehabilitation of accused persons or criminal offenders. "Administration of criminal justice" also includes criminal identification activities and the collection, storage, and dissemination of criminal history record information.

(B)(1) The superintendent of the bureau of criminal identification and investigation may do all of the following:

(a) Establish and maintain a state DNA laboratory to perform DNA analyses of DNA specimens;

(b) Establish and maintain a DNA database;

(c) Establish and maintain an unidentified person database to aid in the establishment of the identity of unknown human corpses, human remains, or living individuals;

(d) Establish and maintain a relatives of missing persons database for comparison with the unidentified person database to aid in the establishment of the identity of unknown human corpses, human remains, and living individuals.

(2) If the bureau of criminal identification and investigation establishes and maintains a DNA laboratory and a DNA database, the bureau may use or disclose information regarding DNA records for the following purposes:

(a) The bureau may disclose information to a law enforcement agency for the administration of criminal justice.

(b) The bureau shall disclose pursuant to a court order issued under section 3111.09 of the Revised Code any information necessary to determine the existence of a parent and child relationship in an action brought under sections 3111.01 to 3111.18 of the Revised Code.

(c) The bureau may use or disclose information from the population statistics database, for identification research and protocol development, or for quality control purposes.

(3) If the bureau of criminal identification and investigation establishes and maintains a relatives of missing persons database, all of the following apply:

(a) If a person has disappeared and has been continuously absent from the person's place of last domicile for a thirty-day or longer period of time without being heard from during the period, persons related by consanguinity to the missing person may submit to the bureau a DNA specimen, the bureau may include the DNA record of the specimen in the relatives of missing persons database, and, if the bureau does not include the DNA record of the specimen in the relatives of missing persons database, the bureau shall retain the DNA record for future reference and inclusion as appropriate in that database.

(b) The bureau shall not charge a fee for the submission of a DNA specimen pursuant to division (B)(3)(a) of this section.

(c) If the DNA specimen submitted pursuant to division (B)(3)(a) of this section is collected by withdrawing blood from the person or a similarly invasive procedure, a physician, registered nurse, licensed practical nurse, duly licensed clinical laboratory technician, or other qualified medical practitioner shall conduct the collection procedure for the DNA specimen submitted pursuant to division (B)(3)(a) of this section and shall collect the DNA specimen in a medically approved manner. If the DNA specimen is collected by swabbing for buccal cells or a similarly noninvasive procedure, division (B)(3)(c) of this section does not require that the DNA specimen be collected by a qualified medical practitioner of that nature. No later than fifteen days after the date of the collection of the DNA specimen, the person conducting the DNA specimen collection procedure shall cause the DNA specimen to be forwarded to the bureau of criminal identification and investigation in accordance with procedures established by the superintendent of the bureau under division (H) of this section. The bureau may provide the specimen vials, mailing tubes, labels, postage, and instruction needed for the collection and forwarding of the DNA specimen to the bureau.

(d) The superintendent, in the superintendent's discretion, may compare DNA records in the relatives of missing persons database with the DNA records in the unidentified person database.

(4) If the bureau of criminal identification and investigation establishes and maintains an unidentified person database and if the superintendent of the bureau identifies a matching DNA record for the DNA record of a person or deceased person whose DNA record is contained in the unidentified person database, the superintendent shall inform the coroner who submitted or the law enforcement agency that submitted the DNA specimen to the bureau of the match and, if possible, of the identity of the unidentified person.

(5) The bureau of criminal identification and investigation may enter into a contract with a qualified public or private laboratory to perform DNA analyses, DNA specimen maintenance, preservation, and storage, DNA record keeping, and other duties required of the bureau under this section. A public or private laboratory under contract with the bureau shall follow quality assurance and privacy requirements established by the superintendent of the bureau.

(C) The superintendent of the bureau of criminal identification and investigation shall establish procedures for entering into the DNA database the DNA records submitted pursuant to sections 2152.74 and 2901.07 of the Revised Code and for determining an order of priority for entry of the DNA records based on the types of offenses committed by the persons whose records are submitted and the available resources of the bureau.

(D) When a DNA record is derived from a DNA specimen provided pursuant to section 2152.74 or 2901.07 of the Revised Code, the bureau of criminal identification and investigation shall attach to the DNA record personal identification information that identifies the person from whom the DNA specimen was taken. The personal identification information may include the subject person's fingerprints and any other information the bureau determines necessary. The DNA record and personal identification information attached to it shall be used only for the purpose of personal identification or for a purpose specified in this section.

(E) DNA records, DNA specimens, fingerprints, and photographs that the bureau of criminal identification and investigation receives pursuant to this section and sections 313.08, 2152.74, and 2901.07 of the Revised Code and personal identification information attached to a DNA record are not public records under section 149.43 of the Revised Code.

(F) The bureau of criminal identification and investigation may charge a reasonable fee for providing information pursuant to this section to any law enforcement agency located in another state.

(G)(1) No person who because of the person's employment or official position has access to a DNA specimen, a DNA record, or other information contained in the DNA database that identifies an individual shall knowingly disclose that specimen, record, or information to any person or agency not entitled to receive it or otherwise shall misuse that specimen, record, or information.

(2) No person without authorization or privilege to obtain information contained in the DNA database that identifies an individual person shall purposely obtain that information.

(H) The superintendent of the bureau of criminal identification and investigation shall establish procedures for all of the following:

(1) The forwarding to the bureau of DNA specimens collected pursuant to division (H) of this section and sections 313.08, 2152.74, and 2901.07 of the Revised Code and of fingerprints and photographs collected pursuant to section 313.08 of the Revised Code;

(2) The collection, maintenance, preservation, and analysis of DNA specimens;

(3) The creation, maintenance, and operation of the DNA database;

(4) The use and dissemination of information from the DNA database;

(5) The creation, maintenance, and operation of the unidentified person database;

(6) The use and dissemination of information from the unidentified person database;

(7) The creation, maintenance, and operation of the relatives of missing persons database;

(8) The use and dissemination of information from the relatives of missing persons database;

(9) The verification of entities requesting DNA records and other DNA information from the bureau and the authority of the entity to receive the information;

(10) The operation of the bureau and responsibilities of employees of the bureau with respect to the activities described in this section.

(I) In conducting DNA analyses of DNA specimens, the state DNA laboratory and any laboratory with which the bureau has entered into a contract pursuant to division (B)(5) of this section shall give DNA analyses of DNA specimens that relate to ongoing criminal investigations or prosecutions priority over DNA analyses of DNA specimens that relate to applications made pursuant to section 2953.73 or 2953.82 of the Revised Code.

(2004 H 525, eff. 5–18–05; 2003 S 11, eff. 10–29–03; 2002 H 427, eff. 8–29–02; 2000 S 179, § 3, eff. 1–1–02; 2000 S 180, eff. 3–22–01; 1998 S 140, eff. 5–21–98; 1996 H 124, eff. 3–31–97; 1995 H 5, eff. 8–30–95)

Note: See also preceding version of this section, in effect until 5–18–05.

109.574 Definitions

As used in sections 109.574 to 109.577 of the Revised Code:

(A) "Organization or entity" means a religious, charitable, scientific, educational, athletic, or service institution or organization or local government entity that provides care, treatment, education, training, instruction, supervision, or recreation to children.

(B) "Unsupervised access to a child" means that the person in question has access to a child and that either of the following applies:

(1) No other person eighteen years of age or older is present in the same room with the child.

(2) If outdoors, no other person eighteen years of age or older is within a thirty-yard radius of the child or has visual contact with the child.

(2000 S 187, eff. 3–22–01)

109.575 Notification to volunteers of fingerprinting or criminal background checks

At the time of a person's initial application to an organization or entity to be a volunteer in a position in which the person on a regular basis will have unsupervised access to a child, the organization or entity shall inform the person that, at any time, the person might be required to provide a set of impressions of the person's fingerprints and a criminal records check might be conducted with respect to the person. Not later than thirty days after the effective date of this section, each organization or entity shall notify each current volunteer who is in a position in which the person on a regular basis has unsupervised access to a child that, at any time, the volunteer might be required to provide a set of impressions of the volunteer's fingerprints and a criminal records check might be conducted with respect to the volunteer.

(2000 S 187, eff. 3–22–01)

109.576 Notification of parent or guardian of convictions of volunteers

(A) If a person has applied to an organization or entity to be a volunteer in a position in which the person on a regular basis has unsupervised access to a child, if the organization or entity subjects the person to a criminal records check, if the report of the results of the criminal records check indicates that the person has been convicted of or pleaded guilty to any of the offenses described in division (A)(1) of section 109.572 of the Revised Code, and if the organization or entity accepts the person as a volunteer in a position in which the person on a regular basis has unsupervised access to a child, the organization or entity shall notify the parent or guardian of each child for whom it provides services that the volunteer has been convicted of one or more of those offenses but that, nonetheless, the person will be serving the organization or entity in that position. The notification required by this division shall be in writing, and the organization or entity shall send the notice to the parent or guardian on the date the organization or entity commences providing services to the child or on the date the organization or entity decides to accept the person as a volunteer after receiving the report of the results of the criminal records check, whichever is later.

(B) If a person is serving an organization or entity as a volunteer in a position in which the person on a regular basis has unsupervised access to a child, if the organization or entity subjects the person to a criminal records check, if the report of the results of the criminal records check indicates that the person has been convicted of or pleaded guilty to any of the offenses described in division (A)(1) of section 109.572 of the Revised Code, and if the organization or entity retains the person as a volunteer in the same position or in any other position in which the person on a regular basis has unsupervised access to a child, the organization or entity shall notify the parent or guardian of each child for whom it provides services that the volunteer has been convicted of one or more of those offenses but that, nonetheless, the person will be retained by the organization or entity in that position. The notification required by this division shall be in writing, and the organization or entity shall send the notice to the parent or guardian on the date the organization or entity commences providing services to the child or on the date the organization or entity decides to retain the person after receiving the report of the results of the criminal records check, whichever is later.

(C) A notification to a parent or guardian of a child that is required by division (A) or (B) of this section shall identify by name the person who is accepted or retained as a volunteer in a position in which the person on a regular basis has unsupervised access to a child, shall state the fact that the person has been convicted of or pleaded guilty to one or more of the offenses described in division (A)(1) of section 109.572 of the Revised Code, but shall not identify the offense or offenses in question.

(D) Divisions (A) to (C) of this section apply regarding any criminal records check performed by the bureau of criminal identification and investigation pursuant to section 109.57, section 109.572, or rules adopted under division (E) of section 109.57 of the Revised Code, any criminal records check performed in any manner by the organization or entity or any of its officers or employees, or any criminal records check performed in any manner by any person upon the request of the organization or entity or any of its officers or employees.

(2000 S 187, eff. 3–22–01)

109.577 Immunity of organizations and employees

(A) If an organization or entity uses a volunteer in a position in which the person on a regular basis has unsupervised access to a child and if the volunteer has been subjected to a criminal records check performed by the bureau of criminal identification and investigation pursuant to section 109.57, section 109.572, or rules adopted under division (E) of section 109.57 of the Revised Code, the organization or entity, and its officials and employees, are immune from civil liability that might otherwise be incurred or imposed for any death or any injury or loss to person or property that is caused by any act or omission of the volunteer and that results from or is related to the volunteer having unsupervised access to a child on a regular basis. This immunity does not apply to a person, organization, or entity that has immunity from civil liability in accordance with section 9.86, 2744.02, or 2744.03 of the Revised Code for the good faith compliance, attempted compliance, or failure to comply.

(B) This section does not create a new cause of action or substantive legal right against a person, organization, or entity and does not affect any immunities from civil liability or defenses established by another section of the Revised Code or available at common law, to which a person, organization, or entity may be entitled under circumstances not covered by this section.

(2000 S 187, eff. 3–22–01)

109.578 Criminal records check; form; fingerprint impressions

(A) On receipt of a request pursuant to section 505.381, 737.081, 737.221, or 4765.301 of the Revised Code, a completed form prescribed pursuant to division (C)(1) of this section, and a set of fingerprint impressions obtained in the manner described in division (C)(2) of this section, the superintendent of the bureau of criminal identification and investigation shall conduct a criminal records check in the manner described in division (B) of this section to determine whether any information exists that indicates that the person who is the subject of the request previously has been convicted of or pleaded guilty to any of the following:

(1) A felony;

(2) A violation of section 2909.03 of the Revised Code;

(3) A violation of an existing or former law of this state, any other state, or the United States that is substantially equivalent to any of the offenses listed in division (A)(1) or (2) of this section.

(B) The superintendent shall conduct any criminal records check pursuant to division (A) of this section as follows:

(1) The superintendent shall review or cause to be reviewed any relevant information gathered and compiled by the bureau under division (A) of section 109.57 of the Revised Code that relates to the person who is the subject of the request, including any relevant information contained in records that have been sealed under section 2953.32 of the Revised Code.

(2) If the request received by the superintendent asks for information from the federal bureau of investigation, the superintendent shall request from the federal bureau of investigation any information it has with respect to the person who is the subject of the request and shall review or cause to be reviewed any information the superintendent receives from that bureau.

(C)(1) The superintendent shall prescribe a form to obtain the information necessary to conduct a criminal records check from any person for whom a criminal records check is requested pursuant to section 505.381, 737.081, 737.221, or 4765.301 of the Revised Code. The form that the superintendent prescribes pursuant to this division may be in a tangible format, in an electronic format, or in both tangible and electronic formats.

(2) The superintendent shall prescribe standard impression sheets to obtain the fingerprint impressions of any person for whom a criminal records check is requested pursuant to section 505.381, 737.081, 737.221, or 4765.301 of the Revised Code. Any person for whom a records check is requested pursuant to any of those sections shall obtain the fingerprint impressions at a county sheriff's office, a municipal police department, or any other entity with the ability to make fingerprint impressions on the standard impression sheets prescribed by the superintendent. The office, department, or entity may charge the person a reasonable fee for making the impressions. The standard impression sheets the superintendent prescribes pursuant to this division may be in a tangible format, in an electronic format, or in both tangible and electronic formats.

(3) Subject to division (D) of this section, the superintendent shall prescribe and charge a reasonable fee for providing a criminal records check requested under section 505.381, 737.081, 737.221, or 4765.301 of the Revised Code. The person making the criminal records request shall pay the fee prescribed pursuant to this division.

(4) The superintendent may prescribe methods of forwarding fingerprint impressions and information necessary to conduct a criminal records check. The methods shall include, but are not limited to, an electronic method.

(D) A determination whether any information exists that indicates that a person previously has been convicted of or pleaded guilty to any offense listed or described in division (A) of this section and that the superintendent made with respect to information considered in a criminal records check in accordance with this section is valid for the person who is the subject of the criminal records check for a period of one year from the date upon which the superintendent makes the determination. During the period in which the determination in regard to a person is valid, if another request under this section is made for a criminal records check for that person, the superintendent shall provide the information that is the basis for the superintendent's initial determination at a lower fee than the fee prescribed for the initial criminal records check.

(E) As used in this section, "criminal records check" means any criminal records check conducted by the superintendent of the bureau of criminal identification and investigation in accordance with division (B) of this section.

(2002 S 258, eff. 4–9–03)

109.58 Superintendent shall prepare a standard fingerprint impression sheet; may provide to schools

The superintendent of the bureau of criminal identification and investigation shall prepare standard impression sheets on which fingerprints may be made in accordance with the fingerprint system of identification. The impression sheets may provide for other descriptive matter that the superintendent may prescribe. The superintendent shall furnish the impression sheets to each sheriff, chief of police, and person in charge of every county, multicounty, municipal, municipal-county, or multicounty-municipal jail or workhouse, community-based correctional facility, halfway house, alternative residential facility, or state correctional institution within the state. Upon the request of the board of education of a school district or of the principal or chief administrative officer of a nonpublic school, the superintendent shall provide standard impression sheets to the district or school for use in their fingerprinting programs under section 3313.96 of the Revised Code.

(1997 H 342, eff. 12–31–97; 1994 H 571, eff. 10–6–94; 1984 S 321, eff. 4–9–85; 130 v H 263)

109.59 Fingerprint impression and descriptive measurement records

The sheriff, chief of police, or other person in charge of each prison, workhouse, or state correctional institution shall send to the bureau of criminal identification and investigation, on forms furnished by the superintendent of the bureau, any fingerprint impressions and other descriptive measurements that the superintendent may require. The information shall be filed, classified, and preserved by the bureau.

(1994 H 571, eff. 10–6–94; 130 v H 263, eff. 9–24–63)

109.60 Duty of sheriffs and chiefs of police to take fingerprints; report; exception

(A)(1) The sheriffs of the several counties and the chiefs of police of cities, immediately upon the arrest of any person for any felony, on suspicion of any felony, for a crime constituting a misdemeanor on the first offense and a felony on subsequent offenses, or for any misdemeanor described in division (A)(1)(a) of section 109.572 of the Revised Code, and immediately upon the arrest or taking into custody of any child under eighteen years of age for committing an act that would be a felony or an offense of violence if committed by an adult or upon probable cause to believe that a child of that age may have committed an act that would be a felony or an offense of violence if committed by an adult, shall take the person's or child's fingerprints, or cause the same to be taken, according to the fingerprint system of identification on the forms furnished by the superintendent of the bureau of criminal identification and investigation, and immediately shall forward copies of the completed forms, any other description that may be required, and the history of the offense committed to the bureau to be classified and filed and to the clerk of the court having jurisdiction over the prosecution of the offense or over the adjudication relative to the act.

(2) If a sheriff or chief of police has not taken, or caused to be taken, a person's or child's fingerprints in accordance with division (A)(1) of this section by the time of the arraignment or first appearance of the person or child, the court shall order the person or child to appear before the sheriff or chief of police within twenty-four hours to have the person's or child's fingerprints taken. The sheriff or chief of police shall take the person's or child's fingerprints, or cause the fingerprints to be taken, according to the fingerprint system of identification on the forms furnished by the superintendent of the bureau of criminal identification and investigation and, immediately after the person's or child's arraignment or first appearance, forward copies of the completed forms, any other description that may be required, and the history of the offense committed to the bureau to be classified and filed and to the clerk of the court.

(3) Every court with jurisdiction over a case involving a person or child with respect to whom division (A)(1) of this section requires a sheriff or chief of police to take the person's or child's fingerprints shall inquire at the time of the person's or child's sentencing or adjudication whether or not the person or child has been fingerprinted pursuant to division (A)(1) or (2) of this section for the original arrest upon which the sentence or adjudication is based. If the person or child was not fingerprinted for the original arrest upon which the sentence or adjudication is based, the court shall order the person or child to appear before the sheriff or chief of police within twenty-four hours to have the person's or child's fingerprints taken. The sheriff or chief of police shall take the person's or child's fingerprints, or cause the

fingerprints to be taken, according to the fingerprint system of identification on the forms furnished by the superintendent of the bureau of criminal identification and investigation and immediately forward copies of the completed forms, any other description that may be required, and the history of the offense committed to the bureau to be classified and filed and to the clerk of the court.

(4) If a person or child is in the custody of a law enforcement agency or a detention facility, as defined in section 2921.01 of the Revised Code, and the chief law enforcement officer or chief administrative officer of the detention facility discovers that a warrant has been issued or a bill of information has been filed alleging the person or child to have committed an offense or act other than the offense or act for which the person or child is in custody, and the other alleged offense or act is one for which fingerprints are to be taken pursuant to division (A)(1) of this section, the law enforcement agency or detention facility shall take the fingerprints of the person or child, or cause the fingerprints to be taken, according to the fingerprint system of identification on the forms furnished by the superintendent of the bureau of criminal identification and investigation and immediately forward copies of the completed forms, any other description that may be required, and the history of the offense committed to the bureau to be classified and filed and to the clerk of the court that issued the warrant or with which the bill of information was filed.

(5) If an accused is found not guilty of the offense charged or a nolle prosequi is entered in any case, or if any accused child under eighteen years of age is found not to be a delinquent child for committing an act that would be a felony or an offense of violence if committed by an adult or not guilty of the felony or offense of violence charged or a nolle prosequi is entered in that case, the fingerprints and description shall be given to the accused upon the accused's request.

(6) The superintendent shall compare the description received with those already on file in the bureau, and, if the superintendent finds that the person arrested or taken into custody has a criminal record or a record as a delinquent child for having committed an act that would be a felony or an offense of violence if committed by an adult or is a fugitive from justice or wanted by any jurisdiction in this or another state, the United States, or a foreign country for any offense, the superintendent at once shall inform the arresting officer, the officer taking the person into custody, or the chief administrative officer of the county, multicounty, municipal, municipal-county, or multicounty-municipal jail or workhouse, community-based correctional facility, halfway house, alternative residential facility, or state correctional institution in which the person or child is in custody of that fact and give appropriate notice to the proper authorities in the jurisdiction in which the person is wanted, or, if that jurisdiction is a foreign country, give appropriate notice to federal authorities for transmission to the foreign country. The names, under which each person whose identification is filed is known, shall be alphabetically indexed by the superintendent.

(B) This section does not apply to a violator of a city ordinance unless the officers have reason to believe that the violator is a past offender or the crime is one constituting a misdemeanor on the first offense and a felony on subsequent offenses, or unless it is advisable for the purpose of subsequent identification. This section does not apply to any child under eighteen years of age who was not arrested or otherwise taken into custody for committing an act that would be a felony or an offense of violence if committed by an adult or upon probable cause to believe that a child of that age may have committed an act that would be a felony or an offense of violence if committed by an adult, except as provided in section 2151.313 of the Revised Code.

(1998 H 2, eff. 1–1–99; 1997 H 342, eff. 12–31–97; 1996 H 124, eff. 3–31–97; 1995 H 1, eff. 1–1–96; 1977 S 170, eff. 11–16–77; 1970 H 956; 130 v H 263)

109.61 Descriptions, fingerprints, and photographs sent to bureau by sheriffs and chiefs of police

Each sheriff or chief of police shall furnish the bureau of criminal identification and investigation with descriptions, fingerprints, photographs, and measurements of the following:

(A)(1) Persons arrested who in that sheriff's or chief of police's judgment are wanted for serious offenses, are fugitives from justice, or in whose possession at the time of arrest are found goods or property reasonably believed to have been stolen;

(2) Children arrested or otherwise taken into custody who in that sheriff's or chief of police's judgment are under eighteen years of age and have committed an act that would be a felony or an offense of violence if committed by an adult.

(B) All persons in whose possession are found burglar outfits, burglar tools, or burglar keys, or who have in their possession high power explosives reasonably believed to be intended to be used for unlawful purposes;

(C) Persons who are in possession of infernal machines or other contrivances in whole or in part and reasonably believed by the sheriff or chief of police to be intended to be used for unlawful purposes;

(D) All persons carrying concealed firearms or other deadly weapons reasonably believed to be carried for unlawful purposes;

(E) All persons who have in their possession inks, dies, paper, or other articles necessary in the making of counterfeit bank notes or in the alteration of bank notes, or dies, molds, or other articles necessary in the making of counterfeit money and reasonably believed to be intended to be used by them for those types of unlawful purposes.

(1998 H 2, eff. 1–1–99; 1996 H 124, eff. 3–31–97; 1995 H 1, eff. 1–1–96; 130 v H 263, eff. 9–24–63)

109.62 Interstate, national, and international co-operation

The superintendent of the bureau of criminal identification and investigation shall co-operate with bureaus in other states and with the federal bureau of investigation to develop and carry on a complete interstate, national, and international system of criminal identification and investigation.

(130 v H 263, eff. 9–24–63)

109.63 Superintendent and assistants may testify in court

The superintendent of the bureau of criminal identification and investigation and his assistants employed in accordance with section 109.51 of the Revised Code may testify in any court in this state to the same extent as any law enforcement officer in this state.

(130 v H 263, eff. 9–24–63)

MISSING CHILDREN

109.64 Information bulletin concerning missing children

The bureau of criminal identification and investigation shall prepare a periodic information bulletin concerning missing children whom it determines may be present in this state. The bureau shall compile the bulletin from information contained in the national crime information center computer. The bulletin shall indicate the names and addresses of these minors who are the subject of missing children cases and other information that the superintendent of the bureau considers appropriate. The bulletin shall contain a reminder to law enforcement agencies of their responsibilities under section 2901.30 of the Revised Code.

The bureau shall send a copy of each periodic information bulletin to the missing children clearinghouse established under section 109.65 of the Revised Code for use in connection with its responsibilities under division (E) of that section. Upon receipt of each periodic information bulletin from the bureau, the missing children clearinghouse shall send a copy of the bulletin to each sheriff, marshal, police department of a municipal corporation, police force of a township police district or joint township police district, and township constable in this state, to the board of education of each school district in this state, and to each nonpublic school in this state. The bureau shall provide a copy of the bulletin, upon request, to other persons or entities. The superintendent of the bureau, with the approval of the attorney general, may establish a reasonable fee for a copy of a bulletin provided to persons or entities other than law enforcement agencies in this or other states or of the federal government, the department of education, governmental entities of this state, and libraries in this state. The superintendent shall deposit all fees collected by him into the missing children fund created by section 109.65 of the Revised Code.

As used in this section, "missing children," "information," and "minor" have the same meanings as in section 2901.30 of the Revised Code.

(1993 S 63, eff. 10–1–93; 1984 S 321)

109.69 Reciprocity agreements regarding concealed handguns

(A)(1) The attorney general shall negotiate and enter into a reciprocity agreement with any other license-issuing state under which a license to carry a concealed handgun that is issued by the other state is recognized in this state if the attorney general determines that both of the following apply:

(a) The eligibility requirements imposed by that license-issuing state for that license are substantially comparable to the eligibility requirements for a license to carry a concealed handgun issued under section 2923.125 of the Revised Code.

(b) That license-issuing state recognizes a license to carry a concealed handgun issued under section 2923.125 of the Revised Code.

(2) A reciprocity agreement entered into under division (A)(1) of this section also may provide for the recognition in this state of a license to carry a concealed handgun issued on a temporary or emergency basis by the other license-issuing state, if the eligibility requirements imposed by that license-issuing state for the temporary or emergency license are substantially comparable to the eligibility requirements for a license or temporary emergency license to carry a concealed handgun issued under section 2923.125 or 2923.1213 of the Revised Code and if that license-issuing state recognizes a temporary emergency license to carry a concealed handgun issued under section 2923.1213 of the Revised Code.

(3) The attorney general shall not negotiate any agreement with any other license-issuing state under which a license to carry a concealed handgun that is issued by the other state is recognized in this state other than as provided in divisions (A)(1) and (2) of this section.

(B) As used in this section:

(1) "Handgun" has the same meaning as in section 2923.11 of the Revised Code.

(2) "License–issuing state" means a state other than this state that, pursuant to law, provides for the issuance of a license to carry a concealed handgun.

(2004 H 12, eff. 4–8–04)

OHIO PEACE OFFICER TRAINING COMMISSION

109.71 Peace officer training commission

There is hereby created in the office of the attorney general the Ohio peace officer training commission. The commission shall consist of nine members appointed by the governor with the advice and consent of the senate and selected as follows: one member representing the public; two members who are incumbent sheriffs; two members who are incumbent chiefs of police; one member from the bureau of criminal identification and investigation; one member from the state highway patrol; one member who is the special agent in charge of a field office of the federal bureau of investigation in this state; and one member from the department of education, trade and industrial education services, law enforcement training.

As used in sections 109.71 to 109.77 of the Revised Code:

(A) "Peace officer" means:

(1) A deputy sheriff, marshal, deputy marshal, member of the organized police department of a township or municipal corporation, member of a township police district or joint township police district police force, member of a police force employed by a metropolitan housing authority under division (D) of section 3735.31 of the Revised Code, or township constable, who is commissioned and employed as a peace officer by a political subdivision of this state or by a metropolitan housing authority, and whose primary duties are to preserve the peace, to protect life and property, and to enforce the laws of this state, ordinances of a municipal corporation, resolutions of a township, or regulations of a board of county commissioners or board of township trustees, or any of those laws, ordinances, resolutions, or regulations;

(2) A police officer who is employed by a railroad company and appointed and commissioned by the governor pursuant to sections 4973.17 to 4973.22 of the Revised Code;

(3) Employees of the department of taxation engaged in the enforcement of Chapter 5743. of the Revised Code and designated by the tax commissioner for peace officer training for purposes of the delegation of investigation powers under section 5743.45 of the Revised Code;

(4) An undercover drug agent;

(5) Enforcement agents of the department of public safety whom the director of public safety designates under section 5502.14 of the Revised Code;

(6) An employee of the department of natural resources who is a natural resources law enforcement staff officer designated pursuant to section 1501.013, a park officer designated pursuant to section 1541.10, a forest officer designated pursuant to section 1503.29, a preserve officer designated pursuant to section 1517.10, a wildlife officer designated pursuant to section 1531.13, or a state watercraft officer designated pursuant to section 1547.521 of the Revised Code;

(7) An employee of a park district who is designated pursuant to section 511.232 or 1545.13 of the Revised Code;

(8) An employee of a conservancy district who is designated pursuant to section 6101.75 of the Revised Code;

(9) A police officer who is employed by a hospital that employs and maintains its own proprietary police department or security department, and who is appointed and commissioned by the governor pursuant to sections 4973.17 to 4973.22 of the Revised Code;

(10) Veterans' homes police officers designated under section 5907.02 of the Revised Code;

(11) A police officer who is employed by a qualified nonprofit corporation police department pursuant to section 1702.80 of the Revised Code;

(12) A state university law enforcement officer appointed under section 3345.04 of the Revised Code or a person serving as a state university law enforcement officer on a permanent basis on June 19, 1978, who has been awarded a certificate by the executive director of the Ohio peace officer training commission attesting to the person's satisfactory completion of an approved state, county, municipal, or department of natural resources peace officer basic training program;

(13) A special police officer employed by the department of mental health pursuant to section 5119.14 of the Revised Code or the department of mental retardation and developmental disabilities pursuant to section 5123.13 of the Revised Code;

(14) A member of a campus police department appointed under section 1713.50 of the Revised Code;

(15) A member of a police force employed by a regional transit authority under division (Y) of section 306.35 of the Revised Code;

(16) Investigators appointed by the auditor of state pursuant to section 117.091 of the Revised Code and engaged in the enforcement of Chapter 117. of the Revised Code;

(17) A special police officer designated by the superintendent of the state highway patrol pursuant to section 5503.09 of the Revised Code or a person who was serving as a special police officer pursuant to that section on a permanent basis on October 21, 1997, and who has been awarded a certificate by the executive director of the Ohio peace officer training commission attesting to the person's satisfactory completion of an approved state, county, municipal, or department of natural resources peace officer basic training program;

(18) A special police officer employed by a port authority under section 4582.04 or 4582.28 of the Revised Code or a person serving as a special police officer employed by a port authority on a permanent basis on May 17, 2000, who has been awarded a certificate by the executive director of the Ohio peace officer training commission attesting to the person's satisfactory completion of an approved state, county, municipal, or department of natural resources peace officer basic training program;

(19) A special police officer employed by a municipal corporation who has been awarded a certificate by the executive director of the Ohio peace officer training commission for satisfactory completion of an approved peace officer basic training program and who is employed on a permanent basis on or after the effective date of this amendment at a municipal airport, or other municipal air navigation facility, that has scheduled operations, as defined in section 119.3 of Title 14 of the Code of Federal Regulations, 14 C.F.R. 119.3, as amended, and that is required to be under a security program and is governed by aviation security rules of the transportation security administration of the United States department of transportation as provided in Parts 1542. and 1544. of Title 49 of the Code of Federal Regulations, as amended.

(B) "Undercover drug agent" has the same meaning as in division (B)(2) of section 109.79 of the Revised Code.

(C) "Crisis intervention training" means training in the use of interpersonal and communication skills to most effectively and sensitively interview victims of rape.

(D) "Missing children" has the same meaning as in section 2901.30 of the Revised Code.

(2002 H 675, eff. 3–14–03; 2002 H 545, eff. 3–19–03; 2000 S 137, eff. 5–17–00; 1999 H 163, eff. 6–30–99; 1998 S 187, eff. 3–18–99; 1998 S 213, eff. 7–29–98; 1997 S 60, eff. 10–21–97; 1996 S 285, eff. 3–13–97; 1996 H 670, eff. 12–2–96; 1996 H 351, eff. 1–14–97; 1996 H 445, eff. 9–3–96; 1995 S 2, eff. 7–1–96; 1995 S 162, eff. 10–29–95; 1994 S 182, eff. 10–20–94; 1992 H 758, eff. 1–15–93; 1992 S 49; 1991 H 77; 1990 H 669, H 271, H 110; 1988 H 708, § 1)

109.72 Membership; appointment; term; meetings; expenses

Ohio peace officer training commission member terms shall be for three years, commencing on the twentieth day of September and ending on the nineteenth day of September. Each member shall hold office from the date of appointment until the end of the term to which the member was appointed. Any member appointed to fill a vacancy occurring prior to the expiration of the term for which the member's predecessor was appointed shall hold office for the remainder of such term. Any member shall continue in office subsequent to the expiration date of the member's term until the member's successor takes office, or until a period of sixty days has elapsed, whichever occurs first. An interim chairperson shall be appointed by the governor until such time as the commission elects a permanent chairperson.

Any member of the commission appointed pursuant to section 109.71 of the Revised Code as an incumbent sheriff, incumbent chief of police, representative of the state highway patrol, state department of education, federal bureau of investigation, and bureau of criminal identification and investigation, shall immediately, upon termination of holding such office, cease to be a member of the commission, and a successor shall be appointed.

The commission shall meet at least four times each year. Special meetings may be called by the chairperson and shall be called by the chairperson at the request of the attorney general or upon the written request of five members of the commission. The commission may establish its own requirements as to quorum and its own procedures with respect to the conduct of its meetings and other affairs; provided, that all recommendations by the commission to the attorney general pursuant to section 109.74 of the Revised Code shall require the affirmative vote of five members of the commission.

Membership on the commission does not constitute the holding of an office, and members of the commission shall not be required to take and file oaths of office before serving on the commission. The commission shall not exercise any portion of the sovereign power of the state.

The members of the commission shall receive no compensation for their services but shall be allowed their actual and necessary expenses incurred in the performance of their duties.

No member of the commission shall be disqualified from holding any public office or employment, nor shall the member forfeit any such office or employment, by reason of appointment to the commission, notwithstanding any general, special, or local law, ordinance, or city charter to the contrary.

(1996 H 670, eff. 12–2–96; 1973 S 131, eff. 8–21–73; 131 v H 363)

109.73 Powers and duties

(A) The Ohio peace officer training commission shall recommend rules to the attorney general with respect to all of the following:

(1) The approval, or revocation of approval, of peace officer training schools administered by the state, counties, municipal

corporations, public school districts, technical college districts, and the department of natural resources;

(2) Minimum courses of study, attendance requirements, and equipment and facilities to be required at approved state, county, municipal, and department of natural resources peace officer training schools;

(3) Minimum qualifications for instructors at approved state, county, municipal, and department of natural resources peace officer training schools;

(4) The requirements of minimum basic training that peace officers appointed to probationary terms shall complete before being eligible for permanent appointment, which requirements shall include a minimum of fifteen hours of training in the handling of the offense of domestic violence, other types of domestic violence-related offenses and incidents, and protection orders and consent agreements issued or approved under section 2919.26 or 3113.31 of the Revised Code, a minimum of six hours of crisis intervention training, and a specified amount of training in the handling of missing children and child abuse and neglect cases, and the time within which such basic training shall be completed following such appointment to a probationary term;

(5) The requirements of minimum basic training that peace officers not appointed for probationary terms but appointed on other than a permanent basis shall complete in order to be eligible for continued employment or permanent appointment, which requirements shall include a minimum of fifteen hours of training in the handling of the offense of domestic violence, other types of domestic violence-related offenses and incidents, and protection orders and consent agreements issued or approved under section 2919.26 or 3113.31 of the Revised Code, a minimum of six hours of crisis intervention training, and a specified amount of training in the handling of missing children and child abuse and neglect cases, and the time within which such basic training shall be completed following such appointment on other than a permanent basis;

(6) Categories or classifications of advanced in-service training programs for peace officers, including programs in the handling of the offense of domestic violence, other types of domestic violence-related offenses and incidents, and protection orders and consent agreements issued or approved under section 2919.26 or 3113.31 of the Revised Code, in crisis intervention, and in the handling of missing children and child abuse and neglect cases, and minimum courses of study and attendance requirements with respect to such categories or classifications;

(7) Permitting persons who are employed as members of a campus police department appointed under section 1713.50 of the Revised Code, who are employed as police officers by a qualified nonprofit corporation police department pursuant to section 1702.80 of the Revised Code, or who are appointed and commissioned as railroad police officers or hospital police officers pursuant to sections 4973.17 to 4973.22 of the Revised Code to attend approved peace officer training schools, including the Ohio peace officer training academy, and to receive certificates of satisfactory completion of basic training programs, if the private college or university that established the campus police department, qualified nonprofit corporation police department, railroad company, or hospital sponsoring the police officers pays the entire cost of the training and certification and if trainee vacancies are available;

(8) Permitting undercover drug agents to attend approved peace officer training schools, other than the Ohio peace officer training academy, and to receive certificates of satisfactory completion of basic training programs, if, for each undercover drug agent, the county, township, or municipal corporation that employs that undercover drug agent pays the entire cost of the training and certification;

(9)(a) The requirements for basic training programs for bailiffs and deputy bailiffs of courts of record of this state and for criminal investigators employed by the state public defender that those persons shall complete before they may carry a firearm while on duty;

(b) The requirements for any training received by a bailiff or deputy bailiff of a court of record of this state or by a criminal investigator employed by the state public defender prior to June 6, 1986, that is to be considered equivalent to the training described in division (A)(9)(a) of this section.

(10) Establishing minimum qualifications and requirements for certification for dogs utilized by law enforcement agencies;

(11) Establishing minimum requirements for certification of persons who are employed as correction officers in a full-service jail, five-day facility, or eight-hour holding facility or who provide correction services in such a jail or facility;

(12) Establishing requirements for the training of agents of a county humane society under section 1717.06 of the Revised Code, including, without limitation, a requirement that the agents receive instruction on traditional animal husbandry methods and training techniques, including customary owner-performed practices.

(B) The commission shall appoint an executive director, with the approval of the attorney general, who shall hold office during the pleasure of the commission. The executive director shall perform such duties as may be assigned by the commission. The executive director shall receive a salary fixed pursuant to Chapter 124. of the Revised Code and reimbursement for expenses within the amounts available by appropriation. The executive director may appoint officers, employees, agents, and consultants as the executive director considers necessary, prescribe their duties, and provide for reimbursement of their expenses within the amounts available for reimbursement by appropriation and with the approval of the commission.

(C) The commission may do all of the following:

(1) Recommend studies, surveys, and reports to be made by the executive director regarding the carrying out of the objectives and purposes of sections 109.71 to 109.77 of the Revised Code;

(2) Visit and inspect any peace officer training school that has been approved by the executive director or for which application for approval has been made;

(3) Make recommendations, from time to time, to the executive director, the attorney general, and the general assembly regarding the carrying out of the purposes of sections 109.71 to 109.77 of the Revised Code;

(4) Report to the attorney general from time to time, and to the governor and the general assembly at least annually, concerning the activities of the commission;

(5) Establish fees for the services the commission offers under sections 109.71 to 109.79 of the Revised Code, including, but not limited to, fees for training, certification, and testing;

(6) Perform such other acts as are necessary or appropriate to carry out the powers and duties of the commission as set forth in sections 109.71 to 109.77 of the Revised Code.

(D) In establishing the requirements, under division (A)(12) of this section, the commission may consider any portions of the curriculm[1] for instruction on the topic of animal husbandry practices, if any, of the Ohio state university college of veterinary medicine. No person or entity that fails to provide instruction on traditional animal husbandry methods and training techniques, including customary owner-performed practices, shall qualify to train a humane agent for appointment under section 1717.06 of the Revised Code.

(2002 S 221, eff. 4–9–03; 1996 H 670, eff. 12–2–96; 1992 H 758, eff. 1–15–93; 1992 S 359; 1990 H 669, S 3, H 110; 1986 S 364, S 149; 1984 S 321, H 435, H 759; 1981 H 44; 1978 H 835; 1976 S 272; 1971 S 396; 132 v H 93; 131 v H 363)

[1] So in original; 2002 S 221.

109.731 Powers and duties; concealed handguns

(A) The Ohio peace officer training commission shall prescribe, and shall make available to sheriffs, all of the following:

(1) An application form that is to be used under section 2923.125 of the Revised Code by a person who applies for a license to carry a concealed handgun or for the renewal of a license of that nature and that conforms substantially to the form prescribed in section 2923.1210 of the Revised Code;

(2) A form for the license to carry a concealed handgun that is to be issued by sheriffs to persons who qualify for a license to carry a concealed handgun under section 2923.125 of the Revised Code and that conforms to the following requirements:

(a) It has space for the licensee's full name, residence address, and date of birth and for a color photograph of the licensee.

(b) It has space for the date of issuance of the license, its expiration date, its county of issuance, the name of the sheriff who issues the license, and the unique combination of letters and numbers that identify the county of issuance and the license given to the licensee by the sheriff in accordance with division (A)(4) of this section.

(c) It has space for the signature of the licensee and the signature or a facsimile signature of the sheriff who issues the license.

(d) It does not require the licensee to include serial numbers of handguns, other identification related to handguns, or similar data that is not pertinent or relevant to obtaining the license and that could be used as a de facto means of registration of handguns owned by the licensee.

(3) A series of three-letter county codes that identify each county in this state;

(4) A procedure by which a sheriff shall give each license, replacement license, or renewal license to carry a concealed handgun and each temporary emergency license or replacement temporary emergency license to carry a concealed handgun the sheriff issues under section 2923.125 or 2923.1213 of the Revised Code a unique combination of letters and numbers that identifies the county in which the license or temporary emergency license was issued and that uses the county code and a unique number for each license and each temporary emergency license the sheriff of that county issues;

(5) A form for the temporary emergency license to carry a concealed handgun that is to be issued by sheriffs to persons who qualify for a temporary emergency license under section 2923.1213 of the Revised Code, which form shall conform to all the requirements set forth in divisions (A)(2)(a) to (d) of this section and shall additionally conspicuously specify that the license is a temporary emergency license and the date of its issuance.

(B)(1) The Ohio peace officer training commission, in consultation with the attorney general, shall prepare a pamphlet that does all of the following, in everyday language:

(a) Explains the firearms laws of this state;

(b) Instructs the reader in dispute resolution and explains the laws of this state related to that matter;

(c) Provides information to the reader regarding all aspects of the use of deadly force with a firearm, including, but not limited to, the steps that should be taken before contemplating the use of, or using, deadly force with a firearm, possible alternatives to using deadly force with a firearm, and the law governing the use of deadly force with a firearm.

(2) The attorney general shall consult with and assist the commission in the preparation of the pamphlet described in division (B)(1) of this section and, as necessary, shall recommend to the commission changes in the pamphlet to reflect changes in the law that are relevant to it. The commission shall make copies of the pamphlet available to any person, public entity, or private entity that operates or teaches a training course, class, or program described in division (B)(3)(a), (b), (c), and (e) of section 2923.125 of the Revised Code and requests copies for distribution to persons who take the course, class, or program, and to sheriffs for distribution to applicants under section 2923.125 of the Revised Code for a license to carry a concealed handgun and applicants under that section for the renewal of a license to carry a concealed handgun.

(C)(1) The Ohio peace officer training commission, in consultation with the attorney general, shall prescribe a fee to be paid by an applicant under section 2923.125 of the Revised Code for a license to carry a concealed handgun or for the renewal of a license to carry a concealed handgun as follows:

(a) For an applicant who has been a resident of this state for five or more years, an amount that does not exceed the lesser of the actual cost of issuing the license, including, but not limited to, the cost of conducting the criminal records check, or forty-five dollars;

(b) For an applicant who has been a resident of this state for less than five years, an amount that shall consist of the actual cost of having a criminal background check performed by the federal bureau of investigation, if one is so performed, plus the lesser of the actual cost of issuing the license, including, but not limited to, the cost of conducting the criminal records check, or forty-five dollars.

(2) The commission, in consultation with the attorney general, shall specify the portion of the fee prescribed under division (C)(1) of this section that will be used to pay each particular cost of the issuance of the license. The sheriff shall deposit all fees paid by an applicant under section 2923.125 of the Revised Code into the sheriff's concealed handgun license issuance expense fund established pursuant to section 311.42 of the Revised Code.

(D) The Ohio peace officer training commission shall maintain statistics with respect to the issuance, renewal, suspension, revocation, and denial of licenses to carry a concealed handgun and the suspension of processing of applications for those licenses, and with respect to the issuance, suspension, revocation, and denial of temporary emergency licenses to carry a concealed handgun, as reported by the sheriffs pursuant to division (C) of section 2923.129 of the Revised Code. Not later than the first day of March in each year, the commission shall submit a statistical report to the governor, the president of the senate, and the speaker of the house of representatives indicating the number of licenses to carry a concealed handgun that were issued, renewed, suspended, revoked, and denied in the previous calendar year, the number of applications for those licenses for which processing was suspended in accordance with division (D)(3) of section 2923.125 of the Revised Code in the previous calendar year, and the number of temporary emergency licenses to carry a concealed handgun that were issued, suspended, revoked, or denied in the previous calendar year. Nothing in the statistics or the statistical report shall identify, or enable the identification of, any individual who was issued or denied a license, for whom a license was renewed, whose license was suspended or revoked, or for whom application processing was suspended. The statistics and the statistical report are public records for the purpose of section 149. 43 of the Revised Code.

(E) As used in this section, "handgun" has the same meaning as in section 2923.11 of the Revised Code.

(2004 H 12, eff. 4–8–04)

109.74 Promulgation of rules and regulations by attorney general

The attorney general, in accordance with Chapter 119. of the Revised Code, has discretion to adopt and promulgate any or all of the rules and regulations recommended by the Ohio peace officer training commission to the attorney general pursuant to section 109.73 of the Revised Code. When the attorney general promulgates any rule or regulation recommended by the commission, the attorney general shall transmit a certified copy thereof to the secretary of state.

(1996 H 670, eff. 12–2–96; 131 v H 363, eff. 9–6–65)

109.741 Training in handling children's cases

The attorney general shall adopt, in accordance with Chapter 119. or pursuant to section 109.74 of the Revised Code, rules governing the training of peace officers in the handling of missing children and child abuse and neglect cases. The rules shall specify the amount of that training necessary for the satisfactory completion of basic training programs at approved peace officer training schools, other than the Ohio peace officer training academy and the time within which a peace officer is required to receive that training, if he receives his appointment as a peace officer before receiving that training.

(1985 S 84, eff. 4–9–85; 1984 S 321)

109.742 Rules on training in crisis intervention

The attorney general shall adopt, in accordance with Chapter 119. or pursuant to section 109.74 of the Revised Code, rules governing the training of peace officers in crisis intervention. The rules shall specify six or more hours of that training for the satisfactory completion of basic training programs at approved peace officer training schools, other than the Ohio peace officer training academy.

(1984 H 435, eff. 4–4–85)

109.743 Rules governing firearms requalification programs

The attorney general shall adopt, in accordance with Chapter 119. of the Revised Code or pursuant to section 109.74 of the Revised Code, rules governing firearms requalification programs that are required by section 109.801 of the Revised Code. At a minimum, the rules shall prohibit a firearms requalification program from being used to fulfill the requirements of section 109.801 of the Revised Code until after the program is approved by the executive director of the Ohio peace officer training commission pursuant to section 109.75 of the Revised Code.

(1996 H 670, eff. 12–2–96; 1990 H 271, eff. 4–10–91)

109.744 Rules for officer training in domestic violence offenses

The attorney general shall adopt, in accordance with Chapter 119. of the Revised Code or pursuant to section 109.74 of the Revised Code, rules governing the training of peace officers in the handling of the offense of domestic violence, other types of domestic violence-related offenses and incidents, and protection orders and consent agreements issued or approved under section 2919.26 or 3113.31 of the Revised Code. The provisions of the rules shall include, but shall not be limited to, all of the following:

(A) A specification that fifteen or more hours of that training is required for the satisfactory completion of basic training programs at approved peace officer training schools, other than the Ohio peace officer training academy;

(B) A requirement that the training include, but not be limited to, training in all of the following:

(1) All recent amendments to domestic violence-related laws;

(2) Notifying a victim of domestic violence of his rights;

(3) Processing protection orders and consent agreements issued or approved under section 2919.26 or 3113.31 of the Revised Code.

(1990 S 3, eff. 4–11–91)

109.75 Executive director

The executive director of the Ohio peace officer training commission, on behalf of the commission, shall have the following powers and duties, which shall be exercised with the general advice of the commission and only in accordance with section 109.751 of the Revised Code and the rules adopted pursuant to that section, and with the rules adopted by the attorney general pursuant to sections 109.74, 109.741, 109.742, and 109.743 of the Revised Code:

(A) To approve peace officer training schools and firearms requalification programs administered by the state, counties, municipal corporations, and the department of natural resources, to issue certificates of approval to approved schools, and to revoke an approval or certificate;

(B) To certify, as qualified, instructors at approved peace officer training schools, to issue appropriate certificates to these instructors, and to revoke for good cause shown certificates of these instructors;

(C) To certify, as qualified, commanders at approved peace officer training schools, to issue appropriate certificates to these commanders, and to revoke for good cause shown certificates of these commanders. As used in this division, "commander" means the director or other head of an approved peace officer training school.

(D) To certify peace officers and sheriffs who have satisfactorily completed basic training programs and to issue appropriate certificates to these peace officers and sheriffs;

(E) To cause studies and surveys to be made relating to the establishment, operation, and approval of state, county, and municipal peace officer training schools;

(F) To consult and cooperate with state, county, and municipal peace officer training schools for the development of advanced in-service training programs for peace officers;

(G) To consult and cooperate with universities, colleges, and institutes for the development of specialized courses of study in the state for peace officers in police science and police administration;

(H) To consult and cooperate with other departments and agencies of the state and federal government concerned with peace officer training;

(I) To perform any other acts that may be necessary or appropriate to carry out the executive director's powers and duties as set forth in sections 109.71 to 109.77 of the Revised Code;

(J) To report to the commission at each regular meeting of the commission and at any other times that the commission may require;

(K) To certify persons who have satisfactorily completed approved training programs for correction officers in full-service jails, five-day facilities, or eight-hour holding facilities or approved training programs for others who provide correction services in those jails or facilities and to issue appropriate certificates to those persons;

(L) To maintain any records associated with the powers and duties set forth in this section. Certification examinations, either before or after completion, are not public records for purposes of section 149.43 of the Revised Code, but the results of such examinations are public records under that section.

(2002 H 545, eff. 3–19–03; 1996 H 670, eff. 12–2–96; 1996 H 566, eff. 10–16–96; 1990 H 669, eff. 1–10–91; 1990 H 271; 1986 H 428; 1984 S 321, H 435, H 759; 1981 H 44; 131 v H 363)

109.751 Approval of schools; attendance of undercover drug agents

(A) The executive director of the Ohio peace officer training commission shall neither approve nor issue a certificate of approval to a peace officer training school pursuant to section 109.75 of the Revised Code unless the school agrees to permit, in accordance with rules adopted by the attorney general pursuant to division (C) of this section, undercover drug agents to attend its basic training programs. The executive director shall revoke approval, and the certificate of approval of, a peace officer training school that does not permit, in accordance with rules adopted by the attorney general pursuant to division (C) of this section, undercover drug agents to attend its basic training programs.

This division does not apply to peace officer training schools for employees of conservancy districts who are designated pursuant to section 6101.75 of the Revised Code or for a natural resources law enforcement staff officer, park officers, forest officers, preserve officers, wildlife officers, or state watercraft officers of the department of natural resources.

(B)(1) A peace officer training school is not required to permit an undercover drug agent, a bailiff or deputy bailiff of a court of record of this state, or a criminal investigator employed by the state public defender to attend its basic training programs if either of the following applies:

(a) In the case of the Ohio peace officer training academy, the employer county, township, municipal corporation, court, or state public defender or the particular undercover drug agent, bailiff, deputy bailiff, or criminal investigator has not paid the tuition costs of training in accordance with section 109.79 of the Revised Code;

(b) In the case of other peace officer training schools, the employer county, township, municipal corporation, court, or state public defender fails to pay the entire cost of the training and certification.

(2) A training school shall not permit a bailiff or deputy bailiff of a court of record of this state or a criminal investigator employed by the state public defender to attend its basic training programs unless the employing court of the bailiff or deputy bailiff or the state public defender, whichever is applicable, has authorized the bailiff, deputy bailiff, or investigator to attend the school.

(C) The attorney general shall adopt, in accordance with Chapter 119. or pursuant to section 109.74 of the Revised Code, rules governing the attendance of undercover drug agents at approved peace officer training schools, other than the Ohio peace officer training academy, and the certification of the agents upon their satisfactory completion of basic training programs.

(1998 S 187, eff. 3–18–99; 1996 H 670, eff. 12–2–96; 1994 S 182, eff. 10–20–94; 1986 H 428, eff. 12–23–86; 1986 S 278, S 149; 1984 H 759; 1981 H 44)

109.752 Completion of basic training programs by sheriffs

Any sheriff may attend and be awarded a certificate by the executive director of the Ohio peace officer training commission attesting to the satisfactory completion of any state, county, municipal, or department of natural resources peace officer basic training program that has been approved by the executive director under section 109.75 of the Revised Code or is offered at the Ohio peace officer training academy.

(1996 H 670, eff. 12–2–96; 1990 H 669, eff. 1–10–91; 1990 H 271)

109.76 Construction of act

Nothing in sections 109.71 to 109.77 of the Revised Code shall be construed to except any peace officer, or other officer or employee from the provisions of Chapter 124. of the Revised Code.

(1977 H 1, eff. 8–26–77; 131 v H 363)

109.761 Reports to peace officer training commission

(A)(1) Each agency or entity that appoints or employs one or more peace officers shall report to the Ohio peace officer training commission all of the following that occur on or after the effective date of this section:

(a) The appointment or employment of any person to serve the agency or entity as a peace officer in any full-time, part-time, reserve, auxiliary, or other capacity;

(b) The termination, resignation, felony conviction, or death of any person who has been appointed to or employed by the agency or entity as a peace officer in any full-time, part-time, reserve, auxiliary, or other capacity and is serving the agency or entity in any of those peace officer capacities.

(2) An agency or entity shall make each report required by this division not later than ten days after the occurrence of the event being reported. The agency or entity shall make the report in the manner and format prescribed by the executive director of the Ohio peace officer training commission.

(B) Each agency or entity that appoints or employs one or more peace officers shall annually provide to the Ohio peace officer training commission a roster of all persons who have been appointed to or employed by the agency or entity as peace officers in any full-time, part-time, reserve, auxiliary, or other capacity and are serving, or during the year covered by the report have served, the agency or entity in any of those peace officer capacities. The agency or entity shall provide the roster in the manner and format, and by the date, prescribed by the executive director of the Ohio peace officer training commission.

(C) The Ohio peace officer training commission shall prescribe the manner and format of making reports under division (A) of this section and providing annual rosters under division (B) of this section and shall prescribe the date by which the annual rosters must be provided.

(2001 S 119, eff. 2–20–02)

109.77 Certificate of training for peace officer, liquor control investigator, bailiff, or criminal investigator; training in domestic matters, crisis intervention; exceptions; prohibition

(A) As used in this section, "felony" has the same meaning as in section 109.511 of the Revised Code.

(B)(1) Notwithstanding any general, special, or local law or charter to the contrary, and except as otherwise provided in this section, no person shall receive an original appointment on a permanent basis as any of the following unless the person previously has been awarded a certificate by the executive director of the Ohio peace officer training commission attesting to the person's satisfactory completion of an approved state, county, municipal, or department of natural resources peace officer basic training program:

(a) A peace officer of any county, township, municipal corporation, regional transit authority, or metropolitan housing authority;

(b) A natural resources law enforcement staff officer, park officer, forest officer, preserve officer, wildlife officer, or state watercraft officer of the department of natural resources;

(c) An employee of a park district under section 511.232 or 1545.13 of the Revised Code;

(d) An employee of a conservancy district who is designated pursuant to section 6101.75 of the Revised Code;

(e) A state university law enforcement officer;

(f) A special police officer employed by the department of mental health pursuant to section 5119.14 of the Revised Code or the department of mental retardation and developmental disabilities pursuant to section 5123.13 of the Revised Code;

(g) An enforcement agent of the department of public safety whom the director of public safety designates under section 5502.14 of the Revised Code;

(h) A special police officer employed by a port authority under section 4582.04 or 4582.28 of the Revised Code;

(i) A special police officer employed by a municipal corporation at a municipal airport, or other municipal air navigation facility, that has scheduled operations, as defined in section 119.3 of Title 14 of the Code of Federal Regulations, 14 C.F.R. 119.3, as amended, and that is required to be under a security program and is governed by aviation security rules of the transportation security administration of the United States department of transportation as provided in Parts 1542. and 1544. of Title 49 of the Code of Federal Regulations, as amended.

(2) Every person who is appointed on a temporary basis or for a probationary term or on other than a permanent basis as any of the following shall forfeit the appointed position unless the person previously has completed satisfactorily or, within the time prescribed by rules adopted by the attorney general pursuant to section 109.74 of the Revised Code, satisfactorily completes a state, county, municipal, or department of natural resources peace officer basic training program for temporary or probationary officers and is awarded a certificate by the director attesting to the satisfactory completion of the program:

(a) A peace officer of any county, township, municipal corporation, regional transit authority, or metropolitan housing authority;

(b) A natural resources law enforcement staff officer, park officer, forest officer, preserve officer, wildlife officer, or state watercraft officer of the department of natural resources;

(c) An employee of a park district under section 511.232 or 1545.13 of the Revised Code;

(d) An employee of a conservancy district who is designated pursuant to section 6101.75 of the Revised Code;

(e) A special police officer employed by the department of mental health pursuant to section 5119.14 of the Revised Code or the department of mental retardation and developmental disabilities pursuant to section 5123.13 of the Revised Code;

(f) An enforcement agent of the department of public safety whom the director of public safety designates under section 5502.14 of the Revised Code;

(g) A special police officer employed by a port authority under section 4582.04 or 4582.28 of the Revised Code;

(h) A special police officer employed by a municipal corporation at a municipal airport, or other municipal air navigation facility, that has scheduled operations, as defined in section 119.3 of Title 14 of the Code of Federal Regulations, 14 C.F.R. 119.3, as amended, and that is required to be under a security program and is governed by aviation security rules of the transportation security administration of the United States department of transportation as provided in Parts 1542. and 1544. of Title 49 of the Code of Federal Regulations, as amended.

(3) For purposes of division (B) of this section, a state, county, municipal, or department of natural resources peace officer basic training program, regardless of whether the program is to be completed by peace officers appointed on a permanent or temporary, probationary, or other nonpermanent basis, shall include at least fifteen hours of training in the handling of the offense of domestic violence, other types of domestic violence-related offenses and incidents, and protection orders and consent agreements issued or approved under section 2919.26 or 3113.31 of the Revised Code and at least six hours of crisis intervention training. The requirement to complete fifteen hours of training in the handling of the offense of domestic violence, other types of domestic violence-related offenses and incidents, and protection orders and consent agreements issued or approved under section 2919.26 or 3113.31 of the Revised Code does not apply to any person serving as a peace officer on March 27, 1979, and the requirement to complete six hours of training in crisis intervention does not apply to any person serving as a peace officer on April 4, 1985. Any person who is serving as a peace officer on April 4, 1985, who terminates that employment after that date, and who subsequently is hired as a peace officer by the same or another law enforcement agency shall complete the six hours of training in crisis intervention within the time prescribed by rules adopted by the attorney general pursuant to section 109.742 of the Revised Code. No peace officer shall have employment as a peace officer terminated and then be reinstated with intent to circumvent this section.

(4) Division (B) of this section does not apply to any person serving on a permanent basis on March 28, 1985, as a park officer, forest officer, preserve officer, wildlife officer, or state watercraft officer of the department of natural resources or as an employee of a park district under section 511.232 or 1545.13 of the Revised Code, to any person serving on a permanent basis on March 6, 1986, as an employee of a conservancy district designated pursuant to section 6101.75 of the Revised Code, to any person serving on a permanent basis on January 10, 1991, as a preserve officer of the department of natural resources, to any person employed on a permanent basis on July 2, 1992, as a special police officer by the department of mental health pursuant to section 5119.14 of the Revised Code or by the department of mental retardation and developmental disabilities pursuant to section 5123.13 of the Revised Code, to any person serving on a permanent basis on May 17, 2000, as a special police officer employed by a port authority under section 4582.04 or 4582.28 of the Revised Code, to any person serving on a permanent basis on the effective date of this amendment as a special police officer employed by a municipal corporation at a municipal airport or other municipal air navigation facility described in division (A)(19) of section 109.71 of the Revised Code, to any person [1] serving on a permanent basis on June 19, 1978, as a state university law enforcement officer pursuant to section 3345.04 of the Revised Code and who, immediately prior to June 19, 1978, was serving as a special police officer designated under authority of that section, or to any person serving on a permanent basis on September 20, 1984, as a liquor control investigator, known after June 30, 1999, as an enforcement agent of the department of public safety, engaged in the enforcement of Chapters 4301. and 4303. of the Revised Code.

(5) Division (B) of this section does not apply to any person who is appointed as a regional transit authority police officer pursuant to division (Y) of section 306.35 of the Revised Code if, on or before July 1, 1996, the person has completed satisfactorily an approved state, county, municipal, or department of natural resources peace officer basic training program and has been awarded a certificate by the executive director of the Ohio peace officer training commission attesting to the person's satisfactory completion of such an approved program and if, on July 1, 1996, the person is performing peace officer functions for a regional transit authority.

(C) No person, after September 20, 1984, shall receive an original appointment on a permanent basis as a veterans' home police officer designated under section 5907.02 of the Revised Code unless the person previously has been awarded a certificate by the executive director of the Ohio peace officer training commission attesting to the person's satisfactory completion of an approved police officer basic training program. Every person who is appointed on a temporary basis or for a probationary term or on other than a permanent basis as a veterans' home police officer designated under section 5907.02 of the Revised Code shall forfeit that position unless the person previously has completed satisfactorily or, within one year from the time of appointment, satisfactorily completes an approved police officer basic training program.

(D) No bailiff or deputy bailiff of a court of record of this state and no criminal investigator who is employed by the state public defender shall carry a firearm, as defined in section 2923.11 of the Revised Code, while on duty unless the bailiff, deputy bailiff, or criminal investigator has done or received one of the following:

(1) Has been awarded a certificate by the executive director of the Ohio peace officer training commission, which certificate attests to satisfactory completion of an approved state, county, or municipal basic training program for bailiffs and deputy bailiffs of courts of record and for criminal investigators employed by the state public defender that has been recommended by the Ohio peace officer training commission;

(2) Has successfully completed a firearms training program approved by the Ohio peace officer training commission prior to employment as a bailiff, deputy bailiff, or criminal investigator;

(3) Prior to June 6, 1986, was authorized to carry a firearm by the court that employed the bailiff or deputy bailiff or, in the case of a criminal investigator, by the state public defender and has received training in the use of firearms that the Ohio peace officer training commission determines is equivalent to the training that otherwise is required by division (D) of this section.

(E)(1) Before a person seeking a certificate completes an approved peace officer basic training program, the executive director of the Ohio peace officer training commission shall request the person to disclose, and the person shall disclose, any previous criminal conviction of or plea of guilty of that person to a felony.

(2) Before a person seeking a certificate completes an approved peace officer basic training program, the executive director shall request a criminal history records check on the person. The executive director shall submit the person's fingerprints to the bureau of criminal identification and investigation, which shall submit the fingerprints to the federal bureau of investigation for a national criminal history records check.

Upon receipt of the executive director's request, the bureau of criminal identification and investigation and the federal bureau of investigation shall conduct a criminal history records check on the person and, upon completion of the check, shall provide a copy of the criminal history records check to the executive director. The executive director shall not award any certificate prescribed in this section unless the executive director has received a copy of the criminal history records check on the person to whom the certificate is to be awarded.

(3) The executive director of the commission shall not award a certificate prescribed in this section to a person who has been convicted of or has pleaded guilty to a felony or who fails to disclose any previous criminal conviction of or plea of guilty to a felony as required under division (E)(1) of this section.

(4) The executive director of the commission shall revoke the certificate awarded to a person as prescribed in this section, and that person shall forfeit all of the benefits derived from being certified as a peace officer under this section, if the person, before completion of an approved peace officer basic training program, failed to disclose any previous criminal conviction of or plea of guilty to a felony as required under division (E)(1) of this section.

(F)(1) Regardless of whether the person has been awarded the certificate or has been classified as a peace officer prior to, on, or after October 16, 1996, the executive director of the Ohio peace officer training commission shall revoke any certificate that has been awarded to a person as prescribed in this section if the person does either of the following:

(a) Pleads guilty to a felony committed on or after January 1, 1997;

(b) Pleads guilty to a misdemeanor committed on or after January 1, 1997, pursuant to a negotiated plea agreement as provided in division (D) of section 2929.43 of the Revised Code in which the person agrees to surrender the certificate awarded to the person under this section.

(2) The executive director of the commission shall suspend any certificate that has been awarded to a person as prescribed in this section if the person is convicted, after trial, of a felony committed on or after January 1, 1997. The executive director shall suspend the certificate pursuant to division (F)(2) of this section pending the outcome of an appeal by the person from that conviction to the highest court to which the appeal is taken or until the expiration of the period in which an appeal is required to be filed. If the person files an appeal that results in that person's acquittal of the felony or conviction of a misdemeanor, or in the dismissal of the felony charge against that person, the executive director shall reinstate the certificate awarded to the person under this section. If the person files an appeal from that person's conviction of the felony and the conviction is upheld by the highest court to which the appeal is taken or if the person does not file a timely appeal, the executive director shall revoke the certificate awarded to the person under this section.

(G)(1) If a person is awarded a certificate under this section and the certificate is revoked pursuant to division (E)(4) or (F) of this section, the person shall not be eligible to receive, at any time, a certificate attesting to the person's satisfactory completion of a peace officer basic training program.

(2) The revocation or suspension of a certificate under division (E)(4) or (F) of this section shall be in accordance with Chapter 119. of the Revised Code.

(H)(1) A person who was employed as a peace officer of a county, township, or municipal corporation of the state on January 1, 1966, and who has completed at least sixteen years of full-time active service as such a peace officer may receive an original appointment on a permanent basis and serve as a peace officer of a county, township, or municipal corporation, or as a state university law enforcement officer, without complying with the requirements of division (B) of this section.

(2) Any person who held an appointment as a state highway trooper on January 1, 1966, may receive an original appointment on a permanent basis and serve as a peace officer of a county, township, or municipal corporation, or as a state university law enforcement officer, without complying with the requirements of division (B) of this section.

(I) No person who is appointed as a peace officer of a county, township, or municipal corporation on or after April 9, 1985, shall serve as a peace officer of that county, township, or municipal corporation unless the person has received training in the handling of missing children and child abuse and neglect cases from an approved state, county, township, or municipal police officer basic training program or receives the training within the time prescribed by rules adopted by the attorney general pursuant to section 109.741 of the Revised Code.

(J) No part of any approved state, county, or municipal basic training program for bailiffs and deputy bailiffs of courts of record and no part of any approved state, county, or municipal basic training program for criminal investigators employed by the state public defender shall be used as credit toward the completion by a peace officer of any part of the approved state, county, or municipal peace officer basic training program that the peace officer is required by this section to complete satisfactorily.

(K) This section does not apply to any member of the police department of a municipal corporation in an adjoining state serving in this state under a contract pursuant to section 737.04 of the Revised Code.

(2002 H 675, eff. 3–14–03; 2002 H 490, eff. 1–1–04; 2002 H 545, eff. 3–19–03; 2000 S 137, eff. 5–17–00; 1999 H 148, eff. 7–15–99; 1999 H 163, eff. 6–30–99; 1998 S 187, eff. 3–18–99; 1996 S 285, eff. 3–13–97; 1996 H 670, eff. 12–2–96; 1996 H 566, eff. 10–16–96; 1996 S 269, eff. 7–1–96; 1995 S 2, eff. 7–1–96; 1995 S 162, eff. 10–29–95; 1994 S 182, eff. 10–20–94; 1992 S 49, eff. 7–21–92; 1990 H 669, S 3, H 271; 1988 H 708, § 1)

[1] Prior and current versions differ; although no amendment to this language was indicated in 2002 H 545, H 490, or H 675, "to any person" appeared as "or to any person" in 2000 S 137.

109.78 Certification as special police officer or security guard; payment of cost; firearms training; peace officer private security fund

(A) The executive director of the Ohio peace officer training commission, on behalf of the commission and in accordance with rules promulgated by the attorney general, shall certify persons who have satisfactorily completed approved training programs designed to qualify persons for positions as special police, security guards, or persons otherwise privately employed in a police capacity and issue appropriate certificates to such persons. Application for approval of a training program designed to qualify persons for such positions shall be made to the commission. An application for approval shall be submitted to the commission with a fee of one hundred twenty-five dollars, which fee shall be refunded if the application is denied. Such programs shall cover only duties and jurisdiction of such security guards and special police privately employed in a police capacity when such officers do not qualify for training under section 109.71 of the Revised Code. A person attending an approved basic training program administered by the state shall pay to the agency administering the program the cost of the person's participation in the program as determined by the agency. A person attending an approved basic training program administered by a county or municipal corporation shall pay the cost of the person's participation in the program, as determined by the administering subdivision, to the county or the municipal corporation. A person who is issued a certificate for satisfactory completion of an approved basic training program shall pay to the commission a fee of fifteen dollars. A duplicate of a lost, spoliated, or destroyed certificate may be issued upon application and payment of a fee of fifteen dollars. Such certificate or the completion of twenty years of active duty as a peace officer shall satisfy the educational requirements for appointment or commission as a special police officer or special deputy of a political subdivision of this state.

(B)(1) The executive director of the Ohio peace officer training commission, on behalf of the commission and in accordance with rules promulgated by the attorney general, shall certify basic firearms training programs, and shall issue certificates to class A, B, or C licensees or prospective class A, B, or C licensees under Chapter 4749. of the Revised Code and to registered or prospective employees of such class A, B, or C licensees who have satisfactorily completed a basic firearms training program of the type described in division (A)(1) of section 4749.10 of the Revised Code.

Application for approval of a basic firearms training program shall be made to the commission. An application shall be submitted to the commission with a fee of one hundred dollars, which fee shall be refunded if the application is denied.

A person who is issued a certificate for satisfactory completion of an approved basic firearms training program shall pay a fee of ten dollars to the commission. A duplicate of a lost, spoliated, or destroyed certificate may be issued upon application and payment of a fee of five dollars.

(2) The executive director, on behalf of the commission and in accordance with rules promulgated by the attorney general, also shall certify firearms requalification training programs and instructors for the annual requalification of class A, B, or C licensees under Chapter 4749. of the Revised Code and registered or prospective employees of such class A, B, or C licensees who are authorized to carry a firearm under section 4749.10 of the Revised Code. Application for approval of a training program or instructor for such purpose shall be made to the commission. Such an application shall be submitted to the commission with a fee of fifty dollars, which fee shall be refunded if the application is denied.

(3) The executive director, upon request, also shall review firearms training received within three years prior to November 23, 1985, by any class A, B, or C licensee or prospective class A, B, or C licensee, or by any registered or prospective employee of any class A, B, or C licensee under Chapter 4749. of the Revised Code to determine if the training received is equivalent to a basic firearms training program that includes twenty hours of handgun training and five hours of training in the use of other firearms, if any other firearm is to be used. If the executive director determines the training was received within the three-year period and that it is equivalent to such a program, the executive director shall issue written evidence of approval of the equivalency training to the licensee or employee.

(C) There is hereby established in the state treasury the peace officer private security fund, which shall be used by the Ohio peace officer training commission to administer the training program to qualify persons for positions as special police, security guards, or other private employment in a police capacity, as described in division (A) of this section, and the training program in basic firearms and the training program for firearms requalification, both as described in division (B) of this section. All fees paid to the commission by applicants for approval of a training program designed to qualify persons for such private police positions, basic firearms training program, or a firearms requalification training program or instructor, as required by division (A) or (B) of this section, by persons who satisfactorily complete a private police training program or a basic firearms training program, as required by division (A) or (B) of this section, or by persons who satisfactorily requalify in firearms use, as required by division (B)(2) of section 4749.10 of the Revised Code, shall be transmitted to the treasurer of state for deposit in the fund. The fund shall be used only for the purpose set forth in this division.

(D) No public or private educational institution or superintendent of the state highway patrol shall employ a person as a special police officer, security guard, or other position in which such person goes armed while on duty, who has not received a certificate of having satisfactorily completed an approved basic peace officer training program, unless the person has completed twenty years of active duty as a peace officer.

(2000 S 137, eff. 5–17–00; 1996 H 670, eff. 12–2–96; 1995 S 2, eff. 7–1–96; 1987 H 419, eff. 7–1–87; 1986 H 428; 1985 H 402; 1977 S 194; 1974 S 192; 1972 H 633; 1971 H 1; 1969 H 575)

109.79 Ohio peace officer training academy

(A) The Ohio peace officer training commission shall establish and conduct a training school for law enforcement officers of any political subdivision of the state or of the state public defender's office. The school shall be known as the Ohio peace officer training academy. No bailiff or deputy bailiff of a court of record of this state and no criminal investigator employed by the state public defender shall be permitted to attend the academy for training unless the employing court of the bailiff or deputy bailiff or the state public defender, whichever is applicable, has authorized the bailiff, deputy bailiff, or investigator to attend the academy.

The Ohio peace officer training commission shall develop the training program, which shall include courses in both the civil and criminal functions of law enforcement officers, a course in crisis intervention with six or more hours of training, and training in the handling of missing children and child abuse and neglect cases, and shall establish rules governing qualifications for admission to the academy. The commission may require competitive examinations to determine fitness of prospective trainees, so long as the examinations or other criteria for admission to the academy are consistent with the provisions of Chapter 124. of the Revised Code.

The Ohio peace officer training commission shall determine tuition costs which shall be sufficient in the aggregate to pay the costs of operating the academy. The costs of acquiring and equipping the academy shall be paid from appropriations made by the general assembly to the Ohio peace officer training commission for that purpose, or from gifts or grants received for that purpose.

The law enforcement officers, during the period of their training, shall receive compensation as determined by the political subdivision that sponsors them or, if the officer is a criminal investigator employed by the state public defender, as determined by the state public defender. The political subdivision may pay the tuition costs of the law enforcement officers they sponsor and the state public defender may pay the tuition costs of criminal investigators of that office who attend the academy.

If trainee vacancies exist, the academy may train and issue certificates of satisfactory completion to peace officers who are employed by a campus police department pursuant to section 1713.50 of the Revised Code, by a qualified nonprofit corporation police department pursuant to section 1702.80 of the Revised Code, or by a railroad company or who are hospital police officers appointed and commissioned by the governor pursuant to sections 4973.17 to 4973.22 of the Revised Code, provided that no such officer shall be trained at the academy unless the officer meets the qualifications established for admission to the academy and the qualified nonprofit corporation police department, railroad company, or hospital or the private college or university that established the campus police department prepays the entire cost of the training. A qualified nonprofit corporation police department, railroad company, or hospital or a private college or university that has established a campus police department is not entitled to reimbursement from the state for any amount paid for the cost of training the railroad company's peace officers or the peace officers of the qualified nonprofit corporation police department, campus police department, or hospital.

The academy shall permit investigators employed by the state medical board to take selected courses that the board determines are consistent with its responsibilities for initial and continuing training of investigators as required under sections 4730.26 and 4731.05 of the Revised Code. The board shall pay the entire cost of training that investigators receive at the academy.

(B) As used in this section:

(1) "Law enforcement officers" include any undercover drug agent, any bailiff or deputy bailiff of a court of record, and any criminal investigator who is employed by the state public defender.

(2) "Undercover drug agent" means any person who:

(a) Is employed by a county, township, or municipal corporation for the purposes set forth in division (B)(2)(b) of this section but who is not an employee of a county sheriff's department, of a township constable, or of the police department of a municipal corporation or township;

(b) In the course of the person's employment by a county, township, or municipal corporation, investigates and gathers information pertaining to persons who are suspected of violating Chapter 2925. or 3719. of the Revised Code, and generally does not wear a uniform in the performance of the person's duties.

(3) "Crisis intervention training" has the same meaning as in section 109.71 of the Revised Code.

(4) "Missing children" has the same meaning as in section 2901.30 of the Revised Code.

(1998 H 606, eff. 3–9–99; 1996 H 670, eff. 12–2–96; 1992 H 758, eff. 1–15–93; 1990 H 110; 1988 H 708; 1986 S 364, H 769, S 149; 1984 S 321, H 435; 1981 H 44; 1979 H 83; 1976 S 272; 1970 H 1160)

109.80 Basic training course for sheriffs; continuing education

(A) The Ohio peace officer training commission shall develop and conduct a basic training course lasting at least three weeks for appointed and newly elected sheriffs appointed or elected on or after January 1, 1988, and shall establish criteria for what constitutes successful completion of the course. The basic training course shall include instruction in contemporary law enforcement, criminal investigations, the judicial process, civil rules, corrections, and other topics relevant to the duties and operations of the office of sheriff. The commission shall offer the course every four years within six months after the general election of sheriffs in each county and at other times when it is needed to permit sheriffs to attend within six months after appointment or election. The course shall be conducted by the Ohio peace officer training academy. The council shall provide that not less than two weeks of the course conducted within six months after the general election of sheriffs in each county shall be conducted prior to the first Monday in January next after that general election.

(B) The attorney general shall appoint a continuing education committee, consisting of not fewer than five nor more than seven members, including but not limited to, members of the Ohio peace officer training commission and sheriffs. The commission and the committee jointly shall determine the type of continuing education required for sheriffs to complete the requirements of division (E) of section 311.01 of the Revised Code and shall establish criteria for what constitutes successful completion of the requirement. The committee shall approve the courses that sheriffs may attend to complete the continuing education requirement and shall publish an approved list of those courses. The commission shall maintain a list of approved training schools that sheriffs may attend to complete the continuing education requirement. Upon request, the committee may approve courses other than those courses conducted as part of a certified law enforcement manager program.

(C) Upon presentation of evidence by a sheriff that because of medical disability or for other good cause that the sheriff is unable to complete the basic or continuing education requirement, the commission may waive the requirement until the disability or cause terminates.

(D) As used in this section, "newly elected sheriff" means a person who did not hold the office of sheriff of a county on the date the person was elected sheriff of that county.

(1996 H 670, eff. 12–2–96; 1996 H 351, eff. 1–14–97; 1988 H 708, eff. 4–19–88; 1986 H 683)

109.801 Firearms requalification program

(A)(1) Each year the following persons shall complete successfully a firearms requalification program approved by the executive director of the Ohio peace officer training commission in accordance with rules adopted by the attorney general pursuant to section 109.743 of the Revised Code: any sheriff, deputy sheriff, marshal, deputy marshal, township constable, chief of police or member of an organized police department of a municipal corporation or township, chief of police or member of a township police district police force, superintendent of the state highway patrol, state highway patrol trooper, special police officer of the state highway patrol designated under section 5503.09 of the Revised Code, enforcement agent employed under section 5502.14 of the Revised Code, or chief of police of a university or college police department or state university law enforcement officer appointed under section 3345.04 of the Revised Code; any parole or probation officer who carries a firearm in the course of official duties; any employee of the department of natural resources who is a natural resources law enforcement staff officer, park officer, forest officer, preserve officer, wildlife officer, or state watercraft officer who carries a firearm in the course of official duties; the house of representatives sergeant at arms if the house of representatives sergeant at arms has arrest authority pursuant to division (E)(1) of section 101.311 of the Revised Code; any assistant house of representatives sergeant at arms; any employee of the department of youth services who is designated pursuant to division (A)(2) of section 5139.53 of the Revised Code as being authorized to carry a firearm while on duty as described in that division; or a special police officer employed by a municipal corporation at a municipal airport or other municipal air navigation facility described in division (A)(19) of section 109.71 of the Revised Code.

(2) No person listed in division (A)(1) of this section shall carry a firearm during the course of official duties if the person does not comply with division (A)(1) of this section.

(B) The hours that a sheriff spends attending a firearms requalification program required by division (A) of this section are in addition to the sixteen hours of continuing education that are required by division (E) of section 311.01 of the Revised Code.

(C) As used in this section, "firearm" has the same meaning as in section 2923.11 of the Revised Code.

(2004 H 230, eff. 9–16–04; 2002 H 545, eff. 3–19–03; 2000 S 317, eff. 3–22–01; 1998 S 187, eff. 3–18–99; 1997 H 1, eff. 7–1–98; 1996 H 670, eff. 12–2–96; 1994 H 406, eff. 11–11–94; 1994 S 182, eff. 10–20–94; 1990 H 271, eff. 4–10–91)

109.802 Law enforcement assistance fund; disbursement of moneys

(A) There is hereby created in the state treasury the law enforcement assistance fund. The fund shall be used to pay reimbursements for law enforcement training as provided in this section and section 109.803 of the Revised Code, the compensation of any employees of the attorney general required to administer those sections, and any other administrative costs incurred by the attorney general to administer those sections.

(B) The attorney general shall adopt rules in accordance with Chapter 119. of the Revised Code establishing application procedures, standards, and guidelines, and prescribing an application form, for the reimbursement of sheriffs, constables, chiefs of police of organized municipal and township police departments, chiefs of police of township police district police forces, and chiefs of police of university or college police departments for the costs of peace officer basic training programs, advanced peace officer training programs, basic jailer training programs, and firearms requalification programs successfully completed by them or the peace officers under their supervision, for the reimbursement of the superintendent of the state highway patrol and the director of natural resources for the costs of peace officer basic training programs, advanced peace officer training programs, and basic jailer training programs successfully completed by them or the peace officers under their supervision, and for the reimbursement of the chief of the adult parole authority and the chief probation officer of a county probation department, multicounty probation department, and municipal court department of probation for the costs of basic firearm training programs and firearms requalification programs successfully completed by them or by parole or probation officers under their supervision. The rules shall include, but are not limited to, all of the following:

(1) A requirement that applications for reimbursement be submitted on a fiscal year basis;

(2) The documentation required to substantiate any costs for which the applicant seeks reimbursement;

(3) The procedure for prorating reimbursements if the amount of money appropriated for reimbursement for any fiscal year is not sufficient to pay all of the costs approved for reimbursement for that fiscal year;

(4) Any other requirements necessary for the proper administration of the reimbursement program.

(C) Each sheriff, constable, and chief of police of an organized municipal or township police department, township police district police force, or university or college police department may apply each fiscal year to the peace officer training commission for reimbursement for the costs of peace officer basic training programs, advanced peace officer training programs, basic jailer training programs, and firearms requalification training programs that are successfully completed by the sheriff, constable, or chief or a peace officer under the sheriff's, constable's, or chief's supervision. The superintendent of the state highway patrol and the director of natural resources may apply each fiscal year to the peace officer training commission for reimbursement for the costs of peace officer basic training programs, advanced peace officer training programs, and basic jailer training programs successfully completed by the superintendent or director or the peace officers under the superintendent's or director's supervision. The chief of the adult parole authority and each chief probation officer of a county probation department, multicounty probation department, or municipal court department of probation may apply each fiscal year to the peace officer training commission for reimbursement for the costs of basic firearm training programs and firearms requalification programs successfully completed by that chief or by parole or probation officers under the chief's supervision. Each application shall be made in accordance with, on an application form prescribed in, and be supported by the documentation required by, the rules adopted by the attorney general pursuant to division (B) of this section.

(D) As used in this section and section 109.803 of the Revised Code:

(1) "Peace officer" includes a sheriff, deputy sheriff, marshal, deputy marshal, chief of police and member of a municipal or township police department, chief of police and member of a township police district police force, chief of police of a university or college police department, state university law enforcement officer appointed under section 3345.04 of the Revised Code, superintendent of the state highway patrol, state highway patrol trooper, and employee of the department of natural resources who is a natural resources law enforcement staff officer, park officer, forest officer, preserve officer, wildlife officer, or state watercraft officer.

(2) "Chief of police of an organized municipal police department" includes the chief of police of a village police department.

(3) "Chief of police of a village police department" means the village marshal.

(4) "Chief of police of a university or college police department" means the person who has direct supervisory authority over the state university law enforcement officers who are appointed for the university or college pursuant to section 3345.04

of the Revised Code by the board of trustees of the university or college.

(1998 S 187, eff. 3–18–99; 1996 H 670, eff. 12–2–96; 1996 H 566, eff. 10–16–96; 1994 H 406, eff. 11–11–94; 1994 S 182, eff. 10–20–94; 1990 H 271, eff. 4–10–91)

109.803 Program for reimbursement of peace officers for training costs

(A) The Ohio peace officer training commission shall administer a program for reimbursing sheriffs, constables, and chiefs of police of organized municipal and township police departments, township police district police forces, and university and college police departments for the costs of peace officer basic training programs, advanced peace officer training programs, basic jailer training programs, and firearms requalification training programs that are successfully completed by them or by peace officers under their supervision, for reimbursing the superintendent of the state highway patrol and the director of natural resources for the costs of peace officer basic training programs, advanced peace officer training programs, and basic jailer training programs that are successfully completed by them or the peace officers under their supervision, and for reimbursing the chief of the adult parole authority and the chief probation officer of a county probation department, multicounty probation department, or municipal court department of probation for the costs of basic firearm training programs and firearms requalification programs that are successfully completed by them or by parole or probation officers under their supervision. The commission shall administer the reimbursement program in accordance with rules adopted by the attorney general pursuant to division (B) of section 109.802 of the Revised Code.

(B)(1) The commission, in accordance with the rules of the attorney general, shall review each application for reimbursement to determine if the applicant is entitled to reimbursement for the programs for which the applicant seeks reimbursement. It shall approve for reimbursement any program for which reimbursement is authorized in the rules of the attorney general, if the program was successfully completed by the applicant or a peace officer, parole officer, or probation officer supervised by the applicant. The actual amount of reimbursement for each authorized program shall be determined pursuant to divisions (B)(2), (3), (4), and (5) of this section.

(2) The commission shall prepare a basic peace officer training reimbursement voucher for each applicant for whom it approves reimbursement for all or some of the peace officer basic training programs, basic jailer training programs, basic firearms training programs, and firearms requalification programs for which the applicant applied for reimbursement. To compute the amount of the voucher for each applicant, the commission shall do all of the following:

(a) For each application for reimbursement for a peace officer basic training program, the commission shall approve an amount equal to seventy-five per cent of the costs, not to exceed eight hundred dollars, of each approved program successfully completed by the applicant or a peace officer under the applicant's supervision.

(b) For each application for reimbursement for a basic jailer training program, the commission shall approve an amount equal to seventy-five per cent of the costs, not to exceed four hundred dollars, for each approved program successfully completed by the applicant or a peace officer under the applicant's supervision.

(c) For each application by a sheriff, constable, or chief of police for reimbursement for a firearms requalifications program, the commission shall approve an amount equal to the full amount of the costs, not to exceed fifty dollars, for each approved program successfully completed by the applicant or a peace officer under the applicant's supervision.

(d) For each application by the chief of the adult parole authority or a chief probation officer of a county probation department, multicounty probation department, or municipal court department of probation for reimbursement for a basic firearm training program or a firearms requalification program, the commission shall approve an amount equal to the full amount of the costs, not to exceed fifty dollars, for each approved program successfully completed by the applicant or a parole or probation officer under the applicant's supervision.

(e) Add the total of all amounts approved under divisions (B)(2)(a), (b), (c), and (d) of this section for all approved programs for each applicant and, subject to division (B)(3) of this section, prepare a peace officer training reimbursement voucher for the applicant for that total amount.

(3) If the amount of money appropriated by the general assembly in any fiscal year to reimburse the costs of basic peace officer training programs, basic jailer training programs, basic firearm training programs, and firearms requalification programs is not sufficient to pay all peace officer training reimbursement vouchers prepared pursuant to division (B)(2)(e) of this section, the commission shall reduce all of the vouchers by a pro rata amount.

(4) The commission shall prepare an advanced peace officer training reimbursement voucher for each applicant for whom it approves reimbursement for all or some of the advanced peace officer training programs for which the applicant applied for reimbursement. To compute the amount of the voucher for each applicant, the commission shall do all of the following:

(a) Determine the number of full-time peace officers, parole officers, or probation officers working for each applicant;

(b) For a twenty-six week period designated by the attorney general in the rules adopted pursuant to division (B) of section 109.802 of the Revised Code, determine the total number of hours worked by peace officers, parole officers, or probation officers who are under the supervision of the applicant, are not considered full-time peace officers, parole officers, or probation officers, and are not included in division (B)(4)(a) of this section and divide that number by five hundred twenty.

(c) Determine a total number of shares for each applicant by adding the two numbers determined for the applicant in divisions (B)(4)(a) and (b) of this section.

(d) Determine the reimbursement amount to be paid per share by dividing the total amount of money appropriated in the fiscal year for the reimbursement of the costs of advanced training programs by the total number of all shares receivable by all applicants for the fiscal year.

(e) Subject to division (B)(5) of this section, determine the amount of the advanced peace officer training reimbursement voucher by multiplying the total number of shares for each applicant determined under division (B)(4)(c) of this section by the reimbursement amount per share determined under division (B)(4)(d) of this section.

(5) The advanced peace officer training reimbursement voucher for each applicant shall not exceed seventy-five per cent of the total costs expended by the applicant for all advanced peace officer training programs that were approved under division (B)(4) of this section and were successfully completed by the applicant and the peace officers under the applicant's supervision.

(1996 H 670, eff. 12–2–96; 1994 H 406, eff. 11–11–94; 1990 H 271, eff. 4–10–91)

MISCELLANEOUS INVESTIGATORY POWERS AND DUTIES

109.83 Investigation of organized crime; referral to prosecuting attorney or grand jury

(A) When directed by the governor or general assembly, the attorney general may investigate any organized criminal activity in this state. When it appears to the attorney general, as a result of an investigation conducted pursuant to this division, that there is cause to prosecute for the commission of a crime, the attorney general shall refer the evidence to the prosecuting attorney having jurisdiction of the matter, to a regular grand jury drawn and impaneled pursuant to sections 2939.01 to 2939.24 of the Revised Code, or to a special grand jury drawn and impaneled pursuant to section 2939.17 of the Revised Code. When the crime or the elements of the crime were committed in two or more counties, the referral shall be to the prosecuting attorney, the regular grand jury, or a special grand jury of the county in which the most significant portion of the crime or the elements of the crime occurred or, if it is not possible to determine that county, the county with the largest population. When evidence is referred directly to a grand jury pursuant to this section, the attorney general and any assistant or special counsel designated by the attorney general has the exclusive right to appear at any time before the grand jury to give information relative to a legal matter cognizable by it, or to advise upon a legal matter when required, and may exercise all rights, privileges, and powers of prosecuting attorneys in such cases.

(B)(1) When information is referred to the attorney general by an organized crime task force or the organized crime investigations commission pursuant to section 177.03 of the Revised Code, the attorney general shall review the information so referred and upon a determination that there is cause to prosecute for the commission of a crime, the attorney general either shall refer the information as evidence to a regular or special grand jury in the manner described in, and in the county determined in accordance with the provisions of, division (A) of this section or shall initiate a criminal action or proceeding in a court of proper jurisdiction. If an indictment is returned by a grand jury pursuant to a referral made under this division, the attorney general has sole responsibility to prosecute the accused offender.

(2) The attorney general, and any assistant or special counsel designated by the attorney general who appears under this division in any county for the prosecution of any crime has the same powers and authority as a prosecuting attorney, including, but not limited to, powers relating to attendance before the courts and grand juries of the county, preparation and trial of indictments for crimes, and representation of the state in any criminal proceeding, in any civil proceeding related to the crime, or in any appeal from a criminal case or from a civil case related to the crime in any court of this state.

(C) When proceeding under the authority of this section, the attorney general may appear for the state in any court or tribunal of proper jurisdiction for the purpose of conducting investigations under division (A) of this section, or for the purpose of conducting criminal proceedings, civil proceedings, or any other proceeding that is necessary to promote and safeguard the public interests of the citizens of this state.

(D) This section shall not be construed to prevent the attorney general and prosecuting attorneys or special prosecutors from cooperating in the investigation and prosecution of offenses under this section. However, in cases in which information was referred to the attorney general by an organized crime task force because the office of a prosecuting attorney was implicated by an investigation conducted by the task force, the attorney general shall not inform the implicated prosecutor of the investigation or referral and shall not cooperate with the prosecutor on the matter.

(E) As used in this section, "organized criminal activity" has the same meaning as in section 177.01 of the Revised Code.

(1998 H 2, eff. 1–1–99; 1986 S 74, eff. 9–3–86; 1970 H 956)

109.84 Powers regarding workers' compensation

(A) Upon the written request of the governor, the industrial commission, the administrator of workers' compensation, or upon the attorney general's becoming aware of criminal or improper activity related to Chapter 4121. or 4123. of the Revised Code, the attorney general shall investigate any criminal or civil violation of law related to Chapter 4121. or 4123. of the Revised Code.

(B) When it appears to the attorney general, as a result of an investigation under division (A) of this section, that there is cause to prosecute for the commission of a crime or to pursue a civil remedy, he may refer the evidence to the prosecuting attorney having jurisdiction of the matter, or to a regular grand jury drawn and impaneled pursuant to sections 2939.01 to 2939.24 of the Revised Code, or to a special grand jury drawn and impaneled pursuant to section 2939.17 of the Revised Code, or he may initiate and prosecute any necessary criminal or civil actions in any court or tribunal of competent jurisdiction in this state. When proceeding under this section, the attorney general has all rights, privileges, and powers of prosecuting attorneys, and any assistant or special counsel designated by him for that purpose has the same authority.

(C) The attorney general shall be reimbursed by the bureau of workers' compensation for all actual and necessary costs incurred in conducting investigations requested by the governor, the commission, or the administrator and all actual and necessary costs in conducting the prosecution arising out of such investigation.

(1989 H 222, eff. 11–3–89; 1976 S 545)

109.85 Investigations and prosecutions for excess medicaid payments

(A) Upon the written request of the governor, the general assembly, the auditor of state, the director of job and family services, the director of health, or the director of budget and management, or upon the attorney general's becoming aware of criminal or improper activity related to Chapter 3721. and the medical assistance program established under section 5111.01 of the Revised Code, the attorney general shall investigate any criminal or civil violation of law related to Chapter 3721. of the Revised Code or the medical assistance program.

(B) When it appears to the attorney general, as a result of an investigation under division (A) of this section, that there is cause to prosecute for the commission of a crime or to pursue a civil remedy, the attorney general may refer the evidence to the prosecuting attorney having jurisdiction of the matter, or to a regular grand jury drawn and impaneled pursuant to sections 2939.01 to 2939.24 of the Revised Code, or to a special grand jury drawn and impaneled pursuant to section 2939.17 of the Revised Code, or the attorney general may initiate and prosecute any necessary criminal or civil actions in any court or tribunal of competent jurisdiction in this state. When proceeding under this section, the attorney general, and any assistant or special counsel designated by the attorney general for that purpose, have all rights, privileges, and powers of prosecuting attorneys. The attorney general shall have exclusive supervision and control of all investigations and prosecutions initiated by the attorney general under this section. The forfeiture provisions of sections 2933.71 to 2933.75 of the Revised Code apply in relation to any such criminal action initiated and prosecuted by the attorney general.

(C) Nothing in this section shall prevent a county prosecuting attorney from investigating and prosecuting criminal activity related to Chapter 3721. of the Revised Code and the medical assistance program established under section 5111.01 of the Revised Code. The forfeiture provisions of sections 2933.71 to 2933.75 of the Revised Code apply in relation to any prosecution of criminal activity related to the medical assistance program undertaken by the prosecuting attorney.

(1999 H 471, eff. 7–1–00; 1993 H 152, eff. 7–1–93; 1989 H 672; 1985 H 201; 1979 H 176; 1978 S 159)

109.86 Investigation and prosecution of patient abuse

(A) The attorney general shall investigate any activity the attorney general has reasonable cause to believe is in violation of section 2903.34 of the Revised Code. Upon written request of the governor, the general assembly, the auditor of state, or the director of health, job and family services, aging, mental health, or mental retardation and developmental disabilities, the attorney general shall investigate any activity these persons believe is in violation of section 2903.34 of the Revised Code. If after an investigation the attorney general has probable cause to prosecute for the commission of a crime, the attorney general shall refer the evidence to the prosecuting attorney, director of law, or other similar chief legal officer having jurisdiction over the matter. If the prosecuting attorney decides to present the evidence to a grand jury, the prosecuting attorney shall notify the attorney general in writing of the decision within thirty days after referral of the matter and shall present the evidence prior to the discharge of the next regular grand jury. If the director of law or other chief legal officer decides to prosecute the case, the director or officer shall notify the attorney general in writing of the decision within thirty days and shall initiate prosecution within sixty days after the matter was referred to the director or officer.

(B) If the prosecuting attorney, director of law, or other chief legal officer fails to notify the attorney general or to present evidence or initiate prosecution in accordance with division (A) of this section, the attorney general may present the evidence to a regular grand jury drawn and impaneled pursuant to sections 2939.01 to 2939.24 of the Revised Code, or to a special grand jury drawn and impaneled pursuant to section 2939.17 of the Revised Code, or the attorney general may initiate and prosecute any action in any court or tribunal of competent jurisdiction in this state. The attorney general, and any assistant or special counsel designated by the attorney general, have all the powers of a prosecuting attorney, director of law, or other chief legal officer when proceeding under this section. Nothing in this section shall limit or prevent a prosecuting attorney, director of law, or other chief legal officer from investigating and prosecuting criminal activity committed against a resident or patient of a care facility.

(1999 H 471, eff. 7–1–00; 1986 H 566, eff. 9–17–86)

109.87 Investigations and civil actions regarding telemarketing practices

(A)(1) As used in this section, "federal act or rule" means the "Telemarketing and Consumer Fraud and Abuse Prevention Act," 108 Stat. 1545 to 1551, 15 U.S.C. 6101 to 6108, the "Telephone Consumer Protection Act of 1991," 105 Stat. 2395, 47 U.S.C. 227, any amendment or reenactment of either of those acts, any rule adopted or issued pursuant to either of those acts, or any amendment of that rule.

(2) The terms that are used in this section have the same meanings as in the applicable federal act or rule.

(B)(1) No seller or telemarketer shall engage in any act or practice in violation of any provision of a federal act or rule.

(2) The attorney general, in any proceedings under this section, shall recognize any exemptions recognized by the federal communications commission under the "Telephone Consumer Protection Act of 1991," 105 Stat. 2395, 47 U.S.C. 227, any amendment or reenactment of that act, any rule adopted or issued pursuant to that act, or any amendment of that rule.

(C)(1) If the attorney general, as a result of complaints or the attorney general's own inquiries, has reason to believe that a person has engaged, is engaging, or is preparing to engage in a violation of any provision of a federal act or rule, the attorney general may investigate the alleged violation. For purposes of an investigation under division (C)(1) of this section, the attorney general may administer oaths, subpoena witnesses, adduce evidence, and require the production of any relevant matter.

(2) If the matter to be produced under division (C)(1) of this section is located outside this state, the attorney general may designate any representative, including any official of the state in which the matter is located, to inspect the matter on the behalf of the attorney general. The person subpoenaed may make the matter available to the attorney general at a convenient location within the state or pay the reasonable and necessary expenses for the attorney general or the attorney general's representative to examine the matter at the place where it is located, provided that those expenses shall not be charged to a party that subsequently is not found to have engaged in a violation of any provision of a federal act or rule.

(3) A person subpoenaed under division (C)(1) of this section may file a motion to extend the day on which the subpoena is to be returned or to modify or quash the subpoena, for good cause shown, in the court of common pleas of Franklin county or of the county in this state in which the person resides or in which the person's principal place of business is located. The person may file the motion not later than twenty days after the service of the subpoena.

(4) A person subpoenaed under division (C)(1) of this section shall comply with the terms of the subpoena unless the parties agree to modify the terms of the subpoena or unless the court has modified or quashed the subpoena, extended the day on which the subpoena is to be returned, or issued any other order with respect to the subpoena prior to the day on which the subpoena is to be returned. If a person fails without lawful excuse to testify or to produce relevant matter pursuant to a subpoena, the attorney general may apply to the court of common pleas of the county in which the person subpoenaed resides or in which the person's principal place of business is located for an order that compels compliance with the subpoena.

(5) If an individual subpoenaed under division (C)(1) of this section refuses to testify or to produce relevant matter pursuant to the subpoena on the ground that the testimony or matter may incriminate the individual, the attorney general may request the court to order the individual to provide the testimony or matter. With the exception of a prosecution for perjury or a civil action for damages under division (D)(1) of this section, an individual who complies with a court order to provide testimony or matter, after asserting a privilege against self-incrimination to which the individual is entitled by law, shall not be subjected to a criminal proceeding or a civil penalty or forfeiture on the basis of the testimony or matter required to be disclosed or testimony or matter discovered through that testimony or matter required to be disclosed.

(6) The attorney general may do either of the following:

(a) During an investigation under division (C) of this section, afford the person who is the subject of the investigation, in a manner considered appropriate to that person, an opportunity to cease and desist from any suspected violation of any provision of a federal act or rule. The attorney general may suspend the investigation during the period that the attorney general permits the person to cease and desist from that suspected violation. The suspension of the investigation or the affording of an opportunity to cease and desist shall not prejudice or prohibit any further investigation by the attorney general under division (C) of this section.

(b) Terminate an investigation under division (C) of this section upon acceptance of a written assurance of voluntary compliance from a person who is suspected of a violation of any provision of a federal act or rule. The acceptance of an assurance under division (C)(6)(b) of this section may be conditioned upon an undertaking to reimburse or to take other appropriate corrective action with respect to identifiable telephone service subscribers who are damaged by an alleged violation of any provision of a federal act or rule. An assurance of compliance given by a person under division (C)(6)(b) of this section is not evidence of a violation of any provision of a federal act or rule. The attorney general, at any time, may reopen an investigation terminated by the acceptance of an assurance of voluntary compliance, if the attorney general believes that further proceedings are in the public interest. Evidence of a violation of an assurance of voluntary compliance is prima-facie evidence of an act or practice in violation of the applicable provision of a federal act or rule if the evidence is presented after the violation in a civil action brought under division (D)(1) of this section. An assurance of voluntary compliance may be filed with the court and if approved by the court, entered as a consent judgment in the action.

(7) The procedures that are available to the attorney general under division (C) of this section are cumulative and concurrent, and the exercise of one procedure by the attorney general does not preclude or require the exercise of any other procedure.

(D)(1) If, by the attorney general's own inquiries or as a result of complaints or an investigation conducted under division (C) of this section, the attorney general has reasonable cause to believe that a person has engaged or is engaging in a violation of any provision of this section or of a federal act or rule, the attorney general, subject to division (D)(2) or (3) of this section, may bring in the appropriate court of common pleas of this state or in the appropriate district court of the United States, but not in both courts, a civil action against the alleged violator for injunctive relief or a civil action against the alleged violator for damages, or both, pursuant to the federal act or rule, on behalf of the residents of this state who have been subjected to telemarketing acts or practices in violation of this section. The attorney general may bring the action under this section or under the applicable federal act or rule, but the attorney general shall not plead a violation of both this section and the applicable federal act or rule in the action. On the motion of the attorney general or on its own motion, a court may impose a civil penalty for a violation of the provision of this section or of the federal act or rule that is the subject of the action. The amount of any award of damages made or civil penalty imposed under division (D)(1) of this section shall not exceed any maximum allowable amount of damages or civil penalty that is specified in the applicable federal act or rule. An award of damages or civil penalties may be recovered under this section or under the applicable federal act or rule, but an award of damages or civil penalties shall not be recovered under both this section and the applicable federal act or rule.

(2) If a civil action has been instituted by or on behalf of the federal trade commission or the federal communications commission for a violation of any provision of an applicable federal act or rule, the attorney general, during the pendency of that action, shall not institute any civil action under division (D)(1) of this section against any defendant that is named in the complaint in the civil action that has been instituted by or on behalf of the federal trade commission or the federal communications commission, whichever is applicable, for any violation that is alleged in that complaint.

(3) If a civil action that has been instituted by or on behalf of the federal trade commission or the federal communications commission for a violation of any provision of an applicable federal act or rule affecting the residents of this state is litigated to its conclusion and the federal trade commission or the federal communications commission recovers an award of damages or civil penalties or obtains any relief under the applicable federal act or rule, the attorney general shall not institute any civil action under division (D)(1) of this section for any violation within the same time period that is alleged in the civil action that was instituted as described in division (D)(3) of this section and in which the federal trade commission or federal communications commission has recovered the damages or civil penalties or obtained the relief.

(E) Any civil action that the attorney general brings in a federal court under division (D)(1) of this section shall comply with the applicable provisions of the federal act or rule the violation of which is the subject of the action.

(F) The attorney general shall deposit any civil penalties that are imposed under division (D)(1) of this section to the credit of the telephone solicitation protection fund, which is hereby created in the state treasury, to be used to pay the costs of the office of the attorney general in investigating any violation of, and in enforcing, any federal act or rule or this section.

(2003 S 28, eff. 4–13–04)

VICTIMS ASSISTANCE

109.91 Crime victims assistance office; state victims assistance advisory committee; duties

(A) There is hereby established within the office of the attorney general the crime victims assistance office.

(B) There is hereby established the state victims assistance advisory committee. The committee shall consist of a chairperson, to be appointed by the attorney general, four ex officio members, and fifteen members to be appointed by the attorney general as follows: one member who represents the Ohio victim-witness association; three members who represent local victim assistance programs, including one from a municipally operated program and one from a county-operated program; one member who represents the interests of elderly victims; one member who is a board member of any statewide or local organization that exists primarily to aid victims of domestic violence, or who is an employee of, or counselor for, such an organization; one member who is an employee or officer of a county probation department or a probation department operated by the department of rehabilitation and correction; one member who is a county prosecuting attorney; one member who is a city law director; one member who is a county sheriff; one member who is a member or officer of a township or municipal police department; one member who is a court of common pleas judge; one member who is a municipal court judge or county court judge; and two members who are private citizens and are not government employees.

The committee shall include the following ex officio, nonvoting members: the chief justice of the supreme court, the attorney general, one member of the senate to be designated by the president of the senate, and one member of the house of representatives to be designated by the speaker of the house.

Members of the committee shall serve without compensation, but shall be reimbursed for travel and other necessary expenses that are incurred in the conduct of their official duties as members of the committee. The chairperson and members of the committee appointed by the attorney general shall serve at the pleasure of the attorney general. The chief justice of the supreme court and the attorney general shall serve on the committee until the end of the term of office that qualified them for membership on the committee. The member of the senate and the member of the house of representatives shall serve at the pleasure of the president of the senate and the speaker of the house of representatives, respectively.

(C) The victims assistance advisory committee shall perform both of the following duties:

(1) Advise the crime victims assistance office in determining crime and delinquency victim service needs, determining crime and delinquency victim policies for the state, and improving and exercising leadership in the quality of crime and delinquency victim programs in the state;

(2) Review and recommend to the crime victims assistance office the victim assistance programs that should be considered for the receipt of state financial assistance pursuant to section

109.92 of the Revised Code. The financial assistance allocation recommendations of the committee shall be based on the following priorities:

(a) Programs in existence on July 1, 1985, shall be given first priority;

(b) Programs offering or proposing to offer the broadest range of services and referrals to the community served, including medical, psychological, financial, educational, vocational, and legal services that were not in existence on July 1, 1985, shall be given second priority;

(c) Other qualified programs shall be given last priority.

(D) As used in this section and section 109.92 of the Revised Code, "victim assistance program" includes, but is not limited to a program that provides at least one of the following:

(1) Services to victims of any offense of violence or delinquent act that would be an offense of violence if committed by an adult;

(2) Financial assistance or property repair services to victims of crime or delinquent acts;

(3) Assistance to victims of crime or delinquent acts in judicial proceedings;

(4) Assistance to victims of crime or delinquent acts under the operation of any political subdivision of the state or a branch of the criminal justice system set forth in division (B)(1), (2), or (3) of section 181.51 of the Revised Code;

(5) Technical assistance to persons or organizations that provide services to victims of crime or delinquent acts under the operation of a branch of the criminal justice system set forth in divisions (B)(1), (2), and (3) of section 181.51 of the Revised Code.

A victim assistance program does not include the program for the reparation of crime victims established pursuant to Chapter 2743. of the Revised Code.

(1996 H 670, eff. 12–2–96; 1993 H 152, eff. 7–1–93; 1987 H 231, H 171; 1984 S 195)

109.92 State financial assistance to victims assistance programs; procedures

(A) Appropriations may be made by the general assembly to the office of the attorney general for the purpose of providing state financial assistance to victim assistance programs that operate in the state. All amounts so appropriated shall be used to provide financial assistance to victim assistance programs in accordance with section 109.91 of the Revised Code and this section. The program for the provision of such financial assistance shall be administered by the crime victims assistance office established pursuant to section 109.91 of the Revised Code.

(B) A victim assistance program may apply to the crime victims assistance office for state financial assistance out of funds appropriated to the office of the attorney general for that purpose by the general assembly. Each application for such financial assistance shall include all of the following information:

(1) Evidence that the program is incorporated in this state as a nonprofit corporation or is a program established by a unit of state or local government;

(2) The proposed budget of the program for the period during which the financial assistance is sought;

(3) A summary of services offered by the program;

(4) An estimate of the number of persons served by the program.

(C) Within thirty days of receipt of an application for financial assistance from a victim assistance program in accordance with division (B) of this section, the crime victims assistance office, based in part on the recommendations of the victim assistance advisory board made pursuant to section 109.91 of the Revised Code, shall notify the program in writing whether it is eligible for financial assistance and, if eligible, estimate the amount that will be made available to the program and the time when the financial assistance will be made available.

(D) Each victim assistance program that receives any financial assistance pursuant to this section shall use the financial assistance only to provide the services identified in its application for such assistance as being services it offered and to cover a reasonable cost of administration of the program. Each victim assistance program that receives any such financial assistance shall make a good faith effort to minimize its costs of administration.

(2000 S 153, eff. 7–1–00; 1989 H 111, eff. 7–1–89; 1984 S 195)

MISCELLANEOUS PROVISIONS

109.97 Capital case status reports

(A) As used in this section:

(1) "Commutation," "pardon," "prisoner," and "state correctional institution" have the same meanings as in section 2967.01 of the Revised Code.

(2) "Individual's present legal status" means whichever of the following circumstances apply on the thirty-first day of December of the calendar year covered by a capital case status report described in divisions (B) and (C) of this section to an individual who was sentenced to death pursuant to sections 2929.02 to 2929.04 or section 2929.06 of the Revised Code for an aggravated murder committed on or after October 19, 1981:

(a) The individual was executed in accordance with section 2949.22 of the Revised Code for the aggravated murder, or the individual otherwise is deceased.

(b) The individual continues to be confined in a state correctional institution waiting for the execution of the sentence of death.

(c) The individual has been released from confinement in a state correctional institution pursuant to a pardon granted in connection with the aggravated murder, or the individual has been granted a commutation in connection with the aggravated murder and has been released from confinement or is serving a prison term or sentence of imprisonment pursuant to the commutation.

(d) The individual has had the sentence of death vacated or reversed on appeal or pursuant to division (C) of section 2929.05 of the Revised Code or otherwise has been relieved of the sentence of death by a court of this state or the United States.

(e) The individual has had the sentence of death vacated as described in section 2929.06 of the Revised Code or otherwise, the individual has been resentenced pursuant to that section or otherwise to a sentence other than a sentence of death, and the individual is a prisoner serving a prison term or sentence of imprisonment in a state correctional institution.

(f) The individual is confined in a correctional institution of another state or the United States for the commission of another offense or has been executed in accordance with a sentence of death imposed by a court of another state or the United States for the commission of another offense.

(g) The individual has escaped from confinement in a state correctional institution or a correctional institution of another state or the United States and currently is at-large.

(B) The attorney general annually shall prepare or cause to be prepared a capital case status report that pertains to all individuals who were sentenced to death pursuant to sections 2929.02 to 2929.04 or section 2929.06 of the Revised Code for an aggravated murder committed on or after October 19, 1981, and that contains for each of those individuals the information described in division (C)(1) of this section. The attorney general shall file a copy of each annual capital case status report with the governor, the chief justice of the supreme court, the president of the senate, and the speaker of the house of representatives no later than the first day of April of the calendar year following the calendar year covered by the report. Each annual capital case status report shall be a public record subject to inspection and copying in accordance with section 149.43 of the Revised Code.

(C)(1) An annual capital case status report prepared pursuant to division (B) of this section shall contain all of the following information that pertains as of the thirty-first day of December of the calendar year covered by the report to each individual who was sentenced to death pursuant to sections 2929.02 to 2929.04 or 2929.06 of the Revised Code for an aggravated murder committed on or after October 19, 1981:

(a) A citation to and brief summary of the facts of each case in which the individual was sentenced to death pursuant to sections 2929.02 to 2929.04 or section 2929.06 of the Revised Code for an aggravated murder committed on or after October 19, 1981;

(b) A statement as to the individual's present legal status;

(c) A summary history of the individual's legal actions to vacate, reverse, or otherwise be relieved from the sentence of death described in division (C)(1)(a) of this section, including, but not limited to, motions to vacate the sentence of death, appeals, petitions for postconviction relief, and petitions for habeas corpus relief filed with a court of this state or a court of the United States under section 2929.05, 2953.21, or another section of the Revised Code, the Ohio Constitution, federal statutes, or the United States Constitution;

(d) Any other information that the attorney general determines is relevant, including, but not limited to, a tentatively scheduled date for the execution of the individual's sentence of death in accordance with section 2949.22 of the Revised Code.

(2) In each annual capital case status report prepared pursuant to division (B) of this section, the attorney general shall set forth or cause to be set forth the information described in division (C)(1) of this section in the form that the attorney general considers most appropriate to present that information, including, but not limited to, charts, tables, graphs, and narrative summaries.

(D) All officers and employees of the government of this state and its political subdivisions shall cooperate, upon request of the attorney general, in providing information that facilitates the attorney general in the performance of the attorney general's responsibilities under this section.

(1997 H 18, eff. 1–30–98)

PENALTIES

109.99 Penalties

(A) Whoever violates section 109.26 of the Revised Code shall be fined not less than five hundred nor more than ten thousand dollars or be imprisoned not less than one month nor more than one year, or both.

(B) Whoever violates division (G)(1) of section 109.573 of the Revised Code is guilty of unlawful disclosure of DNA database information, a misdemeanor of the first degree.

(C) Whoever violates division (G)(2) of section 109.573 of the Revised Code is guilty of unlawful possession of DNA database information, a misdemeanor of the first degree.

(D)(1) Whoever violates division (G)(1) of section 109.35 of the Revised Code is guilty of entering into a transaction involving a nonprofit health care entity without the approval of the attorney general, a felony of the third degree.

(2) Whoever violates division (G)(2) of section 109.35 of the Revised Code is guilty of receiving improper compensation relating to a transaction involving a nonprofit health care entity, a felony of the third degree.

(1997 H 242, eff. 5–7–97; 1995 H 5, eff. 8–30–95; 125 v 351, eff. 10–14–53)

CHAPTER 117

AUDITOR OF STATE

117.29 Criminal proceedings instituted

Where an audit report sets forth any malfeasance or gross neglect of duty on the part of any public official for which a criminal penalty is provided, a certified copy of the report shall be filed with the prosecuting attorney of the county in which the offense is committed, and the prosecuting attorney shall, within one hundred twenty days, institute criminal proceedings against the public official.

(1985 H 201, eff. 7–1–85)

117.52 Auditor shall make adjustment of damage amount for wrongful imprisonment

The auditor of state shall make the adjustment, as described in section 2743.49 of the Revised Code, of the amount that a wrongfully imprisoned individual, in an action brought in the court of claims pursuant to section 2743.48 of the Revised Code, may receive for each full year or part of a year of imprisonment and shall perform all of the functions relating to that adjustment as specified in section 2743.49 of the Revised Code.

(2002 S 149, eff. 4–9–03)

CHAPTER 120

PUBLIC DEFENDERS

OHIO PUBLIC DEFENDER COMMISSION

120.01 Ohio public defender commission created; members

There is hereby created the Ohio public defender commission to provide, supervise, and coordinate legal representation at state expense for indigent and other persons. The commission shall consist of nine members, one of whom shall be chairman. The chairman shall be appointed by the governor with the advice and consent of the senate. Four members shall be appointed by the governor, two of whom shall be from each of the two major political parties. Four members shall be appointed by the supreme court, two of whom shall be from each of the two major political parties. The chairman, and not less than two of the members appointed by the governor, and not less than two of the members appointed by the supreme court shall be attorneys admitted to the practice of law in this state.

Within thirty days after the effective date of this section, the governor and the supreme court shall make initial appointments to the commission. Of the initial appointments made to the commission by the governor, the appointment of the chairman shall be for a term of two years. Of the other four appointments, one shall be for a term ending one year after the effective date of this section, one shall be for a term ending two years after that date, one shall be for a term ending three years after that date, and one shall be for a term ending four years after that date. Of the initial appointments made to the commission by the supreme court, one shall be for a term ending one year after the effective date of this section, one shall be for a term ending two years after that date, one shall be for a term ending three years after that date, and one shall be for a term ending four years after that date. Thereafter, terms of office shall be for four years, each term ending on the same day of the same month of the year as did the term which it succeeds. Any member appointed to fill a vacancy occurring prior to the expiration of the term for which his predecessor was appointed shall hold office for the remainder of such term. Any member shall continue in office subsequent to the expiration date of his term until his successor takes office or until a period of sixty days has elapsed, whichever occurs first.

(1975 H 164, eff. 1–13–76)

120.02 Meetings; compensation

The members of the Ohio public defender commission shall meet at least quarterly, and shall meet at other times pursuant to the call of the chairman of the commission or at the request of the state public defender. The members of the commission shall receive an amount fixed pursuant to section 124.14 of the Revised Code per diem for every meeting of the commission that they attend, together with the actual and necessary expenses that they incur, and mileage for each mile necessarily traveled, in connection with every meeting of the commission that they attend.

(1992 H 210, eff. 5–1–92; 1975 H 164)

120.03 Powers and duties of commission; state public defender; rules; training fund; attorney general providing representation

(A) The Ohio public defender commission shall appoint the state public defender, who shall serve at the pleasure of the commission.

(B) The Ohio public defender commission shall establish rules for the conduct of the offices of the county and joint county public defenders and for the conduct of county appointed counsel systems in the state. These rules shall include, but are not limited to, the following:

(1) Standards of indigency and minimum qualifications for legal representation by a public defender or appointed counsel. In establishing standards of indigency and determining who is eligible for legal representation by a public defender or appointed counsel, the commission shall consider an indigent person to be an individual who at the time his need is determined is unable to provide for the payment of an attorney and all other necessary expenses of representation. Release on bail shall not prevent a person from being determined to be indigent.

(2) Standards for the hiring of outside counsel;

(3) Standards for contracts by a public defender with law schools, legal aid societies, and nonprofit organizations for providing counsel;

(4) Standards for the qualifications, training, and size of the legal and supporting staff for a public defender, facilities, and other requirements needed to maintain and operate an office of a public defender;

(5) Minimum caseload standards;

(6) Procedures for the assessment and collection of the costs of legal representation that is provided by public defenders or appointed counsel;

(7) Standards and guidelines for determining whether a client is able to make an up-front contribution toward the cost of his legal representation;

(8) Procedures for the collection of up-front contributions from clients who are able to contribute toward the cost of their legal representation, as determined pursuant to the standards and guidelines developed under division (B)(7) of this section. All of such up-front contributions shall be paid into the appropriate county fund.

(9) Standards for contracts between a board of county commissioners, a county public defender commission, or a joint county public defender commission and a municipal corporation for the legal representation of indigent persons charged with violations of the ordinances of the municipal corporation.

(C) The Ohio public defender commission shall adopt rules prescribing minimum qualifications of counsel appointed pursuant to this chapter or appointed by the courts. Without limiting its general authority to prescribe different qualifications for different categories of appointed counsel, the commission shall prescribe, by rule, special qualifications for counsel and co-counsel appointed in capital cases.

(D) In administering the office of the Ohio public defender commission:

(1) The commission shall do the following:

(a) Approve an annual operating budget;

(b) Make an annual report to the governor, the general assembly, and the supreme court of Ohio on the operation of the state public defender's office, the county appointed counsel systems, and the county and joint county public defenders' offices.

(2) The commission may do the following:

(a) Accept the services of volunteer workers and consultants at no compensation other than reimbursement of actual and necessary expenses;

(b) Prepare and publish statistical and case studies and other data pertinent to the legal representation of indigent persons;

(c) Conduct programs having a general objective of training and educating attorneys and others in the legal representation of indigent persons.

(E) There is hereby established in the state treasury the public defender training fund for the deposit of fees received by the Ohio public defender commission from educational seminars, and the sale of publications, on topics concerning criminal law and procedure. Expenditures from this fund shall be made only for the operation of activities authorized by division (D)(2)(c) of this section.

(F)(1) In accordance with sections 109.02, 109.07, and 109.361 to 109.366 of the Revised Code, but subject to division (E) of section 120.06 of the Revised Code, the attorney general shall represent or provide for the representation of the Ohio public defender commission, the state public defender, assistant state public defenders, and other employees of the commission or the state public defender.

(2) Subject to division (E) of section 120.06 of the Revised Code, the attorney general shall represent or provide for the representation of attorneys described in division (C) of section 120.41 of the Revised Code in malpractice or other civil actions or proceedings that arise from alleged actions or omissions related to responsibilities derived pursuant to this chapter, or in civil actions that are based upon alleged violations of the constitution or statutes of the United States, including section 1983 of Title 42 of the United States Code, 93 Stat. 1284 (1979), 42 U.S.C.A. 1983, as amended, and that arise from alleged actions or omissions related to responsibilities derived pursuant to this chapter. For purposes of the representation, sections 109.361 to 109.366 of the Revised Code shall apply to an attorney described in division (C) of section 120.41 of the Revised Code as if he were an officer or employee, as defined in section 109.36 of the Revised Code, and the Ohio public defender commission or the state public defender, whichever contracted with the attorney, shall be considered his employer.

(1993 H 152, eff. 7–1–93; 1992 H 210; 1985 H 201; 1984 S 271; 1983 H 291; 1981 H 694; 1979 H 204; 1975 H 164)

STATE PUBLIC DEFENDER

120.04 Powers and duties of state public defender; funds

(A) The state public defender shall serve at the pleasure of the Ohio public defender commission and shall be an attorney with a minimum of four years of experience in the practice of law and be admitted to the practice of law in this state at least one year prior to appointment.

(B) The state public defender shall do all of the following:

(1) Maintain a central office in Columbus. The central office shall be provided with a library of adequate size, considering the needs of the office and the accessibility of other libraries, and other necessary facilities and equipment.

(2) Appoint assistant state public defenders, all of whom shall be attorneys admitted to the practice of law in this state, and other personnel necessary for the operation of the state public defender office. Assistant state public defenders shall be appointed on a full-time basis. The state public defender, assistant state public defenders, and employees appointed by the state public defender shall not engage in the private practice of law.

(3) Supervise the compliance of county public defender offices, joint county public defender offices, and county appointed counsel systems with standards established by rules of the Ohio public defender commission pursuant to division (B) of section 120.03 of the Revised Code;

(4) Keep and maintain financial records of all cases handled and develop records for use in the calculation of direct and indirect costs, in the operation of the office, and report periodically, but not less than annually, to the commission on all relevant data on the operations of the office, costs, projected needs, and recommendations for legislation or amendments to court rules, as may be appropriate to improve the criminal justice system;

(5) Collect all moneys due the state for reimbursement for legal services under this chapter and under section 2941.51 of the Revised Code and institute any actions in court on behalf of the state for the collection of such sums that the state public defender considers advisable. Except as provided otherwise in division (D) of section 120.06 of the Revised Code, all moneys collected by the state public defender under this chapter and section 2941.51 of the Revised Code shall be deposited in the state treasury to the credit of the client payment fund, which is hereby created. All moneys credited to the fund shall be used by the state public defender to appoint assistant state public defenders and to provide other personnel, equipment, and facilities necessary for the operation of the state public defender office, to reimburse counties for the operation of county public defender offices, joint county public defender offices, and county appointed counsel systems pursuant to sections 120.18, 120.28, and 120.33 of the Revised Code, or to provide assistance to counties in the operation of county indigent defense systems.

(6) With respect to funds appropriated to the commission to pay criminal costs, perform the duties imposed by sections 2949.19 and 2949.201 of the Revised Code;

(7) Establish standards and guidelines for the reimbursement, pursuant to sections 120.18, 120.28, 120.33, 2941.51, and 2949.19 of the Revised Code, of counties for the operation of county public defender offices, joint county public defender offices, and county appointed counsel systems and for other costs related to felony prosecutions;

(8) Establish maximum amounts that the state will reimburse the counties pursuant to sections 120.18, 120.28, 120.33, and 2941.51 of the Revised Code;

(9) Establish maximum amounts that the state will reimburse the counties pursuant to section 120.33 of the Revised Code for each specific type of legal service performed by a county appointed counsel system;

(10) Administer sections 120.18, 120.28, 120.33, 2941.51, and 2949.19 of the Revised Code and make reimbursements pursuant to those sections;

(11) Administer the program established pursuant to sections 120.51 to 120.55 of the Revised Code for the charitable public purpose of providing financial assistance to legal aid societies. Neither the state public defender nor any of the state public defender's employees who is responsible in any way for the administration of that program and who performs those administrative responsibilities in good faith is in any manner liable if a legal aid society that is provided financial assistance under the program uses the financial assistance other than in accordance with sections 120.51 to 120.55 of the Revised Code or fails to comply with the requirements of those sections.

(12) Establish an office for the handling of appeal and post-conviction matters;

(13) Provide technical aid and assistance to county public defender offices, joint county public defender offices, and other local counsel providing legal representation to indigent persons, including representation and assistance on appeals.

(C) The state public defender may do any of the following:

(1) In providing legal representation, conduct investigations, obtain expert testimony, take depositions, use other discovery methods, order transcripts, and make all other preparations which are appropriate and necessary to an adequate defense or the prosecution of appeals and other legal proceedings;

(2) Seek, solicit, and apply for grants for the operation of programs for the defense of indigent persons from any public or private source, and may receive donations, grants, awards, and similar funds from any lawful source. Such funds shall be deposited in the state treasury to the credit of the public defender gifts and grants fund, which is hereby created.

(3) Make all the necessary arrangements to coordinate the services of the office with any federal, county, or private programs established to provide legal representation to indigent persons and others, and to obtain and provide all funds allowable under any such programs;

(4) Consult and cooperate with professional groups concerned with the causes of criminal conduct, the reduction of crime, the rehabilitation and correction of persons convicted of crime, the administration of criminal justice, and the administration and operation of the state public defender's office;

(5) Accept the services of volunteer workers and consultants at no compensation other than reimbursement for actual and necessary expenses;

(6) Prescribe any forms that are necessary for the uniform operation of this chapter;

(7) Contract with a county public defender commission or a joint county public defender commission to provide all or any part of the services that a county public defender or joint county public defender is required or permitted to provide by this chapter, or contract with a board of county commissioners of a county that is not served by a county public defender commission or a joint county public defender commission for the provision of services in accordance with section 120.33 of the Revised Code. All money received by the state public defender pursuant to such a contract shall be credited to either the multi–county: county share fund or, if received as a result of a contract with Trumbull county, the Trumbull county: county share fund.

(8) Authorize persons employed as criminal investigators to attend the Ohio peace officer training academy or any other peace officer training school for training;

(9) Procure a policy or policies of malpractice insurance that provide coverage for the state public defender and assistant state public defenders in connection with malpractice claims that may arise from their actions or omissions related to responsibilities derived pursuant to this chapter.

(D) No person employed by the state public defender as a criminal investigator shall attend the Ohio peace officer training academy or any other peace officer training school unless authorized to do so by the state public defender.

(1999 H 283, eff. 9–29–99; 1997 H 215, eff. 9–29–97; 1992 H 210, eff. 5–1–92; 1987 H 171; 1986 H 428, S 149; 1985 H 201; 1984 S 219, S 271; 1983 H 291; 1981 H 694; 1979 H 204; 1975 H 164)

120.05 Determination of indigency

(A) The determination of indigency shall be made by the state public defender, subject to review by the court. This section does not apply in relation to sections 120.51 to 120.55 of the Revised Code.

(B) The state public defender shall investigate the financial status of each person to be represented, at the earliest time the circumstances permit, and may require the person represented to disclose the records of public or private income sources and property, otherwise confidential, which may be of aid in determining indigency. The state public defender may obtain information from any public record contained in any office of the state, or any political subdivision or agency thereof, on request without payment of any fees ordinarily required by law. He shall make the results of the investigation available to the court upon request. The court, before whom a person seeking representation is taken, may determine the person's eligibility for legal representation by the state public defender.

(C) If a determination of eligibility cannot be made before the time when the first services are to be rendered by the state public defender, he shall render such services on a provisional basis. If the state public defender, or the court on review, subsequently determines that the person receiving the services is ineligible, the public defender shall notify the person of the termination of his services.

(D) Where the person represented has, or may reasonably be expected to have, the means to meet some part of the cost of the services rendered to him, he shall reimburse the state public defender in an amount which he can reasonably be expected to pay.

(E) If it is determined by the state public defender, or by the court, that the legal representation was provided to a person not entitled thereto, the person may be required to reimburse the public defender for the costs of the representation provided. Any action filed by the state public defender to collect legal fees hereunder, must be brought within two years from the last date legal representation was provided.

(1984 S 219, eff. 1–8–85; 1975 H 164)

120.06 Powers of representation; county representation fund; representation by private counsel

(A)(1) The state public defender, when designated by the court or requested by a county public defender or joint county public defender, may provide legal representation in all courts throughout the state to indigent adults and juveniles who are charged with the commission of an offense or act for which the penalty or any possible adjudication includes the potential loss of liberty.

(2) The state public defender may provide legal representation to any indigent person who, while incarcerated in any state correctional institution, is charged with a felony offense, for which the penalty or any possible adjudication that may be imposed by a court upon conviction includes the potential loss of liberty.

(3) The state public defender may provide legal representation to any person incarcerated in any correctional institution of the state, in any matter in which the person asserts the person is unlawfully imprisoned or detained.

(4) The state public defender, in any case in which the state public defender has provided legal representation or is requested to do so by a county public defender or joint county public defender, may provide legal representation on appeal.

(5) The state public defender, when designated by the court or requested by a county public defender, joint county public defender, or the director of rehabilitation and correction, shall provide legal representation in parole and probation revocation matters or matters relating to the revocation of community control or post-release control under a community control sanction or post-release control sanction, unless the state public defender finds that the alleged parole or probation violator or alleged violator of a community control sanction or post-release control sanction has the financial capacity to retain the alleged violator's own counsel.

(6) If the state public defender contracts with a county public defender commission, a joint county public defender commission, or a board of county commissioners for the provision of services, under authority of division (C)(7) of section 120.04 of the Revised Code, the state public defender shall provide legal representation in accordance with the contract.

(B) The state public defender shall not be required to prosecute any appeal, postconviction remedy, or other proceeding pursuant to division (A)(3), (4), or (5) of this section, unless the state public defender first is satisfied that there is arguable merit to the proceeding.

(C) A court may appoint counsel or allow an indigent person to select the indigent's own personal counsel to assist the state public defender as co-counsel when the interests of justice so require. When co-counsel is appointed to assist the state public defender, the co-counsel shall receive any compensation that the court may approve, not to exceed the amounts provided for in section 2941.51 of the Revised Code.

(D) When the state public defender is designated by the court or requested by a county public defender or joint county public defender to provide legal representation for an indigent person in any case, other than pursuant to a contract entered into under authority of division (C)(7) of section 120.04 of the Revised Code, the state public defender shall send to the county in which the case is filed an itemized bill for fifty per cent of the actual cost of the representation. The county, upon receipt of an itemized bill from the state public defender pursuant to this division, shall pay fifty per cent of the actual cost of the legal representation as set forth in the itemized bill. There is hereby created in the state treasury the county representation fund for the deposit of moneys received from counties under this division. All moneys credited to the fund shall be used by the state public defender to provide legal representation for indigent persons when designated by the court or requested by a county or joint county public defender.

(E)(1) Notwithstanding any contrary provision of sections 109.02, 109.07, 109.361 to 109.366, and 120.03 of the Revised Code that pertains to representation by the attorney general, an assistant attorney general, or special counsel of an officer or employee, as defined in section 109.36 of the Revised Code, or of an entity of state government, the state public defender may elect to contract with, and to have the state pay pursuant to division (E)(2) of this section for the services of, private legal counsel to represent the Ohio public defender commission, the state public defender, assistant state public defenders, other employees of the commission or the state public defender, and attorneys described in division (C) of section 120.41 of the Revised Code in a malpractice or other civil action or proceeding that arises from alleged actions or omissions related to responsibilities derived pursuant to this chapter, or in a civil action that is based upon alleged violations of the constitution or statutes of the United States, including section 1983 of Title 42 of the United States Code, 93 Stat. 1284 (1979), 42 U.S.C.A. 1983, as amended, and that arises from alleged actions or omissions related to responsibilities derived pursuant to this chapter, if the state public defender determines, in good faith, that the defendant in the civil action or proceeding did not act manifestly outside the scope of the defendant's employment or official responsibilities, with malicious purpose, in bad faith, or in a wanton or reckless manner. If the state public defender elects not to contract pursuant to this division for private legal counsel in a civil action or proceeding, then, in accordance with sections 109.02, 109.07, 109.361 to 109.366, and 120.03 of the Revised Code, the attorney general shall represent or provide for the representation of the Ohio public defender commission, the state public defender, assistant state public defenders, other employees of the commission or the state public defender, or attorneys described in division (C) of section 120.41 of the Revised Code in the civil action or proceeding.

(2)(a) Subject to division (E)(2)(b) of this section, payment from the state treasury for the services of private legal counsel with whom the state public defender has contracted pursuant to division (E)(1) of this section shall be accomplished only through the following procedure:

(i) The private legal counsel shall file with the attorney general a copy of the contract; a request for an award of legal fees, court costs, and expenses earned or incurred in connection with the defense of the Ohio public defender commission, the state public defender, an assistant state public defender, an employee, or an attorney in a specified civil action or proceeding; a written itemization of those fees, costs, and expenses, including the signature of the state public defender and the state public defender's attestation that the fees, costs, and expenses were earned or incurred pursuant to division (E)(1) of this section to the best of the state public defender's knowledge and information; a written statement whether the fees, costs, and expenses are for all legal services to be rendered in connection with that defense, are only for legal services rendered to the date of the request and additional legal services likely will have to be provided in connection with that defense, or are for the final legal services rendered in connection with that defense; a written statement indicating whether the private legal counsel previously submitted a request for an award under division (E)(2) of this section in connection with that defense and, if so, the date and the amount of each award granted; and, if the fees, costs, and expenses are for all legal services to be rendered in connection with that defense or are for the final legal services rendered in connection with that defense, a certified copy of any judgment entry in the civil action or proceeding or a signed copy of any settlement agreement entered into between the parties to the civil action or proceeding.

(ii) Upon receipt of a request for an award of legal fees, court costs, and expenses and the requisite supportive documentation described in division (E)(2)(a)(i) of this section, the attorney general shall review the request and documentation; determine whether any of the limitations specified in division (E)(2)(b) of this section apply to the request; and, if an award of legal fees, court costs, or expenses is permissible after applying the limitations, prepare a document awarding legal fees, court costs, or expenses to the private legal counsel. The document shall name the private legal counsel as the recipient of the award; specify the total amount of the award as determined by the attorney general; itemize the portions of the award that represent legal fees, court costs, and expenses; specify any limitation applied pursuant to division (E)(2)(b) of this section to reduce the amount of the award sought by the private legal counsel; state that the award is payable from the state treasury pursuant to division (E)(2)(a)(iii) of this section; and be approved by the inclusion of the signatures of the attorney general, the state public defender, and the private legal counsel.

(iii) The attorney general shall forward a copy of the document prepared pursuant to division (E)(2)(a)(ii) of this section to the director of budget and management. The award of legal fees, court costs, or expenses shall be paid out of the state public defender's appropriations, to the extent there is a sufficient available balance in those appropriations. If the state public defender does not have a sufficient available balance in the state public defender's appropriations to pay the entire award of legal fees, court costs, or expenses, the director shall make application for a transfer of appropriations out of the emergency purposes account or any other appropriation for emergencies or contingencies in an amount equal to the portion of the award that exceeds the sufficient available balance in the state public defender's appropriations. A transfer of appropriations out of the emergency purposes account or any other appropriation for emergencies or contingencies shall be authorized if there are sufficient moneys greater than the sum total of then pending emergency purposes account requests, or requests for releases from the other appropriation. If a transfer of appropriations out of the emergency purposes account or other appropriation for emergencies or contingencies is made to pay an amount equal to the portion of the award that exceeds the sufficient available balance in the state public defender's appropriations, the director shall cause the payment to be made to the private legal counsel. If sufficient moneys do not exist in the emergency purposes account or other appropriation for emergencies or contingencies to pay an amount equal to the portion of the award that exceeds the sufficient available balance in the state public defender's appropriations, the private legal counsel shall request the general assembly to make an appropriation sufficient to pay an amount equal to the portion of the award that exceeds the sufficient available balance in the state public defender's appropriations, and no payment in that amount shall be made until the appropriation has been made. The private legal counsel shall make the request during the current biennium and during each succeeding biennium until a sufficient appropriation is made.

(b) An award of legal fees, court costs, and expenses pursuant to division (E) of this section is subject to the following limitations:

(i) The maximum award or maximum aggregate of a series of awards of legal fees, court costs, and expenses to the private legal counsel in connection with the defense of the Ohio public defender commission, the state public defender, an assistant state public defender, an employee, or an attorney in a specified civil action or proceeding shall not exceed fifty thousand dollars.

(ii) The private legal counsel shall not be awarded legal fees, court costs, or expenses to the extent the fees, costs, or expenses are covered by a policy of malpractice or other insurance.

(iii) The private legal counsel shall be awarded legal fees and expenses only to the extent that the fees and expenses are reasonable in light of the legal services rendered by the private legal counsel in connection with the defense of the Ohio public defender commission, the state public defender, an assistant state public defender, an employee, or an attorney in a specified civil action or proceeding.

(c) If, pursuant to division (E)(2)(a) of this section, the attorney general denies a request for an award of legal fees, court costs, or expenses to private legal counsel because of the application of a limitation specified in division (E)(2)(b) of this section, the attorney general shall notify the private legal counsel in writing of the denial and of the limitation applied.

(d) If, pursuant to division (E)(2)(c) of this section, a private legal counsel receives a denial of an award notification or if a private legal counsel refuses to approve a document under division (E)(2)(a)(ii) of this section because of the proposed application of a limitation specified in division (E)(2)(b) of this section, the private legal counsel may commence a civil action against the attorney general in the court of claims to prove the private legal counsel's entitlement to the award sought, to prove that division (E)(2)(b) of this section does not prohibit or otherwise limit the award sought, and to recover a judgment for the amount of the award sought. A civil action under division (E)(2)(d) of this section shall be commenced no later than two years after receipt of a denial of award notification or, if the private legal counsel refused to approve a document under division (E)(2)(a)(ii) of this section because of the proposed application of a limitation specified in division (E)(2)(b) of this section, no later than two years after the refusal. Any judgment of the court of claims in favor of the private legal counsel shall be paid from the state treasury in accordance with division (E)(2)(a) of this section.

(F) If a court appoints the office of the state public defender to represent a petitioner in a postconviction relief proceeding under section 2953.21 of the Revised Code, the petitioner has received a sentence of death, and the proceeding relates to that sentence, all of the attorneys who represent the petitioner in the proceeding pursuant to the appointment, whether an assistant state public defender, the state public defender, or another attorney, shall be certified under Rule 20 of the Rules of Superintendence for the Courts of Ohio to represent indigent defendants charged with or convicted of an offense for which the death penalty can be or has been imposed.

(G) As used in this section:

(1) "Community control sanction" has the same meaning as in section 2929.01 of the Revised Code.

(2) "Post–release control sanction" has the same meaning as in section 2967.01 of the Revised Code.

(2002 H 490, eff. 1–1–04; 2001 H 94, eff. 9–5–01; 1999 H 283, eff. 9–29–99; 1996 S 258, eff. 10–16–96; 1994 H 571, eff. 10–6–94; 1992 H 210, eff. 5–1–92; 1985 H 201; 1984 S 271; 1983 H 291; 1981 H 694; 1979 H 204; 1975 H 164)

COUNTY PUBLIC DEFENDER COMMISSION

120.13 County public defender commission

(A) The county commissioners in any county may establish a county public defender commission. The commission shall have five members, three of whom shall be appointed by the board of county commissioners, and two by the judge, or the presiding judge if there is one, of the court of common pleas of the county. At least one member appointed by each of these appointing bodies shall be an attorney admitted to the practice of law in this state.

(B) The board of county commissioners shall select a specific day for the county public defender commission to be established and on which all members' appointments shall take effect, and shall notify the Ohio public defender commission of the date.

(C) Of the initial appointments made to the county public defender commission, two appointments by the county commissioners and one appointment by the court shall be for a term of two years ending two years after the date the commission is established, and one appointment by each of the appointing bodies shall be for a term ending four years after the date the commission is established. Thereafter, terms of office shall be for four years, each term ending on the same day of the same month of the year as did the term which it succeeds. Each member shall hold office from the date of his appointment until the end of the term for which he was appointed. Any member appointed to fill a vacancy occurring prior to the expiration of the term for which his predecessor was appointed shall hold office for the remainder of such term. Any member shall continue in office subsequent to the expiration date of his term until his successor takes office, or until a period of sixty days has elapsed, whichever occurs first.

(D) The members of the commission shall choose as chairman one of the commission members, who shall serve as chairman for two years. Meetings shall be held at least quarterly and at such other times as called by the chairman or by request of the county public defender. Members of the commission may receive an amount fixed by the county commissioners, but not in excess of the amounts set for the members of the Ohio public defender commission pursuant to section 124.14 of the Revised Code per diem for every meeting of the board they attend, and necessary expenses including mileage for each mile necessarily traveled.

(E) The county commissioners may terminate the county public defender commission at any time if at least ninety days prior to termination, the commissioners notify the Ohio public defender commission in writing of the termination date. Upon the termination date all pending county public defender matters shall be transferred to the state public defender, a joint county public defender, or appointed counsel.

(F) Fifty per cent of the cost of representation in all matters assumed by the state public defender shall be charged to the counties in accordance with division (D) of section 120.06 of the Revised Code.

(1981 H 694, eff. 11–15–81; 1975 H 164)

120.14 Powers and duties

(A)(1) Except as provided in division (A)(2) of this section, the county public defender commission shall appoint the county public defender and may remove him from office only for good cause.

(2) If a county public defender commission contracts with the state public defender or with one or more nonprofit organizations for the state public defender or the organizations to provide all of the services that the county public defender is required or permitted to provide by this chapter, the commission shall not appoint a county public defender.

(B) The commission shall determine the qualifications and size of the supporting staff and facilities and other requirements needed to maintain and operate the office of the county public defender.

(C) In administering the office of county public defender, the commission shall:

(1) Recommend to the county commissioners an annual operating budget which is subject to the review, amendment, and approval of the board of county commissioners;

(2)(a) Make an annual report to the county commissioners and the Ohio public defender commission on the operation of the county public defender's office, including complete and detailed information on finances and costs that separately states costs and expenses that are reimbursable under section 120.35 of the Revised Code, and any other data and information requested by the state public defender;

(b) Make monthly reports relating to reimbursement and associated case data pursuant to the rules of the Ohio public defender commission to the board of county commissioners and the Ohio public defender commission on the total costs of the public defender's office.

(3) Cooperate with the Ohio public defender commission in maintaining the standards established by rules of the Ohio public defender commission pursuant to divisions (B) and (C) of section 120.03 of the Revised Code, and cooperate with the state public defender in his programs providing technical aid and assistance to county systems.

(D) The commission may accept the services of volunteer workers and consultants at no compensation except reimbursement for actual and necessary expenses.

(E) The commission may contract with any municipal corporation, within the county served by the county public defender, for the county public defender to provide legal representation for indigent persons who are charged with a violation of the ordinances of the municipal corporation.

(F) A county public defender commission, with the approval of the board of county commissioners regarding all provisions that pertain to the financing of defense counsel for indigent persons, may contract with the state public defender or with any nonprofit organization, the primary purpose of which is to provide legal representation to indigent persons, for the state public defender or the organization to provide all or any part of the services that a county public defender is required or permitted to provide by this chapter. A contract entered into pursuant to this division may provide for payment for the services provided on a per case, hourly, or fixed contract basis. The state public defender and any nonprofit organization that contracts with a county public defender commission pursuant to this division shall do all of the following:

(1) Comply with all standards established by the rules of the Ohio public defender commission;

(2) Comply with all standards established by the state public defender;

(3) Comply with all statutory duties and other laws applicable to county public defenders.

(1984 S 271, eff. 9–26–84; 1983 H 291; 1975 H 164)

COUNTY PUBLIC DEFENDER

120.15 County public defender; powers and duties

(A) The county public defender shall be appointed by the county public defender commission for a term not to exceed four years. He shall be an attorney with a minimum of two years experience in the practice of law and be admitted to the practice of law in Ohio at least one year prior to his appointment.

(B) In carrying out the responsibilities and performing the duties of his office, the county public defender shall:

(1) Maintain an office, approved by the commission, provided with a library of adequate size, considering the needs of the office and the accessibility of other libraries, and other necessary facilities and equipment;

(2) Keep and maintain financial records of all cases handled and develop records for use in the calculation of direct and indirect costs in the operation of the office and report monthly pursuant to the rules of the Ohio public defender commission to the county public defender commission and to the Ohio public defender commission on all relevant data on the operations of the office, costs, projected needs, and recommendations for legislation or amendments to court rules, as may be appropriate to improve the criminal justice system;

(3) Collect all moneys due from contracts with municipal corporations or for reimbursement for legal services under this chapter and institute such actions in court for the collection of

such sums as he considers advisable. All moneys collected or received by the public defender shall be paid into the county treasury to the credit of the general revenue fund.

(4) Appoint assistant county public defenders and all other personnel necessary to the functioning of the county public defender's office, subject to the authority of the county public defender commission to determine the size and qualifications of the staff pursuant to division (B) of section 120.14 of the Revised Code. All assistant county public defenders shall be admitted to the practice of law in Ohio, and may be appointed on a full or part-time basis.

(C) The county public defender may exercise the rights authorized in division (C) of section 120.04 of the Revised Code.

(D) The county public defender shall determine indigency of persons, subject to review by the court, in the same manner as provided in section 120.05 of the Revised Code. Each monthly report submitted to the board of county commissioners and the state public defender shall include a certification by the county public defender that all persons provided representation by the county public defender's office during the month covered by the report were indigent under the standards of the Ohio public defender commission.

(1984 S 271, eff. 9–26–84; 1975 H 164)

120.16 Powers of representation by county public defenders

(A)(1) The county public defender shall provide legal representation to indigent adults and juveniles who are charged with the commission of an offense or act that is a violation of a state statute and for which the penalty or any possible adjudication includes the potential loss of liberty and in postconviction proceedings as defined in this section.

(2) The county public defender may provide legal representation to indigent adults and juveniles charged with the violation of an ordinance of a municipal corporation for which the penalty or any possible adjudication includes the potential loss of liberty, if the county public defender commission has contracted with the municipal corporation to provide legal representation for indigent persons charged with a violation of an ordinance of the municipal corporation.

(B) The county public defender shall provide the legal representation authorized by division (A) of this section at every stage of the proceedings following arrest, detention, service of summons, or indictment.

(C) The county public defender may request the state public defender to prosecute any appeal or other remedy before or after conviction that the county public defender decides is in the interests of justice, and may provide legal representation in parole and probation revocation matters and matters relating to the revocation of community control or post-release control under a community control sanction or post-release control sanction.

(D) The county public defender shall not be required to prosecute any appeal, postconviction remedy, or other proceeding, unless the county public defender is first satisfied there is arguable merit to the proceeding.

(E) Nothing in this section shall prevent a court from appointing counsel other than the county public defender or from allowing an indigent person to select the indigent person's own personal counsel to represent the indigent person. A court may also appoint counsel or allow an indigent person to select the indigent person's own personal counsel to assist the county public defender as co-counsel when the interests of justice so require.

(F) Information as to the right to legal representation by the county public defender or assigned counsel shall be afforded to an accused person immediately upon arrest, when brought before a magistrate, or when formally charged, whichever occurs first.

(G) If a court appoints the office of the county public defender to represent a petitioner in a postconviction relief proceeding under section 2953.21 of the Revised Code, the petitioner has received a sentence of death, and the proceeding relates to that sentence, all of the attorneys who represent the petitioner in the proceeding pursuant to the appointment, whether an assistant county public defender or the county public defender, shall be certified under Rule 20 of the Rules of Superintendence for the Courts of Ohio to represent indigent defendants charged with or convicted of an offense for which the death penalty can be or has been imposed.

(H) As used in this section:

(1) "Community control sanction" has the same meaning as in section 2929.01 of the Revised Code.

(2) "Post–release control sanction" has the same meaning as in section 2967.01 of the Revised Code.

(2002 H 490, eff. 1–1–04; 2001 H 94, eff. 9–5–01; 1996 S 258, eff. 10–16–96; 1984 S 271, eff. 9–26–84; 1979 H 204; 1975 H 164)

120.17 Effect on state public defender's obligations

In any county in which the county commissioners choose to establish a county public defender's office, the Ohio public defender shall not be required to defend indigent persons in that county, except as set forth in division (A) of section 120.06 of the Revised Code, or if the court finds that it is required in the interests of justice.

(1975 H 164, eff. 1–13–76)

120.18 State subsidy to county; maintenance of standards

(A) The county public defender commission's report to the board of county commissioners shall be audited by the county auditor. The board of county commissioners, after review and approval of the audited report, may then certify it to the state public defender for reimbursement. If a request for the reimbursement of any operating expenditure incurred by a county public defender office is not received by the state public defender within sixty days after the end of the calendar month in which the expenditure is incurred, the state public defender shall not pay the requested reimbursement, unless the county has requested, and the state public defender has granted, an extension of the sixty-day time limit. Each request for reimbursement shall include a certification by the county public defender that the persons provided representation by the county public defender's office during the period covered by the report were indigent and, for each person provided representation during that period, a financial disclosure form completed by the person on a form prescribed by the state public defender. The state public defender shall also review the report and, in accordance with the standards, guidelines, and maximums established pursuant to divisions (B)(7) and (8) of section 120.04 of the Revised Code, prepare a voucher for fifty per cent of the total cost of each county public defender's office for the period of time covered by the certified report and a voucher for fifty per cent of the costs and expenses that are reimbursable under section 120.35 of the Revised Code, if any, or, if the amount of money appropriated by the general assembly to reimburse counties for the operation of county public defender offices, joint county public defender offices, and county appointed counsel systems is not sufficient to pay fifty per cent of the total cost of all of the offices and systems, for the lesser amount required by section 120.34 of the Revised Code. For the purposes of this section, total cost means total expenses minus costs and expenses reimbursable under section 120.35 of the Revised Code and any funds received by the county public defender commission pursuant to a contract, except a contract entered into with a municipal corporation pursuant to division (E) of section 120.14 of the Revised Code, gift, or grant.

(B) If the county public defender fails to maintain the standards for the conduct of the office established by rules of the Ohio public defender commission pursuant to divisions (B) and (C) of section 120.03 or the standards established by the state public defender pursuant to division (B)(7) of section 120.04 of the Revised Code, the Ohio public defender commission shall notify the county public defender commission and the board of county commissioners of the county that the county public defender has failed to comply with its rules or the standards of the state public defender. Unless the county public defender commission or the county public defender corrects the conduct of the county public defender's office to comply with the rules and standards within ninety days after the date of the notice, the state public defender may deny payment of all or part of the county's reimbursement from the state provided for in division (A) of this section.

(1999 H 283, eff. 9–29–99; 1995 H 117, eff. 6–30–95; 1985 H 201, eff. 7–1–85; 1984 S 271; 1983 H 291; 1981 H 694; 1979 H 204; 1975 H 164)

JOINT COUNTY PUBLIC DEFENDER COMMISSION

120.23 Joint county public defender commission

(A) The boards of county commissioners in two or more adjoining or neighboring counties may form themselves into a joint board and proceed to organize a district for the establishment of a joint county public defender commission. The commission shall have three members from each county, who shall be appointed by the board of county commissioners of the county.

(B) The boards shall agree on a specific date for the joint county public defender commission to be established, on which date the appointments of all members shall take effect. The joint board shall notify the Ohio public defender commission of the date.

(C) Of the initial appointments made by each county to the joint county public defender commission, one appointment shall be for a term of one year ending one year after the date the commission is established, one appointment shall be for a term of two years ending two years after the date the commission is established, and one appointment shall be for a period of three years, ending three years after the date the commission is established. Thereafter, terms of office shall be for three years, each term ending on the same day of the same month of the year as did the term which it succeeds. Each member shall hold office from the date of his appointment until the end of the term for which he was appointed. Any member appointed to fill a vacancy occurring prior to the expiration of the term for which his predecessor was appointed shall hold office for the remainder of the term. Any member shall continue in office subsequent to the expiration date of his term until his successor takes office, or until a period of sixty days has elapsed, whichever occurs first.

(D) The members of the commission shall choose as chairman one of the commission members, who shall serve as chairman for two years. Meetings shall be held at least quarterly and at such other times as called by the chairman or by request of the joint county public defender. Members of the commission may receive an amount fixed by the agreement of the boards of commissioners of the counties in the district, but not in excess of the amount set for the members of the Ohio public defender commission pursuant to section 124.14 of the Revised Code per diem for every meeting of the commission they attend, and necessary expenses including mileage for each mile necessarily traveled.

(E) The agreement of the boards of county commissioners establishing the joint county public defender commission shall provide for the allocation of the proportion of expenses to be paid by each county, which may be based upon population, number of cases, or such other factors as the commissioners determine to be appropriate. The county commissioners may amend their agreement from time to time to provide for a different allocation of the proportion of expenses to be paid by each county.

(F) The county auditor of the county, with the greatest population is hereby designated as the fiscal officer of a joint county public defender district organized under this section. The county auditors of the several counties composing the joint county public defender commission district shall meet at the commission office not less than once in each six months, to adjust accounts and to transact such other duties in connection with the commission as pertain to the business of their office.

(G) Each member of the board of county commissioners who meets by appointment to consider the organization of a joint county public defender commission shall, upon presentation of properly certified accounts, be paid his necessary expenses upon a warrant drawn by the county auditor of his county.

(H) The board of county commissioners of any county within a joint county public defender commission district may withdraw from the district. Such withdrawal shall not be effective until at least ninety days after the board has notified the Ohio public defender commission, the joint county public defender commission of the district, and each board of county commissioners in the district, in writing of the termination date. The failure of a board of county commissioners to approve an annual operating budget for the office of the joint county public defender as provided in division (C)(1) of section 120.24 of the Revised Code constitutes a notice of withdrawal by the county from the district, effective on the ninetieth day after commencement of the next fiscal year. Upon the termination date, all joint county public defender matters relating to the withdrawing county shall be transferred to the state public defender, a county public defender, or appointed counsel.

(I) Fifty per cent of the cost of representation in all matters assumed by the state public defender shall be charged to the counties in accordance with division (D) of section 120.06 of the Revised Code.

Members of the joint county public defender commission who are residents of a county withdrawing from such district are deemed to have resigned their positions upon the completion of the withdrawal procedure provided by this section. Vacancies thus created shall not be filled.

If two or more counties remain within the district after the withdrawal, the boards of county commissioners of the remaining adjoining or neighboring counties may agree to continue the operation of the joint county public defender commission and to reallocate the proportionate share of expenses to be paid by each participating county.

(1981 H 694, eff. 11–15–81; 1975 H 164)

JOINT COUNTY PUBLIC DEFENDER

120.24 Joint county public defender, powers and duties

(A)(1) Except as provided in division (A)(2) of this section, the joint county public defender commission shall appoint the joint county public defender and may remove him from office only for good cause.

(2) If a joint county public defender commission contracts with the state public defender or with one or more nonprofit organizations for the state public defender or the organizations to provide all of the services that the joint county public defender is required

or permitted to provide by this chapter, the commission shall not appoint a joint county public defender.

(B) The commission shall determine the qualifications and size of the supporting staff and facilities and other requirements needed to maintain and operate the office.

(C) In administering the office of joint county public defender, the commission shall:

(1) Recommend to the boards of county commissioners in the district an annual operating budget which is subject to the review, amendment, and approval of the boards of county commissioners in the district;

(2)(a) Make an annual report to the boards of county commissioners in the district and the Ohio public defender commission on the operation of the public defender's office, including complete and detailed information on finances and costs that separately states costs and expenses that are reimbursable under section 120.35 of the Revised Code, and such other data and information requested by the state public defender;

(b) Make monthly reports relating to reimbursement and associated case data pursuant to the rules of the Ohio public defender commission to the boards of county commissioners in the district and the Ohio public defender commission on the total costs of the public defender's office.

(3) Cooperate with the Ohio public defender commission in maintaining the standards established by rules of the Ohio public defender commission pursuant to divisions (B) and (C) of section 120.03 of the Revised Code, and cooperate with the state public defender in his programs providing technical aid and assistance to county systems.

(D) The commission may accept the services of volunteer workers and consultants at no compensation except reimbursement for actual and necessary expenses.

(E) The commission may contract with any municipal corporation, within the counties served by the joint county public defender, for the joint county public defender to provide legal representation for indigent persons who are charged with a violation of the ordinances of the municipal corporation.

(F) A joint county public defender commission, with the approval of each participating board of county commissioners regarding all provisions that pertain to the financing of defense counsel for indigent persons, may contract with the state public defender or with any nonprofit organization, the primary purpose of which is to provide legal representation to indigent persons, for the state public defender or the organization to provide all or any part of the services that a joint county public defender is required or permitted to provide by this chapter. A contract entered into pursuant to this division may provide for payment for the services provided on a per case, hourly, or fixed contract basis. The state public defender and any nonprofit organization that contracts with a joint county public defender commission pursuant to this division shall do all of the following:

(1) Comply with all standards established by the rules of the Ohio public defender commission;

(2) Comply with all standards established by the Ohio public defender;

(3) Comply with all statutory duties and other laws applicable to joint county public defenders.

(1984 S 271, eff. 9–26–84; 1983 H 291; 1975 H 164)

120.25 Additional powers and duties

(A) The joint county public defender shall be appointed by the joint county public defender commission for a term not to exceed four years. He shall be an attorney with a minimum of two years experience in the practice of law and be admitted to the practice of law in Ohio at least one year prior to his appointment.

(B) In carrying out the responsibilities and performing the duties of his office, the joint county public defender shall:

(1) Maintain an office, approved by the commission, provided with a library of adequate size, considering the needs of the office and the accessibility of other libraries, and other necessary facilities and equipment;

(2) Keep and maintain financial records of all cases handled and develop records for use in the calculation of direct and indirect costs in the operation of the office, and report monthly pursuant to the rules of the Ohio public defender commission to the joint county defender commission and to the Ohio public defender commission on all relevant data on the operations of the office, costs, projected needs, and recommendations for legislation or amendments to court rules, as may be appropriate to improve the criminal justice system;

(3) Collect all moneys due from contracts with municipal corporations or for reimbursement for legal services under this chapter and institute such actions in court for the collection of such sums as he considers advisable. The public defender shall pay into the treasury of each county in the district, to the credit of the general revenue fund, the county's proportionate share of all moneys collected or received by him.

(4) Appoint assistant joint county public defenders and all other personnel necessary to the functioning of the joint county public defender office, subject to the authority of the joint county public defender commission to determine the size and qualifications of the staff pursuant to division (B) of section 120.24 of the Revised Code. All assistant joint county public defenders shall be admitted to the practice of law in Ohio, and may be appointed on a full or part-time basis.

(C) The joint county public defender may exercise the rights authorized in division (C) of section 120.04 of the Revised Code.

(D) The joint county public defender shall determine indigency of persons, subject to review by the court, in the same manner as provided in section 120.05 of the Revised Code. Each monthly report submitted to the board of county commissioners and the state public defender shall include a certification by the joint county public defender that all persons provided representation by the joint county public defender's office during the month covered by the report were indigent under the standards of the Ohio public defender commission.

(1984 S 271, eff. 9–26–84; 1975 H 164)

120.26 Powers of representation by joint county public defender

(A)(1) The joint county public defender shall provide legal representation to indigent adults and juveniles who are charged with the commission of an offense or act that is a violation of a state statute and for which the penalty or any possible adjudication includes the potential loss of liberty and in postconviction proceedings as defined in this section.

(2) The joint county public defender may provide legal representation to indigent adults and juveniles charged with the violation of an ordinance of a municipal corporation for which the penalty or any possible adjudication includes the potential loss of liberty, if the joint county public defender commission has contracted with the municipal corporation to provide legal representation for indigent persons charged with a violation of an ordinance of the municipal corporation.

(B) The joint county public defender shall provide the legal representation authorized by division (A) of this section at every stage of the proceedings following arrest, detention, service of summons, or indictment.

(C) The joint county public defender may request the Ohio public defender to prosecute any appeal or other remedy before or after conviction that the joint county public defender decides is in the interests of justice and may provide legal representation in parole and probation revocation matters and matters relating to the revocation of community control or post-release control under a community control sanction or post-release control sanction.

(D) The joint county public defender shall not be required to prosecute any appeal, postconviction remedy, or other proceeding, unless the joint county public defender is first satisfied that there is arguable merit to the proceeding.

(E) Nothing in this section shall prevent a court from appointing counsel other than the joint county public defender or from allowing an indigent person to select the indigent person's own personal counsel to represent the indigent person. A court may also appoint counsel or allow an indigent person to select the indigent person's own personal counsel to assist the joint county public defender as co-counsel when the interests of justice so require.

(F) Information as to the right to legal representation by the joint county public defender or assigned counsel shall be afforded to an accused person immediately upon arrest, when brought before a magistrate, or when formally charged, whichever occurs first.

(G) If a court appoints the office of the joint county public defender to represent a petitioner in a postconviction relief proceeding under section 2953.21 of the Revised Code, the petitioner has received a sentence of death, and the proceeding relates to that sentence, all of the attorneys who represent the petitioner in the proceeding pursuant to the appointment, whether an assistant joint county defender or the joint county public defender, shall be certified under Rule 20 of the Rules of Superintendence for the Courts of Ohio to represent indigent defendants charged with or convicted of an offense for which the death penalty can be or has been imposed.

(H) As used in this section:

(1) "Community control sanction" has the same meaning as in section 2929.01 of the Revised Code.

(2) "Post–release control sanction" has the same meaning as in section 2967.01 of the Revised Code.

(2002 H 490, eff. 1–1–04; 2001 H 94, eff. 9–5–01; 1996 S 258, eff. 10–16–96; 1984 S 271, eff. 9–26–84; 1979 H 204; 1975 H 164)

120.27 Effect on state public defender's obligation

In any counties in which the boards of county commissioners choose to establish a joint county public defender's office, the Ohio public defender shall not be required to defend indigent persons in those counties, except as set forth in division (A) of section 120.06 of the Revised Code, or if the court finds that it is required in the interests of justice.

(1975 H 164, eff. 1–13–76)

120.28 State subsidy to districts; maintenance of standards

(A) The joint county public defender commission's report to the joint board of county commissioners shall be audited by the fiscal officer of the district. The joint board of county commissioners, after review and approval of the audited report, may then certify it to the state public defender for reimbursement. If a request for the reimbursement of any operating expenditure incurred by a joint county public defender office is not received by the state public defender within sixty days after the end of the calendar month in which the expenditure is incurred, the state public defender shall not pay the requested reimbursement, unless the joint board of county commissioners has requested, and the state public defender has granted, an extension of the sixty-day time limit. Each request for reimbursement shall include a certification by the joint county public defender that all persons provided representation by the joint county public defender's office during the period covered by the request were indigent and, for each person provided representation during that period, a financial disclosure form completed by the person on a form prescribed by the state public defender. The state public defender shall also review the report and, in accordance with the standards, guidelines, and maximums established pursuant to divisions (B)(7) and (8) of section 120.04 of the Revised Code, prepare a voucher for fifty per cent of the total cost of each joint county public defender's office for the period of time covered by the certified report and a voucher for fifty per cent of the costs and expenses that are reimbursable under section 120.35 of the Revised Code, if any, or, if the amount of money appropriated by the general assembly to reimburse counties for the operation of county public defender offices, joint county public defender offices, and county appointed counsel systems is not sufficient to pay fifty per cent of the total cost of all of the offices and systems, for the lesser amount required by section 120.34 of the Revised Code. For purposes of this section, total cost means total expenses minus costs and expenses reimbursable under section 120.35 of the Revised Code and any funds received by the joint county public defender commission pursuant to a contract, except a contract entered into with a municipal corporation pursuant to division (E) of section 120.24 of the Revised Code, gift, or grant. Each county in the district shall be entitled to a share of such state reimbursement in proportion to the percentage of the total cost it has agreed to pay.

(B) If the joint county public defender fails to maintain the standards for the conduct of the office established by the rules of the Ohio public defender commission pursuant to divisions (B) and (C) of section 120.03 or the standards established by the state public defender pursuant to division (B)(7) of section 120.04 of the Revised Code, the Ohio public defender commission shall notify the joint county public defender commission and the board of county commissioners of each county in the district that the joint county public defender has failed to comply with its rules or the standards of the state public defender. Unless the joint public defender commission or the joint county public defender corrects the conduct of the joint county public defender's office to comply with the rules and standards within ninety days after the date of the notice, the state public defender may deny all or part of the counties' reimbursement from the state provided for in division (A) of this section.

(1999 H 283, eff. 9–29–99; 1995 H 117, eff. 6–30–95; 1985 H 201, eff. 7–1–85; 1984 S 271; 1983 H 291; 1981 H 694; 1979 H 204; 1975 H 164)

MISCELLANEOUS PROVISIONS

120.33 Court–appointed or selected counsel; payment

(A) In lieu of using a county public defender or joint county public defender to represent indigent persons in the proceedings set forth in division (A) of section 120.16 of the Revised Code, the board of county commissioners of any county may adopt a resolution to pay counsel who are either personally selected by the indigent person or appointed by the court. The resolution shall include those provisions the board of county commissioners considers necessary to provide effective representation of indigent persons in any proceeding for which counsel is provided under this section. The resolution shall include provisions for contracts with any municipal corporation under which the municipal corporation shall reimburse the county for counsel appointed to represent indigent persons charged with violations of the ordinances of the municipal corporation.

(1) In a county that adopts a resolution to pay counsel, an indigent person shall have the right to do either of the following:

(a) To select the person's own personal counsel to represent the person in any proceeding included within the provisions of the resolution;

(b) To request the court to appoint counsel to represent the person in such a proceeding.

(2) The court having jurisdiction over the proceeding in a county that adopts a resolution to pay counsel shall, after determining that the person is indigent and entitled to legal representation under this section, do either of the following:

(a) By signed journal entry recorded on its docket, enter the name of the lawyer selected by the indigent person as counsel of record;

(b) Appoint counsel for the indigent person if the person has requested the court to appoint counsel and, by signed journal entry recorded on its dockets, enter the name of the lawyer appointed for the indigent person as counsel of record.

(3) The board of county commissioners shall establish a schedule of fees by case or on an hourly basis to be paid to counsel for legal services provided pursuant to a resolution adopted under this section. Prior to establishing the schedule, the board of county commissioners shall request the bar association or associations of the county to submit a proposed schedule. The schedule submitted shall be subject to the review, amendment, and approval of the board of county commissioners.

(4) Counsel selected by the indigent person or appointed by the court at the request of an indigent person in a county that adopts a resolution to pay counsel, except for counsel appointed to represent a person charged with any violation of an ordinance of a municipal corporation that has not contracted with the county commissioners for the payment of appointed counsel, shall be paid by the county and shall receive the compensation and expenses the court approves. Each request for payment shall be accompanied by a financial disclosure form and an affidavit of indigency that are completed by the indigent person on forms prescribed by the state public defender. Compensation and expenses shall not exceed the amounts fixed by the board of county commissioners in the schedule adopted pursuant to division (A)(3) of this section. No court shall approve compensation and expenses that exceed the amount fixed pursuant to division (A)(3) of this section.

The fees and expenses approved by the court shall not be taxed as part of the costs and shall be paid by the county. However, if the person represented has, or may reasonably be expected to have, the means to meet some part of the cost of the services rendered to the person, the person shall pay the county an amount that the person reasonably can be expected to pay. Pursuant to section 120.04 of the Revised Code, the county shall pay to the state public defender a percentage of the payment received from the person in an amount proportionate to the percentage of the costs of the person's case that were paid to the county by the state public defender pursuant to this section. The money paid to the state public defender shall be credited to the client payment fund created pursuant to division (B)(5) of section 120.04 of the Revised Code.

The county auditor shall draw a warrant on the county treasurer for the payment of counsel in the amount fixed by the court, plus the expenses the court fixes and certifies to the auditor. The county auditor shall report periodically, but not less than annually, to the board of county commissioners and to the Ohio public defender commission the amounts paid out pursuant to the approval of the court. The board of county commissioners, after review and approval of the auditor's report, may then certify it to the state public defender for reimbursement. If a request for reimbursement is not accompanied by a financial disclosure form and an affidavit of indigency completed by the indigent person on forms prescribed by the state public defender, the state public defender shall not pay the requested reimbursement. If a request for the reimbursement of the cost of counsel in any case is not received by the state public defender within ninety days after the end of the calendar month in which the case is finally disposed of by the court, unless the county has requested and the state public defender has granted an extension of the ninety-day limit, the state public defender shall not pay the requested reimbursement. The state public defender shall also review the report and, in accordance with the standards, guidelines, and maximums established pursuant to divisions (B)(7) and (8) of section 120.04 of the Revised Code, prepare a voucher for fifty per cent of the total cost of each county appointed counsel system in the period of time covered by the certified report and a voucher for fifty per cent of the costs and expenses that are reimbursable under section 120.35 of the Revised Code, if any, or, if the amount of money appropriated by the general assembly to reimburse counties for the operation of county public defender offices, joint county public defender offices, and county appointed counsel systems is not sufficient to pay fifty per cent of the total cost of all of the offices and systems other than costs and expenses that are reimbursable under section 120.35 of the Revised Code, for the lesser amount required by section 120.34 of the Revised Code.

(5) If any county appointed counsel system fails to maintain the standards for the conduct of the system established by the rules of the Ohio public defender commission pursuant to divisions (B) and (C) of section 120.03 or the standards established by the state public defender pursuant to division (B)(7) of section 120.04 of the Revised Code, the Ohio public defender commission shall notify the board of county commissioners of the county that the county appointed counsel system has failed to comply with its rules or the standards of the state public defender. Unless the board of county commissioners corrects the conduct of its appointed counsel system to comply with the rules and standards within ninety days after the date of the notice, the state public defender may deny all or part of the county's reimbursement from the state provided for in division (A)(4) of this section.

(B) In lieu of using a county public defender or joint county public defender to represent indigent persons in the proceedings set forth in division (A) of section 120.16 of the Revised Code, and in lieu of adopting the resolution and following the procedure described in division (A) of this section, the board of county commissioners of any county may contract with the state public defender for the state public defender's legal representation of indigent persons. A contract entered into pursuant to this division may provide for payment for the services provided on a per case, hourly, or fixed contract basis.

(C) If a court appoints an attorney pursuant to this section to represent a petitioner in a postconviction relief proceeding under section 2953.21 of the Revised Code, the petitioner has received a sentence of death, and the proceeding relates to that sentence, the attorney who represents the petitioner in the proceeding pursuant to the appointment shall be certified under Rule 20 of the Rules of Superintendence for the Courts of Ohio to represent indigent defendants charged with or convicted of an offense for which the death penalty can be or has been imposed.

(2001 H 94, eff. 9–5–01; 1999 H 283, eff. 9–29–99; 1997 H 215, eff. 9–29–97; 1996 S 258, eff. 10–16–96; 1995 H 117, eff. 6–30–95; 1985 H 201, eff. 7–1–85; 1984 S 271; 1983 H 291; 1981 H 694; 1979 H 204; 1975 H 164)

120.34 Reimbursements limited to appropriated amounts; adjustments required

The total amount of money paid to all counties in any fiscal year pursuant to sections 120.18, 120.28, and 120.33 of the Revised Code for the reimbursement of a percentage of the counties' cost of operating county public defender offices, joint county public defender offices, and county appointed counsel systems shall not exceed the total amount appropriated for that fiscal year by the general assembly for the reimbursement of the counties for the operation of the offices and systems. If the amount appropriated by the general assembly in any fiscal year is insufficient to pay fifty per cent of the total cost in the fiscal year of all county public defender offices, all joint county public defender offices, and all county appointed counsel systems, the amount of money paid in that fiscal year pursuant to sections 120.18, 120.28, and 120.33 of the Revised Code to each county for the fiscal year shall be reduced proportionately so that each county is paid an equal percentage of its total cost in the fiscal year for operating its county public defender system, its joint county public defender system, and its county appointed counsel system.

The total amount of money paid to all counties in any fiscal year pursuant to section 120.35 of the Revised Code for the reimbursement of a percentage of the counties' costs and expenses of conducting the defense in capital cases shall not exceed the total amount appropriated for that fiscal year by the general assembly for the reimbursement of the counties for conducting the defense in capital cases. If the amount appropriated by the general assembly in any fiscal year is insufficient to pay fifty per cent of the counties' total costs and expenses of conducting the defense in capital cases in the fiscal year, the amount of money paid in that fiscal year pursuant to section 120.35 of the Revised Code to each county for the fiscal year shall be reduced proportionately so that each county is paid an equal percentage of its costs and expenses of conducting the defense in capital cases in the fiscal year.

If any county receives an amount of money pursuant to section 120.18, 120.28, 120.33, or 120.35 of the Revised Code that is in excess of the amount of reimbursement it is entitled to receive pursuant to this section, the state public defender shall request the board of county commissioners to return the excess payment and the board of county commissioners, upon receipt of the request, shall direct the appropriate county officer to return the excess payment to the state.

Within thirty days of the end of each fiscal quarter, the state public defender shall provide to the office of budget and management and the legislative budget office of the legislative service commission an estimate of the amount of money that will be required for the balance of the fiscal year to make the payments required by sections 120.18, 120.28, 120.33, and 120.35 of the Revised Code.

(1983 H 291, eff. 7–1–83; 1979 H 204)

120.35 State reimbursement in capital cases

The state public defender shall, pursuant to section 120.18, 120.28, 120.33, or 2941.51 of the Revised Code, reimburse fifty per cent of all costs and expenses of conducting the defense in capital cases. If appropriations are insufficient to pay fifty per cent of such costs and expenses, the state public defender shall reimburse such costs and expenses as provided in section 120.34 of the Revised Code.

(1983 H 291, eff. 7–1–83)

120.38 Confidentiality; privilege

(A) All information obtained by a public defender when determining if a person is indigent, shall be held confidential within the ethical standards of attorney-client communications, unless previously on public record, or made available to the court as provided in section 120.05 of the Revised Code.

(B) All communications between the individual defendant and a public defender shall be fully protected by the attorney-client privilege to the same extent and degree as though counsel had been privately engaged.

(1975 H 164, eff. 1–13–76)

120.39 Conflicts prohibited

(A) Except as provided in division (B) of this section, counsel appointed by the court, co-counsel appointed to assist the state public defender or a county or joint county public defender, and any public defender, county public defender, or joint county defender, or member of their offices, shall not be a partner or employee of any prosecuting attorney, city director of law, village solicitor, or similar chief legal officer.

(B) A partner or employee of a village solicitor or of a law firm, legal professional association, or legal clinic with which the village solicitor is affiliated may be appointed by the court, assist a public defender, or serve as public defender in any criminal proceedings in which the village solicitor is not acting as prosecuting attorney.

(C) No prosecuting attorney, city director of law or similar officer or their assistants and employees, and no judge or court employee shall serve on the state public defender commission, or any county or joint county public defender commission.

(1981 S 38, eff. 3–15–82; 1977 H 219; 1975 H 164)

120.40 Pay ranges

The pay ranges established by the board of county commissioners for the county public defender and staff, and those established by the joint board of county commissioners for the joint county public defender and staff, shall not exceed the pay ranges assigned under section 124.14 of the Revised Code for comparable positions of the Ohio public defender and staff.

(1975 H 164, eff. 1–13–76)

120.41 Malpractice actions; indemnification

(A) In connection with any malpractice action filed against a state, county, or joint county public defender or assistant public defender, the state, or the county or district in which the defender office is located when the action is brought against a county or joint county public defender or assistant public defender, shall indemnify the attorney, if he acted in good faith and in the scope of his employment, for any judgment awarded in the malpractice action or amount negotiated in settlement of the malpractice claim asserted in the action, and for any court costs or legal fees incurred in the defense of the malpractice claim asserted in the action.

(B)(1) In connection with any malpractice action filed against an attorney who was either personally selected by an indigent person or appointed by a court pursuant to section 120.33 of the Revised Code, the attorney shall be indemnified in accordance with division (B) of this section for any judgment awarded in the malpractice action or amount negotiated in settlement of the malpractice claim asserted in the action, and for any court costs or legal fees incurred in defense of the malpractice claim asserted in the action.

(2) Subject to division (B)(3) of this section, an indemnification as described in division (B)(1) of this section shall be accomplished only through the following procedure:

(a) The attorney who was either personally selected by an indigent person or appointed by a court pursuant to section 120.33 of the Revised Code, or his counsel in the malpractice action, shall file with the attorney general a request for indemnification pursuant to division (B)(1) of this section, which shall be accompanied by the following types of supportive documentation to the extent that they relate to the request for indemnification:

(i) A certified copy of the judgment entry in the malpractice action;

(ii) A signed copy of any settlement agreement entered into between the parties to the malpractice action;

(iii) A written itemization of all court costs and legal fees incurred in the defense of the malpractice claim asserted in the action.

(b) Upon receipt of a request for indemnification and the requisite supportive documentation required by division (B)(2)(a) of this section, the attorney general shall review the request and documentation; determine whether any of the limitations specified in division (B)(3) of this section apply to the requested indemnification; and, if an indemnification in any amount is permitted under division (B)(1) of this section after applying those limitations, prepare an indemnity agreement. The indemnity agreement shall specify whether the indemnification will be for a judgment awarded in a malpractice action, an amount negotiated in settlement of the malpractice claim asserted in a malpractice action, court costs or legal fees incurred in the defense of the malpractice claim asserted in a malpractice action, or a combination of those items. The indemnity agreement additionally shall specify the total amount of permissible indemnification as determined by the attorney general; itemize the portions of the permissible indemnification that represent the judgment, settlement, court costs, or legal fees covered by the indemnity agreement; specify any limitations applied pursuant to division (B)(3) of this section to reduce the amount of indemnification sought by the attorney involved; name the persons to whom the entire permissible indemnification or portions of it will be paid; state that the permissible indemnification is payable from the state treasury pursuant to division (B)(2)(c) of this section; and be approved by the inclusion of the signatures of the attorney general and the attorney involved.

(c) The attorney general shall forward a copy of the indemnity agreement prepared pursuant to division (B)(2)(b) of this section to the director of budget and management. The director shall make application for the payment of the amount of the permissible indemnification out of the emergency purposes account or any other appropriation for emergencies or contingencies, and payment out of that account or any other appropriation for emergencies or contingencies shall be authorized if there are sufficient moneys greater than the sum total of then pending emergency purposes account requests, or requests for releases from the other appropriation. If sufficient moneys exist in the emergency purposes account or any other appropriation for emergencies or contingencies to pay the permissible indemnification, the director shall cause payment of the appropriate amounts specified in the indemnity agreement to be made to the persons named in it. If sufficient moneys do not exist in the emergency purposes account or any other appropriation for emergencies or contingencies to pay the permissible indemnification, the attorney involved or his counsel in the malpractice action shall request the general assembly to make an appropriation sufficient to pay the indemnification, and no payment shall be made until the appropriation has been made. The attorney involved or his counsel in the malpractice action shall make the request during the current biennium and during each succeeding biennium until a sufficient appropriation is made.

(3) An indemnification pursuant to divisions (B)(1) and (2) of this section is subject to the following limitations:

(a) The maximum aggregate amount of the indemnification, whether paid to or on behalf of the attorney who was either personally selected by an indigent person or appointed by a court pursuant to section 120.33 of the Revised Code, shall be one million dollars per occurrence, regardless of the number of persons who suffer injury, death, or loss to person or property as a result of the malpractice involved.

(b) The attorney described in division (B)(3)(a) of this section shall not be indemnified to the extent of any amounts covered by a policy of malpractice insurance, for any portion of a judgment that represents punitive or exemplary damages, for any portion of an amount negotiated in settlement of a malpractice claim that is unreasonable, or for any amount described in division (B)(1) of this section unless he acted in good faith and in the scope of his employment.

(c) The attorney described in division (B)(3)(a) of this section shall be indemnified only for the portion of legal fees that is reasonable.

(4) If, pursuant to division (B)(2) of this section, the attorney general denies any indemnification to an attorney who was either personally selected by an indigent person or appointed by a court pursuant to section 120.33 of the Revised Code because of the application of a limitation specified in division (B)(3) of this section, he shall notify that attorney or his counsel in the malpractice action in writing of the denial and of the limitation applied.

(5) If, pursuant to division (B)(4) of this section, an attorney who was either personally selected by an indigent person or appointed by a court pursuant to section 120.33 of the Revised Code or his counsel in the malpractice action receives a denial of indemnification notification, or if that attorney refuses to approve an indemnity agreement under division (B)(2) of this section because of the proposed application of a limitation specified in division (B)(3) of this section, the attorney may commence a civil action against the attorney general in the court of claims to prove his entitlement to the indemnification sought, to prove that division (B)(3) of this section does not prohibit or otherwise limit the indemnification sought, and to recover a judgment for the amount of indemnification sought. A civil action under this division shall be commenced no later than two years after the receipt of a denial of indemnification notification or, if the attorney refused to approve an indemnity agreement under division (B)(2) of this section because of the proposed application of a limitation specified in division (B)(3) of this section, no later than two years after the refusal. Any judgment of the court of claims in favor of the attorney shall be paid from the state treasury in accordance with division (B)(2) of this section.

(C) In connection with any malpractice action filed against an attorney who has contracted with the Ohio public defender commission or the state public defender, pursuant to authority granted by this chapter, to provide legal services to indigent or other persons, the state shall indemnify the attorney, if he acted in good faith and in the scope of his employment, for any judgment awarded in the malpractice action or amount negotiated in settlement of the malpractice claim asserted in the action, and for any court costs or legal fees incurred in the defense of the malpractice claim asserted in the action.

(1992 H 210, eff. 5–1–92; 1981 H 694)

FINANCIAL ASSISTANCE TO LEGAL AID SOCIETIES

120.51 Definitions

As used in sections 120.51 to 120.55 of the Revised Code:

(A) "Legal aid society" means a nonprofit corporation that satisfies all of the following:

(1) It is chartered to provide general legal services to the poor, it is incorporated and operated exclusively in this state, its primary purpose or function is to provide civil legal services, without charge, to indigents, and, in addition to providing civil legal services to indigents, it may provide legal training or legal technical assistance to other legal aid societies in this state.

(2) It has a board of trustees, a majority of its board of trustees are attorneys, and at least one-third of its board of

trustees, when selected, are eligible to receive legal services from the legal aid society.

(3) It receives funding from the legal services corporation or otherwise provides civil legal services to indigents.

(B) "Indigent" means a person or persons whose income is not greater than one hundred twenty-five per cent of the current poverty threshold established by the United States office of management and budget.

(C) "Fee generating case" means any case or matter which, if undertaken on behalf of an indigent by an attorney in private practice, reasonably would be expected to result in payment of a fee for legal services from an award to a client, from public funds, or from the opposing party. A case shall not be considered a fee generating case if adequate representation is unavailable or if any of the following circumstances exist concerning the case:

(1) The legal aid society that represents the indigent in the case has determined that free referral is not possible for any of the following reasons:

(a) The case has been rejected by the local lawyer referral service, or if there is no such service, by two attorneys in private practice who have experience in the subject matter of the case.

(b) Neither the local lawyer referral service, if one exists, nor any attorney will consider the case without payment of a consultation fee.

(c) The case is of a type that attorneys in private practice in the area ordinarily do not accept, or do not accept without prepayment of a fee.

(d) Emergency circumstances compel immediate action before referral can be made, but the client is advised that, if appropriate and consistent with professional responsibility, referral will be attempted at a later time.

(2) Recovery of damages is not the principal object of the case and a request for damages is merely ancillary to an action for equitable or other nonpecuniary relief, or inclusion of a counterclaim requesting damages is necessary for effective defense or because of applicable rules governing joinder of counterclaims.

(3) A court has appointed a legal aid society or its employee to represent the indigent in the case pursuant to a statute, or a court rule or practice of equal applicability to all attorneys in the jurisdiction.

(4) The case involves the rights of a claimant under a publicly supported benefit program for which entitlement is based on need.

(1995 H 151, eff. 12–4–95; 1993 H 152, eff. 7–1–93; 1984 S 219)

120.52 Legal aid fund; legal assistance foundation

There is hereby established in the state treasury the legal aid fund, which shall be for the charitable public purpose of providing financial assistance to legal aid societies that provide civil legal services to indigents. The fund shall contain all funds credited to it by the treasurer of state pursuant to sections 1901.26, 1907.24, 2303.201, 4705.09 and 4705.10 of the Revised Code and income from investment credited to it by the treasurer of state in accordance with this section.

The treasurer of state may invest moneys contained in the legal aid fund in any manner authorized by the Revised Code for the investment of state moneys. However, no such investment shall interfere with any apportionment, allocation, or payment of moneys in January and July of each calendar year, as required by section 120.53 of the Revised Code. All income earned as a result of any such investment shall be credited to the fund.

The state public defender, through the Ohio legal assistance foundation, shall administer the payment of moneys out of the fund. Four and one-half per cent of the moneys in the fund shall be reserved for the actual, reasonable costs of administering sections 120.51 to 120.55 and sections 4705.09 and 4705.10 of the Revised Code. Moneys that are reserved for administrative costs but that are not used for actual, reasonable administrative costs shall be set aside for use in the manner described in division (A) of section 120.521 of the Revised Code. The remainder of the moneys in the fund shall be distributed in accordance with section 120.53 of the Revised Code. The Ohio legal assistance foundation shall establish rules governing the administration of the legal aid fund, including the program established under sections 4705.09 and 4705.10 of the Revised Code regarding interest on interest-bearing trust accounts of an attorney, law firm, or legal professional association.

(1995 H 151, eff. 12–4–95; 1995 H 117, eff. 6–30–95; 1993 H 152, eff. 7–1–93; 1988 H 708; 1985 H 201, § 1, 12; 1984 S 219, § 1, 3)

120.53 Legal aid society may receive financial aid

(A) A legal aid society that operates within the state may apply to the Ohio legal assistance foundation for financial assistance from the legal aid fund established by section 120.52 of the Revised Code to be used for the funding of the society during the calendar year following the calendar year in which application is made.

(B) An application for financial assistance made under division (A) of this section shall be submitted by the first day of November of the calendar year preceding the calendar year for which financial assistance is desired and shall include all of the following:

(1) Evidence that the applicant is incorporated in this state as a nonprofit corporation;

(2) A list of the trustees of the applicant;

(3) The proposed budget of the applicant for these funds for the following calendar year;

(4) A summary of the services to be offered by the applicant in the following calendar year;

(5) A specific description of the territory or constituency served by the applicant;

(6) An estimate of the number of persons to be served by the applicant during the following calendar year;

(7) A general description of the additional sources of the applicant's funding;

(8) The amount of the applicant's total budget for the calendar year in which the application is filed that it will expend in that calendar year for legal services in each of the counties it serves;

(9) A specific description of any services, programs, training, and legal technical assistance to be delivered by the applicant or by another person pursuant to a contract with the applicant, including, but not limited to, by private attorneys or through reduced fee plans, judicare panels, organized pro bono programs, and mediation programs.

(C) The Ohio legal assistance foundation shall determine whether each applicant that filed an application for financial assistance under division (A) of this section in a calendar year is eligible for financial assistance under this section. To be eligible for such financial assistance, an applicant shall satisfy the criteria for being a legal aid society and shall be in compliance with the provisions of sections 120.51 to 120.55 of the Revised Code and with the rules and requirements the foundation establishes pursuant to section 120.52 of the Revised Code. The Ohio legal assistance foundation then, on or before the fifteenth day of December of the calendar year in which the application is filed, shall notify each such applicant, in writing, whether it is eligible for financial assistance under this section, and if it is eligible, estimate the amount that will be available for that applicant for each six-month distribution period, as determined under division (D) of this section.

(D) The Ohio legal assistance foundation shall allocate moneys contained in the legal aid fund twice each year for distribution to applicants that filed their applications in the previous calendar year and were determined to be eligible applicants.

All moneys contained in the fund on the first day of January of a calendar year shall be allocated, after deduction of the costs of administering sections 120.51 to 120.55 and sections 4705.09 and 4705.10 of the Revised Code that are authorized by section 120.52 of the Revised Code, according to this section and shall be distributed accordingly on the thirty-first day of January of that calendar year, and all moneys contained in the fund on the first day of July of that calendar year shall be allocated, after deduction of the costs of administering those sections that are authorized by section 120.52 of the Revised Code, according to this section and shall be distributed accordingly on the thirty-first day of July of that calendar year. In making the allocations under this section, the moneys in the fund that were generated pursuant to sections 1901.26, 1907.24, 2303.201, 4705.09 and 4705.10 of the Revised Code and all income generated from the investment of such moneys shall be apportioned as follows:

(1) After deduction of the amount authorized and used for actual, reasonable administrative costs under section 120.52 of the Revised Code:

(a) Five per cent of the moneys remaining in the fund, plus any moneys reserved for administrative costs under that section that are not used for actual, reasonable administrative costs, shall be reserved for distribution to legal aid societies that provide assistance to special population groups of their eligible clients, engage in special projects that have a substantial impact on their local service area or on significant segments of the state's poverty population, or provide legal training or support to other legal aid societies in the state;

(b) After deduction of the amount described in division (D)(1)(a) of this section, one and three-quarters per cent of the moneys remaining in the fund shall be apportioned among entities that received financial assistance from the legal aid fund prior to the effective date of this amendment but that, on and after the effective date of this amendment, no longer qualify as a legal aid society that is eligible for financial assistance under this section.

(2) After deduction of the actual, reasonable administrative costs under section 120.52 of the Revised Code and after deduction of the amounts identified in division (D)(1)(a) and (b) of this section, the remaining moneys shall be apportioned among the counties that are served by eligible legal aid societies that have applied for financial assistance under this section so that each such county is apportioned a portion of those moneys, based upon the ratio of the number of indigents who reside in that county to the total number of indigents who reside in all counties of this state that are served by eligible legal aid societies that have applied for financial assistance under this section. Subject to division (E) of this section, the moneys apportioned to a county under this division then shall be allocated to the eligible legal aid society that serves the county and that has applied for financial assistance under this section. For purposes of this division, the source of data identifying the number of indigent persons who reside in a county shall be the most recent decennial census figures from the United States department of commerce, division of census.

(E) If the Ohio legal assistance foundation, in attempting to make an allocation of moneys under division (D)(2) of this section, determines that a county that has been apportioned money under that division is served by more than one eligible legal aid society that has applied for financial assistance under this section, the Ohio legal assistance foundation shall allocate the moneys that have been apportioned to that county under division (D)(2) of this section among all eligible legal aid societies that serve that county and that have applied for financial assistance under this section on a pro rata basis, so that each such eligible society is allocated a portion based upon the amount of its total budget expended in the prior calendar year for legal services in that county as compared to the total amount expended in the prior calendar year for legal services in that county by all eligible legal aid societies that serve that county and that have applied for financial assistance under this section.

(F) Moneys allocated to eligible applicants under this section shall be paid twice annually, on the thirty-first day of January and on the thirty-first day of July of the calendar year following the calendar year in which the application is filed.

(G)(1) A legal aid society that receives financial assistance in any calendar year under this section shall file an annual report with the Ohio legal assistance foundation detailing the number and types of cases handled, and the amount and types of legal training, legal technical assistance, and other service provided, by means of that financial assistance. No information contained in the report shall identify or enable the identification of any person served by the legal aid society or in any way breach client confidentiality.

(2) The Ohio legal assistance foundation shall make an annual report to the governor, the general assembly, and the supreme court on the distribution and use of the legal aid fund. The foundation also shall include in the annual report an audited financial statement of all gifts, bequests, donations, contributions, and other moneys the foundation receives. No information contained in the report shall identify or enable the identification of any person served by a legal aid society, or in any way breach confidentiality.

(H) A legal aid society may enter into agreements for the provision of services, programs, training, or legal technical assistance for the legal aid society or to indigent persons.

(1995 H 117, eff. 6–30–95; 1993 H 152, eff. 7–1–93; 1988 H 708; 1985 H 201, § 17)

120.54 Use of state aid limited

(A) A legal aid society that receives financial assistance from the legal aid fund under section 120.53 of the Revised Code shall use the financial assistance for only the following purposes:

(1) To defray the costs of providing legal services to indigents;

(2) To provide legal training and legal technical assistance to other eligible legal aid societies; and

(3) If the legal aid society has entered into an agreement pursuant to division (H) of section 120.53 of the Revised Code and in accordance with the description and list of conditions set forth in its application pursuant to division (B)(9) of that section, to provide funds for the services, programs, training, and legal technical assistance provided to the legal aid society under the contract.

(B) No financial assistance received by a legal aid society from the legal aid fund pursuant to section 120.53 of the Revised Code shall be used for the provision of legal services in relation to any criminal case or proceeding or in relation to the provision of legal assistance in any fee generating case.

(1995 H 117, eff. 6–30–95; 1993 H 152, eff. 7–1–93; 1984 S 219)

120.55 Standards to be maintained

In providing legal assistance, each legal aid society that receives financial assistance from the legal aid fund under section 120.53 of the Revised Code shall ensure all of the following:

(A) The maintenance of quality service and professional standards;

(B) That no person shall interfere with any attorney funded in whole or in part by sections 120.51 to 120.55 of the Revised Code in carrying out his professional responsibility to his client as established by the rules of professional responsibility;

(C) The expenditure of the financial assistance only in accordance with sections 120.51 to 120.55 of the Revised Code;

(D) The preservation of client confidentiality.

(1995 H 117, eff. 6–30–95; 1984 S 219, eff. 1–8–85)

CHAPTER 121

STATE DEPARTMENTS

121.401 Recommended best practices regarding volunteers with unsupervised access to minors

(A) As used in this section and section 121.402 of the Revised Code, "organization or entity" and "unsupervised access to a child" have the same meanings as in section 109.574 of the Revised Code.

(B) The governor's community service council shall adopt a set of "recommended best practices" for organizations or entities to follow when one or more volunteers of the organization or entity have unsupervised access to one or more children or otherwise interact with one or more children. The "recommended best practices" shall focus on, but shall not be limited to, the issue of the safety of the children and, in addition, the screening and supervision of volunteers. The "recommended best practices" shall include as a recommended best practice that the organization or entity subject to a criminal records check performed by the bureau of criminal identification and investigation pursuant to section 109.57, section 109.572, or rules adopted under division (E) of section 109.57 of the Revised Code, all of the following:

(1) All persons who apply to serve as a volunteer in a position in which the person will have unsupervised access to a child on a regular basis.

(2) All volunteers who are in a position in which the person will have unsupervised access to a child on a regular basis and who the organization or entity has not previously subjected to a criminal records check performed by the bureau of criminal identification and investigation.

(C) The set of "recommended best practices" required to be adopted by this section are in addition to the educational program required to be adopted under section 121.402 of the Revised Code.

(2000 S 187, eff. 3–22–01)

121.402 Educational program regarding volunteers having unsupervised access to minors

(A) The governor's community service council shall establish and maintain an educational program that does all of the following:

(1) Makes available to parents and guardians of children notice about the provisions of sections 109.574 to 109.577, section 121.401, and section 121.402 of the Revised Code and information about how to keep children safe when they are under the care, custody, or control of a person other than the parent or guardian;

(2) Makes available to organizations and entities information regarding the best methods of screening and supervising volunteers, how to obtain a criminal records check of a volunteer, confidentiality issues relating to reports of criminal records checks, and record keeping regarding the reports;

(3) Makes available to volunteers information regarding the possibility of being subjected to a criminal records check and displaying appropriate behavior to minors;

(4) Makes available to children advice on personal safety and information on what action to take if someone takes inappropriate action towards a child.

(B) The program shall begin making the materials described in this section available not later than one year after the effective date of this section.

(2000 S 187, eff. 3–22–01)

CHAPTER 149

DOCUMENTS, REPORTS, AND RECORDS

149.43 Availability of public records; mandamus action; bulk commercial special extraction requests

Note: See also following versions, eff. 4–27–05, 7–1–05 and 10–29–05, respectively.

(A) As used in this section:

(1) "Public record" means records kept by any public office, including, but not limited to, state, county, city, village, township, and school district units, and records pertaining to the delivery of educational services by an alternative school in Ohio kept by a nonprofit or for profit entity operating such alternative school pursuant to section 3313.533 of the Revised Code. "Public record" does not mean any of the following:

(a) Medical records;

(b) Records pertaining to probation and parole proceedings or to proceedings related to the imposition of community control sanctions and post-release control sanctions;

(c) Records pertaining to actions under section 2151.85 and division (C) of section 2919.121 of the Revised Code and to appeals of actions arising under those sections;

(d) Records pertaining to adoption proceedings, including the contents of an adoption file maintained by the department of health under section 3705.12 of the Revised Code;

(e) Information in a record contained in the putative father registry established by section 3107.062 of the Revised Code, regardless of whether the information is held by the department of job and family services or, pursuant to section 3111.69 of the Revised Code, the office of child support in the department or a child support enforcement agency;

(f) Records listed in division (A) of section 3107.42 of the Revised Code or specified in division (A) of section 3107.52 of the Revised Code;

(g) Trial preparation records;

(h) Confidential law enforcement investigatory records;

(i) Records containing information that is confidential under section 2317.023 or 4112.05 of the Revised Code;

(j) DNA records stored in the DNA database pursuant to section 109.573 of the Revised Code;

(k) Inmate records released by the department of rehabilitation and correction to the department of youth services or a court of record pursuant to division (E) of section 5120.21 of the Revised Code;

(*l*) Records maintained by the department of youth services pertaining to children in its custody released by the department of youth services to the department of rehabilitation and correction pursuant to section 5139.05 of the Revised Code;

(m) Intellectual property records;

(n) Donor profile records;

(*o*) Records maintained by the department of job and family services pursuant to section 3121.894 of the Revised Code;

(p) Peace officer, firefighter, or EMT residential and familial information;

(q) In the case of a county hospital operated pursuant to Chapter 339. of the Revised Code, information that constitutes a trade secret, as defined in section 1333.61 of the Revised Code;

(r) Information pertaining to the recreational activities of a person under the age of eighteen;

(s) Records provided to, statements made by review board members during meetings of, and all work products of a child fatality review board acting under sections 307.621 to 307.629 of the Revised Code, other than the report prepared pursuant to section 307.626 of the Revised Code;

(t) Records provided to and statements made by the executive director of a public children services agency or a prosecuting attorney acting pursuant to section 5153.171 of the Revised Code other than the information released under that section;

(u) Test materials, examinations, or evaluation tools used in an examination for licensure as a nursing home administrator that the board of examiners of nursing home administrators administers under section 4751.04 of the Revised Code or contracts under that section with a private or government entity to administer;

(v) Records the release of which is prohibited by state or federal law;

(w) Proprietary information of or relating to any person that is submitted to or compiled by the Ohio venture capital authority created under section 150.01 of the Revised Code;

(x) Information reported and evaluations conducted pursuant to section 3701.072 of the Revised Code.

(2) "Confidential law enforcement investigatory record" means any record that pertains to a law enforcement matter of a criminal, quasi-criminal, civil, or administrative nature, but only to the extent that the release of the record would create a high probability of disclosure of any of the following:

(a) The identity of a suspect who has not been charged with the offense to which the record pertains, or of an information source or witness to whom confidentiality has been reasonably promised;

(b) Information provided by an information source or witness to whom confidentiality has been reasonably promised, which information would reasonably tend to disclose the source's or witness's identity;

(c) Specific confidential investigatory techniques or procedures or specific investigatory work product;

(d) Information that would endanger the life or physical safety of law enforcement personnel, a crime victim, a witness, or a confidential information source.

(3) "Medical record" means any document or combination of documents, except births, deaths, and the fact of admission to or discharge from a hospital, that pertains to the medical history, diagnosis, prognosis, or medical condition of a patient and that is generated and maintained in the process of medical treatment.

(4) "Trial preparation record" means any record that contains information that is specifically compiled in reasonable anticipation of, or in defense of, a civil or criminal action or proceeding, including the independent thought processes and personal trial preparation of an attorney.

(5) "Intellectual property record" means a record, other than a financial or administrative record, that is produced or collected by or for faculty or staff of a state institution of higher learning in the conduct of or as a result of study or research on an educational, commercial, scientific, artistic, technical, or scholarly issue, regardless of whether the study or research was sponsored by the institution alone or in conjunction with a governmental body or private concern, and that has not been publicly released, published, or patented.

(6) "Donor profile record" means all records about donors or potential donors to a public institution of higher education except the names and reported addresses of the actual donors and the date, amount, and conditions of the actual donation.

(7) "Peace officer, firefighter, or EMT residential and familial information" means either of the following:

(a) Any information maintained in a personnel record of a peace officer, firefighter, or EMT that discloses any of the following:

(i) The address of the actual personal residence of a peace officer, firefighter, or EMT, except for the state or political subdivision in which the peace officer, firefighter, or EMT resides;

(ii) Information compiled from referral to or participation in an employee assistance program;

(iii) The social security number, the residential telephone number, any bank account, debit card, charge card, or credit card number, or the emergency telephone number of, or any medical information pertaining to, a peace officer, firefighter, or EMT;

(iv) The name of any beneficiary of employment benefits, including, but not limited to, life insurance benefits, provided to a peace officer, firefighter, or EMT by the peace officer's, firefighter's, or EMT's employer;

(v) The identity and amount of any charitable or employment benefit deduction made by the peace officer's, firefighter's, or EMT's employer from the peace officer's, firefighter's, or EMT's compensation unless the amount of the deduction is required by state or federal law;

(vi) The name, the residential address, the name of the employer, the address of the employer, the social security number, the residential telephone number, any bank account, debit card, charge card, or credit card number, or the emergency telephone number of the spouse, a former spouse, or any child of a peace officer, firefighter, or EMT.

(b) Any record that identifies a person's occupation as a peace officer, firefighter, or EMT other than statements required to include the disclosure of that fact under the campaign finance law.

As used in divisions (A)(7) and (B)(5) of this section, "peace officer" has the same meaning as in section 109.71 of the Revised Code and also includes the superintendent and troopers of the state highway patrol; it does not include the sheriff of a county or a supervisory employee who, in the absence of the sheriff, is authorized to stand in for, exercise the authority of, and perform the duties of the sheriff.

As used in divisions (A)(7) and (B)(5) of this section, "firefighter" means any regular, paid or volunteer, member of a lawfully constituted fire department of a municipal corporation, township, fire district, or village.

As used in divisions (A)(7) and (B)(5) of this section, "EMT" means EMTs-basic, EMTs–I, and paramedics that provide emergency medical services for a public emergency medical service organization. "Emergency medical service organization," "EMT-basic," "EMT-I," and "paramedic" have the same meanings as in section 4765.01 of the Revised Code.

(8) "Information pertaining to the recreational activities of a person under the age of eighteen" means information that is kept in the ordinary course of business by a public office, that pertains to the recreational activities of a person under the age of eighteen years, and that discloses any of the following:

(a) The address or telephone number of a person under the age of eighteen or the address or telephone number of that person's parent, guardian, custodian, or emergency contact person;

(b) The social security number, birth date, or photographic image of a person under the age of eighteen;

(c) Any medical record, history, or information pertaining to a person under the age of eighteen;

(d) Any additional information sought or required about a person under the age of eighteen for the purpose of allowing that person to participate in any recreational activity conducted or sponsored by a public office or to use or obtain admission privileges to any recreational facility owned or operated by a public office.

(9) "Community control sanction" has the same meaning as in section 2929.01 of the Revised Code.

(10) "Post–release control sanction" has the same meaning as in section 2967.01 of the Revised Code.

(B)(1) Subject to division (B)(4) of this section, all public records shall be promptly prepared and made available for inspection to any person at all reasonable times during regular business hours. Subject to division (B)(4) of this section, upon request, a public office or person responsible for public records shall make copies available at cost, within a reasonable period of time. In order to facilitate broader access to public records, public offices shall maintain public records in a manner that they can be made available for inspection in accordance with this division.

(2) If any person chooses to obtain a copy of a public record in accordance with division (B)(1) of this section, the public office or person responsible for the public record shall permit that person to choose to have the public record duplicated upon paper, upon the same medium upon which the public office or person responsible for the public record keeps it, or upon any other medium upon which the public office or person responsible for the public record determines that it reasonably can be duplicated as an integral part of the normal operations of the public office or person responsible for the public record. When the person seeking the copy makes a choice under this division, the public office or person responsible for the public record shall provide a copy of it in accordance with the choice made by the person seeking the copy.

(3) Upon a request made in accordance with division (B)(1) of this section, a public office or person responsible for public records shall transmit a copy of a public record to any person by United States mail within a reasonable period of time after receiving the request for the copy. The public office or person responsible for the public record may require the person making the request to pay in advance the cost of postage and other supplies used in the mailing.

Any public office may adopt a policy and procedures that it will follow in transmitting, within a reasonable period of time after receiving a request, copies of public records by United States mail pursuant to this division. A public office that adopts a policy and procedures under this division shall comply with them in performing its duties under this division.

In any policy and procedures adopted under this division, a public office may limit the number of records requested by a person that the office will transmit by United States mail to ten per month, unless the person certifies to the office in writing that the person does not intend to use or forward the requested records, or the information contained in them, for commercial purposes. For purposes of this division, "commercial" shall be narrowly construed and does not include reporting or gathering news, reporting or gathering information to assist citizen oversight or understanding of the operation or activities of government, or nonprofit educational research.

(4) A public office or person responsible for public records is not required to permit a person who is incarcerated pursuant to a criminal conviction or a juvenile adjudication to inspect or to obtain a copy of any public record concerning a criminal investigation or prosecution or concerning what would be a criminal investigation or prosecution if the subject of the investigation or prosecution were an adult, unless the request to inspect or to obtain a copy of the record is for the purpose of acquiring information that is subject to release as a public record under this section and the judge who imposed the sentence or made the adjudication with respect to the person, or the judge's successor in office, finds that the information sought in the public record is necessary to support what appears to be a justiciable claim of the person.

(5) Upon written request made and signed by a journalist on or after December 16, 1999, a public office, or person responsible for public records, having custody of the records of the agency employing a specified peace officer, firefighter, or EMT shall disclose to the journalist the address of the actual personal residence of the peace officer, firefighter or EMT and, if the peace officer's, firefighter's or EMT's spouse, former spouse, or child is employed by a public office, the name and address of the employer of the peace officer's, firefighter's, or EMT's spouse, former spouse, or child. The request shall include the journal-

ist's name and title and the name and address of the journalist's employer and shall state that disclosure of the information sought would be in the public interest.

As used in division (B)(5) of this section, "journalist" means a person engaged in, connected with, or employed by any news medium, including a newspaper, magazine, press association, news agency, or wire service, a radio or television station, or a similar medium, for the purpose of gathering, processing, transmitting, compiling, editing, or disseminating information for the general public.

(C) If a person allegedly is aggrieved by the failure of a public office to promptly prepare a public record and to make it available to the person for inspection in accordance with division (B) of this section, or if a person who has requested a copy of a public record allegedly is aggrieved by the failure of a public office or the person responsible for the public record to make a copy available to the person allegedly aggrieved in accordance with division (B) of this section, the person allegedly aggrieved may commence a mandamus action to obtain a judgment that orders the public office or the person responsible for the public record to comply with division (B) of this section and that awards reasonable attorney's fees to the person that instituted the mandamus action. The mandamus action may be commenced in the court of common pleas of the county in which division (B) of this section allegedly was not complied with, in the supreme court pursuant to its original jurisdiction under Section 2 of Article IV, Ohio Constitution, or in the court of appeals for the appellate district in which division (B) of this section allegedly was not complied with pursuant to its original jurisdiction under Section 3 of Article IV, Ohio Constitution.

(D) Chapter 1347. of the Revised Code does not limit the provisions of this section.

(E)(1) The bureau of motor vehicles may adopt rules pursuant to Chapter 119. of the Revised Code to reasonably limit the number of bulk commercial special extraction requests made by a person for the same records or for updated records during a calendar year. The rules may include provisions for charges to be made for bulk commercial special extraction requests for the actual cost of the bureau, plus special extraction costs, plus ten per cent. The bureau may charge for expenses for redacting information, the release of which is prohibited by law.

(2) As used in divisions (B)(3) and (E)(1) of this section:

(a) "Actual cost" means the cost of depleted supplies, records storage media costs, actual mailing and alternative delivery costs, or other transmitting costs, and any direct equipment operating and maintenance costs, including actual costs paid to private contractors for copying services.

(b) "Bulk commercial special extraction request" means a request for copies of a record for information in a format other than the format already available, or information that cannot be extracted without examination of all items in a records series, class of records, or data base by a person who intends to use or forward the copies for surveys, marketing, solicitation, or resale for commercial purposes. "Bulk commercial special extraction request" does not include a request by a person who gives assurance to the bureau that the person making the request does not intend to use or forward the requested copies for surveys, marketing, solicitation, or resale for commercial purposes.

(c) "Commercial" means profit-seeking production, buying, or selling of any good, service, or other product.

(d) "Special extraction costs" means the cost of the time spent by the lowest paid employee competent to perform the task, the actual amount paid to outside private contractors employed by the bureau, or the actual cost incurred to create computer programs to make the special extraction. "Special extraction costs" include any charges paid to a public agency for computer or records services.

(3) For purposes of divisions (E)(1) and (2) of this section, "commercial surveys, marketing, solicitation, or resale" shall be narrowly construed and does not include reporting or gathering news, reporting or gathering information to assist citizen oversight or understanding of the operation or activities of government, or nonprofit educational research.

(2003 H 6, eff. 2–12–04; 2002 S 258, eff. 4–9–03; 2002 H 490, eff. 1–1–04; 2002 S 180, eff. 4–9–03; 2001 H 196, eff. 11–20–01; 2000 S 180, eff. 3–22–01; 2000 H 448, eff. 10–5–00; 2000 H 640, eff. 9–14–00; 2000 H 539, eff. 6–21–00; 1999 H 471, eff. 7–1–00; 1999 S 78, eff. 12–16–99; 1999 S 55, eff. 10–26–99; 1998 H 421, eff. 5–6–98; 1997 H 352, eff. 1–1–98; 1996 S 277, § 6, eff. 7–1–97; 1996 S 277, § 1, eff. 3–31–97; 1996 H 438, eff. 7–1–97; 1996 S 269, eff. 7–1–96; 1996 H 353, eff. 9–17–96; 1996 H 419, eff. 9–18–96; 1995 H 5, eff. 8–30–95; 1993 H 152, eff. 7–1–93; 1987 S 275; 1985 H 319, H 238; 1984 H 84; 1979 S 62; 130 v H 187)

Note: See also following versions, eff. 4–27–05, 7–1–05 and 10–29–05, respectively.

149.43 Availability of public records; mandamus action; bulk commercial special extraction requests (later effective date)

Note: See also preceding version, in effect until 4–27–05, and following versions, eff. 7–1–05 and 10–29–05, respectively.

(A) As used in this section:

(1) "Public record" means records kept by any public office, including, but not limited to, state, county, city, village, township, and school district units, and records pertaining to the delivery of educational services by an alternative school in Ohio kept by a nonprofit or for profit entity operating such alternative school pursuant to section 3313.533 of the Revised Code. "Public record" does not mean any of the following:

(a) Medical records;

(b) Records pertaining to probation and parole proceedings or to proceedings related to the imposition of community control sanctions and post-release control sanctions;

(c) Records pertaining to actions under section 2151.85 and division (C) of section 2919.121 of the Revised Code and to appeals of actions arising under those sections;

(d) Records pertaining to adoption proceedings, including the contents of an adoption file maintained by the department of health under section 3705.12 of the Revised Code;

(e) Information in a record contained in the putative father registry established by section 3107.062 of the Revised Code, regardless of whether the information is held by the department of job and family services or, pursuant to section 3111.69 of the Revised Code, the office of child support in the department or a child support enforcement agency;

(f) Records listed in division (A) of section 3107.42 of the Revised Code or specified in division (A) of section 3107.52 of the Revised Code;

(g) Trial preparation records;

(h) Confidential law enforcement investigatory records;

(i) Records containing information that is confidential under section 2317.023 or 4112.05 of the Revised Code;

(j) DNA records stored in the DNA database pursuant to section 109.573 of the Revised Code;

(k) Inmate records released by the department of rehabilitation and correction to the department of youth services or a court of record pursuant to division (E) of section 5120.21 of the Revised Code;

(*l*) Records maintained by the department of youth services pertaining to children in its custody released by the department of youth services to the department of rehabilitation and correction pursuant to section 5139.05 of the Revised Code;

(m) Intellectual property records;

(n) Donor profile records;

(*o*) Records maintained by the department of job and family services pursuant to section 3121.894 of the Revised Code;

(p) Peace officer, firefighter, or EMT residential and familial information;

(q) In the case of a county hospital operated pursuant to Chapter 339. of the Revised Code or a municipal hospital operated pursuant to Chapter 749. of the Revised Code, information that constitutes a trade secret, as defined in section 1333.61 of the Revised Code;

(r) Information pertaining to the recreational activities of a person under the age of eighteen;

(s) Records provided to, statements made by review board members during meetings of, and all work products of a child fatality review board acting under sections 307.621 to 307.629 of the Revised Code, other than the report prepared pursuant to section 307.626 of the Revised Code;

(t) Records provided to and statements made by the executive director of a public children services agency or a prosecuting attorney acting pursuant to section 5153.171 of the Revised Code other than the information released under that section;

(u) Test materials, examinations, or evaluation tools used in an examination for licensure as a nursing home administrator that the board of examiners of nursing home administrators administers under section 4751.04 of the Revised Code or contracts under that section with a private or government entity to administer;

(v) Records the release of which is prohibited by state or federal law;

(w) Proprietary information of or relating to any person that is submitted to or compiled by the Ohio venture capital authority created under section 150.01 of the Revised Code;

(x) Information reported and evaluations conducted pursuant to section 3701.072 of the Revised Code.

(2) "Confidential law enforcement investigatory record" means any record that pertains to a law enforcement matter of a criminal, quasi-criminal, civil, or administrative nature, but only to the extent that the release of the record would create a high probability of disclosure of any of the following:

(a) The identity of a suspect who has not been charged with the offense to which the record pertains, or of an information source or witness to whom confidentiality has been reasonably promised;

(b) Information provided by an information source or witness to whom confidentiality has been reasonably promised, which information would reasonably tend to disclose the source's or witness's identity;

(c) Specific confidential investigatory techniques or procedures or specific investigatory work product;

(d) Information that would endanger the life or physical safety of law enforcement personnel, a crime victim, a witness, or a confidential information source.

(3) "Medical record" means any document or combination of documents, except births, deaths, and the fact of admission to or discharge from a hospital, that pertains to the medical history, diagnosis, prognosis, or medical condition of a patient and that is generated and maintained in the process of medical treatment.

(4) "Trial preparation record" means any record that contains information that is specifically compiled in reasonable anticipation of, or in defense of, a civil or criminal action or proceeding, including the independent thought processes and personal trial preparation of an attorney.

(5) "Intellectual property record" means a record, other than a financial or administrative record, that is produced or collected by or for faculty or staff of a state institution of higher learning in the conduct of or as a result of study or research on an educational, commercial, scientific, artistic, technical, or scholarly issue, regardless of whether the study or research was sponsored by the institution alone or in conjunction with a governmental body or private concern, and that has not been publicly released, published, or patented.

(6) "Donor profile record" means all records about donors or potential donors to a public institution of higher education except the names and reported addresses of the actual donors and the date, amount, and conditions of the actual donation.

(7) "Peace officer, firefighter, or EMT residential and familial information" means either of the following:

(a) Any information maintained in a personnel record of a peace officer, firefighter, or EMT that discloses any of the following:

(i) The address of the actual personal residence of a peace officer, firefighter, or EMT, except for the state or political subdivision in which the peace officer, firefighter, or EMT resides;

(ii) Information compiled from referral to or participation in an employee assistance program;

(iii) The social security number, the residential telephone number, any bank account, debit card, charge card, or credit card number, or the emergency telephone number of, or any medical information pertaining to, a peace officer, firefighter, or EMT;

(iv) The name of any beneficiary of employment benefits, including, but not limited to, life insurance benefits, provided to a peace officer, firefighter, or EMT by the peace officer's, firefighter's, or EMT's employer;

(v) The identity and amount of any charitable or employment benefit deduction made by the peace officer's, firefighter's, or EMT's employer from the peace officer's, firefighter's, or EMT's compensation unless the amount of the deduction is required by state or federal law;

(vi) The name, the residential address, the name of the employer, the address of the employer, the social security number, the residential telephone number, any bank account, debit card, charge card, or credit card number, or the emergency telephone number of the spouse, a former spouse, or any child of a peace officer, firefighter, or EMT.

(b) Any record that identifies a person's occupation as a peace officer, firefighter, or EMT other than statements required to include the disclosure of that fact under the campaign finance law.

As used in divisions (A)(7) and (B)(5) of this section, "peace officer" has the same meaning as in section 109.71 of the Revised Code and also includes the superintendent and troopers of the state highway patrol; it does not include the sheriff of a county or a supervisory employee who, in the absence of the sheriff, is authorized to stand in for, exercise the authority of, and perform the duties of the sheriff.

As used in divisions (A)(7) and (B)(5) of this section, "firefighter" means any regular, paid or volunteer, member of a lawfully constituted fire department of a municipal corporation, township, fire district, or village.

As used in divisions (A)(7) and (B)(5) of this section, "EMT" means EMTs-basic, EMTs–I, and paramedics that provide emergency medical services for a public emergency medical service organization. "Emergency medical service organization," "EMT-basic," "EMT-I," and "paramedic" have the same meanings as in section 4765.01 of the Revised Code.

(8) "Information pertaining to the recreational activities of a person under the age of eighteen" means information that is kept in the ordinary course of business by a public office, that pertains to the recreational activities of a person under the age of eighteen years, and that discloses any of the following:

(a) The address or telephone number of a person under the age of eighteen or the address or telephone number of that person's parent, guardian, custodian, or emergency contact person;

(b) The social security number, birth date, or photographic image of a person under the age of eighteen;

(c) Any medical record, history, or information pertaining to a person under the age of eighteen;

(d) Any additional information sought or required about a person under the age of eighteen for the purpose of allowing that person to participate in any recreational activity conducted or sponsored by a public office or to use or obtain admission privileges to any recreational facility owned or operated by a public office.

(9) "Community control sanction" has the same meaning as in section 2929.01 of the Revised Code.

(10) "Post–release control sanction" has the same meaning as in section 2967.01 of the Revised Code.

(B)(1) Subject to division (B)(4) of this section, all public records shall be promptly prepared and made available for inspection to any person at all reasonable times during regular business hours. Subject to division (B)(4) of this section, upon request, a public office or person responsible for public records shall make copies available at cost, within a reasonable period of time. In order to facilitate broader access to public records, public offices shall maintain public records in a manner that they can be made available for inspection in accordance with this division.

(2) If any person chooses to obtain a copy of a public record in accordance with division (B)(1) of this section, the public office or person responsible for the public record shall permit that person to choose to have the public record duplicated upon paper, upon the same medium upon which the public office or person responsible for the public record keeps it, or upon any other medium upon which the public office or person responsible for the public record determines that it reasonably can be duplicated as an integral part of the normal operations of the public office or person responsible for the public record. When the person seeking the copy makes a choice under this division, the public office or person responsible for the public record shall provide a copy of it in accordance with the choice made by the person seeking the copy.

(3) Upon a request made in accordance with division (B)(1) of this section, a public office or person responsible for public records shall transmit a copy of a public record to any person by United States mail within a reasonable period of time after receiving the request for the copy. The public office or person responsible for the public record may require the person making the request to pay in advance the cost of postage and other supplies used in the mailing.

Any public office may adopt a policy and procedures that it will follow in transmitting, within a reasonable period of time after receiving a request, copies of public records by United States mail pursuant to this division. A public office that adopts a policy and procedures under this division shall comply with them in performing its duties under this division.

In any policy and procedures adopted under this division, a public office may limit the number of records requested by a person that the office will transmit by United States mail to ten per month, unless the person certifies to the office in writing that the person does not intend to use or forward the requested records, or the information contained in them, for commercial purposes. For purposes of this division, "commercial" shall be narrowly construed and does not include reporting or gathering news, reporting or gathering information to assist citizen oversight or understanding of the operation or activities of government, or nonprofit educational research.

(4) A public office or person responsible for public records is not required to permit a person who is incarcerated pursuant to a criminal conviction or a juvenile adjudication to inspect or to obtain a copy of any public record concerning a criminal investigation or prosecution or concerning what would be a criminal investigation or prosecution if the subject of the investigation or prosecution were an adult, unless the request to inspect or to obtain a copy of the record is for the purpose of acquiring information that is subject to release as a public record under this section and the judge who imposed the sentence or made the adjudication with respect to the person, or the judge's successor in office, finds that the information sought in the public record is necessary to support what appears to be a justiciable claim of the person.

(5) Upon written request made and signed by a journalist on or after December 16, 1999, a public office, or person responsible for public records, having custody of the records of the agency employing a specified peace officer, firefighter, or EMT shall disclose to the journalist the address of the actual personal residence of the peace officer, firefighter or EMT and, if the peace officer's, firefighter's or EMT's spouse, former spouse, or child is employed by a public office, the name and address of the employer of the peace officer's, firefighter's, or EMT's spouse, former spouse, or child. The request shall include the journalist's name and title and the name and address of the journalist's employer and shall state that disclosure of the information sought would be in the public interest.

As used in division (B)(5) of this section, "journalist" means a person engaged in, connected with, or employed by any news medium, including a newspaper, magazine, press association, news agency, or wire service, a radio or television station, or a similar medium, for the purpose of gathering, processing, transmitting, compiling, editing, or disseminating information for the general public.

(C) If a person allegedly is aggrieved by the failure of a public office to promptly prepare a public record and to make it available to the person for inspection in accordance with division (B) of this section, or if a person who has requested a copy of a public record allegedly is aggrieved by the failure of a public office or the person responsible for the public record to make a copy available to the person allegedly aggrieved in accordance with division (B) of this section, the person allegedly aggrieved may commence a mandamus action to obtain a judgment that orders the public office or the person responsible for the public record to comply with division (B) of this section and that awards reasonable attorney's fees to the person that instituted the mandamus action. The mandamus action may be commenced in the court of common pleas of the county in which division (B) of this section allegedly was not complied with, in the supreme court pursuant to its original jurisdiction under Section 2 of Article IV, Ohio Constitution, or in the court of appeals for the appellate district in which division (B) of this section allegedly was not complied with pursuant to its original jurisdiction under Section 3 of Article IV, Ohio Constitution.

(D) Chapter 1347. of the Revised Code does not limit the provisions of this section.

(E)(1) The bureau of motor vehicles may adopt rules pursuant to Chapter 119. of the Revised Code to reasonably limit the number of bulk commercial special extraction requests made by a person for the same records or for updated records during a calendar year. The rules may include provisions for charges to be made for bulk commercial special extraction requests for the actual cost of the bureau, plus special extraction costs, plus ten per cent. The bureau may charge for expenses for redacting information, the release of which is prohibited by law.

(2) As used in divisions (B)(3) and (E)(1) of this section:

(a) "Actual cost" means the cost of depleted supplies, records storage media costs, actual mailing and alternative delivery costs, or other transmitting costs, and any direct equipment operating and maintenance costs, including actual costs paid to private contractors for copying services.

(b) "Bulk commercial special extraction request" means a request for copies of a record for information in a format other than the format already available, or information that cannot be extracted without examination of all items in a records series, class of records, or data base by a person who intends to use or forward the copies for surveys, marketing, solicitation, or resale for commercial purposes. "Bulk commercial special extraction request" does not include a request by a person who gives assurance to the bureau that the person making the request does not intend to use or forward the requested copies for surveys, marketing, solicitation, or resale for commercial purposes.

(c) "Commercial" means profit-seeking production, buying, or selling of any good, service, or other product.

(d) "Special extraction costs" means the cost of the time spent by the lowest paid employee competent to perform the task, the actual amount paid to outside private contractors employed by the bureau, or the actual cost incurred to create computer programs to make the special extraction. "Special extraction costs" include any charges paid to a public agency for computer or records services.

(3) For purposes of divisions (E)(1) and (2) of this section, "commercial surveys, marketing, solicitation, or resale" shall be narrowly construed and does not include reporting or gathering news, reporting or gathering information to assist citizen oversight or understanding of the operation or activities of government, or nonprofit educational research.

(2004 S 222, eff 4–27–05; 2003 H 6, eff. 2-12–04; 2002 S 258, eff. 4–9–03; 2002 H 490, eff. 1–1–04; 2002 S 180, eff. 4–9–03; 2001 H 196, eff. 11–20–01; 2000 S 180, eff. 3–22–01; 2000 H 448, eff. 10–5–00; 2000 H 640, eff. 9–14–00; 2000 H 539, eff. 6–21–00; 1999 H 471, eff. 7 1 00; 1999 S 78, eff. 12–16–99; 1999 S 55, eff. 10–26–99; 1998 H 421, eff. 5–6–98; 1997 H 352, eff. 1–1–98; 1996 S 277, § 6, eff. 7–1–97; 1996 S 277, § 1, eff. 3–31–97; 1996 H 438, eff. 7-1–97; 1996 S 269, eff. 7–1–96; 1996 H 353, eff. 9–17–96; 1996 H 419, eff. 9–18–96; 1995 H 5, eff. 8–30–95; 1993 H 152, eff. 7–1–93; 1987 S 275; 1985 H 319, H 238; 1984 H 84; 1979 S 62; 130 v H 187)

Note: See also preceding version, in effect until 4–27–05, and following versions, eff. 7–1–05 and 10–29–05, respectively.

149.43 Availability of public records; mandamus action; bulk commercial special extraction requests (later effective date)

Note: See also preceding versions, in effect until 4–27–05 and 7–1–05, respectively, and following version, eff. 10–29–05.

(A) As used in this section:

(1) "Public record" means records kept by any public office, including, but not limited to, state, county, city, village, township, and school district units, and records pertaining to the delivery of educational services by an alternative school in Ohio kept by a nonprofit or for profit entity operating such alternative school pursuant to section 3313.533 of the Revised Code. "Public record" does not mean any of the following:

(a) Medical records;

(b) Records pertaining to probation and parole proceedings or to proceedings related to the imposition of community control sanctions and post-release control sanctions;

(c) Records pertaining to actions under section 2151.85 and division (C) of section 2919.121 of the Revised Code and to appeals of actions arising under those sections;

(d) Records pertaining to adoption proceedings, including the contents of an adoption file maintained by the department of health under section 3705.12 of the Revised Code;

(e) Information in a record contained in the putative father registry established by section 3107.062 of the Revised Code, regardless of whether the information is held by the department of job and family services or, pursuant to section 3111.69 of the Revised Code, the office of child support in the department or a child support enforcement agency;

(f) Records listed in division (A) of section 3107.42 of the Revised Code or specified in division (A) of section 3107.52 of the Revised Code;

(g) Trial preparation records;

(h) Confidential law enforcement investigatory records;

(i) Records containing information that is confidential under section 2317.023 or 4112.05 of the Revised Code;

(j) DNA records stored in the DNA database pursuant to section 109.573 of the Revised Code;

(k) Inmate records released by the department of rehabilitation and correction to the department of youth services or a court of record pursuant to division (E) of section 5120.21 of the Revised Code;

(*l*) Records maintained by the department of youth services pertaining to children in its custody released by the department of youth services to the department of rehabilitation and correction pursuant to section 5139.05 of the Revised Code;

(m) Intellectual property records;

(n) Donor profile records;

(*o*) Records maintained by the department of job and family services pursuant to section 3121.894 of the Revised Code;

(p) Peace officer, firefighter, or EMT residential and familial information;

(q) In the case of a county hospital operated pursuant to Chapter 339. of the Revised Code or a municipal hospital operated pursuant to Chapter 749. of the Revised Code, information that constitutes a trade secret, as defined in section 1333.61 of the Revised Code;

(r) Information pertaining to the recreational activities of a person under the age of eighteen;

(s) Records provided to, statements made by review board members during meetings of, and all work products of a child fatality review board acting under sections 307.621 to 307.629 of the Revised Code, other than the report prepared pursuant to section 307.626 of the Revised Code;

(t) Records provided to and statements made by the executive director of a public children services agency or a prosecuting attorney acting pursuant to section 5153.171 of the Revised Code other than the information released under that section;

(u) Test materials, examinations, or evaluation tools used in an examination for licensure as a nursing home administrator that the board of examiners of nursing home administrators administers under section 4751.04 of the Revised Code or contracts under that section with a private or government entity to administer;

(v) Records the release of which is prohibited by state or federal law;

(w) Proprietary information of or relating to any person that is submitted to or compiled by the Ohio venture capital authority created under section 150.01 of the Revised Code;

(x) Information reported and evaluations conducted pursuant to section 3701.072 of the Revised Code;

(y) Financial statements and data any person submits for any purpose to the Ohio housing finance agency or the controlling board in connection with applying for, receiving, or accounting for financial assistance from the agency, and information that identifies any individual who benefits directly or indirectly from financial assistance from the agency.

(2) "Confidential law enforcement investigatory record" means any record that pertains to a law enforcement matter of a criminal, quasi-criminal, civil, or administrative nature, but only to the extent that the release of the record would create a high probability of disclosure of any of the following:

(a) The identity of a suspect who has not been charged with the offense to which the record pertains, or of an information source or witness to whom confidentiality has been reasonably promised;

(b) Information provided by an information source or witness to whom confidentiality has been reasonably promised, which information would reasonably tend to disclose the source's or witness's identity;

(c) Specific confidential investigatory techniques or procedures or specific investigatory work product;

(d) Information that would endanger the life or physical safety of law enforcement personnel, a crime victim, a witness, or a confidential information source.

(3) "Medical record" means any document or combination of documents, except births, deaths, and the fact of admission to or discharge from a hospital, that pertains to the medical history, diagnosis, prognosis, or medical condition of a patient and that is generated and maintained in the process of medical treatment.

(4) "Trial preparation record" means any record that contains information that is specifically compiled in reasonable anticipation of, or in defense of, a civil or criminal action or proceeding, including the independent thought processes and personal trial preparation of an attorney.

(5) "Intellectual property record" means a record, other than a financial or administrative record, that is produced or collected by or for faculty or staff of a state institution of higher learning in the conduct of or as a result of study or research on an educational, commercial, scientific, artistic, technical, or scholarly issue, regardless of whether the study or research was sponsored by the institution alone or in conjunction with a governmental body or private concern, and that has not been publicly released, published, or patented.

(6) "Donor profile record" means all records about donors or potential donors to a public institution of higher education except the names and reported addresses of the actual donors and the date, amount, and conditions of the actual donation.

(7) "Peace officer, firefighter, or EMT residential and familial information" means either of the following:

(a) Any information maintained in a personnel record of a peace officer, firefighter, or EMT that discloses any of the following:

(i) The address of the actual personal residence of a peace officer, firefighter, or EMT, except for the state or political subdivision in which the peace officer, firefighter, or EMT resides;

(ii) Information compiled from referral to or participation in an employee assistance program;

(iii) The social security number, the residential telephone number, any bank account, debit card, charge card, or credit card number, or the emergency telephone number of, or any medical information pertaining to, a peace officer, firefighter, or EMT;

(iv) The name of any beneficiary of employment benefits, including, but not limited to, life insurance benefits, provided to a peace officer, firefighter, or EMT by the peace officer's, firefighter's, or EMT's employer;

(v) The identity and amount of any charitable or employment benefit deduction made by the peace officer's, firefighter's, or EMT's employer from the peace officer's, firefighter's, or EMT's compensation unless the amount of the deduction is required by state or federal law;

(vi) The name, the residential address, the name of the employer, the address of the employer, the social security number, the residential telephone number, any bank account, debit card, charge card, or credit card number, or the emergency telephone number of the spouse, a former spouse, or any child of a peace officer, firefighter, or EMT.

(b) Any record that identifies a person's occupation as a peace officer, firefighter, or EMT other than statements required to include the disclosure of that fact under the campaign finance law.

As used in divisions (A)(7) and (B)(5) of this section, "peace officer" has the same meaning as in section 109.71 of the Revised Code and also includes the superintendent and troopers of the state highway patrol; it does not include the sheriff of a county or a supervisory employee who, in the absence of the sheriff, is authorized to stand in for, exercise the authority of, and perform the duties of the sheriff.

As used in divisions (A)(7) and (B)(5) of this section, "firefighter" means any regular, paid or volunteer, member of a lawfully constituted fire department of a municipal corporation, township, fire district, or village.

As used in divisions (A)(7) and (B)(5) of this section, "EMT" means EMTs-basic, EMTs–I, and paramedics that provide emergency medical services for a public emergency medical service organization. "Emergency medical service organization," "EMT-basic," "EMT-I," and "paramedic" have the same meanings as in section 4765.01 of the Revised Code.

(8) "Information pertaining to the recreational activities of a person under the age of eighteen" means information that is kept in the ordinary course of business by a public office, that pertains to the recreational activities of a person under the age of eighteen years, and that discloses any of the following:

(a) The address or telephone number of a person under the age of eighteen or the address or telephone number of that person's parent, guardian, custodian, or emergency contact person;

(b) The social security number, birth date, or photographic image of a person under the age of eighteen;

(c) Any medical record, history, or information pertaining to a person under the age of eighteen;

(d) Any additional information sought or required about a person under the age of eighteen for the purpose of allowing that person to participate in any recreational activity conducted or sponsored by a public office or to use or obtain admission privileges to any recreational facility owned or operated by a public office.

(9) "Community control sanction" has the same meaning as in section 2929.01 of the Revised Code.

(10) "Post–release control sanction" has the same meaning as in section 2967.01 of the Revised Code.

(B)(1) Subject to division (B)(4) of this section, all public records shall be promptly prepared and made available for inspection to any person at all reasonable times during regular business hours. Subject to division (B)(4) of this section, upon request, a public office or person responsible for public records shall make copies available at cost, within a reasonable period of time. In order to facilitate broader access to public records, public offices shall maintain public records in a manner that they can be made available for inspection in accordance with this division.

(2) If any person chooses to obtain a copy of a public record in accordance with division (B)(1) of this section, the public office or person responsible for the public record shall permit that person to choose to have the public record duplicated upon paper, upon the same medium upon which the public office or person responsible for the public record keeps it, or upon any other medium upon which the public office or person responsible for the public record determines that it reasonably can be duplicated as an integral part of the normal operations of the public office or person responsible for the public record. When the person seeking the copy makes a choice under this division, the public office or person responsible for the public record shall provide a copy of it in accordance with the choice made by the person seeking the copy.

(3) Upon a request made in accordance with division (B)(1) of this section, a public office or person responsible for public records shall transmit a copy of a public record to any person by United States mail within a reasonable period of time after receiving the request for the copy. The public office or person responsible for the public record may require the person making the request to pay in advance the cost of postage and other supplies used in the mailing.

Any public office may adopt a policy and procedures that it will follow in transmitting, within a reasonable period of time after receiving a request, copies of public records by United States mail pursuant to this division. A public office that adopts a policy and procedures under this division shall comply with them in performing its duties under this division.

In any policy and procedures adopted under this division, a public office may limit the number of records requested by a person that the office will transmit by United States mail to ten per month, unless the person certifies to the office in writing that the person does not intend to use or forward the requested records, or the information contained in them, for commercial purposes. For purposes of this division, "commercial" shall be narrowly construed and does not include reporting or gathering news, reporting or gathering information to assist citizen oversight or understanding of the operation or activities of government, or nonprofit educational research.

(4) A public office or person responsible for public records is not required to permit a person who is incarcerated pursuant to a criminal conviction or a juvenile adjudication to inspect or to obtain a copy of any public record concerning a criminal investigation or prosecution or concerning what would be a criminal investigation or prosecution if the subject of the investigation or prosecution were an adult, unless the request to inspect or to obtain a copy of the record is for the purpose of acquiring information that is subject to release as a public record under this section and the judge who imposed the sentence or made the adjudication with respect to the person, or the judge's successor in office, finds that the information sought in the public record is necessary to support what appears to be a justiciable claim of the person.

(5) Upon written request made and signed by a journalist on or after December 16, 1999, a public office, or person responsible for public records, having custody of the records of the agency employing a specified peace officer, firefighter, or EMT shall disclose to the journalist the address of the actual personal residence of the peace officer, firefighter or EMT and, if the peace officer's, firefighter's or EMT's spouse, former spouse, or child is employed by a public office, the name and address of the employer of the peace officer's, firefighter's, or EMT's spouse, former spouse, or child. The request shall include the journalist's name and title and the name and address of the journalist's employer and shall state that disclosure of the information sought would be in the public interest.

As used in division (B)(5) of this section, "journalist" means a person engaged in, connected with, or employed by any news medium, including a newspaper, magazine, press association, news agency, or wire service, a radio or television station, or a similar medium, for the purpose of gathering, processing, transmitting, compiling, editing, or disseminating information for the general public.

(C) If a person allegedly is aggrieved by the failure of a public office to promptly prepare a public record and to make it available to the person for inspection in accordance with division (B) of this section, or if a person who has requested a copy of a public record allegedly is aggrieved by the failure of a public office or the person responsible for the public record to make a copy available to the person allegedly aggrieved in accordance with division (B) of this section, the person allegedly aggrieved may commence a mandamus action to obtain a judgment that orders the public office or the person responsible for the public record to comply with division (B) of this section and that awards reasonable attorney's fees to the person that instituted the mandamus action. The mandamus action may be commenced in the court of common pleas of the county in which division (B) of this section allegedly was not complied with, in the supreme court pursuant to its original jurisdiction under Section 2 of Article IV, Ohio Constitution, or in the court of appeals for the appellate district in which division (B) of this section allegedly was not complied with pursuant to its original jurisdiction under Section 3 of Article IV, Ohio Constitution.

(D) Chapter 1347. of the Revised Code does not limit the provisions of this section.

(E)(1) The bureau of motor vehicles may adopt rules pursuant to Chapter 119. of the Revised Code to reasonably limit the number of bulk commercial special extraction requests made by a person for the same records or for updated records during a calendar year. The rules may include provisions for charges to be made for bulk commercial special extraction requests for the actual cost of the bureau, plus special extraction costs, plus ten per cent. The bureau may charge for expenses for redacting information, the release of which is prohibited by law.

(2) As used in divisions (B)(3) and (E)(1) of this section:

(a) "Actual cost" means the cost of depleted supplies, records storage media costs, actual mailing and alternative delivery costs, or other transmitting costs, and any direct equipment operating and maintenance costs, including actual costs paid to private contractors for copying services.

(b) "Bulk commercial special extraction request" means a request for copies of a record for information in a format other than the format already available, or information that cannot be extracted without examination of all items in a records series, class of records, or data base by a person who intends to use or forward the copies for surveys, marketing, solicitation, or resale for commercial purposes. "Bulk commercial special extraction request" does not include a request by a person who gives assurance to the bureau that the person making the request does not intend to use or forward the requested copies for surveys, marketing, solicitation, or resale for commercial purposes.

(c) "Commercial" means profit-seeking production, buying, or selling of any good, service, or other product.

(d) "Special extraction costs" means the cost of the time spent by the lowest paid employee competent to perform the task, the actual amount paid to outside private contractors employed by the bureau, or the actual cost incurred to create computer programs to make the special extraction. "Special extraction costs" include any charges paid to a public agency for computer or records services.

(3) For purposes of divisions (E)(1) and (2) of this section, "commercial surveys, marketing, solicitation, or resale" shall be narrowly construed and does not include reporting or gathering news, reporting or gathering information to assist citizen oversight or understanding of the operation or activities of government, or nonprofit educational research.

(2004 H 431, eff. 7–1–05; 2004 S 222, eff. 4–27–05; 2003 H 6, eff. 2–12–04; 2002 S 258, eff. 4–9–03; 2002 H 490, eff. 1–1–04; 2002 S 180, eff. 4–9–03; 2001 H 196, eff. 11–20–01; 2000 S 180, eff. 3–22–01; 2000 H 448, eff. 10–5–00; 2000 H 640, eff. 9–14–00; 2000 H 539, eff. 6–21–00; 1999 H 471, eff. 7–1–00; 1999 S 78, eff. 12–16–99; 1999 S 55, eff. 10–26–99; 1998 H 421, eff. 5–6–98; 1997 H 352, eff. 1–1–98; 1996 S 277, § 6, eff. 7–1–97; 1996 S 277, § 1, eff. 3–31–97; 1996 H 438, eff. 7–1–97; 1996 S 269, eff. 7–1–96; 1996 H 353, eff. 9–17–96; 1996 H 419, eff. 9–18–96; 1995 H 5, eff. 8–30–95; 1993 H 152, eff. 7–1–93; 1987 S 275; 1985 H 319, H 238; 1984 H 84; 1979 S 62; 130 v H 187)

Note: See also preceding versions, in effect until 4–27–05 and 7–1–05, respectively, and following version, eff. 10–29–05.

149.43 Availability of public records; mandamus action; bulk commercial special extraction requests (later effective date)

Note: See also preceding versions, in effect until 4–27–05, 7–1–05, and 10–29–05, respectively.

(A) As used in this section:

(1) "Public record" means records kept by any public office, including, but not limited to, state, county, city, village, township, and school district units, and records pertaining to the delivery of educational services by an alternative school in Ohio kept by a nonprofit or for profit entity operating such alternative school pursuant to section 3313.533 of the Revised Code. "Public record" does not mean any of the following:

(a) Medical records;

(b) Records pertaining to probation and parole proceedings or to proceedings related to the imposition of community control sanctions and post-release control sanctions;

(c) Records pertaining to actions under section 2151.85 and division (C) of section 2919.121 of the Revised Code and to appeals of actions arising under those sections;

(d) Records pertaining to adoption proceedings, including the contents of an adoption file maintained by the department of health under section 3705.12 of the Revised Code;

(e) Information in a record contained in the putative father registry established by section 3107.062 of the Revised Code, regardless of whether the information is held by the department of job and family services or, pursuant to section 3111.69 of the Revised Code, the office of child support in the department or a child support enforcement agency;

(f) Records listed in division (A) of section 3107.42 of the Revised Code or specified in division (A) of section 3107.52 of the Revised Code;

(g) Trial preparation records;

(h) Confidential law enforcement investigatory records;

(i) Records containing information that is confidential under section 2710.03 or 4112.05 of the Revised Code;

(j) DNA records stored in the DNA database pursuant to section 109.573 of the Revised Code;

(k) Inmate records released by the department of rehabilitation and correction to the department of youth services or a court of record pursuant to division (E) of section 5120.21 of the Revised Code;

(*l*) Records maintained by the department of youth services pertaining to children in its custody released by the department of youth services to the department of rehabilitation and correction pursuant to section 5139.05 of the Revised Code;

(m) Intellectual property records;

(n) Donor profile records;

(*o*) Records maintained by the department of job and family services pursuant to section 3121.894 of the Revised Code;

(p) Peace officer, firefighter, or EMT residential and familial information;

(q) In the case of a county hospital operated pursuant to Chapter 339. of the Revised Code or a municipal hospital operated pursuant to Chapter 749. of the Revised Code, information that constitutes a trade secret, as defined in section 1333.61 of the Revised Code;

(r) Information pertaining to the recreational activities of a person under the age of eighteen;

(s) Records provided to, statements made by review board members during meetings of, and all work products of a child fatality review board acting under sections 307.621 to 307.629 of the Revised Code, other than the report prepared pursuant to section 307.626 of the Revised Code;

(t) Records provided to and statements made by the executive director of a public children services agency or a prosecuting attorney acting pursuant to section 5153.171 of the Revised Code other than the information released under that section;

(u) Test materials, examinations, or evaluation tools used in an examination for licensure as a nursing home administrator that the board of examiners of nursing home administrators administers under section 4751.04 of the Revised Code or contracts under that section with a private or government entity to administer;

(v) Records the release of which is prohibited by state or federal law;

(w) Proprietary information of or relating to any person that is submitted to or compiled by the Ohio venture capital authority created under section 150.01 of the Revised Code;

(x) Information reported and evaluations conducted pursuant to section 3701.072 of the Revised Code;

(y) Financial statements and data any person submits for any purpose to the Ohio housing finance agency or the controlling board in connection with applying for, receiving, or accounting for financial assistance from the agency, and information that identifies any individual who benefits directly or indirectly from financial assistance from the agency.

(2) "Confidential law enforcement investigatory record" means any record that pertains to a law enforcement matter of a criminal, quasi-criminal, civil, or administrative nature, but only to the extent that the release of the record would create a high probability of disclosure of any of the following:

(a) The identity of a suspect who has not been charged with the offense to which the record pertains, or of an information source or witness to whom confidentiality has been reasonably promised;

(b) Information provided by an information source or witness to whom confidentiality has been reasonably promised, which information would reasonably tend to disclose the source's or witness's identity;

(c) Specific confidential investigatory techniques or procedures or specific investigatory work product;

(d) Information that would endanger the life or physical safety of law enforcement personnel, a crime victim, a witness, or a confidential information source.

(3) "Medical record" means any document or combination of documents, except births, deaths, and the fact of admission to or discharge from a hospital, that pertains to the medical history, diagnosis, prognosis, or medical condition of a patient and that is generated and maintained in the process of medical treatment.

(4) "Trial preparation record" means any record that contains information that is specifically compiled in reasonable anticipation of, or in defense of, a civil or criminal action or proceeding, including the independent thought processes and personal trial preparation of an attorney.

(5) "Intellectual property record" means a record, other than a financial or administrative record, that is produced or collected by or for faculty or staff of a state institution of higher learning in the conduct of or as a result of study or research on an educational, commercial, scientific, artistic, technical, or scholarly issue, regardless of whether the study or research was sponsored by the institution alone or in conjunction with a governmental body or private concern, and that has not been publicly released, published, or patented.

(6) "Donor profile record" means all records about donors or potential donors to a public institution of higher education except the names and reported addresses of the actual donors and the date, amount, and conditions of the actual donation.

(7) "Peace officer, firefighter, or EMT residential and familial information" means either of the following:

(a) Any information maintained in a personnel record of a peace officer, firefighter, or EMT that discloses any of the following:

(i) The address of the actual personal residence of a peace officer, firefighter, or EMT, except for the state or political subdivision in which the peace officer, firefighter, or EMT resides;

(ii) Information compiled from referral to or participation in an employee assistance program;

(iii) The social security number, the residential telephone number, any bank account, debit card, charge card, or credit card number, or the emergency telephone number of, or any medical information pertaining to, a peace officer, firefighter, or EMT;

(iv) The name of any beneficiary of employment benefits, including, but not limited to, life insurance benefits, provided to a peace officer, firefighter, or EMT by the peace officer's, firefighter's, or EMT's employer;

(v) The identity and amount of any charitable or employment benefit deduction made by the peace officer's, firefighter's, or EMT's employer from the peace officer's, firefighter's, or EMT's compensation unless the amount of the deduction is required by state or federal law;

(vi) The name, the residential address, the name of the employer, the address of the employer, the social security number, the residential telephone number, any bank account, debit card, charge card, or credit card number, or the emergency telephone number of the spouse, a former spouse, or any child of a peace officer, firefighter, or EMT.

(b) Any record that identifies a person's occupation as a peace officer, firefighter, or EMT other than statements required to include the disclosure of that fact under the campaign finance law.

As used in divisions (A)(7) and (B)(5) of this section, "peace officer" has the same meaning as in section 109.71 of the Revised Code and also includes the superintendent and troopers of the state highway patrol; it does not include the sheriff of a county or a supervisory employee who, in the absence of the sheriff, is authorized to stand in for, exercise the authority of, and perform the duties of the sheriff.

As used in divisions (A)(7) and (B)(5) of this section, "firefighter" means any regular, paid or volunteer, member of a lawfully constituted fire department of a municipal corporation, township, fire district, or village.

As used in divisions (A)(7) and (B)(5) of this section, "EMT" means EMTs-basic, EMTs–I, and paramedics that provide emergency medical services for a public emergency medical service organization. "Emergency medical service organization," "EMT-basic," "EMT-I," and "paramedic" have the same meanings as in section 4765.01 of the Revised Code.

(8) "Information pertaining to the recreational activities of a person under the age of eighteen" means information that is kept in the ordinary course of business by a public office, that pertains to the recreational activities of a person under the age of eighteen years, and that discloses any of the following:

(a) The address or telephone number of a person under the age of eighteen or the address or telephone number of that person's parent, guardian, custodian, or emergency contact person;

(b) The social security number, birth date, or photographic image of a person under the age of eighteen;

(c) Any medical record, history, or information pertaining to a person under the age of eighteen;

(d) Any additional information sought or required about a person under the age of eighteen for the purpose of allowing that person to participate in any recreational activity conducted or sponsored by a public office or to use or obtain admission privileges to any recreational facility owned or operated by a public office.

(9) "Community control sanction" has the same meaning as in section 2929.01 of the Revised Code.

(10) "Post-release control sanction" has the same meaning as in section 2967.01 of the Revised Code.

(B)(1) Subject to division (B)(4) of this section, all public records shall be promptly prepared and made available for inspection to any person at all reasonable times during regular business hours. Subject to division (B)(4) of this section, upon request, a public office or person responsible for public records shall make copies available at cost, within a reasonable period of time. In order to facilitate broader access to public records, public offices shall maintain public records in a manner that they can be made available for inspection in accordance with this division.

(2) If any person chooses to obtain a copy of a public record in accordance with division (B)(1) of this section, the public office or person responsible for the public record shall permit that person to choose to have the public record duplicated upon paper, upon the same medium upon which the public office or person responsible for the public record keeps it, or upon any other medium upon which the public office or person responsible for the public record determines that it reasonably can be duplicated as an integral part of the normal operations of the public office or person responsible for the public record. When the person seeking the copy makes a choice under this division, the public office or person responsible for the public record shall provide a copy of it in accordance with the choice made by the person seeking the copy.

(3) Upon a request made in accordance with division (B)(1) of this section, a public office or person responsible for public records shall transmit a copy of a public record to any person by United States mail within a reasonable period of time after receiving the request for the copy. The public office or person responsible for the public record may require the person making the request to pay in advance the cost of postage and other supplies used in the mailing.

Any public office may adopt a policy and procedures that it will follow in transmitting, within a reasonable period of time after receiving a request, copies of public records by United States mail pursuant to this division. A public office that adopts a policy and procedures under this division shall comply with them in performing its duties under this division.

In any policy and procedures adopted under this division, a public office may limit the number of records requested by a person that the office will transmit by United States mail to ten per month, unless the person certifies to the office in writing that the person does not intend to use or forward the requested records, or the information contained in them, for commercial purposes. For purposes of this division, "commercial" shall be narrowly construed and does not include reporting or gathering news, reporting or gathering information to assist citizen oversight or understanding of the operation or activities of government, or nonprofit educational research.

(4) A public office or person responsible for public records is not required to permit a person who is incarcerated pursuant to a criminal conviction or a juvenile adjudication to inspect or to obtain a copy of any public record concerning a criminal investigation or prosecution or concerning what would be a criminal investigation or prosecution if the subject of the investigation or prosecution were an adult, unless the request to inspect or to obtain a copy of the record is for the purpose of acquiring information that is subject to release as a public record under this section and the judge who imposed the sentence or made the adjudication with respect to the person, or the judge's successor in office, finds that the information sought in the public record is necessary to support what appears to be a justiciable claim of the person.

(5) Upon written request made and signed by a journalist on or after December 16, 1999, a public office, or person responsible for public records, having custody of the records of the agency employing a specified peace officer, firefighter, or EMT shall disclose to the journalist the address of the actual personal residence of the peace officer, firefighter or EMT and, if the peace officer's, firefighter's or EMT's spouse, former spouse, or child is employed by a public office, the name and address of the employer of the peace officer's, firefighter's, or EMT's spouse, former spouse, or child. The request shall include the journalist's name and title and the name and address of the journalist's employer and shall state that disclosure of the information sought would be in the public interest.

As used in division (B)(5) of this section, "journalist" means a person engaged in, connected with, or employed by any news medium, including a newspaper, magazine, press association, news agency, or wire service, a radio or television station, or a similar medium, for the purpose of gathering, processing, transmitting, compiling, editing, or disseminating information for the general public.

(C) If a person allegedly is aggrieved by the failure of a public office to promptly prepare a public record and to make it available to the person for inspection in accordance with division (B) of this section, or if a person who has requested a copy of a public record allegedly is aggrieved by the failure of a public office or the person responsible for the public record to make a copy available to the person allegedly aggrieved in accordance with division (B) of this section, the person allegedly aggrieved may commence a mandamus action to obtain a judgment that orders the public office or the person responsible for the public record to comply with division (B) of this section and that awards reasonable attorney's fees to the person that instituted the mandamus action. The mandamus action may be commenced in the court of common pleas of the county in which division (B) of this section allegedly was not complied with, in the supreme court pursuant to its original jurisdiction under Section 2 of Article IV, Ohio Constitution, or in the court of appeals for the appellate district in which division (B) of this section allegedly was not complied with pursuant to its original jurisdiction under Section 3 of Article IV, Ohio Constitution.

(D) Chapter 1347. of the Revised Code does not limit the provisions of this section.

(E)(1) The bureau of motor vehicles may adopt rules pursuant to Chapter 119. of the Revised Code to reasonably limit the number of bulk commercial special extraction requests made by a person for the same records or for updated records during a calendar year. The rules may include provisions for charges to be made for bulk commercial special extraction requests for the actual cost of the bureau, plus special extraction costs, plus ten per cent. The bureau may charge for expenses for redacting information, the release of which is prohibited by law.

(2) As used in divisions (B)(3) and (E)(1) of this section:

(a) "Actual cost" means the cost of depleted supplies, records storage media costs, actual mailing and alternative delivery costs, or other transmitting costs, and any direct equipment operating and maintenance costs, including actual costs paid to private contractors for copying services.

(b) "Bulk commercial special extraction request" means a request for copies of a record for information in a format other than the format already available, or information that cannot be extracted without examination of all items in a records series, class of records, or data base by a person who intends to use or forward the copies for surveys, marketing, solicitation, or resale for commercial purposes. "Bulk commercial special extraction request" does not include a request by a person who gives assurance to the bureau that the person making the request does not intend to use or forward the requested copies for surveys, marketing, solicitation, or resale for commercial purposes.

(c) "Commercial" means profit-seeking production, buying, or selling of any good, service, or other product.

(d) "Special extraction costs" means the cost of the time spent by the lowest paid employee competent to perform the task, the actual amount paid to outside private contractors employed by the bureau, or the actual cost incurred to create computer programs to make the special extraction. "Special extraction costs" include any charges paid to a public agency for computer or records services.

(3) For purposes of divisions (E)(1) and (2) of this section, "commercial surveys, marketing, solicitation, or resale" shall be narrowly construed and does not include reporting or gathering news, reporting or gathering information to assist citizen oversight or understanding of the operation or activities of government, or nonprofit educational research.

(2004 H 303, eff. 10–29–05; 2004 H 431, eff. 7–1–05; 2004 S 222, eff. 4–27–05; 2003 H 6, eff. 2–12–04; 2002 S 258, eff. 4–9–03; 2002 H 490, eff. 1–1–04; 2002 S 180, eff. 4–9–03; 2001 H 196, eff. 11–20–01; 2000 S 180, eff. 3–22–01; 2000 H 448, eff. 10–5–00; 2000 H 640, eff. 9–14–00; 2000 H 539, eff. 6–21–00; 1999 H 471, eff. 7–1–00; 1999 S 78, eff. 12–16–99; 1999 S 55, eff. 10–26–99; 1998 H 421, eff. 5–6–98; 1997 H 352, eff. 1–1–98; 1996 S 277, § 6, eff. 7–1–97; 1996 S 277, § 1, eff. 3–31–97; 1996 H 438, eff. 7–1–97; 1996 S 269, eff. 7–1–96; 1996 H 353, eff. 9–17–96; 1996 H 419, eff. 9–18–96; 1995 H 5, eff. 8–30–95; 1993 H 152, eff. 7–1–93; 1987 S 275; 1985 H 319, H 238; 1984 H 84; 1979 S 62; 130 v H 187)

Note: See also preceding versions, in effect until 4–27–05, 7–1–05, and 10–29–05, respectively.

149.432 Confidentiality of library records

(A) As used in this section:

(1) "Library" means a library that is open to the public, including any of the following:

(a) A library that is maintained and regulated under section 715.13 of the Revised Code;

(b) A library that is created, maintained, and regulated under Chapter 3375. of the Revised Code;

(c) A library that is created and maintained by a public or private school, college, university, or other educational institution;

(d) A library that is created and maintained by a historical or charitable organization, institution, association, or society.

"Library" includes the members of the governing body and the employees of a library.

(2) "Library record" means a record in any form that is maintained by a library and that contains any of the following types of information:

(a) Information that the library requires an individual to provide in order to be eligible to use library services or borrow materials;

(b) Information that identifies an individual as having requested or obtained specific materials or materials on a particular subject;

(c) Information that is provided by an individual to assist a library staff member to answer a specific question or provide information on a particular subject.

"Library record" does not include information that does not identify any individual and that is retained for the purpose of studying or evaluating the use of a library and its materials and services.

(3) Subject to division (B)(5) of this section, "patron information" means personally identifiable information about an individual who has used any library service or borrowed any library materials.

(B) A library shall not release any library record or disclose any patron information except in the following situations:

(1) If a library record or patron information pertaining to a minor child is requested from a library by the minor child's parent, guardian, or custodian, the library shall make that record or information available to the parent, guardian, or custodian in accordance with division (B) of section 149.43 of the Revised Code.

(2) Library records or patron information shall be released in the following situations:

(a) In accordance with a subpoena, search warrant, or other court order;

(b) To a law enforcement officer who is acting in the scope of the officer's law enforcement duties and who is investigating a matter involving public safety in exigent circumstances.

(3) A library record or patron information shall be released upon the request or with the consent of the individual who is the subject of the record or information.

(4) Library records may be released for administrative library purposes, including establishment or maintenance of a system to manage the library records or to assist in the transfer of library records from one records management system to another, compilation of statistical data on library use, and collection of fines and penalties.

(5) A library may release under division (B) of section 149.43 of the Revised Code records that document improper use of the internet at the library so long as any patron information is removed from those records. As used in division (B)(5) of this section, "patron information" does not include information about the age or gender of an individual.

(2004 H 204, eff. 11–5–04; 2000 H 389, eff. 10–5–00)

149.433 Definitions

(A) As used in this section:

(1) "Act of terrorism" has the same meaning as in section 2909.21 of the Revised Code.

(2) "Infrastructure record" means any record that discloses the configuration of a public office's critical systems including, but not limited to, communication, computer, electrical, mechanical, ventilation, water, and plumbing systems, security codes, or the infrastructure or structural configuration of the building in which a public office is located. "Infrastructure record" does not mean a simple floor plan that discloses only the spatial relationship of components of a public office or the building in which a public office is located.

(3) "Security record" means either of the following:

(a) Any record that contains information directly used for protecting or maintaining the security of a public office against attack, interference, or sabotage;

(b) Any record assembled, prepared, or maintained by a public office or public body to prevent, mitigate, or respond to acts of terrorism, including any of the following:

(i) Those portions of records containing specific and unique vulnerability assessments or specific and unique response plans either of which is intended to prevent or mitigate acts of terrorism, and communication codes or deployment plans of law enforcement or emergency response personnel;

(ii) Specific intelligence information and specific investigative records shared by federal and international law enforcement agencies with state and local law enforcement and public safety agencies;

(iii) National security records classified under federal executive order and not subject to public disclosure under federal law that are shared by federal agencies, and other records related to national security briefings to assist state and local government with domestic preparedness for acts of terrorism.

(B) A record kept by a public office that is a security record or an infrastructure record is not a public record under section 149.43 of the Revised Code and is not subject to mandatory release or disclosure under that section.

(C) Notwithstanding any other section of the Revised Code, a public office's or a public employee's disclosure of a security record or infrastructure record that is necessary for construction, renovation, or remodeling work on any public building or project does not constitute public disclosure for purposes of waiving division (B) of this section and does not result in that record becoming a public record for purposes of section 149.43 of the Revised Code.

(2002 S 184, eff. 5–15–02)

CHAPTER 177

INVESTIGATION AND PROSECUTION OF ORGANIZED CRIMINAL ACTIVITY

177.01 Organized crime investigations commission; terms; chairman; compensation; definitions

(A) The organized crime investigations commission, consisting of seven members, is hereby established in the office of the attorney general. One of the members shall be the attorney general. Of the remaining members, each of whom shall be appointed by the governor with the advice and consent of the senate, two shall be prosecuting attorneys, two shall be county sheriffs, and two shall be chief municipal law enforcement officers. No more than four members of the commission shall be members of the same political party.

Of the initial appointments to the commission, one member who is a prosecuting attorney and one who is a county sheriff each shall be appointed for terms ending September 3, 1987, one member who is a prosecuting attorney and one who is a chief municipal law enforcement officer each shall be appointed for terms ending September 3, 1988, and one member who is a county sheriff and one who is a chief municipal law enforcement officer each shall be appointed for terms ending September 3, 1989. Thereafter, terms of office of persons appointed to the commission shall be for three years, with each term ending on the same day of the same month of the year as did the term that it succeeds. Members may be reappointed. Each appointed member shall hold office from the date of the member's appointment until the end of the term for which the member was appointed, except that an appointed member who ceases to hold the office or position of prosecuting attorney, county sheriff, or chief municipal law enforcement officer prior to the expiration of the member's term of office on the commission shall cease to be a member of the commission on the date that the member ceases to hold the office or position. Vacancies shall be filled in the manner provided for original appointments. Any member appointed to fill a vacancy occurring prior to the expiration of the term for which the member's predecessor was appointed shall take office on the commission when the member is confirmed by the senate and shall hold office for the remainder of such term. Any member shall continue in office subsequent to the expiration date of the member's term until the member's successor takes office, or until a period of sixty days has elapsed, whichever occurs first.

The attorney general shall become a member of the commission on September 3, 1986. Successors in office to that attorney general shall become members of the commission on the day they assume the office of attorney general. An attorney general's term of office as a member of the commission shall continue for as long as the person in question holds the office of attorney general.

Each member of the commission may designate, in writing, another person to represent the member on the commission. If a member makes such a designation, either the member or the designee may perform the member's duties and exercise the member's authority on the commission. If a member makes such a designation, the member may revoke the designation by sending written notice of the revocation to the commission. Upon such a revocation, the member may designate a different person to represent the member on the commission by sending written notice of the designation to the commission at least two weeks prior to the date on which the new designation is to take effect.

The attorney general or a person the attorney general designates pursuant to this division to represent the attorney general on the commission shall serve as chairperson of the commission. The commission shall meet within two weeks after all appointed members have been appointed, at a time and place determined by the governor. The commission shall organize by selecting a vice-chairperson and other officers who are necessary and shall adopt rules to govern its procedures. Thereafter, the commission shall meet at least once every six months, or more often upon the call of the chairperson or the written request of two or more members. Each member of the commission shall have one vote. Four members constitute a quorum, and four votes are required to validate an action of the commission.

The members of the commission shall serve without compensation, but each member shall be reimbursed for actual and necessary expenses incurred in the performance of official duties. In the absence of the chairperson, the vice-chairperson shall perform the duties of the chairperson.

(B) The commission shall coordinate investigations of organized criminal activity and perform all of the functions and duties relative to the investigations that are set forth in section 177.02 of the Revised Code, and it shall cooperate with departments and officers of the government of the United States in the suppression of organized criminal activity.

(C) The commission shall appoint and fix the compensation of a director and such technical and clerical employees who are necessary to exercise the powers and carry out the duties of the commission, may enter into contracts with one or more consultants to assist in exercising those powers and carrying out those duties, and may enter into contracts and purchase any equipment necessary to the performance of its duties. The director and employees of the commission shall be members of the unclassified service as defined in section 124.11 of the Revised Code. The commission shall require the director and each employee, prior to commencing employment with the commission, to undergo an investigation for the purpose of obtaining a security clearance and, after the initial investigation, may require the director and each employee to undergo an investigation for that purpose at any time during the director's or employee's employment with the commission. The commission may require any consultant with whom it contracts to undergo an investigation for the purpose of obtaining a security clearance. An investigation under this division may include, but is not limited to, a polygraph examination and shall be conducted by an organization designated by the commission.

(D) An appointed commission member may be removed from office as a member of the commission by the vote of four members of the commission or by the governor for any of the following reasons:

(1) Neglect of duty, misconduct, incompetence, or malfeasance in office;

(2) Conviction of or a plea of guilty to a felony or an offense of moral turpitude;

(3) Being mentally ill or mentally incompetent;

(4) Being the subject of an investigation by a task force established by the commission or another law enforcement agency, where the proof of criminal activity is evident or the presumption great;

(5) Engaging in any activity or associating with any persons or organization inappropriate to the member's position as a member of the commission.

(E) As used in sections 177.01 to 177.03 of the Revised Code:

(1) "Organized criminal activity" means any combination or conspiracy to engage in activity that constitutes "engaging in a pattern of corrupt activity;" any violation, combination of viola-

tions, or conspiracy to commit one or more violations of section 2925.03, 2925.04, 2925.05, 2925.06, or 2925.11 of the Revised Code other than a violation of section 2925.11 of the Revised Code that is a minor drug possession offense; or any criminal activity that relates to the corruption of a public official, as defined in section 2921.01 of the Revised Code, or of a public servant of the type described in division (B)(3) of that section.

(2) A person is engaging in an activity that constitutes "engaging in a pattern of corrupt activity" if any of the following apply:

(a) The person is or was employed by, or associated with, an enterprise and the person conducts or participates in, directly or indirectly, the affairs of the enterprise through a pattern of corrupt activity or the collection of an unlawful debt.

(b) The person, through a pattern of corrupt activity or the collection of an unlawful debt, acquires or maintains, directly or indirectly, an interest in, or control of, an enterprise or real property.

(c) The person knowingly has received proceeds derived, directly or indirectly, from a pattern of corrupt activity or the collection of an unlawful debt and the person uses or invests, directly or indirectly, a part of those proceeds, or proceeds derived from the use or investment of any of those proceeds, in the acquisition of title to, or a right, interest, or equity in, real property or the establishment or operation of an enterprise. A purchase of securities on the open market with intent to make an investment, without intent to control or participate in the control of the issuer, and without intent to assist another to do so is not an activity that constitutes "engaging in a pattern of corrupt activity" if the securities of the issuer held after the purchase by the purchaser, the members of the purchaser's immediate family, and the purchaser's or members' accomplices in any pattern of corrupt activity or the collection of an unlawful debt, do not aggregate one per cent of the outstanding securities of any one class of the issuer and do not confer, in law or in fact, the power to elect one or more directors of the issuer.

(3) "Pattern of corrupt activity" means two or more incidents of corrupt activity, whether or not there has been a prior conviction, that are related to the affairs of the same enterprise, are not isolated, and are not so closely related to each other and connected in time and place that they constitute a single event. At least one of the incidents forming the pattern shall occur on or after September 3, 1986. Unless any incident was an aggravated murder or murder, the most recent of the incidents forming the pattern shall occur within six years after the commission of any prior incident forming the pattern, excluding any period of imprisonment served by any person engaging in the corrupt activity.

(4) "Corrupt activity," "unlawful debt," "enterprise," "person," "real property," and "beneficial interest" have the same meanings as in section 2923.31 of the Revised Code.

(5) "Minor drug possession offense" has the same meaning as in section 2925.01 of the Revised Code.

(1998 H 2, eff. 1-1-99; 1995 S 2, eff. 7-1-96; 1991 H 298, eff. 7-26-91; 1990 H 215; 1988 H 708; 1986 S 74)

177.011 Organized crime commission fund

There is hereby created in the state treasury the organized crime commission fund. The fund shall consist of moneys paid to the treasurer of state pursuant to the judgment of a court in a criminal case as reimbursement of expenses that the organized crime investigations commission or an organized crime task force established by the commission incurred in the investigation of the criminal activity upon which the prosecution of the criminal case was based. All investment earnings on moneys in the fund shall be credited to the fund. The organized crime investigations commission shall use the moneys in the fund to reimburse political subdivisions for the expenses the political subdivisions incur when their law enforcement officers participate in an organized crime task force.

(1997 H 215, eff. 6-30-97)

177.02 Filing of complaint; organized crime task force; director; staff; prosecuting attorney implicated in organized criminal activity

(A) Any person may file with the organized crime investigations commission a complaint that alleges that organized criminal activity has occurred in a county. A person who files a complaint under this division also may file with the commission information relative to the complaint.

(B) Upon the filing of a complaint under division (A) of this section or upon its own initiative, the commission may establish an organized crime task force to investigate organized criminal activity in a single county or in two or more counties if it determines, based upon the complaint filed and the information relative to it or based upon any information that it may have received, that there is reason to believe that organized criminal activity has occurred and continues to occur in that county or in each of those counties. The commission shall not establish an organized crime task force to investigate organized criminal activity in any single county unless it makes the determination required under this division relative to that county and shall not establish an organized crime task force to investigate organized criminal activity in two or more counties unless it makes the determination required under this division relative to each of those counties. The commission, at any time, may terminate an organized crime task force it has established under this section.

(C)(1) If the commission establishes an organized crime task force to investigate organized criminal activity in a single county or in two or more counties pursuant to division (B) of this section, the commission initially shall appoint a task force director to directly supervise the investigation. The task force director shall be either the sheriff or a deputy sheriff of any county in the state, the chief law enforcement officer or a member of a law enforcement agency of any municipal corporation or township in the state, or an agent of the bureau of criminal identification and investigation. No person shall be appointed as task force director without the person's consent and, if applicable, the consent of the person's employing sheriff or law enforcement agency or of the superintendent of the bureau of criminal identification and investigation if the person is an employee of the bureau. Upon appointment of a task force director, the commission shall meet with the director and establish the scope and limits of the investigation to be conducted by the task force and the size of the task force investigatory staff to be appointed by the task force director. The commission, at any time, may remove a task force director appointed under this division and may replace any director so removed according to the guidelines for the initial appointment of a director.

(2) A task force director appointed under this section shall assemble a task force investigatory staff, of a size determined by the commission and the director, to conduct the investigation. Unless it appears to the commission and the director, based upon the complaint filed and any information relative to it or based upon any information that the commission may have received, that there is reason to believe that the office of the prosecuting attorney of the county or one of the counties served by the task force is implicated in the organized criminal activity to be investigated, one member of the investigatory staff shall be the prosecuting attorney or an assistant prosecuting attorney of the county or one of the counties served by the task force. If a prosecuting attorney or assistant prosecuting attorney is not a participating member of the task force, the office of the attorney general shall provide legal assistance to the task force upon request. Each of the other members of the investigatory staff shall be either the sheriff or a deputy sheriff of any county in the state, the chief law

enforcement officer or a member of a law enforcement agency of any municipal corporation or township in the state, or an agent of the bureau of criminal identification and investigation. No person shall be appointed to the investigatory staff without the person's consent and, if applicable, the consent of the person's employing sheriff or law enforcement agency or the superintendent of the bureau of criminal identification and investigation if the person is an employee of the bureau. To the extent possible, the investigatory staff shall be composed of persons familiar with investigatory techniques that generally would be utilized in an investigation of organized criminal activity. To the extent practicable, the investigatory staff shall be assembled in such a manner that numerous law enforcement agencies within the county or the counties served by the task force are represented on the investigatory staff. The investigatory staff shall be assembled in such a manner that at least one sheriff, deputy sheriff, municipal corporation law enforcement officer, or township law enforcement officer from each of the counties served by the task force is represented on the investigatory staff. A task force director, at any time, may remove any member of the investigatory staff the task force director has assembled under this division and may replace any member so removed according to the guidelines for the initial assembly of the investigatory staff.

(3) The commission may provide an organized crime task force established under this section with technical and clerical employees and with equipment necessary to efficiently conduct its investigation into organized criminal activity.

(4) Upon the establishment of a task force, the commission shall issue to the task force director and each member of the task force investigatory staff appropriate credentials stating the person's identity, position, and authority.

(D) A task force investigatory staff, during the period of the investigation for which it is assembled, is responsible only to the task force director and shall operate under the direction and control of the task force director. Any necessary and actual expenses incurred by a task force director or investigatory staff, including any such expenses incurred for food, lodging, or travel, and any other necessary and actual expenses of an investigation into organized criminal activity conducted by a task force, shall be paid by the commission. For purposes of workers' compensation and the allocation of liability for any death, injury, or damage they may cause in the performance of their duties, a task force director and investigatory staff, during the period of the investigation for which the task force is assembled, shall be considered to be employees of the commission and of the state. However, for purposes of compensation, pension or indemnity fund rights, and other rights and benefits to which they may be entitled, a task force director and investigatory staff, during the period of the performance of their duties as director and investigatory staff, shall be considered to be performing their duties in their normal capacity as prosecuting attorney, assistant prosecuting attorney, sheriff, deputy sheriff, chief law enforcement officer or member of a law enforcement agency of a municipal corporation or township, or agent of the bureau of criminal identification and investigation.

(E) Except as provided in this division, upon the establishment of a task force, the commission shall provide the prosecuting attorney of each of the counties served by the task force with written notice that the task force has been established to investigate organized criminal activity in that county. Such notice shall not be provided to a prosecuting attorney if it appears to the commission, based upon the complaint filed and any information relative to it or based upon any information that the commission may have received, that there is reason to believe that the office of that prosecuting attorney is implicated in the organized criminal activity to be investigated.

(F) The filing of a complaint alleging organized criminal activity, the establishment of an organized crime task force, the appointment of a task force director and the identity of the task force director, the assembly of an investigatory staff and the identity of its members, the conduct of an investigation into organized criminal activity, and the identity of any person who is being or is expected to be investigated by the task force shall be kept confidential by the commission and its director and employees, and by the task force and its director, investigatory staff, and employees until an indictment is returned or a criminal action or proceeding is initiated in a court of proper jurisdiction.

(G) For purposes of divisions (C) and (E) of this section, the office of a prosecuting attorney shall be considered as being implicated in organized criminal activity only if the prosecuting attorney, one or more of the prosecuting attorney's assistants, or one or more of the prosecuting attorney's employees has committed or attempted or conspired to commit, is committing or attempting or conspiring to commit, or has engaged in or is engaging in complicity in the commission of, organized criminal activity.

(1998 H 2, eff. 1–1–99; 1986 S 74, eff. 9–3–86)

177.03 Investigations by organized crime task force; cooperation with other law enforcement agencies; referral of information; commission to review information; implication of attorney general or prosecuting attorney; reports

(A) An organized crime task force established under section 177.02 of the Revised Code to investigate organized criminal activity in a single county or in two or more counties shall investigate organized criminal activity within the county or counties in accordance with the scope and limits established by the organized crime investigations commission and the task force director. For purposes of the investigation, the task force director and investigatory staff shall have the powers of a peace officer throughout the county or counties in which the investigation is to be undertaken. However, the authority and powers granted to the director and investigatory staff under this section do not supplant or diminish the authority and power provided by the Revised Code to other law enforcement agencies or their officers or investigators.

An organized crime task force, in the conduct of its investigation, may issue subpoenas and subpoenas duces tecum. The task force may compel the attendance of witnesses and the production of records and papers of all kinds and description that are relevant to the investigation, including, but not limited to, any books, accounts, documents, and memoranda pertaining to the subject of the investigation. Upon the failure of any person to comply with any lawful order of the task force, the task force may apply to the court of common pleas of the proper county for a contempt order, as in the case of disobedience of the requirements of a subpoena issued from the court of common pleas, or a refusal to testify thereon.

(B) This section and section 177.02 of the Revised Code do not prevent an organized crime task force from cooperating with other law enforcement agencies of this state, a political subdivision of this state, another state, a political subdivision of another state, or the United States, or their officers or investigators in the investigation and prosecution of any offenses comprising organized criminal activity.

(C)(1) If an organized crime task force, either prior to the commencement of or during the course of its investigation of organized criminal activity in a single county or in two or more counties, has reason to believe that the investigation will require it to engage in substantial investigative activities in a particular municipal corporation or township in the county or any of the counties, the task force director shall notify the commission chairperson of that belief and the reasons for that belief. The chairperson shall present that belief and those reasons to the commission, and, if the commission determines that there is a compelling reason to notify a local law enforcement agency that has jurisdiction within that municipal corporation or township that the task force will be engaging in investigative activities in the municipal corporation or township, the commission, subject to division (C)(2) of this section, shall provide written notice of that fact as follows:

(a) If the investigative activities will be engaged in in a township or in a municipal corporation that does not have a police department or similar law enforcement agency, the commission shall provide the notice to the sheriff of the county in which the township or municipal corporation is located.

(b) If the investigative activities will be engaged in in a municipal corporation that has a police department or similar law enforcement agency, the commission shall provide the notice to the chief law enforcement officer of the department or agency.

(2) The notice described in division (C)(1) of this section shall not be provided to a sheriff or chief law enforcement officer if it appears to the commission, based upon the complaint filed and any information relative to it or based upon any information that the commission may have received, that there is reason to believe that the office of that sheriff or chief law enforcement officer is implicated in the organized criminal activity being investigated.

(D)(1) If an organized crime task force determines, pursuant to its investigation of organized criminal activity in a single county or in two or more counties, that there is not reasonable cause to believe that organized criminal activity has occurred or is occurring in the county or in any of the counties, it shall report its determination to the commission, terminate its task force activities, and disband.

(2)(a) If a task force determines, pursuant to its investigation of organized criminal activity in a single county or in two or more counties, that there is reasonable cause to believe that organized criminal activity has occurred or is occurring in the county or in any of the counties, it shall report its determination to the commission and, except as provided in division (D)(3) of this section, shall refer a copy of all of the information gathered during the course of the investigation to the prosecuting attorney who has jurisdiction over the matter and inform the prosecuting attorney that the prosecuting attorney has thirty days to decide whether the prosecuting attorney should present the information to a grand jury and that, if the prosecuting attorney intends to make a presentation of the information to the grand jury, the prosecuting attorney has to give the commission written notice of that intention. If the organized criminal activity occurred or is occurring in two or more counties, the referral of the information shall be to the prosecuting attorney of the county in which the most significant portion of the activity occurred or is occurring or, if it is not possible to determine that county, the county with the largest population.

If a prosecuting attorney who has been referred information under this division fails to notify the commission in writing, within thirty days after the referral, that the prosecuting attorney will present the information to the grand jury of the prosecuting attorney's county, the task force, except as provided in division (D)(2)(b) of this section, shall refer a copy of all of the information to the attorney general, who shall proceed according to division (B) of section 109.83 of the Revised Code. If the prosecuting attorney fails to notify the commission in writing within that time that the prosecuting attorney will present the information to the grand jury, the prosecuting attorney promptly shall return all of the information that the task force referred to the prosecuting attorney under this division.

If a prosecuting attorney who has been referred information under this division notifies the commission in writing, within thirty days after the referral, of the prosecuting attorney's intention to present the information referred to the prosecuting attorney to the grand jury of the prosecuting attorney's county, the prosecuting attorney shall proceed promptly to present the information as evidence to the grand jury and shall notify the commission of the grand jury's final actions, findings of indictments, or reports. The prosecuting attorney may disclose to the attorney general any matters occurring before the grand jury that are disclosed to the prosecuting attorney for use in the performance of the prosecuting attorney's duties. The prosecuting attorney shall present the information as evidence to the grand jury prior to the discharge of the next regular grand jury. If the prosecuting attorney fails to present the information as evidence within that time, the commission, except as provided in division (D)(2)(b) of this section, shall notify the attorney general, the task force shall refer a copy of all of the information to the attorney general, and the attorney general may proceed as if the prosecuting attorney had declined under this division to accept the matter. If the prosecuting attorney fails to present the information as evidence within that time, the prosecuting attorney promptly shall return to the task force all of the information that the task force had referred to the prosecuting attorney under this division.

(b) If a prosecuting attorney who has been referred information under division (D)(2)(a) of this section fails to notify the commission in accordance with that division that the prosecuting attorney will present the information to the grand jury, and the task force that conducted the investigation determines, pursuant to its investigation, that the office of the attorney general is implicated in organized criminal activity, the task force shall not contact or refer any information to the attorney general but shall report its determinations and refer all of the information to the commission. If a prosecuting attorney who has been referred information under division (D)(2)(a) of this section notifies the commission in accordance with that division that the prosecuting attorney intends to present the information to the grand jury but fails to do so prior to the discharge of the next regular grand jury, and the task force that conducted the investigation determines, pursuant to the investigation, that the office of the attorney general is implicated in organized criminal activity, neither the commission nor the task force shall contact or refer any information to the attorney general. Instead, the task force shall report its determinations and refer all of the information gathered during the course of the investigation to the commission.

In either such case, the commission shall review the information, and, if a majority of the members of the commission determine that the office of the attorney general is implicated, the chairperson of the commission shall appear before the presiding judge of the court of common pleas or of the court of appeals for the county in which the prosecuting attorney who was referred the information serves and request the appointment of a special prosecutor to handle the matter. If the presiding judge finds that there is reasonable cause to believe that organized criminal activity has occurred or is occurring in the county or in any of the counties served by the task force and that the office of the attorney general is implicated, the judge shall appoint a special prosecutor to perform the functions of prosecuting attorney of the county in relation to the matter. The commission shall refer a copy of all of the information gathered during the course of the investigation to the special prosecutor. The special prosecutor shall review the information so referred and, upon a determination that there is cause to prosecute for the commission of a crime, the special prosecutor shall proceed promptly to present the information so referred to the grand jury and shall notify the commission of the grand jury's final actions, findings of indictments, or reports. A special prosecutor appointed under this division shall not inform the attorney general of the investigation or referral of information and shall not cooperate with the attorney general on the matter.

(3) If a task force determines, pursuant to its investigation of organized criminal activity in a single county or in two or more counties, that there is reasonable cause to believe that organized criminal activity has occurred or is occurring in the county or in any of the counties, and that the office of a prosecuting attorney who normally would be referred the information gathered during the course of the investigation pursuant to division (D)(2) of this

section is implicated by the information in organized criminal activity, the task force shall not contact or refer any information to the prosecuting attorney. Instead it shall report its determinations and refer all of the information gathered during the course of the investigation to the commission. The commission shall review the information, and if a majority of the members of the commission determine that the office of the prosecuting attorney is implicated in organized criminal activity, the chairperson of the commission shall appear before the presiding judge of the court of common pleas or of the court of appeals for the county in which that prosecuting attorney serves and request the appointment of a special prosecutor to handle the matter. If the presiding judge finds that there is reasonable cause to believe that organized criminal activity has occurred or is occurring in the county or in any of the counties served by the task force and that the office of the prosecuting attorney in question is implicated in organized criminal activity, the judge shall appoint a special prosecutor to perform the functions of prosecuting attorney of the county in relation to the matter, and the commission shall refer a copy of all of the information gathered during the course of the investigation to the special prosecutor. It shall inform the special prosecutor that the special prosecutor has thirty days to decide whether the special prosecutor should present the information to a grand jury and that if the special prosecutor intends to make a presentation of the information to the grand jury, the special prosecutor has to give the commission written notice of that intention. A special prosecutor appointed under this division shall not inform the implicated prosecuting attorney of the investigation or referral of information and shall not cooperate with the prosecutor on the matter.

If a special prosecutor who has been referred information under this division fails to notify the commission in writing, within thirty days after the referral, that the special prosecutor will present the information to the grand jury of the county, or if the presiding judge is requested pursuant to this division to appoint a special prosecutor but the judge does not do so, the commission shall refer a copy of all of the information to the attorney general, who shall proceed according to division (B) of section 109.83 of the Revised Code. Upon such a failure of a special prosecutor to notify the commission, the special prosecutor promptly shall return to the commission all of the information that the commission had referred to the special prosecutor under this division.

If a special prosecutor who has been referred information under this division notifies the commission in writing, within thirty days after the referral, of the special prosecutor's intention to present the information referred to the special prosecutor to the grand jury of the county, the special prosecutor shall proceed promptly to present the information as evidence to the grand jury and shall notify the commission of the grand jury's final actions, findings of indictments, or reports. The special prosecutor may disclose to the attorney general any matters occurring before the grand jury that are disclosed to the special prosecutor for use in the performance of the special prosecutor's duties. The information shall be presented as evidence to the grand jury prior to the discharge of the next regular grand jury. If the special prosecutor fails to present the information as evidence within that time, the commission shall notify the attorney general and refer a copy of all of the information to the attorney general, the attorney general may proceed as if the special prosecutor had declined under this division to accept the matter, and the special prosecutor promptly shall return to the commission all of the information that the commission had referred to the special prosecutor under this division.

(4) The referral of information by a task force to a prosecuting attorney, to the attorney general, to the commission, or to a special prosecutor under this division, the content, scope, and subject of any information so referred, and the identity of any person who was investigated by the task force shall be kept confidential by the task force and its director, investigatory staff, and employees, by the commission and its director, employees, and consultants, by the prosecuting attorney and the prosecuting attorney's assistants and employees, by the special prosecutor and the special prosecutor's assistants and employees, and by the attorney general and the attorney general's assistants and employees until an indictment is returned or a criminal action or proceeding is initiated in a court of proper jurisdiction.

(5) Any information gathered by a task force during the course of its investigation that is in the possession of the task force, a prosecuting attorney, the attorney general, the commission, or a special prosecutor, and any record that pertains to any such information and that is maintained by the task force, a prosecuting attorney, the attorney general, the commission, or a special prosecutor is a confidential law enforcement investigatory record for purposes of section 149.43 of the Revised Code. However, no provision contained in this division or that section affects or limits or shall be construed as affecting or limiting any right of discovery granted to any person under the Revised Code, the Rules of Criminal Procedure, or the Rules of Juvenile Procedure.

(6) In no case shall the commission, a task force, a prosecuting attorney, a special prosecutor, or the attorney general publicly issue a report or summary that identifies or enables the identification of any person who has been or is being investigated under sections 177.01 to 177.03 of the Revised Code unless an indictment is returned against the person or a criminal action or proceeding is initiated against the person in a court of proper jurisdiction.

(7) For purposes of divisions (C) and (D) of this section, the office of a prosecuting attorney, the attorney general, a sheriff, or a chief law enforcement officer shall be considered as being implicated in organized criminal activity only if the prosecuting attorney, attorney general, sheriff, or chief law enforcement officer, one or more of the assistants, deputies, or officers thereof, or one or more of the employees thereof has committed or attempted or conspired to commit, is committing or attempting or conspiring to commit, or has engaged in or is engaging in complicity in the commission of, organized criminal activity.

(8) For purposes of this section, notification by a prosecuting attorney or special prosecutor may be accomplished by certified mail or any other documentation that is agreed upon by the prosecuting attorney or special prosecutor and the commission or their representatives. Notice by certified mail is complete upon mailing.

(E) If an organized crime task force has probable cause to believe, pursuant to its investigation of organized criminal activity in a single county or in two or more counties, that a law of another state or the United States has been or is being violated, the task force director shall notify the commission chairperson of that belief and the reasons for that belief. The chairperson shall present that belief and those reasons to the commission and, if the commission determines that there is probable cause to believe that such a law has been or is being violated, the commission may refer the matter to the attorney general of the other state or to the appropriate United States attorney, whichever is applicable, and provide that attorney general or United States attorney with a copy of relevant information.

(1998 H 2, eff. 1–1–99; 1986 S 74, eff. 9–3–86)

CHAPTER 181

CRIMINAL SENTENCING COUNCIL; CRIMINAL JUSTICE SERVICES

CRIMINAL SENTENCING COUNCIL

CRIMINAL SENTENCING COUNCIL

181.21 Criminal sentencing commission

(A) There is hereby created within the supreme court the state criminal sentencing commission, consisting of thirty-one members. One member shall be the chief justice of the supreme court, who shall be the chairperson of the commission. The following ten members of the commission, no more than six of whom shall be members of the same political party, shall be appointed by the chief justice: one judge of a court of appeals, three judges of courts of common pleas who are not juvenile court judges, three judges of juvenile courts, and three judges of municipal courts or county courts. Four members shall be the superintendent of the state highway patrol, the state public defender, the director of youth services, and the director of rehabilitation and correction, or their individual designees. The following twelve members, no more than seven of whom shall be members of the same political party, shall be appointed by the governor after consulting with the appropriate state associations, if any, that are represented by these members: one sheriff; two county prosecuting attorneys, at least one of whom shall be experienced in the prosecution of cases in juvenile court involving alleged delinquent children, unruly children, and juvenile traffic offenders; two peace officers of a municipal corporation or township, at least one of whom shall be experienced in the investigation of cases involving juveniles; one former victim of a violation of Title XXIX of the Revised Code; one attorney whose practice of law primarily involves the representation of criminal defendants; one member of the Ohio state bar association; one attorney whose practice of law primarily involves the representation in juvenile court of alleged delinquent children, unruly children, and juvenile traffic offenders; one full-time city prosecuting attorney; one county commissioner; and one mayor, city manager, or member of a legislative authority of a municipal corporation. Two members shall be members of the senate, one appointed by the president of the senate and one appointed by the minority leader of the senate. Two members shall be members of the house of representatives, one appointed by the speaker of the house of representatives and one appointed by the minority leader of the house of representatives.

The chief justice shall become a member of the commission on August 22, 1990, and the chief justice's successors in office shall become members of the commission on the day that they assume the office of chief justice. The term of office of the chief justice as a member of the commission shall continue for as long as that person holds the office of chief justice. The term of office of the member who is an attorney whose practice of law primarily involves the representation of criminal defendants, the term of office of the member who is an attorney whose practice of law primarily involves the representation in juvenile court of alleged delinquent children, unruly children, and juvenile traffic offenders, and the term of office of the former victim of a violation of Title XXIX of the Revised Code shall be four years. The term of office of the superintendent of the state highway patrol, the state public defender, the director of youth services, and the director of rehabilitation and correction, or their individual designees, as members of the commission shall continue for as long as they hold the office of superintendent of the state highway patrol, state public defender, director of youth services, or director of rehabilitation and correction. The term of office of a municipal corporation or township peace officer as a member of the commission shall be the lesser of four years or until that person ceases to be a peace officer of a municipal corporation or township. Unless the full-time city prosecuting attorney is an elected official, the term of office of the full-time city prosecuting attorney shall be the lesser of four years or until the full-time city prosecuting attorney ceases to be a full-time city prosecuting attorney. All of the members of the commission who are elected officials shall serve the lesser of four years or until the expiration of their term of office. Any vacancy on the commission shall be filled in the same manner as the original appointment.

When the chief justice and governor make their appointments to the commission, they shall consider adequate representation by race and gender.

(B) The commission shall select a vice-chairperson and any other necessary officers and adopt rules to govern its proceedings. The commission shall meet as necessary at the call of the chairperson or on the written request of eight or more of its members. Sixteen members of the commission constitute a quorum, and the votes of a majority of the quorum present shall be required to validate any action of the commission. All business of the commission shall be conducted in public meetings.

The members of the commission shall serve without compensation, but each member shall be reimbursed for the member's actual and necessary expenses incurred in the performance of the member's official duties on the commission. In the absence of the chairperson, the vice-chairperson shall perform the duties of the chairperson.

(C) The commission shall establish an office and shall appoint and fix the compensation of a project director and any other employees necessary to assist the commission in the execution of its authority under sections 181.21 to 181.26 of the Revised Code. The project director shall have a thorough understanding of the criminal laws of this state and experience in committee-oriented research. The other employees may include a research coordinator with experience and training in policy-oriented research; professional staff employees with backgrounds in criminal law, criminal justice, political science, or related fields of expertise; administrative assistants; and secretaries. The commission also may appoint and fix the compensation of part-time data collectors, clerical employees, and other temporary employees as needed to enable the commission to execute its authority under sections 181.21 to 181.26 of the Revised Code.

(D) The sentencing commission shall establish a standing juvenile committee. The committee shall consist of the following commission members: the chief justice of the supreme court or the chief justice's designee, the director of youth services, the three juvenile court judges, one court of common pleas judge who is not a juvenile court judge, one county prosecuting attorney who is experienced in the prosecution of cases in juvenile court involving alleged delinquent children, unruly children, and juvenile traffic offenders, the attorney whose practice of law primarily involves the representation in juvenile court of alleged delinquent children, unruly children, and juvenile traffic offenders, the former victim of a violation of Title XXIX of the Revised Code, the county commissioner, one legislator from each political party, the sheriff, and one municipal corporation or township peace officer who is experienced in the investigation of cases involving juveniles. The members of the commission may serve on the committee by designation of the chief justice. The chief justice shall designate a member to serve as chairperson of the committee. The committee shall meet as necessary at the call of the chairperson or on the written request of four or more of the committee's members. A majority of the members of the committee shall constitute a quorum, and the votes of a majority of the quorum present shall be required to validate any action of the committee, including recommendations to the commission. The committee and the commission shall comply with section 181.26 of the Revised Code.

(1999 S 107, eff. 3–23–00; 1996 H 670, eff. 12–2–96; 1996 H 591, eff. 3–13–97; 1994 H 21, eff. 2–4–94; 1993 H 152, eff. 7–1–93; 1990 S 258)

181.22 Criminal sentencing advisory committee

There is hereby created the criminal sentencing advisory committee. The committee shall be comprised of the chairperson of the parole board, the director of the office of the correctional institution inspection committee, a juvenile detention facility operator, a provider of juvenile probation or community control services, a provider of juvenile parole or aftercare services, a superintendent of a state institution operated by the department of youth services, a community-based juvenile services provider, a person who is a member of a youth advocacy organization, a victim of a violation of Title XXIX of the Revised Code that was committed by a juvenile offender, a representative of community corrections programming appointed by the governor, and any other members appointed by the chairperson of the state criminal sentencing commission upon the advice of the commission. The committee shall serve as an advisory body to the state criminal sentencing commission and to the commission's standing juvenile committee.

The members of the committee shall serve without compensation, but each member shall be reimbursed for the member's actual and necessary expenses incurred in the performance of the member's official duties.

(2000 S 179, § 3, eff. 1–1–02; 1999 S 107, eff. 3–23–00; 1996 H 670, eff. 12–2–96; 1996 H 591, eff. 3–13–97; 1994 H 21, eff. 2–4–94; 1993 H 152, eff. 7–1–93; 1991 H 298; 1990 S 258)

181.23 Study of criminal statutes, sentencing patterns, and available correctional resources

(A) The state criminal sentencing commission shall study the existing criminal statutes and law of this state, sentencing patterns throughout the state, and available correctional resources. The commission shall use the results of its study to develop and recommend to the general assembly a comprehensive criminal sentencing structure. As part of its study, the commission shall do all of the following:

(1) Evaluate the effectiveness of the sentencing structure of the state;

(2) Systematically review each criminal statute to determine if the penalty provided is proportional to the seriousness of the offense committed and to penalties provided for other offenses;

(3) Review any existing sentencing guidelines;

(4) Determine the number, capacity, and quality of all available state, regional, and local correctional facilities and resources, including, but not limited to, detention facilities, probation services, pretrial diversion programs, and other nonfacility correctional programs;

(5) Collect a profile of the populations of state, regional, and local correctional facilities, services, and programs;

(6) Coordinate available correctional facilities, services, and programs with the criminal sentencing goals of the state, including, but not limited to, punishment, deterrence, fairness, rehabilitation, and treatment;

(7) Identify any additional correctional resources that are necessary to balance the needs of criminal sentencing and the available correctional resources.

(B) The commission shall develop a sentencing policy for the state that is based upon the findings and conclusions of its study under division (A) of this section. The policy shall be designed to enhance public safety by achieving certainty in sentencing, deterrence, and a reasonable use of correctional facilities, programs, and services and shall be designed to achieve fairness in sentencing.

(1999 S 107, eff. 3–23–00; 1996 H 670, eff. 12–2–96; 1990 S 258, eff. 8–22–90)

181.24 Recommendation of comprehensive criminal sentencing structure

(A) No later than July 1, 1993, the state criminal sentencing commission shall recommend to the general assembly a comprehensive criminal sentencing structure for the state that is consistent with the sentencing policy developed pursuant to division (B) of section 181.23 of the Revised Code and the conclusions of the study conducted pursuant to division (A) of that section. The sentencing structure shall be designed to enhance public safety, to assist in the management of prison overcrowding and correctional resources, to simplify the sentencing structure of the state that is in existence on August 22, 1990, and to result in a new sentencing structure that is readily understandable by the citizens of the state, to simplify the criminal code of the state, to assure proportionality, uniformity, and other fairness in criminal sentencing, and to provide increased certainty in criminal sentencing.

(B) The comprehensive criminal sentencing structure recommended by the commission shall provide for all of the following:

(1) Proportionate sentences, with increased penalties for offenses based upon the seriousness of the offense and the criminal history of the offender;

(2) Procedures for ensuring that the penalty imposed for a criminal offense upon similar offenders is uniform in all jurisdictions in the state;

(3) Retention of reasonable judicial discretion within established limits that are consistent with the goals of the overall criminal sentencing structure;

(4) Procedures for matching criminal penalties with the available correctional facilities, programs, and services;

(5) A structure and procedures that control the use and duration of a full range of sentencing options that is consistent with public safety, including, but not limited to, long terms of imprisonment, probation, fines, and other sanctions that do not involve incarceration;

(6) Appropriate reasons for judicial discretion in departing from the general sentencing structure.

(C) The commission shall project the impact of all aspects of the comprehensive criminal sentencing structure upon the capacities of existing correctional facilities. It also shall project the effect of parole release patterns and patterns of release from regional and local jails, workhouses, and other correctional facilities upon the sentencing structure. Additionally, the commission shall determine whether any additional correctional facilities are necessary to implement the sentencing structure.

(D) The commission shall determine whether any special appellate procedures are necessary for reviewing departures from, or the misapplication of, the general sentencing structure recommended pursuant to this section.

(E) The commission shall submit a draft version of the comprehensive criminal sentencing structure to selected judges, prosecuting attorneys, defense attorneys, law enforcement officials, correctional officials, bar associations, and other persons with experience or expertise in criminal sentencing and solicit their comments on the draft.

(1999 S 107, eff. 3-23-00; 1996 H 670, eff. 12-2-96; 1992 S 273, eff. 3-6-92; 1990 S 258)

181.25 Duties upon implementation of sentencing structure

(A) If the comprehensive criminal sentencing structure that it recommends to the general assembly pursuant to section 181.24 of the Revised Code or any aspects of that sentencing structure are enacted into law, the state criminal sentencing commission shall do all of the following:

(1) Assist the general assembly in the implementation of those aspects of the sentencing structure that are enacted into law;

(2) Monitor the operation of the aspects of the sentencing structure that are enacted into law and report to the general assembly no later than January 1, 1997, and biennially thereafter, on all of the following matters:

(a) The impact of the sentencing structure in effect on and after July 1, 1996, on political subdivisions and other relevant aspects of local government in this state, including all of the following information:

(i) The number and type of offenders who were being imprisoned in a state correctional institution under the law in effect prior to July 1, 1996, but who are being punished under a community control sanction, as defined in section 2929.01 of the Revised Code, under the law in effect on and after July 1, 1996;

(ii) The fiscal and other impact of the law in effect on and after July 1, 1996, on political subdivisions and other relevant aspects of local government in this state, including law enforcement agencies, the court system, prosecutors, as defined in section 2935.01 of the Revised Code, the public defender and assigned counsel system, jails and workhouses, probation departments, the drug and alcohol abuse intervention and treatment system, and the mental health intervention and treatment system.

(b) The impact of the sentencing structure in effect on and after July 1, 1996, on the population of state correctional institutions, including information regarding the number and types of offenders who are being imprisoned under the law in effect on and after July 1, 1996, and the amount of space in state correctional institutions that is necessary to house those offenders;

(c) The impact of the sentencing structure and the sentence appeal provisions in effect on and after July 1, 1996, on the appellate courts of this state, including information regarding the number of sentence-based appeals, the cost of reviewing appeals of that nature, whether a special court should be created to review sentences, and whether changes should be made to ensure that sentence-based appeals are conducted expeditiously.

(3) Review all bills that are introduced in the general assembly that provide for new criminal offenses or that change the penalty for any criminal offense, determine if those bills are consistent with the sentencing policy adopted under division (B) of section 181.23 of the Revised Code, determine the impact of those bills upon the correctional resources of the state, and recommend to the general assembly any necessary amendments to those bills. When the commission recommends any amendment for a bill before the general assembly, it shall do so in a manner that is consistent with the requirements of section 181.24 of the Revised Code.

(4) Study criminal sentencing structures in this state, other states, and the federal government, recommend necessary changes to the sentencing structure of the state, and determine the costs and effects of any proposed changes in the sentencing structure of the state;

(5) Collect and maintain data that pertains to the cost to counties of the felony sentence appeal provisions set forth in section 2953.08 of the Revised Code, of the postconviction relief proceeding provisions set forth in division (A)(2) of section 2953.21 of the Revised Code, and of appeals from judgments entered in such postconviction relief proceedings. The data so collected and maintained shall include, but shall not be limited to, the increase in expenses that counties experience as a result of those provisions and those appeals and the number of felony sentence appeals made, postconviction relief proceedings filed, and appeals of postconviction relief proceeding judgments made in each county under those provisions. The commission periodically shall provide to the felony sentence appeal cost oversight committee, in accordance with division (I) of section 2953.08 of the Revised Code, all data the commission collects pursuant to this division.

(B) In addition to its duties set forth in section 181.24 of the Revised Code and division (A) of this section, the state criminal sentencing commission shall review all forfeiture statutes in Titles XXIX and XLV of the Revised Code and, not later than July 1, 2002, recommend to the general assembly any necessary changes to those statutes.

(2002 H 327, eff. 7-8-02; 1999 S 107, eff. 3-23-00; 1996 H 670, eff. 12-2-96; 1995 S 2, eff. 7-1-96; 1990 S 258, eff. 8-22-90)

181.26 Comprehensive plan regarding disposition of juvenile matters

(A) In addition to its duties set forth in sections 181.23 to 181.25 of the Revised Code, the state criminal sentencing commission shall do all of the following:

(1) Review all statutes governing delinquent child, unruly child, and juvenile traffic offender dispositions in this state;

(2) Review state and local resources, including facilities and programs, used for delinquent child, unruly child, and juvenile traffic offender dispositions and profile the populations of youthful offenders in the facilities and programs;

(3) Report to the general assembly no later than October 1, 1999, a comprehensive plan containing recommendations based on the reviews required under divisions (A)(1) and (2) of this section. The recommendations shall do all of the following:

(a) Assist in the managing of the number of persons in, and costs of, the facilities, the programs, and other resources used in delinquent child, unruly child, and juvenile traffic offender dispositions;

(b) Foster rehabilitation, public safety, sanctions, accountability, and other reasonable goals;

(c) Provide greater certainty, proportionality, uniformity, fairness, and simplicity in delinquent child, unruly child, and juvenile traffic offender dispositions while retaining reasonable judicial discretion;

(d) Provide for the restoration of victims of juvenile offenses.

(B) The commission shall project the impact of the comprehensive plan recommended by the commission under this section on state and local resources used in delinquent child, unruly child, and juvenile traffic offender dispositions. The commission shall determine whether any additional facilities, programs, or other resources are needed to implement the comprehensive plan.

(C) If the general assembly enacts all or a substantial part of the comprehensive plan recommended by the commission under this section, the commission shall do all of the following:

(1) Assist in the implementation of the enacted plan;

(2) Monitor the operation of the plan, periodically report to the general assembly on the plan's operation and the plan's impact on resources used in delinquent child, unruly child, and juvenile traffic offender dispositions, and periodically recommend changes in the plan to the general assembly based on this monitoring;

(3) Review all bills that are introduced in the general assembly that relate to delinquent child, unruly child, and juvenile traffic offender dispositions and assist the general assembly in making legislation consistent with the plan.

(1998 H 484, eff. 3–18–99; 1997 H 1, eff. 11–25–97; 1996 H 591, eff. 3–13–97)

CRIMINAL SENTENCING COUNCIL; CRIMINAL JUSTICE SERVICES

181.51 Definitions

As used in sections 181.51 to 181.56 of the Revised Code:

(A) "Federal criminal justice acts" means any federal law that authorizes financial assistance and other forms of assistance to be given by the federal government to the states to be used for the improvement of the criminal and juvenile justice systems of the states.

(B)(1) "Criminal justice system" includes all of the functions of the following:

(a) The state highway patrol, county sheriff offices, municipal and township police departments, and all other law enforcement agencies;

(b) The courts of appeals, courts of common pleas, municipal courts, county courts, and mayor's courts, when dealing with criminal cases;

(c) The prosecuting attorneys, city directors of law, village solicitors, and other prosecuting authorities when prosecuting or otherwise handling criminal cases and the county and joint county public defenders and other public defender agencies or offices;

(d) The department of rehabilitation and correction, probation departments, county and municipal jails and workhouses, and any other department, agency, or facility that is concerned with the rehabilitation or correction of criminal offenders;

(e) Any public or private agency whose purposes include the prevention of crime or the diversion, adjudication, detention, or rehabilitation of criminal offenders;

(f) Any public or private agency, the purposes of which include assistance to crime victims or witnesses.

(2) The inclusion of any public or private agency, the purposes of which include assistance to crime victims or witnesses, as part of the criminal justice system pursuant to division (B)(1) of this section does not limit, and shall not be construed as limiting, the discretion or authority of the attorney general with respect to crime victim assistance and criminal justice programs.

(C) "Juvenile justice system" includes all of the functions of the juvenile courts, the department of youth services, any public or private agency whose purposes include the prevention of delinquency or the diversion, adjudication, detention, or rehabilitation of delinquent children, and any of the functions of the criminal justice system that are applicable to children.

(D) "Comprehensive plan" means a document that coordinates, evaluates, and otherwise assists, on an annual or multi-year basis, any of the functions of the criminal and juvenile justice systems of the state or a specified area of the state, that conforms to the priorities of the state with respect to criminal and juvenile justice systems, and that conforms with the requirements of all federal criminal justice acts. These functions may include, but are not limited to, any of the following:

(1) Crime and delinquency prevention;

(2) Identification, detection, apprehension, and detention of persons charged with criminal offenses or delinquent acts;

(3) Assistance to crime victims or witnesses, except that the comprehensive plan does not include the functions of the attorney general pursuant to sections 109.91 and 109.92 of the Revised Code;

(4) Adjudication or diversion of persons charged with criminal offenses or delinquent acts;

(5) Custodial treatment of criminal offenders, delinquent children, or both;

(6) Institutional and noninstitutional rehabilitation of criminal offenders, delinquent children, or both.

(E) "Metropolitan county criminal justice services agency" means an agency that is established pursuant to division (A) of section 181.54 of the Revised Code.

(F) "Administrative planning district" means a district that is established pursuant to division (A) or (B) of section 181.56 of the Revised Code.

(G) "Criminal justice coordinating council" means a criminal justice services agency that is established pursuant to division (D) of section 181.56 of the Revised Code.

(H) "Local elected official" means any person who is a member of a board of county commissioners or township trustees or of a city or village council, judge of the court of common pleas, a municipal court, or a county court, sheriff, county coroner, prosecuting attorney, city director of law, village solicitor, or mayor.

(I) "Juvenile justice coordinating council" means a juvenile justice services agency that is established pursuant to division (D) of section 181.56 of the Revised Code.

(2001 H 94, eff. 9–5–01; 1993 H 152, eff. 7–1–93)

181.52 Criminal justice services office; federal purposes fund

(A) There is hereby created an office of criminal justice services. The governor shall appoint a director of the office, and the director may appoint, within the office, any professional and technical personnel and other employees that are necessary to enable the office to comply with sections 181.51 to 181.56 of the Revised Code. The director and the assistant director of the office, and all professional and technical personnel employed within the office who are not public employees as defined in section 4117.01 of the Revised Code, shall be in the unclassified civil service, and all other persons employed within the office shall be in the classified civil service. The director may enter into any contracts, except contracts governed by Chapter 4117. of the Revised Code, that are necessary for the operation of the office.

(B) Subject to division (E) of this section and subject to divisions (D) to (F) of section 5120.09 of the Revised Code insofar as those divisions relate to federal criminal justice acts that the governor requires the department of rehabilitation and correction to administer, the office of criminal justice services shall do all of the following:

(1) Serve as the state criminal justice services agency and perform criminal justice system planning in the state, including any planning that is required by any federal law;

(2) Collect, analyze, and correlate information and data concerning the criminal justice system in the state;

(3) Cooperate with and provide technical assistance to state departments, administrative planning districts, metropolitan county criminal justice services agencies, criminal justice coordinating councils, agencies, offices, and departments of the criminal justice system in the state, and other appropriate organizations and persons;

(4) Encourage and assist agencies, offices, and departments of the criminal justice system in the state and other appropriate organizations and persons to solve problems that relate to the duties of the office;

(5) Administer within the state any federal criminal justice acts that the governor requires it to administer;

(6) Administer funds received under the "Family Violence Prevention and Services Act," 98 Stat. 1757 (1984), 42 U.S.C.A. 10401, as amended, with all powers necessary for the adequate administration of those funds, including the authority to establish a family violence prevention and services program.

(7) Implement the state comprehensive plans;

(8) Audit grant activities of agencies, offices, organizations, and persons that are financed in whole or in part by funds granted through the office;

(9) Monitor or evaluate the performance of criminal justice system projects and programs in the state that are financed in whole or in part by funds granted through the office;

(10) Apply for, allocate, disburse, and account for grants that are made available pursuant to federal criminal justice acts, or made available from other federal, state, or private sources, to improve the criminal justice system in the state. All money from such federal grants shall, if the terms under which the money is received require that the money be deposited into an interest-bearing fund or account, be deposited in the state treasury to the credit of the federal program purposes fund, which is hereby created. All investment earnings of the fund shall be credited to the fund.

(11) Contract with federal, state, and local agencies, foundations, corporations, businesses, and persons when necessary to carry out the duties of the office;

(12) Oversee the activities of metropolitan county criminal justice services agencies, administrative planning districts, and criminal justice coordinating councils in the state;

(13) Advise the general assembly and governor on legislation and other significant matters that pertain to the improvement and reform of criminal and juvenile justice systems in the state;

(14) Prepare and recommend legislation to the general assembly and governor for the improvement of the criminal and juvenile justice systems in the state;

(15) Assist, advise, and make any reports that are requested or required by the governor, attorney general, or general assembly;

(16) Adopt rules pursuant to Chapter 119. of the Revised Code.

(C) Upon the request of the governor, the office of criminal justice services may do any of the following:

(1) Collect, analyze, or correlate information and data concerning the juvenile justice system in the state;

(2) Cooperate with and provide technical assistance to state departments, administrative planning districts, metropolitan county criminal justice service agencies, criminal justice coordinating councils, agency offices, and the departments of the juvenile justice system in the state and other appropriate organizations and persons;

(3) Encourage and assist agencies, offices, and departments of the juvenile justice system in the state and other appropriate organizations and persons to solve problems that relate to the duties of the office.

(D) Divisions (B) and (C) of this section do not limit the discretion or authority of the attorney general with respect to crime victim assistance and criminal justice programs.

(E) Nothing in this section is intended to diminish or alter the status of the office of the attorney general as a criminal justice services agency.

(2001 H 94, eff. 6–6–01; 1999 H 283, eff. 9–29–99; 1997 H 215, eff. 9–29–97; 1994 H 715, eff. 7–22–94; 1993 H 152, eff. 7–1–93)

181.53 Advisory committees

The governor may appoint any advisory committees to assist the office of criminal justice services that he considers appropriate or that are required under any state or federal law.

(1993 H 152, eff. 7–1–93)

181.54 Metropolitan county criminal justice services agencies

(A) A county may enter into an agreement with the largest city within the county to establish a metropolitan county criminal justice services agency, if the population of the county exceeds five hundred thousand or the population of the city exceeds two hundred fifty thousand.

(B) A metropolitan county criminal justice services agency shall do all of the following:

(1) Accomplish criminal and juvenile justice systems planning within its services area;

(2) Collect, analyze, and correlate information and data concerning the criminal and juvenile justice systems within its services area;

(3) Cooperate with and provide technical assistance to all criminal and juvenile justice agencies and systems and other appropriate organizations and persons within its services area;

(4) Encourage and assist agencies of the criminal and juvenile justice systems and other appropriate organizations and persons to solve problems that relate to its duties;

(5) Administer within its services area any federal criminal justice acts or juvenile justice acts that the office of criminal justice services pursuant to section 5139.11 of the Revised Code or the department of youth services administers within the state;

(6) Implement the comprehensive plans for its services area;

(7) Monitor or evaluate, within its services area, the performance of the criminal and juvenile justice systems projects and programs that are financed in whole or in part by funds granted through it;

(8) Apply for, allocate, and disburse grants that are made available pursuant to any federal criminal justice acts, or pursuant to any other federal, state, or private sources for the purpose of improving the criminal and juvenile justice systems;

(9) Contract with federal, state, and local agencies, foundations, corporations, and other businesses or persons to carry out the duties of the agency.

(2001 H 94, eff. 9–5–01; 1993 H 152, eff. 7–1–93)

181.55 Comprehensive plans

(A)(1) When funds are available for criminal justice purposes pursuant to section 181.54 of the Revised Code, the office of criminal justice services shall provide funds to metropolitan county criminal justice services agencies for the purpose of developing, coordinating, evaluating, and implementing comprehensive plans within their respective counties. The office of criminal justice services shall provide funds to an agency only if it complies with the conditions of division (B) of this section.

(2) When funds are available for juvenile justice purposes pursuant to section 181.54 of the Revised Code, the department of youth services shall provide funds to metropolitan county criminal justice services agencies for the purpose of developing, coordinating, evaluating, and implementing comprehensive plans within their respective counties. The department shall provide funds to an agency only if it complies with the conditions of division (B) of this section.

(B) A metropolitan county criminal justice services agency shall do all of the following:

(1) Submit, in a form that is acceptable to the office of criminal justice services or the department of youth services pursuant to section 5139.01 of the Revised Code, a comprehensive plan for the county;

(2) Establish a metropolitan county criminal justice services supervisory board whose members shall include a majority of the local elected officials in the county and representatives from law enforcement agencies, courts, prosecuting authorities, public defender agencies, rehabilitation and correction agencies, community organizations, juvenile justice services agencies, professionals, and private citizens in the county, and that shall have the authority set forth in division (C) of this section;

(3) Organize in the manner provided in sections 167.01 to 167.03, 302.21 to 302.24, or 713.21 to 713.27 of the Revised Code, unless the board created pursuant to division (B)(2) of this section organizes pursuant to these sections.

(C) A metropolitan county criminal justice services supervisory board shall do all of the following:

(1) Exercise leadership in improving the quality of the criminal and juvenile justice systems in the county;

(2) Review, approve, and maintain general oversight of the comprehensive plans for the county and the implementation of the plans;

(3) Review and comment on the overall needs and accomplishments of the criminal and juvenile justice systems in the county;

(4) Establish, as required to comply with this division, task forces, ad hoc committees, and other committees, whose members shall be appointed by the chairperson of the board;

(5) Establish any rules that the board considers necessary and that are consistent with the federal criminal justice acts and section 181.52 of the Revised Code.

(2001 H 94, eff. 9–5–01; 1993 H 152, eff. 7–1–93)

181.56 Administrative planning districts; criminal justice coordinating councils or juvenile justice coordinating councils

(A) In counties in which a metropolitan county criminal justice services agency does not exist, the office of criminal justice services shall discharge the office's duties that the governor requires it to administer by establishing administrative planning districts for criminal justice programs. An administrative planning district shall contain a group of contiguous counties in which no county has a metropolitan county criminal justice services agency.

(B) In counties in which a metropolitan county criminal justice services agency does not exist, the department of youth services shall discharge pursuant to section 5139.11 of the Revised Code the department's duty by establishing administrative planning districts for juvenile justice programs.

(C) All administrative planning districts shall contain a group of contiguous counties in which no county has a metropolitan county criminal justice services agency.

(D) Any county or any combination of contiguous counties within an administrative planning district may form a criminal justice coordinating council or a juvenile justice coordinating council for its respective programs, if the county or the group of counties has a total population in excess of two hundred fifty thousand. The council shall comply with the conditions set forth in divisions (B) and (C) of section 181.55 of the Revised Code, and exercise within its jurisdiction the powers and duties set forth in division (B) of section 181.54 of the Revised Code.

(2001 H 94, eff. 9–5–01; 1993 H 152, eff. 7–1–93)

CHAPTER 306

REGIONAL TRANSIT AUTHORITY

306.35 Powers and duties

Upon the creation of a regional transit authority as provided by section 306.32 of the Revised Code, and upon the qualifying of its board of trustees and the election of a president and a vice-president, the authority shall exercise in its own name all the rights, powers, and duties vested in and conferred upon it by sections 306.30 to 306.53 of the Revised Code. Subject to any reservations, limitations, and qualifications that are set forth in those sections, the regional transit authority:

(A) May sue or be sued in its corporate name;

(B) May make contracts in the exercise of the rights, powers, and duties conferred upon it;

(C) May adopt and at will alter a seal and use such seal by causing it to be impressed, affixed, reproduced, or otherwise used, but failure to affix the seal shall not affect the validity of any instrument;

(D)(1) May adopt, amend, and repeal bylaws for the administration of its affairs and rules for the control of the administration and operation of transit facilities under its jurisdiction, and for the exercise of all of its rights of ownership in those transit facilities;

(2) The regional transit authority also may adopt bylaws and rules for the following purposes:

(a) To prohibit selling, giving away, or using any beer or intoxicating liquor on transit vehicles or transit property;

(b) For the preservation of good order within or on transit vehicles or transit property;

(c) To provide for the protection and preservation of all property and life within or on transit vehicles or transit property;

(d) To regulate and enforce the collection of fares.

(3) Before a bylaw or rule adopted under division (D)(2) of this section takes effect, the regional transit authority shall provide for a notice of its adoption to be published once a week for two consecutive weeks in a newspaper of general circulation within the territorial boundaries of the regional transit authority.

(4) No person shall violate any bylaw or rule of a regional transit authority adopted under division (D)(2) of this section.

(E) May fix, alter, and collect fares, rates, and rentals and other charges for the use of transit facilities under its jurisdiction to be determined exclusively by it for the purpose of providing for the payment of the expenses of the regional transit authority, the acquisition, construction, improvement, extension, repair, maintenance, and operation of transit facilities under its jurisdiction, the payment of principal and interest on its obligations, and to fulfill the terms of any agreements made with purchasers or holders of any such obligations, or with any person or political subdivision;

(F) Shall have jurisdiction, control, possession, and supervision of all property, rights, easements, licenses, moneys, contracts, accounts, liens, books, records, maps, or other property rights and interests conveyed, delivered, transferred, or assigned to it;

(G) May acquire, construct, improve, extend, repair, lease, operate, maintain, or manage transit facilities within or without its territorial boundaries, considered necessary to accomplish the purposes of its organization and make charges for the use of transit facilities;

(H) May levy and collect taxes as provided in sections 306.40 and 306.49 of the Revised Code;

(I) May issue bonds secured by its general credit as provided in section 306.40 of the Revised Code;

(J) May hold, encumber, control, acquire by donation, by purchase for cash or by installment payments, by lease-purchase agreement, by lease with option to purchase, or by condemnation, and may construct, own, lease as lessee or lessor, use, and sell, real and personal property, or any interest or right in real and personal property, within or without its territorial boundaries, for the location or protection of transit facilities and improvements and access to transit facilities and improvements, the relocation of buildings, structures, and improvements situated on lands acquired by the regional transit authority, or for any other necessary purpose, or for obtaining or storing materials to be used in constructing, maintaining, and improving transit facilities under its jurisdiction;

(K) May exercise the power of eminent domain to acquire property or any interest in property, within or without its territorial boundaries, that is necessary or proper for the construction or efficient operation of any transit facility or access to any transit facility under its jurisdiction in accordance with section 306.36 of the Revised Code;

(L) May provide by agreement with any county, including the counties within its territorial boundaries, or any municipal corporation or any combination of counties or municipal corporations for the making of necessary surveys, appraisals, and examinations preliminary to the acquisition or construction of any transit facility and the amount of the expense for the surveys, appraisals, and examinations to be paid by each such county or municipal corporation;

(M) May provide by agreement with any county, including the counties within its territorial boundaries, or any municipal corporation or any combination of those counties or municipal corporations for the acquisition, construction, improvement, extension, maintenance, or operation of any transit facility owned or to be owned and operated by it or owned or to be owned and operated by any such county or municipal corporation and the terms on which it shall be acquired, leased, constructed, maintained, or operated, and the amount of the cost and expense of the acquisition, lease, construction, maintenance, or operation to be paid by each such county or municipal corporation;

(N) May issue revenue bonds for the purpose of acquiring, replacing, improving, extending, enlarging, or constructing any facility or permanent improvement that it is authorized to acquire, replace, improve, extend, enlarge, or construct, including all costs in connection with and incidental to the acquisition, replacement, improvement, extension, enlargement, or construction, and their financing, as provided by section 306.37 of the Revised Code;

(O) May enter into and supervise franchise agreements for the operation of a transit system;

(P) May accept the assignment of and supervise an existing franchise agreement for the operation of a transit system;

(Q) May exercise a right to purchase a transit system in accordance with the acquisition terms of an existing franchise agreement; and in connection with the purchase the regional transit authority may issue revenue bonds as provided by section 306.37 of the Revised Code or issue bonds secured by its general credit as provided in section 306.40 of the Revised Code;

(R) May apply for and accept grants or loans from the United States, the state, or any other public body for the purpose of providing for the development or improvement of transit facilities, mass transportation facilities, equipment, techniques, methods, or services, and grants or loans needed to exercise a right to purchase a transit system pursuant to agreement with the owner of those transit facilities, or for providing lawful financial assistance to existing transit systems; and may provide any consideration that may be required in order to obtain those grants or loans from the United States, the state, or other public body, either of which grants or loans may be evidenced by the issuance of revenue bonds as provided by section 306.37 of the Revised Code or general obligation bonds as provided by section 306.40 of the Revised Code;

(S) May employ and fix the compensation of consulting engineers, superintendents, managers, and such other engineering, construction, accounting and financial experts, attorneys, and other employees and agents necessary for the accomplishment of its purposes;

(T) May procure insurance against loss to it by reason of damages to its properties resulting from fire, theft, accident, or other casualties or by reason of its liability for any damages to persons or property occurring in the construction or operation of transit facilities under its jurisdiction or the conduct of its activities;

(U) May maintain funds that it considers necessary for the efficient performance of its duties;

(V) May direct its agents or employees, when properly identified in writing, after at least five days' written notice, to enter upon lands within or without its territorial boundaries in order to make surveys and examinations preliminary to the location and construction of transit facilities, without liability to it or its agents or employees except for actual damage done;

(W) On its own motion, may request the appropriate zoning board, as defined in section 4563.03 of the Revised Code, to establish and enforce zoning regulations pertaining to any transit facility under its jurisdiction in the manner prescribed by sections 4563.01 to 4563.21 of the Revised Code;

(X) If it acquires any existing transit system, shall assume all the employer's obligations under any existing labor contract between the employees and management of the system. If the board acquires, constructs, controls, or operates any such facilities, it shall negotiate arrangements to protect the interests of employees affected by the acquisition, construction, control, or operation. The arrangements shall include, but are not limited to:

(1) The preservation of rights, privileges, and benefits under existing collective bargaining agreements or otherwise, the preservation of rights and benefits under any existing pension plans covering prior service, and continued participation in social security in addition to participation in the public employees retirement system as required in Chapter 145. of the Revised Code;

(2) The continuation of collective bargaining rights;

(3) The protection of individual employees against a worsening of their positions with respect to their employment;

(4) Assurances of employment to employees of those transit systems and priority reemployment of employees terminated or laid off;

(5) Paid training or retraining programs;

(6) Signed written labor agreements.

The arrangements may include provisions for the submission of labor disputes to final and binding arbitration.

(Y) May provide for and maintain security operations, including a transit police department, subject to section 306.352 of the Revised Code. Regional transit authority police officers shall have the power and duty to act as peace officers within transit facilities owned, operated, or leased by the transit authority to protect the transit authority's property and the person and property of passengers, to preserve the peace, and to enforce all laws of the state and ordinances and regulations of political subdivisions in which the transit authority operates. Regional transit authority police officers also shall have the power and duty to act as peace officers when they render emergency assistance outside their jurisdiction to any other peace officer who is not a regional transit authority police officer and who has arrest authority under section 2935.03 of the Revised Code. Regional transit authority police officers may render emergency assistance if there is a threat of imminent physical danger to the peace officer, a threat of physical harm to another person, or any other serious emergency situation and if either the peace officer who is assisted requests emergency assistance or it appears that the peace officer who is assisted is unable to request emergency assistance and the circumstances observed by the regional transit authority police officer reasonably indicate that emergency assistance is appropriate.

Before exercising powers of arrest and the other powers and duties of a peace officer, each regional transit authority police officer shall take an oath and give bond to the state in a sum that the board of trustees prescribes for the proper performance of the officer's duties.

Persons employed as regional transit authority police officers shall complete training for the position to which they have been appointed as required by the Ohio peace officer training commission as authorized in section 109.77 of the Revised Code, or be otherwise qualified. The cost of the training shall be provided by the regional transit authority.

(Z) May procure a policy or policies insuring members of its board of trustees against liability on account of damages or injury to persons and property resulting from any act or omission of a member in the member's official capacity as a member of the board or resulting solely out of the member's membership on the board;

(AA) May enter into any agreement for the sale and leaseback or lease and leaseback of transit facilities, which agreement may contain all necessary covenants for the security and protection of any lessor or the regional transit authority including, but not limited to, indemnification of the lessor against the loss of anticipated tax benefits arising from acts, omissions, or misrepresentations of the regional transit authority. In connection with that transaction, the regional transit authority may contract for insurance and letters of credit and pay any premiums or other charges for the insurance and letters of credit. The fiscal officer shall not be required to furnish any certificate under section 5705.41 of the Revised Code in connection with the execution of any such agreement.

(BB) In regard to any contract entered into on or after March 19, 1993, for the rendering of services or the supplying of materials or for the construction, demolition, alteration, repair, or reconstruction of transit facilities in which a bond is required for the faithful performance of the contract, may permit the person awarded the contract to utilize a letter of credit issued by a bank or other financial institution in lieu of the bond;

(CC) May enter into agreements with municipal corporations located within the territorial jurisdiction of the regional transit authority permitting regional transit authority police officers employed under division (Y) of this section to exercise full arrest powers, as provided in section 2935.03 of the Revised Code, for the purpose of preserving the peace and enforcing all laws of the state and ordinances and regulations of the municipal corporation within the areas that may be agreed to by the regional transit authority and the municipal corporation.

(2003 H 95, eff. 9–26–03; 1997 H 228, eff. 5–7–97; 1996 H 670, eff. 12–2–96; 1996 H 566, eff. 10–16–96; 1996 S 269, eff. 7–1–96; 1995 S 2, eff. 7–1–96; 1992 S 164, eff. 3–19–93; 1982 S 543; 1977 S 194; 1976 S 427; 1970 S 125; 131 v H 421)

306.352 Offenses affecting employment eligibility of regional transit authority police officers

(A) As used in this section, "felony" has the same meaning as in section 109.511 of the Revised Code.

(B)(1) In the exercise of its authority under division (Y) of section 306.35 of the Revised Code, a regional transit authority shall not employ a person as a regional transit authority police officer on a permanent basis, on a temporary basis, for a probationary term, or on other than a permanent basis if the person previously has been convicted of or has pleaded guilty to a felony.

(2)(a) The transit authority shall terminate the employment of a person as a regional transit authority police officer if the person does either of the following:

(i) Pleads guilty to a felony;

(ii) Pleads guilty to a misdemeanor pursuant to a negotiated plea agreement as provided in division (D) of section 2929.43 of the Revised Code in which the police officer agrees to surrender the certificate awarded to that police officer under section 109.77 of the Revised Code.

(b) The transit authority shall suspend from employment a person designated as a regional transit authority police officer if that person is convicted, after trial, of a felony. If the police officer files an appeal from that conviction and the conviction is upheld by the highest court to which the appeal is taken or if the police officer does not file a timely appeal, the transit authority shall terminate the employment of that police officer. If the police officer files an appeal that results in the police officer's acquittal of the felony or conviction of a misdemeanor, or in the dismissal of the felony charge against the police officer, the transit authority shall reinstate that police officer. A police officer who is reinstated under division (B)(2)(b) of this section shall not receive any back pay unless that officer's conviction of the felony was reversed on appeal, or the felony charge was dismissed, because the court found insufficient evidence to convict the police officer of the felony.

(3) Division (B) of this section does not apply regarding an offense that was committed prior to January 1, 1997.

(4) The suspension from employment, or the termination of the employment, of a regional transit authority police officer under division (B)(2) of this section shall be in accordance with Chapter 119. of the Revised Code.

(2002 H 490, eff. 1–1–04; 1996 H 566, eff. 10–16–96)

CHAPTER 307

BOARD OF COUNTY COMMISSIONERS—POWERS

CHILD FATALITY REVIEW

307.621 Child fatality review board; regional child fatality review board

A board of county commissioners shall appoint a health commissioner of the board of health of a city or general health district that is entirely or partially located in the county in which the board of county commissioners is located to establish a child fatality review board to review the deaths of children under eighteen years of age. The boards of county commissioners of two or more counties may, by adopting a joint resolution passed by a majority of the members of each participating board of county commissioners, create a regional child fatality review board to serve all participating counties. The joint resolution shall appoint, for each county participating as part of the regional review board, one health commissioner from a board of health of a city or general health district located at least in part in each county. The health commissioners appointed shall select one of their number as the health commissioner to establish the regional review board. The regional review board shall be established in the same manner as provided for single county review boards.

In any county that has a body acting as a child fatality review board on the effective date of this section, the board of county commissioners of that county, in lieu of having a health commissioner establish a child fatality review board, shall appoint that body to function as the child fatality review board for the county. The body shall have the same duties, obligations, and protections as a child fatality review board appointed by a health commissioner. The board of county commissioners or an individual designated by the board shall convene the body as required by section 307.624 of the Revised Code.

(2000 H 448, eff. 10–5–00)

307.622 Members

(A) The health commissioner of the board of health of a city or a general health district who is appointed under section 307.621 of the Revised Code to establish the child fatality review board shall select six members to serve on the child fatality review board along with the commissioner. The review board shall consist of the following:

(1) A county coroner or designee;

(2) The chief of police of a police department or the sheriff that serves the greatest population in the county or region or a designee of the chief or sheriff;

(3) The executive director of a public children services agency or designee;

(4) A public health official or designee;

(5) The executive director of a board of alcohol, drug addiction, and mental health services or designee;

(6) A physician who holds a certificate issued pursuant to Chapter 4731. of the Revised Code authorizing the practice of medicine and surgery or osteopathic medicine and surgery, specializes in pediatric or family medicine, and currently practices pediatric or family medicine.

(B) The majority of the members of a review board may invite additional members to serve on the board. The additional members invited under this division shall serve for a period of time determined by a majority of the members described in division (A) of this section. An additional member shall have the same authority, duties, and responsibilities as members described in division (A) of this section.

(C) A vacancy in a child fatality review board shall be filled in the same manner as the original appointment.

(D) A child fatality review board member shall not receive any compensation for, and shall not be paid for any expenses incurred pursuant to, fulfilling the member's duties on the board unless compensation for, or payment for expenses incurred pursuant to, those duties is received pursuant to a member's regular employment.

(2000 H 448, eff. 10–5–00)

307.623 Purpose of child fatality review board

The purpose of the child fatality review board is to decrease the incidence of preventable child deaths by doing all of the following:

(A) Promoting cooperation, collaboration, and communication between all groups, professions, agencies, or entities that serve families and children;

(B) Maintaining a comprehensive database of all child deaths that occur in the county or region served by the child fatality review board in order to develop an understanding of the causes and incidence of those deaths;

(C) Recommending and developing plans for implementing local service and program changes and changes to the groups, professions, agencies, or entities that serve families and children that might prevent child deaths;

(D) Advising the department of health of aggregate data, trends, and patterns concerning child deaths.

(2000 H 448, eff. 10–5–00)

307.624 Chairperson

The board of county commissioners, or if a regional child fatality review board is established, the group of health commissioners appointed to select the health commissioner to establish the regional review board, shall designate either the health commissioner that establishes the review board or a representative of the health commissioner to convene meetings and be the chairperson of the review board. If a regional review board includes a county with more than one health district, the regional review board meeting shall be convened in that county. If more than one of the counties participating on the regional review board has more than one health district, the person convening the meeting shall select one of the counties with more than one health district as the county in which to convene the meeting. The person designated to convene the review board shall convene it at least once a year to review, in accordance with this section and the rules adopted by the department of health under section 3701.045 of the Revised Code, the deaths of all children under eighteen years of age who, at the time of death, were residents of the county or, if a regional review board, one of the participating counties.

(2000 H 448, eff. 10–5–00)

307.625 Review of death of child prohibited while investigation or prosecution pending

A child fatality review board may not conduct a review of the death of a child described in section 307.624 of the Revised Code while an investigation of the death or prosecution of a person for causing the death is pending unless the prosecuting attorney agrees to allow the review. The law enforcement agency conducting the criminal investigation, on the conclusion of the investigation, and the prosecuting attorney prosecuting the case, on the conclusion of the prosecution, shall notify the chairperson of the review board of the conclusion.

(2000 H 448, eff. 10–5–00)

307.626 Report

(A) By the first day of April of each year, the person convening the child fatality review board shall prepare and submit to the Ohio department of health a report that includes all of the following information with respect to each child death that was reviewed by the review board in the previous calendar year:

(1) The cause of death;

(2) Factors contributing to death;

(3) Age;

(4) Sex;

(5) Race;

(6) The geographic location of death;

(7) The year of death.

The report shall specify the number of child deaths that have not been reviewed since the effective date of this section.

The report may include recommendations for actions that might prevent other deaths, as well as any other information the review board determines should be included.

(B) Reports prepared under this section shall be considered public records under section 149.43 of the Revised Code.

(2000 H 448, eff. 10–5–00)

307.627 Summary sheet of information

(A) Notwithstanding section 3701.243 and any other section of the Revised Code pertaining to confidentiality, any individual; public children services agency, private child placing agency, or agency that provides services specifically to individuals or families; law enforcement agency; or other public or private entity that provided services to a child whose death is being reviewed by a child fatality review board, on the request of the review board, shall submit to the review board a summary sheet of information. With respect to a request made to a health care entity, the summary sheet shall contain only information available and reasonably drawn from the child's medical record created by the health care entity. With respect to a request made to any other individual or entity, the summary shall contain only information available and reasonably drawn from any record involving the child that the individual or entity develops in the normal course of business. On the request of the review board, an individual or entity may, at the individual or entity's discretion, make any additional information, documents, or reports available to the review board. For purposes of the review, the review board shall have access to confidential information provided to the review board under this division or division (H)(4) of section 2151.421 of the Revised Code, and each member of the review board shall preserve the confidentiality of that information.

(B) Notwithstanding division (A) of this section, no person, entity, law enforcement agency, or prosecuting attorney shall provide any information regarding the death of a child to a child fatality review board while an investigation of the death or prosecution of a person for causing the death is pending unless the prosecuting attorney has agreed pursuant to section 307.625 of the Revised Code to allow review of the death.

(2000 H 448, eff. 10–5–00)

307.628 Immunity from liability

(A) An individual or public or private entity providing information, documents, or reports to a child fatality review board is immune from any civil liability for injury, death, or loss to person or property that otherwise might be incurred or imposed as a result of providing the information, documents, or reports to the review board.

(B) Each member of a review board is immune from any civil liability for injury, death, or loss to person or property that might otherwise be incurred or imposed as a result of the member's participation on the review board.

(2000 H 448, eff. 10–5–00)

307.629 Confidentiality

(A) Except as provided in sections 5153.171 to 5153.173 of the Revised Code, any information, document, or report presented to a child fatality review board, all statements made by review board members during meetings of the review board, and all work products of the review board, other than the report prepared pursuant to section 307.626 of the Revised Code, are confidential and shall be used by the review board and its members only in the exercise of the proper functions of the review board.

(B) No person shall permit or encourage the unauthorized dissemination of the confidential information described in division (A) of this section.

(C) Whoever violates division (B) of this section is guilty of a misdemeanor of the second degree.

(2000 H 448, eff. 10–5–00)

MISCELLANEOUS POWERS

307.71 Curfew for persons under eighteen

(A) Whenever the adoption of a curfew for persons under eighteen years of age is deemed necessary by the board of county commissioners for the immediate preservation of the public peace, health, or safety in any of the unincorporated areas of such county, the board of county commissioners may adopt a resolution setting forth the provisions of such curfew and the necessity for such curfew together with a statement of the reasons for such necessity, and providing for its enforcement within such unincorporated areas of the county. Upon adoption of the resolution by a majority of the commissioners, the resolution shall become effective immediately.

(B) Any person under the age of eighteen years who violates the provisions of a curfew adopted in accordance with division (A) of this section shall be apprehended and charged as being an unruly child and taken before the juvenile court in the county in which the violation occurred as provided in Chapter 2151. of the Revised Code.

(1970 H 1018, eff. 6–23–70)

MULTICOUNTY CORRECTIONAL CENTER; PRISONERS

307.93 Multicounty, municipal-county, or multicounty-municipal correctional center; contract; building commission; reimbursement by prisoner

(A) The boards of county commissioners of two or more adjacent counties may contract for the joint establishment of a multicounty correctional center, and the board of county commissioners of a county or the boards of two or more counties may contract with any municipal corporation or municipal corporations located in that county or those counties for the joint establishment of a municipal-county or multicounty-municipal correctional center. The center shall augment county and, where applicable, municipal jail programs and facilities by providing custody and rehabilitative programs for those persons under the charge of the sheriff of any of the contracting counties or of the officer or officers of the contracting municipal corporation or municipal corporations having charge of persons incarcerated in the municipal jail, workhouse, or other correctional facility who, in the opinion of the sentencing court, need programs of custody and rehabilitation not available at the county or municipal jail and by providing custody and rehabilitative programs in accordance with division (C) of this section, if applicable. The contract may include, but need not be limited to, provisions regarding the acquisition, construction, maintenance, repair, termination of operations, and administration of the center. The contract shall prescribe the manner of funding of, and debt assumption for, the center and the standards and procedures to be followed in the operation of the center. Except as provided in division (H) of this section, the contracting counties and municipal corporations shall form a corrections commission to oversee the administration of the center. Members of the commission shall consist of the sheriff of each participating county, the president of the board of county commissioners of each participating county, the presiding judge of the court of common pleas of each participating county, or, if the court of common pleas of a participating county has only one judge, then that judge, the chief of police of each participating municipal corporation, the mayor or city manager of each participating municipal corporation, and the presiding judge or the sole judge of the municipal court of each participating municipal corporation. Any of the foregoing officers may appoint a designee to serve in the officer's place on the corrections commission. The standards and procedures shall be formulated and agreed to by the commission and may be amended at any time during the life of the contract by agreement of the parties to the contract upon the advice of the commission. The standards and procedures formulated by the commission shall include, but need not be limited to, designation of the person in charge of the center, the categories of employees to be employed at the center, the appointing authority of the center, and the standards of treatment and security to be maintained at the center. The person in charge of, and all persons employed to work at, the center shall have all the powers of police officers that are necessary for the proper performance of the duties relating to their positions at the center.

(B) Each board of county commissioners that enters a contract under division (A) of this section may appoint a building commission pursuant to section 153.21 of the Revised Code. If any commissions are appointed, they shall function jointly in the construction of a multicounty or multicounty-municipal correctional center with all the powers and duties authorized by law.

(C) Prior to the acceptance for custody and rehabilitation into a center established under this section of any persons who are designated by the department of rehabilitation and correction, who plead guilty to or are convicted of a felony of the fourth or fifth degree, and who satisfy the other requirements listed in section 5120.161 of the Revised Code, the corrections commission of a center established under this section shall enter into an agreement with the department of rehabilitation and correction under section 5120.161 of the Revised Code for the custody and rehabilitation in the center of persons who are designated by the department, who plead guilty to or are convicted of a felony of the fourth or fifth degree, and who satisfy the other requirements listed in that section, in exchange for a per diem fee per person. Persons incarcerated in the center pursuant to an agreement entered into under this division shall be subject to supervision and control in the manner described in section 5120.161 of the Revised Code. This division does not affect the authority of a court to directly sentence a person who is convicted of or pleads guilty to a felony to the center in accordance with section 2929.16 of the Revised Code.

(D) Pursuant to section 2929.37 of the Revised Code, each board of county commissioners and the legislative authority of each municipal corporation that enters into a contract under division (A) of this section may require a person who was convicted of an offense, who is under the charge of the sheriff of their county or of the officer or officers of the contracting municipal corporation or municipal corporations having charge of persons incarcerated in the municipal jail, workhouse, or other correctional facility, and who is confined in the multicounty, municipal-county, or multicounty-municipal correctional center as provided in that division, to reimburse the applicable county or municipal corporation for its expenses incurred by reason of the person's confinement in the center.

(E) Notwithstanding any contrary provision in this section or section 2929.18, 2929.28, or 2929.37 of the Revised Code, the corrections commission of a center may establish a policy that complies with section 2929.38 of the Revised Code and that requires any person who is not indigent and who is confined in the multicounty, municipal-county, or multicounty-municipal correctional center to pay a reception fee, a fee for medical treatment or service requested by and provided to that person, or the fee for a random drug test assessed under division (E) of section 341.26 of the Revised Code.

(F)(1) The corrections commission of a center established under this section may establish a commissary for the center. The commissary may be established either in-house or by another arrangement. If a commissary is established, all persons incarcerated in the center shall receive commissary privileges. A person's purchases from the commissary shall be deducted from the person's account record in the center's business office. The commissary shall provide for the distribution to indigent persons incarcerated in the center of necessary hygiene articles and writing materials.

(2) If a commissary is established, the corrections commission of a center established under this section shall establish a commissary fund for the center. The management of funds in the commissary fund shall be strictly controlled in accordance with procedures adopted by the auditor of state. Commissary fund revenue over and above operating costs and reserve shall be considered profits. All profits from the commissary fund shall be used to purchase supplies and equipment for the benefit of persons incarcerated in the center and to pay salary and benefits for employees of the center, or for any other persons, who work in or are employed for the sole purpose of providing service to the commissary. The corrections commission shall adopt rules and regulations for the operation of any commissary fund it establishes.

(G) In lieu of forming a corrections commission to administer a multicounty correctional center or a municipal-county or multicounty-municipal correctional center, the boards of county commissioners and the legislative authorities of the municipal corporations contracting to establish the center may also agree to contract for the private operation and management of the center as provided in section 9.06 of the Revised Code, but only if the center houses only misdemeanant inmates. In order to enter into a contract under section 9.06 of the Revised Code, all the boards and legislative authorities establishing the center shall approve and be parties to the contract.

(H) If a person who is convicted of or pleads guilty to an offense is sentenced to a term in a multicounty correctional center or a municipal-county or multicounty-municipal correctional center or is incarcerated in the center in the manner described in division (C) of this section, or if a person who is arrested for an offense, and who has been denied bail or has had bail set and has not been released on bail is confined in a multicounty correctional center or a municipal-county or multicounty-municipal correctional center pending trial, at the time of reception and at other times the officer, officers, or other person in charge of the operation of the center determines to be appropriate, the officer, officers, or other person in charge of the operation of the center may cause the convicted or accused offender to be examined and tested for tuberculosis, HIV infection, hepatitis, including but not limited to hepatitis A, B, and C, and other contagious diseases. The officer, officers, or other person in charge of the operation of the center may cause a convicted or accused offender in the center who refuses to be tested or treated for tuberculosis, HIV infection, hepatitis, including but not limited to hepatitis A, B, and C, or another contagious disease to be tested and treated involuntarily.

(I) As used in this section, "multicounty-municipal" means more than one county and a municipal corporation, or more than one municipal corporation and a county, or more than one municipal corporation and more than one county.

(2003 H 95, § 3.13, eff. 1–1–04; 2003 H 95, § 1, eff. 9–26–03; 2002 H 490, eff. 1–1–04; 2002 H 170, eff. 9–6–02; 2000 H 349, eff. 9–22–00; 1997 S 111, eff. 3–17–98; 1996 H 480, eff. 10–16–96; 1996 S 269, eff. 7–1–96; 1995 S 2, eff. 7–1–96; 1995 H 117, eff. 9–29–95; 1987 H 455, eff. 7–20–87; 1984 H 363; 1982 H 269, § 4, S 199; 1979 S 17)

307.931 Health insurance claims of persons confined in correctional institutions

(A) For each person who is confined in a multicounty, municipal-county, or multicounty-municipal correctional center as provided in section 307.93 of the Revised Code, the applicable county or municipal corporation may make a determination as to whether the person is covered under a health insurance or health care policy, contract, or plan and, if the person has such coverage, what terms and conditions are imposed by it for the filing and payment of claims.

(B) If, pursuant to division (A) of this section, it is determined that the person is covered under a policy, contract, or plan and, while that coverage is in force, the correctional center renders or arranges for the rendering of health care services to the person in accordance with the terms and conditions of the policy, contract, or plan, then the person, county, municipal corporation, or provider of the health care services, as appropriate under the terms and conditions of the policy, contract, or plan, shall promptly submit a claim for payment for the health care services to the appropriate third-party payer and shall designate, or make any other arrangement necessary to ensure, that payment of any amount due on the claim be made to the county, municipal corporation, or provider, as the case may be.

(C) Any payment made to the county or municipal corporation pursuant to division (B) of this section shall be paid into the treasury of the governmental entity that incurred the expenses.

(D) This section also applies to any person who is under the custody of a law enforcement officer, as defined in section 2901.01 of the Revised Code, prior to the person's confinement in the correctional center.

(1996 S 163, eff. 10–16–96)

CHAPTER 309

PROSECUTING ATTORNEY

Section

309.01 Prosecuting attorney

There shall be elected quadrennially in each county, a prosecuting attorney, who shall hold his office for four years, beginning on the first Monday of January next after his election.

(1953 H 1, eff. 10–1–53; GC 2909)

309.02 Qualifications of candidate for prosecuting attorney

No person shall be eligible as a candidate for the office of prosecuting attorney, or shall be elected to such office, who is not an attorney at law licensed to practice law in this state. No prosecuting attorney shall be a member of the general assembly of this state or mayor of a municipal corporation.

(1992 S 243, eff. 8–19–92; 1953 H 1; GC 2910)

309.03 Bond of prosecuting attorney; oath

Before entering upon the discharge of his duties, the prosecuting attorney shall give a bond, signed by a bonding or surety company approved by the court of common pleas or the probate court and authorized to do business in this state, or, at his option, signed by two or more freeholders having real estate in the value of double the amount of the bond over and above all encumbrances to the state. Such bond shall be in a sum not less than one thousand dollars, to be fixed by the court of common pleas or the probate court and conditioned that such prosecuting attorney will faithfully discharge all the duties enjoined upon him by law, and pay over all moneys received by him in his official capacity. The expense or premium for such bond shall be paid by the board of county commissioners, and shall be charged to the general fund of the county. Such bond, with the approval of such court and the oath of office required by sections 3.22 and 3.23 of the Revised Code indorsed thereon, shall be deposited with the county treasurer.

(1953 H 1, eff. 10–1–53; GC 2911)

309.05 Removal of prosecuting attorney for neglect or misconduct

On complaint, in writing, signed by one or more taxpayers, containing distinct charges and specifications of wanton and willful neglect of duty or gross misconduct in office by the prosecuting attorney, supported by affidavit and filed in the court of common pleas, the court shall assign the complaint for hearing and shall cause reasonable notice of the hearing to be given to the prosecuting attorney of the time fixed by the court for the hearing. At the time so fixed, or to which the court adjourns the hearing, the court shall hear the evidence adduced by the complainants and the prosecuting attorney. The court may consider motions for judgment on the pleadings made pursuant to Civil Rule 12, motions to dismiss made pursuant to Civil Rule 41, and motions for summary judgment made pursuant to Civil Rule 56 that are filed before the hearing. If it appears that the prosecuting attorney has willfully and wantonly neglected to perform the prosecuting attorney's duties, or has been guilty of gross misconduct in office, the court shall remove the prosecuting attorney from office and declare the office vacant. Otherwise the complaint shall be dismissed, and the court shall render judgment against the losing party for costs.

If a complaint to remove a prosecuting attorney is dismissed because the complainant or complainants failed to file an affidavit in support of the complaint, the dismissal shall be without prejudice.

(2004 H 252, eff. 9–16–04; 1953 H 1, eff. 10–1–53; GC 2913)

309.06 Assistant prosecuting attorneys; clerks; stenographers

(A) On or before the first Monday in January of each year, the judge of the court of common pleas or, if there is more than one judge, the judges of the court of common pleas in joint session may fix an aggregate sum to be expended for the incoming year for the compensation of assistants, clerks, and stenographers of the prosecuting attorney's office.

The prosecuting attorney may appoint any assistants, clerks, and stenographers who are necessary for the proper performance of the duties of his office and fix their compensation, not to exceed, in the aggregate, the amount fixed by the judges of the court of common pleas. The compensation, after being so fixed, shall be paid to the assistants, clerks, and stenographers biweekly from the general fund of the county treasury, upon the warrant of the county auditor.

(B) Subject to section 2921.421 of the Revised Code, a prosecuting attorney may appoint, as an assistant prosecuting attorney, clerk, stenographer, or other employee, a person who is an associate or partner of, or who is employed by, the prosecuting attorney or an assistant prosecuting attorney in the private practice of law in a partnership, professional association, or other law business arrangement.

(1994 H 285, eff. 3–2–94; 1992 S 359, eff. 12–22–92; 1981 S 114; 1953 H 1; GC 2914, 2915)

309.07 Appointment of secret service officer

The prosecuting attorney may appoint secret service officers whose duty it shall be to aid him in the collection and discovery of evidence to be used in the trial of criminal cases and matters of a criminal nature. Such appointment shall be made for such term as the prosecuting attorney deems advisable, and subject to termination at any time by such prosecuting attorney. The compensation of said officers shall be fixed by the judge of the court of common pleas, or, if there is more than one judge, such compensation shall be fixed by the judges of such court in joint session, and shall not be less than one hundred twenty-five dollars per month for the time actually occupied in such service nor more than seventy-five per cent of the salary of the prosecuting attorney for a year. Such salary shall be payable monthly, out of the county fund, upon the warrant of the county auditor.

(1969 S 94, eff. 10–24–69; 1953 H 1; GC 2915–1; Source—GC 6184 to 6186)

309.08 Powers and duties of prosecuting attorney; organized crime task force membership; rewards for information about drug-related offenses

(A) The prosecuting attorney may inquire into the commission of crimes within the county. The prosecuting attorney shall prosecute, on behalf of the state, all complaints, suits, and controversies in which the state is a party, except for those required to be prosecuted by a special prosecutor pursuant to section 177.03 of the Revised Code or by the attorney general pursuant to section 109.83 of the Revised Code, and other suits, matters, and controversies that the prosecuting attorney is required to prosecute within or outside the county, in the probate court, court of common pleas, and court of appeals. In conjunction with the attorney general, the prosecuting attorney shall prosecute in the supreme court cases arising in the prosecuting attorney's county, except for those cases required to be prosecuted by a special prosecutor pursuant to section 177.03 of the Revised Code or by the attorney general pursuant to section 109.83 of the Revised Code.

In every case of conviction, the prosecuting attorney forthwith shall cause execution to be issued for the fine and costs, or costs only, as the case may be, and faithfully shall urge the collection until it is effected or found to be impracticable to collect. The prosecuting attorney forthwith shall pay to the county treasurer all moneys belonging to the state or county which come into the prosecuting attorney's possession.

The prosecuting attorney or an assistant prosecuting attorney of a county may participate, as a member of the investigatory staff of an organized crime task force established under section 177.02 of the Revised Code that has jurisdiction in that county, in an investigation of organized criminal activity under sections 177.01 to 177.03 of the Revised Code.

(B) The prosecuting attorney may pay a reward to a person who has volunteered any tip or information to a law enforcement agency in the county concerning a drug-related offense that is planned to occur, is occurring, or has occurred, in whole or in part, in the county. The prosecuting attorney may provide for the payment, out of the following sources, of rewards to a person who has volunteered tips and information to a law enforcement agency in the county concerning a drug-related offense that is planned to occur, is occurring, or has occurred, in whole or in part, in the county:

(1) The law enforcement trust fund established by the prosecuting attorney pursuant to division (D)(1)(c) of section 2933.43 of the Revised Code;

(2) The portion of any mandatory fines imposed pursuant to divisions (B)(1) and (2) of section 2929.18 or Chapter 2925. of the Revised Code that is paid to the prosecuting attorney pursuant to that division or chapter, the portion of any additional fines imposed under division (B)(5) of section 2929.18 of the Revised Code that is paid to the prosecuting attorney pursuant to that division, or the portion of any double fines imposed pursuant to division (B)(5) of section 2925.42 of the Revised Code that is paid to the prosecuting attorney pursuant to that division;

(3) The furtherance of justice fund allowed to the prosecuting attorney under section 325.12 of the Revised Code or any additional funds allowed to the prosecuting attorney under section 325.13 of the Revised Code;

(4) Any other moneys lawfully in the possession or control of the prosecuting attorney.

(C) As used in division (B) of this section, "drug–related offense" means any violation of Chapter 2925. or 3719. of the Revised Code or any violation of a municipal ordinance that is substantially equivalent to any section in either of those chapters.

(1996 S 166, eff. 10–17–96; 1995 S 2, eff. 7–1–96; 1993 H 152, eff. 7–1–93; 1990 S 258; 1986 S 74; 1953 H 1; GC 2916)

309.09 Legal adviser; additional counsel; legal services for park districts

(A) The prosecuting attorney shall be the legal adviser of the board of county commissioners, board of elections, and all other county officers and boards, including all tax-supported public libraries, and any of them may require written opinions or instructions from the prosecuting attorney in matters connected with their official duties. The prosecuting attorney shall prosecute and defend all suits and actions which any such officer or board directs or to which it is a party, and no county officer may employ any other counsel or attorney at the expense of the county, except as provided in section 305.14 of the Revised Code.

(B) The prosecuting attorney shall be the legal adviser for all township officers, boards, and commissions, unless the township has adopted a limited home rule government pursuant to Chapter 504. of the Revised Code and has not entered into a contract to have the prosecuting attorney serve as the township law director, in which case the township law director, whether serving full-time or part-time, shall be the legal adviser for all township officers, boards, and commissions. When the board of township trustees finds it advisable or necessary to have additional legal counsel, it may employ an attorney other than the township law director or the prosecuting attorney of the county, either for a particular matter or on an annual basis, to represent the township and its officers, boards, and commissions in their official capacities and to advise them on legal matters. No such legal counsel may be employed, except on the order of the board of township trustees, duly entered upon its journal, in which the compensation to be paid for the legal services shall be fixed. The compensation shall be paid from the township fund.

Nothing in this division confers any of the powers or duties of a prosecuting attorney under section 309.08 of the Revised Code upon a township law director.

(C) Whenever the board of county commissioners employs an attorney other than the prosecuting attorney of the county, without the authorization of the court of common pleas as provided in section 305.14 of the Revised Code, either for a particular matter or on an annual basis, to represent the board in its official capacity and to advise it on legal matters, the board shall enter upon its journal an order of the board in which the compensation to be paid for the legal services shall be fixed. The compensation shall be paid from the county general fund. The total compensation paid, in any year, by the board for legal services under this division shall not exceed the total annual compensation of the prosecuting attorney for that county.

(D) The prosecuting attorney and the board of county commissioners jointly may contract with a board of park commissioners under section 1545.07 of the Revised Code for the prosecuting attorney to provide legal services to the park district the board of park commissioners operates. All moneys received pursuant to the contract shall be deposited into the prosecuting attorney's legal services fund, which shall be established in the county treasury of each county in which the contract exists. Moneys in that fund may be appropriated only to the prosecuting attorney for the purpose of providing legal services under a contract entered into under this division.

(E) The prosecuting attorney may be, in the prosecuting attorney's discretion, the legal adviser of a joint fire district created under section 505.371 of the Revised Code, at no cost to the district.

(2004 H 299, eff. 6–10–04; 1999 H 187, eff. 9–20–99; 1998 S 201, eff. 12–21–98; 1996 H 501, eff. 11–6–96; 1996 H 268, eff. 5–8–96; 1991 H 77, eff. 9–17–91; 1986 H 428; 1978 H 316; 129 v 1557; 128 v 597; 125 v 235; 1953 H 1; GC 2917; Source—GC 2917–1)

309.10 Provisions for other counsel

Sections 309.08 and 309.09 of the Revised Code do not prevent a school board from employing counsel to represent it, but when counsel is employed, the counsel shall be paid by the school board from the school fund. Sections 309.08 and 309.09 of the Revised Code do not prevent a county board of mental retardation and developmental disabilities from employing counsel to represent it, but that counsel shall be employed in accordance with division (C) of section 305.14 and paid in accordance with division (A)(7) of section 5126.05 of the Revised Code.

Sections 309.08 and 309.09 of the Revised Code do not prevent a board of county hospital trustees from employing counsel with the approval of the county commissioners to bring legal action for the collection of delinquent accounts of the hospital, but when counsel is employed, the counsel shall be paid from the hospital's funds. Sections 309.08 and 309.09 of the Revised Code do not prevent a board of library trustees from employing counsel to represent it, but when counsel is employed, the counsel shall be paid from the library's funds. Sections 309.08 and 309.09 of the Revised Code do not prevent the appointment and employment of assistants, clerks, and stenographers to assist the prosecuting attorney as provided in sections 309.01 to 309.16 of the Revised Code, or the appointment by the court of common pleas or the court of appeals of an attorney to assist the prosecuting attorney in the trial of a criminal cause pending in that court, or the board of county commissioners from paying for those services.

(2000 H 400, eff. 8–29–00; 1996 H 629, eff. 3–13–97; 1994 H 694, eff. 11–11–94; 1990 H 569, eff. 11–11–90; 1988 S 155; 128 v 597; 127 v 440; 1953 H 1; GC 2918)

309.11 Official bonds

The prosecuting attorney shall prepare, in legal form, the official bonds for all county officers, and shall see that the acceptance of such bonds by the proper authorities, the signing thereof, and all the indorsements thereon, are in conformity to law, and that they are deposited with the proper officer. No bond shall be accepted or approved for any county officer by the person or tribunal authorized to approve it, until the prosecuting attorney has inspected it, and certified thereon that such bond is sufficient. In case of a vacancy in the office of prosecuting attorney or of the absence or disability of the prosecuting attorney, such duties shall be discharged by the probate judge.

(1953 H 1, eff. 10–1–53; GC 2920)

309.12 Protection of public funds

Upon being satisfied that funds of the county, or public moneys in the hands of the county treasurer or belonging to the county, are about to be or have been misapplied, or that any such public moneys have been illegally drawn or withheld from the county treasury, or that a contract, in contravention of law, has been executed or is about to be entered into, or that such a contract was procured by fraud or corruption, or that any property, real or personal, belonging to the county is being illegally used or occupied, or that such property is being used or occupied in violation of contract, or that the terms of a contract made by or on behalf of the county are being or have been violated, or that money is due the county, the prosecuting attorney may, by civil action in the name of the state, apply to a court of competent jurisdiction, to restrain such contemplated misapplication of funds, or the completion of such illegal contract, or to recover, for the use of the county, all public moneys so misapplied or illegally drawn or withheld from the county treasury, or to recover damages, for the benefit of the county, resulting from the execution of such illegal contract, or to recover, for the benefit of the county, such real or personal property so used or occupied, or to recover for the benefit of the county, damages resulting from the nonperformance of the terms of such contract, or to otherwise enforce it, or to recover such money as is due the county.

(1953 H 1, eff. 10–1–53; GC 2921)

309.13 Taxpayer's suit

If the prosecuting attorney fails, upon the written request of a taxpayer of the county, to make the application or institute the civil action contemplated in section 309.12 of the Revised Code, the taxpayer may make such application or institute such civil action in the name of the state, or, in any case wherein the prosecuting attorney is authorized to make such application, such taxpayer may bring any suit or institute any such proceedings against any county officer or person who holds or has held a county office, for misconduct in office or neglect of his duty, to recover money illegally drawn or illegally withheld from the county treasury, and to recover damages resulting from the execution of such illegal contract.

If such prosecuting attorney fails upon the written request of a taxpayer of the county, to bring such suit or institute such proceedings, or if for any reason the prosecuting attorney cannot bring such action, or if he has received and unlawfully withheld moneys belonging to the county, or has received or drawn public moneys out of the county treasury which he is not lawfully entitled to demand and receive, a taxpayer, upon securing the costs, may bring such suit or institute such proceedings, in the name of the state. Such action shall be for the benefit of the county, as if brought by the prosecuting attorney.

If the court hearing such case is satisfied that such taxpayer is entitled to the relief prayed for in his petition, and judgment is ordered in his favor, he shall be allowed his costs, including a reasonable compensation to his attorney.

(1953 H 1, eff. 10–1–53; GC 2922, 2923)

309.14 Injuries to timber

When trees standing or growing on any land belonging to the state, or to any school district, are, without lawful authority, cut down, or in any way injured, the prosecuting attorney shall prosecute the wrongdoer, and shall seize all timber so cut down, if it can be found, and sell it at public vendue, on five days' notice. The prosecuting attorney shall pay the proceeds of such sale into the state treasury to the credit of the general revenue fund, or into the county treasury to the credit of the school district, as the case may be.

(1985 H 201, eff. 7–1–85; 1953 H 1; GC 2924)

309.15 Annual report to attorney general

On or before the first day of September in each year, if so required by the attorney general by a written notice given on or before the first day of August, the prosecuting attorney shall transmit to the attorney general a report of all crimes prosecuted by indictment or information in his county for the year ending the first day of July, specifying:

(A) Under the head of felonies:

(1) The number convicted;

(2) The number acquitted;

(3) The amount of costs incurred;

(4) The amount of costs collected.

(B) Under the head of misdemeanors:

(1) The number convicted;

(2) The number acquitted;

(3) The amount of fines imposed;

(4) The amount of fines collected;

(5) The amount of costs incurred;

(6) The amount of costs collected.

(C) Such other information as the attorney general requires.

The attorney general may prepare and forward to the prosecuting attorney the necessary blanks and instructions for such annual reports. Prosecuting attorneys shall furnish to the attorney general any information he requires in the execution of his office, whenever such information is requested by him.

(1953 H 1, eff. 10–1–53; GC 2925)

309.16 Report to board of county commissioners; reports relating to arson

(A) On the first Monday of September in each year, each prosecuting attorney shall make a certified statement to the board of county commissioners specifying:

(1) The number of criminal prosecutions pursued to final conviction and sentence under his official care, during the year next preceding the time of making such statement. In such statement the prosecuting attorney shall name the parties to each prosecution, the amount of fine assessed in each case, the number of recognizances forfeited, and the amount of money collected in each case.

(2) With respect to the offenses set forth in sections 2909.02 and 2909.03 of the Revised Code, such statement shall also include the following information:

(a) The number of fires occurring in the county for which the state fire marshal or an assistant state fire marshal has determined there was evidence sufficient to charge a person with aggravated arson or arson;

(b) The number of cases under sections 2909.02 and 2909.03 of the Revised Code presented by the prosecuting attorney to the grand jury for indictment;

(c) The number of indictments under such sections returned by the grand jury;

(d) The number of cases under such sections prosecuted either by indictment or by information by the prosecuting attorney;

(e) The number of cases under such sections resulting in final conviction and sentence and the number of cases resulting in acquittals;

(f) The number of cases under such sections dismissed or terminated without a final adjudication as to guilt or innocence.

(B) The prosecuting attorney shall also transmit to the state fire marshal on or before the first Monday of September in each year all information relative to the crimes under such sections required to be reported to the board of county commissioners pursuant to division (A)(2) of this section.

(C) For purposes of divisions (A)(2) and (B) of this section, sections 2909.02 and 2909.03 of the Revised Code include a conspiracy or attempt to commit, or complicity in the commission of, arson or aggravated arson under sections 2923.01 to 2923.03 of the Revised Code.

(D) If the prosecuting attorney fails to make reports at the time and in the manner required by this section, he shall forfeit and pay not less than one hundred nor more than five hundred dollars, to be recovered in a civil action in the name of the board.

(1980 S 198, eff. 7–31–80; 1953 H 1; GC 2926; Source—GC 2505)

309.17 Action to reclaim property

When the prosecuting attorney of a county is informed that a person has in his possession money or other property belonging to a person found dead within such county, upon whose estate no letters of administration have been issued, the prosecuting attorney, by notice in writing, shall require the person having such money or other property to deposit it with the probate court. If within fifteen days such person does not comply with such requirement, the prosecuting attorney shall bring suit in the court of common pleas, in the name of the state, for the recovery thereof, and, when recovered, it shall be at the disposition of the probate court.

(1953 H 1, eff. 10–1–53; GC 2865)

309.18 Notice to victim of criminal's escape; failure to notify

If a prosecuting attorney of a county receives notice from the department of rehabilitation and correction pursuant to section 5120.14 of the Revised Code that a person indicted in that county for an offense of violence that is a felony has escaped from a correctional institution under the control of the department or otherwise has escaped from the custody of the department, receives notice from the sheriff of the county pursuant to section 341.011 of the Revised Code that a person indicted for or otherwise charged with an offense of violence that is a felony and that was committed in the county has escaped from the county jail or workhouse or otherwise has escaped from the custody of the sheriff, or receives notice from a chief of police or other chief law enforcement officer of a municipal corporation pursuant to section 753.19 of the Revised Code that a person indicted for or otherwise charged with an offense of violence that is a felony and that was committed in the county has escaped from a jail or workhouse of that municipal corporation or otherwise has escaped from the custody of that municipal corporation, the prosecuting attorney shall notify each victim of an offense of violence that is a felony committed by that person of the person's escape and, if applicable, of his subsequent apprehension. The notice of escape shall be given as soon as possible after receipt of the notice from the department, sheriff, or chief law enforcement officer of the municipal corporation and shall be given by telephone or in person, except that, if a prosecuting attorney tries and fails to give the notice of escape by telephone at the victim's last known telephone number or tries and fails to give the notice of escape in person at the victim's last known address, the notice of escape shall be given to the victim at his last known address by certified mail, return receipt requested. The notice of apprehension shall be given as soon as possible after the person is apprehended and shall be given in the same manner as is the notice of escape.

Any prosecuting attorney who fails to give any notice required by this section is immune from civil liability for any injury, death, or loss to person or property that might be incurred as a result of that failure to give notice.

(1994 H 571, eff. 10–6–94; 1987 H 207, eff. 9–24–87)

CHAPTER 311

SHERIFF

QUALIFICATIONS AND DUTIES

QUALIFICATIONS AND DUTIES

311.01 Election of sheriff; qualifications; basic training; continuing education

(A) A sheriff shall be elected quadrennially in each county. A sheriff shall hold office for a term of four years, beginning on the first Monday of January next after the sheriff's election.

(B) Except as otherwise provided in this section, no person is eligible to be a candidate for sheriff, and no person shall be elected or appointed to the office of sheriff, unless that person meets all of the following requirements:

(1) The person is a citizen of the United States.

(2) The person has been a resident of the county in which the person is a candidate for or is appointed to the office of sheriff for at least one year immediately prior to the qualification date.

(3) The person has the qualifications of an elector as specified in section 3503.01 of the Revised Code and has complied with all applicable election laws.

(4) The person has been awarded a high school diploma or a certificate of high school equivalence issued for achievement of specified minimum scores on the general educational development test of the American council on education.

(5) The person has not been convicted of or pleaded guilty to a felony or any offense involving moral turpitude under the laws of this or any other state or the United States, and has not been convicted of or pleaded guilty to an offense that is a misdemeanor of the first degree under the laws of this state or an offense under the laws of any other state or the United States that carries a penalty that is substantially equivalent to the penalty for a misdemeanor of the first degree under the laws of this state.

(6) The person has been fingerprinted and has been the subject of a search of local, state, and national fingerprint files to disclose any criminal record. Such fingerprints shall be taken under the direction of the administrative judge of the court of common pleas who, prior to the applicable qualification date, shall notify the board of elections, board of county commissioners, or county central committee of the proper political party, as applicable, of the judge's findings.

(7) The person has prepared a complete history of the person's places of residence for a period of six years immediately preceding the qualification date and a complete history of the person's places of employment for a period of six years immediately preceding the qualification date, indicating the name and address of each employer and the period of time employed by that employer. The residence and employment histories shall be filed with the administrative judge of the court of common pleas of the county, who shall forward them with the findings under division (D)(6) of this section to the appropriate board of elections, board of county commissioners, or county central committee of the proper political party prior to the applicable qualification date.

(8) The person meets at least one of the following conditions:

(a) Has obtained or held, within the four-year period ending immediately prior to the qualification date, a valid basic peace officer certificate of training issued by the Ohio peace officer training commission or has been issued a certificate of training pursuant to section 5503.05 of the Revised Code, and, within the four-year period ending immediately prior to the qualification date, has been employed as an appointee pursuant to section 5503.01 of the Revised Code or as a full-time peace officer as defined in section 109.71 of the Revised Code performing duties related to the enforcement of statutes, ordinances, or codes;

(b) Has obtained or held, within the three-year period ending immediately prior to the qualification date, a valid basic peace officer certificate of training issued by the Ohio peace officer training commission and has been employed for at least the last three years prior to the qualification date as a full-time law enforcement officer, as defined in division (A)(11) of section 2901.01 of the Revised Code, performing duties related to the enforcement of statutes, ordinances, or codes.

(9) The person meets at least one of the following conditions:

(a) Has at least two years of supervisory experience as a peace officer at the rank of corporal or above, or has been appointed pursuant to section 5503.01 of the Revised Code and served at the rank of sergeant or above, in the five-year period ending immediately prior to the qualification date;

(b) Has completed satisfactorily at least two years of post-secondary education or the equivalent in semester or quarter hours in a college or university authorized to confer degrees by the Ohio board of regents or the comparable agency of another state in which the college or university is located or in a school that holds a certificate of registration issued by the state board of career colleges and schools under Chapter 3332. of the Revised Code.

(C) Persons who meet the requirements of division (B) of this section, except the requirement of division (B)(2) of this section, may take all actions otherwise necessary to comply with division (B) of this section. If, on the applicable qualification date, no person has met all the requirements of division (B) of this section, then persons who have complied with and meet the requirements of division (B) of this section, except the requirement of division (B)(2) of this section, shall be considered qualified candidates under division (B) of this section.

(D) Newly elected sheriffs shall attend a basic training course conducted by the Ohio peace officer training commission pursuant to division (A) of section 109.80 of the Revised Code. A newly elected sheriff shall complete not less than two weeks of this course before the first Monday in January next after the sheriff's election. While attending the basic training course, a newly elected sheriff may, with the approval of the board of county commissioners, receive compensation, paid for from funds established by the sheriff's county for this purpose, in the same manner and amounts as if carrying out the powers and duties of the office of sheriff.

Appointed sheriffs shall attend the first basic training course conducted by the Ohio peace officer training commission pursuant to division (A) of section 109.80 of the Revised Code within six months following the date of appointment or election to the office of sheriff. While attending the basic training course, appointed sheriffs shall receive regular compensation in the same manner and amounts as if carrying out their regular powers and duties.

Five days of instruction at the basic training course shall be considered equal to one week of work. The costs of conducting the basic training course and the costs of meals, lodging, and travel of appointed and newly elected sheriffs attending the course shall be paid from state funds appropriated to the commission for this purpose.

(E) In each calendar year, each sheriff shall attend and successfully complete at least sixteen hours of continuing education approved under division (B) of section 109.80 of the Revised Code. A sheriff who receives a waiver of the continuing education requirement from the commission under division (C) of section 109.80 of the Revised Code because of medical disability or for other good cause shall complete the requirement at the earliest time after the disability or cause terminates.

(F)(1) Each person who is a candidate for election to or who is under consideration for appointment to the office of sheriff shall swear before the administrative judge of the court of common pleas as to the truth of any information the person provides to verify the person's qualifications for the office. A person who violates this requirement is guilty of falsification under section 2921.13 of the Revised Code.

(2) Each board of elections shall certify whether or not a candidate for the office of sheriff who has filed a declaration of candidacy, a statement of candidacy, or a declaration of intent to be a write-in candidate meets the qualifications specified in divisions (B) and (C) of this section.

(G) The office of a sheriff who is required to comply with division (D) or (E) of this section and who fails to successfully complete the courses pursuant to those divisions is hereby deemed to be vacant.

(H) As used in this section:

(1) "Qualification date" means the last day on which a candidate for the office of sheriff can file a declaration of candidacy, a statement of candidacy, or a declaration of intent to be a write-in candidate, as applicable, in the case of a primary election for the

office of sheriff; the last day on which a person may be appointed to fill a vacancy in a party nomination for the office of sheriff under Chapter 3513. of the Revised Code, in the case of a vacancy in the office of sheriff; or a date thirty days after the day on which a vacancy in the office of sheriff occurs, in the case of an appointment to such a vacancy under section 305.02 of the Revised Code.

(2) "Newly elected sheriff" means a person who did not hold the office of sheriff of a county on the date the person was elected sheriff of that county.

(2003 H 75, eff. 12–9–03; 1999 H 283, eff. 9–29–99; 1996 H 670, eff. 12–2–96; 1996 H 351, eff. 1–14–97; 1995 S 2, eff. 7–1–96; 1986 H 683, eff. 3–11–87; 1953 H 1; GC 2823)

311.02 Bond of sheriff

The sheriff shall, within ten days after receiving his commission and before the first Monday of January next after his election, give a bond, signed by a bonding or surety company authorized to do business in this state and to be approved by the board of county commissioners, or, at the option of such sheriff, signed by two or more freeholders having real estate in the value of double the amount of the bond, over and above all encumbrances to the state, in a sum not less than five thousand nor more than fifty thousand dollars, which sum shall be fixed by the board, and such bond shall be conditioned for the faithful performance of the duties of his office. The expense or premium for such bond shall be paid by the board and charged to the general fund of the county. Such bonds, with the approval of the board and the oath of office required by sections 3.22 and 3.23 of the Revised Code, and Section 7 of Article XV, Ohio Constitution, indorsed thereon, shall be filed with the county auditor and kept in his office.

The board may require the sheriff, at any time during his term of office, to give additional sureties on his bond, or to give a new bond.

No judge or clerk of any court or attorney at law shall be received as surety on such bond.

If the sheriff fails to give a bond within the time required, or fails to give additional sureties on such bond or a new bond within ten days after he has received written notice that the board so requires, the board shall declare the office of such sheriff vacant.

(129 v 1365, eff. 10–12–61; 1953 H 1; GC 2824 to 2827)

311.03 Disability or absence

When the sheriff, by reason of absence, sickness, or other disability, is incapable of serving any process required to be served, or by reason of interest is incompetent to serve it, the court of common pleas, if in session, or, if not in session, a judge of such court may appoint a suitable person to serve such process or to perform the duties of sheriff during the continuance of such disability. Such appointee shall give such bond as the court or judge requires, conditioned for the faithful performance of his duties, and take the oath of office.

(129 v 1365, eff. 10–12–61; 129 v 582; 126 v 205; 1953 H 1; GC 2828)

311.04 Deputy sheriffs; disqualification from employment

(A) As used in this section, "felony" has the same meaning as in section 109.511 of the Revised Code.

(B)(1) Subject to division (C) of this section, the sheriff may appoint, in writing, one or more deputies. At the time of the appointment, the sheriff shall file the writing upon which the appointment is made with the clerk of the court of common pleas, and the clerk of the court shall enter it upon the journal of the court. The sheriff shall pay the clerk's fees for the filing and journal entry of the writing. In cases of emergency, the sheriff may request of the sheriff of another county the aid of qualified deputies serving in those other counties of the state, and, if the consent of the sheriff of that other county is received, the deputies while so assigned shall be considered to be the deputies of the sheriff of the county requesting aid. No judge of a county court or mayor shall be appointed a deputy.

(2) Notwithstanding section 2335.33 of the Revised Code, the sheriff shall retain the fee charged pursuant to division (B) of section 311.37 of the Revised Code for the purpose of training deputies appointed pursuant to this section.

(C)(1) The sheriff shall not appoint a person as a deputy sheriff pursuant to division (B)(1) of this section on a permanent basis, on a temporary basis, for a probationary term, or on other than a permanent basis if the person previously has been convicted of or has pleaded guilty to a felony.

(2)(a) The sheriff shall terminate the employment of a deputy sheriff appointed under division (B)(1) of this section if the deputy sheriff does either of the following:

(i) Pleads guilty to a felony;

(ii) Pleads guilty to a misdemeanor pursuant to a negotiated plea agreement as provided in division (D) of section 2929.43 of the Revised Code in which the deputy sheriff agrees to surrender the certificate awarded to the deputy sheriff under section 109.77 of the Revised Code.

(b) The sheriff shall suspend from employment any deputy sheriff appointed under division (B)(1) of this section if the deputy sheriff is convicted, after trial, of a felony. If the deputy sheriff files an appeal from that conviction and the conviction is upheld by the highest court to which the appeal is taken or if the deputy sheriff does not file a timely appeal, the sheriff shall terminate the employment of that deputy sheriff. If the deputy sheriff files an appeal that results in that deputy sheriff's acquittal of the felony or conviction of a misdemeanor, or in the dismissal of the felony charge against the deputy sheriff, the sheriff shall reinstate that deputy sheriff. A deputy sheriff who is reinstated under division (C)(2)(b) of this section shall not receive any back pay unless that deputy sheriff's conviction of the felony was reversed on appeal, or the felony charge was dismissed, because the court found insufficient evidence to convict the deputy sheriff of the felony.

(3) Division (C) of this section does not apply regarding an offense that was committed prior to January 1, 1997.

(4) The suspension from employment, or the termination of the employment, of a deputy sheriff under division (C)(2) of this section shall be in accordance with Chapter 119. of the Revised Code.

(2002 H 490, eff. 1–1–04; 1996 H 566, eff. 10–16–96; 1986 S 247, eff. 7–9–86; 1970 H 1106; 128 v 688; 127 v 1039; 1953 H 1; GC 2830)

311.05 Limited liability of sheriff for deputies' misconduct

The sheriff shall only be responsible for the neglect of duty or misconduct in office of any of his deputies if he orders, has prior knowledge of, participates in, acts in reckless disregard of, or ratifies the neglect of duty or misconduct in office of the deputy.

(1983 H 273, eff. 10–5–83; 1953 H 1; GC 2831)

311.06 Location of sheriff's office

The sheriff's office shall be maintained at the seat of justice, in such rooms as the board of county commissioners provides for that purpose. Such office shall be furnished with all necessary furniture, blankbooks, stationery, and blanks at the expense of the county.

(1953 H 1, eff. 10–1–53; GC 2832)

311.07 General powers and duties of the sheriff; cooperation with other agencies in emergency; organized crime task force membership

(A) Each sheriff shall preserve the public peace and cause all persons guilty of any breach of the peace, within the sheriff's knowledge or view, to enter into recognizance with sureties to keep the peace and to appear at the succeeding term of the court of common pleas, and the sheriff shall commit such persons to jail in case they refuse to do so. The sheriff shall return a transcript of all the sheriff's proceedings with the recognizance so taken to such court. The sheriff shall, except as provided in division (C) of this section, execute all warrants, writs, and other process directed to the sheriff by any proper and lawful authority of this state, and those issued by a proper and lawful authority of any other state. The sheriff shall attend upon the court of common pleas and the court of appeals during their sessions, and, when required, shall attend upon the probate court. In the execution of official duties of the sheriff, the sheriff may call to the sheriff's aid such persons or power of the county as is necessary. Under the direction and control of the board of county commissioners, such sheriff shall have charge of the court house. A sheriff or deputy sheriff of a county may participate, as the director of an organized crime task force established under section 177.02 of the Revised Code or as a member of the investigatory staff of such a task force, in an investigation of organized criminal activity in any county or counties in this state under sections 177.01 to 177.03 of the Revised Code.

(B) The sheriff of a county may call upon the sheriff of any other county, the mayor or other chief executive of any municipal corporation, and the chairperson of the board of township trustees of any township within this state, to furnish such law enforcement or fire protection personnel, or both, together with appropriate equipment and apparatus, as may be necessary to preserve the public peace and protect persons and property in the requesting sheriff's county. Such aid shall be furnished to the sheriff requesting it, insofar as possible without withdrawing from the political subdivision furnishing such aid the minimum police and fire protection appearing necessary under the circumstances. Law enforcement and fire protection personnel acting outside the territory of their regular employment shall be considered as performing services within the territory of their regular employment for the purposes of compensation, pension or indemnity fund rights, workers' compensation, and other rights or benefits to which they may be entitled as incidents of their regular employment. The county receiving aid shall reimburse, as provided in this section, the political subdivision furnishing it the cost of furnishing such aid, including compensation of personnel, expenses incurred by reason of the injury or death of any such personnel while rendering such aid, expenses of furnishing equipment and apparatus, compensation for damage to or loss of equipment or apparatus while in service outside the territory of its regular use, and such other reasonable expenses as may be incurred by any such political subdivision in furnishing aid. The cost of furnishing such aid may be paid from the sheriff's furtherance of justice fund created pursuant to section 325.071 of the Revised Code or from the law enforcement trust fund created pursuant to section 2933.43 of the Revised Code, or from the county general fund to the extent moneys have been appropriated for such purposes pursuant to section 5705.38 of the Revised Code unless the board of county commissioners adopts a resolution restricting or prohibiting the use of general fund moneys without the prior approval of the board of county commissioners. Nothing in this section shall be construed as superseding or modifying in any way any provision of a contract entered into pursuant to section 311.29 of the Revised Code. Law enforcement officers acting pursuant to this section outside the territory of their regular employment have the same authority to enforce the law as when acting within the territory of their regular employment.

(C) The sheriff shall not execute process that is issued in a state other than this state, unless the process contains either of the following:

(1) A certification by the judge of the court that issued the process stating that the issuing court has jurisdiction to issue the process and that the documents being forwarded conform to the laws of the state in which the court is located;

(2) If the process is an initial summons to appear and defend issued after the filing of a complaint commencing an action, a certification by the clerk of the court that issued the process stating that the process was issued in conformance with the laws of the state in which the court is located.

(D) As used in this section and section 311.08 of the Revised Code, "proper and lawful authority" means any authority authorized by law to issue any process and "process" means those documents issued in this state in accordance with section 7.01 of the Revised Code and those documents, other than executions of judgments or decrees, issued in a state other than this state that conform to the laws of the state of issuance governing the issuance of process in that state.

(1997 H 342, eff. 12–31–97; 1986 S 74, eff. 9–3–86; 1983 S 23; 1980 H 278; 1976 S 545; 132 v H 996; 1953 H 1; GC 2833)

311.08 Execution and return of process

(A) The sheriff shall, except as provided in division (B) of this section, execute every summons, order, or other process directed to him by a proper and lawful authority of this state or issued by a proper and lawful authority of any other state, make return thereof, and exercise the powers conferred and perform the duties enjoined upon him by statute and by the common law.

In an action in which the sheriff is a party, or is interested, process shall be directed to and executed by a person appointed by the court of common pleas or a judge of the court of common pleas.

(B) The sheriff shall not execute process that is issued in a state other than this state, unless the process contains either of the following:

(1) A certification by the judge of the court that issued the process stating that the issuing court has jurisdiction to issue th [sic.] process and that the documents being forwarded conform to the laws of the state in which the court is located;

(2) If the process is an initial summons to appear and defend issued after the filing of a complaint commencing an action, a certification by the clerk of the court that issued the process stating that the process was issued in conformance with the laws of the state in which the court is located.

(1981 S 114, eff. 10–27–81; 1980 H 278; 1953 H 1; GC 2834, 2835)

311.09 Indorsement on writs

The sheriff shall indorse upon every writ or order the day and hour such writ or order was received by him.

(1953 H 1, eff. 10–1–53; GC 2836)

MISCELLANEOUS PROVISIONS

311.29 Contract with sheriff for police service; reimbursement of county; contract to provide services to Chautauqua assembly; contract for return of prisoner from outside of state

(A) As used in this section, "Chautauqua assembly" has the same meaning as in section 4511.90 of the Revised Code.

(B) The sheriff may, from time to time, enter into contracts with any municipal corporation, township, township police district, metropolitan housing authority, port authority, water or sewer district, school district, library district, health district, park district created pursuant to section 511.18 or 1545.01 of the Revised Code, soil and water conservation district, water conservancy district, or other taxing district or with the board of county commissioners of any contiguous county with the concurrence of the sheriff of the other county, and such subdivisions, authorities, and counties may enter into agreements with the sheriff pursuant to which the sheriff undertakes and is authorized by the contracting subdivision, authority, or county to perform any police function, exercise any police power, or render any police service in behalf of the contracting subdivision, authority, or county, or its legislative authority, that the subdivision, authority, or county, or its legislative authority, may perform, exercise, or render.

Upon the execution of an agreement under this division and within the limitations prescribed by it, the sheriff may exercise the same powers as the contracting subdivision, authority, or county possesses with respect to such policing that by the agreement the sheriff undertakes to perform or render, and all powers necessary or incidental thereto, as amply as such powers are possessed and exercised by the contracting subdivision, authority, or county directly.

Any agreement authorized by division (A), (B), or (C) of this section shall not suspend the possession by a contracting subdivision, authority, or county of any police power performed or exercised or police service rendered in pursuance to the agreement nor limit the authority of the sheriff.

(C) The sheriff may enter into contracts with any Chautauqua assembly that has grounds located within the county, and the Chautauqua assembly may enter into agreements with the sheriff pursuant to which the sheriff undertakes to perform any police function, exercise any police power, or render any police service upon the grounds of the Chautauqua assembly that the sheriff is authorized by law to perform, exercise, or render in any other part of the county within the sheriff's territorial jurisdiction. Upon the execution of an agreement under this division, the sheriff may, within the limitations prescribed by the agreement, exercise such powers with respect to such policing upon the grounds of the Chautauqua assembly, provided that any limitation contained in the agreement shall not be construed to limit the authority of the sheriff.

(D) Contracts entered into under division (A), (B), or (C) of this section shall provide for the reimbursement of the county for the costs incurred by the sheriff for such policing including, but not limited to, the salaries of deputy sheriffs assigned to such policing, the current costs of funding retirement pensions and of providing workers' compensation, the cost of training, and the cost of equipment and supplies used in such policing, to the extent that such equipment and supplies are not directly furnished by the contracting subdivision, authority, county, or Chautauqua assembly. Each such contract shall provide for the ascertainment of such costs and shall be of any duration, not in excess of four years, and may contain any other terms that may be agreed upon. All payments pursuant to any such contract in reimbursement of the costs of such policing shall be made to the treasurer of the county to be credited to a special fund to be known as the "sheriff's policing revolving fund," hereby created. Any moneys coming into the fund shall be used for the purposes provided in divisions (A) to (D) of this section and paid out on vouchers by the county commissioners as other funds coming into their possession. Any moneys credited to the fund and not obligated at the termination of the contract shall be credited to the county general fund.

The sheriff shall assign the number of deputies as may be provided for in any contract made pursuant to division (A), (B), or (C) of this section. The number of deputies regularly assigned to such policing shall be in addition to and an enlargement of the sheriff's regular number of deputies. Nothing in divisions (A) to (D) of this section shall preclude the sheriff from temporarily increasing or decreasing the deputies so assigned as emergencies indicate a need for shifting assignments to the extent provided by the contracts.

All such deputies shall have the same powers and duties, the same qualifications, and be appointed and paid and receive the same benefits and provisions and be governed by the same laws as all other deputy sheriffs.

Contracts under division (A), (B), or (C) of this section may be entered into jointly with the board of county commissioners, and sections 307.14 to 307.19 of the Revised Code apply to this section insofar as they may be applicable.

(E)(1) As used in division (E) of this section:

(a) "Ohio prisoner" has the same meaning as in section 5120.64 of the Revised Code.

(b) "Out–of–state prisoner" and "private contractor" have the same meanings as in section 9.07 of the Revised Code.

(2) The sheriff may enter into a contract with a private person or entity for the return of Ohio prisoners who are the responsibility of the sheriff from outside of this state to a location in this state specified by the sheriff, if there are adequate funds appropriated by the board of county commissioners and there is a certification pursuant to division (D) of section 5705.41 of the Revised Code that the funds are available for this purpose. A contract entered into under this division is within the coverage of section 325.07 of the Revised Code. If a sheriff enters into a contract as described in this division, subject to division (E)(3) of this section, the private person or entity in accordance with the contract may return Ohio prisoners from outside of this state to locations in this state specified by the sheriff. A contract entered into under this division shall include all of the following:

(a) Specific provisions that assign the responsibility for costs related to medical care of prisoners while they are being returned that is not covered by insurance of the private person or entity;

(b) Specific provisions that set forth the number of days, not exceeding ten, within which the private person or entity, after it receives the prisoner in the other state, must deliver the prisoner to the location in this state specified by the sheriff, subject to the exceptions adopted as described in division (E)(2)(c) of this section;

(c) Any exceptions to the specified number of days for delivery specified as described in division (E)(2)(b) of this section;

(d) A requirement that the private person or entity immediately report all escapes of prisoners who are being returned to this state, and the apprehension of all prisoners who are being returned and who have escaped, to the sheriff and to the local law enforcement agency of this state or another state that has jurisdiction over the place at which the escape occurs;

(e) A schedule of fines that the sheriff shall impose upon the private person or entity if the private person or entity fails to perform its contractual duties, and a requirement that, if the private person or entity fails to perform its contractual duties, the sheriff shall impose a fine on the private person or entity from the schedule of fines and, in addition, may exercise any other rights the sheriff has under the contract.

(f) If the contract is entered into on or after the effective date of the rules adopted by the department of rehabilitation and correction under section 5120.64 of the Revised Code, specific provisions that comport with all applicable standards that are contained in those rules.

(3) If the private person or entity that enters into the contract fails to perform its contractual duties, the sheriff shall impose upon the private person or entity a fine from the schedule, the money paid in satisfaction of the fine shall be paid into the county treasury, and the sheriff may exercise any other rights the sheriff has under the contract. If a fine is imposed under this division, the sheriff may reduce the payment owed to the private person or entity pursuant to any invoice in the amount of the fine.

(4) Upon the effective date of the rules adopted by the department of rehabilitation and correction under section 5120.64 of the Revised Code, notwithstanding the existence of a contract entered into under division (E)(2) of this section, in no case shall the private person or entity that is a party to the contract return Ohio prisoners from outside of this state into this state for a sheriff unless the private person or entity complies with all applicable standards that are contained in the rules.

(5) Divisions (E)(1) to (4) of this section do not apply regarding any out-of-state prisoner who is brought into this state to be housed pursuant to section 9.07 of the Revised Code in a correctional facility in this state that is managed and operated by a private contractor.

(2000 H 661, eff. 3–15–01; 1993 S 200, eff. 12–7–93; 1992 S 174; 1980 H 948; 1977 S 221; 1976 S 545; 1969 H 1; 130 v H 1; 129 v 1362)

311.30 Parking enforcement unit; parking enforcement officers

(A) The board of county commissioners may establish, by resolution, a parking enforcement unit within the office of the sheriff to operate in the unincorporated areas of the county, and may provide for the regulation of parking enforcement officers. The sheriff shall be the executive head of the parking enforcement unit, shall make all appointments and removals of parking enforcement officers, subject to any general rules prescribed by the board of county commissioners by resolution, and shall prescribe rules for the organization, training, administration, control, and conduct of the parking enforcement unit. The sheriff may appoint parking enforcement officers who agree to serve for nominal compensation, and persons with physical disabilities may receive appointments as parking enforcement officers.

(B) The authority of the parking enforcement officers shall be limited to the enforcement of section 4511.69 of the Revised Code and any other parking laws specified in the resolution creating the parking enforcement unit. Parking enforcement officers shall have no other powers.

(C) The training the parking enforcement officers shall receive shall include instruction in general administrative rules and procedures governing the parking enforcement unit, the role of the judicial system as it relates to parking regulation and enforcement, proper techniques and methods relating to the enforcement of parking laws, human interaction skills, and first aid.

(1990 S 174, eff. 7–13–90)

311.31 Voluntary motor vehicle decal registration program

(A) The board of county commissioners of a county may establish, by resolution, a voluntary motor vehicle decal registration program to be controlled and conducted by the sheriff within the unincorporated areas of the county. The board may establish a fee for participation in the program in an amount sufficient to cover the cost of administering the program and the cost of the decals. The board shall coordinate its program with any preexisting program established by a township located within the county under section 505.67 of the Revised Code.

(B) Any resident of the county may enroll a motor vehicle that he owns in the program by signing a consent form, displaying the decal issued under this section, and paying the prescribed fee. The motor vehicle owner shall remove the decal to withdraw from the program and also prior to the sale or transfer of ownership of the vehicle. Any law enforcement officer may conduct, at any place within this state at which the officer would be permitted to arrest the person operating the vehicle, an investigatory stop of any motor vehicle displaying a decal issued under this section when the vehicle is being driven between the hours of one a.m. and five a.m. A law enforcement officer may conduct an investigatory stop under this division regardless of whether the officer observes a violation of law involving the vehicle or whether he has probable cause to believe that any violation of law involving the vehicle has occurred.

(C) The consent form required under division (B) of this section shall:

(1) Describe the conditions for participation in the program, including a description of an investigatory stop and a statement that any law enforcement officer may conduct, at any place within this state at which the officer would be permitted to arrest the person operating the vehicle, an investigatory stop of the motor vehicle when it is being driven between the hours of one a.m. and five a.m.

(2) Contain other information identifying the vehicle and owner as the sheriff considers necessary.

(D) The state director of public safety, in accordance with Chapter 119. of the Revised Code, shall adopt rules governing the color, size, and design of decals issued under this section and the location where the decals shall be displayed on vehicles that are enrolled in the program.

(E) Divisions (A) to (D) of this section do not require a law enforcement officer to conduct an investigatory stop of a vehicle displaying a decal issued under this section.

(F) As used in this section:

(1) "Investigatory stop" means a temporary stop of a motor vehicle and its operator and occupants for purposes of determining the identity of the person who is operating the vehicle and, if the person who is operating it is not its owner, whether any violation of law has occurred or is occurring. An "investigatory stop" is not an arrest, but, if an officer who conducts an investigatory stop determines that illegal conduct has occurred or is occuring [sic.], an "investigatory stop" may be the basis for an arrest.

(2) "Law enforcement officer" means a sheriff, deputy sheriff, constable, police officer of a township or joint township police district, marshal, deputy marshal, municipal police officer, or state highway patrol trooper.

(1994 S 75, eff. 10–20–94)

311.37 Transient vendor to file information with county sheriff; bond

(A) No transient vendor, as defined in section 5739.17 of the Revised Code, who obtains a transient vendor's license pursuant to section 5739.17 of the Revised Code, intending to provide goods and services of a retail value of more than five hundred dollars, shall negligently fail to file with the county sheriff all of the following before doing business as a transient vendor anywhere in that county:

(1) Proof of the transient vendor's identity and proof that a transient vendor's license has been obtained in this state;

(2) A statement describing the goods or services to be provided by the transient vendor and an estimate of the amount of the goods or services that the vendor expects to sell in that county, as documented by invoices indicating the wholesale value of goods to be sold;

(3) The transient vendor's permanent business address;

(4) The times and days during which, and the temporary places of business, as defined in section 5739.17 of the Revised Code, at which the transient vendor plans to do business in that county.

(B) The sheriff shall maintain a record of the information required under division (A) of this section for a period of two years, which shall be open to the inspection of any person. The sheriff shall be allowed a fee of up to one hundred dollars for collection of the bond required by this section. The bond shall be fifty per cent of the wholesale value of the goods and services provided, but in no case shall the bond exceed ten thousand dollars. The bond shall be in a form approved by the attorney general. The bond shall remain in effect for two years after the transient vendor last does business in that county.

(C) No transient vendor, as defined in section 5739.17 of the Revised Code, intending to provide goods and services of a retail value of more than five hundred dollars, shall negligently fail to file a bond within ten days before doing business as a transient vendor anywhere in that county.

(D) The bond filed by any transient vendor pursuant to this section shall be given to the attorney general by the county sheriff within ten working days after a transient vendor ceases to do business in that county, and shall be in favor of the state for the benefit of any person who suffers loss or damage as a result of the purchase of goods from the transient vendor or as the result of the negligent or intentionally tortious acts of the transient vendor in the conduct of business in the county. The bond may be used to compensate any state or local agency for damages caused by the transient vendor, for costs incurred by the agency for the illegal acts of the transient vendor, or for failure to pay any amount owed by the transient vendor to the state or local agency. The bond also may be used to compensate the state for any sales tax not paid by the transient vendor. Except for the amount of unpaid sales taxes to be deducted from the bond, if any, the attorney general shall pay any portion of the bond to any person or agency in accordance with the order of a court without making an independent finding as to the amount of the bond that is payable to that person or agency.

(E) This section does not apply to any of the following:

(1) A transient vendor making retail sales at a temporary exhibition, show, fair, world trade center, flea market, or similar event, as permitted by section 5739.17 of the Revised Code;

(2) Any nonprofit corporation, community chest, fund, or foundation organized and operated exclusively for religious, charitable, scientific, literary, or educational purposes when no part of the entity's earnings benefit any private shareholder or individual;

(3) Any person who operates a permanent business in this state, occupies temporary premises, and prominently displays the permanent business' name and permanent address while business is conducted from the temporary premises.

(4) Any person who sells goods by sample, brochure, or catalog for future delivery or any person who makes sales as the result of the invitation of an owner or occupant of a residence to the person.

(5) Any person who sells handmade or handcrafted items, or who sells fresh farm produce.

Nothing in this section shall prohibit the legislative authority of a municipal corporation from adopting an ordinance regulating transient vendors, as defined in section 5739.17 of the Revised Code, except that a municipal corporation may not require a transient vendor who obtains a bond in compliance with this section to obtain or pay for any additional bond or require that persons exempt pursuant to division (E) of this section obtain a bond. A municipal corporation may require that a transient vendor exhibit the transient vendor's license and any proof of bond required to such officer or employee of the municipal corporation as the municipal corporation designates by ordinance.

(2002 S 143, eff. 6–21–02; 1987 H 153, eff. 10–20–87; 1986 S 247)

311.41 Criminal records check and incompetency records check; destruction of records; failure to destroy records

(A)(1) Upon receipt of an application for a license to carry a concealed handgun under division (C) of section 2923.125 of the Revised Code, an application to renew a license to carry a concealed handgun under division (F) of that section, or an application for a temporary emergency license to carry a concealed handgun under section 2923.1213 of the Revised Code, the sheriff shall conduct a criminal records check and an incompetency check of the applicant to determine whether the applicant fails to meet the criteria described in division (D)(1) of section 2923.125 of the Revised Code. The sheriff shall conduct the criminal records check and the incompetency records check required by this division through use of an electronic fingerprint reading device or, if the sheriff does not possess and does not have ready access to the use of an electronic fingerprint reading device, by requesting the bureau of criminal identification and investigation to conduct the checks as described in this division. In order to conduct the criminal records check and the incompetency records check, the sheriff shall obtain the fingerprints of not more than four fingers of the applicant by using an electronic fingerprint reading device for the purpose of conducting the criminal records check and the incompetency records check or, if the sheriff does not possess and does not have ready access to the use of an electronic fingerprint reading device, shall obtain from the applicant a completed standard fingerprint impression sheet prescribed pursuant to division (C)(2) of section 109.572 of the Revised Code. The fingerprints so obtained, along with the applicant's social security number, shall be used to conduct the criminal records check and the incompetency records check. If the sheriff does not use an electronic fingerprint reading device to obtain the fingerprints and conduct the records checks, the sheriff shall submit the completed standard fingerprint impression sheet of the applicant, along with the applicant's social security number, to the superintendent of the bureau of criminal identification and investigation and shall request the bureau to conduct the criminal records check and the incompetency records check of the applicant and, if necessary, shall request the superintendent of the bureau to obtain information from the federal bureau of investigation as part of the criminal records check for the applicant. If it is not possible to use an electronic fingerprint reading device to conduct an incompetency records check, the sheriff shall submit the completed standard fingerprint impression sheet of the applicant, along with the applicant's social security number, to the superintendent of the bureau of criminal identification and investigation and shall request the bureau to conduct the incompetency records check. The sheriff shall not retain the applicant's fingerprints as part of the application.

(2) Except as otherwise provided in this division, if at any time the applicant decides not to continue with the application process, the sheriff immediately shall cease any investigation that is being conducted under division (A)(1) of this section. The sheriff shall not cease that investigation if, at the time of the applicant's decision not to continue with the application process, the sheriff had determined from any of the sheriff's investigations that the applicant then was engaged in activity of a criminal nature.

(B) If a criminal records check and an incompetency records check conducted under division (A) of this section do not indicate that the applicant fails to meet the criteria described in division (D)(1) of section 2923.125 of the Revised Code, except as otherwise provided in this division, the sheriff shall destroy or cause a designated employee to destroy all records other than the application for a license to carry a concealed handgun, the application to renew a license to carry a concealed handgun, or the affidavit submitted regarding an application for a temporary emergency license to carry a concealed handgun that were made in connection with the criminal records check and incompetency records check within twenty days after conducting the criminal records check and incompetency records check. If an applicant appeals a denial of an application as described in division (D) (2) of section 2923.125 of the Revised Code or challenges the results of a criminal records check pursuant to section 2923.127 of the Revised Code, records of fingerprints of the applicant shall not be destroyed during the pendency of the appeal or the challenge and review. When an applicant appeals a denial as described in that division, the twenty-day period described in this division commences regarding the fingerprints upon the determination of the appeal. When required as a result of a challenge and review performed pursuant to section 2923.127 of the Revised Code, the source the sheriff used in conducting the criminal records check shall destroy or the chief operating officer of the source shall cause an employee of the source designated by the chief to destroy all records other than the application for a license to carry a concealed handgun, the application to renew a license to carry a concealed handgun, or the affidavit submitted regarding an application for a temporary emergency license to carry a concealed handgun that were made in connection with the criminal records check within twenty days after completion of that challenge and review.

(C) If division (B) of this section applies to a particular criminal records check or incompetency records check, no sheriff, employee of a sheriff designated by the sheriff to destroy records under that division, source the sheriff used in conducting the criminal records check or incompetency records check, or employee of the source designated by the chief operating officer of the source to destroy records under that division shall fail to destroy or cause to be destroyed within the applicable twenty-day period specified in that division all records other than the application for a license to carry a concealed handgun, the application to renew a license to carry a concealed handgun, or the affidavit submitted regarding an application for a temporary emergency license to carry a concealed handgun made in connection with the particular criminal records check or incompetency records check.

(D) Whoever violates division (C) of this section is guilty of failure to destroy records, a misdemeanor of the second degree.

(E) As used in this section, "handgun" has the same meaning as in section 2923.11 of the Revised Code.

(2004 H 12, eff. 4–8–04)

311.42 Sheriff's concealed handgun license issuance expense fund

(A) Each county shall establish in the county treasury a sheriff's concealed handgun license issuance expense fund. The sheriff of that county shall deposit into that fund all fees paid by applicants for the issuance or renewal of a license or duplicate license to carry a concealed handgun under section 2923.125 of the Revised Code and all fees paid by the person seeking a temporary emergency license to carry a concealed handgun under section 2923.1213 of the Revised Code. The county shall distribute the fees deposited into the fund in accordance with the specifications prescribed by the Ohio peace officer training commission under division (C) of section 109.731 of the Revised Code.

(B) The sheriff, with the approval of the board of county commissioners, may expend any county portion of the fees deposited into the sheriff's concealed handgun license issuance expense fund for any costs incurred by the sheriff in connection with performing any administrative functions related to the issuance of licenses or temporary emergency licenses to carry a concealed handgun under section 2923.125 or 2923.1213 of the Revised Code, including, but not limited to, personnel expenses and the costs of any handgun safety education program that the sheriff chooses to fund.

(2004 H 12, eff. 4–8–04)

311.99 Penalties

(A) Whoever violates section 311.13 of the Revised Code shall be fined not more than one thousand dollars and imprisoned in the county jail not less than thirty days or more than two years.

(B) Whoever violates division (A) or (C) of section 311.37 of the Revised Code is guilty of failure to file a transient vendor's information or bond, a minor misdemeanor. If the offender previously has been convicted of a violation of division (A) of section 311.37 of the Revised Code, failure to file a transient vendor's information or bond is a misdemeanor of the second degree. If the offender previously has been convicted of two or more violations of division (A) of section 311.37 of the Revised Code, failure to file a transient vendor's information or bond is a misdemeanor of the first degree. A sheriff or police officer in a municipal corporation may enforce this division. The prosecuting attorney of a county shall inform the tax commissioner of any instance when a complaint is brought against a transient vendor pursuant to this division.

(2002 S 143, eff. 6–21–02; 1995 S 2, eff. 7–1–96; 1986 H 683, eff. 3–11–87; 1986 S 247; 1971 H 24; 1970 H 920; 1969 H 625; 1953 H 1; Source—GC 2840)

CHAPTER 313

CORONER

QUALIFICATIONS, DUTIES AND RECORDS

NOTIFICATION AND AUTOPSY

QUALIFICATIONS, DUTIES AND RECORDS

313.09 Records

The coroner shall keep a complete record of and shall fill in the cause of death on the death certificate, in all cases coming under his jurisdiction. All records shall be kept in the office of the coroner, but, if no such office is maintained, then such records shall be kept in the office of the clerk of the court of common pleas. Such records shall be properly indexed, and shall state the name, if known, of every deceased person as described in section 313.12 of the Revised Code, the place where the body was found, date of death, cause of death, and all other available information. The report of the coroner and the detailed findings of the autopsy shall be attached to the report of each case. The coroner shall promptly deliver, to the prosecuting attorney of the county in which such death occurred, copies of all necessary records relating to every death in which, in the judgment of the coroner or prosecuting attorney, further investigation is advisable. The sheriff of the county, the police of the city, the constable of the township, or marshal of the village in which the death occurred may be requested to furnish more information or make further investigation when requested by the coroner or his deputy. The prosecuting attorney may obtain copies of records and such other information as is necessary from the office of the coroner. All records of the coroner are the property of the county.

(1975 H 750, eff. 8–26–75; 1953 H 1; GC 2855–10)

313.091 Inspection and receipt of medical and psychiatric records of deceased

In connection with the performance of duties under this chapter, a coroner, deputy coroner, or representative of a coroner or deputy coroner may request, in writing, to inspect and receive a copy of the deceased person's medical and psychiatric records. The person to whom the request is delivered shall make such records in the person's custody available during normal business hours to the coroner, deputy coroner, or representative for purposes of inspection and copying. A person who provides copies of medical or psychiatric records pursuant to a request made under this section may request, in writing, reimbursement in a specified amount for the necessary and reasonable costs of copying the records, in which case the coroner, deputy coroner, or representative shall remit that amount to the person upon receipt of the copies.

Any medical or psychiatric record provided to a coroner, deputy coroner, or representative of a coroner or deputy coroner under this section is not a public record subject to section 149.43 of the Revised Code. The release of a deceased person's medical or psychiatric records to a coroner, deputy coroner, or representative of a coroner or deputy coroner in accordance with this section does not violate division (B)(4) of section 4731.22 or section 5122.31 of the Revised Code.

As used in this section and section 313.10 of the Revised Code, "medical record" has the same meaning as in division (A)(3) of section 149.43 of the Revised Code.

(2001 H 94, eff. 9–5–01; 2000 H 499, eff. 2–13–01)

313.10 Records to be public; exceptions; certified copies as evidence

The records of the coroner, made personally by the coroner or by anyone acting under the coroner's direction or supervision, are public records, and those records, or transcripts or photostatic copies of them, certified by the coroner, shall be received as evidence in any criminal or civil court in this state, as to the facts contained in those records.

Except for medical and psychiatric records provided to the coroner, a deputy coroner, or a representative of the coroner or a deputy coroner under section 313.091 of the Revised Code, all records in the coroner's office shall be open to inspection by the public, and any person may receive a copy of any such record or part of it upon demand in writing, accompanied by payment of the transcript fee, at the rate of fifteen cents per hundred words, or a minimum fee of one dollar.

(2000 H 499, eff. 2–13–01; 1953 H 1, eff. 10–1–53; GC 2855–11; Source—GC 2855–17)

NOTIFICATION AND AUTOPSY

313.11 Disturbance of certain bodies prohibited

(A) No person, without an order from the coroner, any deputy coroner, or an investigator or other person designated by the coroner as having authority to issue an order under this section, shall purposely remove or disturb the body of any person who has died in the manner described in section 313.12 of the Revised Code, or purposely and without such an order disturb the clothing or any article upon or near such a body or any of the possessions that the coroner has a duty to store under section 313.14 of the Revised Code.

(B) It is an affirmative defense to a charge under this section that the offender attempted in good faith to rescue or administer life-preserving assistance to the deceased person, even though it is established he was dead at the time of the attempted rescue or assistance.

(C) Whoever violates this section is guilty of unlawfully disturbing a body, a misdemeanor of the fourth degree.

(1990 H 639, eff. 9–26–90; 1982 H 55; 1975 H 750)

313.12 Notification of coroner in case of death by violence, casualty, suicide, or suspicious or unusual manner

(A) When any person dies as a result of criminal or other violent means, by casualty, by suicide, or in any suspicious or unusual manner, when any person, including a child under two years of age, dies suddenly when in apparent good health, or when any mentally retarded person or developmentally disabled person dies regardless of the circumstances, the physician called in attendance, or any member of an ambulance service, emergency squad, or law enforcement agency who obtains knowledge thereof arising from the person's duties, shall immediately notify the office of the coroner of the known facts concerning the time, place, manner, and circumstances of the death, and any other information that is required pursuant to sections 313.01 to 313.22 of the Revised Code. In such cases, if a request is made for cremation, the funeral director called in attendance shall immediately notify the coroner.

(B) As used in this section, "mentally retarded person" and "developmentally disabled person" have the same meanings as in section 5123.01 of the Revised Code.

(2004 S 178, eff. 1–30–04; 1992 H 244, eff. 11–1–92; 1975 H 750; 1953 H 1; GC 2855–5)

313.121 Autopsy of child under two years of age dying suddenly when in apparent good health

(A) As used in this section, "parent" means either parent, except that if one parent has been designated the residential parent and legal custodian of the child, "parent" means the designated residential parent and legal custodian, and if a person other than a parent is the child's legal guardian, "parent" means the legal guardian.

(B) If a child under two years of age dies suddenly when in apparent good health, the death shall be reported immediately to the coroner of the county in which the death occurred, as required by section 313.12 of the Revised Code. Except as provided in division (C) of this section, the coroner or deputy coroner shall perform an autopsy on the child. The autopsy shall be performed in accordance with public health council rules adopted under section 313.122 of the Revised Code. The coroner or deputy coroner may perform research procedures and tests when performing the autopsy.

(C) A coroner or deputy coroner is not required to perform an autopsy if the coroner of the county in which the death occurred or a court with jurisdiction over the deceased body determines under section 313.131 of the Revised Code that an autopsy is contrary to the religious beliefs of the child. If the coroner or the court makes such a determination, the coroner shall notify the health district or department of health with jurisdiction in the area in which the child's parent resides. For purposes of this division, the religious beliefs of the parents of a child shall be considered to be the religious beliefs of the child.

(D) If the child's parent makes a written or verbal request for the preliminary results of the autopsy after the results are available, the coroner, or a person designated by him, shall give the parent an oral statement of the preliminary results.

The coroner, within a reasonable time after the final results of the autopsy are reported, shall send written notice of the results to the state department of health, the health district or department with jurisdiction in the area in which the child's parent resides, and, upon the request of a parent of the child, to the child's attending physician. Upon the written request of a parent of the child and the payment of the transcript fee required by section 313.10 of the Revised Code, the coroner shall send written notice of the final results to that parent. The notice sent to the state department of health shall include all of the information specified by rule of the public health council adopted under section 313.122 of the Revised Code.

(E) On the occurrence of any of the following, the health district or department with jurisdiction in the area in which the child's parent resides shall offer the parent any counseling or other supportive services it has available:

(1) When it learns through any source that an autopsy is being performed on a child under two years of age who died suddenly when in apparent good health;

(2) When it receives notice that the final result of an autopsy performed pursuant to this section concluded that the child died of sudden infant death syndrome;

(3) When it is notified by the coroner that, pursuant to division (C) of this section, an autopsy was not performed.

(F) When a health district or department receives notice that the final result of an autopsy performed pursuant to this section concluded that the child died of sudden infant death syndrome or that, pursuant to division (C) of this section, an autopsy was not performed but sudden infant death syndrome may have been the cause of death, it shall offer the child's parent information about sudden infant death syndrome. The state department of health shall ensure that current information on sudden infant death syndrome is available for distribution by health districts and departments.

(1992 H 244, eff. 11–1–92)

313.122 Protocol governing autopsies

The public health council, after reviewing and considering any recommendations made by the Ohio state coroners association, shall adopt rules in accordance with Chapter 119. of the Revised Code establishing a protocol governing the performance of autopsies under section 313.121 of the Revised Code. The rules shall specify the information derived from an autopsy that a coroner is required to report to the state department of health. The public health council shall not amend the rules adopted under this section unless it notifies the Ohio state coroners association of the proposed changes and consults with the association.

(1992 H 244, eff. 11–1–92)

313.13 Autopsy; waiver of right to donated body parts; blood test for alcohol and drug content

(A) The coroner, any deputy coroner, an investigator appointed pursuant to section 313.05 of the Revised Code, or any other person the coroner designates as having the authority to act under this section may go to the dead body and take charge of it. Whether and when an autopsy is performed shall be determined under sections 313.121 and 313.131 of the Revised Code. If an autopsy is performed by the coroner, deputy coroner, or pathologists, a detailed description of the observations written during the progress of such autopsy, or as soon after such autopsy as reasonably possible, and the conclusions drawn from the observations shall be filed in the office of the coroner.

If he takes charge of and decides to perform, or performs, an autopsy on a dead body under section 313.121 or 313.131 of the Revised Code, the coroner, or in his absence, any deputy coroner, under division (E) of section 2108.02 of the Revised Code, may waive his paramount right to any donated part of the dead body.

(B) If the office of the coroner is notified that a person who was the operator of a motor vehicle that was involved in an accident or crash was killed in the accident or crash or died as a result of injuries suffered in it, the coroner, deputy coroner, or pathologist shall go to the dead body and take charge of it and administer a chemical test to the blood of the deceased person to determine the alcohol, drug, or alcohol and drug content of the blood. This division does not authorize the coroner, deputy coroner, or pathologist to perform an autopsy, and does not affect and shall not be construed as affecting the provisions of section 313.131 of the Revised Code that govern the determination of whether and when an autopsy is to be performed.

(1992 H 244, eff. 11–1–92; 1990 H 639, S 131; 1986 S 283; 1976 H 1182; 1953 H 1; GC 2855–6)

313.131 Autopsy contrary to deceased's religious beliefs; injunctions

(A) As used in this section:

(1) "Friend" means any person who maintained regular contact with the deceased person, and who was familiar with the deceased person's activities, health, and religious beliefs at the time of the deceased person's death, any person who assumes custody of the body for burial, and any person authorized by

written instrument, executed by the deceased person to make burial arrangements.

(2) "Relative" means any of the following persons: the deceased person's surviving spouse, children, parents, or siblings.

(B) The coroner, deputy coroner, or pathologist shall perform an autopsy if, in the opinion of the coroner, or, in his absence, in the opinion of the deputy coroner, an autopsy is necessary, except for certain circumstances provided for in this section where a relative or friend of the deceased person informs the coroner that an autopsy is contrary to the deceased person's religious beliefs, or the coroner otherwise has reason to believe that an autopsy is contrary to the deceased person's religious beliefs. The coroner has such reason to believe an autopsy is contrary to the deceased person's religious beliefs if a document signed by the deceased and stating an objection to an autopsy is found on the deceased's person or in his effects. For the purposes of this division, a person is a relative or friend of the deceased person if the person presents an affidavit stating that he is a relative or friend as defined in division (A) of this section.

(C)(1) Except as provided in division (F) of this section, if a relative or friend of the deceased person informs the coroner that an autopsy is contrary to the deceased person's religious beliefs, or the coroner otherwise has reason to believe that an autopsy is contrary to the deceased person's religious beliefs, and the coroner concludes the autopsy is a compelling public necessity, no autopsy shall be performed for forty-eight hours after the coroner takes charge of the deceased person. An autopsy is a compelling public necessity if it is necessary to the conduct of an investigation by law enforcement officials of a homicide or suspected homicide, or any other criminal investigation, or is necessary to establish the cause of the deceased person's death for the purpose of protecting against an immediate and substantial threat to the public health. During the forty-eight hour period, the objecting relative or friend may file suit to enjoin the autopsy, and shall give notice of any such filing to the coroner. The coroner may seek an order waiving the forty-eight hour waiting period. If the coroner seeks such an order, the court shall give notice of the coroner's motion, by telephone if necessary, to the objecting relative or friend, or, if none objected, to all of the deceased person's relatives whose addresses or telephone numbers can be obtained through the exercise of reasonable diligence. The court may grant the coroner's motion if the court determines that no friend or relative of the deceased person objects to the autopsy or if the court is satisfied that any objections of a friend or relative have been heard, and if it also determines that the delay may prejudice the accuracy of the autopsy, or if law enforcement officials are investigating the deceased person's death as a homicide and suspect the objecting party committed the homicide or aided or abetted in the homicide. If no friend or relative files suit within the forty-eight hour period, the coroner may proceed with the autopsy.

(2) The court shall hear a petition to enjoin an autopsy within forty-eight hours after the filing of the petition. The Rules of Civil Procedure shall govern all aspects of the proceedings, except as otherwise provided in division (C)(2) of this section. The court is not bound by the rules of evidence in the conduct of the hearing. The court shall order the autopsy if the court finds that under the circumstances the coroner has demonstrated a need for the autopsy. If the court enjoins the autopsy, the coroner shall immediately proceed under section 313.14 of the Revised Code.

(D)(1) If a relative or friend of the decedent informs the coroner that an autopsy is contrary to the deceased person's religious beliefs, or the coroner otherwise has reason to believe that an autopsy is contrary to the deceased person's religious beliefs, and the coroner concludes the autopsy is necessary, but not a compelling public necessity, the coroner may file a petition in a court of common pleas seeking a declaratory judgment authorizing the autopsy. Upon the filing of the petition, the court shall schedule a hearing on the petition, and shall issue a summons to the objecting relative or friend, or, if none objected, to all of the deceased person's relatives whose addresses can be obtained through the exercise of reasonable diligence. The court shall hold the hearing no later than forty-eight hours after the filing of the petition. The court shall conduct the hearing in the manner provided in division (C)(2) of this section.

(2) Each person claiming to be a relative or friend of the deceased person shall immediately upon receipt of the summons file an affidavit with the court stating the facts upon which the claim is based. If the court finds that any person is falsely representing himself as a relative or friend of the deceased person, the court shall dismiss the person from the action. If after dismissal no objecting party remains, and the coroner does not have reason to believe that an autopsy is contrary to the deceased person's religious beliefs, the court shall dismiss the action and the coroner may proceed with the autopsy. The court shall order the autopsy after hearing the petition if the court finds that under the circumstances the coroner has demonstrated a need for the autopsy. The court shall waive the payment of all court costs in the action. If the petition is denied, the coroner shall immediately proceed under section 313.14 of the Revised Code.

Any autopsy performed pursuant to a court order granting an autopsy shall be performed using the least intrusive procedure.

(E) For purposes of divisions (B), (C)(1), and (D)(1) of this section, any time the friends or relatives of a deceased person disagree about whether an autopsy is contrary to the deceased person's religious beliefs, the coroner shall consider only the information provided to him by the person of highest priority, as determined by which is listed first among the following:

(1) The deceased person's surviving spouse;

(2) An adult son or daughter of the deceased person;

(3) Either parent of the deceased person;

(4) An adult brother or sister of the deceased person;

(5) The guardian of the person of the deceased person at the time of death;

(6) A person other than those listed in divisions (E)(1) to (5) of this section who is a friend as defined in division (A) of this section.

If two or more persons of equal priority disagree about whether an autopsy is contrary to the deceased person's religious beliefs, and those persons are also of the highest priority among those who provide the coroner with information the coroner has reason to believe that an autopsy is contrary to the deceased person's religious beliefs.

(F)(1) Divisions (C)(1) and (2) of this section do not apply in any case involving aggravated murder, suspected aggravated murder, murder, suspected murder, manslaughter offenses, or suspected manslaughter offenses.

(2) This section does not prohibit the coroner, deputy coroner, or pathologist from administering a chemical test to the blood of a deceased person to determine the alcohol, drug, or alcohol and drug content of the blood, when required by division (B) of section 313.13 of the Revised Code, and does not limit the coroner, deputy coroner, or pathologist in the performance of his duties in administering a chemical test under that division.

(1990 S 131, eff. 7–25–90; 1986 S 283)

313.14 Notice to relatives; disposition of property

The coroner shall notify any known relatives of a deceased person who meets death in the manner described by section 313.12 of the Revised Code by letter or otherwise. The next of kin, other relatives, or friends of the deceased person, in the order named, shall have prior right as to disposition of the body of such deceased person. If relatives of the deceased are unknown, the coroner shall make a diligent effort to ascertain the next of kin, other relatives, or friends of the deceased person. The coroner shall take charge and possession of all moneys, clothing, and other valuable personal effects of such deceased person, found in connection with or pertaining to such body, and shall store such possessions in the county coroner's office or such other suitable place as is provided for such storage by the board of county commissioners. If the coroner considers it advisable, he may after taking adequate precautions for the security of such possessions, store the possessions where he finds them until other storage space becomes available. After using such of the clothing as is necessary in the burial of the body, in case the cost of the burial is paid by the county, the coroner shall sell at public auction the valuable personal effects of such deceased persons, found in connection with or pertaining to the unclaimed dead body, except firearms, which shall be disposed of as provided by section 313.141 of the Revised Code, and he shall make a verified inventory of such effects. Such effects shall be sold within eighteen months after burial, or after delivery of such body in accordance with section 1713.34 of the Revised Code. All moneys derived from such sale shall be deposited in the county treasury. A notice of such sale shall be given in one newspaper of general circulation in the county, for five days in succession, and the sale shall be held immediately thereafter. The cost of such advertisement and notices shall be paid by the board upon the submission of a verified statement therefor, certified to the coroner.

This section does not invalidate section 1713.34 of the Revised Code.

(1982 H 55, eff. 8–19–82; 1976 H 1182; 1975 H 750; 1953 H 1; GC 2855–13)

313.141 Delivery of firearms to police chief or sheriff; disposition

If firearms are included in the valuable personal effects of a deceased person who met death in the manner described by section 313.12 of the Revised Code, the coroner shall deliver the firearms to the chief of police of the municipal corporation within which the body is found, or to the sheriff of the county if the body is not found within a municipal corporation. The firearms shall be used for law enforcement purposes only or they shall be destroyed. Upon delivery of the firearms to the chief of police or the sheriff, the law enforcement officer to whom the delivery is made shall give the coroner a receipt for the firearms that states the date of delivery and an accurate description of the firearms.

(1976 H 1182, eff. 8–1–76)

313.15 Body held until diagnosis made

All dead bodies in the custody of the coroner shall be held until such time as the coroner, after consultation with the prosecuting attorney, or with the police department of a municipal corporation, if the death occurred in a municipal corporation, or with the sheriff, has decided that it is no longer necessary to hold such body to enable him to decide on a diagnosis giving a reasonable and true cause of death, or to decide that such body is no longer necessary to assist any of such officials in his duties.

(1953 H 1, eff. 10–1–53; GC 2855–14)

313.16 Laboratory examinations by coroner of another county

In counties where no coroner's laboratory has been established or where the coroner's laboratory does not have the equipment or personnel to follow the protocol established by rule of the public health council adopted under section 313.122 of the Revised Code, the coroner may request a coroner of a county in which such a laboratory is established or that has a laboratory able to follow the public health council's protocol to perform necessary laboratory examinations, the cost of which shall be no greater than the actual value of the services of technicians and the materials used in performing such examination. Money derived from the fees paid for these examinations shall be kept in a special fund, for the use of the coroner's laboratory, from which fund replacements can be made. Such funds shall be used to purchase necessary supplies and equipment for the laboratory.

(1992 H 244, eff. 11–1–92; 1953 H 1; GC 2855–15)

INQUEST

313.17 Subpoenas; oath and testimony of witnesses

The coroner or deputy coroner may issue subpoenas for such witnesses as are necessary, administer to such witnesses the usual oath, and proceed to inquire how the deceased came to his death, whether by violence to self or from any other persons, by whom, whether as principals or accessories before or after the fact, and all circumstances relating thereto. The testimony of such witnesses shall be reduced to writing and subscribed to by them, and with the findings and recognizances mentioned in this section, shall be kept on file in the coroner's office, unless the county fails to provide such an office, in which event all such records, findings and recognizances shall be kept on file in the office of the clerk of the court of common pleas. The coroner may cause such witnesses to enter into recognizance, in such sum as is proper, for their appearance to give testimony concerning the matter. He may require any such witnesses to give security for their attendance, and, if any of them fails to comply with his requirements he shall commit such person to the county jail until discharged by due course of law. In case of the failure of any person to comply with such subpoena, or on the refusal of a witness to testify to any matter regarding which he may lawfully be interrogated, the probate judge, or a judge of the court of common pleas, on application of the coroner, shall compel obedience to such subpoena by attachment proceedings as for contempt. A report shall be made from the personal observation by the coroner or his deputy of the corpse, from the statements of relatives or other persons having any knowledge of the facts, and from such other sources of information as are available, or from the autopsy.

(1976 H 390, eff. 8–6–76; 1953 H 1; GC 2855–7)

313.18 Disinterment of body

The prosecuting attorney or coroner may order the disinterment of any dead body, under the direction and supervision of the coroner, and may authorize the removal of such body by the coroner to the quarters established for the use of such coroner, for the purpose of examination and autopsy.

(1953 H 1, eff. 10–1–53; GC 2855–8)

313.19 Coroner's verdict the legally accepted cause of death

The cause of death and the manner and mode in which the death occurred, as delivered by the coroner and incorporated in the coroner's verdict and in the death certificate filed with the division of vital statistics, shall be the legally accepted manner and mode in which such death occurred, and the legally accepted cause of death, unless the court of common pleas of the county in which the death occurred, after a hearing, directs the coroner to change his decision as to such cause and manner and mode of death.

(1953 H 1, eff. 10–1–53; GC 2855–16)

313.20 Coroner's writs

The coroner may issue any writ required by sections 313.01 to 313.22 of the Revised Code, to any constable of the county in which a body is found as described in section 313.12 of the Revised Code, or if the emergency so requires, to any discreet person of the county, and such person is entitled to receive for the services rendered the same fees as elected constables. Every constable, or other person so appointed, who fails to execute any warrant directed to him, shall forfeit and pay twenty-five dollars, which amount shall be recovered upon the complaint of the coroner, before any court having jurisdiction thereof. All such forfeitures shall be for the use of the county.

(1975 H 750, eff. 8–26–75; 1953 H 1; GC 2858)

313.21 Use of laboratory for emergency or law enforcement purposes; coroner's record

(A) The coroner may use or may allow the use of the coroner's laboratory and facilities for tests in an emergency involving suspected toxic substances or for law enforcement-related testing, and may direct his assistants and other personnel to perform such testing in addition to testing performed in execution of their duties as set forth in sections 313.01 to 313.22 of the Revised Code. Nothing in this division shall permit such testing except in compliance with state and federal quality assurance requirements for medical laboratories.

(B) The coroner shall keep a complete record of all chemical tests and other tests performed each fiscal year pursuant to division (A) of this section, the public agency, hospital, or person for whom the test was performed, and the cost incurred for each test. This record shall be kept in the office of the coroner.

(1991 S 233, § 1, eff. 11–15–91; 1991 S 233, § 4, 5; 1989 H 332, § 1, 6, 22, H 24, § 2; 1987 H 499, § 1, 3; 1978 H 1118)

CHAPTER 341

JAILS

341.01 Sheriff to have charge of jail; minimum standards

The sheriff shall have charge of the county jail and all persons confined therein. He shall keep such persons safely, attend to the jail, and govern and regulate the jail according to the minimum standards for jails in Ohio promulgated by the department of rehabilitation and correction.

The sheriff's responsibilities under this section do not extend to a jail or workhouse that is the subject of a contract entered into under section 9.06 of the Revised Code.

(1995 H 117, eff. 9–29–95; 1982 S 23, eff. 7–6–82; 1953 H 1; GC 3157)

341.011 Sheriff to notify law enforcement agencies, prosecutor, and newspaper when criminal escapes

(A) If a person who was convicted of or pleaded guilty to an offense or was indicted or otherwise charged with the commission of an offense escapes from a county jail or workhouse or otherwise escapes from the custody of a sheriff, the sheriff immediately after the escape shall report the escape, by telephone and in writing, to all local law enforcement agencies with jurisdiction over the place where the person escaped from custody, to the state highway patrol, to the department of rehabilitation and correction if the escaped person is a prisoner under the custody of the department who is in the jail or workhouse, to the prosecuting attorney of the county, and to a newspaper of general circulation in the county. The written notice may be by either facsimile transmission or mail. A failure to comply with this requirement is a violation of section 2921.22 of the Revised Code.

(B) Upon the apprehension of the escaped person, the sheriff shall give notice of the apprehension of the escaped person by telephone and in writing to the persons notified under division (A) of this section.

(1999 H 283, eff. 6–30–99; 1987 H 207, eff. 9–24–87)

341.02 County jail register; written operational policies

The sheriff shall make the following entries in a suitable book, which shall be known as the "jail register," kept in the office of the jailer, and delivered to the successor in office of such jailer:

(A) The name of each prisoner, and the date and cause of his commitment;

(B) The date and manner of his discharge.

The sheriff or jail administrator shall prepare written operational policies and procedures and prisoner rules of conduct, and maintain the records prescribed by these policies and procedures in accordance with the minimum standards for jails in Ohio promulgated by the department of rehabilitation and correction.

The court of common pleas shall review the jail's operational policies and procedures and prisoner rules of conduct. If the court approves the policies, procedures, and rules of conduct, they shall be adopted.

(1982 S 23, eff. 7–6–82; 131 v S 187; 1953 H 1; GC 3158)

341.04 Sheriff shall visit jail

The sheriff shall visit the county jail and examine the condition of each prisoner, at least once during each month.

(1982 S 23, eff. 7–6–82; 1981 S 114; 1953 H 1; GC 3160)

341.05 Jail staff

(A) The sheriff shall assign sufficient staff to ensure the safe and secure operation of the county jail, but staff shall be assigned only to the extent such staff can be provided with funds appropriated to the sheriff at the discretion of the board of county commissioners. The staff may include any of the following:

(1) An administrator for the jail;

(2) Jail officers, including civilian jail officers who are not sheriff's deputies, to conduct security duties;

(3) Other necessary employees to assist in the operation of the county jail.

(B) The sheriff shall employ a sufficient number of female staff to be available to perform all reception and release procedures for female prisoners. These female employees shall be on duty for the duration of the confinement of the female prisoners.

(C) The jail administrator and civilian jail officers appointed by the sheriff shall have all the powers of police officers on the jail grounds as are necessary for the proper performance of the duties relating to their positions at the jail and as are consistent with their level of training.

(D) The sheriff may authorize civilian jail officers to wear a standard uniform consistent with their prescribed authority, in accordance with section 311.281 of the Revised Code. Civilian jail officer uniforms shall be differentiated clearly from the uniforms worn by sheriff's deputies.

(E) Except as provided in division (B) of section 341.25 of the Revised Code, the compensation of jail staff shall be payable from the general fund of the county, upon the warrant of the auditor, in accordance with standard county payroll procedures.

(2003 H 95, eff. 9–26–03; 1996 H 480, eff. 10–16–96; 1982 S 23, eff. 7–6–82; 1953 H 1; GC 3161)

341.07 Copies of minimum standards; rules of conduct; posting or delivery

The department of rehabilitation and correction shall provide a copy of the minimum standards for jails in Ohio to the board of county commissioners, the common pleas court, and the sheriff.

The sheriff shall ensure that the prisoner rules of conduct are placed in a conspicuous location within each jail confinement area or are given to each prisoner in written form.

(1982 S 23, eff. 7–6–82; 1953 H 1; GC 3163, 3164)

341.08 Standards may be revised; distribution

The department of rehabilitation and correction may, by rule, revise, alter, or amend the minimum standards for jails in Ohio to reflect changes in case law or public policy. Such revised, altered, or amended standards shall be printed and distributed to the board of county commissioners, the court of common pleas, and the sheriff in the manner directed by section 341.07 of the Revised Code.

(1982 S 23, eff. 7–6–82; 1953 H 1; GC 3165)

341.09 Separation of prisoners in county jails

When the design of a county jail will permit, the separation of prisoners shall be as required in the minimum standards for jails in Ohio.

The department of rehabilitation and correction shall, when necessary, initiate appropriate judicial proceedings for the enforcement of this section.

(1982 S 23, eff. 7–6–82; 1953 H 1; GC 3166, 3167)

341.10 Separate confinement in new county jails

County officers having charge of the construction of a new jail shall provide for the separate confinement of prisoners, as required by section 341.09 of the Revised Code.

(1953 H 1, eff. 10–1–53; GC 3168)

341.11 Confinement of minors

Except as provided in division (C) of section 2151.311 of the Revised Code, no child taken into custody shall be held in a county, multicounty, or municipal jail or workhouse or other place for the confinement of adults convicted of crime, under arrest, or charged with crime.

Except as provided in division (C) of section 2151.311 of the Revised Code, a child confined pursuant to section 2151.311 of the Revised Code shall be held in a room or cell totally separate and removed by sight and sound from all adult prisoners.

(1996 H 480, eff. 10–16–96; 1989 H 166, eff. 2–14–90; 1982 S 23; 1953 H 1; GC 3169)

341.12 Confinement of persons in custody in jail of another county

In a county not having a sufficient jail or staff, the sheriff shall convey any person charged with the commission of an offense, sentenced to imprisonment in the county jail, or in custody upon civil process, to a jail in any county which the sheriff considers most convenient and secure.

The sheriff may call such aid as is necessary in guarding, transporting, or returning such person. Whoever neglects or refuses to render such aid, when so called upon, shall forfeit and pay the sum of ten dollars, to be recovered by an action in the name and for the use of the county.

Such sheriff and his assistants shall receive such compensation for their services as the county auditor of the county from which such person was removed considers reasonable. The compensation shall be paid from the county treasury on the warrant of the auditor.

(1982 S 23, eff. 7–6–82; 1953 H 1; GC 3170)

341.13 Sheriffs of adjoining counties to receive prisoners

The sheriff of the county to which a prisoner has been removed as provided by section 341.12 of the Revised Code, shall, on being furnished a copy of the process or commitment, receive such prisoner into his custody, and shall be liable for escapes or other neglect of duty in relation to such prisoner, as in other cases. Such sheriff shall receive from the treasury of the county from which the prisoner was removed, such fees as are allowed in other cases.

(1953 H 1, eff. 10–1–53; GC 3171)

341.14 Fees to be advanced; reimbursement by prisoner; testing for contagious diseases

(A) The sheriff of an adjoining county shall not receive prisoners as provided by section 341.12 of the Revised Code unless there is deposited weekly with the sheriff an amount equal to the actual cost of keeping and feeding each prisoner so committed for the use of the jail of that county, and the same amount for a period of time less than one week. If a prisoner is discharged before the expiration of the term for which the prisoner was committed, the excess of the amount advanced shall be refunded.

(B) Pursuant to section 2929.37 of the Revised Code, the board of county commissioners of the county that receives pursuant to section 341.12 of the Revised Code for confinement in its jail, a prisoner who was convicted of an offense, may require the prisoner to reimburse the county for its expenses incurred by reason of the prisoner's confinement.

(C) Notwithstanding any contrary provision in this section or section 2929.18, 2929.28, or 2929.37 of the Revised Code, the board of county commissioners may establish a policy that complies with section 2929.38 of the Revised Code and that requires any prisoner who is not indigent and who is confined in the county's jail under this section to pay a reception fee, a fee for medical treatment or service requested by and provided to that prisoner, or the fee for a random drug test assessed under division (E) of section 341.26 of the Revised Code.

(D) If a county receives pursuant to section 341.12 of the Revised Code for confinement in its jail a person who has been convicted of or pleaded guilty to an offense and has been sentenced to a term in a jail or a person who has been arrested for an offense, who has been denied bail or has had bail set and has not been released on bail, and who is confined in jail pending trial, at the time of reception and at other times the sheriff or other person in charge of the operation of the jail determines to be appropriate, the sheriff or other person in charge of the operation of the jail may cause the convicted or accused offender to be examined and tested for tuberculosis, HIV infection, hepatitis, including but not limited to hepatitis A, B, and C, and other contagious diseases. The sheriff or other person in charge of the operation of the jail may cause a convicted or accused offender in the jail who refuses to be tested or treated for tuberculosis, HIV infection, hepatitis, including but not limited to hepatitis A, B, and C, or another contagious disease to be tested and treated involuntarily.

(2002 H 490, eff. 1–1–04; 2002 H 170, eff. 9–6–02; 1997 S 111, eff. 3–17–98; 1996 H 480, eff. 10–16–96; 1996 S 269, eff. 7–1–96; 1995 S 2, eff. 7–1–96; 1984 H 363, eff. 9–26–84; 1953 H 1; GC 3172)

341.15 Quarterly account of fees of sheriff

At the end of each quarter, of each calendar year, the sheriff shall account for and pay to the county treasurer all money received by him as provided by sections 341.13 and 341.14 of the Revised Code.

(1953 H 1, eff. 10–1–53; GC 3173)

341.16 Process for the return of prisoner

The prosecuting attorney of the county from which a person charged with the commission of an offense has been removed for safekeeping, may file a praecipe with the clerk of the court of common pleas thereof, directing that a warrant be issued to the sheriff having the custody of such person, and commanding him to deliver the prisoner to the sheriff of the county from which the prisoner was removed, or to the sheriff of the county in which the trial is to take place upon change of venue.

(1953 H 1, eff. 10–1–53; GC 3174)

341.17 Payment of costs of habeas corpus

When a writ of habeas corpus is issued for a person removed and confined in a county jail as provided by section 341.12 of the Revised Code, the county from which such person was sent shall pay all the costs of such proceeding. Upon the presentation of the certificate of the clerk of the court of common pleas, showing the amount of such costs, to the county auditor of the county from which such person was sent, the auditor shall draw his order for such costs on the county treasurer in favor of such clerk, or in favor of such person as the clerk orders, and the clerk shall pay such costs to the persons entitled to them.

(1953 H 1, eff. 10–1–53; GC 3175)

341.18 County using jail of another county liable for damages

The county in which a prisoner was confined as provided by sections 341.12 and 341.13 of the Revised Code, shall have a right of action against the county from which such prisoner was sent, for damages done by him to the jail or other property of the county.

(1953 H 1, eff. 10–1–53; GC 3176)

341.19 Board of county commissioners may require prisoners to reimburse county for expenses of confinement; testing for contagious diseases

(A) Pursuant to section 2929.37 of the Revised Code, the board of county commissioners may require a person who was convicted of an offense and who is confined in the county jail to reimburse the county for its expenses incurred by reason of the person's confinement.

(B) Notwithstanding any contrary provision in this section or section 2929.18, 2929.28, or 2929.37 of the Revised Code, the board of county commissioners may establish a policy that complies with section 2929.38 of the Revised Code and that requires any prisoner who is not indigent and who is confined in the county's jail under this section to pay a reception fee, a fee for any medical treatment or service requested by and provided to that prisoner, or the fee for a random drug test assessed under division (E) of section 341.26 of the Revised Code.

(C) If a person who is convicted of or pleads guilty to an offense is sentenced to a term in a jail, or if a person who has been arrested for an offense, and who has been denied bail or has had bail set and has not been released on bail is confined in jail pending trial, at the time of reception and at other times the sheriff or other person in charge of the operation of the jail determines to be appropriate, the sheriff or other person in charge of the operation of the jail may cause the convicted or accused offender to be examined and tested for tuberculosis, HIV infection, hepatitis, including but not limited to hepatitis A, B, and C, and other contagious diseases. The sheriff or other person in charge of the operation of the jail may cause a convicted or accused offender in the jail who refuses to be tested or treated for tuberculosis, HIV infection, hepatitis, including but not limited to hepatitis A, B, and C, or another contagious disease to be tested and treated involuntarily.

(2002 H 490, eff. 1–1–04; 2002 H 170, eff. 9–6–02; 1997 S 111, eff. 3–17–98; 1996 H 480, eff. 10–16–96; 1996 S 269, eff. 7–1–96; 1995 S 2, eff. 7–1–96; 1984 H 363, eff. 9–26–84; 131 v S 187; 1953 H 1; GC 3177)

341.191 Health insurance claims of persons confined in county jail

(A) For each person who is confined in a county jail, the county may make a determination as to whether the person is covered under a health insurance or health care policy, contract, or plan and, if the person has such coverage, what terms and conditions are imposed by it for the filing and payment of claims.

(B) If, pursuant to division (A) of this section, it is determined that the person is covered under a policy, contract, or plan and, while that coverage is in force, the county jail renders or arranges for the rendering of health care services to the person in accordance with the terms and conditions of the policy, contract, or plan, then the person, county, or provider of the health care services, as appropriate under the terms and conditions of the policy, contract, or plan, shall promptly submit a claim for payment for the health care services to the appropriate third-party payer and shall designate, or make any other arrangement necessary to ensure, that payment of any amount due on the claim be made to the county or the provider, as the case may be.

(C) Any payment made to the county pursuant to division (B) of this section shall be paid into the county treasury.

(D) This section also applies to any person who is under the custody of a law enforcement officer, as defined in section 2901.01 of the Revised Code, prior to the person's confinement in the county jail.

(1996 S 163, eff. 10–16–96)

341.20 Food service

The board of county commissioners, with the consent of the sheriff, may contract with commercial providers for the provision to prisoners and other persons of food services, medical services, and other programs and services necessary for the care and welfare of prisoners and other persons placed in the sheriff's charge.

In the absence of a commercial food service contract, the sheriff shall appoint a cook who shall have charge over the preparation of food for the feeding of prisoners and other persons placed in the sheriff's charge. The cook need not, but may be, required to perform other staff duties provided for in this section. The compensation of the cook shall be payable semimonthly from the general fund of the county, upon the warrant of the county auditor.

(1996 H 480, eff. 10–16–96; 1982 S 23, eff. 7–6–82; 1980 H 965; 132 v S 117; 131 v S 187; 125 v 103; 1953 H 1; GC 3178)

341.21 Prisoners of the United States confined in county jails; testing for contagious diseases

(A) The board of county commissioners may direct the sheriff to receive into custody prisoners charged with or convicted of crime by the United States, and to keep those prisoners until discharged.

The board of the county in which prisoners charged with or convicted of crime by the United States may be so committed may negotiate and conclude any contracts with the United States for the use of the jail as provided by this section and as the board sees fit.

A prisoner so committed shall be supported at the expense of the United States during the prisoner's confinement in the county jail. No greater compensation shall be charged by a sheriff for the subsistence of that type of prisoner than is provided by section 311.20 of the Revised Code to be charged for the subsistence of state prisoners.

A sheriff or jailer who neglects or refuses to perform the services and duties directed by the board by reason of this division, shall be liable to the same penalties, forfeitures, and actions as if the prisoner had been committed under the authority of this state.

(B) Prior to the acceptance for housing into the county jail of persons who are designated by the department of rehabilitation and correction, who plead guilty to or are convicted of a felony of the fourth or fifth degree, and who satisfy the other requirements listed in section 5120.161 of the Revised Code, the board of county commissioners shall enter into an agreement with the department of rehabilitation and correction under section 5120.161 of the Revised Code for the housing in the county jail of persons designated by the department who plead guilty to or are convicted of a felony of the fourth or fifth degree and who satisfy the other requirements listed in that section in exchange for a per diem fee per person. Persons incarcerated in the county jail pursuant to an agreement entered into under this division shall be subject to supervision and control in the manner described in section 5120.161 of the Revised Code. This division does not affect the authority of a court to directly sentence a person who is convicted of or pleads guilty to a felony to the county jail in accordance with section 2929.16 of the Revised Code.

(C) Notwithstanding any contrary provision in section 2929.18, 2929.28, or 2929.37 or in any other section of the Revised Code, the board of county commissioners may establish a policy that complies with section 2929.38 of the Revised Code and that requires any person who is not indigent and who is confined in the jail under division (B) of this section to pay a reception fee, a fee for any medical treatment or service requested by and provided to that person, or the fee for a random drug test assessed under division (E) of section 341.26 of the Revised Code.

(D) If a sheriff receives into custody a prisoner convicted of crime by the United States as described in division (A) of this section, if a person who has been convicted of or pleaded guilty to an offense is incarcerated in the jail in the manner described in division (B) of this section, if a sheriff receives into custody a prisoner charged with a crime by the United States and the prisoner has had bail denied or has had bail set, has not been released on bail, and is confined in jail pending trial, or if a person who has been arrested for an offense, and who has been denied bail or has had bail set and has not been released on bail is confined in jail pending trial, at the time of reception and at other times the sheriff or other person in charge of the operation of the jail determines to be appropriate, the sheriff or other person in charge of the operation of the jail may cause the convicted or accused offender to be examined and tested for tuberculosis, HIV infection, hepatitis, including, but not limited to, hepatitis A, B, and C, and other contagious diseases. The sheriff or other person in charge of the operation of the jail may cause a convicted or accused offender in the jail who refuses to be tested or treated for tuberculosis, HIV infection, hepatitis, including, but not limited to, hepatitis A, B, and C, or another contagious disease to be tested and treated involuntarily.

(2002 H 490, eff. 1–1–04; 2002 H 170, eff. 9–6–02; 2000 H 349, eff. 9–22–00; 1997 S 111, eff. 3–17–98; 1996 H 480, eff. 10–16–96; 1995 S 2, eff. 7–1–96; 1982 H 269, § 4, eff. 7–1–83; 1982 S 199; 1953 H 1; GC 3179)

341.22 Religious service and welfare work in county jail

Each administrative board or other authority in the state, having control of a county jail, shall provide for the holding of religious services and the conducting of other welfare work in such jail, by such persons or organizations, and at such times, as the probate judge directs.

(1953 H 1, eff. 10–1–53; GC 3180)

341.23 Care of prisoners by municipal corporations and counties having no workhouse; reimbursement by prisoner; testing for contagious diseases

(A) The board of county commissioners of any county or the legislative authority of any municipal corporation in which there is no workhouse may agree with the legislative authority of any municipal corporation or other authority having control of the workhouse of any other city, or with the directors of any district of a joint city and county workhouse or county workhouse, upon terms on which persons convicted of a misdemeanor by any court or magistrate of a county or municipal corporation having no workhouse, may be received into that workhouse, under sentence of the court or magistrate. The board or legislative authority may pay the expenses incurred under the agreement out of the general fund of that county or municipal corporation, upon the certificate of the proper officer of the workhouse.

(B) The sheriff or other officer transporting any person to the workhouse described in division (A) of this section shall receive six cents per mile for the sheriff or officer, going and returning, five cents per mile for transporting the convict, and five cents per mile, going and coming, for the service of each deputy, to be allowed as in cases in which a person is transported to a state correctional institution. The number of miles shall be computed by the usual routes of travel and, in state cases, shall be paid out of the general fund of the county, on the allowance of the board, and for the violation of the ordinances of any municipal corporation, shall be paid by that municipal corporation on the order of its legislative authority.

(C) Pursuant to section 2929.37 of the Revised Code, the board of county commissioners, the directors of the district of a joint city and county workhouse or county workhouse, or the legislative authority of the municipal corporation may require a person who was convicted of an offense and who is confined in a workhouse as provided in division (A) of this section, to reimburse the county, district, or municipal corporation, as the case may be, for its expenses incurred by reason of the person's confinement.

(D) Notwithstanding any contrary provision in this section or section 2929.18, 2929.28, or 2929.37 of the Revised Code, the appropriate board of county commissioners and legislative authorities may include in their agreement entered into under division (A) of this section a policy that complies with section 2929.38 of the Revised Code and that requires any person who is not indigent and who is confined in the county, city, district, or joint city and county workhouse under this section to pay a reception fee, a fee for any medical treatment or service requested by and provided to that person, or the fee for a random drug test assessed under division (E) of section 341.26 of the Revised Code.

(E) If a person who has been convicted of or pleaded guilty to an offense is incarcerated in the workhouse as provided in division (A) of this section, at the time of reception and at other times the person in charge of the operation of the workhouse determines to be appropriate, the person in charge of the operation of the workhouse may cause the convicted offender to be examined and tested for tuberculosis, HIV infection, hepatitis, including but not limited to hepatitis A, B, and C, and other contagious diseases. The person in charge of the operation of the workhouse may cause a convicted offender in the workhouse who refuses to be tested or treated for tuberculosis, HIV infection, hepatitis, including but not limited to hepatitis A, B, and C, or another contagious disease to be tested and treated involuntarily.

(2002 H 490, eff. 1–1–04; 2002 H 170, eff. 9–6–02; 2000 H 349, eff. 9–22–00; 1997 S 111, eff. 3–17–98; 1996 H 480, eff. 10–16–96; 1996 S 269, eff. 7–1–96; 1995 S 2, eff. 7–1–96; 1994 H 571, eff. 10–6–94; 1984 H 363, eff. 9–26–84; 1953 H 1; GC 14564)

341.24 Health insurance claims of persons confined in workhouse

(A) For each person who is confined in a workhouse as provided in section 341.23 of the Revised Code, the county, district, or municipal corporation, as the case may be, may make a determination as to whether the person is covered under a health insurance or health care policy, contract, or plan and, if the person has such coverage, what terms and conditions are imposed by it for the filing and payment of claims.

(B) If, pursuant to division (A) of this section, it is determined that the person is covered under a policy, contract, or plan and, while that coverage is in force, the workhouse renders or arranges for the rendering of health care services to the person in accordance with the terms and conditions of the policy, contract, or plan, then the person, county, district, municipal corporation, or provider of the health care services, as appropriate under the terms and conditions of the policy, contract, or plan, shall promptly submit a claim for payment for the health care services to the appropriate third-party payer and shall designate, or make any other arrangement necessary to ensure, that payment of any amount due on the claim be made to the county, district, municipal corporation, or provider, as the case may be.

(C) Any payment made to the county, district, or municipal corporation pursuant to division (B) of this section shall be paid into the treasury of the governmental entity that incurred the expenses.

(D) This section also applies to any person who is under the custody of a law enforcement officer, as defined in section 2901.01 of the Revised Code, prior to the person's confinement in the workhouse.

(1996 S 163, eff. 10–16–96)

341.25 Commissary

(A) The sheriff may establish a commissary for the jail. The commissary may be established either in-house or by another arrangement. If a commissary is established, all persons incarcerated in the jail shall receive commissary privileges. A person's purchases from the commissary shall be deducted from the person's account record in the jail's business office. The commissary shall provide for the distribution to indigent persons incarcerated in the jail necessary hygiene articles and writing materials.

(B) If a commissary is established, the sheriff shall establish a commissary fund for the jail. The management of funds in the commissary fund shall be strictly controlled in accordance with procedures adopted by the auditor of state. Commissary fund revenue over and above operating costs and reserve shall be considered profits. All profits from the commissary fund shall be used to purchase supplies and equipment, and to provide life skills training and education or treatment services, or both, for the benefit of persons incarcerated in the jail, and to pay salary and benefits for employees of the sheriff who work in or are employed for the purpose of providing service to the commissary. The sheriff shall adopt rules for the operation of any commissary fund the sheriff establishes.

(2003 H 95, eff. 9–26–03; 1997 H 215, eff. 6–30–97; 1996 H 480, eff. 10–16–96)

341.26 Random drug testing of prisoners

(A) As used in this section:

(1) "Random drug testing" has the same meaning as in section 5120.63 of the Revised Code.

(2) "Prisoner" means a person confined in a jail or multicounty correctional center following a conviction of or plea of guilty to a criminal offense.

(B) The board of county commissioners of the county, with the consent of the sheriff of the county, or the boards of county commissioners of two or more adjacent counties that have jointly established a multicounty correctional center pursuant to section 307.93 of the Revised Code, with the consent of the sheriffs of those adjacent counties, may enter into a contract with a laboratory or entity to perform blood or urine specimen collection, documentation, maintenance, transportation, preservation, storage, and analyses and other duties required in the performance of random drug testing of prisoners. The terms of any contract entered into under this division shall include a requirement that the laboratory or entity and its employees, the sheriff, deputy sheriffs, the corrections commission or the administrator of the multicounty correctional center specified in division (D) of this section, the employees of the jail and multicounty correctional center, and all other persons comply with the standards for the performance of random drug testing as specified in rules adopted under division (C) of this section.

(C) Prior to entering into a contract with a laboratory or entity under division (B) of this section, a board of county commissioners or, in the case of a multicounty correctional center, the boards of county commissioners of the counties that have established the center shall adopt rules for the random drug testing of prisoners. The rules shall include, but are not limited to, provisions that do the following:

(1) Require the laboratory or entity to seek, obtain, and maintain accreditation from the national institute on drug abuse;

(2) Establish standards for the performance of random drug testing that include, but are not limited to, standards governing the following:

(a) The collection by the laboratory or entity of blood or urine specimens of individuals in a scientifically or medically approved manner and under reasonable and sanitary conditions;

(b) The collection and testing by the laboratory or entity of blood or urine specimens with due regard for the privacy of the individual being tested and in a manner reasonably calculated to prevent substitutions or interference with the collection and testing of the specimens;

(c) The documentation of blood or urine specimens collected by the laboratory or entity and documentation procedures that reasonably preclude the possibility of erroneous identification of test results and that provide the individual being tested an opportunity to furnish information identifying any prescription or nonprescription drugs used by the individual in connection with a medical condition;

(d) The collection, maintenance, storage, and transportation by the laboratory or entity of blood or urine specimens in a manner that reasonably precludes the possibility of contamination or adulteration of the specimens;

(e) The testing by the laboratory or entity of a blood or urine specimen of an individual to determine whether the individual ingested or was injected with a drug of abuse, in a manner that conforms to scientifically accepted analytical methods and procedures and that may include verification or confirmation of any positive test result by a reliable analytical method;

(f) The analysis of an individual's blood or urine specimen by an employee of the laboratory or entity who is qualified by education, training, and experience to perform that analysis and whose regular duties include the analysis of blood or urine specimens to determine the presence of a drug of abuse and whether the individual who is the subject of the test ingested or was injected with a drug of abuse.

(3) Specify the frequency of performing random drug testing on prisoners in the jail or multicounty correctional center;

(4) Prescribe procedures for the automatic, random selection of prisoners in the jail or multicounty correctional center to submit to random drug testing under this section;

(5) Provide for reasonable safeguards for transmitting the results of the random drug testing of prisoners in the jail or multicounty correctional center from the contracting laboratory or entity to the sheriff, the corrections commission, or the administrator of the multicounty correctional center pursuant to division (E) of this section;

(6) Establish a reasonable fee to cover the costs associated with random drug testing and analysis performed by a contracting laboratory or entity under this section and establish procedures pursuant to division (E) of this section for the collection of those fees from the prisoners subjected to the drug tests.

(D) If a board of county commissioners enters into a contract pursuant to division (B) of this section, the sheriff of that county, pursuant to the terms of the contract and the rules adopted under division (C) of this section, shall facilitate the collection, documentation, maintenance, and transportation by the contracting laboratory or entity of the blood or urine specimens of the prisoners who are confined in the jail and who are subject to random drug testing. If the boards of county commissioners that have jointly established a multicounty correctional center enter into a contract pursuant to division (B) of this section, the corrections commission or the administrator of the multicounty correctional center, pursuant to the terms of the contract and the rules adopted under division (C) of this section, shall facilitate the collection, documentation, maintenance, and transportation by the contracting laboratory or entity of the blood or urine specimens of the prisoners who are confined in the multicounty correctional center and who are subject to random drug testing.

(E) If a county or two or more adjacent counties enter into a contract pursuant to division (B) of this section and the contracting laboratory or entity performs the random drug testing as provided in the contract, the laboratory or entity shall transmit the results of the drug tests to the sheriff, corrections commission, or administrator who facilitated the collection, documentation, maintenance, and transportation of blood or urine specimens under division (D) of this section. The sheriff, corrections commission, or administrator shall file for record the results of the random drug tests that indicate whether or not each prisoner who is confined in the jail or multicounty correctional center and who was subjected to the drug test ingested or was injected with a drug of abuse. The sheriff, corrections commission, or administrator shall give appropriate notice of the drug test results to each prisoner who was subjected to the drug test and whose drug test results indicate that the prisoner ingested or was injected with a drug of abuse. The sheriff, corrections commission, or administrator shall afford that prisoner an opportunity to be heard regarding the results of the drug test and to present contrary evidence at a hearing held before the sheriff, corrections commission, or administrator within thirty days after notification of the prisoner under this division. After the hearing, if a hearing is held, the sheriff, corrections commission, or administrator shall make a determination regarding any evidence presented by the prisoner. If the sheriff, corrections commission, or administrator rejects the evidence presented by the prisoner at the hearing or if no hearing is held under this division, the sheriff, corrections commission, or administrator may assess a reasonable fee, determined pursuant to division (C) of this section, for the costs associated with the random drug test to be paid by the prisoner whose drug test results indicate that the prisoner ingested or was injected with a drug of abuse. The sheriff, corrections commission, or administrator may collect the fee pursuant to section 307.93, 341.14, 341.19, 341.21, or 341.23 of the Revised Code.

(2002 H 170, eff. 9–6–02; 2000 H 349, eff. 9–22–00)

341.27. Immunity from civil liability for death of prisoner on work detail

(A) As used in this section:

(1) "County correctional facility" has the same meaning as in section 341.42 of the Revised Code.

(2) "County correctional officer" has the same meaning as in section 341.41 of the Revised Code.

(B) If all the prisoners or adult offenders working on a work detail administered by a county correctional facility and outside the facility have volunteered for the work detail and are imprisoned or reside in that facility for an offense other than a felony of the first or second degree and if the applicable county correctional officer complies with division (C) of this section, both of the following apply:

(1) No sheriff, deputy sheriff, or county correctional officer is liable for civil damages for injury, death, or loss to person or property caused or suffered by a prisoner or adult offender working on the work detail unless the injury, death, or loss results from malice or wanton or reckless misconduct of the sheriff, deputy sheriff, or county correctional officer.

(2) The county in which the prisoners or adult offenders work on the work detail and that employs the sheriff, deputy sheriff, or county correctional officer is not liable for civil damages for injury, death, or loss to person or property caused or suffered by a prisoner or adult offender working on the work detail unless the injury, death, or loss results from malice or wanton or reckless misconduct of the sheriff or any deputy sheriff or county correctional officer.

(C) To qualify for the immunity described in division (B)(1) of this section regarding a work detail, a county correctional officer, prior to having the prisoners or adult offenders of the county correctional facility, work outside the facility on the work detail, shall inform each prisoner or adult offender on the work detail of the provisions of this section, including notifying the prisoner or adult offender that, by volunteering for the work detail, the prisoner or adult offender cannot hold the sheriff, deputy sheriff, or county correctional officer or the county liable for civil damages for injury, death, or loss to person or property unless the injury, death, or loss results from malice or wanton or reckless misconduct of the sheriff, deputy sheriff, or county correctional officer.

(2004 H 316, eff. 3–31–05)

341.31 County rehabilitation work camps

In addition to its other powers, the board of county commissioners of any county may construct, maintain, equip, furnish, appoint the necessary personnel of, and supervise the operation of county rehabilitation work camps for the purpose of the rehabilitation of persons who have been sentenced to imprisonment for a misdemeanor.

(1990 S 258, eff. 8–22–90; 128 v 1043)

341.32 Agreement with other counties and municipal corporations

The board of county commissioners of any county not having a county rehabilitation work camp or the legislative authority of any municipal corporation may agree upon the terms on which persons convicted of a misdemeanor by any court or magistrate of such county or municipal corporation may be received into a county rehabilitation work camp under sentence of such court or magistrate. Such board or legislative authority may pay the expenses, including the cost of transportation of prisoners, incurred under such agreement out of the general fund of such county or municipal corporation, upon the certificate of the proper officer of such county work rehabilitation camp.

(128 v 1043, eff. 11–5–59)

341.33 Use of county rehabilitation work camps by municipal corporations

Imprisonment under the ordinances of a municipal corporation, in addition to the manner provided for in section 1905.35 of the Revised Code, may be in a county rehabilitation work camp, provided an agreement for the use of such camp has been entered into between the board of county commissioners of the county wherein such camp is located and the legislative authority of such municipal corporation.

(128 v 1043, eff. 11–5–59)

341.34 Minimum security misdemeanant jails; testing for contagious diseases

(A) As used in this section, "building or structure" includes, but is not limited to, a modular unit, building, or structure and a movable unit, building, or structure.

(B)(1) The board of county commissioners of any county, by resolution, may dedicate and permit the use, as a minimum security jail, of any vacant or abandoned public building or structure owned by the county that has not been dedicated to or is not then in use for any county or other public purpose, or any building or structure rented or leased by the county. The board of county commissioners of any county, by resolution, also may dedicate and permit the use, as a minimum security jail, of any building or structure purchased by or constructed by or for the county. Subject to divisions (B)(3) and (C) of this section, upon the effective date of such a resolution, the specified building or structure shall be used, in accordance with this section, for the confinement of persons who meet one of the following conditions:

(a) The person is sentenced to a term of imprisonment for a traffic violation or a misdemeanor or is sentenced to a residential sanction in the jail for a felony of the fourth or fifth degree pursuant to sections 2929.11 to 2929.19 of the Revised Code, and the jail administrator or the jail administrator's designee has classified the person as a minimal security risk. In determining the person's classification under this division, the administrator or designee shall consider all relevant factors, including, but not limited to, the person's escape risk and propensity for assaultive or violent behavior, based upon the person's prior and current behavior.

(b) The person is an inmate transferred by order of a judge of the sentencing court upon the request of the sheriff, administrator, jailer, or other person responsible for operating the jail other than a contractor as defined in section 9.06 of the Revised Code, who is named in the request as being suitable for confinement in a minimum security facility.

(2) The board of county commissioners of any county, by resolution, may affiliate with one or more adjacent counties, or with one or more municipal corporations located within the county or within an adjacent county, and dedicate and permit the use, as a minimum security jail, of any vacant or abandoned public building or structure owned by any of the affiliating counties or municipal corporations that has not been dedicated to or is not then in use for any public purpose, or any building or structure rented or leased by any of the affiliating counties or municipal corporations. The board of county commissioners of any county, by resolution, also may affiliate with one or more adjacent counties or with one or more municipal corporations located within the county or within an adjacent county and dedicate and permit the use, as a minimum security jail, of any building or structure purchased by or constructed by or for any of the affiliating counties or municipal corporations. Any counties and municipal corporations that affiliate for purposes of this division shall enter into an agreement that establishes the responsibilities for the operation and for the cost of operation of the minimum security jail. Subject to divisions (B)(3) and (C) of this section, upon the effective date of a resolution adopted under this division, the specified building or structure shall be used, in accordance with this section, for the confinement of persons who meet one of the following conditions:

(a) The person is sentenced to a term of imprisonment for a traffic violation, a misdemeanor, or a violation of an ordinance of any municipal corporation, or is sentenced to a residential sanction in the jail for a felony of the fourth or fifth degree pursuant to sections 2929.11 to 2929.19 of the Revised Code, and the jail administrator or the jail administrator's designee has classified the person as a minimal security risk. In determining the person's classification under this division, the administrator or designee shall consider all relevant factors, including, but not limited to, the person's escape risk and propensity for assaultive or violent behavior, based upon the person's prior and current behavior.

(b) The person is an inmate transferred by order of a judge of the sentencing court upon the request of the sheriff, administrator, jailer, or other person responsible for operating the jail other than a contractor as defined in section 9.06 of the Revised Code, who is named in the request as being suitable for confinement in a minimum security facility.

(3) No person shall be confined in a building or structure dedicated as a minimum security jail under division (B)(1) or (2) of this section unless the judge who sentenced the person to the term of imprisonment for the traffic violation or the misdemeanor specifies that the term of imprisonment is to be served in that jail, and division (B)(1) or (2) of this section permits the confinement of the person in that jail or unless the judge who sentenced the person to the residential sanction for the felony specifies that the residential sanction is to be served in a jail, and division (B)(1) or (2) of this section permits the confinement of the person in that jail. If a rented or leased building or structure is so dedicated, the building or structure may be used as a minimum security jail only during the period that it is rented or leased by the county or by an affiliated county or municipal corporation. If a person convicted of a misdemeanor is confined to a building or structure dedicated as a minimum security jail under division (B)(1) or (2) of this section and the sheriff, administrator, jailer, or other person responsible for operating the jail other than a contractor as defined in section 9.06 of the Revised Code determines that it would be more appropriate for the person so confined to be confined in another jail or workhouse facility, the sheriff, administrator, jailer, or other person may transfer the person so confined to a more appropriate jail or workhouse facility.

(C) All of the following apply to a building or structure that is dedicated pursuant to division (B)(1) or (2) of this section for use as a minimum security jail:

(1) To the extent that the use of the building or structure as a minimum security jail requires a variance from any county, municipal corporation, or township zoning regulations or ordinances, the variance shall be granted.

(2) Except as provided in this section, the building or structure shall not be used to confine any person unless it is in substantial compliance with any applicable housing, fire prevention, sanitation, health, and safety codes, regulations, or standards.

(3) Unless such satisfaction or compliance is required under the standards described in division (C)(4) of this section, and notwithstanding any other provision of state or local law to the contrary, the building or structure need not satisfy or comply with any state or local building standard or code in order to be used to confine a person for the purposes specified in division (B) of this section.

(4) The building or structure shall not be used to confine any person unless it is in compliance with all minimum standards and minimum renovation, modification, and construction criteria for minimum security jails that have been proposed by the department of rehabilitation and correction, through its bureau of adult detention, under section 5120.10 of the Revised Code.

(5) The building or structure need not be renovated or modified into a secure detention facility in order to be used solely to confine a person for the purposes specified in divisions (B)(1)(a) and (B)(2)(a) of this section.

(6) The building or structure shall be used, equipped, furnished, and staffed in the manner necessary to provide adequate and suitable living, sleeping, food service or preparation, drinking, bathing and toilet, sanitation, and other necessary facilities, furnishings, and equipment.

(D) Except as provided in this section, a minimum security jail dedicated and used under this section shall be considered to be part of the jail, workhouse, or other correctional facilities of the county or the affiliated counties and municipal corporations for all purposes under the law. All persons confined in such a minimum security jail shall be and shall remain, in all respects, under the control of the county authority that has responsibility for the management and operation of the jail, workhouse, or other correctional facilities of the county or, if it is operated by any affiliation of counties or municipal corporations, under the control of the specified county or municipal corporation with that authority, provided that, if the person was convicted of a felony and is serving a residential sanction in the facility, all provisions of law that pertain to persons convicted of a felony that would not by their nature clearly be inapplicable apply regarding the person. A minimum security jail dedicated and used under this section shall be managed and maintained in accordance with policies and procedures adopted by the board of county commissioners or the affiliated counties and municipal corporations governing the safe and healthful operation of the jail, the confinement and supervision of the persons sentenced to it, and their participation in work release or similar rehabilitation programs. In addition to other rules of conduct and discipline, the rights of ingress and egress of persons confined in a minimum security jail dedicated and used under this section shall be subject to reasonable restrictions. Every person confined in a minimum security jail dedicated and used under this section shall be given verbal and written notification, at the time of the person's admission to the jail, that purposely leaving, or purposely failing to return to, the jail without proper authority or permission constitutes the felony offense of escape.

(E) If a person who has been convicted of or pleaded guilty to an offense is sentenced to a term of imprisonment or a residential sanction in a minimum security jail as described in division (B)(1)(a) or (B)(2)(a) of this section, or if a person is an inmate transferred to a minimum security jail by order of a judge of the sentencing court as described in division (B)(1)(b) or (2)(b) of this section, at the time of reception and at other times the person in charge of the operation of the jail determines to be appropriate, the sheriff or other person in charge of the operation of the jail may cause the convicted offender to be examined and tested for tuberculosis, HIV infection, hepatitis, including but not limited to hepatitis A, B, and C, and other contagious diseases. The person in charge of the operation of the jail may cause a convicted offender in the jail who refuses to be tested or treated for tuberculosis, HIV infection, hepatitis, including but not limited to hepatitis A, B, and C, or another contagious disease to be tested and treated involuntarily.

(1998 H 293, eff. 3–17–98; 1997 S 111, eff. 3–17–98; 1996 H 480, eff. 10–16–96; 1996 S 269, eff. 7–1–96; 1995 H 117, eff. 9–29–95; 1992 S 351, eff. 7–1–92; 1990 S 258, H 837, S 131)

341.35 Contract for private management of facility

The board of county commissioners of a county with a county jail, workhouse, minimum security misdemeanant jail, or other correctional facility may enter into a contract under section 9.06 of the Revised Code for the private operation and management of that facility, but only if the facility is used to house only misdemeanant inmates.

(1995 H 117, eff. 9–29–95)

341.41 Weight exercise equipment and boxing, wrestling, or martial arts training prohibited

(A) As used in this section:

(1) "Free weight exercise equipment" means any equipment or device that is designed to increase the muscle mass and physical strength of the person using it. "Free weight exercise equipment" includes, but is not limited to, barbells, dumbbells, weight plates, and similar free weight-type equipment and other devices that the department of rehabilitation and correction, in rules adopted under section 5120.423 of the Revised Code, designates as enabling a person to increase muscle mass and physical strength.

(2) "Fixed weight exercise equipment" means any equipment, machine, or device that is not designed primarily to increase muscle mass and physical strength but rather to keep a person in relatively good physical condition. "Fixed weight exercise equipment" includes, but is not limited to, weight machines that utilize weight plates, tension bands, or similar devices that provide weight training resistance like universal and nautilus equipment. "Fixed weight exercise equipment" includes machines that are usually assembled as a unit, are not readily dismantled, and have been specifically modified for prison use so as to make them secure and immobile.

(3) "County correctional officer" means a person who is employed by a county as an employee or officer of a county jail, county workhouse, minimum security jail, joint city and county workhouse, municipal-county correctional center, multicounty-municipal correctional center, municipal-county jail or workhouse, or multicounty-municipal jail or workhouse.

(4) A person is "employed by a county" if the person is employed by, or receives any compensation or benefits from, any official, officer, office, agency, board, commission, department, or other entity that is a branch of county government, that is established by a county, or that serves a county, including, but not limited to, a sheriff.

(5) "Multicounty–municipal" has the same meaning as in section 307.93 of the Revised Code.

(B) No county correctional officer shall do any of the following:

(1) Provide a prisoner access to free weight or fixed weight exercise equipment;

(2) Allow a prisoner to provide or receive instruction in boxing, wrestling, karate, judo, or another form of martial arts, or any other program that the department of rehabilitation and correction, in rules adopted under section 5120.423 of the Revised Code, designates as enabling a person to improve fighting skills.

(C) Nothing in this section prohibits a county correctional officer from allowing a prisoner to participate in jogging, basketball, stationary exercise bicycling, supervised calisthenics, or other physical activities that are not designed to increase muscle mass and physical strength or improve fighting skills.

(1998 H 293, eff. 3–17–98; 1996 H 152, eff. 10–4–96)

341.42 Internet access for prisoners; improper internet access

(A) As used in this section:

(1) "County correctional officer" has the same meaning as in section 341.41 of the Revised Code.

(2) "Computer," "computer network," "computer system," "computer services," "telecommunications service," and "information service" have the same meanings as in section 2913.01 of the Revised Code.

(3) "County correctional facility" means a county jail, county workhouse, minimum security jail, joint city and county workhouse, municipal-county correctional center, multicounty-municipal correctional center, municipal-county jail or workhouse, or multicounty-municipal jail or workhouse.

(B) No county correctional officer shall provide a prisoner access to or permit a prisoner to have access to the internet through the use of a computer, computer network, computer system, computer services, telecommunications service, or information service unless both of the following apply:

(1) The prisoner is participating in an approved educational program with direct supervision that requires the use of the internet for training or research purposes.

(2) The provision of and access to the internet is in accordance with rules promulgated by the department of rehabilitation and correction pursuant to section 5120.62 of the Revised Code.

(C)(1) No prisoner in a county correctional facility under the control of a county shall access the internet through the use of a computer, computer network, computer system, computer services, telecommunications service, or information service unless both of the following apply:

(a) The prisoner is participating in an approved educational program with direct supervision that requires the use of the internet for training or research purposes.

(b) The provision of and access to the internet is in accordance with rules promulgated by the department of rehabilitation and correction pursuant to section 5120.62 of the Revised Code.

(2) Whoever violates division (C)(1) of this section is guilty of improper internet access, a misdemeanor of the first degree.

(2004 H 204, eff. 11–5–04; 2000 S 12, eff. 6–8–00)

CHAPTER 351

CONVENTION FACILITIES AUTHORITIES—SPECIAL POLICEMEN

Section

351.07 Employees; special police officers

(A)(1) A convention facilities authority shall employ and fix the qualifications, duties, and compensation of employees and enter into contracts for professional services as it may require to conduct the business of the authority, provided that no full-time employees shall be employed until the authority adopts and implements a policy regarding hiring preferences for veterans. The authority at any time may suspend or dismiss any employee or terminate any contract for professional services.

(2) "Veteran" means either of the following:

(a) An individual who has served in the active military or naval service of the United States and who was discharged or released under circumstances other than dishonorable;

(b) An individual who has served as a member of the United States merchant marine and to whom either of the following applies:

(i) The individual has an honorable report of separation from the active duty military service, form DD214 or DD215.

(ii) The individual served in the United States merchant marine between December 7, 1941, and December 31, 1946, and died on active duty while serving in a war zone during that period of service.

(3) "United States merchant marine" includes the United States army transport service and the United States naval transport service.

(B) A convention facilities authority may provide for the administration and enforcement of the laws of the state by employing special police officers, and may seek the assistance of other appropriate law enforcement officers to enforce its rules and maintain order. Special police officers employed by an authority shall serve as a security force with respect to the property, grounds, buildings, equipment, and facilities under the authority's control to protect the authority's property, suppress nuisances and disturbances and breaches of the peace, and enforce laws for the preservation of good order. In performing their duties, special police officers are vested with the same powers of arrest as police officers are given under divisions (A) and (B) of section 2935.03 of the Revised Code while on the grounds of the authority's facilities, and under division (D) of such section when off of the grounds of the authority's facilities.

(1999 H 118, eff. 3–17–00; 1991 H 77, eff. 9–17–91; 1986 H 583)

CHAPTER 503

GENERAL PROVISIONS

Section

503.51 Definitions

As used in sections 503.51 to 503.59 of the Revised Code:

(A) "Adult cabaret" means a nightclub, bar, restaurant, or similar establishment in which persons appear in a state of nudity in the performance of their duties.

(B) "Nudity" means the showing of either of the following:

(1) The human male or female genitals, pubic area, or buttocks with less than a fully opaque covering;

(2) The female breast with less than a fully opaque covering on any part of the nipple.

(1993 H 3, eff. 10–1–93)

503.53 Prohibitions

If a board of township trustees has adopted a resolution under section 503.52 of the Revised Code:

(A) No person shall engage in, conduct or carry on, or permit to be engaged in, conducted or carried on in the unincorporated areas of the township, the operation of an adult cabaret without first having obtained a permit from the board of township trustees as provided in section 503.54 of the Revised Code.

(B) No owner or operator of an adult cabaret located in the unincorporated areas of the township shall knowingly do any of the following:

(1) Refuse to allow appropriate state or local authorities, including police officers, access to the adult cabaret for any health or safety inspection, or any other inspection conducted to ensure compliance with sections 503.52 to 503.59 of the Revised Code and regulations adopted by the township under sections 503.52 or 503.56 of the Revised Code;

(2) Operate during the hours designated as prohibited hours of operation by the board of township trustees;

(3) Employ any person under the age of eighteen;

(4) Establish or operate an adult cabaret within five hundred feet from the boundaries of a parcel of real estate having situated on it a school, church, library, public playground, or township park.

(C) No person employed in an adult cabaret located in the unincorporated area of the township shall knowingly do any of the following in the performance of duties at the adult cabaret:

(1) Place his or her hand upon, touch with any part of his or her body, fondle in any manner, or massage the genitals, pubic area, or buttocks of any other person or the breasts of any female or, if the employee is a female, of any other female;

(2) Perform, offer, or agree to perform any act that would require the touching of the genitals, pubic area, or buttocks of any other person or the breasts of any female or, if the employee is a female, of any other female;

(3) Uncover the genitals, pubic area, or buttocks of any other person or the breasts of any female or, if the employee is a female, of any other female.

(1993 H 3, eff. 10–1–93)

503.59 Penalties

(A) Whoever violates division (A) of section 503.53 of the Revised Code is guilty of a misdemeanor of the first degree for a first offense, and a felony of the fourth degree for a second offense.

(B) Whoever violates division (B) or (C) of section 503.53 of the Revised Code is guilty of a misdemeanor of the third degree.

(1993 H 3, eff. 10–1–93)

CHAPTER 504

TOWNSHIPS—OPTIONAL LIMITED HOME RULE GOVERNMENT

Section

504.04 Powers of limited home rule townships

Note: See also following version of this section, eff. 5–6–05.

(A) A township that adopts a limited home rule government may do all of the following by resolution, provided that any of these resolutions, other than a resolution to supply water or sewer services in accordance with sections 504.18 to 504.20 of the Revised Code, may be enforced only by the imposition of civil fines as authorized in this chapter:

(1) Exercise all powers of local self-government within the unincorporated area of the township, other than powers that are in conflict with general laws, except that the township shall comply with the requirements and prohibitions of this chapter, and shall enact no taxes other than those authorized by general law, and except that no resolution adopted pursuant to this chapter shall encroach upon the powers, duties, and privileges of elected township officers or change, alter, combine, eliminate, or otherwise modify the form or structure of the township government unless the change is required or permitted by this chapter;

(2) Adopt and enforce within the unincorporated area of the township local police, sanitary, and other similar regulations that are not in conflict with general laws or otherwise prohibited by division (B) of this section;

(3) Supply water and sewer services to users within the unincorporated area of the township in accordance with sections 504.18 to 504.20 of the Revised Code.

(B) No resolution adopted pursuant to this chapter shall do any of the following:

(1) Create a criminal offense or impose criminal penalties, except as authorized by division (A) of this section;

(2) Impose civil fines other than as authorized by this chapter;

(3) Establish or revise subdivision regulations, road construction standards, urban sediment rules, or storm water and drainage regulations;

(4) Establish or revise building standards, building codes, and other standard codes except as provided in section 504.13 of the Revised Code;

(5) Increase, decrease, or otherwise alter the powers or duties of a township under any other chapter of the Revised Code pertaining to agriculture or the conservation or development of natural resources;

(6) Establish regulations affecting hunting, trapping, fishing, or the possession, use, or sale of firearms;

(7) Establish or revise water or sewer regulations, except in accordance with sections 504.18 and 504.19 of the Revised Code.

Nothing in this chapter shall be construed as affecting the powers of counties with regard to the subjects listed in divisions (B)(3) to (5) of this section.

(C) Under a limited home rule government, all officers shall have the qualifications, and be nominated, elected, or appointed, as provided in Chapter 505. of the Revised Code, except that the board of township trustees shall appoint a full-time or part-time law director pursuant to section 504.15 of the Revised Code, and except that a five-member board of township trustees approved for the township before the effective date of this amendment shall continue to serve as the legislative authority with successive members serving for four-year terms of office until a termination of a limited home rule government under section 504.03 of the Revised Code.

(D) In case of conflict between resolutions enacted by a board of township trustees and municipal ordinances or resolutions, the ordinance or resolution enacted by the municipal corporation prevails. In case of conflict between resolutions enacted by a board of township trustees and any county resolution, the resolution enacted by the board of township trustees prevails.

(2003 H 95, eff. 9–26–03; 2001 H 94, eff. 9–5–01; 1999 H 187, eff. 9–20–99; 1994 H 579, eff. 7–13–94; 1991 H 77, eff. 9–17–91)

Note: See also following version of this section, eff. 5–6–05.

504.04 Powers of limited home rule townships (later effective date)

Note: See also preceding version of this section, in effect until 5–6–05.

(A) A township that adopts a limited home rule government may do all of the following by resolution, provided that any of these resolutions, other than a resolution to supply water or sewer services in accordance with sections 504.18 to 504.20 of the Revised Code, may be enforced only by the imposition of civil fines as authorized in this chapter:

(1) Exercise all powers of local self-government within the unincorporated area of the township, other than powers that are in conflict with general laws, except that the township shall comply with the requirements and prohibitions of this chapter, and shall enact no taxes other than those authorized by general law, and except that no resolution adopted pursuant to this chapter shall encroach upon the powers, duties, and privileges of elected township officers or change, alter, combine, eliminate, or otherwise modify the form or structure of the township government unless the change is required or permitted by this chapter;

(2) Adopt and enforce within the unincorporated area of the township local police, sanitary, and other similar regulations that are not in conflict with general laws or otherwise prohibited by division (B) of this section;

(3) Supply water and sewer services to users within the unincorporated area of the township in accordance with sections 504.18 to 504.20 of the Revised Code.

(B) No resolution adopted pursuant to this chapter shall do any of the following:

(1) Create a criminal offense or impose criminal penalties, except as authorized by division (A) of this section;

(2) Impose civil fines other than as authorized by this chapter;

(3) Establish or revise subdivision regulations, road construction standards, urban sediment rules, or storm water and drainage regulations, except as provided in section 504.21 of the Revised Code;

(4) Establish or revise building standards, building codes, and other standard codes except as provided in section 504.13 of the Revised Code;

(5) Increase, decrease, or otherwise alter the powers or duties of a township under any other chapter of the Revised Code pertaining to agriculture or the conservation or development of natural resources;

(6) Establish regulations affecting hunting, trapping, fishing, or the possession, use, or sale of firearms;

(7) Establish or revise water or sewer regulations, except in accordance with section 504.18 , 504.19, or 504.21 of the Revised Code.

Nothing in this chapter shall be construed as affecting the powers of counties with regard to the subjects listed in divisions (B)(3) to (5) of this section.

(C) Under a limited home rule government, all officers shall have the qualifications, and be nominated, elected, or appointed, as provided in Chapter 505. of the Revised Code, except that the board of township trustees shall appoint a full-time or part-time law director pursuant to section 504.15 of the Revised Code, and except that a five-member board of township trustees approved for the township before September 26, 2003, shall continue to serve as the legislative authority with successive members serving for four-year terms of office until a termination of a limited home rule government under section 504.03 of the Revised Code.

(D) In case of conflict between resolutions enacted by a board of township trustees and municipal ordinances or resolutions, the ordinance or resolution enacted by the municipal corporation prevails. In case of conflict between resolutions enacted by a board of township trustees and any county resolution, the resolution enacted by the board of township trustees prevails.

(2004 H 411, eff. 5–6–05; 2003 H 95, eff. 9–26–03; 2001 H 94, eff. 9–5–01; 1999 H 187, eff. 9–20–99; 1994 H 579, eff. 7–13–94; 1991 H 77, eff. 9–17–91)

Note: See also preceding version of this section, in effect until 5–6–05.

504.05 Civil fines

The board of township trustees may impose a civil fine for a violation of a resolution adopted pursuant to this chapter, and may graduate the amount of the fine based on the number of previous violations of the resolution. No fine shall exceed one thousand dollars. Any resolution that imposes a fine shall clearly state the amount of the fine for the first and for subsequent violations.

(1991 H 77, eff. 9–17–91)

504.06 Citations

(A) Peace officers serving the township pursuant to section 504.16 of the Revised Code may issue citations to persons who violate township resolutions adopted pursuant to this chapter. Each such citation shall contain provisions that:

(1) Advise the person upon whom it is served that the person must answer in relation to the violation charged in the citation within fourteen days after the citation is served upon him;

(2) Indicate the allowable answers that may be made and that the person will be afforded a court hearing if he denies in his answer that he committed the violation;

(3) Specify that the answer must be made in person or by mail to the township clerk;

(4) Indicate the amount of the fine that arises from the violation.

(B) A peace officer who issues a citation for a violation of a township resolution shall complete the citation by identifying the violation charged and by indicating the date, time, and place of the violation charged. The officer shall sign the citation, affirm the facts that it contains, and without unnecessary delay file the original citation with the court having jurisdiction over the violation. A copy of a citation issued pursuant to this section shall be served pursuant to the Rules of Civil Procedure upon the person who violated the resolution. No peace officer is entitled to receive witness fees in a cause prosecuted under a township resolution adopted pursuant to this chapter.

(1991 H 77, eff. 9–17–91)

504.07 Citation proceedings

(A)(1) A person who is served with a citation pursuant to division (B) of section 504.06 of the Revised Code shall answer the charge by personal appearance before, or by mail addressed to, the township clerk, who shall immediately notify the township law director. An answer shall be made within fourteen days after the citation is served upon the person and shall be in one of the following forms:

(a) An admission that the person committed the violation, by payment of any fine arising from the violation. Payment of a fine pursuant to division (A)(1)(a) of this section shall be payable to the clerk of the township and deposited by the clerk into the township general fund.

(b) A denial that the person committed the violation.

(2) Whenever a person pays a fine pursuant to division (A)(1)(a) of this section or whenever a person answers by denying the violation or does not submit payment of the fine within the time required by division (A)(1) of this section, the township clerk shall notify the court having jurisdiction over the violation.

(B) If a person answers by denying the violation or does not submit payment of the fine within the time required by division (A)(1) of this section, the court having jurisdiction over the violation shall, upon receiving the notification required by division (A)(2) of this section, schedule a hearing on the violation and send notice of the date and time of the hearing to the person charged with the violation and to the township law director. If the person charged with the violation fails to appear for the scheduled hearing, the court may hold him in contempt, or issue a summons or a warrant for his arrest pursuant to Criminal Rule 4. If the court issues a summons and the person charged with the violation fails to appear, the court may enter a default judgment against the person and require him to pay the fine arising from the violation.

(C) The court shall hold the scheduled hearing in accordance with the Rules of Civil Procedure and the rules of the court, and shall determine whether the township has established, by a preponderance of the evidence, that the person committed the violation. If the court determines that the person committed the violation, it shall enter a judgment against the person requiring him to pay the fine arising from the violation.

If the court determines that the township has not established, by a preponderance of the evidence, that the person committed the violation, the court shall enter judgment against the township whose resolution allegedly was violated, shall dismiss the charge of the violation against the person, and shall assess costs against the township.

(D) Payment of any judgment or default judgment entered against a person pursuant to this section shall be made to the clerk of the court that entered the judgment, within ten days after the date of entry. All money paid in satisfaction of a judgment or default judgment shall be disbursed by the clerk as required by law and the clerk shall enter the fact of payment of the money and its disbursement in the records of the court. If payment of a judgment or default judgment is not made within this time period, execution may be levied, and such other measures may be taken for its collection as are authorized for the collection of an unpaid money judgment in a civil action rendered in that court. The municipal or county court shall assess costs against the judgment debtor, to be paid upon satisfaction of the judgment.

(E) Any person against whom a judgment or default judgment is entered pursuant to this section and any township against which a judgment is entered pursuant to this section may appeal the judgment or default judgment to the court of appeals within whose territorial jurisdiction the resolution allegedly was violated. An appeal shall be made by filing a notice of appeal with the trial court and with the court of appeals within thirty days after the entry of judgment by the trial court and by the payment of such reasonable costs as the court requires. Upon the filing of an appeal, the court shall schedule a hearing date and notify the parties of the date, time, and place of the hearing. The hearing shall be held by the court in accordance with the rules of the court. Service of a notice of appeal under this division does not stay enforcement and collection of the judgment or default judgment from which appeal is taken by the person unless the person who files the appeal posts bond with the trial court, in the amount of the judgment, plus court costs, at or before service of the notice of appeal.

Notwithstanding any other provision of law, the judgment on appeal of the court of appeals is final.

(1991 H 77, eff. 9–17–91)

504.151 Assistant law directors and employees

Subject to section 2921.421 of the Revised Code, a township law director appointed under section 504.15 of the Revised Code may appoint, as an assistant law director, prosecutor, clerk, stenographer, or other employee, a person who is an associate or partner of, or who is employed by, the township law director, assistant law director, or prosecutor in the private practice of law in a partnership, professional association, or other law business arrangement.

(1994 H 285, eff. 3–2–94)

504.16 Police

(A) Each township that adopts a limited home rule government shall promptly do one of the following:

(1) Establish a police district pursuant to section 505.48 of the Revised Code, except that the district shall include all of the unincorporated area of the township and no other territory;

(2) Establish a joint township police district pursuant to section 505.481 of the Revised Code;

(3) Contract pursuant to section 311.29, 505.43, or 505.50 of the Revised Code to obtain police protection services, including the enforcement of township resolutions adopted under this chapter, on a regular basis.

(B) A township that has taken an action described in division (A) of this section before adopting a limited home rule government need not take any other such action upon adopting that government.

(C) The requirement that a township take one of the actions described in divisions (A)(1), (2), and (3) of this section does not prevent a township that acts under division (A)(1) or (2) of this section from contracting under division (A)(3) of this section to obtain additional police protection services on a regular basis.

(1999 H 187, eff. 9–20–99; 1992 S 125, eff. 4–16–93; 1991 H 77)

CHAPTER 505

TOWNSHIP TRUSTEES

ORGANIZATION, POWERS, AND DUTIES

505.105 Deposit of stolen property by police or constable; inventory

Stolen or other property recovered by members of an organized police department of a township, a township police district, a joint township police district, or the office of a township constable shall be deposited and kept in a place designated by the head of the department, district, or office. Each article of property shall be entered in a book kept for that purpose, with the name of its owner, if ascertained, the person from whom it was taken, the place where it was found with general circumstances, the date of its receipt, and the name of the officer receiving it.

An inventory of all money or other property shall be given to the party from whom it was taken, and, if it is not claimed by some person within thirty days after arrest and seizure, it shall be delivered to the person from whom it was taken, and to no other person, either attorney, agent, factor, or clerk, except by special order of the head of the department, district, or office.

(1999 H 55, eff. 9–29–99)

505.106 Neglect or refusal to deposit stolen property

No officer, or other member of an organized police department of a township, a township police district, a joint township police district, or the office of a township constable shall neglect or refuse to deposit property taken or found by the officer or other member in possession of a person arrested. Any conviction for a violation of this section shall vacate the office of the person so convicted.

(1999 H 55, eff. 9–29–99)

505.107 Claims to stolen property

If, within thirty days, the money or property recovered under section 505.105 of the Revised Code is claimed by any other person, it shall be retained by its custodian until after the discharge or conviction of the person from whom it was taken and as long as it is required as evidence in any case in court. If that claimant establishes to the satisfaction of the court that the claimant is the rightful owner, the money or property shall be restored to the claimant; otherwise, it shall be returned to the accused person, personally, and not to any attorney, agent, factor, or clerk of the accused person, except upon special order of the head of the organized police department of the township, township police district, joint township police district, or office of a township constable, as the case may be, after all liens and claims in favor of the township have first been discharged and satisfied.

(1999 H 55, eff. 9–29–99)

505.108 Sale or contribution of unclaimed stolen property

Except as otherwise provided in this section and unless the property involved is required to be disposed of pursuant to another section of the Revised Code, property that is unclaimed for ninety days or more shall be sold by the chief of police or other head of the organized police department of the township, township police district, joint township police district, or office of a township constable at public auction, after notice of the sale has been provided by publication once a week for three successive weeks in a newspaper of general circulation in the county, or counties, if appropriate, in the case of a joint township police district. The proceeds of the sale shall be paid to the clerk of the township and credited to the township general fund, except that, in the case of a joint township police district, the proceeds of a sale shall be paid to the clerk of the most populous participating township and credited to the appropriate township general fund or funds according to agreement of the participating townships.

If authorized to do so by a resolution adopted by the board of township trustees or, in the case of a joint township police district, each participating board of township trustees, and if the property involved is not required to be disposed of pursuant to another section of the Revised Code, the head of the department, district, or office may contribute property that is unclaimed for ninety days or more to one or more public agencies, to one or more nonprofit organizations no part of the net income of which inures to the benefit of any private shareholder or individual and no substantial part of the activities of which consists of carrying on propaganda or otherwise attempting to influence legislation, or to one or more organizations satisfying section 501(c)(3) or (c)(19) of the Internal Revenue Code of 1986.

(1999 H 55, eff. 9–29–99)

505.109 Expenses of removal or storage of stolen property

Upon the sale of any unclaimed property as provided in section 505.108 of the Revised Code, if any of the unclaimed property was ordered removed to a place of storage or stored, or both, by or under the direction of the head of the organized police department of the township, township police district, joint township police district, or office of a township constable, any expenses or charges for the removal or storage, or both, and costs of sale, provided they are approved by the head of the department, district, or office, shall first be paid from the proceeds of the sale. Notice shall be given by certified mail, thirty days before the date of the sale, to the owner and mortgagee, or other lienholder, at their last known addresses.

(1999 H 55, eff. 9–29–99)

505.17 Noise control; regulations for vehicle parking; snow–emergency authorization; vehicle in violation may be stored; disposition of fines

(A) Except in a township or portion thereof that is within the limits of a municipal corporation, the board of township trustees may make such regulations and orders as are necessary to control passenger car, motorcycle, and internal combustion engine noise, as permitted under section 4513.221 of the Revised Code, and all vehicle parking in the township. This authorization includes, among other powers, the power to regulate parking on established roadways proximate to buildings on private property as necessary to provide access to the property by public safety vehicles and equipment, if the property is used for commercial purposes, the public is permitted to use such parking area, and accommodation for more than ten motor vehicles is provided, and the power to authorize the issuance of orders limiting or prohibiting parking on any township street or highway during a snow emergency declared pursuant to a snow-emergency authorization adopted under this division. All such regulations and orders shall be subject to the limitations, restrictions, and exceptions in sections 4511.01 to 4511.76 and 4513.02 to 4513.37 of the Revised Code.

A board of township trustees may adopt a general snow-emergency authorization, which becomes effective under division (B)(1) of this section, allowing the president of the board or some other person specified in the authorization to issue an order declaring a snow emergency and limiting or prohibiting parking on any township street or highway during the snow emergency. Any such order becomes effective under division (B)(2) of this section. Each general snow-emergency authorization adopted under this division shall specify the weather conditions under which a snow emergency may be declared in that township.

(B)(1) All regulations and orders, including any snow-emergency authorization established by the board under this section, except for an order declaring a snow emergency as provided in division (B)(2) of this section, shall be posted by the township clerk in five conspicuous public places in the township for thirty days before becoming effective, and shall be published in a newspaper of general circulation in the township for three consecutive weeks. In addition to these requirements, no general snow-emergency authorization shall become effective until permanent signs giving notice that parking is limited or prohibited during a snow emergency are properly posted, in accordance with any applicable standards adopted by the department of transportation, along streets or highways specified in the authorization.

(2) Pursuant to the adoption of a snow-emergency authorization under this section, an order declaring a snow emergency becomes effective two hours after the president of the board or the other person specified in the general snow-emergency authorization makes an announcement of a snow emergency to the local news media. The president or other specified person shall request the local news media to announce that a snow emergency has been declared, the time the declaration will go into effect, and whether the snow emergency will remain in effect for a specified period of time or indefinitely until canceled by a subsequent announcement to the local news media by the president or other specified person.

(C) Such regulations and orders may be enforced where traffic control devices conforming to section 4511.09 of the Revised Code are prominently displayed. Parking regulations authorized by this section do not apply to any state highway unless the parking regulations are approved by the director of transportation.

(D) A board of township trustees or its designated agent may order into storage any vehicle parked in violation of a township parking regulation or order, if the violation is not one that is required to be handled pursuant to Chapter 4521. of the Revised Code. The owner or any lienholder of a vehicle ordered into storage may claim the vehicle upon presentation of proof of ownership, which may be evidenced by a certificate of title to the vehicle, and payment of all expenses, charges, and fines incurred as a result of the parking violation and removal and storage of the vehicle.

(E) Whoever violates any regulation or order adopted pursuant to this section is guilty of a minor misdemeanor, unless the township has enacted a regulation pursuant to division (A) of section 4521.02 of the Revised Code, that specifies that the violation shall not be considered a criminal offense and shall be handled pursuant to Chapter 4521. of the Revised Code. Fines levied and collected under this section shall be paid into the township general revenue fund.

(1988 H 113, eff. 6–20–88; 1986 H 131; 1982 H 707; 1980 S 257; 1973 H 300, H 200; 1953 H 1; GC 3287)

505.171 Regulations concerning visibility of drive-in theater screen from highways

(A) Except in a township or portion thereof that is within the limits of a municipal corporation, the board of township trustees may adopt regulations necessary to require an owner or operator of a drive-in theater located in the township, to erect the theater screen in such a manner and location that the images projected on the screen are not clearly visible to persons driving on any road, street, or highway located within a radius of one-third mile from the theater screen.

(B) Except in a township or portion thereof that is within the limits of a municipal corporation, the board of township trustees may adopt regulations necessary to require an owner or operator of a drive-in theater located in the township to construct and maintain a fence, wall, or tangible or intangible barrier which shall, to the maximum extent practicable in view of the topography of the site and location of the screen, conceal or obscure X-rated or obscene images projected on the screen from the ordinary view of persons driving on any road, street, or highway located within a radius of one-third mile from the theater screen.

(C) The township constable or police district chief shall inspect each drive-in theater located in the township, but not within the limits of a municipal corporation; furnish the owner or operator thereof with a copy of the regulations adopted pursuant to divisions (A) and (B) of this section; and notify in writing the owner or operator if he finds there is a violation of the regulations.

(D) Whoever violates any regulation adopted pursuant to division (A) or (B) of this section is guilty of a minor misdemeanor.

(1978 H 662, eff. 3–14–79)

505.172 Noise control at premises to which liquor permits issued or in residential areas; exemptions

(A) Except as otherwise provided in this section and section 505.17 of the Revised Code, a board of township trustees may adopt regulations and orders that are necessary to control noise within the unincorporated territory of the township that is generated at any premises to which a D permit has been issued by the division of liquor control or that is generated within any areas zoned for residential use.

(B) Any person who engages in any of the activities described in section 1.61 of the Revised Code is exempt from any regulation or order adopted under division (A) of this section if the noise is attributed to an activity described in section 1.61 of the Revised Code. Any person who engages in coal mining and reclamation operations, as defined in division (B) of section 1513.01 of the Revised Code, or surface mining, as defined in division (A) of section 1514.01 of the Revised Code, is exempt from any regulation or order adopted under division (A) of this section if the noise is attributed to coal mining and reclamation or surface mining activities. Noise resulting from the drilling, completion, operation, maintenance, or construction of any crude oil or natural gas wells or pipelines or any appurtenances to those wells or pipelines or from the distribution, transportation, gathering, or storage of crude oil or natural gas is exempt from any regulation or order adopted under division (A) of this section.

(C) With the exception of any business operating at any premises to which a D permit has been issued by the division of liquor control, no regulation or order adopted under division (A) of this section shall apply to any business or industry in existence and operating on the effective date of this amendment, except that a regulation or order so adopted shall apply to any new operation or expansion of that business or industry that results in substantially increased noise levels from those generated by that business or industry on the effective date of this amendment.

(D) Whoever violates any regulation or order adopted under division (A) of this section is guilty of a minor misdemeanor. Fines levied and collected under this section shall be paid into the township general revenue fund.

(E) Any person allegedly aggrieved by another person's violation of a regulation or order adopted under division (A) of this section may seek in a civil action a declaratory judgment , an injunction, or other appropriate relief against the other person for committing the act or practice that violates that resolution or order. The court involved in the civil action may award to the prevailing party reasonable attorney's fees limited to the work reasonably performed.

(1999 S 42, eff. 10–20–99; 1995 S 162, eff. 7–1–97; 1990 H 737, eff. 4–11–91)

505.173 Storage of junk motor vehicles

(A) Notwithstanding sections 4513.60 to 4513.65 of the Revised Code, the board of township trustees may adopt resolutions as the board considers necessary to regulate the storage of junk motor vehicles on private or public property within the unincorporated area of the township. No resolution shall restrict the operation of a scrap metal processing facility licensed under authority of sections 4737.05 to 4737.12 of the Revised Code; the operation as a motor vehicle salvage dealer, salvage motor vehicle auction, or salvage motor vehicle pool of a person licensed under Chapter 4738. of the Revised Code; or the provision of towing and recovery services conducted under sections 4513.60 to 4513.63 of the Revised Code, including the storage and disposal of junk motor vehicles removed from public or private property in accordance with those sections. Except for a case in which division (C) of this section applies, no resolution shall prevent a person from storing or keeping, or restrict a person in the method of storing or keeping, any collector's vehicle on private property with the permission of the person having the right to the possession of the property, except that a person having such permission may be required to conceal, by means of buildings, fences, vegetation, terrain, or other suitable screening, any unlicensed collector's vehicle stored in the open.

(B) In addition to other remedies provided by law, the board of township trustees may institute an action for injunction, mandamus, or abatement, or any other appropriate action or proceeding to prohibit the storage of junk motor vehicles in violation of this section.

(C) Regardless of whether it is licensed or unlicensed, a collector's vehicle is a "junk motor vehicle" for purposes of this section if the collector's vehicle meets all of the criteria contained in division (E) of this section. If a collector's vehicle meets all of the criteria contained in division (E) of this section, a board of township trustees, in accordance with division (A) of this section, may regulate the storage of that motor vehicle on private or public property in the same manner that the board may regulate the storage of any other junk motor vehicle and, in case of a violation of this section, may pursue any remedy provided by law, including any remedy provided in division (B) of this section.

(D) Whoever violates any resolution adopted under this section is guilty of a minor misdemeanor. Each day that a violation of this section continues constitutes a separate offense. Fines levied and collected under this section shall be paid into the township general revenue fund.

(E) As used in this section, "junk motor vehicle" means a motor vehicle that meets all of the following criteria:

(1) Three model years old, or older;

(2) Apparently inoperable;

(3) Extensively damaged, including, but not limited to, any of the following: missing wheels, tires, engine, or transmission.

(1996 S 121, eff. 11–19–96; 1992 S 125, eff. 4–16–93)

FIRE AND POLICE PROTECTION

505.373 Adoption of standard fire code; procedure

The township board of trustees may, by resolution, adopt by incorporation by reference a standard code pertaining to fire, fire hazards, and fire prevention prepared and promulgated by the state or any department, board, or other agency of the state, or any such code prepared and promulgated by a public or private organization that publishes a model or standard code.

After the adoption of such a code by the board, a notice clearly identifying the code, stating the purpose of the code, and stating that a complete copy of the code is on file with the township clerk for inspection by the public and also on file in the law library of the county in which the township is located and that the clerk has copies available for distribution to the public at cost, shall be posted by the township clerk in five conspicuous places in the township for thirty days before becoming effective. The notice required by this section shall also be published in a newspaper of general circulation in the township once a week for three consecutive weeks. If the adopting township amends or deletes any provision of the code, the notice shall contain a brief summary of the deletion or amendment.

If the agency that originally promulgated or published the code thereafter amends the code, any township that has adopted the code pursuant to this section may adopt the amendment or change by incorporation by reference in the same manner as provided for adoption of the original code.

(1999 H 187, eff. 9–20–99; 1974 H 739, eff. 7–26–74)

505.374 Prohibitions

No person shall violate a provision of a standard code or regulation adopted under section 505.373 or division (C) of section 505.375 of the Revised Code. Each day of continued violation of this section shall constitute a separate offense.

(1995 H 192, eff. 11–21–95; 1974 H 739, eff. 7–26–74)

505.381 Criminal records check for firefighters or volunteer firefighters

(A) The fire chief of a township or fire district may request the superintendent of BCII to conduct a criminal records check with respect to any person who is under consideration for appointment or employment as a permanent, full-time paid firefighter or any person who is under consideration for appointment as a volunteer firefighter.

(B)(1) The fire chief of the township or fire district may request that the superintendent of BCII obtain information from the federal bureau of investigation as a part of the criminal records check requested pursuant to division (A) of this section.

(2) A fire chief authorized by division (A) of this section to request a criminal records check shall provide to each person for

whom the fire chief intends to request a criminal records check a copy of the form prescribed pursuant to division (C)(1) of section 109.578 of the Revised Code and a standard impression sheet to obtain fingerprint impressions prescribed pursuant to division (C)(2) of section 109.578 of the Revised Code, obtain the completed form and impression sheet from the person, and forward the completed form and impression sheet to the superintendent of BCII at the time the criminal records check is requested.

(3) Any person subject to a criminal records check who receives a copy of the form and a copy of the impression sheet pursuant to division (B)(2) of this section and who is requested to complete the form and provide a set of fingerprint impressions shall complete the form or provide all the information necessary to complete the form and shall provide the impression sheet with the impressions of the person's fingerprints. If a person fails to provide the information necessary to complete the form or fails to provide impressions of the person's fingerprints, the appointing authority shall not appoint or employ the person as a permanent, full-time paid firefighter or a volunteer firefighter.

(C)(1) Except as otherwise provided in division (C)(2) of this section, an appointing authority shall not appoint or employ a person as a permanent, full-time paid firefighter or a volunteer firefighter if the fire chief has requested a criminal records check pursuant to division (A) of this section and the criminal records check indicates that the person previously has been convicted of or pleaded guilty to any of the following:

(a) A felony;

(b) A violation of section 2909.03 of the Revised Code;

(c) A violation of an existing or former law of this state, any other state, or the United States that is substantially equivalent to any of the offenses described in division (C)(1)(a) or (b) of this section.

(2) Notwithstanding division (C)(1) of this section, an appointing authority may appoint or employ a person as a permanent, full-time paid firefighter or a volunteer firefighter if all of the following apply:

(a) The fire chief has requested a criminal records check pursuant to division (A) of this section.

(b) The criminal records check indicates that the person previously has been convicted of or pleaded guilty to any of the offenses described in division (C)(1) of this section.

(c) The person meets rehabilitation standards established in rules adopted under division (E) of this section.

(3) If a fire chief requests a criminal records check pursuant to division (A) of this section, an appointing authority may appoint or employ a person as a permanent, full-time paid firefighter or volunteer firefighter conditionally until the criminal records check is completed and the fire chief receives the results. If the results of the criminal records check indicate that, pursuant to division (C)(1) of this section, the person subject to the criminal records check does not qualify for appointment or employment, the fire chief shall release the person from appointment or employment.

(D) The fire chief shall pay to the bureau of criminal identification and investigation the fee prescribed pursuant to division (C)(3) of section 109.578 of the Revised Code for each criminal records check conducted in accordance with that section. The fire chief may charge the applicant who is subject to the criminal records check a fee for the costs the fire chief incurs in obtaining the criminal records check. A fee charged under this division shall not exceed the amount of fees the fire chief pays for the criminal records check. If a fee is charged under this division, the fire chief shall notify the applicant at the time of the applicant's initial application for appointment or employment of the amount of the fee and that, unless the fee is paid, the applicant will not be considered for appointment or employment.

(E) The appointing authority shall adopt rules in accordance with Chapter 119. of the Revised Code to implement this section. The rules shall include rehabilitation standards a person who has been convicted of or pleaded guilty to an offense listed in division (C)(1) of this section must meet for the appointing authority to appoint or employ the person as a permanent, full-time paid firefighter or a volunteer firefighter.

(F) A fire chief who intends to request a criminal records check for an applicant shall inform the applicant, at the time of the person's initial application for appointment or employment, that the applicant is required to provide a set of impressions of the applicant's fingerprints and that the fire chief requires a criminal records check to be conducted and satisfactorily completed in accordance with section 109.578 of the Revised Code.

(G) As used in this section:

(1) "Appointing authority" means any person or body that has the authority to hire, appoint, or employ permanent, full-time paid firefighters and volunteer firefighters under section 505.38 of the Revised Code.

(2) "Criminal records check" has the same meaning as in section 109.578 of the Revised Code.

(3) "Superintendent of BCII" has the same meaning as in section 2151.86 of the Revised Code.

(2002 S 258, eff. 4–9–03)

505.43 Contract for police protection; status of police department members

In order to obtain police protection, or to obtain additional police protection, any township may enter into a contract with one or more townships, municipal corporations, park districts created pursuant to section 511.18 or 1545.01 of the Revised Code, or county sheriffs or with a governmental entity of an adjoining state upon any terms that are agreed to by them, for services of police departments or use of police equipment, or the interchange of the service of police departments or use of police equipment within the several territories of the contracting subdivisions, if the contract is first authorized by respective boards of township trustees or other legislative bodies. The cost of the contract may be paid for from the township general fund or from funds received pursuant to the passage of a levy authorized pursuant to division (J) of section 5705.19 and section 5705.25 of the Revised Code.

Chapter 2744. of the Revised Code, insofar as it is applicable to the operation of police departments, applies to the contracting political subdivisions and police department members when the members are rendering service outside their own subdivision pursuant to the contract.

Police department members acting outside the subdivision in which they are employed may participate in any pension or indemnity fund established by their employer to the same extent as while acting within the employing subdivision, and are entitled to all the rights and benefits of Chapter 4123. of the Revised Code, to the same extent as while performing service within the subdivision.

The contract may provide for a fixed annual charge to be paid at the times agreed upon and stipulated in the contract.

(1997 H 342, eff. 12–31–97; 1992 S 174, eff. 7–31–92; 1985 H 176; 1980 S 98)

505.431 Providing police protection to other subdivisions without contract; liability; rights of members participating

The police department of any township or township police district may provide police protection to any county, municipal corporation, or township of this state, to a park district created pursuant to section 511.18 or 1545.01 of the Revised Code, or to a governmental entity of an adjoining state without a contract to provide police protection, upon the approval, by resolution, of the board of township trustees of the township in which the department is located and upon authorization by an officer or employee of the police department providing the police protection who is designated by title of office or position, pursuant to the resolution of the board of township trustees, to give such authorization.

Chapter 2744. of the Revised Code, insofar as it applies to the operation of police departments, shall apply to any township police department or township police district and to its members when such members are rendering police services pursuant to this section outside the township or township police district by which they are employed.

Police department members acting, as provided in this section, outside the township or township police district by which they are employed shall be entitled to participate in any pension or indemnity fund established by their employer to the same extent as while acting within the township or township police district by which they are employed. Those members shall be entitled to all the rights and benefits of Chapter 4123. of the Revised Code to the same extent as while performing services within the township or township police district by which they are employed.

(1992 S 174, eff. 7–31–92; 1985 H 176; 1982 H 103; 1980 S 98)

505.432 Contract for police protection with port authority or Chautauqua assembly

As used in this section, "Chautauqua assembly" has the same meaning as in section 4511.90 of the Revised Code.

Upon the approval, by resolution, of the board of township trustees of the township or township police district in which the department or office is located, the police department of any township or township police district or the office of any township police constable may contract with any port authority or Chautauqua assembly, and any port authority or Chautauqua assembly may contract with any such department or office, to have the department's members or the office's constables provide police protection to the port authority or Chautauqua assembly with which the deparment *[sic.]* or office has contracted.

Chapter 2744. of the Revised Code, insofar as it applies to the operation of police departments, applies to any township police department, township police district, or township police constable's office, and to its members or constables when they are rendering service outside their own subdivision pursuant to a contract entered into under this section.

Police department members and constables acting outside the subdivision in which they are employed may participate in any pension or indemnity fund established by their employer to the same extent as while acting within the employing subdivision, and are entitled to all the rights and benefits of Chapter 4123. of the Revised Code, to the same extent as while performing service within the subdivision.

(1995 S 93, eff. 12–5–95)

POLICE DISTRICTS

505.48 Township police district; composition; territorial limits; additions to district imposing tax

(A) The board of township trustees of any township may, by resolution adopted by two-thirds of the members of the board, create a township police district comprised of all or a portion of the unincorporated territory of the township as the resolution may specify. If the township police district does not include all of the unincorporated territory of the township, the resolution creating the district shall contain a complete and accurate description of the territory of the district and a separate and distinct name for the district.

At any time not less than one hundred twenty days after a township police district is created and operative, the territorial limits of the district may be altered in the manner provided in division (B) of this section or, if applicable, as provided in section 505.482 of the Revised Code.

(B) Except as otherwise provided in section 505.482 of the Revised Code, the territorial limits of a township police district may be altered by a resolution adopted by a two-thirds vote of the board of township trustees. If the township police district imposes a tax, any territory proposed for addition to the district shall become part of the district only after all of the following have occurred:

(1) Adoption by two-thirds vote of the board of township trustees of a resolution approving the expansion of the territorial limits of the district;

(2) Adoption by a two-thirds vote of the board of township trustees of a resolution recommending the extension of the tax to the additional territory;

(3) Approval of the tax by the electors of the territory proposed for addition to the district.

Each resolution of the board adopted under division (B)(2) of this section shall state the name of the township police district, a description of the territory to be added, and the rate and termination date of the tax, which shall be the rate and termination date of the tax currently in effect in the district.

The board of trustees shall certify each resolution adopted under division (B)(2) of this section to the board of elections in accordance with section 5705.19 of the Revised Code. The election required under division (B)(3) of this section shall be held, canvassed, and certified in the manner provided for the submission of tax levies under section 5705.25 of the Revised Code, except that the question appearing on the ballot shall read:

"Shall the territory within........................ (description of the proposed territory to be added) be added to............... (name) township police district, and a property tax at a rate of taxation not exceeding......... (here insert tax rate) be in effect for......... (here insert the number of years the tax is to be in effect or "a continuing period of time," as applicable)?"

If the question is approved by at least a majority of the electors voting on it, the joinder shall be effective as of the first day of January of the year following approval, and, on that date, the township police district tax shall be extended to the taxable property within the territory that has been added.

(2004 H 148, eff. 11–5–04; 1986 H 743, eff. 3–10–87; 130 v H 744)

505.481 Joint township police districts

The boards of township trustees of any two or more contiguous townships, whether or not within the same county, may, by a two-thirds favorable vote of each such board, form themselves into a joint township police district board, and such townships shall be a part of a joint township police district.

Such joint township police district board shall organize within thirty days after the favorable vote by the last board of trustees joining itself into the joint township police district board. The president of the board of township trustees of the most populous participating township shall give notice of the time and place of organization to each member of the board of township trustees of each participating township. Such notice shall be signed by the president of the board of township trustees of the most populous participating township, and shall be sent by certified mail to each member of the board of township trustees of each participating township, at least five days prior to the organization meeting, which meeting shall be held in one of the participating townships. All members of the boards of township trustees of the participating townships constitute the joint township police district board. Two–thirds of all the township trustees of the participating townships constitutes a quorum. Such members of the boards of township trustees shall, at the organization meeting of the joint township police district board, proceed with the election of a president, a secretary, and a treasurer, and such other officers as they consider necessary and proper, and shall transact such other business as properly comes before the board.

In the formation of such a police district, such action may be taken by or on behalf of part of a township, by excluding that portion of the township lying within a municipal corporation. The joint township police district board may exercise the same powers as are granted to a board of township trustees in the operation of a township police district under sections 505.49 to 505.55 of the Revised Code, including, but not limited to, the power to employ, train, and discipline personnel, to acquire equipment and buildings, to levy a tax, to issue bonds and notes, and to dissolve the district.

(1991 H 77, eff. 9–17–91)

505.482 Resolution for expansion of district

(A) If a township police district does not include all the unincorporated territory of the township, the remaining unincorporated territory of the township may be added to the district by a resolution adopted by a unanimous vote of the board of township trustees to place the issue of expansion of the district on the ballot for the electors of the entire unincorporated territory of the township. The resolution shall state whether the proposed township police district initially will hire personnel as provided in section 505.49 of the Revised Code or contract for the provision of police protection services or additional police protection services as provided in section 505.43 or 505.50 of the Revised Code.

The ballot measure shall provide for the addition into a new district of all the unincorporated territory of the township not already included in the township police district and for the levy of any tax then imposed by the district throughout the unincorporated territory of the township. The measure shall state the rate of the tax, if any, to be imposed in the district resulting from approval of the measure, which need not be the same rate of any tax imposed by the existing district, and the last year in which the tax will be levied or that it will be levied for a continuous period of time.

(B) The election on the measure shall be held, canvassed, and certified in the manner provided for the submission of tax levies under section 5705.25 of the Revised Code, except that the question appearing on the ballot shall read substantially as follows:

"Shall the unincorporated territory within .... (name of the township) not already included within the .... (name of township police district) be added to the township police district to create the .... (name of new township police district) township police district?"

The name of the proposed township police district shall be separate and distinct from the name of the existing township police district.

If a tax is imposed in the existing township police district, the question shall be modified by adding, at the end of the question, the following: ", and shall a property tax be levied in the new township police district, replacing the tax in the existing township police district, at a rate not exceeding .... mills per dollar of taxable valuation, which amounts to .... (rate expressed in dollars and cents per one thousand dollars in taxable valuation), for .... (number of years the tax will be levied, or "a continuing period of time")."

If the measure is not approved by a majority of the electors voting on it, the township police district shall continue to occupy its existing territory until altered as provided in this section or section 505.48 of the Revised Code, and any existing tax imposed under section 505.51 of the Revised Code shall remain in effect in the existing district at the existing rate and for as long as provided in the resolution under the authority of which the tax is levied.

(2004 H 148, eff. 11–5–04)

505.49 Rules, regulation and appointment of police officers; exception; organized crime task force membership

(A) As used in this section, "felony" has the same meaning as in section 109.511 of the Revised Code.

(B)(1) The township trustees by a two-thirds vote of the board may adopt rules necessary for the operation of the township police district, including a determination of the qualifications of the chief of police, patrol officers, and others to serve as members of the district police force.

(2) Except as otherwise provided in division (E) of this section and subject to division (D) of this section, the township trustees by a two-thirds vote of the board shall appoint a chief of police for the district, determine the number of patrol officers and other personnel required by the district, and establish salary schedules and other conditions of employment for the employees of the township police district. The chief of police of the district shall serve at the pleasure of the township trustees and shall appoint patrol officers and other personnel that the district may require, subject to division (D) of this section and to the rules and limits as to qualifications, salary ranges, and numbers of personnel established by the board of township trustees. The township trustees may include in the township police district and under the direction and control of the chief of police any constable appointed pursuant to section 509.01 of the Revised Code, or may designate the chief of police or any patrol officer appointed by the chief of police as a constable, as provided for in section 509.01 of the Revised Code, for the township police district.

(3) Except as provided in division (D) of this section, a patrol officer, other police district employee, or police constable, who has been awarded a certificate attesting to the satisfactory completion of an approved state, county, or municipal police basic training program, as required by section 109.77 of the Revised Code, may be removed or suspended only under the conditions and by the procedures in sections 505.491 to 505.495 of the Revised Code. Any other patrol officer, police district employee, or police constable shall serve at the pleasure of the township trustees. In case of removal or suspension of an appointee by the board of township trustees, that appointee may appeal the decision of the board to the court of common pleas of the county in which the district is situated to determine the sufficiency of the cause of removal or suspension. The appointee shall take the appeal within ten days of written notice to the appointee of the decision of the board.

(C)(1) Division (B) of this section does not apply to a township that has a population of ten thousand or more persons residing within the township and outside of any municipal corporation, that has its own police department employing ten or more full-time paid employees, and that has a civil service commission established under division (B) of section 124.40 of the Revised Code. The township shall comply with the procedures for the employment, promotion, and discharge of police personnel provided by Chapter 124. of the Revised Code, except as otherwise provided in divisions (C)(2) and (3) of this section.

(2) The board of township trustees of the township may appoint the chief of police, and a person so appointed shall be in the unclassified service under section 124.11 of the Revised Code

and shall serve at the pleasure of the board. A person appointed chief of police under these conditions who is removed by the board or who resigns from the position shall be entitled to return to the classified service in the township police department, in the position that person held previous to the person's appointment as chief of police.

(3) The appointing authority of an urban township, as defined in section 504.01 of the Revised Code, may appoint to a vacant position any one of the three highest scorers on the eligible list for a promotional examination.

(4) The board of township trustees shall determine the number of personnel required and establish salary schedules and conditions of employment not in conflict with Chapter 124. of the Revised Code.

(5) Persons employed as police personnel in a township described in this division on the date a civil service commission is appointed pursuant to division (B) of section 124.40 of the Revised Code, without being required to pass a competitive examination or a police training program, shall retain their employment and any rank previously granted them by action of the township trustees or otherwise, but those persons are eligible for promotion only by compliance with Chapter 124. of the Revised Code.

(6) This division does not apply to constables appointed pursuant to section 509.01 of the Revised Code. This division is subject to division (D) of this section.

(D)(1) The board of township trustees shall not appoint or employ a person as a chief of police, and the chief of police shall not appoint or employ a person as a patrol officer or other peace officer of a township police district or a township police department, on a permanent basis, on a temporary basis, for a probationary term, or on other than a permanent basis if the person previously has been convicted of or has pleaded guilty to a felony.

(2)(a) The board of township trustees shall terminate the appointment or employment of a chief of police, patrol officer, or other peace officer of a township police district or township police department who does either of the following:

(i) Pleads guilty to a felony;

(ii) Pleads guilty to a misdemeanor pursuant to a negotiated plea agreement as provided in division (D) of section 2929.43 of the Revised Code in which the chief of police, patrol officer, or other peace officer of a township police district or township police department agrees to surrender the certificate awarded to that chief of police, patrol officer, or other peace officer under section 109.77 of the Revised Code.

(b) The board shall suspend the appointment or employment of a chief of police, patrol officer, or other peace officer of a township police district or township police department who is convicted, after trial, of a felony. If the chief of police, patrol officer, or other peace officer of a township police district or township police department files an appeal from that conviction and the conviction is upheld by the highest court to which the appeal is taken or if no timely appeal is filed, the board shall terminate the appointment or employment of that chief of police, patrol officer, or other peace officer. If the chief of police, patrol officer, or other peace officer of a township police district or township police department files an appeal that results in that chief of police's, patrol officer's, or other peace officer's acquittal of the felony or conviction of a misdemeanor, or in the dismissal of the felony charge against the chief of police, patrol officer, or other peace officer, the board shall reinstate that chief of police, patrol officer, or other peace officer. A chief of police, patrol officer, or other peace officer of a township police district or township police department who is reinstated under division (D)(2)(b) of this section shall not receive any back pay unless the conviction of that chief of police, patrol officer, or other peace officer of the felony was reversed on appeal, or the felony charge was dismissed, because the court found insufficient evidence to convict the chief of police, patrol officer, or other peace officer of the felony.

(3) Division (D) of this section does not apply regarding an offense that was committed prior to January 1, 1997.

(4) The suspension or termination of the appointment or employment of a chief of police, patrol officer, or other peace officer under division (D)(2) of this section shall be in accordance with Chapter 119. of the Revised Code.

(E) The board of township trustees may enter into a contract under section 505.43 or 505.50 of the Revised Code to obtain all police protection for the township police district from one or more municipal corporations, county sheriffs, or other townships. If the board enters into such a contract, subject to division (D) of this section, it may, but is not required to, appoint a police chief for the district.

(F) The members of the police force of a township police district of a township that adopts the limited self-government form of township government shall serve as peace officers for the township territory included in the district.

(G) A chief of police or patrol officer of a township police district, or of a township police department, may participate, as the director of an organized crime task force established under section 177.02 of the Revised Code or as a member of the investigatory staff of that task force, in an investigation of organized criminal activity in any county or counties in this state under sections 177.01 to 177.03 of the Revised Code.

(2002 H 515, eff. 3–31–03; 2002 H 490, eff. 1–1–04; 1996 H 566, eff. 10–16–96; 1992 S 125, eff. 4–16–93; 1991 H 77; 1986 S 74; 1978 H 1074; 1977 H 671; 1974 H 513; 132 v H 191; 130 v H 744)

505.491 Trustees to prefer charges against delinquent police personnel

Except as provided in division (D) of section 505.49 or in division (C) of section 509.01 of the Revised Code, if the board of trustees of a township has reason to believe that a chief of police, patrol officer, or other township police district employee appointed under division (B) of section 505.49 of the Revised Code or a police constable appointed under division (B) of section 509.01 of the Revised Code has been guilty, in the performance of the official duty of that chief of police, patrol officer, other township police district employee, or police constable, of bribery, misfeasance, malfeasance, nonfeasance, misconduct in office, neglect of duty, gross immorality, habitual drunkenness, incompetence, or failure to obey orders given that person by the proper authority, the board immediately shall file written charges against that person, setting forth in detail a statement of the alleged guilt and, at the same time, or as soon thereafter as possible, serve a true copy of those charges upon the person against whom they are made. The service may be made on the person or by leaving a copy of the charges at the office or residence of that person. Return of the service shall be made to the board in the same manner that is provided for the return of the service of summons in a civil action.

(1996 H 566, eff. 10–16–96; 1974 H 513, eff. 8–9–74; 1969 H 1; 132 v H 191)

505.492 Hearing of charges; action of township trustees

Charges filed by the township trustees under section 505.491 of the Revised Code shall be heard at the next regular meeting thereof, unless the board extends the time for the hearing, which shall be done only on the application of the accused. The accused may appear in person and by counsel, examine all witnesses, and answer all charges against him.

(132 v H 191, eff. 11–24–67)

505.493 Suspension of accused pending hearing

Pending any proceedings under sections 505.491 and 505.492 of the Revised Code, an accused person may be suspended by the board of township trustees, but such suspension shall be for a period not longer than fifteen days, unless the hearing of such charges is extended upon the application of the accused, in which event the suspension shall not exceed thirty days.

(132 v H 191, eff. 11–24–67)

505.494 Power of township trustees as to process

For the purpose of investigating charges filed pursuant to section 505.491 of the Revised Code, the board of township trustees may issue subpoenas or compulsory process to compel the attendance of persons and the production of books and papers before it and provide by resolution for exercising and enforcing this section.

(132 v H 191, eff. 11–24–67)

505.495 Oaths; compulsory testimony; costs

In all cases in which the attendance of witnesses may be compelled for an investigation, under section 505.494 of the Revised Code, any member of the board of township trustees may administer the requisite oaths. The board has the same power to compel the giving of testimony by attending witnesses as is conferred upon courts. In all such cases, witnesses shall be entitled to the same privileges, immunities, and compensation as are allowed witnesses in civil cases, and the costs of all such proceedings shall be payable from the general fund of the township.

(132 v H 191, eff. 11–24–67)

505.50 Acquisition of equipment and buildings; emergency police protection

The board of township trustees of a township or a township police district may purchase, lease, lease with an option to purchase, or otherwise acquire any police apparatus, equipment, including a public communications system, or materials that the township or township police district requires and may build, purchase, lease, or lease with an option to purchase any building or buildings and site of the building or buildings that are necessary for the police operations of the township or district.

The boards of trustees of any two or more contiguous townships, may, by joint agreement, unite in the joint purchase, lease, lease with an option to purchase, maintenance, use, and operation of police equipment for any other police purpose designated in sections 505.48 to 505.55 of the Revised Code, and to prorate the expense of that joint action on terms mutually agreed upon by the trustees in each affected township.

The board of trustees of a township or a township police district may enter into a contract with one or more townships, a municipal corporation, a park district created pursuant to section 511.18 or 1545.01 of the Revised Code, or the county sheriff upon any terms that are mutually agreed upon for the provision of police protection services or additional police protection services either on a regular basis or for additional protection in times of emergency. The contract shall be agreed to in each instance by the respective board or boards of township trustees, the board of county commissioners, the board of park commissioners, or the legislative authority of the municipal corporation involved. The contract may provide for a fixed annual charge to be paid at the time agreed upon in the contract.

Chapter 2744. of the Revised Code, insofar as it is applicable to the operation of police departments, applies to the contracting political subdivisions and police department members when the members are serving outside their own political subdivision pursuant to such a contract. Police department members acting outside the political subdivision in which they are employed may participate in any pension or indemnity fund established by their employer and are entitled to all the rights and benefits of Chapter 4123. of the Revised Code, to the same extent as while performing services within the political subdivision.

(2004 H 148, eff. 11–5–04; 2003 H 97, eff. 10–21–03; 1992 S 174, eff. 7–31–92; 1986 H 743; 1985 H 176; 130 v H 744)

505.51 Police district tax levy authorized

The board of trustees of a township police district may levy a tax upon all of the taxable property in the township police district pursuant to sections 5705.19 and 5705.25 of the Revised Code to defray all or a portion of expenses of the district in providing police protection.

(130 v H 744, eff. 9–24–63)

505.511 False security alarm; charges assessed

(A) A board of township trustees that operates a township police department or the board of township trustees of a township police district may, after police constables, the township police, a law enforcement agency with which the township contracts for police services, and the county sheriff or the sheriff's deputy have answered a combined total of three false alarms from the same commercial or residential security alarm system within the township in the same calendar year, cause the township clerk to mail the manager of the commercial establishment or the occupant, lessee, agent, or tenant of the residence a bill for each subsequent false alarm from the same alarm system during that year, to defray the costs incurred. The bill's amount shall be as follows:

(1) For the fourth false alarm of that year $50.00;

(2) For the fifth false alarm of that year $100.00;

(3) For all false alarms in that year occurring after the fifth false alarm ....$150.00.

If payment of the bill is not received within thirty days, the township clerk shall send a notice by certified mail to the manager and to the owner, if different, of the real estate of which the commercial establishment is a part, or to the occupant, lessee, agent, or tenant and to the owner, if different, of the real estate of which the residence is a part, indicating that failure to pay the bill within thirty days, or to show just cause why the bill should not be paid, will result in the assessment of a lien upon the real estate in the amount of the bill. If payment is not received within those thirty days or if just cause is not shown, the amount of the bill shall be entered upon the tax duplicate, shall be a lien upon the real estate from the date of the entry, and shall be collected as other taxes and returned to the township treasury to be earmarked for use for police services.

The board of township trustees shall not cause the township clerk to send a bill pursuant to this division if a bill has already been sent pursuant to division (B) of this section for the same false alarm.

(B) The county sheriff may, after the county sheriff or the sheriff's deputy, police constables, the township police, and a law enforcement agency with which the township contracts for police services have answered a combined total of three false alarms from the same commercial or residential security alarm system within the unincorporated area of the county in the same calendar year, mail the manager of the commercial establishment or the occupant, lessee, agent, or tenant of the residence a bill for each subsequent false alarm from the same alarm system during that year, to defray the costs incurred. The bill's amount shall be as follows:

(1) For the fourth false alarm of that year $50.00;

(2) For the fifth false alarm of that year $100.00;

(3) For all false alarms in that year occurring after the fifth false alarm ....$150.00.

If payment of the bill is not received within thirty days, the sheriff shall send a notice by certified mail to the manager and to the owner, if different, of the real estate of which the commercial establishment is a part, or to the occupant, lessee, agent, or tenant and to the owner, if different, of the real estate of which the residence is a part, indicating that failure to pay the bill within thirty days, or to show just cause why the bill should not be paid, will result in the assessment of a lien upon the real estate in the amount of the bill. If payment is not received within those thirty days or if just cause is not shown, the amount of the bill shall be entered upon the tax duplicate, shall be a lien upon the real estate from the date of the entry, and shall be collected as other taxes and returned to the county treasury.

The sheriff shall not send a bill pursuant to this division if a bill has already been sent pursuant to division (A) of this section for the same false alarm.

(C) As used in this section, "commercial establishment" has the same meaning as in section 505.391 of the Revised Code.

(2004 H 255, eff. 3–31–05; 1997 H 259, eff. 12–18–97; 1988 H 420, eff. 6–14–88; 1986 H 150)

505.52 Bond issues by police district

The board of trustees of a township police district may issue bonds for the purpose of buying police equipment in the manner provided for in section 133.18 and pursuant to Chapter 133. of the Revised Code. The proceeds of the bonds issued under this section, other than any premium and accrued interest which is credited to the sinking fund, shall be placed in the township treasury to the credit of a fund to be known as the police equipment fund. Money from the police equipment fund shall be paid out only upon order of the township board of trustees of the township police district.

(1989 H 230, eff. 10–30–89; 130 v H 744)

505.53 Issuance of notes by police district

The board of trustees of a township police district may issue notes for a period not to exceed three years for the purpose of buying police equipment or a building or site to house police equipment. One–third of the purchase price of the equipment, building, or site shall be paid at the time of purchase, and the remainder of the purchase price shall be covered by notes maturing in two and three years respectively. Notes may bear interest not to exceed the rate determined as provided in section 9.95 of the Revised Code, and shall not be subject to Chapter 133. of the Revised Code. Such notes shall be offered for sale on the open market or given to a vendor if no sale is made.

(1989 H 230, eff. 10–30–89; 1981 H 95; 1979 H 275; 130 v H 744)

505.54 Additional training for police district personnel

The board of trustees of the township may, upon nomination by the chief of police, send one or more of the officers, patrolmen, or other employees of the township police district to a school of instruction designed to provide additional training or skills related to the employees work assignment in the district. The trustees may make advance tuition payments for any employee so nominated and may defray all or a portion of the employee's expenses while receiving this instruction.

(130 v H 744, eff. 9–24–63)

505.541 Parking enforcement unit; parking enforcement officers

(A) The board of township trustees may establish, by resolution, a parking enforcement unit within a township police district, and provide for the regulation of parking enforcement officers. The chief of police of the district shall be the executive head of the parking enforcement unit, shall make all appointments and removals of parking enforcement officers, subject to any general rules prescribed by the board of township trustees by resolution, and shall prescribe rules for the organization, training, administration, control, and conduct of the parking enforcement unit. The chief of police may appoint parking enforcement officers who agree to serve for nominal compensation, and persons with physical disabilities may receive appointments as parking enforcement officers.

(B) The authority of the parking enforcement officers shall be limited to the enforcement of section 4511.69 of the Revised Code and any other parking laws specified in the resolution creating the parking enforcement unit. Parking enforcement officers shall have no other powers.

(C) The training the parking enforcement officers shall receive shall include instruction in general administrative rules and procedures governing the parking enforcement unit, the role of the judicial system as it relates to parking regulation and enforcement, proper techniques and methods relating to the enforcement of parking laws, human interaction skills, and first aid.

(1990 S 174, eff. 7–13–90)

505.55 Dissolution of police district

In the event that need for a township police district ceases to exist, the township trustees by a two-thirds vote of the board shall adopt a resolution specifying the date that the township police district shall cease to exist and provide for the disposal of all property belonging to the district by public sale. Such sale must be by public auction and upon notice thereof being published once a week for three weeks in a newspaper published, or of general circulation in such township, the last of such publications to be at least five days before the date of the sale. Any moneys remaining after the dissolution of the district or received from the public sale of property shall be paid into the treasury of the township and may be expended for any public purpose when duly authorized by the township board of trustees.

(130 v H 744, eff. 9–24–63)

MISCELLANEOUS PROVISIONS

505.67 Voluntary motor vehicle decal registration program

(A) If the board of county commissioners of the county in which a township is located has not established a motor vehicle decal registration program under section 311.31 of the Revised Code, the board of township trustees may establish, by resolution, a voluntary motor vehicle decal registration program to be controlled and conducted by the chief law enforcement officer of the township within the unincorporated areas of the township. The board may establish a fee for participation in the program in an amount sufficient to cover the cost of administering the program and the cost of the decals.

(B) Any resident of the township may enroll a motor vehicle that he owns in the program by signing a consent form, displaying the decal issued under this section, and paying the prescribed fee. The motor vehicle owner shall remove the decal to withdraw from the program and also prior to the sale or transfer of ownership of the vehicle. Any law enforcement officer may conduct, at any place within this state at which the officer would be permitted to arrest the person operating the vehicle, an investigatory stop of any motor vehicle displaying a decal issued under this section when the vehicle is being driven between the hours of one a.m. and five a.m. A law enforcement officer may conduct an investigatory stop under this division regardless of whether the officer observes a violation of law involving the vehicle or whether he has probable cause to believe that any violation of law involving the vehicle has occurred.

(C) The consent form required under division (B) of this section shall:

(1) Describe the conditions for participation in the program, including a description of an investigatory stop and a statement that any law enforcement officer may conduct, at any place within this state at which the officer would be permitted to arrest the person operating the vehicle, an investigatory stop of the motor vehicle when it is being driven between the hours of one a.m. and five a.m.

(2) Contain other information identifying the vehicle and owner as the chief law enforcement officer of the township considers necessary.

(D) The state director of public safety, in accordance with Chapter 119. of the Revised Code, shall adopt rules governing the color, size, and design of decals issued under this section and the location where the decals shall be displayed on vehicles that are enrolled in the program.

(E) Divisions (A) to (D) of this section do not require a law enforcement officer to conduct an investigatory stop of a vehicle displaying a decal issued under this section.

(F) As used in this section:

(1) "Investigatory stop" means a temporary stop of a motor vehicle and its operator and occupants for purposes of determining the identity of the person who is operating the vehicle and, if the person who is operating it is not its owner, whether any violation of law has occurred or is occurring. An "investigatory stop" is not an arrest, but, if an officer who conducts an investigatory stop determines that illegal conduct has occurred or is occuring [sic.], an "investigatory stop" may be the basis for an arrest.

(2) "Law enforcement officer" means a sheriff, deputy sheriff, constable, police officer of a township or joint township police district, marshal, deputy marshal, municipal police officer, or state highway patrol trooper.

(1994 S 75, eff. 10–20–94)

505.93 Boxing matches may be prohibited

A board of township trustees may adopt a resolution prohibiting in the unincorporated area of the township boxing matches or exhibitions to which sections 3773.31 to 3773.58 of the Revised Code apply.

(1981 S 60, eff. 7–27–81)

505.94 Transient vendors; registration may be required

Note: See also following version of this section, eff. 5–6–05.

(A) A board of township trustees may, by resolution, require the registration of all transient vendors within the unincorporated territory of the township and may regulate the time, place, and manner in which these vendors may sell, offer for sale, or solicit orders for future delivery of goods, or the board may, by resolution, prohibit these activities within that territory. If the board requires the registration of all transient vendors, it may establish a reasonable registration fee, not to exceed seventy-five dollars for a registration period, and this registration shall be valid for a period of at least ninety days after the date of registration. Any board of township trustees that provides for the registration and regulation, or prohibition, of transient vendors under this section shall notify the prosecuting attorney of the county in which the township is located of its registration and regulatory requirements or prohibition. No transient vendor shall fail to register or to comply with regulations or prohibitions established by a board of township trustees under this division.

This division does not authorize a board of township trustees to apply a resolution it adopts under this division to any person invited by an owner or tenant to visit the owner's or tenant's premises to sell, offer for sale, or solicit orders for future delivery of goods.

(B) As used in this section:

(1) "Goods" means goods, wares, services, merchandise, periodicals, and other articles or publications.

(2) "Transient vendor" means any person who opens a temporary place of business for the sale of goods or who, on the streets or while traveling about the township, either sells or offers for sale goods, or solicits orders for future delivery of goods where payment is required prior to the delivery of the goods. "Transient vendor" does not include any person who represents any entity exempted from taxation under section 5709.04 of the Revised Code, that notifies the board of township trustees that its representatives are present in the township for the purpose of either selling or offering for sale goods, or soliciting orders for future delivery of goods, and does not include an auction or an auctioneer company licensed under Chapter 4707. of the Revised Code.

(1998 H 657, eff. 3–30–99; 1990 H 318, eff. 6–27–90; 1981 S 80)

Note: See also following version of this section, eff. 5–6–05.

505.94 Transient vendors; registration may be required (later effective date)

Note: See also preceding version of this section, in effect until 5–6–05.

(A) A board of township trustees may, by resolution, require the registration of all transient vendors within the unincorporated territory of the township and may regulate the time, place, and manner in which these vendors may sell, offer for sale, or solicit orders for future delivery of goods, or the board may, by resolution, prohibit these activities within that territory. If the board requires the registration of all transient vendors, it may establish a reasonable registration fee, not to exceed seventy-five dollars for a registration period, and this registration shall be valid for a period of at least ninety days after the date of registration. Any board of township trustees that provides for the registration and regulation, or prohibition, of transient vendors under this section shall notify the prosecuting attorney of the county in which the township is located of its registration and regulatory requirements or prohibition. No transient vendor shall fail to register or to comply with regulations or prohibitions established by a board of township trustees under this division.

This division does not authorize a board of township trustees to apply a resolution it adopts under this division to any person invited by an owner or tenant to visit the owner's or tenant's premises to sell, offer for sale, or solicit orders for future delivery of goods.

(B) As used in this section:

(1) "Goods" means goods, wares, services, merchandise, periodicals, and other articles or publications.

(2) "Transient vendor" means any person who opens a temporary place of business for the sale of goods or who, on the streets or while traveling about the township, either sells or offers for sale goods, or solicits orders for future delivery of goods where payment is required prior to the delivery of the goods. "Transient vendor" does not include any person who represents any entity exempted from taxation under section 5709.04 of the Revised Code, that notifies the board of township trustees that its representatives are present in the township for the purpose of either selling or offering for sale goods, or soliciting orders for future delivery of goods, and does not include a person licensed under Chapter 4707. of the Revised Code.

(2004 S 209, eff. 5–6–05; 1998 H 657, eff. 3–30–99; 1990 H 318, eff. 6–27–90; 1981 S 80)

Note: See also preceding version of this section, in effect until 5–6–05.

505.95 Regulation of resale of tickets to theatrical or sporting events

(A) A board of township trustees may adopt a resolution to regulate in the unincorporated area of the township, by license or otherwise, the resale, by parties not acting as agents of those issuing them, of tickets to theatrical or sporting events or to other public amusements.

(B) The board of township trustees may establish a fine of not more than one hundred dollars for each separate violation of any resolution adopted under division (A) of this section. Fifty per cent of the moneys arising from the collection of the fine shall be deposited in the township's general fund. The remaining fifty per cent of those moneys shall be deposited in the county's general fund.

(C) Any person allegedly aggrieved by a violation of a resolution adopted under division (A) of this section may seek injunctive or other appropriate relief in connection with the act or practice that violates that resolution.

(1999 S 52, eff. 11–2–99)

PENALTIES

505.99 Penalty

Whoever violates section 505.374, 505.74, 505.75, 505.76, 505.77, or 505.94 of the Revised Code is guilty of a minor misdemeanor.

(1995 S 2, eff. 7–1–96; 1987 H 285, eff. 10–20–87; 1985 H 85; 1981 S 80; 1977 S 155; 1974 H 739)

505.991 Penalty for neglect or refusal to deposit stolen property

Whoever violates section 505.106 of the Revised Code shall be fined not less than twice the value of any property not deposited as provided by that section, but not more than three thousand dollars, or imprisoned not more than thirty days, or both.

(1999 H 55, eff. 9–29–99)

CHAPTER 509

TOWNSHIP CONSTABLES

Section

509.01 Constables; suspension or removal; compensation

(A) As used in this section, "felony" has the same meaning as in section 109.511 of the Revised Code.

(B) Subject to division (C) of this section, the board of township trustees may designate any qualified persons as police constables and may provide them with the automobiles, communication systems, uniforms, and police equipment that the board considers necessary. Except as provided in division (C) of this section, police constables designated under this division, who have been awarded a certificate attesting to the satisfactory completion of an approved state, county, or municipal police basic training program, as required by section 109.77 of the Revised Code, may be removed or suspended only under the conditions and by the procedures in sections 505.491 to 505.495 of the Revised Code. Any other police constable shall serve at the pleasure of the township trustees. In case of removal or suspension of a police constable by the board of township trustees, that police constable may appeal the decision of the board to the court of common pleas of the county to determine the sufficiency of the cause of removal or suspension. The police constable shall take the appeal within ten days of written notice to the police constable of the decision of the board. The board may pay each police constable, from the general funds of the township, the compensation that the board by resolution prescribes for the time actually spent in keeping the peace, protecting property, and performing duties as a police constable, including duties as an ex officio deputy bailiff of a municipal court pursuant to section 1901.32 of the Revised Code and duties as a ministerial officer of a county court. The police constable shall not be paid fees in addition to the compensation allowed by the board for services rendered as a police constable, including services as an ex officio deputy bailiff of a municipal court pursuant to section 1901.32 of the Revised Code and as a ministerial officer of a county court. All constable fees provided for by section 509.15 of the Revised Code, if due for services rendered while the police constable performing those services is being compensated as a police constable for that performance, shall be paid into the general fund of the township.

(C)(1) The board of township trustees shall not designate a person as a police constable pursuant to division (B) of this section on a permanent basis, on a temporary basis, for a probationary term, or on other than a permanent basis if the person previously has been convicted of or has pleaded guilty to a felony.

(2)(a) The board of township trustees shall terminate the employment of a police constable designated under division (B) of this section if the police constable does either of the following:

(i) Pleads guilty to a felony;

(ii) Pleads guilty to a misdemeanor pursuant to a negotiated plea agreement as provided in division (D) of section 2929.43 of the Revised Code in which the police constable agrees to surrender the certificate awarded to the police constable under section 109.77 of the Revised Code.

(b) The board shall suspend from employment a police constable designated under division (B) of this section if the police constable is convicted, after trial, of a felony. If the police constable files an appeal from that conviction and the conviction is upheld by the highest court to which the appeal is taken or if the police constable does not file a timely appeal, the board shall terminate the employment of that police constable. If the police constable files an appeal that results in that police constable's acquittal of the felony or conviction of a misdemeanor, or in the dismissal of the felony charge against the police constable, the board shall reinstate that police constable. A police constable who is reinstated under division (C)(2)(b) of this section shall not receive any back pay unless that police constable's conviction of the felony was reversed on appeal, or the felony charge was dismissed, because the court found insufficient evidence to convict the police constable of the felony.

(3) Division (C) of this section does not apply regarding an offense that was committed prior to January 1, 1997.

(4) The suspension from employment, or the termination of the employment, of a police constable under division (C)(2) of this section shall be in accordance with Chapter 119. of the Revised Code.

(2002 H 490, eff. 1–1–04; 1996 H 566, eff. 10–16–96; 1986 H 159, eff. 3–19–87; 132 v H 191; 128 v 823)

509.02 Bond

Each constable, before entering upon the discharge of his duties, shall give bond to the state in a sum of not less than five hundred nor more than two thousand dollars, conditioned for the faithful and diligent discharge of his duties, and with sureties resident of the township. The amount of such bond and its sureties shall be approved by the board of township trustees. Such bond shall be deposited with the township clerk.

(1953 H 1, eff. 10–1–53; GC 3328)

509.04 Parking enforcement unit; parking enforcement officers

(A) The board of township trustees may establish, by resolution, a parking enforcement unit within the office of a township constable, and provide for the regulation of parking enforcement officers. The board of township trustees shall appoint a police constable as executive head of the parking enforcement unit, who shall make all appointments and removals of parking enforcement officers, subject to any general rules prescribed by the board of township trustees by resolution, and shall prescribe rules for the organization, training, administration, control, and conduct of the parking enforcement unit. The executive head of the parking enforcement unit may appoint parking enforcement officers who agree to serve for nominal compensation, and persons with physical disabilities may receive appointments as parking enforcement officers.

(B) The authority of the parking enforcement officers shall be limited to the enforcement of section 4511.69 of the Revised Code and any other parking laws specified in the resolution creating the parking enforcement unit. Parking enforcement officers shall have no other powers.

(C) The training the parking enforcement officers shall receive shall include instruction in general administrative rules and procedures governing the parking enforcement unit, the role of the judicial system as it relates to parking regulation and enforcement, proper techniques and medthods [sic.] relating to the enforcement of parking laws, human interaction skills, and first aid.

(1990 S 174, eff. 7–13–90)

509.05 Sheriffs and constables ministerial officers of county court; powers and duties of constables; organized crime task force membership

In addition to the county sheriff, constables shall be ministerial officers of the county court in all cases in their respective townships, and in criminal cases, they shall be such officers within the county. They shall apprehend and bring to justice felons and disturbers of the peace, suppress riots, and keep and preserve the peace within the county. They may execute all writs and process, in criminal cases, throughout the county in which they reside, and in which they were elected or appointed. If a person charged with the commission of a crime or offense flees from justice, any constable of the county wherein such crime or offense was committed shall pursue and arrest such fugitive in any other county of the state and convey him before the county court of the county where such crime or offense was committed.

Such constables shall serve and execute all warrants, writs, precepts, executions, and other process directed and delivered to them, and shall do all things pertaining to the office of constable.

The authority of a constable in serving any process, either civil or criminal, and in doing his duties generally shall extend throughout the county in which he is appointed, and in executing and serving process issued by a judge of the county court, he may exercise the same authority and powers over goods and chattels, and the persons of parties, as is granted to a sheriff or coroner, under like process issued from courts of record.

A constable may participate, as the director of an organized crime task force established under section 177.02 of the Revised Code or as a member of the investigatory staff of such a task force, in an investigation of organized criminal activity in any county or counties in this state under sections 177.01 to 177.03 of the Revised Code.

(1986 S 74, eff. 9–3–86; 127 v 1039; 1953 H 1; GC 3334, 3335, 3341, 3345)

509.06 Aid of sheriff

Constables, marshals, chiefs of police, and other police officers, in discharging their duties, may call the sheriff or a deputy sheriff to their aid in state cases.

(1953 H 1, eff. 10–1–53; GC 3336)

509.07 Return of process

Each constable shall, at the proper office and on the proper return day, make due return of all process directed and delivered to him. If the judgment upon which such constable has an execution is docketed in the court of common pleas, appealed, or stayed, on notice to return the execution, he shall state such fact on the execution.

(1953 H 1, eff. 10–1–53; GC 3337)

509.08 Time of receiving writ

Each constable, on the receipt of any writ or other process, except subpoenas, shall note thereon the time of receiving it. He shall also state in his return on such writ or process the time and manner of executing it.

(1953 H 1, eff. 10–1–53; GC 3338)

509.09 Return of "not found"

No constable shall make a return on any process of "not found," as to any defendant, unless he has been to the usual place of residence of the defendant at least once, if such defendant has a residence in the county.

(1953 H 1, eff. 10–1–53; GC 3339)

509.10 Arrest on view or warrant; keep the peace

Each constable shall apprehend, on view or warrant, and bring to justice, all felons, disturbers, and violators of the criminal laws of this state, and shall suppress all riots, affrays, and unlawful assemblies which come to his knowledge, and shall generally keep the peace in his township.

(128 v 823, eff. 11–6–59; 1953 H 1; GC 3340)

509.11 Copy of process to be left with jailer

When it becomes the duty of the constable to take a person to the county jail, such constable shall deliver to the sheriff or jailer a certified copy of the execution, commitment, or other process, whereby he holds such person in custody, and shall return the original to the judge who issued it. Such copy is sufficient authority to the sheriff or jailer to keep the prisoner in jail until discharged.

(132 v H 2, eff. 2–14–67; 1953 H 1; GC 3342)

509.12 Payment of moneys

A constable shall pay over to the party entitled thereto, all moneys received by such constable in his official capacity, if demand is made by such party, his agent, or attorney, at any time before the constable returns the writ upon which he has received such moneys. If the money is not paid over by that time, the constable shall pay it to the judge of the county court when he returns the writ.

(128 v 823, eff. 11–6–59; 1953 H 1; GC 3343)

509.13 Forfeiture

Constables shall be liable to a ten per cent forfeiture upon the amount of damages for which judgment may be entered against them, for failing to make return, making a false return, or failing to pay over money collected or received by them in their official capacity. Such judgment must include, in addition to the damages and costs, the forfeiture provided by this section.

(1953 H 1, eff. 10–1–53; GC 3344)

509.15 Fees of constables and police officers

The following fees and expenses shall be taxed as costs, collected from the judgment debtor, and paid to the general fund of the appropriate township or district as compensation due for services rendered by township constables or members of the police force of a township police district or joint police district:

(A) Serving and making return of each of the following:

(1) Order to commit to jail, order on jailer for prisoner, or order of ejectment, including copies to complete service, one dollar for each defendant named therein;

(2) Search warrant or warrant of arrest, for each person named in the writ, five dollars;

(3) Writ of attachment of property, except for purpose of garnishment, twenty dollars;

(4) Writ of attachment for the purpose of garnishment, five dollars;

(5) Writ of possession or restitution, twenty dollars;

(6) Attachment for contempt, for each person named in the writ, three dollars;

(7) Writ of replevin, twenty dollars;

(8) Summons and writs, subpoena, venire, and notice to garnishee, including copies to complete service, three dollars for each person named therein;

(9) Execution against property or person, eighty cents, and six per cent of all money thus collected;

(10) Any other writ, order, or notice required by law, for each person named therein, including copies to complete service, three dollars for the first name and fifty cents for each additional name.

(B) Mileage for the distance actually and necessarily traveled in serving and returning any of the preceding writs, orders, and notices, fifty cents for the first mile and for each additional mile, twenty cents;

(C) For attending a criminal case during the trial or hearing and having charge of prisoners, each case, two dollars and fifty cents, but, when so acting, such constable shall not be entitled to a witness fee if called upon to testify;

(D) For attending civil court during a jury trial, each case, two dollars;

(E) For attending civil court during a trial without jury, each case, one dollar and fifty cents;

(F) The actual amount paid solely for the transportation, meals, and lodging of prisoners, and for the moving and storage of goods and the care of animals taken on any legal process, such expense shall be specifically itemized on the back of the writs and sworn to;

(G) For summoning and swearing appraisers, each case, two dollars;

(H) For advertising property for sale, by posting, taken on any legal process, one dollar;

(I) For taking and making return of any bond required by law, eighty cents.

Notwithstanding anything to the contrary in this section, if any comparable fee or expense specified under section 311.17 of the Revised Code is increased to an amount greater than that set forth in this section, the board of township trustees, board of trustees of the township police district, or joint township police district board, as appropriate, may require that the amount taxed as costs under this section equal the amount specified under section 311.17 of the Revised Code.

(1995 H 56, eff. 8–23–95; 130 v S 68, eff. 8–19–63; 1953 H 1; GC 3347)

CHAPTER 511

TOWNSHIP PARKS

511.235 Contracts for park district law enforcement officers to render police services to political subdivisions

The board of park commissioners of a township park district may enter into contracts with one or more townships, township police districts, municipal corporations, or county sheriffs of this state, with one or more park districts created pursuant to section 1545.01 of the Revised Code or other township park districts, or with a contiguous political subdivision of an adjoining state, and a township, township police district, municipal corporation, county sheriff, park district, or other township park district of this state may enter into a contract with a township park district upon any terms that are agreed to by them, to allow the use of the township park district law enforcement officers designated under section 511.232 of the Revised Code to perform any police function, exercise any police power, or render any police service in behalf of the contracting political subdivision that the subdivision may perform, exercise, or render.

Chapter 2744. of the Revised Code, insofar as it applies to the operation of police departments, shall apply to the contracting political subdivisions and to the members of their police force or law enforcement department when they are rendering service outside their own subdivisions pursuant to that contract.

Any members of the police force or law enforcement department acting pursuant to that contract outside the political subdivision in which they are employed shall be entitled to participate in any indemnity fund established by their employer to the same extent as while acting within the employing subdivision. Those members shall be entitled to all the rights and benefits of Chapter 4123. of the Revised Code, to the same extent as while performing service within the subdivision.

The contracts entered into pursuant to this section may provide for the following:

(A) A fixed annual charge to be paid at the times agreed upon and stipulated in the contract;

(B) Compensation based upon the following:

(1) A stipulated price for each call or emergency;

(2) The number of members or pieces of equipment employed;

(3) The elapsed time of service required in each call or emergency.

(C) Compensation for loss or damage to equipment while engaged in rendering police services outside the limits of the subdivision that owns and furnishes the equipment;

(D) Reimbursement of the subdivision in which the police force or law enforcement department members are employed, for any indemnity award or premium contribution assessed against the employing subdivision for workers' compensation benefits for injuries or death to members of its police force or law enforcement department occurring while engaged in rendering service pursuant to the contract.

(1992 S 174, eff. 7–31–92)

511.236 Park district law enforcement departments providing police services to political subdivisions without contract

The police force or law enforcement department of any township park district may provide police protection to any county, municipal corporation, township, or township police district of this state, to any other township park district or any park district created pursuant to section 1545.01 of the Revised Code, or to a governmental entity of an adjoining state without a contract to provide police protection, upon the approval, by resolution, of the board of park commissioners of the township park district in which the police force or law enforcement department is located and upon authorization by an officer or employee of the police force or department providing the police protection who is designated by title of office or position, pursuant to the resolution of the board of park commissioners, to give the authorization.

Chapter 2744. of the Revised Code, insofar as it applies to the operation of police departments, shall apply to any township park district and to members of its police force or law enforcement department when those members are rendering police services pursuant to this section outside the township park district by which they are employed.

Police force or law enforcement department members acting, as provided in this section, outside the township park district by which they are employed shall be entitled to participate in any pension or indemnity fund established by their employer to the same extent as while acting within the township park district by which they are employed. Those members shall be entitled to all rights and benefits of Chapter 4123. of the Revised Code to the same extent as while performing services within the township park district by which they are employed.

(1992 S 174, eff. 7–31–92)

CHAPTER 715

MUNICIPAL CORPORATIONS—GENERAL POWERS

STREETS AND PARKS

715.23 Impounding animals

Except as otherwise provided in section 955.221 of the Revised Code regarding dogs, a municipal corporation may regulate, restrain, or prohibit the running at large, within the municipal corporation, of cattle, horses, swine, sheep, goats, geese, chickens, or other fowl or animals, impound and hold the fowl or animals, and, on notice to the owners, authorize the sale of the fowl or animals for the penalty imposed by any ordinance, and the cost and expenses of the proceedings.

(1987 H 352, eff. 7–10–87; 1953 H 1; GC 3633)

HEALTH AND SANITATION; INSPECTION

715.44 Power to abate nuisance and prevent injury

A municipal corporation may:

(A) Abate any nuisance and prosecute in any court of competent jurisdiction, any person who creates, continues, contributes to, or suffers such nuisance to exist;

(B) Regulate and prevent the emission of dense smoke, prohibit the careless or negligent emission of dense smoke from locomotive engines, declare each of such acts a nuisance, and prescribe and enforce regulations for the prevention of such acts;

(C) Prevent injury and annoyance from any nuisance;

(D) Regulate and prohibit the use of steam whistles;

(E) Provide for the regulation of the installation and inspection of steam boilers and steam boiler plants.

(1953 H 1, eff. 10–1–53; GC 3650)

PEACE AND MORALS

715.48 Regulation by license of shows and games; trafficking in tickets; exceptions

Any municipal corporation may:

(A) Regulate, by license or otherwise, restrain, or prohibit theatrical exhibitions, public shows, and athletic games, of whatever name or nature, for which money or other reward is demanded or received;

(B) Regulate, by license or otherwise, the business of trafficking in theatrical tickets, or other tickets of licensed amusements, by parties not acting as agents of those issuing them.

Public school entertainments, lecture courses, and lectures on historic, literary, or scientific subjects do not come within this section.

(1953 H 1, eff. 10–1–53; GC 3657)

715.49 Preservation of peace and protection of property

(A) Any municipal corporation may prevent riot, gambling, noise and disturbance, and indecent and disorderly conduct or assemblages, preserve the peace and good order, and protect the property of the municipal corporation and its inhabitants.

(B) Anytime a noise ordinance of a municipal corporation is violated, but the source of the noise is located outside the borders of that municipal corporation in an adjoining municipal corporation, the municipal corporation with the ordinance may enforce the ordinance against that source as long as there is a written agreement between the two municipal corporations permitting such enforcement.

(1994 S 264, eff. 9–29–94; 1953 H 1, eff. 10–1–53; GC 3658)

715.50 Police jurisdiction outside municipal corporation

A municipal corporation owning and using lands beyond its limits for a municipal purpose may provide, by ordinance or resolution, all needful police or sanitary regulations for the protection of such property and may prosecute violations thereof in the municipal court of such municipal corporation.

(1975 H 205, eff. 1–1–76; 1953 H 1; GC 3658–1)

715.51 Billiards, pool, and gambling

Any municipal corporation may:

(A) Regulate billiard and pool tables, nine or ten pin alleys or tables, and shooting and ball alleys;

(B) Authorize the destruction of instruments or devices used for the purpose of gambling.

(1953 H 1, eff. 10–1–53; GC 3659)

715.52 Houses of ill fame; lewd and lascivious behavior

Any municipal corporation may:

(A) Suppress and restrain disorderly houses and houses of ill fame;

(B) Provide for the punishment of all lewd and lascivious behavior in the streets and other public places.

(1953 H 1, eff. 10–1–53; GC 3660)

715.53 Taverns

Any municipal corporation may regulate taverns and other houses for public entertainment.

(1953 H 1, eff. 10–1–53; GC 3662)

715.54 Vicious literature

Any municipal corporation may restrain and prohibit the distribution, sale, and exposure for sale of books, papers, pictures, and periodicals or advertising matters of an obscene or immoral nature.

(1953 H 1, eff. 10–1–53; GC 3663)

IMPRISONMENT

715.59 Hospitals for diseased prisoners

The legislative authority of a municipal corporation may provide suitable hospitals for the reception and care of such prisoners as are diseased or disabled, under such regulations and the charge of such persons as the legislative authority directs.

(1953 H 1, eff. 10–1–53; GC 3668)

LICENSING

715.60 Regulation of explosives

Any municipal corporation may regulate the transportation, keeping, and sale of gunpowder and other explosives or dangerous combustibles and materials, and provide or license magazines therefor.

(1953 H 1, eff. 10–1–53; GC 3669)

715.61 Regulation of manufacturers, dealers, peddlers, and amusements

Any municipal corporation may regulate and license manufacturers and dealers in explosives, chattel mortgage and salary loan brokers, peddlers, public ballrooms, scavengers, intelligence officers, billiard rooms, bowling alleys, livery, sale, and boarding stables, dancing or riding academies or schools, race courses, ball grounds, street musicians, secondhand dealers, junk shops, and all persons engaged in the trade, business, or profession of manicuring, massaging, or chiropody. In the granting of any license a municipal corporation may charge such fees as the legislative authority deems proper and expedient.

(1994 H 376, eff. 7–22–94; 1953 H 1, eff. 10–1–53; GC 3670)

715.62 Evidence

In the trial of any action brought under section 715.61 of the Revised Code, the fact that any party to such action represented himself as engaged in any business or occupation, for the transaction of which a license is required, or as the keeper, proprietor, or manager of the thing for which a license is required, or that such party exhibits a sign indicating such business or calling, or such proprietorship or management, shall be conclusive evidence of the liability of the party to pay such license fee.

(1953 H 1, eff. 10–1–53; GC 3671)

715.63 License power; exception

Any municipal corporation may license exhibitors of shows or performances of any kind, hawkers, peddlers, auctioneers of horses and other animals on the highways or public grounds of the municipal corporation, vendors of gunpowder and other explosives, taverns, houses of public entertainment, and hucksters in the public streets or markets. The municipal corporation may, in granting such license, charge such fee as is reasonable. No municipal corporation may require of the owner of any product of his own raising, or the manufacturer of any article manufactured by him, a license to vend or sell, by himself or his agent, any such article or product. The legislative authority of such municipal corporation may delegate to the mayor of the municipal corporation the authority to grant, issue, and revoke licenses.

(1953 H 1, eff. 10–1–53; GC 3672)

715.64 Licensing transient dealers and solicitors; exceptions

Any municipal corporation may license transient dealers, persons who temporarily open stores or places for the sale of goods, wares, or merchandise, and each person who, on the streets or traveling from place to place about such municipal corporation, sells, bargains to sell, or solicits orders for goods, wares, or merchandise by retail. Such license shall be granted as provided by section 715.63 of the Revised Code.

This section does not apply to persons selling by sample only, nor to any agricultural articles or products offered or exposed for sale by the producer.

(1953 H 1, eff. 10–1–53; GC 3673, 3676)

715.65 Licensing of advertising mediums and matters

Any municipal corporation may license bill-posters, advertising sign painters, bill distributors, card tackers, and advertising matter of any article or compound which has not been manufactured or compounded within such municipal corporation. In granting such license the legislative authority of such municipal corporation may fix such license fees as are expedient, and may delegate to the mayor thereof the authority to grant, issue, and revoke such license.

This section does not authorize such legislative authority to charge merchants doing business therein a license fee for advertising their own business.

(1953 H 1, eff. 10–1–53; GC 3674)

715.66 Vehicle license; money to be used for street repairs

Any municipal corporation may license the owners of vehicles used for the transportation of persons or property, for hire, and all undertakers and owners of hearses.

The owners of such vehicles may be made liable for the breach of any ordinance regulating the conduct of the drivers thereof.

All moneys and receipts, in any municipal corporation, which are derived from the enforcement of any ordinance or law requiring the payment of a vehicle license fee, shall be credited and paid into a separate fund, which fund shall be known as "the public service street repair fund." All moneys and receipts credited to such fund shall be used for the sole purpose of repairing streets, avenues, alleys, and lanes within such municipal corporation.

(1953 H 1, eff. 10–1–53; GC 3675)

MISCELLANEOUS PROVISIONS

715.67 Misdemeanor

Any municipal corporation may make the violation of any of its ordinances a misdemeanor, and provide for the punishment thereof by fine or imprisonment, or both. The fine, imposed under authority of this section, shall not exceed five hundred dollars and imprisonment shall not exceed six months.

(1953 H 1, eff. 10–1–53; GC 3628)

CHAPTER 733

MUNICIPAL OFFICERS

CITY DIRECTOR OF LAW

733.51 Powers and duties

The city director of law shall prepare all contracts, bonds, and other instruments in writing in which the city is concerned, and shall serve the several directors and officers provided in Title VII of the Revised Code as legal counsel and attorney.

The director of law shall be prosecuting attorney of the mayor's court. When the legislative authority of the city allows assistants to the director of law, he may designate the assistants to act as prosecuting attorneys of the mayor's court. The person designated shall be subject to the approval of the legislative authority.

(1977 H 219, eff. 11–1–77; 1975 H 205; 1953 H 1; GC 4305, 4306)

733.52 Prosecuting attorney of mayor's court

The city director of law as prosecuting attorney of the mayor's court shall prosecute all cases brought before the court, and perform the same duties, as far as they are applicable thereto, as required of the prosecuting attorney of the county.

The director of law or the assistants whom he designates to act as prosecuting attorneys of the mayor's court shall receive such compensation for the service provided by this section as the legislative authority of the city prescribes, and such additional compensation as the board of county commissioners allows.

(1977 H 219, eff. 11–1–77; 1975 H 205; 1953 H 1; GC 4307)

733.53 Duties as to suits

The city director of law, when required to do so by resolution of the legislative authority of the city, shall prosecute or defend on behalf of the city, all complaints, suits, and controversies in which the city is a party, and such other suits, matters, and controversies as he is, by resolution or ordinance, directed to prosecute. He shall not be required to prosecute any action before the mayor of the city for the violation of an ordinance without first advising such action.

(1977 H 219, eff. 11–1–77; 1953 H 1; GC 4308)

733.54 City director of law shall give opinions

When an officer of a city entertains doubts concerning the law in any matter before him in his official capacity, and desires the opinion of the city director of law, he shall clearly state to the director of law, in writing, the question upon which the opinion is desired, and thereupon the director of law shall, within a reasonable time, reply orally or in writing to such inquiry. The right conferred upon such officers by this section extends to the legislative authority of the city, and to each board provided for in Title VII of the Revised Code.

(1977 H 219, eff. 11–1–77; 1953 H 1; GC 4309)

MISCONDUCT IN OFFICE

733.72 Charges against municipal officers filed with probate judge; proceedings

When a complaint under oath is filed with the probate judge of the county in which a municipal corporation or the larger part thereof is situated, by any elector of the municipal corporation, signed and approved by four other electors thereof, the judge shall forthwith issue a citation to any person charged in the complaint for his appearance before the judge within ten days from the filing thereof, and shall also furnish the accused and the village solicitor or city director of law with a copy thereof. The complaint shall charge any of the following:

(A) That a member of the legislative authority of the municipal corporation has received, directly or indirectly, compensation for his services as a member thereof, as a committeeman, or otherwise, contrary to law;

(B) That a member of the legislative authority or an officer of the municipal corporation is or has been interested, directly or indirectly, in the profits of a contract, job, work, or service, or is or has been acting as a commissioner, architect, superintendent, or engineer in work undertaken or prosecuted by the municipal corporation, contrary to law;

(C) That a member of the legislative authority or an officer of the municipal corporation has been guilty of misfeasance or malfeasance in office.

Before acting upon such complaint, the judge shall require the party complaining to furnish sufficient security for costs.

(1977 H 219, eff. 11–1–77; 1953 H 1; GC 4670)

CHAPTER 737

MUNICIPAL CORPORATIONS—PUBLIC SAFETY

DEPARTMENT OF PUBLIC SAFETY—CITIES

737.01 Director of public safety

In each city there shall be a department of public safety, which shall be administered by a director of public safety. The director shall be appointed by the mayor and need not be a resident of the city at the time of his appointment but shall become a resident thereof within six months after his appointment unless such residence requirement is waived by ordinance.

(1969 H 279, eff. 10–2–69; 1953 H 1; GC 4367)

737.02 General duties; records; contracts

Under the direction of the mayor, the director of public safety shall be the executive head of the police and fire departments and the chief administrative authority of the charity, correction, and building departments. He shall have all powers and duties connected with and incident to the appointment, regulation, and government of such departments except as otherwise provided by law. He shall keep a record of his proceedings, a copy of which, certified by him, shall be competent evidence in all courts.

Such director shall make all contracts in the name of the city with reference to the management of such departments, for the erection or repair of all buildings or improvements in connection therewith, and for the purchase of all supplies necessary for such departments.

(1953 H 1, eff. 10–1–53; GC 4368, 4369)

737.021 Division of traffic engineering and safety

The legislative authority of a city may create and abolish, by ordinance, a division of traffic engineering and safety within the department of public safety. The director of public safety of such city shall be the executive head of such division. He shall have all powers and duties connected with and incident to the appointment, regulation, and government of such division, and shall make such rules and regulations as he may deem necessary for the government and operation of the division. He shall keep a record of all his proceedings in connection with the administration of such division. A copy of such proceedings, when certified by him, shall be competent evidence in all courts. Such division may be staffed by traffic and safety engineers and such other employees as determined by the legislative authority.

(131 v H 927, eff. 11–1–65)

737.022 Rules and regulations

When authorized by ordinance of the legislative authority of a city, and in order to expedite the flow and direction of traffic, to eliminate congestion on streets, alleys, and highways, and to provide for the safety of passengers in motor vehicles and pedestrians, the director of public safety may make and issue rules and regulations concerning:

(A) The number, type, and location of traffic control devices and signs;

(B) The regulation or prohibition of parking on streets, alleys, highways, or public property;

(C) The regulation of the right-of-way at intersections of streets, alleys, and highways;

(D) The regulation or prohibition of turns at intersections;

(E) The creation, abolition, and regulation of through routes and truck routes;

(F) The creation, abolition, and regulation of pedestrian crosswalk and safety zones;

(G) The creation, abolition, and regulation of bus loading and unloading zones and business loading zones;

(H) The creation, abolition, and regulation of traffic lanes, and passing zones;

(I) The regulation of the direction of traffic on streets, alleys, and highways and the creation and abolition of one way streets;

(J) Such other subjects as may be provided by ordinance, which shall not be limited by the specific enumeration of subjects by this section.

Such rules and regulations shall be issued in the manner and subject to the conditions and limitations as prescribed by ordinance of the legislative authority of such city. Copies of such rules and regulations, when certified by the director of public safety, shall be competent evidence in all courts. Violation of such rules and regulations shall be a misdemeanor and shall be punishable as provided by the ordinances of such city.

(131 v H 927, eff. 11–1–65)

737.03 Management of certain institutions; contracts

Note: See also following version of this section, eff. 4–27–05.

The director of public safety shall manage and make all contracts with reference to police stations, fire houses, reform schools, infirmaries, hospitals, workhouses, farms, pesthouses, and all other charitable and reformatory institutions. In the control and supervision of those institutions, the director shall be governed by the provisions of Title VII of the Revised Code relating to those institutions.

The director may make all contracts and expenditures of money for acquiring lands for the erection or repairing of station houses, police stations, fire department buildings, fire cisterns, and plugs, that are required, for the purchase of engines, apparatus, and all other supplies necessary for the police and fire departments, and for other undertakings and departments under the director's supervision, but no obligation involving an expenditure of more than twenty-five thousand dollars shall be created unless first authorized and directed by ordinance. In making, altering, or modifying those contracts, the director shall be governed by sections 735.05 to 735.09 of the Revised Code, except that all bids shall be filed with and opened by the director. The director shall make no sale or disposition of any property belonging to the city without first being authorized by resolution or ordinance of the city legislative authority.

(2003 H 95, eff. 9–26–03; 2001 H 94, eff. 9–5–01; 1988 H 527, eff. 3–17–89; 1979 H 371; 1975 H 8; 132 v S 378; 1953 H 1; GC 4370, 4371)

Note: See also following version of this section, eff. 4–27–05.

737.03 Management of certain institutions; contracts (later effective date)

Note: See also preceding version of this section, in effect until 4–27–05.

The director of public safety shall manage and make all contracts with reference to police stations, fire houses, reform schools, infirmaries, hospitals other than municipal hospitals operated pursuant to Chapter 749. of the Revised Code, workhouses, farms, pesthouses, and all other charitable and reformatory institutions. In the control and supervision of those institutions, the director shall be governed by the provisions of Title VII of the Revised Code relating to those institutions.

The director may make all contracts and expenditures of money for acquiring lands for the erection or repairing of station houses, police stations, fire department buildings, fire cisterns, and plugs, that are required, for the purchase of engines, apparatus, and all other supplies necessary for the police and fire departments, and for other undertakings and departments under the director's supervision, but no obligation involving an expenditure of more than twenty-five thousand dollars shall be created unless first authorized and directed by ordinance. In making, altering, or modifying those contracts, the director shall be governed by sections 735.05 to 735.09 of the Revised Code, except that all bids shall be filed with and opened by the director. The director shall make no sale or disposition of any property belonging to the city without first being authorized by resolution or ordinance of the city legislative authority.

(2004 S 222, eff. 4–27–05; 2003 H 95, eff. 9–26–03; 2001 H 94, eff. 9–5–01; 1988 H 527, eff. 3–17–89; 1979 H 371; 1975 H 8; 132 v S 378; 1953 H 1; GC 4370, 4371)

Note: See also preceding version of this section, in effect until 4–27–05.

737.04 Contract between municipal corporations for police protection; adjoining state

The legislative authority of any municipal corporation, in order to obtain police protection or to obtain additional police protection, or to allow its police officers to work in multijurisdictional drug, gang, or career criminal task forces, may enter into contracts with one or more municipal corporations, townships, township police districts, or county sheriffs in this state, with one or more park districts created pursuant to section 511.18 or 1545.01 of the Revised Code, or with a contiguous municipal corporation in an adjoining state, upon any terms that are agreed upon, for services of police departments or the use of police equipment or for the interchange of services of police departments or police equipment within the several territories of the contracting subdivisions.

Chapter 2744. of the Revised Code, insofar as it applies to the operation of police departments, shall apply to the contracting political subdivisions and to the police department members when they are rendering service outside their own subdivisions pursuant to the contracts.

Police department members acting outside the subdivision in which they are employed, pursuant to a contract entered into under this section, shall be entitled to participate in any indemnity fund established by their employer to the same extent as while acting within the employing subdivision. Those members shall be entitled to all the rights and benefits of Chapter 4123. of the Revised Code, to the same extent as while performing service within the subdivision.

The contracts may provide for:

(A) A fixed annual charge to be paid at the times agreed upon and stipulated in the contract;

(B) Compensation based upon:

(1) A stipulated price for each call or emergency;

(2) The number of members or pieces of equipment employed;

(3) The elapsed time of service required in each call or emergency.

(C) Compensation for loss or damage to equipment while engaged in rendering police services outside the limits of the subdivision owning and furnishing the equipment;

(D) Reimbursement of the subdivision in which the police department members are employed for any indemnity award or premium contribution assessed against the employing subdivision for workers' compensation benefits for injuries or death of its police department members occurring while engaged in rendering police services pursuant to the contract.

(1997 H 342, eff. 12–31–97; 1992 S 174, eff. 7–31–92; 1985 H 176, H 201; 1982 H 738; 1979 H 279; 1976 S 545; 1953 H 1; GC 4371–1)

737.041 Providing police protection to other subdivisions without contract; liability; rights of members participating

The police department of any municipal corporation may provide police protection to any county, municipal corporation, township, or township police district of this state, to a park district created pursuant to section 511.18 or 1545.01 of the Revised Code, to any multijurisdictional drug, gang, or career criminal task force, or to a governmental entity of an adjoining state without a contract to provide police protection, upon the approval, by resolution, of the legislative authority of the municipal corporation in which the department is located and upon authorization by an officer or employee of the police department providing the police protection who is designated by title of office or position, pursuant to the resolution of the legislative authority of the municipal corporation, to give the authorization.

Chapter 2744. of the Revised Code, insofar as it applies to the operation of police departments, shall apply to any municipal corporation and to members of its police department when the members are rendering police services pursuant to this section outside the municipal corporation by which they are employed.

Police department members acting, as provided in this section, outside the municipal corporation by which they are employed shall be entitled to participate in any pension or indemnity fund established by their employer to the same extent as while acting within the municipal corporation by which they are employed. Those members shall be entitled to all the rights and benefits of Chapter 4123. of the Revised Code to the same extent as while performing services within the municipal corporation by which they are employed.

(1997 H 342, eff. 12–31–97; 1992 S 174, eff. 7–31–92; 1985 H 176; 1982 H 103; 1980 S 98)

CITIES—POLICE AND FIRE DEPARTMENTS

737.05 Composition and control of police department

The police department of each city shall be composed of a chief of police and such other officers, patrolmen, and employees as the legislative authority thereof provides by ordinance.

The director of public safety of such city shall have the exclusive management and control of all other officers, surgeons, secretaries, clerks, and employees in the police department as provided by ordinances or resolution of such legislative authority. He may commission private policemen, who may not be in the classified list of the department, under such rules and regulations as the legislative authority prescribes.

(1953 H 1, eff. 10–1–53; GC 4374, 4375)

737.051 City auxiliary police; rules; parking enforcement unit; parking enforcement officers

(A) The legislative authority of a city may establish, by ordinance, an auxiliary police unit within the police department of the city, and provide for the regulation of auxiliary police officers. The director of public safety shall be the executive head of the auxiliary police unit, shall make all appointments and removals of auxiliary police officers, subject to any general rules prescribed by the legislative authority by ordinance, and shall prescribe rules for the organization, training, administration, control, and conduct of the auxiliary police unit. Members of the auxiliary police unit shall not be in the classified service of the city.

(B)(1) The legislative authority of a city may establish, by ordinance, a parking enforcement unit within the police department of the city, and provide for the regulation of parking enforcement officers. The director of public safety shall be the executive head of the parking enforcement unit, shall make all appointments and removals of parking enforcement officers, subject to any general rules prescribed by the legislative authority by ordinance, and shall prescribe rules for the organization, training, administration, control, and conduct of the parking enforcement unit. The director may appoint parking enforcement officers who agree to serve for nominal compensation, and persons with physical disabilities may receive appointments as parking enforcement officers.

(2) The authority of the parking enforcement officers shall be limited to the enforcement of ordinances governing parking in handicapped parking locations and fire lanes and any other parking ordinances specified in the ordinance creating the parking enforcement unit. Parking enforcement officers shall have no other powers.

(3) The training the parking enforcement officers shall receive shall include instruction in general administrative rules and procedures governing the parking enforcement unit, the role of the judicial system as it relates to parking regulation and enforcement, proper techniques and methods relating to the enforcement of parking ordinances, human interaction skills, and first aid.

(1990 S 174, eff. 7–13–90; 1985 H 201; 130 v H 121)

737.052 Offenses affecting employment eligibility of chief of police, police department members, and auxiliary police officers

(A) As used in this section, "felony" has the same meaning as in section 109.511 of the Revised Code.

(B)(1) The director of public safety shall not appoint a person as a chief of police, a member of the police department of the municipal corporation, or an auxiliary police officer on a permanent basis, on a temporary basis, for a probationary term, or on other than a permanent basis if the person previously has been convicted of or has pleaded guilty to a felony.

(2)(a) The director of public safety shall terminate the employment of a chief of police, member of the police department, or auxiliary police officer who does either of the following:

(i) Pleads guilty to a felony;

(ii) Pleads guilty to a misdemeanor pursuant to a negotiated plea agreement as provided in division (D) of section 2929.43 of the Revised Code in which the chief of police, member of the police department, or auxiliary police officer agrees to surrender the certificate awarded to the chief of police, member of the police department, or auxiliary police officer under section 109.77 of the Revised Code.

(b) The director shall suspend from employment a chief of police, member of the police department, or auxiliary police officer who is convicted, after trial, of a felony. If the chief of police, member of the police department, or auxiliary police officer files an appeal from that conviction and the conviction is upheld by the highest court to which the appeal is taken or if the chief of police, member of the police department, or auxiliary police officer does not file a timely appeal, the director shall terminate that person's employment. If the chief of police, member of the police department, or auxiliary police officer files an appeal that results in that person's acquittal of the felony or conviction of a misdemeanor, or in the dismissal of the felony charge against that person, the director shall reinstate that person. A chief of police, member of the police department, or auxiliary police officer who is reinstated under division (B)(2)(b) of this section shall not receive any back pay unless that person's conviction of the felony was reversed on appeal, or the felony charge was dismissed, because the court found insufficient evidence to convict that person of the felony.

(3) Division (B) of this section does not apply regarding an offense that was committed prior to January 1, 1997.

(4) The suspension from employment, or the termination of the employment, of the chief of police, member of the police department, or auxiliary police officer under division (B)(2) of this section shall be in accordance with Chapter 119. of the Revised Code.

(2002 H 490, eff. 1–1–04; 1996 H 566, eff. 10–16–96)

737.06 Chief of police

The chief of police shall have exclusive control of the stationing and transfer of all patrolmen, auxiliary police officers, and other officers and employees in the police department, and police auxiliary unit, under such general rules and regulations as the director of public safety prescribes.

(130 v H 121, eff. 5–6–63; 1953 H 1; GC 4372)

737.07 Hours of work for police officer in cities; leave of absence

In each city, except in case of necessary appearances in court and emergency special duty assignments, not to exceed eight hours constitute a day's work and not to exceed forty-four hours constitute a week's work for policemen. Annually, in each city, each policeman shall be given not less than two weeks' leave of absence with full pay.

(1969 S 28, eff. 11–19–69; 1953 H 1; GC 4374–1)

737.08 Composition and control of city fire department

(A) The fire department of each city shall be composed of a chief of the fire department and other officers, firefighters, and employees provided for by ordinance. Neither this section nor any other section of the Revised Code requires, or shall be construed to require, that the fire chief be a resident of the city.

(B) No person shall be appointed as a permanent full-time paid member, whose duties include fire fighting, of the fire department of any city, unless either of the following applies:

(1) The person has received a certificate issued under former section 3303.07 of the Revised Code or division (C)(1) or (2) of section 4765.55 of the Revised Code evidencing satisfactory completion of a firefighter training program.

(2) The person began serving as a permanent full-time paid firefighter with the fire department of a village or other city prior to July 2, 1970, and receives a certificate issued under division (C)(3) of section 4765.55 of the Revised Code.

(C) No person who is appointed as a volunteer firefighter of a city fire department shall remain in that position, unless either of the following applies:

(1) Within one year of the appointment, the person has received a certificate issued under former section 3303.07 of the Revised Code or division (C)(1) or (2) of section 4765.55 of the Revised Code evidencing satisfactory completion of a firefighter training program.

(2) The person began serving as a permanent full-time paid firefighter with the fire department of a village or other city prior to July 2, 1970, or as a volunteer firefighter with the fire department of a township, fire district, village, or other city prior to July 2, 1979, and receives a certificate issued under division (C)(3) of section 4765.55 of the Revised Code.

(D) The director of public safety shall have the exclusive management and control of other surgeons, secretaries, clerks, and employees provided for by ordinance or resolution of the legislative authority of the city.

(2001 H 143, eff. 1–25–02; 1996 H 405, eff. 10–1–96; 1992 S 98, eff. 11–12–92; 1978 H 590; 1969 S 226; 1953 H 1; GC 4377)

737.081 Criminal records check for city firefighters or volunteer firefighters

(A) The fire chief of a city fire department may request the superintendent of BCII to conduct a criminal records check with respect to any person who is under consideration for appointment or employment as a permanent, full-time paid firefighter or any person who is under consideration for appointment as a volunteer firefighter.

(B)(1) The fire chief of the city fire department may request that the superintendent of BCII obtain information from the federal bureau of investigation as a part of the criminal records check requested pursuant to division (A) of this section.

(2) A fire chief authorized by division (A) of this section to request a criminal records check shall provide to each person for whom the fire chief intends to request a criminal records check a copy of the form prescribed pursuant to division (C)(1) of section 109.578 of the Revised Code and a standard impression sheet to obtain fingerprint impressions prescribed pursuant to division (C)(2) of section 109.578 of the Revised Code, obtain the completed form and impression sheet from the person, and forward the completed form and impression sheet to the superintendent of BCII at the time the criminal records check is requested.

(3) Any person subject to a criminal records check who receives a copy of the form and a copy of the impression sheet pursuant to division (B)(2) of this section and who is requested to complete the form and provide a set of fingerprint impressions shall complete the form or provide all the information necessary to complete the form and shall provide the impression sheet with the impressions of the person's fingerprints. If a person fails to provide the information necessary to complete the form or fails to provide impressions of the person's fingerprints, the appointing authority shall not appoint or employ the person as a permanent full-time paid firefighter or a volunteer firefighter.

(C)(1) Except as otherwise provided in division (C)(2) of this section, an appointing authority shall not appoint or employ a person as a permanent, full-time paid firefighter or a volunteer firefighter if the fire chief has requested a criminal records check pursuant to division (A) of this section and the criminal records check indicates that the person previously has been convicted of or pleaded guilty to any of the following:

(a) A felony;

(b) A violation of section 2909.03 of the Revised Code;

(c) A violation of an existing or former law of this state, any other state, or the United States that is substantially equivalent to any of the offenses described in division (C)(1)(a) or (b) of this section.

(2) Notwithstanding division (C)(1) of this section, an appointing authority may appoint or employ a person as a permanent, full-time paid firefighter or a volunteer firefighter if all of the following apply:

(a) The fire chief has requested a criminal records check pursuant to division (A) of this section.

(b) The criminal records check indicates that the person previously has been convicted of or pleaded guilty to any of the offenses described in division (C)(1) of this section.

(c) The person meets rehabilitation standards established in rules adopted under division (E) of this section.

(3) If a fire chief requests a criminal records check pursuant to division (A) of this section, an appointing authority may appoint or employ a person as a permanent, full-time paid firefighter or volunteer firefighter conditionally until the criminal records check is completed and the fire chief receives the results. If the results of the criminal records check indicate that, pursuant to division (C)(1) of this section, the person subject to the criminal records check is disqualified from appointment or employment, the fire chief shall release the person from appointment or employment.

(D) The fire chief shall pay to the bureau of criminal identification and investigation the fee prescribed pursuant to division (C)(3) of section 109.578 of the Revised Code for each criminal records check conducted in accordance with that section. The fire chief may charge the applicant who is subject to the criminal records check a fee for the costs the fire chief incurs in obtaining the criminal records check. A fee charged under this division shall not exceed the amount of fees the fire chief pays for the criminal records check. If a fee is charged under this division, the fire chief shall notify the applicant at the time of the applicant's initial application for appointment or employment of the amount of the fee and that, unless the fee is paid, the applicant will not be considered for appointment or employment.

(E) The appointing authority shall adopt rules in accordance with Chapter 119. of the Revised Code to implement this section. The rules shall include rehabilitation standards a person who has been convicted of or pleaded guilty to an offense listed in division (C)(1) of this section must meet for the appointing authority to appoint or employ the person as a permanent, full-time paid firefighter or a volunteer firefighter.

(F) A fire chief who intends to request a criminal records check for an applicant shall inform each applicant, at the time of the person's initial application for appointment or employment, that the applicant is required to provide a set of impressions of the person's fingerprints and that the fire chief requires a criminal records check to be conducted and satisfactorily completed in accordance with section 109.578 of the Revised Code.

(G) As used in this section:

(1) "Appointing authority" means any person or body that has the authority to hire, appoint, or employ permanent, full-time paid firefighters and volunteer firefighters under section 737.08 of the Revised Code.

(2) "Criminal records check" has the same meaning as in section 109.578 of the Revised Code.

(3) "Superintendent of BCII" has the same meaning as in section 2151.86 of the Revised Code.

(2002 S 258, eff. 4–9–03)

737.09 Chief of fire department

The chief of the fire department shall have exclusive control of the stationing and transferring of all firemen and other officers and employees in the department, under such general rules and regulations as the director of public safety prescribes.

(1953 H 1, eff. 10–1–53; GC 4376)

737.10 Emergency patrolmen and firemen; cooperation with other agencies

In case of riot or other like emergency, the mayor may appoint additional patrolmen and officers for temporary service in the police department, or additional firemen and officers for temporary service in the fire department, who need not be in the classified list of such department. Such additional persons shall be employed only for the time during which the emergency exists.

The mayor may call upon the sheriff of the county in which all or part of the municipal corporation lies or the sheriff of any adjoining county, the mayor or other chief executive of any municipal corporation in the same or any adjoining county, and the chairman of the board of township trustees of any township in the same or any adjoining county, to furnish such law enforcement or fire protection personnel, or both, together with appropriate equipment and apparatus, as may be necessary to preserve the public peace and protect persons and property in the requesting municipal corporation in the event of riot. Such aid shall be furnished to the mayor requesting it, insofar as possible without withdrawing from the political subdivision furnishing such aid the minimum police and fire protection appearing necessary under the circumstances. In such case, law enforcement and fire protection personnel acting outside the territory of their regular employment shall be considered as performing services within the territory of their regular employment for purposes of compensation, pension or indemnity fund rights, workers' compensation, and other rights or benefits to which they may be entitled as incidents of their regular employment. The municipal corporation receiving such aid shall reimburse the political subdivision furnishing it the cost of furnishing such aid, including compensation of personnel, expenses incurred by reason of the injury or death of any such personnel while rendering such aid, expenses of furnishing equipment and apparatus, compensation for damage to or loss of equipment or apparatus while in service outside the territory of its regular use, and such other reasonable expenses as may be incurred by any such political subdivision in furnishing such aid. Nothing in this section shall be construed as superseding or modifying in any way any provision of a contract entered into pursuant to section 737.04 of the Revised Code. Law enforcement officers acting pursuant to this section outside the territory of their regular employment have the same authority to enforce the law as when acting within the territory of their regular employment.

(1976 S 545, eff. 1–17–77; 132 v H 996; 1953 H 1; GC 4373; Source—GC 4376)

737.11 General duties of police and fire departments; organized crime task force membership

The police force of a municipal corporation shall preserve the peace, protect persons and property, and obey and enforce all ordinances of the legislative authority of the municipal corporation, all criminal laws of the state and the United States, all court orders issued and consent agreements approved pursuant to sections 2919.26 and 3113.31 of the Revised Code, all protection orders issued pursuant to section 2903.213 or 2903.214 of the Revised Code, and protection orders issued by courts of another state, as defined in section 2919.27 of the Revised Code. The fire department shall protect the lives and property of the people in case of fire. Both the police and fire departments shall perform any other duties that are provided by ordinance. The police and fire departments in every city shall be maintained under the civil service system.

A chief or officer of a police force of a municipal corporation may participate, as the director of an organized crime task force established under section 177.02 of the Revised Code or as a member of the investigatory staff of such a task force, in an investigation of organized criminal activity in any county or counties in this state under sections 177.01 to 177.03 of the Revised Code.

(1998 H 302, eff. 7–29–98; 1997 S 1, eff. 10–21–97; 1992 H 536, eff. 11–5–92; 1986 S 74; 1978 H 835; 1953 H 1; GC 4378)

737.111 Police department's fines, rewards, and fees credited to municipality's general fund

All fines imposed as discipline or punishment upon members of the police department of a municipal corporation by the authority having charge or control thereof, all rewards, fees, or proceeds of gifts and emoluments allowed by such authority paid and given for or on account of any extraordinary service of any member of the department, and moneys arising from the sale of unclaimed property or money, after deducting all expenses incident thereto, shall be credited to the general fund of the municipal corporation.

(1985 H 201, eff. 7–1–85)

737.112 Fire department's fines, penalties and fees credited to municipality's general fund

All fines imposed as discipline or punishment upon members of the fire department of a municipal corporation by the authority having charge or control thereof, the proceeds of all suits for penalties for the violation of state statutes and municipal ordinances with the execution of which such department is charged, license fees or other fees payable thereunder, and fees received by such municipal corporation for any services performed or inspections made by the fire department, except fees charged and received by the municipal corporation from other subdivisions for fire protection or fire fighting therein shall be credited to the general fund of the municipal corporation.

(1985 H 201, eff. 7–1–85)

737.12 Suspension of police and fire personnel

Except as provided in section 737.052 of the Revised Code, the chief of police and the chief of the fire department have the exclusive right to suspend any of the deputies, officers, or employees in their respective departments and under their management and control, for incompetence, gross neglect of duty, gross immorality, habitual drunkenness, failure to obey orders given them by the proper authority, or for any other reasonable and just cause.

If an employee is suspended under this section, the chief of police or the chief of the fire department, as the case may be, shall forthwith certify that fact in writing, together with the cause for the suspension, to the director of public safety, who, within five days from the receipt of that certification, shall proceed to inquire into the cause of the suspension and render judgment on it. If the charge is sustained, the judgment may be for the person's suspension, reduction in rank, or dismissal from the department. The judgment shall be final except as otherwise provided by law.

The director, in any investigation of charges against a member of the police or fire department, shall have the same powers to administer oaths and to secure the attendance of witnesses and the production of books and papers that are conferred upon the mayor.

(1996 H 566, eff. 10–16–96; 1953 H 1, eff. 10–1–53; GC 4379, 4380)

737.13 Classification of service; rules and regulations

The director of public safety of a city shall classify the service in the police and fire departments in conformity with the ordinance of the legislative authority thereof determining the number of persons to be employed in the departments, and shall make all rules for the regulation and discipline of such departments, except as otherwise provided by law.

(1953 H 1, eff. 10–1–53; GC 4382)

737.14 Relief for members of police or fire department

The legislative authority of a municipal corporation may provide by general ordinance for the relief, out of the police or fire funds, of members of either department temporarily or permanently disabled in the discharge of their duty. This section does not impair, restrict, or repeal any law authorizing the levy of taxes in municipal corporations to provide for firemen, police, and sanitary police pension funds, and to create and perpetuate boards of trustees for the administration of such funds.

(1953 H 1, eff. 10–1–53; GC 4383)

VILLAGES—POLICE PROTECTION

737.15 Appointment of village marshal; physical examination

Each village shall have a marshal, designated chief of police, appointed by the mayor with the advice and consent of the legislative authority of the village, who need not be a resident of the village at the time of appointment but shall become a resident thereof within six months after appointment by the mayor and confirmation by the legislative authority unless such residence requirement is waived by ordinance, and who shall continue in office until removed therefrom as provided by section 737.171 of the Revised Code.

No person shall receive an appointment under this section after January 1, 1970, unless, not more than sixty days prior to receiving such appointment, the person has passed a physical examination, given by a licensed physician, a physician assistant, a clinical nurse specialist, a certified nurse practitioner, or a certified nurse-midwife, showing that the person meets the physical requirements necessary to perform the duties of village marshal as established by the legislative authority of the village. The appointing authority shall, prior to making any such appointment, file with the Ohio police and fire pension fund a copy of the report or findings of said licensed physician, physician assistant, clinical nurse specialist, certified nurse practitioner, or certified nurse-midwife. The professional fee for such physical examination shall be paid for by such legislative authority.

(2002 S 245, eff. 3–31–03; 1999 H 222, eff. 11–2–99; 1969 S 86, eff. 10–24–69; 131 v H 358; 130 v H 528; 1953 H 1; GC 4384)

737.16 Deputy marshals and police officers; physical examination

The mayor shall, when provided for by the legislative authority of a village, and subject to its confirmation, appoint all deputy marshals, police officers, night guards, and special police officers.

All such officers shall continue in office until removed therefrom for the cause and in the manner provided by section 737.19 of the Revised Code.

No person shall receive an appointment under this section after January 1, 1970, unless the person has, not more than sixty days prior to receiving such appointment, passed a physical examination, given by a licensed physician, a physician assistant, a clinical nurse specialist, a certified nurse practitioner, or a certified nurse-midwife, showing that the person meets the physical requirements necessary to perform the duties of the position to which the person is to be appointed as established by the legislative authority of the village. The appointing authority shall, prior to making any such appointment, file with the Ohio police and fire pension fund a copy of the report or findings of said licensed physician, physician assistant, clinical nurse specialist, certified nurse practitioner, or certified nurse-midwife. The professional fee for such physical examination shall be paid for by the legislative authority.

(2002 S 245, eff. 3–31–03; 1999 H 222, eff. 11–2–99; 1978 H 812, eff. 8–1–78; 1969 S 86; 130 v H 528; 1953 H 1; GC 4384–1)

737.161 Village auxiliary police; rules; parking enforcement unit; parking enforcement officers

(A) The legislative authority of a village may establish, by ordinance, an auxiliary police unit within the police department of the village, and provide for the regulation of auxiliary police officers. The mayor shall be the executive head of the auxiliary police unit, shall make all appointments and removals of auxiliary police officers, subject to any general rules prescribed by the legislative authority by ordinance, and shall prescribe rules for the organization, training, administration, control, and conduct of the auxiliary police unit. The village marshal shall have exclusive control of the stationing and transferring of all auxiliary police officers, under such general rules as the mayor prescribes.

(B)(1) The legislative authority of a village may establish, by ordinance, a parking enforcement unit within the police department of the village, and provide for the regulation of parking enforcement officers. The mayor shall be the executive head of the parking enforcement unit, shall make all appointments and removals of parking enforcement officers, subject to any general rules prescribed by the legislative authority by ordinance, and shall prescribe rules for the organization, training, administration, control, and conduct of the parking enforcement unit. The mayor may appoint parking enforcement officers who agree to serve for nominal compensation, and persons with physical disabilities may receive appointments as parking enforcement officers.

(2) The authority of the parking enforcement officers shall be limited to the enforcement of ordinances governing parking in handicapped parking locations and fire lanes and any other parking ordinances specified in the ordinance creating the parking enforcement unit. Parking enforcement officers shall have no other powers.

(3) The training the parking enforcement officers shall receive shall include instruction in general administrative rules and procedures governing the parking enforcement unit, the role of the judicial system as it relates to parking regulation and enforcement, proper techniques and methods relating to the enforcement of parking ordinances, human interaction skills, and first aid.

(1990 S 174, eff. 7–13–90; 1985 H 201; 130 v H 121)

737.162 Offenses affecting employment eligibility of marshals, deputy marshals, police officers, and night watchpersons

(A) As used in this section, "felony" has the same meaning as in section 109.511 of the Revised Code.

(B)(1) The mayor shall not appoint a person as a marshal, a deputy marshal, a police officer, a night watchperson, a special police officer, or an auxiliary police officer on a permanent basis, on a temporary basis, for a probationary term, or on other than a permanent basis if the person previously has been convicted of or has pleaded guilty to a felony.

(2)(a) The mayor shall terminate the employment of a marshal, deputy marshal, police officer, night watchperson, special police officer, or auxiliary police officer who does either of the following:

(i) Pleads guilty to a felony;

(ii) Pleads guilty to a misdemeanor pursuant to a negotiated plea agreement as provided in division (D) of section 2929.43 of the Revised Code in which the marshal, deputy marshal, police officer, night watchperson, special police officer, or auxiliary police officer agrees to surrender the certificate awarded to that person under section 109.77 of the Revised Code.

(b) The mayor shall suspend from employment a marshal, deputy marshal, police officer, night watchperson, special police officer, or auxiliary police officer who is convicted, after trial, of a felony. If the marshal, deputy marshal, police officer, night watchperson, special police officer, or auxiliary police officer files an appeal from that conviction and the conviction is upheld by the highest court to which the appeal is taken or if that person does not file a timely appeal, the mayor shall terminate that person's employment. If the marshal, deputy marshal, police officer, night watchperson, special police officer, or auxiliary police officer files an appeal that results in that person's acquittal of the felony or conviction of a misdemeanor, or in the dismissal of the felony charge against that person, the mayor shall reinstate that person. A marshal, deputy marshal, police officer, night watchperson, special police officer, or auxiliary police officer who is reinstated under division (B)(2)(b) of this section shall not receive any back pay unless that person's conviction of the felony was reversed on appeal, or the felony charge was dismissed, because the court found insufficient evidence to convict that person of the felony.

(3) Division (B) of this section does not apply regarding an offense that was committed prior to January 1, 1997.

(4) The suspension from employment, or the termination of the employment, of a marshal, deputy marshal, police officer, night watchperson, special police officer, or auxiliary police officer under division (B)(2) of this section shall be in accordance with Chapter 119. of the Revised Code.

(2002 H 490, eff. 1–1–04; 1996 H 566, eff. 10–16–96)

737.17 Probationary period; final appointment

All appointments made under sections 737.15 and 737.16 of the Revised Code shall be for a probationary period of six months' continuous service, and none shall be finally made until the appointee has satisfactorily served his probationary period. At the end of the probationary period the mayor shall transmit to the legislative authority of the village a record of such employee's service with his recommendations thereon and he may, with the concurrence of the legislative authority, remove or finally appoint the employee.

(1953 H 1, eff. 10–1–53; GC 4384–2)

737.171 Suspension or removal of marshal

Except as provided in section 737.162 of the Revised Code, if the mayor of a village has reason to believe that a duly appointed marshal of the village has been guilty of incompetency, inefficiency, dishonesty, drunkenness, immoral conduct, insubordination, discourteous treatment of the public, neglect of duty, or any other acts of misfeasance, malfeasance, or nonfeasance in the performance of the marshal's official duty, the mayor shall file with the legislative authority of the village written charges against that person setting forth in detail the reason for the charges and immediately shall serve a true copy of the charges upon the person against whom they are made.

Charges filed under this section shall be heard at the next regular meeting of the legislative authority occurring not less than five days after the date those charges have been served on the person against whom they are made. The person against whom those charges are filed may appear in person and by counsel at the hearing, examine all witnesses, and answer all charges against that person.

At the conclusion of the hearing, the legislative authority may dismiss the charges, suspend the accused from office for not more than sixty days, or remove the accused from office.

Action of the legislative authority removing or suspending the accused from office requires the affirmative vote of two-thirds of all members elected to it.

In the case of removal from office, the person so removed may appeal on questions of law and fact the decision of the legislative authority to the court of common pleas of the county in which the village is situated. The person shall take the appeal within ten days from the date of the finding of the legislative authority.

(1996 H 566, eff. 10–16–96; 1978 H 812, eff. 8–1–78; 130 v Pt 2, H 5; 130 v H 528)

737.18 General powers of village police officers; organized crime task force membership

The marshal shall be the peace officer of a village and the executive head, under the mayor, of the police force. The marshal, and the deputy marshals, policemen, or nightwatchmen under him shall have the powers conferred by law upon police officers in all villages of the state, and such other powers, not inconsistent with the nature of their offices, as are conferred by ordinance.

A marshal, deputy marshal, or police officer of a village may participate, as the director of an organized crime task force established under section 177.02 of the Revised Code or as a member of the investigatory staff of such a task force, in an investigation of organized criminal activity in any county or counties in this state under sections 177.01 to 177.03 of the Revised Code.

(1986 S 74, eff. 9–3–86; 1953 H 1; GC 4385)

737.19 Powers and duties of marshal; control of personnel

(A) The marshal of a village has exclusive authority over the stationing and transfer of all deputies, officers, and employees within the police department of the village, under the general rules that the mayor prescribes.

(B) Except as provided in section 737.162 of the Revised Code, the marshal of a village has the exclusive right to suspend any of the deputies, officers, or employees in the village police department who are under the management and control of the marshal for incompetence, gross neglect of duty, gross immorality, habitual drunkenness, failure to obey orders given them by the proper authority, or for any other reasonable or just cause.

If an employee is suspended under this section, the marshal immediately shall certify this fact in writing, together with the cause for the suspension, to the mayor of the village and immediately shall serve a true copy of the charges upon the person against whom they are made. Within five days after receiving this certification, the mayor shall inquire into the cause of the suspension and shall render a judgment on it. If the mayor sustains the charges, the judgment of the mayor may be for the person's suspension, reduction in rank, or removal from the department.

Suspensions of more than three days, reduction in rank, or removal from the department under this section may be appealed to the legislative authority of the village within five days from the date of the mayor's judgment. The legislative authority shall hear the appeal at its next regularly scheduled meeting. The person against whom the judgment has been rendered may appear in person and by counsel at the hearing, examine all witnesses, and answer all charges against that person.

At the conclusion of the hearing, the legislative authority may dismiss the charges, uphold the mayor's judgment, or modify the judgment to one of suspension for not more than sixty days, reduction in rank, or removal from the department.

Action of the legislative authority removing or suspending the accused from the department requires the affirmative vote of two-thirds of all members elected to it.

In the case of removal from the department, the person so removed may appeal on questions of law and fact the decision of the legislative authority to the court of common pleas of the county in which the village is situated. The person shall take the appeal within ten days from the date of the finding of the legislative authority.

(C) The marshal of a village shall suppress all riots, disturbances, and breaches of the peace, and to that end may call upon the citizens to aid the marshal. The marshal shall arrest all disorderly persons in the village and pursue and arrest any person fleeing from justice in any part of the state. The marshal shall arrest any person in the act of committing an offense against the laws of the state or the ordinances of the village and forthwith bring that person before the mayor or other competent authority for examination or trial. The marshal shall receive and execute proper authority for the arrest and detention of criminals fleeing or escaping from other places or states.

In the discharge of the marshal's duties, the marshal shall have the powers and be subject to the responsibilities of constables, and, for services performed by the marshal or the marshal's deputies, the same fees and expenses shall be taxed as are allowed constables.

(1996 H 566, eff. 10–16–96; 1978 H 812, eff. 8–1–78; 1953 H 1; GC 4386, 4387)

737.20 Disposition of fines and penalties

All fees, costs, fines, and penalties collected by the marshal shall immediately be paid to the mayor, who shall report to the legislative authority of the village monthly the amount thereof, from whom, and for what purpose collected, and when paid to the mayor.

(1953 H 1, eff. 10–1–53; GC 4388)

CITIES AND VILLAGES—FIRE DEPARTMENTS

737.21 Municipal fire department regulations

The legislative authority of a municipal corporation may establish all necessary regulations to guard against the occurrence of fires, protect the property and lives of its citizens against damage and accidents resulting therefrom, and for such purpose may establish and maintain a fire department, provide for the establishment and organization of fire engine and hose companies and rescue units, establish the hours of labor of the members of its fire department who shall not be required to be on duty continuously more than six days in every seven, and provide such bylaws and regulations for the government of such companies and their members as is necessary and proper.

(129 v 1436, eff. 10–23–61; 1953 H 1; GC 4393)

737.221 Criminal records check for village firefighters or volunteer firefighters

(A) The fire chief of a village fire department may request the superintendent of BCII to conduct a criminal records check with respect to any person who is under consideration for appointment or employment as a permanent, full-time paid firefighter or any person who is under consideration for appointment as a volunteer firefighter.

(B)(1) The fire chief of the village fire department may request that the superintendent of BCII obtain information from the federal bureau of investigation as a part of the criminal records check requested pursuant to division (A) of this section.

(2) A fire chief authorized by division (A) of this section to request a criminal records check shall provide to each person for whom the fire chief intends to request a criminal records check a copy of the form prescribed pursuant to division (C)(1) of section 109.578 of the Revised Code and a standard impression sheet to obtain fingerprint impressions prescribed pursuant to division (C)(2) of section 109.578 of the Revised Code, obtain the completed form and impression sheet from the person, and forward the completed form and impression sheet to the superintendent of BCII at the time the criminal records check is requested.

(3) Any person subject to a criminal records check who receives a copy of the form and a copy of the impression sheet pursuant to division (B)(2) of this section and who is requested to complete the form and provide a set of fingerprint impressions shall complete the form or provide all the information necessary to complete the form and shall provide the impression sheet with the impressions of the person's fingerprints. If a person fails to provide the information necessary to complete the form or fails to provide impressions of the person's fingerprints, the appointing authority shall not appoint or employ the person as a permanent full-time paid firefighter or a volunteer firefighter.

(C)(1) Except as otherwise provided in division (C)(2) of this section, an appointing authority shall not appoint or employ a person as a permanent, full-time paid firefighter or a volunteer firefighter if the fire chief has requested a criminal records check pursuant to division (A) of this section and the criminal records check indicates that the person previously has been convicted of or pleaded guilty to any of the following:

(a) A felony;

(b) A violation of section 2909.03 of the Revised Code;

(c) A violation of an existing or former law of this state, any other state, or the United States that is substantially equivalent to any of the offenses described in division (C)(1)(a) or (b) of this section.

(2) Notwithstanding division (C)(1) of this section, an appointing authority may appoint or employ a person as a permanent, full-time paid firefighter or a volunteer firefighter if all of the following apply:

(a) The fire chief has requested a criminal records check pursuant to division (A) of this section.

(b) The criminal records check indicates that the person previously has been convicted of or pleaded guilty to any of the offenses described in division (C)(1) of this section.

(c) The person meets rehabilitation standards established in rules adopted under division (E) of this section.

(3) If a fire chief requests a criminal records check pursuant to division (A) of this section, an appointing authority may appoint or employ a person as a permanent, full-time paid firefighter or volunteer firefighter conditionally until the criminal records check is completed and the fire chief receives the results. If the results of the criminal records check indicate that, pursuant to division (C)(1) of this section, the person subject to the criminal records check is disqualified from appointment or employment, the fire chief shall release the person from appointment or employment.

(D) The fire chief shall pay to the bureau of criminal identification and investigation the fee prescribed pursuant to division (C)(3) of section 109.578 of the Revised Code for each criminal records check conducted in accordance with that section. The fire chief may charge the applicant who is subject to the criminal records check a fee for the costs the fire chief incurs in obtaining the criminal records check. A fee charged under this division shall not exceed the amount of fees the fire chief pays for the criminal records check. If a fee is charged under this division, the fire chief shall notify the applicant at the time of the applicant's initial application for appointment or employment of the amount of the fee and that, unless the fee is paid, the applicant will not be considered for appointment or employment.

(E) The appointing authority shall adopt rules in accordance with Chapter 119. of the Revised Code to implement this section. The rules shall include rehabilitation standards a person who has been convicted of or pleaded guilty to an offense listed in division (C)(1) of this section must meet for the appointing authority to appoint or employ the person as a permanent, full-time paid firefighter or a volunteer firefighter.

(F) A fire chief who intends to request a criminal records check for an applicant shall inform each applicant, at the time of the person's initial application for appointment or employment, that the applicant is required to provide a set of impressions of the person's fingerprints and that the fire chief requires a criminal records check to be conducted and satisfactorily completed in accordance with section 109.578 of the Revised Code.

(G) As used in this section:

(1) "Appointing authority" means any person or body that has the authority to hire, appoint, or employ permanent, full-time paid firefighters and volunteer firefighters under section 737.22 of the Revised Code.

(2) "Criminal records check" has the same meaning as in section 109.578 of the Revised Code.

(3) "Superintendent of BCII" has the same meaning as in section 2151.86 of the Revised Code.

(2002 S 258, eff. 4–9–03)

737.27 Investigation of fires

The legislative authority of a municipal corporation may invest any officer of the fire or police department with the power, and impose on him the duty, to be present at all fires, investigate the cause thereof, examine witnesses, compel the attendance of witnesses and the production of books and papers, and to do and perform all other acts necessary to the effective discharge of such duties.

Such officer may administer oaths, make arrests, and enter, for the purpose of examination, any building which, in his opinion, is in danger from fire. The officer shall report his proceedings to the legislative authority at such times as are required.

(1953 H 1, eff. 10–1–53; GC 4396, 4397)

STOLEN AND UNCLAIMED PROPERTY

737.29 Property recovered by police

Stolen or other property recovered by members of the police force of a municipal corporation shall be deposited and kept in a place designated by the mayor. Each such article shall be entered in a book kept for that purpose, with the name of the owner, if ascertained, the person from whom taken, the place where found with general circumstances, the date of its receipt, and the name of the officer receiving it.

An inventory of all money or other property shall be given to the party from whom taken, and in case it is not claimed by some person within thirty days after arrest and seizure it shall be delivered to the person from whom taken, and to no other person, either attorney, agent, factor, or clerk, except by special order of the mayor.

(1953 H 1, eff. 10–1–53; GC 4398, 4399)

737.31 Disposition to claimant

If, within thirty days, the money or property recovered under section 737.29 of the Revised Code is claimed by any other person, it shall be retained by the custodian thereof until after the discharge or conviction of the person from whom it was taken and so long as it is required as evidence in any case in court. If such claimant establishes to the satisfaction of the court that he is the rightful owner, the money or property shall be restored to him, otherwise it shall be returned to the accused person, personally, and not to any attorney, agent, factor, or clerk of such accused person, except upon special order of the mayor after all liens and claims in favor of the municipal corporation have first been discharged and satisfied.

(1953 H 1, eff. 10–1–53; GC 4400)

737.32 Sale of unclaimed property; disposition of proceeds

Except as otherwise provided in this section and unless the property involved is required to be disposed of pursuant to another section of the Revised Code, property that is unclaimed for ninety days or more shall be sold by the chief of police of the municipal corporation, marshal of the village, or licensed auctioneer at public auction, after notice of the sale has been provided by publication once a week for three successive weeks in a newspaper of general circulation in the county. The proceeds of the sale shall be paid to the treasurer of the municipal corporation and shall be credited to the general fund of the municipal corporation.

If authorized to do so by an ordinance adopted by the legislative authority of the municipal corporation and if the property involved is not required to be disposed of pursuant to another section of the Revised Code, the chief of police or marshal may contribute property that is unclaimed for ninety days or more to one or more public agencies, to one or more nonprofit organizations no part of the net income of which inures to the benefit of any private shareholder or individual and no substantial part of the activities of which consists of carrying on propaganda or otherwise attempting to influence legislation, or to one or more organizations satisfying section 501(c)(3) or (c)(19) of the Internal Revenue Code of 1986.

(1999 H 55, eff. 9–29–99; 1971 H 24, eff. 10–6–71; 1969 H 13; 131 v H 157; 1953 H 1; GC 4401)

737.33 Expenses of storage and sale; notice

Upon the sale of any unclaimed or impounded property as provided in section 737.32 of the Revised Code, if any such unclaimed or impounded property was ordered removed to a place of storage or stored, or both, by or under the direction of a chief of police of the municipal corporation or marshal of the village, any expenses or charges for such removal or storage, or both, and costs of sale, provided the same are approved by such chief of police or marshal, shall first be paid from the proceeds of such sale. Notice shall be given by registered mail, thirty days before the date of such sale, to the owner and mortgagee, or other lien holder, at their last known address.

(1953 H 1, eff. 10–1–53; GC 4401–1)

BUILDING INSPECTION

737.37 Power of legislative authority to regulate

The legislative authority of a municipal corporation may make such regulations pertaining to public buildings as it considers necessary for the public safety.

(1953 H 1, eff. 10–1–53; GC 4664)

MISCELLANEOUS PROVISIONS

737.40 Voluntary motor vehicle decal registration program

(A) The legislative authority of a municipal corporation may establish, by ordinance or resolution, a voluntary motor vehicle decal registration program to be controlled by the director of public safety of the municipal corporation and conducted by the police department of the municipal corporation. The legislative authority may establish a fee for participation in the program in an amount sufficient to cover the cost of administering the program and the cost of the decals.

(B) Any resident of the municipal corporation may enroll a motor vehicle that he owns in the program by signing a consent form, displaying the decal issued under this section, and paying the prescribed fee. The motor vehicle owner shall remove the decal to withdraw from the program and also prior to the sale or transfer of ownership of the vehicle. Any law enforcement officer may conduct, at any place within this state at which the officer would be permitted to arrest the person operating the vehicle, an investigatory stop of any motor vehicle displaying a decal issued under this section when the vehicle is being driven between the hours of one a.m. and five a.m. A law enforcement officer may conduct an investigatory stop under this division regardless of whether the officer observes a violation of law involving the vehicle or whether he has probable cause to believe that any violation of law involving the vehicle has occurred.

(C) The consent form required under division (B) of this section shall:

(1) Describe the conditions for participation in the program, including a description of an investigatory stop and a statement that any law enforcement officer may conduct, at any place within this state at which the officer would be permitted to arrest the person operating the vehicle, an investigatory stop of the motor vehicle when it is being driven between the hours of one a.m. and five a.m.

(2) Contain other information identifying the vehicle and owner as the director of public safety of the municipal corporation or the chief of police considers necessary.

(D) The state director of public safety, in accordance with Chapter 119. of the Revised Code, shall adopt rules governing the color, size, and design of decals issued under this section and the location where the decals shall be displayed on vehicles that are enrolled in the program.

(E) Divisions (A) to (D) and (G) of this section do not require a law enforcement officer to conduct an investigatory stop of a vehicle displaying a decal issued under this section or under a program described in division (G) of this section.

(F) As used in this section:

(1) "Investigatory stop" means a temporary stop of a motor vehicle and its operator and occupants for purposes of determining the identity of the person who is operating the vehicle and, if

the person who is operating it is not its owner, whether any violation of law has occurred or is occurring. An "investigatory stop" is not an arrest, but, if an officer who conducts an investigatory stop determines that illegal conduct has occurred or is occurring, an "investigatory stop" may be the basis for an arrest.

(2) "Law enforcement officer" means a sheriff, deputy sheriff, constable, police officer of a township or joint township police district, marshal, deputy marshal, municipal police officer, or state highway patrol trooper.

(G) Any motor vehicle decal registration program that was in existence on June 1, 1993, and administered by a municipal corporation shall not be required to conform in any manner to this section and may continue to be administered in the manner in which it was administered on that date.

(1994 S 75, eff. 10–20–94)

PROBATION SERVICES

737.41 Municipal probation services fund

(A) The legislative authority of a municipal corporation in which is established a municipal court, other than a county-operated municipal court, that has a department of probation shall establish in the municipal treasury a municipal probation services fund. The fund shall contain all moneys paid to the treasurer of the municipal corporation under section 2951.021 of the Revised Code for deposit into the fund. The treasurer of the municipal corporation shall disburse the money contained in the fund at the request of the municipal court department of probation, for use only by that department for specialized staff, purchase of equipment, purchase of services, reconciliation programs for offenders and victims, other treatment programs, including alcohol and drug addiction programs certified under section 3793.06 of the Revised Code, determined to be appropriate by the chief probation officer, and other similar expenses related to placing offenders under a community control sanction.

(B) Any money in a municipal probation services fund at the end of a fiscal year shall not revert to the treasury of the municipal corporation but shall be retained in the fund.

(C) As used in this section:

(1) "County–operated municipal court" has the same meaning as in section 1901.03 of the Revised Code.

(2) "Community control sanction" has the same meaning as in section 2929.01 of the Revised Code.

(2002 H 490, eff. 1–1–04; 1994 H 406, eff. 11–11–94)

CHAPTER 753

REFORMATORY INSTITUTIONS

IMPRISONMENT

753.02 Maintenance expense; reimbursement by prisoner; testing for contagious diseases

(A) The legislative authority of a municipal corporation shall provide by ordinance for sustaining all persons sentenced to or confined in a prison or station house at the expense of the municipal corporation, and in counties where prisons or station houses are in quarters leased from the board of county commissioners, may contract with the board for the care and maintenance of those persons by the sheriff or other person charged with the care and maintenance of county prisoners. On the presentation of bills for food, sustenance, and necessary supplies, to the proper officer, certified by the person whom the legislative authority designates, the officer shall audit the bills under the rules prescribed by the legislative authority, and draw the officer's order on the treasurer of the municipal corporation in favor of the person presenting the bill.

(B) Pursuant to section 2929.37 of the Revised Code, the legislative authority of the municipal corporation may require a person who was convicted of an offense and who is confined in a prison or station house as provided in division (A) of this section, or a person who was convicted of an offense and who is confined in the county jail as provided in section 1905.35 of the Revised Code, to reimburse the municipal corporation for its expenses incurred by reason of the person's confinement.

(C) Notwithstanding any contrary provision in this section or section 2929.18, 2929.28, or 2929.37 of the Revised Code, the legislative authority of the municipal corporation may establish a policy that complies with section 2929.38 of the Revised Code and that requires any person who is not indigent and who is confined in a prison or station house to pay a reception fee, a fee for any medical treatment or service requested by and provided to that person, or the fee for a random drug test assessed under division (E) of section 753.33 of the Revised Code.

(D) If a person who has been convicted of or pleaded guilty to an offense is sentenced to a term of imprisonment in a prison or station house as described in division (A) of this section, or if a person who has been arrested for an offense, and who has been denied bail or has had bail set and has not been released on bail is confined in a prison or station house as described in division (A) of this section pending trial, at the time of reception and at other times the person in charge of the operation of the prison or station house determines to be appropriate, the person in charge of the operation of the prison or station house may cause the convicted or accused offender to be examined and tested for tuberculosis, HIV infection, hepatitis, including, but not limited to, hepatitis A, B, and C, and other contagious diseases. The person in charge of the operation of the prison or station house may cause a convicted or accused offender in the prison or station house who refuses to be tested or treated for tuberculosis, HIV infection, hepatitis, including, but not limited to, hepatitis A, B, and C, or another contagious disease to be tested and treated involuntarily.

(2002 H 490, eff. 1–1–04; 2002 H 170, eff. 9–6–02; 2000 H 349, eff. 9–22–00; 1997 S 111, eff. 3–17–98; 1996 H 480, eff. 10–16–96; 1996 S 269, eff. 7–1–96; 1995 S 2, eff. 7–1–96; 1984 H 363, eff. 9–26–84; 1971 H 172; 1953 H 1; GC 4126)

753.021 Health insurance claims of persons confined in prison or station house

(A) For each person who is confined in a prison or station house as provided in section 753.02 of the Revised Code or in a county jail as provided in section 1905.35 of the Revised Code, the municipal corporation may make a determination as to whether the person is covered under a health insurance or health care policy, contract, or plan and, if the person has such coverage, what terms and conditions are imposed by it for the filing and payment of claims.

(B) If, pursuant to division (A) of this section, it is determined that the person is covered under a policy, contract, or plan and, while that coverage is in force, the prison, station house, or county jail renders or arranges for the rendering of health care services to the person, in accordance with the terms and conditions of the policy, contract, or plan, then the person, municipal corporation, or provider of the health care services, as appropriate under the terms and conditions of the policy, contract, or plan, shall promptly submit a claim for payment for the health care services to the appropriate third-party payer and shall designate, or make any other arrangement necessary to ensure, that payment of any amount due on the claim be made to the municipal corporation or the provider, as the case may be.

(C) Any payment made to the municipal corporation pursuant to division (B) of this section shall be paid into the treasury of the municipal corporation.

(D) This section also applies to any person who is under the custody of a law enforcement officer, as defined in section 2901.01 of the Revised Code, prior to the person's confinement in the prison, station house, or county jail.

(1996 S 163, eff. 10–16–96)

753.03 Confinement for misdemeanors

A municipal legislative authority may, by ordinance, provide for the keeping of persons convicted and sentenced for misdemeanors, during the term of their imprisonment, at such place as the legislative authority determines, provided that the place selected is in substantial compliance with the minimum standards for jails in Ohio promulgated by the department of rehabilitation and correction. The legislative authority may enter into a contract under section 9.06 of the Revised Code for the private operation and management of any municipal correctional facility, but only if the facility is used to house only misdemeanant inmates.

(1995 H 117, eff. 9–29–95; 1982 S 23, eff. 7–6–82; 1953 H 1; GC 4127)

WORKHOUSES

753.04 Commitment to workhouse; reimbursement by prisoner; testing for contagious diseases

(A) When a person over sixteen years of age is convicted of an offense under the law of this state or an ordinance of a municipal corporation, and the tribunal before which the conviction is had is authorized by law to commit the offender to the county jail or municipal corporation prison, the court, mayor, or judge of the county court, as the case may be, may sentence the offender to a workhouse.

When a commitment is made from a municipal corporation or township in the county, other than in a municipal corporation having a workhouse, the legislative authority of the municipal corporation or the board of township trustees shall transmit with the mittimus a sum of money equal to not less than seventy cents per day for the time of the commitment, to be placed in the hands of the superintendent of a workhouse for the care and maintenance of the prisoner.

(B) Pursuant to section 2929.37 of the Revised Code, the legislative authority of the municipal corporation or the board of township trustees may require a person who is convicted of an offense and who is confined in a workhouse as provided in division (A) of this section, to reimburse the municipal corporation or the township, as the case may be, for its expenses incurred by reason of the person's confinement.

(C) Notwithstanding any contrary provision in this section or section 2929.18, 2929.28, or 2929.37 of the Revised Code, the legislative authority of the municipal corporation or board of township trustees may establish a policy that complies with section 2929.38 of the Revised Code and that requires any person who is not indigent and who is confined in the workhouse under division (A) of this section to pay a reception fee, a fee for any medical treatment or service requested by and provided to that person, or the fee for a random drug test assessed under division (E) of section 753.33 of the Revised Code.

(D) If a person who has been convicted of or pleaded guilty to an offense is incarcerated in a workhouse or if a person who has been arrested for an offense, and who has not been denied bail or has had bail set and has not been released on bail is confined in a workhouse pending trial, at the time of reception and at other times the person in charge of the operation of the workhouse determines to be appropriate, the person in charge of the operation of the workhouse may cause the convicted or accused offender to be examined and tested for tuberculosis, HIV infection, hepatitis, including, but not limited to, hepatitis A, B, and C, and other contagious diseases. The person in charge of the operation of the workhouse may cause a convicted or accused offender in the workhouse who refuses to be tested or treated for tuberculosis, HIV infection, hepatitis, including, but not limited to, hepatitis A, B, and C, or another contagious disease to be tested and treated involuntarily.

(2002 H 490, eff. 1–1–04; 2002 H 170, eff. 9–6–02; 2000 H 349, eff. 9–22–00; 1997 S 111, eff. 3–17–98; 1996 H 480, eff. 10–16–96; 1996 S 269, eff. 7–1–96; 1995 S 2, eff. 7–1–96; 1984 H 363, eff. 9–26–84; 127 v 1039; 126 v 320; 1953 H 1; GC 4128)

753.041 Health insurance claims of persons confined in workhouse

(A) For each person who is confined in a workhouse as provided in section 753.04 of the Revised Code, the municipal corporation or the township, as the case may be, may make a determination as to whether the person is covered under a health insurance or health care policy, contract, or plan and, if the person has such coverage, what terms and conditions are imposed by it for the filing and payment of claims.

(B) If, pursuant to division (A) of this section, it is determined that the person is covered under a policy, contract, or plan and, while that coverage is in force, the workhouse renders or arranges for the rendering of health care services to the person in accordance with the terms and conditions of the policy, contract, or plan, then the person, municipal corporation, township, or provider of the health care services, as appropriate under the terms and conditions of the policy, contract, or plan, shall promptly submit a claim for payment for the health care services to the appropriate third-party payer and shall designate, or make any other arrangement necessary to ensure, that payment of any amount due on the claim be made to the municipal corporation, township, or provider, as the case may be.

(C) Any payment made to the municipal corporation or township pursuant to division (B) of this section shall be paid into the treasury of the governmental entity that incurred the expenses.

(D) This section also applies to any person who is under the custody of a law enforcement officer, as defined in section 2901.01 of the Revised Code, prior to the person's confinement in the workhouse.

(1996 S 163, eff. 10–16–96)

753.05 Employment of prisoners

A person sentenced under section 753.04 of the Revised Code shall be received into the workhouse, and shall be kept and confined at labor therein, or if such labor cannot be furnished he may be employed at labor elsewhere when such employment is authorized by ordinance, and shall be subject to the rules, regulations, and discipline thereof until the expiration of his sentence, when he shall be discharged.

(1953 H 1, eff. 10–1–53; GC 4129)

753.06 Immunity from civil liability for death of prisoner on work detail

(A) As used in this section:

(1) "Municipal correctional facility" has the same meaning as in section 753.32 of the Revised Code.

(2) "Municipal correctional officer" has the same meaning as in section 753.31 of the Revised Code.

(B) If all the prisoners working on a work detail administered by a municipal correctional facility and outside the facility have volunteered for the work detail and are imprisoned in that facility for an offense other than a felony of the first or second degree and if the applicable municipal correctional officer complies with division (C) of this section, both of the following apply:

(1) No member of the organized police department of the municipal corporation and no municipal correctional officer is liable for civil damages for injury, death, or loss to person or property caused or suffered by a prisoner working on the work detail unless the injury, death, or loss results from malice or wanton or reckless misconduct of the member of the organized police department of the municipal corporation or the municipal correctional officer.

(2) A municipal corporation in which the prisoners work on the work detail and that employs the member of the organized police department or the municipal correctional officer or a township in which the prisoners work on the work detail is not liable for civil damages for injury, death, or loss to person or property caused or suffered by a prisoner working on the work detail unless the injury, death, or loss results from malice or wanton or reckless misconduct of the member of the organized police department of the municipal corporation or a municipal correctional officer.

(C) To qualify for the immunity described in division (B)(1) of this section regarding a work detail, a municipal correctional officer, prior to having the prisoners of the municipal correctional facility work outside the facility on the work detail, shall inform each prisoner on the work detail of the provisions of this section, including notifying the prisoner that, by volunteering for the work detail, the prisoner cannot hold any member of the organized police department of the municipal corporation or any municipal correctional officer or the municipal corporation or township liable for civil damages for injury, death, or loss to person or property unless the injury, death, or loss results from malice or wanton or reckless misconduct of the member of the organized police department of the municipal corporation or the municipal correctional officer.

(2004 H 316, eff. 3–31–05)

753.08 Prompt commitment; fees

The officer having the execution of the final sentence of a court, magistrate, or mayor shall cause the convicted person to be conveyed to the workhouse as soon as practicable after the sentence is pronounced, and all officers shall be paid the fees therefor allowed by law for similar services in other cases. Such fees shall be paid, when the sentence is by the court, from the county treasury, and when by the magistrate, from the township treasury.

(1953 H 1, eff. 10–1–53; GC 4132)

753.09 Discharge

The director of public safety may discharge, for good and sufficient cause, a person committed to the workhouse. A record of all such discharges shall be kept and reported to the legislative authority of the municipal corporation in the annual report of such director, with a brief statement of the reasons therefor.

(1953 H 1, eff. 10–1–53; GC 4133)

753.10 Parole of inmates

The director of public safety may establish rules and regulations under which, and specify the conditions on which, a prisoner may be allowed to go upon parole outside of the buildings and enclosures of the workhouse. While on parole such person shall remain in the legal custody and under the control of such director, and subject at any time to be taken back within the enclosure of the institution. Full power to enforce the rules, regulations, and conditions, and to retake and reimprison any convict so paroled, is hereby conferred upon such director, whose written order shall be sufficient warrant for all officers named therein to authorize them to return to actual custody any conditionally released or paroled prisoner. All such officers shall execute such order the same as ordinary criminal process.

No parole shall be granted by such director without previous notice thereof to the trial judge.

(1953 H 1, eff. 10–1–53; GC 4134; Source—GC 4136)

753.11 Violation of parole

The director of public safety may employ or authorize any person to see that the conditions of a parole are not violated, and in case of violation to return to the workhouse any prisoner so violating his parole. The time between the violation of the conditions of such parole, or conditional release by whatever name, as entered by order of such director on the records of the workhouse, and the reimprisonment or return of the prisoner, shall not be counted as any part or portion of time served under his sentence.

(1953 H 1, eff. 10–1–53; GC 4135)

753.13 Joint municipal and county workhouse

The board of county commissioners may unite with any municipal corporation located in the county in the acquisition or erection, management, and maintenance of a workhouse for the joint use of such county and municipal corporation, upon such terms as they may agree, and the board may levy and collect the necessary funds therefor from the taxable property of the county.

(1953 H 1, eff. 10–1–53; GC 4139)

753.14 Withdrawal from support and maintenance of joint workhouse

In any county in which, prior to May 20, 1920, there has been constructed and maintained a joint municipal and county workhouse, either the municipal corporation or the county may withdraw therefrom, may decline to further participate in the expense of maintaining such institution, and may sell its interest in such institution.

In the event of a sale thereof by such municipal corporation or county, the proceeds thereof shall be used in the payment of such indebtedness as was incurred in behalf of such municipal corporation or county in the management, control, and operation of such workhouse, and any balance remaining shall be placed in the general fund of such municipal corporation or county.

(1953 H 1, eff. 10–1–53; GC 4139–1)

753.15 Workhouses

(A) Except as provided in division (B) of this section, in a city, a workhouse erected for the joint use of the city and the county in which such city is located shall be managed and controlled by a joint board composed of the board of county commissioners and the board of control of the city, and in a village by the board of county commissioners and the board of trustees of public affairs. Such joint board shall have all the powers and duties in the management, control, and maintenance of such workhouse as are conferred upon the director of public safety in cities, and in addition thereto it may construct sewers for such workhouse and pay therefor from funds raised by taxation for the maintenance of such institution.

The joint board may lease or purchase suitable property and buildings for a workhouse, or real estate for the purpose of erecting and maintaining a workhouse thereon, but it shall not expend more than ten thousand dollars for any such purpose unless such amount is approved by a majority of the voters of the county, exclusive of the municipal corporation, voting at a general election.

(B) In lieu of forming a joint board to manage and control a workhouse erected for the joint use of the city and the county in which the city is located, the board of county commissioners and the legislative authority of the city may enter into a contract for the private operation and management of the workhouse as provided in section 9.06 of the Revised Code, but only if the workhouse is used solely for misdemeanant inmates. In order to enter into a contract under section 9.06 of the Revised Code, both the board and the legislative authority shall approve and be parties to the contract.

(1995 H 117, eff. 9–29–95; 1953 H 1, eff. 10–1–53; GC 4140)

753.16 Agreements to accept prisoners from other jurisdictions; reimbursement by prisoner; testing for contagious diseases

(A) Any city or district having a workhouse may receive as inmates of the workhouse persons sentenced or committed to it from counties other than the one in which the workhouse is situated, upon the terms and during the length of time agreed upon by the boards of county commissioners of those counties, or by the legislative authority of a municipal corporation in those counties and the legislative authority of the city, or the board of the district workhouse, or other authority having the management and control of the workhouse. Prisoners so received shall in all respects be and remain under the control of that authority, and shall be subject to the rules and discipline of the workhouse to which the other prisoners detained in the workhouse are subject.

(B) Prior to the acceptance for housing into a jail or workhouse of persons who are designated by the department of rehabilitation and correction, who plead guilty to or are convicted of a felony of the fourth or fifth degree, and who satisfy the other requirements listed in section 5120.161 of the Revised Code, the legislative authority of a municipal corporation having a jail or workhouse, or the joint board managing and controlling a workhouse for the joint use of a municipal corporation and a county shall enter into an agreement with the department of rehabilitation and correction under section 5120.161 of the Revised Code for the housing in the jail or workhouse of persons who are designated by the department, who plead guilty to or are convicted of a felony of the fourth or fifth degree, and who satisfy the other requirements listed in that section, in exchange for a per diem fee per person. Persons incarcerated in the jail or workhouse pursuant to an agreement of that nature shall be subject to supervision and control in the manner described in section 5120.161 of the Revised Code. This division does not affect the authority of a court to directly sentence a person who is convicted of or pleads guilty to a felony to the jail or workhouse in accordance with section 2929.16 of the Revised Code.

(C) Pursuant to section 2929.37 of the Revised Code, the board of county commissioners, the legislative authority of the municipal corporation, or the board or other managing authority of the district workhouse may require a person who was convicted of an offense and who is confined in the workhouse as provided in division (A) of this section, to reimburse the county, municipal corporation, or district, as the case may be, for its expenses incurred by reason of the person's confinement.

(D) Notwithstanding any contrary provision in this section or section 2929.18, 2929.28, or 2929.37 of the Revised Code, the board of county commissioners, the legislative authority of a municipal corporation, or the board or other managing authority of the district workhouse may establish a policy that complies with section 2929.38 of the Revised Code and that requires any person who is not indigent and who is confined in the jail or workhouse under division (A) or (B) of this section to pay a reception fee, a fee for any medical treatment or service requested by and provided to that person, or the fee for a random drug test assessed under division (E) of section 753.33 of the Revised Code.

(E) If a person who has been convicted of or pleaded guilty to an offense is confined in the workhouse as provided in division (A) of this section or is incarcerated in the workhouse in the manner described in division (B) of this section, or if a person who has been arrested for an offense, and who has been denied bail or has had bail set and has not been released on bail is confined in the workhouse pending trial, at the time of reception and at other times the person in charge of the operation of the workhouse determines to be appropriate, the person in charge of the operation of the workhouse may cause the convicted or accused offender to be examined and tested for tuberculosis, HIV infection, hepatitis, including but not limited to hepatitis A, B, and C, and other contagious diseases. The person in charge of the operation of the workhouse may cause a convicted or accused offender in the workhouse who refuses to be tested or treated for tuberculosis, HIV infection, hepatitis, including but not limited to hepatitis A, B, and C, or another contagious disease to be tested and treated involuntarily.

(2002 H 490, eff. 1–1–04; 2002 H 170, eff. 9–6–02; 2000 H 349, eff. 9–22–00; 1997 S 111, eff. 3–17–98; 1996 H 480, eff. 10–16–96; 1996 S 269, eff. 7–1–96; 1995 S 2, eff. 7–1–96; 1984 H 363, eff. 9–26–84; 1982 H 269, § 4, S 199, S 23; 1953 H 1; GC 4141)

753.161 Health insurance claims of persons from other jurisdictions who are confined in workhouse

(A) For each person who is confined in a workhouse as provided in section 753.16 of the Revised Code, the county, municipal corporation, or district, as the case may be, may make a determination as to whether the person is covered under a health insurance or health care policy, contract, or plan and, if the person has such coverage, what terms and conditions are imposed by it for the filing and payment of claims.

(B) If, pursuant to division (A) of this section, it is determined that the person is covered under a policy, contract, or plan and, while that coverage is in force, the workhouse renders or arranges for the rendering of health care services to the person in accordance with the terms and conditions of the policy, contract, or plan, then the person, county, municipal corporation, district, or provider of the health care services, as appropriate under the terms and conditions of the policy, contract, or plan, shall promptly submit a claim for payment for the health care services to the appropriate third-party payer and shall designate, or make any other arrangement necessary to ensure, that payment of any amount due on the claim be made to the county, municipal corporation, district, or provider, as the case may be.

(C) Any payment made to the county, municipal corporation, or district pursuant to division (B) of this section shall be paid into the treasury of the governmental entity that incurred the expenses.

(D) This section also applies to any person who is under the custody of a law enforcement officer, as defined in section 2901.01 of the Revised Code, prior to the person's confinement in the workhouse.

(1996 S 163, eff. 10–16–96)

753.17 Officers to have police powers

The superintendent, assistant superintendent, and each guard of a workhouse shall have such powers of policemen as are necessary for the proper performance of the duties of their positions.

(1953 H 1, eff. 10–1–53; GC 4137)

MISCELLANEOUS PROVISIONS

753.18 Religious services in prison or workhouse

Each administrative board or other authority in the state having charge or control of a city jail or workhouse shall provide for holding religious services therein each week, and may employ a clergyman or religious organization to conduct such services. Any expense so incurred by such board or authority shall be paid from the general fund of the city.

(1982 S 23, eff. 7–6–82; 1953 H 1; GC 4153)

753.19 Chief law enforcement officer to notify law enforcement agencies, prosecutor, and newspaper when criminal escapes

(A) If a person who was convicted of or pleaded guilty to an offense or was indicted or otherwise charged with the commission of an offense escapes from a jail or workhouse of a municipal corporation or otherwise escapes from the custody of a municipal corporation, the chief of police or other chief law enforcement officer of that municipal corporation immediately after the escape shall report the escape, by telephone and in writing, to all local law enforcement agencies with jurisdiction over the place where the person escaped from custody, to the state highway patrol, to the department of rehabilitation and correction if the escaped person is a prisoner under the custody of the department who is in the jail or workhouse, to the prosecuting attorney of the county, and to a newspaper of general circulation in the municipal corporation in a newspaper of general circulation in each county in which part of the municipal corporation is located. The written notice may be by either facsimile transmission or mail. A failure to comply with this requirement is a violation of section 2921.22 of the Revised Code.

(B) Upon the apprehension of the escaped person, the chief law enforcement officer shall give notice of the apprehension of the escaped person by telephone and in writing to the persons notified under division (A) of this section.

(1999 H 283, eff. 6–30–99; 1987 H 207, eff. 9–24–87)

753.21 Minimum security misdemeanant jails; testing for contagious diseases

(A) As used in this section, "building or structure" includes, but is not limited to, a modular unit, building, or structure and a movable unit, building, or structure.

(B)(1) The legislative authority of a municipal corporation, by ordinance, may dedicate and permit the use, as a minimum security jail, of any vacant or abandoned public building or structure owned by the municipal corporation that has not been dedicated to or is not then in use for any municipal or other public purpose, or any building or structure rented or leased by the municipal corporation. The legislative authority of a municipal corporation, by ordinance, also may dedicate and permit the use, as a minimum security jail, of any building or structure purchased by or constructed by or for the municipal corporation. Subject to divisions (B)(3) and (C) of this section, upon the effective date of such an ordinance, the specified building or structure shall be used, in accordance with this section, for the confinement of persons who meet one of the following conditions:

(a) The person is sentenced to a term of imprisonment for a traffic violation, a misdemeanor, or a violation of a municipal ordinance and is under the jurisdiction of the municipal corporation or is sentenced to a residential sanction in the jail for a felony of the fourth or fifth degree pursuant to sections 2929.11 to 2929.19 of the Revised Code, and the jail administrator or the jail administrator's designee has classified the person as a minimal security risk. In determining the person's classification under this division, the administrator or designee shall consider all relevant factors, including, but not limited to, the person's escape risk and propensity for assaultive or violent behavior, based upon the person's prior and current behavior.

(b) The person is an inmate transferred by order of a judge of the sentencing court upon the request of the sheriff, administrator, jailer, or other person responsible for operating the jail other than a contractor as defined in section 9.06 of the Revised Code, who is named in the request as being suitable for confinement in a minimum security facility.

(2) The legislative authority of a municipal corporation, by ordinance, may affiliate with the county in which it is located, with one or more counties adjacent to the county in which it is located, or with one or more municipal corporations located within the county in which it is located or within an adjacent county, and dedicate and permit the use, as a minimum security jail, of any vacant or abandoned public building or structure owned by any of the affiliating counties or municipal corporations that has not been dedicated to or is not then in use for any public purpose, or any building or structure rented or leased by any of the affiliating counties or municipal corporations. The legislative authority of a municipal corporation, by ordinance, also may affiliate with one or more counties adjacent to the county in which it is located or with one or more municipal corporations located within the county in which it is located or within an adjacent county and dedicate and permit the use, as a minimum security jail, of any building or structure purchased by or constructed by or for any of the affiliating counties or municipal corporations. Any counties and municipal corporations that affiliate for purposes of this division shall enter into an agreement that establishes the responsibilities for the operation and for the cost of operation of the minimum security jail. Subject to divisions (B)(3) and (C) of this section, upon the effective date of an ordinance adopted under this division, the specified building or structure shall be used, in accordance with this section, for the confinement of persons who meet one of the following conditions:

(a) The person is sentenced to a term of imprisonment for a traffic violation, a misdemeanor, or a violation of an ordinance of a municipal corporation and is under the jurisdiction of any of the affiliating counties or municipal corporations or is sentenced to a residential sanction in the jail for a felony of the fourth or fifth degree pursuant to sections 2929.11 to 2929.19 of the Revised Code, and the jail administrator or the jail administrator's designee has classified the person as a minimal security risk. In determining the person's classification under this division, the administrator or designee shall consider all relevant factors, including, but not limited to, the person's escape risk and propensity for assaultive or violent behavior, based upon the person's prior and current behavior.

(b) The person is an inmate transferred by order of a judge of the sentencing court upon the request of the sheriff, administrator, jailer, or other person responsible for operating the jail other than a contractor as defined in section 9.06 of the Revised Code, who is named in the request as being suitable for confinement in a minimum security facility.

(3) No person shall be confined in a building or structure dedicated as a minimum security jail under division (B)(1) or (2) of this section unless the judge who sentenced the person to the term of imprisonment for the traffic violation or the misdemeanor specifies that the term of imprisonment is to be served in that jail, and division (B)(1) or (2) of this section permits the confinement of the person in that jail or unless the judge who sentenced the person to the residential sanction for the felony specifies that the residential sanction is to be served in a jail, and division (B)(1) or (2) of this section permits the confinement of the person in that jail. If a rented or leased building or structure is so dedicated, the building or structure may be used as a minimum security jail only during the period that it is rented or leased by the municipal corporation or by an affiliated county or municipal corporation. If a person convicted of a misdemeanor is confined to a building or structure dedicated as a minimum security jail under division (B)(1) or (2) of this section and the sheriff, administrator, jailer, or other person responsible for operating the jail other than a contractor as defined in division (H) of section 9.06 of the Revised Code determines that it would be more appropriate for the person so confined to be confined in another jail or workhouse facility, the sheriff, administrator, jailer, or other person may transfer the person so confined to a more appropriate jail or workhouse facility.

(C) All of the following apply in relation to a building or structure that is dedicated pursuant to division (B)(1) or (2) of this section for use as a minimum security jail:

(1) To the extent that the use of the building or structure as a minimum security jail requires a variance from any municipal corporation, county, or township zoning ordinances or regulations, the variance shall be granted.

(2) Except as provided in this section, the building or structure shall not be used to confine any person unless it is in substantial compliance with any applicable housing, fire prevention, sanitation, health, and safety codes, regulations, or standards.

(3) Unless such satisfaction or compliance is required under the standards described in division (C)(4) of this section, and notwithstanding any other provision of state or local law to the contrary, the building or structure need not satisfy or comply with any state or local building standard or code in order to be used to confine a person for the purposes specified in division (B) of this section.

(4) The building or structure shall not be used to confine any person unless it is in compliance with all minimum standards and minimum renovation, modification, and construction criteria for minimum security jails that have been proposed by the department of rehabilitation and correction, through its bureau of adult detention, under section 5120.10 of the Revised Code.

(5) The building or structure need not be renovated or modified into a secure detention facility in order to be used solely to confine a person for the purposes specified in divisions (B)(1)(a) and (B)(2)(a) of this section.

(6) The building or structure shall be used, equipped, furnished, and staffed to provide adequate and suitable living, sleeping, food service or preparation, drinking, bathing and toilet, sanitation, and other necessary facilities, furnishings, and equipment.

(D) Except as provided in this section, a minimum security jail dedicated and used under this section shall be considered to be part of the jail, workhouse, or other correctional facilities of the municipal corporation or the affiliated counties and municipal corporations for all purposes under the law. All persons confined in such a minimum security jail shall be and shall remain, in all respects, under the control of the authority of the municipal corporation that has responsibility for the management and operation of the jail, workhouse, or other correctional facilities of the municipal corporation or, if it is operated by any affiliation of counties or municipal corporations, under the control of the specified county or municipal corporation with that authority, provided that, if the person was convicted of a felony and is serving a residential sanction in the facility, all provisions of law that pertain to persons convicted of a felony that would not by their nature clearly be inapplicable apply regarding the person. A minimum security jail dedicated and used under this section shall be managed and maintained in accordance with policies and procedures adopted by the legislative authority of the municipal corporation or the affiliated counties and municipal corporations governing the safe and healthful operation of the jail, the confinement and supervision of the persons sentenced to it, and their participation in work release or similar rehabilitation programs. In addition to other rules of conduct and discipline, the rights of ingress and egress of persons confined in a minimum security jail dedicated and used under this section shall be subject to reasonable restrictions. Every person confined in a minimum security jail dedicated and used under this section shall be given verbal and written notification, at the time of the person's admission to the jail, that purposely leaving, or purposely failing to return to, the jail without proper authority or permission constitutes the felony offense of escape.

(E) If a person who has been convicted of or pleaded guilty to an offense is sentenced to a term of imprisonment or a residential sanction in a minimum security jail as described in division (B)(1)(a) or (B)(2)(a) of this section, or if a person is an inmate transferred to a minimum security jail by order of a judge of the sentencing court as described in division (B)(1)(b) or (2)(b) of this section, at the time of reception and at other times the person in charge of the operation of the jail determines to be appropriate, the person in charge of the operation of the jail may cause the convicted offender to be examined and tested for tuberculosis, HIV infection, hepatitis, including but not limited to hepatitis A, B, and C, and other contagious diseases. The person in charge of the operation of the jail may cause a convicted offender in the jail who refuses to be tested or treated for tuberculosis, HIV infection, hepatitis, including but not limited to hepatitis A, B, and C, or another contagious disease to be tested and treated involuntarily.

(1998 H 293, eff. 3–17–98; 1997 S 111, eff. 3–17–98; 1996 H 480, eff. 10–16–96; 1996 S 269, eff. 7–1–96; 1995 H 117, eff. 9–29–95; 1992 S 351, eff. 7–1–92; 1990 S 258, H 837, S 131)

753.22 Commissary

(A) The director of public safety or the joint board established pursuant to section 753.15 of the Revised Code may establish a commissary for the workhouse. The commissary may be established either in-house or by another arrangement. If a commissary is established, all persons incarcerated in the workhouse shall receive commissary privileges. A person's purchases from the commissary shall be deducted from the person's account record in the workhouse's business office. The commissary shall provide for the distribution to indigent persons incarcerated in the workhouse necessary hygiene articles and writing materials.

(B) If a commissary is established, the director of public safety or the joint board established pursuant to section 753.15 of the Revised Code shall establish a commissary fund for the workhouse. The management of funds in the commissary fund shall be strictly controlled in accordance with procedures adopted by the auditor of state. Commissary fund revenue over and above operating costs and reserve shall be considered profits. All profits from the commissary fund shall be used to purchase supplies and equipment for the benefit of persons incarcerated in the workhouse and to pay salary and benefits for employees of the workhouse, or for any other persons, who work in or are employed for the sole purpose of providing service to the commissary. The director of public safety or the joint board established pursuant to section 753.15 of the Revised Code shall adopt rules and regulations for the operation of any commissary fund the director or the joint board establishes.

(2003 H 95, eff. 9–26–03; 1996 H 480, eff. 10–16–96)

753.31 Weight exercise equipment and boxing, wrestling, or martial arts training prohibited

(A) As used in this section:

(1) "Free weight exercise equipment" means any equipment or device that is designed to increase the muscle mass and physical strength of the person using it. "Free weight exercise equipment" includes, but is not limited to, barbells, dumbbells, weight plates, and similar free weight-type equipment and other devices that the department of rehabilitation and correction, in rules adopted under section 5120.423 of the Revised Code, designates as enabling a person to increase muscle mass and physical strength.

(2) "Fixed weight exercise equipment" means any equipment, machine, or device that is not designed primarily to increase muscle mass and physical strength but rather to keep a person in relatively good physical condition. "Fixed weight exercise equipment" includes, but is not limited to, weight machines that utilize weight plates, tension bands, or similar devices that provide weight training resistance like universal and nautilus equipment. "Fixed weight exercise equipment" includes machines that are usually assembled as a unit, are not readily dismantled, and have been specifically modified for prison use so as to make them secure and immobile.

(3) "Municipal correctional officer" means a person who is employed by a municipal corporation as an employee or officer of a municipal jail, municipal workhouse, minimum security jail, joint city and county workhouse, municipal-county correctional center, multicounty-municipal correctional center, municipal-county jail or workhouse, or multicounty-municipal jail or workhouse.

(4) A person is "employed by a municipal corporation" if the person is employed by, or receives any compensation or benefits from, any official, officer, office, agency, board, commission, department, or other entity that is a branch of municipal government, that is established by a municipal corporation, or that serves a municipal corporation, including, but not limited to, a chief law enforcement officer of a municipal corporation.

(5) "Multicounty–municipal" has the same meaning as in section 307.93 of the Revised Code.

(B) No municipal correctional officer shall do any of the following:

(1) Provide a prisoner access to free weight or fixed weight exercise equipment;

(2) Allow a prisoner to provide or receive instruction in boxing, wrestling, karate, judo, or another form of martial arts, or any other program that the department of rehabilitation and correction, in rules adopted under section 5120.423 of the Revised Code, designates as enabling a person to improve fighting skills.

(C) Nothing in this section prohibits a municipal correctional officer from allowing a prisoner to participate in jogging, basketball, stationary exercise bicycling, supervised calisthenics, or other physical activities that are not designed to increase muscle mass and physical strength or improve fighting skills.

(1998 H 293, eff. 3–17–98; 1996 H 152, eff. 10–4–96)

753.32 Internet access for prisoners; improper internet access

(A) As used in this section:

(1) "Municipal correctional officer" has the same meaning as in section 753.31 of the Revised Code.

(2) "Computer," "computer network," "computer system," "computer services," "telecommunications service," and "information service" have the same meanings as in section 2913.01 of the Revised Code.

(3) "Municipal correctional facility" means a municipal jail, municipal workhouse, minimum security jail, joint city and county workhouse, municipal-county correctional center, multicounty-municipal correctional center, municipal-county jail or workhouse, or multicounty-municipal jail or workhouse.

(B) No municipal correctional officer shall provide a prisoner access to or permit a prisoner to have access to the internet through the use of a computer, computer network, computer system, computer services, telecommunications service, or information service unless both of the following apply:

(1) The prisoner is participating in an approved educational program with direct supervision that requires the use of the internet for training or research purposes.

(2) The provision of and access to the internet is in accordance with rules promulgated by the department of rehabilitation and correction pursuant to section 5120.62 of the Revised Code.

(C)(1) No prisoner in a municipal correctional facility under the control of a municipal corporation shall access the internet through the use of a computer, computer network, computer system, computer services, telecommunications service, or information service unless both of the following apply:

(a) The prisoner is participating in an approved educational program with direct supervision that requires the use of the internet for training or research purposes.

(b) The provision of and access to the internet is in accordance with rules promulgated by the department of rehabilitation and correction pursuant to section 5120.62 of the Revised Code.

(2) Whoever violates division (C)(1) of this section is guilty of improper internet access, a misdemeanor of the first degree.

(2004 H 204, eff. 11–5–04; 2000 S 12, eff. 6–8–00)

753.33 Random drug testing of municipal prisoners

(A) As used in this section:

(1) "Joint board" means the joint board established pursuant to section 753.15 of the Revised Code.

(2) "Municipal prisoner" means a prisoner who is confined in a municipal jail, municipal workhouse, minimum security jail, joint city and county workhouse, municipal-county correctional center, multicounty-municipal correctional center, municipal-county jail or workhouse, or multicounty-municipal jail or workhouse for being convicted of or pleading guilty to a criminal offense.

(3) "Multicounty–municipal" has the same meaning as in section 307.93 of the Revised Code.

(4) "Random drug testing" has the same meaning as in section 5120.63 of the Revised Code.

(B) The director of public safety or a joint board may enter into a contract with a laboratory or entity to perform blood or urine specimen collection, documentation, maintenance, transportation, preservation, storage, and analyses and other duties required in the performance of random drug testing of municipal prisoners. The terms of any contract entered into under this division shall include a requirement that the laboratory or entity and its employees, the director of public safety or the joint board, the superintendent or chief administrative officer specified in division (D) of this section, the employees of the correctional facilities listed in division (A)(1) of this section, and all other persons comply with the standards for the performance of random drug testing as specified in rules adopted under division (C) of this section.

(C) Prior to entering into a contract with a laboratory or entity under division (B) of this section, a director of public safety or a joint board shall adopt rules for the random drug testing of municipal prisoners. The rules shall include, but are not limited to, provisions that do the following:

(1) Require the laboratory or entity to seek, obtain, and maintain accreditation from the national institute on drug abuse;

(2) Establish standards for the performance of random drug testing of municipal prisoners that include, but are not limited to, standards governing the following:

(a) The collection by the laboratory or entity of blood or urine specimens of individuals in a scientifically or medically approved manner and under reasonable and sanitary conditions;

(b) The collection and testing by the laboratory or entity of blood or urine specimens with due regard for the privacy of the individual being tested and in a manner reasonably calculated to prevent substitutions or interference with the collection and testing of the specimens;

(c) The documentation of blood or urine specimens collected by the laboratory or entity and documentation procedures that reasonably preclude the possibility of erroneous identification of test results and that provide the individual being tested an opportunity to furnish information identifying any prescription or nonprescription drugs used by the individual in connection with a medical condition;

(d) The collection, maintenance, storage, and transportation by the laboratory or entity of blood or urine specimens in a manner that reasonably precludes the possibility of contamination or adulteration of the specimens;

(e) The testing by the laboratory or entity of a blood or urine specimen of an individual to determine whether the individual ingested or was injected with a drug of abuse, in a manner that conforms to scientifically accepted analytical methods and procedures and that may include verification or confirmation of any positive test result by a reliable analytical method;

(f) The analysis of an individual's blood or urine specimen by an employee of the laboratory or entity who is qualified by education, training, and experience to perform that analysis and whose regular duties include the analysis of blood or urine specimens to determine the presence of a drug of abuse and whether the individual who is the subject of the test ingested or was injected with a drug of abuse.

(3) Specify the frequency of performing random drug testing on municipal prisoners;

(4) Prescribe procedures for the automatic, random selection of municipal prisoners to submit to random drug testing under this section;

(5) Provide for reasonable safeguards for the transmittal of the results of the random drug testing of municipal prisoners from the contracting laboratory or entity to the director of public safety or the joint board pursuant to division (E) of this section;

(6) Establish a reasonable fee to cover the costs associated with random drug testing and analysis performed by a contracting laboratory or entity under this section and establish procedures pursuant to division (E) of this section for the collection of those fees from the municipal prisoners subjected to the drug tests.

(D) If a director of public safety or a joint board enters into a contract pursuant to division (B) of this section, the superintendent or chief administrative officer of a correctional facility listed in division (A)(2) of this section in which municipal prisoners are confined, pursuant to the terms of the contract and the rules adopted under division (C) of this section, shall facilitate the collection, documentation, maintenance, and transportation by the contracting laboratory or entity of the blood or urine specimens of the municipal prisoners who are confined in that correctional facility and who are subject to random drug testing.

(E) If a director of public safety or a joint board enters into a contract pursuant to division (B) of this section and the contracting laboratory or entity performs the random drug testing as provided in the contract, the laboratory or entity shall transmit the results of the drug test to the director of public safety or the joint board, as appropriate, that entered into the contract. The director or the joint board shall file for record the results of the random drug tests that indicate whether or not each municipal prisoner who was subjected to the drug test ingested or was injected with a drug of abuse. The director or the joint board shall give appropriate notice of the drug test results to each municipal prisoner who was subjected to a drug test and whose drug test results indicate that the municipal prisoner ingested or was injected with a drug of abuse. The director or the joint board shall afford that municipal prisoner an opportunity to be heard regarding the results of the drug test and to present contrary evidence at a hearing held before the director or the joint board within thirty days after notification of the municipal prisoner under this division. After the hearing, if a hearing is held, the director or the joint board shall make a determination regarding any evidence presented by the municipal prisoner. If the director or the joint board rejects the evidence presented by the municipal prisoner at the hearing or if no hearing is held under this division, the director or the joint board may assess a reasonable fee, determined pursuant to division (C) of this section, for the costs associated with the random drug test to be paid by the municipal prisoner whose drug test results indicate that the prisoner ingested or was injected with a drug of abuse. The director or the joint board may collect the fee pursuant to section 753.02, 753.04, or 753.16 of the Revised Code.

(2000 H 349, eff. 9–22–00)

CHAPTER 765

NONCRIMINAL LAND USE INFRACTIONS

Section

765.01 Definitions

As used in this chapter:

(A) "Land use infraction" means a violation of any municipal zoning code provisions that regulate parking on private property, a motor vehicle service or repair business in residential districts, or signage and other graphics displays, and any municipal ordinance, resolution, or other regulation dealing with the display of house numbers on buildings.

(B) "Law enforcement officer" means a law enforcement officer as defined in section 2901.01 of the Revised Code, code enforcement officer, building inspector, or other officer authorized to enforce any code, ordinance, resolution, or regulation described in division (A) of this section.

(1998 S 83, eff. 3–30–99)

765.02 Ordinance establishing noncriminal land use infraction; adoption of ticket

(A) A municipal corporation within the jurisdiction of the environmental division of a municipal court may enact an ordinance stating that specified land use infractions shall not be considered a criminal offense for any purpose if a ticket is issued for the specific land use infraction under Chapter 765. of the Revised Code, that a person who commits any infraction specified on the ticket shall not be arrested as a result of the commission of the infraction, and that ticketed infractions shall be handled pursuant to this chapter. Adoption of an ordinance under this section does not preclude the enforcement of any land use infraction code, ordinance, resolution, or regulation in any manner otherwise provided by law as long as no ticket is issued under this chapter, but instead provides an additional method of enforcing such laws.

(B) Each municipal corporation that enacts an ordinance under this section shall adopt a ticket to be used by its law enforcement officers in all cases in which a person is issued a ticket for committing a land use infraction in its jurisdiction. This ticket shall consist of two parts. The first part shall be notice of the land use infraction charged, and shall include the information specified in division (A) of section 765.03 of the Revised Code. The notice shall specify a reasonable time period within which the infraction must be corrected or a summons and complaint will be served. The first part of the ticket shall also state that if the person corrects the infraction within the specified time period, the ticket will be voided. The second part of the ticket shall be the summons and complaint for purposes of this chapter, to be issued if the infraction is not corrected within the time period specified in the first part of the ticket. The second part of each ticket shall contain provisions that advise the person upon whom it is served that the person must answer in relation to the infraction charged in the ticket and that certain civil penalties may result from a failure to timely answer, indicate that the person will be afforded a hearing if the person denies in the answer that the person committed the infraction, specify the entity to which, the time within which, and the allowable manners in which the answer must be made, indicate the penalties that may result from failure to timely answer and the fine that arises from the land use infraction, warn that failure to timely answer or to appear at a requested hearing will be considered an admission of the land use infraction, and warn that a default civil judgment potentially may be entered against the person.

(1998 S 83, eff. 3–30–99)

765.03 Issuance of ticket; evidence; fines and penalties; immunity from arrest

(A) A law enforcement officer who issues a ticket for a land use infraction under this chapter shall complete the ticket by identifying the land use infraction charged and indicating the date, time, and place of the infraction. The officer shall sign the ticket and affirm the facts it contains. If the offender is present, the officer also shall record on the ticket the name of the offender in a space provided on the ticket for identification of the offender, and then shall serve the first part of the ticket in accordance with the service requirements of the Rules of Civil Procedure. If the infraction is not corrected within the time period specified on the first part of the ticket, the law enforcement officer shall serve the second part of the ticket in accordance with the service requirements of the Rules of Civil Rrocedure [sic.].

(B) The original of a ticket issued under this section or any true copy of it shall be considered a record kept in the ordinary course of business of the municipal corporation and of the law enforcement agency whose officer issued it, and shall be prima-facie evidence of the facts it contains.

(C) When a ticket is issued for a land use infraction and is served under this section, the offender whose act or omission resulted in the infraction for which the ticket was issued is liable for the infraction and for any fine or penalty arising out of the infraction under an ordinance enacted by the municipal corporation under division (A) of section 765.02 of the Revised Code.

(D) No person upon whom a ticket charging a land use infraction is served under this section shall be arrested as a result of the commission of the land use infraction.

(1998 S 83, eff. 3–30–99)

765.04 Provisions in addition to jurisdiction of environmental division of municipal court

The provisions of this chapter are in addition to, and not in abrogation of, any other jurisdiction the environmental division of any municipal court has to enforce any code, ordinance, resolution, or regulation described in division (A) of section 765.01 of the Revised Code.

(1998 S 83, eff. 3–30–99)

CHAPTER 951

ANIMALS RUNNING AT LARGE; STRAYS

951.01 Certain animals not permitted out of enclosure

No person, who is the owner or keeper of a stallion, jackass, bull, boar, ram, or buck, shall permit it to go or be at large out of its own enclosure.

(1978 H 531, eff. 11–3–78; 129 v 582; 1953 H 1; GC 5808)

951.02 Animals not to be permitted to run at large

No person, who is the owner or keeper of horses, mules, cattle, sheep, goats, swine, or geese, shall permit them to run at large in the public road, highway, street, lane, or alley, or upon unenclosed land, or cause such animals to be herded, kept, or detained for the purpose of grazing on premises other than those owned or lawfully occupied by the owner or keeper of such animals.

The running at large of any such animal in or upon any of the places mentioned in this section is prima-facie evidence that it is running at large in violation of this section.

(1978 H 531, eff. 11–3–78; 1953 H 1; GC 5809, 5818)

951.99 Penalty

Whoever violates section 951.01 or 951.02 of the Revised Code is guilty of a misdemeanor of the fourth degree.

(1978 H 531, eff. 11–3–78; 1953 H 1)

CHAPTER 955

DOGS

955.22 Confinement of dogs; dangerous or vicious dogs; debarked or surgically silenced vicious dogs

(A) As used in this section, "dangerous dog" and "vicious dog" have the same meanings as in section 955.11 of the Revised Code.

(B) No owner, keeper, or harborer of any female dog shall permit it to go beyond the premises of the owner, keeper, or harborer at any time the dog is in heat unless the dog is properly in leash.

(C) Except when a dog is lawfully engaged in hunting and accompanied by the owner, keeper, harborer, or handler of the dog, no owner, keeper, or harborer of any dog shall fail at any time to do either of the following:

(1) Keep the dog physically confined or restrained upon the premises of the owner, keeper, or harborer by a leash, tether, adequate fence, supervision, or secure enclosure to prevent escape;

(2) Keep the dog under the reasonable control of some person.

(D) Except when a dangerous or vicious dog is lawfully engaged in hunting or training for the purpose of hunting and is accompanied by the owner, keeper, harborer, or handler of the dog, no owner, keeper, or harborer of a dangerous or vicious dog shall fail to do either of the following:

(1) While that dog is on the premises of the owner, keeper, or harborer, securely confine it at all times in a locked pen that has a top, locked fenced yard, or other locked enclosure that has a top, except that a dangerous dog may, in the alternative, be tied with a leash or tether so that the dog is adequately restrained;

(2) While that dog is off the premises of the owner, keeper, or harborer, keep that dog on a chain-link leash or tether that is not more than six feet in length and additionally do at least one of the following:

(a) Keep that dog in a locked pen that has a top, locked fenced yard, or other locked enclosure that has a top;

(b) Have the leash or tether controlled by a person who is of suitable age and discretion or securely attach, tie, or affix the leash or tether to the ground or a stationary object or fixture so that the dog is adequately restrained and station such a person in close enough proximity to that dog so as to prevent it from causing injury to any person;

(c) Muzzle that dog.

(E) No owner, keeper, or harborer of a vicious dog shall fail to obtain liability insurance with an insurer authorized to write liability insurance in this state providing coverage in each occurrence, subject to a limit, exclusive of interest and costs, of not less than one hundred thousand dollars because of damage or bodily injury to or death of a person caused by the vicious dog.

(F) No person shall do any of the following:

(1) Debark or surgically silence a dog that the person knows or has reason to believe is a vicious dog;

(2) Possess a vicious dog if the person knows or has reason to believe that the dog has been debarked or surgically silenced;

(3) Falsely attest on a waiver form provided by the veterinarian under division (G) of this section that the person's dog is not a vicious dog or otherwise provide false information on that written waiver form.

(G) Before a veterinarian debarks or surgically silences a dog, the veterinarian may give the owner of the dog a written waiver form that attests that the dog is not a vicious dog. The written waiver form shall include all of the following:

(1) The veterinarian's license number and current business address;

(2) The number of the license of the dog if the dog is licensed;

(3) A reasonable description of the age, coloring, and gender of the dog as well as any notable markings on the dog;

(4) The signature of the owner of the dog attesting that the owner's dog is not a vicious dog;

(5) A statement that division (F) of section 955.22 of the Revised Code prohibits any person from doing any of the following:

(a) Debarking or surgically silencing a dog that the person knows or has reason to believe is a vicious dog;

(b) Possessing a vicious dog if the person knows or has reason to believe that the dog has been debarked or surgically silenced;

(c) Falsely attesting on a waiver form provided by the veterinarian under division (G) of section 955.22 of the Revised Code that the person's dog is not a vicious dog or otherwise provide false information on that written waiver form.

(H) It is an affirmative defense to a charge of a violation of division (F) of this section that the veterinarian who is charged with the violation obtained, prior to debarking or surgically silencing the dog, a written waiver form that complies with division (G) of this section and that attests that the dog is not a vicious dog.

(2000 H 350, eff. 10–10–00; 1987 H 352, eff. 7–10–87; 131 v H 388; 1953 H 1; GC 5652–14a)

955.221 County, township, and municipal corporation ordinances to control dogs

(A) For the purposes of this section, ordinances or resolutions to control dogs include, but are not limited to, ordinances or resolutions concerned with the ownership, keeping, or harboring of dogs, the restraint of dogs, dogs as public nuisances, and dogs as a threat to public health, safety, and welfare, except that such ordinances or resolutions as permitted in division (B) of this section shall not prohibit the use of any dog which is lawfully engaged in hunting or training for the purpose of hunting while accompanied by a licensed hunter. However, such dogs at all other times and in all other respects shall be subject to the ordinance or resolution permitted by this section, unless actually in the field and engaged in hunting or in legitimate training for such purpose.

(B)(1) A board of county commissioners may adopt and enforce resolutions to control dogs within the unincorporated areas of the county that are not otherwise in conflict with any other provision of the Revised Code.

(2) A board of township trustees may adopt and enforce resolutions to control dogs within the township that are not otherwise in conflict with any other provision of the Revised Code, if the township is located in a county where the board of county commissioners has not adopted resolutions to control dogs within the unincorporated areas of the county under this section. In the event that the board of county commissioners adopts resolutions to control dogs in the county after a board of township trustees has adopted resolutions to control dogs within the township, the resolutions adopted by the county board of commissioners prevail over the resolutions adopted by the board of township trustees.

(3) A municipal corporation may adopt and enforce ordinances to control dogs within the municipal corporation that are not otherwise in conflict with any other provision of the Revised Code.

(C) No person shall violate any resolution or ordinance adopted under this section.

(1990 H 291, eff. 6–21–90; 1987 H 352)

CHAPTER 959

OFFENSES RELATING TO DOMESTIC ANIMALS

CRUELTY TO ANIMALS

959.02 Injuring animals

No person shall maliciously, or willfully, and without the consent of the owner, kill or injure a horse, mare, foal, filly, jack, mule, sheep, goat, cow, steer, bull, heifer, ass, ox, swine, dog, cat, or other domestic animal that is the property of another. This section does not apply to a licensed veterinarian acting in an official capacity.

(1953 H 1, eff. 10–1–53; GC 13361)

959.03 Poisoning animals

No person shall maliciously, or willfully and without the consent of the owner, administer poison, except a licensed veterinarian acting in such capacity, to a horse, mare, foal, filly, jack, mule, sheep, goat, cow, steer, bull, heifer, ass, ox, swine, dog, cat, poultry, or any other domestic animal that is the property of another; and no person shall, willfully and without the consent of the owner, place any poisoned food where it may be easily found and eaten by any of such animals, either upon his own lands or the lands of another.

(1953 H 1, eff. 10–1–53; GC 13362)

SPECIFIC OFFENSES

959.12 Alteration of brands

No person shall maliciously alter or deface an artificial earmark or brand upon a horse, mare, foal, filly, jack, mule, sheep, goat, cow, steer, bull, heifer, ass, ox, swine, that is the property of another.

(1953 H 1, eff. 10–1–53; GC 13375)

959.13 Cruelty to animals

(A) No person shall:

(1) Torture an animal, deprive one of necessary sustenance, unnecessarily or cruelly beat, needlessly mutilate or kill, or impound or confine an animal without supplying it during such confinement with a sufficient quantity of good wholesome food and water;

(2) Impound or confine an animal without affording it, during such confinement, access to shelter from wind, rain, snow, or excessive direct sunlight if it can reasonably be expected that the animal would otherwise become sick or in some other way suffer. Division (A)(2) of this section does not apply to animals impounded or confined prior to slaughter. For the purpose of this section, shelter means a man-made enclosure, windbreak, sunshade, or natural windbreak or sunshade that is developed from the earth's contour, tree development, or vegetation.

(3) Carry or convey an animal in a cruel or inhuman manner;

(4) Keep animals other than cattle, poultry or fowl, swine, sheep, or goats in an enclosure without wholesome exercise and change of air, nor or [sic.] feed cows on food that produces impure or unwholesome milk;

(5) Detain livestock in railroad cars or compartments longer than twenty-eight hours after they are so placed without supplying them with necessary food, water, and attention, nor permit such stock to be so crowded as to overlie, crush, wound, or kill each other.

(B) Upon the written request of the owner or person in custody of any particular shipment of livestock, which written request shall be separate and apart from any printed bill of lading or other railroad form, the length of time in which such livestock may be detained in any cars or compartments without food, water, and attention, may be extended to thirty-six hours without penalty therefor. This section does not prevent the dehorning of cattle.

(C) All fines collected for violations of this section shall be paid to the society or association for the prevention of cruelty to animals, if there be such in the county, township, or municipal corporation where such violation occurred.

(1976 H 858, eff. 1–17–77; 1953 H 1; GC 13376)

959.131 Cruelty against companion animal

(A) As used in this section:

(1) "Companion animal" means any animal that is kept inside a residential dwelling and any dog or cat regardless of where it is kept. "Companion animal" does not include livestock or any wild animal.

(2) "Cruelty," "torment," and "torture" have the same meanings as in section 1717.01 of the Revised Code.

(3) "Residential dwelling" means a structure or shelter or the portion of a structure or shelter that is used by one or more humans for the purpose of a habitation.

(4) "Practice of veterinary medicine" has the same meaning as in section 4741.01 of the Revised Code.

(5) "Wild animal" has the same meaning as in section 1531.01 of the Revised Code.

(6) "Federal animal welfare act" means the "Laboratory Animal Act of 1966," Pub. L. No. 89–544, 80 Stat. 350 (1966), 7 U.S.C.A. 2131 et seq., as amended by the "Animal Welfare Act of 1970," Pub. L. No. 91–579, 84 Stat. 1560 (1970), the "Animal Welfare Act Amendments of 1976," Pub. L. No. 94–279, 90 Stat. 417 (1976), and the "Food Security Act of 1985," Pub. L. No. 99–198, 99 Stat. 1354 (1985), and as it may be subsequently amended.

(B) No person shall knowingly torture, torment, needlessly mutilate or maim, cruelly beat, poison, needlessly kill, or commit an act of cruelty against a companion animal.

(C) No person who confines or who is the custodian or caretaker of a companion animal shall negligently do any of the following:

(1) Torture, torment, needlessly mutilate or maim, cruelly beat, poison, needlessly kill, or commit an act of cruelty against the companion animal;

(2) Deprive the companion animal of necessary sustenance, confine the companion animal without supplying it during the confinement with sufficient quantities of good, wholesome food and water, or impound or confine the companion animal without affording it, during the impoundment or confinement, with access to shelter from heat, cold, wind, rain, snow, or excessive direct sunlight, if it can reasonably be expected that the companion animal would become sick or suffer in any other way as a result of or due to the deprivation, confinement, or impoundment or confinement in any of those specified manners.

(D) Divisions (B) and (C) of this section do not apply to any of the following:

(1) A companion animal used in scientific research conducted by an institution in accordance with the federal animal welfare act and related regulations;

(2) The lawful practice of veterinary medicine by a person who has been issued a license, temporary permit, or registration certificate to do so under Chapter 4741. of the Revised Code;

(3) Dogs being used or intended for use for hunting or field trial purposes, provided that the dogs are being treated in accordance with usual and commonly accepted practices for the care of hunting dogs;

(4) The use of common training devices, if the companion animal is being treated in accordance with usual and commonly accepted practices for the training of animals;

(5) The administering of medicine to a companion animal that was properly prescribed by a person who has been issued a license, temporary permit, or registration certificate under Chapter 4741. of the Revised Code.

(E) Notwithstanding any section of the Revised Code that otherwise provides for the distribution of fine moneys, the clerk of court shall forward all fines the clerk collects that are so imposed for any violation of this section to the treasurer of the political subdivision or the state, whose county humane society or law enforcement agency is to be paid the fine money as determined under this division. The treasurer to whom the fines are forwarded shall pay the fine moneys to the county humane society or the county, township, municipal corporation, or state law enforcement agency in this state that primarily was responsible for or involved in the investigation and prosecution of the violation. If a county humane society receives any fine moneys under this division, the county humane society shall use the fine moneys to provide the training that is required for humane agents under section 1717.06 of the Revised Code.

(2002 S 221, eff. 4–9–03)

959.132 Impoundment of companion animal; written request for hearing; deposit to cover costs

(A) As used in this section:

(1) "Agent of a county humane society" means a person appointed by a county humane society pursuant to section 1717.06 of the Revised Code.

(2) "Companion animal" has the same meaning as in section 959.131 of the Revised Code.

(3) "Impounding agency" means the county humane society, animal shelter, or law enforcement agency that, in accordance with division (B) or (C) of this section, either has impounded a companion animal or has made regular visits to the place where a companion animal is kept to determine whether it is provided with necessities.

(4) "Officer" means any law enforcement officer, agent of a county humane society, dog warden, assistant dog warden, or other person appointed to act as an animal control officer for a county, municipal corporation, or township in accordance with state law, an ordinance, or a resolution.

(B) Except as otherwise provided in this division, an officer may impound a companion animal if the officer has probable cause to believe that it or other companion animals that are kept by the same person on the premises are the subject of a violation of section 959.131 of the Revised Code and if the officer has lawful access to the companion animal at the time of the impoundment. The officer shall give written notice of the impoundment by posting the notice on the door of the residence on the premises at which the companion animal was impounded, by giving it in person to the owner, custodian, or caretaker of the companion animal, or by otherwise posting the notice in a conspicuous place on the premises where the companion animal was seized. No officer or impounding agency shall impound a companion animal that is the subject of a violation of section 959.131 of the Revised Code in a shelter owned, operated, or controlled by a board of county commissioners pursuant to Chapter 955. of the Revised Code unless the board, by resolution, authorizes the impoundment of companion animals in a shelter owned, operated, or controlled by that board and has executed, in the case when the officer is other than a dog warden or assistant dog warden, a contract specifying the terms and conditions of the impoundment.

(C) If charges are filed under section 959.131 of the Revised Code against the custodian or caretaker of a companion animal, but the companion animal that is the subject of the charges is not impounded, the court in which the charges are pending may order the owner or person having custody of the companion animal to provide to the companion animal the necessities described in divisions (C)(2) to (6) of section 959.131 of the Revised Code until the final disposition of the charges. If the court issues an order of that nature, the court also may authorize an officer or another person to visit the place where the companion animal is being kept, at the times and under the conditions that the court may set, to determine whether the companion animal is receiving those necessities and to remove and impound the companion animal if the companion animal is not receiving those necessities.

(D) An owner, custodian, or caretaker of one or more companion animals that have been impounded under this section may file a written request for a hearing with the clerk of the court in which charges are pending that were filed under section 959.131 of the Revised Code and that involve the impounded companion animals. If a hearing is requested, the court shall conduct a hearing not later than twenty-one days following receipt of the request. At the hearing, the impounding agency has the burden of proving by a preponderance of the evidence that probable cause exists to find that the defendant is guilty of a violation of section 959.131 of the Revised Code, unless probable cause has previously been established in a judicial proceeding, in which case the court shall take notice that probable cause exists and shall not require further proof of probable cause. A hearing that is conducted under division (D) of this section shall be combined whenever possible with any hearing involving the same pending charges that is authorized and conducted under division (E) of this section.

If the court finds at the conclusion of the hearing that probable cause does not exist for finding that the defendant committed a violation and that the defendant otherwise has a right to possession of the impounded companion animals, the court shall order the animals to be returned to the defendant.

If the court finds at the conclusion of the hearing that probable cause exists for finding the defendant guilty of a violation with respect to one or more of the impounded companion animals, the court shall do one of the following with respect to each impounded companion animal:

(1) Allow the impounding agency to retain custody of the companion animal pending resolution of the underlying charges;

(2) Order the companion animal to be returned to the defendant under any conditions and restrictions that the court determines are appropriate to ensure that the companion animal receives humane and adequate care and treatment.

(E)(1) At any time that one or more charges are pending under section 959.131 of the Revised Code, an impounding agency may file a motion in the court in which the charges are pending requesting that the defendant post a deposit to cover the costs of caring, during the pendency of the charges, for any impounded companion animals seized or removed from the defendant's custody if the reasonably necessary projected costs of the care that will be provided prior to the final resolution of the charges are estimated to be in excess of one thousand five hundred dollars. The motion shall be accompanied by an affidavit that sets forth an estimate of the reasonably necessary costs that the impounding agency expects to incur in providing that care, which may include, but are not limited to, the necessary cost of veterinary care, medications, food, water, and board for the companion animals during the pendency of the charges.

(2) Within ten days after the date on which a motion is filed under division (E)(1) of this section, the court shall conduct a hearing. Except as otherwise provided in division (E)(5) of this section, at the hearing, the impounding agency has the burden of proving by a preponderance of the evidence that there is probable cause to find that the defendant is guilty of a violation of section 959.131 of the Revised Code, unless probable cause has previously been established in a judicial proceeding, in which case the court shall take notice that probable cause exists and shall not require further proof of probable cause, and that the reasonably necessary cumulative costs of caring during the pendency of the charges for the companion animals seized or removed from the defendant's custody or control are reasonably projected to exceed one thousand five hundred dollars.

(3) If the court finds at the conclusion of the hearing that probable cause does not exist for finding that the defendant committed a violation of section 959.131 of the Revised Code and that the defendant otherwise has a right to possession of the companion animals, the court shall order the animals to be returned to the defendant. If the court finds at the conclusion of the hearing that probable cause exists for finding that the defendant committed a violation of that section, but that the reasonably necessary costs for caring during the pendency of the charges for the companion animals seized or removed from the defendant's custody or control are reasonably projected to be one thousand five hundred dollars or less, the court shall deny the petitioner's motion to require the defendant to pay a deposit.

If the court finds at the conclusion of the hearing that probable cause exists for finding the defendant guilty of the violation with respect to one or more of the impounded companion animals and for determining that the reasonably necessary projected costs of caring for the companion animals exceed one thousand five hundred dollars during the pendency of the charges, the court shall do one of the following:

(a) Order the defendant to post a deposit with the clerk of the court in a form and in an amount that the court determines is sufficient to cover the cost of care of the companion animals from the date of impoundment until the date of the disposition of the charges;

(b) Order one or more of the companion animals to be returned to the defendant under any conditions and restrictions that the court determines to be appropriate to ensure that the companion animals receive humane and adequate care and treatment;

(c) Deny the motion of the impounding agency requesting the defendant to post a deposit, but permit the impounding agency to retain custody of one or more of the companion animals pending resolution of the underlying charges.

(4) The court may order the defendant to forfeit the right of possession and ownership in one or more of the companion animals to the impounding agency if the defendant fails to comply with the conditions set forth in an order of the court that is rendered under division (E)(3) of this section. If the order that was not complied with required the defendant to post a deposit, forfeiture of the companion animals relieves the defendant of any further obligation to post the deposit.

(5)(a) A hearing that is conducted under division (D) of this section shall be combined whenever possible with any hearing involving the same pending charges that is authorized and conducted under division (E) of this section. However, division (E)(5)(b) of this section applies when both of the hearings are conducted and combining them is not possible.

(b) At a hearing conducted under division (E) of this section, an impounding agency shall not be required to prove that there is probable cause to find that the defendant is guilty of a violation of section 959.131 of the Revised Code if the court already has made a finding concerning probable cause at a separate hearing conducted under division (D) of this section. In such an event, the probable cause finding made at the hearing conducted under division (D) of this section shall be used for purposes of the hearing conducted under division (E) of this section.

(F)(1) If the defendant is found guilty of violating section 959.131 of the Revised Code or any other offense relating to the care or treatment of a companion animal and the defendant posted a deposit pursuant to division (E) of this section, the court shall determine the amount of the reasonably necessary costs that the impounding agency incurred in caring for the companion animal during the pendency of the charges. The court shall order the clerk of the court to pay that amount of the deposit to the impounding agency and to dispose of any amount of the deposit that exceeds that amount in the following order:

(a) Pay any fine imposed on the defendant relative to the violation;

(b) Pay any costs ordered against the defendant relative to the violation;

(c) Return any remaining amount to the defendant.

(2) If the defendant is found not guilty of violating section 959.131 of the Revised Code or any other offense relating to the care or treatment of a companion animal, the court shall order the clerk of court to return the entire amount of the deposit to the defendant, and the impounding agency shall return the companion animal to the defendant. If the companion animal cannot be returned, the court shall order the impounding agency to pay to the defendant an amount determined by the court to be equal to the reasonable market value of the companion animal at the time that it was impounded plus statutory interest as defined in section 1343.03 of the Revised Code from the date of the impoundment. In determining the reasonable market value of the companion animal, the court may consider the condition of the companion animal at the time that the companion animal was impounded and any change in the condition of the companion animal after it was impounded.

(G) An impounding agency that impounds a companion animal under this section shall pay a person who provides veterinary care to the companion animal during the impoundment for the cost of the veterinary care regardless of whether the impounding agency is reimbursed for the payment under this section or section 959.99 of the Revised Code.

(2002 S 221, eff. 4–9–03)

959.15 Animal fights

No person shall knowingly engage in or be employed at cockfighting, bearbaiting, or pitting an animal against another; no person shall receive money for the admission of another to a place kept for such purpose; no person shall use, train, or possess any animal for seizing, detaining, or maltreating a domestic animal. Any person who knowingly purchases a ticket of admission to such place, or is present thereat, or witnesses such spectacle, is an aider and abettor.

(1980 S 233, eff. 6–10–80; 1953 H 1; GC 13378)

959.16 Dogfighting

(A) No person shall knowingly do any of the following:

(1) Promote, engage in, or be employed at dogfighting;

(2) Receive money for the admission of another person to a place kept for dogfighting;

(3) Sell, purchase, possess, or train a dog for dogfighting;

(4) Use, train, or possess a dog for seizing, detaining, or maltreating a domestic animal;

(5) Purchase a ticket of admission to or be present at a dogfight;

(6) Witness a dogfight if it is presented as a public spectacle.

(B) The department of agriculture may investigate complaints and follow up rumors of dogfighting activities and may report any information so gathered to an appropriate prosecutor or law enforcement agency.

(C) Any peace officer, as defined in section 2935.01 of the Revised Code, shall confiscate any dogs that have been, are, or are intended to be used in dogfighting and any equipment or devices used in training such dogs or as part of dogfights.

(1980 S 233, eff. 6–10–80)

PENALTIES

959.99 Penalties; forfeiture of animals or livestock; forfeiture of companion animals

(A) Whoever violates section 959.18 or 959.19 of the Revised Code is guilty of a minor misdemeanor.

(B) Except as otherwise provided in this division, whoever violates section 959.02 of the Revised Code is guilty of a misdemeanor of the second degree. If the value of the animal killed or the injury done amounts to three hundred dollars or more, whoever violates section 959.02 of the Revised Code is guilty of a misdemeanor of the first degree.

(C) Whoever violates section 959.03, 959.06, 959.12, 959.15, or 959.17 of the Revised Code is guilty of a misdemeanor of the fourth degree.

(D) Whoever violates division (A) of section 959.13 of the Revised Code is guilty of a misdemeanor of the second degree. In addition, the court may order the offender to forfeit the animal or livestock and may provide for its disposition, including, but not limited to, the sale of the animal or livestock. If an animal or livestock is forfeited and sold pursuant to this division, the proceeds from the sale first shall be applied to pay the expenses incurred with regard to the care of the animal from the time it was taken from the custody of the former owner. The balance of the proceeds from the sale, if any, shall be paid to the former owner of the animal.

(E)(1) Whoever violates division (B) of section 959.131 of the Revised Code is guilty of a misdemeanor of the first degree on a first offense and a felony of the fifth degree on each subsequent offense.

(2) Whoever violates section 959.01 of the Revised Code or division (C) of section 959.131 of the Revised Code is guilty of a misdemeanor of the second degree on a first offense and a misdemeanor of the first degree on each subsequent offense.

(3)(a) A court may order a person who is convicted of or pleads guilty to a violation of section 959.131 of the Revised Code to forfeit to an impounding agency, as defined in section 959.132 of the Revised Code, any or all of the companion animals in that person's ownership or care. The court also may prohibit or place limitations on the person's ability to own or care for any companion animals for a specified or indefinite period of time.

(b) A court may order a person who is convicted of or pleads guilty to a violation of section 959.131 of the Revised Code to reimburse an impounding agency for the reasonably necessary costs incurred by the agency for the care of a companion animal that the agency impounded as a result of the investigation or prosecution of the violation, provided that the costs were not otherwise paid under section 959.132 of the Revised Code.

(4) If a court has reason to believe that a person who is convicted of or pleads guilty to a violation of section 959.131 of the Revised Code suffers from a mental or emotional disorder that contributed to the violation, the court may impose as a community control sanction or as a condition of probation a requirement that the offender undergo psychological evaluation or counseling. The court shall order the offender to pay the costs of the evaluation or counseling.

(F) Whoever violates section 959.14 of the Revised Code is guilty of a misdemeanor of the second degree on a first offense and a misdemeanor of the first degree on each subsequent offense.

(G) Whoever violates section 959.05 or 959.20 of the Revised Code is guilty of a misdemeanor of the first degree.

(H) Whoever violates section 959.16 of the Revised Code is guilty of a felony of the fourth degree for a first offense and a felony of the third degree on each subsequent offense.

(2002 S 221, eff. 4–9–03; 2000 H 350, eff. 10–10–00; 1998 H 219, eff. 6–1–98; 1995 S 2, eff. 7–1–96; 1989 H 12, eff. 9–15–89; 1982 H 269, § 4, S 199; 1980 H 854, S 233; 1976 H 894; 1972 H 511; 132 v H 1, H 842; 131 v H 541; 125 v 215; 1953 H 1)

CHAPTER 1345

CONSUMER SALES PRACTICES

UNAUTHORIZED CHANGE IN PROVIDER OF UTILITY SERVICES

1345.18 Unauthorized change in consumer's provider of natural gas or public telecommunications services

(A) As used in this section:

(1) "Consumer," "person," and "supplier" have the same meanings as in section 1345.01 of the Revised Code.

(2) "Consumer transaction" has the same meaning as in section 1345.01 of the Revised Code except that the sale, lease, assignment, award by chance, or other transfer of an item of goods, a service, a franchise, or an intangible, or solicitation to supply any of those things, to an individual is for purposes that are primarily other than personal, family, or household.

(3) "Natural gas service" means the sale of natural gas, exclusive of any distribution or ancillary service.

(4) "Public telecommunications service" means the transmission by electromagnetic or other means, other than by a telephone company as defined in section 4927.01 of the Revised Code, of signs, signals, writings, images, sounds, messages, or data originating in this state regardless of actual call routing. "Public telecommunications service" excludes a system, including its construction, maintenance, or operation, for the provision of telecommunications service, or any portion of such service, by any entity for the sole and exclusive use of that entity, its parent, a subsidiary, or an affiliated entity, and not for resale, directly or indirectly; the provision of terminal equipment used to originate telecommunications service; broadcast transmission by radio, television, or satellite broadcast stations regulated by the federal government; or cable television service.

(B)(1) No supplier, in connection with a consumer transaction involving natural gas service or public telecommunications service to a consumer in this state, shall request or submit, or cause to be requested or submitted, a change in the consumer's provider of natural gas service or public telecommunications service, without first obtaining, or causing to be obtained, the verified consent of the consumer. For the purpose of this division and with respect to public telecommunications service only, the procedures necessary for verifying the consent of a consumer shall be those prescribed by rule by the public utilities commission for public telecommunications service under division (D) of section 4905.72 of the Revised Code. Also, for the purpose of this division, the act, omission, or failure of any officer, agent, or other individual, acting for or employed by another person, while acting within the scope of that authority or employment, is the act or failure of that other person.

(2) Consistent with the exclusion, under 47 C.F.R. 64.1100(a)(3), of commercial mobile radio service providers from the verification requirements adopted in 47 C.F.R. 64.1100, 64.1150, 64.1160, 64.1170, 64.1180, and 64.1190 by the federal communications commission, division (B)(1) of this section does not apply to a provider of commercial mobile radio service insofar as such provider is engaged in the provision of commercial mobile radio service. However, when that exclusion no longer is in effect, division (B)(1) of this section shall apply to such a provider.

(2000 H 177, eff. 5–17–00)

1345.19 Jurisdiction; cumulative nature of powers

(A) The courts of common pleas, and municipal or county courts within their respective jurisdictions, have jurisdiction over any supplier with respect to a violation of section 1345.18 of the Revised Code or any claim arising from a consumer transaction subject to that section.

(B) The power, remedies, forfeitures, and penalties provided by sections 1345.18 to 1345.20 and division (C) of section 1345.99 of the Revised Code are in addition to any other power, remedy, forfeiture, or penalty provided by law.

(2000 H 177, eff. 5–17–00)

1345.20 Private right of action; remedies

(A) An aggrieved consumer may bring an action for a declaratory judgment, an injunction, or other appropriate relief against a supplier that is violating or has violated section 1345.18 of the Revised Code. The court may issue any order or enter a judgment as necessary to ensure compliance with section 1345.18 of the Revised Code or prevent any act or practice that violates that section. In addition, upon a preponderance of the evidence, the court:

(1) Shall issue an order providing for all of the following:

(a) Rescinding the aggrieved consumer's change in service provider;

(b) Requiring the supplier to absolve the aggrieved consumer of any liability for any charges assessed the consumer, or refund to the aggrieved consumer any charges collected from the consumer, by the supplier during such period, after the violation occurred, that is determined reasonable by the court;

(c) Requiring the supplier to refund or pay to the aggrieved consumer any fees paid or costs incurred by the consumer resulting from the change of the consumer's service provider or providers, or from the resumption of the consumer's service with the service provider or providers from which the consumer was switched;

(d) Requiring the supplier to make the consumer whole regarding any bonuses or benefits, such as airline mileage or product discounts, to which the consumer is entitled, by restoring bonuses or benefits the consumer lost as a result of the violation and providing bonuses or benefits the consumer would have earned if not for the violation, or by providing something of equal value.

(2) May issue an order providing for any of the following:

(a) Requiring the supplier to comply or undertake any necessary corrective action;

(b) Assessing upon the supplier forfeitures of not more than one thousand dollars for each day of each violation. However, if the preponderance of the evidence shows that the supplier has engaged or is engaging in a pattern or practice of committing any such violations, the court may assess upon the supplier forfeitures of not more than five thousand dollars for each day of each violation. Upon collection, one-half of any such forfeiture assessed under this division shall be paid to the treasurer of the county in which the action was brought and one-half shall be paid into the state treasury to the credit of the general revenue fund.

(B) Upon a finding in an action under division (A) of this section that a supplier is violating or has violated section 1345.18 of the Revised Code, a service provider or providers of natural gas service or public telecommunications service from whom the aggrieved consumer was switched may bring an action seeking the relief authorized by this division. Upon the filing of such action, the court may issue an order providing for either of the following:

(1) Requiring the supplier to compensate the service provider or providers from which the aggrieved consumer was switched in the amount of all charges the consumer would have paid that particular service provider for the same or comparable service had the violation or failure to comply not occurred;

(2) Requiring the supplier to compensate the service provider or providers from which the aggrieved consumer was switched for any costs that the particular service provider incurs as a result of making the consumer whole as provided in division (A)(1)(d) of this section or of effecting the resumption of the consumer's service.

(C) No action may be brought under division (A) of this section to recover for a transaction more than two years after the occurrence of a violation. No action may be brought under division (B) of this section more than one year after the date on which a ruling in an action brought under division (A) of this section was rendered.

(2000 H 177, eff. 5–17–00)

HOME SOLICITATION SALES

1345.23 Writing required; contents, warning

(A) Every home solicitation sale shall be evidenced by a written agreement or offer to purchase in the same language as that principally used in the oral sales presentation and shall contain the name and address of the seller. The seller shall present the writing to the buyer and obtain the buyer's signature to it. The writing shall state the date on which the buyer actually signs. The seller shall leave with the buyer a copy of the writing which has been signed by the seller and complies with division (B) of this section.

(B) In connection with every home solicitation sale:

(1) The following statement shall appear clearly and conspicuously on the copy of the contract left with the buyer in bold-face type of the minimum size of ten points, in substantially the following form and in immediate proximity to the space reserved in the contract for the signature of the buyer: "You, the buyer, may cancel this transaction at any time prior to midnight of the third business day after the date of this transaction. See the attached notice of cancellation for an explanation of this right."

(2) A completed form, in duplicate, captioned "notice of cancellation", shall be attached to the contract signed by the buyer and be easily detachable, and and shall contain in ten-point, bold-face type, the following information and statements in the same language as that used in the contract:

NOTICE OF CANCELLATION

___[(enter day of transaction)] ___

(Date)

You may cancel this transaction, without any penalty or obligation, within three business days from the above date.

If you cancel, any property traded in, any payments made by you under the contract or sale, and any negotiable instrument executed by you will be returned within ten business days following receipt by the seller of your cancellation notice, and any security interest arising out of the transaction will be cancelled.

If you cancel, you must make available to the seller at your residence, in substantially as good condition as when received, any goods delivered to you under this contract or sale; or you may if you wish, comply with the instructions of the seller regarding the return shipment of the goods at the seller's expense and risk.

If you do make the goods available to the seller and the seller does not pick them up within twenty days of the date of your notice of cancellation, you may retain or dispose of the goods without any further obligation. If you fail to make the goods available to the seller, or if you agree to return the goods to the seller and fail to do so, then you remain liable for performance of all obligations under the contract.

To cancel this transaction, mail or deliver a signed and dated copy of this cancellation notice or any other written notice, or send a telegram, to ___[(Name of seller),]___ at ___[(address of seller's place of business)]___ not later than midnight of ___[(Date)]___

I hereby cancel this transaction.

___[(Date)]___

___[(Buyer's signature)]___

(3) Before furnishing copies of the notice of cancellation to the buyer, the seller shall complete both copies by entering the name of the seller, the address of the seller's place of business, the date of the transaction which is the date the buyer signed the contract and the date, not earlier than the third business day following the date of the transaction, by which the buyer may give notice of cancellation.

(4) A home solicitation sales contract which contains the notice of buyer's right to cancel and notice of cancellation in the form and language provided in the federal trade commission's trade regulation rule providing a cooling-off period for door-to-door sales shall be deemed to comply with the requirements of divisions (B)(1), (2), and (3) of this section with respect to the form and language of such notices so long as the federal trade commission language provides at least equal information to the consumer concerning his right to cancel as is required by divisions (B)(1), (2), and (3) of this section.

(C) Until the seller has complied with divisions (A) and (B) of this section the buyer may cancel the home solicitation sale by notifying the seller by mailing, delivering, or telegraphing written notice to the seller of his intention to cancel. The three day period prescribed by section 1345.22 of the Revised Code begins to run from the time the seller complies with divisions (A) and (B) of this section.

(D) In connection with any home solicitation sale, no seller shall:

(1) Include in any home solicitation sales contract, any confession of judgment or any waiver of any rights to which the buyer is entitled under this section, including specifically his right to cancel the sale in accordance with this section.

(2) Fail to inform each buyer orally, at the time he signs the contract for the goods or services, of his right to cancel.

(3) Misrepresent in any manner the buyer's right to cancel.

(4) Fail or refuse to honor any valid notice of cancellation by a buyer and within ten business days after receipt of such notice to:

(a) Refund all payments made under the contract or sale;

(b) Return any goods or property traded in, in substantially as good condition as when received by the seller;

(c) Cancel and return any note, negotiable instrument, or other evidence of indebtedness executed by the buyer in connection with the contract or sale and take any action necessary or appropriate to reflect the termination of any security interest or lien created under the sale or offer to purchase.

(5) Negotiate, transfer, sell, or assign any note or other evidence of indebtedness to a finance company or other third party prior to midnight of the fifth business day following the day the contract for the goods or services was signed.

(6) Fail to notify the buyer, within ten business days of receipt of the buyer's notice of cancellation, whether the seller intends to repossess or abandon any shipped or delivered goods.

(1974 H 241, eff. 9–30–74; 1972 S 24)

1345.24 Seller to retain notice of cancellation and envelope

In a home solicitation sale, the seller shall retain, for the period in which an action to enforce the sale could be commenced, any notice of cancellation made pursuant to section 1345.22 of the Revised Code. The seller shall also retain the envelope in which any notice of cancellation is sent or delivered. If the date of delivery is not indicated or recorded on the notice of cancellation or on the envelope, the seller shall record the date of delivery on the notice of cancellation.

(1974 H 241, eff. 9–30–74; 1972 S 24)

PENALTIES

1345.99 Penalties

(A) Whoever violates section 1345.23 or 1345.24 of the Revised Code is guilty of a minor misdemeanor.

(B) Whoever violates division (D) of section 1345.76 of the Revised Code shall be fined not more than one thousand dollars.

(C) Whoever knowingly violates division (E) of section 1345.02 or knowingly violates section 1345.18 of the Revised Code is guilty of a misdemeanor of the third degree for a first offense and a misdemeanor of the second degree for any subsequent offense.

(2000 H 177, eff. 5–17–00; 1999 H 21, eff. 9–15–99; 1974 H 241, eff. 9–30–74; 1972 S 24)

CHAPTER 1501

DEPARTMENT OF NATURAL RESOURCES—LAW ENFORCEMENT STAFF OFFICERS

1501.013 Natural resources law enforcement staff officers

(A) Subject to division (B) of this section, the director of natural resources may designate an employee of the department of natural resources as a natural resources law enforcement staff officer. Such an officer may do any or all of the following:

(1) Coordinate the law enforcement activities, training, and policies of the department;

(2) Serve as the department's liaison with other law enforcement agencies and jurisdictions and as the director's representative regarding law enforcement activities;

(3) Conduct internal investigations of employees of the department as necessary;

(4) Perform other functions related to the department's law enforcement activities, training, and policies that the director assigns to the officer.

A natural resources law enforcement staff officer, on any lands or waters owned, controlled, maintained, or administered by the department, has the authority specified under section 2935.03 of the Revised Code for peace officers of the department of natural resources to keep the peace, to enforce all laws and rules governing those lands and waters, and to make arrests for violation of those laws and rules.

The governor, upon the recommendation of the director, shall issue to a natural resources law enforcement staff officer a commission indicating authority to make arrests as provided in division (A) of this section.

The director shall furnish a suitable badge to a commissioned natural resources law enforcement staff officer as evidence of that officer's authority.

(B)(1) As used in division (B) of this section, "felony" has the same meaning as in section 109.511 of the Revised Code.

(2) The director shall not designate a person as a natural resources law enforcement staff officer under division (A) of this section on a permanent basis, on a temporary basis, for a probationary term, or on other than a permanent basis if the person previously has been convicted of or has pleaded guilty to a felony.

(3) The director shall terminate the employment as a natural resources law enforcement staff officer of a person designated as such an officer if that person does either of the following:

(a) Pleads guilty to a felony;

(b) Pleads guilty to a misdemeanor pursuant to a negotiated plea agreement as provided in division (D) of section 2929.43 of the Revised Code in which the natural resources law enforcement staff officer agrees to surrender the certificate awarded to that officer under section 109.77 of the Revised Code.

(4) The director shall suspend from employment as a natural resources law enforcement staff officer a person designated as such an officer if that person is convicted, after trial, of a felony. If the natural resources law enforcement staff officer files an appeal from that conviction and the conviction is upheld by the highest court to which the appeal is taken, or if the officer does not file a timely appeal, the director shall terminate the employment of the natural resources law enforcement staff officer. If the natural resources law enforcement staff officer files an appeal that results in the officer's acquittal of the felony or conviction of a misdemeanor, or in the dismissal of the felony charge against the officer, the director shall reinstate the natural resources law enforcement staff officer. A natural resources law enforcement staff officer who is reinstated under division (B)(4) of this section shall not receive any back pay unless the officer's conviction of the felony was reversed on appeal, or the felony charge was dismissed, because the court found insufficient evidence to convict the officer of the felony.

(5) Division (B) of this section does not apply regarding an offense that was committed prior to January 1, 1999.

(6) The suspension from employment, or the termination of the employment, of a natural resources law enforcement staff officer under division (B)(3) or (4) of this section shall be in accordance with Chapter 119. of the Revised Code.

(2002 H 490, eff. 1–1–04; 1998 S 187, eff. 3–18–99)

CHAPTER 1503

DIVISION OF FORESTRY

FOREST FIRES

1503.27 Agreement with federal government

The chief of the division of forestry may take such action as is necessary to provide for the prevention and control of forest fires in groups of districts and, with the approval of the director of natural resources, may enter into an agreement with the secretary of agriculture of the United States under authority of the act of congress of March 1, 1911, 36 Stat. 961, or acts amendatory or supplementary thereto or others having a similar purpose, for the protection of forested watersheds of navigable streams in this state.

(1992 H 167, eff. 10–8–92; 1976 H 972; 1973 S 217; 130 v Pt 2, H 26; 1953 H 1; GC 1177–10bb)

FOREST OFFICERS

1503.29 Forest officer

(A) As used in this section, "felony" has the same meaning as in section 109.511 of the Revised Code.

(B)(1) Subject to division (D) of this section, any person employed by the chief of the division of forestry for administrative service in a state forest may be designated by the chief and known as a forest officer. A forest officer, on any lands or waters owned, controlled, maintained, or administered by the department of natural resources and on highways, as defined in section 4511.01 of the Revised Code, adjacent to lands and waters owned, controlled, maintained, or administered by the division of forestry, has the authority specified under section 2935.03 of the Revised Code for peace officers of the department of natural resources to keep the peace, to enforce all laws and rules governing those lands and waters, and to make arrests for violation of those laws and rules, provided that the authority shall be exercised on lands or waters administered by another division of the department only pursuant to an agreement with the chief of that division or to a request for assistance by an enforcement officer of that division in an emergency.

(2) A forest officer, in or along any watercourse within, abutting, or upstream from the boundary of any area administered by the department, has the authority to enforce section 3767.32 of the Revised Code and other laws prohibiting the dumping of refuse into or along waters and to make arrests for violation of those laws. The jurisdiction of forest officers shall be concurrent with that of the peace officers of the county, township, or municipal corporation in which the violation occurs.

(3) A forest officer may enter upon private and public lands to investigate an alleged violation of, and may enforce, this chapter and sections 2909.02, 2909.03, and 2909.06 of the Revised Code when the alleged violation or other act pertains to forest fires.

(C)(1) A forest officer may render assistance to a state or local law enforcement officer at the request of that officer or may render assistance to a state or local law enforcement officer in the event of an emergency. Forest officers serving outside the division of forestry under this section or serving under the terms of a mutual aid compact authorized under section 1501.02 of the Revised Code shall be considered as performing services within their regular employment for the purposes of compensation, pension or indemnity fund rights, workers' compensation, and other rights or benefits to which they may be entitled as incidents of their regular employment.

(2) Forest officers serving outside the division of forestry under this section or under a mutual aid compact retain personal immunity from civil liability as specified in section 9.86 of the Revised Code and shall not be considered an employee of a political subdivision for purposes of Chapter 2744. of the Revised Code. A political subdivision that uses forest officers under this section or under the terms of a mutual aid compact authorized under section 1501.02 of the Revised Code is not subject to civil liability under Chapter 2744. of the Revised Code as the result of any action or omission of any forest officer acting under this section or under a mutual aid compact.

(D)(1) The chief of the division of forestry shall not designate a person as a forest officer pursuant to division (B)(1) of this section on a permanent basis, on a temporary basis, for a probationary term, or on other than a permanent basis if the person previously has been convicted of or has pleaded guilty to a felony.

(2)(a) The chief of the division of forestry shall terminate the employment as a forest officer of a person designated as a forest officer under division (B)(1) of this section if that person does either of the following:

(i) Pleads guilty to a felony;

(ii) Pleads guilty to a misdemeanor pursuant to a negotiated plea agreement as provided in division (D) of section 2929.43 of the Revised Code in which the forest officer agrees to surrender the certificate awarded to the forest officer under section 109.77 of the Revised Code.

(b) The chief shall suspend from employment as a forest officer a person designated as a forest officer under division (B)(1) of this section if that person is convicted, after trial, of a felony. If the forest officer files an appeal from that conviction and the conviction is upheld by the highest court to which the appeal is taken or if the forest officer does not file a timely appeal, the chief shall terminate the employment of that forest officer. If the forest officer files an appeal that results in that forest officer's acquittal of the felony or conviction of a misdemeanor, or in the dismissal of the felony charge against the forest officer, the chief shall reinstate that forest officer. A forest officer who is reinstated under division (D)(2)(b) of this section shall not receive any back pay unless that forest officer's conviction of the felony was reversed on appeal, or the felony charge was dismissed, because the court found insufficient evidence to convict the forest officer of the felony.

(3) Division (D) of this section does not apply regarding an offense that was committed prior to January 1, 1997.

(4) The suspension from employment, or the termination of the employment, of a forest officer under division (D)(2) of this section shall be in accordance with Chapter 119. of the Revised Code.

(2002 H 490, eff. 1–1–04; 1998 S 187, eff. 3–18–99; 1996 H 566, eff. 10–16–96; 1992 H 167, eff. 10–8–92; 1990 H 669; 1988 H 699; 1976 H 972; 1973 S 217; 1972 S 247; 1970 S 113; 132 v S 345, H 198; 130 v Pt 2, H 26; 1953 H 1; GC 1177–10ee)

1503.30 Commission of forest officer

The chief of the division of forestry shall furnish each forest officer, as an evidence of his authority, a badge which has impressed thereon "Forest Officer."

The governor shall issue to each forest officer a commission indicating such officer's authority to make arrests as provided by section 1503.29 of the Revised Code.

(1976 H 972, eff. 9–1–76; 1973 S 217; 130 v Pt 2, H 26; 1953 H 1; GC 1177–10ff)

1503.31 Forest officer is not entitled to any fines collected

No forest officer shall be entitled to any portion of any fine imposed upon any person for any breach of the peace or violation of rules and regulations of the public forest. When the proceeding is initiated by the forest officer, all such fines shall be paid into the state treasury to the credit of the general revenue fund.

(1953 H 1, eff. 10–1–53; GC 1177–10gg)

CHAPTER 1517
DIVISION OF NATURAL AREAS AND PRESERVES

1517.10 Preserve officers

(A) As used in this section, "felony" has the same meaning as in section 109.511 of the Revised Code.

(B)(1) Any person selected by the chief of the division of natural areas and preserves for custodial or patrol service on the lands and waters operated or administered by the division shall be employed in conformity with the law applicable to the classified civil service of the state. Subject to division (C) of this section, the chief may designate that person as a preserve officer. A preserve officer, in any nature preserve, in any natural area owned or managed through easement, license, or lease by the department of natural resources and administered by the division, and on lands owned or managed through easement, license, or lease by the department and administered by the division that are within or adjacent to any wild, scenic, or recreational river area established under this chapter and along any trail established under Chapter 1519. of the Revised Code, has the authority specified under section 2935.03 of the Revised Code for peace officers of the department of natural resources to keep the peace, to enforce all laws and rules governing those lands and waters, and to make arrests for violation of those laws and rules, provided that the authority shall be exercised on lands or waters administered by another division of the department only pursuant to an agreement with the chief of that division or to a request for assistance by an enforcement officer of that division in an emergency. A preserve officer, in or along any watercourse within, abutting, or upstream from the boundary of any area administered by the department, has the authority to enforce section 3767.32 of the Revised Code and any other laws prohibiting the dumping of refuse into or along waters and to make arrests for violation of those laws. The jurisdiction of a preserve officer shall be concurrent with that of the peace officers of the county, township, or municipal corporation in which the violation occurs.

The governor, upon the recommendation of the chief, shall issue to each preserve officer a commission indicating authority to make arrests as provided in this section.

The chief shall furnish a suitable badge to each commissioned preserve officer as evidence of the preserve officer's authority.

(2) If any person employed under this section is designated by the chief to act as an agent of the state in the collection of money resulting from the sale of licenses, fees of any nature, or other money belonging to the state, the chief shall require a surety bond from the person in an amount not less than one thousand dollars.

(C)(1) The chief of the division of natural areas and preserves shall not designate a person as a preserve officer pursuant to division (B)(1) of this section on a permanent basis, on a temporary basis, for a probationary term, or on other than a permanent basis if the person previously has been convicted of or has pleaded guilty to a felony.

(2)(a) The chief of the division of natural areas and preserves shall terminate the employment as a preserve officer of a person designated as a preserve officer under division (B)(1) of this section if that person does either of the following:

(i) Pleads guilty to a felony;

(ii) Pleads guilty to a misdemeanor pursuant to a negotiated plea agreement as provided in division (D) of section 2929.43 of the Revised Code in which the preserve officer agrees to surrender the certificate awarded to the preserve officer under section 109.77 of the Revised Code.

(b) The chief shall suspend from employment as a preserve officer a person designated as a preserve officer under division (B)(1) of this section if that person is convicted, after trial, of a felony. If the preserve officer files an appeal from that conviction and the conviction is upheld by the highest court to which the appeal is taken or if the preserve officer does not file a timely appeal, the chief shall terminate the employment of that preserve officer. If the preserve officer files an appeal that results in the preserve officer's acquittal of the felony or conviction of a misdemeanor, or in the dismissal of the felony charge against the preserve officer, the chief shall reinstate that preserve officer. A preserve officer who is reinstated under division (C)(2)(b) of this section shall not receive any back pay unless that preserve officer's conviction of the felony was reversed on appeal, or the felony charge was dismissed, because the court found insufficient evidence to convict the preserve officer of the felony.

(3) Division (C) of this section does not apply regarding an offense that was committed prior to January 1, 1997.

(4) The suspension from employment, or the termination of the employment, of a preserve officer under division (C)(2) of this section shall be in accordance with Chapter 119. of the Revised Code.

(2002 H 490, eff. 1–1–04; 1998 S 187, eff. 3–18–99; 1996 H 566, eff. 10–16–96; 1994 S 182, eff. 10–20–94; 1990 H 669, eff. 1–10–91; 1976 H 972)

CHAPTER 1531
DIVISION OF WILDLIFE

GAME PROTECTORS; MISCELLANEOUS RIGHTS OF ENTRY AND REMOVAL

1531.13 Wildlife officers

The law enforcement officers of the division of wildlife shall be known as "wildlife officers." The chief of the division of wildlife, wildlife officers, and such other employees of the division as the chief of the division of wildlife designates, and other officers who are given like authority, shall enforce all laws pertaining to the taking, possession, protection, preservation, management, and propagation of wild animals and all division rules. They shall enforce all laws against hunting without permission of the owner or authorized agent of the land on which the hunting is done. They may arrest on view and without issuance of a warrant. They may inspect any container or package at any time except when within a building and the owner or person in charge of the building objects. The inspection shall be only for bag limits of wild animals taken in open season or for wild animals taken during the closed season, or for any kind or species of those wild animals.

The chief may visit all parts of the state and direct and assist wildlife officers and other employees in the discharge of their duties. The owners or tenants of private lands or waters are not liable to wildlife officers for injuries suffered while carrying out their duties while on the lands or waters of the owners or tenants unless the injuries are caused by the willful or wanton misconduct of the owners or tenants. Any regularly employed salaried wildlife officer may enter any private lands or waters if the wildlife officer has good cause to believe and does believe that a law is being violated.

A wildlife officer, sheriff, deputy sheriff, constable, or officer having a similar authority may search any place which the officer has good reason to believe contains a wild animal or any part of a wild animal taken or had in possession contrary to law or division rule, or a boat, gun, net, seine, trap, ferret, or device used in the violation, and seize any the officer finds so taken or possessed. If the owner or person in charge of the place to be searched refuses to permit the search, upon filing an affidavit in accordance with law with a court having jurisdiction of the offense and upon receiving a search warrant issued, the officer forcibly may search the place described, and if in the search the officer finds any wild animal or part of a wild animal, or any boat, gun, net, seine, trap, ferret, or device in the possession of the owner or person in charge, contrary to this chapter or Chapter 1533. of the Revised Code or division rule, the officer shall seize it and arrest the person in whose custody or possession it was found. The wild animal or parts of a wild animal or boat, gun, net, seine, trap, ferret, or device so found shall escheat to the state.

Each wildlife officer shall post a bond in a sum not less than one thousand dollars executed by a surety company authorized to transact business in this state for the faithful performance of the duties of the wildlife officer's office.

The chief and wildlife officers have the authority specified under section 2935.03 of the Revised Code for peace officers of the department of natural resources for the purpose of enforcing the criminal laws of the state on any property owned, controlled, maintained, or administered by the department of natural resources and may enforce sections 2923.12, 2923.15, and 2923.16 of the Revised Code throughout the state and may arrest without warrant any person who, in the presence of the chief or any wildlife officer, is engaged in the violation of any of those laws.

A wildlife officer may render assistance to a state or local law enforcement officer at the request of that officer or may render assistance to a state or local law enforcement officer in the event of an emergency. Wildlife officers serving outside the division of wildlife under this section shall be considered as performing services within their regular employment for the purposes of compensation, pension or indemnity fund rights, workers' compensation, and other rights or benefits to which they may be entitled as incidents of their regular employment.

Wildlife officers serving outside the division of wildlife under this section retain personal immunity from civil liability as specified in section 9.86 of the Revised Code and shall not be considered an employee of a political subdivision for purposes of Chapter 2744. of the Revised Code. A political subdivision that uses wildlife officers under this section is not subject to civil liability under Chapter 2744. of the Revised Code as the result of any action or omission of any wildlife officer acting under this section.

(1998 S 187, eff. 3–18–99; 1994 S 182, eff. 10–20–94; 1990 H 669, eff. 1–10–91; 1982 H 424; 1973 H 453; 130 v Pt 2, H 5; 130 v H 573; 1953 H 1; GC 1441)

1531.131 Enforcement of dumping prohibitions

A wildlife officer shall enforce section 3767.32 of the Revised Code and any other laws prohibiting the dumping of refuse into or along waters, the rules of the department of natural resources adopted under section 1517.02 of the Revised Code, and the rules of the director of natural resources adopted under Chapter 1519. of the Revised Code and shall make arrests for violation of those laws and rules. The jurisdiction of a wildlife officer is concurrent with that of the peace officers of the county, township, or municipal corporation in which the violation occurs.

(1994 S 182, eff. 10–20–94; 1972 S 247, eff. 10–20–72; 1970 S 113; 132 v S 345)

1531.132 Offenses affecting employment eligibility of game protectors

(A) As used in this section, "felony" has the same meaning as in section 109.511 of the Revised Code.

(B)(1) The chief of the division of wildlife shall not designate a person as a game protector on a permanent basis, on a temporary basis, for a probationary term, or on other than a permanent basis if the person previously has been convicted of or has pleaded guilty to a felony.

(2)(a) The chief of the division of wildlife shall terminate the employment of a person as a game protector if that person does either of the following:

(i) Pleads guilty to a felony;

(ii) Pleads guilty to a misdemeanor pursuant to a negotiated plea agreement as provided in division (D) of section 2929.43 of the Revised Code in which the game protector agrees to surrender the certificate awarded to the game protector under section 109.77 of the Revised Code.

(b) The chief shall suspend from employment as a game protector a person designated as a game protector if that person is convicted, after trial, of a felony. If the game protector files an appeal from that conviction and the conviction is upheld by the highest court to which the appeal is taken or if the game protector does not file a timely appeal, the chief shall terminate the employment of that game protector. If the game protector files an appeal that results in the game protector's acquittal of the felony or conviction of a misdemeanor, or in the dismissal of the felony charge against the game protector, the chief shall reinstate that game protector. A game protector who is reinstated under division (B)(2)(b) of this section shall not receive any back pay unless that game protector's conviction of the felony was reversed on appeal, or the felony charge was dismissed, because the court found insufficient evidence to convict the game protector of the felony.

(3) Division (B) of this section does not apply regarding an offense that was committed prior to January 1, 1997.

(4) The suspension from employment, or the termination of the employment, of a game protector under division (B)(2) of this section shall be in accordance with Chapter 119. of the Revised Code.

(2002 H 490, eff. 1–1–04; 1996 H 566, eff. 10–16–96)

1531.14 Right to enter privately owned lands

Any person regularly employed by the division of wildlife for the purpose of conducting research and investigation of game or fish or their habitat conditions or engaged in restocking game or fish or in any type of work involved in or incident to game or fish restoration projects or in the enforcement of laws or division rules relating to game or fish, or in the enforcement of section 1531.29 or 3767.32 of the Revised Code, other laws prohibiting the dumping of refuse in or along streams, or watercraft laws, while in the normal, lawful, and peaceful pursuit of such investigation, work, or enforcement may enter upon, cross over, be upon, and remain upon privately owned lands for such purposes and shall not be subject to arrest for trespass while so engaged or for such cause thereafter.

Any such person, upon demand, shall identify himself to the owner, tenant, or manager of such privately owned lands by means of a badge or card bearing his name and certifying his employment by the division.

(1994 S 182, eff. 10–20–94; 1971 S 304, eff. 12–10–71; 132 v S 345; 130 v H 573; 1953 H 1; GC 1441–1)

1531.15 Division of wildlife may take fish

The division of wildlife may take fish at any time or place, in any manner, for the maintenance or cultivation of fish in hatcheries, or for the purpose of stocking ponds, lakes, rivers, or creeks, or for the purpose of exterminating rough fish in any waters. The division may set aside any waters for the propagation of fish or waterfowl.

(1953 H 1, eff. 10–1–53; GC 1447)

VIOLATIONS—PROCEDURE

1531.16 Prosecution for offenses not committed in presence of officers

Sheriffs, deputy sheriffs, constables, and other police officers shall enforce the laws and division rules for the taking, possession, protection, preservation, and propagation of wild animals and for this purpose shall have the power conferred upon wildlife officers. Prosecution for offenses not committed in the presence of an officer shall be instituted only upon the approval of the prosecuting attorney of the county in which the offense is committed, or a municipal legal officer within his territorial jurisdiction, or upon the approval of the attorney general, and when the services of counsel are necessary, the attorney authorized by this section to approve the action and who does so shall act as attorney for the prosecution of the case.

(1994 S 182, eff. 10–20–94; 132 v H 811, eff. 12–1–67; 130 v H 573; 1953 H 1; GC 1444)

1531.20 Seizure of device used in the unlawful taking of wild animals

Any motor vehicle, all-terrain vehicle, or boat used in the unlawful taking or transporting of wild animals, and any net, seine, trap, ferret, gun, or other device used in the unlawful taking of wild animals, is a public nuisance. Each wildlife officer, or other officer with like authority, shall seize and safely keep such property and the illegal results of its use, and unless otherwise ordered by the chief of the division of wildlife shall institute, within five days, proceedings in a proper court of the county for its forfeiture. A writ of replevin shall not lie to take the property from the officer's custody or from the custody or jurisdiction of the court in which the proceeding is instituted, nor shall the proceeding affect a criminal prosecution for the unlawful use or possession of the property.

An action for the forfeiture of any such property shall be commenced by the filing of an affidavit describing the property seized and stating the unlawful use made of it, the time and place of seizure, and the name of the person owning or using it at the time of seizure. If the name is unknown, that fact shall be stated. Upon the filing of the affidavit, the court shall issue a summons setting forth the facts stated in the affidavit and fixing a time and place for the hearing of the complaint. A copy of the summons shall be served on the owner or person using the property at the time of its seizure, if the owner or user is known, or by leaving a copy thereof at the owner's or user's usual residence or place of business in the county, at least three days before the time fixed for the hearing of the complaint. If the owner or user is unknown or a nonresident of the county or cannot be found therein, a copy of the summons shall be posted at a suitable place nearest the place of seizure, but if the owner's or user's address is known, a copy of the summons shall be mailed to the owner or user at least three days before the time fixed for the hearing of the complaint. On the date fixed for the hearing, the officer making the service shall make a return of the time and manner of making the service. Upon the proper cause shown, the court may postpone the hearing.

If the owner or person unlawfully using the property at the time of its seizure is arrested, pleads guilty, and confesses that the property at the time of its seizure was being used by the owner or user in violation of law or division rule, no proceeding of forfeiture shall be instituted, but the court in imposing sentence shall order the property so seized forfeited to the state, to be disposed of thereafter as the chief of the division of wildlife directs.

Notwithstanding any other provision of this section to the contrary, a proceeding of forfeiture shall not be instituted under this section unless the owner of the property or the person unlawfully using the property is convicted of a violation of law or division rule.

(1998 S 187, eff. 3–18–99; 1994 S 182, eff. 10–20–94; 1988 S 256, eff. 7–20–88; 1976 H 1316; 130 v H 573; 1953 H 1; GC 1450)

1531.21 Rules of criminal procedure to apply

The defendant in a proceeding for forfeiture or condemnation under a division rule or this chapter or Chapter 1533. of the Revised Code shall be tried under the Rules of Criminal Procedure and according to law.

(1994 S 182, eff. 10–20–94; 1973 H 453, eff. 11–20–73; 130 v Pt 2, H 5; 1953 H 1; GC 1451)

PENALTIES

1531.99 Penalties; restitution for illegally taken or possessed wild animal

(A) Whoever violates section 1531.02 of the Revised Code, or any division rule, other than a rule adopted under section 1531.25 of the Revised Code, is guilty of a misdemeanor of the fourth degree.

(B) Whoever violates section 1531.02 of the Revised Code concerning the taking or possession of deer or violates division (K) of section 1531.06 or section 1531.07 or 1531.29 of the Revised Code is guilty of a misdemeanor of the third degree on a first offense; on each subsequent offense, that person is guilty of a misdemeanor of the first degree.

(C) Whoever violates section 1531.25 of the Revised Code is guilty of a misdemeanor of the first degree.

(D) Whoever violates section 1531.02 of the Revised Code concerning the selling or offering for sale of any wild animals or parts of wild animals, the minimum value of which animals or parts, in the aggregate, is more than one thousand dollars as established under section 1531.201 of the Revised Code, is guilty of a felony of the fifth degree.

(E) A court that imposes sentence for a violation of any section of this chapter governing the holding, taking, or possession of wild animals, including, without limitation, section 1531.11 of the Revised Code, shall require the person who is convicted of or pleads guilty to the offense, in addition to any fine, term of imprisonment, seizure, and forfeiture imposed, to make restitution for the minimum value of the wild animal illegally held, taken, or possessed as established under section 1531.201 of the Revised Code. An officer who collects moneys paid as restitution under this section shall pay those moneys to the treasurer of state who shall deposit them in the state treasury to the credit of the wildlife fund established under section 1531.17 of the Revised Code.

(1998 S 187, eff. 3–18–99; 1995 S 2, eff. 7–1–96; 1994 S 182, eff. 10–20–94; 1986 H 848, eff. 2–27–87; 1976 H 1316; 1973 S 35, H 453; 1969 H 503; 131 v H 896, H 291; 129 v 1310; 1953 H 1)

CHAPTER 1541

DIVISION OF PARKS AND RECREATION

LAKES AND PARKS

1541.10 Park officers

Any person selected by the chief of the division of parks and recreation for custodial or patrol service on the lands and waters operated or administered by the division of parks and recreation shall be employed in conformity with the law applicable to the classified civil service of the state. Subject to section 1541.11 of the Revised Code, the chief may designate that person as a park officer. A park officer, on any lands and waters owned, controlled, maintained, or administered by the department of natural resources and on highways, as defined in section 4511.01 of the Revised Code, adjacent to lands and waters owned, controlled, maintained, or administered by the division, has the authority specified under section 2935.03 of the Revised Code for peace officers of the department of natural resources to keep the peace, to enforce all laws and rules governing those lands and waters, and to make arrests for violation of those laws and rules, provided that the authority shall be exercised on lands or waters administered by another division of the department only pursuant to an agreement with the chief of that division or to a request for assistance by an enforcement officer of that division in an emergency. A park officer, in or along any watercourse within, abutting, or upstream from the boundary of any area administered by the department, has the authority to enforce section 3767.32 of the Revised Code and any other laws prohibiting the dumping of refuse into or along waters and to make arrests for violation of those laws. The jurisdiction of park officers shall be concurrent with that of the peace officers of the county, township, or municipal corporation in which the violation occurs. A state park, for purposes of this section, is any area that is administered as a state park by the division of parks and recreation.

The secretary of state, upon the recommendation of the chief, shall issue to each park officer a commission indicating authority to make arrests as provided in this section.

The chief shall furnish a suitable badge to each commissioned park officer as evidence of that park officer's authority.

If any person employed under this section is designated by the chief to act as an agent of the state in the collection of moneys resulting from the sale of licenses, fees of any nature, or other moneys belonging to the state, the chief shall require a surety bond from that person in an amount not less than one thousand dollars.

A park officer may render assistance to a state or local law enforcement officer at the request of that officer or may render assistance to a state or local law enforcement officer in the event of an emergency.

Park officers serving outside the division of parks and recreation under this section or serving under the terms of a mutual aid compact authorized under section 1501.02 of the Revised Code shall be considered as performing services within their regular employment for the purposes of compensation, pension or indemnity fund rights, workers' compensation, and other rights or benefits to which they may be entitled as incidents of their regular employment.

Park officers serving outside the division of parks and recreation under this section or under a mutual aid compact retain personal immunity from civil liability as specified in section 9.86 of the Revised Code and shall not be considered an employee of a political subdivision for purposes of Chapter 2744. of the Revised Code. A political subdivision that uses park officers under this section or under the terms of a mutual aid compact authorized under section 1501.02 of the Revised Code is not subject to civil liability under Chapter 2744. of the Revised Code as the result of any action or omission of any park officer acting under this section or under a mutual aid compact.

(2003 H 95, eff. 9–26–03; 1998 S 187, eff. 3–18–99; 1996 H 566, eff. 10–16–96; 1990 H 669, eff. 1–10–91; 1972 S 247; 1970 S 113; 132 v S 345; 131 v H 331; 130 v H 573; 1953 H 1; GC 476)

WATERCRAFT

1541.11 Offenses affecting employment eligibility of park officers

(A) As used in this section, "felony" has the same meaning as in section 109.511 of the Revised Code.

(B)(1) The chief of the division of parks and recreation shall not designate a person as a park officer under section 1541.10 of the Revised Code on a permanent basis, on a temporary basis, for a probationary term, or on other than a permanent basis if the person previously has been convicted of or has pleaded guilty to a felony.

(2)(a) The chief of the division of parks and recreation shall terminate the employment as a park officer of a person designated as a park officer under section 1541.10 of the Revised Code if that person does either of the following:

(i) Pleads guilty to a felony;

(ii) Pleads guilty to a misdemeanor pursuant to a negotiated plea agreement as provided in division (D) of section 2929.43 of the Revised Code in which the park officer agrees to surrender the certificate awarded to the park officer under section 109.77 of the Revised Code.

(b) The chief shall suspend from employment as a park officer a person designated as a park officer if that person is convicted, after trial, of a felony. If the park officer files an appeal from that conviction and the conviction is upheld by the highest court to which the appeal is taken or if the park officer does not file a timely appeal, the chief shall terminate the employment of that park officer. If the park officer files an appeal that results in the park officer's acquittal of the felony or conviction of a misdemeanor, or in the dismissal of the felony charge against the park officer, the chief shall reinstate that park officer. A park officer who is reinstated under division (B)(2)(b) of this section shall not receive any back pay unless that park officer's conviction of the felony was reversed on appeal, or the felony charge was dismissed, because the court found insufficient evidence to convict the park officer of the felony.

(3) Division (B) of this section does not apply regarding an offense that was committed prior to January 1, 1997.

(4) The suspension from employment, or the termination of the employment, of a park officer under division (B)(2) of this section shall be in in [1] accordance with Chapter 119. of the Revised Code.

(2002 H 490, eff. 1–1–04; 1996 H 566, eff. 10–16–96)

[1] So in original.

1541.18 Park police patrolman may take possession of boat

A reservoir park police patrolman may take possession of and hold a boat or other property if such action appears necessary in the course of making an arrest of a person violating section 1541.09 to 1541.17, inclusive, of the Revised Code. He shall not be held liable for the loss of or any damage done to such boat or other property taken and held by reason of the failure to comply with such sections, provided ordinary care is exercised in the handling of such property. No person shall take possession of a boat or other property which has been taken in charge by a police patrolman or other officer as provided in this section, until such patrolman or officer has released same.

(1953 H 1, eff. 10–1–53; GC 483)

MISCELLANEOUS PROVISIONS

1541.19 Prohibition against use of firearms or fireworks in state parks; exceptions

No person shall engage in the hunting of wildlife, either with a gun or with a bow and arrow, on lands or waters operated or administered by the division of parks and recreation, except on such lands or waters as are exempted by the chief of the division of parks and recreation, under specific orders adopted in conformity with sections 119.01 to 119.13 of the Revised Code. No person shall engage in the discharge of firearms except during open season for hunting of wildlife on lands or waters exempted as provided in this section, or except in such places where there is provided by the division, skeet, trap shooting, or other shooting ranges. No person shall engage in the discharge of fireworks on lands or waters operated or administered by the division, except a licensed exhibitor of fireworks who is acting in accordance with sections 3743.50 to 3743.55 of the Revised Code and who has obtained the written permission of the chief of the division of parks and recreation for a particular public fireworks exhibition.

(1986 S 61, eff. 5–30–86; 130 v H 573; 1953 H 1; GC 482)

1541.20 Care of state property

No person shall injure, alter, destroy, remove, or change any tree, building, dock, or land, or part thereof, within a state reservoir park or other body of water under the supervision and control of the division of parks and recreation, or construct any building or dock within such reservoir park, without the written permission of the chief of the division of parks and recreation. All lessees of state lands or lots shall keep the premises in good condition and free of weeds, inflammable substances, garbage, and all other unsightly or dangerous things. Proof that any state premises under lease are used for illegal or immoral purposes shall be just cause for the chief to cancel the leasehold for such state property.

(130 v H 573, eff. 9–30–63; 1953 H 1; GC 483–1)

PENALTIES

1541.99 Penalties

Whoever violates sections 1541.09 to 1541.20 of the Revised Code or any rules of the division of parks and recreation shall be fined not less than ten nor more than one hundred dollars.

(2000 S 198, eff. 9–22–00; 132 v H 196, eff. 8–24–67; 1953 H 1; Source—GC 479–4, 483–3)

CHAPTER 1545

PARK DISTRICTS—BOARD OF PARK COMMISSIONERS; POLICE POWERS

PARK COMMISSIONERS; POWERS AND DUTIES

Section

PARK COMMISSIONERS; POWERS AND DUTIES

1545.13 Police powers; offenses affecting employment eligibility

(A) As used in this section, "felony" has the same meaning as in section 109.511 of the Revised Code.

(B) The employees that the board of park commissioners designates for that purpose may exercise all the powers of police officers within and adjacent to the lands under the jurisdiction and control of the board or when acting as authorized by section 1545.131 or 1545.132 of the Revised Code. Before exercising the powers of police officers, the designated employees shall comply with the certification requirement established in section 109.77 of the Revised Code, take an oath, and give a bond to the state in the sum that the board prescribes, for the proper performance of their duties in that respect. This division is subject to division (C) of this section.

(C)(1) The board of park commissioners shall not designate an employee as provided in division (B) of this section on a permanent basis, on a temporary basis, for a probationary term, or on other than a permanent basis if the employee previously has been convicted of or has pleaded guilty to a felony.

(2)(a) The board of park commissioners shall terminate the employment of an employee designated as provided in division (B) of this section if the employee does either of the following:

(i) Pleads guilty to a felony;

(ii) Pleads guilty to a misdemeanor pursuant to a negotiated plea agreement as provided in division (D) of section 2929.43 of the Revised Code in which the employee agrees to surrender the certificate awarded to the employee under section 109.77 of the Revised Code.

(b) The board shall suspend from employment an employee designated as provided in division (B) of this section if the employee is convicted, after trial, of a felony. If the employee files an appeal from that conviction and the conviction is upheld by the highest court to which the appeal is taken or if the employee does not file a timely appeal, the board shall terminate the employment of that employee. If the employee files an appeal that results in the employee's acquittal of the felony or conviction of a misdemeanor, or in the dismissal of the felony charge against the employee, the board shall reinstate that employee. An employee who is reinstated under division (C)(2)(b) of this section shall not receive any back pay unless that employee's conviction of the felony was reversed on appeal, or the felony charge was dismissed, because the court found insufficient evidence to convict the employee of the felony.

(3) Division (C) of this section does not apply regarding an offense that was committed prior to January 1, 1995.

(4) The suspension from employment, or the termination of the employment, of an employee under division (C)(2) of this section shall be in accordance with Chapter 119. of the Revised Code.

(2002 H 490, eff. 1–1–04; 1996 H 566, eff. 10–16–96; 1992 S 174, eff. 7–31–92; 1984 H 759; 1953 H 1; GC 2976–10h)

1545.131 Contracts for park district law enforcement officers to render police services to political subdivisions or state universities or colleges

The board of park commissioners of a park district may enter into contracts with one or more townships, township police districts, municipal corporations, or county sheriffs of this state, with one or more township park districts created pursuant to section 511.18 of the Revised Code or other park districts, with one or more state universities or colleges, as defined in section 3345.12 of the Revised Code, or with a contiguous political subdivision of an adjoining state, and a township, township police district, municipal corporation, county sheriff, township park district, other park district, or state university or college may enter into a contract with a park district upon any terms that are agreed to by them, to allow the use of the park district police or law enforcement officers designated under section 1545.13 of the Revised Code to perform any police function, exercise any police power, or render any police service on behalf of the contracting entity that the entity may perform, exercise, or render.

Chapter 2744. of the Revised Code, insofar as it applies to the operation of police departments, applies to the contracting entities and to the members of the police force or law enforcement department when they are rendering service outside their own subdivisions pursuant to that contract.

Members of the police force or law enforcement department acting outside the political subdivision in which they are employed, pursuant to that contract, shall be entitled to participate in any indemnity fund established by their employer to the same extent as while acting within the employing subdivision. Those members shall be entitled to all the rights and benefits of Chapter 4123. of the Revised Code, to the same extent as while performing service within the subdivision.

The contracts entered into pursuant to this section may provide for the following:

(A) A fixed annual charge to be paid at the times agreed upon and stipulated in the contract;

(B) Compensation based upon the following:

(1) A stipulated price for each call or emergency;

(2) The number of members or pieces of equipment employed;

(3) The elapsed time of service required in each call or emergency.

(C) Compensation for loss or damage to equipment while engaged in rendering police services outside the limits of the subdivision that owns and furnishes the equipment;

(D) Reimbursement of the subdivision in which the police force or law enforcement department members are employed for any indemnity award or premium contribution assessed against the employing subdivision for workers' compensation benefits for injuries or death of its police force or law enforcement department members occurring while engaged in rendering police services pursuant to the contract.

(1996 H 268, eff. 5–8–96; 1992 S 174, eff. 7–31–92)

1545.132 Park district law enforcement departments providing police services to political subdivisions without contract

The police force or law enforcement department of any park district may provide police protection to any county, municipal corporation, township, or township police district of this state, to any other park district or any township park district created pursuant to section 511.18 of the Revised Code, or to a governmental entity of an adjoining state without a contract to provide police protection, upon the approval, by resolution, of the board of park commissioners of the park district in which the police force or law enforcement department is located and upon authorization by an officer or employee of the police force or department providing the police protection who is designated by title of office or position, pursuant to the resolution of the board of park commissioners, to give the authorization.

Chapter 2744. of the Revised Code, insofar as it applies to the operation of police departments, shall apply to any park district and to members of its police force or law enforcement department when those members are rendering police services pursuant to this section outside the park district by which they are employed.

Police force or law enforcement department members acting, as provided in this section, outside the park district by which they are employed shall be entitled to participate in any pension or indemnity fund established by their employer to the same extent as while acting within the park district by which they are employed. Those members shall be entitled to all rights and benefits of Chapter 4123. of the Revised Code to the same extent as while performing services within the park district by which they are employed.

(1992 S 174, eff. 7–31–92)

CHAPTER 1547

WATERCRAFT, VESSELS, AND WATERWAYS

DEFINITIONS

1547.01 Definitions

(A) As used in sections 1541.03, 1547.26, 1547.39, 1547.40, 1547.53, 1547.54, 1547.541, 1547.542, 1547.543, 1547.56, 1547.57, 1547.66, 3733.21, and 5311.01 of the Revised Code, "watercraft" means any of the following when used or capable of being used for transportation on the water:

(1) A vessel operated by machinery either permanently or temporarily affixed;

(2) A sailboat other than a sailboard;

(3) An inflatable, manually propelled boat that is required by federal law to have a hull identification number meeting the requirements of the United States coast guard;

(4) A canoe or rowboat.

"Watercraft" does not include ferries as referred to in Chapter 4583. of the Revised Code.

Watercraft subject to section 1547.54 of the Revised Code shall be divided into five classes as follows:

Class A: Less than sixteen feet in length;

Class 1: At least sixteen feet, but less than twenty-six feet in length;

Class 2: At least twenty-six feet, but less than forty feet in length;

Class 3: At least forty feet, but less than sixty-five feet in length;

Class 4: At least sixty-five feet in length.

(B) As used in this chapter:

(1) "Vessel" includes every description of craft, including nondisplacement craft and seaplanes, designed to be used as a means of transportation on water.

(2) "Rowboat" means any vessel, except a canoe, that is designed to be rowed and that is propelled by human muscular effort by oars or paddles and upon which no mechanical propulsion device, electric motor, internal combustion engine, or sail has been affixed or is used for the operation of the vessel.

(3) "Sailboat" means any vessel, equipped with mast and sails, dependent upon the wind to propel it in the normal course of operation.

(a) Any sailboat equipped with an inboard engine is deemed a powercraft with auxiliary sail.

(b) Any sailboat equipped with a detachable motor is deemed a sailboat with auxiliary power.

(c) Any sailboat being propelled by mechanical power, whether under sail or not, is deemed a powercraft and subject to all laws and rules governing powercraft operation.

(4) "Powercraft" means any vessel propelled by machinery, fuel, rockets, or similar device.

(5) "Person" includes any legal entity defined as a person in section 1.59 of the Revised Code and any body politic, except the United States and this state, and includes any agent, trustee, executor, receiver, assignee, or other representative thereof.

(6) "Owner" includes any person who claims lawful possession of a vessel by virtue of legal title or equitable interest therein that entitled the person to that possession.

(7) "Operator" includes any person who navigates or has under the person's control a vessel, or vessel and detachable motor, on the waters in this state.

(8) "Visible" means visible on a dark night with clear atmosphere.

(9) "Waters in this state" means all streams, rivers, lakes, ponds, marshes, watercourses, waterways, and other bodies of water, natural or humanmade, that are situated wholly or partially within this state or within its jurisdiction and are used for recreational boating.

(10) "Navigable waters" means waters that come under the jurisdiction of the department of the army of the United States and any waterways within or adjacent to this state, except inland lakes having neither a navigable inlet nor outlet.

(11) "In operation" in reference to a vessel means that the vessel is being navigated or otherwise used on the waters in this state.

(12) "Sewage" means human body wastes and the wastes from toilets and other receptacles intended to receive or retain body waste.

(13) "Canoe" means a narrow vessel of shallow draft, pointed at both ends and propelled by human muscular effort, and includes kayaks, racing shells, and rowing sculls.

(14) "Coast guard approved" means bearing an approval number assigned by the United States coast guard.

(15) "Type one personal flotation device" means a device that is designed to turn an unconscious person floating in water from a face downward position to a vertical or slightly face upward position and that has at least nine kilograms, approximately twenty pounds, of buoyancy.

(16) "Type two personal flotation device" means a device that is designed to turn an unconscious person in the water from a face downward position to a vertical or slightly face upward position and that has at least seven kilograms, approximately fifteen and four-tenths pounds, of buoyancy.

(17) "Type three personal flotation device" means a device that is designed to keep a conscious person in a vertical or slightly face upward position and that has at least seven kilograms, approximately fifteen and four-tenths pounds, of buoyancy.

(18) "Type four personal flotation device" means a device that is designed to be thrown to a person in the water and not worn and that has at least seven and five-tenths kilograms, approximately sixteen and five-tenths pounds, of buoyancy.

(19) "Type five personal flotation device" means a device that, unlike other personal flotation devices, has limitations on its approval by the United States coast guard, including, without limitation, all of the following:

(a) The approval label on the type five personal flotation device indicates that the device is approved for the activity in which the vessel is being used or as a substitute for a personal flotation device of the type required on the vessel in use.

(b) The personal flotation device is used in accordance with any requirements on the approval label.

(c) The personal flotation device is used in accordance with requirements in its owner's manual if the approval label refers to such a manual.

(20) "Inflatable watercraft" means any vessel constructed of rubber, canvas, or other material that is designed to be inflated with any gaseous substance, constructed with two or more air cells, and operated as a vessel. Inflatable watercraft propelled by a motor shall be classified as powercraft and shall be registered by length. Inflatable watercraft propelled by a sail shall be classified as a sailboat and shall be registered by length.

(21) "Idle speed" means the slowest possible speed needed to maintain steerage or maneuverability.

(22) "Diver's flag" means a red flag not less than one foot square having a diagonal white stripe extending from the masthead to the opposite lower corner that when displayed indicates that divers are in the water.

(23) "Muffler" means an acoustical suppression device or system that is designed and installed to abate the sound of exhaust gases emitted from an internal combustion engine and that prevents excessive or unusual noise.

(24) "Law enforcement vessel" means any vessel used in law enforcement and under the command of a law enforcement officer.

(25) "Personal watercraft" means a vessel, less than sixteen feet in length, that is propelled by machinery and designed to be operated by an individual sitting, standing, or kneeling on the vessel rather than by an individual sitting or standing inside the vessel.

(26) "No wake" has the same meaning as "idle speed."

(27) "Watercraft dealer" means any person who is regularly engaged in the business of manufacturing, selling, displaying, offering for sale, or dealing in vessels at an established place of business. "Watercraft dealer" does not include a person who is a marine salvage dealer or any other person who dismantles, salvages, or rebuilds vessels using used parts.

(28) "Electronic" includes electrical, digital, magnetic, optical, electromagnetic, or any other form of technology that entails capabilities similar to these technologies.

(29) "Electronic record" means a record generated, communicated, received, or stored by electronic means for use in an information system or for transmission from one information system to another.

(30) "Electronic signature" means a signature in electronic form attached to or logically associated with an electronic record.

(C) Unless otherwise provided, this chapter applies to all vessels operating on the waters in this state. Nothing in this chapter shall be construed in contravention of any valid federal act or regulation, but is in addition to the act or regulation where not inconsistent.

The state reserves to itself the exclusive right to regulate the minimum equipment requirements of watercraft and vessels operated on the waters in this state.

(2002 S 150, eff. 7–5–02; 2000 S 242, eff. 9–14–00; 1999 H 306, eff. 11–22–99; 1998 S 187, eff. 3–18–99; 1996 S 295, eff. 3–18–97; 1995 H 117, eff. 6–30–95; 1990 H 522, eff. 6–13–90; 1985 H 400; 1984 H 682; 1982 H 782; 1979 S 65; 1978 S 387; 1976 H 957; 1970 H 1002; 129 v 1350, 582; 128 v 1004)

OPERATING REGULATIONS

1547.07 Reckless operation; unsafe vessel operation

(A) Any person who operates any vessel or manipulates any water skis, aquaplane, or similar device on the waters in this state carelessly or heedlessly, or in disregard of the rights or safety of any person, vessel, or property, or without due caution, at a rate of speed or in a manner so as to endanger any person, vessel, or property is guilty of reckless operation of the vessel or other device.

(B) No person shall operate or permit the operation of a vessel in an unsafe manner. A vessel shall be operated in a reasonable and prudent manner at all times.

Unsafe vessel operation includes, without limitation, any of the following:

(1) A vessel becoming airborne or completely leaving the water while crossing the wake of another vessel at a distance of less than one hundred feet, or at an unsafe distance, from the vessel creating the wake;

(2) Operating at such a speed and proximity to another vessel or to a person attempting to ride on one or more water skis, surfboard, inflatable device, or similar device being towed by a vessel so as to require the operator of either vessel to swerve or turn abruptly to avoid collision;

(3) Operating less than two hundred feet directly behind a person water skiing or attempting to water ski;

(4) Weaving through congested traffic.

(1996 S 295, eff. 3–18–97; 1990 H 522, eff. 6–13–90; 1982 H 782; 1970 H 1002; 128 v 1004)

1547.071 Officer determining vessel being operated under unsafe conditions

(A) If a law enforcement officer observes a vessel being used and determines that at least one of the unsafe conditions identified in division (C) of this section is present and that an especially hazardous condition exists, the officer may direct the operator of the vessel to take whatever immediate and reasonable actions are necessary for the safety of the persons aboard the vessel, including directing the operator to return the vessel to mooring and remain there until the situation creating the hazardous condition is corrected or has ended.

For the purposes of this section, an especially hazardous condition is one in which a reasonably prudent person would believe that the continued operation of a vessel would create a special hazard to the safety of the persons aboard the vessel.

(B) The refusal by an operator of a vessel to terminate use of the vessel after being ordered to do so by a law enforcement officer under division (A) of this section is prima-facie evidence of a violation of section 1547.07 of the Revised Code.

(C) For the purposes of this section, any of the following is an unsafe condition:

(1) Insufficient personal flotation devices;

(2) Insufficient fire extinguishers;

(3) Overloaded, insufficient freeboard for the water conditions in which the vessel is operating;

(4) Improper display of navigation lights;

(5) Fuel leaks, including fuel leaking from either the engine or the fuel system;

(6) Accumulation of or an abnormal amount of fuel in the bilges;

(7) Inadequate backfire flame control;

(8) Improper ventilation.

(D) This section does not apply to any of the following:

(1) Foreign vessels temporarily using waters that are subject to the jurisdiction of the United States;

(2) Military vessels, vessels owned by the state or a political subdivision, or other public vessels, except those that are used for recreation;

(3) A ship's lifeboats, as defined in section 1548.01 of the Revised Code;

(4) Vessels that are solely commercial and that are carrying more than six passengers for hire.

(1996 S 295, eff. 3–18–97)

1547.10 Information to be given by operator of vessel involved in accident; procedures

In case of accident to or collision with persons or property on the waters of this state, due to the operation of any vessel, the operator having knowledge of the accident or collision shall immediately stop the vessel at the scene of the accident or collision, to the extent that it is safe and practical, and shall remain at the scene of the accident or collision until he has given his name and address and, if he is not the owner, the name and address of the owner of the vessel, together with the registration number of the vessel, if any, to any person injured in the accident or collision or to the operator, occupant, owner, or attendant of any vessel damaged in the accident or collision, or to any law enforcement officer at the scene of the accident or collision.

If the injured person is unable to comprehend and record the information required to be given by this section, the other operator involved in the accident or collision shall forthwith notify the nearest law enforcement agency having authority concerning the location of the accident or collision, and his name, address, and the registration number, if any, of the vessel he was operating, and then remain at the scene of the accident or collision or at the nearest location from which notification is possible until a law enforcement officer arrives, unless removed from the scene by an emergency vehicle operated by the state or a political subdivision or by an ambulance.

If the accident or collision is with an unoccupied or unattended vessel, the operator so colliding with the vessel shall securely attach the information required to be given in this section, in writing, to a conspicuous place in or on the unoccupied or unattended vessel.

(1990 H 522, eff. 6–13–90; 1984 H 682)

1547.11 Operating under influence of alcohol or drugs prohibited; evidence; immunity from liability for person drawing blood; testimony and evidence regarding field sobriety test

(A) No person shall operate or be in physical control of any vessel underway or shall manipulate any water skis, aquaplane, or similar device on the waters in this state if, at the time of the operation, control, or manipulation, any of the following applies:

(1) The person is under the influence of alcohol, a drug of abuse, or a combination of them.

(2) The person has a concentration of eight-hundredths of one per cent or more by weight of alcohol per unit volume in the person's whole blood.

(3) The person has a concentration of ninety-six-thousandths of one per cent or more by weight per unit volume of alcohol in the person's blood serum or plasma.

(4) The person has a concentration of eleven-hundredths of one gram or more by weight of alcohol per one hundred milliliters of the person's urine.

(5) The person has a concentration of eight-hundredths of one gram or more by weight of alcohol per two hundred ten liters of the person's breath.

(B) No person under twenty-one years of age shall operate or be in physical control of any vessel underway or shall manipulate any water skis, aquaplane, or similar device on the waters in this state if, at the time of the operation, control, or manipulation, any of the following applies:

(1) The person has a concentration of at least two-hundredths of one per cent, but less than eight-hundredths of one per cent by weight per unit volume of alcohol in the person's whole blood.

(2) The person has a concentration of at least three-hundredths of one per cent but less than ninety-six-thousandths of one per cent by weight per unit volume of alcohol in the person's blood serum or plasma.

(3) The person has a concentration of at least twenty-eight one-thousandths of one gram, but less than eleven-hundredths of one gram by weight of alcohol per one hundred milliliters of the person's urine.

(4) The person has a concentration of at least two-hundredths of one gram, but less than eight-hundredths of one gram by weight of alcohol per two hundred ten liters of the person's breath.

(C) In any proceeding arising out of one incident, a person may be charged with a violation of division (A)(1) and a violation of division (B)(1), (2), (3), or (4) of this section, but the person shall not be convicted of more than one violation of those divisions.

(D)(1) In any criminal prosecution or juvenile court proceeding for a violation of division (A) or (B) of this section or for an equivalent violation, the court may admit evidence on the concentration of alcohol, drugs of abuse, or a combination of them in the defendant's or child's whole blood, blood serum or plasma, urine, or breath at the time of the alleged violation as shown by chemical analysis of the substance withdrawn, or specimen taken within two hours of the time of the alleged violation.

When a person submits to a blood test, only a physician, a registered nurse, or a qualified technician, chemist, or phlebotomist shall withdraw blood for the purpose of determining the alcohol, drug, or alcohol and drug content of the whole blood, blood serum, or blood plasma. This limitation does not apply to the taking of breath or urine specimens. A person authorized to withdraw blood under this division may refuse to withdraw blood under this division if, in that person's opinion, the physical welfare of the defendant or child would be endangered by withdrawing blood.

The whole blood, blood serum or plasma, urine, or breath shall be analyzed in accordance with methods approved by the director of health by an individual possessing a valid permit issued by the director pursuant to section 3701.143 of the Revised Code.

(2) In a criminal prosecution or juvenile court proceeding for a violation of division (A) of this section or for a violation of a prohibition that is substantially equivalent to division (A) of this section, if there was at the time the bodily substance was taken a concentration of less than the applicable concentration of alcohol specified for a violation of division (A)(2), (3), (4), or (5) of this section, that fact may be considered with other competent evidence in determining the guilt or innocence of the defendant or in making an adjudication for the child. This division does not limit or affect a criminal prosecution or juvenile court proceeding for a violation of division (B) of this section or for a violation of a prohibition that is substantially equivalent to that division.

(3) Upon the request of the person who was tested, the results of the chemical test shall be made available to the person or the person's attorney immediately upon completion of the test analysis.

The person tested may have a physician, a registered nurse, or a qualified technician, chemist, or phlebotomist of the person's own choosing administer a chemical test or tests in addition to any administered at the direction of a law enforcement officer, and shall be so advised. The failure or inability to obtain an additional test by a person shall not preclude the admission of evidence relating to the test or tests taken at the direction of a law enforcement officer.

(E)(1) In any criminal prosecution or juvenile court proceeding for a violation of division (A) or (B) of this section or for an equivalent violation, if a law enforcement officer has administered a field sobriety test to the operator or person found to be in physical control of the vessel underway involved in the violation or the person manipulating the water skis, aquaplane, or similar device involved in the violation and if it is shown by clear and convincing evidence that the officer administered the test in substantial compliance with the testing standards for reliable, credible, and generally accepted field sobriety tests for vehicles that were in effect at the time the tests were administered, including, but not limited to, any testing standards then in effect that have been set by the national highway traffic safety administration, that by their nature are not clearly inapplicable regarding the operation or physical control of vessels underway or the manipulation of water skis, aquaplanes, or similar devices, all of the following apply:

(a) The officer may testify concerning the results of the field sobriety test so administered.

(b) The prosecution may introduce the results of the field sobriety test so administered as evidence in any proceedings in the criminal prosecution or juvenile court proceeding.

(c) If testimony is presented or evidence is introduced under division (E)(1)(a) or (b) of this section and if the testimony or evidence is admissible under the Rules of Evidence, the court shall admit the testimony or evidence, and the trier of fact shall give it whatever weight the trier of fact considers to be appropriate.

(2) Division (E)(1) of this section does not limit or preclude a court, in its determination of whether the arrest of a person was supported by probable cause or its determination of any other matter in a criminal prosecution or juvenile court proceeding of a type described in that division, from considering evidence or testimony that is not otherwise disallowed by division (E)(1) of this section.

(F)(1) Subject to division (F)(3) of this section, in any criminal prosecution or juvenile court proceeding for a violation of this section or for an equivalent violation, the court shall admit as prima-facie evidence a laboratory report from any forensic laboratory certified by the department of health that contains an analysis of the whole blood, blood serum or plasma, breath, urine, or other bodily substance tested and that contains all of the information specified in this division. The laboratory report shall contain all of the following:

(a) The signature, under oath, of any person who performed the analysis;

(b) Any findings as to the identity and quantity of alcohol, a drug of abuse, or a combination of them that was found;

(c) A copy of a notarized statement by the laboratory director or a designee of the director that contains the name of each certified analyst or test performer involved with the report, the analyst's or test performer's employment relationship with the laboratory that issued the report, and a notation that performing an analysis of the type involved is part of the analyst's or test performer's regular duties;

(d) An outline of the analyst's or test performer's education, training, and experience in performing the type of analysis involved and a certification that the laboratory satisfies appropriate quality control standards in general and, in this particular analysis, under rules of the department of health.

(2) Notwithstanding any other provision of law regarding the admission of evidence, a report of the type described in division (F)(1) of this section is not admissible against the defendant or child to whom it pertains in any proceeding, other than a preliminary hearing or a grand jury proceeding, unless the prosecutor has served a copy of the report on the defendant's or child's attorney or, if the defendant or child has no attorney, on the defendant or child.

(3) A report of the type described in division (F)(1) of this section shall not be prima-facie evidence of the contents, identity, or amount of any substance if, within seven days after the defendant or child to whom the report pertains or the defendant's or child's attorney receives a copy of the report, the defendant or child or the defendant's or child's attorney demands the testimony of the person who signed the report. The judge in the case may extend the seven-day time limit in the interest of justice.

(G) Except as otherwise provided in this division, any physician, registered nurse, or qualified technician, chemist, or phlebotomist who withdraws blood from a person pursuant to this section, and a hospital, first-aid station, or clinic at which blood is withdrawn from a person pursuant to this section, is immune from criminal and civil liability based upon a claim of assault and battery or any other claim that is not a claim of malpractice, for any act performed in withdrawing blood from the person. The immunity provided in this division is not available to a person who withdraws blood if the person engages in willful or wanton misconduct.

(H) As used in this section and section 1547.111 of the Revised Code:

(1) "Equivalent violation" means a violation of a municipal ordinance, law of another state, or law of the United States that is substantially equivalent to division (A) or (B) of this section.

(2) "National highway traffic safety administration" has the same meaning as in section 4511.19 of the Revised Code.

(3) "Operate" means that a vessel is being used on the waters in this state when the vessel is not securely affixed to a dock or to shore or to any permanent structure to which the vessel has the right to affix or that a vessel is not anchored in a designated anchorage area or boat camping area that is established by the United States coast guard, this state, or a political subdivision and in which the vessel has the right to anchor.

(2004 H 163, eff. 9–23–04; 2003 H 87, § 4, eff. 1–1–04; 2003 H 87, § 1, eff. 6–30–03; 2002 S 163, § 3, eff. 1–1–04; 2002 S 163, § 1, eff. 4–9–03; 2002 S 123, eff. 1–1–04; 1996 S 295, eff. 3–18–97; 1990 H 522, eff. 6–13–90; 1986 H 265; 1982 H 782; 1976 H 957; 1970 H 1002; 128 v 1004)

Notes of Decisions

Ed. Note: *See notes of decisions at RC 4511.19 regarding construction of the terms "under the influence" and "intoxicating liquor."*

1547.111 Testing for presence of alcohol or drugs; refusal to submit to test; suspension of registration

(A)(1) Any person who operates or is in physical control of a vessel or manipulates any water skis, aquaplane, or similar device upon any waters in this state shall be deemed to have given consent to a chemical test or tests to determine the alcohol, drug of abuse, or alcohol and drug of abuse content of the person's whole blood, blood serum or plasma, breath, or urine if arrested for operating or being in physical control of a vessel or manipulating any water skis, aquaplane, or similar device in violation of section 1547.11 of the Revised Code or a substantially equivalent municipal ordinance.

(2) The test or tests under division (A) of this section shall be administered at the direction of a law enforcement officer having reasonable grounds to believe the person was operating or in physical control of a vessel or manipulating any water skis, aquaplane, or similar device in violation of section 1547.11 of the Revised Code or a substantially equivalent municipal ordinance. The law enforcement agency by which the officer is employed shall designate which test or tests shall be administered.

(B) Any person who is dead or unconscious or who otherwise is in a condition rendering the person incapable of refusal shall be deemed to have consented as provided in division (A)(1) of this section, and the test or tests may be administered, subject to sections 313.12 to 313.16 of the Revised Code.

(C) Any person under arrest for violating section 1547.11 of the Revised Code or a substantially equivalent municipal ordinance shall be advised of the consequences of refusing to submit to a chemical test or tests designated as provided in division (A) of this section. The advice shall be in a written form prescribed by the chief of the division of watercraft and shall be read to the person. The form shall contain a statement that the form was shown to the person under arrest and read to the person by the arresting officer. The reading of the form shall be witnessed by one or more persons, and the witnesses shall certify to this fact by signing the form.

(D) If a law enforcement officer asks a person under arrest for violating section 1547.11 of the Revised Code or a substantially equivalent municipal ordinance to submit to a chemical test or tests as provided in division (A) of this section, if the arresting officer advises the person of the consequences of the person's refusal as provided in division (C) of this section, and if the person refuses to submit, no chemical test shall be given. Upon receipt of a sworn statement of the officer that the arresting law enforcement officer had reasonable grounds to believe the arrested person violated section 1547.11 of the Revised Code or a substantially equivalent municipal ordinance and that the person refused to submit to the chemical test upon the request of the officer, and upon receipt of the form as provided in division (C) of this section certifying that the arrested person was advised of the consequences of the refusal, the chief of the division of watercraft shall inform the person by written notice that the person is prohibited from operating or being in physical control of a vessel, from manipulating any water skis, aquaplane, or similar device, and from registering any watercraft in accordance with section 1547.54 of the Revised Code, for one year following the date of the alleged violation. The suspension of these operation, physical control, manipulation, and registration privileges shall continue for the entire one-year period, subject to review as provided in this section.

If the person under arrest is the owner of the vessel involved in the alleged violation, the law enforcement officer who arrested the person shall seize the watercraft registration certificate and tags from the vessel involved in the violation and forward them to the chief. The chief shall retain the impounded registration certificate and tags and shall impound all other registration certificates and tags issued to the person in accordance with sections 1547.54 and 1547.57 of the Revised Code, for a period of one year following the date of the alleged violation, subject to review as provided in this section.

If the arrested person fails to surrender the registration certificate because it is not on the person of the arrested person or in the watercraft, the law enforcement officer who made the arrest shall order the person to surrender it within twenty-four hours to the law enforcement officer or the law enforcement agency that employs the law enforcement officer. If the person fails to do so, the law enforcement officer shall notify the chief of that fact in the statement the officer submits to the chief under this division.

(E) Upon suspending a person's operation, physical control, manipulation, and registration privileges in accordance with division (D) of this section, the chief shall notify the person in writing, at the person's last known address, and inform the person that the person may petition for a hearing in accordance with division (F) of this section. If a person whose operation, physical control, manipulation, and registration privileges have been suspended petitions for a hearing or appeals any adverse decision, the suspension shall begin at the termination of any hearing or appeal unless the hearing or appeal results in a decision favorable to the person.

(F) Any person who has been notified by the chief that the person is prohibited from operating or being in physical control of a vessel or manipulating any water skis, aquaplane, or similar device and from registering any watercraft in accordance with section 1547.54 of the Revised Code, or who has had the registration certificate and tags of the person's watercraft impounded pursuant to division (D) of this section, within twenty days of the notification or impoundment, may file a petition in the municipal court or the county court, or if the person is a minor in juvenile court, with jurisdiction over the place at which the arrest occurred, agreeing to pay the cost of the proceedings and alleging error in the action taken by the chief under division (D) of this section or alleging one or more of the matters within the scope of the hearing as provided in this section, or both. The petitioner shall notify the chief of the filing of the petition and send the chief a copy of the petition.

The scope of the hearing is limited to the issues of whether the law enforcement officer had reasonable grounds to believe the petitioner was operating or in physical control of a vessel or manipulating any water skis, aquaplane, or similar device in violation of section 1547.11 of the Revised Code or a substantially equivalent municipal ordinance, whether the petitioner was placed under arrest, whether the petitioner refused to submit to the chemical test upon request of the officer, and whether the petitioner was advised of the consequences of the petitioner's refusal.

(G)(1) The chief shall furnish the court a copy of the affidavit as provided in division (C) of this section and any other relevant information requested by the court.

(2) In hearing the matter and in determining whether the person has shown error in the decision taken by the chief as provided in division (D) of this section, the court shall decide the issue upon the relevant, competent, and material evidence submitted by the chief or the person whose operation, physical control, manipulation, and registration privileges have been suspended.

In the proceedings, the chief shall be represented by the prosecuting attorney of the county in which the petition is filed if the petition is filed in a county court or juvenile court, except that if the arrest occurred within a city or village within the jurisdiction of the county court in which the petition is filed, the city director of law or village solicitor of that city or village shall represent the chief. If the petition is filed in the municipal court, the chief shall be represented as provided in section 1901.34 of the Revised Code.

(3) If the court finds from the evidence submitted that the person has failed to show error in the action taken by the chief under division (D) of this section or in one or more of the matters within the scope of the hearing as provided in division (F) of this section, or both, the court shall assess the cost of the proceeding against the person and shall uphold the suspension of the operation, physical control, use, and registration privileges provided in division (D) of this section. If the court finds that the person has shown error in the action taken by the chief under division (D) of this section or in one or more of the matters within the scope of the hearing as provided in division (F) of this section, or both, the cost of the proceedings shall be paid out of the county treasury of the county in which the proceedings were held, the chief shall reinstate the operation, physical control, manipulation, and registration privileges of the person without charge, and the chief shall return the registration certificate and tags, if impounded, without charge.

(4) The court shall give information in writing of any action taken under this section to the chief.

(H) At the end of any period of suspension or impoundment imposed under this section, and upon request of the person whose operation, physical control, use, and registration privileges were suspended or whose registration certificate and tags were impounded, the chief shall reinstate the person's operation, physical control, manipulation, and registration privileges by written notice and return the certificate and tags.

(I) No person who has received written notice from the chief that the person is prohibited from operating or being in physical control of a vessel, from manipulating any water skis, aquaplane, or similar device, and from registering a watercraft, or who has had the registration certificate and tags of the person's watercraft impounded, in accordance with division (D) of this section, shall operate or be in physical control of a vessel or manipulate any water skis, aquaplane, or similar device for a period of one year following the date of the person's alleged violation of section 1547.11 of the Revised Code or the substantially equivalent municipal ordinance.

(2002 S 163, § 3, eff. 1–1–04; 2002 S 163, § 1, eff. 4–9–03; 2002 S 123, eff. 1–1–04; 1998 S 187, eff. 3–18–99; 1990 H 522, eff. 6–13–90; 1986 H 265)

Notes of Decisions

Ed. Note: *See notes of decisions and opinions at RC 4511.19 regarding construction of the terms "under the influence" and "intoxicating liquor."*

1547.13 Failure to comply with order of law enforcement officer; eluding or fleeing from law enforcement officer

(A) No person shall fail to comply with any lawful order or direction of any law enforcement officer having authority to direct, control, or regulate the operation or use of vessels.

(B) No person shall operate any vessel so as to purposely elude or flee from a law enforcement officer after receiving a visible or audible signal from a law enforcement officer to bring the vessel to a stop.

(C) No person shall operate or permit to be operated any vessel on the waters in this state in violation of this section.

(1998 S 187, eff. 3–18–99; 1990 H 522, eff. 6–13–90)

1547.131 Stopping for or yielding to law enforcement vessel

Upon the approach of a law enforcement vessel with at least one flashing, rotating, or oscillating light of a color conforming with the requirements of federal law, the operator of any vessel shall stop if followed or give way in any crossing, head-on, or overtaking situation and shall remain in that position until the law enforcement vessel has passed, except when otherwise directed by a law enforcement officer. If traffic conditions warrant, a siren or other sound producing device also may be operated as an additional signaling device. This section does not relieve the operator of any law enforcement vessel from the duty to operate with due regard for the safety of all persons and property on the waters in this state.

No person shall operate or permit to be operated any vessel on the waters in this state in violation of this section.

(1998 S 187, eff. 3–18–99; 1990 H 522, eff. 6–13–90)

REQUIRED EQUIPMENT; ABANDONMENT OF VESSELS

1547.30 Abandonment of vessels or outboard motors upon private property; mooring of vessels at private docks or mooring facilities

(A) As used in this section and sections 1547.301, 1547.302, and 1547.304 of the Revised Code:

(1) "Vessel or outboard motor" excludes an abandoned junk vessel or outboard motor, as defined in section 1547.303 of the Revised Code, or any watercraft or outboard motor under section 4585.31 of the Revised Code.

(2) "Law enforcement agency" means any organization or unit comprised of law enforcement officers, as defined in section 2901.01 of the Revised Code.

(B)(1) The sheriff of a county, chief of police of a municipal corporation, township, or township police district, or other chief of a law enforcement agency, within the sheriff's or chief's respective territorial jurisdiction, upon complaint of any person adversely affected, may order into storage any vessel or outboard motor that has been left on private property, other than a private dock or mooring facility or structure, for at least seventy-two hours without the permission of the person having the right to the possession of the property. The sheriff or chief, upon complaint of the owner of a marine repair facility or place of storage, may order into storage any vessel or outboard motor that has been left at the facility or place of storage for a longer period than that agreed upon. The place of storage shall be designated by the sheriff or chief. When ordering a vessel or motor into storage under division (B)(1) of this section, a sheriff or chief, whenever possible, shall arrange for the removal of the vessel or motor by a private tow truck operator or towing company.

(2)(a) Except as provided in division (B)(2)(d) of this section, no person, without the consent of the owner or other person authorized to give consent, shall moor, anchor, or tie a vessel or outboard motor at a private dock or mooring facility or structure owned by another person if the owner has posted, in a conspicuous manner, a prohibition against the mooring, anchoring, or tying of vessels or outboard motors at the dock, facility, or structure by any person not having the consent of the owner or other person authorized to give consent.

(b) If the owner of a private dock or mooring facility or structure has posted at the dock, facility, or structure, in a conspicuous manner, conditions and regulations under which the mooring, anchoring, or tying of vessels or outboard motors is permitted at the dock, facility, or structure, no person, except as provided in division (B)(2)(d) of this section, shall moor, anchor, or tie a vessel or outboard motor at the dock, facility, or structure in violation of the posted conditions and regulations.

(c) The owner of a private dock or mooring facility or structure may order towed into storage any vessel or outboard motor found moored, anchored, or tied in violation of division (B)(2)(a) or (b) of this section, provided that the owner of the dock, facility, or structure posts on it a sign that states that the dock, facility, or structure is private, is visible from all entrances to the dock, facility, or structure, and contains all of the following information:

(i) The information specified in division (B)(2)(a) or (b) of this section, as applicable;

(ii) A notice that violators will be towed and that violators are responsible for paying the cost of the towing;

(iii) The telephone number of the person from whom a towed vessel or outboard motor may be recovered, and the address of the place to which the vessel or outboard motor will be taken and the place from which it may be recovered.

(d) Divisions (B)(2)(a) and (b) of this section do not prohibit a person from mooring, anchoring, or tying a vessel or outboard motor at a private dock or mooring facility or structure if either of the following applies:

(i) The vessel or outboard motor is disabled due to a mechanical or structural malfunction, provided that the person immediately removes the vessel or outboard motor from the dock, facility, or structure when the malfunction is corrected or when a reasonable attempt has been made to correct it;

(ii) Weather conditions are creating an imminent threat to safe operation of the vessel or outboard motor, provided that the person immediately removes the vessel or outboard motor from the dock, facility, or structure when the weather conditions permit safe operation of the vessel or outboard motor.

(e) A person whose vessel or outboard motor is towed into storage under division (B)(2)(c) of this section either shall pay the costs of the towing of the vessel or outboard motor or shall reimburse the owner of the dock or mooring facility or structure for the costs that the owner incurs in towing the vessel or outboard motor.

(3) Subject to division (C) of this section, the owner of a vessel or motor that has been removed under division (B) of this section may recover the vessel or motor only in accordance with division (F) of this section.

(C) If the owner or operator of a vessel or outboard motor that has been ordered into storage under division (B) of this section arrives after the vessel or motor has been prepared for removal, but prior to its actual removal from the property, the owner or operator shall be given the opportunity to pay a fee of not more than one-half of the charge for the removal of vessels or motors under division (B) of this section that normally is assessed by the person who has prepared the vessel or motor for removal, in order to obtain release of the vessel or motor. Upon payment of that fee, the vessel or motor shall be released to the owner or operator, and upon its release, the owner or operator immediately shall move it so that it is not on the private property without the permission of the person having the right to possession of the property, or is not at the facility or place of storage without the permission of the owner, whichever is applicable.

(D) Each county sheriff, each chief of police of a municipal corporation, township, or township police district, and each other chief of a law enforcement agency shall maintain a record of vessels or outboard motors that are ordered into storage under division (B)(1) of this section. The record shall include an entry for each such vessel or motor that identifies the vessel's hull identification number or serial number, if any, the vessel's or motor's make, model, and color, the location from which it was removed, the date and time of its removal, the telephone number of the person from whom it may be recovered, and the address of the place to which it has been taken and from which it may be recovered. Any information in the record that pertains to a particular vessel or motor shall be provided to any person who, pursuant to a statement the person makes either in person or by telephone, is identified as the owner or operator of the vessel or motor and requests information pertaining to its location.

(E) Any person who registers a complaint that is the basis of a sheriff's or chief's order for the removal and storage of a vessel or outboard motor under division (B)(1) of this section shall provide the identity of the law enforcement agency with which the complaint was registered to any person who, pursuant to a statement the person makes, is identified as the owner or operator of the vessel or motor and requests information pertaining to its location.

(F)(1) The owner of a vessel or outboard motor that is ordered into storage under division (B) of this section may reclaim it upon payment of any expenses or charges incurred in its removal, in an amount not to exceed two hundred dollars, and storage, in an amount not to exceed five dollars per twenty-four-hour period, and upon presentation of proof of ownership, which may be evidenced by a certificate of title to the vessel or motor, certificate of United States coast guard documentation, or certificate of registration if the vessel or motor is not subject to titling under section 1548.01 of the Revised Code.

(2) If a vessel or outboard motor that is ordered into storage under division (B)(1) of this section remains unclaimed by the owner for thirty days, the procedures established by sections 1547.301 and 1547.302 of the Revised Code shall apply.

(3) If a vessel or outboard motor ordered into storage under division (B)(2) of this section remains unclaimed for seventy-two hours after being stored, the tow truck operator or towing company that removed the vessel or outboard motor shall provide notice of the removal and storage to the sheriff of a county, chief of police of a municipal corporation, township, or township police district, or other chief of a law enforcement agency within whose territorial jurisdiction the vessel or outboard motor had been moored, anchored, or tied in violation of division (B)(2) of this section. The notice shall be in writing and include the vessel's hull identification number or serial number, if any, the vessel's or outboard motor's make, model, and color, the location from which it was removed, the date and time of its removal, the telephone number of the person from whom it may be recovered, and the address of the place to which it has been taken and from which it may be recovered.

Upon receipt of the notice, the sheriff or chief immediately shall cause a search to be made of the records of the division of watercraft to ascertain the owner and any lienholder of the vessel or outboard motor, and, if known, shall send notice to the owner and lienholder, if any, at the owner's and lienholder's last known address by certified mail, return receipt requested, that the vessel or outboard motor will be declared a nuisance and disposed of if not claimed not later than thirty days after the date of the mailing of the notice.

If the owner or lienholder makes no claim to the vessel or outboard motor within thirty days of the date of the mailing of the notice, the sheriff or chief shall file with the clerk of courts of the county in which the place of storage is located an affidavit showing compliance with the requirements of division (F)(3) of this section, and the vessel or outboard motor shall be disposed of in accordance with section 1547.302 of the Revised Code.

(G) No person shall remove, or cause the removal of, any vessel or outboard motor from private property other than in accordance with division (B) of this section or section 1547.301 of the Revised Code.

(1998 S 187, eff. 3–18–99; 1997 H 101, eff. 9–16–97; 1996 S 239, eff. 9–6–96; 1990 H 522, eff. 6–13–90)

1547.301 Abandonment of vessels or outboard motors upon public property

The sheriff of a county, chief of police of a municipal corporation, township, or township police district, or other chief of a law enforcement agency, within his respective territorial jurisdiction, or a state highway patrol trooper, upon notification to the sheriff or chief of such action and of the location of the place of storage, may order into storage any vessel or outboard motor that has been left in a sunken, beached, or drifting condition for any period of time, or in a docked condition, on a public street or other property open to the public, or upon or within the right-of-way of any waterway, road, or highway, for forty-eight hours or longer without notification to the sheriff or chief of the reasons for leaving the vessel or motor in any such place or condition. The sheriff or chief shall designate the place of storage of any vessel or motor ordered removed by him.

The sheriff or chief shall immediately cause a search to be made of the records of the division of watercraft to ascertain the owner and any lienholder of a vessel or outboard motor ordered into storage by the sheriff or chief, and, if known, shall send notice to the owner and lienholder, if any, at his last known address by certified mail, return receipt requested, that the vessel or motor will be declared a nuisance and disposed of if not claimed within ten days of the date of mailing of the notice. The owner or lienholder of the vessel or motor may reclaim it upon payment of any expenses or charges incurred in its removal and storage, and presentation of proof of ownership, which may be evidenced by a certificate of title to the vessel or motor, certificate of United States coast guard documentation, or certificate of registration if the vessel or motor is not subject to titling under section 1548.01 of the Revised Code.

If the owner or lienholder makes no claim to the vessel or outboard motor within ten days of the date of mailing of the notice, and if the vessel or motor is to be disposed of at public auction as provided in section 1547.302 of the Revised Code, the sheriff or chief shall file with the clerk of courts of the county in which the place of storage is located an affidavit showing compliance with the requirements of this section. Upon presentation of the affidavit, the clerk of courts shall without charge issue a salvage certificate of title, free and clear of all liens and encumbrances, to the sheriff or chief and shall send a copy of the affidavit to the chief of the division of watercraft. If the vessel or motor is to be disposed of to a marine salvage dealer or other facility as provided in section 1547.302 of the Revised Code, the sheriff or chief shall execute in triplicate an affidavit, as prescribed by the chief of the division of watercraft, describing the vessel or motor and the manner in which it was disposed of, and that all requirements of this section have been complied with. The sheriff or chief shall retain the original of the affidavit for his records and shall furnish two copies to the marine salvage dealer or other facility. Upon presentation of a copy of the affidavit by the marine salvage dealer or other facility, the clerk of courts shall issue to such owner a salvage certificate of title, free and clear of all liens and encumbrances.

Whenever the marine salvage dealer or other facility receives an affidavit for the disposal of a vessel or outboard motor as provided in this section, such owner shall not be required to obtain an Ohio certificate of title to the vessel or motor in his own name if the vessel or motor is dismantled or destroyed and both copies of the affidavit are delivered to the clerk of courts. Upon receipt of such an affidavit, the clerk of courts shall send one copy of it to the chief of the division of watercraft.

(1991 S 144, eff. 8–8–91; 1990 H 522)

1547.302 Disposition of unclaimed abandoned vessels or outboard motors

(A) Unclaimed vessels or outboard motors ordered into storage under division (B) of section 1547.30 or section 1547.301 of the Revised Code shall be disposed of at the order of the sheriff of the county, the chief of police of the municipal corporation, township, or township police district, or another chief of a law enforcement agency in any of the following ways:

(1) To a marine salvage dealer;

(2) To any other facility owned, operated, or under contract with the state or the county, municipal corporation, township, or other political subdivision;

(3) To a charitable organization, religious organization, or similar organization not used and operated for profit;

(4) By sale at public auction by the sheriff, the chief, or an auctioneer licensed under Chapter 4707. of the Revised Code, after giving notice of the auction by advertisement, published once a week for two consecutive weeks in a newspaper of general circulation in the county.

(B) Any moneys accruing from the disposition of an unclaimed vessel or motor that are in excess of the expenses resulting from the removal and storage of the vessel or motor shall be credited to the general revenue fund or to the general fund of the county, municipal corporation, township, or other political subdivision, as appropriate.

(C) As used in this section, "charitable organization" has the same meaning as in section 1716.01 of the Revised Code.

(1998 S 187, eff. 3–18–99; 1990 H 522, eff. 6–13–90)

1547.303 Disposition of abandoned junk vessels or outboard motors

(A) As used in this section and section 1547.304 of the Revised Code:

(1) "Abandoned junk vessel or outboard motor" means any vessel or outboard motor meeting all of the following requirements:

(a) It has been left on private property for at least seventy-two hours without the permission of the person having the right to the possession of the property; left in a sunken, beached, or drifting condition for any period of time; or left in a docked condition, on a public street or other property open to the public, or upon or within the right-of-way of any waterway, road, or highway, for forty-eight hours or longer without notification to the sheriff of the county, the chief of police of the municipal corporation, township, or township police district, or other chief of a law enforcement agency, having territorial jurisdiction with respect to the location of the vessel or motor, of the reasons for leaving the vessel or motor in any such place or condition;

(b) It is three years old, or older;

(c) It is extensively damaged, such damage including but not limited to any of the following: missing deck, hull, transom, gunwales, motor, or outdrive;

(d) It is apparently inoperable;

(e) It has a fair market value of two hundred dollars or less.

(2) "Law enforcement agency" means any organization or unit comprised of law enforcement officers, as defined in section 2901.01 of the Revised Code.

(B) The sheriff of a county, chief of police of a municipal corporation, township, or township police district, or other chief of a law enforcement agency, within the sheriff's or chief's respective territorial jurisdiction, or a state highway patrol trooper, upon notification to the sheriff or chief of such action, shall order any abandoned junk vessel or outboard motor to be photographed by a law enforcement officer. The officer shall record the make of vessel or motor, the hull identification number or serial number when available, and shall also detail the damage or missing equipment to substantiate the value of two hundred dollars or less. The sheriff or chief shall thereupon immediately dispose of the abandoned junk vessel or outboard motor to a marine salvage dealer or other facility owned, operated, or under contract to the state, the county, township, or municipal corporation for the destruction of such vessels or motors. The records and photographs relating to the abandoned junk vessel or outboard motor shall be retained by the law enforcement agency ordering the disposition of the vessel or motor for a period of at least two years. The law enforcement agency shall execute in quadruplicate an affidavit, as prescribed by the chief of the division of watercraft, describing the vessel or motor and the manner in which it was disposed of, and that all requirements of this section have been complied with, and shall sign and file the same with the clerk of courts of the county in which the vessel or motor was abandoned. The clerk of courts shall retain the original of the affidavit for the clerk's files, shall furnish one copy thereof to the chief of the division of watercraft, one copy to the marine salvage dealer or other facility handling the disposal of the vessel or motor, and one copy to the law enforcement agency ordering the disposal, who shall file such copy with the records and photographs relating to the disposal. Any moneys arising from the disposal of an abandoned junk vessel or outboard motor shall be credited to the general revenue fund, or to the general fund of the county, township, municipal corporation, or other political subdivision, as appropriate.

Notwithstanding section 1547.301 of the Revised Code, any vessel or outboard motor meeting the requirements of divisions (A)(1)(c) to (e) of this section which has remained unclaimed by the owner or lienholder for a period of ten days or longer following notification as provided in section 1547.301 of the Revised Code may be disposed of as provided in this section.

(1996 S 239, eff. 9–6–96; 1991 S 144, eff. 8–8–91; 1990 H 522)

1547.304 Leaving abandoned junk vessels or outboard motors without permission or notification

No person shall purposely leave an abandoned junk vessel or outboard motor on private property for more than seventy-two hours without the permission of the person having the right to the possession of the property; in a sunken, beached, or drifting condition for any period of time; or in a docked condition, on a public street or other property open to the public, or upon or within the right-of-way of any waterway, road, or highway, for forty-eight hours or longer without notification to the sheriff of the county, chief of police of the municipal corporation, township, or township police district, or other chief of a law enforcement agency, having territorial jurisdiction with respect to the location of the vessel or motor, of the reasons for leaving the vessel or motor in any such place or condition.

For purposes of this section, the fact that an abandoned junk vessel or outboard motor has been so left without permission or notification is prima-facie evidence of abandonment.

Nothing in sections 1547.30, 1547.301, and 1547.303 of the Revised Code invalidates the provisions of any ordinance of a municipal corporation regulating or prohibiting the abandonment of vessels or outboard motors on waterways, beaches, docks, streets, highways, public property, or private property within the boundaries of the municipal corporation.

(1990 H 522, eff. 6–13–90)

DIVISION OF WATERCRAFT; NUMBERING AND REGISTRATION

1547.51 Division of watercraft; duties

There is hereby created within the department of natural resources the division of watercraft. The division shall administer and enforce all laws relative to the identification, numbering, registration, titling, use, and operation of vessels operated on the waters in this state.

(1990 H 522, eff. 6–13–90; 1982 H 782; 1973 S 232; 1971 S 350; 1970 H 1002; 131 v H 317; 130 v H 289; 129 v 582)

1547.52 Chief of division of watercraft

(A) The division of watercraft shall be administered by the chief of the division of watercraft. The chief may adopt, amend, and rescind:

(1) Rules considered necessary by the chief to supplement the identification, operation, titling, use, registration, and numbering of watercraft or vessels as provided in this chapter and Chapter 1548. of the Revised Code;

(2) Rules governing the navigation of vessels on waters in this state, including, but not limited to, rules regarding steering and sailing, the conduct of vessels in sight of one another or in restricted visibility, lights and shapes of lights used on vessels, and sound and light signals. As the chief considers necessary, these navigational rules shall be consistent with and equivalent to the regulations and interpretive rulings governing inland waters adopted or issued under the "Inland Navigational Rules Act of 1980," 94 Stat. 3415, 33 U.S.C.A. 151, 1604, 1605, 1608, 2001 to 2008, and 2071 to 2073.

(3) Rules establishing fees and charges for all of the following:

(a) Boating skill development classes and other educational classes;

(b) Law enforcement services provided at special events when the services are in addition to normal enforcement duties;

(c) Inspections of vessels or motors conducted under this chapter or Chapter 1548. of the Revised Code.

All rules adopted by the chief under division (A) of this section shall be adopted in accordance with Chapter 119. of the Revised Code and are subject to the prior approval of the director of natural resources.

(B) The chief, with the approval of the director, may employ such clerical and technical help as the chief considers necessary.

(C) The chief may designate license agents with the approval of the director.

(D) The division is hereby designated as the agency to administer the Ohio boating safety program and allocated federal funds under, and the chief shall prepare and submit reports in such form as may be required by, the "Federal Boat Safety Act of 1971," 85 Stat. 222, 46 U.S.C.A. 1475(a)(6), as amended.

(E) The chief may sell any of the following:

(1) Items related to or that promote boating safety, including, but not limited to, pins, badges, books, bulletins, maps, publications, calendars, and other educational articles;

(2) Artifacts pertaining to boating;

(3) Confiscated or forfeited items;

(4) Surplus equipment.

(1998 S 187, eff. 3–18–99; 1990 H 522, eff. 6–13–90; 1973 S 232; 130 v H 573; 129 v 582)

1547.521 Duties of chief and state watercraft officers

(A) The law enforcement officers of the division of watercraft shall be known as "state watercraft officers." The chief of the division of watercraft and state watercraft officers:

(1) Shall develop and conduct educational programs in vessel safety, sanitation, and operation and in other related subjects that the chief considers appropriate or necessary;

(2) Shall enforce this chapter and Chapter 1548. of the Revised Code and rules adopted under them, and may enforce laws prohibiting the dumping of refuse, trash, or litter into the waters in this state and Chapters 2925. and 3719. of the Revised Code on all waters in the state;

(3) On any lands owned, controlled, maintained, or administered by the department of natural resources and on any waters in this state, shall have the authority specified under section 2935.03 of the Revised Code for peace officers of the department of natural resources to keep the peace, to enforce all laws and rules governing those lands and waters, and to make arrests for violation of those laws and rules, provided that the authority shall be exercised on lands or waters administered by another division of the department only pursuant to an agreement with the chief of that division or to a request for assistance by an enforcement officer of that division in an emergency. The jurisdiction of state watercraft officers shall be concurrent with that of the peace officers of the county, township, or municipal corporation in which the violation occurs.

(4) For the purpose of enforcing the laws and rules that they have the authority to enforce, may stop, board, and conduct a safety inspection of any vessel;

(5) May serve and execute any citation, summons, warrant, or other process issued with respect to any law that they have the authority to enforce.

(B) A state watercraft officer may render assistance to a state or local law enforcement officer at the request of that officer or may render assistance to a state or local law enforcement officer in the event of an emergency.

State watercraft officers serving outside the division of watercraft under this section or serving under the terms of a mutual aid compact authorized under section 1501.02 of the Revised Code shall be considered as performing services within their regular employment for the purposes of compensation, pension or indemnity fund rights, workers' compensation, and other rights or benefits to which they may be entitled as incidents of their regular employment.

State watercraft officers serving outside the division of watercraft under this section or under a mutual aid compact retain personal immunity from civil liability as specified in section 9.86 of the Revised Code and shall not be considered an employee of a political subdivision for purposes of Chapter 2744. of the Revised Code. A political subdivision that uses state watercraft officers under this section or under the terms of a mutual aid compact authorized under section 1501.02 of the Revised Code is not subject to civil liability under Chapter 2744. of the Revised Code as the result of any action or omission of any state watercraft officer acting under this section or under a mutual aid compact.

(1998 S 187, eff. 3–18–99; 1990 H 669, eff. 1–10–91; 1990 H 522; 1984 H 682; 1982 H 782; 1976 H 957; 1973 S 232)

1547.522 Officer's bond; uniform and badge

(A) Each state watercraft officer, upon his appointment and before entering upon his duties, shall execute a bond in a sum not less than one thousand dollars.

(B) The chief of the division of watercraft shall prescribe a uniform and badge, which shall be worn by each state watercraft officer while on duty, except as otherwise ordered by the chief.

(1973 S 232, eff. 8–15–73)

1547.523 Offenses affecting employment eligibility of state watercraft officer

(A) As used in this section, "felony" has the same meaning as in section 109.511 of the Revised Code.

(B)(1) The chief of the division of watercraft shall not appoint a person as a state watercraft officer on a permanent basis, on a temporary basis, for a probationary term, or on other than a permanent basis if the person previously has been convicted of or has pleaded guilty to a felony.

(2)(a) The chief of the division of watercraft shall terminate the employment of a state watercraft officer who does either of the following:

(i) Pleads guilty to a felony;

(ii) Pleads guilty to a misdemeanor pursuant to a negotiated plea agreement as provided in division (D) of section 2929.43 of the Revised Code in which the state watercraft officer agrees to surrender the certificate awarded to that officer under section 109.77 of the Revised Code.

(b) The chief shall suspend from employment a state watercraft officer who is convicted, after trial, of a felony. If the state watercraft officer files an appeal from that conviction and the conviction is upheld by the highest court to which the appeal is taken or if the state watercraft officer does not file a timely appeal, the chief shall terminate the employment of that state watercraft officer. If the state watercraft officer files an appeal that results in the state watercraft officer's acquittal of the felony or conviction of a misdemeanor, or in the dismissal of the felony charge against the state watercraft officer, the chief shall reinstate that state watercraft officer. A state watercraft officer who is reinstated under division (B)(2)(b) of this section shall not receive any back pay unless that state watercraft officer's conviction of the felony was reversed on appeal, or the felony charge was dismissed, because the court found insufficient evidence to convict the state watercraft officer of the felony.

(3) Division (B) of this section does not apply regarding an offense that was committed prior to January 1, 1997.

(4) The suspension from employment, or the termination of the employment, of a state watercraft officer under division (B)(2) of this section shall be in accordance with Chapter 119. of the Revised Code.

(2002 H 490, eff. 1–1–04; 1996 H 566, eff. 10–16–96)

GENERAL PROVISIONS

1547.63 Enforcement

Every sheriff, deputy sheriff, marshal, deputy marshal, member of the organized police department of any municipal corporation, police constable of any township, wildlife officer, park officer, preserve officer, conservancy district police officer, and other law enforcement officer, within the area of his authority, may enforce this chapter and rules adopted by the chief of the division of watercraft and, in the exercise thereof, may stop and board any vessel subject to this chapter and rules adopted under it.

(1994 S 182, eff. 10–20–94; 1990 H 522, eff. 6–13–90; 131 v H 296; 129 v 582)

1547.65 Permanently displayed hull identification number

(A) A watercraft constructed on or after November 1, 1972, shall have a hull identification number permanently displayed and affixed to it in accordance with federal law.

(B) A watercraft constructed before November 1, 1972, shall have a hull identification number assigned to it by the chief of the division of watercraft at the time of registration, at the time of application for title, after transfer of ownership, or at the time of a change to this state as the principal location of operation. The number shall be permanently displayed and affixed as prescribed by rules adopted under section 1547.52 of the Revised Code.

(C) A person who builds a watercraft or imports a watercraft from another country for personal use and not for the purpose of sale shall request a hull identification number from the chief and permanently display and affix the number as prescribed by rules adopted under section 1547.52 of the Revised Code.

(D) No person shall operate or permit to be operated any watercraft on the waters in this state in violation of this section.

(2002 S 150, eff. 7–5–02)

1547.69 Firearm restrictions and prohibitions; affirmative defenses; exemptions

(A) As used in this section:

(1) "Firearm" and "handgun" have the same meanings as in section 2923.11 of the Revised Code.

(2) "Unloaded" has the same meaning as in section 2923.16 of the Revised Code.

(B) No person shall knowingly discharge a firearm while in or on a vessel.

(C) No person shall knowingly transport or have a loaded firearm in a vessel in a manner that the firearm is accessible to the operator or any passenger.

(D) No person shall knowingly transport or have a firearm in a vessel unless it is unloaded and is carried in one of the following ways:

(1) In a closed package, box, or case;

(2) In plain sight with the action opened or the weapon stripped, or, if the firearm is of a type on which the action will not stay open or that cannot easily be stripped, in plain sight.

(E)(1) The affirmative defenses authorized in divisions (D)(1) and (2) of section 2923.12 of the Revised Code are affirmative defenses to a charge under division (C) or (D) of this section that involves a firearm other than a handgun. It is an affirmative defense to a charge under division (C) or (D) of this section of transporting or having a firearm of any type, including a handgun, in a vessel that the actor transported or had the firearm in the vessel for any lawful purpose and while the vessel was on the actor's own property, provided that this affirmative defense is not available unless the actor, prior to arriving at the vessel on the actor's own property, did not transport or possess the firearm in the vessel or in a motor vehicle in a manner prohibited by this section or division (B) or (C) of section 2923.16 of the Revised Code while the vessel was being operated on a waterway that was not on the actor's own property or while the motor vehicle was being operated on a street, highway, or other public or private property used by the public for vehicular traffic.

(2) No person who is charged with a violation of division (C) or (D) of this section shall be required to obtain a license or temporary emergency license to carry a concealed handgun under section 2923.125 or 2923.1213 of the Revised Code as a condition for the dismissal of the charge.

(F) Divisions (B), (C), and (D) of this section do not apply to the possession or discharge of a United States coast guard approved signaling device required to be carried aboard a vessel under section 1547.251 of the Revised Code when the signaling device is possessed or used for the purpose of giving a visual distress signal. No person shall knowingly transport or possess any signaling device of that nature in or on a vessel in a loaded condition at any time other than immediately prior to the discharge of the signaling device for the purpose of giving a visual distress signal.

(G) No person shall operate or permit to be operated any vessel on the waters in this state in violation of this section.

(H) This section does not apply to officers, agents, or employees of this or any other state or of the United States, or to law enforcement officers, when authorized to carry or have loaded or accessible firearms in a vessel and acting within the scope of their duties, and this section does not apply to persons legally engaged in hunting. Divisions (C) and (D) of this section do not apply to a person who transports or possesses a handgun in a vessel and who, at the time of that transportation or possession, is carrying a valid license or temporary emergency license to carry a concealed handgun issued to the person under section 2923.125 or 2923.1213 of the Revised Code or a license to carry a concealed handgun that was issued by another state with which the attorney general has entered into a reciprocity agreement under section 109.69 of the Revised Code, unless the person knowingly is in a place on the vessel described in division (B) of section 2923.126 of the Revised Code.

(I) If a law enforcement officer stops a vessel for a violation of this section or any other law enforcement purpose, if any person on the vessel surrenders a firearm to the officer, either voluntarily or pursuant to a request or demand of the officer, and if the officer does not charge the person with a violation of this section or arrest the person for any offense, the person is not otherwise prohibited by law from possessing the firearm, and the firearm is not contraband, the officer shall return the firearm to the person at the termination of the stop.

(2004 H 12, eff. 4–8–04; 1998 S 187, eff. 3–18–99; 1990 H 522, eff. 6–13–90)

1547.91 Wrecking

No person, with purpose to unlawfully damage, ground, or sink a vessel afloat, shall do any of the following:

(A) Employ any false signal, buoy, or other aid to navigation;

(B) Tamper with any signal, buoy, or other aid to navigation;

(C) Do any act which creates an imminent and substantial risk that any vessel afloat will be damaged, grounded, sunk, or scuttled.

(1990 H 522, eff. 6–13–90; 1972 H 511)

PROHIBITIONS AND PENALTIES

1547.92 Prohibitions

No person shall knowingly:

(A) Damage, remove, or tamper with any signal, buoy, or other aid to navigation;

(B) Sever the mooring lines of, set adrift, or tamper with any vessel that is moored or tied up on the waters in this state.

(1990 H 522, eff. 6–13–90; 1982 H 782)

1547.99 Penalties

(A) Whoever violates section 1547.91 of the Revised Code is guilty of a felony of the fourth degree.

(B) Whoever violates section 1547.10, division (I) of section 1547.111, section 1547.13, or section 1547.66 of the Revised Code is guilty of a misdemeanor of the first degree.

(C) Whoever violates a provision of this chapter or a rule adopted thereunder, for which no penalty is otherwise provided, is guilty of a minor misdemeanor.

(D) Whoever violates section 1547.07 or 1547.12 of the Revised Code without causing injury to persons or damage to property is guilty of a misdemeanor of the fourth degree.

(E) Whoever violates section 1547.07 or 1547.12 of the Revised Code causing injury to persons or damage to property is guilty of a misdemeanor of the third degree.

(F) Whoever violates division (M) of section 1547.54, division (G) of section 1547.30, or section 1547.131, 1547.25, 1547.33, 1547.38, 1547.39, 1547.40, 1547.65, 1547.69, or 1547.92 of the Revised Code or a rule adopted under division (A)(2) of section 1547.52 of the Revised Code is guilty of a misdemeanor of the fourth degree.

(G) Whoever violates section 1547.11 of the Revised Code is guilty of a misdemeanor of the first degree and shall be punished as provided in division (G)(1), (2), or (3) of this section.

(1) Except as otherwise provided in division (G)(2) or (3) of this section, the court shall sentence the offender to a jail term of three consecutive days and may sentence the offender pursuant to section 2929.24 of the Revised Code to a longer jail term. In addition, the court shall impose upon the offender a fine of not less than one hundred fifty nor more than one thousand dollars.

The court may suspend the execution of the mandatory jail term of three consecutive days that it is required to impose by division (G)(1) of this section if the court, in lieu of the suspended jail term, places the offender under a community control sanction pursuant to section 2929.25 of the Revised Code and requires the offender to attend, for three consecutive days, a drivers' intervention program that is certified pursuant to section 3793.10 of the Revised Code. The court also may suspend the execution of any part of the mandatory jail term of three consecutive days that it is required to impose by division (G)(1) of this section if the court places the offender under a community control sanction pursuant to section 2929.25 of the Revised Code for part of the three consecutive days; requires the offender to attend, for that part of the three consecutive days, a drivers' intervention program that is certified pursuant to section 3793.10 of the Revised Code; and sentences the offender to a jail term equal to the remainder of the three consecutive days that the offender does not spend attending the drivers' intervention program. The court may require the offender, as a condition of community control, to attend and satisfactorily complete any treatment or education programs, in addition to the required attendance at a drivers' intervention program, that the operators of the drivers' intervention program determine that the offender should attend and to report periodically to the court on the offender's progress in the programs. The court also may impose any other conditions of community control on the offender that it considers necessary.

(2) If, within six years of the offense, the offender has been convicted of or pleaded guilty to one violation of section 1547.11 of the Revised Code, of a municipal ordinance relating to operating a watercraft or manipulating any water skis, aquaplane, or similar device while under the influence of alcohol, a drug of abuse, or a combination of them, of a municipal ordinance relating to operating a watercraft or manipulating any water skis, aquaplane, or similar device with a prohibited concentration of alcohol in the whole blood, blood serum or plasma, breath, or urine, of division (A)(1) of section 2903.06 of the Revised Code, or of division (A)(2), (3), or (4) of section 2903.06 of the Revised Code or section 2903.06 or 2903.07 of the Revised Code as they existed prior to March 23, 2000, in a case in which the jury or judge found that the offender was under the influence of alcohol, a drug of abuse, or a combination of them, the court shall sentence the offender to a jail term of ten consecutive days and may sentence the offender pursuant to section 2929.24 of the Revised Code to a longer jail term. In addition, the court shall impose upon the offender a fine of not less than one hundred fifty nor more than one thousand dollars.

In addition to any other sentence that it imposes upon the offender, the court may require the offender to attend a drivers' intervention program that is certified pursuant to section 3793.10 of the Revised Code.

(3) If, within six years of the offense, the offender has been convicted of or pleaded guilty to more than one violation identified in division (G)(2) of this section, the court shall sentence the offender to a jail term of thirty consecutive days and may sentence the offender to a longer jail term of not more than one year. In addition, the court shall impose upon the offender a fine of not less than one hundred fifty nor more than one thousand dollars.

In addition to any other sentence that it imposes upon the offender, the court may require the offender to attend a drivers' intervention program that is certified pursuant to section 3793.10 of the Revised Code.

(4) Upon a showing that serving a jail term would seriously affect the ability of an offender sentenced pursuant to division (G)(1), (2), or (3) of this section to continue the offender's employment, the court may authorize that the offender be granted work release after the offender has served the mandatory jail term of three, ten, or thirty consecutive days that the court is required by division (G)(1), (2), or (3) of this section to impose. No court shall authorize work release during the mandatory jail term of three, ten, or thirty consecutive days that the court is required by division (G)(1), (2), or (3) of this section to impose. The duration of the work release shall not exceed the time necessary each day for the offender to commute to and from the place of employment and the place in which the jail term is served and the time actually spent under employment.

(5) Notwithstanding any section of the Revised Code that authorizes the suspension of the imposition or execution of a sentence or the placement of an offender in any treatment program in lieu of being imprisoned or serving a jail term, no court shall suspend the mandatory jail term of ten or thirty consecutive days required to be imposed by division (G)(2) or (3) of this section or place an offender who is sentenced pursuant to division (G)(2) or (3) of this section in any treatment program in lieu of being imprisoned or serving a jail term until after the offender has served the mandatory jail term of ten or thirty consecutive days required to be imposed pursuant to division (G)(2) or (3) of this section. Notwithstanding any section of the Revised Code that authorizes the suspension of the imposition or execution of a sentence or the placement of an offender in any treatment program in lieu of being imprisoned or serving a jail term, no court, except as specifically authorized by division (G)(1) of this section, shall suspend the mandatory jail term of three consecutive days required to be imposed by division (G)(1) of this section or place an offender who is sentenced pursuant to division (G)(1) of this section in any treatment program in lieu of imprisonment until after the offender has served the mandatory jail term of three consecutive days required to be imposed pursuant to division (G)(1) of this section.

(6) As used in division (G) of this section, "jail term" and "mandatory jail term" have the same meanings as in section 2929.01 of the Revised Code.

(H) Whoever violates section 1547.304 of the Revised Code is guilty of a misdemeanor of the fourth degree and also shall be assessed any costs incurred by the state or a county, township, municipal corporation, or other political subdivision in disposing of an abandoned junk vessel or outboard motor, less any money accruing to the state, county, township, municipal corporation, or other political subdivision from that disposal.

(I) Whoever violates division (B) or (C) of section 1547.49 of the Revised Code is guilty of a minor misdemeanor.

(J) Whoever violates section 1547.31 of the Revised Code is guilty of a misdemeanor of the fourth degree on a first offense. On each subsequent offense, the person is guilty of a misdemeanor of the third degree.

(K) Whoever violates section 1547.05 or 1547.051 of the Revised Code is guilty of a misdemeanor of the fourth degree if the violation is not related to a collision, injury to a person, or damage to property and a misdemeanor of the third degree if the violation is related to a collision, injury to a person, or damage to property.

(L) The sentencing court, in addition to the penalty provided under this section for a violation of this chapter or a rule adopted under it that involves a powercraft powered by more than ten horsepower and that, in the opinion of the court, involves a threat to the safety of persons or property, shall order the offender to complete successfully a boating course approved by the national association of state boating law administrators before the offender is allowed to operate a powercraft powered by more than ten horsepower on the waters in this state. Violation of a court order entered under this division is punishable as contempt under Chapter 2705. of the Revised Code.

(2002 H 490, eff. 1–1–04; 2002 S 123, eff. 1–1–04; 2002 S 150, eff. 7–5–02; 1999 S 107, eff. 3–23–00; 1998 H 502, eff. 1–1–00; 1996 S 295, eff. 3–18–97; 1995 S 2, eff. 7–1–96; 1990 H 522, eff. 6–13–90; 1989 H 317; 1986 H 428, H 265; 1984 H 682; 1982 H 782; 1977 H 1; 1972 S 397, H 511; 131 v H 296; 129 v 1388, 582; 128 v 1004)

Notes of Decisions

Ed. Note: *See notes of decisions and opinions at RC 4511.19 regarding construction of the terms "under the influence" and "intoxicating liquor."*

CHAPTER 1548

WATERCRAFT CERTIFICATES OF TITLE

Section

1548.01 Definitions; application of chapter

(A) As used in this chapter, "electronic" and "watercraft" have the same meanings as in section 1547.01 of the Revised Code.

(B) This chapter does not apply to any of the following:

(1) A watercraft covered by a marine document in effect that has been assigned to it by the United States government pursuant to federal law;

(2) A watercraft from a country other than the United States temporarily using the waters in this state;

(3) A watercraft whose owner is the United States, a state, or a political subdivision of a state;

(4) A ship's lifeboat. As used in division (B)(4) of this section, "lifeboat" means a watercraft that is held aboard another vessel and used exclusively for emergency purposes.

(5) A canoe;

(6) A watercraft less than fourteen feet in length without a permanently affixed mechanical means of propulsion;

(7) A watercraft less than fourteen feet in length with a permanently fixed mechanical means of propulsion of less than ten horsepower as determined by the manufacturer's rating;

(8) Outboard motors of less than ten horsepower as determined by the manufacturer's rating.

(C) The various certificates, applications, and assignments necessary to provide certificates of title for watercraft and outboard motors shall be made on appropriate forms approved by the chief of the division of watercraft.

(2001 S 59, eff. 10–31–01; 1999 H 163, § 19, eff. (see Uncodified Law below); 1998 S 187, eff. 3–18–99; 1996 S 295, eff. 3–18–97; 1994 S 182, eff. 10–20–94; 1990 H 522, eff. 6–13–90; 1982 H 782; 1971 S 350; 131 v H 317; 130 v H 289)

Uncodified Law

1999 H 163, § 19, eff. 3–31–99, reads:

During the period commencing on the effective date of this section and expiring January 1, 2000, the operation of sections 1548.01 and 1548.06 of the Revised Code, as amended by Am. Sub. S.B. 187 of the 122nd General Assembly, is suspended insofar as those sections subject watercraft less than fourteen feet in length to Chapter 1548. of the Revised Code, the Watercraft Certificates of Title Law. Upon the expiration of that period of suspension, sections 1548.01 and 1548.06 of the Revised Code, in either the present form of those sections or as they are amended or reenacted after the effective date of this section, again become fully operational.

This section is not subject to the referendum. Therefore, under Ohio Constitution, Article II, Section 1d and section 1.471 of the Revised Code, this section goes into immediate effect when this act becomes law.

1548.03 Certificate of title

No person, except as provided in section 1548.05 of the Revised Code, shall sell or otherwise dispose of a watercraft or outboard motor without delivering to the purchaser or transferee a physical certificate of title with an assignment on it as is necessary to show title in the purchaser or transferee; nor shall any person purchase or otherwise acquire a watercraft or outboard motor without obtaining a certificate of title for it in the person's name in accordance with this chapter; however, a purchaser may take possession of and operate a watercraft or outboard motor on the waters in this state without a certificate of title for a period not exceeding thirty days if the purchaser has been issued and has in the purchaser's possession a dealer's dated bill of sale or, in the case of a casual sale, a notarized bill of sale.

(2001 S 59, eff. 10–31–01; 1990 H 522, eff. 6–13–90; 1982 H 782; 1979 S 65; 1978 S 387; 1973 S 251; 130 v H 289)

1548.04 Evidence of ownership

No person acquiring a watercraft or outboard motor from the owner thereof, whether such owner is a manufacturer, importer, dealer, or otherwise, shall acquire any right, title, claim, or interest in or to such watercraft or outboard motor until such person has had issued to him a certificate of title to such watercraft or outboard motor, or delivered to him a manufacturer's or importer's certificate for it. Nor shall any waiver or estoppel operate in favor of such person against a person having possession of such certificate of title, or manufacturer's or importer's certificate for such watercraft or outboard motor, for a valuable consideration.

No court in any case at law or in equity shall recognize the right, title, claim, or interest of any person in or to any watercraft or outboard motor sold or disposed of, or mortgaged or encumbered, unless evidenced:

(A) By a certificate of title or a manufacturer's or importer's certificate issued in accordance with Chapter 1548. of the Revised Code;

(B) By admission in the pleadings or stipulation of the parties.

(1979 S 65, eff. 1–1–80; 1978 S 387; 1973 S 251; 130 v H 289)

1548.17 Reports and records of watercraft thefts

Every peace officer, sheriff, watercraft officer, division of parks and recreation officer, division of wildlife officer, conservancy district officer, constable, or state highway patrol trooper, having knowledge of a stolen watercraft or outboard motor, shall immediately furnish the chief of the division of watercraft with full information concerning the theft.

The chief, whenever a report of the theft or conversion of a watercraft or outboard motor is received, shall make a distinctive record of it, including the make of the stolen watercraft or outboard motor and its manufacturer's or assigned serial number, and shall file the record in the numerical order of the manufacturer's or assigned serial number with the index records of the watercraft or outboard motors of such make. The chief shall prepare a report listing watercraft and outboard motors stolen and recovered as disclosed by the reports submitted to the chief, to be distributed as the chief deems advisable.

If, under section 1548.02 of the Revised Code, the chief learns of the issuance of a certificate of title to such a watercraft or outboard motor, the chief shall immediately notify the rightful owner of the watercraft or outboard motor and the clerk who issued the certificate of title, and if, upon investigation, it appears that the certificate of title was improperly issued, the chief shall immediately cancel it.

In the event of the recovery of a stolen or converted watercraft or outboard motor, the owner shall immediately notify the chief, who shall remove the record of the theft or conversion from the chief's file.

(2001 S 59, eff. 10–31–01; 1991 S 144, eff. 8–8–91; 1973 S 232; 1971 S 350; 1969 H 1; 131 v H 317; 130 v H 289)

1548.18 Prohibitions

No person shall do any of the following:

(A) Operate in this state a watercraft for which a certificate of title is required or a watercraft powered by an outboard motor for which a certificate of title is required without having the certificate, or a valid temporary permit and number, in accordance with this chapter or, if a physical certificate of title has not been issued for it, operate the watercraft or outboard motor in this state knowing that the ownership information relating to the watercraft or outboard motor has not been entered into the automated title processing system by a clerk of a court of common pleas;

(B) Operate in this state a watercraft for which a certificate of title is required or a watercraft powered by an outboard motor for which a certificate of title is required upon which the certificate of title has been canceled;

(C) Fail to surrender any certificate of title upon cancellation of it by the chief of the division of watercraft and notice of the cancellation as prescribed in this chapter;

(D) Fail to surrender the certificate of title to a clerk of a court of common pleas as provided in this chapter, in case of the destruction or dismantling or change of a watercraft or outboard motor in such respect that it is not the watercraft or outboard motor described in the certificate of title;

(E) Violate any provision of this chapter for which no penalty is otherwise provided, or any lawful rules adopted pursuant to this chapter;

(F) Operate in this state a watercraft or outboard motor knowing that the certificate of title to or ownership of the watercraft or outboard motor as otherwise reflected in the automated title processing system has been canceled.

(2001 S 59, eff. 10–31–01; 1973 S 251, eff. 1–1–74; 1971 S 350; 131 v H 317; 130 v H 289)

1548.19 Altered or false certificate; false information; sale without certificate

No person shall do any of the following:

(A) Procure or attempt to procure a certificate of title to a watercraft or outboard motor, or pass or attempt to pass a certificate of title or any assignment of a certificate of title to a watercraft or outboard motor, or in any other manner gain or attempt to gain ownership of a watercraft or outboard motor, knowing or having reason to believe that the watercraft or outboard motor has been stolen;

(B) Sell or offer for sale in this state a watercraft or outboard motor on which the manufacturer's or assigned serial number has been destroyed, removed, covered, altered, or defaced with knowledge of the destruction, removal, covering, alteration, or defacement of the manufacturer's or assigned serial number;

(C) Sell or transfer a watercraft or outboard motor without delivering to the purchaser or transferee of it a certificate of title, or a manufacturer's or importer's certificate to it, assigned to the purchaser as provided for in this chapter, except as otherwise provided in this chapter.

(2001 S 59, eff. 10–31–01; 1979 S 65, eff. 1–1–80; 1978 S 387; 1973 S 251; 1972 H 511; 130 v H 289)

1548.99 Penalties

(A) Whoever violates section 1548.18 of the Revised Code is guilty of a misdemeanor of the fourth degree.

(B) Whoever violates section 1548.19 of the Revised Code is guilty of a felony of the fifth degree.

(1995 S 2, eff. 7–1–96; 1990 H 522, eff. 6–13–90; 130 v H 289)

CHAPTER 1702

NONPROFIT CORPORATION LAW

1702.80 Qualified nonprofit corporation police departments

(A) As used in this section:

(1) "Qualified nonprofit corporation" means a nonprofit corporation that is established under this chapter and to which all of the following apply:

(a) The nonprofit corporation is a tax-exempt charitable organization;

(b) The nonprofit corporation has other organizations as members, and at least twenty of its members are tax-exempt charitable organizations;

(c) The nonprofit corporation, together with its members that are organizations, owns, leases, occupies, or uses an area of not less than three hundred acres within which its police department established under division (B) of this section will provide police services;

(d) The chief of police of each municipal corporation within which the police department of the nonprofit corporation will be eligible to provide police services has given approval for persons who are appointed as police officers of that department to carry out their powers and duties as police officers.

(2) "Authorizing agreement" means the written agreement entered into between a qualified nonprofit corporation and a municipal corporation pursuant to division (B) of this section for the provision of police services within the municipal corporation by the police department of the nonprofit corporation established under division (B) of this section.

(3) "Tax exempt" means that a corporation or organization is exempt from federal income taxation under subsection 501(a) and is described in subsection 501(c)(3) of the Internal Revenue Code, and that the corporation or organization has received from the internal revenue service a determination letter that currently is in effect stating that the corporation or organization is exempt from federal income taxation under that subsection and is described in that subsection.

(4) "Internal Revenue Code" means the "Internal Revenue Code of 1986," 100 Stat. 2085, 26 U.S.C.A. 1, as amended.

(5) "Felony" has the same meaning as in section 109.511 of the Revised Code.

(B) A qualified nonprofit corporation may establish a police department to provide police services, subject to the requirements and limitations set forth in this division and divisions (C) and (D) of this section, within one or more municipal corporations. Subject to division (E) of this section, the board of trustees of a qualified nonprofit corporation that establishes a police department may appoint persons as police officers of the department, and the corporation may employ the persons so appointed as police officers.

A person so appointed and employed as a police officer is authorized to act as a police officer only to the extent and in the manner described in this section and only when directly engaged in the discharge of that person's duties as a police officer for the qualified nonprofit corporation. No person so appointed and employed as a police officer shall engage in any duties or activities as a police officer for a police department established by a qualified nonprofit corporation unless both of the following apply:

(1) The person successfully has completed a training program approved by the Ohio peace officer training commission and has been certified by the commission as having successfully completed the training program, or the person previously has successfully completed a police officer basic training program certified by the commission and has been awarded a certificate to that effect by the commission.

(2) The qualified nonprofit corporation has entered into a written authorizing agreement, as described in division (C) of this section, with the chief of police of each municipal corporation within which the police department of the qualified nonprofit corporation will provide police services.

(C) An authorizing agreement entered into between a qualified nonprofit corporation and a chief of police of a municipal corporation shall apply only to the agreeing municipal corporation, and a separate authorizing agreement shall be entered into for each municipal corporation within which the police department of the qualified nonprofit corporation will provide police services. An authorizing agreement shall not require, or contain any provision granting authority to, the chief of police or any other officer, official, or employee of the municipal corporation that enters into the agreement, to appoint or to approve or disapprove the appointment of any police officer appointed and employed by the qualified nonprofit corporation police department under division (B) of this section. An authorizing agreement shall comply with any statutes and with any municipal charter provisions, ordinances, or resolutions that may apply to it. An authorizing agreement may prescribe, but is not limited to, any of the following:

(1) The geographical territory within the municipal corporation in which the police department established by the qualified nonprofit corporation under division (B) of this section may provide police services;

(2) The standards and criteria to govern the interaction between the police officers employed by the police department established by the qualified nonprofit corporation under division (B) of this section and the law enforcement officers employed by the municipal corporation, which standards and criteria may include, but are not limited to, either of the following:

(a) Provisions governing the reporting of offenses discovered by the police officers employed by the qualified nonprofit corporation police department to the police department of the municipal corporation;

(b) Provisions governing the processing and confinement of persons arrested by police officers of the qualified nonprofit corporation police department.

(3) Any limitation on the qualified nonprofit corporation police department's enforcement of municipal traffic ordinances and regulations;

(4) The duration, if any, of the agreement.

(D) If a qualified nonprofit corporation establishes a police department under this section, the qualified nonprofit corporation, within the geographical territory specified for each municipal corporation that has entered into an authorizing agreement with it, concurrently with the municipal corporation, shall preserve the peace, protect persons and property, enforce the laws of the state, and enforce the charter provisions, ordinances, and regulations of the political subdivisions of the state that apply within that territory. Except as limited by the terms of any applicable authorizing agreement, each police officer who is employed by a police department established by a qualified nonprofit corporation and who satisfies the requirement set forth in division (B)(1) of this section is vested, while directly in the discharge of that police officer's duties as a police officer, with the same powers and authority as are vested in a police officer of a municipal corporation under Title XXIX of the Revised Code and the Rules of Criminal Procedure, and with the same powers and authority, including the operation of a public safety vehicle, as are vested in a police officer of a municipal corporation under Chapter 4511. of the Revised Code.

(E)(1) The board of trustees of a qualified nonprofit corporation that establishes a police department shall not appoint a person as a police officer of the department pursuant to division (B) of this section on a permanent basis, on a temporary basis, for a probationary term, or on other than a permanent basis if the person previously has been convicted of or has pleaded guilty to a felony.

(2)(a) The board of trustees of a qualified nonprofit corporation shall terminate the employment of a police officer of its police department appointed under division (B) of this section if the police officer does either of the following:

(i) Pleads guilty to a felony;

(ii) Pleads guilty to a misdemeanor pursuant to a negotiated plea agreement as provided in division (D) of section 2929.43 of the Revised Code in which the police officer agrees to surrender the certificate awarded to the police officer under section 109.77 of the Revised Code.

(b) The board of trustees of a qualified nonprofit corporation shall suspend from employment a police officer of its police department appointed under division (B) of this section if the police officer is convicted, after trial, of a felony. If the police officer files an appeal from that conviction and the conviction is upheld by the highest court to which the appeal is taken or if the police officer does not file a timely appeal, the board shall terminate the employment of that police officer. If the police officer files an appeal that results in the police officer's acquittal of the felony or conviction of a misdemeanor, or in the dismissal of the felony charge against the police officer, the board shall reinstate that police officer. A police officer who is reinstated under division (E)(2)(b) of this section shall not receive any back pay unless that police officer's conviction of the felony was reversed on appeal, or the felony charge was dismissed, because the court found insufficient evidence to convict the police officer of the felony.

(3) Division (E) of this section does not apply regarding an offense that was committed prior to January 1, 1997.

(4) The suspension from employment, or the termination of the employment, of a police officer under division (E)(2) of this section shall be in accordance with Chapter 119. of the Revised Code.

(2002 H 490, eff. 1–1–04; 1996 H 670, eff. 12–2–96; 1996 H 566, eff. 10–16–96; 1990 H 110, eff. 5–31–90)

CHAPTER 1711

AGRICULTURAL CORPORATIONS; SPECIAL CONSTABLES

1711.35 Special constables

On the application of a state, county, township, or independent agricultural society, of an industrial association, or of any other association or meeting of citizens for the purpose of promoting social or literary intercourse, a judge of a county court or judge of a municipal court having jurisdiction may appoint a suitable number of special constables to assist in keeping the peace during the time when such society or assembly is holding its annual fair or meeting. He shall make an entry in his docket of the number and names of all persons so appointed.

Constables so appointed have all the power of constables to suppress riots, disturbances, and breaches of the peace. Upon view they may arrest any person guilty of a violation of any law of the state, and pursue and arrest any person fleeing from justice in any part of the state. They may apprehend any person in the act of committing an offense; on reasonable information, supported by affidavit, they may procure process for the arrest of any person charged with a breach of the peace and forthwith bring him before a competent authority; and they may enforce all laws for the preservation of order.

(129 v 582, eff. 1–10–61; 127 v 1039; 1953 H 1; GC 9912, 9913)

CHAPTER 1713

EDUCATIONAL CORPORATIONS—CAMPUS POLICE DEPARTMENTS

CAMPUS POLICE DEPARTMENTS

CAMPUS POLICE DEPARTMENTS

1713.50 Campus police departments

(A) As used in this section:

(1) "Political subdivision" means a county, municipal corporation, or township.

(2) "Private college or university" means a college or university that has all of the following characteristics:

(a) It is not owned or controlled by the state or any political subdivision of the state.

(b) It provides a program of education in residence leading to a baccalaureate degree or provides a program of education in residence, for which the baccalaureate degree is a prerequisite, leading to an academic or professional degree.

(c) It is accredited by the north central association or another nationally recognized agency that accredits colleges and universities.

(3) "Felony" has the same meaning as in section 109.511 of the Revised Code.

(B) The board of trustees of a private college or university may establish a campus police department and appoint members of the campus police department to act as police officers. The board shall assign duties to the members of a campus police department that shall include the enforcement of the regulations of the college or university. Subject to division (E) of this section, the board shall appoint as members of a campus police department only those persons who have successfully completed a training program approved by the Ohio peace officer training commission and have been certified as having done so or who have previously successfully completed a police officer basic training program certified by the commission and have been awarded a certificate to that effect by the commission.

Members of a campus police department shall not be reimbursed with state funds for any training they receive or be eligible to participate in any state or municipal retirement system. The uniforms, vehicles, and badges of members of a campus police department shall be distinct from those of the law enforcement agencies of the political subdivisions in which the private college or university that established the campus police department is located.

(C) Each member of a campus police department appointed under division (B) of this section is vested, while directly in the discharge of that member's duties as a police officer, with the same powers and authority that are vested in a police officer of a municipal corporation or a county sheriff under Title XXIX of the Revised Code and the Rules of Criminal Procedure, including the same powers and authority relating to the operation of a public safety vehicle that are vested in a police officer of a municipal corporation or a county sheriff under Chapter 4511. of the Revised Code. Except as otherwise provided in this division, members of a campus police department may exercise, concurrently with the law enforcement officers of the political subdivisions in which the private college or university is located, the powers and authority granted to them under this division in order to preserve the peace, protect persons and property, enforce the laws of this state, and enforce the ordinances and regulations of the political subdivisions in which the private college or university is located, but only on the property of the private college or university that employs them. The board of trustees of a private college or university may enter into an agreement with any political subdivision pursuant to which the members of the campus police department of the college or university may exercise within that political subdivision, but outside the property of the college or university, the powers and authority granted to them under this division. A member of a campus police department has no authority to serve civil process.

(D) Except as otherwise provided in this division, the board of trustees of a private college or university shall provide to each member of a campus police department appointed under division (B) of this section, without cost to the member, liability insurance coverage that insures the member against any liability that may arise out of or in the course of the member's employment and that is in an amount of not less than two hundred fifty thousand dollars. A board of trustees may provide the liability coverage required by this division by self-insurance.

(E)(1) The board of trustees of a private college or university that establishes a campus police department shall not appoint a person as a member of the campus police department pursuant to division (B) of this section on a permanent basis, on a temporary basis, for a probationary term, or on other than a permanent basis if the person previously has been convicted of or has pleaded guilty to a felony.

(2)(a) The board of trustees of a private college or university shall terminate the employment of a member of its campus police department appointed under division (B) of this section if the member does either of the following:

(i) Pleads guilty to a felony;

(ii) Pleads guilty to a misdemeanor pursuant to a negotiated plea agreement as provided in division (D) of section 2929.43 of the Revised Code in which the member agrees to surrender the certificate awarded to that member under section 109.77 of the Revised Code.

(b) The board of trustees of a private college or university shall suspend from employment a member of its campus police department appointed under division (B) of this section if the member is convicted, after trial, of a felony. If the member of the campus police department files an appeal from that conviction and the conviction is upheld by the highest court to which the appeal is taken or if the member does not file a timely appeal, the board shall terminate the employment of that member. If the member of the campus police department files an appeal that results in that member's acquittal of the felony or conviction of a misdemeanor, or in the dismissal of the felony charge against that member, the board shall reinstate that member. A member of a campus police department who is reinstated under division (E)(2)(b) of this section shall not receive any back pay unless that member's conviction of the felony was reversed on appeal, or the felony charge was dismissed, because the court found insufficient evidence to convict the member of the felony.

(3) Division (E) of this section does not apply regarding an offense that was committed prior to January 1, 1997.

(4) The suspension from employment, or the termination of the employment, of a member of a campus police department under division (E)(2) of this section shall be in accordance with Chapter 119. of the Revised Code.

(2002 H 490, eff. 1–1–04; 1996 H 670, eff. 12–2–96; 1996 H 566, eff. 10–16–96; 1992 H 758, eff. 1–15–93)

CHAPTER 1717

HUMANE SOCIETIES; POLICE POWERS

1717.08 Police powers of officers, agents, and members

An officer, agent, or member of the Ohio humane society or of a county humane society may interfere to prevent the perpetration of any act of cruelty to animals in his presence, may use such force as is necessary to prevent it, and to that end may summon to his aid any bystanders.

(1953 H 1, eff. 10–1–53; GC 10073)

1717.09 Member may require police to act

A member of the Ohio humane society or of a county humane society may require the sheriff of any county, the constable of any township, the marshal or a policeman of any municipal corporation, or any agent of such a society, to arrest any person found violating the laws in relation to cruelty to persons or animals, and to take possession of any animal cruelly treated in their respective counties or municipal corporations, and deliver such animal to the proper officers of the society.

(1953 H 1, eff. 10–1–53; GC 10075)

CHAPTER 1721

CEMETERY ASSOCIATIONS; POLICE OFFICERS

1721.14 Cemetery policemen

The trustees, directors, or other officers of a cemetery company or association, whether it is incorporated or unincorporated, and a board of township trustees having charge of township cemeteries, may appoint day and night watchmen for their grounds. All such watchmen, and all superintendents, gardeners, and agents of such company or association or of such board, who are stationed on the cemetery grounds may take and subscribe, before any judge of a county court or judge of a municipal court having jurisdiction in the township where the grounds are situated, an oath of office similar to the oath required by law of constables. Upon taking such oath, such watchmen, superintendents, gardeners, or agents shall have, within and adjacent to the cemetery grounds, all the powers of police officers.

(129 v 582, eff. 1–10–61; 1953 H 1; GC 10108)

CHAPTER 1901

MUNICIPAL COURT

Publisher's Note: Until 1968, when the Modern Courts Amendment to the Ohio Constitution was adopted, Ohio court procedure was governed entirely by statute and case law. The Modern Courts Amendment required the Supreme Court of Ohio, subject to the approval of the General Assembly, to "prescribe rules governing practice and procedure in all courts of the state." Rules of practice and procedure are the Civil, Criminal, Appellate, and Juvenile Rules, Rules of the Court of Claims, and the Ohio Rules of Evidence. Pursuant to Ohio Constitution Article IV, Section 5(B), such rules "shall not abridge, enlarge, or modify any substantive right," and " [a]ll laws in conflict with such rules shall be of no further force or effect." Provisions of Chapter 1901 should be read with this in mind.

SUBJECT MATTER JURISDICTION; MONETARY LIMITS; CRIMINAL JURISDICTION

1901.183 Additional jurisdiction of environmental division

In addition to jurisdiction otherwise granted in this chapter, the environmental division of a municipal court shall have jurisdiction within its territory in all of the following actions or proceedings and to perform all of the following functions:

(A) Notwithstanding any monetary limitations in section 1901.17 of the Revised Code, in all actions and proceedings for the sale of real or personal property under lien of a judgment of the environmental division of the municipal court, or a lien for machinery, material, fuel furnished, or labor performed, irrespective of amount, and, in those cases, the environmental division may proceed to foreclose and marshal all liens and all vested or contingent rights, to appoint a receiver, and to render personal judgment irrespective of amount in favor of any party;

(B) When in aid of execution of a judgment of the environmental division of the municipal court, in all actions for the foreclosure of a mortgage on real property given to secure the payment of money, or the enforcement of a specific lien for money or other encumbrance or charge on real property, when the real property is situated within the territory, and, in those cases, the environmental division may proceed to foreclose all liens and all vested and contingent rights and proceed to render judgments, and make findings and orders, between the parties, in the same manner and to the same extent as in similar cases in the court of common pleas;

(C) When in aid of execution of a judgment of the environmental division of the municipal court, in all actions for the recovery of real property situated within the territory to the same extent as courts of common pleas have jurisdiction;

(D) In all actions for injunction to prevent or terminate violations of the ordinances and regulations of any municipal corporation within its territory enacted or promulgated under the police power of that municipal corporation pursuant to Section 3 of Article XVIII, Ohio Constitution, over which the court of common pleas has or may have jurisdiction, and, in those cases, the environmental division of the municipal court may proceed to render judgments, and make findings and orders, in the same manner and to the same extent as in similar cases in the court of common pleas;

(E) In all actions for injunction to prevent or terminate violations of the resolutions and regulations of any political subdivision within its territory enacted or promulgated under the power of that political subdivision pursuant to Article X of the Ohio Constitution, over which the court of common pleas has or may have jurisdiction, and, in those cases, the environmental division of the municipal court may proceed to render judgments, and make findings and orders, in the same manner and to the same extent as in similar cases in the court of common pleas;

(F) In any civil action to enforce any provision of Chapter 3704., 3714., 3734., 3737., 3767., or 6111. of the Revised Code over which the court of common pleas has or may have jurisdiction, and, in those actions, the environmental division of the municipal court may proceed to render judgments, and make findings and orders, in the same manner and to the same extent as in similar actions in the court of common pleas;

(G) In all actions and proceedings in the nature of creditors' bills, and in aid of execution to subject the interests of a judgment debtor in real or personal property to the payment of a judgment of the division, and, in those actions and proceedings, the environmental division may proceed to marshal and foreclose all liens on the property irrespective of the amount of the lien, and all vested or contingent rights in the property;

(H) Concurrent jurisdiction with the court of common pleas of all criminal actions or proceedings related to the pollution of the air, ground, or water within the territory of the environmental division of the municipal court, for which a sentence of death cannot be imposed under Chapter 2903. of the Revised Code;

(I) In any review or appeal of any final order of any administrative officer, agency, board, department, tribunal, commission, or other instrumentality that relates to a local building, housing, air pollution, sanitation, health, fire, zoning, or safety code, ordinance, or regulation, in the same manner and to the same extent as in similar appeals in the court of common pleas.

(1999 S 89, eff. 8–3–99; 1998 S 83, eff. 3 30 99)

1901.184 Jurisdiction over campsite use

In addition to jurisdiction otherwise granted by this chapter, a municipal court shall have jurisdiction in actions filed under section 3729.13 of the Revised Code.

(2004 H 368, eff. 10–13–04; 2002 H 520, eff. 4–3–03)

1901.20 Criminal jurisdiction; appeals from noncriminal traffic violations

(A)(1) The municipal court has jurisdiction of the violation of any ordinance of any municipal corporation within its territory, unless the violation is required to be handled by a parking violations bureau or joint parking violations bureau pursuant to Chapter 4521. of the Revised Code, and of the violation of any misdemeanor committed within the limits of its territory. The municipal court has jurisdiction of the violation of a vehicle parking or standing resolution or regulation if a local authority, as defined in division (D) of section 4521.01 of the Revised Code, has specified that it is not to be considered a criminal offense, if the violation is committed within the limits of the court's territory, and if the violation is not required to be handled by a parking violations bureau or joint parking violations bureau pursuant to Chapter 4521. of the Revised Code. The municipal court, if it has a housing or environmental division, has jurisdiction of any criminal action over which the housing or environmental division is given jurisdiction by section 1901.181 of the Revised Code, provided that, except as specified in division (B) of that section, no judge of the court other than the judge of the division shall hear or determine any action over which the division has jurisdiction. In all such prosecutions and cases, the court shall proceed to a final determination of the prosecution or case.

(2) A judge of a municipal court does not have the authority to dismiss a criminal complaint, charge, information, or indictment solely at the request of the complaining witness and over the objection of the prosecuting attorney, village solicitor, city director of law, or other chief legal officer who is responsible for the prosecution of the case.

(B) The municipal court has jurisdiction to hear felony cases committed within its territory. In all felony cases, the court may conduct preliminary hearings and other necessary hearings prior to the indictment of the defendant or prior to the court's finding that there is probable and reasonable cause to hold or recognize the defendant to appear before a court of common pleas and may discharge, recognize, or commit the defendant.

(C) A municipal court has jurisdiction of an appeal from a judgment or default judgment entered pursuant to Chapter 4521. of the Revised Code, as authorized by division (D) of section 4521.08 of the Revised Code. The appeal shall be placed on the regular docket of the court and shall be determined by a judge of the court.

(2001 S 108, § 6, eff. 7–6–01; 2001 S 108, § 2.02, eff. 7–6–01; 1997 S 98, eff. 3–17–98; 1996 H 350, § 13, eff. 7–1–97, § 1, eff. 1–27–97 [1]*; 1996 H 438, eff. 7–1–97; 1992 S 105, eff. 3–24–92; 1986 H 159; 1982 H 707; 128 v 823; 1953 H 1; GC 1598)*

[1] See Notes of Decisions and Opinions, *State ex rel. Ohio Academy of Trial Lawyers v. Sheward* (Ohio 1999), 86 Ohio St.3d 451, 715 N.E.2d 1062.

Notes of Decisions

6. Constitutional issues

1996 H 350, which amended more than 100 statutes and a variety of rules relating to tort and other civil actions, and which was an attempt to reenact provisions of law previously held unconstitutional by the Supreme Court of Ohio, is an act of usurpation of judicial power in violation of the doctrine of separation of powers; for that reason, and because of violation of the one-subject rule of the Ohio Constitution, 1996 H 350 is unconstitutional. State ex rel. Ohio Academy of Trial Lawyers v. Sheward (Ohio, 08-16-1999) 86 Ohio St.3d 451, 715 N.E.2d 1062, 1999-Ohio-123, reconsideration denied 87 Ohio St.3d 1409, 716 N.E.2d 1170.

PRACTICE AND PROCEDURE

1901.21 Criminal and civil procedure; bonds; costs

(A) In a criminal case or proceeding, the practice, procedure, and mode of bringing and conducting prosecutions for offenses shall be as provided in the Criminal Rules, and the power of the court in relation to the prosecution is the same as the power that is conferred upon county courts.

In any civil case or proceeding for which no special provision is made in this chapter, the practice and procedure in the case or proceeding shall be the same as in courts of common pleas. If no practice or procedure for the case or proceeding is provided for in the courts of common pleas, then the practice or procedure of county courts shall apply.

(B) In the Cleveland municipal court, all bonds for the appearance of a defendant charged with an offense, when the offense is bailable, shall be entered into before the clerk of the municipal court and approved by him; and the surety in them shall be qualified by the clerk.

One surety in every such bond shall be a resident within the jurisdiction of the court; the sureties shall own property worth double the sum to be secured and shall have real estate within Cuyahoga county liable to execution of a value equal to the sum to be secured; and when two or more sureties are offered to the same bond, they shall have in the aggregate the qualification prescribed. The bond shall require the defendant to appear before the court to answer the charge against him, or before the court of common pleas when the defendant is held to the grand jury.

The bond shall clearly disclose the full name of each surety, together with the residence address, and there shall be indorsed on it a brief, but pertinent, description of the real estate owned by each surety.

When the bond is entered into, approved, and accepted, it becomes a subsisting lien on the real estate of the surety in it, upon which he has qualified, until the bond has been exonerated or discharged.

A copy of every such bond, certified under the seal of the court by the clerk as a true copy, shall be filed by him with the county recorder of Cuyahoga county forthwith unless in the meantime the defendant has been acquitted or discharged by the court. The recorder shall provide a suitable record book, properly indexed, in which he shall record all bonds certified to him. The recorder shall be entitled to receive from the clerk, such fees and record charges as are now authorized by law for recording deeds and mortgages; and such fees and charges shall be taxed by the clerk in the costs of the respective cases, and shall be paid to the recorder by the clerk from funds in his hands upon certified vouchers or bills rendered by the recorder.

The clerk shall transmit to the recorder each day a certified list, under the seal of the court, of all bonds which have been exonerated or discharged, and the recorder shall note on the margin of the record of each bond the discharge or satisfaction of it, and the lien on the real estate of the surety in such bond shall thereby be canceled and discharged.

The clerk shall not approve or accept as surety, on any such bond, any person who is then liable on any bond previously executed in the municipal court, unless it appears to the satisfaction of the clerk that the person offering himself as surety has sufficient equity in his real estate over and above his liability on the prior bonds, to justify the subsequent bond, or unless the prior bonds have been exonerated and discharged.

The clerk may tax in the costs of the case, such fees for making the copies and certificates required in this section as the court by rule provides.

In all misdemeanor cases, the clerk, in lieu of the sureties required by this section, may accept a deposit of money, in United States legal tender, in an amount equal to the penal sum stipulated in the bond, and in any felony case a judge of the municipal court may direct the clerk to accept such a deposit in an amount fixed by the judge, which amount shall be the sum stipulated in the bond, and such deposit shall be retained by the clerk as security on it until the bond has been exonerated and discharged. If any such bond is forfeited, the clerk shall apply the money so deposited in satisfaction of any judgment that may be rendered on the bond, and the depositor of such fund shall surrender and forfeit all right in and to the deposit to the extent of such judgment.

(1988 H 708, eff. 4–19–88; 1986 H 159, H 412; 1975 H 205; 1973 H 1; 129 v 423; 128 v 823; 125 v 903; 1953 H 1; GC 1599)

1901.23 Issuance of writs and process

Writs and process in a municipal court shall be served, returned, and publication made in the manner provided for service, return, and publication of summons, writs, and process in the court of common pleas.

In any civil action or proceeding in which the subject matter of the action or proceeding is located within the territory or a defendant resides or is served with summons within the territory, the court may issue summons, orders of interpleader, all other writs, and mesne and final process, including executions necessary or proper for the complete adjudication of the issues and determination of the action, to the bailiff for service in the county or counties in which the court is situated and to the sheriff of any other county against one or more of the remaining defendants.

All warrants, executions, subpoenas, writs, and processes in all criminal and quasi-criminal cases may be issued to the bailiff of the court, a police officer of the appropriate municipal corporation, or to the sheriff of the appropriate county.

In any civil action in which the bailiff is a party or is interested, writs and process shall be directed to the sheriff. If both of these officers are interested, the writs and process shall be directed to and executed by a person appointed by the court or a judge of the court, and that person has the same power to execute the writs and process that the bailiff has. The return of the appointee shall be verified by affidavit, and he is entitled to the fees allowed to the bailiff for similar service.

(1986 H 159, eff. 3–19–87; 128 v 823; 1953 H 1; GC 1603)

1901.24 Jury trials governed by civil rules of procedure

(A) A jury trial in a municipal court shall be demanded in the manner prescribed in the Rules of Civil Procedure or the Rules of Criminal Procedure. The number of persons composing a jury and the verdicts of jurors shall be governed by those rules.

(B) The right of a person to a jury trial in a municipal court is waived under the circumstances prescribed in the Rules of Civil Procedure or the Rules of Criminal Procedure.

(1986 H 159, eff. 3–19–87)

1901.25 Selection and impaneling of jury

A municipal court may provide by rule the manner in which jurors shall be chosen, and may provide that jurors to be used in the court may be chosen and summoned by the jury commissioners of the county as provided in sections 2313.01 to 2313.26 of the Revised Code. Selection shall be made from residents within the territory and those appearing to reside outside the territory shall be returned to the jury wheel, to the automation data processing storage drawer, or to any other automated data processing information storage device used pursuant to division (C) of section 2313.21 of the Revised Code. Jurors shall be impaneled in the same manner, shall have the same qualifications, shall be challenged for the same causes, and shall receive the same fees as jurors in the court of common pleas. The fees of jurors in any criminal case involving the violation of state law shall be paid out of the county treasury. The fees of jurors in any criminal case involving a violation of a municipal ordinance shall be paid out of the treasury of the municipal corporation in which the violation occurred.

(1986 H 159, eff. 3–19–87; 1969 H 424; 131 v S 20; 1953 H 1; GC 1604)

1901.26 Costs

(A) Subject to division (E) of this section, costs in a municipal court shall be fixed and taxed as follows:

(1) The municipal court shall require an advance deposit for the filing of any new civil action or proceeding when required by division (A)(9) of this section, and in all other cases, by rule, shall establish a schedule of fees and costs to be taxed in any civil or criminal action or proceeding.

(2) The municipal court, by rule, may require an advance deposit for the filing of any civil action or proceeding and publication fees as provided in section 2701.09 of the Revised Code. The court may waive the requirement for advance deposit upon affidavit or other evidence that a party is unable to make the required deposit.

(3) When a jury trial is demanded in any civil action or proceeding, the party making the demand may be required to make an advance deposit as fixed by rule of court, unless, upon affidavit or other evidence, the court concludes that the party is unable to make the required deposit. If a jury is called, the fees of a jury shall be taxed as costs.

(4) In any civil or criminal action or proceeding, witnesses' fees shall be fixed in accordance with sections 2335.06 and 2335.08 of the Revised Code.

(5) A reasonable charge for driving, towing, carting, storing, keeping, and preserving motor vehicles and other personal property recovered or seized in any proceeding may be taxed as part

of the costs in a trial of the cause, in an amount that shall be fixed by rule of court.

(6) Chattel property seized under any writ or process issued by the court shall be preserved pending final disposition for the benefit of all persons interested and may be placed in storage when necessary or proper for that preservation. The custodian of any chattel property so stored shall not be required to part with the possession of the property until a reasonable charge, to be fixed by the court, is paid.

(7) The municipal court, as it determines, may refund all deposits and advance payments of fees and costs, including those for jurors and summoning jurors, when they have been paid by the losing party.

(8) Charges for the publication of legal notices required by statute or order of court may be taxed as part of the costs, as provided by section 7.13 of the Revised Code.

(B)(1) The municipal court may determine that, for the efficient operation of the court, additional funds are necessary to acquire and pay for special projects of the court including, but not limited to, the acquisition of additional facilities or the rehabilitation of existing facilities, the acquisition of equipment, the hiring and training of staff, community service programs, mediation or dispute resolution services, the employment of magistrates, the training and education of judges, acting judges, and magistrates, and other related services. Upon that determination, the court by rule may charge a fee, in addition to all other court costs, on the filing of each criminal cause, civil action or proceeding, or judgment by confession.

If the municipal court offers a special program or service in cases of a specific type, the municipal court by rule may assess an additional charge in a case of that type, over and above court costs, to cover the special program or service. The municipal court shall adjust the special assessment periodically, but not retroactively, so that the amount assessed in those cases does not exceed the actual cost of providing the service or program.

All moneys collected under division (B) of this section shall be paid to the county treasurer if the court is a county-operated municipal court or to the city treasurer if the court is not a county-operated municipal court for deposit into either a general special projects fund or a fund established for a specific special project. Moneys from a fund of that nature shall be disbursed upon an order of the court in an amount no greater than the actual cost to the court of a project. If a specific fund is terminated because of the discontinuance of a program or service established under division (B) of this section, the municipal court may order that moneys remaining in the fund be transferred to an account established under this division for a similar purpose.

(2) As used in division (B) of this section:

(a) "Criminal cause" means a charge alleging the violation of a statute or ordinance, or subsection of a statute or ordinance, that requires a separate finding of fact or a separate plea before disposition and of which the defendant may be found guilty, whether filed as part of a multiple charge on a single summons, citation, or complaint or as a separate charge on a single summons, citation, or complaint. "Criminal cause" does not include separate violations of the same statute or ordinance, or subsection of the same statute or ordinance, unless each charge is filed on a separate summons, citation, or complaint.

(b) "Civil action or proceeding" means any civil litigation that must be determined by judgment entry.

(C) The municipal court shall collect in all its divisions except the small claims division the sum of fifteen dollars as additional filing fees in each new civil action or proceeding for the charitable public purpose of providing financial assistance to legal aid societies that operate within the state. The municipal court shall collect in its small claims division the sum of seven dollars as additional filing fees in each new civil action or proceeding for the charitable public purpose of providing financial assistance to legal aid societies that operate within the state. This division does not apply to any execution on a judgment, proceeding in aid of execution, or other post-judgment proceeding arising out of a civil action. The filing fees required to be collected under this division shall be in addition to any other court costs imposed in the action or proceeding and shall be collected at the time of the filing of the action or proceeding. The court shall not waive the payment of the additional filing fees in a new civil action or proceeding unless the court waives the advanced payment of all filing fees in the action or proceeding. All such moneys shall be transmitted on the first business day of each month by the clerk of the court to the treasurer of state. The moneys then shall be deposited by the treasurer of state to the credit of the legal aid fund established under section 120.52 of the Revised Code.

The court may retain up to one per cent of the moneys it collects under this division to cover administrative costs, including the hiring of any additional personnel necessary to implement this division.

(D) In the Cleveland municipal court, reasonable charges for investigating titles of real estate to be sold or disposed of under any writ or process of the court may be taxed as part of the costs.

(E) Under the circumstances described in sections 2969.21 to 2969.27 of the Revised Code, the clerk of the municipal court shall charge the fees and perform the other duties specified in those sections.

(2001 H 94, eff. 9–5–01; 1998 H 507, eff. 3–22–99; 1996 H 438, eff. 7–1–97; 1996 H 423, eff. 10–31–96; 1996 H 455, eff. 10–17–96; 1992 H 405, eff. 1–1–93; 1991 H 298; 1989 H 111; 1987 H 171; 1986 H 159, § 3; 1985 H 201, § 14)

1901.262 Dispute resolution procedures; fees

(A) A municipal court may establish by rule procedures for the resolution of disputes between parties. Any procedures so adopted shall include, but are not limited to, mediation. If the court establishes any procedures under this division, the court may include in the court's schedule of fees and costs under section 1901.26 of the Revised Code a reasonable fee, that is to be collected on the filing of each civil or criminal action or proceeding, and that is to be used to implement the procedures, and the court shall direct the clerk of the court to charge the fee.

(B) All fees collected under division (A) of this section shall be paid to the county treasurer if the court is a county-operated municipal court or to the city treasurer if the court is not a county-operated municipal court. The treasurer shall place the funds from the fees in a separate fund to be disbursed upon an order of the court.

(C) If the court determines that the amount of the moneys in the fund described in division (B) of this section is more than the amount sufficient to satisfy the purpose for which the additional fee described in division (A) of this section was imposed, the court may declare a surplus in the fund and expend the surplus moneys for other appropriate expenses of the court.

(2001 S 108, § 6, eff. 7–6–01; 2001 S 108, § 2.02, eff. 7–6–01; 1996 H 627, § 10, eff. 1–1–97; 1996 H 350, § 13, eff. 7–1–97, § 1, eff. 1–27–97 [1]; 1996 H 438, eff. 1–1–97)

[1] See Notes of Decisions and Opinions, *State ex rel. Ohio Academy of Trial Lawyers v. Sheward* (Ohio 1999), 86 Ohio St.3d 451, 715 N.E.2d 1062.

Notes of Decisions

1. Constitutional issues

1996 H 350, which amended more than 100 statutes and a variety of rules relating to tort and other civil actions, and which was an attempt to reenact provisions of law previously held unconstitutional by the Supreme Court of Ohio, is an act of usurpation of judicial power in violation of the doctrine of separation of powers; for that reason, and because of violation of the one-subject rule of the Ohio Constitution, 1996 H 350 is unconstitutional. State ex rel. Ohio Academy of Trial Lawyers v. Sheward (Ohio, 08-

16-1999) 86 Ohio St.3d 451, 715 N.E.2d 1062, 1999-Ohio-123, reconsideration denied 87 Ohio St.3d 1409, 716 N.E.2d 1170.

APPEALS

1901.30 Appeals

Appeals from the municipal court may be taken as follows:

(A) To the court of appeals in accordance with the Rules of Appellate Procedure and any relevant sections of the Revised Code, including, but not limited to, Chapter 2505. of the Revised Code to the extent it is not in conflict with those rules.

(B) When an appeal is taken from the municipal court, the clerk of the municipal court shall transmit, pursuant to the Rules of Appellate Procedure, the record on appeal to the clerk of the appellate court to be filed.

(C) In all appeal proceedings relating to judgments or orders of a municipal court, the reviewing courts shall take judicial notice of all rules relating to pleadings, practice, or procedure of the municipal court.

(1988 H 708, eff. 4–19–88; 1986 H 159, H 412; 1978 H 1168; 1970 S 530; 131 v H 231; 128 v 823; 1953 H 1; GC 1609)

COURT OFFICIALS

1901.32 Bailiffs; deputy bailiffs; court reporters

(A) The bailiffs and deputy bailiffs of a municipal court shall be provided for, and their duties are, as follows:

(1) Except for the Hamilton county municipal court, the court shall appoint a bailiff who shall receive the annual compensation that the court prescribes payable in semimonthly installments from the same sources and in the same manner as provided in section 1901.11 of the Revised Code. The court may provide that the chief of police of the municipal corporation or a member of the police force be appointed by the court to be the bailiff of the court. Before entering upon his duties, the bailiff shall take an oath to faithfully perform the duties of the office and shall give a bond of not less than three thousand dollars, as the legislative authority prescribes, conditioned for the faithful performance of his duties as bailiff.

(2) Except for the Hamilton county municipal court, deputy bailiffs may be appointed by the court. Deputy bailiffs shall receive the compensation payable in semimonthly installments out of the city treasury that the court prescribes, except that the compensation of deputy bailiffs in a county-operated municipal court shall be paid out of the treasury of the county in which the court is located. Each deputy bailiff shall give a bond in an amount not less than one thousand dollars, and, when so qualified, he may perform the duties pertaining to the office of bailiff of the court.

(3) The bailiff and all deputy bailiffs of the Hamilton county municipal court shall be appointed by the clerk and shall receive the compensation payable in semimonthly installments out of the treasury of Hamilton county that the clerk prescribes. Each judge of the Hamilton county municipal court may appoint a courtroom bailiff, each of whom shall receive the compensation payable in semimonthly installments out of the treasury of Hamilton county that the court prescribes.

(4) The legislative authority may purchase motor vehicles for the use of the bailiffs and deputy bailiffs as the court determines they need to perform the duties of their office. All expenses, maintenance, and upkeep of the vehicles shall be paid by the legislative authority upon approval by the court. Any allowances, costs, and expenses for the operation of private motor vehicles by bailiffs and deputy bailiffs for official duties, including the cost of oil, gasoline, and maintenance, shall be prescribed by the court and, subject to the approval of the legislative authority, shall be paid from the city treasury, except that the allowances, costs, and expenses for the bailiffs and deputy bailiffs of a county-operated municipal court shall be paid from the treasury of the county in which the court is located.

(5) Every police officer of any municipal corporation and police constable of a township within the territory of the court is ex officio a deputy bailiff of the court in and for the municipal corporation or township within which he is commissioned as a police officer or police constable, and shall perform any duties in respect to cases within his jurisdiction that are required of him by a judge of the court, or by the clerk or a bailiff or deputy bailiff of the court, without additional compensation.

(6) The bailiff and deputy bailiffs shall perform for the court services similar to those performed by the sheriff for the court of common pleas and shall perform any other duties that are requested by rule of court.

The bailiff or deputy bailiff may administer oaths to witnesses and jurors and receive verdicts in the same manner and form and to the same extent as the clerk or deputy clerks of the court. The bailiff may approve all undertakings and bonds given in actions of replevin and all redelivery bonds in attachments.

(B) In the Cleveland municipal court, the chief clerks and all deputy clerks are in the classified civil service of the city of Cleveland. The clerk, the chief deputy clerks, the probation officers, one private secretary, one personal stenographer to the clerk, and one personal bailiff to each judge are in the unclassified civil service of the city of Cleveland. Upon demand of the clerk, the civil service commission of the city of Cleveland shall certify a list of those eligible for the position of deputy clerk. From the list, the clerk shall designate chief clerks and the number of deputy clerks that the legislative authority determines are necessary.

Except as otherwise provided in this division, the bailiff, chief deputy bailiffs, and all deputy bailiffs of the Cleveland municipal court appointed after January 1, 1968, and the chief housing specialist, housing specialists, and housing division referees of the housing division of the Cleveland municipal court appointed under section 1901.331 of the Revised Code are in the unclassified civil service of the city of Cleveland. All deputy bailiffs of the housing division of the Cleveland municipal court appointed pursuant to that section are in the classified civil service of the city of Cleveland. Upon the demand of the judge of the housing division of the Cleveland municipal court, the civil service commission of the city of Cleveland shall certify a list of those eligible for the position of deputy bailiff of the housing division. From the list, the judge of the housing division shall designate the number of deputy bailiffs that he determines are necessary.

The chief deputy clerks, the chief clerks, and all other deputy clerks of the Cleveland municipal court shall receive the compensation that the clerk prescribes. Except as provided in division (A)(4)(a) of section 1901.331 of the Revised Code with respect to officers and employees of the housing division of the Cleveland municipal court, the bailiff, all deputy bailiffs, and assignment room personnel of the Cleveland municipal court shall receive the compensation that the court prescribes.

Any appointee under sections 1901.01 to 1901.37 of the Revised Code may be dismissed or discharged by the same power that appointed him. In the case of the removal of any civil service appointee under those sections, an appeal may be taken from the decision of the civil service commission to the court of common pleas of Cuyahoga county to determine the sufficiency of the cause of removal. The appeal shall be taken within ten days of the finding of the commission.

In the Cleveland municipal court, the presiding judge may appoint on a full-time, per diem, or contractual basis any official court reporters for the civil branch of the court that the business of the court requires. The compensation of official court reporters shall be determined by the presiding judge of the court. The compensation shall be payable from the city treasury and from the treasury of Cuyahoga county in the same proportion as designated in section 1901.11 of the Revised Code for the payment of compensation of municipal judges. In every trial in which the services of a court reporter so appointed are requested by the judge, any party, or the attorney for any party, there shall be taxed for each day's services of the court reporter a fee in the same amount as may be taxed for similar services in the court of common pleas under section 2301.21 of the Revised Code, to be collected as other costs in the case. The fees so collected shall be paid quarterly by the clerk into the city treasury and the treasury of Cuyahoga county in the same proportion as the compensation for the court reporters is paid from the city and county treasuries and shall be credited to the general funds of the city and county treasuries.

(C) In the Hamilton county municipal court, all employees, including the bailiff, deputy bailiff, and courtroom bailiffs, are in the unclassified civil service.

(1994 H 8, eff. 6–8–94; 1986 H 159, eff. 3–19–87; 1980 H 640; 1977 H 517; 1976 S 387; 1975 H 205; 1973 H 1; 1972 H 529; 132 v H 507, H 354; 131 v H 667; 130 v H 408; 128 v 823; 126 v 170; 1953 H 1; GC 1611)

1901.33 Court aides and probation officers; administrative assistants

(A) The judge or judges of a municipal court may appoint one or more interpreters, one or more mental health professionals, one or more probation officers, an assignment commissioner, deputy assignment commissioners, and other court aides on a full-time, part-time, hourly, or other basis. Each appointee shall receive the compensation out of the city treasury that the legislative authority prescribes, except that in a county-operated municipal court they shall receive the compensation out of the treasury of the county in which the court is located that the board of county commissioners prescribes. Probation officers have all the powers of regular police officers and shall perform any duties that are designated by the judge or judges of the court. Assignment commissioners shall assign cases for trial and perform any other duties that the court directs.

The judge or judges may appoint one or more typists, stenographers, statistical clerks, and official court reporters, each of whom shall be paid the compensation out of the city treasury that the legislative authority prescribes, except that in a county-operated municipal court they shall be paid the compensation out of the treasury of the county in which the court is located that the board of county commissioners prescribes.

(B) If a municipal court appoints one or more probation officers, those officers shall constitute the municipal court department of probation unless the court designates other employees as the department of probation for the court.

(C) The chief probation officer may grant permission to a probation officer to carry firearms when required in the discharge of the probation officer's official duties if the probation officer has successfully completed a basic firearm training program that is approved by the executive director of the Ohio peace officer training commission. A probation officer who has been granted permission to carry a firearm in the discharge of the probation officer's official duties annually shall successfully complete a firearms requalification program in accordance with section 109.801 of the Revised Code.

(D) The judge or judges of a municipal court in which the clerk of the court is elected as provided in division (A)(1)(a) or (d) or (A)(2)(b) of section 1901.31 of the Revised Code may appoint an administrative assistant. The administrative assistant shall have charge of personnel related matters of the court and shall perform any other administrative duties assigned by the court. The administrative assistant shall receive the compensation out of the city treasury that the court prescribes, except that, in a county-operated municipal court, the administrative assistant shall receive the compensation out of the treasury of the county in which the court is located that the court prescribes.

(2002 H 510, eff. 3–31–03; 2000 S 325, eff. 4–9–01; 1996 H 438, eff. 7–1–97; 1996 H 670, eff. 12–2–96; 1994 H 406, eff. 11–11–94; 1986 H 159, eff. 3–19–87; 1977 H 517; 125 v 903; 1953 H 1; GC 1612)

MISCELLANEOUS PROVISIONS

1901.34 Criminal prosecution; compensation of prosecuting officers; agreement with prosecuting attorney

(A) Except as provided in divisions (B) and (D) of this section, the village solicitor, city director of law, or similar chief legal officer for each municipal corporation within the territory of a municipal court shall prosecute all cases brought before the municipal court for criminal offenses occurring within the municipal corporation for which that person is the solicitor, director of law, or similar chief legal officer. Except as provided in division (B) of this section, the village solicitor, city director of law, or similar chief legal officer of the municipal corporation in which a municipal court is located shall prosecute all criminal cases brought before the court arising in the unincorporated areas within the territory of the municipal court.

(B) The Auglaize county, Brown county, Clermont county, Hocking county, Jackson county, Morrow county, Ottawa county, and Portage county prosecuting attorneys shall prosecute in municipal court all violations of state law arising in their respective counties. The Crawford county, Hamilton county, Madison county, and Wayne county prosecuting attorneys shall prosecute all violations of state law arising within the unincorporated areas of their respective counties. The Columbiana county prosecuting attorney shall prosecute in the Columbiana county municipal court all violations of state law arising in the county, except for violations arising in the municipal corporation of East Liverpool, Liverpool township, or St. Clair township. The Darke county prosecuting attorney shall prosecute in the Darke county municipal court all violations of state law arising in the county, except for violations of state law arising in the municipal corporation of Greenville and violations of state law arising in the village of Versailles.

The prosecuting attorney of any county given the duty of prosecuting in municipal court violations of state law shall receive no additional compensation for assuming these additional duties, except that the prosecuting attorney of Hamilton, Portage, and Wayne counties shall receive compensation at the rate of four thousand eight hundred dollars per year, and the prosecuting attorney of Auglaize county shall receive compensation at the rate of one thousand eight hundred dollars per year, each payable from the county treasury of the respective counties in semimonthly installments.

(C) The village solicitor, city director of law, or similar chief legal officer shall perform the same duties, insofar as they are applicable to the village solicitor, city director of law, or similar chief legal officer, as are required of the prosecuting attorney of the county. The village solicitor, city director of law, similar chief legal officer or any assistants who may be appointed shall receive for such services additional compensation to be paid from the treasury of the county as the board of county commissioners prescribes.

(D) The prosecuting attorney of any county, other than Auglaize, Brown, Clermont, Hocking, Jackson, Morrow, Ottawa, or Portage county, may enter into an agreement with any municipal corporation in the county in which the prosecuting attorney serves pursuant to which the prosecuting attorney prosecutes all criminal cases brought before the municipal court that has territorial jurisdiction over that municipal corporation for criminal offenses occurring within the municipal corporation. The prosecuting attorney of Auglaize, Brown, Clermont, Hocking, Jackson, Morrow, Ottawa, or Portage county may enter into an agreement with any municipal corporation in the county in which the prosecuting attorney serves pursuant to which the respective prosecuting attorney prosecutes all cases brought before the Auglaize county, Brown county, Clermont county, Hocking county, Jackson county, Morrow county, Ottawa county, or Portage county municipal court for violations of the ordinances of the municipal corporation or for criminal offenses other than violations of state law occurring within the municipal corporation. For prosecuting these cases, the prosecuting attorney and the municipal corporation may agree upon a fee to be paid by the municipal corporation, which fee shall be paid into the county treasury, to be used to cover expenses of the office of the prosecuting attorney.

(2004 H 38, eff. 6–17–04; 2002 H 530, eff. 12–18–02; 2000 H 599, eff. 1–1–02; 1994 H 21, eff. 2–4–94; 1991 H 200, eff. 7–8–91; 1986 H 159; 1981 H 1; 1980 S 357, H 961; 1977 H 517, H 312, H 219; 1976 H 1558; 1975 H 205; 1969 H 749; 132 v S 493, H 361; 125 v 496; 1953 H 1; GC 1613)

CHAPTER 1905

MAYOR'S COURT

JURISDICTION; EDUCATIONAL AND PROCEDURAL STANDARDS

1905.01 Jurisdiction in ordinance cases, traffic violations, OMVI cases, driving under suspension cases, and domestic violence cases

(A) In Georgetown in Brown county, in Mount Gilead in Morrow county, and in all other municipal corporations having a population of more than one hundred, other than Batavia in Clermont county, not being the site of a municipal court nor a place where a judge of the Auglaize county, Crawford county, Jackson county, Miami county, Portage county, or Wayne county municipal court sits as required pursuant to section 1901.021 of the Revised Code or by designation of the judges pursuant to section 1901.021 of the Revised Code, the mayor of the municipal corporation has jurisdiction, except as provided in divisions (B), (C), and (E) of this section and subject to the limitation contained in section 1905.03 and the limitation contained in section 1905.031 of the Revised Code, to hear and determine any prosecution for the violation of an ordinance of the municipal corporation, to hear and determine any case involving a violation of a vehicle parking or standing ordinance of the municipal corporation unless the violation is required to be handled by a parking violations bureau or joint parking violations bureau pursuant to Chapter 4521. of the Revised Code, and to hear and determine all criminal causes involving any moving traffic violation occurring on a state highway located within the boundaries of the municipal corporation, subject to the limitations of sections 2937.08 and 2938.04 of the Revised Code.

(B)(1) In Georgetown in Brown county, in Mount Gilead in Morrow county, and in all other municipal corporations having a population of more than one hundred, other than Batavia in Clermont county, not being the site of a municipal court nor a place where a judge of a court listed in division (A) of this section sits as required pursuant to section 1901.021 of the Revised Code or by designation of the judges pursuant to section 1901.021 of the Revised Code, the mayor of the municipal corporation has jurisdiction, subject to the limitation contained in section 1905.03 of the Revised Code, to hear and determine prosecutions involving a violation of an ordinance of the municipal corporation relating to operating a vehicle while under the influence of alcohol, a drug of abuse, or a combination of them or relating to operating a vehicle with a prohibited concentration of alcohol in the whole blood, blood serum or plasma, breath, or urine, and to hear and determine criminal causes involving a violation of section 4511.19 of the Revised Code that occur on a state highway located within the boundaries of the municipal corporation, subject to the limitations of sections 2937.08 and 2938.04 of the Revised Code, only if the person charged with the violation, within six years of the date of the violation charged, has not been convicted of or pleaded guilty to any of the following:

(a) A violation of an ordinance of any municipal corporation relating to operating a vehicle while under the influence of alcohol, a drug of abuse, or a combination of them or relating to operating a vehicle with a prohibited concentration of alcohol in the whole blood, blood serum or plasma, breath, or urine;

(b) A violation of section 4511.19 of the Revised Code;

(c) A violation of any ordinance of any municipal corporation or of any section of the Revised Code that regulates the operation of vehicles, streetcars, and trackless trolleys upon the highways or streets, to which all of the following apply:

(i) The person, in the case in which the conviction was obtained or the plea of guilty was entered, had been charged with a violation of an ordinance of a type described in division (B)(1)(a) of this section, or with a violation of section 4511.19 of the Revised Code;

(ii) The charge of the violation described in division (B)(1)(c)(i) of this section was dismissed or reduced;

(iii) The violation of which the person was convicted or to which the person pleaded guilty arose out of the same facts and circumstances and the same act as did the charge that was dismissed or reduced.

(d) A violation of a statute of the United States or of any other state or a municipal ordinance of a municipal corporation located in any other state that is substantially similar to section 4511.19 of the Revised Code.

(2) The mayor of a municipal corporation does not have jurisdiction to hear and determine any prosecution or criminal cause involving a violation described in division (B)(1)(a) or (b) of this section, regardless of where the violation occurred, if the person charged with the violation, within six years of the violation charged, has been convicted of or pleaded guilty to any violation listed in division (B)(1)(a), (b), (c), or (d) of this section.

If the mayor of a municipal corporation, in hearing a prosecution involving a violation of an ordinance of the municipal corporation the mayor serves relating to operating a vehicle while under the influence of alcohol, a drug of abuse, or a combination of them or relating to operating a vehicle with a prohibited concentration of alcohol in the whole blood, blood serum or plasma, breath, or urine, or in hearing a criminal cause involving a violation of section 4511.19 of the Revised Code, determines that the person charged, within six years of the violation charged, has been convicted of or pleaded guilty to any violation listed in division (B)(1)(a), (b), (c), or (d) of this section, the mayor immediately shall transfer the case to the county court or municipal court with jurisdiction over the violation charged, in accordance with section 1905.032 of the Revised Code.

(C)(1) In Georgetown in Brown county, in Mount Gilead in Morrow county, and in all other municipal corporations having a population of more than one hundred, other than Batavia in Clermont county, not being the site of a municipal court and not being a place where a judge of a court listed in division (A) of this section sits as required pursuant to section 1901.021 of the Revised Code or by designation of the judges pursuant to section 1901. 021 of the Revised Code, the mayor of the municipal corporation, subject to sections 1901.031, 2937.08, and 2938.04 of the Revised Code, has jurisdiction to hear and determine prosecutions involving a violation of a municipal ordinance that is substantially equivalent to division (A) of section 4510.14 or section 4510.16 of the Revised Code and to hear and determine criminal causes that involve a moving traffic violation, that involve a violation of division (A) of section 4510.14 or section 4510.16 of the Revised Code, and that occur on a state highway located within the boundaries of the municipal corporation only if all of the following apply regarding the violation and the person charged:

(a) Regarding a violation of section 4510.16 of the Revised Code or a violation of a municipal ordinance that is substantially equivalent to that division, the person charged with the violation, within six years of the date of the violation charged, has not been convicted of or pleaded guilty to any of the following:

(i) A violation of section 4510.16 of the Revised Code;

(ii) A violation of a municipal ordinance that is substantially equivalent to section 4510.16 of the Revised Code;

(iii) A violation of any municipal ordinance or section of the Revised Code that regulates the operation of vehicles, streetcars, and trackless trolleys upon the highways or streets, in a case in which, after a charge against the person of a violation of a type described in division (C)(1)(a)(i) or (ii) of this section was dismissed or reduced, the person is convicted of or pleads guilty to a violation that arose out of the same facts and circumstances and the same act as did the charge that was dismissed or reduced.

(b) Regarding a violation of division (A) of section 4510.14 of the Revised Code or a violation of a municipal ordinance that is substantially equivalent to that division, the person charged with the violation, within six years of the date of the violation charged, has not been convicted of or pleaded guilty to any of the following:

(i) A violation of division (A) of section 4510.14 of the Revised Code;

(ii) A violation of a municipal ordinance that is substantially equivalent to division (A) of section 4510.14 of the Revised Code;

(iii) A violation of any municipal ordinance or section of the Revised Code that regulates the operation of vehicles, streetcars, and trackless trolleys upon the highways or streets in a case in which, after a charge against the person of a violation of a type described in division (C)(1)(b)(i) or (ii) of this section was dismissed or reduced, the person is convicted of or pleads guilty to a violation that arose out of the same facts and circumstances and the same act as did the charge that was dismissed or reduced.

(2) The mayor of a municipal corporation does not have jurisdiction to hear and determine any prosecution or criminal cause involving a violation described in division (C)(1)(a)(i) or (ii) of this section if the person charged with the violation, within six years of the violation charged, has been convicted of or pleaded guilty to any violation listed in division (C)(1)(a)(i), (ii), or (iii) of this section and does not have jurisdiction to hear and determine any prosecution or criminal cause involving a violation described in division (C)(1)(b)(i) or (ii) of this section if the person charged with the violation, within six years of the violation charged, has been convicted of or pleaded guilty to any violation listed in division (C)(1)(b)(i), (ii), or (iii) of this section.

(3) If the mayor of a municipal corporation, in hearing a prosecution involving a violation of an ordinance of the municipal corporation the mayor serves that is substantially equivalent to division (A) of section 4510.14 or section 4510.16 of the Revised Code or a violation of division (A) of section 4510.14 or section 4510.16 of the Revised Code, determines that, under division (C)(2) of this section, mayors do not have jurisdiction of the prosecution, the mayor immediately shall transfer the case to the county court or municipal court with jurisdiction over the violation in accordance with section 1905.032 of the Revised Code.

(D) If the mayor of a municipal corporation has jurisdiction pursuant to division (B)(1) of this section to hear and determine a prosecution or criminal cause involving a violation described in division (B)(1)(a) or (b) of this section, the authority of the mayor to hear or determine the prosecution or cause is subject to the limitation contained in division (C) of section 1905.03 of the Revised Code. If the mayor of a municipal corporation has jurisdiction pursuant to division (A) or (C) of this section to hear and determine a prosecution or criminal cause involving a violation other than a violation described in division (B)(1)(a) or (b) of this section, the authority of the mayor to hear or determine the prosecution or cause is subject to the limitation contained in division (C) of section 1905. 031 of the Revised Code.

(E)(1) The mayor of a municipal corporation does not have jurisdiction to hear and determine any prosecution or criminal cause involving any of the following:

(a) A violation of section 2919.25 or 2919.27 of the Revised Code;

(b) A violation of section 2903.11, 2903.12, 2903.13, 2903.211, or 2911.211 of the Revised Code that involves a person who was a family or household member of the defendant at the time of the violation;

(c) A violation of a municipal ordinance that is substantially equivalent to an offense described in division (E)(1)(a) or (b) of this section and that involves a person who was a family or household member of the defendant at the time of the violation.

(2) The mayor of a municipal corporation does not have jurisdiction to hear and determine a motion filed pursuant to section 2919.26 of the Revised Code or filed pursuant to a municipal ordinance that is substantially equivalent to that sec-

tion or to issue a protection order pursuant to that section or a substantially equivalent municipal ordinance.

(3) As used in this section, "family or household member" has the same meaning as in section 2919.25 of the Revised Code.

(F) In keeping a docket and files, the mayor, and a mayor's court magistrate appointed under section 1905.05 of the Revised Code, shall be governed by the laws pertaining to county courts.

(2003 H 24, § 3, eff. 1–1–04; 2003 H 24, § 1, eff. 8–29–03; 2002 H 530, § 3, eff. 1–1–04; 2002 H 530, § 1, eff. 12–18–02; 2002 S 123, eff. 1–1–04; 1999 H 105, eff. 7–29–99; 1997 S 60, eff. 10–21–97; 1997 S 1, eff. 10–21–97; 1996 H 670, eff. 12–2–96; 1996 H 353, eff. 9–17–96; 1993 S 62, eff. 9–1–93; 1990 H 837, S 131; 1982 H 707; 1977 H 312; 1975 H 205; 132 v H 361; 130 v H 269; 128 v 823; 1953 H 1; GC 4527)

1905.03 Educational standards for mayors hearing OMVI cases; basic training and periodic continuing education courses

(A) The supreme court may adopt rules prescribing educational standards for mayors of municipal corporations who conduct a mayor's court and who wish to exercise the jurisdiction granted by section 1905.01 of the Revised Code over a prosecution or criminal cause involving a violation of section 4511.19 of the Revised Code, a violation of any ordinance of the municipal corporation relating to operating a vehicle while under the influence of alcohol, a drug of abuse, or alcohol and a drug of abuse, or a violation of any ordinance of the municipal corporation relating to operating a vehicle with a prohibited concentration of alcohol in the blood, breath, or urine. Any educational standards prescribed by rule under authority of this division shall be for the purpose of assisting mayors of municipal corporations who conduct a mayor's court and who wish to exercise the jurisdiction granted by section 1905.01 of the Revised Code over such a prosecution or cause in the handling of such a prosecution or cause, and shall include, but shall not be limited to, all of the following:

(1) Provisions for basic training in the general principles of law that apply to the hearing and determination of such prosecutions and causes and provisions for periodic continuing education in those general principles;

(2) Provisions for basic training in the laws of this state that apply relative to persons who are convicted of or plead guilty to any such violation, particularly as those laws apply relative to a person who is convicted of or pleads guilty to any such violation in a prosecution or cause that is within the jurisdiction of a mayor's court as specified in section 1905.01 of the Revised Code, and provisions for periodic continuing education in those laws;

(3) Provisions specifying whether periodic continuing education for a mayor who conducts a mayor's court, who wishes to exercise the jurisdiction granted by section 1905.01 of the Revised Code over such a prosecution or cause, and who has received basic training in the principles and laws described in divisions (A)(1) and (2) of this section will be required on an annual or biennial basis;

(4) Provisions specifying the number of hours of basic training that a mayor who conducts a mayor's court and who wishes to exercise the jurisdiction granted by section 1905.01 of the Revised Code over such a prosecution or cause will have to obtain to comply with the educational standards and provisions specifying the number of hours of periodic continuing education that such a mayor will have to obtain within each time period specified under authority of division (A)(3) of this section to comply with the educational standards;

(5) Provisions establishing an exemption, for a reasonable period of time, from the basic training requirements for mayors who initially take office on or after July 1, 1991, and who wish to conduct a mayor's court and exercise the jurisdiction granted by section 1905.01 of the Revised Code over such a prosecution or cause.

(B) If the supreme court adopts rules under authority of division (A) of this section prescribing educational standards for mayors of municipal corporations who conduct a mayor's court and who wish to exercise the jurisdiction granted by section 1905.01 of the Revised Code over a prosecution or criminal cause involving a violation described in division (A) of this section, the court may formulate a basic training course and a periodic continuing education course that such a mayor may complete to satisfy those educational standards, and may offer or provide for the offering of the basic training course and the periodic continuing education course to mayors of municipal corporations.

If the supreme court offers or provides for the offering of a basic training course and a periodic continuing education course formulated under this division, the court may prescribe a reasonable fee to cover the cost associated with formulating, offering, and teaching the particular course, which fee would have to be paid by each mayor who attends the particular course or the municipal corporation served by the mayor.

If the supreme court offers or provides for the offering of a basic training course and a periodic continuing education course formulated under this division, the court or other entity that offers either course shall issue to each mayor who successfully completes the particular course a certificate attesting to the mayor's satisfactory completion of the particular course.

(C) Notwithstanding section 1905.01 of the Revised Code, if the supreme court adopts rules under authority of division (A) of this section, if the supreme court formulates a basic training course and a periodic continuing education course under division (B) of this section, and if the supreme court offers or provides for the offering of the basic training course and the periodic continuing education course to mayors, a mayor shall not hear or determine, on or after July 1, 1991, any prosecution or criminal cause involving a violation described in division (A) of this section unless the exemption under the provisions described in division (A)(5) of this section applies to the mayor, or unless, prior to hearing the prosecution or criminal cause, the mayor successfully has completed the basic training course offered or provided for by the supreme court and has been issued a certificate attesting to satisfactory completion of the basic training course and also successfully has completed any periodic continuing education course offered or provided for by the supreme court that is applicable to the mayor under the rules and has been issued a certificate attesting to satisfactory completion of the periodic continuing education course.

This division does not affect and shall not be construed as affecting the authority of a mayor to appoint a mayor's court magistrate under section 1905.05 of the Revised Code. If a mayor is prohibited from hearing or determining a prosecution or criminal cause involving a violation described in division (A) of this section due to the operation of this division, the prohibition against the mayor hearing or determining the prosecution or cause does not affect and shall not be construed as affecting the jurisdiction or authority of a mayor's court magistrate appointed under that section to hear and determine the prosecution or cause in accordance with that section.

(1996 H 670, eff. 12–2–96; 1990 H 211, eff. 4–11–91; 1990 S 131)

1905.031 Standards for mayors hearing non-OMVI cases; basic training and periodic continuing education courses

(A) The supreme court may adopt rules prescribing educational standards and procedural and operational standards for mayors of municipal corporations who conduct a mayor's court and who wish to exercise the jurisdiction granted by section 1905.01 of the

Revised Code over a prosecution or criminal cause other than a prosecution or cause within the scope of the standards described in section 1905.03 of the Revised Code. Any educational standards and procedural and operational standards prescribed by rule under authority of this division shall be for the purpose of assisting mayors of municipal corporations who conduct a mayor's court, and shall include, but shall not be limited to, all of the following:

(1) Provisions for basic training in the general principles of law that apply to the hearing and determination of prosecutions and causes that are within the jurisdiction of a mayor's court as specified in section 1905.01 of the Revised Code, other than prosecutions and causes that are within the scope of the standards described in section 1905.03 of the Revised Code, provisions for basic training in the procedural and operational standards prescribed by the court under this division, and provisions for periodic continuing education in those general principles and in those procedural and operational standards;

(2) Provisions for basic training in the laws of this state that apply relative to persons who are convicted of or plead guilty to any violation of a statute or ordinance, particularly as those laws apply relative to a person who is convicted of or pleads guilty to any such violation in a prosecution or cause that is within the jurisdiction of a mayor's court as specified in section 1905.01 of the Revised Code, other than prosecutions and causes that are within the scope of the standards described in section 1905.03 of the Revised Code, and provisions for periodic continuing education in those laws;

(3) Provisions specifying whether periodic continuing education for a mayor who conducts a mayor's court, who wishes to exercise the jurisdiction granted by section 1905.01 of the Revised Code over a prosecution or cause, and who has received basic training in the principles and laws described in divisions (A)(1) and (2) of this section will be required on an annual or biennial basis;

(4) Provisions specifying the number of hours of basic training that a mayor who conducts a mayor's court and who wishes to exercise the jurisdiction granted by section 1905.01 of the Revised Code over a prosecution or cause, other than a prosecution or cause that is within the scope of the standards described in section 1905.03 of the Revised Code, will have to obtain to comply with the educational standards and provisions specifying the number of hours of periodic continuing education that such a mayor will have to obtain within each time period specified under authority of division (A)(3) of this section to comply with the educational standards;

(5) Provisions establishing an exemption, for a reasonable period of time, from the basic training requirements for mayors who initially take office on or after July 1, 1992, and who wish to conduct a mayor's court and exercise the jurisdiction granted by section 1905.01 of the Revised Code over a prosecution or cause other than a prosecution or cause within the scope of the standards described in section 1905.03 of the Revised Code;

(6) Provisions establishing procedural and operational standards for mayor's courts.

(B) If the supreme court adopts rules under authority of division (A) of this section prescribing educational standards and procedural and operational standards for mayors of municipal corporations who conduct a mayor's court and who wish to exercise the jurisdiction granted by section 1905.01 of the Revised Code over a prosecution or criminal cause, other than a prosecution or cause that is within the scope of the standards described in section 1905.03 of the Revised Code, the court may formulate a basic training course and a periodic continuing education course that such a mayor may complete to satisfy the basic training and periodic continuing education required relative to those standards, and may offer or provide for the offering of the basic training course and the periodic continuing education course to mayors of municipal corporations.

If the supreme court offers or provides for the offering of a basic training course and a periodic continuing education course formulated under this division, the court may prescribe a reasonable fee to cover the cost associated with formulating, offering, and teaching the particular course, which fee would have to be paid by each mayor who attends the particular course or the municipal corporation served by the mayor.

If the supreme court offers or provides for the offering of a basic training course and a periodic continuing education course formulated under this division, the court or other entity that offers either course shall issue to each mayor who successfully completes the particular course a certificate attesting to the mayor's satisfactory completion of the particular course.

(C) Notwithstanding section 1905.01 of the Revised Code, if the supreme court adopts rules under authority of division (A) of this section on or before July 1, 1991, if the supreme court formulates a basic training course and a periodic continuing education course under division (B) of this section, and if the supreme court offers or provides for the offering of the basic training course and the periodic continuing education course to mayors within a reasonable period of time after the adoption of the rules, a mayor shall not hear or determine, on or after July 1, 1992, any prosecution or criminal cause involving a violation described in division (A) of this section unless the exemption under the provisions described in division (A)(5) of this section applies to the mayor, or unless, prior to hearing the prosecution or criminal cause, the mayor has successfully completed the basic training course offered or provided for by the supreme court and has been issued a certificate attesting to satisfactory completion of the basic training course and also has successfully completed any periodic continuing education course offered or provided for by the supreme court that is applicable to the mayor under the rules and has been issued a certificate attesting to satisfactory completion of the periodic continuing education course.

This division does not affect and shall not be construed as affecting the authority of a mayor to appoint a mayor's court magistrate under section 1905.05 of the Revised Code. If a mayor is prohibited from hearing or determining a prosecution or criminal cause involving a violation described in division (A) of this section due to the operation of this division, the prohibition against the mayor hearing or determining the prosecution or cause does not affect and shall not be construed as affecting the jurisdiction or authority of a mayor's court magistrate appointed under that section to hear and determine the prosecution or cause in accordance with that section.

(1996 H 670, eff. 12–2–96; 1990 H 211, eff. 4–11–91; 1990 H 837, S 131)

CLERKS, MAYOR AND MAGISTRATES; POWERS AND DUTIES

1905.04 Clerk and deputy must be disinterested

Neither the clerk of a mayor's court, nor his deputy, nor a mayor's court magistrate, shall be concerned as counsel or agent in the prosecution or defense of any case before the mayor's court.

(1990 S 131, eff. 7–25–90; 1953 H 1; GC 4529)

1905.05 Mayor's court magistrates

(A) A mayor of a municipal corporation that has a mayor's court may appoint a person as mayor's court magistrate to hear and determine prosecutions and criminal causes in the mayor's court that are within the jurisdiction of the mayor's court, as set forth in section 1905.01 of the Revised Code. No person shall be appointed as a mayor's court magistrate unless the person has been admitted to the practice of law in this state and, for a total of at least three years preceding the person's appointment or the commencement of the person's service as magistrate, has been engaged in the practice of law in this state or served as a judge of a court of record in any jurisdiction in the United States, or both.

A person appointed as a mayor's court magistrate under this division is entitled to hear and determine prosecutions and criminal causes in the mayor's court that are within the jurisdiction of the mayor's court, as set forth in section 1905.01 of the Revised Code. If a mayor is prohibited from hearing or determining a prosecution or cause that charges a person with a violation of section 4511.19 of the Revised Code or with a violation of a municipal ordinance relating to operating a vehicle while under the influence of alcohol, a drug of abuse, or alcohol and a drug of abuse or relating to operating a vehicle with a prohibited concentration of alcohol in the blood, breath, or urine due to the operation of division (C) of section 1905.03 of the Revised Code, or is prohibited from hearing or determining any other prosecution or cause due to the operation of division (C) of section 1905.031 of the Revised Code, the prohibition against the mayor hearing or determining the prosecution or cause does not affect and shall not be construed as affecting the jurisdiction or authority of a person appointed as a mayor's court magistrate under this division to hear and determine the prosecution or cause in accordance with this section. In hearing and determining such prosecutions and causes, the magistrate has the same powers, duties, and authority as does a mayor who conducts a mayor's court to hear and determine prosecutions and causes in general, including, but not limited to, the power and authority to decide the prosecution or cause, enter judgment, and impose sentence; the powers, duties, and authority granted to mayors of mayor's courts by this chapter, in relation to the hearing and determination of prosecutions and causes in mayor's courts; and the powers, duties, and authority granted to mayors of mayor's courts by any other provision of the Revised Code, in relation to the hearing and determination of prosecutions and causes in mayor's courts. A judgment entered and a sentence imposed by a mayor's court magistrate do not have to be reviewed or approved by the mayor who appointed the magistrate, and have the same force and effect as if they had been entered or imposed by the mayor.

A person appointed as a mayor's court magistrate under this division is not entitled to hear or determine any prosecution or criminal cause other than prosecutions and causes that are within the jurisdiction of the mayor's court, as set forth in section 1905.01 of the Revised Code.

A municipal corporation that a mayor's court magistrate serves shall pay the compensation for the services of the magistrate, which shall be either a fixed annual salary set by the legislative authority of the municipal corporation or a fixed annual amount or fees for services rendered set under a contract the magistrate and the municipal corporation enter into.

(B) The appointment of a person as a mayor's court magistrate under division (A) of this section does not preclude the mayor that appointed the magistrate, subject to the limitation contained in section 1905.03 and the limitation contained in section 1905.031 of the Revised Code, from also hearing and determining prosecutions and criminal causes in the mayor's court that are within the jurisdiction of the mayor's court, as set forth in section 1905.01 of the Revised Code.

(1998 S 201, eff. 12–21–98; 1996 H 670, eff. 12–2–96; 1990 S 131, eff. 7–25–90)

1905.08 Duties of police chief or marshal; fees

The chief of police of the city or village or a police officer of the city or village designated by him, or the marshal of a village shall attend the sittings of the mayor's court to execute the orders and process of the court, and to preserve order in it. The chief of police, other police officer, or marshal shall execute and return all writs and process directed to him by the mayor. The jurisdiction of the chief of police, other police officer, or marshal in the execution of such writs and process is coextensive with the county in criminal cases and in cases of violations of ordinances of the municipal corporation. In serving such writs and process and taxing costs on them, the chief of police, other police officer, or marshal shall be governed by the laws pertaining to constables. The fees of the mayor are the same as those allowed in the municipal or county court within whose jurisdiction the municipal corporation is located. There shall be allowed and taxed for services of the chief of police, other police officer, or marshal, the same fees and expense as those allowed constables.

(1986 H 158, eff. 3–17–87; 130 v H 269; 128 v 823; 1953 H 1; GC 4534)

1905.20 Powers of mayor and mayor's court magistrate in criminal matters

(A) The mayor of a municipal corporation has, within the corporate limits, all the powers conferred upon sheriffs to suppress disorder and keep the peace.

(B) The mayor of a municipal corporation shall award and issue all writs and process that are necessary to enforce the administration of justice throughout the municipal corporation. The mayor shall subscribe his name and affix his official seal to all writs, process, transcripts, and other official papers. A mayor's court magistrate, in hearing and determining prosecutions and criminal causes that are within the scope of his authority under section 1905.05 of the Revised Code, has the same powers and duties as are granted to or imposed upon a mayor under this division.

(C) The mayor of a municipal corporation shall be disqualified in any criminal case in which he was the arresting officer, assisted in the arrest, or was present at the time of arrest, and shall not hear the case.

(1990 S 131, eff. 7–25–90; 1986 H 158; 128 v 823; 125 v 297; 1953 H 1; GC 4549)

1905.201 Mayor's and mayor's court magistrate's power in OMVI cases to suspend driver's or commercial driver's license

The mayor of a municipal corporation that has a mayor's court, and a mayor's court magistrate, are entitled to suspend, and shall suspend, in accordance with sections 4510.02, 4510.07, and 4511.19 of the Revised Code, the driver's or commercial driver's license or permit or nonresident operating privilege of any person who is convicted of or pleads guilty to a violation of division (A) of section 4511.19 of the Revised Code, of a municipal ordinance relating to operating a vehicle while under the influence of alcohol, a drug of abuse, or a combination of them, or of a municipal ordinance relating to operating a vehicle with a prohibited concentration of alcohol in the whole blood, blood serum or plasma, breath, or urine that is substantially equivalent to division (A) of section 4511.19 of the Revised Code. The mayor of a municipal corporation that has a mayor's court, and a mayor's court magistrate, are entitled to suspend, and shall suspend, in accordance with sections 4510.02, 4510.07, and 4511.19 of the Revised Code, the driver's, or commercial driver's license or permit or nonresident operating privilege of any person who is convicted of or pleads guilty to a violation of division (B) of section 4511.19 of the Revised Code or of a municipal ordinance relating to operating a vehicle with a prohibited concentration of alcohol in the whole blood, blood serum or plasma, breath, or urine that is substantially equivalent to division (B) of section 4511.19 of the Revised Code.

Suspension of a commercial driver's license under this section shall be concurrent with any period of disqualification or suspension under section 3123.58 or 4506.16 of the Revised Code. No person who is disqualified for life from holding a commercial driver's license under section 4506.16 of the Revised Code shall be issued a driver's license under Chapter 4507. of the Revised Code during the period for which the commercial driver's license was suspended under this section, and no person whose commercial driver's license is suspended under this section shall be issued a driver's license under Chapter 4507. of the Revised Code during the period of the suspension.

(2002 S 123, eff. 1–1–04; 2000 S 180, eff. 3–22–01; 1995 H 167, eff. 5–15–97; 1994 S 82, eff. 5–4–94; 1993 S 62, § 4, eff. 9–1–93; 1992 S 275; 1990 S 131; 1989 H 381; 1987 H 303)

MISCELLANEOUS PROVISIONS

1905.28 Contempt; rules

The mayor or mayor's court magistrate presiding at any trial under this chapter may punish contempts, compel the attendance of jurors and witnesses, and establish rules for the examination and trial of all cases brought before him, in the same manner as judges of county courts.

(1990 S 131, eff. 7–25–90; 128 v 823; 1953 H 1; GC 4557)

1905.29 Temporary confinement of dangerous criminals from township in municipal prison

The mayor of a municipal corporation, and in his absence, the president of the legislative authority of the municipal corporation, may grant to officials of adjoining or contiguous townships the temporary use of the municipal corporation prison, station house, or watchhouse to confine criminals or other persons dangerous to the peace of the community, until they can be safety [sic.] removed to the county jail, or other place of security.

(1990 S 131, eff. 7–25–90; 1953 H 1; GC 4558)

1905.30 Confinement until fine paid

When a fine is the whole or part of a sentence, the mayor's court may order the person sentenced to remain confined in the county jail, workhouse, or prison of the municipal corporation, until the fine is paid or secured to be paid, or the offender is legally discharged.

(1970 S 460, eff. 9–3–70; 1953 H 1; GC 4559)

1905.32 Fines and forfeitures recovered

Fines, penalties, and forfeitures may, in all cases, and in addition to any other mode provided, be recovered by action before any judge of a county court, or other court of competent jurisdiction, in the name of the proper municipal corporation, and for its use. In any action in which a pleading is necessary, it is sufficient if the petition sets forth generally the amount claimed to be due in respect to the violation of the ordinance of the municipal corporation. Such petition shall refer to the title of such ordinance, state the date of its adoption or passage, and show, as near as is practicable, the true time of the alleged violation.

(128 v 823, eff. 11–6–59; 1953 H 1; GC 4561)

1905.34 Party committed in default of payment of fine

When a fine imposed for the violation of an ordinance of a municipal corporation is not paid, the party convicted may, by order of the mayor of the municipal corporation, or other proper authority, or on process issued for the purpose, be committed until such fine and the costs of prosecution are paid, or until the party convicted is legally discharged.

(1975 H 205, eff. 8–19–75; 1953 H 1; GC 4563)

1905.35 Imprisonment

Imprisonment under the ordinances of a municipal corporation shall be in the workhouse or other jail of the municipal corporation. Any municipal corporation not provided with a workhouse, or other jail, may, for the purpose of imprisonment, use the county jail, at the expense of the municipal corporation, until the municipal corporation is provided with a prison, house of correction, or workhouse. Persons so imprisoned in the county jail are under the charge of the sheriff. Such sheriff shall receive and hold such persons in the manner prescribed by the ordinances of the municipal corporation, until such persons are legally discharged.

(1953 H 1, eff. 10–1–53; GC 4564)

1905.36 Use of county jail prohibited

The board of county commissioners, at such board's discretion, on giving ninety days' written notice to the legislative authority of any municipal corporation, may prohibit the use of the county jail for the purpose authorized in section 1905.35 of the Revised Code.

(1953 H 1, eff. 10–1–53; GC 4565)

1905.37 Limit of prohibition

If, within ninety days after the notice mentioned in section 1905.36 of the Revised Code is given, the legislative authority of the municipal corporation provides by ordinance and the necessary contracts for the immediate erection of a prison, workhouse, or house of correction, the municipal corporation, notwithstanding the notice and prohibition provided for in such section, shall continue to have the use of the county jail for the purpose of imprisonment, until such prison, workhouse, or house of correction is erected and ready for use.

(1953 H 1, eff. 10–1–53; GC 4566)

CHAPTER 1907

COUNTY COURT—GENERAL PROVISIONS

Publisher's Note: Until 1968, when the Modern Courts Amendment to the Ohio Constitution was adopted, Ohio court procedure was governed entirely by statute and case law. The Modern Courts Amendment required the Supreme Court of Ohio, subject to the approval of the General Assembly, to "prescribe rules governing practice and procedure in all courts of the state." Rules of practice and procedure are the Civil, Criminal, Appellate, and Juvenile Rules, Rules of the Court of Claims, and the Ohio Rules of Evidence. Pursuant to Ohio Constitution Article IV, Section 5(B), such rules "shall not abridge, enlarge, or modify any substantive right," and " [a]ll laws in conflict with such rules shall be of no further force or effect." Provisions of Chapter 1907 should be read with this in mind.

JURISDICTION

1907.01 County court created; territorial jurisdiction; court of record

There is hereby created in each county of the state, in which the territorial jurisdiction of a municipal court or municipal courts is not coextensive with the boundaries of the county, a court to be known as the county court. The county court shall have jurisdiction throughout a county court district that shall consist of all territory within the county not subject to the territorial jurisdiction of any municipal court.

County courts are courts of record for all purposes of law.

(1986 H 158, eff. 3–17–87)

1907.011 Concurrent jurisdiction over Ohio River

In addition to the territorial jurisdiction conferred by section 1907.01 of the Revised Code, the county courts of Adams, Belmont, Jefferson, Meigs, and Monroe counties have jurisdiction beyond the north or northwest shore of the Ohio river extending to the opposite shore line, between the boundary lines of any adjacent municipal courts or adjacent county courts. Each of the county courts that is given jurisdiction on the Ohio river by this section has concurrent jurisdiction on the Ohio river with any adjacent municipal courts or adjacent county courts that border on that river and with any court of Kentucky or of West Virginia that borders on the Ohio river and that has jurisdiction on the Ohio river under the law of Kentucky or the law of West Virginia, whichever is applicable, or under federal law.

(2002 H 530, eff. 12–18–02; 2000 H 599, eff. 1–1–02; 1992 S 371, eff. 1–17–93; 1992 S 284)

1907.02 Jurisdiction, criminal cases, parking violations

(A)(1) In addition to other jurisdiction granted a county court in the Revised Code, a county court has jurisdiction of all misdemeanor cases. A county court has jurisdiction to conduct preliminary hearings in felony cases, to bind over alleged felons to the court of common pleas, and to take other action in felony cases as authorized by Criminal Rule 5.

(2) A judge of a county court does not have the authority to dismiss a criminal complaint, charge, information, or indictment solely at the request of the complaining witness and over the objection of the prosecuting attorney, village solicitor, city director of law, or other chief legal officer who is responsible for the prosecution of the case.

(B) A county court has jurisdiction of the violation of a vehicle parking or standing ordinance, resolution, or regulation if a local authority, as defined in division (D) of section 4521.01 of the Revised Code, has specified that it is not to be considered a criminal offense, if the violation is committed within the limits of the court's territory, and if the violation is not required to be handled by a parking violations bureau or joint parking violations bureau pursuant to Chapter 4521. of the Revised Code. A county court does not have jurisdiction over violations of ordinances, resolutions, or regulations that are required to be handled by a parking violations bureau or joint parking violations bureau pursuant to that chapter.

A county court also has jurisdiction of an appeal from a judgment or default judgment entered pursuant to Chapter 4521. of the Revised Code, as authorized by division (D) of section 4521.08 of the Revised Code. Any such appeal shall be placed on the regular docket of the court and shall be determined by a judge of the court.

(1997 S 98, eff. 3–17–98; 1986 H 158, eff. 3–17–87)

1907.032 Jurisdiction over campsite use

In addition to the jurisdiction authorized in other sections of this chapter, a county court has original jurisdiction in actions filed under section 3729.13 of the Revised Code.

(2004 H 368, eff. 10–13–04; 2002 H 520, eff. 4–3–03)

1907.10 Mayors' criminal jurisdiction

Mayors retain jurisdiction in all criminal cases involving the violation of ordinances of their respective municipal corporations and in all criminal cases involving moving traffic violations occurring on state highways located within their respective municipal corporations, to be exercised concurrently with the county court.

(1986 H 158, eff. 3–17–87)

COURT ADMINISTRATION

1907.231 Retention of documentation regarding criminal convictions and guilty pleas

Notwithstanding section 149.38 of the Revised Code, each clerk of a county court shall retain documentation regarding each criminal conviction and plea of guilty involving a case that is or was before the court. The documentation shall be in a form that is admissible as evidence in a criminal proceeding as evidence of a prior conviction or that is readily convertible to or producible in a form that is admissible as evidence in a criminal proceeding as evidence of a prior conviction and may be retained in any form authorized by section 9.01 of the Revised Code. The clerk shall retain this documentation for a period of fifty years after the entry of judgment in the case, except that documentation regarding cases solely concerned with minor misdemeanor offenses or minor misdemeanor traffic offenses shall be retained as provided in divisions (A) and (B) of section 1901.41 of the Revised Code, and documentation regarding other misdemeanor traffic offenses shall be retained for a period of twenty-five years after the entry of judgment in the case. This section shall apply to records currently retained and to records created on or after September 23, 2004.

(2004 H 30, eff. 3–23–05; 2004 H 163, eff. 9–23–04)

FEES AND COSTS

1907.24 Schedule of fees and costs; advance deposits; charitable public purpose fee

(A) Subject to division (C) of this section, a county court shall fix and tax fees and costs as follows:

(1) The county court shall require an advance deposit for the filing of any new civil action or proceeding when required by division (C) of this section and, in all other cases, shall establish a schedule of fees and costs to be taxed in any civil or criminal action or proceeding.

(2) The county court by rule may require an advance deposit for the filing of a civil action or proceeding and publication fees as provided in section 2701.09 of the Revised Code. The court may waive an advance deposit requirement upon the presentation of an affidavit or other evidence that establishes that a party is unable to make the requisite deposit.

(3) When a party demands a jury trial in a civil action or proceeding, the county court may require the party to make an advance deposit as fixed by rule of court, unless the court concludes, on the basis of an affidavit or other evidence presented by the party, that the party is unable to make the requisite deposit. If a jury is called, the county court shall tax the fees of a jury as costs.

(4) In a civil or criminal action or proceeding, the county court shall fix the fees of witnesses in accordance with sections 2335.06 and 2335.08 of the Revised Code.

(5) A county court may tax as part of the costs in a trial of the cause, in an amount fixed by rule of court, a reasonable charge for driving, towing, carting, storing, keeping, and preserving motor vehicles and other personal property recovered or seized in a proceeding.

(6) The court shall preserve chattel property seized under a writ or process issued by the court pending final disposition for the benefit of all interested persons. The court may place the chattel property in storage when necessary or proper for its preservation. The custodian of chattel property so stored shall not be required to part with the possession of the property until a reasonable charge, to be fixed by the court, is paid.

(7) The county court, as it determines, may refund all deposits and advance payments of fees and costs, including those for jurors and summoning jurors, when they have been paid by the losing party.

(8) The court may tax as part of costs charges for the publication of legal notices required by statute or order of court, as provided by section 7.13 of the Revised Code.

(B)(1) The county court may determine that, for the efficient operation of the court, additional funds are necessary to acquire and pay for special projects of the court including, but not limited to, the acquisition of additional facilities or the rehabilitation of existing facilities, the acquisition of equipment, the hiring and training of staff, community service programs, mediation or dispute resolution services, the employment of magistrates, the training and education of judges, acting judges, and magistrates, and other related services. Upon that determination, the court by rule may charge a fee, in addition to all other court costs, on the filing of each criminal cause, civil action or proceeding, or judgment by confession.

If the county court offers a special program or service in cases of a specific type, the county court by rule may assess an additional charge in a case of that type, over and above court costs, to cover the special program or service. The county court shall adjust the special assessment periodically, but not retroactively, so that the amount assessed in those cases does not exceed the actual cost of providing the service or program.

All moneys collected under division (B) of this section shall be paid to the county treasurer for deposit into either a general special projects fund or a fund established for a specific special project. Moneys from a fund of that nature shall be disbursed upon an order of the court in an amount no greater than the actual cost to the court of a project. If a specific fund is terminated because of the discontinuance of a program or service established under division (B) of this section, the county court may order that moneys remaining in the fund be transferred to an account established under this division for a similar purpose.

(2) As used in division (B) of this section:

(a) "Criminal cause" means a charge alleging the violation of a statute or ordinance, or subsection of a statute or ordinance, that requires a separate finding of fact or a separate plea before disposition and of which the defendant may be found guilty, whether filed as part of a multiple charge on a single summons, citation, or complaint or as a separate charge on a single summons, citation, or complaint. "Criminal cause" does not include separate violations of the same statute or ordinance, or subsection of the same statute or ordinance, unless each charge is filed on a separate summons, citation, or complaint.

(b) "Civil action or proceeding" means any civil litigation that must be determined by judgment entry.

(C) Subject to division (E) of this section, the county court shall collect in all its divisions except the small claims division the sum of fifteen dollars as additional filing fees in each new civil action or proceeding for the charitable public purpose of providing financial assistance to legal aid societies that operate within the state. Subject to division (E) of this section, the county court shall collect in its small claims division the sum of seven dollars as additional filing fees in each new civil action or proceeding for the charitable public purpose of providing financial assistance to legal aid societies that operate within the state. This division does not apply to any execution on a judgment, proceeding in aid of execution, or other post-judgment proceeding arising out of a civil action. The filing fees required to be collected under this division shall be in addition to any other court costs imposed in the action or proceeding and shall be collected at the time of the filing of the action or proceeding. The court shall not waive the payment of the additional filing fees in a new civil action or proceeding unless the court waives the advanced payment of all filing fees in the action or proceeding. All such moneys collected during a month shall be transmitted on or before the twentieth day of the following month by the clerk of the court to the treasurer of state. The moneys then shall be deposited by the treasurer of state to the credit of the legal aid fund established under section 120.52 of the Revised Code.

The court may retain up to one per cent of the moneys it collects under this division to cover administrative costs, including the hiring of any additional personnel necessary to implement this division.

(D) The county court shall establish by rule a schedule of fees for miscellaneous services performed by the county court or any of its judges in accordance with law. If judges of the court of common pleas perform similar services, the fees prescribed in the schedule shall not exceed the fees for those services prescribed by the court of common pleas.

(E) Under the circumstances described in sections 2969.21 to 2969.27 of the Revised Code, the clerk of the county court shall charge the fees and perform the other duties specified in those sections.

(2001 H 94, eff. 9–5–01; 1998 H 507, eff. 3–22–99; 1998 H 426, eff. 7–22–98; 1996 H 438, eff. 7–1–97; 1996 H 423, eff. 10–31–96; 1996 H 455, eff. 10–17–96; 1992 H 405, eff. 1–1–93; 1991 H 298; 1989 H 111; 1987 H 171; 1986 H 158)

1907.27 Witness fees

Witness fees in relation to civil and criminal actions and proceedings shall be determined in accordance with Chapter 2335. of the Revised Code.

(1986 H 158, eff. 3–17–87)

PRACTICE AND PROCEDURE

1907.29 Jury trials; procedure

(A) A jury trial shall be demanded in the manner prescribed in the Rules of Civil Procedure or the Rules of Criminal Procedure. The number of persons composing a jury and the verdicts of jurors shall be governed by those rules.

(B) The right of a person to a jury trial is waived under the circumstances prescribed in the Rules of Civil Procedure or the Rules of Criminal Procedure.

(C) If, as a result of challenges or other causes, a jury panel is not full, the deputy sheriff or constable who is in attendance at a trial before a county court may fill the panel in the same manner as the sheriff fills a panel in the court of common pleas.

(D) The judge of the county court involved in a case shall administer an oath to the jury to try the matters in difference between the parties that are to be determined by the jury, and to give a verdict in accordance with the evidence.

(E) After the jurors are sworn in a case before a county court, they shall sit together and hear the proofs and allegations of the parties. After the hearing, the jury shall be kept together in a convenient place until they have agreed upon their verdict or have been discharged by the county court judge involved in the case.

(F) If an action being tried to a jury in a county court is continued, the jurors shall attend at the time and place appointed for trial without further notice.

(G) The judge of a county court involved in a case may punish as for contempt any juror who neglects or refuses to attend when properly summoned or who, although in attendance, refuses to serve.

(H) If, in a civil action before a county court, the judge is satisfied that the number of jurors required by Civil Rule 48 for concurrence purposes cannot concur in a verdict, and the jury has deliberated upon the verdict for a reasonable time, the judge may discharge the jury and continue the action. If either party requests a new jury, the judge shall cause the selection of another jury. If the action is continued, it shall be continued to a time that the judge considers reasonable unless the parties or their attorneys agree on a longer or shorter time.

(1986 H 158, eff. 3–17–87)

1907.31 Applicability of rules of procedure

(A) The Rules of Civil Procedure, the Rules of Criminal Procedure, and the Rules of Evidence apply in civil and criminal actions and proceedings before a county court unless otherwise specifically provided in the Revised Code.

(B) The Rules of Appellate Procedure govern appeals from a county court to the court of appeals.

(1986 H 158, eff. 3–17–87)

WITNESSES

1907.37 Warrant for arrest of witness

When it appears to a judge of a county court that a witness was served with a subpoena to appear and give testimony before him in any matter in which he has authority to require the witness to appear and testify, that the testimony of that witness is material, and that he refuses or neglects to attend in conformity with the subpoena, the judge shall issue a warrant to arrest the witness for the purpose of compelling his attendance and punishing his disobedience.

(1986 H 158, eff. 3–17–87)

1907.38 Punishment of witness

When a witness arrested under section 1907.37 of the Revised Code is brought before the judge of the county court, or when a person in attendance refuses to testify as a witness, and no valid excuse is shown, the judge may punish the person as for contempt, and, if he does so, the judge shall enter any fine or imprisonment imposed on the docket. An entry indicating a fine has the effect of a judgment in favor of this state against the witness or person, and it may be enforced against his person or property.

(1986 H 158, eff. 3–17–87)

MISCELLANEOUS PROVISIONS

1907.53 Bailiffs; ex officio bailiffs; attendance of deputy sheriffs and constables during trials

(A)(1) Each judge of a county court may appoint a bailiff on a full-time or part-time basis. The bailiff shall receive compensation as prescribed by the appointing judge, and the compensation is payable in semimonthly installments from the treasury of the county or other authorized fund. Before entering upon the duties of the office, a bailiff shall take an oath to faithfully perform those duties and shall give a bond of not less than three thousand dollars, as the appointing judge prescribes, conditioned on the faithful performance of the duties as bailiff.

(2) The board of county commissioners may purchase motor vehicles for the use of the bailiff that the court determines necessary to perform the duties of the office. The board, upon approval by the court, shall pay all expenses, maintenance, and upkeep of the vehicles from the county treasury or other authorized fund. Any allowances, costs, and expenses for the operation of private motor vehicles by the bailiffs for official duties, including the cost of oil, gasoline, and maintenance, shall be prescribed by the court and subject to the approval of the board and shall be paid from the county treasury or other authorized fund.

(B)(1) In a county court district in which no bailiff is appointed pursuant to division (A)(1) of this section, every deputy sheriff of the county, every police officer of a municipal corporation within the jurisdiction of the court, every member of a township or joint township police district police force, and every police constable of a township within the county court district is ex officio a bailiff of the court in and for the county, municipal corporation, or township within which the deputy sheriff, police officer, police force member, or police constable is commissioned and shall perform, in respect to cases within that jurisdiction and without additional compensation, any duties that are required by a judge of the court or by the clerk of the court.

(2) At the request of a county court judge, a deputy sheriff or constable shall attend the county court while a trial is in progress.

(C)(1) A bailiff and an ex officio bailiff shall perform for the county court services similar to those performed by the sheriff for the court of common pleas and shall perform any other duties that are required by rule of court.

(2) The bailiff may administer oaths to witnesses and jurors and receive verdicts in the same manner and form and to the same extent as the clerk or deputy clerks of the county court. The bailiff may approve all undertakings and bonds given in actions of replevin and all redelivery bonds in attachments.

(D) Bailiffs and deputy bailiffs are in the unclassified civil service.

(1996 H 438, eff. 7–1–97; 1986 H 158, eff. 3–17–87)

1907.54 Appointment of special constables

Upon the written application of the director of administrative services or of three freeholders of the county in which a county court judge resides, the judge may appoint one or more electors of the county as special constables. In order to be eligible to serve as a special constable, an elector shall hold a valid certificate issued by the Ohio peace officer training commission.

The special constables shall guard and protect the property of this state, or the property of such freeholders and the property of this state under lease to such freeholders, designated in general terms in the application, from all unlawful acts, and, so far as necessary for that purpose, a special constable has the same authority and is subject to the same obligations as other constables.

(1996 H 670, eff. 12–2–96; 1994 H 136, eff. 11–9–94; 1986 H 158, eff. 3–17–87)

1907.55 Memorandum of appointment of special constable; compensation; reappointment

The judge of a county court appointing a special constable pursuant to section 1907.54 of the Revised Code, shall make a memorandum of the appointment upon the judge's docket. The appointment shall continue in force for one year, unless the judge revokes it sooner. A special constable shall be paid in full for the special constable's services by the freeholders for whose benefit the special constable was appointed, and shall receive no compensation except from those freeholders.

If a county court judge wishes to reappoint an elector for a successive one-year period, before the elector may be appointed the elector shall have successfully completed a firearms requalification program approved by the executive director of the Ohio peace officer training commission in accordance with rules adopted by the attorney general under section 109.743 of the Revised Code.

(1996 H 670, eff. 12–2–96; 1994 H 136, eff. 11–9–94; 1986 H 158, eff. 3–17–87)

1907.57 Prohibition against failure to deliver official dockets and papers

No judge of a county court shall refuse, upon lawful demand, to deliver any docket, papers, files, or other matter to the person entitled to them.

(1986 H 158, eff. 3–17–87)

CHAPTER 1923

FORCIBLE ENTRY AND DETAINER

JURISDICTION

JURISDICTION

1923.02 Persons subject to forcible entry and detainer action

(A) Proceedings under this chapter may be had as follows:

(1) Against tenants or manufactured home park residents holding over their terms;

(2) Against tenants or manufactured home park residents in possession under an oral tenancy, who are in default in the payment of rent as provided in division (B) of this section;

(3) In sales of real estate, on executions, orders, or other judicial process, when the judgment debtor was in possession at the time of the rendition of the judgment or decree, by virtue of which the sale was made;

(4) In sales by executors, administrators, or guardians, and on partition, when any of the parties to the complaint were in possession at the commencement of the action, after the sales, so made on execution or otherwise, have been examined by the proper court and adjudged legal;

(5) When the defendant is an occupier of lands or tenements, without color of title, and the complainant has the right of possession to them;

(6) In any other case of the unlawful and forcible detention of lands or tenements. For purposes of this division, in addition to any other type of unlawful and forcible detention of lands or tenements, such a detention may be determined to exist when both of the following apply:

(a) A tenant fails to vacate residential premises within three days after both of the following occur:

(i) The tenant's landlord has actual knowledge of or has reasonable cause to believe that the tenant, any person in the tenant's household, or any person on the premises with the consent of the tenant previously has or presently is engaged in a violation of Chapter 2925. or 3719. of the Revised Code, or of a municipal ordinance that is substantially similar to any section in either of those chapters, which involves a controlled substance and which occurred in, is occurring in, or otherwise was or is connected with the premises, whether or not the tenant or other person has been charged with, has pleaded guilty to or been convicted of, or has been determined to be a delinquent child for an act that, if committed by an adult, would be a violation as described in this division. For purposes of this division, a landlord has "actual knowledge of or has reasonable cause to believe" that a tenant, any person in the tenant's household, or any person on the premises with the consent of the tenant previously has or presently is engaged in a violation as described in this division if a search warrant was issued pursuant to Criminal Rule 41 or Chapter 2933. of the Revised Code; the affidavit presented to obtain the warrant named or described the tenant or person as the individual to be searched and particularly described the tenant's premises as the place to be searched, named or described one or more controlled substances to be searched for and seized, stated substantially the offense under Chapter 2925. or 3719. of the Revised Code or the substantially similar municipal ordinance that occurred in, is occurring in, or otherwise was or is connected with the tenant's premises, and states the factual basis for the affiant's belief that the controlled substances are located on the tenant's premises; the warrant was properly executed by a law enforcement officer and any controlled substance described in the affidavit was found by that officer during the search and seizure; and, subsequent to the search and seizure, the landlord was informed by that or another law enforcement officer of the fact that the tenant or person has or presently is engaged in a violation as described in this division and it occurred in, is occurring in, or otherwise was or is connected with the tenant's premises.

(ii) The landlord gives the tenant the notice required by division (C) of section 5321.17 of the Revised Code.

(b) The court determines, by a preponderance of the evidence, that the tenant, any person in the tenant's household, or any person on the premises with the consent of the tenant previously has or presently is engaged in a violation as described in division (A)(6)(a)(i) of this section.

(7) In cases arising out of Chapter 5313. of the Revised Code. In those cases, the court has the authority to declare a forfeiture of the vendee's rights under a land installment contract and to grant any other claims arising out of the contract.

(8) Against tenants who have breached an obligation that is imposed by section 5321.05 of the Revised Code, other than the obligation specified in division (A)(9) of that section, and that materially affects health and safety. Prior to the commencement of an action under this division, notice shall be given to the tenant and compliance secured with section 5321.11 of the Revised Code.

(9) Against tenants who have breached an obligation imposed upon them by a written rental agreement;

(10) Against manufactured home park residents who have defaulted in the payment of rent or breached the terms of a rental agreement with a manufactured home park operator. Nothing in this division precludes the commencement of an action under division (A)(12) of this section when the additional circumstances described in that division apply.

(11) Against manufactured home park residents who have committed two material violations of the rules of the manufactured home park, of the public health council, or of applicable state and local health and safety codes and who have been notified of the violations in compliance with section 3733.13 of the Revised Code;

(12) Against a manufactured home park resident, or the estate of a manufactured home park resident, who has been absent from the manufactured home park for a period of thirty consecutive days prior to the commencement of an action under this division and whose manufactured home or mobile home, or recreational vehicle that is parked in the manufactured home park, has been left unoccupied for that thirty-day period, without notice to the park operator and without payment of rent due under the rental agreement with the park operator;

(13) Against occupants of self-service storage facilities, as defined in division (A) of section 5322.01 of the Revised Code, who have breached the terms of a rental agreement or violated section 5322.04 of the Revised Code;

(14) Against any resident or occupant who, pursuant to a rental agreement, resides in or occupies residential premises located within one thousand feet of any school premises and to whom both of the following apply:

(a) The resident's or occupant's name appears on the state registry of sex offenders and child-victim offenders maintained under section 2950.13 of the Revised Code.

(b) The state registry of sex offenders and child-victim offenders indicates that the resident or occupant was convicted of or pleaded guilty to either a sexually oriented offense that is not a registration-exempt sexually oriented offense or a child-victim oriented offense in a criminal prosecution and was not sentenced to a serious youthful offender dispositional sentence for that offense.

(15) Against any tenant who permits any person to occupy residential premises located within one thousand feet of any school premises if both of the following apply to the person:

(a) The person's name appears on the state registry of sex offenders and child-victim offenders maintained under section 2950.13 of the Revised Code.

(b) The state registry of sex offenders and child-victim offenders indicates that the person was convicted of or pleaded guilty to either a sexually oriented offense that is not a registration-exempt sexually oriented offense or a child-victim oriented offense in a criminal prosecution and was not sentenced to a serious youthful offender dispositional sentence for that offense.

(B) If a tenant or manufactured home park resident holding under an oral tenancy is in default in the payment of rent, the tenant or resident forfeits the right of occupancy, and the landlord may, at the landlord's option, terminate the tenancy by notifying the tenant or resident, as provided in section 1923.04 of the Revised Code, to leave the premises, for the restitution of which an action may then be brought under this chapter.

(C)(1) If a tenant or any other person with the tenant's permission resides in or occupies residential premises that are located within one thousand feet of any school premises and is a resident or occupant of the type described in division (A)(14) of this section or a person of the type described in division (A)(15) of this section, the landlord for those residential premises, upon discovery that the tenant or other person is a resident, occupant, or person of that nature, may terminate the rental agreement or tenancy for those residential premises by notifying the tenant and all other occupants, as provided in section 1923.04 of the Revised Code, to leave the premises.

(2) If a landlord is authorized to terminate a rental agreement or tenancy pursuant to division (C)(1) of this section but does not so terminate the rental agreement or tenancy, the landlord is not liable in a tort or other civil action in damages for any injury, death, or loss to person or property that allegedly result from that decision.

(D) This chapter does not apply to a student tenant as defined by division (H) of section 5321.01 of the Revised Code when the college or university proceeds to terminate a rental agreement pursuant to section 5321. 031 of the Revised Code.

(2003 S 5, eff. 7–31–03; 2002 H 520, eff. 4–3–03; 1994 H 438, eff. 10–12–94; 1990 S 258, eff. 8–22–90; 1988 H 708; 1986 H 158, H 495; 1984 S 231; 1980 H 410, S 227; 1977 H 29; 1974 S 103; 1969 S 156; 1953 H 1; GC 10449)

ACTIONS AND PROCEDURES

1923.04 Notice; content; service; alternative in case of land contract

(A) Except as provided in division (B) of this section, a party desiring to commence an action under this chapter shall notify the adverse party to leave the premises, for the possession of which the action is about to be brought, three or more days before beginning the action, by certified mail, return receipt requested, or by handing a written copy of the notice to the defendant in person, or by leaving it at his usual place of abode or at the premises from which the defendant is sought to be evicted.

Every notice given under this section by a landlord to recover residential premises shall contain the following language printed or written in a conspicuous manner: "You are being asked to leave the premises. If you do not leave, an eviction action may be initiated against you. If you are in doubt regarding your legal rights and obligations as a tenant, it is recommended that you seek legal assistance."

(B) The service of notice pursuant to section 5313.06 of the Revised Code constitutes compliance with the notice requirement of division (A) of this section. The service of the notice required by division (C) of section 5321.17 of the Revised Code constitutes compliance with the notice requirement of division (A) of this section.

(1990 S 258, eff. 8–22–90; 1986 H 158; 1980 S 312; 1979 H 76; 1974 S 103; 131 v H 405; 1953 H 1; GC 10451)

1923.05 Complaint filed and recorded

The summons shall not issue in an action under this chapter until the plaintiff files his complaint in writing with the court. The complaint shall particularly describe the premises so entered upon and detained, and set forth either an unlawful and forcible entry and detention, or an unlawful and forcible detention after a peacable *[sic.]* or lawful entry of the described premises. The complaint shall be copied into, and made a part of the record.

(1986 H 158, eff. 3–17–87; 127 v 1039; 1953 H 1; GC 10452)

1923.051 Actions based on controlled substance violations

(A) Notwithstanding the time-for-service of a summons provision of division (A) of section 1923.06 of the Revised Code, if the complaint described in section 1923.05 of the Revised Code that is filed by a landlord in an action under this chapter states that the landlord seeks a judgment of restitution based on the grounds specified in divisions (A)(6)(a) and (b) of section 1923.02 of the Revised Code, then the clerk of the municipal court, county court, or court of common pleas in which the complaint is filed shall cause both of the following to occur:

(1) The service and return of the summons in the action in accordance with the Rules of Civil Procedure, which service shall be made, if possible, within three working days after the filing of the complaint;

(2) The action to be set for trial not later than the thirtieth calendar day after the date that the tenant is served with a copy of the summons in accordance with division (A)(1) of this section.

(B) The tenant in an action under this chapter as described in division (A) of this section is not required to file an answer to the complaint of the landlord, and may present any defenses that the tenant may possess at the trial of the action in accordance with section 1923.061 of the Revised Code.

(C) No continuances of an action under this chapter as described in division (A) of this section shall be permitted under section 1923.08 of the Revised Code, and if the tenant in the action does not appear at the trial and the summons in the action was properly served in accordance with division (A)(1) of this section, then the court shall try the action in accordance with section 1923.07 of the Revised Code.

(D) All provisions of this chapter that are not inconsistent with this section shall apply to an action under this chapter as described in division (A) of this section.

(2003 S 5, eff. 7–31–03; 1990 S 258, eff. 8–22–90)

1923.06 Summons; content; service

(A) Any summons in an action, including a claim for possession, pursuant to this chapter shall be issued, be in the form specified, and be served and returned as provided in this section. Such service shall be at least seven days before the day set for trial.

(B) Every summons issued under this section to recover residential premises shall contain the following language printed in a conspicuous manner: "A complaint to evict you has been filed with this court. No person shall be evicted unless the person's right to possession has ended and no person shall be evicted in retaliation for the exercise of the person's lawful rights. If you are depositing rent with the clerk of this court you shall continue to deposit such rent until the time of the court hearing. The failure to continue to deposit such rent may result in your eviction. You may request a trial by jury. You have the right to seek legal assistance. If you cannot afford a lawyer, you may contact your local legal aid or legal service office. If none is available, you may contact your local bar association."

(C) The clerk of the court in which a complaint to evict is filed shall mail any summons by ordinary mail, along with a copy of the complaint, document, or other process to be served, to the defendant at the address set forth in the caption of the summons and to any address set forth in any written instructions furnished to the clerk. The mailing shall be evidenced by a certificate of mailing which the clerk shall complete and file.

In addition to this ordinary mail service, the clerk also shall cause service of that process to be completed under division (D) or (E) of this section or both, depending upon which of those two methods of service is requested by the plaintiff upon filing the complaint to evict.

(D)(1) If requested, the clerk shall deliver sufficient copies of the summons, complaint, document, or other process to be served to, and service shall be made by, one of the following persons:

(a) The sheriff of the county in which the premises are located when the process issues from a court of common pleas or county court;

(b) The bailiff of the court for service when process issues from a municipal court;

(c) Any person who is eighteen years of age or older, who is not a party, and who has been designated by order of the court to make service of process when process issues from any of the courts referred to in divisions (D)(1)(a) and (b) of this section.

(2) The person serving process shall effect service at the premises that are the subject of the forcible entry and detainer action by one of the following means:

(a) By locating the person to be served at the premises to tender a copy of the process and accompanying documents to that person;

(b) By leaving a copy of the summons, complaint, document, or other process with a person of suitable age and discretion found at the premises if the person to be served cannot be found at the time the person making service attempts to serve the summons pursuant to division (D)(2)(a) of this section;

(c) By posting a copy in a conspicuous place on the subject premises if service cannot be made pursuant to divisions (D)(2)(a) and (b) of this section.

(3) Within five days after receiving the summons, complaint, document, or other process from the clerk for service, the person making service shall return the process to the clerk. The person

shall indicate on the process which method described in division (D)(2) of this section was used to serve the summons. The clerk shall make the appropriate entry on the appearance docket.

(E) If requested, the clerk shall mail by certified mail, return receipt requested, a copy of the summons, complaint, document, or other process to be served to the address set forth in the caption of the summons and to any address set forth in any written instructions furnished to the clerk.

(F) Service of process shall be deemed complete on the date that any of the following has occurred:

(1) Service is made pursuant to division (D)(2)(a) or (b) of this section.

(2) Both ordinary mail service under division (C) and service by posting pursuant to division (D)(2)(c) of this section have been made.

(3) For service performed pursuant to division (E) of this section, on the date of mailing, if on the date of the hearing either of the following applies:

(a) The certified mail has not been returned for any reason other than refused or unclaimed.

(b) The certified mail has not been endorsed, and the ordinary mail has not been returned.

(G)(1) The claim for restitution of the premises shall be scheduled for hearing in accordance with local court rules, but in no event sooner than the seventh day from the date service is complete.

(2) Answer day for any other claims filed with the claim for possession shall be twenty-eight days from the date service is deemed complete under this section.

(1999 S 30, eff. 9–29–99; 1998 S 83, eff. 3–30–99; 1986 H 158, eff. 3–17–87; 1974 S 103; 1953 H 1; GC 10453)

1923.062 Stay of proceedings or adjustment of rental obligation for tenant on active duty or immediate family member of tenant on active duty

(A) In an action under this chapter for possession of residential premises of a tenant or manufactured home park resident who is deployed on active duty or of any member of the tenant's or resident's immediate family, if the tenant or resident entered into the rental agreement on or after the effective date of this section, the court may, on its own motion, and shall, upon motion made by or on behalf of the tenant or resident, do either of the following if the tenant's or resident's ability to pay the agreed rent is materially affected by the deployment on active duty:

(1) Stay the proceedings for a period of ninety days, unless, in the opinion of the court, justice and equity require a longer or shorter period of time;

(2) Adjust the obligation under the rental agreement to preserve the interest of all parties to it.

(B) If a stay is granted under division (A) of this section, the court may grant the landlord or park operator such relief as equity may require.

(C) This section does not apply to landlords or park operators operating less than four residential premises.

(D) As used in this section, "active duty" means active duty pursuant to an executive order of the president of the United States, an act of the congress of the United States, or section 5919.29 or 5923.21 of the Revised Code.

(2004 H 426, eff. 5–18–05)

CHAPTER 2101

PROBATE COURT—JURISDICTION; PROCEDURE

2101.26 Abuse of elderly or wards or theft from estates; referral of information to law enforcement agency

If the probate judge receives information of the alleged abuse or financial exploitation of a person of advanced age or of an incompetent or minor under guardianship, or receives information of an alleged theft from the estate of a decedent, the judge may refer the information to the appropriate law enforcement agency of the political subdivision in which the abuse, exploitation, or theft allegedly occurred, which agency shall conduct an investigation to determine whether there is probable cause to believe that a violation of any section of the Revised Code that sets forth a criminal offense, or of any ordinance, resolution, or regulation of a municipal corporation or other political subdivision of the state that sets forth a criminal offense, has occurred. Upon completion of the investigation, the law enforcement agency involved shall file with the judge a report that summarizes its findings and indicates whether an indictment will be sought or charges will be filed as a result of the investigation.

(1989 S 46, eff. 1–1–90)

CHAPTER 2108

HUMAN BODIES OR PARTS THEREOF

2108.30 Determination that death has occurred; immunity of physician

An individual is dead if he has sustained either irreversible cessation of circulatory and respiratory functions or irreversible cessation of all functions of the brain, including the brain stem, as determined in accordance with accepted medical standards. If the respiratory and circulatory functions of a person are being artificially sustained, under accepted medical standards a determination that death has occurred is made by a physician by observing and conducting a test to determine that the irreversible cessation of all functions of the brain has occurred.

A physician who makes a determination of death in accordance with this section and accepted medical standards is not liable for damages in any civil action or subject to prosecution in any criminal proceeding for his acts or the acts of others based on that determination.

Any person who acts in good faith in reliance on a determination of death made by a physician in accordance with this section and accepted medical standards is not liable for damages in any civil action or subject to prosecution in any criminal proceeding for his actions.

(1981 S 98, eff. 3–15–82)

CHAPTER 2151

JUVENILE COURTS—GENERAL PROVISIONS

Publisher's Note: Until 1968, when the Modern Courts Amendment to the Ohio Constitution was adopted, Ohio court procedure was governed entirely by statute and case law. The Modern Courts Amendment required the Supreme Court of Ohio, subject to the approval of the General Assembly, to "prescribe rules governing practice and procedure in all courts of the state." Rules of practice and procedure are the Civil, Criminal, Appellate, and Juvenile Rules, Rules of the Court of Claims, and the Ohio Rules of Evidence. Pursuant to Ohio Constitution Article IV, Section 5(B), such rules "shall not abridge, enlarge, or modify any substantive right," and " [a]ll laws in conflict with such rules shall be of no further force or effect." Provisions of Chapter 2151 should be read with this in mind.

CONSTRUCTION; DEFINITIONS

2151.01 Construction; purpose

The sections in Chapter 2151. of the Revised Code, with the exception of those sections providing for the criminal prosecution of adults, shall be liberally interpreted and construed so as to effectuate the following purposes:

(A) To provide for the care, protection, and mental and physical development of children subject to Chapter 2151. of the Revised Code, whenever possible, in a family environment, separating the child from the child's parents only when necessary for the child's welfare or in the interests of public safety;

(B) To provide judicial procedures through which Chapters 2151. and 2152. of the Revised Code are executed and enforced, and in which the parties are assured of a fair hearing, and their constitutional and other legal rights are recognized and enforced.

(2000 S 179, § 3, eff. 1–1–02; 1969 H 320, eff. 11–19–69)

2151.011 Definitions

Note: See also following version of this section, eff. 5–18–05.

(A) As used in the Revised Code:

(1) "Juvenile court" means whichever of the following is applicable that has jurisdiction under this chapter and Chapter 2152. of the Revised Code:

(a) The division of the court of common pleas specified in section 2101.022 or 2301.03 of the Revised Code as having jurisdiction under this chapter and Chapter 2152. of the Revised Code or as being the juvenile division or the juvenile division combined with one or more other divisions;

(b) The juvenile court of Cuyahoga county or Hamilton county that is separately and independently created by section 2151.08 or Chapter 2153. of the Revised Code and that has jurisdiction under this chapter and Chapter 2152. of the Revised Code;

(c) If division (A)(1)(a) or (b) of this section does not apply, the probate division of the court of common pleas.

(2) "Juvenile judge" means a judge of a court having jurisdiction under this chapter.

(3) "Private child placing agency" means any association, as defined in section 5103.02 of the Revised Code, that is certified under section 5103.03 of the Revised Code to accept temporary, permanent, or legal custody of children and place the children for either foster care or adoption.

(4) "Private noncustodial agency" means any person, organization, association, or society certified by the department of job and family services that does not accept temporary or permanent legal custody of children, that is privately operated in this state, and that does one or more of the following:

(a) Receives and cares for children for two or more consecutive weeks;

(b) Participates in the placement of children in certified foster homes;

(c) Provides adoption services in conjunction with a public children services agency or private child placing agency.

(B) As used in this chapter:

(1) "Adequate parental care" means the provision by a child's parent or parents, guardian, or custodian of adequate food, clothing, and shelter to ensure the child's health and physical safety and the provision by a child's parent or parents of specialized services warranted by the child's physical or mental needs.

(2) "Adult" means an individual who is eighteen years of age or older.

(3) "Agreement for temporary custody" means a voluntary agreement authorized by section 5103.15 of the Revised Code that transfers the temporary custody of a child to a public children services agency or a private child placing agency.

(4) "Certified foster home" means a foster home, as defined in section 5103.02 of the Revised Code, certified under section 5103.03 of the Revised Code.

(5) "Child" means a person who is under eighteen years of age, except that the juvenile court has jurisdiction over any person who is adjudicated an unruly child prior to attaining eighteen years of age until the person attains twenty-one years of age, and, for purposes of that jurisdiction related to that adjudication, a person who is so adjudicated an unruly child shall be deemed a "child" until the person attains twenty-one years of age.

(6) "Child day camp," "child day-care," "child day-care center," "part-time child day-care center," "type A family day-care home," "certified type B family day-care home," "type B home," "administrator of a child day-care center," "administrator of a type A family day-care home," "in-home aide," and "authorized provider" have the same meanings as in section 5104.01 of the Revised Code.

(7) "Child day-care provider" means an individual who is a child-care staff member or administrator of a child day-care center, a type A family day-care home, or a type B family day-care home, or an in-home aide or an individual who is licensed, is regulated, is approved, operates under the direction of, or otherwise is certified by the department of job and family services, department of mental retardation and developmental disabilities, or the early childhood programs of the department of education.

(8) "Chronic truant" has the same meaning as in section 2152.02 of the Revised Code.

(9) "Commit" means to vest custody as ordered by the court.

(10) "Counseling" includes both of the following:

(a) General counseling services performed by a public children services agency or shelter for victims of domestic violence to assist a child, a child's parents, and a child's siblings in alleviating identified problems that may cause or have caused the child to be an abused, neglected, or dependent child.

(b) Psychiatric or psychological therapeutic counseling services provided to correct or alleviate any mental or emotional illness or disorder and performed by a licensed psychiatrist, licensed psychologist, or a person licensed under Chapter 4757. of the Revised Code to engage in social work or professional counseling.

(11) "Custodian" means a person who has legal custody of a child or a public children services agency or private child placing agency that has permanent, temporary, or legal custody of a child.

(12) "Delinquent child" has the same meaning as in section 2152.02 of the Revised Code.

(13) "Detention" means the temporary care of children pending court adjudication or disposition, or execution of a court order, in a public or private facility designed to physically restrict the movement and activities of children.

(14) "Developmental disability" has the same meaning as in section 5123. 01 of the Revised Code.

(15) "Foster caregiver" has the same meaning as in section 5103.02 of the Revised Code.

(16) "Guardian" means a person, association, or corporation that is granted authority by a probate court pursuant to Chapter 2111. of the Revised Code to exercise parental rights over a child to the extent provided in the court's order and subject to the residual parental rights of the child's parents.

(17) "Habitual truant" means any child of compulsory school age who is absent without legitimate excuse for absence from the public school the child is supposed to attend for five or more consecutive school days, seven or more school days in one school month, or twelve or more school days in a school year.

(18) "Juvenile traffic offender" has the same meaning as in section 2152.02 of the Revised Code.

(19) "Legal custody" means a legal status that vests in the custodian the right to have physical care and control of the child and to determine where and with whom the child shall live, and the right and duty to protect, train, and discipline the child and to provide the child with food, shelter, education, and medical care, all subject to any residual parental rights, privileges, and responsibilities. An individual granted legal custody shall exercise the

rights and responsibilities personally unless otherwise authorized by any section of the Revised Code or by the court.

(20) A "legitimate excuse for absence from the public school the child is supposed to attend" includes, but is not limited to, any of the following:

(a) The fact that the child in question has enrolled in and is attending another public or nonpublic school in this or another state;

(b) The fact that the child in question is excused from attendance at school for any of the reasons specified in section 3321.04 of the Revised Code;

(c) The fact that the child in question has received an age and schooling certificate in accordance with section 3331.01 of the Revised Code.

(21) "Mental illness" and "mentally ill person subject to hospitalization by court order" have the same meanings as in section 5122.01 of the Revised Code.

(22) "Mental injury" means any behavioral, cognitive, emotional, or mental disorder in a child caused by an act or omission that is described in section 2919.22 of the Revised Code and is committed by the parent or other person responsible for the child's care.

(23) "Mentally retarded person" has the same meaning as in section 5123. 01 of the Revised Code.

(24) "Nonsecure care, supervision, or training" means care, supervision, or training of a child in a facility that does not confine or prevent movement of the child within the facility or from the facility.

(25) "Of compulsory school age" has the same meaning as in section 3321. 01 of the Revised Code.

(26) "Organization" means any institution, public, semipublic, or private, and any private association, society, or agency located or operating in the state, incorporated or unincorporated, having among its functions the furnishing of protective services or care for children, or the placement of children in certified foster homes or elsewhere.

(27) "Out-of-home care" means detention facilities, shelter facilities, certified foster homes, placement in a prospective adoptive home prior to the issuance of a final decree of adoption, organizations, certified organizations, child day-care centers, type A family day-care homes, child day-care provided by type B family day-care home providers and by in-home aides, group home providers, group homes, institutions, state institutions, residential facilities, residential care facilities, residential camps, day camps, public schools, chartered nonpublic schools, educational service centers, hospitals, and medical clinics that are responsible for the care, physical custody, or control of children.

(28) "Out-of-home care child abuse" means any of the following when committed by a person responsible for the care of a child in out-of-home care:

(a) Engaging in sexual activity with a child in the person's care;

(b) Denial to a child, as a means of punishment, of proper or necessary subsistence, education, medical care, or other care necessary for a child's health;

(c) Use of restraint procedures on a child that cause injury or pain;

(d) Administration of prescription drugs or psychotropic medication to the child without the written approval and ongoing supervision of a licensed physician;

(e) Commission of any act, other than by accidental means, that results in any injury to or death of the child in out-of-home care or commission of any act by accidental means that results in an injury to or death of a child in out-of-home care and that is at variance with the history given of the injury or death.

(29) "Out-of-home care child neglect" means any of the following when committed by a person responsible for the care of a child in out-of-home care:

(a) Failure to provide reasonable supervision according to the standards of care appropriate to the age, mental and physical condition, or other special needs of the child;

(b) Failure to provide reasonable supervision according to the standards of care appropriate to the age, mental and physical condition, or other special needs of the child, that results in sexual or physical abuse of the child by any person;

(c) Failure to develop a process for all of the following:

(i) Administration of prescription drugs or psychotropic drugs for the child;

(ii) Assuring that the instructions of the licensed physician who prescribed a drug for the child are followed;

(iii) Reporting to the licensed physician who prescribed the drug all unfavorable or dangerous side effects from the use of the drug.

(d) Failure to provide proper or necessary subsistence, education, medical care, or other individualized care necessary for the health or well-being of the child;

(e) Confinement of the child to a locked room without monitoring by staff;

(f) Failure to provide ongoing security for all prescription and nonprescription medication;

(g) Isolation of a child for a period of time when there is substantial risk that the isolation, if continued, will impair or retard the mental health or physical well-being of the child.

(30) "Permanent custody" means a legal status that vests in a public children services agency or a private child placing agency, all parental rights, duties, and obligations, including the right to consent to adoption, and divests the natural parents or adoptive parents of all parental rights, privileges, and obligations, including all residual rights and obligations.

(31) "Permanent surrender" means the act of the parents or, if a child has only one parent, of the parent of a child, by a voluntary agreement authorized by section 5103.15 of the Revised Code, to transfer the permanent custody of the child to a public children services agency or a private child placing agency.

(32) "Person responsible for a child's care in out-of-home care" means any of the following:

(a) Any foster caregiver, in-home aide, or provider;

(b) Any administrator, employee, or agent of any of the following: a public or private detention facility; shelter facility; organization; certified organization; child day-care center; type A family day-care home; certified type B family day-care home; group home; institution; state institution; residential facility; residential care facility; residential camp; day camp; school district; community school; chartered nonpublic school; educational service center; hospital; or medical clinic;

(c) Any person who supervises or coaches children as part of an extracurricular activity sponsored by a school district, public school, or chartered nonpublic school;

(d) Any other person who performs a similar function with respect to, or has a similar relationship to, children.

(33) "Physically impaired" means having one or more of the following conditions that substantially limit one or more of an individual's major life activities, including self-care, receptive and expressive language, learning, mobility, and self-direction:

(a) A substantial impairment of vision, speech, or hearing;

(b) A congenital orthopedic impairment;

(c) An orthopedic impairment caused by disease, rheumatic fever or any other similar chronic or acute health problem, or amputation or another similar cause.

(34) "Placement for adoption" means the arrangement by a public children services agency or a private child placing agency with a person for the care and adoption by that person of a child of whom the agency has permanent custody.

(35) "Placement in foster care" means the arrangement by a public children services agency or a private child placing agency for the out-of-home care of a child of whom the agency has temporary custody or permanent custody.

(36) "Planned permanent living arrangement" means an order of a juvenile court pursuant to which both of the following apply:

(a) The court gives legal custody of a child to a public children services agency or a private child placing agency without the termination of parental rights.

(b) The order permits the agency to make an appropriate placement of the child and to enter into a written agreement with a foster care provider or with another person or agency with whom the child is placed.

(37) "Practice of social work" and "practice of professional counseling" have the same meanings as in section 4757.01 of the Revised Code.

(38) "Sanction, service, or condition" means a sanction, service, or condition created by court order following an adjudication that a child is an unruly child that is described in division (A)(4) of section 2152.19 of the Revised Code.

(39) "Protective supervision" means an order of disposition pursuant to which the court permits an abused, neglected, dependent, or unruly child to remain in the custody of the child's parents, guardian, or custodian and stay in the child's home, subject to any conditions and limitations upon the child, the child's parents, guardian, or custodian, or any other person that the court prescribes, including supervision as directed by the court for the protection of the child.

(40) "Psychiatrist" has the same meaning as in section 5122.01 of the Revised Code.

(41) "Psychologist" has the same meaning as in section 4732.01 of the Revised Code.

(42) "Residential camp" means a program in which the care, physical custody, or control of children is accepted overnight for recreational or recreational and educational purposes.

(43) "Residential care facility" means an institution, residence, or facility that is licensed by the department of mental health under section 5119.22 of the Revised Code and that provides care for a child.

(44) "Residential facility" means a home or facility that is licensed by the department of mental retardation and developmental disabilities under section 5123.19 of the Revised Code and in which a child with a developmental disability resides.

(45) "Residual parental rights, privileges, and responsibilities" means those rights, privileges, and responsibilities remaining with the natural parent after the transfer of legal custody of the child, including, but not necessarily limited to, the privilege of reasonable visitation, consent to adoption, the privilege to determine the child's religious affiliation, and the responsibility for support.

(46) "School day" means the school day established by the state board of education pursuant to section 3313.48 of the Revised Code.

(47) "School month" and "school year" have the same meanings as in section 3313.62 of the Revised Code.

(48) "Secure correctional facility" means a facility under the direction of the department of youth services that is designed to physically restrict the movement and activities of children and used for the placement of children after adjudication and disposition.

(49) "Sexual activity" has the same meaning as in section 2907.01 of the Revised Code.

(50) "Shelter" means the temporary care of children in physically unrestricted facilities pending court adjudication or disposition.

(51) "Shelter for victims of domestic violence" has the same meaning as in section 3113.33 of the Revised Code.

(52) "Temporary custody" means legal custody of a child who is removed from the child's home, which custody may be terminated at any time at the discretion of the court or, if the legal custody is granted in an agreement for temporary custody, by the person who executed the agreement.

(C) For the purposes of this chapter, a child shall be presumed abandoned when the parents of the child have failed to visit or maintain contact with the child for more than ninety days, regardless of whether the parents resume contact with the child after that period of ninety days.

(2004 H 106, eff. 9–16–04; 2002 H 400, eff. 4–3–03; 2000 S 179, § 3, eff. 1–1–02; 2000 H 332, eff. 1–1–01; 2000 H 448, eff. 10–5–00; 2000 S 181, eff. 9–4–00; 1999 H 470, eff. 7–1–00; 1998 H 484, eff. 3–18–99; 1998 S 212, eff. 9–30–98; 1997 H 408, eff. 10–1–97; 1996 S 223, eff. 3–18–97; 1996 H 124, eff. 3–31–97; 1996 H 265, eff. 3–3–97; 1996 H 274, § 4, eff. 8–8–96; 1996 H 274, § 1, eff. 8–8–96; 1995 S 2, eff. 7–1–96; 1995 H 1, eff. 1–1–96; 1994 H 715, eff. 7–22–94; 1993 S 21, eff. 10–29–93; 1993 H 152, eff. 7–1–93; 1992 H 356; 1991 H 155; 1990 H 38; 1989 H 257; 1988 H 403)

Note: See also following version of this section, eff. 5–18–05.

2151.011 Definitions (later effective date)

Note: See also preceding version of this section, in effect until 5–18–05.

(A) As used in the Revised Code:

(1) "Juvenile court" means whichever of the following is applicable that has jurisdiction under this chapter and Chapter 2152. of the Revised Code:

(a) The division of the court of common pleas specified in section 2101.022 or 2301.03 of the Revised Code as having jurisdiction under this chapter and Chapter 2152. of the Revised Code or as being the juvenile division or the juvenile division combined with one or more other divisions;

(b) The juvenile court of Cuyahoga county or Hamilton county that is separately and independently created by section 2151.08 or Chapter 2153. of the Revised Code and that has jurisdiction under this chapter and Chapter 2152. of the Revised Code;

(c) If division (A)(1)(a) or (b) of this section does not apply, the probate division of the court of common pleas.

(2) "Juvenile judge" means a judge of a court having jurisdiction under this chapter.

(3) "Private child placing agency" means any association, as defined in section 5103.02 of the Revised Code, that is certified under section 5103.03 of the Revised Code to accept temporary, permanent, or legal custody of children and place the children for either foster care or adoption.

(4) "Private noncustodial agency" means any person, organization, association, or society certified by the department of job and family services that does not accept temporary or permanent legal custody of children, that is privately operated in this state, and that does one or more of the following:

(a) Receives and cares for children for two or more consecutive weeks;

(b) Participates in the placement of children in certified foster homes;

(c) Provides adoption services in conjunction with a public children services agency or private child placing agency.

(B) As used in this chapter:

(1) "Adequate parental care" means the provision by a child's parent or parents, guardian, or custodian of adequate food, clothing, and shelter to ensure the child's health and physical safety and the provision by a child's parent or parents of specialized services warranted by the child's physical or mental needs.

(2) "Adult" means an individual who is eighteen years of age or older.

(3) "Agreement for temporary custody" means a voluntary agreement authorized by section 5103.15 of the Revised Code that transfers the temporary custody of a child to a public children services agency or a private child placing agency.

(4) "Certified foster home" means a foster home, as defined in section 5103.02 of the Revised Code, certified under section 5103. 03 of the Revised Code.

(5) "Child" means a person who is under eighteen years of age, except that the juvenile court has jurisdiction over any person who is adjudicated an unruly child prior to attaining eighteen years of age until the person attains twenty-one years of age, and, for purposes of that jurisdiction related to that adjudication, a person who is so adjudicated an unruly child shall be deemed a "child" until the person attains twenty-one years of age.

(6) "Child day camp," "child care," "child day-care center," "part-time child day-care center," "type A family day-care home," "certified type B family day-care home," "type B home," "administrator of a child day-care center," "administrator of a type A family day-care home," "in- home aide," and "authorized provider" have the same meanings as in section 5104.01 of the Revised Code.

(7) "Child care provider" means an individual who is a child-care staff member or administrator of a child day-care center, a type A family day-care home, or a type B family day-care home, or an in-home aide or an individual who is licensed, is regulated, is approved, operates under the direction of, or otherwise is certified by the department of job and family services, department of mental retardation and developmental disabilities, or the early childhood programs of the department of education.

(8) "Chronic truant" has the same meaning as in section 2152.02 of the Revised Code.

(9) "Commit" means to vest custody as ordered by the court.

(10) "Counseling" includes both of the following:

(a) General counseling services performed by a public children services agency or shelter for victims of domestic violence to assist a child, a child's parents, and a child's siblings in alleviating identified problems that may cause or have caused the child to be an abused, neglected, or dependent child.

(b) Psychiatric or psychological therapeutic counseling services provided to correct or alleviate any mental or emotional illness or disorder and performed by a licensed psychiatrist, licensed psychologist, or a person licensed under Chapter 4757. of the Revised Code to engage in social work or professional counseling.

(11) "Custodian" means a person who has legal custody of a child or a public children services agency or private child placing agency that has permanent, temporary, or legal custody of a child.

(12) "Delinquent child" has the same meaning as in section 2152.02 of the Revised Code.

(13) "Detention" means the temporary care of children pending court adjudication or disposition, or execution of a court order, in a public or private facility designed to physically restrict the movement and activities of children.

(14) "Developmental disability" has the same meaning as in section 5123. 01 of the Revised Code.

(15) "Foster caregiver" has the same meaning as in section 5103.02 of the Revised Code.

(16) "Guardian" means a person, association, or corporation that is granted authority by a probate court pursuant to Chapter 2111. of the Revised Code to exercise parental rights over a child to the extent provided in the court's order and subject to the residual parental rights of the child's parents.

(17) "Habitual truant" means any child of compulsory school age who is absent without legitimate excuse for absence from the public school the child is supposed to attend for five or more consecutive school days, seven or more school days in one school month, or twelve or more school days in a school year.

(18) "Juvenile traffic offender" has the same meaning as in section 2152.02 of the Revised Code.

(19) "Legal custody" means a legal status that vests in the custodian the right to have physical care and control of the child and to determine where and with whom the child shall live, and the right and duty to protect, train, and discipline the child and to provide the child with food, shelter, education, and medical care, all subject to any residual parental rights, privileges, and responsibilities. An individual granted legal custody shall exercise the rights and responsibilities personally unless otherwise authorized by any section of the Revised Code or by the court.

(20) A "legitimate excuse for absence from the public school the child is supposed to attend" includes, but is not limited to, any of the following:

(a) The fact that the child in question has enrolled in and is attending another public or nonpublic school in this or another state;

(b) The fact that the child in question is excused from attendance at school for any of the reasons specified in section 3321.04 of the Revised Code;

(c) The fact that the child in question has received an age and schooling certificate in accordance with section 3331.01 of the Revised Code.

(21) "Mental illness" and "mentally ill person subject to hospitalization by court order" have the same meanings as in section 5122.01 of the Revised Code.

(22) "Mental injury" means any behavioral, cognitive, emotional, or mental disorder in a child caused by an act or omission that is described in section 2919.22 of the Revised Code and is committed by the parent or other person responsible for the child's care.

(23) "Mentally retarded person" has the same meaning as in section 5123. 01 of the Revised Code.

(24) "Nonsecure care, supervision, or training" means care, supervision, or training of a child in a facility that does not confine or prevent movement of the child within the facility or from the facility.

(25) "Of compulsory school age" has the same meaning as in section 3321. 01 of the Revised Code.

(26) "Organization" means any institution, public, semipublic, or private, and any private association, society, or agency located or operating in the state, incorporated or unincorporated, having among its functions the furnishing of protective services or care for children, or the placement of children in certified foster homes or elsewhere.

(27) "Out–of–home care" means detention facilities, shelter facilities, certified foster homes, placement in a prospective adoptive home prior to the issuance of a final decree of adoption, organizations, certified organizations, child day-care centers, type

A family day-care homes, child care provided by type B family day-care home providers and by in-home aides, group home providers, group homes, institutions, state institutions, residential facilities, residential care facilities, residential camps, day camps, public schools, chartered nonpublic schools, educational service centers, hospitals, and medical clinics that are responsible for the care, physical custody, or control of children.

(28) "Out–of–home care child abuse" means any of the following when committed by a person responsible for the care of a child in out-of-home care:

(a) Engaging in sexual activity with a child in the person's care;

(b) Denial to a child, as a means of punishment, of proper or necessary subsistence, education, medical care, or other care necessary for a child's health;

(c) Use of restraint procedures on a child that cause injury or pain;

(d) Administration of prescription drugs or psychotropic medication to the child without the written approval and ongoing supervision of a licensed physician;

(e) Commission of any act, other than by accidental means, that results in any injury to or death of the child in out-of-home care or commission of any act by accidental means that results in an injury to or death of a child in out-of-home care and that is at variance with the history given of the injury or death.

(29) "Out–of–home care child neglect" means any of the following when committed by a person responsible for the care of a child in out-of-home care:

(a) Failure to provide reasonable supervision according to the standards of care appropriate to the age, mental and physical condition, or other special needs of the child;

(b) Failure to provide reasonable supervision according to the standards of care appropriate to the age, mental and physical condition, or other special needs of the child, that results in sexual or physical abuse of the child by any person;

(c) Failure to develop a process for all of the following:

(i) Administration of prescription drugs or psychotropic drugs for the child;

(ii) Assuring that the instructions of the licensed physician who prescribed a drug for the child are followed;

(iii) Reporting to the licensed physician who prescribed the drug all unfavorable or dangerous side effects from the use of the drug.

(d) Failure to provide proper or necessary subsistence, education, medical care, or other individualized care necessary for the health or well-being of the child;

(e) Confinement of the child to a locked room without monitoring by staff;

(f) Failure to provide ongoing security for all prescription and nonprescription medication;

(g) Isolation of a child for a period of time when there is substantial risk that the isolation, if continued, will impair or retard the mental health or physical well-being of the child.

(30) "Permanent custody" means a legal status that vests in a public children services agency or a private child placing agency, all parental rights, duties, and obligations, including the right to consent to adoption, and divests the natural parents or adoptive parents of all parental rights, privileges, and obligations, including all residual rights and obligations.

(31) "Permanent surrender" means the act of the parents or, if a child has only one parent, of the parent of a child, by a voluntary agreement authorized by section 5103.15 of the Revised Code, to transfer the permanent custody of the child to a public children services agency or a private child placing agency.

(32) "Person responsible for a child's care in out-of-home care" means any of the following:

(a) Any foster caregiver, in-home aide, or provider;

(b) Any administrator, employee, or agent of any of the following: a public or private detention facility; shelter facility; organization; certified organization; child day-care center; type A family day-care home; certified type B family day-care home; group home; institution; state institution; residential facility; residential care facility; residential camp; day camp; school district; community school; chartered nonpublic school; educational service center; hospital; or medical clinic;

(c) Any person who supervises or coaches children as part of an extracurricular activity sponsored by a school district, public school, or chartered nonpublic school;

(d) Any other person who performs a similar function with respect to, or has a similar relationship to, children.

(33) "Physically impaired" means having one or more of the following conditions that substantially limit one or more of an individual's major life activities, including self-care, receptive and expressive language, learning, mobility, and self–direction:

(a) A substantial impairment of vision, speech, or hearing;

(b) A congenital orthopedic impairment;

(c) An orthopedic impairment caused by disease, rheumatic fever or any other similar chronic or acute health problem, or amputation or another similar cause.

(34) "Placement for adoption" means the arrangement by a public children services agency or a private child placing agency with a person for the care and adoption by that person of a child of whom the agency has permanent custody.

(35) "Placement in foster care" means the arrangement by a public children services agency or a private child placing agency for the out-of-home care of a child of whom the agency has temporary custody or permanent custody.

(36) "Planned permanent living arrangement" means an order of a juvenile court pursuant to which both of the following apply:

(a) The court gives legal custody of a child to a public children services agency or a private child placing agency without the termination of parental rights.

(b) The order permits the agency to make an appropriate placement of the child and to enter into a written agreement with a foster care provider or with another person or agency with whom the child is placed.

(37) "Practice of social work" and "practice of professional counseling" have the same meanings as in section 4757.01 of the Revised Code.

(38) "Sanction, service, or condition" means a sanction, service, or condition created by court order following an adjudication that a child is an unruly child that is described in division (A)(4) of section 2152.19 of the Revised Code.

(39) "Protective supervision" means an order of disposition pursuant to which the court permits an abused, neglected, dependent, or unruly child to remain in the custody of the child's parents, guardian, or custodian and stay in the child's home, subject to any conditions and limitations upon the child, the child's parents, guardian, or custodian, or any other person that the court prescribes, including supervision as directed by the court for the protection of the child.

(40) "Psychiatrist" has the same meaning as in section 5122.01 of the Revised Code.

(41) "Psychologist" has the same meaning as in section 4732.01 of the Revised Code.

(42) "Residential camp" means a program in which the care, physical custody, or control of children is accepted overnight for recreational or recreational and educational purposes.

(43) "Residential care facility" means an institution, residence, or facility that is licensed by the department of mental health under section 5119.22 of the Revised Code and that provides care for a child.

(44) "Residential facility" means a home or facility that is licensed by the department of mental retardation and developmental disabilities under section 5123.19 of the Revised Code and in which a child with a developmental disability resides.

(45) "Residual parental rights, privileges, and responsibilities" means those rights, privileges, and responsibilities remaining with the natural parent after the transfer of legal custody of the child, including, but not necessarily limited to, the privilege of reasonable visitation, consent to adoption, the privilege to determine the child's religious affiliation, and the responsibility for support.

(46) "School day" means the school day established by the state board of education pursuant to section 3313.48 of the Revised Code.

(47) "School month" and "school year" have the same meanings as in section 3313.62 of the Revised Code.

(48) "Secure correctional facility" means a facility under the direction of the department of youth services that is designed to physically restrict the movement and activities of children and used for the placement of children after adjudication and disposition.

(49) "Sexual activity" has the same meaning as in section 2907.01 of the Revised Code.

(50) "Shelter" means the temporary care of children in physically unrestricted facilities pending court adjudication or disposition.

(51) "Shelter for victims of domestic violence" has the same meaning as in section 3113.33 of the Revised Code.

(52) "Temporary custody" means legal custody of a child who is removed from the child's home, which custody may be terminated at any time at the discretion of the court or, if the legal custody is granted in an agreement for temporary custody, by the person who executed the agreement.

(C) For the purposes of this chapter, a child shall be presumed abandoned when the parents of the child have failed to visit or maintain contact with the child for more than ninety days, regardless of whether the parents resume contact with the child after that period of ninety days.

(2004 H 11, eff. 5–18–05; 2004 H 106, eff. 9–16–04; 2002 H 400, eff. 4–3–03; 2000 S 179, § 3, eff. 1–1–02; 2000 H 332, eff. 1–1–01; 2000 H 448, eff. 10–5–00; 2000 S 181, eff. 9–4–00; 1999 H 470, eff. 7–1–00; 1998 H 484, eff. 3–18–99; 1998 S 212, eff. 9–30–98; 1997 H 408, eff. 10–1–97; 1996 S 223, eff. 3–18–97; 1996 H 124, eff. 3–31–97; 1996 H 265, eff. 3–3–97; 1996 H 274, § 4, eff. 8–8–96; 1996 H 274, § 1, eff. 8–8–96; 1995 S 2, eff. 7–1–96; 1995 H 1, eff. 1–1–96; 1994 H 715, eff. 7–22–94; 1993 S 21, eff. 10–29–93; 1993 H 152, eff. 7–1–93; 1992 H 356; 1991 H 155; 1990 H 38; 1989 H 257; 1988 H 403)

Note: See also preceding version of this section, in effect until 5–18–05.

2151.022 "Unruly child" defined

As used in this chapter, "unruly child" includes any of the following:

(A) Any child who does not submit to the reasonable control of the child's parents, teachers, guardian, or custodian, by reason of being wayward or habitually disobedient;

(B) Any child who is an habitual truant from school and who previously has not been adjudicated an unruly child for being an habitual truant;

(C) Any child who behaves in a manner as to injure or endanger the child's own health or morals or the health or morals of others;

(D) Any child who violates a law, other than division (A) of section 2923.211 or section 2151.87 of the Revised Code, that is applicable only to a child.

(2000 S 179, § 3, eff. 1–1–02; 2000 S 218, eff. 3–15–01; 2000 S 181, eff. 9–4–00; 1995 H 4, eff. 11–9–95; 1969 H 320, eff. 11–19–69)

2151.03 "Neglected child" defined

(A) As used in this chapter, "neglected child" includes any child:

(1) Who is abandoned by the child's parents, guardian, or custodian;

(2) Who lacks adequate parental care because of the faults or habits of the child's parents, guardian, or custodian;

(3) Whose parents, guardian, or custodian neglects the child or refuses to provide proper or necessary subsistence, education, medical or surgical care or treatment, or other care necessary for the child's health, morals, or well being;

(4) Whose parents, guardian, or custodian neglects the child or refuses to provide the special care made necessary by the child's mental condition;

(5) Whose parents, legal guardian, or custodian have placed or attempted to place the child in violation of sections 5103.16 and 5103.17 of the Revised Code;

(6) Who, because of the omission of the child's parents, guardian, or custodian, suffers physical or mental injury that harms or threatens to harm the child's health or welfare;

(7) Who is subjected to out-of-home care child neglect.

(B) Nothing in this chapter shall be construed as subjecting a parent, guardian, or custodian of a child to criminal liability when, solely in the practice of religious beliefs, the parent, guardian, or custodian fails to provide adequate medical or surgical care or treatment for the child. This division does not abrogate or limit any person's responsibility under section 2151.421 of the Revised Code to report known or suspected child abuse, known or suspected child neglect, and children who are known to face or are suspected of facing a threat of suffering abuse or neglect and does not preclude any exercise of the authority of the state, any political subdivision, or any court to ensure that medical or surgical care or treatment is provided to a child when the child's health requires the provision of medical or surgical care or treatment.

(1996 H 274, eff. 8–8–96; 1989 H 257, eff. 8–3–89; 1969 H 320; 1953 H 1; GC 1639–3)

2151.031 "Abused child" defined

As used in this chapter, an "abused child" includes any child who:

(A) Is the victim of "sexual activity" as defined under Chapter 2907. of the Revised Code, where such activity would constitute an offense under that chapter, except that the court need not find that any person has been convicted of the offense in order to find that the child is an abused child;

(B) Is endangered as defined in section 2919.22 of the Revised Code, except that the court need not find that any person has been convicted under that section in order to find that the child is an abused child;

(C) Exhibits evidence of any physical or mental injury or death, inflicted other than by accidental means, or an injury or death which is at variance with the history given of it. Except as provided in division (D) of this section, a child exhibiting evidence of corporal punishment or other physical disciplinary measure by a parent, guardian, custodian, person having custody or control, or person in loco parentis of a child is not an abused child under this division if the measure is not prohibited under section 2919.22 of the Revised Code.

(D) Because of the acts of his parents, guardian, or custodian, suffers physical or mental injury that harms or threatens to harm the child's health or welfare.

(E) Is subjected to out-of-home care child abuse.

(1989 H 257, eff. 8–3–89; 1988 S 89; 1975 H 85)

2151.04 "Dependent child" defined

As used in this chapter, "dependent child" means any child:

(A) Who is homeless or destitute or without adequate parental care, through no fault of the child's parents, guardian, or custodian;

(B) Who lacks adequate parental care by reason of the mental or physical condition of the child's parents, guardian, or custodian;

(C) Whose condition or environment is such as to warrant the state, in the interests of the child, in assuming the child's guardianship;

(D) To whom both of the following apply:

(1) The child is residing in a household in which a parent, guardian, custodian, or other member of the household committed an act that was the basis for an adjudication that a sibling of the child or any other child who resides in the household is an abused, neglected, or dependent child.

(2) Because of the circumstances surrounding the abuse, neglect, or dependency of the sibling or other child and the other conditions in the household of the child, the child is in danger of being abused or neglected by that parent, guardian, custodian, or member of the household.

(1996 H 274, eff. 8–8–96; 1988 S 89, eff. 1–1–89; 1969 H 320; 129 v 1778; 1953 H 1; GC 1639–4)

2151.05 Child without proper parental care

Under sections 2151.01 to 2151.54 of the Revised Code, a child whose home is filthy and unsanitary; whose parents, stepparents, guardian, or custodian permit him to become dependent, neglected, abused, or delinquent; whose parents, stepparents, guardian, or custodian, when able, refuse or neglect to provide him with necessary care, support, medical attention, and educational facilities; or whose parents, stepparents, guardian, or custodian fail to subject such child to necessary discipline is without proper parental care or guardianship.

(1975 H 85, eff. 11–28–75; 1953 H 1; GC 1639–5)

2151.06 Residence or legal settlement

Under sections 2151.01 to 2151.54, inclusive, of the Revised Code, a child has the same residence or legal settlement as his parents, legal guardian of his person, or his custodian who stands in the relation of loco parentis.

(1953 H 1, eff. 10–1–53; GC 1639–6)

ADMINISTRATION, OFFICIALS,
AND JURISDICTION

2151.07 Creation and powers of juvenile court; assignment of judge

The juvenile court is a court of record within the court of common pleas. The juvenile court has and shall exercise the powers and jurisdiction conferred in Chapters 2151. and 2152. of the Revised Code.

Whenever the juvenile judge of the juvenile court is sick, is absent from the county, or is unable to attend court, or the volume of cases pending in court necessitates it, upon the request of the administrative juvenile judge, the presiding judge of the court of common pleas pursuant to division (DD) of section 2301.03 of the Revised Code shall assign a judge of any division of the court of common pleas of the county to act in the juvenile judge's place or in conjunction with the juvenile judge. If no judge of the court of common pleas is available for that purpose, the chief justice of the supreme court shall assign a judge of the court of common pleas, a juvenile judge, or a probate judge from a different county to act in the place of that juvenile judge or in conjunction with that juvenile judge. The assigned judge shall receive the compensation and expenses for so serving that is provided by law for judges assigned to hold court in courts of common pleas.

(2003 H 86, eff. 11–13–03; 2003 H 26, eff. 8–8–03; 2001 H 11, § 3, eff. 1–1–02; 2000 S 179, § 3, eff. 1–1–02; 1972 H 574, eff. 6–29–72; 1969 H 320; 127 v 847; 1953 H 1; GC 1639–7)

2151.08 Juvenile court in Hamilton county

In Hamilton county, the powers and jurisdiction of the juvenile court as conferred by Chapters 2151. and 2152. of the Revised Code shall be exercised by the judge of the court of common pleas whose term begins on January 1, 1957, and that judge's successors and by the judge of the court of common pleas whose term begins on February 14, 1967, and that judge's successors as provided by section 2301.03 of the Revised Code. This conferral of powers and jurisdiction on the specified judges shall be deemed a creation of a separately and independently created and established juvenile court in Hamilton county, Ohio. The specified judges shall serve in each and every position where the statutes permit or require a juvenile judge to serve.

(2000 S 179, § 3, eff. 1–1–02; 131 v H 165, eff. 11–16–65; 127 v 84)

2151.09 Separate building and site may be purchased or leased

Upon the advice and recommendation of the juvenile judge, the board of county commissioners may provide by purchase, lease, or otherwise a separate building and site to be known as "the juvenile court" at a convenient location within the county which shall be appropriately constructed, arranged, furnished, and maintained for the convenient and efficient transaction of the business of the court and all parts thereof and its employees, including adequate facilities to be used as laboratories, dispensaries, or clinics for the use of scientific specialists connected with the court.

(1953 H 1, eff. 10–1–53; GC 1639–15)

2151.10 Appropriation for expenses of the court and maintenance of children; hearing; action in court of appeals; limitation of contempt power

The juvenile judge shall annually submit a written request for an appropriation to the board of county commissioners that shall set forth estimated administrative expenses of the juvenile court that the judge considers reasonably necessary for the operation of the court, including reasonably necessary expenses of the judge and such officers and employees as the judge may designate in attending conferences at which juvenile or welfare problems are discussed, and such sum each year as will provide for the maintenance and operation of the detention facility, the care, maintenance, education, and support of neglected, abused, dependent, and delinquent children, other than children eligible to participate in the Ohio works first program established under Chapter 5107. of the Revised Code, and for necessary orthopedic, surgical, and medical treatment, and special care as may be ordered by the court for any neglected, abused, dependent, or delinquent children. The board shall conduct a public hearing with respect to the written request submitted by the judge and shall appropriate such sum of money each year as it determines, after conducting the public hearing and considering the written request of the judge, is reasonably necessary to meet all the administrative expenses of the court. All disbursements from such appropriations shall be upon specifically itemized vouchers, certified to by the judge.

If the judge considers the appropriation made by the board pursuant to this section insufficient to meet all the administrative expenses of the court, the judge shall commence an action under Chapter 2731. of the Revised Code in the court of appeals for the judicial district for a determination of the duty of the board of county commissioners to appropriate the amount of money in dispute. The court of appeals shall give priority to the action filed by the juvenile judge over all cases pending on its docket. The burden shall be on the juvenile judge to prove that the appropriation requested is reasonably necessary to meet all administrative expenses of the court. If, prior to the filing of an action under Chapter 2731. of the Revised Code or during the pendency of the action, the judge exercises the judge's contempt power in order to obtain the sum of money in dispute, the judge shall not order the imprisonment of any member of the board of county commissioners notwithstanding sections 2705.02 to 2705.06 of the Revised Code.

(2000 S 179, § 3, eff. 1–1–02; 1997 H 408, eff. 10–1–97; 1979 S 63, eff. 7–26–79; 1975 H 85; 1953 H 1; GC 1639–57)

2151.12 Clerk; judge as clerk; bond

(A) Except as otherwise provided in this division, whenever a court of common pleas, division of domestic relations, exercises the powers and jurisdictions conferred in Chapters 2151. and 2152. of the Revised Code, the judge or judges of that division or, if applicable, the judge of that division who specifically is designated by section 2301.03 of the Revised Code as being responsible for administering sections 2151.13, 2151.16, 2151.17, 2151.18, and 2152.71 of the Revised Code shall be the clerk of the court for all records filed with the court pursuant to Chapter 2151. or 2152. of the Revised Code or pursuant to any other section of the Revised Code that requires documents to be filed with a juvenile judge or a juvenile court. If, in a division of domestic relations of a court of common pleas that exercises the powers and jurisdiction conferred in Chapters 2151. and 2152. of the Revised Code, the judge of the division, both judges in a two-judge division, or a majority of the judges in a division with three or more judges and the clerk of the court of common pleas agree in an agreement that is signed by the agreeing judge or judges and the clerk and entered into formally in the journal of the court, the clerk of courts of common pleas shall keep the records filed with the court pursuant to Chapter 2151. or 2152. of the Revised Code or pursuant to any other section of the Revised Code that requires documents to be filed with a juvenile judge or a juvenile court.

Whenever the juvenile judge, or a majority of the juvenile judges of a multi-judge juvenile division, of a court of common pleas, juvenile division, and the clerk of the court of common pleas agree in an agreement that is signed by the judge and the clerk and entered formally in the journal of the court, the clerks of courts of common pleas shall keep the records of those courts. In all other cases, the juvenile judge shall be the clerk of the judge's own court.

(B) In counties in which the juvenile judge is clerk of the judge's own court, before entering upon the duties of office as the clerk, the judge shall execute and file with the county treasurer a bond in a sum to be determined by the board of county commissioners, with sufficient surety to be approved by the board, conditioned for the faithful performance of duties as clerk. The bond shall be given for the benefit of the county, the state, or any person who may suffer loss by reason of a default in any of the conditions of the bond.

(2000 S 179, § 3, eff. 1–1–02; 1996 H 423, eff. 10–31–96; 1977 S 336, eff. 3–3–78; 1953 H 1; GC 1639–17)

2151.13 Employees; compensation; bond

The juvenile judge may appoint such bailiffs, probation officers, and other employees as are necessary and may designate their titles and fix their duties, compensation, and expense allowances. The juvenile court may by entry on its journal authorize any deputy clerk to administer oaths when necessary in the discharge of his duties. Such employees shall serve during the pleasure of the judge.

The compensation and expenses of all employees and the salary and expenses of the judge shall be paid in semimonthly installments by the county treasurer from the money appropriated for the operation of the court, upon the warrant of the county auditor, certified to by the judge.

The judge may require any employee to give bond in the sum of not less than one thousand dollars, conditioned for the honest and faithful performance of his duties. The sureties on such bonds shall be approved in the manner provided by section 2151.12 of the Revised Code. The judge shall not be personally liable for the default, misfeasance, or nonfeasance of any employee from whom a bond has been required.

(1953 H 1, eff. 10–1–53; GC 1639–18)

2151.14 Duties and powers of probation department; records; command assistance; notice to victim of accused sex offender's communicable disease; order to provide copies of records

(A) The chief probation officer, under the direction of the juvenile judge, shall have charge of the work of the probation department. The department shall make any investigations that the judge directs, keep a written record of the investigations, and submit the record to the judge or deal with them as the judge directs. The department shall furnish to any person placed on community control a statement of the conditions of community control and shall instruct the person regarding them. The department shall keep informed concerning the conduct and condition of each person under its supervision and shall report on their conduct and condition to the judge as the judge directs. Each probation officer shall use all suitable methods to aid persons on community control and to bring about improvement in their conduct and condition. The department shall keep full records of its work, keep accurate and complete accounts of money collected from persons under its supervision, give receipts for the money, and make reports on the money as the judge directs.

(B) Except as provided in this division or in division (C) or (D) of this section, the reports and records of the department shall be considered confidential information and shall not be made public. If an officer is preparing pursuant to section 2947.06 or 2951.03 of the Revised Code or Criminal Rule 32.2 a presentence investigation report pertaining to a person, the department shall make available to the officer, for use in preparing the report, any reports and records it possesses regarding any adjudications of that person as a delinquent child or regarding the dispositions made relative to those adjudications. A probation officer may serve the process of the court within or without the county, make arrests without warrant upon reasonable information or upon view of the violation of this chapter or Chapter 2152. of the Revised Code, detain the person arrested pending the issuance of a warrant, and perform any other duties, incident to the office, that the judge directs. All sheriffs, deputy sheriffs, constables, marshals, deputy marshals, chiefs of police, municipal corporation and township police officers, and other peace officers shall render assistance to probation officers in the performance of their duties when requested to do so by any probation officer.

(C) When a complaint has been filed alleging that a child is delinquent by reason of having committed an act that would constitute a violation of section 2907.02, 2907.03, 2907.05, or 2907.06 of the Revised Code if committed by an adult and the arresting authority, a court, or a probation officer discovers that the child or a person whom the child caused to engage in sexual activity, as defined in section 2907.01 of the Revised Code, has a communicable disease, the arresting authority, court, or probation officer immediately shall notify the victim of the delinquent act of the nature of the disease.

(D)(1) In accordance with division (D)(2) of this section, subject to the limitation specified in division (D)(4) of this section, and in connection with a disposition pursuant to section 2151.354 of the Revised Code when a child has been found to be an unruly child, a disposition pursuant to sections 2152.19 and 2152.20 of the Revised Code when a child has been found to be a delinquent child, or a disposition pursuant to sections 2152.20 and 2152.21 of the Revised Code when a child has been found to be a juvenile traffic offender, the court may issue an order requiring boards of education, governing bodies of chartered nonpublic schools, public children services agencies, private child placing agencies, probation departments, law enforcement agencies, and prosecuting attorneys that have records related to the child in question to provide copies of one or more specified records, or specified information in one or more specified records, that the individual or entity has with respect to the child to any of the following individuals or entities that request the records in accordance with division (D)(3)(a) of this section:

(a) The child;

(b) The attorney or guardian ad litem of the child;

(c) A parent, guardian, or custodian of the child;

(d) A prosecuting attorney;

(e) A board of education of a public school district;

(f) A probation department of a juvenile court;

(g) A public children services agency or private child placing agency that has custody of the child, is providing services to the child or the child's family, or is preparing a social history or performing any other function for the juvenile court;

(h) The department of youth services when the department has custody of the child or is performing any services for the child that are required by the juvenile court or by statute;

(i) The individual in control of a juvenile detention or rehabilitation facility to which the child has been committed;

(j) An employee of the juvenile court that found the child to be an unruly child, a delinquent child, or a juvenile traffic offender;

(k) Any other entity that has custody of the child or is providing treatment, rehabilitation, or other services for the child pursuant to a court order, statutory requirement, or other arrangement.

(2) Any individual or entity listed in divisions (D)(1)(a) to (k) of this section may file a motion with the court that requests the court to issue an order as described in division (D)(1) of this section. If such a motion is filed, the court shall conduct a hearing on it. If at the hearing the movant demonstrates a need for one or more specified records, or for information in one or more specified records, related to the child in question and additionally demonstrates the relevance of the information sought to be obtained from those records, and if the court determines that the limitation specified in division (D)(4) of this section does not preclude the provision of a specified record or specified information to the movant, then the court may issue an order to a designated individual or entity to provide the movant with copies of one or more specified records or with specified information contained in one or more specified records.

(3)(a) Any individual or entity that is authorized by an order issued pursuant to division (D)(1) of this section to obtain copies of one or more specified records, or specified information, related to a particular child may file a written request for copies of the records or for the information with any individual or entity required by the order to provide copies of the records or the information. The request shall be in writing, describe the type of records or the information requested, explain the need for the records or the information, and be accompanied by a copy of the order.

(b) If an individual or entity that is required by an order issued pursuant to division (D)(1) of this section to provide one or more specified records, or specified information, related to a child receives a written request for the records or information in accordance with division (D)(3)(a) of this section, the individual or entity immediately shall comply with the request to the extent it is able to do so, unless the individual or entity determines that it is unable to comply with the request because it is prohibited by law from doing so, or unless the requesting individual or entity does not have authority to obtain the requested records or information. If the individual or entity determines that it is unable to comply with the request, it shall file a motion with the court that issued the order requesting the court to determine the extent to which it is required to comply with the request for records or information. Upon the filing of the motion, the court immediately shall hold a hearing on the motion, determine the extent to which the movant is required to comply with the request for records or information, and issue findings of fact and conclusions of law in support of its determination. The determination of the court shall be final. If the court determines that the movant is required to comply with the request for records or information, it shall identify the specific records or information that must be supplied to the individual or entity that requested the records or information.

(c) If an individual or entity is required to provide copies of one or more specified records pursuant to division (D) of this section, the individual or entity may charge a fee for the copies that does not exceed the cost of supplying them.

(4) Division (D) of this section does not require, authorize, or permit the dissemination of any records or any information contained in any records if the dissemination of the records or information generally is prohibited by any provision of the Revised Code and a specific provision of the Revised Code does not specifically authorize or permit the dissemination of the records or information pursuant to division (D) of this section.

(2002 H 247, eff. 5–30–02; 2000 S 179, § 3, eff. 1–1–02; 2000 H 442, eff. 10–17–00; 1996 H 445, eff. 9–3–96; 1990 S 258, eff. 8–22–90; 1986 H 468; 1953 H 1; GC 1639–19)

2151.141 Requests for copies of records

(A) If a complaint filed with respect to a child pursuant to section 2151.27 of the Revised Code alleges that a child is an abused, neglected, or dependent child, any individual or entity that is listed in divisions (D)(1)(a) to (k) of section 2151.14 of the Revised Code and that is investigating whether the child is an abused, neglected, or dependent child, has custody of the child, is preparing a social history for the child, or is providing any services for the child may request any board of education, governing body of a chartered nonpublic school, public children services agency, private child placing agency, probation department, law enforcement agency, or prosecuting attorney that has any records related to the child to provide the individual or entity with a copy of the records. The request shall be in writing, describe the type of records requested, explain the need for the records, be accompanied by a copy of the complaint, and describe the relationship of the requesting individual or entity to the child. The individual or entity shall provide a copy of the request to the child in question, the attorney or guardian ad litem of the child, and the parent, guardian, or custodian of the child.

(B)(1) Any board of education, governing body of a chartered nonpublic school, public children services agency, private child placing agency, probation department, law enforcement agency, or prosecuting attorney that has any records related to a child who is the subject of a complaint as described in division (A) of this section and that receives a request for a copy of the records pursuant to division (A) of this section shall comply with the request, unless the individual or entity determines that it is unable to do so because it is prohibited by law from complying with the request, the request does not comply with division (A) of this section, or a complaint as described in division (A) of this section has not been filed with respect to the child who is the subject of the requested records. If the individual or entity determines that it is unable to comply with the request, it shall file a motion with the court in which the complaint as described in division (A) of this section was filed or was alleged to have been filed requesting the court to determine the extent to which it is required to comply with the request for records. Upon the filing of the motion, the court immediately shall hold a hearing on the motion, determine the extent to which the movant is required to comply with the request for records, and issue findings of fact and conclusions of law in support of its determination. The determination of the court shall be final. If the court determines that the movant is required to comply with the request for records, it shall identify the specific records that must be supplied to the individual or entity that requested them.

(2) In addition to or in lieu of the motion described in division (B)(1) of this section, a law enforcement agency or prosecuting attorney that receives a request for a copy of records pursuant to division (A) of this section may file a motion for a protective order as described in this division with the court in which the complaint as described in division (A) of this section was filed or alleged to have been filed. Upon the filing of a motion of that nature, the court shall conduct a hearing on the motion. If at the hearing the law enforcement agency or prosecuting attorney demonstrates that any of the following applies and if, after considering the purposes for which the records were requested pursuant to division (A) of this section, the best interest of the child, and any demonstrated need to prevent specific information in the records from being disclosed, the court determines that the issuance of a protective order is necessary, then the court shall issue a protective order that appropriately limits the disclosure of one or more specified records or specified information in one or more specified records:

(a) The records or information in the records relate to a case in which the child is alleged to be a delinquent child or a case in which a child is transferred for trial as an adult pursuant to section 2152.12 of the Revised Code and Juvenile Rule 30, and the adjudication hearing in the case, the trial in the case, or other disposition of the case has not been concluded.

(b) The records in question, or the records containing the information in question, are confidential law enforcement investigatory records, as defined in section 149.43 of the Revised Code.

(c) The records or information in the records relate to a case in which the child is or was alleged to be a delinquent child or to a case in which a child is or was transferred for trial as an adult pursuant to section 2152.12 of the Revised Code and Juvenile Rule 30; another case is pending against any child or any adult in which the child is alleged to be a delinquent child, the child is so transferred for trial as an adult, or the adult is alleged to be a criminal offender; the allegations in the case to which the records or information relate and the allegations in the other case are based on the same act or transaction, are based on two or more connected transactions or constitute parts of a common scheme or plan, or are part of a course of criminal conduct; and the adjudication hearing in, trial in, or other disposition of the other case has not been concluded.

(C) If an individual or entity is required to provide copies of records pursuant to this section, the individual or entity may charge a fee for the copies that does not exceed the cost of supplying them.

(D) This section does not require, authorize, or permit the dissemination of any records or any information contained in any records if the dissemination of the records or information generally is prohibited by section 2151.142 or another section of the Revised Code and a waiver as described in division (B)(1) of section 2151.142 of the Revised Code or a specific provision of the Revised Code does not specifically authorize or permit the dissemination of the records or information pursuant to this section.

(2000 S 179, § 3, eff. 1–1–02; 2000 H 412, eff. 4–10–01; 1990 S 258, eff. 8–22–90)

2151.142 Confidentiality of residential addresses; exceptions

(A) As used in this section, "public record" and "journalist" have the same meanings as in section 149.43 of the Revised Code.

(B) Both of the following apply to the residential address of each officer or employee of a public children services agency or a private child placing agency who performs official responsibilities or duties described in section 2151.14, 2151.141, 2151.33, 2151.353, 2151.412, 2151.413, 2151.414, 2151.415, 2151.416, 2151.417, or 2151.421 or another section of the Revised Code and to the residential address of persons related to that officer or employee by consanguinity or affinity:

(1) Other officers and employees of a public children services agency, private child placing agency, juvenile court, or law enforcement agency shall consider those residential addresses to be confidential information. The officer or employee of the public children services agency or private child placing agency may waive the confidentiality of those residential addresses by giving express permission for their disclosure to other officers or employees of a public children services agency, private child placing agency, juvenile court, or law enforcement agency.

(2) To the extent that those residential addresses are contained in public records kept by a public children services agency, private child placing agency, juvenile court, or law enforcement agency, they shall not be considered to be information that is subject to inspection or copying as part of a public record under section 149.43 of the Revised Code.

(C) Except as provided in division (D) of this section, in the absence of a waiver as described in division (B)(1) of this section, no officer or employee of a public children services agency, private child placing agency, juvenile court, or law enforcement agency shall disclose the residential address of an officer or employee of a public children services agency or private child placing agency, or the residential address of a person related to that officer or employee by consanguinity or affinity, that is confidential information under division (B)(1) of this section to any person, when the disclosing officer or employee knows that the person is or may be a subject of an investigation, interview, examination, criminal case, other case, or other matter with which the officer or employee to whom the residential address relates currently is or has been associated.

(D) If, on or after the effective date of this section, a journalist requests a public children services agency, private child placing agency, juvenile court, or law enforcement agency to disclose a residential address that is confidential information under division (B)(1) of this section, the agency or juvenile court shall disclose to the journalist the residential address if all of the following apply:

(1) The request is in writing, is signed by the journalist, includes the journalist's name and title, and includes the name and address of the journalist's employer.

(2) The request states that disclosure of the residential address would be in the public interest.

(3) The request adequately identifies the person whose residential address is requested.

(4) The public children services agency, private child placing agency, juvenile court, or law enforcement agency receiving the request is one of the following:

(a) The agency or juvenile court with which the official in question serves or with which the employee in question is employed;

(b) The agency or juvenile court that has custody of the records of the agency with which the official in question serves or with which the employee in question is employed.

(2000 H 412, eff. 4–10–01)

2151.15 Powers and duties vested in county department of probation

When a county department of probation has been established in the county and the juvenile judge does not establish a probation department within the juvenile court as provided in section 2151.14 of the Revised Code, all powers and duties of the probation department provided for in sections 2151.01 to 2151.54, inclusive, of the Revised Code, shall vest in and be imposed upon such county department of probation.

In counties in which a county department of probation has been or is hereafter established the judge may transfer to such department all or any part of the powers and duties of his own probation department; provided that all juvenile cases shall be handled within a county department of probation exclusively by an officer or division separate and distinct from the officers or division handling adult cases.

(1953 H 1, eff. 10–1–53; GC 1639–20)

2151.151 Juvenile court may contract for services to children on probation

(A) The juvenile judge may contract with any agency, association, or organization, which may be of a public or private, or profit or nonprofit nature, or with any individual for the provision of supervisory or other services to children placed on probation who are under the custody and supervision of the juvenile court.

(B) The juvenile judges of two or more adjoining or neighboring counties may join together for purposes of contracting with any agency, association, or organization, which may be of a public or private, or profit or nonprofit nature, or with any individual for the provision of supervisory or other services to children placed on probation who are under the custody and supervision of the juvenile court of any of the counties that joins [sic.] together.

(1981 H 440, eff. 11–23–81)

2151.152 Agreement to reimburse juvenile court for foster care maintenance costs and associated administrative and training costs

The juvenile judge may enter into an agreement with the department of job and family services pursuant to section 5101.11 of the Revised Code for the purpose of reimbursing the court for foster care maintenance costs and associated administrative and training costs incurred on behalf of a child eligible for payments under Title IV–E of the "Social Security Act," 94 Stat. 501, 42 U.S.C.A. 670 (1980) and who is in the temporary or permanent custody of the court or subject to a disposition issued under division (A)(5) of section 2151.354 or division (A)(7) (a)(ii) or (A)(8) of section 2152.19 of the Revised Code. The agreement shall govern the responsibilities and duties the court shall perform in providing services to the child.

(2002 H 400, eff. 4–3–03; 2001 H 57, eff. 2–19–02; 1999 H 471, eff. 7–1–00; 1996 H 274, eff. 8–8–96)

2151.16 Referees; powers and duties

The juvenile judge may appoint and fix the compensation of referees who shall have the usual power of masters in chancery cases, provided, in all such cases submitted to them by the juvenile court, they shall hear the testimony of witnesses and certify to the judge their findings upon the case submitted to them, together with their recommendation as to the judgment or order to be made in the case in question. The court, after notice to the parties in the case of the presentation of such findings and recommendation, may make the order recommended by the referee, or any other order in the judgment of the court required by the findings of the referee, or may hear additional testimony, or may set aside said findings and hear the case anew. In appointing a referee for the trial of females, a female referee shall be appointed where possible.

(1953 H 1, eff. 10–1–53; GC 1639–21)

2151.17 Rules governing practice and procedure

Except as otherwise provided by rules promulgated by the supreme court, the juvenile court may prescribe rules regulating the docketing and hearing of causes, motions, and demurrers, and such other matters as are necessary for the orderly conduct of its business and the prevention of delay, and for the government of its officers and employees, including their conduct, duties, hours, expenses, leaves of absence, and vacations.

(1969 H 320, eff. 11–19–69; 1953 H 1; GC 1639–11)

2151.18 Records of cases; annual report

(A) The juvenile court shall maintain records of all official cases brought before it, including, but not limited to, an appearance docket, a journal, and records of the type required by division (A)(2) of section 2151.35 of the Revised Code. The parents, guardian, or other custodian of any child affected, if living, or the nearest of kin of the child, if the parents would be entitled to inspect the records but are deceased, may inspect these records, either in person or by counsel, during the hours in which the court is open.

(B) Not later than June of each year, the court shall prepare an annual report covering the preceding calendar year showing the number and kinds of cases that have come before it, the disposition of the cases, and any other data pertaining to the work of the court that the juvenile judge directs. The court shall file copies of the report with the board of county commissioners. With the approval of the board, the court may print or cause to be printed copies of the report for distribution to persons and agencies interested in the court or community program for dependent, neglected, abused, or delinquent children and juvenile traffic offenders. The court shall include the number of copies ordered printed and the estimated cost of each printed copy on each copy of the report printed for distribution.

(2002 H 393, eff. 7–5–02; 2000 S 179, § 3, eff. 1–1–02)

2151.19 Summons; expense

The summons, warrants, citations, subpoenas, and other writs of the juvenile court may issue to a probation officer of any such court or to the sheriff of any county or any marshal, constable, or police officer, and the provisions of law relating to the subpoenaing of witnesses in other cases shall apply in so far as they are applicable.

When a summons, warrant, citation, subpoena, or other writ is issued to any such officer, other than a probation officer, the expense in serving the same shall be paid by the county, township, or municipal corporation in the manner prescribed for the payment of sheriffs, deputies, assistants, and other employees.

(1953 H 1, eff. 10–1–53; GC 1639–52, 1639–53)

2151.20 Seal of court; dimensions

Juvenile courts within the probate court shall have a seal which shall consist of the coat of arms of the state within a circle one and one-fourth inches in diameter and shall be surrounded by the words "juvenile court ________ county."

The seal of other courts exercising the powers and jurisdiction conferred in sections 2151.01 to 2151.54, inclusive, of the Revised Code, shall be attached to all writs and processes.

(132 v H 164, eff. 12–15–67; 1953 H 1; GC 1639–9)

2151.21 Jurisdiction in contempt

The juvenile court has the same jurisdiction in contempt as courts of common pleas.

(1953 H 1, eff. 10–1–53; GC 1639–10)

2151.211 Employee's attendance at proceeding; employer may not penalize

No employer shall discharge or terminate from employment, threaten to discharge or terminate from employment, or otherwise punish or penalize any employee because of time lost from regular employment as a result of the employee's attendance at any proceeding pursuant to a subpoena under this chapter or Chapter 2152. of the Revised Code. This section generally does not require and shall not be construed to require an employer to pay an employee for time lost as a result of attendance at any proceeding under either chapter. However, if an employee is subpoenaed to appear at a proceeding under either chapter and the proceeding pertains to an offense against the employer or an offense involving the employee during the course of the employee's employment, the employer shall not decrease or withhold the employee's pay for any time lost as a result of compliance with the subpoena. Any employer who knowingly violates this section is in contempt of court.

(2000 S 179, § 3, eff. 1–1–02; 1984 S 172, eff. 9–26–84)

2151.22 Terms of court; sessions

The term of any juvenile or domestic relations court, whether a division of the court of common pleas or an independent court, is one calendar year. All actions and other business pending at the expiration of any term of court is automatically continued without further order. The judge may adjourn court or continue any case whenever, in his opinion, such continuance is warranted.

Sessions of the court may be held at such places throughout the county as the judge shall from time to time determine.

(1976 H 390, eff. 8–6–76; 1953 H 1; GC 1639–12)

2151.23 Jurisdiction of juvenile court; orders for child support

(A) The juvenile court has exclusive original jurisdiction under the Revised Code as follows:

(1) Concerning any child who on or about the date specified in the complaint, indictment, or information is alleged to have violated section 2151.87 of the Revised Code or an order issued under that section or to be a juvenile traffic offender or a delinquent, unruly, abused, neglected, or dependent child and, based on and in relation to the allegation pertaining to the child, concerning the parent, guardian, or other person having care of a child who is alleged to be an unruly or delinquent child for being an habitual or chronic truant;

(2) Subject to divisions (G) and (V) of section 2301.03 of the Revised Code, to determine the custody of any child not a ward of another court of this state;

(3) To hear and determine any application for a writ of habeas corpus involving the custody of a child;

(4) To exercise the powers and jurisdiction given the probate division of the court of common pleas in Chapter 5122. of the Revised Code, if the court has probable cause to believe that a child otherwise within the jurisdiction of the court is a mentally ill person subject to hospitalization by court order, as defined in section 5122.01 of the Revised Code;

(5) To hear and determine all criminal cases charging adults with the violation of any section of this chapter;

(6) To hear and determine all criminal cases in which an adult is charged with a violation of division (C) of section 2919.21, division (B)(1) of section 2919.22, section 2919.222, division (B) of section 2919.23, or section 2919.24 of the Revised Code, provided the charge is not included in an indictment that also charges the alleged adult offender with the commission of a felony arising out of the same actions that are the basis of the alleged violation of division (C) of section 2919.21, division (B)(1) of section 2919.22, section 2919.222, division (B) of section 2919.23, or section 2919.24 of the Revised Code;

(7) Under the interstate compact on juveniles in section 2151.56 of the Revised Code;

(8) Concerning any child who is to be taken into custody pursuant to section 2151.31 of the Revised Code, upon being notified of the intent to take the child into custody and the reasons for taking the child into custody;

(9) To hear and determine requests for the extension of temporary custody agreements, and requests for court approval of permanent custody agreements, that are filed pursuant to section 5103.15 of the Revised Code;

(10) To hear and determine applications for consent to marry pursuant to section 3101.04 of the Revised Code;

(11) Subject to divisions (G) and (V) of section 2301.03 of the Revised Code, to hear and determine a request for an order for the support of any child if the request is not ancillary to an action for divorce, dissolution of marriage, annulment, or legal separa-

tion, a criminal or civil action involving an allegation of domestic violence, or an action for support brought under Chapter 3115. of the Revised Code;

(12) Concerning an action commenced under section 121.38 of the Revised Code;

(13) To hear and determine violations of section 3321.38 of the Revised Code;

(14) To exercise jurisdiction and authority over the parent, guardian, or other person having care of a child alleged to be a delinquent child, unruly child, or juvenile traffic offender, based on and in relation to the allegation pertaining to the child;

(15) To conduct the hearings, and to make the determinations, adjudications, and orders authorized or required under sections 2152.82 to 2152.85 and Chapter 2950. of the Revised Code regarding a child who has been adjudicated a delinquent child and to refer the duties conferred upon the juvenile court judge under sections 2152.82 to 2152.85 and Chapter 2950. of the Revised Code to magistrates appointed by the juvenile court judge in accordance with Juvenile Rule 40.

(B) Except as provided in divisions (G) and (I) of section 2301.03 of the Revised Code, the juvenile court has original jurisdiction under the Revised Code:

(1) To hear and determine all cases of misdemeanors charging adults with any act or omission with respect to any child, which act or omission is a violation of any state law or any municipal ordinance;

(2) To determine the paternity of any child alleged to have been born out of wedlock pursuant to sections 3111.01 to 3111.18 of the Revised Code;

(3) Under the uniform interstate family support act in Chapter 3115. of the Revised Code;

(4) To hear and determine an application for an order for the support of any child, if the child is not a ward of another court of this state;

(5) To hear and determine an action commenced under section 3111.28 of the Revised Code;

(6) To hear and determine a motion filed under section 3119.961 of the Revised Code;

(7) To receive filings under section 3109.74 of the Revised Code, and to hear and determine actions arising under sections 3109.51 to 3109.80 of the Revised Code.

(8) To enforce an order for the return of a child made under the Hague Convention on the Civil Aspects of International Child Abduction pursuant to section 3127.32 of the Revised Code;

(9) To grant any relief normally available under the laws of this state to enforce a child custody determination made by a court of another state and registered in accordance with section 3127.35 of the Revised Code.

(C) The juvenile court, except as to juvenile courts that are a separate division of the court of common pleas or a separate and independent juvenile court, has jurisdiction to hear, determine, and make a record of any action for divorce or legal separation that involves the custody or care of children and that is filed in the court of common pleas and certified by the court of common pleas with all the papers filed in the action to the juvenile court for trial, provided that no certification of that nature shall be made to any juvenile court unless the consent of the juvenile judge first is obtained. After a certification of that nature is made and consent is obtained, the juvenile court shall proceed as if the action originally had been begun in that court, except as to awards for spousal support or support due and unpaid at the time of certification, over which the juvenile court has no jurisdiction.

(D) The juvenile court, except as provided in divisions (G) and (I) of section 2301.03 of the Revised Code, has jurisdiction to hear and determine all matters as to custody and support of children duly certified by the court of common pleas to the juvenile court after a divorce decree has been granted, including jurisdiction to modify the judgment and decree of the court of common pleas as the same relate to the custody and support of children.

(E) The juvenile court, except as provided in divisions (G) and (I) of section 2301.03 of the Revised Code, has jurisdiction to hear and determine the case of any child certified to the court by any court of competent jurisdiction if the child comes within the jurisdiction of the juvenile court as defined by this section.

(F)(1) The juvenile court shall exercise its jurisdiction in child custody matters in accordance with sections 3109.04, 3127.01 to 3127.53, and 5103.20 to 5103.28 of the Revised Code.

(2) The juvenile court shall exercise its jurisdiction in child support matters in accordance with section 3109.05 of the Revised Code.

(G) Any juvenile court that makes or modifies an order for child support shall comply with Chapters 3119., 3121., 3123., and 3125. of the Revised Code. If any person required to pay child support under an order made by a juvenile court on or after April 15, 1985, or modified on or after December 1, 1986, is found in contempt of court for failure to make support payments under the order, the court that makes the finding, in addition to any other penalty or remedy imposed, shall assess all court costs arising out of the contempt proceeding against the person and require the person to pay any reasonable attorney's fees of any adverse party, as determined by the court, that arose in relation to the act of contempt.

(H) If a child who is charged with an act that would be an offense if committed by an adult was fourteen years of age or older and under eighteen years of age at the time of the alleged act and if the case is transferred for criminal prosecution pursuant to section 2152.12 of the Revised Code, the juvenile court does not have jurisdiction to hear or determine the case subsequent to the transfer. The court to which the case is transferred for criminal prosecution pursuant to that section has jurisdiction subsequent to the transfer to hear and determine the case in the same manner as if the case originally had been commenced in that court, including, but not limited to, jurisdiction to accept a plea of guilty or another plea authorized by Criminal Rule 11 or another section of the Revised Code and jurisdiction to accept a verdict and to enter a judgment of conviction pursuant to the Rules of Criminal Procedure against the child for the commission of the offense that was the basis of the transfer of the case for criminal prosecution, whether the conviction is for the same degree or a lesser degree of the offense charged, for the commission of a lesser-included offense, or for the commission of another offense that is different from the offense charged.

(I) If a person under eighteen years of age allegedly commits an act that would be a felony if committed by an adult and if the person is not taken into custody or apprehended for that act until after the person attains twenty-one years of age, the juvenile court does not have jurisdiction to hear or determine any portion of the case charging the person with committing that act. In those circumstances, divisions (A) and (B) of section 2152.12 of the Revised Code do not apply regarding the act, and the case charging the person with committing the act shall be a criminal prosecution commenced and heard in the appropriate court having jurisdiction of the offense as if the person had been eighteen years of age or older when the person committed the act. All proceedings pertaining to the act shall be within the jurisdiction of the court having jurisdiction of the offense, and that court has all the authority and duties in the case that it has in other criminal cases in that court.

(2004 S 185, eff. 4–11–05; 2004 H 38, eff. 6–17–04; 2001 S 3, eff. 1–1–02; 2000 S 179, § 3, eff. 1–1–02; 2000 S 180, eff. 3–22–01; 2000 S 218, eff. 3–15–01; 2000 H 583, eff. 6–14–00; 2000 S 181, eff. 9–4–00; 1997 H 352, eff. 1–1–98; 1997 H 215, eff. 6–30–97; 1996 H 124, eff. 3–31–97; 1996 H 377, eff. 10–17–96; 1996 S 269, eff. 7–1–96; 1996 H 274, eff. 8–8–96; 1995 H 1, eff. 1–1–96; 1993 H 173, eff. 12–31–93; 1993 S 21; 1992 S 10; 1990 S 3, H 514, S 258, H 591; 1988 S 89; 1986 H 428, H 509, H 476; 1984 H 614; 1983 H 93; 1982 H 515; 1981 H 1; 1977 S 135; 1976 H 244; 1975 H 85; 1970 H 931; 1969 H 320)

2151.231 Action for child support order

The parent, guardian, or custodian of a child, the person with whom a child resides, or the child support enforcement agency of the county in which the child, parent, guardian, or custodian of the child resides may bring an action in a juvenile court or other court with jurisdiction under section 2101.022 or 2301.03 of the Revised Code under this section requesting the court to issue an order requiring a parent of the child to pay an amount for the support of the child without regard to the marital status of the child's parents. No action may be brought under this section against a person presumed to be the parent of a child based on an acknowledgment of paternity that has not yet become final under former section 3111.211 or 5101.314 or section 2151.232, 3111.25, or 3111.821 of the Revised Code.

The parties to an action under this section may raise the issue of the existence or nonexistence of a parent-child relationship, unless a final and enforceable determination of the issue has been made with respect to the parties pursuant to Chapter 3111. of the Revised Code or an acknowledgment of paternity signed by the child's parents has become final pursuant to former section 3111.211 or 5101.314 or section 2151.232, 3111.25, or 3111.821 of the Revised Code. If a complaint is filed under this section and an issue concerning the existence or nonexistence of a parent-child relationship is raised, the court shall treat the action as an action pursuant to sections 3111.01 to 3111.18 of the Revised Code. An order issued in an action under this section does not preclude a party to the action from bringing a subsequent action pursuant to sections 3111.01 to 3111.18 of the Revised Code if the issue concerning the existence or nonexistence of the parent-child relationship was not determined with respect to the party pursuant to a proceeding under this section, a proceeding under Chapter 3111. of the Revised Code, or an acknowledgment of paternity that has become final under former section 3111.211 or 5101.314 or section 2151.232, 3111.25, or 3111.821 of the Revised Code. An order issued pursuant to this section shall remain effective until an order is issued pursuant to sections 3111.01 to 3111.18 of the Revised Code that a parent-child relationship does not exist between the alleged father of the child and the child or until the occurrence of an event described in section 3119.88 of the Revised Code that would require the order to terminate.

The court, in accordance with sections 3119.29 to 3119.56 of the Revised Code, shall include in each support order made under this section the requirement that one or both of the parents provide for the health care needs of the child to the satisfaction of the court.

(2002 H 657, eff. 12–13–02; 2000 S 180, eff. 3–22–01; 1997 H 352, eff. 1–1–98; 1996 H 710, § 7, eff. 6–11–96; 1995 H 167, eff. 6–11–96; 1992 S 10, eff. 7–15–92)

2151.232 Action for child support order before acknowledgment becomes final

If an acknowledgment has been filed and entered into the birth registry pursuant to section 3111.24 of the Revised Code but has not yet become final, either parent who signed the acknowledgment may bring an action in the juvenile court or other court with jurisdiction under section 2101.022 or 2301.03 of the Revised Code under this section requesting that the court issue an order requiring a parent of the child to pay an amount for the support of the child in accordance with Chapters 3119., 3121., 3123., and 3125. of the Revised Code.

The parties to an action under this section may raise the issue of the existence or nonexistence of a parent-child relationship. If an action is commenced pursuant to this section and the issue of the existence or nonexistence of a parent-child relationship is raised, the court shall treat the action as an action commenced pursuant to sections 3111.01 to 3111.18 of the Revised Code. If the issue is raised, the court shall promptly notify the office of child support in the department of job and family services that it is conducting proceedings in compliance with sections 3111.01 to 3111.18 of the Revised Code. On receipt of the notice by the office, the acknowledgment of paternity signed by the parties and filed pursuant to section 3111.23 of the Revised Code shall be considered rescinded.

If the parties do not raise the issue of the existence or nonexistence of a parent-child relationship in the action and an order is issued pursuant to this section prior to the date the acknowledgment filed and entered on the birth registry becomes final, the acknowledgment shall be considered final as of the date of the issuance of the order. An order issued pursuant to this section shall not affect an acknowledgment that becomes final pursuant to section 3111.25 of the Revised Code prior to the issuance of the order.

(2000 S 180, eff. 3–22–01; 1999 H 471, eff. 7–1–00; 1997 H 352, eff. 1–1–98)

2151.24 Separate room for hearings

(A) Except as provided in division (B) of this section, the board of county commissioners shall provide a special room not used for the trial of criminal or adult cases, when available, for the hearing of the cases of dependent, neglected, abused, and delinquent children.

(B) Division (A) of this section does not apply to the case of an alleged delinquent child when the case is one in which the prosecuting attorney seeks a serious youthful offender disposition under section 2152.13 of the Revised Code.

(2000 S 179, § 3, eff. 1–1–02; 1975 H 85, eff. 11–28–75; 1953 H 1; GC 1639–14)

PRACTICE AND PROCEDURE

2151.27 Complaint

(A)(1) Subject to division (A)(2) of this section, any person having knowledge of a child who appears to have violated section 2151.87 of the Revised Code or to be a juvenile traffic offender or to be an unruly, abused, neglected, or dependent child may file a sworn complaint with respect to that child in the juvenile court of the county in which the child has a residence or legal settlement or in which the violation, unruliness, abuse, neglect, or dependency allegedly occurred. If an alleged abused, neglected, or dependent child is taken into custody pursuant to division (D) of section 2151.31 of the Revised Code or is taken into custody pursuant to division (A) of section 2151.31 of the Revised Code without the filing of a complaint and placed into shelter care pursuant to division (C) of that section, a sworn complaint shall be filed with respect to the child before the end of the next day after the day on which the child was taken into custody. The sworn complaint may be upon information and belief, and, in addition to the allegation that the child committed the violation or is an unruly, abused, neglected, or dependent child, the complaint shall allege the particular facts upon which the allegation that the child committed the violation or is an unruly, abused, neglected, or dependent child is based.

(2) Any person having knowledge of a child who appears to be an unruly child for being an habitual truant may file a sworn complaint with respect to that child and the parent, guardian, or other person having care of the child in the juvenile court of the county in which the child has a residence or legal settlement or in which the child is supposed to attend public school. The sworn complaint may be upon information and belief and shall contain the following allegations:

(a) That the child is an unruly child for being an habitual truant and, in addition, the particular facts upon which that allegation is based;

(b) That the parent, guardian, or other person having care of the child has failed to cause the child's attendance at school in violation of section 3321.38 of the Revised Code and, in addition, the particular facts upon which that allegation is based.

(B) If a child, before arriving at the age of eighteen years, allegedly commits an act for which the child may be adjudicated an unruly child and if the specific complaint alleging the act is not filed or a hearing on that specific complaint is not held until after the child arrives at the age of eighteen years, the court has jurisdiction to hear and dispose of the complaint as if the complaint were filed and the hearing held before the child arrived at the age of eighteen years.

(C) If the complainant in a case in which a child is alleged to be an abused, neglected, or dependent child desires permanent custody of the child or children, temporary custody of the child or children, whether as the preferred or an alternative disposition, or the placement of the child in a planned permanent living arrangement, the complaint shall contain a prayer specifically requesting permanent custody, temporary custody, or the placement of the child in a planned permanent living arrangement.

(D) Any person with standing under applicable law may file a complaint for the determination of any other matter over which the juvenile court is given jurisdiction by section 2151.23 of the Revised Code. The complaint shall be filed in the county in which the child who is the subject of the complaint is found or was last known to be found.

(E) A public children services agency, acting pursuant to a complaint or an action on a complaint filed under this section, is not subject to the requirements of section 3127.23 of the Revised Code.

(F) Upon the filing of a complaint alleging that a child is an unruly child, the court may hold the complaint in abeyance pending the child's successful completion of actions that constitute a method to divert the child from the juvenile court system. The method may be adopted by a county pursuant to divisions (D) and (E) of section 121.37 of the Revised Code or it may be another method that the court considers satisfactory. If the child completes the actions to the court's satisfaction, the court may dismiss the complaint. If the child fails to complete the actions to the court's satisfaction, the court may consider the complaint.

(2004 S 185, eff. 4–11–05; 2001 H 57, eff. 2–19–02; 2000 S 179, § 3, eff. 1–1–02; 2000 S 218, eff. 3–15–01; 2000 S 181, eff. 9–4–00; 1998 H 484, eff. 3–18–99; 1996 H 445, eff. 9–3–96; 1996 H 274, § 4, eff. 8–8–96; 1996 H 274, § 1, eff. 8–8–96; 1995 S 2, eff. 7–1–96; 1992 H 154, eff. 7–31–92; 1988 S 89; 1984 S 5; 1975 H 85; 1969 H 320)

2151.271 Transfer to juvenile court of another county

Except in a case in which the child is alleged to be a serious youthful offender under section 2152.13 of the Revised Code, if the child resides in a county of the state and the proceeding is commenced in a juvenile court of another county, that court, on its own motion or a motion of a party, may transfer the proceeding to the county of the child's residence upon the filing of the complaint or after the adjudicatory, or dispositional hearing, for such further proceeding as required. The court of the child's residence shall then proceed as if the original complaint had been filed in that court. Transfer may also be made if the residence of the child changes. The proceeding shall be so transferred if other proceedings involving the child are pending in the juvenile court of the county of the child's residence.

Whenever a case is transferred to the county of the child's residence and it appears to the court of that county that the interests of justice and the convenience of the parties requires that the adjudicatory hearing be had in the county in which the complaint was filed, the court may return the proceeding to the county in which the complaint was filed for the purpose of the adjudicatory hearing. The court may thereafter proceed as to the transfer to the county of the child's legal residence as provided in this section.

Certified copies of all legal and social records pertaining to the case shall accompany the transfer.

(2000 S 179, § 3, eff. 1–1–02; 1969 H 320, eff. 11–19–69)

2151.28 Summons

(A) No later than seventy-two hours after the complaint is filed, the court shall fix a time for an adjudicatory hearing. The court shall conduct the adjudicatory hearing within one of the following periods of time:

(1) Subject to division (C) of section 2152.13 of the Revised Code and division (A)(3) of this section, if the complaint alleged that the child violated section 2151.87 of the Revised Code or is a delinquent or unruly child or a juvenile traffic offender, the adjudicatory hearing shall be held and may be continued in accordance with the Juvenile Rules.

(2) If the complaint alleged that the child is an abused, neglected, or dependent child, the adjudicatory hearing shall be held no later than thirty days after the complaint is filed, except that, for good cause shown, the court may continue the adjudicatory hearing for either of the following periods of time:

(a) For ten days beyond the thirty-day deadline to allow any party to obtain counsel;

(b) For a reasonable period of time beyond the thirty-day deadline to obtain service on all parties or any necessary evaluation, except that the adjudicatory hearing shall not be held later than sixty days after the date on which the complaint was filed.

(3) If the child who is the subject of the complaint is in detention and is charged with violating a section of the Revised Code that may be violated by an adult, the hearing shall be held not later than fifteen days after the filing of the complaint. Upon a showing of good cause, the adjudicatory hearing may be continued and detention extended.

(B) At an adjudicatory hearing held pursuant to division (A)(2) of this section, the court, in addition to determining whether the child is an abused, neglected, or dependent child, shall determine whether the child should remain or be placed in shelter care until the dispositional hearing. When the court makes the shelter care determination, all of the following apply:

(1) The court shall determine whether there are any relatives of the child who are willing to be temporary custodians of the child. If any relative is willing to be a temporary custodian, the child otherwise would remain or be placed in shelter care, and the appointment is appropriate, the court shall appoint the relative as temporary custodian of the child, unless the court appoints another relative as custodian. If it determines that the appointment of a relative as custodian would not be appropriate, it shall issue a written opinion setting forth the reasons for its determination and give a copy of the opinion to all parties and the guardian ad litem of the child.

The court's consideration of a relative for appointment as a temporary custodian does not make that relative a party to the proceedings.

(2) The court shall comply with section 2151.419 of the Revised Code.

(3) The court shall schedule the date for the dispositional hearing to be held pursuant to section 2151.35 of the Revised Code. The parents of the child have a right to be represented by counsel; however, in no case shall the dispositional hearing be held later than ninety days after the date on which the complaint was filed.

(C)(1) The court shall direct the issuance of a summons directed to the child except as provided by this section, the parents, guardian, custodian, or other person with whom the child may be, and any other persons that appear to the court to be proper or necessary parties to the proceedings, requiring them to appear before the court at the time fixed to answer the allegations of the complaint. The summons shall contain the name and telephone number of the court employee designated by the court pursuant to section 2151.314 of the Revised Code to arrange for the prompt appointment of counsel for indigent persons. A child alleged to be an abused, neglected, or dependent child shall not be summoned unless the court so directs. A summons issued for a child who is under fourteen years of age and who is alleged to be a delinquent child, unruly child, or a juvenile traffic offender shall be served on the parent, guardian, or custodian of the child in the child's behalf.

If the person who has physical custody of the child, or with whom the child resides, is other than the parent or guardian, then the parents and guardian also shall be summoned. A copy of the complaint shall accompany the summons.

(2) In lieu of appearing before the court at the time fixed in the summons and prior to the date fixed for appearance in the summons, a child who is alleged to have violated section 2151.87 of the Revised Code and that child's parent, guardian, or custodian may sign a waiver of appearance before the clerk of the juvenile court and pay a fine of one hundred dollars. If the child and that child's parent, guardian, or custodian do not waive the court appearance, the court shall proceed with the adjudicatory hearing as provided in this section.

(D) If the complaint contains a prayer for permanent custody, temporary custody, whether as the preferred or an alternative disposition, or a planned permanent living arrangement in a case involving an alleged abused, neglected, or dependent child, the summons served on the parents shall contain as is appropriate an explanation that the granting of permanent custody permanently divests the parents of their parental rights and privileges, an explanation that an adjudication that the child is an abused, neglected, or dependent child may result in an order of temporary custody that will cause the removal of the child from their legal custody until the court terminates the order of temporary custody or permanently divests the parents of their parental rights, or an explanation that the issuance of an order for a planned permanent living arrangement will cause the removal of the child from the legal custody of the parents if any of the conditions listed in divisions (A)(5)(a) to (c) of section 2151.353 of the Revised Code are found to exist.

(E)(1) Except as otherwise provided in division (E)(2) of this section, the court may endorse upon the summons an order directing the parents, guardian, or other person with whom the child may be to appear personally at the hearing and directing the person having the physical custody or control of the child to bring the child to the hearing.

(2) In cases in which the complaint alleges that a child is an unruly or delinquent child for being an habitual or chronic truant and that the parent, guardian, or other person having care of the child has failed to cause the child's attendance at school, the court shall endorse upon the summons an order directing the parent, guardian, or other person having care of the child to appear personally at the hearing and directing the person having the physical custody or control of the child to bring the child to the hearing.

(F)(1) The summons shall contain a statement advising that any party is entitled to counsel in the proceedings and that the court will appoint counsel or designate a county public defender or joint county public defender to provide legal representation if the party is indigent.

(2) In cases in which the complaint alleges a child to be an abused, neglected, or dependent child and no hearing has been conducted pursuant to division (A) of section 2151.314 of the Revised Code with respect to the child or a parent, guardian, or custodian of the child does not attend the hearing, the summons also shall contain a statement advising that a case plan may be prepared for the child, the general requirements usually contained in case plans, and the possible consequences of failure to comply with a journalized case plan.

(G) If it appears from an affidavit filed or from sworn testimony before the court that the conduct, condition, or surroundings of the child are endangering the child's health or welfare or those of others, that the child may abscond or be removed from the jurisdiction of the court, or that the child will not be brought to the court, notwithstanding the service of the summons, the court may endorse upon the summons an order that a law enforcement officer serve the summons and take the child into immediate custody and bring the child forthwith to the court.

(H) A party, other than the child, may waive service of summons by written stipulation.

(I) Before any temporary commitment is made permanent, the court shall fix a time for hearing in accordance with section 2151.414 of the Revised Code and shall cause notice by summons to be served upon the parent or guardian of the child and the guardian ad litem of the child, or published, as provided in section 2151.29 of the Revised Code. The summons shall contain an explanation that the granting of permanent custody permanently divests the parents of their parental rights and privileges.

(J) Any person whose presence is considered necessary and who is not summoned may be subpoenaed to appear and testify at the hearing. Anyone summoned or subpoenaed to appear who fails to do so may be punished, as in other cases in the court of common pleas, for contempt of court. Persons subpoenaed shall be paid the same witness fees as are allowed in the court of common pleas.

(K) The failure of the court to hold an adjudicatory hearing within any time period set forth in division (A)(2) of this section does not affect the ability of the court to issue any order under this chapter and does not provide any basis for attacking the jurisdiction of the court or the validity of any order of the court.

(L) If the court, at an adjudicatory hearing held pursuant to division (A) of this section upon a complaint alleging that a child is an abused, neglected, dependent, delinquent, or unruly child or a juvenile traffic offender, determines that the child is a dependent child, the court shall incorporate that determination into written findings of fact and conclusions of law and enter those findings of fact and conclusions of law in the record of the case. The court shall include in those findings of fact and conclusions of law specific findings as to the existence of any danger to the child and any underlying family problems that are the basis for the court's determination that the child is a dependent child.

(2002 H 393, eff. 7–5–02; 2002 H 180, eff. 5–16–02; 2000 S 179, § 3, eff. 1–1–02; 2000 S 218, eff. 3–15–01; 2000 S 181, eff. 9–4–00; 1998 H 484, eff. 3–18–99; 1996 H 274, eff. 8–8–96; 1996 H 419, eff. 9–18–96; 1988 S 89, eff. 1–1–89; 1975 H 164, H 85; 1969 H 320)

2151.281 Guardian ad litem

(A) The court shall appoint a guardian ad litem to protect the interest of a child in any proceeding concerning an alleged or adjudicated delinquent child or unruly child when either of the following applies:

(1) The child has no parent, guardian, or legal custodian.

(2) The court finds that there is a conflict of interest between the child and the child's parent, guardian, or legal custodian.

(B)(1) The court shall appoint a guardian ad litem to protect the interest of a child in any proceeding concerning an alleged abused or neglected child and in any proceeding held pursuant to section 2151.414 of the Revised Code. The guardian ad litem so appointed shall not be the attorney responsible for presenting the evidence alleging that the child is an abused or neglected child and shall not be an employee of any party in the proceeding.

(2) The guardian ad litem appointed for an alleged or adjudicated abused or neglected child may bring a civil action against any person, who is required by division (A)(1) of section 2151.421 of the Revised Code to file a report of known or suspected child abuse or child neglect, if that person knows or suspects that the child for whom the guardian ad litem is appointed is the subject of child abuse or child neglect and does not file the required report and if the child suffers any injury or harm as a result of the known or suspected child abuse or child neglect or suffers additional injury or harm after the failure to file the report.

(C) In any proceeding concerning an alleged or adjudicated delinquent, unruly, abused, neglected, or dependent child in which the parent appears to be mentally incompetent or is under eighteen years of age, the court shall appoint a guardian ad litem to protect the interest of that parent.

(D) The court shall require the guardian ad litem to faithfully discharge the guardian ad litem's duties and, upon the guardian ad litem's failure to faithfully discharge the guardian ad litem's duties, shall discharge the guardian ad litem and appoint another guardian ad litem. The court may fix the compensation for the service of the guardian ad litem, which compensation shall be paid from the treasury of the county.

(E) A parent who is eighteen years of age or older and not mentally incompetent shall be deemed sui juris for the purpose of any proceeding relative to a child of the parent who is alleged or adjudicated to be an abused, neglected, or dependent child.

(F) In any case in which a parent of a child alleged or adjudicated to be an abused, neglected, or dependent child is under eighteen years of age, the parents of that parent shall be summoned to appear at any hearing respecting the child, who is alleged or adjudicated to be an abused, neglected, or dependent child.

(G) In any case involving an alleged or adjudicated abused or neglected child or an agreement for the voluntary surrender of temporary or permanent custody of a child that is made in accordance with section 5103.15 of the Revised Code, the court shall appoint the guardian ad litem in each case as soon as possible after the complaint is filed, the request for an extension of the temporary custody agreement is filed with the court, or the request for court approval of the permanent custody agreement is filed. In any case involving an alleged dependent child in which the parent of the child appears to be mentally incompetent or is under eighteen years of age, there is a conflict of interest between the child and the child's parents, guardian, or custodian, or the court believes that the parent of the child is not capable of representing the best interest of the child, the court shall appoint a guardian ad litem for the child. The guardian ad litem or the guardian ad litem's replacement shall continue to serve until any of the following occur:

(1) The complaint is dismissed or the request for an extension of a temporary custody agreement or for court approval of the permanent custody agreement is withdrawn or denied;

(2) All dispositional orders relative to the child have terminated;

(3) The legal custody of the child is granted to a relative of the child, or to another person;

(4) The child is placed in an adoptive home or, at the court's discretion, a final decree of adoption is issued with respect to the child;

(5) The child reaches the age of eighteen if the child is not mentally retarded, developmentally disabled, or physically impaired or the child reaches the age of twenty-one if the child is mentally retarded, developmentally disabled, or physically impaired;

(6) The guardian ad litem resigns or is removed by the court and a replacement is appointed by the court.

If a guardian ad litem ceases to serve a child pursuant to division (G)(4) of this section and the petition for adoption with respect to the child is denied or withdrawn prior to the issuance of a final decree of adoption or prior to the date an interlocutory order of adoption becomes final, the juvenile court shall reappoint a guardian ad litem for that child. The public children services agency or private child placing agency with permanent custody of the child shall notify the juvenile court if the petition for adoption is denied or withdrawn.

(H) If the guardian ad litem for an alleged or adjudicated abused, neglected, or dependent child is an attorney admitted to the practice of law in this state, the guardian ad litem also may serve as counsel to the ward. If a person is serving as guardian ad litem and counsel for a child and either that person or the court finds that a conflict may exist between the person's roles as guardian ad litem and as counsel, the court shall relieve the person of duties as guardian ad litem and appoint someone else as guardian ad litem for the child. If the court appoints a person who is not an attorney admitted to the practice of law in this state to be a guardian ad litem, the court also may appoint an attorney admitted to the practice of law in this state to serve as counsel for the guardian ad litem.

(I) The guardian ad litem for an alleged or adjudicated abused, neglected, or dependent child shall perform whatever functions are necessary to protect the best interest of the child, including, but not limited to, investigation, mediation, monitoring court proceedings, and monitoring the services provided the child by the public children services agency or private child placing agency that has temporary or permanent custody of the child, and shall file any motions and other court papers that are in the best interest of the child.

The guardian ad litem shall be given notice of all hearings, administrative reviews, and other proceedings in the same manner as notice is given to parties to the action.

(J)(1) When the court appoints a guardian ad litem pursuant to this section, it shall appoint a qualified volunteer whenever one is available and the appointment is appropriate.

(2) Upon request, the department of job and family services shall provide for the training of volunteer guardians ad litem.

(1999 H 471, eff. 7–1–00; 1996 H 274, eff. 8–8–96; 1996 H 419, eff. 9–18–96; 1988 S 89, eff. 1–1–89; 1986 H 529; 1984 S 321; 1980 H 695; 1975 H 85; 1969 H 320)

2151.29 Service of summons

Service of summons, notices, and subpoenas, prescribed by section 2151.28 of the Revised Code, shall be made by delivering a copy to the person summoned, notified, or subpoenaed, or by leaving a copy at the person's usual place of residence. If the juvenile judge is satisfied that such service is impracticable, the juvenile judge may order service by registered or certified mail. If the person to be served is without the state but the person can be found or the person's address is known, or the person's whereabouts or address can with reasonable diligence be ascertained, service of the summons may be made by delivering a copy to the person personally or mailing a copy to the person by registered or certified mail.

Whenever it appears by affidavit that after reasonable effort the person to be served with summons cannot be found or the person's post-office address ascertained, whether the person is within or without a state, the clerk shall publish such summons once in a newspaper of general circulation throughout the county. The summons shall state the substance and the time and place of the hearing, which shall be held at least one week later than the date of the publication. A copy of the summons and the complaint, indictment, or information shall be sent by registered or certified mail to the last known address of the person summoned unless it is shown by affidavit that a reasonable effort has been made, without success, to obtain such address.

A copy of the advertisement, the summons, and the complaint, indictment, or information, accompanied by the certificate of the clerk that such publication has been made and that the summons and the complaint, indictment, or information have been mailed as required by this section, is sufficient evidence of publication and mailing. When a period of one week from the time of publication has elapsed, the juvenile court shall have full jurisdiction to deal with such child as provided by sections 2151.01 to 2151.99 of the Revised Code.

(2000 S 179, § 3, eff. 1–1–02; 1969 H 320, eff. 11–19–69)

2151.30 Issuance of warrant

In any case when it is made to appear to the juvenile judge that the service of a citation under section 2151.29 of the Revised Code will be ineffectual or the welfare of the child requires that he be brought forthwith into the custody of the juvenile court, a warrant may be issued against the parent, custodian, or guardian, or against the child himself.

(1953 H 1, eff. 10–1–53; GC 1639–26)

2151.31 Apprehension, custody, and detention

(A) A child may be taken into custody in any of the following ways:

(1) Pursuant to an order of the court under this chapter or pursuant to an order of the court upon a motion filed pursuant to division (B) of section 2930.05 of the Revised Code;

(2) Pursuant to the laws of arrest;

(3) By a law enforcement officer or duly authorized officer of the court when any of the following conditions are present:

(a) There are reasonable grounds to believe that the child is suffering from illness or injury and is not receiving proper care, as described in section 2151.03 of the Revised Code, and the child's removal is necessary to prevent immediate or threatened physical or emotional harm;

(b) There are reasonable grounds to believe that the child is in immediate danger from the child's surroundings and that the child's removal is necessary to prevent immediate or threatened physical or emotional harm;

(c) There are reasonable grounds to believe that a parent, guardian, custodian, or other household member of the child's household has abused or neglected another child in the household and to believe that the child is in danger of immediate or threatened physical or emotional harm from that person.

(4) By an enforcement official, as defined in section 4109.01 of the Revised Code, under the circumstances set forth in section 4109.08 of the Revised Code;

(5) By a law enforcement officer or duly authorized officer of the court when there are reasonable grounds to believe that the child has run away from the child's parents, guardian, or other custodian;

(6) By a law enforcement officer or duly authorized officer of the court when any of the following apply:

(a) There are reasonable grounds to believe that the conduct, conditions, or surroundings of the child are endangering the health, welfare, or safety of the child.

(b) A complaint has been filed with respect to the child under section 2151.27 or 2152.021 of the Revised Code or the child has been indicted under division (A) of section 2152.13 of the Revised Code or charged by information as described in that section and there are reasonable grounds to believe that the child may abscond or be removed from the jurisdiction of the court.

(c) The child is required to appear in court and there are reasonable grounds to believe that the child will not be brought before the court when required.

(d) There are reasonable grounds to believe that the child committed a delinquent act and that taking the child into custody is necessary to protect the public interest and safety.

(B)(1) The taking of a child into custody is not and shall not be deemed an arrest except for the purpose of determining its validity under the constitution of this state or of the United States.

(2) Except as provided in division (C) of section 2151.311 of the Revised Code, a child taken into custody shall not be held in any state correctional institution, county, multicounty, or municipal jail or workhouse, or any other place where any adult convicted of crime, under arrest, or charged with crime is held.

(C)(1) Except as provided in division (C)(2) of this section, a child taken into custody shall not be confined in a place of juvenile detention or placed in shelter care prior to the implementation of the court's final order of disposition, unless detention or shelter care is required to protect the child from immediate or threatened physical or emotional harm, because the child is a danger or threat to one or more other persons and is charged with violating a section of the Revised Code that may be violated by an adult, because the child may abscond or be removed from the jurisdiction of the court, because the child has no parents, guardian, or custodian or other person able to provide supervision and care for the child and return the child to the court when required, or because an order for placement of the child in detention or shelter care has been made by the court pursuant to this chapter.

(2) A child alleged to be a delinquent child who is taken into custody may be confined in a place of juvenile detention prior to the implementation of the court's final order of disposition if the confinement is authorized under section 2152.04 of the Revised Code or if the child is alleged to be a serious youthful offender under section 2152.13 of the Revised Code and is not released on bond.

(D) Upon receipt of notice from a person that the person intends to take an alleged abused, neglected, or dependent child into custody pursuant to division (A)(3) of this section, a juvenile judge or a designated referee may grant by telephone an ex parte emergency order authorizing the taking of the child into custody if there is probable cause to believe that any of the conditions set forth in divisions (A)(3)(a) to (c) of this section are present. The judge or referee shall journalize any ex parte emergency order issued pursuant to this division. If an order is issued pursuant to this division and the child is taken into custody pursuant to the order, a sworn complaint shall be filed with respect to the child before the end of the next business day after the day on which the child is taken into custody and a hearing shall be held pursuant to division (E) of this section and the Juvenile Rules. A juvenile judge or referee shall not grant an emergency order by telephone pursuant to this division until after the judge or referee determines that reasonable efforts have been made to notify the parents, guardian, or custodian of the child that the child may be placed into shelter care and of the reasons for placing the child into shelter care, except that, if the requirement for notification would jeopardize the physical or emotional safety of the child or result in the child being removed from the court's jurisdiction, the judge or referee may issue the order for taking the child into custody and placing the child into shelter care prior to giving notice to the parents, guardian, or custodian of the child.

(E) If a judge or referee pursuant to division (D) of this section issues an ex parte emergency order for taking a child into custody, the court shall hold a hearing to determine whether there is probable cause for the emergency order. The hearing shall be held before the end of the next business day after the day on which the emergency order is issued, except that it shall not be held later than seventy-two hours after the emergency order is issued.

If the court determines at the hearing that there is not probable cause for the issuance of the emergency order issued pursuant to division (D) of this section, it shall order the child released to the custody of the child's parents, guardian, or custodian. If the court determines at the hearing that there is probable cause for the issuance of the emergency order issued pursuant to division (D) of this section, the court shall do all of the following:

(1) Ensure that a complaint is filed or has been filed;

(2) Comply with section 2151.419 of the Revised Code;

(3) Hold a hearing pursuant to section 2151.314 of the Revised Code to determine if the child should remain in shelter care.

(F) If the court determines at the hearing held pursuant to division (E) of this section that there is probable cause to believe that the child is an abused child, as defined in division (A) of section 2151.031 of the Revised Code, the court may do any of the following:

(1) Upon the motion of any party, the guardian ad litem, the prosecuting attorney, or an employee of the public children services agency, or its own motion, issue reasonable protective orders with respect to the interviewing or deposition of the child;

(2) Order that the child's testimony be videotaped for preservation of the testimony for possible use in any other proceedings in the case;

(3) Set any additional conditions with respect to the child or the case involving the child that are in the best interest of the child.

(G) This section is not intended, and shall not be construed, to prevent any person from taking a child into custody, if taking the child into custody is necessary in an emergency to prevent the physical injury, emotional harm, or neglect of the child.

(2002 H 180, eff. 5–16–02; 2000 S 179, § 3, eff. 1–1–02; 1999 H 3, eff. 11–22–99; 1999 H 176, eff. 10–29–99; 1998 H 484, eff. 3–18–99; 1997 H 408, eff. 10–1–97; 1994 H 571, eff. 10–6–94; 1989 H 166, eff. 2–14–90; 1988 S 89; 1978 H 883; 1969 H 320)

2151.311 Procedure upon apprehension

(A) A person taking a child into custody shall, with all reasonable speed and in accordance with division (C) of this section, either:

(1) Release the child to the child's parents, guardian, or other custodian, unless the child's detention or shelter care appears to be warranted or required as provided in section 2151.31 of the Revised Code;

(2) Bring the child to the court or deliver the child to a place of detention or shelter care designated by the court and promptly give notice thereof, together with a statement of the reason for taking the child into custody, to a parent, guardian, or other custodian and to the court.

(B) If a parent, guardian, or other custodian fails, when requested by the court, to bring the child before the court as provided by this section, the court may issue its warrant directing that the child be taken into custody and brought before the court.

(C)(1) Before taking any action required by division (A) of this section, a person taking a child into custody may hold the child for processing purposes in a county, multicounty, or municipal jail or workhouse, or other place where an adult convicted of crime, under arrest, or charged with crime is held for either of the following periods of time:

(a) For a period not to exceed six hours, if all of the following apply:

(i) The child is alleged to be a delinquent child for the commission of an act that would be a felony if committed by an adult;

(ii) The child remains beyond the range of touch of all adult detainees;

(iii) The child is visually supervised by jail or workhouse personnel at all times during the detention;

(iv) The child is not handcuffed or otherwise physically secured to a stationary object during the detention.

(b) For a period not to exceed three hours, if all of the following apply:

(i) The child is alleged to be a delinquent child for the commission of an act that would be a misdemeanor if committed by an adult, is alleged to be a delinquent child for being a chronic truant or an habitual truant who previously has been adjudicated an unruly child for being an habitual truant, or is alleged to be an unruly child or a juvenile traffic offender;

(ii) The child remains beyond the range of touch of all adult detainees;

(iii) The child is visually supervised by jail or workhouse personnel at all times during the detention;

(iv) The child is not handcuffed or otherwise physically secured to a stationary object during the detention.

(2) If a child has been transferred to an adult court for prosecution for the alleged commission of a criminal offense, subsequent to the transfer, the child may be held as described in division (F) of section 2152.26 or division (B) of section 5120.16 of the Revised Code.

(D) As used in division (C)(1) of this section, "processing purposes" means all of the following:

(1) Fingerprinting, photographing, or fingerprinting and photographing the child in a secure area of the facility;

(2) Interrogating the child, contacting the child's parent or guardian, arranging for placement of the child, or arranging for transfer or transferring the child, while holding the child in a nonsecure area of the facility.

(2000 S 179, § 3, eff. 1–1–02; 2000 S 181, eff. 9–4–00; 1996 H 124, eff. 3–31–97; 1996 H 480, eff. 10–16–96; 1994 H 571, eff. 10–6–94, 1989 H 166, eff. 2–14–90; 1972 S 445; 1970 H 931; 1969 H 320)

2151.312 Place of detention

(A) A child alleged to be or adjudicated an unruly child may be held only in the following places:

(1) A certified family foster home or a home approved by the court;

(2) A facility operated by a certified child welfare agency;

(3) Any other suitable place designated by the court.

(B)(1) Except as provided under division (C)(1) of section 2151.311 of the Revised Code, a child alleged to be or adjudicated a neglected child, an abused child, a dependent child, or an unruly child may not be held in any of the following facilities:

(a) A state correctional institution, county, multicounty, or municipal jail or workhouse, or other place in which an adult convicted of a crime, under arrest, or charged with a crime is held;

(b) A secure correctional facility.

(2) Except as provided under sections 2151.26 to 2151.61 of the Revised Code and division (B)(3) of this section, a child alleged to be or adjudicated an unruly child may not be held for more than twenty-four hours in a detention facility. A child alleged to be or adjudicated a neglected child, an abused child, or a dependent child shall not be held in a detention facility.

(3) A child who is alleged to be or adjudicated an unruly child and who is taken into custody on a Saturday, Sunday, or legal holiday, as listed in section 1.14 of the Revised Code, may be held in a detention facility until the next succeeding day that is not a Saturday, Sunday, or legal holiday.

(2000 S 179, § 3, eff. 1–1–02)

2151.313 Fingerprinting or photographing child in an investigation

(A)(1) Except as provided in division (A)(2) of this section and in sections 109.57, 109.60, and 109.61 of the Revised Code, no child shall be fingerprinted or photographed in the investigation of any violation of law without the consent of the juvenile judge.

(2) Subject to division (A)(3) of this section, a law enforcement officer may fingerprint and photograph a child without the consent of the juvenile judge when the child is arrested or otherwise taken into custody for the commission of an act that would be an offense, other than a traffic offense or a minor misdemeanor, if committed by an adult, and there is probable cause to believe that the child may have been involved in the commission of the act. A law enforcement officer who takes fingerprints or photographs of a child under division (A)(2) of this section immediately shall inform the juvenile court that the fingerprints or photographs were taken and shall provide the court with the identity of the child, the number of fingerprints and photographs taken, and the name and address of each person who has custody and control of the fingerprints or photographs or copies of the fingerprints or photographs.

(3) This section does not apply to a child to whom either of the following applies:

(a) The child has been arrested or otherwise taken into custody for committing, or has been adjudicated a delinquent child for committing, an act that would be a felony if committed by an adult or has been convicted of or pleaded guilty to committing a felony.

(b) There is probable cause to believe that the child may have committed an act that would be a felony if committed by an adult.

(B)(1) Subject to divisions (B)(4), (5), and (6) of this section, all fingerprints and photographs of a child obtained or taken under division (A)(1) or (2) of this section, and any records of the arrest or custody of the child that was the basis for the taking of the fingerprints or photographs, initially may be retained only until the expiration of thirty days after the date taken, except that the court may limit the initial retention of fingerprints and photographs of a child obtained under division (A)(1) of this section to a shorter period of time and except that, if the child is adjudicated a delinquent child for the commission of an act described in division (B)(3) of this section or is convicted of or pleads guilty to a criminal offense for the commission of an act described in division (B)(3) of this section, the fingerprints and photographs, and the records of the arrest or custody of the child that was the basis for the taking of the fingerprints and photographs, shall be retained in accordance with division (B)(3) of this section. During the initial period of retention, the fingerprints and photographs of a child, copies of the fingerprints and photographs, and records of the arrest or custody of the child shall be used or released only in accordance with division (C) of this section. At the expiration of the initial period for which fingerprints and photographs of a child, copies of fingerprints and photographs of a child, and records of the arrest or custody of a child may be retained under this division, if no complaint, indictment, or information is pending against the child in relation to the act for which the fingerprints and photographs originally were obtained or taken and if the child has neither been adjudicated a delinquent child for the commission of that act nor been convicted of or pleaded guilty to a criminal offense based on that act subsequent to a transfer of the child's case for criminal prosecution pursuant to section 2152.12 of the Revised Code, the fingerprints and photographs of the child, all copies of the fingerprints and photographs, and all records of the arrest or custody of the child that was the basis of the taking of the fingerprints and photographs shall be removed from the file and delivered to the juvenile court.

(2) If, at the expiration of the initial period of retention set forth in division (B)(1) of this section, a complaint, indictment, or information is pending against the child in relation to the act for which the fingerprints and photographs originally were obtained or the child either has been adjudicated a delinquent child for the commission of an act other than an act described in division (B)(3) of this section or has been convicted of or pleaded guilty to a criminal offense for the commission of an act other than an act described in division (B)(3) of this section subsequent to transfer of the child's case, the fingerprints and photographs of the child, copies of the fingerprints and photographs, and the records of the arrest or custody of the child that was the basis of the taking of the fingerprints and photographs may further be retained, subject to division (B)(4) of this section, until the earlier of the expiration of two years after the date on which the fingerprints or photographs were taken or the child attains eighteen years of age, except that, if the child is adjudicated a delinquent child for the commission of an act described in division (B)(3) of this section or is convicted of or pleads guilty to a criminal offense for the commission of an act described in division (B)(3) of this section, the fingerprints and photographs, and the records of the arrest or custody of the child that was the basis for the taking of the fingerprints and photographs, shall be retained in accordance with division (B)(3) of this section.

Except as otherwise provided in division (B)(3) of this section, during this additional period of retention, the fingerprints and photographs of a child, copies of the fingerprints and photographs of a child, and records of the arrest or custody of a child shall be used or released only in accordance with division (C) of this section. At the expiration of the additional period, if no complaint, indictment, or information is pending against the child in relation to the act for which the fingerprints originally were obtained or taken or in relation to another act for which the fingerprints were used as authorized by division (C) of this section and that would be a felony if committed by an adult, the fingerprints of the child, all copies of the fingerprints, and all records of the arrest or custody of the child that was the basis of the taking of the fingerprints shall be removed from the file and delivered to the juvenile court, and, if no complaint, indictment, or information is pending against the child concerning the act for which the photographs originally were obtained or taken or concerning an act that would be a felony if committed by an adult, the photographs and all copies of the photographs, and, if no fingerprints were taken at the time the photographs were taken, all records of the arrest or custody that was the basis of the taking of the photographs shall be removed from the file and delivered to the juvenile court. In either case, if, at the expiration of the applicable additional period, such a complaint, indictment, or information is pending against the child, the photographs and copies of the photographs of the child, or the fingerprints and copies of the fingerprints of the child, whichever is applicable, and the records of the arrest or custody of the child may be retained, subject to division (B)(4) of this section, until final disposition of the complaint, indictment, or information, and, upon final disposition of the complaint, indictment, or information, they shall be removed from the file and delivered to the juvenile court, except that, if the child is adjudicated a delinquent child for the commission of an act described in division (B)(3) of this section or is convicted of or pleads guilty to a criminal offense for the commission of an act described in division (B)(3) of this section, the fingerprints and photographs, and the records of the arrest or custody of the child that was the basis for the taking of the fingerprints and photographs, shall be retained in accordance with division (B)(3) of this section.

(3) If a child is adjudicated a delinquent child for violating section 2923.42 of the Revised Code or for committing an act that would be a misdemeanor offense of violence if committed by an adult, or is convicted of or pleads guilty to a violation of section 2923.42 of the Revised Code, a misdemeanor offense of violence, or a violation of an existing or former municipal ordinance or law of this state, another state, or the United States that is substantially equivalent to section 2923.42 of the Revised Code or any misdemeanor offense of violence, both of the following apply:

(a) Originals and copies of fingerprints and photographs of the child obtained or taken under division (A)(1) of this section, and any records of the arrest or custody that was the basis for the taking of the fingerprints or photographs, may be retained for the period of time specified by the juvenile judge in that judge's grant of consent for the taking of the fingerprints or photographs. Upon the expiration of the specified period, all originals and copies of the fingerprints, photographs, and records shall be delivered to the juvenile court or otherwise disposed of in accordance with any instructions specified by the juvenile judge in that judge's grant of consent. During the period of retention of the photographs and records, all originals and copies of them shall be retained in a file separate and apart from all photographs taken of adults. During the period of retention of the fingerprints, all originals and copies of them may be maintained in the files of fingerprints taken of adults. If the juvenile judge who grants consent for the taking of fingerprints and photographs under division (A)(1) of this section does not specify a period of retention in that judge's grant of consent, originals and copies of the fingerprints, photographs, and records may be retained in accordance with this section as if the fingerprints and photographs had been taken under division (A)(2) of this section.

(b) Originals and copies of fingerprints and photographs taken under division (A)(2) of this section, and any records of the arrest or custody that was the basis for the taking of the fingerprints or photographs, may be retained for the period of time and in the manner specified in division (B)(3)(b) of this section. Prior to the child's attainment of eighteen years of age, all originals and copies of the photographs and records shall be retained and shall be kept in a file separate and apart from all photographs taken of adults. During the period of retention of the fingerprints, all originals and copies of them may be maintained in the files of fingerprints taken of adults. Upon the child's attainment of eighteen years of age, all originals and copies of the fingerprints, photographs, and records shall be disposed of as follows:

(i) If the juvenile judge issues or previously has issued an order that specifies a manner of disposition of the originals and copies of the fingerprints, photographs, and records, they shall be delivered to the juvenile court or otherwise disposed of in accordance with the order.

(ii) If the juvenile judge does not issue and has not previously issued an order that specifies a manner of disposition of the originals and copies of the fingerprints not maintained in adult files, photographs, and records, the law enforcement agency, in its discretion, either shall remove all originals and copies of them from the file in which they had been maintained and transfer them to the files that are used for the retention of fingerprints and photographs taken of adults who are arrested for, otherwise taken into custody for, or under investigation for the commission of a criminal offense or shall remove them from the file in which they had been maintained and deliver them to the juvenile court. If the originals and copies of any fingerprints of a child who attains eighteen years of age are maintained in the files of fingerprints taken of adults or if pursuant to division (B)(3)(b)(ii) of this section the agency transfers the originals and copies of any fingerprints not maintained in adult files, photographs, or records to the files that are used for the retention of fingerprints and photographs taken of adults who are arrested for, otherwise taken into custody for, or under investigation for the commission of a criminal offense, the originals and copies of the fingerprints, photographs, and records may be maintained, used, and released after they are maintained in the adult files or after the transfer as if the fingerprints and photographs had been taken of, and as if the records pertained to, an adult who was arrested for, otherwise taken into custody for, or under investigation for the commission of a criminal offense.

(4) If a sealing or expungement order issued under section 2151.358 of the Revised Code requires the sealing or destruction of any fingerprints or photographs of a child obtained or taken under division (A)(1) or (2) of this section or of the records of an arrest or custody of a child that was the basis of the taking of the fingerprints or photographs prior to the expiration of any period for which they otherwise could be retained under division (B)(1), (2), or (3) of this section, the fingerprints, photographs, and arrest or custody records that are subject to the order and all copies of the fingerprints, photographs, and arrest or custody records shall be sealed or destroyed in accordance with the order.

(5) All fingerprints of a child, photographs of a child, records of an arrest or custody of a child, and copies delivered to a juvenile court in accordance with division (B)(1), (2), or (3) of this section shall be destroyed by the court, provided that, if a complaint is filed against the child in relation to any act to which the records pertain, the court shall maintain all records of an arrest or custody of a child so delivered for at least three years after the final disposition of the case or after the case becomes inactive.

(6)(a) All photographs of a child and records of an arrest or custody of a child retained pursuant to division (B) of this section and not delivered to a juvenile court shall be kept in a file separate and apart from fingerprints, photographs, and records of an arrest or custody of an adult. All fingerprints of a child retained pursuant to division (B) of this section and not delivered to a juvenile court may be maintained in the files of fingerprints taken of adults.

(b) If a child who is the subject of photographs or fingerprints is adjudicated a delinquent child for the commission of an act that would be an offense, other than a traffic offense or a minor misdemeanor, if committed by an adult or is convicted of or pleads guilty to a criminal offense, other than a traffic offense or a minor misdemeanor, all fingerprints not maintained in the files of fingerprints taken of adults and all photographs of the child, and all records of the arrest or custody of the child that is the basis of the taking of the fingerprints or photographs, that are retained pursuant to division (B) of this section and not delivered to a juvenile court shall be kept in a file separate and apart from fingerprints, photographs, and arrest and custody records of children who have not been adjudicated a delinquent child for the commission of an act that would be an offense, other than a traffic offense or a minor misdemeanor, if committed by an adult and have not been convicted of or pleaded guilty to a criminal offense other than a traffic offense or a minor misdemeanor.

(C) Until they are delivered to the juvenile court or sealed, transferred in accordance with division (B)(3)(b) of this section, or destroyed pursuant to a sealing or expungement order, the originals and copies of fingerprints and photographs of a child that are obtained or taken pursuant to division (A)(1) or (2) of this section, and the records of the arrest or custody of the child that was the basis of the taking of the fingerprints or photographs, shall be used or released only as follows:

(1) During the initial thirty-day period of retention, originals and copies of fingerprints and photographs of a child, and records

of the arrest or custody of a child, shall be used, prior to the filing of a complaint or information against or the obtaining of an indictment of the child in relation to the act for which the fingerprints and photographs were originally obtained or taken, only for the investigation of that act and shall be released, prior to the filing of the complaint, only to a court that would have jurisdiction of the child's case under this chapter. Subsequent to the filing of a complaint or information or the obtaining of an indictment, originals and copies of fingerprints and photographs of a child, and records of the arrest or custody of a child, shall be used or released during the initial thirty-day period of retention only as provided in division (C)(2)(a), (b), or (c) of this section.

(2) Originals and copies of fingerprints and photographs of a child, and records of the arrest or custody of a child, that are retained beyond the initial thirty-day period of retention subsequent to the filing of a complaint or information or the obtaining of an indictment, a delinquent child adjudication, or a conviction of or guilty plea to a criminal offense shall be used or released only as follows:

(a) Originals and copies of photographs of a child, and, if no fingerprints were taken at the time the photographs were taken, records of the arrest or custody of the child that was the basis of the taking of the photographs, may be used only as follows:

(i) They may be used for the investigation of the act for which they originally were obtained or taken; if the child who is the subject of the photographs is a suspect in the investigation, for the investigation of any act that would be an offense if committed by an adult; and for arresting or bringing the child into custody.

(ii) If the child who is the subject of the photographs is adjudicated a delinquent child for the commission of an act that would be a felony if committed by an adult or is convicted of or pleads guilty to a criminal offense that is a felony as a result of the arrest or custody that was the basis of the taking of the photographs, a law enforcement officer may use the photographs for a photo line-up conducted as part of the investigation of any act that would be a felony if committed by an adult, whether or not the child who is the subject of the photographs is a suspect in the investigation.

(b) Originals and copies of fingerprints of a child, and records of the arrest or custody of the child that was the basis of the taking of the fingerprints, may be used only for the investigation of the act for which they originally were obtained or taken; if a child is a suspect in the investigation, for the investigation of another act that would be an offense if committed by an adult; and for arresting or bringing the child into custody.

(c) Originals and copies of fingerprints, photographs, and records of the arrest or custody that was the basis of the taking of the fingerprints or photographs shall be released only to the following:

(i) Law enforcement officers of this state or a political subdivision of this state, upon notification to the juvenile court of the name and address of the law enforcement officer or agency to whom or to which they will be released;

(ii) A court that has jurisdiction of the child's case under Chapters 2151. and 2152. of the Revised Code or subsequent to a transfer of the child's case for criminal prosecution pursuant to section 2152.12 of the Revised Code.

(D) No person shall knowingly do any of the following:

(1) Fingerprint or photograph a child in the investigation of any violation of law other than as provided in division (A)(1) or (2) of this section or in sections 109.57, 109.60, and 109.61 of the Revised Code;

(2) Retain fingerprints or photographs of a child obtained or taken under division (A)(1) or (2) of this section, copies of fingerprints or photographs of that nature, or records of the arrest or custody that was the basis of the taking of fingerprints or photographs of that nature other than in accordance with division (B) of this section;

(3) Use or release fingerprints or photographs of a child obtained or taken under division (A)(1) or (2) of this section, copies of fingerprints or photographs of that nature, or records of the arrest or custody that was the basis of the taking of fingerprints or photographs of that nature other than in accordance with division (B) or (C) of this section.

(2000 S 179, § 3, eff. 1–1–02; 2000 S 181, eff. 9–4–00; 1998 H 2, eff. 1–1–99; 1996 H 124, eff. 3–31–97; 1996 H 445, eff. 9–3–96; 1995 H 1, eff. 1–1–96; 1992 H 198, eff. 10–6–92; 1984 H 258; 1977 H 315; 1973 S 1; 1969 H 320)

2151.314 Detention hearing

(A) When a child is brought before the court or delivered to a place of detention or shelter care designated by the court, the intake or other authorized officer of the court shall immediately make an investigation and shall release the child unless it appears that the child's detention or shelter care is warranted or required under section 2151.31 of the Revised Code.

If the child is not so released, a complaint under section 2151.27 or 2152.021 or an information under section 2152.13 of the Revised Code shall be filed or an indictment under division (B) of section 2152.13 of the Revised Code shall be sought and an informal detention or shelter care hearing held promptly, not later than seventy-two hours after the child is placed in detention or shelter care, to determine whether detention or shelter care is required. Reasonable oral or written notice of the time, place, and purpose of the detention or shelter care hearing shall be given to the child and, if they can be found, to the child's parents, guardian, or custodian. In cases in which the complaint alleges a child to be an abused, neglected, or dependent child, the notice given the parents, guardian, or custodian shall inform them that a case plan may be prepared for the child, the general requirements usually contained in case plans, and the possible consequences of the failure to comply with a journalized case plan.

Prior to the hearing, the court shall inform the parties of their right to counsel and to appointed counsel or to the services of the county public defender or joint county public defender, if they are indigent, of the child's right to remain silent with respect to any allegation of delinquency, and of the name and telephone number of a court employee who can be contacted during the normal business hours of the court to arrange for the prompt appointment of counsel for any party who is indigent. Unless it appears from the hearing that the child's detention or shelter care is required under the provisions of section 2151.31 of the Revised Code, the court shall order the child's release as provided by section 2151.311 of the Revised Code. If a parent, guardian, or custodian has not been so notified and did not appear or waive appearance at the hearing, upon the filing of an affidavit stating these facts, the court shall rehear the matter without unnecessary delay.

(B) When the court conducts a hearing pursuant to division (A) of this section, all of the following apply:

(1) The court shall determine whether an alleged abused, neglected, or dependent child should remain or be placed in shelter care;

(2) The court shall determine whether there are any relatives of the child who are willing to be temporary custodians of the child. If any relative is willing to be a temporary custodian, the child would otherwise be placed or retained in shelter care, and the appointment is appropriate, the court shall appoint the relative as temporary custodian of the child, unless the court appoints another relative as temporary custodian. If it determines that the appointment of a relative as custodian would not be appropriate, it shall issue a written opinion setting forth the

reasons for its determination and give a copy of the opinion to all parties and to the guardian ad litem of the child.

The court's consideration of a relative for appointment as a temporary custodian does not make that relative a party to the proceedings.

(3) The court shall comply with section 2151.419 of the Revised Code.

(C) If a child is in shelter care following the filing of a complaint pursuant to section 2151.27 or 2152.021 of the Revised Code, the filing of an information, or the obtaining of an indictment or following a hearing held pursuant to division (A) of this section, any party, including the public children services agency, and the guardian ad litem of the child may file a motion with the court requesting that the child be released from shelter care. The motion shall state the reasons why the child should be released from shelter care and, if a hearing has been held pursuant to division (A) of this section, any changes in the situation of the child or the parents, guardian, or custodian of the child that have occurred since that hearing and that justify the release of the child from shelter care. Upon the filing of the motion, the court shall hold a hearing in the same manner as under division (A) of this section.

(D) Each juvenile court shall designate at least one court employee to assist persons who are indigent in obtaining appointed counsel. The court shall include in each notice given pursuant to division (A) or (C) of this section and in each summons served upon a party pursuant to this chapter, the name and telephone number at which each designated employee can be contacted during the normal business hours of the court to arrange for prompt appointment of counsel for indigent persons.

(2002 H 393, eff. 7–5–02; 2000 S 179, § 3, eff. 1–1–02; 1999 H 176, eff. 10–29–99; 1998 H 484, eff. 3–18–99; 1996 H 274, eff. 8–8–96; 1988 S 89, eff. 1–1–89; 1975 H 164; 1969 H 320)

2151.32 Selection of custodian

In placing a child under any guardianship or custody other than that of its parent, the juvenile court shall, when practicable, select a person or an institution or agency governed by persons of like religious faith as that of the parents of such child, or in case of a difference in the religious faith of the parents, then of the religious faith of the child, or if the religious faith of the child is not ascertained, then of either of the parents.

(1953 H 1, eff. 10–1–53; GC 1639–33)

2151.33 Temporary care; emergency medical treatment; reimbursement

(A) Pending hearing of a complaint filed under section 2151.27 of the Revised Code or a motion filed or made under division (B) of this section and the service of citations, the juvenile court may make any temporary disposition of any child that it considers necessary to protect the best interest of the child and that can be made pursuant to division (B) of this section. Upon the certificate of one or more reputable practicing physicians, the court may summarily provide for emergency medical and surgical treatment that appears to be immediately necessary to preserve the health and well-being of any child concerning whom a complaint or an application for care has been filed, pending the service of a citation upon the child's parents, guardian, or custodian. The court may order the parents, guardian, or custodian, if the court finds the parents, guardian, or custodian able to do so, to reimburse the court for the expense involved in providing the emergency medical or surgical treatment. Any person who disobeys the order for reimbursement may be adjudged in contempt of court and punished accordingly.

If the emergency medical or surgical treatment is furnished to a child who is found at the hearing to be a nonresident of the county in which the court is located and if the expense of the medical or surgical treatment cannot be recovered from the parents, legal guardian, or custodian of the child, the board of county commissioners of the county in which the child has a legal settlement shall reimburse the court for the reasonable cost of the emergency medical or surgical treatment out of its general fund.

(B)(1) After a complaint, petition, writ, or other document initiating a case dealing with an alleged or adjudicated abused, neglected, or dependent child is filed and upon the filing or making of a motion pursuant to division (C) of this section, the court, prior to the final disposition of the case, may issue any of the following temporary orders to protect the best interest of the child:

(a) An order granting temporary custody of the child to a particular party;

(b) An order for the taking of the child into custody pursuant to section 2151.31 of the Revised Code pending the outcome of the adjudicatory and dispositional hearings;

(c) An order granting, limiting, or eliminating parenting time or visitation rights with respect to the child;

(d) An order requiring a party to vacate a residence that will be lawfully occupied by the child;

(e) An order requiring a party to attend an appropriate counseling program that is reasonably available to that party;

(f) Any other order that restrains or otherwise controls the conduct of any party which conduct would not be in the best interest of the child.

(2) Prior to the final disposition of a case subject to division (B)(1) of this section, the court shall do both of the following:

(a) Issue an order pursuant to Chapters 3119. to 3125. of the Revised Code requiring the parents, guardian, or person charged with the child's support to pay support for the child.

(b) Issue an order requiring the parents, guardian, or person charged with the child's support to continue to maintain any health insurance coverage for the child that existed at the time of the filing of the complaint, petition, writ, or other document, or to obtain health insurance coverage in accordance with sections 3119.29 to 3119.56 of the Revised Code.

(C)(1) A court may issue an order pursuant to division (B) of this section upon its own motion or if a party files a written motion or makes an oral motion requesting the issuance of the order and stating the reasons for it. Any notice sent by the court as a result of a motion pursuant to this division shall contain a notice that any party to a juvenile proceeding has the right to be represented by counsel and to have appointed counsel if the person is indigent.

(2) If a child is taken into custody pursuant to section 2151.31 of the Revised Code and placed in shelter care, the public children services agency or private child placing agency with which the child is placed in shelter care shall file or make a motion as described in division (C)(1) of this section before the end of the next day immediately after the date on which the child was taken into custody and, at a minimum, shall request an order for temporary custody under division (B)(1)(a) of this section.

(3) A court that issues an order pursuant to division (B)(1)(b) of this section shall comply with section 2151.419 of the Revised Code.

(D) The court may grant an ex parte order upon its own motion or a motion filed or made pursuant to division (C) of this section requesting such an order if it appears to the court that the best interest and the welfare of the child require that the court issue the order immediately. The court, if acting on its own motion, or the person requesting the granting of an ex parte order, to the extent possible, shall give notice of its intent or of the request to the parents, guardian, or custodian of the child who is the subject of the request. If the court issues an ex parte order, the court shall hold a hearing to review the order within seventy-two hours after it is issued or before the end of the next day after the day on which it is issued, whichever occurs first. The court shall give written notice of the hearing to all parties to the action and shall appoint a guardian ad litem for the child prior to the hearing.

The written notice shall be given by all means that are reasonably likely to result in the party receiving actual notice and shall include all of the following:

(1) The date, time, and location of the hearing;

(2) The issues to be addressed at the hearing;

(3) A statement that every party to the hearing has a right to counsel and to court-appointed counsel, if the party is indigent;

(4) The name, telephone number, and address of the person requesting the order;

(5) A copy of the order, except when it is not possible to obtain it because of the exigent circumstances in the case.

If the court does not grant an ex parte order pursuant to a motion filed or made pursuant to division (C) of this section or its own motion, the court shall hold a shelter care hearing on the motion within ten days after the motion is filed. The court shall give notice of the hearing to all affected parties in the same manner as set forth in the Juvenile Rules.

(E) The court, pending the outcome of the adjudicatory and dispositional hearings, shall not issue an order granting temporary custody of a child to a public children services agency or private child placing agency pursuant to this section, unless the court determines and specifically states in the order that the continued residence of the child in the child's current home will be contrary to the child's best interest and welfare and the court complies with section 2151.419 of the Revised Code.

(F) Each public children services agency and private child placing agency that receives temporary custody of a child pursuant to this section shall maintain in the child's case record written documentation that it has placed the child, to the extent that it is consistent with the best interest, welfare, and special needs of the child, in the most family-like setting available and in close proximity to the home of the parents, custodian, or guardian of the child.

(G) For good cause shown, any court order that is issued pursuant to this section may be reviewed by the court at any time upon motion of any party to the action or upon the motion of the court.

(2002 H 657, eff. 12–13–02; 2000 S 180, eff. 3–22–01; 1999 H 176, eff. 10–29–99; 1998 H 484, eff. 3–18–99; 1997 H 352, eff. 1–1–98; 1996 H 274, eff. 8–8–96; 1988 S 89, eff. 1–1–89; 1953 H 1; GC 1639–28)

2151.331 Detention in certified foster home; arrangement for temporary care; alternative diversion programs

A child alleged to be or adjudicated an abused, neglected, dependent, or unruly child or a juvenile traffic offender may be detained after a complaint is filed in a certified foster home for a period not exceeding sixty days or until the final disposition of the case, whichever comes first. The court also may arrange with a public children services agency or private child placing agency to receive, or with a private noncustodial agency for temporary care of, the child within the jurisdiction of the court. A child alleged to be or adjudicated an unruly child also may be assigned to an alternative diversion program established by the court for a period not exceeding sixty days after a complaint is filed or until final disposition of the case, whichever comes first.

If the court arranges for the board of a child temporarily detained in a certified foster home or arranges for the board of a child through a private child placing agency, the board of county commissioners shall pay a reasonable sum, which the court shall fix, for the board of the child. In order to have certified foster homes available for service, an agreed monthly subsidy may be paid in addition to a fixed rate per day for care of a child actually residing in the certified foster home.

(2000 H 332, eff. 1–1–01; 2000 H 448, eff. 10–5–00; 1996 H 265, eff. 3–3–97)

HEARING AND DISPOSITION

2151.35 Hearing procedure; findings; record

(A)(1) Except as otherwise provided by division (A)(3) of this section or in section 2152.13 of the Revised Code, the juvenile court may conduct its hearings in an informal manner and may adjourn its hearings from time to time. The court may exclude the general public from its hearings in a particular case if the court holds a separate hearing to determine whether that exclusion is appropriate. If the court decides that exclusion of the general public is appropriate, the court still may admit to a particular hearing or all of the hearings relating to a particular case those persons who have a direct interest in the case and those who demonstrate that their need for access outweighs the interest in keeping the hearing closed.

Except cases involving children who are alleged to be unruly or delinquent children for being habitual or chronic truants and except as otherwise provided in section 2152.13 of the Revised Code, all cases involving children shall be heard separately and apart from the trial of cases against adults. The court may excuse the attendance of the child at the hearing in cases involving abused, neglected, or dependent children. The court shall hear and determine all cases of children without a jury, except cases involving serious youthful offenders under section 2152.13 of the Revised Code.

If a complaint alleges a child to be a delinquent child, unruly child, or juvenile traffic offender, the court shall require the parent, guardian, or custodian of the child to attend all proceedings of the court regarding the child. If a parent, guardian, or custodian fails to so attend, the court may find the parent, guardian, or custodian in contempt.

If the court finds from clear and convincing evidence that the child violated section 2151.87 of the Revised Code, the court shall proceed in accordance with divisions (F) and (G) of that section.

If the court at the adjudicatory hearing finds from clear and convincing evidence that the child is an abused, neglected, or dependent child, the court shall proceed, in accordance with division (B) of this section, to hold a dispositional hearing and hear the evidence as to the proper disposition to be made under section 2151.353 of the Revised Code. If the court at the adjudicatory hearing finds beyond a reasonable doubt that the child is a delinquent or unruly child or a juvenile traffic offender, the court shall proceed immediately, or at a postponed hearing, to hear the evidence as to the proper disposition to be made under section 2151.354 or Chapter 2152. of the Revised Code. If the court at the adjudicatory hearing finds beyond a reasonable doubt that the child is an unruly child for being an habitual truant, or that the child is an unruly child for being an habitual truant and that the parent, guardian, or other person having care of the child has failed to cause the child's attendance at school in violation of section 3321.38 of the Revised Code, the court shall proceed to hold a hearing to hear the evidence as to the proper disposition to be made in regard to the child under division (C)(1) of section 2151.354 of the Revised Code and the proper action to take in regard to the parent, guardian, or other person having care of the child under division (C)(2) of section 2151.354 of the Revised Code. If the court at the adjudicatory hearing finds beyond a reasonable doubt that the child is a delinquent child for being a chronic truant or for being an habitual truant who previously has been adjudicated an unruly child for being an habitual truant, or that the child is a delinquent child for either of those reasons and the parent, guardian, or other person having care of the child has failed to cause the child's attendance at school in violation of section 3321.38 of the Revised Code, the court shall proceed to hold a hearing to hear the evidence as to the proper disposition to be made in regard to the child under division (A)(7) (a) of section 2152.19 of the Revised Code and the proper action to take in regard to the parent, guardian, or other person having care of the child under division (A)(7) (b) of section 2152.19 of the Revised Code.

If the court does not find the child to have violated section 2151.87 of the Revised Code or to be an abused, neglected, dependent, delinquent, or unruly child or a juvenile traffic offender, it shall order that the case be dismissed and that the child be discharged from any detention or restriction theretofore ordered.

(2) A record of all testimony and other oral proceedings in juvenile court shall be made in all proceedings that are held pursuant to section 2151.414 of the Revised Code or in which an order of disposition may be made pursuant to division (A)(4) of section 2151.353 of the Revised Code, and shall be made upon request in any other proceedings. The record shall be made as provided in section 2301.20 of the Revised Code.

(3) The authority of a juvenile court to exclude the general public from its hearings that is provided by division (A)(1) of this section does not limit or affect any right of a victim of a crime or delinquent act, or of a victim's representative, under Chapter 2930. of the Revised Code.

(B)(1) If the court at an adjudicatory hearing determines that a child is an abused, neglected, or dependent child, the court shall not issue a dispositional order until after the court holds a separate dispositional hearing. The court may hold the dispositional hearing for an adjudicated abused, neglected, or dependent child immediately after the adjudicatory hearing if all parties were served prior to the adjudicatory hearing with all documents required for the dispositional hearing. The dispositional hearing may not be held more than thirty days after the adjudicatory hearing is held. The court, upon the request of any party or the guardian ad litem of the child, may continue a dispositional hearing for a reasonable time not to exceed the time limits set forth in this division to enable a party to obtain or consult counsel. The dispositional hearing shall not be held more than ninety days after the date on which the complaint in the case was filed.

If the dispositional hearing is not held within the period of time required by this division, the court, on its own motion or the motion of any party or the guardian ad litem of the child, shall dismiss the complaint without prejudice.

(2) The dispositional hearing shall be conducted in accordance with all of the following:

(a) The judge or referee who presided at the adjudicatory hearing shall preside, if possible, at the dispositional hearing;

(b) The court may admit any evidence that is material and relevant, including, but not limited to, hearsay, opinion, and documentary evidence;

(c) Medical examiners and each investigator who prepared a social history shall not be cross-examined, except upon consent of the parties, for good cause shown, or as the court in its discretion may direct. Any party may offer evidence supplementing, explaining, or disputing any information contained in the social history or other reports that may be used by the court in determining disposition.

(3) After the conclusion of the dispositional hearing, the court shall enter an appropriate judgment within seven days and shall schedule the date for the hearing to be held pursuant to section 2151.415 of the Revised Code. The court may make any order of disposition that is set forth in section 2151.353 of the Revised Code. A copy of the judgment shall be given to each party and to the child's guardian ad litem. If the judgment is conditional, the order shall state the conditions of the judgment. If the child is not returned to the child's own home, the court shall determine which school district shall bear the cost of the child's education and shall comply with section 2151.36 of the Revised Code.

(4) As part of its dispositional order, the court may issue any order described in division (B) of section 2151.33 of the Revised Code.

(C) The court shall give all parties to the action and the child's guardian ad litem notice of the adjudicatory and dispositional hearings in accordance with the Juvenile Rules.

(D) If the court issues an order pursuant to division (A)(4) of section 2151.353 of the Revised Code committing a child to the permanent custody of a public children services agency or a private child placing agency, the parents of the child whose parental rights were terminated cease to be parties to the action upon the issuance of the order. This division is not intended to eliminate or restrict any right of the parents to appeal the permanent custody order issued pursuant to division (A)(4) of section 2151.353 of the Revised Code.

(E) Each juvenile court shall schedule its hearings in accordance with the time requirements of this chapter.

(F) In cases regarding abused, neglected, or dependent children, the court may admit any statement of a child that the court determines to be excluded by the hearsay rule if the proponent of the statement informs the adverse party of the proponent's intention to offer the statement and of the particulars of the statement, including the name of the declarant, sufficiently in advance of the hearing to provide the party with a fair opportunity to prepare to challenge, respond to, or defend against the statement, and the court determines all of the following:

(1) The statement has circumstantial guarantees of trustworthiness;

(2) The statement is offered as evidence of a material fact;

(3) The statement is more probative on the point for which it is offered than any other evidence that the proponent can procure through reasonable efforts;

(4) The general purposes of the evidence rules and the interests of justice will best be served by the admission of the statement into evidence.

(G) If a child is alleged to be an abused child, the court may order that the testimony of the child be taken by deposition. On motion of the prosecuting attorney, guardian ad litem, or any party, or in its own discretion, the court may order that the deposition be videotaped. Any deposition taken under this division shall be taken with a judge or referee present.

If a deposition taken under this division is intended to be offered as evidence at the hearing, it shall be filed with the court. Part or all of the deposition is admissible in evidence if counsel for all parties had an opportunity and similar motive at the time of the taking of the deposition to develop the testimony by direct, cross, or redirect examination and the judge determines that there is reasonable cause to believe that if the child were to testify in person at the hearing, the child would experience emotional trauma as a result of participating at the hearing.

(2002 H 400, eff. 4–3–03; 2000 S 179, § 3, eff. 1–1–02; 2000 S 179, § 1, eff. 4–9–01; 2000 S 218, eff. 3–15–01; 2000 S 181, eff. 9–4–00; 1996 H 124, eff. 3–31–97; 1996 H 274, eff. 8–8–96; 1995 H 1, eff. 1–1–96; 1988 S 89, eff. 1–1–89; 1980 H 695; 1975 H 85; 1969 H 320)

2151.352 Right to counsel

A child, or the child's parents, custodian, or other person in loco parentis of such child is entitled to representation by legal counsel at all stages of the proceedings under this chapter or Chapter 2152. of the Revised Code and if, as an indigent person, any such person is unable to employ counsel, to have counsel provided for the person pursuant to Chapter 120. of the Revised Code. If a party appears without counsel, the court shall ascertain whether the party knows of the party's right to counsel and of the party's right to be provided with counsel if the party is an indigent person. The court may continue the case to enable a party to obtain counsel or to be represented by the county public defender or the joint county public defender and shall provide counsel upon request pursuant to Chapter 120. of the Revised Code. Counsel must be provided for a child not represented by the child's parent, guardian, or custodian. If the interests of two or more such parties conflict, separate counsel shall be provided for each of them.

Section 2935.14 of the Revised Code applies to any child taken into custody. The parents, custodian, or guardian of a child taken into custody, and any attorney at law representing them or the child, shall be entitled to visit the child at any reasonable time, be present at any hearing involving the child, and be given reasonable notice of the hearing.

Any report or part of a report concerning the child, which is used in the hearing and is pertinent to the hearing, shall for good cause shown be made available to any attorney at law representing the child and to any attorney at law representing the parents, custodian, or guardian of the child, upon written request prior to any hearing involving the child.

(2003 H 95, eff. 9–26–03; 2000 S 179, § 3, eff. 1–1–02; 1975 H 164, eff. 1–13–76; 1969 H 320)

2151.353 Disposition of abused, neglected, or dependent child

(A) If a child is adjudicated an abused, neglected, or dependent child, the court may make any of the following orders of disposition:

(1) Place the child in protective supervision;

(2) Commit the child to the temporary custody of a public children services agency, a private child placing agency, either parent, a relative residing within or outside the state, or a probation officer for placement in a certified foster home, or in any other home approved by the court;

(3) Award legal custody of the child to either parent or to any other person who, prior to the dispositional hearing, files a motion requesting legal custody of the child;

(4) Commit the child to the permanent custody of a public children services agency or private child placing agency, if the court determines in accordance with division (E) of section 2151.414 of the Revised Code that the child cannot be placed with one of the child's parents within a reasonable time or should not be placed with either parent and determines in accordance with division (D) of section 2151.414 of the Revised Code that the permanent commitment is in the best interest of the child. If the court grants permanent custody under this division, the court, upon the request of any party, shall file a written opinion setting forth its findings of fact and conclusions of law in relation to the proceeding.

(5) Place the child in a planned permanent living arrangement with a public children services agency or private child placing agency, if a public children services agency or private child placing agency requests the court to place the child in a planned permanent living arrangement and if the court finds, by clear and convincing evidence, that a planned permanent living arrangement is in the best interest of the child and that one of the following exists:

(a) The child, because of physical, mental, or psychological problems or needs, is unable to function in a family-like setting and must remain in residential or institutional care.

(b) The parents of the child have significant physical, mental, or psychological problems and are unable to care for the child because of those problems, adoption is not in the best interest of the child, as determined in accordance with division (D) of section 2151.414 of the Revised Code, and the child retains a significant and positive relationship with a parent or relative.

(c) The child is sixteen years of age or older, has been counseled on the permanent placement options available to the child, is unwilling to accept or unable to adapt to a permanent placement, and is in an agency program preparing the child for independent living.

(6) Order the removal from the child's home until further order of the court of the person who committed abuse as described in section 2151.031 of the Revised Code against the child, who caused or allowed the child to suffer neglect as described in section 2151.03 of the Revised Code, or who is the parent, guardian, or custodian of a child who is adjudicated a dependent child and order any person not to have contact with the child or the child's siblings.

(B) No order for permanent custody or temporary custody of a child or the placement of a child in a planned permanent living arrangement shall be made pursuant to this section unless the complaint alleging the abuse, neglect, or dependency contains a prayer requesting permanent custody, temporary custody, or the placement of the child in a planned permanent living arrangement as desired, the summons served on the parents of the child contains as is appropriate a full explanation that the granting of an order for permanent custody permanently divests them of their parental rights, a full explanation that an adjudication that the child is an abused, neglected, or dependent child may result in an order of temporary custody that will cause the removal of the child from their legal custody until the court terminates the order of temporary custody or permanently divests the parents of their parental rights, or a full explanation that the granting of an order for a planned permanent living arrangement will result in the removal of the child from their legal custody if any of the conditions listed in divisions (A)(5)(a) to (c) of this section are found to exist, and the summons served on the parents contains a full explanation of their right to be represented by counsel and to have counsel appointed pursuant to Chapter 120. of the Revised Code if they are indigent.

If after making disposition as authorized by division (A)(2) of this section, a motion is filed that requests permanent custody of the child, the court may grant permanent custody of the child to the movant in accordance with section 2151.414 of the Revised Code.

(C) If the court issues an order for protective supervision pursuant to division (A)(1) of this section, the court may place any reasonable restrictions upon the child, the child's parents, guardian, or custodian, or any other person, including, but not limited to, any of the following:

(1) Order a party, within forty-eight hours after the issuance of the order, to vacate the child's home indefinitely or for a specified period of time;

(2) Order a party, a parent of the child, or a physical custodian of the child to prevent any particular person from having contact with the child;

(3) Issue an order restraining or otherwise controlling the conduct of any person which conduct would not be in the best interest of the child.

(D) As part of its dispositional order, the court shall journalize a case plan for the child. The journalized case plan shall not be changed except as provided in section 2151.412 of the Revised Code.

(E)(1) The court shall retain jurisdiction over any child for whom the court issues an order of disposition pursuant to division (A) of this section or pursuant to section 2151.414 or 2151.415 of the Revised Code until the child attains the age of eighteen years if the child is not mentally retarded, developmentally disabled, or physically impaired, the child attains the age of twenty-one years if the child is mentally retarded, developmentally disabled, or physically impaired, or the child is adopted and a final decree of adoption is issued, except that the court may retain jurisdiction over the child and continue any order of disposition under division (A) of this section or under section 2151.414 or 2151.415 of the Revised Code for a specified period of time to enable the child to graduate from high school or vocational school. The court shall make an entry continuing its jurisdiction under this division in the journal.

(2) Any public children services agency, any private child placing agency, the department of job and family services, or any party, other than any parent whose parental rights with respect to the child have been terminated pursuant to an order issued under division (A)(4) of this section, by filing a motion with the court, may at any time request the court to modify or terminate any order of disposition issued pursuant to division (A) of this section or section 2151.414 or 2151.415 of the Revised Code. The court shall hold a hearing upon the motion as if the hearing were the original dispositional hearing and shall give all parties to the action and the guardian ad litem notice of the hearing pursuant to the Juvenile Rules. If applicable, the court shall comply with section 2151.42 of the Revised Code.

(F) Any temporary custody order issued pursuant to division (A) of this section shall terminate one year after the earlier of the date on which the complaint in the case was filed or the child was first placed into shelter care, except that, upon the filing of a motion pursuant to section 2151.415 of the Revised Code, the temporary custody order shall continue and not terminate until the court issues a dispositional order under that section.

(G)(1) No later than one year after the earlier of the date the complaint in the case was filed or the child was first placed in shelter care, a party may ask the court to extend an order for protective supervision for six months or to terminate the order. A party requesting extension or termination of the order shall file a written request for the extension or termination with the court and give notice of the proposed extension or termination in writing before the end of the day after the day of filing it to all parties and the child's guardian ad litem. If a public children services agency or private child placing agency requests termination of the order, the agency shall file a written status report setting out the facts supporting termination of the order at the time it files the request with the court. If no party requests extension or termination of the order, the court shall notify the parties that the court will extend the order for six months or terminate it and that it may do so without a hearing unless one of the parties requests a hearing. All parties and the guardian ad litem shall have seven days from the date a notice is sent pursuant to this division to object to and request a hearing on the proposed extension or termination.

(a) If it receives a timely request for a hearing, the court shall schedule a hearing to be held no later than thirty days after the request is received by the court. The court shall give notice of the date, time, and location of the hearing to all parties and the guardian ad litem. At the hearing, the court shall determine whether extension or termination of the order is in the child's best interest. If termination is in the child's best interest, the court shall terminate the order. If extension is in the child's best interest, the court shall extend the order for six months.

(b) If it does not receive a timely request for a hearing, the court may extend the order for six months or terminate it without a hearing and shall journalize the order of extension or termination not later than fourteen days after receiving the request for extension or termination or after the date the court notifies the parties that it will extend or terminate the order. If the court does not extend or terminate the order, it shall schedule a hearing to be held no later than thirty days after the expiration of the applicable fourteen-day time period and give notice of the date, time, and location of the hearing to all parties and the child's guardian ad litem. At the hearing, the court shall determine whether extension or termination of the order is in the child's best interest. If termination is in the child's best interest, the court shall terminate the order. If extension is in the child's best interest, the court shall issue an order extending the order for protective supervision six months.

(2) If the court grants an extension of the order for protective supervision pursuant to division (G)(1) of this section, a party may, prior to termination of the extension, file with the court a request for an additional extension of six months or for termination of the order. The court and the parties shall comply with division (G)(1) of this section with respect to extending or terminating the order.

(3) If a court grants an extension pursuant to division (G)(2) of this section, the court shall terminate the order for protective supervision at the end of the extension.

(H) The court shall not issue a dispositional order pursuant to division (A) of this section that removes a child from the child's home unless the court complies with section 2151.419 of the Revised Code and includes in the dispositional order the findings of fact required by that section.

(I) If a motion or application for an order described in division (A)(6) of this section is made, the court shall not issue the order unless, prior to the issuance of the order, it provides to the person all of the following:

(1) Notice and a copy of the motion or application;

(2) The grounds for the motion or application;

(3) An opportunity to present evidence and witnesses at a hearing regarding the motion or application;

(4) An opportunity to be represented by counsel at the hearing.

(J) The jurisdiction of the court shall terminate one year after the date of the award or, if the court takes any further action in the matter subsequent to the award, the date of the latest further action subsequent to the award, if the court awards legal custody of a child to either of the following:

(1) A legal custodian who, at the time of the award of legal custody, resides in a county of this state other than the county in which the court is located;

(2) A legal custodian who resides in the county in which the court is located at the time of the award of legal custody, but moves to a different county of this state prior to one year after the date of the award or, if the court takes any further action in the matter subsequent to the award, one year after the date of the latest further action subsequent to the award.

The court in the county in which the legal custodian resides then shall have jurisdiction in the matter.

(2004 S 185, eff. 4–11–05; 2000 H 332, eff. 1–1–01; 2000 H 448, eff. 10–5–00; 1999 H 471, eff. 7–1–00; 1998 H 484, eff. 3–18–99; 1996 H 265, eff. 3–3–97; 1996 H 274, eff. 8–8–96; 1996 H 419, eff. 9–18–96; 1993 H 152, eff. 7–1–93; 1988 S 89; 1986 H 428; 1981 H 440; 1980 H 695; 1975 H 85; 1969 H 320)

2151.354 Disposition of unruly child; driver's license suspension; habitual truants

(A) If the child is adjudicated an unruly child, the court may:

(1) Make any of the dispositions authorized under section 2151.353 of the Revised Code;

(2) Place the child on community control under any sanctions, services, and conditions that the court prescribes, as described in division (A)(4) of section 2152.19 of the Revised Code, provided that, if the court imposes a period of community service upon the child, the period of community service shall not exceed one hundred seventy-five hours;

(3) Suspend the driver's license, probationary driver's license, or temporary instruction permit issued to the child for a period of time prescribed by the court and suspend the registration of all motor vehicles registered in the name of the child for a period of time prescribed by the court. A child whose license or permit is so suspended is ineligible for issuance of a license or permit during the period of suspension. At the end of the period of suspension, the child shall not be reissued a license or permit until the child has paid any applicable reinstatement fee and complied with all requirements governing license reinstatement.

(4) Commit the child to the temporary or permanent custody of the court;

(5) Make any further disposition the court finds proper that is consistent with sections 2151.312 and 2151.56 to 2151.61 of the Revised Code;

(6) If, after making a disposition under division (A)(1), (2), or (3) of this section, the court finds upon further hearing that the child is not amenable to treatment or rehabilitation under that disposition, make a disposition otherwise authorized under divisions (A)(1), (4), (5), and (8) of section 2152.19 of the Revised Code that is consistent with sections 2151.312 and 2151.56 to 2151.61 of the Revised Code.

(B) If a child is adjudicated an unruly child for committing any act that, if committed by an adult, would be a drug abuse offense, as defined in section 2925.01 of the Revised Code, or a violation of division (B) of section 2917.11 of the Revised Code, in addition to imposing, in its discretion, any other order of disposition authorized by this section, the court shall do both of the following:

(1) Require the child to participate in a drug abuse or alcohol abuse counseling program;

(2) Suspend the temporary instruction permit, probationary driver's license, or driver's license issued to the child for a period of time prescribed by the court. The court, in its discretion, may terminate the suspension if the child attends and satisfactorily completes a drug abuse or alcohol abuse education, intervention, or treatment program specified by the court. During the time the child is attending a program as described in this division, the court shall retain the child's temporary instruction permit, probationary driver's license, or driver's license, and the court shall return the permit or license if it terminates the suspension.

(C)(1) If a child is adjudicated an unruly child for being an habitual truant, in addition to or in lieu of imposing any other order of disposition authorized by this section, the court may do any of the following:

(a) Order the board of education of the child's school district or the governing board of the educational service center in the child's school district to require the child to attend an alternative school if an alternative school has been established pursuant to section 3313.533 of the Revised Code in the school district in which the child is entitled to attend school;

(b) Require the child to participate in any academic program or community service program;

(c) Require the child to participate in a drug abuse or alcohol abuse counseling program;

(d) Require that the child receive appropriate medical or psychological treatment or counseling;

(e) Make any other order that the court finds proper to address the child's habitual truancy, including an order requiring the child to not be absent without legitimate excuse from the public school the child is supposed to attend for five or more consecutive days, seven or more school days in one school month, or twelve or more school days in a school year and including an order requiring the child to participate in a truancy prevention mediation program.

(2) If a child is adjudicated an unruly child for being an habitual truant and the court determines that the parent, guardian, or other person having care of the child has failed to cause the child's attendance at school in violation of section 3321.38 of the Revised Code, in addition to any order of disposition authorized by this section, all of the following apply:

(a) The court may require the parent, guardian, or other person having care of the child to participate in any community service program, preferably a community service program that requires the involvement of the parent, guardian, or other person having care of the child in the school attended by the child.

(b) The court may require the parent, guardian, or other person having care of the child to participate in a truancy prevention mediation program.

(c) The court shall warn the parent, guardian, or other person having care of the child that any subsequent adjudication of the child as an unruly or delinquent child for being an habitual or chronic truant may result in a criminal charge against the parent, guardian, or other person having care of the child for a violation of division (C) of section 2919.21 or section 2919.24 of the Revised Code.

(2002 H 400, § 4, eff. 1–1–04; 2002 H 400, § 1, eff. 4–3–03; 2002 S 123, eff. 1–1–04; 2002 H 393, eff. 7–5–02; 2001 H 57, eff. 2–19–02; 2000 S 179, § 3, eff. 1–1–02; 2000 S 181, eff. 9–4–00; 1997 S 35, eff. 1–1–99; 1996 H 265, eff. 3–3–97; 1996 H 274, eff. 8–8–96; 1992 H 154, eff. 7–31–92; 1990 S 258, S 131; 1989 H 381, H 330, H 329; 1988 H 643; 1969 H 320)

2151.355 Orders of disposition for delinquent child; records; notice to victims; electronically monitored house detention; notice to school districts; searches authorized—Repealed (first version)

Note: See also following version, Publisher's Note, and Uncodified Law.

(2000 S 179, § 4, eff. 1–1–02; 2002 H 130, eff. 4–7–03; 2000 S 222, eff. 3–22–01; 2000 S 181, eff. 9–4–00; 1999 H 3, eff. 11–22–99; 1998 H 526, § 4, eff. 1–1–99; 1998 H 526, § 1, eff. 9–1–98; 1998 H 2, eff. 1–1–99; 1997 S 35, eff. 1–1–99; 1997 H 1, eff. 7–1–98; 1997 H 215, § 7, eff. 9–30–97; 1997 H 215, § 1, eff. 9–29–97; 1996 H 124, eff. 9–30–97; 1996 S 269, eff. 7–1–96; 1996 H 445, eff. 9–3–96; 1996 H 274, § 4, eff. 8–8–96; 1996 H 274, § 1, eff. 8–8–96; 1995 S 2, eff. 7–1–96; 1995 H 1, eff. 1–1–96; 1995 H 4, eff. 11–9–95; 1994 H 571, eff. 10–6–94; 1992 H 725, eff. 4–16–93; 1992 S 331, H 154; 1990 S 258, H 51, H 266, H 513, S 131; 1989 H 166, H 381, H 330, H 329; 1988 H 643; 1983 S 210; 1982 H 209; 1981 H 440; 1978 H 565, S 119; 1977 H 1; 1976 H 1196; 1974 H 1067; 1973 S 324; 1972 H 494; 1970 H 931; 1969 H 320)

Note: See also following version, Publisher's Note, and Uncodified Law.

2151.355 Disposition where child adjudicated delinquent (second version)

Note: See also preceding repeal, Publisher's Note, and Uncodified Law.

(A) If a child is adjudicated a delinquent child, the court may make any of the following orders of disposition:

(1) Any order that is authorized by section 2151.353 of the Revised Code;

(2) Place the child on probation under any conditions that the court prescribes. If the child is adjudicated a delinquent child for violating section 2909.05, 2909.06, or 2909.07 of the Revised Code and if restitution is appropriate under the circumstances of the case, the court shall require the child to make restitution for the property damage caused by the child's violation as a condition of the child's probation. If the child is adjudicated a delinquent child because the child violated any other section of the Revised Code, the court may require the child as a condition of the child's probation to make restitution for the property damage caused by the child's violation and for the value of the property that was the subject of the violation the child committed if it would be a theft offense, as defined in division (K) of section 2913.01 of the Revised Code, if committed by an adult. The restitution may be in the form of a cash reimbursement paid in a lump sum or in installments, the performance of repair work to restore any damaged property to its original condition, the performance of a reasonable amount of labor for the victim approximately equal to the value of the property damage caused by the child's violation or to the value of the property that is the subject of the violation if it would be a theft offense if committed by an adult, the performance of community service or community work, any other form of restitution devised by the court, or any combination of the previously described forms of restitution.

If the child is adjudicated a delinquent child for violating a law of this state or the United States, or an ordinance or regulation of a political subdivision of this state, that would be a crime if committed by an adult or for violating division (A) of section 2923.211 of the Revised Code, the court, in addition to all other required or permissive conditions of probation that the court imposes upon the delinquent child pursuant to division (A)(2) of this section, shall require the child as a condition of the child's probation to abide by the law during the period of probation, including, but not limited to, complying with the provisions of Chapter 2923. of the Revised Code relating to the possession, sale, furnishing, transfer, disposition, purchase, acquisition, carrying, conveying, or use of, or other conduct involving, a firearm or dangerous ordnance, as defined in section 2923.11 of the Revised Code.

(3) Commit the child to the temporary custody of any school, camp, institution, or other facility operated for the care of delinquent children by the county, by a district organized under section 2151.34 or 2151.65 of the Revised Code, or by a private agency or organization, within or without the state, that is authorized and qualified to provide the care, treatment, or placement required;

(4) If the child is adjudicated a delinquent child for committing an act that would be a felony of the third, fourth, or fifth degree if committed by an adult or for violating division (A) of section 2923.211 of the Revised Code, commit the child to the legal custody of the department of youth services for institutionalization for an indefinite term consisting of a minimum period of six months and a maximum period not to exceed the child's attainment of twenty-one years of age;

(5)(a) If the child is adjudicated a delinquent child for violating section 2903.03, 2905.01, 2909.02, or 2911.01 or division (A) of section 2903.04 of the Revised Code or for violating any provision of section 2907.02 of the Revised Code other than division (A)(1)(b) of that section when the sexual conduct or insertion involved was consensual and when the victim of the violation of division (A)(1)(b) of that section was older than the delinquent child, was the same age as the delinquent child, or was less than three years younger than the delinquent child, commit the child to the legal custody of the department of youth services for institutionalization in a secure facility for an indefinite term consisting of a minimum period of one to three years, as prescribed by the court, and a maximum period not to exceed the child's attainment of twenty-one years of age;

(b) If the child is adjudicated a delinquent child for violating section 2923.02 of the Revised Code and if the violation involves an attempt to commit a violation of section 2903.01 or 2903.02 of the Revised Code, commit the child to the legal custody of the department of youth services for institutionalization in a secure facility for an indefinite term consisting of a minimum period of six to seven years, as prescribed by the court, and a maximum period not to exceed the child's attainment of twenty-one years of age;

(c) If the child is adjudicated a delinquent child for committing an act that is not described in division (A)(5)(a) or (b) of this section and that would be a felony of the first or second degree if committed by an adult, commit the child to the legal custody of the department of youth services for institutionalization in a secure facility for an indefinite term consisting of a minimum period of one year and a maximum period not to exceed the child's attainment of twenty-one years of age.

(6) If the child is adjudicated a delinquent child for committing a violation of section 2903.01 or 2903.02 of the Revised Code, commit the child to the legal custody of the department of youth services for institutionalization in a secure facility until the child's attainment of twenty-one years of age;

(7)(a) If the child is adjudicated a delinquent child for committing an act, other than a violation of section 2923.12 of the Revised Code, that would be a felony if committed by an adult and is committed to the legal custody of the department of youth services pursuant to division (A)(4), (5), or (6) of this section and if the court determines that the child, if the child was an adult, would be guilty of a specification of the type set forth in section 2941.141, 2941.144, 2941.145, 2941.146, or 2941.1412 of the Revised Code in relation to the act for which the child was adjudicated a delinquent child, commit the child to the legal custody of the department of youth services for institutionalization in a secure facility for the following period of time, subject to division (A)(7)(d) of this section:

(i) If the child would be guilty of a specification of the type set forth in section 2941.141 of the Revised Code, a period of one year;

(ii) If the child would be guilty of a specification of the type set forth in section 2941.144, 2941.145, 2941.146, or 2941.1412 of the Revised Code, a period of three years.

(b) If the child is adjudicated a delinquent child for committing a category one offense or a category two offense and is committed to the legal custody of the department of youth services pursuant to division (A)(5) or (6) of this section and if the court determines that the child, if the child was an adult, would be guilty of a specification of the type set forth in section 2941.142 of the Revised Code in relation to the act for which the child was adjudicated a delinquent child, the court shall commit the child to the legal custody of the department of youth services for institutionalization in a secure facility for a period of not less than one year or more than three years, subject to division (A)(7)(d) of this section.

(c) If the child is adjudicated a delinquent child for committing an act that would be an offense of violence that is a felony if committed by an adult and is committed to the legal custody of the department of youth services pursuant to division (A)(4), (5), or (6) of this section and if the court determines that the child, if the child was an adult, would be guilty of a specification of the type set forth in section 2941.1411 of the Revised Code in relation to the act for which the child was adjudicated a delinquent child, the court may commit the child to the custody of the department of youth services for institutionalization in a secure facility for two years, subject to division (A)(7)(d) of this section.

(d) A court that imposes a period of commitment under division (A)(7)(a) of this section is not precluded from imposing an additional period of commitment under division (A)(7)(b) or (c) of this section, a court that imposes a period of commitment under division (A)(7)(b) of this section is not precluded from imposing an additional period of commitment under division (A)(7)(a) or (c) of this section, and a court that imposes a period of commitment under division (A)(7)(c) of this section is not precluded from imposing an additional period of commitment under division (A)(7)(a) or (b) of this section. The court shall not commit a child to the legal custody of the department of youth services pursuant to division (A)(7)(a), (b), or (c) of this section for a period of time that exceeds three years. The period of commitment imposed pursuant to division (A)(7)(a), (b), or (c) of this section shall be in addition to, and shall be served consecutively with and prior to, a period of commitment ordered pursuant to division (A)(4), (5), or (6) of this section, provided that the total of all the periods of commitment shall not exceed the child's attainment of twenty-one years of age.

(8) Impose a fine and costs in accordance with the schedule set forth in section 2151.3512 of the Revised Code;

(9) Require the child to make restitution for all or part of the property damage caused by the child's delinquent act and for all or part of the value of the property that was the subject of any delinquent act the child committed that would be a theft offense, as defined in division (K) of section 2913.01 of the Revised Code, if committed by an adult. If the court determines that the victim of the child's delinquent act was sixty-five years of age or older or permanently and totally disabled at the time of the commission of the act, the court, regardless of whether or not the child knew the age of the victim, shall consider that fact in favor of imposing restitution, but that fact shall not control the decision of the court. The restitution may be in the form of a cash reimbursement paid in a lump sum or in installments, the performance of repair work to restore any damaged property to its original condition, the performance of a reasonable amount of labor for the victim, the performance of community service or community work, any other form of restitution devised by the court, or any combination of the previously described forms of restitution.

(10) Subject to division (D) of this section, suspend or revoke the driver's license, probationary driver's license, or temporary instruction permit issued to the child or suspend or revoke the registration of all motor vehicles registered in the name of the child. A child whose license or permit is so suspended or revoked is ineligible for issuance of a license or permit during the period of suspension or revocation. At the end of the period of suspension or revocation, the child shall not be reissued a license or permit until the child has paid any applicable reinstatement fee and complied with all requirements governing license reinstatement.

(11) If the child is adjudicated a delinquent child for committing an act that, if committed by an adult, would be a criminal offense that would qualify the adult as an eligible offender pursuant to division (A)(3) of section 2929.23 of the Revised Code, impose a period of electronically monitored house detention in accordance with division (J) of this section that does not exceed the maximum sentence of imprisonment that could be imposed upon an adult who commits the same act;

(12) Impose a period of day reporting in which the child is required each day to report to and leave a center or other approved reporting location at specified times in order to participate in work, education or training, treatment, and other approved programs at the center or outside the center;

(13) Impose a period of electronically monitored house arrest in accordance with division (J) of this section;

(14) Impose a period of community service of up to five hundred hours;

(15) Impose a period in an alcohol or drug treatment program with a level of security for the child as determined necessary by the court;

(16) Impose a period of intensive supervision, in which the child is required to maintain frequent contact with a person appointed by the court to supervise the child while the child is seeking or maintaining employment and participating in training, education, and treatment programs as the order of disposition;

(17) Impose a period of basic supervision, in which the child is required to maintain contact with a person appointed to supervise the child in accordance with sanctions imposed by the court;

(18) Impose a period of drug and alcohol use monitoring;

(19) Impose a period in which the court orders the child to observe a curfew that may involve daytime or evening hours;

(20) Require the child to obtain a high school diploma, a certificate of high school equivalence, or employment;

(21) If the court obtains the assent of the victim of the criminal act committed by the child, require the child to participate in a reconciliation or mediation program that includes a meeting in which the child and the victim may discuss the criminal act, discuss restitution, and consider other sanctions for the criminal act;

(22) Commit the child to the temporary or permanent custody of the court;

(23) Require the child to not be absent without legitimate excuse from the public school the child is supposed to attend for five or more consecutive days, seven or more school days in one school month, or twelve or more school days in a school year;

(24)(a) If a child is adjudicated a delinquent child for being a chronic truant or an habitual truant who previously has been adjudicated an unruly child for being an habitual truant, do either or both of the following:

(i) Require the child to participate in a truancy prevention mediation program;

(ii) Make any order of disposition as authorized by this section, except that the court shall not commit the child to a facility described in division (A)(3) of this section unless the court determines that the child violated a lawful court order made pursuant to division (C)(1)(e) of section 2151.354 of the Revised Code or division (A)(23) of this section.

(b) If a child is adjudicated a delinquent child for being a chronic truant or an habitual truant who previously has been adjudicated an unruly child for being an habitual truant and the court determines that the parent, guardian, or other person having care of the child has failed to cause the child's attendance at school in violation of section 3321.38 of the Revised Code, do either or both of the following:

(i) Require the parent, guardian, or other person having care of the child to participate in a truancy prevention mediation program;

(ii) Require the parent, guardian, or other person having care of the child to participate in any community service program, preferably a community service program that requires the involvement of the parent, guardian, or other person having care of the child in the school attended by the child.

(25) Make any further disposition that the court finds proper, except that the child shall not be placed in any state correctional institution, county, multicounty, or municipal jail or workhouse, or other place in which an adult convicted of a crime, under arrest, or charged with a crime is held.

(B)(1) If a child is adjudicated a delinquent child for violating section 2923.32 of the Revised Code, the court, in addition to any order of disposition it makes for the child under division (A) of this section, shall enter an order of criminal forfeiture against the child in accordance with divisions (B)(3), (4), (5), and (6) and (C) to (F) of section 2923.32 of the Revised Code.

(2) If a child is adjudicated a delinquent child for being a chronic truant or an habitual truant who previously has been adjudicated an unruly child for being an habitual truant and the court determines that the parent, guardian, or other person having care of the child has failed to cause the child's attendance at school in violation of section 3321.38 of the Revised Code, in addition to any order of disposition it makes under this section, the court shall warn the parent, guardian, or other person having care of the child that any subsequent adjudication of the child as an unruly or delinquent child for being an habitual or chronic truant may result in a criminal charge against the parent, guardian, or other person having care of the child for a violation of division (C) of section 2919.21 or section 2919.24 of the Revised Code.

(3) If a child is adjudicated a delinquent child for committing two or more acts that would be felonies if committed by an adult and if the court entering the delinquent child adjudication orders the commitment of the child, for two or more of those acts, to the legal custody of the department of youth services for institutionalization or institutionalization in a secure facility pursuant to division (A)(4), (5), or (6) of this section, the court may order that all of the periods of commitment imposed under those divisions for those acts be served consecutively in the legal custody of the department of youth services and, if applicable, be in addition to and commence immediately following the expiration of all periods of commitment that the court imposes pursuant to division (A)(7)(a), (b), or (c) of this section. A court shall not commit a delinquent child to the legal custody of the department of youth services under division (B)(2) of this section for a period that exceeds the child's attainment of twenty-one years of age.

(C) If a child is adjudicated a delinquent child for committing an act that, if committed by an adult, would be a drug abuse offense, as defined in section 2925.01 of the Revised Code, or for violating division (B) of section 2917.11 of the Revised Code, in addition to imposing in its discretion any other order of disposition authorized by this section, the court shall do both of the following:

(1) Require the child to participate in a drug abuse or alcohol abuse counseling program;

(2) Suspend or revoke the temporary instruction permit, probationary driver's license, or driver's license issued to the child for a period of time prescribed by the court or, at the discretion of the court, until the child attends and satisfactorily completes, a drug abuse or alcohol abuse education, intervention, or treatment program specified by the court. During the time the child is attending the program, the court shall retain any temporary instruction permit, probationary driver's license, or driver's license issued to the child, and the court shall return the permit or license when the child satisfactorily completes the program.

(D) If a child is adjudicated a delinquent child for violating section 2923.122 of the Revised Code, the court, in addition to any order of disposition it makes for the child under division (A), (B), or (C) of this section, shall revoke the temporary instruction permit and deny the child the issuance of another temporary instruction permit in accordance with division (F)(1)(b) of section 2923.122 of the Revised Code or shall suspend the probationary driver's license, restricted license, or nonresident operating privilege of the child or deny the child the issuance of a probationary driver's license, restricted license, or temporary instruction permit in accordance with division (F)(1)(a), (c), (d), or (e) of section 2923.122 of the Revised Code.

(E)(1) At the dispositional hearing and prior to making any disposition pursuant to division (A) of this section, the court shall determine whether a victim of the delinquent act committed by the child was five years of age or younger at the time the delinquent act was committed, whether a victim of the delinquent act sustained physical harm to the victim's person during the commission of or otherwise as a result of the delinquent act, whether a victim of the delinquent act was sixty-five years of age or older or permanently and totally disabled at the time the delinquent act was committed, and whether the delinquent act would have been an offense of violence if committed by an adult. If the victim was five years of age or younger at the time the delinquent act was committed, sustained physical harm to the victim's person during the commission of or otherwise as a result of the delinquent act, or was sixty-five years of age or older or permanently and totally disabled at the time the act was committed, regardless of whether the child knew the age of the victim, and if the act would have been an offense of violence if committed by an adult, the court shall consider those facts in favor of imposing commitment under division (A)(3), (4), (5), or (6) of this section, but those facts shall not control the court's decision.

(2) At the dispositional hearing and prior to making any disposition pursuant to division (A)(4), (5), or (6) of this section, the court shall determine whether the delinquent child previously has been adjudicated a delinquent child for a violation of a law or ordinance. If the delinquent child previously has been adjudicated a delinquent child for a violation of a law or ordinance, the court, for purposes of entering an order of disposition for the delinquent child under this section, shall consider the previous delinquent child adjudication as a conviction of a violation of the law or ordinance in determining the degree of offense the current delinquent act would be had it been committed by an adult.

(F)(1) When a juvenile court commits a delinquent child to the custody of the department of youth services pursuant to this section, the court shall not designate the specific institution in which the department is to place the child but instead shall specify that the child is to be institutionalized or that the institutionalization is to be in a secure facility if that is required by division (A) of this section.

(2) When a juvenile court commits a delinquent child to the custody of the department of youth services, the court shall provide the department with the child's medical records, a copy of the report of any mental examination of the child ordered by the court, the section or sections of the Revised Code violated by the child and the degree of the violation, the warrant to convey the child to the department, a copy of the court's journal entry ordering the commitment of the child to the legal custody of the department, a copy of the arrest record pertaining to the act for which the child was adjudicated a delinquent child, a copy of any victim impact statement pertaining to the act, and any other information concerning the child that the department reasonably requests. The court also shall complete the form for the standard disposition investigation report that is developed and furnished by the department of youth services pursuant to section 5139.04 of the Revised Code and provide the department with the completed form. The department may refuse to accept physical custody of a delinquent child who is committed to the legal custody of the department until the court provides to the department the documents specified in division (F)(2) of this section. No officer or employee of the department who refuses to accept physical custody of a delinquent child who is committed to the legal custody of the department shall be subject to prosecution or contempt of court for the refusal if the court fails to provide the documents specified in division (F)(2) of this section at the time the court transfers the physical custody of the child to the department.

(3) Within twenty working days after the department of youth services receives physical custody of a delinquent child from a juvenile court, the court shall provide the department with a certified copy of the child's birth certificate or the child's social security number, or, if the court made all reasonable efforts to obtain the information but was unsuccessful, the court shall provide the department with documentation of the efforts it made to obtain the information.

(4) When a juvenile court commits a delinquent child to the custody of the department of youth services, the court shall give notice to the school attended by the child of the child's commitment by sending to that school a copy of the court's journal entry ordering the commitment. As soon as possible after receipt of the notice described in this division, the school shall provide the department with the child's school transcript. However, the department shall not refuse to accept a child committed to it, and a child committed to it shall not be held in a county or district detention home, because of a school's failure to provide the school transcript that it is required to provide under division (F)(4) of this section.

(5) The department of youth services shall provide the court and the school with an updated copy of the child's school transcript and shall provide the court with a summary of the institutional record of the child when it releases the child from institutional care. The department also shall provide the court with a copy of any portion of the child's institutional record that the court specifically requests within five working days of the request.

(6) When a juvenile court commits a delinquent child to the custody of the department of youth services pursuant to division (A)(4) or (5) of this section, the court shall state in the order of commitment the total number of days that the child has been held, as of the date of the issuance of the order, in detention in connection with the delinquent child complaint upon which the order of commitment is based. The department shall reduce the minimum period of institutionalization or minimum period of institutionalization in a secure facility specified in division (A)(4) or (5) of this section by both the total number of days that the child has been so held in detention as stated by the court in the order of commitment and the total number of any additional days that the child has been held in detention subsequent to the order of commitment but prior to the transfer of physical custody of the child to the department.

(G)(1) At any hearing at which a child is adjudicated a delinquent child or as soon as possible after the hearing, the court shall notify all victims of the delinquent act, who may be entitled to a recovery under any of the following sections, of the right of the victims to recover, pursuant to section 3109.09 of the Revised Code, compensatory damages from the child's parents; of the right of the victims to recover, pursuant to section 3109.10 of the Revised Code, compensatory damages from the child's parents for willful and malicious assaults committed by the child; and of the right of the victims to recover an award of reparations pursuant to sections 2743.51 to 2743.72 of the Revised Code.

(2) If a child is adjudicated a delinquent child for committing an act that, if committed by an adult, would be aggravated murder, murder, rape, felonious sexual penetration in violation of former section 2907.12 of the Revised Code, involuntary manslaughter, a felony of the first or second degree resulting in the death of or physical harm to a person, complicity in or an attempt to commit any of those offenses, or an offense under an existing or former law of this state that is or was substantially equivalent to any of those offenses and if the court in its order of disposition for that act commits the child to the custody of the department of youth services, the court may make a specific finding that the adjudication should be considered a conviction for purposes of a determination in the future, pursuant to Chapter 2929. of the Revised Code, as to whether the child is a repeat violent offender as defined in section 2929.01 of the Revised Code. If the court makes a specific finding as described in this division, it shall include the specific finding in its order of disposition and in the record in the case.

(H)(1) If a child is adjudicated a delinquent child for committing an act that would be a felony or offense of violence if committed by an adult, the court, prior to issuing an order of disposition under this section, shall order the preparation of a victim impact statement by the probation department of the county in which the victim of the act resides, by the court's own probation department, or by a victim assistance program that is operated by the state, a county, a municipal corporation, or another governmental entity. The court shall consider the victim impact statement in determining the order of disposition to issue for the child.

(2) Each victim impact statement shall identify the victim of the act for which the child was adjudicated a delinquent child, itemize any economic loss suffered by the victim as a result of the act, identify any physical injury suffered by the victim as a result of the act and the seriousness and permanence of the injury, identify any change in the victim's personal welfare or familial relationships as a result of the act and any psychological impact experienced by the victim or the victim's family as a result of the act, and contain any other information related to the impact of the act upon the victim that the court requires.

(3) A victim impact statement shall be kept confidential and is not a public record, as defined in section 149.43 of the Revised Code. However, the court may furnish copies of the statement to the department of youth services pursuant to division (F)(3) of this section or to both the adjudicated delinquent child or the adjudicated delinquent child's counsel and the prosecuting attorney. The copy of a victim impact statement furnished by the court to the department pursuant to division (F)(3) of this section shall be kept confidential and is not a public record, as defined in section 149.43 of the Revised Code. The copies of a victim impact statement that are made available to the adjudicated delinquent child or the adjudicated delinquent child's counsel and the prosecuting attorney pursuant to division (H)(3) of this section shall be returned to the court by the person to whom they were made available immediately following the imposition of an order of disposition for the child under this section.

(I)(1) Sections 2925.41 to 2925.45 of the Revised Code apply to children who are adjudicated or could be adjudicated by a juvenile court to be delinquent children for an act that, if committed by an adult, would be a felony drug abuse offense. Subject to division (B) of section 2925.42 and division (E) of section 2925.43 of the Revised Code, a delinquent child of that nature loses any right to the possession of, and forfeits to the state any right, title, and interest that the delinquent child may have in, property as defined in section 2925.41 and further described in section 2925.42 or 2925.43 of the Revised Code.

(2) Sections 2923.44 to 2923.47 of the Revised Code apply to children who are adjudicated or could be adjudicated by a juvenile court to be delinquent children for an act in violation of section 2923.42 of the Revised Code. Subject to division (B) of section 2923.44 and division (E) of section 2923.45 of the Revised Code, a delinquent child of that nature loses any right to the possession of, and forfeits to the state any right, title, and interest that the delinquent child may have in, property as defined in section 2923.41 of the Revised Code and further described in section 2923.44 or 2923.45 of the Revised Code.

(J)(1) A juvenile court, pursuant to division (A)(11) of this section, may impose a period of electronically monitored house detention upon a child who is adjudicated a delinquent child for committing an act that, if committed by an adult, would be a criminal offense that would qualify the adult as an eligible offender pursuant to division (A)(3) of section 2929.23 of the Revised Code. The court may impose a period of electronically monitored house detention in addition to or in lieu of any other dispositional order imposed upon the child, except that any period of electronically monitored house detention shall not extend beyond the child's eighteenth birthday. If a court imposes a period of electronically monitored house detention upon a child, it shall require the child to wear, otherwise have attached to the child's person, or otherwise be subject to monitoring by a certified electronic monitoring device or to participate in the operation of and monitoring by a certified electronic monitoring system; to remain in the child's home or other specified premises for the entire period of electronically monitored house detention except when the court permits the child to leave those premises to go to school or to other specified premises; to be monitored by a central system that monitors the certified electronic monitoring device that is attached to the child's person or that otherwise is being used to monitor the child and that can monitor and determine the child's location at any time or at a designated point in time or to be monitored by the certified electronic monitoring system; to report periodically to a person designated by the court; and, in return for receiving a dispositional order of electronically monitored house detention, to enter into a written contract with the court agreeing to comply with all restrictions and requirements imposed by the court, agreeing to pay any fee imposed by the court for the costs of the electronically monitored house detention imposed by the court pursuant to division (E) of section 2929.23 of the Revised Code, and agreeing to waive the right to receive credit for any time served on electronically monitored house detention toward the period of any other dispositional order imposed upon the child for the act for which the dispositional order of electronically monitored house detention was imposed if the child violates any of the restrictions or requirements of the dispositional order of electronically monitored house detention. The court also may impose other reasonable restrictions and requirements upon the child.

(2) If a child violates any of the restrictions or requirements imposed upon the child as part of the child's dispositional order of electronically monitored house detention, the child shall not receive credit for any time served on electronically monitored house detention toward any other dispositional order imposed upon the child for the act for which the dispositional order of electronically monitored house detention was imposed.

(K)(1) Within ten days after completion of the adjudication, the court shall give written notice of an adjudication that a child is a delinquent child to the superintendent of a city, local, exempted village, or joint vocational school district, and to the principal of the school the child attends, if the basis of the adjudication was the commission of an act that would be a criminal offense if committed by an adult, if the act was committed by the delinquent child when the child was fourteen years of age or older, and if the act is any of the following:

(a) An act that would be a felony or an offense of violence if committed by an adult, an act in the commission of which the child used or brandished a firearm, or an act that is a violation of section 2907.04, 2907.06, 2907.07, 2907.08, 2907.09, 2907.24, or 2907.241 of the Revised Code and that would be a misdemeanor if committed by an adult;

(b) A violation of section 2923.12 of the Revised Code or of a substantially similar municipal ordinance that would be a misdemeanor if committed by an adult and that was committed on property owned or controlled by, or at an activity held under the auspices of, the board of education of that school district;

(c) A violation of division (A) of section 2925.03 or 2925.11 of the Revised Code that would be a misdemeanor if committed by an adult, that was committed on property owned or controlled by, or at an activity held under the auspices of, the board of education of that school district, and that is not a minor drug possession offense;

(d) Complicity in any violation described in division (K)(1)(a) of this section, or complicity in any violation described in division (K)(1)(b) or (c) of this section that was alleged to have been committed in the manner described in division (K)(1)(b) or (c) of this section, and regardless of whether the act of complicity was committed on property owned or controlled by, or at an activity held under the auspices of, the board of education of that school district.

(2) The notice given pursuant to division (K)(1) of this section shall include the name of the child who was adjudicated to be a delinquent child, the child's age at the time the child committed the act that was the basis of the adjudication, and identification of the violation of the law or ordinance that was the basis of the adjudication.

(L) During the period of a delinquent child's probation granted under division (A)(2) of this section, authorized probation officers who are engaged within the scope of their supervisory duties or responsibilities may search, with or without a warrant, the person of the delinquent child, the place of residence of the delinquent child, and a motor vehicle, another item of tangible or intangible personal property, or other real property in which the delinquent child has a right, title, or interest or for which the delinquent child has the express or implied permission of a person with a right, title, or interest to use, occupy, or possess if the probation officers have reasonable grounds to believe that the delinquent child is not abiding by the law or otherwise is not complying with the conditions of the delinquent child's probation. The court that places a delinquent child on probation under division (A)(2) of this section shall provide the delinquent child with a written notice that informs the delinquent child that authorized probation officers who are engaged within the scope of their supervisory duties or responsibilities may conduct those types of searches during the period of probation if they have reasonable grounds to believe that the delinquent child is not abiding by the law or otherwise is not complying with the conditions of the delinquent child's probation. The court also shall provide the written notice described in division (C)(2)(b) of section 2151.411 of the Revised Code to each parent, guardian, or custodian of the delinquent child who is described in division (C)(2)(a) of that section.

(M) As used in this section:

(1) "Certified electronic monitoring device," "certified electronic monitoring system," "electronic monitoring device," and "electronic monitoring system" have the same meanings as in section 2929.23 of the Revised Code.

(2) "Electronically monitored house detention" means a period of confinement of a child in the child's home or in other premises specified by the court, during which period of confinement all of the following apply:

(a) The child wears, otherwise has attached to the child's person, or otherwise is subject to monitoring by a certified electronic monitoring device or is subject to monitoring by a certified electronic monitoring system.

(b) The child is required to remain in the child's home or other premises specified by the court for the specified period of confinement, except for periods of time during which the child is at school or at other premises as authorized by the court.

(c) The child is subject to monitoring by a central system that monitors the certified electronic monitoring device that is attached to the child's person or that otherwise is being used to monitor the child and that can monitor and determine the child's location at any time or at a designated point in time, or the child is required to participate in monitoring by a certified electronic monitoring system.

(d) The child is required by the court to report periodically to a person designated by the court.

(e) The child is subject to any other restrictions and requirements that may be imposed by the court.

(3) "Felony drug abuse offense" and "minor drug possession offense" have the same meanings as in section 2925.01 of the Revised Code.

(4) "Firearm" has the same meaning as in section 2923.11 of the Revised Code.

(5) "Sexually oriented offense" has the same meaning as in section 2950.01 of the Revised Code.

(6) "Theft offense" has the same meaning as in section 2913.01 of the Revised Code.

(2002 H 130, eff. 4–7–03; 2000 S 179, § 4, eff. 1–1–02; 2000 S 222, eff. 3–22–01; 2000 S 181, eff. 9–4–00; 1999 H 3, eff. 11–22–99; 1998 H 526, § 4, eff. 1–1–99; 1998 H 526, § 1, eff. 9–1–98; 1998 H 2, eff. 1–1–99; 1997 S 35, eff. 1–1–99; 1997 H 1, eff. 7–1–98; 1997 H 215, § 7, eff. 9–30–97; 1997 H 215, § 1, eff. 9–29–97; 1996 H 124, eff. 9–30–97; 1996 S 269, eff. 7–1–96; 1996 H 445, eff. 9–3–96; 1996 H 274, § 4, eff. 8–8–96; 1996 H 274, § 1, eff. 8–8–96; 1995 S 2, eff. 7–1–96; 1995 H 1, eff. 1–1–96; 1995 H 4, eff. 11–9–95; 1994 H 571, eff. 10–6–94; 1992 H 725, eff. 4–16–93; 1992 S 331, H 154; 1990 S 258, H 51, H 266, H 513, S 131; 1989 H 166, H 381, H 330, H 329; 1988 H 643; 1983 S 210; 1982 H 209; 1981 H 440; 1978 H 565, S 119; 1977 H 1; 1976 H 1196; 1974 H 1067; 1973 S 324; 1972 H 494; 1970 H 931; 1969 H 320)

Note: See also preceding repeal, Publisher's Note, and Uncodified Law.

Uncodified Law

2002 H 130, § 4, eff. 4–7–03, reads:

The amendment of section 2151.355 of the Revised Code is not intended to supersede the earlier repeal, with delayed effective date, of that section.

Historical and Statutory Notes

Publisher's Note: 2151.355 was repealed by 2000 S 179, § 4, eff. 1–1–02, and amended by 2002 H 130, eff. 4–7–03. The legal effect of these actions, pursuant to 2002 H 130, § 4, is in question. See *Baldwin's Ohio Legislative Service Annotated*, 2000, page 11/L–3793, and 2002, page 12/L–2943, or the OH–LEGIS or OH–LEGIS–OLD database on Westlaw, for original versions of these Acts.

2151.357 Cost of education

In the manner prescribed by division (C)(2) of section 3313.64 of the Revised Code, the court, at the time of making any order that removes a child from the child's own home or that vests legal or permanent custody of the child in a person other than the child's parent or a government agency, shall determine the school district that is to bear the cost of educating the child. The court shall make the determination a part of the order that provides for the child's placement or commitment.

Whenever a child is placed in a detention facility established under section 2152.41 of the Revised Code or a juvenile facility established under section 2151.65 of the Revised Code, the child's school district as determined by the court shall pay the cost of educating the child based on the per capita cost of the educational facility within the detention home or juvenile facility.

Whenever a child is placed by the court in a private institution, school, or residential treatment center or any other private facility, the state shall pay to the court a subsidy to help defray the expense of educating the child in an amount equal to the product of the daily per capita educational cost of the private facility, as determined pursuant to this section, and the number of days the child resides at the private facility, provided that the subsidy shall not exceed twenty-five hundred dollars per year per child. The daily per capita educational cost of a private facility shall be determined by dividing the actual program cost of the private facility or twenty-five hundred dollars, whichever is less, by three hundred sixty-five days or by three hundred sixty-six days for years that include February twenty-ninth. The state shall pay seventy-five per cent of the total subsidy for each year quarterly to the court. The state may adjust the remaining twenty-five per cent of the total subsidy to be paid to the court for each year to an amount that is less than twenty-five per cent of the total subsidy for that year based upon the availability of funds appropriated to the department of education for the purpose of subsidizing courts that place a child in a private institution, school, or residential treatment center or any other private facility and shall pay that adjusted amount to the court at the end of the year.

(2000 S 179, § 3, eff. 1–1–02; 1995 H 117, eff. 6–30–95; 1981 S 140, eff. 7–1–81; 1970 S 518; 1969 H 320)

2151.358 Under what conditions records are to be sealed or expunged; procedures; effects; offense of divulging confidential information

(A) As used in this section, "seal a record" means to remove a record from the main file of similar records and to secure it in a separate file that contains only sealed records and that is accessible only to the juvenile court. A record that is sealed shall be destroyed by all persons and governmental bodies except the juvenile court.

(B) The department of youth services and any other institution or facility that unconditionally discharges a person who has been adjudicated a delinquent child, an unruly child, or a juvenile traffic offender shall immediately give notice of the discharge to the court that committed the person. The court shall note the date of discharge on a separate record of discharges of those natures.

(C)(1)(a) Two years after the termination of any order made by the court or two years after the unconditional discharge of a person from the department of youth services or another institution or facility to which the person may have been committed, the court that issued the order or committed the person shall do whichever of the following is applicable:

(i) If the person was adjudicated an unruly child, order the record of the person sealed;

(ii) If the person was adjudicated a delinquent child for committing an act other than a violation of section 2903.01, 2903.02, 2907.02, 2907.03, or 2907.05 of the Revised Code or was adjudicated a juvenile traffic offender, either order the record of the person sealed or send the person notice of the person's right to have that record sealed.

(b) Division (C)(1)(a) of this section does not apply regarding a person who was adjudicated a delinquent child for committing a violation of section 2903.01, 2903.02, 2907.02, 2907.03, or 2907.05 of the Revised Code.

(2) The court shall send the notice described in division (C)(1)(a)(ii) of this section within ninety days after the expiration of the two-year period described in division (C)(1)(a) of this section by certified mail, return receipt requested, to the person's last known address. The notice shall state that the person may apply to the court for an order to seal the person's record, explain what sealing a record means, and explain the possible consequences of not having the person's record sealed.

(D)(1) At any time after the two-year period described in division (C)(1)(a) of this section has elapsed, any person who has been adjudicated a delinquent child for committing an act other than a violation of section 2903.01, 2903.02, 2907.02, 2907.03, or 2907.05 of the Revised Code or who has been adjudicated a juvenile traffic offender may apply to the court for an order to seal the person's record. The court shall hold a hearing on each application within sixty days after the application is received. Notice of the hearing on the application shall be given to the prosecuting attorney and to any other public office or agency known to have a record of the prior adjudication. If the court finds that the rehabilitation of the person who was adjudicated a delinquent child or a juvenile traffic offender has been attained to a satisfactory degree, the court may order the record of the person sealed.

(2) Division (D)(1) of this section does not apply regarding a person who was adjudicated a delinquent child for committing a violation of section 2903.01, 2903.02, 2907.02, 2907.03, or 2907.05 of the Revised Code.

(3) If a child who was charged with violating division (E)(1) of section 4301.69 of the Revised Code successfully completes a diversion program under division (E)(2)(a) of section 4301.69 of the Revised Code with respect to that charge, the court shall order the person's record in that case sealed.

(E)(1) If the court orders the adjudication record or other record of a person sealed pursuant to division (C) or (D) of this section, the court, except as provided in division (K) of this section, shall order that the proceedings in the case in which the person was adjudicated a juvenile traffic offender, a delinquent child, or an unruly child, or in which the person was the subject of a complaint alleging the person to have violated division (E)(1) of section 4301.69 of the Revised Code, be deemed never to have occurred. Except as provided in division (G)(2) of this section, all index references to the case and the person shall be deleted, and the person and the court properly may reply that no record exists with respect to the person upon any inquiry in the matter.

(2) Inspection of records that have been ordered sealed under division (E)(1) of this section may be made only by the following persons or for the following purposes:

(a) If the records in question pertain to an act that would be an offense of violence that would be a felony if committed by an adult, by any law enforcement officer or any prosecutor, or the assistants of a law enforcement officer or prosecutor, for any valid law enforcement or prosecutorial purpose;

(b) Upon application by the person who is the subject of the sealed records, by the persons that are named in that application;

(c) If the records in question pertain to an alleged violation of division (E)(1) of section 4301.69 of the Revised Code, by any law enforcement officer or any prosecutor, or the assistants of a law enforcement officer or prosecutor, for the purpose of determining whether the person is eligible for diversion under division (E)(2) of section 4301.69 of the Revised Code.

(F) Any person who has been arrested and charged with being a delinquent child or a juvenile traffic offender and who is adjudicated not guilty of the charges in the case or has the charges in the case dismissed may apply to the court for an expungement of the record in the case. The application may be filed at any time after the person is adjudicated not guilty or the charges against the person are dismissed. The court shall give notice to the prosecuting attorney of any hearing on the application. The court may initiate the expungement proceedings on its own motion.

Any person who has been arrested and charged with being an unruly child and who is adjudicated not guilty of the charges in the case or has the charges in the case dismissed may apply to the court for an expungement of the record in the case. The court shall initiate the expungement proceedings on its own motion if an application for expungement is not filed.

If the court upon receipt of an application for expungement or upon its own motion determines that the charges against any person in any case were dismissed or that any person was adjudicated not guilty in any case, the court shall order that the records of the case be expunged and that the proceedings in the case be deemed never to have occurred. If the applicant for the expungement order, with the written consent of the applicant's parents or guardian if the applicant is a minor and with the written approval of the court, waives in writing the applicant's right to bring any civil action based on the arrest for which the expungement order is applied, the court shall order the appropriate persons and governmental agencies to delete all index references to the case; destroy or delete all court records of the case; destroy all copies of any pictures and fingerprints taken of the person pursuant to the expunged arrest; and destroy, erase, or delete any reference to the arrest that is maintained by the state or any political subdivision of the state, except a record of the arrest that is maintained for compiling statistical data and that does not contain any reference to the person.

If the applicant for an expungement order does not waive in writing the right to bring any civil action based on the arrest for which the expungement order is applied, the court, in addition to ordering the deletion, destruction, or erasure of all index references and court records of the case and of all references to the arrest that are maintained by the state or any political subdivision of the state, shall order that a copy of all records of the case, except fingerprints held by the court or a law enforcement agency, be delivered to the court. The court shall seal all of the records delivered to the court in a separate file in which only sealed records are maintained. The sealed records shall be kept by the court until the statute of limitations expires for any civil action based on the arrest, any pending litigation based on the arrest is terminated, or the applicant files a written waiver of the right to bring a civil action based on the arrest. After the expiration of the statute of limitations, the termination of the pending litigation, or the filing of the waiver, the court shall destroy the sealed records.

After the expungement order has been issued, the court shall, and the person may properly, reply that no record of the case with respect to the person exists.

(G)(1) The court shall send notice of the order to expunge or seal to any public office or agency that the court has reason to believe may have a record of the expunged or sealed record. Except as provided in division (K) of this section, an order to seal or expunge under this section applies to every public office or agency that has a record of the prior adjudication or arrest, regardless of whether it receives notice of the hearing on the expungement or sealing of the record or a copy of the order to expunge or seal the record. Except as provided in division (K) of this section, upon the written request of a person whose record has been expunged and the presentation of a copy of the order to expunge, a public office or agency shall destroy its record of the prior adjudication or arrest, except a record of the adjudication or arrest that is maintained for compiling statistical data and that does not contain any reference to the person who is the subject of the order to expunge.

(2) The person, or the public office or agency, that maintains sealed records pertaining to an adjudication of a child as a delinquent child may maintain a manual or computerized index to the sealed records. The index shall contain only the name of, and alphanumeric identifiers that relate to, the persons who are the subject of the sealed records, the word "sealed," and the name of the person, or the public office or agency that has custody of the sealed records and shall not contain the name of the delinquent act committed. The person who has custody of the sealed records shall make the index available only for the purposes set forth in divisions (E)(2) and (H) of this section.

(H) The judgment rendered by the court under this chapter shall not impose any of the civil disabilities ordinarily imposed by conviction of a crime in that the child is not a criminal by reason of the adjudication and no child shall be charged with or convicted of a crime in any court except as provided by this chapter. The disposition of a child under the judgment rendered or any evidence given in court shall not operate to disqualify a child in any future civil service examination, appointment, or application. Evidence of a judgment rendered and the disposition of a child under the judgment is not admissible to impeach the credibility of the child in any action or proceeding. Otherwise, the disposition of a child under the judgment rendered or any evidence given in court is admissible as evidence for or against the child in any action or proceeding in any court in accordance with the Rules of Evidence and also may be considered by any court as to the matter of sentence or to the granting of probation, and a court may consider the judgment rendered and the disposition of a child under that judgment for purposes of determining whether the child, for a future criminal conviction or guilty plea, is a repeat violent offender, as defined in section 2929.01 of the Revised Code.

(I) In any application for employment, license, or other right or privilege, any appearance as a witness, or any other inquiry, a person may not be questioned with respect to any arrest for which the records were expunged. If an inquiry is made in violation of this division, the person may respond as if the expunged arrest did not occur, and the person shall not be subject to any adverse action because of the arrest or the response.

(J) An officer or employee of the state or any of its political subdivisions who knowingly releases, disseminates, or makes available for any purpose involving employment, bonding, licensing, or education to any person or to any department, agency, or other instrumentality of the state or of any of its political subdivisions any information or other data concerning any arrest, complaint, indictment, information, trial, hearing, adjudication, or correctional supervision, the records of which have been expunged or sealed pursuant to this section and the release, dissemination, or making available of which is not expressly permitted by this section, is guilty of divulging confidential information, a misdemeanor of the fourth degree.

(K) Notwithstanding any provision of this section that requires otherwise, a board of education of a city, local, exempted village, or joint vocational school district that maintains records of an individual who has been permanently excluded under sections 3301.121 and 3313.662 of the Revised Code is permitted to maintain records regarding an adjudication that the individual is a delinquent child that was used as the basis for the individual's permanent exclusion, regardless of a court order to seal the record. An order issued under this section to seal the record of an adjudication that an individual is a delinquent child does not revoke the adjudication order of the superintendent of public instruction to permanently exclude the individual who is the subject of the sealing order. An order issued under this section to seal the record of an adjudication that an individual is a delinquent child may be presented to a district superintendent as evidence to support the contention that the superintendent should recommend that the permanent exclusion of the individual who is the subject of the sealing order be revoked. Except as otherwise authorized by this division and sections 3301.121 and 3313.662 of the Revised Code, any school employee in possession of or having access to the sealed adjudication records of an individual that were the basis of a permanent exclusion of the individual is subject to division (J) of this section.

(2002 H 17, eff. 10–11–02; 2000 S 179, § 3, eff. 1–1–02; 2000 S 181, eff. 9–4–00; 1995 S 2, eff. 7–1–96; 1995 H 1, eff. 1–1–96; 1992 H 154, eff. 7–31–92; 1991 H 27; 1984 H 37; 1981 H 440; 1977 H 315; 1969 H 320)

2151.359 Control of conduct of parent, guardian, or custodian; contempt

(A)(1) In any proceeding in which a child has been adjudicated an unruly, abused, neglected, or dependent child, on the application of a party, or on the court's own motion, the court may make an order restraining or otherwise controlling the conduct of any parent, guardian, or other custodian in the relationship of that individual to the child if the court finds that an order of that type is necessary to do either of the following:

(a) Control any conduct or relationship that will be detrimental or harmful to the child.

(b) Control any conduct or relationship that will tend to defeat the execution of the order of disposition made or to be made.

(2) The court shall give due notice of the application or motion under division (A) of this section, the grounds for the application or motion, and an opportunity to be heard to the person against whom an order under this division is directed. The order may include a requirement that the child's parent, guardian, or other custodian enter into a recognizance with sufficient surety, conditioned upon the faithful discharge of any conditions or control required by the court.

(B) The authority to make an order under division (A) of this section and any order made under that authority is in addition to the authority to make an order pursuant to division (C)(2) of section 2151.354 or division (A)(7) (b) of section 2152.19 of the Revised Code and to any order made under either division.

(C) A person's failure to comply with any order made by the court under this section is contempt of court under Chapter 2705. of the Revised Code.

(2002 H 400, eff. 4–3–03; 2000 S 179, § 3, eff. 1–1–02; 2000 S 181, eff. 9–4–00; 1975 H 85, eff. 11–28–75; 1969 H 320)

2151.3510 Notice of intended dispositional order

Before a juvenile court issues an order of disposition pursuant to division (A)(1) of section 2151.354 or 2152.19 of the Revised Code committing an unruly or delinquent child to the custody of a public children services agency, it shall give the agency notice in the manner prescribed by the Juvenile Rules of the intended dispositional order.

(2000 S 179, § 3, eff. 1–1–02; 1996 H 274, eff. 8–8–96; 1991 H 298, eff. 7–26–91)

2151.3514 Orders requiring alcohol and drug addiction assessment, treatment, and testing of parents or caregivers

(A) As used in this section:

(1) "Alcohol and drug addiction program" has the same meaning as in section 3793.01 of the Revised Code;

(2) "Chemical dependency" means either of the following:

(a) The chronic and habitual use of alcoholic beverages to the extent that the user no longer can control the use of alcohol or endangers the user's health, safety, or welfare or that of others;

(b) The use of a drug of abuse to the extent that the user becomes physically or psychologically dependent on the drug or endangers the user's health, safety, or welfare or that of others.

(3) "Drug of abuse" has the same meaning as in section 3719.011 of the Revised Code.

(4) "Medicaid" means the program established under Chapter 5111. of the Revised Code.

(B) If the juvenile court issues an order of temporary custody or protective supervision under division (A) of section 2151.353 of the Revised Code with respect to a child adjudicated to be an abused, neglected, or dependent child and the alcohol or other drug addiction of a parent or other caregiver of the child was the basis for the adjudication of abuse, neglect, or dependency, the court shall issue an order requiring the parent or other caregiver to submit to an assessment and, if needed, treatment from an alcohol and drug addiction program certified by the department of alcohol and drug addiction services. The court may order the parent or other caregiver to submit to alcohol or other drug testing during, after, or both during and after, the treatment. The court shall send any order issued pursuant to this division to the public children services agency that serves the county in which the court is located for use as described in section 340.15 of the Revised Code.

(C) Any order requiring alcohol or other drug testing that is issued pursuant to division (B) of this section shall require one alcohol or other drug test to be conducted each month during a period of twelve consecutive months beginning the month immediately following the month in which the order for alcohol or other drug testing is issued. Arrangements for administering the alcohol or other drug tests, as well as funding the costs of the tests, shall be locally determined in accordance with sections 340.033 and 340.15 of the Revised Code. If a parent or other caregiver required to submit to alcohol or other drug tests under this section is not a recipient of medicaid, the agency that refers the parent or caregiver for the tests may require the parent or caregiver to reimburse the agency for the cost of conducting the tests.

(D) The certified alcohol and drug addiction program that conducts any alcohol or other drug tests ordered in accordance with divisions (B) and (C) of this section shall send the results of the tests, along with the program's recommendations as to the benefits of continued treatment, to the court and to the public children services agency providing services to the involved family, according to federal regulations set forth in 42 C.F.R. Part 2, and division (B) of section 340.15 of the Revised Code. The court shall consider the results and the recommendations sent to it under this division in any adjudication or review by the court, according to section 2151.353, 2151.414, or 2151.419 of the Revised Code.

(1998 H 484, eff. 3–18–99)

2151.3515 Definitions

As used in sections 2151.3515 to 2151.3530 of the Revised Code:

(A) "Deserted child" means a child whose parent has voluntarily delivered the child to an emergency medical service worker, peace officer, or hospital employee without expressing an intent to return for the child.

(B) "Emergency medical service organization," "emergency medical technician–basic," "emergency medical technician–intermediate," "first responder," and "paramedic" have the same meanings as in section 4765.01 of the Revised Code.

(C) "Emergency medical service worker" means a first responder, emergency medical technician-basic, emergency medical technician-intermediate, or paramedic.

(D) "Hospital" has the same meaning as in section 3727.01 of the Revised Code.

(E) "Hospital employee" means any of the following persons:

(1) A physician who has been granted privileges to practice at the hospital;

(2) A nurse, physician assistant, or nursing assistant employed by the hospital;

(3) An authorized person employed by the hospital who is acting under the direction of a physician described in division (E)(1) of this section.

(F) "Law enforcement agency" means an organization or entity made up of peace officers.

(G) "Nurse" means a person who is licensed under Chapter 4723. of the Revised Code to practice as a registered nurse or licensed practical nurse.

(H) "Nursing assistant" means a person designated by a hospital as a nurse aide or nursing assistant whose job is to aid nurses, physicians, and physician assistants in the performance of their duties.

(I) "Peace officer" means a sheriff, deputy sheriff, constable, police officer of a township or joint township police district, marshal, deputy marshal, municipal police officer, or a state highway patrol trooper.

(J) "Physician" and "physician assistant" have the same meanings as in section 4730.01 of the Revised Code.

(2000 H 660, eff. 4–9–01)

2151.3516 Persons authorized to take possession of deserted child

The following persons, while acting in an official capacity, shall take possession of a child who is seventy-two hours old or younger if that child's parent has voluntarily delivered the child to that person without the parent expressing an intent to return for the child:

(A) A peace officer on behalf of the law enforcement agency that employs the officer;

(B) A hospital employee on behalf of the hospital that has granted the person privilege to practice at the hospital or that employs the person;

(C) An emergency medical service worker on behalf of the emergency medical service organization that employs the worker or for which the worker provides services.

(2000 H 660, eff. 4–9–01)

2151.3517 Duties of persons taking possession of deserted child

(A) On taking possession of a child pursuant to section 2151.3516 of the Revised Code, a law enforcement agency, hospital, or emergency medical service organization shall do all the following:

(1) Perform any act necessary to protect the child's health or safety;

(2) Notify the public children services agency of the county in which the agency, hospital, or organization is located that the child has been taken into possession;

(3) If possible, make available to the parent who delivered the child forms developed under section 2151.3529 of the Revised Code that are designed to gather medical information concerning the child and the child's parents;

(4) If possible, make available to the parent who delivered the child written materials developed under section 2151.3529 of the Revised Code that describe services available to assist parents and newborns;

(5) If the child has suffered a physical or mental wound, injury, disability, or condition of a nature that reasonably indicates abuse or neglect of the child, attempt to identify and pursue the person who delivered the child.

(B) An emergency medical service worker who takes possession of a child shall, in addition to any act performed under division (A)(1) of this section, perform any medical service the worker is authorized to perform that is necessary to protect the physical health or safety of the child.

(2000 H 660, eff. 4–9–01)

2151.3518 Duties of public children services agencies

On receipt of a notice given pursuant to section 2151.3517 of the Revised Code that an emergency medical service organization, a law enforcement agency, or hospital has taken possession of a child and in accordance with rules of the department of job and family services, a public children services agency shall do all of the following:

(A) Consider the child to be in need of public care and protective services;

(B) Accept and take emergency temporary custody of the child;

(C) Provide temporary emergency care for the child, without agreement or commitment;

(D) Make an investigation concerning the child;

(E) File a motion with the juvenile court of the county in which the agency is located requesting that the court grant temporary custody of the child to the agency or to a private child placing agency;

(F) Provide any care for the child that the public children services agency considers to be in the best interest of the child, including placing the child in shelter care;

(G) Provide any care and perform any duties that are required of public children services agencies under section 5153.16 of the Revised Code;

(H) Prepare and keep written records of the investigation of the child, of the care and treatment afforded the child, and any other records required by the department of job and family services.

(2000 H 660, eff. 4–9–01)

2151.3519 Emergency hearings; adjudications

When a public children services agency files a motion pursuant to division (E) of section 2151.3518 of the Revised Code, the juvenile court shall hold an emergency hearing as soon as possible to determine whether the child is a deserted child. The court is required to give notice to the parents of the child only if the court has knowledge of the names of the parents. If the court determines at the initial hearing or at any other hearing that a child is a deserted child, the court shall adjudicate the child a deserted child and enter its findings in the record of the case.

(2000 H 660, eff. 4–9–01)

2151.3520 Temporary custody orders

If a juvenile court adjudicates a child a deserted child, the court shall commit the child to the temporary custody of a public children services agency or a private child placing agency. The court shall consider the order committing the child to the temporary custody of the agency to be an order of disposition issued under division (A)(2) of section 2151.353 of the Revised Code with respect to a child adjudicated a neglected child.

(2000 H 660, eff. 4–9–01)

2151.3521 Deserted child treated as neglected child

A court that issues an order pursuant to section 2151.3520 of the Revised Code shall treat the child who is the subject of the order the same as a child adjudicated a neglected child when performing duties under Chapter 2151. of the Revised Code with respect to the child, except that there is a rebuttable presumption that it is not in the child's best interest to return the child to the natural parents.

(2000 H 660, eff. 4–9–01)

2151.3522 Case plans, investigations, administrative reviews, and services

A public children services agency or private child placing agency that receives temporary custody of a child adjudicated a deserted child shall prepare case plans, conduct investigations, conduct periodic administrative reviews of case plans, and provide services for the deserted child as if the child were adjudicated a neglected child and shall follow the same procedures under this chapter in performing those functions as if the deserted child was a neglected child.

(2000 H 660, eff. 4–9–01)

2151.3523 Immunity from criminal liability; exceptions

(A) A parent does not commit a criminal offense under the laws of this state and shall not be subject to criminal prosecution in this state for the act of voluntarily delivering a child under section 2151.3516 of the Revised Code.

(B) A person who delivers or attempts to deliver a child who has suffered any physical or mental wound, injury, disability, or condition of a nature that reasonably indicates abuse or neglect of the child is not immune from civil or criminal liability for abuse or neglect.

(C) A person or governmental entity that takes possession of a child pursuant to section 2151.3516 of the Revised Code or takes emergency temporary custody of and provides temporary emergency care for a child pursuant to section 2151.3518 of the Revised Code is immune from any civil liability that might otherwise be incurred or imposed as a result of these actions, unless the person or entity has acted in bad faith or with malicious purpose. The immunity provided by this division does not apply if the person or governmental entity has immunity from civil liability under section 9.86, 2744.02, or 2744.03 of the Revised Code for the action in question.

(D) A person or governmental entity that takes possession of a child pursuant to section 2151.3516 of the Revised Code or takes emergency temporary custody of and provides temporary emergency care for a child pursuant to section 2151.3518 of the Revised Code is immune from any criminal liability that might otherwise be incurred or imposed as a result of these actions, unless the person or entity has acted in bad faith or with malicious purpose.

(E) Divisions (C) and (D) of this section do not create a new cause of action or substantive legal right against a person or governmental entity, and do not affect any immunities from civil liability or defenses established by another section of the Revised Code or available at common law, to which a person or governmental entity may be entitled under circumstances not covered by this section.

(2000 H 660, eff. 4–9–01)

2151.3524 Anonymity of parent; exceptions

(A) A parent who voluntarily delivers a child under section 2151.3516 of the Revised Code has the absolute right to remain anonymous. The anonymity of a parent who voluntarily delivers a child does not affect any duty imposed under sections 2151.3516 or 2151.3517 of the Revised Code. A parent who voluntarily delivers a child may leave the place at which the parent delivers the child at any time after the delivery of the child.

(B) Notwithstanding division (A) of this section, a parent who delivers or attempts to deliver a child who has suffered any physical or mental wound, injury, disability, or condition of a nature that reasonably indicates abuse or neglect of the child does not have the right to remain anonymous and may be subject to arrest pursuant to Chapter 2935. of the Revised Code.

(2000 H 660, eff. 4–9–01)

2151.3525 Completion of medical information forms by parents

A parent who voluntarily delivers a child under section 2151.3516 of the Revised Code may complete all or any part of the medical information forms the parent receives under division (A)(3) of section 2151.3517 of the Revised Code. The parent may deliver the fully or partially completed forms at the same time as delivering the child or at a later time. The parent is not required to complete all or any part of the forms.

(2000 H 660, eff. 4–9–01)

2151.3526 Refusal of parents to accept written materials

A parent who voluntarily delivers a child under section 2151.3516 of the Revised Code may refuse to accept the materials made available under division (A)(4) of section 2151.3517 of the Revised Code.

(2000 H 660, eff. 4–9–01)

2151.3527 Coercion prohibited

(A) No person described in section 2151.3516 of the Revised Code shall do the following with respect to a parent who voluntarily delivers a child under that section:

(1) Coerce or otherwise try to force the parent into revealing the identity of the child's parents;

(2) Pursue or follow the parent after the parent leaves the place at which the child was delivered;

(3) Coerce or otherwise try to force the parent not to desert the child;

(4) Coerce or otherwise try to force the parent to complete all or any part of the medical information forms received under division (A)(3) of section 2151.3517 of the Revised Code;

(5) Coerce or otherwise try to force the parent to accept the materials made available under division (A)(4) of section 2151.3517 of the Revised Code.

(B) Divisions (A)(1) and (2) of this section do not apply to a person who delivers or attempts to deliver a child who has suffered any physical or mental wound, injury, disability, or condition of a nature that reasonably indicates abuse or neglect of the child.

(2000 H 660, eff. 4–9–01)

2151.3528 DNA testing of parents

If a child is adjudicated a deserted child and a person indicates to the court that the person is the parent of the child and that the person seeks to be reunited with the child, the court that adjudicated the child shall require the person, at the person's expense, to submit to a DNA test to verify that the person is a parent of the child.

(2000 H 660, eff. 4–9–01)

2151.3529 Medical information forms; written materials

(A) The director of job and family services shall promulgate forms designed to gather pertinent medical information concerning a deserted child and the child's parents. The forms shall clearly and unambiguously state on each page that the information requested is to facilitate medical care for the child, that the forms may be fully or partially completed or left blank, that completing the forms or parts of the forms is completely voluntary, and that no adverse legal consequence will result from failure to complete any part of the forms.

(B) The director shall promulgate written materials to be given to the parents of a child delivered pursuant to section 2151.3516 of the Revised Code. The materials shall describe services available to assist parents and newborns and shall include information directly relevant to situations that might cause parents to desert a child and information on the procedures for a person to follow in order to reunite with a child the person delivered under section 2151.3516 of the Revised Code, including notice that the person will be required to submit to a DNA test, at that person's expense, to prove that the person is the parent of the child.

(C) If the department of job and family services determines that money in the putative father registry fund created under section 2101.16 of the Revised Code is more than is needed for its duties related to the putative father registry, the department may use surplus moneys in the fund for costs related to the development and publication of forms and materials promulgated pursuant to divisions (A) and (B) of this section.

(2003 H 95, eff. 6–26–03; 2000 H 660, eff. 4–9–01)

2151.3530 Distribution of forms and materials by job and family services department

(A) The director of job and family services shall distribute the medical information forms and written materials promulgated under section 2151.3529 of the Revised Code to entities permitted to receive a deserted child, to public children services agencies, and to other public or private agencies that, in the discretion of the director, are best able to disseminate the forms and materials to the persons who are most in need of the forms and materials.

(B) If the department of job and family services determines that money in the putative father registry fund created under section 2101.16 of the Revised Code is more than is needed to perform its duties related to the putative father registry, the department may use surplus moneys in the fund for costs related to the distribution of forms and materials pursuant to this section.

(2003 H 95, eff. 6–26–03; 2000 H 660, eff. 4–9–01)

2151.36 Support of child

Except as provided in section 2151.361 of the Revised Code, when a child has been committed as provided by this chapter or Chapter 2152. of the Revised Code, the juvenile court shall issue an order pursuant to Chapters 3119., 3121., 3123., and 3125. of the Revised Code requiring that the parent, guardian, or person charged with the child's support pay for the care, support, maintenance, and education of the child. The juvenile court shall order that the parents, guardian, or person pay for the expenses involved in providing orthopedic, medical, or surgical treatment for, or for special care of, the child, enter a judgment for the amount due, and enforce the judgment by execution as in the court of common pleas.

Any expenses incurred for the care, support, maintenance, education, orthopedic, medical, or surgical treatment, and special care of a child who has a legal settlement in another county shall be at the expense of the county of legal settlement if the consent of the juvenile judge of the county of legal settlement is first obtained. When the consent is obtained, the board of county commissioners of the county in which the child has a legal settlement shall reimburse the committing court for the expenses out of its general fund. If the department of job and family services considers it to be in the best interest of any delinquent, dependent, unruly, abused, or neglected child who has a legal settlement in a foreign state or country that the child be returned to the state or country of legal settlement, the juvenile court may commit the child to the department for the child's return to that state or country.

Any expenses ordered by the court for the care, support, maintenance, education, orthopedic, medical, or surgical treatment, or special care of a dependent, neglected, abused, unruly, or delinquent child or of a juvenile traffic offender under this chapter or Chapter 2152. of the Revised Code, except the part of the expense that may be paid by the state or federal government or paid by the parents, guardians, or person charged with the child's support pursuant to this section, shall be paid from the county treasury upon specifically itemized vouchers, certified to by the judge. The court shall not be responsible for any expenses resulting from the commitment of children to any home, public children services agency, private child placing agency, or other institution, association, or agency, unless the court authorized the expenses at the time of commitment.

(2001 S 27, § 3, eff. 3–15–02; 2001 S 27, § 1, eff. 3–15–02; 2000 S 179, § 3, eff. 1–1–02; 2000 S 180, eff. 3–22–01; 1999 H 471, eff. 7–1–00; 1996 H 274, eff. 8–8–96; 1988 S 89, eff. 1–1–89; 1986 H 428; 1975 H 85; 1969 S 49, H 320; 1953 H 1; GC 1639–34)

2151.361 Payment for care, support, maintenance, and education of child

(A) If the parents of a child enter into an agreement with a public children services agency or private child placing agency to place the child into the temporary custody of the agency or the child is committed as provided by this chapter, the juvenile court, at its discretion, may issue an order pursuant to Chapters 3119., 3121., 3123., and 3125. of the Revised Code requiring that the parents pay for the care, support, maintenance, and education of the child if the parents adopted the child.

(B) When determining whether to issue an order under division (A) of this section, the juvenile court shall consider all pertinent issues, including, but not limited to, all of the following:

(1) The ability of the parents to pay for the care, support, maintenance, and education of the child;

(2) The chances for reunification of the parents and child;

(3) Whether issuing the order will encourage the reunification of the parents and child or undermine that reunification;

(4) Whether the problem underlying the agreement to place the child into temporary custody existed prior to the parents' adoption of the child and whether the parents were informed of the problem prior to that adoption;

(5) Whether the problem underlying the agreement to place the child into temporary custody began after the parents' adoption of the child;

(6) Whether the parents have contributed to the child's problems;

(7) Whether the parents are part of the solution to the child's problems.

(2001 S 27, eff. 3–15–02)

2151.37 Institution receiving children required to make report

At any time the juvenile judge may require from an association receiving or desiring to receive children, such reports, information, and statements as he deems necessary. He may at any time require from an association or institution reports, information, or statements concerning any child committed to it by such judge under sections 2151.01 to 2151.54, inclusive, of the Revised Code.

(1953 H 1, eff. 10–1–53; GC 1639–36)

2151.38 Temporary nature of dispositional orders

Subject to sections 2151.353 and 2151.412 to 2151.421 of the Revised Code, and any other provision of law that specifies a different duration for a dispositional order, all dispositional orders made by the court under this chapter shall be temporary and shall continue for a period that is designated by the court in its order, until terminated or modified by the court or until the child attains twenty-one years of age.

(2002 H 393, eff. 7–5–02; 2000 S 179, § 3, eff. 1–1–02; 1999 H 3, eff. 11–22–99; 1998 H 526, eff. 9–1–98; 1997 H 1, eff. 7–1–98; 1996 H 124, eff. 3–31–97; 1995 H 1, eff. 1–1–96; 1994 H 314, eff. 9–29–94; 1994 H 715, eff. 7–22–94; 1993 H 152, eff. 7–1–93; 1992 S 241; 1988 S 89; 1986 H 428; 1983 H 291; 1981 H 440, H 1; 1980 H 695; 1969 H 320, S 49; 130 v H 299; 1953 H 1; GC 1639–35)

2151.39 Placement of children from other states

No person, association or agency, public or private, of another state, incorporated or otherwise, shall place a child in a family home or with an agency or institution within the boundaries of this state, either for temporary or permanent care or custody or for adoption, unless such person or association has furnished the department of job and family services with a medical and social history of the child, pertinent information about the family, agency, association, or institution in this state with whom the sending party desires to place the child, and any other information or financial guaranty required by the department to determine whether the proposed placement will meet the needs of the child. The department may require the party desiring the placement to agree to promptly receive and remove from the state a child brought into the state whose placement has not proven satisfactorily responsive to the needs of the child at any time until the child is adopted, reaches majority, becomes self-supporting or is discharged with the concurrence of the department. All placements proposed to be made in this state by a party located in a state which is a party to the interstate compact on the placement of children shall be made according to the provisions of sections 5103.20 to 5103.28 of the Revised Code.

(1999 H 471, eff. 7–1–00; 1986 H 428, eff. 12–23–86; 1975 H 247; 126 v 1165; 1953 H 1; GC 1639–37)

2151.40 Cooperation with court

Every county, township, or municipal official or department, including the prosecuting attorney, shall render all assistance and co-operation within his jurisdictional power which may further the objects of sections 2151.01 to 2151.54 of the Revised Code. All institutions or agencies to which the juvenile court sends any child shall give to the court or to any officer appointed by it such information concerning such child as said court or officer requires. The court may seek the co-operation of all societies or organizations having for their object the protection or aid of children.

On the request of the judge, when the child is represented by an attorney, or when a trial is requested the prosecuting attorney shall assist the court in presenting the evidence at any hearing or proceeding concerning an alleged or adjudicated delinquent, unruly, abused, neglected, or dependent child or juvenile traffic offender.

(1975 H 85, eff. 11–28–75; 1969 H 320; 1953 H 1; GC 1639–55)

GENERAL PROVISIONS

2151.412 Case plans

(A) Each public children services agency and private child placing agency shall prepare and maintain a case plan for any child to whom the agency is providing services and to whom any of the following applies:

(1) The agency filed a complaint pursuant to section 2151.27 of the Revised Code alleging that the child is an abused, neglected, or dependent child;

(2) The agency has temporary or permanent custody of the child;

(3) The child is living at home subject to an order for protective supervision;

(4) The child is in a planned permanent living arrangement.

Except as provided by division (A)(2) of section 5103.153 of the Revised Code, a private child placing agency providing services to a child who is the subject of a voluntary permanent custody surrender agreement entered into under division (B)(2) of section 5103.15 of the Revised Code is not required to prepare and maintain a case plan for that child.

(B)(1) The director of job and family services shall adopt rules pursuant to Chapter 119. of the Revised Code setting forth the content and format of case plans required by division (A) of this section and establishing procedures for developing, implementing, and changing the case plans. The rules shall at a minimum comply with the requirements of Title IV–E of the "Social Security Act," 94 Stat. 501, 42 U.S.C. 671 (1980), as amended.

(2) The director of job and family services shall adopt rules pursuant to Chapter 119. of the Revised Code requiring public children services agencies and private child placing agencies to maintain case plans for children and their families who are receiving services in their homes from the agencies and for whom case plans are not required by division (A) of this section. The agencies shall maintain case plans as required by those rules; however, the case plans shall not be subject to any other provision of this section except as specifically required by the rules.

(C) Each public children services agency and private child placing agency that is required by division (A) of this section to maintain a case plan shall file the case plan with the court prior to the child's adjudicatory hearing but no later than thirty days after the earlier of the date on which the complaint in the case was filed or the child was first placed into shelter care. If the agency does not have sufficient information prior to the adjudicatory hearing to complete any part of the case plan, the agency shall specify in the case plan the additional information necessary to complete each part of the case plan and the steps that will be taken to obtain that information. All parts of the case plan shall be completed by the earlier of thirty days after the adjudicatory hearing or the date of the dispositional hearing for the child.

(D) Any agency that is required by division (A) of this section to prepare a case plan shall attempt to obtain an agreement among all parties, including, but not limited to, the parents, guardian, or custodian of the child and the guardian ad litem of the child regarding the content of the case plan. If all parties agree to the content of the case plan and the court approves it, the court shall journalize it as part of its dispositional order. If the agency cannot obtain an agreement upon the contents of the case plan or the court does not approve it, the parties shall present evidence on the contents of the case plan at the dispositional hearing. The court, based upon the evidence presented at the dispositional hearing and the best interest of the child, shall determine the contents of the case plan and journalize it as part of the dispositional order for the child.

(E)(1) All parties, including the parents, guardian, or custodian of the child, are bound by the terms of the journalized case plan. A party that fails to comply with the terms of the journalized case plan may be held in contempt of court.

(2) Any party may propose a change to a substantive part of the case plan, including, but not limited to, the child's placement and the visitation rights of any party. A party proposing a change to the case plan shall file the proposed change with the court and give notice of the proposed change in writing before the end of the day after the day of filing it to all parties and the child's guardian ad litem. All parties and the guardian ad litem shall have seven days from the date the notice is sent to object to and request a hearing on the proposed change.

(a) If it receives a timely request for a hearing, the court shall schedule a hearing pursuant to section 2151.417 of the Revised Code to be held no later than thirty days after the request is received by the court. The court shall give notice of the date, time, and location of the hearing to all parties and the guardian ad litem. The agency may implement the proposed change after the hearing, if the court approves it. The agency shall not implement the proposed change unless it is approved by the court.

(b) If it does not receive a timely request for a hearing, the court may approve the proposed change without a hearing. If the court approves the proposed change without a hearing, it shall journalize the case plan with the change not later than fourteen days after the change is filed with the court. If the court does not approve the proposed change to the case plan, it shall schedule a hearing to be held pursuant to section 2151.417 of the Revised Code no later than thirty days after the expiration of the fourteen-day time period and give notice of the date, time, and location of the hearing to all parties and the guardian ad litem of the child. If, despite the requirements of division (E)(2) of this section, the court neither approves and journalizes the proposed change nor conducts a hearing, the agency may implement the proposed change not earlier than fifteen days after it is submitted to the court.

(3) If an agency has reasonable cause to believe that a child is suffering from illness or injury and is not receiving proper care and that an appropriate change in the child's case plan is necessary to prevent immediate or threatened physical or emotional harm, to believe that a child is in immediate danger from the child's surroundings and that an immediate change in the child's case plan is necessary to prevent immediate or threatened physical or emotional harm to the child, or to believe that a parent, guardian, custodian, or other member of the child's household has abused or neglected the child and that the child is in danger of immediate or threatened physical or emotional harm from that person unless the agency makes an appropriate change in the child's case plan, it may implement the change without prior agreement or a court hearing and, before the end of the next day after the change is made, give all parties, the guardian ad litem of the child, and the court notice of the change. Before the end of the third day after implementing the change in the case plan, the agency shall file a statement of the change with the court and give notice of the filing accompanied by a copy of the statement to all parties and the guardian ad litem. All parties and the guardian ad litem shall have ten days from the date the notice is sent to object to and request a hearing on the change.

(a) If it receives a timely request for a hearing, the court shall schedule a hearing pursuant to section 2151.417 of the Revised Code to be held no later than thirty days after the request is received by the court. The court shall give notice of the date, time, and location of the hearing to all parties and the guardian ad litem. The agency shall continue to administer the case plan with the change after the hearing, if the court approves the change. If the court does not approve the change, the court shall make appropriate changes to the case plan and shall journalize the case plan.

(b) If it does not receive a timely request for a hearing, the court may approve the change without a hearing. If the court approves the change without a hearing, it shall journalize the case plan with the change within fourteen days after receipt of the change. If the court does not approve the change to the case plan, it shall schedule a hearing under section 2151.417 of the Revised Code to be held no later than thirty days after the expiration of the fourteen-day time period and give notice of the date, time, and location of the hearing to all parties and the guardian ad litem of the child.

(F)(1) All case plans for children in temporary custody shall have the following general goals:

(a) Consistent with the best interest and special needs of the child, to achieve a safe out-of-home placement in the least restrictive, most family-like setting available and in close proximity to the home from which the child was removed or the home in which the child will be permanently placed;

(b) To eliminate with all due speed the need for the out-of-home placement so that the child can safely return home.

(2) The director of job and family services shall adopt rules pursuant to Chapter 119. of the Revised Code setting forth the general goals of case plans for children subject to dispositional orders for protective supervision, a planned permanent living arrangement, or permanent custody.

(G) In the agency's development of a case plan and the court's review of the case plan, the child's health and safety shall be the paramount concern. The agency and the court shall be guided by the following general priorities:

(1) A child who is residing with or can be placed with the child's parents within a reasonable time should remain in their legal custody even if an order of protective supervision is required for a reasonable period of time;

(2) If both parents of the child have abandoned the child, have relinquished custody of the child, have become incapable of supporting or caring for the child even with reasonable assistance, or have a detrimental effect on the health, safety, and best interest of the child, the child should be placed in the legal custody of a suitable member of the child's extended family;

(3) If a child described in division (G)(2) of this section has no suitable member of the child's extended family to accept legal custody, the child should be placed in the legal custody of a suitable nonrelative who shall be made a party to the proceedings after being given legal custody of the child;

(4) If the child has no suitable member of the child's extended family to accept legal custody of the child and no suitable nonrelative is available to accept legal custody of the child and, if the child temporarily cannot or should not be placed with the child's parents, guardian, or custodian, the child should be placed in the temporary custody of a public children services agency or a private child placing agency;

(5) If the child cannot be placed with either of the child's parents within a reasonable period of time or should not be placed with either, if no suitable member of the child's extended family or suitable nonrelative is available to accept legal custody of the child, and if the agency has a reasonable expectation of placing the child for adoption, the child should be committed to the permanent custody of the public children services agency or private child placing agency;

(6) If the child is to be placed for adoption or foster care, the placement shall not be delayed or denied on the basis of the child's or adoptive or foster family's race, color, or national origin.

(H) The case plan for a child in temporary custody shall include at a minimum the following requirements if the child is or has been the victim of abuse or neglect or if the child witnessed the commission in the child's household of abuse or neglect against a sibling of the child, a parent of the child, or any other person in the child's household:

(1) A requirement that the child's parents, guardian, or custodian participate in mandatory counseling;

(2) A requirement that the child's parents, guardian, or custodian participate in any supportive services that are required by or provided pursuant to the child's case plan.

(I) A case plan may include, as a supplement, a plan for locating a permanent family placement. The supplement shall not be considered part of the case plan for purposes of division (D) of this section.

(1999 H 471, eff. 7–1–00; 1998 H 484, eff. 3–18–99; 1996 H 274, eff. 8–8–96; 1996 H 419, eff. 9–18–96; 1988 H 403, eff. 1–1–89)

2151.413 Motion for permanent custody

(A) A public children services agency or private child placing agency that, pursuant to an order of disposition under division (A)(2) of section 2151.353 of the Revised Code or under any version of section 2151.353 of the Revised Code that existed prior to January 1, 1989, is granted temporary custody of a child who is not abandoned or orphaned may file a motion in the court that made the disposition of the child requesting permanent custody of the child.

(B) A public children services agency or private child placing agency that, pursuant to an order of disposition under division (A)(2) of section 2151.353 of the Revised Code or under any version of section 2151.353 of the Revised Code that existed prior to January 1, 1989, is granted temporary custody of a child who is orphaned may file a motion in the court that made the disposition of the child requesting permanent custody of the child whenever it can show that no relative of the child is able to take legal custody of the child.

(C) A public children services agency or private child placing agency that, pursuant to an order of disposition under division (A)(5) of section 2151.353 of the Revised Code, places a child in a planned permanent living arrangement may file a motion in the court that made the disposition of the child requesting permanent custody of the child.

(D)(1) Except as provided in division (D)(3) of this section, if a child has been in the temporary custody of one or more public children services agencies or private child placing agencies for twelve or more months of a consecutive twenty-two month period ending on or after March 18, 1999, the agency with custody shall file a motion requesting permanent custody of the child. The motion shall be filed in the court that issued the current order of temporary custody. For the purposes of this division, a child shall be considered to have entered the temporary custody of an agency on the earlier of the date the child is adjudicated pursuant to section 2151.28 of the Revised Code or the date that is sixty days after the removal of the child from home.

(2) Except as provided in division (D)(3) of this section, if a court makes a determination pursuant to division (A)(2) of section 2151.419 of the Revised Code, the public children services agency or private child placing agency required to develop the permanency plan for the child under division (K) of section 2151.417 of the Revised Code shall file a motion in the court that made the determination requesting permanent custody of the child.

(3) An agency shall not file a motion for permanent custody under division (D)(1) or (2) of this section if any of the following apply:

(a) The agency documents in the case plan or permanency plan a compelling reason that permanent custody is not in the best interest of the child.

(b) If reasonable efforts to return the child to the child's home are required under section 2151.419 of the Revised Code, the agency has not provided the services required by the case plan to the parents of the child or the child to ensure the safe return of the child to the child's home.

(c) The agency has been granted permanent custody of the child.

(d) The child has been returned home pursuant to court order in accordance with division (A)(3) of section 2151.419 of the Revised Code.

(E) Any agency that files a motion for permanent custody under this section shall include in the case plan of the child who is the subject of the motion, a specific plan of the agency's actions to seek an adoptive family for the child and to prepare the child for adoption.

(F) The department of job and family services may adopt rules pursuant to Chapter 119. of the Revised Code that set forth the time frames for case reviews and for filing a motion requesting permanent custody under division (D)(1) of this section.

(1999 H 471, eff. 7–1–00; 1999 H 176, eff. 10–29–99; 1998 H 484, eff. 3–18–99; 1996 H 419, eff. 9–18–96; 1988 S 89, eff. 1–1–89; 1980 H 695)

2151.414 Procedures upon motion

(A)(1) Upon the filing of a motion pursuant to section 2151.413 of the Revised Code for permanent custody of a child, the court shall schedule a hearing and give notice of the filing of the motion and of the hearing, in accordance with section 2151.29 of the Revised Code, to all parties to the action and to the child's guardian ad litem. The notice also shall contain a full explanation that the granting of permanent custody permanently divests the parents of their parental rights, a full explanation of their right to be represented by counsel and to have counsel appointed pursuant to Chapter 120. of the Revised Code if they are indigent, and the name and telephone number of the court employee designated by the court pursuant to section 2151.314 of the Revised Code to arrange for the prompt appointment of counsel for indigent persons.

The court shall conduct a hearing in accordance with section 2151.35 of the Revised Code to determine if it is in the best interest of the child to permanently terminate parental rights and grant permanent custody to the agency that filed the motion. The adjudication that the child is an abused, neglected, or dependent child and any dispositional order that has been issued in the case under section 2151.353 of the Revised Code pursuant to the adjudication shall not be readjudicated at the hearing and shall not be affected by a denial of the motion for permanent custody.

(2) The court shall hold the hearing scheduled pursuant to division (A)(1) of this section not later than one hundred twenty days after the agency files the motion for permanent custody, except that, for good cause shown, the court may continue the hearing for a reasonable period of time beyond the one-hundred-twenty-day deadline. The court shall issue an order that grants, denies, or otherwise disposes of the motion for permanent custody, and journalize the order, not later than two hundred days after the agency files the motion.

If a motion is made under division (D)(2) of section 2151.413 of the Revised Code and no dispositional hearing has been held in the case, the court may hear the motion in the dispositional hearing required by division (B) of section 2151.35 of the Revised Code. If the court issues an order pursuant to section 2151.353 of the Revised Code granting permanent custody of the child to the agency, the court shall immediately dismiss the motion made under division (D)(2) of section 2151.413 of the Revised Code.

The failure of the court to comply with the time periods set forth in division (A)(2) of this section does not affect the authority of the court to issue any order under this chapter and does not provide any basis for attacking the jurisdiction of the court or the validity of any order of the court.

(B)(1) Except as provided in division (B)(2) of this section, the court may grant permanent custody of a child to a movant if the court determines at the hearing held pursuant to division (A) of this section, by clear and convincing evidence, that it is in the best interest of the child to grant permanent custody of the child to the agency that filed the motion for permanent custody and that any of the following apply:

(a) The child is not abandoned or orphaned or has not been in the temporary custody of one or more public children services agencies or private child placing agencies for twelve or more months of a consecutive twenty-two month period ending on or after March 18, 1999, and the child cannot be placed with either of the child's parents within a reasonable time or should not be placed with the child's parents.

(b) The child is abandoned.

(c) The child is orphaned, and there are no relatives of the child who are able to take permanent custody.

(d) The child has been in the temporary custody of one or more public children services agencies or private child placing agencies for twelve or more months of a consecutive twenty-two month period ending on or after March 18, 1999.

For the purposes of division (B)(1) of this section, a child shall be considered to have entered the temporary custody of an agency on the earlier of the date the child is adjudicated pursuant to section 2151.28 of the Revised Code or the date that is sixty days after the removal of the child from home.

(2) With respect to a motion made pursuant to division (D)(2) of section 2151.413 of the Revised Code, the court shall grant permanent custody of the child to the movant if the court determines in accordance with division (E) of this section that the child cannot be placed with one of the child's parents within a reasonable time or should not be placed with either parent and determines in accordance with division (D) of this section that permanent custody is in the child's best interest.

(C) In making the determinations required by this section or division (A)(4) of section 2151.353 of the Revised Code, a court shall not consider the effect the granting of permanent custody to the agency would have upon any parent of the child. A written report of the guardian ad litem of the child shall be submitted to the court prior to or at the time of the hearing held pursuant to division (A) of this section or section 2151.35 of the Revised Code but shall not be submitted under oath.

If the court grants permanent custody of a child to a movant under this division, the court, upon the request of any party, shall file a written opinion setting forth its findings of fact and conclusions of law in relation to the proceeding. The court shall not deny an agency's motion for permanent custody solely because the agency failed to implement any particular aspect of the child's case plan.

(D) In determining the best interest of a child at a hearing held pursuant to division (A) of this section or for the purposes of division (A)(4) or (5) of section 2151.353 or division (C) of section 2151.415 of the Revised Code, the court shall consider all relevant factors, including, but not limited to, the following:

(1) The interaction and interrelationship of the child with the child's parents, siblings, relatives, foster caregivers and out-of-home providers, and any other person who may significantly affect the child;

(2) The wishes of the child, as expressed directly by the child or through the child's guardian ad litem, with due regard for the maturity of the child;

(3) The custodial history of the child, including whether the child has been in the temporary custody of one or more public children services agencies or private child placing agencies for twelve or more months of a consecutive twenty-two month period ending on or after March 18, 1999;

(4) The child's need for a legally secure permanent placement and whether that type of placement can be achieved without a grant of permanent custody to the agency;

(5) Whether any of the factors in divisions (E)(7) to (11) of this section apply in relation to the parents and child.

For the purposes of this division, a child shall be considered to have entered the temporary custody of an agency on the earlier of the date the child is adjudicated pursuant to section 2151.28 of the Revised Code or the date that is sixty days after the removal of the child from home.

(E) In determining at a hearing held pursuant to division (A) of this section or for the purposes of division (A)(4) of section 2151.353 of the Revised Code whether a child cannot be placed with either parent within a reasonable period of time or should not be placed with the parents, the court shall consider all relevant evidence. If the court determines, by clear and convincing evidence, at a hearing held pursuant to division (A) of this section or for the purposes of division (A)(4) of section 2151.353 of the Revised Code that one or more of the following exist as to each of the child's parents, the court shall enter a finding that the child cannot be placed with either parent within a reasonable time or should not be placed with either parent:

(1) Following the placement of the child outside the child's home and notwithstanding reasonable case planning and diligent efforts by the agency to assist the parents to remedy the problems that initially caused the child to be placed outside the home, the parent has failed continuously and repeatedly to substantially remedy the conditions causing the child to be placed outside the child's home. In determining whether the parents have substantially remedied those conditions, the court shall consider parental utilization of medical, psychiatric, psychological, and other social and rehabilitative services and material resources that were made available to the parents for the purpose of changing parental conduct to allow them to resume and maintain parental duties.

(2) Chronic mental illness, chronic emotional illness, mental retardation, physical disability, or chemical dependency of the parent that is so severe that it makes the parent unable to provide an adequate permanent home for the child at the present time and, as anticipated, within one year after the court holds the hearing pursuant to division (A) of this section or for the purposes of division (A)(4) of section 2151.353 of the Revised Code;

(3) The parent committed any abuse as described in section 2151.031 of the Revised Code against the child, caused the child to suffer any neglect as described in section 2151.03 of the Revised Code, or allowed the child to suffer any neglect as described in section 2151.03 of the Revised Code between the date that the original complaint alleging abuse or neglect was filed and the date of the filing of the motion for permanent custody;

(4) The parent has demonstrated a lack of commitment toward the child by failing to regularly support, visit, or communicate with the child when able to do so, or by other actions showing an unwillingness to provide an adequate permanent home for the child;

(5) The parent is incarcerated for an offense committed against the child or a sibling of the child;

(6) The parent has been convicted of or pleaded guilty to an offense under division (A) or (C) of section 2919.22 or under section 2903.16, 2903.21, 2903.34, 2905.01, 2905.02, 2905.03, 2905.04, 2905.05, 2907.07, 2907.08, 2907.09, 2907.12, 2907.21, 2907.22, 2907.23, 2907.25, 2907.31, 2907.32, 2907.321, 2907.322, 2907.323, 2911.01, 2911.02, 2911.11, 2911.12, 2919.12, 2919.24, 2919.25, 2923.12, 2923.13, 2923.161, 2925.02, or 3716.11 of the Revised Code and the child or a sibling of the child was a victim of the offense or the parent has been convicted of or pleaded guilty to an offense under section 2903.04 of the Revised Code, a sibling of the child was the victim of the offense, and the parent who committed the offense poses an ongoing danger to the child or a sibling of the child.

(7) The parent has been convicted of or pleaded guilty to one of the following:

(a) An offense under section 2903.01, 2903.02, or 2903.03 of the Revised Code or under an existing or former law of this state, any other state, or the United States that is substantially equivalent to an offense described in those sections and the victim of the offense was a sibling of the child or the victim was another child who lived in the parent's household at the time of the offense;

(b) An offense under section 2903.11, 2903.12, or 2903.13 of the Revised Code or under an existing or former law of this state, any other state, or the United States that is substantially equivalent to an offense described in those sections and the victim of the offense is the child, a sibling of the child, or another child who lived in the parent's household at the time of the offense;

(c) An offense under division (B)(2) of section 2919.22 of the Revised Code or under an existing or former law of this state, any other state, or the United States that is substantially equivalent to the offense described in that section and the child, a sibling of the child, or another child who lived in the parent's household at the time of the offense is the victim of the offense;

(d) An offense under section 2907.02, 2907.03, 2907.04, 2907.05, or 2907.06 of the Revised Code or under an existing or former law of this state, any other state, or the United States that is substantially equivalent to an offense described in those sections and the victim of the offense is the child, a sibling of the child, or another child who lived in the parent's household at the time of the offense;

(e) A conspiracy or attempt to commit, or complicity in committing, an offense described in division (E)(7)(a) or (d) of this section.

(8) The parent has repeatedly withheld medical treatment or food from the child when the parent has the means to provide the treatment or food, and, in the case of withheld medical treatment, the parent withheld it for a purpose other than to treat the physical or mental illness or defect of the child by spiritual means through prayer alone in accordance with the tenets of a recognized religious body.

(9) The parent has placed the child at substantial risk of harm two or more times due to alcohol or drug abuse and has rejected treatment two or more times or refused to participate in further treatment two or more times after a case plan issued pursuant to section 2151.412 of the Revised Code requiring treatment of the parent was journalized as part of a dispositional order issued with respect to the child or an order was issued by any other court requiring treatment of the parent.

(10) The parent has abandoned the child.

(11) The parent has had parental rights involuntarily terminated pursuant to this section or section 2151.353 or 2151.415 of the Revised Code with respect to a sibling of the child.

(12) The parent is incarcerated at the time of the filing of the motion for permanent custody or the dispositional hearing of the child and will not be available to care for the child for at least eighteen months after the filing of the motion for permanent custody or the dispositional hearing.

(13) The parent is repeatedly incarcerated, and the repeated incarceration prevents the parent from providing care for the child.

(14) The parent for any reason is unwilling to provide food, clothing, shelter, and other basic necessities for the child or to prevent the child from suffering physical, emotional, or sexual abuse or physical, emotional, or mental neglect.

(15) The parent has committed abuse as described in section 2151.031 of the Revised Code against the child or caused or allowed the child to suffer neglect as described in section 2151.03 of the Revised Code, and the court determines that the seriousness, nature, or likelihood of recurrence of the abuse or neglect makes the child's placement with the child's parent a threat to the child's safety.

(16) Any other factor the court considers relevant.

(F) The parents of a child for whom the court has issued an order granting permanent custody pursuant to this section, upon the issuance of the order, cease to be parties to the action. This division is not intended to eliminate or restrict any right of the parents to appeal the granting of permanent custody of their child to a movant pursuant to this section.

(2000 H 448, eff. 10–5–00; 1999 H 176, eff. 10–29–99; 1998 H 484, eff. 3–18–99; 1996 H 274, eff. 8–8–96; 1996 H 419, eff. 9–18–96; 1988 S 89, eff. 1–1–89; 1980 H 695)

2151.415 Motions for dispositional orders; procedure

(A) Except for cases in which a motion for permanent custody described in division (D)(1) of section 2151.413 of the Revised Code is required to be made, a public children services agency or private child placing agency that has been given temporary custody of a child pursuant to section 2151.353 of the Revised Code, not later than thirty days prior to the earlier of the date for the termination of the custody order pursuant to division (F) of section 2151.353 of the Revised Code or the date set at the dispositional hearing for the hearing to be held pursuant to this section, shall file a motion with the court that issued the order of disposition requesting that any of the following orders of disposition of the child be issued by the court:

(1) An order that the child be returned home and the custody of the child's parents, guardian, or custodian without any restrictions;

(2) An order for protective supervision;

(3) An order that the child be placed in the legal custody of a relative or other interested individual;

(4) An order permanently terminating the parental rights of the child's parents;

(5) An order that the child be placed in a planned permanent living arrangement;

(6) In accordance with division (D) of this section, an order for the extension of temporary custody.

(B) Upon the filing of a motion pursuant to division (A) of this section, the court shall hold a dispositional hearing on the date set at the dispositional hearing held pursuant to section 2151.35 of the Revised Code, with notice to all parties to the action in accordance with the Juvenile Rules. After the dispositional hearing or at a date after the dispositional hearing that is not later than one year after the earlier of the date on which the complaint in the case was filed or the child was first placed into shelter care, the court, in accordance with the best interest of the child as supported by the evidence presented at the dispositional hearing, shall issue an order of disposition as set forth in division (A) of this section, except that all orders for permanent custody shall be made in accordance with sections 2151.413 and 2151.414 of the Revised Code. In issuing an order of disposition under this section, the court shall comply with section 2151.42 of the Revised Code.

(C)(1) If an agency pursuant to division (A) of this section requests the court to place a child into a planned permanent living arrangement, the agency shall present evidence to indicate why a planned permanent living arrangement is appropriate for the child, including, but not limited to, evidence that the agency has tried or considered all other possible dispositions for the child. A court shall not place a child in a planned permanent living arrangement, unless it finds, by clear and convincing evidence, that a planned permanent living arrangement is in the best interest of the child and that one of the following exists:

(a) The child, because of physical, mental, or psychological problems or needs, is unable to function in a family-like setting and must remain in residential or institutional care.

(b) The parents of the child have significant physical, mental, or psychological problems and are unable to care for the child because of those problems, adoption is not in the best interest of the child, as determined in accordance with division (D) of section 2151.414 of the Revised Code, and the child retains a significant and positive relationship with a parent or relative;

(c) The child is sixteen years of age or older, has been counseled on the permanent placement options available, is unwilling to accept or unable to adapt to a permanent placement, and is in an agency program preparing for independent living.

(2) If the court issues an order placing a child in a planned permanent living arrangement, both of the following apply:

(a) The court shall issue a finding of fact setting forth the reasons for its finding;

(b) The agency may make any appropriate placement for the child and shall develop a case plan for the child that is designed to assist the child in finding a permanent home outside of the home of the parents.

(D)(1) If an agency pursuant to division (A) of this section requests the court to grant an extension of temporary custody for a period of up to six months, the agency shall include in the motion an explanation of the progress on the case plan of the child and of its expectations of reunifying the child with the child's family, or placing the child in a permanent placement, within the extension period. The court shall schedule a hearing on the motion, give notice of its date, time, and location to all parties and the guardian ad litem of the child, and at the hearing consider the evidence presented by the parties and the guardian ad litem. The court may extend the temporary custody order of the child for a period of up to six months, if it determines at the hearing, by clear and convincing evidence, that the extension is in the best interest of the child, there has been significant progress on the case plan of the child, and there is reasonable cause to believe that the child will be reunified with one of the parents or otherwise permanently placed within the period of extension. In determining whether to extend the temporary custody of the child pursuant to this division, the court shall comply with section 2151.42 of the Revised Code. If the court extends the temporary custody of the child pursuant to this division, upon request it shall issue findings of fact.

(2) Prior to the end of the extension granted pursuant to division (D)(1) of this section, the agency that received the extension shall file a motion with the court requesting the issuance of one of the orders of disposition set forth in divisions (A)(1) to (5) of this section or requesting the court to extend the temporary custody order of the child for an additional period of up to six months. If the agency requests the issuance of an order of disposition under divisions (A)(1) to (5) of this section or does not file any motion prior to the expiration of the extension period, the court shall conduct a hearing in accordance with division (B) of this section and issue an appropriate order of disposition. In issuing an order of disposition, the court shall comply with section 2151.42 of the Revised Code.

If the agency requests an additional extension of up to six months of the temporary custody order of the child, the court shall schedule and conduct a hearing in the manner set forth in division (D)(1) of this section. The court may extend the temporary custody order of the child for an additional period of up to six months if it determines at the hearing, by clear and convincing evidence, that the additional extension is in the best interest of the child, there has been substantial additional progress since the original extension of temporary custody in the case plan of the child, there has been substantial additional progress since the original extension of temporary custody toward reunifying the child with one of the parents or otherwise permanently placing the child, and there is reasonable cause to believe that the child will be reunified with one of the parents or otherwise placed in a permanent setting before the expiration of the additional extension period. In determining whether to grant an additional extension, the court shall comply with section 2151.42 of the Revised Code. If the court extends the temporary custody of the child for an additional period pursuant to this division, upon request it shall issue findings of fact.

(3) Prior to the end of the extension of a temporary custody order granted pursuant to division (D)(2) of this section, the agency that received the extension shall file a motion with the court requesting the issuance of one of the orders of disposition set forth in divisions (A)(1) to (5) of this section. Upon the filing of the motion by the agency or, if the agency does not file the motion prior to the expiration of the extension period, upon its own motion, the court, prior to the expiration of the extension period, shall conduct a hearing in accordance with division (B) of this section and issue an appropriate order of disposition. In issuing an order of disposition, the court shall comply with section 2151.42 of the Revised Code.

(4) No court shall grant an agency more than two extensions of temporary custody pursuant to division (D) of this section.

(E) After the issuance of an order pursuant to division (B) of this section, the court shall retain jurisdiction over the child until the child attains the age of eighteen if the child is not mentally retarded, developmentally disabled, or physically impaired, the child attains the age of twenty-one if the child is mentally retarded, developmentally disabled, or physically impaired, or the child is adopted and a final decree of adoption is issued, unless the court's jurisdiction over the child is extended pursuant to division (E) of section 2151.353 of the Revised Code.

(F) The court, on its own motion or the motion of the agency or person with legal custody of the child, the child's guardian ad litem, or any other party to the action, may conduct a hearing with notice to all parties to determine whether any order issued pursuant to this section should be modified or terminated or whether any other dispositional order set forth in divisions (A)(1) to (5) of this section should be issued. After the hearing and consideration of all the evidence presented, the court, in accordance with the best interest of the child, may modify or terminate any order issued pursuant to this section or issue any dispositional order set forth in divisions (A)(1) to (5) of this section. In rendering a decision under this division, the court shall comply with section 2151.42 of the Revised Code.

(G) If the court places a child in a planned permanent living arrangement with a public children services agency or a private child placing agency pursuant to this section, the agency with which the child is placed in a planned permanent living arrangement shall not remove the child from the residential placement in which the child is originally placed pursuant to the case plan for the child or in which the child is placed with court approval pursuant to this division, unless the court and the guardian ad litem are given notice of the intended removal and the court issues an order approving the removal or unless the removal is necessary to protect the child from physical or emotional harm and the agency gives the court notice of the removal and of the reasons why the removal is necessary to protect the child from physical or emotional harm immediately after the removal of the child from the prior setting.

(H) If the hearing held under this section takes the place of an administrative review that otherwise would have been held under section 2151.416 of the Revised Code, the court at the hearing held under this section shall do all of the following in addition to any other requirements of this section:

(1) Determine the continued necessity for and the appropriateness of the child's placement;

(2) Determine the extent of compliance with the child's case plan;

(3) Determine the extent of progress that has been made toward alleviating or mitigating the causes necessitating the child's placement in foster care;

(4) Project a likely date by which the child may be returned to the child's home or placed for adoption or legal guardianship;

(5) Approve the permanency plan for the child consistent with section 2151.417 of the Revised Code.

(1999 H 176, eff. 10–29–99; 1998 H 484, eff. 3–18–99; 1996 H 274, eff. 8–8–96; 1988 S 89, eff. 1–1–89)

2151.416 Administrative review of case plans

(A) Each agency that is required by section 2151.412 of the Revised Code to prepare a case plan for a child shall complete a semiannual administrative review of the case plan no later than six months after the earlier of the date on which the complaint in the case was filed or the child was first placed in shelter care. After the first administrative review, the agency shall complete semiannual administrative reviews no later than every six months. If the court issues an order pursuant to section 2151.414 or 2151.415 of the Revised Code, the agency shall complete an administrative review no later than six months after the court's order and continue to complete administrative reviews no later than every six months after the first review, except that the court hearing held pursuant to section 2151.417 of the Revised Code may take the place of any administrative review that would otherwise be held at the time of the court hearing. When conducting a review, the child's health and safety shall be the paramount concern.

(B) Each administrative review required by division (A) of this section shall be conducted by a review panel of at least three persons, including, but not limited to, both of the following:

(1) A caseworker with day-to-day responsibility for, or familiarity with, the management of the child's case plan;

(2) A person who is not responsible for the management of the child's case plan or for the delivery of services to the child or the parents, guardian, or custodian of the child.

(C) Each semiannual administrative review shall include, but not be limited to, a joint meeting by the review panel with the parents, guardian, or custodian of the child, the guardian ad litem of the child, and the child's foster care provider and shall include an opportunity for those persons to submit any written materials to be included in the case record of the child. If a parent, guardian, custodian, guardian ad litem, or foster care provider of the child cannot be located after reasonable efforts to do so or declines to participate in the administrative review after being contacted, the agency does not have to include them in the joint meeting.

(D) The agency shall prepare a written summary of the semiannual administrative review that shall include, but not be limited to, all of the following:

(1) A conclusion regarding the safety and appropriateness of the child's foster care placement;

(2) The extent of the compliance with the case plan of all parties;

(3) The extent of progress that has been made toward alleviating the circumstances that required the agency to assume temporary custody of the child;

(4) An estimated date by which the child may be returned to and safely maintained in the child's home or placed for adoption or legal custody;

(5) An updated case plan that includes any changes that the agency is proposing in the case plan;

(6) The recommendation of the agency as to which agency or person should be given custodial rights over the child for the six-month period after the administrative review;

(7) The names of all persons who participated in the administrative review.

(E) The agency shall file the summary with the court no later than seven days after the completion of the administrative review. If the agency proposes a change to the case plan as a result of the administrative review, the agency shall file the proposed change with the court at the time it files the summary. The agency shall give notice of the summary and proposed change in writing before the end of the next day after filing them to all parties and the child's guardian ad litem. All parties and the guardian ad litem shall have seven days after the date the notice is sent to object to and request a hearing on the proposed change.

(1) If the court receives a timely request for a hearing, the court shall schedule a hearing pursuant to section 2151.417 of the Revised Code to be held not later than thirty days after the court receives the request. The court shall give notice of the date, time, and location of the hearing to all parties and the guardian ad litem. The agency may implement the proposed change after the hearing, if the court approves it. The agency shall not implement the proposed change unless it is approved by the court.

(2) If the court does not receive a timely request for a hearing, the court may approve the proposed change without a hearing. If the court approves the proposed change without a hearing, it shall journalize the case plan with the change not later than fourteen days after the change is filed with the court. If the court does not approve the proposed change to the case plan, it shall schedule a review hearing to be held pursuant to section 2151.417 of the Revised Code no later than thirty days after the expiration of the fourteen-day time period and give notice of the date, time, and location of the hearing to all parties and the guardian ad litem of the child. If, despite the requirements of this division and division (D) of section 2151.417 of the Revised Code, the court neither approves and journalizes the proposed change nor conducts a hearing, the agency may implement the proposed change not earlier than fifteen days after it is submitted to the court.

(F) The director of job and family services may adopt rules pursuant to Chapter 119. of the Revised Code for procedures and standard forms for conducting administrative reviews pursuant to this section.

(G) The juvenile court that receives the written summary of the administrative review, upon determining, either from the written summary, case plan, or otherwise, that the custody or care arrangement is not in the best interest of the child, may terminate the custody of an agency and place the child in the custody of another institution or association certified by the department of job and family services under section 5103.03 of the Revised Code.

(H) The department of job and family services shall report annually to the public and to the general assembly on the results of the review of case plans of each agency and on the results of the summaries submitted to the department under section 3107.10 of the Revised Code. The annual report shall include any information that is required by the department, including, but not limited to, all of the following:

(1) A statistical analysis of the administrative reviews conducted pursuant to this section and section 2151.417 of the Revised Code;

(2) The number of children in temporary or permanent custody for whom an administrative review was conducted, the number of children whose custody status changed during the period, the number of children whose residential placement changed during the period, and the number of residential placement changes for each child during the period;

(3) An analysis of the utilization of public social services by agencies and parents or guardians, and the utilization of the adoption listing service of the department pursuant to section 5103.154 of the Revised Code;

(4) A compilation and analysis of data submitted to the department under section 3107.10 of the Revised Code.

(1999 H 471, eff. 7–1–00; 1998 H 484, eff. 3–18–99; 1996 H 274, eff. 8–8–96; 1996 H 419, eff. 9–18–96; 1988 S 89, eff. 1–1–89)

2151.417 Review by court issuing dispositional orders

(A) Any court that issues a dispositional order pursuant to section 2151.353, 2151.414, or 2151.415 of the Revised Code may review at any time the child's placement or custody arrangement, the case plan prepared for the child pursuant to section 2151.412 of the Revised Code, the actions of the public children services agency or private child placing agency in implementing that case plan, the child's permanency plan, if the child's permanency plan has been approved and any other aspects of the child's placement or custody arrangement. In conducting the review, the court shall determine the appropriateness of any agency actions, the safety and appropriateness of continuing the child's placement or custody arrangement, and whether any changes should be made with respect to the child's permanency plan or placement or custody arrangement or with respect to the actions of the agency under the child's placement or custody arrangement. Based upon the evidence presented at a hearing held after notice to all parties and the guardian ad litem of the child, the court may require the agency, the parents, guardian, or custodian of the child, and the physical custodians of the child to take any reasonable action that the court determines is necessary and in the best interest of the child or to discontinue any action that it determines is not in the best interest of the child.

(B) If a court issues a dispositional order pursuant to section 2151.353, 2151.414, or 2151.415 of the Revised Code, the court has continuing jurisdiction over the child as set forth in division (E)(1) of section 2151.353 of the Revised Code. The court may amend a dispositional order in accordance with division (E)(2) of section 2151.353 of the Revised Code at any time upon its own motion or upon the motion of any interested party. The court shall comply with section 2151.42 of the Revised Code in amending any dispositional order pursuant to this division.

(C) Any court that issues a dispositional order pursuant to section 2151.353, 2151.414, or 2151.415 of the Revised Code shall hold a review hearing one year after the earlier of the date on which the complaint in the case was filed or the child was first placed into shelter care to review the case plan prepared pursuant to section 2151.412 of the Revised Code and the child's placement or custody arrangement, to approve or review the permanency plan for the child, and to make changes to the case plan and placement or custody arrangement consistent with the permanency plan. The court shall schedule the review hearing at the time that it holds the dispositional hearing pursuant to section 2151.35 of the Revised Code.

The court shall hold a similar review hearing no later than every twelve months after the initial review hearing until the child is adopted, returned to the parents, or the court otherwise terminates the child's placement or custody arrangement, except that the dispositional hearing held pursuant to section 2151.415 of the Revised Code shall take the place of the first review hearing to be held under this section. The court shall schedule each subsequent review hearing at the conclusion of the review hearing immediately preceding the review hearing to be scheduled.

(D) If, within fourteen days after a written summary of an administrative review is filed with the court pursuant to section 2151.416 of the Revised Code, the court does not approve the proposed change to the case plan filed pursuant to division (E) of section 2151.416 of the Revised Code or a party or the guardian ad litem requests a review hearing pursuant to division (E) of that section, the court shall hold a review hearing in the same manner that it holds review hearings pursuant to division (C) of this section, except that if a review hearing is required by this division and if a hearing is to be held pursuant to division (C) of this section or section 2151.415 of the Revised Code, the hearing held pursuant to division (C) of this section or section 2151.415 of the Revised Code shall take the place of the review hearing required by this division.

(E) If a court determines pursuant to section 2151.419 of the Revised Code that a public children services agency or private child placing agency is not required to make reasonable efforts to prevent the removal of a child from the child's home, eliminate the continued removal of a child from the child's home, and return the child to the child's home, and the court does not return the child to the child's home pursuant to division (A)(3) of section 2151.419 of the Revised Code, the court shall hold a review hearing to approve the permanency plan for the child and, if appropriate, to make changes to the child's case plan and the child's placement or custody arrangement consistent with the permanency plan. The court may hold the hearing immediately following the determination under section 2151.419 of the Revised Code and shall hold it no later than thirty days after making that determination.

(F) The court shall give notice of the review hearings held pursuant to this section to every interested party, including, but not limited to, the appropriate agency employees who are responsible for the child's care and planning, the child's parents, any person who had guardianship or legal custody of the child prior to the custody order, the child's guardian ad litem, and the child. The court shall summon every interested party to appear at the review hearing and give them an opportunity to testify and to present other evidence with respect to the child's custody arrangement, including, but not limited to, the following: the case plan for the child the *[sic]* permanency plan, if one exists; the actions taken by the child's custodian; the need for a change in the child's custodian or caseworker; and the need for any specific action to be taken with respect to the child. The court shall require any interested party to testify or present other evidence when necessary to a proper determination of the issues presented at the review hearing.

(G) After the review hearing, the court shall take the following actions based upon the evidence presented:

(1) If an administrative review has been conducted, determine whether the conclusions of the review are supported by a preponderance of the evidence and approve or modify the case plan based upon that evidence;

(2) If the hearing was held under division (C) or (E) of this section, approve a permanency plan for the child that specifies whether and, if applicable, when the child will be safely returned home or placed for adoption, for legal custody, or in a planned permanent living arrangement. a permanency plan approved after a hearing under division (E) of this section shall not include any provision requiring the child to be returned to the child's home.

(3) If the child is in temporary custody, do all of the following:

(a) Determine whether the child can and should be returned home with or without an order for protective supervision;

(b) If the child can and should be returned home with or without an order for protective supervision, terminate the order for temporary custody;

(c) If the child cannot or should not be returned home with an order for protective supervision, determine whether the agency currently with custody of the child should retain custody or whether another public children services agency, private child placing agency, or an individual should be given custody of the child.

The court shall comply with section 2151.42 of the Revised Code in taking any action under this division.

(4) If the child is in permanent custody, determine what actions are required by the custodial agency and of any other organizations or persons in order to facilitate an adoption of the child and make any appropriate orders with respect to the custody arrangement or conditions of the child, including, but not limited to, a transfer of permanent custody to another public children services agency or private child placing agency;

(5) Journalize the terms of the updated case plan for the child.

(H) The court may appoint a referee or a citizens review board to conduct the review hearings that the court is required by this section to conduct, subject to the review and approval by the court of any determinations made by the referee or citizens review board. If the court appoints a citizens review board to conduct the review hearings, the board shall consist of one member representing the general public and four members who are trained or experienced in the care or placement of children and have training or experience in the fields of medicine, psychology, social work, education, or any related field. Of the initial appointments to the board, two shall be for a term of one year, two shall be for a term of two years, and one shall be for a term of three years, with all the terms ending one year after the date on which the appointment was made. Thereafter, all terms of the board members shall be for three years and shall end on the same day of the same month of the year as did the term that they succeed. Any member appointed to fill a vacancy occurring prior to the expiration of the term for which the member's predecessor was appointed shall hold office for the remainder of the term.

(I) A copy of the court's determination following any review hearing held pursuant to this section shall be sent to the custodial agency, the guardian ad litem of the child who is the subject of the review hearing, and, if that child is not the subject of a permanent commitment hearing, the parents of the child.

(J) If the hearing held under this section takes the place of an administrative review that otherwise would have been held under section 2151.416 of the Revised Code, the court at the hearing held under this section shall do all of the following in addition to any other requirements of this section:

(1) Determine the continued necessity for and the safety and appropriateness of the child's placement;

(2) Determine the extent of compliance with the child's case plan;

(3) Determine the extent of progress that has been made toward alleviating or mitigating the causes necessitating the child's placement in foster care;

(4) Project a likely date by which the child may be safely returned home or placed for adoption or legal custody.

(K)(1) Whenever the court is required to approve a permanency plan under this section or section 2151.415 of the Revised Code, the public children services agency or private child placing agency that filed the complaint in the case, has custody of the child, or will be given custody of the child shall develop a permanency plan for the child. The agency must file the plan with the court prior to the hearing under this section or section 2151.415 of the Revised Code.

(2) The permanency plan developed by the agency must specify whether and, if applicable, when the child will be safely returned home or placed for adoption or legal custody. If the agency determines that there is a compelling reason why returning the child home or placing the child for adoption or legal custody is not in the best interest of the child, the plan shall provide that the child will be placed in a planned permanent living arrangement. A permanency plan developed as a result of a determination made under division (A)(2) of section 2151.419 of the Revised Code may not include any provision requiring the child to be returned home.

(1998 H 484, eff. 3–18–99; 1996 H 274, eff. 8–8–96; 1988 S 89, eff. 1–1–89)

2151.419 Hearings on efforts of agencies to prevent removal of children from homes

(A)(1) Except as provided in division (A)(2) of this section, at any hearing held pursuant to section 2151.28, division (E) of section 2151.31, or section 2151.314, 2151.33, or 2151.353 of the Revised Code at which the court removes a child from the child's home or continues the removal of a child from the child's home, the court shall determine whether the public children services agency or private child placing agency that filed the complaint in the case, removed the child from home, has custody of the child, or will be given custody of the child has made reasonable efforts to prevent the removal of the child from the child's home, to eliminate the continued removal of the child from the child's home, or to make it possible for the child to return safely home. The agency shall have the burden of proving that it has made those reasonable efforts. If the agency removed the child from home during an emergency in which the child could not safely remain at home and the agency did not have prior contact with the child, the court is not prohibited, solely because the agency did not make reasonable efforts during the emergency to prevent the removal of the child, from determining that the agency made those reasonable efforts. In determining whether reasonable efforts were made, the child's health and safety shall be paramount.

(2) If any of the following apply, the court shall make a determination that the agency is not required to make reasonable efforts to prevent the removal of the child from the child's home, eliminate the continued removal of the child from the child's home, and return the child to the child's home:

(a) The parent from whom the child was removed has been convicted of or pleaded guilty to one of the following:

(i) An offense under section 2903.01, 2903.02, or 2903.03 of the Revised Code or under an existing or former law of this state, any other state, or the United States that is substantially equivalent to an offense described in those sections and the victim of the offense was a sibling of the child or the victim was another child who lived in the parent's household at the time of the offense;

(ii) An offense under section 2903.11, 2903.12, or 2903.13 of the Revised Code or under an existing or former law of this state, any other state, or the United States that is substantially equivalent to an offense described in those sections and the victim of the offense is the child, a sibling of the child, or another child who lived in the parent's household at the time of the offense;

(iii) An offense under division (B)(2) of section 2919.22 of the Revised Code or under an existing or former law of this state, any other state, or the United States that is substantially equivalent to the offense described in that section and the child, a sibling of the child, or another child who lived in the parent's household at the time of the offense is the victim of the offense;

(iv) An offense under section 2907.02, 2907.03, 2907.04, 2907.05, or 2907.06 of the Revised Code or under an existing or former law of this state, any other state, or the United States that is substantially equivalent to an offense described in those sections and the victim of the offense is the child, a sibling of the child, or another child who lived in the parent's household at the time of the offense;

(v) A conspiracy or attempt to commit, or complicity in committing, an offense described in division (A)(2)(a)(i) or (iv) of this section.

(b) The parent from whom the child was removed has repeatedly withheld medical treatment or food from the child when the parent has the means to provide the treatment or food. If the parent has withheld medical treatment in order to treat the physical or mental illness or defect of the child by spiritual means through prayer alone, in accordance with the tenets of a recognized religious body, the court or agency shall comply with the requirements of division (A)(1) of this section.

(c) The parent from whom the child was removed has placed the child at substantial risk of harm two or more times due to alcohol or drug abuse and has rejected treatment two or more times or refused to participate in further treatment two or more times after a case plan issued pursuant to section 2151.412 of the Revised Code requiring treatment of the parent was journalized as part of a dispositional order issued with respect to the child or an order was issued by any other court requiring such treatment of the parent.

(d) The parent from whom the child was removed has abandoned the child.

(e) The parent from whom the child was removed has had parental rights involuntarily terminated pursuant to section 2151.353, 2151.414, or 2151.415 of the Revised Code with respect to a sibling of the child.

(3) At any hearing in which the court determines whether to return a child to the child's home, the court may issue an order that returns the child in situations in which the conditions described in divisions (A)(2)(a) to (e) of this section are present.

(B)(1) A court that is required to make a determination as described in division (A)(1) or (2) of this section shall issue written findings of fact setting forth the reasons supporting its determination. If the court makes a written determination under division (A)(1) of this section, it shall briefly describe in the findings of fact the relevant services provided by the agency to the family of the child and why those services did not prevent the removal of the child from the child's home or enable the child to return safely home.

(2) If a court issues an order that returns the child to the child's home in situations in which division (A)(2)(a), (b), (c), (d), or (e) of this section applies, the court shall issue written findings of fact setting forth the reasons supporting its determination.

(C) If the court makes a determination pursuant to division (A)(2) of this section, the court shall conduct a review hearing pursuant to section 2151.417 of the Revised Code to approve a permanency plan with respect to the child, unless the court issues an order returning the child home pursuant to division (A)(3) of this section. The hearing to approve the permanency plan may be held immediately following the court's determination pursuant to division (A)(2) of this section and shall be held no later than thirty days following that determination.

(1999 H 176, eff. 10–29–99; 1998 H 484, eff. 3–18–99; 1988 S 89, eff. 1–1–89)

2151.42 Modification or termination of dispositional order

(A) At any hearing in which a court is asked to modify or terminate an order of disposition issued under section 2151.353, 2151.415, or 2151.417 of the Revised Code, the court, in determining whether to return the child to the child's parents, shall consider whether it is in the best interest of the child.

(B) An order of disposition issued under division (A)(3) of section 2151.353, division (A)(3) of section 2151.415, or section 2151.417 of the Revised Code granting legal custody of a child to a person is intended to be permanent in nature. A court shall not modify or terminate an order granting legal custody of a child unless it finds, based on facts that have arisen since the order was issued or that were unknown to the court at that time, that a change has occurred in the circumstances of the child or the person who was granted legal custody, and that modification or termination of the order is necessary to serve the best interest of the child.

(1999 H 176, eff. 10–29–99; 1998 H 484, eff. 3–18–99)

2151.421 Persons required to report injury or neglect; procedures on receipt of report

Note: See also following version, eff. 5–6–05.

(A)(1)(a) No person described in division (A)(1)(b) of this section who is acting in an official or professional capacity and knows or suspects that a child under eighteen years of age or a mentally retarded, developmentally disabled, or physically impaired child under twenty-one years of age has suffered or faces a threat of suffering any physical or mental wound, injury, disability, or condition of a nature that reasonably indicates abuse or neglect of the child, shall fail to immediately report that knowledge or suspicion to the entity or persons specified in this division. Except as provided in section 5120.173 of the Revised Code, the person making the report shall make it to the public children services agency or a municipal or county peace officer in the county in which the child resides or in which the abuse or neglect is occurring or has occurred. In the circumstances described in section 5120.173 of the Revised Code, the person making the report shall make it to the entity specified in that section.

(b) Division (A)(1)(a) of this section applies to any person who is an attorney; physician, including a hospital intern or resident; dentist; podiatrist; practitioner of a limited branch of medicine as specified in section 4731.15 of the Revised Code; registered nurse; licensed practical nurse; visiting nurse; other health care professional; licensed psychologist; licensed school psychologist; independent marriage and family therapist or marriage and family therapist; speech pathologist or audiologist; coroner; administrator or employee of a child day-care center; administrator or employee of a residential camp or child day camp; administrator or employee of a certified child care agency or other public or private children services agency; school teacher; school employee; school authority; person engaged in social work or the practice of professional counseling; agent of a county humane society; person rendering spiritual treatment through prayer in accordance with the tenets of a well-recognized religion; superintendent, board member, or employee of a county board of mental retardation; investigative agent contracted with by a county board of mental retardation; or employee of the department of mental retardation and developmental disabilities.

(2) An attorney or a physician is not required to make a report pursuant to division (A)(1) of this section concerning any communication the attorney or physician receives from a client or patient in an attorney-client or physician-patient relationship, if, in accordance with division (A) or (B) of section 2317.02 of the Revised Code, the attorney or physician could not testify with respect to that communication in a civil or criminal proceeding, except that the client or patient is deemed to have waived any testimonial privilege under division (A) or (B) of section 2317.02 of the Revised Code with respect to that communication and the attorney or physician shall make a report pursuant to division (A)(1) of this section with respect to that communication, if all of the following apply:

(a) The client or patient, at the time of the communication, is either a child under eighteen years of age or a mentally retarded, developmentally disabled, or physically impaired person under twenty-one years of age.

(b) The attorney or physician knows or suspects, as a result of the communication or any observations made during that communication, that the client or patient has suffered or faces a threat of suffering any physical or mental wound, injury, disability, or condition of a nature that reasonably indicates abuse or neglect of the client or patient.

(c) The attorney-client or physician-patient relationship does not arise out of the client's or patient's attempt to have an abortion without the notification of her parents, guardian, or custodian in accordance with section 2151.85 of the Revised Code.

(B) Anyone, who knows or suspects that a child under eighteen years of age or a mentally retarded, developmentally disabled, or physically impaired person under twenty-one years of age has suffered or faces a threat of suffering any physical or mental wound, injury, disability, or other condition of a nature that reasonably indicates abuse or neglect of the child may report or cause reports to be made of that knowledge or suspicion to the entity or persons specified in this division. Except as provided in section 5120.173 of the Revised Code, a person making a report or causing a report to be made under this division shall make it or cause it to be made to the public children services agency or to a municipal or county peace officer. In the circumstances described in section 5120.173 of the Revised Code, a person making a report or causing a report to be made under this division shall make it or cause it to be made to the entity specified in that section.

(C) Any report made pursuant to division (A) or (B) of this section shall be made forthwith either by telephone or in person and shall be followed by a written report, if requested by the receiving agency or officer. The written report shall contain:

(1) The names and addresses of the child and the child's parents or the person or persons having custody of the child, if known;

(2) The child's age and the nature and extent of the child's known or suspected injuries, abuse, or neglect or of the known or suspected threat of injury, abuse, or neglect, including any evidence of previous injuries, abuse, or neglect;

(3) Any other information that might be helpful in establishing the cause of the known or suspected injury, abuse, or neglect or of the known or suspected threat of injury, abuse, or neglect.

Any person, who is required by division (A) of this section to report known or suspected child abuse or child neglect, may take or cause to be taken color photographs of areas of trauma visible on a child and, if medically indicated, cause to be performed radiological examinations of the child.

(D)(1) When a municipal or county peace officer receives a report concerning the possible abuse or neglect of a child or the possible threat of abuse or neglect of a child, upon receipt of the report, the municipal or county peace officer who receives the report shall refer the report to the appropriate public children services agency.

(2) When a public children services agency receives a report pursuant to this division or division (A) or (B) of this section, upon receipt of the report, the public children services agency shall comply with section 2151.422 of the Revised Code.

(E) No township, municipal, or county peace officer shall remove a child about whom a report is made pursuant to this section from the child's parents, stepparents, or guardian or any other persons having custody of the child without consultation with the public children services agency, unless, in the judgment of the officer, and, if the report was made by physician, the physician, immediate removal is considered essential to protect the child from further abuse or neglect. The agency that must be consulted shall be the agency conducting the investigation of the report as determined pursuant to section 2151.422 of the Revised Code.

(F)(1) Except as provided in section 2151.422 of the Revised Code, the public children services agency shall investigate, within twenty-four hours, each report of known or suspected child abuse or child neglect and of a known or suspected threat of child abuse or child neglect that is referred to it under this section to determine the circumstances surrounding the injuries, abuse, or neglect or the threat of injury, abuse, or neglect, the cause of the injuries, abuse, neglect, or threat, and the person or persons responsible. The investigation shall be made in cooperation with the law enforcement agency and in accordance with the memorandum of understanding prepared under division (J) of this section. A representative of the public children services agency shall, at the time of initial contact with the person subject to the investigation, inform the person of the specific complaints or allegations made against the person. The information shall be given in a manner that is consistent with division (H)(1) of this section and protects the rights of the person making the report under this section.

A failure to make the investigation in accordance with the memorandum is not grounds for, and shall not result in, the dismissal of any charges or complaint arising from the report or the suppression of any evidence obtained as a result of the report and does not give, and shall not be construed as giving, any rights or any grounds for appeal or post-conviction relief to any person. The public children services agency shall report each case to a central registry which the department of job and family services shall maintain in order to determine whether prior reports have been made in other counties concerning the child or other principals in the case. The public children services agency shall submit a report of its investigation, in writing, to the law enforcement agency.

(2) The public children services agency shall make any recommendations to the county prosecuting attorney or city director of law that it considers necessary to protect any children that are brought to its attention.

(G)(1)(a) Except as provided in division (H)(3) of this section, anyone or any hospital, institution, school, health department, or agency participating in the making of reports under division (A) of this section, anyone or any hospital, institution, school, health department, or agency participating in good faith in the making of reports under division (B) of this section, and anyone participating in good faith in a judicial proceeding resulting from the reports, shall be immune from any civil or criminal liability for injury, death, or loss to person or property that otherwise might be incurred or imposed as a result of the making of the reports or the participation in the judicial proceeding.

(b) Notwithstanding section 4731.22 of the Revised Code, the physician-patient privilege shall not be a ground for excluding evidence regarding a child's injuries, abuse, or neglect, or the cause of the injuries, abuse, or neglect in any judicial proceeding resulting from a report submitted pursuant to this section.

(2) In any civil or criminal action or proceeding in which it is alleged and proved that participation in the making of a report under this section was not in good faith or participation in a judicial proceeding resulting from a report made under this section was not in good faith, the court shall award the prevailing party reasonable attorney's fees and costs and, if a civil action or proceeding is voluntarily dismissed, may award reasonable attorney's fees and costs to the party against whom the civil action or proceeding is brought.

(H)(1) Except as provided in divisions (H)(4) and (M) of this section, a report made under this section is confidential. The information provided in a report made pursuant to this section and the name of the person who made the report shall not be released for use, and shall not be used, as evidence in any civil action or proceeding brought against the person who made the report. In a criminal proceeding, the report is admissible in evidence in accordance with the Rules of Evidence and is subject to discovery in accordance with the Rules of Criminal Procedure.

(2) No person shall permit or encourage the unauthorized dissemination of the contents of any report made under this section.

(3) A person who knowingly makes or causes another person to make a false report under division (B) of this section that alleges that any person has committed an act or omission that resulted in a child being an abused child or a neglected child is guilty of a violation of section 2921.14 of the Revised Code.

(4) If a report is made pursuant to division (A) or (B) of this section and the child who is the subject of the report dies for any reason at any time after the report is made, but before the child attains eighteen years of age, the public children services agency or municipal or county peace officer to which the report was made or referred, on the request of the child fatality review board, shall submit a summary sheet of information providing a summary of the report to the review board of the county in which the deceased child resided at the time of death. On the request of the review board, the agency or peace officer may, at its discretion, make the report available to the review board.

(5) A public children services agency shall advise a person alleged to have inflicted abuse or neglect on a child who is the subject of a report made pursuant to this section in writing of the disposition of the investigation. The agency shall not provide to the person any information that identifies the person who made the report, statements of witnesses, or police or other investigative reports.

(I) Any report that is required by this section, other than a report that is made to the state highway patrol as described in section 5120.173 of the Revised Code, shall result in protective services and emergency supportive services being made available by the public children services agency on behalf of the children about whom the report is made, in an effort to prevent further neglect or abuse, to enhance their welfare, and, whenever possible, to preserve the family unit intact. The agency required to provide the services shall be the agency conducting the investigation of the report pursuant to section 2151.422 of the Revised Code.

(J)(1) Each public children services agency shall prepare a memorandum of understanding that is signed by all of the following:

(a) If there is only one juvenile judge in the county, the juvenile judge of the county or the juvenile judge's representative;

(b) If there is more than one juvenile judge in the county, a juvenile judge or the juvenile judges' representative selected by the juvenile judges or, if they are unable to do so for any reason, the juvenile judge who is senior in point of service or the senior juvenile judge's representative;

(c) The county peace officer;

(d) All chief municipal peace officers within the county;

(e) Other law enforcement officers handling child abuse and neglect cases in the county;

(f) The prosecuting attorney of the county;

(g) If the public children services agency is not the county department of job and family services, the county department of job and family services;

(h) The county humane society.

(2) A memorandum of understanding shall set forth the normal operating procedure to be employed by all concerned officials in the execution of their respective responsibilities under this section and division (C) of section 2919.21, division (B)(1) of section 2919.22, division (B) of section 2919.23, and section 2919.24 of the Revised Code and shall have as two of its primary goals the elimination of all unnecessary interviews of children who are the subject of reports made pursuant to division (A) or (B) of this section and, when feasible, providing for only one interview of a child who is the subject of any report made pursuant to division (A) or (B) of this section. A failure to follow the procedure set forth in the memorandum by the concerned officials is not grounds for, and shall not result in, the dismissal of any charges or complaint arising from any reported case of abuse or neglect or the suppression of any evidence obtained as a result of any reported child abuse or child neglect and does not give, and shall not be construed as giving, any rights or any grounds for appeal or post-conviction relief to any person.

(3) A memorandum of understanding shall include all of the following:

(a) The roles and responsibilities for handling emergency and nonemergency cases of abuse and neglect;

(b) Standards and procedures to be used in handling and coordinating investigations of reported cases of child abuse and reported cases of child neglect, methods to be used in interviewing the child who is the subject of the report and who allegedly was abused or neglected, and standards and procedures addressing the categories of persons who may interview the child who is the subject of the report and who allegedly was abused or neglected.

(K)(1) Except as provided in division (K)(4) of this section, a person who is required to make a report pursuant to division (A) of this section may make a reasonable number of requests of the public children services agency that receives or is referred the report to be provided with the following information:

(a) Whether the agency has initiated an investigation of the report;

(b) Whether the agency is continuing to investigate the report;

(c) Whether the agency is otherwise involved with the child who is the subject of the report;

(d) The general status of the health and safety of the child who is the subject of the report;

(e) Whether the report has resulted in the filing of a complaint in juvenile court or of criminal charges in another court.

(2) A person may request the information specified in division (K)(1) of this section only if, at the time the report is made, the person's name, address, and telephone number are provided to the person who receives the report.

When a municipal or county peace officer or employee of a public children services agency receives a report pursuant to division (A) or (B) of this section the recipient of the report shall inform the person of the right to request the information described in division (K)(1) of this section. The recipient of the report shall include in the initial child abuse or child neglect report that the person making the report was so informed and, if provided at the time of the making of the report, shall include the person's name, address, and telephone number in the report.

Each request is subject to verification of the identity of the person making the report. If that person's identity is verified, the agency shall provide the person with the information described in division (K)(1) of this section a reasonable number of times, except that the agency shall not disclose any confidential information regarding the child who is the subject of the report other than the information described in those divisions.

(3) A request made pursuant to division (K)(1) of this section is not a substitute for any report required to be made pursuant to division (A) of this section.

(4) If an agency other than the agency that received or was referred the report is conducting the investigation of the report pursuant to section 2151.422 of the Revised Code, the agency conducting the investigation shall comply with the requirements of division (K) of this section.

(L) The director of job and family services shall adopt rules in accordance with Chapter 119. of the Revised Code to implement this section. The department of job and family services may enter into a plan of cooperation with any other governmental entity to aid in ensuring that children are protected from abuse and neglect. The department shall make recommendations to the attorney general that the department determines are necessary to protect children from child abuse and child neglect.

(M)(1) As used in this division:

(a) "Out–of–home care" includes a nonchartered nonpublic school if the alleged child abuse or child neglect, or alleged threat of child abuse or child neglect, described in a report received by a public children services agency allegedly occurred in or involved the nonchartered nonpublic school and the alleged perpetrator named in the report holds a certificate, permit, or license issued by the state board of education under section 3301.071 or Chapter 3319. of the Revised Code.

(b) "Administrator, director, or other chief administrative officer" means the superintendent of the school district if the out-of-home care entity subject to a report made pursuant to this section is a school operated by the district.

(2) No later than the end of the day following the day on which a public children services agency receives a report of alleged child abuse or child neglect, or a report of an alleged threat of child abuse or child neglect, that allegedly occurred in or involved an out-of-home care entity, the agency shall provide written notice of the allegations contained in and the person named as the alleged perpetrator in the report to the administrator, director, or other chief administrative officer of the out-of-home care entity that is the subject of the report unless the administrator, director, or other chief administrative officer is named as an alleged perpetrator in the report. If the administrator, director, or other chief administrative officer of an out-of-home care entity is named as an alleged perpetrator in a report of alleged child abuse or child neglect, or a report of an alleged threat of child abuse or child neglect, that allegedly occurred in or involved the out-of-home care entity, the agency shall provide the written notice to the owner or governing board of the out-of-home care entity that is the subject of the report. The agency shall not provide witness statements or police or other investigative reports.

(3) No later than three days after the day on which a public children services agency that conducted the investigation as determined pursuant to section 2151.422 of the Revised Code makes a disposition of an investigation involving a report of alleged child abuse or child neglect, or a report of an alleged threat of child abuse or child neglect, that allegedly occurred in or involved an out-of-home care entity, the agency shall send written notice of the disposition of the investigation to the administrator, director, or other chief administrative officer and the owner or governing board of the out-of-home care entity. The agency shall not provide witness statements or police or other investigative reports.

(2004 S 185, eff. 4–11–05; 2004 H 106, eff. 9–16–04; 2004 S 178, eff. 1–30–04; 2002 S 221, eff. 4–9–03; 2002 H 374, eff. 4–7–03; 2002 H 510, eff. 3–31–03; 2000 H 448, eff. 10–5–00; 1999 H 471, eff. 7–1–00; 1998 H 606, eff. 3–9–99; 1998 S 212, eff. 9–30–98; 1997 H 408, eff. 10–1–97; 1997 H 215, eff. 6–30–97; 1996 S 223, eff. 3–18–97; 1996 S 269, eff. 7–1–96; 1996 H 274, eff. 8–8–96; 1992 H 154, eff. 7–31–92; 1990 S 3, H 44; 1989 H 257; 1986 H 529, H 528; 1985 H 349; 1984 S 321; 1977 H 219; 1975 H 85; 1969 H 338, S 49; 131 v H 218; 130 v H 765)

Note: See also following version, eff. 5–6–05.

2151.421 Persons required to report injury or neglect; procedures on receipt of report (later effective date)

Note: See also preceding version, in effect until 5–6–05.

(A)(1)(a) No person described in division (A)(1)(b) of this section who is acting in an official or professional capacity and knows or suspects that a child under eighteen years of age or a mentally retarded, developmentally disabled, or physically impaired child under twenty-one years of age has suffered or faces a threat of suffering any physical or mental wound, injury, disability, or condition of a nature that reasonably indicates abuse or neglect of the child, shall fail to immediately report that knowledge or suspicion to the entity or persons specified in this division. Except as provided in section 5120.173 of the Revised Code, the person making the report shall make it to the public children services agency or a municipal or county peace officer in the county in which the child resides or in which the abuse or neglect is occurring or has occurred. In the circumstances described in section 5120.173 of the Revised Code, the person making the report shall make it to the entity specified in that section.

(b) Division (A)(1)(a) of this section applies to any person who is an attorney; physician, including a hospital intern or resident; dentist; podiatrist; practitioner of a limited branch of medicine as specified in section 4731.15 of the Revised Code; registered nurse; licensed practical nurse; visiting nurse; other health care professional; licensed psychologist; licensed school psychologist; independent marriage and family therapist or marriage and family therapist; speech pathologist or audiologist; coroner; administrator or employee of a child day-care center; administrator or employee of a residential camp or child day camp; administrator or employee of a certified child care agency or other public or private children services agency; school teacher; school employee; school authority; person engaged in social work or the practice of professional counseling; agent of a county humane society; person rendering spiritual treatment through prayer in accordance with the tenets of a well-recognized religion; superintendent, board member, or employee of a county board of mental retardation; investigative agent contracted with by a county board of mental retardation; or employee of the department of mental retardation and developmental disabilities.

(2) An attorney or a physician is not required to make a report pursuant to division (A)(1) of this section concerning any communication the attorney or physician receives from a client or patient in an attorney-client or physician-patient relationship, if, in accordance with division (A) or (B) of section 2317.02 of the Revised Code, the attorney or physician could not testify with respect to that communication in a civil or criminal proceeding, except that the client or patient is deemed to have waived any testimonial privilege under division (A) or (B) of section 2317.02 of the Revised Code with respect to that communication and the attorney or physician shall make a report pursuant to division (A)(1) of this section with respect to that communication, if all of the following apply:

(a) The client or patient, at the time of the communication, is either a child under eighteen years of age or a mentally retarded, developmentally disabled, or physically impaired person under twenty-one years of age.

(b) The attorney or physician knows or suspects, as a result of the communication or any observations made during that communication, that the client or patient has suffered or faces a threat of suffering any physical or mental wound, injury, disability, or condition of a nature that reasonably indicates abuse or neglect of the client or patient.

(c) The attorney-client or physician-patient relationship does not arise out of the client's or patient's attempt to have an abortion without the notification of her parents, guardian, or custodian in accordance with section 2151.85 of the Revised Code.

(B) Anyone, who knows or suspects that a child under eighteen years of age or a mentally retarded, developmentally disabled, or physically impaired person under twenty-one years of age has suffered or faces a threat of suffering any physical or mental wound, injury, disability, or other condition of a nature that reasonably indicates abuse or neglect of the child may report or cause reports to be made of that knowledge or suspicion to the entity or persons specified in this division. Except as provided in section 5120.173 of the Revised Code, a person making a report or causing a report to be made under this division shall make it or cause it to be made to the public children services agency or to a municipal or county peace officer. In the circumstances described in section 5120.173 of the Revised Code, a person making a report or causing a report to be made under this division shall make it or cause it to be made to the entity specified in that section.

(C) Any report made pursuant to division (A) or (B) of this section shall be made forthwith either by telephone or in person and shall be followed by a written report, if requested by the receiving agency or officer. The written report shall contain:

(1) The names and addresses of the child and the child's parents or the person or persons having custody of the child, if known;

(2) The child's age and the nature and extent of the child's known or suspected injuries, abuse, or neglect or of the known or suspected threat of injury, abuse, or neglect, including any evidence of previous injuries, abuse, or neglect;

(3) Any other information that might be helpful in establishing the cause of the known or suspected injury, abuse, or neglect or of the known or suspected threat of injury, abuse, or neglect.

Any person, who is required by division (A) of this section to report known or suspected child abuse or child neglect, may take or cause to be taken color photographs of areas of trauma visible on a child and, if medically indicated, cause to be performed radiological examinations of the child.

(D) As used in this division, "children's advocacy center" and "sexual abuse of a child" have the same meanings as in section 2151.425 of the Revised Code.

(1) When a municipal or county peace officer receives a report concerning the possible abuse or neglect of a child or the possible threat of abuse or neglect of a child, upon receipt of the report, the municipal or county peace officer who receives the report shall refer the report to the appropriate public children services agency.

(2) When a public children services agency receives a report pursuant to this division or division (A) or (B) of this section, upon receipt of the report, the public children services agency shall do both of the following:

(a) Comply with section 2151.422 of the Revised Code;

(b) If the county served by the agency is also served by a children's advocacy center and the report alleges sexual abuse of a child or another type of abuse of a child that is specified in the memorandum of understanding that creates the center as being within the center's jurisdiction, comply regarding the report with the protocol and procedures for referrals and investigations, with the coordinating activities, and with the authority or responsibility for performing or providing functions, activities, and services stipulated in the interagency agreement entered into under section 2151.428 of the Revised Code relative to that center.

(E) No township, municipal, or county peace officer shall remove a child about whom a report is made pursuant to this section from the child's parents, stepparents, or guardian or any other persons having custody of the child without consultation with the public children services agency, unless, in the judgment of the officer, and, if the report was made by physician, the physician, immediate removal is considered essential to protect the child from further abuse or neglect. The agency that must be consulted shall be the agency conducting the investigation of the report as determined pursuant to section 2151.422 of the Revised Code.

(F)(1) Except as provided in section 2151.422 of the Revised Code or in an interagency agreement entered into under section 2151.428 of the Revised Code that applies to the particular report, the public children services agency shall investigate, within twenty-four hours, each report of known or suspected child abuse or child neglect and of a known or suspected threat of child abuse or child neglect that is referred to it under this section to determine the circumstances surrounding the injuries, abuse, or neglect or the threat of injury, abuse, or neglect, the cause of the injuries, abuse, neglect, or threat, and the person or persons responsible. The investigation shall be made in cooperation with the law enforcement agency and in accordance with the memorandum of understanding prepared under division (J) of this section. A representative of the public children services agency shall, at the time of initial contact with the person subject to the investigation, inform the person of the specific complaints or allegations made against the person. The information shall be given in a manner that is consistent with division (H)(1) of this section and protects the rights of the person making the report under this section.

A failure to make the investigation in accordance with the memorandum is not grounds for, and shall not result in, the dismissal of any charges or complaint arising from the report or the suppression of any evidence obtained as a result of the report and does not give, and shall not be construed as giving, any rights or any grounds for appeal or post-conviction relief to any person. The public children services agency shall report each case to a central registry which the department of job and family services shall maintain in order to determine whether prior reports have been made in other counties concerning the child or other principals in the case. The public children services agency shall submit a report of its investigation, in writing, to the law enforcement agency.

(2) The public children services agency shall make any recommendations to the county prosecuting attorney or city director of law that it considers necessary to protect any children that are brought to its attention.

(G)(1)(a) Except as provided in division (H)(3) of this section, anyone or any hospital, institution, school, health department, or agency participating in the making of reports under division (A) of this section, anyone or any hospital, institution, school, health department, or agency participating in good faith in the making of reports under division (B) of this section, and anyone participating in good faith in a judicial proceeding resulting from the reports, shall be immune from any civil or criminal liability for injury, death, or loss to person or property that otherwise might be incurred or imposed as a result of the making of the reports or the participation in the judicial proceeding.

(b) Notwithstanding section 4731.22 of the Revised Code, the physician-patient privilege shall not be a ground for excluding evidence regarding a child's injuries, abuse, or neglect, or the cause of the injuries, abuse, or neglect in any judicial proceeding resulting from a report submitted pursuant to this section.

(2) In any civil or criminal action or proceeding in which it is alleged and proved that participation in the making of a report under this section was not in good faith or participation in a judicial proceeding resulting from a report made under this section was not in good faith, the court shall award the prevailing party reasonable attorney's fees and costs and, if a civil action or proceeding is voluntarily dismissed, may award reasonable attorney's fees and costs to the party against whom the civil action or proceeding is brought.

(H)(1) Except as provided in divisions (H)(4) and (M) of this section, a report made under this section is confidential. The information provided in a report made pursuant to this section and the name of the person who made the report shall not be released for use, and shall not be used, as evidence in any civil action or proceeding brought against the person who made the report. In a criminal proceeding, the report is admissible in evidence in accordance with the Rules of Evidence and is subject to discovery in accordance with the Rules of Criminal Procedure.

(2) No person shall permit or encourage the unauthorized dissemination of the contents of any report made under this section.

(3) A person who knowingly makes or causes another person to make a false report under division (B) of this section that alleges that any person has committed an act or omission that resulted in a child being an abused child or a neglected child is guilty of a violation of section 2921.14 of the Revised Code.

(4) If a report is made pursuant to division (A) or (B) of this section and the child who is the subject of the report dies for any reason at any time after the report is made, but before the child attains eighteen years of age, the public children services agency or municipal or county peace officer to which the report was made or referred, on the request of the child fatality review board, shall submit a summary sheet of information providing a summary of the report to the review board of the county in which the deceased child resided at the time of death. On the request of the review board, the agency or peace officer may, at its discretion, make the report available to the review board. If the county served by the public children services agency is also served by a children's advocacy center and the report of alleged sexual abuse of a child or another type of abuse of a child is specified in the memorandum of understanding that creates the center as being within the center's jurisdiction, the agency or center shall perform the duties and functions specified in this division in accordance with the interagency agreement entered into under section 2151.428 of the Revised Code relative to that advocacy center.

(5) A public children services agency shall advise a person alleged to have inflicted abuse or neglect on a child who is the subject of a report made pursuant to this section, including a report alleging sexual abuse of a child or another type of abuse of a child referred to a children's advocacy center pursuant to an interagency agreement entered into under section 2151.428 of the Revised Code, in writing of the disposition of the investigation. The agency shall not provide to the person any information that identifies the person who made the report, statements of witnesses, or police or other investigative reports.

(I) Any report that is required by this section, other than a report that is made to the state highway patrol as described in section 5120.173 of the Revised Code, shall result in protective services and emergency supportive services being made available by the public children services agency on behalf of the children about whom the report is made, in an effort to prevent further neglect or abuse, to enhance their welfare, and, whenever possible, to preserve the family unit intact. The agency required to provide the services shall be the agency conducting the investigation of the report pursuant to section 2151.422 of the Revised Code.

(J)(1) Each public children services agency shall prepare a memorandum of understanding that is signed by all of the following:

(a) If there is only one juvenile judge in the county, the juvenile judge of the county or the juvenile judge's representative;

(b) If there is more than one juvenile judge in the county, a juvenile judge or the juvenile judges' representative selected by the juvenile judges or, if they are unable to do so for any reason, the juvenile judge who is senior in point of service or the senior juvenile judge's representative;

(c) The county peace officer;

(d) All chief municipal peace officers within the county;

(e) Other law enforcement officers handling child abuse and neglect cases in the county;

(f) The prosecuting attorney of the county;

(g) If the public children services agency is not the county department of job and family services, the county department of job and family services;

(h) The county humane society;

(i) If the public children services agency participated in the execution of a memorandum of understanding under section 2151.426 of the Revised Code establishing a children's advocacy center, each participating member of the children's advocacy center established by the memorandum.

(2) A memorandum of understanding shall set forth the normal operating procedure to be employed by all concerned officials in the execution of their respective responsibilities under this section and division (C) of section 2919.21, division (B)(1) of section 2919.22, division (B) of section 2919.23, and section 2919.24 of the Revised Code and shall have as two of its primary goals the elimination of all unnecessary interviews of children who are the subject of reports made pursuant to division (A) or (B) of this section and, when feasible, providing for only one interview of a child who is the subject of any report made pursuant to division (A) or (B) of this section. A failure to follow the procedure set forth in the memorandum by the concerned officials is not grounds for, and shall not result in, the dismissal of any charges or complaint arising from any reported case of abuse or neglect or the suppression of any evidence obtained as a result of any reported child abuse or child neglect and does not give, and shall not be construed as giving, any rights or any grounds for appeal or post-conviction relief to any person.

(3) A memorandum of understanding shall include all of the following:

(a) The roles and responsibilities for handling emergency and nonemergency cases of abuse and neglect;

(b) Standards and procedures to be used in handling and coordinating investigations of reported cases of child abuse and reported cases of child neglect, methods to be used in interviewing the child who is the subject of the report and who allegedly was abused or neglected, and standards and procedures addressing the categories of persons who may interview the child who is the subject of the report and who allegedly was abused or neglected.

(4) If a public children services agency participated in the execution of a memorandum of understanding under section 2151.426 of the Revised Code establishing a children's advocacy center, the agency shall incorporate the contents of that memorandum in the memorandum prepared pursuant to this section.

(K)(1) Except as provided in division (K)(4) of this section, a person who is required to make a report pursuant to division (A) of this section may make a reasonable number of requests of the public children services agency that receives or is referred the report, or of the children's advocacy center that is referred the report if the report is referred to a children's advocacy center pursuant to an interagency agreement entered into under section 2151.428 of the Revised Code, to be provided with the following information:

(a) Whether the agency or center has initiated an investigation of the report;

(b) Whether the agency or center is continuing to investigate the report;

(c) Whether the agency or center is otherwise involved with the child who is the subject of the report;

(d) The general status of the health and safety of the child who is the subject of the report;

(e) Whether the report has resulted in the filing of a complaint in juvenile court or of criminal charges in another court.

(2) A person may request the information specified in division (K)(1) of this section only if, at the time the report is made, the person's name, address, and telephone number are provided to the person who receives the report.

When a municipal or county peace officer or employee of a public children services agency receives a report pursuant to division (A) or (B) of this section the recipient of the report shall inform the person of the right to request the information described in division (K)(1) of this section. The recipient of the report shall include in the initial child abuse or child neglect report that the person making the report was so informed and, if provided at the time of the making of the report, shall include the person's name, address, and telephone number in the report.

Each request is subject to verification of the identity of the person making the report. If that person's identity is verified, the agency shall provide the person with the information described in division (K)(1) of this section a reasonable number of times, except that the agency shall not disclose any confidential information regarding the child who is the subject of the report other than the information described in those divisions.

(3) A request made pursuant to division (K)(1) of this section is not a substitute for any report required to be made pursuant to division (A) of this section.

(4) If an agency other than the agency that received or was referred the report is conducting the investigation of the report pursuant to section 2151.422 of the Revised Code, the agency conducting the investigation shall comply with the requirements of division (K) of this section.

(L) The director of job and family services shall adopt rules in accordance with Chapter 119. of the Revised Code to implement this section. The department of job and family services may enter into a plan of cooperation with any other governmental entity to aid in ensuring that children are protected from abuse and neglect. The department shall make recommendations to the attorney general that the department determines are necessary to protect children from child abuse and child neglect.

(M)(1) As used in this division:

(a) "Out-of-home care" includes a nonchartered nonpublic school if the alleged child abuse or child neglect, or alleged threat of child abuse or child neglect, described in a report received by a public children services agency allegedly occurred in or involved the nonchartered nonpublic school and the alleged perpetrator named in the report holds a certificate, permit, or license issued by the state board of education under section 3301.071 or Chapter 3319. of the Revised Code.

(b) "Administrator, director, or other chief administrative officer" means the superintendent of the school district if the out-of-home care entity subject to a report made pursuant to this section is a school operated by the district.

(2) No later than the end of the day following the day on which a public children services agency receives a report of alleged child abuse or child neglect, or a report of an alleged threat of child abuse or child neglect, that allegedly occurred in or involved an out-of-home care entity, the agency shall provide written notice of the allegations contained in and the person named as the alleged perpetrator in the report to the administrator, director, or other chief administrative officer of the out-of-home care entity that is the subject of the report unless the administrator, director, or other chief administrative officer is named as an alleged perpetrator in the report. If the administrator, director, or other chief administrative officer of an out-of-home care entity is named as an alleged perpetrator in a report of alleged child abuse or child neglect, or a report of an alleged threat of child abuse or child neglect, that allegedly occurred in or involved the out-of-home care entity, the agency shall provide the written notice to the owner or governing board of the out-of-home care entity that is the subject of the report. The agency shall not provide witness statements or police or other investigative reports.

(3) No later than three days after the day on which a public children services agency that conducted the investigation as determined pursuant to section 2151.422 of the Revised Code makes a disposition of an investigation involving a report of alleged child abuse or child neglect, or a report of an alleged threat of child abuse or child neglect, that allegedly occurred in or involved an out-of-home care entity, the agency shall send written notice of the disposition of the investigation to the administrator, director, or other chief administrative officer and the owner or governing board of the out-of-home care entity. The agency shall not

provide witness statements or police or other investigative reports.

(2004 S 66, eff. 5–6–05; 2004 S 185, eff. 4–11–05; 2004 H 106, eff. 9–16–04; 2004 S 178, eff. 1–30–04; 2002 S 221, eff. 4–9–03; 2002 H 374, eff. 4–7–03; 2002 H 510, eff. 3–31–03; 2000 H 448, eff. 10–5–00; 1999 H 471, eff. 7–1–00; 1998 H 606, eff. 3–9–99; 1998 S 212, eff. 9–30–98; 1997 H 408, eff. 10–1–97; 1997 H 215, eff. 6–30–97; 1996 S 223, eff. 3–18–97; 1996 S 269, eff. 7–1–96; 1996 H 274, eff. 8–8–96; 1992 H 154, eff. 7–31–92; 1990 S 3, H 44; 1989 H 257; 1986 H 529, H 528; 1985 H 349; 1984 S 321; 1977 H 219; 1975 H 85; 1969 H 338, S 49; 131 v H 218; 130 v H 765)

Note: See also preceding version, in effect until 5–6–05.

2151.422 Investigations concerning children in domestic violence or homeless shelters; services; custody; confidentiality of information

(A) As used in this section, "homeless shelter" means a facility that provides accommodations to homeless individuals.

(B) On receipt of a notice pursuant to division (A), (B), or (D) of section 2151.421 of the Revised Code, the public children services agency shall determine whether the child subject to the report is living in a shelter for victims of domestic violence or a homeless shelter and whether the child was brought to that shelter pursuant to an agreement with a shelter in another county. If the child is living in a shelter and was brought there from another county, the agency shall immediately notify the public children services agency of the county from which the child was brought of the report and all the information contained in the report. On receipt of the notice pursuant to this division, the agency of the county from which the child was brought shall conduct the investigation of the report required pursuant to section 2151.421 of the Revised Code and shall perform all duties required of the agency under this chapter with respect to the child who is the subject of the report. If the child is not living in a shelter or the child was not brought to the shelter from another county, the agency that received the report pursuant to division (A), (B), or (D) of section 2151.421 of the Revised Code shall conduct the investigation required pursuant to section 2151.421 of the Revised Code and shall perform all duties required of the agency under this chapter with respect to the child who is the subject of the report. The agency of the county in which the shelter is located in which the child is living and the agency of the county from which the child was brought may ask the shelter to provide information concerning the child's residence address and county of residence to the agency.

(C) If a child is living in a shelter for victims of domestic violence or a homeless shelter and the child was brought to that shelter pursuant to an agreement with a shelter in another county, the public children services agency of the county from which the child was brought shall provide services to or take custody of the child if services or custody are needed or required under this chapter or section 5153.16 of the Revised Code.

(D) When a homeless shelter provides accommodations to a person, the shelter, on admitting the person to the shelter, shall determine, if possible, the person's last known residential address and county of residence. The information concerning the address and county of residence is confidential and may only be released to a public children services agency pursuant to this section.

(1997 H 215, eff. 6–30–97)

2151.424 Notice of dispositional hearings

(A) If a child has been placed in a certified foster home or is in the custody of a relative of the child, other than a parent of the child, a court, prior to conducting any hearing pursuant to division (E)(2) or (3) of section 2151.412 or section 2151.28, 2151.33, 2151.35, 2151.414, 2151.415, 2151.416, or 2151.417 of the Revised Code with respect to the child, shall notify the foster caregiver or relative of the date, time, and place of the hearing. At the hearing, the foster caregiver or relative may present evidence.

(B) If a public children services agency or private child placing agency has permanent custody of a child and a petition to adopt the child has been filed under Chapter 3107. of the Revised Code, the agency, prior to conducting a review under section 2151.416 of the Revised Code, or a court, prior to conducting a hearing under division (E)(2) or (3) of section 2151.412 or section 2151.416 or 2151.417 of the Revised Code, shall notify the prospective adoptive parent of the date, time, and place of the review or hearing. At the review or hearing, the prospective adoptive parent may present evidence.

(C) The notice and the opportunity to present evidence do not make the foster caregiver, relative, or prospective adoptive parent a party in the action or proceeding pursuant to which the review or hearing is conducted.

(2000 H 448, eff. 10–5–00; 1998 H 484, eff. 3–18–99)

CHILDREN'S ADVOCACY CENTERS

2151.425 Definitions

As used in sections 2151.426 to 2151.428 of the Revised Code:

(A) "Children's advocacy center" means a center operated by participating entities within a county or two or more contiguous counties to perform functions and activities and provide services, in accordance with the interagency agreement entered into under section 2151.428 of the Revised Code, regarding reports received under section 2151.421 of the Revised Code of alleged sexual abuse of a child or another type of abuse of a child that is specified in the memorandum of understanding that creates the center as being within the center's jurisdiction and regarding the children who are the subjects of the report.

(B) "Sexual abuse of a child" means unlawful sexual conduct or sexual contact, as those terms are defined in section 2907.01 of the Revised Code, with a person under eighteen years of age or a mentally retarded, developmentally disabled, or physically impaired person under twenty-one years of age.

(2004 S 66, eff. 5–6–05)

2151.426 Children's advocacy center; memorandum of understanding with other entities regarding child abuse

(A)(1) A children's advocacy center may be established to serve a single county by execution of a memorandum of understanding regarding the participation in the operation of the center by any of the following entities in the county to be served by the center:

(a) The public children services agency;

(b) Representatives of any county or municipal law enforcement agencies serving the county that investigate any of the types of abuse specified in the memorandum of understanding creating the center as being within the center's jurisdiction;

(c) The prosecuting attorney of the county or a village solicitor, city director of law, or similar chief legal officer of a municipal corporation in the county who prosecutes any of the types of abuse specified in the memorandum of understanding creating the center as being within the center's jurisdiction in the area to be served by the center;

(d) Any other entity considered appropriate by all of the other entities executing the memorandum.

(2) A children's advocacy center may be established to serve two or more contiguous counties if a memorandum of understanding regarding the participation in the operation of the center is executed by any of the entities described in division (A)(1) of this section in each county to be served by the center.

(3) Any memorandum of understanding executed under this section may include a provision that specifies types of abuse of a child, in addition to sexual abuse of a child, that are to be within the jurisdiction of the children's advocacy center created as a result of the execution of the memorandum. If a memorandum of understanding executed under this section does not include any provision of that nature, the children's advocacy center created as a result of the execution of the memorandum has jurisdiction only in relation to reports of alleged sexual abuse of a child.

(B) Each entity that participates in the execution of a memorandum of understanding under this section shall cooperate in all of the following:

(1) Developing a multidisciplinary team pursuant to section 2151.427 of the Revised Code to perform the functions and activities and provide the services specified in the interagency agreement entered into under section 2151.428 of the Revised Code, regarding reports received under section 2151.421 of the Revised Code of alleged sexual abuse of a child and reports of allegations of another type of abuse of a child that is specified in the memorandum of understanding that creates the center as being within the center's jurisdiction, and regarding the children who are the subjects of the reports;

(2) Participating in the operation of the center in compliance with standards for full membership established by the national children's alliance;

(3) Employing the center's staff.

(C) A center shall do both of the following:

(1) Operate in accordance with sections 2151.427 and 2151.428 of the Revised Code, the interagency agreement entered into under section 2151.428 of the Revised Code relative to the center, and the standards for full membership established by the national children's alliance;

(2) Register annually with the attorney general.

(2004 S 66, eff. 5–6–05)

2151.427 Multidisciplinary team; members; powers and duties

(A) The entities that participate in a memorandum of understanding executed under section 2151.426 of the Revised Code establishing a children's advocacy center shall assemble the center's multidisciplinary team.

(B)(1) The multidisciplinary team for a single county center shall consist of the following members who serve the county:

(a) Any county or municipal law enforcement officer;

(b) The executive director of the public children services agency or a designee of the executive director;

(c) The prosecuting attorney of the county or the prosecuting attorney's designee;

(d) A mental health professional;

(e) A medical health professional;

(f) A victim advocate;

(g) A center staff member;

(h) Any other person considered appropriate by all of the entities that executed the memorandum.

(2) If the center serves two or more contiguous counties, the multidisciplinary team shall consist of the members described in division (B)(1) of this section from the counties to be served by the center, with each county to be served by the center being represented on the multidisciplinary team by at least one member described in that division.

(C) The multidisciplinary team shall perform the functions and activities and provide the services specified in the interagency agreement entered into under section 2151.428 of the Revised Code, regarding reports received under section 2151.421 of the Revised Code of alleged sexual abuse of a child and reports of allegations of another type of abuse of a child that is specified in the memorandum of understanding that creates the center as being within the center's jurisdiction and regarding the children who are the subjects of the reports.

(2004 S 66, eff. 5–6–05)

2151.428 Interagency agreements relating to child abuse

(A) If a children's advocacy center is established under section 2151.426 of the Revised Code, in addition to the memorandum of understanding executed under that section, each public children services agency that participates in the execution of the memorandum of understanding, the children's advocacy center, and the children's advocacy center's multidisciplinary team assembled under section 2151.427 of the Revised Code shall enter into an interagency agreement that stipulates all of the following regarding reports received under section 2151.421 of the Revised Code of alleged sexual abuse of a child and reports of allegations of another type of abuse of a child that is specified in the memorandum of understanding that creates the center as being within the center's jurisdiction:

(1) The protocol and procedures for any and all referrals and investigations of the reports;

(2) Any and all coordinating activities between the parties that enter into the agreement;

(3) The authority or responsibility for performing any and all functions and activities, and providing any and all services, regarding the reports and the children who are the subjects of the reports.

(B) The parties that enter into an interagency agreement under division (A) of this section shall comply with the agreement in referring the reports, investigating the reports, coordinating the activities between the parties, and performing and providing the functions, activities, and services relative to the reports and the children who are the subjects of the reports.

(C) Nothing in this section, section 2151.421, or sections 2151.425 to 2151.427 of the Revised Code pertaining to the operation of a children's advocacy center shall relieve any public official or agency from any legal obligation or responsibility.

(2004 S 66, eff. 5–6–05)

ADULT CASES

2151.43 Charges against adults; defendant bound over to grand jury

In cases against an adult under sections 2151.01 to 2151.54 of the Revised Code, any person may file an affidavit with the clerk of the juvenile court setting forth briefly, in plain and ordinary language, the charges against the accused who shall be tried thereon. When the child is a recipient of aid pursuant to Chapter 5107. or 5115. of the Revised Code, the county department of job and family services shall file charges against any person who fails to provide support to a child in violation of section 2919.21 of the Revised Code, unless the department files charges under section 3113.06 of the Revised Code, or unless charges of nonsupport are filed by a relative or guardian of the child, or unless action to enforce support is brought under Chapter 3115. of the Revised Code.

In such prosecution an indictment by the grand jury or information by the prosecuting attorney shall not be required. The clerk shall issue a warrant for the arrest of the accused, who, when arrested, shall be taken before the juvenile judge and tried according to such sections.

The affidavit may be amended at any time before or during the trial.

The judge may bind such adult over to the grand jury, where the act complained of constitutes a felony.

(1999 H 471, eff. 7–1–00; 1995 H 249, eff. 7–17–95; 1991 H 298, eff. 7–26–91; 1986 H 428; 1972 H 511; 1969 H 361; 132 v H 390; 127 v 847; 1953 H 1; GC 1639–39)

2151.44 Complaint after hearing

If it appears at the hearing of a child that any person has abused or has aided, induced, caused, encouraged, or contributed to the dependency, neglect, or delinquency of a child or acted in a way tending to cause delinquency in such child, or that a person charged with the care, support, education, or maintenance of any child has failed to support or sufficiently contribute toward the support, education, and maintenance of such child, the juvenile judge may order a complaint filed against such person and proceed to hear and dispose of the case as provided in sections 2151.01 to 2151.54, inclusive, of the Revised Code.

On the request of the judge, the prosecuting attorney shall prosecute all adults charged with violating such sections.

(1953 H 1, eff. 10–1–53; GC 1639–40, 1639–42)

2151.49 Suspension of sentence

In every case of conviction under sections 2151.01 to 2151.54 of the Revised Code, where imprisonment is imposed as part of the punishment, the juvenile judge may suspend sentence, before or during commitment, upon such condition as the juvenile judge imposes. In the case of conviction for nonsupport of a child who is receiving aid under Chapter 5107. or 5115. of the Revised Code, if the juvenile judge suspends sentence on condition that the person make payments for support, the payment shall be made to the county department of job and family services rather than to the child or custodian of the child.

The court, in accordance with sections 3119.29 to 3119.56 of the Revised Code, shall include in each support order made under this section the requirement that one or both of the parents provide for the health care needs of the child to the satisfaction of the court.

(2002 H 657, eff. 12–13–02; 2000 S 180, eff. 3–22–01; 1999 H 471, eff. 7-1-00; 1997 H 352, eff. 1–1–98; 1995 H 249, eff. 7–17–95; 1991 H 298, eff. 7–26–91; 1986 H 428; 132 v H 390; 1953 H 1; GC 1639–49)

2151.50 Forfeiture of bond

When, as a condition of suspension of sentence under section 2151.49 of the Revised Code, bond is required and given, upon the failure of a person giving such bond to comply with the conditions thereof, such bond may be forfeited, the suspension terminated by the juvenile judge, the original sentence executed as though it had not been suspended, and the term of any sentence imposed in such case shall commence from the date of imprisonment of such person after such forfeiture and termination of suspension. Any part of such sentence which may have been served shall be deducted from any such period of imprisonment. When such bond is forfeited the judge may issue execution thereon without further proceedings.

(1953 H 1, eff. 10–1–53; GC 1639–50)

2151.52 Appeals on questions of law

The sections of the Revised Code and rules relating to appeals on questions of law from the court of common pleas shall apply to prosecutions of adults under this chapter, and from such prosecutions an appeal on a question of law may be taken to the court of appeals of the county under laws or rules governing appeals in other criminal cases to such court of appeals.

(1986 H 412, eff. 3–17–87; 129 v 290; 1953 H 1; GC 1639–51)

2151.53 Physical and mental examinations; records of examination; expenses

Any person coming within sections 2151.01 to 2151.54 of the Revised Code may be subjected to a physical examination by competent physicians, physician assistants, clinical nurse specialists, and certified nurse practitioners, and a mental examination by competent psychologists, psychiatrists, and clinical nurse specialists that practice the specialty of mental health or psychiatric mental health to be appointed by the juvenile court. Whenever any child is committed to any institution by virtue of such sections, a record of such examinations shall be sent with the commitment to such institution. The compensation of such physicians, physician assistants, clinical nurse specialists, certified nurse practitioners, psychologists, and psychiatrists and the expenses of such examinations shall be paid by the county treasurer upon specifically itemized vouchers, certified by the juvenile judge.

(2002 S 245, eff. 3–31–03; 1953 H 1, eff. 10–1–53; GC 1639–54)

FEES AND COSTS

2151.54 Fees and costs; waiver

The juvenile court shall tax and collect the same fees and costs as are allowed the clerk of the court of common pleas for similar services. No fees or costs shall be taxed in cases of delinquent, unruly, dependent, abused, or neglected children except as required by section 2743.70 or 2949.091 of the Revised Code or when specifically ordered by the court. The expense of transportation of children to places to which they have been committed, and the transportation of children to and from another state by police or other officers, acting upon order of the court, shall be paid from the county treasury upon specifically itemized vouchers certified to by the judge.

If a child is adjudicated to be a delinquent child or a juvenile traffic offender and the juvenile court specifically is required, by section 2743.70 or 2949.091 of the Revised Code or any other section of the Revised Code, to impose a specified sum of money as court costs in addition to any other court costs that the court is required or permitted by law to impose, the court shall not waive the payment of the specified additional court costs that the section of the Revised Code specifically requires the court to impose unless the court determines that the child is indigent and the court either waives the payment of all court costs or enters an order in its journal stating that no court costs are to be taxed in the case.

(1990 S 131, eff. 7–25–90; 1980 H 238; 1975 H 85; 1970 H 931; 1953 H 1; GC 1639–56)

2151.541 Additional fees for computer services

(A)(1) The juvenile judge may determine that, for the efficient operation of the juvenile court, additional funds are required to computerize the court, to make available computerized legal research services, or both. Upon making a determination that additional funds are required for either or both of those purposes, the judge shall do one of the following:

(a) If he is clerk of the court, charge one additional fee not to exceed three dollars on the filing of each cause of action or appeal under division (A), (Q), or (U) of section 2303.20 of the Revised Code;

(b) If the clerk of the court of common pleas serves as the clerk of the juvenile court pursuant to section 2151.12 of the Revised Code, authorize and direct the clerk to charge one additional fee not to exceed three dollars on the filing of each cause of action or appeal under division (A), (Q), or (U) of section 2303.20 of the Revised Code.

(2) All moneys collected under division (A)(1) of this section shall be paid to the county treasurer. The treasurer shall place the moneys from the fees in a separate fund to be disbursed, upon an order of the juvenile judge, in an amount no greater than the actual cost to the court of procuring and maintaining computerization of the court, computerized legal research services, or both.

(3) If the court determines that the funds in the fund described in division (A)(2) of this section are more than sufficient to satisfy the purpose for which the additional fee described in division (A)(1) of this section was imposed, the court may declare a surplus in the fund and expend those surplus funds for other appropriate technological expenses of the court.

(B)(1) If the juvenile judge is the clerk of the juvenile court, he may determine that, for the efficient operation of his court, additional funds are required to computerize the clerk's office and, upon that determination, may charge an additional fee, not to exceed ten dollars, on the filing of each cause of action or appeal, on the filing, docketing, and endorsing of each certificate of judgment, or on the docketing and indexing of each aid in execution or petition to vacate, revive, or modify a judgment under divisions (A), (P), (Q), (T), and (U) of section 2303.20 of the Revised Code. Subject to division (B)(2) of this section, all moneys collected under this division shall be paid to the county treasurer to be disbursed, upon an order of the juvenile judge and subject to appropriation by the board of county commissioners, in an amount no greater than the actual cost to the juvenile court of procuring and maintaining computer systems for the clerk's office.

(2) If the juvenile judge makes the determination described in division (B)(1) of this section, the board of county commissioners may issue one or more general obligation bonds for the purpose of procuring and maintaining the computer systems for the office of the clerk of the juvenile court. In addition to the purposes stated in division (B)(1) of this section for which the moneys collected under that division may be expended, the moneys additionally may be expended to pay debt charges on and financing costs related to any general obligation bonds issued pursuant to this division as they become due. General obligation bonds issued pursuant to this division are Chapter 133. securities.

(1992 S 246, eff. 3–24–93; 1992 H 405)

PLACEMENT OF CHILDREN IN FOSTER HOMES OUTSIDE COUNTIES OF RESIDENCE

2151.55 Persons entitled to oral communication of intended placement

When a private or governmental entity intends to place a child in a certified foster home in a county other than the county in which the child resided at the time of being removed from home, a representative of the placing entity shall orally communicate the intended placement to the foster caregiver with whom the child is to be placed and, if the child will attend the schools of the district in which the certified foster home is located, a representative of the school district's board of education.

(2000 H 332, eff. 1–1–01; 2000 H 448, eff. 10–5–00; 1999 H 283, eff. 9–29–99)

2151.551 Requirements of oral communication of intended placement

During the oral communication described in section 2151.55 of the Revised Code, the representative of the placing entity shall do the following:

(A) Discuss safety and well-being concerns regarding the child and, if the child attends school, the students, teachers, and personnel of the school;

(B) Provide the following information:

(1) A brief description of the reasons the child was removed from home;

(2) Services the child is receiving;

(3) The name of the contact person for the placing entity that is directly responsible for monitoring the child's placement;

(4) The telephone number of the placing entity and, if the child is in the temporary, permanent, or legal custody of a private or government entity other than the placing entity, the telephone number of the entity with custody;

(5) The previous school district attended by the child;

(6) The last known address of the child's parents.

(1999 H 283, eff. 9–29–99)

2151.552 Time for provision of written information

No later than five days after a child described in section 2151.55 of the Revised Code is enrolled in school in the district described in that section, the placing entity shall provide in writing the information described in division (B) of section 2151.551 of the Revised Code to the school district and the child's foster caregiver.

(1999 H 283, eff. 9–29–99)

2151.553 School district procedures for receiving information

Each school district board of education shall implement a procedure for receiving the information described in section 2151.552 of the Revised Code.

(1999 H 283, eff. 9–29–99)

2151.554 Provision of written information to juvenile court

When a private or governmental entity places a child who has been adjudicated to be an unruly or delinquent child in a certified foster home in a county other than the county in which the child resided at the time of being removed from home, the placing entity shall provide the following information in writing to the juvenile court of the county in which the certified foster home is located:

(A) The information listed in divisions (B)(2) to (4) of section 2151.551 of the Revised Code;

(B) A brief description of the facts supporting the adjudication that the child is unruly or delinquent;

(C) The name and address of the foster caregiver;

(D) Safety and well-being concerns with respect to the child and community.

(2000 H 332, eff. 1–1–01; 2000 H 448, eff. 10–5–00; 1999 H 283, eff. 9–29–99)

INTERSTATE COMPACT ON JUVENILES

2151.56 Interstate compact on juveniles

The governor is hereby authorized to execute a compact on behalf of this state with any other state or states legally joining therein in the form substantially as follows:

THE INTERSTATE COMPACT ON JUVENILES

The contracting states solemnly agree:

Article I —Findings and Purposes

That juveniles who are not under proper supervision and control, or who have absconded, escaped or run away, are likely to endanger their own health, morals and welfare, and the health, morals and welfare of others. The cooperation of the states party to this compact is therefore necessary to provide for the welfare and protection of juveniles and of the public with respect to (1) cooperative supervision of delinquent juveniles on probation or parole; (2) the return, from one state to another, of delinquent juveniles who have escaped or absconded; (3) the return, from one state to another, of nondelinquent juveniles who have run away from home; and (4) additional measures for the protection of juveniles and of the public, which any two or more of the party states may find desirable to undertake cooperatively. In carrying out the provisions of this compact the party states shall be guided by the noncriminal, reformative and protective policies which guide their laws concerning delinquent, neglected or dependent juveniles generally. It shall be the policy of the states party to this compact to cooperate and observe their respective responsibilities for the prompt return and acceptance of juveniles and delinquent juveniles who become subject to the provisions of this compact. The provisions of this compact shall be reasonably and liberally construed to accomplish the foregoing purposes.

Article II —Existing Rights and Remedies

That all remedies and procedures provided by this compact shall be in addition to and not in substitution for other rights, remedies and procedures, and shall not be in derogation of parental rights and responsibilities.

Article III —Definitions

That, for the purposes of this compact, "delinquent juvenile" means any juvenile who has been adjudged delinquent and who, at the time the provisions of this compact are invoked, is still subject to the jurisdiction of the court that has made such adjudication or to the jurisdiction or supervision of an agency or institution pursuant to an order of such court; "probation or parole" means any kind of conditional release of juveniles authorized under the laws of the states party hereto; "court" means any court having jurisdiction over delinquent, neglected or dependent children; "state" means any state, territory or possessions of the United States, the District of Columbia, and the Commonwealth of Puerto Rico; and "residence" or any variant thereof means a place at which a home or regular place of abode is maintained.

Article IV —Return of Runaways

(a) That the parent, guardian, person or agency entitled to legal custody of a juvenile who has not been adjudged delinquent but who has run away without the consent of such parent, guardian, person or agency may petition the appropriate court in the demanding state for the issuance of a requisition for his return. The petition shall state the name and age of the juvenile, the name of the petitioner and the basis of entitlement to the juvenile's custody, the circumstances of his running away, his location if known at the time application is made, and such other facts as may tend to show that the juvenile who has run away is endangering his own welfare or the welfare of others and is not an emancipated minor. The petition shall be verified by affidavit, shall be executed in duplicate, and shall be accompanied by two certified copies of the document or documents on which the petitioner's entitlement to the juvenile's custody is based, such as birth records, letters of guardianship, or custody decrees. Such further affidavits and other documents as may be deemed proper may be submitted with such petition. The judge of the court to which this application is made may hold a hearing thereon to determine whether for the purposes of this compact the petitioner is entitled to the legal custody of the juvenile, whether or not it appears that the juvenile has in fact run away without consent, whether or not he is an emancipated minor, and whether or not it is in the best interest of the juvenile to compel his return to the state. If the judge determines, either with or without a hearing, that the juvenile should be returned, he shall present to the appropriate court or to the executive authority of the state where the juvenile is alleged to be located a written requisition for the return of such juvenile. Such requisition shall set forth the name and age of the juvenile, the determination of the court that the juvenile has run away without the consent of a parent, guardian, person or agency entitled to his legal custody, and that it is in the best interest and for the protection of such juvenile that he be returned. In the event that a proceeding for the adjudication of the juvenile as a delinquent, neglected or dependent juvenile is pending in the court at the time when such juvenile runs away, the court may issue a requisition for the return of such juvenile upon its own motion, regardless of the consent of the parent, guardian, person or agency entitled to legal custody, reciting therein the nature and circumstances of the pending proceeding. The requisition shall in every case be executed in duplicate and shall be signed by the judge. One copy of the requisition shall be filed with the compact administrator of the demanding state, there to remain on file subject to the provisions of law governing records of such court. Upon the receipt of a requisition demanding the return of a juvenile who has run away, the court or the executive authority to whom the requisition is addressed shall issue an order to any peace officer or other appropriate person directing him to take into custody and detain such juvenile. Such detention order must substantially recite the facts necessary to the validity of its issuance hereunder. No juvenile detained upon such order shall be delivered over to the officer whom the court demanding him shall have appointed to receive him, unless he shall first be taken forthwith before a judge of a court in the state, who shall inform him of the demand made for his return, and who may appoint counsel or guardian ad litem for him. If the judge of such court shall find that the requisition is in order, he shall deliver such juvenile over to the officer whom the court demanding him shall have appointed to receive him. The judge, however, may fix a reasonable time to be allowed for the purpose of testing the legality of the proceeding.

Upon reasonable information that a person is a juvenile who has run away from another state party to this compact without the consent of a parent, guardian, person or agency entitled to his legal custody, such juvenile may be taken into custody without a requisition and brought forthwith before a judge of the appropriate court who may appoint counsel or guardian ad litem for such juvenile and who shall determine after a hearing whether sufficient cause exists to hold the person, subject to the order of the court, for his own protection and welfare, for such a time not exceeding ninety days as will enable his return to another state party to this compact pursuant to a requisition for his return from a court of that state. If, at the time when a state seeks the return of a juvenile who has run away, there is pending in the state wherein he is found any criminal charge, or any proceeding to have him adjudicated a delinquent juvenile for an act committed in such state, or if he is suspected of having committed within such state a criminal offense or an act of juvenile delinquency, he shall not be returned without the consent of such state until discharged from prosecution or other form of proceeding, imprisonment, detention or supervision for such offense or juvenile delinquency. The duly accredited officers of any state party to this compact, upon the establishment of their authority and the identity of the juvenile being returned, shall be permitted to transport such juvenile through any and all states party to this compact, without interference. Upon his return to the state from which he ran away, the juvenile shall be subject to such further proceedings as may be appropriate under the laws of that state.

(b) That the state to which a juvenile is returned under this Article shall be responsible for payment of the transportation costs of such return.

(c) That "juvenile" as used in this Article means any person who is a minor under the law of the state of residence of the parent, guardian, person or agency entitled to the legal custody of such minor.

Article V —Return of Escapees and Absconders

(a) That the appropriate person or authority from whose probation or parole supervision a delinquent juvenile has absconded or from whose institutional custody he has escaped shall present to the appropriate court or to the executive authority of the state where the delinquent juvenile is alleged to be located a written requisition for the return of such delinquent juvenile. Such requisition shall state the name and age of the delinquent juvenile, the particulars of his adjudication as a delinquent juvenile, the circumstances of the breach of the terms of his probation or parole or of his escape from an institution or agency vested with his legal custody or supervision, and the location of such delinquent juvenile, if known, at the time the requisition is made. The requisition shall be verified by affidavit, shall be executed in duplicate, and shall be accompanied by two certified copies of the judgment, formal adjudication, or order of commitment which subjects such delinquent juvenile to probation or parole or to the legal custody of the institution or agency concerned. Such further affidavits and other documents as may be deemed proper may be submitted with such requisition. One copy of the requisition shall be filed with the compact administrator of the demanding state, there to remain on file subject to the provisions of law governing records of the appropriate court. Upon the receipt of a requisition demanding the return of a delinquent juvenile who has absconded or escaped, the court or the executive authority to whom the requisition is addressed shall issue an order to any peace officer or other appropriate person directing him to take into custody and detain such delinquent juvenile. Such detention order must substantially recite the facts necessary to the validity of its issuance hereunder. No delinquent juvenile detained upon such order shall be delivered over to the officer whom the appropriate person or authority demanding him shall have appointed to receive him, unless he shall first be taken forthwith before a judge of an appropriate court in the state, who shall inform him of the demand made for his return and who may appoint counsel or guardian ad litem for him. If the judge of such court shall find that the requisition is in order, he shall deliver such delinquent juvenile over to the officer whom the appropriate person or authority demanding him shall have appointed to receive him. The judge, however, may fix a reasonable time to be allowed for the purpose of testing the legality of the proceeding.

Upon reasonable information that a person is a delinquent juvenile who has absconded while on probation or parole, or escaped from an institution or agency vested with his legal custody or supervision in any state party to this compact, such person may be taken into custody in any other state party to this compact without a requisition. But in such event, he must be taken forthwith before a judge of the appropriate court, who may appoint counsel or guardian ad litem for such person and who shall determine, after a hearing, whether sufficient cause exists to hold the person subject to the order of the court for such a time, not exceeding ninety days, as will enable his detention under a detention order issued on a requisition pursuant to this Article. If, at the time when a state seeks the return of a delinquent juvenile who has either absconded while on probation or parole or escaped from an institution or agency vested with his legal custody or supervision, there is pending in the state wherein he is detained any criminal charge or any proceeding to have him adjudicated a delinquent juvenile for an act committed in such state, or if he is suspected of having committed within such state a criminal offense or an act of juvenile delinquency, he shall not be returned without the consent of such state until discharged from prosecution or other form of proceeding, imprisonment, detention or supervision for such offense or juvenile delinquency. The duly accredited officers of any state party to this compact, upon the establishment of their authority and the identity of the delinquent juvenile being returned, shall be permitted to transport such delinquent juvenile through any and all states party to this compact, without interference. Upon his return to the state from which he escaped or absconded, the delinquent juvenile shall be subject to such further proceedings as may be appropriate under the laws of that state.

(b) That the state to which a delinquent juvenile is returned under this Article shall be responsible for the payment of the transportation costs of such return.

Article VI —Voluntary Return Procedure

That any delinquent juvenile who has absconded while on probation or parole, or escaped from an institution or agency vested with his legal custody or supervision in any state party to this compact, and any juvenile who has run away from any state party to this compact, who is taken into custody without a requisition in another state party to this compact under the provisions of Article IV (a) or of Article V (a), may consent to his immediate return to the state from which he absconded, escaped or ran away. Such consent shall be given by the juvenile or delinquent juvenile and his counsel or guardian ad litem if any, by executing or subscribing a writing, in the presence of a judge of the appropriate court, which states that the juvenile or delinquent juvenile and his counsel or guardian ad litem, if any, consent to his return to the demanding state. Before such consent shall be executed or subscribed, however, the judge, in the presence of counsel or guardian ad litem, if any, shall inform the juvenile or delinquent juvenile of his rights under this compact. When the consent has been duly executed, it shall be forwarded to and filed with the compact administrator of the state in which the court is located and the judge shall direct the officer having the juvenile or delinquent juvenile in custody to deliver him to the duly accredited officer or officers of the state demanding his return, and shall cause to be delivered to such officer or officers a copy of the consent. The court may, however, upon the request of the state to which the juvenile or delinquent juvenile is being returned, order him to return unaccompanied to such state and shall provide him with a copy of such court order; in such event a copy of the consent shall be forwarded to the compact administrator of the state to which said juvenile or delinquent juvenile is ordered to return.

Article VII —Cooperative Supervision of Probationers and Parolees

(a) That the duly constituted judicial and administrative authorities of a state party to this compact (herein called "sending state") may permit any delinquent juvenile within such state, placed on probation or parole, to reside in any other state party to this compact (herein called "receiving state") while on probation or parole, and the receiving state shall accept such delinquent juvenile, if the parent, guardian or person entitled to the legal custody of such delinquent juvenile is residing or undertakes to reside within the receiving state. Before granting such permission, opportunity shall be given to the receiving state to make such investigations as it deems necessary. The authorities of the sending state shall send to the authorities of the receiving state copies of pertinent court orders, social case studies and all other available information which may be of value to and assist the receiving state in supervising a probationer or parolee under this compact. A receiving state, in its discretion, may agree to accept supervision of a probationer or parolee in cases where the parent, guardian or person entitled to the legal custody of the delinquent juvenile is not a resident of the receiving state, and if so accepted the sending state may transfer supervision accordingly.

(b) That each receiving state will assume the duties of visitation and of supervision over any such delinquent juvenile and in the exercise of those duties will be governed by the same standards of visitation and supervision that prevail for its own delinquent juveniles released on probation or parole.

(c) That, after consultation between the appropriate authorities of the sending state and of the receiving state as to the desirability and necessity of returning such a delinquent juvenile, the duly accredited officers of a sending state may enter a receiving state and there apprehend and retake any such delinquent juvenile on probation or parole. For that purpose, no formalities will be required, other than establishing the authority of the officer and the identity of the delinquent juvenile to be retaken and returned. The decision of the sending state to retake a delinquent juvenile on probation or parole shall be conclusive upon and not reviewable within the receiving state, but if, at the time the sending state seeks to retake a delinquent juvenile on probation or parole, there is pending against him within the receiving state any criminal charge or any proceeding to have him adjudicated a delinquent juvenile for any act committed in such state, or if he is suspected of having committed within such state a criminal offense or an act of juvenile delinquency, he shall not be returned without the consent of the receiving state until discharged from prosecution or other form of proceeding, imprisonment, detention or supervision for such offense or juvenile delinquency. The duly accredited officers of the sending state shall be permitted to transport delinquent juveniles being so returned through any and all states party to this compact, without interference.

(d) That the sending state shall be responsible under this Article for paying the costs of transporting any delinquent juvenile to the receiving state or of returning any delinquent juvenile to the sending state.

Article VIII —Responsibility for Costs

(a) That the provisions of Articles IV(b), V(b) and VII(d) of this compact shall not be construed to alter or affect any internal relationship among the departments, agencies and officers of and in the government of a party state, or between a party state and its subdivisions, as to the payment of costs, or responsibilities therefor.

(b) That nothing in this compact shall be construed to prevent any party state or subdivision thereof from asserting any right against any person, agency or other entity in regard to costs for which such party state or subdivision thereof may be responsible pursuant to Articles IV(b), V(b) or VII(d) of this compact.

Article IX —Detention Practices

That, to every extent possible, it shall be the policy of states party to this compact that no juvenile or delinquent juvenile shall be placed or detained in any prison, jail or lockup nor be detained or transported in association with criminal, vicious or dissolute persons.

Article X —Supplementary Agreements

That the duly constituted administrative authorities of a state party to this compact may enter into supplementary agreements with any other state or states party hereto for the cooperative care, treatment and rehabilitation of delinquent juveniles whenever they shall find that such agreements will improve the facilities or programs available for such care, treatment and rehabilitation. Such care, treatment and rehabilitation may be provided in an institution located within any state entering into such supplementary agreement. Such supplementary agreements shall (1) provide the rates to be paid for the care, treatment and custody of such delinquent juveniles, taking into consideration the character of facilities, services and subsistence furnished; (2) provide that the delinquent juvenile shall be given a court hearing prior to his being sent to another state for care, treatment and custody; (3) provide that the state receiving such a delinquent juvenile in one of its institutions shall act solely as agent for the state sending such delinquent juvenile; (4) provide that the sending state shall at all times retain jurisdiction over delinquent juveniles sent to an institution in another state; (5) provide for reasonable inspection of such institutions by the sending state; (6) provide that the consent of the parent, guardian, person or agency entitled to the legal custody of said delinquent juvenile shall be secured prior to his being sent to another state; and (7) make provision for such other matters and details as shall be necessary to protect the rights and equities of such delinquent juveniles and of the cooperating states.

Article XI —Acceptance of Federal and Other Aid

That any state party to this compact may accept any and all donations, gifts and grants of money, equipment and services from the federal or any local government, or any agency thereof and from any person, firm or corporation, for any of the purposes and functions of this compact, and may receive and utilize the same subject to the terms, conditions and regulations governing such donations, gifts and grants.

Article XII —Compact Administrators

That the governor of each state party to this compact shall designate an officer who, acting jointly with like officers of other party states, shall promulgate rules and regulations to carry out more effectively the terms and provisions of this compact.

Article XIII —Execution of Compact

That this compact shall become operative immediately upon its execution by any state as between it and any other state or states so executing. When executed it shall have the full force and effect of law within such state, the form of execution to be in accordance with the laws of the executing state.

Article XIV —Renunciation

That this compact shall continue in force and remain binding upon each executing state until renounced by it. Renunciation of this compact shall be by the same authority which executed it, by sending six months' notice in writing of its intention to withdraw from the compact to the other states party hereto. The duties and obligations of a renouncing state under Article VII hereof shall continue as to parolees and probationers residing therein at the time of withdrawal until retaken or finally discharged. Supplementary agreements entered into under Article X hereof shall be subject to renunciation as provided by such supplementary agreements, and shall not be subject to the six months' renunciation notice of the present Article.

Article XV —Severability

That the provisions of this compact shall be severable and if any phrase, clause, sentence or provision of this compact is declared to be contrary to the constitution of any participating state or of the United States or the applicability thereof to any government, agency, person or circumstance is held invalid, the validity of the remainder of this compact and the applicability thereof to any government, agency, person or circumstance shall not be affected thereby. If this compact shall be held contrary to the constitution of any state participating therein, the compact shall remain in full force and effect as to the remaining states and in full force and effect as to the state affected as to all severable matters.

(1988 H 790, eff. 3–16–89; 127 v 530)

2151.57 Compact administrator; powers and duties

Pursuant to section 2151.56 of the Revised Code, the governor is hereby authorized and empowered, with the advice and consent of the senate, to designate an officer who shall be the compact administrator and who, acting jointly with like officers of other party states, shall promulgate rules and regulations to carry out more effectively the terms of the compact. Such compact administrator shall serve subject to the pleasure of the governor. The compact administrator is hereby authorized, empowered and directed to cooperate with all departments, agencies and officers of and in the government of this state and its subdivisions in facilitating the proper administration of the compact or of any supplementary agreement or agreements entered into by this state thereunder.

(127 v 530, eff. 9–17–57)

2151.58 Supplementary agreements

The compact administrator is hereby authorized and empowered to enter into supplementary agreements with appropriate officials of other states pursuant to the compact. In the event that such supplementary agreement shall require or contemplate the use of any institution or facility of this state or require or contemplate the provision of any service by this state, said supplementary agreement shall have no force or effect until approved by the head of the department or agency under whose jurisdiction the institution or facility is operated or whose department or agency will be charged with the rendering of such service.

(127 v 530, eff. 9–17–57)

2151.59 Discharge of financial obligations

The compact administrator, subject to the approval of the director of budget and management, may make or arrange for any payments necessary to discharge any financial obligations imposed upon this state by the compact or by any supplementary agreement entered into thereunder.

(1985 H 201, eff. 7–1–85; 127 v 530)

2151.60 Enforcement by agencies of state and subdivisions

The courts, departments, agencies and officers of this state and its subdivisions shall enforce this compact and shall do all things appropriate to the effectuation of its purposes and intent which may be within their respective jurisdictions.

(127 v 530, eff. 9–17–57)

2151.61 Additional article

In addition to any procedure provided in Articles IV and VI of the compact for the return of any runaway juvenile, the particular states, the juvenile or his parents, the courts, or other legal custodian involved may agree upon and adopt any other plan or procedure legally authorized under the laws of this state and the other respective party states for the return of any such runaway juvenile.

Article XVI —Additional Article

The governor is hereby authorized and directed to execute, with any other state or states legally joining in the same, an amendment to the interstate compact on juveniles in substantially the following form:

"(a) That this Article shall provide additional remedies, and shall be binding only as among and between those party states which specifically execute the same.

(b) For the purposes of Article XVI(c), "child", as used herein, means any minor within the jurisdictional age limits of any court in the home state.

(c) When any child is brought before a court of a state of which such child is not a resident, and such state is willing to permit such child's return to the home state of such child, such home state, upon being so advised by the state in which such proceeding is pending, shall immediately institute proceedings to determine the residence and jurisdictional facts as to such child in such home state, and upon finding that such child is in fact a resident of said state and subject to the jurisdiction of the court thereof, shall within five days authorize the return of such child to the home state, and to the parent or custodial agency legally authorized to accept such custody in such home state, and at the expense of such home state, to be paid from such funds as such home state may procure, designate, or provide, prompt action being of the essence.

(d) All provisions and procedures of Articles V and VI of the interstate compact on juveniles shall be construed to apply to any juvenile charged with being a delinquent juvenile for the violation of any criminal law. Any juvenile charged with being a delinquent juvenile for violating any criminal law shall be returned to the requesting state upon a requisition to the state where the juvenile may be found. A petition in the case shall be filed in a court of competent jurisdiction in the requesting state where the violation of criminal law is alleged to have been committed. The petition may be filed regardless of whether the juvenile has left the state before or after the filing of the petition. The requisition described in Article V of the compact shall be forwarded by the judge of the county in which the petition has been filed."

(1992 H 154, eff. 7–31–92; 127 v 530)

FACILITIES FOR TRAINING, TREATMENT, AND REHABILITATION OF JUVENILES

2151.65 Facilities for treatment of juveniles; joint boards; admission

Upon the advice and recommendation of the juvenile judge, the board of county commissioners may provide by purchase, lease, construction, or otherwise a school, forestry camp, or other facility or facilities where delinquent children, as defined in section 2152.02 of the Revised Code, dependent children, abused children, unruly children, as defined in section 2151.022 of the Revised Code, or neglected children or juvenile traffic offenders may be held for training, treatment, and rehabilitation. Upon the joint advice and recommendation of the juvenile judges of two or more adjoining or neighboring counties, the boards of county commissioners of such counties may form themselves into a joint board and proceed to organize a district for the establishment and support of a school, forestry camp, or other facility or facilities for the use of the juvenile courts of such counties, where delinquent, dependent, abused, unruly, or neglected children, or juvenile traffic offenders may be held for treatment, training, and rehabilitation, by using a site or buildings already established in one such county, or by providing for the purchase of a site and the erection of the necessary buildings thereon. Such county or district school, forestry camp, or other facility or facilities shall be maintained as provided in Chapters 2151. and 2152. of the Revised Code. Children who are adjudged to be delinquent, dependent, neglected, abused, unruly, or juvenile traffic offenders may be committed to and held in any such school, forestry camp, or other facility or facilities for training, treatment, and rehabilitation.

The juvenile court shall determine:

(A) The children to be admitted to any school, forestry camp, or other facility maintained under this section;

(B) The period such children shall be trained, treated, and rehabilitated at such facility;

(C) The removal and transfer of children from such facility.

(2000 S 179, § 3, eff. 1–1–02; 1980 S 168, eff. 10–2–80; 1975 H 85; 130 v H 879)

2151.651 Application for financial assistance for acquisition or construction of facilities

The board of county commissioners of a county which, either separately or as part of a district, is planning to establish a school, forestry camp, or other facility under section 2151.65 of the Revised Code, to be used exclusively for the rehabilitation of children between the ages of twelve to eighteen years, other than psychotic or mentally retarded children, who are designated delinquent children, as defined in section 2152.02 of the Revised Code, or unruly children, as defined in section 2151.022 of the Revised Code, by order of a juvenile court, may make application to the department of youth services, created under section 5139.01 of the Revised Code, for financial assistance in defraying the county's share of the cost of acquisition or construction of such school, camp, or other facility, as provided in section 5139.27 of the Revised Code. Such application shall be made on forms prescribed and furnished by the department.

(2000 S 179, § 3, eff. 1–1–02; 1981 H 440, eff. 11–23–81; 1980 S 168; 131 v H 943)

2151.653 Program of education; teachers

The board of county commissioners of a county or the board of trustees of a district maintaining a school, forestry camp, or other facility established under section 2151.65 of the Revised Code, shall provide a program of education for the youths admitted to such school, forestry camp, or other facility. Either of such boards and the board of education of any school district may enter into an agreement whereby such board of education provides teachers for such school, forestry camp, or other facility, or permits youths admitted to such school, forestry camp, or other facility to attend a school or schools within such school district, or both. Either of such boards may enter into an agreement with the appropriate authority of any university, college, or vocational institution to assist in providing a program of education for the youths admitted to such school, forestry camp, or other facility.

(131 v H 943, eff. 8–10–65)

2151.654 Agreements for admission of children from counties not maintaining facilities

The board of county commissioners of a county or the board of trustees of a district maintaining a school, forestry camp, or other facility established under section 2151.65 of the Revised Code, may enter into an agreement with the board of county commissioners of a county which does not maintain such a school, forestry camp, or other facility, to admit to such school, forestry camp, or other facility a child from the county not maintaining such a school, forestry camp, or other facility.

(131 v H 943, eff. 8–10–65)

2151.655 County taxing authority may submit securities issue to electors for support of schools, detention homes, forestry camps, or other facilities

(A) The taxing authority of a county may issue general obligation securities of the county under Chapter 133. of the Revised Code to pay such county's share, either separately or as a part of a district, of the cost of acquiring schools, detention facilities, forestry camps, or other facilities, or any combination thereof, under section 2152.41 or 2151.65 of the Revised Code, or of acquiring sites for and constructing, enlarging, or otherwise improving such schools, detention facilities, forestry camps, other facilities, or combinations thereof.

(B) The taxing authority of a detention facility district, or a district organized under section 2151.65 of the Revised Code, or of a combined district organized under sections 2152.41 and 2151.65 of the Revised Code, may submit to the electors of the district the question of issuing general obligation bonds of the district to pay the cost of acquiring, constructing, enlarging, or otherwise improving sites, buildings, and facilities for any purposes for which the district was organized. The election on such question shall be submitted and held under section 133.18 of the Revised Code.

(2000 S 179, § 3, eff. 1–1–02; 1989 H 230, eff. 10–30–89)

2151.66 Annual tax assessments

The joint boards of county commissioners of district schools, forestry camps, or other facility or facilities created under section 2151.65 of the Revised Code, shall make annual assessments of taxes sufficient to support and defray all necessary expenses of such school, forestry camp, or other facility or facilities.

(130 v H 879, eff. 10–14–63)

2151.67 Receipt and use of gifts, grants, devises, bequests and public moneys

The board of county commissioners of a county or the board of trustees of a district maintaining a school, forestry camp, or other facility established or to be established under section 2151.65 of the Revised Code may receive gifts, grants, devises, and bequests, either absolutely or in trust, and may receive any public moneys made available to it. Each of such boards shall use such gifts, grants, devises, bequests, and public moneys in whatever manner it determines is most likely to carry out the purposes for which such school, forestry camp, or other facility was or is to be established.

(132 v H 1, eff. 2–21–67; 131 v H 943)

2151.68 Board of trustees

Immediately upon the organization of the joint board of county commissioners as provided by section 2151.65 of the Revised Code, or so soon thereafter as practicable, such joint board of county commissioners shall appoint a board of not less than five trustees, which shall hold office and perform its duties until the first annual meeting after the choice of an established site and buildings, or after the selection and purchase of a building site, at which time such joint board of county commissioners shall appoint a board of not less than five trustees, one of whom shall hold office for a term of one year, one for the term of two years, one for the term of three years, half of the remaining number for the term of four years, and the remainder for the term of five years. Annually thereafter, the joint board of county commissioners shall appoint one or more trustees, each of whom shall hold office for the term of five years, to succeed any trustee whose term of office expires. A trustee may be appointed to succeed himself upon such board of trustees, and all appointments to such board of trustees shall be made from persons who are recommended and approved by the juvenile court judge or judges of the county of which such person is a resident. The annual meeting of the board of trustees shall be held on the first Tuesday in May in each year.

(130 v H 879, eff. 10–14–63)

2151.69 Board meetings; compensation

A majority of the trustees appointed under section 2151.68 of the Revised Code constitutes a quorum. Board meetings shall be held at least quarterly. The presiding juvenile court judge of each of the counties of the district organized pursuant to section 2151.65 of the Revised Code shall attend such meetings, or shall designate a member of his staff to do so. The members of the board shall receive no compensation for their services, except their actual traveling expenses, which, when properly certified, shall be allowed and paid by the treasurer.

(130 v H 879, eff. 10–14–63)

2151.70 Appointment of superintendent; bond; compensation; duties

The judge, in a county maintaining a school, forestry camp, or other facility or facilities created under section 2151.65 of the Revised Code, shall appoint the superintendent of any such facility. In the case of a district facility created under such section, the board of trustees shall appoint the superintendent. A superintendent, before entering upon his duties, shall give bond with sufficient surety to the judge or to the board, as the case may be, in such amount as may be fixed by the judge or the board, such bond being conditioned upon the full and faithful accounting of the funds and properties coming into his hands.

Compensation of the superintendent and other necessary employees of a school, forestry camp, or other facility or facilities shall be fixed by the judge in the case of a county facility, or by the board of trustees in the case of a district facility. Such compensation and other expenses of maintaining the facility shall be paid in the manner prescribed in section 2151.13 of the Revised Code in the case of a county facility, or in accordance with rules and regulations provided for in section 2151.77 of the Revised Code in the case of a district facility.

The superintendent of a facility shall appoint all employees of such facility. All such employees, except the superintendent, shall be in the classified civil service.

The superintendent of a school, forestry camp, or other facility shall have entire executive charge of such facility, under supervision of the judge, in the case of a county facility, or under supervision of the board of trustees, in the case of a district facility. The superintendent shall control, manage, and operate the facility, and shall have custody of its property, files, and records.

(130 v H 879, eff. 10–14–63)

2151.71 Operation of facilities

District schools, forestry camps, or other facilities created under section 2151.65 of the Revised Code shall be established, operated, maintained, and managed in the same manner, so far as applicable, as county schools, forestry camps, or other facilities.

(130 v H 879, eff. 10–14–63)

2151.72 Selection of site for district facility

When the board of trustees appointed under section 2151.68 of the Revised Code does not choose an established institution in one of the counties of the district, it may select a suitable site for the erection of a district school, forestry camp, or other facility or facilities created under section 2151.65 of the Revised Code.

(130 v H 879, eff. 10–14–63)

2151.73 Apportionment of trustees; executive committee

Each county in the district, organized under section 2151.65 of the Revised Code, shall be entitled to one trustee, and in districts composed of but two counties, each county shall be entitled to not less than two trustees. In districts composed of more than four counties, the number of trustees shall be sufficiently increased so that there shall always be an uneven number of trustees constituting such board. The county in which a district school, forestry camp, or other facility created under section 2151.65 of the Revised Code is located shall have not less than two trustees, who, in the interim period between the regular meetings of the board of trustees, shall act as an executive committee in the discharge of all business pertaining to the school, forestry camp, or other facility.

(130 v H 879, eff. 10–14–63)

2151.74 Removal of trustee

The joint board of county commissioners organized under section 2151.65 of the Revised Code may remove any trustee appointed under section 2151.68 of the Revised Code, but no such removal shall be made on account of the religious or political convictions of such trustee. The trustee appointed to fill any vacancy shall hold his office for the unexpired term of his predecessor.

(130 v H 879, eff. 10–14–63)

2151.75 Interim duties of trustees; trustees fund; reports

In the interim, between the selection and purchase of a site, and the erection and occupancy of a district school, forestry camp, or other facility or facilities created under section 2151.65 of the Revised Code, the joint board of county commissioners provided by section 2151.65 of the Revised Code may delegate to a board of trustees appointed under section 2151.68 of the Revised Code, such powers and duties as, in its judgment, will be of general interest or aid to the institution. Such joint board of county commissioners may appropriate a trustees' fund, to be expended by the board of trustees in payment of such contracts, purchases, or other expenses necessary to the wants or requirements of the school, forestry camp, or other facility or facilities which are not otherwise provided for. The board of trustees shall make a complete settlement with the joint board of county commissioners once each six months, or quarterly if required, and shall make a full report of the condition of the school, forestry camp, or other facility or facilities and inmates, to the board of county commissioners, and to the juvenile court of each of the counties.

(130 v H 879, eff. 10–14–63)

2151.76 Authority for choice, construction, and furnishing of district facility

The choice of an established site and buildings, or the purchase of a site, stock, implements, and general farm equipment, should there be a farm, the erection of buildings, and the completion and furnishing of the district school, forestry camp, or other facility or facilities for occupancy, shall be in the hands of the joint board of county commissioners organized under section 2151.65 of the Revised Code. Such joint board of county commissioners may delegate all or a portion of these duties to the board of trustees provided for under section 2151.68 of the Revised Code, under such restrictions and regulations as the joint board of county commissioners imposes.

(130 v H 879, eff. 10–14–63)

2151.77 Capital and current expenses of district

When an established site and buildings are used for a district school, forestry camp, or other facility or facilities created under section 2151.65 of the Revised Code the joint board of county commissioners organized under section 2151.65 of the Revised Code shall cause the value of such site and buildings to be properly appraised. This appraisal value, or in case of the purchase of a site, the purchase price and the cost of all betterments and additions thereto, shall be paid by the counties comprising the district, in proportion to the taxable property of each county, as shown by its tax duplicate. The current expenses of maintaining the school, forestry camp, or other facility or facilities and the cost of ordinary repairs thereto shall be paid by each such county in accordance with one of the following methods as approved by the joint board of county commissioners:

(A) In proportion to the number of children from such county who are maintained in the school, forestry camp, or other facility or facilities during the year;

(B) By a levy submitted by the joint board of county commissioners under division (A) of section 5705.19 of the Revised Code and approved by the electors of the district;

(C) In proportion to the taxable property of each county, as shown by its tax duplicate;

(D) In any combination of the methods for payment described in division (A), (B), or (C) of this section.

The board of trustees shall, with the approval of the joint board of county commissioners, adopt rules for the management of funds used for the current expenses of maintaining the school, forestry camp, or other facility or facilities.

(1988 H 365, eff. 6–14–88; 1972 H 258; 130 v H 879)

2151.78 Withdrawal of county from district; continuity of district tax levy

The board of county commissioners of any county within a school, forestry camp, or other facility or facilities district may, upon the recommendation of the juvenile court of such county, withdraw from such district and dispose of its interest in such school, forestry camp, or other facility or facilities selling or leasing its right, title, and interest in the site, buildings, furniture, and equipment to any counties in the district, at such price and upon such terms as are agreed upon among the boards of county commissioners of the counties concerned. Section 307.10 of the Revised Code does not apply to this section. The net proceeds of any such sale or lease shall be paid into the treasury of the withdrawing county.

Any county withdrawing from such district or from a combined district organized under sections 2152.41 and 2151.65 of the Revised Code shall continue to have levied against its tax duplicate any tax levied by the district during the period in which the county was a member of the district for current operating expenses, permanent improvements, or the retirement of bonded indebtedness. Such levy shall continue to be a levy against such duplicate of the county until such time that it expires or is renewed.

Members of the board of trustees of a district school, forestry camp, or other facility or facilities who are residents of a county withdrawing from such district are deemed to have resigned their positions upon the completion of the withdrawal procedure provided by this section. Vacancies then created shall be filled according to sections 2151.68 and 2151.74 of the Revised Code.

(2000 S 179, § 3, eff. 1–1–02; 1972 H 258, eff. 1–27–72; 130 v H 879)

2151.79 Designation of fiscal officer of district; duties of county auditors

The county auditor of the county having the greatest population, or, with the unanimous concurrence of the county auditors of the counties composing a facilities district, the auditor of the county wherein the facility is located, shall be the fiscal officer of a district organized under section 2151.65 of the Revised Code or a combined district organized under sections 2152.41 and 2151.65 of the Revised Code. The county auditors of the several counties composing a school, forestry camp, or other facility or facilities district, shall meet at the district school, forestry camp, or other facility or facilities not less than once in each six months, to review accounts and to transact such other duties in connection with the institution as pertain to the business of their office.

(2000 S 179, § 3, eff. 1–1–02; 1974 H 1033, eff. 10–2–74; 1972 H 258; 130 v H 879)

2151.80 Expenses of members of boards of county commissioners

Each member of the board of county commissioners who meets by appointment to consider the organization of a district school, forestry camp, or other facility or facilities shall, upon presentation of properly certified accounts, be paid his necessary expenses upon a warrant drawn by the county auditor of his county.

(130 v H 879, eff. 10–14–63)

INDEPENDENT LIVING SERVICES

2151.81 Definitions

As used in sections 2151.82 to 2151.84 of the Revised Code:

(A) "Independent living services" means services and other forms of support designed to aid children and young adults to successfully make the transition to independent adult living and to achieve emotional and economic self-sufficiency. "Independent living services" may include the following:

(1) Providing housing;

(2) Teaching decision-making skills;

(3) Teaching daily living skills such as securing and maintaining a residence, money management, utilization of community services and systems, personal health care, hygiene and safety, and time management;

(4) Assisting in obtaining education, training, and employment skills;

(5) Assisting in developing positive adult relationships and community supports.

(B) "Young adult" means a person eighteen years of age or older but under twenty-one years of age who was in the temporary or permanent custody of, or was provided care in a planned permanent living arrangement by, a public children services agency or private child placing agency on the date the person attained age eighteen.

(2002 H 38, eff. 11–1–02)

2151.82 Independent living services

A public children services agency or private child placing agency, that has temporary or permanent custody of, or is providing care in a planned permanent living arrangement to, a child who is sixteen or seventeen years of age, shall provide independent living services to the child. The services to be provided shall be determined based on an evaluation of the strengths and weaknesses of the child, completed or obtained by the agency. If housing is provided as part of the services, the child shall be placed in housing that is supervised or semi-supervised by an adult.

The services shall be included as part of the case plan established for the child pursuant to section 2151.412 of the Revised Code.

(2002 H 38, eff. 11–1–02)

2151.83 Joint agreement for provision of independent living services

(A) A public children services agency or private child placing agency, on the request of a young adult, shall enter into a jointly prepared written agreement with the young adult that obligates the agency to ensure that independent living services are provided to the young adult and sets forth the responsibilities of the young adult regarding the services. The agreement shall be developed based on the young adult's strengths, needs, and circumstances. The agreement shall be designed to promote the young adult's successful transition to independent adult living and emotional and economic self-sufficiency.

(B) If the young adult appears to be eligible for services from one or more of the following entities, the agency must contact the appropriate entity to determine eligibility:

(1) An entity, other than the agency, that is represented on a county family and children first council established pursuant to section 121.37 of the Revised Code. If the entity is a board of alcohol, drug addiction, and mental health services, an alcohol and drug addiction services board, or a community mental health board, the agency shall contact the provider of alcohol, drug addiction, or mental health services that has been designated by the board to determine the young adult's eligibility for services.

(2) The rehabilitation services commission;

(3) A metropolitan housing authority established pursuant to section 3735.27 of the Revised Code.

If an entity described in this division determines that the young adult qualifies for services from the entity, that entity, the young adult, and the agency to which the young adult made the request for independent living services shall enter into a written addendum to the jointly prepared agreement entered into under division (A) of this section. The addendum shall indicate how services under the agreement and addendum are to be coordinated and allocate the service responsibilities among the entities and agency that signed the addendum.

(2003 H 95, eff. 9–26–03; 2002 H 38, eff. 11–1–02)

2151.84 Model agreements

The department of job and family services shall establish model agreements that may be used by public children services agencies and private child placing agencies required to provide services under an agreement with a young adult pursuant to section 2151.83 of the Revised Code. The model agreements shall include provisions describing the specific independent living services to be provided, the duration of the services and the agreement, the duties and responsibilities of each party under the agreement, and grievance procedures regarding disputes that arise regarding the agreement or services provided under it.

(2003 H 95, eff. 9–26–03; 2002 H 38, eff. 11–1–02)

MISCELLANEOUS PROVISIONS

2151.85 Minor female's complaint for abortion; hearing; appeal

(A) A woman who is pregnant, unmarried, under eighteen years of age, and unemancipated and who wishes to have an abortion without the notification of her parents, guardian, or custodian may file a complaint in the juvenile court of the county in which she has a residence or legal settlement, in the juvenile court of any county that borders to any extent the county in which she has a residence or legal settlement, or in the juvenile court of the county in which the hospital, clinic, or other facility in which the abortion would be performed or induced is located, requesting the issuance of an order authorizing her to consent to the performance or inducement of an abortion without the notification of her parents, guardian, or custodian.

The complaint shall be made under oath and shall include all of the following:

(1) A statement that the complainant is pregnant;

(2) A statement that the complainant is unmarried, under eighteen years of age, and unemancipated;

(3) A statement that the complainant wishes to have an abortion without the notification of her parents, guardian, or custodian;

(4) An allegation of either or both of the following:

(a) That the complainant is sufficiently mature and well enough informed to intelligently decide whether to have an abortion without the notification of her parents, guardian, or custodian;

(b) That one or both of her parents, her guardian, or her custodian was engaged in a pattern of physical, sexual, or emotional abuse against her, or that the notification of her parents, guardian, or custodian otherwise is not in her best interest.

(5) A statement as to whether the complainant has retained an attorney and, if she has retained an attorney, the name, address, and telephone number of her attorney.

(B)(1) The court shall fix a time for a hearing on any complaint filed pursuant to division (A) of this section and shall keep a record of all testimony and other oral proceedings in the action. The court shall hear and determine the action and shall not refer any portion of it to a referee. The hearing shall be held at the earliest possible time, but not later than the fifth business day after the day that the complaint is filed. The court shall enter judgment on the complaint immediately after the hearing is concluded. If the hearing required by this division is not held by the fifth business day after the complaint is filed, the failure to hold the hearing shall be considered to be a constructive order of the court authorizing the complainant to consent to the performance or inducement of an abortion without the notification of her parent, guardian, or custodian, and the complainant and any other person may rely on the constructive order to the same extent as if the court actually had issued an order under this section authorizing the complainant to consent to the performance or inducement of an abortion without such notification.

(2) The court shall appoint a guardian ad litem to protect the interests of the complainant at the hearing that is held pursuant to this section. If the complainant has not retained an attorney, the court shall appoint an attorney to represent her. If the guardian ad litem is an attorney admitted to the practice of law in this state, the court also may appoint him to serve as the complainant's attorney.

(C)(1) If the complainant makes only the allegation set forth in division (A)(4)(a) of this section and if the court finds, by clear and convincing evidence, that the complainant is sufficiently mature and well enough informed to decide intelligently whether to have an abortion, the court shall issue an order authorizing the complainant to consent to the performance or inducement of an abortion without the notification of her parents, guardian, or custodian. If the court does not make the finding specified in this division, it shall dismiss the complaint.

(2) If the complainant makes only the allegation set forth in division (A)(4)(b) of this section and if the court finds, by clear and convincing evidence, that there is evidence of a pattern of physical, sexual, or emotional abuse of the complainant by one or both of her parents, her guardian, or her custodian, or that the notification of the parents, guardian, or custodian of the complainant otherwise is not in the best interest of the complainant, the court shall issue an order authorizing the complainant to consent to the performance or inducement of an abortion without the notification of her parents, guardian, or custodian. If the court does not make the finding specified in this division, it shall dismiss the complaint.

(3) If the complainant makes both of the allegations set forth in divisions (A)(4)(a) and (b) of this section, the court shall proceed as follows:

(a) The court first shall determine whether it can make the finding specified in division (C)(1) of this section and, if so, shall issue an order pursuant to that division. If the court issues such an order, it shall not proceed pursuant to division (C)(3)(b) of this section. If the court does not make the finding specified in division (C)(1) of this section, it shall proceed pursuant to division (C)(3)(b) of this section.

(b) If the court pursuant to division (C)(3)(a) of this section does not make the finding specified in division (C)(1) of this section, it shall proceed to determine whether it can make the finding specified in division (C)(2) of this section and, if so, shall issue an order pursuant to that division. If the court does not make the finding specified in division (C)(2) of this section, it shall dismiss the complaint.

(D) The court shall not notify the parents, guardian, or custodian of the complainant that she is pregnant or that she wants to have an abortion.

(E) If the court dismisses the complaint, it immediately shall notify the complainant that she has a right to appeal under section 2505.073 of the Revised Code.

(F) Each hearing under this section shall be conducted in a manner that will preserve the anonymity of the complainant. The complaint and all other papers and records that pertain to an action commenced under this section shall be kept confidential and are not public records under section 149.43 of the Revised Code.

(G) The clerk of the supreme court shall prescribe complaint and notice of appeal forms that shall be used by a complainant filing a complaint under this section and by an appellant filing an appeal under section 2505.073 of the Revised Code. The clerk of each juvenile court shall furnish blank copies of the forms, without charge, to any person who requests them.

(H) No filing fee shall be required of, and no court costs shall be assessed against, a complainant filing a complaint under this section or an appellant filing an appeal under section 2505.073 of the Revised Code.

(I) As used in this section, "unemancipated" means that a woman who is unmarried and under eighteen years of age has not entered the armed services of the United States, has not become employed and self-subsisting, or has not otherwise become independent from the care and control of her parent, guardian, or custodian.

(1985 H 319, eff. 3–24–86)

2151.86 Criminal records check; disqualification from employment

(A)(1) The appointing or hiring officer of any entity that appoints or employs any person responsible for a child's care in out-of-home care shall request the superintendent of BCII to conduct a criminal records check with respect to any person who is under final consideration for appointment or employment as a person responsible for a child's care in out-of-home care, except that section 3319.39 of the Revised Code shall apply instead of this section if the out-of-home care entity is a public school, educational service center, or chartered nonpublic school.

(2) The administrative director of an agency, or attorney, who arranges an adoption for a prospective adoptive parent shall request the superintendent of BCII to conduct a criminal records check with respect to that prospective adoptive parent and all persons eighteen years of age or older who reside with the prospective adoptive parent.

(3) Before a recommending agency submits a recommendation to the department of job and family services on whether the department should issue a certificate to a foster home under section 5103.03 of the Revised Code, the administrative director of the agency shall request that the superintendent of BCII conduct a criminal records check with respect to the prospective foster caregiver and all other persons eighteen years of age or older who reside with the foster caregiver.

(B) If a person subject to a criminal records check does not present proof that the person has been a resident of this state for the five-year period immediately prior to the date upon which the criminal records check is requested or does not provide evidence that within that five-year period the superintendent of BCII has requested information about the person from the federal bureau of investigation in a criminal records check, the appointing or hiring officer, administrative director, or attorney shall request that the superintendent of BCII obtain information from the federal bureau of investigation as a part of the criminal records check. If the person subject to the criminal records check presents proof that the person has been a resident of this state for that five-year period, the officer, director, or attorney may request that the superintendent of BCII include information from the federal bureau of investigation in the criminal records check.

An appointing or hiring officer, administrative director, or attorney required by division (A) of this section to request a criminal records check shall provide to each person subject to a criminal records check a copy of the form prescribed pursuant to division (C)(1) of section 109.572 of the Revised Code and a standard impression sheet to obtain fingerprint impressions prescribed pursuant to division (C)(2) of section 109.572 of the Revised Code, obtain the completed form and impression sheet from the person, and forward the completed form and impression sheet to the superintendent of BCII at the time the criminal records check is requested.

Any person subject to a criminal records check who receives pursuant to this division a copy of the form prescribed pursuant to division (C)(1) of section 109.572 of the Revised Code and a copy of an impression sheet prescribed pursuant to division (C)(2) of that section and who is requested to complete the form and provide a set of fingerprint impressions shall complete the form or provide all the information necessary to complete the form and shall provide the impression sheet with the impressions of the person's fingerprints. If a person subject to a criminal records check, upon request, fails to provide the information necessary to complete the form or fails to provide impressions of the person's fingerprints, the appointing or hiring officer shall not appoint or employ the person as a person responsible for a child's care in out-of-home care, a probate court may not issue a final decree of adoption or an interlocutory order of adoption making the person an adoptive parent, and the department of job and family services shall not issue a certificate authorizing the prospective foster caregiver to operate a foster home.

(C)(1) No appointing or hiring officer shall appoint or employ a person as a person responsible for a child's care in out-of-home care, the department of job and family services shall not issue a certificate under section 5103.03 of the Revised Code authorizing a prospective foster caregiver to operate a foster home, and no probate court shall issue a final decree of adoption or an interlocutory order of adoption making a person an adoptive parent if the person or, in the case of a prospective foster caregiver or prospective adoptive parent, any person eighteen years of age or older who resides with the prospective foster caregiver or prospective adoptive parent previously has been convicted of or pleaded guilty to any of the following, unless the person meets rehabilitation standards established in rules adopted under division (F) of this section:

(a) A violation of section 2903.01, 2903.02, 2903.03, 2903.04, 2903.11, 2903.12, 2903.13, 2903.16, 2903.21, 2903.34, 2905.01, 2905.02, 2905.05, 2907. 02, 2907.03, 2907.04, 2907.05, 2907.06, 2907.07, 2907.08, 2907.09, 2907.21, 2907.22, 2907.23, 2907.25, 2907.31, 2907.32, 2907.321, 2907.322, 2907.323, 2909.02, 2909.03, 2911.01, 2911.02, 2911.11, 2911.12, 2919.12, 2919.22, 2919.24, 2919.25, 2923. 12, 2923.13, 2923.161, 2925.02, 2925.03, 2925.04, 2925.05, 2925.06, or 3716.11 of the Revised Code, a violation of section 2905.04 of the Revised Code as it existed prior to July 1, 1996, a violation of section 2919.23 of the Revised Code that would have been a violation of section 2905.04 of the Revised Code as it existed prior to July 1, 1996, had the violation been committed prior to that date, a violation of section 2925.11 of the Revised Code that is not a minor drug possession offense, or felonious sexual penetration in violation of former section 2907.12 of the Revised Code;

(b) A violation of an existing or former law of this state, any other state, or the United States that is substantially equivalent to any of the offenses described in division (C)(1)(a) of this section.

(2) The appointing or hiring officer may appoint or employ a person as a person responsible for a child's care in out-of-home care conditionally until the criminal records check required by this section is completed and the officer receives the results of the criminal records check. If the results of the criminal records check indicate that, pursuant to division (C)(1) of this section, the person subject to the criminal records check does not qualify for appointment or employment, the officer shall release the person from appointment or employment.

(D) The appointing or hiring officer, administrative director, or attorney shall pay to the bureau of criminal identification and investigation the fee prescribed pursuant to division (C)(3) of section 109.572 of the Revised Code for each criminal records check conducted in accordance with that section upon a request pursuant to division (A) of this section. The officer, director, or attorney may charge the person subject to the criminal records check a fee for the costs the officer, director, or attorney incurs in obtaining the criminal records check. A fee charged under this division shall not exceed the amount of fees the officer, director, or attorney pays for the criminal records check. If a fee is charged under this division, the officer, director, or attorney shall notify the person who is the applicant at the time of the person's initial application for appointment or employment, an adoption to be arranged, or a certificate to operate a foster home of the amount of the fee and that, unless the fee is paid, the person who is the applicant will not be considered for appointment or employment or as an adoptive parent or foster caregiver.

(E) The report of any criminal records check conducted by the bureau of criminal identification and investigation in accordance with section 109.572 of the Revised Code and pursuant to a request made under division (A) of this section is not a public record for the purposes of section 149.43 of the Revised Code and shall not be made available to any person other than the person who is the subject of the criminal records check or the person's representative; the appointing or hiring officer, administrative director, or attorney requesting the criminal records check or the officer's, director's, or attorney's representative; the department of job and family services or a county department of job and family services; and any court, hearing officer, or other necessary individual involved in a case dealing with the denial of employment, a final decree of adoption or interlocutory order of adoption, or a foster home certificate.

(F) The director of job and family services shall adopt rules in accordance with Chapter 119. of the Revised Code to implement this section. The rules shall include rehabilitation standards a person who has been convicted of or pleaded guilty to an offense listed in division (C)(1) of this section must meet for an appointing or hiring officer to appoint or employ the person as a person responsible for a child's care in out-of-home care, a probate court to issue a final decree of adoption or interlocutory order of adoption making the person an adoptive parent, or the department to issue a certificate authorizing the prospective foster caregiver to operate a foster home.

(G) An appointing or hiring officer, administrative director, or attorney required by division (A) of this section to request a criminal records check shall inform each person who is the applicant, at the time of the person's initial application for appointment or employment, an adoption to be arranged, or a foster home certificate, that the person subject to the criminal records check is required to provide a set of impressions of the person's fingerprints and that a criminal records check is required to be conducted and satisfactorily completed in accordance with section 109.572 of the Revised Code.

(H) The department of job and family services may waive the requirement that a criminal records check based on fingerprints be conducted for an adult resident of a prospective adoptive or foster home or the home of a foster caregiver if the recommending agency documents to the department's satisfaction that the adult resident is physically unable to comply with the fingerprinting requirement and poses no danger to foster children or adoptive children who may be placed in the home. In such cases, the recommending or approving agency shall request that the bureau of criminal identification and investigation conduct a criminal records check using the person's name and social security number.

(I) As used in this section:

(1) "Children's hospital" means any of the following:

(a) A hospital registered under section 3701.07 of the Revised Code that provides general pediatric medical and surgical care, and in which at least seventy-five per cent of annual inpatient discharges for the preceding two calendar years were individuals less than eighteen years of age;

(b) A distinct portion of a hospital registered under section 3701.07 of the Revised Code that provides general pediatric medical and surgical care, has a total of at least one hundred fifty registered pediatric special care and pediatric acute care beds, and in which at least seventy-five per cent of annual inpatient discharges for the preceding two calendar years were individuals less than eighteen years of age;

(c) A distinct portion of a hospital, if the hospital is registered under section 3701.07 of the Revised Code as a children's hospital and the children's hospital meets all the requirements of division (I)(3)(a) of this section.

(2) "Criminal records check" has the same meaning as in section 109.572 of the Revised Code.

(3) "Minor drug possession offense" has the same meaning as in section 2925.01 of the Revised Code.

(4) "Person responsible for a child's care in out-of-home care" has the same meaning as in section 2151.011 of the Revised Code, except that it does not include a prospective employee of the department of youth services or a person responsible for a child's care in a hospital or medical clinic other than a children's hospital.

(5) "Person subject to a criminal records check" means the following:

(a) A person who is under final consideration for appointment or employment as a person responsible for a child's care in out-of-home care;

(b) A prospective adoptive parent;

(c) A prospective foster caregiver;

(d) A person eighteen years old or older who resides with a prospective foster caregiver or a prospective adoptive parent.

(6) "Recommending agency" means a public children services agency, private child placing agency, or private noncustodial agency to which the department of job and family services has delegated a duty to inspect and approve foster homes.

(7) "Superintendent of BCII" means the superintendent of the bureau of criminal identification and investigation.

(2004 H 106, eff. 9–16–04; 2004 H 117, eff. 9–3–04; 2000 H 448, eff. 10–5–00; 1999 H 471, eff. 7–1–00; 1998 H 446, eff. 8–5–98; 1996 S 269, eff. 7–1–96; 1996 H 445, eff. 9–3–96; 1995 S 2, eff. 7–1–96; 1993 S 38, eff. 10–29–93)

2151.861 Random sampling of registered child day camps; effect of noncompliance relating to criminal records check

(A) The department of job and family services may periodically conduct a random sampling of registered child day camps to determine compliance with section 2151.86 of the Revised Code.

(B)(1) No child day camp shall fail to comply with section 2151.86 of the Revised Code in regards to a person it appoints or employs.

(2) If the department determines that a child day camp has violated division (B)(1) of this section, the department shall do both of the following:

(a) Consider imposing a civil penalty on the child day camp in an amount that shall not exceed ten per cent of the camp's gross revenues for the full month immediately preceding the month in which the violation occurred. If the camp was not operating for the entire calendar month preceding the month in which the violation occurred, the penalty shall be five hundred dollars.

(b) Order the child day camp to initiate a criminal records check of the person who is the subject of the violation within a specified period of time.

(3) If, within the specified period of time, the child day camp fails to comply with an order to initiate a criminal records check of the person who is the subject of the violation or to release the person from the appointment or employment, the department shall do both of the following:

(a) Impose a civil penalty in an amount not less than the amount previously imposed and that shall not exceed twice the amount permitted by division (B)(2)(a) of this section;

(b) Order the child day camp to initiate a criminal records check of the person who is the subject of the violation within a specified period of time.

(C) If the department determines that a child day camp has violated division (B)(1) of this section, the department may post a notice at a prominent place at the camp that states that the camp has failed to conduct criminal records checks of its appointees or employees as required by section 2151.86 of the Revised Code. Once the camp demonstrates to the department that the camp is in compliance with that section, the department shall permit the camp to remove the notice.

(D) The department shall include on the department's web site a list of child day camps that the department has determined from a random sample to be not in compliance with the criminal records check requirements of section 2151.86 of the Revised Code. The department shall remove a camp's name from the list when the camp demonstrates to the department that the camp is in compliance with that section.

(E) For the purposes of divisions (C) and (D) of this section, a child day camp will be considered to be in compliance with section 2151.86 of the Revised Code by doing any of the following:

(1) Requesting that the bureau of criminal identification and investigation conduct a criminal records check regarding the person who is the subject of the violation of division (B)(1) of this section and, if the person does not qualify for the appointment or employment, releasing the person from the appointment or employment;

(2) Releasing the person who is the subject of the violation from the appointment or employment.

(F) The attorney general shall commence and prosecute to judgment a civil action in a court of competent jurisdiction to collect any civil penalty imposed under this section that remains unpaid.

(G) A child day camp may appeal any action the department takes under divisions (B) to (D) of this section to the court of common pleas of the county in which the camp is located.

(2004 H 11, eff. 5–18–05)

2151.87 Prohibitions relating to cigarettes or tobacco products

(A) As used in this section:

(1) "Cigarette" and "tobacco product" have the same meanings as in section 2927.02 of the Revised Code.

(2) "Youth smoking education program" means a private or public agency program that is related to tobacco use, prevention, and cessation, that is carried out or funded by the tobacco use prevention and control foundation pursuant to section 183.07 of the Revised Code, that utilizes educational methods focusing on the negative health effects of smoking and using tobacco products, and that is not more than twelve hours in duration.

(B) No child shall do any of the following unless accompanied by a parent, spouse who is eighteen years of age or older, or legal guardian of the child:

(1) Use, consume, or possess cigarettes, other tobacco products, or papers used to roll cigarettes;

(2) Purchase or attempt to purchase cigarettes, other tobacco products, or papers used to roll cigarettes;

(3) Order, pay for, or share the cost of cigarettes, other tobacco products, or papers used to roll cigarettes;

(4) Except as provided in division (E) of this section, accept or receive cigarettes, other tobacco products, or papers used to roll cigarettes.

(C) No child shall knowingly furnish false information concerning that child's name, age, or other identification for the purpose of obtaining cigarettes, other tobacco products, or papers used to roll cigarettes.

(D) A juvenile court shall not adjudicate a child a delinquent or unruly child for a violation of division (B)(1), (2), (3), or (4) or (C) of this section.

(E)(1) It is not a violation of division (B)(4) of this section for a child to accept or receive cigarettes, other tobacco products, or papers used to roll cigarettes if the child is required to do so in the performance of the child's duties as an employee of that child's employer and the child's acceptance or receipt of cigarettes, other tobacco products, or papers used to roll cigarettes occurs exclusively within the scope of the child's employment.

(2) It is not a violation of division (B)(1), (2), (3), or (4) of this section if the child possesses, purchases or attempts to purchase, orders, pays for, shares the cost of, or accepts or receives cigarettes, other tobacco products, or papers used to roll cigarettes while participating in an inspection or compliance check conducted by a federal, state, local, or corporate entity at a location at which cigarettes, other tobacco products, or papers used to roll cigarettes are sold or distributed.

(3) It is not a violation of division (B)(1) or (4) of this section for a child to accept, receive, use, consume, or possess cigarettes, other tobacco products, or papers used to roll cigarettes while participating in a research protocol if all of the following apply:

(a) The parent, guardian, or legal custodian of the child has consented in writing to the child participating in the research protocol.

(b) An institutional human subjects protection review board, or an equivalent entity, has approved the research protocol.

(c) The child is participating in the research protocol at the facility or location specified in the research protocol.

(F) If a juvenile court finds that a child violated division (B)(1), (2), (3), or (4) or (C) of this section, the court may do either or both of the following:

(1) Require the child to attend a youth smoking education program or other smoking treatment program approved by the court, if one is available;

(2) Impose a fine of not more than one hundred dollars.

(G) If a child disobeys a juvenile court order issued pursuant to division (F) of this section, the court may do any or all of the following:

(1) Increase the fine imposed upon the child under division (F)(2) of this section;

(2) Require the child to perform not more than twenty hours of community service;

(3) Suspend for a period of thirty days the temporary instruction permit, probationary driver's license, or driver's license issued to the child.

(H) A child alleged or found to have violated division (B) or (C) of this section shall not be detained under any provision of this chapter or any other provision of the Revised Code.

(2002 H 393, eff. 7–5–02; 2000 S 218, eff. 3–15–01)

PENALTIES

2151.99 Penalties

(A) Whoever violates division (D)(2) or (3) of section 2151.313 or division (A)(1) or (H)(2) of section 2151.421 of the Revised Code is guilty of a misdemeanor of the fourth degree.

(B) Whoever violates division (D)(1) of section 2151.313 of the Revised Code is guilty of a minor misdemeanor.

(2000 S 179, § 3, eff. 1–1–02; 1998 H 173, eff. 7–29–98; 1989 H 257, eff. 8–3–89; 1986 H 529; 1985 H 349; 1984 H 258; 1972 H 511; 1969 H 320; 130 v H 765; 1953 H 1)

CHAPTER 2152

JUVENILE COURTS—CRIMINAL PROVISIONS

GENERAL PROVISIONS

GENERAL PROVISIONS

2152.01 Purposes; applicability of law

(A) The overriding purposes for dispositions under this chapter are to provide for the care, protection, and mental and physical development of children subject to this chapter, protect the public interest and safety, hold the offender accountable for the offender's actions, restore the victim, and rehabilitate the offender. These purposes shall be achieved by a system of graduated sanctions and services.

(B) Dispositions under this chapter shall be reasonably calculated to achieve the overriding purposes set forth in this section, commensurate with and not demeaning to the seriousness of the delinquent child's or the juvenile traffic offender's conduct and its impact on the victim, and consistent with dispositions for similar acts committed by similar delinquent children and juvenile traffic offenders. The court shall not base the disposition on the race, ethnic background, gender, or religion of the delinquent child or juvenile traffic offender.

(C) To the extent they do not conflict with this chapter, the provisions of Chapter 2151. of the Revised Code apply to the proceedings under this chapter.

(2000 S 179, § 3, eff. 1–1–02)

2152.02 Definitions

As used in this chapter:

(A) "Act charged" means the act that is identified in a complaint, indictment, or information alleging that a child is a delinquent child.

(B) "Admitted to a department of youth services facility" includes admission to a facility operated, or contracted for, by the department and admission to a comparable facility outside this state by another state or the United States.

(C)(1) "Child" means a person who is under eighteen years of age, except as otherwise provided in divisions (C)(2) to (6) of this section.

(2) Subject to division (C)(3) of this section, any person who violates a federal or state law or a municipal ordinance prior to attaining eighteen years of age shall be deemed a "child" irrespective of that person's age at the time the complaint with respect to that violation is filed or the hearing on the complaint is held.

(3) Any person who, while under eighteen years of age, commits an act that would be a felony if committed by an adult and who is not taken into custody or apprehended for that act until after the person attains twenty-one years of age is not a child in relation to that act.

(4) Any person whose case is transferred for criminal prosecution pursuant to section 2152.12 of the Revised Code shall be deemed after the transfer not to be a child in the transferred case.

(5) Any person whose case is transferred for criminal prosecution pursuant to section 2152.12 of the Revised Code and who subsequently is convicted of or pleads guilty to a felony in that case, and any person who is adjudicated a delinquent child for the commission of an act, who has a serious youthful offender dispositional sentence imposed for the act pursuant to section 2152.13 of the Revised Code, and whose adult portion of the dispositional sentence is invoked pursuant to section 2152.14 of the Revised Code, shall be deemed after the transfer or invocation not to be a child in any case in which a complaint is filed against the person.

(6) The juvenile court has jurisdiction over a person who is adjudicated a delinquent child or juvenile traffic offender prior to attaining eighteen years of age until the person attains twenty-one years of age, and, for purposes of that jurisdiction related to that adjudication, except as otherwise provided in this division, a person who is so adjudicated a delinquent child or juvenile traffic offender shall be deemed a "child" until the person attains twenty-one years of age. If a person is so adjudicated a delinquent child or juvenile traffic offender and the court makes a disposition of the person under this chapter, at any time after the person attains eighteen years of age, the places at which the person may be held under that disposition are not limited to places authorized under this chapter solely for confinement of children, and the person may be confined under that disposition, in accordance with division (F)(2) of section 2152.26 of the Revised Code, in places other than those authorized under this chapter solely for confinement of children.

(D) "Chronic truant" means any child of compulsory school age who is absent without legitimate excuse for absence from the public school the child is supposed to attend for seven or more consecutive school days, ten or more school days in one school month, or fifteen or more school days in a school year.

(E) "Community corrections facility," "public safety beds," "release authority," and "supervised release" have the same meanings as in section 5139.01 of the Revised Code.

(F) "Delinquent child" includes any of the following:

(1) Any child, except a juvenile traffic offender, who violates any law of this state or the United States, or any ordinance of a political subdivision of the state, that would be an offense if committed by an adult;

(2) Any child who violates any lawful order of the court made under this chapter or under Chapter 2151. of the Revised Code other than an order issued under section 2151.87 of the Revised Code;

(3) Any child who violates division (A) of section 2923.211 of the Revised Code;

(4) Any child who is a habitual truant and who previously has been adjudicated an unruly child for being a habitual truant;

(5) Any child who is a chronic truant.

(G) "Discretionary serious youthful offender" means a person who is eligible for a discretionary SYO and who is not transferred to adult court under a mandatory or discretionary transfer.

(H) "Discretionary SYO" means a case in which the juvenile court, in the juvenile court's discretion, may impose a serious youthful offender disposition under section 2152.13 of the Revised Code.

(I) "Discretionary transfer" means that the juvenile court has discretion to transfer a case for criminal prosecution under division (B) of section 2152.12 of the Revised Code.

(J) "Drug abuse offense," "felony drug abuse offense," and "minor drug possession offense" have the same meanings as in section 2925.01 of the Revised Code.

(K) "Electronic monitoring" and "electronic monitoring device" have the same meanings as in section 2929.01 of the Revised Code.

(L) "Economic loss" means any economic detriment suffered by a victim of a delinquent act or juvenile traffic offense as a direct and proximate result of the delinquent act or juvenile traffic offense and includes any loss of income due to lost time at work because of any injury caused to the victim and any property loss, medical cost, or funeral expense incurred as a result of the delinquent act or juvenile traffic offense. "Economic loss" does not include non-economic loss or any punitive or exemplary damages.

(M) "Firearm" has the same meaning as in section 2923.11 of the Revised Code.

(N) "Juvenile traffic offender" means any child who violates any traffic law, traffic ordinance, or traffic regulation of this state, the United States, or any political subdivision of this state, other than a resolution, ordinance, or regulation of a political subdivision of this state the violation of which is required to be handled by a parking violations bureau or a joint parking violations bureau pursuant to Chapter 4521. of the Revised Code.

(O) A "legitimate excuse for absence from the public school the child is supposed to attend" has the same meaning as in section 2151.011 of the Revised Code.

(P) "Mandatory serious youthful offender" means a person who is eligible for a mandatory SYO and who is not transferred to adult court under a mandatory or discretionary transfer.

(Q) "Mandatory SYO" means a case in which the juvenile court is required to impose a mandatory serious youthful offender disposition under section 2152.13 of the Revised Code.

(R) "Mandatory transfer" means that a case is required to be transferred for criminal prosecution under division (A) of section 2152.12 of the Revised Code.

(S) "Mental illness" has the same meaning as in section 5122.01 of the Revised Code.

(T) "Mentally retarded person" has the same meaning as in section 5123.01 of the Revised Code.

(U) "Monitored time" and "repeat violent offender" have the same meanings as in section 2929.01 of the Revised Code.

(V) "Of compulsory school age" has the same meaning as in section 3321.01 of the Revised Code.

(W) "Public record" has the same meaning as in section 149.43 of the Revised Code.

(X) "Serious youthful offender" means a person who is eligible for a mandatory SYO or discretionary SYO but who is not transferred to adult court under a mandatory or discretionary transfer.

(Y) "Sexually oriented offense," "habitual sex offender," "juvenile offender registrant," " sexual predator," "presumptive registration-exempt sexually oriented offense," "registration-exempt sexually oriented offense," "child-victim oriented offense," " habitual child-victim offender," and "child-victim predator" have the same meanings as in section 2950.01 of the Revised Code.

(Z) "Traditional juvenile" means a case that is not transferred to adult court under a mandatory or discretionary transfer, that is eligible for a disposition under sections 2152.16, 2152.17, 2152.19, and 2152.20 of the Revised Code, and that is not eligible for a disposition under section 2152.13 of the Revised Code.

(AA) "Transfer" means the transfer for criminal prosecution of a case involving the alleged commission by a child of an act that would be an offense if committed by an adult from the juvenile court to the appropriate court that has jurisdiction of the offense.

(BB) "Category one offense" means any of the following:

(1) A violation of section 2903.01 or 2903.02 of the Revised Code;

(2) A violation of section 2923.02 of the Revised Code involving an attempt to commit aggravated murder or murder.

(CC) "Category two offense" means any of the following:

(1) A violation of section 2903.03, 2905.01, 2907.02, 2909.02, 2911.01, or 2911.11 of the Revised Code;

(2) A violation of section 2903.04 of the Revised Code that is a felony of the first degree;

(3) A violation of section 2907.12 of the Revised Code as it existed prior to September 3, 1996.

(DD) "Non–economic loss" means nonpecuniary harm suffered by a victim of a delinquent act or juvenile traffic offense as a result of or related to the delinquent act or juvenile traffic offense, including, but not limited to, pain and suffering; loss of society, consortium, companionship, care, assistance, attention, protection, advice, guidance, counsel, instruction, training, or education; mental anguish; and any other intangible loss.

(2004 H 52, eff. 6–1–04; 2003 S 5, § 3, eff. 1–1–04; 2003 S 5, § 1, eff. 7–31–03; 2002 H 490, eff. 1–1–04; 2002 H 400, eff. 4–3–03; 2001 S 3, eff. 1–1–02; 2000 S 179, § 3, eff. 1–1–02)

2152.021 Complaint; indictment

(A)(1) Subject to division (A)(2) of this section, any person having knowledge of a child who appears to be a juvenile traffic offender or to be a delinquent child may file a sworn complaint with respect to that child in the juvenile court of the county in which the child has a residence or legal settlement or in which the traffic offense or delinquent act allegedly occurred. The sworn complaint may be upon information and belief, and, in addition to the allegation that the child is a delinquent child or a juvenile traffic offender, the complaint shall allege the particular facts upon which the allegation that the child is a delinquent child or a juvenile traffic offender is based.

If a child appears to be a delinquent child who is eligible for a serious youthful offender dispositional sentence under section 2152.11 of the Revised Code and if the prosecuting attorney desires to seek a serious youthful offender dispositional sentence under section 2152.13 of the Revised Code in regard to the child, the prosecuting attorney of the county in which the alleged delinquency occurs may initiate a case in the juvenile court of the county by presenting the case to a grand jury for indictment, by charging the child in a bill of information as a serious youthful offender pursuant to section 2152.13 of the Revised Code, by requesting a serious youthful offender dispositional sentence in the original complaint alleging that the child is a delinquent child, or by filing with the juvenile court a written notice of intent to seek a serious youthful offender dispositional sentence.

(2) Any person having knowledge of a child who appears to be a delinquent child for being an habitual or chronic truant may file a sworn complaint with respect to that child and the parent, guardian, or other person having care of the child in the juvenile court of the county in which the child has a residence or legal settlement or in which the child is supposed to attend public school. The sworn complaint may be upon information and belief and shall contain the following allegations:

(a) That the child is a delinquent child for being a chronic truant or an habitual truant who previously has been adjudicated an unruly child for being a habitual truant and, in addition, the particular facts upon which that allegation is based;

(b) That the parent, guardian, or other person having care of the child has failed to cause the child's attendance at school in violation of section 3321.38 of the Revised Code and, in addition, the particular facts upon which that allegation is based.

(B) Any person with standing under applicable law may file a complaint for the determination of any other matter over which the juvenile court is given jurisdiction by section 2151.23 of the Revised Code. The complaint shall be filed in the county in which the child who is the subject of the complaint is found or was last known to be found.

(C) Within ten days after the filing of a complaint or the issuance of an indictment, the court shall give written notice of the filing of the complaint or the issuance of an indictment and of the substance of the complaint or indictment to the superintendent of a city, local, exempted village, or joint vocational school district if the complaint or indictment alleges that a child committed an act that would be a criminal offense if committed by an adult, that the child was sixteen years of age or older at the time of the commission of the alleged act, and that the alleged act is any of the following:

(1) A violation of section 2923.122 of the Revised Code that relates to property owned or controlled by, or to an activity held under the auspices of, the board of education of that school district;

(2) A violation of section 2923.12 of the Revised Code, of a substantially similar municipal ordinance, or of section 2925.03 of the Revised Code that was committed on property owned or controlled by, or at an activity held under the auspices of, the board of education of that school district;

(3) A violation of section 2925.11 of the Revised Code that was committed on property owned or controlled by, or at an activity held under the auspices of, the board of education of that school district, other than a violation of that section that would be a minor drug possession offense if committed by an adult;

(4) A violation of section 2903.01, 2903.02, 2903.03, 2903.04, 2903.11, 2903.12, 2907.02, or 2907.05 of the Revised Code, or a violation of former section 2907.12 of the Revised Code, that was committed on property owned or controlled by, or at an activity held under the auspices of, the board of education of that school district, if the victim at the time of the commission of the alleged act was an employee of the board of education of that school district;

(5) Complicity in any violation described in division (C)(1), (2), (3), or (4) of this section that was alleged to have been committed in the manner described in division (C)(1), (2), (3), or (4) of this section, regardless of whether the act of complicity was committed on property owned or controlled by, or at an activity held under the auspices of, the board of education of that school district.

(D) A public children services agency, acting pursuant to a complaint or an action on a complaint filed under this section, is not subject to the requirements of section 3127.23 of the Revised Code.

(E) For purposes of the record to be maintained by the clerk under division (B) of section 2152.71 of the Revised Code, when a complaint is filed that alleges that a child is a delinquent child, the court shall determine if the victim of the alleged delinquent act was sixty-five years of age or older or permanently and totally disabled at the time of the alleged commission of the act.

(2004 S 185, eff. 4–11–05; 2000 S 179, § 3, eff. 1–1–02)

2152.03 Transfer of cases to juvenile court

When a child is arrested under any charge, complaint, affidavit, or indictment for a felony or a misdemeanor, proceedings regarding the child initially shall be in the juvenile court in accordance with this chapter. If the child is taken before a judge of a county court, a mayor, a judge of a municipal court, or a judge of a court of common pleas other than a juvenile court, the judge of the county court, mayor, judge of the municipal court, or judge of the court of common pleas shall transfer the case to the juvenile court, and, upon the transfer, the proceedings shall be in accordance with this chapter. Upon the transfer, all further proceedings under the charge, complaint, information, or indictment shall be discontinued in the court of the judge of the county court, mayor, municipal judge, or judge of the court of common pleas other than a juvenile court subject to section 2152.12 of the Revised Code. The case relating to the child then shall be within the exclusive jurisdiction of the juvenile court, subject to section 2152.12 of the Revised Code.

(2000 S 179, § 3, eff. 1–1–02)

2152.04 Social histories of delinquent children

A child who is alleged to be, or who is adjudicated, a delinquent child may be confined in a place of juvenile detention provided under section 2152.41 of the Revised Code for a period not to exceed ninety days, during which time a social history may be prepared to include court record, family history, personal history, school and attendance records, and any other pertinent studies and material that will be of assistance to the juvenile court in its disposition of the charges against that alleged or adjudicated delinquent child.

(2000 S 179, § 3, eff. 1–1–02)

DISPOSITIONAL ORDERS

2152.10 Mandatory transfer; discretionary transfer

(A) A child who is alleged to be a delinquent child is eligible for mandatory transfer and shall be transferred as provided in section 2152.12 of the Revised Code in any of the following circumstances:

(1) The child is charged with a category one offense and either of the following apply:

(a) The child was sixteen years of age or older at the time of the act charged.

(b) The child was fourteen or fifteen years of age at the time of the act charged and previously was adjudicated a delinquent child for committing an act that is a category one or category two offense and was committed to the legal custody of the department of youth services upon the basis of that adjudication.

(2) The child is charged with a category two offense, other than a violation of section 2905.01 of the Revised Code, the child was sixteen years of age or older at the time of the commission of the act charged, and either or both of the following apply:

(a) The child previously was adjudicated a delinquent child for committing an act that is a category one or a category two offense and was committed to the legal custody of the department of youth services on the basis of that adjudication.

(b) The child is alleged to have had a firearm on or about the child's person or under the child's control while committing the act charged and to have displayed the firearm, brandished the firearm, indicated possession of the firearm, or used the firearm to facilitate the commission of the act charged.

(3) Division (A)(2) of section 2152.12 of the Revised Code applies.

(B) Unless the child is subject to mandatory transfer, if a child is fourteen years of age or older at the time of the act charged and if the child is charged with an act that would be a felony if committed by an adult, the child is eligible for discretionary transfer to the appropriate court for criminal prosecution. In determining whether to transfer the child for criminal prosecution, the juvenile court shall follow the procedures in section 2152.12 of the Revised Code. If the court does not transfer the child and if the court adjudicates the child to be a delinquent child for the act charged, the court shall issue an order of disposition in accordance with section 2152.11 of the Revised Code.

(2002 H 393, eff. 7–5–02; 2000 S 179, § 3, eff. 1–1–02)

2152.11 More restrictive dispositions for commission of enhanced acts

(A) A child who is adjudicated a delinquent child for committing an act that would be a felony if committed by an adult is eligible for a particular type of disposition under this section if the child was not transferred under section 2152.12 of the Revised Code. If the complaint, indictment, or information charging the act includes one or more of the following factors, the act is considered to be enhanced, and the child is eligible for a more restrictive disposition under this section;

(1) The act charged against the child would be an offense of violence if committed by an adult.

(2) During the commission of the act charged, the child used a firearm, displayed a firearm, brandished a firearm, or indicated that the child possessed a firearm and actually possessed a firearm.

(3) The child previously was admitted to a department of youth services facility for the commission of an act that would have been aggravated murder, murder, a felony of the first or second degree if committed by an adult, or an act that would have been a felony of the third degree and an offense of violence if committed by an adult.

(B) If a child is adjudicated a delinquent child for committing an act that would be aggravated murder or murder if committed by an adult, the child is eligible for whichever of the following is appropriate:

(1) Mandatory SYO, if the act allegedly was committed when the child was fourteen or fifteen years of age;

(2) Discretionary SYO, if the act was committed when the child was ten, eleven, twelve, or thirteen years of age;

(3) Traditional juvenile, if divisions (B)(1) and (2) of this section do not apply.

(C) If a child is adjudicated a delinquent child for committing an act that would be attempted aggravated murder or attempted murder if committed by an adult, the child is eligible for whichever of the following is appropriate:

(1) Mandatory SYO, if the act allegedly was committed when the child was fourteen or fifteen years of age;

(2) Discretionary SYO, if the act was committed when the child was ten, eleven, twelve, or thirteen years of age;

(3) Traditional juvenile, if divisions (C)(1) and (2) of this section do not apply.

(D) If a child is adjudicated a delinquent child for committing an act that would be a felony of the first degree if committed by an adult, the child is eligible for whichever of the following is appropriate:

(1) Mandatory SYO, if the act allegedly was committed when the child was sixteen or seventeen years of age, and the act is enhanced by the factors described in division (A)(1) and either division (A)(2) or (3) of this section;

(2) Discretionary SYO, if any of the following applies:

(a) The act was committed when the child was sixteen or seventeen years of age, and division (D)(1) of this section does not apply.

(b) The act was committed when the child was fourteen or fifteen years of age.

(c) The act was committed when the child was twelve or thirteen years of age, and the act is enhanced by any factor described in division (A)(1), (2), or (3) of this section.

(d) The act was committed when the child was ten or eleven years of age, and the act is enhanced by the factors described in division (A)(1) and either division (A)(2) or (3) of this section.

(3) Traditional juvenile, if divisions (D)(1) and (2) of this section do not apply.

(E) If a child is adjudicated a delinquent child for committing an act that would be a felony of the second degree if committed by an adult, the child is eligible for whichever of the following is appropriate:

(1) Discretionary SYO, if the act was committed when the child was fourteen, fifteen, sixteen, or seventeen years of age;

(2) Discretionary SYO, if the act was committed when the child was twelve or thirteen years of age, and the act is enhanced by any factor described in division (A)(1), (2), or (3) of this section;

(3) Traditional juvenile, if divisions (E)(1) and (2) of this section do not apply.

(F) If a child is adjudicated a delinquent child for committing an act that would be a felony of the third degree if committed by an adult, the child is eligible for whichever of the following is appropriate:

(1) Discretionary SYO, if the act was committed when the child was sixteen or seventeen years of age;

(2) Discretionary SYO, if the act was committed when the child was fourteen or fifteen years of age, and the act is enhanced by any factor described in division (A)(1), (2), or (3) of this section;

(3) Traditional juvenile, if divisions (F)(1) and (2) of this section do not apply.

(G) If a child is adjudicated a delinquent child for committing an act that would be a felony of the fourth or fifth degree if committed by an adult, the child is eligible for whichever of the following dispositions is appropriate:

(1) Discretionary SYO, if the act was committed when the child was sixteen or seventeen years of age, and the act is enhanced by any factor described in division (A)(1), (2), or (3) of this section;

(2) Traditional juvenile, if division (G)(1) of this section does not apply.

(H) The following table describes the dispositions that a juvenile court may impose on a delinquent child:

OFFENSE CATEGORY (Enhancement factors)	AGE 16 & 17	AGE 14 & 15	AGE 12 & 13	AGE 10 & 11
Murder/aggravated Murder	N/A	MSYO, TJ	DSYO, TJ	DSYO, TJ
Attempted Murder/Attempted Aggravated Murder	N/A	MSYO, TJ	DSYO, TJ	DSYO, TJ
F1 (enhanced by offense of violence factor and either disposition firearm factor or previous DYS admission factor)	MSYO,	DSYO, TJ	DSYO, TJ	DSYO, TJ
F1 (enhanced by any single or other combination of enhancement factors)	DSYO, TJ	DSYO, TJ	DSYO, TJ	TJ
F1 (not enhanced)	DSYO, TJ	DSYO, TJ	TJ	TJ
F2 (enhanced by any enhancement factor)	DSYO, TJ	DSYO, TJ	DSYO, TJ	TJ
F2 (not enhanced)	DSYO, TJ	DSYO, TJ	TJ	TJ
F3 (enhanced by any enhancement factor)	DSYO, TJ	DSYO, TJ	TJ	TJ
F3 (not enhanced)	DSYO, TJ	TJ	TJ	TJ
F4 (enhanced by any enhancement factor)	DSYO, TJ	TJ	TJ	TJ
F4 (not enhanced)	TJ	TJ	TJ	TJ
F5 (enhanced by any enhancement factor)	DSYO, TJ	TJ	TJ	TJ
F5 (not enhanced)	TJ	TJ	TJ	TJ

(I) The table in division (H) of this section is for illustrative purposes only. If the table conflicts with any provision of divisions (A) to (G) of this section, divisions (A) to (G) of this section shall control.

(J) Key for table in division (H) of this section:

(1) "Any enhancement factor" applies when the criteria described in division (A)(1), (2), or (3) of this section apply.

(2) The "disposition firearm factor" applies when the criteria described in division (A)(2) of this section apply.

(3) "DSYO" refers to discretionary serious youthful offender disposition.

(4) "F1" refers to an act that would be a felony of the first degree if committed by an adult.

(5) "F2" refers to an act that would be a felony of the second degree if committed by an adult.

(6) "F3" refers to an act that would be a felony of the third degree if committed by an adult.

(7) "F4" refers to an act that would be a felony of the fourth degree if committed by an adult.

(8) "F5" refers to an act that would be a felony of the fifth degree if committed by an adult.

(9) "MSYO" refers to mandatory serious youthful offender disposition.

(10) The "offense of violence factor" applies when the criteria described in division (A)(1) of this section apply.

(11) The "previous DYS admission factor" applies when the criteria described in division (A)(3) of this section apply.

(12) "TJ" refers to traditional juvenile.

(2000 S 179, § 3, eff. 1–1–02)

2152.12 Transfer of cases from juvenile court

(A)(1)(a) After a complaint has been filed alleging that a child is a delinquent child for committing an act that would be aggravated murder, murder, attempted aggravated murder, or attempted murder if committed by an adult, the juvenile court at a hearing shall transfer the case if the child was sixteen or seventeen years of age at the time of the act charged and there is probable cause to believe that the child committed the act charged. The juvenile court also shall transfer the case at a hearing if the child was fourteen or fifteen years of age at the time of the act charged, if section 2152.10 of the Revised Code provides that the child is eligible for mandatory transfer, and if there is probable cause to believe that the child committed the act charged.

(b) After a complaint has been filed alleging that a child is a delinquent child by reason of committing a category two offense, the juvenile court at a hearing shall transfer the case if section 2152.10 of the Revised Code requires the mandatory transfer of the case and there is probable cause to believe that the child committed the act charged.

(2) The juvenile court also shall transfer a case in the circumstances described in division (C)(5) of section 2152.02 of the Revised Code or if either of the following applies:

(a) A complaint is filed against a child who is eligible for a discretionary transfer under section 2152.10 of the Revised Code and who previously was convicted of or pleaded guilty to a felony in a case that was transferred to a criminal court.

(b) A complaint is filed against a child who is domiciled in another state alleging that the child is a delinquent child for committing an act that would be a felony if committed by an adult, and, if the act charged had been committed in that other state, the child would be subject to criminal prosecution as an adult under the law of that other state without the need for a transfer of jurisdiction from a juvenile, family, or similar noncriminal court to a criminal court.

(B) Except as provided in division (A) of this section, after a complaint has been filed alleging that a child is a delinquent child for committing an act that would be a felony if committed by an adult, the juvenile court at a hearing may transfer the case if the court finds all of the following:

(1) The child was fourteen years of age or older at the time of the act charged.

(2) There is probable cause to believe that the child committed the act charged.

(3) The child is not amenable to care or rehabilitation within the juvenile system, and the safety of the community may require that the child be subject to adult sanctions. In making its decision under this division, the court shall consider whether the applicable factors under division (D) of this section indicating that the case should be transferred outweigh the applicable factors under division (E) of this section indicating that the case should not be transferred. The record shall indicate the specific factors that were applicable and that the court weighed.

(C) Before considering a transfer under division (B) of this section, the juvenile court shall order an investigation, including a mental examination of the child by a public or private agency or a person qualified to make the examination. The child may waive the examination required by this division if the court finds that the waiver is competently and intelligently made. Refusal to submit to a mental examination by the child constitutes a waiver of the examination.

(D) In considering whether to transfer a child under division (B) of this section, the juvenile court shall consider the following relevant factors, and any other relevant factors, in favor of a transfer under that division:

(1) The victim of the act charged suffered physical or psychological harm, or serious economic harm, as a result of the alleged act.

(2) The physical or psychological harm suffered by the victim due to the alleged act of the child was exacerbated because of the physical or psychological vulnerability or the age of the victim.

(3) The child's relationship with the victim facilitated the act charged.

(4) The child allegedly committed the act charged for hire or as a part of a gang or other organized criminal activity.

(5) The child had a firearm on or about the child's person or under the child's control at the time of the act charged, the act charged is not a violation of section 2923.12 of the Revised Code, and the child, during the commission of the act charged, allegedly used or displayed the firearm, brandished the firearm, or indicated that the child possessed a firearm.

(6) At the time of the act charged, the child was awaiting adjudication or disposition as a delinquent child, was under a community control sanction, or was on parole for a prior delinquent child adjudication or conviction.

(7) The results of any previous juvenile sanctions and programs indicate that rehabilitation of the child will not occur in the juvenile system.

(8) The child is emotionally, physically, or psychologically mature enough for the transfer.

(9) There is not sufficient time to rehabilitate the child within the juvenile system.

(E) In considering whether to transfer a child under division (B) of this section, the juvenile court shall consider the following relevant factors, and any other relevant factors, against a transfer under that division:

(1) The victim induced or facilitated the act charged.

(2) The child acted under provocation in allegedly committing the act charged.

(3) The child was not the principal actor in the act charged, or, at the time of the act charged, the child was under the negative influence or coercion of another person.

(4) The child did not cause physical harm to any person or property, or have reasonable cause to believe that harm of that nature would occur, in allegedly committing the act charged.

(5) The child previously has not been adjudicated a delinquent child.

(6) The child is not emotionally, physically, or psychologically mature enough for the transfer.

(7) The child has a mental illness or is a mentally retarded person.

(8) There is sufficient time to rehabilitate the child within the juvenile system and the level of security available in the juvenile system provides a reasonable assurance of public safety.

(F) If one or more complaints are filed alleging that a child is a delinquent child for committing two or more acts that would be offenses if committed by an adult, if a motion is made alleging that division (A) of this section applies and requires that the case or cases involving one or more of the acts charged be transferred for, and if a motion also is made requesting that the case or cases involving one or more of the acts charged be transferred pursuant to division (B) of this section, the juvenile court, in deciding the motions, shall proceed in the following manner:

(1) Initially, the court shall decide the motion alleging that division (A) of this section applies and requires that the case or cases involving one or more of the acts charged be transferred.

(2) If the court determines that division (A) of this section applies and requires that the case or cases involving one or more of the acts charged be transferred, the court shall transfer the case or cases in accordance with the that division. After the transfer pursuant to division (A) of this section, the court shall decide, in accordance with division (B) of this section, whether to grant the motion requesting that the case or cases involving one or more of the acts charged be transferred pursuant to that division. Notwithstanding division (B) of this section, prior to transferring a case pursuant to division (A) of this section, the court is not required to consider any factor specified in division (D) or (E) of this section or to conduct an investigation under division (C) of this section.

(3) If the court determines that division (A) of this section does not require that the case or cases involving one or more of the acts charged be transferred, the court shall decide in accordance with division (B) of this section whether to grant the motion requesting that the case or cases involving one or more of the acts charged be transferred pursuant to that division.

(G) The court shall give notice in writing of the time, place, and purpose of any hearing held pursuant to division (A) or (B) of this section to the child's parents, guardian, or other custodian and to the child's counsel at least three days prior to the hearing.

(H) No person, either before or after reaching eighteen years of age, shall be prosecuted as an adult for an offense committed prior to becoming eighteen years of age, unless the person has been transferred as provided in division (A) or (B) of this section or unless division (J) of this section applies. Any prosecution that is had in a criminal court on the mistaken belief that the person who is the subject of the case was eighteen years of age or older at the time of the commission of the offense shall be deemed a nullity, and the person shall not be considered to have been in jeopardy on the offense.

(I) Upon the transfer of a case under division (A) or (B) of this section, the juvenile court shall state the reasons for the transfer on the record, and shall order the child to enter into a recognizance with good and sufficient surety for the child's appearance before the appropriate court for any disposition that the court is authorized to make for a similar act committed by an adult. The transfer abates the jurisdiction of the juvenile court with respect to the delinquent acts alleged in the complaint, and, upon the transfer, all further proceedings pertaining to the act charged shall be discontinued in the juvenile court, and the case then shall be within the jurisdiction of the court to which it is transferred as described in division (H) of section 2151.23 of the Revised Code.

(J) If a person under eighteen years of age allegedly commits an act that would be a felony if committed by an adult and if the person is not taken into custody or apprehended for that act until after the person attains twenty-one years of age, the juvenile court does not have jurisdiction to hear or determine any portion of the case charging the person with committing that act. In those circumstances, divisions (A) and (B) of this section do not apply regarding the act, and the case charging the person with committing the act shall be a criminal prosecution commenced and heard in the appropriate court having jurisdiction of the offense as if the person had been eighteen years of age or older when the person committed the act. All proceedings pertaining to the act shall be within the jurisdiction of the court having jurisdiction of the offense, and that court has all the authority and duties in the case as it has in other criminal cases in that court.

(2000 S 179, § 3, eff. 1–1–02)

2152.13 Serious youthful offender dispositional sentence

(A) A juvenile court may impose a serious youthful offender dispositional sentence on a child only if the prosecuting attorney of the county in which the delinquent act allegedly occurred initiates the process against the child in accordance with this division, and the child is an alleged delinquent child who is eligible for the dispositional sentence. The prosecuting attorney may initiate the process in any of the following ways:

(1) Obtaining an indictment of the child as a serious youthful offender;

(2) The child waives the right to indictment, charging the child in a bill of information as a serious youthful offender;

(3) Until an indictment or information is obtained, requesting a serious youthful offender dispositional sentence in the original complaint alleging that the child is a delinquent child;

(4) Until an indictment or information is obtained, if the original complaint does not request a serious youthful offender dispositional sentence, filing with the juvenile court a written notice of intent to seek a serious youthful offender dispositional sentence within twenty days after the later of the following, unless the time is extended by the juvenile court for good cause shown:

(a) The date of the child's first juvenile court hearing regarding the complaint;

(b) The date the juvenile court determines not to transfer the case under section 2152.12 of the Revised Code.

After a written notice is filed under division (A)(4) of this section, the juvenile court shall serve a copy of the notice on the child and advise the child of the prosecuting attorney's intent to seek a serious youthful offender dispositional sentence in the case.

(B) If an alleged delinquent child is not indicted or charged by information as described in division (A)(1) or (2) of this section and if a notice or complaint as described in division (A)(3) or (4) of this section indicates that the prosecuting attorney intends to pursue a serious youthful offender dispositional sentence in the case, the juvenile court shall hold a preliminary hearing to determine if there is probable cause that the child committed the act charged and is by age eligible for, or required to receive, a serious youthful offender dispositional sentence.

(C) (1) A child for whom a serious youthful offender dispositional sentence is sought has the right to a grand jury determination of probable cause that the child committed the act charged and that the child is eligible by age for a serious youthful offender dispositional sentence. The grand jury may be impaneled by the court of common pleas or the juvenile court.

Once a child is indicted, or charged by information or the juvenile court determines that the child is eligible for a serious youthful offender dispositional sentence, the child is entitled to an open and speedy trial by jury in juvenile court and to be provided with a transcript of the proceedings. The time within which the trial is to be held under Title XXIX of the Revised Code commences on whichever of the following dates is applicable:

(a) If the child is indicted or charged by information, on the date of the filing of the indictment or information.

(b) If the child is charged by an original complaint that requests a serious youthful offender dispositional sentence, on the date of the filing of the complaint.

(c) If the child is not charged by an original complaint that requests a serious youthful offender dispositional sentence, on the date that the prosecuting attorney files the written notice of intent to seek a serious youthful offender dispositional sentence.

(2) If the child is detained awaiting adjudication, upon indictment or being charged by information, the child has the same right to bail as an adult charged with the offense the alleged delinquent act would be if committed by an adult. Except as provided in division (D) of section 2152.14 of the Revised Code, all provisions of Title XXIX of the Revised Code and the Criminal Rules shall apply in the case and to the child. The juvenile court shall afford the child all rights afforded a person who is prosecuted for committing a crime including the right to counsel and the right to raise the issue of competency. The child may not waive the right to counsel.

(D) (1) If a child is adjudicated a delinquent child for committing an act under circumstances that require the juvenile court to impose upon the child a serious youthful offender dispositional sentence under section 2152.11 of the Revised Code, all of the following apply:

(a) The juvenile court shall impose upon the child a sentence available for the violation, as if the child were an adult, under Chapter 2929. of the Revised Code, except that the juvenile court shall not impose on the child a sentence of death or life imprisonment without parole.

(b) The juvenile court also shall impose upon the child one or more traditional juvenile dispositions under sections 2152.16, 2152.19, and 2152.20, and, if applicable, section 2152.17 of the Revised Code.

(c) The juvenile court shall stay the adult portion of the serious youthful offender dispositional sentence pending the successful completion of the traditional juvenile dispositions imposed.

(2)(a) If a child is adjudicated a delinquent child for committing an act under circumstances that allow, but do not require, the juvenile court to impose on the child a serious youthful offender dispositional sentence under section 2152.11 of the Revised Code, all of the following apply:

(i) If the juvenile court on the record makes a finding that, given the nature and circumstances of the violation and the history of the child, the length of time, level of security, and types of programming and resources available in the juvenile system alone are not adequate to provide the juvenile court with a reasonable expectation that the purposes set forth in section 2152.01 of the Revised Code will be met, the juvenile court may impose upon the child a sentence available for the violation, as if the child were an adult, under Chapter 2929. of the Revised Code, except that the juvenile court shall not impose on the child a sentence of death or life imprisonment without parole.

(ii) If a sentence is imposed under division (D) (2)(a)(i) of this section, the juvenile court also shall impose upon the child one or more traditional juvenile dispositions under sections 2152.16, 2152.19, and 2152.20 and, if applicable, section 2152.17 of the Revised Code.

(iii) The juvenile court shall stay the adult portion of the serious youthful offender dispositional sentence pending the successful completion of the traditional juvenile dispositions imposed.

(b) If the juvenile court does not find that a sentence should be imposed under division (D) (2)(a)(i) of this section, the juvenile court may impose one or more traditional juvenile dispositions under sections 2152.16, 2152.19, 2152.20, and, if applicable, section 2152.17 of the Revised Code.

(3) A child upon whom a serious youthful offender dispositional sentence is imposed under division (D) (1) or (2) of this section has a right to appeal under division (A)(1), (3), (4), (5), or (6) of section 2953.08 of the Revised Code the adult portion of the serious youthful offender dispositional sentence when any of those divisions apply. The child may appeal the adult portion, and the court shall consider the appeal as if the adult portion were not stayed.

(2002 H 393, eff. 7–5–02; 2000 S 179, § 3, eff. 1–1–02)

2152.14 Invoking adult portion of sentence

(A)(1) The director of youth services may request the prosecuting attorney of the county in which is located the juvenile court that imposed a serious youthful offender dispositional sentence upon a person to file a motion with that juvenile court to invoke the adult portion of the dispositional sentence if all of the following apply to the person:

(a) The person is at least fourteen years of age.

(b) The person is in the institutional custody, or an escapee from the custody, of the department of youth services.

(c) The person is serving the juvenile portion of the serious youthful offender dispositional sentence.

(2) The motion shall state that there is reasonable cause to believe that either of the following misconduct has occurred and shall state that at least one incident of misconduct of that nature occurred after the person reached fourteen years of age:

(a) The person committed an act that is a violation of the rules of the institution and that could be charged as any felony or as a first degree misdemeanor offense of violence if committed by an adult.

(b) The person has engaged in conduct that creates a substantial risk to the safety or security of the institution, the community, or the victim.

(B) If a person is at least fourteen years of age, is serving the juvenile portion of a serious youthful offender dispositional sentence, and is on parole or aftercare from a department of youth services facility, or on community control, the director of youth services, the juvenile court that imposed the serious youthful offender dispositional sentence on the person, or the probation department supervising the person may request the prosecuting attorney of the county in which is located the juvenile court to file a motion with the juvenile court to invoke the adult portion of the dispositional sentence. The prosecuting attorney may file a motion to invoke the adult portion of the dispositional sentence even if no request is made. The motion shall state that there is reasonable cause to believe that either of the following occurred and shall state that at least one incident of misconduct of that nature occurred after the person reached fourteen years of age:

(1) The person committed an act that is a violation of the conditions of supervision and that could be charged as any felony or as a first degree misdemeanor offense of violence if committed by an adult.

(2) The person has engaged in conduct that creates a substantial risk to the safety or security of the community or of the victim.

(C) If the prosecuting attorney declines a request to file a motion that was made by the department of youth services or the supervising probation department under division (A) or (B) of this section or fails to act on a request made under either division by the department within a reasonable time, the department of youth services or the supervising probation department may file a motion of the type described in division (A) or (B) of this section with the juvenile court to invoke the adult portion of the serious youthful offender dispositional sentence. If the prosecuting attorney declines a request to file a motion that was made by the juvenile court under division (B) of this section or fails to act on a request from the court under that division within a reasonable time, the juvenile court may hold the hearing described in division (D) of this section on its own motion.

(D) Upon the filing of a motion described in division (A), (B), or (C) of this section, the juvenile court may hold a hearing to determine whether to invoke the adult portion of a person's serious juvenile offender dispositional sentence. The juvenile court shall not invoke the adult portion of the dispositional sentence without a hearing. At the hearing the person who is the subject of the serious youthful offender disposition has the right to be present, to receive notice of the grounds upon which the adult sentence portion is sought to be invoked, to be represented by counsel including counsel appointed under Juvenile Rule 4(A), to be advised on the procedures and protections set forth in the Juvenile Rules, and to present evidence on the person's own behalf, including evidence that the person has a mental illness or is a mentally retarded person. The person may not waive the right to counsel. The hearing shall be open to the public. If the person presents evidence that the person has a mental illness or is a mentally retarded person, the juvenile court shall consider that evidence in determining whether to invoke the adult portion of the serious youthful offender dispositional sentence.

(E)(1) The juvenile court may invoke the adult portion of a person's serious youthful offender dispositional sentence if the juvenile court finds all of the following on the record by clear and convincing evidence:

(a) The person is serving the juvenile portion of a serious youthful offender dispositional sentence.

(b) The person is at least fourteen years of age and has been admitted to a department of youth services facility, or criminal charges are pending against the person.

(c) The person engaged in the conduct or acts charged under division (A), (B), or (C) of this section, and the person's conduct demonstrates that the person is unlikely to be rehabilitated during the remaining period of juvenile jurisdiction.

(2) The court may modify the adult sentence the court invokes to consist of any lesser prison term that could be imposed for the offense and, in addition to the prison term or in lieu of the prison term if the prison term was not mandatory, any community control sanction that the offender was eligible to receive at sentencing.

(F) If a juvenile court issues an order invoking the adult portion of a serious youthful offender dispositional sentence under division (E) of this section, the juvenile portion of the dispositional sentence shall terminate, and the department of youth services shall transfer the person to the department of rehabilitation and correction or place the person under another sanction imposed as part of the sentence. The juvenile court shall state in its order the total number of days that the person has been held in detention or in a facility operated by, or under contract with, the department of youth services under the juvenile portion of the dispositional sentence. The time the person must serve on a prison term imposed under the adult portion of the dispositional sentence shall be reduced by the total number of days specified in the order plus any additional days the person is held in a juvenile facility or in detention after the order is issued and before the person is transferred to the custody of the department of rehabilitation and correction. In no case shall the total prison term as calculated under this division exceed the maximum prison term available for an adult who is convicted of violating the same sections of the Revised Code.

Any community control imposed as part of the adult sentence or as a condition of a judicial release from prison shall be under the supervision of the entity that provides adult probation services in the county. Any post-release control imposed after the offender otherwise is released from prison shall be supervised by the adult parole authority.

(2002 H 393, eff. 7–5–02; 2000 S 179, § 3, eff. 1–1–02)

2152.16 Commitment of delinquent children to custody of youth services department

(A)(1) If a child is adjudicated a delinquent child for committing an act that would be a felony if committed by an adult, the juvenile court may commit the child to the legal custody of the department of youth services for secure confinement as follows:

(a) For an act that would be aggravated murder or murder if committed by an adult, until the offender attains twenty-one years of age;

(b) For a violation of section 2923.02 of the Revised Code that involves an attempt to commit an act that would be aggravated murder or murder if committed by an adult, a minimum period of six to seven years as prescribed by the court and a maximum period not to exceed the child's attainment of twenty-one years of age;

(c) For a violation of section 2903.03, 2905.01, 2909.02, or 2911.01 or division (A) of section 2903.04 of the Revised Code or for a violation of any provision of section 2907.02 of the Revised Code other than division (A)(1)(b) of that section when the sexual conduct or insertion involved was consensual and when the victim of the violation of division (A)(1)(b) of that section was older than the delinquent child, was the same age as the delinquent child, or was less than three years younger than the delinquent child, for an indefinite term consisting of a minimum period of one to three years, as prescribed by the court, and a maximum period not to exceed the child's attainment of twenty-one years of age;

(d) If the child is adjudicated a delinquent child for committing an act that is not described in division (A)(1)(b) or (c) of this section and that would be a felony of the first or second degree if committed by an adult, for an indefinite term consisting of a minimum period of one year and a maximum period not to exceed the child's attainment of twenty-one years of age.

(e) For committing an act that would be a felony of the third, fourth, or fifth degree if committed by an adult or for a violation of division (A) of section 2923.211 of the Revised Code, for an indefinite term consisting of a minimum period of six months and a maximum period not to exceed the child's attainment of twenty-one years of age.

(2) In each case in which a court makes a disposition under this section, the court retains control over the commitment for the minimum period specified by the court in divisions (A)(1)(a) to (e) of this section. During the minimum period, the department of youth services shall not move the child to a nonsecure setting without the permission of the court that imposed the disposition.

(B) (1) Subject to division (B)(2) of this section, if a delinquent child is committed to the department of youth services under this section, the department may release the child at any time after the minimum period specified by the court in division (A)(1) of this section ends.

(2) A commitment under this section is subject to a supervised release or to a discharge of the child from the custody of the department for medical reasons pursuant to section 5139.54 of the Revised Code, but, during the minimum period specified by the court in division (A)(1) of this section, the department shall obtain court approval of a supervised release or discharge under that section.

(C) If a child is adjudicated a delinquent child, at the dispositional hearing and prior to making any disposition pursuant to this section, the court shall determine whether the delinquent child previously has been adjudicated a delinquent child for a violation of a law or ordinance. If the delinquent child previously has been adjudicated a delinquent child for a violation of a law or ordinance, the court, for purposes of entering an order of disposition of the delinquent child under this section, shall consider the previous delinquent child adjudication as a conviction of a violation of the law or ordinance in determining the degree of the offense the current act would be had it been committed by an adult. This division also shall apply in relation to the imposition of any financial sanction under section 2152.19 of the Revised Code.

(2002 H 393, eff. 7–5–02; 2000 S 179, § 3, eff. 1–1–02)

2152.17 Felony specifications

(A) Subject to division (D) of this section, if a child is adjudicated a delinquent child for committing an act, other than a violation of section 2923.12 of the Revised Code, that would be a felony if committed by an adult and if the court determines that, if the child was an adult, the child would be guilty of a specification of the type set forth in section 2941.141, 2941.144, 2941.145, 2941.146, 2941.1412, 2941.1413[1], or 2941.1414[2] of the Revised Code, in addition to any commitment or other disposition the court imposes for the underlying delinquent act, all of the following apply:

(1) If the court determines that the child would be guilty of a specification of the type set forth in section 2941.141 of the Revised Code, the court may commit the child to the department of youth services for the specification for a definite period of up to one year.

(2) If the court determines that the child would be guilty of a specification of the type set forth in section 2941.145 of the Revised Code or if the delinquent act is a violation of division (A)(1) or (2) of section 2903.06 of the Revised Code and the court determines that the child would be guilty of a specification of the type set forth in section 2941.1414[2] of the Revised Code, the court shall commit the child to the department of youth services for the specification for a definite period of not less than one and not more than three years, and the court also shall commit the child to the department for the underlying delinquent act under sections 2152.11 to 2152.16 of the Revised Code.

(3) If the court determines that the child would be guilty of a specification of the type set forth in section 2941.144, 2941.146, or 2941.1412 of the Revised Code or if the delinquent act is a violation of division (A)(1) or (2) of section 2903.06 of the Revised Code and the court determines that the child would be guilty of a specification of the type set forth in section 2941.1413[1] of the Revised Code, the court shall commit the child to the department of youth services for the specification for a definite period of not less than one and not more than five years, and the court also shall commit the child to the department for the underlying delinquent act under sections 2152.11 to 2152.16 of the Revised Code.

(B) Division (A) of this section also applies to a child who is an accomplice to the same extent the firearm specifications would apply to an adult accomplice in a criminal proceeding.

(C) If a child is adjudicated a delinquent child for committing an act that would be aggravated murder, murder, or a first, second, or third degree felony offense of violence if committed by an adult and if the court determines that, if the child was an adult, the child would be guilty of a specification of the type set forth in section 2941.142 of the Revised Code in relation to the act for which the child was adjudicated a delinquent child, the court shall commit the child for the specification to the legal custody of the department of youth services for institutionalization in a secure facility for a definite period of not less than one and not more than three years, subject to division (D)(2) of this section, and the court also shall commit the child to the department for the underlying delinquent act.

(D)(1) If the child is adjudicated a delinquent child for committing an act that would be an offense of violence that is a felony if committed by an adult and is committed to the legal custody of the department of youth services pursuant to division (A)(1) of section 2152.16 of the Revised Code and if the court determines that the child, if the child was an adult, would be guilty of a specification of the type set forth in section 2941.1411 of the Revised Code in relation to the act for which the child was adjudicated a delinquent child, the court may commit the child to the custody of the department of youth services for institutionalization in a secure facility for up to two years, subject to division (D)(2) of this section.

(2) A court that imposes a period of commitment under division (A) of this section is not precluded from imposing an additional period of commitment under division (C) or (D)(1) of this section, a court that imposes a period of commitment under division (C) of this section is not precluded from imposing an additional period of commitment under division (A) or (D)(1) of this section, and a court that imposes a period of commitment

under division (D)(1) of this section is not precluded from imposing an additional period of commitment under division (A) or (C) of this section.

(E) The court shall not commit a child to the legal custody of the department of youth services for a specification pursuant to this section for a period that exceeds five years for any one delinquent act. Any commitment imposed pursuant to division (A), (B), (C), or (D)(1) of this section shall be in addition to, and shall be served consecutively with and prior to, a period of commitment ordered under this chapter for the underlying delinquent act, and each commitment imposed pursuant to division (A), (B), (C), or (D)(1) of this section shall be in addition to, and shall be served consecutively with, any other period of commitment imposed under those divisions. If a commitment is imposed under division (A) or (B) of this section and a commitment also is imposed under division (C) of this section, the period imposed under division (A) or (B) of this section shall be served prior to the period imposed under division (C) of this section.

In each case in which a court makes a disposition under this section, the court retains control over the commitment for the entire period of the commitment.

The total of all the periods of commitment imposed for any specification under this section and for the underlying offense shall not exceed the child's attainment of twenty-one years of age.

(F) If a child is adjudicated a delinquent child for committing two or more acts that would be felonies if committed by an adult and if the court entering the delinquent child adjudication orders the commitment of the child for two or more of those acts to the legal custody of the department of youth services for institutionalization in a secure facility pursuant to section 2152.13 or 2152.16 of the Revised Code, the court may order that all of the periods of commitment imposed under those sections for those acts be served consecutively in the legal custody of the department of youth services, provided that those periods of commitment shall be in addition to and commence immediately following the expiration of a period of commitment that the court imposes pursuant to division (A), (B), (C), or (D)(1) of this section. A court shall not commit a delinquent child to the legal custody of the department of youth services under this division for a period that exceeds the child's attainment of twenty-one years of age.

(G) If a child is adjudicated a delinquent child for committing an act that if committed by an adult would be aggravated murder, murder, rape, felonious sexual penetration in violation of former section 2907.12 of the Revised Code, involuntary manslaughter, a felony of the first or second degree resulting in the death of or physical harm to a person, complicity in or an attempt to commit any of those offenses, or an offense under an existing or former law of this state that is or was substantially equivalent to any of those offenses and if the court in its order of disposition for that act commits the child to the custody of the department of youth services, the adjudication shall be considered a conviction for purposes of a future determination pursuant to Chapter 2929. of the Revised Code as to whether the child, as an adult, is a repeat violent offender.

(2004 H 52, eff. 6–1–04; 2002 H 130, § 3, eff. 1–1–02[3]*; 2002 H 393, eff. 7–5–02; 2000 S 179, § 3, eff. 1–1–02)*

1 RC 2941.1413 renumbered to RC 2941.1414 by the Legislative Service Commission.

2 RC 2941.1414 renumbered to RC 2941.1415 by the Legislative Service Commission.

3 O Const Art II, § 1c and 1d, and RC 1.471, state that codified sections of law are subject to the referendum unless providing for tax levies, state appropriations, or are emergency in nature. Since this Act is apparently not an exception, and 1–1–02 is within the ninety-day period, the effective date should probably be 4–7–03.

2152.18 Place and duration of institutionalization; records; notice to schools and victims

(A) When a juvenile court commits a delinquent child to the custody of the department of youth services pursuant to this chapter, the court shall not designate the specific institution in which the department is to place the child but instead shall specify that the child is to be institutionalized in a secure facility.

(B) When a juvenile court commits a delinquent child to the custody of the department of youth services pursuant to this chapter, the court shall state in the order of commitment the total number of days that the child has been held in detention in connection with the delinquent child complaint upon which the order of commitment is based. The department shall reduce the minimum period of institutionalization that was ordered by both the total number of days that the child has been so held in detention as stated by the court in the order of commitment and the total number of any additional days that the child has been held in detention subsequent to the order of commitment but prior to the transfer of physical custody of the child to the department.

(C)(1) When a juvenile court commits a delinquent child to the custody of the department of youth services pursuant to this chapter, the court shall provide the department with the child's medical records, a copy of the report of any mental examination of the child ordered by the court, the Revised Code section or sections the child violated and the degree of each violation, the warrant to convey the child to the department, a copy of the court's journal entry ordering the commitment of the child to the legal custody of the department, a copy of the arrest record pertaining to the act for which the child was adjudicated a delinquent child, a copy of any victim impact statement pertaining to the act, and any other information concerning the child that the department reasonably requests. The court also shall complete the form for the standard predisposition investigation report that the department furnishes pursuant to section 5139.04 of the Revised Code and provide the department with the completed form.

The department may refuse to accept physical custody of a delinquent child who is committed to the legal custody of the department until the court provides to the department the documents specified in this division. No officer or employee of the department who refuses to accept physical custody of a delinquent child who is committed to the legal custody of the department shall be subject to prosecution or contempt of court for the refusal if the court fails to provide the documents specified in this division at the time the court transfers the physical custody of the child to the department.

(2) Within twenty working days after the department of youth services receives physical custody of a delinquent child from a juvenile court, the court shall provide the department with a certified copy of the child's birth certificate and the child's social security number or, if the court made all reasonable efforts to obtain the information but was unsuccessful, with documentation of the efforts it made to obtain the information.

(3) If an officer is preparing pursuant to section 2947.06 or 2951.03 of the Revised Code or Criminal Rule 32.2 a presentence investigation report pertaining to a person, the department shall make available to the officer, for use in preparing the report, any records or reports it possesses regarding that person that it received from a juvenile court pursuant to division (C)(1) of this section or that pertain to the treatment of that person after the person was committed to the custody of the department as a delinquent child.

(D)(1) Within ten days after an adjudication that a child is a delinquent child, the court shall give written notice of the adjudication to the superintendent of a city, local, exempted village, or joint vocational school district, and to the principal of the school the child attends, if the basis of the adjudication was the commission of an act that would be a criminal offense if committed by an adult, if the act was committed by the delinquent child when the child was fourteen years of age or older, and if the act is any of the following:

(a) An act that would be a felony or an offense of violence if committed by an adult, an act in the commission of which the child used or brandished a firearm, or an act that is a violation of section 2907.06, 2907.07, 2907.08, 2907.09, 2907.24, or 2907.241 of the Revised Code and that would be a misdemeanor if committed by an adult;

(b) A violation of section 2923.12 of the Revised Code or of a substantially similar municipal ordinance that would be a misdemeanor if committed by an adult and that was committed on property owned or controlled by, or at an activity held under the auspices of, the board of education of that school district;

(c) A violation of division (A) of section 2925.03 or 2925.11 of the Revised Code that would be a misdemeanor if committed by an adult, that was committed on property owned or controlled by, or at an activity held under the auspices of, the board of education of that school district, and that is not a minor drug possession offense;

(d) An act that would be a criminal offense if committed by an adult and that results in serious physical harm to persons or serious physical harm to property while the child is at school, on any other property owned or controlled by the board, or at an interscholastic competition, an extracurricular event, or any other school program or activity;

(e) Complicity in any violation described in division (D)(1)(a), (b), (c), or (d) of this section that was alleged to have been committed in the manner described in division (D)(1)(a), (b), (c), or (d) of this section, regardless of whether the act of complicity was committed on property owned or controlled by, or at an activity held under the auspices of, the board of education of that school district.

(2) The notice given pursuant to division (D)(1) of this section shall include the name of the child who was adjudicated to be a delinquent child, the child's age at the time the child committed the act that was the basis of the adjudication, and identification of the violation of the law or ordinance that was the basis of the adjudication.

(3) Within fourteen days after committing a delinquent child to the custody of the department of youth services, the court shall give notice to the school attended by the child of the child's commitment by sending to that school a copy of the court's journal entry ordering the commitment. As soon as possible after receipt of the notice described in this division, the school shall provide the department with the child's school transcript. However, the department shall not refuse to accept a child committed to it, and a child committed to it shall not be held in a county or district detention facility, because of a school's failure to provide the school transcript that it is required to provide under this division.

(4) Within fourteen days after discharging or releasing a child from an institution under its control, the department of youth services shall provide the court and the superintendent of the school district in which the child is entitled to attend school under section 3313.64 or 3313.65 of the Revised Code with the following:

(a) An updated copy of the child's school transcript;

(b) A report outlining the child's behavior in school while in the custody of the department;

(c) The child's current individualized education program, as defined in section 3323.01 of the Revised Code, if such a program has been developed for the child;

(d) A summary of the institutional record of the child's behavior.

The department also shall provide the court with a copy of any portion of the child's institutional record that the court specifically requests, within five working days of the request.

(E) At any hearing at which a child is adjudicated a delinquent child or as soon as possible after the hearing, the court shall notify all victims of the delinquent act who may be entitled to a recovery under any of the following sections of the right of the victims to recover, pursuant to section 3109.09 of the Revised Code, compensatory damages from the child's parents; of the right of the victims to recover, pursuant to section 3109.10 of the Revised Code, compensatory damages from the child's parents for willful and malicious assaults committed by the child; and of the right of the victims to recover an award of reparations pursuant to sections 2743.51 to 2743.72 of the Revised Code.

(2004 H 106, eff. 9–16–04; 2002 H 393, eff. 7–5–02; 2002 H 247, eff. 5–30–02; 2000 S 179, § 3, eff. 1–1–02)

2152.19 Additional disposition orders for delinquent children

(A) If a child is adjudicated a delinquent child, the court may make any of the following orders of disposition, in addition to any other disposition authorized or required by this chapter:

(1) Any order that is authorized by section 2151.353 of the Revised Code for the care and protection of an abused, neglected, or dependent child;

(2) Commit the child to the temporary custody of any school, camp, institution, or other facility operated for the care of delinquent children by the county, by a district organized under section 2152.41 or 2151.65 of the Revised Code, or by a private agency or organization, within or without the state, that is authorized and qualified to provide the care, treatment, or placement required, including, but not limited to, a school, camp, or facility operated under section 2151.65 of the Revised Code;

(3) Place the child in a detention facility or district detention facility operated under section 2152.41 of the Revised Code, for up to ninety days;

(4) Place the child on community control under any sanctions, services, and conditions that the court prescribes. As a condition of community control in every case and in addition to any other condition that it imposes upon the child, the court shall require the child to abide by the law during the period of community control. As referred to in this division, community control includes, but is not limited to, the following sanctions and conditions:

(a) A period of basic probation supervision in which the child is required to maintain contact with a person appointed to supervise the child in accordance with sanctions imposed by the court;

(b) A period of intensive probation supervision in which the child is required to maintain frequent contact with a person appointed by the court to supervise the child while the child is seeking or maintaining employment and participating in training, education, and treatment programs as the order of disposition;

(c) A period of day reporting in which the child is required each day to report to and leave a center or another approved reporting location at specified times in order to participate in work, education or training, treatment, and other approved programs at the center or outside the center;

(d) A period of community service of up to five hundred hours for an act that would be a felony or a misdemeanor of the first degree if committed by an adult, up to two hundred hours for an act that would be a misdemeanor of the second, third, or fourth degree if committed by an adult, or up to thirty hours for an act that would be a minor misdemeanor if committed by an adult;

(e) A requirement that the child obtain a high school diploma, a certificate of high school equivalence, vocational training, or employment;

(f) A period of drug and alcohol use monitoring;

(g) A requirement of alcohol or drug assessment or counseling, or a period in an alcohol or drug treatment program with a level of security for the child as determined necessary by the court;

(h) A period in which the court orders the child to observe a curfew that may involve daytime or evening hours;

(i) A requirement that the child serve monitored time;

(j) A period of house arrest without electronic monitoring or continuous alcohol monitoring;

(k) A period of electronic monitoring or continuous alcohol monitoring without house arrest, or house arrest with electronic monitoring or continuous alcohol monitoring or both electronic monitoring and continuous alcohol monitoring, that does not exceed the maximum sentence of imprisonment that could be imposed upon an adult who commits the same act.

A period of house arrest with electronic monitoring or continuous alcohol monitoring or both electronic monitoring and continuous alcohol monitoring, imposed under this division shall not extend beyond the child's twenty-first birthday. If a court imposes a period of house arrest with electronic monitoring or continuous alcohol monitoring or both electronic monitoring and continuous alcohol monitoring, upon a child under this division, it shall require the child: to remain in the child's home or other specified premises for the entire period of house arrest with electronic monitoring or continuous alcohol monitoring or both except when the court permits the child to leave those premises to go to school or to other specified premises. Regarding electronic monitoring, the court also shall require the child to be monitored by a central system that can determine the child's location at designated times; to report periodically to a person designated by the court; and to enter into a written contract with the court agreeing to comply with all requirements imposed by the court, agreeing to pay any fee imposed by the court for the costs of the house arrest with electronic monitoring, and agreeing to waive the right to receive credit for any time served on house arrest with electronic monitoring toward the period of any other dispositional order imposed upon the child if the child violates any of the requirements of the dispositional order of house arrest with electronic monitoring. The court also may impose other reasonable requirements upon the child.

Unless ordered by the court, a child shall not receive credit for any time served on house arrest with electronic monitoring or continuous alcohol monitoring or both toward any other dispositional order imposed upon the child for the act for which was imposed the dispositional order of house arrest with electronic monitoring or continuous alcohol monitoring. As used in this division and division (A)(4)(*l*) of this section, "continuous alcohol monitoring" has the same meaning as in section 2929.01 of the Revised Code.

(*l*) A suspension of the driver's license, probationary driver's license, or temporary instruction permit issued to the child for a period of time prescribed by the court, or a suspension of the registration of all motor vehicles registered in the name of the child for a period of time prescribed by the court. A child whose license or permit is so suspended is ineligible for issuance of a license or permit during the period of suspension. At the end of the period of suspension, the child shall not be reissued a license or permit until the child has paid any applicable reinstatement fee and complied with all requirements governing license reinstatement.

(5) Commit the child to the custody of the court;

(6) Require the child to not be absent without legitimate excuse from the public school the child is supposed to attend for five or more consecutive days, seven or more school days in one school month, or twelve or more school days in a school year;

(7)(a) If a child is adjudicated a delinquent child for being a chronic truant or a habitual truant who previously has been adjudicated an unruly child for being a habitual truant, do either or both of the following:

(i) Require the child to participate in a truancy prevention mediation program;

(ii) Make any order of disposition as authorized by this section, except that the court shall not commit the child to a facility described in division (A)(2) or (3) of this section unless the court determines that the child violated a lawful court order made pursuant to division (C)(1)(e) of section 2151.354 of the Revised Code or division (A)(6) of this section.

(b) If a child is adjudicated a delinquent child for being a chronic truant or a habitual truant who previously has been adjudicated an unruly child for being a habitual truant and the court determines that the parent, guardian, or other person having care of the child has failed to cause the child's attendance at school in violation of section 3321.38 of the Revised Code, do either or both of the following:

(i) Require the parent, guardian, or other person having care of the child to participate in a truancy prevention mediation program;

(ii) Require the parent, guardian, or other person having care of the child to participate in any community service program, preferably a community service program that requires the involvement of the parent, guardian, or other person having care of the child in the school attended by the child.

(8) Make any further disposition that the court finds proper, except that the child shall not be placed in any of the following:

(a) A state correctional institution, a county, multicounty, or municipal jail or workhouse, or another place in which an adult convicted of a crime, under arrest, or charged with a crime is held;

(b) A community corrections facility, if the child would be covered by the definition of public safety beds for purposes of sections 5139.41 to 5139.43 of the Revised Code if the court exercised its authority to commit the child to the legal custody of the department of youth services for institutionalization or institutionalization in a secure facility pursuant to this chapter.

(B) If a child is adjudicated a delinquent child, in addition to any order of disposition made under division (A) of this section, the court, in the following situations and for the specified periods of time, shall suspend the child's temporary instruction permit, restricted license, probationary driver's license, or nonresident operating privilege, or suspend the child's ability to obtain such a permit:

(1) If the child is adjudicated a delinquent child for violating section 2923.122 of the Revised Code, impose a class four suspension of the child's license, permit, or privilege from the range specified in division (A)(4) of section 4510.02 of the Revised Code or deny the child the issuance of a license or permit in accordance with division (F)(1) of section 2923.122 of the Revised Code.

(2) If the child is adjudicated a delinquent child for committing an act that if committed by an adult would be a drug abuse offense or for violating division (B) of section 2917.11 of the Revised Code, suspend the child's license, permit, or privilege for a period of time prescribed by the court. The court, in its discretion, may terminate the suspension if the child attends and satisfactorily completes a drug abuse or alcohol abuse education, intervention, or treatment program specified by the court. During the time the child is attending a program described in this division, the court shall retain the child's temporary instruction permit, probationary driver's license, or driver's license, and the

court shall return the permit or license if it terminates the suspension as described in this division.

(C) The court may establish a victim-offender mediation program in which victims and their offenders meet to discuss the offense and suggest possible restitution. If the court obtains the assent of the victim of the delinquent act committed by the child, the court may require the child to participate in the program.

(D)(1) If a child is adjudicated a delinquent child for committing an act that would be a felony if committed by an adult and if the child caused, attempted to cause, threatened to cause, or created a risk of physical harm to the victim of the act, the court, prior to issuing an order of disposition under this section, shall order the preparation of a victim impact statement by the probation department of the county in which the victim of the act resides, by the court's own probation department, or by a victim assistance program that is operated by the state, a county, a municipal corporation, or another governmental entity. The court shall consider the victim impact statement in determining the order of disposition to issue for the child.

(2) Each victim impact statement shall identify the victim of the act for which the child was adjudicated a delinquent child, itemize any economic loss suffered by the victim as a result of the act, identify any physical injury suffered by the victim as a result of the act and the seriousness and permanence of the injury, identify any change in the victim's personal welfare or familial relationships as a result of the act and any psychological impact experienced by the victim or the victim's family as a result of the act, and contain any other information related to the impact of the act upon the victim that the court requires.

(3) A victim impact statement shall be kept confidential and is not a public record. However, the court may furnish copies of the statement to the department of youth services if the delinquent child is committed to the department or to both the adjudicated delinquent child or the adjudicated delinquent child's counsel and the prosecuting attorney. The copy of a victim impact statement furnished by the court to the department pursuant to this section shall be kept confidential and is not a public record. If an officer is preparing pursuant to section 2947.06 or 2951.03 of the Revised Code or Criminal Rule 32.2 a presentence investigation report pertaining to a person, the court shall make available to the officer, for use in preparing the report, a copy of any victim impact statement regarding that person. The copies of a victim impact statement that are made available to the adjudicated delinquent child or the adjudicated delinquent child's counsel and the prosecuting attorney pursuant to this division shall be returned to the court by the person to whom they were made available immediately following the imposition of an order of disposition for the child under this chapter.

The copy of a victim impact statement that is made available pursuant to this division to an officer preparing a criminal presentence investigation report shall be returned to the court by the officer immediately following its use in preparing the report.

(4) The department of youth services shall work with local probation departments and victim assistance programs to develop a standard victim impact statement.

(E) If a child is adjudicated a delinquent child for being a chronic truant or a habitual truant who previously has been adjudicated an unruly child for being a habitual truant and the court determines that the parent, guardian, or other person having care of the child has failed to cause the child's attendance at school in violation of section 3321.38 of the Revised Code, in addition to any order of disposition it makes under this section, the court shall warn the parent, guardian, or other person having care of the child that any subsequent adjudication of the child as an unruly or delinquent child for being a habitual or chronic truant may result in a criminal charge against the parent, guardian, or other person having care of the child for a violation of division (C) of section 2919.21 or section 2919.24 of the Revised Code.

(F)(1) During the period of a delinquent child's community control granted under this section, authorized probation officers who are engaged within the scope of their supervisory duties or responsibilities may search, with or without a warrant, the person of the delinquent child, the place of residence of the delinquent child, and a motor vehicle, another item of tangible or intangible personal property, or other real property in which the delinquent child has a right, title, or interest or for which the delinquent child has the express or implied permission of a person with a right, title, or interest to use, occupy, or possess if the probation officers have reasonable grounds to believe that the delinquent child is not abiding by the law or otherwise is not complying with the conditions of the delinquent child's community control. The court that places a delinquent child on community control under this section shall provide the delinquent child with a written notice that informs the delinquent child that authorized probation officers who are engaged within the scope of their supervisory duties or responsibilities may conduct those types of searches during the period of community control if they have reasonable grounds to believe that the delinquent child is not abiding by the law or otherwise is not complying with the conditions of the delinquent child's community control. The court also shall provide the written notice described in division (E)(2) of this section to each parent, guardian, or custodian of the delinquent child who is described in that division.

(2) The court that places a child on community control under this section shall provide the child's parent, guardian, or other custodian with a written notice that informs them that authorized probation officers may conduct searches pursuant to division (E)(1) of this section. The notice shall specifically state that a permissible search might extend to a motor vehicle, another item of tangible or intangible personal property, or a place of residence or other real property in which a notified parent, guardian, or custodian has a right, title, or interest and that the parent, guardian, or custodian expressly or impliedly permits the child to use, occupy, or possess.

(G) If a juvenile court commits a delinquent child to the custody of any person, organization, or entity pursuant to this section and if the delinquent act for which the child is so committed is a sexually oriented offense that is not a registration-exempt sexually oriented offense or is a child-victim oriented offense, the court in the order of disposition shall do one of the following:

(1) Require that the child be provided treatment as described in division (A)(2) of section 5139.13 of the Revised Code;

(2) Inform the person, organization, or entity that it is the preferred course of action in this state that the child be provided treatment as described in division (A)(2) of section 5139.13 of the Revised Code and encourage the person, organization, or entity to provide that treatment.

(2004 H 163, eff. 9–23–04; 2003 S 5, § 3, eff. 1–1–04; 2003 S 5, § 1, eff. 7–31–03; 2003 H 95, § 3.13, eff. 1–1–04; 2003 H 95, § 1, eff. 9–26–03; 2002 H 490, eff. 1–1–04; 2002 H 400, § 4, eff. 1–1–04; 2002 H 400, § 1, eff. 4–3–03; 2002 S 123, eff. 1–1–04; 2002 H 393, eff. 7–5–02; 2002 H 247, eff. 5–30–02; 2001 S 3, eff. 1–1–02; 2000 S 179, § 3, eff. 1–1–02)

2152.191 Application of certain sections of Revised Code to child adjudicated a delinquent child for committing sexually oriented offense

If a child is adjudicated a delinquent child for committing a sexually oriented offense that is not a registration-exempt sexually oriented offense or for committing a child-victim oriented offense, if the child is fourteen years of age or older at the time of committing the offense, and if the child committed the offense on or after January 1, 2002, both of the following apply:

(A) Sections 2152.82 to 2152.85 and Chapter 2950. of the Revised Code apply to the child and the adjudication.

(B) In addition to any order of disposition it makes of the child under this chapter, the court may make any determination, adjudication, or order authorized under sections 2152.82 to 2152.85 and Chapter 2950. of the Revised Code and shall make any determination, adjudication, or order required under those sections and that chapter.

(2003 S 5, eff. 7–31–03; 2001 S 3, eff. 1–1–02)

2152.20 Fines; costs; restitution; forfeitures

(A) If a child is adjudicated a delinquent child or a juvenile traffic offender, the court may order any of the following dispositions, in addition to any other disposition authorized or required by this chapter:

(1) Impose a fine in accordance with the following schedule:

(a) For an act that would be a minor misdemeanor or an unclassified misdemeanor if committed by an adult, a fine not to exceed fifty dollars;

(b) For an act that would be a misdemeanor of the fourth degree if committed by an adult, a fine not to exceed one hundred dollars;

(c) For an act that would be a misdemeanor of the third degree if committed by an adult, a fine not to exceed one hundred fifty dollars;

(d) For an act that would be a misdemeanor of the second degree if committed by an adult, a fine not to exceed two hundred dollars;

(e) For an act that would be a misdemeanor of the first degree if committed by an adult, a fine not to exceed two hundred fifty dollars;

(f) For an act that would be a felony of the fifth degree or an unclassified felony if committed by an adult, a fine not to exceed three hundred dollars;

(g) For an act that would be a felony of the fourth degree if committed by an adult, a fine not to exceed four hundred dollars;

(h) For an act that would be a felony of the third degree if committed by an adult, a fine not to exceed seven hundred fifty dollars;

(i) For an act that would be a felony of the second degree if committed by an adult, a fine not to exceed one thousand dollars;

(j) For an act that would be a felony of the first degree if committed by an adult, a fine not to exceed one thousand five hundred dollars;

(k) For an act that would be aggravated murder or murder if committed by an adult, a fine not to exceed two thousand dollars.

(2) Require the child to pay costs;

(3) Unless the child's delinquent act or juvenile traffic offense would be a minor misdemeanor if committed by an adult or could be disposed of by the juvenile traffic violations bureau serving the court under Traffic Rule 13.1 if the court has established a juvenile traffic violations bureau, require the child to make restitution to the victim of the child's delinquent act or juvenile traffic offense or, if the victim is deceased, to a survivor of the victim in an amount based upon the victim's economic loss caused by or related to the delinquent act or juvenile traffic offense. The court may not require a child to make restitution pursuant to this division if the child's delinquent act or juvenile traffic offense would be a minor misdemeanor if committed by an adult or could be disposed of by the juvenile traffic violations bureau serving the court under Traffic Rule 13.1 if the court has established a juvenile traffic violations bureau. If the court requires restitution under this division, the restitution shall be made directly to the victim in open court or to the probation department that serves the jurisdiction or the clerk of courts on behalf of the victim.

If the court requires restitution under this division, the restitution may be in the form of a cash reimbursement paid in a lump sum or in installments, the performance of repair work to restore any damaged property to its original condition, the performance of a reasonable amount of labor for the victim or survivor of the victim, the performance of community service work, any other form of restitution devised by the court, or any combination of the previously described forms of restitution.

If the court requires restitution under this division, the court may base the restitution order on an amount recommended by the victim or survivor of the victim, the delinquent child, the juvenile traffic offender, a presentence investigation report, estimates or receipts indicating the cost of repairing or replacing property, and any other information, provided that the amount the court orders as restitution shall not exceed the amount of the economic loss suffered by the victim as a direct and proximate result of the delinquent act or juvenile traffic offense. If the court decides to order restitution under this division and the amount of the restitution is disputed by the victim or survivor or by the delinquent child or juvenile traffic offender, the court shall hold a hearing on the restitution. If the court requires restitution under this division, the court shall determine, or order the determination of, the amount of restitution to be paid by the delinquent child or juvenile traffic offender. All restitution payments shall be credited against any recovery of economic loss in a civil action brought by or on behalf of the victim against the delinquent child or juvenile traffic offender or the delinquent child's or juvenile traffic offender's parent, guardian, or other custodian.

If the court requires restitution under this division, the court may order that the delinquent child or juvenile traffic offender pay a surcharge, in an amount not exceeding five per cent of the amount of restitution otherwise ordered under this division, to the entity responsible for collecting and processing the restitution payments.

The victim or the survivor of the victim may request that the prosecuting authority file a motion, or the delinquent child or juvenile traffic offender may file a motion, for modification of the payment terms of any restitution ordered under this division. If the court grants the motion, it may modify the payment terms as it determines appropriate.

(4) Require the child to reimburse any or all of the costs incurred for services or sanctions provided or imposed, including, but not limited to, the following:

(a) All or part of the costs of implementing any community control imposed as a disposition under section 2152.19 of the Revised Code, including a supervision fee;

(b) All or part of the costs of confinement in a residential facility described in section 2152.19 of the Revised Code or in a department of youth services institution, including, but not limited to, a per diem fee for room and board, the costs of medical and dental treatment provided, and the costs of repairing property the delinquent child damaged while so confined. The amount of reimbursement ordered for a child under this division shall not exceed the total amount of reimbursement the child is able to pay as determined at a hearing and shall not exceed the actual cost of the confinement. The court may collect any reimbursement ordered under this division. If the court does not order reimbursement under this division, confinement costs may be assessed pursuant to a repayment policy adopted under section 2929.37 of the Revised Code and division (D) of section 307.93, division (A) of section 341.19, division (C) of section 341.23 or 753.16, or division (B) of section 341.14, 753.02, 753.04, 2301.56, or 2947.19 of the Revised Code.

(B)(1) If a child is adjudicated a delinquent child for violating section 2923.32 of the Revised Code, the court shall enter an order of criminal forfeiture against the child in accordance with divisions (B)(3), (4), (5), and (6) and (C) to (F) of section 2923.32 of the Revised Code.

(2) Sections 2925.41 to 2925.45 of the Revised Code apply to children who are adjudicated or could be adjudicated by a juvenile court to be delinquent children for an act that, if committed by an adult, would be a felony drug abuse offense. Subject to division (B) of section 2925.42 and division (E) of section 2925.43 of the Revised Code, a delinquent child of that nature loses any right to the possession of, and forfeits to the state any right, title, and interest that the delinquent child may have in, property as defined in section 2925.41 of the Revised Code and further described in section 2925.42 or 2925.43 of the Revised Code.

(3) Sections 2923.44 to 2923.47 of the Revised Code apply to children who are adjudicated or could be adjudicated by a juvenile court to be delinquent children for an act in violation of section 2923.42 of the Revised Code. Subject to division (B) of section 2923.44 and division (E) of section 2923. 45 of the Revised Code, a delinquent child of that nature loses any right to the possession of, and forfeits to the state any right, title, and interest that the delinquent child may have in, property as defined in section 2923.41 of the Revised Code and further described in section 2923.44 or 2923. 45 of the Revised Code.

(C) The court may hold a hearing if necessary to determine whether a child is able to pay a sanction under this section.

(D) If a child who is adjudicated a delinquent child is indigent, the court shall consider imposing a term of community service under division (A) of section 2152.19 of the Revised Code in lieu of imposing a financial sanction under this section. If a child who is adjudicated a delinquent child is not indigent, the court may impose a term of community service under that division in lieu of, or in addition to, imposing a financial sanction under this section. The court may order community service for an act that if committed by an adult would be a minor misdemeanor.

If a child fails to pay a financial sanction imposed under this section, the court may impose a term of community service in lieu of the sanction.

(E) The clerk of the court, or another person authorized by law or by the court to collect a financial sanction imposed under this section, may do any of the following:

(1) Enter into contracts with one or more public agencies or private vendors for the collection of the amounts due under the financial sanction, which amounts may include interest from the date of imposition of the financial sanction;

(2) Permit payment of all, or any portion of, the financial sanction in installments, by credit or debit card, by another type of electronic transfer, or by any other reasonable method, within any period of time, and on any terms that the court considers just, except that the maximum time permitted for payment shall not exceed five years. The clerk may pay any fee associated with processing an electronic transfer out of public money and may charge the fee to the delinquent child.

(3) To defray administrative costs, charge a reasonable fee to a child who elects a payment plan rather than a lump sum payment of a financial sanction.

(2004 H 52, eff. 6–1–04; 2002 H 490, eff. 1–1–04; 2002 H 170, eff. 9–6–02; 2000 S 179, § 3, eff. 1–1–02)

2152.201 Recovery of costs where offense constitutes act of terrorism

(A) In addition to any other dispositions authorized or required by this chapter, the juvenile court making disposition of a child adjudicated a delinquent child for committing a violation of section 2909.22, 2909.23, or 2909.24 of the Revised Code or a violation of section 2921.32 of the Revised Code when the offense or act committed by the person aided or to be aided as described in that section is an act of terrorism may order the child to pay to the state, municipal, or county law enforcement agencies that handled the investigation and prosecution all of the costs that the state, municipal corporation, or county reasonably incurred in the investigation and prosecution of the violation. The court shall hold a hearing to determine the amount of costs to be imposed under this section. The court may hold the hearing as part of the dispositional hearing for the child.

(B) If a child is adjudicated a delinquent child for committing a violation of section 2909.23 or 2909.24 of the Revised Code and if any political subdivision incurred any response costs as a result of, or in making any response to, the threat of the specified offense involved in the violation of section 2909.23 of the Revised Code or the actual specified offense involved in the violation of section 2909.24 of the Revised Code, in addition to any other dispositions authorized or required by this chapter, the juvenile court making disposition of the child for the violation may order the child to reimburse the involved political subdivision for the response costs it so incurred.

(C) As used in this section, "response costs" and "act of terrorism" have the same meanings as in section 2909.21 of the Revised Code.

(2002 S 184, eff. 5–15–02)

2152.21 Disposition of juvenile traffic offender

(A) Unless division (C) of this section applies, if a child is adjudicated a juvenile traffic offender, the court may make any of the following orders of disposition:

(1) Impose costs and one or more financial sanctions in accordance with section 2152.20 of the Revised Code;

(2) Suspend the child's driver's license, probationary driver's license, or temporary instruction permit for a definite period not exceeding two years or suspend the registration of all motor vehicles registered in the name of the child for a definite period not exceeding two years. A child whose license or permit is so suspended is ineligible for issuance of a license or permit during the period of suspension. At the end of the period of suspension, the child shall not be reissued a license or permit until the child has paid any applicable reinstatement fee and complied with all requirements governing license reinstatement.

(3) Place the child on community control;

(4) If the child is adjudicated a juvenile traffic offender for an act other than an act that would be a minor misdemeanor if committed by an adult and other than an act that could be disposed of by the juvenile traffic violations bureau serving the court under Traffic Rule 13.1 if the court has established a juvenile traffic violations bureau, require the child to make restitution pursuant to division (A)(3) of section 2152.20 of the Revised Code;

(5)(a) If the child is adjudicated a juvenile traffic offender for committing a violation of division (A) of section 4511.19 of the Revised Code or of a municipal ordinance that is substantially equivalent to that division, commit the child, for not longer than five days, to either of the following:

(i) The temporary custody of a detention facility or district detention facility established under section 2152.41 of the Revised Code;

(ii) The temporary custody of any school, camp, institution, or other facility for children operated in whole or in part for the care of juvenile traffic offenders of that nature by the county, by a district organized under section 2151.65 or 2152.41 of the Revised Code, or by a private agency or organization within the state that is authorized and qualified to provide the care, treatment, or placement required.

(b) If an order of disposition committing a child to the temporary custody of a home, school, camp, institution, or other facility of that nature is made under division (A)(5)(a) of this section, the length of the commitment shall not be reduced or diminished as a credit for any time that the child was held in a place of detention or shelter care, or otherwise was detained, prior to entry of the order of disposition.

(6) If, after making a disposition under divisions (A)(1) to (5) of this section, the court finds upon further hearing that the child has failed to comply with the orders of the court and the child's operation of a motor vehicle constitutes the child a danger to the child and to others, the court may make any disposition authorized by divisions (A)(1), (4), (5), and (8) of section 2152.19 of the Revised Code, except that the child may not be committed to or placed in a secure correctional facility unless authorized by division (A)(5) of this section, and commitment to or placement in a detention facility may not exceed twenty-four hours.

(B) If a child is adjudicated a juvenile traffic offender for violating division (A) or (B) of section 4511.19 of the Revised Code, in addition to any order of disposition made under division (A) of this section, the court shall impose a class six suspension of the temporary instruction permit, probationary driver's license, or driver's license issued to the child from the range specified in division (A)(6) of section 4510.02 of the Revised Code. The court, in its discretion, may terminate the suspension if the child attends and satisfactorily completes a drug abuse or alcohol abuse education, intervention, or treatment program specified by the court. During the time the child is attending a program as described in this division, the court shall retain the child's temporary instruction permit, probationary driver's license, or driver's license issued, and the court shall return the permit or license if it terminates the suspension as described in this division.

(C) If a child is adjudicated a juvenile traffic offender for violating division (B)(1) of section 4513.263 of the Revised Code, the court shall impose the appropriate fine set forth in division (G) of that section. If a child is adjudicated a juvenile traffic offender for violating division (B)(3) of section 4513.263 of the Revised Code and if the child is sixteen years of age or older, the court shall impose the fine set forth in division (G)(2) of that section. If a child is adjudicated a juvenile traffic offender for violating division (B)(3) of section 4513.263 of the Revised Code and if the child is under sixteen years of age, the court shall not impose a fine but may place the child on probation or community control.

(D) A juvenile traffic offender is subject to sections 4509.01 to 4509.78 of the Revised Code.

(2004 H 52, eff. 6–1–04; 2002 H 400, § 4, eff. 1–1–04; 2002 H 400, § 1, eff. 4–3–03; 2002 S 123, eff. 1–1–04; 2000 S 179, § 3, eff. 1–1–02)

2152.22 Relinquishment of juvenile court control; judicial release

(A) When a child is committed to the legal custody of the department of youth services under this chapter, the juvenile court relinquishes control with respect to the child so committed, except as provided in divisions (B), (C), and (G) of this section or in sections 2152.82 to 2152.85 of the Revised Code. Subject to divisions (B) and (C) of this section, sections 2151.353 and 2151.412 to 2151.421 of the Revised Code, sections 2152.82 to 2152.85 of the Revised Code, and any other provision of law that specifies a different duration for a dispositional order, all other dispositional orders made by the court under this chapter shall be temporary and shall continue for a period that is designated by the court in its order, until terminated or modified by the court or until the child attains twenty-one years of age.

The department shall not release the child from a department facility and as a result shall not discharge the child or order the child's release on supervised release prior to the expiration of the minimum period specified by the court in division (A)(1) of section 2152.16 of the Revised Code and any term of commitment imposed under section 2152.17 of the Revised Code or prior to the child's attainment of twenty-one years of age, except upon the order of a court pursuant to division (B) or (C) of this section or in accordance with section 5139.54 of the Revised Code.

(B)(1) The court that commits a delinquent child to the department may grant judicial release of the child to court supervision under this division during the first half of the prescribed minimum term for which the child was committed to the department or, if the child was committed to the department until the child attains twenty-one years of age, during the first half of the prescribed period of commitment that begins on the first day of commitment and ends on the child's twenty-first birthday, provided any commitment imposed under division (A), (B), (C), or (D) of section 2152.17 of the Revised Code has ended.

(2) If the department of youth services desires to release a child during a period specified in division (B)(1) of this section, it shall request the court that committed the child to grant a judicial release of the child to court supervision. During whichever of those periods is applicable, the child or the parents of the child also may request that court to grant a judicial release of the child to court supervision. Upon receipt of a request for a judicial release to court supervision from the department, the child, or the child's parent, or upon its own motion, the court that committed the child shall do one of the following: approve the release by journal entry; schedule within thirty days after the request is received a time for a hearing on whether the child is to be released; or reject the request by journal entry without conducting a hearing.

If the court rejects an initial request for a release under this division by the child or the child's parent, the child or the child's parent may make one additional request for a judicial release to court supervision within the applicable period. The additional request may be made no earlier than thirty days after the filing of the prior request for a judicial release to court supervision. Upon the filing of a second request for a judicial release to court supervision, the court shall either approve or disapprove the release by journal entry or schedule within thirty days after the request is received a time for a hearing on whether the child is to be released.

(3) If a court schedules a hearing under division (B)(2) of this section, it may order the department to deliver the child to the court on the date set for the hearing and may order the department to present to the court a report on the child's progress in the institution to which the child was committed and recommendations for conditions of supervision of the child by the court after release. The court may conduct the hearing without the child being present. The court shall determine at the hearing whether the child should be granted a judicial release to court supervision.

If the court approves the release, it shall order its staff to prepare a written treatment and rehabilitation plan for the child that may include any conditions of the child's release that were recommended by the department and approved by the court. The committing court shall send the juvenile court of the county in which the child is placed a copy of the recommended plan. The court of the county in which the child is placed may adopt the recommended conditions set by the committing court as an order of the court and may add any additional consistent conditions it considers appropriate. If a child is granted a judicial release to court supervision, the release discharges the child from the custody of the department of youth services.

(C)(1) The court that commits a delinquent child to the department may grant judicial release of the child to department of youth services supervision under this division during the second half of the prescribed minimum term for which the child was committed to the department or, if the child was committed to the department until the child attains twenty-one years of age, during the second half of the prescribed period of commitment that begins on the first day of commitment and ends on the child's twenty-first birthday, provided any commitment imposed under division (A), (B), (C), or (D) of section 2152.17 of the Revised Code has ended.

(2) If the department of youth services desires to release a child during a period specified in division (C)(1) of this section, it shall request the court that committed the child to grant a judicial release to department of youth services supervision. During whichever of those periods is applicable, the child or the child's parent also may request the court that committed the child to grant a judicial release to department of youth services supervision. Upon receipt of a request for judicial release to department of youth services supervision, the child, or the child's parent, or upon its own motion at any time during that period, the court shall do one of the following: approve the release by journal entry; schedule a time within thirty days after receipt of the request for a hearing on whether the child is to be released; or reject the request by journal entry without conducting a hearing.

If the court rejects an initial request for release under this division by the child or the child's parent, the child or the child's parent may make one or more subsequent requests for a release within the applicable period, but may make no more than one request during each period of ninety days that the child is in a secure department facility after the filing of a prior request for early release. Upon the filing of a request for release under this division subsequent to an initial request, the court shall either approve or disapprove the release by journal entry or schedule a time within thirty days after receipt of the request for a hearing on whether the child is to be released.

(3) If a court schedules a hearing under division (C)(2) of this section, it may order the department to deliver the child to the court on the date set for the hearing and shall order the department to present to the court at that time a treatment plan for the child's post-institutional care. The court may conduct the hearing without the child being present. The court shall determine at the hearing whether the child should be granted a judicial release to department of youth services supervision.

If the court approves the judicial release to department of youth services supervision, the department shall prepare a written treatment and rehabilitation plan for the child pursuant to division (E) of this section that shall include the conditions of the child's release. It shall send the committing court and the juvenile court of the county in which the child is placed a copy of the plan. The court of the county in which the child is placed may adopt the conditions set by the department as an order of the court and may add any additional consistent conditions it considers appropriate, provided that the court may not add any condition that decreases the level or degree of supervision specified by the department in its plan, that substantially increases the financial burden of supervision that will be experienced by the department, or that alters the placement specified by the department in its plan. If the court of the county in which the child is placed adds to the department's plan any additional conditions, it shall enter those additional conditions in its journal and shall send to the department a copy of the journal entry of the additional conditions.

If the court approves the judicial release to department of youth services supervision, the actual date on which the department shall release the child is contingent upon the department finding a suitable placement for the child. If the child is to be returned to the child's home, the department shall return the child on the date that the court schedules for the child's release or shall bear the expense of any additional time that the child remains in a department facility. If the child is unable to return to the child's home, the department shall exercise reasonable diligence in finding a suitable placement for the child, and the child shall remain in a department facility while the department finds the suitable placement.

(D) If a child is released under division (B) or (C) of this section and the court of the county in which the child is placed has reason to believe that the child's deportment is not in accordance with the conditions of the child's judicial release, the court of the county in which the child is placed shall schedule a time for a hearing to determine whether the child violated any of the post-release conditions, and, if the child was released under division (C) of this section, divisions (A) to (E) of section 5139.52 of the Revised Code apply regarding the child.

If that court determines at the hearing that the child violated any of the post-release conditions, the court, if it determines that the violation was a serious violation, may order the child to be returned to the department for institutionalization, consistent with the original order of commitment of the child, or in any case may make any other disposition of the child authorized by law that the court considers proper. If the court of the county in which the child is placed orders the child to be returned to a department of youth services institution, the time during which the child was held in a secure department facility prior to the child's judicial release shall be considered as time served in fulfilling the prescribed period of institutionalization that is applicable to the child under the child's original order of commitment. If the court orders the child returned to a department institution, the child shall remain in institutional care for a minimum of three months or until the child successfully completes a revocation program of a duration of not less than thirty days operated either by the department or by an entity with which the department has contracted to provide a revocation program.

(E) The department of youth services, prior to the release of a child pursuant to division (C) of this section, shall do all of the following:

(1) After reviewing the child's rehabilitative progress history and medical and educational records, prepare a written treatment and rehabilitation plan for the child that includes conditions of the release;

(2) Completely discuss the conditions of the plan prepared pursuant to division (E)(1) of this section and the possible penalties for violation of the plan with the child and the child's parents, guardian, or legal custodian;

(3) Have the plan prepared pursuant to division (E)(1) of this section signed by the child, the child's parents, legal guardian, or custodian, and any authority or person that is to supervise, control, and provide supportive assistance to the child at the time of the child's release pursuant to division (C) of this section;

(4) Prior to the child's release, file a copy of the treatment plan prepared pursuant to division (E)(1) of this section with the committing court and the juvenile court of the county in which the child is to be placed.

(F) The department of youth services shall file a written progress report with the committing court regarding each child released pursuant to division (C) of this section at least once every thirty days unless specifically directed otherwise by the court. The report shall indicate the treatment and rehabilitative progress of the child and the child's family, if applicable, and shall include any suggestions for altering the program, custody, living arrangements, or treatment. The department shall retain legal custody of a child so released until it discharges the child or until the custody is terminated as otherwise provided by law.

(G) When a child is committed to the legal custody of the department of youth services, the court retains jurisdiction to perform the functions specified in section 5139.51 of the Revised Code with respect to the granting of supervised release by the release authority and to perform the functions specified in section 5139.52 of the Revised Code with respect to violations of the conditions of supervised release granted by the release authority and to the revocation of supervised release granted by the release authority.

(2002 H 393, eff. 7–5–02; 2001 S 3, eff. 1–1–02; 2000 S 179, § 3, eff. 1–1–02)

PLACE OF DETENTION

2152.26 Delinquent child or juvenile traffic offender to be held only in specified places

(A) Except as provided in divisions (B) and (F) of this section, a child alleged to be or adjudicated a delinquent child or a juvenile traffic offender may be held only in the following places:

(1) A certified foster home or a home approved by the court;

(2) A facility operated by a certified child welfare agency;

(3) Any other suitable place designated by the court.

(B) In addition to the places listed in division (A) of this section, a child alleged to be or adjudicated a delinquent child may be held in a detention facility for delinquent children that is under the direction or supervision of the court or other public authority or of a private agency and approved by the court and a child adjudicated a delinquent child may be held in accordance with division (F)(2) of this section in a facility of a type specified in that division. Division (B) of this section does not apply to a child alleged to be or adjudicated a delinquent child for chronic truancy, unless the child violated a lawful court order made pursuant to division (A)(6) of section 2152.19 of the Revised Code. Division (B) of this section also does not apply to a child alleged to be or adjudicated a delinquent child for being an habitual truant who previously has been adjudicated an unruly child for being an habitual truant, unless the child violated a lawful court order made pursuant to division (C)(1)(e) of section 2151.354 of the Revised Code.

(C)(1) Except as provided under division (C)(1) of section 2151.311 of the Revised Code or division (A)(5) of section 2152.21 of the Revised Code, a child alleged to be or adjudicated a juvenile traffic offender may not be held in any of the following facilities:

(a) A state correctional institution, county, multicounty, or municipal jail or workhouse, or other place in which an adult convicted of crime, under arrest, or charged with a crime is held.

(b) A secure correctional facility.

(2) Except as provided under this section, sections 2151.56 to 2151.61, and divisions (A)(5) and (6) of section 2152.21 of the Revised Code, a child alleged to be or adjudicated a juvenile traffic offender may not be held for more than twenty-four hours in a detention facility.

(D) Except as provided in division (F) of this section or in division (C) of section 2151.311, in division (C)(2) of section 5139.06 and section 5120.162, or in division (B) of section 5120.16 of the Revised Code, a child who is alleged to be or is adjudicated a delinquent child may not be held in a state correctional institution, county, multicounty, or municipal jail or workhouse, or other place where an adult convicted of crime, under arrest, or charged with crime is held.

(E) Unless the detention is pursuant to division (F) of this section or division (C) of section 2151.311, division (C)(2) of section 5139.06 and section 5120.162, or division (B) of section 5120.16 of the Revised Code, the official in charge of the institution, jail, workhouse, or other facility shall inform the court immediately when a child, who is or appears to be under the age of eighteen years, is received at the facility, and shall deliver the child to the court upon request or transfer the child to a detention facility designated by the court.

(F)(1) If a case is transferred to another court for criminal prosecution pursuant to section 2152.12 of the Revised Code, the child may be transferred for detention pending the criminal prosecution in a jail or other facility in accordance with the law governing the detention of persons charged with crime. Any child so held shall be confined in a manner that keeps the child beyond the range of touch of all adult detainees. The child shall be supervised at all times during the detention.

(2) If a person is adjudicated a delinquent child or juvenile traffic offender and the court makes a disposition of the person under this chapter, at any time after the person attains eighteen years of age, the person may be held under that disposition in places other than those specified in division (A) of this section, including, but not limited to, a county, multicounty, or municipal jail or workhouse, or other place where an adult convicted of crime, under arrest, or charged with crime is held.

(3)(a) A person alleged to be a delinquent child may be held in places other than those specified in division (A) of this section, including, but not limited to, a county, multicounty, or municipal jail, if the delinquent act that the child allegedly committed would be a felony if committed by an adult, and if either of the following applies:

(i) The person attains eighteen years of age before the person is arrested or apprehended for that act.

(ii) The person is arrested or apprehended for that act before the person attains eighteen years of age, but the person attains eighteen years of age before the court orders a disposition in the case.

(b) If, pursuant to division (F)(3)(a) of this section, a person is held in a place other than a place specified in division (A) of this section, the person has the same rights to bail as an adult charged with the same offense who is confined in a jail pending trial.

(2002 H 400, eff. 4–3–03; 2000 S 179, § 3, eff. 1–1–02)

DETENTION FACILITIES

2152.41 Juvenile detention facility

(A) Upon the recommendation of the judge, the board of county commissioners shall provide, by purchase, lease, construction, or otherwise, a detention facility that shall be within a convenient distance of the juvenile court. The facility shall not be used for the confinement of adults charged with criminal offenses. The facility may be used to detain alleged delinquent children until final disposition for evaluation pursuant to section 2152.04 of the Revised Code, to confine children who are adjudicated delinquent children and placed in the facility pursuant to division (A)(3) of section 2152.19 of the Revised Code, and to confine children who are adjudicated juvenile traffic offenders and committed to the facility under division (A)(5) or (6) of section 2152.21 of the Revised Code.

(B) Upon the joint recommendation of the juvenile judges of two or more neighboring counties, the boards of county commissioners of the counties shall form themselves into a joint board and proceed to organize a district for the establishment and support of a detention facility for the use of the juvenile courts of those counties, in which alleged delinquent children may be detained as provided in division (A) of this section, by using a site or buildings already established in one of the counties or by providing for the purchase of a site and the erection of the necessary buildings on the site.

A child who is adjudicated to be a juvenile traffic offender for having committed a violation of division (A) of section 4511.19 of the Revised Code or of a municipal ordinance that is substantially comparable to that division may be confined in a detention facility or district detention facility pursuant to division (A)(5) of section 2152.21 of the Revised Code, provided the child is kept separate and apart from alleged delinquent children.

Except as otherwise provided by law, district detention facilities shall be established, operated, maintained, and managed in the same manner so far as applicable as county detention facilities.

Members of the board of county commissioners who meet by appointment to consider the organization of a district detention home, upon presentation of properly certified accounts, shall be paid their necessary expenses upon a warrant drawn by the county auditor of their county.

The county auditor of the county having the greatest population or, with the unanimous concurrence of the county auditors of the counties composing a district, the auditor of the county in which the detention facility is located shall be the fiscal officer of a detention facility district. The county auditors of the several counties composing a detention facility district shall meet at the district detention facility, not less than once in six months, to review accounts and to transact any other duties in connection with the institution that pertain to the business of their office.

(C) In any county in which there is no detention facility or that is not served by a district detention facility, the juvenile court may enter into a contract, subject to the approval of the board of county commissioners, with another juvenile court, another county's detention facility, or a joint county detention facility. Alternately, the board of county commissioners shall provide funds for the boarding of children, who would be eligible for detention under division (A) of this section, temporarily in private homes or in certified foster homes approved by the court for a period not exceeding sixty days or until final disposition of their cases, whichever comes first. The court also may arrange with any public children services agency or private child placing agency to receive, or private noncustodial agency for temporary care of, children within the jurisdiction of the court.

If the court arranges for the board of children temporarily detained in certified foster homes or through any private child placing agency, the county shall pay a reasonable sum to be fixed by the court for the board of those children. In order to have certified foster homes available for service, an agreed monthly subsidy may be paid and a fixed rate per day for care of children actually residing in the certified foster home.

(D) The board of county commissioners of any county within a detention facility district, upon the recommendation of the juvenile court of that county, may withdraw from the district and sell or lease its right, title, and interest in the site, buildings, furniture, and equipment of the facility to any counties in the district, at any price and upon any such terms that are agreed upon among the boards of county commissioners of the counties concerned. Section 307.10 of the Revised Code does not apply to this division. The net proceeds of any sale or lease under this division shall be paid into the treasury of the withdrawing county.

The members of the board of trustees of a district detention facility who are residents of a county withdrawing from the district are deemed to have resigned their positions upon the completion of the withdrawal procedure provided by this division. The vacancies then created shall be filled as provided in this section.

(E) The children to be admitted for care in a county or district detention facility established under this section, the period during which they shall be cared for in the facility, and the removal and transfer of children from the facility shall be determined by the juvenile court that ordered the child's detention.

(2002 H 400, eff. 4–3–03; 2000 S 179, § 3, eff. 1–1–02)

2152.42 Superintendents of facilities

(A) Any detention facility established under section 2152.41 of the Revised Code shall be under the direction of a superintendent. The superintendent shall be appointed by, and under the direction of, the judge or judges or, for a district facility, the board of trustees of the facility. The superintendent serves at the pleasure of the juvenile court or, in a district detention facility, at the pleasure of the board of trustees.

Before commencing work as superintendent, the person appointed shall obtain a bond, with sufficient surety, conditioned upon the full and faithful accounting of the funds and properties under the superintendent's control.

The superintendent, under the supervision and subject to the rules and regulations of the board, shall control, manage, operate, and have general charge of the facility and shall have the custody of its property, files, and records.

(B) For a county facility, the superintendent shall appoint all employees of the facility, who shall be in the unclassified civil service. The salaries shall be paid as provided by section 2151.13 of the Revised Code for other employees of the court, and the necessary expenses incurred in maintaining the facility shall be paid by the county.

For a district facility, the superintendent shall appoint other employees of the facility and fix their compensation, subject to approval of the board of trustees. Employees of a district facility, except for the superintendent, shall be in the classified civil service.

(C) During the school year, when possible, a comparable educational program with competent and trained staff shall be provided for children of school age who are in the facility. A sufficient number of trained recreational personnel shall be included among the staff. Medical and mental health services shall be made available.

(2000 S 179, § 3, eff. 1–1–02)

2152.43 Assistance in operation of facilities from department of youth services; tax assessment

(A) A board of county commissioners that provides a detention facility and the board of trustees of a district detention facility may apply to the department of youth services under section 5139.281 of the Revised Code for assistance in defraying the cost of operating and maintaining the facility. The application shall be made on forms prescribed and furnished by the department.

The board of county commissioners of each county that participates in a district detention facility may apply to the department of youth services for assistance in defraying the county's share of the cost of acquisition or construction of the facility, as provided in section 5139.271 of the Revised Code. Application shall be made in accordance with rules adopted by the department. No county shall be reimbursed for expenses incurred in the acquisition or construction of a district detention facility that serves a district having a population of less than one hundred thousand.

(B)(1) The joint boards of county commissioners of district detention facilities shall defray all necessary expenses of the facility not paid from funds made available under section 5139.281 of the Revised Code, through annual assessments of taxes, through gifts, or through other means.

If any county withdraws from a district under division (D) of section 2152.41 of the Revised Code, it shall continue to have levied against its tax duplicate any tax levied by the district during the period in which the county was a member of the district for current operating expenses, permanent improvements, or the retirement of bonded indebtedness. The levy shall continue to be a levy against the tax duplicate of the county until the time that it expires or is renewed.

(2) The current expenses of maintaining the facility not paid from funds made available under section 5139.281 of the Revised Code or division (C) of this section, and the cost of ordinary repairs to the facility, shall be paid by each county in accordance with one of the following methods as approved by the joint board of county commissioners:

(a) In proportion to the number of children from that county who are maintained in the facility during the year;

(b) By a levy submitted by the joint board of county commissioners under division (A) of section 5705.19 of the Revised Code and approved by the electors of the district;

(c) In proportion to the taxable property of each county, as shown by its tax duplicate;

(d) In any combination of the methods for payment described in division (B)(2)(a), (b), or (c) of this section.

(C) When any person donates or bequeaths any real or personal property to a county or district detention facility, the juvenile court or the trustees of the facility may accept and use the gift, consistent with the best interest of the institution and the conditions of the gift.

(2000 S 179, § 3, eff. 1–1–02)

2152.44 District detention facility trustees

(A) As soon as practical after the organization of the joint board of county commissioners as provided by section 2152.41 of the Revised Code, the joint board shall appoint a board of not less than five trustees. The board shall hold office until the first annual meeting after the choice of an established site and buildings, or after the selection and purchase of a building site. At that time, the joint board of county commissioners shall appoint a board of not less than five trustees, one of whom shall hold office for a term of one year, one for a term of two years, one for a term of three years, half of the remaining number for a term of four years, and the remainder for a term of five years. Annually thereafter, the joint board of county commissioners shall appoint one or more trustees, each of whom shall hold office for a term of five years, to succeed the trustee or trustees whose term of office expires. A trustee may be appointed to successive terms. Any person appointed as a trustee shall be recommended and approved by the juvenile court judge or judges of the county of which the person resides.

At least one trustee shall reside in each county in the district. In districts composed of two counties, each county shall be entitled to not less than two trustees. In districts composed of more than four counties, the number of trustees shall be sufficiently increased, provided that there shall always be an uneven number of trustees on the board. The county in which a district detention facility is located shall have not less than two trustees, who, in the interim period between the regular meetings of the trustees, shall act as an executive committee in the discharge of all business pertaining to the facility.

The joint board of county commissioners may remove any trustee for good cause. The trustee appointed to fill any vacancy shall hold the office for the unexpired term of the predecessor trustee.

(B) The annual meeting of the board of trustees shall be held on the first Tuesday in May in each year.

A majority of the board constitutes a quorum. Other board meetings shall be held at least quarterly. The juvenile court judge of each county of the district, or the judge's designee, shall attend the meetings. The members of the board shall receive no compensation for their services, except their actual and necessary expenses. The treasurer shall pay the member's traveling expenses when properly certified.

(C) When the board of trustees does not choose an established institution in one of the counties of the district, it may select a suitable site for the erection of a district detention facility. The site must be easily accessible, conducive to health, economy in purchasing or in building, and the general interest of the facility and its residents, and be as near as practicable to the geographical center of the district.

In the interim between the selection and purchase of a site, and the erection and occupancy of the district detention facility, the joint board of county commissioners provided under section 2151.41 of the Revised Code may delegate to the board of trustees any powers and duties that, in its judgment, will be of general interest or aid to the institution. The joint board of county commissioners may appropriate a trustees' fund, to be expended by the trustees for contracts, purchases, or other necessary expenses of the facility. The trustees shall make a complete settlement with the joint board of county commissioners once each six months, or quarterly if required, and shall make to the board of county commissioners and to the juvenile court of each of the counties a full report of the condition of the facility and residents.

(D) The choice of an established site and buildings, or the purchase of a site, stock, implements, and general farm equipment, should there be a farm, the erection of buildings, and the completion and furnishing of the district detention facility for occupancy, shall be in the hands of the joint board of county commissioners organized under section 2152.41 of the Revised Code. The joint board of county commissioners may delegate all or a portion of these duties to the board of trustees, under any restrictions that the joint board of county commissioners imposes.

When an established site and buildings are used for a district detention facility, the joint board of county commissioners shall cause the value of that site and those buildings to be properly appraised. This appraisal value, or in case of the purchase of a site, the purchase price and the cost of all improvements thereto, shall be paid by the counties comprising the district, in proportion to the taxable property of each county, as shown by its tax duplicate.

(E) Once a district is established, the trustees shall operate, maintain, and manage the facility as provided in sections 2152.41 to 2152.43 of the Revised Code.

(2000 S 179, § 3, eff. 1–1–02)

ORDERS RESTRAINING PARENTS

2152.61 Orders restraining parents, guardians, or custodians

(A) In any proceeding in which a child has been adjudicated a delinquent child or a juvenile traffic offender, on the application of a party or the court's own motion, the court may make an order restraining or otherwise controlling the conduct of any parent, guardian, or other custodian in the relationship of the individual to the child if the court finds that an order of that type necessary to do either of the following:

(1) Control any conduct or relationship that will be detrimental or harmful to the child;

(2) Control any conduct or relationship that will tend to defeat the execution of the order of disposition made or to be made.

(B) Due notice of the application or motion and the grounds for the application or motion under division (A) of this section, and an opportunity to be heard, shall be given to the person against whom the order under that division is directed. The order may include a requirement that the child's parent, guardian, or other custodian enter into a recognizance with sufficient surety, conditioned upon the faithful discharge of any conditions or control required by the court.

(C) A person's failure to comply with any order made by the court under this section is contempt of court under Chapter 2705. of the Revised Code.

(2000 S 179, § 3, eff. 1–1–02)

JURY TRIALS

2152.67 Jury trial; procedure

Any adult who is arrested or charged under any provision in this chapter and who is charged with a crime may demand a trial by jury, or the juvenile judge upon the judge's own motion may call a jury. A demand for a jury trial shall be made in writing in not less than three days before the date set for trial, or within three days after counsel has been retained, whichever is later. Sections 2945.17 and 2945.23 to 2945.36 of the Revised Code, relating to the drawing and impaneling of jurors in criminal cases in the court of common pleas, other than in capital cases, shall apply to a jury trial under this section. The compensation of jurors and costs of the clerk and sheriff shall be taxed and paid in the same manner as in criminal cases in the court of common pleas.

(2000 S 179, § 3, eff. 1–1–02)

MISCELLANEOUS PROVISIONS

2152.71 Records and reports; statistical summaries

(A)(1) The juvenile court shall maintain records of all official cases brought before it, including, but not limited to, an appearance docket, a journal, and, in cases pertaining to an alleged delinquent child, arrest and custody records, complaints, journal entries, and hearing summaries. The court shall maintain a separate docket for traffic cases and shall record all traffic cases on the separate docket instead of on the general appearance docket. The parents, guardian, or other custodian of any child affected, if they are living, or the nearest of kin of the child, if the parents are deceased, may inspect these records, either in person or by counsel, during the hours in which the court is open. Division (A)(1) of this section does not require the release or authorize the inspection of arrest or incident reports, law enforcement investigatory reports or records, or witness statements.

(2) The juvenile court shall send to the superintendent of the bureau of criminal identification and investigation, pursuant to section 109.57 of the Revised Code, a weekly report containing a summary of each case that has come before it and that involves the disposition of a child who is a delinquent child for committing an act that would be a felony or an offense of violence if committed by an adult.

(B) The clerk of the court shall maintain a statistical record that includes all of the following:

(1) The number of complaints that are filed with, or indictments or information made to, the court that allege that a child is a delinquent child, in relation to which the court determines under division (D) of section 2151.27 of the Revised Code that the victim of the alleged delinquent act was sixty-five years of age or older or permanently and totally disabled at the time of the alleged commission of the act;

(2) The number of complaints, indictments, or information described in division (B)(1) of this section that result in the child being adjudicated a delinquent child;

(3) The number of complaints, indictments, or information described in division (B)(2) of this section in which the act upon which the delinquent child adjudication is based caused property damage or would be a theft offense, as defined in division (K) of section 2913.01 of the Revised Code, if committed by an adult;

(4) The number of complaints, indictments, or information described in division (B)(3) of this section that result in the delinquent child being required as an order of disposition made under division (A) of section 2152.20 of the Revised Code to make restitution for all or part of the property damage caused by the child's delinquent act or for all or part of the value of the property that was the subject of the delinquent act that would be a theft offense if committed by an adult;

(5) The number of complaints, indictments, or information described in division (B)(2) of this section in which the act upon which the delinquent child adjudication is based would have been an offense of violence if committed by an adult;

(6) The number of complaints, indictments, or information described in division (B)(5) of this section that result in the delinquent child being committed as an order of disposition made under section 2152.16, divisions (A) and (B) of section 2152.17, or division (A)(2) of section 2152.19 of the Revised Code to any facility for delinquent children operated by the county, a district, or a private agency or organization or to the department of youth services;

(7) The number of complaints, indictments, or information described in division (B)(1) of this section that result in the case being transferred for criminal prosecution to an appropriate court having jurisdiction of the offense under section 2152.12 of the Revised Code.

(C) The clerk of the court shall compile an annual summary covering the preceding calendar year showing all of the information for that year contained in the statistical record maintained under division (B) of this section. The statistical record and the annual summary shall be public records open for inspection. Neither the statistical record nor the annual summary shall include the identity of any party to a case.

(D) Not later than June of each year, the court shall prepare an annual report covering the preceding calendar year showing the number and kinds of cases that have come before it, the disposition of the cases, and any other data pertaining to the work of the court that the juvenile judge directs. The court shall file copies of the report with the board of county commissioners. With the approval of the board, the court may print or cause to be printed copies of the report for distribution to persons and agencies interested in the court or community program for dependent, neglected, abused, or delinquent children and juvenile traffic offenders. The court shall include the number of copies ordered printed and the estimated cost of each printed copy on each copy of the report printed for distribution.

(E) If an officer is preparing pursuant to section 2947.06 or 2951.03 of the Revised Code or Criminal Rule 32.2 a presentence investigation report pertaining to a person, the court shall make available to the officer, for use in preparing the report, any records it possesses regarding any adjudications of that person as a delinquent child or regarding the dispositions made relative to those adjudications. The records to be made available pursuant to this division include, but are not limited to, any social history or report of a mental or physical examination regarding the person that was prepared pursuant to Juvenile Rule 32.

(2002 H 393, eff. 7–5–02; 2002 H 247, eff. 5–30–02; 2000 S 179, § 3, eff. 1–1–02)

2152.72 Information provided to foster caregivers or prospective adoptive parents regarding delinquent children; psychological examination

(A) This section applies only to a child who is or previously has been adjudicated a delinquent child for an act to which any of the following applies:

(1) The act is a violation of section 2903.01, 2903.02, 2903.03, 2903.04, 2903.11, 2903.12, 2903.13, 2907.02, 2907.03, or 2907.05 of the Revised Code.

(2) The act is a violation of section 2923.01 of the Revised Code and involved an attempt to commit aggravated murder or murder.

(3) The act would be a felony if committed by an adult, and the court determined that the child, if an adult, would be guilty of a specification found in section 2941.141, 2941.144, or 2941.145 of the Revised Code or in another section of the Revised Code that relates to the possession or use of a firearm during the commission of the act for which the child was adjudicated a delinquent child.

(4) The act would be an offense of violence that is a felony if committed by an adult, and the court determined that the child, if an adult, would be guilty of a specification found in section 2941.1411 of the Revised Code or in another section of the Revised Code that relates to the wearing or carrying of body armor during the commission of the act for which the child was adjudicated a delinquent child.

(B)(1) Except as provided in division (E) of this section, a public children services agency, private child placing agency, private noncustodial agency, or court, the department of youth services, or another private or government entity shall not place a child in a certified foster home or for adoption until it provides the foster caregivers or prospective adoptive parents with all of the following:

(a) A written report describing the child's social history;

(b) A written report describing all the acts committed by the child the entity knows of that resulted in the child being adjudicated a delinquent child and the disposition made by the court, unless the records pertaining to the acts have been sealed pursuant to section 2151.358 of the Revised Code;

(c) A written report describing any other violent act committed by the child of which the entity is aware;

(d) The substantial and material conclusions and recommendations of any psychiatric or psychological examination conducted on the child or, if no psychological or psychiatric examination of the child is available, the substantial and material conclusions and recommendations of an examination to detect mental and emotional disorders conducted in compliance with the requirements of Chapter 4757. of the Revised Code by an independent social worker, social worker, professional clinical counselor, or professional counselor licensed under that chapter. The entity shall not provide any part of a psychological, psychiatric, or mental and emotional disorder examination to the foster caregivers or prospective adoptive parents other than the substantial and material conclusions.

(2) Notwithstanding section 2151.358 of the Revised Code, if records of an adjudication that a child is a delinquent child have been sealed pursuant to that section and an entity knows the records have been sealed, the entity shall provide the foster caregivers or prospective adoptive parents a written statement that the records of a prior adjudication have been sealed.

(C)(1) The entity that places the child in a certified foster home or for adoption shall conduct a psychological examination of the child unless either of the following applies:

(a) An entity is not required to conduct the examination if an examination was conducted no more than one year prior to the child's placement, and division (C)(1)(b) of this section does not apply.

(b) An entity is not required to conduct the examination if a foster caregiver seeks to adopt the foster caregiver's foster child, and an examination was conducted no more than two years prior to the date the foster caregiver seeks to adopt the child.

(2) No later than sixty days after placing the child, the entity shall provide the foster caregiver or prospective adoptive parents a written report detailing the substantial and material conclusions and recommendations of the examination conducted pursuant to this division.

(D)(1) Except as provided in divisions (D)(2) and (3) of this section, the expenses of conducting the examinations and preparing the reports and assessment required by division (B) or (C) of this section shall be paid by the entity that places the child in the certified foster home or for adoption.

(2) When a juvenile court grants temporary or permanent custody of a child pursuant to any section of the Revised Code, including section 2151.33, 2151.353, 2151.354, or 2152.19 of the Revised Code, to a public children services agency or private child placing agency, the court shall provide the agency the information described in division (B) of this section, pay the expenses of preparing that information, and, if a new examination is required to be conducted, pay the expenses of conducting the examination described in division (C) of this section. On receipt of the information described in division (B) of this section, the agency shall provide to the court written acknowledgment that the agency received the information. The court shall keep the acknowledgment and provide a copy to the agency. On the motion of the agency, the court may terminate the order granting temporary or permanent custody of the child to that agency, if the court does not provide the information described in division (B) of this section.

(3) If one of the following entities is placing a child in a certified foster home or for adoption with the assistance of or by contracting with a public children services agency, private child placing agency, or a private noncustodial agency, the entity shall provide the agency with the information described in division (B) of this section, pay the expenses of preparing that information, and, if a new examination is required to be conducted, pay the expenses of conducting the examination described in division (C) of this section:

(a) The department of youth services if the placement is pursuant to any section of the Revised Code including section 2152.22, 5139.06, 5139.07, 5139.38, or 5139.39 of the Revised Code;

(b) A juvenile court with temporary or permanent custody of a child pursuant to section 2151.354 or 2152.19 of the Revised Code;

(c) A public children services agency or private child placing agency with temporary or permanent custody of the child.

The agency receiving the information described in division (B) of this section shall provide the entity described in division (D)(3)(a) to (c) of this section that sent the information written acknowledgment that the agency received the information and provided it to the foster caregivers or prospective adoptive parents. The entity shall keep the acknowledgment and provide a copy to the agency. An entity that places a child in a certified foster home or for adoption with the assistance of or by contracting with an agency remains responsible to provide the information described in division (B) of this section to the foster caregivers or prospective adoptive parents unless the entity receives written acknowledgment that the agency provided the information.

(E) If a child is placed in a certified foster home as a result of an emergency removal of the child from home pursuant to division (D) of section 2151.31 of the Revised Code, an emergency change in the child's case plan pursuant to division (E)(3) of section 2151.412 of the Revised Code, or an emergency placement by the department of youth services pursuant to this chapter or Chapter 5139. of the Revised Code, the entity that places the child in the certified foster home shall provide the information described in division (B) of this section no later than ninety-six hours after the child is placed in the certified foster home.

(F) On receipt of the information described in divisions (B) and (C) of this section, the foster caregiver or prospective adoptive parents shall provide to the entity that places the child in the foster caregiver's or prospective adoptive parents' home a written acknowledgment that the foster caregiver or prospective adoptive parents received the information. The entity shall keep the acknowledgment and provide a copy to the foster caregiver or prospective adoptive parents.

(G) No person employed by an entity subject to this section and made responsible by that entity for the child's placement in a certified foster home or for adoption shall fail to provide the foster caregivers or prospective adoptive parents with the information required by divisions (B) and (C) of this section.

(H) It is not a violation of any duty of confidentiality provided for in the Revised Code or a code of professional responsibility for a person or government entity to provide the substantial and material conclusions and recommendations of a psychiatric or psychological examination, or an examination to detect mental and emotional disorders, in accordance with division (B)(1)(d) or (C) of this section.

(I) As used in this section:

(1) "Body armor" has the same meaning as in section 2941.1411 of the Revised Code.

(2) "Firearm" has the same meaning as in section 2923.11 of the Revised Code.

(2001 S 27, eff. 3–15–02; 2000 S 179, § 3, eff. 1–1–02)

2152.73 Court participation in delinquency prevention activities

A juvenile court may participate with other public or private agencies of the county served by the court in programs that have as their objective the prevention and control of juvenile delinquency. The juvenile judge may assign employees of the court, as part of their regular duties, to work with organizations concerned with combatting conditions known to contribute to delinquency, providing adult sponsors for children who have been found to be delinquent children, and developing wholesome youth programs.

The juvenile judge may accept and administer on behalf of the court gifts, grants, bequests, and devises made to the court for the purpose of preventing delinquency.

(2000 S 179, § 3, eff. 1–1–02)

2152.74 DNA specimen collected from juvenile adjudged delinquent

Note: See also following version of this section, eff. 5–18–05.

(A) As used in this section, "DNA analysis" and "DNA specimen" have the same meanings as in section 109.573 of the Revised Code.

(B)(1) A child who is adjudicated a delinquent child for committing an act listed in division (D) of this section and who is committed to the custody of the department of youth services, placed in a detention facility or district detention facility pursuant to division (A)(3) of section 2152.19 of the Revised Code, or placed in a school, camp, institution, or other facility for delinquent children described in division (A)(2) of section 2152.19 of the Revised Code shall submit to a DNA specimen collection procedure administered by the director of youth services if committed to the department or by the chief administrative officer of the detention facility, district detention facility, school, camp, institution, or other facility for delinquent children to which the child was committed or in which the child was placed. If the court commits the child to the department of youth services, the director of youth services shall cause the DNA specimen to be collected from the child during the intake process at an institution operated by or under the control of the department. If the court commits the child to or places the child in a detention facility, district detention facility, school, camp, institution, or other facility for delinquent children, the chief administrative officer of the detention facility, district detention facility, school, camp, institution, or facility to which the child is committed or in which the child is placed shall cause the DNA specimen to be collected from the child during the intake process for the detention facility, district detention facility, school, camp, institution, or facility. In accordance with division (C) of this section, the director or the chief administrative officer shall cause the DNA specimen to be forwarded to the bureau of criminal identification and investigation no later than fifteen days after the date of the collection of the DNA specimen. The DNA specimen shall be collected from the child in accordance with division (C) of this section.

(2) If a child is adjudicated a delinquent child for committing an act listed in division (D) of this section, is committed to or placed in the department of youth services, a detention facility or district detention facility, or a school, camp, institution, or other facility for delinquent children, and does not submit to a DNA specimen collection procedure pursuant to division (B)(1) of this section, prior to the child's release from the custody of the department of youth services, from the custody of the detention facility or district detention facility, or from the custody of the school, camp, institution, or facility, the child shall submit to, and the director of youth services or the chief administrator of the detention facility, district detention facility, school, camp, institution, or facility to which the child is committed or in which the child was placed shall administer, a DNA specimen collection procedure at the institution operated by or under the control of the department of youth services or at the detention facility, district detention facility, school, camp, institution, or facility to which the child is committed or in which the child was placed. In accordance with division (C) of this section, the director or the chief administrative officer shall cause the DNA specimen to be forwarded to the bureau of criminal identification and investigation no later than fifteen days after the date of the collection of the DNA specimen. The DNA specimen shall be collected in accordance with division (C) of this section.

(C) If the DNA specimen is collected by withdrawing blood from the child or a similarly invasive procedure, a physician, registered nurse, licensed practical nurse, duly licensed clinical laboratory technician, or other qualified medical practitioner shall collect in a medically approved manner the DNA specimen required to be collected pursuant to division (B) of this section. If the DNA specimen is collected by swabbing for buccal cells or a similarly noninvasive procedure, this section does not require that the DNA specimen be collected by a qualified medical practitioner of that nature. No later than fifteen days after the date of the collection of the DNA specimen, the director of youth services or the chief administrative officer of the detention facility, district detention facility, school, camp, institution, or other facility for delinquent children to which the child is committed or in which the child was placed shall cause the DNA specimen to be forwarded to the bureau of criminal identification and investigation in accordance with procedures established by the superintendent of the bureau under division (H) of section 109.573 of the Revised Code. The bureau shall provide the specimen vials, mailing tubes, labels, postage, and instruction needed for the collection and forwarding of the DNA specimen to the bureau.

(D) The director of youth services and the chief administrative officer of a detention facility, district detention facility, school, camp, institution, or other facility for delinquent children shall cause a DNA specimen to be collected in accordance with divisions (B) and (C) of this section from each child in its custody who is adjudicated a delinquent child for committing any of the following acts:

(1) A violation of section 2903.01, 2903.02, 2903.11, 2905.01, 2907.02, 2907.03, 2907.05, 2911.01, 2911.02, 2911.11, or 2911.12 of the Revised Code;

(2) A violation of section 2907.12 of the Revised Code as it existed prior to September 3, 1996;

(3) An attempt to commit a violation of section 2903.01, 2903.02, 2907.02, 2907.03, or 2907.05 of the Revised Code or to

commit a violation of section 2907.12 of the Revised Code as it existed prior to September 3, 1996;

(4) A violation of any law that arose out of the same facts and circumstances and same act as did a charge against the child of a violation of section 2903.01, 2903.02, 2905.01, 2907.02, 2907.03, 2907.05, or 2911.11 of the Revised Code that previously was dismissed or amended or as did a charge against the child of a violation of section 2907.12 of the Revised Code as it existed prior to September 3, 1996, that previously was dismissed or amended;

(5) A violation of section 2905.02 or 2919.23 of the Revised Code that would have been a violation of section 2905.04 of the Revised Code as it existed prior to July 1, 1996, had the violation been committed prior to that date;

(6) A felony violation of any law that arose out of the same facts and circumstances and same act as did a charge against the child of a violation of section 2903.11, 2911.01, 2911.02, or 2911.12 of the Revised Code that previously was dismissed or amended;

(7) A violation of section 2923.01 of the Revised Code involving a conspiracy to commit a violation of section 2903.01, 2903.02, 2905.01, 2911.01, 2911.02, 2911.11, or 2911.12 of the Revised Code;

(8) A violation of section 2923.03 of the Revised Code involving complicity in committing a violation of section 2903.01, 2903.02, 2903.11, 2905.01, 2907.02, 2907.03, 2907.04, 2907.05, 2911.01, 2911.02, 2911.11, or 2911.12 of the Revised Code or a violation of section 2907.12 of the Revised Code as it existed prior to September 3, 1996.

(E) The director of youth services and the chief administrative officer of a detention facility, district detention facility, school, camp, institution, or other facility for delinquent children is not required to comply with this section in relation to the following acts until the superintendent of the bureau of criminal identification and investigation gives agencies in the juvenile justice system, as defined in section 181.51 of the Revised Code, in the state official notification that the state DNA laboratory is prepared to accept DNA specimens of that nature:

(1) A violation of section 2903.11, 2911.01, 2911.02, or 2911.12 of the Revised Code;

(2) An attempt to commit a violation of section 2903.01 or 2903.02 of the Revised Code;

(3) A felony violation of any law that arose out of the same facts and circumstances and same act as did a charge against the child of a violation of section 2903.11, 2911.01, 2911.02, or 2911.12 of the Revised Code that previously was dismissed or amended;

(4) A violation of section 2923.01 of the Revised Code involving a conspiracy to commit a violation of section 2903.01, 2903.02, 2905.01, 2911.01, 2911.02, 2911.11, or 2911.12 of the Revised Code;

(5) A violation of section 2923.03 of the Revised Code involving complicity in committing a violation of section 2903.01, 2903.02, 2903.11, 2905.01, 2907.02, 2907.03, 2907.04, 2907.05, 2911.01, 2911.02, 2911.11, or 2911.12 of the Revised Code or a violation of section 2907.12 of the Revised Code as it existed prior to September 3, 1996.

(2002 H 400, eff. 4–3–03; 2002 H 427, eff. 8–29–02; 2000 S 179, § 3, eff. 1–1–02)

Note: See also following version of this section, eff. 5–18–05.

2152.74 DNA specimen collected from juvenile adjudged delinquent (later effective date)

Note: See also preceding version of this section, in effect until 5–18–05.

(A) As used in this section, "DNA analysis" and "DNA specimen" have the same meanings as in section 109.573 of the Revised Code.

(B)(1) A child who is adjudicated a delinquent child for committing an act listed in division (D) of this section and who is committed to the custody of the department of youth services, placed in a detention facility or district detention facility pursuant to division (A)(3) of section 2152.19 of the Revised Code, or placed in a school, camp, institution, or other facility for delinquent children described in division (A)(2) of section 2152.19 of the Revised Code shall submit to a DNA specimen collection procedure administered by the director of youth services if committed to the department or by the chief administrative officer of the detention facility, district detention facility, school, camp, institution, or other facility for delinquent children to which the child was committed or in which the child was placed. If the court commits the child to the department of youth services, the director of youth services shall cause the DNA specimen to be collected from the child during the intake process at an institution operated by or under the control of the department. If the court commits the child to or places the child in a detention facility, district detention facility, school, camp, institution, or other facility for delinquent children, the chief administrative officer of the detention facility, district detention facility, school, camp, institution, or facility to which the child is committed or in which the child is placed shall cause the DNA specimen to be collected from the child during the intake process for the detention facility, district detention facility, school, camp, institution, or facility. The DNA specimen shall be collected from the child in accordance with division (C) of this section.

(2) If a child is adjudicated a delinquent child for committing an act listed in division (D) of this section, is committed to or placed in the department of youth services, a detention facility or district detention facility, or a school, camp, institution, or other facility for delinquent children, and does not submit to a DNA specimen collection procedure pursuant to division (B)(1) of this section, prior to the child's release from the custody of the department of youth services, from the custody of the detention facility or district detention facility, or from the custody of the school, camp, institution, or facility, the child shall submit to, and the director of youth services or the chief administrator of the detention facility, district detention facility, school, camp, institution, or facility to which the child is committed or in which the child was placed shall administer, a DNA specimen collection procedure at the institution operated by or under the control of the department of youth services or at the detention facility, district detention facility, school, camp, institution, or facility to which the child is committed or in which the child was placed. The DNA specimen shall be collected in accordance with division (C) of this section.

(3) If a child is adjudicated a delinquent child for committing an act listed in division (D) of this section, is not committed to or placed in the department of youth services, a detention facility or district detention facility, or a school, camp, institution, or other facility for delinquent children described in division (A)(2) or (3) of section 2152.19 of the Revised Code, and does not provide a DNA specimen pursuant to division (B)(1) or (2) of this section, the juvenile court shall order the child to report to the county probation department immediately after disposition to submit to a DNA specimen collection procedure administered by the chief administrative officer of the county probation department. The DNA specimen shall be collected from the child in accordance with division (C) of this section.

(C) If the DNA specimen is collected by withdrawing blood from the child or a similarly invasive procedure, a physician, registered nurse, licensed practical nurse, duly licensed clinical laboratory technician, or other qualified medical practitioner shall collect in a medically approved manner the DNA specimen required to be collected pursuant to division (B) of this section. If the DNA specimen is collected by swabbing for buccal cells or a similarly noninvasive procedure, this section does not require that the DNA specimen be collected by a qualified medical practitioner of that nature. No later than fifteen days after the date of the collection of the DNA specimen, the director of youth services or the chief administrative officer of the detention facility, district detention facility, school, camp, institution, or other facility for delinquent children to which the child is committed or in which the child was placed shall cause the DNA specimen to be forwarded to the bureau of criminal identification and investigation in accordance with procedures established by the superintendent of the bureau under division (H) of section 109.573 of the Revised Code. The bureau shall provide the specimen vials, mailing tubes, labels, postage, and instruction needed for the collection and forwarding of the DNA specimen to the bureau.

(D) The director of youth services and the chief administrative officer of a detention facility, district detention facility, school, camp, institution, or other facility for delinquent children shall cause a DNA specimen to be collected in accordance with divisions (B) and (C) of this section from each child in its custody who is adjudicated a delinquent child for committing any of the following acts:

(1) An act that would be a felony if committed by an adult;

(2) A violation of any law that would be a misdemeanor if committed by an adult and that arose out of the same facts and circumstances and same act as did a charge against the child of a violation of section 2903.01, 2903.02, 2905.01, 2907.02, 2907.03, 2907.05, or 2911.11 of the Revised Code that previously was dismissed or amended or as did a charge against the child of a violation of section 2907.12 of the Revised Code as it existed prior to September 3, 1996, that previously was dismissed or amended;

(3) A violation of section 2919.23 of the Revised Code that would be a misdemeanor if committed by an adult and that would have been a violation of section 2905.04 of the Revised Code as it existed prior to July 1, 1996, had the violation been committed prior to that date;

(4) A violation of section 2923.03 of the Revised Code involving complicity in committing a violation of section 2907.04 of the Revised Code that would be a misdemeanor if committed by an adult.

(2004 H 525, eff. 5–18–05; 2002 H 400, eff. 4–3–03; 2002 H 427, eff. 8–29–02; 2000 S 179, § 3, eff. 1–1–02)

Note: See also preceding version of this section, in effect until 5–18–05.

SEX OFFENSES

2152.81 Deposition of child sex offense victim

(A)(1) As used in this section, "victim" includes any of the following persons:

(a) A person who was a victim of a violation identified in division (A)(2) of this section or an act that would be an offense of violence if committed by an adult;

(b) A person against whom was directed any conduct that constitutes, or that is an element of, a violation identified in division (A)(2) of this section or an act that would be an offense of violence if committed by an adult.

(2) In any proceeding in juvenile court involving a complaint, indictment, or information in which a child is charged with a violation of section 2905.03, 2905.05, 2907.02, 2907.03, 2907.05, 2907.06, 2907.07, 2907.09, 2907.21, 2907.23, 2907.24, 2907.31, 2907.32, 2907.321, 2907.322, 2907.323, or 2919.22 of the Revised Code or an act that would be an offense of violence if committed by an adult and in which an alleged victim of the violation or act was a child who was less than thirteen years of age when the complaint or information was filed or the indictment was returned, the juvenile judge, upon motion of an attorney for the prosecution, shall order that the testimony of the child victim be taken by deposition. The prosecution also may request that the deposition be videotaped in accordance with division (A)(3) of this section. The judge shall notify the child victim whose deposition is to be taken, the prosecution, and the attorney for the child who is charged with the violation or act of the date, time, and place for taking the deposition. The notice shall identify the child victim who is to be examined and shall indicate whether a request that the deposition be videotaped has been made. The child who is charged with the violation or act shall have the right to attend the deposition and the right to be represented by counsel. Depositions shall be taken in the manner provided in civil cases, except that the judge in the proceeding shall preside at the taking of the deposition and shall rule at that time on any objections of the prosecution or the attorney for the child charged with the violation or act. The prosecution and the attorney for the child charged with the violation or act shall have the right, as at an adjudication hearing, to full examination and cross-examination of the child victim whose deposition is to be taken. If a deposition taken under this division is intended to be offered as evidence in the proceeding, it shall be filed in the juvenile court in which the action is pending and is admissible in the manner described in division (B) of this section. If a deposition of a child victim taken under this division is admitted as evidence at the proceeding under division (B) of this section, the child victim shall not be required to testify in person at the proceeding. However, at any time before the conclusion of the proceeding, the attorney for the child charged with the violation or act may file a motion with the judge requesting that another deposition of the child victim be taken because new evidence material to the defense of the child charged has been discovered that the attorney for the child charged could not with reasonable diligence have discovered prior to the taking of the admitted deposition. Any motion requesting another deposition shall be accompanied by supporting affidavits. Upon the filing of the motion and affidavits, the court may order that additional testimony of the child victim relative to the new evidence be taken by another deposition. If the court orders the taking of another deposition under this provision, the deposition shall be taken in accordance with this division; if the admitted deposition was a videotaped deposition taken in accordance with division (A)(3) of this section, the new deposition also shall be videotaped in accordance with that division, and, in other cases, the new deposition may be videotaped in accordance with that division.

(3) If the prosecution requests that a deposition to be taken under division (A)(2) of this section be videotaped, the juvenile judge shall order that the deposition be videotaped in accordance with this division. If a juvenile judge issues an order to video tape the deposition, the judge shall exclude from the room in which the deposition is to be taken every person except the child victim giving the testimony, the judge, one or more interpreters if needed, the attorneys for the prosecution and the child who is charged with the violation or act, any person needed to operate the equipment to be used, one person chosen by the child victim giving the deposition, and any person whose presence the judge determines would contribute to the welfare and well-being of the child victim giving the deposition. The person chosen by the child victim shall not be a witness in the proceeding and, both before and during the deposition, shall not discuss the testimony of the child victim with any other witness in the proceeding. To the extent feasible, any person operating the recording equipment shall be restricted to a room adjacent to the room in which the deposition is being taken, or to a location in the room in which the deposition is being taken that is behind a screen or mirror so

that the person operating the recording equipment can see and hear, but cannot be seen or heard by, the child victim giving the deposition during the deposition. The child who is charged with the violation or act shall be permitted to observe and hear the testimony of the child victim giving the deposition on a monitor, shall be provided with an electronic means of immediate communication with the attorney of the child who is charged with the violation or act during the testimony, and shall be restricted to a location from which the child who is charged with the violation or act cannot be seen or heard by the child victim giving the deposition, except on a monitor provided for that purpose. The child victim giving the deposition shall be provided with a monitor on which the child victim can observe, while giving testimony, the child who is charged with the violation or act. The judge, at the judge's discretion, may preside at the deposition by electronic means from outside the room in which the deposition is to be taken; if the judge presides by electronic means, the judge shall be provided with monitors on which the judge can see each person in the room in which the deposition is to be taken and with an electronic means of communication with each person in that room, and each person in the room shall be provided with a monitor on which that person can see the judge and with an electronic means of communication with the judge. A deposition that is videotaped under this division shall be taken and filed in the manner described in division (A)(2) of this section and is admissible in the manner described in this division and division (B) of this section, and, if a deposition that is videotaped under this division is admitted as evidence at the proceeding, the child victim shall not be required to testify in person at the proceeding. No deposition videotaped under this division shall be admitted as evidence at any proceeding unless division (B) of this section is satisfied relative to the deposition and all of the following apply relative to the recording:

(a) The recording is both aural and visual and is recorded on film or videotape, or by other electronic means.

(b) The recording is authenticated under the Rules of Evidence and the Rules of Criminal Procedure as a fair and accurate representation of what occurred, and the recording is not altered other than at the direction and under the supervision of the judge in the proceeding.

(c) Each voice on the recording that is material to the testimony on the recording or the making of the recording, as determined by the judge, is identified.

(d) Both the prosecution and the child who is charged with the violation or act are afforded an opportunity to view the recording before it is shown in the proceeding.

(B)(1) At any proceeding in relation to which a deposition was taken under division (A) of this section, the deposition or a part of it is admissible in evidence upon motion of the prosecution if the testimony in the deposition or the part to be admitted is not excluded by the hearsay rule and if the deposition or the part to be admitted otherwise is admissible under the Rules of Evidence. For purposes of this division, testimony is not excluded by the hearsay rule if the testimony is not hearsay under Evidence Rule 801; if the testimony is within an exception to the hearsay rule set forth in Evidence Rule 803; if the child victim who gave the testimony is unavailable as a witness, as defined in Evidence Rule 804, and the testimony is admissible under that rule; or if both of the following apply:

(a) The child who is charged with the violation or act had an opportunity and similar motive at the time of the taking of the deposition to develop the testimony by direct, cross, or redirect examination.

(b) The judge determines that there is reasonable cause to believe that, if the child victim who gave the testimony in the deposition were to testify in person at the proceeding, the child victim would experience serious emotional trauma as a result of the child victim's participation at the proceeding.

(2) Objections to receiving in evidence a deposition or a part of it under division (B) of this section shall be made as provided in civil actions.

(3) The provisions of divisions (A) and (B) of this section are in addition to any other provisions of the Revised Code, the Rules of Juvenile Procedure, the Rules of Criminal Procedure, or the Rules of Evidence that pertain to the taking or admission of depositions in a juvenile court proceeding and do not limit the admissibility under any of those other provisions of any deposition taken under division (A) of this section or otherwise taken.

(C) In any proceeding in juvenile court involving a complaint, indictment, or information in which a child is charged with a violation listed in division (A)(2) of this section or an act that would be an offense of violence if committed by an adult and in which an alleged victim of the violation or offense was a child who was less than thirteen years of age when the complaint or information was filed or indictment was returned, the prosecution may file a motion with the juvenile judge requesting the judge to order the testimony of the child victim to be taken in a room other than the room in which the proceeding is being conducted and be televised, by closed circuit equipment, into the room in which the proceeding is being conducted to be viewed by the child who is charged with the violation or act and any other persons who are not permitted in the room in which the testimony is to be taken but who would have been present during the testimony of the child victim had it been given in the room in which the proceeding is being conducted. Except for good cause shown, the prosecution shall file a motion under this division at least seven days before the date of the proceeding. The juvenile judge may issue the order upon the motion of the prosecution filed under this division, if the judge determines that the child victim is unavailable to testify in the room in which the proceeding is being conducted in the physical presence of the child charged with the violation or act, due to one or more of the reasons set forth in division (E) of this section. If a juvenile judge issues an order of that nature, the judge shall exclude from the room in which the testimony is to be taken every person except a person described in division (A)(3) of this section. The judge, at the judge's discretion, may preside during the giving of the testimony by electronic means from outside the room in which it is being given, subject to the limitations set forth in division (A)(3) of this section. To the extent feasible, any person operating the televising equipment shall be hidden from the sight and hearing of the child victim giving the testimony, in a manner similar to that described in division (A)(3) of this section. The child who is charged with the violation or act shall be permitted to observe and hear the testimony of the child victim giving the testimony on a monitor, shall be provided with an electronic means of immediate communication with the attorney of the child who is charged with the violation or act during the testimony, and shall be restricted to a location from which the child who is charged with the violation or act cannot be seen or heard by the child victim giving the testimony, except on a monitor provided for that purpose. The child victim giving the testimony shall be provided with a monitor on which the child victim can observe, while giving testimony, the child who is charged with the violation or act.

(D) In any proceeding in juvenile court involving a complaint, indictment, or information in which a child is charged with a violation listed in division (A)(2) of this section or an act that would be an offense of violence if committed by an adult and in which an alleged victim of the violation or offense was a child who was less than thirteen years of age when the complaint or information was filed or the indictment was returned, the prosecution may file a motion with the juvenile judge requesting the judge to order the testimony of the child victim to be taken outside of the room in which the proceeding is being conducted and be recorded for showing in the room in which the proceeding is being conducted before the judge, the child who is charged with the violation or act, and any other persons who would have been present during the testimony of the child victim had it been given in the room in which the proceeding is being conducted. Except for good cause shown, the prosecution shall file a motion under this division at least seven days before the date of the proceeding. The juvenile judge may issue the order upon the motion of the prosecution filed under this division, if the judge determines that the child victim is unavailable to testify in the room in which the proceeding is being conducted in the physical presence of the child charged with the violation or act, due to one or more of the reasons set forth in division (E) of this section. If a juvenile judge issues an order of that nature, the judge shall exclude from the room in which the testimony is to be taken every person except a person described in division (A)(3) of this section. To the extent feasible, any person operating the recording equipment shall be hidden from the sight and hearing of the child victim giving the testimony, in a manner similar to that described in division (A)(3) of this section. The child who is charged with the violation or act shall be permitted to observe and hear the testimony of the child victim giving the testimony on a monitor, shall be provided with an electronic means of immediate communication with the attorney of the child who is charged with the violation or act during the testimony, and shall be restricted to a location from which the child who is charged with the violation or act cannot be seen or heard by the child victim giving the testimony, except on a monitor provided for that purpose. The child victim giving the testimony shall be provided with a monitor on which the child victim can observe, while giving testimony, the child who is charged with the violation or act. No order for the taking of testimony by recording shall be issued under this division unless the provisions set forth in divisions (A)(3)(a), (b), (c), and (d) of this section apply to the recording of the testimony.

(E) For purposes of divisions (C) and (D) of this section, a juvenile judge may order the testimony of a child victim to be taken outside of the room in which a proceeding is being conducted if the judge determines that the child victim is unavailable to testify in the room in the physical presence of the child charged with the violation or act due to one or more of the following circumstances:

(1) The persistent refusal of the child victim to testify despite judicial requests to do so;

(2) The inability of the child victim to communicate about the alleged violation or offense because of extreme fear, failure of memory, or another similar reason;

(3) The substantial likelihood that the child victim will suffer serious emotional trauma from so testifying.

(F)(1) If a juvenile judge issues an order pursuant to division (C) or (D) of this section that requires the testimony of a child victim in a juvenile court proceeding to be taken outside of the room in which the proceeding is being conducted, the order shall specifically identify the child victim to whose testimony it applies, the order applies only during the testimony of the specified child victim, and the child victim giving the testimony shall not be required to testify at the proceeding other than in accordance with the order. The authority of a judge to close the taking of a deposition under division (A)(3) of this section or a proceeding under division (C) or (D) of this section is in addition to the authority of a judge to close a hearing pursuant to section 2151.35 of the Revised Code.

(2) A juvenile judge who makes any determination regarding the admissibility of a deposition under divisions (A) and (B) of this section, the videotaping of a deposition under division (A)(3) of this section, or the taking of testimony outside of the room in which a proceeding is being conducted under division (C) or (D) of this section, shall enter the determination and findings on the record in the proceeding.

(2000 S 179, § 3, eff. 1–1–02)

JUVENILE OFFENDER REGISTRANTS

2152.811 Child adjudicated a child delinquent for committing a sexually oriented offense

If a court adjudicates a child a delinquent child for committing a presumptive registration-exempt sexually oriented offense, the court may determine pursuant to section 2950.021 of the Revised Code, prior to making an order of disposition for the child, that the child potentially should be subjected to classification as a juvenile offender registrant under sections 2152.82, 2152.83, 2152.84, or 2152.85 of the Revised Code and to registration under section 2950.04 of the Revised Code and all other duties and responsibilities generally imposed under Chapter 2950. of the Revised Code upon persons who are adjudicated delinquent children for committing a sexually oriented offense other than a presumptive registration-exempt sexually oriented offense. If the court so determines, divisions (B)(1) and (3) of section 2950.021 of the Revised Code apply, and the court shall proceed as described in those divisions.

(2003 S 5, eff. 7–31–03)

2152.82 Juvenile offender registrant

(A) The court that adjudicates a child a delinquent child shall issue as part of the dispositional order an order that classifies the child a juvenile offender registrant and specifies that the child has a duty to comply with sections 2950.04, 2950.041, 2950.05, and 2950.06 of the Revised Code if all of the following apply:

(1) The act for which the child is adjudicated a delinquent child is a sexually oriented offense that is not a registration-exempt sexually oriented offense or is a child-victim oriented offense that the child committed on or after January 1, 2002.

(2) The child was fourteen, fifteen, sixteen, or seventeen years of age at the time of committing the offense.

(3) The court has determined that the child previously was convicted of, pleaded guilty to, or was adjudicated a delinquent child for committing any sexually oriented offense or child-victim oriented offense, regardless of when the prior offense was committed and regardless of the child's age at the time of committing the offense.

(B) An order required under division (A) of this section shall be issued at the time the judge makes the orders of disposition for the delinquent child. Prior to issuing the order required by division (A) of this section, the judge shall conduct the hearing and make the determinations required by division (B) of section 2950.09 of the Revised Code regarding a sexually oriented offense that is not a registration-exempt sexually oriented offense or division (B) of section 2950.091 of the Revised Code regarding a child-victim oriented offense to determine if the child is to be classified a sexual predator or a child-victim predator, shall make the determinations required by division (E) of section 2950.09 of the Revised Code regarding a sexually oriented offense that is not a registration-exempt sexually oriented offense or division (E) of section 2950.091 of the Revised Code regarding a child-victim oriented offense to determine if the child is to be classified a habitual sex offender or a habitual child-victim offender, and shall otherwise comply with those divisions. When a judge issues an order under division (A) of this section, all of the following apply:

(1) The judge shall include in the order any determination that the delinquent child is, or is not, a sexual predator or child-victim predator or is, or is not, a habitual sex offender or habitual child-victim offender that the judge makes pursuant to division (B) or (E) of section 2950.09 or 2950.091 of the Revised Code and any related information required or authorized under the division under which the determination is made, including, but not limited to, any requirement imposed by the court subjecting a child who

is a habitual sex offender or habitual child-victim offender to community notification provisions as described in division (E) of section 2950.09 or 2950.091 of the Revised Code.

(2) The judge shall include in the order a statement that, upon completion of the disposition of the delinquent child that was made for the sexually oriented offense or child-victim oriented offense upon which the order is based, a hearing will be conducted, and the order and any determinations included in the order are subject to modification or termination pursuant to sections 2152.84 and 2152.85 of the Revised Code.

(3) The judge shall provide to the delinquent child and to the delinquent child's parent, guardian, or custodian the notice required under divisions (A) and (B) of section 2950.03 of the Revised Code and shall provide as part of that notice a copy of the order.

(4) The judge shall include the order in the delinquent child's dispositional order and shall specify in the dispositional order that the order issued under division (A) of this section was made pursuant to this section.

(C) An order issued under division (A) of this section and any determinations included in the order shall remain in effect for the period of time specified in section 2950.07 of the Revised Code, subject to a modification or termination of the order under section 2152.84 or 2152.85 of the Revised Code, and section 2152.851 of the Revised Code applies regarding the order and the determinations. If an order is issued under division (A) of this section, the child's attainment of eighteen or twenty-one years of age does not affect or terminate the order, and the order remains in effect for the period of time described in this division.

(D) A court that adjudicates a child a delinquent child for a sexually oriented offense that is a registration-exempt sexually oriented offense shall not issue based on that adjudication an order under this section that classifies the child a juvenile offender registrant and specifies that the child has a duty to comply with sections 2950.04, 2950.041, 2950.05, and 2950.06 of the Revised Code.

(2003 S 5, eff. 7–31–03; 2002 H 393, eff. 7–5–02; 2001 S 3, eff. 1–1–02)

2152.821 Testimony of mentally retarded or developmentally disabled victim

(A) As used in this section:

(1) "Mentally retarded person" and "developmentally disabled person" have the same meanings as in section 5123.01 of the Revised Code.

(2) "Mentally retarded or developmentally disabled victim" includes any of the following persons:

(a) A mentally retarded person or developmentally disabled person who was a victim of a violation identified in division (B)(1) of this section or an act that would be an offense of violence if committed by an adult;

(b) A mentally retarded person or developmentally disabled person against whom was directed any conduct that constitutes, or that is an element of, a violation identified in division (B)(1) of this section or an act that would be an offense of violence if committed by an adult.

(B)(1) In any proceeding in juvenile court involving a complaint, indictment, or information in which a child is charged with a violation of section 2903.16, 2903.34, 2903.341, 2907.02, 2907.03, 2907.05, 2907.21, 2907. 23, 2907.24, 2907.32, 2907.321, 2907.322, or 2907.323 of the Revised Code or an act that would be an offense of violence if committed by an adult and in which an alleged victim of the violation or act was a mentally retarded person or developmentally disabled person, the juvenile judge, upon motion of the prosecution, shall order that the testimony of the mentally retarded or developmentally disabled victim be taken by deposition. The prosecution also may request that the deposition be videotaped in accordance with division (B)(2) of this section. The judge shall notify the mentally retarded or developmentally disabled victim whose deposition is to be taken, the prosecution, and the attorney for the child who is charged with the violation or act of the date, time, and place for taking the deposition. The notice shall identify the mentally retarded or developmentally disabled victim who is to be examined and shall indicate whether a request that the deposition be videotaped has been made. The child who is charged with the violation or act shall have the right to attend the deposition and the right to be represented by counsel. Depositions shall be taken in the manner provided in civil cases, except that the judge in the proceeding shall preside at the taking of the deposition and shall rule at that time on any objections of the prosecution or the attorney for the child charged with the violation or act. The prosecution and the attorney for the child charged with the violation or act shall have the right, as at an adjudication hearing, to full examination and cross-examination of the mentally retarded or developmentally disabled victim whose deposition is to be taken.

If a deposition taken under this division is intended to be offered as evidence in the proceeding, it shall be filed in the juvenile court in which the action is pending and is admissible in the manner described in division (C) of this section. If a deposition of a mentally retarded or developmentally disabled victim taken under this division is admitted as evidence at the proceeding under division (C) of this section, the mentally retarded or developmentally disabled victim shall not be required to testify in person at the proceeding.

At any time before the conclusion of the proceeding, the attorney for the child charged with the violation or act may file a motion with the judge requesting that another deposition of the mentally retarded or developmentally disabled victim be taken because new evidence material to the defense of the child charged has been discovered that the attorney for the child charged could not with reasonable diligence have discovered prior to the taking of the admitted deposition. Any motion requesting another deposition shall be accompanied by supporting affidavits. Upon the filing of the motion and affidavits, the court may order that additional testimony of the mentally retarded or developmentally disabled victim relative to the new evidence be taken by another deposition. If the court orders the taking of another deposition under this provision, the deposition shall be taken in accordance with this division. If the admitted deposition was a videotaped deposition taken in accordance with division (B)(2) of this section, the new deposition also shall be videotaped in accordance with that division. In other cases, the new deposition may be videotaped in accordance with that division.

(2) If the prosecution requests that a deposition to be taken under division (B)(1) of this section be videotaped, the juvenile judge shall order that the deposition be videotaped in accordance with this division. If a juvenile judge issues an order to video tape the deposition, the judge shall exclude from the room in which the deposition is to be taken every person except the mentally retarded or developmentally disabled victim giving the testimony, the judge, one or more interpreters if needed, the attorneys for the prosecution and the child who is charged with the violation or act, any person needed to operate the equipment to be used, one person chosen by the mentally retarded or developmentally disabled victim giving the deposition, and any person whose presence the judge determines would contribute to the welfare and well-being of the mentally retarded or developmentally disabled victim giving the deposition. The person chosen by the mentally retarded or developmentally disabled victim shall not be a witness in the proceeding and, both before and during the deposition, shall not discuss the testimony of the victim with any other witness in the proceeding. To the extent feasible, any person operating the recording equipment shall be restricted to a room adjacent to the room in which the deposition

is being taken, or to a location in the room in which the deposition is being taken that is behind a screen or mirror so that the person operating the recording equipment can see and hear, but cannot be seen or heard by, the mentally retarded or developmentally disabled victim giving the deposition during the deposition.

The child who is charged with the violation or act shall be permitted to observe and hear the testimony of the mentally retarded or developmentally disabled victim giving the deposition on a monitor, shall be provided with an electronic means of immediate communication with the attorney of the child who is charged with the violation or act during the testimony, and shall be restricted to a location from which the child who is charged with the violation or act cannot be seen or heard by the mentally retarded or developmentally disabled victim giving the deposition, except on a monitor provided for that purpose. The mentally retarded or developmentally disabled victim giving the deposition shall be provided with a monitor on which the mentally retarded or developmentally disabled victim can observe, while giving testimony, the child who is charged with the violation or act. The judge, at the judge's discretion, may preside at the deposition by electronic means from outside the room in which the deposition is to be taken; if the judge presides by electronic means, the judge shall be provided with monitors on which the judge can see each person in the room in which the deposition is to be taken and with an electronic means of communication with each person in that room, and each person in the room shall be provided with a monitor on which that person can see the judge and with an electronic means of communication with the judge. A deposition that is videotaped under this division shall be taken and filed in the manner described in division (B)(1) of this section and is admissible in the manner described in this division and division (C) of this section. If a deposition that is videotaped under this division is admitted as evidence at the proceeding, the mentally retarded or developmentally disabled victim shall not be required to testify in person at the proceeding. No deposition videotaped under this division shall be admitted as evidence at any proceeding unless division (C) of this section is satisfied relative to the deposition and all of the following apply relative to the recording:

(a) The recording is both aural and visual and is recorded on film or videotape, or by other electronic means.

(b) The recording is authenticated under the Rules of Evidence and the Rules of Criminal Procedure as a fair and accurate representation of what occurred, and the recording is not altered other than at the direction and under the supervision of the judge in the proceeding.

(c) Each voice on the recording that is material to the testimony on the recording or the making of the recording, as determined by the judge, is identified.

(d) Both the prosecution and the child who is charged with the violation or act are afforded an opportunity to view the recording before it is shown in the proceeding.

(C)(1) At any proceeding in relation to which a deposition was taken under division (B) of this section, the deposition or a part of it is admissible in evidence upon motion of the prosecution if the testimony in the deposition or the part to be admitted is not excluded by the hearsay rule and if the deposition or the part to be admitted otherwise is admissible under the Rules of Evidence. For purposes of this division, testimony is not excluded by the hearsay rule if the testimony is not hearsay under Evidence Rule 801; the testimony is within an exception to the hearsay rule set forth in Evidence Rule 803; the mentally retarded or developmentally disabled victim who gave the testimony is unavailable as a witness, as defined in Evidence Rule 804, and the testimony is admissible under that rule; or both of the following apply:

(a) The child who is charged with the violation or act had an opportunity and similar motive at the time of the taking of the deposition to develop the testimony by direct, cross, or redirect examination.

(b) The judge determines that there is reasonable cause to believe that, if the mentally retarded or developmentally disabled victim who gave the testimony in the deposition were to testify in person at the proceeding, the mentally retarded or developmentally disabled victim would experience serious emotional trauma as a result of the mentally retarded or developmentally disabled victim's participation at the proceeding.

(2) Objections to receiving in evidence a deposition or a part of it under division (C) of this section shall be made as provided in civil actions.

(3) The provisions of divisions (B) and (C) of this section are in addition to any other provisions of the Revised Code, the Rules of Juvenile Procedure, the Rules of Criminal Procedure, or the Rules of Evidence that pertain to the taking or admission of depositions in a juvenile court proceeding and do not limit the admissibility under any of those other provisions of any deposition taken under division (B) of this section or otherwise taken.

(D) In any proceeding in juvenile court involving a complaint, indictment, or information in which a child is charged with a violation listed in division (B)(1) of this section or an act that would be an offense of violence if committed by an adult and in which an alleged victim of the violation or offense was a mentally retarded or developmentally disabled person, the prosecution may file a motion with the juvenile judge requesting the judge to order the testimony of the mentally retarded or developmentally disabled victim to be taken in a room other than the room in which the proceeding is being conducted and be televised, by closed circuit equipment, into the room in which the proceeding is being conducted to be viewed by the child who is charged with the violation or act and any other persons who are not permitted in the room in which the testimony is to be taken but who would have been present during the testimony of the mentally retarded or developmentally disabled victim had it been given in the room in which the proceeding is being conducted. Except for good cause shown, the prosecution shall file a motion under this division at least seven days before the date of the proceeding. The juvenile judge may issue the order upon the motion of the prosecution filed under this division, if the judge determines that the mentally retarded or developmentally disabled victim is unavailable to testify in the room in which the proceeding is being conducted in the physical presence of the child charged with the violation or act for one or more of the reasons set forth in division (F) of this section. If a juvenile judge issues an order of that nature, the judge shall exclude from the room in which the testimony is to be taken every person except a person described in division (B)(2) of this section. The judge, at the judge's discretion, may preside during the giving of the testimony by electronic means from outside the room in which it is being given, subject to the limitations set forth in division (B)(2) of this section. To the extent feasible, any person operating the televising equipment shall be hidden from the sight and hearing of the mentally retarded or developmentally disabled victim giving the testimony, in a manner similar to that described in division (B)(2) of this section. The child who is charged with the violation or act shall be permitted to observe and hear the testimony of the mentally retarded or developmentally disabled victim giving the testimony on a monitor, shall be provided with an electronic means of immediate communication with the attorney of the child who is charged with the violation or act during the testimony, and shall be restricted to a location from which the child who is charged with the violation or act cannot be seen or heard by the mentally retarded or developmentally disabled victim giving the testimony, except on a monitor provided for that purpose. The mentally retarded or developmentally disabled victim giving the testimony shall be provided with a monitor on which the mentally retarded or developmentally disabled victim can observe, while giving testimony, the child who is charged with the violation or act.

(E) In any proceeding in juvenile court involving a complaint, indictment, or information in which a child is charged with a violation listed in division (B)(1) of this section or an act that would be an offense of violence if committed by an adult and in which an alleged victim of the violation or offense was a mentally retarded or developmentally disabled person, the prosecution may file a motion with the juvenile judge requesting the judge to order the testimony of the mentally retarded or developmentally disabled victim to be taken outside of the room in which the proceeding is being conducted and be recorded for showing in the room in which the proceeding is being conducted before the judge, the child who is charged with the violation or act, and any other persons who would have been present during the testimony of the mentally retarded or developmentally disabled victim had it been given in the room in which the proceeding is being conducted. Except for good cause shown, the prosecution shall file a motion under this division at least seven days before the date of the proceeding. The juvenile judge may issue the order upon the motion of the prosecution filed under this division, if the judge determines that the mentally retarded or developmentally disabled victim is unavailable to testify in the room in which the proceeding is being conducted in the physical presence of the child charged with the violation or act, due to one or more of the reasons set forth in division (F) of this section. If a juvenile judge issues an order of that nature, the judge shall exclude from the room in which the testimony is to be taken every person except a person described in division (B)(2) of this section. To the extent feasible, any person operating the recording equipment shall be hidden from the sight and hearing of the mentally retarded or developmentally disabled victim giving the testimony, in a manner similar to that described in division (B)(2) of this section. The child who is charged with the violation or act shall be permitted to observe and hear the testimony of the mentally retarded or developmentally disabled victim giving the testimony on a monitor, shall be provided with an electronic means of immediate communication with the attorney of the child who is charged with the violation or act during the testimony, and shall be restricted to a location from which the child who is charged with the violation or act cannot be seen or heard by the mentally retarded or developmentally disabled victim giving the testimony, except on a monitor provided for that purpose. The mentally retarded or developmentally disabled victim giving the testimony shall be provided with a monitor on which the mentally retarded or developmentally disabled victim can observe, while giving testimony, the child who is charged with the violation or act. No order for the taking of testimony by recording shall be issued under this division unless the provisions set forth in divisions (B)(2)(a), (b), (c), and (d) of this section apply to the recording of the testimony.

(F) For purposes of divisions (D) and (E) of this section, a juvenile judge may order the testimony of a mentally retarded or developmentally disabled victim to be taken outside of the room in which a proceeding is being conducted if the judge determines that the mentally retarded or developmentally disabled victim is unavailable to testify in the room in the physical presence of the child charged with the violation or act due to one or more of the following circumstances:

(1) The persistent refusal of the mentally retarded or developmentally disabled victim to testify despite judicial requests to do so;

(2) The inability of the mentally retarded or developmentally disabled victim to communicate about the alleged violation or offense because of extreme fear, failure of memory, or another similar reason;

(3) The substantial likelihood that the mentally retarded or developmentally disabled victim will suffer serious emotional trauma from so testifying.

(G)(1) If a juvenile judge issues an order pursuant to division (D) or (E) of this section that requires the testimony of a mentally retarded or developmentally disabled victim in a juvenile court proceeding to be taken outside of the room in which the proceeding is being conducted, the order shall specifically identify the mentally retarded or developmentally disabled victim to whose testimony it applies, the order applies only during the testimony of the specified mentally retarded or developmentally disabled victim, and the mentally retarded or developmentally disabled victim giving the testimony shall not be required to testify at the proceeding other than in accordance with the order. The authority of a judge to close the taking of a deposition under division (B)(2) of this section or a proceeding under division (D) or (E) of this section is in addition to the authority of a judge to close a hearing pursuant to section 2151.35 of the Revised Code.

(2) A juvenile judge who makes any determination regarding the admissibility of a deposition under divisions (B) and (C) of this section, the videotaping of a deposition under division (B)(2) of this section, or the taking of testimony outside of the room in which a proceeding is being conducted under division (D) or (E) of this section shall enter the determination and findings on the record in the proceeding.

(2004 S 178, eff. 1–30–04)

2152.83 Order classifying child as juvenile offender registrant; hearing to review effectiveness of disposition and treatment

(A)(1) The court that adjudicates a child a delinquent child shall issue as part of the dispositional order or, if the court commits the child for the delinquent act to the custody of a secure facility, shall issue at the time of the child's release from the secure facility, an order that classifies the child a juvenile offender registrant and specifies that the child has a duty to comply with sections 2950.04, 2950.041, 2950.05, and 2950.06 of the Revised Code if all of the following apply:

(a) The act for which the child is or was adjudicated a delinquent child is a sexually oriented offense that is not a registration-exempt sexually oriented offense or is a child-victim oriented offense that the child committed on or after January 1, 2002.

(b) The child was sixteen or seventeen years of age at the time of committing the offense.

(c) The court was not required to classify the child a juvenile offender registrant under section 2152.82 of the Revised Code.

(2) Prior to issuing the order required by division (A)(2) of this section, the judge shall conduct the hearing and make the determinations required by division (B) of section 2950.09 of the Revised Code regarding a sexually oriented offense that is not a registration-exempt sexually oriented offense or division (B) of section 2950.091 of the Revised Code regarding a child-victim oriented offense to determine if the child is to be classified a sexual predator or a child-victim predator, shall make the determinations required by division (E) of section 2950.09 of the Revised Code regarding a sexually oriented offense that is not a registration-exempt sexually oriented offense or division (E) of section 2950.091 of the Revised Code regarding a child-victim oriented offense to determine if the child is to be classified a habitual sex offender or a habitual child-victim offender, and shall otherwise comply with those divisions. When a judge issues an order under division (A)(1) of this section, the judge shall include in the order all of the determinations and information identified in division (B)(1) of section 2152. 82 of the Revised Code that are relevant.

(B)(1) The court that adjudicates a child a delinquent child, on the judge's own motion, may conduct at the time of disposition of the child or, if the court commits the child for the delinquent act to the custody of a secure facility, may conduct at the time of the child's release from the secure facility, a hearing for the purposes described in division (B)(2) of this section if all of the following apply:

(a) The act for which the child is adjudicated a delinquent child is a sexually oriented offense that is not a registration-exempt sexually oriented offense or is a child-victim oriented offense that the child committed on or after January 1, 2002.

(b) The child was fourteen or fifteen years of age at the time of committing the offense.

(c) The court was not required to classify the child a juvenile offender registrant under section 2152.82 of the Revised Code.

(2) A judge shall conduct a hearing under division (B)(1) of this section to review the effectiveness of the disposition made of the child and of any treatment provided for the child placed in a secure setting and to determine whether the child should be classified a juvenile offender registrant. The judge may conduct the hearing on the judge's own initiative or based upon a recommendation of an officer or employee of the department of youth services, a probation officer, an employee of the court, or a prosecutor or law enforcement officer. If the judge conducts the hearing, upon completion of the hearing, the judge, in the judge's discretion and after consideration of the factors listed in division (E) of this section, shall do either of the following:

(a) Decline to issue an order that classifies the child a juvenile offender registrant and specifies that the child has a duty to comply with sections 2950.04, 2950.041, 2950.05, and 2950.06 of the Revised Code;

(b) Issue an order that classifies the child a juvenile offender registrant and specifies that the child has a duty to comply with sections 2950.04, 2950.041, 2950.05, and 2950.06 of the Revised Code and, if the judge conducts a hearing as described in division (C) of this section to determine whether the child is a sexual predator or child-victim predator or a habitual sex offender or habitual child-victim offender, include in the order a statement that the judge has determined that the child is, or is not, a sexual predator , child-victim predator, habitual sex offender, or habitual child-victim offender, whichever is applicable.

(C) A judge may issue an order under division (B) of this section that contains a determination that a delinquent child is a sexual predator or child-victim predator only if the judge, in accordance with the procedures specified in division (B) of section 2950.09 of the Revised Code regarding sexual predators or division (B) of section 2950.091 of the Revised Code regarding child-victim predators, determines at the hearing by clear and convincing evidence that the child is a sexual predator or a child-victim predator. A judge may issue an order under division (B) of this section that contains a determination that a delinquent child is a habitual sex offender or a habitual child-victim offender only if the judge at the hearing determines as described in division (E) of section 2950.09 of the Revised Code regarding habitual sex offenders or division (E) of section 2950.091 of the Revised Code regarding habitual child-victim offenders that the child is a habitual sex offender or a habitual child-victim offender. If the judge issues an order under division (B) of this section that contains a determination that a delinquent child is a habitual sex offender or a habitual child-victim offender, the judge may impose a requirement subjecting the child to community notification provisions as described in division (E) of section 2950.09 or 2950.091 of the Revised Code, whichever is applicable. If the court conducts a hearing as described in this division to determine whether the child is a sexual predator or child-victim predator or a habitual sex offender or habitual child-victim offender, the judge shall comply with division (B) or (E) of section 2950.09 or 2950.091 of the Revised Code, whichever is applicable, in all regards.

(D) If a judge issues an order under division (A) or (B) of this section, the judge shall provide to the delinquent child and to the delinquent child's parent, guardian, or custodian a copy of the order and a notice containing the information described in divisions (A) and (B) of section 2950.03 of the Revised Code. The judge shall provide the notice at the time of the issuance of the order and shall comply with divisions (B) and (C) of that section regarding that notice and the provision of it.

The judge also shall include in the order a statement that, upon completion of the disposition of the delinquent child that was made for the sexually oriented offense or child-victim oriented offense upon which the order is based, a hearing will be conducted and the order is subject to modification or termination pursuant to section 2152.84 of the Revised Code.

(E) In making a decision under division (B) of this section as to whether a delinquent child should be classified a juvenile offender registrant and, if so, whether the child also is a sexual predator or child-victim predator or a habitual sex offender or habitual child-victim offender, a judge shall consider all relevant factors, including, but not limited to, all of the following:

(1) The nature of the sexually oriented offense that is not a registration-exempt sexually oriented offense or the child-victim oriented offense committed by the child;

(2) Whether the child has shown any genuine remorse or compunction for the offense;

(3) The public interest and safety;

(4) The factors set forth in division (B)(3) of section 2950.09 or 2950.091 of the Revised Code, whichever is applicable;

(5) The factors set forth in divisions (B) and (C) of section 2929.12 of the Revised Code as those factors apply regarding the delinquent child, the offense, and the victim;

(6) The results of any treatment provided to the child and of any follow-up professional assessment of the child.

(F) An order issued under division (A) or (B) of this section and any determinations included in the order shall remain in effect for the period of time specified in section 2950.07 of the Revised Code, subject to a modification or termination of the order under section 2152.84 of the Revised Code, and section 2152.851 of the Revised Code applies regarding the order and the determinations. The child's attainment of eighteen or twenty-one years of age does not affect or terminate the order, and the order remains in effect for the period of time described in this division.

(G) A court that adjudicates a child a delinquent child for a sexually oriented offense that is a registration-exempt sexually oriented offense shall not issue based on that adjudication an order under this section that classifies the child a juvenile offender registrant and specifies that the child has a duty to comply with sections 2950.04, 2950.041, 2950.05, and 2950.06 of the Revised Code.

(H) As used in the section, "secure facility" has the same meaning as in section 2950.01 of the Revised Code.

(2003 S 5, eff. 7–31–03; 2002 H 393, eff. 7–5–02; 2001 S 3, eff. 1–1–02)

2152.84 Hearings; orders

(A)(1) When a juvenile court judge issues an order under section 2152.82 or division (A) or (B) of section 2152.83 of the Revised Code that classifies a delinquent child a juvenile offender registrant and specifies that the child has a duty to comply with sections 2950.04, 2950.041, 2950.05, and 2950.06 of the Revised Code, upon completion of the disposition of that child made for the sexually oriented offense that is not a registration-exempt sexually oriented offense or the child-victim oriented offense on which the juvenile offender registrant order was based, the judge or the judge's successor in office shall conduct a hearing to review the effectiveness of the disposition and of any treatment provided for the child, to determine the risks that the child might re-offend, and to determine whether the prior classification of the child as a juvenile offender registrant and, if applicable, as a sexual predator or child-victim predator or as a habitual sex offender or habitual child-victim offender should be continued, modified, or terminated as provided under division (A)(2) of this section.

(2) Upon completion of a hearing under division (A)(1) of this section, the judge, in the judge's discretion and after consideration of the factors listed in division (E) of section 2152.83 of the Revised Code, shall do one of the following, as applicable:

(a) Enter an order that continues the classification of the delinquent child made in the prior order issued under section 2152.82 or division (A) or (B) of section 2152.83 of the Revised Code, and any sexual predator, child-victim predator, habitual sex offender, or habitual child-victim offender determination included in the order;

(b) If the prior order was issued under section 2152.82 or division (A) of section 2152.83 of the Revised Code and includes a determination by the judge that the delinquent child is a sexual predator or child-victim predator, enter, as applicable, an order that contains a determination that the child no longer is a sexual predator, the reason or reasons for that determination, and either a determination that the child is a habitual sex offender or a determination that the child remains a juvenile offender registrant but is not a sexual predator or habitual sex offender, or an order that contains a determination that the child no longer is a child-victim predator, the reason or reasons for that determination, and either a determination that the child is a habitual child-victim offender or a determination that the child remains a juvenile offender registrant but is not a child-victim predator or habitual child-victim offender;

(c) If the prior order was issued under section 2152.82 or division (A) of section 2152.83 of the Revised Code and does not include a sexual predator or child-victim predator determination as described in division (A)(2)(b) of this section but includes a determination by the judge that the delinquent child is a habitual sex offender or a habitual child-victim offender, enter, as applicable, an order that contains a determination that the child no longer is a habitual sex offender and a determination that the child remains a juvenile sex offender registrant but is not a habitual offender, or an order that contains a determination that the child no longer is a habitual child-victim offender and a determination that the child remains a juvenile offender registrant but is not a habitual child-victim offender;

(d) If the prior order was issued under division (B) of section 2152.83 of the Revised Code and includes a determination by the judge that the delinquent child is a sexual predator or child-victim predator, enter, as applicable, an order that contains a determination that the child no longer is a sexual predator, the reason or reasons for that determination, and either a determination that the child is a habitual sex offender, a determination that the child remains a juvenile offender registrant but is not a sexual predator or habitual sex offender, or a determination that the child no longer is a juvenile offender registrant and no longer has a duty to comply with sections 2950.04, 2950.05, and 2950.06 of the Revised Code, or an order that contains a determination that the child no longer is a child-victim predator, the reason or reasons for that determination, and either a determination that the child is a habitual child-victim offender, a determination that the child remains a juvenile offender registrant but is not a child-victim predator or habitual child-victim offender, or a determination that the child no longer is a juvenile offender registrant and no longer has a duty to comply with sections 2950.041, 2950.05, and 2950.06 of the Revised Code;

(e) If the prior order was issued under division (B) of section 2152.83 of the Revised Code and does not include a sexual predator or child-victim predator determination as described in division (A)(2)(d) of this section but includes a determination by the judge that the delinquent child is a habitual sex offender or habitual child-victim offender, enter, as applicable, an order that contains a determination that the child no longer is a habitual sex offender and either a determination that the child remains a juvenile offender registrant but is not a sexual predator or habitual sex offender or a determination that the child no longer is a juvenile offender registrant and no longer has a duty to comply with sections 2950.04, 2950.05, and 2950.06 of the Revised Code, or an order that contains a determination that the child no longer is a habitual child-victim offender and either a determination that the child remains a juvenile offender registrant but is not a child-victim predator or habitual child-victim offender or a determination that the child no longer is a juvenile offender registrant and no longer has a duty to comply with sections 2950.041, 2950.05, and 2950.06 of the Revised Code;

(f) If the prior order was issued under division (B) of section 2152.83 of the Revised Code and does not include a sexual predator or child-victim predator determination or a habitual sex offender or habitual child-victim offender determination as described in divisions (A)(2)(d) and (e) of this section, enter, as applicable, an order that contains a determination that the delinquent child no longer is a juvenile offender registrant and no longer has a duty to comply with sections 2950.04, 2950.05, and 2950.06 of the Revised Code, or an order that contains a determination that the delinquent child no longer is a juvenile offender registrant and no longer has a duty to comply with sections 2950.041, 2950.05, and 2950.06 of the Revised Code.

(B) If a judge issues an order under division (A)(2)(a) of this section that continues the prior classification of the delinquent child as a juvenile offender registrant and any sexual predator or habitual sex offender determination included in the order, or that continues the prior classification of the delinquent child as a juvenile offender registrant and any child-victim predator or habitual child-victim offender determination included in the order, the prior classification and the prior determination, if applicable, shall remain in effect.

A judge may issue an order under division (A)(2) of this section that contains a determination that a child no longer is a sexual predator or no longer is a child-victim predator only if the judge, in accordance with the procedures specified in division (D)(1) of section 2950.09 of the Revised Code regarding a sexual predator, determines at the hearing by clear and convincing evidence that the delinquent child is unlikely to commit a sexually oriented offense in the future, or the judge, in accordance with the procedures specified in division (D)(1) of section 2950.091 of the Revised Code regarding a child-victim predator, determines at the hearing by clear and convincing evidence that the delinquent child is unlikely to commit a child-victim oriented offense in the future. If the judge issues an order of that type, the judge shall provide the notifications described in division (D)(1) of section 2950.09 or 2950.091 of the Revised Code, whichever is applicable, and the recipient of the notification shall comply with the provisions of that division.

If a judge issues an order under division (A)(2) of this section that otherwise reclassifies the delinquent child, the judge shall provide a copy of the order to the bureau of criminal identification and investigation, and the bureau, upon receipt of the copy of the order, promptly shall notify the sheriff with whom the child most recently registered under section 2950.04 or 2950.041 of the Revised Code of the reclassification.

(C) If a judge issues an order under any provision of division (A)(2) of this section, the judge shall provide to the delinquent child and to the delinquent child's parent, guardian, or custodian a copy of the order and a notice containing the information described in divisions (A) and (B) of section 2950.03 of the Revised Code. The judge shall provide the notice at the time of the issuance of the order and shall comply with divisions (B) and (C) of that section regarding that notice and the provision of it.

(D) In making a decision under division (A) of this section, a judge shall consider all relevant factors, including, but not limited to, the factors listed in division (E) of section 2152.83 of the Revised Code.

(E) An order issued under division (A)(2) of this section and any determinations included in the order shall remain in effect for the period of time specified in section 2950.07 of the Revised Code, subject to a modification or termination of the order under section 2152.85 of the Revised Code, and section 2152.851 of the Revised Code applies regarding the order and the determinations. If an order is issued under division (A)(2) of this section, the child's attainment of eighteen or twenty-one years of age does not affect or terminate the order, and the order remains in effect for the period of time described in this division.

(2003 S 5, eff. 7–31–03; 2002 H 393, eff. 7–5–02; 2001 S 3, eff. 1–1–02)

2152.85 Petitioning of judge by juvenile offender registrant

(A) Upon the expiration of the applicable period of time specified in division (B)(1) or (2) of this section, a delinquent child who has been classified pursuant to this section or section 2152.82 or 2152.83 of the Revised Code a juvenile offender registrant may petition the judge who made the classification, or that judge's successor in office, to do one of the following:

(1) If the order containing the juvenile offender registrant classification also includes a determination by the juvenile court judge that the delinquent child is a sexual predator or child-victim predator in the manner described in section 2152.82 or 2152.83 of the Revised Code and that determination remains in effect, to enter, as applicable, an order that contains a determination that the child no longer is a sexual predator, the reason or reasons for that determination, and either a determination that the child is a habitual sex offender or a determination that the child remains a juvenile offender registrant but is not a sexual predator or habitual sex offender, or an order that contains a determination that the child no longer is a child-victim predator, the reason or reasons for that determination, and either a determination that the child is a habitual child-victim offender or a determination that the child remains a juvenile offender registrant but is not a child-victim predator or habitual child-victim offender;

(2) If the order containing the juvenile offender registrant classification under section 2152.82 or 2152.83 of the Revised Code or under division (C)(2) of this section pursuant to a petition filed under division (A) of this section does not include a sexual predator or child-victim predator determination as described in division (A)(1) of this section but includes a determination by the juvenile court judge that the delinquent child is a habitual sex offender or a habitual child-victim offender in the manner described in section 2152.82 or 2152.83 of the Revised Code, or in this section, and that determination remains in effect, to enter, as applicable, an order that contains a determination that the child no longer is a habitual sex offender and either a determination that the child remains a juvenile offender registrant or a determination that the child no longer is a juvenile offender registrant and no longer has a duty to comply with sections 2950.04, 2950.05, and 2950.06 of the Revised Code, or an order that contains a determination that the child no longer is a habitual child-victim offender and either a determination that the child remains a juvenile offender registrant or a determination that the child no longer is a juvenile offender registrant and no longer has a duty to comply with sections 2950.041, 2950.05, and 2950.06 of the Revised Code;

(3) If the order containing the juvenile offender registrant classification under section 2152.82 or 2152.83 of the Revised Code or under division (C)(2) of this section pursuant to a petition filed under division (A) of this section does not include a sexual predator or child-victim predator determination or a habitual sex offender or habitual child-victim offender determination as described in division (A)(1) or (2) of this section, to enter, as applicable, an order that contains a determination that the child no longer is a juvenile offender registrant and no longer has a duty to comply with sections 2950.04, 2950.05, and 2950.06 of the Revised Code, or an order that contains a determination that the child no longer is a juvenile offender registrant and no longer has a duty to comply with sections 2950.041, 2950.05, and 2950.06 of the Revised Code.

(B) A delinquent child who has been adjudicated a delinquent child for committing on or after January 1, 2002, a sexually oriented offense that is not a registration-exempt sexually oriented offense and who has been classified a juvenile offender registrant relative to that offense or who has been adjudicated a delinquent child for committing on or after that date a child-victim oriented offense and who has been classified a juvenile offender registrant relative to that offense may file a petition under division (A) of this section requesting reclassification or declassification as described in that division after the expiration of one of the following periods of time:

(1) The delinquent child initially may file a petition not earlier than three years after the entry of the juvenile court judge's order after the mandatory hearing conducted under section 2152.84 of the Revised Code.

(2) After the delinquent child's initial filing of a petition under division (B)(1) of this section, the child may file a second petition not earlier than three years after the judge has entered an order deciding the petition under division (B)(1) of this section.

(3) After the delinquent child's filing of a petition under division (B)(2) of this section, thereafter, the delinquent child may file a petition under this division upon the expiration of five years after the judge has entered an order deciding the petition under division (B)(2) of this section or the most recent petition the delinquent child has filed under this division.

(C) Upon the filing of a petition under divisions (A) and (B) of this section, the judge may review the prior classification or determination in question and, upon consideration of all relevant factors and information, including, but not limited to the factors listed in division (E) of section 2152.83 of the Revised Code, the judge, in the judge's discretion, shall do one of the following:

(1) Enter an order denying the petition;

(2) Issue an order that reclassifies or declassifies the delinquent child, in the requested manner specified in division (A)(1), (2), or (3) of this section.

(D) If a judge issues an order under division (C) of this section that denies a petition, the prior classification of the delinquent child as a juvenile offender registrant, and the prior determination that the child is a sexual predator, child-victim predator, habitual sex offender, or habitual child-victim offender, if applicable, shall remain in effect.

A judge may issue an order under division (C) of this section that contains a determination that a child no longer is a sexual predator or no longer is a child-victim predator only if the judge conducts a hearing and, in accordance with the procedures specified in division (D)(1) of section 2950.09 of the Revised Code regarding a sexual predator, determines at the hearing by clear and convincing evidence that the delinquent child is unlikely to commit a sexually oriented offense in the future, or, in accordance with the procedures specified in division (D)(1) of section 2950.091 of the Revised Code regarding a child-victim predator, determines at the hearing by clear and convincing evidence that the delinquent child is unlikely to commit a child-victim oriented offense in the future. If the judge issues an order of that type, the judge shall provide the notifications described in division (D)(1) of section 2950.09 or 2950.091 of the Revised Code, whichever is applicable, and the recipient of the notification shall comply with the provisions of that division.

A judge may issue an order under division (C) of this section that contains a determination that a delinquent child is a habitual sex offender or a habitual child-victim offender only if the judge conducts a hearing and determines at the hearing as described in division (E) of section 2950.09 of the Revised Code regarding habitual sex offenders or division (E) of section 2950.091 of the Revised Code regarding habitual child-victim offenders that the child is a habitual sex offender or a habitual child-victim offender. If the judge issues an order that contains a determination that a delinquent child is a habitual sex offender or a habitual child-victim offender, the judge may impose a requirement subjecting the child to community notification provisions as described in that division.

(E) If a judge issues an order under division (C) of this section, the judge shall provide to the delinquent child and to the delinquent child's parent, guardian, or custodian a copy of the order and a notice containing the information described in divisions (A) and (B) of section 2950.03 of the Revised Code. The judge shall provide the notice at the time of the issuance of the order and shall comply with divisions (B) and (C) of that section regarding that notice and the provision of it.

(F) An order issued under division (C) of this section shall remain in effect for the period of time specified in section 2950.07 of the Revised Code, subject to a further modification or a termination of the order under this section, and section 2152.851 of the Revised Code applies regarding the order and the determinations. If an order is issued under division (C) of this section, the child's attainment of eighteen or twenty-one years of age does not affect or terminate the order, and the order remains in effect for the period of time described in this division.

(2003 S 5, eff. 7–31–03; 2001 S 3, eff. 1–1–02)

2152.851 Effect of redesignation of offense on existing order

(A) If, prior to the effective date of this section, a judge issues an order under section 2152.82, 2152.83, 2152.84, or 2152.85 of the Revised Code that classifies a delinquent child a juvenile offender registrant and if, on and after the effective date of this section, the sexually oriented offense upon which the order was based no longer is considered a sexually oriented offense but instead is a child-victim oriented offense, notwithstanding the redesignation of the offense, the order shall remain in effect for the period described in the section under which it was issued, the order shall be considered for all purposes to be an order that classifies the child a juvenile offender registrant, division (A)(2)(b) of section 2950.041 of the Revised Code applies regarding the child, and the duty to register imposed pursuant to that division shall be considered, for purposes of section 2950.07 of the Revised Code and for all other purposes, to be a continuation of the duty imposed upon the child prior to the effective date of this section under the order issued under section 2152.82, 2152.83, 2152.84, or 2152.85 and Chapter 2950. of the Revised Code.

(B) If an order of the type described in division (A) of this section included a classification or determination that the delinquent child was a sexual predator or habitual sex offender, notwithstanding the redesignation of the offense upon which the determination was based, all of the following apply:

(1) Divisions (A)(1) and (2) or (E)(1) and (2) of section 2950.091 of the Revised Code apply regarding the child and the judge's order made prior to the effective date of this section shall be considered for all purposes to be an order that classifies the child as described in those divisions;

(2) The child's classification or determination under divisions (A)(1) and (2) or (E)(1) and (2) of section 2950.091 of the Revised Code shall be considered, for purposes of section 2950.07 of the Revised Code and for all other purposes, to be a continuation of classification or determination made prior to the effective date of this section;

(3) The child's duties under Chapter 2950. of the Revised Code relative to that classification or determination shall be considered for all purposes to be a continuation of the duties related to that classification or determination as they existed prior to the effective date of this section.

(2003 S 5, eff 7–31–03)

PENALTIES

2152.99 Penalties

Whoever violates division (G) of section 2152.72 of the Revised Code is guilty of a minor misdemeanor.

(2000 S 179, § 3, eff. 1 1 02)

CHAPTER 2301

COMMON PLEAS COURTS—ORGANIZATION

GENERAL PROVISIONS

2301.141 Retention of documents

Notwithstanding section 149.38 of the Revised Code, each clerk of a court of common pleas shall retain documentation regarding each criminal conviction and plea of guilty involving a case that is or was before the court. The documentation shall be in a form that is admissible as evidence in a criminal proceeding as evidence of a prior conviction or that is readily convertible to or producible in a form that is admissible as evidence in a criminal proceeding as evidence of a prior conviction and may be retained in any form authorized by section 9.01 of the Revised Code. The clerk shall retain this documentation for a period of fifty years after the entry of judgment in the case, except that documentation regarding cases solely concerned with minor misdemeanor offenses or minor misdemeanor traffic offenses shall be retained as provided in divisions (A) and (B) of section 1901.41 of the Revised Code, and documentation regarding other misdemeanor traffic offenses shall be retained for a period of twenty-five years after the entry of judgment in the case. This section shall apply to records currently retained and to records created on or after September 23, 2004.

(2004 H 30, eff. 3–23–05; 2004 H 163, eff. 9–23–04)

BAILIFF

2301.15 Duties of criminal bailiff; costs

The criminal bailiff shall act for the sheriff in criminal cases and matters of a criminal nature in the court of common pleas and the probate court of the county. Under the direction of the sheriff, he shall be present during trials of criminal cases in those courts and during such trials perform all the duties as are performed by the sheriff. The criminal bailiff shall conduct prisoners to and from the jail of the county and for that purpose shall have access to the jail and to the courtroom, whenever ordered by such courts, and have care and charge of such prisoners when so doing. Under the direction of the sheriff, the criminal bailiff shall convey to state correctional institutions all persons sentenced thereto. He shall receive and collect from the treasurer of state all costs in such criminal cases in the same manner as the sheriff is required to do, and pay the amount so collected to the sheriff of such county.

(1994 H 571, eff. 10–6–94; 1953 H 1, eff. 10–1–53; GC 1543)

2301.16 Bailiff shall give bond

Before entering upon the discharge of his duties, the criminal bailiff shall give a bond to the sheriff in the sum of five thousand dollars, with good and sufficient sureties, conditioned for the faithful discharge of his duties. The judges of the court of common pleas shall fix a compensation for his services, payable monthly from the fee fund, upon the warrant of the county auditor.

(1953 H 1, eff. 10–1–53; GC 1545)

2301.17 Additional temporary bailiff

On the application of the sheriff, in a criminal case, if the court of common pleas is satisfied that the administration of justice requires an additional criminal bailiff to execute process, it may appoint such additional bailiff, whose powers and duties shall cease when such case is determined.

(1953 H 1, eff. 10–1–53; GC 1544)

PROBATION DEPARTMENT; RESTRICTION OF JUDGES

2301.27 Probation departments; probation services; probation officers carrying firearms

(A)(1) The court of common pleas may establish a county department of probation. The establishment of the department shall be entered upon the journal of the court, and the clerk of the court of common pleas shall certify a copy of the journal entry establishing the department to each elective officer and board of the county. The department shall consist of a chief probation officer and the number of other probation officers and employees, clerks, and stenographers that is fixed from time to time by the court. The court shall appoint those individuals, fix their salaries, and supervise their work. The court shall not appoint as a probation officer any person who does not possess the training, experience, and other qualifications prescribed by the adult parole authority created by section 5149.02 of the Revised Code. Probation officers have all the powers of regular police officers and shall perform any duties that are designated by the judge or judges of the court. All positions within the department of probation shall be in the classified service of the civil service of the county.

(2) If two or more counties desire to jointly establish a probation department for those counties, the judges of the courts of common pleas of those counties may establish a probation department for those counties. If a probation department is established pursuant to division (A)(2) of this section to serve more than one county, the judges of the courts of common pleas that established the department shall designate the county treasurer of one of the counties served by the department as the treasurer to whom probation fees paid under section 2951.021 of the Revised Code are to be appropriated and transferred under division (A)(2) of section 321.44 of the Revised Code for deposit into the multicounty probation services fund established under division (B) of section 321.44 of the Revised Code.

The cost of the administration and operation of a probation department established for two or more counties shall be prorated to the respective counties on the basis of population.

(3) Probation officers shall receive, in addition to their respective salaries, their necessary and reasonable travel and other expenses incurred in the performance of their duties. Their salaries and expenses shall be paid monthly from the county treasury in the manner provided for the payment of the compensation of other appointees of the court.

(B)(1) In lieu of establishing a county department of probation under division (A) of this section and in lieu of entering into an agreement with the adult parole authority as described in division (B) of section 2301.32 of the Revised Code, the court of common pleas may request the board of county commissioners to contract with, and upon that request the board may contract with, any nonprofit, public or private agency, association, or organization for the provision of probation services and supervisory services for persons placed under community control sanctions. The contract shall specify that each individual providing the probation services and supervisory services shall possess the training, experience, and other qualifications prescribed by the adult parole authority. The individuals who provide the probation services and supervisory services shall not be included in the classified or unclassified civil service of the county.

(2) In lieu of establishing a county department of probation under division (A) of this section and in lieu of entering into an agreement with the adult parole authority as described in division (B) of section 2301.32 of the Revised Code, the courts of common pleas of two or more adjoining counties jointly may request the boards of county commissioners of those counties to contract with, and upon that request the boards of county commissioners of two or more adjoining counties jointly may contract

with, any nonprofit, public or private agency, association, or organization for the provision of probation services and supervisory services for persons placed under community control sanctions for those counties. The contract shall specify that each individual providing the probation services and supervisory services shall possess the training, experience, and other qualifications prescribed by the adult parole authority. The individuals who provide the probation services and supervisory services shall not be included in the classified or unclassified civil service of any of those counties.

(C) The chief probation officer may grant permission to a probation officer to carry firearms when required in the discharge of official duties if the probation officer has successfully completed a basic firearm training program that is approved by the executive director of the Ohio peace officer training commission. A probation officer who has been granted permission to carry a firearm in the discharge of official duties, annually shall successfully complete a firearms requalification program in accordance with section 109.801 of the Revised Code.

(D) As used in this section and sections 2301.28 to 2301.32 of the Revised Code, "community control sanction" has the same meaning as in section 2929.01 of the Revised Code.

(2002 H 490, eff. 1–1–04; 2002 H 510, eff. 3–31–03; 1996 H 670, eff. 12–2–96; 1996 S 269, eff. 7–1–96; 1994 H 406, eff. 11–11–94; 1993 H 152, eff. 7–1–93; 130 v Pt 2, H 28, H 1; 129 v 481; 125 v 327; 1953 H 1; GC 1554–1)

2301.28 Supervision over person on probation, conditionally pardoned, or paroled

The court of common pleas of a county in which a county department of probation has been established under division (A) of section 2301.27 of the Revised Code, in addition to employing the department in investigation and in the administration of its own orders imposing community control sanctions, shall receive into the legal control or supervision of the department any person who is a resident of the county and who has been placed under a community control sanction by order of any other court exercising criminal jurisdiction in this state, whether within or without the county in which the department of probation is located, upon the request of the other court and subject to its continuing jurisdiction. The court of common pleas also shall receive into the legal custody or supervision of the department any person who is paroled, released under a post-release control sanction, or conditionally pardoned from a state correctional institution and who resides or remains in the county, if requested by the adult parole authority created by section 5149.02 of the Revised Code or any other authority having power to parole or release from any institution of that nature.

As used in this section and section 2301.30 of the Revised Code, "post–release control sanction" has the same meaning as in section 2967.01 of the Revised Code.

(2002 H 490, eff. 1–1–04; 1994 H 571, eff. 10–6–94; 1993 H 152, eff. 7–1–93; 130 v Pt 2, H 28; 129 v 481; 1953 H 1; GC 1554–2)

2301.29 Rules and regulations of the adult parole authority applicable

In all cases in which the county department of probation provided for in division (A) of section 2301.27 of the Revised Code acquires legal custody of or supervision over a person who is granted a conditional pardon or a parole from a state correctional institution, the court of common pleas and the department shall be governed by the rules of the adult parole authority created by section 5149.02 of the Revised Code that are applicable to those cases and by the laws of the state applicable to those cases. In the case of other persons placed in its legal control or under its supervision, the department shall administer the orders and conditions of the authority so placing those persons. The court may exercise supervision over the department by adopting rules that are not inconsistent with law or with the rules of the adult parole authority and that shall be observed and enforced by the probation officers of the department.

As used in this section "pardon," "parole," and "state correctional institution" have the same meanings as in section 2967.01 of the Revised Code.

(1994 H 571, eff. 10–6–94; 1993 H 152, eff. 7–1–93; 130 v Pt 2, H 28; 1953 H 1; GC 1554–3)

2301.30 Conditions of probation or parole

The court of common pleas of a county in which a county department of probation is established under division (A) of section 2301.27 of the Revised Code shall require the department, in the rules through which the supervision of the department is exercised or otherwise, to do all of the following:

(A) Furnish to each person under a community control sanction or post-release control sanction or on parole under its supervision or in its custody, a written statement of the conditions of the community control sanction, post-release control sanction, or parole and instruct the person regarding the conditions;

(B) Keep informed concerning the conduct and condition of each person in its custody or under its supervision by visiting, the requiring of reports, and otherwise;

(C) Use all suitable methods, not inconsistent with the conditions of the community control sanction, post-release control sanction, or parole, to aid and encourage the persons under its supervision or in its custody and to bring about improvement in their conduct and condition;

(D) Keep detailed records of the work of the department, keep accurate and complete accounts of all moneys collected from persons under its supervision or in its custody, and keep or give receipts for those moneys;

(E) Make reports to the adult parole authority created by section 5149.02 of the Revised Code that it requires.

(2002 H 490, eff. 1–1–04; 1993 H 152, eff. 7–1–93; 130 v Pt 2, H 28; 1953 H 1; GC 1554–5)

2301.31 Arrest of person violating parole

(A) If a person on parole is in the custody of a county department of probation provided for in division (A) of section 2301.27 of the Revised Code, any probation officer of that department may arrest the person without a warrant for any violation of any condition of parole, as defined in section 2967.01 of the Revised Code, or of any rule governing persons on parole. If a person on parole is in the custody of a county department of probation provided for in division (A) of section 2301.27 of the Revised Code, any probation officer or peace officer shall arrest the person without a warrant for any violation of any condition of parole or any rule governing persons on parole upon the written order of the chief probation officer of that department. Any peace officer may arrest the person without a warrant, in accordance with section 2941.46 of the Revised Code, if the peace officer has reasonable ground to believe that the person has violated or is violating any of the following that is a condition of the person's parole:

(1) A condition that prohibits ownership, possession, or use of a firearm, deadly weapon, ammunition, or dangerous ordnance;

(2) A condition that prohibits the person from being within a specified structure or geographic area;

(3) A condition that confines the person to a residence, facility, or other structure;

(4) A condition that prohibits the person from contacting or communicating with any specified individual;

(5) A condition that prohibits the person from associating with a specified individual.

(B) A person who is arrested as provided in this section may be confined in the jail or juvenile detention facility, as the case may be, of the county in which the person is arrested, until released or removed to the proper institution. Upon making an arrest under this section, the arresting probation officer or peace officer or the arresting officer's department or agency promptly shall notify the chief probation officer of the county department of probation with custody of the person or the chief probation officer's designee that the person has been arrested.

Upon the written order of the chief probation officer of the county department with custody of the person, the person may be released on parole or reimprisoned or recommitted to the proper institution. An appeal from an order of reimprisonment or recommitment may be taken to the adult parole authority created by section 5149.02 of the Revised Code, and the decision of the authority on the appeal shall be final. The manner of taking an appeal of that nature and the disposition of the appellant pending the making and determination of the appeal shall be governed by the rules and orders of the adult parole authority.

(C) Nothing in this section limits the powers of arrest granted to certain law enforcement officers and citizens under sections 2935.03 and 2935.04 of the Revised Code.

(D) As used in this section:

(1) "Peace officer" has the same meaning as in section 2935.01 of the Revised Code.

(2) "Firearm," "deadly weapon," and "dangerous ordnance" have the same meanings as in section 2923.11 of the Revised Code.

(2000 S 179, § 3, eff. 1–1–02; 1993 H 152, eff. 7–1–93; 1992 S 49; 130 v Pt 2, H 28; 1953 H 1; GC 1554–6)

2301.32 Agreement for supplemental investigation or supervisory services; agreement for supervision of persons on probation

(A) In any county in which a county department of probation has been established under division (A) of section 2301.27 of the Revised Code and complies with standards and conditions prescribed by the adult parole authority created by section 5149.02 of the Revised Code, an agreement may be entered into between the court of common pleas and the authority under which the county department of probation correctional[1] may receive supplemental investigation or supervisory services from the authority.

(B) In any county in which a county department of probation has not been established under division (A) of section 2301.27 of the Revised Code, an agreement may be entered into between the court of common pleas of that county and the adult parole authority under which the court of common pleas may place defendants under a community control sanction in charge of the authority, and, in consideration of those placements, the county shall pay to the state from time to time the amounts that are provided for in the agreement.

(2002 H 490, eff. 1–1–04; 1994 H 406, eff. 11–11–94; 1994 H 571, eff. 10–6–94; 1993 H 152, eff. 7–1–93; 130 v Pt 2, H 28; 129 v 481; 128 v 959; 1953 H 1; GC 1554–7)

[1] Language appears as the result of harmonization of 1994 H 406 and 1994 H 571.

COMMUNITY–BASED AND DISTRICT COMMUNITY–BASED CORRECTIONAL FACILITIES AND PROGRAMS

2301.51 Community based correctional proposal; approval; dissolution

(A)(1) The court of common pleas of any county that has a population of two hundred thousand or more may formulate a community-based correctional proposal that, upon implementation, would provide a community-based correctional facility and program for the use of that court in accordance with sections 2301.51 to 2301.56 of the Revised Code. Upon the approval of the director of rehabilitation and correction, the court of common pleas of any county that has a population of two hundred thousand or more may formulate more than one community-based correctional proposal. In determining whether to grant approval to a court to formulate more than one proposal, the director shall consider the rate at which the county served by the court commits felony offenders to the state correctional system. If a court formulates more than one proposal, each proposal shall be for a separate community-based correctional facility and program.

For each community-based correctional proposal formulated under this division, the fact that the proposal has been formulated and the fact of any subsequent establishment of a community-based correctional facility and program pursuant to the proposal shall be entered upon the journal of the court. A county's community-based correctional facilities and programs shall be administered by a judicial corrections board. The presiding judge of the court or, if the presiding judge is not a judge of the general division of the court, the administrative judge of the general division shall designate the members of the board, who shall be judges of the court. The total number of members of the board shall not exceed eleven. The judge who is authorized to designate the members of the board shall serve as chairperson of the board.

(2) The courts of common pleas of two or more adjoining or neighboring counties that have an aggregate population of two hundred thousand or more may form a judicial corrections board and proceed to organize a district and formulate a district community-based correctional proposal that, upon implementation, would provide a district community-based correctional facility and program for the use of the member courts in accordance with sections 2301.51 to 2301.56 of the Revised Code. Upon the approval of the director of rehabilitation and correction, a judicial corrections board may formulate more than one district community-based correctional proposal. In determining whether to grant approval to a judicial corrections board to formulate more than one proposal, the director shall consider the rate at which the counties that formed the board commit felony offenders to the state correctional system. If a judicial corrections board formulates more than one proposal, each proposal shall be for a separate district community-based correctional facility and program. The judicial corrections board shall consist of not more than eleven judges of the member courts of common pleas, and each member court shall be represented on the board by at least one judge. The presiding judge of the court of common pleas of the county with the greatest population or, if that presiding judge is not a judge of the general division of that court, the administrative judge of the general division of that court shall serve as chairperson of the board. The fact of the formation of a board and district, and, for each district community-based correctional proposal formulated under this division, the fact that the proposal has been formulated and the fact of any subsequent establishment of a district community-based correctional facility and program shall be entered upon the journal of each member court of common pleas.

(B)(1) Each proposal for the establishment of a community-based correctional facility and program or district community-based correctional facility and program that is formulated pursuant to division (A) of this section shall be submitted by the judicial corrections board to the division of parole and community services for its approval under section 5120.10 of the Revised Code.

(2) No person shall be sentenced to or placed in a community-based correctional facility and program or to a district community-based correctional facility and program by a court pursuant to section 2929.16 or 2929.17 of the Revised Code or by the parole board pursuant to section 2967.28 of the Revised Code, or otherwise committed or admitted to a facility and program of that type until after the proposal for the establishment of the facility and program has been approved by the division of parole and community services under section 5120.10 of the Revised Code. A person shall be sentenced to a facility and program of that type only pursuant to a sanction imposed by a court pursuant to section 2929.16 or 2929.17 of the Revised Code as the sentence or as any part of the sentence of the person or otherwise shall be committed or referred to a facility and program of that type only when authorized by law.

(C) Upon the approval by the division of parole and community services of a proposal for the establishment of a community-based correctional facility and program or district community-based correctional facility and program submitted to it under division (B) of this section, the judicial corrections board that submitted the proposal may establish and operate the facility and program addressed by the proposal in accordance with the approved proposal and division (B)(2) of this section. The judicial corrections board may submit a request for funding of some or all of its community-based correctional facilities and programs or district community-based correctional facilities and programs to the board of county commissioners of the county, if the judicial corrections board serves a community-based correctional facility and program, or to the boards of county commissioners of all of the member counties, if the judicial corrections board serves a district community based correctional facility and program. The board or boards may appropriate, but are not required to appropriate, a sum of money for funding all aspects of each facility and program as outlined in sections 2301.51 to 2301.56 of the Revised Code. The judicial corrections board has no recourse against a board or boards of county commissioners, either under Chapter 2731. of the Revised Code, under its contempt power, or under any other authority, if the board or boards of county commissioners do not appropriate money for funding any facility or program or if they appropriate money for funding a facility and program in an amount less than the total amount of the submitted request for funding.

(D)(1) If a court of common pleas that is being served by any community-based correctional facility and program established pursuant to division (C) of this section determines that it no longer wants to be served by the facility and program, the court may dissolve the facility and program by entering upon the journal of the court the fact of the determination to dissolve the facility and program and by notifying, in writing, the division of parole and community services of the determination to dissolve the facility and program. If the court is served by more than one community-based correctional facility and program, it may dissolve some or all of the facilities and programs and, if it does not dissolve all of the facilities and programs, it shall continue the operation of the remaining facilities and programs.

(2) If all of the courts of common pleas being served by any district community-based correctional facility and program established pursuant to division (C) of this section determine that they no longer want to be served by the facility and program, the courts may dissolve the facility and program by entering upon the journal of each court the fact of the determination to dissolve the facility and program and by the judge who serves as chairperson of the judicial corrections board notifying, in writing, the division of parole and community services of the determination to dissolve the facility and program. If the courts are served by more than one community-based correctional facility and program, they may dissolve some or all of the facilities and programs and, if they do not dissolve all of the facilities and programs, they shall continue the operation of the remaining facilities and programs.

(3) If at least one, but not all, of the courts of common pleas being served by one or more district community-based correctional facilities and programs established pursuant to division (C) of this section determines that it no longer wants to be served by the facilities and programs, the court may terminate its involvement with each of the facilities and programs by entering upon the journal of the court the fact of the determination to terminate its involvement with the facilities and programs and by the court notifying, in writing, the division of parole and community services of the determination to terminate its involvement with the facilities and programs.

If at least one, but not all, of the courts of common pleas being served by one or more district community-based correctional facilities and programs terminates its involvement with each of the facilities and programs in accordance with this division, the other courts of common pleas being served by the facilities and programs may continue to be served by each of the facilities and programs if the other counties are adjoining or neighboring counties and have an aggregate population of two hundred thousand or more.

(E) Nothing in this section, sections 2301.52 to 2301.56, or section 5120.10, 5120.111, or 5120.122 of the Revised Code modifies or affects or shall be interpreted as modifying or affecting sections 5149.30 to 5149.37 of the Revised Code.

(1998 H 602, eff. 3–30–99; 1997 S 111, eff. 3–17–98; 1995 S 2, eff. 7–1–96; 1994 H 571, eff. 10–6–94; 1993 H 152, eff. 7–1–93; 1992 S 331; 1980 H 1000)

2301.52 Minimum standards

Each proposal for a community-based correctional facility and program or a district community-based correctional facility and program shall provide for or contain at least the following:

(A) The designation of a physical facility that will be used for the confinement of persons sentenced to the facility and program by a court pursuant to section 2929.16 or 2929.17 of the Revised Code or persons otherwise committed or admitted pursuant to law to the facility and program. The designate facility shall satisfy all of the following:

(1) Be a secure facility that contains lockups and other measures sufficient to ensure the safety of the surrounding community;

(2) Provide living space and accommodations that are suitable and adequate for the housing upon release, sentencing, or other commitment or admission of the following number of persons:

(a) For a facility that became operational prior to July 1, 1993, at least twenty, but not more than two hundred, persons;

(b) For a facility that becomes operational on or after July 1, 1993, at least fifty, but not more than two hundred, persons.

(3) Be constructed or modified, and maintained and operated, so that it complies with the rules adopted pursuant to Chapter 119. of the Revised Code by the division of parole and community services in the department of rehabilitation and correction for community-based correctional facilities and programs and district community-based correctional facilities and programs.

(B) The designation of a general treatment program that will be applied individually to each person sentenced to the facility and program by a court pursuant to section 2929.16 or 2929.17 of the Revised Code or otherwise committed or admitted pursuant to law to the facility and program. The designated general treatment program shall not be limited to, but at a minimum shall include, provisions to ensure that:

(1) Each person sentenced by a court or otherwise committed or admitted to a facility is provided an orientation period of at least thirty days, during which period the person is not permitted to leave the facility and is evaluated in relation to the person's placement in rehabilitative programs;

(2) Each person sentenced by a court or otherwise committed or admitted to a facility is placed in a release program whereby the person will be released temporarily for the purpose of employment in a manner consistent with the applicable work-release program established under section 5147.28 of the Revised Code, for vocational training, or for other educational or rehabilitative programs;

(3) All suitable community resources that are available are utilized in the treatment of each person sentenced by a court or otherwise committed or admitted to the facility.

(C) Provisions to ensure that the facility and program will be staffed and operated by persons who satisfy the minimum educational and experience requirements that are prescribed by rule by the department of rehabilitation and correction;

(D) Provisions for an intake officer to screen each felony offender who is sentenced by the court or courts that the facility and program serve and to make recommendations to the sentencing court concerning the admission or referral of each felony offender to the facility and program within fourteen days after notification of sentencing;

(E) Written screening standards that are to be used by an intake officer in screening an offender under the provisions described in division (D) of this section and that at a minimum include provisions to ensure that the intake officer will not make a recommendation to a sentencing court in support of the sentencing of a person to the facility and program if the person is ineligible for placement in the facility and program under rules adopted by the facility's and program's judicial corrections board.

(F) A statement that a good faith effort will be made to ensure that the persons who staff and operate the facility and program proportionately represent the racial, ethnic, and cultural diversity of the persons released, sentenced, or otherwise committed or admitted to the facility and program; [1]

(1997 S 111, eff. 3–17–98; 1995 S 2, eff. 7–1–96; 1994 H 571, eff. 10–6–94; 1993 H 152, eff. 7–1–93; 1992 S 331; 1990 S 258; 1980 H 1000)

[1] So in original; 1997 S 111.

2301.53 Citizens advisory board

(A) Upon the approval of the division of parole and community services of a proposal for the establishment of a community-based correctional facility and program or for the establishment of a district community-based correctional facility and program, the judicial corrections board that submitted the proposal shall appoint a citizens advisory board comprised of an uneven number of members, but not more than fifteen or less than five members. In the case of a community-based correctional facility and program, the county commissioners of the county in which the facility and program is established shall appoint one-third of the members of the advisory board, and the remaining members shall be appointed by the judicial corrections board. In the case of a district community-based correctional facility and program, the county commissioners of all of the counties that comprise the district shall appoint one-third of the members of the advisory board, but the number of members appointed by each county in the district shall reflect and be in proportion to, as nearly as possible, the population of the county. The remaining members shall be appointed by the judicial corrections board. If the board or boards of county commissioners do not make the appointments under this section within thirty days of approval of the proposal by the division of parole and community services, the judicial corrections board shall make those appointments. Of the initial appointments to the advisory board, one-third of the members shall be appointed for a term of one year; another one-third of the members shall be appointed for a term of two years; and the remaining one-third, or portion thereof, of the members shall be appointed for a term of three years. Thereafter, terms of persons appointed to the advisory board shall be for three years, with each term ending on the same day of the same month of the year as did the term that it succeeds. A member may be reappointed to the advisory board.

If a judicial corrections board submits more than one proposal for the establishment of a community-based correctional facility and program or for the establishment of a district community-based correctional facility and program, and if more than one of the proposals are approved by the division of parole and community services, the judicial corrections board shall appoint only one citizens advisory board under this section. The citizens advisory board shall perform the duties specified in section 2301.54 of the Revised Code for each of the community-based correctional facilities and programs or district community-based correctional facilities and programs that was contained in a proposal submitted by the judicial corrections board that appointed it and that was so approved.

The members of the advisory board shall not receive compensation for their services but shall be reimbursed for their necessary expenses incurred in the performance of their duties.

(B) Each county whose court of common pleas is served by any district community-based correctional facility and program shall be entitled to at least one member on the citizens advisory board. In districts that are comprised of only two counties, each county shall be entitled to at least two members on the advisory board. Each county in which is located a facility to which persons are committed or referred shall have not less than two members on the advisory board.

(C) A judicial corrections board may remove any member of a citizens advisory board whom it appointed under this section. Vacancies on an advisory board shall be filled in the same manner as provided for original appointments. Any member of an advisory board who is appointed to fill a vacancy occurring prior to the expiration of the term for which his predecessor was appointed shall hold office for the remainder of the predecessor's term.

(1994 H 571, eff. 10–6–94; 1993 H 152, eff. 7–1–93; 1980 H 1000)

2301.54 Duties of board

Each citizens advisory board appointed under section 2301.53 of the Revised Code shall do all of the following, for each community-based correctional facility and program or district community-based correctional facility and program that was contained in a proposal submitted by the judicial corrections board that appointed it and that was approved by the division of parole and community services:

(A) Recommend physical facilities for the use and operation of the facility and program;

(B) Provide community relations services for the facility and program;

(C) Regularly conduct public meetings in the communities that are served by the facility and program, accept recommendations from the public that are offered at the meetings and that relate to the operation of the facility and program, and refer the recommendations to the judicial corrections board;

(D) Encourage the provision of community services by persons, agencies, organizations, or groups in the area served by the facility and program, and seek out persons, agencies, organizations, or groups to provide community services, to the facility and program;

(E) Perform other duties relating to the operation of the facility and program that are prescribed by the judicial corrections board.

(2002 H 510, eff. 3–31–03; 1993 H 152, eff. 7–1–93; 1980 H 1000)

2301.55 Judicial corrections board; duties; powers

(A) If a judicial corrections board establishes one or more community-based correctional facilities and programs or district community-based correctional facilities and programs, all of the following apply, for each facility and program so established:

(1) The judicial corrections board shall appoint and fix the compensation of the director of the facility and program and other professional, technical, and clerical employees who are necessary to properly maintain and operate the facility and program.

The director, under the supervision of the judicial corrections board and subject to the rules of the judicial corrections board that are prescribed under division (B) of this section, shall control, manage, operate, and have general charge of the facility and program, and shall have the custody of its property, files, and records.

(2) The judicial corrections board may enter into contracts with the board of county commissioners of the county in which the facility and program is located or, in the case of a district facility and program, with the county commissioners of any county included in the district, whereby the county is to provide buildings, goods, and services to the facility and program.

(3) The judicial corrections board shall adopt rules for the sentencing or other commitment or admission pursuant to law of persons to, and the operation of, the facility and program. The rules shall provide procedures that conform to sections 2301.51 to 2301.56, 5120.10, 5120.111, and 5120.112 of the Revised Code. The rules adopted under this division shall be entered upon the journal of the court of each member court of a district.

(B) A judicial corrections board that establishes one or more community-based correctional facilities and programs or district community-based correctional facilities and programs may accept any gift, donation, devise, or bequest of real or personal property made to it by any person, or any grant or appropriation made to it by any federal, state, or local governmental unit or agency, and use the gift, donation, devise, bequest, grant, or appropriation in any manner that is consistent with any conditions of the gift, donation, devise, bequest, grant, or appropriation and that it considers to be in the interests of the facility and program. The judicial corrections board may sell, lease, convey, or otherwise transfer any real or personal property that it accepts pursuant to this division following the procedures specified in sections 307.09, 307.10, and 307.12 of the Revised Code.

(C) A judicial corrections board that establishes one or more community-based correctional facilities and programs or district community-based correctional facilities and programs shall provide the citizens advisory board of the facilities and programs with the staff assistance that the citizens advisory board requires to perform the duties imposed by section 2301.54 of the Revised Code.

(1997 S 111, eff. 3–17–98; 1995 S 2, eff. 7–1–96; 1994 H 571, eff. 10–6–94; 1993 H 152, eff. 7–1–93; 1980 H 1000)

2301.56 State financial assistance; application; procedures; reimbursement by confined person; testing for contagious diseases

(A) A judicial corrections board that proposes or establishes one or more community-based correctional facilities and programs or district community-based correctional facilities and programs may apply to the division of parole and community services for state financial assistance for the cost of renovation, maintenance, and operation of any of the facilities and programs. If the judicial corrections board has proposed or established more than one facility and program and if it desires state financial assistance for more than one of the facilities and programs, the board shall submit a separate application for each facility and program for which it desires the financial assistance.

An application for state financial assistance under this section may be made when the judicial corrections board submits for the approval of the section its proposal for the establishment of the facility and program in question to the division of parole and community services under division (B) of section 2301.51 of the Revised Code, or at any time after the section has approved the proposal. All applications for state financial assistance for proposed or approved facilities and programs shall be made on forms that are prescribed and furnished by the department of rehabilitation and correction, and in accordance with section 5120.112 of the Revised Code.

The judicial corrections board may submit a request for funding of some or all of its community-based correctional facilities and programs or district community-based correctional facilities and programs to the board of county commissioners of the county, if the judicial corrections board serves a community-based correctional facility and program, or to the boards of county commissioners of all of the member counties, if the judicial corrections board serves a district community-based correctional facility and program. The board or boards may appropriate, but are not required to appropriate, a sum of money for funding all aspects of each facility and program as outlined in sections 2301.51 to 2301.56 of the Revised Code. The judicial corrections board has no recourse against a board or boards of county commissioners, either under Chapter 2731. of the Revised Code, under its contempt power, or under any other authority, if the board or boards of county commissioners do not appropriate money for funding any facility or program or if they appropriate money for funding a facility and program in an amount less than the total amount of the submitted request for funding.

(B) Pursuant to section 2929.37 of the Revised Code, a board of county commissioners may require a person who was convicted of an offense and who is confined in a community-based correctional facility or district community-based correctional facility as provided in sections 2301.51 to 2301.56 of the Revised Code, to reimburse the county for its expenses incurred by reason of the person's confinement.

(C) Notwithstanding any contrary provision in this section or section 2929.18, 2929.28, or 2929.37 of the Revised Code, the judicial corrections board may establish a policy that complies with section 2929.38 of the Revised Code and that requires any person who is not indigent and who is confined in the community-based correctional facility or district community-based correctional facility to pay a reception fee or a fee for any medical treatment or service requested by and provided to that person.

(D) If a person who has been convicted of or pleaded guilty to an offense is confined in a community-based correctional facility or district community-based correctional facility, at the time of reception and at other times the person in charge of the operation of the facility determines to be appropriate, the person in charge of the operation of the facility may cause the convicted offender to be examined and tested for tuberculosis, HIV infection, hepatitis, including but not limited to hepatitis A, B, and C, and other contagious diseases. The person in charge of the operation of the facility may cause a convicted offender in the facility who refuses to be tested or treated for tuberculosis, HIV infection, hepatitis, including but not limited to hepatitis A, B, and C, or another contagious disease to be tested and treated involuntarily.

(E)(1) Community-based correctional facilities and programs and district community-based correctional facilities and programs are public offices under section 117.01 of the Revised Code and are subject to audit under section 117.10 of the Revised Code. The audits of the facilities and programs shall include financial audits and, in addition, in the circumstances specified in this division, performance audits by the auditor of state. If a private or nonprofit entity performs the day-to-day operation of any community-based correctional facility and program or district community-based correctional facility and program, the private or nonprofit entity also is subject to financial audits under section 117.10 of the Revised Code, and, in addition, in the circumstances specified in this division, to performance audits by the auditor of state. The auditor of state shall conduct the performance audits of a facility and program and of an entity required under section 117.10 of the Revised Code and this division and, notwithstanding the time period for audits specified in section 117.11 of the Revised Code, shall conduct the financial audits of a facility and program and of an entity required under section 117.10 of the Revised Code and this division, in accordance with the following criteria:

(a) For each facility and program and each entity, the auditor of state shall conduct the initial financial audit within two years after the effective date of this amendment or, if the facility and program in question is established on or after the effective date of this amendment, within two years after the date on which it is established.

(b) After the initial financial audit described in division (E)(1)(a) of this section, for each facility and program and each entity, the auditor of state shall conduct the financial audits of the facility and program or the entity at least once every two fiscal years.

(c) At any time after the effective date of this amendment regarding a facility and program or regarding an entity that performs the day-to-day operation of a facility and program, the department of rehabilitation and correction or the judicial corrections board that established the facility and program may request, or the auditor of state on its own initiative may undertake, a performance audit of the facility and program or the entity. Upon the receipt of the request, or upon the auditor of state's own initiative as described in this division, the auditor of state shall conduct a performance audit of the facility and program or the entity.

(2) The department of rehabilitation and correction shall prepare and provide to the auditor of state quarterly financial reports for each community-based correctional facility and program, for each district community-based correctional facility and program, and, to the extent that information is available, for each private or nonprofit entity that performs the day-to-day operation of any community-based correctional facility and program or district community-based correctional facility and program. Each report shall cover a three-month period and shall be provided to the auditor of state not later than fifteen days after the end of the period covered by the report.

(2002 H 490, eff. 1–1–04; 2002 H 510, eff. 3–31–03; 2002 H 170, eff. 9–6–02; 1997 S 111, eff. 3–17–98; 1996 H 480, eff. 10–16–96; 1996 S 269, eff. 7–1–96; 1995 S 2, eff. 7–1–96; 1994 H 571, eff. 10–6–94; 1993 H 152, eff. 7–1–93; 1984 H 363; 1980 H 1000)

PENALTIES

2301.99 Penalties

Whoever violates section 2301.33 of the Revised Code shall be fined not less than fifty nor more than two hundred dollars and imprisoned not less than ten nor more than thirty days.

(2000 S 180, eff. 3–22–01; 1978 S 87, eff. 1–1–79; 1953 H 1)

CHAPTER 2305

COMMON PLEAS COURTS—JURISDICTION; LIMITATION OF ACTIONS

JURISDICTION

2305.02 Jurisdiction to hear action for wrongful imprisonment

A court of common pleas has exclusive, original jurisdiction to hear and determine an action or proceeding that is commenced by an individual who satisfies divisions (A)(1) to (4) of section 2743.48 of the Revised Code and that seeks a determination by the court that the offense of which he was found guilty, including all lesser-included offenses, either was not committed by him or was not committed by any person. If the court enters the requested determination, it shall comply with division (B) of that section.

(1988 H 623, eff. 3–17–89; 1986 H 609)

LIMITATIONS—MISCELLANEOUS

2305.114 Limitation of action for partial birth feticide

A civil action pursuant to section 2307.53 of the Revised Code for partial birth feticide shall be commenced within one year after the commission of that offense.

(2000 H 351, eff. 8–18–00)

2305.115 Limitation of action for assault or battery against mental health professional; sexual contact or conduct

(A) An action for assault or battery shall be brought within two years after the cause of action accrues, except as provided in division (B) of this section, if all of the following apply regarding the action, the cause of the action, and the parties to the action:

(1) The action is brought against a mental health professional.

(2) The assault or battery claim asserted in the action is that, while the plaintiff was a mental health client or patient of the mental health professional, the mental health professional engaged in sexual conduct with, had sexual contact with, or caused one or more other persons to have sexual contact with the plaintiff.

(3) At the time of the sexual conduct or sexual contact described in division (A)(2) of this section, the plaintiff was not the spouse of the mental health professional.

(B) If the mental health service relationship between the plaintiff in an action for assault or battery that is described in division (A) of this section and the mental health professional continues after the date on which the cause of action accrues, the two-year period specified in division (A) of this section does not begin to run until the date on which that mental health service relationship is terminated by either or both of the parties.

(C) Unless division (A) or (B) of this section applies, an action for assault or battery shall be brought as provided in section 2305.111 of the Revised Code.

(D) As used in this section:

(1) "Mental health client or patient" and "mental health service" have the same meanings as in section 2305.51 of the Revised Code.

(2) "Mental health professional" has the same meaning as in section 2305.51 of the Revised Code and also includes an individual who is not licensed, certified, or registered under the Revised Code, or otherwise authorized in this state, but who regularly provides or purports to provide mental health services for compensation or remuneration at an established place of business.

(3) "Mental health service relationship" means the relationship between a mental health professional and a mental health client or patient of the mental health professional that exists for purposes of the mental health professional's provision of mental health services to the mental health client or patient.

(4) "Sexual conduct" and "sexual contact" have the same meanings as in section 2907.01 of the Revised Code.

(2002 S 9, eff. 5–14–02)

MISCELLANEOUS PROVISIONS

2305.23 Liability for emergency care

No person shall be liable in civil damages for administering emergency care or treatment at the scene of an emergency outside of a hospital, doctor's office, or other place having proper medical equipment, for acts performed at the scene of such emergency, unless such acts constitute willful or wanton misconduct.

Nothing in this section applies to the administering of such care or treatment where the same is rendered for remuneration, or with the expectation of remuneration, from the recipient of such care or treatment or someone on his behalf. The administering of such care or treatment by one as a part of his duties as a paid member of any organization of law enforcement officers or fire fighters does not cause such to be a rendering for remuneration or expectation of remuneration.

(1977 S 209, eff. 8–18–77; 130 v S 14)

2305.232 Civil immunity for persons assisting in cleanup of hazardous material

(A) No person who gives aid or advice in an emergency situation relating to the prevention of an imminent release of hazardous material, to the clean-up or disposal of hazardous material that has been released, or to the related mitigation of the effects of a release of hazardous material, nor the public or private employer of such a person, is liable in civil damages as a result of the aid or advice if all of the following apply:

(1) The aid or advice was given at the request of:

(a) A sheriff, the chief of police or other chief officer of the law enforcement agency of a municipal corporation, the chief of police of a township police district, the chief of a fire department, the state fire marshal, the director of environmental protection, the chairperson of the public utilities commission, the superintendent of the state highway patrol, the executive director of the emergency management agency, the chief executive of a municipal corporation, or the authorized representative of any such official, or the legislative authority of a township or county; or

(b) The owner or manufacturer of the hazardous material, an association of manufacturers of the hazardous material, or a hazardous material mutual aid group.

(2) The person giving the aid or advice acted without anticipating remuneration for self or the person's employer from the governmental official, authority, or agency that requested the aid or advice;

(3) The person giving the aid or advice was specially qualified by training or experience to give the aid or advice;

(4) Neither the person giving the aid or advice nor the public or private employer of the person giving the aid or advice was responsible for causing the release or threat of release nor would otherwise be liable for damages caused by the release;

(5) The person giving the aid or advice did not engage in willful, wanton, or reckless misconduct or grossly negligent conduct in giving the aid or advice;

(6) The person giving the aid or advice notified the emergency response section of the environmental protection agency prior to giving the aid or advice.

(B) The immunity conferred by this section does not limit the liability of any person whose action caused or contributed to the release of hazardous material. That person is liable for any enhancement of damages caused by the person giving aid or advice under this section unless the enhancement of damages was caused by the willful, wanton, or reckless misconduct or grossly negligent conduct of the person giving aid or advice.

(C) This section does not apply to any person rendering care, assistance, or advice in response to a discharge of oil when that person's immunity from liability is subject to determination under section 2305.39 of the Revised Code.

(D) As used in this section:

(1) Hazardous material means any material designated as such under the Hazardous Materials Transportation Act, 88 Stat. 2156 (1975), 49 U.S.C.A. 1803, as amended.

(2) Mutual aid group means any group formed at the federal, state, regional, or local level whose members agree to respond to incidents involving hazardous material whether or not they shipped, transported, manufactured, or were at all connected with the hazardous material involved in a particular incident.

(3) Discharge and oil have the same meanings as in section 2305.39 of the Revised Code.

(1999 H 283, eff. 9–29–99; 1995 H 37, eff. 8–23–95; 1988 H 131, eff. 6–29–88; 1986 H 712)

2305.233 Immunity of officers or employees for fire protection assistance

(A) No officer of employee as defined in section 109.36 of the Revised Code, or employee as defined in section 2744.01 of the Revised Code, rendering fire protection assistance pursuant to a reciprocal fire protection agreement shall be liable in civil damages to any person allegedly harmed by the negligent provision of that assistance.

(B) As used in this section, "reciprocal fire protection agreement" includes any mutual aid agreement for the provision of fire protection entered into pursuant to the "Act of May 23, 1955," 69 Stat. 67, 42 U.S.C.A. 1856–1856d, or any intergovernmental firefighting agreement entered into under section 9.60 of the Revised Code.

(1994 S 172, eff. 9–29–94)

2305.236 Definitions

As used in sections 2305.236 to 2305.239 of the Revised Code:

(A) "Conduct" means actions or omissions.

(B) "Domestic violence," "shelter," and "shelter for victims of domestic violence" have the same meanings as in section 3113.33 of the Revised Code.

(C) "Perpetrator" means a person who allegedly has committed domestic violence and who bears one of the relationships specified in division (B) of section 3113.33 of the Revised Code to a victim of domestic violence who is a shelter client.

(D) "Harm" means injury, death, or loss to person or property.

(E) "Political subdivision" has the same meaning as in section 2744.01 of the Revised Code.

(F) "Tort action" means a civil action for damages for injury, death, or loss to person or property other than a civil action for damages for a breach of contract or another agreement between persons.

(G) "Volunteer" means an individual who provides any service at a shelter for victims of domestic violence without the expectation of receiving and without receiving any compensation or other form of remuneration, either directly or indirectly, for the provision of the service.

(H) "Shelter client" means a person who is a victim of domestic violence and who is seeking to use or is using the services or facilities of a shelter for victims of domestic violence.

(I) "Victim advocate" means a person from a crime victim service organization who provides support and assistance for a victim of a crime during court proceedings and recovery efforts related to the crime.

(J) "Crime victim service organization" means any organization that is not organized for profit and that is organized and operated to provide, or to contribute to the support of organizations or institutions organized and operated to provide, services and assistance for victims of crime.

(2002 S 131, eff. 8–14–02)

2305.237 Qualified immunity for injury suffered on premises of domestic violence shelter

(A) Except as provided in division (B) of this section and subject to section 2305.239 of the Revised Code, a shelter for victims of domestic violence and a director, owner, trustee, officer, employee, victim advocate, or volunteer of the shelter are not liable in damages in a tort action for harm that a shelter client or other person who is on the shelter's premises allegedly sustains as a result of tortious conduct of a perpetrator that is committed on the shelter's premises if the perpetrator is not a director, owner, trustee, officer, employee, victim advocate, or volunteer of the shelter and if any of the following situations applies:

(1) The perpetrator illegally entered and illegally remained on the premises at the time the perpetrator's tortious conduct allegedly caused the harm sustained by a shelter client or other person who is on the premises.

(2) The perpetrator legally entered the premises; a director, owner, trustee, officer, employee, victim advocate, or volunteer of the shelter instructed the perpetrator to leave the premises, and took reasonable steps under the circumstances to cause the perpetrator to leave the premises, before the perpetrator allegedly caused the harm sustained by a shelter client or other person who is on the premises; and, despite those reasonable steps, the perpetrator remained on the premises and committed the tortious conduct that allegedly caused the harm sustained by a shelter client or other person who is on the premises.

(3) The perpetrator legally entered the premises; a director, owner, trustee, officer, employee, victim advocate, or volunteer of the shelter granted the perpetrator permission to remain on the premises after taking either of the following precautionary steps; and, despite taking either of those steps, the perpetrator committed the tortious conduct that allegedly caused the harm sustained by a shelter client or other person who is on the premises:

(a) The director, owner, trustee, officer, employee, victim advocate, or volunteer of the shelter asks a person entering the premises whether the person is related by consanguinity or affinity to or has resided with a shelter client; the person responds that the person is not so related and has not so resided; and the director, owner, trustee, officer, employee, victim advocate, or volunteer, in exercising the reasonable judgment and discretion of a prudent person under similar circumstances, believes that the person is not so related and has not so resided.

(b) The director, owner, trustee, officer, employee, victim advocate, or volunteer of the shelter asks a person entering the premises whether the person is related by consanguinity or affinity to or has resided with a shelter client; the person responds that the person is so related or has so resided; and the director, owner, trustee, officer, employee, victim advocate, or volunteer, in exercising the reasonable judgment and discretion of a prudent person under similar circumstances, determines that granting the person permission to remain on the premises does not appear to pose a threat of harm to a shelter client or other person who is on the premises.

(B) The immunity from tort liability conferred by division (A) of this section is not available to a shelter for victims of domestic violence or a director, owner, trustee, officer, employee, victim advocate, or volunteer of the shelter if the plaintiff in a tort action establishes, by clear and convincing evidence, that a director, owner, trustee, officer, employee, victim advocate, or volunteer of the shelter contributed to the harm sustained by a shelter client or other person who is on the shelter's premises, by an action or omission that involved malicious purpose, bad faith, or wanton or reckless conduct. For purposes of this division, "reckless conduct" includes the release of confidential information that pertains to a shelter client.

(2002 S 131, eff. 8–14–02)

2305.238 Qualified immunity for injury suffered off premises of domestic violence shelter

(A) Except as provided in division (B) of this section and subject to section 2305.239 of the Revised Code, a shelter for victims of domestic violence and a director, owner, trustee, officer, employee, victim advocate, or volunteer of the shelter are not liable in damages in a tort action for harm that a shelter client or other person who is on the premises allegedly sustains as a result of tortious conduct of a perpetrator that is committed on premises other than the shelter's premises if the perpetrator is not a director, owner, trustee, officer, employee, victim advocate, or volunteer of the shelter and if both of the following apply when the harm is caused:

(1) A director, owner, trustee, officer, employee, victim advocate, or volunteer of the shelter is providing assistance to a shelter client, including, but not limited to, accompanying the client to a health care practitioner's or attorney's office.

(2) The director, owner, trustee, officer, employee, victim advocate, or volunteer of the shelter is engaged in the course of that director's, owner's, trustee's, officer's, employee's, victim advocate's, or volunteer's employment, official responsibilities, or authorized services for the shelter.

(B) The immunity from tort liability conferred by division (A) of this section is not available to a shelter for victims of domestic violence or a director, owner, trustee, officer, employee, victim advocate, or volunteer of the shelter if the plaintiff in a tort action establishes, by clear and convincing evidence, that a director, owner, trustee, officer, employee, victim advocate, or volunteer of the shelter contributed to the harm sustained by a shelter client or other person who is on the premises, by an action or omission that involved malicious purpose, bad faith, or wanton or reckless conduct. For purposes of this division, "reckless conduct" includes the release of confidential information that pertains to a shelter client.

(2002 S 131, eff. 8–14–02)

2305.239 No new cause of action or legal right created

(A) Sections 2305.237 and 2305.238 of the Revised Code do not create a new cause of action or substantive legal right against a shelter for victims of domestic violence or a director, owner, trustee, officer, employee, victim advocate, or volunteer of the shelter.

(B) Sections 2305.237 and 2305.238 of the Revised Code do not affect any immunities from civil liability or defenses established under section 2305.234, 2744.02, or 2744.03 or another section of the Revised Code or available at common law to which a shelter for victims of domestic violence, a director, owner, trustee, officer, employee, victim advocate, or volunteer of the shelter, or a political subdivision associated with the shelter may be entitled in connection with alleged tort liability of third parties or in connection with circumstances not covered by section 2305.237 or 2305.238 of the Revised Code.

(2002 S 131, eff. 8–14–02)

2305.40 Immunity from liability to trespassers

(A) As used in this section:

(1) "Firearm" has the same meaning as in section 2923.11 of the Revised Code.

(2) "Tort action" means a civil action for damages for injury, death, or loss to person or property other than a civil action for damages for a breach of contract or another agreement between persons.

(3) "Vehicle" has the same meaning as in section 4501.01 of the Revised Code.

(B)(1) The owner, lessee, or renter of real property or a member of the owner's, lessee's, or renter's family who resides on the property is not liable in damages to a trespasser on the property, to a member of the family of the trespasser, or to any other person in a tort action for injury, death, or loss to person or property of the trespasser that allegedly is caused by the owner, lessee, renter, or family member if, at the time the injury, death, or loss to person or property allegedly is caused, all of the following apply:

(a) The owner, lessee, renter, or family member is inside a building or other structure on the property that is maintained as a permanent or temporary dwelling;

(b) The trespasser has made, is making, or is attempting to make an unlawful entry into the building or other structure described in division (B)(1)(a) of this section;

(c) The owner, lessee, renter, or family member uses reasonably necessary force to repel the trespasser from the building or other structure described in division (B)(1)(a) of this section or to prevent the trespasser from making the unlawful entry into that building or other structure.

(2) For purposes of the immunity created by division (B)(1) of this section, reasonably necessary force to repel a trespasser from a building or other structure that is maintained as a permanent or temporary dwelling or to prevent a trespasser from making an unlawful entry into a building or other structure of that nature may include the taking of or attempting to take the trespasser's life, or causing or attempting to cause physical harm or serious physical harm to the person of the trespasser, if the owner, lessee, or renter of real property or a member of the owner's, lessee's, or renter's family who resides on the property has a reasonable good faith belief that the owner, lessee, or renter or a member of the owner's, lessee's, or renter's family is in imminent danger of death or serious physical harm to person and that the only means to escape from the imminent danger is to use deadly force or other force that likely will cause physical harm or serious physical harm to the person of the trespasser, even if the owner, lessee, renter, or family member is mistaken as to the existence or imminence of the danger of death or serious physical harm to person.

(3) In order to qualify for the immunity created by division (B)(1) of this section, an owner, lessee, or renter of real property or a member of the owner's, lessee's, or renter's family who resides on the property is not required to retreat from a building or other structure that is maintained as a permanent or temporary dwelling prior to using reasonably necessary force to repel a trespasser from the building or other structure or to prevent a trespasser from making an unlawful entry into the building or other structure.

(C) The owner, lessee, or renter of real property or a member of the owner's, lessee's, or renter's family who resides on the property is not liable in damages to a trespasser on the property, to a member of the family of the trespasser, or to any other person in a tort action for injury, death, or loss to person or property of the trespasser that allegedly is caused by the owner, lessee, renter, or family member under circumstances not covered by division (B)(1) of this section if, at the time the injury, death, or loss to person or property allegedly is caused, none of the following applies:

(1) The injury, death, or loss to person or property is caused by a physical assault of the owner, lessee, renter, or family member upon the trespasser other than in self-defense or defense of a third person.

(2) Self-defense or defense of a third person is not involved, and the injury, death, or loss to person or property is caused by a vehicle driven or otherwise set in motion, a firearm shot, or any other item of tangible personal property held, driven, set in

motion, projected, or thrown by the owner, lessee, renter, or family member with the intent to cause injury, death, or loss to person or property of the trespasser or with the intent to cause the trespasser to believe that the owner, lessee, renter, or family member would cause injury, death, or loss to person or property of the trespasser.

(3) Under circumstances not described in division (C)(1) or (2) of this section, self-defense or defense of a third person is not involved, and the owner, lessee, renter, or family member intends to create a risk of injury, death, or loss to person or property of any trespasser by direct or indirect means, including, but not limited to, the use of spring guns, traps, or other dangerous instrumentalities.

(D)(1) This section does not create a new cause of action or substantive legal right against the owner, lessee, or renter of real property or a member of the owner's, lessee's, or renter's family who resides on the property.

(2) This section does not affect any civil liability under another section of the Revised Code or the common law of this state of an owner, lessee, or renter of real property or a member of the owner's, lessee's, or renter's family who resides on the property with respect to individuals other than trespassers, including, but not limited to, civil liability to invitees or licensees.

(3) This section does not affect any immunities from or defenses to civil liability established by another section of the Revised Code or available at common law to which the owner, lessee, or renter of real property or a member of the owner's, lessee's, or renter's family who resides on the property may be entitled with respect to individuals other than trespassers, including, but not limited to, immunities from or defenses to civil liability to invitees or licensees.

(4) This section does not affect any criminal liability that the owner, lessee, or renter of real property or a member of the owner's, lessee's, or renter's family who resides on the property may have for injury, death, or loss to person or property of a trespasser, invitee, or licensee on the property.

(5) This section does not affect any immunities from or defenses to civil liability established by another section of the Revised Code or available at common law to which an individual other than the owner, lessee, or renter of real property or a member of the owner's, lessee's, or renter's family who resides on the property may be entitled in connection with injury, death, or loss to person or property of a trespasser on real property owned, leased, or rented by another person, including, but not limited to, self-defense or defense of third persons.

(1996 H 447, eff. 3–18–97)

CHAPTER 2307

CIVIL ACTIONS

MISCELLANEOUS PROVISIONS

MISCELLANEOUS PROVISIONS

2307.53 Civil action for partial birth feticide

(A) As used in this section:

(1) "Frivolous conduct" has the same meaning as in section 2323.51 of the Revised Code.

(2) "Partial birth procedure" has the same meaning as in section 2919.151 of the Revised Code.

(B) A woman upon whom a partial birth procedure is performed in violation of division (B) or (C) of section 2919.151 of the Revised Code, the father of the child if the child was not conceived by rape, or the parent of the woman if the woman is not eighteen years of age or older at the time of the violation has and may commence a civil action for compensatory damages, punitive or exemplary damages if authorized by section 2315.21 of the Revised Code, and court costs and reasonable attorney's fees against the person who committed the violation.

(C) If a judgment is rendered in favor of the defendant in a civil action commenced pursuant to division (B) of this section and the court finds, upon the filing of a motion under section 2323.51 of the Revised Code, that the commencement of the civil action constitutes frivolous conduct and that the defendant was adversely affected by the frivolous conduct, the court shall award in accordance with section 2323.51 of the Revised Code reasonable attorney's fees to the defendant.

(2000 H 351, eff. 8–18–00)

2307.61 Damages recoverable for willful damage or theft; demand; agreement for payment; procedure

(A) If a property owner brings a civil action pursuant to division (A) of section 2307.60 of the Revised Code to recover damages from any person who willfully damages the owner's property or who commits a theft offense, as defined in section 2913.01 of the Revised Code, involving the owner's property, the property owner may recover as follows:

(1) In the civil action, the property owner may elect to recover moneys as described in division (A)(1)(a) or (b) of this section:

(a) Compensatory damages that may include, but are not limited to, the value of the property and liquidated damages in whichever of the following amounts applies:

(i) Fifty dollars, if the value of the property was fifty dollars or less at the time it was willfully damaged or was the subject of a theft offense;

(ii) One hundred dollars, if the value of the property was more than fifty dollars, but not more than one hundred dollars, at the time it was willfully damaged or was the subject of a theft offense;

(iii) One hundred fifty dollars, if the value of the property was more than one hundred dollars at the time it was willfully damaged or was the subject of a theft offense.

(b) Liquidated damages in whichever of the following amounts is greater:

(i) Two hundred dollars;

(ii) Three times the value of the property at the time it was willfully damaged or was the subject of a theft offense, irrespective of whether the property is recovered by way of replevin or otherwise, is destroyed or otherwise damaged, is modified or otherwise altered, or is resalable at its full market price. This division does not apply to a check, negotiable order of withdrawal, share draft, or other negotiable instrument that was returned or dishonored for insufficient funds by a financial institution if the check, negotiable order of withdrawal, share draft, or other negotiable instrument was presented by an individual borrower to a check-cashing business licensed pursuant to sections 1315.35 to 1315.44 of the Revised Code for a check-cashing loan transaction.

(2) In a civil action in which the value of the property that was willfully damaged or was the subject of a theft offense is less than five thousand dollars, the property owner may recover damages as described in division (A)(1)(a) or (b) of this section and additionally may recover the reasonable administrative costs, if any, of the property owner that were incurred in connection with actions taken pursuant to division (A)(2) of this section, the cost of maintaining the civil action, and reasonable attorney's fees, if all of the following apply:

(a) The property owner, at least thirty days prior to the filing of the civil action, serves a written demand for payment of moneys as described in division (A)(1)(a) of this section and the reasonable administrative costs, if any, of the property owner that have been incurred in connection with actions taken pursuant to division (A)(2) of this section, upon the person who willfully damaged the property or committed the theft offense.

(b) The demand conforms to the requirements of division (C) of this section and is sent by certified mail, return receipt requested.

(c) Either the person who willfully damaged the property or committed the theft offense does not make payment to the property owner of the amount specified in the demand within thirty days after the date of its service upon that person and does not enter into an agreement with the property owner during that thirty-day period for that payment or the person who willfully damaged the property or committed the theft offense enters into an agreement with the property owner during that thirty-day period for that payment but does not make that payment in accordance with the agreement.

(B) If a property owner who brings a civil action pursuant to division (A) of section 2307.60 of the Revised Code to recover damages for willful damage to property or for a theft offense attempts to collect the reasonable administrative costs, if any, of the property owner that have been incurred in connection with actions taken pursuant to division (A)(2) of this section, the cost of maintaining the civil action, and reasonable attorney's fees under authority of that division and if the defendant prevails in the civil action, the defendant may recover from the property owner reasonable attorney's fees, the cost of defending the civil action, and any compensatory damages that may be proven.

(C) For purposes of division (A)(2) of this section, a written demand for payment shall include a conspicuous notice to the person upon whom the demand is to be served that indicates all of the following:

(1) The willful property damage or theft offense that the person allegedly committed;

(2) That, if the person makes payment of the amount specified in the demand within thirty days after its service upon the person or enters into an agreement with the property owner during that thirty-day period for that payment and makes that payment in accordance with the agreement, the person cannot be sued by the property owner in a civil action in relation to the willful property damage or theft offense;

(3) That, if the person fails to make payment of the amount specified in the demand within thirty days after the date of its service upon the person and fails to enter into an agreement for that payment with the property owner during that thirty-day period or enters into an agreement for that payment with the property owner during that thirty-day period but does not make that payment in accordance with the agreement, the person may be sued in a civil action in relation to the willful property damage or theft offense;

(4) The potential judgment that the person may be required to pay if the person is sued in a civil action in relation to the willful property damage or theft offense and judgment is rendered against the person in that civil action;

(5) That, if the person is sued in a civil action by the property owner in relation to the willful property damage or theft offense, if the civil action requests that the person be required to pay the reasonable administrative costs, if any, of the property owner that have been incurred in connection with actions taken pursuant to division (A)(2) of this section, the cost of maintaining the action, and reasonable attorney's fees, and if the person prevails in the civil action, the person may recover from the property owner reasonable attorney's fees, the cost of defending the action, and any compensatory damages that can be proved.

(D) If a property owner whose property was willfully damaged or was the subject of a theft offense serves a written demand for payment upon a person who willfully damaged the property or committed the theft offense and if the person makes payment of the amount specified in the demand within thirty days after the date of its service upon the person or the person enters into an agreement with the property owner during that thirty-day period for that payment and makes payment in accordance with the agreement, the property owner shall not file a civil action against the person in relation to the willful property damage or theft offense.

(E) If a property owner whose property was willfully damaged or was the subject of a theft offense serves a written demand for payment upon a person who willfully damaged the property or committed the theft offense and if the person, within thirty days after the date of service of the demand upon the person, enters into an agreement with the property owner for the payment of the amount specified in the demand but does not make that payment in accordance with the agreement, the time between the entering of the agreement and the failure to make that payment shall not be computed as any part of the period within which a civil action based on the willful property damage or theft offense must be brought under the Revised Code.

(F) A civil action to recover damages for willful property damage or for a theft offense may be joined with a civil action that is brought pursuant to Chapter 2737. of the Revised Code to recover the property. If the two actions are joined, any compensatory damages recoverable by the property owner shall be limited to the value of the property.

(G)(1) In a civil action to recover damages for willful property damage or for a theft offense, the trier of fact may determine that an owner's property was willfully damaged or that a theft offense involving the owner's property has been committed, whether or not any person has pleaded guilty to or has been convicted of any criminal offense or has been adjudicated a delinquent child in relation to any act involving the owner's property.

(2) This section does not affect the prosecution of any criminal action or proceeding or any action to obtain a delinquent child adjudication in connection with willful property damage or a theft offense.

(H) As used in this section:

(1) "Administrative costs" includes the costs of written demands for payment and associated postage under division (A)(2) of this section.

(2) "Value of the property" means one of the following:

(a) The retail value of any property that is offered for sale by a mercantile establishment, irrespective of whether the property is destroyed or otherwise damaged, is modified or otherwise altered, or otherwise is not resalable at its full market price;

(b) The face value of any check or other negotiable instrument that is not honored due to insufficient funds in the drawer's account, the absence of any drawer's account, or another reason, and all charges imposed by a bank, savings and loan association, credit union, or other financial institution upon the holder of the check or other negotiable instrument;

(c) The replacement value of any property not described in division (H)(1) or (2) of this section.

(2002 S 107, eff. 6–28–02; 2001 S 108, § 2.01, eff. 7–6–01; 2000 H 294, eff. 8–29–00; 1996 H 350, eff. 1–27–97 [1]*; 1992 S 105, eff. 6–23–92; 1984 H 426)*

[1] See Notes of Decisions and Opinions, *State ex rel. Ohio Academy of Trial Lawyers v. Sheward* (Ohio 1999), 86 Ohio St.3d 451, 715 N.E.2d 1062.

Notes of Decisions

4. Constitutional issues

1996 H 350, which amended more than 100 statutes and a variety of rules relating to tort and other civil actions, and which was an attempt to reenact provisions of law previously held unconstitutional by the Supreme Court of Ohio, is an act of usurpation of judicial power in violation of the doctrine of separation of powers; for that reason, and because of violation of the one-subject rule of the Ohio Constitution, 1996 H 350 is unconstitutional. State ex rel. Ohio Academy of Trial Lawyers v. Sheward (Ohio, 08-16-1999) 86 Ohio St.3d 451, 715 N.E.2d 1062, 1999-Ohio-123, reconsideration denied 87 Ohio St.3d 1409, 716 N.E.2d 1170.

2307.62 Civil action by owner or operator of cable television or communications system

(A) As used in this section:

(1) "Cable service" and "cable system" have the same meanings as in section 2913.04 of the Revised Code.

(2) "Trier of fact" means the jury or, in a nonjury trial, the court.

(3) "Profits" derived from a violation of division (B) of section 2913.04 or division (A) or (B) of section 2913.041 of the Revised Code are equal to whichever of the following applies:

(a) The gross revenue derived from the violation by the persons who violated division (B) of section 2913.04 or division (A) or (B) of section 2913.041 of the Revised Code, as established by a preponderance of the evidence by the owner or operator of the cable service, cable system, cable television system, or other similar closed circuit coaxial cable communications system who is aggrieved by the violation;

(b) The gross revenue derived from the violation by the persons who violated division (B) of section 2913.04 or division (A) or (B) of section 2913.041 of the Revised Code, as established by a preponderance of the evidence by the owner or operator of the cable service, cable system, cable television system, or other similar closed circuit coaxial cable communications system who is aggrieved by the violation, minus deductible expenses and other elements of profit that are not attributable to the violation of division (B) of section 2913.04 or division (A) or (B) of section 2913.041 of the Revised Code, as established by a preponderance of the evidence by the persons who violated either or both of those divisions.

(B)(1) An owner or operator of a cable service, cable system, cable television system, or other similar closed circuit coaxial cable communications system who is aggrieved by conduct that is prohibited by division (B) of section 2913.04 or division (A) or (B) of section 2913.041 of the Revised Code may elect to commence a civil action for damages in accordance with division (A) of section 2307.60 or section 2307.61 of the Revised Code or to commence a civil action under this section in the appropriate municipal court, county court, or court of common pleas to recover damages and other specified moneys described in division (B)(1)(a), (b), or (c) of this section and, if applicable, damages described in division (B)(2) of this section from the persons who violated division (B) of section 2913.04 or division (A) or (B) of section 2913.041 of the Revised Code. If the owner or operator elects to commence a civil action for damages and other specified moneys under this section, the owner or operator shall specify in its complaint which of the following categories of damages and other specified moneys the owner or operator seeks to recover from the persons who violated division (B) of section 2913.04 or division (A) or (B) of section 2913.041 of the Revised Code:

(a) Full compensatory damages, punitive or exemplary damages if authorized by section 2315.21 of the Revised Code, and the reasonable attorney's fees, court costs, and other reasonable expenses incurred in maintaining the civil action under this section.

(b) Damages equal to the actual loss suffered by the owner or operator as a proximate result of the conduct that violated division (B) of section 2913.04 or division (A) or (B) of section 2913.041 of the Revised Code and, in addition, damages equal to the profits derived by the persons who violated one or more of those divisions as a proximate result of the prohibited conduct.

(c) Regarding a violation of division (A) or (B) of section 2913.041 of the Revised Code, liquidated damages in an amount of not less than two hundred fifty dollars and not more than ten thousand dollars, as determined by the trier of fact, for each separate violation of division (A) or (B) of section 2913.041 of the Revised Code as described in division (D) of that section. Division (B)(1)(c) of this section does not apply regarding a violation of division (B) of section 2913.04 of the Revised Code.

(2) The trier of fact shall determine the amount of any compensatory damages to be awarded pursuant to division (B)(1)(a) of this section, and the court shall determine the amount of any punitive or exemplary damages authorized by section 2315.21 of the Revised Code and the amount of reasonable attorney's fees, court costs, and other reasonable expenses to be awarded pursuant to division (B)(1)(a) of this section. The trier of fact shall determine the amount of damages to be awarded to the owner or operator under division (B)(1)(b) of this section.

(3) In a civil action under this section, if an owner or operator of a cable service, cable system, cable television system, or other similar closed circuit coaxial cable communications system establishes by a preponderance of the evidence that the persons who violated division (B) of section 2913.04 or division (A) or (B) of section 2913.041 of the Revised Code engaged in the prohibited conduct for the purpose of direct or indirect commercial advantage or private financial gain, the trier of fact may award to the owner or operator damages in an amount not to exceed fifty thousand dollars in addition to any amount recovered pursuant to division (B)(1)(a), (b), or (c) of this section, whichever of those divisions applies to the owner or operator.

(C) A person may join a civil action under this section with a civil action under Chapter 2737. of the Revised Code to recover any property of the owner or operator of a cable service, cable system, cable television system, or other similar closed circuit coaxial cable communications system that was the subject of the violation of division (B) of section 2913.04 or division (A) or (B) of section 2913.041 of the Revised Code. A person may commence a civil action under this section regardless of whether any person who allegedly violated one or more of those divisions has pleaded guilty to or has been convicted of a violation of one or more of those divisions or has been adjudicated a delinquent child for the commission of any act that constitutes a violation of one or more of those divisions.

(2002 H 327, eff. 7–8–02; 2002 S 107, eff. 6–28–02; 1995 S 2, eff. 7–1–96)

2307.63 Consent to sexual conduct or sexual contact as defense to action for assault or battery against mental health professional

(A) In an action for assault or battery brought against a mental health professional that asserts as a claim that, while the plaintiff was a mental health client or patient of the mental health professional, the mental health professional engaged in sexual conduct with, had sexual contact with, or caused one or more other persons to have sexual contact with the plaintiff, the consent of the plaintiff to the sexual conduct or sexual contact is not a defense to the claim unless either of the following applies:

(1) At the time of that sexual conduct or sexual contact, the plaintiff was the spouse of the mental health professional.

(2) The mental health professional proves by a preponderance of the evidence all of the following:

(a) At the time of the sexual conduct or sexual contact, the plaintiff was not emotionally dependent upon the mental health professional.

(b) The plaintiff did not submit to the sexual conduct or sexual contact because of therapeutic deception by the mental health professional or because the mental health professional falsely represented to the plaintiff that the sexual conduct or sexual contact was necessary for medical or mental health purposes.

(B) As used in this section:

(1) "Emotionally dependent" means that the emotional condition of a mental health client or patient of a mental health professional and the treatment provided by the mental health professional to the client or patient are of such a nature that the mental health professional knows or has reason to know that the client or patient is unable to withhold consent to one or more of the following:

(a) Engaging in sexual conduct with the mental health professional;

(b) Having sexual contact with the mental health professional or having sexual contact caused by the mental health professional with one or more other persons.

(2) "Mental health client or patient" has the same meaning as in section 2305.51 of the Revised Code.

(3) "Mental health professional" has the same meaning as in section 2305.115 of the Revised Code.

(4) "Sexual conduct" and "sexual contact" have the same meanings as in section 2907.01 of the Revised Code.

(5) "Therapeutic deception" means a representation by a mental health professional that one or more of the following is consistent with or part of the treatment for a mental health client or patient of the mental health professional:

(a) The client or patient engaging in sexual conduct with the mental health professional;

(b) The client or patient having sexual contact with the mental health professional or having sexual contact caused by the mental health professional with one or more other persons.

(2002 S 9, eff. 5–14–02)

CHAPTER 2313

COMMON PLEAS COURTS—COMMISSIONERS OF JURORS

SUMMONING AND EXCUSE OF JURORS

2313.18 Discharge of employee for jury service prohibited; penalty

Note: See also following version of this section, eff. 5–18–05.

(A) No employer shall discharge or threaten to discharge any permanent employee who is summoned to serve as a juror pursuant to Chapter 2313. of the Revised Code if the employee gives reasonable notice to the employer of the summons prior to the commencement of the employee's service as a juror and if the employee is absent from employment because of the actual jury service.

(B) Whoever violates this section shall be punished as for a contempt of court pursuant to Chapter 2705. of the Revised Code.

(1981 H 41, eff. 10–9–81)

Note: See also following version of this section, eff. 5–18–05.

2313.18 Discharge of employee for jury service prohibited; penalty (later effective date)

Note: See also preceding version of this section, in effect until 5–18–05.

(A) No employer shall discharge, threaten to discharge, or take any disciplinary action that could lead to the discharge of any permanent employee who is summoned to serve as a juror pursuant to Chapter 2313. of the Revised Code if the employee gives reasonable notice to the employer of the summons prior to the commencement of the employee's service as a juror and if the employee is absent from employment because of the actual jury service.

(B) No employer shall require or request an employee to use annual, vacation, or sick leave for time spent responding to a summons for jury duty, time spent participating in the jury selection process, or for time spent actually serving on a jury. Nothing in this division requires an employer to provide annual, vacation, or sick leave to employees under the provisions of this section who otherwise are not entitled to those benefits under the employer's policies.

(C) A court shall automatically postpone and reschedule the service of a summoned juror of an employer with twenty-five or fewer full-time employees,or their equivalent, if another employee of that employer has previously been summoned to appear during the same term or part of a term of that court for which that juror has been summoned and if that employer or employee demonstrates to the sufficiency of the court that the other employee has been so summoned. A postponement under this division does not constitute the excused individual's right to one automatic postponement pursuant to section 2313.13 of the Revised Code.

(D) Whoever violates this section shall be punished as for a contempt of court pursuant to Chapter 2705. of the Revised Code.

(2004 S 71, eff. 5–18–05; 1981 H 41, eff. 10–9–81)

Note: See also preceding version of this section, in effect until 5–18–05.

VIOLATIONS AND PROHIBITIONS

2313.29 Failure of juror to attend; remission of fine; entry of remission

No person whose name is drawn and who is notified to attend a term or part of a term of a court of record as a juror shall fail to attend at the time specified in the notice, or from day to day.

A fine imposed for the violation of this section under division (A) of section 2313.99 of the Revised Code may be wholly or partly remitted by direction of the judge in open court, before the end of the same term, and upon good cause shown; otherwise it shall not be remitted. Each remission so made by the judge, with the reason for the remission, shall be entered on the journal of the court. This section applies to an additional grand juror or a special juror, as well as to the regular petit juror.

(1995 S 2, eff. 7–1–96; 1953 H 1, eff. 10–1–53; GC 11419–32)

2313.30 Arrest for failure to attend

Note: See also following version of this section, eff. 5–18–05.

When a person whose name is drawn and who is notified, fails to attend and serve as a juror at a term of a court of record, without having been excused, the court, besides imposing a fine as prescribed in section 2313.29 of the Revised Code, may direct the sheriff to arrest him and bring him before the court; and when he has been so brought in, it may compel him to serve, or it may punish him as for contempt of court.

(1953 H 1, eff. 10–1–53; GC 11419–33)

Note: See also following version of this section, eff. 5–18–05.

2313.30 Failure to attend (later effective date)

Note: See also preceding version of this section, in effect until 5–18–05.

No person whose name is drawn and who is notified shall fail to attend and serve as a juror at a term of a court of record, without having been excused.

(2004 S 71, eff. 5–18–05; 1953 H 1, eff. 10–1–53; GC 11419–33)

Note: See also preceding version of this section, in effect until 5–18–05.

GENERAL PROVISIONS

2313.37 Alternate jurors; criminal cases

(A) In the trial in the court of common pleas of any civil case, when it appears to the judge presiding that the trial is likely to be protracted, upon direction of the judge after the jury has been impaneled and sworn, an additional or alternate juror shall be selected in the same manner as the regular jurors in the case were selected, but each party is entitled to two peremptory challenges as to the alternate juror.

(B) In all criminal cases, the selection of alternate jurors shall be made pursuant to Criminal Rule 24.

(C) The additional or alternate jurors selected shall be sworn and seated near the regular jurors, with equal opportunity for seeing and hearing the proceedings and shall attend at all times upon the trial with the regular jurors and shall obey all orders and admonitions of the court to the jury, and when the regular jurors are ordered kept together in a criminal case, the alternate jurors shall be kept with them. The additional or alternate jurors shall be liable as regular jurors for failure to attend the trial or to obey any order or admonition of the court to the jury, shall receive the same compensation as other jurors, and except as provided in this section shall be discharged upon the final submission of the case to the jury.

(D) If before the final submission of the case to the jury, which in capital cases includes any hearing required under division (D) of section 2929.03 of the Revised Code, a regular juror becomes unable to perform his duties, incapacitated, or disqualified, he may be discharged by the judge, in which case, or if a regular juror dies, upon the order of the judge, an additional or alternate juror, in the order in which called, shall become one of the jury and serve in all respects as though selected as an original juror.

(1981 S 1, eff. 10–19–81; 1953 H 1; GC 11419–47)

2313.41 Array may be set aside

A challenge to the array may be made and the whole array set aside by the court when the jury, grand or petit, was not selected, drawn, or summoned, or when the officer who executed the venire did not proceed as prescribed by law. No challenge to the array shall be made or the whole array set aside by the court, by reason of the misnomer of a juror; but on challenge, a juror may be set aside by reason of a misnomer in his name; but such challenge shall only be made before the jury is impaneled and sworn, and no indictment shall be quashed or verdict set aside for any such irregularity or misnomer if the jurors who formed the same possessed the requisite qualifications to act as jurors.

(1953 H 1, eff. 10–1–53; GC 11419–50)

VOIR DIRE AND CHALLENGES

2313.42 Examination of jurors; causes for challenge

Any person called as a juror for the trial of any cause shall be examined under oath or upon affirmation as to his qualifications. A person is qualified to serve as a juror if he is an elector of the county and has been certified by the board of elections pursuant to section 2313.06 of the Revised Code. A person also is qualified to serve as a juror if he is eighteen years of age or older, is a resident of the county, would be an elector if he were registered to vote, regardless of whether he actually is registered to vote, and has been certified by the registrar of motor vehicles pursuant to section 2313.06 of the Revised Code or otherwise as having a valid and current driver's or commercial driver's license.

The following are good causes for challenge to any person called as a juror:

(A) That he has been convicted of a crime which by law renders him disqualified to serve on a jury;

(B) That he has an interest in the cause;

(C) That he has an action pending between him and either party;

(D) That he formerly was a juror in the same cause;

(E) That he is the employer, the employee, or the spouse, parent, son, or daughter of the employer or employee, counselor, agent, steward, or attorney of either party;

(F) That he is subpoenaed in good faith as a witness in the cause;

(G) That he is akin by consanguinity or affinity within the fourth degree, to either party, or to the attorney of either party;

(H) That he or his spouse, parent, son, or daughter is a party to another action then pending in any court in which an attorney in the cause then on trial is an attorney, either for or against him;

(I) That he, not being a regular juror of the term, has already served as a talesman in the trial of any cause, in any court of record in the county within the preceding twelve months;

(J) That he discloses by his answers that he cannot be a fair and impartial juror or will not follow the law as given to him by the court.

Each challenge listed in this section shall be considered as a principal challenge, and its validity tried by the court.

(1989 H 381, eff. 7–1–89; 1984 H 183; 1969 H 104; 127 v 419; 1953 H 1; GC 11419–51)

2313.43 Challenge of petit juror

In addition to the causes listed under section 2313.42 of the Revised Code, any petit juror may be challenged on suspicion of prejudice against or partiality for either party, or for want of a competent knowledge of the English language, or other cause that may render him at the time an unsuitable juror. The validity of such challenge shall be determined by the court and be sustained if the court has any doubt as to the juror's being entirely unbiased.

(1953 H 1, eff. 10–1–53; GC 11419–52)

MISCELLANEOUS PROVISIONS

2313.47 Race or color shall not disqualify a juror

No officer or other person charged with a duty in selecting or summoning jurors shall exclude or fail to summon a citizen as a grand or petit juror on account of his race or color, provided such citizen possesses all other qualifications required by law for jurors.

(1953 H 1, eff. 10–1–53; GC 12868)

2313.99 Penalties

Note: See also following version of this section, eff. 5–18–05.

(A) Whoever violates section 2313.29 of the Revised Code may be fined not less than twenty-five nor more than two hundred fifty dollars.

(B) Whoever violates section 2313.47 of the Revised Code shall be fined not less than fifty nor more than five hundred dollars, imprisoned not less than thirty nor more than ninety days, or both.

(1995 S 2, eff. 7–1–96; 125 v 903, eff. 10–1–53; 1953 H 1)

Note: See also following version of this section, eff. 5–18–05.

2313.99 Penalties (later effective date)

Note: See also preceding version of this section, in effect until 5–18–05.

(A) Whoever violates section 2313.10, 2313.11, 2313.29, or 2313.30 of the Revised Code may be fined not less than one hundred nor more than two hundred fifty dollars and may be punished as for contempt of court.

(B) Whoever violates section 2313.47 of the Revised Code shall be fined not less than fifty nor more than five hundred dollars, imprisoned not less than thirty nor more than ninety days, or both.

(2004 S 71, eff. 5–18–05; 1995 S 2, eff. 7–1–96; 125 v 903, eff. 10–1–53; 1953 H 1)

Note: See also preceding version of this section, in effect until 5–18–05.

CHAPTER 2317

COMMON PLEAS COURTS—EVIDENCE

COMPETENCY OF WITNESSES AND EVIDENCE; PRIVILEGED COMMUNICATIONS

SECURING ATTENDANCE OF WITNESSES; OATH OF WITNESSES

COMPETENCY OF WITNESSES AND EVIDENCE; PRIVILEGED COMMUNICATIONS

2317.01 Competent witnesses

All persons are competent witnesses except those of unsound mind and children under ten years of age who appear incapable of receiving just impressions of the facts and transactions respecting which they are examined, or of relating them truly.

In a hearing in an abuse, neglect, or dependency case, any examination made by the court to determine whether a child is a competent witness shall be conducted by the court in an office or room other than a courtroom or hearing room, shall be conducted in the presence of only those individuals considered necessary by the court for the conduct of the examination or the well-being of the child, and shall be conducted with a court reporter present. The court may allow the prosecutor, guardian ad litem, or attorney for any party to submit questions for use by the court in determining whether the child is a competent witness.

(1988 S 89, eff. 1–1–89; 1953 H 1; GC 11493)

2317.02 Privileged communications and acts

The following persons shall not testify in certain respects:

(A) An attorney, concerning a communication made to the attorney by a client in that relation or the attorney's advice to a client, except that the attorney may testify by express consent of the client or, if the client is deceased, by the express consent of the surviving spouse or the executor or administrator of the estate of the deceased client and except that, if the client voluntarily testifies or is deemed by section 2151.421 of the Revised Code to have waived any testimonial privilege under this division, the attorney may be compelled to testify on the same subject;

(B)(1) A physician or a dentist concerning a communication made to the physician or dentist by a patient in that relation or the physician's or dentist's advice to a patient, except as otherwise provided in this division, division (B)(2), and division (B)(3) of this section, and except that, if the patient is deemed by section 2151.421 of the Revised Code to have waived any testimonial privilege under this division, the physician may be compelled to testify on the same subject.

The testimonial privilege established under this division does not apply, and a physician or dentist may testify or may be compelled to testify, in any of the following circumstances:

(a) In any civil action, in accordance with the discovery provisions of the Rules of Civil Procedure in connection with a civil action, or in connection with a claim under Chapter 4123. of the Revised Code, under any of the following circumstances:

(i) If the patient or the guardian or other legal representative of the patient gives express consent;

(ii) If the patient is deceased, the spouse of the patient or the executor or administrator of the patient's estate gives express consent;

(iii) If a medical claim, dental claim, chiropractic claim, or optometric claim, as defined in section 2305.113 of the Revised Code, an action for wrongful death, any other type of civil action, or a claim under Chapter 4123. of the Revised Code is filed by the patient, the personal representative of the estate of the patient if deceased, or the patient's guardian or other legal representative.

(b) In any civil action concerning court-ordered treatment or services received by a patient, if the court-ordered treatment or services were ordered as part of a case plan journalized under section 2151.412 of the Revised Code or the court-ordered treatment or services are necessary or relevant to dependency, neglect, or abuse or temporary or permanent custody proceedings under Chapter 2151. of the Revised Code.

(c) In any criminal action concerning any test or the results of any test that determines the presence or concentration of alcohol, a drug of abuse, or alcohol and a drug of abuse in the patient's blood, breath, urine, or other bodily substance at any time relevant to the criminal offense in question.

(d) In any criminal action against a physician or dentist. In such an action, the testimonial privilege established under this division does not prohibit the admission into evidence, in accordance with the Rules of Evidence, of a patient's medical or dental records or other communications between a patient and the physician or dentist that are related to the action and obtained by subpoena, search warrant, or other lawful means. A court that permits or compels a physician or dentist to testify in such an action or permits the introduction into evidence of patient records or other communications in such an action shall require that appropriate measures be taken to ensure that the confidentiality of any patient named or otherwise identified in the records is maintained. Measures to ensure confidentiality that may be taken by the court include sealing its records or deleting specific information from its records.

(e) In any will contest action under sections 2107.71 to 2107.77 of the Revised Code if all of the following apply:

(i) The patient is deceased.

(ii) A party to the will contest action requests the testimony, demonstrates to the court that that party would be an heir of the patient if the patient died without a will, is a beneficiary under the will that is the subject of the will contest action, or is a beneficiary under another testamentary document allegedly executed by the patient, and demonstrates to the court that the testimony is necessary to establish the party's rights as described in this division.

(2)(a) If any law enforcement officer submits a written statement to a health care provider that states that an official criminal investigation has begun regarding a specified person or that a criminal action or proceeding has been commenced against a specified person, that requests the provider to supply to the officer copies of any records the provider possesses that pertain to any test or the results of any test administered to the specified person to determine the presence or concentration of alcohol, a drug of abuse, or alcohol and a drug of abuse in the person's blood, breath, or urine at any time relevant to the criminal offense in question, and that conforms to section 2317.022 of the Revised Code, the provider, except to the extent specifically prohibited by any law of this state or of the United States, shall supply to the officer a copy of any of the requested records the provider possesses. If the health care provider does not possess any of the requested records, the provider shall give the officer a written statement that indicates that the provider does not possess any of the requested records.

(b) If a health care provider possesses any records of the type described in division (B)(2)(a) of this section regarding the person in question at any time relevant to the criminal offense in question, in lieu of personally testifying as to the results of the test in question, the custodian of the records may submit a certified copy of the records, and, upon its submission, the certified copy is qualified as authentic evidence and may be admitted as evidence in accordance with the Rules of Evidence. Division (A) of section 2317.422 of the Revised Code does not apply to any certified copy of records submitted in accordance with this division. Nothing in this division shall be construed to limit the right of any party to call as a witness the person who administered the test to which the records pertain, the person under whose supervision the test was administered, the custodian of the records, the person who made the records, or the person under whose supervision the records were made.

(3)(a) If the testimonial privilege described in division (B)(1) of this section does not apply as provided in division (B)(1)(a)(iii) of this section, a physician or dentist may be compelled to testify or to submit to discovery under the Rules of Civil Procedure only as to a communication made to the physician or dentist by the patient in question in that relation, or the physician's or dentist's advice to the patient in question, that related causally or historically to physical or mental injuries that are relevant to issues in the medical claim, dental claim, chiropractic claim, or optometric claim, action for wrongful death, other civil action, or claim under Chapter 4123. of the Revised Code.

(b) If the testimonial privilege described in division (B)(1) of this section does not apply to a physician or dentist as provided in division (B)(1)(c) of this section, the physician or dentist, in lieu of personally testifying as to the results of the test in question, may submit a certified copy of those results, and, upon its submission, the certified copy is qualified as authentic evidence and may be admitted as evidence in accordance with the Rules of Evidence. Division (A) of section 2317.422 of the Revised Code does not apply to any certified copy of results submitted in accordance with this division. Nothing in this division shall be construed to limit the right of any party to call as a witness the person who administered the test in question, the person under whose supervision the test was administered, the custodian of the results of the test, the person who compiled the results, or the person under whose supervision the results were compiled.

(c) If the testimonial privilege described in division (B)(1) of this section does not apply as provided in division (B)(1)(e) of this section, a physician or dentist may be compelled to testify or to submit to discovery in the will contest action under sections 2107.71 to 2107.77 of the Revised Code only as to the patient in question on issues relevant to the competency of the patient at the time of the execution of the will. Testimony or discovery conducted pursuant to this division shall be conducted in accordance with the Rules of Civil Procedure.

(4) The testimonial privilege described in division (B)(1) of this section is not waived when a communication is made by a physician to a pharmacist or when there is communication between a patient and a pharmacist in furtherance of the physician-patient relation.

(5)(a) As used in divisions (B)(1) to (4) of this section, "communication" means acquiring, recording, or transmitting any information, in any manner, concerning any facts, opinions, or statements necessary to enable a physician or dentist to diagnose, treat, prescribe, or act for a patient. A "communication" may include, but is not limited to, any medical or dental, office, or hospital communication such as a record, chart, letter, memorandum, laboratory test and results, x-ray, photograph, financial statement, diagnosis, or prognosis.

(b) As used in division (B)(2) of this section, "health care provider" means a hospital, ambulatory care facility, long-term care facility, pharmacy, emergency facility, or health care practitioner.

(c) As used in division (B)(5)(b) of this section:

(i) "Ambulatory care facility" means a facility that provides medical, diagnostic, or surgical treatment to patients who do not require hospitalization, including a dialysis center, ambulatory surgical facility, cardiac catheterization facility, diagnostic imaging center, extracorporeal shock wave lithotripsy center, home health agency, inpatient hospice, birthing center, radiation therapy center, emergency facility, and an urgent care center. "Ambulatory health care facility" does not include the private office of a physician or dentist, whether the office is for an individual or group practice.

(ii) "Emergency facility" means a hospital emergency department or any other facility that provides emergency medical services.

(iii) "Health care practitioner" has the same meaning as in section 4769.01 of the Revised Code.

(iv) "Hospital" has the same meaning as in section 3727.01 of the Revised Code.

(v) "Long-term care facility" means a nursing home, residential care facility, or home for the aging, as those terms are defined in section 3721.01 of the Revised Code; an adult care facility, as defined in section 3722.01 of the Revised Code; a nursing facility or intermediate care facility for the mentally retarded, as those terms are defined in section 5111.20 of the Revised Code; a facility or portion of a facility certified as a skilled nursing facility under Title XVIII of the "Social Security Act," 49 Stat. 286 (1965), 42 U.S.C.A. 1395, as amended.

(vi) "Pharmacy" has the same meaning as in section 4729.01 of the Revised Code.

(6) Divisions (B)(1), (2), (3), (4), and (5) of this section apply to doctors of medicine, doctors of osteopathic medicine, doctors of podiatry, and dentists.

(7) Nothing in divisions (B)(1) to (6) of this section affects, or shall be construed as affecting, the immunity from civil liability conferred by section 307.628 or 2305.33 of the Revised Code upon physicians who report an employee's use of a drug of abuse, or a condition of an employee other than one involving the use of a drug of abuse, to the employer of the employee in accordance with division (B) of that section. As used in division (B)(7) of this section, "employee," "employer," and "physician" have the same meanings as in section 2305.33 of the Revised Code.

(C) A member of the clergy, rabbi, priest, or regularly ordained, accredited, or licensed minister of an established and legally cognizable church, denomination, or sect, when the member of the clergy, rabbi, priest, or minister remains accountable to the authority of that church, denomination, or sect, concerning a confession made, or any information confidentially communicated, to the member of the clergy, rabbi, priest, or minister for a religious counseling purpose in the member of the clergy's, rabbi's, priest's, or minister's professional character; however, the member of the clergy, rabbi, priest, or minister may testify by express consent of the person making the communication, except when the disclosure of the information is in violation of a sacred trust;

(D) Husband or wife, concerning any communication made by one to the other, or an act done by either in the presence of the other, during coverture, unless the communication was made, or act done, in the known presence or hearing of a third person competent to be a witness; and such rule is the same if the marital relation has ceased to exist;

(E) A person who assigns a claim or interest, concerning any matter in respect to which the person would not, if a party, be permitted to testify;

(F) A person who, if a party, would be restricted under section 2317.03 of the Revised Code, when the property or thing is sold or transferred by an executor, administrator, guardian, trustee, heir, devisee, or legatee, shall be restricted in the same manner in any action or proceeding concerning the property or thing.

(G)(1) A school guidance counselor who holds a valid educator license from the state board of education as provided for in section 3319.22 of the Revised Code, a person licensed under Chapter 4757. of the Revised Code as a professional clinical counselor, professional counselor, social worker, independent social worker, marriage and family therapist or independent marriage and family therapist, or registered under Chapter 4757. of the Revised Code as a social work assistant concerning a confidential communication received from a client in that relation or the person's advice to a client unless any of the following applies:

(a) The communication or advice indicates clear and present danger to the client or other persons. For the purposes of this division, cases in which there are indications of present or past child abuse or neglect of the client constitute a clear and present danger.

(b) The client gives express consent to the testimony.

(c) If the client is deceased, the surviving spouse or the executor or administrator of the estate of the deceased client gives express consent.

(d) The client voluntarily testifies, in which case the school guidance counselor or person licensed or registered under Chapter 4757. of the Revised Code may be compelled to testify on the same subject.

(e) The court in camera determines that the information communicated by the client is not germane to the counselor-client, marriage and family therapist-client, or social worker-client relationship.

(f) A court, in an action brought against a school, its administration, or any of its personnel by the client, rules after an in-camera inspection that the testimony of the school guidance counselor is relevant to that action.

(g) The testimony is sought in a civil action and concerns court-ordered treatment or services received by a patient as part of a case plan journalized under section 2151.412 of the Revised Code or the court-ordered treatment or services are necessary or relevant to dependency, neglect, or abuse or temporary or permanent custody proceedings under Chapter 2151. of the Revised Code.

(2) Nothing in division (G)(1) of this section shall relieve a school guidance counselor or a person licensed or registered under Chapter 4757. of the Revised Code from the requirement to report information concerning child abuse or neglect under section 2151.421 of the Revised Code.

(H) A mediator acting under a mediation order issued under division (A) of section 3109.052 of the Revised Code or otherwise issued in any proceeding for divorce, dissolution, legal separation, annulment, or the allocation of parental rights and responsibilities for the care of children, in any action or proceeding, other than a criminal, delinquency, child abuse, child neglect, or dependent child action or proceeding, that is brought by or against either parent who takes part in mediation in accordance with the order and that pertains to the mediation process, to any information discussed or presented in the mediation process, to the allocation of parental rights and responsibilities for the care of the parents' children, or to the awarding of parenting time rights in relation to their children;

(I) A communications assistant, acting within the scope of the communication assistant's authority, when providing telecommunications relay service pursuant to section 4931.35 of the Revised Code or Title II of the "Communications Act of 1934," 104 Stat. 366 (1990), 47 U.S.C. 225, concerning a communication made through a telecommunications relay service. Nothing in this section shall limit the obligation of a communications assistant to divulge information or testify when mandated by federal law or regulation or pursuant to subpoena in a criminal proceeding.

Nothing in this section shall limit any immunity or privilege granted under federal law or regulation.

(J)(1) A chiropractor in a civil proceeding concerning a communication made to the chiropractor by a patient in that relation or the chiropractor's advice to a patient, except as otherwise provided in this division. The testimonial privilege established under this division does not apply, and a chiropractor may testify or may be compelled to testify, in any civil action, in accordance with the discovery provisions of the Rules of Civil Procedure in connection with a civil action, or in connection with a claim under Chapter 4123. of the Revised Code, under any of the following circumstances:

(a) If the patient or the guardian or other legal representative of the patient gives express consent.

(b) If the patient is deceased, the spouse of the patient or the executor or administrator of the patient's estate gives express consent.

(c) If a medical claim, dental claim, chiropractic claim, or optometric claim, as defined in section 2305.113 of the Revised Code, an action for wrongful death, any other type of civil action, or a claim under Chapter 4123. of the Revised Code is filed by the patient, the personal representative of the estate of the patient if deceased, or the patient's guardian or other legal representative.

(2) If the testimonial privilege described in division (J)(1) of this section does not apply as provided in division (J)(1)(c) of this section, a chiropractor may be compelled to testify or to submit to discovery under the Rules of Civil Procedure only as to a communication made to the chiropractor by the patient in question in that relation, or the chiropractor's advice to the patient in question, that related causally or historically to physical or mental injuries that are relevant to issues in the medical claim, dental claim, chiropractic claim, or optometric claim, action for wrongful death, other civil action, or claim under Chapter 4123. of the Revised Code.

(3) The testimonial privilege established under this division does not apply, and a chiropractor may testify or be compelled to testify, in any criminal action or administrative proceeding.

(4) As used in this division, "communication" means acquiring, recording, or transmitting any information, in any manner, concerning any facts, opinions, or statements necessary to enable a chiropractor to diagnose, treat, or act for a patient. A communication may include, but is not limited to, any chiropractic, office, or hospital communication such as a record, chart, letter, memorandum, laboratory test and results, x-ray, photograph, financial statement, diagnosis, or prognosis.

(2002 S 281, eff. 4-11-03; 2002 H 533, eff. 3-31-03; 2002 H 374, eff. 4-7-03; 2001 H 94, eff. 9-5-01; 2000 S 180, eff. 3-22-01; 2000 H 506, eff. 4-10-01; 2000 S 172, eff. 2-12-01; 2000 H 448, eff. 10-5-00; 1998 H 606, eff. 3-9-99; 1996 S 223, eff. 3-18-97; 1996 S 230, eff. 10-29-96; 1994 H 335, eff. 12-9-94; 1993 S 121, eff. 10-29-93; 1992 S 343; 1990 S 3, H 615; 1989 S 2; 1987 H 1; 1986 H 529, H 528; 1984 H 205; 1980 H 284; 1976 H 1426; 1975 H 682; 125 v 313; 1953 H 1; GC 11494)

2317.021 "Client" defined; application of attorney-client privilege to dissolved corporation or association

As used in division (A) of section 2317.02 of the Revised Code:

"Client" means a person, firm, partnership, corporation, or other association that, directly or through any representative, consults an attorney for the purpose of retaining the attorney or securing legal service or advice from him in his professional capacity, or consults an attorney employee for legal service or advice, and who communicates, either directly or through an agent, employee, or other representative, with such attorney; and includes an incompetent whose guardian so consults the attorney in behalf of the incompetent.

Where a corporation or association is a client having the privilege and it has been dissolved, the privilege shall extend to the last board of directors, their successors or assigns, or to the trustees, their successors or assigns.

This section shall be construed as in addition to, and not in limitation of, other laws affording protection to communications under the attorney-client privilege.

(130 v S 225, eff. 10–14–63)

2317.022 Written requests from law enforcement officers to obtain alcohol or drug test results from health care providers

(A) As used in this section, "health care provider" has the same meaning as in section 2317.02 of the Revised Code.

(B) If an official criminal investigation has begun regarding a person or if a criminal action or proceeding is commenced against a person, any law enforcement officer who wishes to obtain from any health care provider a copy of any records the provider possesses that pertain to any test or the result [1] of any test administered to the person to determine the presence or concentration of alcohol, a drug of abuse, or alcohol and a drug of abuse in the person's blood, breath, or urine at any time relevant to the criminal offense in question shall submit to the health care facility a written statement in the following form:

"WRITTEN STATEMENT REQUESTING THE RELEASE OF RECORDS

To: ________ (insert name of the health care provider in question).

I hereby state that an official criminal investigation has begun regarding, or a criminal action or proceeding has been commenced against, ________ (insert the name of the person in question), and that I believe that one or more tests has been administered to that person by this health care provider to determine the presence or concentration of alcohol, a drug of abuse, or alcohol and a drug of abuse in that person's blood, breath, or urine at a time relevant to the criminal offense in question. Therefore, I hereby request that, pursuant to division (B)(2) of section 2317.02 of the Revised Code, this health care provider supply me with copies of any records the provider possesses that pertain to any test or the results of any test administered to the person specified above to determine the presence or concentration of alcohol, a drug of abuse, or alcohol and a drug of abuse in that person's blood, breath, or urine at any time relevant to the criminal offense in question.

____

(Name of officer)

____

(Officer's title)

____

(Officer's employing agency)

____

(Officer's telephone number)

____

____

(Agency's address)

____

(Date written statement submitted)"

(C) A health care provider that receives a written statement of the type described in division (B) of this section shall comply with division (B)(2) of section 2317.02 of the Revised Code relative to the written statement.

(2001 H 94, eff. 9–5–01; 1994 H 335, eff. 12–9–94)

[1] Prior and current versions differ; although no amendment to this language was indicated in 2001 H 94, "or the result" appeared as "or the results" in 1994 H 335.

2317.023 Mediation communications privileged; exceptions

Note: See also following repeal of this section, eff. 10–29–05.

(A) As used in this section:

(1) "Mediation" means a nonbinding process for the resolution of a dispute in which both of the following apply:

(a) A person who is not a party to the dispute serves as mediator to assist the parties to the dispute in negotiating contested issues.

(b) A court, administrative agency, not-for-profit community mediation provider, or other public body appoints the mediator or refers the dispute to the mediator, or the parties engage the mediator.

(2) "Mediation communication" means a communication made in the course of and relating to the subject matter of a mediation.

(B) A mediation communication is confidential. Except as provided in division (C) of this section, no person shall disclose a mediation communication in a civil proceeding or in an administrative proceeding.

(C) Division (B) of this section does not apply in the following circumstances:

(1) Except as provided in division (H) of section 2317.02 and division (C) of section 3109.052 of the Revised Code, to the disclosure by any person of a mediation communication made by a mediator if all parties to the mediation and the mediator consent to the disclosure;

(2) To the disclosure by a person other than the mediator of a mediation communication made by a person other than the mediator if all parties consent to the disclosure;

(3) To the disclosure of a mediation communication if disclosure is required pursuant to section 2921.22 of the Revised Code;

(4) To the disclosure of a mediation communication if a court, after a hearing, determines that the disclosure does not circumvent Evidence Rule 408, that the disclosure is necessary in the particular case to prevent a manifest injustice, and that the necessity for disclosure is of sufficient magnitude to outweigh the importance of protecting the general requirement of confidentiality in mediation proceedings.

(D) This section does not prevent or inhibit the disclosure, discovery, or admission into evidence of a statement, document, or other matter that is a mediation communication but that, prior to its use in a mediation proceeding, was subject to discovery or admission under law or a rule of evidence or was subject to disclosure as a public record pursuant to section 149.43 of the Revised Code. This section does not affect the admissibility of a written settlement agreement signed by the parties to a mediation or the status of a written settlement agreement as a public record under section 149.43 of the Revised Code.

(2001 S 108, § 5.01, eff. 7–1–97; 1996 H 350, § 14, eff. 7–1–97 [1]*; 1996 H 438, eff. 7–1–97)*

[1] See Notes of Decisions and Opinions, *State ex rel. Ohio Academy of Trial Lawyers v. Sheward* (Ohio 1999), 86 Ohio St.3d 451, 715 N.E.2d 1062.

Note: See also following repeal of this section, eff. 10–29–05.

2317.023 Mediation communications privileged; exceptions—Repealed

Note: See also preceding version of this section, in effect until 10–29–05.

(2004 H 303, eff. 10–29–05; 2001 S 108, § 5.01, eff. 7–1–97; 1996 H350, § 14, eff. 7–1–97 [1]*; 1996 H 438, eff. 7–1–97)*

[1] See Notes of Decisions and Opinions, *State ex rel. Ohio Academy of Trial Lawyers v. Sheward* (Ohio 1999), 86 Ohio St.3d 451, 715 N.E.2d 1062.

Historical and Statutory Notes

Ed. Note: The effective date of the enactment of this section by 1996 H 438—as subsequently amended by 1996 H 350—was changed from 1–27–97 to 7–1–97 by 2001 S 108, § 5.01, eff. 7–6–01.

Ed. Note: The effective date of the enactment of this section by 1996 H 438 was changed from 7–1–97 to 1–27–97 by 1996 H 350, § 14, eff. 1–27–97. (Note: 1996 H 350 was ruled unconstitutional in toto by the Ohio Supreme Court in *State ex rel. Ohio Academy of Trial Lawyers v. Sheward* (Ohio 1999), 86 Ohio St.3d 451, 715 N.E.2d 1062.)

Notes of Decisions

3. Constitutional issues

1996 H 350, which amended more than 100 statutes and a variety of rules relating to tort and other civil actions, and which was an attempt to reenact provisions of law previously held unconstitutional by the Supreme Court of Ohio, is an act of usurpation of judicial power in violation of the doctrine of separation of powers; for that reason, and because of violation of the one-subject rule of the Ohio Constitution, 1996 H 350 is unconstitutional. State ex rel. Ohio Academy of Trial Lawyers v. Sheward (Ohio 1999) 86 Ohio St.3d 451, 715 N.E.2d 1062, 1999 -Ohio- 123, reconsideration denied 87 Ohio St.3d 1409, 716 N.E.2d 1170.

2317.03 Cases in which a party shall not testify

A party shall not testify when the adverse party is the guardian or trustee of either a deaf and dumb or an insane person or of a child of a deceased person, or is an executor or administrator, or claims or defends as heir, grantee, assignee, devisee, or legatee of a deceased person except:

(A) As to facts which occurred after the appointment of the guardian or trustee of an insane person, and, in the other cases, after the time the decedent, grantor, assignor, or testator died;

(B) When the action or proceeding relates to a contract made through an agent by a person since deceased, and the agent is competent to testify as a witness, a party may testify on the same subject;

(C) If a party, or one having a direct interest, testifies to transactions or conversations with another party, the latter may testify as to the same transactions or conversations;

(D) If a party offers evidence of conversations or admissions of the opposite party, the latter may testify concerning the same conversations or admissions; and, if evidence of declarations against interest made by an insane, incompetent, or deceased person has been admitted, then any oral or written declaration made by such insane, incompetent, or deceased person concerning the same subject to which any such admitted evidence relates, and which but for this provision would be excluded as self-serving, shall be admitted in evidence if it be proved to the satisfaction of the trial judge that the declaration was made at a time when the declarant was competent to testify, concerning a subject matter in issue, and, when no apparent motive to misrepresent appears;

(E) In an action or proceeding by or against a partner or joint contractor, the adverse party shall not testify to transactions with, or admissions by, a partner or joint contractor since deceased, unless they were made in the presence of the surviving partner or joint contractor, and this rule applies without regard to the character in which the parties sue or are sued;

(F) If the claim or defense is founded on a book account, a party may testify that the book is his account book, that it is a book of original entries, that the entries therein were made in the regular course of business by himself, a person since deceased, or a disinterested person, and the book is then competent evidence in any case, without regard to the parties, upon like proof by any competent witness;

(G) If after testifying orally, a party dies, the evidence may be proved by either party on a further trial of the case, whereupon the opposite party may testify to the same matters;

(H) If a party dies and his deposition is offered in evidence, the opposite party may testify as to all competent matters therein.

This section does not apply to actions for causing death, or actions or proceedings involving the validity of a deed, will or codicil. When a case is plainly within the reason and spirit of this section and sections 2317.01 and 2317.02 of the Revised Code, though not within the strict letter, their principles shall be applied.

(126 v 39, eff. 10–4–55; 1953 H 1; GC 11495)

2317.04 Impartial report of proceedings privileged

The publication of a fair and impartial report of the proceedings before state or municipal legislative bodies, or before state or municipal executive bodies, boards, or officers, or the whole or a fair synopsis of any bill, ordinance, report, resolution, bulletin, notice, petition, or other document presented, filed, or issued in any proceeding before such legislative or executive body, board, or officer, shall be privileged, unless it is proved that such publication was made maliciously.

(1953 H 1, eff. 10–1–53; GC 11343–1)

2317.05 Impartial report of indictment, warrant, affidavit, or arrest privileged

The publication of a fair and impartial report of the return of any indictment, the issuing of any warrant, the arrest of any person accused of crime, or the filing of any affidavit, pleading, or other document in any criminal or civil cause in any court of competent jurisdiction, or of a fair and impartial report of the contents thereof, is privileged, unless it is proved that the same was published maliciously, or that the defendant has refused or neglected to publish in the same manner in which the publication complained of appeared, a reasonable written explanation or contradiction thereof by the plaintiff, or that the publisher has refused, upon request of the plaintiff, to publish the subsequent determination of such suit or action. This section and section 2317.04 of the Revised Code do not authorize the publication of blasphemous or indecent matter.

(1953 H 1, eff. 10–1–53; GC 11343–2)

2317.06 Proving testimony of absent witness; prisoners

(A) If a party or witness, after testifying orally, dies, is beyond the jurisdiction of the court, cannot be found after diligent search, is insane, because of any physical or mental infirmity is unable to testify, or has been summoned but appears to have been kept away by the adverse party and if the evidence of the party or witness has been taken down by an official stenographer, the evidence so taken may be read in evidence by either party on the further trial of the case and shall be prima-facie evidence of what the deceased party or witness testified to orally on the former trial. If the evidence has not been taken by an official stenographer, it may be proved by witnesses who were present at the former trial, having knowledge of the testimony. All testimony so offered shall be open to all objections that might be taken if the witness was personally present.

(B)(1) If it is necessary in a civil action before the court to procure the testimony of a person who is imprisoned in a workhouse, juvenile detention facility, jail, or state correctional institution within this state, or who is in the custody of the department of youth services, the court shall require that the person's testimony be taken by deposition pursuant to the Civil Rules at the place of the person's confinement, unless the court determines that the interests of justice demand that the person be brought before the court for the presentation of his testimony.

(2) If the court determines that the interests of justice demand that a person specified in division (B)(1) of this section be brought before the court for the presentation of his testimony, the court shall order the person to be brought before it under the procedures set forth in division (B) or (C) of section 2945.47 of the Revised Code.

(C) When a person's deposition is taken pursuant to division (B)(1) of this section, the person shall remain in the custody of the officer who is in charge of the person, and the officer shall provide reasonable facilities for the taking of the deposition.

(D) The person requesting the testimony of the person whose deposition is taken pursuant to division (B)(1) of this section shall pay the expense of taking the deposition, except that the court may tax the expense as court costs in appropriate cases.

(1994 H 571, eff. 10–6–94; 1981 H 440, eff. 11–23–81; 1981 H 145; 1953 H 1; GC 11496)

2317.07 Examination by deposition or interrogatory; rebuttal

At the instance of the adverse party, a party may be examined as if under cross-examination, orally, by way of deposition, like any other witness, by way of written interrogatories filed in the action or proceeding, or by any one or more of such methods. The party calling for such examination shall not thereby be concluded but may rebut it by evidence.

(1971 H 602, eff. 6–30–71; 1970 H 1201; 1969 H 1; 132 v S 25; 131 v H 480; 125 v 35; 1953 H 1; GC 11497)

SECURING ATTENDANCE OF WITNESSES; OATH OF WITNESSES

2317.21 Attachment of witness who disobeys subpoena

When a witness, except a witness who has demanded and has not been paid his traveling fees and fee for one day's attendance when a subpoena is served upon him, as authorized by the provisions of section 2317.18 [1] of the Revised Code, fails to obey a subpoena personally served, the court or officer, before whom his attendance is required, may issue to the sheriff or a constable of the county, a writ of attachment, commanding him to arrest and bring the person named in the writ before such court or officer at the time and place the writ fixes, to give his testimony and answer for the contempt. If such writ does not require the witness to be immediately brought, he may give bond for a sum fixed by the court of common pleas or the court which issued the subpoena, with surety, for his appearance, which sum shall be endorsed on the back of the writ, except that, if no sum is so endorsed, it shall be one hundred dollars. When the witness was not personally served, the court, by a rule, may order him to show cause why such writ should not issue against him.

(1981 S 114, eff. 10–27–81; 129 v 325; 1953 H 1; GC 11511)

[1] 2317.18 repealed by 1970 H 1201, eff. 7–1–71; see now Civil Rule 45(C) for provisions analogous to former 2317.18.

2317.22 Punishment for contempt

Punishment for the acts of contempt specified in section 2317.20 [1] of the Revised Code shall be as follows: When the witness fails to attend in obedience to a subpoena, the court or officer may fine him not more than fifty dollars; in other cases, not more than fifty dollars nor less than five dollars; or the court or officer may imprison such witness in the county jail, there to remain until he submits to be sworn, testifies, or gives his deposition.

(1953 H 1, eff. 10–1–53; GC 11512)

[1] 2317.20 repealed by 1970 H 1201, eff. 7–1–71; see now Civil Rule 45(F) for provisions analogous to former 2317.20.

2317.23 Disposition of fines

A fine imposed under section 2317.22 of the Revised Code by the court shall be paid into the county treasury; that imposed by an officer shall be for the use of the party for whom the witness was subpoenaed. The witness also shall be liable to the party injured for any damages occasioned by his failure to attend, or refusal to be sworn, to testify, or to give his deposition.

(1953 H 1, eff. 10–1–53; GC 11513)

2317.24 Release of witness from imprisonment

A witness imprisoned by an officer under section 2317.22 of the Revised Code may apply to a judge of the supreme court, court of appeals, court of common pleas, or probate court, who may discharge him if it appears that such imprisonment is illegal.

(1953 H 1, eff. 10–1–53; GC 11514)

2317.25 Contents of attachment or order to commit

Every attachment for the arrest or order to commit a witness to prison by a court or officer, pursuant to sections 2317.21 and 2317.22 of the Revised Code, must be under seal of the court or official seal of the officer, if he has one, and must particularly specify the cause of the arrest or commitment. When committed for a refusal to answer a question, the question must be stated in the order.

(1953 H 1, eff. 10–1–53; GC 11515)

2317.26 Order of commitment

The order of commitment mentioned in section 2317.25 of the Revised Code may be directed to the sheriff or a constable of the county where the witness resides, or is at the time, and shall be executed by committing him to the jail of such county, and delivering a copy of it to the jailer.

(1981 S 114, eff. 10–27–81; 1953 H 1; GC 11516)

2317.29 May not sue or serve witness out of his county

A witness shall not be liable to be sued, in a county in which he does not reside, by being served with a summons in such county while going, returning or attending in obedience to a subpoena.

(1953 H 1, eff. 10–1–53; GC 11519)

2317.30 Oath of witness

Before testifying, a witness shall be sworn to testify the truth, the whole truth, and nothing but the truth.

(1953 H 1, eff. 10–1–53; GC 11520)

DOCUMENTARY EVIDENCE

2317.36 Admissible reports

A written report or finding of facts prepared by an expert who is not a party to the cause, nor an employee of a party, except for the purpose of making such report or finding, nor financially interested in the result of the controversy, and containing the conclusions resulting wholly or partly from written information furnished by the co-operation of several persons acting for a common purpose, shall, in so far as the same is relevant, be admissible when testified to by the person, or one of the persons, making such report or finding without calling as witnesses the persons furnishing the information, and without producing the books or other writings on which the report or finding is based, if, in the opinion of the court, no substantial injustice will be done the opposite party.

(1953 H 1, eff. 10–1–53; GC 12102–17)

2317.37 Cross–examination by adverse party

Any person who has furnished information on which a report or finding mentioned in section 2317.36 of the Revised Code is based may be cross-examined by the adverse party, but the fact that his testimony is not obtainable shall not render the report or finding inadmissible, unless the trial court finds that substantial injustice would be done to the adverse party by its admission.

(1953 H 1, eff. 10–1–53; GC 12102–18)

2317.38 Notice of intention to offer report

The report or finding mentioned in section 2317.36 of the Revised Code is not admissible unless the party offering it has given notice to the adverse party a reasonable time before trial of his intention to offer it, together with a copy of the report or finding, or so much thereof as relates to the controversy, and has afforded him a reasonable opportunity to inspect and copy any records or other documents in the offering party's possession or control, on which the report or finding was based, and also the names of all persons furnishing facts upon which the report or finding was based.

This section and sections 2317.36 and 2317.37 of the Revised Code shall be so interpreted and construed as to effectuate their general purpose to make the law of this state uniform with those states which enact similar legislation.

(1953 H 1, eff. 10–1–53; GC 12102–19, 12102–20)

2317.39 Report of investigations conducted by court made available to all parties

Whenever an investigation into the facts of any case, civil or criminal, pending at the time of such investigation in any court, is made, conducted, or participated in, directly or indirectly, by any court or any department thereof, through public employees, paid private investigators, social workers, friends of the court, or any other persons, and a report of such investigation is prepared for submission to the court, the contents of such report shall not be considered by any judge of the court wherein such case is pending either before the trial of the case or at any stage of the proceedings prior to final disposition thereof, unless the full contents of such report have been made readily available and accessible to all parties to the case or their counsel. The parties or their counsel shall be notified in writing of the fact that an investigation has been made, that a report has been submitted, and that the contents of the report are available for examination. Such notice shall be given at least five days prior to the time the contents of any report are to be considered by any judge of the court wherein the case is pending. In the event that a report following any investigation is prepared for submission orally, such oral report shall be reduced to writing prior to the issuance of notice of the availability of such report for examination.

This section does not apply only to the utilization of the contents of such reports as testimony, but shall prevent any judge from familiarizing himself with such contents in any manner unless this section has been fully complied with.

(1953 H 1, eff. 10–1–53; GC 11521–1)

2317.40 Records as evidence

As used in this section "business" includes every kind of business, profession, occupation, calling, or operation of institutions, whether carried on for profit or not.

A record of an act, condition, or event, in so far as relevant, is competent evidence if the custodian or the person who made such record or under whose supervision such record was made testifies to its identity and the mode of its preparation, and if it was made in the regular course of business, at or near the time of the act, condition, or event, and if, in the opinion of the court, the sources of information, method, and time of preparation were such as to justify its admission.

This section shall be so interpreted and construed as to effectuate its general purpose to make the law of this state uniform with those states which enact similar legislation.

(127 v 847, eff. 9–16–57; 1953 H 1; GC 12102–22, 12102–23, 12102–24)

2317.41 Photographic copies of records admissible as competent evidence

"Photograph" as used in this section includes but is not limited to microphotograph, a roll or strip of film, a roll or strip of microfilm, a photostatic copy, or an optically-imaged copy.

To the extent that a record would be competent evidence under section 2317.40 of the Revised Code, a photograph of such record shall be competent evidence if the custodian of the photograph or the person who made such photograph or under whose supervision such photograph was made testifies to the identity of and the mode of making such photograph, and if, in the opinion of the trial court, the record has been destroyed or otherwise disposed of in good faith in the regular course of business, and the mode of making such photograph was such as to justify its admission. If a photograph is admissible under this section, the court may admit the whole or a part thereof.

Such photograph shall be admissible only if the party offering it has delivered a copy of it, or so much thereof as relates to the controversy, to the adverse party a reasonable time before trial, unless in the opinion of the court the adverse party has not been unfairly surprised by the failure to deliver such copy. No such photograph need be submitted to the adverse party as prescribed in this section unless the original instrument would be required to be so submitted.

(1996 H 495, eff. 10–4–96; 1953 H 1, eff. 10–1–53; GC 12102–23a)

2317.42 Official reports admitted as evidence

Official reports made by officers of this state, or certified copies of the same, on a matter within the scope of their duty as defined by statute, shall, in so far as relevant, be admitted as evidence of the matters stated therein.

(1971 H 602, eff. 6–30–71; 1970 H 1201; 1953 H 1; GC 12102–26, 12102–27)

2317.421 Admissibility of medical or funeral bills as prima-facie evidence of reasonableness

In an action for damages arising from personal injury or wrongful death, a written bill or statement, or any relevant portion thereof, itemized by date, type of service rendered, and charge, shall, if otherwise admissible, be prima-facie evidence of the reasonableness of any charges and fees stated therein for medication and prosthetic devices furnished, or medical, dental, hospital, and funeral services rendered by the person, firm, or corporation issuing such bill or statement, provided, that such bill or statement shall be prima-facie evidence of reasonableness only if the party offering it delivers a copy of it, or the relevant portion thereof, to the attorney of record for each adverse party not less than five days before trial.

(1970 S 352, eff. 6–1–70)

2317.422 Qualification of records of hospital, nursing or rest home, or adult care facility

(A) Notwithstanding sections 2317.40 and 2317.41 of the Revised Code but subject to division (B) of this section, the records, or copies or photographs of the records, of a hospital, homes required to be licensed pursuant to section 3721.01 and of adult care facilities required to be licensed pursuant to Chapter 3722. of the Revised Code, and community alternative homes licensed pursuant to section 3724.03 of the Revised Code, in lieu of the testimony in open court of their custodian, person who made them, or person under whose supervision they were made, may be qualified as authentic evidence if any such person endorses thereon his verified certification identifying such records, giving the mode and time of their preparation, and stating that they were prepared in the usual course of the business of the institution. Such records, copies, or photographs may not be qualified by certification as provided in this section unless the party intending to offer them delivers a copy of them, or of their relevant portions, to the attorney of record for each adverse party not less than five days before trial. Nothing in this section shall be construed to limit the right of any party to call the custodian, person who made such records, or person under whose supervision they were made, as a witness.

(B) Division (A) of this section does not apply to any certified copy of the results of any test given to determine the presence or concentration of alcohol, a drug of abuse, or alcohol and a drug of abuse in a patient's blood, breath, or urine at any time relevant to a criminal offense that is submitted in a criminal action or proceeding in accordance with division (B)(2)(b) or (B)(3)(b) of section 2317.02 of the Revised Code.

(1994 H 335, eff. 12–9–94; 1989 H 253, eff. 11–15–90; 1989 S 2; 1974 H 614)

MISCELLANEOUS PROVISIONS

2317.47 Blood tests by court order

Whenever it is relevant in a civil or criminal action or proceeding to determine the paternity or identity of any person, the trial court on motion shall order any party to the action and any person involved in the controversy or proceeding to submit to one or more blood-grouping tests, to be made by qualified physicians or other qualified persons not to exceed three, to be selected by the court and under such restrictions or directions as the court or judge deems proper. In cases where exclusion is established, the results of the tests together with the findings of the experts of the fact of nonpaternity are receivable in evidence. Such experts shall be subject to cross-examination by both parties after the court has caused them to disclose their findings to the court or to the court and jury. Whenever the court orders such blood-grouping tests to be taken and one of the parties refuses to submit to such test, such fact shall be disclosed upon the trial unless good cause is shown to the contrary. The court shall determine how and by whom the costs of such examination shall be paid.

(1953 H 1, eff. 10–1–53; GC 12122–2)

2317.48 Action for discovery

When a person claiming to have a cause of action or a defense to an action commenced against him, without the discovery of a fact from the adverse party, is unable to file his complaint or answer, he may bring an action for discovery, setting forth in his complaint in the action for discovery the necessity and the grounds for the action, with any interrogatories relating to the subject matter of the discovery that are necessary to procure the discovery sought. Unless a motion to dismiss the action is filed under Civil Rule 12, the complaint shall be fully and directly answered under oath by the defendant. Upon the final disposition of the action, the costs of the action shall be taxed in the manner the court deems equitable.

(1984 S 47, eff. 4–4–85; 1953 H 1; GC 11555)

2317.52 Cross–examination of agents

When the action or proceeding relates to a transaction or occurrence in which it has been shown or it is admitted that the adverse party acted either in whole or in part through an agent or employee, such agent or employee of the adverse party may be called as a witness and examined as if under cross-examination upon any matters at issue between the parties which are shown or admitted to have been within the scope of such agent's or employee's authority or employment.

The party calling for such examination shall not thereby be concluded but may rebut such agent's or employee's testimony by counter testimony.

The party whose agent or employee is called as a witness by the adverse party and whose agent or employee is examined as if under cross-examination shall not thereby be concluded but may rebut such agent's or employee's testimony by counter testimony.

(127 v 95, eff. 9–13–57)

2317.54 Informed consent; health care facility liability precluded, when; form for written consent

No hospital, home health agency, ambulatory surgical facility, or provider of a hospice care program shall be held liable for a physician's failure to obtain an informed consent from the physician's patient prior to a surgical or medical procedure or course of procedures, unless the physician is an employee of the hospital, home health agency, ambulatory surgical facility, or provider of a hospice care program.

Written consent to a surgical or medical procedure or course of procedures shall, to the extent that it fulfills all the requirements in divisions (A), (B), and (C) of this section, be presumed to be valid and effective, in the absence of proof by a preponderance of the evidence that the person who sought such consent was not acting in good faith, or that the execution of the consent was induced by fraudulent misrepresentation of material facts, or that the person executing the consent was not able to communicate effectively in spoken and written English or any other language in which the consent is written. Except as herein provided, no evidence shall be admissible to impeach, modify, or limit the authorization for performance of the procedure or procedures set forth in such written consent.

(A) The consent sets forth in general terms the nature and purpose of the procedure or procedures, and what the procedures are expected to accomplish, together with the reasonably known risks, and, except in emergency situations, sets forth the names of the physicians who shall perform the intended surgical procedures.

(B) The person making the consent acknowledges that such disclosure of information has been made and that all questions asked about the procedure or procedures have been answered in a satisfactory manner.

(C) The consent is signed by the patient for whom the procedure is to be performed, or, if the patient for any reason including, but not limited to, competence, infancy, or the fact that, at the latest time that the consent is needed, the patient is under the influence of alcohol, hallucinogens, or drugs, lacks legal capacity to consent, by a person who has legal authority to consent on behalf of such patient in such circumstances.

Any use of a consent form that fulfills the requirements stated in divisions (A), (B), and (C) of this section has no effect on the common law rights and liabilities, including the right of a physician to obtain the oral or implied consent of a patient to a medical procedure, that may exist as between physicians and patients on July 28, 1975.

As used in this section the term "hospital" has the same meaning as in section 2305.113 of the Revised Code; "home health agency" has the same meaning as in section 5101.61 of the Revised Code; "ambulatory surgical facility" has the meaning as in division (A) of section 3702.30 of the Revised Code; and "hospice care program" has the same meaning as in section 3712.01 of the Revised Code. The provisions of this division apply to hospitals, doctors of medicine, doctors of osteopathic medicine, and doctors of podiatric medicine.

(2002 S 281, eff. 4–11–03; 2002 S 124, eff. 9–17–02; 1986 S 22, eff. 3–1–87; 1977 H 213; 1976 H 1426; 1975 H 682)

Notes of Decisions

Ed. Note: *See notes of decisions at RC 4511.19 regarding construction of the term "under the influence."*

CHAPTER 2331

EXECUTION AGAINST THE PERSON

PRIVILEGE FROM ARREST

PRIVILEGE FROM ARREST

2331.11 Privilege from arrest

(A) The following persons are privileged from arrest:

(1) Members, the chief administrative officer of the house of representatives, the clerk of the house of representatives, clerks, sergeants at arms, and staff of the senate and house of representatives, during the sessions of the general assembly, and while traveling to and from such sessions;

(2) Electors, while going to, returning from, or in attendance at elections;

(3) Judges of the courts, while attending court, and also during the time necessarily employed in going to, holding, and returning from the court that it is their duty to attend;

(4) Attorneys, bailiffs, clerks of courts, sheriffs, coroners, constables, plaintiffs, defendants, jurors, and witnesses, and other officers or employees of the court, while going to, attending, or returning from court;

(5) Persons who, on their traditional day of worship, are within, going to, or returning from their place of worship, are worshipping at a service, or are going to or returning from a service.

(B) Whoever arrests a person in violation of division (A) of this section shall pay one hundred dollars, to be recovered by civil action, in the name and for the use of the person injured.

(1998 H 649, eff. 3–9–99; 1978 H 349, eff. 10–25–78; 1969 H 121; 1953 H 1; GC 11754)

2331.12 Days on which arrests may not be made

No person shall be arrested during a sitting of the senate or house of representatives, within the hall where such session is being held, or in any court of justice, during the sitting of such court, or on Sunday, or on the fourth day of July.

(1953 H 1, eff. 10–1–53; GC 11755)

2331.13 Application

Sections 2331.11 to 2331.14, inclusive, of the Revised Code do not extend to cases of treason, felony, or breach of the peace, nor do they privilege any person specified in such sections from being served with a summons or notice to appear. Arrests not contrary to such sections made in any place or on any river or watercourse within or bounding upon this state are lawful.

(1953 H 1, eff. 10–1–53; GC 11756)

2331.14 Discharging prisoner

A person arrested contrary to sections 2331.11 to 2331.14, inclusive, of the Revised Code, shall be discharged by a writ of habeas corpus, or in a summary way, by motion before the court from which the process issued, at the cost of the party who sued out the process.

(1953 H 1, eff. 10–1–53; GC 11757)

CHAPTER 2335

FEES; COSTS

FEES

FEES

2335.08 Witness fees in criminal cases

Each witness attending, under recognizance or subpoena issued by order of the prosecuting attorney or defendant, before the grand jury or any court of record, in criminal causes, shall be allowed the same fees as provided by section 2335.06 of the Revised Code in civil causes, to be taxed in only one cause when such witness is attending in more causes than one on the same days, unless otherwise directed by special order of the court. When certified to the county auditor by the clerk of the court, such fees shall be paid from the county treasury, and except as to the grand jury, taxed in the bill of costs. Each witness attending before a judge of a county court, magistrate, or mayor, under subpoena in criminal cases, shall be allowed the fees provided by such section for witnesses in the court of common pleas. In state cases such fees shall be paid out of the county treasury, and in ordinance cases they shall be paid out of the treasury of the municipal corporation, upon the certificates of the judge or magistrate, and they shall be taxed in the bill of costs.

When the fees enumerated by this section have been collected from the judgment debtor, they shall be paid to the public treasury from which such fees were advanced.

(1975 H 205, eff. 1–1–76; 127 v 1039; 1953 H 1; GC 3014)

2335.09 Interpreter

Whenever, in any criminal proceeding or prosecution for the violation of an ordinance, or in a hearing before a coroner, an interpreter is necessary, the judge, magistrate, or coroner may appoint interpreters, who shall receive fees as witnesses in the case or proceeding. Such fees shall be taxed and paid as provided by sections 2335.05 to 2335.08, inclusive, of the Revised Code for other witness fees. This section shall not apply if, by law, an interpreter is otherwise provided.

(1953 H 1, eff. 10–1–53; GC 3014–1)

2335.10 Expenses in pursuit of felon

The board of county commissioners may allow and pay the necessary expenses incurred by an officer in pursuit of a person charged with a felony, who has signed a formal waiver of interstate extradition or fled the country.

(132 v S 447, eff. 2–5–68; 1953 H 1; GC 3015)

2335.11 Payment of fees and costs in felonies and minor state cases

In felony cases in which the defendant is convicted, the fees of the various magistrates and their officers, the witness fees, and interpreter's fees shall be inserted in the judgment of conviction and, when collected shall be disbursed by the clerk of the court of common pleas to the persons entitled thereto. In minor state cases, which have come to the court of common pleas through such magistrate's courts, the fees enumerated by this section shall be inserted in the judgment of conviction and, when collected shall be disbursed by the clerk to the persons entitled thereto. In both felonies and minor state cases, such clerk shall pay the witness and interpreter's fees into the county treasury, monthly.

In all cases in which recognizances are taken, forfeited, and collected, the amount recovered shall be paid into the county treasury, and if no conviction is had, such costs shall be paid by the county upon the allowance of the county auditor.

(1953 H 1, eff. 10–1–53; GC 3016)

2335.17 Witness fees of police officers

No police officer is entitled to witness fees in a cause prosecuted under an ordinance of a city before a magistrate. In all prosecutions under a criminal law of the state involving a felony, municipal police officers shall be allowed the same fees for attendance as are allowed by section 2335.06 of the Revised Code. Such fees shall be taxed in the bill of costs and deposited, by municipal police officers, with the treasurer of the municipal corporation, to the credit of the general fund.

(1985 H 201, eff. 7–1–85; 1953 H 1; GC 3024)

CHAPTER 2701

COURTS OF RECORD—GENERAL PROVISIONS

Section

2701.031 Affidavit of disqualification of municipal or county court judge for prejudice; procedure; removal

(A) If a judge of a municipal or county court allegedly is interested in a proceeding pending before the judge, allegedly is related to or has a bias or prejudice for or against a party to a proceeding pending before the judge or to a party's counsel, or allegedly otherwise is disqualified to preside in a proceeding pending before the judge, any party to the proceeding or the party's counsel may file an affidavit of disqualification with the clerk of the court in which the proceeding is pending.

(B) An affidavit of disqualification shall be filed under this section with the clerk of the court in which the proceeding is pending not less than seven calendar days before the day on which the next hearing in the proceeding is scheduled and shall include all of the following:

(1) The specific allegations on which the claim of interest, bias, prejudice, or disqualification is based and the facts to support each of those allegations;

(2) The jurat of a notary public or another person authorized to administer oaths or affirmations;

(3) A certificate indicating that a copy of the affidavit has been served on the judge of the municipal or county court against whom the affidavit is filed and on all other parties or their counsel;

(4) The date of the next scheduled hearing in the proceeding or, if there is no hearing scheduled, a statement that there is no hearing scheduled.

(C)(1) Except as provided in division (C)(2) of this section, when an affidavit of disqualification is presented to the clerk of a municipal or county court for filing under division (B) of this section, the clerk shall enter the fact of the filing on the docket in that proceeding and shall provide notice of the filing of the affidavit to one of the following:

(a) The presiding judge of the court of common pleas of the county;

(b) If there is no presiding judge of the court of common pleas of the county, a judge of the court of common pleas of the county.

(2) The clerk of the municipal or county court in which a proceeding is pending shall not accept an affidavit of disqualification presented for filing under division (B) of this section if it is not timely presented for filing or does not satisfy the requirements of divisions (B)(2), (3), and (4) of this section.

(D)(1) Except as provided in divisions (D)(2) to (4) of this section, if the clerk of the municipal or county court in which a proceeding is pending accepts an affidavit of disqualification for filing under divisions (B) and (C) of this section, the affidavit deprives the judge of a municipal or county court against whom the affidavit was filed of any authority to preside in the proceeding until the judge who was notified pursuant to division (C)(1) of this section rules on the affidavit pursuant to division (E) of this section.

(2) A judge of a municipal or county court against whom an affidavit of disqualification has been filed under divisions (B) and (C) of this section may preside in the proceeding if, based on the scheduled hearing date, the affidavit was not timely filed.

(3) A judge of a municipal or county court against whom an affidavit of disqualification has been filed under divisions (B) and (C) of this section may determine a matter that does not affect a substantive right of any of the parties.

(4) If the clerk of a municipal or county court accepts an affidavit of disqualification for filing under divisions (B) and (C) of this section, if the judge who is notified pursuant to division (C)(1) of this section of the filing of the affidavit of disqualification denies the affidavit pursuant to division (E) of this section, and if, after the denial, a second or subsequent affidavit of disqualification regarding the same judge and the same proceeding is filed by the same party who filed or on whose behalf was filed the affidavit that was denied or by counsel for the same party who filed or on whose behalf was filed the affidavit that was denied, the judge of a municipal or county court against whom the second or subsequent affidavit is filed may preside in the proceeding prior to the ruling, by the judge who is notified pursuant to division (C)(1) of this section, on the second or subsequent affidavit pursuant to division (E) of this section.

(E) If the clerk of a municipal or county court accepts an affidavit of disqualification for filing under divisions (B) and (C) of this section and if the judge who is notified pursuant to division (C)(1) of this section of the filing of the affidavit determines that the interest, bias, prejudice, or disqualification alleged in the affidavit does not exist, the judge who is so notified shall issue an entry denying the affidavit of disqualification. If the judge who is notified pursuant to division (C)(1) of this section of the filing of the affidavit determines that the interest, bias, prejudice, or disqualification alleged in the affidavit exists, the judge who is so notified shall issue an entry that disqualifies the judge against whom the affidavit was filed from presiding in the proceeding and designate another judge of the municipal or county court, or of the court of common pleas, to preside in the proceeding in place of the disqualified judge.

(1996 S 263, eff. 11–20–96)

2701.07 Court constables; duties

When, in the opinion of the court, the business thereof so requires, each court of common pleas, court of appeals, and, in counties having at the last or any future federal census more than seventy thousand inhabitants, the probate court, may appoint one or more constables to preserve order, attend the assignment of cases in counties where more than two judges of the court of common pleas regularly hold court at the same time, and discharge such other duties as the court requires. When so directed by the court, each constable has the same powers as sheriffs to call and impanel jurors, except in capital cases.

(1953 H 1, eff. 10–1–53; GC 1692)

CHAPTER 2705

CONTEMPT OF COURT

2705.01 Summary punishment for contempt

A court, or judge at chambers, may summarily punish a person guilty of misbehavior in the presence of or so near the court or judge as to obstruct the administration of justice.

(1953 H 1, eff. 10–1–53; GC 12136)

2705.02 Acts in contempt of court

A person guilty of any of the following acts may be punished as for a contempt:

(A) Disobedience of, or resistance to, a lawful writ, process, order, rule, judgment, or command of a court or officer;

(B) Misbehavior of an officer of the court in the performance of official duties, or in official transactions;

(C) A failure to obey a subpoena duly served, or a refusal to be sworn or to answer as a witness, when lawfully required;

(D) The rescue, or attempted rescue, of a person or of property in the custody of an officer by virtue of an order or process of court held by the officer;

(E) A failure upon the part of a person recognized to appear as a witness in a court to appear in compliance with the terms of the person's recognizance;

(F) A failure to comply with an order issued pursuant to section 3109.19 or 3111.81 of the Revised Code;

(G) A failure to obey a subpoena issued by the department of job and family services or a child support enforcement agency pursuant to section 5101.37 of the Revised Code;

(H) A willful failure to submit to genetic testing, or a willful failure to submit a child to genetic testing, as required by an order for genetic testing issued under section 3111.41 of the Revised Code.

(2000 S 180, eff. 3–22–01; 1999 H 470, eff. 7–1–00; 1997 H 352, eff. 1–1–98; 1996 H 710, § 7, eff. 6–11–96; 1995 H 167, eff. 6–11–96; 1953 H 1, eff. 10–1–53; GC 12137)

2705.03 Hearing

In cases under section 2705.02 of the Revised Code, a charge in writing shall be filed with the clerk of the court, an entry thereof made upon the journal, and an opportunity given to the accused to be heard, by himself or counsel. This section does not prevent the court from issuing process to bring the accused into court, or from holding him in custody, pending such proceedings.

(1953 H 1, eff. 10–1–53; GC 12138)

2705.031 Contempt action for failure to pay support, failure to comply with visitation order, or interference with visitation order; summons

(A) As used in this section, "Title IV–D case" has the same meaning as in section 3125.01 of the Revised Code.

(B)(1) Any party who has a legal claim to any support ordered for a child, spouse, or former spouse may initiate a contempt action for failure to pay the support. In Title IV–D cases, the contempt action for failure to pay support also may be initiated by an attorney retained by the party who has the legal claim, the prosecuting attorney, or an attorney of the department of job and family services or the child support enforcement agency.

(2) Any parent who is granted parenting time rights under a parenting time order or decree issued pursuant to section 3109.051 or 3109.12 of the Revised Code, any person who is granted visitation rights under a visitation order or decree issued pursuant to section 3109.051, 3109.11, or 3109.12 of the Revised Code or pursuant to any other provision of the Revised Code, or any other person who is subject to any parenting time or visitation order or decree, may initiate a contempt action for a failure to comply with, or an interference with, the order or decree.

(C) In any contempt action initiated pursuant to division (B) of this section, the accused shall appear upon the summons and order to appear that is issued by the court. The summons shall include all of the following:

(1) Notice that failure to appear may result in the issuance of an order of arrest, and in cases involving alleged failure to pay support, the issuance of an order for the payment of support by withholding an amount from the personal earnings of the accused or by withholding or deducting an amount from some other asset of the accused;

(2) Notice that the accused has a right to counsel, and that if indigent, the accused must apply for a public defender or court appointed counsel within three business days after receipt of the summons;

(3) Notice that the court may refuse to grant a continuance at the time of the hearing for the purpose of the accused obtaining counsel, if the accused fails to make a good faith effort to retain counsel or to obtain a public defender;

(4) Notice of the potential penalties that could be imposed upon the accused, if the accused is found guilty of contempt for failure to pay support or for a failure to comply with, or an interference with, a parenting time or visitation order or decree.

(D) If the accused is served as required by the Rules of Civil Procedure or by any special statutory proceedings that are relevant to the case, the court may order the attachment of the person of the accused upon failure to appear as ordered by the court.

(E) The imposition of any penalty for contempt under section 2705.05 of the Revised Code shall not eliminate any obligation of the accused to pay any past, present, or future support obligation or any obligation of the accused to comply with or refrain from interfering with the parenting time or visitation order or decree. The court shall have jurisdiction to make a finding of contempt for the failure to pay support and to impose the penalties set forth in section 2705.05 of the Revised Code in all cases in which past due support is at issue even if the duty to pay support has terminated, and shall have jurisdiction to make a finding of contempt for a failure to comply with, or an interference with, a parenting time or visitation order or decree and to impose the penalties set forth in section 2705.05 of the Revised Code in all cases in which the failure or interference is at issue even if the parenting time or visitation order or decree no longer is in effect.

(2000 S 180, eff. 3–22–01; 1999 H 471, eff. 7–1–00; 1990 S 3, eff. 4–11–91; 1988 H 708; 1987 H 231; 1986 H 509)

2705.04 Right of accused to bail

In proceedings under section 2705.02 of the Revised Code, if the writ is not returnable forthwith, the court may fix the amount of a bond to be given by the accused, with surety to the satisfaction of the sheriff. Upon the return of a writ, when it is not convenient to hear the charge without delay, the court shall fix the amount of a bond to be given, with surety to the satisfaction of the clerk of the court, for the appearance of the accused to answer the charge.

On the execution of such bond, the accused shall be released from custody.

(1953 H 1, eff. 10–1–53; GC 12139, 12140)

2705.05 Hearing on contempt; penalties; support orders; failure to withhold or deduct money pursuant to support order

(A) In all contempt proceedings, the court shall conduct a hearing. At the hearing, the court shall investigate the charge and hear any answer or testimony that the accused makes or offers and shall determine whether the accused is guilty of the contempt charge. If the accused is found guilty, the court may impose any of the following penalties:

(1) For a first offense, a fine of not more than two hundred fifty dollars, a definite term of imprisonment of not more than thirty days in jail, or both;

(2) For a second offense, a fine of not more than five hundred dollars, a definite term of imprisonment of not more than sixty days in jail, or both;

(3) For a third or subsequent offense, a fine of not more than one thousand dollars, a definite term of imprisonment of not more than ninety days in jail, or both.

(B) In all contempt proceedings initiated pursuant to section 2705.031 of the Revised Code against an employer, the bureau of workers' compensation, an employer that is paying workers' compensation benefits, a board, board of trustees, or other governing entity of a retirement system, person paying or distributing income to an obligor under a support order, or financial institution that is ordered to withhold or deduct an amount of money from the income or other assets of a person required to pay support and that fails to withhold or deduct the amount of money as ordered by the support order, the court also may require the employer, the bureau of workers' compensation, an employer that is paying workers' compensation benefits, a board, board of trustees, or other governing entity of a retirement system, person paying or distributing income to an obligor under a support order, or financial institution to pay the accumulated support arrearages.

(1986 H 509, eff. 12–1–86; 1953 H 1; GC 12141, 12142)

2705.06 Imprisonment until order obeyed

When the contempt consists of the omission to do an act which the accused yet can perform, he may be imprisoned until he performs it.

(1953 H 1, eff. 10–1–53; GC 12143)

2705.07 Proceedings when party released on bail fails to appear

If the party released on bail under section 2705.04 of the Revised Code fails to appear upon the day named, the court may issue another order of arrest, or order the bond for his appearance to be prosecuted, or both. If the bond is prosecuted, the measure of damages in the action is the extent of loss or injury sustained by the aggrieved party by reason of the misconduct for which the contempt was prosecuted, and the costs of the proceeding. Such recovery is for the benefit of the party injured.

(1953 H 1, eff. 10–1–53; GC 12144)

2705.08 Release of prisoner committed for contempt

When a person is committed to jail for contempt, the court or judge who made the order may discharge him from imprisonment when it appears that the public interest will not suffer thereby.

(1953 H 1, eff. 10–1–53; GC 12145)

2705.09 Judgment final

The judgment and orders of a court or officer made in cases of contempt may be reviewed on appeal. Appeal proceedings shall not suspend execution of the order or judgment until the person in contempt files a bond in the court rendering the judgment, or in the court or before the officer making the order, payable to the state, with sureties to the acceptance of the clerk of that court, in an amount fixed by the reviewing court, or a judge thereof, conditioned that if judgment is rendered against such person he will abide by and perform the order or judgment.

(1953 H 1, eff. 10–1–53; GC 12146)

2705.10 Alternative remedy

This chapter furnishes a remedy in cases not provided for by another section of the Revised Code.

(1986 H 158, eff. 3–17–87; 1953 H 1; GC 12147)

CHAPTER 2725

HABEAS CORPUS

GENERAL PROVISIONS

GENERAL PROVISIONS

2725.01 Persons entitled to writ of habeas corpus

Whoever is unlawfully restrained of his liberty, or entitled to the custody of another, of which custody such person is unlawfully deprived, may prosecute a writ of habeas corpus, to inquire into the cause of such imprisonment, restraint, or deprivation.

(1953 H 1, eff. 10–1–53; GC 12161)

2725.02 Courts authorized to grant writ

The writ of habeas corpus may be granted by the supreme court, court of appeals, court of common pleas, probate court, or by a judge of any such court.

(1953 H 1, eff. 10–1–53; GC 12162)

2725.03 Jurisdiction for production or discharge of inmate of institution

If a person restrained of his liberty is an inmate of a state benevolent or correctional institution, the location of which is fixed by statute and at the time is in the custody of the officers of the institution, no court or judge other than the courts or judges of the county in which the institution is located has jurisdiction to issue or determine a writ of habeas corpus for his production or discharge. Any writ issued by a court or judge of another county to an officer or person in charge at the state institution to compel the production or discharge of an inmate thereof is void.

(1994 H 571, eff. 10–6–94; 1953 H 1, eff. 10–1–53; GC 12163)

WRIT OF HABEAS CORPUS

2725.04 Application for writ

Application for the writ of habeas corpus shall be by petition, signed and verified either by the party for whose relief it is intended, or by some person for him, and shall specify:

(A) That the person in whose behalf the application is made is imprisoned, or restrained of his liberty;

(B) The officer, or name of the person by whom the prisoner is so confined or restrained; or, if both are unknown or uncertain, such officer or person may be described by an assumed appellation and the person who is served with the writ is deemed the person intended;

(C) The place where the prisoner is so imprisoned or restrained, if known;

(D) A copy of the commitment or cause of detention of such person shall be exhibited, if it can be procured without impairing the efficiency of the remedy; or, if the imprisonment or detention is without legal authority, such fact must appear.

(1953 H 1, eff. 10–1–53; GC 12164)

2725.05 Writ not allowed

If it appears that a person alleged to be restrained of his liberty is in the custody of an officer under process issued by a court or magistrate, or by virtue of the judgment or order of a court of record, and that the court or magistrate had jurisdiction to issue the process, render the judgment, or make the order, the writ of habeas corpus shall not be allowed. If the jurisdiction appears after the writ is allowed, the person shall not be discharged by reason of any informality or defect in the process, judgment, or order.

(1953 H 1, eff. 10–1–53; GC 12165)

2725.06 Writ must be granted

When a petition for a writ of habeas corpus is presented, if it appears that the writ ought to issue, a court or judge authorized to grant the writ must grant it forthwith.

(1953 H 1, eff. 10–1–53; GC 12166)

2725.07 Clerk shall issue writ

When a writ of habeas corpus is granted, the clerk of the court which granted the writ shall forthwith issue said writ under the seal of such court. In case of emergency, the judge who allowed the writ may issue it under his own hand, and depute any officer or other person to serve it.

(1953 H 1, eff. 10–1–53; GC 12167)

2725.08 Designation of prisoner

The person to be produced upon a writ of habeas corpus shall be designated by his name, if known, and if his name is not known, or is uncertain, such person may be described in any other way so as to make known who is intended.

(1953 H 1, eff. 10–1–53; GC 12168)

2725.09 Requisites of writ

In case of confinement, imprisonment, or detention of a person by an officer, a writ of habeas corpus shall be directed to him, and command him to have such person before the court or judge designated in the writ, at a time and place therein specified.

(1953 H 1, eff. 10–1–53; GC 12169)

2725.10 Form of writ when prisoner not in custody of an officer

In case of confinement, imprisonment, or detention by a person not an officer, the writ of habeas corpus shall be in the following form:

The State of Ohio, ________ County, ss.: To the sheriff of our several counties, greeting:

We command you that the body of ________ of ________, by ________, of ________, imprisoned and restrained of his liberty, as it is said, you take and have before ________, a judge of our ________ court, or, in case of his absence or disability, before some other judge of the same court, at ________, forthwith to do and receive what our said judge shall then and there consider ________ concerning him in his behalf; and summon the said ________ then and there to appear before our said judge, to show the cause of the taking and detention of the said ________.

(Seal) Witness ________, at ________, this ____ day of ________, in the year ____.

(1953 H 1, eff. 10–1–53; GC 12170)

2725.11 Service of writ

The writ of habeas corpus may be served in any county by the sheriff of that or any other county or by a person deputed by the court or judge issuing the writ.

(1953 H 1, eff. 10–1–53; GC 12171)

RETURN

2725.12 Execution and return of writ

The officer or person to whom a writ of habeas corpus is directed shall convey the person imprisoned or detained, and named in the writ, before the judge granting the writ, or, in case of his absence or disability, before some other judge of the same court, on the day specified in the writ. Said officer or person shall make due return of the writ, together with the day and the cause of the caption and detention of such person, according to its command.

(1953 H 1, eff. 10–1–53; GC 12172)

2725.13 Return of writ to another judge

When a writ of habeas corpus is issued by a court in session, if the court has adjourned when the writ is returned, it shall be returned before any judge of the same court. When the writ is returned before one judge, at a time when the court is in session, he may adjourn the case into the court, there to be heard and determined.

(1953 H 1, eff. 10–1–53; GC 12173)

2725.14 Contents of the return

When the person to be produced under a writ of habeas corpus is imprisoned or restrained by an officer, the person who makes the return shall state therein, and in other cases the person in whose custody the prisoner is found shall state, in writing, to the court or judge before whom the writ is returnable, plainly and unequivocally:

(A) Whether or not he has the prisoner in his custody or power or under restraint.

(B) If the prisoner is in his custody or power or under restraint, he shall set forth, at large, the authority, and the true and whole cause, of such imprisonment and restraint, with a copy of the writ, warrant, or other process upon which the prisoner is detained.

(C) If such prisoner was in his custody or power or under restraint, and such custody or restraint was transferred to another, he shall state particularly to whom, at what time, for what cause, and by what authority such transfer was made.

(1953 H 1, eff. 10–1–53; GC 12174)

2725.15 Return must be signed and sworn to

The return or statement referred to in section 2725.14 of the Revised Code shall be signed by the person who makes it, and shall be sworn to by him, unless he is a sworn public officer and makes the return in his official capacity.

(1953 H 1, eff. 10–1–53; GC 12175)

MISCELLANEOUS PROVISIONS

2725.16 Continuance of cause

The court or judge to whom a writ of habeas corpus is returned, or the court into which it is adjourned, for good cause shown, may continue the cause, and, in that event, shall make such order for the safekeeping of the person imprisoned or detained as the nature of the case requires.

(1953 H 1, eff. 10–1–53; GC 12176)

2725.17 Discharge of prisoner

When the judge has examined the cause of caption and detention of a person brought before him as provided in section 2725.12 of the Revised Code, and is satisfied that such person is unlawfully imprisoned or detained, he shall forthwith discharge such person from confinement. On such examination, the judge may disregard matters of form or technicalities in any mittimus or order of commitment by a court or officer authorized by law to commit.

(1953 H 1, eff. 10–1–53; GC 12177)

2725.18 Prisoner may be committed or let to bail

When the person brought before a judge under section 2725.12 of the Revised Code is confined or detained in a legal manner on a charge of having committed a crime or offense which is bailable, the judge may recommit him or let him to bail. If such person is let to bail, the judge shall require him to enter into a recognizance, with sufficient surety, in such sum as the judge finds reasonable, after considering the circumstances of the prisoner and the nature of the offense charged, and conditioned for his appearance at the court where the offense is properly cognizable. The judge forthwith shall certify his proceedings, together with any recognizance, to the proper court. If the person charged fails to give such recognizance, he shall be committed to prison by the judge.

(1953 H 1, eff. 10–1–53; GC 12178)

2725.19 Mandatory commitment for capital offense

If a prisoner brought before a judge under section 2725.12 of the Revised Code was committed by a judge, and is plainly and specifically charged in the warrant of commitment with a felony the punishment for which is capital, he shall not be removed, discharged, or let to bail.

(129 v 582, eff. 1-10-61; 1953 H 1; GC 12179)

2725.20 Return as evidence or plea

If a prisoner brought before a judge under section 2725.12 of the Revised Code is in custody under a warrant or commitment in pursuance of law, the return of the writ of habeas corpus is prima-facie evidence of the cause of detention. If such prisoner is restrained of his liberty by alleged private authority, the return is only a plea of the facts therein set forth, and the party claiming the custody shall be held to make proof of such facts. Upon the final disposition of a case, the court or judge shall make such order as to costs as it requires.

(1953 H 1, eff. 10–1–53; GC 12180)

2725.21 Forfeiture by clerk for refusal to issue writ

A clerk of a court who refuses to issue a writ of habeas corpus, after an allowance of such writ and a demand therefor, shall forfeit to the party aggrieved the sum of five hundred dollars.

(1953 H 1, eff. 10–1–53; GC 12181)

2725.22 Failure to obey writ

No person to whom a writ of habeas corpus is directed shall neglect or refuse to obey or make return of it according to the command thereof, or make a false return, or upon demand made by the prisoner, or by any person on his behalf, refuse to deliver to the person demanding, within six hours after demand therefor, a true copy of the warrant of commitment and detainer of the prisoner.

Whoever violates this section shall forfeit to the party aggrieved two hundred dollars for a first offense; for a second offense such person shall forfeit four hundred dollars, and, if an officer, shall be incapable of holding his office.

(1953 H 1, eff. 10–1–53; GC 12182)

2725.23 Persons at large upon writ not to be again imprisoned

A person who is set at large upon a writ of habeas corpus shall not be imprisoned again for the same offense, unless by the legal order or process of the court in which he is bound by recognizance to appear, or other court having jurisdiction of the cause or offense.

No person shall knowingly, contrary to sections 2725.01 to 2725.28, inclusive, of the Revised Code, recommit, imprison, or cause to be recommitted or imprisoned, for the same offense, or pretended offense, a person so set at large, or knowingly aid or assist therein.

Whoever violates this section shall forfeit to the party aggrieved five hundred dollars, notwithstanding any colorable pretense or variation in the warrant or commitment.

(1953 H 1, eff. 10–1–53; GC 12183)

2725.24 Prisoner shall not be removed from custody of one officer to another

A person committed to prison, or in the custody of an officer for a criminal matter, shall not be removed therefrom into the custody of another officer, unless by legal process, or unless the prisoner is delivered to an inferior officer to be taken to jail, or, by order of the proper court, is removed from one place to another within this state for trial, or in case of fire, infection, or other necessity.

A person who, after such commitment, makes, signs, or countersigns a warrant for such removal contrary to this section shall forfeit to the party aggrieved five hundred dollars.

(1953 H 1, eff. 10–1–53; GC 12184)

2725.25 No prisoner to be sent out of state

No person shall be sent as a prisoner to a place out of this state, for a crime or offense committed within it.

A person imprisoned in violation of this section may maintain an action for false imprisonment against the person by whom he was so imprisoned or transported, and against a person who contrives, writes, signs, seals, or countersigns a writing for such imprisonment or transportation, or aids or assists therein.

(1953 H 1, eff. 10–1–53; GC 12185, 12186)

2725.26 Record of writs

The proceedings upon a writ of habeas corpus must be recorded by the clerk of the court in which such proceedings were had, and may be reviewed on appeal as in other cases.

(1953 H 1, eff. 10–1–53; GC 12187)

2725.27 Recovery of forfeitures; limitations

The forfeitures mentioned in sections 2725.21 to 2725.24, inclusive, of the Revised Code, may be recovered by the party aggrieved or his executors or administrators against the offender or his executors or administrators by civil action in a court having cognizance thereof.

Actions for violations of sections 2725.21 to 2725.25, inclusive, of the Revised Code, shall be brought within two years after the offense is committed, except in cases of imprisonment of the party aggrieved, when action may be brought within two years after his delivery out of prison, or after his decease if he dies in prison.

(1953 H 1, eff. 10–1–53; GC 12188)

2725.28 Fees and costs

The fees of officers and witnesses shall be taxed by the judge, on return of the proceedings on a writ of habeas corpus, and collected as a part of the original costs in the case. When the prisoner is discharged, the costs shall be taxed to the state, and paid out of the county treasury, upon the warrant of the county auditor. No officer or person shall demand payment in advance for any fees to which he is entitled by virtue of the proceedings, when the writ is demanded or issued for the discharge from custody of a person confined under color of proceedings in a criminal case. When a person in custody by virtue or under color of proceedings in a civil case is discharged, costs shall be taxed against the party at whose instance he was so in custody. If he is remanded to custody, costs shall be taxed against him.

(1953 H 1, eff. 10–1–53; GC 12189)

CHAPTER 2743

COURT OF CLAIMS—ASSISTANCE TO VICTIMS OF CRIMES

PRACTICE AND PROCEDURE

2743.43 Competency of medical witnesses

(A) No person shall be deemed competent to give expert testimony on the liability issues in a medical claim, as defined in section 2305.113 of the Revised Code, unless:

(1) Such person is licensed to practice medicine and surgery, osteopathic medicine and surgery, or podiatric medicine and surgery by the state medical board or by the licensing authority of any state;

(2) Such person devotes three-fourths of the person's professional time to the active clinical practice of medicine or surgery, osteopathic medicine and surgery, or podiatric medicine and surgery, or to its instruction in an accredited university;

(3) The person practices in the same or a substantially similar specialty as the defendant. The court shall not permit an expert in one medical specialty to testify against a health care provider in another medical specialty unless the expert shows both that the standards of care and practice in the two specialties are similar and that the expert has substantial familiarity between the specialties.

(4) If the person is certified in a specialty, the person must be certified by a board recognized by the American board of medical specialties or the American board of osteopathic specialties in a specialty having acknowledged expertise and training directly related to the particular health care matter at issue.

(B) Nothing in division (A) of this section shall be construed to limit the power of the trial court to adjudge the testimony of any expert witness incompetent on any other ground.

(C) Nothing in division (A) of this section shall be construed to limit the power of the trial court to allow the testimony of any other witness, on a matter unrelated to the liability issues in the medical claim, when that testimony is relevant to the medical claim involved.

(2004 H 215, eff. 9–13–04; 2002 S 281, eff. 4–11–03; 1976 H 1426, eff. 7–1–76; 1975 H 682)

ACTION AGAINST STATE FOR WRONGFUL IMPRISONMENT

2743.48 Action against state for wrongful imprisonment; notice of rights; amount of damages; eligibility

(A) As used in this section and section 2743.49 of the Revised Code, a "wrongfully imprisoned individual" means an individual who satisfies each of the following:

(1) The individual was charged with a violation of a section of the Revised Code by an indictment or information prior to, or on or after, September 24, 1986, and the violation charged was an aggravated felony or felony.

(2) The individual was found guilty of, but did not plead guilty to, the particular charge or a lesser-included offense by the court or jury involved, and the offense of which the individual was found guilty was an aggravated felony or felony.

(3) The individual was sentenced to an indefinite or definite term of imprisonment in a state correctional institution for the offense of which the individual was found guilty.

(4) The individual's conviction was vacated or was dismissed, or reversed on appeal, the prosecuting attorney in the case cannot or will not seek any further appeal of right or upon leave of court, and no criminal proceeding is pending, can be brought, or will be brought by any prosecuting attorney, city director of law, village solicitor, or other chief legal officer of a municipal corporation against the individual for any act associated with that conviction.

(5) Subsequent to sentencing and during or subsequent to imprisonment, an error in procedure resulted in the individual's release, or it was determined by a court of common pleas that the offense of which the individual was found guilty, including all lesser-included offenses, either was not committed by the individual or was not committed by any person.

(B)(1) When a court of common pleas determines, on or after September 24, 1986, that a person is a wrongfully imprisoned individual, the court shall provide the person with a copy of this section and orally inform the person and the person's attorney of the person's rights under this section to commence a civil action against the state in the court of claims because of the person's wrongful imprisonment and to be represented in that civil action by counsel of the person's own choice.

(2) The court described in division (B)(1) of this section shall notify the clerk of the court of claims, in writing and within seven days after the date of the entry of its determination that the person is a wrongfully imprisoned individual, of the name and proposed mailing address of the person and of the fact that the person has the rights to commence a civil action and to have legal representation as provided in this section. The clerk of the court of claims shall maintain in the clerk's office a list of wrongfully imprisoned individuals for whom notices are received under this section and shall create files in the clerk's office for each such individual.

(C)(1) In a civil action under this section, a wrongfully imprisoned individual has the right to have counsel of the individual's own choice.

(2) If a wrongfully imprisoned individual who is the subject of a court determination as described in division (B)(1) of this section does not commence a civil action under this section within six months after the entry of that determination, the clerk of the court of claims shall send a letter to the wrongfully imprisoned individual, at the address set forth in the notice received from the court of common pleas pursuant to division (B)(2) of this section or to any later address provided by the wrongfully imprisoned individual, that reminds the wrongfully imprisoned individual of the wrongfully imprisoned individual's rights under this section. Until the statute of limitations provided in division (H) of this section expires and unless the wrongfully imprisoned individual commences a civil action under this section, the clerk of the court of claims shall send a similar letter in a similar manner to the wrongfully imprisoned individual at least once each three months after the sending of the first reminder.

(D) Notwithstanding any provisions of this chapter to the contrary, a wrongfully imprisoned individual has and may file a civil action against the state, in the court of claims, to recover a sum of money as described in this section, because of the individual's wrongful imprisonment. The court of claims shall have exclusive, original jurisdiction over such a civil action. The civil action shall proceed, be heard, and be determined as provided in sections 2743.01 to 2743.20 of the Revised Code, except that if a provision of this section conflicts with a provision in any of those sections, the provision in this section controls.

(E)(1) In a civil action as described in division (D) of this section, the complainant may establish that the claimant is a wrongfully imprisoned individual by submitting to the court of claims a certified copy of the judgment entry of the court of common pleas associated with the claimant's conviction and sentencing, and a certified copy of the entry of the determination of a court of common pleas that the claimant is a wrongfully imprisoned individual. No other evidence shall be required of the complainant to establish that the claimant is a wrongfully imprisoned individual, and the claimant shall be irrebuttably presumed to be a wrongfully imprisoned individual.

(2) In a civil action as described in division (D) of this section, upon presentation of requisite proof to the court, a wrongfully imprisoned individual is entitled to receive a sum of money that equals the total of each of the following amounts:

(a) The amount of any fine or court costs imposed and paid, and the reasonable attorney's fees and other expenses incurred by the wrongfully imprisoned individual in connection with all associated criminal proceedings and appeals, and, if applicable, in connection with obtaining the wrongfully imprisoned individual's discharge from confinement in the state correctional institution;

(b) For each full year of imprisonment in the state correctional institution for the offense of which the wrongfully imprisoned individual was found guilty, forty thousand three hundred thirty dollars or the adjusted amount determined by the auditor of state pursuant to section 2743.49 of the Revised Code, and for each part of a year of being so imprisoned, a pro-rated share of forty thousand three hundred thirty dollars or the adjusted amount determined by the auditor of state pursuant to section 2743.49 of the Revised Code;

(c) Any loss of wages, salary, or other earned income that directly resulted from the wrongfully imprisoned individual's arrest, prosecution, conviction, and wrongful imprisonment;

(d) The amount of the following cost debts the department of rehabilitation and correction recovered from the wrongfully imprisoned individual who was in custody of the department or under the department's supervision:

(i) Any user fee or copayment for services at a detention facility, including, but not limited to, a fee or copayment for sick call visits;

(ii) The cost of housing and feeding the wrongfully imprisoned individual in a detention facility;

(iii) The cost of supervision of the wrongfully imprisoned individual;

(iv) The cost of any ancillary services provided to the wrongfully imprisoned individual.

(F)(1) If the court of claims determines in a civil action as described in division (D) of this section that the complainant is a wrongfully imprisoned individual, it shall enter judgment for the wrongfully imprisoned individual in the amount of the sum of money to which the wrongfully imprisoned individual is entitled under division (E)(2) of this section. In determining that sum, the court of claims shall not take into consideration any expenses incurred by the state or any of its political subdivisions in connection with the arrest, prosecution, and imprisonment of the wrongfully imprisoned individual, including, but not limited to, expenses for food, clothing, shelter, and medical services.

(2) If the wrongfully imprisoned individual was represented in the civil action under this section by counsel of the wrongfully imprisoned individual's own choice, the court of claims shall include in the judgment entry referred to in division (F)(1) of this section an award for the reasonable attorney's fees of that counsel. These fees shall be paid as provided in division (G) of this section.

(3) The state consents to be sued by a wrongfully imprisoned individual because the imprisonment was wrongful, and to liability on its part because of that fact, only as provided in this section. However, this section does not affect any liability of the state or of its employees to a wrongfully imprisoned individual on a claim for relief that is not based on the fact of the wrongful imprisonment, including, but not limited to, a claim for relief that arises out of circumstances occurring during the wrongfully imprisoned individual's confinement in the state correctional institution.

(G) The clerk of the court of claims shall forward a certified copy of a judgment under division (F) of this section to the president of the controlling board. The board shall take all actions necessary to cause the payment of the judgment out of the emergency purposes special purpose account of the board.

(H) To be eligible to recover a sum of money as described in this section because of wrongful imprisonment, a wrongfully imprisoned individual shall not have been, prior to September 24, 1986, the subject of an act of the general assembly that authorized an award of compensation for the wrongful imprisonment or have been the subject of an action before the former sundry claims board that resulted in an award of compensation for the wrongful imprisonment. Additionally, to be eligible to so recover, the wrongfully imprisoned individual shall commence a civil action under this section in the court of claims no later than two years after the date of the entry of the determination of a court of common pleas that the individual is a wrongfully imprisoned individual.

(2002 S 149, eff. 4–9–03; 1994 H 571, eff. 10–6–94; 1988 H 623, eff. 3–17–89; 1986 H 609)

2743.49 Adjustment of damage amount for wrongful imprisonment

(A)(1) In January of each odd-numbered year, the auditor of state, in accordance with this division and division (A)(2) of this section, shall adjust the actual dollar figure specified in division (E)(2)(b) of section 2743.48 of the Revised Code or the actual dollar amount determined pursuant to this section. The adjustment shall be based on the yearly average of the previous two years of the consumer price index for all urban consumers or its successive equivalent, as determined by the United States department of labor, bureau of labor statistics, or its successor in responsibility, for all items, Series A. Using the yearly average for the immediately preceding even-numbered year as the base year, the auditor of state shall compare the most current average consumer price index with that determined in the preceding odd-numbered year and shall determine the percentage increase or decrease. The auditor of state shall multiply the percentage increase or decrease by the actual dollar figure specified in division (E)(2)(b) of section 2743.48 of the Revised Code or the actual dollar figure determined for the previous odd-numbered year under this section and shall add the product to or subtract the product from its corresponding actual dollar figure, as applicable, for the previous odd-numbered year.

(2) The auditor of state shall calculate the adjustment under division (A)(1) of this section on or before the thirty-first day of January of each odd-numbered year. The auditor of state shall base the adjustment on the most current consumer price index that is described in division (A)(1) of this section and that is in effect as of the first day of January of each odd-numbered year.

(B)(1) The auditor of state shall certify the calculations made under division (A) of this section on or before the thirty-first day of January of each odd-numbered year.

(2) On or before the fifteenth day of February of each odd-numbered year, the auditor of state shall prepare a report setting forth the amount that a wrongfully imprisoned individual is entitled to for each full year of imprisonment in the state correctional institution for the offense of which the wrongfully imprisoned individual was found guilty as provided in division (E)(2)(b) of section 2743.49 of the Revised Code and as calculated in accordance with this section. The report and all documents relating to the calculations contained in the report are public records. The report shall contain an indication of the period in which the calculated amount applies, a summary of how the amount was calculated, and a statement that the report and all related documents are available for inspection and copying at the office of the auditor of state.

(3) On or before the fifteenth day of February of each odd-numbered year, the auditor of state shall transmit the report to the general assembly and to the court of claims.

(2002 S 149, eff. 4–9–03)

VICTIMS OF CRIMES; REPARATIONS; PROCEDURE

2743.52 Awards of reparations for loss from criminally injurious conduct

(A) The attorney general shall make awards of reparations for economic loss arising from criminally injurious conduct, if satisfied by a preponderance of the evidence that the requirements for an award of reparations have been met.

(B) A court of claims panel of commissioners or a judge of the court of claims has appellate jurisdiction to order awards of reparations for economic loss arising from criminally injurious conduct, if satisfied by a preponderance of the evidence that the requirements for an award of reparations have been met.

(C) A decision of the attorney general, an order of a court of claims panel of commissioners, or the judgment of a judge of the court of claims concerning an OVI violation shall not be used as the basis for any civil or criminal action and shall not be admissible as evidence in any civil or criminal proceeding.

(2002 S 123, eff. 1–1–04; 2000 S 153, eff. 7–1–00; 1990 H 837, eff. 7–3–90; 1976 H 82)

2743.521 Audit of medical payments; provider prohibited from seeking reimbursement from victim

(A) For claims for medical, psychological, dental, chiropractic, hospital, physical therapy, and nursing services, the attorney general may audit fee bill payments and adjust fee bill reimbursements in accordance with appropriate cost containment and reimbursement guidelines adopted by the administrator of workers compensation.

(B) A medical provider that accepts payment for medical care-related allowable expenses as part of an award of reparations shall not seek reimbursement for any part of those allowable expenses from the victim or the claimant who was granted the award. This division does not prohibit the medical provider from seeking reimbursement from a collateral source.

(2000 S 153, eff. 7–1–00)

2743.53 Powers and duties regarding appeals

(A) A court of claims panel of commissioners shall hear and determine all matters relating to appeals from decisions of the attorney general pursuant to sections 2743.51 to 2743.72 of the Revised Code.

(B) A judge of the court of claims shall hear and determine all matters relating to appeals from decisions or orders of a panel of commissioners of the court of claims.

(2000 S 153, eff. 7–1–00; 1996 S 239, eff. 9–6–96; 1976 H 82, eff. 9–29–76)

2743.531 Court of claims victims of crime fund

The court of claims victims of crime fund is hereby created in the state treasury. The fund shall be used to pay the compensation of the court of claims commissioners, the compensation of judges of the court of claims necessary to hear and determine appeals from the commissioners, the compensation of any court of claims personnel needed to administer sections 2743.51 to 2743.72 of the Revised Code, and other administrative expenses of hearing and determining appeals by court of claims commissioners and judges.

At the beginning of each fiscal year, the director of budget and management shall transfer cash from the reparations fund to the court of claims victims of crime fund in an amount sufficient to make the cash balance in the court of claims victims of crime fund equal to the sum of the appropriation for that fiscal year and all prior fiscal year encumbrances. If the appropriation from the court of claims victims of crime fund is increased during the fiscal year, the director shall transfer cash from the reparations fund to the court of claims victims of crime fund in an amount equal to the increase in the appropriation.

(2000 S 153, eff. 7–1–00)

2743.54 Appointment and compensation of commissioners

(A) The supreme court shall appoint at least three court of claims commissioners to hear and determine all matters relating to appeals from decisions of the attorney general pursuant to sections 2743.51 to 2743.72 of the Revised Code. Each commissioner shall be an attorney who has been licensed to practice law in this state for at least three years prior to appointment and shall serve at the pleasure of the supreme court and under the administrative supervision of the clerk of the court of claims.

(B) The supreme court shall fix the compensation of the court of claims commissioners, and the compensation shall be paid out of the court of claims victims of crime fund.

(2000 S 153, eff. 7–1–00; 1985 H 201, eff. 7–1–85; 1977 S 221; 1976 H 82)

2743.55 Powers and duties regarding claims for awards of reparations

(A) The attorney general, a court of claims panel of commissioners, or a judge of the court of claims shall determine all matters relating to claims for an award of reparations. The attorney general, a court of claims panel of commissioners, or a judge of the court of claims may order law enforcement officers to provide copies of any information or data gathered in the investigation of the criminally injurious conduct that is the basis of any claim to enable the attorney general, a court of claims panel of commissioners, or a judge of the court of claims to determine whether, and the extent to which, a claimant qualifies for an award of reparations.

(B) A court of claims panel of commissioners shall sit in Franklin county.

(2000 S 153, eff. 7–1–00; 1997 H 478, eff. 11–26–97; 1986 H 249, eff. 9–24–86; 1982 S 30; 1977 H 149; 1976 H 82)

2743.56 Applications for awards of reparations

(A) A claim for an award of reparations shall be commenced by filing an application for an award of reparations with the attorney general. The application may be filed by mail. If the application is filed by mail, the post-marked date of the application shall be considered the filing date of the application. The application shall be in a form prescribed by the attorney general and shall include a release authorizing the attorney general and the court of claims to obtain any report, document, or information that relates to the determination of the claim for an award of reparations that is requested in the application.

(B) All applications for an award of reparations shall be filed as follows:

(1) If the victim of the criminally injurious conduct was a minor, within two years of the victim's eighteenth birthday or within two years from the date a complaint, indictment, or information is filed against the alleged offender, whichever is later. This division does not require that a complaint, indictment, or information be filed against an alleged offender in order for an application for an award of reparations to be filed pertaining to a victim who was a minor if the application is filed within two years of the victim's eighteenth birthday, and does not affect the provisions of section 2743.64 of the Revised Code.

(2) If the victim of the criminally injurious conduct was an adult, within two years after the occurrence of the criminally injurious conduct.

(2000 S 153, eff. 7–1–00; 1998 H 523, eff. 6–30–98; 1990 H 837, eff. 7–3–90; 1988 S 308, H 708; 1986 H 662; 1976 H 82)

2743.58 Immunities of prosecutors and law enforcement officers

The prosecuting attorney and any officer or employee of the office of the prosecuting attorney or of the law enforcement agency shall be immune from any civil liability that might otherwise be incurred as the result of providing information on criminally injurious conduct and related matters to the attorney general.

(2000 S 153, eff. 7–1–00; 1982 S 30, eff. 3–18–83; 1977 H 149; 1976 H 82)

2743.59 Investigatory powers and duties of attorney general; public may file information

(A) The attorney general shall fully investigate a claim for an award of reparations, regardless of whether any person is prosecuted for or convicted of committing the criminally injurious conduct alleged in the application. After completing the investigation, the attorney general shall make a written finding of fact and decision concerning an award of reparations.

(B)(1) The attorney general may require the claimant to supplement the application for an award of reparations with any further information or documentary materials, including any medical report readily available, that may lead to any relevant facts in the determination of whether, and the extent to which, a claimant qualifies for an award of reparations. The attorney general may depose any witness, including the claimant, pursuant to Civil Rules 28, 30, and 45.

(2)(a) For the purpose of determining whether, and the extent to which, a claimant qualifies for an award of reparations, the attorney general may issue subpoenas and subpoenas duces tecum to compel any person or entity, including any collateral source, that provided, will provide, or would have provided to the victim any income, benefit, advantage, product, service, or accommodation, including any medical care or other income, benefit, advantage, product, service, or accommodation that might qualify as an allowable expense or a funeral expense, to produce materials to the attorney general that are relevant to the income, benefit, advantage, product, service, or accommodation that was, will be, or would have been so provided and to the attorney general's determination.

(b) If the attorney general issues a subpoena or subpoena duces tecum under division (B)(2)(a) of this section and if the materials that the attorney general requires to be produced are located outside this state, the attorney general may designate one or more representatives, including officials of the state in which the materials are located, to inspect the materials on the attorney general's behalf, and the attorney general may respond to similar requests from officials of other states. The person or entity subpoenaed may make the materials available to the attorney general at a convenient location within the state.

(c) At any time before the return day specified in the subpoena or subpoena duces tecum issued under division (B)(2)(a) of this section or within twenty days after the subpoena or subpoena duces tecum has been served, whichever period is shorter, the person or entity subpoenaed may file with a judge of the court of claims a petition to extend the return day or to modify or quash the subpoena or subpoena duces tecum. The petition shall state good cause.

(d) A person or entity who is subpoenaed under division (B)(2)(a) of this section shall comply with the terms of the subpoena or subpoena duces tecum unless otherwise provided by an order of a judge of the court of claims entered prior to the day for return contained in the subpoena or as extended by the court. If a person or entity fails without lawful excuse to obey a subpoena or subpoena duces tecum issued under division (B)(2)(a) of this section or to produce relevant materials, the attorney general may apply to a judge of the court of claims for and obtain an order adjudging the person or entity in contempt of court.

(C) The finding of fact and decision that is issued by the attorney general pursuant to division (A) of this section shall contain all of the following:

(1) Whether the criminally injurious conduct that is the basis for the application did occur, the date on which the conduct occurred, and the exact nature of the conduct;

(2) Whether the criminally injurious conduct was reported to a law enforcement officer or agency, the date on which the conduct was reported, the name of the person who reported the conduct, and the reasons why the conduct was not reported to a law enforcement officer or agency or was not reported to a law enforcement officer or agency within seventy-two hours after the conduct occurred;

(3) The exact nature of the injuries that the victim sustained as a result of the criminally injurious conduct;

(4) A specific list of the economic loss that was sustained as a result of the criminally injurious conduct by the victim, the claimant, or a dependent;

(5) A specific list of any benefits or advantages that the victim, the claimant, or a dependent has received or is entitled to receive from any collateral source for economic loss that resulted from the conduct and whether a collateral source would have reimbursed the claimant for a particular expense if a timely claim had been made, and the extent to which the expenses likely would have been reimbursed by the collateral source;

(6) A description of any evidence in support of contributory misconduct by the claimant or by the victim through whom the claimant claims an award of reparations, whether the victim has been convicted of a felony or has a record of felony arrests under the laws of this state, another state, or the United States, whether disqualifying conditions exist under division (E) of section 2743.60 of the Revised Code, and whether there is evidence that the victim engaged in an ongoing course of criminal conduct within five years or less of the criminally injurious conduct that is the subject of the claim;

(7) Whether the victim of the criminally injurious conduct was a minor;

(8) If the victim of the criminally injurious conduct was a minor, whether a complaint, indictment, or information was filed against the alleged offender and, if such a filing occurred, its date;

(9) Any information that is relevant to the claim for an award of reparations.

(D) The decision that is issued by the attorney general pursuant to division (A) of this section shall contain all of the following:

(1) A statement as to whether a claimant is eligible for an award of reparations, whether payments made pursuant to the award are to be made to the claimant, to a provider, or jointly to the claimant and a provider, and the amount of the payments to the claimant or provider;

(2) A statement as to whether any of the payments made pursuant to the award should be paid in a lump sum or in installments;

(3) If the attorney general decides that an award not be made to the claimant, the reasons for that decision.

(E) The attorney general shall make a written finding of fact and decision in accordance with sections 2743.51 to 2743.72 of the Revised Code within one hundred twenty days after receiving the claim application. The attorney general may extend the one-hundred-twenty-day time limit and shall record in writing specific reasons to justify the extension. The attorney general shall notify the claimant of the extension and of the reasons for the extension. The attorney general shall serve a copy of its written finding of fact and decision upon the claimant.

(2000 S 153, eff. 7–1–00; 1996 H 363, eff. 8–1–96; 1990 H 837, eff. 7–3–90; 1986 H 662; 1982 S 30; 1977 H 149; 1976 H 82)

2743.60 Limitations on claims; limits and exclusions on awards

(A) The attorney general, a court of claims panel of commissioners, or a judge of the court of claims shall not make or order an award of reparations to any claimant who, if the victim of the criminally injurious conduct was an adult, did not file an application for an award of reparations within two years after the date of the occurrence of the criminally injurious conduct that caused the injury or death for which the victim is seeking an award of reparations or who, if the victim of that criminally injurious conduct was a minor, did not file an application for an award of reparations within the period provided by division (B)(1) of section 2743.56 of the Revised Code. An award of reparations shall not be made to a claimant if the criminally injurious conduct upon which the claimant bases a claim was not reported to a law enforcement officer or agency within seventy-two hours after the occurrence of the conduct, unless it is determined that good cause existed for the failure to report the conduct within the seventy-two-hour period.

(B)(1) The attorney general, a panel of commissioners, or a judge of the court of claims shall not make or order an award of reparations to a claimant if any of the following apply:

(a) The claimant is the offender or an accomplice of the offender who committed the criminally injurious conduct, or the award would unjustly benefit the offender or accomplice.

(b) Except as provided in division (B)(2) of this section, both of the following apply:

(i) The victim was a passenger in a motor vehicle and knew or reasonably should have known that the driver was under the influence of alcohol, a drug of abuse, or both.

(ii) The claimant is seeking compensation for injuries proximately caused by the driver described in division (B)(1)(b)(i) of this section being under the influence of alcohol, a drug of abuse, or both.

(c) Both of the following apply:

(i) The victim was under the influence of alcohol, a drug of abuse, or both and was a passenger in a motor vehicle and, if sober, should have reasonably known that the driver was under the influence of alcohol, a drug of abuse, or both.

(ii) The claimant is seeking compensation for injuries proximately caused by the driver described in division (B)(1)(b)(i) of this section being under the influence of alcohol, a drug of abuse, or both.

(2) Division (B)(1)(b) of this section does not apply if on the date of the occurrence of the criminally injurious conduct, the victim was under sixteen years of age or was at least sixteen years of age but less than eighteen years of age and was riding with a parent, guardian, or care-provider.

(C) The attorney general, a panel of commissioners, or a judge of the court of claims, upon a finding that the claimant or victim has not fully cooperated with appropriate law enforcement agencies, may deny a claim or reconsider and reduce an award of reparations.

(D) The attorney general, a panel of commissioners, or a judge of the court of claims shall reduce an award of reparations or deny a claim for an award of reparations that is otherwise payable to a claimant to the extent that the economic loss upon which the claim is based is recouped from other persons, including collateral sources. If an award is reduced or a claim is denied because of the expected recoupment of all or part of the economic loss of the claimant from a collateral source, the amount of the award or the denial of the claim shall be conditioned upon the claimant's economic loss being recouped by the collateral source. If the award or denial is conditioned upon the recoupment of the claimant's economic loss from a collateral source and it is determined that the claimant did not unreasonably fail to present a timely claim to the collateral source and will not receive all or part of the expected recoupment, the claim may be reopened and an award may be made in an amount equal to the amount of expected recoupment that it is determined the claimant will not receive from the collateral source.

If the claimant recoups all or part of the economic loss upon which the claim is based from any other person or entity, including a collateral source, the attorney general may recover pursuant to section 2743.72 of the Revised Code the part of the award that represents the economic loss for which the claimant received the recoupment from the other person or entity.

(E)(1) Except as otherwise provided in division (E)(2) of this section, the attorney general, a panel of commissioners, or a judge of the court of claims shall not make an award to a claimant if any of the following applies:

(a) The victim was convicted of a felony within ten years prior to the criminally injurious conduct that gave rise to the claim or is convicted of a felony during the pendency of the claim.

(b) The claimant was convicted of a felony within ten years prior to the criminally injurious conduct that gave rise to the claim or is convicted of a felony during the pendency of the claim.

(c) It is proved by a preponderance of the evidence that the victim or the claimant engaged, within ten years prior to the criminally injurious conduct that gave rise to the claim or during the pendency of the claim, in an offense of violence, a violation of section 2925.03 of the Revised Code, or any substantially similar offense that also would constitute a felony under the laws of this state, another state, or the United States.

(d) The claimant was convicted of a violation of section 2919.22 or 2919.25 of the Revised Code, or of any state law or municipal ordinance substantially similar to either section, within ten years prior to the criminally injurious conduct that gave rise to the claim or during the pendency of the claim.

(e) It is proved by a preponderance of the evidence that the victim at the time of the criminally injurious conduct that gave rise to the claim engaged in conduct that was a felony violation of section 2925.11 of the Revised Code or engaged in any substantially similar conduct that would constitute a felony under the laws of this state, another state, or the United States.

(2) The attorney general, a panel of commissioners, or a judge of the court of claims may make an award to a minor dependent of a deceased victim for dependent's economic loss or for counseling pursuant to division (F)(2) of section 2743.51 of the Revised Code if the minor dependent is not ineligible under division (E)(1) of this section due to the minor dependent's criminal history and if the victim was not killed while engaging in illegal conduct that contributed to the criminally injurious conduct that gave rise to the claim. For purposes of this section, the use of illegal drugs by the deceased victim shall not be deemed to have contributed to the criminally injurious conduct that gave rise to the claim.

(F) In determining whether to make an award of reparations pursuant to this section, the attorney general or panel of commissioners shall consider whether there was contributory misconduct by the victim or the claimant. The attorney general, a panel of commissioners, or a judge of the court of claims shall reduce an award of reparations or deny a claim for an award of reparations to the extent it is determined to be reasonable because of the contributory misconduct of the claimant or the victim.

When the attorney general decides whether a claim should be denied because of an allegation of contributory misconduct, the burden of proof on the issue of that alleged contributory misconduct shall be upon the claimant, if either of the following apply:

(1) The victim was convicted of a felony more than ten years prior to the criminally injurious conduct that is the subject of the claim or has a record of felony arrests under the laws of this state, another state, or the United States.

(2) There is good cause to believe that the victim engaged in an ongoing course of criminal conduct within five years or less of the criminally injurious conduct that is the subject of the claim.

(G) The attorney general, a panel of commissioners, or a judge of the court of claims shall not make an award of reparations to a claimant if the criminally injurious conduct that caused the injury or death that is the subject of the claim occurred to a victim who was an adult and while the victim, after being convicted of or pleading guilty to an offense, was serving a sentence of imprisonment in any detention facility, as defined in section 2921.01 of the Revised Code.

(H) If a claimant unreasonably fails to present a claim timely to a source of benefits or advantages that would have been a collateral source and that would have reimbursed the claimant for all or a portion of a particular expense, the attorney general, a panel of commissioners, or a judge of the court of claims may reduce an award of reparations or deny a claim for an award of reparations to the extent that it is reasonable to do so.

(I) Reparations payable to a victim and to all other claimants sustaining economic loss because of injury to or the death of that victim shall not exceed fifty thousand dollars in the aggregate. If the attorney general, a panel of commissioners, or a judge of the court of claims reduces an award under division (F) of this section, the maximum aggregate amount of reparations payable under this division shall be reduced proportionately to the reduction under division (F) of this section.

(2003 H 95, eff. 6–26–03; 2000 S 153, eff. 7–1–00; 1996 H 363, eff. 8–1–96; 1990 H 837, eff. 7–3–90; 1988 S 308; 1986 H 662; 1982 S 30; 1981 H 694; 1976 H 82)

2743.61 Reconsiderations; appeals

(A) The attorney general, on the attorney general's own motion or upon request of a claimant or victim, may reconsider a decision to make an award of reparations, the amount of an award of reparations, or a decision to deny a claim for an award of reparations. A claimant may file a request for reconsideration with the attorney general not later than thirty days after the attorney general renders an initial decision. A claimant may submit with the request any additional information that is relevant to the claimant's claim for an award of reparation.

The attorney general shall reconsider the application based upon evidence that is relevant to the application and issue a final decision within sixty days of receiving the request for reconsideration. The attorney general may extend the sixty-day time limit and shall record in writing specific reasons to justify the extension. The attorney general shall notify the claimant of the extension and of the reasons for the extension.

If a claimant does not file a request for reconsideration of a decision of the attorney general to make an award or to deny a claim or of the amount of an award within thirty days after the decision is rendered, the award, the denial of the claim, or the amount of the award is final unless the attorney general in the interest of justice allows the reconsideration after the expiration of that period of time.

(B) A claimant may appeal an award of reparations, the amount of an award of reparations, or the denial of a claim for an award of reparations that is made by a final decision of the attorney general after any reconsideration. If the final decision of the attorney general with respect to any claim for an award of reparations is appealed, a court of claims panel of commissioners, within ninety days of receiving the notice of appeal, shall schedule and conduct a hearing on the appeal. The panel of commissioners shall determine the appeal within sixty days from the date of the hearing on the basis of the record of the hearing before the commissioners, including the original award or denial and the finding of fact of the attorney general, any information or documents that the attorney general used in the investigation, any information or data provided to the attorney general, any briefs or oral arguments that may be requested by a court of claims panel of commissioners, and any additional evidence presented at the hearing. The panel of commissioners may extend the sixty-day time limit and shall record in writing specific reasons to justify the extension. The attorney general shall supply the panel of commissioners with the original decision awarding or denying compensation, the finding of fact of the attorney general, any information or documents that the attorney general used in the investigation, and any information or data provided to the attorney general within fourteen days of the filing of the objection and notice of appeal by the applicant. The panel of commissioners shall notify the claimant and attorney general of the extension and of the reasons for the extension. If upon hearing and consideration of the record and evidence, the court of claims panel of commissioners decides that the decision of the attorney general appealed from is reasonable and lawful, it shall affirm the same. If the court of claims panel of commissioners decides that the decision of the attorney general is not supported by a preponderance of the evidence or is unreasonable or unlawful, it shall reverse and vacate the decision or modify it and enter judgment thereon.

(C) The attorney general or a claimant may appeal an award of reparations, the amount of an award of reparations, or the denial of a claim for an award of reparations that is made by a panel of court of claims commissioners. If the determination of the panel of commissioners with respect to any claim for an award of reparations is appealed, a judge of the court of claims shall hear and determine the appeal on the basis of the record of the hearing before the commissioners, including the original award or denial made by the attorney general, any information or documents presented to the panel of commissioners, and any briefs or oral arguments that may be requested by the judge. If upon hearing and consideration of the record and evidence, the judge decides that the decision of the panel of commissioners is unreasonable or unlawful, the judge shall reverse and vacate the decision or modify it and enter judgment on the claim. The decision of the judge of the court of claims is final.

(D) Notices of an appeal concerning an award of reparations shall be filed within thirty days after the date on which the award or the denial of a claim is made by a final decision of the attorney general. If a notice of appeal is not filed within the thirty-day period, the award or denial of the claim is final unless a court of claims panel of commissioners in the interests of justice allows the appeal.

(E) The attorney general or a claimant shall file a notice of an appeal concerning an order or decision of a panel of commissioners within thirty days after the date on which the award or the denial of a claim is made by the panel of commissioners. If the attorney general or a claimant does not file a notice of appeal with respect to an award or denial within the thirty-day period, the award or denial of the claim is final unless a judge of the court of claims in the interests of justice allows the appeal.

(2000 S 153, eff. 7–1–00; 1982 S 30, eff. 3–18–83; 1976 H 82)

2743.62 Privileges; medical reports

(A)(1) Subject to division (A)(2) of this section, there is no privilege, except the privileges arising from the attorney-client relationship, as to communications or records that are relevant to the physical, mental, or emotional condition of the claimant or victim in a proceeding under sections 2743.51 to 2743.72 of the Revised Code in which that condition is an element.

(2)(a) Except as specified in division (A)(2)(b) of this section, any record or report that a judge of the court of claims, a court of claims panel of commissioners, or the attorney general has obtained prior to, or obtains on or after, June 30, 1998, under the provisions of sections 2743.51 to 2743.72 of the Revised Code and that is confidential or otherwise exempt from public disclosure under section 149.43 of the Revised Code while in the possession of the creator of the record or report shall remain confidential or exempt from public disclosure under section 149.43 of the Revised Code while in the possession of the court of claims or the attorney general.

(b) Notwithstanding division (A)(2)(a) of this section, a judge of the court of claims, a panel of commissioners, a claimant, a claimant's attorney, or the attorney general may disclose or refer to records or reports described in that division in any hearing conducted under sections 2743.51 to 2743.72 of the Revised Code or in the judge's, panel of commissioners', claimant's, or attorney general's written pleadings, findings, recommendations, and decisions.

(B) If the mental, physical, or emotional condition of a victim or claimant is material to a claim for an award of reparations, the attorney general, a panel of commissioners, or a judge of the court of claims may order the victim or claimant to submit to a mental or physical examination and may order an autopsy of a deceased victim. The order may be made for good cause shown and upon notice to the person to be examined and to the claimant. The order shall specify the time, place, manner, conditions, and scope of the examination or autopsy and the person by whom it is to be made. In the case of a mental examination, the person specified may be a physician or psychologist. In the case of a physical examination, the person specified may be a physician, a physician assistant, a clinical nurse specialist, a certified nurse practitioner, or a certified nurse-midwife. In the case of an autopsy, the person specified must be a physician. The order shall require the person who performs the examination or autopsy to file with the attorney general a detailed written report of the examination or autopsy. The report shall set out the findings, including the results of all tests made, diagnoses, prognoses, and other conclusions and reports of earlier examinations of the same conditions.

(C) On request of the person examined, the attorney general shall furnish the person a copy of the report. If the victim is deceased, the attorney general, on request, shall furnish the claimant a copy of the report.

(D) The attorney general, a panel of commissioners, or a judge of the court of claims may require the claimant to supplement the application for an award of reparations with any reasonably available medical or psychological reports relating to the injury for which the award of reparations is claimed.

(E) The attorney general, a panel of commissioners, or a judge of the court of claims, in a claim arising out of a violation of any provision of sections 2907.02 to 2907.07 of the Revised Code, shall not request the victim or the claimant to supply, or permit any person to supply, any evidence of specific instances of the victim's sexual activity, opinion evidence of the victim's sexual activity, or reputation evidence of the victim's sexual activity unless it involves evidence of the origin of semen, pregnancy, or disease or evidence of the victim's past sexual activity with the offender and only to the extent that the judge, the panel of commissioners, or the attorney general finds that the evidence is relevant to a fact at issue in the claim.

(2002 S 245, eff. 3–31–03; 2000 S 153, eff. 7–1–00; 1998 H 523, eff. 6–30–98; 1996 H 445, eff. 9–3–96; 1976 H 82, eff. 9–29–76)

2743.63 Enforcement of orders

If a person refuses to comply with an order under sections 2743.51 to 2743.72 of the Revised Code, or asserts a privilege, except privileges arising from the attorney-client relationship, to withhold or suppress evidence relevant to a claim for an award of reparations, the attorney general may make any just decision including denial of the claim but shall not find the person in contempt. If necessary to carry out any of the attorney general's powers and duties, the attorney general may petition a court of claims panel of commissioners for an appropriate order, including but not limited to a finding of contempt, but a panel of commissioners shall not find a person in contempt for refusal to submit to a mental or physical examination.

(2000 S 153, eff. 7–1–00; 1976 H 82, eff. 9–29–76)

2743.64 Evidence; effect of criminal proceedings

The attorney general, a court of claims panel of commissioners, or a judge of the court of claims may make an award of reparations whether or not any person is prosecuted or convicted for committing the conduct that is the basis of the award. Proof of conviction of a person whose conduct gave rise to a claim is conclusive evidence that the crime was committed, unless an application for rehearing, an appeal of the conviction, or certiorari is pending, or a rehearing or new trial has been ordered.

If the prosecuting attorney of the county in which the criminally injurious conduct allegedly occurred requests the suspension of proceedings in any claim for an award of reparations and if the request is made because of the commencement of a criminal prosecution, the attorney general may suspend, because a criminal prosecution has been commenced or is imminent, the proceedings in any claim for an award of reparations for a definite period of time, and may make an emergency award under section 2743.67 of the Revised Code.

(2000 S 153, eff. 7–1–00; 1990 H 837, eff. 7–3–90; 1988 S 308; 1982 S 30; 1976 H 82)

2743.65 Attorney fees; witness fees

(A) The attorney general shall determine, and the state shall pay, in accordance with this section attorney's fees, commensurate with services rendered, to the attorney representing a claimant under sections 2743.51 to 2743.72 of the Revised Code. The attorney shall submit on an application form an itemized fee bill at the rate of sixty dollars per hour upon receipt of the final decision on the claim. Attorney's fees paid pursuant to this section are subject to the following maximum amounts:

(1) A maximum of seven hundred twenty dollars for claims resolved without the filing of an appeal to the panel of commissioners;

(2) A maximum of one thousand twenty dollars for claims in which an appeal to the panel of commissioners is filed plus, at the request of an attorney whose main office is not in Franklin county, Delaware county, Licking county, Fairfield county, Pickaway county, Madison county, or Union county, an amount for the attorney's travel time to attend the oral hearing before the panel of commissioners at the rate of thirty dollars per hour;

(3) A maximum of one thousand three hundred twenty dollars for claims in which an appeal to a judge of the court of claims is filed plus, at the request of an attorney whose main office is not in Franklin county, Delaware county, Licking county, Fairfield county, Pickaway county, Madison county, or Union county, an amount for the attorney's travel time to attend the oral hearing before the judge at the rate of thirty dollars per hour;

(4) A maximum of seven hundred twenty dollars for a supplemental reparations application;

(5) A maximum of two hundred dollars if the claim is denied on the basis of a claimant's or victim's conviction of a felony offense prior to the filing of the claim. If the claimant or victim is convicted of a felony offense during the pendency of the claim, the two hundred dollars maximum does not apply. If the attorney had knowledge of the claimant's or victim's felony conviction prior to the filing of the application for the claim, the attorney general may determine that the filing of the claim was frivolous and may deny attorney's fees.

(B) The attorney general may determine that an attorney be reimbursed for fees incurred in the creation of a guardianship if the guardianship is required in order for an individual to receive an award of reparations, and those fees shall be reimbursed at a rate of sixty dollars per hour.

(C)(1) The attorney general shall forward an application form for attorney's fees to a claimant's attorney before or when the final decision on a claim is rendered. The application form for attorney's fees shall do all of the following:

(a) Inform the attorney of the requirements of this section;

(b) Require a verification statement comporting with the law prohibiting falsification;

(c) Require an itemized fee statement;

(d) Require a verification statement that the claimant was served a copy of the completed application form;

(e) Include notice that the claimant may oppose the application by notifying the attorney general in writing within ten days.

(2) The attorney general shall forward a copy of this section to the attorney with the application form for attorney's fees. The attorney shall file the application form with the attorney general. The attorney general's decision with respect to an award of attorney's fees is final ten days after the attorney general renders the decision and mails a copy of the decision to the attorney at the address provided by the attorney. The attorney may request reconsideration of the decision on grounds that it is insufficient or calculated incorrectly. The attorney general's decision on the request for reconsideration is final.

(D) The attorney general shall review all application forms for attorney's fees that are submitted by a claimant's attorney and shall issue an order approving the amount of fees to be paid to the attorney within sixty days after receipt of the application form.

(E) No attorney's fees shall be paid for the following:

(1) Estate work or representation of a claimant against a collateral source;

(2) Duplication of investigative work required to be performed by the attorney general;

(3) Performance of unnecessary criminal investigation of the offense;

(4) Presenting or appealing an issue that has been repeatedly ruled upon by the highest appellate authority, unless a unique set of facts or unique issue of law exists that distinguishes it;

(5) A fee request that is unreasonable, is not commensurate with services rendered, violates the Ohio code of professional responsibility, or is based upon services that are determined to be frivolous.

(F)(1) The attorney general may reduce or deny the payment of attorney's fees to an attorney who has filed a frivolous claim. Subject to division (A)(5) of this section, the denial of a claim on the basis of a felony conviction, felony conduct, or contributory misconduct does not constitute a frivolous claim.

(2) As used in this section, "frivolous claim" means a claim in which there is clearly no legal grounds under the existing laws of this state to support the filing of a claim on behalf of the claimant or victim.

(G) The attorney general may determine that a lesser number of hours should have been required in a given case. Additional reimbursement may be made where the attorney demonstrates to the attorney general that the nature of the particular claim required the expenditure of an amount in excess of that allowed.

(H) No attorney shall receive payment under this section for assisting a claimant with an application for an award of reparations under sections 2743.51 to 2743.72 of the Revised Code if that attorney's fees have been allowed as an expense in accordance with division (F)(4) of section 2743.51 of the Revised Code.

(I) A contract or other agreement between an attorney and any person that provides for the payment of attorney's fees or other payments in excess of the attorney's fees allowed under this section for representing a claimant under sections 2743.51 to 2743.72 of the Revised Code shall be void and unenforceable.

(J) Each witness who appears in a hearing on a claim for an award of reparations shall receive compensation in an amount equal to that received by witnesses in civil cases as provided in section 2335.06 of the Revised Code.

(2003 H 95, eff. 6–26–03; 2000 S 153, eff. 7–1–00; 1982 S 30, eff. 3–18–83; 1976 H 82)

2743.66 Payment of awards

(A) A decision of the attorney general, order of a court of claims panel of commissioners, or judgment of a judge of the court of claims granting an award of reparations may provide for the payment of the award in a lump sum or in installments. The part of an award equal to the amount of economic loss accrued to the date of the award shall be paid in a lump sum. An award for allowable expense that would accrue after the award is made shall not be paid in a lump sum. Except as provided in division (B) of this section, the part of an award not paid in a lump sum shall be paid in installments.

(B) Upon the motion of the claimant, the attorney general may commute future economic loss, other than allowable expense, to a lump sum but only upon a finding that either of the following applies:

(1) The award in a lump sum will promote the interests of the claimant.

(2) The present value of all future economic loss, other than allowable expense, does not exceed one thousand dollars.

(C) The attorney general may make an award for future economic loss payable in installments only for a period as to which future economic loss reasonably can be determined. An award for future economic loss payable in installments may be reconsidered and modified upon a finding that a material and substantial change of circumstances has occurred.

(D) An award is not subject to execution, attachment, garnishment, or other process, except that, upon receipt of an award by a claimant:

(1) The part of the award that is for allowable expense or funeral expense is not exempt from such action by a creditor to the extent that the creditor provided products, services, or accommodations the costs of which are included in the award.

(2) The part of the award that is for work loss shall not be exempt from such action to secure payment of spousal support, other maintenance, or child support.

(3) The attorney general may recover the award pursuant to section 2743.72 of the Revised Code if it is discovered that the claimant actually was not eligible for the award or that the award otherwise should not have been made under the standards and criteria set forth in sections 2743.51 to 2743.72 of the Revised Code.

(4) If the claimant receives compensation from any other person or entity, including a collateral source, for an expense that is included within the award, the attorney general may recover pursuant to section 2743.72 of the Revised Code the part of the award that represents the expense for which the claimant received the compensation from the other person or entity.

(E) If a person entitled to an award of reparations is under eighteen years of age and if the amount of the award exceeds one thousand dollars, the order providing for the payment of the award shall specify that the award be paid either to the guardian of the estate of the minor appointed pursuant to Chapter 2111. of the Revised Code or to the person or depository designated by the probate court under section 2111.05 of the Revised Code. If a person entitled to an award of reparations is under eighteen years of age and if the amount of the award is one thousand dollars or less, the order providing for the payment of the award may specify that the award be paid to an adult member of the family of the minor who is legally responsible for the minor's care or to any other person designated by the attorney general or panel of commissioners issuing the decision or order.

(2000 S 153, eff. 7–1–00; 1996 H 363, eff. 8–1–96; 1994 H 390, eff. 11–15–94; 1990 H 514, eff. 1–1–91; 1990 H 837; 1988 S 308; 1985 H 201; 1982 S 30; 1977 H 149; 1976 H 82)

2743.67 Emergency award in case of hardship

The attorney general may make an emergency award if, before acting on an application for an award of reparations under this section, it appears likely that a final award will be made, and the claimant or victim will suffer undue hardship if immediate economic relief is not obtained. An emergency award shall not exceed two thousand dollars. The attorney general or the court of claims panel of commissioners shall deduct an amount of the emergency award from the final award, or the claimant or victim shall repay the amount of the emergency award that exceeds the final award made to the claimant. If no final award is made, the claimant or victim shall repay the entire emergency award.

(2000 S 153, eff. 7–1–00)

2743.68 Supplemental applications; conditions

A claimant may file a supplemental reparations application in a claim if the attorney general, a court of claims panel of commissioners, or judge of the court of claims, within five years prior to the filing of the supplemental application, has made any of the following determinations:

(A) That an award, supplemental award, or installment award be granted;

(B) That an award, supplemental award, or installment award be conditioned or denied because of actual or potential recovery from a collateral source;

(C) That an award, supplemental award, or installment award be denied because the claimant had not incurred any economic loss at that time.

(2000 S 153, eff. 7–1–00; 1982 S 30, eff. 3–18–83; 1977 H 149; 1976 H 82)

2743.69 Annual report of program activities

(A) The attorney general shall prepare and transmit annually to the governor, the president of the senate, the speaker of the house of representatives, and the minority leaders of both houses a report of the activities of the Ohio crime victims compensation program under sections 2743.51 to 2743.72 of the Revised Code. The report shall include all of the following:

(1) The number of claims filed, the number of awards made and the amount of each award, and a statistical summary of awards made and denied, including the average size of awards;

(2) The balance in the reparations fund, with a listing by source and amount of the moneys that have been deposited in the fund;

(3) The amount that has been withdrawn from the fund, including separate listings of the administrative costs incurred by the attorney general and a court of claims panel of commissioners, compensation of judges and court personnel, the amount awarded as attorney's fees, and the amount of payments made pursuant to divisions (A)(1)(k) and (*l*) of section 2743.191 of the Revised Code.

(B) The director of budget and management shall assist the attorney general in the preparation of the report required by this section.

(2003 S 5, eff. 7–31–03; 2000 S 153, eff. 7–1–00; 1985 H 201, eff. 7–1–85; 1982 S 30; 1977 S 221; 1976 H 82)

2743.70 Additional costs in criminal cases in all courts to fund reparations payments

(A)(1) The court, in which any person is convicted of or pleads guilty to any offense other than a traffic offense that is not a moving violation, shall impose the following sum as costs in the case in addition to any other court costs that the court is required by law to impose upon the offender:

(a) Thirty dollars, if the offense is a felony;

(b) Nine dollars, if the offense is a misdemeanor.

The court shall not waive the payment of the thirty or nine dollars court costs, unless the court determines that the offender is indigent and waives the payment of all court costs imposed upon the indigent offender. All such moneys shall be transmitted on the first business day of each month by the clerk of the court to the treasurer of state and deposited by the treasurer in the reparations fund.

(2) The juvenile court in which a child is found to be a delinquent child or a juvenile traffic offender for an act which, if committed by an adult, would be an offense other than a traffic offense that is not a moving violation, shall impose the following sum as costs in the case in addition to any other court costs that the court is required or permitted by law to impose upon the delinquent child or juvenile traffic offender:

(a) Thirty dollars, if the act, if committed by an adult, would be a felony;

(b) Nine dollars, if the act, if committed by an adult, would be a misdemeanor.

The thirty or nine dollars court costs shall be collected in all cases unless the court determines the juvenile is indigent and waives the payment of all court costs, or enters an order on its journal stating that it has determined that the juvenile is indigent, that no other court costs are to be taxed in the case, and that the payment of the thirty or nine dollars court costs is waived. All such moneys collected during a month shall be transmitted on or before the twentieth day of the following month by the clerk of the court to the treasurer of state and deposited by the treasurer in the reparations fund.

(B) Whenever a person is charged with any offense other than a traffic offense that is not a moving violation and posts bail pursuant to sections 2937.22 to 2937.46 of the Revised Code, Criminal Rule 46, or Traffic Rule 4, the court shall add to the amount of the bail the thirty or nine dollars required to be paid by division (A)(1) of this section. The thirty or nine dollars shall be retained by the clerk of the court until the person is convicted, pleads guilty, forfeits bail, is found not guilty, or has the charges dismissed. If the person is convicted, pleads guilty, or forfeits bail, the clerk shall transmit the thirty or nine dollars to the treasurer of state, who shall deposit it in the reparations fund. If the person is found not guilty or the charges are dismissed, the clerk shall return the thirty or nine dollars to the person.

(C) No person shall be placed or held in jail for failing to pay the additional thirty or nine dollars court costs or bail that are required to be paid by this section.

(D) As used in this section:

(1) "Moving violation" means any violation of any statute or ordinance, other than section 4513.263 of the Revised Code or an ordinance that is substantially equivalent to that section, that regulates the operation of vehicles, streetcars, or trackless trolleys on highways or streets or that regulates size or load limitations or fitness requirements of vehicles. "Moving violation" does not include the violation of any statute or ordinance that regulates pedestrians or the parking of vehicles.

(2) "Bail" means cash, a check, a money order, a credit card, or any other form of money that is posted by or for an offender pursuant to sections 2937.22 to 2937.46 of the Revised Code, Criminal Rule 46, or Traffic Rule 4 to prevent the offender from being placed or held in a detention facility, as defined in section 2921.01 of the Revised Code.

(1998 H 426, eff. 7–22–98; 1993 H 152, eff. 7–1–93; 1992 H 725; 1990 S 131; 1985 H 201; 1983 H 291; 1982 S 30, S 550; 1981 H 552, H 694; 1980 H 238; 1977 S 221; 1976 H 82)

2743.71 Duties of law enforcement agencies and prosecutors; publicity materials expenses; limit

(A) Any law enforcement agency that investigates, and any prosecuting attorney, city director of law, village solicitor, or similar prosecuting authority who prosecutes, an offense committed in this state shall, upon first contact with the victim or the victim's family or dependents, give the victim or the victim's family or dependents a copy of an information card or other printed material provided by the attorney general pursuant to division (B) of this section and explain, upon request, the information on the card or material to the victim or the victim's family or dependents.

(B) The attorney general shall have printed, and shall provide to law enforcement agencies, prosecuting attorneys, city directors of law, village solicitors, and similar prosecuting authorities, cards or other materials that contain information explaining awards of reparations. The information on the cards or other materials shall include, but shall not be limited to, the following statements:

(1) Awards of reparations are limited to losses that are caused by physical injury resulting from criminally injurious conduct;

(2) Reparations applications are required to be filed within two years after the date of the criminally injurious conduct if the victim was an adult, or within the period provided by division (C)(1) of section 2743.56 of the Revised Code if the victim of the criminally injurious conduct was a minor;

(3) An attorney who represents an applicant for an award of reparations cannot charge the applicant for the services rendered in relation to that representation but is required to apply to the attorney general for payment for the representation;

(4) Applications for awards of reparations may be obtained from the attorney general, law enforcement agencies, and victim assistance agencies and are to be filed with the attorney general.

(C) The attorney general may order that a reasonable amount of money be paid out of the reparations fund, subject to the limitation imposed by division (D) of this section, for use by the attorney general to publicize the availability of awards of reparations.

(D) During any fiscal year, the total expenditure for the printing and providing of information cards or other materials pursuant to division (B) of this section and for the publicizing of the availability of awards of reparations pursuant to division (C) of this section shall not exceed two per cent of the total of all court costs deposited, in accordance with section 2743.70 of the Revised Code, in the reparations fund during the immediately preceding fiscal year.

(2000 S 153, eff. 7–1–00; 1988 S 308, eff. 3–14–89; 1986 H 662; 1985 H 201; 1980 H 238; 1976 H 82)

2743.711 Attorney general as legal representative of reparations fund

The attorney general is the legal representative of the reparations fund established by section 2743.191 of the Revised Code. The attorney general may institute, prosecute, and settle actions or proceedings for the enforcement of the reparations fund's right of repayment, reimbursement, recovery, and subrogation. The attorney general shall defend all suits, actions, or proceedings brought against the fund.

(2000 S 153, eff. 7–1–00)

2743.72 Repayment, reimbursement, and subrogation of fund; ineligibility of claimant for award

(A) The payment of an award of reparations from the reparations fund established by section 2743.191 of the Revised Code creates a right of reimbursement, repayment, and subrogation in favor of the reparations fund from an individual who is convicted of the offense that is the basis of the award of reparations. For purposes of establishing an individual's liability under this provision, a certified judgment of the individual's conviction together with the related indictment is admissible as evidence to prove the individual's liability.

(B) The payment of an award of reparations from the reparations fund creates a right of reimbursement, repayment, and subrogation in favor of the reparations fund from a third party who, because of an express or implied contractual or other legal relationship, had an obligation to pay any expenses for which an award of reparations was made.

(C) If an award of reparations is made to a claimant under sections 2743.51 to 2743.72 of the Revised Code and if it is discovered that the claimant actually was not eligible for the award or that the award otherwise should not have been made under the standards and criteria set forth in sections 2743.51 to 2743.72 of the Revised Code, the fund is entitled to recover the award from the claimant.

(D) If an award of reparations is made to a claimant under sections 2743.51 to 2743.72 of the Revised Code and if the claimant receives compensation from any other person or entity, including a collateral source, for an expense that is included within the award, the fund is entitled to recover from the claimant the part of the award that represents the expense for which the claimant received the compensation from the other person or entity.

(E) The reparations fund is an eligible recipient for payment of restitution.

(F) The subrogation right of the reparations fund includes the amount of an award of reparations actually paid to a claimant or to another person on the claimant's behalf and a right of prepayment for the anticipated future payment of an award of reparations to be paid by reason of criminally injurious conduct.

(G) The subrogation right of the reparations fund is enforceable through the filing of an action in the Franklin county court of common pleas within six years of the date of the last payment of any part of an award of reparations from the fund. The time of an offender's imprisonment shall not be computed as any part of this period of limitation. This subrogation right may be established and enforced in the Franklin county court of common pleas as against the heirs and assigns of a subrogation debtor.

(H) As a prerequisite to bringing an action to recover an award related to criminally injurious conduct upon which compensation is claimed or awarded, the claimant must give the attorney general prior written notice of the proposed action. If an action is initiated prior to a claimant filing a reparations claim or supplemental reparations claim, the claimant must give the attorney general written notice of the existence of the action. After receiving either notice, the attorney general promptly shall do one of the following:

(1) Join in the action as a party plaintiff to recover any reparations awarded;

(2) Require the claimant to bring the action in the claimant's individual name as trustee on behalf of the state to recover any reparations awarded;

(3) Reserve the rights described in division (H)(1) or (2) of this section.

If, as requested by the attorney general, the claimant brings the action as trustee and the claimant recovers compensation awarded by the reparations fund, the claimant may deduct from the compensation recovered on behalf of the state the reasonable expenses including attorney's fees allocable by the court for that recovery.

(I) A claimant shall not settle or resolve any action arising out of criminally injurious conduct without written authorization from the attorney general to do so. Any attempt by a third party or an offender, or an agent, an insurer, or attorneys of third parties or offenders, to settle an action is void and shall result in no release from liability to the reparations fund.

(J) If there is more than one offender in connection with an instance of criminally injurious conduct, each offender is jointly and severally liable to pay to the reparations fund the full amount of the reparations award.

(K) The right of the reparations fund to repayment, reimbursement, and subrogation under sections 2743.711 and 2743.72 of the Revised Code is automatic, regardless of whether the reparations fund is joined as a party in an action by a claimant against an offender or third party in connection with criminally injurious conduct.

(L) The reparations fund, through the attorney general, may assert its repayment, reimbursement, or subrogation rights through correspondence with the claimant, offender, or third party, or their legal representatives. The assertion is not to be considered the assertion of a consumer debt.

(M) The reparations fund, through the attorney general, may institute and pursue legal proceedings against an offender, third party, or overpaid claimant. In actions against an offender or third party, the claimant and victim are not necessary parties to the action.

(N) The costs and attorney's fees of the attorney general in enforcing the reparations fund's reimbursement, repayment, or subrogation rights are fully recoverable from the liable offender, third party, or overpaid claimant.

(O) All moneys that are collected by the state pursuant to its rights of subrogation as provided in this section or pursuant to the attorney general's authority to recover some or all of an award of reparations that is granted pursuant to this section shall be deposited in the reparations fund.

(2000 S 153, eff. 7–1–00; 1996 H 363, eff. 8–1–96; 1994 H 390, eff. 11–15–94; 1985 H 201, eff. 7–1–85; 1982 S 30; 1977 S 221; 1976 H 82)

TITLE 29
CRIMES—PROCEDURE

CHAPTER 2901

GENERAL PROVISIONS

GENERAL PROVISIONS

2901.01 Definitions

(A) As used in the Revised Code:

(1) "Force" means any violence, compulsion, or constraint physically exerted by any means upon or against a person or thing.

(2) "Deadly force" means any force that carries a substantial risk that it will proximately result in the death of any person.

(3) "Physical harm to persons" means any injury, illness, or other physiological impairment, regardless of its gravity or duration.

(4) "Physical harm to property" means any tangible or intangible damage to property that, in any degree, results in loss to its value or interferes with its use or enjoyment. "Physical harm to property" does not include wear and tear occasioned by normal use.

(5) "Serious physical harm to persons" means any of the following:

(a) Any mental illness or condition of such gravity as would normally require hospitalization or prolonged psychiatric treatment;

(b) Any physical harm that carries a substantial risk of death;

(c) Any physical harm that involves some permanent incapacity, whether partial or total, or that involves some temporary, substantial incapacity;

(d) Any physical harm that involves some permanent disfigurement or that involves some temporary, serious disfigurement;

(e) Any physical harm that involves acute pain of such duration as to result in substantial suffering or that involves any degree of prolonged or intractable pain.

(6) "Serious physical harm to property" means any physical harm to property that does either of the following:

(a) Results in substantial loss to the value of the property or requires a substantial amount of time, effort, or money to repair or replace;

(b) Temporarily prevents the use or enjoyment of the property or substantially interferes with its use or enjoyment for an extended period of time.

(7) "Risk" means a significant possibility, as contrasted with a remote possibility, that a certain result may occur or that certain circumstances may exist.

(8) "Substantial risk" means a strong possibility, as contrasted with a remote or significant possibility, that a certain result may occur or that certain circumstances may exist.

(9) "Offense of violence" means any of the following:

(a) A violation of section 2903.01, 2903.02, 2903.03, 2903.04, 2903.11, 2903.12, 2903.13, 2903.15, 2903.21, 2903.211, 2903.22, 2905.01, 2905.02, 2905.11, 2907.02, 2907.03, 2907.05, 2909.02, 2909.03, 2909.24, 2911.01, 2911.02, 2911.11, 2917.01, 2917.02, 2917.03, 2917.31, 2919.25, 2921.03, 2921.04, 2921.34, or 2923.161, of division (A)(1), (2), or (3) of section 2911.12, or of division (B)(1), (2), (3), or (4) of section 2919.22 of the Revised Code or felonious sexual penetration in violation of former section 2907.12 of the Revised Code;

(b) A violation of an existing or former municipal ordinance or law of this or any other state or the United States, substantially equivalent to any section, division, or offense listed in division (A)(9)(a) of this section;

(c) An offense, other than a traffic offense, under an existing or former municipal ordinance or law of this or any other state or the United States, committed purposely or knowingly, and involving physical harm to persons or a risk of serious physical harm to persons;

(d) A conspiracy or attempt to commit, or complicity in committing, any offense under division (A)(9)(a), (b), or (c) of this section.

(10)(a) "Property" means any property, real or personal, tangible or intangible, and any interest or license in that property. "Property" includes, but is not limited to, cable television service, other telecommunications service, telecommunications devices, information service, computers, data, computer software, financial instruments associated with computers, other documents associated with computers, or copies of the documents, whether in machine or human readable form, trade secrets, trademarks, copyrights, patents, and property protected by a trademark, copyright, or patent. "Financial instruments associated with computers" include, but are not limited to, checks, drafts, warrants, money orders, notes of indebtedness, certificates of deposit, letters of credit, bills of credit or debit cards, financial transaction authorization mechanisms, marketable securities, or any computer system representations of any of them.

(b) As used in division (A)(10) of this section, "trade secret" has the same meaning as in section 1333.61 of the Revised Code, and "telecommunications service" and "information service" have the same meanings as in section 2913.01 of the Revised Code.

(c) As used in divisions (A)(10) and (13) of this section, "cable television service," "computer," "computer software," "computer system," "computer network," "data," and "telecommunications device" have the same meanings as in section 2913.01 of the Revised Code.

(11) "Law enforcement officer" means any of the following:

(a) A sheriff, deputy sheriff, constable, police officer of a township or joint township police district, marshal, deputy marshal, municipal police officer, member of a police force employed by a metropolitan housing authority under division (D) of section 3735.31 of the Revised Code, or state highway patrol trooper;

(b) An officer, agent, or employee of the state or any of its agencies, instrumentalities, or political subdivisions, upon whom, by statute, a duty to conserve the peace or to enforce all or certain laws is imposed and the authority to arrest violators is conferred, within the limits of that statutory duty and authority;

(c) A mayor, in the mayor's capacity as chief conservator of the peace within the mayor's municipal corporation;

(d) A member of an auxiliary police force organized by county, township, or municipal law enforcement authorities, within the scope of the member's appointment or commission;

(e) A person lawfully called pursuant to section 311.07 of the Revised Code to aid a sheriff in keeping the peace, for the purposes and during the time when the person is called;

(f) A person appointed by a mayor pursuant to section 737.01 of the Revised Code as a special patrolling officer during riot or emergency, for the purposes and during the time when the person is appointed;

(g) A member of the organized militia of this state or the armed forces of the United States, lawfully called to duty to aid civil authorities in keeping the peace or protect against domestic violence;

(h) A prosecuting attorney, assistant prosecuting attorney, secret service officer, or municipal prosecutor;

(i) A veterans' home police officer appointed under section 5907.02 of the Revised Code;

(j) A member of a police force employed by a regional transit authority under division (Y) of section 306.35 of the Revised Code;

(k) A special police officer employed by a port authority under section 4582.04 or 4582.28 of the Revised Code;

(*l*) The house sergeant at arms if the house sergeant at arms has arrest authority pursuant to division (E)(1) of section 101.311 of the Revised Code and an assistant house sergeant at arms;

(m) A special police officer employed by a municipal corporation at a municipal airport, or other municipal air navigation facility, that has scheduled operations, as defined in section 119.3 of Title 14 of the Code of Federal Regulations, 14 C.F.R. 119.3, as amended, and that is required to be under a security program and is governed by aviation security rules of the transportation security administration of the United States department of transportation as provided in Parts 1542. and 1544. of Title 49 of the Code of Federal Regulations, as amended.

(12) "Privilege" means an immunity, license, or right conferred by law, bestowed by express or implied grant, arising out of status, position, office, or relationship, or growing out of necessity.

(13) "Contraband" means any property described in the following categories:

(a) Property that in and of itself is unlawful for a person to acquire or possess;

(b) Property that is not in and of itself unlawful for a person to acquire or possess, but that has been determined by a court of this state, in accordance with law, to be contraband because of its use in an unlawful activity or manner, of its nature, or of the circumstances of the person who acquires or possesses it, including, but not limited to, goods and personal property described in division (D) of section 2913.34 of the Revised Code;

(c) Property that is specifically stated to be contraband by a section of the Revised Code or by an ordinance, regulation, or resolution;

(d) Property that is forfeitable pursuant to a section of the Revised Code, or an ordinance, regulation, or resolution, including, but not limited to, forfeitable firearms, dangerous ordnance, obscene materials, and goods and personal property described in division (D) of section 2913.34 of the Revised Code;

(e) Any controlled substance, as defined in section 3719.01 of the Revised Code, or any device, paraphernalia, money as defined in section 1301.01 of the Revised Code, or other means of exchange that has been, is being, or is intended to be used in an attempt or conspiracy to violate, or in a violation of, Chapter 2925. or 3719. of the Revised Code;

(f) Any gambling device, paraphernalia, money as defined in section 1301.01 of the Revised Code, or other means of exchange that has been, is being, or is intended to be used in an attempt or conspiracy to violate, or in the violation of, Chapter 2915. of the Revised Code;

(g) Any equipment, machine, device, apparatus, vehicle, vessel, container, liquid, or substance that has been, is being, or is intended to be used in an attempt or conspiracy to violate, or in the violation of, any law of this state relating to alcohol or tobacco;

(h) Any personal property that has been, is being, or is intended to be used in an attempt or conspiracy to commit, or in the commission of, any offense or in the transportation of the fruits of any offense;

(i) Any property that is acquired through the sale or other transfer of contraband or through the proceeds of contraband, other than by a court or a law enforcement agency acting within the scope of its duties;

(j) Any computer, computer system, computer network, computer software, or other telecommunications device that is used in a conspiracy to commit, an attempt to commit, or the commission of any offense, if the owner of the computer, computer system, computer network, computer software, or other telecommunications device is convicted of or pleads guilty to the offense in which it is used;

(k) Any property that is material support or resources and that has been, is being, or is intended to be used in an attempt or conspiracy to violate, or in the violation of, section 2909.22, 2909.23, or 2909.24 of the Revised Code or of section 2921.32 of the Revised Code when the offense or act committed by the person aided or to be aided as described in that section is an act of terrorism. As used in division (A)(13)(k) of this section, "material support or resources" and "act of terrorism" have the same meanings as in section 2909.21 of the Revised Code.

(14) A person is "not guilty by reason of insanity" relative to a charge of an offense only if the person proves, in the manner specified in section 2901.05 of the Revised Code, that at the time of the commission of the offense, the person did not know, as a result of a severe mental disease or defect, the wrongfulness of the person's acts.

(B)(1)(a) Subject to division (B)(2) of this section, as used in any section contained in Title XXIX of the Revised Code that sets forth a criminal offense, "person" includes all of the following:

(i) An individual, corporation, business trust, estate, trust, partnership, and association;

(ii) An unborn human who is viable.

(b) As used in any section contained in Title XXIX of the Revised Code that does not set forth a criminal offense, "person" includes an individual, corporation, business trust, estate, trust, partnership, and association.

(c) As used in division (B)(1)(a) of this section:

(i) "Unborn human" means an individual organism of the species Homo sapiens from fertilization until live birth.

(ii) "Viable" means the stage of development of a human fetus at which there is a realistic possibility of maintaining and nourishing of a life outside the womb with or without temporary artificial life-sustaining support.

(2) Notwithstanding division (B)(1)(a) of this section, in no case shall the portion of the definition of the term "person" that is set forth in division (B)(1)(a)(ii) of this section be applied or construed in any section contained in Title XXIX of the Revised Code that sets forth a criminal offense in any of the following manners:

(a) Except as otherwise provided in division (B)(2)(a) of this section, in a manner so that the offense prohibits or is construed as prohibiting any pregnant woman or her physician from performing an abortion with the consent of the pregnant woman, with the consent of the pregnant woman implied by law in a medical emergency, or with the approval of one otherwise authorized by law to consent to medical treatment on behalf of the pregnant woman. An abortion that violates the conditions described in the immediately preceding sentence may be punished as a violation of section 2903.01, 2903.02, 2903.03, 2903.04, 2903.05, 2903.06, 2903.08, 2903.11, 2903.12, 2903.13, 2903.14, 2903.21, or 2903.22 of the Revised Code, as applicable. An abortion that does not violate the conditions described in the second immediately preceding sentence, but that does violate section 2919.12, division (B) of section 2919.13, or section 2919.151, 2919.17, or 2919.18 of the Revised Code, may be punished as a violation of section 2919.12, division (B) of section 2919.13, or section 2919.151, 2919.17, or 2919.18 of the Revised Code, as applicable. Consent is sufficient under this division if it is of the type otherwise adequate to permit medical treatment to the pregnant woman, even if it does not comply with section 2919.12 of the Revised Code.

(b) In a manner so that the offense is applied or is construed as applying to a woman based on an act or omission of the woman that occurs while she is or was pregnant and that results in any of the following:

(i) Her delivery of a stillborn baby;

(ii) Her causing, in any other manner, the death in utero of a viable, unborn human that she is carrying;

(iii) Her causing the death of her child who is born alive but who dies from one or more injuries that are sustained while the child is a viable, unborn human;

(iv) Her causing her child who is born alive to sustain one or more injuries while the child is a viable, unborn human;

(v) Her causing, threatening to cause, or attempting to cause, in any other manner, an injury, illness, or other physiological impairment, regardless of its duration or gravity, or a mental illness or condition, regardless of its duration or gravity, to a viable, unborn human that she is carrying.

(C) As used in Title XXIX of the Revised Code:

(1) "School safety zone" consists of a school, school building, school premises, school activity, and school bus.

(2) "School," "school building," and "school premises" have the same meanings as in section 2925.01 of the Revised Code.

(3) "School activity" means any activity held under the auspices of a board of education of a city, local, exempted village, joint vocational, or cooperative education school district; a governing authority of a community school established under Chap-

ter 3314. of the Revised Code; a governing board of an educational service center; or the governing body of a nonpublic school for which the state board of education prescribes minimum standards under section 3301.07 of the Revised Code.

(4) "School bus" has the same meaning as in section 4511.01 of the Revised Code.

(2002 H 675, eff. 3–14–03; 2002 H 364, eff 4–8–03; 2002 H 545, eff. 3–19–03; 2002 S 184, eff. 5–15–02; 2000 S 317, eff. 3–22–01; 2000 H 351, eff. 8–18–00; 2000 S 137, eff. 5–17–00; 1999 S 107, eff. 3–23–00; 1999 H 162, eff. 8–25–99; 1999 S 1, eff. 8–6–99; 1998 H 565, eff. 3–30–99; 1996 S 277, eff. 3–31–97; 1996 S 269, eff. 7–1–96; 1996 S 239, eff. 9–6–96; 1996 H 445, eff. 9–3–96; 1995 S 2, eff. 7–1–96; 1991 S 144, eff. 8–8–91; 1991 H 77; 1990 S 24; 1988 H 708, § 1)

2901.02 Classification of offenses

As used in the Revised Code:

(A) Offenses include aggravated murder, murder, felonies of the first, second, third, fourth, and fifth degree, misdemeanors of the first, second, third, and fourth degree, minor misdemeanors, and offenses not specifically classified.

(B) Aggravated murder when the indictment or the count in the indictment charging aggravated murder contains one or more specifications of aggravating circumstances listed in division (A) of section 2929.04 of Revised Code, and any other offense for which death may be imposed as a penalty, is a capital offense.

(C) Aggravated murder and murder are felonies.

(D) Regardless of the penalty that may be imposed, any offense specifically classified as a felony is a felony, and any offense specifically classified as a misdemeanor is a misdemeanor.

(E) Any offense not specifically classified is a felony if imprisonment for more than one year may be imposed as a penalty.

(F) Any offense not specifically classified is a misdemeanor if imprisonment for not more than one year may be imposed as a penalty.

(G) Any offense not specifically classified is a minor misdemeanor if the only penalty that may be imposed is one of the following:

(1) For an offense committed prior to the effective date of this amendment, a fine not exceeding one hundred dollars;

(2) For an offense committed on or after the effective date of this amendment, a fine not exceeding one hundred fifty dollars, community service under division (C) of section 2929.27 of the Revised Code, or a financial sanction other than a fine under section 2929.28 of the Revised Code.

(2002 H 490, eff. 1–1–04; 1995 S 2, eff. 7–1–96; 1984 H 380, eff. 4–3–84; 1982 H 269, § 4; 1982 S 199; 1972 H 511)

2901.03 Common law offenses abrogated; offense defined; contempt or sanction powers of courts or general assembly not affected

(A) No conduct constitutes a criminal offense against the state unless it is defined as an offense in the Revised Code.

(B) An offense is defined when one or more sections of the Revised Code state a positive prohibition or enjoin a specific duty, and provide a penalty for violation of such prohibition or failure to meet such duty.

(C) This section does not affect any power of the general assembly under section 8 of Article II, Ohio Constitution, nor does it affect the power of a court to punish for contempt or to employ any sanction authorized by law to enforce an order, civil judgment, or decree.

(1972 H 511, eff. 1–1–74)

2901.04 Rules of construction

(A) Except as otherwise provided in division (C) or (D) of this section, sections of the Revised Code defining offenses or penalties shall be strictly construed against the state, and liberally construed in favor of the accused.

(B) Rules of criminal procedure and sections of the Revised Code providing for criminal procedure shall be construed so as to effect the fair, impartial, speedy, and sure administration of justice.

(C) Any provision of a section of the Revised Code that refers to a previous conviction of or plea of guilty to a violation of a section of the Revised Code or of a division of a section of the Revised Code shall be construed to also refer to a previous conviction of or plea of guilty to a substantially equivalent offense under an existing or former law of this state, another state, or the United States or under an existing or former municipal ordinance.

(D) Any provision of the Revised Code that refers to a section, or to a division of a section, of the Revised Code that defines or specifies a criminal offense shall be construed to also refer to an existing or former law of this state, another state, or the United States, to an existing or former municipal ordinance, or to an existing or former division of any such existing or former law or ordinance that defines or specifies, or that defined or specified, a substantially equivalent offense.

(2004 S 146, eff. 9–23–04; 1999 S 107, eff. 3–23–00; 1972 H 511, eff. 1–1–74)

2901.05 Presumption of innocence; proof of offense; of affirmative defense; as to each; reasonable doubt

(A) Every person accused of an offense is presumed innocent until proven guilty beyond a reasonable doubt, and the burden of proof for all elements of the offense is upon the prosecution. The burden of going forward with the evidence of an affirmative defense, and the burden of proof, by a preponderance of the evidence, for an affirmative defense, is upon the accused.

(B) As part of its charge to the jury in a criminal case, the court shall read the definitions of "reasonable doubt" and "proof beyond a reasonable doubt," contained in division (D) of this section.

(C) As used in this section, an "affirmative defense" is either of the following:

(1) A defense expressly designated as affirmative;

(2) A defense involving an excuse or justification peculiarly within the knowledge of the accused, on which he can fairly be required to adduce supporting evidence.

(D) "Reasonable doubt" is present when the jurors, after they have carefully considered and compared all the evidence, cannot say they are firmly convinced of the truth of the charge. It is a doubt based on reason and common sense. Reasonable doubt is not mere possible doubt, because everything relating to human affairs or depending on moral evidence is open to some possible or imaginary doubt. "Proof beyond a reasonable doubt" is proof of such character that an ordinary person would be willing to rely and act upon it in the most important of his own affairs.

(1978 H 1168, eff. 11–1–78; 1972 H 511)

2901.06 Battered woman syndrome

(A) The general assembly hereby declares that it recognizes both of the following, in relation to the "battered woman syndrome:"

(1) That the syndrome currently is a matter of commonly accepted scientific knowledge;

(2) That the subject matter and details of the syndrome are not within the general understanding or experience of a person who is a member of the general populace and are not within the field of common knowledge.

(B) If a person is charged with an offense involving the use of force against another and the person, as a defense to the offense charged, raises the affirmative defense of self-defense, the person may introduce expert testimony of the "battered woman syndrome" and expert testimony that the person suffered from that syndrome as evidence to establish the requisite belief of an imminent danger of death or great bodily harm that is necessary, as an element of the affirmative defense, to justify the person's use of the force in question. The introduction of any expert testimony under this division shall be in accordance with the Ohio Rules of Evidence.

(1990 H 484, eff. 11–5–90)

2901.07 DNA testing of certain prisoners

Note: See also following version of this section, eff. 5–18–05.

(A) As used in this section:

(1) "DNA analysis" and "DNA specimen" have the same meanings as in section 109.573 of the Revised Code.

(2) "Jail" and "community-based correctional facility" have the same meanings as in section 2929.01 of the Revised Code.

(3) "Post-release control" has the same meaning as in section 2967.01 of the Revised Code.

(B)(1) A person who is convicted of or pleads guilty to a felony offense listed in division (D) of this section and who is sentenced to a prison term or to a community residential sanction in a jail or community-based correctional facility pursuant to section 2929.16 of the Revised Code, and a person who is convicted of or pleads guilty to a misdemeanor offense listed in division (D) of this section and who is sentenced to a term of imprisonment shall submit to a DNA specimen collection procedure administered by the director of rehabilitation and correction or the chief administrative officer of the jail or other detention facility in which the person is serving the term of imprisonment. If the person serves the prison term in a state correctional institution, the director of rehabilitation and correction shall cause the DNA specimen to be collected from the person during the intake process at the reception facility designated by the director. If the person serves the community residential sanction or term of imprisonment in a jail, a community-based correctional facility, or another county, multicounty, municipal, municipal-county, or multicounty-municipal detention facility, the chief administrative officer of the jail, community-based correctional facility, or detention facility shall cause the DNA specimen to be collected from the person during the intake process at the jail, community-based correctional facility, or detention facility. In accordance with division (C) of this section, the director or the chief administrative officer shall cause the DNA specimen to be forwarded to the bureau of criminal identification and investigation no later than fifteen days after the date of the collection of the DNA specimen. The DNA specimen shall be collected in accordance with division (C) of this section.

(2) If a person is convicted of or pleads guilty to an offense listed in division (D) of this section, is serving a prison term, community residential sanction, or term of imprisonment for that offense, and does not provide a DNA specimen pursuant to division (B)(1) of this section, prior to the person's release from the prison term, community residential sanction, or imprisonment, the person shall submit to, and the director of rehabilitation and correction or the chief administrative officer of the jail, community-based correctional facility, or detention facility in which the person is serving the prison term, community residential sanction, or term of imprisonment shall administer, a DNA specimen collection procedure at the state correctional institution, jail, community-based correctional facility, or detention facility in which the person is serving the prison term, community residential sanction, or term of imprisonment. In accordance with division (C) of this section, the director or the chief administrative officer shall cause the DNA specimen to be forwarded to the bureau of criminal identification and investigation no later than fifteen days after the date of the collection of the DNA specimen. The DNA specimen shall be collected in accordance with division (C) of this section.

(3) If a person sentenced to a term of imprisonment or serving a prison term or community residential sanction for committing an offense listed in division (D) of this section is on probation, is released on parole, under transitional control, or on another type of release, or is on post-release control, if the person is under the supervision of a probation department or the adult parole authority, if the person is sent to jail or is returned to a jail, community-based correctional facility, or state correctional institution for a violation of the terms and conditions of the probation, parole, transitional control, other release, or post-release control, if the person was or will be serving a term of imprisonment, prison term, or community residential sanction for committing an offense listed in division (D) of this section, and if the person did not provide a DNA specimen pursuant to division (B)(1) or (2) of this section, the person shall submit to, and the director of rehabilitation and correction or the chief administrative officer of the jail or community-based correctional facility shall administer, a DNA specimen collection procedure at the jail, community-based correctional facility, or state correctional institution in which the person is serving the term of imprisonment, prison term, or community residential sanction. In accordance with division (C) of this section, the director or the chief administrative officer shall cause the DNA specimen to be forwarded to the bureau of criminal identification and investigation no later than fifteen days after the date of the collection of the DNA specimen. The DNA specimen shall be collected from the person in accordance with division (C) of this section.

(C) If the DNA specimen is collected by withdrawing blood from the person or a similarly invasive procedure, a physician, registered nurse, licensed practical nurse, duly licensed clinical laboratory technician, or other qualified medical practitioner shall collect in a medically approved manner the DNA specimen required to be collected pursuant to division (B) of this section. If the DNA specimen is collected by swabbing for buccal cells or a similarly noninvasive procedure, this section does not require that the DNA specimen be collected by a qualified medical practitioner of that nature. No later than fifteen days after the date of the collection of the DNA specimen, the director of rehabilitation and correction or the chief administrative officer of the jail, community-based correctional facility, or other county, multicounty, municipal, municipal-county, or multicounty-municipal detention facility, in which the person is serving the prison term, community residential sanction, or term of imprisonment shall cause the DNA specimen to be forwarded to the bureau of criminal identification and investigation in accordance with procedures established by the superintendent of the bureau under division (H) of section 109.573 of the Revised Code. The bureau shall provide the specimen vials, mailing tubes, labels, postage, and instructions needed for the collection and forwarding of the DNA specimen to the bureau.

(D) The director of rehabilitation and correction and the chief administrative officer of the jail, community-based correctional facility, or other county, multicounty, municipal, municipal-county, or multicounty-municipal detention facility shall cause a DNA specimen to be collected in accordance with divisions (B) and (C) of this section from a person in its custody who is convicted of or pleads guilty to any of the following offenses:

(1) A violation of section 2903.01, 2903.02, 2903.11, 2905.01, 2907.02, 2907.03, 2907.04, 2907.05, 2911.01, 2911.02, 2911.11, or 2911.12 of the Revised Code;

(2) A violation of section 2907.12 of the Revised Code as it existed prior to September 3, 1996;

(3) An attempt to commit a violation of section 2903.01, 2903.02, 2907.02, 2907.03, 2907.04, or 2907.05 of the Revised Code or to commit a violation of section 2907.12 of the Revised Code as it existed prior to September 3, 1996;

(4) A violation of any law that arose out of the same facts and circumstances and same act as did a charge against the person of a violation of section 2903.01, 2903.02, 2905.01, 2907.02, 2907.03, 2907.04, 2907.05, or 2911.11 of the Revised Code that previously was dismissed or amended or as did a charge against the person of a violation of section 2907.12 of the Revised Code as it existed prior to September 3, 1996, that previously was dismissed or amended;

(5) A violation of section 2905.02 or 2919.23 of the Revised Code that would have been a violation of section 2905.04 of the Revised Code as it existed prior to July 1, 1996, had it been committed prior to that date;

(6) A sexually oriented offense or a child-victim oriented offense, both as defined in section 2950.01 of the Revised Code, if, in relation to that offense, the offender has been adjudicated a sexual predator or a child-victim predator, both as defined in section 2950. 01 of the Revised Code;

(7) A felony violation of any law that arose out of the same facts and circumstances and same act as did a charge against the person of a violation of section 2903.11, 2911.01, 2911.02, or 2911.12 of the Revised Code that previously was dismissed or amended;

(8) A conspiracy to commit a violation of section 2903.01, 2903.02, 2905.01, 2911.01, 2911.02, 2911.11, or 2911.12 of the Revised Code;

(9) Complicity in committing a violation of section 2903.01, 2903.02, 2903.11, 2905.01, 2907.02, 2907.03, 2907.04, 2907.05, 2911.01, 2911.02, 2911. 11, or 2911.12 of the Revised Code or a violation of section 2907.12 of the Revised Code as it existed prior to September 3, 1996.

(E) The director of rehabilitation and correction or a chief administrative officer of a jail, community-based correctional facility, or other detention facility described in division (B) of this section in relation to the following offenses is not required to comply with this section until the superintendent of the bureau of criminal identification and investigation gives agencies in the criminal justice system, as defined in section 181.51 of the Revised Code, in the state official notification that the state DNA laboratory is prepared to accept DNA specimens of that nature:

(1) A violation of section 2903.11, 2911.01, 2911.02, or 2911.12 of the Revised Code;

(2) An attempt to commit a violation of section 2903.01 or 2903.02 of the Revised Code;

(3) A felony violation of any law that arose out of the same facts and circumstances and same act as did a charge against the person of a violation of section 2903.11, 2911.01, 2911.02, or 2911.12 of the Revised Code that previously was dismissed or amended;

(4) A conspiracy to commit a violation of section 2903.01, 2903.02, 2905.01, 2911.01, 2911.02, 2911.11, or 2911.12 of the Revised Code;

(5) Complicity in committing a violation of section 2903.01, 2903.02, 2903.11, 2905.01, 2907.02, 2907.03, 2907.04, 2907.05, 2911.01, 2911.02, 2911. 11, or 2911.12 of the Revised Code or a violation of section 2907.12 of the Revised Code as it existed prior to September 3, 1996.

(2003 S 5, eff. 7–31–03; 2002 H 427, eff. 8–29–02; 1998 H 526, eff. 9–1–98; 1997 S 111, eff. 3–17–98; 1996 H 124, eff. 3–31–97; 1996 H 180, eff. 1–1–97; 1996 S 269, eff. 7–1–96; 1995 H 5, eff. 8–30–95)

Note: See also following version of this section, eff. 5–18–05.

2901.07 DNA testing of certain prisoners (later effective date)

Note: See also preceding version of this section, in effect until 5–18–05.

(A) As used in this section:

(1) "DNA analysis" and "DNA specimen" have the same meanings as in section 109.573 of the Revised Code.

(2) "Jail" and "community-based correctional facility" have the same meanings as in section 2929.01 of the Revised Code.

(3) "Post–release control" has the same meaning as in section 2967.01 of the Revised Code.

(B)(1) A person who is convicted of or pleads guilty to a felony offense and who is sentenced to a prison term or to a community residential sanction in a jail or community-based correctional facility pursuant to section 2929.16 of the Revised Code, and a person who is convicted of or pleads guilty to a misdemeanor offense listed in division (D) of this section and who is sentenced to a term of imprisonment shall submit to a DNA specimen collection procedure administered by the director of rehabilitation and correction or the chief administrative officer of the jail or other detention facility in which the person is serving the term of imprisonment. If the person serves the prison term in a state correctional institution, the director of rehabilitation and correction shall cause the DNA specimen to be collected from the person during the intake process at the reception facility designated by the director. If the person serves the community residential sanction or term of imprisonment in a jail, a community-based correctional facility, or another county, multicounty, municipal, municipal-county, or multicounty-municipal detention facility, the chief administrative officer of the jail, community-based correctional facility, or detention facility shall cause the DNA specimen to be collected from the person during the intake process at the jail, community-based correctional facility, or detention facility. The DNA specimen shall be collected in accordance with division (C) of this section.

(2) If a person is convicted of or pleads guilty to a felony offense or a misdemeanor offense listed in division (D) of this section, is serving a prison term, community residential sanction, or term of imprisonment for that offense, and does not provide a DNA specimen pursuant to division (B)(1) of this section, prior to the person's release from the prison term, community residential sanction, or imprisonment, the person shall submit to, and the director of rehabilitation and correction or the chief administrative officer of the jail, community-based correctional facility, or detention facility in which the person is serving the prison term, community residential sanction, or term of imprisonment shall administer, a DNA specimen collection procedure at the state correctional institution, jail, community-based correctional facility, or detention facility in which the person is serving the prison term, community residential sanction, or term of imprisonment. The DNA specimen shall be collected in accordance with division (C) of this section.

(3)(a) If a person is convicted of or pleads guilty to a felony offense or a misdemeanor offense listed in division (D) of this section and the person is on probation, released on parole, under transitional control, on community control, on post-release control, or under any other type of supervised release under the supervision of a probation department or the adult parole authority, the person shall submit to a DNA specimen collection procedure administered by the chief administrative officer of the probation department or the adult parole authority. The DNA specimen shall be collected in accordance with division (C) of this section. If the person refuses to submit to a DNA specimen collection procedure as provided in this division, the person may be subject to the provisions of section 2967.15 of the Revised Code.

(b) If the person is sent to jail or is returned to a jail, community-based correctional facility, or state correctional institution for a violation of the terms and conditions of the probation, parole, transitional control, other release, or post-release control, if the person was or will be serving a term of imprisonment, prison term, or community residential sanction for committing a felony offense or for committing a misdemeanor offense listed in division (D) of this section, and if the person did not provide a DNA specimen pursuant to division (B)(1), (2) or (3)(a) of this section, the person shall submit to, and the director of rehabilitation and correction or the chief administrative officer of the jail or community-based correctional facility shall administer, a DNA specimen collection procedure at the jail, community-based correctional facility, or state correctional institution in which the person is serving the term of imprisonment, prison term, or community residential sanction. The DNA specimen shall be collected from the person in accordance with division (C) of this section.

(4) If a person is convicted of or pleads guilty to a felony offense or a misdemeanor offense listed in division (D) of this section, the person is not sentenced to a prison term, a community residential sanction in a jail or community-based correctional facility, a term of imprisonment, or any type of supervised release under the supervision of a probation department or the adult parole authority, and the person does not provide a DNA specimen pursuant to division (B)(1), (2), (3)(a), or (3)(b) of this section, the sentencing court shall order the person to report to the county probation department immediately after sentencing to submit to a DNA specimen collection procedure administered by the chief administrative officer of the county probation office. If the person is incarcerated at the time of sentencing, the person shall submit to a DNA specimen collection procedure administered by the director of rehabilitation and correction or the chief administrative officer of the jail or other detention facility in which the person is incarcerated. The DNA specimen shall be collected in accordance with division (C) of this section.

(C) If the DNA specimen is collected by withdrawing blood from the person or a similarly invasive procedure, a physician, registered nurse, licensed practical nurse, duly licensed clinical laboratory technician, or other qualified medical practitioner shall collect in a medically approved manner the DNA specimen required to be collected pursuant to division (B) of this section. If the DNA specimen is collected by swabbing for buccal cells or a similarly noninvasive procedure, this section does not require that the DNA specimen be collected by a qualified medical practitioner of that nature. No later than fifteen days after the date of the collection of the DNA specimen, the director of rehabilitation and correction or the chief administrative officer of the jail, community-based correctional facility, or other county, multicounty, municipal, municipal-county, or multicounty-municipal detention facility, in which the person is serving the prison term, community residential sanction, or term of imprisonment shall cause the DNA specimen to be forwarded to the bureau of criminal identification and investigation in accordance with procedures established by the superintendent of the bureau under division (H) of section 109.573 of the Revised Code. The bureau shall provide the specimen vials, mailing tubes, labels, postage, and instructions needed for the collection and forwarding of the DNA specimen to the bureau.

(D) The director of rehabilitation and correction, the chief administrative officer of the jail, community-based correctional facility, or other county, multicounty, municipal, municipal-county, or multicounty-municipal detention facility, or the chief administrative officer of a county probation department or the adult parole authority shall cause a DNA specimen to be collected in accordance with divisions (B) and (C) of this section from a person in its custody or under its supervision who is convicted of or pleads guilty to any felony offense or to any of the following misdemeanor offenses:

(1) A misdemeanor violation, an attempt to commit a misdemeanor violation, or complicity in committing a misdemeanor violation of section 2907.04 of the Revised Code;

(2) A misdemeanor violation of any law that arose out of the same facts and circumstances and same act as did a charge against the person of a violation of section 2903.01, 2903.02, 2905.01, 2907.02, 2907.03, 2907.04, 2907.05, or 2911.11 of the Revised Code that previously was dismissed or amended or as did a charge against the person of a violation of section 2907. 12 of the Revised Code as it existed prior to September 3, 1996, that previously was dismissed or amended;

(3) A misdemeanor violation of section 2919.23 of the Revised Code that would have been a violation of section 2905. 04 of the Revised Code as it existed prior to July 1, 1996, had it been committed prior to that date;

(4) A sexually oriented offense or a child-victim oriented offense, both as defined in section 2950.01 of the Revised Code, that is a misdemeanor, if, in relation to that offense, the offender has been adjudicated a sexual predator, child-victim predator, habitual sex offender, or habitual child-victim offender, all as defined in section 2950.01 of the Revised Code.

(E) The director of rehabilitation and correction may prescribe rules in accordance with Chapter 119. of the Revised Code to collect a DNA specimen, as provided in this section, from an offender whose supervision is transferred from another state to this state in accordance with the interstate compact for adult offender supervision described in section 5149.21 of the Revised Code.

(2004 H 525, eff. 5–18–05; 2003 S 5, eff. 7–31–03; 2002 H 427, eff. 8–29–02; 1998 H 526, eff. 9–1–98; 1997 S 111, eff. 3–17–98; 1996 H 124, eff. 3–31–97; 1996 H 180, eff. 1–1–97; 1996 S 269, eff. 7–1–96; 1995 H 5, eff. 8–30–95)

Note: See also preceding version of this section, in effect until 5–18–05.

2901.08 Delinquency adjudications deemed convictions

If a person is alleged to have committed an offense and if the person previously has been adjudicated a delinquent child or juvenile traffic offender for a violation of a law or ordinance, the adjudication as a delinquent child or as a juvenile traffic offender is a conviction for a violation of the law or ordinance for purposes of determining the offense with which the person should be charged and, if the person is convicted of or pleads guilty to an offense, the sentence to be imposed upon the person relative to the conviction or guilty plea.

(1995 H 1, eff. 1–1–96)

JURISDICTION, VENUE, AND LIMITATIONS OF PROSECUTIONS

2901.11 Criminal law jurisdiction

(A) A person is subject to criminal prosecution and punishment in this state if any of the following occur:

(1) The person commits an offense under the laws of this state, any element of which takes place in this state.

(2) While in this state, the person conspires or attempts to commit, or is guilty of complicity in the commission of, an offense in another jurisdiction, which offense is an offense under both the laws of this state and the other jurisdiction.

(3) While out of this state, the person conspires or attempts to commit, or is guilty of complicity in the commission of, an offense in this state.

(4) While out of this state, the person omits to perform a legal duty imposed by the laws of this state, which omission affects a legitimate interest of the state in protecting, governing, or regulating any person, property, thing, transaction, or activity in this state.

(5) While out of this state, the person unlawfully takes or retains property and subsequently brings any of the unlawfully taken or retained property into this state.

(6) While out of this state, the person unlawfully takes or entices another and subsequently brings the other person into this state.

(7) The person, by means of a computer, computer system, computer network, telecommunication, telecommunications device, telecommunications service, or information service, causes or knowingly permits any writing, data, image, or other telecommunication to be disseminated or transmitted into this state in violation of the law of this state.

(B) In homicide, the element referred to in division (A)(1) of this section is either the act that causes death, or the physical contact that causes death, or the death itself. If any part of the body of a homicide victim is found in this state, the death is presumed to have occurred within this state.

(C)(1) This state includes the land and water within its boundaries and the air space above that land and water, with respect to which this state has either exclusive or concurrent legislative jurisdiction. Where the boundary between this state and another state or foreign country is disputed, the disputed territory is conclusively presumed to be within this state for purposes of this section.

(2) The courts of common pleas of Adams, Athens, Belmont, Brown, Clermont, Columbiana, Gallia, Hamilton, Jefferson, Lawrence, Meigs, Monroe, Scioto, and Washington counties have jurisdiction beyond the north or northwest shore of the Ohio river extending to the opposite shore line, between the extended boundary lines of any adjacent counties or adjacent state. Each of those courts of common pleas has concurrent jurisdiction on the Ohio river with any adjacent court of common pleas that borders on that river and with any court of Kentucky or of West Virginia that borders on the Ohio river and that has jurisdiction on the Ohio river under the law of Kentucky or the law of West Virginia, whichever is applicable, or under federal law.

(D) When an offense is committed under the laws of this state, and it appears beyond a reasonable doubt that the offense or any element of the offense took place either in this state or in another jurisdiction or jurisdictions, but it cannot reasonably be determined in which it took place, the offense or element is conclusively presumed to have taken place in this state for purposes of this section.

(E) As used in this section, "computer," "computer system," "computer network," "information service," "telecommunication," "telecommunications device," "telecommunications service," "data," and "writing" have the same meanings as in section 2913.01 of the Revised Code.

(1998 H 565, eff. 3–30–99; 1992 S 371, eff. 1–17–93; 1972 H 511)

2901.12 Venue

(A) The trial of a criminal case in this state shall be held in a court having jurisdiction of the subject matter, and in the territory of which the offense or any element of the offense was committed.

(B) When the offense or any element of the offense was committed in an aircraft, motor vehicle, train, watercraft, or other vehicle, in transit, and it cannot reasonably be determined in which jurisdiction the offense was committed, the offender may be tried in any jurisdiction through which the aircraft, motor vehicle, train, watercraft, or other vehicle passed.

(C) When the offense involved the unlawful taking or receiving of property or the unlawful taking or enticing of another, the offender may be tried in any jurisdiction from which or into which the property or victim was taken, received, or enticed.

(D) When the offense is conspiracy, attempt, or complicity cognizable under division (A)(2) of section 2901.11 of the Revised Code, the offender may be tried in any jurisdiction in which the conspiracy, attempt, complicity, or any of its elements occurred.

(E) When the offense is conspiracy or attempt cognizable under division (A)(3) of section 2901.11 of the Revised Code, the offender may be tried in any jurisdiction in which the offense that was the object of the conspiracy or attempt, or any element of that offense, was intended to or could have taken place. When the offense is complicity cognizable under division (A)(3) of section 2901.11 of the Revised Code, the offender may be tried in any jurisdiction in which the principal offender may be tried.

(F) When an offense is considered to have been committed in this state while the offender was out of this state, and the jurisdiction in this state in which the offense or any material element of the offense was committed is not reasonably ascertainable, the offender may be tried in any jurisdiction in which the offense or element reasonably could have been committed.

(G) When it appears beyond a reasonable doubt that an offense or any element of an offense was committed in any of two or more jurisdictions, but it cannot reasonably be determined in which jurisdiction the offense or element was committed, the offender may be tried in any of those jurisdictions.

(H) When an offender, as part of a course of criminal conduct, commits offenses in different jurisdictions, the offender may be tried for all of those offenses in any jurisdiction in which one of those offenses or any element of one of those offenses occurred. Without limitation on the evidence that may be used to establish the course of criminal conduct, any of the following is prima-facie evidence of a course of criminal conduct:

(1) The offenses involved the same victim, or victims of the same type or from the same group.

(2) The offenses were committed by the offender in the offender's same employment, or capacity, or relationship to another.

(3) The offenses were committed as part of the same transaction or chain of events, or in furtherance of the same purpose or objective.

(4) The offenses were committed in furtherance of the same conspiracy.

(5) The offenses involved the same or a similar modus operandi.

(6) The offenses were committed along the offender's line of travel in this state, regardless of the offender's point of origin or destination.

(I)(1) When the offense involves a computer, computer system, computer network, telecommunication, telecommunications device, telecommunications service, or information service, the offender may be tried in any jurisdiction containing any location of the computer, computer system, or computer network of the victim of the offense, in any jurisdiction from which or into which, as part of the offense, any writing, data, or image is disseminated or transmitted by means of a computer, computer system, computer network, telecommunication, telecommunications device, telecommunications service, or information service, or in any jurisdiction in which the alleged offender commits any activity that is an essential part of the offense.

(2) As used in this section, "computer," "computer system," "computer network," "information service," "telecommunication," "telecommunications device," "telecommunications service," "data," and "writing" have the same meanings as in section 2913.01 of the Revised Code.

(J) When the offense involves the death of a person, and it cannot reasonably be determined in which jurisdiction the offense was committed, the offender may be tried in the jurisdiction in which the dead person's body or any part of the dead person's body was found.

(K) Notwithstanding any other requirement for the place of trial, venue may be changed, upon motion of the prosecution, the defense, or the court, to any court having jurisdiction of the subject matter outside the county in which trial otherwise would be held, when it appears that a fair and impartial trial cannot be held in the jurisdiction in which trial otherwise would be held, or when it appears that trial should be held in another jurisdiction for the convenience of the parties and in the interests of justice.

(1998 H 565, eff. 3–30–99; 1989 S 64, eff. 10–26–89; 1986 H 49; 1972 H 511)

2901.13 Limitation of criminal prosecutions

(A)(1) Except as provided in division (A)(2) or (3) of this section or as otherwise provided in this section, a prosecution shall be barred unless it is commenced within the following periods after an offense is committed:

(a) For a felony, six years;

(b) For a misdemeanor other than a minor misdemeanor, two years;

(c) For a minor misdemeanor, six months.

(2) There is no period of limitation for the prosecution of a violation of section 2903.01 or 2903.02 of the Revised Code.

(3) Except as otherwise provided in divisions (B) to (H) of this section, a prosecution of any of the following offenses shall be barred unless it is commenced within twenty years after the offense is committed:

(a) A violation of section 2903.03, 2903.04, 2905.01, 2907.02, 2907.03, 2907.04, 2907.05, 2907.21, 2909.02, 2911.01, 2911.02, 2911.11, 2911.12, or 2917.02 of the Revised Code, a violation of section 2903.11 or 2903.12 of the Revised Code if the victim is a peace officer, a violation of section 2903.13 of the Revised Code that is a felony, or a violation of former section 2907.12 of the Revised Code;

(b) A conspiracy to commit, attempt to commit, or complicity in committing a violation set forth in division (A)(3)(a) of this section.

(B) If the period of limitation provided in division (A)(1) or (3) of this section has expired, prosecution shall be commenced for an offense of which an element is fraud or breach of a fiduciary duty, within one year after discovery of the offense either by an aggrieved person, or by the aggrieved person's legal representative who is not a party to the offense.

(C) If the period of limitation provided in division (A)(1) or (3) of this section has expired, prosecution shall be commenced for an offense involving misconduct in office by a public servant as defined in section 2921.01 of the Revised Code, at any time while the accused remains a public servant, or within two years thereafter.

(D) An offense is committed when every element of the offense occurs. In the case of an offense of which an element is a continuing course of conduct, the period of limitation does not begin to run until such course of conduct or the accused's accountability for it terminates, whichever occurs first.

(E) A prosecution is commenced on the date an indictment is returned or an information filed, or on the date a lawful arrest without a warrant is made, or on the date a warrant, summons, citation, or other process is issued, whichever occurs first. A prosecution is not commenced by the return of an indictment or the filing of an information unless reasonable diligence is exercised to issue and execute process on the same. A prosecution is not commenced upon issuance of a warrant, summons, citation, or other process, unless reasonable diligence is exercised to execute the same.

(F) The period of limitation shall not run during any time when the corpus delicti remains undiscovered.

(G) The period of limitation shall not run during any time when the accused purposely avoids prosecution. Proof that the accused departed this state or concealed the accused's identity or whereabouts is prima-facie evidence of the accused's purpose to avoid prosecution.

(H) The period of limitation shall not run during any time a prosecution against the accused based on the same conduct is pending in this state, even though the indictment, information, or process which commenced the prosecution is quashed or the proceedings thereon are set aside or reversed on appeal.

(I) As used in this section, "peace officer" has the same meaning as in section 2935.01 of the Revised Code.

(1998 H 49, eff. 3–9–99; 1972 H 511, eff. 1–1–74)

CRIMINAL LIABILITY

2901.21 Requirements for criminal liability; voluntary intoxication

(A) Except as provided in division (B) of this section, a person is not guilty of an offense unless both of the following apply:

(1) The person's liability is based on conduct that includes either a voluntary act, or an omission to perform an act or duty that the person is capable of performing;

(2) The person has the requisite degree of culpability for each element as to which a culpable mental state is specified by the section defining the offense.

(B) When the section defining an offense does not specify any degree of culpability, and plainly indicates a purpose to impose strict criminal liability for the conduct described in the section, then culpability is not required for a person to be guilty of the offense. When the section neither specifies culpability nor plainly indicates a purpose to impose strict liability, recklessness is sufficient culpability to commit the offense.

(C) Voluntary intoxication may not be taken into consideration in determining the existence of a mental state that is an element of a criminal offense. Voluntary intoxication does not relieve a person of a duty to act if failure to act constitutes a criminal offense. evidence that a person was voluntarily intoxicated may be admissible to show whether or not the person was physically capable of performing the act with which the person is charged.

(D) As used in this section:

(1) Possession is a voluntary act if the possessor knowingly procured or received the thing possessed, or was aware of the possessor's control of the thing possessed for a sufficient time to have ended possession.

(2) Reflexes, convulsions, body movements during unconsciousness or sleep, and body movements that are not otherwise a product of the actor's volition, are involuntary acts.

(3) "Culpability" means purpose, knowledge, recklessness, or negligence, as defined in section 2901.22 of the Revised Code.

(4) "Intoxication" includes, but is not limited to, intoxication resulting from the ingestion of alcohol, a drug, or alcohol and a drug.

(2000 H 318, eff. 10–27–00; 1972 H 511, eff. 1–1–74)

2901.22 Culpable mental states

(A) A person acts purposely when it is his specific intention to cause a certain result, or, when the gist of the offense is a prohibition against conduct of a certain nature, regardless of what the offender intends to accomplish thereby, it is his specific intention to engage in conduct of that nature.

(B) A person acts knowingly, regardless of his purpose, when he is aware that his conduct will probably cause a certain result or will probably be of a certain nature. A person has knowledge of circumstances when he is aware that such circumstances probably exist.

(C) A person acts recklessly when, with heedless indifference to the consequences, he perversely disregards a known risk that his conduct is likely to cause a certain result or is likely to be of a certain nature. A person is reckless with respect to circumstances when, with heedless indifference to the consequences, he perversely disregards a known risk that such circumstances are likely to exist.

(D) A person acts negligently when, because of a substantial lapse from due care, he fails to perceive or avoid a risk that his conduct may cause a certain result or may be of a certain nature. A person is negligent with respect to circumstances when, because of a substantial lapse from due care, he fails to perceive or avoid a risk that such circumstances may exist.

(E) When the section defining an offense provides that negligence suffices to establish an element thereof, then recklessness, knowledge, or purpose is also sufficient culpability for such element. When recklessness suffices to establish an element of an offense, then knowledge or purpose is also sufficient culpability for such element. When knowledge suffices to establish an element of an offense, then purpose is also sufficient culpability for such element.

(1972 H 511, eff. 1–1–74)

2901.23 Organizational criminal liability

(A) An organization may be convicted of an offense under any of the following circumstances:

(1) The offense is a minor misdemeanor committed by an officer, agent, or employee of the organization acting in its behalf and within the scope of his office or employment, except that if the section defining the offense designates the officers, agents, or employees for whose conduct the organization is accountable or the circumstances under which it is accountable, such provisions shall apply.

(2) A purpose to impose organizational liability plainly appears in the section defining the offense, and the offense is committed by an officer, agent, or employee of the organization acting in its behalf and within the scope of his office or employment, except that if the section defining the offense designates the officers, agents, or employees for whose conduct the organization is accountable or the circumstances under which it is accountable, such provisions shall apply.

(3) The offense consists of an omission to discharge a specific duty imposed by law on the organization.

(4) If, acting with the kind of culpability otherwise required for the commission of the offense, its commission was authorized, requested, commanded, tolerated, or performed by the board of directors, trustees, partners, or by a high managerial officer, agent, or employee acting in behalf of the organization and within the scope of his office or employment.

(B) When strict liability is imposed for the commission of an offense, a purpose to impose organizational liability shall be presumed, unless the contrary plainly appears.

(C) In a prosecution of an organization for an offense other than one for which strict liability is imposed, it is a defense that the high managerial officer, agent, or employee having supervisory responsibility over the subject matter of the offense exercised due diligence to prevent its commission. This defense is not available if it plainly appears inconsistent with the purpose of the section defining the offense.

(D) As used in this section, "organization" means a corporation for profit or not for profit, partnership, limited partnership, joint venture, unincorporated association, estate, trust, or other commercial or legal entity. "Organization" does not include an entity organized as or by a governmental agency for the execution of a governmental program.

(1972 H 511, eff. 1–1–74)

2901.24 Personal accountability for organizational conduct

(A) An officer, agent, or employee of an organization as defined in section 2901.23 of the Revised Code may be prosecuted for an offense committed by such organization, if he acts with the kind of culpability required for the commission of the offense, and any of the following apply:

(1) In the name of the organization or in its behalf, he engages in conduct constituting the offense, or causes another to engage in such conduct, or tolerates such conduct when it is of a type for which he has direct responsibility;

(2) He has primary responsibility to discharge a duty imposed on the organization by law, and such duty is not discharged.

(B) When a person is convicted of an offense by reason of this section, he is subject to the same penalty as if he had acted in his own behalf.

(1972 H 511, eff. 1–1–74)

MISSING CHILDREN

2901.30 Police handling of missing child case

(A) As used in sections 2901.30 to 2901.32 of the Revised Code:

(1) "Information" means information that can be integrated into the computer system and that relates to the physical or mental description of a minor including, but not limited to, height, weight, color of hair and eyes, use of eyeglasses or contact lenses, skin coloring, physical or mental handicaps, special medical conditions or needs, abnormalities, problems, scars and marks, and distinguishing characteristics, and other information that could assist in identifying a minor including, but not limited to, full name and nickname, date and place of birth, age, names and addresses of parents and other relatives, fingerprints, dental records, photographs, social security number, driver's license number, credit card numbers, bank account numbers, and clothing.

(2) "Minor" means a person under eighteen years of age.

(3) "Missing children" or "missing child" means either of the following:

(a) A minor who has run away from or who otherwise is missing from the home of, or the care, custody, and control of, the minor's parents, parent who is the residential parent and legal custodian, guardian, legal custodian, or other person having responsibility for the care of the minor;

(b) A minor who is missing and about whom there is reason to believe the minor could be the victim of a violation of section 2905.01, 2905.02, 2905.03, or 2919.23 of the Revised Code or of a violation of section 2905.04 of the Revised Code as it existed prior to the effective date of this amendment.

(B) When a law enforcement agency in this state that has jurisdiction in the matter is informed that a minor is or may be a missing child and that the person providing the information wishes to file a missing child report, the law enforcement agency shall take that report. Upon taking the report, the law enforcement agency shall take prompt action upon it, including, but not limited to, concerted efforts to locate the missing child. No law enforcement agency in this state shall have a rule or policy that prohibits or discourages the filing of or the taking of action upon a missing child report, within a specified period following the discovery or formulation of a belief that a minor is or could be a missing child.

(C) If a missing child report is made to a law enforcement agency in this state that has jurisdiction in the matter, the law enforcement agency shall gather readily available information about the missing child and integrate it into the national crime information center computer within twelve hours following the making of the report. The law enforcement agency shall make reasonable efforts to acquire additional information about the missing child following the transmittal of the initially available information, and promptly integrate any additional information acquired into such computer systems.

Whenever a law enforcement agency integrates information about a missing child into the national crime information center computer, the law enforcement agency promptly shall notify the missing child's parents, parent who is the residential parent and legal custodian, guardian, or legal custodian, or any other person responsible for the care of the missing child, that it has so integrated the information.

The parents, parent who is the residential parent and legal custodian, guardian, legal custodian, or other person responsible for the care of the missing child shall provide available information upon request, and may provide information voluntarily, to the law enforcement agency during the information gathering process. The law enforcement agency also may obtain available information about the missing child from other persons, subject to constitutional and statutory limitations.

(D) Upon the filing of a missing child report, the law enforcement agency involved promptly shall make a reasonable attempt to notify other law enforcement agencies within its county and, if the agency has jurisdiction in a municipal corporation or township that borders another county, to notify the law enforcement agency for the municipal corporation or township in the other county with which it shares the border, that it has taken a missing child report and may be requesting assistance or cooperation in the case, and provide relevant information to the other law enforcement agencies. The agency may notify additional law enforcement agencies, appropriate public children services agencies, about the case, request their assistance or cooperation in the case, and provide them with relevant information.

Upon request from a law enforcement agency, a public children services agency shall grant the law enforcement agency access to all information concerning a missing child that the agency possesses that may be relevant to the law enforcement agency in investigating a missing child report concerning that child. The information obtained by the law enforcement agency shall be used only to further the investigation to locate the missing child.

(E) Upon request, law enforcement agencies in this state shall provide assistance to, and cooperate with, other law enforcement agencies in their investigation of missing child cases.

The information in any missing child report made to a law enforcement agency shall be made available, upon request, to law enforcement personnel of this state, other states, and the federal government when the law enforcement personnel indicate that the request is to aid in identifying or locating a missing child or the possible identification of a deceased minor who, upon discovery, cannot be identified.

(F) When a missing child has not been located within thirty days after the date on which the missing child report pertaining to the child was filed with a law enforcement agency, that law enforcement agency shall request the missing child's parents, parent who is the residential parent and legal custodian, guardian, or legal custodian, or any other person responsible for the care of the missing child, to provide written consent for the law enforcement agency to contact the missing child's dentist and request the missing child's dental records. Upon receipt of such written consent, the dentist shall release a copy of the missing child's dental records to the law enforcement agency and shall provide and encode the records in such form as requested by the law enforcement agency. The law enforcement agency then shall integrate information in the records into the national crime information center computer in order to compare the records to those of unidentified deceased persons. This division does not prevent a law enforcement agency from seeking consent to obtain copies of a missing child's dental records, or prevent a missing child's parents, parent who is the residential parent and legal custodian, guardian, or legal custodian, or any other person responsible for the care of the missing child, from granting consent for the release of copies of the missing child's dental records to a law enforcement agency, at any time.

(G) A missing child's parents, parent who is the residential parent and legal custodian, guardian, or legal custodian, or any other persons responsible for the care of a missing child, immediately shall notify the law enforcement agency with which they filed the missing child report whenever the child has returned to their home or to their care, custody, and control, has been released if the missing child was the victim of an offense listed in division (A)(3)(b) of this section, or otherwise has been located. Upon such notification or upon otherwise learning that a missing child has returned to the home of, or to the care, custody, and control of the missing child's parents, parent who is the residential parent and legal custodian, guardian, legal custodian, or other person responsible for the missing child's care, has been released if the missing child was the victim of an offense listed in division (A)(3)(b) of this section, or otherwise has been located, the law enforcement agency involved promptly shall integrate the fact that the minor no longer is a missing child into the national crime information center computer.

(H) Nothing contained in this section shall be construed to impair the confidentiality of services provided to runaway minors by shelters for runaway minors pursuant to sections 5119.64 to 5119.68 of the Revised Code.

(1997 H 408, eff. 10–1–97; 1995 S 2, eff. 7–1–96; 1990 S 3, eff. 4–11–91; 1984 S 321)

2901.31 Cooperation in national information efforts

Law enforcement agencies in this state shall cooperate fully with the United States attorney general in the collection of information that would assist in the identification of unidentified deceased persons and information that would assist in the location of missing persons under the "Federal Missing Children Act of 1982," 96 Stat. 1259, 28 U.S.C.A. 534, as amended.

Law enforcement agencies in this state that are investigating missing children cases shall utilize the records and information compiled by the United States attorney general pursuant to that act when the circumstances of an investigation indicate that the records and information may be of assistance and when the act authorizes it.

(1984 S 321, eff. 4-9-85)

2901.32 Regulation of solicitations for missing child information distribution

(A) No organization shall solicit contributions for the purpose of distributing materials containing information relating to missing children unless it complies with all of the following requirements:

(1) It has been incorporated under Chapter 1702. of the Revised Code or the nonprofit corporation law of another state for a period of two years prior to the time of the solicitation of contributions.

(2) It has been exempt from federal income taxation under subsection 501(a) and described in subsection 501(c)(3), 501(c)(4), 501(c)(8), 501(c)(10), or 501(c)(19) of the Internal Revenue Code of 1954, 68A Stat. 3, 26 U.S.C. 1, as now or hereafter amended, for a period of two years prior to the time of the solicitation of contributions.

(3) It does not use fund-raising counsel, professional solicitors, commercial co-venturers, or other charitable organizations, as these terms are defined in section 1716.01 of the Revised Code, to solicit such contributions.

(B) No organization that solicits contributions for the purpose of distributing materials containing information relating to missing children shall expressly state or imply in any way that it is affiliated with, or is soliciting contributions on behalf of, an organization established to assist in the location of missing children without the express written consent of that organization.

(C) Whoever violates division (A) or (B) of this section is guilty of improper solicitation of contributions for missing children, a misdemeanor of the third degree.

(1990 H 486, eff. 11-7-90; 1984 S 321)

CHAPTER 2903

HOMICIDE AND ASSAULT

HOMICIDE

2903.01 Aggravated murder

(A) No person shall purposely, and with prior calculation and design, cause the death of another or the unlawful termination of another's pregnancy.

(B) No person shall purposely cause the death of another or the unlawful termination of another's pregnancy while committing or attempting to commit, or while fleeing immediately after committing or attempting to commit, kidnapping, rape, aggravated arson, arson, aggravated robbery, robbery, aggravated burglary, burglary, terrorism, or escape.

(C) No person shall purposely cause the death of another who is under thirteen years of age at the time of the commission of the offense.

(D) No person who is under detention as a result of having been found guilty of or having pleaded guilty to a felony or who breaks that detention shall purposely cause the death of another.

(E) No person shall purposely cause the death of a law enforcement officer whom the offender knows or has reasonable cause to know is a law enforcement officer when either of the following applies:

(1) The victim, at the time of the commission of the offense, is engaged in the victim's duties.

(2) It is the offender's specific purpose to kill a law enforcement officer.

(F) Whoever violates this section is guilty of aggravated murder, and shall be punished as provided in section 2929.02 of the Revised Code.

(G) As used in this section:

(1) "Detention" has the same meaning as in section 2921.01 of the Revised Code.

(2) "Law enforcement officer" has the same meaning as in section 2911.01 of the Revised Code.

(2002 S 184, eff. 5–15–02; 1998 S 193, eff. 12–29–98; 1998 H 5, eff. 6–30–98; 1997 S 32, eff. 8–6–97; 1996 S 239, eff. 9–6–96; 1981 S 1, eff. 10–19–81; 1972 H 511)

2903.02 Murder

(A) No person shall purposely cause the death of another or the unlawful termination of another's pregnancy.

(B) No person shall cause the death of another as a proximate result of the offender's committing or attempting to commit an offense of violence that is a felony of the first or second degree and that is not a violation of section 2903.03 or 2903.04 of the Revised Code.

(C) Division (B) of this section does not apply to an offense that becomes a felony of the first or second degree only if the offender previously has been convicted of that offense or another specified offense.

(D) Whoever violates this section is guilty of murder, and shall be punished as provided in section 2929.02 of the Revised Code.

(1998 H 5, eff. 6–30–98; 1996 S 239, eff. 9–6–96; 1972 H 511, eff. 1–1–74)

2903.03 Voluntary manslaughter

(A) No person, while under the influence of sudden passion or in a sudden fit of rage, either of which is brought on by serious provocation occasioned by the victim that is reasonably sufficient to incite the person into using deadly force, shall knowingly cause the death of another or the unlawful termination of another's pregnancy.

(B) Whoever violates this section is guilty of voluntary manslaughter, a felony of the first degree.

(1996 S 239, eff. 9–6–96; 1995 S 2, eff. 7–1–96; 1982 H 269, § 4, eff. 7–1–83; 1982 S 199, H 103; 1972 H 511)

2903.04 Involuntary manslaughter

(A) No person shall cause the death of another or the unlawful termination of another's pregnancy as a proximate result of the offender's committing or attempting to commit a felony.

(B) No person shall cause the death of another or the unlawful termination of another's pregnancy as a proximate result of the offender's committing or attempting to commit a misdemeanor of any degree, a regulatory offense, or a minor misdemeanor other than a violation of any section contained in Title XLV of the Revised Code that is a minor misdemeanor and other than a violation of an ordinance of a municipal corporation that, regardless of the penalty set by ordinance for the violation, is substantially equivalent to any section contained in Title XLV of the Revised Code that is a minor misdemeanor.

(C) Whoever violates this section is guilty of involuntary manslaughter. Violation of division (A) of this section is a felony of the first degree. Violation of division (B) of this section is a felony of the third degree.

(D) If an offender is convicted of or pleads guilty to a violation of division (A) or (B) of this section and if the felony, misdemeanor, or regulatory offense that the offender committed or attempted to commit, that proximately resulted in the death of the other person or the unlawful termination of another's pregnancy, and that is the basis of the offender's violation of division (A) or (B) of this section was a violation of division (A) or (B) of section 4511.19 of the Revised Code or of a substantially equivalent municipal ordinance or included, as an element of that felony, misdemeanor, or regulatory offense, the offender's operation or participation in the operation of a snowmobile, locomotive, watercraft, or aircraft while the offender was under the influence of alcohol, a drug of abuse, or alcohol and a drug of abuse, both of the following apply:

(1) The court shall impose a class one suspension of the offender's driver's or commercial driver's license or permit or nonresident operating privilege as specified in division (A)(1) of section 4510.02 of the Revised Code.

(2) The court shall impose a mandatory prison term for the violation of division (A) or (B) of this section from the range of prison terms authorized for the level of the offense under section 2929.14 of the Revised Code.

(2002 S 123, eff. 1–1–04; 1999 S 107, eff. 3–23–00; 1996 S 269, eff. 7–1–96; 1996 S 239, eff. 9–6–96; 1995 S 2, eff. 7–1–96; 1994 H 236, eff. 9–29–94; 1993 S 62, § 4, eff. 9–1–93; 1992 S 275; 1982 H 269, § 4, S 199; 1972 H 511)

2903.041 Reckless homicide

(A) No person shall recklessly cause the death of another or the unlawful termination of another's pregnancy.

(B) Whoever violates this section is guilty of reckless homicide, a felony of the third degree.

(1999 H 37, eff. 9–29–99)

2903.05 Negligent homicide

(A) No person shall negligently cause the death of another or the unlawful termination of another's pregnancy by means of a deadly weapon or dangerous ordnance as defined in section 2923.11 of the Revised Code.

(B) Whoever violates this section is guilty of negligent homicide, a misdemeanor of the first degree.

(1996 S 239, eff. 9–6–96; 1972 H 511, eff. 1–1–74)

2903.06 Aggravated vehicular homicide; vehicular homicide; vehicular manslaughter; effect of prior convictions; penalties

(A) No person, while operating or participating in the operation of a motor vehicle, motorcycle, snowmobile, locomotive, watercraft, or aircraft, shall cause the death of another or the unlawful termination of another's pregnancy in any of the following ways:

(1)(a) As the proximate result of committing a violation of division (A) of section 4511.19 of the Revised Code or of a substantially equivalent municipal ordinance;

(b) As the proximate result of committing a violation of division (A) of section 1547.11 of the Revised Code or of a substantially equivalent municipal ordinance;

(c) As the proximate result of committing a violation of division (A)(3) of section 4561.15 of the Revised Code or of a substantially equivalent municipal ordinance.

(2) In one of the following ways:

(a) Recklessly;

(b) As the proximate result of committing, while operating or participating in the operation of a motor vehicle or motorcycle in a construction zone, a reckless operation offense, provided that this division applies only if the person whose death is caused or whose pregnancy is unlawfully terminated is in the construction zone at the time of the offender's commission of the reckless operation offense in the construction zone and does not apply as described in division (F) of this section.

(3) In one of the following ways:

(a) Negligently;

(b) As the proximate result of committing, while operating or participating in the operation of a motor vehicle or motorcycle in a construction zone, a speeding offense, provided that this division applies only if the person whose death is caused or whose pregnancy is unlawfully terminated is in the construction zone at the time of the offender's commission of the speeding offense in the construction zone and does not apply as described in division (F) of this section.

(4) As the proximate result of committing a violation of any provision of any section contained in Title XLV of the Revised Code that is a minor misdemeanor or of a municipal ordinance that, regardless of the penalty set by ordinance for the violation, is substantially equivalent to any provision of any section contained in Title XLV of the Revised Code that is a minor misdemeanor.

(B)(1) Whoever violates division (A)(1) or (2) of this section is guilty of aggravated vehicular homicide and shall be punished as provided in divisions (B)(2) and (3) of this section.

(2)(a) Except as otherwise provided in this division, aggravated vehicular homicide committed in violation of division (A)(1) of this section is a felony of the second degree. Aggravated vehicular homicide committed in violation of division (A)(1) of this section is a felony of the first degree if any of the following apply:

(i) At the time of the offense, the offender was driving under a suspension imposed under Chapter 4510. or any other provision of the Revised Code.

(ii) The offender previously has been convicted of or pleaded guilty to a violation of this section.

(iii) The offender previously has been convicted of or pleaded guilty to any traffic-related homicide, manslaughter, or assault offense.

(iv) The offender previously has been convicted of or pleaded guilty to three or more prior violations of section 4511.19 of the Revised Code or of a substantially equivalent municipal ordinance within the previous six years.

(v) The offender previously has been convicted of or pleaded guilty to three or more prior violations of division (A) of section 1547.11 of the Revised Code or of a substantially equivalent municipal ordinance within the previous six years.

(vi) The offender previously has been convicted of or pleaded guilty to three or more prior violations of division (A)(3) of section 4561.15 of the Revised Code or of a substantially equivalent municipal ordinance within the previous six years.

(vii) The offender previously has been convicted of or pleaded guilty to three or more violations of any combination of the offenses listed in division (B)(2)(a)(iv), (v), or (vi) of this section.

(viii) The offender previously has been convicted of or pleaded guilty to a second or subsequent felony violation of division (A) of section 4511.19 of the Revised Code.

(b) In addition to any other sanctions imposed pursuant to division (B)(2)(a) of this section for aggravated vehicular homicide committed in violation of division (A)(1) of this section, the court shall impose upon the offender a class one suspension of the offender's driver's license, commercial driver's license, temporary instruction permit, probationary license, or nonresident operating privilege as specified in division (A)(1) of section 4510.02 of the Revised Code.

(3) Except as otherwise provided in this division, aggravated vehicular homicide committed in violation of division (A)(2) of this section is a felony of the third degree. Aggravated vehicular homicide committed in violation of division (A)(2) of this section is a felony of the second degree if, at the time of the offense, the offender was driving under a suspension imposed under Chapter 4510. or any other provision of the Revised Code or if the offender previously has been convicted of or pleaded guilty to a violation of this section or any traffic-related homicide, manslaughter, or assault offense.

In addition to any other sanctions imposed pursuant to this division for a violation of division (A)(2) of this section, the court shall impose upon the offender a class two suspension of the offender's driver's license, commercial driver's license, temporary instruction permit, probationary license, or nonresident operating privilege from the range specified in division (A)(2) of section 4510.02 of the Revised Code.

(C) Whoever violates division (A)(3) of this section is guilty of vehicular homicide. Except as otherwise provided in this division, vehicular homicide is a misdemeanor of the first degree. Vehicular homicide committed in violation of division (A)(3) of this section is a felony of the fourth degree if, at the time of the offense, the offender was driving under a suspension or revocation imposed under Chapter 4507. or any other provision of the Revised Code or if the offender previously has been convicted of or pleaded guilty to a violation of this section or any traffic-related homicide, manslaughter, or assault offense.

In addition to any other sanctions imposed pursuant to this division, the court shall impose upon the offender a class four suspension of the offender's driver's license, commercial driver's license, temporary instruction permit, probationary license, or nonresident operating privilege from the range specified in division (A)(4) of section 4510.02 of the Revised Code or, if the offender previously has been convicted of or pleaded guilty to a violation of this section or any traffic-related homicide, manslaughter, or assault offense, a class three suspension of the offender's driver's license, commercial driver's license, temporary instruction permit, probationary license, or nonresident operating privilege from the range specified in division (A)(3) of that section.

(D) Whoever violates division (A)(4) of this section is guilty of vehicular manslaughter. Except as otherwise provided in this division, vehicular manslaughter is a misdemeanor of the second degree. Vehicular manslaughter is a misdemeanor of the first degree if, at the time of the offense, the offender was driving under a suspension imposed under Chapter 4510. or any other provision of the Revised Code or if the offender previously has been convicted of or pleaded guilty to a violation of this section or any traffic-related homicide, manslaughter, or assault offense.

In addition to any other sanctions imposed pursuant to this division, the court shall impose upon the offender a class six suspension of the offender's driver's license, commercial driver's license, temporary instruction permit, probationary license, or nonresident operating privilege from the range specified in division (A)(6) of section 4510.02 of the Revised Code or, if the offender previously has been convicted of or pleaded guilty to a violation of this section or any traffic-related homicide, manslaughter, or assault offense, a class four suspension of the offender's driver's license, commercial driver's license, temporary instruction permit, probationary license, or nonresident operating privilege from the range specified in division (A)(4) of that section.

(E) The court shall impose a mandatory prison term on an offender who is convicted of or pleads guilty to a violation of division (A)(1) of this section. The court shall impose a mandatory jail term of at least fifteen days on an offender who is convicted of or pleads guilty to a misdemeanor violation of division (A)(3)(b) of this section and may impose upon the offender a longer jail term as authorized pursuant to section 2929.24 of the Revised Code. The court shall impose a mandatory prison term on an offender who is convicted of or pleads guilty to a violation of division (A)(2) or (3)(a) of this section or a felony violation of division (A)(3)(b) of this section if either of the following applies:

(1) The offender previously has been convicted of or pleaded guilty to a violation of this section or section 2903.08 of the Revised Code.

(2) At the time of the offense, the offender was driving under suspension under Chapter 4510. or any other provision of the Revised Code.

(F) Divisions (A)(2)(b) and (3)(b) of this section do not apply in a particular construction zone unless signs of the type described in section 2903.081 of the Revised Code are erected in that construction zone in accordance with the guidelines and design specifications established by the director of transportation under section 5501.27 of the Revised Code. The failure to erect signs of the type described in section 2903.081 of the Revised Code in a particular construction zone in accordance with those guidelines and design specifications does not limit or affect the application of division (A)(1), (A)(2)(a), (A)(3)(a), or (A)(4) of this section in that construction zone or the prosecution of any person who violates any of those divisions in that construction zone.

(G)(1) As used in this section:

(a) "Mandatory prison term" and "mandatory jail term" have the same meanings as in section 2929.01 of the Revised Code.

(b) "Traffic–related homicide, manslaughter, or assault offense" means a violation of section 2903.04 of the Revised Code in circumstances in which division (D) of that section applies, a violation of section 2903.06 or 2903.08 of the Revised Code, or a violation of section 2903.06, 2903.07, or 2903.08 of the Revised Code as they existed prior to March 23, 2000.

(c) "Construction zone" has the same meaning as in section 5501.27 of the Revised Code.

(d) "Reckless operation offense" means a violation of section 4511.20 of the Revised Code or a municipal ordinance substantially equivalent to section 4511.20 of the Revised Code.

(e) "Speeding offense" means a violation of section 4511.21 of the Revised Code or a municipal ordinance pertaining to speed.

(2) For the purposes of this section, when a penalty or suspension is enhanced because of a prior or current violation of a specified law or a prior or current specified offense, the reference to the violation of the specified law or the specified offense includes any violation of any substantially equivalent municipal ordinance, former law of this state, or current or former law of another state or the United States.

(2004 H 52, eff. 6–1–04; 2003 H 50, § 4, eff. 1–1–04; 2003 H 50, § 1, eff. 10–21–03; 2002 S 123, eff. 1–1–04; 1999 S 107, eff. 3–23–00; 1996 S 269, eff. 7–1–96; 1996 S 239, eff. 9–6–96; 1995 S 2, eff. 7–1–96; 1993 S 62, § 4, eff. 9–1–93; 1992 S 275; 1990 S 131; 1989 S 49, H 381; 1986 S 262, H 428, S 356, H 265; 1982 S 432; 1973 H 716; 1972 H 511)

Notes of Decisions

Ed. Note: *See notes of decisions and opinions at RC 4511.19 regarding construction of the term "under the influence."*

2903.08 Aggravated vehicular assault; enhancement of penalty; prior convictions; penalties

(A) No person, while operating or participating in the operation of a motor vehicle, motorcycle, snowmobile, locomotive, watercraft, or aircraft, shall cause serious physical harm to another person or another's unborn in any of the following ways:

(1)(a) As the proximate result of committing a violation of division (A) of section 4511.19 of the Revised Code or of a substantially equivalent municipal ordinance;

(b) As the proximate result of committing a violation of division (A) of section 1547.11 of the Revised Code or of a substantially equivalent municipal ordinance;

(c) As the proximate result of committing a violation of division (A)(3) of section 4561.15 of the Revised Code or of a substantially equivalent municipal ordinance.

(2) In one of the following ways:

(a) As the proximate result of committing, while operating or participating in the operation of a motor vehicle or motorcycle in a construction zone, a reckless operation offense, provided that this division applies only if the person to whom the serious physical harm is caused or to whose unborn the serious physical harm is caused is in the construction zone at the time of the offender's commission of the reckless operation offense in the construction zone and does not apply as described in division (E) of this section;

(b) Recklessly.

(3) As the proximate result of committing, while operating or participating in the operation of a motor vehicle or motorcycle in a construction zone, a speeding offense, provided that this division applies only if the person to whom the serious physical harm is caused or to whose unborn the serious physical harm is caused is in the construction zone at the time of the offender's commission of the speeding offense in the construction zone and does not apply as described in division (E) of this section.

(B)(1) Whoever violates division (A)(1) of this section is guilty of aggravated vehicular assault. Except as otherwise provided in this division, aggravated vehicular assault is a felony of the third degree. Aggravated vehicular assault is a felony of the second degree if any of the following apply:

(a) At the time of the offense, the offender was driving under a suspension imposed under Chapter 4510. or any other provision of the Revised Code.

(b) The offender previously has been convicted of or pleaded guilty to a violation of this section.

(c) The offender previously has been convicted of or pleaded guilty to any traffic-related homicide, manslaughter, or assault offense.

(d) The offender previously has been convicted of or pleaded guilty to three or more prior violations of section 4511.19 of the Revised Code or a substantially equivalent municipal ordinance within the previous six years.

(e) The offender previously has been convicted of or pleaded guilty to three or more prior violations of division (A) of section 1547.11 of the Revised Code or of a substantially equivalent municipal ordinance within the previous six years.

(f) The offender previously has been convicted of or pleaded guilty to three or more prior violations of division (A)(3) of section 4561.15 of the Revised Code or of a substantially equivalent municipal ordinance within the previous six years.

(g) The offender previously has been convicted of or pleaded guilty to three or more prior violations of any combination of the offenses listed in division (B)(1)(d), (e), or (f) of this section.

(h) The offender previously has been convicted of or pleaded guilty to a second or subsequent felony violation of division (A) of section 4511.19 of the Revised Code.

(2) In addition to any other sanctions imposed pursuant to division (B)(1) of this section, the court shall impose upon the offender a class three suspension of the offender's driver's license, commercial driver's license, temporary instruction permit, probationary license, or nonresident operating privilege from the range specified in division (A)(3) of section 4510.02 of the Revised Code or, if the offender previously has been convicted of or pleaded guilty to a violation of this section or any traffic-related homicide, manslaughter, or assault offense, a class two suspension of the offender's driver's license, commercial driver's license, temporary instruction permit, probationary license, or nonresident operating privilege from the range specified in division (A)(2) of that section.

(C)(1) Whoever violates division (A)(2) or (3) of this section is guilty of vehicular assault and shall be punished as provided in divisions (C)(2) and (3) of this section.

(2) Except as otherwise provided in this division, vehicular assault committed in violation of division (A)(2) of this section is a felony of the fourth degree. Vehicular assault committed in violation of division (A)(2) of this section is a felony of the third degree if, at the time of the offense, the offender was driving under a suspension imposed under Chapter 4510. or any other provision of the Revised Code, if the offender previously has been convicted of or pleaded guilty to a violation of this section or any traffic-related homicide, manslaughter, or assault offense, or if, in the same course of conduct that resulted in the violation of division (A)(2) of this section, the offender also violated section 4549.02, 4549.021, or 4549.03 of the Revised Code.

In addition to any other sanctions imposed, the court shall impose upon the offender a class four suspension of the offender's driver's license, commercial driver's license, temporary instruction permit, probationary license, or nonresident operating privilege from the range specified in division (A)(4) of section 4510.02 of the Revised Code or, if the offender previously has been convicted of or pleaded guilty to a violation of this section or any traffic-related homicide, manslaughter, or assault offense, a class three suspension of the offender's driver's license, commercial driver's license, temporary instruction permit, probationary license, or nonresident operating privilege from the range specified in division (A)(3) of that section.

(3) Except as otherwise provided in this division, vehicular assault committed in violation of division (A)(3) of this section is a misdemeanor of the first degree. Vehicular assault committed in violation of division (A)(3) of this section is a felony of the fourth degree if, at the time of the offense, the offender was driving under a suspension imposed under Chapter 4510. or any other provision of the Revised Code or if the offender previously has been convicted of or pleaded guilty to a violation of this section or any traffic-related homicide, manslaughter, or assault offense.

In addition to any other sanctions imposed, the court shall impose upon the offender a class four suspension of the offender's driver's license, commercial driver's license, temporary instruction permit, probationary license, or nonresident operating privilege from the range specified in division (A)(4) of section 4510.02 of the Revised Code or, if the offender previously has been convicted of or pleaded guilty to a violation of this section or any traffic-related homicide, manslaughter, or assault offense, a class three suspension of the offender's driver's license, commercial driver's license, temporary instruction permit, probationary license, or nonresident operating privilege from the range specified in division (A)(3) of section 4510.02 of the Revised Code.

(D)(1) The court shall impose a mandatory prison term on an offender who is convicted of or pleads guilty to a violation of division (A)(1) of this section.

(2) The court shall impose a mandatory prison term on an offender who is convicted of or pleads guilty to a violation of division (A)(2) of this section or a felony violation of division (A)(3) of this section if either of the following applies:

(a) The offender previously has been convicted of or pleaded guilty to a violation of this section or section 2903.06 of the Revised Code.

(b) At the time of the offense, the offender was driving under suspension under Chapter 4510. or any other provision of the Revised Code.

(3) The court shall impose a mandatory jail term of at least seven days on an offender who is convicted of or pleads guilty to a misdemeanor violation of division (A)(3) of this section and may impose upon the offender a longer jail term as authorized pursuant to section 2929.24 of the Revised Code.

(E) Divisions (A)(2)(a) and (3) of this section do not apply in a particular construction zone unless signs of the type described in section 2903.081 of the Revised Code are erected in that construction zone in accordance with the guidelines and design specifications established by the director of transportation under section 5501.27 of the Revised Code. The failure to erect signs of the type described in section 2903.081 of the Revised Code in a particular construction zone in accordance with those guidelines and design specifications does not limit or affect the application of division (A)(1) or (2)(b) of this section in that construction zone or the prosecution of any person who violates either of those divisions in that construction zone.

(F) As used in this section:

(1) "Mandatory prison term" and "mandatory jail term" have the same meanings as in section 2929.01 of the Revised Code.

(2) "Traffic-related homicide, manslaughter, or assault offense" has the same meaning as in section 2903.06 of the Revised Code.

(3) "Construction zone" has the same meaning as in section 5501.27 of the Revised Code.

(4) "Reckless operation offense" and "speeding offense" have the same meanings as in section 2903.06 of the Revised Code.

(G) For the purposes of this section, when a penalty or suspension is enhanced because of a prior or current violation of a specified law or a prior or current specified offense, the reference to the violation of the specified law or the specified offense includes any violation of any substantially equivalent municipal ordinance, former law of this state, or current or former law of another state or the United States.

(2004 H 163, eff. 9–23–04; 2004 H 52, eff. 6–1–04; 2003 H 50, § 4, eff. 1–1–04; 2003 H 50, § 1, eff. 10–21–03; 2002 S 123, eff. 1–1–04; 1999 S 107, eff. 3–23–00; 1996 S 269, eff. 7–1–96; 1996 S 239, eff. 9–6–96; 1995 S 2, eff. 7–1–96; 1994 H 236, eff. 9–29–94; 1993 S 62, § 4, eff. 9–1–93; 1992 S 275; 1990 S 131)

2903.081 Signs in construction zones to provide notice to motorists of prohibitions regarding reckless operation or speeding offense in construction zones

(A) As used in this section:

(1) "Construction zone" has the same meaning as in section 5501.27 of the Revised Code.

(2) "Reckless operation offense" and "speeding offense" have the same meanings as in section 2903.06 of the Revised Code.

(B) The director of transportation, board of county commissioners, or board of township trustees shall cause signs to be erected in construction zones notifying motorists of the prohibitions set forth in sections 2903.06 and 2903.08 of the Revised Code regarding the death of or injury to any person in the construction zone as a proximate result of a reckless operation offense or speeding offense in the construction zone. The prohibitions set forth in divisions (A)(2)(b) and (3)(b) of section 2903.06 and divisions (A)(2)(a) and (3) of section 2903.08 of the Revised Code apply to persons who commit a reckless operation offense or speeding offense in a particular construction zone only when signs of that nature are erected in that construction zone in accordance with the guidelines and design specifications established by the director under section 5501.27 of the Revised Code. The failure to erect signs of that nature in a particular construction zone in accordance with those guidelines and design specifications does not limit or affect the application of division (A)(1), (A)(2)(a), (A)(3)(a), or (A)(4) of section 2903.06 or division (A)(1) or (2)(b) of section 2903.08 of the Revised Code in that construction zone or the prosecution of any person who violates either of those divisions in that construction zone.

(2004 H 52, eff. 6–1–04)

2903.09 "Unlawful termination of another's pregnancy", "another's unborn", and "such other person's unborn" defined

As used in sections 2903.01 to 2903.08, 2903.11 to 2903.14, 2903.21, and 2903.22 of the Revised Code:

(A) "Unlawful termination of another's pregnancy" means causing the death of an unborn member of the species homo sapiens, who is or was carried in the womb of another, as a result of injuries inflicted during the period that begins with fertilization and that continues unless and until live birth occurs.

(B) "Another's unborn" or "such other person's unborn" means a member of the species homo sapiens, who is or was carried in the womb of another, during a period that begins with fertilization and that continues unless and until live birth occurs.

(C) Notwithstanding divisions (A) and (B) of this section, in no case shall the definitions of the terms "unlawful termination of another's pregnancy," "another's unborn," and "such other person's unborn" that are set forth in division (A) of this section be applied or construed in any of the following manners:

(1) Except as otherwise provided in division (C)(1) of this section, in a manner so that the offense prohibits or is construed as prohibiting any pregnant woman or her physician from performing an abortion with the actual consent of the pregnant woman, with the consent of the pregnant woman implied by law in a medical emergency, or with the approval of one otherwise authorized by law to consent to medical treatment on behalf of the pregnant woman. An abortion that violates the conditions described in the immediately preceding sentence may be punished as a violation of section 2903.01, 2903.02, 2903.03, 2903.04, 2903.05, 2903.06, 2903.08, 2903.11, 2903.12, 2903.13, 2903.14, 2903.21, or 2903.22 of the Revised Code, as applicable. An abortion that does not violate the conditions described in the second immediately preceding sentence, but that does violate section 2919.12, division (B) of section 2919.13, or section 2919.151, 2919.17, or 2919.18 of the Revised Code, may be punished as a violation of section 2919.12, division (B) of section 2919.13, or section 2919.151, 2919.17, or 2919.18 of the Revised Code, as applicable.

(2) In a manner so that the offense is applied or is construed as applying to a woman based on an act or omission of the woman that occurs while she is or was pregnant and that results in any of the following:

(a) Her delivery of a stillborn baby;

(b) Her causing, in any other manner, the death in utero of an unborn that she is carrying;

(c) Her causing the death of her child who is born alive but who dies from one or more injuries that are sustained while the child is an unborn;

(d) Her causing her child who is born alive to sustain one or more injuries while the child is an unborn;

(e) Her causing, threatening to cause, or attempting to cause, in any other manner, an injury, illness, or other physiological impairment, regardless of its duration or gravity, or a mental illness or condition, regardless of its duration or gravity, to an unborn that she is carrying.

(2000 H 351, eff. 8–18–00; 1999 S 107, eff. 3–23–00; 1996 S 239, eff. 9–6–96)

ASSAULT

2903.10 Definitions

As used in sections 2903.13 and 2903.16 of the Revised Code:

(A) "Functionally impaired person" means any person who has a physical or mental impairment that prevents him from providing for his own care or protection or whose infirmities caused by aging prevent him from providing for his own care or protection.

(B) "Caretaker" means a person who assumes the duty to provide for the care and protection of a funtionally [sic.] impaired person on a voluntary basis, by contract, through receipt of payment for care and protection, as a result of a family relationship, or by order of a court of competent jurisdiction. "Caretaker" does not include a person who owns, operates, or administers, or who is an agent or employee of, a care facility, as defined in section 2903.33 of the Revised Code.

(1988 H 642, eff. 3–17–89)

2903.11 Felonious assault

(A) No person shall knowingly do either of the following:

(1) Cause serious physical harm to another or to another's unborn;

(2) Cause or attempt to cause physical harm to another or to another's unborn by means of a deadly weapon or dangerous ordnance.

(B) No person, with knowledge that the person has tested positive as a carrier of a virus that causes acquired immunodeficiency syndrome, shall knowingly do any of the following:

(1) Engage in sexual conduct with another person without disclosing that knowledge to the other person prior to engaging in the sexual conduct;

(2) Engage in sexual conduct with a person whom the offender knows or has reasonable cause to believe lacks the mental capacity to appreciate the significance of the knowledge that the offender has tested positive as a carrier of a virus that causes acquired immunodeficiency syndrome;

(3) Engage in sexual conduct with a person under eighteen years of age who is not the spouse of the offender.

(C) The prosecution of a person under this section does not preclude prosecution of that person under section 2907.02 of the Revised Code.

(D) Whoever violates this section is guilty of felonious assault, a felony of the second degree. If the victim of a violation of division (A) of this section is a peace officer, felonious assault is a felony of the first degree. If the victim of the offense is a peace officer, as defined in section 2935.01 of the Revised Code, and if the victim suffered serious physical harm as a result of the commission of the offense, felonious assault is a felony of the first degree, and the court, pursuant to division (F) of section 2929.13 of the Revised Code, shall impose as a mandatory prison term one of the prison terms prescribed for a felony of the first degree.

(E) As used in this section:

(1) "Deadly weapon" and "dangerous ordnance" have the same meanings as in section 2923.11 of the Revised Code.

(2) "Peace officer" has the same meaning as in section 2935.01 of the Revised Code.

(3) "Sexual conduct" has the same meaning as in section 2907.01 of the Revised Code, except that, as used in this section, it does not include the insertion of an instrument, apparatus, or other object that is not a part of the body into the vaginal or anal cavity of another, unless the offender knew at the time of the

insertion that the instrument, apparatus, or other object carried the offender's bodily fluid.

(1999 H 100, eff. 3–23–00; 1999 S 142, eff. 2–3–00; 1996 S 239, eff. 9–6–96; 1995 S 2, eff. 7–1–96; 1983 S 210, eff. 7–1–83; 1982 H 269, S 199; 1972 H 511)

2903.12 Aggravated assault

(A) No person, while under the influence of sudden passion or in a sudden fit of rage, either of which is brought on by serious provocation occasioned by the victim that is reasonably sufficient to incite the person into using deadly force, shall knowingly:

(1) Cause serious physical harm to another or to another's unborn;

(2) Cause or attempt to cause physical harm to another or to another's unborn by means of a deadly weapon or dangerous ordnance, as defined in section 2923.11 of the Revised Code.

(B) Whoever violates this section is guilty of aggravated assault, a felony of the fourth degree. If the victim of the offense is a peace officer, as defined in section 2935.01 of the Revised Code, aggravated assault is a felony of the third degree. If the victim of the offense is a peace officer, as defined in section 2935.01 of the Revised Code, and if the victim suffered serious physical harm as a result of the commission of the offense, aggravated assault is a felony of the third degree, and the court, pursuant to division (F) of section 2929.13 of the Revised Code, shall impose as a mandatory prison term one of the prison terms prescribed for a felony of the third degree.

(1999 S 142, eff. 2–3–00; 1996 S 239, eff. 9–6–96; 1984 H 37, eff. 6–22–84; 1983 S 210; 1982 H 269, S 199, H 103; 1972 H 511)

2903.13 Assault

(A) No person shall knowingly cause or attempt to cause physical harm to another or to another's unborn.

(B) No person shall recklessly cause serious physical harm to another or to another's unborn.

(C) Whoever violates this section is guilty of assault. Except as otherwise provided in division (C)(1), (2), (3), (4), or (5) of this section, assault is a misdemeanor of the first degree.

(1) Except as otherwise provided in this division, if the offense is committed by a caretaker against a functionally impaired person under the caretaker's care, assault is a felony of the fourth degree. If the offense is committed by a caretaker against a functionally impaired person under the caretaker's care, if the offender previously has been convicted of or pleaded guilty to a violation of this section or section 2903.11 or 2903.16 of the Revised Code, and if in relation to the previous conviction the offender was a caretaker and the victim was a functionally impaired person under the offender's care, assault is a felony of the third degree.

(2) If the offense is committed in any of the following circumstances, assault is a felony of the fifth degree:

(a) The offense occurs in or on the grounds of a state correctional institution or an institution of the department of youth services, the victim of the offense is an employee of the department of rehabilitation and correction, the department of youth services, or a probation department or is on the premises of the particular institution for business purposes or as a visitor, and the offense is committed by a person incarcerated in the state correctional institution, by a person institutionalized in the department of youth services institution pursuant to a commitment to the department of youth services, by a parolee, by an offender under transitional control, under a community control sanction, or on an escorted visit, by a person under post-release control, or by an offender under any other type of supervision by a government agency.

(b) The offense occurs in or on the grounds of a local correctional facility, the victim of the offense is an employee of the local correctional facility or a probation department or is on the premises of the facility for business purposes or as a visitor, and the offense is committed by a person who is under custody in the facility subsequent to the person's arrest for any crime or delinquent act, subsequent to the person's being charged with or convicted of any crime, or subsequent to the person's being alleged to be or adjudicated a delinquent child.

(c) The offense occurs off the grounds of a state correctional institution and off the grounds of an institution of the department of youth services, the victim of the offense is an employee of the department of rehabilitation and correction, the department of youth services, or a probation department, the offense occurs during the employee's official work hours and while the employee is engaged in official work responsibilities, and the offense is committed by a person incarcerated in a state correctional institution or institutionalized in the department of youth services who temporarily is outside of the institution for any purpose, by a parolee, by an offender under transitional control, under a community control sanction, or on an escorted visit, by a person under post-release control, or by an offender under any other type of supervision by a government agency.

(d) The offense occurs off the grounds of a local correctional facility, the victim of the offense is an employee of the local correctional facility or a probation department, the offense occurs during the employee's official work hours and while the employee is engaged in official work responsibilities, and the offense is committed by a person who is under custody in the facility subsequent to the person's arrest for any crime or delinquent act, subsequent to the person being charged with or convicted of any crime, or subsequent to the person being alleged to be or adjudicated a delinquent child and who temporarily is outside of the facility for any purpose or by a parolee, by an offender under transitional control, under a community control sanction, or on an escorted visit, by a person under post-release control, or by an offender under any other type of supervision by a government agency.

(e) The victim of the offense is a school teacher or administrator or a school bus operator, and the offense occurs in a school, on school premises, in a school building, on a school bus, or while the victim is outside of school premises or a school bus and is engaged in duties or official responsibilities associated with the victim's employment or position as a school teacher or administrator or a school bus operator, including, but not limited to, driving, accompanying, or chaperoning students at or on class or field trips, athletic events, or other school extracurricular activities or functions outside of school premises.

(3) If the victim of the offense is a peace officer, a firefighter, or a person performing emergency medical service, while in the performance of their official duties, assault is a felony of the fourth degree.

(4) If the victim of the offense is a peace officer and if the victim suffered serious physical harm as a result of the commission of the offense, assault is a felony of the fourth degree, and the court, pursuant to division (F) of section 2929.13 of the Revised Code, shall impose as a mandatory prison term one of the prison terms prescribed for a felony of the fourth degree that is at least twelve months in duration.

(5) If the victim of the offense is an officer or employee of a public children services agency or a private child placing agency and the offense relates to the officer's or employee's performance or anticipated performance of official responsibilities or duties, assault is either a felony of the fifth degree or, if the offender previously has been convicted of or pleaded guilty to an offense of violence, the victim of that prior offense was an officer or employee of a public children services agency or private child

placing agency, and that prior offense related to the officer's or employee's performance or anticipated performance of official responsibilities or duties, a felony of the fourth degree.

(D) As used in this section:

(1) "Peace officer" has the same meaning as in section 2935.01 of the Revised Code.

(2) "Firefighter" has the same meaning as in section 3937.41 of the Revised Code.

(3) "Emergency medical service" has the same meaning as in section 4765.01 of the Revised Code.

(4) "Local correctional facility" means a county, multicounty, municipal, municipal-county, or multicounty-municipal jail or workhouse, a minimum security jail established under section 341.23 or 753.21 of the Revised Code, or another county, multicounty, municipal, municipal-county, or multicounty-municipal facility used for the custody of persons arrested for any crime or delinquent act, persons charged with or convicted of any crime, or persons alleged to be or adjudicated a delinquent child.

(5) "Employee of a local correctional facility" means a person who is an employee of the political subdivision or of one or more of the affiliated political subdivisions that operates the local correctional facility and who operates or assists in the operation of the facility.

(6) "School teacher or administrator" means either of the following:

(a) A person who is employed in the public schools of the state under a contract described in section 3319.08 of the Revised Code in a position in which the person is required to have a certificate issued pursuant to sections 3319.22 to 3319.311 of the Revised Code.

(b) A person who is employed by a nonpublic school for which the state board of education prescribes minimum standards under section 3301.07 of the Revised Code and who is certificated in accordance with section 3301.071 of the Revised Code.

(7) "Community control sanction" has the same meaning as in section 2929.01 of the Revised Code.

(8) "Escorted visit" means an escorted visit granted under section 2967.27 of the Revised Code.

(9) "Post-release control" and "transitional control" have the same meanings as in section 2967.01 of the Revised Code.

(2002 H 490, eff. 1-1-04; 2000 H 412, eff. 4-10-01; 1999 S 142, eff. 2-3-00; 1999 S 1, eff. 8-6-99; 1997 S 111, eff. 3-17-98; 1997 H 106, eff. 11-21-97; 1996 H 480, eff. 10-16-96; 1996 S 239, eff. 9-6-96; 1995 S 2, eff. 7-1-96; 1994 H 571, eff. 10-6-94; 1994 S 116, eff. 9-29-94; 1992 H 561, eff. 4-9-93; 1988 H 642; 1972 H 511)

2903.14 Negligent assault

(A) No person shall negligently, by means of a deadly weapon or dangerous ordnance as defined in section 2923.11 of the Revised Code, cause physical harm to another or to another's unborn.

(B) Whoever violates this section is guilty of negligent assault, a misdemeanor of the third degree.

(1996 S 239, eff. 9-6-96; 1972 H 511, eff. 1-1-74)

2903.15 Permitting child abuse

(A) No parent, guardian, custodian, or person having custody of a child under eighteen years of age or of a mentally or physically handicapped child under twenty-one years of age shall cause serious physical harm to the child, or the death of the child, as a proximate result of permitting the child to be abused, to be tortured, to be administered corporal punishment or other physical disciplinary measure, or to be physically restrained in a cruel manner or for a prolonged period.

(B) It is an affirmative defense to a charge under this section that the defendant did not have readily available a means to prevent the harm to the child or the death of the child and that the defendant took timely and reasonable steps to summon aid.

(C) Whoever violates this section is guilty of permitting child abuse. If the violation of this section causes serious physical harm to the child, permitting child abuse is a felony of the third degree. If the violation of this section causes the death of the child, permitting child abuse is a felony of the first degree.

(1999 H 162, eff. 8-25-99)

2903.16 Failing to provide for functionally impaired person

(A) No caretaker shall knowingly fail to provide a functionally impaired person under the caretaker's care with any treatment, care, goods, or service that is necessary to maintain the health or safety of the functionally impaired person when this failure results in physical harm or serious physical harm to the functionally impaired person.

(B) No caretaker shall recklessly fail to provide a functionally impaired person under the caretaker's care with any treatment, care, goods, or service that is necessary to maintain the health or safety of the functionally impaired person when this failure results in serious physical harm to the functionally impaired person.

(C)(1) Whoever violates division (A) of this section is guilty of knowingly failing to provide for a functionally impaired person, a misdemeanor of the first degree. If the functionally impaired person under the offender's care suffers serious physical harm as a result of the violation of this section, a violation of division (A) of this section is a felony of the fourth degree.

(2) Whoever violates division (B) of this section is guilty of recklessly failing to provide for a functionally impaired person, a misdemeanor of the second degree. If the functionally impaired person under the offender's care suffers serious physical harm as a result of the violation of this section, a violation of division (B) of this section is a felony of the fourth degree.

(1995 S 2, eff. 7-1-96; 1988 H 642, eff. 3-17-89)

MENACING; STALKING

2903.21 Aggravated menacing

(A) No person shall knowingly cause another to believe that the offender will cause serious physical harm to the person or property of the other person, the other person's unborn, or a member of the other person's immediate family.

(B) Whoever violates this section is guilty of aggravated menacing. Except as otherwise provided in this division, aggravated menacing is a misdemeanor of the first degree. If the victim of the offense is an officer or employee of a public children services agency or a private child placing agency and the offense relates to the officer's or employee's performance or anticipated performance of official responsibilities or duties, aggravated menacing is a felony of the fifth degree or, if the offender previously has been convicted of or pleaded guilty to an offense of violence, the victim of that prior offense was an officer or employee of a public children services agency or private child placing agency, and that prior offense related to the officer's or employee's performance or anticipated performance of official responsibilities or duties, a felony of the fourth degree.

(2000 H 412, eff. 4–10–01; 1996 S 239, eff. 9–6–96; 1972 H 511, eff. 1–1–74)

2903.211 Menacing by stalking

(A)(1) No person by engaging in a pattern of conduct shall knowingly cause another person to believe that the offender will cause physical harm to the other person or cause mental distress to the other person.

(2) No person, through the use of any electronic method of remotely transferring information, including, but not limited to, any computer, computer network, computer program, or computer system, shall post a message with purpose to urge or incite another to commit a violation of division (A)(1) of this section.

(B) Whoever violates this section is guilty of menacing by stalking.

(1) Except as otherwise provided in divisions (B)(2) and (3) of this section, menacing by stalking is a misdemeanor of the first degree.

(2) Menacing by stalking is a felony of the fourth degree if any of the following applies:

(a) The offender previously has been convicted of or pleaded guilty to a violation of this section or a violation of section 2911.211 of the Revised Code.

(b) In committing the offense under division (A)(1) or (2) of this section, the offender made a threat of physical harm to or against the victim, or as a result of an offense committed under division (A)(2) of this section, a third person induced by the offender's posted message made a threat of physical harm to or against the victim.

(c) In committing the offense under division (A)(1) or (2) of this section, the offender trespassed on the land or premises where the victim lives, is employed, or attends school, or as a result of an offense committed under division (A)(2) of this section, a third person induced by the offender's posted message trespassed on the land or premises where the victim lives, is employed, or attends school.

(d) The victim of the offense is a minor.

(e) The offender has a history of violence toward the victim or any other person or a history of other violent acts toward the victim or any other person.

(f) While committing the offense under division (A)(1) of this section, the offender had a deadly weapon on or about the offender's person or under the offender's control. Division (B)(2)(f) of this section does not apply in determining the penalty for a violation of division (A)(2) of this section.

(g) At the time of the commission of the offense, the offender was the subject of a protection order issued under section 2903.213 or 2903.214 of the Revised Code, regardless of whether the person to be protected under the order is the victim of the offense or another person.

(h) In committing the offense under division (A)(1) or (2) of this section, the offender caused serious physical harm to the premises at which the victim resides, to the real property on which that premises is located, or to any personal property located on that premises, or as a result of an offense committed under division (A)(2) of this section, a third person induced by the offender's posted message caused serious physical harm to that premises, that real property, or any personal property on that premises.

(i) Prior to committing the offense, the offender had been determined to represent a substantial risk of physical harm to others as manifested by evidence of then-recent homicidal or other violent behavior, evidence of then-recent threats that placed another in reasonable fear of violent behavior and serious physical harm, or other evidence of then-present dangerousness.

(3) If the victim of the offense is an officer or employee of a public children services agency or a private child placing agency and the offense relates to the officer's or employee's performance or anticipated performance of official responsibilities or duties, menacing by stalking is either a felony of the fifth degree or, if the offender previously has been convicted of or pleaded guilty to an offense of violence, the victim of that prior offense was an officer or employee of a public children services agency or private child placing agency, and that prior offense related to the officer's or employee's performance or anticipated performance of official responsibilities or duties, a felony of the fourth degree.

(C) Section 2919.271 of the Revised Code applies in relation to a defendant charged with a violation of this section.

(D) As used in this section:

(1) "Pattern of conduct" means two or more actions or incidents closely related in time, whether or not there has been a prior conviction based on any of those actions or incidents. Actions or incidents that prevent, obstruct, or delay the performance by a public official, firefighter, rescuer, emergency medical services person, or emergency facility person of any authorized act within the public official's, firefighter's, rescuer's, emergency medical services person's, or emergency facility person's official capacity, or the posting of messages or receipt of information or data through the use of an electronic method of remotely transferring information, including, but not limited to, a computer, computer network, computer program, computer system, or telecommunications device, may constitute a "pattern of conduct."

(2) "Mental distress" means any of the following:

(a) Any mental illness or condition that involves some temporary substantial incapacity;

(b) Any mental illness or condition that would normally require psychiatric treatment, psychological treatment, or other mental health services, whether or not any person requested or received psychiatric treatment, psychological treatment, or other mental health services.

(3) "Emergency medical services person" is the singular of "emergency medical services personnel" as defined in section 2133.21 of the Revised Code.

(4) "Emergency facility person" is the singular of " emergency facility personnel" as defined in section 2909.04 of the Revised Code.

(5) "Public official" has the same meaning as in section 2921.01 of the Revised Code.

(6) "Computer," "computer network,' ' "computer program," "computer system," and "telecommunications device" have the same meanings as in section 2913.01 of the Revised Code.

(7) "Post a message" means transferring, sending, posting, publishing, disseminating, or otherwise communicating, or attempting to transfer, send, post, publish, disseminate, or otherwise communicate, any message or information, whether truthful or untruthful, about an individual, and whether done under one's own name, under the name of another, or while impersonating another.

(8) "Third person" means, in relation to conduct as described in division (A)(2) of this section, an individual who is neither the offender nor the victim of the conduct.

(E) The state does not need to prove in a prosecution under this section that a person requested or received psychiatric treatment, psychological treatment, or other mental health services in order to show that the person was caused mental distress as described in division (D)(2)(b) of this section.

(F)(1) This section does not apply to a person solely because the person provided access or connection to or from an electronic method of remotely transferring information not under that person's control, including having provided capabilities that are incidental to providing access or connection to or from the electronic method of remotely transferring the information, and that do not include the creation of the content of the material that is the subject of the access or connection. In addition, any person providing access or connection to or from an electronic method of remotely transferring information not under that person's control shall not be liable for any action voluntarily taken in good faith to block the receipt or transmission through its service of any information that it believes is, or will be sent, in violation of this section.

(2) Division (F)(1) of this section does not create an affirmative duty for any person providing access or connection to or from an electronic method of remotely transferring information not under that person's control to block the receipt or transmission through its service of any information that it believes is, or will be sent, in violation of this section except as otherwise provided by law.

(3) Division (F)(1) of this section does not apply to a person who conspires with a person actively involved in the creation or knowing distribution of material in violation of this section or who knowingly advertises the availability of material of that nature.

(2003 S 8, eff. 8–29–03; 2001 S 40, eff. 1–25–02; 2000 H 412, eff. 4–10–01; 1999 H 202, § 3, eff. 3–10–00; 1999 H 137, eff. 3–10–00; 1998 S 215, eff. 3–30–99; 1995 S 2, eff. 7–1–96; 1992 H 536, eff. 11–5–92)

2903.212 Bail

(A) Except when the complaint involves a person who is a family or household member as defined in section 2919.25 of the Revised Code, if a person is charged with a violation of section 2903.21, 2903.211, 2903.22, or 2911.211 of the Revised Code or a violation of a municipal ordinance that is substantially similar to one of those sections and if the person, at the time of the alleged violation, was subject to the terms of any order issued pursuant to section 2903.213, 2933.08, or 2945.04 of the Revised Code or previously had been convicted of or pleaded guilty to a violation of section 2903.21, 2903.211, 2903.22, or 2911.211 of the Revised Code that involves the same complainant or a violation of a municipal ordinance that is substantially similar to one of those sections and that involves the same complainant, the court shall consider all of the following, in addition to any other circumstances considered by the court and notwithstanding any provisions to the contrary contained in Criminal Rule 46, before setting the amount and conditions of the bail for the person:

(1) Whether the person has a history of violence toward the complainant or a history of other violent acts;

(2) The mental health of the person;

(3) Whether the person has a history of violating the orders of any court or governmental entity;

(4) Whether the person is potentially a threat to any other person;

(5) Whether setting bail at a high level will interfere with any treatment or counseling that the person is undergoing.

(B) Any court that has jurisdiction over violations of section 2903.21, 2903.211, 2903.22, or 2911.211 of the Revised Code or violations of a municipal ordinance that is substantially similar to one of those sections may set a schedule for bail to be used in cases involving those violations. The schedule shall require that a judge consider all of the factors listed in division (A) of this section and may require judges to set bail at a certain level or impose other reasonable conditions related to a release on bail or on recognizance if the history of the alleged offender or the circumstances of the alleged offense meet certain criteria in the schedule.

(1992 H 536, eff. 11–5–92)

2903.213 Protection order as pretrial condition of release

(A) Except when the complaint involves a person who is a family or household member as defined in section 2919.25 of the Revised Code, upon the filing of a complaint that alleges a violation of section 2903.11, 2903.12, 2903.13, 2903.21, 2903.211, 2903.22, or 2911.211 of the Revised Code or a violation of a municipal ordinance substantially similar to section 2903.13, 2903.21, 2903.211, 2903.22, or 2911.211 of the Revised Code, the complainant, the alleged victim, or a family or household member of an alleged victim may file a motion that requests the issuance of a protection order as a pretrial condition of release of the alleged offender, in addition to any bail set under Criminal Rule 46. The motion shall be filed with the clerk of the court that has jurisdiction of the case at any time after the filing of the complaint. If the complaint involves a person who is a family or household member, the complainant, the alleged victim, or the family or household member may file a motion for a temporary protection order pursuant to section 2919.26 of the Revised Code.

(B) A motion for a protection order under this section shall be prepared on a form that is provided by the clerk of the court, and the form shall be substantially as follows:

"Motion for Protection Order

____

Name and address of court

State of Ohio

v. No. _____

____

Name of Defendant

(Name of person), moves the court to issue a protection order containing terms designed to ensure the safety and protection of the complainant or the alleged victim in the above-captioned case, in relation to the named defendant, pursuant to its authority to issue a protection order under section 2903.213 of the Revised Code.

A complaint, a copy of which has been attached to this motion, has been filed in this court charging the named defendant with a violation of section 2903.11, 2903.12, 2903.13, 2903.21, 2903.211, 2903.22, or 2911.211 of the Revised Code or a violation of a municipal ordinance substantially similar to section 2903.13, 2903.21, 2903.211, 2903.22, or 2911.211 of the Revised Code.

I understand that I must appear before the court, at a time set by the court not later than the next day that the court is in session after the filing of this motion, for a hearing on the motion, and that any protection order granted pursuant to this motion is a pretrial condition of release and is effective only until the disposition of the criminal proceeding arising out of the attached complaint or until the issuance under section 2903.214 of the Revised Code of a protection order arising out of the same activities as those that were the basis of the attached complaint.

____

Signature of person

____

Address of person"

(C)(1) As soon as possible after the filing of a motion that requests the issuance of a protection order under this section, but not later than the next day that the court is in session after the filing of the motion, the court shall conduct a hearing to determine whether to issue the order. The person who requested the order shall appear before the court and provide the court with the information that it requests concerning the basis of the motion. If the court finds that the safety and protection of the complainant or the alleged victim may be impaired by the continued presence of the alleged offender, the court may issue a protection order under this section, as a pretrial condition of release, that contains terms designed to ensure the safety and protection of the complainant or the alleged victim, including a requirement that the alleged offender refrain from entering the residence, school, business, or place of employment of the complainant or the alleged victim.

(2)(a) If the court issues a protection order under this section that includes a requirement that the alleged offender refrain from entering the residence, school, business, or place of employment of the complainant or the alleged victim, the order shall clearly state that the order cannot be waived or nullified by an invitation to the alleged offender from the complainant, the alleged victim, or a family or household member to enter the residence, school, business, or place of employment or by the alleged offender's entry into one of those places otherwise upon the consent of the complainant, the alleged victim, or a family or household member.

(b) Division (C)(2)(a) of this section does not limit any discretion of a court to determine that an alleged offender charged with a violation of section 2919.27 of the Revised Code, with a violation of a municipal ordinance substantially equivalent to that section, or with contempt of court, which charge is based on an alleged violation of a protection order issued under this section, did not commit the violation or was not in contempt of court.

(D)(1) Except when the complaint involves a person who is a family or household member as defined in section 2919.25 of the Revised Code, upon the filing of a complaint that alleges a violation specified in division (A) of this section, the court, upon its own motion, may issue a protection order under this section as a pretrial condition of release of the alleged offender if it finds that the safety and protection of the complainant or the alleged victim may be impaired by the continued presence of the alleged offender.

(2) If the court issues a protection order under this section as an ex parte order, it shall conduct, as soon as possible after the issuance of the order but not later than the next day that the court is in session after its issuance, a hearing to determine whether the order should remain in effect, be modified, or be revoked. The hearing shall be conducted under the standards set forth in division (C) of this section.

(3) If a municipal court or a county court issues a protection order under this section and if, subsequent to the issuance of the order, the alleged offender who is the subject of the order is bound over to the court of common pleas for prosecution of a felony arising out of the same activities as those that were the basis of the complaint upon which the order is based, notwithstanding the fact that the order was issued by a municipal court or county court, the order shall remain in effect, as though it were an order of the court of common pleas, while the charges against the alleged offender are pending in the court of common pleas, for the period of time described in division (E)(2) of this section, and the court of common pleas has exclusive jurisdiction to modify the order issued by the municipal court or county court. This division applies when the alleged offender is bound over to the court of common pleas as a result of the person waiving a preliminary hearing on the felony charge, as a result of the municipal court or county court having determined at a preliminary hearing that there is probable cause to believe that the felony has been committed and that the alleged offender committed it, as a result of the alleged offender having been indicted for the felony, or in any other manner.

(E) A protection order that is issued as a pretrial condition of release under this section:

(1) Is in addition to, but shall not be construed as a part of, any bail set under Criminal Rule 46;

(2) Is effective only until the disposition, by the court that issued the order or, in the circumstances described in division (D)(3) of this section, by the court of common pleas to which the alleged offender is bound over for prosecution, of the criminal proceeding arising out of the complaint upon which the order is based or until the issuance under section 2903.214 of the Revised Code of a protection order arising out of the same activities as those that were the basis of the complaint filed under this section;

(3) Shall not be construed as a finding that the alleged offender committed the alleged offense and shall not be introduced as evidence of the commission of the offense at the trial of the alleged offender on the complaint upon which the order is based.

(F) A person who meets the criteria for bail under Criminal Rule 46 and who, if required to do so pursuant to that rule, executes or posts bond or deposits cash or securities as bail, shall not be held in custody pending a hearing before the court on a motion requesting a protection order under this section.

(G)(1) A copy of a protection order that is issued under this section shall be issued by the court to the complainant, to the alleged victim, to the person who requested the order, to the defendant, and to all law enforcement agencies that have jurisdiction to enforce the order. The court shall direct that a copy of the order be delivered to the defendant on the same day that the order is entered. If a municipal court or a county court issues a protection order under this section and if, subsequent to the issuance of the order, the defendant who is the subject of the order is bound over to the court of common pleas for prosecution as described in division (D)(3) of this section, the municipal court or county court shall direct that a copy of the order be delivered to the court of common pleas to which the defendant is bound over.

(2) All law enforcement agencies shall establish and maintain an index for the protection orders delivered to the agencies pursuant to division (G)(1) of this section. With respect to each order delivered, each agency shall note on the index the date and time of the agency's receipt of the order.

(3) Regardless of whether the petitioner has registered the protection order in the county in which the officer's agency has jurisdiction, any officer of a law enforcement agency shall enforce a protection order issued pursuant to this section in accordance with the provisions of the order.

(H) Upon a violation of a protection order issued pursuant to this section, the court may issue another protection order under this section, as a pretrial condition of release, that modifies the terms of the order that was violated.

(I) Notwithstanding any provision of law to the contrary and regardless of whether a protection order is issued or a consent agreement is approved by a court of another county or by a court of another state, no court or unit of state or local government shall charge any fee, cost, deposit, or money in connection with the filing of a motion pursuant to this section, in connection with the filing, issuance, registration, or service of a protection order or consent agreement, or for obtaining certified copies of a protection order or consent agreement.

(2002 H 548, eff. 3–31–03; 1999 H 137, eff. 3–10–00; 1998 H 302, eff. 7–29–98; 1997 S 98, eff. 3–17–98; 1997 H 93, eff. 12–31–97; 1993 S 31, eff. 9–27–93; 1992 H 536)

2903.214 Protection orders; persons who may seek relief; ex parte orders

(A) As used in this section:

(1) "Court" means the court of common pleas of the county in which the person to be protected by the protection order resides.

(2) "Victim advocate" means a person who provides support and assistance for a person who files a petition under this section.

(3) "Family or household member" has the same meaning as in section 3113.31 of the Revised Code.

(4) "Protection order issued by a court of another state" has the same meaning as in section 2919.27 of the Revised Code.

(B) The court has jurisdiction over all proceedings under this section.

(C) A person may seek relief under this section for the person, or any parent or adult household member may seek relief under this section on behalf of any other family or household member, by filing a petition with the court. The petition shall contain or state both of the following:

(1) An allegation that the respondent engaged in a violation of section 2903.211 of the Revised Code against the person to be protected by the protection order, including a description of the nature and extent of the violation;

(2) A request for relief under this section.

(D)(1) If a person who files a petition pursuant to this section requests an ex parte order, the court shall hold an ex parte hearing as soon as possible after the petition is filed, but not later than the next day that the court is in session after the petition is filed. The court, for good cause shown at the ex parte hearing, may enter any temporary orders, with or without bond, that the court finds necessary for the safety and protection of the person to be protected by the order. Immediate and present danger to the person to be protected by the protection order constitutes good cause for purposes of this section. Immediate and present danger includes, but is not limited to, situations in which the respondent has threatened the person to be protected by the protection order with bodily harm or in which the respondent previously has been convicted of or pleaded guilty to a violation of section 2903.211 of the Revised Code against the person to be protected by the protection order.

(2)(a) If the court, after an ex parte hearing, issues a protection order described in division (E) of this section, the court shall schedule a full hearing for a date that is within ten court days after the ex parte hearing. The court shall give the respondent notice of, and an opportunity to be heard at, the full hearing. The court shall hold the full hearing on the date scheduled under this division unless the court grants a continuance of the hearing in accordance with this division. Under any of the following circumstances or for any of the following reasons, the court may grant a continuance of the full hearing to a reasonable time determined by the court:

(i) Prior to the date scheduled for the full hearing under this division, the respondent has not been served with the petition filed pursuant to this section and notice of the full hearing.

(ii) The parties consent to the continuance.

(iii) The continuance is needed to allow a party to obtain counsel.

(iv) The continuance is needed for other good cause.

(b) An ex parte order issued under this section does not expire because of a failure to serve notice of the full hearing upon the respondent before the date set for the full hearing under division (D)(2)(a) of this section or because the court grants a continuance under that division.

(3) If a person who files a petition pursuant to this section does not request an ex parte order, or if a person requests an ex parte order but the court does not issue an ex parte order after an ex parte hearing, the court shall proceed as in a normal civil action and grant a full hearing on the matter.

(E)(1) After an ex parte or full hearing, the court may issue any protection order, with or without bond, that contains terms designed to ensure the safety and protection of the person to be protected by the protection order, including, but not limited to, a requirement that the respondent refrain from entering the residence, school, business, or place of employment of the petitioner or family or household member. If the court includes a requirement that the respondent refrain from entering the residence, school, business, or place of employment of the petitioner or family or household member in the order, it also shall include in the order provisions of the type described in division (E)(5) of this section.

(2)(a) Any protection order issued pursuant to this section shall be valid until a date certain but not later than five years from the date of its issuance.

(b) Any protection order issued pursuant to this section may be renewed in the same manner as the original order was issued.

(3) A court may not issue a protection order that requires a petitioner to do or to refrain from doing an act that the court may require a respondent to do or to refrain from doing under division (E)(1) of this section unless all of the following apply:

(a) The respondent files a separate petition for a protection order in accordance with this section.

(b) The petitioner is served with notice of the respondent's petition at least forty-eight hours before the court holds a hearing with respect to the respondent's petition, or the petitioner waives the right to receive this notice.

(c) If the petitioner has requested an ex parte order pursuant to division (D) of this section, the court does not delay any hearing required by that division beyond the time specified in that division in order to consolidate the hearing with a hearing on the petition filed by the respondent.

(d) After a full hearing at which the respondent presents evidence in support of the request for a protection order and the petitioner is afforded an opportunity to defend against that evidence, the court determines that the petitioner has committed a violation of section 2903.211 of the Revised Code against the person to be protected by the protection order issued pursuant to this section or has violated a protection order issued pursuant to section 2903.213 of the Revised Code relative to the person to be protected by the protection order issued pursuant to this section.

(4) No protection order issued pursuant to this section shall in any manner affect title to any real property.

(5)(a) If the court issues a protection order under this section that includes a requirement that the alleged offender refrain from entering the residence, school, business, or place of employment of the petitioner or a family or household member, the order shall clearly state that the order cannot be waived or nullified by an invitation to the alleged offender from the complainant to enter the residence, school, business, or place of employment or by the alleged offender's entry into one of those places otherwise upon the consent of the petitioner or family or household member.

(b) Division (E)(5)(a) of this section does not limit any discretion of a court to determine that an alleged offender charged with a violation of section 2919.27 of the Revised Code, with a violation of a municipal ordinance substantially equivalent to that section, or with contempt of court, which charge is based on an alleged violation of a protection order issued under this section, did not commit the violation or was not in contempt of court.

(F)(1) The court shall cause the delivery of a copy of any protection order that is issued under this section to the petitioner, to the respondent, and to all law enforcement agencies that have jurisdiction to enforce the order. The court shall direct that a copy of the order be delivered to the respondent on the same day that the order is entered.

(2) All law enforcement agencies shall establish and maintain an index for the protection orders delivered to the agencies pursuant to division (F)(1) of this section. With respect to each order delivered, each agency shall note on the index the date and time that it received the order.

(3) Regardless of whether the petitioner has registered the protection order in the county in which the officer's agency has jurisdiction pursuant to division (M) of this section, any officer of a law enforcement agency shall enforce a protection order issued pursuant to this section by any court in this state in accordance with the provisions of the order, including removing the respondent from the premises, if appropriate.

(G) Any proceeding under this section shall be conducted in accordance with the Rules of Civil Procedure, except that a protection order may be obtained under this section with or without bond. An order issued under this section, other than an ex parte order, that grants a protection order, or that refuses to grant a protection order, is a final, appealable order. The remedies and procedures provided in this section are in addition to, and not in lieu of, any other available civil or criminal remedies.

(H) The filing of proceedings under this section does not excuse a person from filing any report or giving any notice required by section 2151.421 of the Revised Code or by any other law.

(I) Any law enforcement agency that investigates an alleged violation of section 2903.211 of the Revised Code shall provide information to the victim and the family or household members of the victim regarding the relief available under this section and section 2903.213 of the Revised Code.

(J) Notwithstanding any provision of law to the contrary and regardless of whether a protection order is issued or a consent agreement is approved by a court of another county or by a court of another state, no court or unit of state or local government shall charge any fee, cost, deposit, or money in connection with the filing of a petition pursuant to this section, in connection with the filing, issuance, registration, or service of a protection order or consent agreement, or for obtaining a certified copy of a protection order or consent agreement.

(K)(1) A person who violates a protection order issued under this section is subject to the following sanctions:

(a) Criminal prosecution for a violation of section 2919.27 of the Revised Code, if the violation of the protection order constitutes a violation of that section;

(b) Punishment for contempt of court.

(2) The punishment of a person for contempt of court for violation of a protection order issued under this section does not bar criminal prosecution of the person for a violation of section 2919.27 of the Revised Code. However, a person punished for contempt of court is entitled to credit for the punishment imposed upon conviction of a violation of that section, and a person convicted of a violation of that section shall not subsequently be punished for contempt of court arising out of the same activity.

(L) In all stages of a proceeding under this section, a petitioner may be accompanied by a victim advocate.

(M)(1) A petitioner who obtains a protection order under this section or a protection order under section 2903.213 of the Revised Code may provide notice of the issuance or approval of the order to the judicial and law enforcement officials in any county other than the county in which the order is issued by registering that order in the other county pursuant to division (M)(2) of this section and filing a copy of the registered order with a law enforcement agency in the other county in accordance with that division. A person who obtains a protection order issued by a court of another state may provide notice of the issuance of the order to the judicial and law enforcement officials in any county of this state by registering the order in that county pursuant to section 2919.272 of the Revised Code and filing a copy of the registered order with a law enforcement agency in that county.

(2) A petitioner may register a protection order issued pursuant to this section or section 2903.213 of the Revised Code in a county other than the county in which the court that issued the order is located in the following manner:

(a) The petitioner shall obtain a certified copy of the order from the clerk of the court that issued the order and present that certified copy to the clerk of the court of common pleas or the clerk of a municipal court or county court in the county in which the order is to be registered.

(b) Upon accepting the certified copy of the order for registration, the clerk of the court of common pleas, municipal court, or county court shall place an endorsement of registration on the order and give the petitioner a copy of the order that bears that proof of registration.

(3) The clerk of each court of common pleas, municipal court, or county court shall maintain a registry of certified copies of protection orders that have been issued by courts in other counties pursuant to this section or section 2903.213 of the Revised Code and that have been registered with the clerk.

(2002 H 548, eff. 3–31–03; 1998 H 302, eff. 7–29–98)

2903.22 Menacing

(A) No person shall knowingly cause another to believe that the offender will cause physical harm to the person or property of the other person, the other person's unborn, or a member of the other person's immediate family.

(B) Whoever violates this section is guilty of menacing. Except as otherwise provided in this division, menacing is a misdemeanor of the fourth degree. If the victim of the offense is an officer or employee of a public children services agency or a private child placing agency and the offense relates to the officer's or employee's performance or anticipated performance of official responsibilities or duties, menacing is a misdemeanor of the first degree or, if the offender previously has been convicted of or pleaded guilty to an offense of violence, the victim of that prior offense was an officer or employee of a public children services agency or private child placing agency, and that prior offense related to the officer's or employee's performance or anticipated performance of official responsibilities or duties, a felony of the fourth degree.

(2000 H 412, eff. 4–10–01; 1996 S 239, eff. 9–6–96; 1972 H 511, eff. 1–1–74)

HAZING

2903.31 Hazing; recklessly participating or permitting

(A) As used in this section, "hazing" means doing any act or coercing another, including the victim, to do any act of initiation into any student or other organization that causes or creates a substantial risk of causing mental or physical harm to any person.

(B)(1) No person shall recklessly participate in the hazing of another.

(2) No administrator, employee, or faculty member of any primary, secondary, or post-secondary school or of any other educational institution, public or private, shall recklessly permit the hazing of any person.

(C) Whoever violates this section is guilty of hazing, a misdemeanor of the fourth degree.

(1982 H 444, eff. 3–3–83)

PATIENT ABUSE OR NEGLECT

2903.33 Definitions

As used in sections 2903.33 to 2903.36 of the Revised Code:

(A) "Care facility" means any of the following:

(1) Any "home" as defined in section 3721.10 or 5111.20 of the Revised Code;

(2) Any "residential facility" as defined in section 5123.19 of the Revised Code;

(3) Any institution or facility operated or provided by the department of mental health or by the department of mental retardation and developmental disabilities pursuant to sections 5119.02 and 5123.03 of the Revised Code;

(4) Any "residential facility" as defined in section 5119.22 of the Revised Code;

(5) Any unit of any hospital, as defined in section 3701.01 of the Revised Code, that provides the same services as a nursing home, as defined in section 3721.01 of the Revised Code;

(6) Any institution, residence, or facility that provides, for a period of more than twenty-four hours, whether for a consideration or not, accommodations to one individual or two unrelated individuals who are dependent upon the services of others;

(7) Any "adult care facility" as defined in section 3722.01 of the Revised Code;

(8) Any adult foster home certified by the department of aging or its designee under section 173.36 of the Revised Code;

(9) Any "community alternative home" as defined in section 3724.01 of the Revised Code.

(B) "Abuse" means knowingly causing physical harm or recklessly causing serious physical harm to a person by physical contact with the person or by the inappropriate use of a physical or chemical restraint, medication, or isolation on the person.

(C)(1) "Gross neglect" means knowingly failing to provide a person with any treatment, care, goods, or service that is necessary to maintain the health or safety of the person when the failure results in physical harm or serious physical harm to the person.

(2) "Neglect" means recklessly failing to provide a person with any treatment, care, goods, or service that is necessary to maintain the health or safety of the person when the failure results in serious physical harm to the person.

(D) "Inappropriate use of a physical or chemical restraint, medication, or isolation" means the use of physical or chemical restraint, medication, or isolation as punishment, for staff convenience, excessively, as a substitute for treatment, or in quantities that preclude habilitation and treatment.

(1995 S 2, eff. 7–1–96; 1993 S 21, eff. 10–29–93; 1993 H 152; 1989 H 253, S 2; 1988 S 156; 1986 H 566)

2903.34 Patient abuse or neglect; spiritual treatment; defense

(A) No person who owns, operates, or administers, or who is an agent or employee of, a care facility shall do any of the following:

(1) Commit abuse against a resident or patient of the facility;

(2) Commit gross neglect against a resident or patient of the facility;

(3) Commit neglect against a resident or patient of the facility.

(B)(1) A person who relies upon treatment by spiritual means through prayer alone, in accordance with the tenets of a recognized religious denomination, shall not be considered neglected under division (A)(3) of this section for that reason alone.

(2) It is an affirmative defense to a charge of gross neglect or neglect under this section that the actor's conduct was committed in good faith solely because the actor was ordered to commit the conduct by a person with supervisory authority over the actor.

(C) Whoever violates division (A)(1) of this section is guilty of patient abuse, a felony of the fourth degree. If the offender previously has been convicted of, or pleaded guilty to, any violation of this section, patient abuse is a felony of the third degree.

(D) Whoever violates division (A)(2) of this section is guilty of gross patient neglect, a misdemeanor of the first degree. If the offender previously has been convicted of, or pleaded guilty to, any violation of this section, gross patient neglect is a felony of the fifth degree.

(E) Whoever violates division (A)(3) of this section is guilty of patient neglect, a misdemeanor of the second degree. If the offender previously has been convicted of or pleaded guilty to any violation of this section, patient neglect is a felony of the fifth degree.

(1995 S 2, eff. 7–1–96; 1986 H 566, eff. 9–17–86)

2903.341 Patient endangerment; affirmative defenses

(A) As used in this section:

(1) "MR/DD caretaker" means any MR/DD employee or any person who assumes the duty to provide for the care and protection of a mentally retarded person or a developmentally disabled person on a voluntary basis, by contract, through receipt of payment for care and protection, as a result of a family relationship, or by order of a court of competent jurisdiction. "MR/DD caretaker" includes a person who is an employee of a care facility and a person who is an employee of an entity under contract with a provider. "MR/DD caretaker" does not include a person who owns, operates, or administers a care facility or who is an agent of a care facility unless that person also personally provides care to persons with mental retardation or a developmental disability.

(2) "Mentally retarded person" and "developmentally disabled person" have the same meanings as in section 5123.01 of the Revised Code.

(3) "MR/DD employee" has the same meaning as in section 5123.50 of the Revised Code.

(B) No MR/DD caretaker shall create a substantial risk to the health or safety of a mentally retarded person or a developmentally disabled person. An MR/DD caretaker does not create a substantial risk to the health or safety of a mentally retarded person or a developmentally disabled person under this division when the MR/DD caretaker treats a physical or mental illness or defect of the mentally retarded person or developmentally disabled person by spiritual means through prayer alone, in accordance with the tenets of a recognized religious body.

(C) No person who owns, operates, or administers a care facility or who is an agent of a care facility shall condone, or knowingly permit, any conduct by an MR/DD caretaker who is employed by or under the control of the owner, operator, administrator, or agent that is in violation of division (B) of this section and that involves a mentally retarded person or a developmentally disabled person who is under the care of the owner, operator, administrator, or agent. A person who relies upon treatment by spiritual means through prayer alone, in accordance with the tenets of a recognized religious denomination, shall not be considered endangered under this division for that reason alone.

(D)(1) It is an affirmative defense to a charge of a violation of division (B) or (C) of this section that the actor's conduct was committed in good faith solely because the actor was ordered to commit the conduct by a person to whom one of the following applies:

(a) The person has supervisory authority over the actor.

(b) The person has authority over the actor's conduct pursuant to a contract for the provision of services.

(2) It is an affirmative defense to a charge of a violation of division (C) of this section that the person who owns, operates, or administers a care facility or who is an agent of a care facility and who is charged with the violation is following the individual service plan for the involved mentally retarded person or a developmentally disabled person or that the admission, discharge, and transfer rule set forth in the Administrative Code is being followed.

(3) It is an affirmative defense to a charge of a violation of division (C) of this section that the actor did not have readily available a means to prevent either the harm to the person with mental retardation or a developmental disability or the death of such a person and the actor took reasonable steps to summon aid.

(E)(1) Except as provided in division (E)(2) or (E)(3) of this section, whoever violates division (B) or (C) of this section is guilty of patient endangerment, a misdemeanor of the first degree.

(2) If the offender previously has been convicted of, or pleaded guilty to, a violation of this section, patient endangerment is a felony of the fourth degree.

(3) If the violation results in serious physical harm to the person with mental retardation or a developmental disability, patient endangerment is a felony of the third degree.

(2004 S 178, eff. 1–30–04)

2903.35 False statements

(A) No person shall knowingly make a false statement, or knowingly swear or affirm the truth of a false statement previously made, alleging a violation of section 2903.34 of the Revised Code, when the statement is made with purpose to incriminate another.

(B) Whoever violates this section is guilty of filing a false patient abuse or neglect complaint, a misdemeanor of the first degree.

(1986 H 566, eff. 9–17–86)

2903.36 Retaliation against person reporting patient abuse or neglect

No care facility shall discharge or in any manner discriminate or retaliate against any person solely because such person, in good faith, filed a complaint, affidavit, or other document alleging a violation of section 2903.34 of the Revised Code.

(1986 H 566, eff. 9–17–86)

2903.37 Revocation of license

Any individual, who owns, operates, or administers, or who is an agent or employee of, a care facility, who is convicted of a felony violation of section 2903.34 of the Revised Code, and who is required to be licensed under any law of this state, shall have his license revoked in accordance with Chapter 119. of the Revised Code.

(1986 H 566, eff. 9–17–86)

CHAPTER 2905

KIDNAPPING AND EXTORTION

KIDNAPPING AND RELATED OFFENSES

2905.01 Kidnapping

(A) No person, by force, threat, or deception, or, in the case of a victim under the age of thirteen or mentally incompetent, by any means, shall remove another from the place where the other person is found or restrain the liberty of the other person, for any of the following purposes:

(1) To hold for ransom, or as a shield or hostage;

(2) To facilitate the commission of any felony or flight thereafter;

(3) To terrorize, or to inflict serious physical harm on the victim or another;

(4) To engage in sexual activity, as defined in section 2907.01 of the Revised Code, with the victim against the victim's will;

(5) To hinder, impede, or obstruct a function of government, or to force any action or concession on the part of governmental authority.

(B) No person, by force, threat, or deception, or, in the case of a victim under the age of thirteen or mentally incompetent, by any means, shall knowingly do any of the following, under circumstances that create a substantial risk of serious physical harm to the victim or, in the case of a minor victim, under circumstances that either create a substantial risk of serious physical harm to the victim or cause physical harm to the victim:

(1) Remove another from the place where the other person is found;

(2) Restrain another of his liberty;

(3) Hold another in a condition of involuntary servitude.

(C) Whoever violates this section is guilty of kidnapping, a felony of the first degree. If the offender releases the victim in a safe place unharmed, kidnapping is a felony of the second degree.

(1995 S 2, eff. 7–1–96; 1982 H 269, § 4, eff. 7–1–83; 1982 S 199; 1972 H 511)

2905.02 Abduction

(A) No person, without privilege to do so, shall knowingly do any of the following:

(1) By force or threat, remove another from the place where the other person is found;

(2) By force or threat, restrain the liberty of another person, under circumstances which create a risk of physical harm to the victim, or place the other person in fear;

(3) Hold another in a condition of involuntary servitude.

(B) Whoever violates this section is guilty of abduction, a felony of the third degree.

(1995 S 2, eff. 7–1–96; 1982 H 269, § 4, eff. 7–1–83; 1982 S 199; 1972 H 511)

2905.03 Unlawful restraint

(A) No person, without privilege to do so, shall knowingly restrain another of his liberty.

(B) Whoever violates this section is guilty of unlawful restraint, a misdemeanor of the third degree.

(1972 H 511, eff. 1–1–74)

2905.05 Criminal child enticement

(A) No person, by any means and without privilege to do so, shall knowingly solicit, coax, entice, or lure any child under fourteen years of age to accompany the person in any manner, including entering into any vehicle or onto any vessel, whether or not the offender knows the age of the child, if both of the following apply:

(1) The actor does not have the express or implied permission of the parent, guardian, or other legal custodian of the child in undertaking the activity.

(2) The actor is not a law enforcement officer, medic, firefighter, or other person who regularly provides emergency services, and is not an employee or agent of, or a volunteer acting under the direction of, any board of education, or the actor is any of such persons, but, at the time the actor undertakes the activity, the actor is not acting within the scope of the actor's lawful duties in that capacity.

(B) It is an affirmative defense to a charge under division (A) of this section that the actor undertook the activity in response to a bona fide emergency situation or that the actor undertook the activity in a reasonable belief that it was necessary to preserve the health, safety, or welfare of the child.

(C) Whoever violates this section is guilty of criminal child enticement, a misdemeanor of the first degree. If the offender previously has been convicted of a violation of this section, section 2907.02, 2907.03, or 2907.12 of the Revised Code, or section 2905.01 or 2907.05 of the Revised Code when the victim of that prior offense was under seventeen years of age at the time of the offense, criminal child enticement is a felony of the fifth degree.

(D) As used in this section:

(1) "Vehicle" has the same meaning as in section 4501.01 of the Revised Code.

(2) "Vessel" has the same meaning as in section 1547.01 of the Revised Code.

(2004 S 160, eff. 4 11 05; 2000 S 312, eff. 4–9–01; 1995 S 2, eff. 7–1–96; 1984 S 321, eff. 4–9–85)

EXTORTION

2905.11 Extortion

(A) No person, with purpose to obtain any valuable thing or valuable benefit or to induce another to do an unlawful act, shall do any of the following:

(1) Threaten to commit any felony;

(2) Threaten to commit any offense of violence;

(3) Violate section 2903.21 or 2903.22 of the Revised Code;

(4) Utter or threaten any calumny against any person;

(5) Expose or threaten to expose any matter tending to subject any person to hatred, contempt, or ridicule, or to damage any person's personal or business repute, or to impair any person's credit.

(B) Whoever violates this section is guilty of extortion, a felony of the third degree.

(C) As used in this section, "threat" includes a direct threat and a threat by innuendo.

(1995 S 2, eff. 7–1–96; 1982 H 269, § 4, eff. 7–1–83; 1982 S 199; 1972 H 511)

2905.12 Coercion

(A) No person, with purpose to coerce another into taking or refraining from action concerning which the other person has a legal freedom of choice, shall do any of the following:

(1) Threaten to commit any offense;

(2) Utter or threaten any calumny against any person;

(3) Expose or threaten to expose any matter tending to subject any person to hatred, contempt, or ridicule, to damage any person's personal or business repute, or to impair any person's credit;

(4) Institute or threaten criminal proceedings against any person;

(5) Take, withhold, or threaten to take or withhold official action, or cause or threaten to cause official action to be taken or withheld.

(B) Divisions (A)(4) and (5) of this section shall not be construed to prohibit a prosecutor or court from doing any of the following in good faith and in the interests of justice:

(1) Offering or agreeing to grant, or granting immunity from prosecution pursuant to section 2945.44 of the Revised Code;

(2) In return for a plea of guilty to one or more offenses charged or to one or more other or lesser offenses, or in return for the testimony of the accused in a case to which the accused is not a party, offering or agreeing to dismiss, or dismissing one or more charges pending against an accused, or offering or agreeing to impose, or imposing a certain sentence or modification of sentence;

(3) Imposing a community control sanction on certain conditions, including without limitation requiring the offender to make restitution or redress to the victim of the offense.

(C) It is an affirmative defense to a charge under division (A)(3), (4), or (5) of this section that the actor's conduct was a reasonable response to the circumstances that occasioned it, and that the actor's purpose was limited to any of the following:

(1) Compelling another to refrain from misconduct or to desist from further misconduct;

(2) Preventing or redressing a wrong or injustice;

(3) Preventing another from taking action for which the actor reasonably believed the other person to be disqualified;

(4) Compelling another to take action that the actor reasonably believed the other person to be under a duty to take.

(D) Whoever violates this section is guilty of coercion, a misdemeanor of the second degree.

(E) As used in this section:

(1) "Threat" includes a direct threat and a threat by innuendo.

(2) "Community control sanction" has the same meaning as in section 2929.01 of the Revised Code.

(2002 H 490, eff. 1–1–04; 1972 H 511, eff. 1–1–74)

EXTORTIONATE EXTENSION OF CREDIT

2905.21 Definitions

As used in sections 2905.21 to 2905.24 of the Revised Code:

(A) "To extend credit" means to make or renew any loan, or to enter into any agreement, express or implied, for the repayment or satisfaction of any debt or claim, regardless of whether the extension of credit is acknowledged or disputed, valid or invalid, and however arising.

(B) "Creditor" means any person who extends credit, or any person claiming by, under, or through such a person.

(C) "Debtor" means any person who receives an extension of credit, any person who guarantees the repayment of an extension of credit, or any person who in any manner undertakes to indemnify the creditor against loss resulting from the failure of any recipient to repay an extension of credit.

(D) "Repayment" of an extension of credit means the repayment, satisfaction, or discharge in whole or in part of any debt or claim, acknowledged or disputed, valid or invalid, resulting from or in connection with that extension of credit.

(E) "Collect an extension of credit" means an attempt to collect from a debtor all or part of an amount due from the extension of credit.

(F) "Extortionate extension of credit" means any extension of credit with respect to which it is the understanding of the creditor and the debtor at the time it is made that delay in making repayment or failure to make repayment will result in the use of an extortionate means or if the debtor at a later time learns that failure to make repayment will result in the use of extortionate means.

(G) "Extortionate means" is any means that involves the use, or an express or implicit threat of use, of violence or other criminal means to cause harm to the person or property of the debtor or any member of his family.

(H) "Criminal usury" means illegally charging, taking, or receiving any money or other property as interest on an extension of credit at a rate exceeding twenty-five per cent per annum or the equivalent rate for a longer or shorter period, unless either:

(1) The rate of interest is otherwise authorized by law;

(2) The creditor and the debtor, or all the creditors and all the debtors are members of the same immediate family.

(I) "Immediate family" means a person's spouse residing in the person's household, brothers and sisters of the whole or of the half blood, and children, including adopted children.

(1978 H 88, eff. 10–9–78)

2905.22 Criminally usurious transactions prohibited

(A) No person shall:

(1) Knowingly make or participate in an extortionate extension of credit;

(2) Knowingly engage in criminal usury;

(3) Possess any writing, paper, instrument, or article used to record criminally usurious transactions, knowing that the contents record a criminally usurious transaction.

(B) Whoever violates division (A)(1) or (2) of this section is guilty of a felony of the fourth degree. Whoever violates division (A)(3) of this section is guilty of a misdemeanor of the first degree.

(1995 S 2, eff. 7–1–96; 1978 H 88, eff. 10–9–78)

2905.23 Evidence establishing probable cause of extortionate intent

In any prosecution under sections 2905.21 to 2905.24 of the Revised Code, if it is shown that any of the following factors were present in connection with the extension of credit, there is probable cause to believe that the extension of credit was extortionate:

(A) The extension of credit was made at a rate of interest in excess of that established for criminal usury;

(B) At the time credit was extended, the debtor reasonably believed that:

(1) One or more extensions of credit by the creditor were collected or attempted to be collected by extortionate means, or the nonrepayment thereof was punished by extortionate means;

(2) The creditor had a reputation for the use of extortionate means to collect extensions of credit or punish the nonrepayment thereof.

(1978 H 88, eff. 10–9–78)

2905.24 Proof of implicit threat

In any prosecution under sections 2905.21 to 2905.24 of the Revised Code, for the purpose of showing an implicit threat as a means of collection, evidence may be introduced tending to show that one or more extensions of credit by the creditor were, to the knowledge of the person against whom the implicit threat is alleged to have been made, collected, or attempted to be collected by extortionate means or that the nonrepayment thereof was punished by extortionate means.

(1978 H 88, eff. 10–9–78)

CHAPTER 2907

SEX OFFENSES

DEFINITIONS

2907.01 Definitions

As used in sections 2907.01 to 2907.37 of the Revised Code:

(A) "Sexual conduct" means vaginal intercourse between a male and female; anal intercourse, fellatio, and cunnilingus between persons regardless of sex; and, without privilege to do so, the insertion, however slight, of any part of the body or any instrument, apparatus, or other object into the vaginal or anal cavity of another. Penetration, however slight, is sufficient to complete vaginal or anal intercourse.

(B) "Sexual contact" means any touching of an erogenous zone of another, including without limitation the thigh, genitals, buttock, pubic region, or, if the person is a female, a breast, for the purpose of sexually arousing or gratifying either person.

(C) "Sexual activity" means sexual conduct or sexual contact, or both.

(D) "Prostitute" means a male or female who promiscuously engages in sexual activity for hire, regardless of whether the hire is paid to the prostitute or to another.

(E) "Harmful to juveniles" means that quality of any material or performance describing or representing nudity, sexual conduct, sexual excitement, or sado-masochistic abuse in any form to which all of the following apply:

(1) The material or performance, when considered as a whole, appeals to the prurient interest in sex of juveniles.

(2) The material or performance is patently offensive to prevailing standards in the adult community as a whole with respect to what is suitable for juveniles.

(3) The material or performance, when considered as a whole, lacks serious literary, artistic, political, and scientific value for juveniles.

(F) When considered as a whole, and judged with reference to ordinary adults or, if it is designed for sexual deviates or other specially susceptible group, judged with reference to that group, any material or performance is "obscene" if any of the following apply:

(1) Its dominant appeal is to prurient interest;

(2) Its dominant tendency is to arouse lust by displaying or depicting sexual activity, masturbation, sexual excitement, or nudity in a way that tends to represent human beings as mere objects of sexual appetite;

(3) Its dominant tendency is to arouse lust by displaying or depicting bestiality or extreme or bizarre violence, cruelty, or brutality;

(4) Its dominant tendency is to appeal to scatological interest by displaying or depicting human bodily functions of elimination in a way that inspires disgust or revulsion in persons with ordinary sensibilities, without serving any genuine scientific, educational, sociological, moral, or artistic purpose;

(5) It contains a series of displays or descriptions of sexual activity, masturbation, sexual excitement, nudity, bestiality, extreme or bizarre violence, cruelty, or brutality, or human bodily functions of elimination, the cumulative effect of which is a dominant tendency to appeal to prurient or scatological interest, when the appeal to such an interest is primarily for its own sake or for commercial exploitation, rather than primarily for a genuine scientific, educational, sociological, moral, or artistic purpose.

(G) "Sexual excitement" means the condition of human male or female genitals when in a state of sexual stimulation or arousal.

(H) "Nudity" means the showing, representation, or depiction of human male or female genitals, pubic area, or buttocks with less than a full, opaque covering, or of a female breast with less than a full, opaque covering of any portion thereof below the top of the nipple, or of covered male genitals in a discernibly turgid state.

(I) "Juvenile" means an unmarried person under the age of eighteen.

(J) "Material" means any book, magazine, newspaper, pamphlet, poster, print, picture, figure, image, description, motion picture film, phonographic record, or tape, or other tangible thing capable of arousing interest through sight, sound, or touch and includes an image or text appearing on a computer monitor, television screen, liquid crystal display, or similar display device or an image or text recorded on a computer hard disk, computer floppy disk, compact disk, magnetic tape, or similar data storage device.

(K) "Performance" means any motion picture, preview, trailer, play, show, skit, dance, or other exhibition performed before an audience.

(L) "Spouse" means a person married to an offender at the time of an alleged offense, except that such person shall not be considered the spouse when any of the following apply:

(1) When the parties have entered into a written separation agreement authorized by section 3103.06 of the Revised Code;

(2) During the pendency of an action between the parties for annulment, divorce, dissolution of marriage, or legal separation;

(3) In the case of an action for legal separation, after the effective date of the judgment for legal separation.

(M) "Minor" means a person under the age of eighteen.

(N) "Mental health client or patient" has the same meaning as in section 2305.51 of the Revised Code.

(O) "Mental health professional" has the same meaning as in section 2305.115 of the Revised Code.

(P) "Sado–masochistic abuse" means flagellation or torture by or upon a person or the condition of being fettered, bound, or otherwise physically restrained.

(2002 H 490, eff. 1–1–04; 2002 H 8, eff. 8–5–02; 2002 S 9, eff. 5–14–02; 1997 H 32, eff. 3–10–98; 1996 H 445, eff. 9–3–96; 1990 H 514, eff. 1–1–91; 1988 H 51; 1975 S 144; 1972 H 511)

SEXUAL ASSAULTS

2907.02 Rape; evidence; marriage or cohabitation not defenses to rape charges

(A)(1) No person shall engage in sexual conduct with another who is not the spouse of the offender or who is the spouse of the offender but is living separate and apart from the offender, when any of the following applies:

(a) For the purpose of preventing resistance, the offender substantially impairs the other person's judgment or control by administering any drug, intoxicant, or controlled substance to the other person surreptitiously or by force, threat of force, or deception.

(b) The other person is less than thirteen years of age, whether or not the offender knows the age of the other person.

(c) The other person's ability to resist or consent is substantially impaired because of a mental or physical condition or because of advanced age, and the offender knows or has reasonable cause to believe that the other person's ability to resist or consent is substantially impaired because of a mental or physical condition or because of advanced age.

(2) No person shall engage in sexual conduct with another when the offender purposely compels the other person to submit by force or threat of force.

(B) Whoever violates this section is guilty of rape, a felony of the first degree. If the offender under division (A)(1)(a) of this section substantially impairs the other person's judgment or control by administering any controlled substance described in section 3719.41 of the Revised Code to the other person surreptitiously or by force, threat of force, or deception, the prison term imposed upon the offender shall be one of the prison terms prescribed for a felony of the first degree in section 2929.14 of the Revised Code that is not less than five years. If the offender under division (A)(1)(b) of this section purposely compels the victim to submit by force or threat of force or if the victim under division (A)(1)(b) of this section is less than ten years of age, whoever violates division (A)(1)(b) of this section shall be imprisoned for life. If the offender under division (A)(1)(b) of this section previously has been convicted of or pleaded guilty to violating division (A)(1)(b) of this section or to violating a law of another state or the United States that is substantially similar to division (A)(1)(b) of this section or if the offender during or immediately after the commission of the offense caused serious physical harm to the victim, whoever violates division (A)(1)(b) of this section shall be imprisoned for life or life without parole.

(C) A victim need not prove physical resistance to the offender in prosecutions under this section.

(D) Evidence of specific instances of the victim's sexual activity, opinion evidence of the victim's sexual activity, and reputation evidence of the victim's sexual activity shall not be admitted under this section unless it involves evidence of the origin of semen, pregnancy, or disease, or the victim's past sexual activity with the offender, and only to the extent that the court finds that the evidence is material to a fact at issue in the case and that its inflammatory or prejudicial nature does not outweigh its probative value.

Evidence of specific instances of the defendant's sexual activity, opinion evidence of the defendant's sexual activity, and reputation evidence of the defendant's sexual activity shall not be admitted under this section unless it involves evidence of the origin of semen, pregnancy, or disease, the defendant's past sexual activity with the victim, or is admissible against the defendant under section 2945.59 of the Revised Code, and only to the extent that the court finds that the evidence is material to a fact at issue in the case and that its inflammatory or prejudicial nature does not outweigh its probative value.

(E) Prior to taking testimony or receiving evidence of any sexual activity of the victim or the defendant in a proceeding under this section, the court shall resolve the admissibility of the proposed evidence in a hearing in chambers, which shall be held at or before preliminary hearing and not less than three days before trial, or for good cause shown during the trial.

(F) Upon approval by the court, the victim may be represented by counsel in any hearing in chambers or other proceeding to resolve the admissibility of evidence. If the victim is indigent or otherwise is unable to obtain the services of counsel, the court, upon request, may appoint counsel to represent the victim without cost to the victim.

(G) It is not a defense to a charge under division (A)(2) of this section that the offender and the victim were married or were cohabiting at the time of the commission of the offense.

(2002 H 485, eff. 6–13–02; 1997 H 32, eff. 3–10–98; 1995 S 2, eff. 7–1–96; 1993 S 31, eff. 9–27–93; 1985 H 475; 1982 H 269, § 4, S 199; 1975 S 144; 1972 H 511)

2907.03 Sexual battery

(A) No person shall engage in sexual conduct with another, not the spouse of the offender, when any of the following apply:

(1) The offender knowingly coerces the other person to submit by any means that would prevent resistance by a person of ordinary resolution.

(2) The offender knows that the other person's ability to appraise the nature of or control the other person's own conduct is substantially impaired.

(3) The offender knows that the other person submits because the other person is unaware that the act is being committed.

(4) The offender knows that the other person submits because the other person mistakenly identifies the offender as the other person's spouse.

(5) The offender is the other person's natural or adoptive parent, or a stepparent, or guardian, custodian, or person in loco parentis of the other person.

(6) The other person is in custody of law or a patient in a hospital or other institution, and the offender has supervisory or disciplinary authority over the other person.

(7) The offender is a teacher, administrator, coach, or other person in authority employed by or serving in a school for which the state board of education prescribes minimum standards pursuant to division (D) of section 3301.07 of the Revised Code, the other person is enrolled in or attends that school, and the offender is not enrolled in and does not attend that school.

(8) The other person is a minor, the offender is a teacher, administrator, coach, or other person in authority employed by or serving in an institution of higher education, and the other person is enrolled in or attends that institution.

(9) The other person is a minor, and the offender is the other person's athletic or other type of coach, is the other person's instructor, is the leader of a scouting troop of which the other person is a member, or is a person with temporary or occasional disciplinary control over the other person.

(10) The offender is a mental health professional, the other person is a mental health client or patient of the offender, and the offender induces the other person to submit by falsely representing to the other person that the sexual conduct is necessary for mental health treatment purposes.

(11) The other person is confined in a detention facility, and the offender is an employee of that detention facility.

(B) Whoever violates this section is guilty of sexual battery, a felony of the third degree.

(C) As used in this section:

(1) "Detention facility" has the same meaning as in section 2921.01 of the Revised Code.

(2) "Institution of higher education" means a state institution of higher education defined in section 3345.011 of the Revised Code, a private nonprofit college or university located in this state that possesses a certificate of authorization issued by the Ohio board of regents pursuant to Chapter 1713. of the Revised Code, or a school certified under Chapter 3332. of the Revised Code.

(2002 H 510, eff. 3–31–03; 2002 S 9, eff. 5–14–02; 1997 H 32, eff. 3–10–98; 1997 S 6, eff. 6–20–97; 1995 S 2, eff. 7–1–96; 1994 H 454, eff. 7–19–94; 1972 H 511, eff. 1–1–74)

2907.04 Unlawful sexual conduct with a minor

(A) No person who is eighteen years of age or older shall engage in sexual conduct with another, who is not the spouse of the offender, when the offender knows the other person is thirteen years of age or older but less than sixteen years of age, or the offender is reckless in that regard.

(B) Whoever violates this section is guilty of unlawful sexual conduct with a minor.

(1) Except as otherwise provided in divisions (B)(2), (3), and (4) of this section, unlawful sexual conduct with a minor is a felony of the fourth degree.

(2) Except as otherwise provided in division (B)(4) of this section, if the offender is less than four years older than the other person, unlawful sexual conduct with a minor is a misdemeanor of the first degree.

(3) Except as otherwise provided in division (B)(4) of this section, if the offender is ten or more years older than the other person, unlawful sexual conduct with a minor is a felony of the third degree.

(4) If the offender previously has been convicted of or pleaded guilty to a violation of section 2907.02, 2907.03, or 2907.04 of the Revised Code or a violation of former section 2907.12 of the Revised Code, unlawful sexual conduct with a minor is a felony of the second degree.

(2000 H 442, eff. 10–17–00; 1995 S 2, eff. 7–1–96; 1990 H 44, eff. 7–24–90; 1972 H 511)

2907.05 Gross sexual imposition

(A) No person shall have sexual contact with another, not the spouse of the offender; cause another, not the spouse of the offender, to have sexual contact with the offender; or cause two or more other persons to have sexual contact when any of the following applies:

(1) The offender purposely compels the other person, or one of the other persons, to submit by force or threat of force.

(2) For the purpose of preventing resistance, the offender substantially impairs the judgment or control of the other person or of one of the other persons by administering any drug, intoxicant, or controlled substance to the other person surreptitiously or by force, threat of force, or deception.

(3) The offender knows that the judgment or control of the other person or of one of the other persons is substantially impaired as a result of the influence of any drug or intoxicant administered to the other person with the other person's consent for the purpose of any kind of medical or dental examination, treatment, or surgery.

(4) The other person, or one of the other persons, is less than thirteen years of age, whether or not the offender knows the age of that person.

(5) The ability of the other person to resist or consent or the ability of one of the other persons to resist or consent is substantially impaired because of a mental or physical condition or because of advanced age, and the offender knows or has reasonable cause to believe that the ability to resist or consent of the other person or of one of the other persons is substantially impaired because of a mental or physical condition or because of advanced age.

(B) Whoever violates this section is guilty of gross sexual imposition. Except as otherwise provided in this section, a violation of division (A)(1), (2), (3), or (5) of this section is a felony of the fourth degree. If the offender under division (A)(2) of this section substantially impairs the judgment or control of the other person or one of the other persons by administering any controlled substance described in section 3719.41 of the Revised Code to the person surreptitiously or by force, threat of force, or deception, a violation of division (A)(2) of this section is a felony of the third degree. A violation of division (A)(4) of this section is a felony of the third degree.

(C) A victim need not prove physical resistance to the offender in prosecutions under this section.

(D) Evidence of specific instances of the victim's sexual activity, opinion evidence of the victim's sexual activity, and reputation evidence of the victim's sexual activity shall not be admitted under this section unless it involves evidence of the origin of semen, pregnancy, or disease, or the victim's past sexual activity with the offender, and only to the extent that the court finds that the evidence is material to a fact at issue in the case and that its inflammatory or prejudicial nature does not outweigh its probative value.

Evidence of specific instances of the defendant's sexual activity, opinion evidence of the defendant's sexual activity, and reputation evidence of the defendant's sexual activity shall not be admitted under this section unless it involves evidence of the origin of semen, pregnancy, or disease, the defendant's past sexual activity with the victim, or is admissible against the defendant under section 2945.59 of the Revised Code, and only to the extent that the court finds that the evidence is material to a fact at issue in the case and that its inflammatory or prejudicial nature does not outweigh its probative value.

(E) Prior to taking testimony or receiving evidence of any sexual activity of the victim or the defendant in a proceeding under this section, the court shall resolve the admissibility of the proposed evidence in a hearing in chambers, which shall be held at or before preliminary hearing and not less than three days before trial, or for good cause shown during the trial.

(F) Upon approval by the court, the victim may be represented by counsel in any hearing in chambers or other proceeding to resolve the admissibility of evidence. If the victim is indigent or otherwise is unable to obtain the services of counsel, the court, upon request, may appoint counsel to represent the victim without cost to the victim.

(1997 H 32, eff. 3–10–98; 1993 S 31, eff. 9–27–93; 1990 H 208; 1977 H 134; 1975 S 144; 1972 H 511)

2907.06 Sexual imposition

(A) No person shall have sexual contact with another, not the spouse of the offender; cause another, not the spouse of the offender, to have sexual contact with the offender; or cause two or more other persons to have sexual contact when any of the following applies:

(1) The offender knows that the sexual contact is offensive to the other person, or one of the other persons, or is reckless in that regard.

(2) The offender knows that the other person's, or one of the other person's, ability to appraise the nature of or control the offender's or touching person's conduct is substantially impaired.

(3) The offender knows that the other person, or one of the other persons, submits because of being unaware of the sexual contact.

(4) The other person, or one of the other persons, is thirteen years of age or older but less than sixteen years of age, whether or not the offender knows the age of such person, and the offender is at least eighteen years of age and four or more years older than such other person.

(5) The offender is a mental health professional, the other person or one of the other persons is a mental health client or patient of the offender, and the offender induces the other person who is the client or patient to submit by falsely representing to the other person who is the client or patient that the sexual contact is necessary for mental health treatment purposes.

(B) No person shall be convicted of a violation of this section solely upon the victim's testimony unsupported by other evidence.

(C) Whoever violates this section is guilty of sexual imposition, a misdemeanor of the third degree. If the offender previously has been convicted of a violation of this section or of section 2907.02, 2907.03, 2907.04, 2907.05, or 2907.12 of the Revised Code, a violation of this section is a misdemeanor of the first degree.

(2002 S 9, eff. 5–14–02; 1995 S 2, eff. 7–1–96; 1990 H 44, eff. 7–24–90; 1977 H 134; 1972 H 511)

2907.07 Importuning

(A) No person shall solicit a person who is less than thirteen years of age to engage in sexual activity with the offender, whether or not the offender knows the age of such person.

(B) No person shall solicit another, not the spouse of the offender, to engage in sexual conduct with the offender, when the offender is eighteen years of age or older and four or more years older than the other person, and the other person is thirteen years of age or older but less than sixteen years of age, whether or not the offender knows the age of the other person.

(C) No person shall solicit another by means of a telecommunications device, as defined in section 2913.01 of the Revised Code, to engage in sexual activity with the offender when the offender is eighteen years of age or older and either of the following applies:

(1) The other person is less than thirteen years of age, and the offender knows that the other person is less than thirteen years of age or is reckless in that regard.

(2) The other person is a law enforcement officer posing as a person who is less than thirteen years of age, and the offender believes that the other person is less than thirteen years of age or is reckless in that regard.

(D) No person shall solicit another by means of a telecommunications device, as defined in section 2913.01 of the Revised Code, to engage in sexual activity with the offender when the offender is eighteen years of age or older and either of the following applies:

(1) The other person is thirteen years of age or older but less than sixteen years of age, the offender knows that the other person is thirteen years of age or older but less than sixteen years of age or is reckless in that regard, and the offender is four or more years older than the other person.

(2) The other person is a law enforcement officer posing as a person who is thirteen years of age or older but less than sixteen years of age, the offender believes that the other person is thirteen years of age or older but less than sixteen years of age or is reckless in that regard, and the offender is four or more years older than the age the law enforcement officer assumes in posing as the person who is thirteen years of age or older but less than sixteen years of age.

(E) Divisions (C) and (D) of this section apply to any solicitation that is contained in a transmission via a telecommunications device that either originates in this state or is received in this state.

(F) Whoever violates this section is guilty of importuning. A violation of division (A) or (C) of this section is a felony of the fourth degree on a first offense and a felony of the third degree on each subsequent offense. A violation of division (B) or (D) of this section is a felony of the fifth degree on a first offense and a felony of the fourth degree on each subsequent offense.

(2003 S 5, eff. 7–31–03; 2002 S 175, eff. 5–7–02; 2000 H 724, eff. 3–22–01; 1972 H 511, eff. 1–1–74)

2907.08 Voyeurism

(A) No person, for the purpose of sexually arousing or gratifying the person's self, shall commit trespass or otherwise surreptitiously invade the privacy of another, to spy or eavesdrop upon another.

(B) No person, for the purpose of sexually arousing or gratifying the person's self, shall commit trespass or otherwise surreptitiously invade the privacy of another to photograph the other person in a state of nudity.

(C) No person, for the purpose of sexually arousing or gratifying the person's self, shall commit trespass or otherwise surreptitiously invade the privacy of another to photograph the other person in a state of nudity if the other person is a minor.

(D) No person, for the purpose of sexually arousing or gratifying the person's self, shall commit trespass or otherwise surreptitiously invade the privacy of another to photograph the other person in a state of nudity if the other person is a minor and any of the following applies:

(1) The offender is the minor's natural or adoptive parent, stepparent, guardian, or custodian, or person in loco parentis of the minor.

(2) The minor is in custody of law or is a patient in a hospital or other institution, and the offender has supervisory or disciplinary authority over the minor.

(3) The offender is a teacher, administrator, coach, or other person in authority employed by or serving in a school for which the state board of education prescribes minimum standards pursuant to division (D) of section 3301.07 of the Revised Code, the minor is enrolled in or attends that school, and the offender is not enrolled in and does not attend that school.

(4) The offender is a teacher, administrator, coach, or other person in authority employed by or serving in an institution of higher education, and the minor is enrolled in or attends that institution.

(5) The offender is a caregiver, administrator, or other person in authority employed by or serving in a child day-care center, type A family day-care home, or type B family day-care home, and the minor is enrolled in or attends that center or home.

(6) The offender is the minor's athletic or other type of coach, is the minor's instructor, is the leader of a scouting troop of which the minor is a member, provides babysitting care for the minor, or is a person with temporary or occasional disciplinary control over the minor.

(E) No person shall secretly or surreptitiously videotape, film, photograph, or otherwise record another person under or through the clothing being worn by that other person for the purpose of viewing the body of, or the undergarments worn by, that other person.

(F)(1) Whoever violates this section is guilty of voyeurism.

(2) A violation of division (A) of this section is a misdemeanor of the third degree.

(3) A violation of division (B) of this section is a misdemeanor of the second degree.

(4) A violation of division (C) or (E) of this section is a misdemeanor of the first degree.

(5) A violation of division (D) of this section is a felony of the fifth degree.

(G) As used in this section:

(1) "Institution of higher education" means a state institution of higher education as defined in section 3345.031 of the Revised Code, a private nonprofit college or university located in this state that possesses a certificate of authorization issued by the Ohio board of regents pursuant to Chapter 1713. of the Revised Code, or a school certified under Chapter 3332. of the Revised Code.

(2) "Child day-care center," "type A family day-care home," and "type B family day-care home" have the same meanings as in section 5104.01 of the Revised Code.

(3) "Babysitting care" means care provided for a child while the parents, guardian, or legal custodian of the child is are [1] temporarily away.

(2000 H 332, eff. 1–1–01; 2000 H 504, eff. 10–10–00; 2000 H 448, eff. 10–5–00; 1997 S 82, eff. 1–30–98; 1972 H 511, eff. 1–1–74)

[1] So in original; language appears as the result of the harmonization of 2000 H 332 and 2000 H 448.

2907.09 Public indecency

(A) No person shall recklessly do any of the following, under circumstances in which his or her conduct is likely to be viewed by and affront others, not members of his or her household:

(1) Expose his or her private parts, or engage in masturbation;

(2) Engage in sexual conduct;

(3) Engage in conduct that to an ordinary observer would appear to be sexual conduct or masturbation.

(B) Whoever violates this section is guilty of public indecency. Except as otherwise provided in this division, public indecency is a misdemeanor of the fourth degree. If the offender previously has been convicted of or pleaded guilty to one violation of this section, public indecency is a misdemeanor of the third degree. If the offender previously has been convicted of or pleaded guilty to two violations of this section, public indecency is a misdemeanor of the second degree. If the offender previously has been convicted of or pleaded guilty to three or more violations of this section, public indecency is a misdemeanor of the first degree.

(1995 S 2, eff. 7–1–96; 1990 H 214, eff. 4–13–90; 1972 H 511)

2907.11 Suppression of certain information

Upon the request of the victim or offender in a prosecution under any provision of sections 2907.02 to 2907.07 of the Revised Code, the judge before whom any person is brought on a charge of having committed an offense under a provision of one of those sections shall order that the names of the victim and offender and the details of the alleged offense as obtained by any law enforcement officer be suppressed until the preliminary hearing, the accused is arraigned in the court of common pleas, the charge is dismissed, or the case is otherwise concluded, whichever occurs first. Nothing in this section shall be construed to deny to either party in the case the name and address of the other party or the details of the alleged offense.

(1996 H 445, eff. 9–3–96; 1975 S 144, eff. 8–27–75)

2907.15 Restitution from offender's government deferred compensation program or public retirement system

(A) As used in this section:

(1) "Public retirement system" means the public employees retirement system, state teachers retirement system, school employees retirement system, Ohio police and fire pension fund, state highway patrol retirement system, or a municipal retirement system of a municipal corporation of this state.

(2) "Government deferred compensation program" means such a program offered by the Ohio public employees deferred compensation board; a municipal corporation; or a governmental unit, as defined in section 148.06 of the Revised Code.

(3) "Deferred compensation program participant" means a "participating employee" or "continuing member," as defined in section 148.01 of the Revised Code, or any other public employee who has funds in a government deferred compensation program.

(4) "Alternative retirement plan" means an alternative retirement plan provided pursuant to Chapter 3305. of the Revised Code.

(5) "Prosecutor" has the same meaning as in section 2935.01 of the Revised Code.

In any case in which a sentencing court orders restitution to the victim under section 2929.18 or 2929.28 of the Revised Code for a violation of section 2907.02, 2907.03, 2907.04, or 2907.05 of the Revised Code and in which the offender is a government deferred compensation program participant, is an electing employee, as defined in section 3305.01 of the Revised Code, or is a member of, or receiving a pension, benefit, or allowance, other than a survivorship benefit, from, a public retirement system and committed the offense against a child, student, patient, or other person with whom the offender had contact in the context of the offender's public employment, at the request of the victim the prosecutor shall file a motion with the sentencing court specifying the government deferred compensation program, alternative retirement plan, or public retirement system and requesting that the court issue an order requiring the government deferred compensation program, alternative retirement plan, or public retirement system to withhold the amount required as restitution from one or more of the following: any payment to be made from a government deferred compensation program, any payment or benefit under an alternative retirement plan, or under a pension, annuity, allowance, or any other benefit, other than a survivorship benefit, that has been or is in the future granted to the offender; from any payment of accumulated employee contributions standing to the offender's credit with the government deferred compensation program, alternative retirement plan, or public retirement system; or from any payment of any other amounts to be paid to the offender pursuant to Chapter 145., 148., 742., 3307., 3309., or 5505. of the Revised Code on withdrawal of contributions. The motion may be filed at any time subsequent to the conviction of the offender or entry of a guilty plea. On the filing of the motion, the clerk of the court in which the motion is filed shall notify the offender and the government deferred compensation program, alternative retirement plan, or public retirement system, in writing, of all of the following: that the motion was filed; that the offender will be granted a hearing on the issuance of the requested order if the offender files a written request for a hearing with the clerk prior to the expiration of thirty days after the offender receives the notice; that, if a hearing is requested, the court will schedule a hearing as soon as possible and notify the offender and the government deferred compensation program, alternative retirement plan, or public retirement system of the date, time, and place of the hearing; that, if a hearing is conducted, it will be limited to a consideration of whether the offender can show good cause why the order should not be issued; that, if a hearing is conducted, the court will not issue the order if the court determines, based on evidence presented at the hearing by the offender, that there is good cause for the order not to be issued; that the court will issue the order if a hearing is not requested or if a hearing is conducted but the court does not determine, based on evidence presented at the hearing by the offender, that there is good cause for the order not to be issued; and that, if the order is issued, the government deferred compensation program, alternative retirement plan, or public retirement system specified in the motion will be required to withhold the amount required as restitution from payments to the offender.

(B) In any case in which a motion requesting the issuance of a withholding order as described in division (A) of this section is filed, the offender may receive a hearing on the motion by delivering a written request for a hearing to the court prior to the expiration of thirty days after the offender's receipt of the notice provided pursuant to division (A) of this section. If the offender requests a hearing within the prescribed time, the court shall schedule a hearing as soon as possible after the request is made and notify the offender and the government deferred compensation program, alternative retirement plan, or public retirement system of the date, time, and place of the hearing. A hearing scheduled under this division shall be limited to a consideration of whether there is good cause, based on evidence presented by the offender, for the requested order not to be issued. If the court determines, based on evidence presented by the offender, that there is good cause for the order not to be issued, the court shall deny the motion and shall not issue the order. Good cause for not issuing the order includes a determination by the court that the order would severely impact the offender's ability to support the offender's dependents.

If the offender does not request a hearing within the prescribed time or the court conducts a hearing but does not determine, based on evidence presented by the offender, that there is good cause for the order not to be issued, the court shall order the government deferred compensation program, alternative retirement plan, or public retirement system to withhold the amount required as restitution from one or more of the following: any payments to be made from a government deferred compensation program, any payment or benefit under an alternative retirement plan, or under a pension, annuity, allowance, or under any other benefit, other than a survivorship benefit, that has been or is in the future granted to the offender; from any payment of accumulated employee contributions standing to the offender's credit with the government deferred compensation program, alternative retirement plan, or public retirement system; or from any payment of any other amounts to be paid to the offender upon withdrawal of contributions pursuant to Chapter 145., 148., 742., 3307., 3309., or 5505. of the Revised Code and to continue the withholding for that purpose, in accordance with the order, out of each payment to be made on or after the date of issuance of the order, until further order of the court. On receipt of an order issued under this division, the government deferred compensation program, alternative retirement plan, or public retirement system shall withhold the amount required as restitution, in accordance with the order, from any such payments and immediately forward the amount withheld to the clerk of the court in which the order was issued for payment to the person to whom restitution is to be made. The order shall not apply to any portion of payments made from a government deferred compensation program, alternative retirement plan, or public retirement system to a person other than the offender pursuant to a previously issued domestic court order.

(C) Service of a notice required by division (A) or (B) of this section shall be effected in the same manner as provided in the Rules of Civil Procedure for the service of process.

(D) Upon the filing of charges under section 2907.02, 2907.03, 2907.04, or 2907.05 of the Revised Code against a person who is a deferred compensation program participant, an electing employee participating in an alternative retirement plan, or a member of, or receiving a pension benefit, or allowance, other than a survivorship benefit, from a public retirement system for an offense against a child, student, patient, or other person with whom the offender had contact in the context of the offender's public employment, the prosecutor shall send written notice that charges have been filed against that person to the appropriate government deferred compensation program, alternative retirement plan, or public retirement system. The notice shall specifically identify the person charged.

(2002 H 490, eff. 1–1–04; 2000 H 535, eff. 4–1–01; 2000 H 628, eff. 9–21–00; 1999 H 222, eff. 11–2–99; 1996 H 668, eff. 12–6–96)

2907.17 Notice to licensing board or agency upon indictment of mental health professional

If a mental health professional is indicted or charged and bound over to the court of common pleas for trial for an alleged violation of division (A)(10) of section 2907.03 or division (A)(5) of section 2907.06 of the Revised Code, the prosecuting attorney handling the case shall send written notice of the indictment or the charge and bind over to the regulatory or licensing board or agency, if any, that has the administrative authority to suspend or revoke the mental health professional's professional license, certification, registration, or authorization.

(2002 S 9, eff. 5–14–02)

2907.171 Effect of failure to give notice

The failure of the prosecuting attorney to give the notice required by section 2907.17 of the Revised Code does not give rise to a claim for damages against the prosecuting attorney or the county. The failure of the prosecuting attorney to give the notice does not constitute grounds for declaring a mistrial or new trial, for setting aside a conviction or sentence, or for granting postconviction relief to a defendant.

(2002 S 9, eff. 5–14–02)

2907.18 Notice to licensing board or agency upon conviction or guilty plea of mental health professional

If a mental health professional is convicted of or pleads guilty to a violation of division (A)(10) of section 2907.03 or division (A)(5) of section 2907.06 of the Revised Code, the court shall transmit a certified copy of the judgment entry of conviction to the regulatory or licensing board or agency, if any, that has the administrative authority to suspend or revoke the mental health professional's professional license, certification, registration, or authorization.

(2002 S 9, eff. 5–14–02)

PROSTITUTION

2907.21 Compelling prostitution

(A) No person shall knowingly do any of the following:

(1) Compel another to engage in sexual activity for hire;

(2) Induce, procure, encourage, solicit, request, or otherwise facilitate a minor to engage in sexual activity for hire, whether or not the offender knows the age of the minor;

(3) Pay or agree to pay a minor, either directly or through the minor's agent, so that the minor will engage in sexual activity, whether or not the offender knows the age of the minor;

(4) Pay a minor, either directly or through the minor's agent, for the minor having engaged in sexual activity, pursuant to a prior agreement, whether or not the offender knows the age of the minor;

(5) Allow a minor to engage in sexual activity for hire if the person allowing the child to engage in sexual activity for hire is the parent, guardian, custodian, person having custody or control, or person in loco parentis of the minor.

(B) Whoever violates this section is guilty of compelling prostitution. Except as otherwise provided in this division, compelling prostitution is a felony of the third degree. If the offender commits a violation of division (A)(1) of this section and the person compelled to engage in sexual activity for hire in violation of that division is less than sixteen years of age, compelling prostitution is a felony of the second degree.

(1995 S 2, eff. 7–1–96; 1988 H 51, eff. 3–17–89; 1972 H 511)

2907.22 Promoting prostitution

(A) No person shall knowingly:

(1) Establish, maintain, operate, manage, supervise, control, or have an interest in a brothel;

(2) Supervise, manage, or control the activities of a prostitute in engaging in sexual activity for hire;

(3) Transport another, or cause another to be transported across the boundary of this state or of any county in this state, in order to facilitate the other person's engaging in sexual activity for hire;

(4) For the purpose of violating or facilitating a violation of this section, induce or procure another to engage in sexual activity for hire.

(B) Whoever violates this section is guilty of promoting prostitution, a felony of the fourth degree. If any prostitute in the brothel involved in the offense, or the prostitute whose activities are supervised, managed, or controlled by the offender, or the person transported, induced, or procured by the offender to engage in sexual activity for hire, is a minor, whether or not the offender knows the age of the minor, then promoting prostitution is a felony of the third degree.

(1995 S 2, eff. 7–1–96; 1988 H 51, eff. 3–17–89; 1972 H 511)

2907.23 Procuring

(A) No person, knowingly and for gain, shall do either of the following:

(1) Entice or solicit another to patronize a prostitute or brothel;

(2) Procure a prostitute for another to patronize, or take or direct another at his or her request to any place for the purpose of patronizing a prostitute.

(B) No person, having authority or responsibility over the use of premises, shall knowingly permit such premises to be used for the purpose of engaging in sexual activity for hire.

(C) Whoever violates this section is guilty of procuring, a misdemeanor of the first degree.

(1972 H 511, eff. 1–1–74)

2907.24 Soliciting; solicitation after positive HIV test

(A) No person shall solicit another to engage with such other person in sexual activity for hire.

(B) No person, with knowledge that the person has tested positive as a carrier of a virus that causes acquired immunodeficiency syndrome, shall engage in conduct in violation of division (A) of this section.

(C)(1) Whoever violates division (A) of this section is guilty of soliciting, a misdemeanor of the third degree.

(2) Whoever violates division (B) of this section is guilty of engaging in solicitation after a positive HIV test. If the offender commits the violation prior to July 1, 1996, engaging in solicitation after a positive HIV test is a felony of the second degree. If the offender commits the violation on or after July 1, 1996, engaging in solicitation after a positive HIV test is a felony of the third degree.

(D) If a person is convicted of or pleads guilty to a violation of any provision of this section, an attempt to commit a violation of any provision of this section, or a violation of or an attempt to commit a violation of a municipal ordinance that is substantially equivalent to any provision of this section and if the person, in committing or attempting to commit the violation, was in, was on, or used a motor vehicle, the court, in addition to or independent of all other penalties imposed for the violation, shall impose upon the offender a class six suspension of the person's driver's license, commercial driver's license, temporary instruction permit, probationary license, or nonresident operating privilege from the range specified in division (A)(6) of section 4510.02 of the Revised Code.

(2002 S 123, eff. 1–1–04; 1996 H 40, eff. 5–30–96; 1972 H 511, eff. 1–1–74)

2907.241 Loitering to engage in solicitation; loitering to engage in solicitation after positive HIV test

(A) No person, with purpose to solicit another to engage in sexual activity for hire and while in or near a public place, shall do any of the following:

(1) Beckon to, stop, or attempt to stop another;

(2) Engage or attempt to engage another in conversation;

(3) Stop or attempt to stop the operator of a vehicle or approach a stationary vehicle;

(4) If the offender is the operator of or a passenger in a vehicle, stop, attempt to stop, beckon to, attempt to beckon to, or entice another to approach or enter the vehicle of which the offender is the operator or in which the offender is the passenger;

(5) Interfere with the free passage of another.

(B) No person, with knowledge that the person has tested positive as a carrier of a virus that causes acquired immunodeficiency syndrome, shall engage in conduct in violation of division (A) of this section.

(C) As used in this section:

(1) "Vehicle" has the same meaning as in section 4501.01 of the Revised Code.

(2) "Public place" means any of the following:

(a) A street, road, highway, thoroughfare, bikeway, walkway, sidewalk, bridge, alley, alleyway, plaza, park, driveway, parking lot, or transportation facility;

(b) A doorway or entrance way to a building that fronts on a place described in division (C)(2)(a) of this section;

(c) A place not described in division (C)(2)(a) or (b) of this section that is open to the public.

(D)(1) Whoever violates division (A) of this section is guilty of loitering to engage in solicitation, a misdemeanor of the third degree.

(2) Whoever violates division (B) of this section is guilty of loitering to engage in solicitation after a positive HIV test. If the offender commits the violation prior to July 1, 1996, loitering to engage in solicitation after a positive HIV test is a felony of the fourth degree. If the offender commits the violation on or after July 1, 1996, loitering to engage in solicitation after a positive HIV test is a felony of the fifth degree.

(1996 H 40, eff. 5–30–96)

2907.25 Prostitution; prostitution after positive HIV test

(A) No person shall engage in sexual activity for hire.

(B) No person, with knowledge that the person has tested positive as a carrier of a virus that causes acquired immunodeficiency syndrome, shall engage in sexual activity for hire.

(C)(1) Whoever violates division (A) of this section is guilty of prostitution, a misdemeanor of the third degree.

(2) Whoever violates division (B) of this section is guilty of engaging in prostitution after a positive HIV test. If the offender commits the violation prior to July 1, 1996, engaging in prostitution after a positive HIV test is a felony of the second degree. If the offender commits the violation on or after July 1, 1996, engaging in prostitution after a positive HIV test is a felony of the third degree.

(1996 H 40, eff. 5–30–96; 1972 H 511, eff. 1–1–74)

2907.26 Rules of evidence in prostitution cases

(A) In any case in which it is necessary to prove that a place is a brothel, evidence as to the reputation of such place and as to the reputation of the persons who inhabit or frequent it, is admissible on the question of whether such place is or is not a brothel.

(B) In any case in which it is necessary to prove that a person is a prostitute, evidence as to the reputation of such person is admissible on the question of whether such person is or is not a prostitute.

(C) In any prosecution for a violation of sections 2907.21 to 2907.25 of the Revised Code, proof of a prior conviction of the accused of any such offense or substantially equivalent offense is admissible in support of the charge.

(D) The prohibition contained in division (D) of section 2317.02 of the Revised Code against testimony by a husband or wife concerning communications between them does not apply, and the accused's spouse may testify concerning any such communication, in any of the following cases:

(1) When the husband or wife is charged with a violation of section 2907.21 of the Revised Code, and the spouse testifying was the victim of the offense;

(2) When the husband or wife is charged with a violation of section 2907.22 of the Revised Code, and the spouse testifying was the prostitute involved in the offense, or the person transported, induced, or procured by the offender to engage in sexual activity for hire;

(3) When the husband or wife is charged with a violation of section 2907.23 of the Revised Code, and the spouse testifying was the prostitute involved in the offense or the person who used the offender's premises to engage in sexual activity for hire;

(4) When the husband or wife is charged with a violation of section 2907.24 or 2907.25 of the Revised Code.

(1977 H 1, eff. 8–26–77; 1972 H 511)

2907.27 Examination and treatment for venereal disease and AIDS

(A)(1) If a person is charged with a violation of section 2907.02, 2907.03, 2907.04, 2907.24, 2907.241, or 2907.25 of the Revised Code or with a violation of a municipal ordinance that is substantially equivalent to any of those sections, the arresting authorities or a court, upon the request of the prosecutor in the case or upon the request of the victim, shall cause the accused to submit to one or more appropriate tests to determine if the accused is suffering from a venereal disease.

(2) If the accused is found to be suffering from a venereal disease in an infectious stage, the accused shall be required to submit to medical treatment for that disease. The cost of the medical treatment shall be charged to and paid by the accused who undergoes the treatment. If the accused is indigent, the court shall order the accused to report to a facility operated by a city health district or a general health district for treatment. If the accused is convicted of or pleads guilty to the offense with which the accused is charged and is placed under a community control sanction, a condition of community control shall be that the offender submit to and faithfully follow a course of medical treatment for the venereal disease. If the offender does not seek the required medical treatment, the court may revoke the offender's community control and order the offender to undergo medical treatment during the period of the offender's incarceration and to pay the cost of that treatment.

(B)(1)(a) Notwithstanding the requirements for informed consent in section 3701.242 of the Revised Code, if a person is charged with a violation of division (B) of section 2903.11 or of section 2907.02, 2907.03, 2907.04, 2907.05, 2907.12, 2907.24,

2907.241, or 2907.25 of the Revised Code or with a violation of a municipal ordinance that is substantially equivalent to that division or any of those sections, the court, upon the request of the prosecutor in the case, upon the request of the victim, or upon the request of any other person whom the court reasonably believes had contact with the accused in circumstances related to the violation that could have resulted in the transmission to that person of a virus that causes acquired immunodeficiency syndrome, shall cause the accused to submit to one or more tests designated by the director of health under section 3701.241 of the Revised Code to determine if the accused is a carrier of a virus that causes acquired immunodeficiency syndrome. The court, upon the request of the prosecutor in the case, upon the request of the victim with the agreement of the prosecutor, or upon the request of any other person with the agreement of the prosecutor, may cause an accused who is charged with a violation of any other section of the Revised Code or with a violation of any other municipal ordinance to submit to one or more tests so designated by the director of health if the circumstances of the violation indicate probable cause to believe that the accused, if the accused is infected with the virus that causes acquired immunodeficiency syndrome, might have transmitted the virus to any of the following persons in committing the violation:

(i) In relation to a request made by the prosecuting attorney, to the victim or to any other person;

(ii) In relation to a request made by the victim, to the victim making the request;

(iii) In relation to a request made by any other person, to the person making the request.

(b) The results of a test performed under division (B)(1)(a) of this section shall be communicated in confidence to the court, and the court shall inform the accused of the result. The court shall inform the victim that the test was performed and that the victim has a right to receive the results on request. If the test was performed upon the request of a person other than the prosecutor in the case and other than the victim, the court shall inform the person who made the request that the test was performed and that the person has a right to receive the results upon request. Additionally, regardless of who made the request that was the basis of the test being performed, if the court reasonably believes that, in circumstances related to the violation, a person other than the victim had contact with the accused that could have resulted in the transmission of the virus to that person, the court may inform that person that the test was performed and that the person has a right to receive the results of the test on request. If the accused tests positive for a virus that causes acquired immunodeficiency syndrome, the test results shall be reported to the department of health in accordance with section 3701.24 of the Revised Code and to the sheriff, head of the state correctional institution, or other person in charge of any jail or prison in which the accused is incarcerated. If the accused tests positive for a virus that causes acquired immunodeficiency syndrome and the accused was charged with, and was convicted of or pleaded guilty to, a violation of section 2907.24, 2907.241, or 2907.25 of the Revised Code or a violation of a municipal ordinance that is substantially equivalent to any of those sections, the test results also shall be reported to the law enforcement agency that arrested the accused, and the law enforcement agency may use the test results as the basis for any future charge of a violation of division (B) of any of those sections or a violation of a municipal ordinance that is substantially equivalent to division (B) of any of those sections. No other disclosure of the test results or the fact that a test was performed shall be made, other than as evidence in a grand jury proceeding or as evidence in a judicial proceeding in accordance with the Rules of Evidence. If the test result is negative, and the charge has not been dismissed or if the accused has been convicted of the charge or a different offense arising out of the same circumstances as the offense charged, the court shall order that the test be repeated not earlier than three months nor later than six months after the original test.

(2) If an accused who is free on bond refuses to submit to a test ordered by the court pursuant to division (B)(1) of this section, the court may order that the accused's bond be revoked and that the accused be incarcerated until the test is performed. If an accused who is incarcerated refuses to submit to a test ordered by the court pursuant to division (B)(1) of this section, the court shall order the person in charge of the jail or prison in which the accused is incarcerated to take any action necessary to facilitate the performance of the test, including the forcible restraint of the accused for the purpose of drawing blood to be used in the test.

(3) A state agency, a political subdivision of the state, or an employee of a state agency or of a political subdivision of the state is immune from liability in a civil action to recover damages for injury, death, or loss to person or property allegedly caused by any act or omission in connection with the performance of the duties required under division (B)(2) of this section unless the acts or omissions are with malicious purpose, in bad faith, or in a wanton or reckless manner.

(C) As used in this section, "community control sanction" has the same meaning as in section 2929.01 of the Revised Code.

(2002 H 490, eff. 1–1–04; 1999 H 100, eff. 3–23–00; 1996 H 40, eff. 5–30–96; 1994 H 571, eff. 10–6–94; 1989 S 2, eff. 11–1–89; 1989 S 94; 1972 H 511)

ASSISTANCE TO VICTIMS OF SEXUAL ASSAULT

2907.28 Medical examination of victim; costs

(A) Any cost incurred by a hospital or emergency medical facility in conducting a medical examination of a victim of an offense under any provision of sections 2907.02 to 2907.06 of the Revised Code for the purpose of gathering physical evidence for a possible prosecution, including the cost of any antibiotics administered as part of the examination, shall be paid out of the reparations fund established pursuant to section 2743.191 of the Revised Code, subject to the following conditions:

(1) The hospital or emergency facility shall follow a protocol for conducting such medical examinations that is identified by the attorney general in rule adopted in accordance with Chapter 119. of the Revised Code.

(2) The hospital or emergency facility shall submit requests for payment to the attorney general on a monthly basis, through a procedure determined by the attorney general and on forms approved by the attorney general. The requests shall identify the number of sexual assault examinations performed and shall verify that all required protocols were met for each examination form submitted for payment in the request.

(3) The attorney general shall review all requests for payment that are submitted under division (A)(2) of this section and shall submit for payment as described in division (A)(5) of this section all requests that meet the requirements of this section.

(4) The hospital or emergency facility shall accept a flat fee payment for conducting each examination in the amount determined by the attorney general pursuant to Chapter 119. of the Revised Code as payment in full for any cost incurred in conducting a medical examination and test of a victim of an offense under any provision of sections 2907.02 to 2907.06 of the Revised Code for the purpose of gathering physical evidence for a possible prosecution of a person. The attorney general shall determine a flat fee payment amount to be paid under this division that is reasonable.

(5) In approving a payment under this section, the attorney general shall order the payment against the state. The payment shall be accomplished only through the following procedure, and

the procedure may be enforced through a mandamus action and a writ of mandamus directed to the appropriate official:

(a) The attorney general shall provide for payment in the amount set forth in the order.

(b) The expense of the payment of the amount described in this section shall be charged against all available unencumbered moneys in the reparations fund.

(B) No costs incurred by a hospital or emergency facility in conducting a medical examination and test of any victim of an offense under any provision of sections 2907.02 to 2907.06 of the Revised Code for the purpose of gathering physical evidence for a possible prosecution of a person shall be billed or charged directly or indirectly to the victim or the victim's insurer.

(C) Any cost incurred by a hospital or emergency medical facility in conducting a medical examination and test of any person who is charged with a violation of division (B) of section 2903.11 or of section 2907.02, 2907.03, 2907.04, 2907.05, 2907.24, 2907.241, or 2907.25 of the Revised Code or with a violation of a municipal ordinance that is substantially equivalent to that division or any of those sections, pursuant to division (B) of section 2907.27 of the Revised Code, shall be charged to and paid by the accused who undergoes the examination and test, unless the court determines that the accused is unable to pay, in which case the cost shall be charged to and paid by the municipal corporation in which the offense allegedly was committed, or charged to and paid by the county if the offense allegedly was committed within an unincorporated area. If separate counts of an alleged offense or alleged separate offenses under section 2907.02, 2907.03, 2907.04, 2907.05, 2907.24, 2907.241, or 2907.25 of the Revised Code or under a municipal ordinance that is substantially equivalent to any of those sections took place in more than one municipal corporation or more than one unincorporated area, or both, the local governments shall share the cost of the examination and test. If a hospital or other emergency medical facility has submitted charges for the cost of a medical examination and test to an accused and has been unable to collect payment for the charges after making good faith attempts to collect for a period of six months or more, the cost shall be charged to and paid by the appropriate municipal corporation or county as specified in division (C) of this section.

(2000 S 153, eff. 7–1–00; 1999 H 100, eff. 3–23–00; 1996 H 445, eff. 9–3–96; 1996 H 40, eff. 5–30–96; 1989 S 2, eff. 11–1–89; 1975 S 144)

2907.29 Emergency medical services for victims; information to be given victim; consent of minor

Every hospital of this state that offers organized emergency services shall provide that a physician, a physician assistant, a clinical nurse specialist, a certified nurse practitioner, or a certified nurse-midwife is available on call twenty-four hours each day for the examination of persons reported to any law enforcement agency to be victims of sexual offenses cognizable as violations of any provision of sections 2907.02 to 2907.06 of the Revised Code. The physician, physician assistant, clinical nurse specialist, certified nurse practitioner, or certified nurse-midwife, upon the request of any peace officer or prosecuting attorney and with the consent of the reported victim or upon the request of the reported victim, shall examine the person for the purposes of gathering physical evidence and shall complete any written documentation of the physical examination. The public health council shall establish procedures for gathering evidence under this section.

Each reported victim shall be informed of available venereal disease, pregnancy, medical, and psychiatric services.

Notwithstanding any other provision of law, a minor may consent to examination under this section. The consent is not subject to disaffirmance because of minority, and consent of the parent, parents, or guardian of the minor is not required for an examination under this section. However, the hospital shall give written notice to the parent, parents, or guardian of a minor that an examination under this section has taken place. The parent, parents, or guardian of a minor giving consent under this section are not liable for payment for any services provided under this section without their consent.

(2002 S 245, eff. 3–31–03; 1996 H 445, eff. 9–3–96; 1975 S 144, eff. 8–27–75)

2907.30 Right to interview by one with crisis intervention training; notice to victim of accused sex offender's communicable disease

(A) A victim of a sexual offense cognizable as a violation of section 2907.02 of the Revised Code who is interviewed by a law enforcement agency shall be interviewed by a peace officer employed by the agency who has had crisis intervention training, if any of the peace officers employed by the agency who have had crisis intervention training is reasonably available.

(B) When a person is charged with a violation of section 2907.02, 2907.03, 2907.04, 2907.05, or 2907.06 of the Revised Code and the law enforcement agency that arrested the person or a court discovers that the person arrested or a person whom the person arrested caused to engage in sexual activity has a communicable disease, the law enforcement agency that arrested the person or the court immediately shall notify the victim of the nature of the disease.

(C) As used in this section, "crisis intervention training" has the same meaning as in section 109.71 of the Revised Code.

(1996 H 445, eff. 9–3–96; 1986 H 468, eff. 9–17–86; 1984 H 435)

OBSCENITY

2907.31 Disseminating matter harmful to juveniles

(A) No person, with knowledge of its character or content, shall recklessly do any of the following:

(1) Directly sell, deliver, furnish, disseminate, provide, exhibit, rent, or present to a juvenile, a group of juveniles, a law enforcement officer posing as a juvenile, or a group of law enforcement officers posing as juveniles any material or performance that is obscene or harmful to juveniles;

(2) Directly offer or agree to sell, deliver, furnish, disseminate, provide, exhibit, rent, or present to a juvenile, a group of juveniles, a law enforcement officer posing as a juvenile, or a group of law enforcement officers posing as juveniles any material or performance that is obscene or harmful to juveniles;

(3) While in the physical proximity of the juvenile or law enforcement officer posing as a juvenile, allow any juvenile or law enforcement officer posing as a juvenile to review or peruse any material or view any live performance that is harmful to juveniles.

(B) The following are affirmative defenses to a charge under this section that involves material or a performance that is harmful to juveniles but not obscene:

(1) The defendant is the parent, guardian, or spouse of the juvenile involved.

(2) The juvenile involved, at the time of the conduct in question, was accompanied by the juvenile's parent or guardian who, with knowledge of its character, consented to the material or performance being furnished or presented to the juvenile.

(3) The juvenile exhibited to the defendant or to the defendant's agent or employee a draft card, driver's license, birth record, marriage license, or other official or apparently official

document purporting to show that the juvenile was eighteen years of age or over or married, and the person to whom that document was exhibited did not otherwise have reasonable cause to believe that the juvenile was under the age of eighteen and unmarried.

(C)(1) It is an affirmative defense to a charge under this section, involving material or a performance that is obscene or harmful to juveniles, that the material or performance was furnished or presented for a bona fide medical, scientific, educational, governmental, judicial, or other proper purpose, by a physician, psychologist, sociologist, scientist, teacher, librarian, clergyman, prosecutor, judge, or other proper person.

(2) Except as provided in division (B)(3) of this section, mistake of age is not a defense to a charge under this section.

(D)(1) A person directly sells, delivers, furnishes, disseminates, provides, exhibits, rents, or presents or directly offers or agrees to sell, deliver, furnish, disseminate, provide, exhibit, rent, or present material or a performance to a juvenile, a group of juveniles, a law enforcement officer posing as a juvenile, or a group of law enforcement officers posing as juveniles in violation of this section by means of an electronic method of remotely transmitting information if the person knows or has reason to believe that the person receiving the information is a juvenile or the group of persons receiving the information are juveniles.

(2) A person remotely transmitting information by means of a method of mass distribution does not directly sell, deliver, furnish, disseminate, provide, exhibit, rent, or present or directly offer or agree to sell, deliver, furnish, disseminate, provide, exhibit, rent, or present the material or performance in question to a juvenile, a group of juveniles, a law enforcement officer posing as a juvenile, or a group of law enforcement officers posing as juveniles in violation of this section if either of the following applies:

(a) The person has inadequate information to know or have reason to believe that a particular recipient of the information or offer is a juvenile.

(b) The method of mass distribution does not provide the person the ability to prevent a particular recipient from receiving the information.

(E) If any provision of this section, or the application of any provision of this section to any person or circumstance, is held invalid, the invalidity does not affect other provisions or applications of this section or related sections that can be given effect without the invalid provision or application. To this end, the provisions are severable.

(F) Whoever violates this section is guilty of disseminating matter harmful to juveniles. If the material or performance involved is harmful to juveniles, except as otherwise provided in this division, a violation of this section is a misdemeanor of the first degree. If the material or performance involved is obscene, except as otherwise provided in this division, a violation of this section is a felony of the fifth degree. If the material or performance involved is obscene and the juvenile to whom it is sold, delivered, furnished, disseminated, provided, exhibited, rented, or presented, the juvenile to whom the offer is made or who is the subject of the agreement, or the juvenile who is allowed to review, peruse, or view it is under thirteen years of age, violation of this section is a felony of the fourth degree.

(2002 H 490, eff. 1–1–04; 1995 S 2, eff. 7–1–96; 1988 H 790, eff. 3–16–89; 1988 H 51; 1972 H 511)

2907.311 Displaying matter harmful to juveniles

(A) No person who has custody, control, or supervision of a commercial establishment, with knowledge of the character or content of the material involved, shall display at the establishment any material that is harmful to juveniles and that is open to view by juveniles as part of the invited general public.

(B) It is not a violation of division (A) of this section if the material in question is displayed by placing it behind "blinder racks" or similar devices that cover at least the lower two-thirds of the material, if the material in question is wrapped or placed behind the counter, or if the material in question otherwise is covered or located so that the portion that is harmful to juveniles is not open to the view of juveniles.

(C) Whoever violates this section is guilty of displaying matter harmful to juveniles, a misdemeanor of the first degree. Each day during which the offender is in violation of this section constitutes a separate offense.

(1988 H 51, eff. 3–17–89)

2907.32 Pandering obscenity

(A) No person, with knowledge of the character of the material or performance involved, shall do any of the following:

(1) Create, reproduce, or publish any obscene material, when the offender knows that the material is to be used for commercial exploitation or will be publicly disseminated or displayed, or when the offender is reckless in that regard;

(2) Promote or advertise for sale, delivery, or dissemination; sell, deliver, publicly disseminate, publicly display, exhibit, present, rent, or provide; or offer or agree to sell, deliver, publicly disseminate, publicly display, exhibit, present, rent, or provide, any obscene material;

(3) Create, direct, or produce an obscene performance, when the offender knows that it is to be used for commercial exploitation or will be publicly presented, or when the offender is reckless in that regard;

(4) Advertise or promote an obscene performance for presentation, or present or participate in presenting an obscene performance, when the performance is presented publicly, or when admission is charged;

(5) Buy, procure, possess, or control any obscene material with purpose to violate division (A)(2) or (4) of this section.

(B) It is an affirmative defense to a charge under this section, that the material or performance involved was disseminated or presented for a bona fide medical, scientific, educational, religious, governmental, judicial, or other proper purpose, by or to a physician, psychologist, sociologist, scientist, teacher, person pursuing bona fide studies or research, librarian, clergyman, prosecutor, judge, or other person having a proper interest in the material or performance.

(C) Whoever violates this section is guilty of pandering obscenity, a felony of the fifth degree. If the offender previously has been convicted of a violation of this section or of section 2907.31 of the Revised Code, then pandering obscenity is a felony of the fourth degree.

(1995 S 2, eff. 7–1–96; 1988 H 51, eff. 3–17–89; 1972 H 511)

2907.321 Pandering obscenity involving a minor

(A) No person, with knowledge of the character of the material or performance involved, shall do any of the following:

(1) Create, reproduce, or publish any obscene material that has a minor as one of its participants or portrayed observers;

(2) Promote or advertise for sale or dissemination; sell, deliver, disseminate, display, exhibit, present, rent, or provide; or offer or agree to sell, deliver, disseminate, display, exhibit, present, rent, or provide, any obscene material that has a minor as one of its participants or portrayed observers;

(3) Create, direct, or produce an obscene performance that has a minor as one of its participants;

(4) Advertise or promote for presentation, present, or participate in presenting an obscene performance that has a minor as one of its participants;

(5) Buy, procure, possess, or control any obscene material, that has a minor as one of its participants;

(6) Bring or cause to be brought into this state any obscene material that has a minor as one of its participants or portrayed observers.

(B)(1) This section does not apply to any material or performance that is sold, disseminated, displayed, possessed, controlled, brought or caused to be brought into this state, or presented for a bona fide medical, scientific, educational, religious, governmental, judicial, or other proper purpose, by or to a physician, psychologist, sociologist, scientist, teacher, person pursuing bona fide studies or research, librarian, clergyman, prosecutor, judge, or other person having a proper interest in the material or performance.

(2) Mistake of age is not a defense to a charge under this section.

(3) In a prosecution under this section, the trier of fact may infer that a person in the material or performance involved is a minor if the material or performance, through its title, text, visual representation, or otherwise, represents or depicts the person as a minor.

(C) Whoever violates this section is guilty of pandering obscenity involving a minor. Violation of division (A)(1), (2), (3), (4), or (6) of this section is a felony of the second degree. Violation of division (A)(5) of this section is a felony of the fourth degree. If the offender previously has been convicted of or pleaded guilty to a violation of this section or section 2907.322 or 2907.323 of the Revised Code, pandering obscenity involving a minor in violation of division (A)(5) of this section is a felony of the third degree.

(1988 H 51, eff. 3–17–89; 1984 H 44; 1977 S 243)

2907.322 Pandering sexually oriented matter involving a minor

(A) No person, with knowledge of the character of the material or performance involved, shall do any of the following:

(1) Create, record, photograph, film, develop, reproduce, or publish any material that shows a minor participating or engaging in sexual activity, masturbation, or bestiality;

(2) Advertise for sale or dissemination, sell, distribute, transport, disseminate, exhibit, or display any material that shows a minor participating or engaging in sexual activity, masturbation, or bestiality;

(3) Create, direct, or produce a performance that shows a minor participating or engaging in sexual activity, masturbation, or bestiality;

(4) Advertise for presentation, present, or participate in presenting a performance that shows a minor participating or engaging in sexual activity, masturbation, or bestiality;

(5) Knowingly solicit, receive, purchase, exchange, possess, or control any material that shows a minor participating or engaging in sexual activity, masturbation, or bestiality;

(6) Bring or cause to be brought into this state any material that shows a minor participating or engaging in sexual activity, masturbation, or bestiality, or bring, cause to be brought, or finance the bringing of any minor into or across this state with the intent that the minor engage in sexual activity, masturbation, or bestiality in a performance or for the purpose of producing material containing a visual representation depicting the minor engaged in sexual activity, masturbation, or bestiality.

(B)(1) This section does not apply to any material or performance that is sold, disseminated, displayed, possessed, controlled, brought or caused to be brought into this state, or presented for a bona fide medical, scientific, educational, religious, governmental, judicial, or other proper purpose, by or to a physician, psychologist, sociologist, scientist, teacher, person pursuing bona fide studies or research, librarian, clergyman, prosecutor, judge, or other person having a proper interest in the material or performance.

(2) Mistake of age is not a defense to a charge under this section.

(3) In a prosecution under this section, the trier of fact may infer that a person in the material or performance involved is a minor if the material or performance, through its title, text, visual representation, or otherwise, represents or depicts the person as a minor.

(C) Whoever violates this section is guilty of pandering sexually oriented matter involving a minor. Violation of division (A)(1), (2), (3), (4), or (6) of this section is a felony of the second degree. Violation of division (A)(5) of this section is a felony of the fourth degree. If the offender previously has been convicted of or pleaded guilty to a violation of this section or section 2907.321 or 2907.323 of the Revised Code, pandering sexually oriented matter involving a minor in violation of division (A)(5) of this section is a felony of the third degree.

(2000 H 724, eff. 3–22–01; 1995 S 2, eff. 7–1–96; 1988 H 51, eff. 3–17–89; 1984 H 44)

2907.323 Illegal use of a minor in nudity-oriented material or performance

(A) No person shall do any of the following:

(1) Photograph any minor who is not the person's child or ward in a state of nudity, or create, direct, produce, or transfer any material or performance that shows the minor in a state of nudity, unless both of the following apply:

(a) The material or performance is, or is to be, sold, disseminated, displayed, possessed, controlled, brought or caused to be brought into this state, or presented for a bona fide artistic, medical, scientific, educational, religious, governmental, judicial, or other proper purpose, by or to a physician, psychologist, sociologist, scientist, teacher, person pursuing bona fide studies or research, librarian, clergyman, prosecutor, judge, or other person having a proper interest in the material or performance;

(b) The minor's parents, guardian, or custodian consents in writing to the photographing of the minor, to the use of the minor in the material or performance, or to the transfer of the material and to the specific manner in which the material or performance is to be used.

(2) Consent to the photographing of the person's minor child or ward, or photograph the person's minor child or ward, in a state of nudity or consent to the use of the person's minor child or ward in a state of nudity in any material or performance, or use or transfer a material or performance of that nature, unless the material or performance is sold, disseminated, displayed, possessed, controlled, brought or caused to be brought into this state, or presented for a bona fide artistic, medical, scientific, educational, religious, governmental, judicial, or other proper purpose, by or to a physician, psychologist, sociologist, scientist, teacher, person pursuing bona fide studies or research, librarian, clergyman, prosecutor, judge, or other person having a proper interest in the material or performance;

(3) Possess or view any material or performance that shows a minor who is not the person's child or ward in a state of nudity, unless one of the following applies:

(a) The material or performance is sold, disseminated, displayed, possessed, controlled, brought or caused to be brought into this state, or presented for a bona fide artistic, medical, scientific, educational, religious, governmental, judicial, or other proper purpose, by or to a physician, psychologist, sociologist, scientist, teacher, person pursuing bona fide studies or research, librarian, clergyman, prosecutor, judge, or other person having a proper interest in the material or performance.

(b) The person knows that the parents, guardian, or custodian has consented in writing to the photographing or use of the minor in a state of nudity and to the manner in which the material or performance is used or transferred.

(B) Whoever violates this section is guilty of illegal use of a minor in a nudity-oriented material or performance. Whoever violates division (A)(1) or (2) of this section is guilty of a felony of the second degree. Whoever violates division (A)(3) of this section is guilty of a felony of the fifth degree. If the offender previously has been convicted of or pleaded guilty to a violation of this section or section 2907.321 or 2907.322 of the Revised Code, illegal use of a minor in a nudity-oriented material or performance in violation of division (A)(3) of this section is a felony of the fourth degree.

(1995 S 2, eff. 7–1–96; 1988 H 51, eff. 3–17–89; 1984 S 321, H 44)

2907.33 Deception to obtain matter harmful to juveniles

(A) No person, for the purpose of enabling a juvenile to obtain any material or gain admission to any performance which is harmful to juveniles, shall do either of the following:

(1) Falsely represent that he is the parent, guardian, or spouse of such juvenile;

(2) Furnish such juvenile with any identification or document purporting to show that such juvenile is eighteen years of age or over or married.

(B) No juvenile, for the purpose of obtaining any material or gaining admission to any performance which is harmful to juveniles, shall do either of the following:

(1) Falsely represent that he is eighteen years of age or over or married;

(2) Exhibit any identification or document purporting to show that he is eighteen years of age or over or married.

(C) Whoever violates this section is guilty of deception to obtain matter harmful to juveniles, a misdemeanor of the second degree. A juvenile who violates division (B) of this section shall be adjudged an unruly child, with such disposition of the case as may be appropriate under Chapter 2151. of the Revised Code.

(1972 H 511, eff. 1–1–74)

2907.34 Compelling acceptance of objectionable materials

(A) No person, as a condition to the sale, allocation, consignment, or delivery of any material or goods of any kind, shall require the purchaser or consignee to accept any other material reasonably believed to be obscene, or which if furnished or presented to a juvenile would be in violation of section 2907.31 of the Revised Code.

(B) No person shall deny or threaten to deny any franchise or impose or threaten to impose any financial or other penalty upon any purchaser or consignee because the purchaser or consignee failed or refused to accept any material reasonably believed to be obscene as a condition to the sale, allocation, consignment, or delivery of any other material or goods or because the purchaser or consignee returned any material believed to be obscene that the purchaser or consignee initially accepted.

(C) Whoever violates this section is guilty of compelling acceptance of objectionable materials, a felony of the fifth degree.

(1995 S 2, eff. 7–1–96; 1988 H 51, eff. 3–17–89; 1972 H 511)

2907.35 Presumptions; notice; defense

(A) An owner or manager, or agent or employee of an owner or manager, of a bookstore, newsstand, theater, or other commercial establishment engaged in selling materials or exhibiting performances, who, in the course of business:

(1) Possesses five or more identical or substantially similar obscene articles, having knowledge of their character, is presumed to possess them in violation of division (A)(5) of section 2907.32 of the Revised Code;

(2) Does any of the acts prohibited by section 2907.31 or 2907.32 of the Revised Code, is presumed to have knowledge of the character of the material or performance involved, if the owner, manager, or agent or employee of the owner or manager has actual notice of the nature of such material or performance, whether or not the owner, manager, or agent or employee of the owner or manager has precise knowledge of its contents.

(B) Without limitation on the manner in which such notice may be given, actual notice of the character of material or a performance may be given in writing by the chief legal officer of the jurisdiction in which the person to whom the notice is directed does business. Such notice, regardless of the manner in which it is given, shall identify the sender, identify the material or performance involved, state whether it is obscene or harmful to juveniles, and bear the date of such notice.

(C) Sections 2907.31 and 2907.32 of the Revised Code do not apply to a motion picture operator or projectionist acting within the scope of employment as an employee of the owner or manager of a theater or other place for the showing of motion pictures to the general public, and having no managerial responsibility or financial interest in the operator's or projectionist's place of employment, other than wages.

(D)(1) Sections 2907.31, 2907.311, 2907.32, 2907.321, 2907.322, 2907.323, and 2907.34 and division (A) of section 2907.33 of the Revised Code do not apply to a person solely because the person provided access or connection to or from an electronic method of remotely transferring information not under that person's control, including having provided capabilities that are incidental to providing access or connection to or from the electronic method of remotely transferring the information, and that do not include the creation of the content of the material that is the subject of the access or connection.

(2) Division (D)(1) of this section does not apply to a person who conspires with an entity actively involved in the creation or knowing distribution of material in violation of section 2907.31, 2907.311, 2907.32, 2907.321, 2907.322, 2907.323, 2907.33, or 2907.34 of the Revised Code or who knowingly advertises the availability of material of that nature.

(3) Division (D)(1) of this section does not apply to a person who provides access or connection to an electronic method of remotely transferring information that is engaged in the violation of section 2907.31, 2907.311, 2907.32, 2907.321, 2907.322, 2907.323, 2907.33, or 2907.34 of the Revised Code and that contains content that person has selected and introduced into the electronic method of remotely transferring information or content over which that person exercises editorial control.

(E) An employer is not guilty of a violation of section 2907.31, 2907.311, 2907.32, 2907.321, 2907.322, 2907.323, 2907.33, or 2907.34 of the Revised Code based on the actions of an employee or agent of the employer unless the employee's or agent's conduct is within the scope of employee's or agent's employment or agency, and the employer does either of the following:

(1) With knowledge of the employee's or agent's conduct, the employer authorizes or ratifies the conduct.

(2) The employer recklessly disregards the employee's or agent's conduct.

(F) It is an affirmative defense to a charge under section 2907.31 or 2907.311 of the Revised Code as the section applies to an image transmitted through the internet or another electronic method of remotely transmitting information that the person charged with violating the section has taken, in good faith, reasonable, effective, and appropriate actions under the circumstances to restrict or prevent access by juveniles to material that is harmful to juveniles, including any method that is feasible under available technology.

(G) If any provision of this section, or the application of any provision of this section to any person or circumstance, is held invalid, the invalidity does not affect other provisions or applications of this section or related sections that can be given effect without the invalid provision or application. To this end, the provisions are severable.

(2002 H 490, eff. 1–1–04; 2002 H 8, eff. 8–5–02; 1973 S 62, eff. 1–1–74; 1972 H 511)

2907.36 Declaratory judgment

(A) Without limitation on the persons otherwise entitled to bring an action for a declaratory judgment pursuant to Chapter 2721. of the Revised Code, involving the same issue, the following persons have standing to bring a declaratory judgment action to determine whether particular materials or performances are obscene or harmful to juveniles:

(1) The chief legal officer of the jurisdiction in which there is reasonable cause to believe that section 2907.31 or 2907.32 of the Revised Code is being or is about to be violated;

(2) Any person who, pursuant to division (B) of section 2907.35 of the Revised Code, has received notice in writing from a chief legal officer stating that particular materials or performances are obscene or harmful to juveniles.

(B) Any party to an action for a declaratory judgment pursuant to division (A) of this section is entitled, upon the party's request, to trial on the merits within five days after joinder of the issues, and the court shall render judgment within five days after trial is concluded.

(C) An action for a declaratory judgment pursuant to division (A) of this section shall not be brought during the pendency of any civil action or criminal prosecution, when the character of the particular materials or performances involved is at issue in the pending case, and either of the following applies:

(1) Either of the parties to the action for a declaratory judgment is a party to the pending case.

(2) A judgment in the pending case will necessarily constitute res judicata as to the character of the materials or performances involved.

(D) A civil action or criminal prosecution in which the character of particular materials or performances is at issue, brought during the pendency of an action for a declaratory judgment involving the same issue, shall be stayed during the pendency of the action for a declaratory judgment.

(E) The fact that a violation of section 2907.31 or 2907.32 of the Revised Code occurs prior to a judicial determination of the character of the material or performance involved in the violation does not relieve the offender of criminal liability for the violation, even though prosecution may be stayed pending the judicial determination.

(1999 H 58, eff. 9–24–99; 1972 H 511, eff. 1–1–74)

2907.37 Injunction

(A) Where it appears that section 2907.31 or 2907.32 of the Revised Code is being or is about to be violated, the chief legal officer of the jurisdiction in which the violation is taking place or is about to take place may bring an action to enjoin the violation. The defendant, upon his request, is entitled to trial on the merits within five days after joinder of the issues, and the court shall render judgment within five days after trial is concluded.

(B) Premises used or occupied for repeated violations of section 2907.31 or 2907.32 of the Revised Code constitute a nuisance subject to abatement pursuant to sections 3767.01 to 3767.99 of the Revised Code.

(1972 H 511, eff. 1–1–74)

CHAPTER 2909

ARSON AND RELATED OFFENSES

2909.01 Definitions

As used in sections 2909.01 to 2909.07 of the Revised Code:

(A) To "create a substantial risk of serious physical harm to any person" includes the creation of a substantial risk of serious physical harm to any emergency personnel.

(B) "Emergency personnel" means any of the following persons:

(1) A peace officer, as defined in section 2935.01 of the Revised Code;

(2) A member of a fire department or other firefighting agency of a municipal corporation, township, township fire district, joint fire district, other political subdivision, or combination of political subdivisions;

(3) A member of a private fire company, as defined in section 9.60 of the Revised Code, or a volunteer firefighter;

(4) A member of a joint ambulance district or joint emergency medical services district;

(5) An emergency medical technician-basic, emergency medical technician-intermediate, emergency medical technician-paramedic, ambulance operator, or other member of an emergency medical service that is owned or operated by a political subdivision or a private entity;

(6) The state fire marshal, the chief deputy state fire marshal, or an assistant state fire marshal;

(7) A fire prevention officer of a political subdivision or an arson, fire, or similar investigator of a political subdivision.

(C) "Occupied structure" means any house, building, outbuilding, watercraft, aircraft, railroad car, truck, trailer, tent, or other structure, vehicle, or shelter, or any portion thereof, to which any of the following applies:

(1) It is maintained as a permanent or temporary dwelling, even though it is temporarily unoccupied and whether or not any person is actually present.

(2) At the time, it is occupied as the permanent or temporary habitation of any person, whether or not any person is actually present.

(3) At the time, it is specially adapted for the overnight accommodation of any person, whether or not any person is actually present.

(4) At the time, any person is present or likely to be present in it.

(D) "Political subdivision" and "state" have the same meanings as in section 2744.01 of the Revised Code.

(E) "Computer," "computer hacking," "computer network," "computer program," "computer software," "computer system," "data," and "telecommunications device" have the same meanings as in section 2913.01 of the Revised Code.

(F) "Computer contaminant" means a computer program that is designed to modify, damage, destroy, disable, deny or degrade access to, allow unauthorized access to, functionally impair, record, or transmit information within a computer, computer system, or computer network without the express or implied consent of the owner or other person authorized to give consent and that is of a type or kind described in divisions (F)(1) to (4) of this section or of a type or kind similar to a type or kind described in divisions (F)(1) to (4) of this section:

(1) A group of computer programs commonly known as " viruses" and "worms" that are self- replicating or self-propagating and that are designed to contaminate other computer programs, compromise computer security, consume computer resources, modify, destroy, record, or transmit data, or disrupt the normal operation of the computer, computer system, or computer network;

(2) A group of computer programs commonly known as " Trojans" or "Trojan horses" that are not self-replicating or self-propagating and that are designed to compromise computer security, consume computer resources, modify, destroy, record, or transmit data, or disrupt the normal operation of the computer, computer system, or computer network;

(3) A group of computer programs commonly known as " zombies" that are designed to use a computer without the knowledge and consent of the owner, or other person authorized to give consent, and that are designed to send large quantities of data to a targeted computer network for the purpose of degrading the targeted computer's or network's performance, or denying access through the network to the targeted computer or network, resulting in what is commonly known as "Denial of Service" or "Distributed Denial of Service" attacks;

(4) A group of computer programs commonly know as "trap doors," "back doors," or "root kits" that are designed to bypass standard authentication software and that are designed to allow access to or use of a computer without the knowledge or consent of the owner, or other person authorized to give consent.

(G) "Internet" has the same meaning as in section 341.42 of the Revised Code.

(2004 S 146, eff. 9–23–04; 2002 S 115, eff. 3–19–03; 1998 S 30, eff. 5–6–98; 1995 S 150, eff. 11–24–95; 1992 H 675, eff. 3–19–93; 1972 H 511)

ARSON

2909.02 Aggravated arson

(A) No person, by means of fire or explosion, shall knowingly do any of the following:

(1) Create a substantial risk of serious physical harm to any person other than the offender;

(2) Cause physical harm to any occupied structure;

(3) Create, through the offer or acceptance of an agreement for hire or other consideration, a substantial risk of physical harm to any occupied structure.

(B)(1) Whoever violates this section is guilty of aggravated arson.

(2) A violation of division (A)(1) or (3) of this section is a felony of the first degree.

(3) A violation of division (A)(2) of this section is a felony of the second degree.

(1996 S 269, eff. 7–1–96; 1995 S 2, eff. 7–1–96; 1982 H 269, § 4, eff. 7–1–83; 1982 S 199; 1976 S 282; 1972 H 511)

2909.03 Arson

(A) No person, by means of fire or explosion, shall knowingly do any of the following:

(1) Cause, or create a substantial risk of, physical harm to any property of another without the other person's consent;

(2) Cause, or create a substantial risk of, physical harm to any property of the offender or another, with purpose to defraud;

(3) Cause, or create a substantial risk of, physical harm to the statehouse or a courthouse, school building, or other building or structure that is owned or controlled by the state, any political subdivision, or any department, agency, or instrumentality of the state or a political subdivision, and that is used for public purposes;

(4) Cause, or create a substantial risk of, physical harm, through the offer or the acceptance of an agreement for hire or other consideration, to any property of another without the other person's consent or to any property of the offender or another with purpose to defraud;

(5) Cause, or create a substantial risk of, physical harm to any park, preserve, wildlands, brush-covered land, cut-over land, forest, timberland, greenlands, woods, or similar real property that is owned or controlled by another person, the state, or a political

subdivision without the consent of the other person, the state, or the political subdivision;

(6) With purpose to defraud, cause, or create a substantial risk of, physical harm to any park, preserve, wildlands, brush-covered land, cut-over land, forest, timberland, greenlands, woods, or similar real property that is owned or controlled by the offender, another person, the state, or a political subdivision.

(B)(1) Whoever violates this section is guilty of arson.

(2) A violation of division (A)(1) of this section is one of the following:

(a) Except as otherwise provided in division (B)(2)(b) of this section, a misdemeanor of the first degree;

(b) If the value of the property or the amount of the physical harm involved is five hundred dollars or more, a felony of the fourth degree.

(3) A violation of division (A)(2), (3), (5), or (6) of this section is a felony of the fourth degree.

(4) A violation of division (A)(4) of this section is a felony of the third degree.

(1995 S 2, eff. 7–1–96; 1992 H 675, eff. 3–19–93; 1982 H 269, § 4, S 199; 1976 S 282; 1972 H 511)

DISRUPTION, VANDALISM, DAMAGING, AND ENDANGERING

2909.04 Disrupting public services

(A) No person, purposely by any means or knowingly by damaging or tampering with any property, shall do any of the following:

(1) Interrupt or impair television, radio, telephone, telegraph, or other mass communications service; police, fire, or other public service communications; radar, loran, radio, or other electronic aids to air or marine navigation or communications; or amateur or citizens band radio communications being used for public service or emergency communications;

(2) Interrupt or impair public transportation, including without limitation school bus transportation, or water supply, gas, power, or other utility service to the public;

(3) Substantially impair the ability of law enforcement officers, firefighters, rescue personnel, emergency medical services personnel, or emergency facility personnel to respond to an emergency or to protect and preserve any person or property from serious physical harm.

(B) No person shall knowingly use any computer, computer system, computer network, telecommunications device, or other electronic device or system or the internet so as to disrupt, interrupt, or impair the functions of any police, fire, educational, commercial, or governmental operations.

(C) Whoever violates this section is guilty of disrupting public services, a felony of the fourth degree.

(D) As used in this section:

(1) "Emergency medical services personnel" has the same meaning as in section 2133.21 of the Revised Code.

(2) "Emergency facility personnel" means any of the following:

(a) Any of the following individuals who perform services in the ordinary course of their professions in an emergency facility:

(i) Physicians authorized under Chapter 4731. of the Revised Code to practice medicine and surgery or osteopathic medicine and surgery;

(ii) Registered nurses and licensed practical nurses licensed under Chapter 4723. of the Revised Code;

(iii) Physician assistants authorized to practice under Chapter 4730. of the Revised Code;

(iv) Health care workers;

(v) Clerical staffs.

(b) Any individual who is a security officer performing security services in an emergency facility;

(c) Any individual who is present in an emergency facility, who was summoned to the facility by an individual identified in division (D)(2)(a) or (b) of this section.

(3) "Emergency facility" means a hospital emergency department or any other facility that provides emergency medical services.

(4) "Hospital" has the same meaning as in section 3727.01 of the Revised Code.

(5) "Health care worker" means an individual, other than an individual specified in division (D)(2)(a), (b), or (c) of this section, who provides medical or other health-related care or treatment in an emergency facility, including medical technicians, medical assistants, orderlies, aides, or individuals acting in similar capacities.

(2004 S 146, eff. 9–23–04; 2001 S 40, eff. 1–25–02; 1999 H 137, eff. 3–10–00; 1995 S 2, eff. 7–1–96; 1972 H 511, eff. 1–1–74)

2909.05 Vandalism

(A) No person shall knowingly cause serious physical harm to an occupied structure or any of its contents.

(B)(1) No person shall knowingly cause physical harm to property that is owned or possessed by another, when either of the following applies:

(a) The property is used by its owner or possessor in the owner's or possessor's profession, business, trade, or occupation, and the value of the property or the amount of physical harm involved is five hundred dollars or more;

(b) Regardless of the value of the property or the amount of damage done, the property or its equivalent is necessary in order for its owner or possessor to engage in the owner's or possessor's profession, business, trade, or occupation.

(2) No person shall knowingly cause serious physical harm to property that is owned, leased, or controlled by a governmental entity. A governmental entity includes, but is not limited to, the state or a political subdivision of the state, a school district, the board of trustees of a public library or public university, or any other body corporate and politic responsible for governmental activities only in geographical areas smaller than that of the state.

(C) No person, without privilege to do so, shall knowingly cause serious physical harm to any tomb, monument, gravestone, or other similar structure that is used as a memorial for the dead; to any fence, railing, curb, or other property that is used to protect, enclose, or ornament any cemetery; or to a cemetery.

(D) No person, without privilege to do so, shall knowingly cause physical harm to a place of burial by breaking and entering into a tomb, crypt, casket, or other structure that is used as a memorial for the dead or as an enclosure for the dead.

(E) Whoever violates this section is guilty of vandalism. Except as otherwise provided in this division, vandalism is a felony of the fifth degree that is punishable by a fine of up to two thousand five hundred dollars in addition to the penalties specified for a felony of the fifth degree in sections 2929.11 to 2929.18 of the Revised Code. If the value of the property or the amount of physical harm involved is five thousand dollars or more but less than one hundred thousand dollars, vandalism is a felony of the fourth degree. If the value of the property or the amount of physical harm involved is one hundred thousand dollars or more, vandalism is a felony of the third degree.

(F) For purposes of this section:

(1) "Cemetery" means any place of burial and includes burial sites that contain American Indian burial objects placed with or containing American Indian human remains.

(2) "Serious physical harm" means physical harm to property that results in loss to the value of the property of five hundred dollars or more.

(1998 H 429, eff. 9–30–98; 1995 S 2, eff. 7–1–96; 1992 H 675, eff. 3–19–93; 1986 S 316; 1982 H 269, S 199; 1980 H 618; 1978 H 741; 1972 H 511)

2909.06 Criminal damaging or endangering

(A) No person shall cause, or create a substantial risk of physical harm to any property of another without the other person's consent:

(1) Knowingly, by any means;

(2) Recklessly, by means of fire, explosion, flood, poison gas, poison, radioactive material, caustic or corrosive material, or other inherently dangerous agency or substance.

(B) Whoever violates this section is guilty of criminal damaging or endangering, a misdemeanor of the second degree. If a violation of this section creates a risk of physical harm to any person, criminal damaging or endangering is a misdemeanor of the first degree. If the property involved in a violation of this section is an aircraft, an aircraft engine, propeller, appliance, spare part, or any other equipment or implement used or intended to be used in the operation of an aircraft and if the violation creates a risk of physical harm to any person, criminal damaging or endangering is a felony of the fifth degree. If the property involved in a violation of this section is an aircraft, an aircraft engine, propeller, appliance, spare part, or any other equipment or implement used or intended to be used in the operation of an aircraft and if the violation creates a substantial risk of physical harm to any person or if the property involved in a violation of this section is an occupied aircraft, criminal damaging or endangering is a felony of the fourth degree.

(1995 S 2, eff. 7–1–96; 1984 H 570, eff. 3–28–85; 1972 H 511)

2909.07 Criminal mischief; safety device defined

(A) No person shall:

(1) Without privilege to do so, knowingly move, deface, damage, destroy, or otherwise improperly tamper with the property of another;

(2) With purpose to interfere with the use or enjoyment of property of another, employ a tear gas device, stink bomb, smoke generator, or other device releasing a substance that is harmful or offensive to persons exposed or that tends to cause public alarm;

(3) Without privilege to do so, knowingly move, deface, damage, destroy, or otherwise improperly tamper with a bench mark, triangulation station, boundary marker, or other survey station, monument, or marker;

(4) Without privilege to do so, knowingly move, deface, damage, destroy, or otherwise improperly tamper with any safety device, the property of another, or the property of the offender when required or placed for the safety of others, so as to destroy or diminish its effectiveness or availability for its intended purpose;

(5) With purpose to interfere with the use or enjoyment of the property of another, set a fire on the land of another or place personal property that has been set on fire on the land of another, which fire or personal property is outside and apart from any building, other structure, or personal property that is on that land;

(6) Without privilege to do so, and with intent to impair the functioning of any computer, computer system, computer network, computer software, or computer program, knowingly do any of thc following:

(a) In any manner or by any means, including, but not limited to, computer hacking, alter, damage, destroy, or modify a computer, computer system, computer network, computer software, or computer program or data contained in a computer, computer system, computer network, computer software, or computer program;

(b) Introduce a computer contaminant into a computer, computer system, computer network, computer software, or computer program.

(B) As used in this section, "safety device" means any fire extinguisher, fire hose, or fire axe, or any fire escape, emergency exit, or emergency escape equipment, or any life line, life-saving ring, life preserver, or life boat or raft, or any alarm, light, flare, signal, sign, or notice intended to warn of danger or emergency, or intended for other safety purposes, or any guard railing or safety barricade, or any traffic sign or signal, or any railroad grade crossing sign, signal, or gate, or any first aid or survival equipment, or any other device, apparatus, or equipment intended for protecting or preserving the safety of persons or property.

(C)(1) Whoever violates this section is guilty of criminal mischief, and shall be punished as provided in division (C)(2) or (3) of this section.

(2) Except as otherwise provided in this division, criminal mischief committed in violation of division (A)(1), (2), (3), (4), or (5) of this section is a misdemeanor of the third degree. Except as otherwise provided in this division, if the violation of division (A)(1), (2), (3), (4), or (5) of this section creates a risk of physical harm to any person, criminal mischief committed in violation of division (A)(1), (2), (3), (4), or (5) of this section is a misdemeanor of the first degree. If the property involved in the violation of division (A)(1), (2), (3), (4), or (5) of this section is an aircraft, an aircraft engine, propeller, appliance, spare part, fuel, lubricant, hydraulic fluid, any other equipment, implement, or material used or intended to be used in the operation of an aircraft, or any cargo carried or intended to be carried in an aircraft , criminal mischief committed in violation of division (A)(1), (2), (3), (4), or (5) of this section is one of the following:

(a) If the violation creates a risk of physical harm to any person, except as otherwise provided in division (C)(2)(b) of this section, criminal mischief committed in violation of division (A)(1), (2), (3), (4), or (5) of this section is a felony of the fifth degree.

(b) If the violation creates a substantial risk of physical harm to any person or if the property involved in a violation of this section is an occupied aircraft, criminal mischief committed in violation of division (A)(1), (2), (3), (4), or (5) of this section is a felony of the fourth degree.

(3) Except as otherwise provided in this division, criminal mischief committed in violation of division (A)(6) of this section is a misdemeanor of the first degree. Except as otherwise provided in this division, if the value of the computer, computer system, computer network, computer software, computer program, or data involved in the violation of division (A)(6) of this section or the loss to the victim resulting from the violation is one thousand dollars or more and less than ten thousand dollars, or if the computer, computer system, computer network, computer software, computer program, or data involved in the violation of division (A)(6) of this section is used or intended to be used in the operation of an aircraft and the violation creates a risk of physical harm to any person, criminal mischief committed in violation of division (A)(6) of this section is a felony of the fifth degree. If the value of the computer, computer system, computer network, computer software, computer program, or data involved in the violation of division (A)(6) of this section or the loss to the victim resulting from the violation is ten thousand

dollars or more, or if the computer, computer system, computer network, computer software, computer program, or data involved in the violation of division (A)(6) of this section is used or intended to be used in the operation of an aircraft and the violation creates a substantial risk of physical harm to any person or the aircraft in question is an occupied aircraft, criminal mischief committed in violation of division (A)(6) of this section is a felony of the fourth degree.

(2004 S 146, eff. 9–23–04; 1995 S 2, eff. 7–1–96; 1986 S 316, eff. 3–19–87; 1984 H 570; 1973 H 89; 1972 H 511)

2909.08 Endangering aircraft or airport operations

(A) As used in this section:

(1) "Air gun" means a hand pistol or rifle that propels its projectile by means of releasing compressed air, carbon dioxide, or other gas.

(2) "Firearm" has the same meaning as in section 2923.11 of the Revised Code.

(3) "Spring–operated gun" means a hand pistol or rifle that propels a projectile not less than four or more than five millimeters in diameter by means of a spring.

(4) "Airport operational surface" means any surface of land or water that is developed, posted, or marked so as to give an observer reasonable notice that the surface is designed and developed for the purpose of storing, parking, taxiing, or operating aircraft, or any surface of land or water that is actually being used for any of those purposes.

(B) No person shall do either of the following:

(1) Knowingly throw an object at, or drop an object upon, any moving aircraft;

(2) Knowingly shoot with a bow and arrow, or knowingly discharge a firearm, air gun, or spring-operated gun, at or toward any aircraft.

(C) No person shall knowingly or recklessly shoot with a bow and arrow, or shall knowingly or recklessly discharge a firearm, air gun, or spring-operated gun, upon or over any airport operational surface. This division does not apply to the following:

(1) An officer, agent, or employee of this or any other state or the United States, or a law enforcement officer, authorized to discharge firearms and acting within the scope of the officer's, agent's, or employee's duties;

(2) A person who, with the consent of the owner or operator of the airport operational surface or the authorized agent of either, is lawfully engaged in any hunting or sporting activity or is otherwise lawfully discharging a firearm.

(D) Whoever violates division (B) of this section is guilty of endangering aircraft, a misdemeanor of the first degree. If the violation creates a risk of physical harm to any person, endangering aircraft is a felony of the fifth degree. If the violation creates a substantial risk of physical harm to any person or if the aircraft that is the subject of the violation is occupied, endangering aircraft is a felony of the fourth degree.

(E) Whoever violates division (C) of this section is guilty of endangering airport operations, a misdemeanor of the second degree. If the violation creates a risk of physical harm to any person, endangering airport operations is a felony of the fifth degree. If the violation creates a substantial risk of physical harm to any person, endangering airport operations is a felony of the fourth degree. In addition to any other penalty or sanction imposed for the violation, the hunting license or permit of a person who violates division (C) of this section while hunting shall be suspended or revoked pursuant to section 1533.68 of the Revised Code.

(F) Any bow and arrow, air gun, spring-operated gun, or firearm that has been used in a felony violation of this section shall be seized or forfeited, and shall be disposed of pursuant to section 2933.41 of the Revised Code.

(1995 S 2, eff. 7–1–96; 1984 H 570, eff. 3–28–85)

2909.09 Vehicular vandalism

(A) As used in this section:

(1) "Highway" means any highway as defined in section 4511.01 of the Revised Code or any lane, road, street, alley, bridge, or overpass.

(2) "Alley," "street," "streetcar," "trackless trolley," and "vehicle" have the same meanings as in section 4511.01 of the Revised Code.

(3) "Vessel" and "waters in this state" have the same meanings as in section 1547.01 of the Revised Code.

(B) No person shall knowingly, and by any means, drop or throw any object at, onto, or in the path of any of the following:

(1) Any vehicle, streetcar, or trackless trolley on a highway;

(2) Any boat or vessel on any of the waters in this state.

(C) Whoever violates this section is guilty of vehicular vandalism. Except as otherwise provided in this division, vehicular vandalism is a misdemeanor of the first degree. Except as otherwise provided in this division, if the violation of this section creates a substantial risk of physical harm to any person or the violation of this section causes serious physical harm to property, vehicular vandalism is a felony of the fourth degree. Except as otherwise provided in this division, if the violation of this section causes physical harm to any person, vehicular vandalism is a felony of the third degree. If the violation of this section causes serious physical harm to any person, vehicular vandalism is a felony of the second degree.

(2002 S 163, eff. 4–9–03)

2909.10 Railroad vandalism; criminal trespass on locomotive, engine, railroad car, or other railroad vehicle; interference with operation of train; criminal trespass on land or premises of railroad company

(A) No person shall knowingly, and by any means, drop or throw any object at, onto, or in the path of, any railroad rail, railroad track, locomotive, engine, railroad car, or other vehicle of a railroad company while such vehicle is on a railroad track.

(B) No person, without privilege to do so, shall climb upon or into any locomotive, engine, railroad car, or other vehicle of a railroad company when it is on a railroad track.

(C) No person, without privilege to do so, shall disrupt, delay, or prevent the operation of any train or other vehicle of a railroad company while such vehicle is on a railroad track.

(D) No person, without privilege to do so, shall knowingly enter or remain on the land or premises of a railroad company.

(E) Whoever violates division (A) of this section is guilty of railroad vandalism. Whoever violates division (B) of this section is guilty of criminal trespass on a locomotive, engine, railroad car, or other railroad vehicle. Whoever violates division (C) of this section is guilty of interference with the operation of a train.

Except as otherwise provided in this division, railroad vandalism; criminal trespass on a locomotive, engine, railroad car, or other railroad vehicle; and interference with the operation of a train each is a misdemeanor of the first degree. Except as otherwise provided in this division, if the violation of division (A),

(B), or (C) of this section causes serious physical harm to property or creates a substantial risk of physical harm to any person, the violation is a felony of the fourth degree. Except as otherwise provided in this division, if the violation of division (A), (B), or (C) of this section causes physical harm to any person, the violation is a felony of the third degree. If the violation of division (A), (B), or (C) of this section causes serious physical harm to any person, the violation is a felony of the second degree.

(F) Whoever violates division (D) of this section is guilty of criminal trespass on the land or premises of a railroad company, a misdemeanor of the fourth degree.

(2002 S 163, eff. 4–9–03)

2909.101 Railroad grade crossing device vandalism

(A) No person shall knowingly deface, damage, obstruct, remove, or otherwise impair the operation of any railroad grade crossing warning signal or other protective device, including any gate, bell, light, crossbuck, stop sign, yield sign, advance warning sign, or advance pavement marking.

(B) Whoever violates this section is guilty of railroad grade crossing device vandalism. Except as otherwise provided in this division, railroad grade crossing device vandalism is a misdemeanor of the first degree. Except as otherwise provided in this division, if the violation of this section causes serious physical harm to property or creates a substantial risk of physical harm to any person, railroad grade crossing device vandalism is a felony of the fourth degree. Except as otherwise provided in this division, if the violation of this section causes physical harm to any person, railroad grade crossing device vandalism is a felony of the third degree. If the violation of this section causes serious physical harm to any person, railroad grade crossing device vandalism is a felony of the second degree.

(2002 S 163, eff. 4–9–03)

2909.11 Determining property value or amount of physical harm

(A) When a person is charged with a violation of division (A)(1) of section 2909.03 of the Revised Code involving property value or an amount of physical harm of five hundred dollars or more or with a violation of section 2909.05 of the Revised Code involving property value or an amount of physical harm of five hundred dollars or more, the jury or court trying the accused shall determine the value of the property or amount of physical harm and, if a guilty verdict is returned, shall return the finding as part of the verdict. In any such case, it is unnecessary to find or return the exact value or amount of physical harm, section 2945.75 of the Revised Code applies, and it is sufficient if either of the following applies, as appropriate, relative to the finding and return of the value or amount of physical harm:

(1) If the finding and return relate to a violation of division (A)(1) of section 2909.03 of the Revised Code and are that the value or amount of the physical harm was five hundred dollars or more, the finding and return shall include a statement that the value or amount was five hundred dollars or more.

(2) If the finding and return relate to a violation of division section [sic.] 2909.05 of the Revised Code and are that the value or amount of the physical harm was in any of the following categories, the finding and return shall include one of the following statements, as appropriate:

(a) If the finding and return are that the value or amount was one hundred thousand dollars or more, a statement that the value or amount was one hundred thousand dollars or more;

(b) If the finding and return are that the value or amount was five thousand dollars or more but less than one hundred thousand dollars a statement that the value or amount was five thousand dollars or more but less than one hundred thousand dollars;

(c) If the finding and return are that the value or amount was five hundred dollars or more but less than five thousand dollars, a statement that the value or amount was five hundred dollars or more but less than five thousand dollars.

(B) The following criteria shall be used in determining the value of property or amount of physical harm involved in a violation of division (A)(1) of section 2909.03 or section 2909.05 of the Revised Code:

(1) If the property is an heirloom, memento, collector's item, antique, museum piece, manuscript, document, record, or other thing that is either irreplaceable or is replaceable only on the expenditure of substantial time, effort, or money, the value of the property or the amount of physical harm involved is the amount that would compensate the owner for its loss.

(2) If the property is not covered under division (B)(1) of this section and the physical harm is such that the property can be restored substantially to its former condition, the amount of physical harm involved is the reasonable cost of restoring the property.

(3) If the property is not covered under division (B)(1) of this section and the physical harm is such that the property cannot be restored substantially to its former condition, the value of the property, in the case of personal property, is the cost of replacing the property with new property of like kind and quality, and, in the case of real property or real property fixtures, is the difference in the fair market value of the property immediately before and immediately after the offense.

(C) As used in this section, "fair market value" has the same meaning as in section 2913.61 of the Revised Code.

(D) Prima–facie evidence of the value of property, as provided in division (E) of section 2913.61 of the Revised Code, may be used to establish the value of property pursuant to this section.

(1995 S 2, eff. 7–1–96; 1992 H 675, eff. 3–19–93; 1982 H 269, S 199; 1980 H 618; 1978 H 741; 1972 H 511)

TERRORISM

2909.21 Definitions

As used in sections 2909.21 to 2909.25 of the Revised Code:

(A) "Act of terrorism" means an act that is committed within or outside the territorial jurisdiction of this state or the United States, that constitutes a specified offense if committed in this state or constitutes an offense in any jurisdiction within or outside the territorial jurisdiction of the United States containing all of the essential elements of a specified offense, and that is intended to do one or more of the following:

(1) Intimidate or coerce a civilian population;

(2) Influence the policy of any government by intimidation or coercion;

(3) Affect the conduct of any government by the act that constitutes the offense.

(B) "Material support or resources" means currency, payment instruments, other financial securities, financial services, lodging, training, safehouses, false documentation or identification, communications equipment, facilities, weapons, lethal substances, explosives, personnel, transportation, and other physical assets, except medicine or religious materials.

(C) "Payment instrument" means a check, draft, money order, traveler's check, cashier's check, teller's check, or other instrument or order for the transmission or payment of money, regardless of whether the item in question is negotiable.

(D) "Response costs" means all costs a political subdivision incurs as a result of, or in making any response to, a threat of a specified offense made as described in section 2909.23 of the Revised Code or a specified offense committed as described in section 2909.24 of the Revised Code, including, but not limited to, all costs so incurred by any law enforcement officers, firefighters, rescue personnel, or emergency medical services personnel of the political subdivision and all costs so incurred by the political subdivision that relate to laboratory testing or hazardous material cleanup.

(E) "Specified offense" means any of the following:

(1) A felony offense of violence, a violation of section 2909.04 or 2927.24 of the Revised Code, or a felony of the first degree that is not a violation of any provision in Chapter 2925. or 3719. of the Revised Code;

(2) An attempt to commit, complicity in committing, or a conspiracy to commit an offense listed in division (E)(1) of this section.

(2002 S 184, eff. 5–15–02)

2909.22 Support of terrorism

(A) No person shall raise, solicit, collect, donate, or provide any material support or resources, with purpose that the material support or resources will be used in whole or in part to plan, prepare, carry out, or aid in either an act of terrorism or the concealment of, or an escape from, an act of terrorism.

(B) Whoever violates this section is guilty of soliciting or providing support for an act of terrorism, a felony of the third degree. Section 2909.25 of the Revised Code applies regarding an offender who is convicted of or pleads guilty to a violation of this section.

(C) A prosecution for a violation of this section does not preclude a prosecution for a violation of any other section of the Revised Code. One or more acts, a series of acts, or a course of behavior that can be prosecuted under this section or any other section of the Revised Code may be prosecuted under this section, the other section, or both sections.

(2002 S 184, eff. 5–15–02)

2909.23 Terroristic threats

(A) No person shall threaten to commit or threaten to cause to be committed a specified offense when both of the following apply:

(1) The person makes the threat with purpose to do any of the following:

(a) Intimidate or coerce a civilian population;

(b) Influence the policy of any government by intimidation or coercion;

(c) Affect the conduct of any government by the threat or by the specified offense.

(2) As a result of the threat, the person causes a reasonable expectation or fear of the imminent commission of the specified offense.

(B) It is not a defense to a charge of a violation of this section that the defendant did not have the intent or capability to commit the threatened specified offense or that the threat was not made to a person who was a subject of the threatened specified offense.

(C) Whoever violates this section is guilty of making a terroristic threat, a felony of the third degree. Section 2909.25 of the Revised Code applies regarding an offender who is convicted of or pleads guilty to a violation of this section.

(2002 S 184, eff. 5–15–02)

2909.24 Terrorism

(A) No person shall commit a specified offense with purpose to do any of the following:

(1) Intimidate or coerce a civilian population;

(2) Influence the policy of any government by intimidation or coercion;

(3) Affect the conduct of any government by the specified offense.

(B)(1) Whoever violates this section is guilty of terrorism.

(2) Except as otherwise provided in divisions (B)(3) and (4) of this section, terrorism is an offense one degree higher than the most serious underlying specified offense the defendant committed.

(3) If the most serious underlying specified offense the defendant committed is a felony of the first degree or murder, the person shall be sentenced to life imprisonment without parole.

(4) If the most serious underlying specified offense the defendant committed is aggravated murder, the offender shall be sentenced to life imprisonment without parole or death pursuant to sections 2929.02 to 2929.06 of the Revised Code.

(5) Section 2909.25 of the Revised Code applies regarding an offender who is convicted of or pleads guilty to a violation of this section.

(2002 S 184, eff. 5–15–02)

2909.25 Recovery of costs of investigation and prosecution of act of terrorism

(A) In addition to the financial sanctions authorized under section 2929.18 of the Revised Code, the court imposing sentence upon an offender who is convicted of or pleads guilty to a violation of section 2909.22, 2909.23, or 2909.24 of the Revised Code or to a violation of section 2921.32 of the Revised Code when the offense or act committed by the person aided or to be aided as described in that section is an act of terrorism may order the offender to pay to the state, municipal, or county law enforcement agencies that handled the investigation and prosecution all of the costs that the state, municipal corporation, or county reasonably incurred in the investigation and prosecution of the violation. The court shall hold a hearing to determine the amount of costs to be imposed under this section. The court may hold the hearing as part of the sentencing hearing for the offender.

(B) If a person is convicted of or pleads guilty to a violation of section 2909.23 or 2909.24 of the Revised Code and if any political subdivision incurred any response costs as a result of, or in making any response to, the threat of the specified offense involved in the violation of section 2909.23 of the Revised Code or the actual specified offense involved in the violation of section 2909.24 of the Revised Code, in addition to the financial sanctions authorized under section 2929.18 of the Revised Code, the court imposing sentence upon the offender for the violation may order the offender to reimburse the involved political subdivision for the response costs it so incurred.

(2002 S 184, eff. 5–15–02)

CHAPTER 2911

ROBBERY, BURGLARY, AND TRESPASS

ROBBERY

2911.01 Aggravated robbery

(A) No person, in attempting or committing a theft offense, as defined in section 2913.01 of the Revised Code, or in fleeing immediately after the attempt or offense, shall do any of the following:

(1) Have a deadly weapon on or about the offender's person or under the offender's control and either display the weapon, brandish it, indicate that the offender possesses it, or use it;

(2) Have a dangerous ordnance on or about the offender's person or under the offender's control;

(3) Inflict, or attempt to inflict, serious physical harm on another.

(B) No person, without privilege to do so, shall knowingly remove or attempt to remove a deadly weapon from the person of a law enforcement officer, or shall knowingly deprive or attempt to deprive a law enforcement officer of a deadly weapon, when both of the following apply:

(1) The law enforcement officer, at the time of the removal, attempted removal, deprivation, or attempted deprivation, is acting within the course and scope of the officer's duties;

(2) The offender knows or has reasonable cause to know that the law enforcement officer is a law enforcement officer.

(C) Whoever violates this section is guilty of aggravated robbery, a felony of the first degree.

(D) As used in this section:

(1) "Deadly weapon" and "dangerous ordnance" have the same meanings as in section 2923.11 of the Revised Code.

(2) "Law enforcement officer" has the same meaning as in section 2901.01 of the Revised Code and also includes employees of the department of rehabilitation and correction who are authorized to carry weapons within the course and scope of their duties.

(1997 H 151, eff. 9–16–97; 1995 S 2, eff. 7–1–96; 1983 S 210, eff. 7–1–83; 1982 H 269, § 4, S 199; 1972 H 511)

2911.02 Robbery

(A) No person, in attempting or committing a theft offense or in fleeing immediately after the attempt or offense, shall do any of the following:

(1) Have a deadly weapon on or about the offender's person or under the offender's control;

(2) Inflict, attempt to inflict, or threaten to inflict physical harm on another;

(3) Use or threaten the immediate use of force against another.

(B) Whoever violates this section is guilty of robbery. A violation of division (A)(1) or (2) of this section is a felony of the second degree. A violation of division (A)(3) of this section is a felony of the third degree.

(C) As used in this section:

(1) "Deadly weapon" has the same meaning as in section 2923.11 of the Revised Code.

(2) "Theft offense" has the same meaning as in section 2913.01 of the Revised Code.

(1996 S 269, eff. 7–1–96; 1995 S 2, eff. 7–1–96; 1982 H 269, § 4, eff. 7–1–83; 1982 S 199; 1972 H 511)

BURGLARY

2911.11 Aggravated burglary

(A) No person, by force, stealth, or deception, shall trespass in an occupied structure or in a separately secured or separately occupied portion of an occupied structure, when another person other than an accomplice of the offender is present, with purpose to commit in the structure or in the separately secured or separately occupied portion of the structure any criminal offense, if any of the following apply:

(1) The offender inflicts, or attempts or threatens to inflict physical harm on another;

(2) The offender has a deadly weapon or dangerous ordnance on or about the offender's person or under the offender's control.

(B) Whoever violates this section is guilty of aggravated burglary, a felony of the first degree.

(C) As used in this section:

(1) "Occupied structure" has the same meaning as in section 2909.01 of the Revised Code.

(2) "Deadly weapon" and "dangerous ordnance" have the same meanings as in section 2923.11 of the Revised Code.

(1996 S 269, eff. 7–1–96; 1995 S 2, eff. 7–1–96; 1983 S 210, eff. 7–1–83; 1982 H 269, § 4, S 199; 1972 H 511)

2911.12 Burglary

(A) No person, by force, stealth, or deception, shall do any of the following:

(1) Trespass in an occupied structure or in a separately secured or separately occupied portion of an occupied structure, when another person other than an accomplice of the offender is present, with purpose to commit in the structure or in the separately secured or separately occupied portion of the structure any criminal offense;

(2) Trespass in an occupied structure or in a separately secured or separately occupied portion of an occupied structure that is a permanent or temporary habitation of any person when any person other than an accomplice of the offender is present or likely to be present, with purpose to commit in the habitation any criminal offense;

(3) Trespass in an occupied structure or in a separately secured or separately occupied portion of an occupied structure, with purpose to commit in the structure or separately secured or separately occupied portion of the structure any criminal offense;

(4) Trespass in a permanent or temporary habitation of any person when any person other than an accomplice of the offender is present or likely to be present.

(B) As used in this section, "occupied structure" has the same meaning as in section 2909.01 of the Revised Code.

(C) Whoever violates this section is guilty of burglary. A violation of division (A)(1) or (2) of this section is a felony of the second degree. A violation of division (A)(3) of this section is a felony of the third degree. A violation of division (A)(4) of this section is a felony of the fourth degree.

(1996 S 269, eff. 7–1–96; 1995 S 2, eff. 7–1–96; 1990 H 837, eff. 7–3–90; 1982 H 269, § 4, S 199; 1972 H 511)

2911.13 Breaking and entering

(A) No person by force, stealth, or deception, shall trespass in an unoccupied structure, with purpose to commit therein any theft offense, as defined in section 2913.01 of the Revised Code, or any felony.

(B) No person shall trespass on the land or premises of another, with purpose to commit a felony.

(C) Whoever violates this section is guilty of breaking and entering, a felony of the fifth degree.

(1995 S 2, eff. 7–1–96; 1972 H 511, eff. 1–1–74)

TRESPASS

2911.21 Criminal trespass

(A) No person, without privilege to do so, shall do any of the following:

(1) Knowingly enter or remain on the land or premises of another;

(2) Knowingly enter or remain on the land or premises of another, the use of which is lawfully restricted to certain persons, purposes, modes, or hours, when the offender knows the offender is in violation of any such restriction or is reckless in that regard;

(3) Recklessly enter or remain on the land or premises of another, as to which notice against unauthorized access or presence is given by actual communication to the offender, or in a manner prescribed by law, or by posting in a manner reasonably calculated to come to the attention of potential intruders, or by fencing or other enclosure manifestly designed to restrict access;

(4) Being on the land or premises of another, negligently fail or refuse to leave upon being notified by signage posted in a conspicuous place or otherwise being notified to do so by the owner or occupant, or the agent or servant of either.

(B) It is no defense to a charge under this section that the land or premises involved was owned, controlled, or in custody of a public agency.

(C) It is no defense to a charge under this section that the offender was authorized to enter or remain on the land or premises involved, when such authorization was secured by deception.

(D) Whoever violates this section is guilty of criminal trespass, a misdemeanor of the fourth degree.

(E) As used in this section, "land or premises" includes any land, building, structure, or place belonging to, controlled by, or in custody of another, and any separate enclosure or room, or portion thereof.

(2004 H 12, eff. 4–8–04; 1972 H 511, eff. 1–1–74)

2911.211 Aggravated trespass

(A) No person shall enter or remain on the land or premises of another with purpose to commit on that land or those premises a misdemeanor, the elements of which involve causing physical harm to another person or causing another person to believe that the offender will cause physical harm to him.

(B) Whoever violates this section is guilty of aggravated trespass, a misdemeanor of the first degree.

(1992 H 536, eff. 11–5–92)

SAFECRACKING

2911.31 Safecracking

(A) No person, with purpose to commit an offense, shall knowingly enter, force an entrance into, or tamper with any vault, safe, or strongbox.

(B) Whoever violates this section is guilty of safecracking, a felony of the fourth degree.

(1995 S 2, eff. 7–1–96; 1972 H 511, eff. 1–1–74)

2911.32 Tampering with coin machines

(A) No person, with purpose to commit theft or to defraud, shall knowingly enter, force an entrance into, tamper with, or insert any part of an instrument into any coin machine.

(B) Whoever violates this section is guilty of tampering with coin machines, a misdemeanor of the first degree. If the offender previously has been convicted of a violation of this section or of any theft offense as defined in section 2913.01 of the Revised Code, tampering with coin machines is a felony of the fifth degree.

(1995 S 2, eff. 7–1–96; 1972 H 511, eff. 1–1–74)

CHAPTER 2913

THEFT AND FRAUD

DEFINITIONS

2913.01 Definitions

Note: See also following version, eff. 5–6–05.

As used in this chapter, unless the context requires that a term be given a different meaning:

(A) "Deception" means knowingly deceiving another or causing another to be deceived by any false or misleading representation, by withholding information, by preventing another from acquiring information, or by any other conduct, act, or omission that creates, confirms, or perpetuates a false impression in another, including a false impression as to law, value, state of mind, or other objective or subjective fact.

(B) "Defraud" means to knowingly obtain, by deception, some benefit for oneself or another, or to knowingly cause, by deception, some detriment to another.

(C) "Deprive" means to do any of the following:

(1) Withhold property of another permanently, or for a period that appropriates a substantial portion of its value or use, or with purpose to restore it only upon payment of a reward or other consideration;

(2) Dispose of property so as to make it unlikely that the owner will recover it;

(3) Accept, use, or appropriate money, property, or services, with purpose not to give proper consideration in return for the money, property, or services, and without reasonable justification or excuse for not giving proper consideration.

(D) "Owner" means, unless the context requires a different meaning, any person, other than the actor, who is the owner of, who has possession or control of, or who has any license or interest in property or services, even though the ownership, possession, control, license, or interest is unlawful.

(E) "Services" include labor, personal services, professional services, public utility services, common carrier services, and food, drink, transportation, entertainment, and cable television services and, for purposes of section 2913.04 of the Revised Code, include cable services as defined in that section.

(F) "Writing" means any computer software, document, letter, memorandum, note, paper, plate, data, film, or other thing having in or upon it any written, typewritten, or printed matter, and any token, stamp, seal, credit card, badge, trademark, label, or other symbol of value, right, privilege, license, or identification.

(G) "Forge" means to fabricate or create, in whole or in part and by any means, any spurious writing, or to make, execute, alter, complete, reproduce, or otherwise purport to authenticate any writing, when the writing in fact is not authenticated by that conduct.

(H) "Utter" means to issue, publish, transfer, use, put or send into circulation, deliver, or display.

(I) "Coin machine" means any mechanical or electronic device designed to do both of the following:

(1) Receive a coin, bill, or token made for that purpose;

(2) In return for the insertion or deposit of a coin, bill, or token, automatically dispense property, provide a service, or grant a license.

(J) "Slug" means an object that, by virtue of its size, shape, composition, or other quality, is capable of being inserted or deposited in a coin machine as an improper substitute for a genuine coin, bill, or token made for that purpose.

(K) "Theft offense" means any of the following:

(1) A violation of section 2911.01, 2911.02, 2911.11, 2911.12, 2911.13, 2911.31, 2911.32, 2913.02, 2913.03, 2913.04, 2913.041, 2913.05, 2913.06, 2913.11, 2913.21, 2913.31, 2913.32, 2913.33, 2913.34, 2913.40, 2913.42, 2913. 43, 2913.44, 2913.45, 2913.47, former section 2913.47 or 2913.48, or section 2913.51, 2915.05, or 2921.41 of the Revised Code;

(2) A violation of an existing or former municipal ordinance or law of this or any other state, or of the United States, substantially equivalent to any section listed in division (K)(1) of this section or a violation of section 2913.41, 2913.81, or 2915.06 of the Revised Code as it existed prior to July 1, 1996;

(3) An offense under an existing or former municipal ordinance or law of this or any other state, or of the United States, involving robbery, burglary, breaking and entering, theft, embezzlement, wrongful conversion, forgery, counterfeiting, deceit, or fraud;

(4) A conspiracy or attempt to commit, or complicity in committing, any offense under division (K)(1), (2), or (3) of this section.

(L) "Computer services" includes, but is not limited to, the use of a computer system, computer network, computer program, data that is prepared for computer use, or data that is contained within a computer system or computer network.

(M) "Computer" means an electronic device that performs logical, arithmetic, and memory functions by the manipulation of electronic or magnetic impulses. "Computer" includes, but is not limited to, all input, output, processing, storage, computer program, or communication facilities that are connected, or related, in a computer system or network to an electronic device of that nature.

(N) "Computer system" means a computer and related devices, whether connected or unconnected, including, but not limited to, data input, output, and storage devices, data communications links, and computer programs and data that make the system capable of performing specified special purpose data processing tasks.

(O) "Computer network" means a set of related and remotely connected computers and communication facilities that includes more than one computer system that has the capability to transmit among the connected computers and communication facilities through the use of computer facilities.

(P) "Computer program" means an ordered set of data representing coded instructions or statements that, when executed by a computer, cause the computer to process data.

(Q) "Computer software" means computer programs, procedures, and other documentation associated with the operation of a computer system.

(R) "Data" means a representation of information, knowledge, facts, concepts, or instructions that are being or have been prepared in a formalized manner and that are intended for use in a computer, computer system, or computer network. For purposes of section 2913.47 of the Revised Code, "data" has the additional meaning set forth in division (A) of that section.

(S) "Cable television service" means any services provided by or through the facilities of any cable television system or other similar closed circuit coaxial cable communications system, or any microwave or similar transmission service used in connection with any cable television system or other similar closed circuit coaxial cable communications system.

(T) "Gain access" means to approach, instruct, communicate with, store data in, retrieve data from, or otherwise make use of any resources of a computer, computer system, or computer network, or any cable service or cable system both as defined in section 2913.04 of the Revised Code.

(U) "Credit card" includes, but is not limited to, a card, code, device, or other means of access to a customer's account for the purpose of obtaining money, property, labor, or services on credit, or for initiating an electronic fund transfer at a point-of-sale terminal, an automated teller machine, or a cash dispensing machine. It also includes a county procurement card issued under section 301.29 of the Revised Code.

(V) "Electronic fund transfer" has the same meaning as in 92 Stat. 3728, 15 U.S.C.A. 1693a, as amended.

(W) "Rented property" means personal property in which the right of possession and use of the property is for a short and possibly indeterminate term in return for consideration; the rentee generally controls the duration of possession of the property, within any applicable minimum or maximum term; and the amount of consideration generally is determined by the duration of possession of the property.

(X) "Telecommunication" means the origination, emission, dissemination, transmission, or reception of data, images, signals, sounds, or other intelligence or equivalence of intelligence of any nature over any communications system by any method, including, but not limited to, a fiber optic, electronic, magnetic, optical, digital, or analog method.

(Y) "Telecommunications device" means any instrument, equipment, machine, or other device that facilitates telecommunication, including, but not limited to, a computer, computer network, computer chip, computer circuit, scanner, telephone, cellular telephone, pager, personal communications device, transponder, receiver, radio, modem, or device that enables the use of a modem.

(Z) "Telecommunications service" means the providing, allowing, facilitating, or generating of any form of telecommunication through the use of a telecommunications device over a telecommunications system.

(AA) "Counterfeit telecommunications device" means a telecommunications device that, alone or with another telecommunications device, has been altered, constructed, manufactured, or programmed to acquire, intercept, receive, or otherwise facilitate the use of a telecommunications service or information service without the authority or consent of the provider of the telecommunications service or information service. "Counterfeit telecommunications device" includes, but is not limited to, a clone telephone, clone microchip, tumbler telephone, or tumbler microchip; a wireless scanning device capable of acquiring, intercepting, receiving, or otherwise facilitating the use of telecommunications service or information service without immediate detection; or a device, equipment, hardware, or software designed for, or capable of, altering or changing the electronic serial number in a wireless telephone.

(BB)(1) "Information service" means, subject to division (BB)(2) of this section, the offering of a capability for generating, acquiring, storing, transforming, processing, retrieving, utilizing, or making available information via telecommunications, including, but not limited to, electronic publishing.

(2) "Information service" does not include any use of a capability of a type described in division (BB)(1) of this section for the management, control, or operation of a telecommunications system or the management of a telecommunications service.

(CC) "Elderly person" means a person who is sixty-five years of age or older.

(DD) "Disabled adult" means a person who is eighteen years of age or older and has some impairment of body or mind that makes the person unable to work at any substantially remunerative employment that the person otherwise would be able to perform and that will, with reasonable probability, continue for a period of at least twelve months without any present indication of recovery from the impairment, or who is eighteen years of age or older and has been certified as permanently and totally disabled by an agency of this state or the United States that has the function of so classifying persons.

(EE) "Firearm" and "dangerous ordnance' ' have the same meanings as in section 2923.11 of the Revised Code.

(FF) "Motor vehicle" has the same meaning as in section 4501.01 of the Revised Code.

(GG) "Dangerous drug" has the same meaning as in section 4729.01 of the Revised Code.

(HH) "Drug abuse offense" has the same meaning as in section 2925.01 of the Revised Code.

(II)(1) "Computer hacking" means any of the following:

(a) Gaining access or attempting to gain access to all or part of a computer, computer system, or a computer network without express or implied authorization with the intent to defraud or with intent to commit a crime;

(b) Misusing computer or network services including, but not limited to, mail transfer programs, file transfer programs, proxy servers, and web servers by performing functions not authorized by the owner of the computer, computer system, or computer network or other person authorized to give consent. As used in this division, "misuse of computer and network services" includes, but is not limited to, the unauthorized use of any of the following:

(i) Mail transfer programs to send mail to persons other than the authorized users of that computer or computer network;

(ii) File transfer program proxy services or proxy servers to access other computers, computer systems, or computer networks;

(iii) Web servers to redirect users to other web pages or web servers.

(c)(i) Subject to division (II)(1)(c)(ii) of this section, using a group of computer programs commonly known as "port scanners" or "probes" to intentionally access any computer, computer system, or computer network without the permission of the owner of the computer, computer system, or computer network or other person authorized to give consent. The group of computer programs referred to in this division includes, but is not limited to, those computer programs that use a computer network to access a computer, computer system, or another computer network to determine any of the following: the presence or types of computers or computer systems on a network; the computer network's facilities and capabilities; the availability of computer or network services; the presence or versions of computer software including, but not limited to, operating systems, computer services, or computer contaminants; the presence of a known computer software deficiency that can be used to gain unauthorized access to a computer, computer system, or computer network; or any other information about a computer, computer system, or computer network not necessary for the normal and lawful operation of the computer initiating the access.

(ii) The group of computer programs referred to in division (II)(1)(c)(i) of this section does not include standard computer software used for the normal operation, administration, management, and test of a computer, computer system, or computer network including, but not limited to, domain name services, mail transfer services, and other operating system services, computer programs commonly called "ping," "tcpdump," and "traceroute" and other network monitoring and management computer software, and computer programs commonly known as "nslookup" and "whois" and other systems administration computer software.

(d) The intentional use of a computer, computer system, or a computer network in a manner that exceeds any right or permission granted by the owner of the computer, computer system, or computer network or other person authorized to give consent.

(2) "Computer hacking" does not include the introduction of a computer contaminant, as defined in section 2909.02 of the Revised Code, into a computer, computer system, computer program, or computer network.

(JJ) "Police dog or horse" and "service dog" have the same meanings as in section 2921.321 of the Revised Code.

(KK) "Anhydrous ammonia" is a compound formed by the combination of two gaseous elements, nitrogen and hydrogen, in the manner described in this division. Anhydrous ammonia is one part nitrogen to three parts hydrogen (NH3). Anhydrous ammonia by weight is fourteen parts nitrogen to three parts hydrogen, which is approximately eighty-two per cent nitrogen to eighteen per cent hydrogen.

(2004 H 536, eff. 4–15–05; 2004 H 369, eff. 11–26–04; 2004 S 146, eff. 9–23–04; 2003 S 82, eff. 2–12–04; 2002 H 327, eff. 7–8–02; 1999 H 2, eff. 11–10–99; 1998 H 565, eff. 3–30–99; 1996 S 277, eff. 3–31–97; 1995 S 2, eff. 7–1–96; 1990 H 347, eff. 7–18–90; 1987 H 182; 1986 H 49, H 340; 1984 S 183; 1983 H 97; 1982 H 437; 1972 H 511)

Note: See also following version, eff. 5–6–05.

2913.01 Definitions (later effective date)

Note: See also preceding version, in effect until 5–6–05.

As used in this chapter, unless the context requires that a term be given a different meaning:

(A) "Deception" means knowingly deceiving another or causing another to be deceived by any false or misleading representation, by withholding information, by preventing another from acquiring information, or by any other conduct, act, or omission that creates, confirms, or perpetuates a false impression in another, including a false impression as to law, value, state of mind, or other objective or subjective fact.

(B) "Defraud" means to knowingly obtain, by deception, some benefit for oneself or another, or to knowingly cause, by deception, some detriment to another.

(C) "Deprive" means to do any of the following:

(1) Withhold property of another permanently, or for a period that appropriates a substantial portion of its value or use, or with purpose to restore it only upon payment of a reward or other consideration;

(2) Dispose of property so as to make it unlikely that the owner will recover it;

(3) Accept, use, or appropriate money, property, or services, with purpose not to give proper consideration in return for the money, property, or services, and without reasonable justification or excuse for not giving proper consideration.

(D) "Owner" means, unless the context requires a different meaning, any person, other than the actor, who is the owner of, who has possession or control of, or who has any license or interest in property or services, even though the ownership, possession, control, license, or interest is unlawful.

(E) "Services" include labor, personal services, professional services, public utility services, including wireless service as defined in division (F)(1) of section 4931.40 of the Revised Code, common carrier services, and food, drink, transportation, entertainment, and cable television services and, for purposes of section 2913.04 of the Revised Code, include cable services as defined in that section.

(F) "Writing" means any computer software, document, letter, memorandum, note, paper, plate, data, film, or other thing having in or upon it any written, typewritten, or printed matter, and any token, stamp, seal, credit card, badge, trademark, label, or other symbol of value, right, privilege, license, or identification.

(G) "Forge" means to fabricate or create, in whole or in part and by any means, any spurious writing, or to make, execute, alter, complete, reproduce, or otherwise purport to authenticate any writing, when the writing in fact is not authenticated by that conduct.

(H) "Utter" means to issue, publish, transfer, use, put or send into circulation, deliver, or display.

(I) "Coin machine" means any mechanical or electronic device designed to do both of the following:

(1) Receive a coin, bill, or token made for that purpose;

(2) In return for the insertion or deposit of a coin, bill, or token, automatically dispense property, provide a service, or grant a license.

(J) "Slug" means an object that, by virtue of its size, shape, composition, or other quality, is capable of being inserted or deposited in a coin machine as an improper substitute for a genuine coin, bill, or token made for that purpose.

(K) "Theft offense" means any of the following:

(1) A violation of section 2911.01, 2911.02, 2911.11, 2911.12, 2911.13, 2911.31, 2911.32, 2913.02, 2913.03, 2913.04, 2913.041, 2913.05, 2913.06, 2913.11, 2913.21, 2913.31, 2913.32, 2913.33, 2913.34, 2913.40, 2913.42, 2913. 43, 2913.44, 2913.45, 2913.47, former section 2913.47 or 2913.48, or section 2913.51, 2915.05, or 2921.41 of the Revised Code;

(2) A violation of an existing or former municipal ordinance or law of this or any other state, or of the United States, substantially equivalent to any section listed in division (K)(1) of this section or a violation of section 2913.41, 2913.81, or 2915.06 of the Revised Code as it existed prior to July 1, 1996;

(3) An offense under an existing or former municipal ordinance or law of this or any other state, or of the United States, involving robbery, burglary, breaking and entering, theft, embezzlement, wrongful conversion, forgery, counterfeiting, deceit, or fraud;

(4) A conspiracy or attempt to commit, or complicity in committing, any offense under division (K)(1), (2), or (3) of this section.

(L) "Computer services" includes, but is not limited to, the use of a computer system, computer network, computer program, data that is prepared for computer use, or data that is contained within a computer system or computer network.

(M) "Computer" means an electronic device that performs logical, arithmetic, and memory functions by the manipulation of electronic or magnetic impulses. "Computer" includes, but is not limited to, all input, output, processing, storage, computer program, or communication facilities that are connected, or related, in a computer system or network to an electronic device of that nature.

(N) "Computer system" means a computer and related devices, whether connected or unconnected, including, but not limited to, data input, output, and storage devices, data communications links, and computer programs and data that make the system capable of performing specified special purpose data processing tasks.

(O) "Computer network" means a set of related and remotely connected computers and communication facilities that includes more than one computer system that has the capability to transmit among the connected computers and communication facilities through the use of computer facilities.

(P) "Computer program" means an ordered set of data representing coded instructions or statements that, when executed by a computer, cause the computer to process data.

(Q) "Computer software" means computer programs, procedures, and other documentation associated with the operation of a computer system.

(R) "Data" means a representation of information, knowledge, facts, concepts, or instructions that are being or have been prepared in a formalized manner and that are intended for use in a computer, computer system, or computer network. For purposes of section 2913.47 of the Revised Code, "data" has the additional meaning set forth in division (A) of that section.

(S) "Cable television service" means any services provided by or through the facilities of any cable television system or other similar closed circuit coaxial cable communications system, or any microwave or similar transmission service used in connection with any cable television system or other similar closed circuit coaxial cable communications system.

(T) "Gain access" means to approach, instruct, communicate with, store data in, retrieve data from, or otherwise make use of any resources of a computer, computer system, or computer network, or any cable service or cable system both as defined in section 2913.04 of the Revised Code.

(U) "Credit card" includes, but is not limited to, a card, code, device, or other means of access to a customer's account for the purpose of obtaining money, property, labor, or services on credit, or for initiating an electronic fund transfer at a point-of-sale terminal, an automated teller machine, or a cash dispensing machine. It also includes a county procurement card issued under section 301.29 of the Revised Code.

(V) "Electronic fund transfer" has the same meaning as in 92 Stat. 3728, 15 U.S.C.A. 1693a, as amended.

(W) "Rented property" means personal property in which the right of possession and use of the property is for a short and possibly indeterminate term in return for consideration; the rentee generally controls the duration of possession of the property, within any applicable minimum or maximum term; and the amount of consideration generally is determined by the duration of possession of the property.

(X) "Telecommunication" means the origination, emission, dissemination, transmission, or reception of data, images, signals, sounds, or other intelligence or equivalence of intelligence of any nature over any communications system by any method, including, but not limited to, a fiber optic, electronic, magnetic, optical, digital, or analog method.

(Y) "Telecommunications device" means any instrument, equipment, machine, or other device that facilitates telecommunication, including, but not limited to, a computer, computer network, computer chip, computer circuit, scanner, telephone, cellular telephone, pager, personal communications device, transponder, receiver, radio, modem, or device that enables the use of a modem.

(Z) "Telecommunications service" means the providing, allowing, facilitating, or generating of any form of telecommunication through the use of a telecommunications device over a telecommunications system.

(AA) "Counterfeit telecommunications device" means a telecommunications device that, alone or with another telecommunications device, has been altered, constructed, manufactured, or programmed to acquire, intercept, receive, or otherwise facilitate the use of a telecommunications service or information service without the authority or consent of the provider of the telecommunications service or information service. "Counterfeit telecommunications device" includes, but is not limited to, a clone telephone, clone microchip, tumbler telephone, or tumbler microchip; a wireless scanning device capable of acquiring, intercepting, receiving, or otherwise facilitating the use of telecommunications service or information service without immediate detection; or a device, equipment, hardware, or software designed for, or capable of, altering or changing the electronic serial number in a wireless telephone.

(BB)(1) "Information service" means, subject to division (BB)(2) of this section, the offering of a capability for generating, acquiring, storing, transforming, processing, retrieving, utilizing, or making available information via telecommunications, including, but not limited to, electronic publishing.

(2) "Information service" does not include any use of a capability of a type described in division (BB)(1) of this section for the management, control, or operation of a telecommunications system or the management of a telecommunications service.

(CC) "Elderly person" means a person who is sixty-five years of age or older.

(DD) "Disabled adult" means a person who is eighteen years of age or older and has some impairment of body or mind that makes the person unable to work at any substantially remunerative employment that the person otherwise would be able to perform and that will, with reasonable probability, continue for a period of at least twelve months without any present indication of recovery from the impairment, or who is eighteen years of age or older and has been certified as permanently and totally disabled by an agency of this state or the United States that has the function of so classifying persons.

(EE) "Firearm" and "dangerous ordnance' ' have the same meanings as in section 2923.11 of the Revised Code.

(FF) "Motor vehicle" has the same meaning as in section 4501.01 of the Revised Code.

(GG) "Dangerous drug" has the same meaning as in section 4729.01 of the Revised Code.

(HH) "Drug abuse offense" has the same meaning as in section 2925.01 of the Revised Code.

(II)(1) "Computer hacking" means any of the following:

(a) Gaining access or attempting to gain access to all or part of a computer, computer system, or a computer network without express or implied authorization with the intent to defraud or with intent to commit a crime;

(b) Misusing computer or network services including, but not limited to, mail transfer programs, file transfer programs, proxy servers, and web servers by performing functions not authorized by the owner of the computer, computer system, or computer network or other person authorized to give consent. As used in this division, "misuse of computer and network services" includes, but is not limited to, the unauthorized use of any of the following:

(i) Mail transfer programs to send mail to persons other than the authorized users of that computer or computer network;

(ii) File transfer program proxy services or proxy servers to access other computers, computer systems, or computer networks;

(iii) Web servers to redirect users to other web pages or web servers.

(c)(i) Subject to division (II)(1)(c)(ii) of this section, using a group of computer programs commonly known as "port scanners" or "probes" to intentionally access any computer, computer system, or computer network without the permission of the owner of the computer, computer system, or computer network or other person authorized to give consent. The group of computer programs referred to in this division includes, but is not limited to, those computer programs that use a computer network to access a computer, computer system, or another computer network to determine any of the following: the presence or types of computers or computer systems on a network; the computer network's facilities and capabilities; the availability of computer or network services; the presence or versions of computer software including, but not limited to, operating systems, computer services, or computer contaminants; the presence of a known computer software deficiency that can be used to gain unauthorized access to a computer, computer system, or computer network; or any other information about a computer, computer system, or computer network not necessary for the normal and lawful operation of the computer initiating the access.

(ii) The group of computer programs referred to in division (II)(1)(c)(i) of this section does not include standard computer software used for the normal operation, administration, management, and test of a computer, computer system, or computer network including, but not limited to, domain name services, mail transfer services, and other operating system services, computer programs commonly called "ping," "tcpdump," and "traceroute" and other network monitoring and management computer software, and computer programs commonly known as "nslookup" and "whois" and other systems administration computer software.

(d) The intentional use of a computer, computer system, or a computer network in a manner that exceeds any right or permission granted by the owner of the computer, computer system, or computer network or other person authorized to give consent.

(2) "Computer hacking" does not include the introduction of a computer contaminant, as defined in section 2909.02 of the Revised Code, into a computer, computer system, computer program, or computer network.

(JJ) "Police dog or horse" and "service dog" have the same meanings as in section 2921.321 of the Revised Code.

(KK) "Anhydrous ammonia" is a compound formed by the combination of two gaseous elements, nitrogen and hydrogen, in the manner described in this division. Anhydrous ammonia is one part nitrogen to three parts hydrogen (NH3). Anhydrous ammonia by weight is fourteen parts nitrogen to three parts hydrogen, which is approximately eighty-two per cent nitrogen to eighteen per cent hydrogen.

(2004 H 361, eff. 5–6–05; 2004 H 536, eff. 4–15–05; 2004 H 369, eff. 11–26–04; 2004 S 146, eff. 9–23–04; 2003 S 82, eff. 2–12–04; 2002 H 327, eff. 7–8–02; 1999 H 2, eff. 11–10–99; 1998 H 565, eff. 3–30–99; 1996 S 277, eff. 3–31–97; 1995 S 2, eff. 7–1–96; 1990 H 347, eff. 7–18–90; 1987 H 182; 1986 H 49, H 340; 1984 S 183; 1983 H 97; 1982 H 437; 1972 H 511)

Note: See also preceding version, in effect until 5–6–05.

THEFT AND RELATED OFFENSES

2913.02 Theft; aggravated theft

(A) No person, with purpose to deprive the owner of property or services, shall knowingly obtain or exert control over either the property or services in any of the following ways:

(1) Without the consent of the owner or person authorized to give consent;

(2) Beyond the scope of the express or implied consent of the owner or person authorized to give consent;

(3) By deception;

(4) By threat;

(5) By intimidation.

(B)(1) Whoever violates this section is guilty of theft.

(2) Except as otherwise provided in this division or division (B)(3), (4), (5), (6), (7), or (8) of this section, a violation of this section is petty theft, a misdemeanor of the first degree. If the value of the property or services stolen is five hundred dollars or more and is less than five thousand dollars or if the property stolen is any of the property listed in section 2913.71 of the Revised Code, a violation of this section is theft, a felony of the fifth degree. If the value of the property or services stolen is five thousand dollars or more and is less than one hundred thousand dollars, a violation of this section is grand theft, a felony of the fourth degree. If the value of the property or services stolen is one hundred thousand dollars or more and is less than five hundred thousand dollars, a violation of this section is aggravated theft, a felony of the third degree. If the value of the property or services is five hundred thousand dollars or more and is less than one million dollars, a violation of this section is aggravated theft, a felony of the second degree. If the value of the property or services stolen is one million dollars or more, a violation of this section is aggravated theft of one million dollars or more, a felony of the first degree.

(3) Except as otherwise provided in division (B)(4), (5), (6), (7), or (8) of this section, if the victim of the offense is an elderly person or disabled adult, a violation of this section is theft from an elderly person or disabled adult, and division (B)(3) of this section applies. Except as otherwise provided in this division, theft from an elderly person or disabled adult is a felony of the fifth degree. If the value of the property or services stolen is five hundred dollars or more and is less than five thousand dollars, theft from an elderly person or disabled adult is a felony of the fourth degree. If the value of the property or services stolen is five thousand dollars or more and is less than twenty-five thousand dollars, theft from an elderly person or disabled adult is a felony of the third degree. If the value of the property or services stolen is twenty-five thousand dollars or more and is less than one hundred thousand dollars, theft from an elderly person or disabled adult is a felony of the second degree. If the value of the property or services stolen is one hundred thousand dollars or more, theft from an elderly person or disabled adult is a felony of the first degree.

(4) If the property stolen is a firearm or dangerous ordnance, a violation of this section is grand theft, a felony of the third degree, and there is a presumption in favor of the court imposing a prison term for the offense. The offender shall serve the prison term consecutively to any other prison term or mandatory prison term previously or subsequently imposed upon the offender.

(5) If the property stolen is a motor vehicle, a violation of this section is grand theft of a motor vehicle, a felony of the fourth degree.

(6) If the property stolen is any dangerous drug, a violation of this section is theft of drugs, a felony of the fourth degree, or, if the offender previously has been convicted of a felony drug abuse offense, a felony of the third degree.

(7) If the property stolen is a police dog or horse or a service dog and the offender knows or should know that the property stolen is a police dog or horse or service dog, a violation of this section is theft of a police dog or horse or service dog, a felony of the third degree.

(8) If the property stolen is anhydrous ammonia, a violation of this section is theft of anhydrous ammonia, a felony of the third degree.

(9) In addition to the penalties described in division (B)(2) of this section, if the offender committed the violation by causing a motor vehicle to leave the premises of an establishment at which gasoline is offered for retail sale without the offender making full payment for gasoline that was dispensed into the fuel tank of the motor vehicle or into another container, the court may do one of the following:

(a) Unless division (B)(9)(b) of this section applies, suspend for not more than six months the offender's driver's license, probationary driver's license, commercial driver's license, temporary instruction permit, or nonresident operating privilege;

(b) If the offender's driver's license, probationary driver's license, commercial driver's license, temporary instruction permit, or nonresident operating privilege has previously been suspended pursuant to division (B)(9)(a) of this section, impose a class seven suspension of the offender's license, permit, or privilege from the range specified in division (A)(7) of section 4510.02 of the Revised Code, provided that the suspension shall be for at least six months.

(C) The sentencing court that suspends an offender's license, permit, or nonresident operating privilege under division (B)(9) of this section may grant the offender limited driving privileges during the period of the suspension in accordance with Chapter 4510. of the Revised Code.

(2004 H 536, eff. 4–15–05; 2004 H 369, eff. 11–26–04; 2004 H 12, eff. 4–8–04; 2003 H 179, eff. 3–9–04; 2003 H 7, eff. 9–16–03; 1999 H 2, eff. 11–10–99; 1998 S 66, eff. 7–22–98; 1995 S 2, eff. 7–1–96; 1995 H 4, eff. 11–9–95; 1990 S 258, eff. 11–20–90; 1990 H 347; 1986 H 49; 1984 H 632; 1982 H 269, § 4, S 199; 1980 S 191; 1972 H 511)

2913.03 Unauthorized use of a vehicle

(A) No person shall knowingly use or operate an aircraft, motor vehicle, motorcycle, motorboat, or other motor-propelled vehicle without the consent of the owner or person authorized to give consent.

(B) No person shall knowingly use or operate an aircraft, motor vehicle, motorboat, or other motor-propelled vehicle without the consent of the owner or person authorized to give consent, and either remove it from this state or keep possession of it for more than forty-eight hours.

(C) The following are affirmative defenses to a charge under this section:

(1) At the time of the alleged offense, the actor, though mistaken, reasonably believed that the actor was authorized to use or operate the property.

(2) At the time of the alleged offense, the actor reasonably believed that the owner or person empowered to give consent would authorize the actor to use or operate the property.

(D)(1) Whoever violates this section is guilty of unauthorized use of a vehicle.

(2) Except as otherwise provided in division (D)(4) of this section, a violation of division (A) of this section is a misdemeanor of the first degree.

(3) Except as otherwise provided in division (D)(4) of this section, a violation of division (B) of this section is a felony of the fifth degree.

(4) If the victim of the offense is an elderly person or disabled adult and if the victim incurs a loss as a result of the violation, a violation of division (A) or (B) of this section is whichever of the following is applicable:

(a) Except as otherwise provided in division (D)(4)(b), (c), (d), or (e) of this section, a felony of the fifth degree;

(b) If the loss to the victim is five hundred dollars or more and is less than five thousand dollars, a felony of the fourth degree;

(c) If the loss to the victim is five thousand dollars or more and is less than twenty-five thousand dollars, a felony of the third degree;

(d) If the loss to the victim is twenty-five thousand dollars or more, a felony of the second degree.

(1999 H 2, eff. 11–10–99; 1995 S 2, eff. 7–1–96; 1972 H 511, eff. 1–1–74)

2913.04 Unauthorized use of property; unauthorized use of computer or telecommunication property; unauthorized use of LEADS information

(A) No person shall knowingly use or operate the property of another without the consent of the owner or person authorized to give consent.

(B) No person, in any manner and by any means, including, but not limited to, computer hacking, shall knowingly gain access to, attempt to gain access to, or cause access to be gained to any computer, computer system, computer network, cable service, cable system, telecommunications device, telecommunications service, or information service without the consent of, or beyond the scope of the express or implied consent of, the owner of the computer, computer system, computer network, cable service, cable system, telecommunications device, telecommunications service, or information service or other person authorized to give consent.

(C) No person shall knowingly gain access to, attempt to gain access to, cause access to be granted to, or disseminate information gained from access to the law enforcement automated database system created pursuant to section 5503.10 of the Revised Code without the consent of, or beyond the scope of the express or implied consent of, the chair of the law enforcement automated data system steering committee.

(D) The affirmative defenses contained in division (C) of section 2913.03 of the Revised Code are affirmative defenses to a charge under this section.

(E)(1) Whoever violates division (A) of this section is guilty of unauthorized use of property.

(2) Except as otherwise provided in division (E)(3) or (4) of this section, unauthorized use of property is a misdemeanor of the fourth degree.

(3) Except as otherwise provided in division (E)(4) of this section, if unauthorized use of property is committed for the purpose of devising or executing a scheme to defraud or to obtain property or services, unauthorized use of property is whichever of the following is applicable:

(a) Except as otherwise provided in division (E)(3)(b), (c), or (d) of this section, a misdemeanor of the first degree.

(b) If the value of the property or services or the loss to the victim is five hundred dollars or more and is less than five thousand dollars, a felony of the fifth degree.

(c) If the value of the property or services or the loss to the victim is five thousand dollars or more and is less than one hundred thousand dollars, a felony of the fourth degree.

(d) If the value of the property or services or the loss to the victim is one hundred thousand dollars or more, a felony of the third degree.

(4) If the victim of the offense is an elderly person or disabled adult, unauthorized use of property is whichever of the following is applicable:

(a) Except as otherwise provided in division (E)(4)(b), (c), or (d) of this section, a felony of the fifth degree;

(b) If the value of the property or services or loss to the victim is five hundred dollars or more and is less than five thousand dollars, a felony of the fourth degree;

(c) If the value of the property or services or loss to the victim is five thousand dollars or more and is less than twenty-five thousand dollars, a felony of the third degree;

(d) If the value of the property or services or loss to the victim is twenty-five thousand dollars or more, a felony of the second degree.

(F)(1) Whoever violates division (B) of this section is guilty of unauthorized use of computer, cable, or telecommunication property, and shall be punished as provided in division (F)(2), (3), or (4) of this section.

(2) Except as otherwise provided in division (F)(3) or (4) of this section, unauthorized use of computer, cable, or telecommunication property is a felony of the fifth degree.

(3) Except as otherwise provided in division (F)(4) of this section, if unauthorized use of computer, cable, or telecommunication property is committed for the purpose of devising or executing a scheme to defraud or to obtain property or services, for obtaining money, property, or services by false or fraudulent pretenses, or for committing any other criminal offense, unauthorized use of computer, cable, or telecommunication property is whichever of the following is applicable:

(a) Except as otherwise provided in division (F)(3)(b) of this section, if the value of the property or services involved or the loss to the victim is five thousand dollars or more and less than one hundred thousand dollars, a felony of the fourth degree;

(b) If the value of the property or services involved or the loss to the victim is one hundred thousand dollars or more, a felony of the third degree.

(4) If the victim of the offense is an elderly person or disabled adult, unauthorized use of computer, cable, or telecommunication property is whichever of the following is applicable:

(a) Except as otherwise provided in division (F)(4)(b), (c), or (d) of this section, a felony of the fifth degree;

(b) If the value of the property or services or loss to the victim is five hundred dollars or more and is less than five thousand dollars, a felony of the fourth degree;

(c) If the value of the property or services or loss to the victim is five thousand dollars or more and is less than twenty-five thousand dollars, a felony of the third degree;

(d) If the value of the property or services or loss to the victim is twenty-five thousand dollars or more, a felony of the second degree.

(G) Whoever violates division (C) of this section is guilty of unauthorized use of the law enforcement automated database system, a felony of the fifth degree.

(H) As used in this section:

(1) "Cable operator" means any person or group of persons that does either of the following:

(a) Provides cable service over a cable system and directly or through one or more affiliates owns a significant interest in that cable system;

(b) Otherwise controls or is responsible for, through any arrangement, the management and operation of a cable system.

(2) "Cable service" means any of the following:

(a) The one-way transmission to subscribers of video programming or of information that a cable operator makes available to all subscribers generally;

(b) Subscriber interaction, if any, that is required for the selection or use of video programming or of information that a cable operator makes available to all subscribers generally, both as described in division (H)(2)(a) of this section;

(c) Any cable television service.

(3) "Cable system" means any facility, consisting of a set of closed transmission paths and associated signal generation, reception, and control equipment that is designed to provide cable service that includes video programming and that is provided to multiple subscribers within a community. "Cable system" does not include any of the following:

(a) Any facility that serves only to retransmit the television signals of one or more television broadcast stations;

(b) Any facility that serves subscribers without using any public right-of-way;

(c) Any facility of a common carrier that, under 47 U.S.C.A. 522(7)(c), is excluded from the term "cable system" as defined in 47 U.S.C.A. 522(7);

(d) Any open video system that complies with 47 U.S.C.A. 573;

(e) Any facility of any electric utility used solely for operating its electric utility system.

(2004 S 146, eff. 9–23–04; 2004 H 12, eff. 4–8–04; 2002 H 327, eff. 7–8–02; 1999 H 2, eff. 11–10–99; 1998 H 565, eff. 3–30–99; 1996 S 269, eff. 7–1–96; 1995 S 2, eff. 7–1–96; 1986 H 49, eff. 6–26–86; 1972 H 511)

2913.041 Possession or sale of unauthorized device

(A) No person shall knowingly possess any device, including any instrument, apparatus, computer chip, equipment, decoder, descrambler, converter, software, or other device specially adapted, modified, or remanufactured for gaining access to cable television service, without securing authorization from or paying the required compensation to the owner or operator of the system that provides the cable television service.

(B) No person shall knowingly sell, distribute, or manufacture any device, including any instrument, apparatus, computer chip, equipment, decoder, descrambler, converter, software, or other device specially adapted, modified, or remanufactured for gaining access to cable television service, without securing authorization from or paying the required compensation to the owner or operator of the system that provides the cable television service.

(C) Whoever violates division (A) of this section is guilty of possession of an unauthorized device, a felony of the fifth degree.

Whoever violates division (B) of this section is guilty of sale of an unauthorized device, a felony of the fourth degree.

(D) A person commits a separate violation of this section with regard to each device that is sold, distributed, manufactured, or possessed in violation of division (A) or (B) of this section.

(1995 S 2, eff. 7–1–96)

2913.05 Telecommunications fraud

(A) No person, having devised a scheme to defraud, shall knowingly disseminate, transmit, or cause to be disseminated or transmitted by means of a wire, radio, satellite, telecommunication, telecommunications device, or telecommunications service any writing, data, sign, signal, picture, sound, or image with purpose to execute or otherwise further the scheme to defraud.

(B) Whoever violates this section is guilty of telecommunications fraud. Except as otherwise provided in this division, telecommunications fraud is a felony of the fifth degree. If the value of the benefit obtained by the offender or of the detriment to the victim of the fraud is five thousand dollars or more but less than one hundred thousand dollars, telecommunications fraud is a felony of the fourth degree. If the value of the benefit obtained by the offender or of the detriment to the victim of the fraud is one hundred thousand dollars or more, telecommunications fraud is a felony of the third degree.

(1998 H 565, eff. 3–30–99)

2913.06 Unlawful use of telecommunications device

(A) No person shall knowingly manufacture, possess, deliver, offer to deliver, or advertise a counterfeit telecommunications device with purpose to use it criminally.

(B) No person shall knowingly manufacture, possess, deliver, offer to deliver, or advertise a counterfeit telecommunications device with purpose to use that device or to allow that device to be used, or knowing or having reason to know that another person may use that device, to do any of the following:

(1) Obtain or attempt to obtain telecommunications service or information service with purpose to avoid a lawful charge for that service or aid or cause another person to obtain or attempt to obtain telecommunications service or information service with purpose to avoid a lawful charge for that service;

(2) Conceal the existence, place of origin, or destination of a telecommunications service or information service.

(C) Whoever violates this section is guilty of unlawful use of a telecommunications device, a felony of the fifth degree.

(D) This section does not prohibit or restrict a person who holds an amateur service license issued by the federal communications commission from possessing a radio receiver or transceiver that is intended primarily or exclusively for use in the amateur radio service and is used for lawful purposes.

(E) This section does not preclude a person from disputing charges imposed for telecommunications service or information service by the provider of that service.

(1998 H 565, eff. 3–30–99)

2913.07 Motion picture piracy (first version)

Note: See also following version of this section, and Publisher's Note.

(A) As used in this section:

(1) "Audiovisual recording function" means the capability of a device to record or transmit a motion picture or any part of a motion picture by means of any technology existing on, or developed after, the effective date of this section.

(2) "Facility" includes all retail establishments and movie theaters.

(B) No person, without the written consent of the owner or lessee of the facility and of the licensor of the motion picture, shall knowingly operate an audiovisual recording function of a device in a facility in which a motion picture is being shown.

(C) Whoever violates division (B) of this section is guilty of motion picture piracy, a misdemeanor of the first degree on the first offense and a felony of the fifth degree on each subsequent offense.

(D) This section does not prohibit or restrict a lawfully authorized investigative, law enforcement, protective, or intelligence gathering employee or agent of the government of this state or a political subdivision of this state, or of the federal government, when acting in an official capacity, from operating an audiovisual recording function of a device in any facility in which a motion picture is being shown.

(E) Division (B) of this section does not limit or affect the application of any other prohibition in the Revised Code. Any act that is a violation of both division (B) of this section and another provision of the Revised Code may be prosecuted under this section, under the other provision of the Revised Code, or under both this section and the other provision of the Revised Code.

(2003 H 179, eff. 3–9–04)

Note: See also following version of this section, and Publisher's Note.

Historical and Statutory Notes

Pub. Note: RC 2913.07 was enacted by 2003 H 179, eff. 3–9–04, and amended by 2003 S 57, eff. 1–1–04. The legal effect of these actions is in question. See *Baldwin's Ohio Legislative Service Annotated*, 2003, pages 11/L–2273 and 11/L–2364, or the OH-LEGIS or OH-LEGIS-OLD databases on Westlaw, for original versions of these Acts.

2913.07 Motion picture piracy (second version)

Note: See also preceding version of this section, and Publisher's Note.

(A) As used in this section:

(1) "Audiovisual recording function" means the capability of a device to record or transmit a motion picture or any part of a motion picture by means of any technology existing on, or developed after, the effective date of this section.

(2) "Facility" means a movie theater.

(B) No person, without the written consent of the owner or lessee of the facility and of the licensor of the motion picture, shall knowingly operate an audiovisual recording function of a device in a facility in which a motion picture is being shown.

(C) Whoever violates division (B) of this section is guilty of motion picture piracy, a misdemeanor of the first degree on the first offense and a felony of the fifth degree on each subsequent offense.

(D) This section does not prohibit or restrict a lawfully authorized investigative, law enforcement, protective, or intelligence gathering employee or agent of the government of this state or a political subdivision of this state, or of the federal government, when acting in an official capacity, from operating an audiovisual recording function of a device in any facility in which a motion picture is being shown.

(E) Division (B) of this section does not limit or affect the application of any other prohibition in the Revised Code. Any act that is a violation of both division (B) of this section and another provision of the Revised Code may be prosecuted under this section, under the other provision of the Revised Code, or under both this section and the other provision of the Revised Code.

(2003 S 57, eff. 1–1–04)

Note: See also preceding version of this section, and Publisher's Note.

COUNTERFEITING; BAD CHECKS; CREDIT CARDS

2913.11 Passing bad checks

Note: See also following version of this section, eff. 5–18–05.

(A) No person, with purpose to defraud, shall issue or transfer or cause to be issued or transferred a check or other negotiable instrument, knowing that it will be dishonored.

(B) For purposes of this section, a person who issues or transfers a check or other negotiable instrument is presumed to know that it will be dishonored if either of the following occurs:

(1) The drawer had no account with the drawee at the time of issue or the stated date, whichever is later;

(2) The check or other negotiable instrument was properly refused payment for insufficient funds upon presentment within thirty days after issue or the stated date, whichever is later, and the liability of the drawer, indorser, or any party who may be liable thereon is not discharged by payment or satisfaction within ten days after receiving notice of dishonor.

(C) For purposes of this section, a person who issues or transfers a check, bill of exchange, or other draft is presumed to have the purpose to defraud if the drawer fails to comply with section 1349.16 of the Revised Code by doing any of the following when opening a checking account intended for personal, family, or household purposes at a financial institution:

(1) Falsely stating that the drawer has not been issued a valid driver's or commercial driver's license or identification card issued under section 4507.50 of the Revised Code;

(2) Furnishing such license or card, or another identification document that contains false information;

(3) Making a false statement with respect to the drawer's current address or any additional relevant information reasonably required by the financial institution.

(D) Whoever violates this section is guilty of passing bad checks. Except as otherwise provided in this division, passing bad checks is a misdemeanor of the first degree. If the check or other negotiable instrument is for payment of five hundred dollars or more and is for the payment of less than five thousand dollars, passing bad checks is a felony of the fifth degree. If the check or other negotiable instrument is for the payment of five thousand dollars or more and is for the payment of less than one hundred thousand dollars, passing bad checks is a felony of the fourth degree. If the check or other negotiable instrument is for the payment of one hundred thousand dollars or more, passing bad checks is a felony of the third degree.

(1995 S 2, eff. 7–1–96; 1990 H 711, eff. 10–16–90; 1986 H 49; 1982 H 269, S 199; 1972 H 511)

Note: See also following version of this section, eff. 5–18–05.

2913.11 Passing bad checks (later effective date)

Note: See also preceding version of this section, in effect until 5–18–05.

(A) As used in this section:

(1) "Check" includes any form of debit from a demand deposit account, including, but not limited to any of the following:

(a) A check, bill of exchange, draft, order of withdrawal, or similar negotiable or non-negotiable instrument;

(b) An electronic check, electronic transaction, debit card transaction, check card transaction, substitute check, web check, or any form of automated clearing house transaction.

(2) "Issue a check" means causing any form of debit from a demand deposit account.

(B) No person, with purpose to defraud, shall issue or transfer or cause to be issued or transferred a check or other negotiable instrument, knowing that it will be dishonored or knowing that a person has ordered or will order stop payment on the check or other negotiable instrument.

(C) For purposes of this section, a person who issues or transfers a check or other negotiable instrument is presumed to know that it will be dishonored if either of the following occurs:

(1) The drawer had no account with the drawee at the time of issue or the stated date, whichever is later;

(2) The check or other negotiable instrument was properly refused payment for insufficient funds upon presentment within thirty days after issue or the stated date, whichever is later, and the liability of the drawer, indorser, or any party who may be liable thereon is not discharged by payment or satisfaction within ten days after receiving notice of dishonor.

(D) For purposes of this section, a person who issues or transfers a check, bill of exchange, or other draft is presumed to have the purpose to defraud if the drawer fails to comply with section 1349.16 of the Revised Code by doing any of the following when opening a checking account intended for personal, family, or household purposes at a financial institution:

(1) Falsely stating that the drawer has not been issued a valid driver's or commercial driver's license or identification card issued under section 4507.50 of the Revised Code;

(2) Furnishing such license or card, or another identification document that contains false information;

(3) Making a false statement with respect to the drawer's current address or any additional relevant information reasonably required by the financial institution.

(E) In determining the value of the payment for purposes of division (F) of this section, the court may aggregate all checks and other negotiable instruments that the offender issued or transferred or caused to be issued or transferred in violation of division (A) of this section within a period of one hundred eighty consecutive days.

(F) Whoever violates this section is guilty of passing bad checks. Except as otherwise provided in this division, passing bad checks is a misdemeanor of the first degree. If the check or checks or other negotiable instrument or instruments are issued or transferred to a single vendor or single other person for the payment of five hundred dollars or more but less than five thousand dollars or if the check or checks or other negotiable instrument or instruments are issued or transferred to multiple vendors or persons for the payment of one thousand dollars or more but less than five thousand dollars, passing bad checks is a felony of the fifth degree. If the check or checks or other negotiable instrument or instruments are for the payment of five thousand dollars or more but less than one hundred thousand dollars, passing bad checks is a felony of the fourth degree. If the check or checks or other negotiable instrument or instruments are for the payment of one hundred thousand dollars or more, passing bad checks is a felony of the third degree.

(2004 H 401, eff. 5–18–05; 1995 S 2, eff. 7–1–96; 1990 H 711, eff. 10–16–90; 1986 H 49; 1982 H 269, S 199; 1972 H 511)

Note: See also preceding version of this section, in effect until 5–18–05.

2913.21 Misuse of credit cards

(A) No person shall do any of the following:

(1) Practice deception for the purpose of procuring the issuance of a credit card, when a credit card is issued in actual reliance thereon;

(2) Knowingly buy or sell a credit card from or to a person other than the issuer.

(B) No person, with purpose to defraud, shall do any of the following:

(1) Obtain control over a credit card as security for a debt;

(2) Obtain property or services by the use of a credit card, in one or more transactions, knowing or having reasonable cause to believe that the card has expired or been revoked, or was obtained, is retained, or is being used in violation of law;

(3) Furnish property or services upon presentation of a credit card, knowing that the card is being used in violation of law;

(4) Represent or cause to be represented to the issuer of a credit card that property or services have been furnished, knowing that the representation is false.

(C) No person, with purpose to violate this section, shall receive, possess, control, or dispose of a credit card.

(D)(1) Whoever violates this section is guilty of misuse of credit cards.

(2) Except as otherwise provided in division (D)(4) of this section, a violation of division (A), (B)(1), or (C) of this section is a misdemeanor of the first degree.

(3) Except as otherwise provided in this division or division (D)(4) of this section, a violation of division (B)(2), (3), or (4) of this section is a misdemeanor of the first degree. If the cumulative retail value of the property and services involved in one or more violations of division (B)(2), (3), or (4) of this section, which violations involve one or more credit card accounts and occur within a period of ninety consecutive days commencing on the date of the first violation, is five hundred dollars or more and is less than five thousand dollars, misuse of credit cards in violation of any of those divisions is a felony of the fifth degree. If the cumulative retail value of the property and services involved in one or more violations of division (B)(2), (3), or (4) of this section, which violations involve one or more credit card accounts and occur within a period of ninety consecutive days commencing on the date of the first violation, is five thousand dollars or more and is less than one hundred thousand dollars, misuse of credit cards in violation of any of those divisions is a felony of the fourth degree. If the cumulative retail value of the property and services involved in one or more violations of division (B)(2), (3), or (4) of this section, which violations involve one or more credit card accounts and occur within a period of ninety consecutive days commencing on the date of the first violation, is one hundred thousand dollars or more, misuse of credit cards in violation of any of those divisions is a felony of the third degree.

(4) If the victim of the offense is an elderly person or disabled adult, and if the offense involves a violation of division (B)(1) or (2) of this section, division (D)(4) of this section applies. Except as otherwise provided in division (D)(4) of this section, a violation of division (B)(1) or (2) of this section is a felony of the fifth degree. If the debt for which the card is held as security or the cumulative retail value of the property or services involved in the violation is five hundred dollars or more and is less than five thousand dollars, a violation of either of those divisions is a felony of the fourth degree. If the debt for which the card is held as security or the cumulative retail value of the property or services involved in the violation is five thousand dollars or more and is less than twenty-five thousand dollars, a violation of either of those divisions is a felony of the third degree. If the debt for which the card is held as security or the cumulative retail value of the property or services involved in the violation is twenty-five thousand dollars or more, a violation of either of those divisions is a felony of the second degree.

(1999 H 2, eff. 11–10–99; 1995 S 2, eff. 7–1–96; 1986 H 49, eff. 6–26–86; 1983 S 210; 1982 S 199, H 269; 1978 S 289; 1972 H 511)

FORGERY

2913.31 Forgery; forging identification cards

(A) No person, with purpose to defraud, or knowing that the person is facilitating a fraud, shall do any of the following:

(1) Forge any writing of another without the other person's authority;

(2) Forge any writing so that it purports to be genuine when it actually is spurious, or to be the act of another who did not authorize that act, or to have been executed at a time or place or with terms different from what in fact was the case, or to be a copy of an original when no such original existed;

(3) Utter, or possess with purpose to utter, any writing that the person knows to have been forged.

(B) No person shall knowingly do either of the following:

(1) Forge an identification card;

(2) Sell or otherwise distribute a card that purports to be an identification card, knowing it to have been forged.

As used in this division, "identification card" means a card that includes personal information or characteristics of an individual, a purpose of which is to establish the identity of the bearer described on the card, whether the words "identity," "identification," "identification card," or other similar words appear on the card.

(C)(1)(a) Whoever violates division (A) of this section is guilty of forgery.

(b) Except as otherwise provided in this division or division (C)(1)(c) of this section, forgery is a felony of the fifth degree. If property or services are involved in the offense or the victim suffers a loss, forgery is one of the following:

(i) If the value of the property or services or the loss to the victim is five thousand dollars or more and is less than one hundred thousand dollars, a felony of the fourth degree;

(ii) If the value of the property or services or the loss to the victim is one hundred thousand dollars or more, a felony of the third degree.

(c) If the victim of the offense is an elderly person or disabled adult, division (C)(1)(c) of this section applies to the forgery. Except as otherwise provided in division (C)(1)(c) of this section, forgery is a felony of the fifth degree. If property or services are involved in the offense or if the victim suffers a loss, forgery is one of the following:

(i) If the value of the property or services or the loss to the victim is five hundred dollars or more and is less than five thousand dollars, a felony of the fourth degree;

(ii) If the value of the property or services or the loss to the victim is five thousand dollars or more and is less than twenty-five thousand dollars, a felony of the third degree;

(iii) If the value of the property or services or the loss to the victim is twenty-five thousand dollars or more, a felony of the second degree.

(2) Whoever violates division (B) of this section is guilty of forging identification cards or selling or distributing forged identification cards. Except as otherwise provided in this division, forging identification cards or selling or distributing forged identification cards is a misdemeanor of the first degree. If the offender previously has been convicted of a violation of division (B) of this section, forging identification cards or selling or distributing forged identification cards is a misdemeanor of the first degree and, in addition, the court shall impose upon the offender a fine of not less than two hundred fifty dollars.

(1999 H 2, eff. 11-10-99; 1995 S 2, eff. 7-1-96; 1991 H 162, eff. 11-11-91; 1972 H 511)

2913.32 Criminal simulation

(A) No person, with purpose to defraud, or knowing that the person is facilitating a fraud, shall do any of the following:

(1) Make or alter any object so that it appears to have value because of antiquity, rarity, curiosity, source, or authorship, which it does not in fact possess;

(2) Practice deception in making, retouching, editing, or reproducing any photograph, movie film, video tape, phonograph record, or recording tape;

(3) Falsely or fraudulently make, simulate, forge, alter, or counterfeit any wrapper, label, stamp, cork, or cap prescribed by the liquor control commission under Chapters 4301. and 4303. of the Revised Code, falsely or fraudulently cause to be made, simulated, forged, altered, or counterfeited any wrapper, label, stamp, cork, or cap prescribed by the liquor control commission under Chapters 4301. and 4303. of the Revised Code, or use more than once any wrapper, label, stamp, cork, or cap prescribed by the liquor control commission under Chapters 4301. and 4303. of the Revised Code.

(4) Utter, or possess with purpose to utter, any object that the person knows to have been simulated as provided in division (A)(1), (2), or (3) of this section.

(B) Whoever violates this section is guilty of criminal simulation. Except as otherwise provided in this division, criminal simulation is a misdemeanor of the first degree. If the loss to the victim is five hundred dollars or more and is less than five thousand dollars, criminal simulation is a felony of the fifth degree. If the loss to the victim is five thousand dollars or more and is less than one hundred thousand dollars, criminal simulation is a felony of the fourth degree. If the loss to the victim is one hundred thousand dollars or more, criminal simulation is a felony of the third degree.

(1995 S 2, eff. 7-1-96; 1972 H 511, eff. 1-1-74)

2913.33 Making or using slugs

(A) No person shall do any of the following:

(1) Insert or deposit a slug in a coin machine, with purpose to defraud;

(2) Make, possess, or dispose of a slug, with purpose of enabling another to defraud by inserting or depositing it in a coin machine.

(B) Whoever violates this section is guilty of making or using slugs, a misdemeanor of the second degree.

(1972 H 511, eff. 1-1-74)

2913.34 Trademark counterfeiting

(A) No person shall knowingly do any of the following:

(1) Attach, affix, or otherwise use a counterfeit mark in connection with the manufacture of goods or services, whether or not the goods or services are intended for sale or resale;

(2) Possess, sell, or offer for sale tools, machines, instruments, materials, articles, or other items of personal property with the knowledge that they are designed for the production or reproduction of counterfeit marks;

(3) Purchase or otherwise acquire goods, and keep or otherwise have the goods in the person's possession, with the knowledge that a counterfeit mark is attached to, affixed to, or otherwise used in connection with the goods and with the intent to sell or otherwise dispose of the goods;

(4) Sell, offer for sale, or otherwise dispose of goods with the knowledge that a counterfeit mark is attached to, affixed to, or otherwise used in connection with the goods;

(5) Sell, offer for sale, or otherwise provide services with the knowledge that a counterfeit mark is used in connection with that sale, offer for sale, or other provision of the services.

(B)(1) Whoever violates this section is guilty of trademark counterfeiting.

(2) Except as otherwise provided in this division, a violation of division (A)(1) of this section is a felony of the fifth degree. Except as otherwise provided in this division, if the cumulative sales price of the goods or services to which or in connection with which the counterfeit mark is attached, affixed, or otherwise used in the offense is five thousand dollars or more but less than one hundred thousand dollars or if the number of units of goods to which or in connection with which the counterfeit mark is attached, affixed, or otherwise used in the offense is more than one hundred units but less than one thousand units, a violation of division (A)(1) of this section is a felony of the fourth degree. If the cumulative sales price of the goods or services to which or in connection with which the counterfeit mark is attached, affixed, or otherwise used in the offense is one hundred thousand dollars or more or if the number of units of goods to which or in connection with which the counterfeit mark is attached, affixed, or otherwise used in the offense is one thousand units or more, a violation of division (A)(1) of this section is a felony of the third degree.

(3) Except as otherwise provided in this division, a violation of division (A)(2) of this section is a misdemeanor of the first degree. If the circumstances of the violation indicate that the tools, machines, instruments, materials, articles, or other items of personal property involved in the violation were intended for use in the commission of a felony, a violation of division (A)(2) of this section is a felony of the fifth degree.

(4) Except as otherwise provided in this division, a violation of division (A)(3), (4), or (5) of this section is a misdemeanor of the first degree. Except as otherwise provided in this division, if the cumulative sales price of the goods or services to which or in connection with which the counterfeit mark is attached, affixed, or otherwise used in the offense is five hundred dollars or more but less than five thousand dollars, a violation of division (A)(3), (4), or (5) of this section is a felony of the fifth degree. Except as otherwise provided in this division, if the cumulative sales price of the goods or services to which or in connection with which the counterfeit mark is attached, affixed, or otherwise used in the offense is five thousand dollars or more but less than one hundred thousand dollars or if the number of units of goods to which or in connection with which the counterfeit mark is attached, affixed, or otherwise used in the offense is more than one hundred units but less than one thousand units, a violation of division (A)(3), (4), or (5) of this section is a felony of the fourth degree. If the cumulative sales price of the goods or services to which or in connection with which the counterfeit mark is at-

tached, affixed, or otherwise used in the offense is one hundred thousand dollars or more or if the number of units of goods to which or in connection with which the counterfeit mark is attached, affixed, or otherwise used in the offense is one thousand units or more, a violation of division (A)(3), (4), or (5) of this section is a felony of the third degree.

(C) A defendant may assert as an affirmative defense to a charge of a violation of this section defenses, affirmative defenses, and limitations on remedies that would be available in a civil, criminal, or administrative action or proceeding under the "Lanham Act," 60 Stat. 427–443 (1946), 15 U.S.C. 1051–1127, as amended, "The Trademark Counterfeiting Act of 1984," 98 Stat. 2178, 18 U.S.C. 2320, as amended, Chapter 1329. or another section of the Revised Code, or common law.

(D)(1) Law enforcement officers may seize pursuant to Criminal Rule 41 or Chapter 2933. of the Revised Code either of the following:

(a) Goods to which or in connection with which a person attached, affixed, otherwise used, or intended to attach, affix, or otherwise use a counterfeit mark in violation of this section;

(b) Tools, machines, instruments, materials, articles, vehicles, or other items of personal property that are possessed, sold, offered for sale, or used in a violation of this section or in an attempt to commit or complicity in the commission of a violation of this section.

(2) Notwithstanding any contrary provision of sections 2923.31 to 2923.35 or 2933.41 to 2933.43 of the Revised Code, if a person is convicted of or pleads guilty to a violation of this section, an attempt to violate this section, or complicity in a violation of this section, the court involved shall declare that the goods described in division (D)(1)(a) of this section and the personal property described in division (D)(1)(b) of this section are contraband and are forfeited. Prior to the court's entry of judgment under Criminal Rule 32, the owner of a registered trademark or service mark that is the subject of the counterfeit mark may recommend a manner in which the forfeited goods and forfeited personal property should be disposed of. If that owner makes a timely recommendation of a manner of disposition, the court is not bound by the recommendation. If that owner makes a timely recommendation of a manner of disposition, the court may include in its entry of judgment an order that requires appropriate persons to dispose of the forfeited goods and forfeited personal property in the recommended manner. If that owner fails to make a timely recommendation of a manner of disposition or if that owner makes a timely recommendation of the manner of disposition but the court determines to not follow the recommendation, the court shall include in its entry of judgment an order that requires the law enforcement agency that employs the law enforcement officer who seized the forfeited goods or the forfeited personal property to destroy them or cause their destruction.

(E) This section does not affect the rights of an owner of a trademark or a service mark, or the enforcement in a civil action or in administrative proceedings of the rights of an owner of a trademark or a service mark, under the "Lanham Act," 60 Stat. 427–443 (1946), 15 U.S.C. 1051–1127, as amended, "The Trademark Counterfeiting Act of 1984," 92 Stat. 2178, 18 U.S.C. 2320, as amended, Chapter 1329. or another section of the Revised Code, or common law.

(F) As used in this section:

(1)(a) Except as provided in division (F)(1)(b) of this section, "counterfeit mark" means a spurious trademark or a spurious service mark that satisfies both of the following:

(i) It is identical with or substantially indistinguishable from a mark that is registered on the principal register in the United States patent and trademark office for the same goods or services as the goods or services to which or in connection with which the spurious trademark or spurious service mark is attached, affixed, or otherwise used or from a mark that is registered with the secretary of state pursuant to sections 1329.54 to 1329.67 of the Revised Code for the same goods or services as the goods or services to which or in connection with which the spurious trademark or spurious service mark is attached, affixed, or otherwise used, and the owner of the registration uses the registered mark, whether or not the offender knows that the mark is registered in a manner described in division (F)(1)(a)(i) of this section.

(ii) Its use is likely to cause confusion or mistake or to deceive other persons.

(b) "Counterfeit mark" does not include a mark or other designation that is attached to, affixed to, or otherwise used in connection with goods or services if the holder of the right to use the mark or other designation authorizes the manufacturer, producer, or vendor of those goods or services to attach, affix, or otherwise use the mark or other designation in connection with those goods or services at the time of their manufacture, production, or sale.

(2) "Cumulative sales price" means the product of the lowest single unit sales price charged or sought to be charged by an offender for goods to which or in connection with which a counterfeit mark is attached, affixed, or otherwise used or of the lowest single service transaction price charged or sought to be charged by an offender for services in connection with which a counterfeit mark is used, multiplied by the total number of those goods or services, whether or not units of goods are sold or are in an offender's possession, custody, or control.

(3) "Registered trademark or service mark" means a trademark or service mark that is registered in a manner described in division (F)(1) of this section.

(4) "Trademark" and "service mark" have the same meanings as in section 1329.54 of the Revised Code.

(1996 S 277, eff. 3–31–97)

FRAUDS

2913.40 Medicaid fraud

(A) As used in this section:

(1) "Statement or representation" means any oral, written, electronic, electronic impulse, or magnetic communication that is used to identify an item of goods or a service for which reimbursement may be made under the medical assistance program or that states income and expense and is or may be used to determine a rate of reimbursement under the medical assistance program.

(2) "Medical assistance program" means the program established by the department of job and family services to provide medical assistance under section 5111.01 of the Revised Code and the medicaid program of Title XIX of the "Social Security Act," 49 Stat. 620 (1935), 42 U.S.C. 301, as amended.

(3) "Provider" means any person who has signed a provider agreement with the department of job and family services to provide goods or services pursuant to the medical assistance program or any person who has signed an agreement with a party to such a provider agreement under which the person agrees to provide goods or services that are reimbursable under the medical assistance program.

(4) "Provider agreement" means an oral or written agreement between the department of job and family services and a person in which the person agrees to provide goods or services under the medical assistance program.

(5) "Recipient" means any individual who receives goods or services from a provider under the medical assistance program.

(6) "Records" means any medical, professional, financial, or business records relating to the treatment or care of any recipient, to goods or services provided to any recipient, or to rates paid for goods or services provided to any recipient and any records that are required by the rules of the director of job and family services to be kept for the medical assistance program.

(B) No person shall knowingly make or cause to be made a false or misleading statement or representation for use in obtaining reimbursement from the medical assistance program.

(C) No person, with purpose to commit fraud or knowing that the person is facilitating a fraud, shall do either of the following:

(1) Contrary to the terms of the person's provider agreement, charge, solicit, accept, or receive for goods or services that the person provides under the medical assistance program any property, money, or other consideration in addition to the amount of reimbursement under the medical assistance program and the person's provider agreement for the goods or services and any deductibles or co-payments authorized by rules adopted under section 5111.0112 of the Revised Code or by any rules adopted pursuant to that section.

(2) Solicit, offer, or receive any remuneration, other than any deductibles or co-payments authorized by rules adopted under section 5111.0112 of the Revised Code or by any rules adopted pursuant to that section, in cash or in kind, including, but not limited to, a kickback or rebate, in connection with the furnishing of goods or services for which whole or partial reimbursement is or may be made under the medical assistance program.

(D) No person, having submitted a claim for or provided goods or services under the medical assistance program, shall do either of the following for a period of at least six years after a reimbursement pursuant to that claim, or a reimbursement for those goods or services, is received under the medical assistance program:

(1) Knowingly alter, falsify, destroy, conceal, or remove any records that are necessary to fully disclose the nature of all goods or services for which the claim was submitted, or for which reimbursement was received, by the person;

(2) Knowingly alter, falsify, destroy, conceal, or remove any records that are necessary to disclose fully all income and expenditures upon which rates of reimbursements were based for the person.

(E) Whoever violates this section is guilty of medicaid fraud. Except as otherwise provided in this division, medicaid fraud is a misdemeanor of the first degree. If the value of property, services, or funds obtained in violation of this section is five hundred dollars or more and is less than five thousand dollars, medicaid fraud is a felony of the fifth degree. If the value of property, services, or funds obtained in violation of this section is five thousand dollars or more and is less than one hundred thousand dollars, medicaid fraud is a felony of the fourth degree. If the value of the property, services, or funds obtained in violation of this section is one hundred thousand dollars or more, medicaid fraud is a felony of the third degree.

(F) Upon application of the governmental agency, office, or other entity that conducted the investigation and prosecution in a case under this section, the court shall order any person who is convicted of a violation of this section for receiving any reimbursement for furnishing goods or services under the medical assistance program to which the person is not entitled to pay to the applicant its cost of investigating and prosecuting the case. The costs of investigation and prosecution that a defendant is ordered to pay pursuant to this division shall be in addition to any other penalties for the receipt of that reimbursement that are provided in this section, section 5111.03 of the Revised Code, or any other provision of law.

(G) The provisions of this section are not intended to be exclusive remedies and do not preclude the use of any other criminal or civil remedy for any act that is in violation of this section.

(2002 S 261, eff. 6–5–02, 1999 H 471, eff. 7–1–00; 1995 S 2, eff. 7–1–96; 1989 H 672, eff. 11–14–89; 1986 H 340)

2913.41 Prima facie evidence of purpose to defraud

In a prosecution of a person for a theft offense that alleges that the person, with purpose to defraud or knowing that the person was facilitating a fraud, hired or rented an aircraft, motor vehicle, motorcycle, motorboat, sailboat, camper, trailer, horse, buggy, or other property or equipment, kept or operated any of the same that has been hired or rented, or engaged accommodations at a hotel, motel, inn, campground, or other hostelry, it is prima-facie evidence of purpose to defraud if the person did any of the following:

(A) Used deception to induce the rental agency to furnish the person with the aircraft, motor vehicle, motorcycle, motorboat, sailboat, camper, trailer, horse, buggy, or other property or equipment, or used deception to induce the hostelry to furnish the person with accommodations;

(B) Hired or rented any aircraft, motor vehicle, motorcycle, motorboat, sailboat, camper, trailer, horse, buggy, or other property or equipment, or engaged accommodations, knowing the person was without sufficient means to pay the hire or rental;

(C) Absconded without paying the hire or rental;

(D) Knowingly failed to pay the hire or rental as required by the contract of hire or rental, without reasonable excuse for such failure;

(E) Knowingly failed to return hired or rented property as required by the contract of hire or rental, without reasonable excuse for the failure.

(2000 H 263, eff. 4–10–01; 1995 S 2, eff. 7–1–96; 1972 H 511, eff. 1–1–74)

2913.42 Tampering with records

(A) No person, knowing the person has no privilege to do so, and with purpose to defraud or knowing that the person is facilitating a fraud, shall do any of the following:

(1) Falsify, destroy, remove, conceal, alter, deface, or mutilate any writing, computer software, data, or record;

(2) Utter any writing or record, knowing it to have been tampered with as provided in division (A)(1) of this section.

(B)(1) Whoever violates this section is guilty of tampering with records.

(2) Except as provided in division (B)(4) of this section, if the offense does not involve data or computer software, tampering with records is whichever of the following is applicable:

(a) If division (B)(2)(b) of this section does not apply, a misdemeanor of the first degree;

(b) If the writing or record is a will unrevoked at the time of the offense, a felony of the fifth degree.

(3) Except as provided in division (B)(4) of this section, if the offense involves a violation of division (A) of this section involving data or computer software, tampering with records is whichever of the following is applicable:

(a) Except as otherwise provided in division (B)(3)(b), (c), or (d) of this section, a misdemeanor of the first degree;

(b) If the value of the data or computer software involved in the offense or the loss to the victim is five hundred dollars or more and is less than five thousand dollars, a felony of the fifth degree;

(c) If the value of the data or computer software involved in the offense or the loss to the victim is five thousand dollars or more and is less than one hundred thousand dollars, a felony of the fourth degree;

(d) If the value of the data or computer software involved in the offense or the loss to the victim is one hundred thousand dollars or more or if the offense is committed for the purpose of devising or executing a scheme to defraud or to obtain property or services and the value of the property or services or the loss to the victim is five thousand dollars or more, a felony of the third degree.

(4) If the writing, data, computer software, or record is kept by or belongs to a local, state, or federal governmental entity, a felony of the third degree.

(1998 H 565, eff. 3–30–99; 1995 S 2, eff. 7–1–96; 1986 H 428, eff. 12–23–86; 1986 H 49; 1972 H 511)

2913.421 Illegal transmission of multiple commercial electronic mail messages; unauthorized access of a computer; civil actions by attorney general or electronic mail service provider

(A) As used in this section:

(1) "Computer," "computer network," and "computer system" have the same meanings as in section 2913.01 of the Revised Code.

(2) "Commercial electronic mail message" means any electronic mail message the primary purpose of which is the commercial advertisement or promotion of a commercial product or service, including content on an internet web site operated for a commercial purpose, but does not include a transactional or relationship message. The inclusion of a reference to a commercial entity or a link to the web site of a commercial entity does not, by itself, cause that message to be treated as a commercial electronic mail message for the purpose of this section, if the contents or circumstances of the message indicate a primary purpose other than commercial advertisement or promotion of a commercial product or service.

(3) "Domain name" means any alphanumeric designation that is registered with or assigned by any domain name registrar, domain name registry, or other domain name registration authority as part of an electronic address on the internet.

(4) "Electronic mail," "originating address," and "receiving address" have the same meanings as in section 2307.64 of the Revised Code.

(5) "Electronic mail message" means each electronic mail addressed to a discrete addressee.

(6) "Electronic mail service provider" means any person, including an internet service provider, that is an intermediary in sending and receiving electronic mail and that provides to the public electronic mail accounts or online user accounts from which electronic mail may be sent.

(7) "Header information" means the source, destination, and routing information attached to an electronic mail message, including the originating domain name, the originating address, and technical information that authenticates the sender of an electronic mail message for computer network security or computer network management purposes.

(8) "Initiate the transmission" or "initiated" means to originate or transmit a commercial electronic mail message or to procure the origination or transmission of that message, regardless of whether the message reaches its intended recipients, but does not include actions that constitute routine conveyance of such message.

(9) "Internet" has the same meaning as in section 341.42 of the Revised Code.

(10) "Internet protocol address" means the string of numbers by which locations on the internet are identified by routers or other computers connected to the internet.

(11) "Materially falsify" means to alter or conceal in a manner that would impair the ability of a recipient of an electronic mail message, an electronic mail service provider processing an electronic mail message on behalf of a recipient, a person alleging a violation of this section, or a law enforcement agency to identify, locate, or respond to the person that initiated the electronic mail message or to investigate an alleged violation of this section.

(12) "Multiple" means more than ten commercial electronic mail messages during a twenty-four-hour period, more than one hundred commercial electronic mail messages during a thirty-day period, or more than one thousand commercial electronic mail messages during a one-year period.

(13) "Recipient" means a person who receives a commercial electronic mail message at any one of the following receiving addresses:

(a) A receiving address furnished by an electronic mail service provider that bills for furnishing and maintaining that receiving address to a mailing address within this state;

(b) A receiving address ordinarily accessed from a computer located within this state or by a person domiciled within this state;

(c) Any other receiving address with respect to which this section can be imposed consistent with the United States Constitution.

(14) "Routine conveyance" means the transmission, routing, relaying, handling, or storing, through an automated technical process, of an electronic mail message for which another person has identified the recipients or provided the recipient addresses.

(15) "Transactional or relationship message" means an electronic mail message the primary purpose of which is to do any of the following:

(a) Facilitate, complete, or confirm a commercial transaction that the recipient has previously agreed to enter into with the sender;

(b) Provide warranty information, product recall information, or safety or security information with respect to a commercial product or service used or purchased by the recipient;

(c) Provide notification concerning a change in the terms or features of; a change in the recipient's standing or status with respect to; or, at regular periodic intervals, account balance information or other type of account statement with respect to, a subscription, membership, account, loan, or comparable ongoing commercial relationship involving the ongoing purchase or use by the recipient of products or services offered by the sender;

(d) Provide information directly related to an employment relationship or related benefit plan in which the recipient is currently involved, participating, or enrolled;

(e) Deliver goods or services, including product updates or upgrades, that the recipient is entitled to receive under the terms of a transaction that the recipient has previously agreed to enter into with the sender.

(B) No person, with regard to commercial electronic mail messages sent from or to a computer in this state, shall do any of the following:

(1) Knowingly use a computer to relay or retransmit multiple commercial electronic mail messages, with the intent to deceive or mislead recipients or any electronic mail service provider, as to the origin of those messages;

(2) Knowingly and materially falsify header information in multiple commercial electronic mail messages and purposely initiate the transmission of those messages;

(3) Knowingly register, using information that materially falsifies the identity of the actual registrant, for five or more electronic mail accounts or online user accounts or two or more domain names and purposely initiate the transmission of multiple commercial electronic mail messages from one, or any combination, of those accounts or domain names;

(4) Knowingly falsely represent the right to use five or more internet protocol addresses, and purposely initiate the transmission of multiple commercial electronic mail messages from those addresses.

(C)(1) Whoever violates division (B) of this section is guilty of illegally transmitting multiple commercial electronic mail messages. Except as otherwise provided in division (C)(2) or (E) of this section, illegally transmitting multiple commercial electronic mail messages is a felony of the fifth degree.

(2) Illegally transmitting multiple commercial electronic mail messages is a felony of the fourth degree if any of the following apply:

(a) Regarding a violation of division (B)(3) of this section, the offender, using information that materially falsifies the identity of the actual registrant, knowingly registers for twenty or more electronic mail accounts or online user accounts or ten or more domain names, and purposely initiates, or conspires to initiate, the transmission of multiple commercial electronic mail messages from the accounts or domain names.

(b) Regarding any violation of division (B) of this section, the volume of commercial electronic mail messages the offender transmitted in committing the violation exceeds two hundred and fifty during any twenty-four-hour period, two thousand five hundred during any thirty-day period, or twenty-five thousand during any one-year period.

(c) Regarding any violation of division (B) of this section, during any one-year period the aggregate loss to the victim or victims of the violation is five hundred dollars or more, or during any one-year period the aggregate value of the property or services obtained by any offender as a result of the violation is five hundred dollars or more.

(d) Regarding any violation of division (B) of this section, the offender committed the violation with three or more other persons with respect to whom the offender was the organizer or leader of the activity that resulted in the violation.

(e) Regarding any violation of division (B) of this section, the offender knowingly assisted in the violation through the provision or selection of electronic mail addresses to which the commercial electronic mail message was transmitted, if that offender knew that the electronic mail addresses of the recipients were obtained using an automated means from an internet web site or proprietary online service operated by another person, and that web site or online service included, at the time the electronic mail addresses were obtained, a notice stating that the operator of that web site or online service will not transfer addresses maintained by that web site or online service to any other party for the purposes of initiating the transmission of, or enabling others to initiate the transmission of, electronic mail messages.

(f) Regarding any violation of division (B) of this section, the offender knowingly assisted in the violation through the provision or selection of electronic mail addresses of the recipients obtained using an automated means that generates possible electronic mail addresses by combining names, letters, or numbers into numerous permutations.

(D)(1) No person, with regard to commercial electronic mail messages sent from or to a computer in this state, shall knowingly access a computer without authorization and purposely initiate the transmission of multiple commercial electronic mail messages from or through the computer.

(2) Except as otherwise provided in division (E) of this section, whoever violates division (D)(1) of this section is guilty of unauthorized access of a computer, a felony of the fourth degree.

(E) Illegally transmitting multiple commercial electronic mail messages and unauthorized access of a computer in violation of this section are felonies of the third degree if the offender previously has been convicted of a violation of this section, or a violation of a law of another state or the United States regarding the transmission of electronic mail messages or unauthorized access to a computer, or if the offender committed the violation of this section in the furtherance of a felony.

(F)(1) The attorney general or an electronic mail service provider that is injured by a violation of this section may bring a civil action in an appropriate court of common pleas of this state seeking relief from any person whose conduct violated this section. The civil action may be commenced at any time within one year of the date after the act that is the basis of the civil action.

(2) In a civil action brought by the attorney general pursuant to division (F)(1) of this section for a violation of this section, the court may award temporary, preliminary, or permanent injunctive relief. The court also may impose a civil penalty against the offender, as the court considers just, in an amount that is the lesser of: (a) twenty-five thousand dollars for each day a violation occurs, or (b) not less than two dollars but not more than eight dollars for each commercial electronic mail message initiated in violation of this section.

(3) In a civil action brought by an electronic mail service provider pursuant to division (F)(1) of this section for a violation of this section, the court may award temporary, preliminary, or permanent injunctive relief, and also may award damages in an amount equal to the greater of the following:

(a) The sum of the actual damages incurred by the electronic mail service provider as a result of a violation of this section, plus any receipts of the offender that are attributable to a violation of this section and that were not taken into account in computing actual damages;

(b) Statutory damages, as the court considers just, in an amount that is the lesser of: (i) twenty-five thousand dollars for each day a violation occurs, or (ii) not less than two dollars but not more than eight dollars for each commercial electronic mail message initiated in violation of this section.

(4) In assessing damages awarded under division (F)(3) of this section, the court may consider whether the offender has established and implemented, with due care, commercially reasonable practices and procedures designed to effectively prevent the violation, or the violation occurred despite commercially reasonable efforts to maintain the practices and procedures established.

(G) Any equipment, software, or other technology of a person who violates this section that is used or intended to be used in the commission of a violation of this section, and any real or personal property that constitutes or is traceable to the gross proceeds obtained from the commission of a violation of this section, is contraband and is subject to seizure and forfeiture pursuant to sections 2933.42 and 2933.43 of the Revised Code.

(H) The attorney general may bring a civil action, pursuant to the "CAN-SPAM Act of 2003," Pub. L. No. 108–187, 117 Stat. 2699, 15 U.S.C. 7701 et seq., on behalf of the residents of the state in a district court of the United States that has jurisdiction for a violation of the CAN–SPAM Act of 2003, but the attorney general shall not bring a civil action under both this division and division (F) of this section. If a federal court dismisses a civil action brought under this division for reasons other than upon the merits, a civil action may be brought under division (F) of this section in the appropriate court of common pleas of this state.

(I) Nothing in this section shall be construed:

(1) To require an electronic mail service provider to block, transmit, route, relay, handle, or store certain types of electronic mail messages;

(2) To prevent or limit, in any way, an electronic mail service provider from adopting a policy regarding electronic mail, including a policy of declining to transmit certain types of electronic mail messages, or from enforcing such policy through technical means, through contract, or pursuant to any remedy available under any other federal, state, or local criminal or civil law;

(3) To render lawful any policy adopted under division (I)(2) of this section that is unlawful under any other law.

(2004 H 383, eff. 5–6–05)

2913.43 Securing writings by deception

(A) No person, by deception, shall cause another to execute any writing that disposes of or encumbers property, or by which a pecuniary obligation is incurred.

(B)(1) Whoever violates this section is guilty of securing writings by deception.

(2) Except as otherwise provided in this division or division (B)(3) of this section, securing writings by deception is a misdemeanor of the first degree. If the value of the property or the obligation involved is five hundred dollars or more and less than five thousand dollars, securing writings by deception is a felony of the fifth degree. If the value of the property or the obligation involved is five thousand dollars or more and is less than one hundred thousand dollars, securing writings by deception is a felony of the fourth degree. If the value of the property or the obligation involved is one hundred thousand dollars or more, securing writings by deception is a felony of the third degree.

(3) If the victim of the offense is an elderly person or disabled adult, division (B)(3) of this section applies. Except as otherwise provided in division (B)(3) of this section, securing writings by deception is a felony of the fifth degree. If the value of the property or obligation involved is five hundred dollars or more and is less than five thousand dollars, securing writings by deception is a felony of the fourth degree. If the value of the property or obligation involved is five thousand dollars or more and is less than twenty-five thousand dollars, securing writings by deception is a felony of the third degree. If the value of the property or obligation involved is twenty-five thousand dollars or more, securing writings by deception is a felony of the second degree.

(1999 H 2, eff. 11–10–99; 1995 S 2, eff. 7–1–96; 1986 H 49, eff. 6–26–86; 1982 H 269, S 199; 1972 H 511)

2913.44 Personating an officer

(A) No person, with purpose to defraud or knowing that he is facilitating a fraud, or with purpose to induce another to purchase property or services, shall personate a law enforcement officer, or an inspector, investigator, or agent of any governmental agency.

(B) Whoever violates this section is guilty of personating an officer, a misdemeanor of the first degree.

(1972 H 511, eff. 1–1–74)

2913.441 Unauthorized display of emblems related to law enforcement on motor vehicles

(A) No person who is not entitled to do so shall knowingly display on a motor vehicle the emblem of a law enforcement agency or an organization of law enforcement officers.

(B) Whoever violates this section is guilty of the unlawful display of the emblem of a law enforcement agency or an organization of law enforcement officers, a minor misdemeanor.

(1976 H 1363, eff. 1–11–77)

2913.45 Defrauding creditors

(A) No person, with purpose to defraud one or more of the person's creditors, shall do any of the following:

(1) Remove, conceal, destroy, encumber, convey, or otherwise deal with any of the person's property;

(2) Misrepresent or refuse to disclose to a fiduciary appointed to administer or manage the person's affairs or estate, the existence, amount, or location of any of the person's property, or any other information regarding such property that the person is legally required to furnish to the fiduciary.

(B) Whoever violates this section is guilty of defrauding creditors. Except as otherwise provided in this division, defrauding creditors is a misdemeanor of the first degree. If the value of the property involved is five hundred dollars or more and is less than five thousand dollars, defrauding creditors is a felony of the fifth degree. If the value of the property involved is five thousand dollars or more and is less than one hundred thousand dollars, defrauding creditors is a felony of the fourth degree. If the value of the property involved is one hundred thousand dollars or more, defrauding creditors is a felony of the third degree.

(1995 S 2, eff. 7–1–96; 1972 H 511, eff. 1–1–74)

2913.46 Trafficking in or illegal use of food stamps (first version)

Note: See also following version of this section, and Publisher's Note.

(A)(1) As used in this section:

(a) "Electronically transferred benefit" means the transfer of food stamp program benefits through the use of an access device, which may include an electronic debit card or other means authorized by section 5101.33 of the Revised Code.

(b) "Access device" means any card, plate, code, account number, or other means of access that can be used, alone or in conjunction with another access device, to obtain payments, allotments, benefits, money, goods, or other things of value or that can be used to initiate a transfer of funds pursuant to section 5101.33 of the Revised Code and the "Food Stamp Act of 1977," 91 Stat. 958, 7 U.S.C.A. 2011 et seq., or any supplemental food program administered by any department of this state or any county or local agency pursuant to the "Child Nutrition Act of 1966," 80 Stat. 885, 42 U.S.C.A. 1786, as amended.

(c) "Aggregate face value of the food stamp coupons plus coupons provided under the "Child Nutrition Act of 1966," 80 Stat. 885, 42 U.S.C.A. 1786, as amended, plus the aggregate value of the electronically transferred benefits involved in the violation" means the total face value of any food stamps plus such coupons, plus the total value of any electronically transferred benefit or other access devices, involved in the violation.

(d) "Total value of any electronically transferred benefit or other access device" means the total value of the payments, allotments, benefits, money, goods, or other things of value that may be obtained, or the total value of funds that may be transferred, by use of any electronically transferred benefit or other access device at the time of violation.

(2) If food stamp coupons or electronically transferred benefits or other access devices of various values are used, transferred, bought, acquired, altered, purchased, possessed, presented for redemption, or transported in violation of this section over a

period of twelve months, the course of conduct may be charged as one offense and the values of food stamp coupons or any electronically transferred benefits or other access devices may be aggregated in determining the degree of the offense.

(B) No individual shall knowingly possess, buy, sell, use, alter, accept, or transfer food stamp coupons, any electronically transferred benefit, or any women, infants, and children program coupon in any manner not authorized by the "Food Stamp Act of 1977," 91 Stat. 958, 7 U.S.C.A. 2011, as amended, or the "Child Nutrition Act of 1966," 80 Stat. 885, 42 U.S.C.A. 1786, as amended.

(C) No organization, as defined in division (D) of section 2901.23 of the Revised Code, shall do either of the following:

(1) Knowingly allow an employee to sell, transfer, or trade items or services, the purchase of which is prohibited by the "Food Stamp Act of 1977," 91 Stat. 958, 7 U.S.C.A. 2011, as amended, or the "Child Nutrition Act of 1966," 80 Stat. 885, 42 U.S.C.A. 1786, as amended, in exchange for food stamp coupons, any electronically transferred benefit, or any women, infants, and children program coupon;

(2) Negligently allow an employee to sell, transfer, or exchange food stamp coupons, any electronically transferred benefit, or any women, infants, and children program coupon for anything of value.

(D) Whoever violates this section is guilty of illegal use of food stamps or coupons. Except as otherwise provided in this division, illegal use of food stamps or coupons is a felony of the fifth degree. If the aggregate face value of the food stamp coupons plus coupons provided under the "Child Nutrition Act of 1966," 80 Stat. 885, 42 U.S.C.A. 1786, as amended, plus the aggregate value of the electronically transferred benefits involved in the violation is five hundred dollars or more and is less than five thousand dollars, illegal use of food stamps or coupons is a felony of the fourth degree. If the aggregate face value of the food stamp coupons plus coupons provided under the "Child Nutrition Act of 1966," 80 Stat. 885, 42 U.S.C.A. 1786, as amended, plus the aggregate value of the electronically transferred benefits involved in the violation is five thousand dollars or more and is less than one hundred thousand dollars, illegal use of food stamps or coupons is a felony of the third degree. If the aggregate face value of the food stamp coupons plus coupons provided under the "Child Nutrition Act of 1966," 80 Stat. 885, 42 U.S.C.A. 1786, as amended, plus the aggregate value of the electronically transferred benefits involved in the violation is one hundred thousand dollars or more, illegal use of food stamps or coupons is a felony of the second degree.

(1996 S 269, eff. 7–1–96; 1996 S 107, eff. 5–8–96; 1995 S 162, eff. 10–29–95; 1995 H 239, eff. 11–24–95; 1995 S 2, eff. 7–1–96; 1983 H 291, eff. 7–1–83)

Note: See also following version of this section, and Publisher's Note.

2913.46 Trafficking in or illegal use of food stamps (second version)

Note: See also preceding version of this section, and Publisher's Note.

(A)(1) As used in this section:

(a) "Electronically transferred benefit" means the transfer of food stamp program benefits or WIC program benefits through the use of an access device.

(b) "WIC program benefits" includes money, coupons, delivery verification receipts, other documents, food, or other property received directly or indirectly pursuant to section 17 the "Child Nutrition Act of 1966," 80 Stat. 885, 42 U.S.C.A. 1786, as amended.

(c) "Access device" means any card, plate, code, account number, or other means of access that can be used, alone or in conjunction with another access device, to obtain payments, allotments, benefits, money, goods, or other things of value or that can be used to initiate a transfer of funds pursuant to section 5101.33 of the Revised Code and the "Food Stamp Act of 1977," 91 Stat. 958, 7 U.S.C.A. 2011 et seq., or any supplemental food program administered by any department of this state or any county or local agency pursuant to section 17 of the "Child Nutrition Act of 1966," 80 Stat. 885, 42 U.S.C.A. 1786, as amended. An "access device" may include an electronic debit card or other means authorized by section 5101.33 of the Revised Code.

(d) "Aggregate value of the food stamp coupons, WIC program benefits, and electronically transferred benefits involved in the violation" means the total face value of any food stamps, plus the total face value of WIC program coupons or delivery verification receipts, plus the total value of other WIC program benefits, plus the total value of any electronically transferred benefit or other access device, involved in the violation.

(e) "Total value of any electronically transferred benefit or other access device" means the total value of the payments, allotments, benefits, money, goods, or other things of value that may be obtained, or the total value of funds that may be transferred, by use of any electronically transferred benefit or other access device at the time of violation.

(2) If food stamp coupons, WIC program benefits, or electronically transferred benefits or other access devices of various values are used, transferred, bought, acquired, altered, purchased, possessed, presented for redemption, or transported in violation of this section over a period of twelve months, the course of conduct may be charged as one offense and the values of food stamp coupons, WIC program benefits, or any electronically transferred benefits or other access devices may be aggregated in determining the degree of the offense.

(B) No individual shall knowingly possess, buy, sell, use, alter, accept, or transfer food stamp coupons, WIC program benefits, or any electronically transferred benefit in any manner not authorized by the "Food Stamp Act of 1977," 91 Stat. 958, 7 U.S.C.A. 2011, as amended, or section 17 of the "Child Nutrition Act of 1966," 80 Stat. 885, 42 U.S.C.A. 1786, as amended.

(C) No organization, as defined in division (D) of section 2901.23 of the Revised Code, shall do either of the following:

(1) Knowingly allow an employee or agent to sell, transfer, or trade items or services, the purchase of which is prohibited by the "Food Stamp Act of 1977," 91 Stat. 958, 7 U.S.C.A. 2011, as amended, or section 17 of the "Child Nutrition Act of 1966," 80 Stat. 885, 42 U.S.C.A. 1786, as amended, in exchange for food stamp coupons, WIC program benefits, or any electronically transferred benefit;

(2) Negligently allow an employee or agent to sell, transfer, or exchange food stamp coupons, WIC program benefits, or any electronically transferred benefit for anything of value.

(D) Whoever violates this section is guilty of illegal use of food stamps or WIC program benefits. Except as otherwise provided in this division, illegal use of food stamps or WIC program benefits is a felony of the fifth degree. If the aggregate value of the food stamp coupons, WIC program benefits, and electronically transferred benefits involved in the violation is five hundred dollars or more and is less than five thousand dollars, illegal use of food stamps or WIC program benefits is a felony of the fourth degree. If the aggregate value of the food stamp coupons, WIC program benefits, and electronically transferred benefits involved in the violation is five thousand dollars or more and is less than one hundred thousand dollars, illegal use of food stamps or WIC program benefits is a felony of the third degree. If the aggregate value of the food stamp coupons, WIC program benefits, and electronically transferred benefits involved in the violation is one hundred thousand dollars or more, illegal use of food stamps or WIC program benefits is a felony of the second degree.

(1996 S 293, eff. 9–26–96 (See also Historical and Statutory Notes.); 1996 S 107, eff. 5–8–96; 1995 S 162, eff. 10–29–95; 1995 H 239, eff. 11–24–95; 1995 S 2, eff. 7–1–96; 1983 H 291, eff. 7–1–83)

Note: See also preceding version of this section, and Publisher's Note.

Historical and Statutory Notes

Publisher's Note: 2913.46 was amended by 1996 S 269, eff. 7–1–96, and 1996 S 293, eff. 9–26–96 (see also Historical and Statutory Notes). Harmonization pursuant to section 1.52 of the Revised Code is in question. See *Baldwin's Ohio Legislative Service*, 1996, pages 6/L–955 and 7/L–2170, or the OH–LEGIS or OH–LEGIS–OLD database on WESTLAW, for original versions of these Acts.

Ed. Note: 1996 S 293 Effective Date—The Secretary of State assigned a general effective date of 9–26–96 for 1996 S 293, along with notice that, in accordance with RC 1.471, the General Assembly has not determined which sections go into immediate effect, and that it appears that certain sections provide for appropriations for current expenses, and are immediately effective in accordance with RC 1.471 and O Const Art II, § 1d.

2913.47 Insurance fraud

(A) As used in this section:

(1) "Data" has the same meaning as in section 2913.01 of the Revised Code and additionally includes any other representation of information, knowledge, facts, concepts, or instructions that are being or have been prepared in a formalized manner.

(2) "Deceptive" means that a statement, in whole or in part, would cause another to be deceived because it contains a misleading representation, withholds information, prevents the acquisition of information, or by any other conduct, act, or omission creates, confirms, or perpetuates a false impression, including, but not limited to, a false impression as to law, value, state of mind, or other objective or subjective fact.

(3) "Insurer" means any person that is authorized to engage in the business of insurance in this state under Title XXXIX of the Revised Code, the Ohio fair plan underwriting association created under section 3929.43 of the Revised Code, any health insuring corporation, and any legal entity that is self-insured and provides benefits to its employees or members.

(4) "Policy" means a policy, certificate, contract, or plan that is issued by an insurer.

(5) "Statement" includes, but is not limited to, any notice, letter, or memorandum; proof of loss; bill of lading; receipt for payment; invoice, account, or other financial statement; estimate of property damage; bill for services; diagnosis or prognosis; prescription; hospital, medical, or dental chart or other record; x–ray, photograph, videotape, or movie film; test result; other evidence of loss, injury, or expense; computer–generated document; and data in any form.

(B) No person, with purpose to defraud or knowing that the person is facilitating a fraud, shall do either of the following:

(1) Present to, or cause to be presented to, an insurer any written or oral statement that is part of, or in support of, an application for insurance, a claim for payment pursuant to a policy, or a claim for any other benefit pursuant to a policy, knowing that the statement, or any part of the statement, is false or deceptive;

(2) Assist, aid, abet, solicit, procure, or conspire with another to prepare or make any written or oral statement that is intended to be presented to an insurer as part of, or in support of, an application for insurance, a claim for payment pursuant to a policy, or a claim for any other benefit pursuant to a policy, knowing that the statement, or any part of the statement, is false or deceptive.

(C) Whoever violates this section is guilty of insurance fraud. Except as otherwise provided in this division, insurance fraud is a misdemeanor of the first degree. If the amount of the claim that is false or deceptive is five hundred dollars or more and is less than five thousand dollars, insurance fraud is a felony of the fifth degree. If the amount of the claim that is false or deceptive is five thousand dollars or more and is less than one hundred thousand dollars, insurance fraud is a felony of the fourth degree. If the amount of the claim that is false or deceptive is one hundred thousand dollars or more, insurance fraud is a felony of the third degree.

(D) This section shall not be construed to abrogate, waive, or modify division (A) of section 2317.02 of the Revised Code.

(1997 S 67, eff. 6–4–97; 1996 S 269, eff. 7–1–96; 1995 S 2, eff. 7–1–96; 1990 H 347, eff. 7–18–90)

2913.48 Workers' compensation fraud

(A) No person, with purpose to defraud or knowing that the person is facilitating a fraud shall do any of the following:

(1) Receive workers' compensation benefits to which the person is not entitled;

(2) Make or present or cause to be made or presented a false or misleading statement with the purpose to secure payment for goods or services rendered under Chapter 4121., 4123., 4127., or 4131. of the Revised Code or to secure workers' compensation benefits;

(3) Alter, falsify, destroy, conceal, or remove any record or document that is necessary to fully establish the validity of any claim filed with, or necessary to establish the nature and validity of all goods and services for which reimbursement or payment was received or is requested from, the bureau of workers' compensation, or a self-insuring employer under Chapter 4121., 4123., 4127., or 4131. of the Revised Code;

(4) Enter into an agreement or conspiracy to defraud the bureau or a self-insuring employer by making or presenting or causing to be made or presented a false claim for workers' compensation benefits.

(B) Whoever violates this section is guilty of workers' compensation fraud. Except as otherwise provided in this division, a violation of this section is a misdemeanor of the first degree. If the value of the goods, services, property, or money stolen is five hundred dollars or more and is less than five thousand dollars, a violation of this section is a felony of the fifth degree. If the value of the goods, services, property, or money stolen is five thousand dollars or more and is less than one hundred thousand dollars, a violation of this section is a felony of the fourth degree. If the value of the goods, services, property, or money stolen is one hundred thousand dollars or more, a violation of this section is a felony of the third degree.

(C) Upon application of the governmental body that conducted the investigation and prosecution of a violation of this section, the court shall order the person who is convicted of the violation to pay the governmental body its costs of investigating and prosecuting the case. These costs are in addition to any other costs or penalty provided in the Revised Code or any other section of law.

(D) The remedies and penalties provided in this section are not exclusive remedies and penalties and do not preclude the use of any other criminal or civil remedy or penalty for any act that is in violation of this section.

(E) As used in this section:

(1) "False" means wholly or partially untrue or deceptive.

(2) "Goods" includes, but is not limited to, medical supplies, appliances, rehabilitative equipment, and any other apparatus or

furnishing provided or used in the care, treatment, or rehabilitation of a claimant for workers' compensation benefits.

(3) "Services" includes, but is not limited to, any service provided by any health care provider to a claimant for workers' compensation benefits.

(4) "Claim" means any attempt to cause the bureau, an independent third party with whom the administrator or an employer contracts under section 4121.44 of the Revised Code, or a self-insuring employer to make payment or reimbursement for workers' compensation benefits.

(5) "Employment" means participating in any trade, occupation, business, service, or profession for substantial gainful remuneration.

(6) "Employer," "employee," and "self–insuring employer" have the same meanings as in section 4123.01 of the Revised Code.

(7) "Remuneration" includes, but is not limited to, wages, commissions, rebates, and any other reward or consideration.

(8) "Statement" includes, but is not limited to, any oral, written, electronic, electronic impulse, or magnetic communication notice, letter, memorandum, receipt for payment, invoice, account, financial statement, bill for services; a diagnosis, prognosis, prescription, hospital, medical, or dental chart or other record; and a computer generated document.

(9) "Records" means any medical, professional, financial, or business record relating to the treatment or care of any person, to goods or services provided to any person, or to rates paid for goods or services provided to any person, or any record that the administrator of workers' compensation requires pursuant to rule.

(10) "Workers' compensation benefits" means any compensation or benefits payable under Chapter 4121., 4123., 4127., or 4131. of the Revised Code.

(1995 S 2, eff. 7–1–96; 1993 H 107, eff. 10–20–93)

2913.49 Identity fraud; affirmative defenses

(A) As used in this section, "personal identifying information" includes, but is not limited to, the following: the name, address, telephone number, driver's license, driver's license number, commercial driver's license, commercial driver's license number, state identification card, state identification card number, social security card, social security number, birth certificate, place of employment, employee identification number, mother's maiden name, demand deposit account number, savings account number, money market account number, mutual fund account number, other financial account number, personal identification number, password, or credit card number of a living or dead individual.

(B) No person, without the express or implied consent of the other person, shall use, obtain, or possess any personal identifying information of another person with intent to do either of the following:

(1) Hold the person out to be the other person;

(2) Represent the other person's personal identifying information as the person's own personal identifying information.

(C) No person shall create, obtain, possess, or use the personal identifying information of any person with the intent to aid or abet another person in violating division (B) of this section.

(D) No person, with intent to defraud, shall permit another person to use the person's own personal identifying information.

(E) No person who is permitted to use another person's personal identifying information as described in division (D) of this section shall use, obtain, or possess the other person's personal identifying information with intent to defraud any person by doing any act identified in division (B)(1) or (2) of this section.

(F)(1) It is an affirmative defense to a charge under division (B) of this section that the person using the personal identifying information is acting in accordance with a legally recognized guardianship or conservatorship or as a trustee or fiduciary.

(2) It is an affirmative defense to a charge under division (B), (D), or (E) of this section that either of the following applies:

(a) The person or entity using the personal identifying information is a law enforcement agency, authorized fraud personnel, or a representative of or attorney for a law enforcement agency or authorized fraud personnel and is using the personal identifying information in a bona fide investigation, an information security evaluation, a pretext calling evaluation, or a similar matter.

(b) The personal identifying information was obtained, possessed, or used for a lawful purpose.

(G) It is not a defense to a charge under this section that the person whose personal identifying information was obtained, possessed, or used was deceased at the time of the offense.

(H) (1) If the violation of division (B), (D), or (E) of this section occurs as part of a course of conduct involving other violations of division (B), (D), or (E) of this section or violations of, attempts to violate, conspiracies to violate, or complicity in violations of division (C) of this section or section 2913.02, 2913.04, 2913.11, 2913.21, 2913.31, 2913.42, 2913.43, or 2921.13 of the Revised Code, the court, in determining the degree of the offense pursuant to division (I) of this section, may aggregate all credit, property, or services obtained or sought to be obtained by the offender and all debts or other legal obligations avoided or sought to be avoided by the offender in the violations involved in that course of conduct. The course of conduct may involve one victim or more than one victim.

(2) If the violation of division (C) of this section occurs as part of a course of conduct involving other violations of division (C) of this section or violations of, attempts to violate, conspiracies to violate, or complicity in violations of division (B), (D), or (E) of this section or section 2913.02, 2913.04, 2913.11, 2913.21, 2913.31, 2913.42, 2913.43, or 2921.13 of the Revised Code, the court, in determining the degree of the offense pursuant to division (I) of this section, may aggregate all credit, property, or services obtained or sought to be obtained by the person aided or abetted and all debts or other legal obligations avoided or sought to be avoided by the person aided or abetted in the violations involved in that course of conduct. The course of conduct may involve one victim or more than one victim.

(I) Whoever violates this section is guilty of identity fraud. Except as otherwise provided in this division, identity fraud is a misdemeanor of the first degree. If the value of the credit, property, services, debt, or other legal obligation involved in the violation or course of conduct is five hundred dollars or more and is less than five thousand dollars, identity fraud is a felony of the fourth degree. If the value of the credit, property, services, debt, or other legal obligation involved in the violation or course of conduct is five thousand dollars or more and is less than one hundred thousand dollars, identity fraud is a felony of the third degree. If the value of the credit, property, services, debt, or other legal obligation involved in the violation or course of conduct is one hundred thousand dollars or more, identity fraud is a felony of the second degree.

(2002 H 309, eff. 9–27–02; 1999 S 7, eff. 8–25–99)

MISCELLANEOUS PROVISIONS

2913.51 Receiving stolen property

(A) No person shall receive, retain, or dispose of property of another knowing or having reasonable cause to believe that the property has been obtained through commission of a theft offense.

(B) It is not a defense to a charge of receiving stolen property in violation of this section that the property was obtained by means other than through the commission of a theft offense if the property was explicitly represented to the accused person as being obtained through the commission of a theft offense.

(C) Whoever violates this section is guilty of receiving stolen property. Except as otherwise provided in this division, receiving stolen property is a misdemeanor of the first degree. If the value of the property involved is five hundred dollars or more and is less than five thousand dollars, if the property involved is any of the property listed in section 2913.71 of the Revised Code, receiving stolen property is a felony of the fifth degree. If the property involved is a motor vehicle, as defined in section 4501.01 of the Revised Code, if the property involved is a dangerous drug, as defined in section 4729.01 of the Revised Code, if the value of the property involved is five thousand dollars or more and is less than one hundred thousand dollars, or if the property involved is a firearm or dangerous ordnance, as defined in section 2923.11 of the Revised Code, receiving stolen property is a felony of the fourth degree. If the value of the property involved is one hundred thousand dollars or more, receiving stolen property is a felony of the third degree.

(1999 S 64, eff. 10–29–99; 1998 S 66, eff. 7–22–98; 1995 S 2, eff. 7–1–96; 1995 H 4, eff. 11–9–95; 1986 H 49, eff. 6–26–86; 1983 S 210; 1982 S 199, H 269; 1980 S 191; 1972 H 511)

2913.61 Value of stolen property

(A) When a person is charged with a theft offense, or with a violation of division (A)(1) of section 1716.14 of the Revised Code involving a victim who is an elderly person or disabled adult that involves property or services valued at five hundred dollars or more, property or services valued at five hundred dollars or more and less than five thousand dollars, property or services valued at five thousand dollars or more and less than twenty-five thousand dollars, property or services valued at twenty-five thousand dollars or more and less than one hundred thousand dollars, or property or services valued at one hundred thousand dollars or more, the jury or court trying the accused shall determine the value of the property or services as of the time of the offense and, if a guilty verdict is returned, shall return the finding of value as part of the verdict. In any case in which the jury or court determines that the value of the property or services at the time of the offense was five hundred dollars or more, it is unnecessary to find and return the exact value, and it is sufficient if the finding and return is to the effect that the value of the property or services involved was five hundred dollars or more and less than five thousand dollars, was five thousand dollars or more and less than twenty-five thousand dollars, was twenty-five thousand dollars or more and less than one hundred thousand dollars, or was one hundred thousand dollars or more.

(B) If more than one item of property or services is involved in a theft offense or in a violation of division (A)(1) of section 1716.14 of the Revised Code involving a victim who is an elderly person or disabled adult, the value of the property or services involved for the purpose of determining the value as required by division (A) of this section is the aggregate value of all property or services involved in the offense.

(C)(1) When a series of offenses under section 2913.02 of the Revised Code, or a series of violations of, attempts to commit a violation of, conspiracies to violate, or complicity in violations of division (A)(1) of section 1716.14, section 2913.02, 2913.03, or 2913.04, division (B)(1) or (2) of section 2913.21, or section 2913.31 or 2913.43 of the Revised Code involving a victim who is an elderly person or disabled adult, is committed by the offender in the offender's same employment, capacity, or relationship to another, all of those offenses shall be tried as a single offense. The value of the property or services involved in the series of offenses for the purpose of determining the value as required by division (A) of this section is the aggregate value of all property and services involved in all offenses in the series.

(2) If an offender commits a series of offenses under section 2913.02 of the Revised Code that involves a common course of conduct to defraud multiple victims, all of the offenses may be tried as a single offense. If an offender is being tried for the commission of a series of violations of, attempts to commit a violation of, conspiracies to violate, or complicity in violations of division (A)(1) of section 1716.14, section 2913.02, 2913.03, or 2913.04, division (B)(1) or (2) of section 2913.21, or section 2913.31 or 2913.43 of the Revised Code, whether committed against one victim or more than one victim, involving a victim who is an elderly person or disabled adult, pursuant to a scheme or course of conduct, all of those offenses may be tried as a single offense. If the offenses are tried as a single offense, the value of the property or services involved for the purpose of determining the value as required by division (A) of this section is the aggregate value of all property and services involved in all of the offenses in the course of conduct.

(3) When a series of two or more offenses under section 2921.41 of the Revised Code is committed by the offender in the offender's same employment, capacity, or relationship to another, all of those offenses may be tried as a single offense. If the offenses are tried as a single offense, the value of the property or services involved for the purpose of determining the value as required by division (A) of this section is the aggregate value of all property and services involved in all of the offenses in the series of two or more offenses.

(4) In prosecuting a single offense under division (C)(1), (2), or (3) of this section, it is not necessary to separately allege and prove each offense in the series. Rather, it is sufficient to allege and prove that the offender, within a given span of time, committed one or more theft offenses or violations of section 2921.41 of the Revised Code in the offender's same employment, capacity, or relationship to another as described in division (C)(1) or (3) of this section, or committed one or more theft offenses that involve a common course of conduct to defraud multiple victims or a scheme or course of conduct as described in division (C)(2) of this section.

(D) The following criteria shall be used in determining the value of property or services involved in a theft offense:

(1) The value of an heirloom, memento, collector's item, antique, museum piece, manuscript, document, record, or other thing that has intrinsic worth to its owner and that either is irreplaceable or is replaceable only on the expenditure of substantial time, effort, or money, is the amount that would compensate the owner for its loss.

(2) The value of personal effects and household goods, and of materials, supplies, equipment, and fixtures used in the profession, business, trade, occupation, or avocation of its owner, which property is not covered under division (D)(1) of this section and which retains substantial utility for its purpose regardless of its age or condition, is the cost of replacing the property with new property of like kind and quality.

(3) The value of any real or personal property that is not covered under division (D)(1) or (2) of this section, and the value of services, is the fair market value of the property or services. As used in this section, "fair market value" is the money consideration that a buyer would give and a seller would accept for property or services, assuming that the buyer is willing to buy and the seller is willing to sell, that both are fully informed as to all facts material to the transaction, and that neither is under any compulsion to act.

(E) Without limitation on the evidence that may be used to establish the value of property or services involved in a theft offense:

(1) When the property involved is personal property held for sale at wholesale or retail, the price at which the property was held for sale is prima-facie evidence of its value.

(2) When the property involved is a security or commodity traded on an exchange, the closing price or, if there is no closing price, the asked price, given in the latest market quotation prior to the offense is prima-facie evidence of the value of the security or commodity.

(3) When the property involved is livestock, poultry, or raw agricultural products for which a local market price is available, the latest local market price prior to the offense is prima-facie evidence of the value of the livestock, poultry, or products.

(4) When the property involved is a negotiable instrument, the face value is prima-facie evidence of the value of the instrument.

(5) When the property involved is a warehouse receipt, bill of lading, pawn ticket, claim check, or other instrument entitling the holder or bearer to receive property, the face value or, if there is no face value, the value of the property covered by the instrument less any payment necessary to receive the property is prima-facie evidence of the value of the instrument.

(6) When the property involved is a ticket of admission, ticket for transportation, coupon, token, or other instrument entitling the holder or bearer to receive property or services, the face value or, if there is no face value, the value of the property or services that may be received by the instrument is prima-facie evidence of the value of the instrument.

(7) When the services involved are gas, electricity, water, telephone, transportation, shipping, or other services for which the rate is established by law, the duly established rate is prima-facie evidence of the value of the services.

(8) When the services involved are services for which the rate is not established by law, and the offender has been notified prior to the offense of the rate for the services, either in writing, orally, or by posting in a manner reasonably calculated to come to the attention of potential offenders, the rate contained in the notice is prima-facie evidence of the value of the services.

(2000 H 364, eff. 9–14–00; 1999 S 2, § 3, eff. 11–22–99; 1999 S 2, § 1, eff. 11–22–99; 1999 H 2, eff. 11–10–99; 1998 H 565, eff. 3–30–99; 1995 S 2, eff. 7–1–96; 1982 H 269, eff. 12–17–82; 1982 S 199; 1972 H 511)

2913.71 Degree of offense when certain property involved

Regardless of the value of the property involved and regardless of whether the offender previously has been convicted of a theft offense, a violation of section 2913.02 or 2913.51 of the Revised Code is a felony of the fifth degree if the property involved is any of the following:

(A) A credit card;

(B) A printed form for a check or other negotiable instrument, that on its face identifies the drawer or maker for whose use it is designed or identifies the account on which it is to be drawn, and that has not been executed by the drawer or maker or on which the amount is blank;

(C) A motor vehicle identification license plate as prescribed by section 4503.22 of the Revised Code, a temporary license placard or windshield sticker as prescribed by section 4503.182 of the Revised Code, or any comparable license plate, placard, or sticker as prescribed by the applicable law of another state or the United States;

(D) A blank form for a certificate of title or a manufacturer's or importer's certificate to a motor vehicle, as prescribed by section 4505.07 of the Revised Code;

(E) A blank form for any license listed in section 4507.01 of the Revised Code.

(1995 S 2, eff. 7–1–96; 1995 H 4, eff. 11–9–95; 1984 H 632, eff. 3–28–85; 1980 S 191; 1977 H 1; 1972 H 511)

2913.72 Evidence of intent to commit theft of rented property

(A) Each of the following shall be considered evidence of an intent to commit theft of rented property:

(1) At the time of entering into the rental contract, the rentee presented the renter with identification that was materially false, fictitious, or not current with respect to name, address, place of employment, or other relevant information.

(2) After receiving a notice demanding the return of rented property as provided in division (B) of this section, the rentee neither returned the rented property nor made arrangements acceptable with the renter to return the rented property.

(B) To establish that a rentee has an intent to commit theft of rented property under division (A)(2) of this section, a renter may issue a notice to a rentee demanding the return of rented property. The renter shall mail the notice by certified mail, return receipt requested, to the rentee at the address the rentee gave when the rental contract was executed, or to the rentee at the last address the rentee or the rentee's agent furnished in writing to the renter.

(C) A demand for the return of rented property is not a prerequisite for the prosecution of a rentee for theft of rented property. The evidence specified in division (A) of this section does not constitute the only evidence that may be considered as evidence of intent to commit theft of rented property.

(D) As used in this section:

(1) "Renter" means a person who owns rented property.

(2) "Rentee" means a person who pays consideration to a renter for the use of rented property.

(1995 S 2, eff. 7–1–96)

2913.73 Admissibility of evidence of lack of capacity to consent

In a prosecution for any alleged violation of a provision of this chapter, if the lack of consent of the victim is an element of the provision that allegedly was violated, evidence that, at the time of the alleged violation, the victim lacked the capacity to give consent is admissible to show that the victim did not give consent.

As used in this section, "lacks the capacity to consent" means being impaired for any reason to the extent that the person lacks sufficient understanding or capacity to make and carry out reasonable decisions concerning the person or the person's resources.

(1999 H 2, eff. 11–10–99)

2913.82 Theft involving motor vehicle; offender to pay towing and storage fees

If a person is convicted of a theft offense that involves a motor vehicle, as defined in section 4501.01 of the Revised Code, or any major part of a motor vehicle, and if a local authority, as defined in section 4511.01 of the Revised Code, the owner of the vehicle or major part, or a person, acting on behalf of the owner, was required to pay any towing or storage fees prior to recovering possession of the motor vehicle or major part, the court that sentences the offender, as a part of its sentence, shall require the offender to repay the fees to the local authority, the owner, or the person who paid the fees on behalf of the owner.

As used in this section, "major part" has the same meaning as in the "Motor Vehicle Theft Law Enforcement Act of 1984," 98 Stat. 2754, 15 U.S.C. 2021 (7), as amended.

(1986 H 546, eff. 3–25–87)

CHAPTER 2915

GAMBLING

GENERAL PROVISIONS

GENERAL PROVISIONS

2915.01 Definitions

As used in this chapter:

(A) "Bookmaking" means the business of receiving or paying off bets.

(B) "Bet" means the hazarding of anything of value upon the result of an event, undertaking, or contingency, but does not include a bona fide business risk.

(C) "Scheme of chance" means a slot machine, lottery, numbers game, pool conducted for profit, or other scheme in which a participant gives a valuable consideration for a chance to win a prize, but does not include bingo, a skill-based amusement machine, or a pool not conducted for profit.

(D) "Game of chance" means poker, craps, roulette, or other game in which a player gives anything of value in the hope of gain, the outcome of which is determined largely by chance, but does not include bingo.

(E) "Game of chance conducted for profit" means any game of chance designed to produce income for the person who conducts or operates the game of chance, but does not include bingo.

(F) "Gambling device" means any of the following:

(1) A book, totalizer, or other equipment for recording bets;

(2) A ticket, token, or other device representing a chance, share, or interest in a scheme of chance or evidencing a bet;

(3) A deck of cards, dice, gaming table, roulette wheel, slot machine, or other apparatus designed for use in connection with a game of chance;

(4) Any equipment, device, apparatus, or paraphernalia specially designed for gambling purposes;

(5) Bingo supplies sold or otherwise provided, or used, in violation of this chapter.

(G) "Gambling offense" means any of the following:

(1) A violation of section 2915.02, 2915.03, 2915.04, 2915.05, 2915.07, 2915.08, 2915.081, 2915.082, 2915.09, 2915.091, 2915.092, 2915.10, or 2915.11 of the Revised Code;

(2) A violation of an existing or former municipal ordinance or law of this or any other state or the United States substantially equivalent to any section listed in division (G)(1) of this section or a violation of section 2915.06 of the Revised Code as it existed prior to July 1, 1996;

(3) An offense under an existing or former municipal ordinance or law of this or any other state or the United States, of which gambling is an element;

(4) A conspiracy or attempt to commit, or complicity in committing, any offense under division (G)(1), (2), or (3) of this section.

(H) Except as otherwise provided in this chapter, "charitable organization" means any tax exempt religious, educational, veteran's, fraternal, sporting, service, nonprofit medical, volunteer rescue service, volunteer firefighter's, senior citizen's, historic railroad educational, youth athletic, amateur athletic, or youth athletic park organization. An organization is tax exempt if the organization is, and has received from the internal revenue service a determination letter that currently is in effect stating that the organization is, exempt from federal income taxation under subsection 501(a) and described in subsection 501(c)(3), 501(c)(4), 501(c)(8), 501(c)(10), or 501(c)(19) of the Internal Revenue Code [1], or if the organization is a sporting organization that is exempt from federal income taxation under subsection 501(a) and is described in subsection 501(c)(7) of the Internal Revenue Code. To qualify as a charitable organization, an organization, except a volunteer rescue service or volunteer fire fighter's organization, shall have been in continuous existence as such in this state for a period of two years immediately preceding either the making of an application for a bingo license under section 2915.08 of the Revised Code or the conducting of any game of chance as provided in division (D) of section 2915.02 of the Revised Code. A charitable organization that is exempt from federal income taxation under subsection 501(a) and described in subsection 501(c)(3) of the Internal Revenue Code and that is created by a veteran's organization, a fraternal organization, or a sporting organization does not have to have been in continuous existence as such in this state for a period of two years immediately preceding either the making of an application for a bingo license under section 2915.08 of the Revised Code or the conducting of any game of chance as provided in division (D) of section 2915.02 of the Revised Code.

(I) "Religious organization" means any church, body of communicants, or group that is not organized or operated for profit and that gathers in common membership for regular worship and religious observances.

(J) "Educational organization" means any organization within this state that is not organized for profit, the primary purpose of which is to educate and develop the capabilities of individuals through instruction by means of operating or contributing to the support of a school, academy, college, or university.

(K) "Veteran's organization" means any individual post or state headquarters of a national veteran's association or an auxiliary unit of any individual post of a national veteran's association, which post, state headquarters, or auxiliary unit has been in continuous existence in this state for at least two years and incorporated as a nonprofit corporation and either has received a letter from the state headquarters of the national veteran's association indicating that the individual post or auxiliary unit is in good standing with the national veteran's association or has received a letter from the national veteran's association indicating that the state headquarters is in good standing with the national veteran's association. As used in this division, "national veteran's association" means any veteran's association that has been in continuous existence as such for a period of at least five years and either is incorporated by an act of the United States congress or has a national dues-paying membership of at least five thousand persons.

(L) "Volunteer firefighter's organization" means any organization of volunteer firefighters, as defined in section 146.01 of the Revised Code, that is organized and operated exclusively to provide financial support for a volunteer fire department or a volunteer fire company and that is recognized or ratified by a county, municipal corporation, or township.

(M) "Fraternal organization" means any society, order, state headquarters, or association within this state, except a college or high school fraternity, that is not organized for profit, that is a branch, lodge, or chapter of a national or state organization, that exists exclusively for the common business or sodality of its members, and that has been in continuous existence in this state for a period of five years.

(N) "Volunteer rescue service organization" means any organization of volunteers organized to function as an emergency medical service organization, as defined in section 4765.01 of the Revised Code.

(O) "Service organization" means either of the following:

(1) Any organization, not organized for profit, that is organized and operated exclusively to provide, or to contribute to the support of organizations or institutions organized and operated exclusively to provide, medical and therapeutic services for persons who are crippled, born with birth defects, or have any other mental or physical defect or those organized and operated exclusively to protect, or to contribute to the support of organizations or institutions organized and operated exclusively to protect, animals from inhumane treatment or provide immediate shelter to victims of domestic violence;

(2) Any organization that is described in subsection 509(a)(1), 509(a)(2), or 509(a)(3) of the Internal Revenue Code and is either a governmental unit or an organization that is tax exempt under subsection 501(a) and described in subsection 501(c)(3) of the Internal Revenue Code and that is an organization, not organized for profit, that is organized and operated primarily to provide, or to contribute to the support of organizations or institutions organized and operated primarily to provide, medical and therapeutic services for persons who are crippled, born with birth defects, or have any other mental or physical defect.

(P) "Nonprofit medical organization" means either of the following:

(1) Any organization that has been incorporated as a nonprofit corporation for at least five years and that has continuously operated and will be operated exclusively to provide, or to contribute to the support of organizations or institutions organized and operated exclusively to provide, hospital, medical, research, or therapeutic services for the public;

(2) Any organization that is described and qualified under subsection 501(c)(3) of the Internal Revenue Code, that has been incorporated as a nonprofit corporation for at least five years, and that has continuously operated and will be operated primarily to provide, or to contribute to the support of organizations or institutions organized and operated primarily to provide, hospital, medical, research, or therapeutic services for the public.

(Q) "Senior citizen's organization" means any private organization, not organized for profit, that is organized and operated exclusively to provide recreational or social services for persons who are fifty-five years of age or older and that is described and qualified under subsection 501(c)(3) of the Internal Revenue Code.

(R) "Charitable bingo game" means any bingo game described in division (S)(1) or (2) of this section that is conducted by a charitable organization that has obtained a license pursuant to section 2915. 08 of the Revised Code and the proceeds of which are used for a charitable purpose.

(S) "Bingo" means either of the following:

(1) A game with all of the following characteristics:

(a) The participants use bingo cards or sheets, including paper formats and electronic representation or image formats, that are divided into twenty-five spaces arranged in five horizontal and five vertical rows of spaces, with each space, except the central space, being designated by a combination of a letter and a number and with the central space being designated as a free space.

(b) The participants cover the spaces on the bingo cards or sheets that correspond to combinations of letters and numbers that are announced by a bingo game operator.

(c) A bingo game operator announces combinations of letters and numbers that appear on objects that a bingo game operator selects by chance, either manually or mechanically, from a receptacle that contains seventy-five objects at the beginning of each game, each object marked by a different combination of a letter and a number that corresponds to one of the seventy-five possible combinations of a letter and a number that can appear on the bingo cards or sheets.

(d) The winner of the bingo game includes any participant who properly announces during the interval between the announcements of letters and numbers as described in division (S)(1)(c) of this section, that a predetermined and preannounced pattern of spaces has been covered on a bingo card or sheet being used by the participant.

(2) Instant bingo, punch boards, and raffles.

(T) "Conduct" means to back, promote, organize, manage, carry on, sponsor, or prepare for the operation of bingo or a game of chance.

(U) "Bingo game operator" means any person, except security personnel, who performs work or labor at the site of bingo, including, but not limited to, collecting money from participants, handing out bingo cards or sheets or objects to cover spaces on bingo cards or sheets, selecting from a receptacle the objects that contain the combination of letters and numbers that appear on bingo cards or sheets, calling out the combinations of letters and numbers, distributing prizes, selling or redeeming instant bingo tickets or cards, supervising the operation of a punch board, selling raffle tickets, selecting raffle tickets from a receptacle and announcing the winning numbers in a raffle, and preparing, selling, and serving food or beverages.

(V) "Participant" means any person who plays bingo.

(W) "Bingo session" means a period that includes both of the following:

(1) Not to exceed five continuous hours for the conduct of one or more games described in division (S)(1) of this section, instant bingo, and seal cards;

(2) A period for the conduct of instant bingo and seal cards for not more than two hours before and not more than two hours after the period described in division (W)(1) of this section.

(X) "Gross receipts" means all money or assets, including admission fees, that a person receives from bingo without the deduction of any amounts for prizes paid out or for the expenses of conducting bingo. "Gross receipts" does not include any money directly taken in from the sale of food or beverages by a charitable organization conducting bingo, or by a bona fide auxiliary unit or society of a charitable organization conducting bingo, provided all of the following apply:

(1) The auxiliary unit or society has been in existence as a bona fide auxiliary unit or society of the charitable organization for at least two years prior to conducting bingo.

(2) The person who purchases the food or beverage receives nothing of value except the food or beverage and items customarily received with the purchase of that food or beverage.

(3) The food and beverages are sold at customary and reasonable prices.

(Y) "Security personnel" includes any person who either is a sheriff, deputy sheriff, marshal, deputy marshal, township constable, or member of an organized police department of a municipal corporation or has successfully completed a peace officer's training course pursuant to sections 109.71 to 109.79 of the Revised Code and who is hired to provide security for the premises on which bingo is conducted.

(Z) "Charitable purpose" means that the net profit of bingo, other than instant bingo, is used by, or is given, donated, or otherwise transferred to, any of the following:

(1) Any organization that is described in subsection 509(a)(1), 509(a)(2), or 509(a)(3) of the Internal Revenue Code and is either a governmental unit or an organization that is tax exempt under subsection 501(a) and described in subsection 501(c)(3) of the Internal Revenue Code;

(2) A veteran's organization that is a post, chapter, or organization of veterans, or an auxiliary unit or society of, or a trust or foundation for, any such post, chapter, or organization organized in the United States or any of its possessions, at least seventy-five per cent of the members of which are veterans and substantially all of the other members of which are individuals who are spouses, widows, or widowers of veterans, or such individuals, provided that no part of the net earnings of such post, chapter, or organization inures to the benefit of any private shareholder or individual, and further provided that the net profit is used by the post, chapter, or organization for the charitable purposes set forth in division (B)(12) of section 5739.02 of the Revised Code, is used for awarding scholarships to or for attendance at an institution mentioned in division (B)(12) of section 5739.02 of the Revised Code, is donated to a governmental agency, or is used for nonprofit youth activities, the purchase of United States or Ohio flags that are donated to schools, youth groups, or other bona fide nonprofit organizations, promotion of patriotism, or disaster relief;

(3) A fraternal organization that has been in continuous existence in this state for fifteen years and that uses the net profit exclusively for religious, charitable, scientific, literary, or educational purposes, or for the prevention of cruelty to children or animals, if contributions for such use would qualify as a deductible charitable contribution under subsection 170 of the Internal Revenue Code;

(4) A volunteer firefighter's organization that uses the net profit for the purposes set forth in division (L) of this section.

(AA) "Internal Revenue Code" means the "Internal Revenue Code of 1986," 100 Stat. 2085, 26 U.S.C. 1, as now or hereafter amended.

(BB) "Youth athletic organization" means any organization, not organized for profit, that is organized and operated exclusively to provide financial support to, or to operate, athletic activities for persons who are twenty-one years of age or younger by means of sponsoring, organizing, operating, or contributing to the support of an athletic team, club, league, or association.

(CC) "Youth athletic park organization" means any organization, not organized for profit, that satisfies both of the following:

(1) It owns, operates, and maintains playing fields that satisfy both of the following:

(a) The playing fields are used at least one hundred days per year for athletic activities by one or more organizations, not organized for profit, each of which is organized and operated exclusively to provide financial support to, or to operate, athletic activities for persons who are eighteen years of age or younger by means of sponsoring, organizing, operating, or contributing to the support of an athletic team, club, league, or association.

(b) The playing fields are not used for any profit-making activity at any time during the year.

(2) It uses the proceeds of bingo it conducts exclusively for the operation, maintenance, and improvement of its playing fields of the type described in division (CC)(1) of this section.

(DD) "Amateur athletic organization" means any organization, not organized for profit, that is organized and operated exclusively to provide financial support to, or to operate, athletic activities for persons who are training for amateur athletic competition that is sanctioned by a national governing body as defined in the "Amateur Sports Act of 1978," 90 Stat. 3045, 36 U.S.C.A. 373.

(EE) "Bingo supplies" means bingo cards or sheets; instant bingo tickets or cards; electronic bingo aids; raffle tickets; punch boards; seal cards; instant bingo ticket dispensers; and devices for selecting or displaying the combination of bingo letters and numbers or raffle tickets. Items that are "bingo supplies" are not gambling devices if sold or otherwise provided, and used, in accordance with this chapter. For purposes of this chapter, "bingo supplies' ' are not to be considered equipment used to conduct a bingo game.

(FF) "Instant bingo" means a form of bingo that uses folded or banded tickets or paper cards with perforated break-open tabs, a face of which is covered or otherwise hidden from view to conceal a number, letter, or symbol, or set of numbers, letters, or symbols, some of which have been designated in advance as prize winners. "Instant bingo" includes seal cards. "Instant bingo" does not include any device that is activated by the insertion of a coin, currency, token, or an equivalent, and that contains as one of its components a video display monitor that is capable of displaying numbers, letters, symbols, or characters in winning or losing combinations.

(GG) "Seal card" means a form of instant bingo that uses instant bingo tickets in conjunction with a board or placard that contains one or more seals that, when removed or opened, reveal predesignated winning numbers, letters, or symbols.

(HH) "Raffle" means a form of bingo in which the one or more prizes are won by one or more persons who have purchased a raffle ticket. The one or more winners of the raffle are determined by drawing a ticket stub or other detachable section from a receptacle containing ticket stubs or detachable sections corresponding to all tickets sold for the raffle.

(II) "Punch board" means a board containing a number of holes or receptacles of uniform size in which are placed, mechanically and randomly, serially numbered slips of paper that may be punched or drawn from the hole or receptacle when used in conjunction with instant bingo. A player may punch or draw the numbered slips of paper from the holes or receptacles and obtain the prize established for the game if the number drawn corresponds to a winning number or, if the punch board includes the use of a seal card, a potential winning number.

(JJ) "Gross profit" means gross receipts minus the amount actually expended for the payment of prize awards.

(KK) "Net profit" means gross profit minus expenses.

(LL) "Expenses" means the reasonable amount of gross profit actually expended for all of the following:

(1) The purchase or lease of bingo supplies;

(2) The annual license fee required under section 2915.08 of the Revised Code;

(3) Bank fees and service charges for a bingo session or game account described in section 2915.10 of the Revised Code;

(4) Audits and accounting services;

(5) Safes;

(6) Cash registers;

(7) Hiring security personnel;

(8) Advertising bingo;

(9) Renting premises in which to conduct a bingo session;

(10) Tables and chairs;

(11) Expenses for maintaining and operating a charitable organization's facilities, including, but not limited to, a post home, club house, lounge, tavern, or canteen and any grounds attached to the post home, club house, lounge, tavern, or canteen;

(12) Any other product or service directly related to the conduct of bingo that is authorized in rules adopted by the attorney general under division (B)(1) of section 2915.08 of the Revised Code.

(MM) "Person" has the same meaning as in section 1.59 of the Revised Code and includes any firm or any other legal entity, however organized.

(NN) "Revoke" means to void permanently all rights and privileges of the holder of a license issued under section 2915.08, 2915.081, or 2915.082 of the Revised Code or a charitable gaming license issued by another jurisdiction.

(OO) "Suspend" means to interrupt temporarily all rights and privileges of the holder of a license issued under section 2915.08, 2915.081, or 2915.082 of the Revised Code or a charitable gaming license issued by another jurisdiction.

(PP) "Distributor" means any person who purchases or obtains bingo supplies and who does either of the following:

(1) Sells, offers for sale, or otherwise provides or offers to provide the bingo supplies to another person for use in this state;

(2) Modifies, converts, adds to, or removes parts from the bingo supplies to further their promotion or sale for use in this state.

(QQ) "Manufacturer" means any person who assembles completed bingo supplies from raw materials, other items, or subparts or who modifies, converts, adds to, or removes parts from bingo supplies to further their promotion or sale.

(RR) "Gross annual revenues" means the annual gross receipts derived from the conduct of bingo described in division (S)(1) of this section plus the annual net profit derived from the conduct of bingo described in division (S)(2) of this section.

(SS) "Instant bingo ticket dispenser" means a mechanical device that dispenses an instant bingo ticket or card as the sole item of value dispensed and that has the following characteristics:

(1) It is activated upon the insertion of United States currency.

(2) It performs no gaming functions.

(3) It does not contain a video display monitor or generate noise.

(4) It is not capable of displaying any numbers, letters, symbols, or characters in winning or losing combinations.

(5) It does not simulate or display rolling or spinning reels.

(6) It is incapable of determining whether a dispensed bingo ticket or card is a winning or nonwinning ticket or card and requires a winning ticket or card to be paid by a bingo game operator.

(7) It may provide accounting and security features to aid in accounting for the instant bingo tickets or cards it dispenses.

(8) It is not part of an electronic network and is not interactive.

(TT)(1) "Electronic bingo aid" means an electronic device used by a participant to monitor bingo cards or sheets purchased at the time and place of a bingo session and that does all of the following:

(a) It provides a means for a participant to input numbers and letters announced by a bingo caller.

(b) It compares the numbers and letters entered by the participant to the bingo faces previously stored in the memory of the device.

(c) It identifies a winning bingo pattern.

(2) "Electronic bingo aid" does not include any device into which a coin, currency, token, or an equivalent is inserted to activate play.

(UU) "Deal of instant bingo tickets" means a single game of instant bingo tickets all with the same serial number.

(VV)(1) "Slot" machine means either of the following:

(a) Any mechanical, electronic, video, or digital device that is capable of accepting anything of value, directly or indirectly, from or on behalf of a player who gives the thing of value in the hope of gain, the outcome of which is determined largely or wholly by chance;

(b) Any mechanical, electronic, video, or digital device that is capable of accepting anything of value, directly or indirectly, from or on behalf of a player to conduct or dispense bingo or a scheme or game of chance.

(2) "Slot machine" does not include a skill-based amusement machine.

(WW) "Net profit from the proceeds of the sale of instant bingo" means gross profit minus the ordinary, necessary, and reasonable expense expended for the purchase of instant bingo supplies.

(XX) "Charitable instant bingo organization" means an organization that is exempt from federal income taxation under subsection 501(a) and described in subsection 501(c)(3) of the Internal Revenue Code [2] and is a charitable organization as defined in this section. A "charitable instant bingo organization" does not include a charitable organization that is exempt from federal income taxation under subsection 501(a) and described in subsection 501(c)(3) of the Internal Revenue Code and that is created by a veteran's organization, a fraternal organization, or a sporting organization in regards to bingo conducted or assisted by a veteran's organization, a fraternal organization, or a sporting organization pursuant to section 2915.13 of the Revised Code.

(YY) "Game flare" means the board or placard that accompanies each deal of instant bingo tickets and that has printed on or affixed to it the following information for the game:

(1) The name of the game;

(2) The manufacturer's name or distinctive logo;

(3) The form number;

(4) The ticket count;

(5) The prize structure, including the number of winning instant bingo tickets by denomination and the respective winning symbol or number combinations for the winning instant bingo tickets;

(6) The cost per play;

(7) The serial number of the game.

(ZZ) "Historic railroad educational organization" means an organization that is exempt from federal income taxation under subsection 501(a) and described in subsection 501(c)(3) of the Internal Revenue Code, that owns in fee simple the tracks and the right of way of a historic railroad that the organization restores or maintains and on which the organization provides excursions as part of a program to promote tourism and educate visitors regarding the role of railroad transportation in Ohio history, and that received as donations from a charitable organization that holds a license to conduct bingo under this chapter an amount equal to at least fifty per cent of that licensed charitable organization's net proceeds from the conduct of bingo during each of the five years preceding June 30, 2003. "Historic railroad" means all or a portion of the tracks and right-of-way of a railroad that was owned and operated by a for profit common carrier in this state at any time prior to January 1, 1950.

(AAA)(1) "Skill–based amusement machine" means a skill-based amusement device, such as a mechanical, electronic, video, or digital device, or machine, whether or not the skill-based amusement machine requires payment for use through a coin or bill validator or other payment of consideration or value to participate in the machine's offering or to activate the machine, provided that all of the following apply:

(a) The machine involves a task, game, play, contest, competition, or tournament in which the player actively participates in the task, game, play, contest, competition, or tournament.

(b) The outcome of an individual's play and participation is not determined largely or wholly by chance.

(c) The outcome of play during a game is not controlled by a person not actively participating in the game.

(2) All of the following apply to any machine that is operated as described in division (AAA)(1) of this section:

(a) As used in this section, "task," "game," and "play" mean one event from the initial activation of the machine until the results of play are determined without payment of additional consideration. An individual utilizing a machine that involves a single task, game, play, contest, competition, or tournament may be awarded prizes based on the results of play.

(b) Advance play for a single task, game, play, contest, competition, or tournament participation may be purchased. The cost of the contest, competition, or tournament participation may be greater than a single non-contest, competition, or tournament play.

(c) To the extent that the machine is used in a contest, competition, or tournament, that contest, competition, or tournament has a defined starting and ending date and is open to participants in competition for scoring and ranking results toward the awarding of prizes that are stated prior to the start of the contest, competition, or tournament.

(BBB) "Pool not conducted for profit" means a scheme in which a participant gives a valuable consideration for a chance to win a prize and the total amount of consideration wagered is distributed to a participant or participants.

(CCC) "Sporting organization" means a hunting, fishing, or trapping organization, other than a college or high school fraternity or sorority, that is not organized for profit, that is affiliated with a state or national sporting organization, including but not limited to, the Ohio League of sportsmen, and that has been in continuous existence in this state for a period of three years.

(DDD) "Community action agency" has the same meaning as in section 122.66 of the Revised Code.

(2004 S 146, eff. 9–23–04; 2004 H 325, eff. 9–30–04; 2003 S 37, eff. 10–21–03; 2003 H 95, eff. 7–1–03; 2003 H 87, § 24, eff. 7–1–03; 2002 H 512, eff. 7–1–03; 1996 H 143, § 3, eff. 7–1–96; 1996 H 143, § 1, eff. 5–15–96; 1995 S 2, eff. 7–1–96; 1992 S 98, eff. 11–12–92; 1990 H 573; 1981 S 91; 1977 H 72; 1976 S 398, H 1547; 1975 H 1; 1972 H 511)

[1] 26 U.S.C.A. § 1 et seq.
[2] 26 U.S.C.A. § 1 et seq.

2915.02 Gambling; exceptions for charitable organizations

(A) No person shall do any of the following:

(1) Engage in bookmaking, or knowingly engage in conduct that facilitates bookmaking;

(2) Establish, promote, or operate or knowingly engage in conduct that facilitates any game of chance conducted for profit or any scheme of chance;

(3) Knowingly procure, transmit, exchange, or engage in conduct that facilitates the procurement, transmission, or exchange of information for use in establishing odds or determining winners in connection with bookmaking or with any game of chance conducted for profit or any scheme of chance;

(4) Engage in betting or in playing any scheme or game of chance as a substantial source of income or livelihood;

(5) With purpose to violate division (A)(1), (2), (3), or (4) of this section, acquire, possess, control, or operate any gambling device.

(B) For purposes of division (A)(1) of this section, a person facilitates bookmaking if the person in any way knowingly aids an illegal bookmaking operation, including, without limitation, placing a bet with a person engaged in or facilitating illegal bookmaking. For purposes of division (A)(2) of this section, a person facilitates a game of chance conducted for profit or a scheme of chance if the person in any way knowingly aids in the conduct or operation of any such game or scheme, including, without limitation, playing any such game or scheme.

(C) This section does not prohibit conduct in connection with gambling expressly permitted by law.

(D) This section does not apply to any of the following:

(1) Games of chance, if all of the following apply:

(a) The games of chance are not craps for money or roulette for money.

(b) The games of chance are conducted by a charitable organization that is, and has received from the internal revenue service a determination letter that is currently in effect, stating that the organization is, exempt from federal income taxation under subsection 501(a) and described in subsection 501(c)(3) of the Internal Revenue Code.

(c) The games of chance are conducted at festivals of the charitable organization that are conducted either for a period of four consecutive days or less and not more than twice a year or for a period of five consecutive days not more than once a year, and are conducted on premises owned by the charitable organization for a period of no less than one year immediately preceding the conducting of the games of chance, on premises leased from a governmental unit, or on premises that are leased from a veteran's or fraternal organization and that have been owned by the lessor veteran's or fraternal organization for a period of no less than one year immediately preceding the conducting of the games of chance.

A charitable organization shall not lease premises from a veteran's or fraternal organization to conduct a festival described in division (D)(1)(c) of this section if the veteran's or fraternal organization already has leased the premises four times during the preceding year to charitable organizations for that purpose. If a charitable organization leases premises from a veteran's or fraternal organization to conduct a festival described in division (D)(1)(c) of this section, the charitable organization shall not pay a rental rate for the premises per day of the festival that exceeds the rental rate per bingo session that a charitable organization may pay under division (B)(1) of section 2915.09 of the Revised Code when it leases premises from another charitable organization to conduct bingo games.

(d) All of the money or assets received from the games of chance after deduction only of prizes paid out during the conduct of the games of chance are used by, or given, donated, or otherwise transferred to, any organization that is described in subsection 509(a)(1), 509(a)(2), or 509(a)(3) of the Internal Revenue Code and is either a governmental unit or an organization that is tax exempt under subsection 501(a) and described in subsection 501(c)(3) of the Internal Revenue Code;

(e) The games of chance are not conducted during, or within ten hours of, a bingo game conducted for amusement purposes only pursuant to section 2915.12 of the Revised Code.

No person shall receive any commission, wage, salary, reward, tip, donation, gratuity, or other form of compensation, directly or indirectly, for operating or assisting in the operation of any game of chance.

(2) Any tag fishing tournament operated under a permit issued under section 1533.92 of the Revised Code, as "tag fishing tournament" is defined in section 1531.01 of the Revised Code;

(3) Bingo conducted by a charitable organization that holds a license issued under section 2915.08 of the Revised Code.

(E) Division (D) of this section shall not be construed to authorize the sale, lease, or other temporary or permanent transfer of the right to conduct games of chance, as granted by that division, by any charitable organization that is granted that right.

(F) Whoever violates this section is guilty of gambling, a misdemeanor of the first degree. If the offender previously has been convicted of any gambling offense, gambling is a felony of the fifth degree.

(2003 H 95, eff. 7–1–03; 2003 H 87, § 24, eff. 7–1–03; 2002 H 512, eff. 7–1–03; 1997 S 37, eff. 7–26–97; 1995 S 2, eff. 7–1–96; 1993 H 336, eff. 10–29–93; 1993 H 104; 1990 H 573, H 550; 1988 H 514; 1977 H 72; 1976 S 398, H 1547; 1972 H 511)

2915.03 Operating a gambling house

(A) No person, being the owner or lessee, or having custody, control, or supervision of premises, shall:

(1) Use or occupy such premises for gambling in violation of section 2915.02 of the Revised Code;

(2) Recklessly permit such premises to be used or occupied for gambling in violation of section 2915.02 of the Revised Code.

(B) Whoever violates this section is guilty of operating a gambling house, a misdemeanor of the first degree. If the offender previously has been convicted of a gambling offense, operating a gambling house is a felony of the fifth degree.

(C) Premises used or occupied in violation of this section constitute a nuisance subject to abatement pursuant to sections 3767.01 to 3767.99 of the Revised Code.

(1995 S 2, eff. 7–1–96; 1972 H 511, eff. 1–1–74)

2915.04 Public gaming

(A) No person, while at a hotel, restaurant, tavern, store, arena, hall, or other place of public accommodation, business, amusement, or resort shall make a bet or play any game of chance or scheme of chance.

(B) No person, being the owner or lessee, or having custody, control, or supervision, of a hotel, restaurant, tavern, store, arena, hall, or other place of public accommodation, business, amusement, or resort shall recklessly permit those premises to be used or occupied in violation of division (A) of this section.

(C) Divisions (A) and (B) of this section do not prohibit conduct in connection with gambling expressly permitted by law.

(D) Whoever violates this section is guilty of public gaming. Except as otherwise provided in this division, public gaming is a minor misdemeanor. If the offender previously has been convicted of any gambling offense, public gaming is a misdemeanor of the fourth degree.

(E) Premises used or occupied in violation of division (B) of this section constitute a nuisance subject to abatement under Chapter 3767. of the Revised Code.

(2003 H 87, § 24, eff. 7–1–03; 2002 H 512, eff. 7–1–03; 1972 H 511, eff. 1–1–74)

2915.05 Cheating

(A) No person, with purpose to defraud or knowing that the person is facilitating a fraud, shall engage in conduct designed to corrupt the outcome of any of the following:

(1) The subject of a bet;

(2) A contest of knowledge, skill, or endurance that is not an athletic or sporting event;

(3) A scheme or game of chance;

(4) Bingo.

(B) No person shall knowingly do any of the following:

(1) Offer, give, solicit, or accept anything of value to corrupt the outcome of an athletic or sporting event;

(2) Engage in conduct designed to corrupt the outcome of an athletic or sporting event.

(C)(1) Whoever violates division (A) of this section is guilty of cheating. Except as otherwise provided in this division, cheating is a misdemeanor of the first degree. If the potential gain from the cheating is five hundred dollars or more or if the offender previously has been convicted of any gambling offense or of any theft offense, as defined in section 2913.01 of the Revised Code, cheating is a felony of the fifth degree.

(2) Whoever violates division (B) of this section is guilty of corrupting sports. Corrupting sports is a felony of the fifth degree on a first offense and a felony of the fourth degree on each subsequent offense.

(2003 H 87, § 24, eff. 7–1–03; 2002 H 512, eff. 7–1–03; 1995 S 2, eff. 7–1–96; 1982 H 269, § 4, eff. 1–5–83; 1982 S 199; 1972 H 511)

CHARITABLE BINGO

2915.07 Conducting an illegal bingo game

(A) No person, except a charitable organization that has obtained a license pursuant to section 2915.08 of the Revised Code, shall conduct or advertise bingo. This division does not apply to a raffle that a charitable organization conducts or advertises.

(B) Whoever violates this section is guilty of conducting illegal bingo, a felony of the fourth degree.

(2003 H 87, § 24, eff. 7–1–03; 2002 H 512, eff. 7–1–03; 1995 S 2, eff. 7–1–96; 1976 S 398, eff. 5–26–76)

2915.08 License of charitable organization to conduct bingo or instant bingo games; temporary renewal; notice of issuance; amendment of license; rules

(A)(1) Annually before the first day of January, a charitable organization that desires to conduct bingo, instant bingo at a bingo session, or instant bingo other than at a bingo session shall make out, upon a form to be furnished by the attorney general for that purpose, an application for a license to conduct bingo, instant bingo at a bingo session, or instant bingo other than at a bingo session and deliver that application to the attorney general together with a license fee as follows:

(a) Except as otherwise provided in this division, for a license for the conduct of bingo, two hundred dollars;

(b) For a license for the conduct of instant bingo at a bingo session or instant bingo other than at a bingo session for a charitable organization that previously has not been licensed under this chapter to conduct instant bingo at a bingo session or instant bingo other than at a bingo session, a license fee of five hundred dollars, and for any other charitable organization, a license fee that is based upon the gross profits received by the charitable organization from the operation of instant bingo at a bingo session or instant bingo other than at a bingo session, during the one-year period ending on the thirty-first day of October of the year immediately preceding the year for which the license is sought, and that is one of the following:

(i) Five hundred dollars, if the total is fifty thousand dollars or less;

(ii) One thousand two hundred fifty dollars plus one-fourth per cent of the gross profit, if the total is more than fifty thousand dollars but less than two hundred fifty thousand one dollars;

(iii) Two thousand two hundred fifty dollars plus one-half per cent of the gross profit, if the total is more than two hundred fifty thousand dollars but less than five hundred thousand one dollars;

(iv) Three thousand five hundred dollars plus one per cent of the gross profit, if the total is more than five hundred thousand dollars but less than one million one dollars;

(v) Five thousand dollars plus one per cent of the gross profit, if the total is one million one dollars or more;

(c) A reduced license fee established by the attorney general pursuant to division (G) of this section.

(d) For a license to conduct bingo for a charitable organization that prior to the effective date of this amendment has not been licensed under this chapter to conduct bingo, instant bingo at a bingo session, or instant bingo other than at a bingo session, a license fee established by rule by the attorney general in accordance with division (H) of this section.

(2) The application shall be in the form prescribed by the attorney general, shall be signed and sworn to by the applicant, and shall contain all of the following:

(a) The name and post-office address of the applicant;

(b) A statement that the applicant is a charitable organization and that it has been in continuous existence as a charitable organization in this state for two years immediately preceding the making of the application or for five years in the case of a fraternal organization or a nonprofit medical organization;

(c) The location at which the organization will conduct bingo, which location shall be within the county in which the principal place of business of the applicant is located, the days of the week and the times on each of those days when bingo will be conducted, whether the organization owns, leases, or subleases the premises, and a copy of the rental agreement if it leases or subleases the premises;

(d) A statement of the applicant's previous history, record, and association that is sufficient to establish that the applicant is a charitable organization, and a copy of a determination letter that is issued by the Internal Revenue Service and states that the organization is tax exempt under subsection 501(a) and described in subsection 501(c)(3), 501(c)(4), 501(c)(7), 501(c)(8), 501(c)(10), or 501(c)(19) of the Internal Revenue Code;

(e) A statement as to whether the applicant has ever had any previous application refused, whether it previously has had a license revoked or suspended, and the reason stated by the attorney general for the refusal, revocation, or suspension;

(f) A statement of the charitable purposes for which the net profit derived from bingo, other than instant bingo, will be used, and a statement of how the net profit derived from instant bingo will be distributed in accordance with section 2915.101 of the Revised Code;

(g) Other necessary and reasonable information that the attorney general may require by rule adopted pursuant to section 111.15 of the Revised Code;

(h) If the applicant is a charitable trust as defined in section 109.23 of the Revised Code, a statement as to whether it has registered with the attorney general pursuant to section 109.26 of the Revised Code or filed annual reports pursuant to section 109.31 of the Revised Code, and, if it is not required to do either, the exemption in section 109.26 or 109.31 of the Revised Code that applies to it;

(i) If the applicant is a charitable organization as defined in section 1716.01 of the Revised Code, a statement as to whether it has filed with the attorney general a registration statement pursuant to section 1716.02 of the Revised Code and a financial report pursuant to section 1716.04 of the Revised Code, and, if it is not required to do both, the exemption in section 1716.03 of the Revised Code that applies to it;

(j) In the case of an applicant seeking to qualify as a youth athletic park organization, a statement issued by a board or body vested with authority under Chapter 755. of the Revised Code for the supervision and maintenance of recreation facilities in the territory in which the organization is located, certifying that the playing fields owned by the organization were used for at least one hundred days during the year in which the statement is issued, and were open for use to all residents of that territory, regardless of race, color, creed, religion, sex, or national origin, for athletic activities by youth athletic organizations that do not discriminate on the basis of race, color, creed, religion, sex, or national origin, and that the fields were not used for any profit-making activity at any time during the year. That type of board or body is authorized to issue the statement upon request and shall issue the statement if it finds that the applicant's playing fields were so used.

(3) The attorney general, within thirty days after receiving a timely filed application from a charitable organization that has been issued a license under this section that has not expired and has not been revoked or suspended, shall send a temporary permit to the applicant specifying the date on which the application was filed with the attorney general and stating that, pursuant to section 119.06 of the Revised Code, the applicant may continue to conduct bingo until a new license is granted or, if the application is rejected, until fifteen days after notice of the rejection is mailed to the applicant. The temporary permit does not affect the validity of the applicant's application and does not grant any rights to the applicant except those rights specifically granted in section 119.06 of the Revised Code. The issuance of a

temporary permit by the attorney general pursuant to this division does not prohibit the attorney general from rejecting the applicant's application because of acts that the applicant committed, or actions that the applicant failed to take, before or after the issuance of the temporary permit.

(4) Within thirty days after receiving an initial license application from a charitable organization to conduct bingo, instant bingo at a bingo session, or instant bingo other than at a bingo session, the attorney general shall conduct a preliminary review of the application and notify the applicant regarding any deficiencies. Once an application is deemed complete, or beginning on the thirtieth day after the application is filed, if the attorney general failed to notify the applicant of any deficiencies, the attorney general shall have an additional sixty days to conduct an investigation and either grant or deny the application based on findings established and communicated in accordance with divisions (B) and (E) of this section. As an option to granting or denying an initial license application, the attorney general may grant a temporary license and request additional time to conduct the investigation if the attorney general has cause to believe that additional time is necessary to complete the investigation and has notified the applicant in writing about the specific concerns raised during the investigation.

(B)(1) The attorney general shall adopt rules to enforce sections 2915.01, 2915.02, and 2915.07 to 2915.13 of the Revised Code to ensure that bingo or instant bingo is conducted in accordance with those sections and to maintain proper control over the conduct of bingo or instant bingo. The rules, except rules adopted pursuant to divisions (A)(2)(g) and (G) of this section, shall be adopted pursuant to Chapter 119. of the Revised Code. The attorney general shall license charitable organizations to conduct bingo, instant bingo at a bingo session, or instant bingo other than at a bingo session in conformance with this chapter and with the licensing provisions of Chapter 119. of the Revised Code.

(2) The attorney general may refuse to grant a license to any organization, or revoke or suspend the license of any organization, that does any of the following or to which any of the following applies:

(a) Fails or has failed at any time to meet any requirement of section 109.26, 109.31, or 1716.02, or sections 2915.07 to 2915.11 of the Revised Code, or violates or has violated any provision of sections 2915.02 or 2915.07 to 2915.13 of the Revised Code or any rule adopted by the attorney general pursuant to this section;

(b) Makes or has made an incorrect or false statement that is material to the granting of the license in an application filed pursuant to division (A) of this section;

(c) Submits or has submitted any incorrect or false information relating to an application if the information is material to the granting of the license;

(d) Maintains or has maintained any incorrect or false information that is material to the granting of the license in the records required to be kept pursuant to divisions (A) and (C) of section 2915.10 of the Revised Code, if applicable;

(e) The attorney general has good cause to believe that the organization will not conduct bingo, instant bingo at a bingo session, or instant bingo other than at a bingo session in accordance with sections 2915.07 to 2915.13 of the Revised Code or with any rule adopted by the attorney general pursuant to this section.

(3) For the purposes of division (B) of this section, any action of an officer, trustee, agent, representative, or bingo game operator of an organization is an action of the organization.

(C) The attorney general may grant licenses to charitable organizations that are branches, lodges, or chapters of national charitable organizations.

(D) The attorney general shall send notice in writing to the prosecuting attorney and sheriff of the county in which the organization will conduct bingo, instant bingo at a bingo session, or instant bingo other than at a bingo session, as stated in its application for a license or amended license, and to any other law enforcement agency in that county that so requests, of all of the following:

(1) The issuance of the license;

(2) The issuance of the amended license;

(3) The rejection of an application for and refusal to grant a license;

(4) The revocation of any license previously issued;

(5) The suspension of any license previously issued.

(E) A license issued by the attorney general shall set forth the information contained on the application of the charitable organization that the attorney general determines is relevant, including, but not limited to, the location at which the organization will conduct bingo, instant bingo at a bingo session, or instant bingo other than at a bingo session and the days of the week and the times on each of those days when bingo will be conducted. If the attorney general refuses to grant or revokes or suspends a license, the attorney general shall notify the applicant in writing and specifically identify the reason for the refusal, revocation, or suspension in narrative form and, if applicable, by identifying the section of the Revised Code violated. The failure of the attorney general to give the written notice of the reasons for the refusal, revocation, or suspension or a mistake in the written notice does not affect the validity of the attorney general's refusal to grant, or the revocation or suspension of, a license. If the attorney general fails to give the written notice or if there is a mistake in the written notice, the applicant may bring an action to compel the attorney general to comply with this division or to correct the mistake, but the attorney general's order refusing to grant, or revoking or suspending, a license shall not be enjoined during the pendency of the action.

(F) A charitable organization that has been issued a license pursuant to division (B) of this section but that cannot conduct bingo or instant bingo at the location, or on the day of the week or at the time, specified on the license due to circumstances that make it impractical to do so may apply in writing, together with an application fee of two hundred fifty dollars, to the attorney general, at least thirty days prior to a change in location, day of the week, or time, and request an amended license. The application shall describe the causes making it impractical for the organization to conduct bingo or instant bingo in conformity with its license and shall indicate the location, days of the week, and times on each of those days when it desires to conduct bingo or instant bingo. Except as otherwise provided in this division, the attorney general shall issue the amended license in accordance with division (E) of this section, and the organization shall surrender its original license to the attorney general. The attorney general may refuse to grant an amended license according to the terms of division (B) of this section.

(G) The attorney general, by rule adopted pursuant to section 111.15 of the Revised Code, shall establish a schedule of reduced license fees for charitable organizations that desire to conduct bingo or instant bingo during fewer than twenty-six weeks in any calendar year.

(H) The attorney general, by rule adopted pursuant to section 111.15 of the Revised Code, shall establish license fees for the conduct of bingo, instant bingo at a bingo session, or instant bingo other than at a bingo session for charitable organizations that prior to the effective date of this amendment have not been licensed to conduct bingo, instant bingo at a bingo session, or instant bingo other than at a bingo session under this chapter.

(I) The attorney general may enter into a written contract with any other state agency to delegate to that state agency the powers prescribed to the attorney general under Chapter 2915. of the Revised Code.

(J) The attorney general, by rule adopted pursuant to section 111.15 of the Revised Code, may adopt rules to determine the requirements for a charitable organization that is exempt from federal income taxation under subsection 501(a) and described in subsection 501(c)(3) of the Internal Revenue Code to be in good standing in the state.

(2003 H 95, eff. 7–1–03; 2003 H 87, § 24, eff. 7–1–03; 2002 H 512, eff. 7–1–03; 2000 S 333, eff. 4–1–01; 1993 H 104, eff. 10–7–93; 1983 H 291; 1982 S 550; 1981 S 91; 1977 H 72; 1976 S 398, H 1547)

2915.081 Distributor license for bingo supplies

(A) No distributor shall sell, offer to sell, or otherwise provide or offer to provide bingo supplies to another person, or modify, convert, add to, or remove parts from bingo supplies to further their promotion or sale, for use in this state without having obtained a license from the attorney general under this section.

(B) The attorney general may issue a distributor license to any person that meets the requirements of this section. The application for the license shall be on a form prescribed by the attorney general and be accompanied by the annual fee prescribed by this section. The license is valid for a period of one year, and the annual fee for the license is five thousand dollars.

(C) The attorney general may refuse to issue a distributor license to any person to which any of the following applies, or to any person that has an officer, partner, or other person who has an ownership interest of ten per cent or more and to whom any of the following applies:

(1) The person, officer, or partner has been convicted of a felony under the laws of this state, another state, or the United States.

(2) The person, officer, or partner has been convicted of any gambling offense.

(3) The person, officer, or partner has made an incorrect or false statement that is material to the granting of a license in an application submitted to the attorney general under this section or in a similar application submitted to a gambling licensing authority in another jurisdiction if the statement resulted in license revocation through administrative action in the other jurisdiction.

(4) The person, officer, or partner has submitted any incorrect or false information relating to the application to the attorney general under this section, if the information is material to the granting of the license.

(5) The person, officer, or partner has failed to correct any incorrect or false information that is material to the granting of the license in the records required to be maintained under division (E) of section 2915.10 of the Revised Code.

(6) The person, officer, or partner has had a license related to gambling revoked or suspended under the laws of this state, another state, or the United States.

(D) The attorney general shall not issue a distributor license to any person that is involved in the conduct of bingo on behalf of a charitable organization or that is a lessor of premises used for the conduct of bingo. This division does not prohibit a distributor from advising charitable organizations on the use and benefit of specific bingo supplies or prohibit a distributor from advising a customer on operational methods to improve bingo profitability.

(E)(1) No distributor shall sell, offer to sell, or otherwise provide or offer to provide bingo supplies to any person, or modify, convert, add to, or remove parts from bingo supplies to further their promotion or sale, for use in this state except to or for the use of a charitable organization that has been issued a license under section 2915.08 of the Revised Code or to another distributor that has been issued a license under this section. No distributor shall accept payment for the sale or other provision of bingo supplies other than by check.

(2) No distributor may donate, give, loan, lease, or otherwise provide any bingo supplies or equipment, or modify, convert, add to, or remove parts from bingo supplies to further their promotion or sale, to or for the use of a charitable organization for use in a bingo session conditioned on or in consideration for an exclusive right to provide bingo supplies to the charitable organization. A distributor may provide a licensed charitable organization with free samples of the distributor's products to be used as prizes or to be used for the purpose of sampling.

(3) No distributor shall purchase bingo supplies for use in this state from any person except from a manufacturer issued a license under section 2915.082 of the Revised Code or from another distributor issued a license under this section. Subject to division (D) of section 2915.082 of the Revised Code, no distributor shall pay for purchased bingo supplies other than by check.

(4) No distributor shall participate in the conduct of bingo on behalf of a charitable organization or have any direct or indirect ownership interest in a premises used for the conduct of bingo.

(5) No distributor shall knowingly solicit, offer, pay, or receive any kickback, bribe, or undocumented rebate, directly or indirectly, overtly or covertly, in cash or in kind, in return for providing bingo supplies to any person in this state.

(F) The attorney general may suspend or revoke a distributor license for any of the reasons for which the attorney general may refuse to issue a distributor license specified in division (C) of this section or if the distributor holding the license violates any provision of this chapter or any rule adopted by the attorney general under this chapter.

(G) Whoever violates division (A) or (E) of this section is guilty of illegally operating as a distributor. Except as otherwise provided in this division, illegally operating as a distributor is a misdemeanor of the first degree. If the offender previously has been convicted of a violation of division (A) or (E) of this section, illegally operating as a distributor is a felony of the fifth degree.

(2004 H 325, eff. 9–30–04; 2003 H 95, eff. 7–1–03; 2003 H 87, § 24, eff. 7–1–03; 2002 H 512, eff. 7–1–03)

2915.082 Manufacturer license for bingo supplies

(A) No manufacturer shall sell, offer to sell, or otherwise provide or offer to provide bingo supplies for use in this state without having obtained a license from the attorney general under this section.

(B) The attorney general may issue a manufacturer license to any person that meets the requirements of this section. The application for the license shall be on a form prescribed by the attorney general and be accompanied by the annual fee prescribed by this section. The license is valid for a period of one year, and the annual fee for the license is five thousand dollars.

(C) The attorney general may refuse to issue a manufacturer license to any person to which any of the following applies, or to any person that has an officer, partner, or other person who has an ownership interest of ten per cent or more and to whom any of the following applies:

(1) The person, officer, or partner has been convicted of a felony under the laws of this state, another state, or the United States.

(2) The person, officer, or partner has been convicted of any gambling offense.

(3) The person, officer, or partner has made an incorrect or false statement that is material to the granting of a license in an application submitted to the attorney general under this section or in a similar application submitted to a gambling licensing authority in another jurisdiction if the statement resulted in license revocation through administrative action in the other jurisdiction.

(4) The person, officer, or partner has submitted any incorrect or false information relating to the application to the attorney general under this section, if the information is material to the granting of the license.

(5) The person, officer, or partner has failed to correct any incorrect or false information that is material to the granting of the license in the records required to be maintained under division (F) of section 2915.10 of the Revised Code.

(6) The person, officer, or partner has had a license related to gambling revoked or suspended under the laws of this state, another state, or the United States.

(D)(1) No manufacturer shall sell, offer to sell, or otherwise provide or offer to provide bingo supplies to any person for use in this state except to a distributor that has been issued a license under section 2915.081 of the Revised Code. No manufacturer shall accept payment for the sale of bingo supplies other than by check.

(2) No manufacturer shall knowingly solicit, offer, pay, or receive any kickback, bribe, or undocumented rebate, directly or indirectly, overtly or covertly, in cash or in kind, in return for providing bingo supplies to any person in this state.

(E)(1) The attorney general may suspend or revoke a manufacturer license for any of the reasons for which the attorney general may refuse to issue a manufacturer license specified in division (C) of this section or if the manufacturer holding the license violates any provision of this chapter or any rule adopted by the attorney general under this chapter.

(2) The attorney general may perform an onsite inspection of a manufacturer of bingo supplies that is selling, offering to sell, or otherwise providing or offering to provide bingo supplies or that is applying for a license to sell, offer to sell, or otherwise provide or offer to provide bingo supplies in this state.

(F) Whoever violates division (A) or (D) of this section is guilty of illegally operating as a manufacturer. Except as otherwise provided in this division, illegally operating as a manufacturer is a misdemeanor of the first degree. If the offender previously has been convicted of a violation of division (A) or (D) of this section, illegally operating as a manufacturer is a felony of the fifth degree.

(2003 H 95, eff. 7–1–03; 2003 H 87, § 24, eff. 7–1–03; 2002 H 512, eff. 7–1–03)

2915.09 Methods of conducting a licensed bingo game; prohibitions

(A) No charitable organization that conducts bingo shall fail to do any of the following:

(1) Own all of the equipment used to conduct bingo or lease that equipment from a charitable organization that is licensed to conduct bingo for a rental rate that is not more than is customary and reasonable for that equipment;

(2) Except as otherwise provided in division (A)(3) of this section, use all of the gross receipts from bingo for paying prizes, for reimbursement of expenses for or for renting premises in which to conduct a bingo session, for reimbursement of expenses for or for purchasing or leasing bingo supplies used in conducting bingo, for reimbursement of expenses for or for hiring security personnel, for reimbursement of expenses for or for advertising bingo, or for reimbursement of other expenses or for other expenses listed in division (LL) of section 2915.01 of the Revised Code, provided that the amount of the receipts so spent is not more than is customary and reasonable for a similar purchase, lease, hiring, advertising, or expense. If the building in which bingo is conducted is owned by the charitable organization conducting bingo and the bingo conducted includes a form of bingo described in division (S)(1) of section 2915.01 of the Revised Code, the charitable organization may deduct from the total amount of the gross receipts from each session a sum equal to the lesser of six hundred dollars or forty-five per cent of the gross receipts from the bingo described in that division as consideration for the use of the premises.

(3) Use, or give, donate, or otherwise transfer, all of the net profit derived from bingo, other than instant bingo, for a charitable purpose listed in its license application and described in division (Z) of section 2915.01 of the Revised Code, or distribute all of the net profit from the proceeds of the sale of instant bingo as stated in its license application and in accordance with section 2915.101 of the Revised Code.

(B) No charitable organization that conducts a bingo game described in division (S)(1) of section 2915.01 of the Revised Code shall fail to do any of the following:

(1) Conduct the bingo game on premises that are owned by the charitable organization, on premises that are owned by another charitable organization and leased from that charitable organization for a rental rate not in excess of the lesser of six hundred dollars per bingo session or forty-five per cent of the gross receipts of the bingo session, on premises that are leased from a person other than a charitable organization for a rental rate that is not more than is customary and reasonable for premises that are similar in location, size, and quality but not in excess of four hundred fifty dollars per bingo session, or on premises that are owned by a person other than a charitable organization, that are leased from that person by another charitable organization, and that are subleased from that other charitable organization by the charitable organization for a rental rate not in excess of four hundred fifty dollars per bingo session. If the charitable organization leases from a person other than a charitable organization the premises on which it conducts bingo sessions, the lessor of the premises shall provide only the premises to the organization and shall not provide the organization with bingo game operators, security personnel, concessions or concession operators, bingo supplies, or any other type of service or equipment. A charitable organization shall not lease or sublease premises that it owns or leases to more than one other charitable organization per calendar week for the purpose of conducting bingo sessions on the premises. A person that is not a charitable organization shall not lease premises that it owns, leases, or otherwise is empowered to lease to more than one charitable organization per calendar week for conducting bingo sessions on the premises. In no case shall more than two bingo sessions be conducted on any premises in any calendar week.

(2) Display its license conspicuously at the premises where the bingo session is conducted;

(3) Conduct the bingo session in accordance with the definition of bingo set forth in division (S)(1) of section 2915.01 of the Revised Code.

(C) No charitable organization that conducts a bingo game described in division (S)(1) of section 2915.01 of the Revised Code shall do any of the following:

(1) Pay any compensation to a bingo game operator for operating a bingo session that is conducted by the charitable organization or for preparing, selling, or serving food or beverages at the site of the bingo session, permit any auxiliary unit or society of the charitable organization to pay compensation to any bingo game operator who prepares, sells, or serves food or beverages at a bingo session conducted by the charitable organization, or permit any auxiliary unit or society of the charitable organization to prepare, sell, or serve food or beverages at a bingo session

conducted by the charitable organization, if the auxiliary unit or society pays any compensation to the bingo game operators who prepare, sell, or serve the food or beverages;

(2) Pay consulting fees to any person for any services performed in relation to the bingo session;

(3) Pay concession fees to any person who provides refreshments to the participants in the bingo session;

(4) Except as otherwise provided in division (C)(4) of this section, conduct more than two bingo sessions in any seven-day period. A volunteer firefighter's organization or a volunteer rescue service organization that conducts not more than five bingo sessions in a calendar year may conduct more than two bingo sessions in a seven-day period after notifying the attorney general when it will conduct the sessions.

(5) Pay out more than three thousand five hundred dollars in prizes for bingo games described in division (S)(1) of section 2915.01 of the Revised Code during any bingo session that is conducted by the charitable organization. "Prizes" does not include awards from the conduct of instant bingo.

(6) Conduct a bingo session at any time during the ten-hour period between midnight and ten a.m., at any time during, or within ten hours of, a bingo game conducted for amusement only pursuant to section 2915.12 of the Revised Code, at any premises not specified on its license, or on any day of the week or during any time period not specified on its license. Division (A)(6) of this section does not prohibit the sale of instant bingo tickets beginning at nine a.m. for a bingo session that begins at ten a.m. If circumstances make it impractical for the charitable organization to conduct a bingo session at the premises, or on the day of the week or at the time, specified on its license or if a charitable organization wants to conduct bingo sessions on a day of the week or at a time other than the day or time specified on its license, the charitable organization may apply in writing to the attorney general for an amended license pursuant to division (F) of section 2915.08 of the Revised Code. A charitable organization may apply twice in each calendar year for an amended license to conduct bingo sessions on a day of the week or at a time other than the day or time specified on its license. If the amended license is granted, the organization may conduct bingo sessions at the premises, on the day of the week, and at the time specified on its amended license.

(7) Permit any person whom the charitable organization knows, or should have known, is under the age of eighteen to work as a bingo game operator;

(8) Permit any person whom the charitable organization knows, or should have known, has been convicted of a felony or gambling offense in any jurisdiction to be a bingo game operator;

(9) Permit the lessor of the premises on which the bingo session is conducted, if the lessor is not a charitable organization, to provide the charitable organization with bingo game operators, security personnel, concessions, bingo supplies, or any other type of service or equipment;

(10) Purchase or lease bingo supplies from any person except a distributor issued a license under section 2915.081 of the Revised Code;

(11)(a) Use or permit the use of electronic bingo aids except under the following circumstances:

(i) For any single participant, not more than ninety bingo faces can be played using an electronic bingo aid or aids.

(ii) The charitable organization shall provide a participant using an electronic bingo aid with corresponding paper bingo cards or sheets.

(iii) The total price of bingo faces played with an electronic bingo aid shall be equal to the total price of the same number of bingo faces played with a paper bingo card or sheet sold at the same bingo session but without an electronic bingo aid.

(iv) An electronic bingo aid cannot be part of an electronic network other than a network that includes only bingo aids and devices that are located on the premises at which the bingo is being conducted or be interactive with any device not located on the premises at which the bingo is being conducted.

(v) An electronic bingo aid cannot be used to participate in bingo that is conducted at a location other than the location at which the bingo session is conducted and at which the electronic bingo aid is used.

(vi) An electronic bingo aid cannot be used to provide for the input of numbers and letters announced by a bingo caller other than the bingo caller who physically calls the numbers and letters at the location at which the bingo session is conducted and at which the electronic bingo aid is used.

(b) The attorney general may adopt rules in accordance with Chapter 119. of the Revised Code that govern the use of electronic bingo aids. The rules may include a requirement that an electronic bingo aid be capable of being audited by the attorney general to verify the number of bingo cards or sheets played during each bingo session.

(12) Permit any person the charitable organization knows, or should have known, to be under eighteen years of age to play bingo described in division (S)(1) of section 2915.01 of the Revised Code.

(D)(1) Except as otherwise provided in division (D)(3) of this section, no charitable organization shall provide to a bingo game operator, and no bingo game operator shall receive or accept, any commission, wage, salary, reward, tip, donation, gratuity, or other form of compensation, directly or indirectly, regardless of the source, for conducting bingo or providing other work or labor at the site of bingo during a bingo session.

(2) Except as otherwise provided in division (D)(3) of this section, no charitable organization shall provide to a bingo game operator any commission, wage, salary, reward, tip, donation, gratuity, or other form of compensation, directly or indirectly, regardless of the source, for conducting instant bingo other than at a bingo session at the site of instant bingo other than at a bingo session.

(3) Nothing in division (D) of this section prohibits an employee of a fraternal organization, veteran's organization, or sporting organization from selling instant bingo tickets or cards to the organization's members or invited guests, as long as no portion of the employee's compensation is paid from any receipts of bingo.

(E) Notwithstanding division (B)(1) of this section, a charitable organization that, prior to December 6, 1977, has entered into written agreements for the lease of premises it owns to another charitable organization or other charitable organizations for the conducting of bingo sessions so that more than two bingo sessions are conducted per calendar week on the premises, and a person that is not a charitable organization and that, prior to December 6, 1977, has entered into written agreements for the lease of premises it owns to charitable organizations for the conducting of more than two bingo sessions per calendar week on the premises, may continue to lease the premises to those charitable organizations, provided that no more than four sessions are conducted per calendar week, that the lessor organization or person has notified the attorney general in writing of the organizations that will conduct the sessions and the days of the week and the times of the day on which the sessions will be conducted, that the initial lease entered into with each organization that will conduct the sessions was filed with the attorney general prior to December 6, 1977, and that each organization that will conduct the sessions was issued a license to conduct bingo games by the attorney general prior to December 6, 1977.

(F) This section does not prohibit a bingo licensed charitable organization or a game operator from giving any person an instant bingo ticket as a prize.

(G) Whoever violates division (A)(2) of this section is guilty of illegally conducting a bingo game, a felony of the fourth degree. Except as otherwise provided in this division, whoever violates division (A)(1) or (3), (B)(1), (2), or (3), (C)(1) to (12), or (D) of this section is guilty of a minor misdemeanor. If the offender previously has been convicted of a violation of division (A)(1) or (3), (B)(1), (2), or (3), (C)(1) to (11), or, (D) of this section, a violation of division (A)(1) or (3), (B)(1), (2), or (3), (C), or (D) of this section is a misdemeanor of the first degree. Whoever violates division (C)(12) of this section is guilty of a misdemeanor of the first degree, if the offender previously has been convicted of a violation of division (C)(12) of this section, a felony of the fourth degree.

(2004 H 325, eff. 9–30–04; 2003 H 95, eff. 7–1–03; 2003 H 87, § 24, eff. 7–1–03; 2002 H 512, eff. 7–1–03; 1995 S 2, eff. 7–1–96; 1995 S 70, eff. 3–5–96; 1993 H 104, eff. 10–7–93; 1990 H 573; 1981 S 91; 1977 H 72; 1976 S 398, H 1547)

2915.091 Prohibitions where instant bingo game is conducted

(A) No charitable organization that conducts instant bingo shall do any of the following:

(1) Fail to comply with the requirements of divisions (A)(1), (2), and (3) of section 2915.09 of the Revised Code;

(2) Conduct instant bingo unless either of the following apply:

(a) That organization is, and has received from the internal revenue service a determination letter that is currently in effect stating that the organization is, exempt from federal income taxation under subsection 501(a), is described in subsection 501(c)(3) [1] of the Internal Revenue Code, is a charitable organization as defined in section 2915.01 of the Revised Code, is in good standing in the state pursuant to section 2915.08 of the Revised Code, and is in compliance with Chapter 1716. of the Revised Code;

(b) That organization is, and has received from the internal revenue service a determination letter that is currently in effect stating that the organization is, exempt from federal income taxation under subsection 501(a), is described in subsection 501(c)(7), 501(c)(8), 501(c)(10), or 501(c)(19) or is a veteran's organization described in subsection 501(c)(4) of the Internal Revenue Code, and conducts instant bingo under section 2915.13 of the Revised Code.

(3) Conduct instant bingo on any day, at any time, or at any premises not specified on the organization's license issued pursuant to section 2915.08 of the Revised Code;

(4) Permit any person whom the organization knows or should have known has been convicted of a felony or gambling offense in any jurisdiction to be a bingo game operator in the conduct of instant bingo;

(5) Purchase or lease supplies used to conduct instant bingo or punch board games from any person except a distributor licensed under section 2915. 081 of the Revised Code;

(6) Sell or provide any instant bingo ticket or card for a price different from the price printed on it by the manufacturer on either the instant bingo ticket or card or on the game flare;

(7) Sell an instant bingo ticket or card to a person under eighteen years of age;

(8) Fail to keep unsold instant bingo tickets or cards for less than three years;

(9) Pay any compensation to a bingo game operator for conducting instant bingo that is conducted by the organization or for preparing, selling, or serving food or beverages at the site of the instant bingo game, permit any auxiliary unit or society of the organization to pay compensation to any bingo game operator who prepares, sells, or serves food or beverages at an instant bingo game conducted by the organization, or permit any auxiliary unit or society of the organization to prepare, sell, or serve food or beverages at an instant bingo game conducted by the organization, if the auxiliary unit or society pays any compensation to the bingo game operators who prepare, sell, or serve the food or beverages;

(10) Pay fees to any person for any services performed in relation to an instant bingo game;

(11) Pay fees to any person who provides refreshments to the participants in an instant bingo game;

(12)(a) Allow instant bingo tickets or cards to be sold to bingo game operators at a premises at which the organization sells instant bingo tickets or cards or to be sold to employees of a D permit holder who are working at a premises at which instant bingo tickets or cards are sold;

(b) Division (A)(12)(a) of this section does not prohibit a licensed charitable organization or a bingo game operator from giving any person an instant bingo tickets as a prize.

(13) Fail to display its bingo license, and the serial numbers of the deal of instant bingo tickets or cards to be sold, conspicuously at each premises at which it sells instant bingo tickets or cards;

(14) Possess a deal of instant bingo tickets or cards that was not purchased from a distributor licensed under section 2915.081 of the Revised Code as reflected on an invoice issued by the distributor that contains all of the information required by division (E) of section 2915.10 of the Revised Code;

(15) Fail, once it opens a deal of instant bingo tickets or cards, to continue to sell the tickets or cards in that deal until the tickets or cards with the top two highest tiers of prizes in that deal are sold;

(16) Purchase, lease, or use instant bingo ticket dispensers to sell instant bingo tickets or cards;

(17) Possess bingo supplies that were not obtained in accordance with sections 2915.01 to 2915.13 of the Revised Code.

(B) A charitable organization may conduct instant bingo other than at a bingo session at not more than five separate locations. A charitable organization that is exempt from federal taxation under subsection 501(a) and described in subsection 501(c)(3) [2] of the Internal Revenue Code and that is created by a veteran's organization or a fraternal organization is not limited in the number of separate locations the charitable organization may conduct instant bingo other than at a bingo session.

(C) The attorney general may adopt rules in accordance with Chapter 119. of the Revised Code that govern the conduct of instant bingo by charitable organizations. Before those rules are adopted, the attorney general shall reference the recommended standards for opacity, randomization, minimum information, winner protection, color, and cutting for instant bingo tickets or cards, seal cards, and punch boards established by the North American gaming regulators association.

(D) Whoever violates division (A) of this section or a rule adopted under division (C) of this section is guilty of illegal instant bingo conduct. Except as otherwise provided in this division, illegal instant bingo conduct is a misdemeanor of the first degree. If the offender previously has been convicted of a violation of division (A) of this section or of such a rule, illegal instant bingo conduct is a felony of the fifth degree.

(2003 H 95, eff. 7–1–03; 2003 H 87, § 24, eff. 7–1–03; 2002 H 512, eff. 7–1–03)

1 26 U.S.C.A. § 1 et seq.

2 26 U.S.C.A. § 1 et seq.

2915.092 Raffle drawings

(A)(1) Subject to division (A)(2) of this section, a charitable organization, a public school, a chartered nonpublic school, a community school, or a veteran's organization, fraternal organization, or sporting organization that is exempt from federal income taxation under subsection 501(a) and is described in subsection 501(c)(3), 501(c)(4), 501(c)(7), 501(c)(8), 501(c)(10), or 501(c)(19) of the Internal Revenue Code [1] may conduct a raffle to raise money for the organization or school and does not need a license to conduct bingo in order to conduct a raffle drawing that is not for profit.

(2) If a charitable organization that is described in division (A)(1) of this section, but that is not also described in subsection 501(c)(3) of the Internal Revenue Code, conducts a raffle, the charitable organization shall distribute at least fifty per cent of the net profit from the raffle to a charitable purpose described in division (Z) of section 2915.01 of the Revised Code or to a department or agency of the federal government, the state, or any political subdivision.

(B) Except as provided in division (A) or (B) of this section, no person shall conduct a raffle drawing that is for profit or a raffle drawing that is not for profit.

(C) Whoever violates division (B) of this section is guilty of illegal conduct of a raffle. Except as otherwise provided in this division, illegal conduct of a raffle is a misdemeanor of the first degree. If the offender previously has been convicted of a violation of division (B) of this section, illegal conduct of a raffle is a felony of the fifth degree.

(2004 S 146, eff. 9–23–04; 2004 H 325, eff. 9–30–04; 2003 H 95, eff. 7–1–03; 2003 H 87, § 24, eff. 7–1–03; 2002 H 512, eff. 7–1–03)

[1] 26 U.S.C.A. § 1 et seq.

2915.093 Instant bingo other than at bingo session

(A) As used in this section, "retail income from all commercial activity" means the income that a person receives from the provision of goods, services, or activities that are provided at the location where instant bingo other than at a bingo session is conducted, including the sale of instant bingo tickets. A religious organization that is exempt from federal income taxation under subsection 501(a) and described in subsection 501(c)(3) of the Internal Revenue Code, at not more than one location at which it conducts its charitable programs, may include donations from its members and guests as retail income.

(B) A charitable instant bingo organization may conduct instant bingo other than at a bingo session at not more than five separate locations.

(C)(1) If a charitable instant bingo organization conducts instant bingo other than at a bingo session, the charitable instant bingo organization shall enter into a written contract with the owner or lessor of the location at which the instant bingo is conducted to allow the owner or lessor to assist in the conduct of instant bingo other than at a bingo session, identify each location where the instant bingo other than at a bingo session is being conducted, and identify the owner or lessor of each location.

(2) A charitable instant bingo organization that conducts instant bingo other than at a bingo session is not required to enter into a written contract with the owner or lessor of the location at which the instant bingo is conducted, provided that the owner or lessor is not assisting in the conduct of the instant bingo other than at a bingo session and provided that the conduct of the instant bingo other than at a bingo session at that location is not more than five days per calendar year and not more than ten hours per day.

(D) Except as provided in division (G) of this section, no charitable instant bingo organization shall conduct instant bingo other than at a bingo session at a location where the primary source of retail income from all commercial activity at that location is the sale of instant bingo tickets.

(E) The owner or lessor of a location that enters into a contract pursuant to division (C) of this section shall pay the full gross profit to the charitable instant bingo organization, in return for the deal of instant bingo tickets. The owner or lessor may retain the money that the owner or lessor receives for selling the instant bingo tickets, provided, however, that after the deal has been sold, the owner or lessor shall pay to the charitable instant bingo organization the value of any unredeemed instant bingo prizes remaining in the deal of instant bingo tickets.

As used in this division, "full gross profit" means the amount by which the total receipts of all instant bingo tickets, if the deal had been sold in full, exceeds the amount that would be paid out if all prizes were redeemed.

(F) A charitable instant bingo organization shall provide the attorney general with all of the following information:

(1) That the charitable instant bingo organization has terminated a contract entered into pursuant to division (C) of this section with an owner or lessor of a location;

(2) That the charitable instant bingo organization has entered into a written contract pursuant to division (C) of this section with a new owner or lessor of a location;

(3) That the charitable instant bingo organization is aware of conduct by the owner or lessor of a location at which instant bingo is conducted that is in violation of this chapter.

(G) Division (D) of this section does not apply to a volunteer firefighter's organization that is exempt from federal income taxation under subsection 501(a) and described in subsection 501(c)(3) of the Internal Revenue Code, that conducts instant bingo other than at a bingo session on the premises where the organization conducts firefighter training, that has conducted instant bingo continuously for at least five years prior to July 1, 2003, and that, during each of those five years, had gross receipts of at least one million five hundred thousand dollars.

(2004 H 325, eff. 9–30–04; 2003 H 95, eff. 7–1–03; 2003 H 87, § 24, eff. 7–1–03; 2002 H 512, eff. 7–1–03)

2915.094 Restrictions on owner or lessor of location of instant bingo

(A) No owner or lessor of a location shall assist a charitable instant bingo organization in the conduct of instant bingo other than at a bingo session at that location unless the owner or lessor has entered into a written contract, as described in division (C) of section 2915.093 of the Revised Code, with the charitable instant bingo organization to assist in the conduct of instant bingo other than at a bingo session.

(B) The location of the lessor or owner shall be designated as a location where the charitable instant bingo organization conducts instant bingo other than at a bingo session.

(C) No owner or lessor of a location that enters into a written contract as prescribed in division (A) of this section shall violate any provision of Chapter 2915. of the Revised Code, or permit, aid, or abet any other person in violating any provision of Chapter 2915. of the Revised Code.

(D) No owner or lessor of a location that enters into a written contract as prescribed in division (A) of this section shall violate the terms of the contract.

(E)(1) Whoever violates division (C) or (D) of this section is guilty of illegal instant bingo conduct. Except as otherwise provided in this division, illegal instant bingo conduct is a misdemeanor of the first degree. If the offender previously has been convicted of a violation of division (C) or (D) of this section, illegal instant bingo conduct is a felony of the fifth degree.

(2) If an owner or lessor of a location knowingly, intentionally, or recklessly violates division (C) or (D) of this section, any license that the owner or lessor holds for the retail sale of any goods on the owner's or lessor's premises that is issued by the state or a political subdivision is subject to suspension, revocation, or payment of a monetary penalty at the request of the attorney general.

(2003 H 87, § 24, eff. 7–1–03; 2002 H 512, eff. 7–1–03)

2915.095 Attorney general to establish standard instant bingo contract

The attorney general, by rule adopted pursuant to section 111.15 of the Revised Code, shall establish a standard contract to be used by a charitable instant bingo organization, a veteran's organization,, a fraternal organization, or a sporting organization for the conduct of instant bingo other than at a bingo session. The terms of the contract shall be limited to the provisions in Chapter 2915. of the Revised Code.

(2003 H 95, eff. 7–1–03; 2003 H 87, § 24, eff. 7–1–03; 2002 H 512, eff. 7–1–03)

2915.10 Records to be maintained; enforcement; prohibitions

(A) No charitable organization that conducts bingo or a game of chance pursuant to division (D) of section 2915.02 of the Revised Code shall fail to maintain the following records for at least three years from the date on which the bingo or game of chance is conducted:

(1) An itemized list of the gross receipts of each bingo session, each game of instant bingo by serial number, each raffle, each punch board game, and each game of chance, and an itemized list of the gross profits of each game of instant bingo by serial number;

(2) An itemized list of all expenses, other than prizes, that are incurred in conducting bingo or instant bingo, the name of each person to whom the expenses are paid, and a receipt for all of the expenses;

(3) A list of all prizes awarded during each bingo session, each raffle, each punch board game, and each game of chance conducted by the charitable organization, the total prizes awarded from each game of instant bingo by serial number, and the name, address, and social security number of all persons who are winners of prizes of six hundred dollars or more in value;

(4) An itemized list of the recipients of the net profit of the bingo or game of chance, including the name and address of each recipient to whom the money is distributed, and if the organization uses the net profit of bingo, or the money or assets received from a game of chance, for any charitable or other purpose set forth in division (Z) of section 2915.01, division (D) of section 2915.02, or section 2915.101 of the Revised Code, a list of each purpose and an itemized list of each expenditure for each purpose;

(5) The number of persons who participate in any bingo session or game of chance that is conducted by the charitable organization;

(6) A list of receipts from the sale of food and beverages by the charitable organization or one of its auxiliary units or societies, if the receipts were excluded from gross receipts under division (X) of section 2915.01 of the Revised Code;

(7) An itemized list of all expenses incurred at each bingo session, each raffle, each punch board game, or each game of instant bingo conducted by the charitable organization in the sale of food and beverages by the charitable organization or by an auxiliary unit or society of the charitable organization, the name of each person to whom the expenses are paid, and a receipt for all of the expenses.

(B) A charitable organization shall keep the records that it is required to maintain pursuant to division (A) of this section at its principal place of business in this state or at its headquarters in this state and shall notify the attorney general of the location at which those records are kept.

(C) The gross profit from each bingo session or game described in division (S)(1) or (2) of section 2915.01 of the Revised Code shall be deposited into a checking account devoted exclusively to the bingo session or game. Payments for allowable expenses incurred in conducting the bingo session or game and payments to recipients of some or all of the net profit of the bingo session or game shall be made only by checks drawn on the bingo session or game account.

(D) Each charitable organization shall conduct and record an inventory of all of its bingo supplies as of the first day of November of each year.

(E) The attorney general may adopt rules in accordance with Chapter 119. of the Revised Code that establish standards of accounting, record keeping, and reporting to ensure that gross receipts from bingo or games of chance are properly accounted for.

(F) A distributor shall maintain, for a period of three years after the date of its sale or other provision, a record of each instance of its selling or otherwise providing to another person bingo supplies for use in this state. The record shall include all of the following for each instance:

(1) The name of the manufacturer from which the distributor purchased the bingo supplies and the date of the purchase;

(2) The name and address of the charitable organization or other distributor to which the bingo supplies were sold or otherwise provided;

(3) A description that clearly identifies the bingo supplies;

(4) Invoices that include the nonrepeating serial numbers of all paper bingo cards and sheets and all instant bingo deals sold or otherwise provided to each charitable organization.

(G) A manufacturer shall maintain, for a period of three years after the date of its sale or other provision, a record of each instance of its selling or otherwise providing bingo supplies for use in this state. The record shall include all of the following for each instance:

(1) The name and address of the distributor to whom the bingo supplies were sold or otherwise provided;

(2) A description that clearly identifies the bingo supplies, including serial numbers;

(3) Invoices that include the nonrepeating serial numbers of all paper bingo cards and sheets and all instant bingo deals sold or otherwise provided to each distributor.

(H) The attorney general or any law enforcement agency may do all of the following:

(1) Investigate any charitable organization or any officer, agent, trustee, member, or employee of the organization;

(2) Examine the accounts and records of the organization;

(3) Conduct inspections, audits, and observations of bingo or games of chance;

(4) Conduct inspections of the premises where bingo or games of chance are conducted;

(5) Take any other necessary and reasonable action to determine if a violation of any provision of sections 2915.01 to 2915.13 of the Revised Code has occurred and to determine whether section 2915.11 of the Revised Code has been complied with.

If any law enforcement agency has reasonable grounds to believe that a charitable organization or an officer, agent, trustee, member, or employee of the organization has violated any provision of this chapter, the law enforcement agency may proceed by action in the proper court to enforce this chapter, provided that the law enforcement agency shall give written notice to the attorney general when commencing an action as described in this division.

(I) No person shall destroy, alter, conceal, withhold, or deny access to any accounts or records of a charitable organization that have been requested for examination, or obstruct, impede, or interfere with any inspection, audit, or observation of bingo or a game of chance or premises where bingo or a game of chance is conducted, or refuse to comply with any reasonable request of, or obstruct, impede, or interfere with any other reasonable action undertaken by, the attorney general or a law enforcement agency pursuant to division (H) of this section.

(J) Whoever violates division (A) or (I) of this section is guilty of a misdemeanor of the first degree.

(2003 H 95, eff. 7–1–03; 2003 H 87, § 24, eff. 7–1–03; 2002 H 512, eff. 7–1–03; 1995 S 2, eff. 7–1–96; 1981 S 91, eff. 10–20–81; 1977 H 72; 1976 S 398, H 1547)

2915.101 Distribution of profit from instant bingo

Except as otherwise provided by law, a charitable organization that conducts instant bingo shall distribute the net profit from the proceeds of the sale of instant bingo as follows:

(A)(1) If a veteran's organization, a fraternal organization, or a sporting organization conducted the instant bingo, the organization shall distribute the net profit from the proceeds of the sale of instant bingo, as follows:

(a) For the first seventy-five thousand dollars, or a greater amount prescribed by the attorney general to adjust for changes in prices as measured by the consumer price index as defined in section 325.18 of the Revised Code, or less of net profit from the proceeds of the sale of instant bingo generated in a calendar year:

(i) At least twenty-five per cent shall be distributed to an organization described in division (Z)(1) of section 2915.01 of the Revised Code or to a department or agency of the federal government, the state, or any political subdivision.

(ii) Not more than seventy-five per cent may be deducted and retained by the organization for reimbursement of or for the organization's expenses, as defined in division (LL) of section 2915.01 of the Revised Code, in conducting the instant bingo game.

(b) For any net profit from the proceeds of the sale of instant bingo of more than seventy-five thousand dollars or an adjusted amount generated in a calendar year:

(i) A minimum of fifty per cent shall be distributed to an organization described in division (Z)(1) of section 2915.01 of the Revised Code or to a department or agency of the federal government, the state, or any political subdivision .

(ii) Five per cent may be distributed for the organization's own charitable purposes or to a community action agency.

(iii) Forty–five per cent may be deducted and retained by the organization for reimbursement of or for the organization's expenses, as defined in division (LL) of section 2915.01 of the Revised Code, in conducting the instant bingo game.

(2) If a veteran's organization, a fraternal organization, or a sporting organization does not distribute the full percentages specified in divisions (A)(1) (a) and (b) of this section for the purposes specified in those divisions, the organization shall distribute the balance of the net profit from the proceeds of the sale of instant bingo not distributed or retained for those purposes to an organization described in division (Z)(1) of section 2915.01 of the Revised Code.

(B) If a charitable organization other than a veteran's organization, a fraternal organization, or a sporting organization conducted the instant bingo, the organization shall distribute one hundred per cent of the net profit from the proceeds of the sale of instant bingo to an organization described in division (Z)(1) of section 2915.01 of the Revised Code or to a department or agency of the federal government, the state, or any political subdivision.

(C) Nothing in this section prohibits a veteran's organization, a fraternal organization, or a sporting organization from distributing any net profit from the proceeds of the sale of instant bingo to an organization that is described in subsection 501(c)(3) of the Internal Revenue Code when the organization that is described in subsection 501(c)(3) of the Internal Revenue Code is one that makes donations to other organizations and permits donors to advise or direct such donations so long as the donations comply with requirements established in or pursuant to subsection 501(c)(3) of the Internal Revenue Code.

(2004 H 325, eff. 9–30–04; 2003 H 95, eff. 7–1–03; 2003 H 87, § 24, eff. 7–1–03; 2002 H 512, eff. 7–1–03)

2915.11 Minor and felon not to work at bingo session

(A) No person shall be a bingo game operator unless he is eighteen years of age or older.

(B) No person who has been convicted of a felony or a gambling offense in any jurisdiction shall be a bingo game operator.

(C) Whoever violates division (A) of this section is guilty of a misdemeanor of the third degree.

(D) Whoever violates division (B) of this section is guilty of a misdemeanor of the first degree.

(1977 H 72, eff. 12–15–77; 1976 S 398)

2915.12 Game for amusement only excepted; conditions; enforcement; offense

(A) Sections 2915.07 to 2915.11 of the Revised Code do not apply to bingo games that are conducted for the purpose of amusement only. A bingo game is conducted for the purpose of amusement only if it complies with all of the requirements specified in either division (A)(1) or (2) of this section:

(1)(a) The participants do not pay any money or any other thing of value including an admission fee, or any fee for bingo cards or sheets, objects to cover the spaces, or other devices used in playing bingo, for the privilege of participating in the bingo game, or to defray any costs of the game, or pay tips or make donations during or immediately before or after the bingo game.

(b) All prizes awarded during the course of the game are nonmonetary, and in the form of merchandise, goods, or entitlements to goods or services only, and the total value of all prizes awarded during the game is less than one hundred dollars.

(c) No commission, wages, salary, reward, tip, donation, gratuity, or other form of compensation, either directly or indirectly, and regardless of the source, is paid to any bingo game operator for work or labor performed at the site of the bingo game.

(d) The bingo game is not conducted either during or within ten hours of any of the following:

(i) A bingo session during which a charitable bingo game is conducted pursuant to sections 2915.07 to 2915.11 of the Revised Code;

(ii) A scheme or game of chance, or bingo described in division (S)(2) of section 2915.01 of the Revised Code.

(e) The number of players participating in the bingo game does not exceed fifty.

(2)(a) The participants do not pay money or any other thing of value as an admission fee, and no participant is charged more than twenty-five cents to purchase a bingo card or sheet, objects to cover the spaces, or other devices used in playing bingo.

(b) The total amount of money paid by all of the participants for bingo cards or sheets, objects to cover the spaces, or other devices used in playing bingo does not exceed one hundred dollars.

(c) All of the money paid for bingo cards or sheets, objects to cover spaces, or other devices used in playing bingo is used only to pay winners monetary and nonmonetary prizes and to provide refreshments.

(d) The total value of all prizes awarded during the game does not exceed one hundred dollars.

(e) No commission, wages, salary, reward, tip, donation, gratuity, or other form of compensation, either directly or indirectly, and regardless of the source, is paid to any bingo game operator for work or labor performed at the site of the bingo game.

(f) The bingo game is not conducted during or within ten hours of either of the following:

(i) A bingo session during which a charitable bingo game is conducted pursuant to sections 2915.07 to 2915.11 of the Revised Code;

(ii) A scheme of chance or game of chance, or bingo described in division (S)(2) of section 2915.01 of the Revised Code.

(g) All of the participants reside at the premises where the bingo game is conducted.

(h) The bingo games are conducted on different days of the week and not more than twice in a calendar week.

(B) The attorney general or any local law enforcement agency may investigate the conduct of a bingo game that purportedly is conducted for purposes of amusement only if there is reason to believe that the purported amusement bingo game does not comply with the requirements of either division (A)(1) or (2) of this section. A local law enforcement agency may proceed by action in the proper court to enforce this section if the local law enforcement agency gives written notice to the attorney general when commencing the action.

(2003 H 87, § 24, eff. 7-1-03; 2002 H 512, eff. 7-1-03; 1995 S 2, eff. 7-1-96; 1990 H 573, eff. 4-10-91; 1977 H 72; 1976 S 398)

2915.13 Veteran's or fraternal organization may conduct instant bingo game

(A) A veteran's organization, a fraternal organization, or a sporting organization authorized to conduct a bingo session pursuant to sections 2915. 01 to 2915.12 of the Revised Code may conduct instant bingo other than at a bingo session if all of the following apply:

(1) The veteran's organization, fraternal organization, or sporting organization limits the sale of instant bingo to twelve hours during any day, provided that the sale does not begin earlier than ten a.m. and ends not later than two a.m.

(2) The veteran's organization, fraternal organization, or sporting organization limits the sale of instant bingo to its own premises and to its own members and invited guests.

(3) The veteran's organization, fraternal organization, or sporting organization is raising money for an organization that is described in subsection 509(a)(1), 509(a)(2), or 509(a)(3) of the Internal Revenue Code [1] and is either a governmental unit or an organization that maintains its principal place of business in this state, that is exempt from federal income taxation under subsection 501(a) and described in subsection 501(c)(3) of the Internal Revenue Code, and that is in good standing in this state and executes a written contract with that organization as required in division (B) of this section.

(B) If a veteran's organization, fraternal organization, or sporting organization authorized to conduct instant bingo pursuant to division (A) of this section is raising money for another organization that is described in subsection 509(a)(1), 509(a)(2), or 509(a)(3) of the Internal Revenue Code and is either a governmental unit or an organization that maintains its principal place of business in this state, that is exempt from federal income taxation under subsection 501(a) and described in subsection 501(c)(3) of the Internal Revenue Code, and that is in good standing in this state, the veteran's organization, fraternal organization, or sporting organization shall execute a written contract with the organization that is described in subsection 509(a)(1), 509(a)(2), or 509(a)(3) of the Internal Revenue Code and is either a governmental unit or an organization that maintains its principal place of business in this state, that is exempt from federal income taxation under subsection 501(a) and described in subsection 501(c)(3) of the Internal Revenue Code, and that is in good standing in this state in order to conduct instant bingo. That contract shall include a statement of the percentage of the net proceeds that the veteran's, fraternal, or sporting organization will be distributing to the organization that is described in subsection 509(a)(1), 509(a)(2), or 509(a)(3) of the Internal Revenue Code and is either a governmental unit or an organization that maintains its principal place of business in this state, that is exempt from federal income taxation under subsection 501(a) and described in subsection 501(c)(3) of the Internal Revenue Code, and that is in good standing in this state.

(C)(1) If a veteran's organization, fraternal organization, or sporting organization authorized to conduct instant bingo pursuant to division (A) of this section has been issued a liquor permit under Chapter 4303. of the Revised Code, that permit may be subject to suspension, revocation, or cancellation if the veteran's organization, fraternal organization, or sporting organization violates a provision of this chapter.

(2) No veteran's organization, fraternal organization, or sporting organization that enters into a written contract pursuant to division (B) of this section shall violate any provision of this chapter or permit, aid, or abet any other person in violating any provision of this chapter.

(D) A veteran's organization, fraternal organization, or sporting organization shall give all required proceeds earned from the conduct of instant bingo to the organization with which the veteran's organization, fraternal organization, or sporting organization has entered into a written contract.

(E) Whoever violates this section is guilty of illegal instant bingo conduct. Except as otherwise provided in this division, illegal instant bingo conduct is a misdemeanor of the first degree. If the offender previously has been convicted of a violation of this section, illegal instant bingo conduct is a felony of the fifth degree.

(2004 H 325, eff. 9-30-04; 2003 H 95, eff. 7-1-03; 2003 H 87, § 24, eff. 7-1-03; 2002 H 512, eff. 7-1-03)

[1] 26 U.S.C.A. § 1 et. seq.

CHAPTER 2917

OFFENSES AGAINST THE PUBLIC PEACE

INCITING, RIOT, AND RELATED OFFENSES

2917.01 Inciting to violence

(A) No person shall knowingly engage in conduct designed to urge or incite another to commit any offense of violence, when either of the following apply:

(1) The conduct takes place under circumstances that create a clear and present danger that any offense of violence will be committed;

(2) The conduct proximately results in the commission of any offense of violence.

(B) Whoever violates this section is guilty of inciting to violence. If the offense of violence that the other person is being urged or incited to commit is a misdemeanor, inciting to violence is a misdemeanor of the first degree. If the offense of violence that the other person is being urged or incited to commit is a felony, inciting to violence is a felony of the third degree.

(1995 S 2, eff. 7–1–96; 1972 H 511, eff. 1–1–74)

2917.02 Aggravated riot

(A) No person shall participate with four or more others in a course of disorderly conduct in violation of section 2917.11 of the Revised Code:

(1) With purpose to commit or facilitate the commission of a felony;

(2) With purpose to commit or facilitate the commission of any offense of violence;

(3) When the offender or any participant to the knowledge of the offender has on or about the offender's or participant's person or under the offender's or participant's control, uses, or intends to use a deadly weapon or dangerous ordnance, as defined in section 2923.11 of the Revised Code.

(B)(1) No person, being an inmate in a detention facility, shall violate division (A)(1) or (3) of this section.

(2) No person, being an inmate in a detention facility, shall violate division (A)(2) of this section or section 2917.03 of the Revised Code.

(C) Whoever violates this section is guilty of aggravated riot. A violation of division (A)(1) or (3) of this section is a felony of the fifth degree. A violation of division (A)(2) or (B)(1) of this section is a felony of the fourth degree. A violation of division (B)(2) of this section is a felony of the third degree.

(D) As used in this section, "detention facility" has the same meaning as in section 2921.01 of the Revised Code.

(1995 S 2, eff. 7–1–96; 1983 S 210, eff. 7–1–83; 1982 H 269, § 4, S 199; 1972 H 511)

2917.03 Riot

(A) No person shall participate with four or more others in a course of disorderly conduct in violation of section 2917.11 of the Revised Code:

(1) With purpose to commit or facilitate the commission of a misdemeanor, other than disorderly conduct;

(2) With purpose to intimidate a public official or employee into taking or refraining from official action, or with purpose to hinder, impede, or obstruct a function of government;

(3) With purpose to hinder, impede, or obstruct the orderly process of administration or instruction at an educational institution, or to interfere with or disrupt lawful activities carried on at such institution.

(B) No person shall participate with four or more others with purpose to do an act with unlawful force or violence, even though such act might otherwise be lawful.

(C) Whoever violates this section is guilty of riot, a misdemeanor of the first degree.

(1972 H 511, eff. 1–1–74)

2917.031 Express agreement not required

For the purposes of prosecuting violations of sections 2917.02 and 2917. 03 of the Revised Code, the state is not required to allege or prove that the offender expressly agreed with four or more others to commit any act that constitutes a violation of either section prior to or while committing those acts.

(2003 S 57, eff. 3–22–04)

2917.04 Failure to disperse

(A) Where five or more persons are participating in a course of disorderly conduct in violation of section 2917.11 of the Revised Code, and there are other persons in the vicinity whose presence creates the likelihood of physical harm to persons or property or of serious public inconvenience, annoyance, or alarm, a law enforcement officer or other public official may order the participants and such other persons to disperse. No person shall knowingly fail to obey such order.

(B) Nothing in this section requires persons to disperse who are peaceably assembled for a lawful purpose.

(C)(1) Whoever violates this section is guilty of failure to disperse.

(2) Except as otherwise provided in division (C)(3) of this section, failure to disperse is a minor misdemeanor.

(3) Failure to disperse is a misdemeanor of the fourth degree if the failure to obey the order described in division (A) of this section creates the likelihood of physical harm to persons or is committed at the scene of a fire, accident, disaster, riot, or emergency of any kind.

(2003 S 57, eff. 3–22–04; 1972 H 511, eff. 1–1–74)

2917.05 Justifiable use of force to suppress riot

A law enforcement officer or fireman, engaged in suppressing riot or in protecting persons or property during riot:

(A) Is justified in using force, other than deadly force, when and to the extent he has probable cause to believe such force is necessary to disperse or apprehend rioters;

(B) Is justified in using force, including deadly force, when and to the extent he has probable cause to believe such force is necessary to disperse or apprehend rioters whose conduct is creating a substantial risk of serious physical harm to persons.

(1972 H 511, eff. 1–1–74)

DISORDERLY CONDUCT

2917.11 Disorderly conduct

(A) No person shall recklessly cause inconvenience, annoyance, or alarm to another by doing any of the following:

(1) Engaging in fighting, in threatening harm to persons or property, or in violent or turbulent behavior;

(2) Making unreasonable noise or an offensively coarse utterance, gesture, or display or communicating unwarranted and grossly abusive language to any person;

(3) Insulting, taunting, or challenging another, under circumstances in which that conduct is likely to provoke a violent response;

(4) Hindering or preventing the movement of persons on a public street, road, highway, or right-of-way, or to, from, within, or upon public or private property, so as to interfere with the rights of others, and by any act that serves no lawful and reasonable purpose of the offender;

(5) Creating a condition that is physically offensive to persons or that presents a risk of physical harm to persons or property, by any act that serves no lawful and reasonable purpose of the offender.

(B) No person, while voluntarily intoxicated, shall do either of the following:

(1) In a public place or in the presence of two or more persons, engage in conduct likely to be offensive or to cause inconvenience, annoyance, or alarm to persons of ordinary sensibilities, which conduct the offender, if the offender were not intoxicated, should know is likely to have that effect on others;

(2) Engage in conduct or create a condition that presents a risk of physical harm to the offender or another, or to the property of another.

(C) Violation of any statute or ordinance of which an element is operating a motor vehicle, locomotive, watercraft, aircraft, or other vehicle while under the influence of alcohol or any drug of abuse, is not a violation of division (B) of this section.

(D) If a person appears to an ordinary observer to be intoxicated, it is probable cause to believe that person is voluntarily intoxicated for purposes of division (B) of this section.

(E)(1) Whoever violates this section is guilty of disorderly conduct.

(2) Except as otherwise provided in division (E)(3) of this section, disorderly conduct is a minor misdemeanor.

(3) Disorderly conduct is a misdemeanor of the fourth degree if any of the following applies:

(a) The offender persists in disorderly conduct after reasonable warning or request to desist.

(b) The offense is committed in the vicinity of a school or in a school safety zone.

(c) The offense is committed in the presence of any law enforcement officer, firefighter, rescuer, medical person, emergency medical services person, or other authorized person who is engaged in the person's duties at the scene of a fire, accident, disaster, riot, or emergency of any kind.

(d) The offense is committed in the presence of any emergency facility person who is engaged in the person's duties in an emergency facility.

(F) As used in this section:

(1) "Emergency medical services person" is the singular of "emergency medical services personnel" as defined in section 2133.21 of the Revised Code.

(2) "Emergency facility person" is the singular of "emergency facility personnel" as defined in section 2909.04 of the Revised Code.

(3) "Emergency facility" has the same meaning as in section 2909.04 of the Revised Code.

(4) "Committed in the vicinity of a school" has the same meaning as in section 2925.01 of the Revised Code.

(2001 S 40, eff. 1–25–02; 1999 H 137, eff. 3–10–00; 1999 S 1, eff. 8–6–99; 1995 S 2, eff. 7–1–96; 1990 H 51, eff. 11–8–90; 1972 H 511)

Notes of Decisions

Ed. Note: See notes of decisions at RC 4511.19 regarding construction of the term "under the influence."

2917.12 Disturbing a lawful meeting

(A) No person, with purpose to prevent or disrupt a lawful meeting, procession, or gathering, shall do either of the following:

(1) Do any act which obstructs or interferes with the due conduct of such meeting, procession, or gathering;

(2) Make any utterance, gesture, or display which outrages the sensibilities of the group.

(B) Whoever violates this section is guilty of disturbing a lawful meeting, a misdemeanor of the fourth degree.

(1972 H 511, eff. 1–1–74)

2917.13 Misconduct at an emergency

(A) No person shall knowingly do any of the following:

(1) Hamper the lawful operations of any law enforcement officer, firefighter, rescuer, medical person, emergency medical services person, or other authorized person, engaged in the person's duties at the scene of a fire, accident, disaster, riot, or emergency of any kind;

(2) Hamper the lawful activities of any emergency facility person who is engaged in the person's duties in an emergency facility;

(3) Fail to obey the lawful order of any law enforcement officer engaged in the law enforcement officer's duties at the

scene of or in connection with a fire, accident, disaster, riot, or emergency of any kind.

(B) Nothing in this section shall be construed to limit access or deny information to any news media representative in the lawful exercise of the news media representative's duties.

(C) Whoever violates this section is guilty of misconduct at an emergency. Except as otherwise provided in this division, misconduct at an emergency is a misdemeanor of the fourth degree. If a violation of this section creates a risk of physical harm to persons or property, misconduct at an emergency is a misdemeanor of the first degree.

(D) As used in this section:

(1) "Emergency medical services person" is the singular of "emergency medical services personnel" as defined in section 2133.21 of the Revised Code.

(2) "Emergency facility person" is the singular of "emergency facility personnel" as defined in section 2909.04 of the Revised Code.

(3) "Emergency facility" has the same meaning as in section 2909.04 of the Revised Code.

(2003 S 57, eff. 3–22–04; 2001 S 40, eff. 1–25–02; 1999 H 137, eff. 3–10–00; 1973 H 716, eff. 1–1–74; 1972 H 511)

HARASSMENT

2917.21 Telecommunications harassment

(A) No person shall knowingly make or cause to be made a telecommunication, or knowingly permit a telecommunication to be made from a telecommunications device under the person's control, to another, if the caller does any of the following:

(1) Fails to identify the caller to the recipient of the telecommunication and makes the telecommunication with purpose to harass or abuse any person at the premises to which the telecommunication is made, whether or not actual communication takes place between the caller and a recipient;

(2) Describes, suggests, requests, or proposes that the caller, the recipient of the telecommunication, or any other person engage in sexual activity, and the recipient or another person at the premises to which the telecommunication is made has requested, in a previous telecommunication or in the immediate telecommunication, that the caller not make a telecommunication to the recipient or to the premises to which the telecommunication is made;

(3) During the telecommunication, violates section 2903.21 of the Revised Code;

(4) Knowingly states to the recipient of the telecommunication that the caller intends to cause damage to or destroy public or private property, and the recipient, any member of the recipient's family, or any other person who resides at the premises to which the telecommunication is made owns, leases, resides, or works in, will at the time of the destruction or damaging be near or in, has the responsibility of protecting, or insures the property that will be destroyed or damaged;

(5) Knowingly makes the telecommunication to the recipient of the telecommunication, to another person at the premises to which the telecommunication is made, or to those premises, and the recipient or another person at those premises previously has told the caller not to make a telecommunication to those premises or to any persons at those premises.

(B) No person shall make or cause to be made a telecommunication, or permit a telecommunication to be made from a telecommunications device under the person's control, with purpose to abuse, threaten, or harass another person.

(C)(1) Whoever violates this section is guilty of telecommunications harassment.

(2) A violation of division (A)(1), (2), (3), or (5) or (B) of this section is a misdemeanor of the first degree on a first offense and a felony of the fifth degree on each subsequent offense.

(3) Except as otherwise provided in division (C)(3) of this section, a violation of division (A)(4) of this section is a misdemeanor of the first degree on a first offense and a felony of the fifth degree on each subsequent offense. If a violation of division (A)(4) of this section results in economic harm of five hundred dollars or more but less than five thousand dollars, telecommunications harassment is a felony of the fifth degree. If a violation of division (A)(4) of this section results in economic harm of five thousand dollars or more but less than one hundred thousand dollars, telecommunications harassment is a felony of the fourth degree. If a violation of division (A)(4) of this section results in economic harm of one hundred thousand dollars or more, telecommunications harassment is a felony of the third degree.

(D) No cause of action may be asserted in any court of this state against any provider of a telecommunications service or information service, or against any officer, employee, or agent of a telecommunication service or information service, for any injury, death, or loss to person or property that allegedly arises out of the provider's, officer's, employee's, or agent's provision of information, facilities, or assistance in accordance with the terms of a court order that is issued in relation to the investigation or prosecution of an alleged violation of this section or section 4931.31 of the Revised Code. A provider of a telecommunications service or information service, or an officer, employee, or agent of a telecommunications service or information service, is immune from any civil or criminal liability for injury, death, or loss to person or property that allegedly arises out of the provider's, officer's, employee's, or agent's provision of information, facilities, or assistance in accordance with the terms of a court order that is issued in relation to the investigation or prosecution of an alleged violation of this section or section 4931.31 of the Revised Code.

(E) As used in this section:

(1) "Economic harm" means all direct, incidental, and consequential pecuniary harm suffered by a victim as a result of criminal conduct. "Economic harm" includes, but is not limited to, all of the following:

(a) All wages, salaries, or other compensation lost as a result of the criminal conduct;

(b) The cost of all wages, salaries, or other compensation paid to employees for time those employees are prevented from working as a result of the criminal conduct;

(c) The overhead costs incurred for the time that a business is shut down as a result of the criminal conduct;

(d) The loss of value to tangible or intangible property that was damaged as a result of the criminal conduct.

(2) "Caller" means the person described in division (A) of this section who makes or causes to be made a telecommunication or who permits a telecommunication to be made from a telecommunications device under that person's control.

(3) "Telecommunication" and "telecommunications device" have the same meanings as in section 2913.01 of the Revised Code.

(4) "Sexual activity" has the same meaning as in section 2907.01 of the Revised Code.

(F) Nothing in this section prohibits a person from making a telecommunication to a debtor that is in compliance with the "Fair Debt Collection Practices Act," 91 Stat. 874 (1977), 15

U.S.C. 1692, as amended, or the "Telephone Consumer Protection Act," 105 Stat. 2395 (1991), 47 U.S.C. 227, as amended.

(1998 S 215, eff. 3–30–99; 1998 H 565, eff. 3–30–99; 1997 H 182, eff. 10–1–97; 1995 S 2, eff. 7–1–96; 1980 H 164, eff. 4–9–81; 1972 H 511)

FALSE ALARMS; WEAPONS OF MASS DESTRUCTION

2917.31 Inducing panic

(A) No person shall cause the evacuation of any public place, or otherwise cause serious public inconvenience or alarm, by doing any of the following:

(1) Initiating or circulating a report or warning of an alleged or impending fire, explosion, crime, or other catastrophe, knowing that such report or warning is false;

(2) Threatening to commit any offense of violence;

(3) Committing any offense, with reckless disregard of the likelihood that its commission will cause serious public inconvenience or alarm.

(B) Division (A)(1) of this section does not apply to any person conducting an authorized fire or emergency drill.

(C)(1) Whoever violates this section is guilty of inducing panic.

(2) Except as otherwise provided in division (C)(3), (4), (5), (6), (7), (8), or (9) of this section, inducing panic is a misdemeanor of the first degree.

(3) Except as otherwise provided in division (C)(4), (5), (6), (7), (8), or (9) of this section, if a violation of this section results in physical harm to any person, inducing panic is a felony of the fourth degree.

(4) Except as otherwise provided in division (C)(5), (6), (7), (8), or (9) of this section, if a violation of this section results in economic harm, the penalty shall be determined as follows:

(a) If the violation results in economic harm of five hundred dollars or more but less than five thousand dollars and if division (C)(3) of this section does not apply, inducing panic is a felony of the fifth degree.

(b) If the violation results in economic harm of five thousand dollars or more but less than one hundred thousand dollars, inducing panic is a felony of the fourth degree.

(c) If the violation results in economic harm of one hundred thousand dollars or more, inducing panic is a felony of the third degree.

(5) Except as otherwise provided in division (C) (6), (7), (8), or (9) of this section, if the public place involved in a violation of division (A)(1) of this section is a school, the penalty shall be determined as follows:

(a) Except as otherwise provided in division (C)(5)(b) or (c) of this section, inducing panic is a felony of the fourth degree.

(b) If the violation results in physical harm to any person and if division (C)(5)(c)(iii) of this section does not apply, inducing panic is a felony of the third degree.

(c) If the violation results in economic harm, the penalty shall be determined as follows:

(i) If the violation results in economic harm of five hundred dollars or more but less than five thousand dollars and if division (C)(5)(b) of this section does not apply, inducing panic is a felony of the fourth degree.

(ii) If the violation results in economic harm of five thousand dollars or more but less than one hundred thousand dollars, inducing panic is a felony of the third degree.

(iii) If the violation results in economic harm of one hundred thousand dollars or more, inducing panic is a felony of the second degree.

(6) If the violation pertains to a purported, threatened, or actual use of a weapon of mass destruction, and except as otherwise provided in division (C)(7), (8), or (9) of this section, inducing panic is a felony of the fourth degree.

(7) If the violation pertains to a purported, threatened, or actual use of a weapon of mass destruction, and except as otherwise provided in division (C)(9)(a) or (c) of this section, if a violation of this section results in physical harm to any person, inducing panic is a felony of the third degree.

(8) If the violation pertains to a purported, threatened, or actual use of a weapon of mass destruction, and except as otherwise provided in division (C)(9)(a) or (c) of this section, if a violation of this section results in economic harm of one hundred thousand dollars or more, inducing panic is a felony of the third degree.

(9)(a) If the public place involved in a violation of division (A)(1) of this section is a school, if the violation pertains to a purported, threatened, or actual use of a weapon of mass destruction, and if the violation results in physical harm to any person, inducing panic is a felony of the second degree.

(b) If the public place involved in a violation of division (A)(1) of this section is a school, if the violation pertains to a purported, threatened, or actual use of a weapon of mass destruction, and if the violation results in economic harm of five thousand dollars or more but less than one hundred thousand dollars, and if division (C)(9)(a) of this section does not apply, inducing panic is a felony of the third degree.

(c) If the public place involved in a violation of division (A)(1) of this section is a school, if the violation pertains to a purported, threatened, or actual use of a weapon of mass destruction, and if the violation results in economic harm of one hundred thousand dollars or more, inducing panic is a felony of the second degree.

(D)(1) It is not a defense to a charge under this section that pertains to a purported or threatened use of a weapon of mass destruction that the offender did not possess or have the ability to use a weapon of mass destruction or that what was represented to be a weapon of mass destruction was not a weapon of mass destruction.

(2) Any act that is a violation of this section and any other section of the Revised Code may be prosecuted under this section, the other section, or both sections.

(E) As used in this section:

(1) "Economic harm" means any of the following:

(a) All direct, incidental, and consequential pecuniary harm suffered by a victim as a result of criminal conduct. "Economic harm" as described in this division includes, but is not limited to, all of the following:

(i) All wages, salaries, or other compensation lost as a result of the criminal conduct;

(ii) The cost of all wages, salaries, or other compensation paid to employees for time those employees are prevented from working as a result of the criminal conduct;

(iii) The overhead costs incurred for the time that a business is shut down as a result of the criminal conduct;

(iv) The loss of value to tangible or intangible property that was damaged as a result of the criminal conduct.

(b) All costs incurred by the state or any political subdivision as a result of, or in making any response to, the criminal conduct that constituted the violation of this section or section 2917.32 of the Revised Code, including, but not limited to, all costs so incurred by any law enforcement officers, firefighters, rescue personnel, or emergency medical services personnel of the state or the political subdivision.

(2) "School" means any school operated by a board of education or any school for which the state board of education prescribes minimum standards under section 3301.07 of the Revised Code, whether or not any instruction, extracurricular activities, or training provided by the school is being conducted at the time a violation of this section is committed.

(3) "Weapon of mass destruction" means any of the following:

(a) Any weapon that is designed or intended to cause death or serious physical harm through the release, dissemination, or impact of toxic or poisonous chemicals, or their precursors;

(b) Any weapon involving a disease organism or biological agent;

(c) Any weapon that is designed to release radiation or radioactivity at a level dangerous to human life;

(d) Any of the following, except to the extent that the item or device in question is expressly excepted from the definition of "destructive device" pursuant to 18 U.S.C. 921(a)(4) and regulations issued under that section:

(i) Any explosive, incendiary, or poison gas bomb, grenade, rocket having a propellant charge of more than four ounces, missile having an explosive or incendiary charge of more than one-quarter ounce, mine, or similar device;

(ii) Any combination of parts either designed or intended for use in converting any item or device into any item or device described in division (E)(3)(d)(i) of this section and from which an item or device described in that division may be readily assembled.

(4) "Biological agent" has the same meaning as in section 2917.33 of the Revised Code.

(5) "Emergency medical services personnel" has the same meaning as in section 2133.21 of the Revised Code.

(2002 H 411, eff. 9–27–02; 1998 H 382, eff. 7–22–98; 1997 H 182, eff. 10–1–97; 1972 H 511, eff. 1–1–74)

2917.32 Making false alarms

(A) No person shall do any of the following:

(1) Initiate or circulate a report or warning of an alleged or impending fire, explosion, crime, or other catastrophe, knowing that the report or warning is false and likely to cause public inconvenience or alarm;

(2) Knowingly cause a false alarm of fire or other emergency to be transmitted to or within any organization, public or private, for dealing with emergencies involving a risk of physical harm to persons or property;

(3) Report to any law enforcement agency an alleged offense or other incident within its concern, knowing that such offense did not occur.

(B) This section does not apply to any person conducting an authorized fire or emergency drill.

(C)(1) Whoever violates this section is guilty of making false alarms.

(2) Except as otherwise provided in division (C)(3), (4), (5), or (6) of this section, making false alarms is a misdemeanor of the first degree.

(3) Except as otherwise provided in division (C)(4) of this section, if a violation of this section results in economic harm of five hundred dollars or more but less than five thousand dollars, making false alarms is a felony of the fifth degree.

(4) If a violation of this section pertains to a purported, threatened, or actual use of a weapon of mass destruction, making false alarms is a felony of the third degree.

(5) If a violation of this section results in economic harm of five thousand dollars or more but less than one hundred thousand dollars and if division (C)(4) of this section does not apply, making false alarms is a felony of the fourth degree.

(6) If a violation of this section results in economic harm of one hundred thousand dollars or more, making false alarms is a felony of the third degree.

(D)(1) It is not a defense to a charge under this section that pertains to a purported or threatened use of a weapon of mass destruction that the offender did not possess or have the ability to use a weapon of mass destruction or that what was represented to be a weapon of mass destruction was not a weapon of mass destruction.

(2) Any act that is a violation of this section and any other section of the Revised Code may be prosecuted under this section, the other section, or both sections.

(E) As used in this section, "economic harm" and "weapon of mass destruction" have the same meanings as in section 2917.31 of the Revised Code.

(2002 H 411, eff. 9–27–02; 1997 H 182, eff. 10–1–97; 1972 H 511, eff. 1–1–74)

2917.33 Hoax weapon of mass destruction

(A) No person, without privilege to do so, shall manufacture, possess, sell, deliver, display, use, threaten to use, attempt to use, conspire to use, or make readily accessible to others a hoax weapon of mass destruction with the intent to deceive or otherwise mislead one or more persons into believing that the hoax weapon of mass destruction will cause terror, bodily harm, or property damage.

(B) This section does not apply to any member or employee of the armed forces of the United States, a governmental agency of this state, another state, or the United States, or a private entity, to whom all of the following apply:

(1) The member or employee otherwise is engaged in lawful activity within the scope of the member's or employee's duties or employment.

(2) The member or employee otherwise is duly authorized or licensed to manufacture, possess, sell, deliver, display, or otherwise engage in activity as described in division (A) of this section.

(3) The member or employee is in compliance with applicable federal and state law.

(C) Whoever violates this section is guilty of unlawful possession or use of a hoax weapon of mass destruction, a felony of the fourth degree.

(D) Any act that is a violation of this section and any other section of the Revised Code may be prosecuted under this section, the other section, or both sections.

(E) As used in this section:

(1) "Hoax weapon of mass destruction" means any device or object that by its design, construction, content, or characteristics appears to be, appears to constitute, or appears to contain, or is represented as being, constituting, or containing, a weapon of mass destruction and to which either of the following applies:

(a) It is, in fact, an inoperative facsimile, imitation, counterfeit, or representation of a weapon of mass destruction that does not meet the definition of a weapon of mass destruction.

(b) It does not actually contain or constitute a weapon, biological agent, toxin, vector, or delivery system.

(2) "Biological agent" means any microorganism, virus, infectious substance, or biological product that may be engineered through biotechnology, or any naturally occurring or bioengineered component of any microorganism, virus, infectious substance, or biological product that may be engineered through biotechnology, capable of causing any of the following:

(a) Death, disease, or other biological malfunction in a human, an animal, a plant, or another living organism;

(b) Deterioration of food, water, equipment, supplies, or material of any kind;

(c) Deleterious alteration of the environment.

(3) "Toxin" means the toxic material of plants, animals, microorganisms, viruses, fungi, or infectious substances or a recombinant molecule, whatever its origin or method of reproduction, including, but not limited to, any of the following:

(a) Any poisonous substance or biological product that may be engineered through biotechnology and that is produced by a living organism;

(b) Any poisonous isomer or biological product, homolog, or derivative of any substance or product described in division (D)(3)(a) of this section.

(4) "Delivery system" means any of the following:

(a) Any apparatus, equipment, device, or means of delivery specifically designed to deliver or disseminate a biological agent, toxin, or vector;

(b) Any vector.

(5) "Vector" means a living organism or molecule, including a recombinant molecule or biological product that may be engineered through biotechnology, capable of carrying a biological agent or toxin to a host.

(6) "Weapon of mass destruction" has the same meaning as in section 2917.31 of the Revised Code.

(2002 H 411, eff. 9–27–02)

MISCELLANEOUS OFFENSES

2917.40 Definitions; seating at certain performances; crowd control measures; exemption may be granted by police; contracts for performances; exceptions; offenses

(A) As used in this section:

(1) "Live entertainment performance" means any live speech; any live musical performance, including a concert; any live dramatic performance; any live variety show; and any other live performance with respect to which the primary intent of the audience can be construed to be viewing the performers. A "live entertainment performance" does not include any form of entertainment with respect to which the person purchasing a ticket routinely participates in amusements as well as views performers.

(2) "Restricted entertainment area" means any wholly or partially enclosed area, whether indoors or outdoors, that has limited access through established entrances, or established turnstyles [sic.] or similar devices.

(3) "Concert" means a musical performance of which the primary component is a presentation by persons singing or playing musical instruments, that is intended by its sponsors mainly, but not necessarily exclusively, for the listening enjoyment of the audience, and that is held in a facility. A "concert" does not include any performance in which music is a part of the presentation and the primary component of which is acting, dancing, a motion picture, a demonstration of skills or talent other than singing or playing an instrument, an athletic event, an exhibition, or a speech.

(4) "Facility" means any structure that has a roof or partial roof and that has walls that wholly surround the area on all sides, including, but not limited to, a stadium, hall, arena, armory, auditorium, ballroom, exhibition hall, convention center, or music hall.

(5) "Person" includes, in addition to an individual or entity specified in division (C) of section 1.59 of the Revised Code, any governmental entity.

(B)(1) No person shall sell, offer to sell, or offer in return for a donation any ticket that is not numbered and that does not correspond to a specific seat for admission to either of the following:

(a) A live entertainment performance that is not exempted under division (D) of this section, that is held in a restricted entertainment area, and for which more than eight thousand tickets are offered to the public;

(b) A concert that is not exempted under division (D) of this section and for which more than three thousand tickets are offered to the public.

(2) No person shall advertise any live entertainment performance as described in division (B)(1)(a) of this section or any concert as described in division (B)(1)(b) of this section, unless the advertisement contains the words "Reserved Seats Only."

(C) Unless exempted by division (D)(1) of this section, no person who owns or operates any restricted entertainment area shall fail to open, maintain, and properly staff at least the number of entrances designated under division (E) of this section for a minimum of ninety minutes prior to the scheduled start of any live entertainment performance that is held in the restricted entertainment area and for which more than three thousand tickets are sold, offered for sale, or offered in return for a donation.

(D)(1) A live entertainment performance, other than a concert, is exempted from the provisions of divisions (B) and (C) of this section if both of the following apply:

(a) The restricted entertainment area in which the performance is held has at least eight entrances or, if both entrances and separate admission turnstyles [sic.] or similar devices are used, has at least eight turnstyles [sic.] or similar devices;

(b) The eight entrances or, if applicable, the eight turnstyles [sic.] or similar devices are opened, maintained, and properly staffed at least one hour prior to the scheduled start of the performance.

(2)(a) The chief of the police department of a township police district in the case of a facility located within the district, the officer responsible for public safety within a municipal corporation in the case of a facility located within the municipal corporation, or the county sheriff in the case of a facility located outside the boundaries of a township police district or municipal corporation may, upon application of the sponsor of a concert covered by division (B) of this section, exempt the concert from the provisions of that division if the official finds that the health, safety, and welfare of the participants and spectators would not be substantially affected by failure to comply with the provisions of that division.

In determining whether to grant an exemption, the official shall consider the following factors:

(i) The size and design of the facility in which the concert is scheduled;

(ii) The size, age, and anticipated conduct of the crowd expected to attend the concert;

(iii) The ability of the sponsor to manage and control the expected crowd.

If the sponsor of any concert desires to obtain an exemption under this division, the sponsor shall apply to the appropriate official on a form prescribed by that official. The official shall issue an order that grants or denies the exemption within five days after receipt of the application. The sponsor may appeal any order that denies an exemption to the court of common pleas of the county in which the facility is located.

(b) If an official grants an exemption under division (D)(2)(a) of this section, the official shall designate an on-duty law enforcement officer to be present at the concert. The designated officer has authority to issue orders to all security personnel at the concert to protect the health, safety, and welfare of the participants and spectators.

(3) Notwithstanding division (D)(2) of this section, in the case of a concert held in a facility located on the campus of an educational institution covered by section 3345.04 of the Revised Code, a state university law enforcement officer appointed pursuant to sections 3345.04 and 3345.21 of the Revised Code shall do both of the following:

(a) Exercise the authority to grant exemptions provided by division (D)(2)(a) of this section in lieu of an official designated in that division;

(b) If the officer grants an exemption under division (D)(3)(a) of this section, designate an on-duty state university law enforcement officer to be present at the concert. The designated officer has authority to issue orders to all security personnel at the concert to protect the health, safety, and welfare of the participants and spectators.

(E)(1) Unless a live entertainment performance is exempted by division (D)(1) of this section, the chief of the police department of a township police district in the case of a restricted entertainment area located within the district, the officer responsible for public safety within a municipal corporation in the case of a restricted entertainment area located within the municipal corporation, or the county sheriff in the case of a restricted entertainment area located outside the boundaries of a township police district or municipal corporation shall designate, for purposes of division (C) of this section, the minimum number of entrances required to be opened, maintained, and staffed at each live entertainment performance so as to permit crowd control and reduce congestion at the entrances. The designation shall be based on such factors as the size and nature of the crowd expected to attend the live entertainment performance, the length of time prior to the live entertainment performance that crowds are expected to congregate at the entrances, and the amount of security provided at the restricted entertainment area.

(2) Notwithstanding division (E)(1) of this section, a state university law enforcement officer appointed pursuant to sections 3345.04 and 3345.21 of the Revised Code shall designate the number of entrances required to be opened, maintained, and staffed in the case of a live entertainment performance that is held at a restricted entertainment area located on the campus of an educational institution covered by section 3345.04 of the Revised Code.

(F) No person shall enter into any contract for a live entertainment performance, that does not permit or require compliance with this section.

(G)(1) This section does not apply to a live entertainment performance held in a restricted entertainment area if one admission ticket entitles the holder to view or participate in three or more different games, rides, activities, or live entertainment performances occurring simultaneously at different sites within the restricted entertainment area and if the initial admittance entrance to the restricted entertainment area, for which the ticket is required, is separate from the entrance to any specific live entertainment performance and an additional ticket is not required for admission to the particular live entertainment performance.

(2) This section does not apply to a symphony orchestra performance, a ballet performance, horse races, dances, or fairs.

(H) This section does not prohibit the legislative authority of any municipal corporation from imposing additional requirements, not in conflict with this section, for the promotion or holding of live entertainment performances.

(I) Whoever violates division (B), (C), or (F) of this section is guilty of a misdemeanor of the first degree. If any individual suffers physical harm to his person as a result of a violation of this section, the sentencing court shall consider this factor in favor of imposing a term of imprisonment upon the offender.

(1980 S 320, eff. 3–23–81)

2917.41 Misconduct involving a public transportation system

(A) No person shall evade the payment of the known fares of a public transportation system.

(B) No person shall alter any transfer, pass, ticket, or token of a public transportation system with the purpose of evading the payment of fares or of defrauding the system.

(C) No person shall do any of the following while in any facility or on any vehicle of a public transportation system:

(1) Play sound equipment without the proper use of a private earphone;

(2) Smoke, eat, or drink in any area where the activity is clearly marked as being prohibited;

(3) Expectorate upon a person, facility, or vehicle.

(D) No person shall write, deface, draw, or otherwise mark on any facility or vehicle of a public transportation system.

(E) No person shall fail to comply with a lawful order of a public transportation system police officer, and no person shall resist, obstruct, or abuse a public transportation police officer in the performance of the officer's duties.

(F) Whoever violates this section is guilty of misconduct involving a public transportation system.

(1) Violation of division (A), (B), or (E) of this section is a misdemeanor of the fourth degree.

(2) Violation of division (C) of this section is a minor misdemeanor on a first offense. If a person previously has been convicted of or pleaded guilty to a violation of any division of this section or of a municipal ordinance that is substantially similar to any division of this section, violation of division (C) of this section is a misdemeanor of the fourth degree.

(3) Violation of division (D) of this section is a misdemeanor of the third degree.

(G) Notwithstanding any other provision of law, seventy-five per cent of each fine paid to satisfy a sentence imposed for a violation of this section shall be deposited into the treasury of the county in which the violation occurred and twenty-five per cent shall be deposited with the county transit board, regional transit authority, or regional transit commission that operates the public transportation system involved in the violation, unless the board of county commissioners operates the public transportation system, in which case one hundred per cent of each fine shall be deposited into the treasury of the county.

(H) As used in this section, "public transportation system" means a county transit system operated in accordance with sections 306.01 to 306.13 of the Revised Code, a regional transit authority operated in accordance with sections 306.30 to 306.71 of the Revised Code, or a regional transit commission operated in accordance with sections 306.80 to 306.90 of the Revised Code.

(2003 H 95, eff. 9–26–03; 1995 S 2, eff. 7–1–96; 1995 H 61, eff. 10–25–95; 1986 H 813, eff. 9–17–86; 1984 S 86)

2917.46 Misuse of block parent symbol

(A) No person shall, with intent to identify a building as a block parent home or building, display the block parent symbol adopted by the state board of education pursuant to section 3301.076 of the Revised Code unless authorized in accordance with that section or section 3313.206 of the Revised Code.

(B) No person shall, with intent to identify a building as a block parent home or building, display a symbol that falsely gives the appearance of being the block parent symbol adopted by the board of education.

(C) Whoever violates division (A) or (B) of this section is guilty of unauthorized use of a block parent symbol, a minor misdemeanor.

(1988 H 708, eff. 4–19–88; 1985 H 112)

2917.47 Improperly handling infectious agents

As used in this section, "infectious agent" means a microorganism such as a virus, bacterium, or similar agent that causes disease or death in human beings.

(A) No person shall knowingly possess, send, receive, or cause to be sent or received an isolate or derivative of an isolate of an infectious agent, except as permitted by division (B) of this section.

(B) A person may possess, send, receive, or cause to be sent or received an isolate or derivative of an isolate of an infectious agent as permitted by state or federal law, including for purposes of biomedical or biotechnical research or production, provision of health care services, or investigation of disease by public health agencies.

(C) Whoever violates this section is guilty of improperly handling infectious agents, a felony of the second degree.

(1996 H 456, eff. 9–10–96)

CHAPTER 2919

OFFENSES AGAINST THE FAMILY

BIGAMY

2919.01 Bigamy

(A) No married person shall marry another or continue to cohabit with such other person in this state.

(B) It is an affirmative defense to a charge under this section that the actor's spouse was continuously absent for five years immediately preceding the purported subsequent marriage, and was not known by the actor to be alive within that time.

(C) Whoever violates this section is guilty of bigamy, a misdemeanor of the first degree.

(1972 H 511, eff. 1–1–74)

ABORTION

2919.11 Abortion defined; practice of medicine

As used in the Revised Code, "abortion" means the purposeful termination of a human pregnancy by any person, including the pregnant woman herself, with an intention other than to produce a live birth or to remove a dead fetus or embryo. Abortion is the practice of medicine or surgery for the purposes of section 4731.41 of the Revised Code.

(1974 H 989, eff. 9–16–74)

2919.12 Abortion without informed consent prohibited; unmarried minors

(A) No person shall perform or induce an abortion without the informed consent of the pregnant woman.

(B)(1)(a) No person shall knowingly perform or induce an abortion upon a woman who is pregnant, unmarried, under eighteen years of age, and unemancipated unless at least one of the following applies:

(i) Subject to division (B)(2) of this section, the person has given at least twenty-four hours actual notice, in person or by telephone, to one of the woman's parents, her guardian, or her custodian as to the intention to perform or induce the abortion, provided that if the woman has requested, in accordance with division (B)(1)(b) of this section, that notice be given to a specified brother or sister of the woman who is twenty-one years of age or older or to a specified stepparent or grandparent of the woman instead of to one of her parents, her guardian, or her custodian, and if the person is notified by a juvenile court that affidavits of the type described in that division have been filed with that court, the twenty-four hours actual notice described in this division as to the intention to perform or induce the abortion shall be given, in person or by telephone, to the specified brother, sister, stepparent, or grandparent instead of to the parent, guardian, or custodian;

(ii) One of the woman's parents, her guardian, or her custodian has consented in writing to the performance or inducement of the abortion;

(iii) A juvenile court pursuant to section 2151.85 of the Revised Code issues an order authorizing the woman to consent to the abortion without notification of one of her parents, her guardian, or her custodian;

(iv) A juvenile court or a court of appeals, by its inaction, constructively has authorized the woman to consent to the abortion without notification of one of her parents, her guardian, or her custodian under division (B)(1) of section 2151.85 or division (A) of section 2505.073 of the Revised Code.

(b) If a woman who is pregnant, unmarried, under eighteen years of age, and unemancipated desires notification as to a person's intention to perform or induce an abortion on the woman to be given to a specified brother or sister of the woman who is twenty-one years of age or older or to a specified stepparent or grandparent of the woman instead of to one of her parents, her guardian, or her custodian, the person who intends to perform or induce the abortion shall notify the specified brother, sister, stepparent, or grandparent instead of the parent, guardian, or custodian for purposes of division (B)(1)(a)(i) of this section if all of the following apply:

(i) The woman has requested the person to provide the notification to the specified brother, sister, stepparent, or grandparent, clearly has identified the specified brother, sister, stepparent, or grandparent and her relation to that person, and, if the specified relative is a brother or sister, has indicated the age of the brother or sister;

(ii) The woman has executed an affidavit stating that she is in fear of physical, sexual, or severe emotional abuse from the parent, guardian, or custodian who otherwise would be notified under division (B)(1)(a)(i) of this section, and that the fear is based on a pattern of physical, sexual, or severe emotional abuse of her exhibited by that parent, guardian, or custodian, has filed the affidavit with the juvenile court of the county in which the woman has a residence or legal settlement, the juvenile court of any county that borders to any extent the county in which she has a residence or legal settlement, or the juvenile court of the county in which the hospital, clinic, or other facility in which the abortion would be performed or induced is located, and has given the court written notice of the name and address of the person who intends to perform or induce the abortion;

(iii) The specified brother, sister, stepparent, or grandparent has executed an affidavit stating that the woman has reason to fear physical, sexual, or severe emotional abuse from the parent, guardian, or custodian who otherwise would be notified under division (B)(1)(a)(i) of this section, based on a pattern of physical, sexual, or severe emotional abuse of her by that parent, guardian, or custodian, and the woman or the specified brother, sister, stepparent, or grandparent has filed the affidavit with the juvenile court in which the affidavit described in division (B)(1)(b)(ii) of this section was filed;

(iv) The juvenile court in which the affidavits described in divisions (B)(1)(b)(ii) and (iii) of this section were filed has notified the person that both of those affidavits have been filed with the court.

(c) If an affidavit of the type described in division (B)(1)(b)(ii) of this section and an affidavit of the type described in division (B)(1)(b)(iii) of this section are filed with a juvenile court and the court has been provided with written notice of the name and address of the person who intends to perform or induce an abortion upon the woman to whom the affidavits pertain, the court promptly shall notify the person who intends to perform or induce the abortion that the affidavits have been filed. If possible, the notice to the person shall be given in person or by telephone.

(2) If division (B)(1)(a)(ii), (iii), or (iv) of this section does not apply, and if no parent, guardian, or custodian can be reached for purposes of division (B)(1)(a)(i) of this section after a reasonable effort, or if notification is to be given to a specified brother, sister, stepparent, or grandparent under that division and the specified brother, sister, stepparent, or grandparent cannot be reached for purposes of that division after a reasonable effort, no person shall perform or induce such an abortion without giving at least forty-eight hours constructive notice to one of the woman's parents, her guardian, or her custodian, by both certified and ordinary mail sent to the last known address of the parent, guardian, or custodian, or if notification for purposes of division (B)(1)(a)(i) of this section is to be given to a specified brother, sister, stepparent, or grandparent, without giving at least forty-eight hours constructive notice to that specified brother, sister, stepparent, or grandparent by both certified and ordinary mail sent to the last known address of that specified brother, sister, stepparent, or grandparent. The forty-eight-hour period under this division begins when the certified mail notice is mailed. If a parent, guardian, or custodian of the woman, or if notification under division (B)(1)(a)(i) of this section is to be given to a specified brother, sister, stepparent, or grandparent, the specified brother, sister, stepparent, or grandparent, is not reached within the forty-eight-hour period, the abortion may proceed even if the certified mail notice is not received.

(3) If a parent, guardian, custodian, or specified brother, sister, stepparent, or grandparent who has been notified in accordance with division (B)(1) or (2) of this section clearly and unequivocally expresses that he or she does not wish to consult with a pregnant woman prior to her abortion, then the abortion may proceed without any further waiting period.

(4) For purposes of prosecutions for a violation of division (B)(1) or (2) of this section, it shall be a rebuttable presumption that a woman who is unmarried and under eighteen years of age is unemancipated.

(C)(1) It is an affirmative defense to a charge under division (B)(1) or (2) of this section that the pregnant woman provided the person who performed or induced the abortion with false, misleading, or incorrect information about her age, marital status, or emancipation, about the age of a brother or sister to whom she requested notice be given as a specified relative instead of to one of her parents, her guardian, or her custodian, or about the last known address of either of her parents, her guardian, her custodian, or a specified brother, sister, stepparent, or grandparent to whom she requested notice be given and the person who performed or induced the abortion did not otherwise have reasonable cause to believe the pregnant woman was under eighteen years of age, unmarried, or unemancipated, to believe that the age of a brother or sister to whom she requested notice be given as a specified relative instead of to one of her parents, her guardian, or her custodian was not twenty-one years of age, or to believe that the last known address of either of her parents, her guardian, her custodian, or a specified brother, sister, stepparent, or grandparent to whom she requested notice be given was incorrect.

(2) It is an affirmative defense to a charge under this section that compliance with the requirements of this section was not possible because an immediate threat of serious risk to the life or physical health of the pregnant woman from the continuation of her pregnancy created an emergency necessitating the immediate performance or inducement of an abortion.

(D) Whoever violates this section is guilty of unlawful abortion. A violation of division (A) of this section is a misdemeanor of the first degree on the first offense and a felony of the fourth degree on each subsequent offense. A violation of division (B) of this section is a misdemeanor of the first degree on a first offense and a felony of the fifth degree on each subsequent offense.

(E) Whoever violates this section is liable to the pregnant woman and her parents, guardian, or custodian for civil compensatory and exemplary damages.

(F) As used in this section "unemancipated" means that a woman who is unmarried and under eighteen years of age has not entered the armed services of the United States, has not become employed and self-subsisting, or has not otherwise become independent from the care and control of her parent, guardian, or custodian.

(1995 S 2, eff. 7–1–96; 1985 H 319, eff. 3–24–86; 1974 H 989)

2919.121 Unlawful abortion

(A) For the purpose of this section, a minor shall be considered "emancipated" if the minor has married, entered the armed services of the United States, become employed and self-subsisting, or has otherwise become independent from the care and control of her parent, guardian, or custodian.

(B) No person shall knowingly perform or induce an abortion upon a pregnant minor unless one of the following is the case:

(1) The attending physician has secured the informed written consent of the minor and one parent, guardian, or custodian;

(2) The minor is emancipated and the attending physician has received her written informed consent;

(3) The minor has been authorized to consent to the abortion by a court order issued pursuant to division (C) of this section, and the attending physician has received her informed written consent;

(4) The court has given its consent in accordance with division (C) of this section and the minor is having the abortion willingly.

(C) The right of a minor to consent to an abortion under division (B)(3) of this section or judicial consent to obtain an abortion under division (B)(4) of this section may be granted by a court order pursuant to the following procedures:

(1) The minor or next friend shall make an application to the juvenile court of the county in which the minor has a residence or legal settlement, the juvenile court of any county that borders the county in which she has a residence or legal settlement, or the juvenile court of the county in which the facility in which the abortion would be performed or induced is located. The juvenile court shall assist the minor or next friend in preparing the petition and notices required by this section. The minor or next friend shall thereafter file a petition setting forth all of the following: the initials of the minor; her age; the names and addresses of each parent, guardian, custodian, or, if the minor's parents are deceased and no guardian has been appointed, any other person standing in loco parentis of the minor; that the minor has been fully informed of the risks and consequences of the abortion; that the minor is of sound mind and has sufficient intellectual capacity to consent to the abortion; that the minor has not previously filed a petition under this section concerning the same pregnancy that was denied on the merits; that, if the court does not authorize the minor to consent to the abortion, the court should find that the abortion is in the best interests of the minor and give judicial consent to the abortion; that the court should appoint a guardian ad litem; and if the minor does not have private counsel, that the court should appoint counsel. The petition shall be signed by the minor or the next friend.

(2) A hearing on the merits shall be held on the record as soon as possible within five days of filing the petition. If the minor has not retained counsel, the court shall appoint counsel at least twenty-four hours prior to the hearing. The court shall appoint a guardian ad litem to protect the interests of the minor at the hearing. If the guardian ad litem is an attorney admitted to the practice of law in this state, the court may appoint the guardian ad litem to serve as the minor's counsel. At the hearing, the court shall hear evidence relating to the emotional development, maturity, intellect, and understanding of the minor; the nature, possible consequences, and alternatives to the abortion; and any other evidence that the court may find useful in determining whether the minor should be granted the right to consent to the abortion or whether the abortion is in the best interests of the minor. If the minor or her counsel fail to appear for a scheduled hearing, jurisdiction shall remain with the judge who would have presided at the hearing.

(3) If the court finds that the minor is sufficiently mature and well enough informed to decide intelligently whether to have an abortion, the court shall grant the petition and permit the minor to consent to the abortion.

If the court finds that the abortion is in the best interests of the minor, the court shall give judicial consent to the abortion, setting forth the grounds for its finding.

If the court does not make either of the findings specified in division (C)(3) of this section, the court shall deny the petition, setting forth the grounds on which the petition is denied.

The court shall issue its order not later than twenty four hours after the end of the hearing.

(4) No juvenile court shall have jurisdiction to rehear a petition concerning the same pregnancy once a juvenile court has granted or denied the petition.

(5) If the petition is granted, the informed consent of the minor, pursuant to a court order authorizing the minor to consent to the abortion, or judicial consent to the abortion, shall bar an action by the parents, guardian, or custodian of the minor for battery of the minor against any person performing or inducing the abortion. The immunity granted shall only extend to the performance or inducement of the abortion in accordance with this section and to any accompanying services that are performed in a competent manner.

(6) An appeal from an order issued under this section may be taken to the court of appeals by the minor. The record on appeal shall be completed and the appeal perfected within four days from the filing of the notice of appeal. Because the abortion may need to be performed in a timely manner, the supreme court shall, by rule, provide for expedited appellate review of cases appealed under this section.

(7) All proceedings under this section shall be conducted in a confidential manner and shall be given such precedence over other pending matters as will ensure that the court will reach a decision promptly and without delay.

The petition and all other papers and records that pertain to an action commenced under this section shall be kept confidential and are not public records under section 149.43 of the Revised Code.

(8) No filing fee shall be required of or court costs assessed against a person filing a petition under this section or appealing an order issued under this section.

(D) It is an affirmative defense to any civil, criminal, or professional disciplinary claim brought under this section that compliance with the requirements of this section was not possible because an immediate threat of serious risk to the life or physical health of the minor from the continuation of her pregnancy created an emergency necessitating the immediate performance or inducement of an abortion.

(E) Whoever violates division (B) of this section is guilty of unlawful abortion, a misdemeanor of the first degree. If the offender previously has been convicted of or pleaded guilty to a violation of this section, unlawful abortion is a felony of the fourth degree.

(F) Whoever violates division (B) of this section is liable to the pregnant minor and her parents, guardian, or custodian for civil, compensatory, and exemplary damages.

(1998 H 421, eff. 5–6–98)

2919.122 Compliance with abortion consent statutes as complete defense

Section 2919.121 of the Revised Code applies in lieu of division (B) of section 2919.12 of the Revised Code whenever its operation is not enjoined. If section 2919.121 of the Revised Code is enjoined, division (B) of section 2919.12 of the Revised Code applies.

If a person complies with the requirements of division (B) of section 2919.12 of the Revised Code under the good faith belief that the application or enforcement of section 2919.121 of the Revised Code is subject to a restraining order or injunction, good faith compliance shall constitute a complete defense to any civil, criminal, or professional disciplinary action brought under section 2919.121 of the Revised Code.

If a person complies with the requirements of section 2919.121 of the Revised Code under the good faith belief that it is not subject to a restraining order or injunction, good faith compliance shall constitute a complete defense to any criminal, civil, or professional disciplinary action for failure to comply with the requirements of division (B) of section 2919.12 of the Revised Code.

(1998 H 421, eff. 5–6–98)

2919.123 Provision or use of RU-486; penalty

(A) No person shall knowingly give, sell, dispense, administer, otherwise provide, or prescribe RU–486 (mifepristone) to another for the purpose of inducing an abortion in any person or enabling the other person to induce an abortion in any person, unless the person who gives, sells, dispenses, administers, or otherwise provides or prescribes the RU–486 (mifepristone) is a physician, the physician satisfies all the criteria established by federal law that a physician must satisfy in order to provide RU–486 (mifepristone) for inducing abortions, and the physician provides the RU–486 (mifepristone) to the other person for the purpose of inducing an abortion in accordance with all provisions of federal law that govern the use of RU–486 (mifepristone) for inducing abortions. A person who gives, sells, dispenses, administers, otherwise provides, or prescribes RU–486 (mifepristone) to another as described in division (A) of this section shall not be prosecuted based on a violation of the criteria contained in this division unless the person knows that the person is not a physician, that the person did not satisfy all the specified criteria established by federal law, or that the person did not provide the RU–486 (mifepristone) in accordance with the specified provisions of federal law, whichever is applicable.

(B) No physician who provides RU–486 (mifepristone) to another for the purpose of inducing an abortion as authorized under division (A) of this section shall knowingly fail to comply with the applicable requirements of any federal law that pertain to follow-up examinations or care for persons to whom or for whom RU–486 (mifepristone) is provided for the purpose of inducing an abortion.

(C)(1) If a physician provides RU–486 (mifepristone) to another for the purpose of inducing an abortion as authorized under division (A) of this section and if the physician knows that the person who uses the RU–486 (mifepristone) for the purpose of inducing an abortion experiences during or after the use an incomplete abortion, severe bleeding, or an adverse reaction to the RU–486 (mifepristone) or is hospitalized, receives a transfusion, or experiences any other serious event, the physician promptly must provide a written report of the incomplete abortion, severe bleeding, adverse reaction, hospitalization, transfusion, or serious event to the state medical board. The board shall compile and retain all reports it receives under this division. Except as otherwise provided in this division, all reports the board receives under this division are public records open to inspection under section 149.43 of the Revised Code. In no case shall the board release to any person the name or any other personal identifying information regarding a person who uses RU–486 (mifepristone) for the purpose of inducing an abortion and who is the subject of a report the board receives under this division.

(2) No physician who provides RU–486 (mifepristone) to another for the purpose of inducing an abortion as authorized under division (A) of this section shall knowingly fail to file a report required under division (C)(1) of this section.

(D) Division (A) of this section does not apply to any of the following:

(1) A pregnant woman who obtains or possesses RU–486 (mifepristone) for the purpose of inducing an abortion to terminate her own pregnancy;

(2) The legal transport of RU–486 (mifepristone) by any person or entity and the legal delivery of the RU–486 (mifepristone) by any person to the recipient, provided that this division does not apply regarding any conduct related to the RU–486 (mifepristone) other than its transport and delivery to the recipient;

(3) The distribution, provision, or sale of RU–486 (mifepristone) by any legal manufacturer or distributor of RU–486 (mifepristone), provided the manufacturer or distributor made a good faith effort to comply with any applicable requirements of federal law regarding the distribution, provision, or sale.

(E) Whoever violates this section is guilty of unlawful distribution of an abortion-inducing drug, a felony of the fourth degree. If the offender previously has been convicted of or pleaded guilty to a violation of this section or of section 2919.12, 2919.121, 2919.13, 2919.14, 2919.151, 2919.17, or 2919.18 of the Revised Code, unlawful distribution of an abortion-inducing drug is a felony of the third degree.

If the offender is a professionally licensed person, in addition to any other sanction imposed by law for the offense, the offender is subject to sanctioning as provided by law by the regulatory or licensing board or agency that has the administrative authority to suspend or revoke the offender's professional license, including the sanctioning provided in section 4731.22 of the Revised Code for offenders who have a certificate to practice or certificate of registration issued under that chapter.

(F) As used in this section:

(1) "Federal law" means any law, rule, or regulation of the United States or any drug approval letter of the food and drug administration of the United States that governs or regulates the use of RU–486 (mifepristone) for the purpose of inducing abortions.

(2) "Personal identifying information" has the same meaning as in section 2913.49 of the Revised Code.

(3) "Physician" has the same meaning as in section 2305.113 of the Revised Code.

(4) "Professionally licensed person" has the same meaning as in section 2925.01 of the Revised Code.

(2004 H 126, eff. 9–23–04)

2919.13 Abortion manslaughter

(A) No person shall purposely take the life of a child born by attempted abortion who is alive when removed from the uterus of the pregnant woman.

(B) No person who performs an abortion shall fail to take the measures required by the exercise of medical judgment in light of the attending circumstances to preserve the life of a child who is alive when removed from the uterus of the pregnant woman.

(C) Whoever violates this section is guilty of abortion manslaughter, a felony of the first degree.

(1974 H 989, eff. 9–16–74)

2919.14 Abortion trafficking

(A) No person shall experiment upon or sell the product of human conception which is aborted. Experiment does not include autopsies pursuant to sections 313.13 and 2108.50 of the Revised Code.

(B) Whoever violates this section is guilty of abortion trafficking, a misdemeanor of the first degree.

(1974 H 989, eff. 9–16–74)

2919.151 Partial birth feticide

(A) As used in this section:

(1) "Dilation and evacuation procedure of abortion" does not include the dilation and extraction procedure of abortion.

(2) "From the body of the mother" means that the portion of the fetus' body in question is beyond the mother's vaginal introitus in a vaginal delivery.

(3) "Partial birth procedure" means the medical procedure that includes all of the following elements in sequence:

(a) Intentional dilation of the cervix of a pregnant woman, usually over a sequence of days;

(b) In a breech presentation, intentional extraction of at least the lower torso to the navel, but not the entire body, of an intact fetus from the body of the mother, or in a cephalic presentation, intentional extraction of at least the complete head, but not the entire body, of an intact fetus from the body of the mother;

(c) Intentional partial evacuation of the intracranial contents of the fetus, which procedure the person performing the procedure knows will cause the death of the fetus, intentional compression of the head of the fetus, which procedure the person performing the procedure knows will cause the death of the fetus, or performance of another intentional act that the person performing the procedure knows will cause the death of the fetus;

(d) Completion of the vaginal delivery of the fetus.

(4) "Partially born" means that the portion of the body of an intact fetus described in division (A)(3)(b) of this section has been intentionally extracted from the body of the mother.

(5) "Serious risk of the substantial and irreversible impairment of a major bodily function" means any medically diagnosed condition that so complicates the pregnancy of the woman as to directly or indirectly cause the substantial and irreversible impairment of a major bodily function.

(6) "Viable" has the same meaning as in section 2901.01 of the Revised Code.

(B) When the fetus that is the subject of the procedure is viable, no person shall knowingly perform a partial birth procedure on a pregnant woman when the procedure is not necessary, in reasonable medical judgment, to preserve the life or health of the mother as a result of the mother's life or health being endangered by a serious risk of the substantial and irreversible impairment of a major bodily function.

(C) When the fetus that is the subject of the procedure is not viable, no person shall knowingly perform a partial birth procedure on a pregnant woman when the procedure is not necessary, in reasonable medical judgment, to preserve the life or health of the mother as a result of the mother's life or health being endangered by a serious risk of the substantial and irreversible impairment of a major bodily function.

(D) Whoever violates division (B) or (C) of this section is guilty of partial birth feticide, a felony of the second degree.

(E) A pregnant woman upon whom a partial birth procedure is performed in violation of division (B) or (C) of this section is not guilty of committing, attempting to commit, complicity in the commission of, or conspiracy in the commission of a violation of those divisions.

(F) This section does not prohibit the suction curettage procedure of abortion, the suction aspiration procedure of abortion, or the dilation and evacuation procedure of abortion.

(G) This section does not apply to any person who performs or attempts to perform a legal abortion if the act that causes the death of the fetus is performed prior to the fetus being partially born even though the death of the fetus occurs after it is partially born.

(2000 H 351, eff. 8–18–00)

2919.16 Definitions

As used in sections 2919.16 to 2919.18 of the Revised Code:

(A) "Fertilization" means the fusion of a human spermatozoon with a human ovum.

(B) "Gestational age" means the age of an unborn human as calculated from the first day of the last menstrual period of a pregnant woman.

(C) "Health care facility" means a hospital, clinic, ambulatory surgical treatment center, other center, medical school, office of a physician, infirmary, dispensary, medical training institution, or other institution or location in or at which medical care, treatment, or diagnosis is provided to a person.

(D) "Hospital" has the same meanings as in sections 2108.01, 3701.01, and 5122.01 of the Revised Code.

(E) "Live birth" has the same meaning as in division (A) of section 3705.01 of the Revised Code.

(F) "Medical emergency" means a condition that a pregnant woman's physician determines, in good faith and in the exercise of reasonable medical judgment, so complicates the woman's pregnancy as to necessitate the immediate performance or inducement of an abortion in order to prevent the death of the pregnant woman or to avoid a serious risk of the substantial and irreversible impairment of a major bodily function of the pregnant woman that delay in the performance or inducement of the abortion would create.

(G) "Physician" has the same meaning as in section 2305.113 of the Revised Code.

(H) "Pregnant" means the human female reproductive condition, that commences with fertilization, of having a developing fetus.

(I) "Premature infant" means a human whose live birth occurs prior to thirty-eight weeks of gestational age.

(J) "Serious risk of the substantial and irreversible impairment of a major bodily function" means any medically diagnosed condition that so complicates the pregnancy of the woman as to directly or indirectly cause the substantial and irreversible impairment of a major bodily function, including, but not limited to, the following conditions:

(1) Pre–eclampsia;

(2) Inevitable abortion;

(3) Prematurely ruptured membrane;

(4) Diabetes;

(5) Multiple sclerosis.

(K) "Unborn human" means an individual organism of the species homo sapiens from fertilization until live birth.

(L) "Viable" means the stage of development of a human fetus at which in the determination of a physician, based on the particular facts of a woman's pregnancy that are known to the physician and in light of medical technology and information reasonably available to the physician, there is a realistic possibility of the maintaining and nourishing of a life outside of the womb with or without temporary artificial life-sustaining support.

(2002 S 281, eff. 4–11–03; 1995 H 135, eff. 11–15–95)

2919.17 Terminating a human pregnancy after viability

(A) No person shall purposely perform or induce or attempt to perform or induce an abortion upon a pregnant woman if the unborn human is viable, unless either of the following applies:

(1) The abortion is performed or induced or attempted to be performed or induced by a physician, and that physician determines, in good faith and in the exercise of reasonable medical judgment, that the abortion is necessary to prevent the death of the pregnant woman or a serious risk of the substantial and irreversible impairment of a major bodily function of the pregnant woman.

(2) The abortion is performed or induced or attempted to be performed or induced by a physician and that physician determines, in good faith and in the exercise of reasonable medical judgment, after making a determination relative to the viability of the unborn human in conformity with division (a) of section 2919.18 of the Revised Code, that the unborn human is not viable.

(B)(1) Except as provided in division (B)(2) of this section, no physician shall purposely perform or induce or attempt to perform or induce an abortion upon a pregnant woman when the unborn human is viable and when the physician has determined, in good faith and in the exercise of reasonable medical judgment, that the abortion is necessary to prevent the death of the pregnant woman or a serious risk of the substantial and irreversible impairment of a major bodily function of the pregnant woman, unless each of the following conditions is satisfied:

(a) The physician who performs or induces or attempts to perform or induce the abortion certifies in writing that that physician has determined, in good faith and in the exercise of reasonable medical judgment, that the abortion is necessary to prevent the death of the pregnant woman or a serious risk of the substantial and irreversible impairment of a major bodily function of the pregnant woman.

(b) The determination of the physician who performs or induces or attempts to perform or induce the abortion that is described in division (B)(1)(a) of this section is concurred in by at least one other physician who certifies in writing that the concurring physician has determined, in good faith, in the exercise of reasonable medical judgment, and following a review of the available medical records of and any available tests results pertaining to the pregnant woman, that the abortion is necessary to prevent the death of the pregnant woman or a serious risk of the substantial and irreversible impairment of a major bodily function of the pregnant woman.

(c) The abortion is performed or induced or attempted to be performed or induced in a health care facility that has or has access to appropriate neonatal services for premature infants.

(d) The physician who performs or induces or attempts to perform or induce the abortion terminates or attempts to terminate the pregnancy in the manner that provides the best opportunity for the unborn human to survive, unless that physician determines, in good faith and in the exercise of reasonable medical judgment, that the termination of the pregnancy in that manner poses a significantly greater risk of the death of the pregnant woman or a serious risk of the substantial and irreversible impairment of a major bodily function of the pregnant woman than would other available methods of abortion.

(e) The physician who performs or induces or attempts to perform or induce the abortion has arranged for the attendance in the same room in which the abortion is to be performed or induced or attempted to be performed or induced of at least one other physician who is to take control of, provide immediate medical care for, and take all reasonable steps necessary to preserve the life and health of the unborn human immediately upon the unborn human's complete expulsion or extraction from the pregnant woman.

(2) Division (B)(1) of this section does not prohibit the performance or inducement or an attempted performance or inducement of an abortion without prior satisfaction of each of the conditions described in divisions (B)(1)(a) to (e) of this section if the physician who performs or induces or attempts to perform or induce the abortion determines, in good faith and in the exercise of reasonable medical judgment, that a medical emergency exists that prevents compliance with one or more of those conditions.

(C) For purposes of this section, it shall be rebuttably presumed that an unborn child of at least twenty-four weeks of gestational age is viable.

(D) Whoever violates this section is guilty of terminating or attempting to terminate a human pregnancy after viability, a felony of the fourth degree.

(E) A pregnant woman upon whom an abortion is performed or induced or attempted to be performed or induced in violation of division (A) or (B) of this section is not guilty of an attempt to commit, complicity in the commission of, or conspiracy in the commission of a violation of either of those divisions.

(1995 H 135, eff. 11–15–95)

2919.18 Failure to perform viability testing on fetus

(A)(1) Except as provided in division (A)(3) of this section, no physician shall perform or induce or attempt to perform or induce an abortion upon a pregnant woman after the beginning of her twenty-second week of pregnancy unless, prior to the performance or inducement of the abortion or the attempt to perform or induce the abortion, the physician determines, in good faith and in the exercise of reasonable medical judgment, that the unborn human is not viable, and the physician makes that determination after performing a medical examination of the pregnant woman and after performing or causing the performing of gestational age, weight, lung maturity, or other tests of the unborn human that a reasonable physician making a determination as to whether an unborn human is or is not viable would perform or cause to be performed.

(2) Except as provided in division (A)(3) of this section, no physician shall perform or induce or attempt to perform or induce an abortion upon a pregnant woman after the beginning of her twenty-second week of pregnancy without first entering the determination described in division (A)(1) of this section and the associated findings of the medical examination and tests described in that division in the medical record of the pregnant woman.

(3) Divisions (A)(1) and (2) of this section do not prohibit a physician from performing or inducing or attempting to perform or induce an abortion upon a pregnant woman after the beginning of her twenty-second week of pregnancy without making the determination described in division (A)(1) of this section or without making the entry described in division (A)(2) of this section if a medical emergency exists.

(B) Whoever violates this section is guilty of failure to perform viability testing, a misdemeanor of the fourth degree.

(1995 H 135, eff. 11–15–95)

NONSUPPORT; CHILD ENDANGERING; RELATED OFFENSES

2919.21 Nonsupport of dependents; assessment of court costs and attorney fees in some cases

(A) No person shall abandon, or fail to provide adequate support to:

(1) The person's spouse, as required by law;

(2) The person's child who is under age eighteen, or mentally or physically handicapped child who is under age twenty-one;

(3) The person's aged or infirm parent or adoptive parent, who from lack of ability and means is unable to provide adequately for the parent's own support.

(B) No person shall abandon, or fail to provide support as established by a court order to, another person whom, by court order or decree, the person is legally obligated to support.

(C) No person shall aid, abet, induce, cause, encourage, or contribute to a child or a ward of the juvenile court becoming a dependent child, as defined in section 2151.04 of the Revised Code, or a neglected child, as defined in section 2151.03 of the Revised Code.

(D) It is an affirmative defense to a charge of failure to provide adequate support under division (A) of this section or a charge of failure to provide support established by a court order under division (B) of this section that the accused was unable to provide adequate support or the established support but did provide the support that was within the accused's ability and means.

(E) It is an affirmative defense to a charge under division (A)(3) of this section that the parent abandoned the accused or failed to support the accused as required by law, while the accused was under age eighteen, or was mentally or physically handicapped and under age twenty-one.

(F) It is not a defense to a charge under division (B) of this section that the person whom a court has ordered the accused to support is being adequately supported by someone other than the accused.

(G)(1) Except as otherwise provided in this division, whoever violates division (A) or (B) of this section is guilty of nonsupport of dependents, a misdemeanor of the first degree. If the offender previously has been convicted of or pleaded guilty to a violation of division (A)(2) or (B) of this section or if the offender has failed to provide support under division (A)(2) or (B) of this section for a total accumulated period of twenty-six weeks out of one hundred four consecutive weeks, whether or not the twenty-six weeks were consecutive, then a violation of division (A)(2) or (B) of this section is a felony of the fifth degree. If the offender previously has been convicted of or pleaded guilty to a felony violation of this section, a violation of division (A)(2) or (B) of this section is a felony of the fourth degree. If the offender is guilty of nonsupport of dependents by reason of failing to provide support to the offender's child as required by a child support order issued on or after April 15, 1985, pursuant to section 2151.23, 2151.231, 2151.232, 2151.33, 3105.21, 3109.05, 3111.13, 3113.04, 3113.31, or 3115.31 of the Revised Code, the court, in addition to any other sentence imposed, shall assess all court costs arising out of the charge against the person and require the person to pay any reasonable attorney's fees of any adverse party other than the state, as determined by the court, that arose in relation to the charge.

(2) Whoever violates division (C) of this section is guilty of contributing to the nonsupport of dependents, a misdemeanor of the first degree. Each day of violation of division (C) of this section is a separate offense.

(1997 H 352, eff. 1–1–98; 1996 S 269, eff. 7–1–96; 1996 H 274, § 4, eff. 8–8–96; 1996 H 274, § 1, eff. 8–8–96; 1995 S 2, eff. 7–1–96; 1986 S 136, eff. 9–24–86; 1985 H 349; 1984 H 614; 1972 H 511)

2919.22 Endangering children

(A) No person, who is the parent, guardian, custodian, person having custody or control, or person in loco parentis of a child under eighteen years of age or a mentally or physically handicapped child under twenty-one years of age, shall create a substantial risk to the health or safety of the child, by violating a duty of care, protection, or support. It is not a violation of a duty of care, protection, or support under this division when the parent, guardian, custodian, or person having custody or control of a child treats the physical or mental illness or defect of the child by spiritual means through prayer alone, in accordance with the tenets of a recognized religious body.

(B) No person shall do any of the following to a child under eighteen years of age or a mentally or physically handicapped child under twenty-one years of age:

(1) Abuse the child;

(2) Torture or cruelly abuse the child;

(3) Administer corporal punishment or other physical disciplinary measure, or physically restrain the child in a cruel manner or for a prolonged period, which punishment, discipline, or restraint is excessive under the circumstances and creates a substantial risk of serious physical harm to the child;

(4) Repeatedly administer unwarranted disciplinary measures to the child, when there is a substantial risk that such conduct, if continued, will seriously impair or retard the child's mental health or development;

(5) Entice, coerce, permit, encourage, compel, hire, employ, use, or allow the child to act, model, or in any other way participate in, or be photographed for, the production, presentation, dissemination, or advertisement of any material or performance that the offender knows or reasonably should know is obscene, is sexually oriented matter, or is nudity-oriented matter;

(6) Allow the child to be on the same parcel of real property and within one hundred feet of, or, in the case of more than one housing unit on the same parcel of real property, in the same housing unit and within one hundred feet of, any act in violation of section 2925.04 or 2925.041 of the Revised Code when the person knows that the act is occurring, whether or not any person is prosecuted for or convicted of the violation of section 2925.04 or 2925.041 of the Revised Code that is the basis of the violation of this division.

(C)(1) No person shall operate a vehicle, streetcar, or trackless trolley within this state in violation of division (A) of section

4511.19 of the Revised Code when one or more children under eighteen years of age are in the vehicle, streetcar, or trackless trolley. Notwithstanding any other provision of law, a person may be convicted at the same trial or proceeding of a violation of this division and a violation of division (A) of section 4511.19 of the Revised Code that constitutes the basis of the charge of the violation of this division. For purposes of sections 4511.191 to 4511.197 of the Revised Code and all related provisions of law, a person arrested for a violation of this division shall be considered to be under arrest for operating a vehicle while under the influence of alcohol, a drug of abuse, or a combination of them or for operating a vehicle with a prohibited concentration of alcohol in the whole blood, blood serum or plasma, breath, or urine.

(2) As used in division (C)(1) of this section, " vehicle," "streetcar," and "trackless trolley" have the same meanings as in section 4511.01 of the Revised Code.

(D)(1) Division (B)(5) of this section does not apply to any material or performance that is produced, presented, or disseminated for a bona fide medical, scientific, educational, religious, governmental, judicial, or other proper purpose, by or to a physician, psychologist, sociologist, scientist, teacher, person pursuing bona fide studies or research, librarian, member of the clergy, prosecutor, judge, or other person having a proper interest in the material or performance.

(2) Mistake of age is not a defense to a charge under division (B)(5) of this section.

(3) In a prosecution under division (B)(5) of this section, the trier of fact may infer that an actor, model, or participant in the material or performance involved is a juvenile if the material or performance, through its title, text, visual representation, or otherwise, represents or depicts the actor, model, or participant as a juvenile.

(4) As used in this division and division (B)(5) of this section:

(a) "Material," "performance," " obscene," and "sexual activity" have the same meanings as in section 2907.01 of the Revised Code.

(b) "Nudity–oriented matter" means any material or performance that shows a minor in a state of nudity and that, taken as a whole by the average person applying contemporary community standards, appeals to prurient interest.

(c) "Sexually oriented matter" means any material or performance that shows a minor participating or engaging in sexual activity, masturbation, or bestiality.

(E)(1) Whoever violates this section is guilty of endangering children.

(2) If the offender violates division (A) or (B)(1) of this section, endangering children is one of the following:

(a) Except as otherwise provided in division (E)(2)(b), (c), or (d) of this section, a misdemeanor of the first degree;

(b) If the offender previously has been convicted of an offense under this section or of any offense involving neglect, abandonment, contributing to the delinquency of, or physical abuse of a child, except as otherwise provided in division (E)(2)(c) or (d) of this section, a felony of the fourth degree;

(c) If the violation is a violation of division (A) of this section and results in serious physical harm to the child involved, a felony of the third degree;

(d) If the violation is a violation of division (B)(1) of this section and results in serious physical harm to the child involved, a felony of the second degree.

(3) If the offender violates division (B)(2), (3), (4), or (6) of this section, except as otherwise provided in this division, endangering children is a felony of the third degree. If the violation results in serious physical harm to the child involved, or if the offender previously has been convicted of an offense under this section or of any offense involving neglect, abandonment, contributing to the delinquency of, or physical abuse of a child, endangering children is a felony of the second degree.

(4) If the offender violates division (B)(5) of this section, endangering children is a felony of the second degree.

(5) If the offender violates division (C) of this section, the offender shall be punished as follows:

(a) Except as otherwise provided in division (E)(5)(b) or (c) of this section, endangering children in violation of division (C) of this section is a misdemeanor of the first degree.

(b) If the violation results in serious physical harm to the child involved or the offender previously has been convicted of an offense under this section or any offense involving neglect, abandonment, contributing to the delinquency of, or physical abuse of a child, except as otherwise provided in division (E)(5)(c) of this section, endangering children in violation of division (C) of this section is a felony of the fifth degree.

(c) If the violation results in serious physical harm to the child involved and if the offender previously has been convicted of a violation of division (C) of this section, section 2903.06 or 2903.08 of the Revised Code, section 2903.07 of the Revised Code as it existed prior to March 23, 2000, or section 2903.04 of the Revised Code in a case in which the offender was subject to the sanctions described in division (D) of that section, endangering children in violation of division (C) of this section is a felony of the fourth degree.

(d) In addition to any term of imprisonment, fine, or other sentence, penalty, or sanction it imposes upon the offender pursuant to division (E)(5)(a), (b), or (c) of this section or pursuant to any other provision of law and in addition to any suspension of the offender's driver's or commercial driver's license or permit or nonresident operating privilege under Chapter 4506., 4509., 4510., or 4511. of the Revised Code or under any other provision of law, the court also may impose upon the offender a class seven suspension of the offender's driver's or commercial driver's license or permit or nonresident operating privilege from the range specified in division (A)(7) of section 4510.02 of the Revised Code.

(e) In addition to any term of imprisonment, fine, or other sentence, penalty, or sanction imposed upon the offender pursuant to division (E)(5)(a), (b), (c), or (d) of this section or pursuant to any other provision of law for the violation of division (C) of this section, if as part of the same trial or proceeding the offender also is convicted of or pleads guilty to a separate charge charging the violation of division (A) of section 4511.19 of the Revised Code that was the basis of the charge of the violation of division (C) of this section, the offender also shall be sentenced in accordance with section 4511.19 of the Revised Code for that violation of division (A) of section 4511.19 of the Revised Code.

(F)(1)(a) A court may require an offender to perform not more than two hundred hours of supervised community service work under the authority of an agency, subdivision, or charitable organization. The requirement shall be part of the community control sanction or sentence of the offender, and the court shall impose the community service in accordance with and subject to divisions (F)(1)(a) and (b) of this section. The court may require an offender whom it requires to perform supervised community service work as part of the offender's community control sanction or sentence to pay the court a reasonable fee to cover the costs of the offender's participation in the work, including, but not limited to, the costs of procuring a policy or policies of liability insurance to cover the period during which the offender will perform the work. If the court requires the offender to perform supervised community service work as part of the offender's community control sanction or sentence, the court shall do so in accordance with the following limitations and criteria:

(i) The court shall require that the community service work be performed after completion of the term of imprisonment or jail term imposed upon the offender for the violation of division (C) of this section, if applicable.

(ii) The supervised community service work shall be subject to the limitations set forth in divisions (B)(1), (2), and (3) of section 2951.02 of the Revised Code.

(iii) The community service work shall be supervised in the manner described in division (B)(4) of section 2951.02 of the Revised Code by an official or person with the qualifications described in that division. The official or person periodically shall report in writing to the court concerning the conduct of the offender in performing the work.

(iv) The court shall inform the offender in writing that if the offender does not adequately perform, as determined by the court, all of the required community service work, the court may order that the offender be committed to a jail or workhouse for a period of time that does not exceed the term of imprisonment that the court could have imposed upon the offender for the violation of division (C) of this section, reduced by the total amount of time that the offender actually was imprisoned under the sentence or term that was imposed upon the offender for that violation and by the total amount of time that the offender was confined for any reason arising out of the offense for which the offender was convicted and sentenced as described in sections 2949.08 and 2967.191 of the Revised Code, and that, if the court orders that the offender be so committed, the court is authorized, but not required, to grant the offender credit upon the period of the commitment for the community service work that the offender adequately performed.

(b) If a court, pursuant to division (F)(1)(a) of this section, orders an offender to perform community service work as part of the offender's community control sanction or sentence and if the offender does not adequately perform all of the required community service work, as determined by the court, the court may order that the offender be committed to a jail or workhouse for a period of time that does not exceed the term of imprisonment that the court could have imposed upon the offender for the violation of division (C) of this section, reduced by the total amount of time that the offender actually was imprisoned under the sentence or term that was imposed upon the offender for that violation and by the total amount of time that the offender was confined for any reason arising out of the offense for which the offender was convicted and sentenced as described in sections 2949.08 and 2967.191 of the Revised Code. The court may order that a person committed pursuant to this division shall receive hour-for-hour credit upon the period of the commitment for the community service work that the offender adequately performed. No commitment pursuant to this division shall exceed the period of the term of imprisonment that the sentencing court could have imposed upon the offender for the violation of division (C) of this section, reduced by the total amount of time that the offender actually was imprisoned under that sentence or term and by the total amount of time that the offender was confined for any reason arising out of the offense for which the offender was convicted and sentenced as described in sections 2949.08 and 2967.191 of the Revised Code.

(2) Division (F)(1) of this section does not limit or affect the authority of the court to suspend the sentence imposed upon a misdemeanor offender and place the offender under a community control sanction pursuant to section 2929.25 of the Revised Code, to require a misdemeanor or felony offender to perform supervised community service work in accordance with division (B) of section 2951.02 of the Revised Code, or to place a felony offender under a community control sanction.

(G)(1) If a court suspends an offender's driver's or commercial driver's license or permit or nonresident operating privilege under division (E)(5)(d) of this section, the period of the suspension shall be consecutive to, and commence after, the period of suspension of the offender's driver's or commercial driver's license or permit or nonresident operating privilege that is imposed under Chapter 4506., 4509., 4510., or 4511. of the Revised Code or under any other provision of law in relation to the violation of division (C) of this section that is the basis of the suspension under division (E)(5)(d) of this section or in relation to the violation of division (A) of section 4511.19 of the Revised Code that is the basis for that violation of division (C) of this section.

(2) An offender is not entitled to request, and the court shall not grant to the offender, limited driving privileges if the offender's license, permit, or privilege has been suspended under division (E)(5)(d) of this section and the offender, within the preceding six years, has been convicted of or pleaded guilty to three or more violations of one or more of the following:

(a) Division (C) of this section;

(b) Any equivalent offense, as defined in section 4511.181 of the Revised Code.

(H)(1) If a person violates division (C) of this section and it, at the time of the violation, there were two or more children under eighteen years of age in the motor vehicle involved in the violation, the offender may be convicted of a violation of division (C) of this section for each of the children, but the court may sentence the offender for only one of the violations.

(2)(a) If a person is convicted of or pleads guilty to a violation of division (C) of this section but the person is not also convicted of and does not also plead guilty to a separate charge charging the violation of division (A) of section 4511.19 of the Revised Code that was the basis of the charge of the violation of division (C) of this section, both of the following apply:

(i) For purposes of the provisions of section 4511.19 of the Revised Code that set forth the penalties and sanctions for a violation of division (A) of section 4511.19 of the Revised Code, the conviction of or plea of guilty to the violation of division (C) of this section shall not constitute a violation of division (A) of section 4511.19 of the Revised Code;

(ii) For purposes of any provision of law that refers to a conviction of or plea of guilty to a violation of division (A) of section 4511.19 of the Revised Code and that is not described in division (H)(2)(a)(i) of this section, the conviction of or plea of guilty to the violation of division (C) of this section shall constitute a conviction of or plea of guilty to a violation of division (A) of section 4511.19 of the Revised Code.

(b) If a person is convicted of or pleads guilty to a violation of division (C) of this section and the person also is convicted of or pleads guilty to a separate charge charging the violation of division (A) of section 4511.19 of the Revised Code that was the basis of the charge of the violation of division (C) of this section, the conviction of or plea of guilty to the violation of division (C) of this section shall not constitute, for purposes of any provision of law that refers to a conviction of or plea of guilty to a violation of division (A) of section 4511.19 of the Revised Code, a conviction of or plea of guilty to a violation of division (A) of section 4511.19 of the Revised Code.

(I) As used in this section:

(1) "Community control sanction" has the same meaning as in section 2929.01 of the Revised Code;

(2) "Limited driving privileges" has the same meaning as in section 4501.01 of the Revised Code.

(2004 S 58, eff. 8–11–04; 2002 H 490, eff. 1–1–04; 2002 S 123, eff. 1–1–04; 2000 S 180, eff. 3–22–01; 1999 S 107, eff. 3–23–00; 1999 H 162, eff. 8–25–99; 1997 S 60, eff. 10–21–97; 1996 S 269, § 8, eff. 5–15–97; 1996 S 269, § 1, eff. 7–1–96; 1996 H 353, § 4, eff. 5–15–97; 1996 H 353, § 1, eff. 9–17–96; 1995 H 167, eff. 5–15–97; 1995 S 2, eff. 7–1–96; 1994 H 236, eff. 9–29–94; 1988 H 51, eff. 3–17–89; 1985 H 349; 1984 S 321, H 44; 1977 S 243; 1972 H 511)

2919.222 Parental education neglect

No person required to attend a parental education or training program pursuant to a policy adopted under division (A) or (B) of section 3313.663 of the Revised Code shall fail to attend the program. Whoever violates this section is guilty of parental education neglect, a misdemeanor of the fourth degree.

(1996 H 601, eff. 10–29–96)

MISREPRESENTATION AND NONDISCLOSURE BY CHILDCARE PROVIDER

2919.223 Definitions

As used in sections 2919.223 to 2919.227 of the Revised Code:

(A) "Child care," "child day-care center," "in-home aide," "type A family day-care home," and "type B family day-care home" have the same meanings as in section 5104.01 of the Revised Code.

(B) "Child care center licensee" means the owner of a child day-care center licensed pursuant to Chapter 5104. of the Revised Code who is responsible for ensuring the center's compliance with Chapter 5104. of the Revised Code and rules adopted pursuant to that chapter.

(C) "Child care facility" means a child day-care center, a type A family day-care home, or a type B family day-care home.

(D) "Child care provider" means any of the following:

(1) An owner, provider, administrator, or employee of, or volunteer at, a child care facility;

(2) An in-home aide;

(3) A person who represents that the person provides child care.

(E) "Peace officer" has the same meaning as in section 2935.01 of the Revised Code.

(2004 H 11, eff. 5–18–05)

2919.224 Misrepresentation by child care provider

(A) No child care provider shall knowingly misrepresent any factor or condition that relates to the provision of child care and that substantially affects the health or safety of any child or children in that provider's facility or receiving child care from that provider to any of the following:

(1) A parent, guardian, custodian, or other person responsible for the care of a child in the provider's facility or receiving child care from the provider;

(2) A parent, guardian, custodian, or other person responsible for the care of a child who is considering the provider as a child care provider for the child;

(3) A public official responsible for issuing the provider a license or certificate to provide child care;

(4) A public official investigating or inquiring about the provision of child care by the provider;

(5) A peace officer.

(B) For the purposes of this section, "any factor or condition that relates to the provision of child care" includes, but is not limited to, the following:

(1) The person or persons who will provide child care to the child of the parent, guardian, custodian, or other person responsible for the care of the child, or to the children in general;

(2) The qualifications to provide child care of the child care provider, of a person employed by the provider, or of a person who provides child care as a volunteer;

(3) The number of children to whom child care is provided at one time or the number of children receiving child care in the child care facility at one time;

(4) The conditions or safety features of the child care facility;

(5) The area of the child care facility in which child day-care is provided.

(C) Whoever violates division (A) of this section is guilty of misrepresentation by a child care provider, a misdemeanor of the first degree.

(2004 H 11, eff. 5–18–05)

2919.225 Failure of certain family day-care homes to disclose death or serious injury of child

(A) Subject to division (C) of this section, no owner, provider, or administrator of a type A family day-care home or type B family day-care home, knowing that the event described in division (A)(1) or (2) of this section has occurred, shall accept a child into that home without first disclosing to the parent, guardian, custodian, or other person responsible for the care of that child any of the following that has occurred:

(1) A child died while under the care of the home or while receiving child care from the owner, provider, or administrator or died as a result of injuries suffered while under the care of the home or while receiving child care from the owner, provider, or administrator.

(2) Within the preceding ten years, a child suffered injuries while under the care of the home or while receiving child care from the owner, provider, or administrator, and those injuries led to the child being hospitalized for more than twenty-four hours.

(B)(1) Subject to division (C) of this section, no owner, provider, or administrator of a type A family day-care home or type B family day-care home shall fail to provide notice in accordance with division (B)(3) of this section to the persons and entities specified in division (B)(2) of this section, of any of the following that occurs:

(a) A child who is under the care of the home or is receiving child care from the owner, provider, or administrator dies while under the care of the home or while receiving child care from the owner, provider, or administrator or dies as a result of injuries suffered while under the care of the home or while receiving child day-care from the owner, provider, or administrator.

(b) A child who is under the care of the home or is receiving child care from the owner, provider, or administrator is hospitalized for more than twenty-four hours as a result of injuries suffered while under the care of the home or while receiving child care from the owner, provider, or administrator.

(2) An owner, provider, or administrator of a home shall provide the notices required under division (B)(1) of this section to each of the following:

(a) For each child who, at the time of the injury or death for which the notice is required, is receiving or is enrolled to receive child care at the home or from the owner, provider, or administrator, to the parent, guardian, custodian, or other person responsible for the care of the child;

(b) If the notice is required as the result of the death of a child as described in division (B)(1)(a) of this section, to the public children services agency of the county in which the home is located or the child care was given, a municipal or county peace officer in the county in which the child resides or in which the home is located or the child care was given, and the child fatality review board appointed under section 307.621 of the Revised

Code that serves the county in which the home is located or the child care was given.

(3) An owner, provider, or administrator of a home shall provide the notices required by divisions (B)(1) and (2) of this section not later than forty-eight hours after the child dies or, regarding a child who is hospitalized for more than twenty-four hours as a result of injuries suffered while under the care of the home, not later than forty-eight hours after the child suffers the injuries. If a child is hospitalized for more than twenty-four hours as a result of injuries suffered while under the care of the home, and the child subsequently dies as a result of those injuries, the owner, provider, or administrator shall provide separate notices under divisions (B)(1) and (2) of this section regarding both the injuries and the death. All notices provided under divisions (B)(1) and (2) of this section shall state that the death or injury occurred.

(C) Division (A) of this section does not require more than one person to make disclosures to the same parent, guardian, custodian, or other person responsible for the care of a child regarding any single injury or death for which disclosure is required under that division. Division (B) of this section does not require more than one person to give notices to the same parent, guardian, custodian, other person responsible for the care of the child, public children services agency, peace officer, or child fatality review board regarding any single injury or death for which disclosure is required under division (B)(1) of this section.

(D) An owner, provider, or administrator of a type A family day-care home or type B family day-care home is not subject to civil liability solely for making a disclosure required by this section.

(E) Whoever violates division (A) or (B) of this section is guilty of failure of a type A or type B family day-care home to disclose the death or serious injury of a child, a misdemeanor of the fourth degree.

(2004 H 11, eff. 5–18–05)

2919.226 Providers not subject to prosecution relating to disclosure form; content of form

(A) If a child care provider accurately answers the questions on a child care disclosure form that is in substantially the form set forth in division (B) of this section, presents the form to a person identified in division (A)(1) or (2) of section 2919.224 of the Revised Code, and obtains the person's signature on the acknowledgement in the form, to the extent that the information set forth on the form is accurate, the provider who presents the form is not subject to prosecution under division (A) of section 2919.224 of the Revised Code regarding presentation of that information to that person.

An owner, provider, or administrator of a type A family day-care home or a type B family day-care home may comply with division (A) of section 2919.225 of the Revised Code by accurately answering the questions on a child care disclosure form that is in substantially the form set forth in division (B) of this section, providing a copy of the form to the parent, guardian, custodian, or other person responsible for the care of a child and to whom disclosure is to be made under division (A) of section 2919.225 of the Revised Code, and obtaining the person's signature on the acknowledgement in the form.

The use of the form set forth in division (B) of this section is discretionary and is not required to comply with any disclosure requirement contained in section 2919.225 of the Revised Code or for any purpose related to section 2919.224 of the Revised Code.

(B) To be sufficient for the purposes described in division (A) of this section, a child care disclosure form shall be in substantially the following form:

"CHILD CARE DISCLOSURE FORM

Please Note: This form contains information that is accurate only at the time the form is given to you. The information provided in this form is likely to change over time. It is the duty of the person responsible for the care of the child to monitor the status of child care services to ensure that those services remain satisfactory. If a question on this form is left unanswered, the child care provider makes no assertion regarding the question. Choosing appropriate child care for a child is a serious responsibility, and the person responsible for the care of the child is encouraged to make all appropriate inquiries. Also, in acknowledging receipt of this form, the person responsible for the care of the child acknowledges that in selecting the child care provider the person is not relying on any representations other than those provided in this form unless the child care provider has acknowledged the other representations in writing.

1. What are the names and qualifications to provide child care of: (a) the child care provider, (b) the employee who will provide child care to the applicant child, (c) the volunteer who will provide child care to the applicant child, and (d) any other employees or volunteers of the child care provider? (attach additional sheets if necessary):

....

....

....

2. What is the maximum number of children to whom you provide child care at one time? (If children are divided into groups or classes, please describe the maximum number of children in each group or class and indicate the group or class in which the applicant child will be placed.):

....

....

....

3. Where in the home will you provide child care to the applicant child?:

....

....

....

4. Has a child died while in the care of, or receiving child care from, the child care provider? (Yes/No)

Description/explanation (attach additional sheets if necessary)

....

....

....

5. Has a child died as a result of injuries suffered while under the care of, or receiving child care from, the child day-care provider? (Yes/No)

Description/explanation (attach additional sheets if necessary)

....

....

....

6. Within the preceding ten years, has a child suffered injuries while under the care of, or receiving child care from, the child care provider that led to the child being hospitalized for more than 24 hours? (Yes/No)

Description/explanation (attach additional sheets if necessary)

....

....

....

....

Signature of person completing form Date

....

Name of person completing form

(Typed or printed)

....

Title of person completing form

(Typed or printed)

Acknowledgement:

I hereby acknowledge that I have been given a copy of the preceding document and have read and understood its contents. I further acknowledge that I am not relying on any other representations in selecting the child care provider unless the child care provider has acknowledged the other representations in writing.

....

Person receiving the form Date"

(C) If a child care provider accurately answers the questions on a disclosure form that is substantially similar to the form described in division (B) of this section, presents the form to a person identified in division (A)(1) or (2) of section 2919.224 of the Revised Code, and obtains the person's signature on the acknowledgement in the form, to the extent that the information set forth on the form is accurate, the form is sufficient for the purposes described in division (A) of this section.

An owner, provider, or administrator of a type A family day-care home or a type B family day-care home who accurately answers the questions on a disclosure form that is substantially similar to the form described in division (B) of this section, provides a copy of the completed form to the parent, guardian, custodian, or other person who is responsible for the care of a child and to whom disclosure is to be made under division (A) of section 2919.225 of the Revised Code, and obtains the person's signature on the acknowledgement in the form complies with the requirements of that division. If the owner, provider, or administrator uses the disclosure form, leaving a portion of the disclosure form blank does not constitute a misrepresentation for the purposes of section 2919.224 of the Revised Code but may constitute a violation of section 2919.225 of the Revised Code. The owner, provider, or administrator of a type A family day-care home or type B family day-care home who completes the disclosure form and provides a copy of the form to any person described in section 2919.224 or 2919.225 of the Revised Code may retain a copy of the completed form.

(2004 H 11, eff. 5–18–05)

2919.227 Failure of child care center to disclose death or serious injury of child

(A)(1) No child care center licensee shall accept a child into that center without first providing to the parent, guardian, custodian, or other person responsible for the care of that child the following information, if the parent, guardian, custodian, or other person responsible for the care of the child requests the information:

(a) The types of injuries to children, as reported in accordance with rules adopted under section 5104.011 of the Revised Code, that occurred at the center on or after April 1, 2003, or the date that is two years before the date the information is requested, whichever date is more recent;

(b) The number of each type of injury to children that occurred at the center during that period.

(2) If a death described in division (A)(2)(a) or (A)(2)(b) of this section occurred during the fifteen-year period immediately preceding the date that the parent, guardian, custodian, or other person responsible for the care of a child seeks to enroll that child, no child care center licensee shall accept that child into that center without first providing to the parent, guardian, custodian, or other person responsible for the care of that child a notice that states that the death occurred.

(a) A child died while under the care of the center or while receiving child care from the owner, provider, or administrator of the center;

(b) A child died as a result of injuries suffered while under the care of the center or while receiving child care from the owner, provider, or administrator of the center.

(3) Each child care center licensee shall keep on file at the center a copy of the information provided under this division for at least three years after providing the information.

(B)(1) No child care center licensee shall fail to provide notice in accordance with division (B)(3) of this section to the persons and entities specified in division (B)(2) of this section if a child who is under the care of the center or is receiving child care from the owner, provider, or administrator of the center dies while under the care of the center or while receiving child care from the owner, provider, or administrator or dies as a result of injuries suffered while under the care of the center or while receiving child care from the owner, provider, or administrator.

(2) A child care center licensee shall provide the notice required under division (B)(1) of this section to all of the following:

(a) The parent, guardian, custodian, or other person responsible for the care of each child who, at the time of the death for which notice is required, is receiving or is enrolled to receive child care from the center;

(b) The public children services agency of the county in which the center is located or the child care was given;

(c) A municipal or county peace officer in the county in which the child resides or in which the center is located or the child care was given;

(d) The child fatality review board appointed under section 307.621 of the Revised Code that serves the county in which the center is located or the child care was given.

(3) A child care center licensee shall provide the notice required by division (B)(1) of this section not later than forty-eight hours after the child dies. The notice shall state that the death occurred.

(C) Whoever violates division (A) or (B) of this section is guilty of failure of a child care center to disclose the death or serious injury of a child, a misdemeanor of the fourth degree.

(2004 H 11, eff. 5–18–05)

2919.23 Interference with custody

(A) No person, knowing the person is without privilege to do so or being reckless in that regard, shall entice, take, keep, or harbor a person identified in division (A)(1), (2), or (3) of this section from the parent, guardian, or custodian of the person identified in division (A)(1), (2), or (3) of this section:

(1) A child under the age of eighteen, or a mentally or physically handicapped child under the age of twenty-one;

(2) A person committed by law to an institution for delinquent, unruly, neglected, abused, or dependent children;

(3) A person committed by law to an institution for the mentally ill or mentally retarded.

(B) No person shall aid, abet, induce, cause, or encourage a child or a ward of the juvenile court who has been committed to the custody of any person, department, or public or private institution to leave the custody of that person, department, or institution without legal consent.

(C) It is an affirmative defense to a charge of enticing or taking under division (A)(1) of this section, that the actor reasonably believed that the actor's conduct was necessary to preserve the child's health or safety. It is an affirmative defense to a charge of keeping or harboring under division (A) of this section, that the actor in good faith gave notice to law enforcement or judicial authorities within a reasonable time after the child or committed person came under the actor's shelter, protection, or influence.

(D)(1) Whoever violates this section is guilty of interference with custody.

(2) Except as otherwise provided in this division, a violation of division (A)(1) of this section is a misdemeanor of the first degree. If the child who is the subject of a violation of division (A)(1) of this section is removed from the state or if the offender previously has been convicted of an offense under this section, a violation of division (A)(1) of this section is a felony of the fifth degree. If the child who is the subject of a violation of division (A)(1) of this section suffers physical harm as a result of the violation, a violation of division (A)(1) of this section is a felony of the fourth degree.

(3) A violation of division (A)(2) or (3) of this section is a misdemeanor of the third degree.

(4) A violation of division (B) of this section is a misdemeanor of the first degree. Each day of violation of division (B) of this section is a separate offense.

(1995 S 2, eff. 7–1–96; 1990 S 3, eff. 4–11–91; 1985 H 349; 1975 H 85; 1972 H 511)

2919.231 Interfering with action to issue or modify support order

(A) No person, by using physical harassment or threats of violence against another person, shall interfere with the other person's initiation or continuance of, or attempt to prevent the other person from initiating or continuing, an action to issue or modify a support order under Chapter 3115. or under section 2151.23, 2151.231, 2151.232, 2151.33, 2151.36, 2151.361, 2151.49, 3105.18, 3105.21, 3109.05, 3109.19, 3111.13, 3113.04, 3113.07, or 3113.31 of the Revised Code.

(B) Whoever violates this section is guilty of interfering with an action to issue or modify a support order, a misdemeanor of the first degree. If the offender previously has been convicted of or pleaded guilty to a violation of this section or of section 3111.19 of the Revised Code, interfering with an action to issue or modify a support order is a felony of the fifth degree.

(2001 S 27, eff. 3–15–02; 2000 S 180, eff. 3–22–01; 1997 H 352, eff. 1–1–98; 1996 S 269, eff. 7–1–96; 1996 H 274, eff. 8–8–96; 1995 H 167, eff. 11–15–95; 1992 S 10, eff. 7–15–92)

2919.24 Contributing to unruliness or delinquency

(A) No person, including a parent, guardian, or other custodian of a child, shall do any of the following:

(1) Aid, abet, induce, cause, encourage, or contribute to a child or a ward of the juvenile court becoming an unruly child, as defined in section 2151.022 of the Revised Code, or a delinquent child, as defined in section 2152.02 of the Revised Code;

(2) Act in a way tending to cause a child or a ward of the juvenile court to become an unruly child, as defined in section 2151.022 of the Revised Code, or a delinquent child, as defined in section 2152.02 of the Revised Code;

(3) If the person is the parent, guardian, or custodian of a child who has the duties under Chapters 2152. and 2950. of the Revised Code to register, register a new residence address, and periodically verify a residence address, and, if applicable, to send a notice of intent to reside, and if the child is not emancipated, as defined in section 2919. 121 of the Revised Code, fail to ensure that the child complies with those duties under Chapters 2152. and 2950. of the Revised Code.

(B) Whoever violates this section is guilty of contributing to the unruliness or delinquency of a child, a misdemeanor of the first degree. Each day of violation of this section is a separate offense.

(2003 S 5, eff. 7–31–03; 2001 S 3, eff. 1–1–02; 2000 S 179, § 3, eff. 1–1–02; 1985 H 349, eff. 3–6–86)

DOMESTIC VIOLENCE

2919.25 Domestic violence

(A) No person shall knowingly cause or attempt to cause physical harm to a family or household member.

(B) No person shall recklessly cause serious physical harm to a family or household member.

(C) No person, by threat of force, shall knowingly cause a family or household member to believe that the offender will cause imminent physical harm to the family or household member.

(D)(1) Whoever violates this section is guilty of domestic violence.

(2) Except as otherwise provided in division (D)(3) or (4) of this section, a violation of division (C) of this section is a misdemeanor of the fourth degree, and a violation of division (A) or (B) of this section is a misdemeanor of the first degree.

(3) Except as otherwise provided in division (D)(4) of this section, if the offender previously has pleaded guilty to or been convicted of domestic violence, a violation of an existing or former municipal ordinance or law of this or any other state or the United States that is substantially similar to domestic violence, a violation of section 2903.14, 2909.06, 2909.07, 2911.12, 2911.211, or 2919.22 of the Revised Code if the victim of the violation was a family or household member at the time of the violation, a violation of an existing or former municipal ordinance or law of this or any other state or the United States that is substantially similar to any of those sections if the victim of the violation was a family or household member at the time of the commission of the violation, or any offense of violence if the victim of the offense was a family or household member at the time of the commission of the offense, a violation of division (A) or (B) of this section is a felony of the fourth degree, and a violation of division (C) of this section is a misdemeanor of the second degree.

(4) If the offender previously has pleaded guilty to or been convicted of two or more offenses of domestic violence or two or more violations or offenses of the type described in division (D)(3) of this section involving a person who was a family or household member at the time of the violations or offenses, a violation of division (A) or (B) of this section is a felony of the third degree, and a violation of division (C) of this section is a misdemeanor of the first degree.

(E) Notwithstanding any provision of law to the contrary, no court or unit of state or local government shall charge any fee, cost, deposit, or money in connection with the filing of charges against a person alleging that the person violated this section or a municipal ordinance substantially similar to this section or in connection with the prosecution of any charges so filed.

(F) As used in this section and sections 2919.251 and 2919.26 of the Revised Code:

(1) "Family or household member" means any of the following:

(a) Any of the following who is residing or has resided with the offender:

(i) A spouse, a person living as a spouse, or a former spouse of the offender;

(ii) A parent or a child of the offender, or another person related by consanguinity or affinity to the offender;

(iii) A parent or a child of a spouse, person living as a spouse, or former spouse of the offender, or another person related by consanguinity or affinity to a spouse, person living as a spouse, or former spouse of the offender.

(b) The natural parent of any child of whom the offender is the other natural parent or is the putative other natural parent.

(2) "Person living as a spouse" means a person who is living or has lived with the offender in a common law marital relationship, who otherwise is cohabiting with the offender, or who otherwise has cohabited with the offender within five years prior to the date of the alleged commission of the act in question.

(2003 S 50, eff. 1–8–04; 2002 H 548, eff. 3–31–03; 2002 H 327, eff. 7–8–02; 1997 H 238, eff. 11–5–97; 1997 S 1, eff. 10–21–97; 1995 S 2, eff. 7–1–96; 1994 H 335, eff. 12–9–94; 1992 H 536, eff. 11–5–92; 1990 S 3; 1988 H 172; 1987 S 6; 1984 H 587; 1980 H 920; 1978 H 835)

2919.251 Factors to be considered when setting bail; bail schedule

(A) If a person is charged with the commission of any offense of violence, if the alleged victim of the offense charged was a family or household member at the time of the violation offense, and if the person charged, at the time of the alleged offense, was subject to the terms of a protection order issued or consent agreement approved pursuant to section 2919.26 or 3113.31 of the Revised Code or previously was convicted of or pleaded guilty to a violation of section 2919.25 of the Revised Code or a violation of section 2919.27 of the Revised Code involving a protection order or consent agreement of that type, a violation of an existing or former municipal ordinance or law of this or any other state or the United States that is substantially similar to either section, a violation of section 2909.06, 2909.07, 2911.12, or 2911.211 of the Revised Code if the victim of the violation was a family or household member at the time of the violation a violation of an existing or former municipal ordinance or law of this or any other state or the United States that is substantially similar to any of those sections if the victim of the violation was a family or household member at the time of the commission of the violation, or any offense of violence if the victim of the offense was a family or household member at the time of the offense, the court shall consider all of the following, in addition to any other circumstances considered by the court and notwithstanding any provisions to the contrary contained in Criminal Rule 46, before setting bail for the person:

(1) Whether the person has a history of domestic violence or a history of other violent acts;

(2) The mental health of the person;

(3) Whether the person has a history of violating the orders of any court or governmental entity;

(4) Whether the person is potentially a threat to any other person;

(5) Whether setting bail at a high level will interfere with any treatment or counseling that the person or the family of the person is undergoing.

(B) Any court that has jurisdiction over that involve charges alleging the commission of an offense of violence in circumstances in which the alleged victim of the offense was a family or household member at the time of the offense, may set a schedule for bail to be used in cases involving those offenses. The schedule shall require that a judge consider all of the factors listed in division (A) of this section and may require judges to set bail at a certain level if the history of the alleged offender or the circumstances of the alleged offense meet certain criteria in the schedule.

(2003 S 50, eff. 1–8–04; 1995 S 2, eff. 7–1–96; 1992 H 536, eff. 11–5–92; 1990 S 3; 1985 H 475)

2919.26 Temporary protection orders

(A)(1) Upon the filing of a complaint that alleges a violation of section 2909.06, 2909.07, 2911.12, or 2911.211 of the Revised Code if the alleged victim of the violation was a family or household member at the time of the violation, a violation of a municipal ordinance that is substantially similar to any of those sections if the alleged victim of the violation was a family or household member at the time of the violation, or any offense of violence if the alleged victim of the offense was a family or household member at the time of the commission of the offense, the complainant, the alleged victim, or a family or household member of an alleged victim may file, or, if in an emergency the alleged victim is unable to file, a person who made an arrest for the alleged violation or offense under section 2935.03 of the Revised Code may file on behalf of the alleged victim, a motion that requests the issuance of a temporary protection order as a pretrial condition of release of the alleged offender, in addition to any bail set under Criminal Rule 46. The motion shall be filed with the clerk of the court that has jurisdiction of the case at any time after the filing of the complaint.

(2) For purposes of section 2930.09 of the Revised Code, all stages of a proceeding arising out of a complaint alleging the commission of a violation or offense of violence described in division (A)(1) of this section, including all proceedings on a motion for a temporary protection order, are critical stages of the case, and a victim may be accompanied by a victim advocate or another person to provide support to the victim as provided in that section.

(B) The motion shall be prepared on a form that is provided by the clerk of the court, which form shall be substantially as follows:

"MOTION FOR TEMPORARY PROTECTION ORDER

__________________ Court

Name and address of court

State of Ohio

v. No. . . . .

. . . .

Name of Defendant

(name of person), moves the court to issue a temporary protection order containing terms designed to ensure the safety and protection of the complainant, alleged victim, and other family or household members, in relation to the named defendant, pursuant to its authority to issue such an order under section 2919.26 of the Revised Code.

A complaint, a copy of which has been attached to this motion, has been filed in this court charging the named defendant with .... (name of the specified violation or the offense of violence charged) in circumstances in which the victim was a family or household member in violation of (section of the Revised Code designating the specified violation or offense of violence charged), or charging the named defendant with a violation of a municipal ordinance that is substantially similar to........................ (section of the Revised Code designating the specified violation or offense of violence charged) involving a family or household member.

I understand that I must appear before the court, at a time set by the court within twenty-four hours after the filing of this motion, for a hearing on the motion or that, if I am unable to appear because of hospitalization or a medical condition resulting from the offense alleged in the complaint, a person who can provide information about my need for a temporary protection order must appear before the court in lieu of my appearing in court. I understand that any temporary protection order granted pursuant to this motion is a pretrial condition of release and is effective only until the disposition of the criminal proceeding arising out of the attached complaint, or the issuance of a civil protection order or the approval of a consent agreement, arising out of the same activities as those that were the basis of the complaint, under section 3113.31 of the Revised Code.

____

Signature of person

(or signature of the arresting officer who filed the motion on behalf of the alleged victim)

____

Address of person (or office address of the arresting officer who filed the motion on behalf of the alleged victim)"

(C)(1) As soon as possible after the filing of a motion that requests the issuance of a temporary protection order, but not later than twenty-four hours after the filing of the motion, the court shall conduct a hearing to determine whether to issue the order. The person who requested the order shall appear before the court and provide the court with the information that it requests concerning the basis of the motion. If the person who requested the order is unable to appear and if the court finds that the failure to appear is because of the person's hospitalization or medical condition resulting from the offense alleged in the complaint, another person who is able to provide the court with the information it requests may appear in lieu of the person who requested the order. If the court finds that the safety and protection of the complainant, alleged victim, or any other family or household member of the alleged offender may be impaired by the continued presence of the alleged offender, the court may issue a temporary protection order, as a pretrial condition of release, that contains terms designed to ensure the safety and protection of the complainant, alleged victim, or the family or household member, including a requirement that the alleged offender refrain from entering the residence, school, business, or place of employment of the complainant, alleged victim, or the family or household member.

(2)(a) If the court issues a temporary protection order that includes a requirement that the alleged offender refrain from entering the residence, school, business, or place of employment of the complainant, the alleged victim, or the family or household member, the order shall state clearly that the order cannot be waived or nullified by an invitation to the alleged offender from the complainant, alleged victim, or family or household member to enter the residence, school, business, or place of employment or by the alleged offender's entry into one of those places otherwise upon the consent of the complainant, alleged victim, or family or household member.

(b) Division (C)(2)(a) of this section does not limit any discretion of a court to determine that an alleged offender charged with a violation of section 2919.27 of the Revised Code, with a violation of a municipal ordinance substantially equivalent to that section, or with contempt of court, which charge is based on an alleged violation of a temporary protection order issued under this section, did not commit the violation or was not in contempt of court.

(D)(1) Upon the filing of a complaint that alleges a violation of section 2909.06, 2909.07, 2911.12, or 2911.211 of the Revised Code if the alleged victim of the violation was a family or household member at the time of the violation, a violation of a municipal ordinance that is substantially similar to any of those sections if the alleged victim of the violation was a family or household member at the time of the violation, or any offense of violence if the alleged victim of the offense was a family or household member at the time of the commission of the offense, the court, upon its own motion, may issue a temporary protection order as a pretrial condition of release if it finds that the safety and protection of the complainant, alleged victim, or other family or household member of the alleged offender may be impaired by the continued presence of the alleged offender.

(2) If the court issues a temporary protection order under this section as an ex parte order, it shall conduct, as soon as possible after the issuance of the order, a hearing in the presence of the alleged offender not later than the next day on which the court is scheduled to conduct business after the day on which the alleged offender was arrested or at the time of the appearance of the alleged offender pursuant to summons to determine whether the order should remain in effect, be modified, or be revoked. The hearing shall be conducted under the standards set forth in division (C) of this section.

(3) An order issued under this section shall contain only those terms authorized in orders issued under division (C) of this section.

(4) If a municipal court or a county court issues a temporary protection order under this section and if, subsequent to the issuance of the order, the alleged offender who is the subject of the order is bound over to the court of common pleas for prosecution of a felony arising out of the same activities as those that were the basis of the complaint upon which the order is based, notwithstanding the fact that the order was issued by a municipal court or county court, the order shall remain in effect, as though it were an order of the court of common pleas, while the charges against the alleged offender are pending in the court of common pleas, for the period of time described in division (E)(2) of this section, and the court of common pleas has exclusive jurisdiction to modify the order issued by the municipal court or county court. This division applies when the alleged offender is bound over to the court of common pleas as a result of the person waiving a preliminary hearing on the felony charge, as a result of the municipal court or county court having determined at a preliminary hearing that there is probable cause to believe that the felony has been committed and that the alleged offender committed it, as a result of the alleged offender having been indicted for the felony, or in any other manner.

(E) A temporary protection order that is issued as a pretrial condition of release under this section:

(1) Is in addition to, but shall not be construed as a part of, any bail set under Criminal Rule 46;

(2) Is effective only until the occurrence of either of the following:

(a) The disposition, by the court that issued the order or, in the circumstances described in division (D)(4) of this section, by the court of common pleas to which the alleged offender is bound over for prosecution, of the criminal proceeding arising out of the complaint upon which the order is based;

(b) The issuance of a protection order or the approval of a consent agreement, arising out of the same activities as those that were the basis of the complaint upon which the order is based, under section 3113.31 of the Revised Code;

(3) Shall not be construed as a finding that the alleged offender committed the alleged offense, and shall not be introduced as evidence of the commission of the offense at the trial of the alleged offender on the complaint upon which the order is based.

(F) A person who meets the criteria for bail under Criminal Rule 46 and who, if required to do so pursuant to that rule, executes or posts bond or deposits cash or securities as bail, shall not be held in custody pending a hearing before the court on a motion requesting a temporary protection order.

(G)(1) A copy of any temporary protection order that is issued under this section shall be issued by the court to the complainant, to the alleged victim, to the person who requested the order, to the defendant, and to all law enforcement agencies that have jurisdiction to enforce the order. The court shall direct that a copy of the order be delivered to the defendant on the same day that the order is entered. If a municipal court or a county court issues a temporary protection order under this section and if, subsequent to the issuance of the order, the defendant who is the subject of the order is bound over to the court of common pleas for prosecution as described in division (D)(4) of this section, the municipal court or county court shall direct that a copy of the order be delivered to the court of common pleas to which the defendant is bound over.

(2) All law enforcement agencies shall establish and maintain an index for the temporary protection orders delivered to the agencies pursuant to division (G)(1) of this section. With respect to each order delivered, each agency shall note on the index, the date and time of the receipt of the order by the agency.

(3) A complainant, alleged victim, or other person who obtains a temporary protection order under this section may provide notice of the issuance of the temporary protection order to the judicial and law enforcement officials in any county other than the county in which the order is issued by registering that order in the other county in accordance with division (N) of section 3113.31 of the Revised Code and filing a copy of the registered protection order with a law enforcement agency in the other county in accordance with that division.

(4) Any officer of a law enforcement agency shall enforce a temporary protection order issued by any court in this state in accordance with the provisions of the order, including removing the defendant from the premises, regardless of whether the order is registered in the county in which the officer's agency has jurisdiction as authorized by division (G)(3) of this section.

(H) Upon a violation of a temporary protection order, the court may issue another temporary protection order, as a pretrial condition of release, that modifies the terms of the order that was violated.

(I)(1) As used in divisions (I)(1) and (2) of this section, "defendant" means a person who is alleged in a complaint to have committed a violation or offense of violence of the type described in division (A) of this section.

(2) If a complaint is filed that alleges that a person committed a violation or offense of violence of the type described in division (A) of this section, the court may not issue a temporary protection order under this section that requires the complainant, the alleged victim, or another family or household member of the defendant to do or refrain from doing an act that the court may require the defendant to do or refrain from doing under a temporary protection order unless both of the following apply:

(a) The defendant has filed a separate complaint that alleges that the complainant, alleged victim, or other family or household member in question who would be required under the order to do or refrain from doing the act committed a violation or offense of violence of the type described in division (A) of this section.

(b) The court determines that both the complainant, alleged victim, or other family or household member in question who would be required under the order to do or refrain from doing the act and the defendant acted primarily as aggressors, that neither the complainant, alleged victim, or other family or household member in question who would be required under the order to do or refrain from doing the act nor the defendant acted primarily in self-defense, and, in accordance with the standards and criteria of this section as applied in relation to the separate complaint filed by the defendant, that it should issue the order to require the complainant, alleged victim, or other family or household member in question to do or refrain from doing the act.

(J) Notwithstanding any provision of law to the contrary and regardless of whether a protection order is issued or a consent agreement is approved by a court of another county or a court of another state, no court or unit of state or local government shall charge any fee, cost, deposit, or money in connection with the filing of a motion pursuant to this section, in connection with the filing, issuance, registration, or service of a protection order or consent agreement, or for obtaining a certified copy of a protection order or consent agreement.

(K) As used in this section, "victim advocate" means a person who provides support and assistance for a victim of an offense during court proceedings.

(2003 S 50, eff. 1–8–04; 2002 H 548, eff. 3–31–03; 1999 H 137, eff. 3–10–00; 1997 S 98, eff. 3–17–98; 1997 S 1, eff. 10–21–97; 1994 H 335, eff. 12–9–94; 1992 H 536, eff. 11–5–92; 1990 S 3; 1984 H 587; 1980 H 920; 1978 H 835)

2919.27 Violating a protection order, consent agreement, or anti-stalking protection order; protection order issued by court of another state

(A) No person shall recklessly violate the terms of any of the following:

(1) A protection order issued or consent agreement approved pursuant to section 2919.26 or 3113.31 of the Revised Code;

(2) A protection order issued pursuant to section 2903.213 or 2903.214 of the Revised Code;

(3) A protection order issued by a court of another state.

(B)(1) Whoever violates this section is guilty of violating a protection order.

(2) Except as otherwise provided in division (B) (3) or (4) of this section, violating a protection order is a misdemeanor of the first degree.

(3) If the offender previously has been convicted of or pleaded guilty to a violation of a protection order issued pursuant to section 2903.213 or 2903.214 of the Revised Code, two or more violations of section 2903.21, 2903.211, 2903.22, or 2911.211 of the Revised Code that involved the same person who is the subject of the protection order or consent agreement, or one or more violations of this section, violating a protection order is a felony of the fifth degree.

(4) If the offender violates a protection order or consent agreement while committing a felony offense, violating a protection order is a felony of the third degree.

(C) It is an affirmative defense to a charge under division (A)(3) of this section that the protection order issued by a court of another state does not comply with the requirements specified in 18 U.S.C. 2265(b) for a protection order that must be accorded full faith and credit by a court of this state or that it is not entitled to full faith and credit under 18 U.S.C. 2265(c).

(D) As used in this section, "protection order issued by a court of another state" means an injunction or another order issued by a criminal court of another state for the purpose of preventing violent or threatening acts or harassment against, contact or communication with, or physical proximity to another person, including a temporary order, and means an injunction or order of that nature issued by a civil court of another state, including a temporary order and a final order issued in an independent action or as a pendente lite order in a proceeding for other relief, if the court issued it in response to a complaint, petition, or motion filed by or on behalf of a person seeking protection. "Protection order issued by a court of another state" does not include an order for support or for custody of a child issued pursuant to the divorce and child custody laws of another state, except to the extent that the order for support or for custody of a child is entitled to full faith and credit under the laws of the United States.

(2003 S 50, eff. 1–8–04; 2002 H 548, eff. 3–31–03; 1998 H 302, eff. 7–29–98; 1997 S 1, eff. 10–21–97; 1995 S 2, eff. 7–1–96; 1994 H 335, eff. 12–9–94; 1992 H 536, eff. 11–5–92; 1985 H 475; 1984 H 587)

2919.271 Mental evaluations

(A)(1)(a) If a defendant is charged with a violation of section 2919.27 of the Revised Code or of a municipal ordinance that is substantially similar to that section, the court may order an evaluation of the mental condition of the defendant if the court determines that either of the following criteria apply:

(i) If the alleged violation is a violation of a protection order issued or consent agreement approved pursuant to section 2919.26 or 3113.31 of the Revised Code, that the violation allegedly involves conduct by the defendant that caused physical harm to the person or property of a family or household member covered by the order or agreement, or conduct by the defendant that caused a family or household member to believe that the defendant would cause physical harm to that member or that member's property.

(ii) If the alleged violation is a violation of a protection order issued pursuant to section 2903.213 or 2903.214 of the Revised Code or a protection order issued by a court of another state, that the violation allegedly involves conduct by the defendant that caused physical harm to the person or property of the person covered by the order, or conduct by the defendant that caused the person covered by the order to believe that the defendant would cause physical harm to that person or that person's property.

(b) If a defendant is charged with a violation of section 2903.211 of the Revised Code or of a municipal ordinance that is substantially similar to that section, the court may order an evaluation of the mental condition of the defendant.

(2) An evaluation ordered under division (A)(1) of this section shall be completed no later than thirty days from the date the order is entered pursuant to that division. In that order, the court shall do either of the following:

(a) Order that the evaluation of the mental condition of the defendant be preceded by an examination conducted either by a forensic center that is designated by the department of mental health to conduct examinations and make evaluations of defendants charged with violations of section 2903.211 or 2919.27 of the Revised Code or of substantially similar municipal ordinances in the area in which the court is located, or by any other program or facility that is designated by the department of mental health or the department of mental retardation and developmental disabilities to conduct examinations and make evaluations of defendants charged with violations of section 2903.211 or 2919.27 of the Revised Code or of substantially similar municipal ordinances, and that is operated by either department or is certified by either department as being in compliance with the standards established under division (I) of section 5119.01 of the Revised Code or division (C) of section 5123.04 of the Revised Code.

(b) Designate a center, program, or facility other than one designated by the department of mental health or the department of mental retardation and developmental disabilities, as described in division (A)(2)(a) of this section, to conduct the evaluation and preceding examination of the mental condition of the defendant.

Whether the court acts pursuant to division (A)(2)(a) or (b) of this section, the court may designate examiners other than the personnel of the center, program, facility, or department involved to make the evaluation and preceding examination of the mental condition of the defendant.

(B) If the court considers that additional evaluations of the mental condition of a defendant are necessary following the evaluation authorized by division (A) of this section, the court may order up to two additional similar evaluations. These evaluations shall be completed no later than thirty days from the date the applicable court order is entered. If more than one evaluation of the mental condition of the defendant is ordered under this division, the prosecutor and the defendant may recommend to the court an examiner whom each prefers to perform one of the evaluations and preceding examinations.

(C)(1) The court may order a defendant who has been released on bail to submit to an examination under division (A) or (B) of this section. The examination shall be conducted either at the detention facility in which the defendant would have been confined if the defendant had not been released on bail, or, if so specified by the center, program, facility, or examiners involved, at the premises of the center, program, or facility. Additionally, the examination shall be conducted at the times established by the examiners involved. If such a defendant refuses to submit to an examination or a complete examination as required by the court or the center, program, facility, or examiners involved, the court may amend the conditions of the bail of the defendant and order the sheriff to take the defendant into custody and deliver the defendant to the detention facility in which the defendant would have been confined if the defendant had not been released on bail, or, if so specified by the center, program, facility, or examiners involved, to the premises of the center, program, or facility, for purposes of the examination.

(2) A defendant who has not been released on bail shall be examined at the detention facility in which the defendant is confined or, if so specified by the center, program, facility, or examiners involved, at the premises of the center, program, or facility.

(D) The examiner of the mental condition of a defendant under division (A) or (B) of this section shall file a written report with the court within thirty days after the entry of an order for the evaluation of the mental condition of the defendant. The report shall contain the findings of the examiner; the facts in reasonable detail on which the findings are based; the opinion of the examiner as to the mental condition of the defendant; the opinion of the examiner as to whether the defendant represents a substantial risk of physical harm to other persons as manifested by evidence of recent homicidal or other violent behavior, evidence of recent threats that placed other persons in reasonable fear of violent behavior and serious physical harm, or evidence of present dangerousness; and the opinion of the examiner as to the types of treatment or counseling that the defendant needs. The court shall provide copies of the report to the prosecutor and defense counsel.

(E) The costs of any evaluation and preceding examination of a defendant that is ordered pursuant to division (A) or (B) of this section shall be taxed as court costs in the criminal case.

(F) If the examiner considers it necessary in order to make an accurate evaluation of the mental condition of a defendant, an examiner under division (A) or (B) of this section may request any family or household member of the defendant to provide the examiner with information. A family or household member may, but is not required to, provide information to the examiner upon receipt of the request.

(G) As used in this section:

(1) "Bail" includes a recognizance.

(2) "Examiner" means a psychiatrist, a licensed independent social worker who is employed by a forensic center that is certified as being in compliance with the standards established under division (I) of section 5119.01 or division (C) of section 5123.04 of the Revised Code, a licensed professional clinical counselor who is employed at a forensic center that is certified as being in compliance with such standards, or a licensed clinical psychologist, except that in order to be an examiner, a licensed

clinical psychologist shall meet the criteria of division (I)(1) of section 5122.01 of the Revised Code or be employed to conduct examinations by the department of mental health or by a forensic center certified as being in compliance with the standards established under division (I) of section 5119.01 or division (C) of section 5123.04 of the Revised Code that is designated by the department of mental health.

(3) "Family or household member" has the same meaning as in section 2919.25 of the Revised Code.

(4) "Prosecutor" has the same meaning as in section 2935.01 of the Revised Code.

(5) "Psychiatrist" and "licensed clinical psychologist" have the same meanings as in section 5122.01 of the Revised Code.

(6) "Protection order issued by a court of another state" has the same meaning as in section 2919.27 of the Revised Code.

(2001 H 94, eff. 9–5–01; 1999 H 202, eff. 2–9–00; 1998 H 302, eff. 7–29–98; 1997 S 1, eff. 10–21–97; 1996 S 223, eff. 3–18–97; 1995 S 2, eff. 7–1–96; 1985 H 475, eff. 3–7–86)

2919.272 Protection order issued by court of another state; procedure for registration in Ohio; registry of orders by law enforcement agencies

(A) As used in this section, "protection order issued by a court of another state" has the same meaning as in section 2919.27 of the Revised Code.

(B) A person who has obtained a protection order issued by a court of another state may provide notice of the issuance of the order to judicial and law enforcement officials in any county of this state by registering the order in that county and filing a copy of the registered order with a law enforcement agency in that county. To register the order, the person shall obtain a certified copy of the order from the clerk of the court that issued the order and present that certified copy to the clerk of the court of common pleas or the clerk of a municipal court or county court in the county in which the order is to be registered. Upon accepting the certified copy of the order for registration, the clerk shall place an endorsement of registration on the order and give the person a copy of the order that bears proof of registration. The person then may file with a law enforcement agency in that county a copy of the order that bears proof of registration.

(C) The clerk of each court of common pleas and the clerk of each municipal court and county court shall maintain a registry of certified copies of protection orders issued by courts of another state that have been registered with the clerk. Each law enforcement agency shall establish and maintain a registry for protection orders delivered to the agency pursuant to this section. The agency shall note in the registry the date and time that the agency received an order.

(D) An officer of a law enforcement agency shall enforce a protection order issued by a court of another state in accordance with the provisions of the order, including removing the person allegedly violating the order from the premises, regardless of whether the order is registered as authorized by division (B) of this section in the county in which the officer's agency has jurisdiction.

(E) Notwithstanding any provision of law to the contrary and regardless of whether a protection order is issued or a consent agreement is approved by a court of another county or a court of another state, no court or unit of state or local government shall charge any fee, cost, deposit, or money in connection with the filing, issuance, registration, or service of a protection order or consent agreement or for obtaining a certified copy of a protection order or consent agreement, including a protection order issued by a court of another state.

(2002 H 548, eff. 3–31–03; 1997 S 1, eff. 10–21–97)

CHAPTER 2921

OFFENSES AGAINST JUSTICE AND PUBLIC ADMINISTRATION

DEFINITIONS

2921.01 Definitions

As used in sections 2921.01 to 2921.45 of the Revised Code:

(A) "Public official" means any elected or appointed officer, or employee, or agent of the state or any political subdivision, whether in a temporary or permanent capacity, and includes, but is not limited to, legislators, judges, and law enforcement officers.

(B) "Public servant" means any of the following:

(1) Any public official;

(2) Any person performing ad hoc a governmental function, including, but not limited to, a juror, member of a temporary commission, master, arbitrator, advisor, or consultant;

(3) A person who is a candidate for public office, whether or not the person is elected or appointed to the office for which the person is a candidate. A person is a candidate for purposes of this division if the person has been nominated according to law for election or appointment to public office, or if the person has filed a petition or petitions as required by law to have the person's name placed on the ballot in a primary, general, or special election, or if the person campaigns as a write-in candidate in any primary, general, or special election.

(C) "Party official" means any person who holds an elective or appointive post in a political party in the United States or this state, by virtue of which the person directs, conducts, or participates in directing or conducting party affairs at any level of responsibility.

(D) "Official proceeding" means any proceeding before a legislative, judicial, administrative, or other governmental agency or official authorized to take evidence under oath, and includes any proceeding before a referee, hearing examiner, commissioner, notary, or other person taking testimony or a deposition in connection with an official proceeding.

(E) "Detention" means arrest; confinement in any vehicle subsequent to an arrest; confinement in any public or private facility for custody of persons charged with or convicted of crime in this state or another state or under the laws of the United States or alleged or found to be a delinquent child or unruly child in this state or another state or under the laws of the United States; hospitalization, institutionalization, or confinement in any public or private facility that is ordered pursuant to or under the authority of section 2945.37, 2945.371, 2945.38, 2945.39, 2945.40, 2945.401, or 2945.402 of the Revised Code; confinement in any vehicle for transportation to or from any facility of any of those natures; detention for extradition or deportation; except as provided in this division, supervision by any employee of any facility of any of those natures that is incidental to hospitalization, institutionalization, or confinement in the facility but that occurs outside the facility; supervision by an employee of the department of rehabilitation and correction of a person on any type of release from a state correctional institution; or confinement in any vehicle, airplane, or place while being returned from outside of this state into this state by a private person or entity pursuant to a contract entered into under division (E) of section 311.29 of the Revised Code or division (B) of section 5149.03 of the Revised Code. For a person confined in a county jail who participates in a county jail industry program pursuant to section 5147.30 of the Revised Code, "detention" includes time spent at an assigned work site and going to and from the work site.

(F) "Detention facility" means any public or private place used for the confinement of a person charged with or convicted of any crime in this state or another state or under the laws of the United States or alleged or found to be a delinquent child or unruly child in this state or another state or under the laws of the United States.

(G) "Valuable thing or valuable benefit" includes, but is not limited to, a contribution. This inclusion does not indicate or imply that a contribution was not included in those terms before September 17, 1986.

(H) "Campaign committee," "contribution," "political action committee," "legislative campaign fund," and "political party" have the same meanings as in section 3517.01 of the Revised Code.

(I) "Provider agreement" and "medical assistance program" have the same meanings as in section 2913.40 of the Revised Code.

(2004 H 1 SS, eff. 3–31–05; 2000 H 661, eff. 3–15–01; 1998 S 134, eff. 7–13–98; 1998 H 293, eff. 3–17–98; 1996 S 285, eff. 7–1–97; 1996 H 154, eff. 10–4–96; 1995 S 2, eff. 7–1–96; 1995 S 8, eff. 8–23–95; 1994 H 571, eff. 10–6–94; 1993 H 42, eff. 2–9–94; 1992 S 37; 1990 H 51; 1988 H 708; 1986 H 428, H 300, H 340; 1972 H 511)

BRIBERY, INTIMIDATION, AND RETALIATION

2921.02 Bribery

(A) No person, with purpose to corrupt a public servant or party official, or improperly to influence him with respect to the discharge of his duty, whether before or after he is elected, appointed, qualified, employed, summoned, or sworn, shall promise, offer, or give any valuable thing or valuable benefit.

(B) No person, either before or after he is elected, appointed, qualified, employed, summoned, or sworn as a public servant or party official, shall knowingly solicit or accept for himself or another person any valuable thing or valuable benefit to corrupt or improperly influence him or another public servant or party official with respect to the discharge of his or the other public servant's or party official's duty.

(C) No person, with purpose to corrupt a witness or improperly to influence him with respect to his testimony in an official proceeding, either before or after he is subpoenaed or sworn, shall promise, offer, or give him or another person any valuable thing or valuable benefit.

(D) No person, either before or after he is subpoenaed or sworn as a witness, shall knowingly solicit or accept for himself or another person any valuable thing or valuable benefit to corrupt or improperly influence him with respect to his testimony in an official proceeding.

(E) Whoever violates this section is guilty of bribery, a felony of the third degree.

(F) A public servant or party official who is convicted of bribery is forever disqualified from holding any public office, employment, or position of trust in this state.

(1986 H 300, eff. 9–17–86; 1972 H 511)

2921.03 Intimidation (first version)

Note: See also following version of this section, and Publisher's Note.

(A) No person, knowingly and by force or by unlawful threat of harm to any person or property, shall attempt to influence, intimidate, or hinder a public servant, a party official, or an attorney or witness involved in a civil action or proceeding in the discharge of the duties of the public servant, party official, attorney, or witness.

(B) Whoever violates this section is guilty of intimidation, a felony of the third degree.

(1996 H 88, eff. 9–3–96; 1984 S 172, eff. 9–26–84; 1972 H 511)

Note: See also following version of this section, and Publisher's Note.

2921.03 Intimidation (second version)

Note: See also preceding version of this section, and Publisher's Note.

(A) No person, knowingly and by force, by unlawful threat of harm to any person or property, or by filing, recording, or otherwise using a materially false or fraudulent writing with malicious purpose, in bad faith, or in a wanton or reckless manner, shall attempt to influence, intimidate, or hinder a public servant, party official, or witness in the discharge of the person's duty.

(B) Whoever violates this section is guilty of intimidation, a felony of the third degree.

(C) A person who violates this section is liable in a civil action to any person harmed by the violation for injury, death, or loss to person or property incurred as a result of the commission of the offense and for reasonable attorney's fees, court costs, and other expenses incurred as a result of prosecuting the civil action commenced under this division. A civil action under this division is not the exclusive remedy of a person who incurs injury, death, or loss to person or property as a result of a violation of this section.

(1996 H 644, eff. 11–6–96; 1984 S 172, eff. 9–26–84; 1972 H 511)

Note: See also preceding version of this section, and Publisher's Note.

Historical and Statutory Notes

Publisher's Note: 2921.03 was amended by 1996 H 88, eff. 9–3–96, and 1996 H 644, eff. 11–6–96. Harmonization pursuant to section 1.52 of the Revised Code is in question. See *Baldwin's Ohio Legislative Service*, 1996, pages 6/L–1355 and 7/L–3206, or the OH–LEGIS or OH–LEGIS–OLD database on WESTLAW, for original versions of these Acts.

2921.04 Intimidation of crime victim or witness

(A) No person shall knowingly attempt to intimidate or hinder the victim of a crime in the filing or prosecution of criminal charges or a witness involved in a criminal action or proceeding in the discharge of the duties of the witness.

(B) No person, knowingly and by force or by unlawful threat of harm to any person or property, shall attempt to influence, intimidate, or hinder the victim of a crime in the filing or prosecution of criminal charges or an attorney or witness involved in a criminal action or proceeding in the discharge of the duties of the attorney or witness.

(C) Division (A) of this section does not apply to any person who is attempting to resolve a dispute pertaining to the alleged commission of a criminal offense, either prior to or subsequent to the filing of a complaint, indictment, or information, by participating in the arbitration, mediation, compromise, settlement, or conciliation of that dispute pursuant to an authorization for arbitration, mediation, compromise, settlement, or conciliation of a dispute of that nature that is conferred by any of the following:

(1) A section of the Revised Code;

(2) The Rules of Criminal Procedure, the Rules of Superintendence for Municipal Courts and County Courts, the Rules of Superintendence for Courts of Common Pleas, or another rule adopted by the supreme court in accordance with section 5 of Article IV, Ohio Constitution;

(3) A local rule of court, including, but not limited to, a local rule of court that relates to alternative dispute resolution or other case management programs and that authorizes the referral of disputes pertaining to the alleged commission of certain types of criminal offenses to appropriate and available arbitration, mediation, compromise, settlement, or other conciliation programs;

(4) The order of a judge of a municipal court, county court, or court of common pleas.

(D) Whoever violates this section is guilty of intimidation of an attorney, victim, or witness in a criminal case. A violation of division (A) of this section is a misdemeanor of the first degree. A violation of division (B) of this section is a felony of the third degree.

(1996 H 88, eff. 9–3–96; 1984 S 172, eff. 9–26–84)

2921.05 Retaliation

(A) No person, purposely and by force or by unlawful threat of harm to any person or property, shall retaliate against a public servant, a party official, or an attorney or witness who was involved in a civil or criminal action or proceeding because the public servant, party official, attorney, or witness discharged the duties of the public servant, party official, attorney, or witness.

(B) No person, purposely and by force or by unlawful threat of harm to any person or property, shall retaliate against the victim of a crime because the victim filed or prosecuted criminal charges.

(C) Whoever violates this section is guilty of retaliation, a felony of the third degree.

(1996 H 88, eff. 9–3–96)

PERJURY

2921.11 Perjury

(A) No person, in any official proceeding, shall knowingly make a false statement under oath or affirmation, or knowingly swear or affirm the truth of a false statement previously made, when either statement is material.

(B) A falsification is material, regardless of its admissibility in evidence, if it can affect the course or outcome of the proceeding. It is no defense to a charge under this section that the offender mistakenly believed a falsification to be immaterial.

(C) It is no defense to a charge under this section that the oath or affirmation was administered or taken in an irregular manner.

(D) Where contradictory statements relating to the same material fact are made by the offender under oath or affirmation and within the period of the statute of limitations for perjury, it is not necessary for the prosecution to prove which statement was false, but only that one or the other was false.

(E) No person shall be convicted of a violation of this section where proof of falsity rests solely upon contradiction by testimony of one person other than the defendant.

(F) Whoever violates this section is guilty of perjury, a felony of the third degree.

(1972 H 511, eff. 1–1–74)

2921.12 Tampering with evidence

(A) No person, knowing that an official proceeding or investigation is in progress, or is about to be or likely to be instituted, shall do any of the following:

(1) Alter, destroy, conceal, or remove any record, document, or thing, with purpose to impair its value or availability as evidence in such proceeding or investigation;

(2) Make, present, or use any record, document, or thing, knowing it to be false and with purpose to mislead a public official who is or may be engaged in such proceeding or investigation, or with purpose to corrupt the outcome of any such proceeding or investigation.

(B) Whoever violates this section is guilty of tampering with evidence, a felony of the third degree.

(1972 H 511, eff. 1–1–74)

2921.13 Falsification

(A) No person shall knowingly make a false statement, or knowingly swear or affirm the truth of a false statement previously made, when any of the following applies:

(1) The statement is made in any official proceeding.

(2) The statement is made with purpose to incriminate another.

(3) The statement is made with purpose to mislead a public official in performing the public official's official function.

(4) The statement is made with purpose to secure the payment of unemployment compensation; Ohio works first; prevention, retention, and contingency benefits and services; disability financial assistance; retirement benefits; economic development assistance, as defined in section 9.66 of the Revised Code; or other benefits administered by a governmental agency or paid out of a public treasury.

(5) The statement is made with purpose to secure the issuance by a governmental agency of a license, permit, authorization, certificate, registration, release, or provider agreement.

(6) The statement is sworn or affirmed before a notary public or another person empowered to administer oaths.

(7) The statement is in writing on or in connection with a report or return that is required or authorized by law.

(8) The statement is in writing and is made with purpose to induce another to extend credit to or employ the offender, to confer any degree, diploma, certificate of attainment, award of excellence, or honor on the offender, or to extend to or bestow upon the offender any other valuable benefit or distinction, when the person to whom the statement is directed relies upon it to that person's detriment.

(9) The statement is made with purpose to commit or facilitate the commission of a theft offense.

(10) The statement is knowingly made to a probate court in connection with any action, proceeding, or other matter within its jurisdiction, either orally or in a written document, including, but not limited to, an application, petition, complaint, or other pleading, or an inventory, account, or report.

(11) The statement is made on an account, form, record, stamp, label, or other writing that is required by law.

(12) The statement is made in connection with the purchase of a firearm, as defined in section 2923.11 of the Revised Code, and in conjunction with the furnishing to the seller of the firearm of a fictitious or altered driver's or commercial driver's license or permit, a fictitious or altered identification card, or any other document that contains false information about the purchaser's identity.

(13) The statement is made in a document or instrument of writing that purports to be a judgment, lien, or claim of indebtedness and is filed or recorded with the secretary of state, a county recorder, or the clerk of a court of record.

(14) The statement is made with purpose to obtain an Ohio's best Rx program enrollment card under section 5110.09 of the Revised Code or a payment from the department of job and family services under section 5110.17 of the Revised Code.

(14)[1] The statement is made in an application filed with a county sheriff pursuant to section 2923.125 of the Revised Code in order to obtain or renew a license to carry a concealed handgun or is made in an affidavit submitted to a county sheriff to obtain a temporary emergency license to carry a concealed handgun under section 2923.1213 of the Revised Code.

(B) No person, in connection with the purchase of a firearm, as defined in section 2923.11 of the Revised Code, shall knowingly furnish to the seller of the firearm a fictitious or altered driver's or commercial driver's license or permit, a fictitious or altered identification card, or any other document that contains false information about the purchaser's identity.

(C) No person, in an attempt to obtain a license to carry a concealed handgun under section 2923.125 of the Revised Code, shall knowingly present to a sheriff a fictitious or altered document that purports to be certification of the person's competence in handling a handgun as described in division (B)(3) of section 2923.125 of the Revised Code.

(D) It is no defense to a charge under division (A)(6) of this section that the oath or affirmation was administered or taken in an irregular manner.

(E) If contradictory statements relating to the same fact are made by the offender within the period of the statute of limitations for falsification, it is not necessary for the prosecution to prove which statement was false but only that one or the other was false.

(F)(1) Whoever violates division (A)(1), (2), (3), (4), (5), (6), (7), (8), (10), (11), or (13) of this section is guilty of falsification, a misdemeanor of the first degree.

(2) Whoever violates division (A)(9) of this section is guilty of falsification in a theft offense. Except as otherwise provided in this division, falsification in a theft offense is a misdemeanor of the first degree. If the value of the property or services stolen is five hundred dollars or more and is less than five thousand dollars, falsification in a theft offense is a felony of the fifth degree. If the value of the property or services stolen is five thousand dollars or more and is less than one hundred thousand dollars, falsification in a theft offense is a felony of the fourth degree. If the value of the property or services stolen is one hundred thousand dollars or more, falsification in a theft offense is a felony of the third degree.

(3) Whoever violates division (A)(12) or (B) of this section is guilty of falsification to purchase a firearm, a felony of the fifth degree.

(4) Whoever violates division (A)(14) or (C) of this section is guilty of falsification to obtain a concealed handgun license, a felony of the fourth degree.

(G) A person who violates this section is liable in a civil action to any person harmed by the violation for injury, death, or loss to person or property incurred as a result of the commission of the offense and for reasonable attorney's fees, court costs, and other expenses incurred as a result of prosecuting the civil action commenced under this division. A civil action under this division is not the exclusive remedy of a person who incurs injury, death, or loss to person or property as a result of a violation of this section.

(2004 H 12, eff. 4–8–04; 2003 H 311, eff. 12–18–03; 2003 H 95, eff. 6–26–03; 2001 H 94, eff. 9–5–01; 1997 H 408, eff. 10–1–97; 1996 H 644, eff. 11–6–96; 1996 S 269, eff. 7–1–96; 1995 S 2, eff. 7–1–96; 1995 S 46, eff. 11–15–95; 1995 H 4, eff. 11–9–95; 1995 H 249, eff. 7–17–95; 1993 H 107, eff. 10–20–93; 1993 H 152; 1991 H 298; 1990 S 3, H 347; 1989 S 46; 1988 H 708; 1986 H 340; 1984 H 632; 1976 S 545; 1972 H 511)

[1] So in original; division numbering appears as the result of the harmonization of 2004 H 12, 2003 H 311, and 2003 H 95.

2921.14 False report of child abuse or neglect

(A) No person shall knowingly make or cause another person to make a false report under division (B) of section 2151.421 of the Revised Code alleging that any person has committed an act or omission that resulted in a child being an abused child as defined in section 2151.031 of the Revised Code or a neglected child as defined in section 2151.03 of the Revised Code.

(B) Whoever violates this section is guilty of making or causing a false report of child abuse or child neglect, a misdemeanor of the first degree.

(1990 S 3, eff. 4–11–91)

2921.15 Making false allegation of peace officer misconduct

(A) As used in this section, "peace officer" has the same meaning as in section 2935.01 of the Revised Code.

(B) No person shall knowingly file a complaint against a peace officer that alleges that the peace officer engaged in misconduct in the performance of the officer's duties if the person knows that the allegation is false.

(C) Whoever violates division (B) of this section is guilty of making a false allegation of peace officer misconduct, a misdemeanor of the first degree.

(2000 S 317, eff. 3–22–01)

COMPOUNDING

2921.21 Compounding a crime

(A) No person shall knowingly demand, accept, or agree to accept anything of value in consideration of abandoning or agreeing to abandon a pending criminal prosecution.

(B) It is an affirmative defense to a charge under this section when both of the following apply:

(1) The pending prosecution involved is for a violation of section 2913.02 or 2913.11, division (B)(2) of section 2913.21, or section 2913.47 of the Revised Code, of which the actor under this section was the victim.

(2) The thing of value demanded, accepted, or agreed to be accepted, in consideration of abandoning or agreeing to abandon the prosecution, did not exceed an amount that the actor reasonably believed due him as restitution for the loss caused him by the offense.

(C) When a prosecuting witness abandons or agrees to abandon a prosecution under division (B) of this section, the abandonment or agreement in no way binds the state to abandoning the prosecution.

(D) Whoever violates this section is guilty of compounding a crime, a misdemeanor of the first degree.

(1990 H 347, eff. 7–18–90; 1973 H 716; 1972 H 511)

2921.22 Reporting felony; medical personnel to report gunshot, stabbing, and burn injuries and suspected domestic violence

(A) No person, knowing that a felony has been or is being committed, shall knowingly fail to report such information to law enforcement authorities.

(B) Except for conditions that are within the scope of division (E) of this section, no physician, limited practitioner, nurse, or other person giving aid to a sick or injured person shall negligently fail to report to law enforcement authorities any gunshot or stab wound treated or observed by the physician, limited practitioner, nurse, or person, or any serious physical harm to persons that the physician, limited practitioner, nurse, or person knows or has reasonable cause to believe resulted from an offense of violence.

(C) No person who discovers the body or acquires the first knowledge of the death of a person shall fail to report the death immediately to a physician whom the person knows to be treating the deceased for a condition from which death at such time would not be unexpected, or to a law enforcement officer, an ambulance service, an emergency squad, or the coroner in a political subdivision in which the body is discovered, the death is believed to have occurred, or knowledge concerning the death is obtained.

(D) No person shall fail to provide upon request of the person to whom a report required by division (C) of this section was made, or to any law enforcement officer who has reasonable cause to assert the authority to investigate the circumstances surrounding the death, any facts within the person's knowledge that may have a bearing on the investigation of the death.

(E)(1) As used in this division, "burn injury" means any of the following:

(a) Second or third degree burns;

(b) Any burns to the upper respiratory tract or laryngeal edema due to the inhalation of superheated air;

(c) Any burn injury or wound that may result in death;

(d) Any physical harm to persons caused by or as the result of the use of fireworks, novelties and trick noisemakers, and wire sparklers, as each is defined by section 3743.01 of the Revised Code.

(2) No physician, nurse, or limited practitioner who, outside a hospital, sanitarium, or other medical facility, attends or treats a person who has sustained a burn injury that is inflicted by an explosion or other incendiary device or that shows evidence of having been inflicted in a violent, malicious, or criminal manner shall fail to report the burn injury immediately to the local arson, or fire and explosion investigation, bureau, if there is a bureau of this type in the jurisdiction in which the person is attended or treated, or otherwise to local law enforcement authorities.

(3) No manager, superintendent, or other person in charge of a hospital, sanitarium, or other medical facility in which a person is attended or treated for any burn injury that is inflicted by an explosion or other incendiary device or that shows evidence of having been inflicted in a violent, malicious, or criminal manner shall fail to report the burn injury immediately to the local arson, or fire and explosion investigation, bureau, if there is a bureau of this type in the jurisdiction in which the person is attended or treated, or otherwise to local law enforcement authorities.

(4) No person who is required to report any burn injury under division (E)(2) or (3) of this section shall fail to file, within three working days after attending or treating the victim, a written

report of the burn injury with the office of the state fire marshal. The report shall comply with the uniform standard developed by the state fire marshal pursuant to division (A)(15) of section 3737.22 of the Revised Code.

(5) Anyone participating in the making of reports under division (E) of this section or anyone participating in a judicial proceeding resulting from the reports is immune from any civil or criminal liability that otherwise might be incurred or imposed as a result of such actions. Notwithstanding section 4731.22 of the Revised Code, the physician-patient relationship is not a ground for excluding evidence regarding a person's burn injury or the cause of the burn injury in any judicial proceeding resulting from a report submitted under division (E) of this section.

(F)(1) Any doctor of medicine or osteopathic medicine, hospital intern or resident, registered or licensed practical nurse, psychologist, social worker, independent social worker, social work assistant, professional clinical counselor, or professional counselor who knows or has reasonable cause to believe that a patient or client has been the victim of domestic violence, as defined in section 3113.31 of the Revised Code, shall note that knowledge or belief and the basis for it in the patient's or client's records.

(2) Notwithstanding section 4731.22 of the Revised Code, the doctor-patient privilege shall not be a ground for excluding any information regarding the report containing the knowledge or belief noted under division (F)(1) of this section, and the information may be admitted as evidence in accordance with the Rules of Evidence.

(G) Divisions (A) and (D) of this section do not require disclosure of information, when any of the following applies:

(1) The information is privileged by reason of the relationship between attorney and client; doctor and patient; licensed psychologist or licensed school psychologist and client; member of the clergy, rabbi, minister, or priest and any person communicating information confidentially to the member of the clergy, rabbi, minister, or priest for a religious counseling purpose of a professional character; husband and wife; or a communications assistant and those who are a party to a telecommunications relay service call.

(2) The information would tend to incriminate a member of the actor's immediate family.

(3) Disclosure of the information would amount to revealing a news source, privileged under section 2739.04 or 2739.12 of the Revised Code.

(4) Disclosure of the information would amount to disclosure by a member of the ordained clergy of an organized religious body of a confidential communication made to that member of the clergy in that member's capacity as a member of the clergy by a person seeking the aid or counsel of that member of the clergy.

(5) Disclosure would amount to revealing information acquired by the actor in the course of the actor's duties in connection with a bona fide program of treatment or services for drug dependent persons or persons in danger of drug dependence, which program is maintained or conducted by a hospital, clinic, person, agency, or organization certified pursuant to section 3793.06 of the Revised Code.

(6) Disclosure would amount to revealing information acquired by the actor in the course of the actor's duties in connection with a bona fide program for providing counseling services to victims of crimes that are violations of section 2907.02 or 2907.05 of the Revised Code or to victims of felonious sexual penetration in violation of former section 2907.12 of the Revised Code. As used in this division, "counseling services" include services provided in an informal setting by a person who, by education or experience, is competent to provide those services.

(H) No disclosure of information pursuant to this section gives rise to any liability or recrimination for a breach of privilege or confidence.

(I) Whoever violates division (A) or (B) of this section is guilty of failure to report a crime. Violation of division (A) of this section is a misdemeanor of the fourth degree. Violation of division (B) of this section is a misdemeanor of the second degree.

(J) Whoever violates division (C) or (D) of this section is guilty of failure to report knowledge of a death, a misdemeanor of the fourth degree.

(K)(1) Whoever negligently violates division (E) of this section is guilty of a minor misdemeanor.

(2) Whoever knowingly violates division (E) of this section is guilty of a misdemeanor of the second degree.

(2002 S 115, eff. 3–19–03; 1996 S 223, eff. 3–18–97; 1996 H 445, eff. 9–3–96; 1994 H 335, eff. 12–9–94; 1992 S 343, eff. 3–24–93; 1989 H 317; 1987 H 273; 1980 H 284, 1977 H 1, S 203; 1975 S 283, H 750; 1972 H 511)

2921.23 Failure to aid a law enforcement officer

(A) No person shall negligently fail or refuse to aid a law enforcement officer, when called upon for assistance in preventing or halting the commission of an offense, or in apprehending or detaining an offender, when such aid can be given without a substantial risk of physical harm to the person giving it.

(B) Whoever violates this section is guilty of failure to aid a law enforcement officer, a minor misdemeanor.

(1972 H 511, eff. 1–1–74)

DISCLOSURE OF CONFIDENTIAL INFORMATION

2921.24 Home address of peace officer not to be disclosed during criminal case

(A) No officer or employee of a law enforcement agency or court, or of the office of the clerk of any court, shall disclose during the pendency of any criminal case the home address of any peace officer, as defined in section 2935.01 of the Revised Code, who is a witness or arresting officer in the case.

(B) Division (A) of this section does not prohibit a peace officer from disclosing his own home address, and does not apply to any person who discloses the home address of a peace officer pursuant to a court-ordered disclosure under division (C) of this section.

(C) The court in which any criminal case is pending may order the disclosure of the home address of any peace officer who is a witness or arresting officer in the case, if the court determines after a written request for the disclosure that good cause exists for disclosing the home address of the peace officer.

(D) Whoever violates division (A) of this section is guilty of disclosure of confidential information, a misdemeanor of the fourth degree.

(1984 H 403, eff. 9–26–84)

2921.25 Judge not to order disclosure; exception

No judge of a court of record, or mayor presiding over a mayor's court, shall order a peace officer, as defined in section 2935.01 of the Revised Code, who is a witness in a criminal case, to disclose his home address during his examination in the case, unless the judge or mayor determines that the defendant has a right to the disclosure.

(1984 H 403, eff. 9–26–84)

OBSTRUCTING AND ESCAPE

2921.31 Obstructing official business

(A) No person, without privilege to do so and with purpose to prevent, obstruct, or delay the performance by a public official of any authorized act within the public official's official capacity, shall do any act that hampers or impedes a public official in the performance of the public official's lawful duties.

(B) Whoever violates this section is guilty of obstructing official business. Except as otherwise provided in this division, obstructing official business is a misdemeanor of the second degree. If a violation of this section creates a risk of physical harm to any person, obstructing official business is a felony of the fifth degree.

(1999 H 137, eff. 3–10–00; 1972 H 511, eff. 1–1–74)

2921.32 Obstructing justice

(A) No person, with purpose to hinder the discovery, apprehension, prosecution, conviction, or punishment of another for crime or to assist another to benefit from the commission of a crime, and no person, with purpose to hinder the discovery, apprehension, prosecution, adjudication as a delinquent child, or disposition of a child for an act that if committed by an adult would be a crime or to assist a child to benefit from the commission of an act that if committed by an adult would be a crime, shall do any of the following:

(1) Harbor or conceal the other person or child;

(2) Provide the other person or child with money, transportation, a weapon, a disguise, or other means of avoiding discovery or apprehension;

(3) Warn the other person or child of impending discovery or apprehension;

(4) Destroy or conceal physical evidence of the crime or act, or induce any person to withhold testimony or information or to elude legal process summoning the person to testify or supply evidence;

(5) Communicate false information to any person;

(6) Prevent or obstruct any person, by means of force, intimidation, or deception, from performing any act to aid in the discovery, apprehension, or prosecution of the other person or child.

(B) A person may be prosecuted for, and may be convicted of or adjudicated a delinquent child for committing, a violation of division (A) of this section regardless of whether the person or child aided ultimately is apprehended for, is charged with, is convicted of, pleads guilty to, or is adjudicated a delinquent child for committing the crime or act the person or child aided committed. The crime or act the person or child aided committed shall be used under division (C) of this section in determining the penalty for the violation of division (A) of this section, regardless of whether the person or child aided ultimately is apprehended for, is charged with, is convicted of, pleads guilty to, or is adjudicated a delinquent child for committing the crime or act the person or child aided committed.

(C) (1) Whoever violates this section is guilty of obstructing justice.

(2) If the crime committed by the person aided is a misdemeanor or if the act committed by the child aided would be a misdemeanor if committed by an adult, obstructing justice is a misdemeanor of the same degree as the crime committed by the person aided or a misdemeanor of the same degree that the act committed by the child aided would be if committed by an adult.

(3) Except as otherwise provided in divisions (C)(4) and (5) of this section, if the crime committed by the person aided is a felony or if the act committed by the child aided would be a felony if committed by an adult, obstructing justice is a felony of the fifth degree.

(4) If the crime committed by the person aided is aggravated murder, murder, or a felony of the first or second degree or if the act committed by the child aided would be one of those offenses if committed by an adult and if the offender knows or has reason to believe that the crime committed by the person aided is one of those offenses or that the act committed by the child aided would be one of those offenses if committed by an adult, obstructing justice is a felony of the third degree.

(5) If the crime or act committed by the person or child aided is an act of terrorism, obstructing justice is one of the following:

(a) Except as provided in division (C)(5)(b) of this section, a felony of the second degree;

(b) If the act of terrorism resulted in the death of a person who was not a participant in the act of terrorism, a felony of the first degree.

(D) As used in this section:

(1) "Adult" and "child" have the same meanings as in section 2151.011 of the Revised Code.

(2) "Delinquent child" has the same meaning as in section 2152.02 of the Revised Code.

(3) "Act of terrorism" has the same meaning as in section 2909.21 of the Revised Code.

(2002 S 184, eff. 5–15–02; 2000 S 179, § 3, eff. 1–1–02; 1997 H 161, eff. 12–31–97; 1995 S 2, eff. 7–1–96; 1972 H 511, eff. 1–1–74)

2921.321 Assaulting police dog, horse, or service dog; penalty

(A) No person shall knowingly cause, or attempt to cause, physical harm to a police dog or horse in either of the following circumstances:

(1) The police dog or horse is assisting a law enforcement officer in the performance of the officer's official duties at the time the physical harm is caused or attempted.

(2) The police dog or horse is not assisting a law enforcement officer in the performance of the officer's official duties at the time the physical harm is caused or attempted, but the offender has actual knowledge that the dog or horse is a police dog or horse.

(B) No person shall recklessly do any of the following:

(1) Taunt, torment, or strike a police dog or horse;

(2) Throw an object or substance at a police dog or horse;

(3) Interfere with or obstruct a police dog or horse, or interfere with or obstruct a law enforcement officer who is being assisted by a police dog or horse, in a manner that does any of the following:

(a) Inhibits or restricts the law enforcement officer's control of the police dog or horse;

(b) Deprives the law enforcement officer of control of the police dog or horse;

(c) Releases the police dog or horse from its area of control;

(d) Enters the area of control of the police dog or horse without the consent of the law enforcement officer, including placing food or any other object or substance into that area;

(e) Inhibits or restricts the ability of the police dog or horse to assist a law enforcement officer.

(4) Engage in any conduct that is likely to cause serious physical injury or death to a police dog or horse;

(5) If the person is the owner, keeper, or harborer of a dog, fail to reasonably restrain the dog from taunting, tormenting, chasing, approaching in a menacing fashion or apparent attitude of attack, or attempting to bite or otherwise endanger a police dog or horse that at the time of the conduct is assisting a law enforcement officer in the performance of the officer's duties or that the person knows is a police dog or horse.

(C) No person shall knowingly cause, or attempt to cause, physical harm to a service dog in either of the following circumstances:

(1) The service dog is assisting or serving a blind, deaf, or mobility impaired person or person with a seizure disorder at the time the physical harm is caused or attempted.

(2) The service dog is not assisting or serving a blind, deaf, or mobility impaired person or person with a seizure disorder at the time the physical harm is caused or attempted, but the offender has actual knowledge that the dog is a service dog.

(D) No person shall recklessly do any of the following:

(1) Taunt, torment, or strike a service dog;

(2) Throw an object or substance at a service dog;

(3) Interfere with or obstruct a service dog, or interfere with or obstruct a blind, deaf, or mobility impaired person or person with a seizure disorder who is being assisted or served by a service dog, in a manner that does any of the following:

(a) Inhibits or restricts the assisted or served person's control of the service dog;

(b) Deprives the assisted or served person of control of the service dog;

(c) Releases the service dog from its area of control;

(d) Enters the area of control of the service dog without the consent of the assisted or served person, including placing food or any other object or substance into that area;

(e) Inhibits or restricts the ability of the service dog to assist the assisted or served person.

(4) Engage in any conduct that is likely to cause serious physical injury or death to a service dog;

(5) If the person is the owner, keeper, or harborer of a dog, fail to reasonably restrain the dog from taunting, tormenting, chasing, approaching in a menacing fashion or apparent attitude of attack, or attempting to bite or otherwise endanger a service dog that at the time of the conduct is assisting or serving a blind, deaf, or mobility impaired person or person with a seizure disorder or that the person knows is a service dog.

(E)(1) Whoever violates division (A) of this section is guilty of assaulting a police dog or horse. Except as otherwise provided in this division, assaulting a police dog or horse is a misdemeanor of the second degree. If the violation results in the death of the police dog or horse, assaulting a police dog or horse is a felony of the third degree. If the violation results in serious physical harm to the police dog or horse other than its death, assaulting a police dog or horse is a felony of the fourth degree. If the violation results in physical harm to the police dog or horse other than death or serious physical harm, assaulting a police dog or horse is a misdemeanor of the first degree.

(2) Whoever violates division (B) of this section is guilty of harassing a police dog or horse. Except as otherwise provided in this division, harassing a police dog or horse is a misdemeanor of the second degree. If the violation results in the death of the police dog or horse, harassing a police dog or horse is a felony of the third degree. If the violation results in serious physical harm to the police dog or horse but does not result in its death, harassing a police dog or horse is a felony of the fourth degree. If the violation results in physical harm to the police dog or horse but does not result in its death or in serious physical harm to it, harassing a police dog or horse is a misdemeanor of the first degree.

(3) Whoever violates division (C) of this section is guilty of assaulting a service dog. Except as otherwise provided in this division, assaulting a service dog is a misdemeanor of the second degree. If the violation results in the death of the service dog, assaulting a service dog is a felony of the third degree. If the violation results in serious physical harm to the service dog other than its death, assaulting a service dog is a felony of the fourth degree. If the violation results in physical harm to the service dog other than death or serious physical harm, assaulting a service dog is a misdemeanor of the first degree.

(4) Whoever violates division (D) of this section is guilty of harassing a service dog. Except as otherwise provided in this division, harassing a service dog is a misdemeanor of the second degree. If the violation results in the death of the service dog, harassing a service dog is a felony of the third degree. If the violation results in serious physical harm to the service dog but does not result in its death, harassing a service dog is a felony of the fourth degree. If the violation results in physical harm to the service dog but does not result in its death or in serious physical harm to it, harassing a service dog is a misdemeanor of the first degree.

(5) In addition to any other sanction or penalty imposed for the offense under this section, Chapter 2929., or any other provision of the Revised Code, whoever violates division (A), (B), (C), or (D) of this section is responsible for the payment of all of the following:

(a) Any veterinary bill or bill for medication incurred as a result of the violation by the police department regarding a violation of division (A) or (B) of this section or by the blind, deaf, or mobility impaired person or person with a seizure disorder assisted or served by the service dog regarding a violation of division (C) or (D) of this section;

(b) The cost of any damaged equipment that results from the violation;

(c) If the violation did not result in the death of the police dog or horse or the service dog that was the subject of the violation and if, as a result of that dog or horse being the subject of the violation, the dog or horse needs further training or retraining to be able to continue in the capacity of a police dog or horse or a service dog, the cost of any further training or retraining of that dog or horse by a law enforcement officer or by the blind, deaf, or mobility impaired person or person with a seizure disorder assisted or served by the service dog;

(d) If the violation resulted in the death of the police dog or horse or the service dog that was the subject of the violation or resulted in serious physical harm to that dog or horse to the extent that the dog or horse needs to be replaced on either a temporary or a permanent basis, the cost of replacing that dog or horse and of any further training of a new police dog or horse or a new service dog by a law enforcement officer or by the blind, deaf, or mobility impaired person or person with a seizure disorder assisted or served by the service dog, which replacement or training is required because of the death of or the serious physical harm to the dog or horse that was the subject of the violation.

(F) This section does not apply to a licensed veterinarian whose conduct is in accordance with Chapter 4741. of the Revised Code.

(G) This section only applies to an offender who knows or should know at the time of the violation that the police dog or horse or service dog that is the subject of a violation under this section is a police dog or horse or service dog.

(H) As used in this section:

(1) "Physical harm" means any injury, illness, or other physiological impairment, regardless of its gravity or duration.

(2) "Police dog or horse" means a dog or horse that has been trained, and may be used, to assist law enforcement officers in the performance of their official duties.

(3) "Serious physical harm" means any of the following:

(a) Any physical harm that carries a substantial risk of death;

(b) Any physical harm that causes permanent maiming or that involves some temporary, substantial maiming;

(c) Any physical harm that causes acute pain of a duration that results in substantial suffering.

(4) "Service dog" means a dog that serves as a guide or leader for a blind person, serves as a listener for a deaf person, provides support or assistance for a mobility impaired person, or serves as a seizure assistance, seizure response, or seizure alert dog for a person with any seizure disorder.

(5) "Blind" and "mobility impaired person" have the same meanings as in section 955.011 of the Revised Code.

(2004 H 369, eff. 11–26–04; 2000 H 701, eff. 4–9–01; 1995 S 2, eff. 7–1–96; 1994 S 116, eff. 9–29–94)

2921.33 Resisting arrest

(A) No person, recklessly or by force, shall resist or interfere with a lawful arrest of the person or another.

(B) No person, recklessly or by force, shall resist or interfere with a lawful arrest of the person or another person and, during the course of or as a result of the resistance or interference, cause physical harm to a law enforcement officer.

(C) No person, recklessly or by force, shall resist or interfere with a lawful arrest of the person or another person if either of the following applies:

(1) The offender, during the course of or as a result of the resistance or interference, recklessly causes physical harm to a law enforcement officer by means of a deadly weapon;

(2) The offender, during the course of the resistance or interference, brandishes a deadly weapon.

(D) Whoever violates this section is guilty of resisting arrest. A violation of division (A) of this section is a misdemeanor of the second degree. A violation of division (B) of this section is a misdemeanor of the first degree. A violation of division (C) of this section is a felony of the fourth degree.

(E) As used in this section, "deadly weapon" has the same meaning as in section 2923.11 of the Revised Code.

(1997 H 151, eff. 9–16–97; 1995 S 2, eff. 7–1–96; 1972 H 511, eff. 1–1–74)

2921.331 Failure to comply with order or signal of police officer

(A) No person shall fail to comply with any lawful order or direction of any police officer invested with authority to direct, control, or regulate traffic.

(B) No person shall operate a motor vehicle so as willfully to elude or flee a police officer after receiving a visible or audible signal from a police officer to bring the person's motor vehicle to a stop.

(C)(1) Whoever violates this section is guilty of failure to comply with an order or signal of a police officer.

(2) A violation of division (A) of this section is a misdemeanor of the first degree.

(3) Except as provided in divisions (C)(4) and (5) of this section, a violation of division (B) of this section is a misdemeanor of the first degree.

(4) Except as provided in division (C)(5) of this section, a violation of division (B) of this section is a felony of the fourth degree if the jury or judge as trier of fact finds by proof beyond a reasonable doubt that, in committing the offense, the offender was fleeing immediately after the commission of a felony.

(5)(a) A violation of division (B) of this section is a felony of the third degree if the jury or judge as trier of fact finds any of the following by proof beyond a reasonable doubt:

(i) The operation of the motor vehicle by the offender was a proximate cause of serious physical harm to persons or property.

(ii) The operation of the motor vehicle by the offender caused a substantial risk of serious physical harm to persons or property.

(b) If a police officer pursues an offender who is violating division (B) of this section and division (C)(5)(a) of this section applies, the sentencing court, in determining the seriousness of an offender's conduct for purposes of sentencing the offender for a violation of division (B) of this section, shall consider, along with the factors set forth in sections 2929.12 and 2929.13 of the Revised Code that are required to be considered, all of the following:

(i) The duration of the pursuit;

(ii) The distance of the pursuit;

(iii) The rate of speed at which the offender operated the motor vehicle during the pursuit;

(iv) Whether the offender failed to stop for traffic lights or stop signs during the pursuit;

(v) The number of traffic lights or stop signs for which the offender failed to stop during the pursuit;

(vi) Whether the offender operated the motor vehicle during the pursuit without lighted lights during a time when lighted lights are required;

(vii) Whether the offender committed a moving violation during the pursuit;

(viii) The number of moving violations the offender committed during the pursuit;

(ix) Any other relevant factors indicating that the offender's conduct is more serious than conduct normally constituting the offense.

(D) If an offender is sentenced pursuant to division (C)(4) or (5) of this section for a violation of division (B) of this section, and if the offender is sentenced to a prison term for that violation, the offender shall serve the prison term consecutively to any other prison term or mandatory prison term imposed upon the offender.

(E) In addition to any other sanction imposed for a violation of this section, the court shall impose a class two suspension from the range specified in division (A)(2) of section 4510.02 of the Revised Code. If the offender previously has been found guilty of an offense under this section, the court shall impose a class one suspension as described in division (A)(1) of that section. The court shall not grant limited driving privileges to the offender. No judge shall suspend the first three years of suspension under a class two suspension of an offender's license, permit, or privilege required by this division on any portion of the suspension under a class one suspension of an offender's license, permit, or privilege required by this division.

(F) As used in this section:

(1) "Moving violation" has the same meaning as in section 2743.70 of the Revised Code.

(2) "Police officer" has the same meaning as in section 4511.01 of the Revised Code.

(2002 S 123, eff. 1–1–04; 1999 H 29, eff. 10–29–99; 1989 S 49, eff. 11–3–89)

2921.34 Escape

Note: See also following version of this section, eff. 4–29–05.

(A)(1) No person, knowing the person is under detention or being reckless in that regard, shall purposely break or attempt to break the detention, or purposely fail to return to detention, either following temporary leave granted for a specific purpose or limited period, or at the time required when serving a sentence in intermittent confinement.

(2) No person who is sentenced to a prison term pursuant to division (A)(3) of section 2971.03 of the Revised Code as a sexually violent predator, for whom the requirement that the entire prison term be served in a state correctional institution has been modified pursuant to section 2971.05 of the Revised Code, and who, pursuant to that modification, is restricted to a geographic area, knowing that the person is under a geographic restriction or being reckless in that regard, shall purposely leave the geographic area to which the restriction applies or purposely fail to return to that geographic area following a temporary leave granted for a specific purpose or for a limited period of time.

(B) Irregularity in bringing about or maintaining detention, or lack of jurisdiction of the committing or detaining authority, is not a defense to a charge under this section if the detention is pursuant to judicial order or in a detention facility. In the case of any other detention, irregularity or lack of jurisdiction is an affirmative defense only if either of the following occurs:

(1) The escape involved no substantial risk of harm to the person or property of another.

(2) The detaining authority knew or should have known there was no legal basis or authority for the detention.

(C) Whoever violates this section is guilty of escape.

(1) If the offender, at the time of the commission of the offense, was under detention as an alleged or adjudicated delinquent child or unruly child and if the act for which the offender was under detention would not be a felony if committed by an adult, escape is a misdemeanor of the first degree.

(2) If the offender, at the time of the commission of the offense, was under detention in any other manner or was a sexually violent predator for whom the requirement that the entire prison term imposed pursuant to division (A)(3) of section 2971.03 of the Revised Code be served in a state correctional institution has been modified pursuant to section 2971.05 of the Revised Code, escape is one of the following:

(a) A felony of the second degree, when the most serious offense for which the person was under detention or adjudicated a sexually violent predator is aggravated murder, murder, or a felony of the first or second degree or, if the person was under detention as an alleged or adjudicated delinquent child, when the most serious act for which the person was under detention would be aggravated murder, murder, or a felony of the first or second degree if committed by an adult;

(b) A felony of the third degree, when the most serious offense for which the person was under detention or adjudicated a sexually violent predator is a felony of the third, fourth, or fifth degree or an unclassified felony or, if the person was under detention as an alleged or adjudicated delinquent child, when the most serious act for which the person was under detention would be a felony of the third, fourth, or fifth degree or an unclassified felony if committed by an adult;

(c) A felony of the fifth degree, when any of the following applies:

(i) The most serious offense for which the person was under detention is a misdemeanor.

(ii) The person was found not guilty by reason of insanity, and the person's detention consisted of hospitalization, institutionalization, or confinement in a facility under an order made pursuant to or under authority of section 2945.40, 2945.401, or 2945.402 of the Revised Code.

(d) A misdemeanor of the first degree, when the most serious offense for which the person was under detention is a misdemeanor and when the person fails to return to detention at a specified time following temporary leave granted for a specific purpose or limited period or at the time required when serving a sentence in intermittent confinement.

(1996 S 285, eff. 7–1–97; 1996 H 180, eff. 1–1–97; 1995 S 2, eff. 7–1–96; 1993 H 42, eff. 2–9–94; 1992 H 725, S 37; 1991 H 298; 1972 H 511)

Note: See also following version of this section, eff. 4–29–05.

2921.34 Escape (later effective date)

Note: See also preceding version of this section, in effect until 4–29–05.

(A)(1) No person, knowing the person is under detention or being reckless in that regard, shall purposely break or attempt to break the detention, or purposely fail to return to detention, either following temporary leave granted for a specific purpose or limited period, or at the time required when serving a sentence in intermittent confinement.

(2) No person who is adjudicated a sexually violent predator and is sentenced to a prison term pursuant to division (A)(3) of section 2971.03 of the Revised Code for the sexually violent offense, for whom the requirement that the entire prison term be served in a state correctional institution has been modified pursuant to section 2971.05 of the Revised Code, and who, pursuant to that modification, is restricted to a geographic area, knowing that the person is under a geographic restriction or being reckless in that regard, shall purposely leave the geographic area to which the restriction applies or purposely fail to return to that geographic area following a temporary leave granted for a specific purpose or for a limited period of time.

(B) Irregularity in bringing about or maintaining detention, or lack of jurisdiction of the committing or detaining authority, is not a defense to a charge under this section if the detention is pursuant to judicial order or in a detention facility. In the case of any other detention, irregularity or lack of jurisdiction is an affirmative defense only if either of the following occurs:

(1) The escape involved no substantial risk of harm to the person or property of another.

(2) The detaining authority knew or should have known there was no legal basis or authority for the detention.

(C) Whoever violates this section is guilty of escape.

(1) If the offender, at the time of the commission of the offense, was under detention as an alleged or adjudicated delinquent child or unruly child and if the act for which the offender was under detention would not be a felony if committed by an adult, escape is a misdemeanor of the first degree.

(2) If the offender, at the time of the commission of the offense, was under detention in any other manner or was adjudicated a sexually violent predator for whom the requirement that the entire prison term imposed pursuant to division (A)(3) of section 2971.03 of the Revised Code be served in a state correc-

tional institution has been modified pursuant to section 2971.05 of the Revised Code, escape is one of the following:

(a) A felony of the second degree, when the most serious offense for which the person was under detention or adjudicated a sexually violent predator is aggravated murder, murder, or a felony of the first or second degree or, if the person was under detention as an alleged or adjudicated delinquent child, when the most serious act for which the person was under detention would be aggravated murder, murder, or a felony of the first or second degree if committed by an adult;

(b) A felony of the third degree, when the most serious offense for which the person was under detention or adjudicated a sexually violent predator is a felony of the third, fourth, or fifth degree or an unclassified felony or, if the person was under detention as an alleged or adjudicated delinquent child, when the most serious act for which the person was under detention would be a felony of the third, fourth, or fifth degree or an unclassified felony if committed by an adult;

(c) A felony of the fifth degree, when any of the following applies:

(i) The most serious offense for which the person was under detention is a misdemeanor.

(ii) The person was found not guilty by reason of insanity, and the person's detention consisted of hospitalization, institutionalization, or confinement in a facility under an order made pursuant to or under authority of section 2945.40, 2945.401, or 2945.402 of the Revised Code.

(d) A misdemeanor of the first degree, when the most serious offense for which the person was under detention is a misdemeanor and when the person fails to return to detention at a specified time following temporary leave granted for a specific purpose or limited period or at the time required when serving a sentence in intermittent confinement.

(D) As used in this section:

(1) "Adjudicated a sexually violent predator" has the same meaning as in section 2929.01 of the Revised Code, and a person is " adjudicated a sexually violent predator" in the same manner and the same circumstances as are described in that section.

(2) "Sexually violent offense" has the same meaning as in section 2971.01 of the Revised Code.

(2004 H 473, eff. 4–29–05; 1996 S 285, eff. 7–1–97; 1996 H 180, eff. 1–1–97; 1995 S 2, eff. 7–1–96; 1993 H 42, eff. 2–9–94; 1992 H 725, S 37; 1991 H 298; 1972 H 511)

Note: See also preceding version of this section, in effect until 4–29–05.

2921.35 Aiding escape or resistance to authority

(A) No person, with purpose to promote or facilitate an escape or resistance to lawful authority, shall convey into a detention facility, or provide anyone confined therein with any instrument or thing which may be used for such purposes.

(B) No person who is confined in a detention facility, and with purpose to promote or facilitate an escape or resistance to lawful authority, shall make, procure, conceal, unlawfully possess, or give to another inmate, any instrument or thing which may be used for such purposes.

(C) Whoever violates this section is guilty of aiding escape or resistance to lawful authority, a felony of the fourth degree.

(1995 S 2, eff. 7–1–96; 1972 H 511, eff. 1–1–74)

CONVEYANCE OF PROHIBITED ITEMS

2921.36 Prohibition of conveyance of certain items onto grounds of detention facility or mental health or mental retardation and developmental disabilities facility

(A) No person shall knowingly convey, or attempt to convey, onto the grounds of a detention facility or of an institution that is under the control of the department of mental health or the department of mental retardation and developmental disabilities, any of the following items:

(1) Any deadly weapon or dangerous ordnance, as defined in section 2923.11 of the Revised Code, or any part of or ammunition for use in such a deadly weapon or dangerous ordnance;

(2) Any drug of abuse, as defined in section 3719.011 of the Revised Code;

(3) Any intoxicating liquor, as defined in section 4301.01 of the Revised Code.

(B) Division (A) of this section does not apply to any person who conveys or attempts to convey an item onto the grounds of a detention facility or of an institution under the control of the department of mental health or the department of mental retardation and developmental disabilities pursuant to the written authorization of the person in charge of the detention facility or the institution and in accordance with the written rules of the detention facility or the institution.

(C) No person shall knowingly deliver, or attempt to deliver, to any person who is confined in a detention facility or to any patient in an institution under the control of the department of mental health or the department of mental retardation and developmental disabilities, any item listed in division (A)(1), (2), or (3) of this section.

(D) No person shall knowingly deliver, or attempt to deliver, cash to any person who is confined in a detention facility.

(E) No person shall knowingly deliver, or attempt to deliver, to any person who is confined in a detention facility a cellular telephone, two-way radio, or other electronic communications device.

(F) (1) It is an affirmative defense to a charge under division (A)(1) of this section that the weapon or dangerous ordnance in question was being transported in a motor vehicle for any lawful purpose, that it was not on the actor's person, and, if the weapon or dangerous ordnance in question was a firearm, that it was unloaded and was being carried in a closed package, box, or case or in a compartment that can be reached only by leaving the vehicle.

(2) It is an affirmative defense to a charge under division (C) of this section that the actor was not otherwise prohibited by law from delivering the item to the confined person or the patient and that either of the following applies:

(a) The actor was permitted by the written rules of the detention facility or the institution to deliver the item to the confined person or the patient.

(b) The actor was given written authorization by the person in charge of the detention facility or the institution to deliver the item to the confined person or the patient.

(G) (1) Whoever violates division (A)(1) of this section or commits a violation of division (C) of this section involving an item listed in division (A)(1) of this section is guilty of illegal conveyance of weapons onto the grounds of a detention facility or a mental health or mental retardation and developmental disabilities institution, a felony of the fourth degree. If the offender is an officer or employee of the department of rehabilitation and correction, the court shall impose a mandatory prison term.

(2) Whoever violates division (A)(2) of this section or commits a violation of division (C) of this section involving any drug of abuse is guilty of illegal conveyance of drugs of abuse onto the grounds of a detention facility or a mental health or mental retardation and developmental disabilities institution, a felony of the third degree. If the offender is an officer or employee of the department of rehabilitation and correction or of the department of youth services, the court shall impose a mandatory prison term.

(3) Whoever violates division (A)(3) of this section or commits a violation of division (C) of this section involving any intoxicating liquor is guilty of illegal conveyance of intoxicating liquor onto the grounds of a detention facility or a mental health or mental retardation and developmental disabilities institution, a misdemeanor of the second degree.

(4) Whoever violates division (D) of this section is guilty of illegal conveyance of cash onto the grounds of a detention facility, a misdemeanor of the first degree. If the offender previously has been convicted of or pleaded guilty to a violation of division (D) of this section, illegal conveyance of cash onto the grounds of a detention facility is a felony of the fifth degree.

(5) Whoever violates division (E) of this section is guilty of illegal conveyance of a communications device onto the grounds of a detention facility, a misdemeanor of the first degree, or if the offender previously has been convicted of or pleaded guilty to a violation of division (E) of this section, a felony of the fifth degree.

(2002 H 510, eff. 3–31–03; 2000 H 357, eff. 8–10–00; 1997 S 111, eff. 3–17–98; 1995 S 2, eff. 7–1–96; 1994 H 571, eff. 10–6–94; 1990 S 258, eff. 11–20–90; 1980 H 900; 1978 H 630)

2921.37 Person in charge of detention facility to have powers of peace officer as to prohibited items

The person in charge of a detention facility shall, on the grounds of the detention facility, have the same power as a peace officer, as defined in section 2935.01 of the Revised Code, to arrest a person who violates section 2921.36 of the Revised Code.

(1978 H 630, eff. 5–23–78)

HARASSMENT BY INMATE

2921.38 Harassment by inmate

(A) No person who is confined in a detention facility, with intent to harass, annoy, threaten, or alarm another person, shall cause or attempt to cause the other person to come into contact with blood, semen, urine, feces, or another bodily substance by throwing the bodily substance at the other person, by expelling the bodily substance upon the other person, or in any other manner.

(B) No person who is confined in a detention facility, with knowledge that the person is a carrier of the virus that causes acquired immunodeficiency syndrome, is a carrier of a hepatitis virus, or is infected with tuberculosis and with intent to harass, annoy, threaten, or alarm another person, shall cause or attempt to cause the other person to come into contact with blood, semen, urine, feces, or another bodily substance by throwing the bodily substance at the other person, by expelling the bodily substance upon the other person, or in any other manner.

(C) Whoever violates this section is guilty of harassment by an inmate. A violation of division (A) of this section is a felony of the fifth degree. A violation of division (B) of this section is a felony of the third degree.

(D)(1) The court, on request of the prosecutor, or the law enforcement authority responsible for the investigation of the violation, shall cause a person who allegedly has committed a violation of this section to submit to one or more appropriate tests to determine if the person is a carrier of the virus that causes acquired immunodeficiency syndrome, is a carrier of a hepatitis virus, or is infected with tuberculosis.

(2) The court shall charge the offender with the costs of the test or tests ordered under division (D)(1) of this section unless the court determines that the accused is unable to pay, in which case the costs shall be charged to the entity that operates the detention facility in which the alleged offense occurred.

(E) This section does not apply to a person who is hospitalized, institutionalized, or confined in a facility operated by the department of mental health or the department of mental retardation and developmental disabilities.

(1997 H 37, eff. 6–11–97)

PECULATION AND DERELICTION

2921.41 Theft in office; restitution order against public or party official; withholding from payments by retirement system; procedures

(A) No public official or party official shall commit any theft offense, as defined in division (K) of section 2913.01 of the Revised Code, when either of the following applies:

(1) The offender uses the offender's office in aid of committing the offense or permits or assents to its use in aid of committing the offense;

(2) The property or service involved is owned by this state, any other state, the United States, a county, a municipal corporation, a township, or any political subdivision, department, or agency of any of them, is owned by a political party, or is part of a political campaign fund.

(B) Whoever violates this section is guilty of theft in office. Except as otherwise provided in this division, theft in office is a felony of the fifth degree. If the value of property or services stolen is five hundred dollars or more and is less than five thousand dollars, theft in office is a felony of the fourth degree. If the value of property or services stolen is five thousand dollars or more, theft in office is a felony of the third degree.

(C)(1) A public official or party official who is convicted of or pleads guilty to theft in office is forever disqualified from holding any public office, employment, or position of trust in this state.

(2)(a) A court that imposes sentence for a violation of this section based on conduct described in division (A)(2) of this section shall require the public official or party official who is convicted of or pleads guilty to the offense to make restitution for all of the property or the service that is the subject of the offense, in addition to the term of imprisonment and any fine imposed. A court that imposes sentence for a violation of this section based on conduct described in division (A)(1) of this section and that determines at trial that this state or a political subdivision of this state if the offender is a public official, or a political party in the United States or this state if the offender is a party official, suffered actual loss as a result of the offense shall require the offender to make restitution to the state, political subdivision, or political party for all of the actual loss experienced, in addition to the term of imprisonment and any fine imposed.

(b)(i) In any case in which a sentencing court is required to order restitution under division (C)(2)(a) of this section and in which the offender, at the time of the commission of the offense or at any other time, was a member of the public employees retirement system, the Ohio police and fire pension fund, the state teachers retirement system, the school employees retirement system, or the state highway patrol retirement system; was an electing employee, as defined in section 3305.01 of the Revised Code, participating in an alternative retirement plan provided pursuant to Chapter 3305. of the Revised Code; was a participating employee or continuing member, as defined in section 148.01 of the Revised Code, in a deferred compensation program offered by the Ohio public employees deferred compensation board; was an officer or employee of a municipal corporation who was a participant in a deferred compensation program offered by that municipal corporation; was an officer or employee of a government unit, as defined in section 148.06 of the Revised Code, who was a participant in a deferred compensation program offered by that government unit, or was a participating employee, continuing member, or participant in any deferred compensation program described in this division and a member of a retirement system specified in this division or a retirement system of a municipal corporation, the entity to which restitution is to be made may file a motion with the sentencing court specifying any retirement system, any provider as defined in section 3305.01 of the Revised Code, and any deferred compensation program of which the offender was a member, electing employee, participating employee, continuing member, or participant and requesting the court to issue an order requiring the specified retirement system, the specified provider under the alternative retirement plan, or the specified deferred compensation program, or, if more than one is specified in the motion, the applicable combination of these, to withhold the amount required as restitution from any payment that is to be made under a pension, annuity, or allowance, under an option in the alternative retirement plan, under a participant account, as defined in section 148.01 of the Revised Code, or under any other type of benefit, other than a survivorship benefit, that has been or is in the future granted to the offender, from any payment of accumulated employee contributions standing to the offender's credit with that retirement system, that provider of the option under the alternative retirement plan, or that deferred compensation program, or, if more than one is specified in the motion, the applicable combination of these, and from any payment of any other amounts to be paid to the offender upon the offender's withdrawal of the offender's contributions pursuant to Chapter 145., 148., 742., 3307., 3309., or 5505. of the Revised Code. A motion described in this division may be filed at any time subsequent to the conviction of the offender or entry of a guilty plea. Upon the filing of the motion, the clerk of the court in which the motion is filed shall notify the offender, the specified retirement system, the specified provider under the alternative retirement plan, or the specified deferred compensation program, or, if more than one is specified in the motion, the applicable combination of these, in writing, of all of the following: that the motion was filed; that the offender will be granted a hearing on the issuance of the requested order if the offender files a written request for a hearing with the clerk prior to the expiration of thirty days after the offender receives the notice; that, if a hearing is requested, the court will schedule a hearing as soon as possible and notify the offender, any specified retirement system, any specified provider under an alternative retirement plan, and any specified deferred compensation program of the date, time, and place of the hearing; that, if a hearing is conducted, it will be limited only to a consideration of whether the offender can show good cause why the requested order should not be issued; that, if a hearing is conducted, the court will not issue the requested order if the court determines, based on evidence presented at the hearing by the offender, that there is good cause for the requested order not to be issued; that the court will issue the requested order if a hearing is not requested or if a hearing is conducted but the court does not determine, based on evidence presented at the hearing by the offender, that there is good cause for the requested order not to be issued; and that, if the requested order is issued, any retirement system, any provider under an alternative retirement plan, and any deferred compensation program specified in the motion will be required to withhold the amount required as restitution from payments to the offender.

(ii) In any case in which a sentencing court is required to order restitution under division (C)(2)(a) of this section and in which a motion requesting the issuance of a withholding order as described in division (C)(2)(b)(i) of this section is filed, the offender may receive a hearing on the motion by delivering a written request for a hearing to the court prior to the expiration of thirty days after the offender's receipt of the notice provided pursuant to division (C)(2)(b)(i) of this section. If a request for a hearing is made by the offender within the prescribed time, the court shall schedule a hearing as soon as possible after the request is made and shall notify the offender, the specified retirement system, the specified provider under the alternative retirement plan, or the specified deferred compensation program, or, if more than one is specified in the motion, the applicable combination of these, of the date, time, and place of the hearing. A hearing scheduled under this division shall be limited to a consideration of whether there is good cause, based on evidence presented by the offender, for the requested order not to be issued. If the court determines, based on evidence presented by the offender, that there is good cause for the order not to be issued, the court shall deny the motion and shall not issue the requested order. If the offender does not request a hearing within the prescribed time or if the court conducts a hearing but does not determine, based on evidence presented by the offender, that there is good cause for the order not to be issued, the court shall order the specified retirement system, the specified provider under the alternative retirement plan, or the specified deferred compensation program, or, if more than one is specified in the motion, the applicable combination of these, to withhold the amount required as restitution under division (C)(2)(a) of this section from any payments to be made under a pension, annuity, or allowance, under a participant account, as defined in section 148.01 of the Revised Code, under an option in the alternative retirement plan, or under any other type of benefit, other than a survivorship benefit, that has been or is in the future granted to the offender, from any payment of accumulated employee contributions standing to the offender's credit with that retirement system, that provider under the alternative retirement plan, or that deferred compensation program, or, if more than one is specified in the motion, the applicable combination of these, and from any payment of any other amounts to be paid to the offender upon the offender's withdrawal of the offender's contributions pursuant to Chapter 145., 148., 742., 3307., 3309., or 5505. of the Revised Code, and to continue the withholding for that purpose, in accordance with the order, out of each payment to be made on or after the date of issuance of the order, until further order of the court. Upon receipt of an order issued under this division, the public employees retirement system, the Ohio police and fire pension fund, the state teachers retirement system, the school employees retirement system, the state highway patrol retirement system, a municipal corporation retirement system, the provider under the alternative retirement plan, and the deferred compensation program offered by the Ohio public employees deferred compensation board, a municipal corporation, or a government unit, as defined in section 148.06 of the Revised Code, whichever are applicable, shall withhold the amount required as restitution, in accordance with the order, from any such payments and immediately shall forward the amount withheld to the clerk of the court in which the order was issued for payment to the entity to which restitution is to be made.

(iii) Service of a notice required by division (C)(2)(b)(i) or (ii) of this section shall be effected in the same manner as provided in the Rules of Civil Procedure for the service of process.

(D) Upon the filing of charges against a person under this section, the prosecutor, as defined in section 2935.01 of the Revised Code, who is assigned the case shall send written notice that charges have been filed against that person to the public employees retirement system, the Ohio police and fire pension fund, the state teachers retirement system, the school employees retirement system, the state highway patrol retirement system, the provider under an alternative retirement plan, any municipal corporation retirement system in this state, and the deferred compensation program offered by the Ohio public employees deferred compensation board, a municipal corporation, or a government unit, as defined in section 148.06 of the Revised

Code. The written notice shall specifically identify the person charged.

(2000 H 535, eff. 4–1–01; 2000 H 628, eff. 9–21–00; 1999 H 222, eff. 11–2–99; 1996 H 586, eff. 3–31–97; 1995 S 2, eff. 7–1–96; 1992 S 300, eff. 11–5–92; 1984 H 265; 1972 H 511)

2921.42 Having an unlawful interest in a public contract

(A) No public official shall knowingly do any of the following:

(1) Authorize, or employ the authority or influence of his office to secure authorization of any public contract in which he, a member of his family, or any of his business associates has an interest;

(2) Authorize, or employ the authority or influence of his office to secure the investment of public funds in any share, bond, mortgage, or other security, with respect to which he, a member of his family, or any of his business associates either has an interest, is an underwriter, or receives any brokerage, origination, or servicing fees;

(3) During his term of office or within one year thereafter, occupy any position of profit in the prosecution of a public contract authorized by him or by a legislative body, commission, or board of which he was a member at the time of authorization, unless the contract was let by competitive bidding to the lowest and best bidder;

(4) Have an interest in the profits or benefits of a public contract entered into by or for the use of the political subdivision or governmental agency or instrumentality with which he is connected;

(5) Have an interest in the profits or benefits of a public contract that is not let by competitive bidding if required by law and that involves more than one hundred fifty dollars.

(B) In the absence of bribery or a purpose to defraud, a public official, member of his family, or any of his business associates shall not be considered as having an interest in a public contract or the investment of public funds, if all of the following apply:

(1) The interest of that person is limited to owning or controlling shares of the corporation, or being a creditor of the corporation or other organization, that is the contractor on the public contract involved, or that is the issuer of the security in which public funds are invested;

(2) The shares owned or controlled by that person do not exceed five per cent of the outstanding shares of the corporation, and the amount due that person as creditor does not exceed five per cent of the total indebtedness of the corporation or other organization;

(3) That person, prior to the time the public contract is entered into, files with the political subdivision or governmental agency or instrumentality involved, an affidavit giving his exact status in connection with the corporation or other organization.

(C) This section does not apply to a public contract in which a public official, member of his family, or one of his business associates has an interest, when all of the following apply:

(1) The subject of the public contract is necessary supplies or services for the political subdivision or governmental agency or instrumentality involved;

(2) The supplies or services are unobtainable elsewhere for the same or lower cost, or are being furnished to the political subdivision or governmental agency or instrumentality as part of a continuing course of dealing established prior to the public official's becoming associated with the political subdivision or governmental agency or instrumentality involved;

(3) The treatment accorded the political subdivision or governmental agency or instrumentality is either preferential to or the same as that accorded other customers or clients in similar transactions;

(4) The entire transaction is conducted at arm's length, with full knowledge by the political subdivision or governmental agency or instrumentality involved, of the interest of the public official, member of his family, or business associate, and the public official takes no part in the deliberations or decision of the political subdivision or governmental agency or instrumentality with respect to the public contract.

(D) Division (A)(4) of this section does not prohibit participation by a public employee in any housing program funded by public moneys if the public employee otherwise qualifies for the program and does not use the authority or influence of his office or employment to secure benefits from the program and if the moneys are to be used on the primary residence of the public employee. Such participation does not constitute an unlawful interest in a public contract in violation of this section.

(E) Whoever violates this section is guilty of having an unlawful interest in a public contract. Violation of division (A)(1) or (2) of this section is a felony of the fourth degree. Violation of division (A)(3), (4), or (5) of this section is a misdemeanor of the first degree.

(F) It is not a violation of this section for a prosecuting attorney to appoint assistants and employees in accordance with sections 309.06 and 2921.421 of the Revised Code, for a chief legal officer of a municipal corporation or an official designated as prosecutor in a municipal corporation to appoint assistants and employees in accordance with sections 733.621 and 2921.421 of the Revised Code, or for a township law director appointed under section 504.15 of the Revised Code to appoint assistants and employees in accordance with sections 504.151 and 2921.421 of the Revised Code.

(F) [1] This section does not apply to a public contract in which a township trustee in a township with a population of five thousand or less in its unincorporated area, a member of the township trustee's family, or one of his business associates has an interest, if all of the following apply:

(1) The subject of the public contract is necessary supplies or services for the township and the amount of the contract is less than five thousand dollars per year;

(2) The supplies or services are being furnished to the township as part of a continuing course of dealing established before the township trustee held that office with the township;

(3) The treatment accorded the township is either preferential to or the same as that accorded other customers or clients in similar transactions;

(4) The entire transaction is conducted with full knowledge by the township of the interest of the township trustee, member of his family, or his business associate.

(G) As used in this section:

(1) "Public contract" means any of the following:

(a) The purchase or acquisition, or a contract for the purchase or acquisition, of property or services by or for the use of the state, any of its political subdivisions, or any agency or instrumentality of either, including the employment of an individual by the state, any of its political subdivisions, or any agency or instrumentality of either;

(b) A contract for the design, construction, alteration, repair, or maintenance of any public property.

(2) "Chief legal officer" has the same meaning as in section 733.621 of the Revised Code.

(1994 H 150, eff. 6–23–94; 1994 H 285, eff. 3–2–94; 1993 H 152, eff. 7–1–93; 1992 S 359; 1972 H 511)

1 Subdivision lettering appears as a result of the harmonization of 1994 H 285 and 1994 H 150.

2921.421 Assistants and employees of prosecutors, law directors, and solicitors

(A) As used in this section:

(1) "Chief legal officer" has the same meaning as in section 733.621 of the Revised Code.

(2) "Political subdivision" means a county, a municipal corporation, or a township that adopts a limited home rule government under Chapter 504. of the Revised Code.

(B) A prosecuting attorney may appoint assistants and employees, except a member of the family of the prosecuting attorney, in accordance with division (B) of section 309.06 of the Revised Code, a chief legal officer of a municipal corporation or an official designated as prosecutor in a municipal corporation may appoint assistants and employees, except a member of the family of the chief legal officer or official designated as prosecutor, in accordance with section 733.621 of the Revised Code, and a township law director appointed under section 504.15 of the Revised Code may appoint assistants and employees, except a member of the family of the township law director, in accordance with section 504.151 of the Revised Code, if all of the following apply:

(1) The services to be furnished by the appointee or employee are necessary services for the political subdivision or are authorized by the legislative authority, governing board, or other contracting authority of the political subdivision.

(2) The treatment accorded the political subdivision is either preferential to or the same as that accorded other clients or customers of the appointee or employee in similar transactions, or the legislative authority, governing board, or other contracting authority of the political subdivision, in its sole discretion, determines that the compensation and other terms of appointment or employment of the appointee or employee are fair and reasonable to the political subdivision.

(3) The appointment or employment is made after prior written disclosure to the legislative authority, governing board, or other contracting authority of the political subdivision of the business relationship between the prosecuting attorney, the chief legal officer or official designated as prosecutor in a municipal corporation, or the township law director and the appointee or employee thereof. In the case of a municipal corporation, the disclosure may be made or evidenced in an ordinance, resolution, or other document that does either or both of the following:

(a) Authorizes the furnishing of services as required under division (B)(1) of this section;

(b) Determines that the compensation and other terms of appointment or employment of the appointee or employee are fair and reasonable to the political subdivision as required under division (B)(2) of this section.

(4) The prosecuting attorney, the elected chief legal officer, or the township law director does not receive any distributive share or other portion, in whole or in part, of the earnings of the business associate, partner, or employee paid by the political subdivision to the business associate, partner, or employee for services rendered for the political subdivision.

(C) It is not a violation of this section or of section 102.03 or 2921.42 of the Revised Code for the legislative authority, the governing board, or other contracting authority of a political subdivision to engage the services of any firm that practices the profession of law upon the terms approved by the legislative authority, the governing board, or the contracting authority, or to designate any partner, officer, or employee of that firm as a nonelected public official or employee of the political subdivision, whether the public office or position of employment is created by statute, charter, ordinance, resolution, or other legislative or administrative action.

(1999 H 187, eff. 9–20–99; 1994 H 285, eff. 3–2–94)

2921.43 Soliciting or receiving improper compensation

(A) No public servant shall knowingly solicit or accept, and no person shall knowingly promise or give to a public servant, either of the following:

(1) Any compensation, other than as allowed by divisions (G), (H), and (I) of section 102.03 of the Revised Code or other provisions of law, to perform the public servant's official duties, to perform any other act or service in the public servant's public capacity, for the general performance of the duties of the public servant's public office or public employment, or as a supplement to the public servant's public compensation;

(2) Additional or greater fees or costs than are allowed by law to perform the public servant's official duties.

(B) No public servant for the public servant's own personal or business use, and no person for the person's own personal or business use or for the personal or business use of a public servant or party official, shall solicit or accept anything of value in consideration of either of the following:

(1) Appointing or securing, maintaining, or renewing the appointment of any person to any public office, employment, or agency;

(2) Preferring, or maintaining the status of, any public employee with respect to compensation, duties, placement, location, promotion, or other material aspects of employment.

(C) No person for the benefit of a political party, campaign committee, legislative campaign fund, or political action committee shall coerce any contribution in consideration of either of the following:

(1) Appointing or securing, maintaining, or renewing the appointment of any person to any public office, employment, or agency;

(2) Preferring, or maintaining the status of, any public employee with respect to compensation, duties, placement, location, promotion, or other material aspects of employment.

(D) Whoever violates this section is guilty of soliciting improper compensation, a misdemeanor of the first degree.

(E) A public servant who is convicted of a violation of this section is disqualified from holding any public office, employment, or position of trust in this state for a period of seven years from the date of conviction.

(F) Divisions (A), (B), and (C) of this section do not prohibit a person from making voluntary contributions to a political party, campaign committee, legislative campaign fund, or political action committee or prohibit a political party, campaign committee, legislative campaign fund, or political action committee from accepting voluntary contributions.

(2004 H 1 SS, eff. 3–31–05; 1998 S 134, eff. 7–13–98; 1995 S 8, eff. 8–23–95; 1986 H 300, eff. 9–17–86; 1974 S 46; 1972 H 511)

2921.44 Dereliction of duty

(A) No law enforcement officer shall negligently do any of the following:

(1) Fail to serve a lawful warrant without delay;

(2) Fail to prevent or halt the commission of an offense or to apprehend an offender, when it is in the law enforcement officer's power to do so alone or with available assistance.

(B) No law enforcement, ministerial, or judicial officer shall negligently fail to perform a lawful duty in a criminal case or proceeding.

(C) No officer, having charge of a detention facility, shall negligently do any of the following:

(1) Allow the detention facility to become littered or unsanitary;

(2) Fail to provide persons confined in the detention facility with adequate food, clothing, bedding, shelter, and medical attention;

(3) Fail to control an unruly prisoner, or to prevent intimidation of or physical harm to a prisoner by another;

(4) Allow a prisoner to escape;

(5) Fail to observe any lawful and reasonable regulation for the management of the detention facility.

(D) No public official of the state shall recklessly create a deficiency, incur a liability, or expend a greater sum than is appropriated by the general assembly for the use in any one year of the department, agency, or institution of the state with which the public official is connected.

(E) No public servant shall recklessly fail to perform a duty expressly imposed by law with respect to the public servant's office, or recklessly do any act expressly forbidden by law with respect to the public servant's office.

(F) Whoever violates this section is guilty of dereliction of duty, a misdemeanor of the second degree.

(G) As used in this section, "public servant" includes an officer or employee of a contractor as defined in section 9.08 of the Revised Code.

(2000 S 12, eff. 6–8–00; 1972 H 511, eff. 1–1–74)

2921.45 Interfering with civil rights

(A) No public servant, under color of his office, employment, or authority, shall knowingly deprive, or conspire or attempt to deprive any person of a constitutional or statutory right.

(B) Whoever violates this section is guilty of interfering with civil rights, a misdemeanor of the first degree.

(1972 H 511, eff. 1–1–74)

USING SHAM LEGAL PROCESS

2921.51 Impersonation of certain officers

(A) As used in this section:

(1) "Peace officer" means a sheriff, deputy sheriff, marshal, deputy marshal, member of the organized police department of a municipal corporation, or township constable, who is employed by a political subdivision of this state, a member of a police force employed by a metropolitan housing authority under division (D) of section 3735.31 of the Revised Code, a member of a police force employed by a regional transit authority under division (Y) of section 306.35 of the Revised Code, a state university law enforcement officer appointed under section 3345.04 of the Revised Code, a veterans' home police officer appointed under section 5907.02 of the Revised Code, a special police officer employed by a port authority under section 4582.04 or 4582.28 of the Revised Code, or a state highway patrol trooper and whose primary duties are to preserve the peace, to protect life and property, and to enforce the laws, ordinances, or rules of the state or any of its political subdivisions.

(2) "Private police officer" means any security guard, special police officer, private detective, or other person who is privately employed in a police capacity.

(3) "Impersonate" means to act the part of, assume the identity of, wear the uniform or any part of the uniform of, or display the identification of a particular person or of a member of a class of persons with purpose to make another person believe that the actor is that particular person or is a member of that class of persons.

(B) No person shall impersonate a peace officer or a private police officer.

(C) No person, by impersonating a peace officer or a private police officer, shall arrest or detain any person, search any person, or search the property of any person.

(D) No person, with purpose to commit or facilitate the commission of an offense, shall impersonate a peace officer, a private police officer, or an officer, agent, or employee of the state.

(E) No person shall commit a felony while impersonating a peace officer, a private police officer, or an officer, agent, or employee of the state.

(F) It is an affirmative defense to a charge under division (B) of this section that the impersonation of the peace officer was for a lawful purpose.

(G) Whoever violates division (B) of this section is guilty of a misdemeanor of the fourth degree. Whoever violates division (C) or (D) of this section is guilty of a misdemeanor of the first degree. If the purpose of a violation of division (D) of this section is to commit or facilitate the commission of a felony, a violation of division (D) is a felony of the fourth degree. Whoever violates division (E) of this section is guilty of a felony of the third degree.

(2002 H 675, eff. 3–14–03; 2000 S 137, eff. 5–17–00; 1995 S 2, eff. 7–1–96; 1991 S 144, eff. 8–8–91; 1988 H 708, § 1)

2921.52 Using sham legal process

(A) As used in this section:

(1) "Lawfully issued" means adopted, issued, or rendered in accordance with the United States constitution, the constitution of a state, and the applicable statutes, rules, regulations, and ordinances of the United States, a state, and the political subdivisions of a state.

(2) "State" means a state of the United States, including without limitation, the state legislature, the highest court of the state that has statewide jurisdiction, the offices of all elected state officers, and all departments, boards, offices, commissions, agencies, institutions, and other instrumentalities of the state. "State" does not include the political subdivisions of the state.

(3) "Political subdivisions" means municipal corporations, townships, counties, school districts, and all other bodies corporate and politic that are organized under state law and are responsible for governmental activities only in geographical areas smaller than that of a state.

(4) "Sham legal process" means an instrument that meets all of the following conditions:

(a) It is not lawfully issued.

(b) It purports to do any of the following:

(i) To be a summons, subpoena, judgment, or order of a court, a law enforcement officer, or a legislative, executive, or administrative body.

(ii) To assert jurisdiction over or determine the legal or equitable status, rights, duties, powers, or privileges of any person or property.

(iii) To require or authorize the search, seizure, indictment, arrest, trial, or sentencing of any person or property.

(c) It is designed to make another person believe that it is lawfully issued.

(B) No person shall, knowing the sham legal process to be sham legal process, do any of the following:

(1) Knowingly issue, display, deliver, distribute, or otherwise use sham legal process;

(2) Knowingly use sham legal process to arrest, detain, search, or seize any person or the property of another person;

(3) Knowingly commit or facilitate the commission of an offense, using sham legal process;

(4) Knowingly commit a felony by using sham legal process.

(C) It is an affirmative defense to a charge under division (B)(1) or (2) of this section that the use of sham legal process was for a lawful purpose.

(D) Whoever violates this section is guilty of using sham legal process. A violation of division (B)(1) of this section is a misdemeanor of the fourth degree. A violation of division (B)(2) or (3) of this section is a misdemeanor of the first degree, except that, if the purpose of a violation of division (B)(3) of this section is to commit or facilitate the commission of a felony, a violation of division (B)(3) of this section is a felony of the fourth degree. A violation of division (B)(4) of this section is a felony of the third degree.

(E) A person who violates this section is liable in a civil action to any person harmed by the violation for injury, death, or loss to person or property incurred as a result of the commission of the offense and for reasonable attorney's fees, court costs, and other expenses incurred as a result of prosecuting the civil action commenced under this division. A civil action under this division is not the exclusive remedy of a person who incurs injury, death, or loss to person or property as a result of a violation of this section.

(1996 H 644, eff. 11–6–96)

CHAPTER 2923

CONSPIRACY, ATTEMPT, AND COMPLICITY; WEAPONS CONTROL

CONSPIRACY, ATTEMPT, AND COMPLICITY

2923.01 Conspiracy

Note: See also following version of this section, eff. 5–6–05.

(A) No person, with purpose to commit or to promote or facilitate the commission of aggravated murder, murder, kidnapping, compelling prostitution, promoting prostitution, aggravated arson, arson, aggravated robbery, robbery, aggravated burglary, burglary, engaging in a pattern of corrupt activity, corrupting another with drugs, a felony drug trafficking, manufacturing, processing, or possession offense, theft of drugs, or illegal processing of drug documents, the commission of a felony offense of unauthorized use of a vehicle, or the commission of a violation of any provision of Chapter 3734. of the Revised Code, other than section 3734.18 of the Revised Code, that relates to hazardous wastes, shall do either of the following:

(1) With another person or persons, plan or aid in planning the commission of any of the specified offenses;

(2) Agree with another person or persons that one or more of them will engage in conduct that facilitates the commission of any of the specified offenses.

(B) No person shall be convicted of conspiracy unless a substantial overt act in furtherance of the conspiracy is alleged and proved to have been done by the accused or a person with whom the accused conspired, subsequent to the accused's entrance into the conspiracy. For purposes of this section, an overt act is substantial when it is of a character that manifests a purpose on the part of the actor that the object of the conspiracy should be completed.

(C) When the offender knows or has reasonable cause to believe that a person with whom the offender conspires also has conspired or is conspiring with another to commit the same offense, the offender is guilty of conspiring with that other person, even though the other person's identity may be unknown to the offender.

(D) It is no defense to a charge under this section that, in retrospect, commission of the offense that was the object of the conspiracy was impossible under the circumstances.

(E) A conspiracy terminates when the offense or offenses that are its objects are committed or when it is abandoned by all conspirators. In the absence of abandonment, it is no defense to a charge under this section that no offense that was the object of the conspiracy was committed.

(F) A person who conspires to commit more than one offense is guilty of only one conspiracy when the offenses are the object of the same agreement or continuous conspiratorial relationship.

(G) When a person is convicted of committing or attempting to commit a specific offense or of complicity in the commission of or attempt to commit the specific offense, the person shall not be convicted of conspiracy involving the same offense.

(H)(1) No person shall be convicted of conspiracy upon the testimony of a person with whom the defendant conspired, unsupported by other evidence.

(2) If a person with whom the defendant allegedly has conspired testifies against the defendant in a case in which the defendant is charged with conspiracy and if the testimony is supported by other evidence, the court, when it charges the jury, shall state substantially the following:

"The testimony of an accomplice that is supported by other evidence does not become inadmissible because of the accomplice's complicity, moral turpitude, or self-interest, but the admitted or claimed complicity of a witness may affect the witness' credibility and make the witness' testimony subject to grave suspicion, and require that it be weighed with great caution.

It is for you, as jurors, in the light of all the facts presented to you from the witness stand, to evaluate such testimony and to determine its quality and worth or its lack of quality and worth."

(3) "Conspiracy," as used in division (H)(1) of this section, does not include any conspiracy that results in an attempt to commit an offense or in the commission of an offense.

(I) The following are affirmative defenses to a charge of conspiracy:

(1) After conspiring to commit an offense, the actor thwarted the success of the conspiracy under circumstances manifesting a complete and voluntary renunciation of the actor's criminal purpose.

(2) After conspiring to commit an offense, the actor abandoned the conspiracy prior to the commission of or attempt to commit any offense that was the object of the conspiracy, either by advising all other conspirators of the actor's abandonment, or by informing any law enforcement authority of the existence of the conspiracy and of the actor's participation in the conspiracy.

(J) Whoever violates this section is guilty of conspiracy, which is one of the following:

(1) A felony of the first degree, when one of the objects of the conspiracy is aggravated murder, murder, or an offense for which the maximum penalty is imprisonment for life;

(2) A felony of the next lesser degree than the most serious offense that is the object of the conspiracy, when the most serious offense that is the object of the conspiracy is a felony of the first, second, third, or fourth degree;

(3) A felony punishable by a fine of not more than twenty-five thousand dollars or imprisonment for not more than eighteen months, or both, when the offense that is the object of the conspiracy is a violation of any provision of Chapter 3734. of the Revised Code, other than section 3734.18 of the Revised Code, that relates to hazardous wastes;

(4) A misdemeanor of the first degree, when the most serious offense that is the object of the conspiracy is a felony of the fifth degree.

(K) This section does not define a separate conspiracy offense or penalty where conspiracy is defined as an offense by one or more sections of the Revised Code, other than this section. In such a case, however:

(1) With respect to the offense specified as the object of the conspiracy in the other section or sections, division (A) of this section defines the voluntary act or acts and culpable mental state necessary to constitute the conspiracy;

(2) Divisions (B) to (I) of this section are incorporated by reference in the conspiracy offense defined by the other section or sections of the Revised Code.

(L)(1) In addition to the penalties that otherwise are imposed for conspiracy, a person who is found guilty of conspiracy to engage in a pattern of corrupt activity is subject to divisions (B)(2), (3), (4), and (5) of section 2923.32 of the Revised Code.

(2) If a person is convicted of or pleads guilty to conspiracy and if the most serious offense that is the object of the conspiracy is a felony drug trafficking, manufacturing, processing, or possession offense, in addition to the penalties or sanctions that may be imposed for the conspiracy under division (J)(2) or (4) of this section and Chapter 2929. of the Revised Code, both of the following apply:

(a) The provisions of divisions (D), (F), and (G) of section 2925.03, division (D) of section 2925.04, division (D) of section 2925.05, division (D) of section 2925.06, and division (E) of section 2925.11 of the Revised Code that pertain to mandatory and additional fines, driver's or commercial driver's license or permit suspensions, and professionally licensed persons and that would apply under the appropriate provisions of those divisions to a person who is convicted of or pleads guilty to the felony drug trafficking, manufacturing, processing, or possession offense that is the most serious offense that is the basis of the conspiracy shall apply to the person who is convicted of or pleads guilty to the conspiracy as if the person had been convicted of or pleaded guilty to the felony drug trafficking, manufacturing, processing, or possession offense that is the most serious offense that is the basis of the conspiracy.

(b) The court that imposes sentence upon the person who is convicted of or pleads guilty to the conspiracy shall comply with the provisions identified as being applicable under division (L)(2) of this section, in addition to any other penalty or sanction that it imposes for the conspiracy under division (J)(2) or (4) of this section and Chapter 2929. of the Revised Code.

(M) As used in this section:

(1) " Felony drug trafficking, manufacturing, processing, or possession offense" means any of the following that is a felony:

(a) A violation of section 2925.03, 2925.04, 2925.05, or 2925.06 of the Revised Code;

(b) A violation of section 2925.11 of the Revised Code that is not a minor drug possession offense.

(2) "Minor drug possession offense" has the same meaning as in section 2925.01 of the Revised Code.

(2002 S 123, eff. 1–1–04; 1996 S 269, eff. 7–1–96; 1996 H 125, eff. 7–1–96; 1995 S 2, eff. 7–1–96; 1986 H 428, eff. 12–23–86; 1986 H 338; 1985 H 5; 1984 H 651; 1983 S 210; 1982 H 269, § 4, S 199, H 108; 1975 H 300; 1972 H 511)

Note: See also following version of this section, eff. 5–6–05.

2923.01 Conspiracy (later effective date)

Note: See also preceding version of this section, in effect until 5–6–05.

(A) No person, with purpose to commit or to promote or facilitate the commission of aggravated murder, murder, kidnapping, compelling prostitution, promoting prostitution, aggravated arson, arson, aggravated robbery, robbery, aggravated burglary, burglary, engaging in a pattern of corrupt activity, corrupting another with drugs, a felony drug trafficking, manufacturing, processing, or possession offense, theft of drugs, or illegal processing of drug documents, the commission of a felony offense of unauthorized use of a vehicle, illegally transmitting multiple commercial electronic mail messages or unauthorized access of a computer in violation of section 2923.421 of the Revised Code, or the commission of a violation of any provision of Chapter 3734. of the Revised Code, other than section 3734.18 of the Revised Code, that relates to hazardous wastes, shall do either of the following:

(1) With another person or persons, plan or aid in planning the commission of any of the specified offenses;

(2) Agree with another person or persons that one or more of them will engage in conduct that facilitates the commission of any of the specified offenses.

(B) No person shall be convicted of conspiracy unless a substantial overt act in furtherance of the conspiracy is alleged and proved to have been done by the accused or a person with whom the accused conspired, subsequent to the accused's entrance into the conspiracy. For purposes of this section, an overt act is substantial when it is of a character that manifests a purpose on the part of the actor that the object of the conspiracy should be completed.

(C) When the offender knows or has reasonable cause to believe that a person with whom the offender conspires also has conspired or is conspiring with another to commit the same offense, the offender is guilty of conspiring with that other person, even though the other person's identity may be unknown to the offender.

(D) It is no defense to a charge under this section that, in retrospect, commission of the offense that was the object of the conspiracy was impossible under the circumstances.

(E) A conspiracy terminates when the offense or offenses that are its objects are committed or when it is abandoned by all conspirators. In the absence of abandonment, it is no defense to a charge under this section that no offense that was the object of the conspiracy was committed.

(F) A person who conspires to commit more than one offense is guilty of only one conspiracy, when the offenses are the object of the same agreement or continuous conspiratorial relationship.

(G) When a person is convicted of committing or attempting to commit a specific offense or of complicity in the commission of or attempt to commit the specific offense, the person shall not be convicted of conspiracy involving the same offense.

(H)(1) No person shall be convicted of conspiracy upon the testimony of a person with whom the defendant conspired, unsupported by other evidence.

(2) If a person with whom the defendant allegedly has conspired testifies against the defendant in a case in which the defendant is charged with conspiracy and if the testimony is supported by other evidence, the court, when it charges the jury, shall state substantially the following:

"The testimony of an accomplice that is supported by other evidence does not become inadmissible because of the accomplice's complicity, moral turpitude, or self-interest, but the admitted or claimed complicity of a witness may affect the witness' credibility and make the witness' testimony subject to grave suspicion, and require that it be weighed with great caution.

It is for you, as jurors, in the light of all the facts presented to you from the witness stand, to evaluate such testimony and to determine its quality and worth or its lack of quality and worth."

(3) "Conspiracy," as used in division (H)(1) of this section, does not include any conspiracy that results in an attempt to commit an offense or in the commission of an offense.

(I) The following are affirmative defenses to a charge of conspiracy:

(1) After conspiring to commit an offense, the actor thwarted the success of the conspiracy under circumstances manifesting a complete and voluntary renunciation of the actor's criminal purpose.

(2) After conspiring to commit an offense, the actor abandoned the conspiracy prior to the commission of or attempt to commit any offense that was the object of the conspiracy, either by advising all other conspirators of the actor's abandonment, or by informing any law enforcement authority of the existence of the conspiracy and of the actor's participation in the conspiracy.

(J) Whoever violates this section is guilty of conspiracy, which is one of the following:

(1) A felony of the first degree, when one of the objects of the conspiracy is aggravated murder, murder, or an offense for which the maximum penalty is imprisonment for life;

(2) A felony of the next lesser degree than the most serious offense that is the object of the conspiracy, when the most serious offense that is the object of the conspiracy is a felony of the first, second, third, or fourth degree;

(3) A felony punishable by a fine of not more than twenty-five thousand dollars or imprisonment for not more than eighteen months, or both, when the offense that is the object of the conspiracy is a violation of any provision of Chapter 3734. of the Revised Code, other than section 3734.18 of the Revised Code, that relates to hazardous wastes;

(4) A misdemeanor of the first degree, when the most serious offense that is the object of the conspiracy is a felony of the fifth degree.

(K) This section does not define a separate conspiracy offense or penalty where conspiracy is defined as an offense by one or more sections of the Revised Code, other than this section. In such a case, however:

(1) With respect to the offense specified as the object of the conspiracy in the other section or sections, division (A) of this section defines the voluntary act or acts and culpable mental state necessary to constitute the conspiracy;

(2) Divisions (B) to (I) of this section are incorporated by reference in the conspiracy offense defined by the other section or sections of the Revised Code.

(L)(1) In addition to the penalties that otherwise are imposed for conspiracy, a person who is found guilty of conspiracy to engage in a pattern of corrupt activity is subject to divisions (B)(2), (3), (4), and (5) of section 2923.32 of the Revised Code.

(2) If a person is convicted of or pleads guilty to conspiracy and if the most serious offense that is the object of the conspiracy is a felony drug trafficking, manufacturing, processing, or possession offense, in addition to the penalties or sanctions that may be imposed for the conspiracy under division (J)(2) or (4) of this section and Chapter 2929. of the Revised Code, both of the following apply:

(a) The provisions of divisions (D), (F), and (G) of section 2925.03, division (D) of section 2925.04, division (D) of section 2925.05, division (D) of section 2925.06, and division (E) of section 2925.11 of the Revised Code that pertain to mandatory and additional fines, driver's or commercial driver's license or permit suspensions, and professionally licensed persons and that would apply under the appropriate provisions of those divisions to a person who is convicted of or pleads guilty to the felony drug trafficking, manufacturing, processing, or possession offense that is the most serious offense that is the basis of the conspiracy shall apply to the person who is convicted of or pleads guilty to the conspiracy as if the person had been convicted of or pleaded guilty to the felony drug trafficking, manufacturing, processing, or possession offense that is the most serious offense that is the basis of the conspiracy.

(b) The court that imposes sentence upon the person who is convicted of or pleads guilty to the conspiracy shall comply with the provisions identified as being applicable under division (L)(2) of this section, in addition to any other penalty or sanction that it imposes for the conspiracy under division (J)(2) or (4) of this section and Chapter 2929. of the Revised Code.

(M) As used in this section:

(1) "Felony drug trafficking, manufacturing, processing, or possession offense" means any of the following that is a felony:

(a) A violation of section 2925.03, 2925.04, 2925.05, or 2925.06 of the Revised Code;

(b) A violation of section 2925.11 of the Revised Code that is not a minor drug possession offense.

(2) "Minor drug possession offense" has the same meaning as in section 2925.01 of the Revised Code.

(2004 H 383, eff. 5–6–05; 2002 S 123, eff. 1–1–04; 1996 S 269, eff. 7–1–96; 1996 H 125, eff. 7–1–96; 1995 S 2, eff. 7–1–96; 1986 H 428, eff. 12–23–86; 1986 H 338; 1985 H 5; 1984 H 651; 1983 S 210; 1982 H 269, § 4, S 199, H 108; 1975 H 300; 1972 H 511)

Note: See also preceding version of this section, in effect until 5–6–05.

2923.02 Attempt

(A) No person, purposely or knowingly, and when purpose or knowledge is sufficient culpability for the commission of an offense, shall engage in conduct that, if successful, would constitute or result in the offense.

(B) It is no defense to a charge under this section that, in retrospect, commission of the offense that was the object of the attempt was either factually or legally impossible under the attendant circumstances, if that offense could have been committed had the attendant circumstances been as the actor believed them to be.

(C) No person who is convicted of committing a specific offense, of complicity in the commission of an offense, or of conspiracy to commit an offense shall be convicted of an attempt to commit the same offense in violation of this section.

(D) It is an affirmative defense to a charge under this section that the actor abandoned the actor's effort to commit the offense or otherwise prevented its commission, under circumstances manifesting a complete and voluntary renunciation of the actor's criminal purpose.

(E) Whoever violates this section is guilty of an attempt to commit an offense. An attempt to commit aggravated murder, murder, or an offense for which the maximum penalty is imprisonment for life is a felony of the first degree. An attempt to commit a drug abuse offense for which the penalty is determined by the amount or number of unit doses of the controlled substance involved in the drug abuse offense is an offense of the same degree as the drug abuse offense attempted would be if that drug abuse offense had been committed and had involved an amount or number of unit doses of the controlled substance that is within the next lower range of controlled substance amounts than was involved in the attempt. An attempt to commit any other offense is an offense of the next lesser degree than the offense attempted. In the case of an attempt to commit an offense other than a violation of Chapter 3734. of the Revised Code that is not specifically classified, an attempt is a misdemeanor of the first degree if the offense attempted is a felony, and a misdemeanor of the fourth degree if the offense attempted is a misdemeanor. In the case of an attempt to commit a violation of any provision of Chapter 3734. of the Revised Code, other than section 3734.18 of the Revised Code, that relates to hazardous wastes, an attempt is a felony punishable by a fine of not more than twenty-five thousand dollars or imprisonment for not more than eighteen months, or both. An attempt to commit a minor misdemeanor, or to engage in conspiracy, is not an offense under this section.

(F) As used in this section, "drug abuse offense" has the same meaning as in section 2925.01 of the Revised Code.

(1999 S 107, eff. 3–23–00; 1995 S 2, eff. 7–1–96; 1991 H 225, eff. 10–23–91; 1984 H 651; 1983 S 210; 1972 H 511)

2923.03 Complicity

(A) No person, acting with the kind of culpability required for the commission of an offense, shall do any of the following:

(1) Solicit or procure another to commit the offense;

(2) Aid or abet another in committing the offense;

(3) Conspire with another to commit the offense in violation of section 2923.01 of the Revised Code;

(4) Cause an innocent or irresponsible person to commit the offense.

(B) It is no defense to a charge under this section that no person with whom the accused was in complicity has been convicted as a principal offender.

(C) No person shall be convicted of complicity under this section unless an offense is actually committed, but a person may be convicted of complicity in an attempt to commit an offense in violation of section 2923.02 of the Revised Code.

(D) If an alleged accomplice of the defendant testifies against the defendant in a case in which the defendant is charged with complicity in the commission of or an attempt to commit an offense, an attempt to commit an offense, or an offense, the court, when it charges the jury, shall state substantially the following:

"The testimony of an accomplice does not become inadmissible because of his complicity, moral turpitude, or self-interest, but the admitted or claimed complicity of a witness may affect his credibility and make his testimony subject to grave suspicion, and require that it be weighed with great caution.

It is for you, as jurors, in the light of all the facts presented to you from the witness stand, to evaluate such testimony and to determine its quality and worth or its lack of quality and worth."

(E) It is an affirmative defense to a charge under this section that, prior to the commission of or attempt to commit the offense, the actor terminated his complicity, under circumstances manifesting a complete and voluntary renunciation of his criminal purpose.

(F) Whoever violates this section is guilty of complicity in the commission of an offense, and shall be prosecuted and punished as if he were a principal offender. A charge of complicity may be stated in terms of this section, or in terms of the principal offense.

(1986 H 338, eff. 9–17–86; 1972 H 511)

WEAPONS CONTROL

2923.11 Definitions

As used in sections 2923.11 to 2923.24 of the Revised Code:

(A) "Deadly weapon" means any instrument, device, or thing capable of inflicting death, and designed or specially adapted for use as a weapon, or possessed, carried, or used as a weapon.

(B)(1) "Firearm" means any deadly weapon capable of expelling or propelling one or more projectiles by the action of an explosive or combustible propellant. "Firearm" includes an unloaded firearm, and any firearm that is inoperable but that can readily be rendered operable.

(2) When determining whether a firearm is capable of expelling or propelling one or more projectiles by the action of an explosive or combustible propellant, the trier of fact may rely upon circumstantial evidence, including, but not limited to, the representations and actions of the individual exercising control over the firearm.

(C) "Handgun" means any of the following:

(1) Any firearm that has a short stock and is designed to be held and fired by the use of a single hand;

(2) Any combination of parts from which a firearm of a type described in division (C)(1) of this section can be assembled.

(D) "Semi–automatic firearm" means any firearm designed or specially adapted to fire a single cartridge and automatically chamber a succeeding cartridge ready to fire, with a single function of the trigger.

(E) "Automatic firearm" means any firearm designed or specially adapted to fire a succession of cartridges with a single function of the trigger. "Automatic firearm" also means any semi-automatic firearm designed or specially adapted to fire more than thirty-one cartridges without reloading, other than a firearm chambering only .22 caliber short, long, or long-rifle cartridges.

(F) "Sawed–off firearm" means a shotgun with a barrel less than eighteen inches long, or a rifle with a barrel less than sixteen inches long, or a shotgun or rifle less than twenty-six inches long overall.

(G) "Zip–gun" means any of the following:

(1) Any firearm of crude and extemporized manufacture;

(2) Any device, including without limitation a starter's pistol, that is not designed as a firearm, but that is specially adapted for use as a firearm;

(3) Any industrial tool, signalling device, or safety device, that is not designed as a firearm, but that as designed is capable of use as such, when possessed, carried, or used as a firearm.

(H) "Explosive device" means any device designed or specially adapted to cause physical harm to persons or property by means of an explosion, and consisting of an explosive substance or agency and a means to detonate it. "Explosive device" includes without limitation any bomb, any explosive demolition device, any blasting cap or detonator containing an explosive charge, and any pressure vessel that has been knowingly tampered with or arranged so as to explode.

(I) "Incendiary device" means any firebomb, and any device designed or specially adapted to cause physical harm to persons or property by means of fire, and consisting of an incendiary substance or agency and a means to ignite it.

(J) "Ballistic knife" means a knife with a detachable blade that is propelled by a spring-operated mechanism.

(K) "Dangerous ordnance" means any of the following, except as provided in division (L) of this section:

(1) Any automatic or sawed-off firearm, zip-gun, or ballistic knife;

(2) Any explosive device or incendiary device;

(3) Nitroglycerin, nitrocellulose, nitrostarch, PETN, cyclonite, TNT, picric acid, and other high explosives; amatol, tritonal, tetrytol, pentolite, pecretol, cyclotol, and other high explosive compositions; plastic explosives; dynamite, blasting gelatin, gelatin dynamite, sensitized ammonium nitrate, liquid-oxygen blasting explosives, blasting powder, and other blasting agents; and any other explosive substance having sufficient brisance or power to be particularly suitable for use as a military explosive, or for use in mining, quarrying, excavating, or demolitions;

(4) Any firearm, rocket launcher, mortar, artillery piece, grenade, mine, bomb, torpedo, or similar weapon, designed and manufactured for military purposes, and the ammunition for that weapon;

(5) Any firearm muffler or silencer;

(6) Any combination of parts that is intended by the owner for use in converting any firearm or other device into a dangerous ordnance.

(L) "Dangerous ordnance" does not include any of the following:

(1) Any firearm, including a military weapon and the ammunition for that weapon, and regardless of its actual age, that employs a percussion cap or other obsolete ignition system, or that is designed and safe for use only with black powder;

(2) Any pistol, rifle, or shotgun, designed or suitable for sporting purposes, including a military weapon as issued or as modified, and the ammunition for that weapon, unless the firearm is an automatic or sawed-off firearm;

(3) Any cannon or other artillery piece that, regardless of its actual age, is of a type in accepted use prior to 1887, has no mechanical, hydraulic, pneumatic, or other system for absorbing recoil and returning the tube into battery without displacing the carriage, and is designed and safe for use only with black powder;

(4) Black powder, priming quills, and percussion caps possessed and lawfully used to fire a cannon of a type defined in division (L)(3) of this section during displays, celebrations, organized matches or shoots, and target practice, and smokeless and black powder, primers, and percussion caps possessed and lawfully used as a propellant or ignition device in small-arms or small-arms ammunition;

(5) Dangerous ordnance that is inoperable or inert and cannot readily be rendered operable or activated, and that is kept as a trophy, souvenir, curio, or museum piece.

(6) Any device that is expressly excepted from the definition of a destructive device pursuant to the "Gun Control Act of 1968," 82 Stat. 1213, 18 U.S.C. 921(a)(4), as amended, and regulations issued under that act.

(M) "Explosive" means any chemical compound, mixture, or device, the primary or common purpose of which is to function by explosion. "Explosive" includes all materials that have been classified as class A, class B, or class C explosives by the United States department of transportation in its regulations and includes, but is not limited to, dynamite, black powder, pellet powders, initiating explosives, blasting caps, electric blasting caps, safety fuses, fuse igniters, squibs, cordeau detonant fuses, instantaneous fuses, and igniter cords and igniters. "Explosive" does not include "fireworks," as defined in section 3743.01 of the Revised Code, or any explosive that is not subject to regulation under the rules of the fire marshal adopted pursuant to section 3737.82 of the Revised Code.

(2004 H 12, eff. 4–8–04; 1995 S 2, eff. 7–1–96; 1990 S 96, eff. 6–13–90; 1987 H 24; 1986 H 51; 1978 H 728; 1972 H 511)

2923.12 Carrying concealed weapons; affirmative defenses

(A) No person shall knowingly carry or have, concealed on the person's person or concealed ready at hand, any of the following:

(1) A deadly weapon other than a handgun;

(2) A handgun other than a dangerous ordnance;

(3) A dangerous ordnance.

(B) No person who has been issued a license or temporary emergency license to carry a concealed handgun under section 2923.125 or 2923.1213 of the Revised Code or a license to carry a concealed hangun [sic.] that was issued by another state with which the attorney general has entered into a reciprocity agreement under section 109.69 of the Revised Code, who is stopped for a law enforcement purpose, and who is carrying a concealed handgun shall fail to promptly inform any law enforcement officer who approaches the person after the person has been stopped that the person has been issued a license or temporary emergency license to carry a concealed handgun and that the person then is carrying a concealed handgun.

(C)(1) This section does not apply to officers, agents, or employees of this or any other state or the United States, or to law enforcement officers, authorized to carry concealed weapons or dangerous ordnance and acting within the scope of their duties.

(2) Division (A)(2) of this section does not apply to any of the following:

(a) An officer, agent, or employee of this or any other state or the United States, or a law enforcement officer, who is authorized to carry a handgun and acting within the scope of the officer's, agent's, or employee's duties;

(b) A person who, at the time of the alleged carrying or possession of a handgun, is carrying a valid license or temporary emergency license to carry a concealed handgun issued to the person under section 2923.125 or 2923.1213 of the Revised Code or a license to carry a concealed handgun that was issued by another state with which the attorney general has entered into a reciprocity agreement under section 109.69 of the Revised Code, unless the person knowingly is in a place described in division (B) of section 2923.126 of the Revised Code.

(D) It is an affirmative defense to a charge under division (A)(1) of this section of carrying or having control of a weapon other than a handgun and other than a dangerous ordnance that the actor was not otherwise prohibited by law from having the weapon and that any of the following applies:

(1) The weapon was carried or kept ready at hand by the actor for defensive purposes while the actor was engaged in or was going to or from the actor's lawful business or occupation, which business or occupation was of a character or was necessarily carried on in a manner or at a time or place as to render the actor particularly susceptible to criminal attack, such as would justify a prudent person in going armed.

(2) The weapon was carried or kept ready at hand by the actor for defensive purposes while the actor was engaged in a lawful activity and had reasonable cause to fear a criminal attack upon the actor, a member of the actor's family, or the actor's home, such as would justify a prudent person in going armed.

(3) The weapon was carried or kept ready at hand by the actor for any lawful purpose and while in the actor's own home.

(4) The weapon was being transported in a motor vehicle for any lawful purpose, was not on the actor's person, and, if the weapon was a firearm, was carried in compliance with the applicable requirements of division (C) of section 2923.16 of the Revised Code.

(E) It is an affirmative defense to a charge under division (A) of this section of carrying or having control of a handgun other than a dangerous ordnance that the actor was not otherwise prohibited by law from having the handgun and that the handgun was carried or kept ready at hand by the actor for any lawful purpose and while in the actor's own home, provided that this affirmative defense is not available unless the actor, prior to arriving at the actor's own home, did not transport or possess the handgun in a motor vehicle in a manner prohibited by division (B) or (C) of section 2923.16 of the Revised Code while the motor vehicle was being operated on a street, highway, or other public or private property used by the public for vehicular traffic.

(F) No person who is charged with a violation of this section shall be required to obtain a license or temporary emergency license to carry a concealed handgun under section 2923.125 or 2923.1213 of the Revised Code as a condition for the dismissal of the charge.

(G)(1) Whoever violates this section is guilty of carrying concealed weapons. Except as otherwise provided in this division or division (G)(2) of this section, carrying concealed weapons in violation of division (A) of this section is a misdemeanor of the first degree. Except as otherwise provided in this division or division (G)(2) of this section, if the offender previously has been convicted of a violation of this section or of any offense of violence, if the weapon involved is a firearm that is either loaded or for which the offender has ammunition ready at hand, or if the weapon involved is dangerous ordnance, carrying concealed weapons in violation of division (A) of this section is a felony of the fourth degree. Except as otherwise provided in division (G)(2) of this section, if the weapon involved is a firearm and the violation of this section is committed at premises for which a D permit has been issued under Chapter 4303. of the Revised Code or if the offense is committed aboard an aircraft, or with purpose to carry a concealed weapon aboard an aircraft, regardless of the weapon involved, carrying concealed weapons in violation of division (A) of this section is a felony of the third degree.

(2) If a person being arrested for a violation of division (A)(2) of this section promptly produces a valid license or temporary emergency license to carry a concealed handgun issued under section 2923.125 or 2923.1213 of the Revised Code or a license to carry a concealed handgun that was issued by another state with which the attorney general has entered into a reciprocity agreement under section 109.69 of the Revised Code, and if at the time of the violation the person was not knowingly in a place described in division (B) of section 2923.126 of the Revised Code, the officer shall not arrest the person for a violation of that division. If the person is not able to promptly produce any of those types of license and if the person is not in a place described

in that section, the officer may arrest the person for a violation of that division, and the offender shall be punished as follows:

(a) The offender shall be guilty of a minor misdemeanor if both of the following apply:

(i) Within ten days after the arrest, the offender presents a license or temporary emergency license to carry a concealed handgun issued under section 2923.125 or 2923.1213 of the Revised Code or a license to carry a concealed handgun that was issued by another state with which the attorney general has entered into a reciprocity agreement under section 109.69 of the Revised Code, which license was valid at the time of the arrest to the law enforcement agency that employs the arresting officer.

(ii) At the time of the arrest, the offender was not knowingly in a place described in division (B) of section 2923.126 of the Revised Code.

(b) The offender shall be guilty of a misdemeanor and shall be fined five hundred dollars if all of the following apply:

(i) The offender previously had been issued a license to carry a concealed handgun under section 2923.125 of the Revised Code or a license to carry a concealed handgun that was issued by another state with which the attorney general has entered into a reciprocity agreement under section 109.69 of the Revised Code and that was similar in nature to a license issued under section 2923.125 of the Revised Code, and that license expired within the two years immediately preceding the arrest.

(ii) Within forty-five days after the arrest, the offender presents any type of license identified in division (G)(2)(a)(i) of this section to the law enforcement agency that employed the arresting officer, and the offender waives in writing the offender's right to a speedy trial on the charge of the violation that is provided in section 2945.71 of the Revised Code.

(iii) At the time of the commission of the offense, the offender was not knowingly in a place described in division (B) of section 2923.126 of the Revised Code.

(c) If neither division (G)(2)(a) nor (b) of this section applies, the offender shall be punished under division (G)(1) of this section.

(3) Carrying concealed weapons in violation of division (B) of this section is a misdemeanor of the fourth degree.

(H) If a law enforcement officer stops a person to question the person regarding a possible violation of this section, for a traffic stop, or for any other law enforcement purpose, if the person surrenders a firearm to the officer, either voluntarily or pursuant to a request or demand of the officer, and if the officer does not charge the person with a violation of this section or arrest the person for any offense, the person is not otherwise prohibited by law from possessing the firearm, and the firearm is not contraband, the officer shall return the firearm to the person at the termination of the stop.

(2004 H 12, eff. 4–8–04; 1995 S 2, eff. 7–1–96; 1986 H 51, eff. 7–30–86; 1973 H 716; 1972 H 511)

2923.121 Possessing firearm in liquor permit premises; privileges; defenses

(A) No person shall possess a firearm in any room in which liquor is being dispensed in premises for which a D permit has been issued under Chapter 4303. of the Revised Code or in an open air arena for which a permit of that nature has been issued.

(B)(1) This section does not apply to officers, agents, or employees of this or any other state or the United States, or to law enforcement officers, authorized to carry firearms, and acting within the scope of their duties.

(2) This section does not apply to any room used for the accommodation of guests of a hotel, as defined in section 4301.01 of the Revised Code.

(3) This section does not prohibit any person who is a member of a veteran's organization, as defined in section 2915.01 of the Revised Code, from possessing a rifle in any room in any premises owned, leased, or otherwise under the control of the veteran's organization, if the rifle is not loaded with live ammunition and if the person otherwise is not prohibited by law from having the rifle.

(4) This section does not apply to any person possessing or displaying firearms in any room used to exhibit unloaded firearms for sale or trade in a soldiers' memorial established pursuant to Chapter 345. of the Revised Code, in a convention center, or in any other public meeting place, if the person is an exhibitor, trader, purchaser, or seller of firearms and is not otherwise prohibited by law from possessing, trading, purchasing, or selling the firearms.

(C) It is an affirmative defense to a charge under this section of illegal possession of a firearm in liquor permit premises that involves the possession of a firearm other than a handgun, that the actor was not otherwise prohibited by law from having the firearm, and that any of the following apply:

(1) The firearm was carried or kept ready at hand by the actor for defensive purposes, while the actor was engaged in or was going to or from the actor's lawful business or occupation, which business or occupation was of such character or was necessarily carried on in such manner or at such a time or place as to render the actor particularly susceptible to criminal attack, such as would justify a prudent person in going armed.

(2) The firearm was carried or kept ready at hand by the actor for defensive purposes, while the actor was engaged in a lawful activity, and had reasonable cause to fear a criminal attack upon the actor or a member of the actor's family, or upon the actor's home, such as would justify a prudent person in going armed.

(D) No person who is charged with a violation of this section shall be required to obtain a license or temporary emergency license to carry a concealed handgun under section 2923.125 or 2923.1213 of the Revised Code as a condition for the dismissal of the charge.

(E) Whoever violates this section is guilty of illegal possession of a firearm in liquor permit premises, a felony of the fifth degree.

(2004 H 12, eff. 4–8–04; 1995 S 2, eff. 7–1–96; 1986 H 39, eff. 2–21–87; 1986 H 51)

2923.122 Conveyance or possession of deadly weapons or dangerous ordnance in school safety zone

(A) No person shall knowingly convey, or attempt to convey, a deadly weapon or dangerous ordnance into a school safety zone.

(B) No person shall knowingly possess a deadly weapon or dangerous ordnance in a school safety zone.

(C) No person shall knowingly possess an object in a school safety zone if both of the following apply:

(1) The object is indistinguishable from a firearm, whether or not the object is capable of being fired.

(2) The person indicates that the person possesses the object and that it is a firearm, or the person knowingly displays or brandishes the object and indicates that it is a firearm.

(D)(1) This section does not apply to officers, agents, or employees of this or any other state or the United States, or to law enforcement officers, authorized to carry deadly weapons or dangerous ordnance and acting within the scope of their duties, to any security officer employed by a board of education or governing body of a school during the time that the security officer is on duty pursuant to that contract of employment, or to any other person who has written authorization from the board of education or governing body of a school to convey deadly weapons or dangerous ordnance into a school safety zone or to possess a deadly weapon or dangerous ordnance in a school safety zone and who conveys or possesses the deadly weapon or dangerous ordnance in accordance with that authorization.

(2) Division (C) of this section does not apply to premises upon which home schooling is conducted. Division (C) of this section also does not apply to a school administrator, teacher, or employee who possesses an object that is indistinguishable from a firearm for legitimate school purposes during the course of employment, a student who uses an object that is indistinguishable from a firearm under the direction of a school administrator, teacher, or employee, or any other person who with the express prior approval of a school administrator possesses an object that is indistinguishable from a firearm for a legitimate purpose, including the use of the object in a ceremonial activity, a play, reenactment, or other dramatic presentation, or a ROTC activity or another similar use of the object.

(3) This section does not apply to a person who conveys or attempts to convey a handgun into, or possesses a handgun in, a school safety zone if, at the time of that conveyance, attempted conveyance, or possession of the handgun, all of the following apply:

(a) The person does not enter into a school building or onto school premises and is not at a school activity.

(b) The person is carrying a valid license or temporary emergency license to carry a concealed handgun issued to the person under section 2923. 125 or 2923.1213 of the Revised Code or a license to carry a concealed handgun that was issued by another state with which the attorney general has entered into a reciprocity agreement under section 109.69 of the Revised Code.

(c) The person is in the school safety zone in accordance with 18 U.S.C. 922(q)(2)(B).

(d) The person is not knowingly in a place described in division (B)(1) or (B)(3) to (10) of section 2923.126 of the Revised Code.

(E)(1) Whoever violates division (A) or (B) of this section is guilty of illegal conveyance or possession of a deadly weapon or dangerous ordnance in a school safety zone. Except as otherwise provided in this division, illegal conveyance or possession of a deadly weapon or dangerous ordnance in a school safety zone is a felony of the fifth degree. If the offender previously has been convicted of a violation of this section, illegal conveyance or possession of a deadly weapon or dangerous ordnance in a school safety zone is a felony of the fourth degree.

(2) Whoever violates division (C) of this section is guilty of illegal possession of an object indistinguishable from a firearm in a school safety zone. Except as otherwise provided in this division, illegal possession of an object indistinguishable from a firearm in a school safety zone is a misdemeanor of the first degree. If the offender previously has been convicted of a violation of this section, illegal possession of an object indistinguishable from a firearm in a school safety zone is a felony of the fifth degree.

(F)(1) In addition to any other penalty imposed upon a person who is convicted of or pleads guilty to a violation of this section and subject to division (F)(2) of this section, if the offender has not attained nineteen years of age, regardless of whether the offender is attending or is enrolled in a school operated by a board of education or for which the state board of education prescribes minimum standards under section 3301.07 of the Revised Code, the court shall impose upon the offender a class four suspension of the offender's probationary driver's license, restricted license, driver's license, commercial driver's license, temporary instruction permit, or probationary commercial driver's license that then is in effect from the range specified in division (A)(4) of section 4510.02 of the Revised Code and shall deny the offender the issuance of any permit or license of that type during the period of the suspension.

If the offender is not a resident of this state, the court shall impose a class four suspension of the nonresident operating privilege of the offender from the range specified in division (A)(4) of section 4510.02 of the Revised Code.

(2) If the offender shows good cause why the court should not suspend one of the types of licenses, permits, or privileges specified in division (F)(1) of this section or deny the issuance of one of the temporary instruction permits specified in that division, the court in its discretion may choose not to impose the suspension, revocation, or denial required in that division.

(G) As used in this section, "object that is indistinguishable from a firearm" means an object made, constructed, or altered so that, to a reasonable person without specialized training in firearms, the object appears to be a firearm.

(2004 H 12, § 3, eff. 4–8–04; 2004 H 12, § 1, eff. 4–8–04; 2002 S 123, eff. 1–1–04; 1999 S 1, eff. 8–6–99; 1996 H 72, eff. 3–18–97; 1996 H 124, eff. 9–30–97; 1995 S 2, eff. 7–1–96; 1992 H 154, eff. 7–31–92)

2923.123 Illegal conveyance, possession or control of a deadly weapon or dangerous ordnance in a courthouse

(A) No person shall knowingly convey or attempt to convey a deadly weapon or dangerous ordnance into a courthouse or into another building or structure in which a courtroom is located.

(B) No person shall knowingly possess or have under the person's control a deadly weapon or dangerous ordnance in a courthouse or in another building or structure in which a courtroom is located.

(C) This section does not apply to any of the following:

(1) A judge of a court of record of this state or a magistrate, unless a rule of superintendence or another type of rule adopted by the supreme court pursuant to Article IV, Ohio Constitution, or an applicable local rule of court prohibits all persons from conveying or attempting to convey a deadly weapon or dangerous ordnance into a courthouse or into another building or structure in which a courtroom is located or from possessing or having under one's control a deadly weapon or dangerous ordnance in a courthouse or in another building or structure in which a courtroom is located;

(2) A peace officer, or an officer of a law enforcement agency of another state, a political subdivision of another state, or the United States, who is authorized to carry a deadly weapon or dangerous ordnance, who possesses or has under that individual's control a deadly weapon or dangerous ordnance as a requirement of that individual's duties, and who is acting within the scope of that individual's duties at the time of that possession or control, unless a rule of superintendence or another type of rule adopted by the supreme court pursuant to Article IV, Ohio Constitution, or an applicable local rule of court prohibits all persons from conveying or attempting to convey a deadly weapon or dangerous ordnance into a courthouse or into another building or structure in which a courtroom is located or from possessing or having under one's control a deadly weapon or dangerous ordnance in a courthouse or in another building or structure in which a courtroom is located;

(3) A person who conveys, attempts to convey, possesses, or has under the person's control a deadly weapon or dangerous ordnance that is to be used as evidence in a pending criminal or civil action or proceeding;

(4) A bailiff or deputy bailiff of a court of record of this state who is authorized to carry a firearm pursuant to section 109.77 of the Revised Code, who possesses or has under that individual's control a firearm as a requirement of that individual's duties, and who is acting within the scope of that individual's duties at the time of that possession or control, unless a rule of superintendence or another type of rule adopted by the supreme court pursuant to Article IV, Ohio Constitution, or an applicable local rule of court prohibits all persons from conveying or attempting to convey a deadly weapon or dangerous ordnance into a courthouse or into another building or structure in which a courtroom is located or from possessing or having under one's control a deadly weapon or dangerous ordnance in a courthouse or in another building or structure in which a courtroom is located;

(5) A prosecutor, or a secret service officer appointed by a county prosecuting attorney, who is authorized to carry a deadly weapon or dangerous ordnance in the performance of the individual's duties, who possesses or has under that individual's control a deadly weapon or dangerous ordnance as a requirement of that individual's duties, and who is acting within the scope of that individual's duties at the time of that possession or control, unless a rule of superintendence or another type of rule adopted by the supreme court pursuant to Article IV of the Ohio Constitution or an applicable local rule of court prohibits all persons from conveying or attempting to convey a deadly weapon or dangerous ordnance into a courthouse or into another building or structure in which a courtroom is located or from possessing or having under one's control a deadly weapon or dangerous ordnance in a courthouse or in another building or structure in which a courtroom is located;

(6) A person who conveys or attempts to convey a handgun into a courthouse or into another building or structure in which a courtroom is located, who, at the time of the conveyance or attempt, is carrying a valid license or temporary emergency license to carry a concealed handgun issued to the person under section 2923.125 or 2923.1213 of the Revised Code or a license to carry a concealed handgun that was issued by another state with which the attorney general has entered into a reciprocity agreement under section 109.69 of the Revised Code, and who transfers possession of the handgun to the officer or officer's designee who has charge of the courthouse or building. The officer shall secure the handgun until the licensee is prepared to leave the premises. The exemption described in this division applies only if the officer who has charge of the courthouse or building provides services of the nature described in this division. An officer who has charge of the courthouse or building is not required to offer services of the nature described in this division. The exemption described in this division does not apply if a rule of superintendence or another type of rule adopted by the supreme court pursuant to Article IV, Ohio Constitution, or if an applicable local rule of court prohibits all persons from conveying or attempting to convey a deadly weapon or dangerous ordnance into a courthouse or into another building or structure in which a courtroom is located or from possessing or having under one's control a deadly weapon or dangerous ordnance in a courthouse or in another building or structure in which a courtroom is located.

(D)(1) Whoever violates division (A) of this section is guilty of illegal conveyance of a deadly weapon or dangerous ordnance into a courthouse. Except as otherwise provided in this division, illegal conveyance of a deadly weapon or dangerous ordnance into a courthouse is a felony of the fifth degree. If the offender previously has been convicted of a violation of division (A) or (B) of this section, illegal conveyance of a deadly weapon or dangerous ordnance into a courthouse is a felony of the fourth degree.

(2) Whoever violates division (B) of this section is guilty of illegal possession or control of a deadly weapon or dangerous ordnance in a courthouse. Except as otherwise provided in this division, illegal possession or control of a deadly weapon or dangerous ordnance in a courthouse is a felony of the fifth degree. If the offender previously has been convicted of a violation of division (A) or (B) of this section, illegal possession or control of a deadly weapon or dangerous ordnance in a courthouse is a felony of the fourth degree.

(E) As used in this section:

(1) "Magistrate" means an individual who is appointed by a court of record of this state and who has the powers and may perform the functions specified in Civil Rule 53, Criminal Rule 19, or Juvenile Rule 40.

(2) "Peace officer" and "prosecutor" have the same meanings as in section 2935.01 of the Revised Code.

(2004 H 12, eff. 4–8–04; 1997 H 151, eff. 9–16–97; 1996 H 88, eff. 9–3–96)

2923.124 Definitions

Note: See also following version of this section, eff. 5–18–05.

As used in sections 2923.124 to 2923.1213 of the Revised Code:

(A) "Application form" means the application form prescribed pursuant to division (A)(1) of section 109.731 of the Revised Code and includes a copy of that form.

(B) "Competency certification" and "competency certificate" mean a document of the type described in division (B)(3) of section 2923.125 of the Revised Code.

(C) "Detention facility" has the same meaning as in section 2921.01 of the Revised Code.

(D) "Licensee" means a person to whom a license to carry a concealed handgun has been issued under section 2923.125 of the Revised Code and, except when the context clearly indicates otherwise, includes a person to whom a temporary emergency license to carry a concealed handgun has been issued under section 2923.1213 of the Revised Code.

(E) "License fee" or "license renewal fee" means the fee for a license to carry a concealed handgun or the fee to renew that license that is prescribed pursuant to division (C) of section 109.731 of the Revised Code and that is to be paid by an applicant for a license of that type.

(F) "Peace officer" has the same meaning as in section 2935.01 of the Revised Code.

(G) "State correctional institution" has the same meaning as in section 2967.01 of the Revised Code.

(H) "Valid license" means a license or temporary emergency license to carry a concealed handgun that has been issued under section 2923.125 or 2923.1213 of the Revised Code, that is currently valid, that is not under a suspension under division (A)(1) of section 2923.128 or under sectiom [1] 2923.1213 of the Revised Code, and that has not been revoked under division (B)(1) of section 2923.128 or under section 2923.1213 of the Revised Code.

(I) "Civil protection order" means a protection order issued, or consent agreement approved, under section 2903.214 or 3113.31 of the Revised Code.

(J) "Temporary protection order" means a protection order issued under section 2903.213 or 2919.26 of the Revised Code.

(K) "Protection order issued by a court of another state" has the same meaning as in section 2919.27 of the Revised Code.

(L) "Child day-care center," "type A family day-care home" and "type B family day-care home" have the same meanings as in section 5104.01 of the Revised Code.

(M) "Type C family day-care home" means a family day-care home authorized to provide child day-care by Sub. H.B. 62 of the 121st General Assembly, as amended by Am. Sub. S.B. 160 of the

121st General Assembly and Sub. H.B. 407 of the 123rd General Assembly.

(N) "Foreign air transportation," "interstate air transportation," and "intrastate air transportation" have the same meanings as in 49 U.S.C. 40102, as now or hereafter amended.

(2004 H 12, eff. 4–8–04)

1 So in original; 2004 H 12.

Note: See also following version of this section, eff. 5–18–05.

2923.124 Definitions (later effective date)

Note: See also preceding version of this section, in effect until 5–18–05.

As used in sections 2923.124 to 2923.1213 of the Revised Code:

(A) "Application form" means the application form prescribed pursuant to division (A)(1) of section 109.731 of the Revised Code and includes a copy of that form.

(B) "Competency certification" and "competency certificate" mean a document of the type described in division (B)(3) of section 2923.125 of the Revised Code.

(C) "Detention facility" has the same meaning as in section 2921.01 of the Revised Code.

(D) "Licensee" means a person to whom a license to carry a concealed handgun has been issued under section 2923.125 of the Revised Code and, except when the context clearly indicates otherwise, includes a person to whom a temporary emergency license to carry a concealed handgun has been issued under section 2923.1213 of the Revised Code.

(E) "License fee" or "license renewal fee" means the fee for a license to carry a concealed handgun or the fee to renew that license that is prescribed pursuant to division (C) of section 109.731 of the Revised Code and that is to be paid by an applicant for a license of that type.

(F) "Peace officer" has the same meaning as in section 2935.01 of the Revised Code.

(G) "State correctional institution" has the same meaning as in section 2967.01 of the Revised Code.

(H) "Valid license" means a license or temporary emergency license to carry a concealed handgun that has been issued under section 2923.125 or 2923.1213 of the Revised Code, that is currently valid, that is not under a suspension under division (A)(1) of section 2923.128 or under section 2923.1213 of the Revised Code, and that has not been revoked under division (B)(1) of section 2923.128 or under section 2923.1213 of the Revised Code.

(I) "Civil protection order" means a protection order issued, or consent agreement approved, under section 2903.214 or 3113.31 of the Revised Code.

(J) "Temporary protection order" means a protection order issued under section 2903.213 or 2919.26 of the Revised Code.

(K) "Protection order issued by a court of another state" has the same meaning as in section 2919.27 of the Revised Code.

(L) "Child day-care center," "type A family day-care home" and "type B family day-care home" have the same meanings as in section 5104.01 of the Revised Code.

(M) "Type C family day-care home" means a family day-care home authorized to provide child care by Sub. H.B. 62 of the 121st general assembly, as amended by Am. Sub. S.B. 160 of the 121st general assembly and Sub. H.B. 407 of the 123rd general assembly.

(N) "Foreign air transportation," "interstate air transportation," and "intrastate air transportation" have the same meanings as in 49 U.S.C. 40102, as now or hereafter amended.

(2004 H 11, eff. 5–18–05; 2004 H 12, eff. 4–8–04)

Note: See also preceding version of this section, in effect until 5–18–05.

2923.125 Application; license; denial; appeal; duplicate license; renewal

(A) Upon the request of a person who wishes to obtain a license to carry a concealed handgun or to renew a license to carry a concealed handgun, a sheriff shall provide to the person free of charge an application form and a copy of the pamphlet described in division (B) of section 109.731 of the Revised Code.

(B) An applicant for a license to carry a concealed handgun shall submit a completed application form and all of the following to the sheriff of the county in which the applicant resides or to the sheriff of any county adjacent to the county in which the applicant resides:

(1) A nonrefundable license fee prescribed by the Ohio peace officer training commission pursuant to division (C) of section 109.731 of the Revised Code, except that the sheriff shall waive the payment of the license fee in connection with an initial or renewal application for a license that is submitted by an applicant who is a retired peace officer, a retired person described in division (B)(1)(b) of section 109.77 of the Revised Code, or a retired federal law enforcement officer who, prior to retirement, was authorized under federal law to carry a firearm in the course of duty, unless the retired peace officer, person, or federal law enforcement officer retired as the result of a mental disability;

(2) A color photograph of the applicant that was taken within thirty days prior to the date of the application;

(3) One or more of the following competency certifications, each of which shall reflect that, regarding a certification described in division (B)(3)(a), (b), (c), (e), or (f) of this section, within the three years immediately preceding the application the applicant has performed that to which the competency certification relates and that, regarding a certification described in division (B)(3)(d) of this section, the applicant currently is an active or reserve member of the armed forces of the United States or within the six years immediately preceding the application the honorable discharge or retirement to which the competency certification relates occurred:

(a) An original or photocopy of a certificate of completion of a firearms safety, training, or requalification or firearms safety instructor course, class, or program that was offered by or under the auspices of the national rifle association and that complies with the requirements set forth in division (G) of this section;

(b) An original or photocopy of a certificate of completion of a firearms safety, training, or requalification or firearms safety instructor course, class, or program that satisfies all of the following criteria:

(i) It was open to members of the general public.

(ii) It utilized qualified instructors who were certified by the national rifle association, the executive director of the Ohio peace officer training commission pursuant to section 109.75 or 109.78 of the Revised Code, or a governmental official or entity of another state.

(iii) It was offered by or under the auspices of a law enforcement agency of this or another state or the United States, a public or private college, university, or other similar postsecondary educational institution located in this or another state, a firearms training school located in this or another state, or another type of public or private entity or organization located in this or another state.

(iv) It complies with the requirements set forth in division (G) of this section.

(c) An original or photocopy of a certificate of completion of a state, county, municipal, or department of natural resources peace officer training school that is approved by the executive director of the Ohio peace officer training commission pursuant to section 109.75 of the Revised Code and that complies with the requirements set forth in division (G) of this section, or the applicant has satisfactorily completed and been issued a certificate of completion of a basic firearms training program, a firearms requalification training program, or another basic training program described in section 109.78 or 109.801 of the Revised Code that complies with the requirements set forth in division (G) of this section;

(d) A document that evidences both of the following:

(i) That the applicant is an active or reserve member of the armed forces of the United States, was honorably discharged from military service in the active or reserve armed forces of the United States, is a retired trooper of the state highway patrol, or is a retired peace officer or federal law enforcement officer described in division (B)(1) of this section or a retired person described in division (B)(1)(b) of section 109.77 of the Revised Code and division (B)(1) of this section;

(ii) That, through participation in the military service or through the former employment described in division (B)(3)(d)(i) of this section, the applicant acquired experience with handling handguns or other firearms, and the experience so acquired was equivalent to training that the applicant could have acquired in a course, class, or program described in division (B)(3)(a), (b), or (c) of this section.

(e) A certificate or another similar document that evidences satisfactory completion of a firearms training, safety, or requalification or firearms safety instructor course, class, or program that is not otherwise described in division (B)(3)(a), (b), (c), or (d) of this section, that was conducted by an instructor who was certified by an official or entity of the government of this or another state or the United States or by the national rifle association, and that complies with the requirements set forth in division (G) of this section;

(f) An affidavit that attests to the applicant's satisfactory completion of a course, class, or program described in division (B)(3)(a), (b), (c), or (e) of this section and that is subscribed by the applicant's instructor or an authorized representative of the entity that offered the course, class, or program or under whose auspices the course, class, or program was offered.

(4) A certification by the applicant that the applicant has read the pamphlet prepared by the Ohio peace officer training commission pursuant to section 109.731 of the Revised Code that reviews firearms, dispute resolution, and use of deadly force matters.

(5) A set of fingerprints of the applicant provided as described in section 311.41 of the Revised Code through use of an electronic fingerprint reading device or, if the sheriff to whom the application is submitted does not possess and does not have ready access to the use of such a reading device, on a standard impression sheet prescribed pursuant to division (C)(2) of section 109.572 of the Revised Code.

(C) Upon receipt of an applicant's completed application form, supporting documentation, and, if not waived, license fee, a sheriff shall conduct or cause to be conducted the criminal records check and the incompetency records check described in section 311.41 of the Revised Code.

(D)(1) Except as provided in division (D)(3), (4), or (5) of this section, within forty-five days after receipt of an applicant's completed application form for a license to carry a concealed handgun, the supporting documentation, and, if not waived, license fee, a sheriff shall make available through the law enforcement automated data system in accordance with division (H) of this section the information described in that division and, upon making the information available through the system, shall issue to the applicant a license to carry a concealed handgun that shall expire four years after the date of issuance if all of the following apply:

(a) The applicant has been a resident of this state for at least forty-five days and a resident of the county in which the person seeks the license or a county adjacent to the county in which the person seeks the license for at least thirty days.

(b) The applicant is at least twenty-one years of age.

(c) The applicant is not a fugitive from justice.

(d) The applicant is not under indictment for or otherwise charged with a felony; an offense under Chapter 2925., 3719., or 4729. of the Revised Code that involves the illegal possession, use, sale, administration, or distribution of or trafficking in a drug of abuse; a misdemeanor offense of violence; or a violation of section 2903.14 or 2923.1211 of the Revised Code.

(e) The applicant has not been convicted of or pleaded guilty to a felony or an offense under Chapter 2925., 3719., or 4729. of the Revised Code that involves the illegal possession, use, sale, administration, or distribution of or trafficking in a drug of abuse; has not been adjudicated a delinquent child for committing an act that if committed by an adult would be a felony or would be an offense under Chapter 2925., 3719., or 4729. of the Revised Code that involves the illegal possession, use, sale, administration, or distribution of or trafficking in a drug of abuse; and has not been convicted of, pleaded guilty to, or adjudicated a delinquent child for committing a violation of section 2903.13 of the Revised Code when the victim of the violation is a peace officer, regardless of whether the applicant was sentenced under division (C)(3) of that section.

(f) The applicant, within three years of the date of the application, has not been convicted of or pleaded guilty to a misdemeanor offense of violence other than a misdemeanor violation of section 2921.33 of the Revised Code or a violation of section 2903.13 of the Revised Code when the victim of the violation is a peace officer, or a misdemeanor violation of section 2923.1211 of the Revised Code; and has not been adjudicated a delinquent child for committing an act that if committed by an adult would be a misdemeanor offense of violence other than a misdemeanor violation of section 2921.33 of the Revised Code or a violation of section 2903.13 of the Revised Code when the victim of the violation is a peace officer or for committing an act that if committed by an adult would be a misdemeanor violation of section 2923.1211 of the Revised Code.

(g) Except as otherwise provided in division (D)(1)(e) of this section, the applicant, within five years of the date of the application, has not been convicted of, pleaded guilty to, or adjudicated a delinquent child for committing two or more violations of section 2903.13 or 2903.14 of the Revised Code.

(h) The applicant, within ten years of the date of the application, has not been convicted of, pleaded guilty to, or adjudicated a delinquent child for committing a violation of section 2921.33 of the Revised Code.

(i) The applicant has not been adjudicated as a mental defective, has not been committed to any mental institution, is not under adjudication of mental incompetence, has not been found by a court to be a mentally ill person subject to hospitalization by court order, and is not an involuntary patient other than one who is a patient only for purposes of observation. As used in this division, "mentally ill person subject to hospitalization by court order" and "patient" have the same meanings as in section 5122.01 of the Revised Code.

(j) The applicant is not currently subject to a civil protection order, a temporary protection order, or a protection order issued by a court of another state.

(k) The applicant certifies that the applicant desires a legal means to carry a concealed handgun for defense of the applicant or a member of the applicant's family while engaged in lawful activity.

(*l*) The applicant submits a competency certification of the type described in division (B)(3) of this section and submits a certification of the type described in division (B)(4) of this section regarding the applicant's reading of the pamphlet prepared by the Ohio peace officer training commission pursuant to section 109.731 of the Revised Code.

(2)(a) If a sheriff issues a license under this section, the sheriff shall place on the license a unique combination of letters and numbers identifying the license in accordance with the procedure prescribed by the Ohio peace officer training commission pursuant to section 109.731 of the Revised Code.

(b) If a sheriff denies an application under this section because the applicant does not satisfy the criteria described in division (D)(1) of this section, the sheriff shall specify the grounds for the denial in a written notice to the applicant. The applicant may appeal the denial pursuant to section 119.12 of the Revised Code. If the denial was as a result of the criminal records check conducted pursuant to section 311.41 of the Revised Code and if, pursuant to section 2923.127 of the Revised Code, the applicant challenges the criminal records check results using the appropriate challenge and review procedure specified in that section, the time for filing the appeal pursuant to section 119.12 of the Revised Code is tolled during the pendency of the request or the challenge and review. If the court in an appeal under section 119.12 of the Revised Code enters a judgment sustaining the sheriff's refusal to grant to the applicant a license to carry a concealed handgun, the applicant may file a new application beginning one year after the judgment is entered. If the court enters a judgment in favor of the applicant, that judgment shall not restrict the authority of a sheriff to suspend or revoke the license pursuant to section 2923.128 or 2923.1213 of the Revised Code or to refuse to renew the license for any proper cause that may occur after the date the judgment is entered. In the appeal, the court shall have full power to dispose of all costs.

(3) If the sheriff with whom an application for a license to carry a concealed handgun was filed under this section becomes aware that the applicant has been arrested for or otherwise charged with an offense that would disqualify the applicant from holding the license, the sheriff shall suspend the processing of the application until the disposition of the case arising from the arrest or charge.

(4) If the sheriff determines the applicant is a resident of the county in which the applicant seeks the license or of an adjacent county but does not yet meet the residency requirements described in division (D)(1)(a) of this section, the sheriff shall not deny the license because of the residency requirements but shall not issue the license until the applicant meets those residency requirements.

(E) If a license to carry a concealed handgun issued under this section is lost or is destroyed, the licensee may obtain from the sheriff who issued that license a duplicate license upon the payment of a fee of fifteen dollars and the submission of an affidavit attesting to the loss or destruction of the license. The sheriff, in accordance with the procedures prescribed in section 109.731 of the Revised Code, shall place on the replacement license a combination of identifying numbers different from the combination on the license that is being replaced.

(F) A licensee who wishes to renew a license to carry a concealed handgun issued under this seciton [1] shall do so within thirty days after the expiration date of the license by filing with the sheriff of the county in which the applicant resides or with the sheriff of an adjacent county an application for renewal of the license obtained pursuant to division (D) of this section, a new color photograph of the licensee that was taken within thirty days prior to the date of the renewal application, a certification by the applicant that, subsequent to the issuance of the license, the applicant has reread the pamphlet prepared by the Ohio peace officer training commission pursuant to section 109.731 of the Revised Code that reviews firearms, dispute resolution, and use of deadly force matters, a new set of fingerprints provided in the manner specified in division (D)(4) of section 2923.125 of the Revised Code regarding initial applications for a license to carry a concealed handgun, and a nonrefundable license renewal fee unless the fee is waived. The licensee also shall submit a competency certification of the type described in division (B)(3) of this section that is not older than six years or a renewed competency certification of the type described in division (G)(4) of this section that is not older than six years.

Upon receipt of a completed renewal application, color photograph, certification that the applicant has reread the specified pamphlet prepared by the Ohio peace officer training commission, new set of fingerprints, competency certification or renewed competency certification, and license renewal fee unless the fee is waived, a sheriff shall conduct or cause to be conducted the criminal records check and the incompetency records check described in section 311.41 of the Revised Code. The sheriff shall renew the license if the sheriff determines that the applicant continues to satisfy the requirements described in division (D)(1) of this section, except that the applicant is required to submit a renewed competency certification only in the circumstances described in division (G)(4) of this section. A renewed license shall expire four years after the date of issuance and is subject to division (E) of this section and sections 2923.126 and 2923.128 of the Revised Code. A sheriff shall comply with divisions (D)(2) to (4) of this section when the circumstances described in those divisions apply to a requested license renewal.

(G)(1) Each course, class, or program described in division (B)(3)(a), (b), (c), or (e) of this section shall provide to each person who takes the course, class, or program a copy of the pamphlet prepared by the Ohio peace officer training commission pursuant to section 109.731 of the Revised Code that reviews firearms, dispute resolution, and use of deadly force matters. Each such course, class, or program described in one of those divisions shall include at least twelve hours of training in the safe handling and use of a firearm that shall include all of the following:

(a) At least ten hours of training on the following matters:

(i) The ability to name, explain, and demonstrate the rules for safe handling of a handgun and proper storage practices for handguns and ammunition;

(ii) The ability to demonstrate and explain how to handle ammunition in a safe manner;

(iii) The ability to demonstrate the knowledge, skills, and attitude necessary to shoot a handgun in a safe manner;

(iv) Gun handling training.

(b) At least two hours of training that consists of range time and live-fire training.

(2) To satisfactorily complete the course, class, or program described in division (B)(3)(a), (b), (c), or (e) of this section, the applicant shall pass a competency examination that shall include both of the following:

(a) A written section on the ability to name and explain the rules for the safe handling of a handgun and proper storage practices for handguns and ammunition;

(b) A physical demonstration of competence in the use of a handgun and in the rules for safe handling and storage of a handgun and a physical demonstration of the attitude necessary to shoot a handgun in a safe manner.

(3) The competency certification described in division (B)(3)(a), (b), (c), or (e) of this section shall be dated and shall attest that the course, class, or program the applicant successfully completed met the requirements described in division (G)(1) of

this section and that the applicant passed the competency examination described in division (G)(2) of this section.

(4) A person who has received a competency certification as described in division (B)(3) of this section, or who previously has received a renewed competency certification as described in this division, may obtain a renewed competency certification pursuant to this division. If the person has received a competency certification within the preceding six years, or previously has received a renewed competency certification within the preceding six years, the person may obtain a renewed competency certification from an entity that offers a course, class, or program described in division (B)(3)(a), (b), (c), or (e) of this section by passing a competency examination of the type described in division (G)(2) of this section. In these circumstances, the person is not required to attend the course, class, or program in order to be eligible to take the competency examination for the renewed competency certification. If more than six years has elapsed since the person last received a competency certification or a renewed competency certification, in order for the person to obtain a renewed competency certification, the person shall both satisfactorily complete a course, class, or program described in division (B)(3)(a), (b), (c), or (e) of this section and pass a competency examination of the type described in division (G)(2) of this section. A renewed competency certification issued under this division shall be dated and shall attest that the applicant passed the competency examination of the type described in division (G)(2) of this section and, if applicable, that the person successfully completed a course, class, or program that met the requirements described in division (G)(1) of this section.

(H) Upon deciding to issue a license, deciding to issue a replacement license, or deciding to renew a license to carry a concealed handgun pursuant to this section, and before actually issuing or renewing the license, the sheriff shall make available through the law enforcement automated data system all information contained on the license. If the license subsequently is suspended under division (A)(1) of section 2923.128 of the Revised Code, revoked pursuant to division (B)(1) of section 2923.128 of the Revised Code, or lost or destroyed, the sheriff also shall make available through the law enforcement automated data system a notation of that fact. The superintendent of the state highway patrol shall ensure that the law enforcement automated data system is so configured as to permit the transmission through the system of the information specified in this division.

(2004 H 12, eff. 4–8–04)

1 So in original; 2004 H 12.

2923.126 License expiration; notice to law enforcement upon stop; prohibited places; effect on private employers; immunity; signage; reciprocity

(A) A license to carry a concealed handgun that is issued under section 2923.125 of the Revised Code shall expire four years after the date of issuance. A licensee who has been issued a license under that section shall be granted a grace period of thirty days after the licensee's license expires during which the licensee's license remains valid. Except as provided in divisions (B) and (C) of this section, a licensee who has been issued a license under section 2923.125 or 2923.1213 of the Revised Code may carry a concealed handgun anywhere in this state if the licensee also carries a valid license and valid identification when the licensee is in actual possession of a concealed handgun. The licensee shall give notice of any change in the licensee's residence address to the sheriff who issued the license within forty-five days after that change.

If a licensee is the driver or an occupant of a motor vehicle that is stopped as the result of a traffic stop or a stop for another law enforcement purpose and if the licensee is transporting or has a loaded handgun in the motor vehicle at that time, the licensee shall promptly inform any law enforcement officer who approaches the vehicle while stopped that the licensee has been issued a license or temporary emergency license to carry a concealed handgun and that the licensee currently possesses or has a loaded handgun; the licensee shall comply with lawful orders of a law enforcement officer given while the motor vehicle is stopped, shall remain in the motor vehicle while stopped, and shall keep the licensee's hands in plain sight while any law enforcement officer begins approaching the licensee while stopped and before the officer leaves, unless directed otherwise by a law enforcement officer; and the licensee shall not knowingly remove, attempt to remove, grasp, or hold the loaded handgun or knowingly have contact with the loaded handgun by touching it with the licensee's hands or fingers, in any manner in violation of division (E) of section 2923.16 of the Revised Code, while any law enforcement officer begins approaching the licensee while stopped and before the officer leaves. If a law enforcement officer otherwise approaches a person who has been stopped for a law enforcement purpose, if the person is a licensee, and if the licensee is carrying a concealed handgun at the time the officer approaches, the licensee shall promptly inform the officer that the licensee has been issued a license or temporary emergency license to carry a concealed handgun and that the licensee currently is carrying a concealed handgun.

(B) A valid license issued under section 2923.125 or 2923.1213 of the Revised Code does not authorize the licensee to carry a concealed handgun in any manner prohibited under division (B) of section 2923.12 of the Revised Code or in any manner prohibited under section 2923.16 of the Revised Code. A valid license does not authorize the licensee to carry a concealed handgun into any of the following places:

(1) A police station, sheriff's office, or state highway patrol station, premises controlled by the bureau of criminal identification and investigation, a state correctional institution, jail, workhouse, or other detention facility, an airport passenger terminal, or an institution that is maintained, operated, managed, and governed pursuant to division (A) of section 5119.02 of the Revised Code or division (A)(1) of section 5123.03 of the Revised Code;

(2) A school safety zone, in violation of section 2923.122 of the Revised Code;

(3) A courthouse or another building or structure in which a courtroom is located, in violation of section 2923.123 of the Revised Code;

(4) Any room or open air arena in which liquor is being dispensed in premises for which a D permit has been issued under Chapter 4303. of the Revised Code, in violation of section 2923.121 of the Revised Code;

(5) Any premises owned or leased by any public or private college, university, or other institution of higher education, unless the handgun is in a locked motor vehicle or the licensee is in the immediate process of placing the handgun in a locked motor vehicle;

(6) Any church, synagogue, mosque, or other place of worship, unless the church, synagogue, mosque, or other place of worship posts or permits otherwise;

(7) A child day-care center, a type A family day-care home, a type B family day-care home, or a type C family day-care home, except that this division does not prohibit a licensee who resides in a type A family day-care home, a type B family day-care home, or a type C family day-care home from carrying a concealed handgun at any time in any part of the home that is not dedicated or used for day-care purposes, or from carrying a concealed handgun in a part of the home that is dedicated or used for day-care purposes at any time during which no children, other than children of that licensee, are in the home;

(8) An aircraft that is in, or intended for operation in, foreign air transportation, interstate air transportation, intrastate air transportation, or the transportation of mail by aircraft;

(9) Any building that is owned by this state or any political subdivision of this state, and all portions of any building that is not owned by any governmental entity listed in this division but that is leased by such a governmental entity listed in this division;

(10) A place in which federal law prohibits the carrying of handguns.

(C)(1) Nothing in this section shall negate or restrict a rule, policy, or practice of a private employer that is not a private college, university, or other institution of higher education concerning or prohibiting the presence of firearms on the private employer's premises or property, including motor vehicles owned by the private employer. Nothing in this section shall require a private employer of that nature to adopt a rule, policy, or practice concerning or prohibiting the presence of firearms on the private employer's premises or property, including motor vehicles owned by the private employer.

(2)(a) A private employer shall be immune from liability in a civil action for any injury, death, or loss to person or property that allegedly was caused by or related to a licensee bringing a handgun onto the premises or property of the private employer, including motor vehicles owned by the private employer, unless the private employer acted with malicious purpose. A private employer is immune from liability in a civil action for any injury, death, or loss to person or property that allegedly was caused by or related to the private employer's decision to permit a licensee to bring, or prohibit a licensee from bringing, a handgun onto the premises or property of the private employer. As used in this division, "private employer" includes a private college, university, or other institution of higher education.

(b) A political subdivision shall be immune from liability in a civil action, to the extent and in the manner provided in Chapter 2744. of the Revised Code, for any injury, death, or loss to person or property that allegedly was caused by or related to a licensee bringing a handgun onto any premises or property owned, leased, or otherwise under the control of the political subdivision. As used in this division, "political subdivision" has the same meaning as in section 2744.01 of the Revised Code.

(3) The owner or person in control of private land or premises, and a private person or entity leasing land or premises owned by the state, the United States, or a political subdivision of the state or the United States, may post a sign in a conspicuous location on that land or on those premises prohibiting persons from carrying firearms or concealed firearms on or onto that land or those premises. A person who knowingly violates a posted prohibition of that nature is guilty of criminal trespass in violation of division (A)(4) of section 2911.21 of the Revised Code and is guilty of a misdemeanor of the fourth degree.

(D) A person who holds a license to carry a concealed handgun that was issued pursuant to the law of another state that is recognized by the attorney general pursuant to a reciprocity agreement entered into pursuant to section 109.69 of the Revised Code has the same right to carry a concealed handgun in this state as a person who was issued a license to carry a concealed handgun under section 2923.125 of the Revised Code and is subject to the same restrictions that apply to a person who carries a license issued under that section.

A peace officer has the same right to carry a concealed handgun in this state as a person who was issued a license to carry a concealed handgun under section 2923.125 of the Revised Code. For purposes of reciprocity with other states, a peace officer shall be considered to be a licensee in this state.

(2004 H 12, eff. 4–8–04)

2923.127 Challenge of criminal records check upon denial of license; challenge and review procedure

(A) If a sheriff denies an application for a license to carry a concealed handgun, denies the renewal of a license to carry a concealed handgun, or denies an application for a temporary emergency license to carry a concealed handgun as a result of the criminal records check conducted pursuant to section 311.41 of the Revised Code and if the applicant believes the denial was based on incorrect information reported by the source the sheriff used in conducting the criminal records check, the applicant may challenge the criminal records check results using whichever of the following is applicable:

(1) If the bureau of criminal identification and investigation performed the criminal records check, by using the bureau's existing challenge and review procedures;

(2) If division (A)(1) of this section does not apply, by using the sheriff's existing challenge and review procedure or, if the sheriff does not have a challenge and review procedure, using the challenge and review procedure prescribed by the bureau of criminal identification and investigation pursuant to division (B) of this section.

(B) The bureau of criminal identification and investigation shall prescribe a challenge and review procedure for applicants to use to challenge criminal records checks under division (A)(2) of this section in counties in which the sheriff with whom the application for a license to carry a concealed handgun or for the renewal of a license to carry a concealed handgun was filed or with whom the application for a temporary emergency license to carry a concealed handgun was submitted does not have an existing challenge and review procedure.

(2004 H 12, eff. 4–8–04)

2923.128 Suspension; revocation; notice

(A)(1) If a licensee holding a valid license issued under section 2923.125 or 2923.1213 of the Revised Code is arrested for or otherwise charged with an offense described in division (D)(1)(d) of section 2923.125 of the Revised Code or with a violation of section 2923.15 of the Revised Code or becomes subject to a temporary protection order or to a protection order issued by a court of another state that is substantially equivalent to a temporary protection order, the sheriff who issued the license or temporary emergency license shall suspend it and shall comply with division (A)(3) of this section upon becoming aware of the arrest, charge, or protection order.

(2) A suspension under division (A)(1) of this section shall be considered as beginning on the date that the licensee is arrested for or otherwise charged with an offense described in that division or on the date the appropriate court issued the protection order described in that division, irrespective of when the sheriff notifies the licensee under division (A)(3) of this section. The suspension shall end on the date on which the charges are dismissed or the licensee is found not guilty of the offense described in division (A)(1) of this section or, subject to division (B) of this section, on the date the appropriate court terminates the protection order described in that division. If the suspension so ends, the sheriff shall return the license or temporary emergency license to the licensee.

(3) Upon becoming aware of an arrest, charge, or protection order described in division (A)(1) of this section with respect to a licensee who was issued a license under section 2923.125 or 2923.1213 of the Revised Code, the sheriff who issued the licensee's license or temporary emergency license to carry a concealed handgun shall notify the licensee, by certified mail, return receipt requested, at the licensee's last known residence address that the license or temporary emergency license has been

suspended and that the licensee is required to surrender the license or temporary emergency license at the sheriff's office within ten days of the date on which the notice was mailed.

(B)(1) A sheriff who issues a license or temporary emergency license to carry a concealed handgun to a licensee under section 2923.125 or 2923.1213 of the Revised Code shall revoke the license or temporary emergency license in accordance with division (B)(2) of this section upon becoming aware that the licensee satisfies any of the following:

(a) The licensee is under twenty-one years of age.

(b) At the time of the issuance of the license or temporary emergency license, the licensee did not satisfy the eligibility requirements of division (D)(1)(c), (d), (e), (f), (g), or (h) of section 2923.125 of the Revised Code.

(c) On or after the date on which the license or temporary emergency license was issued, the licensee is convicted of or pleads guilty to a violation of section 2923.15 of the Revised Code or an offense described in division (D)(1)(e), (f), (g), or (h) of section 2923.125 of the Revised Code.

(d) On or after the date on which the license or temporary emergency license was issued, the licensee becomes subject to a civil protection order or to a protection order issued by a court of another state that is substantially equivalent to a civil protection order.

(e) The licensee knowingly carries a concealed handgun into a place that the licensee knows is an unauthorized place specified in division (B) of section 2923.126 of the Revised Code.

(f) On or after the date on which the license or temporary emergency license was issued, the licensee is adjudicated as a mental defective or is committed to a mental institution.

(g) At the time of the issuance of the license or temporary emergency license, the licensee did not meet the residency requirements described in division (D)(1) of section 2923.125 of the Revised Code and currently does not meet the residency requirements described in that division.

(h) Regarding a license issued under section 2923.125 of the Revised Code, the competency certificate the licensee submitted was forged or otherwise was fraudulent.

(2) Upon becoming aware of any circumstance listed in division (B)(1) of this section that applies to a particular licensee who was issued a license under section 2923.125 or 2923.1213 of the Revised Code, the sheriff who issued the license or temporary emergency license to carry a concealed handgun to the licensee shall notify the licensee, by certified mail, return receipt requested, at the licensee's last known residence address that the license or temporary emergency license is subject to revocation and that the licensee may come to the sheriff's office and contest the sheriff's proposed revocation within fourteen days of the date on which the notice was mailed. After the fourteen-day period and after consideration of any information that the licensee provides during that period, if the sheriff determines on the basis of the information of which the sheriff is aware that the licensee is described in division (B)(1) of this section and no longer satisfies the requirements described in division (D)(1) of section 2923.125 of the Revised Code that are applicable to the licensee's type of license, the sheriff shall revoke the license or temporary emergency license, notify the licensee of that fact, and require the licensee to surrender the license or temporary emergency license.

(2004 H 12, eff. 4–8–04)

2923.129 Immunity from liability; confidentiality of records; disclosure of information to journalists; reports; illegal release of confidential concealed handgun license records

(A)(1) If a sheriff, the superintendent of the bureau of criminal identification and investigation, the employees of the bureau, the Ohio peace officer training commission, or the employees of the commission make a good faith effort in performing the duties imposed upon the sheriff, the superintendent, the bureau's employees, the commission, or the commission's employees by sections 109.731, 311.41, and 2923.124 to 2923.1213 of the Revised Code, in addition to the personal immunity provided by section 9.86 of the Revised Code or division (A)(6) of section 2744.03 of the Revised Code and the governmental immunity of sections 2744.02 and 2744.03 of the Revised Code and in addition to any other immunity possessed by the bureau, the commission, and their employees, the sheriff, the sheriff's office, the county in which the sheriff has jurisdiction, the bureau, the superintendent of the bureau, the bureau's employees, the commission, and the commission's employees are immune from liability in a civil action for injury, death, or loss to person or property that allegedly was caused by or related to any of the following:

(a) The issuance, renewal, suspension, or revocation of a license to carry a concealed handgun or the issuance, suspension, or revocation of a temporary emergency license to carry a concealed handgun;

(b) The failure to issue, renew, suspend, or revoke a license to carry a concealed handgun or the failure to issue, suspend, or revoke a temporary emergency license to carry a concealed handgun;

(c) Any action or misconduct with a handgun committed by a licensee.

(2) Any action of a sheriff relating to the issuance, renewal, suspension, or revocation of a license to carry a concealed handgun or the issuance, suspension, or revocation of a temporary emergency license to carry a concealed handgun shall be considered to be a governmental function for purposes of Chapter 2744. of the Revised Code.

(3) An entity that or instructor who provides a competency certification of a type described in division (B)(3) of section 2923.125 of the Revised Code is immune from civil liability that might otherwise be incurred or imposed for any death or any injury or loss to person or property that is caused by or related to a person to whom the entity or instructor has issued the competency certificate if all of the following apply:

(a) The alleged liability of the entity or instructor relates to the training provided in the course, class, or program covered by the competency certificate.

(b) The entity or instructor makes a good faith effort in determining whether the person has satisfactorily completed the course, class, or program and makes a good faith effort in assessing the person in the competency examination conducted pursuant to division (G)(2) of section 2923. 125 of the Revised Code.

(c) The entity or instructor did not issue the competency certificate with malicious purpose, in bad faith, or in a wanton or reckless manner.

(4) An entity that or instructor who provides a renewed competency certification of a type described in division (G)(4) of section 2923.125 of the Revised Code is immune from civil liability that might otherwise be incurred or imposed for any death or any injury or loss to person or property that is caused by or related to a person to whom the entity or instructor has issued the renewed competency certificate if all of the following apply:

(a) The entity or instructor makes a good faith effort in assessing the person in the competency examination conducted pursuant to division (G)(2) of section 2923.125 of the Revised Code.

(b) The entity or instructor did not issue the renewed competency certificate with malicious purpose, in bad faith, or in a wanton or reckless manner.

(5) A law enforcement agency that employs a peace officer is immune from liability in a civil action to recover damages for

injury, death, or loss to person or property allegedly caused by any act of that peace officer if the act occurred while the peace officer carried a concealed handgun and was off duty and if the act allegedly involved the peace officer's use of the concealed handgun. Sections 9.86 and 9.87, and Chapter 2744., of the Revised Code apply to any civil action involving a peace officer's use of a concealed handgun in the performance of the peace officer's official duties while the peace officer is off duty.

(B) (1) Notwithstanding section 149.43 of the Revised Code, except as provided in division (B)(2) of this section, the records that a sheriff keeps relative to the issuance, renewal, suspension, or revocation of a license to carry a concealed handgun or the issuance, suspension, or revocation of a temporary emergency license to carry a concealed handgun, including, but not limited to, completed applications for the issuance or renewal of a license, completed affidavits submitted regarding an application for a temporary emergency license, reports of criminal records checks and incompetency records checks under section 311.41 of the Revised Code, and applicants' social security numbers and fingerprints that are obtained under division (A) of section 311.41 of the Revised Code, are confidential and are not public records. Except as provided in division (B)(2) of this section, no person shall release or otherwise disseminate records that are confidential under this division unless required to do so pursuant to a court order.

(2) Upon a written request made to a sheriff and signed by a journalist on or after the effective date of this section, the sheriff shall disclose to the journalist the name, county of residence, and date of birth of each person to whom the sheriff has issued a license or replacement license to carry a concealed handgun, renewed a license to carry a concealed handgun, or issued a temporary emergency license or replacement temporary emergency license to carry a concealed handgun under section 2923.125 or 2923.1213 of the Revised Code. The request shall include the journalist's name and title, shall include the name and address of the journalist's employer, and shall state that disclosure of the information sought would be in the public interest.

As used in division (B)(2) of this section, "journalist" means a person engaged in, connected with, or employed by any news medium, including a newspaper, magazine, press association, news agency, or wire service, a radio or television station, or a similar medium, for the purpose of gathering, processing, transmitting, compiling, editing, or disseminating information for the general public.

(C) Each sheriff shall report to the Ohio peace officer training commission the number of licenses to carry a concealed handgun that the sheriff issued, renewed, suspended, revoked, or denied during the previous quarter of the calendar year, the number of applications for those licenses for which processing was suspended in accordance with division (D)(3) of section 2923.125 of the Revised Code during the previous quarter of the calendar year, and the number of temporary emergency licenses to carry a concealed handgun that the sheriff issued, suspended, revoked, or denied during the previous quarter of the calendar year. The sheriff shall not include in the report the name or any other identifying information of an applicant or licensee. The sheriff shall report that information in a manner that permits the commission to maintain the statistics described in division (D) of section 109.731 of the Revised Code and to timely prepare the statistical report described in that division. The information that is received by the commission under this division is a public record kept by the commission for the purposes of section 149.43 of the Revised Code.

(D) Law enforcement agencies may use the information a sheriff makes available through the use of the law enforcement automated data system pursuant to division (H) of section 2923.125 or division (B)(2) or (D) of section 2923.1213 of the Revised Code for law enforcement purposes only. The information is confidential and is not a public record. A person who releases or otherwise disseminates this information obtained through the law enforcement automated data system in a manner not described in this division is guilty of a violation of section 2913.04 of the Revised Code.

(E) Whoever violates division (B) of this section is guilty of illegal release of confidential concealed handgun license records, a felony of the fifth degree. In addition to any penalties imposed under Chapter 2929. of the Revised Code for a violation of division (B) of this section or a violation of section 2913.04 of the Revised Code described in division (D) of this section, if the offender is a sheriff, an employee of a sheriff, or any other public officer or employee, and if the violation was willful and deliberate, the offender shall be subject to a civil fine of one thousand dollars. Any person who is harmed by a violation of division (B) or (C) of this section or a violation of section 2913.04 of the Revised Code described in division (D) of this section has a private cause of action against the offender for any injury, death, or loss to person or property that is a proximate result of the violation and may recover court costs and attorney's fees related to the action.

(2004 H 12, eff. 4–8–04)

2923.1210 Form of application

The application for a license to carry a concealed handgun or for the renewal of a license of that nature that is to be used under section 2923.125 of the Revised Code shall conform substantially to the following form:

"Ohio Peace Officer Training Commission

APPLICATION FOR A LICENSE TO CARRY A CONCEALED HANDGUN

Please Type or Print in Ink

SECTION I.

This application will not be processed unless all applicable questions have been answered and until all required supporting documents as described in division (B) or (F) of section 2923.125 of the Ohio Revised Code and, unless waived, a cashier's check, certified check, or money order in the amount of the applicable license fee or license renewal fee have been submitted. FEES ARE NONREFUNDABLE.

SECTION II.

Name:

Last	First	Middle
....	....	....

Social Security Number: ....

Current Residence:

Street	City	State	County	Zip
....	....	....	....	....

Mailing Address (If Different From Above):

Street	City	State	Zip
....	....	....	....

Date of Birth	Place of Birth	Sex	Race	Residence Telephone
.../.../...	....	.....	.....	(...) ......

SECTION III. THE FOLLOWING QUESTIONS ARE TO BE ANSWERED YES OR NO

(1) Have you been a resident of Ohio for at least forty-five days and have you been a resident for thirty days of the county with whose sheriff you are filing this application or of a county adjacent to that county?	.... YES	.... NO
(2) Are you at least twenty-one years of age?	.... YES	.... NO
(3) Are you a fugitive from justice?	.... YES	.... NO

(4) Are you under indictment for a felony, have you ever been convicted of or pleaded guilty to a felony, or have you ever been adjudicated a delinquent child for committing an act that would be a felony if committed by an adult? .... YES .... NO

(5) Are you under indictment for or otherwise charged with, or have you ever been convicted of or pleaded guilty to, an offense under Chapter 2925., 3719., or 4729. of the Ohio Revised Code that involves the illegal possession, use, sale, administration, or distribution of or trafficking in a drug of abuse, or have you ever been adjudicated a delinquent child for committing an act that would be an offense of that nature if committed by an adult? .... YES .... NO

(6) Are you under indictment for or otherwise charged with, or have you been convicted of or pleaded guilty to within three years of the date of this application, a misdemeanor that is an offense of violence or the offense of possessing a revoked or suspended concealed handgun license, or have you been adjudicated a delinquent child within three years of the date of this application for committing an act that would be a misdemeanor of that nature if committed by an adult? .... YES .... NO

(7) Are you under indictment for or otherwise charged with, or have you been convicted of or pleaded guilty to within ten years of the date of this application, resisting arrest, or have you been adjudicated a delinquent child for committing, within ten years of the date of this application an act that if committed by an adult would be the offense of resisting arrest? .... YES .... NO

(8)(a) Are you under indictment for or otherwise charged with assault or negligent assault? .... YES .... NO

(b) Have you been convicted of, pleaded guilty to, or adjudicated a delinquent child two or more times for committing assault or negligent assault within five years of the date of this application? .... YES .... NO

(c) Have you ever been convicted of, pleaded guilty to, or adjudicated a delinquent child for assaulting a peace officer? .... YES .... NO

(9)(a) Have you ever been adjudicated as a mental defective? .... YES .... NO

(b) Have you ever been committed to a mental institution? ....YES .... NO

(10) Are you currently subject to a civil protection order, a temporary protection order, or a protection order issued by a court of another state? .... YES .... NO

SECTION IV. YOU MUST COMPLETE THIS SECTION OF THE APPLICATION BY PROVIDING, TO THE BEST OF YOUR KNOWLEDGE, THE ADDRESS OF EACH PLACE OF RESIDENCE AT WHICH YOU RESIDED AT ANY TIME AFTER YOU ATTAINED EIGHTEEN YEARS OF AGE AND UNTIL YOU COMMENCED YOUR RESIDENCE AT THE LOCATION IDENTIFIED IN SECTION II OF THIS FORM, AND THE DATES OF RESIDENCE AT EACH OF THOSE ADDRESSES. IF YOU NEED MORE SPACE, COMPLETE AN ADDITIONAL SHEET WITH THE relevant INFORMATION, ATTACH IT TO THE APPLICATION, AND NOTE THE ATTACHMENT AT THE END OF THIS SECTION.

Residence 1:

Street	City	State	County	Zip
....	....	....	....	....

Dates of residence at this address ....

Residence 2:

Street	City	State	County	Zip
....	....	....	....	....

Dates of residence at this address ....

Residence 3:

Street	City	State	County	Zip
....	....	....	....	....

Dates of residence at this address ....

Residence 4:

Street	City	State	County	Zip
....	....	....	....	....

Dates of residence at this address ....

SECTION V.

AN APPLICANT WHO KNOWINGLY GIVES A FALSE ANSWER TO ANY QUESTION OR SUBMITS FALSE INFORMATION ON, OR A FALSE DOCUMENT WITH THE APPLICATION MAY BE PROSECUTED FOR FALSIFICATION TO OBTAIN A CONCEALED HANDGUN LICENSE, A FELONY OF THE FOURTH DEGREE, IN VIOLATION OF SECTION 2921.13 OF THE OHIO REVISED CODE.

(1) I have been furnished, and have read, the pamphlet that explains the Ohio firearms laws, that provides instruction in dispute resolution and explains the Ohio laws related to that matter, and that provides information regarding all aspects of the use of deadly force with a firearm, and I am knowledgeable of the provisions of those laws and of the information on those matters.

(2) I desire a legal means to carry a concealed handgun for defense of myself or a member of my family while engaged in lawful activity.

(3) I have never been convicted of or pleaded guilty to a crime of violence in the state of Ohio or elsewhere. I am of sound mind. I hereby certify that the statements contained herein are true and correct to the best of my knowledge and belief. I understand that if I knowingly make any false statements herein I am subject to penalties prescribed by law. I authorize the sheriff or the sheriff's designee to inspect only those records or documents relevant to information required for this application.

(4) The information contained in this application and all attached documents are true and correct to the best of my knowledge.

....

Signature of Applicant"

(2004 H 12, eff. 4–8–04)

2923.1211 Falsification of license; possession of revoked or suspended license

(A) No person shall alter a license or temporary emergency license to carry a concealed handgun that was issued pursuant to section 2923.125 or 2923.1213 of the Revised Code or create a fictitious document that purports to be a license of that nature.

(B) No person, except in the performance of official duties, shall possess a license to carry a concealed handgun that was issued and that has been revoked or suspended pursuant to section 2923.128 of the Revised Code or a temporary emergency license to carry a concealed handgun that was issued and that has been revoked pursuant to section 2923.1213 of the Revised Code.

(C) Whoever violates division (A) of this section is guilty of falsification of a concealed handgun license, a felony of the fifth degree. Whoever violates division (B) of this section is guilty of possessing a revoked or suspended concealed handgun license, a misdemeanor of the third degree.

(2004 H 12, eff. 4–8–04)

2923.1212 Responsibility for posting and location of signs

(A) The following persons, boards, and entities, or designees, shall post in the following locations a sign that contains a statement in substantially the following form: "Unless otherwise authorized by law, pursuant to the Ohio Revised Code, no person shall knowingly possess, have under the person's control, convey, or attempt to convey a deadly weapon or dangerous ordnance onto these premises.":

(1) The director of public safety or the person or board charged with the erection, maintenance, or repair of police stations, municipal jails, and the municipal courthouse and courtrooms in a conspicuous location at all police stations, municipal jails, and municipal courthouses and courtrooms;

(2) The sheriff or sheriff's designee who has charge of the sheriff's office in a conspicuous location in that office;

(3) The superintendent of the state highway patrol or the superintendent's designee in a conspicuous location at all state highway patrol stations;

(4) Each sheriff, chief of police, or person in charge of every county, multicounty, municipal, municipal-county, or multicounty-municipal jail or workhouse, community-based correctional facility, halfway house, alternative residential facility, or other local or state correctional institution or detention facility within the state, or that person's designee, in a conspicuous location at that facility under that person's charge;

(5) The board of trustees of a regional airport authority, chief administrative officer of an airport facility, or other person in charge of an airport facility in a conspicuous location at each airport facility under that person's control;

(6) The officer or officer's designee who has charge of a courthouse or the building or structure in which a courtroom is located in a conspicuous location in that building or structure;

(7) The superintendent of the bureau of criminal identification and investigation or the superintendent's designee in a conspicuous location in all premises controlled by that bureau;

(8) The owner, administrator, or operator of a child day-care center, a type A family day-care home, a type B family day-care home, or a type C family day-care home;

(9) The officer of this state or of the political subdivision of this state, or the officer's designee, who has charge of a building that is owned by this state or the political subdivision of this state, or who has charge of the portion of a building that is not owned by any governmental entity listed in this division but that is leased by a governmental entity listed in this division.

(B) The following boards, bodies, and persons, or designees, shall post in the following locations a sign that contains a statement in substantially the following form: "Unless otherwise authorized by law, pursuant to Ohio Revised Code section 2923.122, no person shall knowingly possess, have under the person's control, convey, or attempt to convey a deadly weapon or dangerous ordnance into a school safety zone.":

(1) A board of education of a city, local, exempted village, or joint vocational school district or that board's designee in a conspicuous location in each building and on each parcel of real property owned or controlled by the board;

(2) A governing body of a school for which the state board of education prescribes minimum standards under section 3301.07 of the Revised Code or that body's designee in a conspicuous location in each building and on each parcel of real property owned or controlled by the school;

(3) The principal or chief administrative officer of a nonpublic school in a conspicuous location on property owned or controlled by that nonpublic school.

(2004 H 12, eff. 4–8–04)

2923.1213 Temporary emergency licenses

(A) As used in this section:

(1) "Evidence of imminent danger" means any of the following:

(a) A statement sworn by the person seeking to carry a concealed handgun that is made under threat of perjury and that states that the person has reasonable cause to fear a criminal attack upon the person or a member of the person's family, such as would justify a prudent person in going armed;

(b) A written document prepared by a governmental entity or public official describing the facts that give the person seeking to carry a concealed handgun reasonable cause to fear a criminal attack upon the person or a member of the person's family, such as would justify a prudent person in going armed. Written documents of this nature include, but are not limited to, any temporary protection order, civil protection order, protection order issued by another state, or other court order, any court report, and any report filed with or made by a law enforcement agency or prosecutor.

(2) "Prosecutor" has the same meaning as in section 2935.01 of the Revised Code.

(B)(1) A person seeking a temporary emergency license to carry a concealed handgun shall submit to the sheriff of the county in which the person resides all of the following:

(a) Evidence of imminent danger to the person or a member of the person's family;

(b) A sworn affidavit that contains all of the information required to be on the license and attesting that the person is at least twenty-one years of age; is not a fugitive from justice; is not under indictment for or otherwise charged with an offense identified in division (D)(1)(d) of section 2923.125 of the Revised Code; has not been convicted of or pleaded guilty to an offense, and has not been adjudicated a delinquent child for committing an act, identified in division (D)(1)(e) of that section; within three years of the date of the submission, has not been convicted of or pleaded guilty to an offense, and has not been adjudicated a delinquent child for committing an act, identified in division (D)(1)(f) of that section; within five years of the date of the submission, has not been convicted of, pleaded guilty, or adjudicated a delinquent child for committing two or more violations identified in division (D)(1)(g) of that section; within ten years of the date of the submission, has not been convicted of, pleaded guilty, or adjudicated a delinquent child for committing a violation identified in division (D)(1)(h) of that section; has not been adjudicated as a mental defective, has not been committed to any mental institution, is not under adjudication of mental incompetence, has not been found by a court to be a mentally ill person subject to hospitalization by court order, and is not an involuntary patient other than one who is a patient only for purposes of observation, as described in division (D)(1)(i) of that section; and is not currently subject to a civil protection order, a temporary protection order, or a protection order issued by a court of another state, as described in division (D)(1)(j) of that section;

(c) A temporary emergency license fee established by the Ohio peace officer training commission for an amount that does not exceed the actual cost of conducting the criminal background check or thirty dollars;

(d) A set of fingerprints of the applicant provided as described in section 311.41 of the Revised Code through use of an electronic fingerprint reading device or, if the sheriff to whom the application is submitted does not possess and does not have ready access to the use of an electronic fingerprint reading device, on a standard impression sheet prescribed pursuant to division (C)(2) of section 109.572 of the Revised Code. If the fingerprints are provided on a standard impression sheet, the person also shall provide the person's social security number to the sheriff.

(2) Upon receipt of the evidence of imminent danger, the sworn affidavit, the fee, and the set of fingerprints required under division (B)(1) of this section, the sheriff immediately shall conduct or cause to be conducted the criminal records check and the incompetency records check described in section 311.41 of the Revised Code. Immediately upon receipt of the results of the records checks, the sheriff shall review the information and shall determine whether the criteria set forth in divisions (D)(1)(a) to (j) of section 2923.125 of the Revised Code apply regarding the person. If the sheriff determines that all of criteria set forth in divisions (D)(1)(a) to (j) of section 2923.125 of the Revised Code apply regarding the person, the sheriff shall immediately make available through the law enforcement automated data system all information that will be contained on the temporary emergency license for the person if one is issued, and the superintendent of the state highway patrol shall ensure that the system is so configured as to permit the transmission through the system of that information. Upon making that information available through the law enforcement automated data system, the sheriff shall immediately issue to the person a temporary emergency license to carry a concealed handgun.

If the sheriff denies the issuance of a temporary emergency license to the person, the sheriff shall specify the grounds for the denial in a written notice to the person. The person may appeal the denial, or challenge criminal records check results that were the basis of the denial if applicable, in the same manners specified in division (D)(2) of section 2923.125 and in section 2923.127 of the Revised Code, regarding the denial of an application for a license to carry a concealed handgun under that section.

The temporary emergency license under this division shall be in the form, and shall include all of the information, described in divisions (A)(2) and (5) of section 109.731 of the Revised Code, and also shall include a unique combination of identifying letters and numbers in accordance with division (A)(4) of that section.

The temporary emergency license issued under this division is valid for ninety days and may not be renewed. A person who has been issued a temporary emergency license under this division shall not be issued another temporary emergency license unless at least four years has expired since the issuance of the prior temporary emergency license.

(C) A person who holds a temporary emergency license to carry a concealed handgun has the same right to carry a concealed handgun as a person who was issued a license to carry a concealed handgun under section 2923.125 of the Revised Code, and any exceptions to the prohibitions contained in section 1547.69 and sections 2923.12 to 2923.16 of the Revised Code for a licensee under section 2923.125 of the Revised Code apply to a licensee under this section. The person is subject to the same restrictions, and to all other procedures, duties, and sanctions, that apply to a person who carries a license issued under section 2923.125 of the Revised Code, other than the license renewal procedures set forth in that section.

(D) A sheriff who issues a temporary emergency license to carry a concealed handgun under this section shall not require a person seeking to carry a concealed handgun in accordance with this section to submit a competency certificate as a prerequisite for issuing the license and shall comply with division (H) of section 2923.125 of the Revised Code in regards to the license. The sheriff shall suspend or revoke the license in accordance with section 2923.128 of the Revised Code. In addition to the suspension or revocation procedures set forth in section 2923.128 of the Revised Code, the sheriff may revoke the license upon receiving information, verifiable by public documents, that the person is not eligible to possess a firearm under either the laws of this state or of the United States or that the person committed perjury in obtaining the license; if the sheriff revokes a license under this additional authority, the sheriff shall notify the person, by certified mail, return receipt requested, at the person's last known residence address that the license has been revoked and that the person is required to surrender the license at the sheriff's office within ten days of the date on which the notice was mailed. Division (H) of section 2923.125 of the Revised Code applies regarding any suspension or revocation of a temporary emergency license to carry a concealed handgun.

(E) A sheriff who issues a temporary emergency license to carry a concealed handgun under this section shall retain, for the entire period during which the temporary emergency license is in effect, the evidence of imminent danger that the person submitted to the sheriff and that was the basis for the license, or a copy of that evidence, as appropriate.

(F) If a temporary emergency license to carry a concealed handgun issued under this section is lost or is destroyed, the licensee may obtain from the sheriff who issued that license a duplicate license upon the payment of a fee of fifteen dollars and the submission of an affidavit attesting to the loss or destruction of the license. The sheriff, in accordance with the procedures prescribed in section 109.731 of the Revised Code, shall place on the replacement license a combination of identifying numbers different from the combination on the license that is being replaced.

(G) The Ohio peace officer training commission shall prescribe, and shall make available to sheriffs, a standard form to be used under division (B) of this section by a person who applies for a temporary emergency license to carry a concealed handgun on the basis of imminent danger of a type described in division (A)(1)(a) of this section.

(H) A sheriff who receives any fees paid by a person under this section shall deposit all fees so paid into the sheriff's concealed handgun license issuance expense fund established under section 311.42 of the Revised Code.

(2004 H 12, eff. 4–8–04)

2923.13 Having weapons while under disability

(A) Unless relieved from disability as provided in section 2923.14 of the Revised Code, no person shall knowingly acquire, have, carry, or use any firearm or dangerous ordnance, if any of the following apply:

(1) The person is a fugitive from justice.

(2) The person is under indictment for or has been convicted of any felony offense of violence or has been adjudicated a delinquent child for the commission of an offense that, if committed by an adult, would have been a felony offense of violence.

(3) The person is under indictment for or has been convicted of any offense involving the illegal possession, use, sale, administration, distribution, or trafficking in any drug of abuse or has been adjudicated a delinquent child for the commission of an

offense that, if committed by an adult, would have been an offense involving the illegal possession, use, sale, administration, distribution, or trafficking in any drug of abuse.

(4) The person is drug dependent, in danger of drug dependence, or a chronic alcoholic.

(5) The person is under adjudication of mental incompetence, has been adjudicated as a mental defective, has been committed to a mental institution, has been found by a court to be a mentally ill person subject to hospitalization by court order, or is an involuntary patient other than one who is a patient only for purposes of observation. As used in this division, "mentally ill person subject to hospitalization by court order" and "patient" have the same meanings as in section 5122.01 of the Revised Code.

(B) Whoever violates this section is guilty of having weapons while under disability, a felony of the third degree.

(2004 H 12, eff. 4–8–04; 1995 S 2, eff. 7–1–96; 1972 H 511, eff. 1–1–74)

2923.131 Possession of deadly weapon while under detention

(A) "Detention" and "detention facility" have the same meanings as in section 2921.01 of the Revised Code.

(B) No person under detention at a detention facility shall possess a deadly weapon.

(C) Whoever violates this section is guilty of possession of a deadly weapon while under detention.

(1) If the offender, at the time of the commission of the offense, was under detention as an alleged or adjudicated delinquent child or unruly child and if at the time the offender commits the act for which the offender was under detention it would not be a felony if committed by an adult, possession of a deadly weapon while under detention is a misdemeanor of the first degree.

(2) If the offender, at the time of the commission of the offense, was under detention in any other manner, possession of a deadly weapon while under detention is one of the following:

(a) A felony of the first degree, when the most serious offense for which the person was under detention is aggravated murder or murder and regardless of when the aggravated murder or murder occurred or, if the person was under detention as an alleged or adjudicated delinquent child, when the most serious act for which the person was under detention would be aggravated murder or murder if committed by an adult and regardless of when that act occurred;

(b) A felony of the second degree if any of the following applies:

(i) The most serious offense for which the person was under detention is a felony of the first degree committed on or after July 1, 1996, or an aggravated felony of the first degree committed prior to July 1, 1996.

(ii) If the person was under detention as an alleged or adjudicated delinquent child, the most serious act for which the person was under detention was committed on or after July 1, 1996, and would be a felony of the first degree if committed by an adult, or was committed prior to July 1, 1996, and would have been an aggravated felony of the first degree if committed by an adult.

(c) A felony of the third degree if any of the following applies:

(i) The most serious offense for which the person was under detention is a felony of the second degree committed on or after July 1, 1996, or is an aggravated felony of the second degree or a felony of the first degree committed prior to July 1, 1996.

(ii) If the person was under detention as an alleged or adjudicated delinquent child, the most serious act for which the person was under detention was committed on or after July 1, 1996, and would be a felony of the second degree if committed by an adult, or was committed prior to July 1, 1996, and would have been an aggravated felony of the second degree or a felony of the first degree if committed by an adult.

(d) A felony of the fourth degree if any of the following applies:

(i) The most serious offense for which the person was under detention is a felony of the third degree committed on or after July 1, 1996, is an aggravated felony of the third degree or a felony of the second degree committed prior to July 1, 1996, or is a felony of the third degree committed prior to July 1, 1996, that, if it had been committed on or after July 1, 1996, also would be a felony of the third degree.

(ii) If the person was under detention as an alleged or adjudicated delinquent child, the most serious act for which the person was under detention was committed on or after July 1, 1996, and would be a felony of the third degree if committed by an adult, was committed prior to July 1, 1996, and would have been an aggravated felony of the third degree or a felony of the second degree if committed by an adult, or was committed prior to July 1, 1996, would have been a felony of the third degree if committed by an adult, and, if it had been committed on or after July 1, 1996, also would be a felony of the third degree if committed by an adult.

(e) A felony of the fifth degree if any of the following applies:

(i) The most serious offense for which the person was under detention is a felony of the fourth or fifth degree committed on or after July 1, 1996, is a felony of the third degree committed prior to July 1, 1996, that, if committed on or after July 1, 1996, would be a felony of the fourth degree, is a felony of the fourth degree committed prior to July 1, 1996, or is an unclassified felony or a misdemeanor regardless of when the unclassified felony or misdemeanor is committed.

(ii) If the person was under detention as an alleged or adjudicated delinquent child, the most serious act for which the person was under detention was committed on or after July 1, 1996, and would be a felony of the fourth or fifth degree if committed by an adult, was committed prior to July 1, 1996, would have been a felony of the third degree if committed by an adult, and, if it had been committed on or after July 1, 1996, would be a felony of the fourth degree if committed by an adult, was committed prior to July 1, 1996, and would have been a felony of the fourth degree if committed by an adult, or would be an unclassified felony if committed by an adult regardless of when the act is committed.

(1996 H 154, eff. 10–4–96)

2923.14 Relief from disability

(A) Any person who, solely by reason of the person's disability under division (A)(2) or (3) of section 2923.13 of the Revised Code, is prohibited from acquiring, having, carrying, or using firearms, may apply to the court of common pleas in the county in which the person resides for relief from such prohibition.

(B) The application shall recite the following:

(1) All indictments, convictions, or adjudications upon which the applicant's disability is based, the sentence imposed and served, and any release granted under a community control sanction, post-release control sanction, or parole, any partial or conditional pardon granted, or other disposition of each case;

(2) Facts showing the applicant to be a fit subject for relief under this section.

(C) A copy of the application shall be served on the county prosecutor. The county prosecutor shall cause the matter to be investigated and shall raise before the court any objections to granting relief that the investigation reveals.

(D) Upon hearing, the court may grant the applicant relief pursuant to this section, if all of the following apply:

(1) The applicant has been fully discharged from imprisonment, community control, post-release control, and parole, or, if the applicant is under indictment, has been released on bail or recognizance.

(2) The applicant has led a law-abiding life since discharge or release, and appears likely to continue to do so.

(3) The applicant is not otherwise prohibited by law from acquiring, having, or using firearms.

(E) Costs of the proceeding shall be charged as in other civil cases, and taxed to the applicant.

(F) Relief from disability granted pursuant to this section:

(1) Applies only with respect to indictments, convictions, or adjudications recited in the application;

(2) Applies only with respect to firearms lawfully acquired, possessed, carried, or used by the applicant;

(3) Does not apply with respect to dangerous ordnance;

(4) May be revoked by the court at any time for good cause shown and upon notice to the applicant;

(5) Is automatically void upon commission by the applicant of any offense set forth in division (A)(2) or (3) of section 2923.13 of the Revised Code, or upon the applicant's becoming one of the class of persons named in division (A)(1), (4), or (5) of that section.

(G) As used in this section:

(1) "Community control sanction" has the same meaning as in section 2929.01 of the Revised Code.

(2) "Post–release control" and "post–release control sanction" have the same meanings as in section 2967.01 of the Revised Code.

(2002 H 490, eff. 1–1–04; 1972 H 511, eff. 1–1–74)

Notes of Decisions

Ed. Note: See notes of decisions at RC 4511.19 regarding construction of the term "under the influence."

2923.15 Using weapons while intoxicated

(A) No person, while under the influence of alcohol or any drug of abuse, shall carry or use any firearm or dangerous ordnance.

(B) Whoever violates this section is guilty of using weapons while intoxicated, a misdemeanor of the first degree.

(1972 H 511, eff. 1–1–74)

2923.16 Improperly handling firearms in a motor vehicle; return of firearm at termination of stop

(A) No person shall knowingly discharge a firearm while in or on a motor vehicle.

(B) No person shall knowingly transport or have a loaded firearm in a motor vehicle in such a manner that the firearm is accessible to the operator or any passenger without leaving the vehicle.

(C) No person shall knowingly transport or have a firearm in a motor vehicle, unless it is unloaded and is carried in one of the following ways:

(1) In a closed package, box, or case;

(2) In a compartment that can be reached only by leaving the vehicle;

(3) In plain sight and secured in a rack or holder made for the purpose;

(4) In plain sight with the action open or the weapon stripped, or, if the firearm is of a type on which the action will not stay open or which cannot easily be stripped, in plain sight.

(D) No person shall knowingly transport or have a loaded handgun in a motor vehicle if, at the time of that transportation or possession, any of the following applies:

(1) The person is under the influence of alcohol, a drug of abuse, or a combination of them.

(2) The person's whole blood, blood serum or plasma, breath, or urine contains a concentration of alcohol prohibited for persons operating a vehicle, as specified in division (A) of section 4511.19 of the Revised Code, regardless of whether the person at the time of the transportation or possession as described in this division is the operator of or a passenger in the motor vehicle.

(E) No person who has been issued a license or temporary emergency license to carry a concealed handgun under section 2923.125 or 2923.1213 of the Revised Code shall do any of the following:

(1) Knowingly transport or have a loaded handgun in a motor vehicle unless the loaded handgun either is in a holster and in plain sight on the person's person or it is securely encased by being stored in a closed, locked glove compartment or in a case that is in plain sight and that is locked;

(2) If the person is transporting or has a loaded handgun in a motor vehicle in a manner authorized under division (E)(1) of this section, knowingly remove or attempt to remove the loaded handgun from the holster, glove compartment, or case, knowingly grasp or hold the loaded handgun, or knowingly have contact with the loaded handgun by touching it with the person's hands or fingers while the motor vehicle is being operated on a street, highway, or public property unless the person removes, attempts to remove, grasps, holds, or has the contact with the loaded handgun pursuant to and in accordance with directions given by a law enforcement officer;

(3) If the person is the driver or an occupant of a motor vehicle that is stopped as a result of a traffic stop or a stop for another law enforcement purpose and if the person is transporting or has a loaded handgun in the motor vehicle in any manner, fail to promptly inform any law enforcement officer who approaches the vehicle while stopped that the person has been issued a license or temporary emergency license to carry a concealed handgun and that the person then possesses or has a loaded handgun in the motor vehicle.

(4) If the person is the driver or an occupant of a motor vehicle that is stopped as a result of a traffic stop or a stop for another law enforcement purpose and if the person is transporting or has a loaded handgun in the motor vehicle in any manner, knowingly disregard or fail to comply with any lawful order of any law enforcement officer given while the motor vehicle is stopped, knowingly fail to remain in the motor vehicle while stopped, or knowingly fail to keep the person's hands in plain sight at any time after any law enforcement officer begins approaching the person while stopped and before the law enforcement officer leaves, unless, regarding a failure to remain in the motor vehicle or to keep the person's hands in plain sight, the failure is pursuant to and in accordance with directions given by a law enforcement officer;

(5) If the person is the driver or an occupant of a motor vehicle that is stopped as a result of a traffic stop or a stop for another law enforcement purpose, if the person is transporting or has a loaded handgun in the motor vehicle in a manner authorized under division (E)(1) of this section, and if the person is approached by any law enforcement officer while stopped, know-

ingly remove or attempt to remove the loaded handgun from the holster, glove compartment, or case, knowingly grasp or hold the loaded handgun, or knowingly have contact with the loaded handgun by touching it with the person's hands or fingers in the motor vehicle at any time after the law enforcement officer begins approaching and before the law enforcement officer leaves, unless the person removes, attempts to remove, grasps, holds, or has contact with the loaded handgun pursuant to and in accordance with directions given by the law enforcement officer.

(F)(1) This section does not apply to officers, agents, or employees of this or any other state or the United States, or to law enforcement officers, when authorized to carry or have loaded or accessible firearms in motor vehicles and acting within the scope of their duties.

(2) Division (A) of this section does not apply to a person if all of the following circumstances apply:

(a) The person discharges a firearm from a motor vehicle at a coyote or groundhog, the discharge is not during the deer gun hunting season as set by the chief of the division of wildlife of the department of natural resources, and the discharge at the coyote or groundhog, but for the operation of this section, is lawful.

(b) The motor vehicle from which the person discharges the firearm is on real property that is located in an unincorporated area of a township and that either is zoned for agriculture or is used for agriculture.

(c) The person owns the real property described in division (F)(2)(b) of this section, is the spouse or a child of another person who owns that real property, is a tenant of another person who owns that real property, or is the spouse or a child of a tenant of another person who owns that real property.

(d) The person does not discharge the firearm in any of the following manners:

(i) While under the influence of alcohol, a drug of abuse, or alcohol and a drug of abuse;

(ii) In the direction of a street, highway, or other public or private property used by the public for vehicular traffic or parking;

(iii) At or into an occupied structure that is a permanent or temporary habitation;

(iv) In the commission of any violation of law, including, but not limited to, a felony that includes, as an essential element, purposely or knowingly causing or attempting to cause the death of or physical harm to another and that was committed by discharging a firearm from a motor vehicle.

(3) Divisions (B) and (C) of this section do not apply to a person if all of the following circumstances apply:

(a) At the time of the alleged violation of either of those divisions, the person is the operator of or a passenger in a motor vehicle.

(b) The motor vehicle is on real property that is located in an unincorporated area of a township and that either is zoned for agriculture or is used for agriculture.

(c) The person owns the real property described in division (D)(3)(b) of this section, is the spouse or a child of another person who owns that real property, is a tenant of another person who owns that real property, or is the spouse or a child of a tenant of another person who owns that real property.

(d) The person, prior to arriving at the real property described in division (D)(3)(b) of this section, did not transport or possess a firearm in the motor vehicle in a manner prohibited by division (B) or (C) of this section while the motor vehicle was being operated on a street, highway, or other public or private property used by the public for vehicular traffic or parking.

(4) Divisions (B) and (C) of this section do not apply to a person who transports or possesses a handgun in a motor vehicle if, at the time of that transportation or possession, all of the following apply:

(a) The person transporting or possessing the handgun is carrying a valid license or temporary emergency license to carry a concealed handgun issued to the person under section 2923.125 or 2923.1213 of the Revised Code or a license to carry a concealed handgun that was issued by another state with which the attorney general has entered into a reciprocity agreement under section 109.69 of the Revised Code.

(b) The person transporting or possessing the handgun is not knowingly in a place described in division (B) of section 2923.126 of the Revised Code.

(c) Either the handgun is in a holster and in plain sight on the person's person or the handgun is securely encased by being stored in a closed, locked glove compartment or in a case that is in plain sight and that is locked.

(G)(1) The affirmative defenses authorized in divisions (D)(1) and (2) of section 2923.12 of the Revised Code are affirmative defenses to a charge under division (B) or (C) of this section that involves a firearm other than a handgun.

(2) It is an affirmative defense to a charge under division (B) or (C) of this section of improperly handling firearms in a motor vehicle that the actor transported or had the firearm in the motor vehicle for any lawful purpose and while the motor vehicle was on the actor's own property, provided that this affirmative defense is not available unless the person, prior to arriving at the actor's own property, did not transport or possess the firearm in a motor vehicle in a manner prohibited by division (B) or (C) of this section while the motor vehicle was being operated on a street, highway, or other public or private property used by the public for vehicular traffic.

(H) No person who is charged with a violation of division (B), (C), or (D) of this section shall be required to obtain a license or temporary emergency license to carry a concealed handgun under section 2923.125 or 2923.1213 of the Revised Code as a condition for the dismissal of the charge.

(I) Whoever violates this section is guilty of improperly handling firearms in a motor vehicle. Violation of division (A) of this section is a felony of the fourth degree. Violation of division (C) of this section is a misdemeanor of the fourth degree. A violation of division (D) of this section is a felony of the fifth degree. A violation of division (E)(3) of this section is a misdemeanor of the fourth degree. A violation of division (E)(1), (2), or (5) of this section is a felony of the fifth degree. A violation of division (E)(4) of this section is a misdemeanor of the first degree or, if the offender previously has been convicted of or pleaded guilty to a violation of division (E)(4) of this section, a felony of the fifth degree. A violation of division (B) of this section is whichever of the following is applicable:

(1) If, at the time of the transportation or possession in violation of division (B) of this section, the offender was carrying a valid license or temporary emergency license to carry a concealed handgun issued to the offender under section 2923.125 or 2923.1213 of the Revised Code or a license to carry a concealed handgun that was issued by another state with which the attorney general has entered into a reciprocity agreement under section 109.69 of the Revised Code and the offender was not knowingly in a place described in division (B) of section 2923.126 of the Revised Code, the violation is a misdemeanor of the first degree or, if the offender previously has been convicted of or pleaded guilty to a violation of division (B) of this section, a felony of the fourth degree.

(2) If division (I)(1) of this section does not apply, a felony of the fourth degree.

(J) If a law enforcement officer stops a motor vehicle for a traffic stop or any other purpose, if any person in the motor vehicle surrenders a firearm to the officer, either voluntarily or pursuant to a request or demand of the officer, and if the officer does not charge the person with a violation of this section or arrest the person for any offense, the person is not otherwise prohibited by law from possessing the firearm, and the firearm is not contraband, the officer shall return the firearm to the person at the termination of the stop.

(K) As used in this section:

(1) "Motor vehicle," "street," and " highway" have the same meanings as in section 4511.01 of the Revised Code.

(2) "Occupied structure" has the same meaning as in section 2909.01 of the Revised Code.

(3) "Agriculture" has the same meaning as in section 519.01 of the Revised Code.

(4) "Tenant" has the same meaning as in section 1531.01 of the Revised Code.

(5) "Unloaded" means, with respect to a firearm employing a percussion cap, flintlock, or other obsolete ignition system, when the weapon is uncapped or when the priming charge is removed from the pan.

(2004 H 12, eff. 4–8–04; 1997 H 275, eff. 12–31–97; 1973 H 716, eff. 1–1–74; 1972 H 511)

2923.161 Improperly discharging firearm at or into habitation or school safety zone

(A) No person, without privilege to do so, shall knowingly do any of the following:

(1) Discharge a firearm at or into an occupied structure that is a permanent or temporary habitation of any individual;

(2) Discharge a firearm at, in, or into a school safety zone;

(3) Discharge a firearm within one thousand feet of any school building or of the boundaries of any school premises, with the intent to do any of the following:

(a) Cause physical harm to another who is in the school, in the school building, or at a function or activity associated with the school;

(b) Cause panic or fear of physical harm to another who is in the school, in the school building, or at a function or activity associated with the school;

(c) Cause the evacuation of the school, the school building, or a function or activity associated with the school.

(B) This section does not apply to any officer, agent, or employee of this or any other state or the United States, or to any law enforcement officer, who discharges the firearm while acting within the scope of the officer's, agent's, or employee's duties.

(C) Whoever violates this section is guilty of improperly discharging a firearm at or into a habitation, in a school safety zone, or with the intent to cause harm or panic to persons in a school, in a school building, or at a school function or the evacuation of a school function, a felony of the second degree.

(D) As used in this section, "occupied structure" has the same meaning as in section 2909.01 of the Revised Code.

(2002 H 442, eff. 10–11–02; 1999 S 1, eff. 8–6–99; 1998 H 5, eff. 6–30–98; 1995 S 2, eff. 7–1–96; 1990 S 258, eff. 11–20–90)

2923.162 Discharge of firearm on or near prohibited premises; penalties

(A) No person shall do any of the following:

(1) Without permission from the proper officials and subject to division (B)(1) of this section, discharge a firearm upon or over a cemetery or within one hundred yards of a cemetery;

(2) Subject to division (B)(2) of this section, discharge a firearm on a lawn, park, pleasure ground, orchard, or other ground appurtenant to a schoolhouse, church, or inhabited dwelling, the property of another, or a charitable institution;

(3) Discharge a firearm upon or over a public road or highway.

(B)(1) Division (A)(1) of this section does not apply to a person who, while on the person's own land, discharges a firearm.

(2) Division (A)(2) of this section does not apply to a person who owns any type of property described in that division and who, while on the person's own enclosure, discharges a firearm.

(C) Whoever violates this section is guilty of discharge of a firearm on or near prohibited premises. A violation of division (A)(1) or (2) of this section is a misdemeanor of the fourth degree. A violation of division (A)(3) of this section shall be punished as follows:

(1) Except as otherwise provided in division (C)(2), (3), or (4) of this section, a violation of division (A)(3) of this section is a misdemeanor of the first degree.

(2) Except as otherwise provided in division (C)(3) or (4) of this section, if the violation created a substantial risk of physical harm to any person or caused serious physical harm to property, a violation of division (A)(3) of this section is a felony of the third degree.

(3) Except as otherwise provided in division (C)(4) of this section, if the violation caused physical harm to any person, a violation of division (A)(3) of this section is a felony of the second degree.

(4) If the violation caused serious physical harm to any person, a violation of division (A)(3) of this section is a felony of the first degree.

(2004 H 52, eff. 6–1–04; 1999 S 107, eff. 3–23–00)

2923.17 Unlawful possession of dangerous ordnance; illegally manufacturing or processing explosives

(A) No person shall knowingly acquire, have, carry, or use any dangerous ordnance.

(B) No person shall manufacture or process an explosive at any location in this state unless the person first has been issued a license, certificate of registration, or permit to do so from a fire official of a political subdivision of this state or from the office of the fire marshal.

(C) Division (A) of this section does not apply to:

(1) Officers, agents, or employees of this or any other state or the United States, members of the armed forces of the United States or the organized militia of this or any other state, and law enforcement officers, to the extent that any such person is authorized to acquire, have, carry, or use dangerous ordnance and is acting within the scope of the person's duties;

(2) Importers, manufacturers, dealers, and users of explosives, having a license or user permit issued and in effect pursuant to the "Organized Crime Control Act of 1970," 84 Stat. 952, 18 U.S.C. 843, and any amendments or additions thereto or reenactments thereof, with respect to explosives and explosive devices lawfully acquired, possessed, carried, or used under the laws of this state and applicable federal law;

(3) Importers, manufacturers, and dealers having a license to deal in destructive devices or their ammunition, issued and in effect pursuant to the "Gun Control Act of 1968," 82 Stat. 1213, 18 U.S.C. 923, and any amendments or additions thereto or reenactments thereof, with respect to dangerous ordnance lawfully acquired, possessed, carried, or used under the laws of this state and applicable federal law;

(4) Persons to whom surplus ordnance has been sold, loaned, or given by the secretary of the army pursuant to 70A Stat. 262 and 263, 10 U.S.C. 4684, 4685, and 4686, and any amendments or additions thereto or reenactments thereof, with respect to dangerous ordnance when lawfully possessed and used for the purposes specified in such section;

(5) Owners of dangerous ordnance registered in the national firearms registration and transfer record pursuant to the act of October 22, 1968, 82 Stat. 1229, 26 U.S.C. 5841, and any amendments or additions thereto or reenactments thereof, and regulations issued thereunder.

(6) Carriers, warehousemen, and others engaged in the business of transporting or storing goods for hire, with respect to dangerous ordnance lawfully transported or stored in the usual course of their business and in compliance with the laws of this state and applicable federal law;

(7) The holders of a license or temporary permit issued and in effect pursuant to section 2923.18 of the Revised Code, with respect to dangerous ordnance lawfully acquired, possessed, carried, or used for the purposes and in the manner specified in such license or permit.

(D) Whoever violates division (A) of this section is guilty of unlawful possession of dangerous ordnance, a felony of the fifth degree.

(E) Whoever violates division (B) of this section is guilty of illegally manufacturing or processing explosives, a felony of the second degree.

(1995 S 2, eff. 7–1–96; 1978 H 728, eff. 8–22–78; 1972 H 511)

2923.18 License or permit to possess dangerous ordnance

(A) Upon application to the sheriff of the county or safety director or police chief of the municipality where the applicant resides or has his principal place of business, and upon payment of the fee specified in division (B) of this section, a license or temporary permit shall be issued to qualified applicants to acquire, possess, carry, or use dangerous ordnance, for the following purposes:

(1) Contractors, wreckers, quarrymen, mine operators, and other persons regularly employing explosives in the course of a legitimate business, with respect to explosives and explosive devices acquired, possessed, carried, or used in the course of such business;

(2) Farmers, with respect to explosives and explosive devices acquired, possessed, carried, or used for agricultural purposes on lands farmed by them;

(3) Scientists, engineers, and instructors, with respect to dangerous ordnance acquired, possessed, carried, or used in the course of bona fide research or instruction;

(4) Financial institution and armored car company guards, with respect to automatic firearms lawfully acquired, possessed, carried, or used by any such person while acting within the scope of his duties;

(5) In the discretion of the issuing authority, any responsible person, with respect to dangerous ordnance lawfully acquired, possessed, carried, or used for a legitimate research, scientific, educational, industrial, or other proper purpose.

(B) Application for a license or temporary permit under this section shall be in writing under oath to the sheriff of the county or safety director or police chief of the municipality where the applicant resides or has his principal place of business. The application shall be accompanied by an application fee of fifty dollars when the application is for a license, and an application fee of five dollars when the application is for a temporary permit. The fees shall be paid into the general revenue fund of the county or municipality. The application shall contain the following information:

(1) The name, age, address, occupation, and business address of the applicant, if he is a natural person, or the name, address, and principal place of business of the applicant, if the applicant is a corporation;

(2) A description of the dangerous ordnance for which a permit is requested;

(3) A description of the place or places where and the manner in which the dangerous ordnance is to be kept, carried, and used;

(4) A statement of the purposes for which the dangerous ordnance is to be acquired, possessed, carried, or used;

(5) Such other information, as the issuing authority may require in giving effect to this section.

(C) Upon investigation, the issuing authority shall issue a license or temporary permit only if all of the following apply:

(1) The applicant is not otherwise prohibited by law from acquiring, having, carrying or using dangerous ordnance;

(2) The applicant is age twenty-one or over, if he is a natural person;

(3) It appears that the applicant has sufficient competence to safely acquire, possess, carry, or use the dangerous ordnance, and that proper precautions will be taken to protect the security of the dangerous ordnance and ensure the safety of persons and property;

(4) It appears that the dangerous ordnance will be lawfully acquired, possessed, carried, and used by the applicant for a legitimate purpose.

(D) The license or temporary permit shall identify the person to whom it is issued, identify the dangerous ordnance involved and state the purposes for which the license or temporary permit is issued, state the expiration date, if any, and list such restrictions on the acquisition, possession, carriage, or use of the dangerous ordnance as the issuing authority considers advisable to protect the security of the dangerous ordnance and ensure the safety of persons and property.

(E) A temporary permit shall be issued for the casual use of explosives and explosive devices, and other consumable dangerous ordnance, and shall expire within thirty days of its issuance. A license shall be issued for the regular use of consumable dangerous ordnance, or for any noncomsumable [sic.] dangerous ordnance, which license need not specify an expiration date, but the issuing authority may specify such expiration date, not earlier than one year from the date of issuance, as it considers advisable in view of the nature of the dangerous ordnance and the purposes for which the license is issued.

(F) The dangerous ordnance specified in a license or temporary permit may be obtained by the holder anywhere in the state. The holder of a license may use such dangerous ordnance anywhere in the state. The holder of a temporary permit may use such dangerous ordnance only within the territorial jurisdiction of the issuing authority.

(G) The issuing authority shall forward to the state fire marshal a copy of each license or temporary permit issued pursuant to this section, and a copy of each record of a transaction in dangerous ordnance and of each report of lost or stolen dangerous ordnance, given to the local law enforcement authority as required by divisions (A)(4) and (5) of section 2923.20 of the Revised Code. The state fire marshal shall keep a permanent file of all licenses and temporary permits issued pursuant to this section, and of all records of transactions in, and losses or thefts of dangerous ordnance forwarded by local law enforcement authorities pursuant to this section.

(1978 H 590, eff. 7–1–79; 1972 H 511)

2923.19 Failure to secure dangerous ordnance

(A) No person, in acquiring, possessing, carrying, or using any dangerous ordnance, shall negligently fail to take proper precautions:

(1) To secure the dangerous ordnance against theft, or against its acquisition or use by any unauthorized or incompetent person;

(2) To insure the safety of persons and property.

(B) Whoever violates this section is guilty of failure to secure dangerous ordnance, a misdemeanor of the second degree.

(1972 H 511, eff. 1–1–74)

2923.20 Unlawful transactions in weapons

(A) No person shall:

(1) Recklessly sell, lend, give, or furnish any firearm to any person prohibited by section 2923.13 or 2923.15 of the Revised Code from acquiring or using any firearm, or recklessly sell, lend, give, or furnish any dangerous ordnance to any person prohibited by section 2923.13, 2923.15, or 2923.17 of the Revised Code from acquiring or using any dangerous ordnance;

(2) Possess any firearm or dangerous ordnance with purpose to dispose of it in violation of division (A) of this section;

(3) Manufacture, possess for sale, sell, or furnish to any person other than a law enforcement agency for authorized use in police work, any brass knuckles, cestus, billy, blackjack, sandbag, switchblade knife, springblade knife, gravity knife, or similar weapon;

(4) When transferring any dangerous ordnance to another, negligently fail to require the transferee to exhibit such identification, license, or permit showing him to be authorized to acquire dangerous ordnance pursuant to section 2923.17 of the Revised Code, or negligently fail to take a complete record of the transaction and forthwith forward a copy of that record to the sheriff of the county or safety director or police chief of the municipality where the transaction takes place;

(5) Knowingly fail to report to law enforcement authorities forthwith the loss or theft of any firearm or dangerous ordnance in the person's possession or under the person's control.

(B) Whoever violates this section is guilty of unlawful transactions in weapons. A violation of division (A)(1) or (2) of this section is a felony of the fourth degree. A violation of division (A)(3) or (4) of this section is a misdemeanor of the second degree. A violation of division (A)(5) of this section is a misdemeanor of the fourth degree.

(1995 S 2, eff. 7–1–96; 1978 H 728, eff. 8–22–78; 1972 H 511)

2923.21 Improperly furnishing firearms to a minor

(A) No person shall do any of the following:

(1) Sell any firearm to a person who is under eighteen years of age;

(2) Subject to division (B) of this section, sell any handgun to a person who is under twenty-one years of age;

(3) Furnish any firearm to a person who is under eighteen years of age or, subject to division (B) of this section, furnish any handgun to a person who is under twenty-one years of age, except for lawful hunting, sporting, or educational purposes, including, but not limited to, instruction in firearms or handgun safety, care, handling, or marksmanship under the supervision or control of a responsible adult;

(4) Sell or furnish a firearm to a person who is eighteen years of age or older if the seller or furnisher knows, or has reason to know, that the person is purchasing or receiving the firearm for the purpose of selling the firearm in violation of division (A)(1) of this section to a person who is under eighteen years of age or for the purpose of furnishing the firearm in violation of division (A)(3) of this section to a person who is under eighteen years of age;

(5) Sell or furnish a handgun to a person who is twenty-one years of age or older if the seller or furnisher knows, or has reason to know, that the person is purchasing or receiving the handgun for the purpose of selling the handgun in violation of division (A)(2) of this section to a person who is under twenty-one years of age or for the purpose of furnishing the handgun in violation of division (A)(3) of this section to a person who is under twenty-one years of age;

(6) Purchase or attempt to purchase any firearm with the intent to sell the firearm in violation of division (A)(1) of this section to a person who is under eighteen years of age or with the intent to furnish the firearm in violation of division (A)(3) of this section to a person who is under eighteen years of age;

(7) Purchase or attempt to purchase any handgun with the intent to sell the handgun in violation of division (A)(2) of this section to a person who is under twenty-one years of age or with the intent to furnish the handgun in violation of division (A)(3) of this section to a person who is under twenty-one years of age.

(B) Divisions (A)(1) and (2) of this section do not apply to the sale or furnishing of a handgun to a person eighteen years of age or older and under twenty-one years of age if the person eighteen years of age or older and under twenty-one years of age is a law enforcement officer who is properly appointed or employed as a law enforcement officer and has received firearms training approved by the Ohio peace officer training council or equivalent firearms training.

(C) Whoever violates this section is guilty of improperly furnishing firearms to a minor, a felony of the fifth degree.

(1996 H 124, eff. 3–31–97; 1996 S 269, eff. 7–1–96; 1995 H 4, eff. 11–9–95; 1972 H 511, eff. 1–1–74)

2923.211 Underage purchase of firearm or handgun

(A) No person under eighteen years of age shall purchase or attempt to purchase a firearm.

(B) No person under twenty-one years of age shall purchase or attempt to purchase a handgun, provided that this division does not apply to the purchase or attempted purchase of a handgun by a person eighteen years of age or older and under twenty-one years of age if the person eighteen years of age or older and under twenty-one years of age is a law enforcement officer who is properly appointed or employed as a law enforcement officer and has received firearms training approved by the Ohio peace officer training council or equivalent firearms training.

(C) Whoever violates division (A) of this section is guilty of underage purchase of a firearm, a delinquent act that would be a felony of the fourth degree if it could be committed by an adult. Whoever violates division (B) of this section is guilty of underage purchase of a handgun, a misdemeanor of the second degree.

(2000 S 179, § 3, eff. 1–1–02; 1996 H 124, eff. 3–31–97; 1995 H 4, eff. 11–9–95)

2923.22 Permitted interstate transactions in firearms

(A) Any resident of Ohio age eighteen or over, and not prohibited by section 2923.13 or 2923.15 of the Revised Code or any applicable law of another state or the United States from acquiring or using firearms, may purchase or obtain a rifle, shotgun, or ammunition therefor in Indiana, Kentucky, Michigan, Pennsylvania, or West Virginia.

(B) Any resident of Indiana, Kentucky, Michigan, Pennsylvania, or West Virginia, age eighteen or over, and not prohibited by section 2923.13 or 2923.15 of the Revised Code or the laws of his domicile or the United States from acquiring or using firearms, may purchase or obtain a rifle, shotgun, or ammunition therefor in Ohio.

(C) Any purchase and sale pursuant to this section shall be for such purposes and under such circumstances and upon such conditions as are prescribed by the "Gun Control Act of 1968," 82 Stat. 1213, 18 U.S.C. 922(b)(3), and any amendments or additions thereto or reenactments thereof.

(1972 H 511, eff. 1–1–74)

2923.23 Immunity from prosecution

(A) No person who acquires, possesses, or carries a firearm or dangerous ordnance in violation of section 2923.13 or 2923.17 of the Revised Code shall be prosecuted for such violation, if he reports his possession of firearms or dangerous ordnance to any law enforcement authority, describes the firearms of [1] dangerous ordnance in his possession and where they may be found, and voluntarily surrenders the firearms or dangerous ordnance to the law enforcement authority. A surrender is not voluntary if it occurs when the person is taken into custody or during a pursuit or attempt to take the person into custody, under circumstances indicating that the surrender is made under threat of force.

(B) No person in violation of section 2923.13 of the Revised Code solely by reason of his being under indictment shall be prosecuted for such violation if, within ten days after service of the indictment, he voluntarily surrenders the firearms and dangerous ordnance in his possession to any law enforcement authority pursuant to division (A) of this section, for safekeeping pending disposition of the indictment or of an application for relief under section 2923.14 of the Revised Code.

(C) Evidence obtained from or by reason of an application or proceeding under section 2923.14 of the Revised Code for relief from disability, shall not be used in a prosecution of the applicant for any violation of section 2923.13 of the Revised Code.

(D) Evidence obtained from or by reason of an application under section 2923.18 of the Revised Code for a permit to possess dangerous ordnance, shall not be used in a prosecution of the applicant for any violation of section 2923.13 or 2923.17 of the Revised Code.

(1972 H 511, eff. 1–1–74)

[1] So in original; should this read "or"?

2923.24 Possessing criminal tools

(A) No person shall possess or have under the person's control any substance, device, instrument, or article, with purpose to use it criminally.

(B) Each of the following constitutes prima-facie evidence of criminal purpose:

(1) Possession or control of any dangerous ordnance, or the materials or parts for making dangerous ordnance, in the absence of circumstances indicating the dangerous ordnance, materials, or parts are intended for legitimate use;

(2) Possession or control of any substance, device, instrument, or article designed or specially adapted for criminal use;

(3) Possession or control of any substance, device, instrument, or article commonly used for criminal purposes, under circumstances indicating the item is intended for criminal use.

(C) Whoever violates this section is guilty of possessing criminal tools. Except as otherwise provided in this division, possessing criminal tools is a misdemeanor of the first degree. If the circumstances indicate that the substance, device, instrument, or article involved in the offense was intended for use in the commission of a felony, possessing criminal tools is a felony of the fifth degree.

(1995 S 2, eff. 7–1–96; 1972 H 511, eff. 1–1–74)

2923.25 Trigger lock or gun locking device to be offered for sale

Each federally licensed firearms dealer who sells any firearm, at the time of the sale of the firearm, shall offer for sale to the purchaser of the firearm a trigger lock, gun lock, or gun locking device that is appropriate for that firearm. Each federally licensed firearms dealer shall post in a conspicuous location in the dealer's place of business the poster furnished to the dealer pursuant to section 181.521 of the Revised Code and shall make available to all purchasers of firearms from the dealer the brochure furnished to the dealer pursuant to that section.

As used in this section, "federally licensed firearms dealer" has the same meaning as in section 181.251 of the Revised Code.

(2004 H 12, eff. 4–8–04)

CORRUPT ACTIVITY

2923.31 Definitions

As used in sections 2923.31 to 2923.36 of the Revised Code:

(A) "Beneficial interest" means any of the following:

(1) The interest of a person as a beneficiary under a trust in which the trustee holds title to personal or real property;

(2) The interest of a person as a beneficiary under any other trust arrangement under which any other person holds title to personal or real property for the benefit of such person;

(3) The interest of a person under any other form of express fiduciary arrangement under which any other person holds title to personal or real property for the benefit of such person.

"Beneficial interest" does not include the interest of a stockholder in a corporation or the interest of a partner in either a general or limited partnership.

(B) "Costs of investigation and prosecution" and "costs of investigation and litigation" mean all of the costs incurred by the state or a county or municipal corporation under sections 2923.31 to 2923.36 of the Revised Code in the prosecution and investigation of any criminal action or in the litigation and investigation of any civil action, and includes, but is not limited to, the costs of resources and personnel.

(C) "Enterprise" includes any individual, sole proprietorship, partnership, limited partnership, corporation, trust, union, government agency, or other legal entity, or any organization, association, or group of persons associated in fact although not a legal entity. "Enterprise" includes illicit as well as licit enterprises.

(D) "Innocent person" includes any bona fide purchaser of property that is allegedly involved in a violation of section 2923.32 of the Revised Code, including any person who establishes a valid claim to or interest in the property in accordance with division (E) of section 2923.32 of the Revised Code, and any victim of an alleged violation of that section or of any underlying offense involved in an alleged violation of that section.

(E) "Pattern of corrupt activity" means two or more incidents of corrupt activity, whether or not there has been a prior conviction, that are related to the affairs of the same enterprise, are not isolated, and are not so closely related to each other and connected in time and place that they constitute a single event.

At least one of the incidents forming the pattern shall occur on or after January 1, 1986. Unless any incident was an aggravated murder or murder, the last of the incidents forming the pattern shall occur within six years after the commission of any prior incident forming the pattern, excluding any period of imprisonment served by any person engaging in the corrupt activity.

For the purposes of the criminal penalties that may be imposed pursuant to section 2923.32 of the Revised Code, at least one of the incidents forming the pattern shall constitute a felony under the laws of this state in existence at the time it was committed or, if committed in violation of the laws of the United States or of any other state, shall constitute a felony under the law of the United States or the other state and would be a criminal offense under the law of this state if committed in this state.

(F) "Pecuniary value" means money, a negotiable instrument, a commercial interest, or anything of value, as defined in section 1.03 of the Revised Code, or any other property or service that has a value in excess of one hundred dollars.

(G) "Person" means any person, as defined in section 1.59 of the Revised Code, and any governmental officer, employee, or entity.

(H) "Personal property" means any personal property, any interest in personal property, or any right, including, but not limited to, bank accounts, debts, corporate stocks, patents, or copyrights. Personal property and any beneficial interest in personal property are deemed to be located where the trustee of the property, the personal property, or the instrument evidencing the right is located.

(I) "Corrupt activity" means engaging in, attempting to engage in, conspiring to engage in, or soliciting, coercing, or intimidating another person to engage in any of the following:

(1) Conduct defined as "racketeering activity" under the "Organized Crime Control Act of 1970," 84 Stat. 941, 18 U.S.C. 1961(1)(B), (1)(C), (1)(D), and (1)(E), as amended;

(2) Conduct constituting any of the following:

(a) A violation of section 1315.55, 1322.02, 2903.01, 2903.02, 2903.03, 2903.04, 2903.11, 2903.12, 2905.01, 2905.02, 2905.11, 2905.22, 2907.321, 2907.322, 2907.323, 2909.02, 2909.03, 2909.22, 2909.23, 2909.24, 2911.01, 2911.02, 2911.11, 2911.12, 2911.13, 2911.31, 2913.05, 2913.06, 2921.02, 2921.03, 2921.04, 2921.11, 2921.12, 2921.32, 2921.41, 2921.42, 2921.43, 2923.12, or 2923.17; division (F)(1)(a), (b), or (c) of section 1315.53; division (A)(1) or (2) of section 1707.042; division (B), (C)(4), (D), (E), or (F) of section 1707.44; division (A)(1) or (2) of section 2923.20; division (J)(1) of section 4712.02; section 4719.02, 4719.05, or 4719.06; division (C), (D), or (E) of section 4719.07; section 4719.08; or division (A) of section 4719.09 of the Revised Code.

(b) Any violation of section 3769.11, 3769.15, 3769.16, or 3769.19 of the Revised Code as it existed prior to July 1, 1996, any violation of section 2915.02 of the Revised Code that occurs on or after July 1, 1996, and that, had it occurred prior to that date, would have been a violation of section 3769.11 of the Revised Code as it existed prior to that date, or any violation of section 2915.05 of the Revised Code that occurs on or after July 1, 1996, and that, had it occurred prior to that date, would have been a violation of section 3769.15, 3769.16, or 3769.19 of the Revised Code as it existed prior to that date.

(c) Any violation of section 2907.21, 2907.22, 2907.31, 2913.02, 2913.11, 2913.21, 2913.31, 2913.32, 2913.34, 2913.42, 2913.47, 2913.51, 2915.03, 2925.03, 2925.04, 2925.05, or 2925.37 of the Revised Code, any violation of section 2925.11 of the Revised Code that is a felony of the first, second, third, or fourth degree and that occurs on or after July 1, 1996, any violation of section 2915.02 of the Revised Code that occurred prior to July 1, 1996, any violation of section 2915.02 of the Revised Code that occurs on or after July 1, 1996, and that, had it occurred prior to that date, would not have been a violation of section 3769.11 of the Revised Code as it existed prior to that date, any violation of section 2915.06 of the Revised Code as it existed prior to July 1, 1996, or any violation of division (B) of section 2915.05 of the Revised Code as it exists on and after July 1, 1996, when the proceeds of the violation, the payments made in the violation, the amount of a claim for payment or for any other benefit that is false or deceptive and that is involved in the violation, or the value of the contraband or other property illegally possessed, sold, or purchased in the violation exceeds five hundred dollars, or any combination of violations described in division (I)(2)(c) of this section when the total proceeds of the combination of violations, payments made in the combination of violations, amount of the claims for payment or for other benefits that is false or deceptive and that is involved in the combination of violations, or value of the contraband or other property illegally possessed, sold, or purchased in the combination of violations exceeds five hundred dollars;

(d) Any violation of section 5743.112 of the Revised Code when the amount of unpaid tax exceeds one hundred dollars;

(e) Any violation or combination of violations of section 2907.32 of the Revised Code involving any material or performance containing a display of bestiality or of sexual conduct, as defined in section 2907.01 of the Revised Code, that is explicit and depicted with clearly visible penetration of the genitals or clearly visible penetration by the penis of any orifice when the total proceeds of the violation or combination of violations, the payments made in the violation or combination of violations, or the value of the contraband or other property illegally possessed, sold, or purchased in the violation or combination of violations exceeds five hundred dollars;

(f) Any combination of violations described in division (I)(2)(c) of this section and violations of section 2907.32 of the Revised Code involving any material or performance containing a display of bestiality or of sexual conduct, as defined in section 2907.01 of the Revised Code, that is explicit and depicted with clearly visible penetration of the genitals or clearly visible penetration by the penis of any orifice when the total proceeds of the combination of violations, payments made in the combination of violations, amount of the claims for payment or for other benefits that is false or deceptive and that is involved in the combination of violations, or value of the contraband or other property illegally possessed, sold, or purchased in the combination of violations exceeds five hundred dollars.

(3) Conduct constituting a violation of any law of any state other than this state that is substantially similar to the conduct described in division (I)(2) of this section, provided the defendant was convicted of the conduct in a criminal proceeding in the other state.

(J) "Real property" means any real property or any interest in real property, including, but not limited to, any lease of, or mortgage upon, real property. Real property and any beneficial interest in it is deemed to be located where the real property is located.

(K) "Trustee" means any of the following:

(1) Any person acting as trustee under a trust in which the trustee holds title to personal or real property;

(2) Any person who holds title to personal or real property for which any other person has a beneficial interest;

(3) Any successor trustee.

"Trustee" does not include an assignee or trustee for an insolvent debtor or an executor, administrator, administrator with the will annexed, testamentary trustee, guardian, or committee, appointed by, under the control of, or accountable to a court.

(L) "Unlawful debt" means any money or other thing of value constituting principal or interest of a debt that is legally unenforceable in this state in whole or in part because the debt was incurred or contracted in violation of any federal or state law relating to the business of gambling activity or relating to the business of lending money at an usurious rate unless the creditor proves, by a preponderance of the evidence, that the usurious rate was not intentionally set and that it resulted from a good faith error by the creditor, notwithstanding the maintenance of procedures that were adopted by the creditor to avoid an error of that nature.

(2002 S 184, eff. 5–15–02; 1998 H 565, eff. 3–30–99; 1996 S 277, eff. 3–31–97; 1996 S 214, § 3, eff. 12–5–96; 1996 S 214, § 1, eff. 12–5–96; 1996 S 269, eff. 7–1–96; 1996 H 333, eff. 9–19–96; 1995 S 2, eff. 7–1–96; 1992 S 323, eff. 4–16–93; 1990 H 347; 1988 H 624, H 708; 1986 S 74; 1985 H 5)

2923.32 Engaging in a pattern of corrupt activity; fines; penalties; forfeiture; records and reports; third–party claims to property subject to forfeiture

(A)(1) No person employed by, or associated with, any enterprise shall conduct or participate in, directly or indirectly, the affairs of the enterprise through a pattern of corrupt activity or the collection of an unlawful debt.

(2) No person, through a pattern of corrupt activity or the collection of an unlawful debt, shall acquire or maintain, directly or indirectly, any interest in, or control of, any enterprise or real property.

(3) No person, who knowingly has received any proceeds derived, directly or indirectly, from a pattern of corrupt activity or the collection of any unlawful debt, shall use or invest, directly or indirectly, any part of those proceeds, or any proceeds derived from the use or investment of any of those proceeds, in the acquisition of any title to, or any right, interest, or equity in, real property or in the establishment or operation of any enterprise.

A purchase of securities on the open market with intent to make an investment, without intent to control or participate in the control of the issuer, and without intent to assist another to do so is not a violation of this division, if the securities of the issuer held after the purchase by the purchaser, the members of the purchaser's immediate family, and the purchaser's or the immediate family members' accomplices in any pattern of corrupt activity or the collection of an unlawful debt do not aggregate one per cent of the outstanding securities of any one class of the issuer and do not confer, in law or in fact, the power to elect one or more directors of the issuer.

(B)(1) Whoever violates this section is guilty of engaging in a pattern of corrupt activity. Except as otherwise provided in this division, engaging in corrupt activity is a felony of the second degree. If at least one of the incidents of corrupt activity is a felony of the first, second, or third degree, aggravated murder, or murder, if at least one of the incidents was a felony under the law of this state that was committed prior to the effective date of this amendment and that would constitute a felony of the first, second, or third degree, aggravated murder, or murder if committed on or after the effective date of this amendment, or if at least one of the incidents of corrupt activity is a felony under the law of the United States or of another state that, if committed in this state on or after the effective date of this amendment, would constitute a felony of the first, second, or third degree, aggravated murder, or murder under the law of this state, engaging in a pattern of corrupt activity is a felony of the first degree. Notwithstanding any other provision of law, a person may be convicted of violating the provisions of this section as well as of a conspiracy to violate one or more of those provisions under section 2923.01 of the Revised Code.

(2) Notwithstanding the financial sanctions authorized by section 2929.18 of the Revised Code, the court may do all of the following with respect to any person who derives pecuniary value or causes property damage, personal injury other than pain and suffering, or other loss through or by the violation of this section:

(a) In lieu of the fine authorized by that section, impose a fine not exceeding the greater of three times the gross value gained or three times the gross loss caused and order the clerk of the court to pay the fine into the corrupt activity investigation and prosecution fund created in section 2923.35 of the Revised Code;

(b) In addition to the fine described in division (B)(2)(a) of this section and the financial sanctions authorized by section 2929.18 of the Revised Code, order the person to pay court costs;

(c) In addition to the fine described in division (B)(2)(a) of this section and the financial sanctions authorized by section 2929.18 of the Revised Code, order the person to pay to the state, municipal, or county law enforcement agencies that handled the investigation and prosecution the costs of investigation and prosecution that are reasonably incurred.

The court shall hold a hearing to determine the amount of fine, court costs, and other costs to be imposed under this division.

(3) In addition to any other penalty or disposition authorized or required by law, the court shall order any person who is convicted of or pleads guilty to a violation of this section or who is adjudicated delinquent by reason of a violation of this section to criminally forfeit to the state any personal or real property in which the person has an interest and that was used in the course of or intended for use in the course of a violation of this section, or that was derived from or realized through conduct in violation of this section, including any property constituting an interest in, means of control over, or influence over the enterprise involved in the violation and any property constituting proceeds derived from the violation, including all of the following:

(a) Any position, office, appointment, tenure, commission, or employment contract of any kind acquired or maintained by the person in violation of this section, through which the person, in violation of this section, conducted or participated in the conduct of an enterprise, or that afforded the person a source of influence or control over an enterprise that the person exercised in violation of this section;

(b) Any compensation, right, or benefit derived from a position, office, appointment, tenure, commission, or employment contract described in division (B)(3)(a) of this section that accrued to the person in violation of this section during the period of the pattern of corrupt activity;

(c) Any interest in, security of, claim against, or property or contractual right affording the person a source of influence or control over the affairs of an enterprise that the person exercised in violation of this section;

(d) Any amount payable or paid under any contract for goods or services that was awarded or performed in violation of this section.

(4)(a) A sentence or disposition of criminal forfeiture pursuant to division (B)(3) of this section shall not be entered unless either of the following applies:

(i) The indictment, count in the indictment, or information charging the offense, or the complaint, indictment, or information filed in juvenile court charging the violation as a delinquent act alleges the extent of the property subject to forfeiture;

(ii) The criminal sentence or delinquency disposition requires the forfeiture of property that was not reasonably foreseen to be subject to forfeiture at the time of the indictment, count in the indictment, or information charging the offense, or the complaint, indictment, or information filed in juvenile court charging the violation as a delinquent act, provided that the prosecuting attorney gave prompt notice to the defendant or the alleged or adjudicated delinquent child of such property not reasonably foreseen to be subject to forfeiture when it is discovered to be forfeitable.

(b) A special verdict shall be returned as to the extent of the property, if any, subject to forfeiture. When the special verdict is returned, a judgment of forfeiture shall be entered.

(5) If any property included in a special verdict of forfeiture returned pursuant to division (B)(4) of this section cannot be located, has been sold to a bona fide purchaser for value, placed beyond the jurisdiction of the court, substantially diminished in value by the conduct of the defendant or adjudicated delinquent child, or commingled with other property that cannot be divided without difficulty or undue injury to innocent persons, or otherwise is unreachable without undue injury to innocent persons, the court shall order forfeiture of any other reachable property of the defendant or adjudicated delinquent child up to the value of the property that is unreachable.

(6) All property ordered forfeited pursuant to this section shall be held by the law enforcement agency that seized it for distribution or disposal pursuant to section 2923.35 of the Revised Code. The agency shall maintain an accurate record of each item of property so seized and held, which record shall include the date on which each item was seized, the manner and date of disposition by the agency, and if applicable, the name of the person who received the item; however, the record shall not identify or enable the identification of the individual officer who seized the property. The record is a public record open for inspection under section 149.43 of the Revised Code. Each law enforcement agency that seizes and holds in any calendar year any item of property that is ordered forfeited pursuant to this section shall prepare a report covering the calendar year that cumulates all of the information contained in all of the records kept by the agency pursuant to this division for that calendar year, and shall send the cumulative report, no later than the first day of March in the calendar year following the calendar year covered by the report, to the attorney general. Each such report so received by the attorney general is a public record open for inspection under section 149.43 of the Revised Code. Not later than the fifteenth day of April in the calendar year in which the reports were received, the attorney general shall send to the president of the senate and the speaker of the house of representatives a written notification that does all of the following:

(a) Indicates that the attorney general has received from law enforcement agencies reports of the type described in this division that cover the previous calendar year and indicates that the reports were received under this division;

(b) Indicates that the reports are open for inspection under section 149.43 of the Revised Code;

(c) Indicates that the attorney general will provide a copy of any or all of the reports to the president of the senate or the speaker of the house of representatives upon request.

(C) Notwithstanding the notice and procedure prescribed by division (E) of this section, an order of criminal forfeiture entered under division (B)(3) of this section shall authorize an appropriate law enforcement agency to seize the property declared forfeited under this section upon the terms and conditions, relating to the time and manner of seizure, that the court determines proper.

(D) Criminal penalties under this section are not mutually exclusive, unless otherwise provided, and do not preclude the application of any other criminal or civil remedy under this or any other section of the Revised Code. A disposition of criminal forfeiture ordered pursuant to division (B)(3) of this section in relation to a child who was adjudicated delinquent by reason of a violation of this section does not preclude the application of any other order of disposition under Chapter 2152. of the Revised Code or any other civil remedy under this or any other section of the Revised Code.

(E)(1) Upon the entry of a judgment of forfeiture pursuant to division (B)(3) of this section, the court shall cause notice of the judgment to be sent by certified mail, return receipt requested, to all persons known to have, or appearing to have, an interest in the property that was acquired prior to the filing of a corrupt activity lien notice or a lis pendens as authorized by section 2923.36 of the Revised Code. If the notices cannot be given to those persons in that manner, the court shall cause publication of the notice of the judgment of forfeiture pursuant to the Rules of Civil Procedure.

(2) Within thirty days after receipt of a notice or after the date of publication of a notice under division (E)(1) of this section, any person, other than the defendant or the adjudicated delinquent child, who claims an interest in the property that is subject to forfeiture may petition the court for a hearing to determine the validity of the claim. The petition shall be signed and sworn to by the petitioner and shall set forth the nature and extent of the petitioner's interest in the property, the date and circumstances of the petitioner's acquisition of the interest, any additional allegations supporting the claim, and the relief sought. The petitioner shall furnish the prosecuting attorney with a copy of the petition.

(3) The court, to the extent practicable and consistent with the interests of justice, shall hold the hearing described under division (E)(2) of this section within thirty days from the filing of the petition. The court may consolidate the hearings on all petitions filed by third party claimants under this section. At the hearing, the petitioner may testify and present evidence on the petitioner's own behalf and cross-examine witnesses. The prosecuting attorney may present evidence and witnesses in rebuttal and in defense of the claim of the state to the property and cross-examine witnesses. The court, in making its determination, shall consider the testimony and evidence presented at the hearing and the relevant portions of the record of the criminal proceeding that resulted in the judgment of forfeiture.

(4) If at a hearing held under division (E)(3) of this section, the court, by a preponderance of the evidence, determines either that the petitioner has a legal right, title, or interest in the property that, at the time of the commission of the acts giving rise to the forfeiture of the property, was vested in the petitioner and not in the defendant or the adjudicated delinquent child or was superior to the right, title, or interest of the defendant or the adjudicated delinquent child, or that the petitioner is a bona fide purchaser for value of the right, title, or interest in the property and was at the time of the purchase reasonably without cause to believe that the property was subject to forfeiture under this section, it shall amend, in accordance with its determination, the judgment of forfeiture to protect the rights of innocent persons.

(F) Except as provided in division (E) of this section, no person claiming an interest in property that is subject to forfeiture under this section shall do either of the following:

(1) Intervene in a trial or appeal of a criminal case or a delinquency case that involves the forfeiture of the property;

(2) File an action against the state concerning the validity of the person's alleged interest in the property subsequent to the filing of the indictment, count in the indictment, or information, or the filing of the complaint, indictment, or information in juvenile court, that alleges that the property is subject to forfeiture under this section.

(G) As used in this section, "law enforcement agency" includes, but is not limited to, the state board of pharmacy.

(2000 S 179, § 3, eff. 1–1–02; 1998 S 164, eff. 1–15–98; 1995 S 2, eff. 7–1–96; 1990 H 266, eff. 9–6–90; 1990 H 215; 1988 H 708; 1986 S 74; 1985 H 5)

2923.33 Property subject to forfeiture; restraining orders

(A) At any time after an indictment is filed alleging a violation of section 2923.32 of the Revised Code or a conspiracy to violate that section or after a complaint, indictment or information is filed in juvenile court alleging a violation of that section or a conspiracy to violate that section as a delinquent act, the prosecuting attorney may file a motion requesting the court to issue an order to preserve the reachability of any property that may be subject to forfeiture. Upon the filing of the motion, the court, after giving notice to any person who will be affected by any order issued by the court pursuant to the motion, shall hold a hearing on the motion at which all affected persons have an opportunity to be heard and, upon a showing by the prosecuting attorney by a preponderance of the evidence that the particular action is necessary to preserve the reachability of any property that may be subject to forfeiture and based upon the indictment, may enter a restraining order or injunction, require the execution of a satisfactory performance bond, or take any other necessary action, including the appointment of a receiver. The prosecuting attorney is not required to show special or irreparable injury to obtain any court action pursuant to this division. Notwithstanding the Rules of Evidence, the court's order or injunction may be based on hearsay testimony.

(B) If no indictment has been filed alleging a violation of section 2923.32 of the Revised Code or a conspiracy to violate that section and no complaint, indictment, or information has been filed in juvenile court alleging a violation of that section or a conspiracy to violate that section as a delinquent act, the court may take any action specified in division (A) of this section if the prosecuting attorney for the county, in addition to the showing that would be required pursuant to division (A) of this section, also shows both of the following by a preponderance of the evidence:

(1) There is probable cause to believe that the property with respect to which the order is sought, in the event of a conviction or a delinquency adjudication, would be subject to criminal forfeiture under section 2923.32 of the Revised Code;

(2) The requested order would not result in irreparable harm to the party against whom the order is to be entered that outweighs the need to preserve the reachability of the property.

No order entered pursuant to this division shall be effective for more than ninety days, unless it is extended pursuant to the procedure provided in this division by the court for good cause shown or an indictment is returned alleging that the property is subject to forfeiture.

(C) Upon application by the prosecuting attorney, the court may grant a temporary restraining order to preserve the reachability of property subject to criminal forfeiture under section 2923.32 of the Revised Code without notice to any party, if all of the following occur:

(1) Either an indictment or a juvenile delinquency complaint, indictment, or information alleging that property is subject to criminal forfeiture has been filed, or the court determines that there is probable cause to believe that property with respect to which the order is sought would be subject, in the event of a conviction or a delinquency adjudication, to criminal forfeiture;

(2) The property is in the possession or control of the party against whom the order is to be entered;

(3) The court determines that the nature of the property is such that it can be concealed, disposed of, or placed beyond the jurisdiction of the court before any party may be heard in opposition to the order.

A temporary restraining order granted without notice to any party under this division shall expire within the time, not to exceed ten days, that the court fixes, unless extended for good cause shown or unless the party against whom it is entered consents to an extension for a longer period. If a temporary restraining order is granted under this division without notice to any party, the court shall hold a hearing concerning the entry of an order under this division at the earliest practicable time prior to the expiration of the temporary order.

(D) Following sentencing and the entry of a judgment against an offender that includes a fine or an order of criminal forfeiture, or both, under section 2923.32 of the Revised Code, or following the entry of a judgment against a delinquent child that includes an order of criminal forfeiture under that section, the court may enter a restraining order or injunction, require the execution of a satisfactory performance bond, or take any other action, including the appointment of a receiver, that the court determines to be proper to protect the interests of the state or an innocent person.

(2000 S 179, § 3, eff. 1–1–02; 1990 H 266, eff. 9–6–90; 1985 H 5)

2923.34 Civil proceedings

(A) The prosecuting attorney of the county in which a violation of section 2923.32 of the Revised Code, or a conspiracy to violate that section, occurs may institute a civil proceeding as authorized by this section in an appropriate court seeking relief from any person whose conduct violated section 2923.32 of the Revised Code or who conspired to violate that section.

(B) Any person who is injured or threatened with injury by a violation of section 2923.32 of the Revised Code may institute a civil proceeding in an appropriate court seeking relief from any person whose conduct violated or allegedly violated section 2923.32 of the Revised Code or who conspired or allegedly conspired to violate that section, except that the pattern of corrupt activity alleged by an injured person or person threatened with injury shall include at least one incident other than a violation of division (A)(1) or (2) of section 1707.042 or division (B), (C)(4), (D), (E), or (F) of section 1707.44 of the Revised Code, of 18 U.S.C. 1341, 18 U.S.C. 1343, 18 U.S.C. 2314, or any other offense involving fraud in the sale of securities.

(C) If the plaintiff in a civil action instituted pursuant to this section proves the violation by a preponderance of the evidence, the court, after making due provision for the rights of innocent persons, may grant relief by entering any appropriate orders to ensure that the violation will not continue or be repeated. The orders may include, but are not limited to, orders that:

(1) Require the divestiture of the defendant's interest in any enterprise or in any real property;

(2) Impose reasonable restrictions upon the future activities or investments of any defendant in the action, including, but not limited to, restrictions that prohibit the defendant from engaging in the same type of endeavor as the enterprise in which the defendant was engaged in violation of section 2923.32 of the Revised Code;

(3) Order the dissolution or reorganization of any enterprise;

(4) Order the suspension or revocation of a license, permit, or prior approval granted to any enterprise by any department or agency of the state;

(5) Order the dissolution of a corporation organized under the laws of this state, or the revocation of the authorization of a foreign corporation to conduct business within this state, upon a finding that the board of directors or an agent acting on behalf of the corporation, in conducting the affairs of the corporation, has authorized or engaged in conduct in violation of section 2923.32 of the Revised Code, and that, for the prevention of future criminal conduct, the public interest requires the corporation to be dissolved or its license revoked.

(D) Relief pursuant to division (C)(3), (4), or (5) of this section shall not be granted in any civil proceeding instituted by an injured person unless the attorney general intervenes in the civil action pursuant to this division.

Upon the filing of a civil proceeding for relief under division (C)(3), (4), or (5) of this section by an allegedly injured person other than a prosecuting attorney, the allegedly injured person immediately shall notify the attorney general of the filing. The attorney general, upon timely application, may intervene in any civil proceeding for relief under division (C)(3), (4), or (5) if the attorney general certifies that, in the attorney general's opinion, the proceeding is of general public interest. In any proceeding brought by an injured person under division (C)(3), (4), or (5) of this section, the attorney general is entitled to the same relief as if the attorney general instituted the proceeding.

(E) In a civil proceeding under division (C) of this section, the court may grant injunctive relief without a showing of special or irreparable injury.

Pending final determination of a civil proceeding initiated under this section, the court may issue a temporary restraining order or a preliminary injunction upon a showing of immediate danger or significant injury to the plaintiff, including the possibility that any judgment for money damages might be difficult to execute, and, in a proceeding initiated by an aggrieved person, upon the execution of proper bond against injury for an improvidently granted injunction.

(F) In a civil proceeding under division (B) of this section, any person directly or indirectly injured by conduct in violation of section 2923.32 of the Revised Code or a conspiracy to violate that section, other than a violator of that section or a conspirator to violate that section, in addition to relief under division (C) of this section, shall have a cause of action for triple the actual damages the person sustained. To recover triple damages, the plaintiff shall prove the violation or conspiracy to violate that section and actual damages by clear and convincing evidence. Damages under this division may include, but are not limited to, competitive injury and injury distinct from the injury inflicted by corrupt activity.

(G) In a civil action in which the plaintiff prevails under division (C) or (F) of this section, the plaintiff shall recover reasonable attorney fees in the trial and appellate courts, and the court shall order the defendant to pay to the state, municipal, or county law enforcement agencies that handled the investigation and litigation the costs of investigation and litigation that reasonably are incurred and that are not ordered to be paid pursuant to division (B)(2) of section 2923.32 of the Revised Code or division (I) of this section.

(H) Upon application, based on the evidence presented in the case by the plaintiff, as the interests of justice may require, the trial court may grant a defendant who prevails in a civil action brought pursuant to this section all or part of the defendant's costs, including the costs of investigation and litigation reasonably incurred, and all or part of the defendant's reasonable attorney fees, unless the court finds that special circumstances, including the relative economic position of the parties, make an award unjust.

(I) If a person, other than an individual, is not convicted of a violation of section 2923.32 of the Revised Code, the prosecuting attorney may institute proceedings against the person to recover a civil penalty for conduct that the prosecuting attorney proves by clear and convincing evidence is in violation of section 2923.32 of the Revised Code. The civil penalty shall not exceed one hundred thousand dollars and shall be paid into the state treasury to the credit of the corrupt activity investigation and prosecution fund created in section 2923.35 of the Revised Code. If a civil penalty is ordered pursuant to this division, the court shall order the defendant to pay to the state, municipal, or county law enforcement agencies that handled the investigation and litigation the costs of investigation and litigation that are reasonably incurred and that are not ordered to be paid pursuant to this section.

(J) A final judgment, decree, or delinquency adjudication rendered against the defendant or the adjudicated delinquent child in a civil action under this section or in a criminal or delinquency action or proceeding for a violation of section 2923.32 of the Revised Code shall estop the defendant or the adjudicated delinquent child in any subsequent civil proceeding or action brought by any person as to all matters as to which the judgment, decree, or adjudication would be an estoppel as between the parties to the civil, criminal, or delinquency proceeding or action.

(K) Notwithstanding any other provision of law providing a shorter period of limitations, a civil proceeding or action under this section may be commenced at any time within five years after the unlawful conduct terminates or the cause of action accrues or within any longer statutory period of limitations that may be applicable. If a criminal proceeding, delinquency proceeding, civil action, or other proceeding is brought or intervened in by the state to punish, prevent, or restrain any activity that is unlawful under section 2923.32 of the Revised Code, the running of the period of limitations prescribed by this division with respect to any civil action brought under this section by a person who is injured by a violation or threatened violation of section 2923.32 of the Revised Code, based in whole or in part upon any matter complained of in the state prosecution, action, or proceeding, shall be suspended during the pendency of the state prosecution, action, or proceeding and for two years following its termination.

(L) Personal service of any process in a proceeding under this section may be made upon any person outside this state if the person was involved in any conduct constituting a violation of section 2923.32 of the Revised Code in this state. The person is deemed by the person's conduct in violation of section 2923.32 of the Revised Code to have submitted to the jurisdiction of the courts of this state for the purposes of this section.

(M) The application of any civil remedy under this section shall not preclude the application of any criminal remedy or criminal forfeiture under section 2923.32 of the Revised Code or any other provision of law, or the application of any delinquency disposition under Chapter 2152. of the Revised Code or any other provision of law.

(N) As used in this section, "law enforcement agency" includes, but is not limited to, the state board of pharmacy.

(2000 S 179, § 3, eff. 1–1–02; 1990 H 266, eff. 9–6–90; 1986 H 428; 1985 H 5)

2923.35 Court orders; rights of prevailing party in civil action; disposal of property; records and reports; funds; written internal control policy on use and disposition of proceeds

(A)(1) With respect to property ordered forfeited under section 2923.32 of the Revised Code, with respect to any fine or civil penalty imposed in any criminal or civil proceeding under section 2923.32 or 2923.34 of the Revised Code, and with respect to any fine imposed for a violation of section 2923.01 of the Revised Code for conspiracy to violate section 2923.32 of the Revised Code, the court, upon petition of the prosecuting attorney, may do any of the following:

(a) Authorize the prosecuting attorney to settle claims;

(b) Award compensation to persons who provide information that results in a forfeiture, fine, or civil penalty under section 2923.32 or 2923.34 of the Revised Code;

(c) Grant petitions for mitigation or remission of forfeiture, fines, or civil penalties, or restore forfeited property, imposed fines, or imposed civil penalties to persons injured by the violation;

(d) Take any other action to protect the rights of innocent persons that is in the interest of justice and that is consistent with the purposes of sections 2923.31 to 2923.36 of the Revised Code.

(2) The court shall maintain an accurate record of the actions it takes under division (A)(1) of this section with respect to the property ordered forfeited or the fine or civil penalty. The record is a public record open for inspection under section 149.43 of the Revised Code.

(B)(1) After the application of division (A) of this section, any person who prevails in a civil action pursuant to section 2923.34

of the Revised Code has a right to any property, or the proceeds of any property, criminally forfeited to the state pursuant to section 2923.32 of the Revised Code or against which any fine under that section or civil penalty under division (I) of section 2923.34 of the Revised Code may be imposed.

The right of any person who prevails in a civil action pursuant to section 2923.34 of the Revised Code, other than a prosecuting attorney performing official duties under that section, to forfeited property, property against which fines and civil penalties may be imposed, and the proceeds of that property is superior to any right of the state, a municipal corporation, or a county to the property or the proceeds of the property, if the civil action is brought within one hundred eighty days after the entry of a sentence of forfeiture or a fine pursuant to section 2923.32 of the Revised Code or the entry of a civil penalty pursuant to division (I) of section 2923.34 of the Revised Code.

The right is limited to the total value of the treble damages, civil penalties, attorney's fees, and costs awarded to the prevailing party in an action pursuant to section 2923.34 of the Revised Code, less any restitution received by the person.

(2) If the aggregate amount of claims of persons who have prevailed in a civil action pursuant to section 2923.34 of the Revised Code against any one defendant is greater than the total value of the treble fines, civil penalties, and forfeited property paid by the person against whom the actions were brought, all of the persons who brought their actions within one hundred eighty days after the entry of a sentence or disposition of forfeiture or a fine pursuant to section 2923.32 of the Revised Code or the entry of a civil penalty pursuant to division (I) of section 2923.34 of the Revised Code, first shall receive a pro rata share of the total amount of the fines, civil penalties, and forfeited property. After the persons who brought their actions within the specified one-hundred-eighty-day period have satisfied their claims out of the fines, civil penalties, and forfeited property, all other persons who prevailed in civil actions pursuant to section 2923.34 of the Revised Code shall receive a pro rata share of the total amount of the fines, civil penalties, and forfeited property that remains in the custody of the law enforcement agency or in the corrupt activity investigation and prosecution fund.

(C)(1) Subject to divisions (A) and (B) of this section and notwithstanding any contrary provision of section 2933.41 of the Revised Code, the prosecuting attorney shall order the disposal of property ordered forfeited in any proceeding under sections 2923.32 and 2923.34 of the Revised Code as soon as feasible, making due provisions for the rights of innocent persons, by any of the following methods:

(a) Transfer to any person who prevails in a civil action pursuant to section 2923.34 of the Revised Code, subject to the limit set forth in division (B)(1) of this section;

(b) Public sale;

(c) Transfer to a state governmental agency for official use;

(d) Sale or transfer to an innocent person;

(e) If the property is contraband and is not needed for evidence in any pending criminal or civil proceeding, pursuant to section 2933.41 or any other applicable section of the Revised Code.

(2) Any interest in personal or real property not disposed of pursuant to this division and not exercisable by, or transferable for value to, the state shall expire and shall not revert to the person found guilty of or adjudicated a delinquent child for a violation of section 2923.32 of the Revised Code. No person found guilty of or adjudicated a delinquent child for a violation of that section and no person acting in concert with a person found guilty of or adjudicated a delinquent child for a violation of that section is eligible to purchase forfeited property from the state.

(3) Upon application of a person, other than the defendant, the adjudicated delinquent child, or a person acting in concert with or on behalf of either the defendant or the adjudicated delinquent child, the court may restrain or stay the disposal of the property pursuant to this division pending the conclusion of any appeal of the criminal case or delinquency case giving rise to the forfeiture or pending the determination of the validity of a claim to or interest in the property pursuant to division (E) of section 2923.32 of the Revised Code, if the applicant demonstrates that proceeding with the disposal of the property will result in irreparable injury, harm, or loss to the applicant.

(4) The prosecuting attorney shall maintain an accurate record of each item of property disposed of pursuant to this division, which record shall include the date on which each item came into the prosecuting attorney's custody, the manner and date of disposition, and, if applicable, the name of the person who received the item. The record shall not identify or enable the identification of the individual officer who seized the property, and the record is a public record open for inspection under section 149.43 of the Revised Code.

Each prosecuting attorney who disposes in any calendar year of any item of property pursuant to this division shall prepare a report covering the calendar year that cumulates all of the information contained in all of the records kept by the prosecuting attorney pursuant to this division for that calendar year and shall send the cumulative report, no later than the first day of March in the calendar year following the calendar year covered by the report, to the attorney general. Each report received by the attorney general is a public record open for inspection under section 149.43 of the Revised Code. Not later than the fifteenth day of April in the calendar year following the calendar year covered by the reports, the attorney general shall send to the president of the senate and the speaker of the house of representatives a written notification that does all of the following:

(a) Indicates that the attorney general has received from prosecuting attorneys reports of the type described in this division that cover the previous calendar year and indicates that the reports were received under this division;

(b) Indicates that the reports are open for inspection under section 149.43 of the Revised Code;

(c) Indicates that the attorney general will provide a copy of any or all of the reports to the president of the senate or the speaker of the house of representatives upon request.

(D)(1)(a) Ten per cent of the proceeds of all property ordered forfeited by a juvenile court pursuant to section 2923.32 of the Revised Code shall be applied to one or more alcohol and drug addiction treatment programs that are certified by the department of alcohol and drug addiction services under section 3793.06 of the Revised Code and that are specified in the order of forfeiture. A juvenile court shall not specify an alcohol or drug addiction treatment program in the order of forfeiture unless the program is a certified alcohol and drug addiction treatment program and, except as provided in division (D)(1)(a) of this section, unless the program is located in the county in which the court that orders the forfeiture is located or in a contiguous county. If no certified alcohol and drug addiction treatment program is located in any of those counties, the juvenile court may specify in the order a certified alcohol and drug addiction treatment program located anywhere within this state. The remaining ninety per cent of the proceeds shall be disposed of as provided in divisions (D)(1)(b) and (D)(2) of this section.

All of the proceeds of all property ordered forfeited by a court other than a juvenile court pursuant to section 2923.32 of the Revised Code shall be disposed of as provided in divisions (D)(1)(b) and (D)(2) of this section.

(b) The remaining proceeds of all property ordered forfeited pursuant to section 2923.32 of the Revised Code, after compliance with division (D)(1)(a) of this section when that division is applicable, and all fines and civil penalties imposed pursuant to sections 2923.32 and 2923.34 of the Revised Code shall be deposited into the state treasury and credited to the corrupt activity investigation and prosecution fund, which is hereby created.

(2) The proceeds, fines, and penalties credited to the corrupt activity investigation and prosecution fund pursuant to division (D)(1) of this section shall be disposed of in the following order:

(a) To a civil plaintiff in an action brought within the one-hundred-eighty-day time period specified in division (B)(1) of this section, subject to the limit set forth in that division;

(b) To the payment of the fees and costs of the forfeiture and sale, including expenses of seizure, maintenance, and custody of the property pending its disposition, advertising, and court costs;

(c) Except as otherwise provided in division (D)(2)(c) of this section, the remainder shall be paid to the law enforcement trust fund of the prosecuting attorney that is established pursuant to division (D)(1)(c) of section 2933.43 of the Revised Code and to the law enforcement trust fund of the county sheriff that is established pursuant to that division if the county sheriff substantially conducted the investigation, to the law enforcement trust fund of a municipal corporation that is established pursuant to that division if its police department substantially conducted the investigation, to the law enforcement trust fund of a township that is established pursuant to that division if the investigation was substantially conducted by a township police department, township police district police force, or office of a township constable, or to the law enforcement trust fund of a park district created pursuant to section 511.18 or 1545.01 of the Revised Code that is established pursuant to that division if the investigation was substantially conducted by its park district police force or law enforcement department. The prosecuting attorney may decline to accept any of the remaining proceeds, fines, and penalties, and, if the prosecuting attorney so declines, they shall be applied to the fund described in division (D)(2)(c) of this section that relates to the appropriate law enforcement agency that substantially conducted the investigation.

If the state highway patrol substantially conducted the investigation, the director of budget and management shall transfer the remaining proceeds, fines, and penalties to the state highway patrol for deposit into the state highway patrol contraband, forfeiture, and other fund that is created by division (D)(1)(c) of section 2933.43 of the Revised Code. If the department of taxation substantially conducted the investigation, the director, shall transfer the remaining proceeds, fines, and penalties to the department for deposit into the department of taxation enforcement fund. If the state board of pharmacy substantially conducted the investigation, the director shall transfer the remaining proceeds, fines, and penalties to the board for deposit into the board of pharmacy drug law enforcement fund that is created by division (B)(1) of section 4729.65 of the Revised Code. If a state law enforcement agency, other than the state highway patrol, the department of taxation, or the state board of pharmacy, substantially conducted the investigation, the director shall transfer the remaining proceeds, fines, and penalties to the treasurer of state for deposit into the peace officer training commission fund.

The remaining proceeds, fines, and penalties that are paid to a law enforcement trust fund or that are deposited into the state highway patrol contraband, forfeiture, and other fund, the department of taxation enforcement fund, the board of pharmacy drug law enforcement fund, or the peace officer training commission fund pursuant to division (D)(2)(c) of this section shall be allocated, used, and expended only in accordance with division (D)(1)(c) of section 2933.43 of the Revised Code, only in accordance with a written internal control policy adopted under division (D)(3) of that section, and, if applicable, only in accordance with division (B) of section 4729.65 of the Revised Code. The annual reports that pertain to the funds and that are required by divisions (D)(1)(c) and (3)(b) of section 2933.43 of the Revised Code also shall address the remaining proceeds, fines, and penalties that are paid or deposited into the funds pursuant to division (D)(2)(c) of this section.

(3) If more than one law enforcement agency substantially conducted the investigation, the court ordering the forfeiture shall equitably divide the remaining proceeds, fines, and penalties among the law enforcement agencies that substantially conducted the investigation, in the manner described in division (D)(2) of section 2933.43 of the Revised Code for the equitable division of contraband proceeds and forfeited moneys. The equitable shares of the proceeds, fines, and penalties so determined by the court shall be paid or deposited into the appropriate funds specified in division (D)(2)(c) of this section.

(E) As used in this section, "law enforcement agency" includes, but is not limited to, the state board of pharmacy and the department of taxation.

(2003 H 95, eff. 9–26–03; 1998 S 164, eff. 1–15–98; 1996 H 670, eff. 12–2–96; 1995 H 1, eff. 1–1–96; 1993 H 152, eff. 7–1–93; 1992 S 174; 1990 S 258, H 266, H 261, H 215; 1986 S 74; 1985 H 5)

2923.36 Corrupt activity lien notice

(A) Upon the institution of any criminal proceeding charging a violation of section 2923.32 of the Revised Code, the filing of any complaint, indictment, or information in juvenile court alleging a violation of that section as a delinquent act, or the institution of any civil proceeding under section 2923.32 or 2923.34 of the Revised Code, the state, at any time during the pendency of the proceeding, may file a corrupt activity lien notice with the county recorder of any county in which property subject to forfeiture may be located. No fee shall be required for filing the notice. The recorder immediately shall record the notice pursuant to section 317.08 of the Revised Code.

(B) A corrupt activity lien notice shall be signed by the prosecuting attorney who files the lien. The notice shall set forth all of the following information:

(1) The name of the person against whom the proceeding has been brought. The prosecuting attorney may specify in the notice any aliases, names, or fictitious names under which the person may be known. The prosecuting attorney also may specify any corporation, partnership, or other entity in which the person has an interest subject to forfeiture under section 2923.32 of the Revised Code and shall describe in the notice the person's interest in the corporation, partnership, or other entity.

(2) If known to the prosecuting attorney, the present residence and business addresses of the person or names set forth in the notice;

(3) A statement that a criminal or delinquency proceeding for a violation of section 2923.32 of the Revised Code or a civil proceeding under section 2923.32 or 2923.34 of the Revised Code has been brought against the person named in the notice, the name of the county in which the proceeding has been brought, and the case number of the proceeding;

(4) A statement that the notice is being filed pursuant to this section;

(5) The name and address of the prosecuting attorney filing the notice;

(6) A description of the real or personal property subject to the notice and of the interest in that property of the person named in the notice, to the extent the property and the interest of the person in it reasonably is known at the time the proceeding is instituted or at the time the notice is filed.

(C) A corrupt activity lien notice shall apply only to one person and, to the extent applicable, any aliases, fictitious names, or other names, including names of corporations, partnerships, or other entities, to the extent permitted in this section. A separate corrupt activity lien notice is required to be filed for any other person.

(D) Within seven days after the filing of each corrupt activity lien notice, the prosecuting attorney who files the notice shall furnish to the person named in the notice by certified mail, return receipt requested, to the last known business or residential address of the person, a copy of the recorded notice with a notation on it of any county in which the notice has been recorded. The failure of the prosecuting attorney to furnish a copy of the notice under this section shall not invalidate or otherwise affect the corrupt activity lien notice when the prosecuting attorney did not know and could not reasonably ascertain the address of the person entitled to notice.

After receipt of a copy of the notice under this division, the person named in the notice may petition the court to authorize the person to post a surety bond in lieu of the lien or to otherwise modify the lien as the interests of justice may require. The bond shall be in an amount equal to the value of the property reasonably known to be subject to the notice and conditioned on the payment of any judgment and costs ordered in an action pursuant to section 2923.32 or 2923.34 of the Revised Code up to the value of the bond.

(E) From the date of filing of a corrupt activity lien notice, the notice creates a lien in favor of the state on any personal or real property or any beneficial interest in the property located in the county in which the notice is filed that then or subsequently is owned by the person named in the notice or under any of the names set forth in the notice.

The lien created in favor of the state is superior and prior to the interest of any other person in the personal or real property or beneficial interest in the property, if the interest is acquired subsequent to the filing of the notice.

(F)(1) Notwithstanding any law or rule to the contrary, in conjunction with any civil proceeding brought pursuant to section 2923.34 of the Revised Code, the prosecuting attorney may file in any county, without prior court order, a lis pendens pursuant to sections 2703.26 and 2703.27 of the Revised Code. In such a case, any person acquiring an interest in the subject property or beneficial interest in the property, if the property interest is acquired subsequent to the filing of the lis pendens, shall take the property or interest subject to the civil proceeding and any subsequent judgment.

(2) If a corrupt activity lien notice has been filed, the prosecuting attorney may name as a defendant in the lis pendens, in addition to the person named in the notice, any person acquiring an interest in the personal or real property or beneficial interest in the property subsequent to the filing of the notice. If a judgment of forfeiture is entered in the criminal or delinquency proceeding pursuant to section 2923.32 of the Revised Code in favor of the state, the interest of any person in the property that was acquired subsequent to the filing of the notice shall be subject to the notice and judgment of forfeiture.

(G) Upon a final judgment of forfeiture in favor of the state pursuant to section 2923.32 of the Revised Code, title of the state to the forfeited property shall do either of the following:

(1) In the case of real property, or a beneficial interest in it, relate back to the date of filing of the corrupt activity lien notice in the county where the property or interest is located. If no corrupt activity lien notice was filed, title of the state relates back to the date of the filing of any lis pendens under division (F) of this section in the records of the county recorder of the county in which the real property or beneficial interest is located. If no corrupt activity lien notice or lis pendens was filed, title of the state relates back to the date of the recording of the final judgment of forfeiture in the records of the county recorder of the county in which the real property or beneficial interest is located.

(2) In the case of personal property or a beneficial interest in it, relate back to the date on which the property or interest was seized by the state, or the date of filing of a corrupt activity lien notice in the county in which the property or beneficial interest is located. If the property was not seized and no corrupt activity lien notice was filed, title of the state relates back to the date of the recording of the final judgment of forfeiture in the county in which the personal property or beneficial interest is located.

(H) If personal or real property, or a beneficial interest in it, that is subject to forfeiture pursuant to section 2923.32 of the Revised Code is conveyed, alienated, disposed of, or otherwise rendered unavailable for forfeiture after the filing of either a corrupt activity lien notice, or a criminal or delinquency proceeding for a violation of section 2923.32 or a civil proceeding under section 2923.32 or 2923.34 of the Revised Code, whichever is earlier, the state may bring an action in any court of common pleas against the person named in the corrupt activity lien notice or the defendant in the criminal, delinquency, or civil proceeding to recover the value of the property or interest. The court shall enter final judgment against the person named in the notice or the defendant for an amount equal to the value of the property or interest together with investigative costs and attorney's fees incurred by the state in the action. If a civil proceeding is pending, an action pursuant to this section shall be filed in the court in which the proceeding is pending.

(I) If personal or real property, or a beneficial interest in it, that is subject to forfeiture pursuant to section 2923.32 of the Revised Code is alienated or otherwise transferred or disposed of after either the filing of a corrupt activity lien notice, or the filing of a criminal or delinquency proceeding for a violation of section 2923.32 or a civil proceeding under section 2923.32 or 2923.34 of the Revised Code, whichever is earlier, the transfer or disposal is fraudulent as to the state and the state shall have all the rights granted a creditor under Chapter 1336. of the Revised Code.

(J) No trustee, who acquires actual knowledge that a corrupt activity lien notice, a criminal or delinquency proceeding for a violation of section 2923.32 or a civil proceeding under section 2923.32 or 2923.34 of the Revised Code has been filed against any person for whom the trustee holds legal or record title to personal or real property, shall recklessly fail to furnish promptly to the prosecuting attorney all of the following:

(1) The name and address of the person, as known to the trustee;

(2) The name and address, as known to the trustee, of all other persons for whose benefit the trustee holds title to the property;

(3) If requested by the prosecuting attorney, a copy of the trust agreement or other instrument under which the trustee holds title to the property.

Any trustee who fails to comply with this division is guilty of failure to provide corrupt activity lien information, a misdemeanor of the first degree.

(K) If a trustee transfers title to personal or real property after a corrupt activity lien notice is filed against the property, the lien is filed in the county in which the property is located, and the lien names a person who holds a beneficial interest in the property, the trustee, if the trustee has actual notice of the notice, shall be liable to the state for the greater of the following:

(1) The proceeds received directly by the person named in the notice as a result of the transfer;

(2) The proceeds received by the trustee as a result of the transfer and distributed to the person named in the notice;

(3) The fair market value of the interest of the person named in the notice in the property transferred.

However, if the trustee transfers property for at least its fair market value and holds the proceeds that otherwise would be paid or distributed to the beneficiary, or at the direction of the beneficiary or the beneficiary's designee, the liability of the trustee shall not exceed the amount of the proceeds held by the trustee.

(L) The filing of a corrupt activity lien notice does not constitute a lien on the record title to personal or real property owned by the trustee, except to the extent the trustee is named in the notice.

The prosecuting attorney for the county may bring a civil action in any court of common pleas to recover from the trustee the amounts set forth in division (H) of this section. The county may recover investigative costs and attorney's fees incurred by the prosecuting attorney.

(M)(1) This section does not apply to any transfer by a trustee under a court order, unless the order is entered in an action between the trustee and the beneficiary.

(2) Unless the trustee has actual knowledge that a person owning a beneficial interest in the trust is named in a corrupt activity lien notice or otherwise is a defendant in a civil proceeding brought pursuant to section 2923.34 of the Revised Code, this section does not apply to either of the following:

(a) Any transfer by a trustee required under the terms of any trust agreement, if the agreement is a matter of public record before the filing of any corrupt activity lien notice;

(b) Any transfer by a trustee to all of the persons who own a beneficial interest in the trust.

(N) The filing of a corrupt activity lien notice does not affect the use to which personal or real property, or a beneficial interest in it, that is owned by the person named in the notice may be put or the right of the person to receive any proceeds resulting from the use and ownership, but not the sale, of the property, until a judgment of forfeiture is entered.

(O) The term of a corrupt activity lien notice is five years from the date the notice is filed, unless a renewal notice has been filed by the prosecuting attorney of the county in which the property or interest is located. The term of any renewal of a corrupt activity lien notice granted by the court is five years from the date of its filing. A corrupt activity lien notice may be renewed any number of times while a criminal or civil proceeding under section 2923.32 or 2923.34 of the Revised Code, or an appeal from either type of proceeding, is pending.

(P) The prosecuting attorney who files the corrupt activity lien notice may terminate, in whole or part, any corrupt activity lien notice or release any personal or real property or beneficial interest in the property upon any terms that the prosecuting attorney determines are appropriate. Any termination or release shall be filed by the prosecuting attorney with each county recorder with whom the notice was filed. No fee shall be imposed for the filing.

(Q)(1) If no civil proceeding has been brought by the prosecuting attorney pursuant to section 2923.34 of the Revised Code against the person named in the corrupt activity lien notice, the acquittal in a criminal or delinquency proceeding for a violation of section 2923.32 of the Revised Code of the person named in the notice or the dismissal of a criminal or delinquency proceeding for such a violation against the person named in the notice terminates the notice. In such a case, the filing of the notice has no effect.

(2) If a civil proceeding has been brought pursuant to section 2923.34 of the Revised Code with respect to any property that is the subject of a corrupt activity lien notice and if the criminal or delinquency proceeding brought against the person named in the notice for a violation of section 2923.32 of the Revised Code has been dismissed or the person named in the notice has been acquitted in the criminal or delinquency proceeding for such a violation, the notice shall continue for the duration of the civil proceeding and any appeals from the civil proceeding, except that it shall not continue any longer than the term of the notice as determined pursuant to division (O) of this section.

(3) If no civil proceeding brought pursuant to section 2923.34 of the Revised Code then is pending against the person named in a corrupt activity lien notice, any person so named may bring an action against the prosecuting attorney who filed the notice, in the county where it was filed, seeking a release of the property subject to the notice or termination of the notice. In such a case, the court of common pleas promptly shall set a date for hearing, which shall be not less than five nor more than ten days after the action is filed. The order and a copy of the complaint shall be served on the prosecuting attorney within three days after the action is filed. At the hearing, the court shall take evidence as to whether any personal or real property, or beneficial interest in it, that is owned by the person bringing the action is covered by the notice or otherwise is subject to forfeiture. If the person bringing the action shows by a preponderance of the evidence that the notice does not apply to the person or that any personal or real property, or beneficial interest in it, that is owned by the person is not subject to forfeiture, the court shall enter a judgment terminating the notice or releasing the personal or real property or beneficial interest from the notice.

At a hearing, the court may release from the notice any property or beneficial interest upon the posting of security, by the person against whom the notice was filed, in an amount equal to the value of the property or beneficial interest owned by the person.

(4) The court promptly shall enter an order terminating a corrupt activity lien notice or releasing any personal or real property or beneficial interest in the property, if a sale of the property or beneficial interest is pending and the filing of the notice prevents the sale. However, the proceeds of the sale shall be deposited with the clerk of the court, subject to the further order of the court.

(R) Notwithstanding any provision of this section, any person who has perfected a security interest in personal or real property or a beneficial interest in the property for the payment of an enforceable debt or other similar obligation prior to the filing of a corrupt activity lien notice or a lis pendens in reference to the property or interest may foreclose on the property or interest as otherwise provided by law. The foreclosure, insofar as practical, shall be made so that it otherwise will not interfere with a forfeiture under section 2923.32 of the Revised Code.

(2000 S 179, § 3, eff. 1–1–02; 1990 H 506, eff. 9–28–90; 1990 H 266; 1989 H 190; 1985 H 5)

CRIMINAL GANG ACTIVITY

2923.41 Definitions

As used in sections 2923.41 to 2923.47 of the Revised Code:

(A) "Criminal gang" means an ongoing formal or informal organization, association, or group of three or more persons to which all of the following apply:

(1) It has as one of its primary activities the commission of one or more of the offenses listed in division (B) of this section.

(2) It has a common name or one or more common, identifying signs, symbols, or colors.

(3) The persons in the organization, association, or group individually or collectively engage in or have engaged in a pattern of criminal gang activity.

(B)(1) "Pattern of criminal gang activity" means, subject to division (B)(2) of this section, that persons in the criminal gang have committed, attempted to commit, conspired to commit, been complicitors in the commission of, or solicited, coerced, or intimidated another to commit, attempt to commit, conspire to commit, or be in complicity in the commission of two or more of any of the following offenses:

(a) A felony or an act committed by a juvenile that would be a felony if committed by an adult;

(b) An offense of violence or an act committed by a juvenile that would be an offense of violence if committed by an adult;

(c) A violation of section 2907.04, 2909.06, 2911.211, 2917.04, 2919.23, or 2919.24 of the Revised Code, section 2921.04 or 2923.16 of the Revised Code, section 2925.03 of the Revised Code if the offense is trafficking in marihuana, or section 2927.12 of the Revised Code.

(2) There is a "pattern of criminal gang activity" if all of the following apply with respect to the offenses that are listed in division (B)(1)(a), (b), or (c) of this section and that persons in the criminal gang committed, attempted to commit, conspired to commit, were in complicity in committing, or solicited, coerced, or intimidated another to commit, attempt to commit, conspire to commit, or be in complicity in committing:

(a) At least one of the two or more offenses is a felony.

(b) At least one of those two or more offenses occurs on or after the effective date of this section.

(c) The last of those two or more offenses occurs within five years after at least one of those offenses.

(d) The two or more offenses are committed on separate occasions or by two or more persons.

(C) "Criminal conduct" means the commission of, an attempt to commit, a conspiracy to commit, complicity in the commission of, or solicitation, coercion, or intimidation of another to commit, attempt to commit, conspire to commit, or be in complicity in the commission of an offense listed in division (B)(1)(a), (b), or (c) of this section or an act that is committed by a juvenile and that would be an offense, an attempt to commit an offense, a conspiracy to commit an offense, complicity in the commission of, or solicitation, coercion, or intimidation of another to commit, attempt to commit, conspire to commit, or be in complicity in the commission of an offense listed in division (B)(1)(a), (b), or (c) of this section if committed by an adult.

(D) "Juvenile" means a person who is under eighteen years of age.

(E) "Law enforcement agency" includes, but is not limited to, the state board of pharmacy and the office of a prosecutor.

(F) "Prosecutor" has the same meaning as in section 2935.01 of the Revised Code.

(G) "Financial institution" means a bank, credit union, savings and loan association, or a licensee or registrant under Chapter 1321. of the Revised Code.

(H) "Property" includes both of the following:

(1) Real property, including, but not limited to, things growing on, affixed to, and found in the real property;

(2) Tangible and intangible personal property, including, but not limited to, rights, privileges, interests, claims, and securities.

(I) "Firearms" and "dangerous ordnance" have the same meanings as in section 2923.11 of the Revised Code.

(J) "Computers," "computer networks," "computer systems," and "computer software" have the same meanings as in section 2913.01 of the Revised Code.

(K) "Vehicle" has the same meaning as in section 4501.01 of the Revised Code.

(1998 H 2, eff. 1–1–99)

2923.42 Criminal gang activity; disposition of fine moneys; report of law enforcement agencies

(A) No person who actively participates in a criminal gang, with knowledge that the criminal gang engages in or has engaged in a pattern of criminal gang activity, shall purposely promote, further, or assist any criminal conduct, as defined in division (C) of section 2923.41 of the Revised Code, or shall purposely commit or engage in any act that constitutes criminal conduct, as defined in division (C) of section 2923.41 of the Revised Code.

(B) Whoever violates this section is guilty of participating in a criminal gang, a felony of the second degree.

(C)(1) Notwithstanding any contrary provision of any section of the Revised Code, the clerk of the court shall pay any fine imposed for a violation of this section pursuant to division (A) of section 2929.18 of the Revised Code to the county, township, municipal corporation, park district, as created pursuant to section 511.18 or 1545.04 of the Revised Code, or state law enforcement agencies in this state that primarily were responsible for or involved in making the arrest of, and in prosecuting, the offender. However, the clerk shall not pay a fine so imposed to a law enforcement agency unless the agency has adopted a written internal control policy under division (C)(2) of this section that addresses the use of the fine moneys that it receives. Each agency shall use the fines so paid in accordance with the written internal control policy adopted by the recipient agency under division (C)(2) of this section to subsidize the agency's law enforcement efforts that pertain to criminal gangs.

(2)(a) Prior to receiving any fine moneys under division (C)(1) of this section or division (B)(5) of section 2923.44 of the Revised Code, a law enforcement agency shall adopt a written internal control policy that addresses the agency's use and disposition of all fine moneys so received and that provides for the keeping of detailed financial records of the receipts of those fine moneys, the general types of expenditures made out of those fine moneys, and the specific amount of each general type of expenditure. The policy shall not provide for or permit the identification of any specific expenditure that is made in an ongoing investigation. All financial records of the receipts of those fine moneys, the general types of expenditures made out of those fine moneys, and the specific amount of each general type of expenditure by an agency are public records open for inspection under section 149.43 of the Revised Code. Additionally, a written internal control policy adopted under division (C)(2)(a) of this section is a public record open for inspection under section 149.43 of the Revised Code, and the agency that adopted the policy shall comply with it.

(b) Each law enforcement agency that receives in any calendar year any fine moneys under division (C)(1) of this section or division (B)(5) of section 2923.44 of the Revised Code shall prepare a report covering the calendar year that cumulates all of the information contained in all of the public financial records kept by the agency pursuant to division (C)(2)(a) of this section for that calendar year and shall send a copy of the cumulative report, no later than the first day of March in the calendar year following the calendar year covered by the report, to the attorney general. Each report received by the attorney general is a public record open for inspection under section 149.43 of the Revised Code. Not later than the fifteenth day of April in the calendar year in which the reports are received, the attorney general shall send the president of the senate and the speaker of the house of representatives a written notice that does all of the following:

(i) Indicates that the attorney general has received from law enforcement agencies reports of the type described in division (C)(2)(b) of this section that cover the previous calendar year and indicates that the reports were received under division (C)(2)(b) of this section;

(ii) Indicates that the reports are open for inspection under section 149.43 of the Revised Code;

(iii) Indicates that the attorney general will provide a copy of any or all reports to the president of the senate or the speaker of the house upon request.

(D) A prosecution for a violation of this section does not preclude a prosecution of a violation of any other section of the Revised Code. One or more acts, a series of acts, or a course of behavior that can be prosecuted under this section or any other section of the Revised Code may be prosecuted under this section, the other section of the Revised Code, or both sections.

(1998 H 2, eff. 1–1–99)

2923.43 Use of property for gang activity; subject to abatement

Any building, premises, or real estate, including vacant land, that is used or occupied by a criminal gang on more than two occasions within a one-year period to engage in a pattern of criminal gang activity constitutes a nuisance subject to abatement pursuant to sections 3767.01 to 3767.11 of the Revised Code.

(1998 H 2, eff. 1–1–99)

2923.44 Criminal forfeiture of property; proceedings; claims of interest

(A)(1) In accordance with division (B) of this section, a person who is convicted of or pleads guilty to a violation of section 2923.42 of the Revised Code, and a juvenile who is found by a juvenile court to be a delinquent child for an act committed in violation of section 2923.42 of the Revised Code, loses any right to the possession of property and forfeits to the state any right, title, and interest the person may have in that property if either of the following applies:

(a) The property constitutes, or is derived directly or indirectly from, any proceeds that the person obtained directly or indirectly from the commission of the violation of section 2923.42 of the Revised Code.

(b) The property was used or intended to be used in any manner to commit, or to facilitate the commission of, the violation of section 2923.42 of the Revised Code.

(2) All right, title, and interest of a person in property described in division (A)(1) of this section vests in the state upon the person's commission of the violation of section 2923.42 of the Revised Code of which the person is convicted or to which the person pleads guilty and that is the basis of the forfeiture, or upon the juvenile's commission of the act that is a violation of section 2923.42 of the Revised Code, that is the basis of the juvenile being found to be a delinquent child, and that is the basis of the forfeiture. Subject to divisions (F)(3)(b) and (5)(b) and (G)(2) of this section, if any right, title, or interest in property is vested in this state under division (A)(2) of this section and subsequently is transferred to a person other than the adult offender or the delinquent child who forfeits the right, title, or interest in the property under division (A)(1) of this section, then, in accordance with division (B) of this section, the right, title, or interest in the property may be the subject of a special verdict of forfeiture and, after any special verdict of forfeiture, shall be ordered forfeited to this state, unless the transferee establishes in a hearing held pursuant to division (F) of this section that the transferee is a bona fide purchaser for value of the right, title, or interest in the property and that, at the time of its purchase, the transferee was reasonably without cause to believe that it was subject to forfeiture under this section.

(3) The provisions of section 2923.45 of the Revised Code that relate to the forfeiture of any right, title, or interest in property associated with a violation of section 2923.42 of the Revised Code pursuant to a civil action to obtain a civil forfeiture do not apply to the forfeiture of any right, title, or interest in property described in division (A)(1) of this section that occurs pursuant to division (B) of this section upon a person's conviction of or guilty plea to a violation of section 2923.42 of the Revised Code or upon a juvenile being found by a juvenile court to be a delinquent child for an act that is a violation of section 2923.42 of the Revised Code.

(4) Nothing in this section precludes a financial institution that has or purports to have a security interest in or lien on property described in division (A)(1) of this section from commencing a civil action or taking other appropriate legal action in connection with the property prior to its disposition in accordance with section 2923.46 of the Revised Code for the purpose of obtaining possession of the property in order to foreclose or otherwise enforce the security interest or lien. A financial institution may commence a civil action or take other appropriate legal action for that purpose prior to the disposition of the property in accordance with section 2923.46 of the Revised Code, even if a prosecution for a violation of section 2923.42 of the Revised Code or a delinquent child proceeding for an act that is a violation of section 2923.42 of the Revised Code has been or could be commenced, even if the property is or could be the subject of an order of forfeiture issued under division (B)(5) of this section, and even if the property has been seized or is subject to seizure pursuant to division (D) or (E) of this section.

If a financial institution commences a civil action or takes any other appropriate legal action as described in division (A)(4) of this section, if the financial institution subsequently causes the sale of the property prior to its seizure pursuant to division (D) or (E) of this section and its disposition pursuant to section 2923.46 of the Revised Code, and if the person responsible for the conduct of the sale has actual knowledge of the commencement of a prosecution for a violation of section 2923.42 of the Revised Code or of a delinquent child proceeding for an act that is a violation of section 2923.42 of the Revised Code, actual knowledge of a pending forfeiture proceeding under division (B) of this section, or actual knowledge of an order of forfeiture issued under division (B)(5) of this section, then the person responsible for the conduct of the sale shall dispose of the proceeds of the sale in the following order:

(a) First, to the payment of the costs of the sale and to the payment of the costs incurred by law enforcement agencies and financial institutions in connection with the seizure of, storage of, maintenance of, and provision of security for the property. As used in this division, "costs" of a financial institution do not include attorney's fees incurred by that institution in connection with the property.

(b) Second, the remaining proceeds of the sale after compliance with division (A)(4)(a) of this section, to the payment in the order of priority of the security interests and liens of valid security interests and liens pertaining to the property that, at the time of the vesting in the state under division (A)(2) of this section of the right, title, or interest of the adult or juvenile, are held by known secured parties and lienholders;

(c) Third, the remaining proceeds of the sale after compliance with division (A)(4)(b) of this section, to the court that has or would have jurisdiction in a prosecution for a violation of section 2923.42 of the Revised Code or a delinquent child proceeding for an act that is a violation of section 2923.42 of the Revised Code for disposition in accordance with section 2923.46 of the Revised Code.

(B)(1) A criminal forfeiture of any right, title, or interest in property described in division (A)(1) of this section is precluded unless one of the following applies:

(a) The indictment, count in the indictment, or information charging the violation of section 2923.42 of the Revised Code specifies the nature of the right, title, or interest of the alleged offender in the property described in division (A)(1) of this section that is potentially subject to forfeiture under this section, or a description of the property of the alleged offender that is potentially subject to forfeiture under this section, to the extent the right, title, or interest in the property or the property reasonably is known at the time of the filing of the indictment or information; or the complaint, indictment, or information charging a juvenile with being a delinquent child for the commission of an act that is a violation of section 2923.42 of the Revised Code specifies the nature of the right, title, or interest of the juvenile in the property described in division (A)(1) of this section that is potentially subject to forfeiture under this section, or a description of the property of the juvenile that is potentially subject to forfeiture under this section, to the extent the right, title, or interest in the property or the property reasonably is known at the time of the filing of the complaint, indictment, or information.

(b) The property in question was not reasonably foreseen to be subject to forfeiture under this section at the time of the filing of the indictment, information, or complaint, the prosecuting attorney gave prompt notice to the alleged offender or juvenile of that property when it was discovered to be subject to forfeiture under this section, and a verdict of forfeiture described in division (B)(3) of this section requires the forfeiture of that property.

(2) The specifications described in division (B)(1) of this section shall be stated at the end of the body of the indictment, count in the indictment, information, or complaint.

(3)(a) If a person is convicted of or pleads guilty to a violation of section 2923.42 of the Revised Code or a juvenile is found to be a delinquent child for an act that is a violation of section 2923.42 of the Revised Code, then a special proceeding shall be conducted in accordance with division (B)(3) of this section to determine whether any property described in division (B)(1)(a) or (b) of this section will be the subject of an order of forfeiture under this section. Except as otherwise provided in division (B)(3)(b) of this section, the jury in the criminal action, the judge in the delinquent child action, or, if the criminal action was a nonjury action, the judge in that action shall hear and consider testimony and other evidence in the proceeding relative to whether any property described in division (B)(1)(a) or (b) of this section is subject to forfeiture under this section. If the jury or judge determines that the prosecuting attorney has established by a preponderance of the evidence that any property so described is subject to forfeiture under this section, the judge or juvenile judge shall render a verdict of forfeiture that specifically describes the right, title, or interest in property or the property that is subject to forfeiture under this section. The Rules of Evidence shall apply in the proceeding.

(b) If the trier of fact in a criminal action for a violation of section 2923.42 of the Revised Code was a jury, then, upon the filing of a motion by the person who was convicted of or pleaded guilty to the violation of section 2923.42 of the Revised Code, the determinations in the proceeding described in division (B)(3) of this section instead shall be made by the judge in the criminal action.

(4) In a criminal action for a violation of section 2923.42 of the Revised Code, if the trier of fact is a jury, the jury shall not be informed of any specification described in division (B)(1)(a) of this section or of any property described in that division or division (B)(1)(b) of this section prior to the alleged offender being convicted of or pleading guilty to the violation of section 2923.42 of the Revised Code.

(5)(a) If a verdict of forfeiture is entered pursuant to division (B)(3) of this section, then the court that imposes sentence upon a person who is convicted of or pleads guilty to a violation of section 2923.42 of the Revised Code, or the juvenile court that finds a juvenile to be a delinquent child for an act that is a violation of section 2923.42 of the Revised Code, in addition to any other sentence imposed upon the offender or order of disposition imposed upon the delinquent child, shall order that the offender or delinquent child forfeit to the state all of the offender's or delinquent child's right, title, and interest in the property described in division (A)(1) of this section. If a person is convicted of or pleads guilty to a violation of section 2923.42 of the Revised Code, or a juvenile is found by a juvenile court to be a delinquent child for an act that is a violation of section 2923.42 of the Revised Code, and derives profits or other proceeds from the offense or act, the court that imposes sentence or an order of disposition upon the offender or delinquent child, in lieu of any fine that the court is otherwise authorized or required to impose, may impose upon the offender or delinquent child a fine of not more than twice the gross profits or other proceeds so derived.

(b) Notwithstanding any contrary provision of the Revised Code, the clerk of the court shall pay all fines imposed pursuant to division (B)(5) of this section to the county, municipal corporation, township, park district created pursuant to section 511.18 or 1545.01 of the Revised Code, or state law enforcement agencies in this state that were primarily responsible for or involved in making the arrest of, and in prosecuting, the offender. However, the clerk shall not pay a fine so imposed to a law enforcement agency unless the agency has adopted a written internal control policy pursuant to division (C)(2) of section 2923.42 of the Revised Code that addresses the use of the fine moneys that it receives under division (B)(5) of this section and division (C)(1) of section 2923.42 of the Revised Code. The law enforcement agencies shall use the fines imposed and paid pursuant to division (B)(5) of this section to subsidize their efforts pertaining to criminal gangs, in accordance with the written internal control policy adopted by the recipient agency pursuant to division (C)(2) of section 2923.42 of the Revised Code.

(6) If any of the property that is described in division (A)(1) of this section and that is the subject of an order of forfeiture issued under division (B)(5) of this section, because of an act of the person who is convicted of or pleads guilty to the violation of section 2923.42 of the Revised Code that is the basis of the order of forfeiture or an act of the juvenile found by a juvenile court to be a delinquent child for an act that is a violation of section 2923.42 of the Revised Code and that is the basis of the forfeiture, cannot be located upon the exercise of due diligence, has been transferred to, sold to, or deposited with a third party, has been placed beyond the jurisdiction of the court, has been substantially diminished in value, or has been commingled with other property that cannot be divided without difficulty, the court that issues the order of forfeiture shall order the forfeiture of any other property of the offender or the delinquent child up to the value of any forfeited property described in division (B)(6) of this section.

(C) There shall be a rebuttable presumption that any right, title, or interest of a person in property described in division (A)(1) of this section is subject to forfeiture under division (B) of this section, if the state proves both of the following by a preponderance of the evidence:

(1) The right, title, or interest in the property was acquired by the offender or delinquent child during the period of the commission of the violation of section 2923.42 of the Revised Code, or within a reasonable time after that period.

(2) There is no likely source for the right, title, or interest in the property other than proceeds obtained from the commission of the violation of section 2923.42 of the Revised Code.

(D)(1) Upon the application of the prosecuting attorney who is prosecuting or has jurisdiction to prosecute the violation of section 2923.42 of the Revised Code, the court of common pleas or juvenile court of the county in which property subject to forfeiture under division (B) of this section is located, whichever is applicable, may issue a restraining order or injunction, an order requiring the execution of a satisfactory performance bond, or an order taking any other reasonable action necessary to preserve the availability of the property, at either of the following times:

(a) Upon the filing of an indictment, complaint, or information charging a person who has any right, title, or interest in the property with the commission of a violation of section 2923.42 of the Revised Code and alleging that the property with respect to which the order is sought will be subject to forfeiture under division (B) of this section if the person is convicted of or pleads guilty to the offense, or upon the filing of a complaint, indictment, or information alleging that a juvenile who has any right, title, or interest in the property is a delinquent child because of the commission of an act that is a violation of section 2923.42 of the Revised Code and alleging that the property with respect to which the order is sought will be subject to forfeiture under division (B) of this section if the juvenile is found to be a delinquent child because of the commission of that act;

(b) Except as provided in division (D)(3) of this section, prior to the filing of an indictment, complaint, or information charging a person who has any right, title, or interest in the property with the commission of a violation of section 2923.42 of the Revised Code, or prior to the filing of a complaint, indictment or information alleging that a juvenile who has any right, title, or interest in the property is a delinquent child because of the commission of an act that is a violation of section 2923.42 of the Revised Code, if, after notice is given to all persons known to have any right, title, or interest in the property and an opportunity to have a hearing on the order is given to those persons, the court determines both of the following:

(i) There is a substantial probability that the state will prevail on the issue of forfeiture and that failure to enter the order will result in the property subject to forfeiture being destroyed, removed from the jurisdiction of the court, or otherwise being made unavailable for forfeiture.

(ii) The need to preserve the availability of the property subject to forfeiture through the entry of the requested order outweighs the hardship on any party against whom the order is to be entered.

(2) Except as provided in division (D)(3) of this section, an order issued under division (D)(1) of this section is effective for not more than ninety days, unless extended by the court for good cause shown or unless an indictment, complaint, or information charging the commission of a violation of section 2923.42 of the Revised Code or a complaint, indictment, or information alleging that a juvenile is a delinquent child because of the commission of an act that is a violation of section 2923.42 of the Revised Code, is filed against any alleged adult offender or alleged delinquent child with any right, title, or interest in the property that is the subject of the order.

(3) A court may issue an order under division (D)(1)(b) of this section without giving notice or an opportunity for a hearing to persons known to have any right, title, or interest in property if the prosecuting attorney who is prosecuting or has jurisdiction to prosecute the violation of section 2923.42 of the Revised Code demonstrates that there is probable cause to believe that the property will be subject to forfeiture under division (B) of this section if a person with any right, title, or interest in the property is convicted of or pleads guilty to a violation of section 2923.42 of the Revised Code or a juvenile with any right, title, or interest in the property is found by a juvenile court to be a delinquent child for an act that is a violation of section 2923.42 of the Revised Code and that giving notice or an opportunity for a hearing to persons with any right, title, or interest in the property will jeopardize its availability for forfeiture. The order shall be a temporary order and shall expire not more than ten days after the date on which it is entered, unless it is extended for good cause shown or unless a person with any right, title, or interest in the property that is the subject of the order consents to an extension for a longer period. A hearing concerning an order issued under division (D)(3) of this section may be requested, and, if it is requested, the court shall hold the hearing at the earliest possible time prior to the expiration of the order.

(4) At any hearing held under division (D) of this section, the court may receive and consider evidence and information that is inadmissible under the Rules of Evidence. Each hearing held under division (D) of this section shall be recorded by shorthand, by stenotype, or by any other mechanical, electronic, or video recording device. If, as a result of a hearing under division (D) of this section, property would be seized, the recording of and any transcript of the recording of that hearing shall not be a public record for purposes of section 149.43 of the Revised Code until that property has been seized pursuant to division (D) of this section. Division (D)(4) of this section does not require, authorize, or permit the making available for inspection, or the copying, under section 149.43 of the Revised Code of any confidential law enforcement investigatory record or trial preparation record, as defined in that section.

(5) A prosecuting attorney or other law enforcement officer may request the court of common pleas of the county in which property subject to forfeiture under this section is located to issue a warrant authorizing the seizure of that property. The request shall be made in the same manner as provided for a search warrant. If the court determines that there is probable cause to believe that the property to be seized will be subject to forfeiture under this section when a person with any right, title, or interest in the property is convicted of or pleads guilty to a violation of section 2923.42 of the Revised Code or when a juvenile with any right, title, or interest in the property is found by a juvenile court to be a delinquent child for an act that is a violation of section 2923.42 of the Revised Code and if the court determines that any order issued under division (D)(1), (2), or (3) of this section may not be sufficient to ensure the availability of the property for forfeiture, the court shall issue a warrant authorizing the seizure of the property.

(E)(1) Upon the entry of an order of forfeiture under this section, the court shall order an appropriate law enforcement officer to seize all of the forfeited property upon the terms and conditions that the court determines are proper. In addition, upon the request of the prosecuting attorney who prosecuted the offense or act in violation of section 2923.42 of the Revised Code, the court shall enter any appropriate restraining orders or injunctions, require the execution of satisfactory performance bonds, appoint receivers, conservators, appraisers, accountants, or trustees, or take any other action to protect the interest of the state in the forfeited property. Any income accruing to or derived from property ordered forfeited under this section may be used to offset ordinary and necessary expenses related to the property that are required by law or that are necessary to protect the interest of the state or third parties.

After forfeited property is seized, the prosecuting attorney who prosecuted the offense or act in violation of section 2923.42 of the Revised Code shall direct its disposition in accordance with section 2923.46 of the Revised Code, making due provision for the rights of any innocent persons. Any right, title, or interest in property not exercisable by, or transferable for value to, the state shall expire and shall not revert to the offender whose conviction or plea of guilty or act as a delinquent child is the basis of the order of forfeiture. Neither the adult offender or delinquent child nor any person acting in concert with or on behalf of the adult offender or delinquent child is eligible to purchase forfeited property at any sale held pursuant to section 2923.46 of the Revised Code.

Upon the application of any person other than the adult offender or delinquent child whose right, title, or interest in the property is the subject of the order of forfeiture or any person acting in concert with or on behalf of the adult offender or delinquent child, the court may restrain or stay the sale or other disposition of the property pursuant to section 2923.46 of the Revised Code pending the conclusion of any appeal of the conviction or of the delinquent child adjudication that is the basis of the order of forfeiture, if the applicant demonstrates that proceeding with the sale or other disposition of the property will result in irreparable injury or loss to the applicant.

(2) With respect to property that is the subject of an order of forfeiture issued under this section, the court that issued the order, upon the petition of the prosecuting attorney who prosecuted the offense or act in violation of section 2923.42 of the Revised Code, may do any of the following:

(a) Grant petitions for mitigation or remission of forfeiture, restore forfeited property to victims of a violation of section

2923.42 of the Revised Code, or take any other action to protect the rights of innocent persons that is in the interest of justice and that is not inconsistent with this section;

(b) Compromise claims that arise under this section;

(c) Award compensation to persons who provide information resulting in a forfeiture under this section;

(d) Direct the disposition by the prosecuting attorney who prosecuted the offense or act in violation of section 2923.42 of the Revised Code, in accordance with section 2923.46 of the Revised Code, of all property ordered forfeited under this section, making due provision for the rights of innocent persons;

(e) Pending the disposition of any property that is the subject of an order of forfeiture under this section, take any appropriate measures that are necessary to safeguard and maintain the property.

(3) To facilitate the identification and location of property that is the subject of an order of forfeiture under this section and to facilitate the disposition of petitions for remission or mitigation issued under division (E)(2) of this section, after the issuance of an order of forfeiture under this section and upon application by the prosecuting attorney who prosecuted the offense or act in violation of section 2923.42 of the Revised Code, the court may order that the testimony of any witness relating to the forfeited property be taken by deposition, and that any designated book, paper, document, record, recording, or other material that is not privileged be produced at the same time and place as the testimony, in the same manner as provided for the taking of depositions under the Rules of Civil Procedure.

(F)(1) Except as provided in divisions (F)(2) to (5) of this section, no person claiming any right, title, or interest in property subject to forfeiture under this section or section 2923.45 of the Revised Code may intervene in a criminal trial or appeal, or a delinquent child proceeding or appeal, involving the forfeiture of the property under this section or in a civil action for a civil forfeiture under section 2923.45 of the Revised Code or may commence an action at law or equity against the state concerning the validity of the person's alleged right, title, or interest in the property subsequent to the filing of an indictment, complaint, or information alleging that the property is subject to forfeiture under this section or subsequent to the filing of a complaint, indictment, or information alleging that a juvenile who has any right, title, or interest in the property is a delinquent child because of the commission of an act that is a violation of section 2923.42 of the Revised Code and alleging that the property is subject to forfeiture under this section.

(2) After the entry of an order of forfeiture under this section, the prosecuting attorney who prosecuted the offense or act in violation of section 2923.42 of the Revised Code shall conduct or cause to be conducted a search of the appropriate public records that relate to the property and shall make or cause to be made reasonably diligent inquiries for the purpose of identifying persons who have any right, title, or interest in the property. The prosecuting attorney then shall cause a notice of the order of forfeiture, of the prosecuting attorney's intent to dispose of the property in accordance with section 2923.46 of the Revised Code, and of the manner of the proposed disposal to be given by certified mail, return receipt requested, or by personal service to each person who is known, because of the conduct of the search, the making of the inquiries, or otherwise, to have any right, title, or interest in the property. Additionally, the prosecuting attorney shall cause a similar notice to be published once a week for two consecutive weeks in a newspaper of general circulation in the county in which the property was seized.

(3)(a) Any person, other than the adult offender whose conviction or guilty plea or the delinquent child whose adjudication is the basis of the order of forfeiture, who asserts a legal right, title, or interest in the property that is the subject of the order may petition the court that issued the order, within thirty days after the earlier of the final publication of notice or the person's receipt of notice under division (F)(2) of this section, for a hearing to adjudicate the validity of the person's alleged right, title, or interest in the property. The petition shall be signed by the petitioner under the penalties for falsification as specified in section 2921.13 of the Revised Code and shall set forth the nature and extent of the petitioner's right, title, or interest in the property, the time and circumstances of the petitioner's acquisition of that right, title, or interest, any additional facts supporting the petitioner's claim, and the relief sought.

(b) In lieu of filing a petition as described in division (F)(3)(a) of this section, a secured party or other lienholder of record that asserts a legal right, title, or interest in the property that is the subject of the order, including, but not limited to, a mortgage, security interest, or other type of lien, may file an affidavit as described in division (F)(3)(b) of this section to establish the validity of the alleged right, title, or interest in the property. The secured party or lienholder shall file the affidavit within thirty days after the earlier of the final publication of notice or the receipt of notice under division (F)(2) of this section and, except as otherwise provided in this section, the affidavit shall constitute prima-facie evidence of the validity of the secured party's or other lienholder's alleged right, title, or interest in the property. Unless the prosecuting attorney files a motion challenging the affidavit within ten days after its filing and unless the prosecuting attorney establishes by a preponderance of the evidence at a subsequent hearing before the court that issued the forfeiture order, that the secured party or other lienholder does not possess the alleged right, title, or interest in the property or that the secured party or other lienholder had actual knowledge of facts pertaining to the violation that was the basis of the forfeiture order, the affidavit shall constitute conclusive evidence of the validity of the secured party's or other lienholder's right, title, or interest in the property and shall have the legal effect described in division (G)(2) of this section. To the extent practicable and consistent with the interests of justice, the court shall hold any hearing held pursuant to division (F)(3)(b) of this section within thirty days after the prosecuting attorney files the motion. At any such hearing, the prosecuting attorney and the secured party or other lienholder may present evidence and witnesses and may cross-examine witnesses.

In order to be valid for the purposes of this division and division (G)(2) of this section, the affidavit of a secured party or other lienholder shall contain averments that the secured party or other lienholder acquired its alleged right, title, or interest in the property in the regular course of its business, for a specified valuable consideration, without actual knowledge of any facts pertaining to the violation that was the basis of the forfeiture order, in good faith and without the intent to prevent or otherwise impede the state from seizing or obtaining a forfeiture of the property under sections 2923.44 to 2923.47 of the Revised Code, and prior to the seizure or forfeiture of the property under those sections.

(4) Upon receipt of a petition filed under division (F)(3) of this section, the court shall hold a hearing to determine the validity of the petitioner's right, title, or interest in the property that is the subject of the order of forfeiture. To the extent practicable and consistent with the interests of justice, the court shall hold the hearing within thirty days after the filing of the petition. The court may consolidate the hearing on the petition with a hearing on any other petition filed by a person other than the offender whose conviction or guilty plea or adjudication as a delinquent child is the basis of the order of forfeiture. At the hearing, the petitioner may testify, present evidence and witnesses on the petitioner's behalf, and cross-examine witnesses for the state. The state may present evidence and witnesses in rebuttal and in defense of its claim to the property and cross-examine witnesses for the petitioner. In addition to evidence and testimony presented at the hearing, the court shall consider the relevant portions of the record in the case that resulted in the order of forfeiture.

(5)(a) The court shall amend its order of forfeiture in accordance with its determination if it determines at the hearing that the petitioner has established either of the following by a preponderance of the evidence:

(i) The petitioner has a legal right, title, or interest in the property that renders the order of forfeiture completely or partially invalid because it was vested in the petitioner, rather than the adult offender whose conviction or guilty plea or the delinquent child whose adjudication is the basis of the order, or was superior to any right, title, or interest of that adult offender or delinquent child, at the time of the commission of the violation that is the basis of the order.

(ii) The petitioner is a bona fide purchaser for value of the right, title, or interest in the property and was at the time of the purchase reasonably without cause to believe that it was subject to forfeiture under this section.

(b) The court also shall amend its order of forfeiture to reflect any right, title, or interest of a secured party or other lienholder of record in the property subject to the order that was established pursuant to division (F)(3)(b) of this section by means of an affidavit, or that was established pursuant to that division by the failure of a prosecuting attorney to establish, in a hearing as described in that division, that the secured party or other lienholder did not possess the alleged right, title, or interest in the property or that the secured party or other lienholder had actual knowledge of facts pertaining to the violation that was the basis of the order.

(G)(1) Subject to division (G)(2) of this section, if the court has disposed of all petitions filed under division (F) of this section or if no petitions are filed under that division and the time for filing petitions under that division has expired, the state shall have clear title to all property that is the subject of an order of forfeiture issued under this section and may warrant good title to any subsequent purchaser or other transferee.

(2) If an affidavit as described in division (F)(3)(b) of this section is filed in accordance with that division, if the affidavit constitutes under the circumstances described in that division conclusive evidence of the validity of the right, title, or interest of a secured party or other lienholder of record in the property subject to a forfeiture order, and if any mortgage, security interest, or other type of lien possessed by the secured party or other lienholder in connection with the property is not satisfied prior to a sale or other disposition of the property pursuant to section 2923.46 of the Revised Code, then the right, title, or interest of the secured party or other lienholder in the property remains valid for purposes of sections 2923.44 to 2923.47 of the Revised Code and any subsequent purchaser or other transferee of the property pursuant to section 2923.46 of the Revised Code shall take the property subject to the continued validity of the right, title, or interest of the secured party or other lienholder in the property.

(2000 S 179, § 3, eff. 1–1–02; 1998 H 2, eff. 1–1–99)

2923.45 Civil forfeiture of property; procedure

(A) The following property is subject to forfeiture to the state in a civil action as described in division (E) of this section, and no person has any right, title, or interest in the following property:

(1) Any property that constitutes, or is derived directly or indirectly from, any proceeds that a person obtained directly or indirectly from the commission of an act that, upon the filing of an indictment, complaint, or information, could be prosecuted as a violation of section 2923.42 of the Revised Code or that, upon the filing of a complaint, indictment, or information, could be the basis for finding a juvenile to be a delinquent child for committing an act that is a violation of section 2923.42 of the Revised Code;

(2) Any property that was used or intended to be used in any manner to commit, or to facilitate the commission of, an act that, upon the filing of an indictment, complaint, or information, could be prosecuted as a violation of section 2923.42 of the Revised Code or that, upon the filing of a complaint, indictment, or information, could be the basis for finding a juvenile to be a delinquent child for committing an act that is a violation of section 2923.42 of the Revised Code.

(B)(1) All right, title, and interest in property described in division (A) of this section shall vest in the state upon the commission of the act giving rise to a civil forfeiture under this section.

(2) The provisions of section 2933.43 of the Revised Code relating to the procedures for the forfeiture of contraband do not apply to a civil action to obtain a civil forfeiture under this section.

(3) Any property taken or detained pursuant to this section is not subject to replevin and is considered to be in the custody of the head of the law enforcement agency that seized the property.

This section does not preclude the head of a law enforcement agency that seizes property from seeking the forfeiture of that property pursuant to federal law. If the head of a law enforcement agency that seizes property does not seek the forfeiture of that property pursuant to federal law and if the property is subject to forfeiture under this section, the property is subject only to the orders of the court of common pleas of the county in which the property is located, and it shall be disposed of in accordance with section 2923.46 of the Revised Code.

(4) Nothing in this section precludes a financial institution that has or purports to have a security interest in or lien on property described in division (A) of this section from commencing a civil action or taking other appropriate legal action in connection with the property, prior to its disposition in accordance with section 2923.46 of the Revised Code, for the purpose of obtaining possession of the property in order to foreclose or otherwise enforce the security interest or lien. A financial institution may commence a civil action or take other appropriate legal action for that purpose prior to the disposition of the property in accordance with section 2923.46 of the Revised Code, even if a civil action to obtain a civil forfeiture has been or could be commenced under this section, even if the property is or could be the subject of an order of civil forfeiture issued under this section, and even if the property has been seized or is subject to seizure pursuant to this section.

If a financial institution commences a civil action or takes any other appropriate legal action as described in this division, if the financial institution subsequently causes the sale of the property prior to its seizure pursuant to this section and its disposition pursuant to section 2923.46 of the Revised Code, and if the person responsible for the conduct of the sale has actual knowledge of the commencement of a civil action to obtain a civil forfeiture under this section or actual knowledge of an order of civil forfeiture issued under this section, then the person responsible for the conduct of the sale shall dispose of the proceeds of the sale in the following order:

(a) First, to the payment of the costs of the sale and to the payment of the costs incurred by law enforcement agencies and financial institutions in connection with the seizure of, storage of, maintenance of, and provision of security for the property. As used in this division, "costs" of a financial institution do not include attorney's fees incurred by that institution in connection with the property.

(b) Second, the remaining proceeds of the sale after compliance with division (B)(4)(a) of this section, to the payment in the order of priority of the security interests and liens of valid security interests and liens pertaining to the property that, at the time of the vesting in the state under division (B)(1) of this section of the right, title, or interest of the adult or juvenile, are held by known secured parties and lienholders;

(c) Third, the remaining proceeds of the sale after compliance with division (B)(4)(b) of this section, to the court that has or would have jurisdiction in a civil action to obtain a civil forfeiture under this section, for disposition in accordance with section 2923.46 of the Revised Code.

(C)(1) A law enforcement officer may seize any property that is subject to civil forfeiture under this section upon process, or a warrant as described in division (C)(2) of this section, issued by a court of common pleas that has jurisdiction over the property. Additionally, a law enforcement officer may seize the property, without process or a warrant being so issued, when any of the following applies:

(a) The seizure is incident to an arrest, a search under a search warrant, a lawful search without a search warrant, or an inspection under an administrative inspection warrant.

(b) The property is the subject of a prior judgment in favor of the state in a restraining order, injunction, or other preservation order proceeding under section 2923.44 of the Revised Code, or is the subject of a forfeiture order issued pursuant to that section.

(c) The law enforcement officer has probable cause to believe that the property is directly or indirectly dangerous to the public health or safety.

(d) The initial intrusion by the law enforcement officer afforded the officer with plain view of personal property that is subject to civil forfeiture in a civil action under this section, the initial intrusion by the law enforcement officer was lawful, the discovery of the personal property by the law enforcement officer was inadvertent, and the incriminating nature of the personal property was immediately apparent to the law enforcement officer.

(2) For purposes of division (C)(1) of this section, the state may request a court of common pleas to issue a warrant that authorizes the seizure of property that is subject to civil forfeiture under this section, in the same manner as provided in Criminal Rule 41 and Chapter 2933. of the Revised Code for the issuance of a search warrant. For purposes of division (C)(1) of this section, any proceeding before a court of common pleas that involves a request for the issuance of process, or a warrant as described in this division, authorizing the seizure of any property that is subject to civil forfeiture under this section shall be recorded by shorthand, by stenotype, or by any other mechanical, electronic, or video recording device. The recording of and any transcript of the recording of such a proceeding shall not be a public record for purposes of section 149.43 of the Revised Code until the property has been seized pursuant to the process or warrant. This division does not require, authorize, or permit the making available for inspection, or the copying, under section 149.43 of the Revised Code of any confidential law enforcement investigatory record or trial preparation record, as defined in that section.

(3) If property is seized pursuant to division (C)(1) of this section and if a civil action to obtain a civil forfeiture under this section, a criminal action that could result in a criminal forfeiture under section 2923.44 of the Revised Code, or a delinquent child proceeding that could result in a criminal forfeiture under that section is not pending at the time of the seizure or previously did not occur in connection with the property, then the prosecuting attorney of the county in which the seizure occurred promptly shall commence a civil action to obtain a civil forfeiture under this section in connection with the property, unless an indictment, complaint, or information alleging the commission of a violation of section 2923.42 of the Revised Code or a complaint, or indictment, or information alleging that a juvenile is a delinquent child because of the commission of an act that is a violation of section 2923.42 of the Revised Code is filed prior to the commencement of the civil action. Nothing in division (C)(3) of this section precludes the filing of an indictment, complaint, or information alleging the commission of a violation of section 2923.42 of the Revised Code or the filing of a complaint, indictment, or information alleging that a juvenile is a delinquent child because of the commission of an act that is a violation of section 2923.42 of the Revised Code, after the commencement of a civil action to obtain a civil forfeiture under this section.

(D)(1) The filing of an indictment, complaint, or information alleging the commission of a violation of section 2923.42 of the Revised Code that also is the basis of a civil action for a civil forfeiture under this section, or the filing of a complaint, indictment, or information alleging that a juvenile is a delinquent child because of the commission of an act that is a violation of section 2923.42 of the Revised Code, and that also is the basis of a civil action for a civil forfeiture under this section, upon the motion of the prosecuting attorney of the county in which the indictment, complaint, or information or the complaint, indictment, or information in the delinquent child proceeding is filed, shall stay the civil action.

(2) A civil action to obtain a civil forfeiture under this section may be commenced as described in division (E) of this section whether or not the adult or juvenile who committed a violation of section 2923.42 of the Revised Code or an act that is a violation of section 2923.42 of the Revised Code has been charged by an indictment, complaint, or information with the commission of a violation of that section, has pleaded guilty to or been found guilty of a violation of that section, has been determined to be a delinquent child for the commission of a violation of that section, has been found not guilty of committing a violation of that section, or has not been determined to be a delinquent child for the alleged commission of a violation of that section.

(E)(1) The prosecuting attorney of the county in which property described in division (A) of this section is located may commence a civil action to obtain a civil forfeiture under this section by filing in the court of common pleas of that county a complaint that requests the issuance of an order of civil forfeiture of the property to the state. Notices of the action shall be served and published in accordance with division (E)(2) of this section.

(2) Prior to or simultaneously with the commencement of the civil action as described in division (E)(1) of this section, the prosecuting attorney shall conduct or cause to be conducted a search of the appropriate public records that relate to the property subject to civil forfeiture, and shall make or cause to be made reasonably diligent inquiries, for the purpose of identifying persons who have any right, title, or interest in the property. The prosecuting attorney then shall cause a notice of the commencement of the civil action, together with a copy of the complaint filed in it, to be given to each person who is known, because of the conduct of the search, the making of the inquiries, or otherwise, to have any right, title, or interest in the property, by certified mail, return receipt requested, or by personal service. Additionally, the prosecuting attorney shall cause a similar notice to be published once a week for two consecutive weeks in a newspaper of general circulation in the county in which the property is located.

(3) The procedures specified in divisions (F)(3) to (5) of section 2923.44 of the Revised Code apply to persons claiming any right, title, or interest in property subject to civil forfeiture under this section. The references in those divisions to the adult offender whose conviction or guilty plea, or the delinquent child whose adjudication, is the basis of an order of criminal forfeiture shall be construed for purposes of this section to mean the adult or juvenile who committed the act that could be the basis of an order of civil forfeiture under this section, and the references in those divisions to an issued order of criminal forfeiture shall be inapplicable.

(4) A hearing shall be held in the civil action described in division (E)(1) of this section at least thirty days after the final publication of notice as required by division (E)(2) of this section and after the date of completion of the service of notice by personal service or certified mail, return receipt requested, as required by that division. Following the hearing, the court shall issue the requested order of civil forfeiture if the court deter-

mines that the prosecuting attorney has proven by clear and convincing evidence that the property in question is property as described in division (A)(1) or (2) of this section and if the court has disposed of all petitions filed under division (E)(3) of this section or no petitions have been so filed and the time for filing them has expired. An order of civil forfeiture so issued shall state that all right, title, and interest in the property in question of the adult or juvenile who committed the act that is the basis of the order is forfeited to the state and shall make due provision for the right, title, or interest in that property of any other person in accordance with any determinations made by the court under division (E)(3) of this section and in accordance with divisions (F)(5)(b) and (G)(2) of section 2923.44 of the Revised Code.

(5) Subject to division (G)(2) of section 2923.44 of the Revised Code, if a court of common pleas enters an order of civil forfeiture in accordance with division (E) of this section, the state shall have clear title to the property that is the subject of the order and may warrant good title to any subsequent purchaser or other transferee.

(2000 S 179, § 3, eff. 1–1–02; 1998 H 2, eff. 1–1–99)

2923.46 Disposition of forfeited property

(A) If property is seized pursuant to section 2923.44 or 2923.45 of the Revised Code, it is considered to be in the custody of the head of the law enforcement agency that seized it, and the head of that agency may do any of the following with respect to that property prior to its disposition in accordance with division (A)(4) or (B) of this section:

(1) Place the property under seal;

(2) Remove the property to a place that the head of that agency designates;

(3) Request the issuance of a court order that requires any other appropriate municipal corporation, county, township, park district created pursuant to section 511.18 or 1545.01 of the Revised Code, or state law enforcement officer or other officer to take custody of the property and, if practicable, remove it to an appropriate location for eventual disposition in accordance with division (B) of this section;

(4)(a) Seek forfeiture of the property pursuant to federal law. If the head of that agency seeks its forfeiture pursuant to federal law, the law enforcement agency shall deposit, use, and account for proceeds from a sale of the property upon its forfeiture, proceeds from another disposition of the property upon its forfeiture, or forfeited moneys it receives, in accordance with the applicable federal law and otherwise shall comply with that law.

(b) If the state highway patrol seized the property and if the superintendent of the state highway patrol seeks its forfeiture pursuant to federal law, the appropriate governmental officials shall deposit into the state highway patrol contraband, forfeiture, and other fund all interest or other earnings derived from the investment of the proceeds from a sale of the property upon its forfeiture, the proceeds from another disposition of the property upon its forfeiture, or the forfeited moneys. The state highway patrol shall use and account for that interest or other earnings in accordance with the applicable federal law.

(c) Division (B) of this section and divisions (D)(1) to (3) of section 2933.43 of the Revised Code do not apply to proceeds or forfeited moneys received pursuant to federal law or to the interest or other earnings that are derived from the investment of proceeds or forfeited moneys received pursuant to federal law and that are described in division (A)(4)(b) of this section.

(B) In addition to complying with any requirements imposed by a court pursuant to section 2923.44 or 2923.45 of the Revised Code, and the requirements imposed by those sections, in relation to the disposition of property forfeited to the state under either of those sections, the prosecuting attorney who is responsible for its disposition shall dispose of the property as follows:

(1) Any vehicle that was used in a violation of section 2923.42 of the Revised Code or in an act of a juvenile that is a violation of section 2923.42 of the Revised Code shall be given to the law enforcement agency of the municipal corporation or county in which the offense or act occurred if that agency desires to have the vehicle, except that, if the offense or act occurred in a township or in a park district created pursuant to section 511.18 or 1545.01 of the Revised Code and a law enforcement officer employed by the township or the park district was involved in the seizure of the vehicle, the vehicle may be given to the law enforcement agency of that township or park district if that agency desires to have the vehicle, and except that, if the state highway patrol made the seizure of the vehicle, the vehicle may be given to the state highway patrol if it desires to have the vehicle.

(2) Drugs shall be disposed of pursuant to section 3719.11 of the Revised Code or placed in the custody of the secretary of the treasury of the United States for disposal or use for medical or scientific purposes under applicable federal law.

(3) Firearms and dangerous ordnance suitable for police work may be given to a law enforcement agency for that purpose. Firearms suitable for sporting use, or as museum pieces or collectors' items, may be disposed of by sale pursuant to division (B)(7) of this section. Other firearms and dangerous ordnance shall be destroyed by a law enforcement agency or shall be sent to the bureau of criminal identification and investigation for destruction by it.

(4) Computers, computer networks, computer systems, and computer software suitable for police work may be given to a law enforcement agency for that purpose. Other computers, computer networks, computer systems, and computer software shall be disposed of by sale pursuant to division (B)(7) of this section or disposed of in another manner that the court that issued the order of forfeiture considers proper under the circumstances.

(5) Obscene materials shall be destroyed.

(6) Beer, intoxicating liquor, and alcohol shall be disposed of in accordance with division (D)(4) of section 2933.41 of the Revised Code.

(7) In the case of property not described in divisions (B)(1) to (6) of this section and of property described in those divisions but not disposed of pursuant to them, the property shall be sold in accordance with division (B)(7) of this section or, in the case of forfeited moneys, disposed of in accordance with division (B)(7) of this section. If the property is to be sold, the prosecuting attorney shall cause a notice of the proposed sale of the property to be given in accordance with law, and the property shall be sold, without appraisal, at a public auction to the highest bidder for cash. The proceeds of a sale and forfeited moneys shall be applied in the following order:

(a) First, to the payment of the costs incurred in connection with the seizure of, storage of, maintenance of, and provision of security for the property, the forfeiture proceeding or civil action, and, if any, the sale;

(b) Second, the remaining proceeds or forfeited moneys after compliance with division (B)(7)(a) of this section, to the payment of the value of any legal right, title, or interest in the property that is possessed by a person who, pursuant to division (F) of section 2923.44 of the Revised Code or division (E) of section 2923.45 of the Revised Code, established the validity of and consequently preserved that legal right, title, or interest, including, but not limited to, any mortgage, perfected or other security interest, or other lien in the property. The value of these rights, titles, or interests shall be paid according to their record or other order of priority.

(c) Third, the remaining proceeds or forfeited moneys after compliance with divisions (B)(7)(a) and (b) of this section, as follows:

(i) If the forfeiture was ordered in a juvenile court, ten per cent to one or more alcohol and drug addiction treatment programs that are certified by the department of alcohol and drug addiction services under section 3793.06 of the Revised Code and that are specified in the order of forfeiture. A juvenile court shall not specify an alcohol or drug addiction treatment program in the order of forfeiture unless the program is a certified alcohol and drug addiction treatment program and, except as provided in division (B)(7)(c)(i) of this section, unless the program is located in the county in which the court that orders the forfeiture is located or in a contiguous county. If no certified alcohol and drug addiction treatment program is located in any of those counties, the juvenile court may specify in the order a certified alcohol and drug addiction treatment program located anywhere within this state.

(ii) If the forfeiture was ordered in a juvenile court, ninety per cent, and if the forfeiture was ordered in a court other than a juvenile court, one hundred per cent to appropriate funds in accordance with divisions (D)(1)(c) and (2) of section 2933.43 of the Revised Code. The remaining proceeds or forfeited moneys so deposited shall be used only for the purposes authorized by those divisions and division (D)(3)(a)(ii) of that section.

(C)(1) Sections 2923.44 to 2923.47 of the Revised Code do not preclude a financial institution that possessed a valid mortgage, security interest, or lien that is not satisfied prior to a sale under division (B)(7) of this section or following a sale by application of division (B)(7)(b) of this section, from commencing a civil action in any appropriate court in this or another state to obtain a deficiency judgment against the debtor if the financial institution otherwise would have been entitled to do so in this or another state.

(2) Any law enforcement agency that obtains any vehicle pursuant to division (B)(1) of this section shall take the vehicle subject to the outstanding amount of any security interest or lien that attaches to the vehicle.

(3) Nothing in this section impairs a mortgage, security interest, lien, or other interest of a financial institution in property that was the subject of a forfeiture order under section 2923.44 or 2923.45 of the Revised Code and that was sold or otherwise disposed of in a manner that does not conform to the requirements of division (B) of this section, or any right of a financial institution of that nature to commence a civil action in any appropriate court in this or another state to obtain a deficiency judgment against the debtor.

(4) Following the sale under division (B)(7) of this section of any property that is required to be titled or registered under the law of this state, the prosecuting attorney responsible for the disposition of the property shall cause the state to issue an appropriate certificate of title or registration to the purchaser of the property. If, in a disposition of property pursuant to division (B) of this section, the state or a political subdivision is given any property that is required to be titled or registered under the law of this state, the prosecuting attorney responsible for the disposition of the property shall cause the state to issue an appropriate certificate of title or registration to itself or to the political subdivision.

(D) Property that has been forfeited to the state pursuant to an order of criminal forfeiture under section 2923.44 of the Revised Code or an order of civil forfeiture under section 2923.45 of the Revised Code shall not be available for use to pay any fine imposed upon a person who is convicted of or pleads guilty to a violation of section 2923.42 of the Revised Code or upon a juvenile who is found by a juvenile court to be a delinquent child for an act that is a violation of section 2923.42 of the Revised Code.

(E) Sections 2923.44 to 2923.47 of the Revised Code do not prohibit a law enforcement officer from seeking the forfeiture of contraband associated with a violation of section 2923.42 of the Revised Code pursuant to section 2933.43 of the Revised Code.

(1998 H 2, eff. 1–1–99)

2923.47 Motion to return seized property; order

(A) Any person who is aggrieved by an alleged unlawful seizure of property that potentially is subject to forfeiture under section 2923.44 or 2923.45 of the Revised Code may file a motion as described in division (B) of this section with whichever of the following courts is appropriate under the circumstances, within the time described in division (C) of this section:

(1) The court of common pleas in which a criminal prosecution for a violation of section 2923.42 of the Revised Code is pending;

(2) The juvenile court in which a delinquent child action for an act that is a violation of section 2923.42 of the Revised Code is pending;

(3) The court of common pleas in which a civil action as described in division (E) of section 2923.45 of the Revised Code is pending;

(4) The court of common pleas of the county in which the property was seized.

(B) A motion filed pursuant to division (A) of this section shall specify that the seizure of specified property was unlawful, state the reasons why the movant believes the seizure was unlawful, state that the movant is lawfully entitled to possession of the seized property, and request the court of common pleas or the juvenile court to issue an order that mandates the law enforcement agency having custody of the seized property to return it to the movant. For purposes of this division, an unlawful seizure of property includes, but is not limited to, a seizure in violation of the Fourth Amendment to the Constitution of the United States or of Section 14 of Article I, Ohio Constitution, and a seizure pursuant to sections 2923.44 to 2923.46 of the Revised Code of property other than potentially forfeitable property as described in division (A)(1) of section 2923.44 or division (A) of section 2923.45 of the Revised Code.

(C)(1) If a motion as described in division (A) of this section is filed prior to the entry of an order of forfeiture under section 2923.44 or 2923.45 of the Revised Code, the court of common pleas or the juvenile court promptly shall schedule a hearing on the motion and cause notice of the date and time of the hearing to be given to the movant and the prosecuting attorney of the county in which the property was seized. At the hearing, the movant and the prosecuting attorney may present witnesses and evidence relative to the issues of whether the property in question was unlawfully seized and whether the movant is lawfully entitled to possession of the property. If, after the hearing, the court of common pleas or the juvenile court determines that the movant has established, by a preponderance of the evidence, that the property in question was unlawfully seized and that the movant is lawfully entitled to possession of it, the court shall issue an order that requires the law enforcement agency having custody of the seized property to return it to the movant.

(2)(a) If a motion is filed in accordance with division (C)(1) of this section and, at the time of filing or of the hearing on the motion, a criminal prosecution for a violation of section 2923.42 of the Revised Code or a delinquent child action for an act that is a violation of section 2923.42 of the Revised Code has been commenced by the filing of an indictment, information, or complaint, then the court of common pleas or the juvenile court shall treat the motion as a motion to suppress evidence.

(b) If an order to return seized property is issued pursuant to division (C)(1) of this section, the returned property shall not be admissible in evidence in any pending or subsequently commenced criminal prosecution for a violation of section 2923.42 of the Revised Code if the prosecution arose or arises out of the unlawful seizure of the property, or in any pending or subsequently commenced delinquent child action for an act that is a violation of section 2923.42 of the Revised Code if the action arose or arises out of the unlawful seizure of the property.

(1998 H 2, eff. 1–1–99)

CHAPTER 2925

DRUG OFFENSES

DEFINITIONS

2925.01 Definitions

Note: See also following version of this section, eff. 5–6–05.

As used in this chapter:

(A) "Administer," "controlled substance," "dispense," " distribute," "hypodermic," " manufacturer," "official written order," "person," "pharmacist," " pharmacy," "sale," "schedule I," "schedule II," "schedule III, " "schedule IV," "schedule V," and "wholesaler" have the same meanings as in section 3719.01 of the Revised Code.

(B) "Drug dependent person" and "drug of abuse" have the same meanings as in section 3719.011 of the Revised Code.

(C) "Drug," "dangerous drug," "licensed health professional authorized to prescribe drugs," and "prescription" have the same meanings as in section 4729.01 of the Revised Code.

(D) "Bulk amount" of a controlled substance means any of the following:

(1) For any compound, mixture, preparation, or substance included in schedule I, schedule II, or schedule III, with the exception of marihuana, cocaine, L.S.D., heroin, and hashish and except as provided in division (D)(2) or (5) of this section, whichever of the following is applicable:

(a) An amount equal to or exceeding ten grams or twenty-five unit doses of a compound, mixture, preparation, or substance that is or contains any amount of a schedule I opiate or opium derivative;

(b) An amount equal to or exceeding ten grams of a compound, mixture, preparation, or substance that is or contains any amount of raw or gum opium;

(c) An amount equal to or exceeding thirty grams or ten unit doses of a compound, mixture, preparation, or substance that is or contains any amount of a schedule I hallucinogen other than tetrahydrocannabinol or lysergic acid amide, or a schedule I stimulant or depressant;

(d) An amount equal to or exceeding twenty grams or five times the maximum daily dose in the usual dose range specified in a standard pharmaceutical reference manual of a compound, mixture, preparation, or substance that is or contains any amount of a schedule II opiate or opium derivative;

(e) An amount equal to or exceeding five grams or ten unit doses of a compound, mixture, preparation, or substance that is or contains any amount of phencyclidine;

(f) An amount equal to or exceeding one hundred twenty grams or thirty times the maximum daily dose in the usual dose range specified in a standard pharmaceutical reference manual of a compound, mixture, preparation, or substance that is or contains any amount of a schedule II stimulant that is in a final dosage form manufactured by a person authorized by the "Federal Food, Drug, and Cosmetic Act," 52 Stat. 1040 (1938), 21 U.S.C.A. 301, as amended, and the federal drug abuse control laws, as defined in section 3719. 01 of the Revised Code, that is or contains any amount of a schedule II depressant substance or a schedule II hallucinogenic substance;

(g) An amount equal to or exceeding three grams of a compound, mixture, preparation, or substance that is or contains any amount of a schedule II stimulant, or any of its salts or isomers, that is not in a final dosage form manufactured by a person authorized by the Federal Food, Drug, and Cosmetic Act and the federal drug abuse control laws.

(2) An amount equal to or exceeding one hundred twenty grams or thirty times the maximum daily dose in the usual dose

range specified in a standard pharmaceutical reference manual of a compound, mixture, preparation, or substance that is or contains any amount of a schedule III or IV substance other than an anabolic steroid or a schedule III opiate or opium derivative;

(3) An amount equal to or exceeding twenty grams or five times the maximum daily dose in the usual dose range specified in a standard pharmaceutical reference manual of a compound, mixture, preparation, or substance that is or contains any amount of a schedule III opiate or opium derivative;

(4) An amount equal to or exceeding two hundred fifty milliliters or two hundred fifty grams of a compound, mixture, preparation, or substance that is or contains any amount of a schedule V substance;

(5) An amount equal to or exceeding two hundred solid dosage units, sixteen grams, or sixteen milliliters of a compound, mixture, preparation, or substance that is or contains any amount of a schedule III anabolic steroid.

(E) "Unit dose" means an amount or unit of a compound, mixture, or preparation containing a controlled substance that is separately identifiable and in a form that indicates that it is the amount or unit by which the controlled substance is separately administered to or taken by an individual.

(F) "Cultivate" includes planting, watering, fertilizing, or tilling.

(G) "Drug abuse offense" means any of the following:

(1) A violation of division (A) of section 2913.02 that constitutes theft of drugs, or a violation of section 2925.02, 2925.03, 2925.04, 2925.041, 2925.05, 2925.06, 2925.11, 2925.12, 2925.13, 2925.22, 2925.23, 2925.24, 2925. 31, 2925.32, 2925.36, or 2925.37 of the Revised Code;

(2) A violation of an existing or former law of this or any other state or of the United States that is substantially equivalent to any section listed in division (G)(1) of this section;

(3) An offense under an existing or former law of this or any other state, or of the United States, of which planting, cultivating, harvesting, processing, making, manufacturing, producing, shipping, transporting, delivering, acquiring, possessing, storing, distributing, dispensing, selling, inducing another to use, administering to another, using, or otherwise dealing with a controlled substance is an element;

(4) A conspiracy to commit, attempt to commit, or complicity in committing or attempting to commit any offense under division (G)(1), (2), or (3) of this section.

(H) "Felony drug abuse offense" means any drug abuse offense that would constitute a felony under the laws of this state, any other state, or the United States.

(I) "Harmful intoxicant" does not include beer or intoxicating liquor but means any of the following:

(1) Any compound, mixture, preparation, or substance the gas, fumes, or vapor of which when inhaled can induce intoxication, excitement, giddiness, irrational behavior, depression, stupefaction, paralysis, unconsciousness, asphyxiation, or other harmful physiological effects, and includes, but is not limited to, any of the following:

(a) Any volatile organic solvent, plastic cement, model cement, fingernail polish remover, lacquer thinner, cleaning fluid, gasoline, or other preparation containing a volatile organic solvent;

(b) Any aerosol propellant;

(c) Any fluorocarbon refrigerant;

(d) Any anesthetic gas.

(2) Gamma Butyrolactone;

(3) 1,4 Butanediol.

(J) "Manufacture" means to plant, cultivate, harvest, process, make, prepare, or otherwise engage in any part of the production of a drug, by propagation, extraction, chemical synthesis, or compounding, or any combination of the same, and includes packaging, repackaging, labeling, and other activities incident to production.

(K) "Possess" or "possession" means having control over a thing or substance, but may not be inferred solely from mere access to the thing or substance through ownership or occupation of the premises upon which the thing or substance is found.

(L) "Sample drug" means a drug or pharmaceutical preparation that would be hazardous to health or safety if used without the supervision of a licensed health professional authorized to prescribe drugs, or a drug of abuse, and that, at one time, had been placed in a container plainly marked as a sample by a manufacturer.

(M) "Standard pharmaceutical reference manual" means the current edition, with cumulative changes if any, of any of the following reference works:

(1) "The National Formulary";

(2) "The United States Pharmacopeia," prepared by authority of the United States Pharmacopeial Convention, Inc.;

(3) Other standard references that are approved by the state board of pharmacy.

(N) "Juvenile" means a person under eighteen years of age.

(O) "Counterfeit controlled substance" means any of the following:

(1) Any drug that bears, or whose container or label bears, a trademark, trade name, or other identifying mark used without authorization of the owner of rights to that trademark, trade name, or identifying mark;

(2) Any unmarked or unlabeled substance that is represented to be a controlled substance manufactured, processed, packed, or distributed by a person other than the person that manufactured, processed, packed, or distributed it;

(3) Any substance that is represented to be a controlled substance but is not a controlled substance or is a different controlled substance;

(4) Any substance other than a controlled substance that a reasonable person would believe to be a controlled substance because of its similarity in shape, size, and color, or its markings, labeling, packaging, distribution, or the price for which it is sold or offered for sale.

(P) An offense is "committed in the vicinity of a school" if the offender commits the offense on school premises, in a school building, or within one thousand feet of the boundaries of any school premises, regardless of whether the offender knows the offense is being committed on school premises, in a school building, or within one thousand feet of the boundaries of any school premises.

(Q) "School" means any school operated by a board of education, any community school established under Chapter 3314. of the Revised Code, or any nonpublic school for which the state board of education prescribes minimum standards under section 3301.07 of the Revised Code, whether or not any instruction, extracurricular activities, or training provided by the school is being conducted at the time a criminal offense is committed.

(R) "School premises" means either of the following:

(1) The parcel of real property on which any school is situated, whether or not any instruction, extracurricular activities, or training provided by the school is being conducted on the premises at the time a criminal offense is committed;

(2) Any other parcel of real property that is owned or leased by a board of education of a school, the governing authority of a community school established under Chapter 3314. of the Re-

vised Code, or the governing body of a nonpublic school for which the state board of education prescribes minimum standards under section 3301.07 of the Revised Code and on which some of the instruction, extracurricular activities, or training of the school is conducted, whether or not any instruction, extracurricular activities, or training provided by the school is being conducted on the parcel of real property at the time a criminal offense is committed.

(S) "School building" means any building in which any of the instruction, extracurricular activities, or training provided by a school is conducted, whether or not any instruction, extracurricular activities, or training provided by the school is being conducted in the school building at the time a criminal offense is committed.

(T) "Disciplinary counsel" means the disciplinary counsel appointed by the board of commissioners on grievances and discipline of the supreme court under the Rules for the Government of the Bar of Ohio.

(U) "Certified grievance committee" means a duly constituted and organized committee of the Ohio state bar association or of one or more local bar associations of the state of Ohio that complies with the criteria set forth in Rule V, section 6 of the Rules for the Government of the Bar of Ohio.

(V) "Professional license" means any license, permit, certificate, registration, qualification, admission, temporary license, temporary permit, temporary certificate, or temporary registration that is described in divisions (W)(1) to (36) of this section and that qualifies a person as a professionally licensed person.

(W) "Professionally licensed person" means any of the following:

(1) A person who has obtained a license as a manufacturer of controlled substances or a wholesaler of controlled substances under Chapter 3719. of the Revised Code;

(2) A person who has received a certificate or temporary certificate as a certified public accountant or who has registered as a public accountant under Chapter 4701. of the Revised Code and who holds an Ohio permit issued under that chapter;

(3) A person who holds a certificate of qualification to practice architecture issued or renewed and registered under Chapter 4703. of the Revised Code;

(4) A person who is registered as a landscape architect under Chapter 4703. of the Revised Code or who holds a permit as a landscape architect issued under that chapter;

(5) A person licensed as an auctioneer or apprentice auctioneer or licensed to operate an auction company under Chapter 4707. of the Revised Code;

(6) A person who has been issued a certificate of registration as a registered barber under Chapter 4709. of the Revised Code;

(7) A person licensed and regulated to engage in the business of a debt pooling company by a legislative authority, under authority of Chapter 4710. of the Revised Code;

(8) A person who has been issued a cosmetologist's license, hair designer's license, manicurist's license, esthetician's license, natural hair stylist's license, managing cosmetologist's license, managing hair designer's license, managing manicurist's license, managing esthetician's license, managing natural hair stylist's license, cosmetology instructor's license, hair design instructor's license, manicurist instructor's license, esthetics instructor's license, natural hair style instructor's license, independent contractor's license, or tanning facility permit under Chapter 4713. of the Revised Code;

(9) A person who has been issued a license to practice dentistry, a general anesthesia permit, a conscious intravenous sedation permit, a limited resident's license, a limited teaching license, a dental hygienist's license, or a dental hygienist's teacher's certificate under Chapter 4715. of the Revised Code;

(10) A person who has been issued an embalmer's license, a funeral director's license, a funeral home license, or a crematory license, or who has been registered for an embalmer's or funeral director's apprenticeship under Chapter 4717. of the Revised Code;

(11) A person who has been licensed as a registered nurse or practical nurse, or who has been issued a certificate for the practice of nurse-midwifery under Chapter 4723. of the Revised Code;

(12) A person who has been licensed to practice optometry or to engage in optical dispensing under Chapter 4725. of the Revised Code;

(13) A person licensed to act as a pawnbroker under Chapter 4727. of the Revised Code;

(14) A person licensed to act as a precious metals dealer under Chapter 4728. of the Revised Code;

(15) A person licensed as a pharmacist, a pharmacy intern, a wholesale distributor of dangerous drugs, or a terminal distributor of dangerous drugs under Chapter 4729. of the Revised Code;

(16) A person who is authorized to practice as a physician assistant under Chapter 4730. of the Revised Code;

(17) A person who has been issued a certificate to practice medicine and surgery, osteopathic medicine and surgery, a limited branch of medicine, or podiatry under Chapter 4731. of the Revised Code;

(18) A person licensed as a psychologist or school psychologist under Chapter 4732. of the Revised Code;

(19) A person registered to practice the profession of engineering or surveying under Chapter 4733. of the Revised Code;

(20) A person who has been issued a license to practice chiropractic under Chapter 4734. of the Revised Code;

(21) A person licensed to act as a real estate broker or real estate salesperson under Chapter 4735. of the Revised Code;

(22) A person registered as a registered sanitarian under Chapter 4736. of the Revised Code;

(23) A person licensed to operate or maintain a junkyard under Chapter 4737. of the Revised Code;

(24) A person who has been issued a motor vehicle salvage dealer's license under Chapter 4738. of the Revised Code;

(25) A person who has been licensed to act as a steam engineer under Chapter 4739. of the Revised Code;

(26) A person who has been issued a license or temporary permit to practice veterinary medicine or any of its branches, or who is registered as a graduate animal technician under Chapter 4741. of the Revised Code;

(27) A person who has been issued a hearing aid dealer's or fitter's license or trainee permit under Chapter 4747. of the Revised Code;

(28) A person who has been issued a class A, class B, or class C license or who has been registered as an investigator or security guard employee under Chapter 4749. of the Revised Code;

(29) A person licensed and registered to practice as a nursing home administrator under Chapter 4751. of the Revised Code;

(30) A person licensed to practice as a speech-language pathologist or audiologist under Chapter 4753. of the Revised Code;

(31) A person issued a license as an occupational therapist or physical therapist under Chapter 4755. of the Revised Code;

(32) A person who is licensed as a professional clinical counselor or professional counselor, licensed as a social worker or independent social worker, or registered as a social work assistant under Chapter 4757. of the Revised Code;

(33) A person issued a license to practice dietetics under Chapter 4759. of the Revised Code;

(34) A person who has been issued a license or limited permit to practice respiratory therapy under Chapter 4761. of the Revised Code;

(35) A person who has been issued a real estate appraiser certificate under Chapter 4763. of the Revised Code;

(36) A person who has been admitted to the bar by order of the supreme court in compliance with its prescribed and published rules.

(X) "Cocaine" means any of the following:

(1) A cocaine salt, isomer, or derivative, a salt of a cocaine isomer or derivative, or the base form of cocaine;

(2) Coca leaves or a salt, compound, derivative, or preparation of coca leaves, including ecgonine, a salt, isomer, or derivative of ecgonine, or a salt of an isomer or derivative of ecgonine;

(3) A salt, compound, derivative, or preparation of a substance identified in division (X)(1) or (2) of this section that is chemically equivalent to or identical with any of those substances, except that the substances shall not include decocainized coca leaves or extraction of coca leaves if the extractions do not contain cocaine or ecgonine.

(Y) "L.S.D." means lysergic acid diethylamide.

(Z) "Hashish" means the resin or a preparation of the resin contained in marihuana, whether in solid form or in a liquid concentrate, liquid extract, or liquid distillate form.

(AA) "Marihuana" has the same meaning as in section 3719.01 of the Revised Code, except that it does not include hashish.

(BB) An offense is "committed in the vicinity of a juvenile" if the offender commits the offense within one hundred feet of a juvenile or within the view of a juvenile, regardless of whether the offender knows the age of the juvenile, whether the offender knows the offense is being committed within one hundred feet of or within view of the juvenile, or whether the juvenile actually views the commission of the offense.

(CC) "Presumption for a prison term" or "presumption that a prison term shall be imposed" means a presumption, as described in division (D) of section 2929.13 of the Revised Code, that a prison term is a necessary sanction for a felony in order to comply with the purposes and principles of sentencing under section 2929.11 of the Revised Code.

(DD) "Major drug offender" has the same meaning as in section 2929.01 of the Revised Code.

(EE) "Minor drug possession offense" means either of the following:

(1) A violation of section 2925.11 of the Revised Code as it existed prior to July 1, 1996;

(2) A violation of section 2925.11 of the Revised Code as it exists on and after July 1, 1996, that is a misdemeanor or a felony of the fifth degree.

(FF) "Mandatory prison term" has the same meaning as in section 2929.01 of the Revised Code.

(GG) "Crack cocaine" means a compound, mixture, preparation, or substance that is or contains any amount of cocaine that is analytically identified as the base form of cocaine or that is in a form that resembles rocks or pebbles generally intended for individual use.

(HH) "Adulterate" means to cause a drug to be adulterated as described in section 3715.63 of the Revised Code.

(II) "Public premises" means any hotel, restaurant, tavern, store, arena, hall, or other place of public accommodation, business, amusement, or resort.

(2004 H 163, eff. 9–23–04; 2002 H 364, § 8, eff. 1–1–04; 2002 H 364, § 1, eff. 4–8–03; 2002 H 415, eff. 4–7–03; 2002 S 123, eff. 1–1–04; 2002 H 273, eff. 7–23–02; 2001 H 7, eff. 8–7–01; 1999 H 202, eff. 2–9–00; 1999 H 18, eff. 10–20–99; 1998 S 200, eff. 3–30–99; 1998 H 606, eff. 3–9–99; 1998 S 117, eff. 8–5–98; 1998 S 66, eff. 7–22–98; 1996 S 223, eff. 3–18–97; 1996 S 269, eff. 7–1–96; 1996 H 125, eff. 7–1–96; 1995 S 143, § 5, eff. 7–1–96; 1995 S 143, § 1, eff. 3–5–96; 1995 S 2, eff. 7–1–96; 1993 H 156, eff. 5–19–93; 1991 H 322, H 62; 1990 S 258, H 215; 1985 H 281; 1982 H 269, § 4, S 199, H 535; 1980 S 378, H 900; 1978 H 565; 1976 S 414; 1975 H 300)

Note: See also following version of this section, eff. 5–6–05.

2925.01 Definitions (later effective date)

Note: See also preceding version of this section, in effect until 5–6–05.

As used in this chapter:

(A) "Administer," "controlled substance," "dispense," "distribute," "hypodermic," "manufacturer," "official written order," "person," "pharmacist," "pharmacy," "sale," "schedule I," "schedule II," "schedule III," "schedule IV," "schedule V," and "wholesaler" have the same meanings as in section 3719.01 of the Revised Code.

(B) "Drug dependent person" and "drug of abuse" have the same meanings as in section 3719.011 of the Revised Code.

(C) "Drug," "dangerous drug," "licensed health professional authorized to prescribe drugs," and "prescription" have the same meanings as in section 4729.01 of the Revised Code.

(D) "Bulk amount" of a controlled substance means any of the following:

(1) For any compound, mixture, preparation, or substance included in schedule I, schedule II, or schedule III, with the exception of marihuana, cocaine, L.S.D., heroin, and hashish and except as provided in division (D)(2) or (5) of this section, whichever of the following is applicable:

(a) An amount equal to or exceeding ten grams or twenty-five unit doses of a compound, mixture, preparation, or substance that is or contains any amount of a schedule I opiate or opium derivative;

(b) An amount equal to or exceeding ten grams of a compound, mixture, preparation, or substance that is or contains any amount of raw or gum opium;

(c) An amount equal to or exceeding thirty grams or ten unit doses of a compound, mixture, preparation, or substance that is or contains any amount of a schedule I hallucinogen other than tetrahydrocannabinol or lysergic acid amide, or a schedule I stimulant or depressant;

(d) An amount equal to or exceeding twenty grams or five times the maximum daily dose in the usual dose range specified in a standard pharmaceutical reference manual of a compound, mixture, preparation, or substance that is or contains any amount of a schedule II opiate or opium derivative;

(e) An amount equal to or exceeding five grams or ten unit doses of a compound, mixture, preparation, or substance that is or contains any amount of phencyclidine;

(f) An amount equal to or exceeding one hundred twenty grams or thirty times the maximum daily dose in the usual dose range specified in a standard pharmaceutical reference manual of a compound, mixture, preparation, or substance that is or contains any amount of a schedule II stimulant that is in a final dosage form manufactured by a person authorized by the "Federal Food, Drug, and Cosmetic Act," 52 Stat. 1040 (1938), 21 U.S.C.A. 301, as amended, and the federal drug abuse control laws, as defined in section 3719. 01 of the Revised Code, that is or contains any amount of a schedule II depressant substance or a schedule II hallucinogenic substance;

(g) An amount equal to or exceeding three grams of a compound, mixture, preparation, or substance that is or contains any amount of a schedule II stimulant, or any of its salts or isomers, that is not in a final dosage form manufactured by a person authorized by the Federal Food, Drug, and Cosmetic Act and the federal drug abuse control laws.

(2) An amount equal to or exceeding one hundred twenty grams or thirty times the maximum daily dose in the usual dose range specified in a standard pharmaceutical reference manual of a compound, mixture, preparation, or substance that is or contains any amount of a schedule III or IV substance other than an anabolic steroid or a schedule III opiate or opium derivative;

(3) An amount equal to or exceeding twenty grams or five times the maximum daily dose in the usual dose range specified in a standard pharmaceutical reference manual of a compound, mixture, preparation, or substance that is or contains any amount of a schedule III opiate or opium derivative;

(4) An amount equal to or exceeding two hundred fifty milliliters or two hundred fifty grams of a compound, mixture, preparation, or substance that is or contains any amount of a schedule V substance;

(5) An amount equal to or exceeding two hundred solid dosage units, sixteen grams, or sixteen milliliters of a compound, mixture, preparation, or substance that is or contains any amount of a schedule III anabolic steroid.

(E) "Unit dose" means an amount or unit of a compound, mixture, or preparation containing a controlled substance that is separately identifiable and in a form that indicates that it is the amount or unit by which the controlled substance is separately administered to or taken by an individual.

(F) "Cultivate" includes planting, watering, fertilizing, or tilling.

(G) "Drug abuse offense" means any of the following:

(1) A violation of division (A) of section 2913.02 that constitutes theft of drugs, or a violation of section 2925.02, 2925.03, 2925.04, 2925.041, 2925.05, 2925.06, 2925.11, 2925.12, 2925.13, 2925.22, 2925.23, 2925.24, 2925.31, 2925.32, 2925.36, or 2925.37 of the Revised Code;

(2) A violation of an existing or former law of this or any other state or of the United States that is substantially equivalent to any section listed in division (G)(1) of this section;

(3) An offense under an existing or former law of this or any other state, or of the United States, of which planting, cultivating, harvesting, processing, making, manufacturing, producing, shipping, transporting, delivering, acquiring, possessing, storing, distributing, dispensing, selling, inducing another to use, administering to another, using, or otherwise dealing with a controlled substance is an element;

(4) A conspiracy to commit, attempt to commit, or complicity in committing or attempting to commit any offense under division (G)(1), (2), or (3) of this section.

(H) "Felony drug abuse offense" means any drug abuse offense that would constitute a felony under the laws of this state, any other state, or the United States.

(I) "Harmful intoxicant" does not include beer or intoxicating liquor but means any of the following:

(1) Any compound, mixture, preparation, or substance the gas, fumes, or vapor of which when inhaled can induce intoxication, excitement, giddiness, irrational behavior, depression, stupefaction, paralysis, unconsciousness, asphyxiation, or other harmful physiological effects, and includes, but is not limited to, any of the following:

(a) Any volatile organic solvent, plastic cement, model cement, fingernail polish remover, lacquer thinner, cleaning fluid, gasoline, or other preparation containing a volatile organic solvent;

(b) Any aerosol propellant;

(c) Any fluorocarbon refrigerant;

(d) Any anesthetic gas.

(2) Gamma Butyrolactone;

(3) 1,4 Butanediol.

(J) "Manufacture" means to plant, cultivate, harvest, process, make, prepare, or otherwise engage in any part of the production of a drug, by propagation, extraction, chemical synthesis, or compounding, or any combination of the same, and includes packaging, repackaging, labeling, and other activities incident to production.

(K) "Possess" or "possession" means having control over a thing or substance, but may not be inferred solely from mere access to the thing or substance through ownership or occupation of the premises upon which the thing or substance is found.

(L) "Sample drug" means a drug or pharmaceutical preparation that would be hazardous to health or safety if used without the supervision of a licensed health professional authorized to prescribe drugs, or a drug of abuse, and that, at one time, had been placed in a container plainly marked as a sample by a manufacturer.

(M) "Standard pharmaceutical reference manual" means the current edition, with cumulative changes if any, of any of the following reference works:

(1) "The National Formulary";

(2) "The United States Pharmacopeia," prepared by authority of the United States Pharmacopeial Convention, Inc.;

(3) Other standard references that are approved by the state board of pharmacy.

(N) "Juvenile" means a person under eighteen years of age.

(O) "Counterfeit controlled substance" means any of the following:

(1) Any drug that bears, or whose container or label bears, a trademark, trade name, or other identifying mark used without authorization of the owner of rights to that trademark, trade name, or identifying mark;

(2) Any unmarked or unlabeled substance that is represented to be a controlled substance manufactured, processed, packed, or distributed by a person other than the person that manufactured, processed, packed, or distributed it;

(3) Any substance that is represented to be a controlled substance but is not a controlled substance or is a different controlled substance;

(4) Any substance other than a controlled substance that a reasonable person would believe to be a controlled substance because of its similarity in shape, size, and color, or its markings, labeling, packaging, distribution, or the price for which it is sold or offered for sale.

(P) An offense is "committed in the vicinity of a school' ' if the offender commits the offense on school premises, in a school building, or within one thousand feet of the boundaries of any school premises, regardless of whether the offender knows the offense is being committed on school premises, in a school building, or within one thousand feet of the boundaries of any school premises.

(Q) "School" means any school operated by a board of education, any community school established under Chapter 3314. of the Revised Code, or any nonpublic school for which the state board of education prescribes minimum standards under section 3301.07 of the Revised Code, whether or not any instruction, extracurricular activities, or training provided by the school is being conducted at the time a criminal offense is committed.

(R) "School premises" means either of the following:

(1) The parcel of real property on which any school is situated, whether or not any instruction, extracurricular activities, or training provided by the school is being conducted on the premises at the time a criminal offense is committed;

(2) Any other parcel of real property that is owned or leased by a board of education of a school, the governing authority of a community school established under Chapter 3314. of the Revised Code, or the governing body of a nonpublic school for which the state board of education prescribes minimum standards under section 3301.07 of the Revised Code and on which some of the instruction, extracurricular activities, or training of the school is conducted, whether or not any instruction, extracurricular activities, or training provided by the school is being conducted on the parcel of real property at the time a criminal offense is committed.

(S) "School building" means any building in which any of the instruction, extracurricular activities, or training provided by a school is conducted, whether or not any instruction, extracurricular activities, or training provided by the school is being conducted in the school building at the time a criminal offense is committed.

(T) "Disciplinary counsel" means the disciplinary counsel appointed by the board of commissioners on grievances and discipline of the supreme court under the Rules for the Government of the Bar of Ohio.

(U) "Certified grievance committee" means a duly constituted and organized committee of the Ohio state bar association or of one or more local bar associations of the state of Ohio that complies with the criteria set forth in Rule V, section 6 of the Rules for the Government of the Bar of Ohio.

(V) "Professional license" means any license, permit, certificate, registration, qualification, admission, temporary license, temporary permit, temporary certificate, or temporary registration that is described in divisions (W)(1) to (36) of this section and that qualifies a person as a professionally licensed person.

(W) "Professionally licensed person" means any of the following:

(1) A person who has obtained a license as a manufacturer of controlled substances or a wholesaler of controlled substances under Chapter 3719. of the Revised Code;

(2) A person who has received a certificate or temporary certificate as a certified public accountant or who has registered as a public accountant under Chapter 4701. of the Revised Code and who holds an Ohio permit issued under that chapter;

(3) A person who holds a certificate of qualification to practice architecture issued or renewed and registered under Chapter 4703. of the Revised Code;

(4) A person who is registered as a landscape architect under Chapter 4703. of the Revised Code or who holds a permit as a landscape architect issued under that chapter;

(5) A person licensed under Chapter 4707. of the Revised Code;

(6) A person who has been issued a certificate of registration as a registered barber under Chapter 4709. of the Revised Code;

(7) A person licensed and regulated to engage in the business of a debt pooling company by a legislative authority, under authority of Chapter 4710. of the Revised Code;

(8) A person who has been issued a cosmetologist's license, hair designer's license, manicurist's license, esthetician's license, natural hair stylist's license, managing cosmetologist's license, managing hair designer's license, managing manicurist's license, managing esthetician's license, managing natural hair stylist's license, cosmetology instructor's license, hair design instructor's license, manicurist instructor's license, esthetics instructor's license, natural hair style instructor's license, independent contractor's license, or tanning facility permit under Chapter 4713. of the Revised Code;

(9) A person who has been issued a license to practice dentistry, a general anesthesia permit, a conscious intravenous sedation permit, a limited resident's license, a limited teaching license, a dental hygienist's license, or a dental hygienist's teacher's certificate under Chapter 4715. of the Revised Code;

(10) A person who has been issued an embalmer's license, a funeral director's license, a funeral home license, or a crematory license, or who has been registered for an embalmer's or funeral director's apprenticeship under Chapter 4717. of the Revised Code;

(11) A person who has been licensed as a registered nurse or practical nurse, or who has been issued a certificate for the practice of nurse-midwifery under Chapter 4723. of the Revised Code;

(12) A person who has been licensed to practice optometry or to engage in optical dispensing under Chapter 4725. of the Revised Code;

(13) A person licensed to act as a pawnbroker under Chapter 4727. of the Revised Code;

(14) A person licensed to act as a precious metals dealer under Chapter 4728. of the Revised Code;

(15) A person licensed as a pharmacist, a pharmacy intern, a wholesale distributor of dangerous drugs, or a terminal distributor of dangerous drugs under Chapter 4729. of the Revised Code;

(16) A person who is authorized to practice as a physician assistant under Chapter 4730. of the Revised Code;

(17) A person who has been issued a certificate to practice medicine and surgery, osteopathic medicine and surgery, a limited branch of medicine, or podiatry under Chapter 4731. of the Revised Code;

(18) A person licensed as a psychologist or school psychologist under Chapter 4732. of the Revised Code;

(19) A person registered to practice the profession of engineering or surveying under Chapter 4733. of the Revised Code;

(20) A person who has been issued a license to practice chiropractic under Chapter 4734. of the Revised Code;

(21) A person licensed to act as a real estate broker or real estate salesperson under Chapter 4735. of the Revised Code;

(22) A person registered as a registered sanitarian under Chapter 4736. of the Revised Code;

(23) A person licensed to operate or maintain a junkyard under Chapter 4737. of the Revised Code;

(24) A person who has been issued a motor vehicle salvage dealer's license under Chapter 4738. of the Revised Code;

(25) A person who has been licensed to act as a steam engineer under Chapter 4739. of the Revised Code;

(26) A person who has been issued a license or temporary permit to practice veterinary medicine or any of its branches, or who is registered as a graduate animal technician under Chapter 4741. of the Revised Code;

(27) A person who has been issued a hearing aid dealer's or fitter's license or trainee permit under Chapter 4747. of the Revised Code;

(28) A person who has been issued a class A, class B, or class C license or who has been registered as an investigator or security guard employee under Chapter 4749. of the Revised Code;

(29) A person licensed and registered to practice as a nursing home administrator under Chapter 4751. of the Revised Code;

(30) A person licensed to practice as a speech-language pathologist or audiologist under Chapter 4753. of the Revised Code;

(31) A person issued a license as an occupational therapist or physical therapist under Chapter 4755. of the Revised Code;

(32) A person who is licensed as a professional clinical counselor or professional counselor, licensed as a social worker or independent social worker, or registered as a social work assistant under Chapter 4757. of the Revised Code;

(33) A person issued a license to practice dietetics under Chapter 4759. of the Revised Code;

(34) A person who has been issued a license or limited permit to practice respiratory therapy under Chapter 4761. of the Revised Code;

(35) A person who has been issued a real estate appraiser certificate under Chapter 4763. of the Revised Code;

(36) A person who has been admitted to the bar by order of the supreme court in compliance with its prescribed and published rules.

(X) "Cocaine" means any of the following:

(1) A cocaine salt, isomer, or derivative, a salt of a cocaine isomer or derivative, or the base form of cocaine;

(2) Coca leaves or a salt, compound, derivative, or preparation of coca leaves, including ecgonine, a salt, isomer, or derivative of ecgonine, or a salt of an isomer or derivative of ecgonine;

(3) A salt, compound, derivative, or preparation of a substance identified in division (X)(1) or (2) of this section that is chemically equivalent to or identical with any of those substances, except that the substances shall not include decocainized coca leaves or extraction of coca leaves if the extractions do not contain cocaine or ecgonine.

(Y) "L.S.D." means lysergic acid diethylamide.

(Z) "Hashish" means the resin or a preparation of the resin contained in marihuana, whether in solid form or in a liquid concentrate, liquid extract, or liquid distillate form.

(AA) "Marihuana" has the same meaning as in section 3719.01 of the Revised Code, except that it does not include hashish.

(BB) An offense is "committed in the vicinity of a juvenile" if the offender commits the offense within one hundred feet of a juvenile or within the view of a juvenile, regardless of whether the offender knows the age of the juvenile, whether the offender knows the offense is being committed within one hundred feet of or within view of the juvenile, or whether the juvenile actually views the commission of the offense.

(CC) "Presumption for a prison term" or "presumption that a prison term shall be imposed" means a presumption, as described in division (D) of section 2929.13 of the Revised Code, that a prison term is a necessary sanction for a felony in order to comply with the purposes and principles of sentencing under section 2929.11 of the Revised Code.

(DD) "Major drug offender" has the same meaning as in section 2929.01 of the Revised Code.

(EE) "Minor drug possession offense" means either of the following:

(1) A violation of section 2925.11 of the Revised Code as it existed prior to July 1, 1996;

(2) A violation of section 2925.11 of the Revised Code as it exists on and after July 1, 1996, that is a misdemeanor or a felony of the fifth degree.

(FF) "Mandatory prison term" has the same meaning as in section 2929.01 of the Revised Code.

(GG) "Crack cocaine" means a compound, mixture, preparation, or substance that is or contains any amount of cocaine that is analytically identified as the base form of cocaine or that is in a form that resembles rocks or pebbles generally intended for individual use.

(HH) "Adulterate" means to cause a drug to be adulterated as described in section 3715.63 of the Revised Code.

(II) "Public premises" means any hotel, restaurant, tavern, store, arena, hall, or other place of public accommodation, business, amusement, or resort.

(2004 S 209, eff. 5–6–05; 2004 H 163, eff. 9–23–04; 2002 H 364, § 8, eff. 1–1–04; 2002 H 364, § 1, eff. 4–8–03; 2002 H 415, eff. 4–7–03; 2002 S 123, eff. 1–1–04; 2002 H 273, eff. 7–23–02; 2001 H 7, eff. 8–7–01; 1999 H 202, eff. 2–9–00; 1999 H 18, eff. 10–20–99; 1998 S 200, eff. 3–30–99; 1998 H 606, eff. 3–9–99; 1998 S 117, eff. 8–5–98; 1998 S 66, eff. 7–22–98; 1996 S 223, eff. 3–18–97; 1996 S 269, eff. 7–1–96; 1996 H 125, eff. 7–1–96; 1995 S 143, § 5, eff. 7–1–96; 1995 S 143, § 1, eff. 3–5–96; 1995 S 2, eff. 7–1–96; 1993 H 156, eff. 5–19–93; 1991 H 322, H 62; 1990 S 258, H 215; 1985 H 281; 1982 H 269, § 4, S 199, H 535; 1980 S 378, H 900; 1978 H 565; 1976 S 414; 1975 H 300)

Note: See also preceding version of this section, in effect until 5–6–05.

DRUG OFFENSES

2925.02 Corrupting another with drugs

(A) No person shall knowingly do any of the following:

(1) By force, threat, or deception, administer to another or induce or cause another to use a controlled substance;

(2) By any means, administer or furnish to another or induce or cause another to use a controlled substance with purpose to cause serious physical harm to the other person, or with purpose to cause the other person to become drug dependent;

(3) By any means, administer or furnish to another or induce or cause another to use a controlled substance, and thereby cause serious physical harm to the other person, or cause the other person to become drug dependent;

(4) By any means, do any of the following:

(a) Furnish or administer a controlled substance to a juvenile who is at least two years the offender's junior, when the offender knows the age of the juvenile or is reckless in that regard;

(b) Induce or cause a juvenile who is at least two years the offender's junior to use a controlled substance, when the offender knows the age of the juvenile or is reckless in that regard;

(c) Induce or cause a juvenile who is at least two years the offender's junior to commit a felony drug abuse offense, when the offender knows the age of the juvenile or is reckless in that regard;

(d) Use a juvenile, whether or not the offender knows the age of the juvenile, to perform any surveillance activity that is intended to prevent the detection of the offender or any other person in the commission of a felony drug abuse offense or to prevent the arrest of the offender or any other person for the commission of a felony drug abuse offense.

(B) Division (A)(1), (3), or (4) of this section does not apply to manufacturers, wholesalers, licensed health professionals authorized to prescribe drugs, pharmacists, owners of pharmacies, and other persons whose conduct is in accordance with Chapters 3719., 4715., 4723., 4729., 4731., and 4741. of the Revised Code.

(C) Whoever violates this section is guilty of corrupting another with drugs. The penalty for the offense shall be determined as follows:

(1) Except as otherwise provided in this division, if the drug involved is any compound, mixture, preparation, or substance included in schedule I or II, with the exception of marihuana, corrupting another with drugs is a felony of the second degree, and, subject to division (E) of this section, the court shall impose as a mandatory prison term one of the prison terms prescribed for a felony of the second degree. If the drug involved is any compound, mixture, preparation, or substance included in schedule I or II, with the exception of marihuana, and if the offense was committed in the vicinity of a school, corrupting another with drugs is a felony of the first degree, and, subject to division (E) of this section, the court shall impose as a mandatory prison term one of the prison terms prescribed for a felony of the first degree.

(2) Except as otherwise provided in this division, if the drug involved is any compound, mixture, preparation, or substance included in schedule III, IV, or V, corrupting another with drugs is a felony of the second degree, and there is a presumption for a prison term for the offense. If the drug involved is any compound, mixture, preparation, or substance included in schedule III, IV, or V and if the offense was committed in the vicinity of a school, corrupting another with drugs is a felony of the second degree, and the court shall impose as a mandatory prison term one of the prison terms prescribed for a felony of the second degree.

(3) Except as otherwise provided in this division, if the drug involved is marihuana, corrupting another with drugs is a felony of the fourth degree, and division (C) of section 2929.13 of the Revised Code applies in determining whether to impose a prison term on the offender. If the drug involved is marihuana and if the offense was committed in the vicinity of a school, corrupting another with drugs is a felony of the third degree, and division (C) of section 2929.13 of the Revised Code applies in determining whether to impose a prison term on the offender.

(D) In addition to any prison term authorized or required by division (C) or (E) of this section and sections 2929.13 and 2929.14 of the Revised Code and in addition to any other sanction imposed for the offense under this section or sections 2929.11 to 2929.18 of the Revised Code, the court that sentences an offender who is convicted of or pleads guilty to a violation of division (A) of this section or the clerk of that court shall do all of the following that are applicable regarding the offender:

(1)(a) If the violation is a felony of the first, second, or third degree, the court shall impose upon the offender the mandatory fine specified for the offense under division (B)(1) of section 2929.18 of the Revised Code unless, as specified in that division, the court determines that the offender is indigent.

(b) Notwithstanding any contrary provision of section 3719.21 of the Revised Code, any mandatory fine imposed pursuant to division (D)(1)(a) of this section and any fine imposed for a violation of this section pursuant to division (A) of section 2929.18 of the Revised Code shall be paid by the clerk of the court in accordance with and subject to the requirements of, and shall be used as specified in, division (F) of section 2925.03 of the Revised Code.

(c) If a person is charged with any violation of this section that is a felony of the first, second, or third degree, posts bail, and forfeits the bail, the forfeited bail shall be paid by the clerk of the court pursuant to division (D)(1)(b) of this section as if it were a fine imposed for a violation of this section.

(2) The court shall suspend for not less than six months nor more than five years the offender's driver's or commercial driver's license or permit. If an offender's driver's or commercial driver's license or permit is suspended pursuant to this division, the offender, at any time after the expiration of two years from the day on which the offender's sentence was imposed or from the day on which the offender finally was released from a prison term under the sentence, whichever is later, may file a motion with the sentencing court requesting termination of the suspension. Upon the filing of the motion and the court's finding of good cause for the termination, the court may terminate the suspension.

(3) If the offender is a professionally licensed person, in addition to any other sanction imposed for a violation of this section, the court immediately shall comply with section 2925.38 of the Revised Code.

(E) Notwithstanding the prison term otherwise authorized or required for the offense under division (C) of this section and sections 2929.13 and 2929.14 of the Revised Code, if the violation of division (A) of this section involves the sale, offer to sell, or possession of a schedule I or II controlled substance, with the exception of marihuana, and if the court imposing sentence upon the offender finds that the offender as a result of the violation is a major drug offender and is guilty of a specification of the type described in section 2941.1410 of the Revised Code, the court, in lieu of the prison term that otherwise is authorized or required, shall impose upon the offender the mandatory prison term specified in division (D)(3)(a) of section 2929.14 of the Revised Code and may impose an additional prison term under division (D)(3)(b) of that section.

(2002 S 123, eff. 1–1–04; 2000 H 241, eff. 5–17–00; 1999 S 107, eff. 3–23–00; 1998 S 66, eff. 7–22–98; 1996 S 269, eff. 7–1–96; 1995 S 2, eff. 7–1–96; 1994 H 391, eff. 7–21–94; 1993 H 377, eff. 9–30–93; 1992 H 591; 1990 S 258, H 215; 1975 H 300)

2925.03 Trafficking offenses

(A) No person shall knowingly do any of the following:

(1) Sell or offer to sell a controlled substance;

(2) Prepare for shipment, ship, transport, deliver, prepare for distribution, or distribute a controlled substance, when the offender knows or has reasonable cause to believe that the controlled substance is intended for sale or resale by the offender or another person.

(B) This section does not apply to any of the following:

(1) Manufacturers, licensed health professionals authorized to prescribe drugs, pharmacists, owners of pharmacies, and other persons whose conduct is in accordance with Chapters 3719., 4715., 4723., 4729., 4731., and 4741. of the Revised Code;

(2) If the offense involves an anabolic steroid, any person who is conducting or participating in a research project involving the use of an anabolic steroid if the project has been approved by the United States food and drug administration;

(3) Any person who sells, offers for sale, prescribes, dispenses, or administers for livestock or other nonhuman species an anabolic steroid that is expressly intended for administration through implants to livestock or other nonhuman species and approved for that purpose under the "Federal Food, Drug, and Cosmetic Act," 52 Stat. 1040 (1938), 21 U.S.C.A. 301, as amended, and is sold, offered for sale, prescribed, dispensed, or administered for that purpose in accordance with that act.

(C) Whoever violates division (A) of this section is guilty of one of the following:

(1) If the drug involved in the violation is any compound, mixture, preparation, or substance included in schedule I or schedule II, with the exception of marihuana, cocaine, L.S.D., heroin, and hashish, whoever violates division (A) of this section is guilty of aggravated trafficking in drugs. The penalty for the offense shall be determined as follows:

(a) Except as otherwise provided in division (C)(1)(b), (c), (d), (e), or (f) of this section, aggravated trafficking in drugs is a felony of the fourth degree, and division (C) of section 2929.13 of the Revised Code applies in determining whether to impose a prison term on the offender.

(b) Except as otherwise provided in division (C)(1)(c), (d), (e), or (f) of this section, if the offense was committed in the vicinity of a school or in the vicinity of a juvenile, aggravated trafficking in drugs is a felony of the third degree, and division (C) of section 2929.13 of the Revised Code applies in determining whether to impose a prison term on the offender.

(c) Except as otherwise provided in this division, if the amount of the drug involved equals or exceeds the bulk amount but is less than five times the bulk amount, aggravated trafficking in drugs is a felony of the third degree, and the court shall impose as a mandatory prison term one of the prison terms prescribed for a felony of the third degree. If the amount of the drug involved is within that range and if the offense was committed in the vicinity of a school or in the vicinity of a juvenile, aggravated trafficking in drugs is a felony of the second degree, and the court shall impose as a mandatory prison term one of the prison terms prescribed for a felony of the second degree.

(d) Except as otherwise provided in this division, if the amount of the drug involved equals or exceeds five times the bulk amount but is less than fifty times the bulk amount, aggravated trafficking in drugs is a felony of the second degree, and the court shall impose as a mandatory prison term one of the prison terms prescribed for a felony of the second degree. If the amount of the drug involved is within that range and if the offense was committed in the vicinity of a school or in the vicinity of a juvenile, aggravated trafficking in drugs is a felony of the first degree, and the court shall impose as a mandatory prison term one of the prison terms prescribed for a felony of the first degree.

(e) If the amount of the drug involved equals or exceeds fifty times the bulk amount but is less than one hundred times the bulk amount and regardless of whether the offense was committed in the vicinity of a school or in the vicinity of a juvenile, aggravated trafficking in drugs is a felony of the first degree, and the court shall impose as a mandatory prison term one of the prison terms prescribed for a felony of the first degree.

(f) If the amount of the drug involved equals or exceeds one hundred times the bulk amount and regardless of whether the offense was committed in the vicinity of a school or in the vicinity of a juvenile, aggravated trafficking in drugs is a felony of the first degree, the offender is a major drug offender, and the court shall impose as a mandatory prison term the maximum prison term prescribed for a felony of the first degree and may impose an additional prison term prescribed for a major drug offender under division (D)(3)(b) of section 2929.14 of the Revised Code.

(2) If the drug involved in the violation is any compound, mixture, preparation, or substance included in schedule III, IV, or V, whoever violates division (A) of this section is guilty of trafficking in drugs. The penalty for the offense shall be determined as follows:

(a) Except as otherwise provided in division (C)(2)(b), (c), (d), or (e) of this section, trafficking in drugs is a felony of the fifth degree, and division (C) of section 2929.13 of the Revised Code applies in determining whether to impose a prison term on the offender.

(b) Except as otherwise provided in division (C)(2)(c), (d), or (e) of this section, if the offense was committed in the vicinity of a school or in the vicinity of a juvenile, trafficking in drugs is a felony of the fourth degree, and division (C) of section 2929.13 of the Revised Code applies in determining whether to impose a prison term on the offender.

(c) Except as otherwise provided in this division, if the amount of the drug involved equals or exceeds the bulk amount but is less than five times the bulk amount, trafficking in drugs is a felony of the fourth degree, and there is a presumption for a prison term for the offense. If the amount of the drug involved is within that range and if the offense was committed in the vicinity of a school or in the vicinity of a juvenile, trafficking in drugs is a felony of the third degree, and there is a presumption for a prison term for the offense.

(d) Except as otherwise provided in this division, if the amount of the drug involved equals or exceeds five times the bulk amount but is less than fifty times the bulk amount, trafficking in drugs is a felony of the third degree, and there is a presumption for a prison term for the offense. If the amount of the drug involved is within that range and if the offense was committed in the vicinity of a school or in the vicinity of a juvenile, trafficking in drugs is a felony of the second degree, and there is a presumption for a prison term for the offense.

(e) Except as otherwise provided in this division, if the amount of the drug involved equals or exceeds fifty times the bulk amount, trafficking in drugs is a felony of the second degree, and the court shall impose as a mandatory prison term one of the prison terms prescribed for a felony of the second degree. If the amount of the drug involved equals or exceeds fifty times the bulk amount and if the offense was committed in the vicinity of a school or in the vicinity of a juvenile, trafficking in drugs is a felony of the first degree, and the court shall impose as a mandatory prison term one of the prison terms prescribed for a felony of the first degree.

(3) If the drug involved in the violation is marihuana or a compound, mixture, preparation, or substance containing marihuana other than hashish, whoever violates division (A) of this section is guilty of trafficking in marihuana. The penalty for the offense shall be determined as follows:

(a) Except as otherwise provided in division (C)(3)(b), (c), (d), (e), (f), or (g) of this section, trafficking in marihuana is a felony of the fifth degree, and division (C) of section 2929.13 of the Revised Code applies in determining whether to impose a prison term on the offender.

(b) Except as otherwise provided in division (C)(3)(c), (d), (e), (f), or (g) of this section, if the offense was committed in the vicinity of a school or in the vicinity of a juvenile, trafficking in marihuana is a felony of the fourth degree, and division (C) of section 2929.13 of the Revised Code applies in determining whether to impose a prison term on the offender.

(c) Except as otherwise provided in this division, if the amount of the drug involved equals or exceeds two hundred grams but is less than one thousand grams, trafficking in marihuana is a felony of the fourth degree, and division (C) of section 2929.13 of the Revised Code applies in determining whether to impose a prison term on the offender. If the amount of the drug involved is within that range and if the offense was committed in the vicinity of a school or in the vicinity of a juvenile, trafficking in marihuana is a felony of the third degree, and division (C) of section 2929.13 of the Revised Code applies in determining whether to impose a prison term on the offender.

(d) Except as otherwise provided in this division, if the amount of the drug involved equals or exceeds one thousand grams but is less than five thousand grams, trafficking in marihuana is a felony of the third degree, and division (C) of section 2929.13 of the Revised Code applies in determining whether to impose a prison term on the offender. If the amount of the drug involved is within that range and if the offense was committed in the vicinity of a school or in the vicinity of a juvenile, trafficking in marihuana is a felony of the second degree, and there is a presumption that a prison term shall be imposed for the offense.

(e) Except as otherwise provided in this division, if the amount of the drug involved equals or exceeds five thousand grams but is less than twenty thousand grams, trafficking in marihuana is a felony of the third degree, and there is a presumption that a prison term shall be imposed for the offense. If the amount of the drug involved is within that range and if the offense was committed in the vicinity of a school or in the vicinity of a juvenile, trafficking in marihuana is a felony of the second degree, and there is a presumption that a prison term shall be imposed for the offense.

(f) Except as otherwise provided in this division, if the amount of the drug involved equals or exceeds twenty thousand grams, trafficking in marihuana is a felony of the second degree, and the court shall impose as a mandatory prison term the maximum prison term prescribed for a felony of the second degree. If the amount of the drug involved equals or exceeds twenty thousand grams and if the offense was committed in the vicinity of a school or in the vicinity of a juvenile, trafficking in marihuana is a felony of the first degree, and the court shall impose as a mandatory prison term the maximum prison term prescribed for a felony of the first degree.

(g) Except as otherwise provided in this division, if the offense involves a gift of twenty grams or less of marihuana, trafficking in marihuana is a minor misdemeanor upon a first offense and a misdemeanor of the third degree upon a subsequent offense. If the offense involves a gift of twenty grams or less of marihuana and if the offense was committed in the vicinity of a school or in the vicinity of a juvenile, trafficking in marihuana is a misdemeanor of the third degree.

(4) If the drug involved in the violation is cocaine or a compound, mixture, preparation, or substance containing cocaine, whoever violates division (A) of this section is guilty of trafficking in cocaine. The penalty for the offense shall be determined as follows:

(a) Except as otherwise provided in division (C)(4)(b), (c), (d), (e), (f), or (g) of this section, trafficking in cocaine is a felony of the fifth degree, and division (C) of section 2929.13 of the Revised Code applies in determining whether to impose a prison term on the offender.

(b) Except as otherwise provided in division (C)(4)(c), (d), (e), (f), or (g) of this section, if the offense was committed in the vicinity of a school or in the vicinity of a juvenile, trafficking in cocaine is a felony of the fourth degree, and division (C) of section 2929.13 of the Revised Code applies in determining whether to impose a prison term on the offender.

(c) Except as otherwise provided in this division, if the amount of the drug involved equals or exceeds five grams but is less than ten grams of cocaine that is not crack cocaine or equals or exceeds one gram but is less than five grams of crack cocaine, trafficking in cocaine is a felony of the fourth degree, and there is a presumption for a prison term for the offense. If the amount of the drug involved is within one of those ranges and if the offense was committed in the vicinity of a school or in the vicinity of a juvenile, trafficking in cocaine is a felony of the third degree, and there is a presumption for a prison term for the offense.

(d) Except as otherwise provided in this division, if the amount of the drug involved equals or exceeds ten grams but is less than one hundred grams of cocaine that is not crack cocaine or equals or exceeds five grams but is less than ten grams of crack cocaine, trafficking in cocaine is a felony of the third degree, and the court shall impose as a mandatory prison term one of the prison terms prescribed for a felony of the third degree. If the amount of the drug involved is within one of those ranges and if the offense was committed in the vicinity of a school or in the vicinity of a juvenile, trafficking in cocaine is a felony of the second degree, and the court shall impose as a mandatory prison term one of the prison terms prescribed for a felony of the second degree.

(e) Except as otherwise provided in this division, if the amount of the drug involved equals or exceeds one hundred grams but is less than five hundred grams of cocaine that is not crack cocaine or equals or exceeds ten grams but is less than twenty-five grams of crack cocaine, trafficking in cocaine is a felony of the second degree, and the court shall impose as a mandatory prison term one of the prison terms prescribed for a felony of the second degree. If the amount of the drug involved is within one of those ranges and if the offense was committed in the vicinity of a school or in the vicinity of a juvenile, trafficking in cocaine is a felony of the first degree, and the court shall impose as a mandatory prison term one of the prison terms prescribed for a felony of the first degree.

(f) If the amount of the drug involved equals or exceeds five hundred grams but is less than one thousand grams of cocaine that is not crack cocaine or equals or exceeds twenty-five grams but is less than one hundred grams of crack cocaine and regardless of whether the offense was committed in the vicinity of a school or in the vicinity of a juvenile, trafficking in cocaine is a felony of the first degree, and the court shall impose as a mandatory prison term one of the prison terms prescribed for a felony of the first degree.

(g) If the amount of the drug involved equals or exceeds one thousand grams of cocaine that is not crack cocaine or equals or exceeds one hundred grams of crack cocaine and regardless of whether the offense was committed in the vicinity of a school or in the vicinity of a juvenile, trafficking in cocaine is a felony of the first degree, the offender is a major drug offender, and the court shall impose as a mandatory prison term the maximum prison term prescribed for a felony of the first degree and may impose an additional mandatory prison term prescribed for a major drug offender under division (D)(3)(b) of section 2929.14 of the Revised Code.

(5) If the drug involved in the violation is L.S.D. or a compound, mixture, preparation, or substance containing L.S.D., whoever violates division (A) of this section is guilty of trafficking in L.S.D. The penalty for the offense shall be determined as follows:

(a) Except as otherwise provided in division (C)(5)(b), (c), (d), (e), (f), or (g) of this section, trafficking in L.S.D. is a felony of the fifth degree, and division (C) of section 2929.13 of the Revised Code applies in determining whether to impose a prison term on the offender.

(b) Except as otherwise provided in division (C)(5)(c), (d), (e), (f), or (g) of this section, if the offense was committed in the vicinity of a school or in the vicinity of a juvenile, trafficking in L.S.D. is a felony of the fourth degree, and division (C) of section 2929.13 of the Revised Code applies in determining whether to impose a prison term on the offender.

(c) Except as otherwise provided in this division, if the amount of the drug involved equals or exceeds ten unit doses but is less than fifty unit doses of L.S.D. in a solid form or equals or exceeds one gram but is less than five grams of L.S.D. in a liquid concentrate, liquid extract, or liquid distillate form, trafficking in L.S.D. is a felony of the fourth degree, and there is a presumption for a prison term for the offense. If the amount of the drug involved is within that range and if the offense was committed in the vicinity of a school or in the vicinity of a juvenile, trafficking in L.S.D. is a felony of the third degree, and there is a presumption for a prison term for the offense.

(d) Except as otherwise provided in this division, if the amount of the drug involved equals or exceeds fifty unit doses but is less than two hundred fifty unit doses of L.S.D. in a solid form or equals or exceeds five grams but is less than twenty-five grams of L.S.D. in a liquid concentrate, liquid extract, or liquid distillate form, trafficking in L.S.D. is a felony of the third degree, and the court shall impose as a mandatory prison term one of the prison terms prescribed for a felony of the third degree. If the amount of the drug involved is within that range and if the offense was committed in the vicinity of a school or in the vicinity of a juvenile, trafficking in L.S.D. is a felony of the second degree, and the court shall impose as a mandatory prison term one of the prison terms prescribed for a felony of the second degree.

(e) Except as otherwise provided in this division, if the amount of the drug involved equals or exceeds two hundred fifty unit doses but is less than one thousand unit doses of L.S.D. in a solid form or equals or exceeds twenty-five grams but is less than one hundred grams of L.S.D. in a liquid concentrate, liquid extract, or liquid distillate form, trafficking in L.S.D. is a felony of the second degree, and the court shall impose as a mandatory prison term one of the prison terms prescribed for a felony of the second degree. If the amount of the drug involved is within that range and if the offense was committed in the vicinity of a school or in the vicinity of a juvenile, trafficking in L.S.D. is a felony of the first degree, and the court shall impose as a mandatory prison term one of the prison terms prescribed for a felony of the first degree.

(f) If the amount of the drug involved equals or exceeds one thousand unit doses but is less than five thousand unit doses of L.S.D. in a solid form or equals or exceeds one hundred grams but is less than five hundred grams of L.S.D. in a liquid concentrate, liquid extract, or liquid distillate form and regardless of whether the offense was committed in the vicinity of a school or in the vicinity of a juvenile, trafficking in L.S.D. is a felony of the first degree, and the court shall impose as a mandatory prison term one of the prison terms prescribed for a felony of the first degree.

(g) If the amount of the drug involved equals or exceeds five thousand unit doses of L.S.D. in a solid form or equals or exceeds five hundred grams of L.S.D. in a liquid concentrate, liquid extract, or liquid distillate form and regardless of whether the offense was committed in the vicinity of a school or in the vicinity of a juvenile, trafficking in L.S.D. is a felony of the first degree, the offender is a major drug offender, and the court shall impose as a mandatory prison term the maximum prison term prescribed for a felony of the first degree and may impose an additional mandatory prison term prescribed for a major drug offender under division (D)(3)(b) of section 2929.14 of the Revised Code.

(6) If the drug involved in the violation is heroin or a compound, mixture, preparation, or substance containing heroin, whoever violates division (A) of this section is guilty of trafficking in heroin. The penalty for the offense shall be determined as follows:

(a) Except as otherwise provided in division (C)(6)(b), (c), (d), (e), (f), or (g) of this section, trafficking in heroin is a felony of the fifth degree, and division (C) of section 2929.13 of the Revised Code applies in determining whether to impose a prison term on the offender.

(b) Except as otherwise provided in division (C)(6)(c), (d), (e), (f), or (g) of this section, if the offense was committed in the vicinity of a school or in the vicinity of a juvenile, trafficking in heroin is a felony of the fourth degree, and division (C) of section 2929.13 of the Revised Code applies in determining whether to impose a prison term on the offender.

(c) Except as otherwise provided in this division, if the amount of the drug involved equals or exceeds ten unit doses but is less than fifty unit doses or equals or exceeds one gram but is less than five grams, trafficking in heroin is a felony of the fourth degree, and there is a presumption for a prison term for the offense. If the amount of the drug involved is within that range and if the offense was committed in the vicinity of a school or in the vicinity of a juvenile, trafficking in heroin is a felony of the third degree, and there is a presumption for a prison term for the offense.

(d) Except as otherwise provided in this division, if the amount of the drug involved equals or exceeds fifty unit doses but is less than one hundred unit doses or equals or exceeds five grams but is less than ten grams, trafficking in heroin is a felony of the third degree, and there is a presumption for a prison term for the offense. If the amount of the drug involved is within that range and if the offense was committed in the vicinity of a school or in the vicinity of a juvenile, trafficking in heroin is a felony of the second degree, and there is a presumption for a prison term for the offense.

(e) Except as otherwise provided in this division, if the amount of the drug involved equals or exceeds one hundred unit doses but is less than five hundred unit doses or equals or exceeds ten grams but is less than fifty grams, trafficking in heroin is a felony of the second degree, and the court shall impose as a mandatory prison term one of the prison terms prescribed for a felony of the second degree. If the amount of the drug involved is within that range and if the offense was committed in the vicinity of a school or in the vicinity of a juvenile, trafficking in heroin is a felony of the first degree, and the court shall impose as a mandatory prison term one of the prison terms prescribed for a felony of the first degree.

(f) If the amount of the drug involved equals or exceeds five hundred unit doses but is less than two thousand five hundred unit doses or equals or exceeds fifty grams but is less than two hundred fifty grams and regardless of whether the offense was committed in the vicinity of a school or in the vicinity of a juvenile, trafficking in heroin is a felony of the first degree, and the court shall impose as a mandatory prison term one of the prison terms prescribed for a felony of the first degree.

(g) If the amount of the drug involved equals or exceeds two thousand five hundred unit doses or equals or exceeds two hundred fifty grams and regardless of whether the offense was committed in the vicinity of a school or in the vicinity of a juvenile, trafficking in heroin is a felony of the first degree, the offender is a major drug offender, and the court shall impose as a mandatory prison term the maximum prison term prescribed for a felony of the first degree and may impose an additional mandatory prison term prescribed for a major drug offender under division (D)(3)(b) of section 2929.14 of the Revised Code.

(7) If the drug involved in the violation is hashish or a compound, mixture, preparation, or substance containing hashish, whoever violates division (A) of this section is guilty of trafficking in hashish. The penalty for the offense shall be determined as follows:

(a) Except as otherwise provided in division (C)(7)(b), (c), (d), (e), or (f) of this section, trafficking in hashish is a felony of the fifth degree, and division (C) of section 2929.13 of the Revised Code applies in determining whether to impose a prison term on the offender.

(b) Except as otherwise provided in division (C)(7)(c), (d), (e), or (f) of this section, if the offense was committed in the vicinity of a school or in the vicinity of a juvenile, trafficking in hashish is a felony of the fourth degree, and division (C) of section 2929.13 of the Revised Code applies in determining whether to impose a prison term on the offender.

(c) Except as otherwise provided in this division, if the amount of the drug involved equals or exceeds ten grams but is less than fifty grams of hashish in a solid form or equals or exceeds two grams but is less than ten grams of hashish in a liquid concentrate, liquid extract, or liquid distillate form, trafficking in hashish is a felony of the fourth degree, and division (C) of section 2929.13 of the Revised Code applies in determining whether to impose a prison term on the offender. If the amount of the drug involved is within that range and if the offense was committed in the vicinity of a school or in the vicinity of a juvenile, trafficking in hashish is a felony of the third degree, and division (C) of section 2929.13 of the Revised Code applies in determining whether to impose a prison term on the offender.

(d) Except as otherwise provided in this division, if the amount of the drug involved equals or exceeds fifty grams but is less than two hundred fifty grams of hashish in a solid form or equals or exceeds ten grams but is less than fifty grams of hashish in a liquid concentrate, liquid extract, or liquid distillate form, trafficking in hashish is a felony of the third degree, and division (C) of section 2929.13 of the Revised Code applies in determining whether to impose a prison term on the offender. If the amount of the drug involved is within that range and if the offense was committed in the vicinity of a school or in the vicinity of a juvenile, trafficking in hashish is a felony of the second degree, and there is a presumption that a prison term shall be imposed for the offense.

(e) Except as otherwise provided in this division, if the amount of the drug involved equals or exceeds two hundred fifty grams but is less than one thousand grams of hashish in a solid form or equals or exceeds fifty grams but is less than two hundred grams of hashish in a liquid concentrate, liquid extract, or liquid distillate form, trafficking in hashish is a felony of the third degree, and there is a presumption that a prison term shall be imposed for the offense. If the amount of the drug involved is within that range and if the offense was committed in the vicinity of a school or in the vicinity of a juvenile, trafficking in hashish is a felony of the second degree, and there is a presumption that a prison term shall be imposed for the offense.

(f) Except as otherwise provided in this division, if the amount of the drug involved equals or exceeds one thousand grams of hashish in a solid form or equals or exceeds two hundred grams of hashish in a liquid concentrate, liquid extract, or liquid distillate form, trafficking in hashish is a felony of the second degree, and the court shall impose as a mandatory prison term the maximum prison term prescribed for a felony of the second degree. If the amount of the drug involved is within that range and if the offense was committed in the vicinity of a school or in the vicinity of a juvenile, trafficking in hashish is a felony of the first degree, and the court shall impose as a mandatory prison term the maximum prison term prescribed for a felony of the first degree.

(D) In addition to any prison term authorized or required by division (C) of this section and sections 2929.13 and 2929.14 of the Revised Code, and in addition to any other sanction imposed for the offense under this section or sections 2929.11 to 2929.18 of the Revised Code, the court that sentences an offender who is convicted of or pleads guilty to a violation of division (A) of this section shall do all of the following that are applicable regarding the offender:

(1) If the violation of division (A) of this section is a felony of the first, second, or third degree, the court shall impose upon the offender the mandatory fine specified for the offense under division (B)(1) of section 2929.18 of the Revised Code unless, as specified in that division, the court determines that the offender is indigent. Except as otherwise provided in division (H)(1) of this section, a mandatory fine or any other fine imposed for a violation of this section is subject to division (F) of this section. If a person is charged with a violation of this section that is a felony of the first, second, or third degree, posts bail, and forfeits the bail, the clerk of the court shall pay the forfeited bail pursuant to divisions (D)(1) and (F) of this section, as if the forfeited bail was a fine imposed for a violation of this section. If any amount of the forfeited bail remains after that payment and if a fine is imposed under division (H)(1) of this section, the clerk of the court shall pay the remaining amount of the forfeited bail pursuant to divisions (H)(2) and (3) of this section, as if that remaining amount was a fine imposed under division (H)(1) of this section.

(2) The court shall suspend the driver's or commercial driver's license or permit of the offender in accordance with division (G) of this section.

(3) If the offender is a professionally licensed person, the court immediately shall comply with section 2925.38 of the Revised Code.

(E) When a person is charged with the sale of or offer to sell a bulk amount or a multiple of a bulk amount of a controlled substance, the jury, or the court trying the accused, shall determine the amount of the controlled substance involved at the time of the offense and, if a guilty verdict is returned, shall return the findings as part of the verdict. In any such case, it is unnecessary to find and return the exact amount of the controlled substance involved, and it is sufficient if the finding and return is to the effect that the amount of the controlled substance involved is the requisite amount, or that the amount of the controlled substance involved is less than the requisite amount.

(F)(1) Notwithstanding any contrary provision of section 3719.21 of the Revised Code and except as provided in division (H) of this section, the clerk of the court shall pay any mandatory fine imposed pursuant to division (D)(1) of this section and any fine other than a mandatory fine that is imposed for a violation of this section pursuant to division (A) or (B)(5) of section 2929.18 of the Revised Code to the county, township, municipal corporation, park district, as created pursuant to section 511.18 or 1545.04 of the Revised Code, or state law enforcement agencies in this state that primarily were responsible for or involved in making the arrest of, and in prosecuting, the offender. However, the clerk shall not pay a mandatory fine so imposed to a law enforcement agency unless the agency has adopted a written internal control policy under division (F)(2) of this section that addresses the use of the fine moneys that it receives. Each agency shall use the mandatory fines so paid to subsidize the agency's law enforcement efforts that pertain to drug offenses, in accordance with the written internal control policy adopted by the recipient agency under division (F)(2) of this section.

(2)(a) Prior to receiving any fine moneys under division (F)(1) of this section or division (B)(5) of section 2925.42 of the Revised Code, a law enforcement agency shall adopt a written internal control policy that addresses the agency's use and disposition of all fine moneys so received and that provides for the keeping of detailed financial records of the receipts of those fine moneys, the general types of expenditures made out of those fine moneys, and the specific amount of each general type of expenditure. The policy shall not provide for or permit the identification of any specific expenditure that is made in an ongoing investigation. All financial records of the receipts of those fine moneys, the general types of expenditures made out of those fine moneys, and the specific amount of each general type of expenditure by an agency are public records open for inspection under section 149.43 of the Revised Code. Additionally, a written internal control policy adopted under this division is such a public record, and the agency that adopted it shall comply with it.

(b) Each law enforcement agency that receives in any calendar year any fine moneys under division (F)(1) of this section or division (B)(5) of section 2925.42 of the Revised Code shall prepare a report covering the calendar year that cumulates all of the information contained in all of the public financial records kept by the agency pursuant to division (F)(2)(a) of this section for that calendar year, and shall send a copy of the cumulative report, no later than the first day of March in the calendar year following the calendar year covered by the report, to the attorney general. Each report received by the attorney general is a public record open for inspection under section 149.43 of the Revised Code. Not later than the fifteenth day of April in the calendar year in which the reports are received, the attorney general shall send to the president of the senate and the speaker of the house of representatives a written notification that does all of the following:

(i) Indicates that the attorney general has received from law enforcement agencies reports of the type described in this division that cover the previous calendar year and indicates that the reports were received under this division;

(ii) Indicates that the reports are open for inspection under section 149.43 of the Revised Code;

(iii) Indicates that the attorney general will provide a copy of any or all of the reports to the president of the senate or the speaker of the house of representatives upon request.

(3) As used in division (F) of this section:

(a) "Law enforcement agencies" includes, but is not limited to, the state board of pharmacy and the office of a prosecutor.

(b) "Prosecutor" has the same meaning as in section 2935.01 of the Revised Code.

(G) When required under division (D)(2) of this section or any other provision of this chapter, the court shall suspend for not less than six months or more than five years the driver's or commercial driver's license or permit of any person who is convicted of or pleads guilty to any violation of this section or any other specified provision of this chapter. If an offender's driver's or commercial driver's license or permit is suspended pursuant to this division, the offender, at any time after the expiration of two years from the day on which the offender's sentence was imposed or from the day on which the offender finally was released from a prison term under the sentence, whichever is later, may file a motion with the sentencing court requesting termination of the suspension; upon the filing of such a motion and the court's finding of good cause for the termination, the court may terminate the suspension.

(H)(1) In addition to any prison term authorized or required by division (C) of this section and sections 2929.13 and 2929.14 of the Revised Code, in addition to any other penalty or sanction imposed for the offense under this section or sections 2929.11 to 2929.18 of the Revised Code, and in addition to the forfeiture of property in connection with the offense as prescribed in sections 2925.42 to 2925.45 of the Revised Code, the court that sentences an offender who is convicted of or pleads guilty to a violation of division (A) of this section may impose upon the offender an additional fine specified for the offense in division (B)(4) of section 2929.18 of the Revised Code. A fine imposed under division (H)(1) of this section is not subject to division (F) of this section and shall be used solely for the support of one or more eligible alcohol and drug addiction programs in accordance with divisions (H)(2) and (3) of this section.

(2) The court that imposes a fine under division (H)(1) of this section shall specify in the judgment that imposes the fine one or more eligible alcohol and drug addiction programs for the support of which the fine money is to be used. No alcohol and drug addiction program shall receive or use money paid or collected in satisfaction of a fine imposed under division (H)(1) of this section unless the program is specified in the judgment that imposes the fine. No alcohol and drug addiction program shall be specified in the judgment unless the program is an eligible alcohol and drug addiction program and, except as otherwise provided in division (H)(2) of this section, unless the program is located in the county in which the court that imposes the fine is located or in a county that is immediately contiguous to the county in which that court is located. If no eligible alcohol and drug addiction program is located in any of those counties, the judgment may specify an eligible alcohol and drug addiction program that is located anywhere within this state.

(3) Notwithstanding any contrary provision of section 3719.21 of the Revised Code, the clerk of the court shall pay any fine imposed under division (H)(1) of this section to the eligible alcohol and drug addiction program specified pursuant to division (H)(2) of this section in the judgment. The eligible alcohol and drug addiction program that receives the fine moneys shall use the moneys only for the alcohol and drug addiction services identified in the application for certification under section 3793.06 of the Revised Code or in the application for a license under section 3793.11 of the Revised Code filed with the department of alcohol and drug addiction services by the alcohol and drug addiction program specified in the judgment.

(4) Each alcohol and drug addiction program that receives in a calendar year any fine moneys under division (H)(3) of this section shall file an annual report covering that calendar year with the court of common pleas and the board of county commissioners of the county in which the program is located, with the court of common pleas and the board of county commissioners of each county from which the program received the moneys if that county is different from the county in which the program is located, and with the attorney general. The alcohol and drug addiction program shall file the report no later than the first day of March in the calendar year following the calendar year in which the program received the fine moneys. The report shall include statistics on the number of persons served by the alcohol and drug addiction program, identify the types of alcohol and drug addiction services provided to those persons, and include a specific accounting of the purposes for which the fine moneys received were used. No information contained in the report shall identify, or enable a person to determine the identity of, any person served by the alcohol and drug addiction program. Each report received by a court of common pleas, a board of county commissioners, or the attorney general is a public record open for inspection under section 149.43 of the Revised Code.

(5) As used in divisions (H)(1) to (5) of this section:

(a) "Alcohol and drug addiction program" and "alcohol and drug addiction services" have the same meanings as in section 3793.01 of the Revised Code.

(b) "Eligible alcohol and drug addiction program" means an alcohol and drug addiction program that is certified under section 3793.06 of the Revised Code or licensed under section 3793.11 of the Revised Code by the department of alcohol and drug addiction services.

(2002 S 123, eff. 1–1–04; 2000 H 528, eff. 2–13–01; 2000 H 241, eff. 5–17–00; 1999 S 107, eff. 3–23–00; 1998 S 66, eff. 7–22–98; 1998 S 164, eff. 1–15–98; 1996 S 166, eff. 10–17–96; 1996 S 269, eff. 7–1–96; 1995 S 2, eff. 7–1–96; 1994 H 391, eff. 7–21–94; 1993 H 377, eff. 9–30–93; 1992 H 591, S 174; 1991 H 62; 1990 S 258, H 266, H 261, H 215; 1986 S 67; 1975 H 300)

2925.04 Illegal manufacture of drugs or cultivation of marihuana

(A) No person shall knowingly cultivate marihuana or knowingly manufacture or otherwise engage in any part of the production of a controlled substance.

(B) This section does not apply to any person listed in division (B)(1), (2), or (3) of section 2925.03 of the Revised Code to the extent and under the circumstances described in those divisions.

(C)(1) Whoever commits a violation of division (A) of this section that involves any drug other than marihuana is guilty of illegal manufacture of drugs, and whoever commits a violation of division (A) of this section that involves marihuana is guilty of illegal cultivation of marihuana.

(2) Except as otherwise provided in this division, if the drug involved in the violation of division (A) of this section is any compound, mixture, preparation, or substance included in schedule I or II, with the exception of marihuana, illegal manufacture of drugs is a felony of the second degree, and, subject to division (E) of this section, the court shall impose as a mandatory prison term one of the prison terms prescribed for a felony of the second degree. If the drug involved in the violation is any compound, mixture, preparation, or substance included in schedule I or II, with the exception of marihuana, and if the offense was committed in the vicinity of a juvenile or in the vicinity of a school, illegal manufacture of drugs is a felony of the first degree, and, subject to division (E) of this section, the court shall impose as a mandatory prison term one of the prison terms prescribed for a felony of the first degree. If the drug involved in the violation is methamphetamine, any salt, isomer, or salt of an isomer of methamphetamine, or any compound, mixture, preparation, or substance containing methamphetamine or any salt, isomer, or salt of an isomer of methamphetamine and if the offense was committed on public premises, illegal manufacture of drugs is a felony of the first degree, and, subject to division (E) of this section, the court shall impose as a mandatory prison term one of the prison terms prescribed for a felony of the first degree.

(3) If the drug involved in the violation of division (A) of this section is any compound, mixture, preparation, or substance included in schedule III, IV, or V, illegal manufacture of drugs is a felony of the third degree or, if the offense was committed in the vicinity of a school or in the vicinity of a juvenile, a felony of

the second degree, and there is a presumption for a prison term for the offense.

(4) If the drug involved in the violation is marihuana, the penalty for the offense shall be determined as follows:

(a) Except as otherwise provided in division (C)(4)(b), (c), (d), (e), or (f) of this section, illegal cultivation of marihuana is a minor misdemeanor or, if the offense was committed in the vicinity of a school or in the vicinity of a juvenile, a misdemeanor of the fourth degree.

(b) If the amount of marihuana involved equals or exceeds one hundred grams but is less than two hundred grams, illegal cultivation of marihuana is a misdemeanor of the fourth degree or, if the offense was committed in the vicinity of a school or in the vicinity of a juvenile, a misdemeanor of the third degree.

(c) If the amount of marihuana involved equals or exceeds two hundred grams but is less than one thousand grams, illegal cultivation of marihuana is a felony of the fifth degree or, if the offense was committed in the vicinity of a school or in the vicinity of a juvenile, a felony of the fourth degree, and division (B) of section 2929.13 of the Revised Code applies in determining whether to impose a prison term on the offender.

(d) If the amount of marihuana involved equals or exceeds one thousand grams but is less than five thousand grams, illegal cultivation of marihuana is a felony of the third degree or, if the offense was committed in the vicinity of a school or in the vicinity of a juvenile, a felony of the second degree, and division (C) of section 2929.13 of the Revised Code applies in determining whether to impose a prison term on the offender.

(e) If the amount of marihuana involved equals or exceeds five thousand grams but is less than twenty thousand grams, illegal cultivation of marihuana is a felony of the third degree or, if the offense was committed in the vicinity of a school or in the vicinity of a juvenile, a felony of the second degree, and there is a presumption for a prison term for the offense.

(f) Except as otherwise provided in this division, if the amount of marihuana involved equals or exceeds twenty thousand grams, illegal cultivation of marihuana is a felony of the second degree, and the court shall impose as a mandatory prison term the maximum prison term prescribed for a felony of the second degree. If the amount of the drug involved equals or exceeds twenty thousand grams and if the offense was committed in the vicinity of a school or in the vicinity of a juvenile, illegal cultivation of marihuana is a felony of the first degree, and the court shall impose as a mandatory prison term the maximum prison term prescribed for a felony of the first degree.

(D) In addition to any prison term authorized or required by division (C) or (E) of this section and sections 2929.13 and 2929.14 of the Revised Code and in addition to any other sanction imposed for the offense under this section or sections 2929.11 to 2929.18 of the Revised Code, the court that sentences an offender who is convicted of or pleads guilty to a violation of division (A) of this section shall do all of the following that are applicable regarding the offender:

(1) If the violation of division (A) of this section is a felony of the first, second, or third degree, the court shall impose upon the offender the mandatory fine specified for the offense under division (B)(1) of section 2929.18 of the Revised Code unless, as specified in that division, the court determines that the offender is indigent. The clerk of the court shall pay a mandatory fine or other fine imposed for a violation of this section pursuant to division (A) of section 2929.18 of the Revised Code in accordance with and subject to the requirements of division (F) of section 2925.03 of the Revised Code. The agency that receives the fine shall use the fine as specified in division (F) of section 2925.03 of the Revised Code. If a person is charged with a violation of this section that is a felony of the first, second, or third degree, posts bail, and forfeits the bail, the clerk shall pay the forfeited bail as if the forfeited bail were a fine imposed for a violation of this section.

(2) The court shall suspend the offender's driver's or commercial driver's license or permit in accordance with division (G) of section 2925.03 of the Revised Code. If an offender's driver's or commercial driver's license or permit is suspended in accordance with that division, the offender may request termination of, and the court may terminate, the suspension in accordance with that division.

(3) If the offender is a professionally licensed person, the court immediately shall comply with section 2925.38 of the Revised Code.

(E) Notwithstanding the prison term otherwise authorized or required for the offense under division (C) of this section and sections 2929.13 and 2929. 14 of the Revised Code, if the violation of division (A) of this section involves the sale, offer to sell, or possession of a schedule I or II controlled substance, with the exception of marihuana, and if the court imposing sentence upon the offender finds that the offender as a result of the violation is a major drug offender and is guilty of a specification of the type described in section 2941.1410 of the Revised Code, the court, in lieu of the prison term otherwise authorized or required, shall impose upon the offender the mandatory prison term specified in division (D)(3)(a) of section 2929.14 of the Revised Code and may impose an additional prison term under division (D)(3)(b) of that section.

(F) It is an affirmative defense, as provided in section 2901.05 of the Revised Code, to a charge under this section for a fifth degree felony violation of illegal cultivation of marihuana that the marihuana that gave rise to the charge is in an amount, is in a form, is prepared, compounded, or mixed with substances that are not controlled substances in a manner, or is possessed or cultivated under any other circumstances that indicate that the marihuana was solely for personal use.

Notwithstanding any contrary provision of division (F) of this section, if, in accordance with section 2901.05 of the Revised Code, a person who is charged with a violation of illegal cultivation of marihuana that is a felony of the fifth degree sustains the burden of going forward with evidence of and establishes by a preponderance of the evidence the affirmative defense described in this division, the person may be prosecuted for and may be convicted of or plead guilty to a misdemeanor violation of illegal cultivation of marihuana.

(G) Arrest or conviction for a minor misdemeanor violation of this section does not constitute a criminal record and need not be reported by the person so arrested or convicted in response to any inquiries about the person's criminal record, including any inquiries contained in an application for employment, a license, or any other right or privilege or made in connection with the person's appearance as a witness.

(2004 S 58, eff. 8–11–04; 2002 S 123, eff. 1–1–04; 2001 H 7, eff. 8–7–01; 1999 S 107, eff. 3–23–00; 1996 S 269, eff. 7–1–96; 1995 S 2, eff. 7–1–96)

2925.041 Assembly or possession of chemicals used to manufacture controlled substance with intent to manufacture controlled substance

(A) No person shall knowingly assemble or possess one or more chemicals that may be used to manufacture a controlled substance in schedule I or II with the intent to manufacture a controlled substance in schedule I or II in violation of section 2925.04 of the Revised Code.

(B) In a prosecution under this section, it is not necessary to allege or prove that the offender assembled or possessed all chemicals necessary to manufacture a controlled substance in schedule I or II. The assembly or possession of a single chemical that may be used in the manufacture of a controlled substance in schedule I or II, with the intent to manufacture a controlled substance in either schedule, is sufficient to violate this section.

(C) Whoever violates this section is guilty of illegal assembly or possession of chemicals for the manufacture of drugs. Except as otherwise provided in this division, illegal assembly or possession of chemicals for the manufacture of drugs is a felony of the third degree, and division (C) of section 2929.13 of the Revised Code applies in determining whether to impose a prison term on the offender. If the offense was committed in the vicinity of a juvenile or in the vicinity of a school, illegal assembly or possession of chemicals for the manufacture of drugs is a felony of the second degree, and division (C) of section 2929.13 of the Revised Code applies in determining whether to impose a prison term on the offender.

(D) In addition to any prison term authorized by division (C) of this section and sections 2929.13 and 2929.14 of the Revised Code and in addition to any other sanction imposed for the offense under this section or sections 2929.11 to 2929.18 of the Revised Code, the court that sentences an offender who is convicted of or pleads guilty to a violation of this section shall do all of the following that are applicable regarding the offender:

(1) The court shall impose upon the offender the mandatory fine specified for the offense under division (B)(1) of section 2929.18 of the Revised Code unless, as specified in that division, the court determines that the offender is indigent. The clerk of the court shall pay a mandatory fine or other fine imposed for a violation of this section under division (A) of section 2929.18 of the Revised Code in accordance with and subject to the requirements of division (F) of section 2925.03 of the Revised Code. The agency that receives the fine shall use the fine as specified in division (F) of section 2925.03 of the Revised Code. If a person charged with a violation of this section posts bail and forfeits the bail, the clerk shall pay the forfeited bail as if the forfeited bail were a fine imposed for a violation of this section.

(2) The court shall revoke or suspend the offender's driver's or commercial driver's license or permit in accordance with division (G) of section 2925.03 of the Revised Code. If an offender's driver's or commercial driver's license or permit is revoked in accordance with that division, the offender may request termination of, and the court may terminate, the revocation in accordance with that division.

(3) If the offender is a professionally licensed person or a person who has been admitted to the bar by order of the supreme court in compliance with its prescribed and published rules, the court shall comply with section 2925.38 of the Revised Code.

(2004 S 58, eff. 8–11–04; 2001 H 7, eff. 8–7–01)

2925.05 Funding of drug or marihuana trafficking

(A) No person shall knowingly provide money or other items of value to another person with the purpose that the recipient of the money or items of value use them to obtain any controlled substance for the purpose of violating section 2925.04 of the Revised Code or for the purpose of selling or offering to sell the controlled substance in the following amount:

(1) If the drug to be sold or offered for sale is any compound, mixture, preparation, or substance included in schedule I or II, with the exception of marihuana, cocaine, L.S.D., heroin, and hashish, or schedule III, IV, or V, an amount of the drug that equals or exceeds the bulk amount of the drug;

(2) If the drug to be sold or offered for sale is marihuana or a compound, mixture, preparation, or substance other than hashish containing marihuana, an amount of the marihuana that equals or exceeds two hundred grams;

(3) If the drug to be sold or offered for sale is cocaine or a compound, mixture, preparation, or substance containing cocaine, an amount of the cocaine that equals or exceeds five grams if the cocaine is not crack cocaine or equals or exceeds one gram if the cocaine is crack cocaine;

(4) If the drug to be sold or offered for sale is L.S.D. or a compound, mixture, preparation, or substance containing L.S.D., an amount of the L.S.D. that equals or exceeds ten unit doses if the L.S.D. is in a solid form or equals or exceeds one gram if the L.S.D. is in a liquid concentrate, liquid extract, or liquid distillate form;

(5) If the drug to be sold or offered for sale is heroin or a compound, mixture, preparation, or substance containing heroin, an amount of the heroin that equals or exceeds ten unit doses or equals or exceeds one gram;

(6) If the drug to be sold or offered for sale is hashish or a compound, mixture, preparation, or substance containing hashish, an amount of the hashish that equals or exceeds ten grams if the hashish is in a solid form or equals or exceeds two grams if the hashish is in a liquid concentrate, liquid extract, or liquid distillate form.

(B) This section does not apply to any person listed in division (B)(1), (2), or (3) of section 2925.03 of the Revised Code to the extent and under the circumstances described in those divisions.

(C)(1) If the drug involved in the violation is any compound, mixture, preparation, or substance included in schedule I or II, with the exception of marihuana, whoever violates division (A) of this section is guilty of aggravated funding of drug trafficking, a felony of the first degree, and, subject to division (E) of this section, the court shall impose as a mandatory prison term one of the prison terms prescribed for a felony of the first degree.

(2) If the drug involved in the violation is any compound, mixture, preparation, or substance included in schedule III, IV, or V, whoever violates division (A) of this section is guilty of funding of drug trafficking, a felony of the second degree, and the court shall impose as a mandatory prison term one of the prison terms prescribed for a felony of the second degree.

(3) If the drug involved in the violation is marihuana, whoever violates division (A) of this section is guilty of funding of marihuana trafficking, a felony of the third degree, and the court shall impose as a mandatory prison term one of the prison terms prescribed for a felony of the third degree.

(D) In addition to any prison term authorized or required by division (C) or (E) of this section and sections 2929.13 and 2929.14 of the Revised Code and in addition to any other sanction imposed for the offense under this section or sections 2929.11 to 2929.18 of the Revised Code, the court that sentences an offender who is convicted of or pleads guilty to a violation of division (A) of this section shall do all of the following that are applicable regarding the offender:

(1) The court shall impose the mandatory fine specified for the offense under division (B)(1) of section 2929.18 of the Revised Code unless, as specified in that division, the court determines that the offender is indigent. The clerk of the court shall pay a mandatory fine or other fine imposed for a violation of this section pursuant to division (A) of section 2929.18 of the Revised Code in accordance with and subject to the requirements of division (F) of section 2925.03 of the Revised Code. The agency that receives the fine shall use the fine in accordance with division (F) of section 2925.03 of the Revised Code. If a person is charged with a violation of this section, posts bail, and forfeits the bail, the forfeited bail shall be paid as if the forfeited bail were a fine imposed for a violation of this section.

(2) The court shall suspend the offender's driver's or commercial driver's license or permit in accordance with division (G) of section 2925.03 of the Revised Code. If an offender's driver's or commercial driver's license or permit is suspended in accordance with that division, the offender may request termination of, and

the court may terminate, the suspension in accordance with that division.

(3) If the offender is a professionally licensed person, the court immediately shall comply with section 2925.38 of the Revised Code.

(E) Notwithstanding the prison term otherwise authorized or required for the offense under division (C) of this section and sections 2929.13 and 2929.14 of the Revised Code, if the violation of division (A) of this section involves the sale, offer to sell, or possession of a schedule I or II controlled substance, with the exception of marihuana, and if the court imposing sentence upon the offender finds that the offender as a result of the violation is a major drug offender and is guilty of a specification of the type described in section 2941.1410 of the Revised Code, the court, in lieu of the prison term otherwise authorized or required, shall impose upon the offender the mandatory prison term specified in division (D)(3)(a) of section 2929.14 of the Revised Code and may impose an additional prison term under division (D)(3)(b) of that section.

(2002 S 123, eff. 1–1–04; 1999 S 107, eff. 3–23–00; 1996 S 269, eff. 7–1–96; 1995 S 2, eff. 7–1–96)

2925.06 Illegal administration or distribution of anabolic steroids

(A) No person shall knowingly administer to a human being, or prescribe or dispense for administration to a human being, any anabolic steroid not approved by the United States food and drug administration for administration to human beings.

(B) This section does not apply to any person listed in division (B)(1), (2), or (3) of section 2925.03 of the Revised Code to the extent and under the circumstances described in those divisions.

(C) Whoever violates division (A) of this section is guilty of illegal administration or distribution of anabolic steroids, a felony of the fourth degree, and division (C) of section 2929.13 of the Revised Code applies in determining whether to impose a prison term on the offender.

(D) In addition to any prison term authorized or required by division (C) of this section and sections 2929.13 and 2929.14 of the Revised Code and in addition to any other sanction imposed for the offense under this section or sections 2929.11 to 2929.18 of the Revised Code, the court that sentences an offender who is convicted of or pleads guilty to a violation of division (A) of this section shall do both of the following:

(1) The court shall suspend the offender's driver's or commercial driver's license or permit in accordance with division (G) of section 2925.03 of the Revised Code. If an offender's driver's or commercial driver's license or permit is suspended in accordance with that division, the offender may request termination of, and the court may terminate, the suspension in accordance with that division.

(2) If the offender is a professionally licensed person, the court immediately shall comply with section 2925.38 of the Revised Code.

(E) If a person commits any act that constitutes a violation of division (A) of this section and that also constitutes a violation of any other provision of the Revised Code, the prosecutor, as defined in section 2935.01 of the Revised Code, using customary prosecutorial discretion, may prosecute the person for a violation of the appropriate provision of the Revised Code.

(2002 S 123, eff. 1–1–04; 1996 S 269, eff. 7–1–96; 1995 S 2, eff. 7–1–96)

2925.09 Sale or use of drugs not approved by Food and Drug Administration

(A) No person shall administer, dispense, distribute, manufacture, possess, sell, or use any drug, other than a controlled substance, that is not approved by the United States food and drug administration, or the United States department of agriculture, unless one of the following applies:

(1) The United States food and drug administration has approved an application for investigational use in accordance with the "Federal Food, Drug, and Cosmetic Act," 52 Stat. 1040 (1938), 21 U.S.C.A. 301, as amended, and the drug is used only for the approved investigational use;

(2) The United States department of agriculture has approved an application for investigational use in accordance with the federal "Virus-Serum-Toxin Act," 37 Stat. 832 (1913), 21 U.S.C.A. 151, as amended, and the drug is used only for the approved investigational use;

(3) A licensed health professional authorized to prescribe drugs, other than a veterinarian, prescribes or combines two or more drugs as a single product for medical purposes;

(4) A pharmacist, pursuant to a prescription, compounds and dispenses two or more drugs as a single product for medical purposes.

(B)(1) As used in this division, "dangerous drug," "prescription," "sale at retail," "wholesale distributor of dangerous drugs," and "terminal distributor of dangerous drugs," have the same meanings as in section 4729.01 of the Revised Code.

(2) Except as provided in division (B)(3) of this section, no person shall administer, dispense, distribute, manufacture, possess, sell, or use any dangerous drug to or for livestock or any animal that is generally used for food or in the production of food, unless the drug is prescribed by a licensed veterinarian by prescription or other written order and the drug is used in accordance with the veterinarian's order or direction.

(3) Division (B)(2) of this section does not apply to a registered wholesale distributor of dangerous drugs, a licensed terminal distributor of dangerous drugs, or a person who possesses, possesses for sale, or sells, at retail, a drug in accordance with Chapters 3719., 4729., or 4741. of the Revised Code.

(C) Whoever violates division (A) or (B)(2) of this section is guilty of a felony of the fifth degree on a first offense and of a felony of the fourth degree on each subsequent offense.

(1998 S 66, eff. 7–22–98; 1996 S 269, eff. 7–1–96)

2925.11 Drug possession offenses

(A) No person shall knowingly obtain, possess, or use a controlled substance.

(B) This section does not apply to any of the following:

(1) Manufacturers, licensed health professionals authorized to prescribe drugs, pharmacists, owners of pharmacies, and other persons whose conduct was in accordance with Chapters 3719., 4715., 4723., 4729., 4731., and 4741. of the Revised Code;

(2) If the offense involves an anabolic steroid, any person who is conducting or participating in a research project involving the use of an anabolic steroid if the project has been approved by the United States food and drug administration;

(3) Any person who sells, offers for sale, prescribes, dispenses, or administers for livestock or other nonhuman species an anabolic steroid that is expressly intended for administration through implants to livestock or other nonhuman species and approved for that purpose under the "Federal Food, Drug, and Cosmetic Act," 52 Stat. 1040 (1938), 21 U.S.C.A. 301, as amended, and is

sold, offered for sale, prescribed, dispensed, or administered for that purpose in accordance with that act;

(4) Any person who obtained the controlled substance pursuant to a prescription issued by a licensed health professional authorized to prescribe drugs.

(C) Whoever violates division (A) of this section is guilty of one of the following:

(1) If the drug involved in the violation is a compound, mixture, preparation, or substance included in schedule I or II, with the exception of marihuana, cocaine, L.S.D., heroin, and hashish, whoever violates division (A) of this section is guilty of aggravated possession of drugs. The penalty for the offense shall be determined as follows:

(a) Except as otherwise provided in division (C)(1)(b), (c), (d), or (e) of this section, aggravated possession of drugs is a felony of the fifth degree, and division (B) of section 2929.13 of the Revised Code applies in determining whether to impose a prison term on the offender.

(b) If the amount of the drug involved equals or exceeds the bulk amount but is less than five times the bulk amount, aggravated possession of drugs is a felony of the third degree, and there is a presumption for a prison term for the offense.

(c) If the amount of the drug involved equals or exceeds five times the bulk amount but is less than fifty times the bulk amount, aggravated possession of drugs is a felony of the second degree, and the court shall impose as a mandatory prison term one of the prison terms prescribed for a felony of the second degree.

(d) If the amount of the drug involved equals or exceeds fifty times the bulk amount but is less than one hundred times the bulk amount, aggravated possession of drugs is a felony of the first degree, and the court shall impose as a mandatory prison term one of the prison terms prescribed for a felony of the first degree.

(e) If the amount of the drug involved equals or exceeds one hundred times the bulk amount, aggravated possession of drugs is a felony of the first degree, the offender is a major drug offender, and the court shall impose as a mandatory prison term the maximum prison term prescribed for a felony of the first degree and may impose an additional mandatory prison term prescribed for a major drug offender under division (D)(3)(b) of section 2929.14 of the Revised Code.

(2) If the drug involved in the violation is a compound, mixture, preparation, or substance included in schedule III, IV, or V, whoever violates division (A) of this section is guilty of possession of drugs. The penalty for the offense shall be determined as follows:

(a) Except as otherwise provided in division (C)(2)(b), (c), or (d) of this section, possession of drugs is a misdemeanor of the third degree or, if the offender previously has been convicted of a drug abuse offense, a misdemeanor of the second degree. If the drug involved in the violation is an anabolic steroid included in schedule III and if the offense is a misdemeanor of the third degree under this division, in lieu of sentencing the offender to a term of imprisonment in a detention facility, the court may place the offender under a community control sanction, as defined in section 2929.01 of the Revised Code, that requires the offender to perform supervised community service work pursuant to division (B) of section 2951.02 of the Revised Code.

(b) If the amount of the drug involved equals or exceeds the bulk amount but is less than five times the bulk amount, possession of drugs is a felony of the fourth degree, and division (C) of section 2929.13 of the Revised Code applies in determining whether to impose a prison term on the offender.

(c) If the amount of the drug involved equals or exceeds five times the bulk amount but is less than fifty times the bulk amount, possession of drugs is a felony of the third degree, and there is a presumption for a prison term for the offense.

(d) If the amount of the drug involved equals or exceeds fifty times the bulk amount, possession of drugs is a felony of the second degree, and the court shall impose upon the offender as a mandatory prison term one of the prison terms prescribed for a felony of the second degree.

(3) If the drug involved in the violation is marihuana or a compound, mixture, preparation, or substance containing marihuana other than hashish, whoever violates division (A) of this section is guilty of possession of marihuana. The penalty for the offense shall be determined as follows:

(a) Except as otherwise provided in division (C)(3)(b), (c), (d), (e), or (f) of this section, possession of marihuana is a minor misdemeanor.

(b) If the amount of the drug involved equals or exceeds one hundred grams but is less than two hundred grams, possession of marihuana is a misdemeanor of the fourth degree.

(c) If the amount of the drug involved equals or exceeds two hundred grams but is less than one thousand grams, possession of marihuana is a felony of the fifth degree, and division (B) of section 2929.13 of the Revised Code applies in determining whether to impose a prison term on the offender.

(d) If the amount of the drug involved equals or exceeds one thousand grams but is less than five thousand grams, possession of marihuana is a felony of the third degree, and division (C) of section 2929.13 of the Revised Code applies in determining whether to impose a prison term on the offender.

(e) If the amount of the drug involved equals or exceeds five thousand grams but is less than twenty thousand grams, possession of marihuana is a felony of the third degree, and there is a presumption that a prison term shall be imposed for the offense.

(f) If the amount of the drug involved equals or exceeds twenty thousand grams, possession of marihuana is a felony of the second degree, and the court shall impose as a mandatory prison term the maximum prison term prescribed for a felony of the second degree.

(4) If the drug involved in the violation is cocaine or a compound, mixture, preparation, or substance containing cocaine, whoever violates division (A) of this section is guilty of possession of cocaine. The penalty for the offense shall be determined as follows:

(a) Except as otherwise provided in division (C)(4)(b), (c), (d), (e), or (f) of this section, possession of cocaine is a felony of the fifth degree, and division (B) of section 2929.13 of the Revised Code applies in determining whether to impose a prison term on the offender.

(b) If the amount of the drug involved equals or exceeds five grams but is less than twenty-five grams of cocaine that is not crack cocaine or equals or exceeds one gram but is less than five grams of crack cocaine, possession of cocaine is a felony of the fourth degree, and there is a presumption for a prison term for the offense.

(c) If the amount of the drug involved equals or exceeds twenty-five grams but is less than one hundred grams of cocaine that is not crack cocaine or equals or exceeds five grams but is less than ten grams of crack cocaine, possession of cocaine is a felony of the third degree, and the court shall impose as a mandatory prison term one of the prison terms prescribed for a felony of the third degree.

(d) If the amount of the drug involved equals or exceeds one hundred grams but is less than five hundred grams of cocaine that is not crack cocaine or equals or exceeds ten grams but is less than twenty-five grams of crack cocaine, possession of cocaine is a felony of the second degree, and the court shall impose as a mandatory prison term one of the prison terms prescribed for a felony of the second degree.

(e) If the amount of the drug involved equals or exceeds five hundred grams but is less than one thousand grams of cocaine that is not crack cocaine or equals or exceeds twenty-five grams but is less than one hundred grams of crack cocaine, possession of cocaine is a felony of the first degree, and the court shall impose as a mandatory prison term one of the prison terms prescribed for a felony of the first degree.

(f) If the amount of the drug involved equals or exceeds one thousand grams of cocaine that is not crack cocaine or equals or exceeds one hundred grams of crack cocaine, possession of cocaine is a felony of the first degree, the offender is a major drug offender, and the court shall impose as a mandatory prison term the maximum prison term prescribed for a felony of the first degree and may impose an additional mandatory prison term prescribed for a major drug offender under division (D)(3)(b) of section 2929.14 of the Revised Code.

(5) If the drug involved in the violation is L.S.D., whoever violates division (A) of this section is guilty of possession of L.S.D. The penalty for the offense shall be determined as follows:

(a) Except as otherwise provided in division (C)(5)(b), (c), (d), (e), or (f) of this section, possession of L.S.D. is a felony of the fifth degree, and division (B) of section 2929.13 of the Revised Code applies in determining whether to impose a prison term on the offender.

(b) If the amount of L.S.D. involved equals or exceeds ten unit doses but is less than fifty unit doses of L.S.D. in a solid form or equals or exceeds one gram but is less than five grams of L.S.D. in a liquid concentrate, liquid extract, or liquid distillate form, possession of L.S.D. is a felony of the fourth degree, and division (C) of section 2929.13 of the Revised Code applies in determining whether to impose a prison term on the offender.

(c) If the amount of L.S.D. involved equals or exceeds fifty unit doses, but is less than two hundred fifty unit doses of L.S.D. in a solid form or equals or exceeds five grams but is less than twenty-five grams of L.S.D. in a liquid concentrate, liquid extract, or liquid distillate form, possession of L.S.D. is a felony of the third degree, and there is a presumption for a prison term for the offense.

(d) If the amount of L.S.D. involved equals or exceeds two hundred fifty unit doses but is less than one thousand unit doses of L.S.D. in a solid form or equals or exceeds twenty-five grams but is less than one hundred grams of L.S.D. in a liquid concentrate, liquid extract, or liquid distillate form, possession of L.S.D. is a felony of the second degree, and the court shall impose as a mandatory prison term one of the prison terms prescribed for a felony of the second degree.

(e) If the amount of L.S.D. involved equals or exceeds one thousand unit doses but is less than five thousand unit doses of L.S.D. in a solid form or equals or exceeds one hundred grams but is less than five hundred grams of L.S.D. in a liquid concentrate, liquid extract, or liquid distillate form, possession of L.S.D. is a felony of the first degree, and the court shall impose as a mandatory prison term one of the prison terms prescribed for a felony of the first degree.

(f) If the amount of L.S.D. involved equals or exceeds five thousand unit doses of L.S.D. in a solid form or equals or exceeds five hundred grams of L.S.D. in a liquid concentrate, liquid extract, or liquid distillate form, possession of L.S.D. is a felony of the first degree, the offender is a major drug offender, and the court shall impose as a mandatory prison term the maximum prison term prescribed for a felony of the first degree and may impose an additional mandatory prison term prescribed for a major drug offender under division (D)(3)(b) of section 2929.14 of the Revised Code.

(6) If the drug involved in the violation is heroin or a compound, mixture, preparation, or substance containing heroin, whoever violates division (A) of this section is guilty of possession of heroin. The penalty for the offense shall be determined as follows:

(a) Except as otherwise provided in division (C)(6)(b), (c), (d), (e), or (f) of this section, possession of heroin is a felony of the fifth degree, and division (B) of section 2929.13 of the Revised Code applies in determining whether to impose a prison term on the offender.

(b) If the amount of the drug involved equals or exceeds ten unit doses but is less than fifty unit doses or equals or exceeds one gram but is less than five grams, possession of heroin is a felony of the fourth degree, and division (C) of section 2929.13 of the Revised Code applies in determining whether to impose a prison term on the offender.

(c) If the amount of the drug involved equals or exceeds fifty unit doses but is less than one hundred unit doses or equals or exceeds five grams but is less than ten grams, possession of heroin is a felony of the third degree, and there is a presumption for a prison term for the offense.

(d) If the amount of the drug involved equals or exceeds one hundred unit doses but is less than five hundred unit doses or equals or exceeds ten grams but is less than fifty grams, possession of heroin is a felony of the second degree, and the court shall impose as a mandatory prison term one of the prison terms prescribed for a felony of the second degree.

(e) If the amount of the drug involved equals or exceeds five hundred unit doses but is less than two thousand five hundred unit doses or equals or exceeds fifty grams but is less than two hundred fifty grams, possession of heroin is a felony of the first degree, and the court shall impose as a mandatory prison term one of the prison terms prescribed for a felony of the first degree.

(f) If the amount of the drug involved equals or exceeds two thousand five hundred unit doses or equals or exceeds two hundred fifty grams, possession of heroin is a felony of the first degree, the offender is a major drug offender, and the court shall impose as a mandatory prison term the maximum prison term prescribed for a felony of the first degree and may impose an additional mandatory prison term prescribed for a major drug offender under division (D)(3)(b) of section 2929.14 of the Revised Code.

(7) If the drug involved in the violation is hashish or a compound, mixture, preparation, or substance containing hashish, whoever violates division (A) of this section is guilty of possession of hashish. The penalty for the offense shall be determined as follows:

(a) Except as otherwise provided in division (C)(7)(b), (c), (d), (e), or (f) of this section, possession of hashish is a minor misdemeanor.

(b) If the amount of the drug involved equals or exceeds five grams but is less than ten grams of hashish in a solid form or equals or exceeds one gram but is less than two grams of hashish in a liquid concentrate, liquid extract, or liquid distillate form, possession of hashish is a misdemeanor of the fourth degree.

(c) If the amount of the drug involved equals or exceeds ten grams but is less than fifty grams of hashish in a solid form or equals or exceeds two grams but is less than ten grams of hashish in a liquid concentrate, liquid extract, or liquid distillate form, possession of hashish is a felony of the fifth degree, and division (B) of section 2929.13 of the Revised Code applies in determining whether to impose a prison term on the offender.

(d) If the amount of the drug involved equals or exceeds fifty grams but is less than two hundred fifty grams of hashish in a solid form or equals or exceeds ten grams but is less than fifty grams of hashish in a liquid concentrate, liquid extract, or liquid distillate form, possession of hashish is a felony of the third degree, and division (C) of section 2929.13 of the Revised Code applies in determining whether to impose a prison term on the offender.

(e) If the amount of the drug involved equals or exceeds two hundred fifty grams but is less than one thousand grams of hashish in a solid form or equals or exceeds fifty grams but is less than two hundred grams of hashish in a liquid concentrate, liquid extract, or liquid distillate form, possession of hashish is a felony of the third degree, and there is a presumption that a prison term shall be imposed for the offense.

(f) If the amount of the drug involved equals or exceeds one thousand grams of hashish in a solid form or equals or exceeds two hundred grams of hashish in a liquid concentrate, liquid extract, or liquid distillate form, possession of hashish is a felony of the second degree, and the court shall impose as a mandatory prison term the maximum prison term prescribed for a felony of the second degree.

(D) Arrest or conviction for a minor misdemeanor violation of this section does not constitute a criminal record and need not be reported by the person so arrested or convicted in response to any inquiries about the person's criminal record, including any inquiries contained in any application for employment, license, or other right or privilege, or made in connection with the person's appearance as a witness.

(E) In addition to any prison term or jail term authorized or required by division (C) of this section and sections 2929.13, 2929.14, 2929.22, 2929.24, and 2929.25 of the Revised Code and in addition to any other sanction that is imposed for the offense under this section, sections 2929.11 to 2929.18, or sections 2929.21 to 2929.28 of the Revised Code, the court that sentences an offender who is convicted of or pleads guilty to a violation of division (A) of this section shall do all of the following that are applicable regarding the offender:

(1)(a) If the violation is a felony of the first, second, or third degree, the court shall impose upon the offender the mandatory fine specified for the offense under division (B)(1) of section 2929.18 of the Revised Code unless, as specified in that division, the court determines that the offender is indigent.

(b) Notwithstanding any contrary provision of section 3719.21 of the Revised Code, the clerk of the court shall pay a mandatory fine or other fine imposed for a violation of this section pursuant to division (A) of section 2929.18 of the Revised Code in accordance with and subject to the requirements of division (F) of section 2925.03 of the Revised Code. The agency that receives the fine shall use the fine as specified in division (F) of section 2925.03 of the Revised Code.

(c) If a person is charged with a violation of this section that is a felony of the first, second, or third degree, posts bail, and forfeits the bail, the clerk shall pay the forfeited bail pursuant to division (E)(1)(b) of this section as if it were a mandatory fine imposed under division (E)(1)(a) of this section.

(2) The court shall suspend for not less than six months or more than five years the offender's driver's or commercial driver's license or permit.

(3) If the offender is a professionally licensed person, in addition to any other sanction imposed for a violation of this section, the court immediately shall comply with section 2925.38 of the Revised Code.

(F) It is an affirmative defense, as provided in section 2901.05 of the Revised Code, to a charge of a fourth degree felony violation under this section that the controlled substance that gave rise to the charge is in an amount, is in a form, is prepared, compounded, or mixed with substances that are not controlled substances in a manner, or is possessed under any other circumstances, that indicate that the substance was possessed solely for personal use. Notwithstanding any contrary provision of this section, if, in accordance with section 2901.05 of the Revised Code, an accused who is charged with a fourth degree felony violation of division (C)(2), (4), (5), or (6) of this section sustains the burden of going forward with evidence of and establishes by a preponderance of the evidence the affirmative defense described in this division, the accused may be prosecuted for and may plead guilty to or be convicted of a misdemeanor violation of division (C)(2) of this section or a fifth degree felony violation of division (C)(4), (5), or (6) of this section respectively.

(G) When a person is charged with possessing a bulk amount or multiple of a bulk amount, division (E) of section 2925.03 of the Revised Code applies regarding the determination of the amount of the controlled substance involved at the time of the offense.

(2002 H 490, eff. 1–1–04; 2002 S 123, eff. 1–1–04; 2000 H 241, eff. 5–17–00; 1999 S 107, eff. 3–23–00; 1998 S 66, eff. 7–22–98; 1997 S 2, eff. 6–20–97; 1996 S 269, eff. 7–1–96; 1995 S 2, eff. 7–1–96; 1995 H 249, eff. 7–17–95; 1994 H 391, eff. 7–21–94; 1993 H 377, eff. 9–30–93; 1991 H 298, H 62; 1990 S 258; 1980 S 184, § 5)

2925.12 Possessing drug abuse instruments

(A) No person shall knowingly make, obtain, possess, or use any instrument, article, or thing the customary and primary purpose of which is for the administration or use of a dangerous drug, other than marihuana, when the instrument involved is a hypodermic or syringe, whether or not of crude or extemporized manufacture or assembly, and the instrument, article, or thing involved has been used by the offender to unlawfully administer or use a dangerous drug, other than marihuana, or to prepare a dangerous drug, other than marihuana, for unlawful administration or use.

(B) This section does not apply to manufacturers, licensed health professionals authorized to prescribe drugs, pharmacists, owners of pharmacies, and other persons whose conduct was in accordance with Chapters 3719., 4715., 4723., 4729., 4731., and 4741. of the Revised Code.

(C) Whoever violates this section is guilty of possessing drug abuse instruments, a misdemeanor of the second degree. If the offender previously has been convicted of a drug abuse offense, a violation of this section is a misdemeanor of the first degree.

(D) In addition to any other sanction imposed upon an offender for a violation of this section, the court shall suspend for not less than six months or more than five years the offender's driver's or commercial driver's license or permit. If the offender is a professionally licensed person, in addition to any other sanction imposed for a violation of this section, the court immediately shall comply with section 2925.38 of the Revised Code.

(2002 S 123, eff. 1–1–04; 2000 H 241, eff. 5–17–00; 1998 S 66, eff. 7–22–98; 1996 S 269, eff. 7–1–96; 1995 S 2, eff. 7–1–96; 1994 H 391, eff. 7–21–94; 1993 H 377, eff. 9–30–93; 1990 S 258; 1975 H 300)

2925.13 Permitting drug abuse

(A) No person who is the owner, operator, or person in charge of a locomotive, watercraft, aircraft, or other vehicle, as defined in division (A) of section 4501.01 of the Revised Code, shall knowingly permit the vehicle to be used for the commission of a felony drug abuse offense.

(B) No person who is the owner, lessee, or occupant, or who has custody, control, or supervision, of premises or real estate, including vacant land, shall knowingly permit the premises or real estate, including vacant land, to be used for the commission of a felony drug abuse offense by another person.

(C)(1) Whoever violates this section is guilty of permitting drug abuse.

(2) Except as provided in division (C)(3) of this section, permitting drug abuse is a misdemeanor of the first degree.

(3) Permitting drug abuse is a felony of the fifth degree, and division (C) of section 2929.13 of the Revised Code applies in determining whether to impose a prison term on the offender, if the felony drug abuse offense in question is a violation of section 2925.02 or 2925.03 of the Revised Code.

(D) In addition to any prison term authorized or required by division (C) of this section and sections 2929.13 and 2929.14 of the Revised Code and in addition to any other sanction imposed for the offense under this section or sections 2929.11 to 2929.18 of the Revised Code, the court that sentences a person who is convicted of or pleads guilty to a violation of division (A) of this section shall do all of the following that are applicable regarding the offender:

(1) The court shall suspend for not less than six months or more than five years the offender's driver's or commercial driver's license or permit.

(2) If the offender is a professionally licensed person, in addition to any other sanction imposed for a violation of this section, the court immediately shall comply with section 2925.38 of the Revised Code.

(E) Notwithstanding any contrary provision of section 3719.21 of the Revised Code, the clerk of the court shall pay a fine imposed for a violation of this section pursuant to division (A) of section 2929.18 of the Revised Code in accordance with and subject to the requirements of division (F) of section 2925.03 of the Revised Code. The agency that receives the fine shall use the fine as specified in division (F) of section 2925.03 of the Revised Code.

(F) Any premises or real estate that is permitted to be used in violation of division (B) of this section constitutes a nuisance subject to abatement pursuant to Chapter 3767. of the Revised Code.

(2002 S 123, eff. 1–1–04; 1999 S 107, eff. 3–23–00; 1996 S 269, eff. 7–1–96; 1995 S 2, eff. 7–1–96; 1993 H 377, eff. 9–30–93; 1992 H 591; 1990 S 258, H 215; 1975 H 300)

2925.14 Use, possession, or sale of drug paraphernalia; exemptions; forfeiture

(A) As used in this section, "drug paraphernalia" means any equipment, product, or material of any kind that is used by the offender, intended by the offender for use, or designed for use, in propagating, cultivating, growing, harvesting, manufacturing, compounding, converting, producing, processing, preparing, testing, analyzing, packaging, repackaging, storing, containing, concealing, injecting, ingesting, inhaling, or otherwise introducing into the human body, a controlled substance in violation of this chapter. "Drug paraphernalia" includes, but is not limited to, any of the following equipment, products, or materials that are used by the offender, intended by the offender for use, or designed by the offender for use, in any of the following manners:

(1) A kit for propagating, cultivating, growing, or harvesting any species of a plant that is a controlled substance or from which a controlled substance can be derived;

(2) A kit for manufacturing, compounding, converting, producing, processing, or preparing a controlled substance;

(3) Any object, instrument, or device for manufacturing, compounding, converting, producing, processing, or preparing methamphetamine or any salt, isomer, or salt of an isomer of methamphetamine;

(4) An isomerization device for increasing the potency of any species of a plant that is a controlled substance;

(5) Testing equipment for identifying, or analyzing the strength, effectiveness, or purity of, a controlled substance;

(6) A scale or balance for weighing or measuring a controlled substance;

(7) A diluent or adulterant, such as quinine hydrochloride, mannitol, mannite, dextrose, or lactose, for cutting a controlled substance;

(8) A separation gin or sifter for removing twigs and seeds from, or otherwise cleaning or refining, marihuana;

(9) A blender, bowl, container, spoon, or mixing device for compounding a controlled substance;

(10) A capsule, balloon, envelope, or container for packaging small quantities of a controlled substance;

(11) A container or device for storing or concealing a controlled substance;

(12) A hypodermic syringe, needle, or instrument for parenterally injecting a controlled substance into the human body;

(13) An object, instrument, or device for ingesting, inhaling, or otherwise introducing into the human body, marihuana, cocaine, hashish, or hashish oil, such as a metal, wooden, acrylic, glass, stone, plastic, or ceramic pipe, with or without a screen, permanent screen, hashish head, or punctured metal bowl; water pipe; carburetion tube or device; smoking or carburetion mask; roach clip or similar object used to hold burning material, such as a marihuana cigarette, that has become too small or too short to be held in the hand; miniature cocaine spoon, or cocaine vial; chamber pipe; carburetor pipe; electric pipe; air driver pipe; chillum; bong; or ice pipe or chiller.

(B) In determining if any equipment, product, or material is drug paraphernalia, a court or law enforcement officer shall consider, in addition to other relevant factors, the following:

(1) Any statement by the owner, or by anyone in control, of the equipment, product, or material, concerning its use;

(2) The proximity in time or space of the equipment, product, or material, or of the act relating to the equipment, product, or material, to a violation of any provision of this chapter;

(3) The proximity of the equipment, product, or material to any controlled substance;

(4) The existence of any residue of a controlled substance on the equipment, product, or material;

(5) Direct or circumstantial evidence of the intent of the owner, or of anyone in control, of the equipment, product, or material, to deliver it to any person whom the owner or person in control of the equipment, product, or material knows intends to use the object to facilitate a violation of any provision of this chapter. A finding that the owner, or anyone in control, of the equipment, product, or material, is not guilty of a violation of any other provision of this chapter does not prevent a finding that the equipment, product, or material was intended or designed by the offender for use as drug paraphernalia.

(6) Any oral or written instruction provided with the equipment, product, or material concerning its use;

(7) Any descriptive material accompanying the equipment, product, or material and explaining or depicting its use;

(8) National or local advertising concerning the use of the equipment, product, or material;

(9) The manner and circumstances in which the equipment, product, or material is displayed for sale;

(10) Direct or circumstantial evidence of the ratio of the sales of the equipment, product, or material to the total sales of the business enterprise;

(11) The existence and scope of legitimate uses of the equipment, product, or material in the community;

(12) Expert testimony concerning the use of the equipment, product, or material.

(C)(1) No person shall knowingly use, or possess with purpose to use, drug paraphernalia.

(2) No person shall knowingly sell, or possess or manufacture with purpose to sell, drug paraphernalia, if the person knows or reasonably should know that the equipment, product, or material will be used as drug paraphernalia.

(3) No person shall place an advertisement in any newspaper, magazine, handbill, or other publication that is published and printed and circulates primarily within this state, if the person knows that the purpose of the advertisement is to promote the illegal sale in this state of the equipment, product, or material that the offender intended or designed for use as drug paraphernalia.

(D) This section does not apply to manufacturers, licensed health professionals authorized to prescribe drugs, pharmacists, owners of pharmacies, and other persons whose conduct is in accordance with Chapters 3719., 4715., 4723., 4729., 4731., and 4741. of the Revised Code. This section shall not be construed to prohibit the possession or use of a hypodermic as authorized by section 3719.172 of the Revised Code.

(E) Notwithstanding sections 2933.42 and 2933.43 of the Revised Code, any drug paraphernalia that was used, possessed, sold, or manufactured in a violation of this section shall be seized, after a conviction for that violation shall be forfeited, and upon forfeiture shall be disposed of pursuant to division (D)(8) of section 2933.41 of the Revised Code.

(F)(1) Whoever violates division (C)(1) of this section is guilty of illegal use or possession of drug paraphernalia, a misdemeanor of the fourth degree.

(2) Except as provided in division (F)(3) of this section, whoever violates division (C)(2) of this section is guilty of dealing in drug paraphernalia, a misdemeanor of the second degree.

(3) Whoever violates division (C)(2) of this section by selling drug paraphernalia to a juvenile is guilty of selling drug paraphernalia to juveniles, a misdemeanor of the first degree.

(4) Whoever violates division (C)(3) of this section is guilty of illegal advertising of drug paraphernalia, a misdemeanor of the second degree.

(G) In addition to any other sanction imposed upon an offender for a violation of this section, the court shall suspend for not less than six months or more than five years the offender's driver's or commercial driver's license or permit. If the offender is a professionally licensed person, in addition to any other sanction imposed for a violation of this section, the court immediately shall comply with section 2925.38 of the Revised Code.

(2002 S 123, eff. 1–1–04; 2001 H 7, eff. 8–7–01; 2000 H 241, eff. 5–17–00; 1998 S 66, eff. 7–22–98; 1996 S 269, eff. 7–1–96; 1995 S 2, eff. 7–1–96; 1994 H 391, eff. 7–21–94; 1993 H 377, eff. 9–30–93; 1990 S 258; 1989 H 182)

2925.22 Deception to obtain a dangerous drug

(A) No person, by deception, as defined in section 2913.01 of the Revised Code, shall procure the administration of, a prescription for, or the dispensing of, a dangerous drug or shall possess an uncompleted preprinted prescription blank used for writing a prescription for a dangerous drug.

(B) Whoever violates this section is guilty of deception to obtain a dangerous drug. The penalty for the offense shall be determined as follows:

(1) If the drug involved is a compound, mixture, preparation, or substance included in schedule I or II, with the exception of marihuana, deception to obtain drugs is a felony of the fourth degree, and division (C) of section 2929.13 of the Revised Code applies in determining whether to impose a prison term on the offender.

(2) If the drug involved is a dangerous drug or a compound, mixture, preparation, or substance included in schedule III, IV, or V or is marihuana, deception to obtain a dangerous drug is a felony of the fifth degree, and division (C) of section 2929.13 of the Revised Code applies in determining whether to impose a prison term on the offender.

(C) In addition to any prison term authorized or required by division (B) of this section and sections 2929.13 and 2929.14 of the Revised Code and in addition to any other sanction imposed for the offense under this section or sections 2929.11 to 2929.18 of the Revised Code, the court that sentences an offender who is convicted of or pleads guilty to a violation of division (A) of this section shall do both of the following:

(1) The court shall suspend for not less than six months or more than five years the offender's driver's or commercial driver's license or permit.

(2) If the offender is a professionally licensed person, in addition to any other sanction imposed for a violation of this section, the court immediately shall comply with section 2925.38 of the Revised Code.

(D) Notwithstanding any contrary provision of section 3719.21 of the Revised Code, the clerk of the court shall pay a fine imposed for a violation of this section pursuant to division (A) of section 2929.18 of the Revised Code in accordance with and subject to the requirements of division (F) of section 2925.03 of the Revised Code. The agency that receives the fine shall use the fine as specified in division (F) of section 2925.03 of the Revised Code.

(2002 S 123, eff. 1–1–04; 1996 S 269, eff. 7–1–96; 1995 S 2, eff. 7–1–96; 1993 H 377, eff. 9–30–93; 1990 H 615, S 258; 1975 H 300)

2925.23 Illegal processing of drug documents

(A) No person shall knowingly make a false statement in any prescription, order, report, or record required by Chapter 3719. or 4729. of the Revised Code.

(B) No person shall intentionally make, utter, or sell, or knowingly possess any of the following that is a false or forged:

(1) Prescription;

(2) Uncompleted preprinted prescription blank used for writing a prescription;

(3) Official written order;

(4) License for a terminal distributor of dangerous drugs as required in section 4729.60 of the Revised Code;

(5) Registration certificate for a wholesale distributor of dangerous drugs as required in section 4729.60 of the Revised Code.

(C) No person, by theft as defined in section 2913.02 of the Revised Code, shall acquire any of the following:

(1) A prescription;

(2) An uncompleted preprinted prescription blank used for writing a prescription;

(3) An official written order;

(4) A blank official written order;

(5) A license or blank license for a terminal distributor of dangerous drugs as required in section 4729.60 of the Revised Code;

(6) A registration certificate or blank registration certificate for a wholesale distributor of dangerous drugs as required in section 4729.60 of the Revised Code.

(D) No person shall knowingly make or affix any false or forged label to a package or receptacle containing any dangerous drugs.

(E) Divisions (A) and (D) of this section do not apply to licensed health professionals authorized to prescribe drugs, pharmacists, owners of pharmacies, and other persons whose conduct is in accordance with Chapters 3719., 4715., 4723., 4725., 4729., 4731., and 4741. of the Revised Code.

(F) Whoever violates this section is guilty of illegal processing of drug documents. If the offender violates division (B)(2), (4), or (5) or division (C)(2), (4), (5), or (6) of this section, illegal processing of drug documents is a felony of the fifth degree. If the offender violates division (A), division (B)(1) or (3), division (C)(1) or (3), or division (D) of this section, the penalty for illegal processing of drug documents shall be determined as follows:

(1) If the drug involved is a compound, mixture, preparation, or substance included in schedule I or II, with the exception of marihuana, illegal processing of drug documents is a felony of the fourth degree, and division (C) of section 2929.13 of the Revised Code applies in determining whether to impose a prison term on the offender.

(2) If the drug involved is a dangerous drug or a compound, mixture, preparation, or substance included in schedule III, IV, or V or is marihuana, illegal processing of drug documents is a felony of the fifth degree, and division (C) of section 2929.13 of the Revised Code applies in determining whether to impose a prison term on the offender.

(G) In addition to any prison term authorized or required by division (F) of this section and sections 2929.13 and 2929.14 of the Revised Code and in addition to any other sanction imposed for the offense under this section or sections 2929.11 to 2929.18 of the Revised Code, the court that sentences an offender who is convicted of or pleads guilty to any violation of divisions (A) to (D) of this section shall do both of the following:

(1) The court shall suspend for not less than six months or more than five years the offender's driver's or commercial driver's license or permit.

(2) If the offender is a professionally licensed person, in addition to any other sanction imposed for a violation of this section, the court immediately shall comply with section 2925.38 of the Revised Code.

(H) Notwithstanding any contrary provision of section 3719.21 of the Revised Code, the clerk of court shall pay a fine imposed for a violation of this section pursuant to division (A) of section 2929.18 of the Revised Code in accordance with and subject to the requirements of division (F) of section 2925.03 of the Revised Code. The agency that receives the fine shall use the fine as specified in division (F) of section 2925.03 of the Revised Code.

(2002 S 123, eff. 1–1–04; 2002 H 327, eff. 7–8–02; 2000 H 241, eff. 5–17–00; 1999 S 107, eff. 3–23–00; 1998 S 66, eff. 7–22–98; 1996 S 269, eff. 7–1–96; 1995 S 2, eff. 7–1–96; 1994 H 391, eff. 7–21–94; 1993 H 377, eff. 9–30–93; 1992 S 110; 1990 S 258; 1975 H 300)

2925.24 Tampering with drugs

(A) No person shall knowingly adulterate or alter any dangerous drug or substitute any dangerous drug with another substance.

(B) No person shall knowingly adulterate or alter any package or receptacle containing any dangerous drug or substitute any package or receptacle containing any dangerous drug with another package or receptacle.

(C) Divisions (A) and (B) of this section do not apply to manufacturers, practitioners, pharmacists, owners of pharmacies, nurses, and other persons, when the conduct of the manufacturer, practitioner, pharmacist, owner of a pharmacy, nurse, or other person is in accordance with Chapters 3719., 4715., 4723., 4729., 4731., and 4741. of the Revised Code.

(D) It is an affirmative defense to a charge under this section alleging that a person altered a dangerous drug that the dangerous drug the person allegedly altered was lawfully prescribed for the person's personal use and that the person did not sell or transfer or intend to sell or transfer the dangerous drug to another person.

(E) Whoever violates this section is guilty of tampering with drugs, a felony of the third degree. if the violation results in physical harm to any person, tampering with drugs is a felony of the second degree.

(1999 H 202, eff. 2–9–00)

2925.31 Abusing harmful intoxicants

(A) Except for lawful research, clinical, medical, dental, or veterinary purposes, no person, with purpose to induce intoxication or similar physiological effects, shall obtain, possess, or use a harmful intoxicant.

(B) Whoever violates this section is guilty of abusing harmful intoxicants, a misdemeanor of the first degree. If the offender previously has been convicted of a drug abuse offense, abusing harmful intoxicants is a felony of the fifth degree.

(C) In addition to any other sanction imposed upon an offender for a violation of this section, the court shall suspend for not less than six months or more than five years the offender's driver's or commercial driver's license or permit. If the offender is a professionally licensed person, in addition to any other sanction imposed for a violation of this section, the court immediately shall comply with section 2925.38 of the Revised Code.

(2002 S 123, eff. 1–1–04; 1996 H 162, eff. 1–1–97; 1995 S 2, eff. 7–1–96; 1993 H 377, eff. 9–30–93; 1990 S 258; 1975 H 300)

2925.32 Trafficking in harmful intoxicants; improperly dispensing or distributing nitrous oxide

(A) Divisions (A)(1) and (2) of this section do not apply to the dispensing or distributing of nitrous oxide.

(1) No person shall knowingly dispense or distribute a harmful intoxicant to a person age eighteen or older if the person who dispenses or distributes it knows or has reason to believe that the harmful intoxicant will be used in violation of section 2925.31 of the Revised Code.

(2) No person shall knowingly dispense or distribute a harmful intoxicant to a person under age eighteen if the person who dispenses or distributes it knows or has reason to believe that the harmful intoxicant will be used in violation of section 2925.31 of the Revised Code. Division (A)(2) of this section does not prohibit either of the following:

(a) Dispensing or distributing a harmful intoxicant to a person under age eighteen if a written order from the juvenile's parent or guardian is provided to the dispenser or distributor;

(b) Dispensing or distributing gasoline or diesel fuel to a person under age eighteen if the dispenser or distributor does not know or have reason to believe the product will be used in violation of section 2925.31 of the Revised Code. Division (A)(2)(a) of this section does not require a person to obtain a written order from the parent or guardian of a person under age eighteen in order to distribute or dispense gasoline or diesel fuel to the person.

(B)(1) No person shall knowingly dispense or distribute nitrous oxide to a person age twenty-one or older if the person who dispenses or distributes it knows or has reason to believe the nitrous oxide will be used in violation of section 2925.31 of the Revised Code.

(2) Except for lawful medical, dental, or clinical purposes, no person shall knowingly dispense or distribute nitrous oxide to a person under age twenty-one.

(3) No person, at the time a cartridge of nitrous oxide is sold to another person, shall sell a device that allows the purchaser to inhale nitrous oxide from cartridges or to hold nitrous oxide released from cartridges for purposes of inhalation. The sale of any such device constitutes a rebuttable presumption that the person knew or had reason to believe that the purchaser intended to abuse the nitrous oxide.

(4) No person who dispenses or distributes nitrous oxide in cartridges shall fail to comply with either of the following:

(a) The record-keeping requirements established under division (F) of this section;

(b) The labeling and transaction identification requirements established under division (G) of this section.

(C) This section does not apply to products used in making, fabricating, assembling, transporting, or constructing a product or structure by manual labor or machinery for sale or lease to another person, or to the mining, refining, or processing of natural deposits.

(D)(1) Whoever violates division (A)(1) or (2) or division (B)(1), (2), or (3) of this section is guilty of trafficking in harmful intoxicants, a felony of the fifth degree. If the offender previously has been convicted of a drug abuse offense, trafficking in harmful intoxicants is a felony of the fourth degree. In addition to any other sanction imposed upon an offender for trafficking in harmful intoxicants, the court shall suspend for not less than six months or more than five years the offender's driver's or commercial driver's license or permit. If the offender is a professionally licensed person, in addition to any other sanction imposed for trafficking in harmful intoxicants, the court immediately shall comply with section 2925.38 of the Revised Code.

(2) Whoever violates division (B)(4)(a) or (b) of this section is guilty of improperly dispensing or distributing nitrous oxide, a misdemeanor of the fourth degree.

(E) It is an affirmative defense to a charge of a violation of division (A)(2) or (B)(2) of this section that:

(1) An individual exhibited to the defendant or an officer or employee of the defendant, for purposes of establishing the individual's age, a driver's license or permit issued by this state, a commercial driver's license or permit issued by this state, an identification card issued pursuant to section 4507.50 of the Revised Code, for another document that purports to be a license, permit, or identification card described in this division;

(2) The document exhibited appeared to be a genuine, unaltered document, to pertain to the individual, and to establish the individual's age;

(3) The defendant or the officer or employee of the defendant otherwise did not have reasonable cause to believe that the individual was under the age represented.

(F) Beginning July 1, 2001, a person who dispenses or distributes nitrous oxide shall record each transaction involving the dispensing or distributing of the nitrous oxide on a separate card. The person shall require the purchaser to sign the card and provide a complete residence address. The person dispensing or distributing the nitrous oxide shall sign and date the card. The person shall retain the card recording a transaction for one year from the date of the transaction. The person shall maintain the cards at the person's business address and make them available during normal business hours for inspection and copying by officers or employees of the state board of pharmacy or of other law enforcement agencies of this state or the United States that are authorized to investigate violations of Chapter 2925., 3719., or 4729. of the Revised Code or the federal drug abuse control laws.

The cards used to record each transaction shall inform the purchaser of the following:

(1) That nitrous oxide cartridges are to be used only for purposes of preparing food;

(2) That inhalation of nitrous oxide can have dangerous health effects;

(3) That it is a violation of state law to distribute or dispense cartridges of nitrous oxide to any person under age twenty-one, punishable as a felony of the fifth degree.

(G)(1) Each cartridge of nitrous oxide dispensed or distributed in this state shall bear the following printed warning:

"Nitrous oxide cartridges are to be used only for purposes of preparing food. Nitrous oxide cartridges may not be sold to persons under age twenty-one. Do not inhale contents. Misuse can be dangerous to your health."

(2) Each time a person dispenses or distributes one or more cartridges of nitrous oxide, the person shall mark the packaging containing the cartridges with a label or other device that identifies the person who dispensed or distributed the nitrous oxide and the person's business address.

(2002 S 123, eff. 1–1–04; 2000 H 331, eff. 10–10–00; 1999 S 55, eff. 10–26–99; 1998 H 122, eff. 7–29–98; 1996 H 162, eff. 1–1–97; 1995 S 2, eff. 7–1–96; 1993 H 377, eff. 9–30–93; 1990 S 258; 1976 S 414)

2925.33 Possessing nitrous oxide in a motor vehicle

(A) As used in this section, "motor vehicle," "street," and "highway" have the same meanings as in section 4511.01 of the Revised Code.

(B) Unless authorized under Chapter 3719., 4715., 4729., 4731., 4741., or 4765. of the Revised Code, no person shall possess an open cartridge of nitrous oxide in either of the following circumstances:

(1) While operating or being a passenger in or on a motor vehicle on a street, highway, or other public or private property open to the public for purposes of vehicular traffic or parking;

(2) While being in or on a stationary motor vehicle on a street, highway, or other public or private property open to the public for purposes of vehicular traffic or parking.

(C) Whoever violates this section is guilty of possessing nitrous oxide in a motor vehicle, a misdemeanor of the fourth degree.

(1996 H 162, eff. 1–1–97)

2925.36 Illegal dispensing of drug samples

(A) No person shall knowingly furnish another a sample drug.

(B) Division (A) of this section does not apply to manufacturers, wholesalers, pharmacists, owners of pharmacies, licensed health professionals authorized to prescribe drugs, and other persons whose conduct is in accordance with Chapters 3719., 4715., 4723., 4725., 4729., 4731., and 4741. of the Revised Code.

(C)(1) Whoever violates this section is guilty of illegal dispensing of drug samples.

(2) If the drug involved in the offense is a compound, mixture, preparation, or substance included in schedule I or II, with the exception of marihuana, the penalty for the offense shall be determined as follows:

(a) Except as otherwise provided in division (C)(2)(b) of this section, illegal dispensing of drug samples is a felony of the fifth degree, and, subject to division (E) of this section, division (C) of section 2929.13 of the Revised Code applies in determining whether to impose a prison term on the offender.

(b) If the offense was committed in the vicinity of a school or in the vicinity of a juvenile, illegal dispensing of drug samples is a felony of the fourth degree, and, subject to division (E) of this section, division (C) of section 2929.13 of the Revised Code applies in determining whether to impose a prison term on the offender.

(3) If the drug involved in the offense is a dangerous drug or a compound, mixture, preparation, or substance included in schedule III, IV, or V, or is marihuana, the penalty for the offense shall be determined as follows:

(a) Except as otherwise provided in division (C)(3)(b) of this section, illegal dispensing of drug samples is a misdemeanor of the second degree.

(b) If the offense was committed in the vicinity of a school or in the vicinity of a juvenile, illegal dispensing of drug samples is a misdemeanor of the first degree.

(D) In addition to any prison term authorized or required by division (C) or (E) of this section and sections 2929.13 and 2929.14 of the Revised Code and in addition to any other sanction imposed for the offense under this section or sections 2929.11 to 2929.18 of the Revised Code, the court that sentences an offender who is convicted of or pleads guilty to a violation of division (A) of this section shall do both of the following:

(1) The court shall suspend for not less than six months or more than five years the offender's driver's or commercial driver's license or permit.

(2) If the offender is a professionally licensed person, in addition to any other sanction imposed for a violation of this section, the court immediately shall comply with section 2925.38 of the Revised Code.

(E) Notwithstanding the prison term authorized or required by division (C) of this section and sections 2929.13 and 2929.14 of the Revised Code, if the violation of division (A) of this section involves the sale, offer to sell, or possession of a schedule I or II controlled substance, with the exception of marihuana, and if the court imposing sentence upon the offender finds that the offender as a result of the violation is a major drug offender and is guilty of a specification of the type described in section 2941.1410 of the Revised Code, the court, in lieu of the prison term otherwise authorized or required, shall impose upon the offender the mandatory prison term specified in division (D)(3)(a) of section 2929.14 of the Revised Code and may impose an additional prison term under division (D)(3)(b) of that section.

(F) Notwithstanding any contrary provision of section 3719.21 of the Revised Code, the clerk of the court shall pay a fine imposed for a violation of this section pursuant to division (A) of section 2929.18 of the Revised Code in accordance with and subject to the requirements of division (F) of section 2925.03 of the Revised Code. The agency that receives the fine shall use the fine as specified in division (F) of section 2925.03 of the Revised Code.

(2002 S 123, eff. 1–1–04; 2000 H 241, eff. 5–17–00; 1999 S 107, eff. 3–23–00; 1996 S 269, eff. 7–1–96; 1995 S 2, eff. 7–1–96; 1994 H 391, eff. 7–21–94; 1993 H 377, eff. 9–30–93; 1992 H 591, S 110; 1990 S 258, H 215; 1975 H 300)

2925.37 Possession of or trafficking in counterfeit controlled substances

(A) No person shall knowingly possess any counterfeit controlled substance.

(B) No person shall knowingly make, sell, offer to sell, or deliver any substance that the person knows is a counterfeit controlled substance.

(C) No person shall make, possess, sell, offer to sell, or deliver any punch, die, plate, stone, or other device knowing or having reason to know that it will be used to print or reproduce a trademark, trade name, or other identifying mark upon a counterfeit controlled substance.

(D) No person shall sell, offer to sell, give, or deliver any counterfeit controlled substance to a juvenile.

(E) No person shall directly or indirectly represent a counterfeit controlled substance as a controlled substance by describing its effects as the physical or psychological effects associated with use of a controlled substance.

(F) No person shall directly or indirectly falsely represent or advertise a counterfeit controlled substance as a controlled substance. As used in this division, "advertise" means engaging in "advertisement," as defined in section 3715.01 of the Revised Code.

(G) Whoever violates division (A) of this section is guilty of possession of counterfeit controlled substances, a misdemeanor of the first degree.

(H) Whoever violates division (B) or (C) of this section is guilty of trafficking in counterfeit controlled substances. Except as otherwise provided in this division, trafficking in counterfeit controlled substances is a felony of the fifth degree, and division (C) of section 2929.13 of the Revised Code applies in determining whether to impose a prison term on the offender. If the offense was committed in the vicinity of a school or in the vicinity of a juvenile, trafficking in counterfeit controlled substances is a felony of the fourth degree, and division (C) of section 2929.13 of the Revised Code applies in determining whether to impose a prison term on the offender.

(I) Whoever violates division (D) of this section is guilty of aggravated trafficking in counterfeit controlled substances. Except as otherwise provided in this division, aggravated trafficking in counterfeit controlled substances is a felony of the fourth degree, and division (C) of section 2929.13 of the Revised Code applies in determining whether to impose a prison term on the offender.

(J) Whoever violates division (E) of this section is guilty of promoting and encouraging drug abuse. Except as otherwise provided in this division, promoting and encouraging drug abuse is a felony of the fifth degree, and division (C) of section 2929.13 of the Revised Code applies in determining whether to impose a prison term on the offender. If the offense was committed in the vicinity of a school or in the vicinity of a juvenile, promoting and encouraging drug abuse is a felony of the fourth degree, and division (C) of section 2929.13 of the Revised Code applies in determining whether to impose a prison term on the offender.

(K) Whoever violates division (F) of this section is guilty of fraudulent drug advertising. Except as otherwise provided in this division, fraudulent drug advertising is a felony of the fifth degree, and division (C) of section 2929.13 of the Revised Code applies in determining whether to impose a prison term on the offender. If the offense was committed in the vicinity of a school or in the vicinity of a juvenile, fraudulent drug advertising is a felony of the fourth degree, and division (C) of section 2929.13 of the Revised Code applies in determining whether to impose a prison term on the offender.

(L) In addition to any prison term authorized or required by divisions (H) to (K) of this section and sections 2929.13 and 2929.14 of the Revised Code and in addition to any other sanction imposed for the offense under this section or sections 2929.11 to 2929.18 of the Revised Code, the court that sentences an offender who is convicted of or pleads guilty to a violation of division (B), (C), (D), (E), or (F) of this section shall do both of the following:

(1) The court shall suspend for not less than six months or more than five years the offender's driver's or commercial driver's license or permit.

(2) If the offender is a professionally licensed person, in addition to any other sanction imposed for a violation of this section, the court immediately shall comply with section 2925.38 of the Revised Code.

(M) Notwithstanding any contrary provision of section 3719.21 of the Revised Code, the clerk of the court shall pay a fine imposed for a violation of this section pursuant to division (A) of section 2929.18 of the Revised Code in accordance with and subject to the requirements of division (F) of section 2925.03 of the Revised Code. The agency that receives the fine shall use the fine as specified in division (F) of section 2925.03 of the Revised Code.

(2002 S 123, eff. 1–1–04; 1996 S 269, eff. 7–1–96; 1995 S 2, eff. 7–1–96; 1993 H 377, eff. 9–30–93; 1990 S 258; 1982 H 535)

2925.38 Convictions of professionally licensed persons

If a person who is convicted of or pleads guilty to a violation of section 2925.02, 2925.03, 2925.04, 2925.041, 2925.05, 2925.06, 2925.11, 2925.12, 2925.13, 2925.14, 2925.22, 2925.23, 2925.31, 2925.32, 2925.36, or 2925.37 of the Revised Code is a professionally licensed person, in addition to any other sanctions imposed for the violation, the court, except as otherwise provided in this section, immediately shall transmit a certified copy of the judgment entry of conviction to the regulatory or licensing board or agency that has the administrative authority to suspend or revoke the offender's professional license. If the professionally licensed person who is convicted of or pleads guilty to a violation of any section listed in this section is a person who has been admitted to the bar by order of the supreme court in compliance with its prescribed and published rules, in addition to any other sanctions imposed for the violation, the court immediately shall transmit a certified copy of the judgment entry of conviction to the secretary of the board of commissioners on grievances and discipline of the supreme court and to either the disciplinary counsel or the president, secretary, and chairperson of each certified grievance committee.

(2002 S 123, eff. 1–1–04; 2001 H 7, eff. 8–7–01; 1995 S 2, eff. 7–1–96; 1990 S 258, eff. 11–20–90)

FORFEITURE OF PROPERTY

2925.41 Definitions

As used in sections 2925.42 to 2925.45 of the Revised Code:

(A) "Financial institution" means a bank, credit union, savings and loan association, or a licensee or registrant under Chapter 1321. of the Revised Code.

(B) "Property" includes both of the following:

(1) Real property, including, but not limited to, things growing on, affixed to, and found in the real property;

(2) Tangible and intangible personal property, including, but not limited to, rights, privileges, interests, claims, and securities.

(1990 S 258, eff. 11–20–90)

2925.42 Criminal forfeiture of property

(A)(1) In accordance with division (B) of this section, a person who is convicted of or pleads guilty to a felony drug abuse offense, and any juvenile who is found by a juvenile court to be a delinquent child for an act that, if committed by an adult, would be a felony drug abuse offense, loses any right to the possession of property and forfeits to the state any right, title, and interest the person may have in that property if either of the following applies:

(a) The property constitutes, or is derived directly or indirectly from, any proceeds that the person obtained directly or indirectly from the commission of the felony drug abuse offense or act.

(b) The property was used or intended to be used in any manner to commit, or to facilitate the commission of, the felony drug abuse offense or act.

(2) All right, title, and interest of a person in property described in division (A)(1) of this section vests in the state upon the person's commission of the felony drug abuse offense of which the person is convicted or to which the person pleads guilty and that is the basis of the forfeiture, or upon the juvenile's commission of the act that, if committed by an adult, would be a felony drug abuse offense, that is the basis of the juvenile being found to be a delinquent child, and that is the basis of the forfeiture. Subject to divisions (F)(3)(b) and (5)(b) and (G)(2) of this section, if any right, title, or interest in property is vested in this state under this division and subsequently is transferred to a person other than the offender who forfeits the right, title, or interest under division (A)(1) of this section, then, in accordance with division (B) of this section, the right, title, or interest in the property may be the subject of a special verdict of forfeiture and, after any special verdict of forfeiture, shall be ordered forfeited to this state, unless the transferee establishes in a hearing held pursuant to division (F) of this section that the transferee is a bona fide purchaser for value of the right, title, or interest in the property and that, at the time of its purchase, the transferee was reasonably without cause to believe that it was subject to forfeiture under this section.

(3) The provisions of section 2925.43 of the Revised Code that relate to the forfeiture of any right, title, or interest in property associated with a felony drug abuse offense pursuant to a civil action to obtain a civil forfeiture do not apply to the forfeiture of any right, title, or interest in property described in division (A)(1) of this section that occurs pursuant to division (B) of this section upon a person's conviction of or guilty plea to a felony drug abuse offense or upon a juvenile being found by a juvenile court to be a delinquent child for an act that, if committed by an adult, would be a felony drug abuse offense.

(4) Nothing in this section precludes a financial institution that has or purports to have a security interest in or lien on property described in division (A)(1) of this section from commencing a civil action or taking other appropriate legal action in connection with the property, prior to its disposition in accordance with section 2925.44 of the Revised Code, for the purpose of obtaining possession of the property in order to foreclose or otherwise enforce the security interest or lien. A financial institution may commence a civil action or take other appropriate legal action for that purpose prior to the disposition of the property in accordance with section 2925.44 of the Revised Code, even if a felony drug abuse offense prosecution or a delinquent child proceeding for an act that, if committed by an adult, would be a felony drug abuse offense has been or could be commenced, even if the property is or could be the subject of an order of forfeiture issued under division (B)(5) of this section, and even if the property has been seized or is subject to seizure pursuant to division (D) or (E) of this section.

If a financial institution commences a civil action or takes any other appropriate legal action as described in this division, if the financial institution subsequently causes the sale of the property prior to its seizure pursuant to division (D) or (E) of this section and its disposition pursuant to section 2925.44 of the Revised Code, and if the person responsible for the conduct of the sale has actual knowledge of the commencement of a felony drug abuse offense prosecution or of a delinquent child proceeding for an act that, if committed by an adult, would be a felony drug abuse offense, actual knowledge of a pending forfeiture proceeding under division (B) of this section, or actual knowledge of an order of forfeiture issued under division (B)(5) of this section, then the person responsible for the conduct of the sale shall dispose of the proceeds of the sale in the following order:

(a) First, to the payment of the costs of the sale and to the payment of the costs incurred by law enforcement agencies and financial institutions in connection with the seizure of, storage of, maintenance of, and provision of security for the property. As used in this division, "costs" of a financial institution do not include attorney's fees incurred by that institution in connection with the property.

(b) Second, the remaining proceeds of the sale after compliance with division (A)(4)(a) of this section, to the payment of valid security interests and liens pertaining to the property that, at the time of the vesting of the right, title, or interest of the adult or juvenile in the state under division (A)(2) of this section, are held by known secured parties and lienholders, in the order of priority of those security interests and liens;

(c) Third, the remaining proceeds of the sale after compliance with division (A)(4)(b) of this section, to the court that has or would have jurisdiction in a felony drug abuse offense prosecution or a delinquent child proceeding for an act that, if committed by an adult, would be a felony drug abuse offense, for disposition in accordance with section 2925.44 of the Revised Code.

(B)(1) A criminal forfeiture of any right, title, or interest in property described in division (A)(1) of this section is precluded unless one of the following applies:

(a) The indictment, count in the indictment, or information charging the felony drug abuse offense specifies the nature of the right, title, or interest of the alleged offender in the property described in division (A)(1) of this section that is potentially subject to forfeiture under this section, or a description of the property of the alleged offender that is potentially subject to forfeiture under this section, to the extent the right, title, or interest in the property or the property reasonably is known at the time of the filing of the indictment or information; or the complaint, indictment, or information charging a juvenile with being a delinquent child for the commission of an act that, if committed by an adult, would be a felony drug abuse offense specifies the nature of the right, title, or interest of the juvenile in the property described in division (A)(1) of this section that is potentially subject to forfeiture under this section, or a description of the property of the juvenile that is potentially subject to forfeiture under this section, to the extent the right, title, or interest in the property or the property reasonably is known at the time of the filing of the complaint, indictment, or information.

(b) The property in question was not reasonably foreseen to be subject to forfeiture under this section at the time of the filing of the indictment, information, or complaint, the prosecuting attorney gave prompt notice to the alleged offender or juvenile of that property when it was discovered to be subject to forfeiture under this section, and a verdict of forfeiture described in division (B)(3) of this section requires the forfeiture of that property.

(2) The specifications described in division (B)(1) of this section shall be stated at the end of the body of the indictment, count in the indictment, information, or complaint.

(3)(a) If a person is convicted of or pleads guilty to a felony drug abuse offense, or a juvenile is found to be a delinquent child for an act that, if committed by an adult, would be a felony drug abuse offense, then a special proceeding shall be conducted in accordance with this division to determine whether any property described in division (B)(1)(a) or (b) of this section will be the subject of an order of forfeiture under this section. Except as otherwise provided in division (B)(3)(b) of this section, the jury in the felony drug abuse offense criminal action or in the delinquent child action or, if that action was a nonjury action, the judge in that action shall hear and consider testimony and other evidence in the proceeding relative to whether any property described in division (B)(1)(a) or (b) of this section is subject to forfeiture under this section. If the jury or judge determines that the prosecuting attorney has established, by a preponderance of the evidence, that any property so described is subject to forfeiture under this section, the judge or juvenile judge shall render a verdict of forfeiture that specifically describes the right, title, or interest in property or the property that is subject to forfeiture under this section. The Rules of Evidence shall apply in the proceeding.

(b) If the trier of fact in a felony drug abuse offense criminal action or in a delinquent child action was a jury, then, upon the filing of a motion by the person who was convicted of or pleaded guilty to the felony drug abuse offense or upon the filing of a motion by the juvenile who was found to be a delinquent child for an act that, if committed by an adult, would be a felony drug abuse offense, the determinations in the proceeding described in this division instead shall be made by the judge in the felony drug abuse offense criminal action or the juvenile judge.

(4) In a felony drug abuse offense criminal action or in a delinquent child action, if the trier of fact is a jury, the jury shall not be informed of any specification described in division (B)(1)(a) of this section or of any property described in that division or division (B)(1)(b) of this section prior to the alleged offender being convicted of or pleading guilty to the felony drug abuse offense or prior to the juvenile being found to be a delinquent child for the commission of an act that, if committed by an adult, would be a felony drug abuse offense.

(5)(a) If a verdict of forfeiture is entered pursuant to division (B)(3) of this section, then the court that imposes sentence upon a person who is convicted of or pleads guilty to a felony drug abuse offense, or the juvenile court that finds a juvenile to be a delinquent child for an act that, if committed by an adult, would be a felony drug abuse offense, in addition to any other sentence imposed upon the offender or order of disposition imposed upon the delinquent child, shall order that the offender or delinquent child forfeit to the state all of the offender's or delinquent child's right, title, and interest in the property described in division (A)(1) of this section. If a person is convicted of or pleads guilty to a felony drug abuse offense, or a juvenile is found by a juvenile court to be a delinquent child for an act that, if committed by an adult, would be a felony drug abuse offense, and derives profits or other proceeds from the offense or act, the court that imposes sentence or an order of disposition upon the offender or delinquent child, in lieu of any fine that the court is otherwise authorized or required to impose, may impose upon the offender or delinquent child a fine of not more than twice the gross profits or other proceeds so derived.

(b) Notwithstanding any contrary provision of section 3719.21 of the Revised Code, all fines imposed pursuant to this division shall be paid by the clerk of the court to the county, municipal corporation, township, park district, as created pursuant to section 511.18 or 1545.01 of the Revised Code, or state law enforcement agencies in this state that were primarily responsible for or involved in making the arrest of, and in prosecuting, the offender. However, no fine so imposed shall be paid to a law enforcement agency unless the agency has adopted a written internal control policy under division (F)(2) of section 2925.03 of the Revised Code that addresses the use of the fine moneys that it receives under this division and division (F)(1) of section 2925.03 of the Revised Code. The fines imposed and paid pursuant to this division shall be used by the law enforcement agencies to subsidize their efforts pertaining to drug offenses, in accordance with the written internal control policy adopted by the recipient agency under division (F)(2) of section 2925.03 of the Revised Code.

(c) As used in division (B)(5) of this section:

(i) "Law enforcement agencies" includes, but is not limited to, the state board of pharmacy and the office of a prosecutor.

(ii) "Prosecutor" has the same meaning as in section 2935.01 of the Revised Code.

(6) If any of the property that is described in division (A)(1) of this section and that is the subject of an order of forfeiture issued

under division (B)(5) of this section, because of an act or omission of the person who is convicted of or pleads guilty to the felony drug abuse offense that is the basis of the order of forfeiture, or an act or omission of the juvenile found by a juvenile court to be a delinquent child for an act that, if committed by an adult, would be a felony drug abuse offense and that is the basis of the forfeiture, cannot be located upon the exercise of due diligence, has been transferred to, sold to, or deposited with a third party, has been placed beyond the jurisdiction of the court, has been substantially diminished in value, or has been commingled with other property that cannot be divided without difficulty, the court that issues the order of forfeiture shall order the forfeiture of any other property of the offender up to the value of any forfeited property described in this division.

(C) There shall be a rebuttable presumption that any right, title, or interest of a person in property described in division (A)(1) of this section is subject to forfeiture under division (B) of this section, if the state proves both of the following by a preponderance of the evidence:

(1) The right, title, or interest in the property was acquired by the offender during the period of the commission of the felony drug abuse offense or act that, if committed by an adult, would be a felony drug abuse offense, or within a reasonable time after that period.

(2) There is no likely source for the right, title, or interest in the property other than proceeds obtained from the commission of the felony drug abuse offense or act.

(D)(1) Upon the application of the prosecuting attorney who is prosecuting or has jurisdiction to prosecute the felony drug abuse offense or act, the court of common pleas or juvenile court of the county in which property subject to forfeiture under division (B) of this section is located, whichever is applicable, may issue a restraining order or injunction, an order requiring the execution of a satisfactory performance bond, or an order taking any other reasonable action necessary to preserve the availability of the property, at either of the following times:

(a) Upon the filing of an indictment, complaint, or information charging a person who has any right, title, or interest in the property with the commission of a felony drug abuse offense and alleging that the property with respect to which the order is sought will be subject to forfeiture under division (B) of this section if the person is convicted of or pleads guilty to the offense, or upon the filing of a complaint, indictment, or information alleging that a juvenile who has any right, title, or interest in the property is a delinquent child because of the commission of an act that, if committed by an adult, would be a felony drug abuse offense and alleging that the property with respect to which the order is sought will be subject to forfeiture under division (B) of this section if the juvenile is found to be a delinquent child because of the commission of that act;

(b) Except as provided in division (D)(3) of this section, prior to the filing of an indictment, complaint, or information charging a person who has any right, title, or interest in the property with the commission of a felony drug abuse offense, or prior to the filing of a complaint, indictment, or information alleging that a juvenile who has any right, title, or interest in the property is a delinquent child because of the commission of an act that, if committed by an adult, would be a felony drug abuse offense, if, after notice is given to all persons known to have any right, title, or interest in the property and an opportunity to have a hearing on the order is given to those persons, the court determines both of the following:

(i) There is a substantial probability that the state will prevail on the issue of forfeiture and that failure to enter the order will result in the property subject to forfeiture being destroyed, removed from the jurisdiction of the court, or otherwise being made unavailable for forfeiture.

(ii) The need to preserve the availability of the property subject to forfeiture through the entry of the requested order outweighs the hardship on any party against whom the order is to be entered.

(2) Except as provided in division (D)(3) of this section, an order issued under division (D)(1) of this section is effective for not more than ninety days, unless extended by the court for good cause shown or unless an indictment, complaint, or information charging the commission of a felony drug abuse offense or a complaint, indictment, or information alleging that a juvenile is a delinquent child because of the commission of an act that, if committed by an adult, would be a felony drug abuse offense, is filed against any alleged adult offender or alleged delinquent child with any right, title, or interest in the property that is the subject of the order.

(3) A court may issue an order under division (D)(1)(b) of this section without giving notice or an opportunity for a hearing to persons known to have any right, title, or interest in property, if the prosecuting attorney who is prosecuting or has jurisdiction to prosecute the felony drug abuse offense or act demonstrates that there is probable cause to believe that the property will be subject to forfeiture under division (B) of this section if a person with any right, title, or interest in the property is convicted of or pleads guilty to a felony drug abuse offense or a juvenile with any right, title, or interest in the property is found by a juvenile court to be a delinquent child for an act that, if committed by an adult, would be a felony drug abuse offense, and that giving notice or an opportunity for a hearing to persons with any right, title, or interest in the property will jeopardize its availability for forfeiture. The order shall be a temporary order and expire not more than ten days after the date on which it is entered, unless it is extended for good cause shown or unless a person with any right, title, or interest in the property that is the subject of the order consents to an extension for a longer period. A hearing concerning an order issued under this division may be requested, and, if it is requested, the court shall hold the hearing at the earliest possible time prior to the expiration of the order.

(4) At any hearing held under division (D) of this section, the court may receive and consider evidence and information that is inadmissible under the Rules of Evidence. However, each hearing held under division (D) of this section shall be recorded by shorthand, by stenotype, or by any other mechanical, electronic, or video recording device. If, as a result of a hearing under division (D) of this section, property would be seized, the recording of and any transcript of the recording of that hearing shall not be a public record for purposes of section 149.43 of the Revised Code until that property has been seized pursuant to division (D) of this section. Division (D)(4) of this section shall not be construed as requiring, authorizing, or permitting, and does not require, authorize, or permit, the making available for inspection, or the copying, under section 149.43 of the Revised Code of any confidential law enforcement investigatory record or trial preparation record, as defined in that section.

(5) A prosecuting attorney or other law enforcement officer may request the court of common pleas of the county in which property subject to forfeiture under this section is located to issue a warrant authorizing the seizure of that property. The request shall be made in the same manner as provided for a search warrant. If the court determines that there is probable cause to believe that the property to be seized will be subject to forfeiture under this section when a person with any right, title, or interest in the property is convicted of or pleads guilty to a felony drug abuse offense or when a juvenile with any right, title, or interest in the property is found by a juvenile court to be a delinquent child for an act that, if committed by an adult, would be a felony drug abuse offense, and if the court determines that any order issued under division (D)(1), (2), or (3) of this section may not be sufficient to ensure the availability of the property for forfeiture, the court shall issue a warrant authorizing the seizure of the property.

(E)(1) Upon the entry of an order of forfeiture under this section, the court shall order an appropriate law enforcement officer to seize all of the forfeited property upon the terms and conditions that the court determines are proper. In addition, upon the request of the prosecuting attorney who prosecuted the felony drug abuse offense or act, the court shall enter any appropriate restraining orders or injunctions, require the execution of satisfactory performance bonds, appoint receivers, conservators, appraisers, accountants, or trustees, or take any other action to protect the interest of the state in the forfeited property. Any income accruing to or derived from property ordered forfeited under this section may be used to offset ordinary and necessary expenses related to the property that are required by law or that are necessary to protect the interest of the state or third parties.

After forfeited property is seized, the prosecuting attorney who prosecuted the felony drug abuse offense or act shall direct its disposition in accordance with section 2925.44 of the Revised Code, making due provision for the rights of any innocent persons. Any right, title, or interest in property not exercisable by, or transferable for value to, the state shall expire and shall not revert to the offender whose conviction or plea of guilty or act as a delinquent child is the basis of the order of forfeiture. Neither the adult offender or delinquent child nor any person acting in concert with or on behalf of the adult offender or delinquent child is eligible to purchase forfeited property at any sale held pursuant to section 2925.44 of the Revised Code.

Upon the application of any person other than the adult offender or delinquent child whose right, title, or interest in the property is the subject of the order of forfeiture or any person acting in concert with or on behalf of the adult offender or delinquent child, the court may restrain or stay the sale or other disposition of the property pursuant to section 2925.44 of the Revised Code pending the conclusion of any appeal of the felony drug abuse offense conviction or of the delinquent child adjudication that is the basis of the order of forfeiture, if the applicant demonstrates that proceeding with the sale or other disposition of the property will result in irreparable injury or loss to the applicant.

(2) With respect to property that is the subject of an order of forfeiture issued under this section, the court that issued the order, upon the petition of the prosecuting attorney who prosecuted the felony drug abuse offense or act, may do any of the following:

(a) Grant petitions for mitigation or remission of forfeiture, restore forfeited property to victims of a felony drug abuse offense, or take any other action to protect the rights of innocent persons that is in the interest of justice and that is not inconsistent with this section;

(b) Compromise claims that arise under this section;

(c) Award compensation to persons who provide information resulting in a forfeiture under this section;

(d) Direct the disposition by the prosecuting attorney who prosecuted the felony drug abuse offense or act, in accordance with section 2925.44 of the Revised Code, of all property ordered forfeited under this section, making due provision for the rights of innocent persons;

(e) Pending the disposition of any property that is the subject of an order of forfeiture under this section, take any appropriate measures that are necessary to safeguard and maintain the property.

(3) To facilitate the identification and location of property that is the subject of an order of forfeiture under this section and to facilitate the disposition of petitions for remission or mitigation issued under division (E)(2) of this section, after the issuance of an order of forfeiture under this section and upon application by the prosecuting attorney who prosecuted the felony drug abuse offense or act, the court may order that the testimony of any witness relating to the forfeited property be taken by deposition, and that any designated book, paper, document, record, recording, or other material that is not privileged be produced at the same time and place as the testimony, in the same manner as provided for the taking of depositions under the Rules of Civil Procedure.

(F)(1) Except as provided in divisions (F)(2) to (5) of this section, no person claiming any right, title, or interest in property subject to forfeiture under this section or section 2925.43 of the Revised Code may intervene in a criminal trial or appeal, or a delinquent child proceeding or appeal, involving the forfeiture of the property under this section or in a civil action for a civil forfeiture under section 2925.43 of the Revised Code, or may commence an action at law or equity against the state concerning the validity of the person's alleged right, title, or interest in the property subsequent to the filing of an indictment, complaint, or information alleging that the property is subject to forfeiture under this section or subsequent to the filing of a complaint, indictment, or information alleging that a juvenile who has any right, title, or interest in the property is a delinquent child because of the commission of an act that, if committed by an adult, would be a felony drug abuse offense and alleging that the property is subject to forfeiture under this section.

(2) After the entry of an order of forfeiture under this section, the prosecuting attorney who prosecuted the felony drug abuse offense or act shall conduct or cause to be conducted a search of the appropriate public records that relate to the property, and make or cause to be made reasonably diligent inquiries, for the purpose of identifying persons who have any right, title, or interest in the property. The prosecuting attorney then shall cause a notice of the order of forfeiture, of the prosecuting attorney's intent to dispose of the property in accordance with section 2925.44 of the Revised Code, and of the manner of the proposed disposal, to be given to each person who is known, because of the conduct of the search, the making of the inquiries, or otherwise, to have any right, title, or interest in the property, by certified mail, return receipt requested, or by personal service. Additionally, the prosecuting attorney shall cause a similar notice to be published once a week for two consecutive weeks in a newspaper of general circulation in the county in which the property was seized.

(3)(a) Any person, other than the adult offender whose conviction or guilty plea or the delinquent child whose adjudication is the basis of the order of forfeiture, who asserts a legal right, title, or interest in the property that is the subject of the order may petition the court that issued the order, within thirty days after the earlier of the final publication of notice or the person's receipt of notice under division (F)(2) of this section, for a hearing to adjudicate the validity of the person's alleged right, title, or interest in the property. The petition shall be signed by the petitioner under the penalties for falsification as specified in section 2921.13 of the Revised Code and shall set forth the nature and extent of the petitioner's right, title, or interest in the property, the time and circumstances of the petitioner's acquisition of that right, title, or interest, any additional facts supporting the petitioner's claim, and the relief sought.

(b) In lieu of filing a petition as described in division (F)(3)(a) of this section, a secured party or other lienholder of record that asserts a legal right, title, or interest in the property that is the subject of the order, including, but not limited to, a mortgage, security interest, or other type of lien, may file an affidavit as described in this division to establish the validity of the alleged right, title, or interest in the property. The affidavit shall be filed within thirty days after the earlier of the final publication of notice or the receipt of notice under division (F)(2) of this section and, except as otherwise provided in this section, shall constitute prima-facie evidence of the validity of the secured party's or other lienholder's alleged right, title, or interest in the property. Unless the prosecuting attorney files a motion challenging the affidavit within ten days after its filing and unless the prosecuting attorney establishes, by a preponderance of the evidence, at a subsequent hearing before the court that issued the forfeiture order, that the secured party or other lienholder does not possess the alleged right, title, or interest in the property or that the secured party or other lienholder had actual knowledge of facts pertaining to the felony drug abuse offense or act that was the basis of the forfeiture order, the affidavit shall constitute conclusive evidence of the validity of the secured party's or other lienholder's right, title, or interest in the property and shall have the legal effect described in division (G)(2) of this section. To the extent practicable and consistent with the interests of justice, any such hearing shall be held within thirty days after the prosecuting attorney files the motion. At any such hearing, the prosecuting attorney and the secured party or other lienholder may present evidence and witnesses and cross-examine witnesses.

In order to be valid for the purposes of this division and division (G)(2) of this section, the affidavit of a secured party or other lienholder shall contain averments that the secured party or other lienholder acquired its alleged right, title, or interest in the property in the regular course of its business, for a specified valuable consideration, without actual knowledge of any facts pertaining to the felony drug abuse offense or act that was the basis of the forfeiture order, in good faith and without the intent to prevent or otherwise impede the state from seizing or obtaining a forfeiture of the property under sections 2925.41 to 2925.45 of the Revised Code, and prior to the seizure or forfeiture of the property under those sections.

(4) Upon receipt of a petition filed under division (F)(3) of this section, the court shall hold a hearing to determine the validity of the petitioner's right, title, or interest in the property that is the subject of the order of forfeiture. To the extent practicable and consistent with the interests of justice, the hearing shall be held within thirty days after the filing of the petition. The court may consolidate the hearing on the petition with a hearing on any other petition filed by a person other than the offender whose conviction or guilty plea or adjudication as a delinquent child is the basis of the order of forfeiture. At the hearing, the petitioner may testify, present evidence and witnesses on the petitioner's behalf, and cross-examine witnesses for the state. The state may present evidence and witnesses in rebuttal and in defense of its claim to the property and cross-examine witnesses for the petitioner. In addition to evidence and testimony presented at the hearing, the court shall consider the relevant portions of the record in the felony drug abuse offense or delinquent child case that resulted in the order of forfeiture.

(5)(a) The court shall amend its order of forfeiture in accordance with its determination if it determines, at the hearing, that the petitioner has established either of the following by a preponderance of the evidence:

(i) The petitioner has a legal right, title, or interest in the property that renders the order of forfeiture completely or partially invalid because it was vested in the petitioner, rather than the adult offender whose conviction or guilty plea or the delinquent child whose adjudication is the basis of the order, or was superior to any right, title, or interest of that offender, at the time of the commission of the felony drug abuse offense or act that is the basis of the order.

(ii) The petitioner is a bona fide purchaser for value of the right, title, or interest in the property and was at the time of the purchase reasonably without cause to believe that it was subject to forfeiture under this section.

(b) The court also shall amend its order of forfeiture to reflect any right, title, or interest of a secured party or other lienholder of record in the property subject to the order that was established pursuant to division (F)(3)(b) of this section by means of an affidavit, or that was established pursuant to that division by the failure of a prosecuting attorney to establish, in a hearing as described in that division, that the secured party or other lienholder did not possess the alleged right, title, or interest in the property or that the secured party or other lienholder had actual knowledge of facts pertaining to the felony drug abuse offense or act that was the basis of the order.

(G)(1) Subject to division (G)(2) of this section, if the court has disposed of all petitions filed under division (F) of this section or if no petitions are filed under that division and the time for filing petitions under that division has expired, the state shall have clear title to all property that is the subject of an order of forfeiture issued under this section and may warrant good title to any subsequent purchaser or other transferee.

(2) If an affidavit as described in division (F)(3)(b) of this section is filed in accordance with that division, if the affidavit constitutes, under the circumstances described in that division, conclusive evidence of the validity of the right, title, or interest of a secured party or other lienholder of record in the property subject to a forfeiture order, and if any mortgage, security interest, or other type of lien possessed by the secured party or other lienholder in connection with the property is not satisfied prior to a sale or other disposition of the property pursuant to section 2925.44 of the Revised Code, then the right, title, or interest of the secured party or other lienholder in the property remains valid for purposes of sections 2925.41 to 2925.45 of the Revised Code and any subsequent purchaser or other transferee of the property pursuant to section 2925.44 of the Revised Code shall take the property subject to the continued validity of the right, title, or interest of the secured party or other lienholder in the property.

(2000 S 179, § 3, eff. 1-1-02; 1995 S 2, eff. 7-1-96; 1992 S 174, eff. 7-31-92; 1990 S 258)

2925.43 Civil forfeiture of property

(A) The following property is subject to forfeiture to the state in a civil action as described in division (E) of this section, and no person has any right, title, or interest in the following property:

(1) Any property that constitutes, or is derived directly or indirectly from, any proceeds that a person obtained directly or indirectly from the commission of an act that, upon the filing of an indictment, complaint, or information, could be prosecuted as a felony drug abuse offense or that, upon the filing of a complaint, indictment, or information, could be the basis for finding a juvenile to be a delinquent child for committing an act that, if committed by an adult, would be a felony drug abuse offense;

(2) Any property that was used or intended to be used in any manner to commit, or to facilitate the commission of, an act that, upon the filing of an indictment, complaint, or information, could be prosecuted as a felony drug abuse offense or that, upon the filing of a complaint, indictment, or information, could be the basis for finding a juvenile to be a delinquent child for committing an act that, if committed by an adult, would be a felony drug abuse offense.

(B)(1) All right, title, and interest in property described in division (A) of this section shall vest in the state upon the commission of the act giving rise to a civil forfeiture under this section.

(2) The provisions of section 2933.43 of the Revised Code relating to the procedures for the forfeiture of contraband do not apply to a civil action to obtain a civil forfeiture under this section.

(3) Any property taken or detained pursuant to this section is not subject to replevin and is deemed to be in the custody of the head of the law enforcement agency that seized the property.

This section does not preclude the head of a law enforcement agency that seizes property from seeking the forfeiture of that property pursuant to federal law. However, if the head of a law enforcement agency that seizes property does not seek the forfeiture of that property pursuant to federal law and if the property is subject to forfeiture under this section, the property is subject only to the orders of the court of common pleas of the county in which the property is located, and it shall be disposed of in accordance with section 2925.44 of the Revised Code.

(4) Nothing in this section precludes a financial institution that has or purports to have a security interest in or lien on property described in division (A) of this section from commencing a civil action or taking other appropriate legal action in connection with the property, prior to its disposition in accordance with section 2925.44 of the Revised Code, for the purpose of obtaining possession of the property in order to foreclose or otherwise enforce the security interest or lien. A financial institution may commence a civil action or take other appropriate legal action for that purpose prior to the disposition of the property in accordance with section 2925.44 of the Revised Code, even if a civil action to obtain a civil forfeiture has been or could be commenced under this section, even if the property is or could be the subject of an order of civil forfeiture issued under this section, and even if the property has been seized or is subject to seizure pursuant to this section.

If a financial institution commences a civil action or takes any other appropriate legal action as described in this division, if the financial institution subsequently causes the sale of the property prior to its seizure pursuant to this section and its disposition pursuant to section 2925.44 of the Revised Code, and if the person responsible for the conduct of the sale has actual knowledge of the commencement of a civil action to obtain a civil forfeiture under this section or actual knowledge of an order of civil forfeiture issued under this section, then the person responsible for the conduct of the sale shall dispose of the proceeds of the sale in the following order:

(a) First, to the payment of the costs of the sale and to the payment of the costs incurred by law enforcement agencies and financial institutions in connection with the seizure of, storage of, maintenance of, and provision of security for the property. As used in this division, "costs" of a financial institution do not include attorney's fees incurred by that institution in connection with the property;

(b) Second, the remaining proceeds of the sale after compliance with division (B)(4)(a) of this section, to the payment of valid security interests and liens pertaining to the property that, at the time of the vesting of the right, title, or interest of the adult or juvenile in the state under division (B)(1) of this section, are held by known secured parties and lienholders, in the order of priority of those security interests and liens;

(c) Third, the remaining proceeds of the sale after compliance with division (B)(4)(b) of this section, to the court that has or would have jurisdiction in a civil action to obtain a civil forfeiture under this section, for disposition in accordance with section 2925.44 of the Revised Code.

(C)(1) Any property that is subject to civil forfeiture under this section may be seized by a law enforcement officer upon process, or a warrant as described in division (C)(2) of this section, issued by a court of common pleas that has jurisdiction over the property. Additionally, a seizure of the property, without process or a warrant being so issued, may be made by a law enforcement officer when any of the following applies:

(a) The seizure is incident to an arrest, a search under a search warrant, a lawful search without a search warrant, or an inspection under an administrative inspection warrant.

(b) The property is the subject of a prior judgment in favor of the state in a restraining order, injunction, or other preservation order proceeding under section 2925.42 of the Revised Code, or is the subject of a forfeiture order issued pursuant to that section.

(c) The law enforcement officer has probable cause to believe that the property is directly or indirectly dangerous to the public health or safety.

(d) The initial intrusion by the law enforcement officer afforded the officer with plain view of personal property that is subject to civil forfeiture in a civil action under this section, the initial intrusion by the law enforcement officer was lawful, the discovery of the personal property by the law enforcement officer was inadvertent, and the incriminating nature of the personal property was immediately apparent to the law enforcement officer.

(2) For purposes of division (C)(1) of this section, the state may request a court of common pleas to issue a warrant that authorizes the seizure of property that is subject to civil forfeiture under this section, in the same manner as provided in Criminal Rule 41 and Chapter 2933. of the Revised Code for the issuance of a search warrant. Additionally, for purposes of division (C)(1) of this section, any proceeding before a court of common pleas that involves a request for the issuance of process, or a warrant as described in this division, authorizing the seizure of any property that is subject to civil forfeiture under this section shall be recorded by shorthand, by stenotype, or by any other mechanical, electronic, or video recording device. The recording of and any transcript of the recording of such a proceeding shall not be a public record for purposes of section 149.43 of the Revised Code until the property has been seized pursuant to the process or warrant. This division shall not be construed as requiring, authorizing, or permitting, and does not require, authorize, or permit, the making available for inspection, or the copying, under section 149.43 of the Revised Code of any confidential law enforcement investigatory record or trial preparation record, as defined in that section.

(3) If property is seized pursuant to division (C)(1) of this section and if a civil action to obtain a civil forfeiture under this section, a criminal action that could result in a criminal forfeiture under section 2925.42 of the Revised Code, or a delinquent child proceeding that could result in a criminal forfeiture under that section is not pending at the time of the seizure or previously did not occur in connection with the property, then the prosecuting attorney of the county in which the seizure occurred promptly shall commence a civil action to obtain a civil forfeiture under this section in connection with the property, unless an indictment, complaint, or information alleging the commission of a felony drug abuse offense or a complaint, indictment, or information alleging that a juvenile is a delinquent child because of the commission of an act that, if committed by an adult, would be a felony drug abuse offense is filed prior to the commencement of the civil action. Nothing in this division precludes, or shall be construed as precluding, the filing of an indictment, complaint, or information alleging the commission of a felony drug abuse offense or the filing of a complaint, indictment, or information alleging that a juvenile is a delinquent child because of the commission of an act that, if committed by an adult, would be a felony drug abuse offense, after the commencement of a civil action to obtain a civil forfeiture under this section.

(D)(1) The filing of an indictment, complaint, or information alleging the commission of a felony drug abuse offense that also is the basis of a civil action for a civil forfeiture under this section, or the filing of a complaint, indictment, or information alleging that a juvenile is a delinquent child because of the commission of an act that, if committed by an adult, would be a felony drug abuse offense, and that also is the basis of a civil action for a civil forfeiture under this section, upon the motion of the prosecuting attorney of the county in which the indictment, complaint, or information or the complaint, indictment, or information in the delinquent child proceeding is filed, shall stay the civil action.

(2) A civil action to obtain a civil forfeiture under this section may be commenced as described in division (E) of this section whether or not the adult or juvenile who committed a felony drug abuse offense or an act that, if committed by an adult, would be a felony drug abuse offense has been charged by an indictment, complaint, or information with the commission of such an offense or such an act, has pleaded guilty to or been found guilty of such an offense, has been determined to be a delinquent child for the commission of such an act, has been found not guilty of commit-

ting such an offense, or has not been determined to be a delinquent child for the alleged commission of such an act.

(E)(1) The prosecuting attorney of the county in which property described in division (A) of this section is located may commence a civil action to obtain a civil forfeiture under this section by filing, in the court of common pleas of that county, a complaint that requests the issuance of an order of civil forfeiture of the property to the state. Notices of the action shall be served and published in accordance with division (E)(2) of this section.

(2) Prior to or simultaneously with the commencement of the civil action as described in division (E)(1) of this section, the prosecuting attorney shall conduct or cause to be conducted a search of the appropriate public records that relate to the property subject to civil forfeiture, and make or cause to be made reasonably diligent inquiries, for the purpose of identifying persons who have any right, title, or interest in the property. The prosecuting attorney then shall cause a notice of the commencement of the civil action, together with a copy of the complaint filed in it, to be given to each person who is known, because of the conduct of the search, the making of the inquiries, or otherwise, to have any right, title, or interest in the property, by certified mail, return receipt requested, or by personal service. Additionally, the prosecuting attorney shall cause a similar notice to be published once a week for two consecutive weeks in a newspaper of general circulation in the county in which the property is located.

(3) The procedures specified in divisions (F)(3) to (5) of section 2925.42 of the Revised Code apply to persons claiming any right, title, or interest in property subject to civil forfeiture under this section. The references in those divisions to the adult offender whose conviction or guilty plea, or the delinquent child whose adjudication, is the basis of an order of criminal forfeiture shall be construed for purposes of this section to mean the adult or juvenile who committed the act that could be the basis of an order of civil forfeiture under this section, and the references in those divisions to an issued order of criminal forfeiture shall be inapplicable.

(4) A hearing shall be held in the civil action described in division (E)(1) of this section at least thirty days after the final publication of notice as required by division (E)(2) of this section and after the date of completion of the service of notice by personal service or certified mail, return receipt requested, as required by that division. Following the hearing, the court shall issue the requested order of civil forfeiture if the court determines that the prosecuting attorney has proven, by clear and convincing evidence, that the property in question is property as described in division (A)(1) or (2) of this section, and if the court has disposed of all petitions filed under division (E)(3) of this section or no petitions have been so filed and the time for filing them has expired. An order of civil forfeiture so issued shall state that all right, title, and interest in the property in question of the adult or juvenile who committed the act that is the basis of the order, is forfeited to the state and shall make due provision for the right, title, or interest in that property of any other person in accordance with any determinations made by the court under division (E)(3) of this section and in accordance with divisions (F)(5)(b) and (G)(2) of section 2925.42 of the Revised Code.

(5) Subject to division (G)(2) of section 2925.42 of the Revised Code, if a court of common pleas enters an order of civil forfeiture in accordance with division (E) of this section, the state shall have clear title to the property that is the subject of the order and may warrant good title to any subsequent purchaser or other transferee.

(2000 S 179, § 3, eff. 1-1-02; 1990 S 258, eff. 11-20-90)

2925.44 Disposition of forfeited property

(A) If property is seized pursuant to section 2925.42 or 2925.43 of the Revised Code, it is deemed to be in the custody of the head of the law enforcement agency that seized it, and the head of that agency may do any of the following with respect to that property prior to its disposition in accordance with division (A)(4) or (B) of this section:

(1) Place the property under seal;

(2) Remove the property to a place that the head of that agency designates;

(3) Request the issuance of a court order that requires any other appropriate municipal corporation, county, township, park district created pursuant to section 511.18 or 1545.01 of the Revised Code, or state law enforcement officer or other officer to take custody of the property and, if practicable, remove it to an appropriate location for eventual disposition in accordance with division (B) of this section;

(4)(a) Seek forfeiture of the property pursuant to federal law. If the head of that agency seeks its forfeiture pursuant to federal law, the law enforcement agency shall deposit, use, and account for proceeds from a sale of the property upon its forfeiture, proceeds from another disposition of the property upon its forfeiture, or forfeited moneys it receives, in accordance with the applicable federal law and otherwise shall comply with that law.

(b) If the state highway patrol seized the property and if the superintendent of the state highway patrol seeks its forfeiture pursuant to federal law, the appropriate governmental officials shall deposit into the state highway patrol contraband, forfeiture, and other fund all interest or other earnings derived from the investment of the proceeds from a sale of the property upon its forfeiture, the proceeds from another disposition of the property upon its forfeiture, or the forfeited moneys. The state highway patrol shall use and account for that interest or other earnings in accordance with the applicable federal law.

(c) If the investigative unit of the department of public safety seized the property and if the director of public safety seeks its forfeiture pursuant to federal law, the appropriate governmental officials shall deposit into the department of public safety investigative unit contraband, forfeiture, and other fund all interest or other earnings derived from the investment of the proceeds from a sale of the property upon its forfeiture, the proceeds from another disposition of the property upon its forfeiture, or the forfeited moneys. The department shall use and account for that interest or other earnings in accordance with the applicable federal law.

(d) If the enforcement division of the department of taxation seized the property and if the tax commissioner seeks its forfeiture pursuant to federal law, the appropriate governmental officials shall, deposit into the department of taxation enforcement fund all interest or other earnings derived from the investment of the proceeds from a sale of the property upon its forfeiture, the proceeds from another disposition of the property upon its forfeiture, or the forfeited moneys. The department shall use and account for that interest or other earnings in accordance with the applicable federal law.

(e) Division (B) of this section and divisions (D)(1) to (3) of section 2933.43 of the Revised Code do not apply to proceeds or forfeited moneys received pursuant to federal law or to the interest or other earnings that are derived from the investment of proceeds or forfeited moneys received pursuant to federal law and that are described in division (A)(4)(b) or (d) of this section.

(B) In addition to complying with any requirements imposed by a court pursuant to section 2925.42 or 2925.43 of the Revised Code, and the requirements imposed by those sections, in relation to the disposition of property forfeited to the state under either of those sections, the prosecuting attorney who is responsible for its disposition shall dispose of the property as follows:

(1) Any vehicle, as defined in section 4501.01 of the Revised Code, that was used in a felony drug abuse offense or in an act that, if committed by an adult, would be a felony drug abuse offense shall be given to the law enforcement agency of the

municipal corporation or county in which the offense occurred if that agency desires to have the vehicle, except that, if the offense occurred in a township or in a park district created pursuant to section 511.18 or 1545.01 of the Revised Code and a law enforcement officer employed by the township or the park district was involved in the seizure of the vehicle, the vehicle may be given to the law enforcement agency of that township or park district if that agency desires to have the vehicle, and except that, if the state highway patrol made the seizure of the vehicle, the vehicle may be given to the state highway patrol if it desires to have the vehicle.

(2) Any drug paraphernalia that was used, possessed, sold, or manufactured in a violation of section 2925.14 of the Revised Code that would be a felony drug abuse offense or in a violation of that section committed by a juvenile that, if committed by an adult, would be a felony drug abuse offense, may be given to the law enforcement agency of the municipal corporation or county in which the offense occurred if that agency desires to have and can use the drug paraphernalia, except that, if the offense occurred in a township or in a park district created pursuant to section 511.18 or 1545.01 of the Revised Code and a law enforcement officer employed by the township or the park district was involved in the seizure of the drug paraphernalia, the drug paraphernalia may be given to the law enforcement agency of that township or park district if that agency desires to have and can use the drug paraphernalia. If the drug paraphernalia is not so given, it shall be disposed of by sale pursuant to division (B)(8) of this section or disposed of in another manner that the court that issued the order of forfeiture considers proper under the circumstances.

(3) Drugs shall be disposed of pursuant to section 3719.11 of the Revised Code or placed in the custody of the secretary of the treasury of the United States for disposal or use for medical or scientific purposes under applicable federal law.

(4) Firearms and dangerous ordnance suitable for police work may be given to a law enforcement agency for that purpose. Firearms suitable for sporting use, or as museum pieces or collectors' items, may be disposed of by sale pursuant to division (B)(8) of this section. Other firearms and dangerous ordnance shall be destroyed by a law enforcement agency or shall be sent to the bureau of criminal identification and investigation for destruction by it. As used in this division, "firearms" and "dangerous ordnance" have the same meanings as in section 2923.11 of the Revised Code.

(5) Computers, computer networks, computer systems, and computer software suitable for police work may be given to a law enforcement agency for that purpose. Other computers, computer networks, computer systems, and computer software shall be disposed of by sale pursuant to division (B)(8) of this section or disposed of in another manner that the court that issued the order of forfeiture considers proper under the circumstances. As used in this division, "computers," "computer networks," "computer systems," and "computer software" have the same meanings as in section 2913.01 of the Revised Code.

(6) Obscene materials shall be destroyed.

(7) Beer, intoxicating liquor, and alcohol shall be disposed of in accordance with division (D)(4) of section 2933.41 of the Revised Code.

(8) In the case of property not described in divisions (B)(1) to (7) of this section and of property described in those divisions but not disposed of pursuant to them, the property shall be sold in accordance with division (B)(8) of this section or, in the case of forfeited moneys, disposed of in accordance with division (B)(8) of this section. If the property is to be sold, the prosecuting attorney shall cause a notice of the proposed sale of the property to be given in accordance with law, and the property shall be sold, without appraisal, at a public auction to the highest bidder for cash. The proceeds of a sale and forfeited moneys shall be applied in the following order:

(a) First, to the payment of the costs incurred in connection with the seizure of, storage of, maintenance of, and provision of security for the property, the forfeiture proceeding or civil action, and, if any, the sale;

(b) Second, the remaining proceeds or forfeited moneys after compliance with division (B)(8)(a) of this section, to the payment of the value of any legal right, title, or interest in the property that is possessed by a person who, pursuant to division (F) of section 2925.42 of the Revised Code or division (E) of section 2925.43 of the Revised Code, established the validity of and consequently preserved that legal right, title, or interest, including, but not limited to, any mortgage, perfected or other security interest, or other lien in the property. The value of these rights, titles, or interests shall be paid according to their record or other order of priority.

(c) Third, the remaining proceeds or forfeited moneys after compliance with divisions (B)(8)(a) and (b) of this section, as follows:

(i) If the forfeiture was ordered in a juvenile court, ten per cent to one or more alcohol and drug addiction treatment programs that are certified by the department of alcohol and drug addiction services under section 3793.06 of the Revised Code and that are specified in the order of forfeiture. A juvenile court shall not specify an alcohol or drug addiction treatment program in the order of forfeiture unless the program is a certified alcohol and drug addiction treatment program and, except as provided in division (B)(8)(c)(i) of this section, unless the program is located in the county in which the court that orders the forfeiture is located or in a contiguous county. If no certified alcohol and drug addiction treatment program is located in any of those counties, the juvenile court may specify in the order a certified alcohol and drug addiction treatment program located anywhere within this state.

(ii) If the forfeiture was ordered in a juvenile court, ninety per cent, and if the forfeiture was ordered in a court other than a juvenile court, one hundred per cent to appropriate funds in accordance with divisions (D)(1)(c) and (2) of section 2933.43 of the Revised Code. The remaining proceeds or forfeited moneys so deposited shall be used only for the purposes authorized by those divisions and division (D)(3)(a)(ii) of that section.

(C)(1) Sections 2925.41 to 2925.45 of the Revised Code do not preclude a financial institution that possessed a valid mortgage, security interest, or lien that is not satisfied prior to a sale under division (B)(8) of this section or following a sale by application of division (B)(8)(b) of this section, from commencing a civil action in any appropriate court in this or another state to obtain a deficiency judgment against the debtor if the financial institution otherwise would have been entitled to do so in this or another state.

(2) Any law enforcement agency that obtains any vehicle pursuant to division (B)(1) of this section shall take the vehicle subject to the outstanding amount of any security interest or lien that attaches to the vehicle.

(3) Nothing in this section impairs a mortgage, security interest, lien, or other interest of a financial institution in property that was the subject of a forfeiture order under section 2925.42 or 2925.43 of the Revised Code and that was sold or otherwise disposed of in a manner that does not conform to the requirements of division (B) of this section, or any right of a financial institution of that nature to commence a civil action in any appropriate court in this or another state to obtain a deficiency judgment against the debtor.

(4) Following the sale under division (B)(8) of this section of any property that is required to be titled or registered under the law of this state, the prosecuting attorney responsible for the disposition of the property shall cause the state to issue an appropriate certificate of title or registration to the purchaser of the property. Additionally, if, in a disposition of property pursuant to division (B) of this section, the state or a political

subdivision is given any property that is required to be titled or registered under the law of this state, the prosecuting attorney responsible for the disposition of the property shall cause the state to issue an appropriate certificate of title or registration to itself or to the political subdivision.

(D) Property that has been forfeited to the state pursuant to an order of criminal forfeiture under section 2925.42 of the Revised Code or an order of civil forfeiture under section 2925.43 of the Revised Code shall not be available for use to pay any fine imposed upon a person who is convicted of or pleads guilty to a felony drug abuse offense or upon any juvenile who is found by a juvenile court to be a delinquent child for an act that, if committed by an adult, would be a felony drug abuse offense.

(E) Sections 2925.41 to 2925.45 of the Revised Code do not prohibit a law enforcement officer from seeking the forfeiture of contraband associated with a felony drug abuse offense pursuant to section 2933.43 of the Revised Code.

(2003 H 95, eff. 9–26–03; 1999 H 163, eff. 6–30–99; 1997 H 210, eff. 6–30–97; 1995 H 1, eff. 1–1–96; 1995 H 107, eff. (See Historical and Statutory Notes); 1992 S 174, eff. 7–31–92; 1991 S 218; 1990 S 258)

Historical and Statutory Notes

Ed. Note: 1995 H 107 Effective Date—The Secretary of State assigned a general effective date of 6–30–95 for 1995 H 107. Pursuant to O Const Art II § 1c and 1d, and RC 1.471, sections of 1995 H 107 that are, or depend for their implementation upon, current expense appropriations are effective 3–31–95; sections of 1995 H 107 that are not, and do not depend for their implementation upon, current expense appropriations are effective 6–30–95.

2925.45 Motion for possession of unlawfully seized property

(A) Any person who is aggrieved by an alleged unlawful seizure of property that potentially is subject to forfeiture under section 2925.42 or 2925.43 of the Revised Code may file a motion as described in division (B) of this section with whichever of the following courts is appropriate under the circumstances, within the time described in division (C) of this section:

(1) The court of common pleas in which a criminal prosecution for a felony drug abuse offense is pending;

(2) The juvenile court in which a delinquent child action for an act that, if committed by an adult, would be a felony drug abuse offense is pending;

(3) The court of common pleas in which a civil action as described in division (E) of section 2925.43 of the Revised Code is pending;

(4) The court of common pleas of the county in which the property was seized.

(B) The motion shall specify that the seizure of specified property was unlawful, state the reasons why the movant believes the seizure was unlawful, state that the movant is lawfully entitled to possession of the seized property, and request the court of common pleas to issue an order that mandates the law enforcement agency having custody of the seized property to return it to the movant. For purposes of this division, an unlawful seizure of property includes, but is not limited to, a seizure in violation of the Fourth Amendment to the Constitution of the United States or of Section 14 of Article I, Ohio Constitution, and a seizure pursuant to sections 2925.41 to 2925.44 of the Revised Code of property other than potentially forfeitable property as described in division (A)(1) of section 2925.42 or division (A) of section 2925.43 of the Revised Code.

(C)(1) If a motion as described in division (A) of this section is filed prior to the entry of an order of forfeiture under section 2925.42 or 2925.43 of the Revised Code, the court of common pleas promptly shall schedule a hearing on the motion and cause notice of the date and time of the hearing to be given to the movant and the prosecuting attorney of the county in which the property was seized. At the hearing, the movant and the prosecuting attorney may present witnesses and evidence relative to the issues of whether the property in question was unlawfully seized and whether the movant is lawfully entitled to possession of it. If, after the hearing, the court of common pleas determines that the movant has established, by a preponderance of the evidence, that the property in question was unlawfully seized and that the movant is lawfully entitled to possession of it, the court shall issue an order that requires the law enforcement agency having custody of the seized property to return it to the movant.

(2)(a) If a motion is filed in accordance with division (C)(1) of this section and, at the time of filing or of the hearing on the motion, a criminal prosecution for a felony drug abuse offense or a delinquent child action for an act that, if committed by an adult, would be a felony drug abuse offense has been commenced by the filing of an indictment, information, or complaint, then the court of common pleas shall treat the motion as a motion to suppress evidence.

(b) If an order to return seized property is issued pursuant to division (C)(1) of this section, the returned property shall not be admissible in evidence in any pending or subsequently commenced criminal prosecution for a felony drug abuse offense if the prosecution arose or arises out of the unlawful seizure of the property, or in any pending or subsequently commenced delinquent child action for an act that, if committed by an adult, would be a felony drug abuse offense if the action arose or arises out of the unlawful seizure of the property.

(1990 S 258, eff. 11–20–90)

MISCELLANEOUS PROVISIONS

2925.50 Federal prosecution acts as bar

If a violation of this chapter is a violation of the federal drug abuse control laws, as defined in section 3719.01 of the Revised Code, a conviction or acquittal under the federal drug abuse control laws for the same act is a bar to prosecution in this state.

(1998 S 66, eff. 7–22–98; 1975 H 300, eff. 7–1–76)

2925.51 Laboratory report as prima-facie evidence of content; weight and identity of substance; rights of accused

(A) In any criminal prosecution for a violation of this chapter or Chapter 3719. of the Revised Code, a laboratory report from the bureau of criminal identification and investigation, a laboratory operated by another law enforcement agency, or a laboratory established by or under the authority of an institution of higher education that has its main campus in this state and that is accredited by the association of American universities or the north central association of colleges and secondary schools, primarily for the purpose of providing scientific services to law enforcement agencies and signed by the person performing the analysis, stating that the substance that is the basis of the alleged offense has been weighed and analyzed and stating the findings as to the content, weight, and identity of the substance and that it contains any amount of a controlled substance and the number and description of unit dosages, is prima-facie evidence of the content, identity, and weight or the existence and number of unit dosages of the substance. In any criminal prosecution for a violation of section 2925.041 of the Revised Code or a violation of this chapter or Chapter 3719. of the Revised Code that is based on the possession of chemicals sufficient to produce a compound, mixture, preparation, or substance included in schedule I, II, III, IV, or V, a laboratory report from the bureau or from any laboratory that is operated or established as described in this division that is signed by the person performing the analysis, stating that the substances that are the basis of the alleged offense have been weighed and analyzed and stating the findings as to the content, weight, and identity of each of the substances, is prima-facie evidence of the content, identity, and weight of the substances.

Attached to that report shall be a copy of a notarized statement by the signer of the report giving the name of the signer and stating that the signer is an employee of the laboratory issuing the report and that performing the analysis is a part of the signer's regular duties, and giving an outline of the signer's education, training, and experience for performing an analysis of materials included under this section. The signer shall attest that scientifically accepted tests were performed with due caution, and that the evidence was handled in accordance with established and accepted procedures while in the custody of the laboratory.

(B) The prosecuting attorney shall serve a copy of the report on the attorney of record for the accused, or on the accused if the accused has no attorney, prior to any proceeding in which the report is to be used against the accused other than at a preliminary hearing or grand jury proceeding where the report may be used without having been previously served upon the accused.

(C) The report shall not be prima-facie evidence of the contents, identity, and weight or the existence and number of unit dosages of the substance if the accused or the accused's attorney demands the testimony of the person signing the report, by serving the demand upon the prosecuting attorney within seven days from the accused or the accused's attorney's receipt of the report. The time may be extended by a trial judge in the interests of justice.

(D) Any report issued for use under this section shall contain notice of the right of the accused to demand, and the manner in which the accused shall demand, the testimony of the person signing the report.

(E) Any person who is accused of a violation of this chapter or of Chapter 3719. of the Revised Code is entitled, upon written request made to the prosecuting attorney, to have a portion of the substance that is, or of each of the substances that are, the basis of the alleged violation preserved for the benefit of independent analysis performed by a laboratory analyst employed by the accused person, or, if the accused is indigent, by a qualified laboratory analyst appointed by the court. Such portion shall be a representative sample of the entire substance that is, or of each of the substances that are, the basis of the alleged violation and shall be of sufficient size, in the opinion of the court, to permit the accused's analyst to make a thorough scientific analysis concerning the identity of the substance or substances. The prosecuting attorney shall provide the accused's analyst with the sample portion at least fourteen days prior to trial, unless the trial is to be held in a court not of record or unless the accused person is charged with a minor misdemeanor, in which case the prosecuting attorney shall provide the accused's analyst with the sample portion at least three days prior to trial. If the prosecuting attorney determines that such a sample portion cannot be preserved and given to the accused's analyst, the prosecuting attorney shall so inform the accused person or his attorney. In such a circumstance, the accused person is entitled, upon written request made to the prosecuting attorney, to have the accused's privately employed or court appointed analyst present at an analysis of the substance that is, or the substances that are, the basis of the alleged violation, and, upon further written request, to receive copies of all recorded scientific data that result from the analysis and that can be used by an analyst in arriving at conclusions, findings, or opinions concerning the identity of the substance or substances subject to the analysis.

(F) In addition to the rights provided under division (E) of this section, any person who is accused of a violation of this chapter or of Chapter 3719. of the Revised Code that involves a bulk amount of a controlled substance, or any multiple thereof, or who is accused of a violation of section 2925.11 of the Revised Code, other than a minor misdemeanor violation, that involves marihuana, is entitled, upon written request made to the prosecuting attorney, to have a laboratory analyst of the accused's choice, or, if the accused is indigent, a qualified laboratory analyst appointed by the court present at a measurement or weighing of the substance that is the basis of the alleged violation. Also, the accused person is entitled, upon further written request, to receive copies of all recorded scientific data that result from the measurement or weighing and that can be used by an analyst in arriving at conclusions, findings, or opinions concerning the weight, volume, or number of unit doses of the substance subject to the measurement or weighing.

(2001 H 7, eff. 8–7–01; 1977 S 201, eff. 11–16–77; 1976 S 541; 1975 H 300)

2925.52 Destruction of chemicals used to produce methamphetamine, salt, isomer or salt of isomer of methamphetamine; preservation of samples

(A) If a person is charged with a violation of section 2925.041 of the Revised Code or with any violation of this chapter or Chapter 3719. of the Revised Code that is based on the possession of chemicals sufficient to produce methamphetamine, any salt, isomer, or salt of an isomer of methamphetamine, or any compound, mixture, preparation, or substance containing methamphetamine or any salt, isomer, or salt of an isomer of methamphetamine, the law enforcement agency that has custody of the chemicals may file a motion with the court in which the charges are pending requesting the court to order the chemicals destroyed in accordance with this division. If a law enforcement agency files a motion of that type with a court, the court may issue an order that requires the containers in which the chemicals are contained be photographed, orders the chemicals forfeited, and requires that the chemicals be destroyed.

(B) If the court issues an order under division (A) of this section, the court may include in the order a requirement that the chemicals be sampled prior to their destruction and that the samples be preserved.

(2001 H 7, eff. 8–7–01)

CHAPTER 2927

MISCELLANEOUS OFFENSES

2927.01 Offenses against human corpse

(A) No person, except as authorized by law, shall treat a human corpse in a way that the person knows would outrage reasonable family sensibilities.

(B) No person, except as authorized by law, shall treat a human corpse in a way that would outrage reasonable community sensibilities.

(C) Whoever violates division (A) of this section is guilty of abuse of a corpse, a misdemeanor of the second degree. Whoever violates division (B) of this section is guilty of gross abuse of a corpse, a felony of the fifth degree.

(1995 S 2, eff. 7–1–96; 1978 H 741, eff. 10–9–78; 1972 H 511)

2927.02 Illegal distribution of cigarettes or other tobacco products; vending machines

(A) As used in this section and section 2927.021 of the Revised Code:

(1) "Child" has the same meaning as in section 2151.011 of the Revised Code.

(2) "Cigarette" includes clove cigarettes and hand-rolled cigarettes.

(3) "Distribute" means to furnish, give, or provide cigarettes, other tobacco products, or papers used to roll cigarettes to the ultimate consumer of the cigarettes, other tobacco products, or papers used to roll cigarettes.

(4) "Proof of age" means a driver's license, a commercial driver's license, a military identification card, a passport, or an identification card issued under sections 4507.50 to 4507.52 of the Revised Code that shows that a person is eighteen years of age or older.

(5) "Tobacco product" means any product that is made from tobacco, including, but not limited to, a cigarette, a cigar, pipe tobacco, chewing tobacco, or snuff.

(6) "Vending machine" has the same meaning as "coin machine" in section 2913.01 of the Revised Code.

(B) No manufacturer, producer, distributor, wholesaler, or retailer of cigarettes, other tobacco products, or papers used to roll cigarettes, no agent, employee, or representative of a manufacturer, producer, distributor, wholesaler, or retailer of cigarettes, other tobacco products, or papers used to roll cigarettes, and no other person shall do any of the following:

(1) Give, sell, or otherwise distribute cigarettes, other tobacco products, or papers used to roll cigarettes to any child;

(2) Give away, sell, or distribute cigarettes, other tobacco products, or papers used to roll cigarettes in any place that does not have posted in a conspicuous place a sign stating that giving, selling, or otherwise distributing cigarettes, other tobacco products, or papers used to roll cigarettes to a person under eighteen years of age is prohibited by law;

(3) Knowingly furnish any false information regarding the name, age, or other identification of any child with purpose to obtain cigarettes, other tobacco products, or papers used to roll cigarettes for that child;

(4) Manufacture, sell, or distribute in this state any pack or other container of cigarettes containing fewer than twenty cigarettes or any package of roll-your-own tobacco containing less than six-tenths of one ounce of tobacco;

(5) Sell cigarettes in a smaller quantity than that placed in the pack or other container by the manufacturer.

(C) No person shall sell or offer to sell cigarettes or other tobacco products by or from a vending machine, except in the following locations:

(1) An area within a factory, business, office, or other place not open to the general public;

(2) An area to which children are not generally permitted access;

(3) Any other place not identified in division (C)(1) or (2) of this section, upon all of the following conditions:

(a) The vending machine is located within the immediate vicinity, plain view, and control of the person who owns or operates the place, or an employee of that person, so that all cigarettes and other tobacco product purchases from the vending machine will be readily observed by the person who owns or operates the place or an employee of that person. For the purpose of this section, a vending machine located in any unmonitored area, including an unmonitored coatroom, restroom, hallway, or outer waiting area, shall not be considered located within the immediate vicinity, plain view, and control of the person who owns or operates the place, or an employee of that person.

(b) The vending machine is inaccessible to the public when the place is closed.

(D) The following are affirmative defenses to a charge under division (B)(1) of this section:

(1) The child was accompanied by a parent, spouse who is eighteen years of age or older, or legal guardian of the child.

(2) The person who gave, sold, or distributed cigarettes, other tobacco products, or papers used to roll cigarettes to a child under division (B)(1) of this section is a parent, spouse who is eighteen years of age or older, or legal guardian of the child.

(E) It is not a violation of division (B)(1) or (2) of this section for a person to give or otherwise distribute to a child cigarettes, other tobacco products, or papers used to roll cigarettes while the child is participating in a research protocol if all of the following apply:

(1) The parent, guardian, or legal custodian of the child has consented in writing to the child participating in the research protocol.

(2) An institutional human subjects protection review board, or an equivalent entity, has approved the research protocol.

(3) The child is participating in the research protocol at the facility or location specified in the research protocol.

(F)(1) Whoever violates division (B)(1), (2), (4), or (5) or (C) of this section is guilty of illegal distribution of cigarettes or other tobacco products, a misdemeanor of the fourth degree. If the offender previously has been convicted of a violation of division (B)(1), (2), (4), or (5) or (C) of this section, illegal distribution of cigarettes or other tobacco products is a misdemeanor of the third degree.

(2) Whoever violates division (B)(3) of this section is guilty of permitting children to use cigarettes or other tobacco products, a misdemeanor of the fourth degree. If the offender previously has been convicted of a violation of division (B)(3) of this section, permitting children to use cigarettes or other tobacco products is a misdemeanor of the third degree.

(G) Any cigarettes, other tobacco products, or papers used to roll cigarettes that are given, sold, or otherwise distributed to a child in violation of this section and that are used, possessed, purchased, or received by a child in violation of section 2151.87

of the Revised Code are subject to seizure and forfeiture as contraband under sections 2933.42 and 2933.43 of the Revised Code.

(2002 S 242, eff. 9–19–02; 2002 H 393, eff. 7–5–02; 2000 S 218, eff. 3–15–01; 1991 S 40, eff. 10–23–91; 1984 H 152)

2927.021 Engaging in illegal tobacco product transaction scan

(A) As used in this section and section 2927.022 of the Revised Code:

(1) "Card holder" means any person who presents a driver's or commercial driver's license or an identification card to a seller, or an agent or employee of a seller, to purchase or receive cigarettes or other tobacco products from the seller, agent, or employee.

(2) "Identification card" means an identification card issued under sections 4507.50 to 4507.52 of the Revised Code.

(3) "Seller" means a seller of cigarettes or other tobacco products and includes any person whose gift of or other distribution of cigarettes or other tobacco products is subject to the prohibitions of section 2927.02 of the Revised Code.

(4) "Transaction scan" means the process by which a seller or an agent or employee of a seller checks, by means of a transaction scan device, the validity of a driver's or commercial driver's license or an identification card that is presented as a condition for purchasing or receiving cigarettes or other tobacco products.

(5) "Transaction scan device" means any commercial device or combination of devices used at a point of sale that is capable of deciphering in an electronically readable format the information encoded on the magnetic strip or bar code of a driver's or commercial driver's license or an identification card.

(B)(1) A seller or an agent or employee of a seller may perform a transaction scan by means of a transaction scan device to check the validity of a driver's or commercial driver's license or identification card presented by a card holder as a condition for selling, giving away, or otherwise distributing to the card holder cigarettes or other tobacco products.

(2) If the information deciphered by the transaction scan performed under division (B)(1) of this section fails to match the information printed on the driver's or commercial driver's license or identification card presented by the card holder, or if the transaction scan indicates that the information so printed is false or fraudulent, neither the seller nor any agent or employee of the seller shall sell, give away, or otherwise distribute any cigarettes or other tobacco products to the card holder.

(3) Division (B)(1) of this section does not preclude a seller or an agent or employee of a seller from using a transaction scan device to check the validity of a document other than a driver's or commercial driver's license or an identification card, if the document includes a bar code or magnetic strip that may be scanned by the device, as a condition for selling, giving away, or otherwise distributing cigarettes or other tobacco products to the person presenting the document.

(C) Rules adopted by the registrar of motor vehicles under division (C) of section 4301.61 of the Revised Code apply to the use of transaction scan devices for purposes of this section and section 2927.022 of the Revised Code.

(D)(1) No seller or agent or employee of a seller shall electronically or mechanically record or maintain any information derived from a transaction scan, except the following:

(a) The name and date of birth of the person listed on the driver's or commercial driver's license or identification card presented by a card holder;

(b) The expiration date and identification number of the driver's or commercial driver's license or identification card presented by a card holder.

(2) No seller or agent or employee of a seller shall use the information that is derived from a transaction scan or that is permitted to be recorded and maintained under division (D)(1) of this section, except for purposes of section 2927.022 of the Revised Code.

(3) No seller or agent or employee of a seller shall use a transaction scan device for a purpose other than the purpose specified in division (B)(1) of this section.

(4) No seller or agent or employee of a seller shall sell or otherwise disseminate the information derived from a transaction scan to any third party, including, but not limited to, selling or otherwise disseminating that information for any marketing, advertising, or promotional activities, but a seller or agent or employee of a seller may release that information pursuant to a court order or as specifically authorized by section 2927.022 or another section of the Revised Code.

(E) Nothing in this section or section 2927.022 of the Revised Code relieves a seller or an agent or employee of a seller of any responsibility to comply with any other applicable state or federal laws or rules governing the sale, giving away, or other distribution of cigarettes or other tobacco products.

(F) Whoever violates division (B)(2) or (D) of this section is guilty of engaging in an illegal tobacco product transaction scan, and the court may impose upon the offender a civil penalty of up to one thousand dollars for each violation. The clerk of the court shall pay each collected civil penalty to the county treasurer for deposit into the county treasury.

(2000 S 200, eff. 9–21–00)

2927.022 Affirmative defenses to illegal distribution of cigarettes or other tobacco products

(A) A seller or an agent or employee of a seller may not be found guilty of a charge of a violation of section 2927.02 of the Revised Code in which the age of the purchaser or other recipient of cigarettes or other tobacco products is an element of the alleged violation, if the seller, agent, or employee raises and proves as an affirmative defense that all of the following occurred:

(1) A card holder attempting to purchase or receive cigarettes or other tobacco products presented a driver's or commercial driver's license or an identification card.

(2) A transaction scan of the driver's or commercial driver's license or identification card that the card holder presented indicated that the license or card was valid.

(3) The cigarettes or other tobacco products were sold, given away, or otherwise distributed to the card holder in reasonable reliance upon the identification presented and the completed transaction scan.

(B) In determining whether a seller or an agent or employee of a seller has proven the affirmative defense provided by division (A) of this section, the trier of fact in the action for the alleged violation of section 2927.02 of the Revised Code shall consider any written policy that the seller has adopted and implemented and that is intended to prevent violations of section 2927.02 of the Revised Code. For purposes of division (A)(3) of this section, the trier of fact shall consider that reasonable reliance upon the identification presented and the completed transaction scan may require a seller or an agent or employee of a seller to exercise reasonable diligence to determine, and that the use of a transaction scan device does not excuse a seller or an agent or employee of a seller from exercising reasonable diligence to determine, the following:

(1) Whether a person to whom the seller or agent or employee of a seller sells, gives away, or otherwise distributes cigarettes or other tobacco products is eighteen years of age or older;

(2) Whether the description and picture appearing on the driver's or commercial driver's license or identification card presented by a card holder is that of the card holder.

(C) In any criminal action in which the affirmative defense provided by division (A) of this section is raised, the registrar of motor vehicles or a deputy registrar who issued an identification card under sections 4507.50 to 4507.52 of the Revised Code shall be permitted to submit certified copies of the records of that issuance in lieu of the testimony of the personnel of or contractors with the bureau of motor vehicles in the action.

(2000 S 200, eff. 9–21–00)

2927.03 Injuring, intimidating, or interfering with housing

(A) No person, whether or not acting under color of law, shall by force or threat of force willfully injure, intimidate, or interfere with, or attempt to injure, intimidate, or interfere with, any of the following:

(1) Any person because of race, color, religion, sex, familial status as defined in section 4112.01 of the Revised Code, national origin, disability as defined in that section, or ancestry and because that person is or has been selling, purchasing, renting, financing, occupying, contracting, or negotiating for the sale, purchase, rental, financing, or occupation of any housing accommodations, or applying for or participating in any service, organization, or facility relating to the business of selling or renting housing accommodations;

(2) Any person because that person is or has been doing, or in order to intimidate that person or any other person or any class of persons from doing, either of the following:

(a) Participating, without discrimination on account of race, color, religion, sex, familial status as defined in section 4112.01 of the Revised Code, national origin, disability as defined in that section, or ancestry, in any of the activities, services, organizations, or facilities described in division (A)(1) of this section;

(b) Affording another person or class of persons opportunity or protection so to participate.

(3) Any person because that person is or has been, or in order to discourage that person or any other person from, lawfully aiding or encouraging other persons to participate, without discrimination on account of race, color, religion, sex, familial status as defined in section 4112.01 of the Revised Code, national origin, disability as defined in that section, or ancestry, in any of the activities, services, organizations, or facilities described in division (A)(1) of this section, or participating lawfully in speech or peaceful assembly opposing any denial of the opportunity to so participate.

(B) Whoever violates division (A) of this section is guilty of a misdemeanor of the first degree.

(1999 H 264, eff. 3–17–00; 1995 S 2, eff. 7–1–96; 1992 H 321, eff. 6–30–92; 1987 H 5)

2927.11 Desecration; fine

(A) No person, without privilege to do so, shall purposely deface, damage, pollute, or otherwise physically mistreat any of the following:

(1) The flag of the United States or of this state;

(2) Any public monument;

(3) Any historical or commemorative marker, or any structure, Indian mound or earthwork, cemetery, thing, or site of great historical or archaeological interest;

(4) A place of worship, its furnishings, or religious artifacts or sacred texts within the place of worship or within the grounds upon which the place of worship is located;

(5) A work of art or museum piece;

(6) Any other object of reverence or sacred devotion.

(B) Whoever violates this section is guilty of desecration. A violation of division (A)(1), (2), (3), (5), or (6) of this section is a misdemeanor of the second degree. Except as otherwise provided in this division, a violation of division (A)(4) of this section is a felony of the fifth degree that is punishable by a fine of up to two thousand five hundred dollars in addition to the penalties specified for a felony of the fifth degree in sections 2929.13 to 2929.18 of the Revised Code. If the value of the property or the amount of physical harm involved in a violation of division (A)(4) of this section is five thousand dollars or more but less than one hundred thousand dollars, a violation of that division is a felony of the fourth degree. If the value of the property or the amount of physical harm involved in a violation of division (A)(4) of this section is one hundred thousand dollars or more, a violation of that division is a felony of the third degree.

(C) As used in this section, "cemetery" means any place of burial and includes burial sites that contain American Indian burial objects placed with or containing American Indian human remains.

(1999 S 51, eff. 9–20–99; 1998 H 429, eff. 9–30–98; 1986 S 316, eff. 3–19–87; 1978 H 741; 1976 H 418; 1972 H 511)

2927.12 Ethnic intimidation

(A) No person shall violate section 2903.21, 2903.22, 2909.06, or 2909.07, or division (A)(3), (4), or (5) of section 2917.21 of the Revised Code by reason of the race, color, religion, or national origin of another person or group of persons.

(B) Whoever violates this section is guilty of ethnic intimidation. Ethnic intimidation is an offense of the next higher degree than the offense the commission of which is a necessary element of ethnic intimidation.

(1986 S 316, eff. 3–19–87)

2927.13 Sale or donation of blood by AIDS carrier

(A) No person, with knowledge that the person is a carrier of a virus that causes acquired immune deficiency syndrome, shall sell or donate the person's blood, plasma, or a product of the person's blood, if the person knows or should know the blood, plasma, or product of the person's blood is being accepted for the purpose of transfusion to another individual.

(B) Whoever violates this section is guilty of selling or donating contaminated blood, a felony of the fourth degree.

(1995 S 2, eff. 7–1–96; 1988 H 571, eff. 3–17–89)

2927.21 Escape of exotic or dangerous animal; report

(A) The owner or keeper of any member of a species of the animal kingdom that escapes from his custody or control and that is not indigenous to this state or presents a risk of serious physical harm to persons or property, or both, shall, within one hour after he discovers or reasonably should have discovered the escape, report it to:

(1) A law enforcement officer of the municipal corporation or township and the sheriff of the county where the escape occurred; and

(2) The clerk of the municipal legislative authority or the township clerk of the township where the escape occurred.

(B) If the office of the clerk of a legislative authority or township clerk is closed to the public at the time a report is required by division (A) of this section, then it is sufficient compliance with division (A)(2) of this section if the owner or keeper makes the report within one hour after the office is next open to the public.

(C) Whoever violates this section is guilty of a misdemeanor of the first degree.

(1985 H 32, eff. 9–11–85)

2927.24 Contaminating substance for human consumption or use; release of hazardous substance; spreading false report of contamination or release

(A) As used in this section:

(1) "Poison" has the same meaning as in section 3719.01 of the Revised Code.

(2) "Drug" has the same meaning as in section 4729.01 of the Revised Code.

(3) "Hazardous chemical, biological, or radioactive substance" means any of the following:

(a) Any toxic or poisonous chemical, the precursor of any toxic or poisonous chemical, or any toxin;

(b) Any disease organism or biological agent;

(c) Any substance or item that releases or is designed to release radiation or radioactivity at a level dangerous to human life.

(4) "Biological agent" means any microorganism, virus, infectious substance, or biological product that may be engineered through biotechnology, or any naturally occurring or bioengineered component of any microorganism, virus, infectious substance, or biological product that may be engineered through biotechnology, capable of causing death, disease, or other biological malfunction in a human, an animal, a plant, or another living organism, deterioration of food, water, equipment, supplies, or material of any kind, or deleterious alteration of the environment.

(5) "Toxin" means the toxic material of plants, animals, microorganisms, viruses, fungi, or infectious substances, or a recombinant molecule, whatever its origin or method of reproduction, including, but not limited to, any poisonous substance or biological product that may be engineered through biotechnology or produced by a living organism and any poisonous isomer or biological product, homolog, or derivative of any substance or product of that nature.

(B) Except as provided in division (D) of this section, no person shall do any of the following:

(1) Knowingly mingle a poison, hazardous chemical, biological, or radioactive substance, or other harmful substance with a food, drink, nonprescription drug, prescription drug, or pharmaceutical product, or knowingly place a poison, hazardous chemical, biological, or radioactive substance, or other harmful substance in a spring, well, reservoir, or public water supply, if the person knows or has reason to know that the food, drink, nonprescription drug, prescription drug, pharmaceutical product, or water may be ingested or used by another person. For purposes of this division, a person does not know or have reason to know that water may be ingested or used by another person if it is disposed of as waste into a household drain including the drain of a toilet, sink, tub, or floor.

(2) Knowingly release into the air, knowingly leave in any public place, or knowingly expose one or more persons to any hazardous chemical, biological, or radioactive substance with the intent to cause, or create a risk of, death or serious physical harm to any person.

(C) No person shall do any of the following:

(1) Inform another person that a poison, hazardous chemical, biological, or radioactive substance, or other harmful substance has been or will be placed in a food, drink, nonprescription drug, prescription drug, or other pharmaceutical product, spring, well, reservoir, or public water supply, if the placement of the poison or substance would be a violation of division (B)(1) of this section, and the person knows both that the information is false and that the information likely will be disseminated to the public.

(2) Inform another person that a hazardous chemical, biological, or radioactive substance has been or will be released into the air or left in a public place, or that one or more persons has been or will be exposed to a hazardous chemical, biological, or radioactive substance, if the release, leaving, or exposure of the hazardous chemical, biological, or radioactive substance would be a violation of division (B)(2) of this section, and the person knows both that the information is false and that the information likely will be disseminated to the general public.

(D)(1) A person may mingle a drug with a food or drink for the purpose of causing the drug to be ingested or used in the quantity described by its labeling or prescription.

(2) A person may place a poison or other harmful substance in a spring, well, reservoir, or public water supply in such quantity as is necessary to treat the spring, well, reservoir, or water supply to make it safe for human consumption and use.

(3) The provisions of division (B) of this section shall not be applied in a manner that conflicts with any other state or federal law or rule relating to substances permitted to be applied to or present in any food, raw or processed, any milk or milk product, any meat or meat product, any type of crop, water, or alcoholic or nonalcoholic beverage.

(E)(1) Whoever violates division (B)(1) or (2) of this section is guilty of contaminating a substance for human consumption or use or contamination with a hazardous chemical, biological, or radioactive substance. Except as otherwise provided in this division, contaminating a substance for human consumption or use or contamination with a hazardous chemical, biological, or radioactive substance is a felony of the first degree. If the offense involved an amount of poison, the hazardous chemical, biological, or radioactive substance, or the other harmful substance sufficient to cause death if ingested or used by a person regarding a violation of division (B)(1) of this section or sufficient to cause death to persons who are exposed to it regarding a violation of division (B)(2) of this section or if the offense resulted in serious physical harm to another person, whoever violates division (B)(1) or (2) of this section shall be imprisoned for life with parole eligibility after serving fifteen years of imprisonment.

(2) Whoever violates division (C)(1) or (2) of this section is guilty of spreading a false report of contamination, a felony of the fourth degree.

(F) Divisions (C)(1) and (2) of this section do not limit or affect the application of sections 2917.31 or 2917.32 of the Revised Code. Any act that is a violation of both division (C)(1) or (2) of this section and of section 2917.31 or 2917.32 of the Revised Code may be prosecuted under this section, section 2917.31 or 2917.32 of the Revised Code, or both this section and section 2917.31 or 2917.32 of the Revised Code.

(2002 S 184, eff. 5–15–02; 1999 S 107, eff. 3–23–00; 1998 S 66, eff. 7–22–98; 1995 S 2, eff. 7–1–96; 1994 H 280, eff. 6–29–94)

2927.27 Apprehension, detention, or arrest of person on bond

(A) No person, other than a law enforcement officer, shall apprehend, detain, or arrest a principal on bond, wherever issued, unless that person meets all of the following criteria:

(1) The person is any of the following:

(a) Qualified, licensed, and appointed as a surety bail bond agent under sections 3905.83 to 3905.95 of the Revised Code;

(b) Licensed as a surety bail bond agent by the state where the bond was written;

(c) Licensed as a private investigator under chapter 4749. of the Revised Code;

(d) Licensed as a private investigator by the state where the bond was written;

(e) An off-duty peace officer, as defined in section 2921.51 of the Revised Code.

(2) The person, prior to apprehending, detaining, or arresting the principal, has entered into a written contract with the surety or with a licensed surety bail bond agent appointed by the surety, which contract sets forth the name of the principal who is to be apprehended, detained, or arrested.

For purposes of division(A) (2) of this section, "surety" has the same meaning as in section 3905.83 of the Revised Code.

(3) The person, prior to apprehending, detaining, or arresting the principal, has notified the local law enforcement agency having jurisdiction over the area in which such activities will be performed and has provided any form of identification or other information requested by the law enforcement agency.

(B) No person shall represent the person's self to be a bail enforcement agent or bounty hunter, or claim any similar title, in this state.

(C)(1) Whoever violates this section is guilty of illegal bail bond agent practices.

(2) A violation of division (A) of this section is a misdemeanor of the first degree or, if the offender previously has been convicted of or pleaded guilty to two or more violations of division (A) of this section, a felony of the third degree.

(3) A violation of division (B) of this section is a misdemeanor of the first degree or, if the offender previously has been convicted of or pleaded guilty to two or more violations of division (B) of this section, a felony of the third degree.

(2000 H 730, eff. 10–9–01)

CHAPTER 2929

PENALTIES AND SENTENCING

DEFINITIONS

2929.01 Definitions

Note: See also following version of this section, eff. 4–29–05.

As used in this chapter:

(A)(1) "Alternative residential facility" means, subject to division (A)(2) of this section, any facility other than an offender's home or residence in which an offender is assigned to live and that satisfies all of the following criteria:

(a) It provides programs through which the offender may seek or maintain employment or may receive education, training, treatment, or habilitation.

(b) It has received the appropriate license or certificate for any specialized education, training, treatment, habilitation, or other service that it provides from the government agency that is responsible for licensing or certifying that type of education, training, treatment, habilitation, or service.

(2) "Alternative residential facility" does not include a community-based correctional facility, jail, halfway house, or prison.

(B) "Bad time" means the time by which the parole board administratively extends an offender's stated prison term or terms pursuant to section 2967.11 of the Revised Code because the parole board finds by clear and convincing evidence that the offender, while serving the prison term or terms, committed an act that is a criminal offense under the law of this state or the United States, whether or not the offender is prosecuted for the commission of that act.

(C) "Basic probation supervision" means a requirement that the offender maintain contact with a person appointed to supervise the offender in accordance with sanctions imposed by the court or imposed by the parole board pursuant to section 2967.28 of the Revised Code. "Basic probation supervision" includes basic parole supervision and basic post-release control supervision.

(D) "Cocaine," "crack cocaine," "hashish," "L.S.D.," and "unit dose" have the same meanings as in section 2925.01 of the Revised Code.

(E) "Community–based correctional facility" means a community-based correctional facility and program or district community-based correctional facility and program developed pursuant to sections 2301.51 to 2301.56 of the Revised Code.

(F) "Community control sanction" means a sanction that is not a prison term and that is described in section 2929.15, 2929.16, 2929. 17, or 2929.18 of the Revised Code or a sanction that is not a jail term and that is described in section 2929.26, 2929.27, or 2929.28 of the Revised Code. "Community control sanction" includes probation if the sentence involved was imposed for a felony that was committed prior to July 1, 1996, or if the sentence involved was imposed for a misdemeanor that was committed prior to January 1, 2004.

(G) "Controlled substance," "marihuana," "schedule I," and "schedule II" have the same meanings as in section 3719.01 of the Revised Code.

(H) "Curfew" means a requirement that an offender during a specified period of time be at a designated place.

(I) "Day reporting" means a sanction pursuant to which an offender is required each day to report to and leave a center or other approved reporting location at specified times in order to participate in work, education or training, treatment, and other approved programs at the center or outside the center.

(J) "Deadly weapon" has the same meaning as in section 2923.11 of the Revised Code.

(K) "Drug and alcohol use monitoring" means a program under which an offender agrees to submit to random chemical analysis of the offender's blood, breath, or urine to determine whether the offender has ingested any alcohol or other drugs.

(L) "Drug treatment program" means any program under which a person undergoes assessment and treatment designed to reduce or completely eliminate the person's physical or emotional reliance upon alcohol, another drug, or alcohol and another drug and under which the person may be required to receive assessment and treatment on an outpatient basis or may be required to reside at a facility other than the person's home or residence while undergoing assessment and treatment.

(M) "Economic loss" means any economic detriment suffered by a victim as a direct and proximate result of the commission of an offense and includes any loss of income due to lost time at work because of any injury caused to the victim, and any property loss, medical cost, or funeral expense incurred as a result of the commission of the offense. "Economic loss" does not include non-economic loss or any punitive or exemplary damages.

(N) "Education or training" includes study at, or in conjunction with a program offered by, a university, college, or technical college or vocational study and also includes the completion of primary school, secondary school, and literacy curricula or their equivalent.

(O) "Firearm" has the same meaning as in section 2923.11 of the Revised Code.

(P) "Halfway house" means a facility licensed by the division of parole and community services of the department of rehabilitation and correction pursuant to section 2967.14 of the Revised Code as a suitable facility for the care and treatment of adult offenders.

(Q) "House arrest" means a period of confinement of an offender that is in the offender's home or in other premises specified by the sentencing court or by the parole board pursuant to section 2967.28 of the Revised Code and during which all of the following apply:

(1) The offender is required to remain in the offender's home or other specified premises for the specified period of confinement, except for periods of time during which the offender is at the offender's place of employment or at other premises as authorized by the sentencing court or by the parole board.

(2) The offender is required to report periodically to a person designated by the court or parole board.

(3) The offender is subject to any other restrictions and requirements that may be imposed by the sentencing court or by the parole board.

(R) "Intensive probation supervision" means a requirement that an offender maintain frequent contact with a person appointed by the court, or by the parole board pursuant to section 2967.28 of the Revised Code, to supervise the offender while the offender is seeking or maintaining necessary employment and participating in training, education, and treatment programs as required in the court's or parole board's order. "Intensive probation supervision" includes intensive parole supervision and intensive post-release control supervision.

(S) "Jail" means a jail, workhouse, minimum security jail, or other residential facility used for the confinement of alleged or convicted offenders that is operated by a political subdivision or a combination of political subdivisions of this state.

(T) "Jail term" means the term in a jail that a sentencing court imposes or is authorized to impose pursuant to section 2929. 24 or 2929.25 of the Revised Code or pursuant to any other provision of the Revised Code that authorizes a term in a jail for a misdemeanor conviction.

(U) "Mandatory jail term" means the term in a jail that a sentencing court is required to impose pursuant to division (G) of section 1547.99 of the Revised Code, division (E) of section 2903.06 or division (D) of section 2903.08 of the Revised Code, division (E) of section 2929.24 of the Revised Code, division (B) of section 4510.14 of the Revised Code, or division (G) of section 4511.19 of the Revised Code or pursuant to any other provision of the Revised Code that requires a term in a jail for a misdemeanor conviction.

(V) "Delinquent child" has the same meaning as in section 2152.02 of the Revised Code.

(W) "License violation report" means a report that is made by a sentencing court, or by the parole board pursuant to section 2967.28 of the Revised Code, to the regulatory or licensing board or agency that issued an offender a professional license or a license or permit to do business in this state and that specifies that the offender has been convicted of or pleaded guilty to an offense that may violate the conditions under which the offender's professional license or license or permit to do business in this state was granted or an offense for which the offender's professional license or license or permit to do business in this state may be revoked or suspended.

(X) "Major drug offender" means an offender who is convicted of or pleads guilty to the possession of, sale of, or offer to sell any drug, compound, mixture, preparation, or substance that consists of or contains at least one thousand grams of hashish; at least one hundred grams of crack cocaine; at least one thousand grams of cocaine that is not crack cocaine; at least two thousand five hundred unit doses or two hundred fifty grams of heroin; at least five thousand unit doses of L.S.D. or five hundred grams of L.S.D. in a liquid concentrate, liquid extract, or liquid distillate form; or at least one hundred times the amount of any other schedule I or II controlled substance other than marihuana that is necessary to commit a felony of the third degree pursuant to section 2925.03, 2925.04, 2925.05, or 2925.11 of the Revised Code that is based on the possession of, sale of, or offer to sell the controlled substance.

(Y) "Mandatory prison term" means any of the following:

(1) Subject to division (Y)(2) of this section, the term in prison that must be imposed for the offenses or circumstances set forth in divisions (F)(1) to (8) or (F)(12) to (14) of section 2929.13 and division (D) of section 2929. 14 of the Revised Code. Except as provided in sections 2925.02, 2925.03, 2925.04, 2925.05, and 2925.11 of the Revised Code, unless the maximum or another specific term is required under section 2929.14 of the Revised Code, a mandatory prison term described in this division may be any prison term authorized for the level of offense.

(2) The term of sixty or one hundred twenty days in prison that a sentencing court is required to impose for a third or fourth degree felony OVI offense pursuant to division (G)(2) of section 2929.13 and division (G)(1)(d) or (e) of section 4511.19 of the Revised Code or the term of one, two, three, four, or five years in prison that a sentencing court is required to impose pursuant to division (G)(2) of section 2929.13 of the Revised Code.

(3) The term in prison imposed pursuant to section 2971.03 of the Revised Code for the offenses and in the circumstances described in division (F)(11) of section 2929.13 of the Revised Code and that term as modified or terminated pursuant to section 2971.05 of the Revised Code.

(Z) "Monitored time" means a period of time during which an offender continues to be under the control of the sentencing court or parole board, subject to no conditions other than leading a law-abiding life.

(AA) "Offender" means a person who, in this state, is convicted of or pleads guilty to a felony or a misdemeanor.

(BB) "Prison" means a residential facility used for the confinement of convicted felony offenders that is under the control of the department of rehabilitation and correction but does not include a violation sanction center operated under authority of section 2967.141 of the Revised Code.

(CC) "Prison term" includes any of the following sanctions for an offender:

(1) A stated prison term;

(2) A term in a prison shortened by, or with the approval of, the sentencing court pursuant to section 2929.20, 2967.26, 5120.031, 5120.032, or 5120.073 of the Revised Code;

(3) A term in prison extended by bad time imposed pursuant to section 2967.11 of the Revised Code or imposed for a violation of post-release control pursuant to section 2967.28 of the Revised Code.

(DD) "Repeat violent offender" means a person about whom both of the following apply:

(1) The person has been convicted of or has pleaded guilty to, and is being sentenced for committing, for complicity in committing, or for an attempt to commit, aggravated murder, murder, involuntary manslaughter, a felony of the first degree other than one set forth in Chapter 2925. of the Revised Code, a felony of the first degree set forth in Chapter 2925. of the Revised Code that involved an attempt to cause serious physical harm to a person or that resulted in serious physical harm to a person, or a felony of the second degree that involved an attempt to cause serious physical harm to a person or that resulted in serious physical harm to a person.

(2) Either of the following applies:

(a) The person previously was convicted of or pleaded guilty to, and previously served or, at the time of the offense was serving, a prison term for, any of the following:

(i) Aggravated murder, murder, involuntary manslaughter, rape, felonious sexual penetration as it existed under section 2907.12 of the Revised Code prior to September 3, 1996, a felony of the first or second degree that resulted in the death of a person or in physical harm to a person, or complicity in or an attempt to commit any of those offenses;

(ii) An offense under an existing or former law of this state, another state, or the United States that is or was substantially equivalent to an offense listed under division (DD)(2)(a)(i) of this section and that resulted in the death of a person or in physical harm to a person.

(b) The person previously was adjudicated a delinquent child for committing an act that if committed by an adult would have been an offense listed in division (DD)(2)(a)(i) or (ii) of this section, the person was committed to the department of youth services for that delinquent act.

(EE) "Sanction" means any penalty imposed upon an offender who is convicted of or pleads guilty to an offense, as punishment for the offense. "Sanction" includes any sanction imposed pursuant to any provision of sections 2929.14 to 2929.18 or 2929.24 to 2929.28 of the Revised Code.

(FF) "Sentence" means the sanction or combination of sanctions imposed by the sentencing court on an offender who is convicted of or pleads guilty to an offense.

(GG) "Stated prison term" means the prison term, mandatory prison term, or combination of all prison terms and mandatory prison terms imposed by the sentencing court pursuant to section 2929.14 or 2971.03 of the Revised Code. "Stated prison term" includes any credit received by the offender for time spent in jail awaiting trial, sentencing, or transfer to prison for the offense and any time spent under house arrest or house arrest with electronic monitoring imposed after earning credits pursuant to section 2967.193 of the Revised Code.

(HH) "Victim–offender mediation" means a reconciliation or mediation program that involves an offender and the victim of the offense committed by the offender and that includes a meeting in which the offender and the victim may discuss the offense, discuss restitution, and consider other sanctions for the offense.

(II) "Fourth degree felony OVI offense" means a violation of division (A) of section 4511.19 of the Revised Code that, under division (G) of that section, is a felony of the fourth degree.

(JJ) "Mandatory term of local incarceration" means the term of sixty or one hundred twenty days in a jail, a community-based correctional facility, a halfway house, or an alternative residential facility that a sentencing court may impose upon a person who is convicted of or pleads guilty to a fourth degree felony OVI offense pursuant to division (G)(1) of section 2929.13 of the Revised Code and division (G)(1)(d) or (e) of section 4511.19 of the Revised Code.

(KK) "Designated homicide, assault, or kidnapping offense," "sexual motivation specification," "sexually violent offense," "sexually violent predator," and "sexually violent predator specification" have the same meanings as in section 2971.01 of the Revised Code.

(LL) "Habitual sex offender," "sexually oriented offense," "sexual predator," "registration-exempt sexually oriented offense," "child-victim oriented offense," "habitual child-victim offender," and "child-victim predator" have the same meanings as in section 2950.01 of the Revised Code.

(MM) An offense is "committed in the vicinity of a child" if the offender commits the offense within thirty feet of or within the same residential unit as a child who is under eighteen years of age, regardless of whether the offender knows the age of the child or whether the offender knows the offense is being committed within thirty feet of or within the same residential unit as the child and regardless of whether the child actually views the commission of the offense.

(NN) "Family or household member" has the same meaning as in section 2919.25 of the Revised Code.

(OO) "Motor vehicle" and "manufactured home" have the same meanings as in section 4501.01 of the Revised Code.

(PP) "Detention" and "detention facility" have the same meanings as in section 2921.01 of the Revised Code.

(QQ) "Third degree felony OVI offense" means a violation of division (A) of section 4511.19 of the Revised Code that, under division (G) of that section, is a felony of the third degree.

(RR) "Random drug testing" has the same meaning as in section 5120.63 of the Revised Code.

(SS) "Felony sex offense" has the same meaning as in section 2967.28 of the Revised Code.

(TT) "Body armor" has the same meaning as in section 2941.1411 of the Revised Code.

(UU) "Electronic monitoring" means monitoring through the use of an electronic monitoring device.

(VV) "Electronic monitoring device" means any of the following:

(1) Any device that can be operated by electrical or battery power and that conforms with all of the following:

(a) The device has a transmitter that can be attached to a person, that will transmit a specified signal to a receiver of the type described in division (VV)(1)(b) of this section if the transmitter is removed from the person, turned off, or altered in any manner without prior court approval in relation to electronic monitoring or without prior approval of the department of rehabilitation and correction in relation to the use of an electronic monitoring device for an inmate on transitional control or otherwise is tampered with, that can transmit continuously and periodically a signal to that receiver when the person is within a specified distance from the receiver, and that can transmit an appropriate signal to that receiver if the person to whom it is attached travels a specified distance from that receiver.

(b) The device has a receiver that can receive continuously the signals transmitted by a transmitter of the type described in division (VV)(1)(a) of this section, can transmit continuously those signals by telephone to a central monitoring computer of the type described in division (VV)(1)(c) of this section, and can transmit continuously an appropriate signal to that central monitoring computer if the receiver is turned off or altered without prior court approval or otherwise tampered with.

(c) The device has a central monitoring computer that can receive continuously the signals transmitted by telephone by a receiver of the type described in division (VV)(1)(b) of this section and can monitor continuously the person to whom an electronic monitoring device of the type described in division (VV)(1)(a) of this section is attached.

(2) Any device that is not a device of the type described in division (VV)(1) of this section and that conforms with all of the following:

(a) The device includes a transmitter and receiver that can monitor and determine the location of a subject person at any time, or at a designated point in time, through the use of a central monitoring computer or through other electronic means.

(b) The device includes a transmitter and receiver that can determine at any time, or at a designated point in time, through the use of a central monitoring computer or other electronic means the fact that the transmitter is turned off or altered in any manner without prior approval of the court in relation to the electronic monitoring or without prior approval of the department of rehabilitation and correction in relation to the use of an electronic monitoring device for an inmate on transitional control or otherwise is tampered with.

(3) Any type of technology that can adequately track or determine the location of a subject person at any time and that is approved by the director of rehabilitation and correction, including, but not limited to, any satellite technology, voice tracking system, or retinal scanning system that is so approved.

(WW) "Non-economic loss" means nonpecuniary harm suffered by a victim of an offense as a result of or related to the commission of the offense, including, but not limited to, pain and suffering; loss of society, consortium, companionship, care, assistance, attention, protection, advice, guidance, counsel, instruction, training, or education; mental anguish; and any other intangible loss.

(XX) "Prosecutor" has the same meaning as in section 2935.01 of the Revised Code.

(WW) [1] "Continuous alcohol monitoring" means the ability to automatically test and periodically transmit alcohol consumption levels and tamper attempts at least every hour, regardless of the location of the person who is being monitored.

(2004 H 163, eff. 9–23–04; 2004 H 52, eff. 6–1–04; 2003 S 57, eff. 1–1–04; 2003 S 5, § 3, eff. 1–1–04; 2003 S 5, § 1, eff. 7–31–03; 2002 H 490, eff. 1–1–04; 2002 S 123, eff. 1–1–04; 2002 H 327, eff. 7–8–02; 2000 S 179, § 3, eff. 1–1–02; 2000 S 222, eff. 3–22–01; 2000 H 349, eff. 9–22–00; 1999 S 22, eff. 5–17–00; 1999 S 107, eff. 3–23–00; 1999 S 9, eff. 3–8–00; 1997 S 111, eff. 3–17–98; 1997 H 378, eff. 3–10–98; 1996 S 166, eff. 10–17–96; 1996 H 180, eff. 1–1–97; 1996 S 269, eff. 7–1–96; 1996 H 480, eff. 10–16–96; 1996 H 445, eff. 9–3–96; 1995 S 2, eff. 7–1–96)

[1] So in original; paragraph designation appears as the result of the harmonization of 2004 H 163 and 2004 H 52.

Note: See also following version of this section, eff. 4–29–05.

2929.01 Definitions (later effective date)

Note: See also preceding version of this section, in effect until 4–29–05.

As used in this chapter:

(A)(1) "Alternative residential facility" means, subject to division (A)(2) of this section, any facility other than an offender's home or residence in which an offender is assigned to live and that satisfies all of the following criteria:

(a) It provides programs through which the offender may seek or maintain employment or may receive education, training, treatment, or habilitation.

(b) It has received the appropriate license or certificate for any specialized education, training, treatment, habilitation, or other service that it provides from the government agency that is responsible for licensing or certifying that type of education, training, treatment, habilitation, or service.

(2) "Alternative residential facility" does not include a community-based correctional facility, jail, halfway house, or prison.

(B) "Bad time" means the time by which the parole board administratively extends an offender's stated prison term or terms pursuant to section 2967.11 of the Revised Code because the parole board finds by clear and convincing evidence that the offender, while serving the prison term or terms, committed an act that is a criminal offense under the law of this state or the United States, whether or not the offender is prosecuted for the commission of that act.

(C) "Basic probation supervision" means a requirement that the offender maintain contact with a person appointed to supervise the offender in accordance with sanctions imposed by the court or imposed by the parole board pursuant to section 2967.28 of the Revised Code. "Basic probation supervision" includes basic parole supervision and basic post-release control supervision.

(D) "Cocaine," "crack cocaine," " hashish," "L.S.D.," and "unit dose" have the same meanings as in section 2925.01 of the Revised Code.

(E) "Community–based correctional facility" means a community-based correctional facility and program or district community-based correctional facility and program developed pursuant to sections 2301.51 to 2301.56 of the Revised Code.

(F) "Community control sanction" means a sanction that is not a prison term and that is described in section 2929.15, 2929.16, 2929. 17, or 2929.18 of the Revised Code or a sanction that is not a jail term and that is described in section 2929.26, 2929.27, or 2929.28 of the Revised Code. "Community control sanction" includes probation if the sentence involved was imposed for a felony that was committed prior to July 1, 1996, or if the sentence involved was imposed for a misdemeanor that was committed prior to January 1, 2004.

(G) "Controlled substance," " marihuana," "schedule I," and "schedule II" have the same meanings as in section 3719.01 of the Revised Code.

(H) "Curfew" means a requirement that an offender during a specified period of time be at a designated place.

(I) "Day reporting" means a sanction pursuant to which an offender is required each day to report to and leave a center or other approved reporting location at specified times in order to participate in work, education or training, treatment, and other approved programs at the center or outside the center.

(J) "Deadly weapon" has the same meaning as in section 2923.11 of the Revised Code.

(K) "Drug and alcohol use monitoring" means a program under which an offender agrees to submit to random chemical analysis of the offender's blood, breath, or urine to determine whether the offender has ingested any alcohol or other drugs.

(L) "Drug treatment program" means any program under which a person undergoes assessment and treatment designed to reduce or completely eliminate the person's physical or emotional reliance upon alcohol, another drug, or alcohol and another drug and under which the person may be required to receive assessment and treatment on an outpatient basis or may be required to reside at a facility other than the person's home or residence while undergoing assessment and treatment.

(M) "Economic loss" means any economic detriment suffered by a victim as a direct and proximate result of the commission of an offense and includes any loss of income due to lost time at work because of any injury caused to the victim, and any property loss, medical cost, or funeral expense incurred as a result of the commission of the offense. "Economic loss" does not include non-economic loss or any punitive or exemplary damages.

(N) "Education or training" includes study at, or in conjunction with a program offered by, a university, college, or technical college or vocational study and also includes the completion of primary school, secondary school, and literacy curricula or their equivalent.

(O) "Firearm" has the same meaning as in section 2923.11 of the Revised Code.

(P) "Halfway house" means a facility licensed by the division of parole and community services of the department of rehabilitation and correction pursuant to section 2967.14 of the Revised Code as a suitable facility for the care and treatment of adult offenders.

(Q) "House arrest" means a period of confinement of an offender that is in the offender's home or in other premises specified by the sentencing court or by the parole board pursuant to section 2967.28 of the Revised Code and during which all of the following apply:

(1) The offender is required to remain in the offender's home or other specified premises for the specified period of confinement, except for periods of time during which the offender is at the offender's place of employment or at other premises as authorized by the sentencing court or by the parole board.

(2) The offender is required to report periodically to a person designated by the court or parole board.

(3) The offender is subject to any other restrictions and requirements that may be imposed by the sentencing court or by the parole board.

(R) "Intensive probation supervision" means a requirement that an offender maintain frequent contact with a person appointed by the court, or by the parole board pursuant to section 2967.28 of the Revised Code, to supervise the offender while the offender is seeking or maintaining necessary employment and participating in training, education, and treatment programs as required in the court's or parole board's order. "Intensive probation supervision" includes intensive parole supervision and intensive post-release control supervision.

(S) "Jail" means a jail, workhouse, minimum security jail, or other residential facility used for the confinement of alleged or convicted offenders that is operated by a political subdivision or a combination of political subdivisions of this state.

(T) "Jail term" means the term in a jail that a sentencing court imposes or is authorized to impose pursuant to section 2929. 24 or 2929.25 of the Revised Code or pursuant to any other provision of the Revised Code that authorizes a term in a jail for a misdemeanor conviction.

(U) "Mandatory jail term" means the term in a jail that a sentencing court is required to impose pursuant to division (G) of section 1547.99 of the Revised Code, division (E) of section 2903.06 or division (D) of section 2903.08 of the Revised Code, division (E) of section 2929.24 of the Revised Code, division (B) of section 4510.14 of the Revised Code, or division (G) of section 4511.19 of the Revised Code or pursuant to any other provision of the Revised Code that requires a term in a jail for a misdemeanor conviction.

(V) "Delinquent child" has the same meaning as in section 2152.02 of the Revised Code.

(W) "License violation report" means a report that is made by a sentencing court, or by the parole board pursuant to section 2967.28 of the Revised Code, to the regulatory or licensing board or agency that issued an offender a professional license or a license or permit to do business in this state and that specifies that the offender has been convicted of or pleaded guilty to an offense that may violate the conditions under which the offender's professional license or license or permit to do business in this state was granted or an offense for which the offender's professional license or license or permit to do business in this state may be revoked or suspended.

(X) "Major drug offender" means an offender who is convicted of or pleads guilty to the possession of, sale of, or offer to sell any drug, compound, mixture, preparation, or substance that consists of or contains at least one thousand grams of hashish; at least one hundred grams of crack cocaine; at least one thousand grams of cocaine that is not crack cocaine; at least two thousand five hundred unit doses or two hundred fifty grams of heroin; at least five thousand unit doses of L.S.D. or five hundred grams of L.S.D. in a liquid concentrate, liquid extract, or liquid distillate form; or at least one hundred times the amount of any other schedule I or II controlled substance other than marihuana that is necessary to commit a felony of the third degree pursuant to section 2925.03, 2925.04, 2925.05, or 2925.11 of the Revised Code that is based on the possession of, sale of, or offer to sell the controlled substance.

(Y) "Mandatory prison term" means any of the following:

(1) Subject to division (Y)(2) of this section, the term in prison that must be imposed for the offenses or circumstances set forth in divisions (F)(1) to (8) or (F)(12) to (14) of section 2929.13 and division (D) of section 2929.14 of the Revised Code. Except as provided in sections 2925.02, 2925.03, 2925.04, 2925.05, and 2925.11 of the Revised Code, unless the maximum or another specific term is required under section 2929.14 of the Revised Code, a mandatory prison term described in this division may be any prison term authorized for the level of offense.

(2) The term of sixty or one hundred twenty days in prison that a sentencing court is required to impose for a third or fourth degree felony OVI offense pursuant to division (G)(2) of section 2929.13 and division (G)(1)(d) or (e) of section 4511.19 of the Revised Code or the term of one, two, three, four, or five years in prison that a sentencing court is required to impose pursuant to division (G)(2) of section 2929.13 of the Revised Code.

(3) The term in prison imposed pursuant to section 2971.03 of the Revised Code for the offenses and in the circumstances described in division (F)(11) of section 2929.13 of the Revised Code and that term as modified or terminated pursuant to section 2971.05 of the Revised Code.

(Z) "Monitored time" means a period of time during which an offender continues to be under the control of the sentencing court or parole board, subject to no conditions other than leading a law-abiding life.

(AA) "Offender" means a person who, in this state, is convicted of or pleads guilty to a felony or a misdemeanor.

(BB) "Prison" means a residential facility used for the confinement of convicted felony offenders that is under the control of the department of rehabilitation and correction but does not include a violation sanction center operated under authority of section 2967.141 of the Revised Code.

(CC) "Prison term" includes any of the following sanctions for an offender:

(1) A stated prison term;

(2) A term in a prison shortened by, or with the approval of, the sentencing court pursuant to section 2929.20, 2967.26, 5120.031, 5120.032, or 5120.073 of the Revised Code;

(3) A term in prison extended by bad time imposed pursuant to section 2967.11 of the Revised Code or imposed for a violation of post-release control pursuant to section 2967.28 of the Revised Code.

(DD) "Repeat violent offender" means a person about whom both of the following apply:

(1) The person has been convicted of or has pleaded guilty to, and is being sentenced for committing, for complicity in committing, or for an attempt to commit, aggravated murder, murder, involuntary manslaughter, a felony of the first degree other than one set forth in Chapter 2925. of the Revised Code, a felony of the first degree set forth in Chapter 2925. of the Revised Code that involved an attempt to cause serious physical harm to a person or that resulted in serious physical harm to a person, or a felony of the second degree that involved an attempt to cause serious physical harm to a person or that resulted in serious physical harm to a person.

(2) Either of the following applies:

(a) The person previously was convicted of or pleaded guilty to, and previously served or, at the time of the offense was serving, a prison term for, any of the following:

(i) Aggravated murder, murder, involuntary manslaughter, rape, felonious sexual penetration as it existed under section 2907.12 of the Revised Code prior to September 3, 1996, a felony of the first or second degree that resulted in the death of a person or in physical harm to a person, or complicity in or an attempt to commit any of those offenses;

(ii) An offense under an existing or former law of this state, another state, or the United States that is or was substantially equivalent to an offense listed under division (DD)(2)(a)(i) of this section and that resulted in the death of a person or in physical harm to a person.

(b) The person previously was adjudicated a delinquent child for committing an act that if committed by an adult would have been an offense listed in division (DD)(2)(a)(i) or (ii) of this section, the person was committed to the department of youth services for that delinquent act.

(EE) "Sanction" means any penalty imposed upon an offender who is convicted of or pleads guilty to an offense, as punishment for the offense. "Sanction" includes any sanction imposed pursuant to any provision of sections 2929.14 to 2929.18 or 2929.24 to 2929.28 of the Revised Code.

(FF) "Sentence" means the sanction or combination of sanctions imposed by the sentencing court on an offender who is convicted of or pleads guilty to an offense.

(GG) "Stated prison term" means the prison term, mandatory prison term, or combination of all prison terms and mandatory prison terms imposed by the sentencing court pursuant to section 2929.14 or 2971.03 of the Revised Code. "Stated prison term" includes any credit received by the offender for time spent in jail awaiting trial, sentencing, or transfer to prison for the offense and any time spent under house arrest or house arrest with electronic monitoring imposed after earning credits pursuant to section 2967.193 of the Revised Code.

(HH) "Victim-offender mediation" means a reconciliation or mediation program that involves an offender and the victim of the offense committed by the offender and that includes a meeting in which the offender and the victim may discuss the offense, discuss restitution, and consider other sanctions for the offense.

(II) "Fourth degree felony OVI offense" means a violation of division (A) of section 4511.19 of the Revised Code that, under division (G) of that section, is a felony of the fourth degree.

(JJ) "Mandatory term of local incarceration" means the term of sixty or one hundred twenty days in a jail, a community-based correctional facility, a halfway house, or an alternative residential facility that a sentencing court may impose upon a person who is convicted of or pleads guilty to a fourth degree felony OVI offense pursuant to division (G)(1) of section 2929.13 of the Revised Code and division (G)(1)(d) or (e) of section 4511.19 of the Revised Code.

(KK) "Designated homicide, assault, or kidnapping offense," "violent sex offense," "sexual motivation specification," "sexually violent offense," "sexually violent predator," and " sexually violent predator specification" have the same meanings as in section 2971.01 of the Revised Code.

(LL) "Habitual sex offender," "sexually oriented offense," "sexual predator," "registration-exempt sexually oriented offense," "child-victim oriented offense," "habitual child-victim offender," and " child-victim predator" have the same meanings as in section 2950.01 of the Revised Code.

(MM) An offense is "committed in the vicinity of a child" if the offender commits the offense within thirty feet of or within the same residential unit as a child who is under eighteen years of age, regardless of whether the offender knows the age of the child or whether the offender knows the offense is being committed within thirty feet of or within the same residential unit as the child and regardless of whether the child actually views the commission of the offense.

(NN) "Family or household member" has the same meaning as in section 2919.25 of the Revised Code.

(OO) "Motor vehicle" and "manufactured home" have the same meanings as in section 4501.01 of the Revised Code.

(PP) "Detention" and "detention facility" have the same meanings as in section 2921.01 of the Revised Code.

(QQ) "Third degree felony OVI offense" means a violation of division (A) of section 4511.19 of the Revised Code that, under division (G) of that section, is a felony of the third degree.

(RR) "Random drug testing" has the same meaning as in section 5120.63 of the Revised Code.

(SS) "Felony sex offense" has the same meaning as in section 2967.28 of the Revised Code.

(TT) "Body armor" has the same meaning as in section 2941.1411 of the Revised Code.

(UU) "Electronic monitoring" means monitoring through the use of an electronic monitoring device.

(VV) "Electronic monitoring device" means any of the following:

(1) Any device that can be operated by electrical or battery power and that conforms with all of the following:

(a) The device has a transmitter that can be attached to a person, that will transmit a specified signal to a receiver of the type described in division (VV)(1)(b) of this section if the transmitter is removed from the person, turned off, or altered in any manner without prior court approval in relation to electronic monitoring or without prior approval of the department of rehabilitation and correction in relation to the use of an electronic monitoring device for an inmate on transitional control or otherwise is tampered with, that can transmit continuously and periodically a signal to that receiver when the person is within a specified distance from the receiver, and that can transmit an appropriate signal to that receiver if the person to whom it is attached travels a specified distance from that receiver.

(b) The device has a receiver that can receive continuously the signals transmitted by a transmitter of the type described in division (VV)(1)(a) of this section, can transmit continuously those signals by telephone to a central monitoring computer of the type described in division (VV)(1)(c) of this section, and can transmit continuously an appropriate signal to that central monitoring computer if the receiver is turned off or altered without prior court approval or otherwise tampered with.

(c) The device has a central monitoring computer that can receive continuously the signals transmitted by telephone by a receiver of the type described in division (VV)(1)(b) of this section and can monitor continuously the person to whom an electronic monitoring device of the type described in division (VV)(1)(a) of this section is attached.

(2) Any device that is not a device of the type described in division (VV)(1) of this section and that conforms with all of the following:

(a) The device includes a transmitter and receiver that can monitor and determine the location of a subject person at any time, or at a designated point in time, through the use of a central monitoring computer or through other electronic means.

(b) The device includes a transmitter and receiver that can determine at any time, or at a designated point in time, through the use of a central monitoring computer or other electronic means the fact that the transmitter is turned off or altered in any manner without prior approval of the court in relation to the electronic monitoring or without prior approval of the department of rehabilitation and correction in relation to the use of an electronic monitoring device for an inmate on transitional control or otherwise is tampered with.

(3) Any type of technology that can adequately track or determine the location of a subject person at any time and that is approved by the director of rehabilitation and correction, including, but not limited to, any satellite technology, voice tracking system, or retinal scanning system that is so approved.

(WW) "Non–economic loss" means nonpecuniary harm suffered by a victim of an offense as a result of or related to the commission of the offense, including, but not limited to, pain and suffering; loss of society, consortium, companionship, care, assistance, attention, protection, advice, guidance, counsel, instruction, training, or education; mental anguish; and any other intangible loss.

(XX) "Prosecutor" has the same meaning as in section 2935.01 of the Revised Code.

(YY) "Continuous alcohol monitoring" means the ability to automatically test and periodically transmit alcohol consumption levels and tamper attempts at least every hour, regardless of the location of the person who is being monitored.

(ZZ) A person is "adjudicated a sexually violent predator" if the person is convicted of or pleads guilty to a violent sex offense and also is convicted of or pleads guilty to a sexually violent predator specification that was included in the indictment, count in the indictment, or information charging that violent sex offense or if the person is convicted of or pleads guilty to a designated homicide, assault, or kidnapping offense and also is convicted of or pleads guilty to both a sexual motivation specification and a sexually violent predator specification that were included in the indictment, count in the indictment, or information charging that designated homicide, assault, or kidnapping offense.

(2004 H 473, eff. 4–29–05; 2004 H 163, eff. 9–23–04; 2004 H 52, eff. 6–1–04; 2003 S 57, eff. 1–1–04; 2003 S 5, § 3, eff. 1–1–04; 2003 S 5, § 1, eff. 7–31–03; 2002 H 490, eff. 1–1–04; 2002 S 123, eff. 1–1–04; 2002 H 327, eff. 7–8–02; 2000 S 179, § 3, eff. 1–1–02; 2000 S 222, eff. 3–22–01; 2000 H 349, eff. 9–22–00; 1999 S 22, eff. 5–17–00; 1999 S 107, eff. 3–23–00; 1999 S 9, eff. 3–8–00; 1997 S 111, eff. 3–17–98; 1997 H 378, eff. 3–10–98; 1996 S 166, eff. 10–17–96; 1996 H 180, eff. 1–1–97; 1996 S 269, eff. 7–1–96; 1996 H 480, eff. 10–16–96; 1996 H 445, eff. 9–3–96; 1995 S 2, eff. 7–1–96)

Note: See also preceding version of this section, in effect until 4–29–05.

PENALTIES FOR MURDER

2929.02 Penalties for murder

(A) Whoever is convicted of or pleads guilty to aggravated murder in violation of section 2903.01 of the Revised Code shall suffer death or be imprisoned for life, as determined pursuant to sections 2929.022, 2929.03, and 2929.04 of the Revised Code, except that no person who raises the matter of age pursuant to section 2929.023 of the Revised Code and who is not found to have been eighteen years of age or older at the time of the commission of the offense shall suffer death. In addition, the offender may be fined an amount fixed by the court, but not more than twenty-five thousand dollars.

(B) Whoever is convicted of or pleads guilty to murder in violation of section 2903.02 of the Revised Code shall be imprisoned for an indefinite term of fifteen years to life, except that, if the offender also is convicted of or pleads guilty to a sexual motivation specification and a sexually violent predator specification that were included in the indictment, count in the indictment, or information that charged the murder, the court shall impose upon the offender a term of life imprisonment without parole that shall be served pursuant to section 2971.03 of the Revised Code. In addition, the offender may be fined an amount fixed by the court, but not more than fifteen thousand dollars.

(C) The court shall not impose a fine or fines for aggravated murder or murder which, in the aggregate and to the extent not suspended by the court, exceeds the amount which the offender is or will be able to pay by the method and within the time allowed without undue hardship to the offender or to the dependents of the offender, or will prevent the offender from making reparation for the victim's wrongful death.

(1998 S 107, eff. 7–29–98; 1996 H 180, eff. 1–1–97; 1981 S 1, eff. 10–19–81; 1972 H 511)

2929.021 Specifications of aggravating circumstance; clerk to notify supreme court of certain facts

(A) If an indictment or a count in an indictment charges the defendant with aggravated murder and contains one or more specifications of aggravating circumstances listed in division (A) of section 2929.04 of the Revised Code, the clerk of the court in which the indictment is filed, within fifteen days after the day on which it is filed, shall file a notice with the supreme court indicating that the indictment was filed. The notice shall be in the form prescribed by the clerk of the supreme court and shall contain, for each charge of aggravated murder with a specification, at least the following information pertaining to the charge:

(1) The name of the person charged in the indictment or count in the indictment with aggravated murder with a specification;

(2) The docket number or numbers of the case or cases arising out of the charge, if available;

(3) The court in which the case or cases will be heard;

(4) The date on which the indictment was filed.

(B) If an indictment or a count in an indictment charges the defendant with aggravated murder and contains one or more specifications of aggravating circumstances listed in division (A) of section 2929.04 of the Revised Code and if the defendant pleads guilty or no contest to any offense in the case or if the indictment or any count in the indictment is dismissed, the clerk of the court in which the plea is entered or the indictment or count is dismissed shall file a notice with the supreme court indicating what action was taken in the case. The notice shall be filed within fifteen days after the plea is entered or the indictment or count is dismissed, shall be in the form prescribed by the clerk of the supreme court, and shall contain at least the following information:

(1) The name of the person who entered the guilty or no contest plea or who is named in the indictment or count that is dismissed;

(2) The docket numbers of the cases in which the guilty or no contest plea is entered or in which the indictment or count is dismissed;

(3) The sentence imposed on the offender in each case.

(1981 S 1, eff. 10–19–81)

2929.022 Elections of defendant as to certain trial procedures

(A) If an indictment or count in an indictment charging a defendant with aggravated murder contains a specification of the aggravating circumstance of a prior conviction listed in division (A)(5) of section 2929.04 of the Revised Code, the defendant may elect to have the panel of three judges, if he waives trial by jury, or the trial judge, if he is tried by jury, determine the existence of that aggravating circumstance at the sentencing hearing held pursuant to divisions (C) and (D) of section 2929.03 of the Revised Code.

(1) If the defendant does not elect to have the existence of the aggravating circumstance determined at the sentencing hearing, the defendant shall be tried on the charge of aggravated murder, on the specification of the aggravating circumstance of a prior conviction listed in division (A)(5) of section 2929.04 of the Revised Code, and on any other specifications of an aggravating circumstance listed in division (A) of section 2929.04 of the Revised Code in a single trial as in any other criminal case in which a person is charged with aggravated murder and specifications.

(2) If the defendant does elect to have the existence of the aggravating circumstance of a prior conviction listed in division (A)(5) of section 2929.04 of the Revised Code determined at the sentencing hearing, then, following a verdict of guilty of the charge of aggravated murder, the panel of three judges or the trial judge shall:

(a) Hold a sentencing hearing pursuant to division (B) of this section, unless required to do otherwise under division (A)(2)(b) of this section;

(b) If the offender raises the matter of age at trial pursuant to section 2929.023 of the Revised Code and is not found at trial to have been eighteen years of age or older at the time of the commission of the offense, conduct a hearing to determine if the specification of the aggravating circumstance of a prior conviction listed in division (A)(5) of section 2929.04 of the Revised Code is proven beyond a reasonable doubt. After conducting the hearing, the panel or judge shall proceed as follows:

(i) If that aggravating circumstance is proven beyond a reasonable doubt or if the defendant at trial was convicted of any other specification of an aggravating circumstance, the panel or judge shall impose sentence according to division (E) of section 2929.03 of the Revised Code;

(ii) If that aggravating circumstance is not proven beyond a reasonable doubt and the defendant at trial was not convicted of any other specification of an aggravating circumstance, the panel or judge shall impose sentence of life imprisonment with parole eligibility after serving twenty years of imprisonment on the offender.

(B) At the sentencing hearing, the panel of judges, if the defendant was tried by a panel of three judges, or the trial judge, if the defendant was tried by jury, shall, when required pursuant to division (A)(2) of this section, first determine if the specification of the aggravating circumstance of a prior conviction listed in division (A)(5) of section 2929.04 of the Revised Code is proven beyond a reasonable doubt. If the panel of judges or the trial judge determines that the specification of the aggravating circumstance of a prior conviction listed in division (A)(5) of section 2929.04 of the Revised Code is proven beyond a reasonable doubt or if they do not determine that the specification is proven beyond a reasonable doubt but the defendant at trial was convicted of a specification of any other aggravating circumstance listed in division (A) of section 2929.04 of the Revised Code, the panel of judges or the trial judge and trial jury shall impose sentence on the offender pursuant to division (D) of section 2929.03 and section 2929.04 of the Revised Code. If the panel of judges or the trial judge does not determine that the specification of the aggravating circumstance of a prior conviction listed in division (A)(5) of section 2929.04 of the Revised Code is proven beyond a reasonable doubt and the defendant at trial was not convicted of any other specification of an aggravating circumstance listed in division (A) of section 2929.04 of the Revised Code, the panel of judges or the trial judge shall terminate the sentencing hearing and impose a sentence of life imprisonment with parole eligibility after serving twenty years of imprisonment on the offender.

(1981 S 1, eff. 10–19–81)

2929.023 Defendant's age; raising issue; burdens relating to matter

A person charged with aggravated murder and one or more specifications of an aggravating circumstance may, at trial, raise the matter of his age at the time of the alleged commission of the offense and may present evidence at trial that he was not eighteen years of age or older at the time of the alleged commission of the offense. The burdens of raising the matter of age, and of going forward with the evidence relating to the matter of age, are upon the defendant. After a defendant has raised the matter of age at trial, the prosecution shall have the burden of proving, by proof beyond a reasonable doubt, that the defendant was eighteen years of age or older at the time of the alleged commission of the offense.

(1981 S 1, eff. 10–19–81)

2929.024 Indigency; services of investigation; experts; payment

If the court determines that the defendant is indigent and that investigation services, experts, or other services are reasonably necessary for the proper representation of a defendant charged with aggravated murder at trial or at the sentencing hearing, the court shall authorize the defendant's counsel to obtain the necessary services for the defendant, and shall order that payment of the fees and expenses for the necessary services be made in the same manner that payment for appointed counsel is made pursuant to Chapter 120. of the Revised Code. If the court determines that the necessary services had to be obtained prior to court authorization for payment of the fees and expenses for the necessary services, the court may, after the services have been obtained, authorize the defendant's counsel to obtain the necessary services and order that payment of the fees and expenses for the necessary services be made as provided in this section.

(1981 S 1, eff. 10–19–81)

2929.03 Imposing sentence for a capital offense; procedures; proof of relevant factors; alternative sentences

(A) If the indictment or count in the indictment charging aggravated murder does not contain one or more specifications of aggravating circumstances listed in division (A) of section 2929.04 of the Revised Code, then, following a verdict of guilty of the charge of aggravated murder, the trial court shall impose sentence on the offender as follows:

(1) Except as provided in division (A)(2) of this section, the trial court shall impose one of the following sentences on the offender:

(a) Life imprisonment without parole;

(b) Life imprisonment with parole eligibility after serving twenty years of imprisonment;

(c) Life imprisonment with parole eligibility after serving twenty-five full years of imprisonment;

(d) Life imprisonment with parole eligibility after serving thirty full years of imprisonment.

(2) If the offender also is convicted of or pleads guilty to a sexual motivation specification and a sexually violent predator specification that are included in the indictment, count in the indictment, or information that charged the aggravated murder, the trial court shall impose upon the offender a sentence of life imprisonment without parole that shall be served pursuant to section 2971.03 of the Revised Code.

(B) If the indictment or count in the indictment charging aggravated murder contains one or more specifications of aggravating circumstances listed in division (A) of section 2929.04 of the Revised Code, the verdict shall separately state whether the accused is found guilty or not guilty of the principal charge and, if guilty of the principal charge, whether the offender was eighteen years of age or older at the time of the commission of the offense, if the matter of age was raised by the offender pursuant to section 2929.023 of the Revised Code, and whether the offender is guilty or not guilty of each specification. The jury shall be instructed on its duties in this regard. The instruction to the jury shall include an instruction that a specification shall be proved beyond a reasonable doubt in order to support a guilty verdict on the specification, but the instruction shall not mention the penalty that may be the consequence of a guilty or not guilty verdict on any charge or specification.

(C)(1) If the indictment or count in the indictment charging aggravated murder contains one or more specifications of aggravating circumstances listed in division (A) of section 2929.04 of the Revised Code, then, following a verdict of guilty of the charge but not guilty of each of the specifications, and regardless of whether the offender raised the matter of age pursuant to section 2929.023 of the Revised Code, the trial court shall impose sentence on the offender as follows:

(a) Except as provided in division (C)(1)(b) of this section, the trial court shall impose one of the following sentences on the offender:

(i) Life imprisonment without parole;

(ii) Life imprisonment with parole eligibility after serving twenty years of imprisonment;

(iii) Life imprisonment with parole eligibility after serving twenty-five full years of imprisonment;

(iv) Life imprisonment with parole eligibility after serving thirty full years of imprisonment.

(b) If the offender also is convicted of or pleads guilty to a sexual motivation specification and a sexually violent predator specification that are included in the indictment, count in the indictment, or information that charged the aggravated murder, the trial court shall impose upon the offender a sentence of life imprisonment without parole that shall be served pursuant to section 2971.03 of the Revised Code.

(2)(a) If the indictment or count in the indictment contains one or more specifications of aggravating circumstances listed in division (A) of section 2929.04 of the Revised Code and if the offender is found guilty of both the charge and one or more of the specifications, the penalty to be imposed on the offender shall be one of the following:

(i) Except as provided in division (C)(2)(a)(ii) of this section, the penalty to be imposed on the offender shall be death, life imprisonment without parole, life imprisonment with parole eligibility after serving twenty-five full years of imprisonment, or life imprisonment with parole eligibility after serving thirty full years of imprisonment.

(ii) If the offender also is convicted of or pleads guilty to a sexual motivation specification and a sexually violent predator specification that are included in the indictment, count in the indictment, or information that charged the aggravated murder, the penalty to be imposed on the offender shall be death or life imprisonment without parole that shall be served pursuant to section 2971.03 of the Revised Code.

(b) A penalty imposed pursuant to division (C)(2)(a)(i) or (ii) of this section shall be determined pursuant to divisions (D) and (E) of this section and shall be determined by one of the following:

(i) By the panel of three judges that tried the offender upon the offender's waiver of the right to trial by jury;

(ii) By the trial jury and the trial judge, if the offender was tried by jury.

(D)(1) Death may not be imposed as a penalty for aggravated murder if the offender raised the matter of age at trial pursuant to section 2929.023 of the Revised Code and was not found at trial to have been eighteen years of age or older at the time of the commission of the offense. When death may be imposed as a penalty for aggravated murder, the court shall proceed under this division. When death may be imposed as a penalty, the court, upon the request of the defendant, shall require a pre-sentence investigation to be made and, upon the request of the defendant, shall require a mental examination to be made, and shall require reports of the investigation and of any mental examination submitted to the court, pursuant to section 2947.06 of the Revised Code. No statement made or information provided by a defendant in a mental examination or proceeding conducted pursuant to this division shall be disclosed to any person, except as provided in this division, or be used in evidence against the defendant on the issue of guilt in any retrial. A pre-sentence investigation or mental examination shall not be made except upon request of the defendant. Copies of any reports prepared under this division shall be furnished to the court, to the trial jury if the offender was tried by a jury, to the prosecutor, and to the offender or the offender's counsel for use under this division. The court, and the trial jury if the offender was tried by a jury, shall consider any report prepared pursuant to this division and furnished to it and any evidence raised at trial that is relevant to the aggravating circumstances the offender was found guilty of committing or to any factors in mitigation of the imposition of the sentence of death, shall hear testimony and other evidence that is relevant to the nature and circumstances of the aggravating circumstances the offender was found guilty of committing, the mitigating factors set forth in division (B) of section 2929.04 of the Revised Code, and any other factors in mitigation of the imposition of the sentence of death, and shall hear the statement, if any, of the offender, and the arguments, if any, of counsel for the defense and prosecution, that are relevant to the penalty that should be imposed on the offender. The defendant shall be given great latitude in the presentation of evidence of the mitigating factors set forth in division (B) of section 2929.04 of the Revised Code and of any other factors in mitigation of the imposition of the sentence of death. If the offender chooses to make a statement, the offender is subject to cross-examination only if the offender consents to make the statement under oath or affirmation.

The defendant shall have the burden of going forward with the evidence of any factors in mitigation of the imposition of the sentence of death. The prosecution shall have the burden of proving, by proof beyond a reasonable doubt, that the aggravating circumstances the defendant was found guilty of committing are sufficient to outweigh the factors in mitigation of the imposition of the sentence of death.

(2) Upon consideration of the relevant evidence raised at trial, the testimony, other evidence, statement of the offender, arguments of counsel, and, if applicable, the reports submitted pursuant to division (D)(1) of this section, the trial jury, if the offender was tried by a jury, shall determine whether the aggravating circumstances the offender was found guilty of committing are sufficient to outweigh the mitigating factors present in the case. If the trial jury unanimously finds, by proof beyond a reasonable doubt, that the aggravating circumstances the offender was found guilty of committing outweigh the mitigating factors, the trial jury shall recommend to the court that the sentence of death be imposed on the offender. Absent such a finding, the jury shall recommend that the offender be sentenced to one of the following:

(a) Except as provided in division (D)(2)(b) of this section, to life imprisonment without parole, life imprisonment with parole eligibility after serving twenty-five full years of imprisonment, or life imprisonment with parole eligibility after serving thirty full years of imprisonment;

(b) If the offender also is convicted of or pleads guilty to a sexual motivation specification and a sexually violent predator specification that are included in the indictment, count in the indictment, or information that charged the aggravated murder, to life imprisonment without parole.

If the trial jury recommends that the offender be sentenced to life imprisonment without parole, life imprisonment with parole eligibility after serving twenty-five full years of imprisonment, or life imprisonment with parole eligibility after serving thirty full years of imprisonment, the court shall impose the sentence recommended by the jury upon the offender. If the sentence is a sentence of life imprisonment without parole imposed under division (D)(2)(b) of this section, the sentence shall be served pursuant to section 2971.03 of the Revised Code. If the trial jury recommends that the sentence of death be imposed upon the offender, the court shall proceed to impose sentence pursuant to division (D)(3) of this section.

(3) Upon consideration of the relevant evidence raised at trial, the testimony, other evidence, statement of the offender, arguments of counsel, and, if applicable, the reports submitted to the court pursuant to division (D)(1) of this section, if, after receiving pursuant to division (D)(2) of this section the trial jury's recommendation that the sentence of death be imposed, the court finds, by proof beyond a reasonable doubt, or if the panel of three judges unanimously finds, by proof beyond a reasonable doubt, that the aggravating circumstances the offender was found guilty of committing outweigh the mitigating factors, it shall impose sentence of death on the offender. Absent such a finding by the court or panel, the court or the panel shall impose one of the following sentences on the offender:

(a) Except as provided in division (D)(3)(b) of this section, one of the following:

(i) Life imprisonment without parole;

(ii) Life imprisonment with parole eligibility after serving twenty-five full years of imprisonment;

(iii) Life imprisonment with parole eligibility after serving thirty full years of imprisonment.

(b) If the offender also is convicted of or pleads guilty to a sexual motivation specification and a sexually violent predator specification that are included in the indictment, count in the indictment, or information that charged the aggravated murder, life imprisonment without parole that shall be served pursuant to section 2971.03 of the Revised Code.

(E) If the offender raised the matter of age at trial pursuant to section 2929.023 of the Revised Code, was convicted of aggravated murder and one or more specifications of an aggravating circumstance listed in division (A) of section 2929.04 of the Revised Code, and was not found at trial to have been eighteen years of age or older at the time of the commission of the offense, the court or the panel of three judges shall not impose a sentence of death on the offender. Instead, the court or panel shall impose one of the following sentences on the offender:

(1) Except as provided in division (E)(2) of this section, one of the following:

facility that a sentencing court may impose upon a person who is convicted of or pleads guilty to a fourth degree felony OVI offense pursuant to division (G)(1) of section 2929.13 of the Revised Code and division (G)(1)(d) or (e) of section 4511.19 of the Revised Code.

(KK) "Designated homicide, assault, or kidnapping offense," "sexual motivation specification," "sexually violent offense," "sexually violent predator," and "sexually violent predator specification" have the same meanings as in section 2971.01 of the Revised Code.

(LL) "Habitual sex offender," "sexually oriented offense," "sexual predator," "registration-exempt sexually oriented offense," "child-victim oriented offense," "habitual child-victim offender," and "child-victim predator" have the same meanings as in section 2950.01 of the Revised Code.

(MM) An offense is "committed in the vicinity of a child" if the offender commits the offense within thirty feet of or within the same residential unit as a child who is under eighteen years of age, regardless of whether the offender knows the age of the child or whether the offender knows the offense is being committed within thirty feet of or within the same residential unit as the child and regardless of whether the child actually views the commission of the offense.

(NN) "Family or household member" has the same meaning as in section 2919.25 of the Revised Code.

(OO) "Motor vehicle" and "manufactured home" have the same meanings as in section 4501.01 of the Revised Code.

(PP) "Detention" and "detention facility" have the same meanings as in section 2921.01 of the Revised Code.

(QQ) "Third degree felony OVI offense" means a violation of division (A) of section 4511.19 of the Revised Code that, under division (G) of that section, is a felony of the third degree.

(RR) "Random drug testing" has the same meaning as in section 5120.63 of the Revised Code.

(SS) "Felony sex offense" has the same meaning as in section 2967.28 of the Revised Code.

(TT) "Body armor" has the same meaning as in section 2941.1411 of the Revised Code.

(UU) "Electronic monitoring" means monitoring through the use of an electronic monitoring device.

(VV) "Electronic monitoring device" means any of the following:

(1) Any device that can be operated by electrical or battery power and that conforms with all of the following:

(a) The device has a transmitter that can be attached to a person, that will transmit a specified signal to a receiver of the type described in division (VV)(1)(b) of this section if the transmitter is removed from the person, turned off, or altered in any manner without prior court approval in relation to electronic monitoring or without prior approval of the department of rehabilitation and correction in relation to the use of an electronic monitoring device for an inmate on transitional control or otherwise is tampered with, that can transmit continuously and periodically a signal to that receiver when the person is within a specified distance from the receiver, and that can transmit an appropriate signal to that receiver if the person to whom it is attached travels a specified distance from that receiver.

(b) The device has a receiver that can receive continuously the signals transmitted by a transmitter of the type described in division (VV)(1)(a) of this section, can transmit continuously those signals by telephone to a central monitoring computer of the type described in division (VV)(1)(c) of this section, and can transmit continuously an appropriate signal to that central monitoring computer if the receiver is turned off or altered without prior court approval or otherwise tampered with.

(c) The device has a central monitoring computer that can receive continuously the signals transmitted by telephone by a receiver of the type described in division (VV)(1)(b) of this section and can monitor continuously the person to whom an electronic monitoring device of the type described in division (VV)(1)(a) of this section is attached.

(2) Any device that is not a device of the type described in division (VV)(1) of this section and that conforms with all of the following:

(a) The device includes a transmitter and receiver that can monitor and determine the location of a subject person at any time, or at a designated point in time, through the use of a central monitoring computer or through other electronic means.

(b) The device includes a transmitter and receiver that can determine at any time, or at a designated point in time, through the use of a central monitoring computer or other electronic means the fact that the transmitter is turned off or altered in any manner without prior approval of the court in relation to the electronic monitoring or without prior approval of the department of rehabilitation and correction in relation to the use of an electronic monitoring device for an inmate on transitional control or otherwise is tampered with.

(3) Any type of technology that can adequately track or determine the location of a subject person at any time and that is approved by the director of rehabilitation and correction, including, but not limited to, any satellite technology, voice tracking system, or retinal scanning system that is so approved.

(WW) "Non-economic loss" means nonpecuniary harm suffered by a victim of an offense as a result of or related to the commission of the offense, including, but not limited to, pain and suffering; loss of society, consortium, companionship, care, assistance, attention, protection, advice, guidance, counsel, instruction, training, or education; mental anguish; and any other intangible loss.

(XX) "Prosecutor" has the same meaning as in section 2935.01 of the Revised Code.

(WW) [1] "Continuous alcohol monitoring" means the ability to automatically test and periodically transmit alcohol consumption levels and tamper attempts at least every hour, regardless of the location of the person who is being monitored.

(2004 H 163, eff. 9–23–04; 2004 H 52, eff. 6–1–04; 2003 S 57, eff. 1–1–04; 2003 S 5, § 3, eff. 1–1–04; 2003 S 5, § 1, eff. 7–31–03; 2002 H 490, eff. 1–1–04; 2002 S 123, eff. 1–1–04; 2002 H 327, eff. 7–8–02; 2000 S 179, § 3, eff. 1–1–02; 2000 S 222, eff. 3–22–01; 2000 H 349, eff. 9–22–00; 1999 S 22, eff. 5–17–00; 1999 S 107, eff. 3–23–00; 1999 S 9, eff. 3–8–00; 1997 S 111, eff. 3–17–98; 1997 H 378, eff. 3–10–98; 1996 S 166, eff. 10–17–96; 1996 H 180, eff. 1–1–97; 1996 S 269, eff. 7–1–96; 1996 H 480, eff. 10–16–96; 1996 H 445, eff. 9–3–96; 1995 S 2, eff. 7–1–96)

[1] So in original; paragraph designation appears as the result of the harmonization of 2004 H 163 and 2004 H 52.

Note: See also following version of this section, eff. 4–29–05.

2929.01 Definitions (later effective date)

Note: See also preceding version of this section, in effect until 4–29–05.

As used in this chapter:

(A)(1) "Alternative residential facility" means, subject to division (A)(2) of this section, any facility other than an offender's home or residence in which an offender is assigned to live and that satisfies all of the following criteria:

that the offender has been convicted of or pleaded guilty to an offense that may violate the conditions under which the offender's professional license or license or permit to do business in this state was granted or an offense for which the offender's professional license or license or permit to do business in this state may be revoked or suspended.

(X) "Major drug offender" means an offender who is convicted of or pleads guilty to the possession of, sale of, or offer to sell any drug, compound, mixture, preparation, or substance that consists of or contains at least one thousand grams of hashish; at least one hundred grams of crack cocaine; at least one thousand grams of cocaine that is not crack cocaine; at least two thousand five hundred unit doses or two hundred fifty grams of heroin; at least five thousand unit doses of L.S.D. or five hundred grams of L.S.D. in a liquid concentrate, liquid extract, or liquid distillate form; or at least one hundred times the amount of any other schedule I or II controlled substance other than marihuana that is necessary to commit a felony of the third degree pursuant to section 2925.03, 2925.04, 2925.05, or 2925.11 of the Revised Code that is based on the possession of, sale of, or offer to sell the controlled substance.

(Y) "Mandatory prison term" means any of the following:

(1) Subject to division (Y)(2) of this section, the term in prison that must be imposed for the offenses or circumstances set forth in divisions (F)(1) to (8) or (F)(12) to (14) of section 2929.13 and division (D) of section 2929.14 of the Revised Code. Except as provided in sections 2925.02, 2925.03, 2925.04, 2925.05, and 2925.11 of the Revised Code, unless the maximum or another specific term is required under section 2929.14 of the Revised Code, a mandatory prison term described in this division may be any prison term authorized for the level of offense.

(2) The term of sixty or one hundred twenty days in prison that a sentencing court is required to impose for a third or fourth degree felony OVI offense pursuant to division (G)(2) of section 2929.13 and division (G)(1)(d) or (e) of section 4511.19 of the Revised Code or the term of one, two, three, four, or five years in prison that a sentencing court is required to impose pursuant to division (G)(2) of section 2929.13 of the Revised Code.

(3) The term in prison imposed pursuant to section 2971.03 of the Revised Code for the offenses and in the circumstances described in division (F)(11) of section 2929.13 of the Revised Code and that term as modified or terminated pursuant to section 2971.05 of the Revised Code.

(Z) "Monitored time" means a period of time during which an offender continues to be under the control of the sentencing court or parole board, subject to no conditions other than leading a law-abiding life.

(AA) "Offender" means a person who, in this state, is convicted of or pleads guilty to a felony or a misdemeanor.

(BB) "Prison" means a residential facility used for the confinement of convicted felony offenders that is under the control of the department of rehabilitation and correction but does not include a violation sanction center operated under authority of section 2967.141 of the Revised Code.

(CC) "Prison term" includes any of the following sanctions for an offender:

(1) A stated prison term;

(2) A term in a prison shortened by, or with the approval of, the sentencing court pursuant to section 2929.20, 2967.26, 5120.031, 5120.032, or 5120.073 of the Revised Code;

(3) A term in prison extended by bad time imposed pursuant to section 2967.11 of the Revised Code or imposed for a violation of post-release control pursuant to section 2967.28 of the Revised Code.

(DD) "Repeat violent offender" means a person about whom both of the following apply:

(1) The person has been convicted of or has pleaded guilty to, and is being sentenced for committing, for complicity in committing, or for an attempt to commit, aggravated murder, murder, involuntary manslaughter, a felony of the first degree other than one set forth in Chapter 2925. of the Revised Code, a felony of the first degree set forth in Chapter 2925. of the Revised Code that involved an attempt to cause serious physical harm to a person or that resulted in serious physical harm to a person, or a felony of the second degree that involved an attempt to cause serious physical harm to a person or that resulted in serious physical harm to a person.

(2) Either of the following applies:

(a) The person previously was convicted of or pleaded guilty to, and previously served or, at the time of the offense was serving, a prison term for, any of the following:

(i) Aggravated murder, murder, involuntary manslaughter, rape, felonious sexual penetration as it existed under section 2907.12 of the Revised Code prior to September 3, 1996, a felony of the first or second degree that resulted in the death of a person or in physical harm to a person, or complicity in or an attempt to commit any of those offenses;

(ii) An offense under an existing or former law of this state, another state, or the United States that is or was substantially equivalent to an offense listed under division (DD)(2)(a)(i) of this section and that resulted in the death of a person or in physical harm to a person.

(b) The person previously was adjudicated a delinquent child for committing an act that if committed by an adult would have been an offense listed in division (DD)(2)(a)(i) or (ii) of this section, the person was committed to the department of youth services for that delinquent act.

(EE) "Sanction" means any penalty imposed upon an offender who is convicted of or pleads guilty to an offense, as punishment for the offense. "Sanction" includes any sanction imposed pursuant to any provision of sections 2929.14 to 2929.18 or 2929.24 to 2929.28 of the Revised Code.

(FF) "Sentence" means the sanction or combination of sanctions imposed by the sentencing court on an offender who is convicted of or pleads guilty to an offense.

(GG) "Stated prison term" means the prison term, mandatory prison term, or combination of all prison terms and mandatory prison terms imposed by the sentencing court pursuant to section 2929.14 or 2971.03 of the Revised Code. "Stated prison term" includes any credit received by the offender for time spent in jail awaiting trial, sentencing, or transfer to prison for the offense and any time spent under house arrest or house arrest with electronic monitoring imposed after earning credits pursuant to section 2967.193 of the Revised Code.

(HH) "Victim–offender mediation" means a reconciliation or mediation program that involves an offender and the victim of the offense committed by the offender and that includes a meeting in which the offender and the victim may discuss the offense, discuss restitution, and consider other sanctions for the offense.

(II) "Fourth degree felony OVI offense" means a violation of division (A) of section 4511.19 of the Revised Code that, under division (G) of that section, is a felony of the fourth degree.

(JJ) "Mandatory term of local incarceration" means the term of sixty or one hundred twenty days in a jail, a community-based correctional facility, a halfway house, or an alternative residential facility that a sentencing court may impose upon a person who is convicted of or pleads guilty to a fourth degree felony OVI offense pursuant to division (G)(1) of section 2929.13 of the Revised Code and division (G)(1)(d) or (e) of section 4511.19 of the Revised Code.

(KK) "Designated homicide, assault, or kidnapping offense," "violent sex offense," "sexual motivation specification," "sexually the offender pursuant to division (D) of section 2929.03 and section 2929.04 of the Revised Code. If the panel of judges or the trial judge does not determine that the specification of the aggravating circumstance of a prior conviction listed in division (A)(5) of section 2929.04 of the Revised Code is proven beyond a reasonable doubt and the defendant at trial was not convicted of any other specification of an aggravating circumstance listed in division (A) of section 2929.04 of the Revised Code, the panel of judges or the trial judge shall terminate the sentencing hearing and impose a sentence of life imprisonment with parole eligibility after serving twenty years of imprisonment on the offender.

(1981 S 1, eff. 10–19–81)

2929.023 Defendant's age; raising issue; burdens relating to matter

A person charged with aggravated murder and one or more specifications of an aggravating circumstance may, at trial, raise the matter of his age at the time of the alleged commission of the offense and may present evidence at trial that he was not eighteen years of age or older at the time of the alleged commission of the offense. The burdens of raising the matter of age, and of going forward with the evidence relating to the matter of age, are upon the defendant. After a defendant has raised the matter of age at trial, the prosecution shall have the burden of proving, by proof beyond a reasonable doubt, that the defendant was eighteen years of age or older at the time of the alleged commission of the offense.

(1981 S 1, eff. 10–19–81)

2929.024 Indigency; services of investigation; experts; payment

If the court determines that the defendant is indigent and that investigation services, experts, or other services are reasonably necessary for the proper representation of a defendant charged with aggravated murder at trial or at the sentencing hearing, the court shall authorize the defendant's counsel to obtain the necessary services for the defendant, and shall order that payment of the fees and expenses for the necessary services be made in the same manner that payment for appointed counsel is made pursuant to Chapter 120. of the Revised Code. If the court determines that the necessary services had to be obtained prior to court authorization for payment of the fees and expenses for the necessary services, the court may, after the services have been obtained, authorize the defendant's counsel to obtain the necessary services and order that payment of the fees and expenses for the necessary services be made as provided in this section.

(1981 S 1, eff. 10–19–81)

2929.03 Imposing sentence for a capital offense; procedures; proof of relevant factors; alternative sentences

(A) If the indictment or count in the indictment charging aggravated murder does not contain one or more specifications of aggravating circumstances listed in division (A) of section 2929.04 of the Revised Code, then, following a verdict of guilty of the charge of aggravated murder, the trial court shall impose sentence on the offender as follows:

(1) Except as provided in division (A)(2) of this section, the trial court shall impose one of the following sentences on the offender:

(a) Life imprisonment without parole;

(b) Life imprisonment with parole eligibility after serving twenty years of imprisonment;

(c) Life imprisonment with parole eligibility after serving twenty-five full years of imprisonment;

(d) Life imprisonment with parole eligibility after serving thirty full years of imprisonment.

(2) If the offender also is convicted of or pleads guilty to a sexual motivation specification and a sexually violent predator specification that are included in the indictment, count in the indictment, or information that charged the aggravated murder, the trial court shall impose upon the offender a sentence of life imprisonment without parole that shall be served pursuant to section 2971.03 of the Revised Code.

(B) If the indictment or count in the indictment charging aggravated murder contains one or more specifications of aggravating circumstances listed in division (A) of section 2929.04 of the Revised Code, the verdict shall separately state whether the accused is found guilty or not guilty of the principal charge and, if guilty of the principal charge, whether the offender was eighteen years of age or older at the time of the commission of the offense, if the matter of age was raised by the offender pursuant to section 2929.023 of the Revised Code, and whether the offender is guilty or not guilty of each specification. The jury shall be instructed on its duties in this regard. The instruction to the jury shall include an instruction that a specification shall be proved beyond a reasonable doubt in order to support a guilty verdict on the specification, but the instruction shall not mention the penalty that may be the consequence of a guilty or not guilty verdict on any charge or specification.

(C)(1) If the indictment or count in the indictment charging aggravated murder contains one or more specifications of aggravating circumstances listed in division (A) of section 2929.04 of the Revised Code, then, following a verdict of guilty of the charge but not guilty of each of the specifications, and regardless of whether the offender raised the matter of age pursuant to section 2929.023 of the Revised Code, the trial court shall impose sentence on the offender as follows:

(a) Except as provided in division (C)(1)(b) of this section, the trial court shall impose one of the following sentences on the offender:

(i) Life imprisonment without parole;

(ii) Life imprisonment with parole eligibility after serving twenty years of imprisonment;

(iii) Life imprisonment with parole eligibility after serving twenty-five full years of imprisonment;

(iv) Life imprisonment with parole eligibility after serving thirty full years of imprisonment.

(b) If the offender also is convicted of or pleads guilty to a sexual motivation specification and a sexually violent predator specification that are included in the indictment, count in the indictment, or information that charged the aggravated murder, the trial court shall impose upon the offender a sentence of life imprisonment without parole that shall be served pursuant to section 2971.03 of the Revised Code.

(2)(a) If the indictment or count in the indictment contains one or more specifications of aggravating circumstances listed in division (A) of section 2929.04 of the Revised Code and if the offender is found guilty of both the charge and one or more of the specifications, the penalty to be imposed on the offender shall be one of the following:

(i) Except as provided in division (C)(2)(a)(ii) of this section, the penalty to be imposed on the offender shall be death, life imprisonment without parole, life imprisonment with parole eligibility after serving twenty-five full years of imprisonment, or life imprisonment with parole eligibility after serving thirty full years of imprisonment.

(ii) If the offender also is convicted of or pleads guilty to a sexual motivation specification and a sexually violent predator specification that are included in the indictment, count in the indictment, or information that charged the aggravated murder, the penalty to be imposed on the offender shall be death or life imprisonment without parole that shall be served pursuant to section 2971.03 of the Revised Code.

(b) A penalty imposed pursuant to division (C)(2)(a)(i) or (ii) of this section shall be determined pursuant to divisions (D) and (E) of this section and shall be determined by one of the following:

(i) By the panel of three judges that tried the offender upon the offender's waiver of the right to trial by jury;

(ii) By the trial jury and the trial judge, if the offender was tried by jury.

(D)(1) Death may not be imposed as a penalty for aggravated murder if the offender raised the matter of age at trial pursuant to section 2929.023 of the Revised Code and was not found at trial to have been eighteen years of age or older at the time of the commission of the offense. When death may be imposed as a penalty for aggravated murder, the court shall proceed under this division. When death may be imposed as a penalty, the court, upon the request of the defendant, shall require a pre-sentence investigation to be made and, upon the request of the defendant, shall require a mental examination to be made, and shall require reports of the investigation and of any mental examination submitted to the court, pursuant to section 2947.06 of the Revised Code. No statement made or information provided by a defendant in a mental examination or proceeding conducted pursuant to this division shall be disclosed to any person, except as provided in this division, or be used in evidence against the defendant on the issue of guilt in any retrial. A pre-sentence investigation or mental examination shall not be made except upon request of the defendant. Copies of any reports prepared under this division shall be furnished to the court, to the trial jury if the offender was tried by a jury, to the prosecutor, and to the offender or the offender's counsel for use under this division. The court, and the trial jury if the offender was tried by a jury, shall consider any report prepared pursuant to this division and furnished to it and any evidence raised at trial that is relevant to the aggravating circumstances the offender was found guilty of committing or to any factors in mitigation of the imposition of the sentence of death, shall hear testimony and other evidence that is relevant to the nature and circumstances of the aggravating circumstances the offender was found guilty of committing, the mitigating factors set forth in division (B) of section 2929.04 of the Revised Code, and any other factors in mitigation of the imposition of the sentence of death, and shall hear the statement, if any, of the offender, and the arguments, if any, of counsel for the defense and prosecution, that are relevant to the penalty that should be imposed on the offender. The defendant shall be given great latitude in the presentation of evidence of the mitigating factors set forth in division (B) of section 2929.04 of the Revised Code and of any other factors in mitigation of the imposition of the sentence of death. If the offender chooses to make a statement, the offender is subject to cross-examination only if the offender consents to make the statement under oath or affirmation.

The defendant shall have the burden of going forward with the evidence of any factors in mitigation of the imposition of the sentence of death. The prosecution shall have the burden of proving, by proof beyond a reasonable doubt, that the aggravating circumstances the defendant was found guilty of committing are sufficient to outweigh the factors in mitigation of the imposition of the sentence of death.

(2) Upon consideration of the relevant evidence raised at trial, the testimony, other evidence, statement of the offender, arguments of counsel, and, if applicable, the reports submitted pursuant to division (D)(1) of this section, the trial jury, if the offender was tried by a jury, shall determine whether the aggravating circumstances the offender was found guilty of committing are sufficient to outweigh the mitigating factors present in the case. If the trial jury unanimously finds, by proof beyond a reasonable doubt, that the aggravating circumstances the offender was found guilty of committing outweigh the mitigating factors, the trial jury shall recommend to the court that the sentence of death be imposed on the offender. Absent such a finding, the jury shall recommend that the offender be sentenced to one of the following:

(a) Except as provided in division (D)(2)(b) of this section, to life imprisonment without parole, life imprisonment with parole eligibility after serving twenty-five full years of imprisonment, or life imprisonment with parole eligibility after serving thirty full years of imprisonment;

(b) If the offender also is convicted of or pleads guilty to a sexual motivation specification and a sexually violent predator specification that are included in the indictment, count in the indictment, or information that charged the aggravated murder, to life imprisonment without parole.

If the trial jury recommends that the offender be sentenced to life imprisonment without parole, life imprisonment with parole eligibility after serving twenty-five full years of imprisonment, or life imprisonment with parole eligibility after serving thirty full years of imprisonment, the court shall impose the sentence recommended by the jury upon the offender. If the sentence is a sentence of life imprisonment without parole imposed under division (D)(2)(b) of this section, the sentence shall be served pursuant to section 2971.03 of the Revised Code. If the trial jury recommends that the sentence of death be imposed upon the offender, the court shall proceed to impose sentence pursuant to division (D)(3) of this section.

(3) Upon consideration of the relevant evidence raised at trial, the testimony, other evidence, statement of the offender, arguments of counsel, and, if applicable, the reports submitted to the court pursuant to division (D)(1) of this section, if, after receiving pursuant to division (D)(2) of this section the trial jury's recommendation that the sentence of death be imposed, the court finds, by proof beyond a reasonable doubt, or if the panel of three judges unanimously finds, by proof beyond a reasonable doubt, that the aggravating circumstances the offender was found guilty of committing outweigh the mitigating factors, it shall impose sentence of death on the offender. Absent such a finding by the court or panel, the court or the panel shall impose one of the following sentences on the offender:

(a) Except as provided in division (D)(3)(b) of this section, one of the following:

(i) Life imprisonment without parole;

(ii) Life imprisonment with parole eligibility after serving twenty-five full years of imprisonment;

(iii) Life imprisonment with parole eligibility after serving thirty full years of imprisonment.

(b) If the offender also is convicted of or pleads guilty to a sexual motivation specification and a sexually violent predator specification that are included in the indictment, count in the indictment, or information that charged the aggravated murder, life imprisonment without parole that shall be served pursuant to section 2971.03 of the Revised Code.

(E) If the offender raised the matter of age at trial pursuant to section 2929.023 of the Revised Code, was convicted of aggravated murder and one or more specifications of an aggravating circumstance listed in division (A) of section 2929.04 of the Revised Code, and was not found at trial to have been eighteen years of age or older at the time of the commission of the offense, the court or the panel of three judges shall not impose a sentence of death on the offender. Instead, the court or panel shall impose one of the following sentences on the offender:

(1) Except as provided in division (E)(2) of this section, one of the following:

(a) Life imprisonment without parole;

(b) Life imprisonment with parole eligibility after serving twenty-five full years of imprisonment;

(c) Life imprisonment with parole eligibility after serving thirty full years of imprisonment.

(2) If the offender also is convicted of or pleads guilty to a sexual motivation specification and a sexually violent predator specification that are included in the indictment, count in the indictment, or information that charged the aggravated murder, life imprisonment without parole that shall be served pursuant to section 2971.03 of the Revised Code.

(F) The court or the panel of three judges, when it imposes sentence of death, shall state in a separate opinion its specific findings as to the existence of any of the mitigating factors set forth in division (B) of section 2929.04 of the Revised Code, the existence of any other mitigating factors, the aggravating circumstances the offender was found guilty of committing, and the reasons why the aggravating circumstances the offender was found guilty of committing were sufficient to outweigh the mitigating factors. The court or panel, when it imposes life imprisonment under division (D) of this section, shall state in a separate opinion its specific findings of which of the mitigating factors set forth in division (B) of section 2929.04 of the Revised Code it found to exist, what other mitigating factors it found to exist, what aggravating circumstances the offender was found guilty of committing, and why it could not find that these aggravating circumstances were sufficient to outweigh the mitigating factors. For cases in which a sentence of death is imposed for an offense committed before January 1, 1995, the court or panel shall file the opinion required to be prepared by this division with the clerk of the appropriate court of appeals and with the clerk of the supreme court within fifteen days after the court or panel imposes sentence. For cases in which a sentence of death is imposed for an offense committed on or after January 1, 1995, the court or panel shall file the opinion required to be prepared by this division with the clerk of the supreme court within fifteen days after the court or panel imposes sentence. The judgment in a case in which a sentencing hearing is held pursuant to this section is not final until the opinion is filed.

(G)(1) Whenever the court or a panel of three judges imposes a sentence of death for an offense committed before January 1, 1995, the clerk of the court in which the judgment is rendered shall deliver the entire record in the case to the appellate court.

(2) Whenever the court or a panel of three judges imposes a sentence of death for an offense committed on or after January 1, 1995, the clerk of the court in which the judgment is rendered shall deliver the entire record in the case to the supreme court.

(2004 H 184, eff. 3–23–05; 1996 H 180, eff. 1–1–97; 1996 S 269, eff. 7–1–96; 1995 S 2, eff. 7–1–96; 1995 S 4, eff. 9–21–95; 1981 S 1, eff. 10–19–81; 1972 H 511)

2929.04 Criteria for imposing death or imprisonment for a capital offense

(A) Imposition of the death penalty for aggravated murder is precluded unless one or more of the following is specified in the indictment or count in the indictment pursuant to section 2941.14 of the Revised Code and proved beyond a reasonable doubt:

(1) The offense was the assassination of the president of the United States or a person in line of succession to the presidency, the governor or lieutenant governor of this state, the president-elect or vice president-elect of the United States, the governor-elect or lieutenant governor-elect of this state, or a candidate for any of the offices described in this division. For purposes of this division, a person is a candidate if the person has been nominated for election according to law, if the person has filed a petition or petitions according to law to have the person's name placed on the ballot in a primary or general election, or if the person campaigns as a write-in candidate in a primary or general election.

(2) The offense was committed for hire.

(3) The offense was committed for the purpose of escaping detection, apprehension, trial, or punishment for another offense committed by the offender.

(4) The offense was committed while the offender was under detention or while the offender was at large after having broken detention. As used in division (A)(4) of this section, "detention" has the same meaning as in section 2921.01 of the Revised Code, except that detention does not include hospitalization, institutionalization, or confinement in a mental health facility or mental retardation and developmentally disabled facility unless at the time of the commission of the offense either of the following circumstances apply:

(a) The offender was in the facility as a result of being charged with a violation of a section of the Revised Code.

(b) The offender was under detention as a result of being convicted of or pleading guilty to a violation of a section of the Revised Code.

(5) Prior to the offense at bar, the offender was convicted of an offense an essential element of which was the purposeful killing of or attempt to kill another, or the offense at bar was part of a course of conduct involving the purposeful killing of or attempt to kill two or more persons by the offender.

(6) The victim of the offense was a law enforcement officer, as defined in section 2911.01 of the Revised Code, whom the offender had reasonable cause to know or knew to be a law enforcement officer as so defined, and either the victim, at the time of the commission of the offense, was engaged in the victim's duties, or it was the offender's specific purpose to kill a law enforcement officer as so defined.

(7) The offense was committed while the offender was committing, attempting to commit, or fleeing immediately after committing or attempting to commit kidnapping, rape, aggravated arson, aggravated robbery, or aggravated burglary, and either the offender was the principal offender in the commission of the aggravated murder or, if not the principal offender, committed the aggravated murder with prior calculation and design.

(8) The victim of the aggravated murder was a witness to an offense who was purposely killed to prevent the victim's testimony in any criminal proceeding and the aggravated murder was not committed during the commission, attempted commission, or flight immediately after the commission or attempted commission of the offense to which the victim was a witness, or the victim of the aggravated murder was a witness to an offense and was purposely killed in retaliation for the victim's testimony in any criminal proceeding.

(9) The offender, in the commission of the offense, purposefully caused the death of another who was under thirteen years of age at the time of the commission of the offense, and either the offender was the principal offender in the commission of the offense or, if not the principal offender, committed the offense with prior calculation and design.

(10) The offense was committed while the offender was committing, attempting to commit, or fleeing immediately after committing or attempting to commit terrorism.

(B) If one or more of the aggravating circumstances listed in division (A) of this section is specified in the indictment or count in the indictment and proved beyond a reasonable doubt, and if the offender did not raise the matter of age pursuant to section 2929.023 of the Revised Code or if the offender, after raising the matter of age, was found at trial to have been eighteen years of age or older at the time of the commission of the offense, the court, trial jury, or panel of three judges shall consider, and weigh against the aggravating circumstances proved beyond a reasonable doubt, the nature and circumstances of the offense, the

history, character, and background of the offender, and all of the following factors:

(1) Whether the victim of the offense induced or facilitated it;

(2) Whether it is unlikely that the offense would have been committed, but for the fact that the offender was under duress, coercion, or strong provocation;

(3) Whether, at the time of committing the offense, the offender, because of a mental disease or defect, lacked substantial capacity to appreciate the criminality of the offender's conduct or to conform the offender's conduct to the requirements of the law;

(4) The youth of the offender;

(5) The offender's lack of a significant history of prior criminal convictions and delinquency adjudications;

(6) If the offender was a participant in the offense but not the principal offender, the degree of the offender's participation in the offense and the degree of the offender's participation in the acts that led to the death of the victim;

(7) Any other factors that are relevant to the issue of whether the offender should be sentenced to death.

(C) The defendant shall be given great latitude in the presentation of evidence of the factors listed in division (B) of this section and of any other factors in mitigation of the imposition of the sentence of death.

The existence of any of the mitigating factors listed in division (B) of this section does not preclude the imposition of a sentence of death on the offender but shall be weighed pursuant to divisions (D)(2) and (3) of section 2929.03 of the Revised Code by the trial court, trial jury, or the panel of three judges against the aggravating circumstances the offender was found guilty of committing.

(2002 S 184, eff. 5–15–02; 1998 S 193, eff. 12–29–98; 1997 H 151, eff. 9–16–97; 1997 S 32, eff. 8–6–97; 1981 S 1, eff. 10–19–81; 1972 H 511)

2929.05 Appeals; procedures

(A) Whenever sentence of death is imposed pursuant to sections 2929.03 and 2929.04 of the Revised Code, the court of appeals, in a case in which a sentence of death was imposed for an offense committed before January 1, 1995, and the supreme court shall review upon appeal the sentence of death at the same time that they review the other issues in the case. The court of appeals and the supreme court shall review the judgment in the case and the sentence of death imposed by the court or panel of three judges in the same manner that they review other criminal cases, except that they shall review and independently weigh all of the facts and other evidence disclosed in the record in the case and consider the offense and the offender to determine whether the aggravating circumstances the offender was found guilty of committing outweigh the mitigating factors in the case, and whether the sentence of death is appropriate. In determining whether the sentence of death is appropriate, the court of appeals, in a case in which a sentence of death was imposed for an offense committed before January 1, 1995, and the supreme court shall consider whether the sentence is excessive or disproportionate to the penalty imposed in similar cases. They also shall review all of the facts and other evidence to determine if the evidence supports the finding of the aggravating circumstances the trial jury or the panel of three judges found the offender guilty of committing, and shall determine whether the sentencing court properly weighed the aggravating circumstances the offender was found guilty of committing and the mitigating factors. The court of appeals, in a case in which a sentence of death was imposed for an offense committed before January 1, 1995, or the supreme court shall affirm a sentence of death only if the particular court is persuaded from the record that the aggravating circumstances the offender was found guilty of committing outweigh the mitigating factors present in the case and that the sentence of death is the appropriate sentence in the case.

A court of appeals that reviews a case in which the sentence of death is imposed for an offense committed before January 1, 1995, shall file a separate opinion as to its findings in the case with the clerk of the supreme court. The opinion shall be filed within fifteen days after the court issues its opinion and shall contain whatever information is required by the clerk of the supreme court.

(B) The court of appeals, in a case in which a sentence of death was imposed for an offense committed before January 1, 1995, and the supreme court shall give priority over all other cases to the review of judgments in which the sentence of death is imposed and, except as otherwise provided in this section, shall conduct the review in accordance with the Rules of Appellate Procedure.

(C) At any time after a sentence of death is imposed pursuant to section 2929.022 or 2929.03 of the Revised Code, the court of common pleas that sentenced the offender shall vacate the sentence if the offender did not present evidence at trial that the offender was not eighteen years of age or older at the time of the commission of the aggravated murder for which the offender was sentenced and if the offender shows by a preponderance of the evidence that the offender was less than eighteen years of age at the time of the commission of the aggravated murder for which the offender was sentenced. The court is not required to hold a hearing on a motion filed pursuant to this division unless the court finds, based on the motion and any supporting information submitted by the defendant, any information submitted by the prosecuting attorney, and the record in the case, including any previous hearings and orders, probable cause to believe that the defendant was not eighteen years of age or older at the time of the commission of the aggravated murder for which the defendant was sentenced to death.

(1998 S 107, eff. 7–29–98; 1995 S 4, eff. 9–21–95; 1981 S 1, eff. 10–19–81)

2929.06 Resentencing after sentence of death is set aside, nullified, or vacated

(A) If a sentence of death imposed upon an offender is set aside, nullified, or vacated because the court of appeals, in a case in which a sentence of death was imposed for an offense committed before January 1, 1995, or the supreme court, in cases in which the supreme court reviews the sentence upon appeal, could not affirm the sentence of death under the standards imposed by section 2929.05 of the Revised Code, is set aside, nullified, or vacated for the sole reason that the statutory procedure for imposing the sentence of death that is set forth in sections 2929.03 and 2929.04 of the Revised Code is unconstitutional, is set aside, nullified, or vacated pursuant to division (C) of section 2929.05 of the Revised Code, or is set aside, nullified, or vacated because a court has determined that the offender is mentally retarded under standards set forth in decisions of the supreme court of this state or the United States supreme court, the trial court that sentenced the offender shall conduct a hearing to resentence the offender. At the resentencing hearing, the court shall impose upon the offender a sentence of life imprisonment that is determined as specified in this division. The sentences of life imprisonment that are available at the hearing, and from which the court shall impose sentence, shall be the same sentences of life imprisonment that were available under division (D) of section 2929.03 or under section 2909.24 of the Revised Code at the time the offender committed the offense for which the sentence of death was imposed. Nothing in this division regarding the resentencing of an offender shall affect the operation of section 2971.03 of the Revised Code.

(B) Whenever any court of this state or any federal court sets aside, nullifies, or vacates a sentence of death imposed upon an offender because of error that occurred in the sentencing phase of the trial and if division (A) of this section does not apply, the trial court that sentenced the offender shall conduct a new hearing to resentence the offender. If the offender was tried by a jury, the trial court shall impanel a new jury for the hearing. If the offender was tried by a panel of three judges, that panel or, if necessary, a new panel of three judges shall conduct the hearing. At the hearing, the court shall follow the procedure set forth in division (D) of section 2929.03 of the Revised Code in determining whether to impose upon the offender a sentence of death or a sentence of life imprisonment. If, pursuant to that procedure, the court determines that it will impose a sentence of life imprisonment, the sentences of life imprisonment that are available at the hearing, and from which the court shall impose sentence, shall be the same sentences of life imprisonment that were available under division (D) of section 2929.03 or under section 2909.24 of the Revised Code at the time the offender committed the offense for which the sentence of death was imposed.

(C) If a sentence of life imprisonment without parole imposed upon an offender pursuant to section 2929.021 or 2929.03 of the Revised Code is set aside, nullified, or vacated for the sole reason that the statutory procedure for imposing the sentence of life imprisonment without parole that is set forth in sections 2929.03 and 2929.04 of the Revised Code is unconstitutional, the trial court that sentenced the offender shall conduct a hearing to resentence the offender to life imprisonment with parole eligibility after serving twenty-five full years of imprisonment or to life imprisonment with parole eligibility after serving thirty full years of imprisonment.

(D) Nothing in this section limits or restricts the rights of the state to appeal any order setting aside, nullifying, or vacating a conviction or sentence of death, when an appeal of that nature otherwise would be available.

(E) This section, as amended by H.B. 184 of the 125th General Assembly, shall apply to all offenders who have been sentenced to death for an aggravated murder that was committed on or after October 19, 1981, or for terrorism that was committed on or after May 15, 2002. This section, as amended by H.B. 184 of the 125th general assembly, shall apply equally to all such offenders sentenced to death prior to, on, or after the effective date of that act, including offenders who, on the effective date of that act, are challenging their sentence of death and offenders whose sentence of death has been set aside, nullified, or vacated by any court of this state or any federal court but who, as of the effective date of that act, have not yet been resentenced.

(2004 H 184, eff. 3–23–05; 1998 S 107, eff. 7–29–98; 1996 H 180, eff. 1–1–97; 1996 S 258, eff. 10–16–96; 1996 S 269, eff. 7–1–96; 1995 S 2, eff. 7–1–96; 1995 S 4, eff. 9–21–95; 1981 S 1, eff. 10–19–81)

FELONY SENTENCING

2929.11 Overriding purposes of felony sentencing

(A) A court that sentences an offender for a felony shall be guided by the overriding purposes of felony sentencing. The overriding purposes of felony sentencing are to protect the public from future crime by the offender and others and to punish the offender. To achieve those purposes, the sentencing court shall consider the need for incapacitating the offender, deterring the offender and others from future crime, rehabilitating the offender, and making restitution to the victim of the offense, the public, or both.

(B) A sentence imposed for a felony shall be reasonably calculated to achieve the two overriding purposes of felony sentencing set forth in division (A) of this section, commensurate with and not demeaning to the seriousness of the offender's conduct and its impact upon the victim, and consistent with sentences imposed for similar crimes committed by similar offenders.

(C) A court that imposes a sentence upon an offender for a felony shall not base the sentence upon the race, ethnic background, gender, or religion of the offender.

(1995 S 2, eff. 7–1–96)

2929.12 Factors to consider in felony sentencing

(A) Unless otherwise required by section 2929.13 or 2929.14 of the Revised Code, a court that imposes a sentence under this chapter upon an offender for a felony has discretion to determine the most effective way to comply with the purposes and principles of sentencing set forth in section 2929.11 of the Revised Code. In exercising that discretion, the court shall consider the factors set forth in divisions (B) and (C) of this section relating to the seriousness of the conduct and the factors provided in divisions (D) and (E) of this section relating to the likelihood of the offender's recidivism and, in addition, may consider any other factors that are relevant to achieving those purposes and principles of sentencing.

(B) The sentencing court shall consider all of the following that apply regarding the offender, the offense, or the victim, and any other relevant factors, as indicating that the offender's conduct is more serious than conduct normally constituting the offense:

(1) The physical or mental injury suffered by the victim of the offense due to the conduct of the offender was exacerbated because of the physical or mental condition or age of the victim.

(2) The victim of the offense suffered serious physical, psychological, or economic harm as a result of the offense.

(3) The offender held a public office or position of trust in the community, and the offense related to that office or position.

(4) The offender's occupation, elected office, or profession obliged the offender to prevent the offense or bring others committing it to justice.

(5) The offender's professional reputation or occupation, elected office, or profession was used to facilitate the offense or is likely to influence the future conduct of others.

(6) The offender's relationship with the victim facilitated the offense.

(7) The offender committed the offense for hire or as a part of an organized criminal activity.

(8) In committing the offense, the offender was motivated by prejudice based on race, ethnic background, gender, sexual orientation, or religion.

(9) If the offense is a violation of section 2919.25 or a violation of section 2903.11, 2903.12, or 2903.13 of the Revised Code involving a person who was a family or household member at the time of the violation, the offender committed the offense in the vicinity of one or more children who are not victims of the offense, and the offender or the victim of the offense is a parent, guardian, custodian, or person in loco parentis of one or more of those children.

(C) The sentencing court shall consider all of the following that apply regarding the offender, the offense, or the victim, and any other relevant factors, as indicating that the offender's conduct is less serious than conduct normally constituting the offense:

(1) The victim induced or facilitated the offense.

(2) In committing the offense, the offender acted under strong provocation.

(3) In committing the offense, the offender did not cause or expect to cause physical harm to any person or property.

(4) There are substantial grounds to mitigate the offender's conduct, although the grounds are not enough to constitute a defense.

(D) The sentencing court shall consider all of the following that apply regarding the offender, and any other relevant factors, as factors indicating that the offender is likely to commit future crimes:

(1) At the time of committing the offense, the offender was under release from confinement before trial or sentencing, under a sanction imposed pursuant to section 2929.16, 2929.17, or 2929.18 of the Revised Code, or under post-release control pursuant to section 2967.28 or any other provision of the Revised Code for an earlier offense or had been unfavorably terminated from post-release control for a prior offense pursuant to division (B) of section 2967.16 or section 2929.141 of the Revised Code.

(2) The offender previously was adjudicated a delinquent child pursuant to Chapter 2151. of the Revised Code prior to January 1, 2002, or pursuant to Chapter 2152. of the Revised Code, or the offender has a history of criminal convictions.

(3) The offender has not been rehabilitated to a satisfactory degree after previously being adjudicated a delinquent child pursuant to Chapter 2151. of the Revised Code prior to January 1, 2002, or pursuant to Chapter 2152. of the Revised Code, or the offender has not responded favorably to sanctions previously imposed for criminal convictions.

(4) The offender has demonstrated a pattern of drug or alcohol abuse that is related to the offense, and the offender refuses to acknowledge that the offender has demonstrated that pattern, or the offender refuses treatment for the drug or alcohol abuse.

(5) The offender shows no genuine remorse for the offense.

(E) The sentencing court shall consider all of the following that apply regarding the offender, and any other relevant factors, as factors indicating that the offender is not likely to commit future crimes:

(1) Prior to committing the offense, the offender had not been adjudicated a delinquent child.

(2) Prior to committing the offense, the offender had not been convicted of or pleaded guilty to a criminal offense.

(3) Prior to committing the offense, the offender had led a law-abiding life for a significant number of years.

(4) The offense was committed under circumstances not likely to recur.

(5) The offender shows genuine remorse for the offense.

(2002 H 327, eff. 7–8–02; 2000 S 179, § 3, eff. 1–1–02; 1999 S 107, eff. 3–23–00; 1999 S 9, eff. 3–8–00; 1996 S 269, eff. 7–1–96; 1995 S 2, eff. 7–1–96)

2929.13 Sentencing guidelines for various specific offenses and degrees of offenses

Note: See also following version of this section, eff. 4–29–05.

(A) Except as provided in division (E), (F), or (G) of this section and unless a specific sanction is required to be imposed or is precluded from being imposed pursuant to law, a court that imposes a sentence upon an offender for a felony may impose any sanction or combination of sanctions on the offender that are provided in sections 2929.14 to 2929.18 of the Revised Code. The sentence shall not impose an unnecessary burden on state or local government resources.

If the offender is eligible to be sentenced to community control sanctions, the court shall consider the appropriateness of imposing a financial sanction pursuant to section 2929.18 of the Revised Code or a sanction of community service pursuant to section 2929.17 of the Revised Code as the sole sanction for the offense. Except as otherwise provided in this division, if the court is required to impose a mandatory prison term for the offense for which sentence is being imposed, the court also may impose a financial sanction pursuant to section 2929.18 of the Revised Code but may not impose any additional sanction or combination of sanctions under section 2929.16 or 2929.17 of the Revised Code.

If the offender is being sentenced for a fourth degree felony OVI offense or for a third degree felony OVI offense, in addition to the mandatory term of local incarceration or the mandatory prison term required for the offense by division (G)(1) or (2) of this section, the court shall impose upon the offender a mandatory fine in accordance with division (B)(3) of section 2929. 18 of the Revised Code and may impose whichever of the following is applicable:

(1) For a fourth degree felony OVI offense for which sentence is imposed under division (G)(1) of this section, an additional community control sanction or combination of community control sanctions under section 2929.16 or 2929.17 of the Revised Code. If the court imposes upon the offender a community control sanction and the offender violates any condition of the community control sanction, the court may take any action prescribed in division (B) of section 2929.15 of the Revised Code relative to the offender, including imposing a prison term on the offender pursuant to that division.

(2) For a third or fourth degree felony OVI offense for which sentence is imposed under division (G)(2) of this section, an additional prison term as described in division (D)(4) of section 2929.14 of the Revised Code or a community control sanction as described in division (G)(2) of this section.

(B)(1) Except as provided in division (B)(2), (E), (F), or (G) of this section, in sentencing an offender for a felony of the fourth or fifth degree, the sentencing court shall determine whether any of the following apply:

(a) In committing the offense, the offender caused physical harm to a person.

(b) In committing the offense, the offender attempted to cause or made an actual threat of physical harm to a person with a deadly weapon.

(c) In committing the offense, the offender attempted to cause or made an actual threat of physical harm to a person, and the offender previously was convicted of an offense that caused physical harm to a person.

(d) The offender held a public office or position of trust and the offense related to that office or position; the offender's position obliged the offender to prevent the offense or to bring those committing it to justice; or the offender's professional reputation or position facilitated the offense or was likely to influence the future conduct of others.

(e) The offender committed the offense for hire or as part of an organized criminal activity.

(f) The offense is a sex offense that is a fourth or fifth degree felony violation of section 2907.03, 2907.04, 2907.05, 2907.22, 2907.31, 2907.321, 2907.322, 2907.323, or 2907.34 of the Revised Code.

(g) The offender at the time of the offense was serving, or the offender previously had served, a prison term.

(h) The offender committed the offense while under a community control sanction, while on probation, or while released from custody on a bond or personal recognizance.

(i) The offender committed the offense while in possession of a firearm.

(2)(a) If the court makes a finding described in division (B)(1)(a), (b), (c), (d), (e), (f), (g), (h), or (i) of this section and if the court, after considering the factors set forth in section 2929.12 of the Revised Code, finds that a prison term is consistent with the purposes and principles of sentencing set forth in section 2929.11 of the Revised Code and finds that the offender is not amenable to an available community control sanction, the court shall impose a prison term upon the offender.

(b) Except as provided in division (E), (F), or (G) of this section, if the court does not make a finding described in division (B)(1)(a), (b), (c), (d), (e), (f), (g), (h), or (i) of this section and if the court, after considering the factors set forth in section 2929.12 of the Revised Code, finds that a community control sanction or combination of community control sanctions is consistent with the purposes and principles of sentencing set forth in section 2929.11 of the Revised Code, the court shall impose a community control sanction or combination of community control sanctions upon the offender.

(C) Except as provided in division (E), (F), or (G) of this section, in determining whether to impose a prison term as a sanction for a felony of the third degree or a felony drug offense that is a violation of a provision of Chapter 2925. of the Revised Code and that is specified as being subject to this division for purposes of sentencing, the sentencing court shall comply with the purposes and principles of sentencing under section 2929.11 of the Revised Code and with section 2929.12 of the Revised Code.

(D) Except as provided in division (E) or (F) of this section, for a felony of the first or second degree and for a felony drug offense that is a violation of any provision of Chapter 2925., 3719., or 4729. of the Revised Code for which a presumption in favor of a prison term is specified as being applicable, it is presumed that a prison term is necessary in order to comply with the purposes and principles of sentencing under section 2929.11 of the Revised Code. Notwithstanding the presumption established under this division, the sentencing court may impose a community control sanction or a combination of community control sanctions instead of a prison term on an offender for a felony of the first or second degree or for a felony drug offense that is a violation of any provision of Chapter 2925., 3719., or 4729. of the Revised Code for which a presumption in favor of a prison term is specified as being applicable if it makes both of the following findings:

(1) A community control sanction or a combination of community control sanctions would adequately punish the offender and protect the public from future crime, because the applicable factors under section 2929.12 of the Revised Code indicating a lesser likelihood of recidivism outweigh the applicable factors under that section indicating a greater likelihood of recidivism.

(2) A community control sanction or a combination of community control sanctions would not demean the seriousness of the offense, because one or more factors under section 2929.12 of the Revised Code that indicate that the offender's conduct was less serious than conduct normally constituting the offense are applicable, and they outweigh the applicable factors under that section that indicate that the offender's conduct was more serious than conduct normally constituting the offense.

(E)(1) Except as provided in division (F) of this section, for any drug offense that is a violation of any provision of Chapter 2925. of the Revised Code and that is a felony of the third, fourth, or fifth degree, the applicability of a presumption under division (D) of this section in favor of a prison term or of division (B) or (C) of this section in determining whether to impose a prison term for the offense shall be determined as specified in section 2925.02, 2925.03, 2925.04, 2925.05, 2925.06, 2925.11, 2925.13, 2925.22, 2925.23, 2925.36, or 2925.37 of the Revised Code, whichever is applicable regarding the violation.

(2) If an offender who was convicted of or pleaded guilty to a felony violates the conditions of a community control sanction imposed for the offense solely by reason of producing positive results on a drug test, the court, as punishment for the violation of the sanction, shall not order that the offender be imprisoned unless the court determines on the record either of the following:

(a) The offender had been ordered as a sanction for the felony to participate in a drug treatment program, in a drug education program, or in narcotics anonymous or a similar program, and the offender continued to use illegal drugs after a reasonable period of participation in the program.

(b) The imprisonment of the offender for the violation is consistent with the purposes and principles of sentencing set forth in section 2929.11 of the Revised Code.

(F) Notwithstanding divisions (A) to (E) of this section, the court shall impose a prison term or terms under sections 2929.02 to 2929.06, section 2929.14, or section 2971.03 of the Revised Code and except as specifically provided in section 2929.20 or 2967.191 of the Revised Code or when parole is authorized for the offense under section 2967.13 of the Revised Code shall not reduce the terms pursuant to section 2929.20, section 2967.193, or any other provision of Chapter 2967. or Chapter 5120. of the Revised Code for any of the following offenses:

(1) Aggravated murder when death is not imposed or murder;

(2) Any rape, regardless of whether force was involved and regardless of the age of the victim, or an attempt to commit rape if, had the offender completed the rape that was attempted, the offender would have been subject to a sentence of life imprisonment or life imprisonment without parole for the rape;

(3) Gross sexual imposition or sexual battery, if the victim is under thirteen years of age, if the offender previously was convicted of or pleaded guilty to rape, the former offense of felonious sexual penetration, gross sexual imposition, or sexual battery, and if the victim of the previous offense was under thirteen years of age;

(4) A felony violation of section 2903.04, 2903.06, 2903.08, 2903.11, 2903.12, or 2903.13 of the Revised Code if the section requires the imposition of a prison term;

(5) A first, second, or third degree felony drug offense for which section 2925.02, 2925.03, 2925.04, 2925.05, 2925.06, 2925.11, 2925.13, 2925.22, 2925.23, 2925.36, 2925.37, 3719.99, or 4729.99 of the Revised Code, whichever is applicable regarding the violation, requires the imposition of a mandatory prison term;

(6) Any offense that is a first or second degree felony and that is not set forth in division (F)(1), (2), (3), or (4) of this section, if the offender previously was convicted of or pleaded guilty to aggravated murder, murder, any first or second degree felony, or an offense under an existing or former law of this state, another state, or the United States that is or was substantially equivalent to one of those offenses;

(7) Any offense that is a third degree felony and that is listed in division (DD)(1) of section 2929.01 of the Revised Code if the offender previously was convicted of or pleaded guilty to any offense that is listed in division (DD)(2)(a)(i) or (ii) of section 2929.01 of the Revised Code;

(8) Any offense, other than a violation of section 2923.12 of the Revised Code, that is a felony, if the offender had a firearm on or about the offender's person or under the offender's control while committing the felony, with respect to a portion of the sentence imposed pursuant to division (D)(1)(a) of section 2929.14 of the Revised Code for having the firearm;

(9) Any offense of violence that is a felony, if the offender wore or carried body armor while committing the felony offense of violence, with respect to the portion of the sentence imposed pursuant to division (D)(1)(d) of section 2929.14 of the Revised Code for wearing or carrying the body armor;

(10) Corrupt activity in violation of section 2923.32 of the Revised Code when the most serious offense in the pattern of

corrupt activity that is the basis of the offense is a felony of the first degree;

(11) Any sexually violent offense for which the offender also is convicted of or pleads guilty to a sexually violent predator specification that was included in the indictment, count in the indictment, or information charging the sexually violent offense;

(12) A violation of division (A)(1) or (2) of section 2921.36 of the Revised Code, or a violation of division (C) of that section involving an item listed in division (A)(1) or (2) of that section, if the offender is an officer or employee of the department of rehabilitation and correction;

(13) A violation of division (A)(1) or (2) of section 2903.06 of the Revised Code if the victim of the offense is a peace officer, as defined in section 2935.01 of the Revised Code, with respect to the portion of the sentence imposed pursuant to division (D)(5) of section 2929.14 of the Revised Code;

(14) A violation of division (A)(1) or (2) of section 2903.06 of the Revised Code if the offender has been convicted of or pleaded guilty to three or more violations of division (A) or (B) of section 4511.19 of the Revised Code or an equivalent offense, as defined in section 2941.1415 of the Revised Code, or three or more violations of any combination of those divisions and offenses, with respect to the portion of the sentence imposed pursuant to division (D)(6) of section 2929.14 of the Revised Code.

(G) Notwithstanding divisions (A) to (E) of this section, if an offender is being sentenced for a fourth degree felony OVI offense or for a third degree felony OVI offense, the court shall impose upon the offender a mandatory term of local incarceration or a mandatory prison term in accordance with the following:

(1) If the offender is being sentenced for a fourth degree felony OVI offense and if the offender has not been convicted of and has not pleaded guilty to a specification of the type described in section 2941.1413 of the Revised Code, the court may impose upon the offender a mandatory term of local incarceration of sixty days or one hundred twenty days as specified in division (G)(1)(d) of section 4511.19 of the Revised Code. The court shall not reduce the term pursuant to section 2929.20, 2967.193, or any other provision of the Revised Code. The court that imposes a mandatory term of local incarceration under this division shall specify whether the term is to be served in a jail, a community-based correctional facility, a halfway house, or an alternative residential facility, and the offender shall serve the term in the type of facility specified by the court. A mandatory term of local incarceration imposed under division (G)(1) of this section is not subject to extension under section 2967.11 of the Revised Code, to a period of post-release control under section 2967.28 of the Revised Code, or to any other Revised Code provision that pertains to a prison term except as provided in division (A)(1) of this section.

(2) If the offender is being sentenced for a third degree felony OVI offense, or if the offender is being sentenced for a fourth degree felony OVI offense and the court does not impose a mandatory term of local incarceration under division (G)(1) of this section, the court shall impose upon the offender a mandatory prison term of one, two, three, four, or five years if the offender also is convicted of or also pleads guilty to a specification of the type described in section 2941.1413 of the Revised Code or shall impose upon the offender a mandatory prison term of sixty days or one hundred twenty days as specified in division (G)(1)(d) or (e) of section 4511.19 of the Revised Code if the offender has not been convicted of and has not pleaded guilty to a specification of that type. The court shall not reduce the term pursuant to section 2929.20, 2967.193, or any other provision of the Revised Code. The offender shall serve the one-, two-, three-, four-, or five-year mandatory prison term consecutively to and prior to the prison term imposed for the underlying offense and consecutively to any other mandatory prison term imposed in relation to the offense. In no case shall an offender who once has been sentenced to a mandatory term of local incarceration pursuant to division (G)(1) of this section for a fourth degree felony OVI offense be sentenced to another mandatory term of local incarceration under that division for any violation of division (A) of section 4511.19 of the Revised Code. In addition to the mandatory prison term described in division (G)(2) of this section, the court may sentence the offender to a community control sanction under section 2929.16 or 2929.17 of the Revised Code, but the offender shall serve the prison term prior to serving the community control sanction. The department of rehabilitation and correction may place an offender sentenced to a mandatory prison term under this division in an intensive program prison established pursuant to section 5120.033 of the Revised Code if the department gave the sentencing judge prior notice of its intent to place the offender in an intensive program prison established under that section and if the judge did not notify the department that the judge disapproved the placement. Upon the establishment of the initial intensive program prison pursuant to section 5120.033 of the Revised Code that is privately operated and managed by a contractor pursuant to a contract entered into under section 9.06 of the Revised Code, both of the following apply:

(a) The department of rehabilitation and correction shall make a reasonable effort to ensure that a sufficient number of offenders sentenced to a mandatory prison term under this division are placed in the privately operated and managed prison so that the privately operated and managed prison has full occupancy.

(b) Unless the privately operated and managed prison has full occupancy, the department of rehabilitation and correction shall not place any offender sentenced to a mandatory prison term under this division in any intensive program prison established pursuant to section 5120.033 of the Revised Code other than the privately operated and managed prison.

(H) If an offender is being sentenced for a sexually oriented offense committed on or after January 1, 1997, the judge shall require the offender to submit to a DNA specimen collection procedure pursuant to section 2901.07 of the Revised Code if either of the following applies:

(1) The offense was a sexually violent offense, and the offender also was convicted of or pleaded guilty to a sexually violent predator specification that was included in the indictment, count in the indictment, or information charging the sexually violent offense.

(2) The judge imposing sentence for the sexually oriented offense determines pursuant to division (B) of section 2950.09 of the Revised Code that the offender is a sexual predator.

(I) If an offender is being sentenced for a sexually oriented offense that is not a registration-exempt sexually oriented offense or for a child-victim oriented offense committed on or after January 1, 1997, the judge shall include in the sentence a summary of the offender's duties imposed under sections 2950.04, 2950.041, 2950.05, and 2950.06 of the Revised Code and the duration of the duties. The judge shall inform the offender, at the time of sentencing, of those duties and of their duration and, if required under division (A)(2) of section 2950.03 of the Revised Code, shall perform the duties specified in that section.

(J)(1) Except as provided in division (J)(2) of this section, when considering sentencing factors under this section in relation to an offender who is convicted of or pleads guilty to an attempt to commit an offense in violation of section 2923.02 of the Revised Code, the sentencing court shall consider the factors applicable to the felony category of the violation of section 2923.02 of the Revised Code instead of the factors applicable to the felony category of the offense attempted.

(2) When considering sentencing factors under this section in relation to an offender who is convicted of or pleads guilty to an attempt to commit a drug abuse offense for which the penalty is determined by the amount or number of unit doses of the controlled substance involved in the drug abuse offense, the

sentencing court shall consider the factors applicable to the felony category that the drug abuse offense attempted would be if that drug abuse offense had been committed and had involved an amount or number of unit doses of the controlled substance that is within the next lower range of controlled substance amounts than was involved in the attempt.

(K) As used in this section, "drug abuse offense" has the same meaning as in section 2925.01 of the Revised Code.

(2004 H 163, eff. 9–23–04; 2004 H 52, eff. 6–1–04; 2003 S 5, § 3, eff. 1–1–04; 2003 S 5, § 1, eff. 7–31–03; 2002 S 123, eff. 1–1–04; 2002 H 485, eff. 6–13–02; 2002 H 327, eff. 7–8–02; 2000 S 222, eff. 3–22–01; 2000 H 528, eff. 2–13–01; 1999 S 22, eff. 5–17–00; 1999 S 107, eff. 3–23–00; 1999 S 142, eff. 2–3–00; 1998 H 122, eff. 7–29–98; 1998 H 293, eff. 3–17–98; 1997 S 111, eff. 3–17–98; 1997 H 32, eff. 3–10–98; 1996 H 180, eff. 1–1–97; 1996 S 166, eff. 10–17–96; 1996 S 269, eff. 7–1–96; 1996 H 445, eff. 9–3–96; 1995 S 2, eff. 7–1–96)

Note: See also following version of this section, eff. 4–29–05.

2929.13 Sentencing guidelines for various specific offenses and degrees of offenses (later effective date)

Note: See also preceding version of this section, in effect until 4–29–05.

(A) Except as provided in division (E), (F), or (G) of this section and unless a specific sanction is required to be imposed or is precluded from being imposed pursuant to law, a court that imposes a sentence upon an offender for a felony may impose any sanction or combination of sanctions on the offender that are provided in sections 2929.14 to 2929.18 of the Revised Code. The sentence shall not impose an unnecessary burden on state or local government resources.

If the offender is eligible to be sentenced to community control sanctions, the court shall consider the appropriateness of imposing a financial sanction pursuant to section 2929.18 of the Revised Code or a sanction of community service pursuant to section 2929.17 of the Revised Code as the sole sanction for the offense. Except as otherwise provided in this division, if the court is required to impose a mandatory prison term for the offense for which sentence is being imposed, the court also may impose a financial sanction pursuant to section 2929.18 of the Revised Code but may not impose any additional sanction or combination of sanctions under section 2929.16 or 2929.17 of the Revised Code.

If the offender is being sentenced for a fourth degree felony OVI offense or for a third degree felony OVI offense, in addition to the mandatory term of local incarceration or the mandatory prison term required for the offense by division (G)(1) or (2) of this section, the court shall impose upon the offender a mandatory fine in accordance with division (B)(3) of section 2929. 18 of the Revised Code and may impose whichever of the following is applicable:

(1) For a fourth degree felony OVI offense for which sentence is imposed under division (G)(1) of this section, an additional community control sanction or combination of community control sanctions under section 2929.16 or 2929.17 of the Revised Code. If the court imposes upon the offender a community control sanction and the offender violates any condition of the community control sanction, the court may take any action prescribed in division (B) of section 2929.15 of the Revised Code relative to the offender, including imposing a prison term on the offender pursuant to that division.

(2) For a third or fourth degree felony OVI offense for which sentence is imposed under division (G)(2) of this section, an additional prison term as described in division (D)(4) of section 2929.14 of the Revised Code or a community control sanction as described in division (G)(2) of this section.

(B)(1) Except as provided in division (B)(2), (E), (F), or (G) of this section, in sentencing an offender for a felony of the fourth or fifth degree, the sentencing court shall determine whether any of the following apply:

(a) In committing the offense, the offender caused physical harm to a person.

(b) In committing the offense, the offender attempted to cause or made an actual threat of physical harm to a person with a deadly weapon.

(c) In committing the offense, the offender attempted to cause or made an actual threat of physical harm to a person, and the offender previously was convicted of an offense that caused physical harm to a person.

(d) The offender held a public office or position of trust and the offense related to that office or position; the offender's position obliged the offender to prevent the offense or to bring those committing it to justice; or the offender's professional reputation or position facilitated the offense or was likely to influence the future conduct of others.

(e) The offender committed the offense for hire or as part of an organized criminal activity.

(f) The offense is a sex offense that is a fourth or fifth degree felony violation of section 2907.03, 2907.04, 2907.05, 2907.22, 2907.31, 2907.321, 2907.322, 2907.323, or 2907.34 of the Revised Code.

(g) The offender at the time of the offense was serving, or the offender previously had served, a prison term.

(h) The offender committed the offense while under a community control sanction, while on probation, or while released from custody on a bond or personal recognizance.

(i) The offender committed the offense while in possession of a firearm.

(2)(a) If the court makes a finding described in division (B)(1)(a), (b), (c), (d), (e), (f), (g), (h), or (i) of this section and if the court, after considering the factors set forth in section 2929.12 of the Revised Code, finds that a prison term is consistent with the purposes and principles of sentencing set forth in section 2929.11 of the Revised Code and finds that the offender is not amenable to an available community control sanction, the court shall impose a prison term upon the offender.

(b) Except as provided in division (E), (F), or (G) of this section, if the court does not make a finding described in division (B)(1)(a), (b), (c), (d), (e), (f), (g), (h), or (i) of this section and if the court, after considering the factors set forth in section 2929.12 of the Revised Code, finds that a community control sanction or combination of community control sanctions is consistent with the purposes and principles of sentencing set forth in section 2929.11 of the Revised Code, the court shall impose a community control sanction or combination of community control sanctions upon the offender.

(C) Except as provided in division (E), (F), or (G) of this section, in determining whether to impose a prison term as a sanction for a felony of the third degree or a felony drug offense that is a violation of a provision of Chapter 2925. of the Revised Code and that is specified as being subject to this division for purposes of sentencing, the sentencing court shall comply with the purposes and principles of sentencing under section 2929.11 of the Revised Code and with section 2929.12 of the Revised Code.

(D) Except as provided in division (E) or (F) of this section, for a felony of the first or second degree and for a felony drug offense that is a violation of any provision of Chapter 2925., 3719., or 4729. of the Revised Code for which a presumption in favor of a prison term is specified as being applicable, it is presumed that a prison term is necessary in order to comply with the purposes and principles of sentencing under section 2929.11 of the Revised Code. Notwithstanding the presumption established under this division, the sentencing court may impose a community control sanction or a combination of community control sanctions instead of a prison term on an offender for a felony of the first or second degree or for a felony drug offense that is a violation of any provision of Chapter 2925., 3719., or 4729. of the Revised Code for which a presumption in favor of a prison term is specified as being applicable if it makes both of the following findings:

(1) A community control sanction or a combination of community control sanctions would adequately punish the offender and protect the public from future crime, because the applicable factors under section 2929.12 of the Revised Code indicating a lesser likelihood of recidivism outweigh the applicable factors under that section indicating a greater likelihood of recidivism.

(2) A community control sanction or a combination of community control sanctions would not demean the seriousness of the offense, because one or more factors under section 2929.12 of the Revised Code that indicate that the offender's conduct was less serious than conduct normally constituting the offense are applicable, and they outweigh the applicable factors under that section that indicate that the offender's conduct was more serious than conduct normally constituting the offense.

(E)(1) Except as provided in division (F) of this section, for any drug offense that is a violation of any provision of Chapter 2925. of the Revised Code and that is a felony of the third, fourth, or fifth degree, the applicability of a presumption under division (D) of this section in favor of a prison term or of division (B) or (C) of this section in determining whether to impose a prison term for the offense shall be determined as specified in section 2925.02, 2925.03, 2925.04, 2925.05, 2925.06, 2925.11, 2925.13, 2925.22, 2925.23, 2925.36, or 2925.37 of the Revised Code, whichever is applicable regarding the violation.

(2) If an offender who was convicted of or pleaded guilty to a felony violates the conditions of a community control sanction imposed for the offense solely by reason of producing positive results on a drug test, the court, as punishment for the violation of the sanction, shall not order that the offender be imprisoned unless the court determines on the record either of the following:

(a) The offender had been ordered as a sanction for the felony to participate in a drug treatment program, in a drug education program, or in narcotics anonymous or a similar program, and the offender continued to use illegal drugs after a reasonable period of participation in the program.

(b) The imprisonment of the offender for the violation is consistent with the purposes and principles of sentencing set forth in section 2929.11 of the Revised Code.

(F) Notwithstanding divisions (A) to (E) of this section, the court shall impose a prison term or terms under sections 2929.02 to 2929.06, section 2929.14, or section 2971.03 of the Revised Code and except as specifically provided in section 2929.20 or 2967.191 of the Revised Code or when parole is authorized for the offense under section 2967.13 of the Revised Code shall not reduce the terms pursuant to section 2929.20, section 2967.193, or any other provision of Chapter 2967. or Chapter 5120. of the Revised Code for any of the following offenses:

(1) Aggravated murder when death is not imposed or murder;

(2) Any rape, regardless of whether force was involved and regardless of the age of the victim, or an attempt to commit rape if, had the offender completed the rape that was attempted, the offender would have been subject to a sentence of life imprisonment or life imprisonment without parole for the rape;

(3) Gross sexual imposition or sexual battery, if the victim is under thirteen years of age, if the offender previously was convicted of or pleaded guilty to rape, the former offense of felonious sexual penetration, gross sexual imposition, or sexual battery, and if the victim of the previous offense was under thirteen years of age;

(4) A felony violation of section 2903.04, 2903.06, 2903.08, 2903.11, 2903.12, or 2903.13 of the Revised Code if the section requires the imposition of a prison term;

(5) A first, second, or third degree felony drug offense for which section 2925.02, 2925.03, 2925.04, 2925.05, 2925.06, 2925.11, 2925.13, 2925.22, 2925.23, 2925.36, 2925.37, 3719.99, or 4729.99 of the Revised Code, whichever is applicable regarding the violation, requires the imposition of a mandatory prison term;

(6) Any offense that is a first or second degree felony and that is not set forth in division (F)(1), (2), (3), or (4) of this section, if the offender previously was convicted of or pleaded guilty to aggravated murder, murder, any first or second degree felony, or an offense under an existing or former law of this state, another state, or the United States that is or was substantially equivalent to one of those offenses;

(7) Any offense that is a third degree felony and that is listed in division (DD)(1) of section 2929.01 of the Revised Code if the offender previously was convicted of or pleaded guilty to any offense that is listed in division (DD)(2)(a)(i) or (ii) of section 2929.01 of the Revised Code;

(8) Any offense, other than a violation of section 2923.12 of the Revised Code, that is a felony, if the offender had a firearm on or about the offender's person or under the offender's control while committing the felony, with respect to a portion of the sentence imposed pursuant to division (D)(1)(a) of section 2929.14 of the Revised Code for having the firearm;

(9) Any offense of violence that is a felony, if the offender wore or carried body armor while committing the felony offense of violence, with respect to the portion of the sentence imposed pursuant to division (D)(1)(d) of section 2929.14 of the Revised Code for wearing or carrying the body armor;

(10) Corrupt activity in violation of section 2923.32 of the Revised Code when the most serious offense in the pattern of corrupt activity that is the basis of the offense is a felony of the first degree;

(11) Any violent sex offense or designated homicide, assault, or kidnapping offense if, in relation to that offense, the offender is adjudicated a sexually violent predator;

(12) A violation of division (A)(1) or (2) of section 2921.36 of the Revised Code, or a violation of division (C) of that section involving an item listed in division (A)(1) or (2) of that section, if the offender is an officer or employee of the department of rehabilitation and correction;

(13) A violation of division (A)(1) or (2) of section 2903.06 of the Revised Code if the victim of the offense is a peace officer, as defined in section 2935.01 of the Revised Code, with respect to the portion of the sentence imposed pursuant to division (D)(5) of section 2929.14 of the Revised Code;

(14) A violation of division (A)(1) or (2) of section 2903.06 of the Revised Code if the offender has been convicted of or pleaded guilty to three or more violations of division (A) or (B) of section 4511.19 of the Revised Code or an equivalent offense, as defined in section 2941.1415 of the Revised Code, or three or more violations of any combination of those divisions and offenses, with respect to the portion of the sentence imposed pursuant to division (D)(6) of section 2929.14 of the Revised Code.

(G) Notwithstanding divisions (A) to (E) of this section, if an offender is being sentenced for a fourth degree felony OVI offense or for a third degree felony OVI offense, the court shall impose upon the offender a mandatory term of local incarceration or a mandatory prison term in accordance with the following:

(1) If the offender is being sentenced for a fourth degree felony OVI offense and if the offender has not been convicted of

and has not pleaded guilty to a specification of the type described in section 2941.1413 of the Revised Code, the court may impose upon the offender a mandatory term of local incarceration of sixty days or one hundred twenty days as specified in division (G)(1)(d) of section 4511.19 of the Revised Code. The court shall not reduce the term pursuant to section 2929.20, 2967.193, or any other provision of the Revised Code. The court that imposes a mandatory term of local incarceration under this division shall specify whether the term is to be served in a jail, a community-based correctional facility, a halfway house, or an alternative residential facility, and the offender shall serve the term in the type of facility specified by the court. A mandatory term of local incarceration imposed under division (G)(1) of this section is not subject to extension under section 2967.11 of the Revised Code, to a period of post-release control under section 2967.28 of the Revised Code, or to any other Revised Code provision that pertains to a prison term except as provided in division (A)(1) of this section.

(2) If the offender is being sentenced for a third degree felony OVI offense, or if the offender is being sentenced for a fourth degree felony OVI offense and the court does not impose a mandatory term of local incarceration under division (G)(1) of this section, the court shall impose upon the offender a mandatory prison term of one, two, three, four, or five years if the offender also is convicted of or also pleads guilty to a specification of the type described in section 2941.1413 of the Revised Code or shall impose upon the offender a mandatory prison term of sixty days or one hundred twenty days as specified in division (G)(1)(d) or (e) of section 4511.19 of the Revised Code if the offender has not been convicted of and has not pleaded guilty to a specification of that type. The court shall not reduce the term pursuant to section 2929.20, 2967.193, or any other provision of the Revised Code. The offender shall serve the one-, two-, three-, four-, or five-year mandatory prison term consecutively to and prior to the prison term imposed for the underlying offense and consecutively to any other mandatory prison term imposed in relation to the offense. In no case shall an offender who once has been sentenced to a mandatory term of local incarceration pursuant to division (G)(1) of this section for a fourth degree felony OVI offense be sentenced to another mandatory term of local incarceration under that division for any violation of division (A) of section 4511.19 of the Revised Code. In addition to the mandatory prison term described in division (G)(2) of this section, the court may sentence the offender to a community control sanction under section 2929.16 or 2929.17 of the Revised Code, but the offender shall serve the prison term prior to serving the community control sanction. The department of rehabilitation and correction may place an offender sentenced to a mandatory prison term under this division in an intensive program prison established pursuant to section 5120.033 of the Revised Code if the department gave the sentencing judge prior notice of its intent to place the offender in an intensive program prison established under that section and if the judge did not notify the department that the judge disapproved the placement. Upon the establishment of the initial intensive program prison pursuant to section 5120.033 of the Revised Code that is privately operated and managed by a contractor pursuant to a contract entered into under section 9.06 of the Revised Code, both of the following apply:

(a) The department of rehabilitation and correction shall make a reasonable effort to ensure that a sufficient number of offenders sentenced to a mandatory prison term under this division are placed in the privately operated and managed prison so that the privately operated and managed prison has full occupancy.

(b) Unless the privately operated and managed prison has full occupancy, the department of rehabilitation and correction shall not place any offender sentenced to a mandatory prison term under this division in any intensive program prison established pursuant to section 5120.033 of the Revised Code other than the privately operated and managed prison.

(H) If an offender is being sentenced for a sexually oriented offense committed on or after January 1, 1997, the judge shall require the offender to submit to a DNA specimen collection procedure pursuant to section 2901.07 of the Revised Code if either of the following applies:

(1) The offense was a violent sex offense or a designated homicide, assault, or kidnapping offense and, in relation to that offense, the offender was adjudicated a sexually violent predator.

(2) The judge imposing sentence for the sexually oriented offense determines pursuant to division (B) of section 2950.09 of the Revised Code that the offender is a sexual predator.

(I) If an offender is being sentenced for a sexually oriented offense that is not a registration-exempt sexually oriented offense or for a child-victim oriented offense committed on or after January 1, 1997, the judge shall include in the sentence a summary of the offender's duties imposed under sections 2950.04, 2950.041, 2950.05, and 2950.06 of the Revised Code and the duration of the duties. The judge shall inform the offender, at the time of sentencing, of those duties and of their duration and, if required under division (A)(2) of section 2950.03 of the Revised Code, shall perform the duties specified in that section.

(J)(1) Except as provided in division (J)(2) of this section, when considering sentencing factors under this section in relation to an offender who is convicted of or pleads guilty to an attempt to commit an offense in violation of section 2923.02 of the Revised Code, the sentencing court shall consider the factors applicable to the felony category of the violation of section 2923.02 of the Revised Code instead of the factors applicable to the felony category of the offense attempted.

(2) When considering sentencing factors under this section in relation to an offender who is convicted of or pleads guilty to an attempt to commit a drug abuse offense for which the penalty is determined by the amount or number of unit doses of the controlled substance involved in the drug abuse offense, the sentencing court shall consider the factors applicable to the felony category that the drug abuse offense attempted would be if that drug abuse offense had been committed and had involved an amount or number of unit doses of the controlled substance that is within the next lower range of controlled substance amounts than was involved in the attempt.

(K) As used in this section, "drug abuse offense" has the same meaning as in section 2925.01 of the Revised Code.

(2004 H 473, eff. 4–29–05; 2004 H 163, eff. 9–23–04; 2004 H 52, eff. 6–1–04; 2003 S 5, § 3, eff. 1–1–04; 2003 S 5, § 1, eff. 7–31–03; 2002 S 123, eff. 1–1–04; 2002 H 485, eff. 6–13–02; 2002 H 327, eff. 7–8–02; 2000 S 222, eff. 3–22–01; 2000 H 528, eff. 2–13–01; 1999 S 22, eff. 5–17–00; 1999 S 107, eff. 3–23–00; 1999 S 142, eff. 2–3–00; 1998 H 122, eff. 7–29–98; 1998 H 293, eff. 3–17–98; 1997 S 111, eff. 3–17–98; 1997 H 32, eff. 3–10–98; 1996 H 180, eff. 1–1–97; 1996 S 166, eff. 10–17–96; 1996 S 269, eff. 7–1–96; 1996 H 445, eff. 9–3–96; 1995 S 2, eff. 7–1–96)

Note: See also preceding version of this section, in effect until 4–29–05.

2929.14 Prison terms

Note: See also following version of this section, eff. 4–29–05.

(A) Except as provided in division (C), (D)(1), (D)(2), (D)(3), (D)(4), (D)(5), (D)(6), or (G) of this section and except in relation to an offense for which a sentence of death or life imprisonment is to be imposed, if the court imposing a sentence upon an offender for a felony elects or is required to impose a prison term on the offender pursuant to this chapter, the court shall impose a definite prison term that shall be one of the following:

(1) For a felony of the first degree, the prison term shall be three, four, five, six, seven, eight, nine, or ten years.

(2) For a felony of the second degree, the prison term shall be two, three, four, five, six, seven, or eight years.

(3) For a felony of the third degree, the prison term shall be one, two, three, four, or five years.

(4) For a felony of the fourth degree, the prison term shall be six, seven, eight, nine, ten, eleven, twelve, thirteen, fourteen, fifteen, sixteen, seventeen, or eighteen months.

(5) For a felony of the fifth degree, the prison term shall be six, seven, eight, nine, ten, eleven, or twelve months.

(B) Except as provided in division (C), (D)(1), (D)(2), (D)(3), (D)(5), (D)(6), or (G) of this section, in section 2907.02 of the Revised Code, or in Chapter 2925. of the Revised Code, if the court imposing a sentence upon an offender for a felony elects or is required to impose a prison term on the offender, the court shall impose the shortest prison term authorized for the offense pursuant to division (A) of this section, unless one or more of the following applies:

(1) The offender was serving a prison term at the time of the offense, or the offender previously had served a prison term.

(2) The court finds on the record that the shortest prison term will demean the seriousness of the offender's conduct or will not adequately protect the public from future crime by the offender or others.

(C) Except as provided in division (G) of this section or in Chapter 2925. of the Revised Code, the court imposing a sentence upon an offender for a felony may impose the longest prison term authorized for the offense pursuant to division (A) of this section only upon offenders who committed the worst forms of the offense, upon offenders who pose the greatest likelihood of committing future crimes, upon certain major drug offenders under division (D)(3) of this section, and upon certain repeat violent offenders in accordance with division (D)(2) of this section.

(D)(1)(a) Except as provided in division (D)(1)(e) of this section, if an offender who is convicted of or pleads guilty to a felony also is convicted of or pleads guilty to a specification of the type described in section 2941. 141, 2941.144, or 2941.145 of the Revised Code, the court shall impose on the offender one of the following prison terms:

(i) A prison term of six years if the specification is of the type described in section 2941.144 of the Revised Code that charges the offender with having a firearm that is an automatic firearm or that was equipped with a firearm muffler or silencer on or about the offender's person or under the offender's control while committing the felony;

(ii) A prison term of three years if the specification is of the type described in section 2941.145 of the Revised Code that charges the offender with having a firearm on or about the offender's person or under the offender's control while committing the offense and displaying the firearm, brandishing the firearm, indicating that the offender possessed the firearm, or using it to facilitate the offense;

(iii) A prison term of one year if the specification is of the type described in section 2941.141 of the Revised Code that charges the offender with having a firearm on or about the offender's person or under the offender's control while committing the felony.

(b) If a court imposes a prison term on an offender under division (D)(1)(a) of this section, the prison term shall not be reduced pursuant to section 2929.20, section 2967.193, or any other provision of Chapter 2967. or Chapter 5120. of the Revised Code. A court shall not impose more than one prison term on an offender under division (D)(1)(a) of this section for felonies committed as part of the same act or transaction.

(c) Except as provided in division (D)(1)(e) of this section, if an offender who is convicted of or pleads guilty to a violation of section 2923. 161 of the Revised Code or to a felony that includes, as an essential element, purposely or knowingly causing or attempting to cause the death of or physical harm to another, also is convicted of or pleads guilty to a specification of the type described in section 2941.146 of the Revised Code that charges the offender with committing the offense by discharging a firearm from a motor vehicle other than a manufactured home, the court, after imposing a prison term on the offender for the violation of section 2923.161 of the Revised Code or for the other felony offense under division (A), (D)(2), or (D)(3) of this section, shall impose an additional prison term of five years upon the offender that shall not be reduced pursuant to section 2929.20, section 2967.193, or any other provision of Chapter 2967. or Chapter 5120. of the Revised Code. A court shall not impose more than one additional prison term on an offender under division (D)(1)(c) of this section for felonies committed as part of the same act or transaction. If a court imposes an additional prison term on an offender under division (D)(1)(c) of this section relative to an offense, the court also shall impose a prison term under division (D)(1)(a) of this section relative to the same offense, provided the criteria specified in that division for imposing an additional prison term are satisfied relative to the offender and the offense.

(d) If an offender who is convicted of or pleads guilty to an offense of violence that is a felony also is convicted of or pleads guilty to a specification of the type described in section 2941.1411 of the Revised Code that charges the offender with wearing or carrying body armor while committing the felony offense of violence, the court shall impose on the offender a prison term of two years. The prison term so imposed shall not be reduced pursuant to section 2929.20, section 2967.193, or any other provision of Chapter 2967. or Chapter 5120. of the Revised Code. A court shall not impose more than one prison term on an offender under division (D)(1)(d) of this section for felonies committed as part of the same act or transaction. If a court imposes an additional prison term under division (D)(1)(a) or (c) of this section, the court is not precluded from imposing an additional prison term under division (D)(1)(d) of this section.

(e) The court shall not impose any of the prison terms described in division (D)(1)(a) of this section or any of the additional prison terms described in division (D)(1)(c) of this section upon an offender for a violation of section 2923.12 or 2923.123 of the Revised Code. The court shall not impose any of the prison terms described in division (D)(1)(a) of this section or any of the additional prison terms described in division (D)(1)(c) of this section upon an offender for a violation of section 2923.13 of the Revised Code unless all of the following apply:

(i) The offender previously has been convicted of aggravated murder, murder, or any felony of the first or second degree.

(ii) Less than five years have passed since the offender was released from prison or post-release control, whichever is later, for the prior offense.

(f) If an offender is convicted of or pleads guilty to a felony that includes, as an essential element, causing or attempting to cause the death of or physical harm to another and also is convicted of or pleads guilty to a specification of the type described in section 2941.1412 of the Revised Code that charges the offender with committing the offense by discharging a firearm at a peace officer as defined in section 2935.01 of the Revised Code or a corrections officer as defined in section 2941.1412 of the Revised Code, the court, after imposing a prison term on the offender for the felony offense under division (A), (D)(2), or (D)(3) of this section, shall impose an additional prison term of seven years upon the offender that shall not be reduced pursuant to section 2929.20, section 2967.193, or any other provision of Chapter 2967. or Chapter 5120. of the Revised Code. A court shall not impose more than one additional prison term on an offender under division (D)(1)(f) of this section for felonies committed as part of the same act or transaction. If a court imposes an additional prison term on an offender under division (D)(1)(f) of this section relative to an offense, the court shall not impose a prison term under division (D)(1)(a) or (c) of this section relative to the same offense.

(2)(a) If an offender who is convicted of or pleads guilty to a felony also is convicted of or pleads guilty to a specification of the type described in section 2941.149 of the Revised Code that the offender is a repeat violent offender, the court shall impose a prison term from the range of terms authorized for the offense under division (A) of this section that may be the longest term in the range and that shall not be reduced pursuant to section 2929.20, section 2967.193, or any other provision of Chapter 2967. or Chapter 5120. of the Revised Code. If the court finds that the repeat violent offender, in committing the offense, caused any physical harm that carried a substantial risk of death to a person or that involved substantial permanent incapacity or substantial permanent disfigurement of a person, the court shall impose the longest prison term from the range of terms authorized for the offense under division (A) of this section.

(b) If the court imposing a prison term on a repeat violent offender imposes the longest prison term from the range of terms authorized for the offense under division (A) of this section, the court may impose on the offender an additional definite prison term of one, two, three, four, five, six, seven, eight, nine, or ten years if the court finds that both of the following apply with respect to the prison terms imposed on the offender pursuant to division (D)(2)(a) of this section and, if applicable, divisions (D)(1) and (3) of this section:

(i) The terms so imposed are inadequate to punish the offender and protect the public from future crime, because the applicable factors under section 2929.12 of the Revised Code indicating a greater likelihood of recidivism outweigh the applicable factors under that section indicating a lesser likelihood of recidivism.

(ii) The terms so imposed are demeaning to the seriousness of the offense, because one or more of the factors under section 2929.12 of the Revised Code indicating that the offender's conduct is more serious than conduct normally constituting the offense are present, and they outweigh the applicable factors under that section indicating that the offender's conduct is less serious than conduct normally constituting the offense.

(3)(a) Except when an offender commits a violation of section 2903.01 or 2907.02 of the Revised Code and the penalty imposed for the violation is life imprisonment or commits a violation of section 2903.02 of the Revised Code, if the offender commits a violation of section 2925.03 or 2925.11 of the Revised Code and that section classifies the offender as a major drug offender and requires the imposition of a ten-year prison term on the offender, if the offender commits a felony violation of section 2925.02, 2925.04, 2925.05, 2925.36, 3719.07, 3719.08, 3719.16, 3719.161, 4729.37, or 4729.61, division (C) or (D) of section 3719.172, division (C) of section 4729.51, or division (J) of section 4729.54 of the Revised Code that includes the sale, offer to sell, or possession of a schedule I or II controlled substance, with the exception of marihuana, and the court imposing sentence upon the offender finds that the offender is guilty of a specification of the type described in section 2941.1410 of the Revised Code charging that the offender is a major drug offender, if the court imposing sentence upon an offender for a felony finds that the offender is guilty of corrupt activity with the most serious offense in the pattern of corrupt activity being a felony of the first degree, or if the offender is guilty of an attempted violation of section 2907.02 of the Revised Code and, had the offender completed the violation of section 2907.02 of the Revised Code that was attempted, the offender would have been subject to a sentence of life imprisonment or life imprisonment without parole for the violation of section 2907.02 of the Revised Code, the court shall impose upon the offender for the felony violation a ten-year prison term that cannot be reduced pursuant to section 2929.20 or Chapter 2967. or 5120. of the Revised Code.

(b) The court imposing a prison term on an offender under division (D)(3)(a) of this section may impose an additional prison term of one, two, three, four, five, six, seven, eight, nine, or ten years, if the court, with respect to the term imposed under division (D)(3)(a) of this section and, if applicable, divisions (D)(1) and (2) of this section, makes both of the findings set forth in divisions (D)(2)(b)(i) and (ii) of this section.

(4) If the offender is being sentenced for a third or fourth degree felony OVI offense under division (G)(2) of section 2929.13 of the Revised Code, the sentencing court shall impose upon the offender a mandatory prison term in accordance with that division. In addition to the mandatory prison term, if the offender is being sentenced for a fourth degree felony OVI offense, the court, notwithstanding division (A)(4) of this section, may sentence the offender to a definite prison term of not less than six months and not more than thirty months, and if the offender is being sentenced for a third degree felony OVI offense, the sentencing court may sentence the offender to an additional prison term of any duration specified in division (A)(3) of this section. In either case, the additional prison term imposed shall be reduced by the sixty or one hundred twenty days imposed upon the offender as the mandatory prison term. The total of the additional prison term imposed under division (D)(4) of this section plus the sixty or one hundred twenty days imposed as the mandatory prison term shall equal a definite term in the range of six months to thirty months for a fourth degree felony OVI offense and shall equal one of the authorized prison terms specified in division (A)(3) of this section for a third degree felony OVI offense. If the court imposes an additional prison term under division (D)(4) of this section, the offender shall serve the additional prison term after the offender has served the mandatory prison term required for the offense. In addition to the mandatory prison term or mandatory and additional prison term imposed as described in division (D)(4) of this section, the court also may sentence the offender to a community control sanction under section 2929.16 or 2929.17 of the Revised Code, but the offender shall serve all of the prison terms so imposed prior to serving the community control sanction.

If the offender is being sentenced for a fourth degree felony OVI offense under division (G)(1) of section 2929.13 of the Revised Code and the court imposes a mandatory term of local incarceration, the court may impose a prison term as described in division (A)(1) of that section.

(5) If an offender is convicted of or pleads guilty to a violation of division (A)(1) or (2) of section 2903.06 of the Revised Code and also is convicted of or pleads guilty to a specification of the type described in section 2941.1414 of the Revised Code that charges that the victim of the offense is a peace officer, as defined in section 2935.01 of the Revised Code, the court shall impose on the offender a prison term of five years. If a court imposes a prison term on an offender under division (D)(5) of this section, the prison term shall not be reduced pursuant to section 2929.20, section 2967.193, or any other provision of Chapter 2967. or Chapter 5120. of the Revised Code. A court shall not impose more than one prison term on an offender under division (D)(5) of this section for felonies committed as part of the same act.

(6) If an offender is convicted of or pleads guilty to a violation of division (A)(1) or (2) of section 2903.06 of the Revised Code and also is convicted of or pleads guilty to a specification of the type described in section 2941.1415 of the Revised Code that charges that the offender previously has been convicted of or pleaded guilty to three or more violations of division (A) or (B) of section 4511.19 of the Revised Code or an equivalent offense, as defined in section 2941.1415 of the Revised Code, or three or more violations of any combination of those divisions and offenses, the court shall impose on the offender a prison term of three years. If a court imposes a prison term on an offender under division (D)(6) of this section, the prison term shall not be reduced pursuant to section 2929.20, section 2967.193, or any

other provision of Chapter 2967. or Chapter 5120. of the Revised Code. A court shall not impose more than one prison term on an offender under division (D)(6) of this section for felonies committed as part of the same act.

(E)(1)(a) Subject to division (E)(1)(b) of this section, if a mandatory prison term is imposed upon an offender pursuant to division (D)(1)(a) of this section for having a firearm on or about the offender's person or under the offender's control while committing a felony, if a mandatory prison term is imposed upon an offender pursuant to division (D)(1)(c) of this section for committing a felony specified in that division by discharging a firearm from a motor vehicle, or if both types of mandatory prison terms are imposed, the offender shall serve any mandatory prison term imposed under either division consecutively to any other mandatory prison term imposed under either division or under division (D)(1)(d) of this section, consecutively to and prior to any prison term imposed for the underlying felony pursuant to division (A), (D)(2), or (D)(3) of this section or any other section of the Revised Code, and consecutively to any other prison term or mandatory prison term previously or subsequently imposed upon the offender.

(b) If a mandatory prison term is imposed upon an offender pursuant to division (D)(1)(d) of this section for wearing or carrying body armor while committing an offense of violence that is a felony, the offender shall serve the mandatory term so imposed consecutively to any other mandatory prison term imposed under that division or under division (D)(1)(a) or (c) of this section, consecutively to and prior to any prison term imposed for the underlying felony under division (A), (D)(2), or (D)(3) of this section or any other section of the Revised Code, and consecutively to any other prison term or mandatory prison term previously or subsequently imposed upon the offender.

(c) If a mandatory prison term is imposed upon an offender pursuant to division (D)(1)(f) of this section, the offender shall serve the mandatory prison term so imposed consecutively to and prior to any prison term imposed for the underlying felony under division (A), (D)(2), or (D)(3) of this section or any other section of the Revised Code, and consecutively to any other prison term or mandatory prison term previously or subsequently imposed upon the offender.

(2) If an offender who is an inmate in a jail, prison, or other residential detention facility violates section 2917.02, 2917.03, 2921.34, or 2921.35 of the Revised Code, if an offender who is under detention at a detention facility commits a felony violation of section 2923.131 of the Revised Code, or if an offender who is an inmate in a jail, prison, or other residential detention facility or is under detention at a detention facility commits another felony while the offender is an escapee in violation of section 2921.34 of the Revised Code, any prison term imposed upon the offender for one of those violations shall be served by the offender consecutively to the prison term or term of imprisonment the offender was serving when the offender committed that offense and to any other prison term previously or subsequently imposed upon the offender.

(3) If a prison term is imposed for a violation of division (B) of section 2911.01 of the Revised Code, a violation of division (A) of section 2913.02 of the Revised Code in which the stolen property is a firearm or dangerous ordnance, or a felony violation of division (B) of section 2921.331 of the Revised Code, the offender shall serve that prison term consecutively to any other prison term or mandatory prison term previously or subsequently imposed upon the offender.

(4) If multiple prison terms are imposed on an offender for convictions of multiple offenses, the court may require the offender to serve the prison terms consecutively if the court finds that the consecutive service is necessary to protect the public from future crime or to punish the offender and that consecutive sentences are not disproportionate to the seriousness of the offender's conduct and to the danger the offender poses to the public, and if the court also finds any of the following:

(a) The offender committed one or more of the multiple offenses while the offender was awaiting trial or sentencing, was under a sanction imposed pursuant to section 2929.16, 2929.17, or 2929.18 of the Revised Code, or was under post-release control for a prior offense.

(b) At least two of the multiple offenses were committed as part of one or more courses of conduct, and the harm caused by two or more of the multiple offenses so committed was so great or unusual that no single prison term for any of the offenses committed as part of any of the courses of conduct adequately reflects the seriousness of the offender's conduct.

(c) The offender's history of criminal conduct demonstrates that consecutive sentences are necessary to protect the public from future crime by the offender.

(5) If a mandatory prison term is imposed upon an offender pursuant to division (D)(5) or (6) of this section, the offender shall serve the mandatory prison term consecutively to and prior to any prison term imposed for the underlying violation of division (A)(1) or (2) of section 2903.06 of the Revised Code pursuant to division (A) of this section. If a mandatory prison term is imposed upon an offender pursuant to division (D)(5) of this section, and if a mandatory prison term also is imposed upon the offender pursuant to division (D)(6) of this section in relation to the same violation, the offender shall serve the mandatory prison term imposed pursuant to division (D)(5) of this section consecutively to and prior to the mandatory prison term imposed pursuant to division (D)(6) of this section and consecutively to and prior to any prison term imposed for the underlying violation of division (A)(1) or (2) of section 2903.06 of the Revised Code pursuant to division (A) of this section.

(6) When consecutive prison terms are imposed pursuant to division (E)(1), (2), (3), (4), or (5) of this section, the term to be served is the aggregate of all of the terms so imposed.

(F) If a court imposes a prison term of a type described in division (B) of section 2967.28 of the Revised Code, it shall include in the sentence a requirement that the offender be subject to a period of post-release control after the offender's release from imprisonment, in accordance with that division. If a court imposes a prison term of a type described in division (C) of that section, it shall include in the sentence a requirement that the offender be subject to a period of post-release control after the offender's release from imprisonment, in accordance with that division, if the parole board determines that a period of post-release control is necessary.

(G) If a person is convicted of or pleads guilty to a sexually violent offense and also is convicted of or pleads guilty to a sexually violent predator specification that was included in the indictment, count in the indictment, or information charging that offense, the court shall impose sentence upon the offender in accordance with section 2971.03 of the Revised Code, and Chapter 2971. of the Revised Code applies regarding the prison term or term of life imprisonment without parole imposed upon the offender and the service of that term of imprisonment.

(H) If a person who has been convicted of or pleaded guilty to a felony is sentenced to a prison term or term of imprisonment under this section, sections 2929.02 to 2929.06 of the Revised Code, section 2971.03 of the Revised Code, or any other provision of law, section 5120.163 of the Revised Code applies regarding the person while the person is confined in a state correctional institution.

(I) If an offender who is convicted of or pleads guilty to a felony that is an offense of violence also is convicted of or pleads guilty to a specification of the type described in section 2941.142 of the Revised Code that charges the offender with having committed the felony while participating in a criminal gang, the court shall impose upon the offender an additional prison term of one, two, or three years.

(J) If an offender who is convicted of or pleads guilty to aggravated murder, murder, or a felony of the first, second, or third degree that is an offense of violence also is convicted of or pleads guilty to a specification of the type described in section 2941.143 of the Revised Code that charges the offender with having committed the offense in a school safety zone or towards a person in a school safety zone, the court shall impose upon the offender an additional prison term of two years. The offender shall serve the additional two years consecutively to and prior to the prison term imposed for the underlying offense.

(K) At the time of sentencing, the court may recommend the offender for placement in a program of shock incarceration under section 5120.031 of the Revised Code or for placement in an intensive program prison under section 5120.032 of the Revised Code, disapprove placement of the offender in a program of shock incarceration or an intensive program prison of that nature, or make no recommendation on placement of the offender. In no case shall the department of rehabilitation and correction place the offender in a program or prison of that nature unless the department determines as specified in section 5120.031 or 5120.032 of the Revised Code, whichever is applicable, that the offender is eligible for the placement.

If the court disapproves placement of the offender in a program or prison of that nature, the department of rehabilitation and correction shall not place the offender in any program of shock incarceration or intensive program prison.

If the court recommends placement of the offender in a program of shock incarceration or in an intensive program prison, and if the offender is subsequently placed in the recommended program or prison, the department shall notify the court of the placement and shall include with the notice a brief description of the placement.

If the court recommends placement of the offender in a program of shock incarceration or in an intensive program prison and the department does not subsequently place the offender in the recommended program or prison, the department shall send a notice to the court indicating why the offender was not placed in the recommended program or prison.

If the court does not make a recommendation under this division with respect to an offender and if the department determines as specified in section 5120.031 or 5120.032 of the Revised Code, whichever is applicable, that the offender is eligible for placement in a program or prison of that nature, the department shall screen the offender and determine if there is an available program of shock incarceration or an intensive program prison for which the offender is suited. If there is an available program of shock incarceration or an intensive program prison for which the offender is suited, the department shall notify the court of the proposed placement of the offender as specified in section 5120.031 or 5120.032 of the Revised Code and shall include with the notice a brief description of the placement. The court shall have ten days from receipt of the notice to disapprove the placement.

(2004 H 163, eff. 9–23–04; 2004 H 52, eff. 6–1–04; 2004 H 12, § 3, eff. 4–8–04; 2004 H 12, § 1, eff. 4–8–04; 2002 H 130, eff. 4–7–03; 2002 S 123, eff. 1–1–04; 2002 H 485, eff. 6–13–02; 2002 H 327, eff. 7–8–02; 2000 S 222, eff. 3–22–01; 1999 S 22, eff. 5–17–00; 1999 S 107, eff. 3–23–00; 1999 H 29, eff. 10–29–99; 1999 S 1, eff. 8–6–99; 1998 H 2, eff. 1–1–99; 1997 S 111, eff. 3–17–98; 1997 H 32, eff. 3–10–98; 1997 H 151, eff. 9–16–97; 1996 H 180, eff. 1–1–97; 1996 S 166, eff. 10–17–96; 1996 H 154, eff. 10–4–96; 1996 S 269, eff. 7–1–96; 1996 H 445, eff. 9–3–96; 1996 H 88, eff. 9–3–96; 1995 S 2, eff. 7–1–96)

Note: See also following version of this section, eff. 4–29–05.

2929.14 Prison terms (later effective date)

Note: See also preceding version of this section, in effect until 4–29–05.

(A) Except as provided in division (C), (D)(1), (D)(2), (D)(3), (D)(4), (D)(5), (D)(6), or (G) of this section and except in relation to an offense for which a sentence of death or life imprisonment is to be imposed, if the court imposing a sentence upon an offender for a felony elects or is required to impose a prison term on the offender pursuant to this chapter, the court shall impose a definite prison term that shall be one of the following:

(1) For a felony of the first degree, the prison term shall be three, four, five, six, seven, eight, nine, or ten years.

(2) For a felony of the second degree, the prison term shall be two, three, four, five, six, seven, or eight years.

(3) For a felony of the third degree, the prison term shall be one, two, three, four, or five years.

(4) For a felony of the fourth degree, the prison term shall be six, seven, eight, nine, ten, eleven, twelve, thirteen, fourteen, fifteen, sixteen, seventeen, or eighteen months.

(5) For a felony of the fifth degree, the prison term shall be six, seven, eight, nine, ten, eleven, or twelve months.

(B) Except as provided in division (C), (D)(1), (D)(2), (D)(3), (D)(5), (D)(6), or (G) of this section, in section 2907.02 of the Revised Code, or in Chapter 2925. of the Revised Code, if the court imposing a sentence upon an offender for a felony elects or is required to impose a prison term on the offender, the court shall impose the shortest prison term authorized for the offense pursuant to division (A) of this section, unless one or more of the following applies:

(1) The offender was serving a prison term at the time of the offense, or the offender previously had served a prison term.

(2) The court finds on the record that the shortest prison term will demean the seriousness of the offender's conduct or will not adequately protect the public from future crime by the offender or others.

(C) Except as provided in division (G) of this section or in Chapter 2925. of the Revised Code, the court imposing a sentence upon an offender for a felony may impose the longest prison term authorized for the offense pursuant to division (A) of this section only upon offenders who committed the worst forms of the offense, upon offenders who pose the greatest likelihood of committing future crimes, upon certain major drug offenders under division (D)(3) of this section, and upon certain repeat violent offenders in accordance with division (D)(2) of this section.

(D)(1)(a) Except as provided in division (D)(1)(e) of this section, if an offender who is convicted of or pleads guilty to a felony also is convicted of or pleads guilty to a specification of the type described in section 2941. 141, 2941.144, or 2941.145 of the Revised Code, the court shall impose on the offender one of the following prison terms:

(i) A prison term of six years if the specification is of the type described in section 2941.144 of the Revised Code that charges the offender with having a firearm that is an automatic firearm or that was equipped with a firearm muffler or silencer on or about the offender's person or under the offender's control while committing the felony;

(ii) A prison term of three years if the specification is of the type described in section 2941.145 of the Revised Code that charges the offender with having a firearm on or about the offender's person or under the offender's control while committing the offense and displaying the firearm, brandishing the firearm, indicating that the offender possessed the firearm, or using it to facilitate the offense;

(iii) A prison term of one year if the specification is of the type described in section 2941.141 of the Revised Code that charges the offender with having a firearm on or about the offender's person or under the offender's control while committing the felony.

(b) If a court imposes a prison term on an offender under division (D)(1)(a) of this section, the prison term shall not be reduced pursuant to section 2929.20, section 2967.193, or any other provision of Chapter 2967. or Chapter 5120. of the Revised Code. A court shall not impose more than one prison term on an offender under division (D)(1)(a) of this section for felonies committed as part of the same act or transaction.

(c) Except as provided in division (D)(1)(e) of this section, if an offender who is convicted of or pleads guilty to a violation of section 2923. 161 of the Revised Code or to a felony that includes, as an essential element, purposely or knowingly causing or attempting to cause the death of or physical harm to another, also is convicted of or pleads guilty to a specification of the type described in section 2941.146 of the Revised Code that charges the offender with committing the offense by discharging a firearm from a motor vehicle other than a manufactured home, the court, after imposing a prison term on the offender for the violation of section 2923.161 of the Revised Code or for the other felony offense under division (A), (D)(2), or (D)(3) of this section, shall impose an additional prison term of five years upon the offender that shall not be reduced pursuant to section 2929.20, section 2967.193, or any other provision of Chapter 2967. or Chapter 5120. of the Revised Code. A court shall not impose more than one additional prison term on an offender under division (D)(1)(c) of this section for felonies committed as part of the same act or transaction. If a court imposes an additional prison term on an offender under division (D)(1)(c) of this section relative to an offense, the court also shall impose a prison term under division (D)(1)(a) of this section relative to the same offense, provided the criteria specified in that division for imposing an additional prison term are satisfied relative to the offender and the offense.

(d) If an offender who is convicted of or pleads guilty to an offense of violence that is a felony also is convicted of or pleads guilty to a specification of the type described in section 2941.1411 of the Revised Code that charges the offender with wearing or carrying body armor while committing the felony offense of violence, the court shall impose on the offender a prison term of two years. The prison term so imposed shall not be reduced pursuant to section 2929.20, section 2967.193, or any other provision of Chapter 2967. or Chapter 5120. of the Revised Code. A court shall not impose more than one prison term on an offender under division (D)(1)(d) of this section for felonies committed as part of the same act or transaction. If a court imposes an additional prison term under division (D)(1)(a) or (c) of this section, the court is not precluded from imposing an additional prison term under division (D)(1)(d) of this section.

(e) The court shall not impose any of the prison terms described in division (D)(1)(a) of this section or any of the additional prison terms described in division (D)(1)(c) of this section upon an offender for a violation of section 2923.12 or 2923.123 of the Revised Code. The court shall not impose any of the prison terms described in division (D)(1)(a) of this section or any of the additional prison terms described in division (D)(1)(c) of this section upon an offender for a violation of section 2923.13 of the Revised Code unless all of the following apply:

(i) The offender previously has been convicted of aggravated murder, murder, or any felony of the first or second degree.

(ii) Less than five years have passed since the offender was released from prison or post-release control, whichever is later, for the prior offense.

(f) If an offender is convicted of or pleads guilty to a felony that includes, as an essential element, causing or attempting to cause the death of or physical harm to another and also is convicted of or pleads guilty to a specification of the type described in section 2941.1412 of the Revised Code that charges the offender with committing the offense by discharging a firearm at a peace officer as defined in section 2935.01 of the Revised Code or a corrections officer as defined in section 2941.1412 of the Revised Code, the court, after imposing a prison term on the offender for the felony offense under division (A), (D)(2), or (D)(3) of this section, shall impose an additional prison term of seven years upon the offender that shall not be reduced pursuant to section 2929.20, section 2967.193, or any other provision of Chapter 2967. or Chapter 5120. of the Revised Code. A court shall not impose more than one additional prison term on an offender under division (D)(1)(f) of this section for felonies committed as part of the same act or transaction. If a court imposes an additional prison term on an offender under division (D)(1)(f) of this section relative to an offense, the court shall not impose a prison term under division (D)(1)(a) or (c) of this section relative to the same offense.

(2)(a) If an offender who is convicted of or pleads guilty to a felony also is convicted of or pleads guilty to a specification of the type described in section 2941.149 of the Revised Code that the offender is a repeat violent offender, the court shall impose a prison term from the range of terms authorized for the offense under division (A) of this section that may be the longest term in the range and that shall not be reduced pursuant to section 2929.20, section 2967.193, or any other provision of Chapter 2967. or Chapter 5120. of the Revised Code. If the court finds that the repeat violent offender, in committing the offense, caused any physical harm that carried a substantial risk of death to a person or that involved substantial permanent incapacity or substantial permanent disfigurement of a person, the court shall impose the longest prison term from the range of terms authorized for the offense under division (A) of this section

(b) If the court imposing a prison term on a repeat violent offender imposes the longest prison term from the range of terms authorized for the offense under division (A) of this section, the court may impose on the offender an additional definite prison term of one, two, three, four, five, six, seven, eight, nine, or ten years if the court finds that both of the following apply with respect to the prison terms imposed on the offender pursuant to division (D)(2)(a) of this section and, if applicable, divisions (D)(1) and (3) of this section:

(i) The terms so imposed are inadequate to punish the offender and protect the public from future crime, because the applicable factors under section 2929.12 of the Revised Code indicating a greater likelihood of recidivism outweigh the applicable factors under that section indicating a lesser likelihood of recidivism.

(ii) The terms so imposed are demeaning to the seriousness of the offense, because one or more of the factors under section 2929.12 of the Revised Code indicating that the offender's conduct is more serious than conduct normally constituting the offense are present, and they outweigh the applicable factors under that section indicating that the offender's conduct is less serious than conduct normally constituting the offense.

(3)(a) Except when an offender commits a violation of section 2903.01 or 2907.02 of the Revised Code and the penalty imposed for the violation is life imprisonment or commits a violation of section 2903.02 of the Revised Code, if the offender commits a violation of section 2925.03 or 2925.11 of the Revised Code and that section classifies the offender as a major drug offender and requires the imposition of a ten-year prison term on the offender, if the offender commits a felony violation of section 2925.02, 2925.04, 2925.05, 2925.36, 3719.07, 3719.08, 3719.16, 3719.161, 4729.37, or 4729.61, division (C) or (D) of section 3719.172, division (C) of section 4729.51, or division (J) of section 4729.54 of the Revised Code that includes the sale, offer to sell, or possession of a schedule I or II controlled substance, with the exception of marihuana, and the court imposing sentence upon the offender finds that the offender is guilty of a specification of the type described in section 2941.1410 of the Revised Code charging that the offender is a major drug offender, if the court imposing sentence upon an offender for a felony finds that the offender is guilty of corrupt activity with the most serious offense in the pattern of corrupt activity being a felony of the first degree, or if the offender is guilty of an attempted violation of section 2907.02 of the Revised Code and, had the offender completed the violation of section 2907.02 of the Revised Code that was attempted, the offender would have been subject to a sentence of life imprisonment or life imprisonment without parole for the violation of section 2907.02 of the Revised Code, the court shall impose upon the offender for the felony violation a ten-year prison term that cannot be reduced pursuant to section 2929.20 or Chapter 2967. or 5120. of the Revised Code.

(b) The court imposing a prison term on an offender under division (D)(3)(a) of this section may impose an additional prison term of one, two, three, four, five, six, seven, eight, nine, or ten years, if the court, with respect to the term imposed under division (D)(3)(a) of this section and, if applicable, divisions (D)(1) and (2) of this section, makes both of the findings set forth in divisions (D)(2)(b)(i) and (ii) of this section.

(4) If the offender is being sentenced for a third or fourth degree felony OVI offense under division (G)(2) of section 2929.13 of the Revised Code, the sentencing court shall impose upon the offender a mandatory prison term in accordance with that division. In addition to the mandatory prison term, if the offender is being sentenced for a fourth degree felony OVI offense, the court, notwithstanding division (A)(4) of this section, may sentence the offender to a definite prison term of not less than six months and not more than thirty months, and if the offender is being sentenced for a third degree felony OVI offense, the sentencing court may sentence the offender to an additional prison term of any duration specified in division (A)(3) of this section. In either case, the additional prison term imposed shall be reduced by the sixty or one hundred twenty days imposed upon the offender as the mandatory prison term. The total of the additional prison term imposed under division (D)(4) of this section plus the sixty or one hundred twenty days imposed as the mandatory prison term shall equal a definite term in the range of six months to thirty months for a fourth degree felony OVI offense and shall equal one of the authorized prison terms specified in division (A)(3) of this section for a third degree felony OVI offense. If the court imposes an additional prison term under division (D)(4) of this section, the offender shall serve the additional prison term after the offender has served the mandatory prison term required for the offense. In addition to the mandatory prison term or mandatory and additional prison term imposed as described in division (D)(4) of this section, the court also may sentence the offender to a community control sanction under section 2929.16 or 2929.17 of the Revised Code, but the offender shall serve all of the prison terms so imposed prior to serving the community control sanction.

If the offender is being sentenced for a fourth degree felony OVI offense under division (G)(1) of section 2929.13 of the Revised Code and the court imposes a mandatory term of local incarceration, the court may impose a prison term as described in division (A)(1) of that section.

(5) If an offender is convicted of or pleads guilty to a violation of division (A)(1) or (2) of section 2903.06 of the Revised Code and also is convicted of or pleads guilty to a specification of the type described in section 2941.1414 of the Revised Code that charges that the victim of the offense is a peace officer, as defined in section 2935.01 of the Revised Code, the court shall impose on the offender a prison term of five years. If a court imposes a prison term on an offender under division (D)(5) of this section, the prison term shall not be reduced pursuant to section 2929.20, section 2967.193, or any other provision of Chapter 2967. or Chapter 5120. of the Revised Code. A court shall not impose more than one prison term on an offender under division (D)(5) of this section for felonies committed as part of the same act.

(6) If an offender is convicted of or pleads guilty to a violation of division (A)(1) or (2) of section 2903.06 of the Revised Code and also is convicted of or pleads guilty to a specification of the type described in section 2941.1415 of the Revised Code that charges that the offender previously has been convicted of or pleaded guilty to three or more violations of division (A) or (B) of section 4511.19 of the Revised Code or an equivalent offense, as defined in section 2941.1415 of the Revised Code, or three or more violations of any combination of those divisions and offenses, the court shall impose on the offender a prison term of three years. If a court imposes a prison term on an offender under division (D)(6) of this section, the prison term shall not be reduced pursuant to section 2929.20, section 2967.193, or any other provision of Chapter 2967. or Chapter 5120. of the Revised Code. A court shall not impose more than one prison term on an offender under division (D)(6) of this section for felonies committed as part of the same act.

(E)(1)(a) Subject to division (E)(1)(b) of this section, if a mandatory prison term is imposed upon an offender pursuant to division (D)(1)(a) of this section for having a firearm on or about the offender's person or under the offender's control while committing a felony, if a mandatory prison term is imposed upon an offender pursuant to division (D)(1)(c) of this section for committing a felony specified in that division by discharging a firearm from a motor vehicle, or if both types of mandatory prison terms are imposed, the offender shall serve any mandatory prison term imposed under either division consecutively to any other mandatory prison term imposed under either division or under division (D)(1)(d) of this section, consecutively to and prior to any prison term imposed for the underlying felony pursuant to division (A), (D)(2), or (D)(3) of this section or any other section of the Revised Code, and consecutively to any other prison term or mandatory prison term previously or subsequently imposed upon the offender.

(b) If a mandatory prison term is imposed upon an offender pursuant to division (D)(1)(d) of this section for wearing or carrying body armor while committing an offense of violence that is a felony, the offender shall serve the mandatory term so imposed consecutively to any other mandatory prison term imposed under that division or under division (D)(1)(a) or (c) of this section, consecutively to and prior to any prison term imposed for the underlying felony under division (A), (D)(2), or (D)(3) of this section or any other section of the Revised Code, and consecutively to any other prison term or mandatory prison term previously or subsequently imposed upon the offender.

(c) If a mandatory prison term is imposed upon an offender pursuant to division (D)(1)(f) of this section, the offender shall serve the mandatory prison term so imposed consecutively to and prior to any prison term imposed for the underlying felony under division (A), (D)(2), or (D)(3) of this section or any other section of the Revised Code, and consecutively to any other prison term or mandatory prison term previously or subsequently imposed upon the offender.

(2) If an offender who is an inmate in a jail, prison, or other residential detention facility violates section 2917.02, 2917.03, 2921.34, or 2921.35 of the Revised Code, if an offender who is under detention at a detention facility commits a felony violation of section 2923.131 of the Revised Code, or if an offender who is an inmate in a jail, prison, or other residential detention facility or is under detention at a detention facility commits another felony while the offender is an escapee in violation of section 2921.34 of the Revised Code, any prison term imposed upon the offender for one of those violations shall be served by the offender consecutively to the prison term or term of imprisonment the offender was serving when the offender committed that offense and to any other prison term previously or subsequently imposed upon the offender.

(3) If a prison term is imposed for a violation of division (B) of section 2911.01 of the Revised Code, a violation of division (A) of section 2913.02 of the Revised Code in which the stolen property is a firearm or dangerous ordnance, or a felony violation

of division (B) of section 2921.331 of the Revised Code, the offender shall serve that prison term consecutively to any other prison term or mandatory prison term previously or subsequently imposed upon the offender.

(4) If multiple prison terms are imposed on an offender for convictions of multiple offenses, the court may require the offender to serve the prison terms consecutively if the court finds that the consecutive service is necessary to protect the public from future crime or to punish the offender and that consecutive sentences are not disproportionate to the seriousness of the offender's conduct and to the danger the offender poses to the public, and if the court also finds any of the following:

(a) The offender committed one or more of the multiple offenses while the offender was awaiting trial or sentencing, was under a sanction imposed pursuant to section 2929.16, 2929.17, or 2929.18 of the Revised Code, or was under post-release control for a prior offense.

(b) At least two of the multiple offenses were committed as part of one or more courses of conduct, and the harm caused by two or more of the multiple offenses so committed was so great or unusual that no single prison term for any of the offenses committed as part of any of the courses of conduct adequately reflects the seriousness of the offender's conduct.

(c) The offender's history of criminal conduct demonstrates that consecutive sentences are necessary to protect the public from future crime by the offender.

(5) If a mandatory prison term is imposed upon an offender pursuant to division (D)(5) or (6) of this section, the offender shall serve the mandatory prison term consecutively to and prior to any prison term imposed for the underlying violation of division (A)(1) or (2) of section 2903.06 of the Revised Code pursuant to division (A) of this section. If a mandatory prison term is imposed upon an offender pursuant to division (D)(5) of this section, and if a mandatory prison term also is imposed upon the offender pursuant to division (D)(6) of this section in relation to the same violation, the offender shall serve the mandatory prison term imposed pursuant to division (D)(5) of this section consecutively to and prior to the mandatory prison term imposed pursuant to division (D)(6) of this section and consecutively to and prior to any prison term imposed for the underlying violation of division (A)(1) or (2) of section 2903.06 of the Revised Code pursuant to division (A) of this section.

(6) When consecutive prison terms are imposed pursuant to division (E)(1), (2), (3), (4), or (5) of this section, the term to be served is the aggregate of all of the terms so imposed.

(F) If a court imposes a prison term of a type described in division (B) of section 2967.28 of the Revised Code, it shall include in the sentence a requirement that the offender be subject to a period of post-release control after the offender's release from imprisonment, in accordance with that division. If a court imposes a prison term of a type described in division (C) of that section, it shall include in the sentence a requirement that the offender be subject to a period of post-release control after the offender's release from imprisonment, in accordance with that division, if the parole board determines that a period of post-release control is necessary.

(G) If a person is convicted of or pleads guilty to a violent sex offense or a designated homicide, assault, or kidnapping offense and, in relation to that offense, the offender is adjudicated a sexually violent predator, the court shall impose sentence upon the offender in accordance with section 2971.03 of the Revised Code, and Chapter 2971. of the Revised Code applies regarding the prison term or term of life imprisonment without parole imposed upon the offender and the service of that term of imprisonment.

(H) If a person who has been convicted of or pleaded guilty to a felony is sentenced to a prison term or term of imprisonment under this section, sections 2929.02 to 2929.06 of the Revised Code, section 2971.03 of the Revised Code, or any other provision of law, section 5120.163 of the Revised Code applies regarding the person while the person is confined in a state correctional institution.

(I) If an offender who is convicted of or pleads guilty to a felony that is an offense of violence also is convicted of or pleads guilty to a specification of the type described in section 2941.142 of the Revised Code that charges the offender with having committed the felony while participating in a criminal gang, the court shall impose upon the offender an additional prison term of one, two, or three years.

(J) If an offender who is convicted of or pleads guilty to aggravated murder, murder, or a felony of the first, second, or third degree that is an offense of violence also is convicted of or pleads guilty to a specification of the type described in section 2941.143 of the Revised Code that charges the offender with having committed the offense in a school safety zone or towards a person in a school safety zone, the court shall impose upon the offender an additional prison term of two years. The offender shall serve the additional two years consecutively to and prior to the prison term imposed for the underlying offense.

(K) At the time of sentencing, the court may recommend the offender for placement in a program of shock incarceration under section 5120.031 of the Revised Code or for placement in an intensive program prison under section 5120.032 of the Revised Code, disapprove placement of the offender in a program of shock incarceration or an intensive program prison of that nature, or make no recommendation on placement of the offender. In no case shall the department of rehabilitation and correction place the offender in a program or prison of that nature unless the department determines as specified in section 5120.031 or 5120.032 of the Revised Code, whichever is applicable, that the offender is eligible for the placement.

If the court disapproves placement of the offender in a program or prison of that nature, the department of rehabilitation and correction shall not place the offender in any program of shock incarceration or intensive program prison.

If the court recommends placement of the offender in a program of shock incarceration or in an intensive program prison, and if the offender is subsequently placed in the recommended program or prison, the department shall notify the court of the placement and shall include with the notice a brief description of the placement.

If the court recommends placement of the offender in a program of shock incarceration or in an intensive program prison and the department does not subsequently place the offender in the recommended program or prison, the department shall send a notice to the court indicating why the offender was not placed in the recommended program or prison.

If the court does not make a recommendation under this division with respect to an offender and if the department determines as specified in section 5120.031 or 5120.032 of the Revised Code, whichever is applicable, that the offender is eligible for placement in a program or prison of that nature, the department shall screen the offender and determine if there is an available program of shock incarceration or an intensive program prison for which the offender is suited. If there is an available program of shock incarceration or an intensive program prison for which the offender is suited, the department shall notify the court of the proposed placement of the offender as specified in section 5120.031 or 5120.032 of the Revised Code and shall include with the notice a brief description of the placement. The court shall have ten days from receipt of the notice to disapprove the placement.

(2004 H 473, eff. 4–29–05; 2004 H 163, eff. 9–23–04; 2004 H 52, eff. 6–1–04; 2004 H 12, § 3, eff. 4–8–04; 2004 H 12, § 1, eff. 4–8–04; 2002 H 130, eff. 4–7–03; 2002 S 123, eff. 1–1–04; 2002 H 485, eff. 6–13–02; 2002 H 327, eff. 7–8–02; 2000 S 222, eff. 3–22–01; 1999 S 22, eff. 5–17–00; 1999 S 107, eff. 3–23–00; 1999 H 29, eff. 10–29–99; 1999 S 1, eff. 8–6–99; 1998 H 2, eff. 1–1–99; 1997 S 111, eff. 3–17–98; 1997 H 32, eff. 3–10–98; 1997 H 151, eff. 9–16–97; 1996 H 180, eff. 1–1–97; 1996 S 166, eff. 10–17–96; 1996 H 154, eff. 10–4–96; 1996 S 269, eff. 7–1–96; 1996 H 445, eff. 9–3–96; 1996 H 88, eff. 9–3–96; 1995 S 2, eff. 7–1–96)

Note: See also preceding version of this section, in effect until 4–29–05.

2929.141 Commission of new offense by parolee or releasee

(A) As used in this section, "person on release" means a "releasee" or "parolee," both as defined in section 2967.01 of the Revised Code.

(B) A person on release who by committing a felony violates any condition of parole, any post-release control sanction, or any conditions described in division (A) of section 2967.131 of the Revised Code that are imposed upon the person may be prosecuted for the new felony. Upon the person's conviction of or plea of guilty to the new felony, the court shall impose sentence for the new felony, the court may terminate the term of post-release control if the person is a releasee and the court may do either or both of the following for a person who is either a releasee or parolee regardless of whether the sentencing court or another court of this state imposed the original prison term for which the person is on parole or is serving a term of post-release control:

(1) In addition to any prison term for the new felony, impose a prison term for the violation. If the person is a releasee, the maximum prison term for the violation shall be the greater of twelve months or the period of post-release control for the earlier felony minus any time the releasee has spent under post-release control for the earlier felony. In all cases, any prison term imposed for the violation shall be reduced by any prison term that is administratively imposed by the parole board or adult parole authority as a post-release control sanction. In all cases, a prison term imposed for the violation shall be served consecutively to any prison term imposed for the new felony. If the person is a releasee, a prison term imposed for the violation, and a prison term imposed for the new felony, shall not count as, or be credited toward, the remaining period of post-release control imposed for the earlier felony.

(2) Impose a sanction under sections 2929.15 to 2929.18 of the Revised Code for the violation that shall be served concurrently or consecutively, as specified by the court, with any community control sanctions for the new felony.

(2002 H 327, eff. 7–8–02)

Ed. Note: RC 2929.141 contains provisions analogous to former RC 2967.28(F)(4), repealed by 2002 H 327, eff. 7–8–02.

2929.15 Community control sanctions

(A)(1) If in sentencing an offender for a felony the court is not required to impose a prison term, a mandatory prison term, or a term of life imprisonment upon the offender, the court may directly impose a sentence that consists of one or more community control sanctions authorized pursuant to section 2929.16, 2929.17, or 2929.18 of the Revised Code. If the court is sentencing an offender for a fourth degree felony OVI offense under division (G)(1) of section 2929.13 of the Revised Code, in addition to the mandatory term of local incarceration imposed under that division and the mandatory fine required by division (B)(3) of section 2929.18 of the Revised Code, the court may impose upon the offender a community control sanction or combination of community control sanctions in accordance with sections 2929.16 and 2929.17 of the Revised Code. If the court is sentencing an offender for a third or fourth degree felony OVI offense under division (G)(2) of section 2929.13 of the Revised Code, in addition to the mandatory prison term or mandatory prison term and additional prison term imposed under that division, the court also may impose upon the offender a community control sanction or combination of community control sanctions under section 2929.16 or 2929.17 of the Revised Code, but the offender shall serve all of the prison terms so imposed prior to serving the community control sanction.

The duration of all community control sanctions imposed upon an offender under this division shall not exceed five years. If the offender absconds or otherwise leaves the jurisdiction of the court in which the offender resides without obtaining permission from the court or the offender's probation officer to leave the jurisdiction of the court, or if the offender is confined in any institution for the commission of any offense while under a community control sanction, the period of the community control sanction ceases to run until the offender is brought before the court for its further action. If the court sentences the offender to one or more nonresidential sanctions under section 2929.17 of the Revised Code, the court shall impose as a condition of the nonresidential sanctions that, during the period of the sanctions, the offender must abide by the law and must not leave the state without the permission of the court or the offender's probation officer. The court may impose any other conditions of release under a community control sanction that the court considers appropriate, including, but not limited to, requiring that the offender not ingest or be injected with a drug of abuse and submit to random drug testing as provided in division (D) of this section to determine whether the offender ingested or was injected with a drug of abuse and requiring that the results of the drug test indicate that the offender did not ingest or was not injected with a drug of abuse.

(2)(a) If a court sentences an offender to any community control sanction or combination of community control sanctions authorized pursuant to section 2929.16, 2929.17, or 2929.18 of the Revised Code, the court shall place the offender under the general control and supervision of a department of probation in the county that serves the court for purposes of reporting to the court a violation of any condition of the sanctions, any condition of release under a community control sanction imposed by the court, a violation of law, or the departure of the offender from this state without the permission of the court or the offender's probation officer. Alternatively, if the offender resides in another county and a county department of probation has been established in that county or that county is served by a multicounty probation department established under section 2301.27 of the Revised Code, the court may request the court of common pleas of that county to receive the offender into the general control and supervision of that county or multicounty department of probation for purposes of reporting to the court a violation of any condition of the sanctions, any condition of release under a community control sanction imposed by the court, a violation of law, or the departure of the offender from this state without the permission of the court or the offender's probation officer, subject to the jurisdiction of the trial judge over and with respect to the person of the offender, and to the rules governing that department of probation.

If there is no department of probation in the county that serves the court, the court shall place the offender, regardless of the offender's county of residence, under the general control and supervision of the adult parole authority for purposes of reporting to the court a violation of any of the sanctions, any condition of release under a community control sanction imposed by the court, a violation of law, or the departure of the offender from this state without the permission of the court or the offender's probation officer.

(b) If the court imposing sentence upon an offender sentences the offender to any community control sanction or combination of community control sanctions authorized pursuant to section 2929.16, 2929.17, or 2929.18 of the Revised Code, and if the offender violates any condition of the sanctions, any condition of release under a community control sanction imposed by the court, violates any law, or departs the state without the permission of the court or the offender's probation officer, the public or private person or entity that operates or administers the sanction or the program or activity that comprises the sanction shall report the violation or departure directly to the sentencing court, or shall report the violation or departure to the county or multicounty department of probation with general control and supervision over the offender under division (A)(2)(a) of this section or the officer of that department who supervises the offender, or, if there is no such department with general control and supervision over the offender under that division, to the adult parole authority. If the public or private person or entity that operates or administers the sanction or the program or activity that comprises the sanction reports the violation or departure to the county or multicounty department of probation or the adult parole authority, the department's or authority's officers may treat the offender as if the offender were on probation and in violation of the probation, and shall report the violation of the condition of the sanction, any condition of release under a community control sanction imposed by the court, the violation of law, or the departure from the state without the required permission to the sentencing court.

(B) If the conditions of a community control sanction are violated or if the offender violates a law or leaves the state without the permission of the court or the offender's probation officer, the sentencing court may impose a longer time under the same sanction if the total time under the sanctions does not exceed the five-year limit specified in division (A) of this section, may impose a more restrictive sanction under section 2929.16, 2929.17, or 2929.18 of the Revised Code, or may impose a prison term on the offender pursuant to section 2929.14 of the Revised Code. The prison term, if any, imposed upon a violator pursuant to this division shall be within the range of prison terms available for the offense for which the sanction that was violated was imposed and shall not exceed the prison term specified in the notice provided to the offender at the sentencing hearing pursuant to division (B)(3) [1] of section 2929.19 of the Revised Code. The court may reduce the longer period of time that the offender is required to spend under the longer sanction, the more restrictive sanction, or a prison term imposed pursuant to this division by the time the offender successfully spent under the sanction that was initially imposed.

(C) If an offender, for a significant period of time, fulfills the conditions of a sanction imposed pursuant to section 2929.16, 2929.17, or 2929.18 of the Revised Code in an exemplary manner, the court may reduce the period of time under the sanction or impose a less restrictive sanction, but the court shall not permit the offender to violate any law or permit the offender to leave the state without the permission of the court or the offender's probation officer.

(D)(1) If a court under division (A)(1) of this section imposes a condition of release under a community control sanction that requires the offender to submit to random drug testing, the department of probation or the adult parole authority that has general control and supervision of the offender under division (A)(2)(a) of this section may cause the offender to submit to random drug testing performed by a laboratory or entity that has entered into a contract with any of the governmental entities or officers authorized to enter into a contract with that laboratory or entity under section 341.26, 753.33, or 5120.63 of the Revised Code.

(2) If no laboratory or entity described in division (D)(1) of this section has entered into a contract as specified in that division, the department of probation or the adult parole authority that has general control and supervision of the offender under division (A)(2)(a) of this section shall cause the offender to submit to random drug testing performed by a reputable public laboratory to determine whether the individual who is the subject of the drug test ingested or was injected with a drug of abuse.

(3) A laboratory or entity that has entered into a contract pursuant to section 341.26, 753.33, or 5120.63 of the Revised Code shall perform the random drug tests under division (D)(1) of this section in accordance with the applicable standards that are included in the terms of that contract. A public laboratory shall perform the random drug tests under division (D)(2) of this section in accordance with the standards set forth in the policies and procedures established by the department of rehabilitation and correction pursuant to section 5120.63 of the Revised Code. An offender who is required under division (A)(1) of this section to submit to random drug testing as a condition of release under a community control sanction and whose test results indicate that the offender ingested or was injected with a drug of abuse shall pay the fee for the drug test if the department of probation or the adult parole authority that has general control and supervision of the offender requires payment of a fee. A laboratory or entity that performs the random drug testing on an offender under division (D)(1) or (2) of this section shall transmit the results of the drug test to the appropriate department of probation or the adult parole authority that has general control and supervision of the offender under division (A)(2)(a) of this section.

(2004 H 163, eff. 9–23–04; 2002 S 123, eff. 1–1–04; 2000 H 349, eff. 9–22–00; 1999 S 22, eff. 5–17–00; 1999 S 107, eff. 3–23–00; 1996 S 166, eff. 10–17–96; 1996 S 269, eff. 7–1–96; 1995 S 2, eff. 7–1–96)

[1] The reference to subsection (B)(3) is held to be a typographical error in *State v Virasaychack*, No. 76782, 2000 WL 1144880 (8th Dist Ct App, Cuyahoga, 8–21–2000), wherein the court states: " [W]e take the extraordinary step of correcting R.C. 2929.15(B) to refer to R.C. 2929.19(B)(5) rather than R.C. 2929.19(B)(3)."

2929.16 Community residential sanctions; testing for contagious diseases

(A) Except as provided in this division, the court imposing a sentence for a felony upon an offender who is not required to serve a mandatory prison term may impose any community residential sanction or combination of community residential sanctions under this section. The court imposing a sentence for a fourth degree felony OVI offense under division (G)(1) or (2) of section 2929.13 of the Revised Code or for a third degree felony OVI offense under division (G)(2) of that section may impose upon the offender, in addition to the mandatory term of local incarceration or mandatory prison term imposed under the applicable division, a community residential sanction or combination of community residential sanctions under this section, and the offender shall serve or satisfy the sanction or combination of sanctions after the offender has served the mandatory term of local incarceration or mandatory prison term required for the offense. Community residential sanctions include, but are not limited to, the following:

(1) A term of up to six months at a community-based correctional facility that serves the county;

(2) Except as otherwise provided in division (A)(3) of this section and subject to division (D) of this section, a term of up to six months in a jail;

(3) If the offender is convicted of a fourth degree felony OVI offense and is sentenced under division (G)(1) of section 2929.13 of the Revised Code, subject to division (D) of this section, a term of up to one year in a jail less the mandatory term of local incarceration of sixty or one hundred twenty consecutive days of imprisonment imposed pursuant to that division;

(4) A term in a halfway house;

(5) A term in an alternative residential facility.

(B) The court that assigns any offender convicted of a felony to a residential sanction under this section may authorize the offender to be released so that the offender may seek or maintain employment, receive education or training, or receive treatment. A release pursuant to this division shall be only for the duration of time that is needed to fulfill the purpose of the release and for travel that reasonably is necessary to fulfill the purposes of the release.

(C) If the court assigns an offender to a county jail that is not a minimum security misdemeanant jail in a county that has established a county jail industry program pursuant to section

5147.30 of the Revised Code, the court shall specify, as part of the sentence, whether the sheriff of that county may consider the offender for participation in the county jail industry program. During the offender's term in the county jail, the court shall retain jurisdiction to modify its specification upon a reassessment of the offender's qualifications for participation in the program.

(D) If a court sentences an offender to a term in jail under division (A)(2) or (3) of this section and if the sentence is imposed for a felony of the fourth or fifth degree that is not an offense of violence, the court may specify that it prefers that the offender serve the term in a minimum security jail established under section 341.34 or 753.21 of the Revised Code. If the court includes a specification of that type in the sentence and if the administrator of the appropriate minimum security jail or the designee of that administrator classifies the offender in accordance with section 341. 34 or 753.21 of the Revised Code as a minimal security risk, the offender shall serve the term in the minimum security jail established under section 341.34 or 753.21 of the Revised Code. Absent a specification of that type and a finding of that type, the offender shall serve the term in a jail other than a minimum security jail established under section 341.34 or 753.21 of the Revised Code.

(E) If a person who has been convicted of or pleaded guilty to a felony is sentenced to a community residential sanction as described in division (A) of this section, at the time of reception and at other times the person in charge of the operation of the community-based correctional facility, jail, halfway house, alternative residential facility, or other place at which the offender will serve the residential sanction determines to be appropriate, the person in charge of the operation of the community-based correctional facility, jail, halfway house, alternative residential facility, or other place may cause the convicted offender to be examined and tested for tuberculosis, HIV infection, hepatitis, including but not limited to hepatitis A, B, and C, and other contagious diseases. The person in charge of the operation of the community-based correctional facility, jail, halfway house, alternative residential facility, or other place at which the offender will serve the residential sanction may cause a convicted offender in the community-based correctional facility, jail, halfway house, alternative residential facility, or other place who refuses to be tested or treated for tuberculosis, HIV infection, hepatitis, including but not limited to hepatitis A, B, and C, or another contagious disease to be tested and treated involuntarily.

(2004 H 163, eff. 9–23–04; 2002 S 123, eff. 1–1–04; 1999 S 22, eff. 5–17–00; 1997 S 111, eff. 3–17–98; 1996 H 72, eff. 3–18–97; 1996 S 166, eff. 10–17–96; 1996 H 480, eff. 10–16–96; 1996 S 269, eff. 7–1–96; 1995 S 2, eff. 7–1–96)

2929.17 Nonresidential sanctions

Except as provided in this section, the court imposing a sentence for a felony upon an offender who is not required to serve a mandatory prison term may impose any nonresidential sanction or combination of nonresidential sanctions authorized under this section. If the court imposes one or more nonresidential sanctions authorized under this section, the court shall impose as a condition of the sanction that, during the period of the nonresidential sanction, the offender shall abide by the law and shall not leave the state without the permission of the court or the offender's probation officer.

The court imposing a sentence for a fourth degree felony OVI offense under division (G)(1) or (2) of section 2929.13 of the Revised Code or for a third degree felony OVI offense under division (G)(2) of that section may impose upon the offender, in addition to the mandatory term of local incarceration or mandatory prison term imposed under the applicable division, a nonresidential sanction or combination of nonresidential sanctions under this section, and the offender shall serve or satisfy the sanction or combination of sanctions after the offender has served the mandatory term of local incarceration or mandatory prison term required for the offense. Nonresidential sanctions include, but are not limited to, the following:

(A) A term of day reporting;

(B) A term of house arrest with electronic monitoring or continuous alcohol monitoring or both electronic monitoring and continuous alcohol monitoring, a term of electronic monitoring or continuous alcohol monitoring without house arrest, or a term of house arrest without electronic monitoring or continuous alcohol monitoring;

(C) A term of community service of up to five hundred hours pursuant to division (B) of section 2951.02 of the Revised Code or, if the court determines that the offender is financially incapable of fulfilling a financial sanction described in section 2929.18 of the Revised Code, a term of community service as an alternative to a financial sanction;

(D) A term in a drug treatment program with a level of security for the offender as determined necessary by the court;

(E) A term of intensive probation supervision;

(F) A term of basic probation supervision;

(G) A term of monitored time;

(H) A term of drug and alcohol use monitoring, including random drug testing;

(I) A curfew term;

(J) A requirement that the offender obtain employment;

(K) A requirement that the offender obtain education or training;

(L) Provided the court obtains the prior approval of the victim, a requirement that the offender participate in victim-offender mediation;

(M) A license violation report;

(N) If the offense is a violation of section 2919.25 or a violation of section 2903.11, 2903.12, or 2903.13 of the Revised Code involving a person who was a family or household member at the time of the violation, if the offender committed the offense in the vicinity of one or more children who are not victims of the offense, and if the offender or the victim of the offense is a parent, guardian, custodian, or person in loco parentis of one or more of those children, a requirement that the offender obtain counseling. This division does not limit the court in requiring the offender to obtain counseling for any offense or in any circumstance not specified in this division.

(2004 H 163, eff. 9–23–04; 2002 H 490, eff. 1–1–04; 2002 S 123, eff. 1–1–04; 2000 H 349, eff. 9–22–00; 1999 S 22, eff. 5–17–00; 1999 S 107, eff. 3–23–00; 1999 S 9, eff. 3–8–00; 1996 S 166, eff. 10–17–96; 1996 S 269, eff. 7–1–96; 1995 S 2, eff. 7–1–96)

2929.18 Financial sanctions

(A) Except as otherwise provided in this division and in addition to imposing court costs pursuant to section 2947.23 of the Revised Code, the court imposing a sentence upon an offender for a felony may sentence the offender to any financial sanction or combination of financial sanctions authorized under this section or, in the circumstances specified in section 2929.32 of the Revised Code, may impose upon the offender a fine in accordance with that section. Financial sanctions that may be imposed pursuant to this section include, but are not limited to, the following:

(1) Restitution by the offender to the victim of the offender's crime or any survivor of the victim, in an amount based on the victim's economic loss. If the court imposes restitution, the court shall order that the restitution be made to the victim in open court, to the adult probation department that serves the county on behalf of the victim, to the clerk of courts, or to

another agency designated by the court. If the court imposes restitution, at sentencing, the court shall determine the amount of restitution to be made by the offender. If the court imposes restitution, the court may base the amount of restitution it orders on an amount recommended by the victim, the offender, a presentence investigation report, estimates or receipts indicating the cost of repairing or replacing property, and other information, provided that the amount the court orders as restitution shall not exceed the amount of the economic loss suffered by the victim as a direct and proximate result of the commission of the offense. If the court decides to impose restitution, the court shall hold a hearing on restitution if the offender, victim, or survivor disputes the amount. All restitution payments shall be credited against any recovery of economic loss in a civil action brought by the victim or any survivor of the victim against the offender.

If the court imposes restitution, the court may order that the offender pay a surcharge of not more than five per cent of the amount of the restitution otherwise ordered to the entity responsible for collecting and processing restitution payments.

The victim or survivor may request that the prosecutor in the case file a motion, or the offender may file a motion, for modification of the payment terms of any restitution ordered. If the court grants the motion, it may modify the payment terms as it determines appropriate.

(2) Except as provided in division (B)(1), (3), or (4) of this section, a fine payable by the offender to the state, to a political subdivision, or as described in division (B)(2) of this section to one or more law enforcement agencies, with the amount of the fine based on a standard percentage of the offender's daily income over a period of time determined by the court and based upon the seriousness of the offense. A fine ordered under this division shall not exceed the maximum conventional fine amount authorized for the level of the offense under division (A)(3) of this section.

(3) Except as provided in division (B)(1), (3), or (4) of this section, a fine payable by the offender to the state, to a political subdivision when appropriate for a felony, or as described in division (B)(2) of this section to one or more law enforcement agencies, in the following amount:

(a) For a felony of the first degree, not more than twenty thousand dollars;

(b) For a felony of the second degree, not more than fifteen thousand dollars;

(c) For a felony of the third degree, not more than ten thousand dollars;

(d) For a felony of the fourth degree, not more than five thousand dollars;

(e) For a felony of the fifth degree, not more than two thousand five hundred dollars.

(4) A state fine or costs as defined in section 2949.111 of the Revised Code.

(5)(a) Reimbursement by the offender of any or all of the costs of sanctions incurred by the government, including the following:

(i) All or part of the costs of implementing any community control sanction, including a supervision fee under section 2951.021 of the Revised Code;

(ii) All or part of the costs of confinement under a sanction imposed pursuant to section 2929.14 or 2929.16 of the Revised Code, provided that the amount of reimbursement ordered under this division shall not exceed the total amount of reimbursement the offender is able to pay as determined at a hearing and shall not exceed the actual cost of the confinement.

(b) If the offender is sentenced to a sanction of confinement pursuant to section 2929.14 or 2929.16 of the Revised Code that is to be served in a facility operated by a board of county commissioners, a legislative authority of a municipal corporation, or another local governmental entity, if, pursuant to section 307.93, 341.14, 341.19, 341.23, 753.02, 753.04, 753.16, 2301.56, or 2947.19 of the Revised Code and section 2929.37 of the Revised Code, the board, legislative authority, or other local governmental entity requires prisoners to reimburse the county, municipal corporation, or other entity for its expenses incurred by reason of the prisoner's confinement, and if the court does not impose a financial sanction under division (A)(5)(a)(ii) of this section, confinement costs may be assessed pursuant to section 2929.37 of the Revised Code. In addition, the offender may be required to pay the fees specified in section 2929.38 of the Revised Code in accordance with that section.

(c) Reimbursement by the offender for costs pursuant to section 2929.71 of the Revised Code.

(B)(1) For a first, second, or third degree felony violation of any provision of Chapter 2925., 3719., or 4729. of the Revised Code, the sentencing court shall impose upon the offender a mandatory fine of at least one-half of, but not more than, the maximum statutory fine amount authorized for the level of the offense pursuant to division (A)(3) of this section. If an offender alleges in an affidavit filed with the court prior to sentencing that the offender is indigent and unable to pay the mandatory fine and if the court determines the offender is an indigent person and is unable to pay the mandatory fine described in this division, the court shall not impose the mandatory fine upon the offender.

(2) Any mandatory fine imposed upon an offender under division (B)(1) of this section and any fine imposed upon an offender under division (A)(2) or (3) of this section for any fourth or fifth degree felony violation of any provision of Chapter 2925., 3719., or 4729. of the Revised Code shall be paid to law enforcement agencies pursuant to division (F) of section 2925.03 of the Revised Code.

(3) For a fourth degree felony OVI offense and for a third degree felony OVI offense, the sentencing court shall impose upon the offender a mandatory fine in the amount specified in division (G)(1)(d) or (e) of section 4511.19 of the Revised Code, whichever is applicable. The mandatory fine so imposed shall be disbursed as provided in the division pursuant to which it is imposed.

(4) Notwithstanding any fine otherwise authorized or required to be imposed under division (A)(2) or (3) or (B)(1) of this section or section 2929.31 of the Revised Code for a violation of section 2925.03 of the Revised Code, in addition to any penalty or sanction imposed for that offense under section 2925.03 or sections 2929.11 to 2929.18 of the Revised Code and in addition to the forfeiture of property in connection with the offense as prescribed in sections 2925.42 to 2925.45 of the Revised Code, the court that sentences an offender for a violation of section 2925.03 of the Revised Code may impose upon the offender a fine in addition to any fine imposed under division (A)(2) or (3) of this section and in addition to any mandatory fine imposed under division (B)(1) of this section. The fine imposed under division (B)(4) of this section shall be used as provided in division (H) of section 2925.03 of the Revised Code. A fine imposed under division (B)(4) of this section shall not exceed whichever of the following is applicable:

(a) The total value of any personal or real property in which the offender has an interest and that was used in the course of, intended for use in the course of, derived from, or realized through conduct in violation of section 2925.03 of the Revised Code, including any property that constitutes proceeds derived from that offense;

(b) If the offender has no interest in any property of the type described in division (B)(4)(a) of this section or if it is not possible to ascertain whether the offender has an interest in any property of that type in which the offender may have an interest, the amount of the mandatory fine for the offense imposed under division (B)(1) of this section or, if no mandatory fine is imposed under division (B)(1) of this section, the amount of the fine authorized for the level of the offense imposed under division (A)(3) of this section.

(5) Prior to imposing a fine under division (B)(4) of this section, the court shall determine whether the offender has an interest in any property of the type described in division (B)(4)(a) of this section. Except as provided in division (B)(6) or (7) of this section, a fine that is authorized and imposed under division (B)(4) of this section does not limit or affect the imposition of the penalties and sanctions for a violation of section 2925.03 of the Revised Code prescribed under those sections or sections 2929.11 to 2929.18 of the Revised Code and does not limit or affect a forfeiture of property in connection with the offense as prescribed in sections 2925.42 to 2925.45 of the Revised Code.

(6) If the sum total of a mandatory fine amount imposed for a first, second, or third degree felony violation of section 2925.03 of the Revised Code under division (B)(1) of this section plus the amount of any fine imposed under division (B)(4) of this section does not exceed the maximum statutory fine amount authorized for the level of the offense under division (A)(3) of this section or section 2929.31 of the Revised Code, the court may impose a fine for the offense in addition to the mandatory fine and the fine imposed under division (B)(4) of this section. The sum total of the amounts of the mandatory fine, the fine imposed under division (B)(4) of this section, and the additional fine imposed under division (B)(6) of this section shall not exceed the maximum statutory fine amount authorized for the level of the offense under division (A)(3) of this section or section 2929.31 of the Revised Code. The clerk of the court shall pay any fine that is imposed under division (B)(6) of this section to the county, township, municipal corporation, park district as created pursuant to section 511.18 or 1545.04 of the Revised Code, or state law enforcement agencies in this state that primarily were responsible for or involved in making the arrest of, and in prosecuting, the offender pursuant to division (F) of section 2925.03 of the Revised Code.

(7) If the sum total of the amount of a mandatory fine imposed for a first, second, or third degree felony violation of section 2925.03 of the Revised Code plus the amount of any fine imposed under division (B)(4) of this section exceeds the maximum statutory fine amount authorized for the level of the offense under division (A)(3) of this section or section 2929.31 of the Revised Code, the court shall not impose a fine under division (B)(6) of this section.

(C)(1) The offender shall pay reimbursements imposed upon the offender pursuant to division (A)(5)(a) of this section to pay the costs incurred by the department of rehabilitation and correction in operating a prison or other facility used to confine offenders pursuant to sanctions imposed under section 2929.14 or 2929.16 of the Revised Code to the treasurer of state. The treasurer of state shall deposit the reimbursements in the confinement cost reimbursement fund that is hereby created in the state treasury. The department of rehabilitation and correction shall use the amounts deposited in the fund to fund the operation of facilities used to confine offenders pursuant to sections 2929.14 and 2929.16 of the Revised Code.

(2) Except as provided in section 2951.021 of the Revised Code, the offender shall pay reimbursements imposed upon the offender pursuant to division (A)(5)(a) of this section to pay the costs incurred by a county pursuant to any sanction imposed under this section or section 2929.16 or 2929.17 of the Revised Code or in operating a facility used to confine offenders pursuant to a sanction imposed under section 2929.16 of the Revised Code to the county treasurer. The county treasurer shall deposit the reimbursements in the sanction cost reimbursement fund that each board of county commissioners shall create in its county treasury. The county shall use the amounts deposited in the fund to pay the costs incurred by the county pursuant to any sanction imposed under this section or section 2929.16 or 2929.17 of the Revised Code or in operating a facility used to confine offenders pursuant to a sanction imposed under section 2929.16 of the Revised Code.

(3) Except as provided in section 2951.021 of the Revised Code, the offender shall pay reimbursements imposed upon the offender pursuant to division (A)(5)(a) of this section to pay the costs incurred by a municipal corporation pursuant to any sanction imposed under this section or section 2929.16 or 2929.17 of the Revised Code or in operating a facility used to confine offenders pursuant to a sanction imposed under section 2929.16 of the Revised Code to the treasurer of the municipal corporation. The treasurer shall deposit the reimbursements in a special fund that shall be established in the treasury of each municipal corporation. The municipal corporation shall use the amounts deposited in the fund to pay the costs incurred by the municipal corporation pursuant to any sanction imposed under this section or section 2929.16 or 2929.17 of the Revised Code or in operating a facility used to confine offenders pursuant to a sanction imposed under section 2929.16 of the Revised Code.

(4) Except as provided in section 2951.021 of the Revised Code, the offender shall pay reimbursements imposed pursuant to division (A)(5)(a) of this section for the costs incurred by a private provider pursuant to a sanction imposed under this section or section 2929.16 or 2929.17 of the Revised Code to the provider.

(D) Except as otherwise provided in this division, a financial sanction imposed pursuant to division (A) or (B) of this section is a judgment in favor of the state or a political subdivision in which the court that imposed the financial sanction is located, and the offender subject to the financial sanction is the judgment debtor. A financial sanction of reimbursement imposed pursuant to division (A)(5)(a)(ii) of this section upon an offender who is incarcerated in a state facility or a municipal jail is a judgment in favor of the state or the municipal corporation, and the offender subject to the financial sanction is the judgment debtor. A financial sanction of reimbursement imposed upon an offender pursuant to this section for costs incurred by a private provider of sanctions is a judgment in favor of the private provider, and the offender subject to the financial sanction is the judgment debtor. A financial sanction of restitution imposed pursuant to this section is an order in favor of the victim of the offender's criminal act that can be collected through execution as described in division (D)(1) of this section or through an order as described in division (D)(2) of this section, and the offender shall be considered for purposes of the collection as the judgment debtor. Imposition of a financial sanction and execution on the judgment does not preclude any other power of the court to impose or enforce sanctions on the offender. Once the financial sanction is imposed as a judgment or order under this division, the victim, private provider, state, or political subdivision may bring an action to do any of the following:

(1) Obtain execution of the judgment or order through any available procedure, including:

(a) An execution against the property of the judgment debtor under Chapter 2329. of the Revised Code;

(b) An execution against the person of the judgment debtor under Chapter 2331. of the Revised Code;

(c) A proceeding in aid of execution under Chapter 2333. of the Revised Code, including:

(i) A proceeding for the examination of the judgment debtor under sections 2333.09 to 2333.12 and sections 2333.15 to 2333.27 of the Revised Code;

(ii) A proceeding for attachment of the person of the judgment debtor under section 2333.28 of the Revised Code;

(iii) A creditor's suit under section 2333.01 of the Revised Code.

(d) The attachment of the property of the judgment debtor under Chapter 2715. of the Revised Code;

(e) The garnishment of the property of the judgment debtor under Chapter 2716. of the Revised Code.

(2) Obtain an order for the assignment of wages of the judgment debtor under section 1321.33 of the Revised Code.

(E) A court that imposes a financial sanction upon an offender may hold a hearing if necessary to determine whether the offender is able to pay the sanction or is likely in the future to be able to pay it.

(F) Each court imposing a financial sanction upon an offender under this section or under section 2929.32 of the Revised Code may designate the clerk of the court or another person to collect the financial sanction. The clerk or other person authorized by law or the court to collect the financial sanction may enter into contracts with one or more public agencies or private vendors for the collection of, amounts due under the financial sanction imposed pursuant to this section or section 2929.32 of the Revised Code. Before entering into a contract for the collection of amounts due from an offender pursuant to any financial sanction imposed pursuant to this section or section 2929.32 of the Revised Code, a court shall comply with sections 307.86 to 307.92 of the Revised Code.

(G) If a court that imposes a financial sanction under division (A) or (B) of this section finds that an offender satisfactorily has completed all other sanctions imposed upon the offender and that all restitution that has been ordered has been paid as ordered, the court may suspend any financial sanctions imposed pursuant to this section or section 2929.32 of the Revised Code that have not been paid.

(H) No financial sanction imposed under this section or section 2929.32 of the Revised Code shall preclude a victim from bringing a civil action against the offender.

(2004 H 52, eff. 6–1–04; 2002 H 490, eff. 1–1–04; 2002 S 123, eff. 1–1–04; 2002 H 170, eff. 9–6–02; 2000 H 528, eff. 2–13–01; 1999 S 22, eff. 5–17–00; 1999 S 107, eff. 3–23–00; 1998 H 122, eff. 7–29–98; 1996 S 166, eff. 10–17–96; 1996 H 480, eff. 10–16–96; 1996 S 269, eff. 7–1–96; 1995 S 2, eff. 7–1–96)

2929.19 Sentencing hearing

Note: See also following version of this section, eff. 4–29–05.

(A)(1) The court shall hold a sentencing hearing before imposing a sentence under this chapter upon an offender who was convicted of or pleaded guilty to a felony and before resentencing an offender who was convicted of or pleaded guilty to a felony and whose case was remanded pursuant to section 2953.07 or 2953.08 of the Revised Code. At the hearing, the offender, the prosecuting attorney, the victim or the victim's representative in accordance with section 2930.14 of the Revised Code, and, with the approval of the court, any other person may present information relevant to the imposition of sentence in the case. The court shall inform the offender of the verdict of the jury or finding of the court and ask the offender whether the offender has anything to say as to why sentence should not be imposed upon the offender.

(2) Except as otherwise provided in this division, before imposing sentence on an offender who is being sentenced for a sexually oriented offense that was committed on or after January 1, 1997, that is not a registration-exempt sexually oriented offense, and that is not a sexually violent offense, and before imposing sentence on an offender who is being sentenced for a sexually violent offense committed on or after January 1, 1997, and who was not charged with a sexually violent predator specification in the indictment, count in the indictment, or information charging the sexually violent offense, and before imposing sentence on or after May 7, 2002, on an offender who is being sentenced for a sexually oriented offense that is not a registration-exempt sexually oriented offense and who was acquitted of a sexually violent predator specification included in the indictment, count in the indictment, or information charging the sexually oriented offense, the court shall conduct a hearing in accordance with division (B) of section 2950.09 of the Revised Code to determine whether the offender is a sexual predator. The court shall not conduct a hearing under that division if the offender is being sentenced for a sexually violent offense, if a sexually violent predator specification was included in the indictment, count in the indictment, or information charging the sexually violent offense, and if the offender was convicted of or pleaded guilty to that sexually violent predator specification. Before imposing sentence on an offender who is being sentenced for a sexually oriented offense that is not a registration-exempt sexually oriented offense, the court also shall comply with division (E) of section 2950.09 of the Revised Code.

Before imposing sentence on or after July 31, 2003, on an offender who is being sentenced for a child-victim oriented offense, regardless of when the offense was committed, the court shall conduct a hearing in accordance with division (B) of section 2950.091 of the Revised Code to determine whether the offender is a child-victim predator. Before imposing sentence on an offender who is being sentenced for a child-victim oriented offense, the court also shall comply with division (E) of section 2950.091 of the Revised Code.

(B)(1) At the sentencing hearing, the court, before imposing sentence, shall consider the record, any information presented at the hearing by any person pursuant to division (A) of this section, and, if one was prepared, the presentence investigation report made pursuant to section 2951.03 of the Revised Code or Criminal Rule 32.2, and any victim impact statement made pursuant to section 2947.051 of the Revised Code.

(2) The court shall impose a sentence and shall make a finding that gives its reasons for selecting the sentence imposed in any of the following circumstances:

(a) Unless the offense is a sexually violent offense for which the court is required to impose sentence pursuant to division (G) of section 2929.14 of the Revised Code, if it imposes a prison term for a felony of the fourth or fifth degree or for a felony drug offense that is a violation of a provision of Chapter 2925. of the Revised Code and that is specified as being subject to division (B) of section 2929.13 of the Revised Code for purposes of sentencing, its reasons for imposing the prison term, based upon the overriding purposes and principles of felony sentencing set forth in section 2929.11 of the Revised Code, and any factors listed in divisions (B)(1)(a) to (i) of section 2929.13 of the Revised Code that it found to apply relative to the offender.

(b) If it does not impose a prison term for a felony of the first or second degree or for a felony drug offense that is a violation of a provision of Chapter 2925. of the Revised Code and for which a presumption in favor of a prison term is specified as being applicable, its reasons for not imposing the prison term and for overriding the presumption, based upon the overriding purposes and principles of felony sentencing set forth in section 2929.11 of the Revised Code, and the basis of the findings it made under divisions (D)(1) and (2) of section 2929.13 of the Revised Code.

(c) If it imposes consecutive sentences under section 2929.14 of the Revised Code, its reasons for imposing the consecutive sentences;

(d) If the sentence is for one offense and it imposes a prison term for the offense that is the maximum prison term allowed for that offense by division (A) of section 2929.14 of the Revised Code, its reasons for imposing the maximum prison term;

(e) If the sentence is for two or more offenses arising out of a single incident and it imposes a prison term for those offenses that is the maximum prison term allowed for the offense of the highest degree by division (A) of section 2929.14 of the Revised Code, its reasons for imposing the maximum prison term.

(3) Subject to division (B)(4) of this section, if the sentencing court determines at the sentencing hearing that a prison term is necessary or required, the court shall do all of the following:

(a) Impose a stated prison term;

(b) Notify the offender that, as part of the sentence, the parole board may extend the stated prison term for certain violations of prison rules for up to one-half of the stated prison term;

(c) Notify the offender that the offender will be supervised under section 2967.28 of the Revised Code after the offender leaves prison if the offender is being sentenced for a felony of the first degree or second degree, for a felony sex offense, or for a felony of the third degree in the commission of which the offender caused or threatened to cause physical harm to a person;

(d) Notify the offender that the offender may be supervised under section 2967.28 of the Revised Code after the offender leaves prison if the offender is being sentenced for a felony of the third, fourth, or fifth degree that is not subject to division (B)(3)(c) of this section;

(e) Notify the offender that, if a period of supervision is imposed following the offender's release from prison, as described in division (B)(3)(c) or (d) of this section, and if the offender violates that supervision or a condition of post-release control imposed under division (B) of section 2967.131 of the Revised Code, the parole board may impose a prison term, as part of the sentence, of up to one-half of the stated prison term originally imposed upon the offender;

(f) Require that the offender not ingest or be injected with a drug of abuse and submit to random drug testing as provided in section 341.26, 753.33, or 5120.63 of the Revised Code, whichever is applicable to the offender who is serving a prison term, and require that the results of the drug test administered under any of those sections indicate that the offender did not ingest or was not injected with a drug of abuse.

(4) If the offender is being sentenced for a sexually violent offense that the offender committed on or after January 1, 1997, and the offender also is convicted of or pleads guilty to a sexually violent predator specification that was included in the indictment, count in the indictment, or information charging the sexually violent offense, if the offender is being sentenced for a sexually oriented offense that is not a registration-exempt sexually oriented offense and that the offender committed on or after January 1, 1997, and the court imposing the sentence has determined pursuant to division (B) of section 2950.09 of the Revised Code that the offender is a sexual predator, if the offender is being sentenced on or after July 31, 2003, for a child-victim oriented offense and the court imposing the sentence has determined pursuant to division (B) of section 2950.091 of the Revised Code that the offender is a child-victim predator, or if the offender is being sentenced for an aggravated sexually oriented offense as defined in section 2950.01 of the Revised Code, the court shall include in the offender's sentence a statement that the offender has been adjudicated a sexual predator, has been adjudicated a child victim predator, or has been convicted of or pleaded guilty to an aggravated sexually oriented offense, whichever is applicable, and shall comply with the requirements of section 2950.03 of the Revised Code. Additionally, in the circumstances described in division (G) of section 2929.14 of the Revised Code, the court shall impose sentence on the offender as described in that division.

(5) If the sentencing court determines at the sentencing hearing that a community control sanction should be imposed and the court is not prohibited from imposing a community control sanction, the court shall impose a community control sanction. The court shall notify the offender that, if the conditions of the sanction are violated, if the offender commits a violation of any law, or if the offender leaves this state without the permission of the court or the offender's probation officer, the court may impose a longer time under the same sanction, may impose a more restrictive sanction, or may impose a prison term on the offender and shall indicate the specific prison term that may be imposed as a sanction for the violation, as selected by the court from the range of prison terms for the offense pursuant to section 2929.14 of the Revised Code.

(6) Before imposing a financial sanction under section 2929.18 of the Revised Code or a fine under section 2929.32 of the Revised Code, the court shall consider the offender's present and future ability to pay the amount of the sanction or fine.

(7) If the sentencing court sentences the offender to a sanction of confinement pursuant to section 2929.14 or 2929.16 of the Revised Code that is to be served in a local detention facility, as defined in section 2929.36 of the Revised Code, and if the local detention facility is covered by a policy adopted pursuant to section 307.93, 341.14, 341.19, 341.21, 341.23, 753.02, 753.04, 753.16, 2301.56, or 2947.19 of the Revised Code and section 2929.37 of the Revised Code, both of the following apply:

(a) The court shall specify both of the following as part of the sentence:

(i) If the offender is presented with an itemized bill pursuant to section 2929.37 of the Revised Code for payment of the costs of confinement, the offender is required to pay the bill in accordance with that section.

(ii) If the offender does not dispute the bill described in division (B)(7)(a)(i) of this section and does not pay the bill by the times specified in section 2929.37 of the Revised Code, the clerk of the court may issue a certificate of judgment against the offender as described in that section.

(b) The sentence automatically includes any certificate of judgment issued as described in division (B)(7)(a)(ii) of this section.

(C)(1) If the offender is being sentenced for a fourth degree felony OVI offense under division (G)(1) of section 2929.13 of the Revised Code, the court shall impose the mandatory term of local incarceration in accordance with that division, shall impose a mandatory fine in accordance with division (B)(3) of section 2929.18 of the Revised Code, and, in addition, may impose additional sanctions as specified in sections 2929.15, 2929.16, 2929.17, and 2929.18 of the Revised Code. The court shall not impose a prison term on the offender except that the court may impose a prison term upon the offender as provided in division (A)(1) of section 2929.13 of the Revised Code.

(2) If the offender is being sentenced for a third or fourth degree felony OVI offense under division (G)(2) of section 2929.13 of the Revised Code, the court shall impose the mandatory prison term in accordance with that division, shall impose a mandatory fine in accordance with division (B)(3) of section 2929.18 of the Revised Code, and, in addition, may impose an additional prison term as specified in section 2929.14 of the Revised Code. In addition to the mandatory prison term or mandatory prison term and additional prison term the court imposes, the court also may impose a community control sanction on the offender, but the offender shall serve all of the prison terms so imposed prior to serving the community control sanction.

(D) The sentencing court, pursuant to division (K) of section 2929.14 of the Revised Code, may recommend placement of the offender in a program of shock incarceration under section 5120.031 of the Revised Code or an intensive program prison under section 5120.032 of the Revised Code, disapprove placement of the offender in a program or prison of that nature, or make no recommendation. If the court recommends or disapproves placement, it shall make a finding that gives its reasons for its recommendation or disapproval.

(2004 H 163, eff. 9–23–04; 2003 S 5, § 3, eff. 1–1–04; 2003 S 5, § 1, eff. 7–31–03; 2002 H 490, eff. 1–1–04; 2002 S 123, eff. 1–1–04; 2002 H 485, eff. 6–13–02; 2002 H 170, eff. 9–6–02; 2002 H 327, eff. 7–8–02; 2000 H 349, eff. 9–22–00; 1999 S 22, eff. 5–17–00; 1999 S 107, eff. 3–23–00; 1996 H 180, eff. 1–1–97; 1996 S 166, eff. 10–17–96; 1996 S 269, eff. 7–1–96; 1995 S 2, eff. 7–1–96)

Note: See also following version of this section, eff. 4–29–05.

2929.19 Sentencing hearing (later effective date)

Note: See also preceding version of this section, in effect until 4–29–05.

(A)(1) The court shall hold a sentencing hearing before imposing a sentence under this chapter upon an offender who was convicted of or pleaded guilty to a felony and before resentencing an offender who was convicted of or pleaded guilty to a felony and whose case was remanded pursuant to section 2953.07 or 2953.08 of the Revised Code. At the hearing, the offender, the prosecuting attorney, the victim or the victim's representative in accordance with section 2930.14 of the Revised Code, and, with the approval of the court, any other person may present information relevant to the imposition of sentence in the case. The court shall inform the offender of the verdict of the jury or finding of the court and ask the offender whether the offender has anything to say as to why sentence should not be imposed upon the offender.

(2) Except as otherwise provided in this division, before imposing sentence on an offender who is being sentenced on or after January 1, 1997, for a sexually oriented offense that is not a registration-exempt sexually oriented offense and who is in any category of offender described in division (B)(1)(a)(i), (ii), or (iii) of section 2950.09 of the Revised Code, the court shall conduct a hearing in accordance with division (B) of section 2950.09 of the Revised Code to determine whether the offender is a sexual predator. The court shall not conduct a hearing under that division if the offender is being sentenced for a violent sex offense or a designated homicide, assault, or kidnapping offense and, in relation to that offense, the offender was adjudicated a sexually violent predator. Before imposing sentence on an offender who is being sentenced for a sexually oriented offense that is not a registration-exempt sexually oriented offense, the court also shall comply with division (E) of section 2950.09 of the Revised Code.

Before imposing sentence on or after July 31, 2003, on an offender who is being sentenced for a child-victim oriented offense, regardless of when the offense was committed, the court shall conduct a hearing in accordance with division (B) of section 2950.091 of the Revised Code to determine whether the offender is a child-victim predator. Before imposing sentence on an offender who is being sentenced for a child-victim oriented offense, the court also shall comply with division (E) of section 2950.091 of the Revised Code.

(B)(1) At the sentencing hearing, the court, before imposing sentence, shall consider the record, any information presented at the hearing by any person pursuant to division (A) of this section, and, if one was prepared, the presentence investigation report made pursuant to section 2951.03 of the Revised Code or Criminal Rule 32.2, and any victim impact statement made pursuant to section 2947.051 of the Revised Code.

(2) The court shall impose a sentence and shall make a finding that gives its reasons for selecting the sentence imposed in any of the following circumstances:

(a) Unless the offense is a violent sex offense or designated homicide, assault, or kidnapping offense for which the court is required to impose sentence pursuant to division (G) of section 2929.14 of the Revised Code, if it imposes a prison term for a felony of the fourth or fifth degree or for a felony drug offense that is a violation of a provision of Chapter 2925. of the Revised Code and that is specified as being subject to division (B) of section 2929.13 of the Revised Code for purposes of sentencing, its reasons for imposing the prison term, based upon the overriding purposes and principles of felony sentencing set forth in section 2929.11 of the Revised Code, and any factors listed in divisions (B)(1)(a) to (i) of section 2929.13 of the Revised Code that it found to apply relative to the offender.

(b) If it does not impose a prison term for a felony of the first or second degree or for a felony drug offense that is a violation of a provision of Chapter 2925. of the Revised Code and for which a presumption in favor of a prison term is specified as being applicable, its reasons for not imposing the prison term and for overriding the presumption, based upon the overriding purposes and principles of felony sentencing set forth in section 2929.11 of the Revised Code, and the basis of the findings it made under divisions (D)(1) and (2) of section 2929.13 of the Revised Code.

(c) If it imposes consecutive sentences under section 2929.14 of the Revised Code, its reasons for imposing the consecutive sentences;

(d) If the sentence is for one offense and it imposes a prison term for the offense that is the maximum prison term allowed for that offense by division (A) of section 2929.14 of the Revised Code, its reasons for imposing the maximum prison term;

(e) If the sentence is for two or more offenses arising out of a single incident and it imposes a prison term for those offenses that is the maximum prison term allowed for the offense of the highest degree by division (A) of section 2929.14 of the Revised Code, its reasons for imposing the maximum prison term.

(3) Subject to division (B)(4) of this section, if the sentencing court determines at the sentencing hearing that a prison term is necessary or required, the court shall do all of the following:

(a) Impose a stated prison term;

(b) Notify the offender that, as part of the sentence, the parole board may extend the stated prison term for certain violations of prison rules for up to one-half of the stated prison term;

(c) Notify the offender that the offender will be supervised under section 2967.28 of the Revised Code after the offender leaves prison if the offender is being sentenced for a felony of the first degree or second degree, for a felony sex offense, or for a felony of the third degree in the commission of which the offender caused or threatened to cause physical harm to a person;

(d) Notify the offender that the offender may be supervised under section 2967.28 of the Revised Code after the offender leaves prison if the offender is being sentenced for a felony of the third, fourth, or fifth degree that is not subject to division (B)(3)(c) of this section;

(e) Notify the offender that, if a period of supervision is imposed following the offender's release from prison, as described in division (B)(3)(c) or (d) of this section, and if the offender violates that supervision or a condition of post-release control imposed under division (B) of section 2967.131 of the Revised Code, the parole board may impose a prison term, as part of the sentence, of up to one-half of the stated prison term originally imposed upon the offender;

(f) Require that the offender not ingest or be injected with a drug of abuse and submit to random drug testing as provided in section 341.26, 753.33, or 5120.63 of the Revised Code, whichever is applicable to the offender who is serving a prison term, and require that the results of the drug test administered under any of those sections indicate that the offender did not ingest or was not injected with a drug of abuse.

(4) If the offender is being sentenced for a violent sex offense or designated homicide, assault, or kidnapping offense that the offender committed on or after January 1, 1997, and the offender is adjudicated a sexually violent predator in relation to that offense, if the offender is being sentenced for a sexually oriented offense that is not a registration-exempt sexually oriented offense and that the offender committed on or after January 1, 1997, and the court imposing the sentence has determined pursuant to division (B) of section 2950.09 of the Revised Code that the offender is a sexual predator, if the offender is being sentenced on or after July 31, 2003, for a child-victim oriented offense and the court imposing the sentence has determined pursuant to division (B) of section 2950.091 of the Revised Code that the offender is a child-victim predator, or if the offender is being

sentenced for an aggravated sexually oriented offense as defined in section 2950.01 of the Revised Code, the court shall include in the offender's sentence a statement that the offender has been adjudicated a sexual predator, has been adjudicated a child victim predator, or has been convicted of or pleaded guilty to an aggravated sexually oriented offense, whichever is applicable, and shall comply with the requirements of section 2950.03 of the Revised Code. Additionally, in the circumstances described in division (G) of section 2929.14 of the Revised Code, the court shall impose sentence on the offender as described in that division.

(5) If the sentencing court determines at the sentencing hearing that a community control sanction should be imposed and the court is not prohibited from imposing a community control sanction, the court shall impose a community control sanction. The court shall notify the offender that, if the conditions of the sanction are violated, if the offender commits a violation of any law, or if the offender leaves this state without the permission of the court or the offender's probation officer, the court may impose a longer time under the same sanction, may impose a more restrictive sanction, or may impose a prison term on the offender and shall indicate the specific prison term that may be imposed as a sanction for the violation, as selected by the court from the range of prison terms for the offense pursuant to section 2929.14 of the Revised Code.

(6) Before imposing a financial sanction under section 2929.18 of the Revised Code or a fine under section 2929.32 of the Revised Code, the court shall consider the offender's present and future ability to pay the amount of the sanction or fine.

(7) If the sentencing court sentences the offender to a sanction of confinement pursuant to section 2929.14 or 2929.16 of the Revised Code that is to be served in a local detention facility, as defined in section 2929.36 of the Revised Code, and if the local detention facility is covered by a policy adopted pursuant to section 307.93, 341.14, 341.19, 341.21, 341.23, 753.02, 753.04, 753.16, 2301.56, or 2947.19 of the Revised Code and section 2929.37 of the Revised Code, both of the following apply:

(a) The court shall specify both of the following as part of the sentence:

(i) If the offender is presented with an itemized bill pursuant to section 2929.37 of the Revised Code for payment of the costs of confinement, the offender is required to pay the bill in accordance with that section.

(ii) If the offender does not dispute the bill described in division (B)(7)(a)(i) of this section and does not pay the bill by the times specified in section 2929.37 of the Revised Code, the clerk of the court may issue a certificate of judgment against the offender as described in that section.

(b) The sentence automatically includes any certificate of judgment issued as described in division (B)(7)(a)(ii) of this section.

(C)(1) If the offender is being sentenced for a fourth degree felony OVI offense under division (G)(1) of section 2929.13 of the Revised Code, the court shall impose the mandatory term of local incarceration in accordance with that division, shall impose a mandatory fine in accordance with division (B)(3) of section 2929.18 of the Revised Code, and, in addition, may impose additional sanctions as specified in sections 2929.15, 2929.16, 2929.17, and 2929.18 of the Revised Code. The court shall not impose a prison term on the offender except that the court may impose a prison term upon the offender as provided in division (A)(1) of section 2929.13 of the Revised Code.

(2) If the offender is being sentenced for a third or fourth degree felony OVI offense under division (G)(2) of section 2929.13 of the Revised Code, the court shall impose the mandatory prison term in accordance with that division, shall impose a mandatory fine in accordance with division (B)(3) of section 2929.18 of the Revised Code, and, in addition, may impose an additional prison term as specified in section 2929.14 of the Revised Code. In addition to the mandatory prison term or mandatory prison term and additional prison term the court imposes, the court also may impose a community control sanction on the offender, but the offender shall serve all of the prison terms so imposed prior to serving the community control sanction.

(D) The sentencing court, pursuant to division (K) of section 2929.14 of the Revised Code, may recommend placement of the offender in a program of shock incarceration under section 5120.031 of the Revised Code or an intensive program prison under section 5120.032 of the Revised Code, disapprove placement of the offender in a program or prison of that nature, or make no recommendation. If the court recommends or disapproves placement, it shall make a finding that gives its reasons for its recommendation or disapproval.

(2004 H 473, eff. 4–29–05; 2004 H 163, eff. 9–23–04; 2003 S 5, § 3, eff. 1–1–04; 2003 S 5, § 1, eff. 7–31–03; 2002 H 490, eff. 1–1–04; 2002 S 123, eff. 1–1–04; 2002 H 485, eff. 6–13–02; 2002 H 170, eff. 9–6–02; 2002 H 327, eff. 7–8–02; 2000 H 349, eff. 9–22–00; 1999 S 22, eff. 5–17–00; 1999 S 107, eff. 3–23–00; 1996 H 180, eff. 1–1–97; 1996 S 166, eff. 10–17–96; 1996 S 269, eff. 7–1–96; 1995 S 2, eff. 7–1–96)

Note: See also preceding version of this section, in effect until 4–29–05.

2929.20 Judicial release

(A) As used in this section, "eligible offender" means any person serving a stated prison term of ten years or less when either of the following applies:

(1) The stated prison term does not include a mandatory prison term.

(2) The stated prison term includes a mandatory prison term, and the person has served the mandatory prison term.

(B) Upon the filing of a motion by the eligible offender or upon its own motion, a sentencing court may reduce the offender's stated prison term through a judicial release in accordance with this section. The court shall not reduce the stated prison term of an offender who is not an eligible offender. An eligible offender may file a motion for judicial release with the sentencing court within the following applicable period of time:

(1)(a) Except as otherwise provided in division (B)(1)(b) or (c) of this section, if the stated prison term was imposed for a felony of the fourth or fifth degree, the eligible offender may file the motion not earlier than thirty days or later than ninety days after the offender is delivered to a state correctional institution.

(b) If the stated prison term is five years and is an aggregate of stated prison terms that are being served consecutively and that were imposed for any combination of felonies of the fourth degree and felonies of the fifth degree, the eligible offender may file the motion after the eligible offender has served four years of the stated prison term.

(c) If the stated prison term is more than five years and not more than ten years and is an aggregate of stated prison terms that are being served consecutively and that were imposed for any combination of felonies of the fourth degree and felonies of the fifth degree, the eligible offender may file the motion after the eligible offender has served five years of the stated prison term.

(2) Except as otherwise provided in division (B)(3) or (4) of this section, if the stated prison term was imposed for a felony of the first, second, or third degree, the eligible offender may file the motion not earlier than one hundred eighty days after the offender is delivered to a state correctional institution.

(3) If the stated prison term is five years, the eligible offender may file the motion after the eligible offender has served four years of the stated prison term.

(4) If the stated prison term is more than five years and not more than ten years, the eligible offender may file the motion after the eligible offender has served five years of the stated prison term.

(5) If the offender's stated prison term includes a mandatory prison term, the offender shall file the motion within the time authorized under division (B)(1), (2), (3), or (4) of this section for the nonmandatory portion of the prison term, but the time for filing the motion does not begin to run until after the expiration of the mandatory portion of the prison term.

(C) Upon receipt of a timely motion for judicial release filed by an eligible offender under division (B) of this section or upon the sentencing court's own motion made within the appropriate time period specified in that division, the court may schedule a hearing on the motion. The court may deny the motion without a hearing but shall not grant the motion without a hearing. If a court denies a motion without a hearing, the court may consider a subsequent judicial release for that eligible offender on its own motion or a subsequent motion filed by that eligible offender. If a court denies a motion after a hearing, the court shall not consider a subsequent motion for that eligible offender. The court shall hold only one hearing for any eligible offender.

A hearing under this section shall be conducted in open court within sixty days after the date on which the motion is filed, provided that the court may delay the hearing for a period not to exceed one hundred eighty additional days. If the court holds a hearing on the motion, the court shall enter a ruling on the motion within ten days after the hearing. If the court denies the motion without a hearing, the court shall enter its ruling on the motion within sixty days after the motion is filed.

(D) If a court schedules a hearing under division (C) of this section, the court shall notify the eligible offender of the hearing. The eligible offender promptly shall give a copy of the notice of the hearing to the head of the state correctional institution in which the eligible offender is confined. If the court schedules a hearing for judicial release, the court promptly shall give notice of the hearing to the prosecuting attorney of the county in which the eligible offender was indicted. Upon receipt of the notice from the court, the prosecuting attorney shall notify the victim of the offense for which the stated prison term was imposed or the victim's representative, pursuant to section 2930.16 of the Revised Code, of the hearing.

(E) Prior to the date of the hearing on a motion for judicial release under this section, the head of the state correctional institution in which the eligible offender in question is confined shall send to the court a report on the eligible offender's conduct in the institution and in any institution from which the eligible offender may have been transferred. The report shall cover the eligible offender's participation in school, vocational training, work, treatment, and other rehabilitative activities and any disciplinary action taken against the eligible offender. The report shall be made part of the record of the hearing.

(F) If the court grants a hearing on a motion for judicial release under this section, the eligible offender shall attend the hearing if ordered to do so by the court. Upon receipt of a copy of the journal entry containing the order, the head of the state correctional institution in which the eligible offender is incarcerated shall deliver the eligible offender to the sheriff of the county in which the hearing is to be held. The sheriff shall convey the eligible offender to the hearing and return the offender to the institution after the hearing.

(G) At the hearing on a motion for judicial release under this section, the court shall afford the eligible offender and the eligible offender's attorney an opportunity to present written information relevant to the motion and shall afford the eligible offender, if present, and the eligible offender's attorney an opportunity to present oral information relevant to the motion. The court shall afford a similar opportunity to the prosecuting attorney, the victim or the victim's representative, as defined in section 2930.01 of the Revised Code, and any other person the court determines is likely to present additional relevant information. The court shall consider any statement of a victim made pursuant to section 2930.14 or 2930.17 of the Revised Code, any victim impact statement prepared pursuant to section 2947.051 of the Revised Code, and any report made under division (E) of this section. After ruling on the motion, the court shall notify the victim of the ruling in accordance with sections 2930.03 and 2930.16 of the Revised Code.

(H)(1) A court shall not grant a judicial release under this section to an eligible offender who is imprisoned for a felony of the first or second degree, or to an eligible offender who committed an offense contained in Chapter 2925. or 3719. of the Revised Code and for whom there was a presumption under section 2929.13 of the Revised Code in favor of a prison term, unless the court, with reference to factors under section 2929.12 of the Revised Code, finds both of the following:

(a) That a sanction other than a prison term would adequately punish the offender and protect the public from future criminal violations by the eligible offender because the applicable factors indicating a lesser likelihood of recidivism outweigh the applicable factors indicating a greater likelihood of recidivism;

(b) That a sanction other than a prison term would not demean the seriousness of the offense because factors indicating that the eligible offender's conduct in committing the offense was less serious than conduct normally constituting the offense outweigh factors indicating that the eligible offender's conduct was more serious than conduct normally constituting the offense.

(2) A court that grants a judicial release to an eligible offender under division (H)(1) of this section shall specify on the record both findings required in that division and also shall list all the factors described in that division that were presented at the hearing.

(I) If the court grants a motion for judicial release under this section, the court shall order the release of the eligible offender, shall place the eligible offender under an appropriate community control sanction, under appropriate community control conditions, and under the supervision of the department of probation serving the court, and shall reserve the right to reimpose the sentence that it reduced pursuant to the judicial release if the offender violates the sanction. If the court reimposes the reduced sentence pursuant to this reserved right, it may do so either concurrently with, or consecutive to, any new sentence imposed upon the eligible offender as a result of the violation that is a new offense. The period of the community control sanction shall be no longer than five years. The court, in its discretion, may reduce the period of the community control sanction by the amount of time the eligible offender spent in jail for the offense and in prison. If the court made any findings pursuant to division (H)(1) of this section, the court shall serve a copy of the findings upon counsel for the parties within fifteen days after the date on which the court grants the motion for judicial release.

Prior to being released pursuant to a judicial release granted under this section, the eligible offender shall serve any extension of sentence that was imposed under section 2967.11 of the Revised Code.

(2002 H 327, eff. 7–8–02; 1999 S 107, eff. 3–23–00; 1997 H 151, eff. 9–16–97; 1996 S 269, eff. 7–1–96; 1995 S 2, eff. 7–1–96)

MISDEMEANOR SENTENCING

2929.21 Sentencing considerations for misdemeanor or municipal ordinance violation similar to misdemeanor or minor misdemeanor

(A) A court that sentences an offender for a misdemeanor or minor misdemeanor violation of any provision of the Revised

Code, or of any municipal ordinance that is substantially similar to a misdemeanor or minor misdemeanor violation of a provision of the Revised Code, shall be guided by the overriding purposes of misdemeanor sentencing. The overriding purposes of misdemeanor sentencing are to protect the public from future crime by the offender and others and to punish the offender. To achieve those purposes, the sentencing court shall consider the impact of the offense upon the victim and the need for changing the offender's behavior, rehabilitating the offender, and making restitution to the victim of the offense, the public, or the victim and the public.

(B) A sentence imposed for a misdemeanor or minor misdemeanor violation of a Revised Code provision or for a violation of a municipal ordinance that is subject to division (A) of this section shall be reasonably calculated to achieve the two overriding purposes of misdemeanor sentencing set forth in division (A) of this section, commensurate with and not demeaning to the seriousness of the offender's conduct and its impact upon the victim, and consistent with sentences imposed for similar offenses committed by similar offenders.

(C) A court that imposes a sentence upon an offender for a misdemeanor or minor misdemeanor violation of a Revised Code provision or for a violation of a municipal ordinance that is subject to division (A) of this section shall not base the sentence upon the race, ethnic background, gender, or religion of the offender.

(D) Divisions (A) and (B) of this section shall not apply to any offense that is disposed of by a traffic violations bureau of any court pursuant to Traffic Rule 13 and shall not apply to any violation of any provision of the Revised Code that is a minor misdemeanor and that is disposed of without a court appearance. Divisions (A) to (C) of this section do not affect any penalties established by a municipal corporation for a violation of its ordinances.

(2004 H 52, eff. 6–1–04; 2002 H 490, eff. 1–1–04)

Historical and Statutory Notes

Ed. Note: Former 2929.21 repealed by 2002 H 490, eff. 1–1–04; 2003 S 5, eff. 7–31–03; 2002 H 170, eff. 9–6–02; 1996 H 180, eff. 1–1–97; 1990 H 51, eff. 11–8–90; 1990 S 131; 1986 H 284; 1978 S 119; 1972 H 511.

2929.22 Imposing sentence for misdemeanor

(A) Unless a mandatory jail term is required to be imposed by division (G) of section 1547.99, division (B) of section 4510.14, division (G) of section 4511.19 of the Revised Code, or any other provision of the Revised Code a court that imposes a sentence under this chapter upon an offender for a misdemeanor or minor misdemeanor has discretion to determine the most effective way to achieve the purposes and principles of sentencing set forth in section 2929.21 of the Revised Code.

Unless a specific sanction is required to be imposed or is precluded from being imposed by the section setting forth an offense or the penalty for an offense or by any provision of sections 2929.23 to 2929.28 of the Revised Code, a court that imposes a sentence upon an offender for a misdemeanor may impose on the offender any sanction or combination of sanctions under sections 2929.24 to 2929.28 of the Revised Code. The court shall not impose a sentence that imposes an unnecessary burden on local government resources.

(B)(1) In determining the appropriate sentence for a misdemeanor, the court shall consider all of the following factors:

(a) The nature and circumstances of the offense or offenses;

(b) Whether the circumstances regarding the offender and the offense or offenses indicate that the offender has a history of persistent criminal activity and that the offender's character and condition reveal a substantial risk that the offender will commit another offense;

(c) Whether the circumstances regarding the offender and the offense or offenses indicate that the offender's history, character, and condition reveal a substantial risk that the offender will be a danger to others and that the offender's conduct has been characterized by a pattern of repetitive, compulsive, or aggressive behavior with heedless indifference to the consequences;

(d) Whether the victim's youth, age, disability, or other factor made the victim particularly vulnerable to the offense or made the impact of the offense more serious;

(e) Whether the offender is likely to commit future crimes in general, in addition to the circumstances described in divisions (B) (1)(b) and (c) of this section.

(2) In determining the appropriate sentence for a misdemeanor, in addition to complying with division (B)(1) of this section, the court may consider any other factors that are relevant to achieving the purposes and principles of sentencing set forth in section 2929.21 of the Revised Code.

(C) Before imposing a jail term as a sentence for a misdemeanor, a court shall consider the appropriateness of imposing a community control sanction or a combination of community control sanctions under sections 2929.25, 2929. 26, 2929.27, and 2929.28 of the Revised Code. A court may impose the longest jail term authorized under section 2929.24 of the Revised Code only upon offenders who commit the worst forms of the offense or upon offenders whose conduct and response to prior sanctions for prior offenses demonstrate that the imposition of the longest jail term is necessary to deter the offender from committing a future crime.

(D)(1) A sentencing court shall consider any relevant oral or written statement made by the victim, the defendant, the defense attorney, or the prosecuting authority regarding sentencing for a misdemeanor. This division does not create any rights to notice other than those rights authorized by Chapter 2930. of the Revised Code.

(2) At the time of sentencing for a misdemeanor or as soon as possible after sentencing, the court shall notify the victim of the offense of the victim's right to file an application for an award of reparations pursuant to sections 2743.51 to 2743.72 of the Revised Code.

(2003 S 57, eff. 1–1–04; 2002 H 490, eff. 1–1–04)

Historical and Statutory Notes

Ed. Note: Former 2929.22 repealed by 2002 H 490, eff. 1–1–04; 1999 S 9, eff. 3–8–00; 1995 S 2, eff. 7–1–96; 1994 S 186, eff. 10–12–94; 1990 S 258, eff. 11–20–90; 1978 S 119; 1972 H 511.

MISCELLANEOUS SENTENCING PROVISIONS

2929.23 Sentencing for sexually oriented offense; sexual predator; registration

(A) If an offender is being sentenced for a sexually oriented offense that is a misdemeanor committed on or after January 1, 1997, and if the judge imposing sentence for the sexually oriented offense determines pursuant to division (B) of section 2950.09 of the Revised Code that the offender is a sexual predator, the judge shall include in the offender's sentence a statement that the offender has been adjudicated a sexual predator, shall comply with the requirements of section 2950.03 of the Revised Code, and shall require the offender to submit to a DNA specimen collection procedure pursuant to section 2901.07 of the Revised Code.

(B) Before imposing sentence on an offender who is being sentenced for a sexually oriented offense that is a misdemeanor, that was committed on or after January 1, 1997, and that is not a registration-exempt sexually oriented offense, the judge shall conduct a hearing in accordance with division (B) of section

2950.09 of the Revised Code to determine whether the offender is a sexual predator. Before imposing sentence on an offender who is being sentenced for a sexually oriented offense that is not a registration-exempt sexually oriented offense, the court also shall comply with division (E) of section 2950.09 of the Revised Code.

Before imposing sentence on or after the effective date of this amendment on an offender who is being sentenced for a child-victim oriented offense that is a misdemeanor, regardless of when the offense was committed, the judge shall conduct a hearing in accordance with division (B) of section 2950.091 of the Revised Code to determine whether the offender is a child-victim predator. Before imposing sentence on an offender who is being sentenced for a child-victim oriented offense, the court also shall comply with division (E) of section 2950.091 of the Revised Code.

(C) If an offender is being sentenced for a sexually oriented offense that is not a registration-exempt sexually oriented offense or for a child-victim oriented offense that is a misdemeanor committed on or after January 1, 1997, the judge shall include in the sentence a summary of the offender's duties imposed under sections 2950.04, 2950.041, 2950.05, and 2950.06 of the Revised Code and the duration of the duties. The judge shall inform the offender, at the time of sentencing, of those duties and of their duration and, if required under division (A)(2) of section 2950.03 of the Revised Code, shall perform the duties specified in that section.

(2003 S 5, § 3, eff. 1–1–04; 2003 S 5, § 1, eff. 7–31–03; 2002 H 490, eff. 1–1–04)

Historical and Statutory Notes

Ed. Note: Former 2929.23 repealed by 2002 H 490, eff. 1–1–04; 2002 S 123, eff. 1–1–04; 2000 S 179, § 3, eff. 1–1–02; 1999 S 22, eff. 5–17–00; 1997 S 111, eff. 3–17–98; 1996 H 72, eff. 3–18–97; 1996 S 166, eff. 10–17–96; 1996 S 269, eff. 7–1–96; 1995 S 2, eff. 7–1–96; 1994 S 82, eff. 5–4–94; 1993 S 62, § 4, eff. 9–1–93; 1992 H 725, S 275, S 351; 1990 H 51, S 131.

2929.24 Misdemeanor jail terms

(A) Except as provided in section 2929.22 or 2929.23 of the Revised Code and unless another term is required or authorized pursuant to law, if the sentencing court imposing a sentence upon an offender for a misdemeanor elects or is required to impose a jail term on the offender pursuant to this chapter, the court shall impose a definite jail term that shall be one of the following:

(1) For a misdemeanor of the first degree, not more than one hundred eighty days;

(2) For a misdemeanor of the second degree, not more than ninety days;

(3) For a misdemeanor of the third degree, not more than sixty days;

(4) For a misdemeanor of the fourth degree, not more than thirty days.

(B) A court that sentences an offender to a jail term under this section may permit the offender to serve the sentence in intermittent confinement or may authorize a limited release of the offender as provided in division (B) of section 2929.26 of the Revised Code.

(C) If a court sentences an offender to a jail term under this section and the court assigns the offender to a county jail that has established a county jail industry program pursuant to section 5147.30 of the Revised Code, the court shall specify, as part of the sentence, whether the offender may be considered for participation in the program. During the offender's term in the county jail, the court retains jurisdiction to modify its specification regarding the offender's participation in the county jail industry program.

(D) If a person is sentenced to a jail term pursuant to this section, the court may impose as part of the sentence pursuant to section 2929.28 of the Revised Code a reimbursement sanction, and, if the local detention facility in which the term is to be served is covered by a policy adopted pursuant to section 307.93, 341.14, 341.19, 341.21, 341.23, 753.02, 753.04, 753.16, 2301. 56, or 2947.19 of the Revised Code and section 2929.37 of the Revised Code, both of the following apply:

(1) The court shall specify both of the following as part of the sentence:

(a) If the person is presented with an itemized bill pursuant to section 2929.37 of the Revised Code for payment of the costs of confinement, the person is required to pay the bill in accordance with that section.

(b) If the person does not dispute the bill described in division (D)(1)(a) of this section and does not pay the bill by the times specified in section 2929.37 of the Revised Code, the clerk of the court may issue a certificate of judgment against the person as described in that section.

(2) The sentence automatically includes any certificate of judgment issued as described in division (D)(1)(b) of this section.

(E) If an offender who is convicted of or pleads guilty to a violation of division (B) of section 4511.19 of the Revised Code also is convicted of or also pleads guilty to a specification of the type described in section 2941.1414 [1] of the Revised Code and if the court imposes a jail term on the offender for the underlying offense, the court shall impose upon the offender an additional definite jail term of not more than six months. The additional jail term shall not be reduced pursuant to any provision of the Revised Code. The offender shall serve the additional jail term consecutively to and prior to the jail term imposed for the underlying offense and consecutively to any other mandatory term imposed in relation to the offense.

(2004 H 163, eff. 9–23–04; 2002 H 490, eff. 1–1–04)

[1] Section renumbered to RC 2941.1416 by the Legislative Service Commission

Historical and Statutory Notes

Ed. Note: Former RC 2929.24 recodified as RC 2929.42 by 2002 H 490, eff. 1–1–04; 2000 H 506, eff. 4–10–01; 1995 S 143, § 5, eff. 7–1–96; 1995 S 2, eff. 7–1–96.

2929.25 Misdemeanor community control sanctions

(A)(1) Except as provided in sections 2929.22 and 2929.23 of the Revised Code or when a jail term is required by law, in sentencing an offender for a misdemeanor, other than a minor misdemeanor, the sentencing court may do either of the following:

(a) Directly impose a sentence that consists of one or more community control sanctions authorized by section 2929.26, 2929.27, or 2929.28 of the Revised Code. The court may impose any other conditions of release under a community control sanction that the court considers appropriate. If the court imposes a jail term upon the offender, the court may impose any community control sanction or combination of community control sanctions in addition to the jail term.

(b) Impose a jail term under section 2929.24 of the Revised Code from the range of jail terms authorized under that section for the offense, suspend all or a portion of the jail term imposed, and place the offender under a community control sanction or combination of community control sanctions authorized under section 2929.26, 2929.27, or 2929.28 of the Revised Code.

(2) The duration of all community control sanctions imposed upon an offender and in effect for an offender at any time shall not exceed five years.

(3) At sentencing, if a court directly imposes a community control sanction or combination of community control sanctions pursuant to division (A)(1)(a) of this section, the court shall state the duration of the community control sanctions imposed and shall notify the offender that if any of the conditions of the community control sanctions are violated the court may do any of the following:

(a) Impose a longer time under the same community control sanction if the total time under all of the offender's community control sanctions does not exceed the five-year limit specified in division (A)(2) of this section;

(b) Impose a more restrictive community control sanction under section 2929.26, 2929.27, or 2929.28 of the Revised Code, but the court is not required to impose any particular sanction or sanctions;

(c) Impose a definite jail term from the range of jail terms authorized for the offense under section 2929.24 of the Revised Code.

(B)(1) If a court sentences an offender to any community control sanction or combination of community control sanctions authorized under section 2929.26, 2929.27, or 2929.28 of the Revised Code, the court shall place the offender under the general control and supervision of the court or of a department of probation in the jurisdiction that serves the court for purposes of reporting to the court a violation of any of the conditions of the sanctions imposed. If the offender resides in another jurisdiction and a department of probation has been established to serve the municipal court or county court in that jurisdiction, the sentencing court may request the municipal court or the county court to receive the offender into the general control and supervision of that department of probation for purposes of reporting to the sentencing court a violation of any of the conditions of the sanctions imposed. The sentencing court retains jurisdiction over any offender whom it sentences for the duration of the sanction or sanctions imposed.

(2) The sentencing court shall require as a condition of any community control sanction that the offender abide by the law and not leave the state without the permission of the court or the offender's probation officer. In the interests of doing justice, rehabilitating the offender, and ensuring the offender's good behavior, the court may impose additional requirements on the offender. The offender's compliance with the additional requirements also shall be a condition of the community control sanction imposed upon the offender.

(C)(1) If the court imposing sentence upon an offender sentences the offender to any community control sanction or combination of community control sanctions authorized under section 2929.26, 2929.27, or 2929.28 of the Revised Code, and if the offender violates any of the conditions of the sanctions, the public or private person or entity that supervises or administers the program or activity that comprises the sanction shall report the violation directly to the sentencing court or to the department of probation or probation officer with general control and supervision over the offender. If the public or private person or entity reports the violation to the department of probation or probation officer, the department or officer shall report the violation to the sentencing court.

(2) If an offender violates any condition of a community control sanction, the sentencing court may impose upon the violator a longer time under the same community control sanction if the total time under all of the community control sanctions imposed on the violator does not exceed the five-year limit specified in division (A)(2) of this section or may impose on the violator a more restrictive community control sanction or combination of community control sanctions, including a jail term. If the court imposes a jail term upon a violator pursuant to this division, the total time spent in jail for the misdemeanor offense and the violation of a condition of the community control sanction shall not exceed the maximum jail term available for the offense for which the sanction that was violated was imposed. The court may reduce the longer period of time that the violator is required to spend under the longer sanction or the more restrictive sanction by all or part of the time the violator successfully spent under the sanction that was initially imposed.

(D) Except as otherwise provided in this division, if an offender, for a significant period of time, fulfills the conditions of a community control sanction imposed pursuant to section 2929.26, 2929.27, or 2929.28 of the Revised Code in an exemplary manner, the court may reduce the period of time under the community control sanction or impose a less restrictive community control sanction. Fulfilling the conditions of a community control sanction does not relieve the offender of a duty to make restitution under section 2929.28 of the Revised Code.

(2003 S 57, eff. 1-1-04; 2002 H 490, eff. 1-1-04)

Historical and Statutory Notes

Ed. Note: Former 2929.25 amended and recodified as 2929.32 by 2002 H 490, eff. 1-1-04; 1996 S 269, eff. 7-1-96; 1995 S 91, eff. 11-15-95.

2929.26 Community residential sanction

(A) Except when a mandatory jail term is required by law, the court imposing a sentence for a misdemeanor, other than a minor misdemeanor, may impose upon the offender any community residential sanction or combination of community residential sanctions under this section. Community residential sanctions include, but are not limited to, the following:

(1) A term of up to one hundred eighty days in a halfway house or a term in a halfway house not to exceed the longest jail term available for the offense, whichever is shorter, if the political subdivision that would have responsibility for paying the costs of confining the offender in a jail has entered into a contract with the halfway house for use of the facility for misdemeanor offenders;

(2) A term of up to one hundred eighty days in an alternative residential facility or a term in an alternative residential facility not to exceed the longest jail term available for the offense, whichever is shorter. The court may specify the level of security in the alternative residential facility that is needed for the offender.

(B) The court that sentences an offender to a community residential sanction under this section may do either or both of the following:

(1) Permit the offender to serve the offender's sentence in intermittent confinement, overnight, on weekends or at any other time or times that will allow the offender to continue at the offender's occupation or care for the offender's family;

(2) Authorize the offender to be released so that the offender may seek or maintain employment, receive education or training, receive treatment, perform community service, or otherwise fulfill an obligation imposed by law or by the court. A release pursuant to this division shall be only for the duration of time that is needed to fulfill the purpose of the release and for travel that reasonably is necessary to fulfill the purposes of the release.

(C) The court may order that a reasonable portion of the income earned by the offender upon a release pursuant to division (B) of this section be applied to any financial sanction imposed under section 2929.28 of the Revised Code.

(D) No court shall sentence any person to a prison term for a misdemeanor or minor misdemeanor or to a jail term for a minor misdemeanor.

(E) If a court sentences a person who has been convicted of or pleaded guilty to a misdemeanor to a community residential sanction as described in division (A) of this section, at the time of reception and at other times the person in charge of the operation of the halfway house, alternative residential facility, or other place at which the offender will serve the residential sanction determines to be appropriate, the person in charge of the operation of the halfway house, alternative residential facility, or other place may cause the convicted offender to be examined and tested for tuberculosis, HIV infection, hepatitis, including, but not limited to, hepatitis A, B, and C, and other contagious diseases. The person in charge of the operation of the halfway house, alternative residential facility, or other place at which the offender will serve the residential sanction may cause a convicted offender in the halfway house, alternative residential facility, or other place who refuses to be tested or treated for tuberculosis, HIV infection, hepatitis, including, but not limited to, hepatitis A, B, and C, or another contagious disease to be tested and treated involuntarily.

(F) A political subdivision may enter into a contract with a halfway house for use of the halfway house to house misdemeanor offenders under a sanction imposed under division (A)(1) of this section.

(2002 H 490, eff. 1–1–04)

2929.27 Nonresidential sanction where jail term not mandatory

(A) Except when a mandatory jail term is required by law, the court imposing a sentence for a misdemeanor, other than a minor misdemeanor, may impose upon the offender any nonresidential sanction or combination of nonresidential sanctions authorized under this division. Nonresidential sanctions include, but are not limited to, the following:

(1) A term of day reporting;

(2) A term of house arrest with electronic monitoring or continuous alcohol monitoring or both electronic monitoring and continuous alcohol monitoring, a term of electronic monitoring or continuous alcohol monitoring without house arrest, or a term of house arrest without electronic monitoring or continuous alcohol monitoring;

(3) A term of community service of up to five hundred hours for a misdemeanor of the first degree or two hundred hours for a misdemeanor of the second, third, or fourth degree;

(4) A term in a drug treatment program with a level of security for the offender as determined necessary by the court;

(5) A term of intensive probation supervision;

(6) A term of basic probation supervision;

(7) A term of monitored time;

(8) A term of drug and alcohol use monitoring, including random drug testing;

(9) A curfew term;

(10) A requirement that the offender obtain employment;

(11) A requirement that the offender obtain education or training;

(12) Provided the court obtains the prior approval of the victim, a requirement that the offender participate in victim-offender mediation;

(13) If authorized by law, suspension of the offender's privilege to operate a motor vehicle, immobilization or forfeiture of the offender's motor vehicle, a requirement that the offender obtain a valid motor vehicle operator's license, or any other related sanction;

(14) A requirement that the offender obtain counseling if the offense is a violation of section 2919.25 or a violation of section 2903.13 of the Revised Code involving a person who was a family or household member at the time of the violation, if the offender committed the offense in the vicinity of one or more children who are not victims of the offense, and if the offender or the victim of the offense is a parent, guardian, custodian, or person in loco parentis of one or more of those children. This division does not limit the court in requiring that the offender obtain counseling for any offense or in any circumstance not specified in this division.

(B) In addition to the sanctions authorized under division (A) of this section, the court imposing a sentence for a misdemeanor, other than a minor misdemeanor, upon an offender who is not required to serve a mandatory jail term may impose any other sanction that is intended to discourage the offender or other persons from committing a similar offense if the sanction is reasonably related to the overriding purposes and principles of misdemeanor sentencing.

(C) The court imposing a sentence for a minor misdemeanor may impose a term of community service in lieu of all or part of a fine. The term of community service imposed for a minor misdemeanor shall not exceed thirty hours.

(2004 H 163, eff. 9–23–04; 2002 H 490, eff. 1–1–04)

2929.28 Financial sanctions

(A) In addition to imposing court costs pursuant to section 2947.23 of the Revised Code, the court imposing a sentence upon an offender for a misdemeanor, including a minor misdemeanor, may sentence the offender to any financial sanction or combination of financial sanctions authorized under this section. If the court in its discretion imposes one or more financial sanctions, the financial sanctions that may be imposed pursuant to this section include, but are not limited to, the following:

(1) Unless the misdemeanor offense is a minor misdemeanor or could be disposed of by the traffic violations bureau serving the court under Traffic Rule 13, restitution by the offender to the victim of the offender's crime or any survivor of the victim, in an amount based on the victim's economic loss. The court may not impose restitution as a sanction pursuant to this division if the offense is a minor misdemeanor or could be disposed of by the traffic violations bureau serving the court under Traffic Rule 13. If the court requires restitution, the court shall order that the restitution be made to the victim in open court or to the adult probation department that serves the jurisdiction or the clerk of the court on behalf of the victim.

If the court imposes restitution, the court shall determine the amount of restitution to be paid by the offender. If the court imposes restitution, the court may base the amount of restitution it orders on an amount recommended by the victim, the offender, a presentence investigation report, estimates or receipts indicating the cost of repairing or replacing property, and other information, provided that the amount the court orders as restitution shall not exceed the amount of the economic loss suffered by the victim as a direct and proximate result of the commission of the offense. If the court decides to impose restitution, the court shall hold an evidentiary hearing on restitution if the offender, victim, or survivor disputes the amount of restitution. If the court holds an evidentiary hearing, at the hearing the victim or survivor has the burden to prove by a preponderance of the evidence the amount of restitution sought from the offender.

All restitution payments shall be credited against any recovery of economic loss in a civil action brought by the victim or any survivor of the victim against the offender.

If the court imposes restitution, the court may order that the offender pay a surcharge, of not more than five per cent of the amount of the restitution otherwise ordered, to the entity responsible for collecting and processing restitution payments.

The victim or survivor may request that the prosecutor in the case file a motion, or the offender may file a motion, for modification of the payment terms of any restitution ordered. If the court grants the motion, it may modify the payment terms as it determines appropriate.

(2) A fine of the type described in divisions (A)(2)(a) and (b) of this section payable to the appropriate entity as required by law:

(a) A fine in the following amount:

(i) For a misdemeanor of the first degree, not more than one thousand dollars;

(ii) For a misdemeanor of the second degree, not more than seven hundred fifty dollars;

(iii) For a misdemeanor of the third degree, not more than five hundred dollars;

(iv) For a misdemeanor of the fourth degree, not more than two hundred fifty dollars;

(v) For a minor misdemeanor, not more than one hundred fifty dollars.

(b) A state fine or cost as defined in section 2949.111 of the Revised Code.

(3)(a) Reimbursement by the offender of any or all of the costs of sanctions incurred by the government, including, but not limited to, the following:

(i) All or part of the costs of implementing any community control sanction, including a supervision fee under section 2951.021 of the Revised Code;

(ii) All or part of the costs of confinement in a jail or other residential facility, including, but not limited to, a per diem fee for room and board, the costs of medical and dental treatment, and the costs of repairing property damaged by the offender while confined.

(b) The amount of reimbursement ordered under division (A)(3)(a) of this section shall not exceed the total amount of reimbursement the offender is able to pay and shall not exceed the actual cost of the sanctions. The court may collect any amount of reimbursement the offender is required to pay under that division. If the court does not order reimbursement under that division, confinement costs may be assessed pursuant to a repayment policy adopted under section 2929.37 of the Revised Code. In addition, the offender may be required to pay the fees specified in section 2929.38 of the Revised Code in accordance with that section.

(B) If the court determines a hearing is necessary, the court may hold a hearing to determine whether the offender is able to pay the financial sanction imposed pursuant to this section or court costs or is likely in the future to be able to pay the sanction or costs.

If the court determines that the offender is indigent and unable to pay the financial sanction or court costs, the court shall consider imposing and may impose a term of community service under division (A) of section 2929.27 of the Revised Code in lieu of imposing a financial sanction or court costs. If the court does not determine that the offender is indigent, the court may impose a term of community service under division (A) of section 2929.27 of the Revised Code in lieu of or in addition to imposing a financial sanction under this section and in addition to imposing court costs. The court may order community service for a minor misdemeanor pursuant to division (C) of section 2929.27 of the Revised Code in lieu of or in addition to imposing a financial sanction under this section and in addition to imposing court costs. If a person fails to pay a financial sanction or court costs, the court may order community service in lieu of the financial sanction or court costs.

(C)(1) The offender shall pay reimbursements imposed upon the offender pursuant to division (A)(3) of this section to pay the costs incurred by a county pursuant to any sanction imposed under this section or section 2929.26 or 2929.27 of the Revised Code or in operating a facility used to confine offenders pursuant to a sanction imposed under section 2929.26 of the Revised Code to the county treasurer. The county treasurer shall deposit the reimbursements in the county's general fund. The county shall use the amounts deposited in the fund to pay the costs incurred by the county pursuant to any sanction imposed under this section or section 2929.26 or 2929.27 of the Revised Code or in operating a facility used to confine offenders pursuant to a sanction imposed under section 2929.26 of the Revised Code.

(2) The offender shall pay reimbursements imposed upon the offender pursuant to division (A)(3) of this section to pay the costs incurred by a municipal corporation pursuant to any sanction imposed under this section or section 2929.26 or 2929.27 of the Revised Code or in operating a facility used to confine offenders pursuant to a sanction imposed under section 2929.26 of the Revised Code to the treasurer of the municipal corporation. The treasurer shall deposit the reimbursements in the municipal corporation's general fund. The municipal corporation shall use the amounts deposited in the fund to pay the costs incurred by the municipal corporation pursuant to any sanction imposed under this section or section 2929.26 or 2929.27 of the Revised Code or in operating a facility used to confine offenders pursuant to a sanction imposed under section 2929.26 of the Revised Code.

(3) The offender shall pay reimbursements imposed pursuant to division (A)(3) of this section for the costs incurred by a private provider pursuant to a sanction imposed under this section or section 2929.26 or 2929.27 of the Revised Code to the provider.

(D) Except as otherwise provided in this division, a financial sanction imposed under division (A) of this section is a judgment in favor of the state or the political subdivision that operates the court that imposed the financial sanction, and the offender subject to the financial sanction is the judgment debtor. A financial sanction of reimbursement imposed pursuant to division (A)(3)(a)(i) of this section upon an offender is a judgment in favor of the entity administering the community control sanction, and the offender subject to the financial sanction is the judgment debtor. A financial sanction of reimbursement imposed pursuant to division (A)(3)(a)(ii) of this section upon an offender confined in a jail or other residential facility is a judgment in favor of the entity operating the jail or other residential facility, and the offender subject to the financial sanction is the judgment debtor. A financial sanction of restitution imposed pursuant to division (A)(1) of this section is an order in favor of the victim of the offender's criminal act that can be collected through execution as described in division (D)(1) of this section or through an order as described in division (D)(2) of this section and the offender shall be considered for purposes of the collection as the judgment debtor.

Once the financial sanction is imposed as a judgment or order under this division, the victim, private provider, state, or political subdivision may bring an action to do any of the following:

(1) Obtain execution of the judgment or order through any available procedure, including any of the procedures identified in divisions (D)(1)(a) to (e) of section 2929.18 of the Revised Code.

(2) Obtain an order for the assignment of wages of the judgment debtor under section 1321.33 of the Revised Code.

(E) The civil remedies authorized under division (D) of this section for the collection of the financial sanction supplement, but do not preclude, enforcement of the criminal sentence.

(F) Each court imposing a financial sanction upon an offender under this section may designate the clerk of the court or another person to collect the financial sanction. The clerk, or another person authorized by law or the court to collect the financial sanction may do the following:

(1) Enter into contracts with one or more public agencies or private vendors for the collection of amounts due under the sanction. Before entering into a contract for the collection of amounts due from an offender pursuant to any financial sanction

imposed pursuant to this section, a court shall comply with sections 307.86 to 307.92 of the Revised Code.

(2) Permit payment of all or any portion of the sanction in installments, by financial transaction device if the court is a county court or a municipal court operated by a county, by credit or debit card or by another electronic transfer if the court is a municipal court not operated by a county, or by any other reasonable method, in any time, and on any terms that court considers just, except that the maximum time permitted for payment shall not exceed five years. If the court is a county court or a municipal court operated by a county, the acceptance of payments by any financial transaction device shall be governed by the policy adopted by the board of county commissioners of the county pursuant to section 301.28 of the Revised Code. If the court is a municipal court not operated by a county, the clerk may pay any fee associated with processing an electronic transfer out of public money or may charge the fee to the offender.

(3) To defray administrative costs, charge a reasonable fee to an offender who elects a payment plan rather than a lump sum payment of any financial sanction.

(G) No financial sanction imposed under this section shall preclude a victim from bringing a civil action against the offender.

(2004 H 52, eff. 6–1–04; 2003 S 57, eff. 1–1–04; 2002 H 490, eff. 1–1–04)

Historical and Statutory Notes

Ed. Note: Former 2929.28 amended and recodified as 2929.71 by 2002 H 490, eff. 1–1–04; 1986 H 284, eff. 3–6–86.

2929.31 Organizational penalties

(A) Regardless of the penalties provided in sections 2929.02, 2929.14 to 2929.18, and 2929.24 to 2929.28 of the Revised Code, an organization convicted of an offense pursuant to section 2901.23 of the Revised Code shall be fined in accordance with this section. The court shall fix the fine as follows:

(1) For aggravated murder, not more than one hundred thousand dollars;

(2) For murder, not more than fifty thousand dollars;

(3) For a felony of the first degree, not more than twenty-five thousand dollars;

(4) For a felony of the second degree, not more than twenty thousand dollars;

(5) For a felony of the third degree, not more than fifteen thousand dollars;

(6) For a felony of the fourth degree, not more than ten thousand dollars;

(7) For a felony of the fifth degree, not more than seventy-five hundred dollars;

(8) For a misdemeanor of the first degree, not more than five thousand dollars;

(9) For a misdemeanor of the second degree, not more than four thousand dollars;

(10) For a misdemeanor of the third degree, not more than three thousand dollars;

(11) For a misdemeanor of the fourth degree, not more than two thousand dollars;

(12) For a minor misdemeanor, not more than one thousand dollars;

(13) For a felony not specifically classified, not more than ten thousand dollars;

(14) For a misdemeanor not specifically classified, not more than two thousand dollars;

(15) For a minor misdemeanor not specifically classified, not more than one thousand dollars.

(B) When an organization is convicted of an offense that is not specifically classified, and the section defining the offense or penalty plainly indicates a purpose to impose the penalty provided for violation upon organizations, then the penalty so provided shall be imposed in lieu of the penalty provided in this section.

(C) When an organization is convicted of an offense that is not specifically classified, and the penalty provided includes a higher fine than the fine that is provided in this section, then the penalty imposed shall be pursuant to the penalty provided for the violation of the section defining the offense.

(D) This section does not prevent the imposition of available civil sanctions against an organization convicted of an offense pursuant to section 2901.23 of the Revised Code, either in addition to or in lieu of a fine imposed pursuant to this section.

(2002 H 490, eff. 1–1–04; 1995 S 2, eff. 7–1–96; 1982 H 269, § 4, eff. 7–1–83; 1982 S 199; 1972 H 511)

2929.32 Crime victims recovery fund

(A)(1) Subject to division (A)(2) of this section, notwithstanding the fines prescribed in section 2929.02 of the Revised Code for a person who is convicted of or pleads guilty to aggravated murder or murder, the fines prescribed in section 2929.18 of the Revised Code for a person who is convicted of or pleads guilty to a felony, the fines prescribed in section 2929.28 of the Revised Code for a person who is convicted of or pleads guilty to a misdemeanor, the fines prescribed in section 2929.31 of the Revised Code for an organization that is convicted of or pleads guilty to an offense, and the fines prescribed in any other section of the Revised Code for a person who is convicted of or pleads guilty to an offense, a sentencing court may impose upon the offender a fine of not more than one million dollars if any of the following applies to the offense and the offender:

(a) There are three or more victims, as defined in section 2969.11 of the Revised Code, of the offense for which the offender is being sentenced.

(b) The offender previously has been convicted of or pleaded guilty to one or more offenses, and, for the offense for which the offender is being sentenced and all of the other offenses, there is a total of three or more victims, as defined in section 2969.11 of the Revised Code.

(c) The offense for which the offender is being sentenced is aggravated murder, murder, or a felony of the first degree that, if it had been committed prior to July 1, 1996, would have been an aggravated felony of the first degree.

(2) If the offense in question is a first, second, or third degree felony violation of any provision of Chapter 2925., 3719., or 4729. of the Revised Code, the court shall impose upon the offender the mandatory fine described in division (B) of section 2929.18 of the Revised Code, and, in addition, may impose a fine under division (A)(1) of this section, provided that the total of the mandatory fine and the fine imposed under division (A)(1) of this section shall not exceed one million dollars. The mandatory fine shall be paid as described in division (D) of section 2929.18 of the Revised Code, and the fine imposed under division (A)(1) of this section shall be deposited pursuant to division (B) of this section.

(B) If a sentencing court imposes a fine upon an offender pursuant to division (A)(1) of this section, all moneys paid in satisfaction of the fine or collected pursuant to division (C)(1) of this section in satisfaction of the fine shall be deposited into the crime victims recovery fund created by division (D) of this section and shall be distributed as described in that division.

(C)(1) Subject to division (C)(2) of this section, notwithstanding any contrary provision of any section of the Revised Code, if a sentencing court imposes a fine upon an offender pursuant to division (A)(1) of this section or pursuant to another section of the Revised Code, the fine shall be a judgment against the offender in favor of the state, and both of the following apply to that judgment:

(a) The state may collect the judgment by garnishing, attaching, or otherwise executing against any income, profits, or other real or personal property in which the offender has any right, title, or interest, including property acquired after the imposition of the fine, in the same manner as if the judgment had been rendered against the offender and in favor of the state in a civil action. If the fine is imposed pursuant to division (A)(1) of this section, the moneys collected as a result of the garnishment, attachment, or other execution shall be deposited and distributed as described in divisions (B) and (D) of this section. If the fine is not imposed pursuant to division (A)(1) of this section, the moneys collected as a result of the garnishment, attachment, or other execution shall be distributed as otherwise provided by law for the distribution of money paid in satisfaction of a fine.

(b) The provisions of Chapter 2329. of the Revised Code relative to the establishment of court judgments and decrees as liens and to the enforcement of those liens apply to the judgment.

(2) Division (C)(1) of this section does not apply to any financial sanction imposed pursuant to section 2929.18 of the Revised Code upon a person who is convicted of or pleads guilty to a felony.

(D) There is hereby created in the state treasury the crime victims recovery fund. If a sentencing court imposes a fine upon an offender pursuant to division (A)(1) of this section, all moneys paid in satisfaction of the fine and all moneys collected in satisfaction of the fine pursuant to division (C)(1) of this section shall be deposited into the fund. The fund shall be administered and the moneys in it shall be distributed in accordance with sections 2969.11 to 2969.14 of the Revised Code.

(2002 H 490, eff. 1–1–04)

Historical and Statutory Notes

Ed. Note: 2929.32 is former 2929.25, amended and recodified by 2002 H 490, eff. 1–1–04; 1996 S 269, eff. 7–1–96; 1995 S 91, eff. 11–15–95.

2929.34 Places of imprisonment according to offenses

(A) A person who is convicted of or pleads guilty to aggravated murder, murder, or an offense punishable by life imprisonment and who is sentenced to a term of life imprisonment or a prison term pursuant to that conviction shall serve that term in an institution under the control of the department of rehabilitation and correction.

(B)(1) A person who is convicted of or pleads guilty to a felony other than aggravated murder, murder, or an offense punishable by life imprisonment and who is sentenced to a term of imprisonment or a prison term pursuant to that conviction shall serve that term as follows:

(a) Subject to divisions (B)(1)(b) and (B)(2) of this section, in an institution under the control of the department of rehabilitation and correction if the term is a prison term or as otherwise determined by the sentencing court pursuant to section 2929.16 of the Revised Code if the term is not a prison term;

(b) In a facility of a type described in division (G)(1) of section 2929.13 of the Revised Code, if the offender is sentenced pursuant to that division.

(2) If the term is a prison term, the person may be imprisoned in a jail that is not a minimum security jail pursuant to agreement under section 5120.161 of the Revised Code between the department of rehabilitation and correction and the local authority that operates the jail.

(C) A person who is convicted of or pleads guilty to one or more misdemeanors and who is sentenced to a jail term or term of imprisonment pursuant to the conviction or convictions shall serve that term in a county, multicounty, municipal, municipal-county, or multicounty-municipal jail or workhouse or, if the misdemeanor or misdemeanors are not offenses of violence, in a minimum security jail.

(D) Nothing in this section prohibits the commitment, referral, or sentencing of a person who is convicted of or pleads guilty to a felony to a community-based correctional facility and program or district community-based correctional facility and program in accordance with sections 2301.51 to 2301.56 of the Revised Code.

(2002 H 490, eff. 1–1–04)

Historical and Statutory Notes

Ed. Note: 2929.34 is former 2929.221, amended and recodified by 2002 H 490, eff. 1–1–04; 1996 S 166, eff. 10–17–96; 1996 S 269, eff. 7–1–96; 1995 S 2, eff. 7–1–96; 1994 H 571, eff. 10–6–94; 1990 S 258, eff. 11–20–90; 1987 H 455; 1983 S 210; 1982 H 269, S 199.

2929.36 Definitions

As used in sections 2929.36 to 2929.38 of the Revised Code:

(A) "Chief legal officer" includes a prosecuting attorney, village solicitor, city director of law, and attorney for a district of a joint city and county workhouse or county workhouse.

(B) "Clerk of the appropriate court" or "appropriate court clerk" means whichever of the following applies:

(1) If the local detention facility in question is a multicounty correctional center, multicounty-municipal correctional center, district community-based correctional facility, or district workhouse, the clerk of the court of common pleas of the most populous county served by the local detention facility;

(2) If the local detention facility in question is a city workhouse, the clerk of the municipal court for that city;

(3) If neither (B)(1) nor (B)(2) of this section applies, the clerk of the court of common pleas of the county in which the local detention facility in question is located.

(C) "Homestead" has the same meaning as in division (A) of section 323.151 of the Revised Code.

(D) "Inmate account" has the same meaning as in section 2969.21 of the Revised Code.

(E) "Local detention facility" means a multicounty correctional center, municipal-county correctional center, multicounty-municipal correctional center, community-based correctional facility, district community-based correctional facility, jail, county jail, municipal or county prison, station house, workhouse, city workhouse, county workhouse, joint city and county workhouse, and district workhouse.

(2002 H 490, eff. 1–1–04)

Historical and Statutory Notes

Ed. Note: 2929.36 is former 2929.35, amended and recodified by 2002 H 490, eff. 1–1–04; 2002 H 170, eff. 9–6–02.

2929.37 Adoption of policy requiring repayment for costs of confinement

(A) A board of county commissioners, in an agreement with the sheriff, a legislative authority of a municipal corporation, a corrections commission, a judicial corrections board, or any other public or private entity that operates a local detention facility at which a prisoner who is convicted of an offense and who is confined in the facility under a sanction or term of imprisonment imposed under section 2929.16, sections 2929.21 to 2929.28, or any other provision of the Revised Code may adopt, pursuant to section 307.93, 341.14, 341.19, 341.21, 341.23, 753.02, 753.04, 753.16, 2301.56, or 2947.19 of the Revised Code, a policy that requires the prisoner to pay all or part of the costs of confinement in that facility. If a board of county commissioners, legislative authority, corrections commission, judicial corrections board, or other entity adopts a policy for a facility pursuant to one of those sections, the person in charge of that facility shall appoint a reimbursement coordinator to administer the facility's policy.

The costs of confinement may include, but are not limited to, the costs of repairing property damaged by the prisoner while confined, a per diem fee for room and board, medical and dental treatment costs, the fee for a random drug test assessed under division (E) of section 341.26 and division (E) of section 753.33 of the Revised Code, and a one-time reception fee for the costs of processing the prisoner into the facility at the time of the prisoner's initial entry into the facility under the confinement in question, minus any fees deducted under section 2929.38 of the Revised Code. Any policy adopted under this section shall be used when a court does not order reimbursement of confinement costs under section 2929.18 or 2929.28 of the Revised Code. The amount assessed under this section shall not exceed the total amount that the prisoner is able to pay.

(B)(1) Each prisoner covered by a repayment policy adopted as described in division (A) of this section shall receive at the end of the prisoner's confinement an itemized bill of the expenses to be reimbursed. The policy shall allow periodic payments on a schedule to be implemented upon a prisoner's release. The bill also shall state that payment shall be made to the person identified in the bill as the reimbursement coordinator and include a notice that specifies that the prisoner has thirty days in which to dispute the bill by filing a written objection with the reimbursement coordinator and that if the prisoner does not dispute the bill in that manner within that period, the prisoner is required to pay the bill and a certificate of judgment may be obtained against the prisoner for the amount of the unpaid expenses. The prisoner shall sign a copy of the bill, and the reimbursement coordinator shall retain that copy. If the prisoner disputes an item on the bill within thirty days after receiving the bill, the reimbursement coordinator may either concede the disputed item or proceed to a hearing under division (B)(2) of this section.

(2) If the prisoner disputes an item on an itemized bill presented to the prisoner under division (B)(1) of this section and the reimbursement coordinator does not concede the item, the reimbursement coordinator shall submit the bill to the court, and the court shall hold a hearing on the disputed items in the bill. At the end of the hearing, the court shall determine how much of the disputed expenses the prisoner shall reimburse the legislative authority or managing authority and shall issue a judgment in favor of the legislative authority or managing authority for any undisputed expenses and the amount of the disputed expenses for which the prisoner must reimburse the legislative authority or managing authority. The reimbursement coordinator shall not seek to enforce the judgment until at least ninety days after the court issues the judgment.

(C) If a prisoner does not dispute the itemized bill presented to the prisoner under division (B) of this section and does not pay the bill within ninety days, the reimbursement coordinator shall send by mail a notice to the prisoner requesting payment of the expenses as stated in the bill. If the prisoner does not respond to the notice by paying the expenses in full within thirty days of the date the notice was mailed, the reimbursement coordinator shall send by mail a second notice to the prisoner requesting payment of the expenses. If one hundred eighty days elapse from the date that the reimbursement coordinator provides the bill and if the prisoner has not paid the full amount of the expenses pursuant to the bill and the notices, the reimbursement coordinator may notify the clerk of the appropriate court of those facts, and the clerk may issue a certificate of judgment against the prisoner for the balance of the expenses remaining unpaid.

(D) The reimbursement coordinator may collect any amounts remaining unpaid on an itemized bill and any costs associated with the enforcement of the judgment and may enter into a contract with one or more public agencies or private vendors to collect any amounts remaining unpaid. For enforcing a judgment issued under this section, the reimbursement coordinator may assess an additional poundage fee of two per cent of the amount remaining unpaid and may collect costs associated with the enforcement of the judgment.

(E) Neither the reimbursement coordinator nor the legislative authority or the managing authority shall enforce any judgment obtained under this section by means of execution against the prisoner's homestead. Any reimbursement received under this section shall be credited to the general fund of the treasury of the political subdivision that incurred the expense, to be used for general fund purposes.

(2002 H 490, eff. 1-1-04; 2002 H 170, eff. 9-6-02)

2929.38 Establishment of policy requiring payment of reception fee, fee for medical or dental treatment, or fee for random drug test

(A) A board of commissioners of a county, in an agreement with the sheriff, a legislative authority of a municipal corporation, a corrections commission, a judicial corrections board, or any other public or private entity that operates a local detention facility described in division (A) of section 2929.37 of the Revised Code, may establish a policy that requires any prisoner who is confined in the facility as a result of pleading guilty to or having been convicted of an offense to pay a one-time reception fee for the costs of processing the prisoner into the facility at the time of the prisoner's initial entry into the facility under the confinement in question, to pay a reasonable fee for any medical or dental treatment or service requested by and provided to that prisoner, and to pay the fee for a random drug test assessed under division (E) of section 341.26, and division (E) of section 753.33 of the Revised Code. The fee for the medical treatment or service shall not exceed the actual cost of the treatment or service provided. No prisoner confined in the local detention facility shall be denied any necessary medical care because of inability to pay the fees.

(B) Upon assessment of a one-time reception fee as described in division (A) of this section, the provision of the requested medical treatment or service, or the assessment of a fee for a random drug test, payment of the required fee may be automatically deducted from the prisoner's inmate account in the business office of the local detention facility in which the prisoner is confined. If there is no money in the account, a deduction may be made at a later date during the prisoner's confinement if the money becomes available in the account. If, after release, the prisoner has an unpaid balance of those fees, the sheriff, legislative authority of the municipal corporation, corrections commission, judicial corrections board, or other entity that operates the local detention facility described in division (A) of section 2929.37 of the Revised Code may bill the prisoner for the payment of the unpaid fees. Fees received for medical or dental treatment or services shall be paid to the commissary fund, if one exists for the facility, or if no commissary fund exists, to the general fund of the treasury of the political subdivision that incurred the expenses, in the same proportion as those expenses were borne by the political subdivision. Fees received for medical treatment or services that are placed in the commissary fund under this division shall be used for the same purposes as profits from the commissary fund, except that they shall not be used to pay any salary or benefits of any person who works in or is employed for the sole purpose of providing service to the commissary.

(C) Any fee paid by a person under this section shall be deducted from any medical or dental costs that the person is ordered to reimburse under a financial sanction imposed pursuant to section 2929.28 of the Revised Code or to repay under a policy adopted under section 2929.37 of the Revised Code.

(D) As used in this section, "inmate account" has the same meaning as in section 2969.21 of the Revised Code.

(2003 H 95, § 3.13, eff. 1-1-04; 2003 H 95, § 1, eff. 9-26-03; 2002 H 490, eff. 1-1-04; 2002 H 170, eff. 9-6-02)

2929.41 Multiple sentences

(A) Except as provided in division (B) of this section, division (E) of section 2929.14, or division (D) or (E) of section 2971.03 of the Revised Code, a prison term, jail term, or sentence of imprisonment shall be served concurrently with any other prison term, jail term, or sentence of imprisonment imposed by a court of this state, another state, or the United States. Except as provided in division (B)(3) of this section, a jail term or sentence of imprisonment for misdemeanor shall be served concurrently with a prison term or sentence of imprisonment for felony served in a state or federal correctional institution.

(B)(1) A jail term or sentence of imprisonment for a misdemeanor shall be served consecutively to any other prison term, jail term, or sentence of imprisonment when the trial court specifies that it is to be served consecutively or when it is imposed for a misdemeanor violation of section 2907.322, 2921.34, or 2923.131 of the Revised Code.

When consecutive sentences are imposed for misdemeanor under this division, the term to be served is the aggregate of the consecutive terms imposed, except that the aggregate term to be served shall not exceed eighteen months.

(2) If a court of this state imposes a prison term upon the offender for the commission of a felony and a court of another state or the United States also has imposed a prison term upon the offender for the commission of a felony, the court of this state may order that the offender serve the prison term it imposes consecutively to any prison term imposed upon the offender by the court of another state or the United States.

(3) A jail term or sentence of imprisonment imposed for a misdemeanor violation of section 4510.11, 4510.14, 4510.16, 4510.21, or 4511.19 of the Revised Code shall be served consecutively to a prison term that is imposed for a felony violation of section 2903.06, 2903.07, 2903.08, or 4511.19 of the Revised Code or a felony violation of section 2903.04 of the Revised Code involving the operation of a motor vehicle by the offender and that is served in a state correctional institution when the trial court specifies that it is to be served consecutively.

When consecutive jail terms or sentences of imprisonment and prison terms are imposed for one or more misdemeanors and one or more felonies under this division, the term to be served is the aggregate of the consecutive terms imposed, and the offender shall serve all terms imposed for a felony before serving any term imposed for a misdemeanor.

(2002 H 490, eff. 1-1-04; 2002 S 123, eff. 1-1-04; 1999 S 22, eff. 5-17-00; 1999 S 107, eff. 3-23-00; 1996 H 180, eff. 1-1-97; 1996 H 154, eff. 10-4-96; 1995 S 2, eff. 7-1-96; 1994 H 571, eff. 10-6-94; 1992 H 561, eff. 4-9-93; 1990 S 258; 1988 H 51; 1983 S 210; 1982 H 269, § 4, S 199; 1981 S 1; 1978 H 202; 1972 H 511)

2929.42 Reports to licensing boards of criminal offenses involving licensed health care professionals

(A) The prosecutor in any case against any person licensed, certified, registered, or otherwise authorized to practice under Chapter 3719., 4715., 4723., 4729., 4730., 4731., 4734., or 4741. of the Revised Code shall notify the appropriate licensing board, on forms provided by the board, of any of the following regarding the person:

(1) A plea of guilty to, or a conviction of, a felony, or a court order dismissing a felony charge on technical or procedural grounds;

(2) A plea of guilty to, or a conviction of, a misdemeanor committed in the course of practice or in the course of business, or a court order dismissing such a misdemeanor charge on technical or procedural grounds;

(3) A plea of guilty to, or a conviction of, a misdemeanor involving moral turpitude, or a court order dismissing such a charge on technical or procedural grounds.

(B) The report required by division (A) of this section shall include the name and address of the person, the nature of the offense, and certified copies of court entries in the action.

(2002 H 490, eff. 1-1-04)

Historical and Statutory Notes

Ed. Note: 2929.42 is former 2929.24, recodified by 2002 H 490, eff. 1-1-04; 2000 H 506, eff. 4-10-01; 1995 S 143, § 5, eff. 7-1-96; 1995 S 2, eff. 7-1-96.

2929.43 Guilty plea or conviction of peace officer of felony charge; notice; report

(A) As used in this section:

(1) "Peace officer" has the same meaning as in section 109.71 of the Revised Code.

(2) "Felony" has the same meaning as in section 109.511 of the Revised Code.

(B)(1) Prior to accepting a plea of guilty to an indictment, information, or complaint charging a felony, the court shall determine whether the defendant is a peace officer. If the court determines that the defendant is a peace officer, it shall address the defendant personally and provide the following advisement to the defendant that shall be entered in the record of the court.

"You are hereby advised that conviction of the felony offense to which you are pleading guilty will result in the termination of your employment as a peace officer and in your decertification as a peace officer pursuant to the laws of Ohio."

Upon the request of the defendant, the court shall allow the defendant additional time to consider the appropriateness of the plea of guilty in light of the advisement described in division (B)(1) of this section.

The court shall not accept a plea of guilty of a defendant who is a peace officer unless, in addition to any other procedures required under the Rules of Criminal Procedure, the court determines that the defendant voluntarily and intelligently enters that plea after being given the advisement described in division (B)(1) of this section.

(2) After accepting under division (B)(1) of this section a plea of guilty to an indictment, information, or complaint charging a felony, the court shall provide to the clerk of the court of common pleas a written notice of the plea of guilty of the defendant peace officer, the name and address of the peace officer, the law enforcement agency or other governmental entity that employs the peace officer and its address, the date of the

plea, the nature of the felony offense, and certified copies of court entries in the action. Upon receiving the written notice required by division (B)(2) of this section, the clerk of the court of common pleas shall transmit to the employer of the peace officer and to the Ohio peace officer training council a report that includes the information contained in the written notice and the certified copies of the court entries in the action.

(C)(1) Upon the conviction of a defendant, after trial, of a felony, the trial judge shall determine whether the defendant is a peace officer. If the judge determines that the defendant is a peace officer or if the defendant states on the record that the defendant is a peace officer, the judge shall provide to the clerk of the court of common pleas a written notice of the conviction of the defendant peace officer, the name and address of the peace officer, the law enforcement agency or other governmental entity that employs the peace officer and its address, the date of the conviction, the nature of the felony offense, and certified copies of court entries in the action. Upon receiving the written notice required by division (C)(1) of this section, the clerk of the court of common pleas shall transmit to the employer of the peace officer and to the Ohio peace officer training council a report that includes the information contained in the written notice and the certified copies of the court entries in the action.

(2) Upon the conclusion of the final appeal of a defendant who is a peace officer and who has been convicted of a felony, upon expiration of the time period within which that peace officer may appeal the conviction if no appeal is taken, or otherwise upon the final disposition of the criminal action against that peace officer, the trial judge shall provide to the clerk of the court of common pleas a written notice of the final disposition of the action that shall include, as appropriate, notice of the final conviction of the peace officer of the felony, the acquittal of the peace officer of the felony, the conviction of the peace officer of a misdemeanor, or the dismissal of the felony charge against the peace officer. The judge also shall provide to the clerk of the court of common pleas certified copies of the court entries in the action. Upon receiving the written notice required by division (C)(2) of this section, the clerk of the court of common pleas shall transmit to the employer of the peace officer and to the Ohio peace officer training council a report that includes the information contained in the written notice and the certified copies of the court entries in the action.

(D) If pursuant to a negotiated plea agreement between a prosecuting attorney and a defendant who is a peace officer and who is charged with a felony, in which the defendant agrees to enter a plea of guilty to a misdemeanor and to surrender the certificate awarded to the defendant under section 109.77 of the Revised Code, the trial judge issues an order to the defendant to surrender that certificate, the trial judge shall provide to the clerk of the court a written notice of the order, the name and address of the peace officer, the law enforcement agency or other governmental entity that employs the peace officer and its address, the date of the plea, the nature of the misdemeanor to which the peace officer pleaded guilty, and certified copies of court entries in the action. Upon receiving the written notice required by this division, the clerk of the court shall transmit to the employer of the peace officer and to the executive director of the Ohio peace officer training council a report that includes the information contained in the written notice and the certified copies of the court entries in the action.

(2002 H 490, eff. 1–1–04)

Historical and Statutory Notes

Ed. Note: 2929.43 is former 2929.29, recodified by 2002 H 490, eff. 1–1–04; 1996 H 566, eff. 10–16–96.

2929.61 Applicable law according to time of offense; may be chosen by person to be sentenced

(A) Persons charged with a capital offense committed prior to January 1, 1974, shall be prosecuted under the law as it existed at the time the offense was committed, and, if convicted, shall be imprisoned for life, except that whenever the statute under which any such person is prosecuted provides for a lesser penalty under the circumstances of the particular case, such lesser penalty shall be imposed.

(B) Persons charged with an offense, other than a capital offense, committed prior to January 1, 1974, shall be prosecuted under the law as it existed at the time the offense was committed. Persons convicted or sentenced on or after January 1, 1974, for an offense committed prior to January 1, 1974, shall be sentenced according to the penalty for commission of the substantially equivalent offense under Amended Substitute House Bill 511 of the 109th General Assembly. If the offense for which sentence is being imposed does not have a substantial equivalent under that act, or if that act provides a more severe penalty than that originally prescribed for the offense of which the person is convicted, then sentence shall be imposed under the law as it existed prior to January 1, 1974.

(C) Persons charged with an offense that is a felony of the third or fourth degree and that was committed on or after January 1, 1974, and before July 1, 1983, shall be prosecuted under the law as it existed at the time the offense was committed. Persons convicted or sentenced on or after July 1, 1983, for an offense that is a felony of the third or fourth degree and that was committed on or after January 1, 1974, and before July 1, 1983, shall be notified by the court sufficiently in advance of sentencing that they may choose to be sentenced pursuant to either the law in effect at the time of the commission of the offense or the law in effect at the time of sentencing. This notice shall be written and shall include the differences between and possible effects of the alternative sentence forms and the effect of the person's refusal to choose. The person to be sentenced shall then inform the court in writing of his choice, and shall be sentenced accordingly. Any person choosing to be sentenced pursuant to the law in effect at the time of the commission of an offense that is a felony of the third or fourth degree shall then be eligible for parole, and this person cannot at a later date have his sentence converted to a definite sentence. If the person refuses to choose between the two possible sentences, the person shall be sentenced pursuant to the law in effect at the time of the commission of the offense.

(D) Persons charged with an offense that was a felony of the first or second degree at the time it was committed, that was committed on or after January 1, 1974, and that was committed prior to July 1, 1983, shall be prosecuted for that offense and, if convicted, shall be sentenced under the law as it existed at the time the offense was committed.

(1983 S 210, eff. 7–1–83; 1982 H 269, S 199; 1975 H 1; 1972 H 511, § 3)

2929.71 Convicted arsonist to make restitution to public agency; hearing

(A) As used in this section:

(1) "Agency" means any law enforcement agency, other public agency, or public official involved in the investigation or prosecution of the offender or in the investigation of the fire or explosion in an aggravated arson, arson, or criminal damaging or endangering case. An "agency" includes, but is not limited to, a sheriff's office, a municipal corporation, township, or township police district police department, the office of a prosecuting attorney, city director of law, village solicitor, or similar chief legal officer of a municipal corporation, the fire marshal's office, a municipal corporation, township, or township fire district fire department,

the office of a fire prevention officer, and any state, county, or municipal corporation crime laboratory.

(2) "Assets" includes all forms of real or personal property.

(3) "Itemized statement" means the statement of costs described in division (B) of this section.

(4) "Offender" means the person who has been convicted of or pleaded guilty to committing, attempting to commit, or complicity in committing a violation of section 2909.02 or 2909.03 of the Revised Code, or, when the means used are fire or explosion, division (A)(2) of section 2909.06 of the Revised Code.

(5) "Costs" means the reasonable value of the time spent by an officer or employee of an agency on the aggravated arson, arson, or criminal damaging or endangering case, any moneys spent by the agency on that case, and the reasonable fair market value of resources used or expended by the agency on that case.

(B) Prior to the sentencing of an offender, the court shall enter an order that directs agencies that wish to be reimbursed by the offender for the costs they incurred in the investigation or prosecution of the offender or in the investigation of the fire or explosion involved in the case, to file with the court within a specified time an itemized statement of those costs. The order also shall require that a copy of the itemized statement be given to the offender or offender's attorney within the specified time. Only itemized statements so filed and given shall be considered at the hearing described in division (C) of this section.

(C) The court shall set a date for a hearing on all the itemized statements filed with it and given to the offender or the offender's attorney in accordance with division (B) of this section. The hearing shall be held prior to the sentencing of the offender, but may be held on the same day as the sentencing. Notice of the hearing date shall be given to the offender or the offender's attorney and to the agencies whose itemized statements are involved. At the hearing, each agency has the burden of establishing by a preponderance of the evidence that the costs set forth in its itemized statement were incurred in the investigation or prosecution of the offender or in the investigation of the fire or explosion involved in the case, and of establishing by a preponderance of the evidence that the offender has assets available for the reimbursement of all or a portion of the costs.

The offender may cross-examine all witnesses and examine all documentation presented by the agencies at the hearing, and the offender may present at the hearing witnesses and documentation the offender has obtained without a subpoena or a subpoena duces tecum or, in the case of documentation, that belongs to the offender. The offender also may issue subpoenas and subpoenas duces tecum for, and present and examine at the hearing, witnesses and documentation, subject to the following applying to the witnesses or documentation subpoenaed:

(1) The testimony of witnesses subpoenaed or documentation subpoenaed is material to the preparation or presentation by the offender of the offender's defense to the claims of the agencies for a reimbursement of costs;

(2) If witnesses to be subpoenaed are personnel of an agency or documentation to be subpoenaed belongs to an agency, the personnel or documentation may be subpoenaed only if the agency involved has indicated, pursuant to this division, that it intends to present the personnel as witnesses or use the documentation at the hearing. The offender shall submit, in writing, a request to an agency as described in this division to ascertain whether the agency intends to present various personnel as witnesses or to use particular documentation. The request shall indicate that the offender is considering issuing subpoenas to personnel of the agency who are specifically named or identified by title or position, or for documentation of the agency that is specifically described or generally identified, and shall request the agency to indicate, in writing, whether it intends to present such personnel as witnesses or to use such documentation at the hearing. The agency shall promptly reply to the request of the offender. An agency is prohibited from presenting personnel as witnesses or from using documentation at the hearing if it indicates to the offender it does not intend to do so in response to a request of the offender under this division, or if it fails to reply or promptly reply to such a request.

(D) Following the hearing, the court shall determine which of the agencies established by a preponderance of the evidence that costs set forth in their itemized statements were incurred as described in division (C) of this section and that the offender has assets available for reimbursement purposes. The court also shall determine whether the offender has assets available to reimburse all such agencies, in whole or in part, for their established costs, and if it determines that the assets are available, it shall order the offender, as part of the offender's sentence, to reimburse the agencies from the offender's assets for all or a specified portion of their established costs.

(2002 H 490, eff. 1–1–04)

Historical and Statutory Notes

Ed. Note: 2929.71 is former 2929.28, amended and recodified by 2002 H 490, eff. 1-1-04; 1986 H 284, eff. 3-6-86.

CHAPTER 2930

RIGHTS OF VICTIMS OF CRIMES

2930.01 Definitions

As used in this chapter:

(A) "Crime" means any of the following:

(1) A felony;

(2) A violation of section 2903.05, 2903.06, 2903.13, 2903.21, 2903.211, 2903.22, 2907.06, 2919.25, or 2921.04 of the Revised Code, a violation of section 2903.07 of the Revised Code as it existed prior to the effective date of this amendment, or a violation of a substantially equivalent municipal ordinance.

(B) "Custodial agency" means one of the following:

(1) The entity that has custody of a defendant or an alleged juvenile offender who is incarcerated for a crime, is under detention for the commission of a specified delinquent act, or who is detained after a finding of incompetence to stand trial or not guilty by reason of insanity relative to a crime, including any of the following:

(a) The department of rehabilitation and correction or the adult parole authority;

(b) A county sheriff;

(c) The entity that administers a jail, as defined in section 2929.01 of the Revised Code;

(d) The entity that administers a community-based correctional facility and program or a district community based correctional facility and program;

(e) The department of mental health or other entity to which a defendant found incompetent to stand trial or not guilty by reason of insanity is committed.

(2) The entity that has custody of an alleged juvenile offender pursuant to an order of disposition of a juvenile court, including the department of youth services or a school, camp, institution, or other facility operated for the care of delinquent children.

(C) "Defendant" means a person who is alleged to be the perpetrator of a crime in a police report or in a complaint, indictment, or information that charges the commission of a crime and that provides the basis for the criminal prosecution and subsequent proceedings to which this chapter makes reference.

(D) "Member of the victim's family" means a spouse, child, stepchild, sibling, parent, stepparent, grandparent, or other relative of a victim but does not include a person who is charged with, convicted of, or adjudicated to be a delinquent child for the crime or specified delinquent act against the victim or another crime or specified delinquent act arising from the same conduct, criminal episode, or plan.

(E) "Prosecutor" means one of the following:

(1) With respect to a criminal case, it has the same meaning as in section 2935.01 of the Revised Code and also includes the attorney general and, when appropriate, the employees of any person listed in section 2935.01 of the Revised Code or of the attorney general.

(2) With respect to a delinquency proceeding, it includes any person listed in division (C) of section 2935.01 of the Revised Code or an employee of a person listed in that division who prosecutes a delinquency proceeding.

(F) "Public agency" means an office, agency, department, bureau, or other governmental entity of the state or of a political subdivision of the state.

(G) "Public official" has the same meaning as in section 2921.01 of the Revised Code.

(H) "Victim" means a person who is identified as the victim of a crime or specified delinquent act in a police report or in a complaint, indictment, or information that charges the commission of a crime and that provides the basis for the criminal prosecution or delinquency proceeding and subsequent proceedings to which this chapter makes reference.

(I) "Victim's representative" means a member of the victim's family or another person who pursuant to the authority of section 2930.02 of the Revised Code exercises the rights of a victim under this chapter.

(J) "Court" means a court of common pleas, juvenile court, municipal court, or county court.

(K) "Delinquency proceeding" means all proceedings in a juvenile court that are related to a case in which a complaint has been filed alleging that a child is a delinquent child.

(L) "Case" means a delinquency proceeding and all related activity or a criminal prosecution and all related activity.

(M) The "defense" means the defense against criminal charges in a criminal prosecution or the defense against a delinquent child complaint in a delinquency proceeding.

(N) The "prosecution" means the prosecution of criminal charges in a criminal prosecution or the prosecution of a delinquent child complaint in a delinquency proceeding.

(O) "Specified delinquent act" means any of the following:

(1) An act committed by a child that if committed by an adult would be a felony;

(2) An act committed by a child that is a violation of a section listed in division (A)(1) or (2) of this section or is a violation of a substantially equivalent municipal ordinance.

(P)(1) "Alleged juvenile offender" means a child who is alleged to have committed a specified delinquent act in a police report or in a complaint in juvenile court that charges the commission of a specified delinquent act and that provides the basis for the delinquency proceeding and all subsequent proceedings to which this chapter makes reference.

(2) As used in divisions (O) and (P)(1) of this section, "child" has the same meaning as in section 2151.011 of the Revised Code.

(1999 S 107, eff. 3–23–00; 1999 H 3, eff. 11–22–99; 1995 S 2, eff. 7–1–96; 1994 S 186, eff. 10–12–94)

2930.02 Representative of victim

(A) If a victim is a minor or is incapacitated, incompetent, or deceased, or if the victim chooses to designate another person, a member of a victim's family or another person may exercise the rights of the victim under this chapter as the victim's representative.

If more than one person seeks to act as the victim's representative for a particular victim, the court in which the criminal prosecution or delinquency proceeding is held shall designate one of those persons as the victim's representative. If a victim does not want to have anyone act as the victim's representative, the court shall order that only the victim may exercise the rights of a victim under this chapter.

(B) If pursuant to division (A) of this section a victim's representative is to exercise the rights of a victim, the victim or victim's representative shall notify the prosecutor or, if it is a delinquency proceeding and a prosecutor is not involved in the case, shall notify the court that the victim's representative is to act for the victim. When a victim or victim's representative has so notified the prosecutor or the court, all notice under this chapter shall be sent only to the victim's representative, all rights under this chapter shall be granted only to the victim's representative, and all references in this chapter to a victim shall be interpreted as being references to the victim's representative unless the victim informs the notifying authority that the victim also wishes to receive the notices or exercise the rights. If division (B) of section 2930.03 of the Revised Code requires a victim to make a request in order to receive any notice of a type described in this division and if a victim's representative is to exercise the rights of the victim, the victim's representative shall make the request.

(1999 H 3, eff. 11–22–99; 1995 S 2, eff. 7–1–96; 1994 S 186, eff. 10–12–94)

2930.03 Method of notice

(A) A person or entity required or authorized under this chapter to give notice to a victim shall give the notice to the victim by any means reasonably calculated to provide prompt actual notice. Except when a provision requires that notice is to be given in a specific manner, a notice may be oral or written.

(B) Except for receipt of the initial information and notice required to be given to a victim under divisions (A) and (B) of section 2930.04, section 2930.05, and divisions (A) and (B) of section 2930.06 of the Revised Code, a victim who wishes to receive any notice authorized by this chapter shall make a request for the notice to the prosecutor or the custodial agency that is to provide the notice, as specified in this chapter. If the victim does not make a request as described in this division, the prosecutor or custodial agency is not required to provide any notice described in this chapter other than the initial information and notice required to be given to a victim under divisions (A) and (B) of section 2930.04, section 2930.05, and divisions (A) and (B) of section 2930.06 of the Revised Code.

(C) A person or agency that is required to furnish notice under this chapter shall give the notice to the victim at the address or telephone number provided to the person or agency by the victim. A victim who requests to receive notice under this chapter as described in division (B) of this section shall inform the person or agency of the name, address, or telephone number of the victim and of any change to that information.

(D) A person or agency that has furnished information to a victim in accordance with any requirement or authorization under this chapter shall notify the victim promptly of any significant changes to that information.

(E) Divisions (A) to (D) of this section do not apply regarding a notice that a prosecutor is required to provide under section 2930.061 of the Revised Code. A prosecutor required to provide notice under that section shall provide the notice as specified in that section.

(2004 S 178, eff. 1–30–04; 1995 S 2, eff. 7–1–96; 1994 S 186, eff. 10–12–94)

2930.04 Information provided by law enforcement agency after initial contact with victim

(A) After its initial contact with a victim of a crime, the law enforcement agency responsible for investigating the crime promptly shall give to the victim, in writing, all of the following information:

(1) An explanation of the victim's rights under this chapter;

(2) Information about medical, counseling, housing, emergency, and any other services that are available to a victim;

(3) Information about compensation for victims under the reparations program in sections 2743.51 to 2743.72 of the Revised Code and the name, street address, and telephone number of the agency to contact to apply for an award of reparations under those sections;

(4) Information about protection that is available to the victim, including protective orders issued by a court.

(B) As soon as practicable after its initial contact with a victim of a crime, the law enforcement agency responsible for investigating the crime shall give to the victim all of the following information:

(1) The business telephone number of the law enforcement officer assigned to investigate the case;

(2) The office address and business telephone number of the prosecutor in the case;

(3) A statement that, if the victim is not notified of the arrest of the offender in the case within a reasonable period of time, the victim may contact the law enforcement agency to learn the status of the case.

(C) To the extent that the information required by this section is provided in the pamphlet prepared pursuant to section 109.42 of the Revised Code or in the information card or other material prepared pursuant to section 2743.71 of the Revised Code, the law enforcement agency may fulfill that portion of its obligations under this section by giving that pamphlet, information card, or other material to the victim.

(1995 S 2, eff. 7–1–96; 1994 S 186, eff. 10–12–94)

2930.05 Information provided by law enforcement agency after arrest or detention of defendant or alleged juvenile offender

(A) Within a reasonable period of time after the arrest or detention of a defendant or an alleged juvenile offender for a crime or specified delinquent act, the law enforcement agency that investigates the crime or specified delinquent act shall give the victim of the crime or specified delinquent act notice of all of the following:

(1) The arrest or detention;

(2) The name of the defendant or alleged juvenile offender;

(3) Whether the defendant or alleged juvenile offender is eligible for pretrial release or for release from detention;

(4) The telephone number of the law enforcement agency;

(5) The victim's right to telephone the agency to ascertain whether the defendant or alleged juvenile offender has been released from custody or from detention.

(B) If a defendant or alleged juvenile offender has been released from custody on a bond or personal recognizance or has been released from detention and the prosecutor in the case has received the affidavit of a victim stating that the defendant or alleged juvenile offender, or someone acting at the defendant's or alleged juvenile offender's direction, has committed or threatened to commit one or more acts of violence or intimidation against the victim, the victim's family, or the victim's representative, the prosecutor may file a motion asking the court to reconsider the conditions of the bond or personal recognizance granted to the defendant or alleged juvenile offender or to consider returning the defendant or alleged juvenile offender to detention.

(1999 H 3, eff. 11–22–99; 1995 S 2, eff. 7–1–96; 1994 S 186, eff. 10–12–94)

2930.06 Information provided by prosecutor

(A) The prosecutor in a case, to the extent practicable, shall confer with the victim in the case before pretrial diversion is granted to the defendant or alleged juvenile offender in the case, before amending or dismissing an indictment, information, or complaint against that defendant or alleged juvenile offender, before agreeing to a negotiated plea for that defendant or alleged juvenile offender, before a trial of that defendant by judge or jury, or before the juvenile court conducts an adjudicatory hearing for that alleged juvenile offender. If the juvenile court disposes of a case prior to the prosecutor's involvement in the case, the court or a court employee shall notify the victim in the case that the alleged juvenile offender will be granted pretrial diversion, the complaint against that alleged juvenile offender will be amended or dismissed, or the court will conduct an adjudicatory hearing for that alleged juvenile offender. If the prosecutor fails to confer with the victim at any of those times, the court, if informed of the failure, shall note on the record the failure and the prosecutor's reasons for the failure. A prosecutor's failure to confer with a victim as required by this division and a court's failure to provide the notice as required by this division do not affect the validity of an agreement between the prosecutor and the defendant or alleged juvenile offender in the case, a pretrial diversion of the defendant or alleged juvenile offender, an amendment or dismissal of an indictment, information, or complaint filed against the defendant or alleged juvenile offender, a plea entered by the defendant or alleged juvenile defender, an admission entered by the defendant or alleged juvenile offender, or any other disposition in the case. A court shall not dismiss a criminal complaint, charge, information, or indictment or a delinquent child complaint solely at the request of the victim and over the objection of the prosecuting attorney, village solicitor, city director of law, or other chief legal officer responsible for the prosecution of the case.

(B) After a prosecution in a case has been commenced, the prosecutor or a designee of the prosecutor other than a court or court employee, to the extent practicable, promptly shall give the victim all of the following information, except that, if the juvenile court disposes of a case prior to the prosecutor's involvement in the case, the court or a court employee, to the extent practicable, promptly shall give the victim all of the following information:

(1) The name of the crime or specified delinquent act with which the defendant or alleged juvenile offender in the case has been charged and the name of the defendant or alleged juvenile offender;

(2) The file number of the case;

(3) A brief statement regarding the procedural steps in a criminal prosecution or delinquency proceeding involving a crime or specified delinquent act similar to the crime or specified delinquent act with which the defendant or alleged juvenile offender has been charged and the right of the victim to be present during all proceedings held throughout the prosecution of the case;

(4) A summary of the rights of a victim under this chapter;

(5) Procedures the victim or the prosecutor may follow if the victim becomes subject to threats or intimidation by the defendant, alleged juvenile offender, or any other person;

(6) The name and business telephone number of a person to contact for further information with respect to the case;

(7) The right of the victim to have a victim's representative exercise the victim's rights under this chapter in accordance with section 2930.02 of the Revised Code and the procedure by which a victim's representative may be designated;

(8) Notice that any notification under division (C) of this section, sections 2930.07 to 2930.19, and section 5139.56 of the Revised Code will be given to the victim only if the victim asks to receive the notification.

(C) Upon the request of the victim, the prosecutor or, if it is a delinquency proceeding and a prosecutor is not involved in the case, the court shall give the victim notice of the date, time, and place of any scheduled criminal or juvenile proceedings in the case and notice of any changes in those proceedings or in the schedule in the case.

(D) A victim who requests notice under division (C) of this section and who elects pursuant to division (B) of section 2930.03 of the Revised Code to receive any further notice from the prosecutor or, if it is a delinquency proceeding and a prosecutor is not involved in the case, the court under this chapter shall keep the prosecutor or the court informed of the victim's current address and telephone number until the case is dismissed or terminated, the defendant is acquitted or sentenced, the delinquent child complaint is dismissed, the defendant is adjudicated a delinquent child, or the appellate process is completed, whichever is the final disposition in the case.

(E) If a defendant is charged with the commission of a misdemeanor offense that is not identified in division (A)(2) of section 2930.01 of the Revised Code and if a police report or a complaint, indictment, or information that charges the commission of that offense and provides the basis for a criminal prosecution of that defendant identifies one or more individuals as individuals against whom that offense was committed, after a prosecution in the case has been commenced, the prosecutor or a designee of the prosecutor other than a court or court employee, to the extent practicable, promptly shall notify each of the individuals so identified in the report, complaint, indictment, or information that, if the defendant is convicted of or pleads guilty to the offense, the individual may make an oral or written statement to the court hearing the case regarding the sentence to be imposed upon the defendant and that the court must consider any statement so made that is relevant. Before imposing sentence in the case, the court shall permit the individuals so identified in the report, complaint, indictment, or information to make an oral or written statement. Division (A) of section 2930.14 of the Revised Code applies regarding any statement so made. The court shall consider a statement so made, in accordance with division (B) of that section and division (D) of section 2929.22 of the Revised Code.

(2002 H 490, eff. 1–1–04; 1999 H 3, eff. 11–22–99; 1997 S 98, eff. 3–17–98; 1996 S 269, eff. 7–1–96; 1995 S 2, eff. 7–1–96; 1994 S 186, eff. 10–12–94)

2930.061 Notice to MRDD department

(A) If a person is charged in a complaint, indictment, or information with any crime or specified delinquent act or with any other violation of law, and if the case involves a victim that the prosecutor in the case knows is a mentally retarded person or a developmentally disabled person, in addition to any other notices required under this chapter or under any other provision of law, the prosecutor in the case shall send written notice of the charges to the department of mental retardation and developmental disabilities. The written notice shall specifically identify the person so charged.

(B) As used in this section, "mentally retarded person' ' and "developmentally disabled person" have the same meanings as in section 5123.01 of the Revised Code.

(2004 S 178, eff. 1–30–04)

2930.07 Protection of victim

(A) If the prosecutor in a case determines that there are reasonable grounds for the victim in a case to be apprehensive regarding acts or threats of violence or intimidation by the defendant or alleged juvenile offender in the case or at the defendant's or alleged juvenile offender's direction against the victim, the victim's family, or the victim's representative, the prosecutor may file a motion with the court requesting that the court issue an order specifying that the victim and other witnesses in the case not be compelled in any phase of the criminal or delinquency proceeding to give testimony that would disclose the victim's or victim's representative's address, place of employment, or similar identifying fact without the victim's or victim's representative's consent. The court shall hold a hearing on the motion in chambers, and a court reporter shall make a record of the proceeding.

(B) If the court, pursuant to division (A) of this section, orders that the victim's or victim's representative's address, telephone number, place of employment, or other identifying fact shall be confidential, the court files or documents shall not contain that information unless it is used to identify the location of the crime or specified delinquent act. The hearing shall be recorded, and the court shall order the transcript sealed.

(1999 H 3, eff. 11–22–99; 1996 S 269, eff. 7–1–96; 1995 S 2, eff. 7–1–96; 1994 S 186, eff. 10–12–94)

2930.08 Notice of potential delays in prosecution of defendant

If a motion, request, or agreement between counsel is made in a case and the motion, request, or agreement might result in a substantial delay in the prosecution of the case, the prosecutor in the case, to the extent practicable and if the victim has requested notice pursuant to division (B) of section 2930.03 of the Revised Code, shall inform the victim that the motion, request, or agreement has been made and that it might result in a delay. If the victim objects to the delay, the prosecutor shall inform the court of the victim's objections, and the court shall consider the victim's objections in ruling on the motion, request, or agreement.

(1995 S 2, eff. 7–1–96; 1994 S 186, eff. 10–12–94)

2930.09 Right of victim to be present

A victim in a case may be present whenever the defendant or alleged juvenile offender in the case is present during any stage of the case against the defendant or alleged juvenile offender that is conducted on the record, other than a grand jury proceeding, unless the court determines that exclusion of the victim is necessary to protect the defendant's or alleged juvenile offender's right to a fair trial or to a fair delinquency proceeding. At any stage of the case at which the victim is present, the court, at the victim's request, shall permit the victim to be accompanied by an individual to provide support to the victim unless the court determines that exclusion of the individual is necessary to protect the defendant's or alleged juvenile offender's right to a fair trial or to a fair delinquency proceeding.

(1999 H 3, eff. 11–22–99; 1996 S 269, eff. 7–1–96; 1995 S 2, eff. 7–1–96; 1994 S 186, eff. 10–12–94)

2930.10 Minimizing contact between victim and defendant or alleged juvenile offender

(A) The court in which a criminal prosecution or delinquency proceeding is held shall make a reasonable effort to minimize any contact between the victim in the case, members of the victim's family, the victim's representative, or witnesses for the prosecution and the defendant or alleged juvenile offender in the case, members of the defendant's or alleged juvenile offender's family, or witnesses for the defense before, during, and immediately after all court proceedings.

(B) The court shall provide a waiting area for the victim, members of the victim's family, the victim's representative, or witnesses for the prosecution that is separate from the waiting area provided for the defendant or alleged juvenile offender, members of the defendant's or alleged juvenile offender's family, and defense witnesses if a separate waiting area is available and the use of the area is practical.

(1999 H 3, eff. 11–22–99; 1995 S 2, eff. 7–1–96; 1994 S 186, eff. 10–12–94)

2930.11 Property of victim

(A) Except as otherwise provided in this section or in sections 2933.41 to 2933.43 of the Revised Code, the law enforcement agency responsible for investigating a crime or specified delinquent act shall promptly return to the victim of the crime or specified delinquent act any property of the victim that was taken in the course of the investigation. In accordance with Criminal Rule 26 or an applicable juvenile rule, the law enforcement agency may take photographs of the property for use as evidence. If the ownership of the property is in dispute, the agency shall not return the property until the dispute is resolved.

(B) The law enforcement agency responsible for investigating a crime or specified delinquent act shall retain any property of the victim of the crime or specified delinquent act that is needed as evidence in the case, including any weapon used in the commission of the crime or specified delinquent act, if the prosecutor certifies to the court a need to retain the property in lieu of a photograph of the property or of another evidentiary substitute for the property itself.

(C) If the defendant or alleged juvenile offender in a case files a motion requesting the court to order the law enforcement agency to retain property of the victim because the property is needed for the defense in the case, the agency shall retain the property until the court rules on the motion. The court, in making a determination on the motion, shall weigh the victim's need for the property against the defendant's or alleged juvenile offender's assertion that the property has evidentiary value for the defense. The court shall rule on the motion in a timely fashion.

(1999 H 3, eff. 11–22–99; 1995 S 2, eff. 7–1–96; 1994 S 186, eff. 10–12–94)

2930.12 Notice of acquittal or conviction of defendant or adjudication of alleged juvenile offender

At the request of the victim in a criminal prosecution, the prosecutor shall give the victim notice of the defendant's acquittal or conviction. At the request of the victim in a delinquency proceeding, the prosecutor shall give the victim notice of the dismissal of the complaint against the alleged juvenile offender or of the adjudication of the alleged juvenile offender as a delinquent child, except that, if the juvenile court dismisses the complaint against the alleged juvenile offender or adjudicates the alleged juvenile offender a delinquent child prior to the prosecutor's involvement in the case, at the request of the victim, the court or a court employee shall give the victim notice of the dismissal or of the adjudication. If the defendant or alleged juvenile offender is convicted or is adjudicated a delinquent child, the notice shall include all of the following:

(A) The crimes or specified delinquent acts of which the defendant was convicted or for which the alleged juvenile offender was adjudicated a delinquent child;

(B) The address and telephone number of the probation office or other person, if any, that is to prepare a presentence investigation report pursuant to section 2951.03 of the Revised Code or Criminal Rule 32.2, the address and telephone number of the person, if any, who is to prepare a disposition investigation report pursuant to division (C)(1) of section 2152.18 of the Revised Code, and the address and telephone number of the person, if any, who is to prepare a victim impact statement pursuant to division (D)(1) of section 2152.19 or section 2947.051 of the Revised Code;

(C) Notice that the victim may make a statement about the impact of the crime or specified delinquent act to the probation officer or other person, if any, who prepares the presentence investigation report or to the person, if any, who prepares a victim impact statement, that a statement of the victim included in the report will be made available to the defendant or alleged juvenile offender unless the court exempts it from disclosure, and that the court may make the victim impact statement available to the defendant or alleged juvenile offender;

(D) Notice of the victim's right under section 2930.14 of the Revised Code to make a statement about the impact of the crime or specified delinquent act before sentencing or disposition;

(E) The date, time, and place of the sentencing hearing or dispositional hearing;

(F) One of the following:

(1) Any sentence imposed upon the defendant and any subsequent modification of that sentence, including modification under section 2929.20 of the Revised Code or as a result of the defendant's appeal of the sentence pursuant to section 2953.08 of the Revised Code;

(2) Any disposition ordered for the defendant and any subsequent modification of that disposition, including judicial release or early release in accordance with section 2151.38 of the Revised Code.

(2000 S 179, § 3, eff. 1-1-02; 1999 H 3, eff. 11-22-99; 1995 S 2, eff. 7-1-96; 1994 S 186, eff. 10-12-94)

2930.13 Victim impact statement; presentence investigation report

(A) If the court orders the preparation of a victim impact statement pursuant to division (D)(1) of section 2152.19 or section 2947.051 of the Revised Code, the victim in the case may make a written or oral statement regarding the impact of the crime or specified delinquent act to the person whom the court orders to prepare the victim impact statement. A statement made by the victim under this section shall be included in the victim impact statement.

(B) If a probation officer or other person is preparing a presentence investigation report pursuant to section 2947.06 or 2951.03 of the Revised Code or Criminal Rule 32.2, or a disposition investigation report pursuant to section 2151.355 of the Revised Code, concerning the defendant or alleged juvenile offender in the case, the victim may make a written or oral statement regarding the impact of the crime or specified delinquent act to the probation officer or other person. The probation officer or other person shall use the statement in preparing the presentence investigation report or disposition investigation report and, upon the victim's request, shall include a written statement submitted by the victim in the presentence investigation report or disposition investigation report.

(C) A statement made by the victim under division (A) or (B) of this section may include the following:

(1) An explanation of the nature and extent of any physical, psychological, or emotional harm suffered by the victim as a result of the crime or specified delinquent act that is the basis of the case;

(2) An explanation of the extent of any property damage or other economic loss suffered by the victim as a result of that crime or specified delinquent act;

(3) An opinion regarding the extent to which, if any, the victim needs restitution for harm caused by the defendant or alleged juvenile offender as a result of that crime or specified delinquent act and information about whether the victim has applied for or received any compensation for loss or damage caused by that crime or specified delinquent act;

(4) The victim's recommendation for an appropriate sanction or disposition for the defendant or alleged juvenile offender regarding that crime or specified delinquent act.

(D) If a statement made by a victim under division (A) of this section is included in a victim impact statement, the provision, receipt, and retention of copies of, the use of, and the confidentiality, nonpublic record character, and sealing of the victim impact statement is governed by division (H) of section 2151.355 or by division (C) of section 2947.051 of the Revised Code, as appropriate. If a statement made by a victim under division (B) of this section is included in a presentence investigation report prepared pursuant to section 2947.06 or 2951.03 of the Revised Code or Criminal Rule 32.2 or in a disposition investigation report pursuant to division (C)(1) of section 2152.18 of the Revised Code, the provision, receipt, and retention of copies of, the use of, and the confidentiality, nonpublic record character, and sealing of the presentence investigation report or disposition investigation report that contains the victim's statement is governed by section 2951.03 of the Revised Code.

(2000 S 179, § 3, eff. 1-1-02; 1999 H 3, eff. 11-22-99; 1996 S 269, eff. 7-1-96; 1995 S 2, eff. 7-1-96; 1994 S 186, eff. 10-12-94)

2930.14 Statement by victim prior to sentencing of defendant or disposition of alleged juvenile offender

(A) Before imposing sentence upon, or entering an order of disposition for, a defendant or alleged juvenile offender for the commission of a crime or specified delinquent act, the court shall permit the victim of the crime or specified delinquent act to make a statement. The court may give copies of any written statement made by a victim to the defendant or alleged juvenile offender and defendant's or alleged juvenile offender's counsel and may give any written statement made by the defendant or alleged juvenile offender to the victim and the prosecutor. The court may redact any information contained in a written statement that the court determines is not relevant to and will not be relied upon in the sentencing or disposition decision. The written statement of the victim or of the defendant or alleged juvenile offender is confidential and is not a public record as used in section 149.43 of the Revised Code. Any person to whom a copy of a written statement was released by the court shall return it to the court immediately following sentencing or disposition.

(B) The court shall consider a victim's statement made under division (A) of this section along with other factors that the court is required to consider in imposing sentence or in determining the order of disposition. If the statement includes new material facts, the court shall not rely on the new material facts unless it continues the sentencing or dispositional proceeding or takes other appropriate action to allow the defendant or alleged juvenile offender an adequate opportunity to respond to the new material facts.

(1999 H 3, eff. 11-22-99; 1995 S 2, eff. 7-1-96; 1994 S 186, eff. 10-12-94)

2930.15 Notice of appeal by defendant or alleged juvenile offender

(A) If a defendant is convicted of committing a crime against a victim or an alleged juvenile offender is adjudicated a delinquent child for committing a specified delinquent act against a victim, if the victim requests notice of the filing of an appeal, and if the defendant or alleged juvenile offender files an appeal, the prosecutor in the case promptly shall notify the victim of the appeal. The prosecutor also shall give the victim all of the following information:

(1) A brief explanation of the appellate process, including the possible disposition of the case;

(2) Whether the defendant or alleged juvenile offender has been released on bail or other recognizance or under conditions

imposed by the juvenile court pending the disposition of the appeal;

(3) The time, place, and location of appellate court proceedings and any subsequent changes in the time, place, or location of those proceedings;

(4) The result of the appeal.

(B) If the appellate court returns the defendant's or alleged juvenile offender's case to the trial court or juvenile court for further proceedings, the victim may exercise all the rights that previously were available to the victim in the trial court or the juvenile court.

(1999 H 3, eff. 11–22–99; 1995 S 2, eff. 7–1–96; 1994 S 186, eff. 10–12–94)

2930.16 Notice of incarceration or release of defendant or custody of alleged juvenile offender

Note: See also following version of this section, eff. 4–29–05.

(A) If a defendant is incarcerated, a victim in a case who has requested to receive notice under this section shall be given notice of the incarceration of the defendant. If an alleged juvenile offender is committed to the temporary custody of a school, camp, institution, or other facility operated for the care of delinquent children or to the legal custody of the department of youth services, a victim in a case who has requested to receive notice under this section shall be given notice of the commitment. Promptly after sentence is imposed upon the defendant or the commitment of the alleged juvenile offender is ordered, the prosecutor in the case shall notify the victim of the date on which the defendant will be released from confinement or the prosecutor's reasonable estimate of that date or the date on which the alleged juvenile offender will have served the minimum period of commitment or the prosecutor's reasonable estimate of that date. The prosecutor also shall notify the victim of the name of the custodial agency of the defendant or alleged juvenile offender and tell the victim how to contact that custodial agency. If the custodial agency is the department of youth services, the prosecutor shall notify the victim of the services provided by the office of victims' services within the release authority of the department pursuant to section 5139.55 of the Revised Code and the victim's right pursuant to section 5139.56 of the Revised Code to submit a written request to the release authority to be notified of actions the release authority takes with respect to the alleged juvenile offender. The victim shall keep the custodial agency informed of the victim's current address and telephone number.

(B)(1) Upon the victim's request, the prosecutor promptly shall notify the victim of any hearing for judicial release of the defendant pursuant to section 2929.20 of the Revised Code or of any hearing for judicial release or early release of the alleged juvenile offender pursuant to section 2151.38 of the Revised Code and of the victim's right to make a statement under those sections. The court shall notify the victim of its ruling in each of those hearings and on each of those applications.

(2) Upon the request of a victim of a crime that is a sexually violent offense and that is committed by a sexually violent predator who is sentenced to a prison term pursuant to division (A)(3) of section 2971.03 of the Revised Code, the prosecutor promptly shall notify the victim of any hearing to be conducted pursuant to section 2971.05 of the Revised Code to determine whether to modify the requirement that the offender serve the entire prison term in a state correctional facility in accordance with division (C) of that section, whether to continue, revise, or revoke any existing modification of that requirement, or whether to terminate the prison term in accordance with division (D) of that section. The court shall notify the victim of any order issued at the conclusion of the hearing. As used in this division, "sexually violent offense" and "sexually violent predator" have the same meanings as in section 2971.01 of the Revised Code.

(C) Upon the victim's request made at any time before the particular notice would be due, the custodial agency of a defendant or alleged juvenile offender shall give the victim any of the following notices that is applicable:

(1) At least three weeks before the adult parole authority recommends a pardon or commutation of sentence for the defendant or at least three weeks prior to a hearing before the adult parole authority regarding a grant of parole to the defendant, notice of the victim's right to submit a statement regarding the impact of the defendant's release in accordance with section 2967.12 of the Revised Code and, if applicable, of the victim's right to appear at a full board hearing of the parole board to give testimony as authorized by section 5149.101 of the Revised Code;

(2) At least three weeks before the defendant is transferred to transitional control under section 2967.26 of the Revised Code, notice of the pendency of the transfer and of the victim's right under that section to submit a statement regarding the impact of the transfer;

(3) At least thirty days before the release authority of the department of youth services holds a release review, release hearing, or discharge review for the alleged juvenile offender, notice of the pendency of the review or hearing, of the victim's right to make an oral or written statement regarding the impact of the crime upon the victim or regarding the possible release or discharge, and, if the notice pertains to a hearing, of the victim's right to attend and make statements or comments at the hearing as authorized by section 5139.56 of the Revised Code;

(4) Prompt notice of the defendant's or alleged juvenile offender's escape from a facility of the custodial agency in which the defendant was incarcerated or in which the alleged juvenile offender was placed after commitment, of the defendant's or alleged juvenile offender's absence without leave from a mental health or mental retardation and developmental disabilities facility or from other custody, and of the capture of the defendant or alleged juvenile offender after an escape or absence;

(5) Notice of the defendant's or alleged juvenile offender's death while in confinement or custody;

(6) Notice of the defendant's or alleged juvenile offender's release from confinement or custody and the terms and conditions of the release.

(1999 H 3, eff. 11–22–99; 1997 S 111, eff. 3–17–98; 1996 H 180, eff. 1–1–97; 1995 S 2, eff. 7–1–96; 1994 S 186, eff. 10–12–94)

Note: See also following version of this section, eff. 4–29–05.

2930.16 Notice of incarceration or release of defendant or custody of alleged juvenile offender (later effective date)

Note: See also preceding version of this section, in effect until 4–29–05.

(A) If a defendant is incarcerated, a victim in a case who has requested to receive notice under this section shall be given notice of the incarceration of the defendant. If an alleged juvenile offender is committed to the temporary custody of a school, camp, institution, or other facility operated for the care of delinquent children or to the legal custody of the department of youth services, a victim in a case who has requested to receive notice under this section shall be given notice of the commitment. Promptly after sentence is imposed upon the defendant or the commitment of the alleged juvenile offender is ordered, the prosecutor in the case shall notify the victim of the date on which the defendant will be released from confinement or the prosecutor's reasonable estimate of that date or the date on which the alleged juvenile offender will have served the minimum period of commitment or the prosecutor's reasonable estimate of that date. The prosecutor also shall notify the victim of the name of the custodial agency of the defendant or alleged juvenile offender and tell the victim how to contact that custodial agency. If the custodial agency is the department of rehabilitation and correction, the prosecutor shall notify the victim of the services offered by the office of victims' services pursuant to section 5120.60 of the Revised Code. If the custodial agency is the department of youth services, the prosecutor shall notify the victim of the services provided by the office of victims' services within the release authority of the department pursuant to section 5139.55 of the Revised Code and the victim's right pursuant to section 5139.56 of the Revised Code to submit a written request to the release authority to be notified of actions the release authority takes with respect to the alleged juvenile offender. The victim shall keep the custodial agency informed of the victim's current address and telephone number.

(B)(1) Upon the victim's request, the prosecutor promptly shall notify the victim of any hearing for judicial release of the defendant pursuant to section 2929.20 of the Revised Code or of any hearing for judicial release or early release of the alleged juvenile offender pursuant to section 2151.38 of the Revised Code and of the victim's right to make a statement under those sections. The court shall notify the victim of its ruling in each of those hearings and on each of those applications.

(2) If an offender is convicted of or pleads guilty to a violent sex offense or designated homicide, assault, or kidnapping offense, if the offender is adjudicated a sexually violent predator in relation to that crime, and if the offender is sentenced to a prison term for that crime pursuant to division (A)(3) of section 2971.03 of the Revised Code, upon the request of the victim of the crime, the prosecutor promptly shall notify the victim of any hearing to be conducted pursuant to section 2971.05 of the Revised Code to determine whether to modify the requirement that the offender serve the entire prison term in a state correctional facility in accordance with division (C) of that section, whether to continue, revise, or revoke any existing modification of that requirement, or whether to terminate the prison term in accordance with division (D) of that section. The court shall notify the victim of any order issued at the conclusion of the hearing. As used in this division:

(a) "Adjudicated a sexually violent predator" has the same meaning as in section 2929.01 of the Revised Code and a person is "adjudicated a sexually violent predator" in the same manner and the same circumstances as are described in that section.

(b) "Designated homicide, assault, or kidnapping offense" and "violent sex offense" have the same meanings as in section 2971.01 of the Revised Code.

(C) Upon the victim's request made at any time before the particular notice would be due, the custodial agency of a defendant or alleged juvenile offender shall give the victim any of the following notices that is applicable:

(1) At least three weeks before the adult parole authority recommends a pardon or commutation of sentence for the defendant or at least three weeks prior to a hearing before the adult parole authority regarding a grant of parole to the defendant, notice of the victim's right to submit a statement regarding the impact of the defendant's release in accordance with section 2967.12 of the Revised Code and, if applicable, of the victim's right to appear at a full board hearing of the parole board to give testimony as authorized by section 5149.101 of the Revised Code;

(2) At least three weeks before the defendant is transferred to transitional control under section 2967.26 of the Revised Code, notice of the pendency of the transfer and of the victim's right under that section to submit a statement regarding the impact of the transfer;

(3) At least thirty days before the release authority of the department of youth services holds a release review, release hearing, or discharge review for the alleged juvenile offender, notice of the pendency of the review or hearing, of the victim's right to make an oral or written statement regarding the impact of the crime upon the victim or regarding the possible release or discharge, and, if the notice pertains to a hearing, of the victim's right to attend and make statements or comments at the hearing as authorized by section 5139.56 of the Revised Code;

(4) Prompt notice of the defendant's or alleged juvenile offender's escape from a facility of the custodial agency in which the defendant was incarcerated or in which the alleged juvenile offender was placed after commitment, of the defendant's or alleged juvenile offender's absence without leave from a mental health or mental retardation and developmental disabilities facility or from other custody, and of the capture of the defendant or alleged juvenile offender after an escape or absence;

(5) Notice of the defendant's or alleged juvenile offender's death while in confinement or custody;

(6) Notice of the defendant's or alleged juvenile offender's release from confinement or custody and the terms and conditions of the release.

(2004 H 375, eff. 4–29–05; 2004 H 473, eff. 4–29–05; 1999 H 3, eff. 11–22–99; 1997 S 111, eff. 3–17–98; 1996 H 180, eff. 1–1–97; 1995 S 2, eff. 7–1–96; 1994 S 186, eff. 10–12–94)

Note: See also preceding version of this section, in effect until 4–29–05.

2930.17 Statement by victim prior to judicial release of defendant or alleged juvenile offender

(A) In determining whether to grant a judicial release to a defendant from a prison term pursuant to section 2929.20 of the Revised Code at a time before the defendant's stated prison term expires or in determining whether to grant a judicial release or early release to an alleged juvenile offender from a commitment to the department of youth services pursuant to section 2151.38 of the Revised Code, the court shall permit a victim of a crime or specified delinquent act for which the defendant or alleged juvenile offender was incarcerated or committed to make a statement, in addition to any other statement made under this chapter, concerning the effects of that crime or specified delinquent act on the victim, the circumstances surrounding the crime or specified delinquent act, the manner in which the crime or specified delinquent act was perpetrated, and the victim's opinion whether the defendant or alleged juvenile offender should be released. The victim may make the statement in writing or orally, at the court's discretion. The court shall give the defendant or alleged juvenile offender and either the adult parole authority or the department of youth services, whichever is applicable, a copy of any written impact statement made by the victim under this division.

(B) In deciding whether to grant a judicial release or early release to the defendant or alleged juvenile offender, the court shall consider a statement made by the victim under division (A) of this section or section 2930.14 or 2947.051 of the Revised Code.

(1999 H 3, eff. 11–22–99; 1995 S 2, eff. 7–1–96; 1994 S 186, eff. 10–12–94)

2930.18 Retaliation by employer against victim

No employer of a victim shall discharge, discipline, or otherwise retaliate against the victim, a member of the victim's family, or a victim's representative for participating, at the prosecutor's request, in preparation for a criminal or delinquency proceeding or for attendance, pursuant to a subpoena, at a criminal or delinquency proceeding if the attendance is reasonably necessary to protect the interests of the victim. This section generally does not require an employer to pay an employee for time lost as a result of attendance at a criminal or delinquency proceeding. An employer who knowingly violates this section is in contempt of court. This section does not limit or affect the application to any person of section 2151.211, 2939.121, or 2945.451 of the Revised Code.

(1999 H 3, eff. 11–22–99; 1995 S 2, eff. 7–1–96; 1994 S 186, eff. 10–12–94)

2930.19 Miscellaneous provisions

(A) In a manner consistent with the duty of a prosecutor to represent the interests of the public as a whole, a prosecutor shall seek compliance with this chapter on behalf of a victim, a member of the victim's family, or the victim's representative.

(B) The failure of a public official or public agency to comply with the requirements of this chapter does not give rise to a claim for damages against that public official or public agency, except that a public agency as an employer may be held responsible for a violation of section 2930.18 of the Revised Code.

(C) The failure of any person or entity to provide a right, privilege, or notice to a victim under this chapter does not constitute grounds for declaring a mistrial or new trial, for setting aside a conviction, sentence, adjudication, or disposition, or for granting postconviction release to a defendant or alleged juvenile offender.

(D) If there is a conflict between a provision in this chapter and a specific statute governing the procedure in a case involving a capital offense, the specific statute supersedes the provision in this chapter.

(E) If the victim of a crime is incarcerated in a state or local correctional facility or is in the legal custody of the department of youth services, the victim's rights under this chapter may be modified by court order to prevent any security risk, hardship, or undue burden upon a public official or public agency with a duty under this chapter.

(1999 H 3, eff. 11–22–99; 1995 S 2, eff. 7–1–96; 1994 S 186, eff. 10–12–94)

CHAPTER 2931

JURISDICTION; VENUE

JURISDICTION

2931.01 Definition of magistrate

As used in Chapters 2931. to 2953. of the Revised Code:

(A) "Magistrate" includes county court judges, police justices, mayors of municipal corporation, and judges of other courts inferior to the court of common pleas.

(B) "Judge" does not include the probate judge.

(C) "Court" does not include the probate court.

(D) "Clerk" does not include the clerk of the probate court.

(1975 H 205, eff. 1–1–76; 127 v 1039; 1953 H 1; GC 13422–1)

2931.02 General jurisdiction of county court judge

A judge of a county court is a conservator of the peace and has jurisdiction in criminal cases throughout his area of jurisdiction. He may hear complaints of the peace and issue search warrants. Judges of county courts have jurisdiction on sworn complaint, to issue a warrant for the arrest of a person charged with the commission of a felony where it is made to appear that such person has fled or is outside this state and it is necessary or desirable to extradite such person. Judges of county courts have jurisdiction within their respective areas of jurisdiction in all cases of violation of any law relating to:

(A) Adulteration or deception in the sale of dairy products and other food, drink, drugs, and medicines;

(B) Prevention of cruelty to animals and children;

(C) The abandonment, nonsupport, or ill treatment of a child under eighteen years of age or a physically and mentally handicapped child under the age of eighteen years by its parents;

(D) The abandonment, or ill treatment of a child under eighteen years of age or a physically and mentally handicapped child under the age of eighteen years by its guardian;

(E) The employment of a child under fourteen years of age in public exhibitions or vocations injurious to health, life, or morals, or which will cause or permit him to suffer unnecessary physical or mental pain;

(F) The regulation, restriction, or prohibition of the employment of females and minors;

(G) The torturing, unlawfully punishing, ill treating, or depriving anyone of necessary food, clothing, or shelter;

(H) Any violation of Chapters 4301. and 4303. of the Revised Code, or keeping a place where intoxicating liquor is sold, given away, or furnished in violation of any law prohibiting such acts;

(I) The shipping, selling, using, permitting the use of, branding, or having unlawful quantities of illuminating oil for or in a mine;

(J) The sale, shipment, or adulteration of commercial feeds;

(K) The use of dust-creating machinery in workshops and factories;

(L) The conducting of a pharmacy, or retail drug or chemical store, or the dispensing or selling of drugs, chemicals, poisons, or pharmaceutical preparations therein;

(M) The failure to place and keep in a sanitary condition a bakery, confectionery, creamery, dairy barn, milk depot, laboratory, hotel, restaurant, eating house, packing house, slaughterhouse, ice cream factory, or place where a food product is manufactured, packed, stored, deposited, collected, prepared, produced, or sold for any purpose, or for the violation of any law relating to public health;

(N) Inspection of steam boilers, and of laws licensing steam engineers and boiler operators;

(O) Prevention of short weighing and measuring and all violations of the weights and measures laws;

(P) Laws relating to the practice of medicine or surgery, or any of its branches;

(Q) Laws relating to the filling or refilling of registered containers by other than the owner, or the defacing of the marks of ownership thereon;

(R) Offenses arising from or growing out of the violation of conservation laws.

(1973 S 1, eff. 1–1–74; 1969 H 1; 132 v S 65; 128 v 823; 127 v 1039; 1953 H 1; GC 13422–2)

2931.03 Jurisdiction of court of common pleas

The court of common pleas has original jurisdiction of all crimes and offenses, except in cases of minor offenses the exclusive jurisdiction of which is vested in courts inferior to the court of common pleas.

A judge of a court of common pleas does not have the authority to dismiss a criminal complaint, charge, information, or indictment solely at the request of the complaining witness and over the objection of the prosecuting attorney or other chief legal officer who is responsible for the prosecution of the case.

(1997 S 98, eff. 3–17–98; 1953 H 1, eff. 10–1–53; GC 13422–5)

2931.04 Jurisdiction of municipal courts not affected

Sections 2931.01 to 2931.03, inclusive, of the Revised Code, do not affect, modify, or limit the jurisdiction of municipal courts. All municipal court judges have jurisdiction within the territory for which they were elected or appointed in all cases of violation of Chapters 4301. and 4303. of the Revised Code and of prosecutions for keeping a place where intoxicating liquor is sold, given away, or furnished, in violation of any law prohibiting such acts.

(128 v 823, eff. 11–6–59; 1953 H 1; GC 13422–6)

PROCEDURE

2931.06 Special constables in certain townships

When the constables in a township situated on and consisting in whole or in part of one or more islands in a lake in this state, or in a township adjoining or abutting on lands belonging to a state or national home for disabled volunteer soldiers or a disabled volunteer soldiers' home, are insufficient to maintain the peace and enforce the laws for the preservation of order therein, a judge of the county court having jurisdiction in township may appoint not more than ten special constables to be conservators of the peace within such township and with powers of constables in criminal causes. The appointing judge shall enter such appointments upon his docket and they shall continue in force for one year unless revoked by him. Such special constables shall receive like fees as are paid for similar services to regular constables.

(127 v 1039, eff. 1–1–58; 1953 H 1; GC 13423–2)

2931.07 Recognizance

Recognizances taken by a judge of a county court or other officer authorized to take them, may be returned to the court of common pleas.

Such recognizances shall be returned to such court forthwith after the commitment of the accused, or after the taking of a recognizance for his appearance before such court. The prosecuting attorney may proceed with the prosecution in such court, and the accused shall appear therein and answer to his recognizance.

(127 v 1039, eff. 1–1–58; 1953 H 1; GC 13423–2a, 13423–2b)

2931.15 New trial

In prosecutions before a magistrate, a defendant who has been found guilty upon the verdict of a jury or by the decision of the magistrate without the intervention of a jury may upon written application filed within three days after the verdict or decision, be granted a new trial in like manner and for like reasons as provided by sections 2945.79 to 2945.83, inclusive, of the Revised Code.

(128 v 141, eff. 1–1–60; 128 v 97; 1953 H 1; GC 13424–5)

2931.18 Humane society may employ attorney and assistants

A humane society or its agent may employ an attorney, and may also employ one or more assistant attorneys to prosecute violations of law relating to:

(A) Prevention of cruelty to animals or children;

(B) Abandonment, nonsupport, or ill-treatment of a child by its parent;

(C) Employment of a child under fourteen years of age in public exhibitions or vocations injurious to health, life, or morals or which cause or permit such child to suffer unnecessary physical or mental pain;

(D) Neglect or refusal of an adult to support destitute parent.

Such attorneys shall be paid out of the county treasury in an amount approved as just and reasonable by the board of county commissioners of that county.

(1988 H 246, eff. 12–12–88; 130 v S 4; 1953 H 1; GC 13424–8)

VENUE

2931.29 Procedure on change of venue

When a change of venue is ordered pursuant to section 2901.12 of the Revised Code, the clerk of the court in which the cause is pending shall make a certified transcript of the proceedings in the case, which, with the original affidavit, complaint, indictment, or information, he shall transmit to the clerk of the court to which said case is sent for trial, and the trial shall be conducted as if the cause had originated in the jurisdiction of the latter court. The prosecuting attorney, city director of law, or other officer who would have prosecuted the case in the court in which the cause originated shall take charge of and try the cause, and the court to which the cause is sent may on application appoint one or more attorneys to assist the prosecutor in the trial, and allow the appointed attorneys reasonable compensation.

(1977 H 219, eff. 11–1–77; 1972 H 511; 1953 H 1; GC 13427–1)

2931.30 Transfer of prisoner on change of venue

When a change of venue is ordered pursuant to section 2901.12 of the Revised Code, and the accused is in jail, a warrant shall be issued by the clerk of the court in which the cause originated, directed to the proper officer, commanding him to convey the prisoner to the jail of the county or municipal corporation where the prisoner is to be tried, there to be kept until discharged. If the accused is charged with a bailable offense, and at the date of the order changing the venue is under bond for his appearance at the court from which the venue is changed, the court may fix in said order the amount of recognizance which said accused shall give for his appearance at the time the court may designate, in the court to which the venue is changed, and the clerk shall take such recognizance as in other cases, and forward the same with the record. The court shall recognize the witnesses of the prosecution to appear before the court in which the accused is to be tried.

(1972 H 511, eff. 1–1–74; 1953 H 1; GC 13427–2)

2931.31 Payment of costs and expenses on change of venue

The reasonable expenses of the officer acting as prosecutor, incurred in consequence of a change of venue under section 2901.12 of the Revised Code, the fees of the clerk of the court to which the venue is changed, the sheriff or bailiff, and of the jury shall be allowed and paid out of the treasury of the county in which said cause originated.

(1972 H 511, eff. 1–1–74; 1953 H 1; GC 13427–3)

CHAPTER 2933

PEACE WARRANTS; SEARCH WARRANTS

PEACE WARRANTS

2933.01 Definition of magistrate

The definition of "magistrate" set forth in section 2931.01 of the Revised Code applies to Chapter 2933. of the Revised Code.

(1953 H 1, eff. 10–1–53)

2933.02 Complaint to keep the peace

When a complaint is made in writing and upon oath, filed with a municipal or county court or a mayor sitting as the judge of a mayor's court, and states that the complainant has just cause to fear and fears that another individual will commit an offense against the person or property of the complainant or his ward or child, a municipal or county court judge or mayor shall issue to the sheriff or to any other appropriate peace officer, as defined in section 2935.01 of the Revised Code, within the territorial jurisdiction of the court, a warrant in the name of the state that commands him forthwith to arrest and take the individual complained of before the court to answer the complaint.

(1986 H 412, eff. 3–17–87; 1953 H 1; GC 13428–1)

2933.03 Form of warrant to keep the peace

Warrants issued under section 2933.02 of the Revised Code shall be substantially in the following form:

The State of Ohio, _____ County, ss:

To the sheriff or other appropriate peace officer, greeting:

Whereas, a complaint has been filed by one C.D., in writing and upon oath, stating that he has just cause to fear and does fear that one E.F. will (here state the threatened injury or violence according to the fact as sworn to).

These are therefore to command you to forthwith arrest E.F. and bring him before this court to show cause why he should not find surety to keep the peace and be of good behavior toward the citizens of the state generally, and C.D. especially, and for his appearance before the proper court.

Given under my hand, this _____ day of ___

A. B., Judge, _____ County Court;
Judge, _____ Municipal Court;
Mayor, ...
Mayor's Court

(1986 H 412, eff. 3–17–87; 127 v 1039; 1953 H 1; GC 13428–2)

2933.04 Arraignment; detention

When the accused in [sic.] brought before the municipal, county, or mayor's court pursuant to sections 2933.02 and 2933.03 of the Revised Code, he shall be heard in his defense. If it is necessary for just cause to adjourn the hearing, the municipal or county court judge or mayor involved may order such adjournment. The judge or mayor also may direct the sheriff or other peace officer having custody of the accused to detain him in the county jail or other appropriate detention facility until the cause of delay is removed, unless a bond in a sum fixed by the judge or mayor but not to exceed five hundred dollars, with sufficient surety, is given by the accused. A delay shall not exceed two days.

(1986 H 412, eff. 3–17–87; 1953 H 1; GC 13428–3)

2933.05 Hearing; discharge or bond; detention upon bond default

The municipal or county court judge or mayor sitting as the judge of a mayor's court, upon the appearance of the parties pursuant to sections 2933.02 to 2933.04 of the Revised Code, shall hear the witnesses under oath and do one of the following:

(A) Discharge the accused, render judgment against the complainant for costs, and award execution for the costs;

(B) Order the accused to enter into a bond of not less than fifty or more than five hundred dollars, with sufficient surety, to keep the peace and be of good behavior for such time as may be just, render judgment against him for costs, and award execution for the costs.

In default of such bond, the judge or mayor shall commit the accused to the county jail or other appropriate detention facility, until such order is complied with or he is discharged.

(1986 H 412, eff. 3–17–87; 1953 H 1; GC 13428–4, 13428–5)

2933.06 Appeal; bond; transcript

The accused under sections 2933.02 to 2933.05 of the Revised Code may appeal from the decision of a municipal or county court judge to the appropriate court of appeals or from the decision of a mayor sitting as the judge of a mayor's court to the appropriate municipal or county court. An appeal from the decision of a municipal or county court judge to the appropriate court of appeals shall be only as to questions of law and, to the extent that sections 2933.06 to 2933.09 of the Revised Code do not contain relevant provisions, shall be made and proceed in accordance with the Rules of Appellate Procedure. An appeal from the decision of a mayor sitting as the judge of a mayor's court to the appropriate municipal or county court shall be as to questions of law and fact, and shall be made and proceed in accordance with sections 2933.06 to 2933.09 of the Revised Code.

In connection with either type of appeal, the accused shall file with the clerk of the municipal, county, or mayor's court, within ten days after the decision is rendered, an appeal bond in a sum to be fixed by the judge or mayor at not less than fifty or more than five hundred dollars, with surety to be approved by the judge or mayor, conditioned that, pending the determination of the appeal, the accused will keep the peace and will be of good behavior generally and especially towards the person named in the complaint. Upon the filing of the appeal bond, the clerk of the municipal, county, or mayor's court forthwith shall make a certified transcript of the proceedings in the action, the appeal bond to be included. Upon the payment by the appellant of the fee for the transcript, the clerk immediately shall file the transcript and all the original papers in the action in the office of the clerk of the appellate court.

(1986 H 412, eff. 3–17–87; 1953 H 1; GC 13428–6)

2933.07 Discharge on failure to prosecute

In the case of an appeal from the decision of a mayor sitting as the judge of a mayor's court to the appropriate municipal or county court, no further pleadings shall be required. If the complainant fails to prosecute in such an appeal, the accused shall be discharged unless good cause to the contrary is shown, and the municipal or county court shall render judgment against the complainant for the costs of prosecution and award execution for the costs.

(1986 H 412, eff. 3–17–87; 1953 H 1; GC 13428–7)

2933.08 Hearing; judgment

In the case of an appeal from the decision of a mayor sitting as the judge of a mayor's court to the appropriate municipal or county court, the municipal or county court shall set a time for the hearing of that appeal and, at that time, shall hear the witnesses under oath, and either discharge the accused, render judgment against the complainant for costs, and award execution for the costs, or order the accused to enter into a bond, for such time as may be just, to keep the peace and be of good behavior, render judgment against him for costs, and award execution for the costs.

(1986 H 412, eff. 3–17–87; 1953 H 1; GC 13428–8)

2933.09 Commitment to jail

In the case of an appeal from the decision of a mayor sitting as the judge of a mayor's court to the appropriate municipal or county court, if the accused fails to enter into a bond ordered pursuant to section 2933.08 of the Revised Code, the municipal or county court shall commit the accused to jail until he enters into a bond or is discharged by law, and shall render judgment against him for costs and award execution for the costs. He shall not be imprisoned longer than one year.

After such a commitment following such an appeal, or after a commitment of not more than one year for not entering into a bond ordered pursuant to section 2933.05 of the Revised Code, if such an appeal was not taken, the court may at any time discharge the accused on his own recognizance.

(1986 H 412, eff. 3–17–87; 1953 H 1; GC 13428–9)

2933.10 Bond without process; commitment upon default

Whoever, in the presence of a municipal or county court judge, or a mayor sitting as the judge of a mayor's court, makes an affray, threatens to beat or kill another or to commit an offense against the person or property of another, or contends with angry words to the disturbance of the peace, may be ordered without process or other proof to enter into a bond under section 2933.05 of the Revised Code. In default of such a bond, the person may be committed under that section.

(1988 H 708, eff. 4–19–88; 1986 H 412; 1953 H 1; GC 13428–10)

SEARCH WARRANTS

2933.21 Search warrant

A judge of a court of record may, within his jurisdiction, issue warrants to search a house or place:

(A) For property stolen, taken by robbers, embezzled, or obtained under false pretense;

(B) For weapons, implements, tools, instruments, articles or property used as a means of the commission of a crime, or when any of the objects or articles are in the possession of another person with the intent to use them as a means of committing crime;

(C) For forged or counterfeit coins, stamps, imprints, labels, trade-marks, bank bills, or other instruments of writing, and dies, plates, stamps, or brands for making them;

(D) For obscene materials and materials harmful to minors involved in a violation of section 2907.31 or 2907.32 of the Revised Code, but only so much of such materials shall be seized as are necessary for evidence in a prosecution of the violation;

(E) For gaming table, establishment, device, or apparatus kept or exhibited for unlawful gaming, or to win or gain money or other property, and for money or property won by unlawful gaming;

(F) For the existence of physical conditions which are or may become hazardous to the public health, safety, or welfare, when governmental inspections of property are authorized or required by law.

The enumeration of certain property and material [1] in this section shall not affect or modify other laws for search and seizure.

(1975 H 1, eff. 6–13–75; 1974 H 989; 1973 H 1; 1972 S 397; 1970 H 84; 1953 H 1; GC 13430–1)

[1] Prior and current versions differ; although no amendment to this language was indicated in 1975 H 1, "material" appeared as "materials" in 1974 H 989.

2933.22 Probable cause

(A) A warrant of search or seizure shall issue only upon probable cause, supported by oath or affirmation particularly describing the place to be searched and the property and things to be seized.

(B) A warrant of search to conduct an inspection of property shall issue only upon probable cause to believe that conditions exist upon such property which are or may become hazardous to the public health, safety, or welfare.

(1972 S 397, eff. 10–23–72; 1953 H 1; GC 13430–2)

2933.23 Affidavit for search warrant

A search warrant shall not be issued until there is filed with the judge or magistrate an affidavit that particularly describes the place to be searched, names or describes the person to be searched, and names or describes the property to be searched for and seized; that states substantially the offense in relation to the property and that the affiant believes and has good cause to believe that the property is concealed at the place or on the person; and that states the facts upon which the affiant's belief is based. The judge or magistrate may demand other and further evidence before issuing the warrant. If the judge or magistrate is satisfied that grounds for the issuance of the warrant exist or that there is probable cause to believe that they exist, he shall issue the warrant, identifying in it the property and naming or describing the person or place to be searched.

A search warrant issued pursuant to this chapter or Criminal Rule 41 also may contain a provision waiving the statutory precondition for nonconsensual entry, as described in division (C) of section 2933.231 of the Revised Code, if the requirements of that section are satisfied.

(1990 S 258, eff. 11–20–90; 130 v H 418; 1953 H 1; GC 13430–3)

2933.231 Waiver of statutory precondition for nonconsensual entry

(A) As used in this section:

(1) "Law enforcement officer" has the same meaning as in section 2901.01 of the Revised Code and in Criminal Rule 2.

(2) "Prosecutor" has the same meaning as in section 2935.01 of the Revised Code, and includes any prosecuting attorney as defined in Criminal Rule 2.

(3) "Statutory precondition for nonconsensual entry" means the precondition specified in section 2935.12 of the Revised Code that requires a law enforcement officer or other authorized individual executing a search warrant to give notice of his intention to execute the warrant and then be refused admittance to a

dwelling house or other building before he legally may break down a door or window to gain entry to execute the warrant.

(B) A law enforcement officer, prosecutor, or other authorized individual who files an affidavit for the issuance of a search warrant pursuant to this chapter or Criminal Rule 41 may include in the affidavit a request that the statutory precondition for nonconsensual entry be waived in relation to the search warrant. A request for that waiver shall contain all of the following:

(1) A statement that the affiant has good cause to believe that there is a risk of serious physical harm to the law enforcement officers or other authorized individuals who will execute the warrant if they are required to comply with the statutory precondition for nonconsensual entry;

(2) A statement setting forth the facts upon which the affiant's belief is based, including, but not limited to, the names of all known persons who the affiant believes pose the risk of serious physical harm to the law enforcement officers or other authorized individuals who will execute the warrant at the particular dwelling house or other building;

(3) A statement verifying the address of the dwelling house or other building proposed to be searched as the correct address in relation to the criminal offense or other violation of law underlying the request for the issuance of the search warrant;

(4) A request that, based on those facts, the judge or magistrate waive the statutory precondition for nonconsensual entry.

(C) If an affidavit for the issuance of a search warrant filed pursuant to this chapter or Criminal Rule 41 includes a request for a waiver of the statutory precondition for nonconsensual entry, if the request conforms with division (B) of this section, if division (E) of this section is satisfied, and if the judge or magistrate issues the warrant, the judge or magistrate shall include in it a provision that waives the statutory precondition for nonconsensual entry for purposes of the search and seizure authorized under the warrant only if he determines there is probable cause to believe that, if the law enforcement officers or other authorized individuals who execute the warrant are required to comply with the statutory precondition for nonconsensual entry, they will be subjected to a risk of serious physical harm and to believe that the address of the dwelling house or other building to be searched is the correct address in relation to the criminal offense or other violation of law underlying the issuance of the warrant.

(D)(1) A waiver of the statutory precondition for nonconsensual entry by a judge or magistrate pursuant to division (C) of this section does not authorize, and shall not be construed as authorizing, a law enforcement officer or other authorized individual who executes a search warrant to enter a building other than a building described in the warrant.

(2) The state or any political subdivision associated with a law enforcement officer or other authorized officer who executes a search warrant that contains a provision waiving the statutory precondition for nonconsensual entry is liable in damages in a tort action for any injury, death, or loss to person or property that is proximately caused by the officer's execution of the warrant in accordance with the waiver at an address of a dwelling house or other building that is not described in the warrant.

(E) Any proceeding before a judge or magistrate that involves a request for a waiver of the statutory precondition for nonconsensual entry shall be recorded by shorthand, by stenotype, or by any other mechanical, electronic, or video recording device. The recording of and any transcript of the recording of such a proceeding shall not be a public record for purposes of section 149.43 of the Revised Code until the search warrant is returned by the law enforcement officer or other authorized officer who executes it. This division shall not be construed as requiring, authorizing, or permitting, and does not require, authorize, or permit, the making available for inspection, or the copying, under section 149.43 of the Revised Code of any confidential law enforcement investigatory record or trial preparation record, as defined in that section.

(1990 S 258, eff. 11–20–90)

2933.24 Contents of search warrant; report of inspection findings

(A) A search warrant shall be directed to the proper law enforcement officer or other authorized individual and, by a copy of the affidavit inserted in it or annexed and referred to in it, shall show or recite all the material facts alleged in the affidavit, and particularly name or describe the property to be searched for and seized, the place to be searched, and the person to be searched. If a waiver of the statutory precondition for nonconsensual entry, as defined in division (A) of section 2933.231 of the Revised Code, has been granted pursuant to that section, the warrant also shall contain a provision as described in division (C) of that section.

The warrant shall command the officer or individual to search the place or person named or described for the property, and to bring them, together with the person, before the judge or magistrate. The command of the warrant shall be that the search be made in the daytime, unless there is urgent necessity for a search in the night, in which case a search in the night may be ordered.

The warrant shall be returned by the officer or individual holding it not later than three days after its issuance. It shall designate the judge or magistrate to whom it shall be returned, if such judge or magistrate is available.

(B) When a search warrant commands a proper law enforcement officer or other authorized individual to inspect physical conditions relating to public health, safety, or welfare, such officer or individual, upon completion of the search, shall complete a report of the conditions and file a copy of such report with his agency headquarters.

(1990 S 258, eff. 11–20–90; 1972 S 397; 130 v H 418; 1953 H 1; GC 13430–4)

2933.241 Inventory of property taken

The officer taking property under a warrant for search shall give to the person from whom or from whose premises the property was taken a copy of the warrant and a receipt for the property taken or shall leave the copy and receipt at the place from which the property was taken. The return shall be made promptly and shall be accompanied by a written inventory of any property taken. The inventory shall be made in the presence of the applicant for the warrant and the person from whose possession or premises the property was taken, if they are present, or in the presence of at least one credible person other than the applicant for the warrant or the person from whose possession or premises the property was taken and shall be verified by the officer. The judge or magistrate shall upon request deliver a copy of the inventory to the person from whom or from whose premises the property was taken and to the applicant for the warrant.

(130 v H 418, eff. 10–14–63)

2933.25 Form of search warrant

Warrants issued under section 2933.21 of the Revised Code shall be substantially in the following form:

State of Ohio, __________ County, ss:

To the sheriff (or other officer) of said County, greeting:

Whereas there has been filed with me an affidavit, of which the following is a copy (here copy the affidavit).

These are, therefore, to command you in the name of the State of Ohio, with the necessary and proper assistance, to enter, in the daytime (or in the nighttime) into (here describe the house or place as in the affidavit) of the said ________ of the township of ________ in the County aforesaid, and there diligently search for the said goods and chattels, or articles, to wit: (here describe the articles as in the affidavit) and that you bring the same or any part thereof, found on such search, and also the body of E. F., forthwith before me, or some other judge or magistrate of the county having cognizance thereof to be disposed of and dealt with according to law.

Given under my hand, this ________ day of ________

A.B., Judge, County Court

(127 v 1039, eff. 1–1–58; 1953 H 1; GC 13430–5)

2933.26 Property seized to be kept by court

When a warrant is executed by the seizure of property or things described therein, such property or things shall be kept by the judge, clerk, or magistrate to be used as evidence.

(1953 H 1, eff. 10–1–53; GC 13430–6)

2933.27 Disposition of property before trial

If, upon examination, the judge or magistrate is satisfied that the offense charged with reference to the things seized under a search warrant has been committed, he shall keep such things or deliver them to the sheriff of the county, to be kept until the accused is tried or the claimant's right is otherwise ascertained.

(1953 H 1, eff. 10–1–53; GC 13430–7)

2933.29 Property seized liable for fines

Upon conviction of a person for keeping a room or place to be used for gambling, or knowingly permitting gambling to be conducted therein, or permitting a game to be played for gain, or a gaming device for gain, money, or other property or for betting, or gambling, or permitting such device to be so used, or for being without a fixed residence and in the habit of gambling, if money or other property won in gaming is found in his possession, such money or other property is subject to seizure and payment of a judgment which may be rendered against him, growing out of such violation.

(1953 H 1, eff. 10–1–53; GC 13430–9)

2933.30 Search for dead bodies

When an affidavit is filed before a judge or magistrate, alleging that affiant has reason to believe and does believe that a dead human body, procured or obtained contrary to law, is secreted in a building or place in the county, therein particularly specified, such judge or magistrate, taking with him a judge of a county court, or if within a municipal corporation, two officers of such corporation, may enter, inspect, and search said building or place for such body. In making such search, they have the powers of officers executing warrants of search.

(127 v 1039, eff. 1–1–58; 1953 H 1; GC 13430–10)

2933.31 Search in case of animals

When complaint is made, on oath or affirmation to a judge or magistrate, that the complainant believes that the law relating to or affecting animals is being, or is about to be violated in a particular building or place, such judge or magistrate shall forthwith issue and deliver a warrant, directed to any sheriff, deputy sheriff, marshal, deputy marshal, watchman, police officer, or agent of a society for the prevention of cruelty to animals, authorizing him to enter and search such building or place and arrest all persons there violating, or attempting to violate, such law, and bring such persons before a judge or magistrate within the county within which such offense has been committed.

An attempt to violate such law relating to animals is a violation thereof.

(1953 H 1, eff. 10–1–53; GC 13430–11)

BODY CAVITY AND STRIP SEARCHES

2933.32 Conduct of body cavity search or strip search; conditions; methods; reports; offense

(A) As used in this section:

(1) "Body cavity search" means an inspection of the anal or vaginal cavity of a person that is conducted visually, manually, by means of any instrument, apparatus, or object, or in any other manner while the person is detained or arrested for the alleged commission of a misdemeanor or traffic offense.

(2) "Strip search" means an inspection of the genitalia, buttocks, breasts, or undergarments of a person that is preceded by the removal or rearrangement of some or all of the person's clothing that directly covers the person's genitalia, buttocks, breasts, or undergarments and that is conducted visually, manually, by means of any instrument, apparatus, or object, or in any other manner while the person is detained or arrested for the alleged commission of a misdemeanor or traffic offense. "Strip search" does not mean the visual observation of a person who was afforded a reasonable opportunity to secure release on bail or recognizance, who fails to secure such release, and who is to be integrated with the general population of any detention facility, while the person is changing into clothing that is required to be worn by inmates in the facility.

(B)(1) Except as authorized by this division, no law enforcement officer, other employee of a law enforcement agency, physician, or registered nurse or licensed practical nurse shall conduct or cause to be conducted a body cavity search or a strip search.

(2) A body cavity search or strip search may be conducted if a law enforcement officer or employee of a law enforcement agency has probable cause to believe that the person is concealing evidence of the commission of a criminal offense, including fruits or tools of a crime, contraband, or a deadly weapon, as defined in section 2923.11 of the Revised Code, that could not otherwise be discovered. In determining probable cause for purposes of this section, a law enforcement officer or employee of a law enforcement agency shall consider the nature of the offense with which the person to be searched is charged, the circumstances of the person's arrest, and, if known, the prior conviction record of the person.

(3) A body cavity search or strip search may be conducted for any legitimate medical or hygienic reason.

(4) Unless there is a legitimate medical reason or medical emergency justifying a warrantless search, a body cavity search shall be conducted only after a search warrant is issued that authorizes the search. In any case, a body cavity search shall be conducted under sanitary conditions and only by a physician, or a registered nurse or licensed practical nurse, who is registered or licensed to practice in this state.

(5) Unless there is a legitimate medical reason or medical emergency that makes obtaining written authorization impracticable, a body cavity search or strip search shall be conducted only after a law enforcement officer or employee of a law enforcement agency obtains a written authorization for the search from the

person in command of the law enforcement agency, or from a person specifically designated by the person in command to give a written authorization for either type of search.

(6) A body cavity search or strip search shall be conducted by a person or persons who are of the same sex as the person who is being searched and the search shall be conducted in a manner and in a location that permits only the person or persons who are physically conducting the search and the person who is being searched to observe the search.

(C)(1) Upon completion of a body cavity search or strip search pursuant to this section, the person or persons who conducted the search shall prepare a written report concerning the search that shall include all of the following:

(a) The written authorization for the search obtained from the person in command of the law enforcement agency or his designee, if required by division (B)(5) of this section;

(b) The name of the person who was searched;

(c) The name of the person or persons who conducted the search, the time and date of the search, and the place at which the search was conducted;

(d) A list of the items, if any, recovered during the search;

(e) The facts upon which the law enforcement officer or employee of the law enforcement agency based his probable cause for the search, including, but not limited to, the officer or employee's review of the nature of the offense with which the searched person is charged, the circumstances of his arrest, and, if known, his prior conviction record;

(f) If the body cavity search was conducted before or without the issuance of a search warrant pursuant to division (B)(4) of this section, or if the body cavity or strip search was conducted before or without the granting of written authorization pursuant to division (B)(5) of this section, the legitimate medical reason or medical emergency that justified the warrantless search or made obtaining written authorization impracticable.

(2) A copy of the written report required by division (C)(1) of this section shall be kept on file in the law enforcement agency, and another copy of it shall be given to the person who was searched.

(D)(1) This section does not preclude the prosecution of a law enforcement officer or employee of a law enforcement agency for the violation of any other section of the Revised Code.

(2) This section does not limit, and shall not be construed to limit, any statutory or common law rights of a person to obtain injunctive relief or to recover damages in a civil action.

(3) If a person is subjected to a body cavity search or strip search in violation of this section, any person may commence a civil action to recover compensatory damages for any injury, death, or loss to person or property or any indignity arising from the violation. In the civil action, the court may award punitive damages to the plaintiffs if they prevail in the action, and it may award reasonable attorney's fees to the parties who prevail in the action.

(4) This section does not apply to body cavity searches or strip searches of persons who have been sentenced to serve a term of imprisonment and who are serving that term in a detention facility, as defined in section 2921.01 of the Revised Code.

(E)(1) Whoever violates division (B) of this section is guilty of conducting an unauthorized search, a misdemeanor of the first degree.

(2) Whoever violates division (C) of this section is guilty of failure to prepare a proper search report, a misdemeanor of the fourth degree.

(1984 H 426, eff. 4–4–85; 1984 S 268)

DISPOSITION OF PROPERTY AND CONTRABAND

2933.41 Disposition of property held by law enforcement agency; written internal control policy; records and reports; funding citizens' reward programs

(A)(1) Any property, other than contraband that is subject to the provisions of section 2913.34 or 2933.43 of the Revised Code, other than property that is subject to section 3719.141 of the Revised Code, other than property that is forfeited under sections 2923.44 to 2923.47 or 2925.41 to 2925.45 of the Revised Code, other than a vehicle that is criminally forfeited under an order issued under section 4503.233 or 4503.234 of the Revised Code and that is to be disposed of under section 4503.234 of the Revised Code, other than property that has been lawfully seized under sections 2933.71 to 2933.75 of the Revised Code in relation to a medicaid fraud offense, and other than property that has been lawfully seized in relation to a violation of section 2923.32 of the Revised Code, that has been lost, abandoned, stolen, seized pursuant to a search warrant, or otherwise lawfully seized or forfeited, and that is in the custody of a law enforcement agency shall be kept safely pending the time it no longer is needed as evidence and shall be disposed of pursuant to this section. Each law enforcement agency that has custody of any property that is subject to this section shall adopt a written internal control policy that addresses the keeping of detailed records as to the amount of property taken in by the agency, that addresses the agency's disposition of the property under this section, that provides for the keeping of detailed records of the disposition of the property, and that provides for the keeping of detailed financial records of the amount and disposition of any proceeds of a sale of the property under division (D)(8) of this section and of the general types of expenditures made out of the proceeds retained by the agency and the specific amount expended on each general type of expenditure. The policy shall not provide for or permit the identification of any specific expenditure that is made in an ongoing investigation. The policy is a public record open for inspection under section 149.43 of the Revised Code.

(2)(a) Every law enforcement agency that has any lost, abandoned, stolen, seized, or forfeited property as described in division (A)(1) of this section in its custody shall comply with its written internal control policy adopted under that division relative to the property. Each agency that has any such property in its custody, except for property to be disposed of under division (D)(4) of this section, shall maintain an accurate record, in accordance with its written internal control policy, of each item of the property. The record shall include the date on which each item of property came into the agency's custody, the manner in which it was disposed of, the date of its disposition, the name of the person who received the property if it was not destroyed, and all other information required by the agency's written internal control policy; however, the record shall not identify or enable the identification of the individual officer who seized any item of property. The record of any property that no longer is needed as evidence, and all financial records of the amount and disposition of any proceeds of a sale under division (D)(8) of this section and of the general types of expenditures made out of the proceeds retained by the agency and the specific amount of each general type of expenditure, shall be open to public inspection during the agency's regular business hours.

Each law enforcement agency that, during any calendar year, has any seized or forfeited property as described in division (A)(1) of this section in its custody shall prepare a report covering the calendar year that cumulates all of the information contained in all of the records kept by the agency pursuant to this division for that calendar year and shall send a copy of the cumulative report, no later than the first day of March in the calendar year following the calendar year covered by the report, to the attorney general. Each report received by the attorney general is a public record open for inspection under section 149.43 of the Revised Code.

(b) Each law enforcement agency that receives in any calendar year any proceeds of a sale under division (D)(8) of this section shall prepare a report covering the calendar year that cumulates all of the information contained in all of the public financial records kept by the agency pursuant to division (D)(2)(a) of this section for that calendar year and shall send a copy of the cumulative report, no later than the first day of March in the calendar year following the calendar year covered by the report, to the attorney general. Each report received by the attorney general is a public record open for inspection under section 149.43 of the Revised Code.

(c) Not later than the fifteenth day of April in the calendar year in which reports are sent to the attorney general under divisions (A)(2)(a) and (b) of this section, the attorney general shall send to the president of the senate and the speaker of the house of representatives a written notification that does all of the following:

(i) Indicates that the attorney general has received from law enforcement agencies reports of the type described in division (A)(2)(a), (A)(2)(b), or both (A)(2)(a) and (b) of this section, whichever is applicable, that cover the previous calendar year and indicates that the reports were received under division (A)(2)(a), (A)(2)(b), or both (A)(2)(a) and (b) of this section, whichever is applicable;

(ii) Indicates that the reports are open for inspection under section 149. 43 of the Revised Code;

(iii) Indicates that the attorney general will provide a copy of any or all of the reports to the president of the senate or the speaker of the house of representatives upon request.

(B) A law enforcement agency that has property in its possession that is required to be disposed of pursuant to this section shall make a reasonable effort to locate the persons entitled to possession of the property in its custody, to notify them of when and where it may be claimed, and to return the property to them at the earliest possible time. In the absence of evidence identifying persons entitled to possession, it is sufficient notice to advertise in a newspaper of general circulation in the county, briefly describing the nature of the property in custody and inviting persons to view and establish their right to it.

(C) A person loses any right that the person may have to the possession, or the possession and ownership, of property if any of the following applies:

(1) The property was the subject, or was used in a conspiracy or attempt to commit, or in the commission, of an offense other than a traffic offense, and the person is a conspirator, accomplice, or offender with respect to the offense.

(2) A court determines that the property should be forfeited because, in light of the nature of the property or the circumstances of the person, it is unlawful for the person to acquire or possess the property.

(D) Unclaimed or forfeited property in the custody of a law enforcement agency, other than contraband that is subject to the provisions of section 2913.34 or 2933.43 of the Revised Code, other than property forfeited under sections 2923.44 to 2923.47 or 2925.41 to 2925.45 of the Revised Code, and other than property that has been lawfully seized in relation to a violation of section 2923.32 of the Revised Code, shall be disposed of on application to and order of any court of record that has territorial jurisdiction over the political subdivision in which the law enforcement agency has jurisdiction to engage in law enforcement activities, as follows:

(1) Drugs shall be disposed of pursuant to section 3719.11 of the Revised Code or placed in the custody of the secretary of the treasury of the United States for disposal or use for medical or scientific purposes under applicable federal law.

(2) Firearms and dangerous ordnance suitable for police work may be given to a law enforcement agency for that purpose. Firearms suitable for sporting use or as museum pieces or collectors' items may be sold at public auction pursuant to division (D)(8) of this section. Other firearms and dangerous ordnance shall be destroyed by the agency or shall be sent to the bureau of criminal identification and investigation for destruction by the bureau.

(3) Obscene materials shall be destroyed.

(4) Except as otherwise provided in division (D)(4) of this section, beer or intoxicating liquor seized by a law enforcement agency shall be destroyed. Intoxicating liquor seized by the investigative unit in the department of public safety may be distributed for training relating to law enforcement activities. Pursuant to rules the department adopts in accordance with Chapter 119. of the Revised Code, the department shall provide for the distribution of seized intoxicating liquor that is not distributed for training relating to its law enforcement activities, to state or local law enforcement agencies, upon their request, for training related to their law enforcement activities.

(5) Money received by an inmate of a correctional institution from an unauthorized source or in an unauthorized manner shall be returned to the sender, if known, or deposited in the inmates' industrial and entertainment fund if the sender is not known.

(6) Vehicles and vehicle parts forfeited under sections 4549.61 to 4549.63 of the Revised Code may be given to a law enforcement agency for use in the performance of its duties. Those parts may be incorporated into any other official vehicle. Parts that do not bear vehicle identification numbers or derivatives of them may be sold or disposed of as provided by rules of the director of public safety. Parts from which a vehicle identification number or derivative of it has been removed, defaced, covered, altered, or destroyed and that are not suitable for police work or incorporation into an official vehicle shall be destroyed and sold as junk or scrap.

(7)(a) Computers, computer networks, computer systems, and computer software suitable for police work may be given to a law enforcement agency for that purpose. Other computers, computer networks, computer systems, and computer software shall be disposed of pursuant to division (D)(8) of this section.

(b) As used in this section, "computers," "computer networks," "computer systems," and "computer software" have the same meanings as in section 2913.01 of the Revised Code.

(8) Other unclaimed or forfeited property, including personal property that is abandoned or relinquished by an inmate of a state correctional institution, with the approval of the court, may be used by the law enforcement agency that has possession of it. If the other unclaimed or forfeited property is not used by the law enforcement agency, it may be sold, without appraisal, at a public auction to the highest bidder for cash, or, in the case of other unclaimed or forfeited moneys, disposed of in another manner that the court considers proper in the circumstances.

(E)(1)(a) If the property was in the possession of the law enforcement agency in relation to a delinquent child proceeding in a juvenile court, ten per cent of the proceeds from property disposed of pursuant to this section shall be applied to one or more alcohol and drug addiction treatment programs that are certified by the department of alcohol and drug addiction services under section 3793.06 of the Revised Code and that are specified by the court in its order issued under division (D) of this section. A juvenile court shall not specify an alcohol or drug addiction treatment program in the order unless the program is a certified alcohol and drug addiction treatment program and, except as provided in division (E)(1)(a) of this section, unless the program is located in the county in which the court that issues the orders is located or in a contiguous county. If no certified alcohol and drug addiction treatment program is located in any of those counties, the juvenile court may specify in the order a certified alcohol and drug addiction treatment program located anywhere within this state. The remaining ninety per cent of the proceeds shall be applied as provided in division (E)(1)(b) of this section.

If the property was in the possession of the law enforcement agency other than in relation to a delinquent child proceeding in a juvenile court, all of the proceeds from property disposed of pursuant to this section shall be applied as provided in division (E)(1)(b) of this section.

(b) Except as provided in divisions (D)(4), (5), and (E)(2) of this section and after compliance with division (E)(1)(a) of this section when that division is applicable, the proceeds from property disposed of pursuant to this section shall be placed in the general fund of the state, the county, the township, or the municipal corporation, of which the law enforcement agency involved is an agency.

(2) Each board of county commissioners that recognizes a citizens' reward program as provided in section 9.92 of the Revised Code shall notify each law enforcement agency of that county and each law enforcement agency of a township or municipal corporation wholly located in that county of the official recognition of the citizens' reward program by filing a copy of its resolution conferring that recognition with each of those law enforcement agencies. When the board of county commissioners of a county recognizes a citizens' reward program and the county includes a part, but not all, of the territory of a municipal corporation, the board shall so notify the law enforcement agency of that municipal corporation of the official recognition of the citizens' reward program only if the county contains the highest percentage of the municipal corporation's population. Upon receipt of a notice described in this division, each law enforcement agency shall pay twenty-five per cent of the proceeds from each sale of property disposed of pursuant to this section to the citizens' reward program for use exclusively for the payment of rewards. No part of those funds may be used to pay for the administrative expenses or any other expenses associated with a citizens' reward program. If a citizens' reward program that operates in more than one county or in another state or states in addition to this state receives funds pursuant to this section, the funds shall be used to pay rewards only for tips and information to law enforcement agencies concerning felonies, offenses of violence, or misdemeanors that have been committed in the county from which the funds were received.

(F) This section does not apply to the collection, storage, or disposal of abandoned junk motor vehicles. This section shall not be construed to rescind or restrict the authority of a municipal law enforcement agency to keep and dispose of lost, abandoned, stolen, seized, or forfeited property under an ordinance of the municipal corporation or under sections 737.29 to 737.33 of the Revised Code, provided that, when a municipal corporation that has received notice as provided in division (E)(2) of this section disposes of property under an ordinance, it shall pay twenty-five per cent of the proceeds from any sale or auction to the citizens' reward program as provided under that division.

(G) The receipt of funds by a citizens' reward program pursuant to division (E) of this section does not make it a governmental unit for purposes of section 149.43 of the Revised Code and does not subject it to the disclosure provisions of that section.

(H) This section does not apply to the disposal of stolen or other property recovered by township law enforcement agencies pursuant to sections 505.105 to 505.109 of the Revised Code.

(I)(1) Subject to divisions (D)(1) to (7) of this section, and otherwise notwithstanding the provisions of this section, personal property that is subject to this section and that is abandoned or relinquished by an inmate of a state correctional institution may be destroyed or used by order of the warden of the institution, if either of the following apply:

(a) The value of the item is one hundred dollars or less, the state correctional institution has attempted to contact or identify the owner of the personal property, and those attempts have been unsuccessful.

(b) The inmate who owns the personal property agrees in writing to the disposal of the personal property in question.

(2) The department of rehabilitation and correction shall record the seizure and disposition of any personal property pursuant to division (I)(1) of this section, any attempts to contact or identify the owner of the personal property pursuant to division (I)(1)(a) of this section, and any agreement made pursuant to division (I)(1)(b) of this section.

(J) For purposes of this section, "law enforcement agency" includes correctional institutions, and "citizens' reward program" has the same meaning as in section 9.92 of the Revised Code. As used in division (H) of this section, "township law enforcement agencies" means an organized police department of a township, a township police district, a joint township police district, or the office of a township constable.

(2004 H 306, eff. 7–23–04; 2002 H 510, eff. 3–31–03; 1999 H 55, eff. 9–29–99; 1998 H 402, eff. 3–30–99; 1998 H 2, eff. 1–1–99; 1998 S 164, eff. 1–15–98; 1996 S 277, § 3, eff. 7–1–97; 1996 S 277, § 1, eff. 3–31–97; 1995 S 162, eff. 7–1–97; 1995 H 1, eff. 1–1–96; 1994 H 715, eff. 7–22–94; 1993 S 62, § 4, eff. 9–1–93; 1992 S 275, S 98; 1990 S 258, H 215; 1986 H 428, S 69, H 49; 1984 S 65, H 632; 1981 H 1; 1980 S 50; 1972 H 511)

2933.42 Possession or conveyance of contraband prohibited; when watercraft, motor vehicle, or aircraft considered contraband; property subject to seizure and forfeiture

(A) No person shall possess, conceal, transport, receive, purchase, sell, lease, rent, or otherwise transfer any contraband.

(B) For purposes of section 2933.43 of the Revised Code, if a watercraft, motor vehicle, aircraft, or other personal property that is not within the scope of the definition of contraband in section 2901.01 of the Revised Code is used in a violation of division (A) of this section, the watercraft, motor vehicle, aircraft, or personal property is contraband and, if the underlying offense involved in the violation of division (A) of this section is a felony, is subject to seizure and forfeiture pursuant to section 2933.43 of the Revised Code. It is rebuttably presumed that a watercraft, motor vehicle, aircraft, or other personal property in or on which contraband is found at the time of seizure has been, is being, or is intended to be used in a violation of division (A) of this section.

(C) For purposes of sections 2901.01 and 2933.41 to 2933.43 of the Revised Code, "offense," "criminal case," "criminal violation," "criminal offense," "felony," and similar terms shall be construed to include acts committed by persons under eighteen years of age that, if committed by an adult, would be within the meaning of those terms. This division shall be liberally construed to give effect to the intent of the general assembly in enacting this division that the forfeiture and contraband provisions of sections 2901.01 and 2933.41 to 2933.43 of the Revised Code apply to property that is possessed, or possessed and owned, by persons under eighteen years of age in the same manner as those provisions apply to property that is possessed, or possessed and owned, by adults.

(1990 S 258, eff. 8–22–90; 1986 S 69)

2933.43 Seizure of contraband; notice; holding period; records and reports; forfeiture proceeding; hearings; disposition; written internal control policy on use or disposition of proceeds

(A)(1) Except as provided in this division or in section 2913.34 or sections 2923.44 to 2923.47 or 2925.41 to 2925.45 of the

Revised Code, a law enforcement officer shall seize any contraband that has been, is being, or is intended to be used in violation of division (A) of section 2933.42 of the Revised Code. A law enforcement officer shall seize contraband that is a watercraft, motor vehicle, or aircraft and that has been, is being, or is intended to be used in violation of division (A) of section 2933.42 of the Revised Code only if the watercraft, motor vehicle, or aircraft is contraband because of its relationship to an underlying criminal offense that is a felony.

Additionally, a law enforcement officer shall seize any watercraft, motor vehicle, aircraft, or other personal property that is classified as contraband under division (B) of section 2933.42 of the Revised Code if the underlying offense involved in the violation of division (A) of that section that resulted in the watercraft, motor vehicle, aircraft, or personal property being classified as contraband, is a felony.

(2) If a law enforcement officer seizes property that is titled or registered under law, including a motor vehicle, pursuant to division (A)(1) of this section, the officer or the officer's employing law enforcement agency shall notify the owner of the seizure. The notification shall be given to the owner at the owner's last known address within seventy-two hours after the seizure, and may be given orally by any means, including telephone, or by certified mail, return receipt requested.

If the officer or the officer's agency is unable to provide the notice required by this division despite reasonable, good faith efforts to do so, the exercise of the reasonable, good faith efforts constitutes fulfillment of the notice requirement imposed by this division.

(B)(1) A motor vehicle seized pursuant to division (A)(1) of this section and the contents of the vehicle may be retained for a reasonable period of time, not to exceed seventy-two hours, for the purpose of inspection, investigation, and the gathering of evidence of any offense or illegal use.

At any time prior to the expiration of the seventy-two-hour period, the law enforcement agency that seized the motor vehicle may petition the court of common pleas of the county that has jurisdiction over the underlying criminal case or administrative proceeding involved in the forfeiture for an extension of the seventy-two-hour period if the motor vehicle or its contents are needed as evidence or if additional time is needed for the inspection, investigation, or gathering of evidence. Upon the filing of such a petition, the court immediately shall schedule a hearing to be held at a time as soon as possible after the filing, but in no event at a time later than the end of the next business day subsequent to the day on which the petition was filed, and upon scheduling the hearing, immediately shall notify the owner of the vehicle, at the address at which notification of the seizure was provided under division (A) of this section, of the date, time, and place of the hearing. If the court, at the hearing, determines that the vehicle or its contents, or both, are needed as evidence or that additional time is needed for the inspection, investigation, or gathering of evidence, the court may grant the petition and issue an order authorizing the retention of the vehicle or its contents, or both, for an extended period as specified by the court in its order. An order extending a period of retention issued under this division may be renewed.

If no petition for the extension of the initial seventy-two-hour period has been filed, prior to the expiration of that period, under this division, if the vehicle was not in the custody and control of the owner at the time of its seizure, and if, at the end of that seventy-two-hour period, the owner of the vehicle has not been charged with an offense or administrative violation that includes the use of the vehicle as an element and has not been charged with any other offense or administrative violation in the actual commission of which the motor vehicle was used, the vehicle and its contents shall be released to its owner or the owner's agent, provided that the law enforcement agency that seized the vehicle may require proof of ownership of the vehicle, proof of ownership or legal possession of the contents, and an affidavit of the owner that the owner neither knew of nor expressly or impliedly consented to the use of the vehicle that resulted in its forfeiture as conditions precedent to release. If a petition for the extension of the initial seventy-two-hour period has been filed, prior to the expiration of that period, under this division but the court does not grant the petition, if the vehicle was not in the custody and control of the owner at the time of its seizure, and if, at the end of that seventy-two-hour period, the owner of the vehicle has not been charged with an offense or administrative violation that includes the use of the vehicle as an element and has not been charged with any other offense or administrative violation in the actual commission of which the motor vehicle was used, the vehicle and its contents shall be released to its owner or the owner's agent, provided that the court may require the proof and affidavit described in the preceding sentence as conditions precedent to release. If the initial seventy-two-hour period has been extended under this division, the vehicle and its contents to which the extension applies may be retained in accordance with the extension order. If, at the end of that extended period, the owner of the vehicle has not been charged with an offense or administrative violation that includes the use of the vehicle as an element and has not been charged with any other offense or administrative violation in the actual commission of which the motor vehicle was used, and if the vehicle was not in the custody and control of the owner at the time of its seizure, the vehicle and its contents shall be released to its owner or the owner's agent, provided that the court may require the proof and affidavit described in the third preceding sentence as conditions precedent to release. In cases in which the court may require proof and affidavits as conditions precedent to release, the court also may require the posting of a bond, with sufficient sureties approved by the court, in an amount equal to the value of the property to be released, as determined by the court, and conditioned upon the return of the property to the court if it is forfeited under this section, as a further condition to release. If, at the end of the initial seventy-two-hour period or at the end of any extended period granted under this section, the owner has been charged with an offense or administrative violation that includes the use of the vehicle as an element or has been charged with another offense or administrative violation in the actual commission of which the motor vehicle was used, or if the vehicle was in the custody and control of the owner at the time of its seizure, the vehicle and its contents shall be retained pending disposition of the charge, provided that upon the filing of a motion for release by the owner, if the court determines that the motor vehicle or its contents, or both, are not needed as evidence in the underlying criminal case or administrative proceeding, the court may permit the release of the property that is not needed as evidence to the owner; as a condition precedent to a release of that nature, the court may require the owner to execute a bond with the court. Any bond so required shall be in an amount equal to the value of the property to be released, as determined by the court, shall have sufficient sureties approved by the court, and shall be conditioned upon the return of the property to the court to which it is forfeited under this section.

The final disposition of a motor vehicle seized pursuant to division (A)(1) of this section shall be determined in accordance with division (C) of this section.

(2) Pending a hearing pursuant to division (C) of this section, and subject to divisions (B)(1) and (C) of this section, any property lawfully seized pursuant to division (A) of this section because it was contraband of a type described in division (A)(13)(b), (d), (e), (f), (g), (h), (i), or (j) of section 2901.01 of the Revised Code shall not be subject to replevin or other action in any court and shall not be subject to release upon request of the owner, and no judgment shall be enforced against the property. Pending the hearing, and subject to divisions (B)(1) and (C) of this section, the property shall be kept in the custody of the law enforcement agency responsible for its seizure.

Pending a hearing pursuant to division (C) of this section, and notwithstanding any provisions of division (B)(1) or (C) of this section to the contrary, any property lawfully seized pursuant to division (A) of this section because it was contraband of a type described in division (A)(13)(a) or (c) of section 2901.01 of the Revised Code shall not be subject to replevin or other action in any court and shall not be subject to release upon request of the owner, and no judgment shall be enforced against the property. Pending the hearing, and notwithstanding any provisions of division (B)(1) or (C) of this section to the contrary, the property shall be kept in the custody of the law enforcement agency responsible for its seizure.

A law enforcement agency that seizes property under division (A) of this section because it was contraband of any type described in division (A)(13) of section 2901.01 or division (B) of section 2933.42 of the Revised Code shall maintain an accurate record of each item of property so seized, which record shall include the date on which each item was seized, the manner and date of its disposition, and if applicable, the name of the person who received the item; however, the record shall not identify or enable the identification of the individual officer who seized the item. The record of property of that nature that no longer is needed as evidence shall be open to public inspection during the agency's regular business hours. Each law enforcement agency that, during any calendar year, seizes property under division (A) of this section because it was contraband shall prepare a report covering the calendar year that cumulates all of the information contained in all of the records kept by the agency pursuant to this division for that calendar year, and shall send a copy of the cumulative report, no later than the first day of March in the calendar year following the calendar year covered by the report, to the attorney general. Each report received by the attorney general is a public record open for inspection under section 149.43 of the Revised Code. Not later than the fifteenth day of April in the calendar year in which the reports are received, the attorney general shall send to the president of the senate and the speaker of the house of representatives a written notification that does all of the following:

(a) Indicates that the attorney general has received from law enforcement agencies reports of the type described in this division that cover the previous calendar year and indicates that the reports were received under this division;

(b) Indicates that the reports are open for inspection under section 149.43 of the Revised Code;

(c) Indicates that the attorney general will provide a copy of any or all of the reports to the president of the senate or the speaker of the house of representatives upon request.

(C) The prosecuting attorney, village solicitor, city director of law, or similar chief legal officer who has responsibility for the prosecution of the underlying criminal case or administrative proceeding, or the attorney general if the attorney general has that responsibility, shall file a petition for the forfeiture, to the seizing law enforcement agency of the contraband seized pursuant to division (A) of this section. The petition shall be filed in the court that has jurisdiction over the underlying criminal case or administrative proceeding involved in the forfeiture. If the property was seized on the basis of both a criminal violation and an administrative regulation violation, the petition shall be filed by the officer and in the court that is appropriate in relation to the criminal case.

The petitioner shall conduct or cause to be conducted a search of the appropriate public records that relate to the seized property for the purpose of determining, and shall make or cause to be made reasonably diligent inquiries for the purpose of determining, any person having an ownership or security interest in the property. The petitioner then shall give notice of the forfeiture proceedings by personal service or by certified mail, return receipt requested, to any persons known, because of the conduct of the search, the making of the inquiries, or otherwise, to have an ownership or security interest in the property, and shall publish notice of the proceedings once each week for two consecutive weeks in a newspaper of general circulation in the county in which the seizure occurred. The notices shall be personally served, mailed, and first published at least four weeks before the hearing. They shall describe the property seized; state the date and place of seizure; name the law enforcement agency that seized the property and, if applicable, that is holding the property; list the time, date, and place of the hearing; and state that any person having an ownership or security interest in the property may contest the forfeiture.

If the property seized was determined by the seizing law enforcement officer to be contraband because of its relationship to an underlying criminal offense or administrative violation, no forfeiture hearing shall be held under this section unless the person pleads guilty to or is convicted of the commission of, or an attempt or conspiracy to commit, the offense or a different offense arising out of the same facts and circumstances or unless the person admits or is adjudicated to have committed the administrative violation or a different violation arising out of the same facts and circumstances; a forfeiture hearing shall be held in a case of that nature no later than forty-five days after the conviction or the admission or adjudication of the violation, unless the time for the hearing is extended by the court for good cause shown. The owner of any property seized because of its relationship to an underlying criminal offense or administrative violation may request the court to release the property to the owner. Upon receipt of a request of that nature, if the court determines that the property is not needed as evidence in the underlying criminal case or administrative proceeding, the court may permit the release of the property to the owner. As a condition precedent to a release of that nature, the court may require the owner to execute a bond with the court. Any bond so required shall have sufficient sureties approved by the court, shall be in a sum equal to the value of the property, as determined by the court, and shall be conditioned upon the return of the property to the court if the property is forfeited under this section. Any property seized because of its relationship to an underlying criminal offense or administrative violation shall be returned to its owner if charges are not filed in relation to that underlying offense or violation within thirty days after the seizure, if charges of that nature are filed and subsequently are dismissed, or if charges of that nature are filed and the person charged does not plead guilty to and is not convicted of the offense or does not admit and is not found to have committed the violation.

If the property seized was determined by the seizing law enforcement officer to be contraband other than because of a relationship to an underlying criminal offense or administrative violation, the forfeiture hearing under this section shall be held no later than forty-five days after the seizure, unless the time for the hearing is extended by the court for good cause shown.

Where possible, a court holding a forfeiture hearing under this section shall follow the Rules of Civil Procedure. When a hearing is conducted under this section, property shall be forfeited upon a showing, by a preponderance of the evidence, by the petitioner that the person from which the property was seized was in violation of division (A) of section 2933.42 of the Revised Code. If that showing is made, the court shall issue an order of forfeiture. If an order of forfeiture is issued in relation to contraband that was released to the owner or the owner's agent pursuant to this division or division (B)(1) of this section, the order shall require the owner to deliver the property, by a specified date, to the law enforcement agency that employed the law enforcement officer who made the seizure of the property, and the court shall deliver a copy of the order to the owner or send a copy of it by certified mail, return receipt requested, to the owner at the address to which notice of the seizure was given under division (A)(2) of this section. Except as otherwise provided in this division, all rights, interest, and title to the forfeited contraband vests in the state, effective from the date of seizure.

No property shall be forfeited pursuant to this division if the owner of the property establishes, by a preponderance of the evidence, that the owner neither knew, nor should have known after a reasonable inquiry, that the property was used, or was likely to be used, in a crime or administrative violation. No bona fide security interest shall be forfeited pursuant to this division if the holder of the interest establishes, by a preponderance of the evidence, that the holder of the interest neither knew, nor should have known after a reasonable inquiry, that the property was used, or likely to be used, in a crime or administrative violation, that the holder of the interest did not expressly or impliedly consent to the use of the property in a crime or administrative violation, and that the security interest was perfected pursuant to law prior to the seizure. If the holder of the interest satisfies the court that these requirements are met, the interest shall be preserved by the court. In a case of that nature, the court shall either order that the agency to which the property is forfeited reimburse the holder of the interest to the extent of the preserved interest or order that the holder be paid for the interest from the proceeds of any sale pursuant to division (D) of this section.

(D)(1) Contraband ordered forfeited pursuant to this section shall be disposed of pursuant to divisions (D)(1) to (7) of section 2933.41 of the Revised Code or, if the contraband is not described in those divisions, may be used, with the approval of the court, by the law enforcement agency that has custody of the contraband pursuant to division (D)(8) of that section. In the case of contraband not described in any of those divisions and of contraband not disposed of pursuant to any of those divisions, the contraband shall be sold in accordance with this division or, in the case of forfeited moneys, disposed of in accordance with this division. If the contraband is to be sold, the prosecuting attorney shall cause a notice of the proposed sale of the contraband to be given in accordance with law, and the property shall be sold, without appraisal, at a public auction to the highest bidder for cash. The proceeds of a sale and forfeited moneys shall be applied in the following order:

(a) First, to the payment of the costs incurred in connection with the seizure of, storage of, maintenance of, and provision of security for the contraband, the forfeiture proceeding, and, if any, the sale;

(b) Second, the remaining proceeds or forfeited moneys after compliance with division (D)(1)(a) of this section, to the payment of the balance due on any security interest preserved pursuant to division (C) of this section;

(c) Third, the remaining proceeds or forfeited moneys after compliance with divisions (D)(1)(a) and (b) of this section, as follows:

(i) If the forfeiture was ordered in a juvenile court, ten per cent to one or more alcohol and drug addiction treatment programs that are certified by the department of alcohol and drug addiction services under section 3793.06 of the Revised Code and that are specified in the order of forfeiture. A juvenile court shall not certify an alcohol or drug addiction treatment program in the order of forfeiture unless the program is a certified alcohol and drug addiction treatment program and, except as provided in division (D)(1)(c)(i) of this section, unless the program is located in the county in which the court that orders the forfeiture is located or in a contiguous county. If no certified alcohol and drug addiction treatment program is located in any of those counties, the juvenile court may specify in the order a certified alcohol and drug addiction treatment program located anywhere within this state.

(ii) If the forfeiture was ordered in a juvenile court, ninety per cent, and if the forfeiture was ordered in a court other than a juvenile court, one hundred per cent to the law enforcement trust fund of the prosecuting attorney and to the law enforcement trust fund of the county sheriff if the county sheriff made the seizure, to the law enforcement trust fund of a municipal corporation if its police department made the seizure, to the law enforcement trust fund of a township if the seizure was made by a township police department, township police district police force, or office of a township constable, to the law enforcement trust fund of a park district created pursuant to section 511.18 or 1545.01 of the Revised Code if the seizure was made by the park district police force or law enforcement department, to the state highway patrol contraband, forfeiture, and other fund if the state highway patrol made the seizure, to the department of public safety investigative unit contraband, forfeiture, and other fund if the investigative unit of the department of public safety made the seizure, to the department of taxation enforcement fund if the department of taxation made the seizure to the board of pharmacy drug law enforcement fund created by division (B)(1) of section 4729.65 of the Revised Code if the board made the seizure, or to the treasurer of state for deposit into the peace officer training commission fund if a state law enforcement agency, other than the state highway patrol, the investigative unit of the department of public safety, the enforcement division of the department of taxation, or the state board of pharmacy, made the seizure. The prosecuting attorney may decline to accept any of the remaining proceeds or forfeited moneys, and, if the prosecuting attorney so declines, the remaining proceeds or forfeited moneys shall be applied to the fund described in this division that relates to the law enforcement agency that made the seizure.

A law enforcement trust fund shall be established by the prosecuting attorney of each county who intends to receive any remaining proceeds or forfeited moneys pursuant to this division, by the sheriff of each county, by the legislative authority of each municipal corporation, by the board of township trustees of each township that has a township police department, township police district police force, or office of the constable, and by the board of park commissioners of each park district created pursuant to section 511.18 or 1545.01 of the Revised Code that has a park district police force or law enforcement department, for the purposes of this division. There is hereby created in the state treasury the state highway patrol contraband, forfeiture, and other fund, the department of public safety investigative unit contraband, forfeiture, and other fund, the department of taxation enforcement fund, and the peace officer training commission fund, for the purposes described in this division.

Proceeds or forfeited moneys distributed to any municipal corporation, township, or park district law enforcement trust fund shall be allocated from the fund by the legislative authority only to the police department of the municipal corporation, by the board of township trustees only to the township police department, township police district police force, or office of the constable, and by the board of park commissioners only to the park district police force or law enforcement department.

Additionally, no proceeds or forfeited moneys shall be allocated to or used by the state highway patrol, the department of public safety, the department of taxation, the state board of pharmacy, or a county sheriff, prosecuting attorney, municipal corporation police department, township police department, township police district police force, office of the constable, or park district police force or law enforcement department unless the state highway patrol, department of public safety, department of taxation, state board of pharmacy, sheriff, prosecuting attorney, municipal corporation police department, township police department, township police district police force, office of the constable, or park district police force or law enforcement department has adopted a written internal control policy under division (D)(3) of this section that addresses the use of moneys received from the state highway patrol contraband, forfeiture, and other fund, the department of public safety investigative unit contraband, forfeiture, and other fund, the department of taxation enforcement fund, the board of pharmacy drug law enforcement fund, or the appropriate law enforcement trust fund.

The state highway patrol contraband, forfeiture, and other fund, the department of public safety investigative unit contraband, forfeiture, and other fund, the department of taxation enforcement fund, and a law enforcement trust fund shall be expended only in accordance with the written internal control policy so adopted by the recipient, and, subject to the requirements specified in division (D)(3)(a)(ii) of this section, only to pay the costs of protracted or complex investigations or prosecutions, to provide reasonable technical training or expertise, to provide matching funds to obtain federal grants to aid law enforcement, in the support of DARE programs or other programs designed to educate adults or children with respect to the dangers associated with the use of drugs of abuse, to pay the costs of emergency action taken under section 3745.13 of the Revised Code relative to the operation of an illegal methamphetamine laboratory if the forfeited property or money involved was that of a person responsible for the operation of the laboratory, or for other law enforcement purposes that the superintendent of the state highway patrol, department of public safety, department of taxation, prosecuting attorney, county sheriff, legislative authority, board of township trustees, or board of park commissioners determines to be appropriate. The board of pharmacy drug law enforcement fund shall be expended only in accordance with the written internal control policy so adopted by the board and only in accordance with section 4729.65 of the Revised Code, except that it also may be expended to pay the costs of emergency action taken under section 3745.13 of the Revised Code relative to the operation of an illegal methamphetamine laboratory if the forfeited property or money involved was that of a person responsible for the operation of the laboratory. The state highway patrol contraband, forfeiture, and other fund, the department of public safety investigative unit contraband, forfeiture, and other fund, the department of taxation enforcement fund, the board of pharmacy drug law enforcement fund, and a law enforcement trust fund shall not be used to meet the operating costs of the state highway patrol, of the investigative unit of the department of public safety, of the department of taxation enforcement division, of the state board of pharmacy, of any political subdivision, or of any office of a prosecuting attorney or county sheriff that are unrelated to law enforcement.

Proceeds and forfeited moneys that are paid into the state treasury to be deposited into the peace officer training commission fund shall be used by the commission only to pay the costs of peace officer training.

Any sheriff or prosecuting attorney who receives proceeds or forfeited moneys pursuant to this division during any calendar year shall file a report with the county auditor, no later than the thirty-first day of January of the next calendar year, verifying that the proceeds and forfeited moneys were expended only for the purposes authorized by this division and division (D)(3)(a)(ii) of this section and specifying the amounts expended for each authorized purpose. Any municipal corporation police department that is allocated proceeds or forfeited moneys from a municipal corporation law enforcement trust fund pursuant to this division during any calendar year shall file a report with the legislative authority of the municipal corporation, no later than the thirty-first day of January of the next calendar year, verifying that the proceeds and forfeited moneys were expended only for the purposes authorized by this division and division (D)(3)(a)(ii) of this section and specifying the amounts expended for each authorized purpose. Any township police department, township police district police force, or office of the constable that is allocated proceeds or forfeited moneys from a township law enforcement trust fund pursuant to this division during any calendar year shall file a report with the board of township trustees of the township, no later than the thirty-first day of January of the next calendar year, verifying that the proceeds and forfeited moneys were expended only for the purposes authorized by this division and division (D)(3)(a)(ii) of this section and specifying the amounts expended for each authorized purpose. Any park district police force or law enforcement department that is allocated proceeds or forfeited moneys from a park district law enforcement trust fund pursuant to this division during any calendar year shall file a report with the board of park commissioners of the park district, no later than the thirty-first day of January of the next calendar year, verifying that the proceeds and forfeited moneys were expended only for the purposes authorized by this division and division (D)(3)(a)(ii) of this section and specifying the amounts expended for each authorized purpose. The superintendent of the state highway patrol shall file a report with the attorney general, no later than the thirty-first day of January of each calendar year, verifying that proceeds and forfeited moneys paid into the state highway patrol contraband, forfeiture, and other fund pursuant to this division during the prior calendar year were used by the state highway patrol during the prior calendar year only for the purposes authorized by this division and specifying the amounts expended for each authorized purpose. The executive director of the state board of pharmacy shall file a report with the attorney general, no later than the thirty-first day of January of each calendar year, verifying that proceeds and forfeited moneys paid into the board of pharmacy drug law enforcement fund during the prior calendar year were used only in accordance with section 4729.65 of the Revised Code and specifying the amounts expended for each authorized purpose. The peace officer training commission shall file a report with the attorney general, no later than the thirty-first day of January of each calendar year, verifying that proceeds and forfeited moneys paid into the peace officer training commission fund pursuant to this division during the prior calendar year were used by the commission during the prior calendar year only to pay the costs of peace officer training and specifying the amount used for that purpose.

The tax commissioner shall file a report with the attorney general, not later than the thirty-first day of January of each calendar year, verifying that proceeds and forfeited moneys paid into the department of taxation enforcement fund pursuant to this division during the prior calendar year were used by the enforcement division during the prior calendar year to pay only the costs of enforcing the tax laws and specifying the amount used for that purpose.

(2) If more than one law enforcement agency is substantially involved in the seizure of contraband that is forfeited pursuant to this section, the court ordering the forfeiture shall equitably divide the proceeds or forfeited moneys, after calculating any distribution to the law enforcement trust fund of the prosecuting attorney pursuant to division (D)(1)(c) of this section, among any county sheriff whose office is determined by the court to be substantially involved in the seizure, any legislative authority of a municipal corporation whose police department is determined by the court to be substantially involved in the seizure, any board of township trustees whose law enforcement agency is determined by the court to be substantially involved in the seizure, any board of park commissioners of a park district whose police force or law enforcement department is determined by the court to be substantially involved in the seizure, the state board of pharmacy if it is determined by the court to be substantially involved in the seizure, the investigative unit of the department of public safety if it is determined by the court to be substantially involved in the seizure, the enforcement division of the department of taxation if it is determined by the court to be substantially involved in the seizure and the state highway patrol if it is determined by the court to be substantially involved in the seizure. The proceeds or forfeited moneys shall be deposited in the respective law enforcement trust funds of the county sheriff, municipal corporation, township, and park district, the board of pharmacy drug law enforcement fund, the department of public safety investigative unit contraband, forfeiture, and other fund, the department of taxation enforcement fund, or the state highway patrol contraband, forfeiture, and other fund, in accordance with division (D)(1)(c) of this section. If a state law enforcement agency, other than the state highway patrol, the investigative unit of the department of public safety, the department of taxation, or the state board of pharmacy, is determined by the court to be substantially involved in the seizure, the state agency's equitable share of the proceeds and forfeited moneys shall be paid to the

treasurer of state for deposit into the peace officer training commission fund.

(3)(a)(i) Prior to being allocated or using any proceeds or forfeited moneys out of the state highway patrol contraband, forfeiture, and other fund, the department of public safety investigative unit contraband, forfeiture, and other fund, the department of taxation enforcement fund, the board of pharmacy drug law enforcement fund, or a law enforcement trust fund under division (D)(1)(c) of this section, the state highway patrol, the department of public safety, the department of taxation, the state board of pharmacy, and a county sheriff, prosecuting attorney, municipal corporation police department, township police department, township police district police force, office of the constable, or park district police force or law enforcement department shall adopt a written internal control policy that addresses the state highway patrol's, department of public safety's, department of taxation's, state board of pharmacy's, sheriff's, prosecuting attorney's, police department's, police force's, office of the constable's, or law enforcement department's use and disposition of all the proceeds and forfeited moneys received and that provides for the keeping of detailed financial records of the receipts of the proceeds and forfeited moneys, the general types of expenditures made out of the proceeds and forfeited moneys, the specific amount of each general type of expenditure, and the amounts, portions, and programs described in division (D)(3)(a)(ii) of this section. The policy shall not provide for or permit the identification of any specific expenditure that is made in an ongoing investigation.

All financial records of the receipts of the proceeds and forfeited moneys, the general types of expenditures made out of the proceeds and forfeited moneys, the specific amount of each general type of expenditure by the state highway patrol, by the department of public safety, by the department of taxation, by the state board of pharmacy, and by a sheriff, prosecuting attorney, municipal corporation police department, township police department, township police district police force, office of the constable, or park district police force or law enforcement department, and the amounts, portions, and programs described in division (D)(3)(a)(ii) of this section are public records open for inspection under section 149.43 of the Revised Code. Additionally, a written internal control policy adopted under this division is a public record of that nature, and the state highway patrol, the department of public safety, the department of taxation, the state board of pharmacy, or the sheriff, prosecuting attorney, municipal corporation police department, township police department, township police district police force, office of the constable, or park district police force or law enforcement department that adopted it shall comply with it.

(ii) The written internal control policy of a county sheriff, prosecuting attorney, municipal corporation police department, township police department, township police district police force, office of the constable, or park district police force or law enforcement department shall provide that at least ten per cent of the first one hundred thousand dollars of proceeds and forfeited moneys deposited during each calendar year in the sheriff's, prosecuting attorney's, municipal corporation's, township's, or park district's law enforcement trust fund pursuant to division (B)(7)(c)(ii) of section 2923.46 or division (B)(8)(c)(ii) of section 2925.44 of the Revised Code, and at least twenty per cent of the proceeds and forfeited moneys exceeding one hundred thousand dollars that are so deposited, shall be used in connection with community preventive education programs. The manner in which the described percentages are so used shall be determined by the sheriff, prosecuting attorney, department, police force, or office of the constable after the receipt and consideration of advice on appropriate community preventive education programs from the county's board of alcohol, drug addiction, and mental health services, from the county's alcohol and drug addiction services board, or through appropriate community dialogue. The financial records described in division (D)(3)(a)(i) of this section shall specify the amount of the proceeds and forfeited moneys deposited during each calendar year in the sheriff's, prosecuting attorney's, municipal corporation's, township's, or park district's law enforcement trust fund pursuant to division (B)(7)(c)(ii) of section 2923.46 or division (B)(8)(c)(ii) of section 2925.44 of the Revised Code, the portion of that amount that was used pursuant to the requirements of this division, and the community preventive education programs in connection with which the portion of that amount was so used.

As used in this division, "community preventive education programs" includes, but is not limited to, DARE programs and other programs designed to educate adults or children with respect to the dangers associated with the use of drugs of abuse.

(b) Each sheriff, prosecuting attorney, municipal corporation police department, township police department, township police district police force, office of the constable, or park district police force or law enforcement department that receives in any calendar year any proceeds or forfeited moneys out of a law enforcement trust fund under division (D)(1)(c) of this section or uses any proceeds or forfeited moneys in its law enforcement trust fund in any calendar year shall prepare a report covering the calendar year that cumulates all of the information contained in all of the public financial records kept by the sheriff, prosecuting attorney, municipal corporation police department, township police department, township police district police force, office of the constable, or park district police force or law enforcement department pursuant to division (D)(3)(a) of this section for that calendar year, and shall send a copy of the cumulative report, no later than the first day of March in the calendar year following the calendar year covered by the report, to the attorney general.

The superintendent of the state highway patrol shall prepare a report covering each calendar year in which the state highway patrol uses any proceeds or forfeited moneys in the state highway patrol contraband, forfeiture, and other fund under division (D)(1)(c) of this section, that cumulates all of the information contained in all of the public financial records kept by the state highway patrol pursuant to division (D)(3)(a) of this section for that calendar year, and shall send a copy of the cumulative report, no later than the first day of March in the calendar year following the calendar year covered by the report, to the attorney general.

The department of public safety shall prepare a report covering each fiscal year in which the department uses any proceeds or forfeited moneys in the department of public safety investigative unit contraband, forfeiture, and other fund under division (D)(1)(c) of this section that cumulates all of the information contained in all of the public financial records kept by the department pursuant to division (D)(3)(a) of this section for that fiscal year. The department shall send a copy of the cumulative report to the attorney general no later than the first day of August in the fiscal year following the fiscal year covered by the report. The director of public safety shall include in the report a verification that proceeds and forfeited moneys paid into the department of public safety investigative unit contraband, forfeiture, and other fund under division (D)(1)(c) of this section during the preceding fiscal year were used by the department during that fiscal year only for the purposes authorized by that division and shall specify the amount used for each authorized purpose.

The tax commissioner shall prepare a report covering each calendar year in which the department of taxation enforcement division uses any proceeds or forfeited moneys in the department of taxation enforcement fund under division (D)(1)(c) of this section, that cumulates all of the information contained in all of the public financial records kept by the department of taxation enforcement division pursuant to division (D)(3)(a) of this section for that calendar year, and shall send a copy of the cumulative report, not later than the first day of March in the calendar year following the calendar year covered by the report, to the attorney general.

The executive director of the state board of pharmacy shall prepare a report covering each calendar year in which the board uses any proceeds or forfeited moneys in the board of pharmacy drug law enforcement fund under division (D)(1)(c) of this section, that cumulates all of the information contained in all of the public financial records kept by the board pursuant to division (D)(3)(a) of this section for that calendar year, and shall send a copy of the cumulative report, no later than the first day of March in the calendar year following the calendar year covered by the report, to the attorney general. Each report received by the attorney general is a public record open for inspection under section 149.43 of the Revised Code. Not later than the fifteenth day of April in the calendar year in which the reports are received, the attorney general shall send to the president of the senate and the speaker of the house of representatives a written notification that does all of the following:

(i) Indicates that the attorney general has received from entities or persons specified in this division reports of the type described in this division that cover the previous calendar year and indicates that the reports were received under this division;

(ii) Indicates that the reports are open for inspection under section 149. 43 of the Revised Code;

(iii) Indicates that the attorney general will provide a copy of any or all of the reports to the president of the senate or the speaker of the house of representatives upon request.

(4)(a) A law enforcement agency that receives pursuant to federal law proceeds from a sale of forfeited contraband, proceeds from another disposition of forfeited contraband, or forfeited contraband moneys shall deposit, use, and account for the proceeds or forfeited moneys in accordance with, and otherwise comply with, the applicable federal law.

(b) If the state highway patrol receives pursuant to federal law proceeds from a sale of forfeited contraband, proceeds from another disposition of forfeited contraband, or forfeited contraband moneys, the appropriate governmental officials shall deposit into the state highway patrol contraband, forfeiture, and other fund all interest or other earnings derived from the investment of the proceeds or forfeited moneys. The state highway patrol shall use and account for that interest or other earnings in accordance with the applicable federal law.

(c) If the investigative unit of the department of public safety receives pursuant to federal law proceeds from a sale of forfeited contraband, proceeds from another disposition of forfeited contraband, or forfeited contraband moneys, the appropriate governmental officials shall deposit into the department of public safety investigative unit contraband, forfeiture, and other fund all interest or other earnings derived from the investment of the proceeds or forfeited moneys. The department shall use and account for that interest or other earnings in accordance with the applicable federal law.

(d) If the tax commissioner receives pursuant to federal law proceeds from a sale of forfeited contraband, proceeds from another disposition of forfeited contraband, or forfeited contraband moneys, the appropriate governmental officials, shall deposit into the department of taxation enforcement fund all interest or other earnings derived from the investment of the proceeds or forfeited moneys. The department shall use and account for that interest or other earnings in accordance with the applicable federal law.

(e) Divisions (D)(1) to (3) of this section do not apply to proceeds or forfeited moneys received pursuant to federal law or to the interest or other earnings that are derived from the investment of proceeds or forfeited moneys received pursuant to federal law and that are described in division (D)(4)(b) of this section.

(E) Upon the sale pursuant to this section of any property that is required to be titled or registered under law, the state shall issue an appropriate certificate of title or registration to the purchaser. If the state is vested with title pursuant to division (C) of this section and elects to retain property that is required to be titled or registered under law, the state shall issue an appropriate certificate of title or registration.

(F) Notwithstanding any provisions of this section to the contrary, any property that is lawfully seized in relation to a violation of section 2923.32 of the Revised Code shall be subject to forfeiture and disposition in accordance with sections 2923.32 to 2923.36 of the Revised Code; any property that is forfeited pursuant to section 2923.44 or 2923.45 of the Revised Code in relation to a violation of section 2923.42 of the Revised Code or in relation to an act of a juvenile that is a violation of section 2923.42 of the Revised Code may be subject to forfeiture and disposition in accordance with sections 2923.44 to 2923.47 of the Revised Code; and any property that is forfeited pursuant to section 2925.42 or 2925.43 of the Revised Code in relation to a felony drug abuse offense, as defined in section 2925.01 of the Revised Code, or in relation to an act that, if committed by an adult, would be a felony drug abuse offense of that nature, may be subject to forfeiture and disposition in accordance with sections 2925.41 to 2925.45 of the Revised Code or this section.

(G) Any failure of a law enforcement officer or agency, a prosecuting attorney, village solicitor, city director of law, or similar chief legal officer, a court, or the attorney general to comply with any duty imposed by this section in relation to any property seized or with any other provision of this section in relation to any property seized does not affect the validity of the seizure of the property, provided the seizure itself was made in accordance with law, and is not and shall not be considered to be the basis for the suppression of any evidence resulting from the seizure of the property, provided the seizure itself was made in accordance with law.

(H) Contraband that has been forfeited pursuant to division (C) of this section shall not be available for use to pay any fine imposed upon a person who is convicted of or pleads guilty to an underlying criminal offense or a different offense arising out of the same facts and circumstances.

(2003 H 95, eff. 9–26–03; 2001 H 7, eff. 8–7–01; 1999 H 163, eff. 6–30–99; 1998 H 2, eff. 1–1–99; 1998 S 164, eff. 1–15–98; 1997 H 210, eff. 6–30–97; 1996 S 277, eff. 3–31–97; 1996 H 670, eff. 12–2–96; 1996 S 239, eff. 9–6–96; 1995 H 1, eff. 1–1–96; 1995 S 162, eff. 10–29–95; 1995 H 107, eff. (See Historical and Statutory Notes); 1992 S 351, eff. 7–1–92; 1992 S 174; 1991 S 218; 1990 S 258, H 261, H 215; 1986 H 428, S 69)

Historical and Statutory Notes

Ed. Note: 1995 H 107 Effective Date—The Secretary of State assigned a general effective date of 6–30–95 for 1995 H 107. Pursuant to O Const Art II § 1c and 1d, and RC 1.471, sections of 1995 H 107 that are, or depend for their implementation upon, current expense appropriations are effective 3–31–95; sections of 1995 H 107 that are not, and do not depend for their implementation upon, current expense appropriations are effective 6–30–95.

2933.44 Reports regarding juvenile-related forfeiture orders by alcohol and drug addiction treatment programs

(A) As used in this section, "juvenile–related forfeiture order" means any order of forfeiture issued by a juvenile court under section 2923.32, 2923.44, 2923.45, 2925.42, 2925.43, or 2933.43 of the Revised Code and any order of disposition of property issued by a court under section 2933.41 of the Revised Code regarding property that was in the possession of a law enforcement agency in relation to a delinquent child proceeding in a juvenile court.

(B) Each certified alcohol and drug addiction treatment program that receives in any calendar year money under division (D)(1)(a) of section 2923.35, division (B)(7)(c)(i) of section 2923.46, division (B)(8)(c)(i) of section 2925.44, division

(E)(1)(a) of section 2933.41, or division (D)(1)(c)(i) of section 2933.43 of the Revised Code subsequent to the issuance of any juvenile-related forfeiture order shall file an annual report for that calendar year with the attorney general and with the court of common pleas and board of county commissioners of the county in which the program is located and of any other county from which the program received money under any of those divisions subsequent to the issuance of the juvenile-related forfeiture order. The program shall file the report on or before the first day of March in the calendar year following the calendar year in which the program received the money. The report shall include statistics on the number of persons the program served, identify the types of treatment services it provided to those persons, and include a specific accounting of the purposes for which it used the money so received. No information contained in the report shall identify, or enable a person to determine the identity of, any person served by the program.

(1998 H 2, eff. 1-1-99; 1995 H 1, eff. 1-1-96)

INTERCEPTION OF COMMUNICATIONS; WARRANTS

2933.51 Definitions

As used in sections 2933.51 to 2933.66 of the Revised Code:

(A) "Wire communication" means an aural transfer that is made in whole or in part through the use of facilities for the transmission of communications by the aid of wires or similar methods of connecting the point of origin of the communication and the point of reception of the communication, including the use of a method of connecting the point of origin and the point of reception of the communication in a switching station, if the facilities are furnished or operated by a person engaged in providing or operating the facilities for the transmission of communications. "Wire communication" includes an electronic storage of a wire communication.

(B) "Oral communication" means an oral communication uttered by a person exhibiting an expectation that the communication is not subject to interception under circumstances justifying that expectation. "Oral communication" does not include an electronic communication.

(C) "Intercept" means the aural or other acquisition of the contents of any wire, oral, or electronic communication through the use of an interception device.

(D) "Interception device" means an electronic, mechanical, or other device or apparatus that can be used to intercept a wire, oral, or electronic communication. "Interception device" does not mean any of the following:

(1) A telephone or telegraph instrument, equipment, or facility, or any of its components, if the instrument, equipment, facility, or component is any of the following:

(a) Furnished to the subscriber or user by a provider of wire or electronic communication service in the ordinary course of its business and being used by the subscriber or user in the ordinary course of its business;

(b) Furnished by a subscriber or user for connection to the facilities of a provider of wire or electronic communication service and used in the ordinary course of that subscriber's or user's business;

(c) Being used by a provider of wire or electronic communication service in the ordinary course of its business or by an investigative or law enforcement officer in the ordinary course of the officer's duties that do not involve the interception of wire, oral, or electronic communications.

(2) A hearing aid or similar device being used to correct subnormal hearing to not better than normal.

(E) "Investigative officer" means any of the following:

(1) An officer of this state or a political subdivision of this state, who is empowered by law to conduct investigations or to make arrests for a designated offense;

(2) A person described in divisions (A)(11)(a) and (b) of section 2901.01 of the Revised Code;

(3) An attorney authorized by law to prosecute or participate in the prosecution of a designated offense;

(4) A secret service officer appointed pursuant to section 309.07 of the Revised Code;

(5) An officer of the United States, a state, or a political subdivision of a state who is authorized to conduct investigations pursuant to the "Electronic Communications Privacy Act of 1986," 100 Stat. 1848–1857, 18 U.S.C. 2510–2521 (1986), as amended.

(F) "Interception warrant" means a court order that authorizes the interception of wire, oral, or electronic communications and that is issued pursuant to sections 2933.53 to 2933.56 of the Revised Code.

(G) "Contents," when used with respect to a wire, oral, or electronic communication, includes any information concerning the substance, purport, or meaning of the communication.

(H) "Communications common carrier" means a person who is engaged as a common carrier for hire in intrastate, interstate, or foreign communications by wire, radio, or radio transmission of energy. "Communications common carrier" does not include, to the extent that the person is engaged in radio broadcasting, a person engaged in radio broadcasting.

(I) "Designated offense" means any of the following:

(1) A felony violation of section 1315.53, 1315.55, 2903.01, 2903.02, 2903.11, 2905.01, 2905.02, 2905.11, 2905.22, 2907.02, 2907.21, 2907.22, 2909.02, 2909.03, 2909.04, 2909.22, 2909.23, 2909.24, 2911.01, 2911.02, 2911.11, 2911.12, 2913.02, 2913.04, 2913.42, 2913.51, 2915.02, 2915.03, 2917.01, 2917.02, 2921.02, 2921.03, 2921.04, 2921.32, 2921.34, 2923.20, 2923.32, 2925.03, 2925.04, 2925.05, or 2925.06 or of division (B) of section 2915.05 of the Revised Code;

(2) A violation of section 2919.23 of the Revised Code that, had it occurred prior to July 1, 1996, would have been a violation of section 2905.04 of the Revised Code as it existed prior to that date;

(3) A felony violation of section 2925.11 of the Revised Code that is not a minor drug possession offense, as defined in section 2925.01 of the Revised Code;

(4) Complicity in the commission of a felony violation of a section listed in division (I)(1), (2), or (3) of this section;

(5) An attempt to commit, or conspiracy in the commission of, a felony violation of a section listed in division (I)(1), (2), or (3) of this section, if the attempt or conspiracy is punishable by a term of imprisonment of more than one year.

(J) "Aggrieved person" means a person who was a party to an intercepted wire, oral, or electronic communication or a person against whom the interception of the communication was directed.

(K) "Person" means a person, as defined in section 1.59 of the Revised Code, or a governmental officer, employee, or entity.

(L) "Special need" means a showing that a licensed physician, licensed practicing psychologist, attorney, practicing cleric, journalist, or either spouse is personally engaging in continuing criminal activity, was engaged in continuing criminal activity over a period of time, or is committing, has committed, or is about to commit, a designated offense, or a showing that specified public facilities are being regularly used by someone who is personally engaging in continuing criminal activity, was engaged in continuing criminal activity over a period of time, or is committing, has committed, or is about to commit, a designated offense.

(M) "Journalist" means a person engaged in, connected with, or employed by, any news media, including a newspaper, magazine, press association, news agency, or wire service, a radio or television station, or a similar media, for the purpose of gathering, processing, transmitting, compiling, editing, or disseminating news for the general public.

(N) "Electronic communication" means a transfer of a sign, signal, writing, image, sound, datum, or intelligence of any nature that is transmitted in whole or in part by a wire, radio, electromagnetic, photoelectronic, or photo-optical system. "Electronic communication" does not mean any of the following:

(1) A wire or oral communication;

(2) A communication made through a tone-only paging device;

(3) A communication from an electronic or mechanical tracking device that permits the tracking of the movement of a person or object.

(O) "User" means a person or entity that uses an electronic communication service and is duly authorized by the provider of the service to engage in the use of the electronic communication service.

(P) "Electronic communications system" means a wire, radio, electromagnetic, photoelectronic, or photo-optical facility for the transmission of electronic communications, and a computer facility or related electronic equipment for the electronic storage of electronic communications.

(Q) "Electronic communication service" means a service that provides to users of the service the ability to send or receive wire or electronic communications.

(R) "Readily accessible to the general public" means, with respect to a radio communication, that the communication is none of the following:

(1) Scrambled or encrypted;

(2) Transmitted using a modulation technique, the essential parameters of which have been withheld from the public with the intention of preserving the privacy of the communication;

(3) Carried on a subcarrier or other signal subsidiary to a radio transmission;

(4) Transmitted over a communications system provided by a communications common carrier, unless the communication is a tone-only paging system communication;

(5) Transmitted on a frequency allocated under part 25, subpart D, E, or F of part 74, or part 94 of the Rules of the Federal Communications Commission, as those provisions existed on July 1, 1996, unless, in the case of a communication transmitted on a frequency allocated under part 74 that is not exclusively allocated to broadcast auxiliary services, the communication is a two-way voice communication by radio.

(S) "Electronic storage" means a temporary, intermediate storage of a wire or electronic communication that is incidental to the electronic transmission of the communication, and a storage of a wire or electronic communication by an electronic communication service for the purpose of backup protection of the communication.

(T) "Aural transfer" means a transfer containing the human voice at a point between and including the point of origin and the point of reception.

(U) "Pen register" means a device that records or decodes electronic impulses that identify the numbers dialed, pulsed, or otherwise transmitted on telephone lines to which the device is attached.

(V) "Trap and trace device" means a device that captures the incoming electronic or other impulses that identify the originating number of an instrument or device from which a wire communication or electronic communication was transmitted but that does not intercept the contents of the wire communication or electronic communication.

(W) "Judge of a court of common pleas" means a judge of that court who is elected or appointed as a judge of general jurisdiction or as a judge who exercises both general jurisdiction and probate, domestic relations, or juvenile jurisdiction. "Judge of a court of common pleas" does not mean a judge of that court who is elected or appointed specifically as a probate, domestic relations, or juvenile judge.

(2002 S 184, eff. 5–15–02; 1998 H 565, eff. 3–30–99; 1996 S 269, eff. 7–1–96; 1996 S 239, eff. 9–6–96; 1996 H 333, eff. 9–19–96; 1996 H 181, § 3, eff. 7–1–96; 1996 H 181, § 1, eff. 6–13–96; 1995 S 2, eff. 7–1–96; 1986 S 222, eff. 3–25–87)

2933.52 Prohibition against interception of communications; exceptions

(A) No person purposely shall do any of the following:

(1) Intercept, attempt to intercept, or procure another person to intercept or attempt to intercept a wire, oral, or electronic communication;

(2) Use, attempt to use, or procure another person to use or attempt to use an interception device to intercept a wire, oral, or electronic communication, if either of the following applies:

(a) The interception device is affixed to, or otherwise transmits a signal through, a wire, cable, satellite, microwave, or other similar method of connection used in wire communications;

(b) The interception device transmits communications by radio, or interferes with the transmission of communications by radio.

(3) Use, or attempt to use, the contents of a wire, oral, or electronic communication, knowing or having reason to know that the contents were obtained through the interception of a wire, oral, or electronic communication in violation of sections 2933.51 to 2933.66 of the Revised Code.

(B) This section does not apply to any of the following:

(1) The interception, disclosure, or use of the contents, or evidence derived from the contents, of an oral, wire, or electronic communication that is obtained through the use of an interception warrant issued pursuant to sections 2933.53 to 2933.56 of the Revised Code, that is obtained pursuant to an oral approval for an interception granted pursuant to section 2933.57 of the Revised Code, or that is obtained pursuant to an order that is issued or an interception that is made in accordance with section 802 of the "Omnibus Crime Control and Safe Streets Act of 1968," 82 Stat. 237, 254, 18 U.S.C. 2510 to 2520 (1968), as amended, the "Electronic Communications Privacy Act of 1986," 100 Stat. 1848–1857, 18 2510–2521 [sic.] (1986), as amended, or the "Foreign Intelligence Surveillance Act," 92 Stat. 1783, 50 U.S.C. 1801.11 (1978), as amended;

(2) An operator of a switchboard, or an officer, employee, or agent of a provider of wire or electronic communication service, whose facilities are used in the transmission of a wire or electronic communication to intercept, disclose, or use that communication in the normal course of employment while engaged in an activity that is necessary to the rendition of service or to the protection of the rights or property of the provider of that service, except that a provider of wire or electronic communication service to the public shall not utilize service observing or random monitoring except for mechanical or service quality control checks;

(3) A law enforcement officer who intercepts a wire, oral, or electronic communication, if the officer is a party to the communication or if one of the parties to the communication has given prior consent to the interception by the officer;

(4) A person who is not a law enforcement officer and who intercepts a wire, oral, or electronic communication, if the person is a party to the communication or if one of the parties to the communication has given the person prior consent to the interception, and if the communication is not intercepted for the purpose of committing a criminal offense or tortious act in violation of the laws or Constitution of the United States or this state or for the purpose of committing any other injurious act;

(5) An officer, employee, or agent of a communications common carrier providing information, facilities, or technical assistance to an investigative officer who is authorized to intercept a wire, oral, or electronic communication pursuant to sections 2933.51 to 2933.66 of the Revised Code;

(6) The use of a pen register in accordance with federal or state law;

(7) The use of a trap and trace device in accordance with federal or state law;

(8) A police, fire, or emergency communications system to intercept wire communications coming into and going out of the communications system of a police department, fire department, or emergency center, if both of the following apply:

(a) The telephone, instrument, equipment, or facility is limited to the exclusive use of the communication system for administrative purposes;

(b) At least one telephone, instrument, equipment, or facility that is not subject to interception is made available for public use at each police department, fire department, or emergency center.

(9) The interception or accessing of an electronic communication made through an electronic communication system that is configured so that the electronic communication is readily accessible to the general public.

(10) The interception of a radio communication that is transmitted by any of the following:

(a) A station for the use of the general public;

(b) Governmental, law enforcement, civil defense, private land mobile, or public safety communications system, including a police or fire system, that is readily accessible to the general public;

(c) A station operating on an authorized frequency within the bands allocated to the amateur, citizen band, or general mobile radio services;

(d) A marine or aeronautical communications system.

(11) The interception of a radio communication that relates to a ship, aircraft, vehicle, or person in distress.

(12) The interception of a wire or electronic communication the transmission of which is causing harmful interference to a lawfully operating station or consumer electronic equipment, to the extent necessary to identify the source of that interference.

(13) Other users of the same frequency to intercept a radio communication made through a system that utilizes frequencies monitored by individuals engaged in the provision or the use of that system, if the communication is not scrambled or encrypted.

(C) Whoever violates this section is guilty of interception of wire, oral, or electronic communications, a felony of the fourth degree.

(1996 H 181, § 3, eff. 7–1–96; 1996 H 181, § 1, eff. 6–13–96; 1995 S 2, eff. 7–1–96; 1987 H 231, eff. 10–5–87; 1986 S 222)

2933.521 Divulging content of communication by provider of electronic communication service

(A) Except as provided in division (B) of this section, no person or entity that provides electronic communication service to the public shall purposely divulge the content of a communication, while it is in transmission on that service, to a person or entity other than an addressee or intended recipient of the communication or an agent of an addressee or intended recipient of the communication.

(B)(1) Division (A) of this section does not apply to a communication being transmitted to the person or entity providing the electronic communication service or to an agent of that person or entity.

(2) Notwithstanding division (A) of this section, a person or entity that provides electronic communication service to the public may divulge the content of a communication that is in transmission on that service in any of the following circumstances:

(a) The divulgence is authorized by division (B)(2) of section 2933.52, by section 2933.581, by division (C) of section 2933.55, or by division (F) or (G) of section 2933.59 of the Revised Code or by a provision of the "Electronic Communications Privacy Act of 1986," 100 Stat. 1848–1857, 18 U.S.C. 2510–2521 (1986), as amended.

(b) The originator or an addressee or intended recipient of the communication has lawfully consented to the divulgence.

(c) The divulgence is made to a person who is employed or authorized, or whose facilities are used, to forward the communication to its destination.

(d) The content of the communication divulged was inadvertently obtained by the provider of the service, the content appears to pertain to the commission of a crime, and the divulgence is made to a law enforcement agency.

(C) Neither division (A) of this section nor any other provision of sections 2933.51 to 2933.66 of the Revised Code prohibits a provider of electronic communication service from recording the fact that a wire or electronic communication was initiated or completed, in order to protect the provider, another provider furnishing service toward the completion of the wire or electronic communication, or a user of the electronic communication service from fraudulent, unlawful, or abusive use of the electronic communication service.

(1996 H 181, eff. 6–13–96)

2933.522 Authority of judges of courts of common pleas

A judge of a court of common pleas, in accordance with sections 2933.51 to 2933.66 of the Revised Code, may accept applications for interception warrants, may issue interception warrants, may accept applications for extensions of interception warrants, may order extensions of interception warrants, may accept applications for grants of oral orders for interceptions, may grant oral orders for interceptions, and may issue other orders, perform other functions, or engage in other activities authorized or required by sections 2933.51 to 2933.66 of the Revised Code.

(1996 H 181, eff. 6–13–96)

2933.53 Application for interception warrant; contents; exemptions

(A) The prosecuting attorney of the county in which an interception is to take place or in which an interception device is to be installed, or an assistant to the prosecuting attorney of that county who is specifically designated by the prosecuting attorney to exercise authority under this section, may authorize an application for an interception warrant to a judge of the court of common pleas of the county in which the interception is to take place or in which the interception device is to be installed. If the prosecuting attorney of a county in which an interception is to take place or in which an interception device is to be installed is the subject of an investigation, a special prosecutor appointed by a judge of the court of common pleas of the county served by the prosecuting attorney, without the knowledge of the prosecuting attorney, may apply the procedures of this section. If the subject of an investigation is employed in the office of the prosecuting attorney of the county in which an interception is to take place or in which an interception device is to be installed or the prosecuting attorney of that county believes that the subject has a conflict of interest, the approval of the prosecuting attorney shall be obtained before a special prosecutor is appointed to authorize the application for an interception warrant.

(B) Each application for an interception warrant shall be made in writing upon oath or affirmation to a judge of the court of common pleas of the county in which the interception is to take place or in which the interception device is to be installed, by a person who has received training that satisfies the minimum standards established by the attorney general and the Ohio peace officer training commission under section 2933.64 of the Revised Code. Each application shall contain all of the following:

(1) The name and office of the applicant and the name and office of the prosecuting attorney or assistant prosecuting attorney authorizing the application;

(2) The identity of the investigative officers or law enforcement agency that will intercept the wire, oral, or electronic communications;

(3) A full and complete statement of the objective in seeking the warrant, and a full and complete statement of the facts and circumstances relied on by the applicant to justify the belief that the warrant should be issued, including, but not limited to the following:

(a) The details regarding the designated offense that has been, is being, or is about to be committed;

(b) The identity of the person, if known, who has committed, is committing, or is about to commit the designated offense and whose communications are to be intercepted and the location at which the communications are sought to be intercepted;

(c) Except as provided in division (G)(1) of this section, a particular description of the nature and location of the facilities from which, or the place at which, the communication is to be intercepted;

(d) A particular description of the type of communication sought to be intercepted, and the basis for believing that evidence relating to a designated offense will be obtained through the interception.

(4) A statement as to whether the applicant, or the prosecuting attorney or assistant prosecuting attorney authorizing the application for an interception warrant, knows or has reason to know that the communications sought to be intercepted are privileged under section 2317.02 of the Revised Code, the nature of any privilege that exists, and the basis of the knowledge of the applicant or authorizing prosecuting attorney or assistant prosecuting attorney of the privileged nature of the communications;

(5) A statement of the use to which the contents of an intercepted wire, oral, or electronic communication, or the evidence derived from the communication, will be put;

(6) A statement of the period of time for which the interception is required to be maintained, and, if the nature of the investigation requires that the authorization for interception not be terminated automatically when the described type of communication first has been intercepted, a particular description of the facts establishing probable cause to believe that additional communications of the same type will occur after the first intercepted communication;

(7) A full and complete statement indicating whether other investigative procedures have been tried and have failed to produce the required evidence or indicating the reason that other investigative procedures reasonably appear to be unlikely to succeed if tried or to be too dangerous to employ in order to obtain evidence;

(8) A full and complete statement of the particular facts concerning all previous applications known to the applicant or the prosecuting attorney or assistant prosecuting attorney authorizing the application for the interception warrant, that have been made to a judge for authorization to intercept wire, oral, or electronic communications involving any of the persons, facilities, or places specified in the application, and the action of the judge with respect to each previous application;

(9) Unless the attorney general is a subject of the investigation, a written statement, signed by the attorney general or an assistant attorney general designated by the attorney general, that the attorney general or assistant attorney general has reviewed the application and either agrees or disagrees with the submission of the application to a judge of the court of common pleas of the county in which the interception is to take place or in which the interception device is to be installed. A disagreement by the attorney general or assistant attorney general does not preclude the making or consideration of an application that otherwise complies with divisions (B)(1) to (8) of this section.

(C) If an application for an interception warrant is for an extension of a warrant, the application shall include, in addition to the information and statements specified in division (B) of this section, a statement setting forth the results thus far obtained from the interceptions of wire, oral, or electronic communications, or a reasonable explanation of the failure to obtain results from the interceptions.

(D) An applicant may submit affidavits of persons other than the applicant in conjunction with the application if the affidavits support a fact or conclusion in the application. The accompanying affidavits shall be based on personal knowledge of the affiant or shall be based on information and belief and specify the source of the information and the reason for the belief. If the applicant or an affiant personally knows of the facts contained in the application or affidavit, the application or affidavit shall state the personal knowledge. If the application or affidavit states the facts based upon information and belief, the application or affidavit shall state that reliance upon information and belief and shall set forth fully the facts supporting the information and belief. If the facts contained in the application or affidavits are derived in whole or in part from the statement of a person other than the applicant or affiant, the application or affidavits shall disclose or describe the sources of the facts and shall contain facts establishing the existence and reliability of the other person or the reliability of the information supplied by the other person. The application also shall state, so far as possible, the basis of the other person's knowledge or belief. If the application or affidavit relies on hearsay to support a fact alleged on information and belief, the application or affidavit shall contain the underlying facts that establish the basis for the conclusions of the source of the hearsay and the factual basis upon which the applicant or the affiant concludes that the source of the hearsay is credible or reliable.

(E) A judge of a court of common pleas to whom an application is made under this section may require the applicant to furnish additional sworn testimony or documentary evidence in support of the application. All sworn testimony furnished shall be recorded and transcribed and shall be made part of the application.

(F) An interception warrant is not required for any of the following:

(1) A pen register used in accordance with federal or state law;

(2) The interception of a wire, oral, or electronic communication by a law enforcement officer if the officer is a party to the communication or if one of the parties to the communication has given prior consent to the interception by the officer;

(3) The interception of a wire, oral, or electronic communication by a person who is not a law enforcement officer if the person is a party to the communication or if one of the parties to the communication has given the person prior consent to the interception, and if the communication is not intercepted for the purpose of committing a criminal offense or tortious act in violation of the laws or constitution of the United States or this state or for the purpose of committing another injurious act.

(4) A trap and trace device used in accordance with federal or state law.

(G)(1) The requirements of division (B)(3)(c) of this section and of division (A)(5) of section 2933.54 of the Revised Code that relate to the specification of facilities from which or the place at which the communication is to be intercepted do not apply if either of the following applies:

(a) In the case of an application with respect to the interception of an oral communication, the application contains a full and complete statement indicating the reason that the specification is not practical and identifies the person committing the designated offense and whose communications are to be intercepted, and the judge of a court of common pleas to whom the application is made finds that the specification is not practical.

(b) In the case of an application with respect to a wire or electronic communication, the application identifies the person believed to be committing the designated offense and whose communications are to be intercepted, the applicant makes a showing of purpose on the part of that person to thwart interception by changing facilities, and the judge of a court of common pleas to whom the application is made finds that that purpose adequately has been shown.

(2) An interception of a communication under an interception warrant with respect to which the requirements of division (B)(3)(c) of this section and division (A)(5) of section 2933.54 of the Revised Code do not apply, due to the application of division (G)(1) of this section, shall not begin until the facilities from which or the place at which the communication is to be intercepted is ascertained by the person implementing the interception warrant.

A provider of wire or electronic communication service that has received an interception warrant that does not specify the facilities from which or the place at which the communication is to be intercepted, due to the application of division (G)(1)(b) of this section, may file a motion with the court requesting the court to modify or quash the interception warrant on the ground that the provider's assistance with respect to the interception cannot be performed in a timely or reasonable manner. The court, upon notice to the applicant for the interception warrant, shall decide the motion expeditiously.

(1996 H 670, eff. 12–2–96; 1996 H 181, eff. 6–13–96; 1986 S 222, eff. 3–25–87)

2933.54 Issuance of interception warrant; hearings

(A) A judge of a court of common pleas to whom an application for an interception warrant is made under section 2933.53 of the Revised Code may issue an interception warrant if the judge determines, on the basis of the facts submitted by the person who made the application and all affiants, that all of the following exist:

(1) The application and affidavits comply with section 2933.53 of the Revised Code.

(2) There is probable cause to believe that a particular person is committing, has committed, or is about to commit a designated offense.

(3) There is probable cause to believe that particular communications concerning the designated offense will be obtained through the interception of wire, oral, or electronic communications.

(4) Normal investigative procedures with respect to the designated offense have been tried and have failed or normal investigative procedures with respect to the designated offense reasonably appear to be unlikely to succeed if tried or to be too dangerous to employ in order to obtain evidence.

(5) Except as provided in division (G)(1) of section 2933.53 of the Revised Code, there is probable cause to believe that the communication facilities from which the communications are to be intercepted, or the place at which oral communications are to be intercepted, are being used or are about to be used in connection with the commission of the designated offense or are leased to, listed in the name of, or commonly used by a person who is the subject of the interception warrant.

(6) The investigative officer has received training that satisfies the minimum standards established by the attorney general and the Ohio peace officer training commission under section 2933.64 of the Revised Code in order to intercept the wire, oral, or electronic communication and is able to execute the interception sought.

(B) If the communication facilities from which a wire or electronic communication is to be intercepted are public facilities, the judge of the court of common pleas to whom the application for an interception warrant is made shall not issue an interception warrant unless the judge, in addition to the findings specified in division (A) of this section, determines that there is a special need to intercept wire or electronic communications made from the facilities.

(C) If the facilities from which, or the place at which, the wire, oral, or electronic communications are to be intercepted are being used by, are about to be used by, are leased to, are listed in the name of, or are commonly used by a licensed physician, a licensed practicing psychologist, an attorney, a practicing clergyman, or a journalist or are used primarily for habitation by a husband and wife, the judge of the court of common pleas to whom the application is made shall not issue an interception warrant unless the judge, in addition to the findings specified in divisions (A) and (B) of this section, determines that there is a special need to intercept wire, oral, or electronic communications over the facilities or in those places. No otherwise privileged wire, oral, or electronic communication shall lose its privileged character because it is intercepted in accordance with or in violation of sections 2933.51 to 2933.66 of the Revised Code.

(D) If an application for an interception warrant does not comply with section 2933.53 of the Revised Code, or if the judge of a court of common pleas with whom an application is filed is not satisfied that grounds exist for issuance of an interception warrant, the judge shall deny the application.

(E) An interception warrant shall terminate when the objective of the warrant has been achieved or upon the expiration of thirty days after the date of commencement of the warrant as specified in this division, whichever occurs first, unless an extension is granted as described in this division. The date of commencement of an interception warrant is the day on which an investigative or law enforcement officer first begins to conduct an interception under the warrant, or the day that is ten days after the warrant is issued, whichever is earlier. A judge of a court of common pleas may grant extensions of a warrant pursuant to section 2933.55 of the Revised Code.

(F) If a judge of a court of common pleas issues an interception warrant, the judge shall make a finding as to the objective of the warrant.

(1996 H 670, eff. 12–2–96; 1996 H 181, eff. 6–13–96; 1988 H 708, eff. 4–19–88; 1986 S 222)

2933.55 Extension of interception warrant; approval of interceptions beyond scope of warrant

(A) At any time prior to the expiration of an interception warrant, the person who made the application for the warrant may apply for an extension of the warrant. The person shall file the application for extension with a judge of the court of common pleas of the county in which the interception under the warrant was to take place. An application for extension shall comply with section 2933.53 of the Revised Code.

(B) A judge of a court of common pleas with whom an application for extension of an interception warrant is filed shall determine whether to order an extension of the interception warrant in accordance with section 2933.54 of the Revised Code and shall order an extension for a period no longer than the judge considers necessary to achieve the purposes of the extension. The extension shall terminate upon the attainment of the authorized objective or thirty days after it is granted, whichever occurs first. All provisions of sections 2933.51 to 2933.66 of the Revised Code that apply to original interception warrants apply to extensions of interception warrants.

(C)(1) When an investigative officer, while intercepting communications pursuant to an interception warrant or pursuant to an oral order for an interception granted under section 2933.57 of the Revised Code, intercepts wire, oral, or electronic communications that pertain to a criminal offense that is other than the designated offense specified in the interception warrant or oral order and that is completely unrelated to the designated offense specified in the interception warrant or oral order, the prosecuting attorney, in order to permit the disclosure or use of the contents, or evidence derived from the contents, of the intercepted communications pursuant to division (G) of section 2933.59 of the Revised Code, may file a motion with the judge who issued the warrant or granted the oral order for an order approving the interception. The judge shall enter an order approving the interception if the judge finds that the communication otherwise was intercepted in accordance with sections 2933.53 to 2933.66 of the Revised Code.

A person may disclose or use the contents, and any evidence derived from the contents, of the intercepted communications dealing with the other, unrelated offense as set forth in division (F) of section 2933.59 of the Revised Code. The person may disclose or use those contents and the evidence derived from those contents as set forth in division (G) of section 2933.59 of the Revised Code only if the issuing judge issues an order approving the interception of the communications concerning the other, unrelated offense.

(2) When an investigative officer, while intercepting communications pursuant to an interception warrant or pursuant to an oral order for an interception granted under section 2933.57 of the Revised Code, intercepts wire, oral, or electronic communications that pertain to a criminal offense that is other than the designated offense specified in the interception warrant or oral order but that is not completely unrelated to the designated offense specified in the interception warrant or oral order, the wire, oral, or electronic communications intercepted shall be treated for all purposes and without the need for further action as if the offense to which they pertain was a designated offense specified in the interception warrant or oral order.

(1996 H 181, eff. 6–13–96; 1986 S 222, eff. 3–25–87)

2933.56 Contents of interception warrant; sealing of records

(A) Any interception warrant or extension of an interception warrant that is issued pursuant to sections 2933.53 to 2933.55 of the Revised Code shall contain all of the following:

(1) The name and court of the judge who issued the warrant and the jurisdiction of that court;

(2) If known, the identity of each person whose communications are to be intercepted or, if the identity is unascertainable, a detailed description of each known person whose communications are to be intercepted;

(3) The nature and location of the communications facilities from which or of the place at which the authority to intercept is granted and, in the case of telephone or telegraph communications, a designation of the particular lines involved;

(4) A statement of the objective of the warrant, as found by the issuing judge, and a statement of the designated offenses for which the authority to intercept is granted;

(5) A description of the particular type of communication sought to be intercepted;

(6) The identity of the investigative officer or law enforcement agency that is authorized to intercept communications pursuant to the interception warrant and the identity of the prosecuting attorney or assistant prosecuting attorney authorizing the application for the interception warrant;

(7) The period of time during which the interception is authorized, including a statement as to whether the interception shall terminate automatically when the described communication is first intercepted;

(8) A statement that the interception warrant shall be executed as soon as practicable;

(9) A statement that the interception shall be conducted in a way that minimizes the interception of communications that are not subject to the interception warrant, provided that if the intercepted communication is in a code or a foreign language and an expert in decoding or in that foreign language is not reasonably available during the interception period, minimization may be accomplished as soon as practicable after the interception;

(10) A statement that the interception shall terminate upon attainment of the authorized objective or upon the expiration of the thirty-day period described in division (F) of section 2933.54 of the Revised Code, whichever occurs first, unless an extension of the interception warrant is granted upon application by the judge who issued the original warrant;

(11) A statement that the person who made the application for the warrant or extension and the investigative officer or law enforcement agency authorized to intercept the communications shall provide oral or written progress reports at seven-day intervals to the judge who issued the warrant showing the progress made toward achievement of the authorized objective of the warrant and the need for continued interception;

(12) An authorization to enter private premises, other than the premises of a provider of wire or electronic communication service, for the sole purposes of installing, or of removing and permanently inactivating, interception devices and, if the entry is necessary to execute the interception warrant, a requirement that the time and date of the entry and name of the individual making the entry be reported to the court;

(13) If applicable, a statement directing a provider of wire or electronic communication service, landlord, custodian, or other person forthwith to furnish the applicant all information, facilities, and technical assistance necessary to accomplish the interception unobtrusively and with a minimum of interference with the services that the provider of wire or electronic communication service, landlord, custodian, or other person is providing to the person whose communications are to be intercepted. This assistance by a provider of wire or electronic communication service shall not include assistance in supplying, installing, or removing and permanently inactivating, interception devices. Any provider of wire or electronic communication service and any landlord, custodian, or other person furnishing the facilities or technical assistance shall be compensated for them at the prevailing rates.

(B) The judge of the court of common pleas to whom the application is made or who issued the warrant shall seal all applications for interception warrants that are made and all interception warrants that are issued pursuant to sections 2933.53 to 2933.55 of the Revised Code.

The judge of a court of common pleas who received the application or issued the warrant shall specify who shall have custody of the sealed application and interception warrant. Copies of the interception warrant, together with a copy of the application, shall be delivered to and retained by the person who made the application for the warrant or extension as authority for the interception authorized by the warrant.

Except as otherwise provided in sections 2933.51 to 2933.66 of the Revised Code, the application and interception warrants shall be disclosed only upon a showing of good cause before a judge who is authorized to issue interception warrants. Upon the termination of the authorized interception, the person who made the application for the warrant or extension shall return all applications made and interception warrants issued under sections 2933.53 to 2933.55 of the Revised Code that pertain to the interception to the issuing judge, and the applications and warrants shall be sealed under the issuing judge's direction.

The applications and warrants shall be kept for at least ten years. At the expiration of the ten-year period, the issuing or denying judge may order that the applications and warrants be destroyed.

(C) A violation of division (B) of this section may be punished as contempt of court.

(1996 H 181, eff. 6–13–96; 1986 S 222, eff. 3–25–87)

2933.57 Oral order for interception without warrant

(A) A judge of the court of common pleas may grant an oral order for an interception without a warrant of a wire, oral, or electronic communication. Upon receipt of an application under this division, the judge of the court of common pleas to whom the application is made may grant an oral order for an interception without a warrant, may include in the order a statement of the type described in division (A)(13) of section 2933.56 of the Revised Code, and shall condition the order upon the filing with the judge, within forty-eight hours, of an application for an interception warrant under section 2933.53 of the Revised Code and division (B) of this section, if the judge determines all of the following:

(1) There appear to be grounds upon which an interception warrant could be issued under section 2933.54 of the Revised Code.

(2) There is probable cause to believe that an emergency situation exists with respect to the investigation of a designated offense.

(3) There is probable cause to believe that the emergency situation involves an immediate danger of death or serious physical harm that justifies the authorization for immediate interception of a private wire, oral, or electronic communication before an application for an interception warrant could, with due diligence, be submitted to the judge and acted upon.

(B) No statement by the attorney general or the attorney general's designee pursuant to division (B)(9) of section 2933.53 is required prior to consideration of an application pursuant to this section.

(C) The judge of a court of common pleas to whom an application is made under division (A) of this section, the applicant, the prosecuting attorney or assistant prosecuting attorney who authorized the application, and any involved provider of wire or electronic communication service may tape record any telephone or other communications between any of them related to the application for, the approval of, and the implementation of an oral order for an interception. All of the provisions of sections 2933.51 to 2933.66 of the Revised Code concerning the sealing, distribution, use, and disclosure of an application for an interception warrant apply to any tape recording between the judge, the applicant, and the prosecuting attorney or the designated assistant concerning the application for and an oral order for an interception.

(D)(1) As soon as possible after granting an oral order for an interception without a warrant, a judge shall place upon the journal of the court an entry nunc pro tunc to record the granting of the oral order. If an interception warrant is issued pursuant to the filing of an application following the granting of an oral order for an interception under this section, the judge shall issue the warrant in accordance with section 2933.54 of the Revised Code, and the warrant shall recite the granting of the oral order and shall be retroactive to the time of the oral order.

(2) Interception pursuant to an oral order under this section shall be made in accordance with section 2933.59 of the Revised Code, except that the interception shall terminate immediately when the communication sought is obtained or when the application for a warrant is denied, whichever is earlier.

(3) If no application for a warrant is made in accordance with this section within forty-eight hours following a grant of an oral order or if an application for a warrant is made in accordance with this section following the grant of an oral order but the application is denied, the content of any private wire, oral, or electronic communication intercepted under the oral order shall be treated as having been obtained in violation of this chapter, and an inventory shall be served in accordance with section 2933.61 of the Revised Code upon the person named in the application. However, a provider of wire or electronic communication service that relies in good faith on the oral order in accordance with division (B) of section 2933.65 of the Revised Code is immune from civil or criminal liability in accordance with that section.

(4) If no application for a warrant is made within forty-eight hours following a grant of an oral order under this section or if an application for a warrant is made but is denied, the judge of a court of common pleas who granted an oral order for the interception shall prepare a journal entry reciting the grant of the oral order that includes as much of the information required to be included in an interception warrant that is practical to include. All of the provisions of sections 2933.51 to 2933.63 of the Revised Code concerning the sealing, distribution, use, and disclosure of an interception warrant apply to the journal entry required by this division. The judge who granted the oral order also shall order the person who received the oral order under this section to prepare an inventory of the recordings and resumes compiled under the oral order and shall require the tape or other recording of the intercepted communication to be delivered to, and sealed by, the judge in accordance with division (B) of section 2933.59 of the Revised Code. The court served by that judge shall retain the evidence, and no person shall use or disclose the evidence in a legal proceeding, other than a civil action brought by an aggrieved person or as otherwise authorized by the order of a judge of the court of common pleas of the county in which the interception took place. In addition to other remedies or penalties provided by law, a failure to deliver a tape or other recording to the judge in accordance with this division shall be punishable as contempt by the judge directing the delivery.

(1996 H 181, eff. 6–13–96; 1986 S 222, eff. 3–25–87)

2933.58 Instruction of investigative officers; privileged communications; validity of warrant

(A) Upon the issuance of an interception warrant pursuant to section 2933.54 of the Revised Code and prior to the execution of the warrant or upon a grant of an oral order for an interception under section 2933.57 of the Revised Code, the prosecuting attorney or assistant prosecuting attorney who authorized the application for the warrant or the oral approval shall instruct the investigative officers who are authorized to intercept the communications regarding the application and interpretation of divisions (A), (B), and (C) of section 2317.02 of the Revised Code. The prosecuting attorney or assistant prosecuting attorney who authorized the application or the oral order also shall instruct the officers to minimize the interception of communications that are not subject to the warrant or oral order and shall inform the officers of the procedures to be followed if communications concerning another offense are intercepted. If individuals operating under a contract to provide interception services as described in section 2933.59 of the Revised Code are involved in the interception, the prosecuting attorney or assistant prosecuting attorney who authorized the application for the warrant or the oral order also shall give the instructions and information under this division to those individuals.

(B) Investigative officers who are authorized to intercept communications pursuant to an interception warrant or pursuant to an oral order for an interception granted under section 2933.57 of the Revised Code and individuals who are operating under a contract to provide interception services as described in section 2933.59 of the Revised Code shall monitor the receiver of the interception device at all times during the time period for which the interception is authorized. All communications shall be intercepted only in accordance with the warrant or the oral order.

(C) An interception warrant issued pursuant to sections 2933.53 to 2933.55 of the Revised Code or an oral order for an interception granted under section 2933.57 of the Revised Code authorizes the interception of wire, oral, or electronic communications or the installation of an interception device within the jurisdiction of the court of common pleas served by the judge who issued the warrant or granted the oral order. The warrant or oral order is valid at any place if the interception device is installed within the jurisdiction of the judge who issued the warrant or granted the oral order and is then moved to another place by persons other than the investigative officers.

(1996 H 181, eff. 6–13–96; 1986 S 222, eff. 3–25–87)

2933.581 Assistance by provider of electronic communication service, landlord, or custodian; prohibition against disclosure of existence of interception

(A) Notwithstanding any other provision of law, a provider of wire or electronic communication service, an officer, employee, or agent of a provider of that type, and a landlord, custodian, or other person is authorized to provide information, facilities, or technical assistance to a person who is authorized by the law of this state or the United States to intercept wire, oral, or electronic communications if both of the following apply:

(1) The provider, officer, employee, agent, landlord, custodian, or person has been provided with either of the following:

(a) An interception warrant or extension of an interception warrant that contains a statement of the type described in division (A)(13) of section 2933.56 of the Revised Code;

(b) A written representation of a judge of a court of common pleas or of a prosecuting attorney or specifically designated assistant prosecuting attorney that an oral order for an interception has been granted pursuant to section 2933.57 of the Revised Code, that no interception warrant is required by law, that all applicable statutory requirements have been satisfied, and that the oral order contains a statement of the type described in division (A)(13) of section 2933.56 of the Revised Code that directs the provision of the specified information, facilities, or technical assistance.

(2) The warrant, extension, or representation sets forth the period of time during which the provision of the information, facilities, or technical assistance is authorized and specifies the information, facilities, or technical assistance required.

(B)(1) Except as provided in division (B)(2) of this section, no provider of wire or electronic communication service, no officer, employee, or agent of a provider of that type, and no landlord, custodian, or other person who is authorized to provide information, facilities, or technical assistance under division (A) of this section shall disclose the existence of an interception or the device used to accomplish the interception with respect to which the person has been furnished an interception warrant, an extension of an interception warrant, or a written representation pursuant to that division. A person that makes a disclosure in violation of this division is liable for civil damages of the type described in section 2933.65 of the Revised Code.

(2) Division (B)(1) of this section does not prohibit the disclosure of the existence of an interception or the disclosure of a device used to accomplish an interception when the disclosure is required by legal process, provided the person making the disclosure gives prior notification of the disclosure to the prosecuting attorney of the county in which the interception takes place or in which the interception device is installed.

(C) Except as provided in this section, a provider of wire or electronic communication service, an officer, employee, or agent of a provider of that type, and a landlord, custodian, or other specified person is immune from civil or criminal liability in any action that arises out of its providing information, facilities, or technical assistance in accordance with division (A) of this section and the terms of the interception warrant, extension of an interception warrant, or written representation provided under that division.

(1996 H 181, eff. 6–13–96)

2933.59 Execution of interception warrant; altering recordings or resumes; disclosure of information

(A) An investigative officer who is, or a member of the law enforcement agency that is, authorized by an interception warrant or a grant of an oral order for an interception pursuant to section 2933.57 of the Revised Code to intercept wire, oral, or electronic communications or an individual who is operating under a contract with that agency and is acting under the supervision of that officer or a member of that agency shall execute the interception warrant or the oral order in accordance with the terms of the warrant or oral order. The officer or member of the law enforcement agency who executes the warrant or oral order or who supervises the execution of the warrant or oral order shall have received training that satisfies the minimum standards established by the attorney general and the Ohio peace officer training commission under section 2933.64 of the Revised Code. The contents of a wire, oral, or electronic communication intercepted pursuant to an interception warrant or pursuant to a grant of an oral order for an interception, if possible, shall be recorded on tape or another similar device. If it is not possible to record the intercepted communication, a detailed resume of that communication immediately shall be reduced to writing. The recording or transcribing of the contents of any wire, oral, or electronic communication pursuant to sections 2933.51 to 2933.66 of the Revised Code shall be done in a way that will protect the recording or transcription from editing or any other alteration.

(B) Immediately upon the expiration of the period of time for which an interception warrant was authorized, or any extensions of that time period, all wire, oral, or electronic communications interceptions shall cease, and any interception device installed pursuant to the interception warrant shall be removed or permanently inactivated as soon as is reasonably practicable. Entry to remove or inactivate an interception device is authorized by the granting of an interception warrant.

Immediately upon the expiration of that period of time or the extension, the recordings or resumes of intercepted communications shall be made available to the issuing judge and shall be sealed under the judge's direction. The issuing judge shall specify who shall have custody of the sealed recordings and resumes. The recordings and resumes shall be kept for at least ten years. At the expiration of the ten-year period, the recordings and resumes may be destroyed upon the order of a judge of the court of common pleas of the county in which the interception took place. Duplicate recordings or resumes may be made for use or disclosure pursuant to divisions (F) and (G) of this section.

(C) No person, with intent to present the altered recording or resume in any judicial proceeding or proceeding under oath or affirmation, shall purposely edit, alter, or tamper with any recording or resume of any intercepted wire, oral, or electronic communications, shall attempt to edit, alter, or tamper with any recording or resume of any intercepted wire, oral, or electronic communications, or shall present or permit the presentation of any altered recording or resume in any judicial proceeding or proceeding under oath or affirmation, without fully indicating the nature of the changes made in the original state of the recording or resume.

(D)(1) Any interception warrant, the existence of lawfully installed interception devices, the application, affidavits, and return prepared in connection with the warrant, and any information concerning the application for, the granting of, or the denial of an interception warrant shall remain secret until they have been disclosed in a criminal trial or in a proceeding that is open to the public or until they have been furnished to the defendant or unless otherwise provided in sections 2933.51 to 2933.66 of the Revised Code.

(2) Any person who violates division (D)(1) of this section may be punished for contempt of court.

(E) When an order for destruction of any documents dealing with an interception warrant is issued, the person directed in the order to destroy the applications, affidavits, interception warrants, any amendments or extensions of the warrants, or recordings or resumes made pursuant to the warrants shall do so in the presence of at least one witness who is not connected with a law enforcement agency. The person who destroys the documents and each witness shall execute affidavits setting forth the facts and circumstances of the destruction. The affidavits shall be filed with and approved by the court having custody of the original materials.

(F) An investigative officer who has obtained knowledge of the contents, or of evidence derived from the contents, of a wire, oral, or electronic communication pursuant to sections 2933.51 to 2933.66 of the Revised Code may disclose the contents or evidence to another investigative officer to the extent that the disclosure is appropriate to the proper performance of the official duties of the officer making or receiving the disclosure and may use the contents or evidence to the extent appropriate to the proper performance of official duties.

(G) A person who has received, pursuant to sections 2933.51 to 2933.66 of the Revised Code, information concerning, or evidence derived from, a wire, oral, or electronic communication intercepted pursuant to an interception warrant may disclose the contents of that communication, or the evidence derived from the contents, while giving testimony under oath or affirmation in a proceeding held under the authority of the United States, this state, another state, or a political subdivision of this state or another state, except that the presence of the seal provided for in division (B) of section 2933.56 of the Revised Code and in division (B) of this section, or a satisfactory explanation of the absence of the seal, shall be a prerequisite for the use or disclosure of the contents of any wire, oral, or electronic communication or evidence derived from the contents. The contents, or evidence derived from the contents, of a wire, oral, or electronic communication intercepted pursuant to an interception warrant and in accordance with sections 2933.51 to 2933.66 of the Revised Code otherwise may be disclosed only upon a showing of good cause before a judge authorized to issue interception warrants.

(H) Whoever violates division (C) of this section is guilty of a felony of the third degree.

(1996 H 670, eff. 12–2–96; 1996 H 181, eff. 6–13–96; 1986 S 222, eff. 3–25–87)

2933.591 Giving warning of possible surveillance

(A) No person who knows that an application for an interception warrant has been authorized or made under section 2933.53 of the Revised Code, that an interception warrant has been issued under section 2933.54 of the Revised Code, that an application for an extension of an interception warrant has been filed under section 2933.53 of the Revised Code, that an extension of an interception warrant has been ordered under that section, that an application for a grant of an oral order for an interception has been made under section 2933.57 of the Revised Code, or that oral order for an interception has been granted under section 2933.57 of the Revised Code, with purpose to obstruct, impede, or prevent the interception in question, shall give notice or attempt to give notice of the possible interception to a person.

(B) Whoever violates division (A) of this section is guilty of giving warning of possible surveillance, a felony of the third degree.

(1996 H 181, eff. 6–13–96)

2933.60 Expiration or denial of interception warrant; reports

(A) Within thirty days after the expiration of an interception warrant, the expiration of an extension of an interception warrant, or the denial of an application for an interception warrant, the judge of a court of common pleas who issued the warrant or extension or denied the application shall report all of the following to the administrative office of the United States courts and to the attorney general of this state:

(1) The fact that an application was made for an interception warrant or extension of an interception warrant;

(2) The kind of interception warrant or extension for which application was made, including a statement of whether the warrant or extension was or was not one to which the requirements of division (B)(3)(c) of section 2933.53 and division (A)(5) of section 2933.54 of the Revised Code did not apply due to the application of division (G)(1) of section 2933.53 of the Revised Code;

(3) The fact that the interception warrant or extension was granted as applied for or was denied;

(4) The period of interception authorized by the interception warrant, and the number and duration of any extensions of the warrant;

(5) The designated offenses specified in the interception warrant, application, or extension;

(6) The identity of the person who made the application, any person who executed any accompanying affidavit to an application, and the prosecuting attorney or assistant prosecuting attorney who authorized the application;

(7) The nature of the facilities from which, or the place at which, communications are to be intercepted.

(B) In January of each year, the prosecuting attorney of each county shall report to the administrative office of the United States courts and to the attorney general of this state all information that is required to be reported by subsection (2) of section 2519 of the "Omnibus Crime Control and Safe Streets Act of 1968," 82 Stat. 197, 18 U.S.C. 2519 (1968), as amended.

(1996 H 181, eff. 6–13–96; 1986 S 222, eff. 3–25–87)

2933.61 Notice to parties to intercepted communications

(A) Within a reasonable time not later than ninety days after the filing of an application for an interception warrant that is denied or after the termination of the period of an interception warrant or any extensions of an interception warrant, the judge of a court of common pleas who issued the warrant or extension or denied the application shall cause to be served on the persons named in the application or the interception warrant, and on any other parties to intercepted wire, oral, or electronic communications that the judge determines in the judge's discretion should be notified in the interest of justice, an inventory that shall include notice of all of the following:

(1) The fact that an interception warrant was issued or that application for one was made;

(2) The date the interception warrant was issued and the period of authorized, approved, or disapproved interception or the date of the denial of the application;

(3) The fact that during the stated period wire, oral, or electronic communications were or were not intercepted.

(B) A judge of the court of common pleas of the county, upon the filing of a motion for inspection, in the judge's discretion, may make available for inspection to the person filing the motion or the person's counsel any portions of intercepted wire, oral, or electronic communications, applications for interception warrants, or interception warrants that the judge determines to be in the interest of justice. Upon an ex parte showing of good cause to a judge of a court of common pleas who denied the issuance of or issued an interception warrant, the judge may postpone the serving of the inventory required by this section for a specified period of time.

(1996 H 181, eff. 6–13–96; 1986 S 222, eff. 3–25–87)

2933.62 Use of intercepted communication in evidence

(A) No part of the contents, and no evidence derived from the contents, of any intercepted wire, oral, or electronic communication shall be received in evidence in any trial, hearing, or other proceedings in or before any court, grand jury, department, officer, agency, regulatory body, legislative committee, or other authority of this state or of a political subdivision of this state, if the disclosure of that information is in violation of sections 2933.51 to 2933.66 of the Revised Code.

(B) The contents, or any evidence derived from the contents, of any wire, oral, or electronic communication intercepted pursuant to sections 2933.51 to 2933.66 of the Revised Code shall not be received in evidence or otherwise disclosed in any trial, hearing, or other proceeding held under the authority of this state, other than a proceeding or session of the grand jury, unless each party has been furnished not less than ten days before the trial, hearing, or proceeding, with a copy of the interception warrant and the related application, or a written representation of a judge of a court of common pleas or of a prosecuting attorney or specifically designated assistant prosecuting attorney that an oral order for an interception has been granted pursuant to section 2933.57 of the Revised Code, under which the interception was authorized or approved. The judge or other officer conducting the trial, hearing, or other proceeding may waive the ten-day period if the judge or officer finds that it was not possible to furnish the party with the above information at least ten days before the trial, hearing, or proceeding, and that the party will not be prejudiced by the delay in receiving the information.

(1996 H 181, eff. 6–13–96; 1986 S 222, eff. 3–25–87)

2933.63 Suppression of contents of intercepted communication

(A) Any aggrieved person in any trial, hearing, or proceeding in or before any court, department, officer, agency, regulatory body, or other authority of this state or of a political subdivision of this state, other than a grand jury, may request the involved court, department, officer, agency, body, or authority, by motion, to suppress the contents, or evidence derived from the contents, of a wire, oral, or electronic communication intercepted pursuant to sections 2933.51 to 2933.66 of the Revised Code for any of the following reasons:

(1) The communication was unlawfully intercepted.

(2) The interception warrant under which the communication was intercepted is insufficient on its face.

(3) The interception was not made in conformity with the interception warrant or an oral order for an interception granted under section 2933.57 of the Revised Code.

(4) The communications are of a privileged character and a special need for their interception is not shown or is inadequate as shown.

(B) Any motion filed pursuant to division (A) of this section shall be made before the trial, hearing, or proceeding at which the contents, or evidence derived from the contents, is to be used, unless there was no opportunity to make the motion or the aggrieved person was not aware of the intercepted communications or the grounds of the motion. Upon the filing of the motion by the aggrieved person, the judge or other officer conducting the trial, hearing, or proceeding may make available to the aggrieved person or the person's counsel for inspection any portions of the intercepted communication or evidence derived from the intercepted communication as the judge or other officer determines to be in the interest of justice. If the judge or other officer grants the motion to suppress evidence pursuant to this section, the contents, or the evidence derived from the contents, of the intercepted wire, oral, or electronic communications shall be treated as having been obtained in violation of the law, and the contents and evidence derived from the contents shall not be received in evidence in any trial, hearing, or proceeding.

(C) In addition to any other right to appeal, the state shall have an appeal as of right from an order granting a motion to suppress the contents, or evidence derived from the contents, of a wire, oral, or electronic communication that was intercepted pursuant to an interception warrant or an oral order for an interception granted under section 2933.57 of the Revised Code, or the denial of an application for an interception warrant, if the state's representative certifies to the judge or other official who granted the motion or denied the application that the appeal is not taken for purposes of delay. Any appeal shall be taken within thirty days after the date the order was entered and shall be diligently prosecuted.

(1996 H 181, eff. 6–13–96; 1986 S 222, eff. 3–25–87)

2933.64 Training of investigative officers

The attorney general and the Ohio peace officer training commission, pursuant to Chapter 109. of the Revised Code, shall establish a course of training in the legal and technical aspects of wiretapping and electronic surveillance, shall establish regulations that they find necessary and proper for the training program, and shall establish minimum standards for certification and periodic recertification for investigative officers to be eligible to conduct wiretapping or electronic surveillance under sections 2933.51 to 2933.66 of the Revised Code. The commission shall charge each investigative officer who enrolls in this training a reasonable enrollment fee to offset the cost of the training.

(1996 H 670, eff. 12–2–96; 1996 H 181, eff. 6–13–96; 1986 S 222, eff. 3–25–87)

2933.65 Civil liability for unlawful interceptions; defenses and immunities

(A) A person whose wire, oral, or electronic communications are intercepted, disclosed, or intentionally used in violation of sections 2933.51 to 2933.66 of the Revised Code may bring a civil action to recover from the person or entity that engaged in the violation any relief that may be appropriate and that includes, but is not limited to, the following:

(1) The preliminary and other equitable or declaratory relief that is appropriate;

(2) Whichever of the following is greater:

(a) Liquidated damages computed at a rate of two hundred dollars per day for each day of violation or liquidated damages of ten thousand dollars, whichever is greater;

(b) The sum of actual damages suffered by the plaintiff and the profits, if any, made as a result of the violation by the person or entity that engaged in the violation.

(3) Punitive damages, if appropriate;

(4) Reasonable attorney's fees and other litigation expenses that are reasonably incurred in bringing the civil action.

(B) Good faith reliance on an interception warrant, extension of an interception warrant, other court order, a grant of an oral order for an interception, a grand jury subpoena, a legislative or statutory authorization, or a good faith determination that divisions (A) and (B) of section 2933.521 of the Revised Code permitted the conduct that is the subject of a complaint is a complete defense to a civil action or criminal action that is brought under the laws of this state and that arises out of the execution of the warrant or the oral order.

(C) A claimant who brings a civil action under division (A) of this section shall commence the civil action within two years after the date on which the claimant first has a reasonable opportunity to discover the violation.

(D) The remedies and sanctions described in sections 2933.51 to 2933.66 of the Revised Code with respect to the interception of wire, oral, or electronic communications are the only judicial remedies and sanctions for violations of those sections involving those types of communications that are not violations of the constitution of the United States or of this state.

(1996 H 181, eff. 6–13–96; 1986 S 222, eff. 3–25–87)

2933.66 Proceedings to conform with constitutional provisions

Notwithstanding any provision of sections 2933.51 to 2933.65 of the Revised Code, a judge of a court of common pleas to whom an application for an interception warrant, an extension of an interception warrant, an oral order for an interception, or another purpose is made pursuant to sections 2933.51 to 2933.65 of the Revised Code may take evidence, make a finding, or issue an order to conform the proceedings or the issuance of an order to the constitution of the United States or of this state.

(1996 H 181, eff. 6–13–96; 1986 S 222, eff. 3–25–87)

MEDICAID FRAUD FORFEITURES

2933.71 Definitions

As used in sections 2933.71 to 2933.75 of the Revised Code:

(A) "Medicaid fraud offense" means any of the following:

(1) Any violation of section 2913.40 of the Revised Code;

(2) Any violation of section 2921.13 of the Revised Code that involves the making of a false statement in relation to the securement of benefits or payments under the medical assistance program established under section 5111.01 of the Revised Code or the swearing or affirming of a false statement previously made in relation to the securement of any such benefits or payments;

(3) Any other criminal violation of law related to the medical assistance program established under section 5111.01 of the Revised Code;

(4) Any conspiracy to commit any violation described in division (A)(1), (2), or (3) of this section.

(B) "Forfeitable property" means any profit, money, or proceeds, and any property, real or personal, tangible, or intangible, including any interest in, security of, claim against, or property or contractual right of any kind affording a source of influence over any enterprise, that is derived from, or that is traceable to any profit, money, or proceeds obtained directly or indirectly from, any medicaid fraud offense.

(C) "Beneficial interest" means any of the following:

(1) The interest of a person as a beneficiary under a trust in which the trustee holds title to personal or real property;

(2) The interest of a person as a beneficiary under any other trust arrangement under which any other person holds title to personal or real property for the benefit of such person;

(3) The interest of a person under any other form of express fiduciary arrangement under which any other person holds title to personal or real property for the benefit of such person.

"Beneficial interest" does not include the interest of a stockholder in a corporation or the interest of a partner in either a general or limited partnership.

(D) "Costs of investigation and prosecution" and "costs of investigation and litigation" mean all of the costs incurred by the state or a county or municipal corporation in the prosecution and investigation of the medicaid fraud offense in question, and includes, but is not limited to, the costs of resources and personnel.

(E) "Innocent person" includes any bona fide purchaser of property that allegedly is forfeitable property, including any person who establishes a valid claim to or interest in the property in accordance with division (F) of section 2933.73 of the Revised Code.

(F) "Personal property" means any personal property, any interest in personal property, or any right, including, but not limited to, bank accounts, debts, corporate stocks, patents, or copyrights. Personal property and any beneficial interest in personal property are deemed to be located where the trustee of the property, the personal property, or the instrument evidencing the right is located.

(G) "Real property" means any real property or any interest in real property, including, but not limited to, any lease of, or mortgage upon, real property. Real property and any beneficial interest in it is deemed to be located where the real property is located.

(H) "Trustee" means any of the following:

(1) Any person acting as trustee under a trust in which the trustee holds title to personal or real property;

(2) Any person who holds title to personal or real property for which any other person has a beneficial interest;

(3) Any successor trustee.

"Trustee" does not include an assignee or trustee for an insolvent debtor or an executor, administrator, administrator with the will annexed, testamentary trustee, guardian, or committee, appointed by, or under the control of, or accountable to, a court.

(1993 H 152, eff. 7–1–93)

2933.72 Orders to preserve reachability of forfeitable property

(A) At any time after an indictment is filed alleging a medicaid fraud offense, the prosecuting attorney who is prosecuting the case or the attorney general, if the attorney general is prosecuting the case, may file a motion requesting the court to issue an order to preserve the reachability of any property that may be forfeitable property. Upon the filing of the motion, the court, after giving notice to any person who will be affected by any order issued by the court pursuant to the motion, shall hold a hearing on the motion at which all affected persons have an opportunity to be heard and, upon a showing by the prosecuting attorney or attorney general by a preponderance of the evidence that the particular action is necessary to preserve the reachability of any property that may be subject to forfeiture and based upon the indictment, may enter a restraining order or injunction, require the execution of a satisfactory performance bond, or take any other necessary action, including the attachment of the property or the appointment of a receiver. The prosecuting attorney or attorney general is not required to show special or irreparable injury to obtain any court action pursuant to this division. Notwithstanding the Rules of Evidence, the court's order or injunction may be based on hearsay testimony.

(B) If no indictment has been filed alleging a medicaid fraud offense, the court may take any action specified in division (A) of this section if the prosecuting attorney for the county or the attorney general, in addition to the showing that would be required pursuant to division (A) of this section, also shows both of the following by a preponderance of the evidence:

(1) There is probable cause to believe that the property with respect to which the order is sought, in the event of a conviction, would be forfeitable property subject to forfeiture under section 2933.73 of the Revised Code;

(2) The requested order would not result in irreparable harm to the party against whom the order is to be entered that outweighs the need to preserve the reachability of the property.

No order entered pursuant to division (B) of this section shall be effective for more than ninety days, unless it is extended pursuant to the procedure provided in division (B) of this section by the court for good cause shown or an indictment is returned alleging that the property is forfeitable property subject to forfeiture.

(C) Upon application by the prosecuting attorney or attorney general, the court may grant a temporary restraining order to preserve the reachability of forfeitable property that is subject to forfeiture under section 2933.73 of the Revised Code without notice to any party, if all of the following occur:

(1) An indictment alleging that property is forfeitable property has been filed, or the court determines that there is probable cause to believe that property with respect to which the order is sought would be forfeitable property subject, in the event of a conviction, to forfeiture under section 2933.73 of the Revised Code;

(2) The property is in the possession or control of the party against whom the order is to be entered;

(3) The court determines that the nature of the property is such that it can be concealed, disposed of, or placed beyond the jurisdiction of the court before any party may be heard in opposition to the order.

A temporary restraining order granted without notice to any party under division (C) of this section shall expire within the time, not to exceed ten days, that the court fixes, unless extended for good cause shown or unless the party against whom it is entered consents to an extension for a longer period. If a temporary restraining order is granted under division (C) of this section without notice to any party, the court shall hold a hearing concerning the entry of an order under division (C) of this section at the earliest practicable time prior to the expiration of the temporary order.

(D) Following sentencing and the entry of a judgment against an offender that includes an order of forfeiture under section 2933.73 of the Revised Code, the court may enter a restraining order or injunction, require the execution of a satisfactory performance bond, or take any other action, including the appointment of a receiver, that the court determines to be proper to protect the interests of the state or an innocent person.

(1994 H 715, eff. 7–22–94; 1993 H 152, eff. 7–1–93)

2933.73 Forfeiture of property

(A) In addition to any other penalty or disposition authorized or required by law, if a person is convicted of or pleads guilty to any medicaid fraud offense, the trial court shall conduct a civil forfeiture hearing to determine whether any property identified in division (B) of this section should be forfeited to the state in relation to the offense. At the hearing, the offender who was convicted of or pleaded guilty to the medicaid fraud offense has the burden of proving, by a preponderance of the evidence, that the property in question is not forfeitable property in relation to the offense. If the offender does not prove by a preponderance of the evidence that the property in question is not forfeitable property in relation to the offense, the court shall issue an order specifying that the forfeitable property is forfeited to the state. If the offender proves by a preponderance of the evidence that the property in question is not forfeitable property in relation to the offense, the court shall not issue an order specifying that the forfeitable property is forfeited to the state and, if the property has been seized, shall order that it be returned to the offender.

(B) A court shall not issue an order under division (A) of this section specifying that forfeitable property is forfeited to the state unless one of the following applies:

(1) The indictment, count in the indictment, or information charging the medicaid fraud offense specifically identified the property as forfeitable property;

(2) The property was not reasonably foreseen to be forfeitable property at the time of the indictment, count in the indictment, or information charging the offense, provided that the prosecuting attorney or attorney general who prosecuted the offense gave prompt notice to the defendant of such property not reasonably foreseen to be forfeitable property when it is discovered to be forfeitable property.

(C) If any forfeitable property included in a forfeiture order issued under division (A) of this section cannot be located, has been sold to a bona fide purchaser for value, placed beyond the jurisdiction of the court, substantially diminished in value by the conduct of the defendant, or commingled with other property that cannot be divided without difficulty or undue injury to innocent persons, or otherwise is unreachable without undue injury to innocent persons, the court shall order forfeiture of any other reachable property of the defendant up to the value of the property that is unreachable.

(D) All property ordered forfeited pursuant to this section shall be held by the law enforcement agency that seized it for distribution or disposal pursuant to section 2933.74 of the Revised Code. The agency shall maintain an accurate record of each item of property so seized and held, which record shall include the date on which each item was seized, the manner and date of disposition by the agency, and if applicable, the name of the person who received the item; however, the record shall not identify or enable the identification of the individual officer who seized the property. The record is a public record open for inspection under section 149.43 of the Revised Code. Each law enforcement agency that seizes and holds in any calendar year any item of property that is ordered forfeited pursuant to this section shall prepare a report covering the calendar year that cumulates all of the information contained in all of the records kept by the agency pursuant to this division for that calendar year, and shall send the cumulative report, no later than the first day of March in the calendar year following the calendar year covered by the report, to the attorney general. Each such report so received by the attorney general is a public record open for inspection under section 149.43 of the Revised Code. The attorney general shall make copies of each such report so received, and, no later than the fifteenth day of April in the calendar year in which the reports were received, shall send a copy of each such report to the office of the president of the senate and the office of the speaker of the house of representatives.

(E) Notwithstanding the notice and procedure prescribed by division (F) of this section, an order of forfeiture entered under division (A) of this section shall authorize an appropriate law enforcement agency to seize the forfeitable property declared forfeited under this section upon the terms and conditions, relating to the time and manner of seizure, that the court determines proper.

(F)(1) Upon the entry of a forfeiture order under division (A) of this section, the court shall cause notice of the issuance of the order to be sent by certified mail, return receipt requested, to all persons known to have, or appearing to have, an interest in the property that was acquired prior to the filing of a medicaid fraud lien notice as authorized by section 2933.75 of the Revised Code. If the notices cannot be given to those persons in that manner, the court shall cause publication of the notice of the forfeiture order pursuant to the Rules of Civil Procedure.

(2) Within thirty days after receipt of a notice or after the date of publication of a notice under division (F)(1) of this section, any person, other than the offender who was convicted of or pleaded guilty to the medicaid fraud offense, who claims an interest in the forfeitable property that is subject to forfeiture may petition the court for a hearing to determine the validity of the claim. The petition shall be signed and sworn to by the petitioner and shall set forth the nature and extent of the petitioner's interest in the property, the date and circumstances of the petitioner's acquisition of the interest, any additional allegations supporting the claim, and the relief sought. The petitioner shall furnish a copy of the petition to the prosecuting attorney or attorney general who prosecuted the offense in relation to which the forfeiture order was issued.

(3) The court, to the extent practicable and consistent with the interests of justice, shall hold the hearing described under division (F)(2) of this section within thirty days from the filing of the petition. The court may consolidate the hearings on all petitions filed by third party claimants under this section. At the hearing, the petitioner may testify and present evidence on his own behalf and cross-examine witnesses. The prosecuting attorney or attorney general who prosecuted the offense may present evidence and witnesses in rebuttal and in defense of the claim of the state to the property and cross-examine witnesses. The court, in making its determination, shall consider the testimony and evidence presented at the hearing and the relevant portions of the record of the criminal proceeding that resulted in the forfeiture order.

(4) If at a hearing held under division (F)(3) of this section, the court, by a preponderance of the evidence, determines either that the petitioner has a legal right, title, or interest in the property that, at the time of the commission of the acts giving rise to the forfeiture of the property, was vested in the petitioner and not in the offender or was superior to the right, title, or interest of the offender, or that the petitioner is a bona fide purchaser for value of the right, title, or interest in the property and was at the time of the purchase reasonably without cause to believe that the property was subject to forfeiture under this section, it shall amend, in accordance with its determination, the order of forfeiture to protect the rights of innocent persons.

(G) Except as provided in division (F) of this section, no person claiming an interest in forfeitable property that is subject to forfeiture under this section shall do either of the following:

(1) Intervene in a trial or appeal of a criminal case that involves the forfeiture of the property;

(2) File an action against the state concerning the validity of his alleged interest in the property subsequent to the filing of the indictment, count in the indictment, or information, that alleges that the property is subject to forfeiture under this section.

(H) As used in this section, "law enforcement agency" includes the state board of pharmacy.

(1994 H 715, eff. 7–22–94; 1993 H 152, eff. 7–1–93)

2933.74 Disposition of forfeited property

(A)(1) With respect to forfeitable property ordered forfeited under section 2933.73 of the Revised Code, the court that issued the order, upon petition of the prosecuting attorney or attorney general who prosecuted the case, may do any of the following:

(a) Authorize the prosecuting attorney or the attorney general to settle claims;

(b) Award compensation to persons who provide information that results in a forfeiture under section 2933.73 of the Revised Code;

(c) Take any other action to protect the rights of innocent persons that is in the interest of justice and that is consistent with the purposes of sections 2933.71 to 2933.75 of the Revised Code. (2)[1] The court shall maintain an accurate record of the actions it takes under division (A)(1) of this section with respect to the forfeitable property ordered forfeited. The record is a public record open for inspection under section 149.43 of the Revised Code.

(B)(1) Subject to division (A) of this section and notwithstanding any contrary provision of section 2933.41 of the Revised Code, the prosecuting attorney or attorney general who prosecuted the case shall order the disposal of forfeitable property ordered forfeited in any proceeding under section 2933.73 of the Revised Code as soon as feasible, making due provisions for the rights of innocent persons, by any of the following methods:

(a) Public sale;

(b) Transfer to a state governmental agency for official use;

(c) Sale or transfer to an innocent person;

(d) If the property is contraband and is not needed for evidence in any pending criminal or civil proceeding, pursuant to section 2933.41 or any other applicable section of the Revised Code.

(2) Any interest in personal or real property not disposed of pursuant to division (B) of this section and not exercisable by, or transferable for value to, the state shall expire and shall not revert to the person who was convicted of or pleaded guilty to the medicaid fraud offense. No person who was convicted of or pleaded guilty to the medicaid fraud offense and no person acting in concert with a person who was convicted of or pleaded guilty

to the medicaid fraud offense is eligible to purchase forfeited property from the state.

(3) Upon application of a person, other than the person who was convicted of or pleaded guilty to the medicaid fraud offense or a person acting in concert with or on behalf of the person who was convicted of or pleaded guilty to the medicaid fraud offense, the court may restrain or stay the disposal of the forfeitable property pursuant to this division pending the conclusion of any appeal of the criminal case giving rise to the forfeiture or pending the determination of the validity of a claim to or interest in the property pursuant to division (F) of section 2933.73 of the Revised Code, if the applicant demonstrates that proceeding with the disposal of the property will result in irreparable injury, harm, or loss to the applicant.

(4) The prosecuting attorney or attorney general who prosecuted the case shall maintain an accurate record of each item of property disposed of pursuant to division (B) of this section, which record shall include the date on which each item came into the prosecuting attorney's or attorney general's custody, the manner and date of disposition, and, if applicable, the name of the person who received the item. The record shall not identify or enable the identification of the individual officer who seized the property, and the record is a public record open for inspection under section 149.43 of the Revised Code.

Each prosecuting attorney who disposes in any calendar year of any item of property pursuant to division (B) of this section shall prepare a report covering the calendar year that cumulates all of the information contained in all of the records the prosecuting attorney kept pursuant to this division for that calendar year and shall send the cumulative report, no later than the first day of March in the calendar year following the calendar year covered by the report, to the attorney general. No later than the first day of March in the calendar year following the calendar year covered by the report, the attorney general shall prepare a report covering the calendar year that cumulates all of the records the attorney general kept pursuant to this division for that calendar year. Each report received or prepared by the attorney general is a public record open for inspection under section 149.43 of the Revised Code. Not later than the fifteenth day of April in the calendar year following the calendar year covered by the reports, the attorney general shall send to the president of the senate and the speaker of the house of representatives a written notification that does all of the following:

(a) Indicates that the attorney general has received from prosecuting attorneys reports of the type described in this division that cover the previous calendar year and indicates that the reports were received under this division;

(b) Lists the attorney general's own cumulative report covering the previous calendar year;

(c) Indicates that the reports are open for inspection under section 149.43 of the Revised Code;

(d) Indicates that the attorney general will provide a copy of any or all of the reports to the president of the senate or the speaker of the house of representatives upon request.

(C)(1) The proceeds of the sale of all forfeitable property ordered forfeited pursuant to section 2933.73 of the Revised Code shall be deposited into the state treasury and credited to the medicaid fraud investigation and prosecution fund, which is hereby created.

(2) The proceeds credited to the medicaid fraud investigation and prosecution fund pursuant to division (C)(1) of this section shall be disposed of in the following order:

(a) To the payment of the fees and costs of the forfeiture and sale, including expenses of seizure, maintenance, and custody of the property pending its disposition, advertising, and court costs;

(b) Except as otherwise provided in division (C)(2)(b) of this section, the remainder shall be paid to the law enforcement trust fund of the prosecuting attorney that is established pursuant to division (D)(1)(c) of section 2933.43 of the Revised Code or to the attorney general, and to the law enforcement trust fund of the county sheriff that is established pursuant to that division if the county sheriff substantially conducted the investigation, to the law enforcement trust fund of a municipal corporation that is established pursuant to that division if its police department substantially conducted the investigation, to the law enforcement trust fund of a township that is established pursuant to that division if the investigation was substantially conducted by a township police department, township police district police force, or office of a township constable, or to the law enforcement trust fund of a park district created pursuant to section 511.18 or 1545.01 of the Revised Code that is established pursuant to that division if the investigation was substantially conducted by its park district police force or law enforcement department. The prosecuting attorney or attorney general may decline to accept any of the remaining proceeds, and, if the prosecuting attorney or attorney general so declines, they shall be applied to the fund described in division (C)(2)(b) of this section that relates to the appropriate law enforcement agency that substantially conducted the investigation.

If the state highway patrol substantially conducted the investigation, the director of budget and management shall transfer the remaining proceeds to the state highway patrol for deposit into the state highway patrol contraband, forfeiture, and other fund that is created by division (D)(1)(c) of section 2933.43 of the Revised Code. If the state board of pharmacy substantially conducted the investigation, the director shall transfer the remaining proceeds to the board for deposit into the board of pharmacy drug law enforcement fund that is created by division (B)(1) of section 4729.65 of the Revised Code. If a state law enforcement agency, other than the state highway patrol, the board, or the attorney general, substantially conducted the investigation, the director shall transfer the remaining proceeds to the treasurer of state for deposit into the peace officer training commission fund that is created by division (D)(1)(c) of section 2933.43 of the Revised Code.

The remaining proceeds that are paid to the attorney general shall be used and expended only in relation to the investigation and prosecution of medicaid fraud offenses or the activities identified in section 109.85 of the Revised Code, and those that are paid to a law enforcement trust fund or that are deposited into the state highway patrol contraband, forfeiture, and other fund, the board of pharmacy drug law enforcement fund, or the peace officer training commission fund pursuant to division (C)(2)(b) of this section shall be allocated, used, and expended only in accordance with division (D)(1)(c) of section 2933.43 of the Revised Code, only in accordance with a written internal control policy adopted under division (D)(3) of that section, and, if applicable, only in accordance with division (B)(1) of section 4729.65 of the Revised Code. The annual reports that pertain to the funds and that are required by divisions (D)(1)(c) and (3)(b) of section 2933.43 of the Revised Code also shall address the remaining proceeds that are paid or deposited into the funds pursuant to division (C)(2)(b) of this section.

(3) If more than one law enforcement agency substantially conducted the investigation, the court ordering the forfeiture shall equitably divide the remaining proceeds among the law enforcement agencies that substantially conducted the investigation, in the manner described in division (D)(2) of section 2933.43 of the Revised Code for the equitable division of contraband proceeds and forfeited moneys. The equitable shares of the proceeds so determined by the court shall be paid or deposited into the appropriate funds specified in division (C)(2)(b) of this section.

(D) As used in this section, "law enforcement agency" includes, but is not limited to, the state board of pharmacy.

(1998 S 164, eff. 1–15–98; 1996 H 670, eff. 12–2–96; 1994 H 715, eff. 7–22–94; 1993 H 152, eff. 7–1–93)

1 So in original.

2933.75 Medicaid fraud liens

(A) Upon the institution of any criminal proceeding charging a medicaid fraud offense, the state, at any time during the pendency of the proceeding, may file a medicaid fraud lien notice with the county recorder of any county in which forfeitable property subject to forfeiture may be located. No fee shall be required for filing the notice. The recorder immediately shall record the notice pursuant to section 317.08 of the Revised Code.

(B) A medicaid fraud lien notice shall be signed by the prosecuting attorney or attorney general who will prosecute the case and who files the lien. The notice shall set forth all of the following information:

(1) The name of the person against whom the proceeding has been brought. The prosecuting attorney or attorney general who will prosecute the case may specify in the notice any aliases, names, or fictitious names under which the person may be known.

(2) If known to the prosecuting attorney or attorney general who will prosecute the case, the present residence and business addresses of the person or names set forth in the notice;

(3) A statement that a criminal proceeding for a medicaid fraud offense has been brought against the person named in the notice, the name of the county in which the proceeding has been brought, and the case number of the proceeding;

(4) A statement that the notice is being filed pursuant to this section;

(5) The name and address of the prosecuting attorney or attorney general filing the notice;

(6) A description of the real or personal property subject to the notice and of the interest in that property of the person named in the notice, to the extent the property and the interest of the person in it reasonably is known at the time the proceeding is instituted or at the time the notice is filed.

(C) A medicaid fraud lien notice shall apply only to one person and, to the extent applicable, any aliases, fictitious names, or other names, including names of corporations, partnerships, or other entities, to the extent permitted in this section. A separate medicaid fraud lien notice is required to be filed for any other person.

(D) Within seven days after the filing of each medicaid fraud lien notice, the prosecuting attorney or attorney general who files the notice shall furnish to the person named in the notice by certified mail, return receipt requested, to the last known business or residential address of the person, a copy of the recorded notice with a notation on it of any county in which the notice has been recorded. The failure of the prosecuting attorney or attorney general to furnish a copy of the notice under this section shall not invalidate or otherwise affect the medicaid fraud lien notice when the prosecuting attorney or attorney general did not know and could not reasonably ascertain the address of the person entitled to notice.

After receipt of a copy of the notice under this division, the person named in the notice may petition the court to authorize the person to post a surety bond in lieu of the lien or to otherwise modify the lien as the interests of justice may require. The bond shall be in an amount equal to the value of the property reasonably known to be subject to the notice and conditioned on the payment of any judgment and costs ordered in an action pursuant to section 2933.73 of the Revised Code up to the value of the bond.

(E) From the date of filing of a medicaid fraud lien notice, the notice creates a lien in favor of the state on any personal or real property or any beneficial interest in the property located in the county in which the notice is filed that then or subsequently is owned by the person named in the notice or under any of the names set forth in the notice.

The lien created in favor of the state is superior and prior to the interest of any other person in the personal or real property or beneficial interest in the property, if the interest is acquired subsequent to the filing of the notice.

(F) If a medicaid fraud lien notice has been filed, and if a forfeiture order is entered subsequent to a conviction or guilty plea in the criminal proceeding pursuant to section 2933.73 of the Revised Code in favor of the state, the interest of any person in the property that was acquired subsequent to the filing of the notice shall be subject to the notice and order of forfeiture.

(G) Upon the issuance of an order of forfeiture in favor of the state pursuant to section 2933.73 of the Revised Code, title of the state to the forfeited property shall do either of the following:

(1) In the case of real property, or a beneficial interest in it, relate back to the date of filing of the medicaid fraud lien notice in the county where the property or interest is located. If no medicaid fraud lien notice was filed, title of the state relates back to the date of the recording of the order of forfeiture in the records of the county recorder of the county in which the real property or beneficial interest is located.

(2) In the case of personal property or a beneficial interest in it, relate back to the date on which the property or interest was seized by the state, or the date of filing of a medicaid fraud lien notice in the county in which the property or beneficial interest is located. If the property was not seized and no medicaid fraud lien notice was filed, title of the state relates back to the date of the recording of the order of forfeiture in the county in which the personal property or beneficial interest is located.

(H) If personal or real property, or a beneficial interest in it, that is forfeitable property and is subject to forfeiture pursuant to section 2933.73 of the Revised Code is conveyed, alienated, disposed of, or otherwise rendered unavailable for forfeiture after the filing of either a medicaid fraud lien notice, or a criminal proceeding for a medicaid fraud offense, whichever is earlier, the state may bring an action in any court of common pleas against the person named in the medicaid fraud lien notice or the defendant in the criminal proceeding to recover the value of the property or interest. The court shall enter final judgment against the person named in the notice or the defendant for an amount equal to the value of the property or interest together with investigative costs and attorney's fees incurred by the state in the action.

(I) If personal or real property, or a beneficial interest in it, that is forfeitable property and is subject to forfeiture pursuant to section 2933.73 of the Revised Code is alienated or otherwise transferred or disposed of after either the filing of a medicaid fraud lien notice, or the filing of a criminal proceeding for a medicaid fraud offense, whichever is earlier, the transfer or disposal is fraudulent as to the state and the state shall have all the rights granted a creditor under Chapter 1336. of the Revised Code.

(J) No trustee, who acquires actual knowledge that a medicaid fraud lien notice or a criminal proceeding for a medicaid fraud offense has been filed against any person for whom he holds legal or record title to personal or real property, shall recklessly fail to furnish promptly to the prosecuting attorney or attorney general who is prosecuting the case all of the following:

(1) The name and address of the person, as known to the trustee;

(2) The name and address, as known to the trustee, of all other persons for whose benefit the trustee holds title to the property;

(3) If requested by the prosecuting attorney or attorney general who is prosecuting the case, a copy of the trust agreement or other instrument under which the trustee holds title to the property.

Any trustee who fails to comply with division (J) of this section is guilty of failure to provide medicaid fraud lien information, a misdemeanor of the first degree.

(K) If a trustee transfers title to personal or real property after a medicaid fraud lien notice is filed against the property, the lien is filed in the county in which the property is located, and the lien names a person who holds a beneficial interest in the property, the trustee, if he has actual notice of the notice, shall be liable to the state for the greater of the following:

(1) The proceeds received directly by the person named in the notice as a result of the transfer;

(2) The proceeds received by the trustee as a result of the transfer and distributed to the person named in the notice;

(3) The fair market value of the interest of the person named in the notice in the property transferred.

However, if the trustee transfers property for at least its fair market value and holds the proceeds that otherwise would be paid or distributed to the beneficiary, or at the direction of the beneficiary or his designee, the liability of the trustee shall not exceed the amount of the proceeds held by the trustee.

(L) The filing of a medicaid fraud lien notice does not constitute a lien on the record title to personal or real property owned by the trustee, except to the extent the trustee is named in the notice.

The prosecuting attorney for the county or the attorney general may bring a civil action in any court of common pleas to recover from the trustee the amounts set forth in division (H) of this section. The county or state may recover investigative costs and attorney's fees incurred by the prosecuting attorney or the attorney general.

(M)(1) This section does not apply to any transfer by a trustee under a court order, unless the order is entered in an action between the trustee and the beneficiary.

(2) Unless the trustee has actual knowledge that a person owning a beneficial interest in the trust is named in a medicaid fraud lien notice, this section does not apply to either of the following:

(a) Any transfer by a trustee required under the terms of any trust agreement, if the agreement is a matter of public record before the filing of any medicaid fraud lien notice;

(b) Any transfer by a trustee to all of the persons who own a beneficial interest in the trust.

(N) The filing of a medicaid fraud lien notice does not affect the use to which personal or real property, or a beneficial interest in it, that is owned by the person named in the notice may be put or the right of the person to receive any proceeds resulting from the use and ownership, but not the sale, of the property, until a judgment of forfeiture is entered.

(O) The term of a medicaid fraud lien notice is five years from the date the notice is filed, unless a renewal notice has been filed by the prosecuting attorney of the county in which the property or interest is located or by the attorney general. The term of any renewal of a medicaid fraud lien notice granted by the court is five years from the date of its filing. A medicaid fraud lien notice may be renewed any number of times while a criminal proceeding for a medicaid fraud offense, or an appeal from such a proceeding, is pending.

(P) The prosecuting attorney or attorney general who files the medicaid fraud lien notice may terminate, in whole or part, the notice or release any personal or real property or beneficial interest in the property upon any terms that he determines are appropriate. Any termination or release shall be filed by the prosecuting attorney or attorney general with each county recorder with whom the notice was filed. No fee shall be imposed for the filing.

(Q) The acquittal in a criminal proceeding for a medicaid fraud offense of the person named in the medicaid fraud lien notice or the dismissal of a criminal proceeding for such an offense against the person named in the notice terminates the notice. In such a case, the filing of the notice has no effect.

A person named in a medicaid fraud lien notice may bring an action against the prosecuting attorney or attorney general who filed the notice, in the county where it was filed, seeking a release of the property subject to the notice or termination of the notice. In such a case, the court of common pleas promptly shall set a date for hearing, which shall be not less than five nor more than ten days after the action is filed. The order and a copy of the complaint shall be served on the prosecuting attorney or attorney general within three days after the action is filed. At the hearing, the court shall take evidence as to whether any personal or real property, or beneficial interest in it, that is owned by the person bringing the action is covered by the notice or otherwise is subject to forfeiture. If the person bringing the action shows by a preponderance of the evidence that the notice does not apply to him or that any personal or real property, or beneficial interest in it, that is owned by him is not subject to forfeiture, the court shall enter a judgment terminating the notice or releasing the personal or real property or beneficial interest from the notice.

At a hearing, the court may release from the notice any property or beneficial interest upon the posting of security, by the person against whom the notice was filed, in an amount equal to the value of the property or beneficial interest owned by the person.

The court promptly shall enter an order terminating a medicaid fraud lien notice or releasing any personal or real property or beneficial interest in the property, if a sale of the property or beneficial interest is pending and the filing of the notice prevents the sale. However, the proceeds of the sale shall be deposited with the clerk of the court, subject to the further order of the court.

(R) Notwithstanding any provision of this section, any person who has perfected a security interest in personal or real property or a beneficial interest in the property for the payment of an enforceable debt or other similar obligation prior to the filing of a medicaid fraud lien notice in reference to the property or interest may foreclose on the property or interest as otherwise provided by law. The foreclosure, insofar as practical, shall be made so that it otherwise will not interfere with a forfeiture under section 2933.73 of the Revised Code.

(1994 H 715, eff. 7–22–94; 1993 H 152, eff. 7–1–93)

PEN REGISTERS; TRAP AND TRACE DEVICES

2933.76 Order authorizing installation and use of pen register or trap and trace device

(A) As used in this section and section 2933.77 of the Revised Code, "electronic communication," "electronic communication service," "investigative officer," "judge of a court of common pleas," "pen register," "trap and trace device," and "wire communication" have the same meanings as in section 2933.51 of the Revised Code.

(B) A judge of a court of common pleas, in accordance with this section, may issue an order authorizing or approving the installation and use, within the jurisdiction of the court, of a pen register or a trap and trace device to obtain information in connection with a criminal investigation.

(C) A law enforcement officer or investigative officer may make an application to a judge of a court of common pleas for an order authorizing the installation and use, within the jurisdiction of the court, of a pen register or a trap and trace device to obtain information in connection with a criminal investigation. The application shall be in writing and shall be under oath or affirmation. Each application shall contain all of the following:

(1) The name of the law enforcement officer or investigative officer making the application and the name of the investigative or law enforcement agency conducting the criminal investigation to which the application relates;

(2) The name, if known, of the person to whom the telephone or other line to which the pen register or trap and trace device is to be attached is leased or in whose name that telephone or other line is listed;

(3) The name, if known, of the person who is the subject of the criminal investigation to which the application relates;

(4) The number and, if known, the physical location of the telephone or other line to which the pen register or the trap and trace device is to be attached;

(5) A statement of the offense to which the information that is likely to be obtained by the installation and use of the pen register or trap and trace device relates;

(6) A certification by the law enforcement officer or investigative officer making the application that the information that is likely to be obtained by the installation and use of the pen register or trap and trace device is relevant to an ongoing criminal investigation being conducted by the investigative or law enforcement agency identified under division (C)(1) of this section.

(D)(1) The judge to whom an application is made under division (C) of this section shall issue and enter an order authorizing the installation and use of a pen register or a trap and trace device if the judge finds that the information relating to an offense that is likely to be obtained by the installation and use of the pen register or trap and trace device is relevant to an ongoing criminal investigation being conducted by the investigative or law enforcement agency identified under division (C)(1) of this section. In the order, the judge shall specify a finding with respect to each of the items required by divisions (C)(1) to (6) of this section to be included in the application.

(2) If the law enforcement officer or investigative officer so requests, the order shall direct the appropriate provider of wire or electronic communication service, landlord, custodian, or other person to furnish the law enforcement officer or investigative officer with all information, facilities, and technical assistance necessary to accomplish the installation and operation of a pen register or trap and trace device unobtrusively and with a minimum of interference of service to the person with respect to whom the installation and operation are to take place. The order further shall direct the person who owns or leases the telephone or other line to which the pen register or trap and trace device is to be attached, or the provider of wire or electronic communication service, landlord, custodian, or other person who is ordered under division (D)(2) of this section to provide information, facilities, or technical assistance, not to disclose the existence of the criminal investigation or of the installation and use of the pen register or trap and trace device to the listed subscriber of the telephone or other line or to another person unless or until otherwise ordered by the court. If the order pertains to a trap and trace device, the order may require the appropriate provider of wire or electronic communication service to install and operate the device. The order shall be sealed until otherwise ordered by the court.

(E) An order issued pursuant to division (D) of this section shall authorize the installation and use of a pen register or a trap and trace device for a period not to exceed sixty days. The court may grant an extension of the sixty-day period upon application for an order in accordance with division (C) of this section and upon the judicial findings required by division (D)(1) of this section. An extension of an order issued under this division shall be in effect for a period not to exceed sixty days. The court may order further extensions of the sixty-day extended period upon compliance with this division.

(F) A good faith reliance on a court order issued under this section, a legislative authorization, or a statutory authorization is a complete defense against any claim in a civil action or any charge in a criminal action alleging a violation of the requirements of this section or section 2933.77 of the Revised Code.

(1998 H 565, eff. 3–30–99; 1996 H 181, eff. 6–13–96)

2933.77 Assistance by provider of electronic communication service, landlord, or custodian

(A) If an order issued under section 2933.76 of the Revised Code authorizing the installation and use of a pen register or a trap and trace device directs a provider of wire or electronic communication service, landlord, custodian, or other person to furnish information, facilities, and technical assistance to accomplish the installation and operation of the pen register or trap and trace device, that provider, landlord, custodian, or other person, in accordance with the order, shall furnish the law enforcement officer or investigative officer with all information, facilities, and technical assistance necessary to accomplish the installation and operation of the pen register or trap and trace device unobtrusively and with a minimum of interference with the service accorded by the provider, landlord, custodian, or other person to the person with respect to whom the installation and operation are to take place. If an order issued under that section requires a provider of wire or electronic communication service to install and operate a trap and trace device, the provider, in accordance with the order, shall install and operate the device.

(B) The investigative or law enforcement agency conducting the criminal investigation to which the order issued under section 2933.76 of the Revised Code for the installation and use of a pen register or a trap and trace device relates shall provide reasonable compensation to a provider of wire or electronic communication service, landlord, custodian, or other person who furnishes facilities or technical assistance in accordance with the order for any reasonable expenses the provider, landlord, custodian, or other person incurs in furnishing the facilities or technical assistance.

(C) A provider of wire or electronic communication service, an officer, employee, or agent of that provider, or a landlord, custodian, or other specified person is immune from civil or criminal liability in any action that arises from the provision of information, facilities, or technical assistance in accordance with the terms of an order of a court issued under section 2933.76 of the Revised Code.

(1998 H 565, eff. 3–30–99; 1996 H 181, eff. 6–13–96)

CHAPTER 2935

ARREST, CITATION, AND DISPOSITION ALTERNATIVES

DEFINITIONS

DEFINITIONS

2935.01 Definitions

As used in this chapter:

(A) "Magistrate" has the same meaning as in section 2931.01 of the Revised Code.

(B) "Peace officer" includes, except as provided in section 2935.081 of the Revised Code, a sheriff; deputy sheriff; marshal; deputy marshal; member of the organized police department of any municipal corporation, including a member of the organized police department of a municipal corporation in an adjoining state serving in Ohio under a contract pursuant to section 737.04 of the Revised Code; member of a police force employed by a metropolitan housing authority under division (D) of section 3735.31 of the Revised Code; member of a police force employed by a regional transit authority under division (Y) of section 306.05 of the Revised Code; state university law enforcement officer appointed under section 3345.04 of the Revised Code; enforcement agent of the department of public safety designated under section 5502.14 of the Revised Code; employee of the department of taxation to whom investigation powers have been delegated under section 5743.45 of the Revised Code; employee of the department of natural resources who is a natural resources law enforcement staff officer designated pursuant to section 1501.013 of the Revised Code, a forest officer designated pursuant to section 1503.29 of the Revised Code, a preserve officer designated pursuant to section 1517.10 of the Revised Code, a wildlife officer designated pursuant to section 1531.13 of the Revised Code, a park officer designated pursuant to section 1541.10 of the Revised Code, or a state watercraft officer designated pursuant to section 1547.521 of the Revised Code; individual designated to perform law enforcement duties under section 511.232, 1545.13, or 6101.75 of the Revised Code; veterans' home police officer appointed under section 5907.02 of the Revised Code; special police officer employed by a port authority under section 4582.04 or 4582.28 of the Revised Code; police constable of any township; police officer of a township or joint township police district; a special police officer employed by a municipal corporation at a municipal airport, or other municipal air navigation facility, that has scheduled operations, as defined in section 119.3 of Title 14 of the Code of Federal Regulations, 14 C.F.R. 119.3, as amended, and that is required to be under a security program and is governed by aviation security rules of the transportation security administration of the United States department of transportation as provided in Parts 1542. and 1544. of Title 49 of the Code of Federal Regulations, as amended; the house sergeant at arms if the house sergeant at arms has arrest authority pursuant to division (E)(1) of section 101.311 of the Revised Code; and an assistant house sergeant at arms; officer or employee of the bureau of criminal identification and investigation established pursuant to section 109.51 of the Revised Code who has been awarded a certificate by the executive director of the Ohio peace officer training commission attesting to the officer's or employee's satisfactory completion of an approved state, county, municipal, or department of natural resources peace officer basic training program and who is providing assistance upon request to a law enforcement officer or emergency assistance to a peace officer pursuant to section 109.54 or 109.541 of the Revised Code; and, for the purpose of arrests within those areas, for the purposes of Chapter 5503. of the Revised Code, and the filing of and service of process relating to those offenses witnessed or investigated by them, the superintendent and troopers of the state highway patrol.

(C) "Prosecutor" includes the county prosecuting attorney and any assistant prosecutor designated to assist the county prosecuting attorney, and, in the case of courts inferior to courts of common pleas, includes the village solicitor, city director of law, or similar chief legal officer of a municipal corporation, any such officer's assistants, or any attorney designated by the prosecuting attorney of the county to appear for the prosecution of a given case.

(D) "Offense," except where the context specifically indicates otherwise, includes felonies, misdemeanors, and violations of ordinances of municipal corporations and other public bodies authorized by law to adopt penal regulations.

(2002 H 675, eff. 3–14–03; 2002 H 545, eff. 3–19–03; 2002 H 427, eff. 8–29–02; 2002 S 200, eff. 9–6–02; 2000 S 317, eff. 3–22–01; 2000 S 137, eff. 5–17–00; 1999 H 163, eff. 6–30–99; 1998 S 187, eff. 3–18–99; 1996 H 72, eff. 3–18–97; 1995 S 162, eff. 10–29–95; 1995 S 2, eff. 7–1–96; 1991 S 144, eff. 8–8–91; 1991 H 77; 1988 H 708, § 1)

2935.011 Officer or employee of bureau of criminal identification as peace officer

If an officer or employee of the bureau of criminal identification and investigation is included as a "peace officer" under division (B) of section 2935.01 of the Revised Code, both of the following apply:

(A) Division (D)(2) of section 109.541 applies to the officer or employee while so included.

(B) The officer or employee is not, as a result of the inclusion, a member of a police department for purposes of Chapter 742. of the Revised Code or a law enforcement officer or peace officer for purposes of any state or local retirement system.

(2002 H 427, eff. 8–29–02)

ARREST

2935.02 Accused may be arrested in any county

If an accused person flees from justice, or is not found in the county where a warrant for his arrest was issued, the officer holding the same may pursue and arrest him in any county in this state, and convey him before the magistrate or court of the county having cognizance of the case.

If such warrant directs the removal of the accused to the county in which the offense was committed, the officer holding the warrant shall deliver the accused to a court or magistrate of such county.

The necessary expense of such removal and reasonable compensation for his time and trouble, shall be paid to such officer out of the treasury of such county, upon the allowance and order of the county auditor.

(1953 H 1, eff. 10–1–53; GC 13432–10)

2935.03 Arrest and detention until warrant can be obtained

(A)(1) A sheriff, deputy sheriff, marshal, deputy marshal, municipal police officer, township constable, police officer of a township or joint township police district, member of a police force employed by a metropolitan housing authority under division (D) of section 3735.31 of the Revised Code, member of a police force employed by a regional transit authority under division (Y) of section 306.35 of the Revised Code, state university law enforcement officer appointed under section 3345.04 of the Revised Code, veterans' home police officer appointed under section 5907.02 of the Revised Code, special police officer employed by a port authority under section 4582.04 or 4582.28 of the Revised Code, or a special police officer employed by a municipal corporation at a municipal airport, or other municipal air navigation facility, that has scheduled operations, as defined in section 119.3 of Title 14 of the Code of Federal Regulations, 14 C.F.R. 119.3, as amended, and that is required to be under a security program and is governed by aviation security rules of the transportation security administration of the United States department of transportation as provided in Parts 1542. and 1544. of Title 49 of the Code of Federal Regulations, as amended, shall arrest and detain, until a warrant can be obtained, a person found violating, within the limits of the political subdivision, metropolitan housing authority housing project, regional transit authority facilities or areas of a municipal corporation that have been agreed to by a regional transit authority and a municipal corporation located within its territorial jurisdiction, college, university, veterans' home operated under Chapter 5907. of the Revised Code, port authority, or municipal airport or other municipal air navigation facility, in which the peace officer is appointed, employed, or elected, a law of this state, an ordinance of a municipal corporation, or a resolution of a township.

(2) A peace officer of the department of natural resources or an individual designated to perform law enforcement duties under section 511.232, 1545.13, or 6101.75 of the Revised Code shall arrest and detain, until a warrant can be obtained, a person found violating, within the limits of the peace officer's or individual's territorial jurisdiction, a law of this state.

(3) The house sergeant at arms if the house sergeant at arms has arrest authority pursuant to division (E)(1) of section 101.311 of the Revised Code and an assistant house sergeant at arms shall arrest and detain, until a warrant can be obtained, a person found violating, within the limits of the sergeant at arms's or assistant sergeant at arms's territorial jurisdiction specified in division (D)(1)(a) of section 101.311 of the Revised Code or while providing security pursuant to division (D)(1)(f) of section 101.311 of the Revised Code, a law of this state, an ordinance of a municipal corporation, or a resolution of a township.

(B)(1) When there is reasonable ground to believe that an offense of violence, the offense of criminal child enticement as defined in section 2905.05 of the Revised Code, the offense of public indecency as defined in section 2907.09 of the Revised Code, the offense of domestic violence as defined in section 2919.25 of the Revised Code, the offense of violating a protection order as defined in section 2919.27 of the Revised Code, the offense of menacing by stalking as defined in section 2903.211 of the Revised Code, the offense of aggravated trespass as defined in section 2911.211 of the Revised Code, a theft offense as defined in section 2913.01 of the Revised Code, or a felony drug abuse offense as defined in section 2925.01 of the Revised Code, has been committed within the limits of the political subdivision, metropolitan housing authority housing project, regional transit authority facilities or those areas of a municipal corporation that have been agreed to by a regional transit authority and a municipal corporation located within its territorial jurisdiction, college, university, veterans' home operated under Chapter 5907. of the Revised Code, port authority, or municipal airport or other municipal air navigation facility, in which the peace officer is appointed, employed, or elected or within the limits of the territorial jurisdiction of the peace officer, a peace officer described in division (A) of this section may arrest and detain until a warrant can be obtained any person who the peace officer has reasonable cause to believe is guilty of the violation.

(2) For purposes of division (B)(1) of this section, the execution of any of the following constitutes reasonable ground to believe that the offense alleged in the statement was committed and reasonable cause to believe that the person alleged in the statement to have committed the offense is guilty of the violation:

(a) A written statement by a person alleging that an alleged offender has committed the offense of menacing by stalking or aggravated trespass;

(b) A written statement by the administrator of the interstate compact on mental health appointed under section 5119.51 of the Revised Code alleging that a person who had been hospitalized, institutionalized, or confined in any facility under an order made pursuant to or under authority of section 2945.37, 2945.371, 2945.38, 2945.39, 2945.40, 2945.401, or 2945.402 of the Revised Code has escaped from the facility, from confinement in a vehicle for transportation to or from the facility, or from supervision by an employee of the facility that is incidental to hospitalization, institutionalization, or confinement in the facility and that occurs outside of the facility, in violation of section 2921.34 of the Revised Code;

(c) A written statement by the administrator of any facility in which a person has been hospitalized, institutionalized, or confined under an order made pursuant to or under authority of section 2945.37, 2945.371, 2945.38, 2945.39, 2945.40, 2945.401, or 2945.402 of the Revised Code alleging that the person has escaped from the facility, from confinement in a vehicle for transportation to or from the facility, or from supervision by an employee of the facility that is incidental to hospitalization, institutionalization, or confinement in the facility and that occurs outside of the facility, in violation of section 2921.34 of the Revised Code.

(3)(a) For purposes of division (B)(1) of this section, a peace officer described in division (A) of this section has reasonable grounds to believe that the offense of domestic violence or the offense of violating a protection order has been committed and reasonable cause to believe that a particular person is guilty of committing the offense if any of the following occurs:

(i) A person executes a written statement alleging that the person in question has committed the offense of domestic violence or the offense of violating a protection order against the person who executes the statement or against a child of the person who executes the statement.

(ii) No written statement of the type described in division (B)(3)(a)(i) of this section is executed, but the peace officer, based upon the peace officer's own knowledge and observation of the facts and circumstances of the alleged incident of the offense of domestic violence or the alleged incident of the offense of violating a protection order or based upon any other information, including, but not limited to, any reasonably trustworthy information given to the peace officer by the alleged victim of the alleged incident of the offense or any witness of the alleged incident of the offense, concludes that there are reasonable grounds to believe that the offense of domestic violence or the offense of violating a protection order has been committed and reasonable cause to believe that the person in question is guilty of committing the offense.

(iii) No written statement of the type described in division (B)(3)(a)(i) of this section is executed, but the peace officer witnessed the person in question commit the offense of domestic violence or the offense of violating a protection order.

(b) If pursuant to division (B)(3)(a) of this section a peace officer has reasonable grounds to believe that the offense of domestic violence or the offense of violating a protection order has been committed and reasonable cause to believe that a particular person is guilty of committing the offense, it is the preferred course of action in this state that the officer arrest and detain that person pursuant to division (B)(1) of this section until a warrant can be obtained.

If pursuant to division (B)(3)(a) of this section a peace officer has reasonable grounds to believe that the offense of domestic violence or the offense of violating a protection order has been committed and reasonable cause to believe that family or household members have committed the offense against each other, it is the preferred course of action in this state that the officer, pursuant to division (B)(1) of this section, arrest and detain until a warrant can be obtained the family or household member who committed the offense and whom the officer has reasonable cause to believe is the primary physical aggressor. There is no preferred course of action in this state regarding any other family or household member who committed the offense and whom the officer does not have reasonable cause to believe is the primary physical aggressor, but, pursuant to division (B)(1) of this section, the peace officer may arrest and detain until a warrant can be obtained any other family or household member who committed the offense and whom the officer does not have reasonable cause to believe is the primary physical aggressor.

(c) If a peace officer described in division (A) of this section does not arrest and detain a person whom the officer has reasonable cause to believe committed the offense of domestic violence or the offense of violating a protection order when it is the preferred course of action in this state pursuant to division (B)(3)(b) of this section that the officer arrest that person, the officer shall articulate in the written report of the incident required by section 2935.032 of the Revised Code a clear statement of the officer's reasons for not arresting and detaining that person until a warrant can be obtained.

(d) In determining for purposes of division (B)(3)(b) of this section which family or household member is the primary physical aggressor in a situation in which family or household members have committed the offense of domestic violence or the offense of violating a protection order against each other, a peace officer described in division (A) of this section, in addition to any other relevant circumstances, should consider all of the following:

(i) Any history of domestic violence or of any other violent acts by either person involved in the alleged offense that the officer reasonably can ascertain;

(ii) If violence is alleged, whether the alleged violence was caused by a person acting in self-defense;

(iii) Each person's fear of physical harm, if any, resulting from the other person's threatened use of force against any person or resulting from the other person's use or history of the use of force against any person, and the reasonableness of that fear;

(iv) The comparative severity of any injuries suffered by the persons involved in the alleged offense.

(e)(i) A peace officer described in division (A) of this section shall not require, as a prerequisite to arresting or charging a person who has committed the offense of domestic violence or the offense of violating a protection order, that the victim of the offense specifically consent to the filing of charges against the person who has committed the offense or sign a complaint against the person who has committed the offense.

(ii) If a person is arrested for or charged with committing the offense of domestic violence or the offense of violating a protection order and if the victim of the offense does not cooperate with the involved law enforcement or prosecuting authorities in the prosecution of the offense or, subsequent to the arrest or the filing of the charges, informs the involved law enforcement or prosecuting authorities that the victim does not wish the prosecution of the offense to continue or wishes to drop charges against the alleged offender relative to the offense, the involved prosecuting authorities, in determining whether to continue with the prosecution of the offense or whether to dismiss charges against the alleged offender relative to the offense and notwithstanding the victim's failure to cooperate or the victim's wishes, shall consider all facts and circumstances that are relevant to the offense, including, but not limited to, the statements and observations of the peace officers who responded to the incident that resulted in the arrest or filing of the charges and of all witnesses to that incident.

(f) In determining pursuant to divisions (B)(3)(a) to (g) of this section whether to arrest a person pursuant to division (B)(1) of this section, a peace officer described in division (A) of this section shall not consider as a factor any possible shortage of cell space at the detention facility to which the person will be taken subsequent to the person's arrest or any possibility that the person's arrest might cause, contribute to, or exacerbate overcrowding at that detention facility or at any other detention facility.

(g) If a peace officer described in division (A) of this section intends pursuant to divisions (B)(3)(a) to (g) of this section to arrest a person pursuant to division (B)(1) of this section and if the officer is unable to do so because the person is not present, the officer promptly shall seek a warrant for the arrest of the person.

(h) If a peace officer described in division (A) of this section responds to a report of an alleged incident of the offense of domestic violence or an alleged incident of the offense of violating a protection order and if the circumstances of the incident involved the use or threatened use of a deadly weapon or any person involved in the incident brandished a deadly weapon during or in relation to the incident, the deadly weapon that was used, threatened to be used, or brandished constitutes contraband, and, to the extent possible, the officer shall seize the deadly weapon as contraband pursuant to section 2933.43 of the Revised Code. Upon the seizure of a deadly weapon pursuant to division (B)(3)(h) of this section, section 2933.43 of the Revised Code shall apply regarding the treatment and disposition of the deadly weapon. For purposes of that section, the "underlying criminal offense" that was the basis of the seizure of a deadly weapon under division (B)(3)(h) of this section and to which the deadly weapon had a relationship is any of the following that is applicable:

(i) The alleged incident of the offense of domestic violence or the alleged incident of the offense of violating a protection order to which the officer who seized the deadly weapon responded;

(ii) Any offense that arose out of the same facts and circumstances as the report of the alleged incident of the offense of domestic violence or the alleged incident of the offense of violating a protection order to which the officer who seized the deadly weapon responded.

(4) If, in the circumstances described in divisions (B)(3)(a) to (g) of this section, a peace officer described in division (A) of this section arrests and detains a person pursuant to division (B)(1) of this section, or if, pursuant to division (B)(3)(h) of this section, a peace officer described in division (A) of this section seizes a deadly weapon, the officer, to the extent described in and in accordance with section 9.86 or 2744.03 of the Revised Code, is immune in any civil action for damages for injury, death, or loss to person or property that arises from or is related to the arrest and detention or the seizure.

(C) When there is reasonable ground to believe that a violation of division (A)(1), (2), or (3) of section 4506.15 or a violation of section 4511.19 of the Revised Code has been committed by a person operating a motor vehicle subject to regulation by the public utilities commission of Ohio under Title XLIX of the Revised Code, a peace officer with authority to enforce that provision of law may stop or detain the person whom the officer has reasonable cause to believe was operating the motor vehicle in violation of the division or section and, after investigating the circumstances surrounding the operation of the vehicle, may arrest and detain the person.

(D) If a sheriff, deputy sheriff, marshal, deputy marshal, municipal police officer, member of a police force employed by a metropolitan housing authority under division (D) of section 3735.31 of the Revised Code, member of a police force employed by a regional transit authority under division (Y) of section 306.35 of the Revised Code, special police officer employed by a port authority under section 4582.04 or 4582.28 of the Revised Code, special police officer employed by a municipal corporation at a municipal airport or other municipal air navigation facility described in division (A) of this section, township constable, police officer of a township or joint township police district, state university law enforcement officer appointed under section 3345.04 of the Revised Code, peace officer of the department of natural resources, individual designated to perform law enforcement duties under section 511.232, 1545.13, or 6101.75 of the Revised Code, the house sergeant at arms if the house sergeant at arms has arrest authority pursuant to division (E)(1) of section 101.311 of the Revised Code, or an assistant house sergeant at arms is authorized by division (A) or (B) of this section to arrest and detain, within the limits of the political subdivision, metropolitan housing authority housing project, regional transit authority facilities or those areas of a municipal corporation that have been agreed to by a regional transit authority and a municipal corporation located within its territorial jurisdiction, port authority, municipal airport or other municipal air navigation facility, college, or university in which the officer is appointed, employed, or elected or within the limits of the territorial jurisdiction of the peace officer, a person until a warrant can be obtained, the peace officer, outside the limits of that territory, may pursue, arrest, and detain that person until a warrant can be obtained if all of the following apply:

(1) The pursuit takes place without unreasonable delay after the offense is committed;

(2) The pursuit is initiated within the limits of the political subdivision, metropolitan housing authority housing project, regional transit authority facilities or those areas of a municipal corporation that have been agreed to by a regional transit authority and a municipal corporation located within its territorial jurisdiction, port authority, municipal airport or other municipal air navigation facility, college, or university in which the peace officer is appointed, employed, or elected or within the limits of the territorial jurisdiction of the peace officer;

(3) The offense involved is a felony, a misdemeanor of the first degree or a substantially equivalent municipal ordinance, a misdemeanor of the second degree or a substantially equivalent municipal ordinance, or any offense for which points are chargeable pursuant to section 4510.036 of the Revised Code.

(E) In addition to the authority granted under division (A) or (B) of this section:

(1) A sheriff or deputy sheriff may arrest and detain, until a warrant can be obtained, any person found violating section 4503.11, 4503.21, or 4549.01, sections 4549.08 to 4549.12, section 4549.62, or Chapter 4511. or 4513. of the Revised Code on the portion of any street or highway that is located immediately adjacent to the boundaries of the county in which the sheriff or deputy sheriff is elected or appointed.

(2) A member of the police force of a township police district created under section 505.48 of the Revised Code, a member of the police force of a joint township police district created under section 505.481 of the Revised Code, or a township constable appointed in accordance with section 509.01 of the Revised Code, who has received a certificate from the Ohio peace officer training commission under section 109.75 of the Revised Code, may arrest and detain, until a warrant can be obtained, any person found violating any section or chapter of the Revised Code listed in division (E)(1) of this section, other than sections 4513.33 and 4513.34 of the Revised Code, on the portion of any street or highway that is located immediately adjacent to the boundaries of the township police district or joint township police district, in the case of a member of a township police district or joint township police district police force, or the unincorporated territory of the township, in the case of a township constable. However, if the population of the township that created the township police district served by the member's police force, or the townships that created the joint township police district served by the member's police force, or the township that is served by the township constable, is sixty thousand or less, the member of the township police district or joint police district police force or the township constable may not make an arrest under division (E)(2) of this section on a state highway that is included as part of the interstate system.

(3) A police officer or village marshal appointed, elected, or employed by a municipal corporation may arrest and detain, until a warrant can be obtained, any person found violating any section or chapter of the Revised Code listed in division (E)(1) of this section on the portion of any street or highway that is located immediately adjacent to the boundaries of the municipal corporation in which the police officer or village marshal is appointed, elected, or employed.

(4) A peace officer of the department of natural resources or an individual designated to perform law enforcement duties under section 511.232, 1545.13, or 6101.75 of the Revised Code may arrest and detain, until a warrant can be obtained, any person found violating any section or chapter of the Revised Code listed in division (E)(1) of this section, other than sections 4513.33 and 4513.34 of the Revised Code, on the portion of any street or highway that is located immediately adjacent to the boundaries of the lands and waters that constitute the territorial jurisdiction of the peace officer.

(F)(1) A department of mental health special police officer or a department of mental retardation and developmental disabilities special police officer may arrest without a warrant and detain until a warrant can be obtained any person found committing on the premises of any institution under the jurisdiction of the particular department a misdemeanor under a law of the state.

A department of mental health special police officer or a department of mental retardation and developmental disabilities special police officer may arrest without a warrant and detain until a warrant can be obtained any person who has been hospitalized, institutionalized, or confined in an institution under the jurisdiction of the particular department pursuant to or under authority of section 2945.37, 2945.371, 2945.38, 2945.39, 2945.40, 2945.401, or 2945.402 of the Revised Code and who is found committing on the premises of any institution under the jurisdiction of the particular department a violation of section 2921.34 of the Revised Code that involves an escape from the premises of the institution.

(2)(a) If a department of mental health special police officer or a department of mental retardation and developmental disabilities special police officer finds any person who has been hospitalized, institutionalized, or confined in an institution under the jurisdiction of the particular department pursuant to or under authority of section 2945.37, 2945.371, 2945.38, 2945.39, 2945.40, 2945.401, or 2945.402 of the Revised Code committing a violation of section 2921.34 of the Revised Code that involves an escape from the premises of the institution, or if there is reasonable ground to believe that a violation of section 2921.34 of the Revised Code has been committed that involves an escape from the premises of an institution under the jurisdiction of the department of mental health or the department of mental retardation and developmental disabilities and if a department of mental health special police officer or a department of mental retardation and developmental disabilities special police officer has reasonable cause to believe that a particular person who has been hospitalized, institutionalized, or confined in the institution pursuant to or under authority of section 2945.37, 2945.371, 2945.38, 2945.39, 2945.40, 2945.401, or 2945.402 of the Revised Code is guilty of the violation, the special police officer, outside of the premises of the institution, may pursue, arrest, and detain that person for that violation of section 2921.34 of the Revised Code, until a warrant can be obtained, if both of the following apply:

(i) The pursuit takes place without unreasonable delay after the offense is committed;

(ii) The pursuit is initiated within the premises of the institution from which the violation of section 2921.34 of the Revised Code occurred.

(b) For purposes of division (F)(2)(a) of this section, the execution of a written statement by the administrator of the institution in which a person had been hospitalized, institutionalized, or confined pursuant to or under authority of section 2945.37, 2945.371, 2945.38, 2945.39, 2945.40, 2945.401, or 2945.402 of the Revised Code alleging that the person has escaped from the premises of the institution in violation of section 2921.34 of the Revised Code constitutes reasonable ground to believe that the violation was committed and reasonable cause to believe that the person alleged in the statement to have committed the offense is guilty of the violation.

(G) As used in this section:

(1) A "department of mental health special police officer" means a special police officer of the department of mental health designated under section 5119.14 of the Revised Code who is certified by the Ohio peace officer training commission under section 109.77 of the Revised Code as having successfully completed an approved peace officer basic training program.

(2) A "department of mental retardation and developmental disabilities special police officer" means a special police officer of the department of mental retardation and developmental disabilities designated under section 5123.13 of the Revised Code who is certified by the Ohio peace officer training council under section 109.77 of the Revised Code as having successfully completed an approved peace officer basic training program.

(3) "Deadly weapon" has the same meaning as in section 2923.11 of the Revised Code.

(4) "Family or household member" has the same meaning as in section 2919.25 of the Revised Code.

(5) "Street" or "highway" has the same meaning as in section 4511.01 of the Revised Code.

(6) "Interstate system" has the same meaning as in section 5516.01 of the Revised Code.

(7) "Peace officer of the department of natural resources" means an employee of the department of natural resources who is a natural resources law enforcement staff officer designated pursuant to section 1501.013, a forest officer designated pursuant to section 1503.29, a preserve officer designated pursuant to section 1517.10, a wildlife officer designated pursuant to section 1531.13, a park officer designated pursuant to section 1541.10, or a state watercraft officer designated pursuant to section 1547.521 of the Revised Code.

(2002 H 675, § 1.04, eff. 1–1–04; 2002 H 675, § 1.01, eff. 3–14–03; 2002 H 545, eff. 3–19–03; 2002 S 123, eff. 1–1–04; 2000 S 317, eff. 3–22–01, 2000 S 137, eff. 5–17–00, 1998 S 187, eff. 3–18–99; 1997 S 1, eff. 10–21–97; 1996 S 285, eff. 7–1–97; 1996 H 670, eff. 12–2–96; 1996 S 269, eff. 7–1–96; 1995 S 2, eff. 7–1–96; 1994 H 335, eff. 12–9–94; 1994 S 82, eff. 5–4–94; 1993 H 42, eff. 2–9–94; 1992 H 536; 1991 H 77; 1990 H 669, H 88; 1988 H 708, § 1)

2935.031 Agencies employing persons with arrest authority to adopt motor vehicle pursuit policies

Any agency, instrumentality, or political subdivision of the state that employs a sheriff, deputy sheriff, constable, marshal, deputy marshal, police officer, member of a metropolitan housing authority police force, state university law enforcement officer, or veterans' home police officer with arrest authority under section 2935.03 of the Revised Code or that employs other persons with arrest authority under the Revised Code, shall adopt a policy for the pursuit in a motor vehicle of any person who violates a law of this state or an ordinance of a municipal corporation. The chief law enforcement officer or other chief official of the agency, instrumentality, or political subdivision shall formally advise each peace officer or other person with arrest authority it employs of the pursuit policy adopted by that agency, instrumentality, or political subdivision pursuant to this section.

(2002 H 675, eff. 3–14–03; 1989 S 49, eff. 11–3–89)

2935.032 Domestic violence arrest policies

(A) Not later than ninety days after the effective date of this amendment, each agency, instrumentality, or political subdivision that is served by any peace officer described in division (B)(1) of section 2935.03 of the Revised Code shall adopt, in accordance with division (E) of this section, written policies, written procedures implementing the policies, and other written procedures for the peace officers who serve it to follow in implementing division (B)(3) of section 2935.03 of the Revised Code and for their appropriate response to each report of an alleged incident of the offense of domestic violence or an alleged incident of the offense of violating a protection order. The policies and procedures shall conform to and be consistent with the provisions of divisions (B)(1) and (B)(3) of section 2935.03 of the Revised Code and divisions (B) to (D) of this section. Each policy adopted under this division shall include, but not be limited to, all of the following:

(1) Provisions specifying that, if a peace officer who serves the agency, instrumentality, or political subdivision responds to an alleged incident of the offense of domestic violence, an alleged incident of the offense of violating a protection order, or an alleged incident of any other offense, both of the following apply:

(a) If the officer determines that there are reasonable grounds to believe that a person knowingly caused serious physical harm to another or to another's unborn or knowingly caused or attempted to cause physical harm to another or to another's unborn by means of a deadly weapon or dangerous ordnance, then, regardless of whether the victim of the offense was a family or household member of the offender, the officer shall treat the incident as felonious assault, shall consider the offender to have committed and the victim to have been the victim of felonious assault, shall consider the offense that was committed to have been felonious assault in determining the manner in which the offender should be treated, and shall comply with whichever of the following is applicable:

(i) Unless the officer has reasonable cause to believe that, during the incident, the offender who committed the felonious assault and one or more other persons committed offenses against each other, the officer shall arrest the offender who committed the felonious assault pursuant to section 2935.03 of the Revised Code and shall detain that offender pursuant to that section until a warrant can be obtained, and the arrest shall be for felonious assault.

(ii) If the officer has reasonable cause to believe that, during the incident, the offender who committed the felonious assault and one or more other persons committed offenses against each other, the officer shall determine in accordance with division (B)(3)(d) of section 2935.03 of the Revised Code which of those persons is the primary physical aggressor. If the offender who committed the felonious assault is the primary physical aggressor, the officer shall arrest that offender for felonious assault pursuant to section 2935.03 of the Revised Code and shall detain that offender pursuant to that section until a warrant can be obtained, and the officer is not required to arrest but may arrest pursuant to section 2935.03 of the Revised Code any other person who committed an offense but who is not the primary physical aggressor. If the offender who committed the felonious assault is not the primary physical aggressor, the officer is not required to arrest that offender or any other person who committed an offense during the incident but may arrest any of them pursuant to section 2935.03 of the Revised Code and detain them pursuant to that section until a warrant can be obtained.

(b) If the officer determines that there are reasonable grounds to believe that a person, while under the influence of sudden passion or in a sudden fit of rage, either of which is brought on by serious provocation occasioned by the victim that is reasonably sufficient to incite the person into using deadly force, knowingly caused serious physical harm to another or to another's unborn or knowingly caused or attempted to cause physical harm to another or to another's unborn by means of a deadly weapon or dangerous ordnance, then, regardless of whether the victim of the offense was a family or household member of the offender, the officer shall treat the incident as aggravated assault, shall consider the offender to have committed and the victim to have been the victim of aggravated assault, shall consider the offense that was committed to have been aggravated assault in determining the manner in which the offender should be treated, and shall comply with whichever of the following is applicable:

(i) Unless the officer has reasonable cause to believe that, during the incident, the offender who committed the aggravated assault and one or more other persons committed offenses against each other, the officer shall arrest the offender who committed the aggravated assault pursuant to section 2935.03 of the Revised Code and shall detain that offender pursuant to that section until a warrant can be obtained, and the arrest shall be for aggravated assault.

(ii) If the officer has reasonable cause to believe that, during the incident, the offender who committed the aggravated assault and one or more other persons committed offenses against each other, the officer shall determine in accordance with division (B)(3)(d) of section 2935.03 of the Revised Code which of those persons is the primary physical aggressor. If the offender who committed the aggravated assault is the primary physical aggressor, the officer shall arrest that offender for aggravated assault pursuant to section 2935.03 of the Revised Code and shall detain that offender pursuant to that section until a warrant can be obtained, and the officer is not required to arrest but may arrest pursuant to section 2935.03 of the Revised Code any other person who committed an offense but who is not the primary physical aggressor. If the offender who committed the aggravated assault is not the primary physical aggressor, the officer is not required to arrest that offender or any other person who committed an offense during the incident but may arrest any of them pursuant to section 2935.03 of the Revised Code and detain them pursuant to that section until a warrant can be obtained.

(2) Provisions requiring the peace officers who serve the agency, instrumentality, or political subdivision to do all of the following:

(a) Respond without undue delay to a report of an alleged incident of the offense of domestic violence or the offense of violating a protection order;

(b) If the alleged offender has been granted pretrial release from custody on a prior charge of the offense of domestic violence or the offense of violating a protection order and has violated one or more conditions of that pretrial release, document the facts and circumstances of the violation in the report to the law enforcement agency that the peace officer makes pursuant to division (D) of this section;

(c) Separate the victim of the offense of domestic violence or the offense of violating a protection order and the alleged offender, conduct separate interviews with the victim and the alleged offender in separate locations, and take a written statement from the victim that indicates the frequency and severity of any prior incidents of physical abuse of the victim by the alleged offender, the number of times the victim has called peace officers for assistance, and the disposition of those calls, if known;

(d) Comply with divisions (B)(1) and (B)(3) of section 2935.03 of the Revised Code and with divisions (B), (C), and (D) of this section.

(3) Sanctions to be imposed upon a peace officer who serves the agency, instrumentality, or political subdivision and who fails to comply with any provision in the policy or with division (B)(1) or (B)(3) of section 2935.03 of the Revised Code or division (B), (C), or (D) of this section.

(4) Examples of reasons that a peace officer may consider for not arresting and detaining until a warrant can be obtained a person who allegedly committed the offense of domestic violence or the offense of violating a protection order when it is the preferred course of action in this state that the officer arrest the alleged offender, as described in division (B)(3)(b) of section 2935.03 of the Revised Code.

(B)(1) Nothing in this section or in division (B)(1) or (B)(3) of section 2935.03 of the Revised Code precludes an agency, instrumentality, or political subdivision that is served by any peace officer described in division (B)(1) of section 2935.03 of the Revised Code from including in the policy it adopts under division (A) of this section either of the following types of provisions:

(a) A provision that requires the peace officers who serve it, if they have reasonable grounds to believe that the offense of domestic violence or the offense of violating a protection order has been committed within the limits of the jurisdiction of the agency, instrumentality, or political subdivision and reasonable cause to believe that a particular person committed the offense, to arrest the alleged offender;

(b) A provision that does not require the peace officers who serve it, if they have reasonable grounds to believe that the offense of domestic violence or the offense of violating a protection order has been committed within the limits of the jurisdiction of the agency, instrumentality, or political subdivision and reasonable cause to believe that a particular person committed the offense, to arrest the alleged offender, but that grants the officers less discretion in those circumstances in deciding whether to arrest the alleged offender than peace officers are granted by divisions (B)(1) and (B)(3) of section 2935.03 of the Revised Code.

(2) If an agency, instrumentality, or political subdivision that is served by any peace officer described in division (B)(1) of section 2935.03 of the Revised Code includes in the policy it adopts under division (A) of this section a provision of the type described in division (B)(1)(a) or (b) of this section, the peace officers who serve the agency, instrumentality, or political subdivision shall comply with the provision in making arrests authorized under division (B)(1) of section 2935.03 of the Revised Code.

(C) When a peace officer described in division (B)(1) of section 2935.03 of the Revised Code investigates a report of an alleged incident of the offense of domestic violence or an alleged incident of the offense of violating a protection order, the officer shall do all of the following:

(1) Complete a domestic violence report in accordance with division (D) of this section;

(2) Advise the victim of the availability of a temporary protection order pursuant to section 2919.26 of the Revised Code or a protection order or consent agreement pursuant to section 3113.31 of the Revised Code;

(3) Give the victim the officer's name, the officer's badge number if the officer has a badge and the badge has a number, the report number for the incident if a report number is available at the time of the officer's investigation, a telephone number that the victim can call for information about the case, the telephone number of a domestic violence shelter in the area, and information on any local victim advocate program.

(D) A peace officer who investigates a report of an alleged incident of the offense of domestic violence or an alleged incident of the offense of violating a protection order shall make a written report of the incident whether or not an arrest is made. The report shall document the officer's observations of the victim and the alleged offender, any visible injuries of the victim or alleged offender, any weapons at the scene, the actions of the alleged offender, any statements made by the victim or witnesses, and any other significant facts or circumstances. If the officer does not arrest and detain until a warrant can be obtained a person who allegedly committed the offense of domestic violence or the offense of violating a protection order when it is the preferred course of action in this state pursuant to division (B)(3)(b) of section 2935.03 of the Revised Code that the alleged offender be arrested, the officer must articulate in the report a clear statement of the officer's reasons for not arresting and detaining that alleged offender until a warrant can be obtained. The officer shall submit the written report to the law enforcement agency to which the officer has been appointed, employed, or elected.

(E) Each agency, instrumentality, or political subdivision that is required to adopt policies and procedures under division (A) of this section shall adopt those policies and procedures in conjunction and consultation with shelters in the community for victims of domestic violence and private organizations, law enforcement agencies, and other public agencies in the community that have expertise in the recognition and handling of domestic violence cases.

(F) To the extent described in and in accordance with section 9.86 or 2744.03 of the Revised Code, a peace officer who arrests an offender for the offense of violating a protection order with respect to a protection order or consent agreement of this state or another state that on its face is valid is immune from liability in a civil action for damages for injury, death, or loss to person or property that allegedly was caused by or related to the arrest.

(G) Each agency, instrumentality, or political subdivision described in division (A) of this section that arrests an offender for an alleged incident of the offense of domestic violence or an alleged incident of the offense of violating a protection order shall consider referring the case to federal authorities for prosecution under 18 U.S.C. 2261 if the incident constitutes a violation of federal law.

(H) As used in this section:

(1) "Another's unborn" has the same meaning as in section 2903.09 of the Revised Code.

(2) "Dangerous ordnance" and "deadly weapon" have the same meanings as in section 2923.11 of the Revised Code.

(3) "The offense of violating a protection order" includes the former offense of violating a protection order or consent agreement or anti-stalking protection order as set forth in section 2919.27 of the Revised Code as it existed prior to the effective date of this amendment.

(1997 S 1, eff. 10–21–97; 1994 H 335, eff. 12–9–94)

2935.04 When any person may arrest

When a felony has been committed, or there is reasonable ground to believe that a felony has been committed, any person without a warrant may arrest another whom he has reasonable cause to believe is guilty of the offense, and detain him until a warrant can be obtained.

(1953 H 1, eff. 10–1–53; GC 13432–2)

2935.041 Detention of shoplifters; rights of museums and libraries; rights of motion picture facility owner or lessee

(A) A merchant, or an employee or agent of a merchant, who has probable cause to believe that items offered for sale by a mercantile establishment have been unlawfully taken by a person, may, for the purposes set forth in division (C) of this section, detain the person in a reasonable manner for a reasonable length of time within the mercantile establishment or its immediate vicinity.

(B) Any officer, employee, or agent of a library, museum, or archival institution may, for the purposes set forth in division (C) of this section or for the purpose of conducting a reasonable investigation of a belief that the person has acted in a manner described in divisions (B)(1) and (2) of this section, detain a person in a reasonable manner for a reasonable length of time within, or in the immediate vicinity of, the library, museum, or archival institution, if the officer, employee, or agent has probable cause to believe that the person has either:

(1) Without privilege to do so, knowingly moved, defaced, damaged, destroyed, or otherwise improperly tempered with property owned by or in the custody of the library, museum, or archival institution; or

(2) With purpose to deprive the library, museum, or archival institution of property owned by it or in its custody, knowingly obtained or exerted control over the property without the consent of the owner or person authorized to give consent, beyond the scope of the express or implied consent of the owner or person authorized to give consent, by deception, or by threat.

(C) An officer, agent, or employee of a library, museum, or archival institution pursuant to division (B) of this section or a merchant or employee or agent of a merchant pursuant to division (A) of this section may detain another person for any of the following purposes:

(1) To recover the property that is the subject of the unlawful taking, criminal mischief, or theft;

(2) To cause an arrest to be made by a peace officer;

(3) To obtain a warrant of arrest.

(D) The owner or lessee of a facility in which a motion picture is being shown, or the owner's or lessee's employee or agent, who has probable cause to believe that a person is or has been operating an audiovisual recording function of a device in violation of section 2913.07 of the Revised Code may, for the purpose of causing an arrest to be made by a peace officer or of obtaining an arrest warrant, detain the person in a reasonable manner for a reasonable length of time within the facility or its immediate vicinity.

(E) The officer, agent, or employee of the library, museum, or archival institution, the merchant or employee or agent of a merchant, or the owner, lessee, employee, or agent of the facility acting under division (A), (B), or (D) of this section shall not search the person detained, search or seize any property belonging to the person detained without the person's consent, or use undue restraint upon the person detained.

(F) Any peace officer may arrest without a warrant any person that the officer has probable cause to believe has committed any act described in division (B)(1) or (2) of this section, that the officer has probable cause to believe has committed an unlawful taking in a mercantile establishment, or that the officer has reasonable cause to believe has committed an act prohibited by section 2913.07 of the Revised Code. An arrest under this division shall be made within a reasonable time after the commission of the act or unlawful taking.

(G) As used in this section:

(1) "Archival institution" means any public or private building, structure, or shelter in which are stored historical documents, devices, records, manuscripts, or items of public interest, which historical materials are stored to preserve the materials or the information in the materials, to disseminate the information contained in the materials, or to make the materials available for public inspection or for inspection by certain persons who have a particular interest in, use for, or knowledge concerning the materials.

(2) "Museum" means any public or private nonprofit institution that is permanently organized for primarily educational or aesthetic purposes, owns or borrows objects or items of public interest, and cares for and exhibits to the public the objects or items.

(3) "Audiovisual recording function" and "facility" have the same meaning as in section 2913.07 of the Revised Code.

(2003 H 179, eff. 3–9–04; 1978 H 403, eff. 7–4–78; 1969 H 49; 131 v H 395; 127 v 765)

2935.05 Affidavit filed in case of arrest without warrant

When a person named in section 2935.03 of the Revised Code has arrested a person without a warrant, he shall, without unnecessary delay, take the person arrested before a court or magistrate having jurisdiction of the offense, and shall file or cause to be filed an affidavit describing the offense for which the person was arrested. Such affidavit shall be filed either with the court or magistrate, or with the prosecuting attorney or other attorney charged by law with prosecution of crimes before such court or magistrate and if filed with such attorney he shall forthwith file with such court or magistrate a complaint, based on such affidavit.

(128 v 97, eff. 1–1–60; 1953 H 1; GC 13432–3)

2935.06 Duty of private person making arrest

A private person who has made an arrest pursuant to section 2935.04 of the Revised Code or detention pursuant to section 2935.041 of the Revised Code shall forthwith take the person arrested before the most convenient judge or clerk of a court of record or before a magistrate, or deliver such person to an officer authorized to execute criminal warrants who shall, without unnecessary delay, take such person before the court or magistrate having jurisdiction of the offense. The officer may, but if he does not, the private person shall file or cause to be filed in such court or before such magistrate an affidavit stating the offense for which the person was arrested.

(128 v 97, eff. 1–1–60; 1953 H 1; GC 13432–4)

2935.07 Person arrested without warrant shall be informed of cause of arrest

When an arrest is made without a warrant by an officer, he shall inform the person arrested of such officer's authority to make the arrest and the cause of the arrest.

When an arrest is made by a private person, he shall, before making the arrest, inform the person to be arrested of the intention to arrest him and the cause of the arrest.

When a person is engaged in the commission of a criminal offense, it is not necessary to inform him of the cause of his arrest.

(1953 H 1, eff. 10–1–53; GC 13432–5)

2935.08 Issuance of warrant

Upon the filing of an affidavit or complaint as provided in sections 2935.05 or 2935.06 of the Revised Code such judge, clerk, or magistrate shall forthwith issue a warrant to the peace officer making the arrest, or if made by a private person, to the most convenient peace officer who shall receive custody of the person arrested. All further detention and further proceedings shall be pursuant to such affidavit or complaint and warrant.

(129 v 582, eff. 1–10–61; 128 v 97; 1953 H 1; GC 13432–6)

2935.081 Administering oaths; acknowledging complaints, summonses, affidavits, and returns of court orders

(A) As used in this section, "peace officer" has the same meaning as in section 2935.01 of the Revised Code, except that "peace officer" does not include, for any purpose, the superintendent or any trooper of the state highway patrol.

(B) A peace officer who has completed a course of in-service training that includes training in the administration of oaths and the acknowledgment of documents and that is approved by the chief legal officer of the political subdivision in which the peace officer is elected or of the political subdivision or other entity in which or by which the peace officer is appointed or employed may administer oaths and acknowledge criminal and juvenile court complaints, summonses, affidavits, and returns of court orders in matters related to the peace officer's official duties.

(C) Except as authorized by division (B) of this section, no peace officer who has completed a course of in-service training of a type described in division (B) of this section shall knowingly perform any act that is specifically required of a notary public unless the peace officer has complied with Chapter 147. of the Revised Code.

(1996 H 72, eff. 3–18–97)

2935.09 Accusation by affidavit to cause arrest or prosecution

In all cases not provided by sections 2935.02 to 2935.08, inclusive, of the Revised Code, in order to cause the arrest or prosecution of a person charged with committing an offense in this state, a peace officer, or a private citizen having knowledge of the facts, shall file with the judge or clerk of a court of record, or with a magistrate, an affidavit charging the offense committed, or shall file such affidavit with the prosecuting attorney or attorney charged by law with the prosecution of offenses in court or before such magistrate, for the purpose of having a complaint filed by such prosecuting or other authorized attorney.

(128 v 97, eff. 1–1–60)

2935.10 Procedure upon filing of affidavit or complaint; withdrawal of unexecuted warrants

(A) Upon the filing of an affidavit or complaint as provided by section 2935.09 of the Revised Code, if it charges the commission of a felony, such judge, clerk, or magistrate, unless he has reason to believe that it was not filed in good faith, or the claim is not meritorious, shall forthwith issue a warrant for the arrest of the person charged in the affidavit, and directed to a peace officer; otherwise he shall forthwith refer the matter to the prosecuting attorney or other attorney charged by law with prosecution for investigation prior to the issuance of warrant.

(B) If the offense charged is a misdemeanor or violation of a municipal ordinance, such judge, clerk, or magistrate may:

(1) Issue a warrant for the arrest of such person, directed to any officer named in section 2935.03 of the Revised Code but in cases of ordinance violation only to a police officer or marshal or deputy marshal of the municipal corporation;

(2) Issue summons, to be served by a peace officer, bailiff, or court constable, commanding the person against whom the affidavit or complaint was filed to appear forthwith, or at a fixed time in the future, before such court or magistrate. Such summons shall be served in the same manner as in civil cases.

(C) If the affidavit is filed by, or the complaint is filed pursuant to an affidavit executed by, a peace officer who has, at his discretion, at the time of commission of the alleged offense, notified the person to appear before the court or magistrate at a specific time set by such officer, no process need be issued unless the defendant fails to appear at the scheduled time.

(D) Any person charged with a misdemeanor or violation of a municipal ordinance may give bail as provided in sections 2937.22 to 2937.46 of the Revised Code, for his appearance, regardless of whether a warrant, summons, or notice to appear has been issued.

(E) Any warrant, summons, or any notice issued by the peace officer shall state the substance of the charge against the person arrested or directed to appear.

(F) When the offense charged is a misdemeanor, and the warrant or summons issued pursuant to this section is not served within two years of the date of issue, a judge or magistrate may order such warrant or summons withdrawn and the case closed, when it does not appear that the ends of justice require keeping the case open.

(1972 H 511, eff. 3–23–73; 129 v 582; 128 v 97)

2935.11 Failure of person summoned to appear

If the person summoned to appear as provided in division (B) of section 2935.10 of the Revised Code fails to appear without just cause and personal service of the summons was had upon him, he may be found guilty of contempt of court, and may be fined not to exceed twenty dollars for such contempt. Upon failure to appear the court or magistrate may forthwith issue a warrant for his arrest.

(128 v 97, eff. 1–1–60)

2935.12 Forcible entry in making arrest; execution of search warrant

(A) When making an arrest or executing an arrest warrant or summons in lieu of an arrest warrant, or when executing a search warrant, the peace officer, law enforcement officer, or other authorized individual making the arrest or executing the warrant or summons may break down an outer or inner door or window of a dwelling house or other building, if, after notice of his intention to make the arrest or to execute the warrant or summons, he is refused admittance, but the law enforcement officer or other authorized individual executing a search warrant shall not enter a house or building not described in the warrant.

(B) The precondition for nonconsensual, forcible entry established by division (A) of this section is subject to waiver, as it applies to the execution of a search warrant, in accordance with section 2933.231 of the Revised Code.

(1990 S 258, eff. 11–20–90; 128 v 97)

2935.13 Proceedings upon arrest

Upon the arrest of any person pursuant to warrant, he shall forthwith be taken before the court or magistrate issuing the same, if such court be in session or such magistrate available, and proceedings had as provided in sections 2937.01 to 2937.46, inclusive, of the Revised Code. If such court be not in session and a misdemeanor or ordinance violation is charged, he shall be taken before the clerk or deputy clerk of the court and let to bail, as provided in sections 2937.22 to 2937.46, inclusive, of the Revised Code, if the magistrate be not available, or if the defendant is arrested in a county other than that of the issuing court or magistrate he shall forthwith be taken before the most convenient magistrate, clerk, or deputy clerk of a court of record, and there let to bail for his appearance before the issuing court or magistrate within a reasonable time to be set by such clerk.

(128 v 97, eff. 1–1–60)

2935.14 Rights of person arrested

If the person arrested is unable to offer sufficient bail or, if the offense charged be a felony, he shall, prior to being confined or removed from the county of arrest, as the case may be, be speedily permitted facilities to communicate with an attorney at law of his own choice, or to communicate with at least one relative or other person for the purpose of obtaining counsel (or in cases of misdemeanors or ordinance violation for the purpose of arranging bail). He shall not thereafter be confined or removed from the county or from the situs of initial detention until such attorney has had reasonable opportunity to confer with him privately, or other person to arrange bail, under such security measures as may be necessary under the circumstances.

Whoever, being a police officer in charge of a prisoner, or the custodian of any jail or place of confinement, violates this section shall be fined not less than one hundred nor more than five hundred dollars or imprisoned not more than thirty days, or both.

(128 v 97, eff. 1–1–60)

2935.15 Amount and disposition of bail

Amount of bail, and nature of security therefor in misdemeanor cases may be set by a schedule fixed by the court or magistrate, or it may be endorsed on the warrant by the magistrate or clerk of the issuing court. If the amount be not endorsed on the warrant, the schedule set by the court or magistrate before whom bail is taken shall prevail. All recognizances taken, or cash received shall be promptly transmitted to the court issuing the warrant, and further proceedings thereon shall be the same as if taken by the issuing court.

(128 v 97, eff. 1–1–60)

WARRANT AND GENERAL PROVISIONS

2935.16 Prisoners held without process

When it comes to the attention of any judge or magistrate that a prisoner is being held in any jail or place of custody in his jurisdiction without commitment from a court or magistrate, he shall forthwith, by summary process, require the officer or person in charge of such jail or place of custody to disclose to such court or magistrate, in writing, whether or not he holds the person described or identified in the process and the court under whose process the prisoner is being held. If it appears from the disclosure that the prisoner is held solely under warrant of arrest from any court or magistrate, the judge or magistrate shall order the custodian to produce the prisoner forthwith before the court or magistrate issuing the warrant and if such be impossible for any reason, to produce him before the inquiring judge or magistrate. If it appears from the disclosure that the prisoner is held without process, such judge or magistrate shall require the custodian to produce the prisoner forthwith before him, there to be charged as provided in section 2935.06 of the Revised Code.

Whoever, being the person in temporary or permanent charge of any jail or place of confinement, violates this section shall be fined not less than one hundred nor more than five hundred dollars or imprisoned not more than ninety days, or both.

(128 v 97, eff. 1–1–60)

2935.17 Affidavit forms; authority of supreme court to prescribe

(A) An affidavit in either of the following forms is sufficient:

(1) "State of Ohio,

_________ County, ss:

Before me, A.B., personally came C.D., who being duly sworn according to law deposes and says that on or about the day of _________, _____, at the county of _________ one E.F. (here describe the offense as nearly according to the nature thereof as the case will admit, in ordinary concise language) C.D.

Sworn to and subscribed before me this _____ day of _________, _____.

A.B., County Judge

Clerk of _________ Court"

(2) "State of Ohio,

_________ County, ss:

Before me, A.B., personally came C.D., who being duly sworn according to law says that on or about the day of _____, _____, one E.F. did: (here listing several common offenses, plainly but tersely described as: fail to stop at stop sign, pass at crest of grade, etc., with a ruled box before each, and then showing an X or distinctive mark in front of the offense claimed to be committed). C.D.

Sworn to before me and subscribed in my presence this _________ day of _________, _____

A.B., County Judge

Clerk of _________ Court"

(B) A complaint in the following form is sufficient:

"State of Ohio,

_________ County, ss:

The undersigned (assistant) prosecuting attorney of _________ County complains that on or about the _________ day of _________, _____, one E.F. did (here describing the offense committed as above) based on affidavit of _________ filed with me.

____

Prosecuting Attorney/City Director of Law"

Provided, that the supreme court of Ohio, may, by rule, provide for the uniform type and language to be used in any affidavit or complaint to be filed in any court inferior to the court of common pleas for violations of the motor vehicle and traffic acts and related ordinances and in any notice to violator to appear in such courts, and may require that such forms and no other, shall be received in such courts, and issued to violators.

(2000 H 495, eff. 5–9–00; 1977 H 219, eff. 11–1–77; 128 v 97)

2935.18 Contents of warrant, summons or notice

A warrant, summons, or notice of a peace officer shall either contain a copy of the affidavit or recite the substance of the accusation. A warrant shall be directed to a specific officer or to a department designated by its chief, and shall command such officer or member of department to take the accused and bring the accused forthwith before the magistrate or court issuing such warrant to be dealt with according to law. A summons shall be directed to the officer or department, and shall command the officer or department to notify the accused by serving a copy of such summons upon the accused. The following form of warrant is sufficient:

"The State of Ohio,

_________ County, ss:

To the Sheriff (other Officer):

Greetings:

Whereas there has been filed with me an affidavit of which the following is a copy (here copy) or the substance, (here set forth the substance, omitting formal parts). These are therefore to command you to take the said E.F., if E.F. is found in your county, or if E.F. is not found in your county, that you pursue after E.F. in any other county in this state and take and safely keep the said E.F. so that you have E.F. forthwith before me or some other magistrate of said county to answer the said complaint and be further dealt with according to law.

Given under my hand this _____ day of _________, _____.

A.B., Judge of _________ Court

Clerk of _________ Court"

The following form of summons is sufficient:

"The State of Ohio, ________ County, ss:

To the Bailiff or ________ Constable:

Whereas there has been filed before me an Affidavit (Complaint) of which the following is a copy (here copy) or the substance (here set forth the substance, omitting formal parts). You are commanded to summon one said E.F. to appear before me on the ____ day of ________, ____, at ____ o'clock, ___. M., at ________ Building, ________, Ohio, to answer to said charge.

You will make due return of this summons forthwith upon service.

A.B., Judge of ________ Court

Clerk of ________ Court"

(2000 H 495, eff. 5–9–00; 128 v 97, eff. 1–1–60)

2935.19 Form of affidavit

An affidavit in the form following is sufficient:

"The State of Ohio,

________ County, ss:

Before me, A.B., personally came C.D., who being duly sworn according to law, deposes and says that on or about the ____ day of ________, ____ at the county of ________, one E.F. (here describe the offense committed as nearly according to the nature thereof as the case will admit, in ordinary and concise language.)

Sworn to and subscribed before me, this ____ day of ________, ____.

A.B., Judge"

(2000 H 495, eff. 5–9–00; 127 v 1039, eff. 1–1–58; 1953 H 1; GC 13432–18)

2935.20 Right of one in custody to be visited by attorney

After the arrest, detention, or any other taking into custody of a person, with or without a warrant, such person shall be permitted forthwith facilities to communicate with an attorney at law of his choice who is entitled to practice in the courts of this state, or to communicate with any other person of his choice for the purpose of obtaining counsel. Such communication may be made by a reasonable number of telephone calls or in any other reasonable manner. Such person shall have a right to be visited immediately by any attorney at law so obtained who is entitled to practice in the courts of this state, and to consult with him privately. No officer or any other agent of this state shall prevent, attempt to prevent, or advise such person against the communication, visit, or consultation provided for by this section.

Whoever violates this section shall be fined not less than twenty-five nor more than one hundred dollars or imprisoned not more than thirty days, or both.

(131 v H 471, eff. 11–1–65)

2935.21 Security for costs

When the offense charged is a misdemeanor, the magistrate or court, before issuing the warrant, may require the complainant, or if the magistrate considers the complainant irresponsible, may require that said complainant procure a person to be liable for the costs if the complaint is dismissed, and the complainant or other person shall acknowledge himself so liable, and such court or magistrate shall enter such acknowledgment on his docket. Such bond shall not be required of an officer authorized to make arrests when in the discharge of his official duty, or other person or officer authorized to assist the prosecuting attorney in the prosecution of offenders.

(1953 H 1, eff. 10–1–53; GC 13432–20)

2935.23 Felony investigation; examination of witnesses

After a felony has been committed, and before any arrest has been made, the prosecuting attorney of the county, or any judge or magistrate, may cause subpoenas to issue, returnable before any court or magistrate, for any person to give information concerning such felony. The subpoenas shall require the witness to appear forthwith. Before such witness is required to give any information, he must be informed of the purpose of the inquiry, and that he is required to tell the truth concerning the same. He shall then be sworn and be examined under oath by the prosecuting attorney, or the court or magistrate, subject to the constitutional rights of the witness. Such examination shall be taken in writing in any form, and shall be filed with the court or magistrate taking the testimony. Witness fees shall be paid to such persons as in other cases.

(1972 H 511, eff. 1–1–74; 1953 H 1; GC 13432–22)

2935.24 Warrants transmitted by teletype or similar means

A judge of a court of record may, by an endorsement under his hand upon a warrant of arrest, authorize the service thereof by telegraph, teletype, wire photo, or other means whereby a written or facsimile copy may be transmitted, and thereafter a copy of such warrant may be sent by any such means to any law enforcement officer. Such copy is effectual in the hands of any law enforcement officer and he shall proceed in the same manner under it as though he held the orginal [sic.] warrant issued by the court making the endorsement, except that a state university law enforcement officer shall not arrest for a minor misdemeanor on the basis of a written or facsimile copy of a warrant of arrest. Every officer causing copies of warrants to be sent pursuant to this section, shall certify as correct and file in the office from which such warrant was sent, a copy of such warrant and endorsement thereon, and shall return the original with a statement of his action thereunder.

(1978 H 588, eff. 6–19–78; 1972 H 511; 1953 H 1; GC 13432–23)

2935.25 Power of arrest

Sections 2935.02 to 2935.24, inclusive, of the Revised Code do not affect or modify the power of arrest vested by law in other persons or officers than those named in section 2935.03 of the Revised Code.

(1953 H 1, eff. 10–1–53; GC 13432–24)

2935.26 When citation must be used rather than arrest; exceptions; procedures

(A) Notwithstanding any other provision of the Revised Code, when a law enforcement officer is otherwise authorized to arrest a person for the commission of a minor misdemeanor, the officer shall not arrest the person, but shall issue a citation, unless one of the following applies:

(1) The offender requires medical care or is unable to provide for his own safety.

(2) The offender cannot or will not offer satisfactory evidence of his identity.

(3) The offender refuses to sign the citation.

(4) The offender has previously been issued a citation for the commission of that misdemeanor and has failed to do one of the following:

(a) Appear at the time and place stated in the citation;

(b) Comply with division (C) of this section.

(B) The citation shall contain all of the following:

(1) The name and address of the offender;

(2) A description of the offense and the numerical designation of the applicable statute or ordinance;

(3) The name of the person issuing the citation;

(4) An order for the offender to appear at a stated time and place;

(5) A notice that the offender may comply with division (C) of this section in lieu of appearing at the stated time and place;

(6) A notice that the offender is required to do one of the following and that he may be arrested if he fails to do one of them:

(a) Appear at the time and place stated in the citation;

(b) Comply with division (C) of this section.

(C) In lieu of appearing at the time and place stated in the citation, the offender may, within seven days after the date of issuance of the citation, do either of the following:

(1) Appear in person at the office of the clerk of the court stated in the citation, sign a plea of guilty and a waiver of trial provision that is on the citation, and pay the total amount of the fine and costs;

(2) Sign the guilty plea and waiver of trial provision of the citation, and mail the citation and a check or money order for the total amount of the fine and costs to the office of the clerk of the court stated in the citation.

Remittance by mail of the fine and costs to the office of the clerk of the court stated in the citation constitutes a guilty plea and waiver of trial whether or not the quilty plea and waiver of trial provision of the citation are signed by the defendant.

(D) A law enforcement officer who issues a citation shall complete and sign the citation form, serve a copy of the completed form upon the offender and, without unnecessary delay, file the original citation with the court having jurisdiction over the offense.

(E) Each court shall establish a fine schedule that shall list the fine for each minor misdemeanor, and state the court costs. The fine schedule shall be prominently posted in the place where minor misdemeanor fines are paid.

(F) If an offender fails to appear and does not comply with division (C) of this section, the court may issue a supplemental citation, or a summons or warrant for the arrest of the offender pursuant to the Criminal Rules. Supplemental citations shall be in the form prescribed by division (B) of this section, but shall be issued and signed by the clerk of the court at which the citation directed the offender to appear and shall be served in the same manner as a summons.

(1978 S 351, eff. 10–25–78)

2935.27 Alternatives for security for appearance

(A)(1) If a law enforcement officer issues a citation to a person pursuant to section 2935.26 of the Revised Code and if the minor misdemeanor offense for which the citation is issued is an act prohibited by Chapter 4511., 4513., or 4549. of the Revised Code or an act prohibited by any municipal ordinance that is substantially similar to any section contained in Chapter 4511., 4513., or 4549. of the Revised Code, the officer shall inform the person, if the person has a current valid Ohio driver's or commercial driver's license, of the possible consequences of the person's actions as required under division (E) of this section, and also shall inform the person that the person is required either to appear at the time and place stated in the citation or to comply with division (C) of section 2935.26 of the Revised Code.

(2) If the person is an Ohio resident but does not have a current valid Ohio driver's or commercial driver's license or if the person is a resident of a state that is not a member of the nonresident violator compact of which this state is a member pursuant to section 4510.71 of the Revised Code, and if the court, by local rule, has prescribed a procedure for the setting of a reasonable security pursuant to division (F) of this section, security shall be set in accordance with that local rule and that division.

A court by local rule may prescribe a procedure for the setting of reasonable security as described in this division. As an alternative to this procedure, a court by local rule may prescribe a procedure for the setting of a reasonable security by the person without the person appearing before the court.

(B) A person who has security set under division (A)(2) of this section shall be given a receipt or other evidence of the deposit of the security by the court.

(C) Upon compliance with division (C) of section 2935.26 of the Revised Code by a person who was issued a citation, the clerk of the court shall notify the court. The court shall immediately return any sum of money, license, or other security deposited in relation to the citation to the person, or to any other person who deposited the security.

(D) If a person who has a current valid Ohio driver's or commercial driver's license and who was issued a citation fails to appear at the time and place specified on the citation, fails to comply with division (C) of section 2935.26 of the Revised Code, or fails to comply with or satisfy any judgment of the court within the time allowed by the court, the court shall declare the forfeiture of the person's license. Thirty days after the declaration of forfeiture, the court shall enter information relative to the forfeiture on a form approved and furnished by the registrar of motor vehicles, and forward the form to the registrar. The registrar shall suspend the person's driver's or commercial driver's license, send written notification of the suspension to the person at the person's last known address, and order the person to surrender the person's driver's or commercial driver's license to the registrar within forty-eight hours. No valid driver's or commercial driver's license shall be granted to the person until the court having jurisdiction of the offense that led to the forfeiture orders that the forfeiture be terminated. The court shall so order if the person, after having failed to appear in court at the required time and place to answer the charge or after having pleaded guilty to or been found guilty of the violation and having failed within the time allowed by the court to pay the fine imposed by the court, thereafter appears to answer the charge and pays any fine imposed by the court or pays the fine originally imposed by the court. The court shall inform the registrar of the termination of the forfeiture by entering information relative to the termination on a form approved and furnished by the registrar and sending the form to the registrar as provided in this division. The person shall pay to the bureau of motor vehicles a fifteen-dollar reinstatement fee to cover the costs of the bureau in administering this section. The registrar shall deposit the fees so paid into the state bureau of motor vehicles fund created by section 4501.25 of the Revised Code.

In addition, upon receipt of the copy of the declaration of forfeiture from the court, neither the registrar nor any deputy registrar shall accept any application for the registration or transfer of registration of any motor vehicle owned or leased by the person named in the declaration of forfeiture until the court having jurisdiction of the offense that led to the forfeiture orders that the forfeiture be terminated. However, for a motor vehicle leased by a person named in a declaration of forfeiture, the registrar shall not implement the preceding sentence until the registrar adopts procedures for that implementation under section 4503.39 of the Revised Code. Upon receipt by the registrar of an order terminating the forfeiture, the registrar shall take such measures as may be necessary to permit the person to register a motor vehicle owned or leased by the person or to transfer the registration of such a motor vehicle, if the person later makes application to take such action and the person otherwise is eligible to register the motor vehicle or to transfer the registration of it.

The registrar is not required to give effect to any declaration of forfeiture or order terminating a forfeiture unless the order is transmitted to the registrar by means of an electronic transfer system. The registrar shall not restore the person's driving or vehicle registration privileges until the person pays the reinstatement fee as provided in this division.

If the person who was issued the citation fails to appear at the time and place specified on the citation and fails to comply with division (C) of section 2935.26 of the Revised Code and the person has deposited a sum of money or other security in relation to the citation under division (A)(2) of this section, the deposit immediately shall be forfeited to the court.

This section does not preclude further action as authorized by division (F) of section 2935.26 of the Revised Code.

(E) A law enforcement officer who issues a person a minor misdemeanor citation for an act prohibited by Chapter 4511., 4513., or 4549. of the Revised Code or an act prohibited by a municipal ordinance that is substantially similar to any section contained in Chapter 4511., 4513., or 4549. of the Revised Code shall inform the person that if the person does not appear at the time and place stated on the citation or does not comply with division (C) of section 2935.26 of the Revised Code, the person's driver's or commercial driver's license will be suspended, the person will not be eligible for the reissuance of the license or the issuance of a new license or the issuance of a certificate of registration for a motor vehicle owned or leased by the person, until the person appears and complies with all orders of the court. The person also is subject to any applicable criminal penalties.

(F) A court setting security under division (A)(2) of this section shall do so in conformity with sections 2937.22 and 2937.23 of the Revised Code and the Rules of Criminal Procedure.

(2004, H 230, eff. 9–16–04; 2002 S 123, eff. 1–1–04; 1997 S 85, eff. 5–15–97; 1996 S 121, eff. 11–19–96; 1996 H 353, eff. 9–17–96; 1994 H 687, eff. 10–12–94; 1993 S 62, § 4, eff. 9–1–93; 1992 S 275; 1990 S 338; 1989 H 381; 1986 S 356; 1978 S 351)

2935.28 Property owners to be provided with names of persons charged with damaging their property

(A) As used in this section, "motor vehicle" has the same meaning as in section 4501.01 of the Revised Code.

(B) If damage is caused to real property by the operation of a motor vehicle in, or during the, violation of any section of the Revised Code or of any municipal ordinance, the law enforcement agency that investigates the case, upon request of the real property owner, shall provide the owner with the names of the persons who are charged with the commission of the offense. If a request for the names is made, the agency shall provide the names as soon as possible after the persons are charged with the offense.

(C) The personnel of law enforcement agencies who act pursuant to division (B) of this section in good faith are not liable in damages in a civil action allegedly arising from their actions taken pursuant to that division. Political subdivisions and the state are not liable in damages in a civil action allegedly arising from the actions of personnel of their law enforcement agencies if the personnel have immunity under this division.

(1984 H 666, eff. 3–14–85)

2935.29 Definition of fresh pursuit and state

As used in sections 2935.30 and 2935.31 of the Revised Code:

(A) "Fresh pursuit" includes fresh pursuit as defined by the common law, and also the pursuit of a person who has committed a felony or who is reasonably suspected of having committed a felony. It includes the pursuit of a person suspected of having committed a supposed felony, though no felony has actually been committed, if there is reasonable ground for believing that a felony has been committed. Fresh pursuit does not necessarily imply instant pursuit, but pursuit without unreasonable delay.

(B) "State" includes the District of Columbia.

(1953 H 1, eff. 10–1–53; GC 13434–7, 13434–8)

2935.30 Authority of foreign police

Any member of an organized state, county, or municipal peace unit of another state of the United States who enters this state in fresh pursuit, and continues within this state in such fresh pursuit, of a person in order to arrest him on the ground that he is believed to have committed a felony in such other state has the same authority to arrest and hold such person in custody as has any member of any organized state, county, or municipal peace unit of this state to arrest and hold in custody a person on the ground that he is believed to have committed a felony in this state.

This section does not make unlawful any arrest in this state which would otherwise be lawful.

(1953 H 1, eff. 10–1–53; GC 13434–4, 13434–6)

2935.31 Hearing before magistrate in county of arrest

If an arrest is made in this state by an officer of another state under section 2935.30 of the Revised Code, he shall without unnecessary delay take the person arrested before a magistrate of the county in which the arrest was made, who shall conduct a hearing for the purpose of determining the lawfulness of the arrest. If the magistrate determines that the arrest was lawful be [1] shall commit the person arrested to await for a reasonable time the issuance of an extradition warrant by the governor of this state, or admit him to bail for such purposes. If the magistrate determines that the arrest was unlawful he shall discharge the person arrested.

(1953 H 1, eff. 10–1–53; GC 13434–5)

1 So in original; should this read "he"?

2935.32 Broadcasting information of crime

The board of county commissioners or the prosecuting attorney of any county, with the consent of the court of common pleas, may contract with any company engaged in broadcasting by radio, for the purpose of immediate broadcasting of information concerning any violent felony, when the perpetrator thereof has escaped. The sheriff and heads of police departments, immediately upon the commission of any such felony and the escape of such perpetrator, shall furnish all information concerning said crime and the perpetrator thereof, to said company with which such contract may be made, for the purpose of broadcasting. The reasonable cost of such broadcasting shall be paid by the county, out of the county treasury, on the order of the board.

(1953 H 1, eff. 10–1–53; GC 13431–1)

2935.33 Commitment of alcoholics and intoxicated persons

(A) If a person charged with a misdemeanor is taken before a judge of a court of record and if it appears to the judge that the person is an alcoholic or is suffering from acute alcohol intoxication and that the person would benefit from services provided by an alcohol and drug addiction program certified under Chapter 3793. of the Revised Code, the judge may place the person temporarily in a program certified under that chapter in the area in which the court has jurisdiction for inpatient care and treatment for an indefinite period not exceeding five days. The commitment does not limit the right to release on bail. The judge may dismiss a charge of a violation of division (B) of section 2917.11 of the Revised Code or of a municipal ordinance substantially equivalent to that division if the defendant complies with all the conditions of treatment ordered by the court.

The court may order that any fines or court costs collected by the court from defendants who have received inpatient care from an alcohol and drug addiction program be paid, for the benefit of the program, to the board of alcohol, drug addiction, and mental health services of the alcohol, drug addiction, and mental health service district in which the program is located or to the director of alcohol and drug addiction services.

(B) If a person is being sentenced for a violation of division (B) of section 2917.11 or section 4511.19 of the Revised Code, a misdemeanor violation of section 2919.25 of the Revised Code, a misdemeanor violation of section 2919.27 of the Revised Code involving a protection order issued or consent agreement approved pursuant to section 2919.26 or 3113.31 of the Revised Code, or a violation of a municipal ordinance substantially equivalent to that division or any of those sections and if it appears to the judge at the time of sentencing that the person is an alcoholic or is suffering from acute alcohol intoxication and that, in lieu of imprisonment, the person would benefit from services provided by an alcohol and drug addiction program certified under Chapter 3793. of the Revised Code, the court may commit the person to close supervision in any facility in the area in which the court has jurisdiction that is, or is operated by, such a program. Such close supervision may include outpatient services and part-time release, except that a person convicted of a violation of division (A) of section 4511.19 of the Revised Code shall be confined to the facility for at least three days and except that a person convicted of a misdemeanor violation of section 2919.25 of the Revised Code, a misdemeanor violation of section 2919.27 of the Revised Code involving a protection order issued or consent agreement approved pursuant to section 2919.26 or 3113.31 of the Revised Code, or a violation of a substantially equivalent municipal ordinance shall be confined to the facility in accordance with the order of commitment. A commitment of a person to a facility for purposes of close supervision shall not exceed the maximum term for which the person could be imprisoned.

(C) A law enforcement officer who finds a person subject to prosecution for violation of division (B) of section 2917.11 of the Revised Code or a municipal ordinance substantially equivalent to that division and who has reasonable cause to believe that the person is an alcoholic or is suffering from acute alcohol intoxication and would benefit from immediate treatment immediately may place the person in an alcohol and drug addiction program certified under Chapter 3793. of the Revised Code in the area in which the person is found, for emergency treatment, in lieu of other arrest procedures, for a maximum period of forty-eight hours. During that time, if the person desires to leave such custody, the person shall be released forthwith.

(D) As used in this section:

(1) "Alcoholic" has the same meaning as in section 3793.01 of the Revised Code;

(2) "Acute alcohol intoxication" means a heavy consumption of alcohol over a relatively short period of time, resulting in dysfunction of the brain centers controlling behavior, speech, and memory and causing characteristic withdrawal symptoms.

(2002 H 490, eff. 1–1–04; 1995 S 2, eff. 7–1–96; 1994 S 82, eff. 5–4–94; 1989 H 317, eff. 10–10–89; 1985 H 475; 1984 H 37; 1976 H 907; 1975 H 1; 1972 H 240)

2935.36 Pre–trial diversion programs for adult offenders; limits; procedure

(A) The prosecuting attorney may establish pre-trial diversion programs for adults who are accused of committing criminal offenses and whom the prosecuting attorney believes probably will not offend again. The prosecuting attorney may require, as a condition of an accused's participation in the program, the accused to pay a reasonable fee for supervision services that include, but are not limited to, monitoring and drug testing. The programs shall be operated pursuant to written standards approved by journal entry by the presiding judge or, in courts with only one judge, the judge of the court of common pleas and shall not be applicable to any of the following:

(1) Repeat offenders or dangerous offenders;

(2) Persons accused of an offense of violence, of a violation of section 2903.06, 2907.04, 2907.05, 2907.21, 2907.22, 2907.31, 2907.32, 2907.34, 2911. 31, 2919.12, 2919.13, 2919.22, 2921.02, 2921.11, 2921.12, 2921.32, or 2923.20 of the Revised Code, or of a violation of section 2905.01, 2905.02, or 2919.23 of the Revised Code that, had it occurred prior to July 1, 1996, would have been a violation of section 2905.04 of the Revised Code as it existed prior to that date, with the exception that the prosecuting attorney may permit persons accused of any such offense to enter a pre-trial diversion program, if the prosecuting attorney finds any of the following:

(a) The accused did not cause, threaten, or intend serious physical harm to any person;

(b) The offense was the result of circumstances not likely to recur;

(c) The accused has no history of prior delinquency or criminal activity;

(d) The accused has led a law-abiding life for a substantial time before commission of the alleged offense;

(e) Substantial grounds tending to excuse or justify the alleged offense.

(3) Persons accused of a violation of Chapter 2925. or 3719. of the Revised Code;

(4) Drug dependent persons or persons in danger of becoming drug dependent persons, as defined in section 3719.011 of the Revised Code. However, this division does not affect the eligibility of such persons for intervention in lieu of conviction pursuant to section 2951.041 of the Revised Code.

(5) Persons accused of a violation of section 4511.19 of the Revised Code or a violation of any substantially similar municipal ordinance.

(B) An accused who enters a diversion program shall do all of the following:

(1) Waive, in writing and contingent upon the accused's successful completion of the program, the accused's right to a speedy trial, the preliminary hearing, the time period within which the grand jury may consider an indictment against the accused, and arraignment, unless the hearing, indictment, or arraignment has already occurred;

(2) Agree, in writing, to the tolling while in the program of all periods of limitation established by statutes or rules of court, that are applicable to the offense with which the accused is charged and to the conditions of the diversion program established by the prosecuting attorney;

(3) Agree, in writing, to pay any reasonable fee for supervision services established by the prosecuting attorney.

(C) The trial court, upon the application of the prosecuting attorney, shall order the release from confinement of any accused who has agreed to enter a pre-trial diversion program and shall discharge and release any existing bail and release any sureties on recognizances and shall release the accused on a recognizance bond conditioned upon the accused's compliance with the terms of the diversion program. The prosecuting attorney shall notify every victim of the crime and the arresting officers of the prosecuting attorney's intent to permit the accused to enter a pre-trial diversion program. The victim of the crime and the arresting officers shall have the opportunity to file written objections with the prosecuting attorney prior to the commencement of the pre-trial diversion program.

(D) If the accused satisfactorily completes the diversion program, the prosecuting attorney shall recommend to the trial court that the charges against the accused be dismissed, and the court, upon the recommendation of the prosecuting attorney, shall dismiss the charges. If the accused chooses not to enter the prosecuting attorney's diversion program, or if the accused violates the conditions of the agreement pursuant to which the accused has been released, the accused may be brought to trial upon the charges in the manner provided by law, and the waiver executed pursuant to division (B)(1) of this section shall be void on the date the accused is removed from the program for the violation.

(E) As used in this section:

(1) "Repeat offender" means a person who has a history of persistent criminal activity and whose character and condition reveal a substantial risk that the person will commit another offense. It is prima-facie evidence that a person is a repeat offender if any of the following applies:

(a) Having been convicted of one or more offenses of violence and having been imprisoned pursuant to sentence for any such offense, the person commits a subsequent offense of violence;

(b) Having been convicted of one or more sexually oriented offenses or child-victim oriented offenses, both as defined in section 2950.01 of the Revised Code, and having been imprisoned pursuant to sentence for one or more of those offenses, the person commits a subsequent sexually oriented offense or child-victim oriented offense;

(c) Having been convicted of one or more theft offenses as defined in section 2913.01 of the Revised Code and having been imprisoned pursuant to sentence for one or more of those theft offenses, the person commits a subsequent theft offense;

(d) Having been convicted of one or more felony drug abuse offenses as defined in section 2925.01 of the Revised Code and having been imprisoned pursuant to sentence for one or more of those felony drug abuse offenses, the person commits a subsequent felony drug abuse offense;

(e) Having been convicted of two or more felonies and having been imprisoned pursuant to sentence for one or more felonies, the person commits a subsequent offense;

(f) Having been convicted of three or more offenses of any type or degree other than traffic offenses, alcoholic intoxication offenses, or minor misdemeanors and having been imprisoned pursuant to sentence for any such offense, the person commits a subsequent offense.

(2) "Dangerous offender" means a person who has committed an offense, whose history, character, and condition reveal a substantial risk that the person will be a danger to others, and whose conduct has been characterized by a pattern of repetitive, compulsive, or aggressive behavior with heedless indifference to the consequences.

(2003 S 5, eff. 7–31–03; 2003 H 95, eff. 9–26–03; 1999 S 107, eff. 3–23–00; 1996 H 180, eff. 7–1–97; 1995 S 2, eff. 7–1–96; 1994 S 82, eff. 5–4–94; 1986 S 262, eff. 3–20–87; 1978 H 473)

CHAPTER 2937

PRELIMINARY EXAMINATION; BAIL

PRELIMINARY EXAMINATION

BAIL

PRELIMINARY EXAMINATION

2937.01 Definitions

The definition of "magistrate" set forth in section 2931.01 of the Revised Code, and the definitions of "peace officer," "prosecutor," and "offense" set forth in section 2935.01 of the Revised Code apply to Chapter 2937. of the Revised Code.

(128 v 97, eff. 1–1–60; 1953 H 1)

2937.02 Announcement of charge and rights of accused by court

When, after arrest, the accused is taken before a court or magistrate, or when the accused appears pursuant to terms of summons or notice, the affidavit or complaint being first filed, the court or magistrate shall, before proceeding further:

(A) Inform the accused of the nature of the charge against him and the identity of the complainant and permit the accused or his counsel to see and read the affidavit or complaint or a copy thereof;

(B) Inform the accused of his right to have counsel and the right to a continuance in the proceedings to secure counsel;

(C) Inform the accused of the effect of pleas of guilty, not guilty, and no contest, of his right to trial by jury, and the necessity of making written demand therefor;

(D) If the charge be a felony, inform the accused of the nature and extent of possible punishment on conviction and of the right to preliminary hearing. Such information may be given to each accused individually or, if at any time there exists any substantial number of defendants to be arraigned at the same session, the judge or magistrate may, by general announcement or by distribution of printed matter, advise all those accused concerning those rights general in their nature, and informing as to individual matters at arraignment.

(128 v 97, eff. 1–1–60)

2937.03 Arraignment; counsel; bail

After the announcement, as provided by section 2937.02 of the Revised Code, the accused shall be arraigned by the magistrate, clerk, or prosecutor of the court reading the affidavit or complaint, or reading its substance, omitting purely formal parts, to the accused unless the reading of the affidavit or complaint is waived. The judge or magistrate shall then inquire of the accused whether the accused understands the nature of the charge. If the accused does not indicate understanding, the judge or magistrate shall give explanation in terms of the statute or ordinance claimed violated. If the accused is not represented by counsel and expresses a desire to consult with an attorney at law, the judge or magistrate shall continue the case for a reasonable time to allow the accused to send for or consult with counsel and shall set bail for the later appearance if the offense is bailable. If the accused is not able to make bail, bail is denied, or the offense is not bailable, the court or magistrate shall require the officer having custody of the accused immediately to take a message to any attorney at law within the municipal corporation where the accused is detained, or immediately to make available to the accused use of a telephone for calling to arrange for legal counsel or bail.

(1999 S 8, eff. 7–29–99; 129 v 582, eff. 1–10–61; 128 v 97)

2937.04 Motion for dismissal

If accused does not desire counsel or, having engaged counsel, appears at the end of granted continuance, he may then raise, by motion to dismiss the affidavit or complaint, any exception thereto which could be asserted against an indictment or information by motion to quash, plea in abatement, or demurrer. Such motion may be made orally and ruled upon by the court or magistrate at the time of presentation, with minute of motion and ruling made in the journal (if a court of record) or on the docket (if a court not of record) or such motion may be presented in writing and set down for argument at later time. Where the motion attacks a defect in the record by facts extrinsic thereto, proof may be offered by testimony or affidavit.

(128 v 97, eff. 1–1–60)

2937.05 Discharge on motion to dismiss; amendment of complaint

If the motion pursuant to section 2937.04 of the Revised Code be sustained, accused shall be discharged unless the court or magistrate finds that the defect can be corrected without changing the nature of the charge, in which case he may order the complaint amended or a proper affidavit filed forthwith and require the accused to plead thereto. The discharge of accused upon the sustaining of a motion to dismiss shall not be considered a bar to further prosecution either of felony or misdemeanor.

(128 v 97, eff. 1–1–60)

2937.06 Pleas

(A) After all motions are disposed of or if no motion is presented, the court or magistrate shall require the accused to plead to the charge.

(1) In cases of felony, only a plea of not guilty or a written plea of guilty shall be received and if the defendant declines to plead, a plea of not guilty shall be entered for the defendant and further proceedings had as set forth in sections 2937.09 to 2937.12 of the Revised Code.

(2) In cases of misdemeanor, the following pleas may be received:

(a) Guilty;

(b) Not guilty;

(c) No contest;

(d) Once in jeopardy, which includes the defenses of former conviction or former acquittal.

(B) Prior to accepting a plea of guilty or a plea of no contest under division (A) of this section, the court shall comply with sections 2943.031 and 2943.032 of the Revised Code.

(C) Entry of any plea pursuant to this section shall constitute a waiver of any objection that could be taken advantage of by motion pursuant to section 2937.04 of the Revised Code.

(1995 S 2, eff. 7–1–96; 1989 S 95, eff. 10–2–89; 128 v 97)

2937.07 Action on pleas of "guilty" and "no contest" in misdemeanor cases

If the offense is a misdemeanor and the accused pleads guilty to the offense, the court or magistrate shall receive and enter the plea unless the court or magistrate believes that it was made through fraud, collusion, or mistake. If the court or magistrate so believes, the court or magistrate shall enter a plea of not guilty and set the matter for trial pursuant to Chapter 2938. of the Revised Code. Upon receiving a plea of guilty, the court or magistrate shall call for an explanation of the circumstances of the offense from the affiant or complainant or the affiant's or complainant's representatives. After hearing the explanation of circumstances, together with any statement of the accused, the court or magistrate shall proceed to pronounce the sentence or shall continue the matter for the purpose of imposing the sentence.

A plea to a misdemeanor offense of "no contest" or words of similar import shall constitute a stipulation that the judge or magistrate may make a finding of guilty or not guilty from the explanation of the circumstances of the offense. If a finding of guilty is made, the judge or magistrate shall impose the sentence or continue the case for sentencing accordingly. A plea of "no contest" or words of similar import shall not be construed as an admission of any fact at issue in the criminal charge in any subsequent civil or criminal action or proceeding.

(2002 H 490, eff. 1–1–04; 128 v 97, eff. 1–1–60)

2937.08 Action on pleas of "not guilty" or "once in jeopardy" in misdemeanor cases

Upon a plea of not guilty or a plea of once in jeopardy, if the charge be a misdemeanor in a court of record, the court shall proceed to set the matter for trial at a future time, pursuant to Chapter 2938. of the Revised Code, and shall let accused to bail pending such trial. Or he may, but only if both prosecutor and accused expressly consent, set the matter for trial forthwith.

Upon the entry of such pleas to a charge of misdemeanor in a court not of record, the magistrate shall forthwith set the matter for future trial or, with the consent of both state and defendant may set trial forthwith, both pursuant to Chapter 2938. of the Revised Code, provided that if the nature of the offense is such that right to jury trial exists, such matter shall not be tried before him unless the accused, by writing subscribed by him, waives a jury and consents to be tried by the magistrate.

If the defendant in such event does not waive right to jury trial, then the magistrate shall require the accused to enter into recognizance to appear before a court of record in the county, set by such magistrate, and the magistrate shall thereupon certify all papers filed, together with transcript of proceedings and accrued costs to date, and such recognizance if given, to such designated court of record. Such transfer shall not require the filing of indictment or information and trial shall proceed in the transferee court pursuant to Chapter 2938. of the Revised Code.

(128 v 97, eff. 1–1–60)

2937.09 Procedure in felony cases

If the charge is a felony, the court or magistrate shall, before receiving a plea of guilty, advise the accused that such plea constitutes an admission which may be used against him at a later trial. If the defendant enters a written plea of guilty or, pleading not guilty, affirmatively waives the right to have the court or magistrate take evidence concerning the offense, the court or magistrate forthwith and without taking evidence may find that the crime has been committed and that there is probable and reasonable cause to hold the defendant for trial pursuant to indictment by the grand jury, and, if the offense is bailable, require the accused to enter into recognizance in such amount as it determines to appear before the court of common pleas pursuant to indictment, otherwise to be confined until the grand jury has considered and reported the matter.

(129 v 582, eff. 1–10–61; 128 v 97)

2937.10 Hearing set in felony cases

If the charge be a felony and there be no written plea of guilty or waiver of examination, or the court or magistrate refuses to receive such waiver, the court or magistrate, with the consent of the prosecutor and the accused, may set the matter for hearing forthwith, otherwise he shall set the matter for hearing at a fixed time in the future and shall notify both prosecutor and defendant promptly of such time of hearing.

(128 v 97, eff. 1–1–60)

2937.11 Presentation of state's case; videotaped or recorded testimony of child victims

(A)(1) As used in this section, "victim" includes any person who was a victim of a felony violation identified in division (B) of this section or a felony offense of violence or against whom was directed any conduct that constitutes, or that is an element of, a felony violation identified in division (B) of this section or a felony offense of violence.

(2) At the preliminary hearing set pursuant to section 2937.10 of the Revised Code and the Criminal Rules, the prosecutor may state, but is not required to state, orally the case for the state and shall then proceed to examine witnesses and introduce exhibits for the state. The accused and the magistrate have full right of cross examination, and the accused has the right of inspection of exhibits prior to their introduction. The hearing shall be conducted under the rules of evidence prevailing in criminal trials generally. On motion of either the state or the accused, witnesses shall be separated and not permitted in the hearing room except when called to testify.

(B) In a case involving an alleged felony violation of section 2905.05, 2907.02, 2907.03, 2907.04, 2907.05, 2907.21, 2907.24, 2907.31, 2907.32, 2907.321, 2907.322, 2907.323, or 2919.22 of the Revised Code or an alleged felony offense of violence and in which an alleged victim of the alleged violation or offense was less than thirteen years of age when the complaint or information was filed, whichever occurred earlier, upon motion of the prosecution, the testimony of the child victim at the preliminary hearing may be taken in a room other than the room in which the preliminary hearing is being conducted and be televised, by closed circuit equipment, into the room in which the preliminary hearing is being conducted, in accordance with division (C) of section 2945.481 of the Revised Code.

(C) In a case involving an alleged felony violation listed in division (B) of this section or an alleged felony offense of violence and in which an alleged victim of the alleged violation or offense was less than thirteen years of age when the complaint or information was filed, whichever occurred earlier, the court, on written motion of the prosecutor in the case filed at least three days prior to the hearing, shall order that all testimony of the child victim be recorded and preserved on videotape, in addition to being recorded for purposes of the transcript of the proceeding. If such an order is issued, it shall specifically identify the child victim concerning whose testimony it pertains, apply only during the testimony of the child victim it specifically identifies, and apply to all testimony of the child victim presented at the hearing, regardless of whether the child victim is called as a witness by the prosecution or by the defense.

(1997 S 53, eff. 10–14–97; 1996 H 445, eff. 9–3–96; 1986 H 108, eff. 10–14–86; 128 v 97)

2937.12 Motion for discharge; presentation on behalf of accused; finding of court

(A) At the conclusion of the presentation of the state's case accused may move for discharge for failure of proof or may offer evidence on his own behalf. Prior to the offering of evidence on behalf of the accused, unless accused is then represented by counsel, the court or magistrate shall advise accused:

(1) That any testimony of witnesses offered by him in the proceeding may, if unfavorable in any particular, be used against him at later trial;

(2) That accused himself may make a statement, not under oath, regarding the charge, for the purpose of explaining the facts in evidence;

(3) That he may refuse to make any statement and such refusal may not be used against him at trials;

(4) That any statement he makes may be used against him at trial.

(B) Upon conclusion of all the evidence and the statement, if any, of the accused, the court or magistrate shall either:

(1) Find that the crime alleged has been committed and that there is probable and reasonable cause to hold or recognize defendant to appear before the court of common pleas of the county or any other county in which venue appears, for trial pursuant to indictment by grand jury;

(2) Find that there is probable cause to hold or recognize defendant to appear before the court of common pleas for trial pursuant to indictment or information on such other charge, felony or misdemeanor, as the evidence indicates was committed by accused;

(3) Find that a misdemeanor was committed and there is probable cause to recognize accused to appear before himself or some other court inferior to the court of common pleas for trial upon such charge;

(4) Order the accused discharged from custody.

(128 v 97, eff. 1–1–60)

2937.13 Basis for finding; no appeal; further prosecution

In entering a finding, pursuant to section 2937.12 of the Revised Code, the court, while weighing credibility of witnesses, shall not be required to pass on the weight of the evidence and any finding requiring accused to stand trial on any charge shall be based solely on the presence of substantial credible evidence thereof. No appeal shall lie from such decision nor shall the discharge of defendant be a bar to further prosecution by indictment or otherwise.

(128 v 97, eff. 1–1–60)

2937.14 Entry of reason for change in charge

In any case in which accused is held or recognized to appear for trial on any charge other than the one on which he was arraigned the court or magistrate shall enter the reason for such charge on the journal of the court (if a court of record) or on the docket (if a court not of record) and shall file with the papers in the case the text of the charge found by him to be sustained by the evidence.

(128 v 97, eff. 1–1–60)

2937.15 Transcript of proceedings

Upon the conclusion of the hearing and finding, the magistrate, or if a court of record, the clerk of such court, shall complete all notations of appearance, motions, pleas, and findings on the criminal docket of the court, and shall transmit a transcript of the appearance docket entries, together with a copy of the original complaint and affidavits, if any, filed with the complaint, the journal or docket entry of reason for changes in the charge, if any, together with the order setting bail and the bail deposit, if any, filed, and together with the videotaped testimony, if any, prepared in accordance with division (C) of section 2937.11 of the Revised Code, to the clerk of the court in which the accused is to appear. Such transcript shall contain an itemized account of the costs accrued.

(1986 H 108, eff. 10–14–86; 128 v 97)

2937.16 When witnesses shall be recognized to appear

When an accused enters into a recognizance or is committed in default thereof, the judge or magistrate shall require such witnesses against the prisoner as he finds necessary, to enter into a recognizance to appear and testify before the proper court at a proper time, and not depart from such court without leave. If the judge or magistrate finds it necessary he may require such witnesses to give sufficient surety to appear at such court.

(1953 H 1, eff. 10–1–53; GC 13433–15)

2937.17 Recognizance for minor

A person may be liable in a recognizance for a minor to appear as a witness, or the judge or magistrate may take the minor's recognizance, in a sufficient sum, which is valid notwithstanding the disability of minority.

(1953 H 1, eff. 10–1–53; GC 13433–16)

2937.18 Detention of material witnesses

If a witness ordered to give recognizance fails to comply with such order, the judge or magistrate shall commit him to such custody or open or close detention as may be appropriate under the circumstances, until he complies with the order or is discharged. Commitment of the witness may be to the custody of any suitable person or public or private agency, or to an appropriate detention facility other than a jail, or to a jail, but the witness shall not be confined in association with prisoners charged with or convicted of crime. The witness, in lieu of the fee ordinarily allowed witnesses, shall be allowed twenty-five dollars for each day of custody or detention under such order, and shall be allowed mileage as provided for other witnesses, calculated on the distance from his home to the place of giving testimony and return. All proceedings in the case or cases in which the witness is held to appear shall be given priority over other cases and had with all due speed.

(1972 H 511, eff. 3–23–73; 1953 H 1; GC 13433–17)

2937.19 Subpoena of witnesses or documents

The magistrate or judge or clerk of the court in which proceedings are being had may issue subpoenas or other process to bring witnesses or documents before the magistrate or court in hearings pending before him either under Chapter 2937. or 2938. of the Revised Code.

In complaints to keep the peace a subpoena must be served within the county, or, in cases of misdemeanors and ordinance offenses, it may be served at any place in this state within one hundred miles of the place where the court or magistrate is scheduled to sit; in felony cases it may be served at any place within this state. In cases where such process is to be served outside the county, it may be issued to be served either by the bailiff or constable of the court or by a sheriff or police officer either by the county in which the court or magistrate sits or in which process is to be served.

(129 v 582, eff. 1–10–61; 128 v 97)

2937.21 Continuance

No continuance at any stage of the proceeding, including that for determination of a motion, shall extend for more than ten days unless both the state and the accused consent thereto. Any continuance or delay in ruling contrary to the provisions of this section shall, unless procured by defendant or his counsel, be grounds for discharge of the defendant forthwith.

(128 v 97, eff. 1–1–60)

BAIL

2937.22 Forms of bail; receipts

Bail is security for the appearance of an accused to appear and answer to a specific criminal or quasi-criminal charge in any court or before any magistrate at a specific time or at any time to which a case may be continued, and not depart without leave. It may take any of the following forms:

(A) The deposit of cash by the accused or by some other person for him;

(B) The deposit by the accused or by some other person for him in form of bonds of the United States, this state, or any political subdivision thereof in a face amount equal to the sum set by the court or magistrate. In case of bonds not negotiable by delivery such bonds shall be properly endorsed for transfer.

(C) The written undertaking by one or more persons to forfeit the sum of money set by the court or magistrate, if the accused is in default for appearance, which shall be known as a recognizance.

All bail shall be received by the clerk of the court, deputy clerk of court, or by the magistrate, or by a special referee appointed by the supreme court pursuant to section 2937.46 of the Revised Code, and, except in cases of recognizances, receipt shall be given therefor by him.

(128 v 97, eff. 1–1–60)

2937.221 Use of driver's or commercial driver's license as bond in certain traffic violation arrests

(A) A person arrested without warrant for any violation listed in division (B) of this section, and having a current valid Ohio driver's or commercial driver's license, if the person has been notified of the possible consequences of the person's actions as required by division (C) of this section, may post bond by depositing the license with the arresting officer if the officer and person so choose, or with the local court having jurisdiction if the court and person so choose. The license may be used as bond only during the period for which it is valid.

When an arresting officer accepts the driver's or commercial driver's license as bond, the officer shall note the date, time, and place of the court appearance on "the violator's notice to appear," and the notice shall serve as a valid Ohio driver's or commercial driver's license until the date and time appearing thereon. The arresting officer immediately shall forward the license to the appropriate court.

When a local court accepts the license as bond or continues the case to another date and time, it shall provide the person with a card in a form approved by the registrar of motor vehicles setting forth the license number, name, address, the date and time of the court appearance, and a statement that the license is being held as bond. The card shall serve as a valid license until the date and time contained in the card.

The court may accept other bond at any time and return the license to the person. The court shall return the license to the person when judgment is satisfied, including, but not limited to, compliance with any court orders, unless a suspension or cancellation is part of the penalty imposed.

Neither "the violator's notice to appear" nor a court- granted card shall continue driving privileges beyond the expiration date of the license.

If the person arrested fails to appear in court at the date and time set by the court or fails to satisfy the judgment of the court, including, but not limited to, compliance with all court orders within the time allowed by the court, the court may declare the forfeiture of the person's license. Thirty days after the declaration of the forfeiture, the court shall forward the person's license to the registrar. The court also shall enter information relative to the forfeiture on a form approved and furnished by the registrar and send the form to the registrar. The registrar shall suspend the person's license and send written notification of the suspension to the person at the person's last known address. No valid driver's or commercial driver's license shall be granted to the person until the court having jurisdiction orders that the forfeiture be terminated. The court shall inform the registrar of the termination of the forfeiture by entering information relative to the termination on a form approved and furnished by the registrar and sending the form to the registrar. Upon the termination, the person shall pay to the bureau of motor vehicles a reinstatement fee of fifteen dollars to cover the costs of the bureau in administering this section. The registrar shall deposit the fees so paid into the state bureau of motor vehicles fund created by section 4501.25 of the Revised Code.

In addition, upon receipt from the court of the copy of the declaration of forfeiture, neither the registrar nor any deputy registrar shall accept any application for the registration or transfer of registration of any motor vehicle owned by or leased in the name of the person named in the declaration of forfeiture until the court having jurisdiction over the offense that led to the suspension issues an order terminating the forfeiture. However, for a motor vehicle leased in the name of a person named in a declaration of forfeiture, the registrar shall not implement the preceding sentence until the registrar adopts procedures for that implementation under section 4503.39 of the Revised Code. Upon receipt by the registrar of such an order, the registrar also shall take the measures necessary to permit the person to register a motor vehicle the person owns or leases or to transfer the registration of a motor vehicle the person owns or leases if the person later makes a proper application and otherwise is eligible to be issued or to transfer a motor vehicle registration.

(B) Division (A) of this section applies to persons arrested for violation of:

(1) Any of the provisions of Chapter 4511. or 4513. of the Revised Code, except sections 4511.19, 4511.20, 4511.251, and 4513.36 of the Revised Code;

(2) Any municipal ordinance substantially similar to a section included in division (B)(1) of this section;

(3) Any bylaw, rule, or regulation of the Ohio turnpike commission substantially similar to a section included in division (B)(1) of this section.

Division (A) of this section does not apply to those persons issued a citation for the commission of a minor misdemeanor under section 2935.26 of the Revised Code.

(C) No license shall be accepted as bond by an arresting officer or by a court under this section until the officer or court has notified the person that, if the person deposits the license with the officer or court and either does not appear on the date and at the time set by the officer or the court, if the court sets a time, or does not satisfy any judgment rendered, including, but not limited to, compliance with all court orders, the license will be suspended, and the person will not be eligible for reissuance of the license or issuance of a new license, or the issuance of a certificate of registration for a motor vehicle owned or leased by the person until the person appears and complies with any order issued by the court. The person also is subject to any criminal penalties that may apply to the person.

(D) The registrar shall not restore the person's driving or vehicle registration privileges until the person pays the reinstatement fee as provided in this section.

(2004 H 230, eff. 9–16–04; 2002 S 123, eff. 1–1–04; 1997 S 85, eff. 5–15–97; 1996 S 121, eff. 11–19–96; 1996 H 353, eff. 9–17–96; 1994 H 687, eff. 10–12–94; 1989 S 49, eff. 11–3–89; 1989 H 381; 1986 S 356; 1978 S 351; 1975 H 1; 1973 H 234)

2937.222 Hearing to deny bail; information to consider

(A) On the motion of the prosecuting attorney or on the judge's own motion, the judge shall hold a hearing to determine whether an accused person charged with aggravated murder when it is not a capital offense, murder, a felony of the first or second degree, a violation of section 2903.06 of the Revised Code, a violation of section 2903.211 of the Revised Code that is a felony, or a felony OVI offense shall be denied bail. The judge shall order that the accused be detained until the conclusion of the hearing. Except for good cause, a continuance on the motion of the state shall not exceed three court days. Except for good cause, a continuance on the motion of the accused shall not exceed five court days unless the motion of the accused waives in writing the five-day limit and states in writing a specific period for which the accused requests a continuance. A continuance granted upon a motion of the accused that waives in writing the five-day limit shall not exceed five court days after the period of continuance requested in the motion.

At the hearing, the accused has the right to be represented by counsel and, if the accused is indigent, to have counsel appointed. The judge shall afford the accused an opportunity to testify, to present witnesses and other information, and to cross-examine witnesses who appear at the hearing. The rules concerning admissibility of evidence in criminal trials do not apply to the presentation and consideration of information at the hearing. Regardless of whether the hearing is being held on the motion of the prosecuting attorney or on the court's own motion, the state has the burden of proving that the proof is evident or the presumption great that the accused committed the offense with which the accused is charged, of proving that the accused poses a substantial risk of serious physical harm to any person or to the community, and of proving that no release conditions will reasonably assure the safety of that person and the community.

The judge may reopen the hearing at any time before trial if the judge finds that information exists that was not known to the movant at the time of the hearing and that that information has a material bearing on whether bail should be denied. If a municipal court or county court enters an order denying bail, a judge of the court of common pleas having jurisdiction over the case may continue that order or may hold a hearing pursuant to this section to determine whether to continue that order.

(B) No accused person shall be denied bail pursuant to this section unless the judge finds by clear and convincing evidence that the proof is evident or the presumption great that the accused committed the offense described in division (A) of this section with which the accused is charged, finds by clear and convincing evidence that the accused poses a substantial risk of serious physical harm to any person or to the community, and finds by clear and convincing evidence that no release conditions will reasonably assure the safety of that person and the community.

(C) The judge, in determining whether the accused person described in division (A) of this section poses a substantial risk of serious physical harm to any person or to the community and whether there are conditions of release that will reasonably assure the safety of that person and the community, shall consider all available information regarding all of the following:

(1) The nature and circumstances of the offense charged, including whether the offense is an offense of violence or involves alcohol or a drug of abuse;

(2) The weight of the evidence against the accused;

(3) The history and characteristics of the accused, including, but not limited to, both of the following:

(a) The character, physical and mental condition, family ties, employment, financial resources, length of residence in the community, community ties, past conduct, history relating to drug or alcohol abuse, and criminal history of the accused;

(b) Whether, at the time of the current alleged offense or at the time of the arrest of the accused, the accused was on probation, parole, post-release control, or other release pending trial, sentencing, appeal, or completion of sentence for the commission of an offense under the laws of this state, another state, or the United States or under a municipal ordinance.

(4) The nature and seriousness of the danger to any person or the community that would be posed by the person's release.

(D)(1) An order of the court of common pleas denying bail pursuant to this section is a final appealable order. In an appeal pursuant to division (D) of this section, the court of appeals shall do all of the following:

(a) Give the appeal priority on its calendar;

(b) Liberally modify or dispense with formal requirements in the interest of a speedy and just resolution of the appeal;

(c) Decide the appeal expeditiously;

(d) Promptly enter its judgment affirming or reversing the order denying bail.

(2) The pendency of an appeal under this section does not deprive the court of common pleas of jurisdiction to conduct further proceedings in the case or to further consider the order denying bail in accordance with this section. If, during the pendency of an appeal under division (D) of this section, the court of common pleas sets aside or terminates the order denying bail, the court of appeals shall dismiss the appeal.

(E) As used in this section:

(1) "Court day" has the same meaning as in section 5122.01 of the Revised Code.

(2) "Felony OVI offense" means a third degree felony OVI offense and a fourth degree felony OVI offense.

(3) "Fourth degree felony OVI offense" and "third degree felony OVI offense" have the same meanings as in section 2929.01 of the Revised Code.

(2002 S 123, eff. 1–1–04; 1999 S 22, eff. 5–17–00; 1999 H 137, eff. 3–10–00; 1999 S 8, eff. 7–29–99)

2937.23 Amount of bail; domestic violence offenders; anti–stalking violations

(A)(1) In a case involving a felony or a violation of section 2903.11, 2903.12, or 2903.13 of the Revised Code when the victim of the offense is a peace officer, the judge or magistrate shall fix the amount of bail.

(2) In a case involving a misdemeanor or a violation of a municipal ordinance and not involving a felony or a violation of section 2903.11, 2903.12, or 2903.13 of the Revised Code when the victim of the offense is a peace officer, the judge, magistrate, or clerk of the court may fix the amount of bail and may do so in accordance with a schedule previously fixed by the judge or magistrate. If the judge, magistrate, or clerk of the court is not readily available, the sheriff, deputy sheriff, marshal, deputy marshal, police officer, or jailer having custody of the person charged may fix the amount of bail in accordance with a schedule previously fixed by the judge or magistrate and shall take the bail only in the county courthouse, the municipal or township building, or the county or municipal jail.

(3) In all cases, the bail shall be fixed with consideration of the seriousness of the offense charged, the previous criminal record of the defendant, and the probability of the defendant appearing at the trial of the case.

(B) In any case involving an alleged violation of section 2903.211 of the Revised Code or of a municipal ordinance that is substantially similar to that section, the court shall determine whether it will order an evaluation of the mental condition of the defendant pursuant to section 2919.271 of the Revised Code and, if it decides to so order, shall issue the order requiring the evaluation before it sets bail for the person charged with the violation. In any case involving an alleged violation of section 2919.27 of the Revised Code or of a municipal ordinance that is substantially similar to that section and in which the court finds that either of the following criteria applies, the court shall determine whether it will order an evaluation of the mental condition of the defendant pursuant to section 2919.271 of the Revised Code and, if it decides to so order, shall issue the order requiring that evaluation before it sets bail for the person charged with the violation:

(1) Regarding an alleged violation of a protection order issued or consent agreement approved pursuant to section 2919.26 or 3113.31 of the Revised Code, that the violation allegedly involves conduct by the defendant that caused physical harm to the person or property of a family or household member covered by the order or agreement or conduct by that defendant that caused a family or household member to believe that the defendant would cause physical harm to that member or that member's property;

(2) Regarding an alleged violation of a protection order issued pursuant to section 2903.213 or 2903.214 of the Revised Code, or a protection order issued by a court of another state, as defined in section 2919.27 of the Revised Code, that the violation allegedly involves conduct by the defendant that caused physical harm to the person or property of the person covered by the order or conduct by that defendant that caused the person covered by the order to believe that the defendant would cause physical harm to that person or that person's property.

(C) As used in this section, "peace officer" has the same meaning as in section 2935.01 of the Revised Code.

(1999 H 202, eff. 2–9–00; 1999 S 142, eff. 2–3–00; 1998 H 302, eff. 7–29–98; 1997 S 1, eff. 10–21–97; 1995 S 2, eff. 7–1–96; 1992 H 536, eff. 11–5–92; 1985 H 475; 129 v 557; 128 v 97)

2937.24 Oath to surety; form of affidavit

When a recognizance is offered under section 2937.22 of the Revised Code, the surety on which recognizance qualifies as a real property owner, the judge or magistrate shall require such surety to pledge to this state real property owned by the surety and located in this state. Whenever such pledge of real property has been given by any such proposed surety, he shall execute the usual form of recognizance, and in addition thereto there shall be filed his affidavit of justification of suretyship, to be attached to said recognizance as a part thereof. The surety may be required in such affidavit to depose as to whether he is, at the time of executing the same, surety upon any other recognizance and as to whether there are any unsatisfied judgments or executions against him. He may also be required to state any other fact which the court thinks relevant and material to a correct determination of the surety's sufficiency to act as bail. Such surety shall state in such affidavit where notices under section 2937.38 of the Revised Code may be served on himself, and service of notice of summons at such place is sufficient service for all purposes.

Such affidavit shall be executed by the proposed surety under an oath and may be in the following form:

"State of Ohio, County of ________, ss:

________ residing at ________, who offers himself as surety for ________ being first duly sworn, says that he owns in his own legal right, real property subject to execution, located in the county of ________, State of Ohio, consisting of ________ and described as follows to wit: ________; that the title to the same is in his own name, that the value of the same is not less than ______ dollars, and is subject to no encumbrances whatever except ________; that he is not surety upon any unpaid or forfeited recognizance, and that he is not party to any unsatisfied judgment upon any recognizance; that he is worth not less than ______ dollars over and above all debts, liabilities, and lawful claims against him, and all liens, encumbrances, and lawful claims against his property."

(1953 H 1, eff. 10–1–53; GC 13435–4)

2937.25 Lien; form

Upon the execution of any recognizance in an amount in excess of two hundred dollars in the usual form, and an affidavit of justification under section 2937.24 of the Revised Code, there shall attach to the real property described in said affidavit of justification, a lien in favor of this state in the penal sum of the recognizance, which lien shall remain in full force and effect during such time as such recognizance remains effective, or until further order of the court. Upon the acceptance by the judge or magistrate of such recognizance, containing such affidavit of justification, the said recognizance shall be immediately filed with the clerk of said court, if there is a clerk, or with the magistrate. The clerk of the court or the magistrate shall forthwith, upon the filing with him of such recognizance, file with the county recorder of the county in which such real property is located, a notice or lien, in writing, in substance as follows:

"To whom it may concern:

Take notice that the hereinafter described real property, located in the county of ________, has been pledged for the sum of ________ dollars, to the state of Ohio, by ________ surety upon the recognizance of _________ in a certain cause pending in the _________ court of the county (or city) of _________, to wit: the state of Ohio, plaintiff, versus _________ defendant, known and identified in such court as cause No. _________

Description of real estate: _________ Clerk of the court for the county of _________ or _________ Magistrate.

Dated _________"

From the time of the filing and recording of such notice it is notice to everyone that the real property therein described has been pledged to this state as security for the performance of the conditions of a criminal recognizance in the penal sum set forth in said recognizance and notice. Such lien does not affect the validity of prior liens on said property.

(1953 H 1, eff. 10–1–53; GC 13435–5)

2937.26 Cancellation of lien; form

Whenever, by the order of a court, a recognizance under sections 2937.24 and 2937.25 of the Revised Code has been canceled, discharged, or set aside, or the cause in which such recognizance is taken has been dismissed or otherwise terminated the clerk of such court shall forthwith file with the county recorder of the county in which the real property is located, a notice of discharge in writing, in substance as follows:

"To whom it may concern:

Take notice that by the order of the court of _________ (naming court) _________ of the county (or city) of _________, the recognizance of _________ as principal, and _____ as surety, given in the cause of the State of Ohio, plaintiff, versus _________, defendant, known and identified as Cause No. _____ in said court, is canceled, discharged, and set aside, and the lien of the State of Ohio on the real property therein pledged as security, is hereby waived, discharged, and set aside.

_________ Clerk of the court.

Dated _____"

(1953 H 1, eff. 10–1–53; GC 13435–6)

2937.27 Duties of county recorder

The county recorder of the county in which the property of a surety on a recognizance is located, shall keep and file all notices of lien and notices of discharge which are filed with him pursuant to section 2937.26 of the Revised Code, and shall keep in addition thereto, a book or record in which he shall index notice of liens and notice of discharges, as they are filed with him. When a lien has been released or discharged for a period of one year, the county recorder may destroy all notices of such lien.

(129 v 1033, eff. 10–26–61; 1953 H 1; GC 13435–7)

2937.28 Transmission of recognizance

All recognizances shall be returnable to and all deposits shall be held by or subject to the order of the court or magistrate before whom the accused is to appear initially, and upon the transfer of the case to any other court or magistrate shall be returnable to and transmitted to the transferee court or magistrate.

It is not necessary for the accused to give new recognizance for appearance in common pleas court for arraignment upon indictment or pending appeal after judgment and sentence, unless the magistrate or judge of the trial court or the court to which appeal is taken, shall, for good cause shown, increase or decrease the amount of the recognizance, but such recognizance shall continue and be in full force until trial and appeal therefrom is finally determined. When two or more charges are filed, or indictments returned, against the same person at or about the same time, the recognizance given may be made to include all offenses charged against the accused.

(128 v 97, eff. 1–1–60)

2937.281 Requirements of recognizance

In cases of felony, the recognizance shall be signed by the accused and one or more adult residents of the county in which the case is pending, who shall own, in the aggregate, real property double the amount set as bail, over and above all encumbrances and liable to execution in at least that amount; or it may be signed by the accused and a surety company authorized to do business in this state.

In cases of misdemeanor, the recognizance may be signed by the accused and one or more adult residents, qualified as set forth above or as to personal property ownership, by the accused and surety company, or, if authorized by judge or magistrate, by the accused alone. In cases of misdemeanors arising under Chapters 4501., 4503., 4505., 4507., 4509., 4511., 4513., 4517., and 4549. of the Revised Code, and related ordinance offenses (except those of driving under the influence of intoxicating liquor or controlled substances and leaving the scene of an accident) the court or magistrate shall accept guaranteed arrest bond with respect to which a surety company has become surety as provided in section 3929.141 of the Revised Code in lieu of cash bail in an amount not to exceed two hundred dollars.

(1975 H 300, eff. 7–1–76; 129 v 1401; 128 v 97)

2937.29 Release of accused on his own recognizance

When from all the circumstances the court is of the opinion that the accused will appear as required, either before or after conviction, the accused may be released on his own recognizance. A failure to appear as required by such recognizance shall constitute an offense subject to the penalty provided in section 2937.99 of the Revised Code.

(131 v H 47, eff. 8–10–65)

2937.30 Recognizance when accused discharged

When a defendant is discharged by the trial court otherwise than on a verdict or finding of acquittal, or when the appellate court reverses a conviction and orders the discharge of the defendant and the state or municipality signifies its intention to appeal therefrom, or the record is certified to the supreme court, the defendant shall not be discharged if he is in jail, nor the surety discharged or deposit released if the defendant is on bail, but the trial court, or the court to which appeal is taken may make order for his release on his own recognizance or bail, or recommit him.

(128 v 97, eff. 1–1–60; 1953 H 1; GC 13435–10)

2937.31 Recognizance or deposit for appearance of accused

If an accused is held to answer and offers sufficient bail, a recognizance or deposit shall be taken for his appearance to answer the charge before such magistrate or before such court to which proceedings may be transferred pursuant to Chapter 2937. of the Revised Code, at a date certain, or from day to day, or in case of the common pleas court on the first day of the next term thereof, and not depart without leave.

(128 v 97, eff. 1–1–60; 1953 H 1; GC 13435–11)

2937.32 Confinement for unbailable offenses, when bail is denied, and lack of sufficient bail

If an offense is not bailable, if the court denies bail to the accused, or if the accused does not offer sufficient bail, the court shall order the accused to be detained.

(1999 S 8, eff. 7–29–99)

2937.33 Receipt of recognizance

When a transcript or recognizance is received by the clerk of the court of common pleas, or of any court of record to which proceedings are transferred, he shall enter the same upon the appearance docket of the court, with the date of the filing of such transcript or recognizance, the date and amount of the recognizance, the names of the sureties, and the costs. Such recognizance is then of record in such court, and is proceeded on by process issuing therefrom, in a like manner as if it had been entered into before such court. When a court having recognizance of an offense takes a recognizance, it is a sufficient record thereof to enter upon the journal of such court the title of the case, the crime charged, the names of the sureties, the amount of the recognizance, and the time therein required for the appearance of the accused. In making the complete record, when required to be made, recognizances whether returned to or taken in such court shall be recorded in full, if required by the prosecutor or the accused.

(128 v 97, eff. 1–1–60; 1953 H 1; GC 13435–13)

2937.34 Accused unlawfully detained; examining court to be held

When a person is committed to jail, charged with an offense for which he has not been indicted, and claims to be unlawfully detained, the sheriff on demand of the accused or his counsel shall forthwith notify the court of common pleas, and the prosecuting attorney, to attend an examining court, the time of which shall be fixed by the judge. The judge shall hear said cause or complaint, examine the witnesses, and make such order as the justice of the case requires, and for such purpose the court may admit to bail, release without bond, or recommit to jail in accordance with the commitment. In the absence of the judge of the court of common pleas, the probate judge shall hold such examining court.

(1953 H 1, eff. 10–1–53; GC 13435–14)

2937.35 Forfeit of bail

Upon the failure of the accused or witness to appear in accordance with its terms the bail may in open court be adjudged forfeit, in whole or in part by the court or magistrate before whom he is to appear. But such court or magistrate may, in its discretion, continue the cause to a later date certain, giving notice of such date to him and the bail depositor or sureties, and adjudge the bail forfeit upon failure to appear at such later date.

(128 v 97, eff. 1–1–60)

2937.36 Forfeiture proceedings

Upon declaration of forfeiture, the magistrate or clerk of the court adjudging forfeiture shall proceed as follows:

(A) As to each bail, he shall proceed forthwith to deal with the sum deposited as if the same were imposed as a fine for the offense charged and distribute and account for the same accordingly provided that prior to so doing, he may satisfy accrued costs in the case out of the fund.

(B) As to any securities deposited, he shall proceed to sell the same, either at public sale advertised in the same manner as sale on chattel execution, or through any state or national bank performing such service upon the over the counter securities market and shall apply proceeds of sale, less costs or brokerage thereof as in cases of forfeited cash bail. Prior to such sale, the clerk shall give notices by ordinary mail to the depositor, at his address listed of record, if any, of his intention so to do, and such sale shall not proceed if the depositor, within ten days of mailing of such notice appears, and redeems said securities by either producing the body of the defendant in open court or posting the amount set in the recognizance in cash, to be dealt with as forfeited cash bail.

(C) As to recognizances he shall notify accused and each surety by ordinary mail at the address shown by them in their affidavits of qualification or on the record of the case, of the default of the accused and the adjudication of forfeiture and require each of them to show cause on or before a date certain to be stated in the notice, and which shall be not less than twenty nor more than thirty days from date of mailing notice, why judgment should not be entered against each of them for the penalty stated in the recognizance. If good cause by production of the body of the accused or otherwise is not shown, the court or magistrate shall thereupon enter judgment against the sureties or either of them, so notified, in such amount, not exceeding the penalty of the bond, as has been set in the adjudication of forfeiture, and shall award execution therefor as in civil cases. The proceeds of sale shall be received by the clerk or magistrate and distributed as on forfeiture of cash bail.

(128 v 97, eff. 1–1–60)

2937.37 Levy on property in judgment against surety

A magistrate or court of record inferior to the court of common pleas may proceed to judgment against a surety on a recognizance, and levy on his personal property, notwithstanding that the bond may exceed the monetary limitations on the jurisdiction of such court in civil cases, and jurisdiction over the person of surety shall attach from the mailing of the notice specified in section 2937.36 of the Revised Code, notwithstanding that such surety may not be within the territorial jurisdiction of the court; but levy on real property shall be made only through issuance, return, and levy made under certificate of judgment issued to the clerk of the court of common pleas pursuant to section 2329.02 of the Revised Code.

(128 v 97, eff. 1–1–60)

2937.38 Minority no defense in forfeiture proceedings

In any matter in which a minor is admitted to bail pursuant to Chapter 2937. of the Revised Code, the minority of the accused shall not be available as a defense to judgment against principal or surety, or against the sale of securities or transfer of cash bail, upon forfeiture.

(128 v 97, eff. 1–1–60)

2937.39 Remission of penalty

After judgment has been rendered against surety or after securities sold or cash bail applied, the court or magistrate, on the appearance, surrender, or re-arrest of the accused on the charge, may remit all or such portion of the penalty as it deems just and in the case of previous application and transfer of cash or proceeds, the magistrate or clerk may deduct an amount equal to the amount so transferred from subsequent payments to the agencies receiving such proceeds of forfeiture until the amount is recouped for the benefit of the person or persons entitled thereto under order or remission.

(128 v 97, eff. 1–1–60)

2937.40 Release of bail and sureties; use to satisfy fine or costs only when deposited by accused

(A) Bail of any type that is deposited under sections 2937.22 to 2937.45 of the Revised Code or Criminal Rule 46 by a person other than the accused shall be discharged and released, and sureties on recognizances shall be released, in any of the following ways:

(1) When a surety on a recognizance or the depositor of cash or securities as bail for an accused desires to surrender the accused before the appearance date, the surety is discharged from further responsibility or the deposit is redeemed in either of the following ways:

(a) By delivery of the accused into open court;

(b) When, on the written request of the surety or depositor, the clerk of the court to which recognizance is returnable or in which deposit is made issues to the sheriff a warrant for the arrest of the accused and the sheriff indicates on the return that he holds the accused in his jail.

(2) By appearance of the accused in accordance with the terms of the recognizance or deposit and the entry of judgment by the court or magistrate;

(3) By payment into court, after default, of the sum fixed in the recognizance or the sum fixed in the order of forfeiture, if it is less.

(B) When cash or securities have been deposited as bail by a person other than the accused and the bail is discharged and released pursuant to division (A) of this section, or when property has been pledged by a surety on recognizance and the surety on recognizance has been released pursuant to division (A) of this section, the court shall not deduct any amount from the cash or securities or declare forfeited and levy or execute against pledged property. The court shall not apply any of the deposited cash or securities toward, or declare forfeited and levy or execute against property pledged for a recognizance for, the satisfaction of any penalty or fine, and court costs, assessed against the accused upon his conviction or guilty plea, except upon express approval of the person who deposited the cash or securities or the surety.

(C) Bail of any type that is deposited under sections 2937.22 to 2937.45 of the Revised Code or Criminal Rule 46 by an accused shall be discharged and released to the accused, and property pledged by an accused for a recognizance shall be discharged, upon the appearance of the accused in accordance with the terms of the recognizance or deposit and the entry of judgment by the court or magistrate, except that, if the defendant is not indigent, the court may apply deposited bail toward the satisfaction of a penalty or fine, and court costs, assessed against the accused upon his conviction or guilty plea, and may declare forfeited and levy or execute against pledged property for the satisfaction of a penalty or fine, and court costs, assessed against the accused upon his conviction or guilty plea.

(D) Notwithstanding any other provision of this section, an Ohio driver's or commercial driver's license that is deposited as bond may be forfeited and otherwise handled as provided in section 2937.221 of the Revised Code.

(1990 S 338, eff. 11–28–90; 1989 H 381; 1986 S 356; 1980 H 402; 128 v 97)

2937.41 Return of bail; notice of discharge of recognizance

On the discharge of bail, the magistrate or clerk of the court shall return, subject to division (B) or (C) of section 2937.40 of the Revised Code, deposited cash or securities to the depositor, but the magistrate or clerk of the court may require presentation of an issued original receipt as a condition to the return. In the case of discharged recognizances, subject to division (B) or (C) of section 2937.40 of the Revised Code, the magistrate or clerk of the court shall endorse the satisfaction on the recognizance and shall forthwith transmit to the county recorder the notice of discharge provided for in section 2937.26 of the Revised Code.

(1980 H 402, eff. 5–13–80; 128 v 97)

2937.42 Defect in form of recognizance

Forfeiture of a recognizance shall not be barred or defeated or a judgment thereon reversed by the neglect or omission to note or record the default, or by a defect in the form of such recognizance, if it appears from the tenor thereof at what court the party or witness was bound to appear and that the court or officer before whom it was taken was authorized to require and take such recognizance.

(128 v 97, eff. 1–1–60; 1953 H 1; GC 13435–22)

2937.43 Arrest for failure to appear; issuance of warrant

Should the accused fail to appear as required, after having been released pursuant to section 2937.29 of the Revised Code, the court having jurisdiction at the time of such failure may, in addition to any other action provided by law, issue a warrant for the arrest of such accused.

(131 v H 47, eff. 8–10–65)

2937.44 Form of recognizance

Recognizances substantially in the forms following are sufficient:

RECOGNIZANCE OF THE ACCUSED

The State of Ohio, ________ County, ss:

Be it remembered, that on the ____ day of ________, in the year ____ E.F. and G.H. personally appeared before me, and jointly and severally acknowledged themselves to owe the state of Ohio, the sum of ________ dollars, to be levied on their goods, chattels, lands, and tenements, if default is made in the condition following, to wit:

The condition of this recognizance is such that if the above bound E.F. personally appears before the court of common pleas on the first day of the next term thereof, then and there to answer a charge of (here name the offense with which the accused is charged) and abide the judgment of the court and not depart without leave, then this recognizance shall be void; otherwise it shall be and remain in full force and virtue in law.

Taken and acknowledged before me, on the day and year above written.

A.B., Judge

RECOGNIZANCE OF WITNESS

The State of Ohio, ________ County, ss:

Be it remembered, that on the ________ day of ______, in the year _____ E.F. and G.H. personally appeared before me and jointly and severally acknowledged themselves to owe the state of Ohio, the sum of ________ dollars, to be levied on their goods, chattels, lands, and tenements, if default is made in the condition following, to wit:

The condition of this recognizance is such that if the above bound E.F. personally appears before the court of common pleas on the first day of the next term thereof then and there to give evidence on behalf of the state, touching such matters as shall then and there be required of him, and not depart the court without leave, then this recognizance shall be void, otherwise it shall remain in full force and virtue in law.

Taken and acknowledged before me, on the day and year above written.

A.B., Judge

TO KEEP THE PEACE

The State of Ohio, ________ County, ss:

Be it remembered, that on the ________ day of ________, in the year of _____ E.F., and G.H. personally appeared before me, and jointly and severally acknowledged themselves to owe the state of Ohio, the sum of ________ dollars, to be levied on their goods, chattels, lands, and tenements, if default is made in the condition following, to wit:

The condition of this recognizance is such that if the above bound E.F. personally appears before the court of common pleas, on the first day of the next term thereof, then and there to answer unto a complaint of C.D. that he has reason to fear, and does fear, that the said E.F. will (here state the charge in the complaint), and abide the order of the court thereon, and in the meantime to keep the peace and be of good behavior toward the citizens of the state generally, and especially toward the said C.D., then this recognizance shall be void; otherwise it shall be and remain in full force and virtue in law.

Taken and acknowledged before me, on the day and year above written.

A.B., Judge

(127 v 1039, eff. 1–1–58; 1953 H 1; GC 13435–24)

2937.45 Forms of commitments

Commitments substantially in the forms following are sufficient:

COMMITMENT AFTER EXAMINATION

The State of Ohio, ________ County, ss:

To the Keeper of the Jail of the County aforesaid, greeting:

Whereas, E.F. has been arrested, on the oath of C.D., for (here describe the offense), and has been examined by me on such charge, and required to give bail in the sum of ________ dollars for his appearance before the court of common pleas with which requisition he has failed to comply. Therefore, in the name of the state of Ohio, I command you to receive the said E.F. into your custody, in the jail of the county aforesaid, there to remain until discharged by due course of law.

Given under my hand, this _____ day of ______

A.B., Judge

COMMITMENT PENDING EXAMINATION

The State of Ohio, ________ County, ss:

To the Keeper of the Jail of the County aforesaid, greeting:

Whereas, E.F. has been arrested on the oath of C.D., for (here describe the offense) and has been brought before me for examination and the same has been necessarily postponed by reason of (here state the cause of delay). Therefore, I command you, in the name of the state of Ohio, to receive the said E.F. into your custody in the jail of the county aforesaid (or in such other place as the justice shall name) there to remain until discharged by due course of law.

Given under my hand, this _____ day of _____

A.B., Judge

(127 v 1039, eff. 1–1–58; 1953 H 1; GC 13435–25)

UNIFORM PROCEDURES IN TRAFFIC CASES

2937.46 Supreme court authorized to set uniform procedures in traffic cases

(A) The supreme court of Ohio, in the interest of uniformity of procedure in the various courts and for the purpose of promoting prompt and efficient disposition of cases arising under the traffic laws of this state and related ordinances, may make uniform rules for practice and procedure in courts inferior to the court of common pleas not inconsistent with the provisions of Chapter 2937. of the Revised Code, including, but not limited to:

(1) Separation of arraignment and trial of traffic and other types of cases;

(2) Consolidation of cases for trial;

(3) Transfer of cases within the same county for the purpose of trial;

(4) Designation of special referees for hearings or for receiving pleas or bail at times when courts are not in session;

(5) Fixing of reasonable bonds, and disposition of cases in which bonds have been forfeited.

(B) Except as otherwise specified in division (L) of section 4511.19 of the Revised Code, all of the rules described in division (A) of this section, when promulgated by the supreme court, shall be fully binding on all courts inferior to the court of common pleas and on the court of common pleas in relation to felony violations of division (A) of section 4511.19 of the Revised Code and shall effect a cancellation of any local court rules inconsistent with the supreme court's rules.

(2002 S 123, eff. 1–1–04; 129 v 582, eff. 1–10–61; 128 v 97)

PENALTY

2937.99 Penalties

(A) No person shall fail to appear as required, after having been released pursuant to section 2937.29 of the Revised Code. Whoever violates this section is guilty of failure to appear and shall be punished as set forth in division (B) or (C) of this section.

(B) If the release was in connection with a felony charge or pending appeal after conviction of a felony, failure to appear is a felony of the fourth degree.

(C) If the release was in connection with a misdemeanor charge or for appearance as a witness, failure to appear is a misdemeanor of the first degree.

(D) This section does not apply to misdemeanors and related ordinance offenses arising under Chapters 4501., 4503., 4505., 4507., 4509., 4510., 4511., 4513., 4517., 4549., and 5577. of the Revised Code, except that this section does apply to violations of sections 4511.19, 4549.02, and 4549.021 of the Revised Code and ordinance offenses related to sections 4511.19, 4549.02, and 4549.021 of the Revised Code.

(2002 S 123, eff. 1–1–04; 1999 S 107, eff. 3–23–00; 1994 H 571, eff. 10–6–94; 131 v H 47, eff. 8–10–65)

CHAPTER 2938

TRIAL—MAGISTRATE COURTS

PRELIMINARY PROVISIONS

2938.01 Definitions

The definition of "magistrate" set forth in section 2931.01 of the Revised Code, and the definition of "peace officer," "prosecutor," and "offense" set forth in section 2935.01 of the Revised Code applies to Chapter 2938 of the Revised Code.

(128 v 97, eff. 1–1–60)

2938.02 Applicability of provisions

The provisions of Chapter 2938. of the Revised Code shall apply to trial on the merits of any misdemeanor, ordinance offense, prosecution for the violation of any rule or regulation of any governmental body authorized to adopt penal regulations, or to complaints to keep the peace, which may be instituted in and retained for trial on the merits in any court or before any magistrate inferior to the court of common pleas; provided that in juvenile courts, where the conduct of any person under the age of eighteen years is made the subject of inquiry and for which special provision is made by Chapter 2151. or 2152. of the Revised Code, such matters shall be tried, adjusted, or disposed of pursuant to Chapter 2151. or 2152. of the Revised Code.

(2000 S 179, § 3, eff. 1–1–02; 128 v 97, eff. 1–1–60)

2938.03 Setting and continuing cases; assignment of additional judges

The magistrate, or judge or clerk of court of record, shall set all criminal cases for a trial at a date not later than thirty days after plea is received, or in those cases in which the charge has been reduced on preliminary hearing or has been certified by another magistrate, then at a date not later than thirty days from fixing of charge or receipt of transcript as the case may be. Continuances beyond such date shall be granted only upon notice to the opposing party and for good cause shown.

Criminal cases shall be given precedence over civil matters in all assignments for trial and if the volume of contested criminal matters in courts of more than one judge is such as to require it, the chief justice or presiding judge of such court shall assign additional judges from other divisions of the court to assist in the trial of such criminal matters; in the case of county courts, the presiding judge of the court of common pleas shall assign county judges from other areas of jurisdiction within the county to assist those county judges whose volume of criminal cases requires assistance.

(128 v 97, eff. 1–1–60)

JURIES

2938.04 Jury trial

In courts of record right to trial by jury as defined in section 2945.17 of the Revised Code shall be claimed by making demand in writing therefor and filing the same with the clerk of the court not less than three days prior to the date set for trial or on the day following receipt of notice whichever is the later. Failure to claim jury trial as provided in this section is a complete waiver of right thereto. In courts not of record jury trial may not be had, but failure to waive jury in writing where right to jury trial may be asserted shall require the magistrate to certify such case to a court of record as provided in section 2937.08 of the Revised Code.

(129 v 582, eff. 1–10–61; 128 v 97)

2938.05 Withdrawal of claim of jury

Claim of jury, once made, may be withdrawn by written waiver of jury but in such case the court may, if a jury has been summoned, require accused to pay all costs of mileage and fees of members of the venire for one day's service, notwithstanding the outcome of the case. No withdrawal of claim for jury shall effect any re-transfer of a case, once it has been certified to a court of record.

(128 v 97, eff. 1–1–60)

2938.06 Number of jurors; challenges

If the number of jurors to be sworn in a case is not stated in the claim, the number to be sworn shall be twelve, but the accused may stipulate for a jury of six, provided in such case the number of pre-emptory [1] challenges shall be limited to two on each side.

(128 v 97, eff. 1–1–60)

[1] So in original.

PRACTICE AND PROCEDURE

2938.07 Authority of magistrate or judge

The magistrate or judge of the trial court shall control all proceedings during a criminal trial and shall limit the introduction of evidence and argument of counsel to relevant and material matters with a view to expeditious and effective ascertainment of truth regarding the matters in issue.

(128 v 97, eff. 1–1–60)

2938.08 Presumption of innocence

A defendant in a criminal action is presumed to be innocent until he is proved guilty of the offense charged, and in case of a reasonable doubt whether his guilt is satisfactorily shown, he shall be acquitted. The presumption of innocence places upon the state (or the municipality) the burden of proving him guilty beyond a reasonable doubt.

In charging a jury the trial court shall state the meaning of the presumption of innocence and of reasonable doubt in each case.

(128 v 97, eff. 1–1–60)

2938.09 Grounds of objection to be stated

In the trial of any criminal case, the grounds of an objection to any ruling or action of the judge or magistrate shall be stated if required by him.

(1986 H 412, eff. 3–17–87; 128 v 97)

2938.10 Territorial jurisdiction

The state or municipality in all cases must prove the offense committed within the territorial jurisdiction of the court, and in ordinance cases within the municipality, except as to those offenses in which the court has county wide jurisdiction created by statute and as to those cases in which certification has been made pursuant to section 2937.08 of the Revised Code.

(128 v 97, eff. 1–1–60)

2938.11 Order of proceedings of trial

The trial of an issue shall proceed before the trial court or jury as follows:

(A) Counsel may state the case for the prosecution, including the evidence by which he expects to sustain it.

(B) Counsel for the defendant may state his defense, including the evidence which he expects to offer.

(C) The prosecution then shall produce all its evidence, and the defendant may follow with his evidence, but the court or magistrate, in the furtherance of justice and for good cause shown, may permit evidence to be offered by either side out of its order and may permit rebuttal evidence to be offered by the prosecution.

(D) When the evidence is concluded, unless the case is submitted without argument, counsel for the prosecution shall commence, defendant or his counsel follow, and counsel for the prosecution conclude his argument either to the court or jury. The judge or magistrate may impose a reasonable time limit on argument.

(E) The judge, after argument is concluded in a jury case, forthwith shall charge the jury on the law pertaining to the case and controlling their deliberations, which charge shall not be reduced to writing and taken into the jury room unless the trial judge in his discretion shall so order.

(F) Any verdict arrived at by the jury, or finding determined by the judge or magistrate in trial to the court, shall be announced and received only in open court as soon as it is determined. Any finding by the judge or magistrate shall be announced in open court not more than forty-eight hours after submission of the case to him.

(1986 H 412, eff. 3–17–87; 128 v 97)

2938.12 When accused may be tried in his absence

A person being tried for a misdemeanor, either to the court, or to a jury, upon request in writing, subscribed by him, may, with the consent of the judge or magistrate, be tried in his absence, but no right shall exist in the defendant to be so tried. If after trial commences a person being tried escapes or departs without leave, the trial shall proceed and verdict or finding be received and sentence passed as if he were personally present.

(128 v 97, eff. 1–1–60)

2938.13 Responsibility for prosecution

In any case prosecuted for violation of a municipal ordinance the village solicitor or city director of law, and for a statute, he or the prosecuting attorney, shall present the case for the municipal corporation and the state respectively, but either may delegate the responsibility to some other attorney in a proper case, or, if the defendant be unrepresented by counsel may with leave of court, withdraw from the case. But the magistrate or judge shall not permit prosecution of any criminal case by private attorney employed or retained by a complaining witness.

(1977 H 219, eff. 11–1–77; 128 v 97)

2938.14 Venires for juries

Venires for juries in courts of record inferior to the court of common pleas shall be drawn and summoned in the manner provided in the various acts creating such courts. But no challenge to the array shall be sustained in any case for the reason that some of the venire are not residents of the territory of the court, if it appears that the venire was regularly drawn and certified by the jury commissioners of county or municipality as the case may be.

(129 v 582, eff. 1–10–61; 128 v 97)

2938.15 Rules of evidence and procedure

The rules of evidence and procedure, including those governing notices, proof of special matters, depositions, and joinder of defendants and offenses set forth in Chapter 2945. of the Revised Code, which are not, by their nature, inapplicable to the trial of misdemeanors, shall prevail in trials under Chapter 2938. of the Revised Code where no special provision is made in such chapter, or where no provision is made by rule of the supreme court adopted pursuant to section 2937.46 of the Revised Code.

(129 v 582, eff. 1–10–61; 128 v 97)

CHAPTER 2939

GRAND JURIES

GRAND JURORS

2939.01 Definition of magistrate

The definition of "magistrate" set forth in section 2931.01 of the Revised Code applies to Chapter 2939. of the Revised Code.

(1953 H 1, eff. 10–1–53)

2939.02 Selection of grand jury

Grand juries shall consist of fifteen persons who satisfy the qualifications of a juror specified in section 2313.42 of the Revised Code. Persons to serve as grand jurors in the court of common pleas of each county shall be selected from the persons whose names are contained in the annual jury list and from the ballots deposited in the jury wheel, or in the automation data processing storage drawer, or from the names contained in an automated data processing information storage device as prescribed by sections 2313.07, 2313.08, and 2313.35 of the Revised Code.

At the time of the selection of the persons who are to constitute the grand jury, the commissioners of jurors shall draw from the jury wheel, or draw by utilizing the automation data processing equipment and procedures described in section 2313.07 of the Revised Code, ballots containing the names of not less than twenty-five persons. The first fifteen persons whose names are drawn shall constitute the grand jury, if they can be located and served by the sheriff, and if they are not excused by the court or a judge of the court. If any of the first fifteen persons whose names are so drawn are not located or are unable to serve and are for that reason excused by the court or by a judge of the court, whose duty it is to supervise the impaneling of the grand jury, the judge shall then designate the person whose name next appears on the list of persons drawn, to serve in the place of the person not found or excused and shall so continue to substitute the names of the persons drawn in the order in which they were drawn, to fill all vacancies resulting from persons not being found or having been excused by the court or the judge of the court, until the necessary fifteen persons are selected to make up the grand jury. If all of the names appearing on the list of persons drawn are exhausted before the grand jury is complete, the judge shall order the commissioners of jurors to draw such additional names as the judge determines, and shall proceed to fill the vacancies from those names in the order in which they are drawn.

The judge of the court of common pleas may select any person who satisfies the qualifications of a juror and whose name is not included in the annual jury list or on a ballot deposited in the jury wheel or automation data processing storage drawer, or whose name is not contained in an automated data processing information storage device, to preside as foreman of the grand jury, in which event the grand jury shall consist of the foreman so selected and fourteen additional grand jurors selected from the jury wheel or by use of the automation data processing equipment and procedures in the manner provided in this section.

(1984 H 183, eff. 10–1–84; 1969 H 424; 131 v S 20; 130 v S 103; 1953 H 1; GC 11419–34)

2939.03 Grand jurors subject to same provisions and regulations as other jurors

A grand jury is drawn and notified by the same persons, from the same jury wheel, automation data processing storage drawer, or automated data processing information storage device, and in the same manner as other jurors are drawn and notified under sections 2939.02 to 2939.04 and 2313.01 to 2313.46 of the Revised Code. Grand jurors so drawn and notified are not entitled to an exemption for any reason but may be excused from service or have their service postponed for the same reasons and in the same manner as other jurors under those sections and not otherwise. Grand jurors are subject to the same fines and penalties for nonattendance and otherwise as are other jurors under those sections. The duties and the powers of courts of common pleas, clerks of courts of common pleas, and commissioners of jurors in regard to grand jurors in all respects are the same as in regard to other jurors.

(1998 S 69, eff. 4–16–98; 1969 H 424, eff. 11–25–69; 131 v S 20; 1953 H 1; GC 11419–35)

2939.031 Alternate juror for grand jury; selection of

When it appears to the judge impaneling a grand jury that the inquiry is likely to be protracted, or upon direction of the judge, an additional or alternate juror shall be selected in the same manner as the regular jurors in the inquiry are selected. The additional or alternate juror shall be sworn and seated near the jury, with equal opportunity for seeing and hearing the proceedings, shall attend the inquiry at all times and shall obey all orders and admonitions of the court or foreman. When the jurors are ordered kept together, the alternate juror shall be kept with them. The additional or alternate juror shall be liable as a regular juror for failure to attend the inquiry or to obey any order or admonition of the court or foreman. He shall receive the same compensation as other jurors, and except as provided in this section shall be discharged upon the final submission of the bill to the foreman.

If before the final submission of the bill to the jury, a juror dies or is discharged by the judge or foreman due to incapacity, absence, or disqualification of such juror, the additional or alternate juror, upon order of the judge or foreman, shall become one of the jury and serve in all respects as though selected as an original juror during the absence or incapacity of an original juror.

(125 v 345, eff. 10–14–53)

2939.04 Grand jurors; compensation

The compensation of grand jurors shall be fixed by resolution of the board of county commissioners, not to exceed forty dollars for each day's attendance, payable out of the county treasury. Except in counties of less than one hundred thousand population according to the last federal census, in which counties the judge of the court of common pleas shall make rules in the judge's own county applicable to subsequent grand juror and petit juror service, a person who has served as a grand juror at a term of court is prohibited from serving again, either as a grand juror or petit juror, in that jury year in which the service is rendered or in the next jury year. The person is entitled to a certificate of excuse or postponement in the same manner as a petit juror. The court of common pleas may order the drawing of a special jury to sit at any time public business requires it.

(1998 S 69, eff. 4–16–98; 1974 S 465, eff. 3–4–75; 1953 H 1; GC 11419–36)

2939.06 Oath to grand jurors

(A) When a grand jury is impaneled, the court of common pleas shall appoint one of the members of the grand jury as foreperson, and shall administer, or cause to be administered, to the jurors an oath in the following words to which the jurors shall respond "I do solemnly swear" or "I do solemnly affirm":

"Do you solemnly swear or affirm that you will diligently inquire into and carefully deliberate all matters that shall come to your attention concerning this service; and do you solemnly swear or affirm that you will keep secret all proceedings of the grand jury unless you are required in a court of justice to make disclosure; and do you solemnly swear or affirm that you will indict no person through malice, hatred, or ill will; and do you solemnly swear or affirm that you will not leave unindicted any person through fear, favor, or affection, or for any reward or hope thereof; and do you solemnly swear or affirm that in all your deliberations you will present the truth, the whole truth, and nothing but the truth, according to the best of your skill and understanding, as you shall answer unto God or under the penalties of perjury?"

(B) If, on or after the effective date of this amendment, a court impaneling a grand jury uses the grand juror's oath that was in effect prior to the effective date of this amendment instead of the oath set forth in division (A) of this section, the court's use of the former oath does not invalidate or affect the validity of the impanelment of the grand jury, any proceeding, inquiry, or presentation of the grand jury, any indictment or other document found, returned, or issued by the grand jury, or any other action taken by the grand jury.

(2002 S 218, eff. 3–24–03; 1953 H 1, eff. 10–1–53; GC 13436–3)

2939.07 Charge of the court

The grand jurors, after being sworn, shall be charged as to their duty by the judge of the court of common pleas, who shall call their attention particularly to the obligation of secrecy which their oaths impose, and explain to them the law applicable to such matters as may be brought before them.

(1953 H 1, eff. 10–1–53; GC 13436–4)

2939.08 Duty of grand jury

After the charge of the court of common pleas, the grand jury shall retire with the officer appointed to attend it, and proceed to inquire of and present all offenses committed within the county.

(1953 H 1, eff. 10–1–53; GC 13436–5)

2939.09 Clerk of grand jury

The grand jury may appoint one of its members to be its clerk to preserve the minutes of its proceedings and actions in all cases pending before it. Such minutes shall be delivered to the prosecuting attorney before the jury is discharged.

(1953 H 1, eff. 10–1–53; GC 13436–6)

OFFICIALS

2939.10 Who shall have access to grand jury

The prosecuting attorney or assistant prosecuting attorney may at all times appear before the grand jury to give information relative to a matter cognizable by it, or advice upon a legal matter when required. The prosecuting attorney may interrogate witnesses before the grand jury when the grand jury or the prosecuting attorney finds it necessary, but no person other than the grand jurors shall be permitted to remain in the room with the jurors while the jurors are expressing their views or giving their votes on a matter before them. In all matters or cases which the attorney general is required to investigate or prosecute by the governor or general assembly, or which a special prosecutor is required by section 177.03 of the Revised Code to investigate and prosecute, the attorney general or the special prosecutor, respectively, shall have and exercise any or all rights, privileges, and powers of prosecuting attorneys, and any assistant or special counsel designated by the attorney general or special prosecutor for that purpose, has the same authority. Proceedings in relation to such matters or cases are under the exclusive supervision and control of the attorney general or the special prosecutor.

(1986 S 74, eff. 9–3–86; 1953 H 1; GC 13436–7)

2939.11 Official reporters

The official shorthand reporter of the county, or any shorthand reporter designated by the court of common pleas, at the request of the prosecuting attorney, or any such reporter designated by the attorney general in investigations conducted by him, may take shorthand notes of testimony before the grand jury, and furnish a transcript to the prosecuting attorney or the attorney general, and to no other person. The shorthand reporter shall withdraw from the jury room before the jurors begin to express their views or take their vote on the matter before them. Such reporter shall take an oath to be administered by the judge after the grand jury is sworn, imposing an obligation of secrecy to not disclose any testimony taken or heard except to the grand jury, prosecuting attorney, or attorney general, unless called upon in court to make disclosures.

(1953 H 1, eff. 10–1–53; GC 13436–8)

2939.12 Clerk to issue subpoenas for witnesses

When required by the grand jury, prosecuting attorney, or judge of the court of common pleas, the clerk of the court of common pleas shall issue subpoenas and other process to any county to bring witnesses to testify before such jury.

(1953 H 1, eff. 10–1–53; GC 13436–9)

WITNESSES

2939.121 Employee's attendance before grand jury under subpoena; employer may not penalize

No employer shall discharge or terminate from employment, threaten to discharge or terminate from employment, or otherwise punish or penalize any employee because of time lost from regular employment as a result of the employee's attendance at any proceeding before a grand jury pursuant to a subpoena. This section generally does not require and shall not be construed to require an employer to pay an employee for time lost resulting from attendance at any grand jury proceeding. However, if an employee is subpoenaed to appear at a grand jury proceeding and the proceeding pertains to an offense against the employer or an offense involving the employee during the course of his employment, the employer shall not decrease or withhold the employee's pay for any time lost as a result of compliance with the subpoena. Any employer who knowingly violates this section is in contempt of court.

(1984 S 172, eff. 9–26–84)

2939.13 Oath to witnesses

Before a witness is examined by the grand jury, an oath shall be administered to him by the foreman of the grand jury or by the judge of the court of common pleas or the clerk of the court of common pleas, truly to testify of such matters and things as may lawfully be inquired of before such jury. A certificate that the oath has been administered shall be indorsed on the subpoena of the witness or otherwise made by the foreman of the grand jury, judge, or clerk certifying the attendance of said witness to the clerk of the court.

(1953 H 1, eff. 10–1–53; GC 13436–10)

2939.14 Proceedings when witness refuses to testify

If a witness before a grand jury refuses to answer an interrogatory, the court of common pleas shall be informed in writing, in which such interrogatory shall be stated, with the excuse for the refusal given by the witness. The court shall determine whether the witness is required to answer, and the grand jury shall be forthwith informed of such decision.

(1953 H 1, eff. 10–1–53; GC 13436–11)

2939.15 Court may proceed against witness for contempt

If the court of common pleas determines that a witness before a grand jury is required to answer an interrogatory and such witness persists in his refusal, he shall be brought before the court, which shall proceed in a like manner as if such witness had been interrogated and refused to answer in open court.

(1953 H 1, eff. 10–1–53; GC 13436–12)

GENERAL PROVISIONS

2939.16 Court may appoint grand juror in case of death

In case of sickness, death, discharge, or nonattendance of a grand juror after the grand jury is sworn, the court may cause another to be sworn in his stead. The court shall charge such juror as required by section 2939.07 of the Revised Code.

(1953 H 1, eff. 10–1–53; GC 13436–13)

2939.17 New grand jury may be summoned

After the grand jury is discharged, the court of common pleas, when necessary, may order the drawing and impaneling of a new grand jury, which shall be summoned and returned as provided by section 2939.03 of the Revised Code and shall be sworn and proceed in the manner provided by sections 2939.06 to 2939.24, inclusive, of the Revised Code. Whenever the governor or general assembly directs the attorney general to conduct any investigation or prosecution, the court of common pleas or any judge thereof, on written request of the attorney general, shall order a special grand jury to be summoned, and such special grand jury may be called and discharge its duties either before, during, or after any session of the regular grand jury, and its proceedings shall be independent of the proceedings of the regular grand jury but of the same force and effect.

Whenever a witness is necessary to a full investigation by the attorney general under this section, or to secure or successfully maintain and conclude a prosecution arising out of any such investigation, the judge of the court of common pleas may grant to such witness immunity from any prosecution based on the testimony or other evidence given by the witness in the course of the investigation or prosecution, other than a prosecution for perjury in giving such testimony or evidence.

(1970 H 956, eff. 9–16–70; 129 v 1201; 1953 H 1; GC 13436–14)

2939.18 Fact of indictment shall be kept secret

No grand juror, officer of the court, or other person shall disclose that an indictment has been found against a person not in custody or under bail, before such indictment is filed and the case docketed, except by the issue of process.

(1953 H 1, eff. 10–1–53; GC 13436–15)

2939.19 Testimony of grand jurors

No grand juror may state or testify in court in what manner any member of the grand jury voted or what opinion was expressed by any juror on any question before the grand jury.

(1953 H 1, eff. 10–1–53; GC 13436–16)

2939.20 Indictment by twelve jurors

At least twelve of the grand jurors must concur in the finding of an indictment. When so found, the foreman shall indorse on such indictment the words "A true bill" and subscribe his name as foreman.

(1953 H 1, eff. 10–1–53; GC 13436–17)

2939.21 Grand jury to visit county jail

Once every three months, the grand jurors shall visit the county jail, examine its condition, and inquire into the discipline and treatment of the prisoners, their habits, diet, and accommodations. They shall report on these matters to the court of common pleas in writing. The clerk of the court of common pleas shall forward a copy of the report to the department of rehabilitation and correction.

(1982 S 23, eff. 7–6–82; 1976 H 390; 1953 H 1; GC 13436–20)

2939.22 Proceedings when indictments are returned

Indictments found by a grand jury shall by presented by the foreman to the court of common pleas, and filed with the clerk of the court of common pleas, who shall indorse thereon the date of such filing and enter each case upon the appearance docket and the trial docket of the term when the persons indicted have been arrested. The court shall assign such indictments for trial under section 2945.02 of the Revised Code, and recognizances of defendants and witnesses shall be taken for their appearance in court. When a case is continued to the next term of court, such recognizance shall require the appearance of the defendants and witnesses at a time designated by the court. Secret indictments shall not be docketed by name until after the apprehension of the accused.

(1953 H 1, eff. 10–1–53; GC 13436–21)

2939.23 Report to court when indictment not found

If an indictment is not found by the grand jury, against an accused who has been held to answer, such fact shall be reported by the foreman to the court of common pleas.

(1953 H 1, eff. 10–1–53; GC 13436–22)

2939.24 Disposition of person in jail and not indicted

If a person held in jail charged with an indictable offense is not indicted at the term of court at which he is held to answer, he shall be discharged unless:

(A) He was committed on such charge after the discharge of the grand jury.

(B) The transcript has not been filed.

(C) There is not sufficient time at such term of court to investigate said cause.

(D) The grand jury, for good cause, continues the hearing of said charge until the next term of court.

(E) It appears to the court of common pleas that a witness for the state has been enticed or kept away, detained, or prevented from attending court by sickness or unavoidable accident.

(1953 H 1, eff. 10–1–53; GC 13436–23)

OUT–OF–STATE WITNESS

2939.25 Definition of witness, state, and summons

As used in sections 2939.25 to 2939.29, inclusive, of the Revised Code:

(A) "Witness" includes a person whose testimony is desired in any proceeding or investigation by a grand jury or in a criminal action, prosecution, or proceeding.

(B) "State" includes any territory of the United States and District of Columbia.

(C) "Summons" includes a subpoena, order, or other notice requiring the appearance of a witness.

(1953 H 1, eff. 10–1–53; GC 13436–24)

2939.26 Foreign court may compel witnesses

If a judge of a court of record in any state which by its laws has made provision for commanding persons within that state to attend and testify in this state, certifies under the seal of such court that there is a criminal prosecution pending in such court, or that a grand jury investigation has commenced or is about to commence, that a person being within this state is a material witness in such prosecution or grand jury investigation, and that his presence will be required for a specified number of days, upon presentation of such certificate to any judge of a court of record in the county in this state in which such person is, such judge shall fix a time and place for a hearing and shall make an order directing the witness to appear at a time and place certain for the hearing.

If at a hearing such judge determines that the witness is material and necessary, that it will not cause undue hardship to the witness to be compelled to attend and testify in the prosecution or grand jury investigation in the other state, and that the laws of the state in which the prosecution is pending, or grand jury investigation has commenced or is about to commence, and of any other state through which the witness may be required to pass by ordinary course of travel, will give to him protection from arrest and the service of civil and criminal process, he shall issue a summons, with a copy of the certificate attached, directing the witness to attend and testify in the court where the prosecution is pending, or where a grand jury investigation has commenced or is about to commence, at a time and place specified in the summons. In any such hearing the certificate is prima-facie evidence of all the facts stated therein.

If said certificate recommends that the witness be taken into immediate custody and delivered to an officer of the requesting state to assure his attendance in the requesting state, such judge may, in lieu of notification of the hearing, direct that such witness be forthwith brought before him for said hearing. If the judge at the hearing is satisfied of the desirability of such custody and delivery, for which determination the certificate is prima-facie proof of such desirability, he may, in lieu of issuing subpoena or summons, order that said witness be forthwith taken into custody and delivered to an officer of the requesting state.

If the witness, who is summoned as provided in this section, after being paid or tendered by some properly authorized person the sum of ten cents a mile for each mile by the ordinary traveled route to and from the court where the prosecution is pending and five dollars for each day, that he is required to travel and attend as a witness, fails without good cause to attend and testify as directed in the summons, he shall be punished in the manner provided for the punishment of any witness who disobeys a summons issued from a court of record in this state.

(1953 H 1, eff. 10–1–53; GC 13436–25)

2939.27 Certificate to specify time witness will be required; mileage and fees

If a person in any state, which by its laws has made provision for commanding persons within its borders to attend and testify in criminal prosecutions or grand jury investigations commenced or about to commence, in this state, is a material witness in a prosecution pending in a court of record in this state, or in a grand jury investigation which has commenced or is about to commence, a judge of such court may issue a certificate under the seal of the court stating these facts and specifying the number of days the witness will be required. Said certificate may include a recommendation that the witness be taken into immediate custody and delivered to an officer of this state to assure his attendance in this state. This certificate shall be presented to a judge of a court of record in the county in which the witness is found.

If the witness is summoned to attend and testify in this state he shall be tendered the sum of ten cents a mile for each mile by the ordinary traveled route to and from the court where the prosecution is pending, and five dollars for each day that he is required to travel and attend as a witness. A witness who has appeared in accordance with the summons shall not be required to remain within this state a longer period of time than the period mentioned in the certificate, unless otherwise ordered by the court. If such witness, after coming into this state, fails without good cause to attend and testify as directed in the summons, he shall be punished in the manner provided for the punishment of any witness who disobeys a summons issued from a court of record in this state.

(1953 H 1, eff. 10–1–53; GC 13436–26)

2939.28 Exemption from arrest

If a person comes into this state in obedience to a summons directing him to attend and testify in this state, while in this state pursuant to such summons he is not subject to arrest or the service of process, civil or criminal, in connection with matters which arose before his entrance into this state under the summons.

If a person passes through this state while going to another state in obedience to a summons to attend and testify in that state or while returning therefrom, while so passing through this state he is not subject to arrest or the service of process, civil or criminal, in connection with matters which arose before his entrance into this state under the summons.

(1953 H 1, eff. 10–1–53; GC 13436–27)

2939.29 Construction

Sections 2939.25 to 2939.28, inclusive, of the Revised Code shall be so interpreted and construed as to effectuate their general purpose, to make the law of this state uniform with the law of other states which enact similar uniform legislation.

(1953 H 1, eff. 10–1–53; GC 13436–28)

CHAPTER 2941

INDICTMENT

MAGISTRATE DEFINED

2941.01 Definition of magistrate

The definition of "magistrate" set forth in section 2931.01 of the Revised Code applies to Chapter 2941. of the Revised Code.

(1953 H 1, eff. 10–1–53)

INDICTMENTS AND INFORMATIONS

2941.02 Informations

All sections of the Revised Code which apply to prosecutions upon indictments, the process thereon, and the issuing and service thereof, to commitments, bails, motions, pleadings, trials, appeals, and punishments, to the execution of any sentence, and all other proceedings in cases of indictments whether in the court of original or appellate jurisdiction, apply to informations, and all prosecutions and proceedings thereon.

(1953 H 1, eff. 10–1–53; GC 13437–1)

2941.021 Prosecution by information

Any criminal offense which is not punishable by death or life imprisonment may be prosecuted by information filed in the common pleas court by the prosecuting attorney if the defendant, after he has been advised by the court of the nature of the charge against him and of his rights under the constitution, is represented by counsel or has affirmatively waived counsel by waiver in writing and in open court, waives in writing and in open court prosecution by indictment.

(128 v 53, eff. 11–9–59)

2941.03 Sufficiency of indictments or informations

An indictment or information is sufficient if it can be understood therefrom:

(A) That it is entitled in a court having authority to receive it, though the name of the court is not stated;

(B) If it is an indictment, that it was found by a grand jury of the county in which the court was held, of [sic.] if it is an information, that it was subscribed and presented to the court by the prosecuting attorney of the county in which the court was held;

(C) That the defendant is named, or, if his name cannot be discovered, that he is described by a fictitious name, with a statement that his true name is unknown to the jury or prosecuting attorney, but no name shall be stated in addition to one necessary to identify the accused;

(D) That an offense was committed at some place within the jurisdiction of the court, except where the act, though done without the local jurisdiction of the county, is triable therein;

(E) That the offense was committed at some time prior to the time of finding of the indictment or filing of the information.

(1953 H 1, eff. 10–1–53; GC 13437–2)

2941.04 Two or more offenses in one indictment

An indictment or information may charge two or more different offenses connected together in their commission, or different statements of the same offense, or two or more different offenses of the same class of crimes or offenses, under separate counts, and if two or more indictments or informations are filed in such cases the court may order them to be consolidated.

The prosecution is not required to elect between the different offenses or counts set forth in the indictment or information, but the defendant may be convicted of any number of the offenses charged, and each offense upon which the defendant is convicted must be stated in the verdict. The court in the interest of justice and for good cause shown, may order different offenses or counts set forth in the indictment or information tried separately or divided into two or more groups and each of said groups tried separately. A verdict of acquittal of one or more counts is not an acquittal of any other count.

(1953 H 1, eff. 10–1–53; GC 13437–3)

2941.05 Statement charging an offense

In an indictment or information charging an offense, each count shall contain, and is sufficient if it contains in substance, a statement that the accused has committed some public offense therein specified. Such statement may be made in ordinary and concise language without any technical averments or any allegations not essential to be proved. It may be in the words of the section of the Revised Code describing the offense or declaring the matter charged to be a public offense, or in any words sufficient to give the accused notice of the offense of which he is charged.

(126 v 392, eff. 3–17–55; 1953 H 1; GC 13437–4)

2941.06 Form of indictment or information

An indictment may be substantially in the following form:

"The State of Ohio,)
ss.
_________ County)

In the Year ____.

The jurors of the Grand Jury of the State of Ohio, within and for the body of the County aforesaid, on their oaths, in the name and by the authority of the State of Ohio, do find and present that A.B., on the ____ day of ________, ____, at the county of ________ aforesaid, did ________ (here insert the name of the offense if it has one, such as murder, arson, or the like, or if a misdemeanor having no general name, insert a brief description of it as given by law) contrary to the form of the statute in such case made and provided, and against the peace and dignity of the State of Ohio.

________ C.D. ________

(Indorsed) A true bill. Prosecuting Attorney

E.F., Foreperson of the Grand Jury."

(2000 H 495, eff. 5–9–00; 1976 H 390, eff. 8–6–76; 1953 H 1; GC 13437–5)

2941.07 Bill of particulars

Upon written request of the defendant made not later than five days prior to the date set for trial, or upon order of the court, the prosecuting attorney shall furnish a bill of particulars setting up specifically the nature of the offense charged and the conduct of the defendant which is alleged to constitute the offense.

(1972 H 511, eff. 1–1–74; 1953 H 1; GC 13437–6)

2941.08 Certain defects do not render indictment invalid

An indictment or information is not made invalid, and the trial, judgment, or other proceedings stayed, arrested, or affected:

(A) By the omission of "with force and arms," or words of similar import, or "as appears by the record";

(B) For omitting to state the time at which the offense was committed, in a case in which time is not of the essence of the offense;

(C) For stating the time imperfectly;

(D) For stating imperfectly the means by which the offense was committed except insofar as means is an element of the offense;

(E) For want of a statement of the value or price of a matter or thing, or the amount of damages or injury, where the value or price or the amount of damages or injury is not of the essence of the offense, and in such case it is sufficient to aver that the value or price of the property is less than, equals, or exceeds the certain value or price which determines the offense or grade thereof;

(F) For the want of an allegation of the time or place of a material fact when the time and place have been once stated therein;

(G) Because dates and numbers are represented by figures;

(H) For an omission to allege that the grand jurors were impaneled, sworn, or charged;

(I) For surplusage or repugnant allegations when there is sufficient matter alleged to indicate the crime and person charged;

(J) For want of averment of matter not necessary to be proved;

(K) For other defects or imperfections which do not tend to prejudice the substantial rights of the defendant upon the merits.

(1953 H 1, eff. 10–1–53; GC 13437–7)

2941.09 Identification of corporation

In any indictment or information it is sufficient for the purpose of identifying any group or association of persons, not incorporated, to state the proper name of such group or association, to state any name or designation by which the group or association has been or is known, to state the names of all persons in such group or association or of one or more of them, or to state the name of one or more persons in such group or association referring to the others as "another" or "others." It is sufficient for the purpose of identifying a corporation to state the corporate name of such corporation, or any name or designation by which such corporation has been or is known.

(1953 H 1, eff. 10–1–53; GC 13437–8)

2941.10 Indictment complete

No indictment or information for any offense created or defined by statute is objectionable for the reason that it fails to negative any exception, excuse, or proviso contained in the statute creating or defining the offense. The fact that the charge is made is an allegation that no legal excuse for the doing of the act exists in the particular case.

(1953 H 1, eff. 10–1–53; GC 13437–9)

PLEADING, AVERMENTS, AND ALLEGATIONS

2941.11 Pleading prior conviction

Whenever it is necessary to allege a prior conviction of the accused in an indictment or information, it is sufficient to allege that the accused was, at a certain stated time, in a certain stated court, convicted of a certain stated offense, giving the name of the offense, or stating the substantial elements thereof.

(1953 H 1, eff. 10–1–53; GC 13437–10)

2941.12 Pleading a statute

In pleading a statute or right derived therefrom it is sufficient to refer to the statute by its title, or in any other manner which identifies the statute. The court must thereupon take judicial notice of such statute.

(1953 H 1, eff. 10–1–53; GC 13437–11)

2941.13 Pleading a judgment

In pleading a judgment or other determination of, or a proceeding before, any court or officer, civil or military, it is not necessary to allege the fact conferring jurisdiction on such court or officer. It is sufficient to allege generally that such judgment or determination was given or made or such proceedings had.

(1953 H 1, eff. 10–1–53; GC 13437–12)

2941.14 Allegations in homicide indictment

(A) In an indictment for aggravated murder, murder, or voluntary or involuntary manslaughter, the manner in which, or the means by which the death was caused need not be set forth.

(B) Imposition of the death penalty for aggravated murder is precluded unless the indictment or count in the indictment charging the offense specifies one or more of the aggravating circumstances listed in division (A) of section 2929.04 of the Revised Code. If more than one aggravating circumstance is specified to an indictment or count, each shall be in a separately numbered specification, and if an aggravating circumstance is specified to a count in an indictment containing more than one count, such specification shall be identified as to the count to which it applies.

(C) A specification to an indictment or count in an indictment charging aggravated murder shall be stated at the end of the body of the indictment or count, and may be in substantially the following form:

"SPECIFICATION (or, SPECIFICATION 1, SPECIFICATION TO THE FIRST COUNT, or SPECIFICATION 1 TO THE FIRST COUNT). The Grand Jurors further find and specify that (set forth the applicable aggravating circumstance listed in divisions (A)(1) to (10) of section 2929.04 of the Revised Code. The aggravating circumstance may be stated in the words of the subdivision in which it appears, or in words sufficient to give the accused notice of the same)."

(2002 S 184, eff. 5–15–02; 1997 S 32, eff. 8–6–97; 1981 S 1, eff. 10–19–81; 1973 H 716; 1972 H 511; 1953 H 1; GC 13437–13)

2941.141 Specification concerning possession of firearm essential to affect sentence

(A) Imposition of a one-year mandatory prison term upon an offender under division (D)(1)(a) of section 2929.14 of the Revised Code is precluded unless the indictment, count in the indictment, or information charging the offense specifies that the offender had a firearm on or about the offender's person or under the offender's control while committing the offense. The specification shall be stated at the end of the body of the indictment, count, or information, and shall be in substantially the following form:

"SPECIFICATION (or, SPECIFICATION TO THE FIRST COUNT). The Grand Jurors (or insert the person's or the prosecuting attorney's name when appropriate) further find and specify that (set forth that the offender had a firearm on or about the offender's person or under the offender's control while committing the offense.)"

(B) Imposition of a one-year mandatory prison term upon an offender under division (D)(1)(a) of section 2929.14 of the Revised Code is precluded if a court imposes a three-year or six-year mandatory prison term on the offender under that division relative to the same felony.

(C) The specification described in division (A) of this section may be used in a delinquent child proceeding in the manner and for the purpose described in section 2152.17 of the Revised Code.

(D) As used in this section, "firearm" has the same meaning as in section 2923.11 of the Revised Code.

(2000 S 179, § 3, eff. 1–1–02; 1999 S 107, eff. 3–23–00; 1995 S 2, eff. 7–1–96; 1990 H 669, eff. 1–10–91; 1990 S 258; 1982 H 269, § 4, S 199)

2941.142 Specification concerning offense of violence while participating in criminal gang activity

(A) Imposition of a mandatory prison term of one, two, or three years pursuant to division (I) of section 2929.14 of the Revised Code upon an offender who committed a felony that is an offense of violence while participating in a criminal gang is precluded unless the indictment, count in the indictment, or information charging the felony specifies that the offender committed the felony that is an offense of violence while participating in a criminal gang. The specification shall be stated at the end of the body of the indictment, count, or information, and shall be in substantially the following form:

"SPECIFICATION (or, SPECIFICATION TO THE FIRST COUNT). The grand jurors (or insert the person's or the prosecuting attorney's name when appropriate) further find and specify that (set forth that the offender committed the felony that is an offense of violence while participating in a criminal gang.)"

(B) The specification described in division (A) of this section may be used in a delinquent child proceeding in the manner and for the purpose described in section 2152.17 of the Revised Code.

(C) As used in this section, "criminal gang" has the same meaning as in section 2923.41 of the Revised Code.

(2000 S 179, § 3, eff. 1–1–02; 1998 H 2, eff. 1–1–99)

2941.143 Specification concerning school safety zone

Imposition of a sentence by a court pursuant to division (J) of section 2929.14 of the Revised Code is precluded unless the indictment, count in the indictment, or information charging aggravated murder, murder, or a felony of the first, second, or third degree that is an offense of violence specifies that the offender committed the offense in a school safety zone or towards a person in a school safty[1] zone. The specification shall be stated at the end of the body of the indictment, count, or information and shall be in substantially the following form:

"SPECIFICATION (or, SPECIFICATION TO THE FIRST COUNT). The grand jurors (or insert the person's or the prosecuting attorney's name when appropriate) further find and specify that (set forth that the offender committed aggravated murder, murder, or the felony of the first, second, or third degree that is an offense of violence in a school safety zone or towards a person in a school safety zone)."

(1999 S 1, eff. 8–6–99)

[1] So in original; 1999 S 1.

2941.144 Specification concerning possession of automatic firearm or firearm with silencer

(A) Imposition of a six-year mandatory prison term upon an offender under division (D)(1)(a) of section 2929.14 of the Revised Code is precluded unless the indictment, count in the indictment, or information charging the offense specifies that the offender had a firearm that is an automatic firearm or that was equipped with a firearm muffler or silencer on or about the offender's person or under the offender's control while committing the offense. The specification shall be stated at the end of the body of the indictment, count, or information and shall be stated in substantially the following form:

"SPECIFICATION (or, SPECIFICATION TO THE FIRST COUNT). The Grand Jurors (or insert the person's or the prosecuting attorney's name when appropriate) further find and specify that (set forth that the offender had a firearm that is an automatic firearm or that was equipped with a firearm muffler or silencer on or about the offender's person or under the offender's control while committing the offense)."

(B) Imposition of a six-year mandatory prison term upon an offender under division (D)(1)(a) of section 2929.14 of the Revised Code is precluded if a court imposes a three-year or one-year mandatory prison term on the offender under that division relative to the same felony.

(C) The specification described in division (A) of this section may be used in a delinquent child proceeding in the manner and for the purpose described in section 2152.17 of the Revised Code.

(D) As used in this section, "firearm" and "automatic firearm" have the same meanings as in section 2923.11 of the Revised Code.

(2000 S 179, § 3, eff. 1–1–02; 1999 S 107, eff. 3–23–00; 1995 S 2, eff. 7–1–96; 1990 S 258, eff. 11–20–90)

2941.145 Specification concerning use of firearm to facilitate offense

(A) Imposition of a three-year mandatory prison term upon an offender under division (D)(1)(a) of section 2929.14 of the Revised Code is precluded unless the indictment, count in the indictment, or information charging the offense specifies that the offender had a firearm on or about the offender's person or under the offender's control while committing the offense and displayed the firearm, brandished the firearm, indicated that the offender possessed the firearm, or used it to facilitate the offense. The specification shall be stated at the end of the body of the indictment, count, or information, and shall be stated in substantially the following form:

"SPECIFICATION (or, SPECIFICATION TO THE FIRST COUNT). The Grand Jurors (or insert the person's or the prosecuting attorney's name when appropriate) further find and specify that (set forth that the offender had a firearm on or about the offender's person or under the offender's control while committing the offense and displayed the firearm, brandished the firearm, indicated that the offender possessed the firearm, or used it to facilitate the offense)."

(B) Imposition of a three-year mandatory prison term upon an offender under division (D)(1)(a) of section 2929.14 of the Revised Code is precluded if a court imposes a one-year or six-year mandatory prison term on the offender under that division relative to the same felony.

(C) The specification described in division (A) of this section may be used in a delinquent child proceeding in the manner and for the purpose described in section 2152.17 of the Revised Code.

(D) As used in this section, "firearm" has the same meaning as in section 2923.11 of the Revised Code.

(2000 S 179, § 3, eff. 1–1–02; 1999 S 107, eff. 3–23–00; 1995 S 2, eff. 7–1–96)

2941.146 Specification concerning discharge of firearm from motor vehicle

(A) Imposition of a mandatory five-year prison term upon an offender under division (D)(1)(c) of section 2929.14 of the Revised Code for committing a violation of section 2923.161 of the Revised Code or for committing a felony that includes, as an essential element, purposely or knowingly causing or attempting to cause the death of or physical harm to another and that was committed by discharging a firearm from a motor vehicle other than a manufactured home is precluded unless the indictment, count in the indictment, or information charging the offender specifies that the offender committed the offense by discharging a firearm from a motor vehicle other than a manufactured home. The specification shall be stated at the end of the body of the indictment, count, or information, and shall be stated in substantially the following form:

"SPECIFICATION (or, SPECIFICATION TO THE FIRST COUNT). The Grand Jurors (or insert the person's or prosecuting attorney's name when appropriate) further find and specify that (set forth that the offender committed the violation of section 2923.161 of the Revised Code or the felony that includes, as an essential element, purposely or knowingly causing or attempting to cause the death of or physical harm to another and that was committed by discharging a firearm from a motor vehicle other than a manufactured home)."

(B) The specification described in division (A) of this section may be used in a delinquent child proceeding in the manner and for the purpose described in section 2152.17 of the Revised Code.

(C) As used in this section:

(1) "Firearm" has the same meaning as in section 2923.11 of the Revised Code;

(2) "Motor vehicle" and "manufactured home" have the same meanings as in section 4501.01 of the Revised Code.

(2000 S 179, § 3, eff. 1–1–02; 1999 S 107, eff. 3–23–00; 1995 S 2, eff. 7–1–96)

2941.147 Sexual motivation specification

(A) Whenever a person is charged with an offense that is a violation of section 2903.01, 2903.02, 2903.11, or 2905.01 of the Revised Code, a violation of division (A) of section 2903.04 of the Revised Code, an attempt to violate or complicity in violating section 2903.01, 2903.02, 2903.11, or 2905.01 of the Revised Code when the attempt or complicity is a felony, or an attempt to violate or complicity in violating division (A) of section 2903.04 of the Revised Code when the attempt or complicity is a felony, the indictment, count in the indictment, information, or complaint charging the offense may include a specification that the person committed the offense with a sexual motivation. The specification shall be stated at the end of the body of the indictment, count, information, or complaint and shall be in substantially the following form:

"SPECIFICATION (OR, SPECIFICATION TO THE FIRST COUNT). The Grand Jurors (or insert the person's or the prosecuting attorney's name when appropriate) further find and specify that the offender committed the offense with a sexual motivation."

(B) As used in this section, "sexual motivation" has the same meaning as in section 2971.01 of the Revised Code.

(1996 H 180, eff. 1–1–97)

2941.148 Sexually violent predator specification

Note: See also following version of this section, eff. 4–29–05.

(A) The application of Chapter 2971. of the Revised Code to an offender is precluded unless the indictment, count in the indictment, or information charging the sexually violent offense or charging the designated homicide, assault, or kidnapping offense also includes a specification that the offender is a sexually violent predator. The specification shall be stated at the end of the body of the indictment, count, or information and shall be stated in substantially the following form:

"SPECIFICATION (OR, SPECIFICATION TO THE FIRST COUNT). The grand jury (or insert the person's or prosecuting attorney's name when appropriate) further find and specify that the offender is a sexually violent predator."

(B) In determining for purposes of this section whether a person is a sexually violent predator, all of the factors set forth in divisions (H)(1) to (6) of section 2971.01 of the Revised Code that apply regarding the person may be considered as evidence tending to indicate that it is likely that the person will engage in the future in one or more sexually violent offenses.

(C) As used in this section, "designated homicide, assault, or kidnapping offense," "sexually violent offense," and "sexually violent predator" have the same meanings as in section 2971.01 of the Revised Code.

(1996 H 180, eff. 1–1–97)

Note: See also following version of this section, eff. 4–29–05.

2941.148 Sexually violent predator specification (later effective date)

Note: See also preceding version of this section, in effect until 4–29–05.

(A) The application of Chapter 2971. of the Revised Code to an offender is precluded unless the indictment, count in the indictment, or information charging the violent sex offense also includes a specification that the offender is a sexually violent predator, or the indictment, count in the indictment, or information charging the designated homicide, assault, or kidnapping offense also includes both a specification of the type described in section 2941.147 of the Revised Code and a specification that the offender is a sexually violent predator. The specification that the offender is a sexually violent predator shall be stated at the end of the body of the indictment, count, or information and shall be stated in substantially the following form:

"Specification (or, specification to the first count). The grand jury (or insert the person's or prosecuting attorney's name when appropriate) further find and specify that the offender is a sexually violent predator."

(B) In determining for purposes of this section whether a person is a sexually violent predator, all of the factors set forth in divisions (H)(1) to (6) of section 2971.01 of the Revised Code that apply regarding the person may be considered as evidence tending to indicate that it is likely that the person will engage in the future in one or more sexually violent offenses.

(C) As used in this section, "designated homicide, assault, or kidnapping offense," "violent sex offense," and "sexually violent predator" have the same meanings as in section 2971.01 of the Revised Code.

(2004 H 473, eff. 4–29–05; 1996 H 180, eff. 1–1–97)

Note: See also preceding version of this section, in effect until 4–29–05.

2941.149 Specification concerning repeat violent offenders

(A) The determination by a court that an offender is a repeat violent offender is precluded unless the indictment, count in the indictment, or information charging the offender specifies that the offender is a repeat violent offender. The specification shall be stated at the end of the body of the indictment, count, or information, and shall be stated in substantially the following form:

"SPECIFICATION (or, SPECIFICATION TO THE FIRST COUNT). The Grand Jurors (or insert the person's or prosecuting attorney's name when appropriate) further find and specify that (set forth that the offender is a repeat violent offender)."

(B) The court shall determine the issue of whether an offender is a repeat violent offender.

(C) As used in this section, "repeat violent offender" has the same meaning as in section 2929.01 of the Revised Code.

(1996 S 269, eff. 7–1–96)

2941.1410 Specification concerning major drug offender

(A) Except as provided in sections 2925.03 and 2925.11 of the Revised Code, the determination by a court that an offender is a major drug offender is precluded unless the indictment, count in the indictment, or information charging the offender specifies that the offender is a major drug offender. The specification shall be stated at the end of the body of the indictment, count, or information, and shall be stated in substantially the following form:

"SPECIFICATION (or, SPECIFICATION TO THE FIRST COUNT). The Grand Jurors (or insert the person's or prosecuting attorney's name when appropriate) further find and specify that (set forth that the offender is a major drug offender)."

(B) The court shall determine the issue of whether an offender is a major drug offender.

(C) As used in this section, "major drug offender" has the same meaning as in section 2929.01 of the Revised Code.

(1999 S 107, eff. 3–23–00; 1996 S 269, eff. 7–1–96)

2941.1411 Specification concerning use of body armor

(A) Imposition of a two-year mandatory prison term upon an offender under division (D)(1)(d) of section 2929.14 of the Revised Code is precluded unless the indictment, count in the indictment, or information charging the offense specifies that the offender wore or carried body armor while committing the offense and that the offense is an offense of violence that is a felony. The specification shall be stated at the end of the body of the indictment, count, or information and shall be stated in substantially the following form:

"SPECIFICATION (or, SPECIFICATION TO THE FIRST COUNT). The Grand Jurors (or insert the person's or the prosecuting attorney's name when appropriate) further find and specify that (set forth that the offender wore or carried body armor while committing the specified offense and that the specified offense is an offense of violence that is a felony)."

(B) As used in this section, "body armor" means any vest, helmet, shield, or similar item that is designed or specifically carried to diminish the impact of a bullet or projectile upon the offender's body.

(2000 S 222, eff. 3–22–01)

2941.1412 Discharging firearm at peace officer or corrections officer

(A) Imposition of a seven-year mandatory prison term upon an offender under division (D)(1)(f) of section 2929.14 of the Revised Code is precluded unless the indictment, count in the indictment, or information charging the offense specifies that the offender discharged a firearm at a peace officer or a corrections officer while committing the offense. The specification shall be stated at the end of the body of the indictment, count, or information and shall be in substantially the following form:

"SPECIFICATION (or, SPECIFICATION TO THE FIRST COUNT).

The Grand Jurors (or insert the person's or the prosecuting attorney's name when appropriate) further find and specify that (set forth that the offender discharged a firearm at a peace officer or a corrections officer while committing the offense)."

(B) As used in this section:

(1) "Firearm" has the same meaning as in section 2923.11 of the Revised Code.

(2) "Peace officer" has the same meaning as in section 2935.01 of the Revised Code.

(3) "Corrections officer" means a person employed by a detention facility as a corrections officer.

(4) "Detention facility" has the same meaning as in section 2921.01 of the Revised Code.

(2002 H 130, eff. 4–7–03)

2941.1413 Specification concerning prior felony OVI offenses

(A) Imposition of a mandatory additional prison term of one, two, three, four, or five years upon an offender under division

(G)(2) of section 2929.13 of the Revised Code is precluded unless the indictment, count in the indictment, or information charging a felony violation of division (A) of section 4511.19 of the Revised Code specifies that the offender, within twenty years of the offense, previously has been convicted of or pleaded guilty to five or more equivalent offenses. The specification shall be stated at the end of the body of the indictment, count, or information and shall be stated in substantially the following form:

"SPECIFICATION (or, SPECIFICATION TO THE FIRST COUNT). The Grand Jurors (or insert the person's or the prosecuting attorney's name when appropriate) further find and specify that (set forth that the offender, within twenty years of committing the offense, previously had been convicted of or pleaded guilty to five or more equivalent offenses)."

(B) As used in division (A) of this section, "equivalent offense" has the same meaning as in section 4511.181 of the Revised Code.

(2004 H 163, eff. 9–23–04)

2941.1414. Specifications concerning drug or alcohol related vehicular homicide of peace officer in construction zone

(A) Imposition of a five-year mandatory prison term upon an offender under division (D)(5) of section 2929.14 of the Revised Code is precluded unless the offender is convicted of or pleads guilty to violating division (A)(1) or (2) of section 2903.06 of the Revised Code and unless the indictment, count in the indictment, or information charging the offense specifies that the victim of the offense is a peace officer. The specification shall be stated at the end of the body of the indictment, count, or information and shall be stated in substantially the following form:

"SPECIFICATION (or, SPECIFICATION TO THE FIRST COUNT). The Grand Jurors (or insert the person's or the prosecuting attorney's name when appropriate) further find and specify that (set forth that the victim of the offense is a peace officer)."

(B) The specification described in division (A) of this section may be used in a delinquent child proceeding in the manner and for the purpose described in section 2152.17 of the Revised Code.

(C) As used in this section, "peace officer" has the same meaning as in section 2935.01 of the Revised Code.

(2004 H 52, eff. 6–1–04)

2941.1415. Specifications concerning drug or alcohol related vehicular homicide of peace officer in construction zone and prior convictions

(A) Imposition of a three-year mandatory prison term upon an offender under division (D)(6) of section 2929.14 of the Revised Code is precluded unless the offender is convicted of or pleads guilty to violating division (A)(1) or (2) of section 2903.06 of the Revised Code and unless the indictment, count in the indictment, or information charging the offense specifies that the offender previously has been convicted of or pleaded guilty to three or more violations of division (A) or (B) of section 4511.19 of the Revised Code or an equivalent offense, or three or more violations of any combination of those divisions and offenses. The specification shall be stated at the end of the body of the indictment, count, or information and shall be stated in substantially the following form:

"SPECIFICATION (or, SPECIFICATION TO THE FIRST COUNT). The Grand Jurors (or insert the person's or the prosecuting attorney's name when appropriate) further find and specify that (set forth that the offender previously has been convicted of or pleaded guilty to three or more violations of division (A) or (B) of section 4511.19 of the Revised Code or an equivalent offense, or three or more violations of any combination of those divisions and offenses)."

(B) The specification described in division (A) of this section may be used in a delinquent child proceeding in the manner and for the purpose described in section 2152.17 of the Revised Code.

(C) As used in this section, "equivalent offense" has the same meaning as in section 4511.181 of the Revised Code.

(2004 H 52, eff. 6–1–04)

2941.1416 Specification concerning prior misdemeanor OVI offenses

(A) Imposition of a mandatory, additional, definite jail term of up to six months upon an offender under division (E) of section 2929.24 of the Revised Code is precluded unless the information charging a violation of division (B) of section 4511.19 of the Revised Code specifies that the offender, within twenty years of the offense, previously has been convicted of or pleaded guilty to five or more equivalent offenses. The specification shall be stated at the end of the body of the information and shall be stated in substantially the following form:

"SPECIFICATION. (Insert the person's or the prosecuting attorney's name as appropriate) further finds and specifies that (set forth that the offender, within twenty years of committing the offense, previously had been convicted of or pleaded guilty to five or more equivalent offenses)."

(B) As used in division (A) of this section, "equivalent offense" has the same meaning as in section 4511.181 of the Revised Code.

(2004 H 163, eff. 9–23–04)

2941.15 Sufficiency of indictment for forgery

In an indictment or information for falsely making, altering, forging, printing, photographing, uttering, disposing of, or putting off an instrument, it is sufficient to set forth the purport and value thereof. Where the instrument is a promise to pay money conditionally, it is not necessary to allege that the condition has been performed.

(1953 H 1, eff. 10–1–53; GC 13437–14)

2941.16 Sufficient description for forgery

In an indictment or information for engraving or making the whole or part of an instrument, matter, or thing, or for using or having the unlawful custody or possession of a plate or other material upon which the whole or part of an instrument, matter, or thing was engraved or made, or for having the unlawful custody or possession of a paper upon which the whole or part of an instrument, matter, or thing was made or printed, it is sufficient to describe such instrument, matter, or thing by any name or designation by which it is usually known.

(1953 H 1, eff. 10–1–53; GC 13437–15)

2941.17 Description by usual name or purport

In all cases when it is necessary to make an averment in an indictment or information as to a writing, instrument, tool, or thing, it is sufficient to describe it by any name or designation by which it is usually known, or by the purport thereof.

(1972 H 511, eff. 1–1–74; 1953 H 1; GC 13437–16)

2941.18 Allegations in perjury indictment

In an indictment or information for perjury or falsification, it is not necessary to set forth any part of a record or proceeding, or the commission or authority of the court or other authority before which perjury or falsification was committed.

(1972 H 511, eff. 1–1–74; 1953 H 1; GC 13437–17)

2941.19 Alleging intent to defraud

It is sufficient in an indictment or information where it is necessary to allege an intent to defraud, to allege that the accused did the act with intent to defraud, without alleging an intent to defraud a particular person or corporation. On the trial of such an indictment or information, an intent to defraud a particular person need not be proved. It is sufficient to prove that the accused did the act charged with intent to defraud.

(1953 H 1, eff. 10–1–53; GC 13437–18)

2941.20 Allegations sufficient for unlawfully selling liquor

An indictment, information, or affidavit charging a violation of law relative to the sale, possession, transportation, buying, or giving intoxicating liquor to any person, need not allege the kind of liquor sold, nor the person by whom bought except that such charge must be sufficient to inform the accused of the particular offense with which he is charged.

(1953 H 1, eff. 10–1–53; GC 13437–19)

2941.21 Averments as to joint ownership

In an indictment or information for an offense committed upon, or in relation to, property belonging to partners or joint owners, it is sufficient to allege the ownership of such property to be in such partnership by its firm name, or in one or more of such partners or owners without naming all of them.

(1953 H 1, eff. 10–1–53; GC 13437–20)

2941.22 Averments as to will or codicil

In an indictment or information for stealing a will, codicil, or other testamentary instrument, or for forgery thereof, or, for a fraudulent purpose, keeping, destroying, or secreting it, whether in relation to real or personal property, or during the life of a testator or after his death, it is not necessary to allege the ownership or value thereof.

(1953 H 1, eff. 10–1–53; GC 13437–21)

2941.23 Averments as to election

In an indictment or information for an offense committed in relation to an election, it is sufficient to allege that such election was authorized by law, without stating the names of the officers holding it or the person voted for or the offices to be filled at the election.

(1953 H 1, eff. 10–1–53; GC 13437–22)

2941.25 Multiple counts

(A) Where the same conduct by defendant can be construed to constitute two or more allied offenses of similar import, the indictment or information may contain counts for all such offenses, but the defendant may be convicted of only one.

(B) Where the defendant's conduct constitutes two or more offenses of dissimilar import, or where his conduct results in two or more offenses of the same or similar kind committed separately or with a separate animus as to each, the indictment or information may contain counts for all such offenses, and the defendant may be convicted of all of them.

(1972 H 511, eff. 1–1–74)

PROCEDURE

2941.26 Variance

When, on the trial of an indictment or information, there appears to be a variance between the statement in such indictment or information and the evidence offered in proof thereof, in the Christian name or surname, or other description of a person therein named or described, or in the name or description of a matter or thing therein named or described, such variance is not ground for an acquittal of the defendant unless the court before which the trial is had finds that such variance is material to the merits of the case or may be prejudicial to the defendant.

(1953 H 1, eff. 10–1–53; GC 13437–25)

2941.27 Proof of dilatory plea

No plea in abatement, or other dilatory plea to the indictment or information, shall be received by any court unless the party offering such plan proves the truth thereof by affidavit, or by some other sworn evidence.

(1953 H 1, eff. 10–1–53; GC 13437–26)

2941.28 Misjoinder of parties or offenses

No indictment or information shall be quashed, set aside, or dismissed for any of the following defects:

(A) That there is a misjoinder of the parties accused;

(B) That there is a misjoinder of the offenses charged in the indictment or information, or duplicity therein;

(C) That any uncertainty exists therein.

If the court is of the opinion that either defect referred to in division (A) or (B) of this section exists in any indictment or information, it may sever such indictment or information into separate indictments or informations or into separate counts.

If the court is of the opinion that the defect referred to in division (C) of this section exists in the indictment or information, it may order the indictment or information amended to cure such defect, provided no change is made in the name or identity of the crime charged.

(1953 H 1, eff. 10–1–53; GC 13437–27)

2941.29 Time for objecting to defect in indictment

No indictment or information shall be quashed, set aside, or dismissed, or motion to quash be sustained, or any motion for delay of sentence for the purpose of review be granted, nor shall any conviction be set aside or reversed on account of any defect in form or substance of the indictment or information, unless the objection to such indictment or information, specifically stating the defect claimed, is made prior to the commencement of the trial, or at such time thereafter as the court permits.

(1953 H 1, eff. 10–1–53; GC 13437–28)

2941.30 Amending an indictment

The court may at any time before, during, or after a trial amend the indictment, information, or bill of particulars, in respect to any defect, imperfection, or omission in form or substance, or of any variance with the evidence, provided no change is made in the name or identity of the crime charged. If any amendment is made to the substance of the indictment or information or to cure a variance between the indictment or information and the proof, the accused is entitled to a discharge of the jury on his motion, if a jury has been impaneled, and to a reasonable continuance of the cause, unless it clearly appears from the whole proceedings that he has not been misled or prejudiced by the defect or variance in respect to which the amendment is made, or that his rights will be fully protected by proceeding with the trial, or by a postponement thereof to a later day with the same or another jury. In case a jury is discharged from further consideration of a case under this section, the accused was not in jeopardy. No action of the court in refusing a continuance or postponement under this section is reviewable except after motion to and refusal by the trial court to grant a new trial therefor, and no appeal based upon such action of the court shall be sustained, nor reversal had, unless from consideration of the whole proceedings, the reviewing court finds that the accused was prejudiced in his defense or that a failure of justice resulted.

(1953 H 1, eff. 10–1–53; GC 13437–29)

2941.31 Record of quashed indictment

In criminal prosecutions, when the indictment or information has been quashed or the prosecuting attorney has entered a nolle prosequi thereon, or the cause or indictment is disposed of otherwise than upon trial, a complete record shall not be made by the clerk of the court of common pleas unless ordered to do so by the court of common pleas.

(1953 H 1, eff. 10–1–53; GC 13437–30)

2941.32 Proceedings when two indictments pending

If two or more indictments or informations are pending against the same defendant for the same criminal act, the prosecuting attorney must elect upon which he will proceed, and upon trial being had upon one of them, the remaining indictments or information shall be quashed.

(1953 H 1, eff. 10–1–53; GC 13437–31)

2941.33 Nolle prosequi

The prosecuting attorney shall not enter a nolle prosequi in any cause without leave of the court, on good cause shown, in open court. A nolle prosequi entered contrary to this section is invalid.

(1953 H 1, eff. 10–1–53; GC 13437–32)

2941.34 Lost or destroyed indictment

If an indictment or information is mutilated, obliterated, lost, mislaid, destroyed, or stolen, or for any other reason cannot be produced at the arraignment or trial of the defendant, the court may substitute a copy.

(127 v 847, eff. 9–16–57; 1953 H 1; GC 13437–33)

MISDEMEANOR

2941.35 Prosecutions for misdemeanor

Prosecutions for misdemeanors may be instituted by a prosecuting attorney by affidavit or such other method as is provided by law in such courts as have original jurisdiction in misdemeanors. Laws as to form, sufficiency, amendments, objections, and exceptions to indictments and as to the service thereof apply to such affidavits and warrants issued thereon.

(1953 H 1, eff. 10–1–53; GC 13437–34)

WARRANTS

2941.36 Warrant for arrest of accused

A warrant may be issued at any time by an order of a court, or on motion of a prosecuting attorney after the indictment, information, or affidavit is filed. When directed to the sheriff of the county where such indictment was found or information or affidavit filed, he may pursue and arrest the accused in any county and commit him to jail or present him in open court, if court is in session.

(1953 H 1, eff. 10–1–53; GC 13438–1)

2941.37 Warrant when accused is nonresident

When an accused resides out of the county in which the indictment was found or information filed, a warrant may issue thereon, directed to the sheriff of the county where such accused resides or is found. Such sheriff shall arrest the accused and convey him to the county from which such warrant was issued, and there commit him to jail or present him in open court, if court is in session.

(1953 H 1, eff. 10–1–53; GC 13438–2)

2941.38 Warrant when accused escapes

When an accused escapes and forfeits his recognizance after the jury is sworn, a warrant reciting the facts may issue at the request of the prosecuting attorney, to the sheriff of any county, who shall pursue, arrest, and commit the accused to the jail of the county from which such warrant issued, until he is discharged.

(1953 H 1, eff. 10–1–53; GC 13438–3)

CONVICTS

2941.39 Indictment of convicts

When a convict in a state correctional institution is indicted for a felony committed while confined in the correctional institution, the convict shall remain in the custody of the department of rehabilitation and correction, subject to sections 2941.40 to 2941.46 of the Revised Code.

(1997 S 111, eff. 3–17–98; 1994 H 571, eff. 10–6–94; 1953 H 1, eff. 10–1–53; GC 13438–4)

2941.40 Convicts removed for sentence or trial

A convict in a state correctional institution, who escaped, forfeited his recognizance before receiving sentence for a felony, or against whom an indictment or information for felony is pending, may be removed to the county in which the conviction was had or the indictment or information was pending for sentence or trial, upon the warrant of the court of common pleas of the county.

(1994 H 571, eff. 10–6–94; 1969 H 508, eff. 10–24–69; 1953 H 1; GC 13438–5)

2941.401 Request by a prisoner for trial on pending charges

When a person has entered upon a term of imprisonment in a correctional institution of this state, and when during the continuance of the term of imprisonment there is pending in this state any untried indictment, information, or complaint against the prisoner, he shall be brought to trial within one hundred eighty days after he causes to be delivered to the prosecuting attorney and the appropriate court in which the matter is pending, written notice of the place of his imprisonment and a request for a final disposition to be made of the matter, except that for good cause shown in open court, with the prisoner or his counsel present, the court may grant any necessary or reasonable continuance. The request of the prisoner shall be accompanied by a certificate of the warden or superintendent having custody of the prisoner, stating the term of commitment under which the prisoner is being held, the time served and remaining to be served on the sentence, the amount of good time earned, the time of parole eligibility of the prisoner, and any decisions of the adult parole authority relating to the prisoner.

The written notice and request for final disposition shall be given or sent by the prisoner to the warden or superintendent having custody of him, who shall promptly forward it with the certificate to the appropriate prosecuting attorney and court by registered or certified mail, return receipt requested.

The warden or superintendent having custody of the prisoner shall promptly inform him in writing of the source and contents of any untried indictment, information, or complaint against him, concerning which the warden or superintendent has knowledge, and of his right to make a request for final disposition thereof.

Escape from custody by the prisoner, subsequent to his execution of the request for final disposition, voids the request.

If the action is not brought to trial within the time provided, subject to continuance allowed pursuant to this section, no court any longer has jurisdiction thereof, the indictment, information, or complaint is void, and the court shall enter an order dismissing the action with prejudice.

This section does not apply to any person adjudged to be mentally ill or who is under sentence of life imprisonment or death, or to any prisoner under sentence of death.

(1994 H 571, eff. 10–6–94; 1969 S 355, eff. 11–18–69)

2941.41 Warrant for removal

A warrant for removal specified in section 2941.40 of the Revised Code shall be in the usual form, except that it shall set forth that the accused is in a state correctional institution. The warrant shall be directed to the sheriff of the county in which the conviction was had or the indictment or information is pending. When a copy of the warrant is presented to the warden or the superintendent of a state correctional institution, he shall deliver the convict to the sheriff who shall convey him to the county and commit him to the county jail. For removing and returning the convict, the sheriff shall receive the fees allowed for conveying convicts to a state correctional institution.

(1994 H 571, eff. 10–6–94; 1981 H 145, eff. 5–28–81; 1953 H 1; GC 13438–6)

2941.42 Convict to be confined

A convict removed as provided by section 2941.41 of the Revised Code shall be kept in jail subject to be taken into court for sentence or trial. If the case is continued or the execution of the sentence is suspended, the court may order him to be returned to the state correctional institution by the sheriff, who shall deliver him, with a certified copy of the order, to the warden, who shall again deliver the convict to the sheriff upon another certified order of the court.

(1994 H 571, eff. 10–6–94; 1953 H 1, eff. 10–1–53; GC 13438–7)

2941.43 Disposition of prisoner following trial for another offense

If the convict referred to in section 2941.40 of the Revised Code is acquitted, he shall forthwith returned [1] by the sheriff to the state correctional institution to serve out the remainder of his sentence. If he is sentenced to imprisonment in a state correctional institution, he shall be returned to the state correctional institution by the sheriff to serve his new term. If he is sentenced to death, the death sentence shall be executed as if he were not under sentence of imprisonment in a state correctional institution.

(1994 H 571, eff. 10–6–94; 1972 H 511, eff. 1–1–74; 131 v H 700; 1953 H 1; GC 13438–8)

[1] So in original; should this read "be returned"?

2941.44 Arrests and return of escaped convicts; expenses

Sheriffs, deputy sheriffs, marshals, deputy marshals, watchmen, police officers, and coroners may arrest a convict escaping from a state correctional institution and forthwith convey him to the institution and deliver him to the warden of the institution. They shall be allowed ten cents per mile going to and returning from the institution and additional compensation that the warden finds reasonable for the necessary expense incurred.

(1994 H 571, eff. 10–6–94; 128 v 542, eff. 7–17–59; 1953 H 1; GC 13438–9)

2941.45 Trial of persons serving sentence

Any person serving a sentence in jail or the workhouse, who is indicted or informed against for another offense, may be brought before the court of common pleas upon warrant for that purpose, for arraignment and trial. Such person shall remain in the custody of the jailer or keeper of the workhouse, but may be temporarily confined in the jail, if a prisoner in the workhouse.

If such prisoner is convicted and sentenced upon trial, he shall be returned to the jail or workhouse to serve out the former sentence before the subsequent sentence is executed.

(1953 H 1, eff. 10–1–53; GC 13438–10)

2941.46 Arrest of convict or prisoner violating pardon or parole

(A) If a convict has been conditionally pardoned or a prisoner has been paroled from any state correctional institution, any peace officer may arrest the convict or prisoner without a warrant if the peace officer has reasonable ground to believe that the convict or prisoner has violated or is violating any rule governing the conduct of paroled prisoners prescribed by the adult parole authority or any of the following that is a condition of his pardon or parole:

(1) A condition that prohibits his ownership, posession, or use of a firearm, deadly weapon, ammunition, or dangerous ordnance;

(2) A condition that prohibits him from being within a specified structure or geographic area;

(3) A condition that confines him to a residence, facility, or other structure;

(4) A condition that prohibits him from contacting or communicating with any specified individual;

(5) A condition that prohibits him from associating with a specified individual.

(B) Upon making an arrest under this section, the arresting peace officer or his department or agency promptly shall notify the authority that the convict or prisoner has been arrested.

(C) Nothing in this section limits, or shall be construed to limit, the powers of arrest granted to certain law enforcement officers and citizens under sections 2935.03 and 2935.04 of the Revised Code.

(D) As used in this section:

(1) "State correctional institution," "pardon," "parole," "convict," and "prisoner" have the same meanings as in section 2967.01 of the Revised Code.

(2) "Peace officer" has the same meaning as in section 2935.01 of the Revised Code.

(3) "Firearm," "deadly weapon," and "dangerous ordnance" have the same meanings as in section 2923.11 of the Revised Code.

(1994 H 571, eff. 10–6–94; 1992 S 49, eff. 7–21–92; 130 v Pt 2, H 28; 1953 H 1; GC 13438–11)

MISCELLANEOUS PROVISIONS

2941.47 Summons on indictments against corporations

When an indictment is returned or information filed against a corporation, a summons commanding the sheriff to notify the accused thereof, returnable on the seventh day after its date, shall issue on praecipe of the prosecuting attorney. Such summons with a copy of the indictment shall be served and returned in the manner provided for service of summons upon corporations in civil actions. If the service cannot be made in the county where the prosecution began, the sheriff may make service in any other county of the state, upon the president, secretary, superintendent, clerk, treasurer, cashier, managing agent, or other chief officer thereof, or by leaving a copy at a general or branch office or usual place of doing business of such corporation, with the person having charge thereof. Such corporation shall appear by one of its officers or by counsel on or before the return day of the summons served and answer to the indictment or information by motion, demurrer, or plea, and upon failure to make such appearance and answer, the clerk of the court of common pleas shall enter a plea of "not guilty." Upon such appearance being made or plea entered, the corporation is before the court until the case is finally disposed of. On said indictment or information no warrant of arrest may issue except for individuals who may be included in such indictment or information.

(1953 H 1, eff. 10–1–53; GC 13438–12)

2941.48 Recognizance of witnesses

In any case pending in the court of common pleas, the court, either before or after indictment, may require any witness designated by the prosecuting attorney to enter into a recognizance, with or without surety, in such sum as the court thinks proper for his appearance to testify in such cause. A witness failing or refusing to comply with such order shall be committed to the county jail until he gives his testimony in such case or is ordered discharged by the court. If a witness is committed to jail upon order of court for want of such recognizance, he shall be paid while so confined like fees as are allowed witnesses by section 2335.08 of the Revised Code. The trial of such case has precedence over other cases and the court shall designate any early day for such trial.

(1953 H 1, eff. 10–1–53; GC 13438–13)

2941.49 Indictment to be served on accused

Within three days after the filing of an indictment for felony and in every other case when requested, the clerk of the court of common pleas shall make and deliver to the sheriff, defendant, or the defendant's counsel, a copy of such indictment. The sheriff, on receiving such copy, shall serve it on the defendant. A defendant, without his assent, shall not be arraigned or called on to answer to an indictment until one day has elapsed after receiving or having an opportunity to receive in person or by counsel, a copy of such indictment.

(1953 H 1, eff. 10–1–53; GC 13439–1)

2941.51 Person represented shall pay for part of costs if able

(A) Counsel appointed to a case or selected by an indigent person under division (E) of section 120.16 or division (E) of section 120.26 of the Revised Code, or otherwise appointed by the court, except for counsel appointed by the court to provide legal representation for a person charged with a violation of an ordinance of a municipal corporation, shall be paid for their services by the county the compensation and expenses that the trial court approves. Each request for payment shall be accompanied by a financial disclosure form and an affidavit of indigency that are completed by the indigent person on forms prescribed by the state public defender. Compensation and expenses shall not exceed the amounts fixed by the board of county commissioners pursuant to division (B) of this section.

(B) The board of county commissioners shall establish a schedule of fees by case or on an hourly basis to be paid by the county for legal services provided by appointed counsel. Prior to establishing such schedule, the board shall request the bar association or associations of the county to submit a proposed schedule. The schedule submitted shall be subject to the review, amendment, and approval of the board of county commissioners.

(C) In a case where counsel have been appointed to conduct an appeal under Chapter 120. of the Revised Code, such compensation shall be fixed by the court of appeals or the supreme court, as provided in divisions (A) and (B) of this section.

(D) The fees and expenses approved by the court under this section shall not be taxed as part of the costs and shall be paid by the county. However, if the person represented has, or reasonably may be expected to have, the means to meet some part of the cost of the services rendered to the person, the person shall pay the county an amount that the person reasonably can be expected to pay. Pursuant to section 120.04 of the Revised Code, the county shall pay to the state public defender a percentage of the payment received from the person in an amount proportionate to the percentage of the costs of the person's case that were paid to the county by the state public defender pursuant to this section. The money paid to the state public defender shall be credited to the client payment fund created pursuant to division (B)(5) of section 120.04 of the Revised Code.

(E) The county auditor shall draw a warrant on the county treasurer for the payment of such counsel in the amount fixed by the court, plus the expenses that the court fixes and certifies to the auditor. The county auditor shall report periodically, but not less than annually, to the board of county commissioners and to the Ohio public defender commission the amounts paid out pursuant to the approval of the court under this section, separately stating costs and expenses that are reimbursable under section 120.35 of the Revised Code. The board, after review and approval of the auditor's report, may then certify it to the state public defender for reimbursement. The request for reimbursement shall be accompanied by a financial disclosure form completed by each indigent person for whom counsel was provided on a form prescribed by the state public defender. The state public defender shall review the report and, in accordance with the standards, guidelines, and maximums established pursuant to divisions (B)(7) and (8) of section 120.04 of the Revised Code, pay fifty per cent of the total cost, other than costs and expenses that are reimbursable under section 120.35 of the Revised Code, if any, of paying appointed counsel in each county and pay fifty per cent of costs and expenses that are reimbursable under section 120.35 of the Revised Code, if any, to the board.

(F) If any county system for paying appointed counsel fails to maintain the standards for the conduct of the system established by the rules of the Ohio public defender commission pursuant to divisions (B) and (C) of section 120.03 of the Revised Code or the standards established by the state public defender pursuant to division (B)(7) of section 120.04 of the Revised Code, the commission shall notify the board of county commissioners of the county that the county system for paying appointed counsel has failed to comply with its rules. Unless the board corrects the conduct of its appointed counsel system to comply with the rules within ninety days after the date of the notice, the state public defender may deny all or part of the county's reimbursement from the state provided for in this section.

(1999 H 283, eff. 9–29–99; 1997 H 215, eff. 9–29–97; 1995 H 117, eff. 6–30–95; 1985 H 201, eff. 7–1–85; 1984 S 271; 1983 H 291; 1975 H 164; 132 v H 1; 131 v H 362; 128 v 54; 1953 H 1; GC 13439–3)

2941.53 Exceptions to an indictment

An accused may except to an indictment by:

(A) A motion to quash;

(B) A plea in abatement;

(C) A demurrer.

(1953 H 1, eff. 10–1–53; GC 13439–5)

DEMURRERS AND MOTIONS

2941.54 Motion to quash

A motion to quash may be made when there is a defect apparent upon the face of the record, within the meaning of sections 2941.02 to 2941.35, inclusive, of the Revised Code, including defects in the form of indictment and in the manner in which an offense is charged.

(1953 H 1, eff. 10–1–53; GC 13439–6)

2941.55 Plea in abatement

Plea in abatement may be made when there is a defect in the record shown by facts extrinsic thereto.

(1953 H 1, eff. 10–1–53; GC 13439–7)

2941.56 Misnomer

If the accused pleads in abatement that he is not indicted by his true name, he must plead his true name which shall be entered on the minutes of the court. After such entry, the trial and proceedings on the indictment shall be had against him by that name, referring also to the name by which he is indicted, as if he had been indicted by his true name.

(1953 H 1, eff. 10–1–53; GC 13439–8)

2941.57 Demurrer

The accused may demur:

(A) When the facts stated in the indictment do not constitute an offense punishable by the laws of this state;

(B) When the intent is not alleged and proof thereof is necessary to make out the offense charged;

(C) When it appears on the face of the indictment that the offense charged is not within the jurisdiction of the court.

(1953 H 1, eff. 10–1–53; GC 13439–9)

2941.58 Accused not discharged when indictment quashed

When a motion to quash or a plea in abatement is adjudged in favor of the accused, the trial court may order the case to be resubmitted to the grand jury, if then pending, or to the next succeeding grand jury. The accused then may be committed to jail or held to bail in such sum as the trial court requires for his appearance to answer at a time to be fixed by the court.

(1953 H 1, eff. 10–1–53; GC 13439–10)

2941.59 Waiver of defects

The accused waives all defects which may be excepted to by a motion to quash or a plea in abatement, by demurring to an indictment, or by pleading in bar or the general issue.

(1953 H 1, eff. 10–1–53; GC 13439–11)

2941.60 Answer to plea in abatement

The prosecuting attorney may demur to a plea in abatement if it is not sufficient in substance, or he may reply, setting forth any facts which may show there is no defect in the record as charged in the plea.

(1953 H 1, eff. 10–1–53; GC 13439–12)

2941.61 After demurrer accused may plead

After a demurrer to an indictment is overruled, the accused may plead under section 2943.03 of the Revised Code.

(1953 H 1, eff. 10–1–53; GC 13439–13)

2941.62 Hearing on motions and demurrers

Motions to quash, pleas in abatement, and demurrers shall be heard immediately upon their filing, unless the trial court, for good cause shown, sets another time for such hearing.

(1953 H 1, eff. 10–1–53; GC 13439–14)

2941.63 Counsel to assist prosecutor

The court of common pleas, or the court of appeals, whenever it is of the opinion that the public interest requires it, may appoint an attorney to assist the prosecuting attorney in the trial of a case pending in such court. The board of county commissioners shall pay said assistant to the prosecuting attorney such compensation for his services as the court approves.

(1953 H 1, eff. 10–1–53; GC 13439–15)

CHAPTER 2943

ARRAIGNMENT; PLEAS

MAGISTRATE DEFINED

2943.01 Definition of magistrate

The definition of "magistrate" set forth in section 2931.01 of the Revised Code applies to Chapter 2943. of the Revised Code.

(1953 H 1, eff. 10–1–53)

ARRAIGNMENT

2943.02 Arraignment

An accused person shall be arraigned by the clerk of the court of common pleas, or his deputy, reading the indictment or information to the accused, unless the accused or his attorney waives the reading thereof. He shall then be asked to plead thereto. Arraignment shall be made immediately after the disposition of exceptions to the indictment, if any are filed, or, if no exceptions are filed, after reasonable opportunity has been given the accused to file such exceptions.

(1953 H 1, eff. 10–1–53; GC 13440–1)

PLEAS

2943.03 Pleas to indictment

Pleas to an indictment or information are:

(A) Guilty;

(B) Not guilty;

(C) A former judgment of conviction or acquittal of the offense;

(D) Once in jeopardy;

(E) Not guilty by reason of insanity.

A defendant who does not plead guilty may enter one or more of the other pleas. A defendant who does not plead not guilty by reason of insanity is conclusively presumed to have been sane at the time of the commission of the offense charged. The court may, for good cause shown, allow a change of plea at any time before the commencement of the trial.

(1953 H 1, eff. 10–1–53; GC 13440–2)

2943.031 Court advising defendants on possibility of deportation, exclusion, or denial of naturalization prior to accepting pleas

(A) Except as provided in division (B) of this section, prior to accepting a plea of guilty or a plea of no contest to an indictment, information, or complaint charging a felony or a misdemeanor other than a minor misdemeanor if the defendant previously has not been convicted of or pleaded guilty to a minor misdemeanor, the court shall address the defendant personally, provide the following advisement to the defendant that shall be entered in the record of the court, and determine that the defendant understands the advisement:

"If you are not a citizen of the United States, you are hereby advised that conviction of the offense to which you are pleading guilty (or no contest, when applicable) may have the consequences of deportation, exclusion from admission to the United States, or denial of naturalization pursuant to the laws of the United States."

Upon request of the defendant, the court shall allow him additional time to consider the appropriateness of the plea in light of the advisement described in this division.

(B) The court is not required to give the advisement described in division (A) of this section if either of the following applies:

(1) The defendant enters a plea of guilty on a written form, the form includes a question asking whether the defendant is a citizen of the United States, and the defendant answers that question in the affirmative;

(2) The defendant states orally on the record that he is a citizen of the United States.

(C) Except as provided in division (B) of this section, the defendant shall not be required at the time of entering a plea to disclose to the court his legal status in the United States.

(D) Upon motion of the defendant, the court shall set aside the judgment and permit the defendant to withdraw a plea of guilty or no contest and enter a plea of not guilty or not guilty by reason of insanity, if, after the effective date of this section, the court fails to provide the defendant the advisement described in division (A) of this section, the advisement is required by that division, and the defendant shows that he is not a citizen of the United States and that the conviction of the offense to which he pleaded guilty or no contest may result in his being subject to deportation, exclusion from admission to the United States, or denial of naturalization pursuant to the laws of the United States.

(E) In the absence of a record that the court provided the advisement described in division (A) of this section and if the advisement is required by that division, the defendant shall be presumed not to have received the advisement.

(F) Nothing in this section shall be construed as preventing a court, in the sound exercise of its discretion pursuant to Criminal Rule 32.1, from setting aside the judgment of conviction and permitting a defendant to withdraw his plea.

(1989 S 95, eff. 10–2–89)

2943.032 Court to inform defendant prison term may be administratively extended for offenses committed during term before accepting plea

Prior to accepting a guilty plea or a plea of no contest to an indictment, information, or complaint that charges a felony, the court shall inform the defendant personally that, if the defendant pleads guilty or no contest to the felony so charged or any other felony and if the court imposes a prison term upon the defendant for the felony, all of the following apply:

(A) The parole board may extend the stated prison term if the defendant commits any criminal offense under the law of this state or the United States while serving the prison term.

(B) Any such extension will be done administratively as part of the defendant's sentence in accordance with section 2967.11 of the Revised Code and may be for thirty, sixty, or ninety days for each violation.

(C) All such extensions of the stated prison term for all violations during the course of the term may not exceed one-half of the term's duration.

(D) The sentence imposed for the felony automatically includes any such extension of the stated prison term by the parole board.

(E) If the offender violates the conditions of a post-release control sanction imposed by the parole board upon the completion of the stated prison term, the parole board may impose upon the offender a residential sanction that includes a new prison term up to nine months.

(1995 S 2, eff. 7–1–96)

2943.04 Form of plea

Pleas of guilty or not guilty may be oral. Pleas in all other cases shall be in writing, subscribed by the defendant or his counsel, and shall immediately be entered upon the minutes of the court.

(1953 H 1, eff. 10–1–53; GC 13440–3)

DOUBLE JEOPARDY

2943.05 Form of plea of former conviction

If a defendant pleads that he has had former judgment of conviction or acquittal, or has been once in jeopardy, he must set forth in his plea the court, time, and place of such conviction, acquittal, or jeopardy. No claim of former judgment of conviction or acquittal, or jeopardy may be given in evidence under the plea of not guilty.

(1953 H 1, eff. 10–1–53; GC 13440–4)

2943.06 Trial of issue on plea of former conviction

If a defendant pleads a judgment of conviction, acquittal, or former jeopardy, the prosecuting attorney may reply that there is no such conviction, acquittal, or jeopardy. The issue thus made shall be tried to a jury, and on such trial the defendant must produce the record of such conviction, acquittal, or jeopardy, and prove that he is the person charged in such record, and he may also introduce other evidence to establish the identity of such offense. If the prosecuting attorney demurs to said plea and said demurrer is overruled, the prosecuting attorney may then reply to said plea.

(1953 H 1, eff. 10–1–53; GC 13440–5)

2943.07 What is not former acquittal

If a defendant was formerly acquitted on the ground of variance between the indictment or information and the proof, or if the indictment or information was dismissed, without a judgment of acquittal, upon an objection to its form or substance, or in order to hold the defendant for a higher offense, it is not an acquittal of the same offense.

(1953 H 1, eff. 10–1–53; GC 13440–6)

2943.08 What is former acquittal

Whenever a defendant is acquitted on the merits, he is acquitted of the same offense, notwithstanding any defect in form or substance in the indictment or information on which the trial was had.

(1953 H 1, eff. 10–1–53; GC 13440–7)

2943.09 Conviction or acquittal of a higher offense

When a defendant has been convicted or acquitted, or has been once in jeopardy upon an indictment or information, the conviction, acquittal, or jeopardy is a bar to another indictment or information for the offense charged in the former indictment or information, or for an attempt to commit the same offense, or for an offense necessarily included therein, of which he might have been convicted under the former indictment or information.

(1953 H 1, eff. 10–1–53; GC 13440–8)

2943.10 Proceedings after verdict on plea in bar

If the issue on the plea in bar under section 2943.06 of the Revised Code is found for the defendant he shall be discharged. If the issue is found against the defendant the case shall proceed and be disposed of upon his other pleas.

(1953 H 1, eff. 10–1–53; GC 13440–9)

CHAPTER 2945

TRIAL

PRELIMINARY PROVISIONS

2945.01 Definition of magistrate

The definition of "magistrate" set forth in section 2931.01 of the Revised Code applies to Chapter 2945. of the Revised Code.

(1953 H 1, eff. 10–1–53)

2945.02 Setting and continuing cases

The court of common pleas shall set all criminal cases for trial for a day not later than thirty days after the date of entry of the plea of the defendant. No continuance of the trial shall be granted except upon affirmative proof in open court, upon reasonable notice, that the ends of justice require a continuance.

No continuance shall be granted for any other time than it is affirmatively proved the ends of justice require.

Whenever any continuance is granted, the court shall enter on the journal the reason for the same.

Criminal cases shall be given precedence over civil matters and proceedings. The failure of the court to set such criminal cases for trial, as required by this section, does not operate as an acquittal, but upon notice of such failure or upon motion of the prosecuting attorney or a defendant, such case shall forthwith be set for trial within a reasonable time, not exceeding thirty days thereafter.

(1953 H 1, eff. 10–1–53; GC 13442–1)

2945.03 Control of trial

The judge of the trial court shall control all proceedings during a criminal trial, and shall limit the introduction of evidence and the argument of counsel to relevant and material matters with a view to expeditious and effective ascertainment of the truth regarding the matters in issue.

(1953 H 1, eff. 10–1–53; GC 13442–2)

2945.04 Protective orders available if it is found likely that intimidation of crime victim or witness or domestic violence will occur; procedures; contempt of court

(A) If a motion is filed with a court before which a criminal case is pending alleging that a person has committed or is reasonably likely to commit any act prohibited by section 2921.04 of the Revised Code in relation to the case, if the court holds a hearing on the motion, and if the court determines that the allegations made in the motion are true, the court may issue an order doing any or any combination of the following, subject to division (C) of this section:

(1) Directing the defendant in the case not to violate or to cease a violation of section 2921.04 of the Revised Code;

(2) Directing a person other than a defendant who is before the court, including, but not limited to, a subpoenaed witness or other person entering the courtroom of the court, not to violate or to cease a violation of section 2921.04 of the Revised Code;

(3) Directing the defendant or a person described in division (A)(2) of this section to maintain a prescribed geographic distance from any specified person who is before the court, including, but not limited to, the victim of the offense that is the basis of the case or a subpoenaed witness in the case;

(4) Directing the defendant or a person described in division (A)(2) of this section not to communicate with any specified person who is before the court, including, but not limited to, the victim of the offense or a subpoenaed witness in the case;

(5) Directing a specified law enforcement agency that serves a political subdivision within the territorial jurisdiction of the court to provide protection for any specified person who is before the court, including, but not limited to, the victim of the offense or a subpoenaed witness in the case;

(6) Any other reasonable order that would assist in preventing or causing the cessation of a violation of section 2921.04 of the Revised Code.

(B) If a motion is filed with a court in which a criminal complaint has been filed alleging that the offender or another person acting in concert with the offender has committed or is reasonably likely to commit any act that would constitute an offense against the person or property of the complainant, his ward, or his child, if the court holds a hearing on the motion, and if the court determines that the allegations made in the motion are true, the court may issue an order doing one or more of the following, subject to division (C) of this section:

(1) Directing the defendant in the case not to commit an act or to cease committing an act that constitutes an offense against the person or property of the complainant, his ward, or child;

(2) Directing a person other than the defendant who is before the court, including, but not limited to, a subpoenaed witness or other person entering the courtroom, not to commit an act or to cease committing an act that constitutes an offense against the person or property of the complainant, his ward, or child;

(3) Directing the defendant or a person described in division (B)(2) of this section to maintain a prescribed geographic distance from any specified person who is before the court, including, but not limited to, the complainant or the victim of the offense, or a subpoenaed witness in the case;

(4) Directing the defendant or a person described in division (B)(2) of this section not to communicate with any specified person who is before the court, including, but not limited to, the complainant, the victim of the offense, or a subpoenaed witness in the case;

(5) Directing a specified law enforcement agency that serves a political subdivision within the territorial jurisdiction of the court to provide protection for any specified person who is before the court, including, but not limited to, the complainant, the victim of the offense, or a subpoenaed witness in the case;

(6) When the complainant and the defendant cohabit with one another but the complainant is not a family or household member, as defined in section 2919.25 of the Revised Code, granting possession of the residence or household to the complainant to the exclusion of the defendant by evicting the defendant when the residence or household is owned or leased solely by the complainant or by ordering the defendant to vacate the premises when the residence or household is jointly owned or leased by the complainant and the defendant;

(7) Any other reasonable order that would assist in preventing or causing the cessation of an act that constitutes an offense against the person or property of the complainant, his ward, or child.

(C) No order issued under authority of division (A) or (B) of this section shall prohibit or be construed as prohibiting any attorney for the defendant in the case or for a person described in division (A)(2) or (B)(2) of this section from conducting any investigation of the pending criminal case, from preparing or conducting any defense of the pending criminal case, or from attempting to zealously represent his client in the pending criminal case within the bounds of the law. However, this division does not exempt any person from the prohibitions contained in section 2921.04 or any section of the Revised Code that constitutes an offense against the person or property of the complainant, his ward, or his child, or provide a defense to a charge of any violation of that section or of an offense of that nature.

(D)(1) A person who violates an order issued pursuant to division (A) of this section is subject to the following sanctions:

(a) Criminal prosecution for a violation of section 2921.04 of the Revised Code, if the violation of the court order constitutes a violation of that section;

(b) Punishment for contempt of court.

(2) A person who violates an order issued pursuant to division (B) of this section is subject to the following sanctions:

(a) Criminal prosecution for a violation of a section of the Revised Code that constitutes an offense against the person or property of the complainant, his ward, or child;

(b) Punishment for contempt of court.

(E)(1) The punishment of a person for contempt of court for violation of an order issued pursuant to division (A) of this section does not bar criminal prosecution of the person for a violation of section 2921.04 of the Revised Code.

(2) The punishment of a person for contempt of court for a violation of an order issued pursuant to division (B) of this section does not bar criminal prosecution of the person for an offense against the person or property of the complainant, his ward, or child.

(3) A person punished for contempt of court under this section is entitled to credit for the punishment imposed upon conviction of a violation of the offense arising out of the same activity, and a person convicted of such a violation shall not subsequently be punished for contempt of court arising out of the same activity.

(1994 H 335, eff. 12–9–94; 1984 S 172, eff. 9–26–84)

TRIAL BY COURT

2945.05 Defendant may waive jury trial

In all criminal cases pending in courts of record in this state, the defendant may waive a trial by jury and be tried by the court without a jury. Such waiver by a defendant, shall be in writing, signed by the defendant, and filed in said cause and made a part of the record thereof. It shall be entitled in the court and cause, and in substance as follows: "I ________, defendant in the above cause, hereby voluntarily waive and relinquish my right to a trial by jury, and elect to be tried by a Judge of the Court in which the said cause may be pending. I fully understand that under the laws of this state, I have a constitutional right to a trial by jury."

Such waiver of trial by jury must be made in open court after the defendant has been arraigned and has had opportunity to consult with counsel. Such waiver may be withdrawn by the defendant at any time before the commencement of the trial.

(1953 H 1, eff. 10–1–53; GC 13442–4)

2945.06 Jurisdiction of judge when jury trial is waived; three–judge court

In any case in which a defendant waives his right to trial by jury and elects to be tried by the court under section 2945.05 of the Revised Code, any judge of the court in which the cause is pending shall proceed to hear, try, and determine the cause in accordance with the rules and in like manner as if the cause were being tried before a jury. If the accused is charged with an offense punishable with death, he shall be tried by a court to be composed of three judges, consisting of the judge presiding at the time in the trial of criminal cases and two other judges to be designated by the presiding judge or chief justice of that court, and in case there is neither a presiding judge nor a chief justice, by the chief justice of the supreme court. The judges or a majority of them may decide all questions of fact and law arising upon the trial; however the accused shall not be found guilty or not guilty of any offense unless the judges unanimously find the accused guilty or not guilty. If the accused pleads guilty of aggravated murder, a court composed of three judges shall examine the witnesses, determine whether the accused is guilty of aggravated murder or any other offense, and pronounce sentence accordingly. The court shall follow the procedures contained in sections 2929.03 and 2929.04 of the Revised Code in all cases in which the accused is charged with an offense punishable by death. If in the composition of the court it is necessary that a judge from another county be assigned by the chief justice, the judge from another county shall be compensated for his services as provided by section 141.07 of the Revised Code.

(1981 S 1, eff. 10–19–81; 1953 H 1; GC 13442–5)

TRIAL PROCEDURE

2945.08 Prosecution in wrong county; proceeding

If it appears, on the trial of a criminal cause, that the offense was committed within the exclusive jurisdiction of another county of this state, the court must direct the defendant to be committed to await a warrant from the proper county for his arrest, but if the offense is a bailable offense the court may admit the defendant to bail with sufficient sureties conditioned, that he will, within such time as the court appoints, render himself amenable to a warrant for his arrest from the proper county, and if not sooner arrested thereon, will appear in court at the time fixed to surrender himself upon the warrant.

The clerk of the court of common pleas shall forthwith notify the prosecuting attorney of the county in which such offense was committed, in order that proper proceedings may be had in the case. A defendant in such case shall not be committed nor held under bond for a period of more than ten days.

(1953 H 1, eff. 10–1–53; GC 13442–6)

2945.09 Grounds of objection to be stated

In the trial of any criminal case, the grounds of an objection to any ruling or action of the court shall be stated if required by the court.

(1986 H 412, eff. 3–17–87; 1953 H 1; GC 13442–7)

2945.10 Order of proceedings of trial

The trial of an issue upon an indictment or information shall proceed before the trial court or jury as follows:

(A) Counsel for the state must first state the case for the prosecution, and may briefly state the evidence by which he expects to sustain it.

(B) The defendant or his counsel must then state his defense, and may briefly state the evidence which he expects to offer in support of it.

(C) The state must first produce its evidence and the defendant shall then produce his evidence.

(D) The state will then be confined to rebutting evidence, but the court, for good reason, in furtherance of justice, may permit evidence to be offered by either side out of its order.

(E) When the evidence is concluded, either party may request instructions to the jury on the points of law, which instructions shall be reduced to writing if either party requests it.

(F) When the evidence is concluded, unless the case is submitted without argument, the counsel for the state shall commence, the defendant or his counsel follow, and the counsel for the state conclude the argument to the jury.

(G) The court, after the argument is concluded and before proceeding with other business, shall forthwith charge the jury. Such charge shall be reduced to writing by the court if either party requests it before the argument to the jury is commenced. Such charge, or other charge or instruction provided for in this section, when so written and given, shall not be orally qualified, modified, or explained to the jury by the court. Written charges and instructions shall be taken by the jury in their retirement and returned with their verdict into court and remain on file with the papers of the case.

The court may deviate from the order of proceedings listed in this section.

(1953 H 1, eff. 10–1–53; GC 13442–8)

2945.11 Charge to the jury as to law and fact

In charging the jury, the court must state to it all matters of law necessary for the information of the jury in giving its verdict. The court must also inform the jury that the jury is the exclusive judge of all questions of fact. The court must state to the jury that in determining the question of guilt, it must not consider the punishment but that punishment rests with the judge except in cases of murder in the first degree or burglary of an inhabited dwelling.

(1953 H 1, eff. 10–1–53; GC 13442–9)

2945.12 When accused may be tried in his absence

A person indicted for a misdemeanor, upon request in writing subscribed by him and entered in the journal, may be tried in his absence by a jury or by the court. No other person shall be tried unless personally present, but if a person indicted escapes or forfeits his recognizance after the jury is sworn, the trial shall proceed and the verdict be received and recorded. If the offense charged is a misdemeanor, judgment and sentence shall be pronounced as if he were personally present. If the offense charged is a felony, the case shall be continued until the accused appears in court, or is retaken.

(1953 H 1, eff. 10–1–53; GC 13442–10)

2945.13 Joint trials in felony cases

When two or more persons are jointly indicted for a felony, except a capital offense, they shall be tried jointly unless the court, for good cause shown on application therefor by the prosecuting attorney or one or more of said defendants, orders one or more of said defendants to be tried separately.

(1953 H 1, eff. 10–1–53; GC 13442–11)

2945.14 Mistake in charging offense

If it appears during the trial and before submission to the jury or court, that a mistake has been made in charging the proper offense in the indictment or information, the court may order a discontinuance of trial without prejudice to the prosecution. The accused, if there is good cause to detain him, may be recognized to appear at the same or next succeeding term of court, or in default thereof committed to jail. In such case the court shall recognize the witnesses for the state to appear at the same time and testify.

(1953 H 1, eff. 10–1–53; GC 13442–12)

2945.15 Discharge of defendant

When two or more persons are tried jointly, before any of the accused has gone into his defense the trial court may direct one or more of such accused to be discharged that he may be a witness for the state.

An accused person, when there is not sufficient evidence to put him upon his defense, may be discharged by the court, but if not so discharged, shall be entitled to the immediate verdict of the jury in his favor. Such order of discharge, in either case, is a bar to another prosecution for the same offense.

(1953 H 1, eff. 10–1–53; GC 13442–13)

2945.16 View of the premises

When it is proper for the jurors to have a view of the place at which a material fact occurred, the trial court may order them to be conducted in a body, under the charge of the sheriff or other officer, to such place, which shall be shown to them by a person designated by the court. While the jurors are absent on such view no person other than such officer and such person so appointed, shall speak to them on any subject connected with the trial. The accused has the right to attend such view by the jury, but may waive this right.

The expense of such view as approved by the court shall be taxed as other costs in the case.

(129 v 1201, eff. 9–11–61; 1953 H 1; GC 13442–14)

TRIAL BY JURY

2945.17 Right of trial by jury

(A) At any trial, in any court, for the violation of any statute of this state, or of any ordinance of any municipal corporation, except as provided in divisions (B) and (C) of this section, the accused has the right to be tried by a jury.

(B) The right to be tried by a jury that is granted under division (A) of this section does not apply to a violation of a statute or ordinance that is any of the following:

(1) A violation that is a minor misdemeanor;

(2) A violation for which the potential penalty does not include the possibility of a prison term or jail term and for which the possible fine does not exceed one thousand dollars.

(C) Division (A) of this section does not apply to, and there is no right to a jury trial for, a person who is the subject of a complaint filed under section 2151.27 of the Revised Code against both a child and the parent, guardian, or other person having care of the child.

(2002 H 490, eff. 1–1–04; 2000 S 179, eff. 4–9–01; 1972 H 511, eff. 1–1–74; 1953 H 1; GC 13443)

2945.171 Verdict in writing

In all criminal cases the verdict of the jury shall be in writing and signed by each of the jurors concurring therein.

(129 v 336, eff. 9–28–61)

2945.20 Separate trial for capital offense

When two or more persons are jointly indicted for a capital offense, each of such persons shall be tried separately. The court, for good cause shown on application therefor by the prosecuting attorney or one or more of the defendants, may order said defendants to be tried jointly.

(1953 H 1, eff. 10–1–53; GC 13443–3)

2945.21 Peremptory challenges in capital cases

(A)(1) In criminal cases in which there is only one defendant, each party, in addition to the challenges for cause authorized by law, may peremptorily challenge three of the jurors in misdemeanor cases and four of the jurors in felony cases other than capital cases. If there is more than one defendant, each defendant may peremptorily challenge the same number of jurors as if he were the sole defendant.

(2) Notwithstanding Criminal Rule 24, in capital cases in which there is only one defendant, each party, in addition to the challenges for cause authorized by law, may peremptorily challenge twelve of the jurors. If there is more than one defendant, each defendant may peremptorily challenge the same number of jurors as if he were the sole defendant.

(3) In any case in which there are multiple defendants, the prosecuting attorney may peremptorily challenge a number of jurors equal to the total number of peremptory challenges allowed to all of the defendants.

(B) If any indictments, informations, or complaints are consolidated for trial, the consolidated cases shall be considered, for purposes of exercising peremptory challenges, as though the defendants or offenses had been joined in the same indictment, information, or complaint.

(C) The exercise of peremptory challenges authorized by this section shall be in accordance with the procedures of Criminal Rule 24.

(1981 S 1, eff. 10–19–81; 1953 H 1; GC 13443–4)

2945.23 When peremptory challenges required

Except by agreement, neither the state nor the defendant shall be required to exercise any peremptory challenge until twelve jurors have been passed for cause and are in the panel.

(1953 H 1, eff. 10–1–53; GC 13443–7)

2945.24 Selecting juries for criminal cases

In all criminal cases, a jury summoned and impaneled under sections 2313.01 to 2313.47 of the Revised Code shall try the accused.

(1993 H 41, eff. 9–27–93; 1981 S 1; 1976 H 133; 1953 H 1; GC 13443–5)

2945.25 Causes of challenging of jurors

A person called as a juror in a criminal case may be challenged for the following causes:

(A) That he was a member of the grand jury that found the indictment in the case;

(B) That he is possessed of a state of mind evincing enmity or bias toward the defendant or the state; but no person summoned as a juror shall be disqualified by reason of a previously formed or expressed opinion with reference to the guilt or innocence of the accused, if the court is satisfied, from examination of the juror or from other evidence, that he will render an impartial verdict according to the law and the evidence submitted to the jury at the trial;

(C) In the trial of a capital offense, that he unequivocally states that under no circumstances will he follow the instructions of a trial judge and consider fairly the imposition of a sentence of death in a particular case. A prospective juror's conscientious or religious opposition to the death penalty in and of itself is not grounds for a challenge for cause. All parties shall be given wide latitude in voir dire questioning in this regard.

(D) That he is related by consanguinity or affinity within the fifth degree to the person alleged to be injured or attempted to be injured by the offense charged, or to the person on whose complaint the prosecution was instituted, or to the defendant;

(E) That he served on a petit jury drawn in the same cause against the same defendant, and that jury was discharged after hearing the evidence or rendering a verdict on the evidence that was set aside;

(F) That he served as a juror in a civil case brought against the defendant for the same act;

(G) That he has been subpoenaed in good faith as a witness in the case;

(H) That he is a chronic alcoholic, or drug dependent person;

(I) That he has been convicted of a crime that by law disqualifies him from serving on a jury;

(J) That he has an action pending between him and the state or the defendant;

(K) That he or his spouse is a party to another action then pending in any court in which an attorney in the cause then on trial is an attorney, either for or against him;

(L) That he is the person alleged to be injured or attempted to be injured by the offense charged, or is the person on whose complaint the prosecution was instituted, or the defendant;

(M) That he is the employer or employee, or the spouse, parent, son, or daughter of the employer or employee, or the counselor, agent, or attorney of any person included in division (L) of this section;

(N) That English is not his native language, and his knowledge of English is insufficient to permit him to understand the facts and law in the case;

(O) That he otherwise is unsuitable for any other cause to serve as a juror.

The validity of each challenge listed in this section shall be determined by the court.

(1981 S 1, eff. 10–19–81; 1980 H 965; 1953 H 1; GC 13443–8)

2945.26 Challenge for cause

Challenges for cause shall be tried by the court on the oath of the person challenged, or other evidence, and shall be made before the jury is sworn.

(1953 H 1, eff., 10–1–53; GC 13443–9)

2945.27 Examination of jurors by the court

The judge of the trial court shall examine the prospective jurors under oath or upon affirmation as to their qualifications to serve as fair and impartial jurors, but he shall permit reasonable examination of such jurors by the prosecuting attorney and by the defendant or his counsel.

(127 v 419, eff. 9–9–57; 1953 H 1; GC 13443–10)

2945.28 Form of oath to jury

Note: See also following version of this section, eff. 5–18–05.

In criminal cases jurors and the jury shall take the following oath to be administered by the trial court or the clerk of the court of common pleas: "You shall well and truly try, and true deliverance make between the State of Ohio and the defendant (giving his name). So help you God."

A juror shall be allowed to make affirmation and the words "this you do as you shall answer under the pains and penalties of perjury" shall be substituted for the words, "So help you God."

(1953 H 1, eff. 10–1–53; GC 13443–11, 13443–12)

Note: See also following version of this section, eff. 5–18–05.

2945.28 Form of oath to jury; effect of form on validity of impanelment (later effective date)

Note: See also preceding version of this section, in effect until 5–18–05.

(A) In criminal cases jurors and the jury shall take the following oath to be administered by the trial court or the clerk of the court of common pleas, and the jurors shall respond to the oath "I do swear" or "I do affirm": " Do you swear or affirm that you will diligently inquire into and carefully deliberate all matters between the State of Ohio and the defendant (giving the defendant's name)? Do you swear or affirm you will do this to the best of your skill and understanding, without bias or prejudice? So help you God."

A juror shall be allowed to make affirmation and the words "this you do as you shall answer under the pains and penalties of perjury" shall be substituted for the words, "So help you God."

(B) If, on or after the effective date of this amendment, a court that impanels a jury in a criminal case uses the oath that was in effect prior to the effective date of this amendment instead of the oath set forth in division (A) of this section, the court's use of the former oath does not invalidate or affect the validity of the impanelment of the jury or any action taken by the jury.

(2004 S 71, eff. 5–18–05; 1953 H 1, eff. 10–1–53; GC 13443–11, 13443–12)

Note: See also preceding version of this section, in effect until 5–18–05.

2945.29 Jurors becoming unable to perform duties

If, before the conclusion of the trial, a juror becomes sick, or for other reason is unable to perform his duty, the court may order him to be discharged. In that case, if alternate jurors have been selected, one of them shall be designated to take the place of the juror so discharged. If, after all alternate jurors have been made regular jurors, a juror becomes too incapacitated to perform his duty, and has been discharged by the court, a new juror may be sworn and the trial begin anew, or the jury may be discharged and a new jury then or thereafter impaneled.

(1953 H 1, eff. 10–1–53; GC 13443–13)

2945.30 Medical attendance of juror

In case of sickness of any juror before the conclusion of the trial, the court may order that such juror receive medical attendance and shall order the payment of a reasonable charge for such medical attendance out of the judiciary fund.

(1953 H 1, eff. 10–1–53; GC 13443–14)

2945.31 Separation of jurors

After the trial has commenced, before or after the jury is sworn, the court may order the jurors to be kept in charge of proper officers, or they may be permitted to separate during the trial. If the jurors are kept in charge of officers of the court, proper arrangements shall be made for their care, maintenance, and comfort, under the orders and direction of the court. In case of necessity the court may permit temporary separation of the jurors.

(1953 H 1, eff. 10–1–53; GC 13443–15)

2945.32 Oath to officers if jury sequestered

When an order has been entered by the court of common pleas in any criminal cause, directing the jurors to be kept in charge of the officers of the court, the following oath shall be administered by the clerk of the court of common pleas to said officers: "You do solemnly swear that you will, to the best of your ability, keep the persons sworn as jurors on this trial, from separating from each other; that you will not suffer any communications to be made to them, or any of them, orally or otherwise; that you will not communicate with them, or any of them, orally or otherwise, except by the order of this court, or to ask them if they have agreed on their verdict, until they shall be discharged, and that you will not, before they render their verdict communicate to any person the state of their deliberations or the verdict they have agreed upon, so help you God." Any officer having taken such oath who willfully violates the same, or permits the same to be violated, is guilty of perjury and shall be imprisoned not less than one nor more than ten years.

(1953 H 1, eff. 10–1–53; GC 13443–16; Source—GC 12842)

2945.33 Keeping and conduct of jury after case submitted

When a cause is finally submitted the jurors must be kept together in a convenient place under the charge of an officer until they agree upon a verdict, or are discharged by the court. The court, except in cases where the offense charged may be punishable by death, may permit the jurors to separate during the adjournment of court overnight, under proper cautions, or under supervision of an officer. Such officer shall not permit a communication to be made to them, nor make any himself except to ask if they have agreed upon a verdict, unless he does so by order of the court. Such officer shall not communicate to any person, before the verdict is delivered, any matter in relation to their deliberation. Upon the trial of any prosecution for misdemeanor, the court may permit the jury to separate during their deliberation, or upon adjournment of the court overnight.

In cases where the offense charged may be punished by death, after the case is finally submitted to the jury, the jurors shall be kept in charge of the proper officer and proper arrangements for their care and maintenance shall be made as under section 2945.31 of the Revised Code.

(131 v H 708, eff. 11–9–65; 1953 H 1; GC 13448–1)

2945.34 Admonition if jurors separate during trial

If the jurors are permitted to separate during a trial, they shall be admonished by the court not to converse with, nor permit themselves to be addressed by any person, nor to listen to any conversation on the subject of the trial, nor form or express any opinion thereon, until the case is finally submitted to them.

(1953 H 1, eff. 10–1–53; GC 13443–17)

2945.35 Papers the jury may take

Upon retiring for deliberation, the jury, at the discretion of the court, may take with it all papers except depositions, and all articles, photographs, and maps which have been offered in evidence. No article or paper identified but not admitted in evidence shall be taken by the jury upon its retirement.

(1953 H 1, eff. 10–1–53; GC 13444–26)

2945.36 For what cause jury may be discharged

The trial court may discharge a jury without prejudice to the prosecution:

(A) For the sickness or corruption of a juror or other accident or calamity;

(B) Because there is no probability of such jurors agreeing;

(C) If it appears after the jury has been sworn that one of the jurors is a witness in the case;

(D) By the consent of the prosecuting attorney and the defendant.

The reason for such discharge shall be entered on the journal.

(1953 H 1, eff. 10–1–53; GC 13443–18)

INSANITY

2945.37 Competence to stand trial; raising of issue; procedures; municipal courts

(A) As used in sections 2945.37 to 2945.402 of the Revised Code:

(1) "Prosecutor" means a prosecuting attorney or a city director of law, village solicitor, or similar chief legal officer of a municipal corporation who has authority to prosecute a criminal case that is before the court or the criminal case in which a defendant in a criminal case has been found incompetent to stand trial or not guilty by reason of insanity.

(2) "Examiner" means either of the following:

(a) A psychiatrist or a licensed clinical psychologist who satisfies the criteria of division (I)(1) of section 5122.01 of the Revised Code or is employed by a certified forensic center designated by the department of mental health to conduct examinations or evaluations.

(b) For purposes of a separate mental retardation evaluation that is ordered by a court pursuant to division (H) of section 2945.371 of the Revised Code, a psychologist designated by the director of mental retardation and developmental disabilities pursuant to that section to conduct that separate mental retardation evaluation.

(3) "Nonsecured status" means any unsupervised, off-grounds movement or trial visit from a hospital or institution, or any conditional release, that is granted to a person who is found incompetent to stand trial and is committed pursuant to section 2945.39 of the Revised Code or to a person who is found not guilty by reason of insanity and is committed pursuant to section 2945.40 of the Revised Code.

(4) "Unsupervised, off-grounds movement" includes only off-grounds privileges that are unsupervised and that have an expectation of return to the hospital or institution on a daily basis.

(5) "Trial visit" means a patient privilege of a longer stated duration of unsupervised community contact with an expectation of return to the hospital or institution at designated times.

(6) "Conditional release" means a commitment status under which the trial court at any time may revoke a person's conditional release and order the rehospitalization or reinstitutionalization of the person as described in division (A) of section 2945.402 of the Revised Code and pursuant to which a person who is found incompetent to stand trial or a person who is found not guilty by reason of insanity lives and receives treatment in the community for a period of time that does not exceed the maximum prison term or term of imprisonment that the person could have received for the offense in question had the person been convicted of the offense instead of being found incompetent to stand trial on the charge of the offense or being found not guilty by reason of insanity relative to the offense.

(7) "Licensed clinical psychologist," "mentally ill person subject to hospitalization by court order," and "psychiatrist" have the same meanings as in section 5122.01 of the Revised Code.

(8) "Mentally retarded person subject to institutionalization by court order" has the same meaning as in section 5123.01 of the Revised Code.

(B) In a criminal action in a court of common pleas, a county court, or a municipal court, the court, prosecutor, or defense may raise the issue of the defendant's competence to stand trial. If the issue is raised before the trial has commenced, the court shall hold a hearing on the issue as provided in this section. If the issue is raised after the trial has commenced, the court shall hold a hearing on the issue only for good cause shown or on the court's own motion.

(C) The court shall conduct the hearing required or authorized under division (B) of this section within thirty days after the issue is raised, unless the defendant has been referred for evaluation in which case the court shall conduct the hearing within ten days after the filing of the report of the evaluation or, in the case of a defendant who is ordered by the court pursuant to division (H) of section 2945.371 of the Revised Code to undergo a separate mental retardation evaluation conducted by a psychologist designated by the director of mental retardation and developmental disabilities, within ten days after the filing of the report of the separate mental retardation evaluation under that division. A hearing may be continued for good cause.

(D) The defendant shall be represented by counsel at the hearing conducted under division (C) of this section. If the defendant is unable to obtain counsel, the court shall appoint counsel under Chapter 120. of the Revised Code or under the authority recognized in division (C) of section 120.06, division (E) of section 120.16, division (E) of section 120.26, or section 2941.51 of the Revised Code before proceeding with the hearing.

(E) The prosecutor and defense counsel may submit evidence on the issue of the defendant's competence to stand trial. A written report of the evaluation of the defendant may be admitted into evidence at the hearing by stipulation, but, if either the prosecution or defense objects to its admission, the report may be admitted under sections 2317.36 to 2317.38 of the Revised Code or any other applicable statute or rule.

(F) The court shall not find a defendant incompetent to stand trial solely because the defendant is receiving or has received treatment as a voluntary or involuntary mentally ill patient under Chapter 5122. or a voluntary or involuntary mentally retarded resident under Chapter 5123. of the Revised Code or because the defendant is receiving or has received psychotropic drugs or other medication, even if the defendant might become incompetent to stand trial without the drugs or medication.

(G) A defendant is presumed to be competent to stand trial. If, after a hearing, the court finds by a preponderance of the evidence that, because of the defendant's present mental condition, the defendant is incapable of understanding the nature and objective of the proceedings against the defendant or of assisting in the defendant's defense, the court shall find the defendant incompetent to stand trial and shall enter an order authorized by section 2945.38 of the Revised Code.

(H) Municipal courts shall follow the procedures set forth in sections 2945.37 to 2945.402 of the Revised Code. Except as provided in section 2945.371 of the Revised Code, a municipal court shall not order an evaluation of the defendant's competence to stand trial or the defendant's mental condition at the time of the commission of the offense to be conducted at any hospital operated by the department of mental health. Those evaluations shall be performed through community resources including, but not limited to, certified forensic centers, court probation departments, and community mental health agencies. All expenses of the evaluations shall be borne by the legislative authority of the municipal court, as defined in section 1901.03 of the Revised Code, and shall be taxed as costs in the case. If a defendant is found incompetent to stand trial or not guilty by reason of insanity, a municipal court may commit the defendant as provided in sections 2945.38 to 2945.402 of the Revised Code [1]

(1996 S 285, eff. 7–1–97; 1988 S 156, eff. 7–1–89; 1981 H 694; 1980 S 297; 1978 H 565)

[1] So in original.

2945.371 Evaluations of mental condition

(A) If the issue of a defendant's competence to stand trial is raised or if a defendant enters a plea of not guilty by reason of insanity, the court may order one or more evaluations of the defendant's present mental condition or, in the case of a plea of not guilty by reason of insanity, of the defendant's mental condition at the time of the offense charged. An examiner shall conduct the evaluation.

(B) If the court orders more than one evaluation under division (A) of this section, the prosecutor and the defendant may recommend to the court an examiner whom each prefers to perform one of the evaluations. If a defendant enters a plea of not guilty by reason of insanity and if the court does not designate an examiner recommended by the defendant, the court shall inform the defendant that the defendant may have independent expert evaluation and that, if the defendant is unable to obtain independent expert evaluation, it will be obtained for the defendant at public expense if the defendant is indigent.

(C) If the court orders an evaluation under division (A) of this section, the defendant shall be available at the times and places established by the examiners who are to conduct the evaluation. The court may order a defendant who has been released on bail or recognizance to submit to an evaluation under this section. If a defendant who has been released on bail or recognizance refuses to submit to a complete evaluation, the court may amend the conditions of bail or recognizance and order the sheriff to take the defendant into custody and deliver the defendant to a center, program, or facility operated or certified by the department of mental health or the department of mental retardation and developmental disabilities where the defendant may be held for evaluation for a reasonable period of time not to exceed twenty days.

(D) A defendant who has not been released on bail or recognizance may be evaluated at the defendant's place of detention. Upon the request of the examiner, the court may order the sheriff to transport the defendant to a program or facility operated by the department of mental health or the department of mental retardation and developmental disabilities, where the defendant may be held for evaluation for a reasonable period of time not to exceed twenty days, and to return the defendant to the place of detention after the evaluation. A municipal court may make an order under this division only upon the request of a certified forensic center examiner.

(E) If a court orders the evaluation to determine a defendant's mental condition at the time of the offense charged, the court shall inform the examiner of the offense with which the defendant is charged.

(F) In conducting an evaluation of a defendant's mental condition at the time of the offense charged, the examiner shall consider all relevant evidence. If the offense charged involves the use of force against another person, the relevant evidence to be considered includes, but is not limited to, any evidence that the defendant suffered, at the time of the commission of the offense, from the "battered woman syndrome."

(G) The examiner shall file a written report with the court within thirty days after entry of a court order for evaluation, and the court shall provide copies of the report to the prosecutor and defense counsel. The report shall include all of the following:

(1) The examiner's findings;

(2) The facts in reasonable detail on which the findings are based;

(3) If the evaluation was ordered to determine the defendant's competence to stand trial, all of the following findings or recommendations that are applicable:

(a) Whether the defendant is capable of understanding the nature and objective of the proceedings against the defendant or of assisting in the defendant's defense;

(b) If the examiner's opinion is that the defendant is incapable of understanding the nature and objective of the proceedings against the defendant or of assisting in the defendant's defense, whether the defendant presently is mentally ill or mentally retarded and, if the examiner's opinion is that the defendant presently is mentally retarded, whether the defendant appears to be a mentally retarded person subject to institutionalization by court order;

(c) If the examiner's opinion is that the defendant is incapable of understanding the nature and objective of the proceedings against the defendant or of assisting in the defendant's defense, the examiner's opinion as to the likelihood of the defendant becoming capable of understanding the nature and objective of the proceedings against the defendant and of assisting in the defendant's defense within one year if the defendant is provided with a course of treatment;

(d) If the examiner's opinion is that the defendant is incapable of understanding the nature and objective of the proceedings against the defendant or of assisting in the defendant's defense and that the defendant presently is mentally ill or mentally retarded, the examiner's recommendation as to the least restrictive treatment alternative, consistent with the defendant's treatment needs for restoration to competency and with the safety of the community.

(4) If the evaluation was ordered to determine the defendant's mental condition at the time of the offense charged, the examiner's findings as to whether the defendant, at the time of the offense charged, did not know, as a result of a severe mental disease or defect, the wrongfulness of the defendant's acts charged.

(H) If the examiner's report filed under division (G) of this section indicates that in the examiner's opinion the defendant is incapable of understanding the nature and objective of the proceedings against the defendant or of assisting in the defendant's defense and that in the examiner's opinion the defendant appears to be a mentally retarded person subject to institutionalization by court order, the court shall order the defendant to undergo a separate mental retardation evaluation conducted by a psychologist designated by the director of mental retardation and developmental disabilities. Divisions (C) to (F) of this section apply in relation to a separate mental retardation evaluation conducted under this division. The psychologist appointed under this division to conduct the separate mental retardation evaluation shall file a written report with the court within thirty days after the entry of the court order requiring the separate mental retardation evaluation, and the court shall provide copies of the report to the prosecutor and defense counsel. The report shall include all of the information described in divisions (G)(1) to (4) of this section. If the court orders a separate mental retardation evaluation of a defendant under this division, the court shall not conduct a hearing under divisions (B) to (H) of section 2945.37 of the Revised Code regarding that defendant until a report of the separate mental retardation evaluation conducted under this division has been filed. Upon the filing of that report, the court shall conduct the hearing within the period of time specified in division (C) of section 2945.37 of the Revised Code.

(I) An examiner appointed under divisions (A) and (B) of this section or under division (H) of this section to evaluate a defendant to determine the defendant's competence to stand trial also may be appointed to evaluate a defendant who has entered a plea of not guilty by reason of insanity, but an examiner of that nature shall prepare separate reports on the issue of competence to stand trial and the defense of not guilty by reason of insanity.

(J) No statement that a defendant makes in an evaluation or hearing under divisions (A) to (H) of this section relating to the defendant's competence to stand trial or to the defendant's mental condition at the time of the offense charged shall be used against the defendant on the issue of guilt in any criminal action or proceeding, but, in a criminal action or proceeding, the prosecutor or defense counsel may call as a witness any person who evaluated the defendant or prepared a report pursuant to a referral under this section. Neither the appointment nor the testimony of an examiner appointed under this section precludes the prosecutor or defense counsel from calling other witnesses or presenting other evidence on competency or insanity issues.

(K) Persons appointed as examiners under divisions (A) and (B) of this section or under division (H) of this section shall be paid a reasonable amount for their services and expenses, as certified by the court. The certified amount shall be paid by the county in the case of county courts and courts of common pleas and by the legislative authority, as defined in section 1901.03 of the Revised Code, in the case of municipal courts.

(2001 S 122, eff. 2–20–02; 1996 S 285, eff. 7–1–97; 1980 H 965, eff. 4–9–81; 1980 H 900, S 297; 1978 H 565)

2945.38 Effect of findings; treatment or continuing evaluation and treatment of incompetent; medication; disposition of defendant; report; additional hearings; discharge

(A) If the issue of a defendant's competence to stand trial is raised and if the court, upon conducting the hearing provided for in section 2945.37 of the Revised Code, finds that the defendant is competent to stand trial, the defendant shall be proceeded against as provided by law. If the court finds the defendant competent to stand trial and the defendant is receiving psychotropic drugs or other medication, the court may authorize the continued administration of the drugs or medication or other appropriate treatment in order to maintain the defendant's competence to stand trial, unless the defendant's attending physician advises the court against continuation of the drugs, other medication, or treatment.

(B)(1)(a) If, after taking into consideration all relevant reports, information, and other evidence, the court finds that the defendant is incompetent to stand trial and that there is a substantial probability that the defendant will become competent to stand trial within one year if the defendant is provided with a course of treatment, the court shall order the defendant to undergo treatment. If the defendant has been charged with a felony offense and if, after taking into consideration all relevant reports, information, and other evidence, the court finds that the defendant is incompetent to stand trial, but the court is unable at that time to determine whether there is a substantial probability that the defendant will become competent to stand trial within one year if the defendant is provided with a course of treatment, the court shall order continuing evaluation and treatment of the defendant for a period not to exceed four months to determine whether there is a substantial probability that the defendant will become competent to stand trial within one year if the defendant is provided with a course of treatment.

(b) The court order for the defendant to undergo treatment or continuing evaluation and treatment under division (B)(1)(a) of this section shall specify that the treatment or continuing evaluation and treatment shall occur at a facility operated by the department of mental health or the department of mental retardation and developmental disabilities, at a facility certified by either of those departments as being qualified to treat mental illness or mental retardation, at a public or private community mental health or mental retardation facility, or by a psychiatrist or another mental health or mental retardation professional. The order may restrict the defendant's freedom of movement as the court considers necessary. The prosecutor in the defendant's case shall send to the chief clinical officer of the hospital or facility, the managing officer of the institution, the director of the program, or the person to which the defendant is committed copies of relevant police reports and other background information that pertains to the defendant and is available to the prosecutor unless the prosecutor determines that the release of any of the information in the police reports or any of the other background information to unauthorized persons would interfere with the effective prosecution of any person or would create a substantial risk of harm to any person.

In determining placement alternatives, the court shall consider the extent to which the person is a danger to the person and to others, the need for security, and the type of crime involved and shall order the least restrictive alternative available that is consistent with public safety and treatment goals. In weighing these factors, the court shall give preference to protecting public safety.

(c) If the defendant is found incompetent to stand trial, if the chief clinical officer of the hospital or facility, the managing officer of the institution, the director of the program, or the person to which the defendant is committed for treatment or continuing evaluation and treatment under division (B)(1)(b) of this section determines that medication is necessary to restore the defendant's competency to stand trial, and if the defendant lacks the capacity to give informed consent or refuses medication, the chief clinical officer, managing officer, director, or person to which the defendant is committed for treatment or continuing evaluation and treatment may petition the court for authorization for the involuntary administration of medication. The court shall hold a hearing on the petition within five days of the filing of the petition if the petition was filed in a municipal court or a county court regarding an incompetent defendant charged with a misdemeanor or within ten days of the filing of the petition if the petition was filed in a court of common pleas regarding an incompetent defendant charged with a felony offense. Following the hearing, the court may authorize the involuntary administration of medication or may dismiss the petition.

(2) If the court finds that the defendant is incompetent to stand trial and that, even if the defendant is provided with a course of treatment, there is not a substantial probability that the defendant will become competent to stand trial within one year, the court shall order the discharge of the defendant, unless upon motion of the prosecutor or on its own motion, the court either seeks to retain jurisdiction over the defendant pursuant to section 2945.39 of the Revised Code or files an affidavit in the probate court for the civil commitment of the defendant pursuant to Chapter 5122. or 5123. of the Revised Code alleging that the defendant is a mentally ill person subject to hospitalization by court order or a mentally retarded person subject to institutionalization by court order. If an affidavit is filed in the probate court, the trial court shall send to the probate court copies of all written reports of the defendant's mental condition that were prepared pursuant to section 2945.371 of the Revised Code.

The trial court may issue the temporary order of detention that a probate court may issue under section 5122.11 or 5123.71 of the Revised Code, to remain in effect until the probable cause or initial hearing in the probate court. Further proceedings in the probate court are civil proceedings governed by Chapter 5122. or 5123. of the Revised Code.

(C) No defendant shall be required to undergo treatment, including any continuing evaluation and treatment, under division (B)(1) of this section for longer than whichever of the following periods is applicable:

(1) One year, if the most serious offense with which the defendant is charged is one of the following offenses:

(a) Aggravated murder, murder, or an offense of violence for which a sentence of death or life imprisonment may be imposed;

(b) An offense of violence that is a felony of the first or second degree;

(c) A conspiracy to commit, an attempt to commit, or complicity in the commission of an offense described in division (C)(1)(a) or (b) of this section if the conspiracy, attempt, or complicity is a felony of the first or second degree.

(2) Six months, if the most serious offense with which the defendant is charged is a felony other than a felony described in division (C)(1) of this section;

(3) Sixty days, if the most serious offense with which the defendant is charged is a misdemeanor of the first or second degree;

(4) Thirty days, if the most serious offense with which the defendant is charged is a misdemeanor of the third or fourth degree, a minor misdemeanor, or an unclassified misdemeanor.

(D) Any defendant who is committed pursuant to this section shall not voluntarily admit the defendant or be voluntarily admitted to a hospital or institution pursuant to section 5122.02, 5122.15, 5123.69, or 5123.76 of the Revised Code.

(E) Except as otherwise provided in this division, a defendant who is charged with an offense and is committed to a hospital or other institution by the court under this section shall not be granted unsupervised on-grounds movement, supervised off-grounds movement, or nonsecured status. The court may grant a defendant supervised off-grounds movement to obtain medical treatment or specialized habilitation treatment services if the person who supervises the treatment or the continuing evaluation and treatment of the defendant ordered under division (B)(1)(a) of this section informs the court that the treatment or continuing evaluation and treatment cannot be provided at the hospital or the institution to which the defendant is committed. The chief clinical officer of the hospital or the managing officer of the institution to which the defendant is committed or a designee of either of those persons may grant a defendant movement to a medical facility for an emergency medical situation with appropriate supervision to ensure the safety of the defendant, staff, and community during that emergency medical situation. The chief clinical officer of the hospital or the managing officer of the institution shall notify the court within twenty-four hours of the defendant's movement to the medical facility for an emergency medical situation under this division.

(F) The person who supervises the treatment or continuing evaluation and treatment of a defendant ordered to undergo treatment or continuing evaluation and treatment under division (B)(1)(a) of this section shall file a written report with the court at the following times:

(1) Whenever the person believes the defendant is capable of understanding the nature and objective of the proceedings against the defendant and of assisting in the defendant's defense;

(2) For a felony offense, fourteen days before expiration of the maximum time for treatment as specified in division (C) of this section and fourteen days before the expiration of the maximum time for continuing evaluation and treatment as specified in division (B)(1)(a) of this section, and, for a misdemeanor offense, ten days before the expiration of the maximum time for treatment, as specified in division (C) of this section;

(3) At a minimum, after each six months of treatment;

(4) Whenever the person who supervises the treatment or continuing evaluation and treatment of a defendant ordered under division (B)(1)(a) of this section believes that there is not a substantial probability that the defendant will become capable of understanding the nature and objective of the proceedings against the defendant or of assisting in the defendant's defense even if the defendant is provided with a course of treatment.

(G) A report under division (F) of this section shall contain the examiner's findings, the facts in reasonable detail on which the findings are based, and the examiner's opinion as to the defendant's capability of understanding the nature and objective of the proceedings against the defendant and of assisting in the defendant's defense. If, in the examiner's opinion, the defendant remains incapable of understanding the nature and objective of the proceedings against the defendant and of assisting in the defendant's defense and there is a substantial probability that the defendant will become capable of understanding the nature and objective of the proceedings against the defendant and of assisting in the defendant's defense if the defendant is provided with a course of treatment, if in the examiner's opinion the defendant remains mentally ill or mentally retarded, and if the maximum time for treatment as specified in division (C) of this section has not expired, the report also shall contain the examiner's recommendation as to the least restrictive treatment alternative that is consistent with the defendant's treatment needs for restoration to competency and with the safety of the community. The court shall provide copies of the report to the prosecutor and defense counsel.

(H) If a defendant is committed pursuant to division (B)(1) of this section, within ten days after the treating physician of the defendant or the examiner of the defendant who is employed or retained by the treating facility advises that there is not a substantial probability that the defendant will become capable of understanding the nature and objective of the proceedings against the defendant or of assisting in the defendant's defense even if the defendant is provided with a course of treatment, within ten days after the expiration of the maximum time for treatment as specified in division (C) of this section, within ten days after the expiration of the maximum time for continuing evaluation and treatment as specified in division (B)(1)(a) of this section, within thirty days after a defendant's request for a hearing that is made after six months of treatment, or within thirty days after being advised by the treating physician or examiner that the defendant is competent to stand trial, whichever is the earliest, the court shall conduct another hearing to determine if the defendant is competent to stand trial and shall do whichever of the following is applicable:

(1) If the court finds that the defendant is competent to stand trial, the defendant shall be proceeded against as provided by law.

(2) If the court finds that the defendant is incompetent to stand trial, but that there is a substantial probability that the defendant will become competent to stand trial if the defendant is provided with a course of treatment, and the maximum time for treatment as specified in division (C) of this section has not expired, the court, after consideration of the examiner's recommendation, shall order that treatment be continued, may change the facility or program at which the treatment is to be continued, and shall specify whether the treatment is to be continued at the same or a different facility or program.

(3) If the court finds that the defendant is incompetent to stand trial, if the defendant is charged with an offense listed in division (C)(1) of this section, and if the court finds that there is not a substantial probability that the defendant will become competent to stand trial even if the defendant is provided with a course of treatment, or if the maximum time for treatment relative to that offense as specified in division (C) of this section has expired, further proceedings shall be as provided in sections 2945.39, 2945.401, and 2945.402 of the Revised Code.

(4) If the court finds that the defendant is incompetent to stand trial, if the most serious offense with which the defendant is charged is a misdemeanor or a felony other than a felony listed in division (C)(1) of this section, and if the court finds that there is not a substantial probability that the defendant will become competent to stand trial even if the defendant is provided with a course of treatment, or if the maximum time for treatment relative to that offense as specified in division (C) of this section has expired, the court shall dismiss the indictment, information, or complaint against the defendant. A dismissal under this division is not a bar to further prosecution based on the same conduct. The court shall discharge the defendant unless the

court or prosecutor files an affidavit in probate court for civil commitment pursuant to Chapter 5122. or 5123. of the Revised Code. If an affidavit for civil commitment is filed, the court may detain the defendant for ten days pending civil commitment. All of the following provisions apply to persons charged with a misdemeanor or a felony other than a felony listed in division (C)(1) of this section who are committed by the probate court subsequent to the court's or prosecutor's filing of an affidavit for civil commitment under authority of this division:

(a) The chief clinical officer of the hospital or facility, the managing officer of the institution, the director of the program, or the person to which the defendant is committed or admitted shall do all of the following:

(i) Notify the prosecutor, in writing, of the discharge of the defendant, send the notice at least ten days prior to the discharge unless the discharge is by the probate court, and state in the notice the date on which the defendant will be discharged;

(ii) Notify the prosecutor, in writing, when the defendant is absent without leave or is granted unsupervised, off-grounds movement, and send this notice promptly after the discovery of the absence without leave or prior to the granting of the unsupervised, off-grounds movement, whichever is applicable;

(iii) Notify the prosecutor, in writing, of the change of the defendant's commitment or admission to voluntary status, send the notice promptly upon learning of the change to voluntary status, and state in the notice the date on which the defendant was committed or admitted on a voluntary status.

(b) Upon receiving notice that the defendant will be granted unsupervised, off-grounds movement, the prosecutor either shall re-indict the defendant or promptly notify the court that the prosecutor does not intend to prosecute the charges against the defendant.

(I) If a defendant is convicted of a crime and sentenced to a jail or workhouse, the defendant's sentence shall be reduced by the total number of days the defendant is confined for evaluation to determine the defendant's competence to stand trial or treatment under this section and sections 2945.37 and 2945.371 of the Revised Code or by the total number of days the defendant is confined for evaluation to determine the defendant's mental condition at the time of the offense charged.

(2001 S 122, eff. 2–20–02; 1996 S 285, eff. 7–1–97; 1996 S 269, eff. 7–1–96; 1988 S 156, eff. 7–1–89; 1980 H 965, H 900, S 297; 1978 H 565; 1975 S 185; 1953 H 1; GC 13441–2)

2945.39 Civil commitment; expiration of time for treatment; jurisdiction; hearing; reports

(A) If a defendant who is charged with an offense described in division (C)(1) of section 2945.38 of the Revised Code is found incompetent to stand trial, after the expiration of the maximum time for treatment as specified in division (C) of that section or after the court finds that there is not a substantial probability that the defendant will become competent to stand trial even if the defendant is provided with a course of treatment, one of the following applies:

(1) The court or the prosecutor may file an affidavit in probate court for civil commitment of the defendant in the manner provided in Chapter 5122. or 5123. of the Revised Code. If the court or prosecutor files an affidavit for civil commitment, the court may detain the defendant for ten days pending civil commitment. If the probate court commits the defendant subsequent to the court's or prosecutor's filing of an affidavit for civil commitment, the chief clinical officer of the hospital or facility, the managing officer of the institution, the director of the program, or the person to which the defendant is committed or admitted shall send to the prosecutor the notices described in divisions (H)(4)(a)(i) to (iii) of section 2945.38 of the Revised Code within the periods of time and under the circumstances specified in those divisions.

(2) On the motion of the prosecutor or on its own motion, the court may retain jurisdiction over the defendant if, at a hearing, the court finds both of the following by clear and convincing evidence:

(a) The defendant committed the offense with which the defendant is charged.

(b) The defendant is a mentally ill person subject to hospitalization by court order or a mentally retarded person subject to institutionalization by court order.

(B) In making its determination under division (A)(2) of this section as to whether to retain jurisdiction over the defendant, the court may consider all relevant evidence, including, but not limited to, any relevant psychiatric, psychological, or medical testimony or reports, the acts constituting the offense charged, and any history of the defendant that is relevant to the defendant's ability to conform to the law.

(C) If the court conducts a hearing as described in division (A)(2) of this section and if the court does not make both findings described in divisions (A)(2)(a) and (b) of this section by clear and convincing evidence, the court shall dismiss the indictment, information, or complaint against the defendant. Upon the dismissal, the court shall discharge the defendant unless the court or prosecutor files an affidavit in probate court for civil commitment of the defendant pursuant to Chapter 5122. or 5123. of the Revised Code. If the court or prosecutor files an affidavit for civil commitment, the court may order that the defendant be detained for up to ten days pending the civil commitment. If the probate court commits the defendant subsequent to the court's or prosecutor's filing of an affidavit for civil commitment, the chief clinical officer of the hospital or facility, the managing officer of the institution, the director of the program, or the person to which the defendant is committed or admitted shall send to the prosecutor the notices described in divisions (H)(4)(a)(i) to (iii) of section 2945.38 of the Revised Code within the periods of time and under the circumstances specified in those divisions. A dismissal of charges under this division is not a bar to further criminal proceedings based on the same conduct.

(D)(1) If the court conducts a hearing as described in division (A)(2) of this section and if the court makes the findings described in divisions (A)(2)(a) and (b) of this section by clear and convincing evidence, the court shall commit the defendant to a hospital operated by the department of mental health, a facility operated by the department of mental retardation and developmental disabilities, or another medical or psychiatric facility, as appropriate. In determining the place and nature of the commitment, the court shall order the least restrictive commitment alternative available that is consistent with public safety and the welfare of the defendant. In weighing these factors, the court shall give preference to protecting public safety.

(2) If a court makes a commitment of a defendant under division (D)(1) of this section, the prosecutor shall send to the place of commitment all reports of the defendant's current mental condition and, except as otherwise provided in this division, any other relevant information, including, but not limited to, a transcript of the hearing held pursuant to division (A)(2) of this section, copies of relevant police reports, and copies of any prior arrest and conviction records that pertain to the defendant and that the prosecutor possesses. The prosecutor shall send the reports of the defendant's current mental condition in every case of commitment, and, unless the prosecutor determines that the release of any of the other relevant information to unauthorized persons would interfere with the effective prosecution of any person or would create a substantial risk of harm to any person, the prosecutor also shall send the other relevant information. Upon admission of a defendant committed under division (D)(1) of this section, the place of commitment shall send to the board of alcohol, drug addiction, and mental health services or the

community mental health board serving the county in which the charges against the defendant were filed a copy of all reports of the defendant's current mental condition and a copy of the other relevant information provided by the prosecutor under this division, including, if provided, a transcript of the hearing held pursuant to division (A)(2) of this section, the relevant police reports, and the prior arrest and conviction records that pertain to the defendant and that the prosecutor possesses.

(3) If a court makes a commitment under division (D)(1) of this section, all further proceedings shall be in accordance with sections 2945.401 and 2945.402 of the Revised Code.

(2001 S 122, eff. 2–20–02; 1996 S 285, eff. 7–1–97)

2945.391 Applicability of not guilty by reason of insanity plea; impairment of reason not defense

For purposes of sections 2945.371, 2945.40, 2945.401, and 2945.402 and Chapters 5122. and 5123. of the Revised Code, a person is "not guilty by reason of insanity" relative to a charge of an offense only as described in division (A)(14) of section 2901.01 of the Revised Code. Proof that a person's reason, at the time of the commission of an offense, was so impaired that the person did not have the ability to refrain from doing the person's act or acts, does not constitute a defense.

(1996 S 285, eff. 7–1–97; 1996 S 239, eff. 9–6–96; 1990 S 24, eff. 7–24–90)

2945.392 Battered woman syndrome

(A) The declarations set forth in division (A) of section 2901.06 of the Revised Code apply in relation to this section.

(B) If a defendant is charged with an offense involving the use of force against another and the defendant enters a plea to the charge of not guilty by reason of insanity, the defendant may introduce expert testimony of the "battered woman syndrome" and expert testimony that the defendant suffered from that syndrome as evidence to establish the requisite impairment of the defendant's reason, at the time of the commission of the offense, that is necessary for a finding that the defendant is not guilty by reason of insanity. The introduction of any expert testimony under this division shall be in accordance with the Ohio Rules of Evidence.

(1996 S 285, eff. 7–1–97; 1990 H 484, eff. 11–5–90)

2945.40 Verdict of not guilty by reason of insanity; effects; procedures; hearings; rights; commitment

(A) If a person is found not guilty by reason of insanity, the verdict shall state that finding, and the trial court shall conduct a full hearing to determine whether the person is a mentally ill person subject to hospitalization by court order or a mentally retarded person subject to institutionalization by court order. Prior to the hearing, if the trial judge believes that there is probable cause that the person found not guilty by reason of insanity is a mentally ill person subject to hospitalization by court order or mentally retarded person subject to institutionalization by court order, the trial judge may issue a temporary order of detention for that person to remain in effect for ten court days or until the hearing, whichever occurs first.

Any person detained pursuant to a temporary order of detention issued under this division shall be held in a suitable facility, taking into consideration the place and type of confinement prior to and during trial.

(B) The court shall hold the hearing under division (A) of this section to determine whether the person found not guilty by reason of insanity is a mentally ill person subject to hospitalization by court order or a mentally retarded person subject to institutionalization by court order within ten court days after the finding of not guilty by reason of insanity. Failure to conduct the hearing within the ten-day period shall cause the immediate discharge of the respondent, unless the judge grants a continuance for not longer than ten court days for good cause shown or for any period of time upon motion of the respondent.

(C) If a person is found not guilty by reason of insanity, the person has the right to attend all hearings conducted pursuant to sections 2945.37 to 2945.402 of the Revised Code. At any hearing conducted pursuant to one of those sections, the court shall inform the person that the person has all of the following rights:

(1) The right to be represented by counsel and to have that counsel provided at public expense if the person is indigent, with the counsel to be appointed by the court under Chapter 120. of the Revised Code or under the authority recognized in division (C) of section 120.06, division (E) of section 120.16, division (E) of section 120.26, or section 2941.51 of the Revised Code;

(2) The right to have independent expert evaluation and to have that independent expert evaluation provided at public expense if the person is indigent;

(3) The right to subpoena witnesses and documents, to present evidence on the person's behalf, and to cross-examine witnesses against the person;

(4) The right to testify in the person's own behalf and to not be compelled to testify;

(5) The right to have copies of any relevant medical or mental health document in the custody of the state or of any place of commitment other than a document for which the court finds that the release to the person of information contained in the document would create a substantial risk of harm to any person.

(D) The hearing under division (A) of this section shall be open to the public, and the court shall conduct the hearing in accordance with the Rules of Civil Procedure. The court shall make and maintain a full transcript and record of the hearing proceedings. The court may consider all relevant evidence, including, but not limited to, any relevant psychiatric, psychological, or medical testimony or reports, the acts constituting the offense in relation to which the person was found not guilty by reason of insanity, and any history of the person that is relevant to the person's ability to conform to the law.

(E) Upon completion of the hearing under division (A) of this section, if the court finds there is not clear and convincing evidence that the person is a mentally ill person subject to hospitalization by court order or a mentally retarded person subject to institutionalization by court order, the court shall discharge the person, unless a detainer has been placed upon the person by the department of rehabilitation and correction, in which case the person shall be returned to that department.

(F) If, at the hearing under division (A) of this section, the court finds by clear and convincing evidence that the person is a mentally ill person subject to hospitalization by court order or a mentally retarded person subject to institutionalization by court order, it shall commit the person to a hospital operated by the department of mental health, a facility operated by the department of mental retardation and developmental disabilities, or another medical or psychiatric facility, as appropriate, and further proceedings shall be in accordance with sections 2945.401 and 2945.402 of the Revised Code. In determining the place and nature of the commitment, the court shall order the least restrictive commitment alternative available that is consistent with public safety and the welfare of the person. In weighing these factors, the court shall give preference to protecting public safety.

(G) If a court makes a commitment of a person under division (F) of this section, the prosecutor shall send to the place of commitment all reports of the person's current mental condition, and, except as otherwise provided in this division, any other relevant information, including, but not limited to, a transcript of the hearing held pursuant to division (A) of this section, copies of relevant police reports, and copies of any prior arrest and conviction records that pertain to the person and that the prosecutor possesses. The prosecutor shall send the reports of the person's current mental condition in every case of commitment, and, unless the prosecutor determines that the release of any of the other relevant information to unauthorized persons would interfere with the effective prosecution of any person or would create a substantial risk of harm to any person, the prosecutor also shall send the other relevant information. Upon admission of a person committed under division (F) of this section, the place of commitment shall send to the board of alcohol, drug addiction, and mental health services or the community mental health board serving the county in which the charges against the person were filed a copy of all reports of the person's current mental condition and a copy of the other relevant information provided by the prosecutor under this division, including, if provided, a transcript of the hearing held pursuant to division (A) of this section, the relevant police reports, and the prior arrest and conviction records that pertain to the person and that the prosecutor possesses.

(H) A person who is committed pursuant to this section shall not voluntarily admit the person or be voluntarily admitted to a hospital or institution pursuant to sections 5122.02, 5122.15, 5123.69, or 5123.76 of the Revised Code.

(1996 S 285, eff. 7–1–97; 1996 H 567, eff. 10–29–96; 1994 H 571, eff. 10–6–94; 1990 S 24, eff. 7–24–90; 1988 S 156; 1981 H 1; 1980 H 965, S 297; 1978 H 565)

2945.401 Nonsecured status or termination of commitment; reports on competence; jurisdiction; hearing

(A) A defendant found incompetent to stand trial and committed pursuant to section 2945.39 of the Revised Code or a person found not guilty by reason of insanity and committed pursuant to section 2945.40 of the Revised Code shall remain subject to the jurisdiction of the trial court pursuant to that commitment, and to the provisions of this section, until the final termination of the commitment as described in division (J)(1) of this section. If the jurisdiction is terminated under this division because of the final termination of the commitment resulting from the expiration of the maximum prison term or term of imprisonment described in division (J)(1)(b) of this section, the court or prosecutor may file an affidavit for the civil commitment of the defendant or person pursuant to Chapter 5122. or 5123. of the Revised Code.

(B) A hearing conducted under any provision of sections 2945.37 to 2945.402 of the Revised Code shall not be conducted in accordance with Chapters 5122. and 5123. of the Revised Code. Any person who is committed pursuant to section 2945.39 or 2945.40 of the Revised Code shall not voluntarily admit the person or be voluntarily admitted to a hospital or institution pursuant to section 5122.02, 5122.15, 5123.69, or 5123.76 of the Revised Code. All other provisions of Chapters 5122. and 5123. of the Revised Code regarding hospitalization or institutionalization shall apply to the extent they are not in conflict with this chapter. A commitment under section 2945.39 or 2945.40 of the Revised Code shall not be terminated and the conditions of the commitment shall not be changed except as otherwise provided in division (D)(2) of this section with respect to a mentally retarded person subject to institutionalization by court order or except by order of the trial court.

(C) The hospital, facility, or program to which a defendant or person has been committed under section 2945.39 or 2945.40 of the Revised Code shall report in writing to the trial court, at the times specified in this division, as to whether the defendant or person remains a mentally ill person subject to hospitalization by court order or a mentally retarded person subject to institutionalization by court order and, in the case of a defendant committed under section 2945.39 of the Revised Code, as to whether the defendant remains incompetent to stand trial. The hospital, facility, or program shall make the reports after the initial six months of treatment and every two years after the initial report is made. The trial court shall provide copies of the reports to the prosecutor and to the counsel for the defendant or person. Within thirty days after its receipt pursuant to this division of a report from a hospital, facility, or program, the trial court shall hold a hearing on the continued commitment of the defendant or person or on any changes in the conditions of the commitment of the defendant or person. The defendant or person may request a change in the conditions of confinement, and the trial court shall conduct a hearing on that request if six months or more have elapsed since the most recent hearing was conducted under this section.

(D)(1) Except as otherwise provided in division (D)(2) of this section, when a defendant or person has been committed under section 2945.39 or 2945.40 of the Revised Code, at any time after evaluating the risks to public safety and the welfare of the defendant or person, the chief clinical officer of the hospital, facility, or program to which the defendant or person is committed may recommend a termination of the defendant's or person's commitment or a change in the conditions of the defendant's or person's commitment.

Except as otherwise provided in division (D)(2) of this section, if the chief clinical officer recommends on-grounds unsupervised movement, off-grounds supervised movement, or nonsecured status for the defendant or person or termination of the defendant's or person's commitment, the following provisions apply:

(a) If the chief clinical officer recommends on-grounds unsupervised movement or off-grounds supervised movement, the chief clinical officer shall file with the trial court an application for approval of the movement and shall send a copy of the application to the prosecutor. Within fifteen days after receiving the application, the prosecutor may request a hearing on the application and, if a hearing is requested, shall so inform the chief clinical officer. If the prosecutor does not request a hearing within the fifteen-day period, the trial court shall approve the application by entering its order approving the requested movement or, within five days after the expiration of the fifteen-day period, shall set a date for a hearing on the application. If the prosecutor requests a hearing on the application within the fifteen-day period, the trial court shall hold a hearing on the application within thirty days after the hearing is requested. If the trial court, within five days after the expiration of the fifteen-day period, sets a date for a hearing on the application, the trial court shall hold the hearing within thirty days after setting the hearing date. At least fifteen days before any hearing is held under this division, the trial court shall give the prosecutor written notice of the date, time, and place of the hearing. At the conclusion of each hearing conducted under this division, the trial court either shall approve or disapprove the application and shall enter its order accordingly.

(b) If the chief clinical officer recommends termination of the defendant's or person's commitment at any time or if the chief clinical officer recommends the first of any nonsecured status for the defendant or person, the chief clinical officer shall send written notice of this recommendation to the trial court and to the local forensic center. The local forensic center shall evaluate the committed defendant or person and, within thirty days after its receipt of the written notice, shall submit to the trial court and the chief clinical officer a written report of the evaluation. The trial court shall provide a copy of the chief clinical officer's written notice and of the local forensic center's written report to the prosecutor and to the counsel for the defendant or person. Upon the local forensic center's submission of the report to the trial court and the chief clinical officer, all of the following apply:

(i) If the forensic center disagrees with the recommendation of the chief clinical officer, it shall inform the chief clinical officer and the trial court of its decision and the reasons for the decision. The chief clinical officer, after consideration of the forensic center's decision, shall either withdraw, proceed with, or modify and proceed with the recommendation. If the chief clinical officer proceeds with, or modifies and proceeds with, the recommendation, the chief clinical officer shall proceed in accordance with division (D)(1)(b)(iii) of this section.

(ii) If the forensic center agrees with the recommendation of the chief clinical officer, it shall inform the chief clinical officer and the trial court of its decision and the reasons for the decision, and the chief clinical officer shall proceed in accordance with division (D)(1)(b)(iii) of this section.

(iii) If the forensic center disagrees with the recommendation of the chief clinical officer and the chief clinical officer proceeds with, or modifies and proceeds with, the recommendation or if the forensic center agrees with the recommendation of the chief clinical officer, the chief clinical officer shall work with the board of alcohol, drug addiction, and mental health services or community mental health board serving the area, as appropriate, to develop a plan to implement the recommendation. If the defendant or person is on medication, the plan shall include, but shall not be limited to, a system to monitor the defendant's or person's compliance with the prescribed medication treatment plan. The system shall include a schedule that clearly states when the defendant or person shall report for a medication compliance check. The medication compliance checks shall be based upon the effective duration of the prescribed medication, taking into account the route by which it is taken, and shall be scheduled at intervals sufficiently close together to detect a potential increase in mental illness symptoms that the medication is intended to prevent.

The chief clinical officer, after consultation with the board of alcohol, drug addiction, and mental health services or the community mental health board serving the area, shall send the recommendation and plan developed under division (D)(1)(b)(iii) of this section, in writing, to the trial court, the prosecutor and the counsel for the committed defendant or person. The trial court shall conduct a hearing on the recommendation and plan developed under division (D)(1)(b)(iii) of this section. Divisions (D)(1)(c) and (d) and (E) to (J) of this section apply regarding the hearing.

(c) If the chief clinical officer's recommendation is for nonsecured status or termination of commitment, the prosecutor may obtain an independent expert evaluation of the defendant's or person's mental condition, and the trial court may continue the hearing on the recommendation for a period of not more than thirty days to permit time for the evaluation.

The prosecutor may introduce the evaluation report or present other evidence at the hearing in accordance with the Rules of Evidence.

(d) The trial court shall schedule the hearing on a chief clinical officer's recommendation for nonsecured status or termination of commitment and shall give reasonable notice to the prosecutor and the counsel for the defendant or person. Unless continued for independent evaluation at the prosecutor's request or for other good cause, the hearing shall be held within thirty days after the trial court's receipt of the recommendation and plan.

(2)(a) Division (D)(1) of this section does not apply to on-grounds unsupervised movement of a defendant or person who has been committed under section 2945.39 or 2945.40 of the Revised Code, who is a mentally retarded person subject to institutionalization by court order, and who is being provided residential habilitation, care, and treatment in a facility operated by the department of mental retardation and developmental disabilities.

(b) If, pursuant to section 2945.39 of the Revised Code, the trial court commits a defendant who is found incompetent to stand trial and who is a mentally retarded person subject to institutionalization by court order, if the defendant is being provided residential habilitation, care, and treatment in a facility operated by the department of mental retardation and developmental disabilities, if an individual who is conducting a survey for the department of health to determine the facility's compliance with the certification requirements of the medicaid program under Chapter 5111. of the Revised Code and Title XIX of the "Social Security Act," 49 Stat. 620 (1935), 42 U.S.C.A. 301, as amended, cites the defendant's receipt of the residential habilitation, care, and treatment in the facility as being inappropriate under the certification requirements, if the defendant's receipt of the residential habilitation, care, and treatment in the facility potentially jeopardizes the facility's continued receipt of federal medicaid moneys, and if as a result of the citation the chief clinical officer of the facility determines that the conditions of the defendant's commitment should be changed, the department of mental retardation and developmental disabilities may cause the defendant to be removed from the particular facility and, after evaluating the risks to public safety and the welfare of the defendant and after determining whether another type of placement is consistent with the certification requirements, may place the defendant in another facility that the department selects as an appropriate facility for the defendant's continued receipt of residential habilitation, care, and treatment and that is a no less secure setting than the facility in which the defendant had been placed at the time of the citation. Within three days after the defendant's removal and alternative placement under the circumstances described in division (D)(2)(b) of this section, the department of mental retardation and developmental disabilities shall notify the trial court and the prosecutor in writing of the removal and alternative placement.

The trial court shall set a date for a hearing on the removal and alternative placement, and the hearing shall be held within twenty-one days after the trial court's receipt of the notice from the department of mental retardation and developmental disabilities. At least ten-days before the hearing is held, the trial court shall give the prosecutor, the department of mental retardation and developmental disabilities, and the counsel for the defendant written notice of the date, time, and place of the hearing. At the hearing, the trial court shall consider the citation issued by the individual who conducted the survey for the department of health to be prima-facie evidence of the fact that the defendant's commitment to the particular facility was inappropriate under the certification requirements of the medicaid program under chapter 5111. of the Revised Code and Title XIX of the "Social Security Act," 49 Stat. 620 (1935), 42 U.S.C.A. 301, as amended, and potentially jeopardizes the particular facility's continued receipt of federal medicaid moneys. At the conclusion of the hearing, the trial court may approve or disapprove the defendant's removal and alternative placement. If the trial court approves the defendant's removal and alternative placement, the department of mental retardation and developmental disabilities may continue the defendant's alternative placement. If the trial court disapproves the defendant's removal and alternative placement, it shall enter an order modifying the defendant's removal and alternative placement, but that order shall not require the department of mental retardation and developmental disabilities to replace the defendant for purposes of continued residential habilitation, care, and treatment in the facility associated with the citation issued by the individual who conducted the survey for the department of health.

(E) In making a determination under this section regarding nonsecured status or termination of commitment, the trial court shall consider all relevant factors, including, but not limited to, all of the following:

(1) Whether, in the trial court's view, the defendant or person currently represents a substantial risk of physical harm to the defendant or person or others;

(2) Psychiatric and medical testimony as to the current mental and physical condition of the defendant or person;

(3) Whether the defendant or person has insight into the dependant's or person's condition so that the defendant or person will continue treatment as prescribed or seek professional assistance as needed;

(4) The grounds upon which the state relies for the proposed commitment;

(5) Any past history that is relevant to establish the defendant's or person's degree of conformity to the laws, rules, regulations, and values of society;

(6) If there is evidence that the defendant's or person's mental illness is in a state of remission, the medically suggested cause and degree of the remission and the probability that the defendant or person will continue treatment to maintain the remissive state of the defendant's or person's illness should the defendant's or person's commitment conditions be altered.

(F) At any hearing held pursuant to division (C) or (D)(1) or (2) of this section, the defendant or the person shall have all the rights of a defendant or person at a commitment hearing as described in section 2945.40 of the Revised Code.

(G) In a hearing held pursuant to division (C) or (D)(1) of this section, the prosecutor has the burden of proof as follows:

(1) For a recommendation of termination of commitment, to show by clear and convincing evidence that the defendant or person remains a mentally ill person subject to hospitalization by court order or a mentally retarded person subject to institutionalization by court order;

(2) For a recommendation for a change in the conditions of the commitment to a less restrictive status, to show by clear and convincing evidence that the proposed change represents a threat to public safety or a threat to the safety of any person.

(H) In a hearing held pursuant to division (C) or (D)(1) or (2) of this section, the prosecutor shall represent the state or the public interest.

(I) At the conclusion of a hearing conducted under division (D)(1) of this section regarding a recommendation from the chief clinical officer of a hospital, program, or facility, the trial court may approve, disapprove, or modify the recommendation and shall enter an order accordingly.

(J)(1) A defendant or person who has been committed pursuant to section 2945.39 or 2945.40 of the Revised Code continues to be under the jurisdiction of the trial court until the final termination of the commitment. For purposes of division (J) of this section, the final termination of a commitment occurs upon the earlier of one of the following:

(a) The defendant or person no longer is a mentally ill person subject to hospitalization by court order or a mentally retarded person subject to institutionalization by court order, as determined by the trial court;

(b) The expiration of the maximum prison term or term of imprisonment that the defendant or person could have received if the defendant or person had been convicted of the most serious offense with which the defendant or person is charged or in relation to which the defendant or person was found not guilty by reason of insanity;

(c) The trial court enters an order terminating the commitment under the circumstances described in division (J)(2)(a)(ii) of this section.

(2)(a) If a defendant is found incompetent to stand trial and committed pursuant to section 2945.39 of the Revised Code, if neither of the circumstances described in divisions (J)(1)(a) and (b) of this section applies to that defendant, and if a report filed with the trial court pursuant to division (C) of this section indicates that the defendant presently is competent to stand trial or if, at any other time during the period of the defendant's commitment, the prosecutor, the counsel for the defendant, or the chief clinical officer of the hospital, facility, or program to which the defendant is committed files an application with the trial court alleging that the defendant presently is competent to stand trial and requesting a hearing on the competency issue or the trial court otherwise has reasonable cause to believe that the defendant presently is competent to stand trial and determines on its own motion to hold a hearing on the competency issue, the trial court shall schedule a hearing on the competency of the defendant to stand trial, shall give the prosecutor, the counsel for the defendant, and the chief clinical officer notice of the date, time, and place of the hearing at least fifteen days before the hearing, and shall conduct the hearing within thirty days of the filing of the application or of its own motion. If, at the conclusion of the hearing, the trial court determines that the defendant presently is capable of understanding the nature and objective of the proceedings against the defendant and of assisting in the defendant's defense, the trial court shall order that the defendant is competent to stand trial and shall be proceeded against as provided by law with respect to the applicable offenses described in division (C)(1) of section 2945.38 of the Revised Code and shall enter whichever of the following additional orders is appropriate:

(i) If the trial court determines that the defendant remains a mentally ill person subject to hospitalization by court order or a mentally retarded person subject to institutionalization by court order, the trial court shall order that the defendant's commitment to the hospital, facility, or program be continued during the pendency of the trial on the applicable offenses described in division (C)(1) of section 2945.38 of the Revised Code.

(ii) If the trial court determines that the defendant no longer is a mentally ill person subject to hospitalization by court order or a mentally retarded person subject to institutionalization by court order, the trial court shall order that the defendant's commitment to the hospital, facility, or program shall not be continued during the pendency of the trial on the applicable offenses described in division (C)(1) of section 2945.38 of the Revised Code. This order shall be a final termination of the commitment for purposes of division (J)(1)(c) of this section.

(b) If, at the conclusion of the hearing described in division (J)(2)(a) of this section, the trial court determines that the defendant remains incapable of understanding the nature and objective of the proceedings against the defendant or of assisting in the defendant's defense, the trial court shall order that the defendant continues to be incompetent to stand trial, that the defendant's commitment to the hospital, facility, or program shall be continued, and that the defendant remains subject to the jurisdiction of the trial court pursuant to that commitment, and to the provisions of this section, until the final termination of the commitment as described in division (J)(1) of this section.

(1996 S 285, eff. 7–1–97)

2945.402 Conditional release

(A) In approving a conditional release, the trial court may set any conditions on the release with respect to the treatment, evaluation, counseling, or control of the defendant or person that the court considers necessary to protect the public safety and the welfare of the defendant or person. The trial court may revoke a defendant's or person's conditional release and order rehospitalization or reinstitutionalization at any time the conditions of the release have not been satisfied, provided that the revocation shall be in accordance with this section.

(B) A conditional release is a commitment. The hearings on continued commitment as described in section 2945.401 of the Revised Code apply to a defendant or person on conditional release.

(C) A person, agency, or facility that is assigned to monitor a defendant or person on conditional release immediately shall notify the trial court on learning that the defendant or person being monitored has violated the terms of the conditional release.

Upon learning of any violation of the terms of the conditional release, the trial court may issue a temporary order of detention or, if necessary, an arrest warrant for the defendant or person. Within ten court days after the defendant's or person's detention or arrest, the trial court shall conduct a hearing to determine whether the conditional release should be modified or terminated. At the hearing, the defendant or person shall have the same rights as are described in division (C) of section 2945.40 of the Revised Code. The trial court may order a continuance of the ten-court-day period for no longer than ten days for good cause shown or for any period on motion of the defendant or person. If the trial court fails to conduct the hearing within the ten-court-day period and does not order a continuance in accordance with this division, the defendant or person shall be restored to the prior conditional release status.

(D) The trial court shall give all parties reasonable notice of a hearing conducted under this section. At the hearing, the prosecutor shall present the case demonstrating that the defendant or person violated the terms of the conditional release. If the court finds by a preponderance of the evidence that the defendant or person violated the terms of the conditional release, the court may continue, modify, or terminate the conditional release and shall enter its order accordingly.

(1996 S 285, eff. 7–1–97)

WITNESSES

2945.41 Rules applicable in criminal cases

The rules of evidence in civil causes, where applicable, govern in all criminal causes.

(1953 H 1, eff. 10–1–53; GC 13444–1)

2945.42 Competency of witnesses

No person is disqualified as a witness in a criminal prosecution by reason of the person's interest in the prosecution as a party or otherwise or by reason of the person's conviction of crime. Husband and wife are competent witnesses to testify in behalf of each other in all criminal prosecutions and to testify against each other in all actions, prosecutions, and proceedings for personal injury of either by the other, bigamy, or failure to provide for, neglect of, or cruelty to their children under eighteen years of age or their physically or mentally handicapped child under twenty-one years of age. A spouse may testify against his or her spouse in a prosecution under a provision of sections 2903.11 to 2903.13, 2919.21, 2919.22, or 2919.25 of the Revised Code for cruelty to, neglect of, or abandonment of such spouse, in a prosecution against his or her spouse under section 2903.211 or 2911.211, of the Revised Code for the commission of the offense against the spouse who is testifying, in a prosecution under section 2919.27 of the Revised Code involving a protection order issued or consent agreement approved pursuant to section 2919.26 or 3113.31 of the Revised Code for the commission of the offense against the spouse who is testifying, or in a prosecution under section 2907.02 of the Revised Code for the commission of rape or under former section 2907.12 of the Revised Code for felonious sexual penetration against such spouse in a case in which the offense can be committed against a spouse. Such interest, conviction, or relationship may be shown for the purpose of affecting the credibility of the witness. Husband or wife shall not testify concerning a communication made by one to the other, or act done by either in the presence of the other, during coverture, unless the communication was made or act done in the known presence or hearing of a third person competent to be a witness, or in case of personal injury by either the husband or wife to the other, or rape or the former offense of felonious sexual penetration in a case in which the offense can be committed against a spouse, or bigamy, or failure to provide for, or neglect or cruelty of either to their children under eighteen years of age or their physically or mentally handicapped child under twenty-one years of age, violation of a protection order or consent agreement, or neglect or abandonment of a spouse under a provision of those sections. The presence or whereabouts of the husband or wife is not an act under this section. The rule is the same if the marital relation has ceased to exist.

(1996 H 445, eff. 9–3–96; 1995 S 2, eff. 7–1–96; 1992 H 536, eff. 11–5–92; 1985 H 475; 1980 H 920; 1975 H 1; 1971 S 312; 1953 H 1; GC 13444–2)

2945.43 Defendant may testify

On the trial of a criminal cause, a person charged with an offense may, at his own request, be a witness, but not otherwise. The failure of such person to testify may be considered by the court and jury and may be made the subject of comment by counsel.

(1953 H 1, eff. 10–1–53; GC 13444–3)

2945.44 Court of common pleas to grant transactional immunity; procedure; exceptions

(A) In any criminal proceeding in this state or in any criminal or civil proceeding brought pursuant to sections 2923.31 to 2923.36 of the Revised Code, if a witness refuses to answer or produce information on the basis of his privilege against self-incrimination, the court of common pleas of the county in which the proceeding is being held, unless it finds that to do so would not further the administration of justice, shall compel the witness to answer or produce the information, if both of the following apply:

(1) The prosecuting attorney of the county in which the proceedings are being held makes a written request to the court of common pleas to order the witness to answer or produce the information, notwithstanding his claim of privilege;

(2) The court of common pleas informs the witness that by answering, or producing the information he will receive immunity under division (B) of this section.

(B) If, but for this section, the witness would have been privileged to withhold an answer or any information given in any criminal proceeding, and he complies with an order under division (A) of this section compelling him to give an answer or produce any information, he shall not be prosecuted or subjected to any criminal penalty in the courts of this state for or on account of any transaction or matter concerning which, in compliance with the order, he gave an answer or produced any information.

(C) A witness granted immunity under this section may be subjected to a criminal penalty for any violation of section 2921.11, 2921.12, or 2921.13 of the Revised Code, or for contempt committed in answering, failing to answer, or failing to produce information in compliance with the order.

(1985 H 5, eff. 1–1–86; 1978 H 491)

2945.45 Subpoenas to issue to any county

In all criminal cases, the clerk of the court of common pleas, upon a praecipe being filed, shall issue writs of subpoena for the witnesses named therein, directed to the sheriff of such county, or the county where such witnesses reside or are found, which shall be served and returned as in other cases. Such sheriff, by writing indorsed on the writs, may depute a disinterested person to serve and return them. The person so deputed to serve such subpoenas shall make a return of the service made, and make oath thereto before a person competent to administer oaths, which shall be indorsed on the writ. The return may be forwarded through the post office, or otherwise.

(1953 H 1, eff. 10–1–53; GC 13444–5)

2945.451 Employee's attendance at proceeding in criminal case under subpoena; employer may not penalize

No employer shall discharge or terminate from employment, threaten to discharge or terminate from employment, or otherwise punish or penalize any employee because of time lost from regular employment as a result of the employee's attendance at any proceeding in a criminal case pursuant to a subpoena. This section generally does not require and shall not be construed to require an employer to pay an employee for time lost as a result of attendance at any criminal proceeding. However, if an employee is subpoenaed to appear at a criminal proceeding and the proceeding pertains to an offense against the employer or an offense involving the employee during the course of his employment, the employer shall not decrease or withhold the employee's pay for any time lost as a result of compliance with the subpoena. Any employer who knowingly violates this section is in contempt of court.

(1984 S 172, eff. 9–26–84)

2945.46 Attendance of witness enforced

Civil procedure relative to compelling the attendance and testimony of witnesses, their examination, the administering of oaths and affirmations, and proceedings for contempt to enforce the remedies and protect the rights of parties, extend to criminal cases as far as applicable.

(1953 H 1, eff. 10–1–53; GC 13444–6)

2945.47 Testimony of prisoners in criminal proceedings

(A)(1) As used in this section, "detention facility" has the same meaning as in section 2921.01 of the Revised Code.

(2) If it is necessary in a criminal proceeding before the court to procure the testimony of a person who is imprisoned in a detention facility or state correctional institution within this state, or who is in the custody of the department of youth services, the court may require that the person's testimony be taken by deposition pursuant to Criminal Rule 15 at the place of the person's confinement, if the person is not a defendant in the case and if the court determines that the interests of justice do not demand that the person be brought before the court for the presentation of the person's testimony. All witnesses for the prosecution shall be brought before the court. The defendant may waive any right to compel the appearance of a person brought before the court pursuant to this division.

(B) Subject to division (C) of this section, if it is necessary in a criminal proceeding before the court to procure the testimony of a person who is imprisoned in a detention facility within this state, the court may order a subpoena to be issued, directed to the keeper of the institution, commanding the keeper to bring the prisoner named in the subpoena before the court.

The keeper, upon receiving the subpoena, shall take the witness before the court at the time and place named in the subpoena, and hold the witness until the witness is discharged by the court. When discharged, the witness shall be returned in the custody of such officer to the place of imprisonment from which the witness was taken, and the officer may command any assistance that the officer considers proper for the transportation of the witness.

(C) If it is necessary in a criminal proceeding before the court to procure the testimony of a person who is imprisoned in a state correctional institution within this state, or who is in the custody of the department of youth services, the court may order a subpoena to be issued directed to the sheriff of the county in which the indictment or grand jury proceeding is pending. When a copy of the subpoena is presented by the sheriff to the warden or superintendent of a state correctional institution, or to the person in charge of the facility in which a juvenile is confined, the witness shall be delivered at the institution or facility to the sheriff who shall take the witness before the court at the time and place named in the subpoena and hold the witness until the witness is discharged by the court. When discharged, the witness shall be returned in the custody of the sheriff to the place of imprisonment from which the witness was taken.

(D) The court, in the manner provided in Chapter 120. of the Revised Code, shall either assign counsel or designate a public defender to represent a juvenile subpoenaed as a witness under this section. Compensation for assigned counsel shall be made pursuant to section 2941.51 of the Revised Code.

(E) When a person's testimony is taken by deposition pursuant to division (A) of this section, the deposition shall be upon oral examination if either the prosecuting authority or the defendant who is taking the deposition requests that the deposition be upon oral examination, and may be videotaped if either the prosecuting authority or the defendant who is taking the deposition requests that it be recorded by means of videotape.

The person requesting the testimony of the person whose deposition is taken pursuant to division (A) of this section shall pay the expense of taking the deposition, except that the court may tax the expense as court costs in appropriate cases.

(1998 H 293, eff. 3–17–98; 1994 H 571, eff. 10–6–94; 1981 H 440, eff. 11–23–81; 1981 H 145; 1976 S 393; 129 v 322; 1953 H 1; GC 13444–7, 13444–8)

2945.48 Witness may be placed in jail

When a witness mentioned in section 2945.47 of the Revised Code is in attendance upon a court he may be placed in the jail of the county. The expenses of the officer in transporting him to and from such court, including compensation for the guard or attendant of such prisoner not exceeding the per diem salary of such guard for the time he is away from said institution, shall be allowed by the court and taxed and paid as other costs against the state.

(1953 H 1, eff. 10–1–53; GC 13444–9)

2945.481 Deposition of child sex offense victim; presence of defendant; additional depositions; videotaped deposition; admissibility of deposition; televised or recorded testimony

(A)(1) As used in this section, "victim" includes any person who was a victim of a violation identified in division (A)(2) of this section or an offense of violence or against whom was directed any conduct that constitutes, or that is an element of, a violation identified in division (A)(2) of this section or an offense of violence.

(2) In any proceeding in the prosecution of a charge of a violation of section 2905.03, 2905.05, 2907.02, 2907.03, 2907.04, 2907.05, 2907.06, 2907.07, 2907.09, 2907.21, 2907.23, 2907.24, 2907.31, 2907.32, 2907.321, 2907.322, 2907.323, or 2919.22 of the Revised Code or an offense of violence and in which an alleged victim of the violation or offense was a child who was less than thirteen years of age when the complaint, indictment, or information was filed, whichever occurred earlier, the judge of the court in which the prosecution is being conducted, upon motion of an

attorney for the prosecution, shall order that the testimony of the child victim be taken by deposition. The prosecution also may request that the deposition be videotaped in accordance with division (A)(3) of this section. The judge shall notify the child victim whose deposition is to be taken, the prosecution, and the defense of the date, time, and place for taking the deposition. The notice shall identify the child victim who is to be examined and shall indicate whether a request that the deposition be videotaped has been made. The defendant shall have the right to attend the deposition and the right to be represented by counsel. Depositions shall be taken in the manner provided in civil cases, except that the judge shall preside at the taking of the deposition and shall rule at that time on any objections of the prosecution or the attorney for the defense. The prosecution and the attorney for the defense shall have the right, as at trial, to full examination and cross-examination of the child victim whose deposition is to be taken. If a deposition taken under this division is intended to be offered as evidence in the proceeding, it shall be filed in the court in which the action is pending and is admissible in the manner described in division (B) of this section. If a deposition of a child victim taken under this division is admitted as evidence at the proceeding under division (B) of this section, the child victim shall not be required to testify in person at the proceeding. However, at any time before the conclusion of the proceeding, the attorney for the defense may file a motion with the judge requesting that another deposition of the child victim be taken because new evidence material to the defense has been discovered that the attorney for the defense could not with reasonable diligence have discovered prior to the taking of the admitted deposition. A motion for another deposition shall be accompanied by supporting affidavits. Upon the filing of a motion for another deposition and affidavits, the court may order that additional testimony of the child victim relative to the new evidence be taken by another deposition. If the court orders the taking of another deposition under this provision, the deposition shall be taken in accordance with this division; if the admitted deposition was a videotaped deposition taken in accordance with division (A)(3) of this section, the new deposition also shall be videotaped in accordance with that division and in other cases, the new deposition may be videotaped in accordance with that division.

(3) If the prosecution requests that a deposition to be taken under division (A)(2) of this section be videotaped, the judge shall order that the deposition be videotaped in accordance with this division. If a judge issues an order that the deposition be videotaped, the judge shall exclude from the room in which the deposition is to be taken every person except the child victim giving the testimony, the judge, one or more interpreters if needed, the attorneys for the prosecution and the defense, any person needed to operate the equipment to be used, one person chosen by the child victim giving the deposition, and any person whose presence the judge determines would contribute to the welfare and well-being of the child victim giving the deposition. The person chosen by the child victim shall not be a witness in the proceeding and, both before and during the deposition, shall not discuss the testimony of the child victim with any other witness in the proceeding. To the extent feasible, any person operating the recording equipment shall be restricted to a room adjacent to the room in which the deposition is being taken, or to a location in the room in which the deposition is being taken that is behind a screen or mirror, so that the person operating the recording equipment can see and hear, but cannot be seen or heard by, the child victim giving the deposition during the deposition. The defendant shall be permitted to observe and hear the testimony of the child victim giving the deposition on a monitor, shall be provided with an electronic means of immediate communication with the defendant's attorney during the testimony, and shall be restricted to a location from which the defendant cannot be seen or heard by the child victim giving the deposition, except on a monitor provided for that purpose. The child victim giving the deposition shall be provided with a monitor on which the child victim can observe, during the testimony, the defendant. The judge, at the judge's discretion, may preside at the deposition by electronic means from outside the room in which the deposition is to be taken; if the judge presides by electronic means, the judge shall be provided with monitors on which the judge can see each person in the room in which the deposition is to be taken and with an electronic means of communication with each person, and each person in the room shall be provided with a monitor on which that person can see the judge and with an electronic means of communication with the judge. A deposition that is videotaped under this division shall be taken and filed in the manner described in division (A)(2) of this section and is admissible in the manner described in this division and division (B) of this section, and, if a deposition that is videotaped under this division is admitted as evidence at the proceeding, the child victim shall not be required to testify in person at the proceeding. No deposition videotaped under this division shall be admitted as evidence at any proceeding unless division (B) of this section is satisfied relative to the deposition and all of the following apply relative to the recording:

(a) The recording is both aural and visual and is recorded on film or videotape, or by other electronic means.

(b) The recording is authenticated under the Rules of Evidence and the Rules of Criminal Procedure as a fair and accurate representation of what occurred, and the recording is not altered other than at the direction and under the supervision of the judge in the proceeding.

(c) Each voice on the recording that is material to the testimony on the recording or the making of the recording, as determined by the judge, is identified.

(d) Both the prosecution and the defendant are afforded an opportunity to view the recording before it is shown in the proceeding.

(B)(1) At any proceeding in a prosecution in relation to which a deposition was taken under division (A) of this section, the deposition or a part of it is admissible in evidence upon motion of the prosecution if the testimony in the deposition or the part to be admitted is not excluded by the hearsay rule and if the deposition or the part to be admitted otherwise is admissible under the Rules of Evidence. For purposes of this division, testimony is not excluded by the hearsay rule if the testimony is not hearsay under Evidence Rule 801; if the testimony is within an exception to the hearsay rule set forth in Evidence Rule 803; if the child victim who gave the testimony is unavailable as a witness, as defined in Evidence Rule 804, and the testimony is admissible under that rule; or if both of the following apply:

(a) The defendant had an opportunity and similar motive at the time of the taking of the deposition to develop the testimony by direct, cross, or redirect examination.

(b) The judge determines that there is reasonable cause to believe that, if the child victim who gave the testimony in the deposition were to testify in person at the proceeding, the child victim would experience serious emotional trauma as a result of the child victim's participation at the proceeding.

(2) Objections to receiving in evidence a deposition or a part of it under division (B) of this section shall be made as provided in civil actions.

(3) The provisions of divisions (A) and (B) of this section are in addition to any other provisions of the Revised Code, the Rules of Criminal Procedure, or the Rules of Evidence that pertain to the taking or admission of depositions in a criminal proceeding and do not limit the admissibility under any of those other provisions of any deposition taken under division (A) of this section or otherwise taken.

(C) In any proceeding in the prosecution of any charge of a violation listed in division (A)(2) of this section or an offense of violence and in which an alleged victim of the violation or offense was a child who was less than thirteen years of age when the complaint, indictment, or information was filed, whichever occurred earlier, the prosecution may file a motion with the judge requesting the judge to order the testimony of the child victim to be taken in a room other than the room in which the proceeding is being conducted and be televised, by closed circuit equipment, into the room in which the proceeding is being conducted to be viewed by the jury, if applicable, the defendant, and any other persons who are not permitted in the room in which the testimony is to be taken but who would have been present during the testimony of the child victim had it been given in the room in which the proceeding is being conducted. Except for good cause shown, the prosecution shall file a motion under this division at least seven days before the date of the proceeding. The judge may issue the order upon the motion of the prosecution filed under this section, if the judge determines that the child victim is unavailable to testify in the room in which the proceeding is being conducted in the physical presence of the defendant, for one or more of the reasons set forth in division (E) of this section. If a judge issues an order of that nature, the judge shall exclude from the room in which the testimony is to be taken every person except a person described in division (A)(3) of this section. The judge, at the judge's discretion, may preside during the giving of the testimony by electronic means from outside the room in which it is being given, subject to the limitations set forth in division (A)(3) of this section. To the extent feasible, any person operating the televising equipment shall be hidden from the sight and hearing of the child victim giving the testimony, in a manner similar to that described in division (A)(3) of this section. The defendant shall be permitted to observe and hear the testimony of the child victim giving the testimony on a monitor, shall be provided with an electronic means of immediate communication with the defendant's attorney during the testimony, and shall be restricted to a location from which the defendant cannot be seen or heard by the child victim giving the testimony, except on a monitor provided for that purpose. The child victim giving the testimony shall be provided with a monitor on which the child victim can observe, during the testimony, the defendant.

(D) In any proceeding in the prosecution of any charge of a violation listed in division (A)(2) of this section or an offense of violence and in which an alleged victim of the violation or offense was a child who was less than thirteen years of age when the complaint, indictment, or information was filed, whichever occurred earlier, the prosecution may file a motion with the judge requesting the judge to order the testimony of the child victim to be taken outside of the room in which the proceeding is being conducted and be recorded for showing in the room in which the proceeding is being conducted before the judge, the jury, if applicable, the defendant, and any other persons who would have been present during the testimony of the child victim had it been given in the room in which the proceeding is being conducted. Except for good cause shown, the prosecution shall file a motion under this division at least seven days before the date of the proceeding. The judge may issue the order upon the motion of the prosecution filed under this division, if the judge determines that the child victim is unavailable to testify in the room in which the proceeding is being conducted in the physical presence of the defendant, for one or more of the reasons set forth in division (E) of this section. If a judge issues an order of that nature, the judge shall exclude from the room in which the testimony is to be taken every person except a person described in division (A)(3) of this section. To the extent feasible, any person operating the recording equipment shall be hidden from the sight and hearing of the child victim giving the testimony, in a manner similar to that described in division (A)(3) of this section. The defendant shall be permitted to observe and hear the testimony of the child victim who is giving the testimony on a monitor, shall be provided with an electronic means of immediate communication with the defendant's attorney during the testimony, and shall be restricted to a location from which the defendant cannot be seen or heard by the child victim giving the testimony, except on a monitor provided for that purpose. The child victim giving the testimony shall be provided with a monitor on which the child victim can observe, during the testimony, the defendant. No order for the taking of testimony by recording shall be issued under this division unless the provisions set forth in divisions (A)(3)(a), (b), (c), and (d) of this section apply to the recording of the testimony.

(E) For purposes of divisions (C) and (D) of this section, a judge may order the testimony of a child victim to be taken outside the room in which the proceeding is being conducted if the judge determines that the child victim is unavailable to testify in the room in the physical presence of the defendant due to one or more of the following:

(1) The persistent refusal of the child victim to testify despite judicial requests to do so;

(2) The inability of the child victim to communicate about the alleged violation or offense because of extreme fear, failure of memory, or another similar reason;

(3) The substantial likelihood that the child victim will suffer serious emotional trauma from so testifying.

(F)(1) If a judge issues an order pursuant to division (C) or (D) of this section that requires the testimony of a child victim in a criminal proceeding to be taken outside of the room in which the proceeding is being conducted, the order shall specifically identify the child victim to whose testimony it applies, the order applies only during the testimony of the specified child victim, and the child victim giving the testimony shall not be required to testify at the proceeding other than in accordance with the order.

(2) A judge who makes any determination regarding the admissibility of a deposition under divisions (A) and (B) of this section, the videotaping of a deposition under division (A)(3) of this section, or the taking of testimony outside of the room in which a proceeding is being conducted under division (C) or (D) of this section, shall enter the determination and findings on the record in the proceeding.

(1997 S 53, eff. 10–14–97)

2945.482 Testimony of mentally retarded or developmentally disabled victim

(A) As used in this section:

(1) "Mentally retarded person" and "developmentally disabled person" have the same meanings as in section 5123.01 of the Revised Code.

(2) "Mentally retarded or developmentally disabled victim" includes a mentally retarded or developmentally disabled person who was a victim of a violation identified in division (B)(1) of this section or an offense of violence or against whom was directed any conduct that constitutes, or that is an element of, a violation identified in division (B)(1) of this section or an offense of violence.

(B)(1) In any proceeding in the prosecution of a charge of a violation of section 2903.16, 2903.34, 2903.341, 2905.03, 2907.02, 2907.03, 2907.05, 2907.06, 2907.09, 2907.21, 2907.23, 2907.24, 2907.32, 2907.321, 2907.322, or 2907.323 of the Revised Code or an offense of violence and in which an alleged victim of the violation or offense was a mentally retarded or developmentally disabled person, the judge of the court in which the prosecution is being conducted, upon motion of an attorney for the prosecution, shall order that the testimony of the mentally retarded or developmentally disabled victim be taken by deposition. The prosecution also may request that the deposition be videotaped in accordance with division (B)(2) of this section. The judge shall notify the mentally retarded or developmentally disabled victim whose deposition is to be taken, the prosecution, and the defense of the date, time, and place for taking the deposition. The notice shall identify the mentally retarded or developmentally disabled victim who is to be examined and shall indicate whether a request that the deposition be videotaped has been made. The defendant shall have the right to attend the deposition and the right to be represented by counsel. Depositions shall be taken in the manner provided in civil cases, except that the judge shall preside at the taking of the deposition and shall rule at the time on any objections of the prosecution or the attorney for the defense. The prosecution and the attorney for the defense shall have the right, as at trial, to full examination and cross-examination of the mentally retarded or developmentally disabled victim whose deposition is to be taken. If a deposition taken under this division is intended to be offered as evidence in the proceeding, it shall be filed in the court in which the action is pending and is admissible in the manner described in division (C) of this section.

If a deposition of a mentally retarded or developmentally disabled victim taken under this division is admitted as evidence at the proceeding under division (C) of this section, the mentally retarded or developmentally disabled victim shall not be required to testify in person at the proceeding.

At any time before the conclusion of the proceeding, the attorney for the defense may file a motion with the judge requesting that another deposition of the mentally retarded or developmentally disabled victim be taken because new evidence material to the defense has been discovered that the attorney for the defense could not with reasonable diligence have discovered prior to the taking of the admitted deposition. If the court orders the taking of another deposition under this provision, the deposition shall be taken in accordance with this division. If the admitted deposition was a videotaped deposition taken in accordance with division (B)(2) of this section, the new deposition shall be videotaped in accordance with that division. In other cases, the new deposition may be videotaped in accordance with that division.

(2) If the prosecution requests that a deposition to be taken under division (B)(2) of this section be videotaped, the judge shall order that the deposition be videotaped in accordance with this division. If a judge issues an order that the deposition be videotaped, the judge shall exclude from the room in which the deposition is to be taken every person except the mentally retarded or developmentally disabled victim giving the testimony, the judge, one or more interpreters if needed, the attorneys for the prosecution and the defense, any person needed to operate the equipment to be used, one person chosen by the mentally retarded or developmentally disabled victim giving the deposition, and any person whose presence the judge determines would contribute to the welfare and well-being of the mentally retarded or developmentally disabled victim giving the deposition. The person chosen by the mentally retarded or developmentally disabled victim shall not be a witness in the proceeding and, both before and during the deposition, shall not discuss the testimony of the mentally retarded or developmentally disabled victim with any other witness in the proceeding. To the extent feasible, any person operating the recording equipment shall be restricted to a room adjacent to the room in which the deposition is being taken, or to a location in the room in which the deposition is being taken that is behind a screen or mirror, so that the person operating the recording equipment can see and hear, but cannot be seen or heard by, the mentally retarded or developmentally disabled victim giving the deposition during the deposition.

The defendant shall be permitted to observe and hear the testimony of the mentally retarded or developmentally disabled victim giving the deposition on a monitor, shall be provided with an electronic means of immediate communication with the defendant's attorney during the testimony, and shall be restricted to a location from which the defendant cannot be seen or heard by the mentally retarded or developmentally disabled victim giving the deposition, except on a monitor provided for that purpose. The mentally retarded or developmentally disabled victim giving the deposition shall be provided with a monitor on which the victim can observe, during the testimony, the defendant. The judge, at the judge's discretion, may preside at the deposition by electronic means from outside the room in which the deposition is to be taken. If the judge presides by electronic means, the judge shall be provided with monitors on which the judge can see each person in the room in which the deposition is to be taken and with an electronic means of communication with each person, and each person in the room shall be provided with a monitor on which that person can see the judge and with an electronic means of communication with the judge. A deposition that is videotaped under this division shall be taken and filed in the manner described in division (B)(1) of this section and is admissible in the manner described in this division and division (C) of this section, and, if a deposition that is videotaped under this division is admitted as evidence at the proceeding, the mentally retarded or developmentally disabled victim shall not be required to testify in person at the proceeding. No deposition videotaped under this division shall be admitted as evidence at any proceeding unless division (C) of this section is satisfied relative to the deposition and all of the following apply relative to the recording:

(a) The recording is both aural and visual and is recorded on film or videotape, or by other electronic means.

(b) The recording is authenticated under the Rules of Evidence and the Rules of Criminal Procedure as a fair and accurate representation of what occurred, and the recording is not altered other than at the direction and under the supervision of the judge in the proceeding.

(c) Each voice on the recording that is material to the testimony on the recording or the making of the recording, as determined by the judge, is identified.

(d) Both the prosecution and the defendant are afforded an opportunity to view the recording before it is shown in the proceeding.

(C)(1) At any proceeding in a prosecution in relation to which a deposition was taken under division (B) of this section, the deposition or a part of it is admissible in evidence upon motion of the prosecution if the testimony in the deposition or the part to be admitted is not excluded by the hearsay rule and if the deposition or the part to be admitted otherwise is admissible under the Rules of Evidence. For purposes of this division, testimony is not excluded by the hearsay rule if the testimony is not hearsay under Evidence Rule 801; the testimony is within an exception to the hearsay rule set forth in Evidence Rule 803; the mentally retarded or developmentally disabled victim who gave the testimony is unavailable as a witness, as defined in Evidence Rule 804, and the testimony is admissible under that rule; or both of the following apply:

(a) The defendant had an opportunity and similar motive at the time of the taking of the deposition to develop the testimony by direct, cross, or redirect examination.

(b) The judge determines that there is reasonable cause to believe that, if the mentally retarded or developmentally disabled victim who gave the testimony in the deposition were to testify in person at the proceeding, the mentally retarded or developmentally disabled victim would experience serious emotional trauma as a result of the mentally retarded or developmentally disabled victim's participation at the proceeding.

(2) Objections to receiving in evidence a deposition or a part of it under division (C) of this section shall be made as provided in civil actions.

(3) The provisions of divisions (B) and (C) of this section are in addition to any other provisions of the Revised Code, the Rules of Criminal Procedure, or the Rules of Evidence that pertain to the taking or admission of depositions in a criminal proceeding and do not limit the admissibility under any of those other provisions of any deposition taken under division (B) of this section or otherwise taken.

(D) In any proceeding in the prosecution of any charge of a violation listed in division (B)(1) of this section or an offense of violence and in which an alleged victim of the violation or offense was a mentally retarded or developmentally disabled person, the prosecution may file a motion with the judge requesting the judge to order the testimony of the mentally retarded or developmentally disabled victim to be taken in a room other than the room in which the proceeding is being conducted and be televised, by closed circuit equipment, into the room in which the proceeding is being conducted to be viewed by the jury, if applicable, the defendant, and any other persons who are not permitted in the room in which the testimony is to be taken but who would have been present during the testimony of the mentally retarded or developmentally disabled victim had it been given in the room in which the proceeding is being conducted. Except for good cause shown, the prosecution shall file a motion under this division at least seven days before the date of the proceeding. The judge may issue the order upon the motion of the prosecution filed under this section, if the judge determines that the mentally retarded or developmentally disabled victim is unavailable to testify in the room in which the proceeding is being conducted in the physical presence of the defendant for one or more of the reasons set forth in division (F) of this section. If a judge issues an order of that nature, the judge shall exclude from the room in which the testimony is to be taken every person except a person described in division (B)(2) of this section. The judge, at the judge's discretion, may preside during the giving of the testimony by electronic means from outside the room in which it is being given, subject to the limitations set forth in division (B)(2) of this section. To the extent feasible, any person operating the televising equipment shall be hidden from the sight and hearing of the mentally retarded or developmentally disabled victim giving the testimony, in a manner similar to that described in division (B)(2) of this section. The defendant shall be permitted to observe and hear the testimony of the mentally retarded or developmentally disabled victim giving the testimony on a monitor, shall be provided with an electronic means of immediate communication with the defendant's attorney during the testimony, and shall be restricted to a location from which the defendant cannot be seen or heard by the mentally retarded or developmentally disabled victim giving the testimony, except on a monitor provided for that purpose. The mentally retarded or developmentally disabled victim giving the testimony shall be provided with a monitor on which the mentally retarded or developmentally disabled victim can observe, during the testimony, the defendant.

(E) In any proceeding in the prosecution of any charge of a violation listed in division (B)(1) of this section or an offense of violence and in which an alleged victim of the violation or offense was a mentally retarded or developmentally disabled victim, the prosecution may file a motion with the judge requesting the judge to order the testimony of the mentally retarded or developmentally disabled victim to be taken outside of the room in which the proceeding is being conducted and be recorded for showing in the room in which the proceeding is being conducted before the judge, the jury, if applicable, the defendant, and any other persons who would have been present during the testimony of the mentally retarded or developmentally disabled victim had it been given in the room in which the proceeding is being conducted. Except for good cause shown, the prosecution shall file a motion under this division at least seven days before the date of the proceeding. The judge may issue the order upon the motion of the prosecution filed under this division, if the judge determines that the mentally retarded or developmentally disabled victim is unavailable to testify in the room in which the proceeding is being conducted in the physical presence of the defendant, for one or more of the reasons set forth in division (F) of this section. If a judge issues an order of that nature, the judge shall exclude from the room in which the testimony is to be taken every person except a person described in division (B)(2) of this section. To the extent feasible, any person operating the recording equipment shall be hidden from the sight and hearing of the mentally retarded or developmentally disabled victim giving the testimony, in a manner similar to that described in division (B)(2) of this section. The defendant shall be permitted to observe and hear the testimony of the mentally retarded or developmentally disabled victim who is giving the testimony on a monitor, shall be provided with an electronic means of immediate communication with the defendant's attorney during the testimony, and shall be restricted to a location from which the defendant cannot be seen or heard by the mentally retarded or developmentally disabled victim giving the testimony, except on a monitor provided for that purpose. The mentally retarded or developmentally disabled victim giving the testimony shall be provided with a monitor on which the victim can observe, during the testimony, the defendant. No order for the taking of testimony by recording shall be issued under this division unless the provisions set forth in divisions (B)(2)(a), (b), (c), and (d) of this section apply to the recording of the testimony.

(F) For purposes of divisions (D) and (E) of this section, a judge may order the testimony of a mentally retarded or developmentally disabled victim to be taken outside the room in which the proceeding is being conducted if the judge determines that the mentally retarded or developmentally disabled victim is unavailable to testify in the room in the physical presence of the defendant due to one or more of the following:

(1) The persistent refusal of the mentally retarded or developmentally disabled victim to testify despite judicial requests to do so;

(2) The inability of the mentally retarded or developmentally disabled victim to communicate about the alleged violation or offense because of extreme fear, failure of memory, or another similar reason;

(3) The substantial likelihood that the mentally retarded or developmentally disabled victim will suffer serious emotional trauma from so testifying.

(G)(1) If a judge issues an order pursuant to division (D) or (E) of this section that requires the testimony of a mentally retarded or developmentally disabled victim in a criminal proceeding to be taken outside of the room in which the proceeding is being conducted, the order shall specifically identify the mentally retarded or developmentally disabled victim to whose testimony it applies, the order applies only during the testimony of the specified mentally retarded or developmentally disabled victim, and the mentally retarded or developmentally disabled victim giving the testimony shall not be required to testify at the proceeding other than in accordance with the order.

(2) A judge who makes any determination regarding the admissibility of a deposition under divisions (B) and (C) of this section, the videotaping of a deposition under division (B)(2) of this section, or the taking of testimony outside of the room in which a proceeding is being conducted under division (D) or (E) of this section shall enter the determination and findings on the record in the proceeding.

(2004 S 178, eff. 1–30–04)

2945.49 Testimony of deceased or absent witness; videotaped testimony of child victim

(A)(1) As used in this section, "victim" includes any person who was a victim of a felony violation identified in division (B)(1) of this section or a felony offense of violence or against whom was directed any conduct that constitutes, or that is an element of, a felony violation identified in division (B)(1) of this section or a felony offense of violence.

(2) Testimony taken at an examination or a preliminary hearing at which the defendant is present, or at a former trial of the cause, or taken by deposition at the instance of the defendant or the state, may be used whenever the witness giving the testimony dies or cannot for any reason be produced at the trial or whenever the witness has, since giving that testimony, become incapacitated to testify. If the former testimony is contained within an authenticated transcript of the testimony, it shall be proven by the transcript, otherwise by other testimony.

(B)(1) At a trial on a charge of a felony violation of section 2905.05, 2907.02, 2907.03, 2907.04, 2907.05, 2907.21, 2907.24, 2907.31, 2907.32, 2907.321, 2907.322, 2907.323, or 2919.22 of the Revised Code or a felony offense of violence and in which an alleged victim of the alleged violation or offense was less than thirteen years of age when the complaint or information was filed, whichever occurred earlier, the court, upon motion of the prosecutor in the case, may admit videotaped preliminary hearing testimony of the child victim as evidence at the trial, in lieu of the child victim appearing as a witness and testifying at the trial, if all of the following apply:

(a) The videotape of the testimony was made at the preliminary hearing at which probable cause of the violation charged was found;

(b) The videotape of the testimony was made in accordance with division (C) of section 2937.11 of the Revised Code;

(c) The testimony in the videotape is not excluded by the hearsay rule and otherwise is admissible under the Rules of Evidence. For purposes of this division, testimony is not excluded by the hearsay rule if the testimony is not hearsay under Evidence Rule 801, if the testimony is within an exception to the hearsay rule set forth in Evidence Rule 803, if the child victim who gave the testimony is unavailable as a witness, as defined in Evidence Rule 804, and the testimony is admissible under that rule, or if both of the following apply:

(i) The accused had an opportunity and similar motive at the preliminary hearing to develop the testimony of the child victim by direct, cross, or redirect examination;

(ii) The court determines that there is reasonable cause to believe that if the child victim who gave the testimony at the preliminary hearing were to testify in person at the trial, the child victim would experience serious emotional trauma as a result of the child victim's participation at the trial.

(2) If a child victim of an alleged felony violation of section 2905.05, 2907.02, 2907.03, 2907.04, 2907.05, 2907.21, 2907.24, 2907.31, 2907.32, 2907.321, 2907.322, 2907.323, or 2919.22 of the Revised Code or an alleged felony offense of violence testifies at the preliminary hearing in the case, if the testimony of the child victim at the preliminary hearing was videotaped pursuant to division (C) of section 2937.11 of the Revised Code, and if the defendant in the case files a written objection to the use, pursuant to division (B)(1) of this section, of the videotaped testimony at the trial, the court, immediately after the filing of the objection, shall hold a hearing to determine whether the videotaped testimony of the child victim should be admissible at trial under division (B)(1) of this section and, if it is admissible, whether the child victim should be required to provide limited additional testimony of the type described in this division. At the hearing held pursuant to this division, the defendant and the prosecutor in the case may present any evidence that is relevant to the issues to be determined at the hearing, but the child victim shall not be required to testify at the hearing.

After the hearing, the court shall not require the child victim to testify at the trial, unless it determines that both of the following apply:

(a) That the testimony of the child victim at trial is necessary for one or more of the following reasons:

(i) Evidence that was not available at the time of the testimony of the child victim at the preliminary hearing has been discovered;

(ii) The circumstances surrounding the case have changed sufficiently to necessitate that the child victim testify at the trial.

(b) That the testimony of the child victim at the trial is necessary to protect the right of the defendant to a fair trial.

The court shall enter its finding and the reasons for it in the journal. If the court requires the child victim to testify at the trial, the testimony of the victim shall be limited to the new evidence and changed circumstances, and the child victim shall not otherwise be required to testify at the trial. The required testimony of the child victim may be given in person or, upon motion of the prosecution, may be taken by deposition in accordance with division (A) of section 2945.481 of the Revised Code provided the deposition is admitted as evidence under division (B) of that section, may be taken outside of the courtroom and televised into the courtroom in accordance with division (C) of that section, or may be taken outside of the courtroom and recorded for showing in the courtroom in accordance with division (D) of that section.

(3) If videotaped testimony of a child victim is admitted at trial in accordance with division (B)(1) of this section, the child victim shall not be compelled in any way to appear as a witness at the trial, except as provided in division (B)(2) of this section.

(C) An order issued pursuant to division (B) of this section shall specifically identify the child victim concerning whose testimony it pertains. The order shall apply only during the testimony of the child victim it specifically identifies.

(D) As used in this section, "prosecutor" has the same meaning as in section 2935.01 of the Revised Code.

(1997 S 53, eff. 10–14–97; 1996 H 445, eff. 9–3–96; 1986 H 108, eff. 10–14–86; 1953 H 1; GC 13444–10)

2945.491 Testimony of mentally retarded or developmentally disabled victim; videotaped testimony

(A) As used in this section:

(1) "Mentally retarded person" and "developmentally disabled person" have the same meanings as in section 5123.01 of the Revised Code.

(2) "Mentally retarded or developmentally disabled victim" includes a mentally retarded or developmentally disabled person who was a victim of a felony violation identified in division (B)(1) of this section or a felony offense of violence or against whom was directed any conduct that constitutes, or that is an element of, a felony violation identified in division (B)(1) of this section or a felony offense of violence.

(B)(1) At a trial on a charge of a felony violation of section 2903.16, 2903.34, 2903.341, 2907.02, 2907.03, 2907.05, 2907.21, 2907.23, 2907.24, 2907.32, 2907.321, 2907.322, or 2907.323 of the Revised Code or an offense of violence and in which an alleged victim of the violation or offense was a mentally retarded or developmentally disabled person, the court, upon motion of the prosecutor in the case, may admit videotaped preliminary hearing testimony of the mentally retarded or developmentally disabled victim as evidence at the trial, in lieu of the mentally retarded or developmentally disabled victim appearing as a witness and testifying at trial, if all of the following apply:

(a) The videotape of the testimony was made at the preliminary hearing at which probable cause of the violation charged was found.

(b) The videotape of the testimony was made in accordance with division (C) of section 2937.11 of the Revised Code.

(c) The testimony in the videotape is not excluded by the hearsay rule and otherwise is admissible under the Rules of Evidence. For purposes of this division, testimony is not excluded by the hearsay rule if the testimony is not hearsay under Evidence Rule 801, the testimony is within an exception to the hearsay rule set forth in Evidence Rule 803, the mentally retarded or developmentally disabled victim who gave the testimony is unavailable as a witness, as defined in Evidence Rule 804, and the testimony is admissible under that rule, or both of the following apply:

(i) The accused had an opportunity and similar motive at the preliminary hearing to develop the testimony of the mentally retarded or developmentally disabled victim by direct, cross, or redirect examination.

(ii) The court determines that there is reasonable cause to believe that if the mentally retarded or developmentally disabled victim who gave the testimony at the preliminary hearing were to testify in person at the trial, the mentally retarded or developmentally disabled victim would experience serious emotional trauma as a result of the victim's participation at the trial.

(2) If a mentally retarded or developmentally disabled victim of an alleged felony violation of section 2903.16, 2903.34, 2903.341, 2907.02, 2907.03, 2907.05, 2907.21, 2907.23, 2907.24, 2907.32, 2907.321, 2907.322, or 2907.323 of the Revised Code or an alleged felony offense of violence testifies at the preliminary hearing in the case, if the testimony of the mentally retarded or developmentally disabled victim at the preliminary hearing was videotaped pursuant to division (C) of section 2937.11 of the Revised Code, and if the defendant in the case files a written objection to the use, pursuant to division (B)(1) of this section, of the videotaped testimony at the trial, the court, immediately after the filing of the objection, shall hold a hearing to determine whether the videotaped testimony of the mentally retarded or developmentally disabled victim should be admissible at trial under division (B)(1) of this section and, if it is admissible, whether the mentally retarded or developmentally disabled victim should be required to provide limited additional testimony of the type described in this division. At the hearing held pursuant to this division, the defendant and the prosecutor in the case may present any evidence that is relevant to the issues to be determined at the hearing, but the mentally retarded or developmentally disabled victim shall not be required to testify at the hearing.

After the hearing, the court shall not require the mentally retarded or developmentally disabled victim to testify at the trial, unless it determines that both of the following apply:

(a) That the testimony of the mentally retarded or developmentally disabled victim at trial is necessary for one or more of the following reasons:

(i) Evidence that was not available at the time of the testimony of the mentally retarded or developmentally disabled victim at the preliminary hearing has been discovered.

(ii) The circumstances surrounding the case have changed sufficiently to necessitate that the mentally retarded or developmentally disabled victim testify at the trial.

(b) That the testimony of the mentally retarded or developmentally disabled victim at the trial is necessary to protect the right of the defendant to a fair trial.

The court shall enter its finding and the reasons for it in the journal. If the court requires the mentally retarded or developmentally disabled victim to testify at the trial, the testimony of the victim shall be limited to the new evidence and changed circumstances, and the mentally retarded or developmentally disabled victim shall not otherwise be required to testify at the trial. The required testimony of the mentally retarded or developmentally disabled victim may be given in person or, upon motion of the prosecution, may be taken by deposition in accordance with division (B) of section 2945.482 of the Revised Code provided the deposition is admitted as evidence under division (C) of that section, may be taken outside of the courtroom and televised into the courtroom in accordance with division (D) of that section, or may be taken outside of the courtroom and recorded for showing in the courtroom in accordance with division (E) of that section.

(3) If videotaped testimony of a mentally retarded or developmentally disabled victim is admitted at trial in accordance with division (B)(1) of this section, the mentally retarded or developmentally disabled victim shall not be compelled in any way to appear as a witness at the trial, except as provided in division (B)(2) of this section.

(C) An order issued pursuant to division (B) of this section shall specifically identify the mentally retarded or developmentally disabled victim concerning whose testimony it pertains. The order shall apply only during the testimony of the mentally retarded or developmentally disabled victim it specifically identifies.

(2004 S 178, eff. 1–30–04)

2945.50 Deposition in criminal cases

At any time after an issue of fact is joined upon an indictment, information, or an affidavit, the prosecution or the defendant may apply in writing to the court in which such indictment, information, or affidavit is pending for a commission to take the depositions of any witness. The court or a judge thereof may grant such commission and make an order stating in what manner and for what length of time notice shall be given to the prosecution or to the defendant, before such witness shall be examined.

(131 v H 153, eff. 10–13–65; 1953 H 1; GC 13444–11)

2945.51 When deposition may be taken; expenses

When a deposition is to be taken in this state, and a commission is granted under section 2945.50 of the Revised Code while the defendant is confined in jail, the sheriff or deputy or other person having custody of the defendant shall be ordered by the court to take the defendant to the place of the taking of the deposition, and have him before the officer at the time of taking such deposition. Such sheriff or deputy or other person having custody of the defendant shall be reimbursed for actual reasonable traveling expenses for himself and the defendant, the bills for the same, upon the approval of the board of county commissioners, to be paid from the county treasury on the warrant of the county auditor. Such sheriff shall receive as fees therefor, one dollar for each day in attendance thereat. Such fees and traveling expenses shall be taxed and collected as other fees and costs in the case.

(131 v H 153, eff. 10–13–65; 1953 H 1; GC 13444–12)

2945.52 Counsel appointed shall represent the defendant

Counsel assigned by the court to represent the defendant may attend upon and represent the defendant at the taking of a deposition under section 2945.50 of the Revised Code, and said counsel shall be paid a reasonable fee for his services in taking such deposition, in addition to the compensation allowed for defending such defendant, to be fixed by the court. He shall also be allowed his actual expenses incurred in going to and from the place of taking the deposition.

(1953 H 1, eff. 10–1–53; GC 13444–13)

2945.53 Right of accused to examine witness

In all cases in which depositions are taken by the state or the accused, to be used by or against the accused, as provided in sections 2945.50 to 2945.52, inclusive, of the Revised Code, the court shall by proper order provide and secure to the accused the means and opportunity to be present in person and with counsel at the taking of such deposition, and to examine the witness face to face, as fully and in the same manner as if in court. All expenses necessarily incurred in the securing of such means and opportunity, and the expenses of the prosecuting attorney in attending the taking of such deposition, shall be paid out of the county treasury upon the certificate of the court making such order.

(1953 H 1, eff. 10–1–53; GC 13444–14)

2945.54 Conduct of examination

The examination of witnesses by deposition in criminal cases shall be taken and certified, and the return thereof to the court made as for taking depositions under sections 2319.05 to 2319.31, inclusive, of the Revised Code. The commissioners appointed under section 2945.50 of the Revised Code to take depositions shall receive such compensation as the court directs, to be paid out of the county treasury and taxed as part of the costs in the case.

(1953 H 1, eff. 10–1–53; GC 13444–15)

2945.55 Testimony of previous identification

When identification of the defendant is an issue, a witness who has on previous occasion identified such person may testify to such previous identification. Such identification may be proved by other witnesses.

(1953 H 1, eff. 10–1–53; GC 13444–16)

2945.56 Rebuttal of defendant's character evidence

When the defendant offers evidence of his character or reputation, the prosecution may offer, in rebuttal thereof, proof of his previous conviction of a crime involving moral turpitude, in addition to other competent evidence.

(1953 H 1, eff. 10–1–53; GC 13444–17)

2945.57 Number of witnesses to character

The number of witnesses who are expected to testify upon the subject of character or reputation, for whom subpoenas are issued, shall be designated upon the praecipe and, except in cases of murder in the first and second degree, manslaughter, rape, assault with intent to commit rape, or selling intoxicating liquor to a person in the habit of becoming intoxicated, shall not exceed ten upon each side, unless a deposit of at least one per diem and mileage fee for each of such additional witnesses is first made with the clerk of the court of common pleas. Not more than ten witnesses upon each side shall be permitted to testify upon the question of character or reputation in a criminal cause unless their full per diem and mileage fees have been deposited or paid by the party in whose behalf they are sworn, and the clerk shall not issue a certificate for compensation to be paid out of the county treasury to a witness who has testified upon the subject of character or reputation, except as provided in this section.

(1953 H 1, eff. 10–1–53; GC 13444–18)

ALIBI

2945.58 Alibi

Whenever a defendant in a criminal cause proposes to offer in his defense, testimony to establish an alibi on his behalf, such defendant shall, not less than three days before the trial of such cause, file and serve upon the prosecuting attorney a notice in writing of his intention to claim such alibi. Notice shall include specific information as to the place at which the defendant claims to have been at the time of the alleged offense. If the defendant fails to file such written notice, the court may exclude evidence offered by the defendant for the purpose of proving such alibi.

(1953 H 1, eff. 10–1–53; GC 13444–20)

PROOF

2945.59 Proof of defendant's motive

In any criminal case in which the defendant's motive or intent, the absence of mistake or accident on his part, or the defendant's scheme, plan, or system in doing an act is material, any acts of the defendant which tend to show his motive or intent, the absence of mistake or accident on his part, or the defendant's scheme, plan, or system in doing the act in question may be proved, whether they are contemporaneous with or prior or subsequent thereto, notwithstanding that such proof may show or tend to show the commission of another crime by the defendant.

(1953 H 1, eff. 10–1–53; GC 13444–19)

2945.64 Prima–facie evidence of embezzlement

Failure or refusal to pay over or produce public money by a person charged with the collection, receipt, transfer, disbursement, or safekeeping of such money, whether belonging to this state, a county, township, municipal corporation, or board of education, or other public money, or to account to or make settlement with a legal authority of the official accounts of such person, is prima-facie evidence of the embezzlement thereof. Upon the trial of such person for the embezzlement of public money, it is sufficient evidence for the purpose of showing a balance against him, to produce a transcript from the records of the auditor of state, director of budget and management, county auditor, or board of county commissioners. The refusal of such person, whether in or out of office, to pay a draft, order, or warrant drawn upon him by an authorized officer, for public money in his hands, or a refusal by a person promptly to pay over to his successor public money or securities on the legal requirement of an authorized officer of the state or county, on the trial of an indictment against him for embezzlement, is prima-facie evidence thereof.

(1985 H 201, eff. 7–1–85; 1953 H 1; GC 13444–25)

BILL OF EXCEPTIONS

2945.67 When prosecutor may appeal; when public defender to oppose

(A) A prosecuting attorney, village solicitor, city director of law, or the attorney general may appeal as a matter of right any decision of a trial court in a criminal case, or any decision of a juvenile court in a delinquency case, which decision grants a motion to dismiss all or any part of an indictment, complaint, or information, a motion to suppress evidence, or a motion for the return of seized property or grants post conviction relief pursuant to sections 2953.21 to 2953.24 of the Revised Code, and may appeal by leave of the court to which the appeal is taken any other decision, except the final verdict, of the trial court in a criminal case or of the juvenile court in a delinquency case. In addition to any other right to appeal under this section or any other provision of law, a prosecuting attorney, city director of law, village solicitor, or similar chief legal officer of a municipal corporation, or the attorney general may appeal, in accordance with section 2953.08 of the Revised Code, a sentence imposed upon a person who is convicted of or pleads guilty to a felony.

(B) In any proceeding brought pursuant to division (A) of this section, the court, in accordance with Chapter 120. of the Revised Code, shall appoint the county public defender, joint county public defender, or other counsel to represent any person who is indigent, is not represented by counsel, and does not waive the person's right to counsel.

(1995 S 2, eff. 7–1–96; 1978 H 1168, eff. 11–1–78)

SCHEDULE OF TRIAL AND HEARINGS

2945.71 Time within which hearing or trial must be held

(A) Subject to division (D) of this section, a person against whom a charge is pending in a court not of record, or against whom a charge of minor misdemeanor is pending in a court of record, shall be brought to trial within thirty days after the person's arrest or the service of summons.

(B) Subject to division (D) of this section, a person against whom a charge of misdemeanor, other than a minor misdemeanor, is pending in a court of record, shall be brought to trial as follows:

(1) Within forty-five days after the person's arrest or the service of summons, if the offense charged is a misdemeanor of the third or fourth degree, or other misdemeanor for which the maximum penalty is imprisonment for not more than sixty days;

(2) Within ninety days after the person's arrest or the service of summons, if the offense charged is a misdemeanor of the first or second degree, or other misdemeanor for which the maximum penalty is imprisonment for more than sixty days.

(C) A person against whom a charge of felony is pending:

(1) Notwithstanding any provisions to the contrary in Criminal Rule 5(B), shall be accorded a preliminary hearing within fifteen consecutive days after the person's arrest if the accused is not held in jail in lieu of bail on the pending charge or within ten consecutive days after the person's arrest if the accused is held in jail in lieu of bail on the pending charge;

(2) Shall be brought to trial within two hundred seventy days after the person's arrest.

(D) A person against whom one or more charges of different degrees, whether felonies, misdemeanors, or combinations of felonies and misdemeanors, all of which arose out of the same act or transaction, are pending shall be brought to trial on all of the charges within the time period required for the highest degree of offense charged, as determined under divisions (A), (B), and (C) of this section.

(E) For purposes of computing time under divisions (A), (B), (C)(2), and (D) of this section, each day during which the accused is held in jail in lieu of bail on the pending charge shall be counted as three days. This division does not apply for purposes of computing time under division (C)(1) of this section.

(F) This section shall not be construed to modify in any way section 2941.401 or sections 2963.30 to 2963.35 of the Revised Code.

(1999 S 49, eff. 10–29–99; 1981 S 119, eff. 3–17–82; 1980 S 288; 1975 S 83; 1973 H 716; 1972 H 511)

2945.72 Extension of time for hearing or trial

The time within which an accused must be brought to trial, or, in the case of felony, to preliminary hearing and trial, may be extended only by the following:

(A) Any period during which the accused is unavailable for hearing or trial, by reason of other criminal proceedings against him, within or outside the state, by reason of his confinement in another state, or by reason of the pendency of extradition proceedings, provided that the prosecution exercises reasonable diligence to secure his availability;

(B) Any period during which the accused is mentally incompetent to stand trial or during which his mental competence to stand trial is being determined, or any period during which the accused is physically incapable of standing trial;

(C) Any period of delay necessitated by the accused's lack of counsel, provided that such delay is not occasioned by any lack of diligence in providing counsel to an indigent accused upon his request as required by law;

(D) Any period of delay occasioned by the neglect or improper act of the accused;

(E) Any period of delay necessitated by reason of a plea in bar or abatement, motion, proceeding, or action made or instituted by the accused;

(F) Any period of delay necessitated by a removal or change of venue pursuant to law;

(G) Any period during which trial is stayed pursuant to an express statutory requirement, or pursuant to an order of another court competent to issue such order;

(H) The period of any continuance granted on the accused's own motion, and the period of any reasonable continuance granted other than upon the accused's own motion;

(I) Any period during which an appeal filed pursuant to section 2945.67 of the Revised Code is pending.

(1978 H 1168, eff. 11–1–78; 1976 S 368; 1975 H 164; 1972 H 511)

2945.73 Discharge for delay in trial

(A) A charge of felony shall be dismissed if the accused is not accorded a preliminary hearing within the time required by sections 2945.71 and 2945.72 of the Revised Code.

(B) Upon motion made at or prior to the commencement of trial, a person charged with an offense shall be discharged if he is not brought to trial within the time required by sections 2945.71 and 2945.72 of the Revised Code.

(C) Regardless of whether a longer time limit may be provided by sections 2945.71 and 2945.72 of the Revised Code, a person charged with misdemeanor shall be discharged if he is held in jail in lieu of bond awaiting trial on the pending charge:

(1) For a total period equal to the maximum term of imprisonment which may be imposed for the most serious misdemeanor charged;

(2) For a total period equal to the term of imprisonment allowed in lieu of payment of the maximum fine which may be imposed for the most serious misdemeanor charged, when the offense or offenses charged constitute minor misdemeanors.

(D) When a charge of felony is dismissed pursuant to division (A) of this section, such dismissal has the same effect as a nolle prosequi. When an accused is discharged pursuant to division (B) or (C) of this section, such discharge is a bar to any further criminal proceedings against him based on the same conduct.

(1972 H 511, eff. 1–1–74)

DEGREE OF OFFENSE

2945.74 Defendant may be convicted of lesser offense

The jury may find the defendant not guilty of the offense charged, but guilty of an attempt to commit it if such attempt is an offense at law. When the indictment or information charges an offense, including different degrees, or if other offenses are included within the offense charged, the jury may find the defendant not guilty of the degree charged but guilty of an inferior degree thereof or lesser included offense.

If the offense charged is murder and the accused is convicted by confession in open court, the court shall examine the witnesses, determine the degree of the crime, and pronounce sentence accordingly.

(1953 H 1, eff. 10–1–53; GC 13448–2)

2945.75 Degree of offense; charge and verdict; prior convictions

(A) When the presence of one or more additional elements makes an offense one of more serious degree:

(1) The affidavit, complaint, indictment, or information either shall state the degree of the offense which the accused is alleged to have committed, or shall allege such additional element or elements. Otherwise, such affidavit, complaint, indictment, or information is effective to charge only the least degree of the offense.

(2) A guilty verdict shall state either the degree of the offense of which the offender is found guilty, or that such additional element or elements are present. Otherwise, a guilty verdict constitutes a finding of guilty of the least degree of the offense charged.

(B) Whenever in any case it is necessary to prove a prior conviction, a certified copy of the entry of judgment in such prior conviction together with evidence sufficient to identify the defendant named in the entry as the offender in the case at bar, is sufficient to prove such prior conviction.

(1972 H 511, eff. 1–1–74)

POST TRIAL PROCEDURE

2945.77 Polling jury

When the jurors agree upon their verdict, they must be conducted into court by the officer having them in charge.

Before the verdict is accepted, the jury may be polled at the request of either the prosecuting attorney or the defendant. If one of the jurors upon being polled declares that said verdict is not his verdict, the jury must further deliberate upon the case.

(1953 H 1, eff. 10–1–53; GC 13448–5)

2945.78 Recording the verdict

When the verdict given is such as the court may receive, it must be immediately entered in full upon the minutes.

(1953 H 1, eff. 10–1–53; GC 13448–6)

2945.79 Causes for new trial

A new trial, after a verdict of conviction, may be granted on the application of the defendant for any of the following causes affecting materially his substantial rights:

(A) Irregularity in the proceedings of the court, jury, prosecuting attorney, or the witnesses for the state, or for any order of the court, or abuse of discretion by which the defendant was prevented from having a fair trial;

(B) Misconduct of the jury, prosecuting attorney, or the witnesses for the state;

(C) Accident or surprise which ordinary prudence could not have guarded against;

(D) That the verdict is not sustained by sufficient evidence or is contrary to law; but if the evidence shows the defendant is not guilty of the degree of crime for which he was convicted, but guilty of a lesser degree thereof, or of a lesser crime included therein, the court may modify the verdict or finding accordingly, without granting or ordering a new trial, and pass sentence on such verdict or finding as modified, provided that this power extends to any court to which the cause may be taken on appeal;

(E) Error of law occurring at the trial;

(F) When new evidence is discovered material to the defendant, which he could not with reasonable diligence have discovered and produced at the trial. When a motion for a new trial is made upon the ground of newly discovered evidence, the defendant must produce at the hearing of said motion, in support thereof, the affidavits of the witnesses by whom such evidence is expected to be given, and if time is required by the defendant to procure such affidavits, the court may postpone the hearing of the motion for such length of time as under all the circumstances of the case is reasonable. The prosecuting attorney may produce affidavits or other evidence to impeach the affidavits of such witnesses.

(1953 H 1, eff. 10–1–53; GC 13449–1)

2945.80 Application for new trial

Application for a new trial shall be made by motion upon written grounds, and except for the cause of newly discovered evidence material for the person applying, which he could not with reasonable diligence have discovered and produced at the trial, shall be filed within three days after the verdict was rendered, or the decision of the court where a trial by jury has been waived, unless it is made to appear by clear and convincing proof that the defendant was unavoidably prevented from filing his motion for new trial in which case it shall be filed within three days from the order of the court finding that he was unavoidably prevented from filing such motion within the time provided herein.

Motions for new trial on account of newly discovered evidence shall be filed within one hundred twenty days following the day upon which the verdict was rendered, or the decision of the court where trial by jury has been waived. If it is made to appear by clear and convincing proof that the defendant was unavoidably prevented from the discovery of the evidence upon which he must rely, such motion shall be filed within three days from an order of the court finding that he was unavoidably prevented from discovering the evidence within the one hundred twenty day period.

(131 v S 389, eff. 11–1–65; 128 v 141; 1953 H 1; GC 13449–2)

2945.81 Causes to be sustained by affidavits

The causes enumerated in divisions (B) and (C) of section 2945.79 of the Revised Code must be sustained by affidavit showing their truth, and may be controverted by affidavits.

(1953 H 1, eff. 10–1–53; GC 13449–3)

2945.82 New trial

When a new trial is granted by the trial court, or when a new trial is awarded on appeal, the accused shall stand for trial upon the indictment or information as though there had been no previous trial thereof.

(1953 H 1, eff. 10–1–53; GC 13449–4)

2945.83 When new trial shall not be granted

No motion for a new trial shall be granted or verdict set aside, nor shall any judgment of conviction be reversed in any court because of:

(A) An inaccuracy or imperfection in the indictment, information, or warrant, provided that the charge is sufficient to fairly and reasonably inform the accused of the nature and cause of the accusation against him;

(B) A variance between the allegations and the proof thereof unless the accused is misled or prejudiced thereby;

(C) The admission or rejection of any evidence offered against or for the accused unless it affirmatively appears on the record that the accused was or may have been prejudiced thereby;

(D) A misdirection of the jury unless the accused was or may have been prejudiced thereby;

(E) Any other cause unless it appears affirmatively from the record that the accused was prejudiced thereby or was prevented from having a fair trial.

(1953 H 1, eff. 10–1–53; GC 13449–5)

2945.831 Motion not necessary for appellate review

A motion for a new trial is not a necessary prerequisite to obtain appellate review of the sufficiency or weight of the evidence in the trial of a criminal case.

(128 v 141, eff. 1–1–60)

CHAPTER 2947

JUDGMENT; SENTENCE

MAGISTRATE DEFINED

2947.01 Definition of magistrate

The definition of "magistrate" set forth in section 2931.01 of the Revised Code applies to Chapter 2947. of the Revised Code.

(1953 H 1, eff. 10–1–53)

ARREST OF JUDGMENT

2947.02 Motion in arrest

A judgment may be arrested by the court upon motion of the defendant, or upon the court's own motion, for either of the following causes:

(A) The offense charged is not within the jurisdiction of the court;

(B) The facts stated in the indictment or information do not constitute an offense.

(1953 H 1, eff. 10–1–53; GC 13450–1)

2947.03 When judgment not arrested

A judgment shall not be arrested for a defect in form. Motions in arrest of judgment shall be made within three days after the verdict is rendered.

(1953 H 1, eff. 10–1–53; GC 13450–2)

2947.04 Effect of arrest of judgment

When a judgment is arrested, it places the defendant in a like position with respect to the prosecution as before the indictment or information was found. If, from the evidence at the trial, there is reason to believe that the defendant is guilty of an offense, the trial court shall order him to enter into a recognizance with sufficient surety for his appearance at the first day of the next term of such court, or the court having jurisdiction of the offense if within this state, otherwise the defendant shall be discharged.

(1953 H 1, eff. 10–1–53; GC 13450–3)

SENTENCING

2947.051 Victim impact statement for use in sentencing

(A) In all criminal cases in which a person is convicted of or pleads guilty to a felony, if the offender, in committing the offense, caused, attempted to cause, threatened to cause, or created a risk of physical harm to the victim of the offense, the court, prior to sentencing the offender, shall order the preparation of a victim impact statement by the department of probation of the county in which the victim of the offense resides, by the court's own regular probation officer, or by a victim assistance program that is operated by the state, any county or municipal corporation, or any other governmental entity. The court, in accordance with sections 2929.13 and 2929.19 of the Revised Code, shall consider the victim impact statement in determining the sentence to be imposed upon the offender.

(B) Each victim impact statement prepared under this section shall identify the victim of the offense, itemize any economic loss suffered by the victim as a result of the offense, identify any physical injury suffered by the victim as a result of the offense and the seriousness and permanence of the injury, identify any change in the victim's personal welfare or familial relationships as a result of the offense and any psychological impact experienced by the victim or the victim's family as a result of the offense, and contain any other information related to the impact of the offense upon the victim that the court requires. Each victim impact statement prepared under this section shall include any statement made by the victim pursuant to section 2930.13 of the Revised Code.

(C) A victim impact statement prepared under this section shall be kept confidential and is not a public record as defined in section 149.43 of the Revised Code. However, the court may furnish copies of the statement to both the defendant or the defendant's counsel and the prosecuting attorney. Immediately following the imposition of sentence upon the defendant, the defendant, the defendant's counsel, and the prosecuting attorney shall return to the court the copies of the victim impact statement that were made available to the defendant, the counsel, or the prosecuting attorney.

(1995 S 2, eff. 7–1–96, 1994 S 186, eff. 10–12–94; 1982 H 269, § 4, eff. 7–1–83; 1982 S 199; 1980 S 384)

2947.06 Testimony after verdict to mitigate penalty; reports confidential

(A)(1) The trial court may hear testimony in mitigation of a sentence at the term of conviction or plea or at the next term. The prosecuting attorney may offer testimony on behalf of the state to give the court a true understanding of the case. The court shall determine whether sentence should immediately be imposed. The court on its own motion may direct the department of probation of the county in which the defendant resides, or its own regular probation officer, to make any inquiries and presentence investigation reports that the court requires concerning the defendant.

(2) The provisions of section 2951.03 of the Revised Code shall govern the preparation of, the provision, receipt, and retention of copies of, the use of, and the confidentiality, nonpublic record character, and sealing of a presentence investigation report prepared pursuant to division (A)(1) of this section.

(B) The court may appoint not more than two psychologists or psychiatrists to make any reports concerning the defendant that the court requires for the purpose of determining the disposition of the case. Each psychologist or psychiatrist shall receive a fee to be fixed by the court and taxed in the costs of the case. The psychologist's or psychiatrist's reports shall be made in writing, in open court, and in the presence of the defendant, except in misdemeanor cases in which sentence may be pronounced in the absence of the defendant. A copy of each report of a psychologist or psychiatrist may be furnished to the defendant, if present, who may examine the persons making the report, under oath, as to any matter or thing contained in the report.

(2002 H 490, eff. 1–1–04; 1996 S 269, eff. 7–1–96; 1995 S 2, eff. 7–1–96; 1987 H 73, § 5, eff. 10–1–89; 1987 H 73, § 1; 1982 H 269, § 4, S 199; 130 v H 686; 1953 H 1; GC 13451–2)

2947.07 When court to pronounce judgment

If a convicted defendant does not show sufficient cause as to why judgment should not be pronounced, the court shall pronounce the judgment.

(1953 H 1, eff. 10–1–53; GC 13451–4)

2947.08 Time of execution in capital cases

In cases where the death sentence is imposed, at least one hundred twenty days shall intervene between the day of sentence and the day appointed for the execution thereof.

(131 v H 24, eff. 8–10–65; 1953 H 1; GC 13451–5)

2947.14 Satisfaction of fine and costs; determination of ability to pay must precede commitment; hearing on change of circumstances

(A) If a fine is imposed as a sentence or a part of a sentence, the court or magistrate that imposed the fine may order that the offender be committed to the jail or workhouse until the fine is paid or secured to be paid, or the offender is otherwise legally discharged, if the court or magistrate determines at a hearing that the offender is able, at that time, to pay the fine but refuses to do so. The hearing required by this section shall be conducted at the time of sentencing.

(B) At the hearing, the offender has the right to be represented by counsel and to testify and present evidence as to the offender's ability to pay the fine. If a court or magistrate determines after considering the evidence presented by an offender, that the offender is able to pay a fine, the determination shall be supported by findings of fact set forth in a judgment entry that indicate the offender's income, assets, and debts, as presented by the offender, and the offender's ability to pay.

(C) If the court or magistrate has found the offender able to pay a fine at a hearing conducted in compliance with divisions (A) and (B) of this section, and the offender fails to pay the fine, a warrant may be issued for the arrest of the offender. Any offender held in custody pursuant to such an arrest shall be entitled to a hearing on the first regularly scheduled court day following the date of arrest in order to inform the court or magistrate of any change of circumstances that has occurred since the time of sentencing and that affects the offender's ability to pay the fine. The right to the hearing on any change of circumstances may be waived by the offender.

At the hearing to determine any change of circumstances, the offender has the right to testify and present evidence as to any portion of the offender's income, assets, or debts that has changed in such a manner as to affect the offender's ability to pay the fine. If a court or magistrate determines, after considering any evidence presented by the offender, that the offender remains able to pay the fine, that determination shall be supported by a judgment entry that includes findings of fact upon which such a determination is based.

(D) No person shall be ordered to be committed to a jail or workhouse or otherwise be held in custody in satisfaction of a fine imposed as the whole or a part of a sentence except as provided in this section. Any person imprisoned pursuant to this section shall receive credit upon the fine at the rate of fifty dollars per day or fraction of a day. If the unpaid fine is less than fifty dollars, the person shall be imprisoned one day.

(E) No commitment pursuant to this section shall exceed six months.

(2002 H 170, eff. 9–6–02; 1984 H 113, eff. 1–8–85; 1984 H 277; 1970 S 460; 1953 H 1; GC 13451–9)

MISCELLANEOUS PROVISIONS

2947.15 Jail limits and proceeds of convict labor; rehabilitation of prisoners

Persons committed to jail by a judge or magistrate for nonpayment of fine, or convicts sentenced to hard labor in the county jail, shall perform labor under the direction of the board of county commissioners within or outside the jail, within the county, and the board shall adopt orders and rules in relation to the performance of labor and the sheriff or other officer having the custody of the persons or convicts shall be governed by the orders and rules. The sheriff of the county shall collect the proceeds of the labor of the persons or convicts, pay it into the county treasury, take the county treasurer's duplicate receipts for the amount paid, and forthwith deposit one of them with the county auditor. The sheriff, with the approval of the board, may provide for the vocational training and rehabilitation of prisoners confined in the county jail.

This section does not apply to prisoners participating in a county jail industry program established under section 5147.30 of the Revised Code.

(1990 H 51, eff. 11–8–90; 1990 H 588; 1970 S 460; 125 v 385; 1953 H 1; GC 13451–10)

2947.151 Reduction of jail sentence

The sheriff in charge of a county jail may, upon a consideration of the quality and amount of work done in the kitchen, in the jail offices, on the jail premises, or elsewhere, allow reductions of inmates' sentences as follows:

(A) On sentences of ninety days or less, up to three days for each thirty days of sentence;

(B) On sentences longer than ninety days but not longer than six months, up to four days for each thirty days of sentence;

(C) On sentences longer than six months, up to five days for each thirty days of sentence.

The reduction of the inmate's sentence, shall become effective only upon the written concurrence of the presiding or sentencing judge or magistrate of the court where the sentence was imposed.

This section shall in no way restrict any other powers vested in the presiding or sentencing judge or magistrate of the court where the sentence was imposed.

(128 v 595, eff. 10–1–59)

2947.16 Recognizance

A person convicted of a misdemeanor may be required by the judge or magistrate to enter into a recognizance, with sufficient surety, in such sum as the judge or magistrate finds proper, to keep the peace and be of good behavior for such time, not exceeding two years, as the court directs. The court may order such person to stand committed until such order is complied with or he is discharged by law, but the court may discharge such person at any time of [1] his own recognizance, or cancel such recognizance.

(1953 H 1, eff. 10–1–53; GC 13451–11)

[1] So in original; should this read "on"?

2947.17 Breach of a condition of a recognizance

In case of a breach of the condition of any recognizance given under section 2947.16 of the Revised Code, the same proceedings shall be had as are prescribed in relation to forfeiture of other recognizances.

(1980 H 736, eff. 10–16–80; 1969 H 228; 1953 H 1; GC 13451–12)

2947.18 Sentence to workhouse for jail offense

Where the board of county commissioners of a county, or legislative authority of a municipal corporation having no workhouse, has made provisions for receiving prisoners into the workhouse of a city in any other county or district in the state, a court or magistrate, where imprisonment in jail may lawfully be imposed in such case, may sentence persons convicted of a misdemeanor, including a violation of a municipal ordinance, to such workhouse.

(1970 S 460, eff. 9–3–70; 1953 H 1; GC 13451–13)

2947.19 Maintenance of prisoners; reimbursement by prisoner; testing for contagious diseases

(A) In a county that has no workhouse but in which is located a city that has a workhouse maintained by the city, the board of county commissioners may agree with the proper authorities of that city upon terms under which persons convicted of misdemeanors shall be maintained in the city workhouse at the expense of the county. In the case of persons committed to the city workhouse for the violation of a law of this state, whether the commitment is from the court of common pleas, magistrate's court, or other court, the cost of maintaining those persons committed shall be paid out of the general fund of the county, on the allowance of the board of county commissioners, provided that all persons committed to the city workhouse for the violation of ordinances of the city shall be maintained in that workhouse at the sole cost of the city.

(B) Pursuant to section 2929.37 of the Revised Code, the board of county commissioners or the legislative authority of the city may require a person who was convicted of an offense and who is confined in the city workhouse as provided in division (A) of this section to reimburse the county or the city, as the case may be, for its expenses incurred by reason of the person's confinement. If a person is convicted of or pleads guilty to a felony and the court imposes a sanction that requires the offender to serve a term in a city workhouse, sections 341.23, 753.02, 753.04, and 753.16 of the Revised Code govern the determination of whether the court may impose a sanction under section 2929.18 of the Revised Code that requires the offender to reimburse the expenses of confinement.

(C) Notwithstanding any contrary provision in this section or section 2929.18, 2929.28, or 2929.37 of the Revised Code, the board of county commissioners or the legislative authority of the city may establish a policy that complies with section 2929.38 of the Revised Code and that requires any person who is not indigent and who is confined in the city workhouse to pay a reception fee or a fee for any medical treatment or service requested by and provided to that person.

(D) If a person who has been convicted of or pleaded guilty to an offense is confined in the workhouse as provided in division (A) of this section, at the time of reception and at other times the person in charge of the operation of the workhouse determines to be appropriate, the person in charge of the operation of the workhouse may cause the convicted offender to be examined and tested for tuberculosis, HIV infection, hepatitis, including but not limited to hepatitis A, B, and C, and other contagious diseases. The person in charge of the operation of the workhouse may cause a convicted offender in the workhouse who refuses to be tested or treated for tuberculosis, HIV infection, hepatitis, including but not limited to hepatitis A, B, and C, or another contagious disease to be tested and treated involuntarily.

(2002 H 490, eff. 1–1–04; 2002 H 170, eff. 9–6–02; 1997 S 111, eff. 3–17–98; 1996 H 480, eff. 10–16–96; 1996 S 269, eff. 7–1–96; 1995 S 2, eff. 7–1–96; 1984 H 363, eff. 9–26–84; 1975 H 205; 1953 H 1; GC 13451–14)

2947.20 Health insurance claims of persons confined in city workhouse

(A) For each person who is confined in a city workhouse as provided in section 2947.19 of the Revised Code, the county or the city, as the case may be, may make a determination as to whether the person is covered under a health insurance or health care policy, contract, or plan and, if the person has such coverage, what terms and conditions are imposed by it for the filing and payment of claims.

(B) If, pursuant to division (A) of this section, it is determined that the person is covered under a policy, contract, or plan and, while that coverage is in force, the workhouse renders or arranges for the rendering of health care services to the person in accordance with the terms and conditions of the policy, contract, or plan, then the person, county, city, or provider of the health care services, as appropriate under the terms and conditions of the policy, contract, or plan, shall promptly submit a claim for payment for the health care services to the appropriate third-party payer and shall designate, or make any other arrangement necessary to ensure, that payment of any amount due on the claim be made to the county, city, or provider, as the case may be.

(C) Any payment made to the county or the city pursuant to division (B) of this section shall be paid into the treasury of the governmental entity that incurred the expenses.

(D) This section also applies to any person who is under the custody of a law enforcement officer, as defined in section 2901.01 of the Revised Code, prior to the person's confinement in the workhouse.

(1996 S 163, eff. 10–16–96)

2947.21 Commitment to workhouse

When a person is sentenced to a workhouse by the court of common pleas, the clerk of the court of common pleas shall make and deliver to the sheriff a certified copy of the judgment. The copy shall describe the crime charged and the sentence of the court. The sheriff shall deliver the copy to the officer in charge of the workhouse, and the copy shall be that officer's warrant for detaining the person in custody. In case of such a conviction by any other court or magistrate, the court or magistrate shall make a certified transcript of the docket in the case, which, in like manner, shall be delivered to the marshal, constable, or sheriff to be delivered by the marshal, constable, or sheriff to the proper officer in charge of the workhouse and be that officer's warrant for detaining the person in custody.

When a person is sentenced to a jail or workhouse under section 2929.24 of the Revised Code, the court shall certify a transcript of the docket in the case, and the court shall deliver the certified transcript to the proper officer in charge of the workhouse or jail, and the certified transcript is the officer's warrant for detaining the person in custody during the prescribed period or periods.

(2002 H 490, eff. 1–1–04; 1995 S 2, eff. 7–1–96; 1980 H 736, eff. 10–16–80; 1969 H 228; 1953 H 1; GC 13451–16)

2947.22 Person may be confined in jail temporarily

A person sentenced to a workhouse may be confined in the jail of the county in which he was convicted, for such period as is necessary to procure the papers and make arrangements to transport him to the workhouse.

(1953 H 1, eff. 10–1–53; GC 13451–17)

2947.23 Judgment for costs and jury fees; community service upon failure to pay

Note: See also following version of this section, eff. 5–18–05.

(A)(1) In all criminal cases, including violations of ordinances, the judge or magistrate shall include in the sentence the costs of prosecution and render a judgment against the defendant for such costs. At the time the judge or magistrate imposes sentence, the judge or magistrate shall notify the defendant of both of the following:

(a) If the defendant fails to pay that judgment or fails to timely make payments towards that judgment under a payment schedule approved by the court, the court may order the defendant to perform community service in an amount of not more than forty hours per month until the judgment is paid or until the court is satisfied that the defendant is in compliance with the approved payment schedule.

(b) If the court orders the defendant to perform the community service, the defendant will receive credit upon the judgment at the specified hourly credit rate per hour of community service performed, and each hour of community service performed will reduce the judgment by that amount.

(2) If a jury has been sworn at the trial of a case, the fees of the jurors shall be included in the costs, which shall be paid to the public treasury from which the jurors were paid.

(B) If a judge or magistrate has reason to believe that a defendant has failed to pay the judgment described in division (A) of this section or has failed to timely make payments towards that judgment under a payment schedule approved by the judge or magistrate, the judge or magistrate shall hold a hearing to determine whether to order the offender to perform community service for that failure. The judge or magistrate shall notify both the defendant and the prosecuting attorney of the place, time, and date of the hearing and shall give each an opportunity to present evidence. If, after the hearing, the judge or magistrate determines that the defendant has failed to pay the judgment or to timely make payments under the payment schedule and that imposition of community service for the failure is appropriate, the judge or magistrate may order the offender to perform community service in an amount of not more than forty hours per month until the judgment is paid or until the judge or magistrate is satisfied that the offender is in compliance with the approved payment schedule. If the judge or magistrate orders the defendant to perform community service under this division, the defendant shall receive credit upon the judgment at the specified hourly credit rate per hour of community service performed, and each hour of community service performed shall reduce the judgment by that amount. Except for the credit and reduction provided in this division, ordering an offender to perform community service under this division does not lessen the amount of the judgment and does not preclude the state from taking any other action to execute the judgment.

(C) As used in this section, "specified hourly credit rate" means the wage rate that is specified in 26 U.S.C.A. 206(a)(1) under the federal Fair Labor Standards Act of 1938, that then is in effect, and that an employer subject to that provision must pay per hour to each of the employer's employees who is subject to that provision.

(2002 H 271, eff. 3–24–03; 1953 H 1, eff. 10–1–53; GC 13451–18)

Note: See also following version of this section, eff. 5–18–05.

2947.23 Judgment for costs and jury fees; community service upon failure to pay (later effective date)

Note: See also preceding version of this section, in effect until 5–18–05.

(A)(1) In all criminal cases, including violations of ordinances, the judge or magistrate shall include in the sentence the costs of prosecution and render a judgment against the defendant for such costs. At the time the judge or magistrate imposes sentence, the judge or magistrate shall notify the defendant of both of the following:

(a) If the defendant fails to pay that judgment or fails to timely make payments towards that judgment under a payment schedule approved by the court, the court may order the defendant to perform community service in an amount of not more than forty hours per month until the judgment is paid or until the court is satisfied that the defendant is in compliance with the approved payment schedule.

(b) If the court orders the defendant to perform the community service, the defendant will receive credit upon the judgment at the specified hourly credit rate per hour of community service performed, and each hour of community service performed will reduce the judgment by that amount.

(2) The following shall apply in all criminal cases:

(a) If a jury has been sworn at the trial of a case, the fees of the jurors shall be included in the costs, which shall be paid to the public treasury from which the jurors were paid.

(b) If a jury has not been sworn at the trial of a case because of a defendant's failure to appear without good cause, the costs incurred in summoning jurors for that particular trial may be included in the costs of prosecution. If the costs incurred in summoning jurors are assessed against the defendant, those costs shall be paid to the public treasury from which the jurors were paid.

(B) If a judge or magistrate has reason to believe that a defendant has failed to pay the judgment described in division (A) of this section or has failed to timely make payments towards that judgment under a payment schedule approved by the judge or magistrate, the judge or magistrate shall hold a hearing to determine whether to order the offender to perform community service for that failure. The judge or magistrate shall notify both the defendant and the prosecuting attorney of the place, time, and date of the hearing and shall give each an opportunity to present evidence. If, after the hearing, the judge or magistrate determines that the defendant has failed to pay the judgment or to timely make payments under the payment schedule and that imposition of community service for the failure is appropriate, the judge or magistrate may order the offender to perform community service in an amount of not more than forty hours per month until the judgment is paid or until the judge or magistrate is satisfied that the offender is in compliance with the approved payment schedule. If the judge or magistrate orders the defendant to perform community service under this division, the defendant shall receive credit upon the judgment at the specified hourly credit rate per hour of community service performed, and each hour of community service performed shall reduce the judgment by that amount. Except for the credit and reduction provided in this division, ordering an offender to perform community service under this division does not lessen the amount of the judgment and does not preclude the state from taking any other action to execute the judgment.

(C) As used in this section, "specified hourly credit rate" means the wage rate that is specified in 26 U.S.C.A. 206(a)(1) under the federal Fair Labor Standards Act of 1938, that then is in effect, and that an employer subject to that provision must pay per hour to each of the employer's employees who is subject to that provision.

(2004 S 71, eff. 5–18–05; 2002 H 271, eff. 3–24–03; 1953 H 1, eff. 10–1–53; GC 13451–18)

Note: See also preceding version of this section, in effect until 5–18–05.

CHAPTER 2949

EXECUTION OF SENTENCE

MAGISTRATE DEFINED

2949.01 Definition of magistrate

The definition of "magistrate" set forth in section 2931.01 of the Revised Code applies to Chapter 2949. of the Revised Code.

(1953 H 1, eff. 10–1–53)

SUSPENSION OF SENTENCE

2949.02 Suspension of execution of sentence or judgment pending appeal to court of appeals; bail; exceptions

(A) If a person is convicted of any bailable offense, including, but not limited to, a violation of an ordinance of a municipal corporation, in a municipal or county court or in a court of common pleas and if the person gives to the trial judge or magistrate a written notice of the person's intention to file or apply for leave to file an appeal to the court of appeals, the trial judge or magistrate may suspend, subject to division (A)(2)(b) of section 2953.09 of the Revised Code, execution of the sentence or judgment imposed for any fixed time that will give the person time either to prepare and file, or to apply for leave to file, the appeal. In all bailable cases, except as provided in division (B) of this section, the trial judge or magistrate may release the person on bail in accordance with Criminal Rule 46, and the bail shall at least be conditioned that the person will appeal without delay and abide by the judgment and sentence of the court.

(B) Notwithstanding any provision of Criminal Rule 46 to the contrary, a trial judge of a court of common pleas shall not release on bail pursuant to division (A) of this section a person who is convicted of a bailable offense if the person is sentenced to imprisonment for life or if that offense is a violation of section 2903.01, 2903.02, 2903.03, 2903.04, 2903.11, 2905.01, 2905.02, 2905.11, 2907.02, 2909.02, 2911.01, 2911.02, or 2911.11 of the Revised Code or is felonious sexual penetration in violation of former section 2907.12 of the Revised Code.

(C) If a trial judge of a court of common pleas is prohibited by division (B) of this section from releasing on bail pursuant to division (A) of this section a person who is convicted of a bailable offense and not sentenced to imprisonment for life, the appropriate court of appeals or two judges of it, upon motion of such a person and for good cause shown, may release the person on bail in accordance with Appellate Rule 8 and Criminal Rule 46, and the bail shall at least be conditioned as described in division (A) of this section.

(1996 H 445, eff. 9–3–96; 1986 H 412, eff. 3–17–87; 1982 H 269, § 4, S 199; 1953 H 1; GC 13453–1)

2949.03 Suspension of execution of sentence or judgment pending appeal to supreme court

If a judgment of conviction by a court of common pleas, municipal court, or county court is affirmed by a court of appeals and remanded to the trial court for execution of the sentence or judgment imposed, and the person so convicted gives notice of his intention to file a notice of appeal to the supreme court, the trial court, on the filing of a motion by such person within three days after the rendition by the court of appeals of the judgment of affirmation, may further suspend, subject to division (A)(2)(b) of section 2953.09 of the Revised Code, the execution of the sentence or judgment imposed for a time sufficient to give such person an opportunity to file a notice of appeal to the supreme court, but the sentence or judgment imposed shall not be suspended more than thirty days for that purpose.

(1986 H 412, eff. 3–17–87; 1953 H 1; GC 13453–2)

2949.04 Increase or decrease of bail

When bail is fixed pursuant to division (B) of section 2953.03 or section 2949.02 or 2953.09 of the Revised Code in connection with an appeal, a reduction or increase in the amount of that bail or other change in that bail shall not be required of the accused during the pendency of the appeal unless the trial judge or magistrate, or the court in which the appeal is being prosecuted, finds that there is good cause to reduce or increase the amount of that bail or good cause for any other change in that bail. If the court in which the appeal is being prosecuted finds there is good cause to reduce or increase the amount of that bail or good cause for any other change in that bail, it shall order the reduction, increase, or other change in accordance with Criminal Rule 46, and the new bail shall be in the amount and form so ordered and otherwise be to the approval of and filed with the clerk of the court in which the appeal is being prosecuted.

(1986 H 412, eff. 3–17–87; 129 v 423; 1953 H 1; GC 13453–3)

EXECUTION OF SENTENCE GENERALLY

2949.05 Execution of sentence or judgment

If no appeal is filed, if leave to file an appeal or certification of a case is denied, if the judgment of the trial court is affirmed on appeal, or if post-conviction relief under section 2953.21 of the Revised Code is denied, the trial court or magistrate shall carry into execution the sentence or judgment which had been pronounced against the defendant.

(1986 H 412, eff. 3–17–87; 1969 S 354; 129 v 423; 1953 H 1; GC 13453–4)

2949.06 Recapture after escape

If a person escapes after sentence and before confinement in a state correctional institution or jail, the clerk of the trial court, upon application of the prosecuting attorney or by order of the court, shall issue a warrant stating the conviction and sentence and commanding the sheriff to pursue the person into any county of this state. The sheriff shall take into custody the person so escaping and shall make return of the warrant to the court if it is in session, and if it is not in session he shall commit the accused to the jail of the county and bring him before the court at the next session of the court. The court shall set aside the former sentence and again pronounce judgment upon the verdict.

(1994 H 571, eff. 10–6–94; 1953 H 1, eff. 10–1–53; GC 13453–5)

2949.07 Computing time served

If a convict escapes from a state correctional institution, the time the convict is absent from the institution because of his escape shall not be credited as a part of the time for which he was sentenced.

(1994 H 571, eff. 10–6–94; 1953 H 1, eff. 10–1–53; GC 13453–6)

2949.08 Confinement of convicts; reduction of sentence for confinement prior to conviction

(A) When a person who is convicted of or pleads guilty to a felony is sentenced to a community residential sanction in a community-based correctional facility pursuant to section 2929.16 of the Revised Code or when a person who is convicted of or pleads guilty to a felony or a misdemeanor is sentenced to a term of imprisonment in a jail, the judge or magistrate shall order the person into the custody of the sheriff or constable, and the sheriff or constable shall deliver the person with the record of the person's conviction to the jailer, administrator, or keeper, in whose custody the person shall remain until the term of imprisonment expires or the person is otherwise legally discharged.

(B) The record of the person's conviction shall specify the total number of days, if any, that the person was confined for any reason arising out of the offense for which the person was convicted and sentenced prior to delivery to the jailer, administrator, or keeper under this section. The record shall be used to determine any reduction of sentence under division (C) of this section.

(C) (1) If the person is sentenced to a jail for a felony or a misdemeanor, the jailer in charge of a jail shall reduce the sentence of a person delivered into the jailer's custody pursuant to division (A) of this section by the total number of days the person was confined for any reason arising out of the offense for which the person was convicted and sentenced, including confinement in lieu of bail while awaiting trial, confinement for examination to determine the person's competence to stand trial or to determine sanity, and confinement while awaiting transportation to the place where the person is to serve the sentence.

(2) If the person is sentenced to a community-based correctional facility for a felony, the total amount of time that a person shall be confined in a community-based correctional facility, in a jail, and for any reason arising out of the offense for which the person was convicted and sentenced prior to delivery to the jailer, administrator, or keeper shall not exceed the maximum prison term available for that offense. Any term in a jail shall be reduced first pursuant to division (C)(1) of this section by the total number of days the person was confined prior to delivery to the jailer, administrator, or keeper. Only after the term in a jail has been entirely reduced may the term in a community-based correctional facility be reduced pursuant to this division. This division does not affect the limitations placed on the duration of a term in a jail or a community-based correctional facility under divisions (A)(1), (2), and (3) of section 2929.16 of the Revised Code.

(D) For purposes of divisions (B) and (C) of this section, a person shall be considered to have been confined for a day if the person was confined for any period or periods of time totaling more than eight hours during that day.

(E) As used in this section, "Community–based correctional facility" and "jail" have the same meanings as in section 2929.01 of the Revised Code.

(1999 S 107, eff. 3–23–00; 1979 S 23, eff. 3–27–80; 1953 H 1; GC 13454–1)

2949.09 Execution for fine

When a judge or magistrate renders judgment for a fine, an execution may issue for such judgment and costs of prosecution, to be levied on the property, or in default thereof, upon the body of the defendant for nonpayment of the fine. The officer holding such writ may arrest such defendant in any county and commit him to the jail of the county in which such writ issued, until such fine is paid or secured to be paid or he is otherwise legally discharged.

(1970 S 460, eff. 9–3–70; 1953 H 1; GC 13454–2)

2949.091 Fees and costs

(A)(1) The court, in which any person is convicted of or pleads guilty to any offense other than a traffic offense that is not a moving violation, shall impose the sum of fifteen dollars as costs in the case in addition to any other court costs that the court is required by law to impose upon the offender. All such moneys collected during a month shall be transmitted on or before the twentieth day of the following month by the clerk of the court to the treasurer of state and deposited by the treasurer of state into the general revenue fund. The court shall not waive the payment of the additional fifteen dollars court costs, unless the court determines that the offender is indigent and waives the payment of all court costs imposed upon the indigent offender.

(2) The juvenile court, in which a child is found to be a delinquent child or a juvenile traffic offender for an act which, if committed by an adult, would be an offense other than a traffic offense that is not a moving violation, shall impose the sum of fifteen dollars as costs in the case in addition to any other court costs that the court is required or permitted by law to impose upon the delinquent child or juvenile traffic offender. All such moneys collected during a month shall be transmitted on or before the twentieth day of the following month by the clerk of the court to the treasurer of state and deposited by the treasurer of state into the general revenue fund. The fifteen dollars court costs shall be collected in all cases unless the court determines the juvenile is indigent and waives the payment of all court costs, or enters an order on its journal stating that it has determined that the juvenile is indigent, that no other court costs are to be taxed in the case, and that the payment of the fifteen dollars court costs is waived.

(B) Whenever a person is charged with any offense other than a traffic offense that is not a moving violation and posts bail, the court shall add to the amount of the bail the fifteen dollars required to be paid by division (A)(1) of this section. The fifteen dollars shall be retained by the clerk of the court until the person is convicted, pleads guilty, forfeits bail, is found not guilty, or has the charges dismissed. If the person is convicted, pleads guilty, or forfeits bail, the clerk shall transmit the fifteen dollars on or before the twentieth day of the month following the month in which the person was convicted, pleaded guilty, or forfeited bail to the treasurer of state, who shall deposit it into the general revenue fund. If the person is found not guilty or the charges are dismissed, the clerk shall return the fifteen dollars to the person.

(C) No person shall be placed or held in a detention facility for failing to pay the additional fifteen dollars court costs or bail that are required to be paid by this section.

(D) As used in this section:

(1) "Moving violation" and "bail" have the same meanings as in section 2743.70 of the Revised Code.

(2) "Detention facility" has the same meaning as in section 2921.01 of the Revised Code.

(2003 H 95, eff. 9–26–03; 1998 H 426, eff. 7–22–98; 1991 H 298, eff. 7–26–91; 1990 S 131; 1989 H 111; 1987 H 171; 1983 H 291)

2949.092 Waiver of additional court costs

If a person is convicted of or pleads guilty to an offense and the court specifically is required, pursuant to section 2743.70 or 2949.091 of the Revised Code or pursuant to any other section of the Revised Code, to impose a specified sum of money as costs in the case in addition to any other costs that the court is required or permitted by law to impose in the case, the court shall not waive the payment of the specified additional court costs that the section of the Revised Code specifically requires the court to impose unless the court determines that the offender is indigent and the court waives the payment of all court costs imposed upon the offender.

(1990 S 131, eff. 7–25–90)

2949.10 Execution for fine to issue to other county

An execution under section 2949.09 of the Revised Code may issue to the sheriff of any county in which the defendant resides, is found, or has property, and the sheriff shall execute the writ. If the defendant is taken, the sheriff shall commit him to the jail of the county in which the writ issued and deliver a certified copy of the writ to the sheriff of such county, who shall detain the offender until he is discharged as provided in such section.

(1953 H 1, eff. 10–1–53; GC 13454–3)

2949.11 Fines paid into county treasury

Unless otherwise required in the Revised Code, an officer who collects a fine shall pay it into the treasury of the county in which such fine was assessed, within twenty days after the receipt of the fine, to the credit of the county general fund. The county treasurer shall issue duplicate receipts for the fine, and the officer making the collection shall deposit one of these receipts with the county auditor.

(1986 S 54, eff. 5–6–86; 125 v 903; 1953 H 1; GC 13454–4)

2949.111 Priority of assignment of payments to satisfaction of costs, restitution, fines, and probation fees

(A) As used in this section:

(1) "Court costs" means any assessment that the court requires an offender to pay to defray the costs of operating the court.

(2) "State fines or costs" means any costs imposed or forfeited bail collected by the court under section 2743.70 of the Revised Code for deposit into the reparations fund or under section 2949.091 of the Revised Code for deposit into the general revenue fund and all fines, penalties, and forfeited bail collected by the court and paid to a law library association under sections 3375.50 to 3375.53 of the Revised Code.

(3) "Reimbursement" means any reimbursement for the costs of confinement that the court orders an offender to pay pursuant to section 2929.28 of the Revised Code, any supervision fee, any fee for the costs of house arrest with electronic monitoring that an offender agrees to pay, any reimbursement for the costs of an investigation or prosecution that the court orders an offender to pay pursuant to section 2929.71 of the Revised Code, or any other costs that the court orders an offender to pay.

(4) "Supervision fees" means any fees that a court, pursuant to sections 2929.18, 2929.28, and 2951.021 of the Revised Code, requires an offender who is under a community control sanction to pay for supervision services.

(5) "Community control sanction" has the same meaning as in section 2929.01 of the Revised Code.

(B) Unless the court, in accordance with division (C) of this section, enters in the record of the case a different method of assigning payments, if a person who is charged with a misdemeanor is convicted of or pleads guilty to the offense, if the court orders the offender to pay any combination of court costs, state fines or costs, restitution, a conventional fine, or any reimbursement, and if the offender makes any payment of any of them to a clerk of court, the clerk shall assign the offender's payment in the following manner:

(1) If the court ordered the offender to pay any court costs, the offender's payment shall be assigned toward the satisfaction of those court costs until they have been entirely paid.

(2) If the court ordered the offender to pay any state fines or costs and if all of the court costs that the court ordered the offender to pay have been paid, the remainder of the offender's payment shall be assigned on a pro rata basis toward the satisfaction of the state fines or costs until they have been entirely paid.

(3) If the court ordered the offender to pay any restitution and if all of the court costs and state fines or costs that the court ordered the offender to pay have been paid, the remainder of the offender's payment shall be assigned toward the satisfaction of the restitution until it has been entirely paid.

(4) If the court ordered the offender to pay any fine and if all of the court costs, state fines or costs, and restitution that the court ordered the offender to pay have been paid, the remainder of the offender's payment shall be assigned toward the satisfaction of the fine until it has been entirely paid.

(5) If the court ordered the offender to pay any reimbursement and if all of the court costs, state fines or costs, restitution, and fines that the court ordered the offender to pay have been paid, the remainder of the offender's payment shall be assigned toward the satisfaction of the reimbursements until they have been entirely paid.

(C) If a person who is charged with a misdemeanor is convicted of or pleads guilty to the offense and if the court orders the offender to pay any combination of court costs, state fines or costs, restitution, fines, or reimbursements, the court, at the time it orders the offender to make those payments, may prescribe an order of payments that differs from the order set forth in division (B) of this section by entering in the record of the case the order so prescribed. If a different order is entered in the record, on receipt of any payment, the clerk of the court shall assign the payment in the manner prescribed by the court.

(2002 H 490, eff. 1–1–04; 2002 H 170, eff. 9–6–02; 1995 S 2, eff. 7–1–96; 1994 H 406, eff. 11–11–94)

COSTS AND TRANSPORTATION OF CONVICTS

2949.12 Conveying convicted felon to reception facility

Unless the execution of sentence is suspended, a convicted felon who is sentenced to serve a term of imprisonment in a state correctional institution shall be conveyed, within five days after sentencing, excluding Saturdays, Sundays, and legal holidays, by the sheriff of the county in which the conviction was had to the facility that is designated by the department of rehabilitation and correction for the reception of convicted felons. The sheriff shall deliver the convicted felon into the custody of the managing officer of the reception facility and, at that time, shall present the managing officer with a copy of the convicted felon's sentence that clearly describes each offense for which the felon was sentenced to a correctional institution, designates each section of the Revised Code that the felon violated and that resulted in the felon's conviction and sentence to a correctional institution, designates the sentence imposed for each offense for which the felon was sentenced to a correctional institution, and, pursuant to section 2967.191 of the Revised Code, specifies the total number of days, if any, that the felon was confined for any reason prior to conviction and sentence. The sheriff, at that time, also shall present the managing officer with a copy of the indictment. The clerk of the court of common pleas shall furnish the copies of the sentence and indictment. In the case of a person under the age of eighteen years who is certified to the court of common pleas by the juvenile court, the clerk of the court of common pleas also shall attach a copy of the certification to the copy of the indictment.

The convicted felon shall be assigned to an institution or designated to be housed in a county, multicounty, municipal, municipal-county, or multicounty-municipal jail or workhouse, if authorized pursuant to section 5120.161 of the Revised Code, shall be conveyed to the institution, jail, or workhouse, and shall be kept within the institution, jail, or workhouse until the term of the felon's imprisonment expires, the felon is pardoned, paroled, or placed under a post-release control sanction, or the felon is transferred under laws permitting the transfer of prisoners. If the execution of the felon's sentence is suspended, and the judgment thereafter affirmed, the felon shall be conveyed, in the same manner as if the execution of the felon's sentence had not been suspended, to the reception facility as soon as practicable after the judge directs the execution of sentence. The trial judge or other judge of the court, in the judge's discretion and for good cause shown, may extend the time of the conveyance.

(1995 S 2, eff. 7–1–96; 1994 H 571, eff. 10–6–94; 1988 H 708, eff. 4–19–88; 1987 H 261, H 455, S 6, § 3; 1984 S 172, § 1, 3; 1983 S 210; 1982 H 269, § 4, S 199; 1976 H 685; 1973 S 254; 1953 H 1; GC 13455–1)

2949.13 Sheriff may require assistance

During the time the sheriff is conveying a convicted felon to an institution for imprisonment therein, he may secure him in a jail and demand the assistance of a sheriff, jailer, or other person in keeping such prisoner, as if he were in his own county. Such sheriff, jailer, or other person is liable, on refusal, to like penalties as if the sheriff making the demand were in his own county.

(1953 H 1, eff. 10–1–53; GC 13455–2)

2949.14 Cost bill in case of felony

Upon conviction of a nonindigent person for a felony, the clerk of the court of common pleas shall make and certify under his hand and seal of the court, a complete itemized bill of the costs made in such prosecution, including the sum paid by the board of county commissioners, certified by the county auditor, for the arrest and return of the person on the requisition of the governor, or on the request of the governor to the president of the United States, or on the return of the fugitive by a designated agent pursuant to a waiver of extradition except in cases of parole violation. Such bill of costs shall be presented by such clerk to the prosecuting attorney, who shall examine each item therein charged and certify to it if correct and legal. Upon certification by the prosecuting attorney, the clerk shall attempt to collect the costs from the person convicted.

(1983 H 291, eff. 7–1–83; 132 v S 447; 1953 H 1; GC 13455–3)

2949.15 Writs of execution to issue

If a nonindigent person convicted of a felony fails to pay the costs of prosecution pursuant to section 2949.14 of the Revised Code, the clerk of the court of common pleas shall forthwith issue to the sheriff of the county in which the indictment was found, and to the sheriff of any other county in which the person has property, executions against his property for fines and the costs of prosecution, which shall be served and returned within ten days, with the proceedings of such sheriff or the certification that there is no property upon which to levy, indorsed thereon.

When a levy is made upon property under such execution, a writ shall forthwith be issued by the clerk for the sale thereof, and such sheriff shall sell the property and make return thereof, and after paying the costs of conviction, execution, and sale, pay the balance to the person authorized to receive it.

(1983 H 291, eff. 7–1–83; 1953 H 1; GC 13455–4)

2949.17 Transportation of prisoners; expenses

(A) The sheriff may take one guard for every two convicted felons to be transported to a correctional institution. The trial judge may authorize a larger number of guards upon written application of the sheriff, in which case a transcript of the order of the judge shall be certified by the clerk of the court of common pleas under the seal of the court, and the sheriff shall deliver the order with the convict to the person in charge of the correctional institution.

(B) In order to obtain reimbursement for the county for the expenses of transportation for indigent convicted felons, the clerk of the court of common pleas shall prepare a transportation cost bill for each indigent convicted felon transported pursuant to this section for an amount equal to ten cents a mile from the county seat to the state correctional institution and return for the sheriff and each of the guards and five cents a mile from the county seat to the state correctional institution for each prisoner. The number of miles shall be computed by the usual route of travel. The clerk's duties under this division are subject to division (B) of section 2949.19 of the Revised Code.

(1999 H 283, eff. 9–29–99; 1994 H 571, eff. 10–6–94; 1983 H 291, eff. 7–1–83; 1981 H 694; 1979 H 204; 128 v 542; 1953 H 1; GC 13455–6)

2949.19 Subsidy by state for certain costs

(A) Subject to division (B) of this section, the clerk of the court of common pleas shall report to the state public defender all cases in which an indigent person was convicted of a felony, all cases in which reimbursement is required by section 2949.20 of the Revised Code, and all cost bills for transportation that are prepared pursuant to section 2949.17 of the Revised Code. The reports shall be filed for each fiscal quarter within thirty days after the end of the quarter on a form prescribed by the state public defender and shall be accompanied by a certification of a judge of the court that in all cases listed in the report the defendant was determined to be indigent and convicted of a felony or that the case is reported pursuant to section 2949.20 of the Revised Code and that for each transportation cost bill submitted pursuant to section 2949.17 of the Revised Code that the convicted felon was determined to be indigent. The state public defender shall review the reports received under this division and prepare a transportation cost voucher and a quarterly subsidy voucher for each county for the amounts the state public defender finds to be correct. To compute the quarterly subsidy, the state public defender first shall subtract the total of all transportation cost vouchers that the state public defender approves for payment for the quarter from one-fourth of the state public defender's total appropriation for criminal costs subsidy for the fiscal year of which the quarter is part. The state public defender then shall compute a base subsidy amount per case by dividing the remainder by the total number of cases from all counties the state public defender approves for subsidy for the quarter. The quarterly subsidy voucher for each county shall then be the product of the base subsidy amount times the number of cases submitted by the county and approved for subsidy for the quarter. Payment shall be made to the clerk.

The clerk shall keep a record of all cases submitted for the subsidy in which the defendant was bound over to the court of common pleas from the municipal court. Upon receipt of the quarterly subsidy, the clerk shall pay to the clerk of the municipal court, for municipal court costs in such cases, an amount that does not exceed fifteen dollars per case, shall pay foreign sheriffs for their services, and shall deposit the remainder of the subsidy to the credit of the general fund of the county. The clerk of the court of common pleas then shall stamp the clerk's records subsidy costs satisfied.

(B) If notified by the state public defender under section 2949.201 of the Revised Code that, for a specified state fiscal year, the general assembly has not appropriated funding for reimbursement payments pursuant to division (A) of this section, the clerk of the court of common pleas is exempt for that state fiscal year from the duties imposed upon the clerk by division (A) of this section and by sections 2949.17 and 2949.20 of the Revised Code. Upon providing the notice described in this division, the state public defender is exempt for that state fiscal year from the duties imposed upon the state public defender by division (A) of this section.

(1999 H 283, eff. 9–29–99; 1987 H 171, eff. 7–1–87; 1985 H 201; 1984 H 462; 1983 H 291; 1981 H 694; 1979 H 204; 130 v S 342; 1953 H 1; GC 13455–8)

2949.20 Reimbursement in case of reversal

In any case of final judgment of reversal as provided in section 2953.07 of the Revised Code, whenever the state of Ohio is the appellee, the clerk of the court of common pleas of the county in which sentence was imposed shall certify the case to the state public defender for reimbursement in the report required by section 2949.19 of the Revised Code, subject to division (B) of section 2949.19 of the Revised Code.

(1999 H 283, eff. 9–29–99; 1983 H 291, eff. 7–1–83; 1981 H 694; 1979 H 204; 1953 H 1; GC 13455–9)

2949.201 State public defender to provide notification regarding reimbursements

(A) On or before the date specified in division (B) of this section, in each state fiscal year, the state public defender shall notify the clerk of the court of common pleas of each county whether the general assembly has, or has not, appropriated funding for that state fiscal year for reimbursement payments pursuant to division (A) of section 2949.19 of the Revised Code.

(B) The state public defender shall provide the notification required by division (A) of this section on or before whichever of the following dates is applicable:

(1) If, on the first day of July of the fiscal year in question, the main operating appropriations act that covers that fiscal year is in effect, on or before the thirty-first day of July;

(2) If, on the first day of July of the fiscal year in question, the main operating appropriations act that covers that fiscal year is not in effect, on or before the day that is thirty days after the effective date of the main operating appropriations act that covers that fiscal year.

(1999 H 283, eff. 9–29–99; 1983 H 291, eff. 7–1–83; 1981 H 694)

2949.21 Conveyance to correctional institution

A writ for the execution of the death penalty shall be directed to the sheriff by the court issuing it, and the sheriff, within thirty days and in a private manner, shall convey the prisoner to the facility designated by the director of rehabilitation and correction for the reception of the prisoner. For conducting the prisoner to the facility, the sheriff shall receive like fees and mileage as in other cases, when approved by the warden of the facility. After the procedures performed at the reception facility are completed, the prisoner shall be assigned to an appropriate correctional institution, conveyed to the institution, and kept within the institution until the execution of his sentence.

(1994 H 571, eff. 10–6–94; 1992 S 359, eff. 12–22–92; 1953 H 1; GC 13456–1)

DEATH SENTENCE

2949.22 Execution of death sentence

(A) Except as provided in division (C) of this section, a death sentence shall be executed by causing the application to the person, upon whom the sentence was imposed, of a lethal injection of a drug or combination of drugs of sufficient dosage to quickly and painlessly cause death. The application of the drug or combination of drugs shall be continued until the person is dead. The warden of the correctional institution in which the sentence is to be executed or another person selected by the director of rehabilitation and correction shall ensure that the death sentence is executed.

(B) A death sentence shall be executed within the walls of the state correctional institution designated by the director of rehabilitation and correction as the location for executions, within an enclosure to be prepared for that purpose, under the direction of the warden of the institution or, in the warden's absence, a deputy warden, and on the day designated by the judge passing sentence or otherwise designated by a court in the course of any appellate or postconviction proceedings. The enclosure shall exclude public view.

(C) If a person is sentenced to death, and if the execution of a death sentence by lethal injection has been determined to be unconstitutional, the death sentence shall be executed by using any different manner of execution prescribed by law subsequent to the effective date of this amendment instead of by causing the application to the person of a lethal injection of a drug or combination of drugs of sufficient dosage to quickly and painlessly cause death, provided that the subsequently prescribed different manner of execution has not been determined to be unconstitutional. The use of the subsequently prescribed different manner of execution shall be continued until the person is dead. The warden of the state correctional institution in which the sentence is to be executed or another person selected by the director of rehabilitation and correction shall ensure that the sentence of death is executed.

(D) No change in the law made by the amendment to this section that took effect on October 1, 1993, or by this amendment constitutes a declaration by or belief of the general assembly that execution of a death sentence by electrocution is a cruel and unusual punishment proscribed by the Ohio Constitution or the United States Constitution.

(2001 H 362, eff. 11–21–01; 1994 H 571, eff. 10–6–94; 1993 H 11, eff. 10–1–93; 1992 S 359; 1953 H 1; GC 13456–2)

2949.24 Execution and return of warrant

Unless a suspension of execution is ordered by the court of appeals in which the cause is pending on appeal or the supreme court for a case in which a sentence of death is imposed for an offense committed before January 1, 1995, or by the supreme court for a case in which a sentence of death is imposed for an offense committed on or after January 1, 1995, or is ordered by two judges or four justices of that court, the warden or another person selected by the director of rehabilitation and correction shall proceed at the time and place named in the warrant to ensure that the death sentence of the prisoner under death sentence is executed in accordance with section 2949.22 of the Revised Code. The warden shall make the return to the clerk of the court of common pleas of the county immediately from which the prisoner was sentenced of the manner of the execution of the warrant. The clerk shall record the warrant and the return in the records of the case.

(1995 S 4, eff. 9–21–95; 1992 S 359, eff. 12–22–92; 1953 H 1; GC 13456–4)

2949.25 Attendance at execution

(A) At the execution of a death sentence, only the following persons may be present:

(1) The warden of the state correctional institution in which the sentence is executed or a deputy warden, any other person selected by the director of rehabilitation and correction to ensure that the death sentence is executed, any persons necessary to

execute the death sentence by lethal injection, and the number of correction officers that the warden thinks necessary;

(2) The sheriff of the county in which the prisoner was tried and convicted;

(3) The director of rehabilitation and correction, or the director's agent;

(4) Physicians of the state correctional institution in which the sentence is executed;

(5) The clergyperson in attendance upon the prisoner, and not more than three other persons, to be designated by the prisoner, who are not confined in any state institution;

(6) Not more than three persons to be designated by the immediate family of the victim;

(7) Representatives of the news media as authorized by the director of rehabilitation and correction.

(B) The director shall authorize at least one representative of a newspaper, at least one representative of a television station, and at least one representative of a radio station to be present at the execution of the sentence under division (A)(7) of this section.

(2001 H 362, eff. 11–21–01; 1994 H 571, eff. 10–6–94; 1993 H 11, eff. 10–1–93; 1992 S 359; 1972 H 494; 125 v 823; 1953 H 1; GC 13456–5)

2949.26 Disposition of body of executed convict

The body of an executed convict shall be returned for burial in any county of the state, to friends who made written request therefor, if made to the warden the day before or on the morning of the execution. The warden may pay the transportation and other funeral expenses, not to exceed fifty dollars.

If no request is made by such friends therefor, such body shall be disposed of as provided by section 1713.34 of the Revised Code and the rules of the director of job and family services.

(1999 H 471, eff. 7–1–00; 1985 H 201, eff. 7–1–85; 1953 H 1; GC 13456–6)

2949.27 Escape, rearrest, and execution

If a convicted felon escapes after sentence of death, and is not retaken before the time fixed for his execution, any sheriff may rearrest and commit him to the county jail, and make return thereof to the court in which the sentence was passed. Such court shall again fix the time for execution, which shall be carried into effect as provided in sections 2949.21 to 2949.26, inclusive, of the Revised Code.

(1953 H 1, eff. 10–1–53; GC 13456–7)

2949.28 Inquiry on sanity of convict

(A) As used in this section and section 2949.29 of the Revised Code, "insane" means that the convict in question does not have the mental capacity to understand the nature of the death penalty and why it was imposed upon the convict.

(B)(1) If a convict sentenced to death appears to be insane, the warden or the sheriff having custody of the convict, the convict's counsel, or a psychiatrist or psychologist who has examined the convict shall give notice of the apparent insanity to whichever of the following is applicable:

(a) If the convict was tried by a jury, to the judge who imposed the sentence upon the convict or, if that judge is unavailable, to another judge of the same court of common pleas;

(b) If the convict was tried by a three-judge panel, to any of the three judges who imposed the sentence upon the convict or, if each of those judges is unavailable, to another judge of the same court of common pleas.

(2) Upon receiving a notice pursuant to division (B)(1) of this section, a judge shall determine, based on the notice and any supporting information, any information submitted by the prosecuting attorney, and the record in the case, including previous hearings and orders, whether probable cause exists to believe that the convict is insane. If the judge finds that probable cause exists to believe that the convict is insane, the judge shall hold a hearing to determine whether the convict is insane. If the judge does not find that probable cause of that nature exists, the judge may dismiss the matter without a hearing.

(3) If the judge who is given notice under division (B)(1) of this section finds probable cause to believe that the convict is insane, the judge shall inquire into the convict's insanity at a time and place to be fixed by the judge and shall give immediate notice of the inquiry to the prosecuting attorney who prosecuted the case, or that prosecuting attorney's successor, and to the convict and the convict's counsel. The judge may hold the inquiry at the place at which the convict is confined. If the convict does not have counsel, the court shall appoint an attorney to represent the convict in the inquiry. The court may appoint one or more psychiatrists or psychologists to examine the convict. The court shall not appoint a psychiatrist or psychologist who is an employee of the department of rehabilitation and correction to examine the convict. The court shall conduct any hearing under this section and section 2949.29 of the Revised Code and issue any ruling in the matter no later than sixty days from the date of the notice given under division (B)(1) of this section.

(4) Execution of the sentence shall be suspended pending completion of the inquiry only upon an order of the supreme court. If the supreme court issues an order granting a stay of execution, the supreme court in that order also may authorize the court of common pleas to continue the stay of execution or to set a new date for execution as provided in this section or section 2949.29 of the Revised Code.

(C) If the court appoints a psychiatrist or psychologist to examine the convict, the court shall inform the psychiatrist or psychologist of the location of the convict and of the purpose of the examination. The examiner shall have access to any available psychiatric or psychological report previously submitted to the court with respect to the mental condition of the convict, including, if applicable, a report regarding the convict's competency to stand trial or the convict's plea of not guilty by reason of insanity. The examiner also shall have access to any available current mental health and medical records of the convict.

The examiner shall conduct a thorough examination of the convict and shall submit a report to the court within thirty days of the examiner's appointment. The report shall contain the examiner's findings as to whether the convict has the mental capacity to understand the nature of the death penalty and why it was imposed upon the convict and the facts, in reasonable detail, upon which the findings are based.

(1998 S 107, eff. 7–29–98; 1969 S 354, eff. 11–18–69; 1953 H 1; GC 13456–8)

2949.29 Proceedings on the insanity inquiry

(A) The prosecuting attorney, the convict, and the convict's counsel shall attend an inquiry commenced as provided in section 2949.28 of the Revised Code. The prosecuting attorney and the convict or the convict's counsel may produce, examine, and cross-examine witnesses, and all findings shall be in writing signed by the judge. If it is found that the convict is not insane, the sentence shall be executed at the time previously appointed, unless that time has passed pending completion of the inquiry, in which case the judge conducting the inquiry, if authorized by the supreme court, shall appoint a time for execution of the sentence to be effective fifteen days from the date of the entry of the judge's findings in the inquiry.

(B) If it is found that the convict is insane and if authorized by the supreme court, the judge shall continue any stay of execution of the sentence previously issued, order the convict to be confined in the area at which other convicts sentenced to death are confined or in a maximum security medical or psychiatric facility operated by the department of rehabilitation and correction, and order treatment of the convict. Thereafter, the court at any time may conduct and, on motion of the prosecuting attorney, shall conduct a hearing pursuant to division (A) of this section to continue the inquiry into the convict's insanity and, as provided in section 2949.28 of the Revised Code, may appoint one or more psychiatrists or psychologists to make a further examination of the convict and to submit a report to the court. If the court finds at the hearing that the convict is not insane and if the time previously appointed for execution of the sentence has not passed, the sentence shall be executed at the previously appointed time. If the court finds at the hearing that the convict is not insane and if the time previously appointed for execution of the sentence has passed, the judge who conducts the hearing, if authorized by the supreme court, shall appoint a new time for execution of the sentence to be effective fifteen days from the date of the entry of the judge's findings in the hearing.

(C) In all proceedings under this section, the convict is presumed not to be insane, and the court shall find that the convict is not insane unless the court finds by a preponderance of the evidence that the convict is insane.

(D) Proceedings for inquiry into the insanity of any convict sentenced to death shall be exclusively pursuant to this section, section 2949.28 of the Revised Code, and the Rules of Evidence. Neither Chapter 5122. or 5123. of the Revised Code nor any other provision of the Revised Code nor any other rule concerning mentally ill persons, mentally retarded persons, or insane persons applies to any proceeding for inquiry into the insanity of any convict sentenced to death.

(1998 S 107, eff. 7–29–98; 1969 S 354, eff. 11–18–69; 1953 H 1; GC 13456–9)

2949.31 Pregnant prisoners

If a female convict sentenced to death appears to be pregnant, the warden or sheriff having custody of the convict, her counsel, or a physician who has examined the convict shall give notice of the apparent pregnancy to the appropriate judge of the appropriate court of common pleas as determined in the same manner as is provided in divisions (B)(1)(a) and (b) of section 2949.28 of the Revised Code, and like proceedings shall be had as are provided under sections 2949.28 and 2949.29 of the Revised Code in case of an insane convict sentenced to death, except to the extent that they by their nature clearly would be inapplicable.

If it is found at the inquiry held in accordance with sections 2949.28 and 2949.29 of the Revised Code that the convict is not pregnant, the sentence shall be executed at the time previously appointed, unless that time has passed pending completion of the inquiry, in which case the judge conducting the inquiry, if authorized by the supreme court, shall appoint a new time for execution of the sentence to be effective fifteen days from the date of the entry of the judge's ruling in the inquiry.

If it is found at the inquiry that the convict is pregnant, the judge shall suspend execution of the sentence and order the convict to be confined in the area at which other convicts sentenced to death are confined or in an appropriate medical facility. When the court finds that the convict no longer is pregnant, if the time previously appointed for execution of the sentence has not passed, the sentence shall be executed at the previously appointed time. When the court finds that the convict no longer is pregnant, if the time previously appointed for execution of the sentence has passed, the judge who conducts the inquiry, if authorized by the supreme court, shall appoint a new time for execution of the sentence to be effective fifteen days from the date of the entry of the judge's ruling in the inquiry.

(1998 S 107, eff. 7–29–98; 1953 H 1, eff. 10–1–53; GC 13456–11)

CHAPTER 2950

SEX OFFENDERS

Section

Section

2950.01 Definitions

Note: See also following version of this section, eff. 4–29–05.

As used in this chapter, unless the context clearly requires otherwise:

(A) "Confinement" includes, but is not limited to, a community residential sanction imposed pursuant to section 2929.16 or 2929.26 of the Revised Code.

(B) "Habitual sex offender" means, except when a juvenile judge removes this classification pursuant to division (A)(2) of section 2152.84 or division (C)(2) of section 2152.85 of the Revised Code, a person to whom both of the following apply:

(1) The person is convicted of or pleads guilty to a sexually oriented offense that is not a registration-exempt sexually oriented offense, or the person is adjudicated a delinquent child for committing on or after January 1, 2002, a sexually oriented offense that is not a registration-exempt sexually oriented offense, was fourteen years of age or older at the time of committing the offense, and is classified a juvenile offender registrant based on that adjudication.

(2) One of the following applies to the person:

(a) Regarding a person who is an offender, the person previously was convicted of or pleaded guilty to one or more sexually oriented offenses or child-victim oriented offenses or previously was adjudicated a delinquent child for committing one or more sexually oriented offenses or child-victim oriented offenses and was classified a juvenile offender registrant or out-of-state juvenile offender registrant based on one or more of those adjudications, regardless of when the offense was committed and regardless of the person's age at the time of committing the offense.

(b) Regarding a delinquent child, the person previously was convicted of, pleaded guilty to, or was adjudicated a delinquent child for committing one or more sexually oriented offenses or child-victim oriented offenses, regardless of when the offense was committed and regardless of the person's age at the time of committing the offense.

(C) "Prosecutor" has the same meaning as in section 2935.01 of the Revised Code.

(D) "Sexually oriented offense" means any of the following:

(1) Any of the following violations or offenses committed by a person eighteen years of age or older:

(a) Regardless of the age of the victim of the offense, a violation of section 2907.02, 2907.03, 2907.05, or 2907.07 of the Revised Code;

(b) Any of the following offenses involving a minor, in the circumstances specified:

(i) A violation of division (A)(4) of section 2905.01 or section 2907.04, 2907.06, or 2907.08 of the Revised Code, when the victim of the offense is under eighteen years of age;

(ii) A violation of section 2907.21 of the Revised Code when the person who is compelled, induced, procured, encouraged, solicited, requested, or facilitated to engage in, paid or agreed to be paid for, or allowed to engage in the sexual activity in question is under eighteen years of age;

(iii) A violation of division (A)(1) or (3) of section 2907.321 or 2907.322 of the Revised Code;

(iv) A violation of division (A)(1) or (2) of section 2907.323 of the Revised Code;

(v) A violation of division (B)(5) of section 2919.22 of the Revised Code when the child who is involved in the offense is under eighteen years of age;

(vi) A violation of division (A)(1), (2), (3), or (5) of section 2905.01, of section 2903.211, 2905.02, 2905.03, or 2905.05, or of former section 2905. 04 of the Revised Code, when the victim of the offense is under eighteen years of age and the offense is committed with a sexual motivation.

(c) Regardless of the age of the victim of the offense, a violation of section 2903.01, 2903.02, 2903.11, or 2905.01 of the Revised Code, or of division (A) of section 2903.04 of the Revised Code, that is committed with a sexual motivation;

(d) A sexually violent offense;

(e) A violation of section 2907.06 or 2907.08 of the Revised Code when the victim of the offense is eighteen years of age or older, or a violation of section 2903.211 of the Revised Code when the victim of the offense is eighteen years of age or older and the offense is committed with a sexual motivation;

(f) A violation of any former law of this state, any existing or former municipal ordinance or law of another state or the United States, any existing or former law applicable in a military court or in an Indian tribal court, or any existing or former law of any nation other than the United States, that is or was substantially equivalent to any offense listed in division (D)(1)(a), (b), (c), (d), or (e) of this section;

(g) An attempt to commit, conspiracy to commit, or complicity in committing any offense listed in division (D)(1)(a), (b), (c), (d), (e), or (f) of this section.

(2) An act committed by a person under eighteen years of age that is any of the following:

(a) Subject to division (D)(2)(i) of this section, regardless of the age of the victim of the violation, a violation of section 2907.02, 2907.03, 2907.05, or 2907.07 of the Revised Code;

(b) Subject to division (D)(2)(i) of this section, any of the following acts involving a minor in the circumstances specified:

(i) A violation of division (A)(4) of section 2905.01 or section 2907.06 or 2907.08 of the Revised Code, when the victim of the violation is under eighteen years of age;

(ii) A violation of section 2907.21 of the Revised Code when the person who is compelled, induced, procured, encouraged, solicited, requested, or facilitated to engage in, paid or agreed to be paid for, or allowed to engage in the sexual activity in question is under eighteen years of age;

(iii) A violation of division (B)(5) of section 2919.22 of the Revised Code when the child who is involved in the violation is under eighteen years of age;

(iv) A violation of division (A)(1), (2), (3), or (5) of section 2905.01, section 2903.211, or former section 2905.04 of the Revised Code, when the victim of the violation is under eighteen years of age and the offense is committed with a sexual motivation.

(c) Subject to division (D)(2)(i) of this section, any sexually violent offense that, if committed by an adult, would be a felony of the first, second, third, or fourth degree;

(d) Subject to division (D)(2)(i) of this section, a violation of section 2903.01, 2903.02, 2903.11, 2905.01, or 2905.02 of the Revised Code, a violation of division (A) of section 2903.04 of the Revised Code, or an attempt to violate any of those sections or that division that is committed with a sexual motivation;

(e) Subject to division (D)(2)(i) of this section, a violation of division (A)(1) or (3) of section 2907.321, division (A)(1) or (3) of section 2907.322, or division (A)(1) or (2) of section 2907.323 of the Revised Code, or an attempt to violate any of those divisions, if the person who violates or attempts to violate the division is four or more years older than the minor who is the victim of the violation;

(f) Subject to division (D)(2)(i) of this section, a violation of section 2907.06 or 2907.08 of the Revised Code when the victim of the violation is eighteen years of age or older, or a violation of section 2903.211 of the Revised Code when the victim of the violation is eighteen years of age or older and the offense is committed with a sexual motivation;

(g) Subject to division (D)(2)(i) of this section, any violation of any former law of this state, any existing or former municipal ordinance or law of another state or the United States, any existing or former law applicable in a military court or in an Indian tribal court, or any existing or former law of any nation other than the United States, that is or was substantially equivalent to any offense listed in division (D)(2)(a), (b), (c), (d), (e), or (f) of this section and that, if committed by an adult, would be a felony of the first, second, third, or fourth degree;

(h) Subject to division (D)(2)(i) of this section, any attempt to commit, conspiracy to commit, or complicity in committing any offense listed in division (D)(2)(a), (b), (c), (d), (e), (f), or (g) of this section;

(i) If the child's case has been transferred for criminal prosecution under section 2152.12 of the Revised Code, the act is any violation listed in division (D)(1)(a), (b), (c), (d), (e), (f), or (g) of this section or would be any offense listed in any of those divisions if committed by an adult.

(E) "Sexual predator" means a person to whom either of the following applies:

(1) The person has been convicted of or pleaded guilty to committing a sexually oriented offense that is not a registration-exempt sexually oriented offense and is likely to engage in the future in one or more sexually oriented offenses.

(2) The person has been adjudicated a delinquent child for committing a sexually oriented offense that is not a registration-exempt sexually oriented offense, was fourteen years of age or older at the time of committing the offense, was classified a juvenile offender registrant based on that adjudication, and is likely to engage in the future in one or more sexually oriented offenses.

(F) "Supervised release" means a release of an offender from a prison term, a term of imprisonment, or another type of confinement that satisfies either of the following conditions:

(1) The release is on parole, a conditional pardon, under a community control sanction, under transitional control, or under a post-release control sanction, and it requires the person to report to or be supervised by a parole officer, probation officer, field officer, or another type of supervising officer.

(2) The release is any type of release that is not described in division (F)(1) of this section and that requires the person to report to or be supervised by a probation officer, a parole officer, a field officer, or another type of supervising officer.

(G) An offender or delinquent child is "adjudicated as being a sexual predator" or "adjudicated a sexual predator" if any of the following applies and if, regarding a delinquent child, that status has not been removed pursuant to section 2152.84, 2152.85, or 2950.09 of the Revised Code:

(1) The offender is convicted of or pleads guilty to committing, on or after January 1, 1997, a sexually oriented offense that is a sexually violent offense and that is not a registration-exempt sexually oriented offense and also is convicted of or pleads guilty to a sexually violent predator specification that was included in the indictment, count in the indictment, or information that charged the sexually violent offense.

(2) Regardless of when the sexually oriented offense was committed, on or after January 1, 1997, the offender is sentenced for a sexually oriented offense that is not a registration-exempt sexually oriented offense, and the sentencing judge determines pursuant to division (B) of section 2950.09 of the Revised Code that the offender is a sexual predator.

(3) The delinquent child is adjudicated a delinquent child for committing a sexually oriented offense that is not a registration-exempt sexually oriented offense, was fourteen years of age or older at the time of committing the offense, and has been classified a juvenile offender registrant based on that adjudication, and the adjudicating judge or that judge's successor in office determines pursuant to division (B) of section 2950.09 or pursuant to section 2152.82, 2152.83, 2152.84, or 2152.85 of the Revised Code that the delinquent child is a sexual predator.

(4) Prior to January 1, 1997, the offender was convicted of or pleaded guilty to, and was sentenced for, a sexually oriented offense that is not a registration-exempt sexually oriented offense, the offender is imprisoned in a state correctional institution on or after January 1, 1997, and the court determines pursuant to division (C) of section 2950.09 of the Revised Code that the offender is a sexual predator.

(5) Regardless of when the sexually oriented offense was committed, the offender or delinquent child is convicted of or pleads guilty to, has been convicted of or pleaded guilty to, or is adjudicated a delinquent child for committing a sexually oriented offense that is not a registration-exempt sexually oriented offense in another state, in a federal court, military court, or Indian tribal court, or in a court in any nation other than the United States, as a result of that conviction, plea of guilty, or adjudication, the offender or delinquent child is required under the law of the jurisdiction in which the offender was convicted or pleaded guilty or the delinquent child was adjudicated to register as a sex offender until the offender's or delinquent child's death, and, on or after July 1, 1997, for offenders or January 1, 2002, for delinquent children, the offender or delinquent child moves to and resides in this state or temporarily is domiciled in this state for more than five days or the offender is required under section 2950.04 of the Revised Code to register a school, institution of higher education, or place of employment address in this state, unless a court of common pleas or juvenile court determines that the offender or delinquent child is not a sexual predator pursuant to division (F) of section 2950.09 of the Revised Code.

(H) "Sexually violent predator specification," "sexually violent offense," "sexual motivation," and "violent sex offense" have the same meanings as in section 2971.01 of the Revised Code.

(I) "Post release control sanction" and "transitional control" have the same meanings as in section 2967.01 of the Revised Code.

(J) "Juvenile offender registrant" means a person who is adjudicated a delinquent child for committing on or after January 1, 2002, a sexually oriented offense that is not a registration-exempt sexually oriented offense or a child-victim oriented offense, who is fourteen years of age or older at the time of committing the offense, and who a juvenile court judge, pursuant to an order issued under section 2152.82, 2152.83, 2152.84, or 2152.85 of the Revised Code, classifies a juvenile offender registrant and specifies has a duty to comply with sections 2950.04, 2950.05, and 2950.06 of the Revised Code if the child committed a sexually oriented offense or with sections 2950.041, 2950.05, and 2950.06 of the Revised Code if the child committed a child-victim oriented offense. "Juvenile offender registrant" includes a person who, prior to July 31, 2003, was a "juvenile sex offender registrant" under the former definition of that former term.

(K) "Secure facility" means any facility that is designed and operated to ensure that all of its entrances and exits are locked and under the exclusive control of its staff and to ensure that, because of that exclusive control, no person who is institutionalized or confined in the facility may leave the facility without permission or supervision.

(L) "Out-of-state juvenile offender registrant" means a person who is adjudicated a delinquent child in a court in another state, in a federal court, military court, or Indian tribal court, or in a court in any nation other than the United States for committing a sexually oriented offense that is not a registration-exempt sexually oriented offense or a child-victim oriented offense, who on or after January 1, 2002, moves to and resides in this state or temporarily is domiciled in this state for more than five days, and who has a duty under section 2950.04 of the Revised Code to register in this state and the duty to otherwise comply with that section and sections 2950.05 and 2950.06 of the Revised Code if the child committed a sexually oriented offense or has a duty under section 2950.041 of the Revised Code to register in this state and the duty to otherwise comply with that section and sections 2950.05 and 2950.06 of the Revised Code if the child committed a child-victim oriented offense. "Out-of-state juvenile offender registrant" includes a person who, prior to July 31, 2003, was an "out-of-state juvenile sex offender registrant" under the former definition of that former term.

(M) "Juvenile court judge" includes a magistrate to whom the juvenile court judge confers duties pursuant to division (A)(15) of section 2151.23 of the Revised Code.

(N) "Adjudicated a delinquent child for committing a sexually oriented offense" includes a child who receives a serious youthful offender dispositional sentence under section 2152.13 of the Revised Code for committing a sexually oriented offense.

(O) "Aggravated sexually oriented offense" means a violation of division (A)(1)(b) of section 2907.02 of the Revised Code committed on or after June 13, 2002, or a violation of division (A)(2) of that section committed on or after July 31, 2003.

(P)(1) "Presumptive registration-exempt sexually oriented offense" means any of the following sexually oriented offenses described in division (P)(1)(a), (b), (c), (d), or (e) of this section, when the offense is committed by a person who previously has not been convicted of, pleaded guilty to, or adjudicated a delinquent child for committing any sexually oriented offense described in division (P)(1)(a), (b), (c), (d), or (e) of this section, any other sexually oriented offense, or any child-victim oriented offense and when the victim or intended victim of the offense is eighteen years of age or older:

(a) Any sexually oriented offense listed in division (D)(1)(e) or (D)(2)(f) of this section committed by a person who is eighteen years of age or older or, subject to division (P)(1)(e) of this section, committed by a person who is under eighteen years of age;

(b) Any violation of any former law of this state, any existing or former municipal ordinance or law of another state or the United States, any existing or former law applicable in a military court or in an Indian tribal court, or any existing or former law of any nation other than the United States that is committed by a person who is eighteen years of age or older and that is or was substantially equivalent to any sexually oriented offense listed in division (P)(1)(a) of this section;

(c) Subject to division (P)(1)(e) of this section, any violation of any former law of this state, any existing or former municipal ordinance or law of another state or the United States, any existing or former law applicable in a military court or in an Indian tribal court, or any existing or former law of any nation other than the United States that is committed by a person who is under eighteen years of age, that is or was substantially equivalent to any sexually oriented offense listed in division (P)(1)(a) of this section, and that would be a felony of the fourth degree if committed by an adult;

(d) Any attempt to commit, conspiracy to commit, or complicity in committing any offense listed in division (P)(1)(a) or (b) of this section if the person is eighteen years of age or older or, subject to division (P)(1)(e) of this section, listed in division (P)(1)(a) or (c) of this section if the person is under eighteen years of age.

(e) Regarding an act committed by a person under eighteen years of age, if the child's case has been transferred for criminal prosecution under section 2152.12 of the Revised Code, the act is any sexually oriented offense listed in division (P)(1)(a), (b), or (d) of this section.

(2) "Presumptive registration-exempt sexually oriented offense" does not include any sexually oriented offense described in division (P)(1)(a), (b), (c), (d), or (e) of this section that is committed by a person who previously has been convicted of, pleaded guilty to, or adjudicated a delinquent child for committing any sexually oriented offense described in division (P)(1)(a), (b), (c), (d), or (e) of this section or any other sexually oriented offense.

(Q)(1) "Registration–exempt sexually oriented offense" means any presumptive registration-exempt sexually oriented offense, if a court does not issue an order under section 2950.021 of the Revised Code that removes the presumptive exemption and subjects the offender who was convicted of or pleaded guilty to the offense to registration under section 2950.04 of the Revised Code and all other duties and responsibilities generally imposed under this chapter upon persons who are convicted of or plead guilty to any sexually oriented offense other than a presumptive registration-exempt sexually oriented offense or that removes the presumptive exemption and potentially subjects the child who was adjudicated a delinquent child for committing the offense to classification as a juvenile offender registrant under section 2152.82, 2152.83, 2152.84, or 2152.85 of the Revised Code and to registration under section 2950.04 of the Revised Code and all other duties and responsibilities generally imposed under this chapter upon persons who are adjudicated delinquent children for committing a sexually oriented offense other than a presumptive registration-exempt sexually oriented offense.

(2) "Registration–exempt sexually oriented offense" does not include a presumptive registration-exempt sexually oriented offense if a court issues an order under section 2950.021 of the Revised Code that removes the presumptive exemption and subjects the offender or potentially subjects the delinquent child to the duties and responsibilities described in division (Q)(1) of this section.

(R) "School" and "school premises" have the same meanings as in section 2925.01 of the Revised Code.

(S)(1) "Child–victim oriented offense" means any of the following:

(a) Subject to division (S)(2) of this section, any of the following violations or offenses committed by a person eighteen years of age or older, when the victim of the violation is under eighteen years of age and is not a child of the person who commits the violation:

(i) A violation of division (A)(1), (2), (3), or (5) of section 2905.01, of section 2905.02, 2905.03, or 2905.05, or of former section 2905.04 of the Revised Code;

(ii) A violation of any former law of this state, any existing or former municipal ordinance or law of another state or the United States, any existing or former law applicable in a military court or in an Indian tribal court, or any existing or former law of any nation other than the United States, that is or was substantially equivalent to any offense listed in division (S)(1)(a)(i) of this section;

(iii) An attempt to commit, conspiracy to commit, or complicity in committing any offense listed in division (S)(1)(a)(i) or (ii) of this section.

(b) Subject to division (S)(2) of this section, an act committed by a person under eighteen years of age that is any of the following, when the victim of the violation is under eighteen years of age and is not a child of the person who commits the violation:

(i) Subject to division (S)(1)(b)(iv) of this section, a violation of division (A)(1), (2), (3), or (5) of section 2905.01 or of former section 2905.04 of the Revised Code;

(ii) Subject to division (S)(1)(b)(iv) of this section, any violation of any former law of this state, any existing or former municipal ordinance or law of another state or the United States, any existing or former law applicable in a military court or in an Indian tribal court, or any existing or former law of any nation other than the United States, that is or was substantially equivalent to any offense listed in division (S)(1)(b)(i) of this section and that, if committed by an adult, would be a felony of the first, second, third, or fourth degree;

(iii) Subject to division (S)(1)(b)(iv) of this section, any attempt to commit, conspiracy to commit, or complicity in committing any offense listed in division (S)(1)(b)(i) or (ii) of this section;

(iv) If the child's case has been transferred for criminal prosecution under section 2152.12 of the Revised Code, the act is any violation listed in division (S)(1)(a)(i), (ii), or (iii) of this section or would be any offense listed in any of those divisions if committed by an adult.

(2) "Child–victim oriented offense" does not include any offense identified in division (S)(1)(a) or (b) of this section that is a sexually violent offense. An offense identified in division (S)(1)(a) or (b) of this section that is a sexually violent offense is within the definition of a sexually oriented offense.

(T)(1) "Habitual child-victim offender" means, except when a juvenile judge removes this classification pursuant to division (A)(2) of section 2152.84 or division (C)(2) of section 2152.85 of the Revised Code, a person to whom both of the following apply:

(a) The person is convicted of or pleads guilty to a child-victim oriented offense, or the person is adjudicated a delinquent child for committing on or after January 1, 2002, a child-victim oriented offense, was fourteen years of age or older at the time of committing the offense, and is classified a juvenile offender registrant based on that adjudication.

(b) One of the following applies to the person:

(i) Regarding a person who is an offender, the person previously was convicted of or pleaded guilty to one or more child-victim oriented offenses or previously was adjudicated a delinquent child for committing one or more child-victim oriented offenses and was classified a juvenile offender registrant or out-of-state juvenile offender registrant based on one or more of those adjudications, regardless of when the offense was committed and regardless of the person's age at the time of committing the offense.

(ii) Regarding a delinquent child, the person previously was convicted of, pleaded guilty to, or was adjudicated a delinquent child for committing one or more child-victim oriented offenses, regardless of when the offense was committed and regardless of the person's age at the time of committing the offense.

(2) "Habitual child-victim offender" includes a person who has been convicted of, pleaded guilty to, or adjudicated a delinquent child for committing, a child-victim oriented offense and who, on and after the effective date of this amendment, is automatically classified a habitual child-victim offender pursuant to division (E) of section 2950.091 of the Revised Code.

(U) "Child–victim predator" means a person to whom either of the following applies:

(1) The person has been convicted of or pleaded guilty to committing a child-victim oriented offense and is likely to engage in the future in one or more child-victim oriented offenses.

(2) The person has been adjudicated a delinquent child for committing a child-victim oriented offense, was fourteen years of age or older at the time of committing the offense, was classified a juvenile offender registrant based on that adjudication, and is likely to engage in the future in one or more child-victim oriented offenses.

(V) An offender or delinquent child is "adjudicated as being a child-victim predator" or "adjudicated a child-victim predator" if any of the following applies and if, regarding a delinquent child, that status has not been removed pursuant to section 2152.84, 2152.85, or 2950.09 of the Revised Code:

(1) The offender or delinquent child has been convicted of, pleaded guilty to, or adjudicated a delinquent child for committing, a child-victim oriented offense and, on and after July 31, 2003, is automatically classified a child-victim predator pursuant to division (A) of section 2950.091 of the Revised Code.

(2) Regardless of when the child-victim oriented offense was committed, on or after July 31, 2003, the offender is sentenced for a child-victim oriented offense, and the sentencing judge determines pursuant to division (B) of section 2950.091 of the Revised Code that the offender is a child-victim predator.

(3) The delinquent child is adjudicated a delinquent child for committing a child-victim oriented offense, was fourteen years of age or older at the time of committing the offense, and has been classified a juvenile offender registrant based on that adjudication, and the adjudicating judge or that judge's successor in office determines pursuant to division (B) of section 2950.09 or pursuant to section 2152.82, 2152.83, 2152.84, or 2152.85 of the Revised Code that the delinquent child is a child-victim predator.

(4) Prior to the effective date of this section, the offender was convicted of or pleaded guilty to a child-victim oriented offense, at the time of the conviction or guilty plea, the offense was considered a sexually oriented offense, on or after July 31, 2003, the offender is serving a term of imprisonment in a state correctional institution, and the court determines pursuant to division (C) of section 2950.091 of the Revised Code that the offender is a child-victim predator.

(5) Regardless of when the child-victim oriented offense was committed, the offender or delinquent child is convicted, pleads guilty, has been convicted, pleaded guilty, or adjudicated a delinquent child in a court in another state, in a federal court, military court, or Indian tribal court, or in a court in any nation other than the United States for committing a child-victim oriented offense, as a result of that conviction, plea of guilty, or adjudication, the offender or delinquent child is required under the law of the jurisdiction in which the offender was convicted or pleaded guilty or the delinquent child was adjudicated, to register as a child-victim offender or sex offender until the offender's or delinquent child's death, and, on or after July 1, 1997, for offenders or January 1, 2002, for delinquent children the offender or delinquent child moves to and resides in this state or temporarily is domiciled in this state for more than five days or the offender is required under section 2950.041 of the Revised Code to register a school, institution of higher education, or place of employment address in this state, unless a court of common pleas or juvenile court determines that the offender or delinquent child is not a child-victim predator pursuant to division (F) of section 2950.091 of the Revised Code.

(W) "Residential premises" means the building in which a residential unit is located and the grounds upon which that building stands, extending to the perimeter of the property. "Residential premises" includes any type of structure in which a residential unit is located, including, but not limited to, multi-unit buildings and mobile and manufactured homes.

(X) "Residential unit" means a dwelling unit for residential use and occupancy, and includes the structure or part of a structure that is used as a home, residence, or sleeping place by one person who maintains a household or two or more persons who maintain a common household. "Residential unit" does not include a halfway house or a community-based correctional facility.

(Y) "Multi–unit building" means a building in which is located more than twelve residential units that have entry doors that open directly into the unit from a hallway that is shared with one or more other units. A residential unit is not considered located in a multi-unit building if the unit does not have an entry door that opens directly into the unit from a hallway that is shared with one or more other units or if the unit is in a building that is not a multi-unit building as described in this division.

(Z) "Community control sanction" has the same meaning as in section 2929.01 of the Revised Code.

(AA) "Halfway house" and "community-based correctional facility" have the same meanings as in section 2929.01 of the Revised Code.

(2003 S 57, eff. 1-1-04; 2003 S 5, § 3, eff. 1-1-04; 2003 S 5, § 1, eff. 7-31-03; 2002 H 490, eff. 1-1-04; 2002 H 485, eff. 6-13-02; 2002 S 175, eff. 5-7-02; 2002 H 393, eff. 7-5-02; 2001 S 3, eff. 1-1-02; 2000 H 502, eff. 3-15-01; 1998 H 565, eff. 3-30-99; 1997 S 111, eff. 3-17-98; 1996 H 180, eff. 1-1-97)

Note: See also following version of this section, eff. 4-29-05.

2950.01 Definitions (later effective date)

Note: See also preceding version of this section, in effect until 4-29-05.

As used in this chapter, unless the context clearly requires otherwise:

(A) "Confinement" includes, but is not limited to, a community residential sanction imposed pursuant to section 2929.16 or 2929.26 of the Revised Code.

(B) "Habitual sex offender" means, except when a juvenile judge removes this classification pursuant to division (A)(2) of section 2152.84 or division (C)(2) of section 2152.85 of the Revised Code, a person to whom both of the following apply:

(1) The person is convicted of or pleads guilty to a sexually oriented offense that is not a registration-exempt sexually oriented offense, or the person is adjudicated a delinquent child for committing on or after January 1, 2002, a sexually oriented offense that is not a registration-exempt sexually oriented offense, was fourteen years of age or older at the time of committing the offense, and is classified a juvenile offender registrant based on that adjudication.

(2) One of the following applies to the person:

(a) Regarding a person who is an offender, the person previously was convicted of or pleaded guilty to one or more sexually oriented offenses or child-victim oriented offenses or previously was adjudicated a delinquent child for committing one or more sexually oriented offenses or child-victim oriented offenses and was classified a juvenile offender registrant or out-of-state juvenile offender registrant based on one or more of those adjudications, regardless of when the offense was committed and regardless of the person's age at the time of committing the offense.

(b) Regarding a delinquent child, the person previously was convicted of, pleaded guilty to, or was adjudicated a delinquent child for committing one or more sexually oriented offenses or child-victim oriented offenses, regardless of when the offense was committed and regardless of the person's age at the time of committing the offense.

(C) "Prosecutor" has the same meaning as in section 2935.01 of the Revised Code.

(D) "Sexually oriented offense" means any of the following:

(1) Any of the following violations or offenses committed by a person eighteen years of age or older:

(a) Regardless of the age of the victim of the offense, a violation of section 2907.02, 2907.03, 2907.05, or 2907.07 of the Revised Code;

(b) Any of the following offenses involving a minor, in the circumstances specified:

(i) A violation of division (A)(4) of section 2905.01 or section 2907.04, 2907.06, or 2907.08 of the Revised Code, when the victim of the offense is under eighteen years of age;

(ii) A violation of section 2907.21 of the Revised Code when the person who is compelled, induced, procured, encouraged, solicited, requested, or facilitated to engage in, paid or agreed to be paid for, or allowed to engage in the sexual activity in question is under eighteen years of age;

(iii) A violation of division (A)(1) or (3) of section 2907.321 or 2907.322 of the Revised Code;

(iv) A violation of division (A)(1) or (2) of section 2907.323 of the Revised Code;

(v) A violation of division (B)(5) of section 2919.22 of the Revised Code when the child who is involved in the offense is under eighteen years of age;

(vi) A violation of division (A)(1), (2), (3), or (5) of section 2905.01, of section 2903.211, 2905.02, 2905.03, or 2905.05, or of former section 2905.04 of the Revised Code, when the victim of the offense is under eighteen years of age and the offense is committed with a sexual motivation.

(c) Regardless of the age of the victim of the offense, a violation of section 2903.01, 2903.02, 2903.11, or 2905.01 of the Revised Code, or of division (A) of section 2903.04 of the Revised Code, that is committed with a sexual motivation;

(d) A violent sex offense, or a designated homicide, assault, or kidnapping offense if the offender also was convicted of or pleaded guilty to a sexual motivation specification that was included in the indictment, count in the indictment, or information charging the designated homicide, assault, or kidnapping offense;

(e) A violation of section 2907.06 or 2907.08 of the Revised Code when the victim of the offense is eighteen years of age or older, or a violation of section 2903.211 of the Revised Code when the victim of the offense is eighteen years of age or older and the offense is committed with a sexual motivation;

(f) A violation of any former law of this state, any existing or former municipal ordinance or law of another state or the United States, any existing or former law applicable in a military court or in an Indian tribal court, or any existing or former law of any nation other than the United States, that is or was substantially equivalent to any offense listed in division (D)(1)(a), (b), (c), (d), or (e) of this section;

(g) An attempt to commit, conspiracy to commit, or complicity in committing any offense listed in division (D)(1)(a), (b), (c), (d), (e), or (f) of this section.

(2) An act committed by a person under eighteen years of age that is any of the following:

(a) Subject to division (D)(2)(i) of this section, regardless of the age of the victim of the violation, a violation of section 2907.02, 2907.03, 2907.05, or 2907.07 of the Revised Code;

(b) Subject to division (D)(2)(i) of this section, any of the following acts involving a minor in the circumstances specified:

(i) A violation of division (A)(4) of section 2905.01 or section 2907.06 or 2907.08 of the Revised Code, when the victim of the violation is under eighteen years of age;

(ii) A violation of section 2907.21 of the Revised Code when the person who is compelled, induced, procured, encouraged, solicited, requested, or facilitated to engage in, paid or agreed to be paid for, or allowed to engage in the sexual activity in question is under eighteen years of age;

(iii) A violation of division (B)(5) of section 2919.22 of the Revised Code when the child who is involved in the violation is under eighteen years of age;

(iv) A violation of division (A)(1), (2), (3), or (5) of section 2905.01, section 2903.211, or former section 2905.04 of the Revised Code, when the victim of the violation is under eighteen years of age and the offense is committed with a sexual motivation.

(c) Subject to division (D)(2)(i) of this section, any of the following:

(i) Any violent sex offense that, if committed by an adult, would be a felony of the first, second, third, or fourth degree;

(ii) Any designated homicide, assault, or kidnapping offense if that offense, if committed by an adult, would be a felony of the first, second, third, or fourth degree and if the court determined that, if the child was an adult, the child would be guilty of a sexual motivation specification regarding that offense.

(d) Subject to division (D)(2)(i) of this section, a violation of section 2903.01, 2903.02, 2903.11, 2905.01, or 2905.02 of the Revised Code, a violation of division (A) of section 2903.04 of the Revised Code, or an attempt to violate any of those sections or that division that is committed with a sexual motivation;

(e) Subject to division (D)(2)(i) of this section, a violation of division (A)(1) or (3) of section 2907.321, division (A)(1) or (3) of section 2907.322, or division (A)(1) or (2) of section 2907.323 of the Revised Code, or an attempt to violate any of those divisions, if the person who violates or attempts to violate the division is four or more years older than the minor who is the victim of the violation;

(f) Subject to division (D)(2)(i) of this section, a violation of section 2907.06 or 2907.08 of the Revised Code when the victim of the violation is eighteen years of age or older, or a violation of section 2903.211 of the Revised Code when the victim of the violation is eighteen years of age or older and the offense is committed with a sexual motivation;

(g) Subject to division (D)(2)(i) of this section, any violation of any former law of this state, any existing or former municipal ordinance or law of another state or the United States, any existing or former law applicable in a military court or in an Indian tribal court, or any existing or former law of any nation other than the United States, that is or was substantially equivalent to any offense listed in division (D)(2)(a), (b), (c), (d), (e), or (f) of this section and that, if committed by an adult, would be a felony of the first, second, third, or fourth degree;

(h) Subject to division (D)(2)(i) of this section, any attempt to commit, conspiracy to commit, or complicity in committing any offense listed in division (D)(2)(a), (b), (c), (d), (e), (f), or (g) of this section;

(i) If the child's case has been transferred for criminal prosecution under section 2152.12 of the Revised Code, the act is any violation listed in division (D)(1)(a), (b), (c), (d), (e), (f), or (g) of this section or would be any offense listed in any of those divisions if committed by an adult.

(E) "Sexual predator" means a person to whom either of the following applies:

(1) The person has been convicted of or pleaded guilty to committing a sexually oriented offense that is not a registration-exempt sexually oriented offense and is likely to engage in the future in one or more sexually oriented offenses.

(2) The person has been adjudicated a delinquent child for committing a sexually oriented offense that is not a registration-exempt sexually oriented offense, was fourteen years of age or older at the time of committing the offense, was classified a juvenile offender registrant based on that adjudication, and is likely to engage in the future in one or more sexually oriented offenses.

(F) "Supervised release" means a release of an offender from a prison term, a term of imprisonment, or another type of confinement that satisfies either of the following conditions:

(1) The release is on parole, a conditional pardon, under a community control sanction, under transitional control, or under a post-release control sanction, and it requires the person to report to or be supervised by a parole officer, probation officer, field officer, or another type of supervising officer.

(2) The release is any type of release that is not described in division (F)(1) of this section and that requires the person to report to or be supervised by a probation officer, a parole officer, a field officer, or another type of supervising officer.

(G) An offender or delinquent child is "adjudicated as being a sexual predator" or "adjudicated a sexual predator" if any of the following applies and if, regarding a delinquent child, that status has not been removed pursuant to section 2152.84, 2152.85, or 2950.09 of the Revised Code:

(1) The offender is convicted of or pleads guilty to committing, on or after January 1, 1997, a sexually oriented offense that is not a registration-exempt sexually oriented offense, the sexually oriented offense is a violent sex offense or a designated homicide, assault, or kidnapping offense, and the offender is adjudicated a sexually violent predator in relation to that offense.

(2) Regardless of when the sexually oriented offense was committed, on or after January 1, 1997, the offender is sentenced for a sexually oriented offense that is not a registration-exempt sexually oriented offense, and the sentencing judge determines pursuant to division (B) of section 2950.09 of the Revised Code that the offender is a sexual predator.

(3) The delinquent child is adjudicated a delinquent child for committing a sexually oriented offense that is not a registration-exempt sexually oriented offense, was fourteen years of age or older at the time of committing the offense, and has been classified a juvenile offender registrant based on that adjudication, and the adjudicating judge or that judge's successor in office determines pursuant to division (B) of section 2950.09 or pursuant to section 2152.82, 2152.83, 2152.84, or 2152.85 of the Revised Code that the delinquent child is a sexual predator.

(4) Prior to January 1, 1997, the offender was convicted of or pleaded guilty to, and was sentenced for, a sexually oriented offense that is not a registration-exempt sexually oriented offense, the offender is imprisoned in a state correctional institution on or after January 1, 1997, and the court determines pursuant to division (C) of section 2950.09 of the Revised Code that the offender is a sexual predator.

(5) Regardless of when the sexually oriented offense was committed, the offender or delinquent child is convicted of or pleads guilty to, has been convicted of or pleaded guilty to, or is adjudicated a delinquent child for committing a sexually oriented offense that is not a registration-exempt sexually oriented offense in another state, in a federal court, military court, or Indian tribal court, or in a court in any nation other than the United States, as a result of that conviction, plea of guilty, or adjudication, the offender or delinquent child is required under the law of the jurisdiction in which the offender was convicted or pleaded guilty or the delinquent child was adjudicated to register as a sex offender until the offender's or delinquent child's death, and, on or after July 1, 1997, for offenders or January 1, 2002, for delinquent children, the offender or delinquent child moves to and resides in this state or temporarily is domiciled in this state for more than five days or the offender is required under section 2950.04 of the Revised Code to register a school, institution of higher education, or place of employment address in this state, unless a court of common pleas or juvenile court determines that the offender or delinquent child is not a sexual predator pursuant to division (F) of section 2950.09 of the Revised Code.

(H) "Sexually violent predator specification," "sexually violent offense," "sexual motivation specification," designated homicide, assault, or kidnapping offense," and "violent sex offense" have the same meanings as in section 2971.01 of the Revised Code.

(I) "Post-release control sanction" and "transitional control" have the same meanings as in section 2967.01 of the Revised Code.

(J) "Juvenile offender registrant" means a person who is adjudicated a delinquent child for committing on or after January 1, 2002, a sexually oriented offense that is not a registration-exempt sexually oriented offense or a child-victim oriented offense, who is fourteen years of age or older at the time of committing the offense, and who a juvenile court judge, pursuant to an order issued under section 2152.82, 2152.83, 2152.84, or 2152.85 of the Revised Code, classifies a juvenile offender registrant and specifies has a duty to comply with sections 2950.04, 2950.05, and 2950.06 of the Revised Code if the child committed a sexually oriented offense or with sections 2950.041, 2950.05, and 2950.06 of the Revised Code if the child committed a child-victim oriented offense. "Juvenile offender registrant" includes a person who, prior to July 31, 2003, was a "juvenile sex offender registrant" under the former definition of that former term.

(K) "Secure facility" means any facility that is designed and operated to ensure that all of its entrances and exits are locked and under the exclusive control of its staff and to ensure that, because of that exclusive control, no person who is institutionalized or confined in the facility may leave the facility without permission or supervision.

(L) "Out–of–state juvenile offender registrant" means a person who is adjudicated a delinquent child in a court in another state, in a federal court, military court, or Indian tribal court, or in a court in any nation other than the United States for committing a sexually oriented offense that is not a registration-exempt sexually oriented offense or a child-victim oriented offense, who on or after January 1, 2002, moves to and resides in this state or temporarily is domiciled in this state for more than five days, and who has a duty under section 2950.04 of the Revised Code to register in this state and the duty to otherwise comply with that section and sections 2950.05 and 2950.06 of the Revised Code if the child committed a sexually oriented offense or has a duty under section 2950.041 of the Revised Code to register in this state and the duty to otherwise comply with that section and sections 2950.05 and 2950.06 of the Revised Code if the child committed a child-victim oriented offense. "Out-of-state juvenile offender registrant" includes a person who, prior to July 31, 2003, was an "out-of-state juvenile sex offender registrant" under the former definition of that former term.

(M) "Juvenile court judge" includes a magistrate to whom the juvenile court judge confers duties pursuant to division (A)(15) of section 2151.23 of the Revised Code.

(N) "Adjudicated a delinquent child for committing a sexually oriented offense" includes a child who receives a serious youthful offender dispositional sentence under section 2152.13 of the Revised Code for committing a sexually oriented offense.

(O) "Aggravated sexually oriented offense" means a violation of division (A)(1)(b) of section 2907.02 of the Revised Code committed on or after June 13, 2002, or a violation of division (A)(2) of that section committed on or after July 31, 2003.

(P)(1) "Presumptive registration-exempt sexually oriented offense" means any of the following sexually oriented offenses described in division (P)(1)(a), (b), (c), (d), or (e) of this section, when the offense is committed by a person who previously has not been convicted of, pleaded guilty to, or adjudicated a delinquent child for committing any sexually oriented offense described in division (P)(1)(a), (b), (c), (d), or (e) of this section, any other sexually oriented offense, or any child-victim oriented offense and when the victim or intended victim of the offense is eighteen years of age or older:

(a) Any sexually oriented offense listed in division (D)(1)(e) or (D)(2)(f) of this section committed by a person who is eighteen years of age or older or, subject to division (P)(1)(e) of this section, committed by a person who is under eighteen years of age;

(b) Any violation of any former law of this state, any existing or former municipal ordinance or law of another state or the United States, any existing or former law applicable in a military court or in an Indian tribal court, or any existing or former law of any nation other than the United States that is committed by a person who is eighteen years of age or older and that is or was substantially equivalent to any sexually oriented offense listed in division (P)(1)(a) of this section;

(c) Subject to division (P)(1)(e) of this section, any violation of any former law of this state, any existing or former municipal ordinance or law of another state or the United States, any existing or former law applicable in a military court or in an Indian tribal court, or any existing or former law of any nation other than the United States that is committed by a person who is under eighteen years of age, that is or was substantially equivalent to any sexually oriented offense listed in division (P)(1)(a) of this section, and that would be a felony of the fourth degree if committed by an adult;

(d) Any attempt to commit, conspiracy to commit, or complicity in committing any offense listed in division (P)(1)(a) or (b) of this section if the person is eighteen years of age or older or, subject to division (P)(1)(e) of this section, listed in division (P)(1)(a) or (c) of this section if the person is under eighteen years of age.

(e) Regarding an act committed by a person under eighteen years of age, if the child's case has been transferred for criminal prosecution under section 2152.12 of the Revised Code, the act is any sexually oriented offense listed in division (P)(1)(a), (b), or (d) of this section.

(2) "Presumptive registration-exempt sexually oriented offense" does not include any sexually oriented offense described in division (P)(1)(a), (b), (c), (d), or (e) of this section that is committed by a person who previously has been convicted of, pleaded guilty to, or adjudicated a delinquent child for committing any sexually oriented offense described in division (P)(1)(a), (b), (c), (d), or (e) of this section or any other sexually oriented offense.

(Q)(1) "Registration–exempt sexually oriented offense" means any presumptive registration-exempt sexually oriented offense, if a court does not issue an order under section 2950.021 of the Revised Code that removes the presumptive exemption and subjects the offender who was convicted of or pleaded guilty to the offense to registration under section 2950.04 of the Revised Code and all other duties and responsibilities generally imposed under this chapter upon persons who are convicted of or plead guilty to any sexually oriented offense other than a presumptive registration-exempt sexually oriented offense or that removes the presumptive exemption and potentially subjects the child who was adjudicated a delinquent child for committing the offense to classification as a juvenile offender registrant under section 2152.82, 2152.83, 2152.84, or 2152.85 of the Revised Code and to registration under section 2950.04 of the Revised Code and all other duties and responsibilities generally imposed under this chapter upon persons who are adjudicated delinquent children for committing a sexually oriented offense other than a presumptive registration-exempt sexually oriented offense.

(2) "Registration–exempt sexually oriented offense" does not include a presumptive registration-exempt sexually oriented offense if a court issues an order under section 2950.021 of the Revised Code that removes the presumptive exemption and subjects the offender or potentially subjects the delinquent child to the duties and responsibilities described in division (Q)(1) of this section.

(R) "School" and "school premises" have the same meanings as in section 2925.01 of the Revised Code.

(S)(1) "Child–victim oriented offense" means any of the following:

(a) Subject to division (S)(2) of this section, any of the following violations or offenses committed by a person eighteen years of age or older, when the victim of the violation is under eighteen years of age and is not a child of the person who commits the violation:

(i) A violation of division (A)(1), (2), (3), or (5) of section 2905.01, of section 2905.02, 2905.03, or 2905.05, or of former section 2905.04 of the Revised Code;

(ii) A violation of any former law of this state, any existing or former municipal ordinance or law of another state or the United States, any existing or former law applicable in a military court or in an Indian tribal court, or any existing or former law of any nation other than the United States, that is or was substantially equivalent to any offense listed in division (S)(1)(a)(i) of this section;

(iii) An attempt to commit, conspiracy to commit, or complicity in committing any offense listed in division (S)(1)(a)(i) or (ii) of this section.

(b) Subject to division (S)(2) of this section, an act committed by a person under eighteen years of age that is any of the following, when the victim of the violation is under eighteen years of age and is not a child of the person who commits the violation:

(i) Subject to division (S)(1)(b)(iv) of this section, a violation of division (A)(1), (2), (3), or (5) of section 2905.01 or of former section 2905.04 of the Revised Code;

(ii) Subject to division (S)(1)(b)(iv) of this section, any violation of any former law of this state, any existing or former municipal ordinance or law of another state or the United States, any existing or former law applicable in a military court or in an Indian tribal court, or any existing or former law of any nation other than the United States, that is or was substantially equivalent to any offense listed in division (S)(1)(b)(i) of this section and that, if committed by an adult, would be a felony of the first, second, third, or fourth degree;

(iii) Subject to division (S)(1)(b)(iv) of this section, any attempt to commit, conspiracy to commit, or complicity in committing any offense listed in division (S)(1)(b)(i) or (ii) of this section;

(iv) If the child's case has been transferred for criminal prosecution under section 2152.12 of the Revised Code, the act is any violation listed in division (S)(1)(a)(i), (ii), or (iii) of this section or would be any offense listed in any of those divisions if committed by an adult.

(2) "Child–victim oriented offense" does not include any offense identified in division (S)(1)(a) or (b) of this section that is a sexually violent offense. An offense identified in division (S)(1)(a) or (b) of this section that is a sexually violent offense is within the definition of a sexually oriented offense.

(T)(1) "Habitual child-victim offender" means, except when a juvenile judge removes this classification pursuant to division (A)(2) of section 2152.84 or division (C)(2) of section 2152.85 of the Revised Code, a person to whom both of the following apply:

(a) The person is convicted of or pleads guilty to a child-victim oriented offense, or the person is adjudicated a delinquent child for committing on or after January 1, 2002, a child-victim oriented offense, was fourteen years of age or older at the time of committing the offense, and is classified a juvenile offender registrant based on that adjudication.

(b) One of the following applies to the person:

(i) Regarding a person who is an offender, the person previously was convicted of or pleaded guilty to one or more child-victim oriented offenses or previously was adjudicated a delinquent child for committing one or more child-victim oriented offenses and was classified a juvenile offender registrant or out-of-state juvenile offender registrant based on one or more of those adjudications, regardless of when the offense was committed and regardless of the person's age at the time of committing the offense.

(ii) Regarding a delinquent child, the person previously was convicted of, pleaded guilty to, or was adjudicated a delinquent child for committing one or more child-victim oriented offenses, regardless of when the offense was committed and regardless of the person's age at the time of committing the offense.

(2) "Habitual child-victim offender" includes a person who has been convicted of, pleaded guilty to, or adjudicated a delinquent child for committing, a child-victim oriented offense and who, on and after July 31, 2003, is automatically classified a habitual child-victim offender pursuant to division (E) of section 2950.091 of the Revised Code.

(U) "Child–victim predator" means a person to whom either of the following applies:

(1) The person has been convicted of or pleaded guilty to committing a child-victim oriented offense and is likely to engage in the future in one or more child-victim oriented offenses.

(2) The person has been adjudicated a delinquent child for committing a child-victim oriented offense, was fourteen years of age or older at the time of committing the offense, was classified a juvenile offender registrant based on that adjudication, and is likely to engage in the future in one or more child-victim oriented offenses.

(V) An offender or delinquent child is "adjudicated as being a child-victim predator" or "adjudicated a child-victim predator" if any of the following applies and if, regarding a delinquent child, that status has not been removed pursuant to section 2152.84, 2152.85, or 2950.09 of the Revised Code:

(1) The offender or delinquent child has been convicted of, pleaded guilty to, or adjudicated a delinquent child for committing, a child-victim oriented offense and, on and after July 31, 2003, is automatically classified a child-victim predator pursuant to division (A) of section 2950.091 of the Revised Code.

(2) Regardless of when the child-victim oriented offense was committed, on or after July 31, 2003, the offender is sentenced for a child victim oriented offense, and the sentencing judge determines pursuant to division (B) of section 2950.091 of the Revised Code that the offender is a child-victim predator.

(3) The delinquent child is adjudicated a delinquent child for committing a child-victim oriented offense, was fourteen years of age or older at the time of committing the offense, and has been classified a juvenile offender registrant based on that adjudication, and the adjudicating judge or that judge's successor in office determines pursuant to division (B) of section 2950.09 or pursuant to section 2152.82, 2152.83, 2152.84, or 2152.85 of the Revised Code that the delinquent child is a child-victim predator.

(4) Prior to July 31, 2003, the offender was convicted of or pleaded guilty to a child-victim oriented offense, at the time of the conviction or guilty plea, the offense was considered a sexually oriented offense, on or after July 31, 2003, the offender is serving a term of imprisonment in a state correctional institution, and the court determines pursuant to division (C) of section 2950.091 of the Revised Code that the offender is a child-victim predator.

(5) Regardless of when the child-victim oriented offense was committed, the offender or delinquent child is convicted, pleads guilty, has been convicted, pleaded guilty, or adjudicated a delinquent child in a court in another state, in a federal court, military court, or Indian tribal court, or in a court in any nation other than the United States for committing a child-victim oriented offense, as a result of that conviction, plea of guilty, or adjudication, the offender or delinquent child is required under the law of the jurisdiction in which the offender was convicted or pleaded guilty or the delinquent child was adjudicated, to register as a child-victim offender or sex offender until the offender's or delinquent child's death, and, on or after July 1, 1997, for offenders or January 1, 2002, for delinquent children the offender or delinquent child moves to and resides in this state or temporarily is domiciled in this state for more than five days or the offender is required under section 2950.041 of the Revised Code to register a school, institution of higher education, or place of employment address in this state, unless a court of common pleas or juvenile court determines that the offender or delinquent child

is not a child-victim predator pursuant to division (F) of section 2950.091 of the Revised Code.

(W) "Residential premises" means the building in which a residential unit is located and the grounds upon which that building stands, extending to the perimeter of the property. "Residential premises" includes any type of structure in which a residential unit is located, including, but not limited to, multi-unit buildings and mobile and manufactured homes.

(X) "Residential unit" means a dwelling unit for residential use and occupancy, and includes the structure or part of a structure that is used as a home, residence, or sleeping place by one person who maintains a household or two or more persons who maintain a common household. "Residential unit" does not include a halfway house or a community-based correctional facility.

(Y) "Multi–unit building" means a building in which is located more than twelve residential units that have entry doors that open directly into the unit from a hallway that is shared with one or more other units. A residential unit is not considered located in a multi-unit building if the unit does not have an entry door that opens directly into the unit from a hallway that is shared with one or more other units or if the unit is in a building that is not a multi-unit building as described in this division.

(Z) "Community control sanction" has the same meaning as in section 2929.01 of the Revised Code.

(AA) "Halfway house" and "community-based correctional facility" have the same meanings as in section 2929.01 of the Revised Code.

(BB) "Adjudicated a sexually violent predator" has the same meaning as in section 2929.01 of the Revised Code, and a person is " adjudicated a sexually violent predator" in the same manner and the same circumstances as are described in that section.

(2004 H 473, eff. 4–29–05; 2003 S 57, eff. 1–1–04; 2003 S 5, § 3, eff. 1–1–04; 2003 S 5, § 1, eff. 7–31–03; 2002 H 490, eff. 1–1–04; 2002 H 485, eff. 6–13–02; 2002 S 175, eff. 5–7–02; 2002 H 393, eff. 7–5–02; 2001 S 3, eff. 1–1–02; 2000 H 502, eff. 3–15–01; 1998 H 565, eff. 3–30–99; 1997 S 111, eff. 3–17–98; 1996 H 180, eff. 1–1–97)

Note: See also preceding version of this section, in effect until 4–29–05.

2950.02 Legislative findings; public policy declaration

(A) The general assembly hereby determines and declares that it recognizes and finds all of the following:

(1) If the public is provided adequate notice and information about offenders and delinquent children who commit sexually oriented offenses that are not registration-exempt sexually oriented offenses or who commit child-victim oriented offenses, members of the public and communities can develop constructive plans to prepare themselves and their children for the offender's or delinquent child's release from imprisonment, a prison term, or other confinement or detention. This allows members of the public and communities to meet with members of law enforcement agencies to prepare and obtain information about the rights and responsibilities of the public and the communities and to provide education and counseling to their children.

(2) Sex offenders and offenders who commit child-victim oriented offenses pose a risk of engaging in further sexually abusive behavior even after being released from imprisonment, a prison term, or other confinement or detention, and protection of members of the public from sex offenders and offenders who commit child-victim oriented offenses is a paramount governmental interest.

(3) The penal, juvenile, and mental health components of the justice system of this state are largely hidden from public view, and a lack of information from any component may result in the failure of the system to satisfy this paramount governmental interest of public safety described in division (A)(2) of this section.

(4) Overly restrictive confidentiality and liability laws governing the release of information about sex offenders and offenders who commit child-victim oriented offenses have reduced the willingness to release information that could be appropriately released under the public disclosure laws and have increased risks of public safety.

(5) A person who is found to be a sex offender or to have committed a child-victim oriented offense has a reduced expectation of privacy because of the public's interest in public safety and in the effective operation of government.

(6) The release of information about sex offenders and offenders who commit child-victim oriented offenses to public agencies and the general public will further the governmental interests of public safety and public scrutiny of the criminal, juvenile, and mental health systems as long as the information released is rationally related to the furtherance of those goals.

(B) The general assembly hereby declares that, in providing in this chapter for registration regarding offenders and certain delinquent children who have committed sexually oriented offenses that are not registration-exempt sexually oriented offenses or who have committed child-victim oriented offenses and for community notification regarding sexual predators , child-victim predators, habitual sex offenders, and habitual child-victim offenders who are about to be or have been released from imprisonment, a prison term, or other confinement or detention and who will live in or near a particular neighborhood or who otherwise will live in or near a particular neighborhood, it is the general assembly's intent to protect the safety and general welfare of the people of this state. The general assembly further declares that it is the policy of this state to require the exchange in accordance with this chapter of relevant information about sex offenders and offenders who commit child-victim oriented offenses among public agencies and officials and to authorize the release in accordance with this chapter of necessary and relevant information about sex offenders and offenders who commit child-victim oriented offenses to members of the general public as a means of assuring public protection and that the exchange or release of that information is not punitive.

(2003 S 5, eff. 7–31–03; 2001 S 3, eff. 1–1–02; 1996 H 180, eff. 7–1–97)

2950.021 Determination of requirement to register as sex offender with sheriff

(A) If an offender is convicted of or pleads guilty to, or a child is adjudicated a delinquent child for committing, any presumptive registration-exempt sexually oriented offense, the court that is imposing sentence on the offender for that offense or the juvenile court that is making the disposition of the delinquent child for that offense may determine, prior to imposing the sentence or making the disposition, that the offender should be subjected to registration under section 2950.04 of the Revised Code and all other duties and responsibilities generally imposed under this chapter upon persons who are convicted of or plead guilty to any sexually oriented offense other than a presumptive registration-exempt sexually oriented offense or that the child potentially should be subjected to classification as a juvenile offender registrant under sections 2152.82, 2152.83, 2152.84, or 2152.85 of the Revised Code and to registration under section 2950.04 of the Revised Code and all other duties and responsibilities generally imposed under this chapter upon persons who are adjudicated delinquent children for committing a sexually oriented offense other than a presumptive registration-exempt sexually oriented offense. The court may make a determination as described in this division without a hearing but may conduct a hearing on the matter. In making a determination under this division, the court shall consider all relevant factors, including, but not limited to, public safety, the interests of justice, and the determinations, findings, and declarations of the general assembly regarding sex offenders and child-victim offenders that are set forth in section 2950.02 of the Revised Code.

(B) If a court determines under division (A) of this section that an offender who has been convicted of or pleaded guilty to a presumptive registration-exempt sexually oriented offense should be subjected to registration under section 2950.04 of the Revised Code and all other duties and responsibilities generally imposed under this chapter upon persons who are convicted of or plead guilty to any sexually oriented offense other than a presumptive registration-exempt sexually oriented offense or that a delinquent child potentially should be subjected to classification as a juvenile offender registrant under sections 2152.82, 2152.83, 2152.84, or 2152.85 of the Revised Code and to registration under section 2950.04 of the Revised Code and all other duties and responsibilities generally imposed under this chapter upon persons who are adjudicated delinquent children for committing a sexually oriented offense other than a presumptive registration-exempt sexually oriented offense, all of the following apply:

(1) The court shall issue an order that contains its determination and that removes the presumptive exemption from registration for the sexually oriented offense, shall include the order in the offender's sentence or in the delinquent child's dispositional order, and shall enter the order in the record in the case.

(2) Regarding an offender, the presumptive exemption from registration is terminated, and the offender is subject to registration under section 2950.04 of the Revised Code and all other duties and responsibilities generally imposed under this chapter upon persons who are convicted of or plead guilty to any sexually oriented offense other than a presumptive registration-exempt sexually oriented offense.

(3) Regarding a delinquent child, the presumptive exemption from registration is terminated, the delinquent child is potentially subject to classification as a juvenile offender registrant under sections 2152.82, 2152.83, 2152.84, or 2152.85 of the Revised Code and to registration under section 2950.04 of the Revised Code and all other duties and responsibilities generally imposed under this chapter upon persons who are adjudicated delinquent children for committing a sexually oriented offense other than a presumptive registration-exempt sexually oriented offense, and the juvenile court shall proceed as required and may proceed as authorized under section 2152.82, 2152.83, 2152.84, or 2152.85 of the Revised Code regarding the child in the same manner as for persons who are adjudicated delinquent children for committing a sexually oriented offense other than a presumptive registration-exempt sexually oriented offense.

(2003 S 5, eff. 7–31–03)

2950.03 Notice of duty to register and related requirements

Note: See also following version of this section, eff. 4–29–05.

(A) Each person who has been convicted of, is convicted of, has pleaded guilty to, or pleads guilty to a sexually oriented offense that is not a registration-exempt sexually oriented offense and who has a duty to register pursuant to section 2950.04 of the Revised Code, each person who is adjudicated a delinquent child for committing a sexually oriented offense that is not a registration-exempt sexually oriented offense and who is classified a juvenile offender registrant based on that adjudication, each person who has been convicted of, is convicted of, has pleaded guilty to, or pleads guilty to a child-victim oriented offense and has a duty to register pursuant to section 2950.041 of the Revised Code, and each person who is adjudicated a delinquent child for committing a child-victim oriented offense and who is classified a juvenile offender registrant based on that adjudication shall be provided notice in accordance with this section of the offender's or delinquent child's duties imposed under sections 2950.04 , 2950.041, 2950.05 , and 2950. 06 of the Revised Code and of the offender's duties to similarly register, provide notice of a change, and verify addresses in another state if the offender resides, is temporarily domiciled, attends a school or institution of higher education, or is employed in a state other than this state. A person who has been convicted of, is convicted of, has pleaded guilty to, or pleads guilty to a sexually oriented offense that is a registration-exempt sexually oriented offense, and a person who is or has been adjudicated a delinquent child for committing a sexually oriented offense that is a registration-exempt sexually oriented offense, does not have a duty to register under section 2950.04 of the Revised Code based on that conviction, guilty plea, or adjudication, and no notice is required to be provided to that person under this division based on that conviction, guilty plea, or adjudication. The following official shall provide the notice required under this division to the specified person at the following time:

(1) Regardless of when the person committed the sexually oriented offense or child-victim oriented offense, if the person is an offender who is sentenced for the sexually oriented offense or child-victim oriented offense to a prison term, a term of imprisonment, or any other type of confinement, and if, on or after January 1, 1997, the offender is serving that term or is under that confinement, the official in charge of the jail, workhouse, state correctional institution, or other institution in which the offender serves the prison term, term of imprisonment, or confinement, or a designee of that official, shall provide the notice to the offender before the offender is released pursuant to any type of supervised release or before the offender otherwise is released from the prison term, term of imprisonment, or confinement. This division applies to a child-victim oriented offense if the offender is sentenced for the offense on or after the effective date of this amendment or if, prior to the effective date of this amendment, the child-victim oriented offense was a sexually oriented offense and the offender was sentenced as described in this division for the child-victim oriented offense when it was designated a sexually oriented offense. If a person was provided notice under this division prior to the effective date of this amendment in relation to an offense that, prior to the effective date of this amendment, was a sexually oriented offense but that, on and after the effective date of this amendment, is a child-victim oriented offense, the notice provided under this division shall suffice for purposes of this section as notice to the offender of the offender's duties under sections 2950.041, 2950.05, and 2950. 06 of the Revised Code imposed as a result of the conviction of or plea of guilty to the child-victim oriented offense.

(2) Regardless of when the person committed the sexually oriented offense or child-victim oriented offense, if the person is an offender who is sentenced for the sexually oriented offense on or after January 1, 1997, or who is sentenced for the child-victim oriented offense on or after the effective date of this amendment and if division (A)(1) of this section does not apply, the judge shall provide the notice to the offender at the time of sentencing. If a person was provided notice under this division prior to the effective date of this amendment in relation to an offense that, prior to the effective date of this amendment, was a sexually oriented offense but that, on and after the effective date of this amendment, is a child-victim oriented offense, the notice so provided under this division shall suffice for purposes of this section as notice to the offender of the offender's duties under sections 2950.041, 2950.05, and 2950. 06 of the Revised Code imposed as a result of the conviction of or plea of guilty to the child-victim oriented offense.

(3) If the person is an offender who committed the sexually oriented offense prior to January 1, 1997, if neither division

(A)(1) nor division (A)(2) of this section applies, and if, immediately prior to January 1, 1997, the offender was a habitual sex offender who was required to register under Chapter 2950. of the Revised Code, the chief of police or sheriff with whom the offender most recently registered under that chapter, in the circumstances described in this division, shall provide the notice to the offender. If the offender has registered with a chief of police or sheriff under Chapter 2950. of the Revised Code as it existed prior to January 1, 1997, the chief of police or sheriff with whom the offender most recently registered shall provide the notice to the offender as soon as possible after January 1, 1997, as described in division (B)(1) of this section. If the offender has not registered with a chief of police or sheriff under that chapter, the failure to register shall constitute a waiver by the offender of any right to notice under this section. If an offender described in this division does not receive notice under this section, the offender is not relieved of the offender's duties imposed under sections 2950.04, 2950.05, and 2950.06 of the Revised Code.

(4) If the person is an offender of the type described in division (A)(1) of this section and if, subsequent to release, the offender is adjudicated a sexual predator pursuant to division (C) of section 2950.09 of the Revised Code or a child-victim predator pursuant to division (C) of section 2950.091 of the Revised Code, the judge shall provide the notice to the offender at the time of adjudication.

(5) If the person is a delinquent child who is classified a juvenile offender registrant, the judge shall provide the notice to the delinquent child at the time specified in division (B) of section 2152.82, division (D) of section 2152.83, division (C) of section 2152.84, or division (E) of section 2152.85 of the Revised Code, whichever is applicable. If a delinquent child was provided notice under this division prior to the effective date of this amendment in relation to an offense that, prior to the effective date of this amendment, was a sexually oriented offense but that, on and after the effective date of this amendment, is a child-victim oriented offense, the notice so provided under this division shall suffice for purposes of this section as notice to the delinquent child of the delinquent child's duties under sections 2950.041, 2950.05, and 2950.06 of the Revised Code imposed as a result of the adjudication as a delinquent child for the child-victim oriented offense.

(6) If the person is an offender in any category described in division (A)(1), (2), (3), or (4) of this section and if, prior to the effective date of this amendment, the offender was provided notice of the offender's duties in accordance with that division, not later than ninety days after the effective date of this amendment, the sheriff with whom the offender most recently registered or verified an address under section 2950.04, 2950.041, 2950.05, or 2950.06 of the Revised Code shall provide notice to the offender of the offender's duties imposed on and after the effective date of this amendment pursuant to any of those sections to register a school, institution of higher education, or place of employment address, provide notice of a change of that address, and verify that address. The sheriff may provide the notice to the offender at the time the offender registers, provides notice of a change in, or verifies a residence, school, institution of higher education, or place of employment address under any of those sections within the specified ninety-day period. If the offender does not so register, provide notice of a change in, or verify an address within the specified ninety-day period, the sheriff shall provide the notice to the offender by sending it to the offender at the most recent residence address available for the offender. If the offender was required to register prior to the effective date of this amendment and failed to do so, the failure to register constitutes a waiver by the offender of any right to notice under this division. If the offender has not registered prior to the effective date of this amendment, the offender is presumed to have knowledge of the law and of the duties referred to in this division that are imposed on and after the effective date of this amendment. If an offender does not receive notice under this division, the offender is not relieved of any of the duties described in this division.

(7) If the person is an offender or delinquent child who has a duty to register in this state pursuant to division (A)(3) of section 2950.04 or 2950.041 of the Revised Code, the offender or delinquent child is presumed to have knowledge of the law and of the offender's or delinquent child's duties imposed under sections 2950.04, 2950.041, 2950.05, and 2950.06 of the Revised Code.

(B)(1) The notice provided under division (A) of this section shall inform the offender or delinquent child of the offender's or delinquent child's duty to register, to provide notice of a change in the offender's or delinquent child's residence address or in the offender's school, institution of higher education, or place of employment address, as applicable, and register the new address, to periodically verify the offender's or delinquent child's residence address or the offender's school, institution of higher education, or place of employment address, as applicable, and, if applicable, to provide notice of the offender's or delinquent child's intent to reside, pursuant to sections 2950.04, 2950.041, 2950.05, and 2950.06 of the Revised Code. The notice shall specify that, for an offender, it applies regarding residence addresses or school, institution of higher education, and place of employment addresses and that, for a delinquent child, it applies regarding residence addresses. Additionally, it shall inform the offender of the offender's duties to similarly register, provide notice of a change in, and verify those addresses in states other than this state as described in division (A) of this section. A notice provided under division (A)(6) of this section shall state the new duties imposed on the offender on and after the effective date of this amendment to register, provide notice of a change in, and periodically verify, a school, institution of higher education, or place of employment address and specify that the new duties are in addition to the prior duties imposed upon the offender. A notice provided under division (A)(1), (2), (3), (4), or (5) of this section shall comport with the following:

(a) If the notice is provided to an offender under division (A)(3) of this section, the notice shall state the offender's duties to register, to file a notice of intent to reside, if applicable, to register a new residence address or new school, institution of higher education, or place of employment address, and to periodically verify those addresses, the offender's duties in other states as described in division (A) of this section, and that, if the offender has any questions concerning these duties, the offender may contact the chief of police or sheriff who sent the form for an explanation of the duties. If the offender appears in person before the chief of police or sheriff, the chief or sheriff shall provide the notice as described in division (B)(1)(a) of this section, and all provisions of this section that apply regarding a notice provided by an official, official's designee, or judge in that manner shall be applicable.

(b) If the notice is provided to an offender under division (A)(1), (2), or (4) of this section, the official, official's designee, or judge shall require the offender to read and sign a form stating that the offender's duties to register, to file a notice of intent to reside, if applicable, to register a new residence address or new school, institution of higher education, or place of employment address, and to periodically verify those addresses, and the offender's duties in other states as described in division (A) of this section have been explained to the offender. If the offender is unable to read, the official, official's designee, or judge shall certify on the form that the official, designee, or judge specifically informed the offender of those duties and that the offender indicated an understanding of those duties.

(c) If the notice is provided to a delinquent child under division (A)(5) of this section, the judge shall require the delinquent child and the delinquent child's parent, guardian, or custodian to read and sign a form stating that the delinquent child's duties to register, to file a notice of intent to reside, if applicable, to register a new residence address, and to periodically verify that address have been explained to the delinquent child and to the delinquent child's parent, guardian, or custodian. If the delinquent child or the delinquent child's parent, guardian, or custodian is unable to read, the judge shall certify on the form that the judge specifically informed the delinquent child or the delinquent child's parent, guardian, or custodian of those duties and that the delinquent child or the delinquent child's parent, guardian, or custodian indicated an understanding of those duties.

(2) The notice provided under divisions (A)(1) to (6) of this section shall be on a form prescribed by the bureau of criminal identification and investigation and shall contain all of the information specified in division (A) of this section and all of the information required by the bureau . The notice provided under divisions (A)(1) to (5) of this section shall include, but is not limited to, all of the following:

(a) For any notice provided under division (A)(1) to (5) of this section, a statement as to whether the offender or delinquent child has been adjudicated a sexual predator or a child-victim predator relative to the sexually oriented offense or child-victim oriented offense in question, a statement as to whether the offender or delinquent child has been determined to be a habitual sex offender or habitual child-victim offender, a statement as to whether the offense for which the offender has the duty to register is an aggravated sexually oriented offense, an explanation of the offender's periodic residence address or periodic school, institution of higher education, or place of employment address verification process or of the delinquent child's periodic residence address verification process, an explanation of the frequency with which the offender or delinquent child will be required to verify those addresses under that process, a statement that the offender or delinquent child must verify those addresses at the times specified under that process or face criminal prosecution or a delinquent child proceeding, and an explanation of the offender's duty to similarly register, verify, and reregister those addresses in another state if the offender resides in another state, attends a school or institution of higher education in another state, or is employed in another state.

(b) If the notice is provided under division (A)(4) of this section, a statement that the notice replaces any notice previously provided to the offender under division (A)(1) of this section, a statement that the offender's duties described in this notice supersede the duties described in the prior notice, and a statement notifying the offender that, if the offender already has registered under section 2950.04 or 2950. 041 of the Revised Code, the offender must register again pursuant to division (A)(6) of that section;

(c) If the notice is provided under division (A)(5) of this section, a statement that the delinquent child has been classified by the adjudicating juvenile court judge or the judge's successor in office a juvenile offender registrant and has a duty to comply with sections 2950.04, 2950.041, 2950.05, and 2950.06 of the Revised Code;

(d) If the notice is provided under division (A)(5) of this section, a statement that, if the delinquent child fails to comply with the requirements of sections 2950.04, 2950.041, 2950.05, and 2950.06 of the Revised Code, both of the following apply:

(i) If the delinquent child's failure occurs while the child is under eighteen years of age, the child is subject to proceedings under Chapter 2152. of the Revised Code based on the failure, but if the failure occurs while the child is eighteen years of age or older, the child is subject to criminal prosecution based on the failure.

(ii) If the delinquent child's failure occurs while the child is under eighteen years of age, unless the child is emancipated, as defined in section 2919.121 of the Revised Code, the failure of the parent, guardian, or custodian to ensure that the child complies with those requirements is a violation of section 2919.24 of the Revised Code and may result in the prosecution of the parent, guardian, or custodian for that violation.

(3)(a) After an offender described in division (A)(1), (2), or (4) of this section has signed the form described in divisions (B)(1) and (2) of this section or the official, official's designee, or judge has certified on the form that the form has been explained to the offender and that the offender indicated an understanding of the duties indicated on it, the official, official's designee, or judge shall give one copy of the form to the offender, within three days shall send one copy of the form to the bureau of criminal identification and investigation in accordance with the procedures adopted pursuant to section 2950.13 of the Revised Code, and shall send one copy of the form to the sheriff of the county in which the offender expects to reside.

(b) After a chief of police or sheriff has sent a form to an offender under division (A)(3) of this section, the chief or sheriff shall send a copy of the form to the bureau of criminal identification and investigation in accordance with the procedures adopted pursuant to section 2950.13 of the Revised Code.

(c) After a delinquent child described in division (A)(5) of this section and the delinquent child's parent, guardian, or custodian have signed the form described in divisions (B)(1) and (2) of this section or the judge has certified on the form that the form has been explained to the delinquent child or the delinquent child's parent, guardian, or custodian and that the delinquent child or the delinquent child's parent, guardian, or custodian indicated an understanding of the duties and information indicated on the form, the judge shall give a copy of the form to both the delinquent child and to the delinquent child's parent, guardian, or custodian, within three days shall send one copy of the form to the bureau of criminal identification and investigation in accordance with the procedures adopted pursuant to section 2950.13 of the Revised Code, and shall send one copy of the form to the sheriff of the county in which the delinquent child expects to reside.

(C) The official, official's designee, judge, chief of police, or sheriff who is required to provide notice to an offender or delinquent child under divisions (A)(1) to (5) of this section shall do all of the following:

(1) If the notice is provided under division (A)(1), (2), (4), or (5) of this section, the official, designee, or judge shall determine the offender's or delinquent child's name, identifying factors, and expected future residence address in this state or any other state, shall obtain the offender's or delinquent child's criminal and delinquency history, and shall obtain a photograph and the fingerprints of the offender or delinquent child. Regarding an offender, the official, designee, or judge also shall obtain from the offender the offender's current or expected future school, institution of higher education, or place of employment address in this state, if any. If the notice is provided by a judge under division (A)(2), (4), or (5) of this section, the sheriff shall provide the offender's or delinquent child's criminal and delinquency history to the judge. The official, official's designee, or judge shall obtain this information and these items prior to giving the notice, except that a judge may give the notice prior to obtaining the offender's or delinquent child's criminal and delinquency history. Within three days after receiving this information and these items, the official, official's designee, or judge shall forward the information and items to the bureau of criminal identification and investigation in accordance with the forwarding procedures adopted pursuant to section 2950.13 of the Revised Code , to the sheriff of the county in which the offender or delinquent child expects to reside, and, regarding an offender, to the sheriff of the county, if any, in which the offender attends or will attend a school or institution of higher education or is or will be employed. If the notice is provided under division (A)(5) of this section and if the delinquent child has been committed to the department of youth services or to a secure facility, the judge, in addition to the other information and items described in this division, also shall forward to the bureau and to the sheriff notification that the child has been so committed. If it has not already done so, the bureau of criminal identification and investi-

gation shall forward a copy of the fingerprints and conviction data received under this division to the federal bureau of investigation.

(2) If the notice is provided under division (A)(3) of this section, the chief of police or sheriff shall determine the offender's name, identifying factors, and residence address in this state or any other state, shall obtain the offender's criminal history from the bureau of criminal identification and investigation, and, to the extent possible, shall obtain a photograph and the fingerprints of the offender. Regarding an offender, the chief or sheriff also shall obtain from the offender the offender's current or expected future school, institution of higher education, or place of employment address in this state, if any. Within three days after receiving this information and these items, the chief or sheriff shall forward the information and items to the bureau of criminal identification and investigation in accordance with the forwarding procedures adopted pursuant to section 2950.13 of the Revised Code and, in relation to a chief of police, to the sheriff of the county in which the offender resides, and, regarding an offender, to the sheriff of the county, if any, in which the offender attends or will attend a school or institution of higher education or is or will be employed. If it has not already done so, the bureau of criminal identification and investigation shall forward a copy of the fingerprints and conviction data so received to the federal bureau of investigation.

(2003 S 5, eff. 7–31–03; 2002 H 485, eff. 6–13–02; 2001 S 3, eff. 1–1–02; 2000 H 502, eff. 3–15–01; 1997 H 93, eff. 12–31–97; 1996 H 180, eff. 1–1–97)

Note: *See also following version of this section, eff. 4–29–05.*

2950.03 Notice of duty to register and related requirements (later effective date)

Note: *See also preceding version of this section, in effect until 4–29–05.*

(A) Each person who has been convicted of, is convicted of, has pleaded guilty to, or pleads guilty to a sexually oriented offense that is not a registration-exempt sexually oriented offense and who has a duty to register pursuant to section 2950.04 of the Revised Code, each person who is adjudicated a delinquent child for committing a sexually oriented offense that is not a registration-exempt sexually oriented offense and who is classified a juvenile offender registrant based on that adjudication, each person who has been convicted of, is convicted of, has pleaded guilty to, or pleads guilty to a child-victim oriented offense and has a duty to register pursuant to section 2950.041 of the Revised Code, and each person who is adjudicated a delinquent child for committing a child-victim oriented offense and who is classified a juvenile offender registrant based on that adjudication shall be provided notice in accordance with this section of the offender's or delinquent child's duties imposed under sections 2950.04, 2950. 041, 2950.05, and 2950.06 of the Revised Code and of the offender's duties to similarly register, provide notice of a change, and verify addresses in another state if the offender resides, is temporarily domiciled, attends a school or institution of higher education, or is employed in a state other than this state. A person who has been convicted of, is convicted of, has pleaded guilty to, or pleads guilty to a sexually oriented offense that is a registration-exempt sexually oriented offense, and a person who is or has been adjudicated a delinquent child for committing a sexually oriented offense that is a registration-exempt sexually oriented offense, does not have a duty to register under section 2950.04 of the Revised Code based on that conviction, guilty plea, or adjudication, and no notice is required to be provided to that person under this division based on that conviction, guilty plea, or adjudication. The following official shall provide the notice required under this division to the specified person at the following time:

(1) Regardless of when the person committed the sexually oriented offense or child-victim oriented offense, if the person is an offender who is sentenced for the sexually oriented offense or child-victim oriented offense to a prison term, a term of imprisonment, or any other type of confinement, and if, on or after January 1, 1997, the offender is serving that term or is under that confinement, the official in charge of the jail, workhouse, state correctional institution, or other institution in which the offender serves the prison term, term of imprisonment, or confinement, or a designee of that official, shall provide the notice to the offender before the offender is released pursuant to any type of supervised release or before the offender otherwise is released from the prison term, term of imprisonment, or confinement. This division applies to a child-victim oriented offense if the offender is sentenced for the offense on or after July 31, 2003, or if, prior to July 31, 2003, the child-victim oriented offense was a sexually oriented offense and the offender was sentenced as described in this division for the child-victim oriented offense when it was designated a sexually oriented offense. If a person was provided notice under this division prior to July 31, 2003, in relation to an offense that, prior to July 31, 2003, was a sexually oriented offense but that, on and after July 31, 2003, is a child-victim oriented offense, the notice provided under this division shall suffice for purposes of this section as notice to the offender of the offender's duties under sections 2950.041, 2950.05, and 2950. 06 of the Revised Code imposed as a result of the conviction of or plea of guilty to the child-victim oriented offense.

(2) Regardless of when the person committed the sexually oriented offense or child-victim oriented offense, if the person is an offender who is sentenced for the sexually oriented offense on or after January 1, 1997, or who is sentenced for the child-victim oriented offense on or after July 31, 2003, and if division (A)(1) of this section does not apply, the judge shall provide the notice to the offender at the time of sentencing. If a person was provided notice under this division prior to July 31, 2003, in relation to an offense that, prior to July 31, 2003,, was a sexually oriented offense but that, on and after July 31, 2003,, is a child-victim oriented offense, the notice so provided under this division shall suffice for purposes of this section as notice to the offender of the offender's duties under sections 2950.041, 2950.05, and 2950. 06 of the Revised Code imposed as a result of the conviction of or plea of guilty to the child-victim oriented offense.

(3) If the person is an offender who committed the sexually oriented offense prior to January 1, 1997, if neither division (A)(1) nor division (A)(2) of this section applies, and if, immediately prior to January 1, 1997, the offender was a habitual sex offender who was required to register under Chapter 2950. of the Revised Code, the chief of police or sheriff with whom the offender most recently registered under that chapter, in the circumstances described in this division, shall provide the notice to the offender. If the offender has registered with a chief of police or sheriff under Chapter 2950. of the Revised Code as it existed prior to January 1, 1997, the chief of police or sheriff with whom the offender most recently registered shall provide the notice to the offender as soon as possible after January 1, 1997, as described in division (B)(1) of this section. If the offender has not registered with a chief of police or sheriff under that chapter, the failure to register shall constitute a waiver by the offender of any right to notice under this section. If an offender described in this division does not receive notice under this section, the offender is not relieved of the offender's duties imposed under sections 2950.04, 2950.05, and 2950.06 of the Revised Code.

(4) If neither division (A)(1), (2), nor (3) of this section applies and if the offender is adjudicated a sexual predator pursuant to division (C) of section 2950.09 of the Revised Code or a child-victim predator pursuant to division (C) of section 2950.091 of the Revised Code, the judge shall provide the notice to the offender at the time of adjudication.

(5) If the person is a delinquent child who is classified a juvenile offender registrant, the judge shall provide the notice to

the delinquent child at the time specified in division (B) of section 2152.82, division (D) of section 2152.83, division (C) of section 2152.84, or division (E) of section 2152.85 of the Revised Code, whichever is applicable. If a delinquent child was provided notice under this division prior to July 31, 2003, in relation to an offense that, prior to July 31, 2003, was a sexually oriented offense but that, on and after July 31, 2003, is a child-victim oriented offense, the notice so provided under this division shall suffice for purposes of this section as notice to the delinquent child of the delinquent child's duties under sections 2950.041, 2950.05, and 2950.06 of the Revised Code imposed as a result of the adjudication as a delinquent child for the child-victim oriented offense.

(6) If the person is an offender in any category described in division (A)(1), (2), (3), or (4) of this section and if, prior to July 31, 2003, the offender was provided notice of the offender's duties in accordance with that division, not later than ninety days after July 31, 2003, the sheriff with whom the offender most recently registered or verified an address under section 2950.04, 2950.041, 2950.05, or 2950.06 of the Revised Code shall provide notice to the offender of the offender's duties imposed on and after July 31, 2003, pursuant to any of those sections to register a school, institution of higher education, or place of employment address, provide notice of a change of that address, and verify that address. The sheriff may provide the notice to the offender at the time the offender registers, provides notice of a change in, or verifies a residence, school, institution of higher education, or place of employment address under any of those sections within the specified ninety-day period. If the offender does not so register, provide notice of a change in, or verify an address within the specified ninety-day period, the sheriff shall provide the notice to the offender by sending it to the offender at the most recent residence address available for the offender. If the offender was required to register prior to July 31, 2003, and failed to do so, the failure to register constitutes a waiver by the offender of any right to notice under this division. If the offender has not registered prior to July 31, 2003, the offender is presumed to have knowledge of the law and of the duties referred to in this division that are imposed on and after July 31, 2003. If an offender does not receive notice under this division, the offender is not relieved of any of the duties described in this division.

(7) If the person is an offender or delinquent child who has a duty to register in this state pursuant to division (A)(3) of section 2950.04 or 2950.041 of the Revised Code, the offender or delinquent child is presumed to have knowledge of the law and of the offender's or delinquent child's duties imposed under sections 2950.04, 2950.041, 2950.05, and 2950.06 of the Revised Code.

(B)(1) The notice provided under division (A) of this section shall inform the offender or delinquent child of the offender's or delinquent child's duty to register, to provide notice of a change in the offender's or delinquent child's residence address or in the offender's school, institution of higher education, or place of employment address, as applicable, and register the new address, to periodically verify the offender's or delinquent child's residence address or the offender's school, institution of higher education, or place of employment address, as applicable, and, if applicable, to provide notice of the offender's or delinquent child's intent to reside, pursuant to sections 2950.04, 2950.041, 2950.05, and 2950.06 of the Revised Code. The notice shall specify that, for an offender, it applies regarding residence addresses or school, institution of higher education, and place of employment addresses and that, for a delinquent child, it applies regarding residence addresses. Additionally, it shall inform the offender of the offender's duties to similarly register, provide notice of a change in, and verify those addresses in states other than this state as described in division (A) of this section. A notice provided under division (A)(6) of this section shall state the new duties imposed on the offender on and after July 31, 2003, to register, provide notice of a change in, and periodically verify, a school, institution of higher education, or place of employment address and specify that the new duties are in addition to the prior duties imposed upon the offender. A notice provided under division (A)(1), (2), (3), (4), or (5) of this section shall comport with the following:

(a) If the notice is provided to an offender under division (A)(3) of this section, the notice shall state the offender's duties to register, to file a notice of intent to reside, if applicable, to register a new residence address or new school, institution of higher education, or place of employment address, and to periodically verify those addresses, the offender's duties in other states as described in division (A) of this section, and that, if the offender has any questions concerning these duties, the offender may contact the chief of police or sheriff who sent the form for an explanation of the duties. If the offender appears in person before the chief of police or sheriff, the chief or sheriff shall provide the notice as described in division (B)(1)(a) of this section, and all provisions of this section that apply regarding a notice provided by an official, official's designee, or judge in that manner shall be applicable.

(b) If the notice is provided to an offender under division (A)(1), (2), or (4) of this section, the official, official's designee, or judge shall require the offender to read and sign a form stating that the offender's duties to register, to file a notice of intent to reside, if applicable, to register a new residence address or new school, institution of higher education, or place of employment address, and to periodically verify those addresses, and the offender's duties in other states as described in division (A) of this section have been explained to the offender. If the offender is unable to read, the official, official's designee, or judge shall certify on the form that the official, designee, or judge specifically informed the offender of those duties and that the offender indicated an understanding of those duties.

(c) If the notice is provided to a delinquent child under division (A)(5) of this section, the judge shall require the delinquent child and the delinquent child's parent, guardian, or custodian to read and sign a form stating that the delinquent child's duties to register, to file a notice of intent to reside, if applicable, to register a new residence address, and to periodically verify that address have been explained to the delinquent child and to the delinquent child's parent, guardian, or custodian. If the delinquent child or the delinquent child's parent, guardian, or custodian is unable to read, the judge shall certify on the form that the judge specifically informed the delinquent child or the delinquent child's parent, guardian, or custodian of those duties and that the delinquent child or the delinquent child's parent, guardian, or custodian indicated an understanding of those duties.

(2) The notice provided under divisions (A)(1) to (6) of this section shall be on a form prescribed by the bureau of criminal identification and investigation and shall contain all of the information specified in division (A) of this section and all of the information required by the bureau. The notice provided under divisions (A)(1) to (5) of this section shall include, but is not limited to, all of the following:

(a) For any notice provided under division (A)(1) to (5) of this section, a statement as to whether the offender or delinquent child has been adjudicated a sexual predator or a child-victim predator relative to the sexually oriented offense or child-victim oriented offense in question, a statement as to whether the offender or delinquent child has been determined to be a habitual sex offender or habitual child-victim offender, a statement as to whether the offense for which the offender has the duty to register is an aggravated sexually oriented offense, an explanation of the offender's periodic residence address or periodic school, institution of higher education, or place of employment address verification process or of the delinquent child's periodic residence address verification process, an explanation of the frequency with which the offender or delinquent child will be required to verify those addresses under that process, a statement that the offender or delinquent child must verify those addresses at the times specified under that process or face criminal prosecution or a delinquent child proceeding, and an explanation of the offender's duty to similarly register, verify, and reregister those addresses in another state if the offender resides in another state, attends a school or institution of higher education in another state, or is employed in another state.

(b) If the notice is provided under division (A)(4) of this section, a statement that the notice replaces any notice previously provided to the offender under division (A)(1) of this section, a statement that the offender's duties described in this notice supersede the duties described in the prior notice, and a statement notifying the offender that, if the offender already has registered under section 2950.04 or 2950.041 of the Revised Code, the offender must register again pursuant to division (A)(6) of that section;

(c) If the notice is provided under division (A)(5) of this section, a statement that the delinquent child has been classified by the adjudicating juvenile court judge or the judge's successor in office a juvenile offender registrant and has a duty to comply with sections 2950.04, 2950.041, 2950.05, and 2950.06 of the Revised Code;

(d) If the notice is provided under division (A)(5) of this section, a statement that, if the delinquent child fails to comply with the requirements of sections 2950.04, 2950.041, 2950.05, and 2950.06 of the Revised Code, both of the following apply:

(i) If the delinquent child's failure occurs while the child is under eighteen years of age, the child is subject to proceedings under Chapter 2152. of the Revised Code based on the failure, but if the failure occurs while the child is eighteen years of age or older, the child is subject to criminal prosecution based on the failure.

(ii) If the delinquent child's failure occurs while the child is under eighteen years of age, unless the child is emancipated, as defined in section 2919.121 of the Revised Code, the failure of the parent, guardian, or custodian to ensure that the child complies with those requirements is a violation of section 2919.24 of the Revised Code and may result in the prosecution of the parent, guardian, or custodian for that violation.

(3)(a) After an offender described in division (A)(1), (2), or (4) of this section has signed the form described in divisions (B)(1) and (2) of this section or the official, official's designee, or judge has certified on the form that the form has been explained to the offender and that the offender indicated an understanding of the duties indicated on it, the official, official's designee, or judge shall give one copy of the form to the offender, within three days shall send one copy of the form to the bureau of criminal identification and investigation in accordance with the procedures adopted pursuant to section 2950.13 of the Revised Code, and shall send one copy of the form to the sheriff of the county in which the offender expects to reside.

(b) After a chief of police or sheriff has sent a form to an offender under division (A)(3) of this section, the chief or sheriff shall send a copy of the form to the bureau of criminal identification and investigation in accordance with the procedures adopted pursuant to section 2950.13 of the Revised Code.

(c) After a delinquent child described in division (A)(5) of this section and the delinquent child's parent, guardian, or custodian have signed the form described in divisions (B)(1) and (2) of this section or the judge has certified on the form that the form has been explained to the delinquent child or the delinquent child's parent, guardian, or custodian and that the delinquent child or the delinquent child's parent, guardian, or custodian indicated an understanding of the duties and information indicated on the form, the judge shall give a copy of the form to both the delinquent child and to the delinquent child's parent, guardian, or custodian, within three days shall send one copy of the form to the bureau of criminal identification and investigation in accordance with the procedures adopted pursuant to section 2950.13 of the Revised Code, and shall send one copy of the form to the sheriff of the county in which the delinquent child expects to reside.

(C) The official, official's designee, judge, chief of police, or sheriff who is required to provide notice to an offender or delinquent child under divisions (A)(1) to (5) of this section shall do all of the following:

(1) If the notice is provided under division (A)(1), (2), (4), or (5) of this section, the official, designee, or judge shall determine the offender's or delinquent child's name, identifying factors, and expected future residence address in this state or any other state, shall obtain the offender's or delinquent child's criminal and delinquency history, and shall obtain a photograph and the fingerprints of the offender or delinquent child. Regarding an offender, the official, designee, or judge also shall obtain from the offender the offender's current or expected future school, institution of higher education, or place of employment address in this state, if any. If the notice is provided by a judge under division (A)(2), (4), or (5) of this section, the sheriff shall provide the offender's or delinquent child's criminal and delinquency history to the judge. The official, official's designee, or judge shall obtain this information and these items prior to giving the notice, except that a judge may give the notice prior to obtaining the offender's or delinquent child's criminal and delinquency history. Within three days after receiving this information and these items, the official, official's designee, or judge shall forward the information and items to the bureau of criminal identification and investigation in accordance with the forwarding procedures adopted pursuant to section 2950.13 of the Revised Code, to the sheriff of the county in which the offender or delinquent child expects to reside, and, regarding an offender, to the sheriff of the county, if any, in which the offender attends or will attend a school or institution of higher education or is or will be employed. If the notice is provided under division (A)(5) of this section and if the delinquent child has been committed to the department of youth services or to a secure facility, the judge, in addition to the other information and items described in this division, also shall forward to the bureau and to the sheriff notification that the child has been so committed. If it has not already done so, the bureau of criminal identification and investigation shall forward a copy of the fingerprints and conviction data received under this division to the federal bureau of investigation.

(2) If the notice is provided under division (A)(3) of this section, the chief of police or sheriff shall determine the offender's name, identifying factors, and residence address in this state or any other state, shall obtain the offender's criminal history from the bureau of criminal identification and investigation, and, to the extent possible, shall obtain a photograph and the fingerprints of the offender. Regarding an offender, the chief or sheriff also shall obtain from the offender the offender's current or expected future school, institution of higher education, or place of employment address in this state, if any. Within three days after receiving this information and these items, the chief or sheriff shall forward the information and items to the bureau of criminal identification and investigation in accordance with the forwarding procedures adopted pursuant to section 2950.13 of the Revised Code and, in relation to a chief of police, to the sheriff of the county in which the offender resides, and, regarding an offender, to the sheriff of the county, if any, in which the offender attends or will attend a school or institution of higher education or is or will be employed. If it has not already done so, the bureau of criminal identification and investigation shall forward a copy of the fingerprints and conviction data so received to the federal bureau of investigation.

(2004 H 473, eff. 4–29–05; 2003 S 5, eff. 7–31–03; 2002 H 485, eff. 6–13–02; 2001 S 3, eff. 1–1–02; 2000 H 502, eff. 3–15–01; 1997 H 93, eff. 12–31–97; 1996 H 180, eff. 1–1–97)

Note: See also preceding version of this section, in effect until 4–29–05.

2950.031 Prohibition against residing near school premises; right of action against violator

Note: See also following version of this section, eff. 4–29–05.

(A) No person who has been convicted of, is convicted of, has pleaded guilty to, or pleads guilty to either a sexually oriented offense that is not a registration-exempt sexually oriented offense or a child-victim oriented offense shall establish a residence or occupy residential premises within one thousand feet of any school premises.

(B) An owner or lessee of real property that is located within one thousand feet of any school premises has a cause of action for injunctive relief against a person who violates division (A) of this section by establishing a residence or occupying residential premises within one thousand feet of those school premises. The owner or lessee shall not be required to prove irreparable harm in order to obtain the relief.

(2003 S 5, eff. 7–31–03)

Note: See also following version of this section, eff. 4–29–05.

2950.031 Prohibition against residing near school premises; right of action against violator (later effective date)

Note: See also preceding version of this section, in effect until 4–29–05.

(A) No person who has been convicted of, is convicted of, has pleaded guilty to, or pleads guilty to either a sexually oriented offense that is not a registration-exempt sexually oriented offense or a child-victim oriented offense shall establish a residence or occupy residential premises within one thousand feet of any school premises.

(B) If a person to whom division (A) of this section applies violates division (A) of this section by establishing a residence or occupying residential premises within one thousand feet of any school premises, an owner or lessee of real property that is located within one thousand feet of those school premises, or the prosecuting attorney, village solicitor, city or township director of law, similar chief legal officer of a municipal corporation or township, or official designated as a prosecutor in a municipal corporation that has jurisdiction over the place at which the person establishes the residence or occupies the residential premises in question, has a cause of action for injunctive relief against the person. The plaintiff shall not be required to prove irreparable harm in order to obtain the relief.

(2004 H 473, eff. 4–29–05; 2003 S 5, eff. 7–31–03)

Note: See also preceding version of this section, in effect until 4–29–05.

2950.04 Manner of registering

Note: See also following version of this section, eff. 4–29–05.

(A)(1) Each of the following types of offender who is convicted of or pleads guilty to, or has been convicted of or pleaded guilty to, a sexually oriented offense that is not a registration-exempt sexually oriented offense shall register personally with the sheriff of the county within five days of the offender's coming into a county in which the offender resides or temporarily is domiciled for more than five days, shall register personally with the sheriff of the county immediately upon coming into a county in which the offender attends a school or institution of higher education on a full-time or part-time basis regardless of whether the offender resides or has a temporary domicile in this state or another state, shall register personally with the sheriff of the county in which the offender is employed if the offender resides or has a temporary domicile in this state and has been employed in that county for more than fourteen days or for an aggregate period of thirty or more days in that calendar year, shall register personally with the sheriff of the county in which the offender then is employed if the offender does not reside or have a temporary domicile in this state and has been employed at any location or locations in this state more than fourteen days or for an aggregate period of thirty or more days in that calendar year, and shall register with the sheriff or other appropriate person of the other state immediately upon entering into any state other than this state in which the offender attends a school or institution of higher education on a full-time or part-time basis or upon being employed in any state other than this state for more than fourteen days or for an aggregate period of thirty or more days in that calendar year regardless of whether the offender resides or has a temporary domicile in this state, the other state, or a different state:

(a) Regardless of when the sexually oriented offense was committed, an offender who is sentenced for the sexually oriented offense to a prison term, a term of imprisonment, or any other type of confinement and, on or after July 1, 1997, is released in any manner from the prison term, term of imprisonment, or confinement;

(b) Regardless of when the sexually oriented offense was committed, an offender who is sentenced for a sexually oriented offense on or after July 1, 1997, and to whom division (A)(1)(a) of this section does not apply;

(c) If the sexually oriented offense was committed prior to July 1, 1997, and neither division (A)(1)(a) nor division (A)(1)(b) of this section applies, an offender who, immediately prior to July 1, 1997, was a habitual sex offender who was required to register under Chapter 2950. of the Revised Code.

(2) Each child who is adjudicated a delinquent child for committing a sexually oriented offense that is not a registration-exempt sexually oriented offense and who is classified a juvenile offender registrant based on that adjudication shall register personally with the sheriff of the county within five days of the delinquent child's coming into a county in which the delinquent child resides or temporarily is domiciled for more than five days. If the delinquent child is committed for the sexually oriented offense that is not a registration-exempt sexually oriented offense to the department of youth services or to a secure facility that is not operated by the department, this duty begins when the delinquent child is discharged or released in any manner from custody in a department of youth services secure facility or from the secure facility that is not operated by the department, if pursuant to the discharge or release the delinquent child is not committed to any other secure facility of the department or any other secure facility. The delinquent child does not have a duty to register under this division while the child is in a department of youth services secure facility or in a secure facility that is not operated by the department.

(3) If divisions (A)(1) and (2) of this section do not apply, each following type of offender and each following type of delinquent child shall register personally with the sheriff of the county within five days of the offender's or delinquent child's coming into a county in which the offender or delinquent child resides or temporarily is domiciled for more than five days, and each following type of offender shall register personally with the sheriff of the county immediately upon coming into a county in which the offender attends a school or institution of higher education on a full-time or part-time basis regardless of whether the offender resides or has a temporary domicile in this state or another state, shall register personally with the sheriff of the county in which the offender is employed if the offender resides or has a temporary domicile in this state and has been employed in that county for more than fourteen days or for an aggregate

period of thirty days or more in that calendar year, and shall register personally with the sheriff of the county in which the offender then is employed if the offender does not reside or have a temporary domicile in this state and has been employed at any location or locations in this state for more than fourteen days or for an aggregate period of thirty or more days in that calendar year:

(a) Regardless of when the sexually oriented offense was committed, a person who is convicted, pleads guilty, or adjudicated a delinquent child in a court in another state, in a federal court, military court, or Indian tribal court, or in a court in any nation other than the United States for committing a sexually oriented offense that is not a registration-exempt sexually oriented offense, if, on or after July 1, 1997, for offenders, or January 1, 2002, for delinquent children, the offender or delinquent child moves to and resides in this state or temporarily is domiciled in this state for more than five days, the offender enters this state to attend any school or institution of higher education on a full-time or part-time basis, or the offender is employed in this state for more than fourteen days or for an aggregate period of thirty or more days in any calendar year, and if, at the time the offender or delinquent child moves to and resides in this state or temporarily is domiciled in this state for more than five days, the offender enters this state to attend the school or institution of higher education, or the offender is employed in this state for more than the specified period of time, the offender or delinquent child has a duty to register as a sex offender or child-victim offender under the law of that other jurisdiction as a result of the conviction, guilty plea, or adjudication.

(b) Regardless of when the sexually oriented offense was committed, a person who is convicted of, pleads guilty to, or is adjudicated a delinquent child in a court in another state, in a federal court, military court, or Indian tribal court, or in a court in any nation other than the United States for committing a sexually oriented offense that is not a registration-exempt sexually oriented offense, if, on or after July 1, 1997, for offenders, or January 1, 2002, for delinquent children, the offender or delinquent child is released from imprisonment, confinement, or detention imposed for that offense, and if, on or after July 1, 1997, for offenders, or January 1, 2002, for delinquent children, the offender or delinquent child moves to and resides in this state or temporarily is domiciled in this state for more than five days, the offender enters this state to attend any school or institution of higher education on a full-time or part-time basis, or the offender is employed in this state for more than fourteen days or for an aggregate period of thirty or more days in any calendar year. The duty to register as described in this division applies to an offender regardless of whether the offender, at the time of moving to and residing in this state or temporarily being domiciled in this state for more than five days, at the time of entering into this state to attend the school or institution of higher education, or at the time of being employed in this state for the specified period of time, has a duty to register as a sex offender or child-victim offender under the law of the jurisdiction in which the conviction or guilty plea occurred. The duty to register as described in this division applies to a delinquent child only if the delinquent child, at the time of moving to and residing in this state or temporarily being domiciled in this state for more than five days, has a duty to register as a sex offender or child-victim offender under the law of the jurisdiction in which the delinquent child adjudication occurred or if, had the delinquent child adjudication occurred in this state, the adjudicating juvenile court judge would have been required to issue an order classifying the delinquent child as a juvenile offender registrant pursuant to section 2152.82 or division (A) of section 2152.83 of the Revised Code.

(4) If division (A)(1)(a) of this section applies and if, subsequent to the offender's release, the offender is adjudicated a sexual predator under division (C) of section 2950.09 of the Revised Code, the offender shall register within five days of the adjudication with the sheriff of the county in which the offender resides or temporarily is domiciled for more than five days, shall register with the sheriff of any county in which the offender subsequently resides or temporarily is domiciled for more than five days within five days of coming into that county, shall register within five days of the adjudication with the sheriff of the county in which the offender attends any school or institution of higher education on a full-time or part-time basis or in which the offender is employed if the offender has been employed in that county for more than fourteen days or for an aggregate period of thirty or more days in that calendar year regardless of whether the offender resides or has temporary domicile in this state or another state, and shall register within five days of the adjudication with the sheriff or other appropriate person of any state other than this state in which the offender attends a school or institution of higher education on a full-time or part-time basis or in which the offender then is employed if the offender has been employed in that state for more than fourteen days or for an aggregate period of thirty or more days in any calendar year regardless of whether the offender resides or has temporary domicile in this state, the other state, or a different state.

(5) A person who is adjudicated a delinquent child for committing a sexually oriented offense that is not a registration-exempt sexually oriented offense is not required to register under division (A)(2) of this section unless the delinquent child committed the offense on or after January 1, 2002, is classified a juvenile offender registrant by a juvenile court judge pursuant to an order issued under section 2152.82, 2152. 83, 2152.84, or 2152.85 of the Revised Code based on that adjudication, and has a duty to register pursuant to division (A)(2) of this section.

(6) A person who has been convicted of, is convicted of, has pleaded guilty to, or pleads guilty to a sexually oriented offense that is a registration-exempt sexually oriented offense, and a person who is or has been adjudicated a delinquent child for committing a sexually oriented offense that is a registration-exempt sexually oriented offense, does not have any duty to register under this section based on that conviction, guilty plea, or adjudication. The exemption of an offender or delinquent child from registration under this division for a conviction of, plea of guilty to, or delinquent child adjudication for a registration-exempt sexually oriented offense does not limit, affect, or supersede any duties imposed upon the offender or delinquent child under this chapter or sections 2152.82 to 2152.85 of the Revised Code for a conviction of, plea of guilty to, or delinquent child adjudication for any other sexually oriented offense or any child-victim oriented offense.

(B) An offender or delinquent child who is required by division (A) of this section to register in this state personally shall obtain from the sheriff or from a designee of the sheriff a registration form that conforms to division (C) of this section, shall complete and sign the form, and shall return the completed form together with the offender's or delinquent child's photograph to the sheriff or the designee. The sheriff or designee shall sign the form and indicate on the form the date on which it is so returned. The registration required under this division is complete when the offender or delinquent child returns the form, containing the requisite information, photograph, signatures, and date, to the sheriff or designee.

(C) The registration form to be used under divisions (A) and (B) of this section shall include the photograph of the offender or delinquent child who is registering and shall contain all of the following:

(1) Regarding an offender or delinquent child who is registering under a duty imposed under division (A)(1), (2), (3), or (4) of this section as a result of the offender or delinquent child residing in this state or temporarily being domiciled in this state for more than five days, the current residence address of the offender or delinquent child who is registering, the name and address of the offender's or delinquent child's employer if the offender or delinquent child is employed at the time of registration or if the offender or delinquent child knows at the time of registration that

the offender or delinquent child will be commencing employment with that employer subsequent to registration, the name and address of the offender's school or institution of higher education if the offender attends one at the time of registration or if the offender knows at the time of registration that the offender will be commencing attendance at that school or institution subsequent to registration, and any other information required by the bureau of criminal identification and investigation.

(2) Regarding an offender who is registering under a duty imposed under division (A)(1), (3), or (4) of this section as a result of the offender attending a school or institution of higher education in this state on a full-time or part-time basis or being employed in this state or in a particular county in this state, whichever is applicable, for more than fourteen days or for an aggregate of thirty or more days in any calendar year, the current address of the school, institution of higher education, or place of employment of the offender who is registering and any other information required by the bureau of criminal identification and investigation.

(3) Regarding an offender or delinquent child who is registering under a duty imposed under division (A)(1), (2), (3), or (4) of this section for any reason, if the offender has been adjudicated a sexual predator relative to the sexually oriented offense in question, if the delinquent child has been adjudicated a sexual predator relative to the sexually oriented offense in question and the court has not subsequently determined pursuant to section 2152.84 or 2152.85 of the Revised Code that the delinquent child no longer is a sexual predator, if the judge determined pursuant to division (C) of section 2950.09 or pursuant to section 2152.82, 2152.83, 2152.84, or 2152.85 of the Revised Code that the offender or delinquent child is a habitual sex offender and the determination has not been removed pursuant to section 2152.84 or 2152.85 of the Revised Code, or if the offender has the duty to register as a result of the conviction of or plea of guilty to an aggravated sexually oriented offense, the offender or delinquent child also shall include on the signed, written registration form all of the following information:

(a) A specific declaration that the person has been adjudicated a sexual predator, has been determined to be a habitual sex offender, or was convicted of or pleaded guilty to an aggravated sexually oriented offense, whichever is applicable;

(b) If the offender or delinquent child has been adjudicated a sexual predator, the identification license plate number of each motor vehicle the offender or delinquent child owns and of each motor vehicle registered in the offender's or delinquent child's name.

(D) After an offender or delinquent child registers with a sheriff pursuant to this section, the sheriff shall forward the signed, written registration form and photograph to the bureau of criminal identification and investigation in accordance with the forwarding procedures adopted pursuant to section 2950.13 of the Revised Code. If an offender registers a school, institution of higher education, or place of employment address, or provides a school or institution of higher education address under division (C)(1) of this section, the sheriff also shall provide notice to the law enforcement agency with jurisdiction over the premises of the school, institution of higher education, or place of employment of the offender's name and that the offender has registered that address as a place at which the offender attends school or an institution of higher education or at which the offender is employed. The bureau shall include the information and materials forwarded to it under this division in the state registry of sex offenders and child victim offenders established and maintained under section 2950.13 of the Revised Code.

(E) No person who is required to register pursuant to divisions (A) and (B) of this section, and no person who is required to send a notice of intent to reside pursuant to division (G) of this section, shall fail to register or send the notice of intent as required in accordance with those divisions or that division.

(F) An offender or delinquent child who is required to register pursuant to divisions (A) and (B) of this section shall register pursuant to this section for the period of time specified in section 2950.07 of the Revised Code.

(G) If an offender or delinquent child who is required by division (A) of this section to register is adjudicated a sexual predator or a habitual sexual offender subject to community notification under division (C)(2) or (E) of section 2950.09 of the Revised Code, or if an offender who is required by division (A) of this section to register has that duty as a result of a conviction of or plea of guilty to an aggravated sexually oriented offense, the offender or delinquent child also shall send the sheriff of the county in which the offender or delinquent child intends to reside written notice of the offender's or delinquent child's intent to reside in the county. The offender or delinquent child shall send the notice of intent to reside at least twenty days prior to the date the offender or delinquent child begins to reside in the county. The notice of intent to reside shall contain the following information:

(1) The offender's or delinquent child's name;

(2) The address or addresses at which the offender or delinquent child intends to reside;

(3) The sexually oriented offense of which the offender was convicted, to which the offender pleaded guilty, or for which the child was adjudicated a delinquent child;

(4) A statement that the offender has been adjudicated a sexual predator, a statement that the delinquent child has been adjudicated a sexual predator and that, as of the date of the notice, the court has not entered a determination that the delinquent child no longer is a sexual predator, a statement that the sentencing or reviewing judge has determined that the offender or delinquent child is a habitual sex offender and that, as of the date of the notice, the determination has not been removed pursuant to section 2152.84 or 2152.85 of the Revised Code, or a statement that the offender was convicted of or pleaded guilty to an aggravated sexually oriented offense.

(H) If, immediately prior to the effective date of this amendment, an offender or delinquent child who was convicted of, pleaded guilty to, or adjudicated a delinquent child for committing a sexually oriented offense was required by division (A) of this section to register and if, on or after the effective date of this amendment, that offense no longer is a sexually oriented offense but instead is designated a child-victim oriented offense, division (A)(1)(c) or (2)(b) of section 2950.041 of the Revised Code applies regarding the offender or delinquent child and the duty to register that is imposed pursuant to that division shall be considered, for purposes of section 2950.07 of the Revised Code and for all other purposes, to be a continuation of the duty imposed upon the offender prior to the effective date of this amendment under this section.

(2003 S 5, eff. 7–31–03; 2002 H 485, eff. 6–13–02; 2002 S 175, eff. 5–7–02; 2002 H 393, eff. 7–5–02; 2001 S 3, eff. 1–1–02; 2000 H 502, eff. 3–15–01; 1998 H 565, eff. 3–30–99; 1996 H 180, eff. 7–1–97)

Note: See also following version of this section, eff. 4–29–05.

2950.04 Manner of registering (later effective date)

Note: See also preceding version of this section, in effect until 4–29–05.

(A)(1) Each of the following types of offender who is convicted of or pleads guilty to, or has been convicted of or pleaded guilty to, a sexually oriented offense that is not a registration-exempt sexually oriented offense shall register personally with the sheriff of the county within five days of the offender's coming into a county in which the offender resides or temporarily is domiciled for more than five days, shall register personally with the sheriff of the county immediately upon coming into a county in which the offender attends a school or institution of higher education on a full-time or part-time basis regardless of whether the offender resides or has a temporary domicile in this state or another state, shall register personally with the sheriff of the county in which the offender is employed if the offender resides or has a temporary domicile in this state and has been employed in that county for more than fourteen days or for an aggregate period of thirty or more days in that calendar year, shall register personally with the sheriff of the county in which the offender then is employed if the offender does not reside or have a temporary domicile in this state and has been employed at any location or locations in this state more than fourteen days or for an aggregate period of thirty or more days in that calendar year, and shall register with the sheriff or other appropriate person of the other state immediately upon entering into any state other than this state in which the offender attends a school or institution of higher education on a full-time or part-time basis or upon being employed in any state other than this state for more than fourteen days or for an aggregate period of thirty or more days in that calendar year regardless of whether the offender resides or has a temporary domicile in this state, the other state, or a different state:

(a) Regardless of when the sexually oriented offense was committed, an offender who is sentenced for the sexually oriented offense to a prison term, a term of imprisonment, or any other type of confinement and, on or after July 1, 1997, is released in any manner from the prison term, term of imprisonment, or confinement;

(b) Regardless of when the sexually oriented offense was committed, an offender who is sentenced for a sexually oriented offense on or after July 1, 1997, and to whom division (A)(1)(a) of this section does not apply;

(c) If the sexually oriented offense was committed prior to July 1, 1997, and neither division (A)(1)(a) nor division (A)(1)(b) of this section applies, an offender who, immediately prior to July 1, 1997, was a habitual sex offender who was required to register under Chapter 2950. of the Revised Code.

(2) Each child who is adjudicated a delinquent child for committing a sexually oriented offense that is not a registration-exempt sexually oriented offense and who is classified a juvenile offender registrant based on that adjudication shall register personally with the sheriff of the county within five days of the delinquent child's coming into a county in which the delinquent child resides or temporarily is domiciled for more than five days. If the delinquent child is committed for the sexually oriented offense that is not a registration-exempt sexually oriented offense to the department of youth services or to a secure facility that is not operated by the department, this duty begins when the delinquent child is discharged or released in any manner from custody in a department of youth services secure facility or from the secure facility that is not operated by the department, if pursuant to the discharge or release the delinquent child is not committed to any other secure facility of the department or any other secure facility. The delinquent child does not have a duty to register under this division while the child is in a department of youth services secure facility or in a secure facility that is not operated by the department.

(3) If divisions (A)(1) and (2) of this section do not apply, each following type of offender and each following type of delinquent child shall register personally with the sheriff of the county within five days of the offender's or delinquent child's coming into a county in which the offender or delinquent child resides or temporarily is domiciled for more than five days, and each following type of offender shall register personally with the sheriff of the county immediately upon coming into a county in which the offender attends a school or institution of higher education on a full-time or part-time basis regardless of whether the offender resides or has a temporary domicile in this state or another state, shall register personally with the sheriff of the county in which the offender is employed if the offender resides or has a temporary domicile in this state and has been employed in that county for more than fourteen days or for an aggregate period of thirty days or more in that calendar year, and shall register personally with the sheriff of the county in which the offender then is employed if the offender does not reside or have a temporary domicile in this state and has been employed at any location or locations in this state for more than fourteen days or for an aggregate period of thirty or more days in that calendar year:

(a) Regardless of when the sexually oriented offense was committed, a person who is convicted, pleads guilty, or adjudicated a delinquent child in a court in another state, in a federal court, military court, or Indian tribal court, or in a court in any nation other than the United States for committing a sexually oriented offense that is not a registration-exempt sexually oriented offense, if, on or after July 1, 1997, for offenders, or January 1, 2002, for delinquent children, the offender or delinquent child moves to and resides in this state or temporarily is domiciled in this state for more than five days, the offender enters this state to attend any school or institution of higher education on a full-time or part-time basis, or the offender is employed in this state for more than fourteen days or for an aggregate period of thirty or more days in any calendar year, and if, at the time the offender or delinquent child moves to and resides in this state or temporarily is domiciled in this state for more than five days, the offender enters this state to attend the school or institution of higher education, or the offender is employed in this state for more than the specified period of time, the offender or delinquent child has a duty to register as a sex offender or child-victim offender under the law of that other jurisdiction as a result of the conviction, guilty plea, or adjudication.

(b) Regardless of when the sexually oriented offense was committed, a person who is convicted of, pleads guilty to, or is adjudicated a delinquent child in a court in another state, in a federal court, military court, or Indian tribal court, or in a court in any nation other than the United States for committing a sexually oriented offense that is not a registration-exempt sexually oriented offense, if, on or after July 1, 1997, for offenders, or January 1, 2002, for delinquent children, the offender or delinquent child is released from imprisonment, confinement, or detention imposed for that offense, and if, on or after July 1, 1997, for offenders, or January 1, 2002, for delinquent children, the offender or delinquent child moves to and resides in this state or temporarily is domiciled in this state for more than five days, the offender enters this state to attend any school or institution of higher education on a full-time or part-time basis, or the offender is employed in this state for more than fourteen days or for an aggregate period of thirty or more days in any calendar year. The duty to register as described in this division applies to an offender regardless of whether the offender, at the time of moving to and residing in this state or temporarily being domiciled in this state for more than five days, at the time of entering into this state to attend the school or institution of higher education, or at the time of being employed in this state for the specified period of time, has a duty to register as a sex offender or child-victim offender under the law of the jurisdiction in which the conviction or guilty plea occurred. The duty to register as described in this division applies to a delinquent child only if the delinquent child, at the time of moving to and residing in this state or temporarily being domiciled in this state for more than five days, has a duty to register as a sex offender or child-victim offender under the law of the jurisdiction in which the delinquent child adjudication occurred or if, had the delinquent child adjudication occurred in this state, the adjudicating juvenile court judge would have been required to issue an order classifying the delinquent child as a juvenile offender registrant pursuant to section 2152.82 or division (A) of section 2152.83 of the Revised Code.

(4) If neither division (A)(1), (2), nor (3) of this section applies and if the offender is adjudicated a sexual predator under division (C) of section 2950. 09 of the Revised Code, the offender shall register within five days of the adjudication with the sheriff of the county in which the offender resides or temporarily is domiciled for more than five days, shall register with the sheriff of any county in which the offender subsequently resides or temporarily is domiciled for more than five days within five days of coming into that county, shall register within five days of the adjudication with the sheriff of the county in which the offender attends any school or institution of higher education on a full-time or part-time basis or in which the offender is employed if the offender has been employed in that county for more than fourteen days or for an aggregate period of thirty or more days in that calendar year regardless of whether the offender resides or has temporary domicile in this state or another state, and shall register within five days of the adjudication with the sheriff or other appropriate person of any state other than this state in which the offender attends a school or institution of higher education on a full-time or part-time basis or in which the offender then is employed if the offender has been employed in that state for more than fourteen days or for an aggregate period of thirty or more days in any calendar year regardless of whether the offender resides or has temporary domicile in this state, the other state, or a different state.

(5) A person who is adjudicated a delinquent child for committing a sexually oriented offense that is not a registration-exempt sexually oriented offense is not required to register under division (A)(2) of this section unless the delinquent child committed the offense on or after January 1, 2002, is classified a juvenile offender registrant by a juvenile court judge pursuant to an order issued under section 2152.82, 2152.83, 2152. 84, or 2152.85 of the Revised Code based on that adjudication, and has a duty to register pursuant to division (A)(2) of this section.

(6) A person who has been convicted of, is convicted of, has pleaded guilty to, or pleads guilty to a sexually oriented offense that is a registration-exempt sexually oriented offense, and a person who is or has been adjudicated a delinquent child for committing a sexually oriented offense that is a registration-exempt sexually oriented offense, does not have any duty to register under this section based on that conviction, guilty plea, or adjudication. The exemption of an offender or delinquent child from registration under this division for a conviction of, plea of guilty to, or delinquent child adjudication for a registration-exempt sexually oriented offense does not limit, affect, or supersede any duties imposed upon the offender or delinquent child under this chapter or sections 2152.82 to 2152.85 of the Revised Code for a conviction of, plea of guilty to, or delinquent child adjudication for any other sexually oriented offense or any child-victim oriented offense.

(B) An offender or delinquent child who is required by division (A) of this section to register in this state personally shall obtain from the sheriff or from a designee of the sheriff a registration form that conforms to division (C) of this section, shall complete and sign the form, and shall return the completed form together with the offender's or delinquent child's photograph to the sheriff or the designee. The sheriff or designee shall sign the form and indicate on the form the date on which it is so returned. The registration required under this division is complete when the offender or delinquent child returns the form, containing the requisite information, photograph, signatures, and date, to the sheriff or designee.

(C) The registration form to be used under divisions (A) and (B) of this section shall include the photograph of the offender or delinquent child who is registering and shall contain all of the following:

(1) Regarding an offender or delinquent child who is registering under a duty imposed under division (A)(1), (2), (3), or (4) of this section as a result of the offender or delinquent child residing in this state or temporarily being domiciled in this state for more than five days, the current residence address of the offender or delinquent child who is registering, the name and address of the offender's or delinquent child's employer if the offender or delinquent child is employed at the time of registration or if the offender or delinquent child knows at the time of registration that the offender or delinquent child will be commencing employment with that employer subsequent to registration, the name and address of the offender's school or institution of higher education if the offender attends one at the time of registration or if the offender knows at the time of registration that the offender will be commencing attendance at that school or institution subsequent to registration, and any other information required by the bureau of criminal identification and investigation.

(2) Regarding an offender who is registering under a duty imposed under division (A)(1), (3), or (4) of this section as a result of the offender attending a school or institution of higher education in this state on a full-time or part-time basis or being employed in this state or in a particular county in this state, whichever is applicable, for more than fourteen days or for an aggregate of thirty or more days in any calendar year, the current address of the school, institution of higher education, or place of employment of the offender who is registering and any other information required by the bureau of criminal identification and investigation.

(3) Regarding an offender or delinquent child who is registering under a duty imposed under division (A)(1), (2), (3), or (4) of this section for any reason, if the offender has been adjudicated a sexual predator relative to the sexually oriented offense in question, if the delinquent child has been adjudicated a sexual predator relative to the sexually oriented offense in question and the court has not subsequently determined pursuant to section 2152.84 or 2152.85 of the Revised Code that the delinquent child no longer is a sexual predator, if the judge determined pursuant to division (C) of section 2950.09 or pursuant to section 2152.82, 2152.83, 2152.84, or 2152.85 of the Revised Code that the offender or delinquent child is a habitual sex offender and the determination has not been removed pursuant to section 2152. 84 or 2152.85 of the Revised Code, or if the offender has the duty to register as a result of the conviction of or plea of guilty to an aggravated sexually oriented offense, the offender or delinquent child also shall include on the signed, written registration form all of the following information:

(a) A specific declaration that the person has been adjudicated a sexual predator, has been determined to be a habitual sex offender, or was convicted of or pleaded guilty to an aggravated sexually oriented offense, whichever is applicable;

(b) If the offender or delinquent child has been adjudicated a sexual predator, the identification license plate number of each motor vehicle the offender or delinquent child owns and of each motor vehicle registered in the offender's or delinquent child's name.

(D) After an offender or delinquent child registers with a sheriff pursuant to this section, the sheriff shall forward the signed, written registration form and photograph to the bureau of criminal identification and investigation in accordance with the forwarding procedures adopted pursuant to section 2950.13 of the Revised Code. If an offender registers a school, institution of higher education, or place of employment address, or provides a school or institution of higher education address under division (C)(1) of this section, the sheriff also shall provide notice to the law enforcement agency with jurisdiction over the premises of the school, institution of higher education, or place of employment of the offender's name and that the offender has registered that address as a place at which the offender attends school or an institution of higher education or at which the offender is employed. The bureau shall include the information and materials forwarded to it under this division in the state registry of sex offenders and child victim offenders established and maintained under section 2950.13 of the Revised Code.

(E) No person who is required to register pursuant to divisions (A) and (B) of this section, and no person who is required to send a notice of intent to reside pursuant to division (G) of this section, shall fail to register or send the notice of intent as required in accordance with those divisions or that division.

(F) An offender or delinquent child who is required to register pursuant to divisions (A) and (B) of this section shall register pursuant to this section for the period of time specified in section 2950.07 of the Revised Code.

(G) If an offender or delinquent child who is required by division (A) of this section to register is adjudicated a sexual predator or a habitual sexual offender subject to community notification under division (C)(2) or (E) of section 2950.09 of the Revised Code, or if an offender who is required by division (A) of this section to register has that duty as a result of a conviction of or plea of guilty to an aggravated sexually oriented offense, the offender or delinquent child also shall send the sheriff of the county in which the offender or delinquent child intends to reside written notice of the offender's or delinquent child's intent to reside in the county. The offender or delinquent child shall send the notice of intent to reside at least twenty days prior to the date the offender or delinquent child begins to reside in the county. The notice of intent to reside shall contain the following information:

(1) The offender's or delinquent child's name;

(2) The address or addresses at which the offender or delinquent child intends to reside;

(3) The sexually oriented offense of which the offender was convicted, to which the offender pleaded guilty, or for which the child was adjudicated a delinquent child;

(4) A statement that the offender has been adjudicated a sexual predator, a statement that the delinquent child has been adjudicated a sexual predator and that, as of the date of the notice, the court has not entered a determination that the delinquent child no longer is a sexual predator, a statement that the sentencing or reviewing judge has determined that the offender or delinquent child is a habitual sex offender and that, as of the date of the notice, the determination has not been removed pursuant to section 2152.84 or 2152.85 of the Revised Code, or a statement that the offender was convicted of or pleaded guilty to an aggravated sexually oriented offense.

(H) If, immediately prior to July 31, 2003, an offender or delinquent child who was convicted of, pleaded guilty to, or adjudicated a delinquent child for committing a sexually oriented offense was required by division (A) of this section to register and if, on or after July 31, 2003, that offense no longer is a sexually oriented offense but instead is designated a child-victim oriented offense, division (A)(1)(c) or (2)(b) of section 2950.041 of the Revised Code applies regarding the offender or delinquent child and the duty to register that is imposed pursuant to that division shall be considered, for purposes of section 2950.07 of the Revised Code and for all other purposes, to be a continuation of the duty imposed upon the offender prior to July 31, 2003, under this section.

(2004 H 473, eff. 4–29–05; 2003 S 5, eff. 7–31–03; 2002 H 485, eff. 6–13–02; 2002 S 175, eff. 5–7–02; 2002 H 393, eff. 7–5–02; 2001 S 3, eff. 1–1–02; 2000 H 502, eff. 3–15–01; 1998 H 565, eff. 3–30–99; 1996 H 180, eff. 7–1–97)

Note: See also preceding version of this section, in effect until 4–29–05.

2950.041 Child-victim oriented offenses; duty of registration of offender or delinquent child

Note: See also following version of this section, eff. 4–29–05.

(A)(1) Each of the following types of offender who is convicted of or pleads guilty to, or has been convicted of or pleaded guilty to, a child-victim oriented offense shall register personally with the sheriff of the county within five days of the offender's coming into a county in which the offender resides or temporarily is domiciled for more than five days, shall register personally with the sheriff of the county immediately upon coming into a county in which the offender attends a school or institution of higher education on a full-time or part-time basis regardless of whether the offender resides or has a temporary domicile in this state or another state, shall register personally with the sheriff of the county in which the offender is employed if the offender resides or has a temporary domicile in this state and has been employed in that county for more than fourteen days or for an aggregate period of thirty or more days in that calendar year, shall register personally with the sheriff of the county in which the offender then is employed if the offender does not reside or have a temporary domicile in this state and has been employed at any location or locations in this state for more than fourteen days or for an aggregate period of thirty or more days in that calendar year, and shall register personally with the sheriff or other appropriate person of the other state immediately upon entering into any state other than this state in which the offender attends a school or institution of higher education on a full-time or part-time basis or upon being employed in any state other than this state for more than fourteen days or for an aggregate period of thirty or more days in that calendar year regardless of whether the offender resides or has a temporary domicile in this state, the other state, or a different state:

(a) Regardless of when the child-victim oriented offense was committed, an offender who is sentenced for the child-victim oriented offense to a prison term, a term of imprisonment, or any other type of confinement and, on or after the effective date of this section, is released in any manner from the prison term, term of imprisonment, or confinement;

(b) Regardless of when the child-victim oriented offense was committed, an offender who is sentenced for a child-victim oriented offense on or after the effective date of this section, and to whom division (A)(1)(a) of this section does not apply;

(c) If the child-victim oriented offense was committed prior to the effective date of this section, if the offense was considered prior to that date to be a sexually oriented offense, and if neither division (A)(1)(a) nor division (A)(1)(b) of this section applies, an offender who, immediately prior to the effective date of this section, was required to register as a result of conviction of or plea of guilty to the commission of that offense under section 2950.04 of the Revised Code. For any offender who is described in this division, the duty imposed under this division shall be considered, for purposes of section 2950.07 of the Revised Code and for all other purposes, to be a continuation of the duty imposed upon the offender prior to the effective date of this section under section 2950.04 of the Revised Code.

(2) Each of the following types of delinquent children shall register personally with the sheriff of the county within five days of the delinquent child's coming into a county in which the delinquent child resides or temporarily is domiciled for more than five days:

(a) Regardless of when the child-victim oriented offense was committed, a child who on or after the effective date of this section is adjudicated a delinquent child for committing a child-victim oriented offense and who is classified a juvenile offender registrant based on that adjudication. If the delinquent child is committed for the child-victim oriented offense to the department of youth services or to a secure facility that is not operated by the department, this duty begins when the delinquent child is discharged or released in any manner from custody in a department of youth services secure facility or from the secure facility that is not operated by the department, if pursuant to the discharge or release the delinquent child is not committed to any other secure facility of the department or any other secure facility. The delinquent child does not have a duty to register under this division while the child is in a department of youth services secure facility or in a secure facility that is not operated by the department.

(b) If the child-victim oriented offense was committed prior to the effective date of this section, if the offense was considered prior to that date to be a sexually oriented offense, and if division (A)(2)(a) of this section does not apply, a delinquent child who, immediately prior to the effective date of this section, was classified a juvenile sex offender registrant and required to register as a result of a delinquent child adjudication for the commission of that offense under section 2950.04 of the Revised Code. For any delinquent child who is described in this division, the duty imposed under this division shall be considered, for purposes of section 2950.07 of the Revised Code and for all other purposes, to be a continuation of the duty imposed upon the delinquent child prior to the effective date of this section under section 2950.04 of the Revised Code. If the delinquent child is committed for the child-victim oriented offense to the department of youth services or to a secure facility that is not operated by the department, the provisions of division (A)(2)(a) of this section regarding the beginning, and tolling, of a duty imposed under that division also apply regarding the beginning, and tolling, of the duty imposed under this division.

(3) If divisions (A)(1) and (2) of this section do not apply, each following type of offender and each following type of delinquent child shall register personally with the sheriff of the county within five days of the offender's or delinquent child's coming into a county in which the offender or delinquent child resides or temporarily is domiciled for more than five days, and each following type of offender shall register personally with the sheriff of the county immediately upon coming into a county in which the offender attends a school or institution of higher education on a full-time or part-time basis regardless of whether the offender resides or has a temporary domicile in this state or another state, shall register personally with the sheriff of the county in which the offender is employed if the offender resides or has a temporary domicile in this state and has been employed in that county for more than fourteen days or for an aggregate period of thirty or more days in that calendar year, and shall register personally with the sheriff of the county in which the offender then is employed if the offender does not reside or have a temporary domicile in this state and has been employed at any location or locations in this state for more than fourteen days or for an aggregate period of thirty or more days in that calendar year:

(a) Regardless of when the child-victim oriented offense was committed, a person who is convicted, pleads guilty, or adjudicated a delinquent child in a court in another state, in a federal court, military court, or Indian tribal court, or in a court in any nation other than the United States for committing a child-victim oriented offense, if, on or after the effective date of this section, the offender or delinquent child moves to and resides in this state or temporarily is domiciled in this state for more than five days, the offender enters this state to attend any school or institution of higher education on a full-time or part-time basis, or the offender is employed in this state for more than fourteen days or for an aggregate period of thirty or more days in any calendar year, and if, at the time the offender or delinquent child moves to and resides in this state or temporarily is domiciled in this state for more than five days, the offender enters this state to attend the school or institution of higher education, or the offender is employed in this state for more than the specified period of time, the offender or delinquent child has a duty to register as a child-victim offender or sex offender under the law of that other jurisdiction as a result of the conviction, guilty plea, or adjudication.

(b) Regardless of when the child-victim oriented offense was committed, a person who is convicted, pleads guilty, or adjudicated a delinquent child in a court in another state, in a federal court, military court, or Indian tribal court, or in a court in any nation other than the United States for committing a child-victim oriented offense, if, on or after the effective date of this section, the offender or delinquent child is released from imprisonment, confinement, or detention imposed for that offense, and if, on or after the effective date of this section, the offender or delinquent child moves to and resides in this state or temporarily is domiciled in this state for more than five days, the offender enters this state to attend any school or institution of higher education on a full-time or part-time basis, or the offender is employed in this state for more than fourteen days or for an aggregate period of thirty or more days in any calendar year. The duty to register as described in this division applies to an offender regardless of whether the offender, at the time of moving to and residing in this state or temporarily being domiciled in this state for more than five days, at the time of entering into this state to attend the school or institution of higher education, or at the time of being employed in this state for more than the specified period of time, has a duty to register as a child-victim offender or sex offender under the law of the jurisdiction in which the conviction or guilty plea occurred. The duty to register as described in this division applies to a delinquent child only if the delinquent child, at the time of moving to and residing in this state or temporarily being domiciled in this state for more than five days, has a duty to register as a child-victim offender or sex offender under the law of the jurisdiction in which the delinquent child adjudication occurred or if, had the delinquent child adjudication occurred in this state, the adjudicating juvenile court judge would have been required to issue an order classifying the delinquent child as a juvenile offender registrant pursuant to section 2152.82 or division (A) of section 2152.83 of the Revised Code.

(4) If division (A)(1)(a) of this section applies and if, subsequent to the offender's release, the offender is adjudicated a child-victim predator under division (C) of section 2950.09 of the Revised Code, the offender shall register within five days of the adjudication with the sheriff of the county in which the offender resides or temporarily is domiciled for more than five days, shall register with the sheriff of any county in which the offender subsequently resides or temporarily is domiciled for more than five days within five days of coming into that county, shall register within five days of the adjudication with the sheriff of the county in which the offender attends any school or institution of higher education on a full-time or part-time basis or in which the offender is employed if the offender has been employed in that county for more than fourteen days or for an aggregate period of thirty or more days in that calendar year regardless of whether the offender resides or has temporary domicile in this state or another state, and shall register within five days of the adjudication with the sheriff or other appropriate person of any state other than this state in which the offender attends a school or institution of higher education on a full-time or part-time basis or in which the offender then is employed if the offender has been employed in this state for more than fourteen days or for an aggregate period of thirty or more days in any calendar year regardless of whether the offender resides or has temporary domicile in this state, the other state, or a different state.

(5) A person who is adjudicated a delinquent child for committing a child-victim oriented offense is not required to register under division (A)(2) of this section unless the delinquent child committed the offense on or after the effective date of this section, is classified a juvenile offender registrant by a juvenile court judge pursuant to an order issued under section 2152.82, 2152.83, 2152.84, or 2152.85 of the Revised Code based on that adjudication, and has a duty to register pursuant to division (A)(2) of this section.

(B) An offender or delinquent child who is required by division (A) of this section to register in this state personally shall do so in the manner described in division (B) of section 2950.04 of the Revised Code, and the registration is complete as described in that division.

(C) The registration form to be used under divisions (A) and (B) of this section shall include the photograph of the offender or delinquent child who is registering and shall contain all of the following:

(1) Regarding an offender or delinquent child who is registering under a duty imposed under division (A)(1), (2), (3), or (4) of this section as a result of the offender or delinquent child residing in this state or temporarily being domiciled in this state for more than five days, all of the information described in division (C)(1) of section 2950.04 of the Revised Code;

(2) Regarding an offender who is registering under a duty imposed under division (A)(1), (3), or (4) of this section as a result of the offender attending a school or institution of higher education on a full-time or part-time basis or being employed in this state or in a particular county in this state, whichever is applicable, for more than fourteen days or for an aggregate of thirty or more days in any calendar year, all of the information described in division (C)(2) of section 2950.04 of the Revised Code;

(3) Regarding an offender or delinquent child who is registering under a duty imposed under division (A)(1), (2), (3), or (4) of this section, if the offender has been adjudicated a child-victim predator relative to the child-victim oriented offense in question, if the delinquent child has been adjudicated a child-victim predator relative to the child-victim oriented offense in question and the court has not subsequently determined pursuant to section 2152.84 or 2152.85 of the Revised Code that the delinquent child no longer is a child-victim predator, if the offender or delinquent child is automatically classified a habitual child-victim offender under division (E) of section 2950.091 of the Revised Code, or if the judge determined pursuant to division (C) or (E) of section 2950.091 or pursuant to section 2152.82, 2152.83, 2152.84, or 2152.85 of the Revised Code that the offender or delinquent child is a habitual child-victim offender and the determination has not been removed pursuant to section 2152.84 or 2152.85 of the Revised Code, the offender or delinquent child shall include on the signed, written registration form all of the information described in division (C)(3) of section 2950.04 of the Revised Code.

(D) Division (D) of section 2950.04 of the Revised Code applies when an offender or delinquent child registers with a sheriff pursuant to this section.

(E) No person who is required to register pursuant to divisions (A) and (B) of this section, and no person who is required to send a notice of intent to reside pursuant to division (G) of this section, shall fail to register or send the notice as required in accordance with those divisions or that division.

(F) An offender or delinquent child who is required to register pursuant to divisions (A) and (B) of this section shall register pursuant to this section for the period of time specified in section 2950.07 of the Revised Code.

(G) If an offender or delinquent child who is required by division (A) of this section to register is adjudicated a child-victim predator or a habitual child-victim offender subject to community notification under division (C)(2) or (E) of section 2950.09 of the Revised Code, the offender or delinquent child also shall send the sheriff of the county in which the offender or delinquent child intends to reside written notice of the offender's or delinquent child's intent to reside in the county. The offender or delinquent child shall send the notice of intent to reside at least twenty days prior to the date the offender or delinquent child begins to reside in the county. The notice of intent to reside shall contain all of the following information:

(1) The information specified in divisions (G)(1) and (2) of section 2950.04 of the Revised Code;

(2) The child-victim oriented offense of which the offender was convicted, to which the offender pleaded guilty, or for which the child was adjudicated a delinquent child;

(3) A statement that the offender has been adjudicated a child-victim predator, a statement that the delinquent child has been adjudicated a child-victim predator and that, as of the date of the notice, the court has not entered a determination that the delinquent child no longer is a child-victim predator, or a statement that the sentencing or reviewing judge has determined that the offender or delinquent child is a habitual child-victim offender and that, as of the date of the notice, the determination has not been removed pursuant to section 2152.84 or 2152.85 of the Revised Code.

(2003 S 5, eff. 7–31–03)

Note: See also following version of this section, eff. 4–29–05.

2950.041 Child-victim oriented offenses; duty of registration of offender or delinquent child (later effective date)

Note: See also preceding version of this section, in effect until 4–29–05.

(A)(1) Each of the following types of offender who is convicted of or pleads guilty to, or has been convicted of or pleaded guilty to, a child-victim oriented offense shall register personally with the sheriff of the county within five days of the offender's coming into a county in which the offender resides or temporarily is domiciled for more than five days, shall register personally with the sheriff of the county immediately upon coming into a county in which the offender attends a school or institution of higher education on a full-time or part-time basis regardless of whether the offender resides or has a temporary domicile in this state or another state, shall register personally with the sheriff of the county in which the offender is employed if the offender resides or has a temporary domicile in this state and has been employed in that county for more than fourteen days or for an aggregate period of thirty or more days in that calendar year, shall register personally with the sheriff of the county in which the offender then is employed if the offender does not reside or have a temporary domicile in this state and has been employed at any location or locations in this state for more than fourteen days or for an aggregate period of thirty or more days in that calendar year, and shall register personally with the sheriff or other appropriate person of the other state immediately upon entering into any state other than this state in which the offender attends a school or institution of higher education on a full-time or part-time basis or upon being employed in any state other than this state for more than fourteen days or for an aggregate period of thirty or more days in that calendar year regardless of whether the offender resides or has a temporary domicile in this state, the other state, or a different state:

(a) Regardless of when the child-victim oriented offense was committed, an offender who is sentenced for the child-victim oriented offense to a prison term, a term of imprisonment, or any other type of confinement and, on or after July 31, 2003, is released in any manner from the prison term, term of imprisonment, or confinement;

(b) Regardless of when the child-victim oriented offense was committed, an offender who is sentenced for a child-victim oriented offense on or after July 31, 2003, and to whom division (A)(1)(a) of this section does not apply;

(c) If the child-victim oriented offense was committed prior to July 31, 2003, if the offense was considered prior to that date to be a sexually oriented offense, and if neither division (A)(1)(a) nor division (A)(1)(b) of this section applies, an offender who, immediately prior to July 31, 2003, was required to register as a result of conviction of or plea of guilty to the commission of that offense under section 2950.04 of the Revised Code. For any offender who is described in this division, the duty imposed under this division shall be considered, for purposes of section 2950.07

of the Revised Code and for all other purposes, to be a continuation of the duty imposed upon the offender prior to July 31, 2003, under section 2950.04 of the Revised Code.

(2) Each of the following types of delinquent children shall register personally with the sheriff of the county within five days of the delinquent child's coming into a county in which the delinquent child resides or temporarily is domiciled for more than five days:

(a) Regardless of when the child-victim oriented offense was committed, a child who on or after July 31, 2003, is adjudicated a delinquent child for committing a child-victim oriented offense and who is classified a juvenile offender registrant based on that adjudication. If the delinquent child is committed for the child-victim oriented offense to the department of youth services or to a secure facility that is not operated by the department, this duty begins when the delinquent child is discharged or released in any manner from custody in a department of youth services secure facility or from the secure facility that is not operated by the department, if pursuant to the discharge or release the delinquent child is not committed to any other secure facility of the department or any other secure facility. The delinquent child does not have a duty to register under this division while the child is in a department of youth services secure facility or in a secure facility that is not operated by the department.

(b) If the child-victim oriented offense was committed prior to July 31, 2003, if the offense was considered prior to that date to be a sexually oriented offense, and if division (A)(2)(a) of this section does not apply, a delinquent child who, immediately prior to July 31, 2003, was classified a juvenile sex offender registrant and required to register as a result of a delinquent child adjudication for the commission of that offense under section 2950.04 of the Revised Code. For any delinquent child who is described in this division, the duty imposed under this division shall be considered, for purposes of section 2950.07 of the Revised Code and for all other purposes, to be a continuation of the duty imposed upon the delinquent child prior to July 31, 2003, under section 2950.04 of the Revised Code. If the delinquent child is committed for the child-victim oriented offense to the department of youth services or to a secure facility that is not operated by the department, the provisions of division (A)(2)(a) of this section regarding the beginning, and tolling, of a duty imposed under that division also apply regarding the beginning, and tolling, of the duty imposed under this division.

(3) If divisions (A)(1) and (2) of this section do not apply, each following type of offender and each following type of delinquent child shall register personally with the sheriff of the county within five days of the offender's or delinquent child's coming into a county in which the offender or delinquent child resides or temporarily is domiciled for more than five days, and each following type of offender shall register personally with the sheriff of the county immediately upon coming into a county in which the offender attends a school or institution of higher education on a full-time or part-time basis regardless of whether the offender resides or has a temporary domicile in this state or another state, shall register personally with the sheriff of the county in which the offender is employed if the offender resides or has a temporary domicile in this state and has been employed in that county for more than fourteen days or for an aggregate period of thirty or more days in that calendar year, and shall register personally with the sheriff of the county in which the offender then is employed if the offender does not reside or have a temporary domicile in this state and has been employed at any location or locations in this state for more than fourteen days or for an aggregate period of thirty or more days in that calendar year:

(a) Regardless of when the child-victim oriented offense was committed, a person who is convicted, pleads guilty, or adjudicated a delinquent child in a court in another state, in a federal court, military court, or Indian tribal court, or in a court in any nation other than the United States for committing a child-victim oriented offense, if, on or after July 31, 2003, the offender or delinquent child moves to and resides in this state or temporarily is domiciled in this state for more than five days, the offender enters this state to attend any school or institution of higher education on a full-time or part-time basis, or the offender is employed in this state for more than fourteen days or for an aggregate period of thirty or more days in any calendar year, and if, at the time the offender or delinquent child moves to and resides in this state or temporarily is domiciled in this state for more than five days, the offender enters this state to attend the school or institution of higher education, or the offender is employed in this state for more than the specified period of time, the offender or delinquent child has a duty to register as a child-victim offender or sex offender under the law of that other jurisdiction as a result of the conviction, guilty plea, or adjudication.

(b) Regardless of when the child-victim oriented offense was committed, a person who is convicted, pleads guilty, or adjudicated a delinquent child in a court in another state, in a federal court, military court, or Indian tribal court, or in a court in any nation other than the United States for committing a child-victim oriented offense, if, on or after July 31, 2003, the offender or delinquent child is released from imprisonment, confinement, or detention imposed for that offense, and if, on or after July 31, 2003, the offender or delinquent child moves to and resides in this state or temporarily is domiciled in this state for more than five days, the offender enters this state to attend any school or institution of higher education on a full-time or part-time basis, or the offender is employed in this state for more than fourteen days or for an aggregate period of thirty or more days in any calendar year. The duty to register as described in this division applies to an offender regardless of whether the offender, at the time of moving to and residing in this state or temporarily being domiciled in this state for more than five days, at the time of entering into this state to attend the school or institution of higher education, or at the time of being employed in this state for more than the specified period of time, has a duty to register as a child-victim offender or sex offender under the law of the jurisdiction in which the conviction or guilty plea occurred. The duty to register as described in this division applies to a delinquent child only if the delinquent child, at the time of moving to and residing in this state or temporarily being domiciled in this state for more than five days, has a duty to register as a child-victim offender or sex offender under the law of the jurisdiction in which the delinquent child adjudication occurred or if, had the delinquent child adjudication occurred in this state, the adjudicating juvenile court judge would have been required to issue an order classifying the delinquent child as a juvenile offender registrant pursuant to section 2152.82 or division (A) of section 2152.83 of the Revised Code.

(4) If neither division (A)(1), (2), nor (3) of this section applies and if the offender is adjudicated a child-victim predator under division (C) of section 2950.091 of the Revised Code, the offender shall register within five days of the adjudication with the sheriff of the county in which the offender resides or temporarily is domiciled for more than five days, shall register with the sheriff of any county in which the offender subsequently resides or temporarily is domiciled for more than five days within five days of coming into that county, shall register within five days of the adjudication with the sheriff of the county in which the offender attends any school or institution of higher education on a full-time or part-time basis or in which the offender is employed if the offender has been employed in that county for more than fourteen days or for an aggregate period of thirty or more days in that calendar year regardless of whether the offender resides or has temporary domicile in this state or another state, and shall register within five days of the adjudication with the sheriff or other appropriate person of any state other than this state in which the offender attends a school or institution of higher education on a full-time or part-time basis or in which the offender then is employed if the offender has been employed in

this state for more than fourteen days or for an aggregate period of thirty or more days in any calendar year regardless of whether the offender resides or has temporary domicile in this state, the other state, or a different state.

(5) A person who is adjudicated a delinquent child for committing a child-victim oriented offense is not required to register under division (A)(2) of this section unless the delinquent child committed the offense on or after July 31, 2003, is classified a juvenile offender registrant by a juvenile court judge pursuant to an order issued under section 2152.82, 2152.83, 2152.84, or 2152.85 of the Revised Code based on that adjudication, and has a duty to register pursuant to division (A)(2) of this section.

(B) An offender or delinquent child who is required by division (A) of this section to register in this state personally shall do so in the manner described in division (B) of section 2950.04 of the Revised Code, and the registration is complete as described in that division.

(C) The registration form to be used under divisions (A) and (B) of this section shall include the photograph of the offender or delinquent child who is registering and shall contain all of the following:

(1) Regarding an offender or delinquent child who is registering under a duty imposed under division (A)(1), (2), (3), or (4) of this section as a result of the offender or delinquent child residing in this state or temporarily being domiciled in this state for more than five days, all of the information described in division (C)(1) of section 2950.04 of the Revised Code;

(2) Regarding an offender who is registering under a duty imposed under division (A)(1), (3), or (4) of this section as a result of the offender attending a school or institution of higher education on a full-time or part-time basis or being employed in this state or in a particular county in this state, whichever is applicable, for more than fourteen days or for an aggregate of thirty or more days in any calendar year, all of the information described in division (C)(2) of section 2950.04 of the Revised Code;

(3) Regarding an offender or delinquent child who is registering under a duty imposed under division (A)(1), (2), (3), or (4) of this section, if the offender has been adjudicated a child-victim predator relative to the child-victim oriented offense in question, if the delinquent child has been adjudicated a child-victim predator relative to the child-victim oriented offense in question and the court has not subsequently determined pursuant to section 2152.84 or 2152.85 of the Revised Code that the delinquent child no longer is a child-victim predator, if the offender or delinquent child is automatically classified a habitual child-victim offender under division (E) of section 2950.091 of the Revised Code, or if the judge determined pursuant to division (C) or (E) of section 2950.091 or pursuant to section 2152.82, 2152.83, 2152.84, or 2152.85 of the Revised Code that the offender or delinquent child is a habitual child-victim offender and the determination has not been removed pursuant to section 2152.84 or 2152.85 of the Revised Code, the offender or delinquent child shall include on the signed, written registration form all of the information described in division (C)(3) of section 2950.04 of the Revised Code.

(D) Division (D) of section 2950.04 of the Revised Code applies when an offender or delinquent child registers with a sheriff pursuant to this section.

(E) No person who is required to register pursuant to divisions (A) and (B) of this section, and no person who is required to send a notice of intent to reside pursuant to division (G) of this section, shall fail to register or send the notice as required in accordance with those divisions or that division.

(F) An offender or delinquent child who is required to register pursuant to divisions (A) and (B) of this section shall register pursuant to this section for the period of time specified in section 2950.07 of the Revised Code.

(G) If an offender or delinquent child who is required by division (A) of this section to register is adjudicated a child-victim predator or a habitual child-victim offender subject to community notification under division (C)(2) or (E) of section 2950.091 of the Revised Code, the offender or delinquent child also shall send the sheriff of the county in which the offender or delinquent child intends to reside written notice of the offender's or delinquent child's intent to reside in the county. The offender or delinquent child shall send the notice of intent to reside at least twenty days prior to the date the offender or delinquent child begins to reside in the county. The notice of intent to reside shall contain all of the following information:

(1) The information specified in divisions (G)(1) and (2) of section 2950. 04 of the Revised Code;

(2) The child-victim oriented offense of which the offender was convicted, to which the offender pleaded guilty, or for which the child was adjudicated a delinquent child;

(3) A statement that the offender has been adjudicated a child-victim predator, a statement that the delinquent child has been adjudicated a child-victim predator and that, as of the date of the notice, the court has not entered a determination that the delinquent child no longer is a child-victim predator, or a statement that the sentencing or reviewing judge has determined that the offender or delinquent child is a habitual child-victim offender and that, as of the date of the notice, the determination has not been removed pursuant to section 2152.84 or 2152.85 of the Revised Code.

(2004 H 473, eff. 4–29–05; 2003 S 5, eff. 7–31–03)

Note: See also preceding version of this section, in effect until 4–29–05.

2950.05 Notice of change of address of residence, school, or place of employment

Note: See also following version of this section, eff. 4–29–05.

(A) If an offender or delinquent child is required to register pursuant to section 2950.04 or 2950.041 of the Revised Code, the offender or delinquent child, at least twenty days prior to changing the offender's or delinquent child's residence address, or the offender, at least twenty days prior to changing the address of the offender's school or institution of higher education and not later than five days after changing the address of the offender's place of employment, during the period during which the offender or delinquent child is required to register, shall provide written notice of the residence, school, institution of higher education, or place of employment address change, as applicable, to the sheriff with whom the offender or delinquent child most recently registered the address under section 2950.04 or 2950.041 of the Revised Code or under division (B) of this section.

(B) If an offender is required to provide notice of a residence, school, institution of higher education, or place of employment address change under division (A) of this section, or a delinquent child is required to provide notice of a residence address change under that division, the offender or delinquent child, at least twenty days prior to changing the residence, school, or institution of higher education address and not later than five days after changing the place of employment address, as applicable, also shall register the new address in the manner described in divisions (B) and (C) of section 2950.04 or 2950.041 of the Revised Code, whichever is applicable, with the sheriff of the county in which the offender's or delinquent child's new address is located, subject to division (C) of this section.

(C) Divisions (A) and (B) of this section apply to a person who is required to register pursuant to section 2950.04 or 2950.041 of the Revised Code regardless of whether the new residence, school, institution of higher education, or place of employment address is in this state or in another state. If the new address is in another state, the person shall register with the appropriate law enforcement officials in that state in the manner required under the law of that state and within the earlier of the period of time required under the law of that state or at least seven days prior to changing the address.

(D)(1) Upon receiving from an offender or delinquent child pursuant to division (A) of this section notice of a change of the offender's residence, school, institution of higher education, or place of employment address or the delinquent child's residence address, a sheriff promptly shall forward the new address to the bureau of criminal identification and investigation in accordance with the forwarding procedures adopted pursuant to section 2950.13 of the Revised Code if the new address is in another state or, if the new address is located in another county in this state, to the sheriff of that county. The bureau shall include all information forwarded to it under this division in the state registry of sex offenders and child-victim offenders established and maintained under section 2950.13 of the Revised Code and shall forward notice of the offender's or delinquent child's new residence, school, institution of higher education, or place of employment address, as applicable, to the appropriate officials in the other state.

(2) When an offender registers a new residence, school, institution of higher education, or place of employment address or a delinquent child registers a new residence address pursuant to division (B) of this section, the sheriff with whom the offender or delinquent child registers and the bureau of criminal identification and investigation shall comply with division (D) of section 2950.04 or 2950.041 of the Revised Code, whichever is applicable.

(E)(1) No person who is required to notify a sheriff of a change of address pursuant to division (A) of this section shall fail to notify the appropriate sheriff in accordance with that division.

(2) No person who is required to register a new residence, school, institution of higher education, or place of employment address with a sheriff or with an official of another state pursuant to divisions (B) and (C) of this section shall fail to register with the appropriate sheriff or official of the other state in accordance with those divisions.

(F) An offender or delinquent child who is required to comply with divisions (A), (B), and (C) of this section shall do so for the period of time specified in section 2950.07 of the Revised Code.

(2003 S 5, eff. 7–31–03; 2002 S 175, eff. 5–7–02; 2001 S 3, eff. 1–1–02; 1996 H 180, eff. 7–1–97)

Note: See also following version of this section, eff. 4–29–05.

2950.05 Notice of change of address of residence, school, or place of employment; affirmative defense (later effective date)

Note: See also preceding version of this section, in effect until 4–29–05.

(A) If an offender or delinquent child is required to register pursuant to section 2950.04 or 2950.041 of the Revised Code, the offender or delinquent child, at least twenty days prior to changing the offender's or delinquent child's residence address, or the offender, at least twenty days prior to changing the address of the offender's school or institution of higher education and not later than five days after changing the address of the offender's place of employment, during the period during which the offender or delinquent child is required to register, shall provide written notice of the residence, school, institution of higher education, or place of employment address change, as applicable, to the sheriff with whom the offender or delinquent child most recently registered the address under section 2950.04 or 2950.041 of the Revised Code or under division (B) of this section. If a residence address change is not to a fixed address, the offender or delinquent child shall include in that notice a detailed description of the place or places at which the offender or delinquent child intends to stay and, not later than the end of the first business day immediately following the day on which the person obtains a fixed residence address, shall provide that sheriff written notice of that fixed residence address. If a person whose residence address change is not to a fixed address describes in a notice under this division the place or places at which the person intends to stay, for purposes of divisions (C) to (H) of this section, sections 2950.06 to 2950.13 of the Revised Code, and sections 311.171 and 2919.24 of the Revised Code, the place or places so described in the notice shall be considered the person's residence address and registered residence address, until the person provides the written notice of a fixed residence address as described in this division.

(B) If an offender is required to provide notice of a residence, school, institution of higher education, or place of employment address change under division (A) of this section, or a delinquent child is required to provide notice of a residence address change under that division, the offender or delinquent child, at least twenty days prior to changing the residence, school, or institution of higher education address and not later than five days after changing the place of employment address, as applicable, also shall register the new address in the manner described in divisions (B) and (C) of section 2950.04 or 2950.041 of the Revised Code, whichever is applicable, with the sheriff of the county in which the offender's or delinquent child's new address is located, subject to division (C) of this section. If a residence address change is not to a fixed address, the offender or delinquent child shall include in the registration a detailed description of the place or places at which the offender or delinquent child intends to stay and, not later than the end of the first business day immediately following the day on which the person obtains a fixed residence address, shall register with that sheriff that fixed residence address. If a person whose residence address change is not to a fixed address describes in a registration under this division the place or places at which the person intends to stay, for purposes of divisions (C) to (H) of this section, sections 2950.06 to 2950.13 of the Revised Code, and sections 311.171 and 2919.24 of the Revised Code, the place or places so described in the registration shall be considered the person's residence address and registered residence address, until the person registers a fixed residence address as described in this division.

(C) Divisions (A) and (B) of this section apply to a person who is required to register pursuant to section 2950.04 or 2950.041 of the Revised Code regardless of whether the new residence, school, institution of higher education, or place of employment address is in this state or in another state. If the new address is in another state, the person shall register with the appropriate law enforcement officials in that state in the manner required under the law of that state and within the earlier of the period of time required under the law of that state or at least seven days prior to changing the address.

(D)(1) Upon receiving from an offender or delinquent child pursuant to division (A) of this section notice of a change of the offender's residence, school, institution of higher education, or place of employment address or the delinquent child's residence address, a sheriff promptly shall forward the new address to the bureau of criminal identification and investigation in accordance with the forwarding procedures adopted pursuant to section 2950.13 of the Revised Code if the new address is in another state or, if the new address is located in another county in this state, to the sheriff of that county. The bureau shall include all information forwarded to it under this division in the state registry of sex offenders and child-victim offenders established and maintained under section 2950.13 of the Revised Code and shall forward notice of the offender's or delinquent child's new residence, school, institution of higher education, or place of employment address, as applicable, to the appropriate officials in the other state.

(2) When an offender registers a new residence, school, institution of higher education, or place of employment address or a delinquent child registers a new residence address pursuant to division (B) of this section, the sheriff with whom the offender or delinquent child registers and the bureau of criminal identification and investigation shall comply with division (D) of section 2950.04 or 2950.041 of the Revised Code, whichever is applicable.

(E)(1) No person who is required to notify a sheriff of a change of address pursuant to division (A) of this section shall fail to notify the appropriate sheriff in accordance with that division.

(2) No person who is required to register a new residence, school, institution of higher education, or place of employment address with a sheriff or with an official of another state pursuant to divisions (B) and (C) of this section shall fail to register with the appropriate sheriff or official of the other state in accordance with those divisions.

(F)(1) It is an affirmative defense to a charge of a violation of division (E)(1) of this section that it was impossible for the person to provide the written notice to the sheriff as required under division (A) of this section because of a lack of knowledge, on the date specified for the provision of the written notice, of a residence, school, institution of higher education, or place of employment address change, and that the person provided notice of the residence, school, institution of higher education, or place of employment address change to the sheriff specified in division (A) of this section as soon as possible, but not later than the end of the first business day, after learning of the address change by doing either of the following:

(a) The person provided notice of the address change to the sheriff specified in division (A) of this section by telephone immediately upon learning of the address change or, if the person did not have reasonable access to a telephone at that time, as soon as possible, but not later than the end of the first business day, after learning of the address change and having reasonable access to a telephone, and the person, as soon as possible, but not later than the end of the first business day, after providing notice of the address change to the sheriff by telephone, provided written notice of the address change to that sheriff.

(b) The person, as soon as possible, but not later than the end of the first business day, after learning of the address change, provided written notice of the address change to the sheriff specified in division (A) of this section.

(2) It is an affirmative defense to a charge of a violation of division (E)(2) of this section that it was impossible for the person to register the new address with the sheriff or the official of the other state as required under division (B) or (C) of this section because of a lack of knowledge, on the date specified for the registration of the new address, of a residence, school, institution of higher education, or place of employment address change, and that the person registered the new residence, school, institution of higher education, or place of employment address with the sheriff or the official of the other state specified in division (B) or (C) of this section as soon as possible, but not later than the end of the first business day, after learning of the address change by doing either of the following:

(a) The person provided notice of the new address to the sheriff or official specified in division (B) or (C) of this section by telephone immediately upon learning of the new address or, if the person did not have reasonable access to a telephone at that time, as soon as possible, but not later than the end of the first business day, after learning of the new address and having reasonable access to a telephone, and the person, as soon as possible, but not later than the end of the first business day, after providing notice of the new address to the sheriff or official by telephone, registered the new address with that sheriff or official in accordance with division (B) or (C) of this section.

(b) The person, as soon as possible, but not later than the end of the first business day, after learning of the new address, registered the new address with the sheriff or official specified in division (B) or (C) of this section, in accordance with that division.

(G) An offender or delinquent child who is required to comply with divisions (A), (B), and (C) of this section shall do so for the period of time specified in section 2950.07 of the Revised Code.

(H) As used in this section, and in all other sections of the Revised Code that refer to the duties imposed on an offender or delinquent child under this section relative to a change in the offender's or delinquent child's residence, school, institution of higher education, or place of employment address, "change in address" includes any circumstance in which the old address for the person in question no longer is accurate, regardless of whether the person in question has a new address.

(2004 H 473, eff. 4–29–05; 2003 S 5, eff. 7–31–03; 2002 S 175, eff. 5–7–02; 2001 S 3, eff. 1–1–02; 1996 H 180, eff. 7–1–97)

Note: See also preceding version of this section, in effect until 4–29–05.

2950.06 Verification of current address of residence, school, or place of employment

(A) An offender or delinquent child who is required to register a residence address pursuant to section 2950.04 or 2950.041 of the Revised Code shall periodically verify the offender's or delinquent child's current residence address, and an offender who is required to register a school, institution of higher education, or place of employment address pursuant to either of those sections shall periodically verify the address of the offender's current school, institution of higher education, or place of employment, in accordance with this section. The frequency of verification shall be determined in accordance with division (B) of this section, and the manner of verification shall be determined in accordance with division (C) of this section.

(B) The frequency with which an offender or delinquent child must verify the offender's or delinquent child's current residence, school, institution of higher education, or place of employment address pursuant to division (A) of this section shall be determined as follows:

(1) Regardless of when the sexually oriented offense or child-victim oriented offense for which the offender or delinquent child is required to register was committed, the offender shall verify the offender's current residence address or current school, institution of higher education, or place of employment address, and the delinquent child shall verify the delinquent child's current residence address, in accordance with division (C) of this section every ninety days after the offender's or delinquent child's initial registration date during the period the offender or delinquent child is required to register if any of the following applies:

(a) The offender or delinquent child is required to register based on a sexually oriented offense, and either the offender has been adjudicated a sexual predator relative to the sexually oriented offense, the delinquent child has been adjudicated a sexual predator relative to the sexually oriented offense and the court has not subsequently entered a determination pursuant to section 2152.84 or 2152.85 of the Revised Code that the delinquent child no longer is a sexual predator, or the offender is required to register as a result of an aggravated sexually oriented offense.

(b) The offender or delinquent child is required to register based on a child-victim oriented offense, and either the offender has been adjudicated a child-victim predator relative to the child-victim oriented offense or the delinquent child has been adjudicated a child-victim predator relative to the child-victim oriented offense and the court has not subsequently entered a determination pursuant to section 2152.84 or 2152.85 of the Revised Code that the delinquent child no longer is a child-victim predator.

(2) In all circumstances not described in division (B)(1) of this section, the offender shall verify the offender's current residence address or current school, institution of higher education, or place of employment address, and the delinquent child shall verify the delinquent child's current residence address, in accordance with division (C) of this section on each anniversary of the offender's or delinquent child's initial registration date during the period the offender or delinquent child is required to register.

If, prior to the effective date of this amendment, an offender or delinquent child registered with a sheriff under a duty imposed under section 2950.04 of the Revised Code as a result of a conviction of, plea of guilty to, or adjudication as a delinquent child for committing a sexually oriented offense and if, on or after the effective date of this amendment, that offense no longer is a sexually oriented offense but instead is a child-victim oriented offense, the duty to register that is imposed on the offender or delinquent child pursuant to section 2950.041 of the Revised Code is a continuation of the duty imposed upon the offender prior to the effective date of this amendment under section 2950.04 of the Revised Code and, for purposes of divisions (B)(1) and (2) of this section, the offender's initial registration date related to that offense is the date on which the offender initially registered under section 2950.04 of the Revised Code.

(C)(1) An offender or delinquent child who is required to verify the offender's or delinquent child's current residence, school, institution of higher education, or place of employment address pursuant to division (A) of this section shall verify the address with the sheriff with whom the offender or delinquent child most recently registered the address by personally appearing before the sheriff or a designee of the sheriff, no earlier than ten days before the date on which the verification is required pursuant to division (B) of this section and no later than the date so required for verification, and completing and signing a copy of the verification form prescribed by the bureau of criminal identification and investigation. The sheriff or designee shall sign the completed form and indicate on the form the date on which it is so completed. The verification required under this division is complete when the offender or delinquent child personally appears before the sheriff or designee and completes and signs the form as described in this division.

(2) To facilitate the verification of an offender's or delinquent child's current residence, school, institution of higher education, or place of employment address, as applicable, under division (C)(1) of this section, the sheriff with whom the offender or delinquent child most recently registered the address may mail a nonforwardable verification form prescribed by the bureau of criminal identification and investigation to the offender's or delinquent child's last reported address and to the last reported address of the parents of the delinquent child, with a notice that conspicuously states that the offender or delinquent child must personally appear before the sheriff or a designee of the sheriff to complete the form and the date by which the form must be so completed. Regardless of whether a sheriff mails a form to an offender or delinquent child and that child's parents, each offender or delinquent child who is required to verify the offender's or delinquent child's current residence, school, institution of higher education, or place of employment address, as applicable, pursuant to division (A) of this section shall personally appear before the sheriff or a designee of the sheriff to verify the address in accordance with division (C)(1) of this section.

(D) The verification form to be used under division (C) of this section shall contain all of the following:

(1) Except as provided in division (D)(2) of this section, the current residence address of the offender or delinquent child, the name and address of the offender's or delinquent child's employer if the offender or delinquent child is employed at the time of verification or if the offender or delinquent child knows at the time of verification that the offender or delinquent child will be commencing employment with that employer subsequent to verification, the name and address of the offender's school or institution of higher education if the offender attends one at the time of verification or if the offender knows at the time of verification that the offender will be commencing attendance at that school or institution subsequent to verification, and any other information required by the bureau of criminal identification and investigation.

(2) Regarding an offender who is verifying a current school, institution of higher education, or place of employment address, the current address of the school, institution of higher education, or place of employment of the offender and any other information required by the bureau of criminal identification and investigation.

(E) Upon an offender's or delinquent child's personal appearance and completion of a verification form under division (C) of this section, a sheriff promptly shall forward a copy of the verification form to the bureau of criminal identification and investigation in accordance with the forwarding procedures adopted by the attorney general pursuant to section 2950.13 of the Revised Code. If an offender verifies a school, institution of higher education, or place of employment address, or provides a school or institution of higher education address under division (D)(1) of this section, the sheriff also shall provide notice to the law enforcement agency with jurisdiction over the premises of the school, institution of higher education, or place of employment of the offender's name and that the offender has verified or provided that address as a place at which the offender attends school or an institution of higher education or at which the offender is employed. The bureau shall include all information forwarded to it under this division in the state registry of sex offenders and child-victim offenders established and maintained under section 2950. 13 of the Revised Code.

(F) No person who is required to verify a current residence, school, institution of higher education, or place of employment address, as applicable, pursuant to divisions (A) to (C) of this section shall fail to verify a current residence, school, institution of higher education, or place of employment address, as applicable, in accordance with those divisions by the date required for the verification as set forth in division (B) of this section, provided that no person shall be prosecuted or subjected to a delinquent child proceeding for a violation of this division, and that no parent, guardian, or custodian of a delinquent child shall be prosecuted for a violation of section 2919.24 of the Revised Code based on the delinquent child's violation of this division, prior to the expiration of the period of time specified in division (G) of this section.

(G)(1) If an offender or delinquent child fails to verify a current residence, school, institution of higher education, or place of employment address, as applicable, as required by divisions (A) to (C) of this section by the date required for the verification as set forth in division (B) of this section, the sheriff with whom the offender or delinquent child is required to verify the current address, on the day following that date required for the verification, shall send a written warning to the offender or to the delinquent child and that child's parents, at the offender's or delinquent child's and that child's parents' last known residence, school, institution of higher education, or place of employment address, as applicable, regarding the offender's or delinquent child's duty to verify the offender's or delinquent child's current residence, school, institution of higher education, or place of employment address, as applicable.

The written warning shall do all of the following:

(a) Identify the sheriff who sends it and the date on which it is sent;

(b) State conspicuously that the offender or delinquent child has failed to verify the offender's current residence, school, institution of higher education, or place of employment address or the delinquent child's current residence address by the date required for the verification;

(c) Conspicuously state that the offender or delinquent child has seven days from the date on which the warning is sent to verify the current residence, school, institution of higher education, or place of employment address, as applicable, with the sheriff who sent the warning;

(d) Conspicuously state that a failure to timely verify the specified current address or addresses is a felony offense;

(e) Conspicuously state that, if the offender verifies the current residence, school, institution of higher education, or place of employment address or the delinquent child verifies the current residence address with that sheriff within that seven-day period, the offender or delinquent child will not be prosecuted or subjected to a delinquent child proceeding for a failure to timely verify a current address and the delinquent child's parent, guardian, or custodian will not be prosecuted based on a failure of the delinquent child to timely verify an address;

(f) Conspicuously state that, if the offender does not verify the current residence, school, institution of higher education, or place of employment address or the delinquent child verifies the current residence address with that sheriff within that seven-day period, the offender or delinquent child will be arrested or taken into custody, as appropriate, and prosecuted or subjected to a delinquent child proceeding for a failure to timely verify a current address and the delinquent child's parent, guardian, or custodian may be prosecuted for a violation of section 2919.24 of the Revised Code based on the delinquent child's failure to timely verify a current residence address.

(2) If an offender or delinquent child fails to verify a current residence, school, institution of higher education, or place of employment address, as applicable, as required by divisions (A) to (C) of this section by the date required for the verification as set forth in division (B) of this section, the offender or delinquent child shall not be prosecuted or subjected to a delinquent child proceeding for a violation of division (F) of this section, and the delinquent child's parent, guardian, or custodian shall not be prosecuted for a violation of section 2919.24 of the Revised Code based on the delinquent child's failure to timely verify a current residence address, as applicable, unless the seven-day period subsequent to that date that the offender or delinquent child is provided under division (G)(1) of this section to verify the current address has expired and the offender or delinquent child, prior to the expiration of that seven-day period, has not verified the current address. Upon the expiration of the seven-day period that the offender or delinquent child is provided under division (G)(1) of this section to verify the current address, if the offender or delinquent child has not verified the current address, all of the following apply:

(a) The sheriff with whom the offender or delinquent child is required to verify the current residence, school, institution of higher education, or place of employment address, as applicable, promptly shall notify the bureau of criminal identification and investigation of the failure.

(b) The sheriff with whom the offender or delinquent child is required to verify the current residence, school, institution of higher education, or place of employment address, as applicable, the sheriff of the county in which the offender or delinquent child resides, the sheriff of the county in which is located the offender's school, institution of higher education, or place of employment address that was to be verified, or a deputy of the appropriate sheriff, shall locate the offender or delinquent child, promptly shall seek a warrant for the arrest or taking into custody, as appropriate, of the offender or delinquent child for the violation of division (F) of this section and shall arrest the offender or take the child into custody, as appropriate.

(c) The offender or delinquent child is subject to prosecution or a delinquent child proceeding for the violation of division (F) of this section, and the delinquent child's parent, guardian, or custodian may be subject to prosecution for a violation of section 2919.24 of the Revised Code based on the delinquent child's violation of that division.

(H) An offender who is required to verify the offender's current residence, school, institution of higher education, or place of employment address pursuant to divisions (A) to (C) of this section and a delinquent child who is required to verify the delinquent child's current residence address pursuant to those divisions shall do so for the period of time specified in section 2950.07 of the Revised Code.

(2003 S 5, eff. 7–31–03; 2002 H 485, eff. 6–13–02; 2001 S 3, eff. 1–1–02; 1998 H 565, eff. 3–30–99; 1996 H 180, eff. 7–1–97)

2950.07 Duration of registration requirements

(A) The duty of an offender who is convicted of or pleads guilty to, or has been convicted of or pleaded guilty to, either a sexually oriented offense that is not a registration-exempt sexually oriented offense or a child-victim oriented offense and the duty of a delinquent child who is adjudicated a delinquent child for committing either a sexually oriented offense that is not a registration-exempt sexually oriented offense or a child-victim oriented offense and is classified a juvenile offender registrant or who is an out-of-state juvenile offender registrant to comply with sections 2950.04, 2950.041, 2950.05, and 2950.06 of the Revised Code commences on whichever of the following dates is applicable:

(1) If the offender's duty to register is imposed pursuant to division (A)(1)(a) of section 2950.04 or division (A)(1)(a) of section 2950.041 of the Revised Code, the offender's duty to comply with those sections commences regarding residence addresses on the date of the offender's release from a prison term, a term of imprisonment, or any other type of confinement or on July 1, 1997, for a duty under section 2950.04 or the effective date of this amendment for a duty under section 2950.041 of the Revised Code, whichever is later, and commences regarding addresses of schools, institutions of higher education, and places of employment on the date of the offender's release from a prison term, term of imprisonment, or any other type of confinement or on the effective date of this amendment, whichever is later.

(2) If the offender's duty to register is imposed pursuant to division (A)(1)(b) of section 2950.04 or division (A)(1)(b) of section 2950.041 of the Revised Code, the offender's duty to comply with those sections commences regarding residence addresses on the date of entry of the judgment of conviction of the sexually oriented offense or child-victim oriented offense or on July 1, 1997, for a duty under section 2950.04 or the effective date of this amendment for a duty under section 2950.041 of the Revised Code, whichever is later, and commences regarding addresses of schools, institutions of higher education, and places of employment on the date of entry of the judgment of conviction of the sexually oriented offense or child-victim oriented offense or on the effective date of this amendment, whichever is later.

(3) If the offender's duty to register is imposed pursuant to division (A)(1)(c) of section 2950.04 of the Revised Code, the offender's duty to comply with those sections commences regarding residence addresses fourteen days after July 1, 1997, and commences regarding addresses of schools, institutions of higher education, and places of employment fourteen days after the effective date of this amendment.

(4) If the offender's or delinquent child's duty to register is imposed pursuant to division (A)(3)(a) or (b) of section 2950.04 or division (A)(3)(a) or (b) of section 2950.041 of the Revised Code, the offender's duty to comply with those sections commences regarding residence addresses on the date that the offender begins to reside or becomes temporarily domiciled in this state or on March 30, 1999, for a duty under section 2950.04 of the Revised Code or the effective date of this amendment for a duty under section 2950.041 of the Revised Code, whichever is

later, the offender's duty regarding addresses of schools, institutions of higher education, and places of employment commences on the effective date of this amendment or on the date the offender begins attending any school or institution of higher education in this state on a full-time or part-time basis or becomes employed in this state, whichever is later, and the delinquent child's duty commences on the date the delinquent child begins to reside or becomes temporarily domiciled in this state or on January 1, 2002, for a duty under section 2950.04 of the Revised Code or the effective date of this amendment for a duty under section 2950.041 of the Revised Code, whichever is later.

(5) If the delinquent child's duty to register is imposed pursuant to division (A)(2) of section 2950.04 or division (A)(2)(a) of section 2950.041 of the Revised Code, if the delinquent child's classification as a juvenile offender registrant is made at the time of the child's disposition for that sexually oriented offense or child-victim oriented offense, whichever is applicable, and if the delinquent child is committed for the sexually oriented offense or child victim oriented offense to the department of youth services or to a secure facility that is not operated by the department, the delinquent child's duty to comply with those sections commences on the date of the delinquent child's discharge or release from custody in the department of youth services secure facility or from the secure facility not operated by the department as described in that division.

(6) If the delinquent child's duty to register is imposed pursuant to division (A)(2) of section 2950.04 or division (A)(2)(a) of section 2950.041 of the Revised Code and if either the delinquent child's classification as a juvenile offender registrant is made at the time of the child's disposition for that sexually oriented offense or child-victim oriented offense, whichever is applicable, and the delinquent child is not committed for the sexually oriented offense or child-victim oriented offense to the department of youth services or to a secure facility that is not operated by the department or the child's classification as a juvenile offender registrant is made pursuant to sections 2152.83 of the Revised Code, the delinquent child's duty to comply with those sections commences on the date of entry of the court's order that classifies the delinquent child a juvenile offender registrant.

(7) If the offender's duty to register is imposed pursuant to division (A)(1)(c) of section 2950.041 of the Revised Code, the offender's duty to comply with those sections regarding residence addresses is a continuation of the offender's former duty to register regarding residence addresses imposed prior to the effective date of this amendment under section 2950.04 of the Revised Code and shall be considered for all purposes as having commenced on the date that the offender's former duty under that section commenced. The offender's duty to comply with those sections commences regarding addresses of schools, institutions of higher education, and places of employment on the effective date of this amendment.

(8) If the delinquent child's duty to register is imposed pursuant to division (A)(2)(b) of section 2950.041 of the Revised Code, the delinquent child's duty to comply with those sections is a continuation of the delinquent child's former duty to register imposed prior to the effective date of this amendment under section 2950.04 of the Revised Code and shall be considered for all purposes as having commenced on the date that the delinquent child's former duty under that section commenced or commences.

(B) The duty of an offender who is convicted of or pleads guilty to, or has been convicted of or pleaded guilty to, either a sexually oriented offense that is not a registration-exempt sexually oriented offense or a child-victim oriented offense and the duty of a delinquent child who is adjudicated a delinquent child for committing either a sexually oriented offense that is not a registration-exempt sexually oriented offense or a child-victim oriented offense and is classified a juvenile offender registrant or who is an out-of-state juvenile offender registrant to comply with sections 2950.04, 2950.041, 2950.05, and 2950.06 of the Revised Code continues, after the date of commencement, for whichever of the following periods is applicable:

(1) Except as otherwise provided in this division, if the offense is a sexually oriented offense that is not a registration-exempt sexually oriented offense and the offender or delinquent child has been adjudicated a sexual predator relative to the sexually oriented offense, if the offense is a sexually oriented offense and the offender has the duty to register as a result of an aggravated sexually oriented offense, or if the offense is a child-victim oriented offense and the offender or delinquent child has been adjudicated a child-victim predator relative to the child-victim oriented offense, the offender's or delinquent child's duty to comply with those sections continues until the offender's or delinquent child's death. Regarding a delinquent child who has been adjudicated a sexual predator relative to the sexually oriented offense or who has been adjudicated a child-victim predator relative to the child-victim oriented offense, if the judge who made the disposition for the delinquent child or that judge's successor in office subsequently enters a determination pursuant to section 2152.84 or 2152.85 of the Revised Code that the delinquent child no longer is a sexual predator or child-victim predator, the delinquent child's duty to comply with those sections continues for the period of time that otherwise would have been applicable to the delinquent child under division (B)(2) or (3) of this section. In no case shall the lifetime duty to comply that is imposed under this division on an offender who is adjudicated a sexual predator or is adjudicated a child-victim predator or is imposed under this division for an aggravated sexually oriented offense, or the adjudication, classification, or conviction that subjects the offender to this division, be removed or terminated.

(2) If the judge who sentenced the offender or made the disposition for the delinquent child for committing the sexually oriented offense that is not a registration-exempt sexually oriented offense or the child-victim oriented offense, or the successor in office of the juvenile court judge who made the delinquent child disposition, determined pursuant to division (E) of section 2950.09 or 2950.091 or pursuant to division (B) of section 2152.83, section 2152.84, or section 2152.85 of the Revised Code that the offender or delinquent child is a habitual sex offender or a habitual child-victim offender, or if the offender or delinquent child is automatically classified a habitual child-victim offender pursuant to division (E) of section 2950.091 of the Revised Code, the offender's duty to comply with those sections continues either until the offender's death or for twenty years, determined as provided in this division, and the delinquent child's duty to comply with those sections continues for twenty years. If a delinquent child is so determined or classified to be a habitual sex offender or a habitual child-victim offender and if the judge who made the disposition for the delinquent child or that judge's successor in office subsequently enters a determination pursuant to section 2152.84 or 2152.85 of the Revised Code that the delinquent child no longer is a habitual sex offender or habitual child-victim offender but remains a juvenile offender registrant, the delinquent child's duty to comply with those sections continues for the period of time that otherwise would have been applicable to the delinquent child under division (B)(3) of this section. Except as otherwise provided in this division, the offender's duty to comply with those sections continues until the offender's death. If a lifetime duty to comply is imposed under this division on an offender, in no case shall that lifetime duty, or the determination that subjects the offender to this division, be removed or terminated. The offender's duty to comply with those sections continues for twenty years if the offender is a habitual sex offender and both of the following apply:

(a) At least one of the sexually oriented offenses of which the offender has been convicted or to which the offender has pleaded guilty and that are included in the habitual sex offender determination is a violation of division (A)(1) or (5) of section 2907.06 of the Revised Code involving a victim who is eighteen years of age or older, a violation of division (A), (B), or (E) of section 2907.08 of the Revised Code involving a victim who is eighteen years of age or older, or a violation of section 2903.211 of the Revised Code that is a misdemeanor;

(b) The total of all the sexually oriented offenses of which the offender has been convicted or to which the offender has pleaded guilty and that are included in the habitual sex offender determination does not include at least two sexually oriented offenses that are not described in division (B)(2)(a) of this section.

(3) If neither division (B)(1) nor (B)(2) of this section applies, the offender's or delinquent child's duty to comply with those sections continues for ten years. If a delinquent child is classified pursuant to section 2152.82 or 2152.83 of the Revised Code a juvenile offender registrant and if the judge who made the disposition for the delinquent child or that judge's successor in office subsequently enters a determination pursuant to section 2152.84 or 2152.85 of the Revised Code that the delinquent child no longer is to be classified a juvenile offender registrant, the delinquent child's duty to comply with those sections terminates upon the court's entry of the determination.

(C)(1) If an offender has been convicted of or pleaded guilty to a sexually oriented offense that is not a registration-exempt sexually oriented offense and the offender subsequently is convicted of or pleads guilty to another sexually oriented offense or a child-victim oriented offense, if an offender has been convicted of or pleaded guilty to a child-victim oriented offense and the offender subsequently is convicted of or pleads guilty to another child-victim oriented offense or a sexually oriented offense, if a delinquent child has been adjudicated a delinquent child for committing a sexually oriented offense that is not a registration-exempt sexually oriented offense and is classified a juvenile offender registrant or is an out-of-state juvenile offender registrant and the child subsequently is adjudicated a delinquent child for committing another sexually oriented offense or a child-victim oriented offense and is classified a juvenile offender registrant relative to that offense or subsequently is convicted of or pleads guilty to another sexually oriented offense or a child-victim oriented offense, or if a delinquent child has been adjudicated a delinquent child for committing a child-victim oriented offense and is classified a juvenile offender registrant or is an out-of-state juvenile offender registrant and the child subsequently is adjudicated a delinquent child for committing another child-victim oriented offense or a sexually oriented offense and is classified a juvenile offender registrant relative to that offense or subsequently is convicted of or pleads guilty to another child-victim oriented offense or a sexually oriented offense, the period of time for which the offender or delinquent child must comply with the sections specified in division (A) of this section shall be separately calculated pursuant to divisions (A)(1) to (8) and (B)(1) to (3) of this section for each of the sexually oriented offenses and child-victim oriented offenses, and the separately calculated periods of time shall be complied with independently.

If a delinquent child has been adjudicated a delinquent child for committing either a sexually oriented offense that is not a registration-exempt sexually oriented offense or a child-victim oriented offense, is classified a juvenile offender registrant or is an out-of-state juvenile offender registrant relative to the offense, and, after attaining eighteen years of age, subsequently is convicted of or pleads guilty to another sexually oriented offense or child-victim oriented offense, the subsequent conviction or guilty plea does not limit, affect, or supersede the duties imposed upon the delinquent child under this chapter relative to the delinquent child's classification as a juvenile offender registrant or as an out-of-state juvenile offender registrant, and the delinquent child shall comply with both those duties and the duties imposed under this chapter relative to the subsequent conviction or guilty plea.

(2) If a delinquent child has been adjudicated a delinquent child for committing on or after January 1, 2002, either a sexually oriented offense that is not a registration-exempt sexually oriented offense or a child-victim oriented offense and is classified a juvenile offender registrant relative to the offense, if the order containing the classification also contains a determination by the juvenile judge that the child is a sexual predator or a habitual sex offender or that the child is a child-victim predator or a habitual child-victim offender, and if the juvenile judge or the judge's successor in office subsequently determines pursuant to section 2152.84 or 2152.85 of the Revised Code that the delinquent child no longer is a sexual predator or habitual sex offender or no longer is a child-victim predator or habitual child-victim offender, whichever is applicable, the judge's subsequent determination does not affect the date of commencement of the delinquent child's duty to comply with sections 2950.04, 2950.041, 2950.05, and 2950.06 of the Revised Code as determined under division (A) of this section.

(D) The duty of an offender or delinquent child to register under this chapter is tolled for any period during which the offender or delinquent child is returned to confinement in a secure facility for any reason or imprisoned for an offense when the confinement in a secure facility or imprisonment occurs subsequent to the date determined pursuant to division (A) of this section. The offender's or delinquent child's duty to register under this chapter resumes upon the offender's or delinquent child's release from confinement in a secure facility or imprisonment.

(E) An offender or delinquent child who has been convicted or pleaded guilty, or has been or is adjudicated a delinquent child , in a court in another state, in a federal court, military court, or Indian tribal court, or in a court of any nation other than the United States for committing either a sexually oriented offense that is not a registration-exempt sexually oriented offense or a child-victim oriented offense may apply to the sheriff of the county in which the offender or delinquent child resides or temporarily is domiciled, or in which the offender attends a school or institution of higher education or is employed, for credit against the duty to register for the time that the offender or delinquent child has complied with the sex offender or child-victim offender registration requirements of another jurisdiction. The sheriff shall grant the offender or delinquent child credit against the duty to register for time for which the offender or delinquent child provides adequate proof that the offender or delinquent child has complied with the sex offender or child-victim offender registration requirements of another jurisdiction. If the offender or delinquent child disagrees with the determination of the sheriff, the offender or delinquent child may appeal the determination to the court of common pleas of the county in which the offender or delinquent child resides or is temporarily domiciled, or in which the offender attends a school or institution of higher education or is employed.

(2003 S 5, eff. 7–31–03; 2002 H 485, eff. 6–13–02; 2001 S 3, eff. 1–1–02; 1998 H 565, eff. 3–30–99; 1996 H 180, eff. 7–1–97)

2950.08 Public inspection of registration data prohibited; exception

(A) Subject to division (B) of this section, the statements, information, photographs, and fingerprints required by sections 2950.04, 2950.041, 2950.05, and 2950.06 of the Revised Code and provided by a person who registers, who provides notice of a change of residence, school, institution of higher education, or place of employment address and registers the new residence, school, institution of higher education, or place of employment address, or who provides verification of a current residence, school, institution of higher education, or place of employment address pursuant to those sections and that are in the possession of the bureau of criminal identification and investigation and the information in the possession of the bureau that was received by the bureau pursuant to section 2950.14 of the Revised Code shall not be open to inspection by the public or by any person other than the following persons:

(1) A regularly employed peace officer or other law enforcement officer;

(2) An authorized employee of the bureau of criminal identification and investigation for the purpose of providing information to a board, administrator, or person pursuant to division (F) or (G) of section 109.57 of the Revised Code;

(3) The registrar of motor vehicles, or an employee of the registrar of motor vehicles, for the purpose of verifying and updating any of the information so provided, upon the request of the bureau of criminal identification and investigation.

(B) Division (A) of this section does not apply to any information that is contained in the internet sex offender and child-victim offender database established by the attorney general under division (A)(11) of section 2950.13 of the Revised Code regarding offenders and that is disseminated as described in that division.

(2003 S 5, eff. 7–31–03; 1996 H 180, eff. 7–1–97; 1996 S 160, eff. 1–27–97; 1989 S 140, eff. 10–2–89; 130 v S 160)

2950.081 Public records; exceptions

(A) Any statements, information, photographs, or fingerprints that are required to be provided, and that are provided, by an offender or delinquent child pursuant to section 2950.04, 2950.041, 2950.05, or 2950.06 of the Revised Code and that are in the possession of a county sheriff are public records open to public inspection under section 149.43 of the Revised Code and shall be included in the internet sex offender and child-victim offender database established and maintained under section 2950.13 of the Revised Code to the extent provided in that section.

(B) Except when the child is classified a juvenile offender registrant and the act that is the basis of the classification is a violation of, or an attempt to commit a violation of, section 2903.01, 2903.02, or 2905.01 of the Revised Code that was committed with a purpose to gratify the sexual needs or desires of the child, a violation of section 2907.02 of the Revised Code, or an attempt to commit a violation of that section, the sheriff shall not cause to be publicly disseminated by means of the internet any statements, information, photographs, or fingerprints that are provided by a juvenile offender registrant who sends a notice of intent to reside, registers, provides notice of a change of residence address and registers the new residence address, or provides verification of a current residence address pursuant to this chapter and that are in the possession of a county sheriff.

(2003 S 5, eff. 7–31–03; 2001 S 3, eff. 1–1–02)

2950.09 Adjudication of offender as sexual predator or as habitual sex offender; exclusion of registration-exempt sexually oriented offense

Note: See also following version of this section, eff. 4–29–05.

(A) If a person is convicted of or pleads guilty to committing, on or after January 1, 1997, a sexually oriented offense that is not a registration-exempt sexually oriented offense and that is a sexually violent offense and also is convicted of or pleads guilty to a sexually violent predator specification that was included in the indictment, count in the indictment, or information charging the sexually violent offense, the conviction of or plea of guilty to the specification automatically classifies the offender as a sexual predator for purposes of this chapter. If a person is convicted, pleads guilty, or adjudicated a delinquent child, in a court in another state, in a federal court, military court, or Indian tribal court, or in a court of any nation other than the United States for committing a sexually oriented offense that is not a registration-exempt sexually oriented offense, and if, as a result of that conviction, plea of guilty, or adjudication, the person is required, under the law of the jurisdiction in which the person was convicted, pleaded guilty, or was adjudicated, to register as a sex offender until the person's death, that conviction, plea of guilty, or adjudication automatically classifies the person as a sexual predator for the purposes of this chapter, but the person may challenge that classification pursuant to division (F) of this section. In all other cases, a person who is convicted of or pleads guilty to, has been convicted of or pleaded guilty to, or is adjudicated a delinquent child for committing, a sexually oriented offense may be classified as a sexual predator for purposes of this chapter only in accordance with division (B) or (C) of this section or, regarding delinquent children, divisions (B) and (C) of section 2152.83 of the Revised Code.

(B)(1)(a) The judge who is to impose sentence on a person who is convicted of or pleads guilty to a sexually oriented offense that is not a registration-exempt sexually oriented offense shall conduct a hearing to determine whether the offender is a sexual predator if any of the following circumstances apply:

(i) Regardless of when the sexually oriented offense was committed, the offender is to be sentenced on or after January 1, 1997, for a sexually oriented offense that is not a registration-exempt sexually oriented offense and that is not a sexually violent offense.

(ii) Regardless of when the sexually oriented offense was committed, the offender is to be sentenced on or after January 1, 1997, for a sexually oriented offense that is not a registration-exempt sexually oriented offense and that is a sexually violent offense, and a sexually violent predator specification was not included in the indictment, count in the indictment, or information charging the sexually violent offense.

(iii) Regardless of when the sexually oriented offense was committed, the offender is to be sentenced on or after May 7, 2002, for a sexually oriented offense that is not a registration-exempt sexually oriented offense, and that offender was acquitted of a sexually violent predator specification that was included in the indictment, count in the indictment, or information charging the sexually oriented offense.

(b) The judge who is to impose or has imposed an order of disposition upon a child who is adjudicated a delinquent child for committing on or after January 1, 2002, a sexually oriented offense that is not a registration-exempt sexually oriented offense shall conduct a hearing as provided in this division to determine whether the child is to be classified as a sexual predator if either of the following applies:

(i) The judge is required by section 2152.82 or division (A) of section 2152.83 of the Revised Code to classify the child a juvenile offender registrant.

(ii) Division (B) of section 2152.83 of the Revised Code applies regarding the child, the judge conducts a hearing under that division for the purposes described in that division, and the judge determines at that hearing that the child will be classified a juvenile offender registrant.

(2) Regarding an offender, the judge shall conduct the hearing required by division (B)(1)(a) of this section prior to sentencing and, if the sexually oriented offense for which sentence is to be imposed is a felony and if the hearing is being conducted under division (B)(1)(a) of this section, the judge may conduct it as part of the sentencing hearing required by section 2929.19 of the Revised Code. Regarding a delinquent child, the judge may conduct the hearing required by division (B)(1)(b) of this section at the same time as, or separate from, the dispositional hearing, as specified in the applicable provision of section 2152.82 or 2152.83 of the Revised Code. The court shall give the offender or delinquent child and the prosecutor who prosecuted the offender or handled the case against the delinquent child for the sexually oriented offense notice of the date, time, and location of the hearing. At the hearing, the offender or delinquent child and the prosecutor shall have an opportunity to testify, present evidence, call and examine witnesses and expert witnesses, and cross-

examine witnesses and expert witnesses regarding the determination as to whether the offender or delinquent child is a sexual predator. The offender or delinquent child shall have the right to be represented by counsel and, if indigent, the right to have counsel appointed to represent the offender or delinquent child.

(3) In making a determination under divisions (B)(1) and (4) of this section as to whether an offender or delinquent child is a sexual predator, the judge shall consider all relevant factors, including, but not limited to, all of the following:

(a) The offender's or delinquent child's age;

(b) The offender's or delinquent child's prior criminal or delinquency record regarding all offenses, including, but not limited to, all sexual offenses;

(c) The age of the victim of the sexually oriented offense for which sentence is to be imposed or the order of disposition is to be made;

(d) Whether the sexually oriented offense for which sentence is to be imposed or the order of disposition is to be made involved multiple victims;

(e) Whether the offender or delinquent child used drugs or alcohol to impair the victim of the sexually oriented offense or to prevent the victim from resisting;

(f) If the offender or delinquent child previously has been convicted of or pleaded guilty to, or been adjudicated a delinquent child for committing an act that if committed by an adult would be, a criminal offense, whether the offender or delinquent child completed any sentence or dispositional order imposed for the prior offense or act and, if the prior offense or act was a sex offense or a sexually oriented offense, whether the offender or delinquent child participated in available programs for sexual offenders;

(g) Any mental illness or mental disability of the offender or delinquent child;

(h) The nature of the offender's or delinquent child's sexual conduct, sexual contact, or interaction in a sexual context with the victim of the sexually oriented offense and whether the sexual conduct, sexual contact, or interaction in a sexual context was part of a demonstrated pattern of abuse;

(i) Whether the offender or delinquent child, during the commission of the sexually oriented offense for which sentence is to be imposed or the order of disposition is to be made, displayed cruelty or made one or more threats of cruelty;

(j) Any additional behavioral characteristics that contribute to the offender's or delinquent child's conduct.

(4) After reviewing all testimony and evidence presented at the hearing conducted under division (B)(1) of this section and the factors specified in division (B)(3) of this section, the court shall determine by clear and convincing evidence whether the subject offender or delinquent child is a sexual predator. If the court determines that the subject offender or delinquent child is not a sexual predator, the court shall specify in the offender's sentence and the judgment of conviction that contains the sentence or in the delinquent child's dispositional order, as appropriate, that the court has determined that the offender or delinquent child is not a sexual predator and the reason or reasons why the court determined that the subject offender or delinquent child is not a sexual predator. If the court determines by clear and convincing evidence that the subject offender or delinquent child is a sexual predator, the court shall specify in the offender's sentence and the judgment of conviction that contains the sentence or in the delinquent child's dispositional order, as appropriate, that the court has determined that the offender or delinquent child is a sexual predator and shall specify that the determination was pursuant to division (B) of this section. In any case in which the sexually oriented offense in question is an aggravated sexually oriented offense, the court shall specify in the offender's sentence and the judgment of conviction that contains the sentence that the offender's offense is an aggravated sexually oriented offense. The offender or delinquent child and the prosecutor who prosecuted the offender or handled the case against the delinquent child for the sexually oriented offense in question may appeal as a matter of right the court's determination under this division as to whether the offender or delinquent child is, or is not, a sexual predator.

(5) A hearing shall not be conducted under division (B) of this section regarding an offender if the sexually oriented offense in question is a sexually violent offense, if the indictment, count in the indictment, or information charging the offense also included a sexually violent predator specification, and if the offender is convicted of or pleads guilty to that sexually violent predator specification.

(C)(1) If a person was convicted of or pleaded guilty to a sexually oriented offense that is not a registration-exempt sexually oriented offense prior to January 1, 1997, if the person was not sentenced for the offense on or after January 1, 1997, and if, on or after January 1, 1997, the offender is serving a term of imprisonment in a state correctional institution, the department of rehabilitation and correction shall do whichever of the following is applicable:

(a) If the sexually oriented offense was an offense described in division (D)(1)(c) of section 2950.01 of the Revised Code or was a violent sex offense, the department shall notify the court that sentenced the offender of this fact, and the court shall conduct a hearing to determine whether the offender is a sexual predator.

(b) If division (C)(1)(a) of this section does not apply, the department shall determine whether to recommend that the offender be adjudicated a sexual predator. In making a determination under this division as to whether to recommend that the offender be adjudicated a sexual predator, the department shall consider all relevant factors, including, but not limited to, all of the factors specified in divisions (B)(2) and (3) of this section. If the department determines that it will recommend that the offender be adjudicated a sexual predator, it immediately shall send the recommendation to the court that sentenced the offender. If the department determines that it will not recommend that the offender be adjudicated a sexual predator, it immediately shall send its determination to the court that sentenced the offender. In all cases, the department shall enter its determination and recommendation in the offender's institutional record, and the court shall proceed in accordance with division (C)(2) of this section.

(2)(a) If the department of rehabilitation and correction sends to a court a notice under division (C)(1)(a) of this section, the court shall conduct a hearing to determine whether the subject offender is a sexual predator. If, pursuant to division (C)(1)(b) of this section, the department sends to a court a recommendation that an offender be adjudicated a sexual predator, the court is not bound by the department's recommendation, and the court shall conduct a hearing to determine whether the offender is a sexual predator. In any case, the court shall not make a determination as to whether the offender is, or is not, a sexual predator without a hearing. The court may hold the hearing and make the determination prior to the offender's release from imprisonment or at any time within one year following the offender's release from that imprisonment.

(b) If, pursuant to division (C)(1)(b) of this section, the department sends to the court a determination that it is not recommending that an offender be adjudicated a sexual predator, the court shall not make any determination as to whether the offender is, or is not, a sexual predator but shall determine whether the offender previously has been convicted of or pleaded guilty to a sexually oriented offense other than the offense in relation to which the department made its determination or previously has been convicted of or pleaded guilty to a child-victim oriented offense.

The court may conduct a hearing to determine whether the offender previously has been convicted of or pleaded guilty to a sexually oriented offense or a child-victim oriented offense but may make the determination without a hearing. However, if the court determines that the offender previously has been convicted of or pleaded guilty to such an offense, it shall not impose a requirement that the offender be subject to the community notification provisions contained in sections 2950.10 and 2950.11 of the Revised Code without a hearing. In determining whether to impose the community notification requirement, the court, in the circumstances described in division (E)(2) of this section, shall apply the presumption specified in that division. The court shall include in the offender's institutional record any determination made under this division as to whether the offender previously has been convicted of or pleaded guilty to a sexually oriented offense or child-victim oriented offense, and, as such, whether the offender is a habitual sex offender.

(c) Upon scheduling a hearing under division (C)(2)(a) or (b) of this section, the court shall give the offender and the prosecutor who prosecuted the offender for the sexually oriented offense, or that prosecutor's successor in office, notice of the date, time, and place of the hearing. If the hearing is scheduled under division (C)(2)(a) of this section to determine whether the offender is a sexual predator, the prosecutor who is given the notice may contact the department of rehabilitation and correction and request that the department provide to the prosecutor all information the department possesses regarding the offender that is relevant and necessary for use in making the determination as to whether the offender is a sexual predator and that is not privileged or confidential under law. If the prosecutor makes a request for that information, the department promptly shall provide to the prosecutor all information the department possesses regarding the offender that is not privileged or confidential under law and that is relevant and necessary for making that determination. A hearing scheduled under division (C)(2)(a) of this section to determine whether the offender is a sexual predator shall be conducted in the manner described in division (B)(1) of this section regarding hearings conducted under that division and, in making a determination under this division as to whether the offender is a sexual predator, the court shall consider all relevant factors, including, but not limited to, all of the factors specified in divisions (B)(2) and (3) of this section. After reviewing all testimony and evidence presented at the sexual predator hearing and the factors specified in divisions (B)(2) and (3) of this section, the court shall determine by clear and convincing evidence whether the offender is a sexual predator. If the court determines at the sexual predator hearing that the offender is not a sexual predator, it also shall determine whether the offender previously has been convicted of or pleaded guilty to a sexually oriented offense other than the offense in relation to which the hearing is being conducted.

Upon making its determinations at the sexual predator hearing, the court shall proceed as follows:

(i) If the court determines that the offender is not a sexual predator and that the offender previously has not been convicted of or pleaded guilty to a sexually oriented offense other than the offense in relation to which the hearing is being conducted and previously has not been convicted of or pleaded guilty to a child-victim oriented offense, it shall include in the offender's institutional record its determinations and the reason or reasons why it determined that the offender is not a sexual predator.

(ii) If the court determines that the offender is not a sexual predator but that the offender previously has been convicted of or pleaded guilty to a sexually oriented offense other than the offense in relation to which the hearing is being conducted or previously has been convicted of or pleaded guilty to a child-victim oriented offense, it shall include in the offender's institutional record its determination that the offender is not a sexual predator but is a habitual sex offender and the reason or reasons why it determined that the offender is not a sexual predator, shall attach the determinations and the reason or reasons to the offender's sentence, shall specify that the determinations were pursuant to division (C) of this section, shall provide a copy of the determinations and the reason or reasons to the offender, to the prosecuting attorney, and to the department of rehabilitation and correction, and may impose a requirement that the offender be subject to the community notification provisions contained in sections 2950.10 and 2950.11 of the Revised Code. In determining whether to impose the community notification requirements, the court, in the circumstances described in division (E)(2) of this section, shall apply the presumption specified in that division. The offender shall not be subject to those community notification provisions relative to the sexually oriented offense in question if the court does not so impose the requirement described in this division. If the court imposes that requirement, the offender may appeal the judge's determination that the offender is a habitual sex offender.

(iii) If the court determines by clear and convincing evidence that the offender is a sexual predator, it shall enter its determination in the offender's institutional record, shall attach the determination to the offender's sentence, shall specify that the determination was pursuant to division (C) of this section, and shall provide a copy of the determination to the offender, to the prosecuting attorney, and to the department of rehabilitation and correction. The offender and the prosecutor may appeal as a matter of right the judge's determination under divisions (C)(2)(a) and (c) of this section as to whether the offender is, or is not, a sexual predator.

If the hearing is scheduled under division (C)(2)(b) of this section to determine whether the offender previously has been convicted of or pleaded guilty to a sexually oriented offense or a child-victim oriented offense or whether to subject the offender to the community notification provisions contained in sections 2950.10 and 2950.11 of the Revised Code, upon making the determination, the court shall attach the determination or determinations to the offender's sentence, shall provide a copy to the offender, to the prosecuting attorney, and to the department of rehabilitation and correction and may impose a requirement that the offender be subject to the community notification provisions. In determining whether to impose the community notification requirements, the court, in the circumstances described in division (E)(2) of this section, shall apply the presumption specified in that division. The offender shall not be subject to the community notification provisions relative to the sexually oriented offense in question if the court does not so impose the requirement described in this division. If the court imposes that requirement, the offender may appeal the judge's determination that the offender is a habitual sex offender.

(3) The changes made in divisions (C)(1) and (2) of this section that take effect on the effective date of this amendment do not require a court to conduct a new hearing under those divisions for any offender regarding a sexually oriented offense if, prior to the effective date of this amendment, the court previously conducted a hearing under those divisions regarding that offense to determine whether the offender was a sexual predator. The changes made in divisions (C)(1) and (2) of this section that take effect on the effective date of this amendment do not require a court to conduct a hearing under those divisions for any offender regarding a sexually oriented offense if, prior to the effective date of this amendment and pursuant to those divisions, the department of rehabilitation and correction recommended that the offender be adjudicated a sexual predator regarding that offense, and the court denied the recommendation and determined that the offender was not a sexual predator without a hearing, provided that this provision does not apply if the sexually oriented offense in question was an offense described in division (D)(1)(c) of section 2950.01 of the Revised Code.

(D)(1) Division (D)(1) of this section does not apply to any person who has been convicted of or pleaded guilty to a sexually oriented offense. Division (D) of this section applies only to delinquent children as provided in Chapter 2152. of the Revised Code. A person who has been adjudicated a delinquent child for committing a sexually oriented offense that is not a registration-exempt sexually oriented offense and who has been classified by a juvenile court judge a juvenile offender registrant or, if applicable, additionally has been determined by a juvenile court judge to be a sexual predator or habitual sex offender, may petition the adjudicating court for a reclassification or declassification pursuant to section 2152.85 of the Revised Code.

A judge who is reviewing a sexual predator determination for a delinquent child under section 2152.84 or 2152.85 of the Revised Code shall comply with this section. At the hearing, the judge shall consider all relevant evidence and information, including, but not limited to, the factors set forth in division (B)(3) of this section. The judge shall not enter a determination that the delinquent child no longer is a sexual predator unless the judge determines by clear and convincing evidence that the delinquent child is unlikely to commit a sexually oriented offense in the future. If the judge enters a determination under this division that the delinquent child no longer is a sexual predator, the judge shall notify the bureau of criminal identification and investigation of the determination and shall include in the notice a statement of the reason or reasons why it determined that the delinquent child no longer is a sexual predator. Upon receipt of the notification, the bureau promptly shall notify the sheriff with whom the delinquent child most recently registered under section 2950.04 or 2950.05 of the Revised Code of the determination that the delinquent child no longer is a sexual predator.

(2) If an offender who has been convicted of or pleaded guilty to a sexually oriented offense is classified a sexual predator pursuant to division (A) of this section or has been adjudicated a sexual predator relative to the offense as described in division (B) or (C) of this section, subject to division (F) of this section, the classification or adjudication of the offender as a sexual predator is permanent and continues in effect until the offender's death and in no case shall the classification or adjudication be removed or terminated.

(E)(1) If a person is convicted of or pleads guilty to committing, on or after January 1, 1997, a sexually oriented offense that is not a registration-exempt sexually oriented offense, the judge who is to impose sentence on the offender shall determine, prior to sentencing, whether the offender previously has been convicted of or pleaded guilty to, or adjudicated a delinquent child for committing, a sexually oriented offense or a child-victim oriented offense and is a habitual sex offender. The judge who is to impose or has imposed an order of disposition upon a child who is adjudicated a delinquent child for committing on or after January 1, 2002, a sexually oriented offense that is not a registration-exempt sexually oriented offense shall determine, prior to entering the order classifying the delinquent child a juvenile offender registrant, whether the delinquent child previously has been convicted of or pleaded guilty to, or adjudicated a delinquent child for committing, a sexually oriented offense or a child-victim oriented offense and is a habitual sex offender, if either of the following applies:

(a) The judge is required by section 2152.82 or division (A) of section 2152.83 of the Revised Code to classify the child a juvenile offender registrant;

(b) Division (B) of section 2152.83 of the Revised Code applies regarding the child, the judge conducts a hearing under that division for the purposes described in that division, and the judge determines at that hearing that the child will be classified a juvenile offender registrant.

(2) If, under division (E)(1) of this section, the judge determines that the offender or delinquent child previously has not been convicted of or pleaded guilty to, or been adjudicated a delinquent child for committing, a sexually oriented offense or a child-victim oriented offense or that the offender otherwise does not satisfy the criteria for being a habitual sex offender, the judge shall specify in the offender's sentence or in the order classifying the delinquent child a juvenile offender registrant that the judge has determined that the offender or delinquent child is not a habitual sex offender.

If, under division (E)(1) of this section, the judge determines that the offender or delinquent child previously has been convicted of or pleaded guilty to, or been adjudicated a delinquent child for committing, a sexually oriented offense or a child-victim oriented offense and that the offender satisfies all other criteria for being a habitual sex offender, the offender or delinquent child is a habitual sex offender or habitual child-victim offender and the court shall determine whether to impose a requirement that the offender or delinquent child be subject to the community notification provisions contained in sections 2950.10 and 2950.11 of the Revised Code. In making the determination regarding the possible imposition of the community notification requirement, if at least two of the sexually oriented offenses or child-victim oriented offenses that are the basis of the habitual sex offender or habitual child-victim offender determination were committed against a victim who was under eighteen years of age, it is presumed that subjecting the offender or delinquent child to the community notification provisions is necessary in order to comply with the determinations, findings, and declarations of the general assembly regarding sex offenders and child-victim offenders that are set forth in section 2950.02 of the Revised Code. When a judge determines as described in this division that an offender or delinquent child is a habitual sex offender or a habitual child-victim offender, the judge shall specify in the offender's sentence and the judgment of conviction that contains the sentence or in the order classifying the delinquent child a juvenile offender registrant that the judge has determined that the offender or delinquent child is a habitual sex offender and may impose a requirement in that sentence and judgment of conviction or in that order that the offender or delinquent child be subject to the community notification provisions contained in sections 2950.10 and 2950.11 of the Revised Code. Unless the habitual sex offender also has been adjudicated a sexual predator relative to the sexually oriented offense in question or the habitual sex offender was convicted of or pleaded guilty to an aggravated sexually oriented offense, the offender or delinquent child shall be subject to those community notification provisions only if the court imposes the requirement described in this division in the offender's sentence and the judgment of conviction or in the order classifying the delinquent child a juvenile offender registrant. If the court determines pursuant to this division or division (C)(2) of this section that an offender is a habitual sex offender, the determination is permanent and continues in effect until the offender's death, and in no case shall the determination be removed or terminated.

If a court in another state, a federal court, military court, or Indian tribal court, or a court in any nation other than the United States determines a person to be a habitual sex offender in that jurisdiction, the person is considered to be determined to be a habitual sex offender in this state. If the court in the other state, the federal court, military court, or Indian tribal court, or the court in the nation other than the United States subjects the habitual sex offender to community notification regarding the person's place of residence, the person, as much as is practicable, is subject to the community notification provisions regarding the person's place of residence that are contained in sections 2950.10 and 2950.11 of the Revised Code, unless the court that so subjected the person to community notification determines that the person no longer is subject to community notification.

(F)(1) An offender or delinquent child classified as a sexual predator may petition the court of common pleas or, for a delinquent child, the juvenile court of the county in which the offender or delinquent child resides or temporarily is domiciled to enter a determination that the offender or delinquent child is not an adjudicated sexual predator in this state for purposes of the registration and other requirements of this chapter or the community notification provisions contained in sections 2950.10 and 2950.11 of the Revised Code if all of the following apply:

(a) The offender or delinquent child was convicted of, pleaded guilty to, or was adjudicated a delinquent child for committing, a sexually oriented offense that is not a registration-exempt sexually oriented offense in another state, in a federal court, a military court, or Indian tribal court, or in a court of any nation other than the United States.

(b) As a result of the conviction, plea of guilty, or adjudication described in division (F)(1)(a) of this section, the offender or delinquent child is required under the law of the jurisdiction under which the offender or delinquent child was convicted, pleaded guilty, or was adjudicated to register as a sex offender until the offender's or delinquent child's death.

(c) The offender or delinquent child was automatically classified a sexual predator under division (A) of this section in relation to the conviction, guilty plea, or adjudication described in division (F)(1)(a) of this section.

(2) The court may enter a determination that the offender or delinquent child filing the petition described in division (F)(1) of this section is not an adjudicated sexual predator in this state for purposes of the registration and other requirements of this chapter or the community notification provisions contained in sections 2950.10 and 2950.11 of the Revised Code only if the offender or delinquent child proves by clear and convincing evidence that the requirement of the other jurisdiction that the offender or delinquent child register as a sex offender until the offender's or delinquent child's death is not substantially similar to a classification as a sexual predator for purposes of this chapter. If the court enters a determination that the offender or delinquent child is not an adjudicated sexual predator in this state for those purposes, the court shall include in the determination a statement of the reason or reasons why it so determined.

(G) If, prior to the effective date of this section, an offender or delinquent child was adjudicated a sexual predator or was determined to be a habitual sex offender under this section or section 2152.82, 2152.83, 2152.84, or 2152.85 of the Revised Code and if, on and after the effective date of this amendment, the sexually oriented offense upon which the classification or determination was based no longer is considered a sexually oriented offense but instead is a child-victim oriented offense, notwithstanding the redesignation of that offense, on and after the effective date of this amendment, all of the following apply:

(1) Divisions (A)(1) or (2) or (E)(1) and (2) of section 2950.091 of the Revised Code apply regarding the offender or child, and the judge's classification or determination made prior to the effective date of this amendment shall be considered for all purposes to be a classification or determination that classifies the offender or child as described in those divisions.

(2) The offender's or child's classification or determination under divisions (A)(1) or (2) or (E)(1) and (2) of section 2950.091 of the Revised Code shall be considered, for purposes of section 2950.07 of the Revised Code and for all other purposes, to be a continuation of the classification or determination made prior to the effective date of this amendment.

(3) The offender's or child's duties under this chapter relative to that classification or determination shall be considered for all purposes to be a continuation of the duties related to that classification or determination as they existed prior to the effective date of this amendment.

(2003 S 5, eff. 7–31–03; 2002 H 485, eff. 6–13–02; 2002 S 175, eff. 5–7–02; 2002 H 393, eff. 7–5–02; 2001 S 3, eff. 1–1–02; 2000 H 502, eff. 3–15–01; 1998 H 565, eff. 3–30–99; 1996 H 180, eff. 1–1–97)

Note: See also following version of this section, eff. 4–29–05.

2950.09 Adjudication of offender as sexual predator or as habitual sex offender; exclusion of registration-exempt sexually oriented offense (later effective date)

Note: See also preceding version of this section, in effect until 4–29–05.

(A) If a person is convicted of or pleads guilty to committing, on or after January 1, 1997, a sexually oriented offense that is not a registration-exempt sexually oriented offense, and if the sexually oriented offense is a violent sex offense or a designated homicide, assault, or kidnapping offense and the offender is adjudicated a sexually violent predator in relation to that offense, the conviction of or plea of guilty to the offense and the adjudication as a sexually violent predator automatically classifies the offender as a sexual predator for purposes of this chapter. If a person is convicted, pleads guilty, or adjudicated a delinquent child, in a court in another state, in a federal court, military court, or Indian tribal court, or in a court of any nation other than the United States for committing a sexually oriented offense that is not a registration-exempt sexually oriented offense, and if, as a result of that conviction, plea of guilty, or adjudication, the person is required, under the law of the jurisdiction in which the person was convicted, pleaded guilty, or was adjudicated, to register as a sex offender until the person's death, that conviction, plea of guilty, or adjudication automatically classifies the person as a sexual predator for the purposes of this chapter, but the person may challenge that classification pursuant to division (F) of this section. In all other cases, a person who is convicted of or pleads guilty to, has been convicted of or pleaded guilty to, or is adjudicated a delinquent child for committing, a sexually oriented offense may be classified as a sexual predator for purposes of this chapter only in accordance with division (B) or (C) of this section or, regarding delinquent children, divisions (B) and (C) of section 2152.83 of the Revised Code.

(B)(1)(a) The judge who is to impose sentence on a person who is convicted of or pleads guilty to a sexually oriented offense that is not a registration-exempt sexually oriented offense shall conduct a hearing to determine whether the offender is a sexual predator if any of the following circumstances apply:

(i) Regardless of when the sexually oriented offense was committed, the offender is to be sentenced on or after January 1, 1997, for a sexually oriented offense that is not a registration-exempt sexually oriented offense and that is not a sexually violent offense.

(ii) Regardless of when the sexually oriented offense was committed, the offender is to be sentenced on or after January 1, 1997, for a sexually oriented offense that is not a registration-exempt sexually oriented offense, and either of the following applies: the sexually oriented offense is a violent sex offense and a sexually violent predator specification was not included in the indictment, count in the indictment, or information charging the violent sex offense; or the sexually oriented offense is a designated homicide, assault, or kidnapping offense and either a sexual motivation specification or a sexually violent predator specification, or both such specifications, were not included in the indictment, count in the indictment, or information charging the designated homicide, assault, or kidnapping offense.

(iii) Regardless of when the sexually oriented offense was committed, the offender is to be sentenced on or after May 7, 2002, for a sexually oriented offense that is not a registration-exempt sexually oriented offense, and that offender was acquitted of a sexually violent predator specification that was included in the indictment, count in the indictment, or information charging the sexually oriented offense.

(b) The judge who is to impose or has imposed an order of disposition upon a child who is adjudicated a delinquent child for committing on or after January 1, 2002, a sexually oriented offense that is not a registration-exempt sexually oriented offense shall conduct a hearing as provided in this division to determine whether the child is to be classified as a sexual predator if either of the following applies:

(i) The judge is required by section 2152.82 or division (A) of section 2152.83 of the Revised Code to classify the child a juvenile offender registrant.

(ii) Division (B) of section 2152.83 of the Revised Code applies regarding the child, the judge conducts a hearing under that division for the purposes described in that division, and the judge determines at that hearing that the child will be classified a juvenile offender registrant.

(2) Regarding an offender, the judge shall conduct the hearing required by division (B)(1)(a) of this section prior to sentencing and, if the sexually oriented offense for which sentence is to be imposed is a felony and if the hearing is being conducted under division (B)(1)(a) of this section, the judge may conduct it as part of the sentencing hearing required by section 2929.19 of the Revised Code. Regarding a delinquent child, the judge may conduct the hearing required by division (B)(1)(b) of this section at the same time as, or separate from, the dispositional hearing, as specified in the applicable provision of section 2152.82 or 2152.83 of the Revised Code. The court shall give the offender or delinquent child and the prosecutor who prosecuted the offender or handled the case against the delinquent child for the sexually oriented offense notice of the date, time, and location of the hearing. At the hearing, the offender or delinquent child and the prosecutor shall have an opportunity to testify, present evidence, call and examine witnesses and expert witnesses, and cross-examine witnesses and expert witnesses regarding the determination as to whether the offender or delinquent child is a sexual predator. The offender or delinquent child shall have the right to be represented by counsel and, if indigent, the right to have counsel appointed to represent the offender or delinquent child.

(3) In making a determination under divisions (B)(1) and (4) of this section as to whether an offender or delinquent child is a sexual predator, the judge shall consider all relevant factors, including, but not limited to, all of the following:

(a) The offender's or delinquent child's age;

(b) The offender's or delinquent child's prior criminal or delinquency record regarding all offenses, including, but not limited to, all sexual offenses;

(c) The age of the victim of the sexually oriented offense for which sentence is to be imposed or the order of disposition is to be made;

(d) Whether the sexually oriented offense for which sentence is to be imposed or the order of disposition is to be made involved multiple victims;

(e) Whether the offender or delinquent child used drugs or alcohol to impair the victim of the sexually oriented offense or to prevent the victim from resisting;

(f) If the offender or delinquent child previously has been convicted of or pleaded guilty to, or been adjudicated a delinquent child for committing an act that if committed by an adult would be, a criminal offense, whether the offender or delinquent child completed any sentence or dispositional order imposed for the prior offense or act and, if the prior offense or act was a sex offense or a sexually oriented offense, whether the offender or delinquent child participated in available programs for sexual offenders;

(g) Any mental illness or mental disability of the offender or delinquent child;

(h) The nature of the offender's or delinquent child's sexual conduct, sexual contact, or interaction in a sexual context with the victim of the sexually oriented offense and whether the sexual conduct, sexual contact, or interaction in a sexual context was part of a demonstrated pattern of abuse;

(i) Whether the offender or delinquent child, during the commission of the sexually oriented offense for which sentence is to be imposed or the order of disposition is to be made, displayed cruelty or made one or more threats of cruelty;

(j) Any additional behavioral characteristics that contribute to the offender's or delinquent child's conduct.

(4) After reviewing all testimony and evidence presented at the hearing conducted under division (B)(1) of this section and the factors specified in division (B)(3) of this section, the court shall determine by clear and convincing evidence whether the subject offender or delinquent child is a sexual predator. If the court determines that the subject offender or delinquent child is not a sexual predator, the court shall specify in the offender's sentence and the judgment of conviction that contains the sentence or in the delinquent child's dispositional order, as appropriate, that the court has determined that the offender or delinquent child is not a sexual predator and the reason or reasons why the court determined that the subject offender or delinquent child is not a sexual predator. If the court determines by clear and convincing evidence that the subject offender or delinquent child is a sexual predator, the court shall specify in the offender's sentence and the judgment of conviction that contains the sentence or in the delinquent child's dispositional order, as appropriate, that the court has determined that the offender or delinquent child is a sexual predator and shall specify that the determination was pursuant to division (B) of this section. In any case in which the sexually oriented offense in question is an aggravated sexually oriented offense, the court shall specify in the offender's sentence and the judgment of conviction that contains the sentence that the offender's offense is an aggravated sexually oriented offense. The offender or delinquent child and the prosecutor who prosecuted the offender or handled the case against the delinquent child for the sexually oriented offense in question may appeal as a matter of right the court's determination under this division as to whether the offender or delinquent child is, or is not, a sexual predator.

(5) A hearing shall not be conducted under division (B) of this section regarding an offender if the sexually oriented offense in question is a sexually violent offense, if the indictment, count in the indictment, or information charging the offense also included a sexually violent predator specification, and if the offender is convicted of or pleads guilty to that sexually violent predator specification.

(C)(1) If a person was convicted of or pleaded guilty to a sexually oriented offense that is not a registration-exempt sexually oriented offense prior to January 1, 1997, if the person was not sentenced for the offense on or after January 1, 1997, and if, on or after January 1, 1997, the offender is serving a term of imprisonment in a state correctional institution, the department of rehabilitation and correction shall do whichever of the following is applicable:

(a) If the sexually oriented offense was an offense described in division (D)(1)(c) of section 2950.01 of the Revised Code or was a violent sex offense, the department shall notify the court that sentenced the offender of this fact, and the court shall conduct a hearing to determine whether the offender is a sexual predator.

(b) If division (C)(1)(a) of this section does not apply, the department shall determine whether to recommend that the offender be adjudicated a sexual predator. In making a determination under this division as to whether to recommend that the offender be adjudicated a sexual predator, the department shall consider all relevant factors, including, but not limited to, all of the factors specified in divisions (B)(2) and (3) of this section. If the department determines that it will recommend that the offender be adjudicated a sexual predator, it immediately shall send the recommendation to the court that sentenced the offender. If the department determines that it will not recommend that the offender be adjudicated a sexual predator, it immediately shall send its determination to the court that sentenced the offender. In all cases, the department shall enter its determination and recommendation in the offender's institutional record, and the court shall proceed in accordance with division (C)(2) of this section.

(2)(a) If the department of rehabilitation and correction sends to a court a notice under division (C)(1)(a) of this section, the court shall conduct a hearing to determine whether the subject offender is a sexual predator. If, pursuant to division (C)(1)(b) of this section, the department sends to a court a recommendation that an offender be adjudicated a sexual predator, the court is not bound by the department's recommendation, and the court shall conduct a hearing to determine whether the offender is a sexual predator. In any case, the court shall not make a determination as to whether the offender is, or is not, a sexual predator without a hearing. The court may hold the hearing and make the determination prior to the offender's release from imprisonment or at any time within one year following the offender's release from that imprisonment.

(b) If, pursuant to division (C)(1)(b) of this section, the department sends to the court a determination that it is not recommending that an offender be adjudicated a sexual predator, the court shall not make any determination as to whether the offender is, or is not, a sexual predator but shall determine whether the offender previously has been convicted of or pleaded guilty to a sexually oriented offense other than the offense in relation to which the department made its determination or previously has been convicted of or pleaded guilty to a child-victim oriented offense.

The court may conduct a hearing to determine whether the offender previously has been convicted of or pleaded guilty to a sexually oriented offense or a child-victim oriented offense but may make the determination without a hearing. However, if the court determines that the offender previously has been convicted of or pleaded guilty to such an offense, it shall not impose a requirement that the offender be subject to the community notification provisions contained in sections 2950.10 and 2950.11 of the Revised Code without a hearing. In determining whether to impose the community notification requirement, the court, in the circumstances described in division (E)(2) of this section, shall apply the presumption specified in that division. The court shall include in the offender's institutional record any determination made under this division as to whether the offender previously has been convicted of or pleaded guilty to a sexually oriented offense or child-victim oriented offense, and, as such, whether the offender is a habitual sex offender.

(c) Upon scheduling a hearing under division (C)(2)(a) or (b) of this section, the court shall give the offender and the prosecutor who prosecuted the offender for the sexually oriented offense, or that prosecutor's successor in office, notice of the date, time, and place of the hearing. If the hearing is scheduled under division (C)(2)(a) of this section to determine whether the offender is a sexual predator, the prosecutor who is given the notice may contact the department of rehabilitation and correction and request that the department provide to the prosecutor all information the department possesses regarding the offender that is relevant and necessary for use in making the determination as to whether the offender is a sexual predator and that is not privileged or confidential under law. If the prosecutor makes a request for that information, the department promptly shall provide to the prosecutor all information the department possesses regarding the offender that is not privileged or confidential under law and that is relevant and necessary for making that determination. A hearing scheduled under division (C)(2)(a) of this section to determine whether the offender is a sexual predator shall be conducted in the manner described in division (B)(1) of this section regarding hearings conducted under that division and, in making a determination under this division as to whether the offender is a sexual predator, the court shall consider all relevant factors, including, but not limited to, all of the factors specified in divisions (B)(2) and (3) of this section. After reviewing all testimony and evidence presented at the sexual predator hearing and the factors specified in divisions (B)(2) and (3) of this section, the court shall determine by clear and convincing evidence whether the offender is a sexual predator. If the court determines at the sexual predator hearing that the offender is not a sexual predator, it also shall determine whether the offender previously has been convicted of or pleaded guilty to a sexually oriented offense other than the offense in relation to which the hearing is being conducted.

Upon making its determinations at the sexual predator hearing, the court shall proceed as follows:

(i) If the court determines that the offender is not a sexual predator and that the offender previously has not been convicted of or pleaded guilty to a sexually oriented offense other than the offense in relation to which the hearing is being conducted and previously has not been convicted of or pleaded guilty to a child-victim oriented offense, it shall include in the offender's institutional record its determinations and the reason or reasons why it determined that the offender is not a sexual predator.

(ii) If the court determines that the offender is not a sexual predator but that the offender previously has been convicted of or pleaded guilty to a sexually oriented offense other than the offense in relation to which the hearing is being conducted or previously has been convicted of or pleaded guilty to a child-victim oriented offense, it shall include in the offender's institutional record its determination that the offender is not a sexual predator but is a habitual sex offender and the reason or reasons why it determined that the offender is not a sexual predator, shall attach the determinations and the reason or reasons to the offender's sentence, shall specify that the determinations were pursuant to division (C) of this section, shall provide a copy of the determinations and the reason or reasons to the offender, to the prosecuting attorney, and to the department of rehabilitation and correction, and may impose a requirement that the offender be subject to the community notification provisions contained in sections 2950.10 and 2950.11 of the Revised Code. In determining whether to impose the community notification requirements, the court, in the circumstances described in division (E)(2) of this section, shall apply the presumption specified in that division. The offender shall not be subject to those community notification provisions relative to the sexually oriented offense in question if the court does not so impose the requirement described in this division. If the court imposes that requirement, the offender may appeal the judge's determination that the offender is a habitual sex offender.

(iii) If the court determines by clear and convincing evidence that the offender is a sexual predator, it shall enter its determination in the offender's institutional record, shall attach the determination to the offender's sentence, shall specify that the determination was pursuant to division (C) of this section, and shall provide a copy of the determination to the offender, to the prosecuting attorney, and to the department of rehabilitation and correction. The offender and the prosecutor may appeal as a matter of right the judge's determination under divisions (C)(2)(a) and (c) of this section as to whether the offender is, or is not, a sexual predator.

If the hearing is scheduled under division (C)(2)(b) of this section to determine whether the offender previously has been convicted of or pleaded guilty to a sexually oriented offense or a child-victim oriented offense or whether to subject the offender to the community notification provisions contained in sections 2950.10 and 2950.11 of the Revised Code, upon making the determination, the court shall attach the determination or determinations to the offender's sentence, shall provide a copy to the offender, to the prosecuting attorney, and to the department of rehabilitation and correction and may impose a requirement that the offender be subject to the community notification provisions. In determining whether to impose the community notification requirements, the court, in the circumstances described in division (E)(2) of this section, shall apply the presumption specified in that division. The offender shall not be subject to the community notification provisions relative to the sexually oriented offense in question if the court does not so impose the requirement described in this division. If the court imposes that requirement, the offender may appeal the judge's determination that the offender is a habitual sex offender.

(3) The changes made in divisions (C)(1) and (2) of this section that take effect on July 31, 2003, do not require a court to conduct a new hearing under those divisions for any offender regarding a sexually oriented offense if, prior to July 31, 2003, the court previously conducted a hearing under those divisions regarding that offense to determine whether the offender was a sexual predator. The changes made in divisions (C)(1) and (2) of this section that take effect on July 31, 2003, do not require a court to conduct a hearing under those divisions for any offender regarding a sexually oriented offense if, prior to July 31, 2003, and pursuant to those divisions, the department of rehabilitation and correction recommended that the offender be adjudicated a sexual predator regarding that offense, and the court denied the recommendation and determined that the offender was not a sexual predator without a hearing, provided that this provision does not apply if the sexually oriented offense in question was an offense described in division (D)(1)(c) of section 2950.01 of the Revised Code.

(D)(1) Division (D)(1) of this section does not apply to any person who has been convicted of or pleaded guilty to a sexually oriented offense. Division (D) of this section applies only to delinquent children as provided in Chapter 2152. of the Revised Code. A person who has been adjudicated a delinquent child for committing a sexually oriented offense that is not a registration-exempt sexually oriented offense and who has been classified by a juvenile court judge a juvenile offender registrant or, if applicable, additionally has been determined by a juvenile court judge to be a sexual predator or habitual sex offender, may petition the adjudicating court for a reclassification or declassification pursuant to section 2152.85 of the Revised Code.

A judge who is reviewing a sexual predator determination for a delinquent child under section 2152.84 or 2152.85 of the Revised Code shall comply with this section. At the hearing, the judge shall consider all relevant evidence and information, including, but not limited to, the factors set forth in division (B)(3) of this section. The judge shall not enter a determination that the delinquent child no longer is a sexual predator unless the judge determines by clear and convincing evidence that the delinquent child is unlikely to commit a sexually oriented offense in the future. If the judge enters a determination under this division that the delinquent child no longer is a sexual predator, the judge shall notify the bureau of criminal identification and investigation of the determination and shall include in the notice a statement of the reason or reasons why it determined that the delinquent child no longer is a sexual predator. Upon receipt of the notification, the bureau promptly shall notify the sheriff with whom the delinquent child most recently registered under section 2950.04 or 2950.05 of the Revised Code of the determination that the delinquent child no longer is a sexual predator.

(2) If an offender who has been convicted of or pleaded guilty to a sexually oriented offense is classified a sexual predator pursuant to division (A) of this section or has been adjudicated a sexual predator relative to the offense as described in division (B) or (C) of this section, subject to division (F) of this section, the classification or adjudication of the offender as a sexual predator is permanent and continues in effect until the offender's death and in no case shall the classification or adjudication be removed or terminated.

(E)(1) If a person is convicted of or pleads guilty to committing, on or after January 1, 1997, a sexually oriented offense that is not a registration-exempt sexually oriented offense, the judge who is to impose sentence on the offender shall determine, prior to sentencing, whether the offender previously has been convicted of or pleaded guilty to, or adjudicated a delinquent child for committing, a sexually oriented offense or a child-victim oriented offense and is a habitual sex offender. The judge who is to impose or has imposed an order of disposition upon a child who is adjudicated a delinquent child for committing on or after January 1, 2002, a sexually oriented offense that is not a registration-exempt sexually oriented offense shall determine, prior to entering the order classifying the delinquent child a juvenile offender registrant, whether the delinquent child previously has been convicted of or pleaded guilty to, or adjudicated a delinquent child for committing, a sexually oriented offense or a child-victim oriented offense and is a habitual sex offender, if either of the following applies:

(a) The judge is required by section 2152.82 or division (A) of section 2152.83 of the Revised Code to classify the child a juvenile offender registrant;

(b) Division (B) of section 2152.83 of the Revised Code applies regarding the child, the judge conducts a hearing under that division for the purposes described in that division, and the judge determines at that hearing that the child will be classified a juvenile offender registrant.

(2) If, under division (E)(1) of this section, the judge determines that the offender or delinquent child previously has not been convicted of or pleaded guilty to, or been adjudicated a delinquent child for committing, a sexually oriented offense or a child-victim oriented offense or that the offender otherwise does not satisfy the criteria for being a habitual sex offender, the judge shall specify in the offender's sentence or in the order classifying the delinquent child a juvenile offender registrant that the judge has determined that the offender or delinquent child is not a habitual sex offender.

If, under division (E)(1) of this section, the judge determines that the offender or delinquent child previously has been convicted of or pleaded guilty to, or been adjudicated a delinquent child for committing, a sexually oriented offense or a child-victim oriented offense and that the offender satisfies all other criteria for being a habitual sex offender, the offender or delinquent child is a habitual sex offender or habitual child-victim offender and the court shall determine whether to impose a requirement that the offender or delinquent child be subject to the community notification provisions contained in sections 2950.10 and 2950.11 of the Revised Code. In making the determination regarding the possible imposition of the community notification requirement, if at least two of the sexually oriented offenses or child-victim oriented offenses that are the basis of the habitual sex offender or habitual child-victim offender determination were committed against a victim who was under eighteen years of age, it is presumed that subjecting the offender or delinquent child to the community notification provisions is necessary in order to comply with the determinations, findings, and declarations of the general assembly regarding sex offenders and child-victim offenders that are set forth in section 2950.02 of the Revised Code. When a judge determines as described in this division that an offender or delinquent child is a habitual sex offender or a habitual child-victim offender, the judge shall specify in the offender's sentence and the judgment of conviction that contains the sentence or in the order classifying the delinquent child a juvenile offender registrant that the judge has determined that the offender or delinquent child is a habitual sex offender and may impose a requirement in that sentence and judgment of conviction or in that order that the offender or delinquent child be subject to the community notification provisions contained in sections 2950.10 and 2950.11 of the Revised Code. Unless the habitual sex offender also has been adjudicated a sexual predator relative to the sexually oriented offense in question or the habitual sex offender was convicted of or pleaded guilty to an aggravated sexually oriented offense, the offender or delinquent child shall be subject to those community notification provisions only if the court imposes the requirement described in this division in the offender's sentence and the judgment of conviction or in the order classifying the delinquent child a juvenile offender registrant. If the court determines pursuant to this division or division (C)(2) of this section that an offender is a habitual sex offender, the determination is permanent and continues in effect until the offender's death, and in no case shall the determination be removed or terminated.

If a court in another state, a federal court, military court, or Indian tribal court, or a court in any nation other than the United States determines a person to be a habitual sex offender in that jurisdiction, the person is considered to be determined to be a habitual sex offender in this state. If the court in the other state, the federal court, military court, or Indian tribal court, or the court in the nation other than the United States subjects the habitual sex offender to community notification regarding the person's place of residence, the person, as much as is practicable, is subject to the community notification provisions regarding the person's place of residence that are contained in sections 2950.10 and 2950.11 of the Revised Code, unless the court that so subjected the person to community notification determines that the person no longer is subject to community notification.

(F)(1) An offender or delinquent child classified as a sexual predator may petition the court of common pleas or, for a delinquent child, the juvenile court of the county in which the offender or delinquent child resides or temporarily is domiciled to enter a determination that the offender or delinquent child is not an adjudicated sexual predator in this state for purposes of the registration and other requirements of this chapter or the community notification provisions contained in sections 2950.10 and 2950.11 of the Revised Code if all of the following apply:

(a) The offender or delinquent child was convicted of, pleaded guilty to, or was adjudicated a delinquent child for committing, a sexually oriented offense that is not a registration-exempt sexually oriented offense in another state, in a federal court, a military court, or Indian tribal court, or in a court of any nation other than the United States.

(b) As a result of the conviction, plea of guilty, or adjudication described in division (F)(1)(a) of this section, the offender or delinquent child is required under the law of the jurisdiction under which the offender or delinquent child was convicted, pleaded guilty, or was adjudicated to register as a sex offender until the offender's or delinquent child's death.

(c) The offender or delinquent child was automatically classified a sexual predator under division (A) of this section in relation to the conviction, guilty plea, or adjudication described in division (F)(1)(a) of this section.

(2) The court may enter a determination that the offender or delinquent child filing the petition described in division (F)(1) of this section is not an adjudicated sexual predator in this state for purposes of the registration and other requirements of this chapter or the community notification provisions contained in sections 2950.10 and 2950.11 of the Revised Code only if the offender or delinquent child proves by clear and convincing evidence that the requirement of the other jurisdiction that the offender or delinquent child register as a sex offender until the offender's or delinquent child's death is not substantially similar to a classification as a sexual predator for purposes of this chapter. If the court enters a determination that the offender or delinquent child is not an adjudicated sexual predator in this state for those purposes, the court shall include in the determination a statement of the reason or reasons why it so determined.

(G) If, prior to the effective date of this section, an offender or delinquent child was adjudicated a sexual predator or was determined to be a habitual sex offender under this section or section 2152.82, 2152.83, 2152.84, or 2152.85 of the Revised Code and if, on and after July 31, 2003, the sexually oriented offense upon which the classification or determination was based no longer is considered a sexually oriented offense but instead is a child-victim oriented offense, notwithstanding the redesignation of that offense, on and after July 31, 2003, all of the following apply:

(1) Divisions (A)(1) or (2) or (E)(1) and (2) of section 2950.091 of the Revised Code apply regarding the offender or child, and the judge's classification or determination made prior to July 31, 2003, shall be considered for all purposes to be a classification or determination that classifies the offender or child as described in those divisions.

(2) The offender's or child's classification or determination under divisions (A)(1) or (2) or (E)(1) and (2) of section 2950.091 of the Revised Code shall be considered, for purposes of section 2950.07 of the Revised Code and for all other purposes, to be a continuation of the classification or determination made prior to July 31, 2003.

(3) The offender's or child's duties under this chapter relative to that classification or determination shall be considered for all purposes to be a continuation of the duties related to that classification or determination as they existed prior to July 31, 2003.

(2004 H 473, eff. 4–29–05; 2003 S 5, eff. 7–31–03; 2002 H 485, eff. 6–13–02; 2002 S 175, eff. 5–7–02; 2002 H 393, eff. 7–5–02; 2001 S 3, eff. 1–1–02; 2000 H 502, eff. 3–15–01; 1998 H 565, eff. 3–30–99; 1996 H 180, eff. 1–1–97)

Note: See also preceding version of this section, in effect until 4–29–05.

2950.091 Determination of offender as child-victim predator; hearing

(A)(1) If, prior to the effective date of this section, a person was convicted of, pleaded guilty to, or was adjudicated a delinquent child for committing, a sexually oriented offense, if, prior to the effective date of this section, the offender or delinquent child was classified a sexual predator in relation to that offense pursuant to division (A) of section 2950.09 of the Revised Code, and if, on and after the effective date of this section, the sexually oriented offense upon which the classification was based no longer is considered a sexually oriented offense but instead is a child-victim oriented offense, notwithstanding the redesignation of the offense, the classification of the offender or child as a sexual predator remains valid and in effect on and after the effective date of this section.

(2) If, prior to the effective date of this section, a person was convicted of, pleaded guilty to, or was adjudicated a delinquent child for committing a sexually oriented offense, if, prior to the effective date of this section, the offender or delinquent child was adjudicated a sexual predator in relation to that offense under section 2950.09 or section 2152.82, 2152.83, 2152.84, or 2152.85 of the Revised Code, if, on and after the effective date of this section, the sexually oriented offense upon which the adjudication was based no longer is considered a sexually oriented offense but instead is a child-victim oriented offense, and if division (A)(1) of this section does not apply, notwithstanding the redesignation of the offense, on and after the effective date of this section, the offender or delinquent child automatically is classified a child-victim predator. If a person is convicted, pleads guilty, or adjudicated a delinquent child in a court of another state, in a federal court, military court, or Indian tribal court, or in a court of any nation other than the United States for committing a child-victim oriented offense, and if, as a result of that conviction, plea of guilty, or adjudication, the person is required under the law of the jurisdiction in which the person was convicted, pleaded guilty, or adjudicated to register as a child-victim offender or sex offender until the person's death, that conviction, plea of guilty, or adjudication automatically classifies the person a child-victim predator for the purposes of this chapter, but the person may challenge that classification pursuant to division (F) of this section.

(3) In all cases not described in division (A)(1) or (2) of this section, a person who is convicted of or pleads guilty to, has been

convicted of or pleaded guilty to, or is adjudicated a delinquent child for committing a child-victim oriented offense may be classified a child-victim predator for purposes of this chapter only in accordance with division (B) or (C) of this section or, regarding delinquent children, divisions (B) and (C) of section 2152.83 of the Revised Code.

(B)(1)(a) Regardless of when the offense was committed, the judge who is to impose sentence on or after the effective date of this section on an offender who has been convicted of or pleaded guilty to a child-victim oriented offense shall conduct a hearing to determine whether the offender is a child-victim predator.

(b) The judge who is to impose or has imposed an order of disposition upon a child who is adjudicated a delinquent child for committing on or after the effective date of this section a child-victim oriented offense shall conduct a hearing as provided in this division to determine whether the child is to be classified as a child-victim predator if either of the following applies:

(i) The judge is required by section 2152.82 or division (A) of section 2152.83 of the Revised Code to classify the child a juvenile offender registrant.

(ii) Division (B) of section 2152.83 of the Revised Code applies regarding the child, the judge conducts a hearing under that division for the purposes described in that division, and the judge determines at that hearing that the child will be classified a juvenile offender registrant.

(2) Regarding an offender, the judge shall conduct the hearing required by division (B)(1)(a) of this section prior to sentencing and, if the child-victim oriented offense is a felony and if the hearing is being conducted under division (B)(1)(a) of this section, the judge may conduct it as part of the sentencing hearing required by section 2929.19 of the Revised Code. Regarding a delinquent child, the judge may conduct the hearing required by division (B)(1)(b) of this section at the same time as, or separate from, the dispositional hearing, as specified in the applicable provision of section 2152.82 or 2152.83 of the Revised Code. The court shall give the offender or delinquent child and the prosecutor who prosecuted the offender or handled the case against the delinquent child for the child-victim oriented offense notice of the date, time, and location of the hearing. At the hearing, the offender or delinquent child and the prosecutor have the same opportunities and rights as described in division (B)(2) of section 2950.09 of the Revised Code regarding sexual predator hearings.

(3) In making a determination under divisions (B)(1) and (4) of this section as to whether an offender or delinquent child is a child-victim predator, the judge shall consider all relevant factors, including, but not limited to, all of the factors identified in division (B)(3) of section 2950. 09 of the Revised Code regarding sexual predator hearings, except that all references in the factors so identified in that division to any "sexual offense" or "sexually oriented offense" shall be construed for purposes of this division as being references to a "child-victim oriented offense" and all references in the factors so identified to "sexual offenders" shall be construed for purposes of this division as being references to "child-victim offenders."

(4) After reviewing all testimony and evidence presented at the hearing conducted under division (B)(1) of this section and the factors specified in division (B)(3) of this section, the court shall determine by clear and convincing evidence whether the subject offender or delinquent child is a child-victim predator. If the court determines that the subject offender or delinquent child is not a child-victim predator, the court shall specify in the offender's sentence and the judgment of conviction that contains the sentence or in the delinquent child's dispositional order, as appropriate, that the court has determined that the offender or delinquent child is not a child-victim predator and the reason or reasons why the court determined that the subject offender or delinquent child is not a child-victim predator. If the court determines by clear and convincing evidence that the subject offender or delinquent child is a child-victim predator, the court shall specify in the offender's sentence and the judgment of conviction that contains the sentence or in the delinquent child's dispositional order, as appropriate, that the court has determined that the offender or delinquent child is a child-victim predator and shall specify that the determination was pursuant to division (B) of this section. The offender or delinquent child and the prosecutor who prosecuted the offender or handled the case against the delinquent child for the child-victim oriented offense in question may appeal as a matter of right the court's determination under this division as to whether the offender or delinquent child is, or is not, a child-victim predator.

(C)(1) If, prior to the effective date of this section, a person was convicted of or pleaded guilty to a sexually oriented offense, if, on and after the effective date of this section, the sexually oriented offense no longer is considered a sexually oriented offense but instead is a child-victim oriented offense, if the person was not sentenced for the offense on or after January 1, 1997, and if, on or after the effective date of this section, the offender is serving a term of imprisonment in a state correctional institution, the department of rehabilitation and correction shall determine whether to recommend that the offender be adjudicated a child-victim predator. In making a determination under this division as to whether to recommend that the offender be adjudicated a child-victim predator, the department shall consider all relevant factors, including, but not limited to, all of the factors specified in divisions (B)(2) and (3) of this section. If the department determines that it will recommend that the offender be adjudicated a child-victim predator or determines that it will not recommend that the offender be adjudicated a child-victim predator, it immediately shall send its recommendation or determination to the court that sentenced the offender. In all cases, the department shall enter its determination and recommendation in the offender's institutional record, and the court shall proceed in accordance with division (C)(2) of this section.

(2)(a) If, pursuant to division (C)(1) of this section, the department of rehabilitation and correction sends to a court a recommendation that an offender be adjudicated a child-victim predator, the court is not bound by the department's recommendation, and the court shall conduct a hearing to determine whether the offender is a child-victim predator. In any case, the court shall not make a determination that the offender is, or is not, a child-victim predator without a hearing. The court may hold the hearing and make the determination prior to the offender's release from imprisonment or at any time within one year following the offender's release from that imprisonment.

(b) If, pursuant to division (C)(1) of this section, the department sends to the court a determination that it is not recommending that an offender be adjudicated a child-victim predator, the court shall not make any determination as to whether the offender is, or is not, a child-victim predator but shall determine whether the offender previously has been convicted of or pleaded guilty to a child-victim oriented offense other than the offense in relation to which the department made its determination.

The court may conduct a hearing to determine whether the offender previously has been convicted of or pleaded guilty to a child-victim oriented offense but may make the determination without a hearing. However, if the court determines that the offender previously has been convicted of or pleaded guilty to an offense of that nature, it shall not impose a requirement that the offender be subject to the community notification provisions contained in sections 2950.10 and 2950.11 of the Revised Code without a hearing. The court shall include in the offender's institutional record any determination made under this division as to whether the offender previously has been convicted of or pleaded guilty to a child-victim oriented offense and whether the offender is a habitual child-victim offender.

(c) Upon scheduling a hearing under division (C)(2)(a) or (b) of this section, the court shall give the offender and the prosecutor who prosecuted the offender for the child-victim oriented offense, or that prosecutor's successor in office, notice of the date, time, and place of the hearing. If the hearing is scheduled under division (C)(2)(a) of this section to determine whether the offender is a child-victim predator, it shall be conducted in the manner described in division (B)(1) of this section regarding hearings conducted under that division, and, in making a determination under this division as to whether the offender is a child-victim predator, the court shall consider all relevant factors, including, but not limited to, all of the factors specified in divisions (B)(2) and (3) of this section. After reviewing all testimony and evidence presented at the child-victim predator hearing and the factors specified in divisions (B)(2) and (3) of this section, the court shall determine by clear and convincing evidence whether the offender is a child-victim predator. If the court determines at the child-victim predator hearing that the offender is not a child-victim predator, it also shall determine whether the offender previously has been convicted of or pleaded guilty to a child-victim oriented offense other than the offense in relation to which the hearing is being conducted.

Upon making its determinations at the child-victim predator hearing, the court shall proceed as follows:

(i) If the court determines that the offender is not a child-victim predator and that the offender previously has not been convicted of or pleaded guilty to a child-victim oriented offense other than the offense in relation to which the hearing is being conducted, it shall include in the offender's institutional record its determinations and the reason or reasons why it determined that the offender is not a child-victim predator.

(ii) If the court determines that the offender is not a child-victim predator but that the offender previously has been convicted of or pleaded guilty to a child-victim oriented offense other than the offense in relation to which the hearing is being conducted, it shall include in the offender's institutional record its determination that the offender is not a child-victim predator but is a habitual child-victim offender and the reason or reasons why it determined that the offender is not a child-victim predator, shall attach the determinations and the reason or reasons to the offender's sentence, shall specify that the determinations were made pursuant to division (C) of this section, shall provide a copy of the determinations and the reason or reasons to the offender, to the prosecuting attorney, and to the department of rehabilitation and correction, and may impose a requirement that the offender be subject to the community notification provisions contained in sections 2950.10 and 2950.11 of the Revised Code. The offender shall not be subject to those community notification provisions relative to the child victim oriented offense in question if the court does not so impose the requirement described in this division. If the court imposes that requirement, the offender may appeal the judge's determination that the offender is a habitual child-victim offender.

(iii) If the court determines by clear and convincing evidence that the offender is a child-victim predator, it shall enter its determination in the offender's institutional record, shall attach the determination to the offender's sentence, shall specify that the determination was made pursuant to division (C) of this section, and shall provide a copy of the determination to the offender, to the prosecuting attorney, and to the department of rehabilitation and correction. The offender and the prosecutor may appeal as a matter of right the judge's determination under this division as to whether the offender is, or is not, a child-victim predator.

If the hearing is scheduled under division (C)(2)(b) of this section to determine whether the offender previously has been convicted of or pleaded guilty to a child-victim oriented offense or whether to subject the offender to the community notification provisions contained in sections 2950.10 and 2950.11 of the Revised Code, upon making the determination, the court shall attach the determination or determinations to the offender's sentence, shall provide a copy to the offender, to the prosecuting attorney, and to the department of rehabilitation and correction and may impose a requirement that the offender be subject to the community notification provisions. The offender shall not be subject to the community notification provisions relative to the child-victim oriented offense in question if the court does not so impose the requirement described in this division. If the court imposes that requirement, the offender may appeal the judge's determination that the offender is a habitual child-victim offender.

(3) Divisions (C)(1) and (2) of this section do not require a court to conduct a new hearing under those divisions for any offender regarding a child-victim oriented offense if, prior to the effective date of this section, the court previously conducted a hearing under divisions (C)(1) and (2) of section 2950.09 of the Revised Code regarding that offense, while it formerly was classified a sexually oriented offense, to determine whether the offender was a sexual predator. Divisions (C)(1) and (2) of this section do not require a court to conduct a hearing under those divisions for any offender regarding a child-victim oriented offense if, prior to the effective date of this section and pursuant to divisions (C)(1) and (2) of section 2950.09 of the Revised Code, the department of rehabilitation and correction recommended that the offender be adjudicated a sexual predator regarding that offense, while it formerly was classified a sexually oriented offense, and the court denied the recommendation and determined that the offender was not a sexual predator without a hearing, provided that this provision does not apply if the child-victim oriented offense in question was an offense described in division (D)(1)(c) of section 2950.01 of the Revised Code.

(D)(1) Division (D) of this section does not apply to any person who has been convicted of or pleaded guilty to a child-victim oriented offense. Division (D) of this section applies only to delinquent children as provided in Chapter 2152. of the Revised Code. A person who has been adjudicated a delinquent child for committing a child-victim oriented offense and who has been classified by a juvenile court judge a juvenile offender registrant or, if applicable, additionally has been determined by a juvenile court judge to be a child-victim predator or habitual child-victim offender, may petition the adjudicating court for a reclassification or declassification pursuant to section 2152.85 of the Revised Code.

A judge who is reviewing a child-victim predator determination for a delinquent child under section 2152.84 or 2152.85 of the Revised Code shall comply with this section. At the hearing, the judge shall consider all relevant evidence and information, including, but not limited to, the factors set forth in division (B)(3) of this section. The judge shall not enter a determination that the delinquent child no longer is a child-victim predator unless the judge determines by clear and convincing evidence that the delinquent child is unlikely to commit a child-victim oriented offense in the future. If the judge enters a determination under this division that the delinquent child no longer is a child-victim predator, the judge shall notify the bureau of criminal identification and investigation of the determination and shall include in the notice a statement of the reason or reasons why it determined that the delinquent child no longer is a child-victim predator. Upon receipt of the notification, the bureau promptly shall notify the sheriff with whom the delinquent child most recently registered under section 2950.04 or 2950.05 of the Revised Code of the determination that the offender no longer is a child-victim predator.

(2) If an offender who has been convicted of or pleaded guilty to a child-victim oriented offense is classified a child-victim predator pursuant to division (A) of this section or has been adjudicated a child-victim predator relative to the offense as described in division (B) or (C) of this section, subject to division (F) of this section, the classification or adjudication of the offender as a child-victim predator is permanent and continues in effect until the offender's death, and in no case shall the classification or adjudication be removed or terminated.

(E)(1) If, prior to the effective date of this section, a person was convicted of, pleaded guilty to, or adjudicated a delinquent child for committing a sexually oriented offense, if, on and after the effective date of this section, the sexually oriented offense no longer is considered a sexually oriented offense but instead is a child-victim oriented offense, if, prior to the effective date of this section, a judge determined that the offender or delinquent child was a habitual sex offender, and if one or more of the offenses that was the basis of the offender or delinquent child being a habitual sex offender remains on and after the effective date of this section a sexually oriented offense, notwithstanding the re-designation of the offense as described in this division, the determination and classification of that person as a habitual sex offender remains valid and in effect on and after the effective date of this section.

(2) If, prior to the effective date of this section, a person was convicted of, pleaded guilty to, or adjudicated a delinquent child for committing a sexually oriented offense, if, on and after the effective date of this section, the sexually oriented offense no longer is considered a sexually oriented offense but instead is a child-victim oriented offense, if, prior to the effective date of this section, a judge determined that the offender or delinquent child was a habitual sex offender, and if none of the offenses that was the basis of the offender or delinquent child being a habitual sex offender remains on and after the effective date of this section a sexually oriented offense, on and after the effective date of this section, the offender or delinquent child automatically is classified a habitual child-victim offender.

(3) If a person is convicted of or pleads guilty to committing a child-victim oriented offense and is to be sentenced for the offense on or after the effective date of this section, the judge who is to impose sentence on the offender shall determine, prior to sentencing, whether the offender previously has been convicted of or pleaded guilty to, or adjudicated a delinquent child for committing, a child-victim oriented offense and is a habitual child-victim offender. The judge who is to impose or has imposed an order of disposition on or after the effective date of this section upon a child who is adjudicated a delinquent child for committing a child-victim oriented offense shall determine, prior to entering the order classifying the delinquent child a juvenile child-victim offender registrant, whether the delinquent child previously has been convicted of or pleaded guilty to, or adjudicated a delinquent child for committing, a child-victim oriented offense and is a habitual child-victim offender, if either of the following applies:

(a) The judge is required by section 2152.82 or division (A) of section 2152.83 of the Revised Code to classify the child a juvenile offender registrant.

(b) Division (B) of section 2152.83 of the Revised Code applies regarding the child, the judge conducts a hearing under that division for the purposes described in that division, and the judge determines at that hearing that the child will be classified a juvenile offender registrant.

(4) If, under division (E)(3) of this section, the judge determines that the offender or delinquent child previously has not been convicted of or pleaded guilty to, or been adjudicated a delinquent child for committing, a child-victim oriented offense or that the offender otherwise does not satisfy the criteria for being a habitual child-victim offender, the judge shall specify in the offender's sentence or in the order classifying the delinquent child a juvenile child-victim offender registrant that the judge has determined that the offender or delinquent child is not a habitual child-victim offender. If the judge determines that the offender or delinquent child previously has been convicted of or pleaded guilty to, or been adjudicated a delinquent child for committing, a child-victim oriented offense and that the offender satisfies all other criteria for being a habitual child-victim offender, the judge shall specify in the offender's sentence and the judgment of conviction that contains the sentence or in the order classifying the delinquent child a juvenile offender registrant that the judge has determined that the offender or delinquent child is a habitual child-victim offender and may impose a requirement in that sentence and judgment of conviction or in that order that the offender or delinquent child be subject to the community notification provisions contained in sections 2950.10 and 2950.11 of the Revised Code. Unless the habitual child-victim offender also has been adjudicated a child-victim predator relative to the child-victim oriented offense in question, the offender or delinquent child shall be subject to those community notification provisions only if the court imposes the requirement described in this division in the offender's sentence and the judgment of conviction or in the order classifying the delinquent child a juvenile offender registrant. If the court determines pursuant to this division or division (C)(2) of this section that an offender is a habitual child-victim offender, the determination is permanent and continues in effect until the offender's death, and in no case shall the determination be removed or terminated.

If a court in another state, a federal court, military court, or Indian tribal court, or a court in any nation other than the United States, determines a person is a habitual child-victim offender in that jurisdiction, the person is considered to be determined a habitual child-victim offender in this state. If the court in the other state, the federal court, military court, or Indian tribal court, or the court in any nation other than the United States subjects the habitual child-victim offender to community notification regarding the person's place of residence, the person, as much as is practicable, is subject to the community notification provisions regarding the person's place of residence that are contained in sections 2950.10 and 2950.11 of the Revised Code, unless the court that so subjected the person to community notification determines that the person no longer is subject to community notification.

(F)(1) An offender or delinquent child classified a child-victim predator may petition the court of common pleas or, for a delinquent child, the juvenile court of the county in which the offender or delinquent child resides or temporarily is domiciled to enter a determination that the offender or delinquent child is not an adjudicated child-victim predator in this state for purposes of the registration and other requirements of this chapter or the community notification provisions contained in sections 2950.10 and 2950.11 of the Revised Code if all of the following apply:

(a) The offender or delinquent child was convicted, pleaded guilty, or adjudicated a delinquent child in a court of another state, in a federal court, a military court, or Indian tribal court, or in a court of any nation other than the United States for committing a child-victim oriented offense.

(b) As a result of the conviction, plea of guilty, or adjudication described in division (F)(1)(a) of this section, the offender or delinquent child is required under the law of the jurisdiction under which the offender or delinquent child was convicted, pleaded guilty, or was adjudicated to register as a child-victim offender until the offender's or delinquent child's death.

(c) The offender or delinquent child was automatically classified a child-victim predator under division (A) of this section in relation to the conviction, guilty plea, or adjudication described in division (F)(1)(a) of this section.

(2) The court may enter a determination that the offender or delinquent child filing the petition described in division (F)(1) of this section is not an adjudicated child-victim predator in this state for purposes of the registration and other requirements of this chapter or the community notification provisions contained in sections 2950.10 and 2950.11 of the Revised Code only if the offender or delinquent child proves by clear and convincing evidence that the requirement of the other jurisdiction that the offender or delinquent child register as a child-victim offender until the offender's or delinquent child's death is not substantially similar to a classification as a child-victim predator for purposes of this chapter. If the court enters a determination that the offender or delinquent child is not an adjudicated child-victim

predator in this state for those purposes, the court shall include in the determination a statement of the reason or reasons why it so determined.

(2003 S 5, eff. 7–31–03)

2950.10 Notices to victim regarding offender

(A)(1) If a person is convicted of or pleads guilty to, or has been convicted of or pleaded guilty to, either a sexually oriented offense that is not a registration-exempt sexually oriented offense or a child-victim oriented offense or a person is adjudicated a delinquent child for committing either a sexually oriented offense that is not a registration-exempt sexually oriented offense or a child-victim oriented offense and is classified a juvenile offender registrant or is an out-of-state juvenile offender registrant based on that adjudication, if the offender or delinquent child is in any category specified in division (B)(1)(a), (b), or (c) of this section, if the offender or delinquent child registers with a sheriff pursuant to section 2950.04, 2950.041, or 2950.05 of the Revised Code, and if the victim of the sexually oriented offense or child-victim oriented offense has made a request in accordance with rules adopted by the attorney general that specifies that the victim would like to be provided the notices described in this section, the sheriff shall notify the victim of the sexually oriented offense or child-victim oriented offense, in writing, that the offender or delinquent child has registered and shall include in the notice the offender's name and the address or addresses of the offender's residence, school, institution of higher education, or place of employment, as applicable, or the delinquent child's name and residence address or addresses. The sheriff shall provide the notice required by this division to the victim at the most recent residence address available for that victim, not later than five days after the offender or delinquent child registers with the sheriff.

(2) If a person is convicted of or pleads guilty to, or has been convicted of or pleaded guilty to, either a sexually oriented offense that is not a registration-exempt sexually oriented offense or a child-victim oriented offense or a person is adjudicated a delinquent child for committing either a sexually oriented offense that is not a registration-exempt sexually oriented offense or a child-victim oriented offense and is classified a juvenile offender registrant or is an out-of-state juvenile offender registrant based on that adjudication, if the offender or delinquent child is in any category specified in division (B)(1)(a), (b), or (c) of this section, if the offender or delinquent child registers with a sheriff pursuant to section 2950.04, 2950.041, or 2950.05 of the Revised Code, if the victim of the sexually oriented offense or child-victim oriented offense has made a request in accordance with rules adopted by the attorney general that specifies that the victim would like to be provided the notices described in this section, and if the offender notifies the sheriff of a change of residence, school, institution of higher education, or place of employment address or the delinquent child notifies the sheriff of a change of residence address pursuant to section 2950.05 of the Revised Code, the sheriff shall notify the victim of the sexually oriented offense or child-victim oriented offense, in writing, that the offender's or delinquent child's address has changed and shall include in the notice the offender's name and the new address or addresses of the offender's residence, school, institution of higher education, or place of employment, as applicable, or the delinquent child's name and new residence address or addresses. The sheriff shall provide the notice required by this division to the victim at the most recent residence address available for that victim, no later than five days after the offender or delinquent child notifies the sheriff of the change in the offender's or delinquent child's residence, school, institution of higher education, or place of employment address.

(3) If a person is convicted of or pleads guilty to, or has been convicted of or pleaded guilty to, either a sexually oriented offense that is not a registration-exempt sexually oriented offense or a child-victim oriented offense or a person is adjudicated a delinquent child for committing either a sexually oriented offense that is not a registration-exempt sexually oriented offense or a child-victim oriented offense and is classified a juvenile offender registrant or is an out-of-state juvenile offender registrant based on that adjudication, and if the offender or delinquent child is in any category specified in division (B)(1)(a), (b), or (c)of this section, the victim of the offense may make a request in accordance with rules adopted by the attorney general pursuant to section 2950.13 of the Revised Code that specifies that the victim would like to be provided the notices described in divisions (A)(1) and (2) of this section. If the victim makes a request in accordance with those rules, the sheriff described in divisions (A)(1) and (2) of this section shall provide the victim with the notices described in those divisions.

(4) If a victim makes a request as described in division (A)(3) of this section that specifies that the victim would like to be provided the notices described in divisions (A)(1) and (2) of this section, all information a sheriff obtains regarding the victim from or as a result of the request is confidential, and the information is not a public record open for inspection under section 149.43 of the Revised Code.

(5) The notices described in divisions (A)(1) and (2) of this section are in addition to any notices regarding the offender or delinquent child that the victim is entitled to receive under Chapter 2930. of the Revised Code.

(B)(1) The duties to provide the notices described in divisions (A)(1) and (2) of this section apply regarding any offender or delinquent child who is in any of the following categories, if the other criteria set forth in division (A)(1) or (2) of this section, whichever is applicable, are satisfied:

(a) The offender or delinquent child has been adjudicated a sexual predator relative to the sexually oriented offense for which the offender or delinquent child has the duty to register under section 2950.04 of the Revised Code or has been adjudicated a child-victim predator relative to the child-victim oriented offense for which the offender or child has the duty to register under section 2950.041 of the Revised Code, and the court has not subsequently determined pursuant to section 2152.84 or 2152.85 of the Revised Code regarding a delinquent child that the delinquent child no longer is a sexual predator or no longer is a child-victim predator, whichever is applicable.

(b) The offender or delinquent child has been determined pursuant to division (C)(2) or (E) of section 2950.09 or 2950.091, division (B) of section 2152.83, section 2152.84, or section 2152.85 of the Revised Code to be a habitual sex offender or a habitual child-victim offender, the court has imposed a requirement under that division or section subjecting the habitual sex offender or habitual child-victim offender to this section, and the determination has not been removed pursuant to section 2152. 84 or 2152.85 of the Revised Code regarding a delinquent child.

(c) The sexually oriented offense for which the offender has the duty to register under section 2950.04 of the Revised Code is an aggravated sexually oriented offense, regardless of whether the offender has been adjudicated a sexual predator relative to the offense or has been determined to be a habitual sex offender and, if the offender has been so determined to be a habitual sex offender, regardless of whether the habitual sex offender determination has not been removed as described in division (A)(1) (b) of this section.

(2) A victim of a sexually oriented offense that is not a registration-exempt sexually oriented offense or of a child-victim oriented offense is not entitled to be provided any notice described in division (A)(1) or (2) of this section unless the offender or delinquent child is in a category specified in division (B)(1)(a), (b), or (c) of this section. A victim of a sexually oriented offense that is not a registration-exempt sexually oriented offense or of a child-victim oriented offense is not entitled to any notice described in division (A)(1) or (2) of this section

unless the victim makes a request in accordance with rules adopted by the attorney general pursuant to section 2950.13 of the Revised Code that specifies that the victim would like to be provided the notices described in divisions (A)(1) and (2) of this section. This division does not affect any rights of a victim of a sexually oriented offense or child-victim oriented offense to be provided notice regarding an offender or delinquent child that are described in Chapter 2930. of the Revised Code.

(2003 S 5, eff. 7–31–03; 2002 H 485, eff. 6–13–02; 2001 S 3, eff. 1–1–02; 1998 H 565, eff. 3–30–99; 1996 H 180, eff. 7–1–97)

2950.11 Community notification of sex offender registration

Note: See also following version of this section, eff. 4–29–05.

(A) As used in this section, "specified geographical notification area" means the geographic area or areas within which the attorney general, by rule adopted under section 2950.13 of the Revised Code, requires the notice described in division (B) of this section to be given to the persons identified in divisions (A)(2) to (8) of this section. If a person is convicted of or pleads guilty to, or has been convicted of or pleaded guilty to, either a sexually oriented offense that is not a registration-exempt sexually oriented offense or a child-victim oriented offense, or a person is adjudicated a delinquent child for committing either a sexually oriented offense that is not a registration-exempt sexually oriented offense or a child-victim oriented offense and is classified a juvenile offender registrant or is an out-of-state juvenile offender registrant based on that adjudication, and if the offender or delinquent child is in any category specified in division (F)(1)(a), (b), or (c) of this section, the sheriff with whom the offender or delinquent child has most recently registered under section 2950.04, 2950.041, or 2950.05 of the Revised Code and the sheriff to whom the offender or delinquent child most recently sent a notice of intent to reside under section 2950.04 or 2950.041 of the Revised Code, within the period of time specified in division (C) of this section, shall provide a written notice containing the information set forth in division (B) of this section to all of the persons described in divisions (A)(1) to (9) of this section. If the sheriff has sent a notice to the persons described in those divisions as a result of receiving a notice of intent to reside and if the offender or delinquent child registers a residence address that is the same residence address described in the notice of intent to reside, the sheriff is not required to send an additional notice when the offender or delinquent child registers. The sheriff shall provide the notice to all of the following persons:

(1)(a) Any occupant of each residential unit that is located within one thousand feet of the offender's or delinquent child's residential premises, that is located within the county served by the sheriff, and that is not located in a multi-unit building. Division (D)(3) of this section applies regarding notices required under this division.

(b) If the offender or delinquent child resides in a multi-unit building, any occupant of each residential unit that is located in that multi-unit building and that shares a common hallway with the offender or delinquent child. For purposes of this division, an occupant's unit shares a common hallway with the offender or delinquent child if the entrance door into the occupant's unit is located on the same floor and opens into the same hallway as the entrance door to the unit the offender or delinquent child occupies. Division (D)(3) of this section applies regarding notices required under this division.

(c) The building manager, or the person the building owner or condominium unit owners association authorizes to exercise management and control, of each multi-unit building that is located within one thousand feet of the offender's or delinquent child's residential premises, including a multi-unit building in which the offender or delinquent child resides, and that is located within the county served by the sheriff. In addition to notifying the building manager or the person authorized to exercise management and control in the multi-unit building under this division, the sheriff shall post a copy of the notice prominently in each common entryway in the building and any other location in the building the sheriff determines appropriate. The manager or person exercising management and control of the building shall permit the sheriff to post copies of the notice under this division as the sheriff determines appropriate. In lieu of posting copies of the notice as described in this division, a sheriff may provide notice to all occupants of the multi-unit building by mail or personal contact; if the sheriff so notifies all the occupants, the sheriff is not required to post copies of the notice in the common entryways to the building. Division (D)(3) of this section applies regarding notices required under this division.

(d) All additional persons who are within any category of neighbors of the offender or delinquent child that the attorney general by rule adopted under section 2950.13 of the Revised Code requires to be provided the notice and who reside within the county served by the sheriff;

(2) The executive director of the public children services agency that has jurisdiction within the specified geographical notification area and that is located within the county served by the sheriff;

(3)(a) The superintendent of each board of education of a school district that has schools within the specified geographical notification area and that is located within the county served by the sheriff;

(b) The principal of the school within the specified geographical notification area and within the county served by the sheriff that the delinquent child attends;

(c) If the delinquent child attends a school outside of the specified geographical notification area or outside of the school district where the delinquent child resides, the superintendent of the board of education of a school district that governs the school that the delinquent child attends and the principal of the school that the delinquent child attends.

(4)(a) The appointing or hiring officer of each chartered nonpublic school located within the specified geographical notification area and within the county served by the sheriff or of each other school located within the specified geographical notification area and within the county served by the sheriff and that is not operated by a board of education described in division (A)(3) of this section;

(b) Regardless of the location of the school, the appointing or hiring officer of a chartered nonpublic school that the delinquent child attends.

(5) The director, head teacher, elementary principal, or site administrator of each preschool program governed by Chapter 3301. of the Revised Code that is located within the specified geographical notification area and within the county served by the sheriff;

(6) The administrator of each child day-care center or type A family day-care home that is located within the specified geographical notification area and within the county served by the sheriff, and the provider of each certified type B family day-care home that is located within the specified geographical notification area and within the county served by the sheriff. As used in this division, "child day-care center," "type A family day-care home," and "certified type B family day-care home" have the same meanings as in section 5104.01 of the Revised Code.

(7) The president or other chief administrative officer of each institution of higher education, as defined in section 2907.03 of the Revised Code, that is located within the specified geographical notification area and within the county served by the sheriff, and the chief law enforcement officer of the state university law enforcement agency or campus police department established

under section 3345.04 or 1713.50 of the Revised Code, if any, that serves that institution;

(8) The sheriff of each county that includes any portion of the specified geographical notification area;

(9) If the offender or delinquent child resides within the county served by the sheriff, the chief of police, marshal, or other chief law enforcement officer of the municipal corporation in which the offender or delinquent child resides or, if the offender or delinquent child resides in an unincorporated area, the constable or chief of the police department or police district police force of the township in which the offender or delinquent child resides.

(B) The notice required under division (A) of this section shall include all of the following information regarding the subject offender or delinquent child:

(1) The offender's or delinquent child's name;

(2) The address or addresses of the offender's residence, school, institution of higher education, or place of employment, as applicable, or the delinquent child's residence address or addresses;

(3) The sexually oriented offense or child-victim oriented offense of which the offender was convicted, to which the offender pleaded guilty, or for which the child was adjudicated a delinquent child;

(4) All of the following statements that are applicable:

(a) A statement that the offender has been adjudicated a sexual predator, a statement that the offender has been convicted of or pleaded guilty to an aggravated sexually oriented offense, a statement that the delinquent child has been adjudicated a sexual predator and that, as of the date of the notice, the court has not entered a determination that the delinquent child no longer is a sexual predator, or a statement that the sentencing or reviewing judge has determined that the offender or delinquent child is a habitual sex offender and that, as of the date of the notice, the determination regarding a delinquent child has not been removed pursuant to section 2152.84 or 2152.85 of the Revised Code;

(b) A statement that the offender has been adjudicated a child-victim predator, a statement that the delinquent child has been adjudicated a child-victim predator and that, as of the date of the notice, the court has not entered a determination that the delinquent child no longer is a child-victim predator, or a statement that the sentencing or reviewing judge has determined that the offender or delinquent child is a habitual child-victim offender and that, as of the date of the notice, the determination regarding a delinquent child has not been removed pursuant to section 2152.84 or 2152.85 of the Revised Code.

(C) If a sheriff with whom an offender or delinquent child registers under section 2950.04, 2950.041, or 2950.05 of the Revised Code or to whom the offender or delinquent child most recently sent a notice of intent to reside under section 2950.04 or 2950.041 of the Revised Code is required by division (A) of this section to provide notices regarding an offender or delinquent child and if, pursuant to that requirement, the sheriff provides a notice to a sheriff of one or more other counties in accordance with division (A)(8) of this section, the sheriff of each of the other counties who is provided notice under division (A)(8) of this section shall provide the notices described in divisions (A)(1) to (7) and (A)(9) of this section to each person or entity identified within those divisions that is located within the specified geographical notification area and within the county served by the sheriff in question.

(D)(1) A sheriff required by division (A) or (C) of this section to provide notices regarding an offender or delinquent child shall provide the notice to the neighbors that are described in division (A)(1) of this section and the notices to law enforcement personnel that are described in divisions (A)(8) and (9) of this section as soon as practicable, but no later than five days after the offender sends the notice of intent to reside to the sheriff and again no later than five days after the offender or delinquent child registers with the sheriff or, if the sheriff is required by division (C) to provide the notices, no later than five days after the sheriff is provided the notice described in division (A)(8) of this section.

A sheriff required by division (A) or (C) of this section to provide notices regarding an offender or delinquent child shall provide the notices to all other specified persons that are described in divisions (A)(2) to (7) of this section as soon as practicable, but not later than seven days after the offender or delinquent child registers with the sheriff or, if the sheriff is required by division (C) to provide the notices, no later than five days after the sheriff is provided the notice described in division (A)(8) of this section.

(2) If an offender or delinquent child in relation to whom division (A) of this section applies verifies the offender's or delinquent child's current residence, school, institution of higher education, or place of employment address, as applicable, with a sheriff pursuant to section 2950.06 of the Revised Code, the sheriff may provide a written notice containing the information set forth in division (B) of this section to the persons identified in divisions (A)(1) to (9) of this section. If a sheriff provides a notice pursuant to this division to the sheriff of one or more other counties in accordance with division (A)(8) of this section, the sheriff of each of the other counties who is provided the notice under division (A)(8) of this section may provide, but is not required to provide, a written notice containing the information set forth in division (B) of this section to the persons identified in divisions (A)(1) to (7) and (A)(9) of this section.

(3) A sheriff may provide notice under division (A)(1)(a) or (b) of this section, and may provide notice under division (A)(1)(c) of this section to a building manager or person authorized to exercise management and control of a building, by mail, by personal contact, or by leaving the notice at or under the entry door to a residential unit. For purposes of divisions (A)(1)(a) and (b) of this section, and the portion of division (A)(1)(c) of this section relating to the provision of notice to occupants of a multi-unit building by mail or personal contact, the provision of one written notice per unit is deemed as providing notice to all occupants of that unit.

(E) All information that a sheriff possesses regarding a sexual predator, a habitual sex offender, a child-victim predator, or a habitual child-victim offender that is described in division (B) of this section and that must be provided in a notice required under division (A) or (C) of this section or that may be provided in a notice authorized under division (D)(2) of this section is a public record that is open to inspection under section 149.43 of the Revised Code.

The sheriff shall not cause to be publicly disseminated by means of the internet any of the information described in this division that is provided by a sexual predator, habitual sex offender, child-victim predator, or habitual child-victim offender who is a juvenile offender registrant, except when the act that is the basis of the child's classification as a juvenile offender registrant is a violation of, or an attempt to commit a violation of, section 2903.01, 2903.02, or 2905.01 of the Revised Code that was committed with a purpose to gratify the sexual needs or desires of the child, a violation of section 2907.02 of the Revised Code, or an attempt to commit a violation of that section.

(F)(1) The duties to provide the notices described in divisions (A) and (C) of this section apply regarding any offender or delinquent child who is in any of the following categories, if the other criteria set forth in division (A) or (C) of this section, whichever is applicable, are satisfied:

(a) The offender or delinquent child has been adjudicated a sexual predator relative to the sexually oriented offense for which the offender or delinquent child has the duty to register under section 2950.04 of the Revised Code or has been adjudicated a child-victim predator relative to the child-victim oriented offense for which the offender or child has the duty to register under section 2950.041 of the Revised Code, and the court has not subsequently determined pursuant to section 2152.84 or 2152.85 of the Revised Code regarding a delinquent child that the delinquent child no longer is a sexual predator or no longer is a child-victim predator, whichever is applicable.

(b) The offender or delinquent child has been determined pursuant to division (C)(2) or (E) of section 2950.09 or 2950.091, division (B) of section 2152.83, section 2152.84, or section 2152.85 of the Revised Code to be a habitual sex offender or a habitual child-victim offender, the court has imposed a requirement under that division or section subjecting the habitual sex offender or habitual child-victim offender to this section, and the determination has not been removed pursuant to section 2152. 84 or 2152.85 of the Revised Code regarding a delinquent child.

(c) The sexually oriented offense for which the offender has the duty to register under section 2950.04 of the Revised Code is an aggravated sexually oriented offense, regardless of whether the offender has been adjudicated a sexual predator relative to the offense or has been determined to be a habitual sex offender.

(2) The notification provisions of this section do not apply regarding a person who is convicted of or pleads guilty to, has been convicted of or pleaded guilty to, or is adjudicated a delinquent child for committing, a sexually oriented offense or a child-victim oriented offense, who is not in the category specified in either division (F)(1)(a) or (c) of this section, and who is determined pursuant to division (C)(2) or (E) of section 2950.09 or 2950.091, division (B) of section 2152.83, section 2152.84, or section 2152.85 of the Revised Code to be a habitual sex offender or habitual child-victim offender unless the sentencing or reviewing court imposes a requirement in the offender's sentence and in the judgment of conviction that contains the sentence or in the delinquent child's adjudication, or imposes a requirement as described in division (C)(2) of section 2950.09 or 2950.091 of the Revised Code, that subjects the offender or the delinquent child to the provisions of this section.

(G) The department of job and family services shall compile, maintain, and update in January and July of each year, a list of all agencies, centers, or homes of a type described in division (A)(2) or (6) of this section that contains the name of each agency, center, or home of that type, the county in which it is located, its address and telephone number, and the name of an administrative officer or employee of the agency, center, or home. The department of education shall compile, maintain, and update in January and July of each year, a list of all boards of education, schools, or programs of a type described in division (A)(3), (4), or (5) of this section that contains the name of each board of education, school, or program of that type, the county in which it is located, its address and telephone number, the name of the superintendent of the board or of an administrative officer or employee of the school or program, and, in relation to a board of education, the county or counties in which each of its schools is located and the address of each such school. The Ohio board of regents shall compile, maintain, and update in January and July of each year, a list of all institutions of a type described in division (A)(7) of this section that contains the name of each such institution, the county in which it is located, its address and telephone number, and the name of its president or other chief administrative officer. A sheriff required by division (A) or (C) of this section, or authorized by division (D)(2) of this section, to provide notices regarding an offender or delinquent child, or a designee of a sheriff of that type, may request the department of job and family services, department of education, or Ohio board of regents, by telephone, in person, or by mail, to provide the sheriff or designee with the names, addresses, and telephone numbers of the appropriate persons and entities to whom the notices described in divisions (A)(2) to (7) of this section are to be provided. Upon receipt of a request, the department or board shall provide the requesting sheriff or designee with the names, addresses, and telephone numbers of the appropriate persons and entities to whom those notices are to be provided.

(H)(1) Upon the motion of the offender or the prosecuting attorney of the county in which the offender was convicted of or pleaded guilty to the sexually oriented offense or child-victim oriented offense for which the offender is subject to community notification under this section, or upon the motion of the sentencing judge or that judge's successor in office, the judge may schedule a hearing to determine whether the interests of justice would be served by suspending the community notification requirement under this section in relation to the offender. The judge may dismiss the motion without a hearing but may not issue an order suspending the community notification requirement without a hearing. At the hearing, all parties are entitled to be heard, and the judge shall consider all of the factors set forth in division (B)(3) of section 2950.09 of the Revised Code. If, at the conclusion of the hearing, the judge finds that the offender has proven by clear and convincing evidence that the offender is unlikely to commit in the future a sexually oriented offense or a child-victim oriented offense and if the judge finds that suspending the community notification requirement is in the interests of justice, the judge may suspend the application of this section in relation to the offender. The order shall contain both of these findings.

The judge promptly shall serve a copy of the order upon the sheriff with whom the offender most recently registered under section 2950.04, 2950.041, or 2950.05 of the Revised Code and upon the bureau of criminal identification and investigation.

An order suspending the community notification requirement does not suspend or otherwise alter an offender's duties to comply with sections 2950.04, 2950.041, 2950.05, and 2950.06 of the Revised Code and does not suspend the victim notification requirement under section 2950.10 of the Revised Code.

(2) A prosecuting attorney, a sentencing judge or that judge's successor in office, and an offender who is subject to the community notification requirement under this section may initially make a motion under division (H)(1) of this section upon the expiration of twenty years after the offender's duty to comply with sections 2950.04, 2950.041, 2950.05, and 2950.06 of the Revised Code begins in relation to the offense for which the offender is subject to community notification. After the initial making of a motion under division (H)(1) of this section, thereafter, the prosecutor, judge, and offender may make a subsequent motion under that division upon the expiration of five years after the judge has entered an order denying the initial motion or the most recent motion made under that division.

(3) The offender and the prosecuting attorney have the right to appeal an order approving or denying a motion made under division (H)(1) of this section.

(4) Division (H) of this section does not apply to any of the following types of offender:

(a) A sexually violent predator;

(b) A habitual sex offender or habitual child-victim oriented offender who is subject to community notification who, subsequent to being subjected to community notification, has pleaded guilty to or been convicted of a sexually oriented offense or a child-victim oriented offense;

(c) A sexual predator or child-victim predator who is not a sexually violent predator who, subsequent to being subjected to community notification, has pleaded guilty to or been convicted of a sexually oriented offense or child-victim oriented offense.

(2003 S 5, eff. 7–31–03; 2002 H 485, eff. 6–13–02; 2002 S 175, eff. 5–7–02; 2001 S 3, eff. 1–1–02; 1999 H 471, eff. 7–1–00; 1998 H 565, eff. 3–30–99; 1997 H 396, eff. 1–30–98; 1996 H 180, eff. 7–1–97)

Note: See also following version of this section, eff. 4–29–05.

2950.11 Community notification of sex offender registration (later effective date)

Note: See also preceding version of this section, in effect until 4–29–05.

(A) As used in this section, "specified geographical notification area" means the geographic area or areas within which the attorney general, by rule adopted under section 2950.13 of the Revised Code, requires the notice described in division (B) of this section to be given to the persons identified in divisions (A)(2) to (8) of this section. If a person is convicted of or pleads guilty to, or has been convicted of or pleaded guilty to, either a sexually oriented offense that is not a registration-exempt sexually oriented offense or a child-victim oriented offense, or a person is adjudicated a delinquent child for committing either a sexually oriented offense that is not a registration-exempt sexually oriented offense or a child-victim oriented offense and is classified a juvenile offender registrant or is an out-of-state juvenile offender registrant based on that adjudication, and if the offender or delinquent child is in any category specified in division (F)(1)(a), (b), or (c) of this section, the sheriff with whom the offender or delinquent child has most recently registered under section 2950.04, 2950.041, or 2950.05 of the Revised Code and the sheriff to whom the offender or delinquent child most recently sent a notice of intent to reside under section 2950.04 or 2950.041 of the Revised Code, within the period of time specified in division (C) of this section, shall provide a written notice containing the information set forth in division (B) of this section to all of the persons described in divisions (A)(1) to (9) of this section. If the sheriff has sent a notice to the persons described in those divisions as a result of receiving a notice of intent to reside and if the offender or delinquent child registers a residence address that is the same residence address described in the notice of intent to reside, the sheriff is not required to send an additional notice when the offender or delinquent child registers. The sheriff shall provide the notice to all of the following persons:

(1)(a) Any occupant of each residential unit that is located within one thousand feet of the offender's or delinquent child's residential premises, that is located within the county served by the sheriff, and that is not located in a multi-unit building. Division (D)(3) of this section applies regarding notices required under this division.

(b) If the offender or delinquent child resides in a multi-unit building, any occupant of each residential unit that is located in that multi-unit building and that shares a common hallway with the offender or delinquent child. For purposes of this division, an occupant's unit shares a common hallway with the offender or delinquent child if the entrance door into the occupant's unit is located on the same floor and opens into the same hallway as the entrance door to the unit the offender or delinquent child occupies. Division (D)(3) of this section applies regarding notices required under this division.

(c) The building manager, or the person the building owner or condominium unit owners association authorizes to exercise management and control, of each multi-unit building that is located within one thousand feet of the offender's or delinquent child's residential premises, including a multi-unit building in which the offender or delinquent child resides, and that is located within the county served by the sheriff. In addition to notifying the building manager or the person authorized to exercise management and control in the multi-unit building under this division, the sheriff shall post a copy of the notice prominently in each common entryway in the building and any other location in the building the sheriff determines appropriate. The manager or person exercising management and control of the building shall permit the sheriff to post copies of the notice under this division as the sheriff determines appropriate. In lieu of posting copies of the notice as described in this division, a sheriff may provide notice to all occupants of the multi-unit building by mail or personal contact; if the sheriff so notifies all the occupants, the sheriff is not required to post copies of the notice in the common entryways to the building. Division (D)(3) of this section applies regarding notices required under this division.

(d) All additional persons who are within any category of neighbors of the offender or delinquent child that the attorney general by rule adopted under section 2950.13 of the Revised Code requires to be provided the notice and who reside within the county served by the sheriff;

(2) The executive director of the public children services agency that has jurisdiction within the specified geographical notification area and that is located within the county served by the sheriff;

(3)(a) The superintendent of each board of education of a school district that has schools within the specified geographical notification area and that is located within the county served by the sheriff;

(b) The principal of the school within the specified geographical notification area and within the county served by the sheriff that the delinquent child attends;

(c) If the delinquent child attends a school outside of the specified geographical notification area or outside of the school district where the delinquent child resides, the superintendent of the board of education of a school district that governs the school that the delinquent child attends and the principal of the school that the delinquent child attends.

(4)(a) The appointing or hiring officer of each chartered nonpublic school located within the specified geographical notification area and within the county served by the sheriff or of each other school located within the specified geographical notification area and within the county served by the sheriff and that is not operated by a board of education described in division (A)(3) of this section;

(b) Regardless of the location of the school, the appointing or hiring officer of a chartered nonpublic school that the delinquent child attends.

(5) The director, head teacher, elementary principal, or site administrator of each preschool program governed by Chapter 3301. of the Revised Code that is located within the specified geographical notification area and within the county served by the sheriff;

(6) The administrator of each child day-care center or type A family day-care home that is located within the specified geographical notification area and within the county served by the sheriff, and the provider of each certified type B family day-care home that is located within the specified geographical notification area and within the county served by the sheriff. As used in this division, "child day-care center," "type A family day-care home," and "certified type B family day-care home" have the same meanings as in section 5104.01 of the Revised Code.

(7) The president or other chief administrative officer of each institution of higher education, as defined in section 2907.03 of the Revised Code, that is located within the specified geographical notification area and within the county served by the sheriff, and the chief law enforcement officer of the state university law enforcement agency or campus police department established under section 3345.04 or 1713.50 of the Revised Code, if any, that serves that institution;

(8) The sheriff of each county that includes any portion of the specified geographical notification area;

(9) If the offender or delinquent child resides within the county served by the sheriff, the chief of police, marshal, or other chief law enforcement officer of the municipal corporation in which the offender or delinquent child resides or, if the offender or delinquent child resides in an unincorporated area, the constable or chief of the police department or police district police force of the township in which the offender or delinquent child resides.

(B) The notice required under division (A) of this section shall include all of the following information regarding the subject offender or delinquent child:

(1) The offender's or delinquent child's name;

(2) The address or addresses of the offender's residence, school, institution of higher education, or place of employment, as applicable, or the delinquent child's residence address or addresses;

(3) The sexually oriented offense or child-victim oriented offense of which the offender was convicted, to which the offender pleaded guilty, or for which the child was adjudicated a delinquent child;

(4) All of the following statements that are applicable:

(a) A statement that the offender has been adjudicated a sexual predator, a statement that the offender has been convicted of or pleaded guilty to an aggravated sexually oriented offense, a statement that the delinquent child has been adjudicated a sexual predator and that, as of the date of the notice, the court has not entered a determination that the delinquent child no longer is a sexual predator, or a statement that the sentencing or reviewing judge has determined that the offender or delinquent child is a habitual sex offender and that, as of the date of the notice, the determination regarding a delinquent child has not been removed pursuant to section 2152.84 or 2152.85 of the Revised Code;

(b) A statement that the offender has been adjudicated a child-victim predator, a statement that the delinquent child has been adjudicated a child-victim predator and that, as of the date of the notice, the court has not entered a determination that the delinquent child no longer is a child-victim predator, or a statement that the sentencing or reviewing judge has determined that the offender or delinquent child is a habitual child-victim offender and that, as of the date of the notice, the determination regarding a delinquent child has not been removed pursuant to section 2152.84 or 2152.85 of the Revised Code.

(C) If a sheriff with whom an offender or delinquent child registers under section 2950.04, 2950.041, or 2950.05 of the Revised Code or to whom the offender or delinquent child most recently sent a notice of intent to reside under section 2950.04 or 2950.041 of the Revised Code is required by division (A) of this section to provide notices regarding an offender or delinquent child and if, pursuant to that requirement, the sheriff provides a notice to a sheriff of one or more other counties in accordance with division (A)(8) of this section, the sheriff of each of the other counties who is provided notice under division (A)(8) of this section shall provide the notices described in divisions (A)(1) to (7) and (A)(9) of this section to each person or entity identified within those divisions that is located within the specified geographical notification area and within the county served by the sheriff in question.

(D)(1) A sheriff required by division (A) or (C) of this section to provide notices regarding an offender or delinquent child shall provide the notice to the neighbors that are described in division (A)(1) of this section and the notices to law enforcement personnel that are described in divisions (A)(8) and (9) of this section as soon as practicable, but no later than five days after the offender sends the notice of intent to reside to the sheriff and again no later than five days after the offender or delinquent child registers with the sheriff or, if the sheriff is required by division (C) to provide the notices, no later than five days after the sheriff is provided the notice described in division (A)(8) of this section.

A sheriff required by division (A) or (C) of this section to provide notices regarding an offender or delinquent child shall provide the notices to all other specified persons that are described in divisions (A)(2) to (7) of this section as soon as practicable, but not later than seven days after the offender or delinquent child registers with the sheriff or, if the sheriff is required by division (C) to provide the notices, no later than five days after the sheriff is provided the notice described in division (A)(8) of this section.

(2) If an offender or delinquent child in relation to whom division (A) of this section applies verifies the offender's or delinquent child's current residence, school, institution of higher education, or place of employment address, as applicable, with a sheriff pursuant to section 2950.06 of the Revised Code, the sheriff may provide a written notice containing the information set forth in division (B) of this section to the persons identified in divisions (A)(1) to (9) of this section. If a sheriff provides a notice pursuant to this division to the sheriff of one or more other counties in accordance with division (A)(8) of this section, the sheriff of each of the other counties who is provided the notice under division (A)(8) of this section may provide, but is not required to provide, a written notice containing the information set forth in division (B) of this section to the persons identified in divisions (A)(1) to (7) and (A)(9) of this section.

(3) A sheriff may provide notice under division (A)(1)(a) or (b) of this section, and may provide notice under division (A)(1)(c) of this section to a building manager or person authorized to exercise management and control of a building, by mail, by personal contact, or by leaving the notice at or under the entry door to a residential unit. For purposes of divisions (A)(1)(a) and (b) of this section, and the portion of division (A)(1)(c) of this section relating to the provision of notice to occupants of a multi-unit building by mail or personal contact, the provision of one written notice per unit is deemed as providing notice to all occupants of that unit.

(E) All information that a sheriff possesses regarding a sexual predator, a habitual sex offender, a child-victim predator, or a habitual child-victim offender that is described in division (B) of this section and that must be provided in a notice required under division (A) or (C) of this section or that may be provided in a notice authorized under division (D)(2) of this section is a public record that is open to inspection under section 149.43 of the Revised Code.

The sheriff shall not cause to be publicly disseminated by means of the internet any of the information described in this division that is provided by a sexual predator, habitual sex offender, child-victim predator, or habitual child-victim offender who is a juvenile offender registrant, except when the act that is the basis of the child's classification as a juvenile offender registrant is a violation of, or an attempt to commit a violation of, section 2903.01, 2903.02, or 2905.01 of the Revised Code that was committed with a purpose to gratify the sexual needs or desires of the child, a violation of section 2907.02 of the Revised Code, or an attempt to commit a violation of that section.

(F)(1) The duties to provide the notices described in divisions (A) and (C) of this section apply regarding any offender or delinquent child who is in any of the following categories, if the other criteria set forth in division (A) or (C) of this section, whichever is applicable, are satisfied:

(a) The offender or delinquent child has been adjudicated a sexual predator relative to the sexually oriented offense for which the offender or delinquent child has the duty to register under section 2950.04 of the Revised Code or has been adjudicated a child-victim predator relative to the child-victim oriented offense for which the offender or child has the duty to register under section 2950.041 of the Revised Code, and the court has not subsequently determined pursuant to section 2152.84 or 2152.85 of the Revised Code regarding a delinquent child that the delinquent child no longer is a sexual predator or no longer is a child-victim predator, whichever is applicable.

(b) The offender or delinquent child has been determined pursuant to division (C)(2) or (E) of section 2950.09 or 2950.091, division (B) of section 2152.83, section 2152.84, or section 2152.85 of the Revised Code to be a habitual sex offender or a habitual child-victim offender, the court has imposed a requirement under that division or section subjecting the habitual sex offender or habitual child-victim offender to this section, and the determination has not been removed pursuant to section 2152.84 or 2152.85 of the Revised Code regarding a delinquent child.

(c) The sexually oriented offense for which the offender has the duty to register under section 2950.04 of the Revised Code is an aggravated sexually oriented offense, regardless of whether the offender has been adjudicated a sexual predator relative to the offense or has been determined to be a habitual sex offender.

(2) The notification provisions of this section do not apply regarding a person who is convicted of or pleads guilty to, has been convicted of or pleaded guilty to, or is adjudicated a delinquent child for committing, a sexually oriented offense or a child-victim oriented offense, who is not in the category specified in either division (F)(1)(a) or (c) of this section, and who is determined pursuant to division (C)(2) or (E) of section 2950.09 or 2950.091, division (B) of section 2152.83, section 2152.84, or section 2152.85 of the Revised Code to be a habitual sex offender or habitual child-victim offender unless the sentencing or reviewing court imposes a requirement in the offender's sentence and in the judgment of conviction that contains the sentence or in the delinquent child's adjudication, or imposes a requirement as described in division (C)(2) of section 2950.09 or 2950.091 of the Revised Code, that subjects the offender or the delinquent child to the provisions of this section.

(G) The department of job and family services shall compile, maintain, and update in January and July of each year, a list of all agencies, centers, or homes of a type described in division (A)(2) or (6) of this section that contains the name of each agency, center, or home of that type, the county in which it is located, its address and telephone number, and the name of an administrative officer or employee of the agency, center, or home. The department of education shall compile, maintain, and update in January and July of each year, a list of all boards of education, schools, or programs of a type described in division (A)(3), (4), or (5) of this section that contains the name of each board of education, school, or program of that type, the county in which it is located, its address and telephone number, the name of the superintendent of the board or of an administrative officer or employee of the school or program, and, in relation to a board of education, the county or counties in which each of its schools is located and the address of each such school. The Ohio board of regents shall compile, maintain, and update in January and July of each year, a list of all institutions of a type described in division (A)(7) of this section that contains the name of each such institution, the county in which it is located, its address and telephone number, and the name of its president or other chief administrative officer. A sheriff required by division (A) or (C) of this section, or authorized by division (D)(2) of this section, to provide notices regarding an offender or delinquent child, or a designee of a sheriff of that type, may request the department of job and family services, department of education, or Ohio board of regents, by telephone, in person, or by mail, to provide the sheriff or designee with the names, addresses, and telephone numbers of the appropriate persons and entities to whom the notices described in divisions (A)(2) to (7) of this section are to be provided. Upon receipt of a request, the department or board shall provide the requesting sheriff or designee with the names, addresses, and telephone numbers of the appropriate persons and entities to whom those notices are to be provided.

(H)(1) Upon the motion of the offender or the prosecuting attorney of the county in which the offender was convicted of or pleaded guilty to the sexually oriented offense or child-victim oriented offense for which the offender is subject to community notification under this section, or upon the motion of the sentencing judge or that judge's successor in office, the judge may schedule a hearing to determine whether the interests of justice would be served by suspending the community notification requirement under this section in relation to the offender. The judge may dismiss the motion without a hearing but may not issue an order suspending the community notification requirement without a hearing. At the hearing, all parties are entitled to be heard, and the judge shall consider all of the factors set forth in division (B)(3) of section 2950.09 of the Revised Code. If, at the conclusion of the hearing, the judge finds that the offender has proven by clear and convincing evidence that the offender is unlikely to commit in the future a sexually oriented offense or a child-victim oriented offense and if the judge finds that suspending the community notification requirement is in the interests of justice, the judge may suspend the application of this section in relation to the offender. The order shall contain both of these findings.

The judge promptly shall serve a copy of the order upon the sheriff with whom the offender most recently registered under section 2950.04, 2950.041, or 2950.05 of the Revised Code and upon the bureau of criminal identification and investigation.

An order suspending the community notification requirement does not suspend or otherwise alter an offender's duties to comply with sections 2950. 04, 2950.041, 2950.05, and 2950.06 of the Revised Code and does not suspend the victim notification requirement under section 2950.10 of the Revised Code.

(2) A prosecuting attorney, a sentencing judge or that judge's successor in office, and an offender who is subject to the community notification requirement under this section may initially make a motion under division (H)(1) of this section upon the expiration of twenty years after the offender's duty to comply with sections 2950.04, 2950.041, 2950.05, and 2950. 06 of the Revised Code begins in relation to the offense for which the offender is subject to community notification. After the initial making of a motion under division (H)(1) of this section, thereafter, the prosecutor, judge, and offender may make a subsequent motion under that division upon the expiration of five years after the judge has entered an order denying the initial motion or the most recent motion made under that division.

(3) The offender and the prosecuting attorney have the right to appeal an order approving or denying a motion made under division (H)(1) of this section.

(4) Division (H) of this section does not apply to any of the following types of offender:

(a) A person who is convicted of or pleads guilty to a violent sex offense or designated homicide, assault, or kidnapping offense and who, in relation to that offense, is adjudicated a sexually violent predator;

(b) A habitual sex offender or habitual child-victim oriented offender who is subject to community notification who, subsequent to being subjected to community notification, has pleaded guilty to or been convicted of a sexually oriented offense or a child-victim oriented offense;

(c) A sexual predator or child-victim predator who is not adjudicated a sexually violent predator who, subsequent to being subjected to community notification, has pleaded guilty to or been convicted of a sexually oriented offense or child-victim oriented offense.

(2004 H 473, eff. 4–29–05; 2003 S 5, eff. 7–31–03; 2002 H 485, eff. 6–13–02; 2002 S 175, eff. 5–7–02; 2001 S 3, eff. 1–1–02; 1999 H 471, eff. 7–1–00; 1998 H 565, eff. 3–30–99; 1997 H 396, eff. 1–30–98; 1996 H 180, eff. 7–1–97)

Note: See also preceding version of this section, in effect until 4–29–05.

2950.111 Confirmation by sheriff of reported residence address

(A) If an offender or delinquent child registers a residence address, provides notice of a change of any residence address, or verifies a current residence address pursuant to section 2950.04,

2950.041, 2950.05, or 2950.06 of the Revised Code, all of the following apply:

(1) At any time after the registration, provision of the notice, or verification, the sheriff with whom the offender or delinquent child so registered or to whom the offender or delinquent child so provided the notice or verified the current address, or a designee of that sheriff, may contact a person who owns, leases, or otherwise has custody, control, or supervision of the premises at the address provided by the offender or delinquent child in the registration, the notice, or the verification and request that the person confirm or deny that the offender or delinquent child currently resides at that address.

(2) Upon receipt of a request under division (A)(1) of this section, notwithstanding any other provision of law, the person who owns, leases, or otherwise has custody, control, or supervision of the premises, or an agent of that person, shall comply with the request and inform the sheriff or designee who made the request whether or not the offender or delinquent child currently resides at that address.

(3) Section 2950.12 of the Revised Code applies to a person who, in accordance with division (A)(2) of this section, provides information of the type described in that division.

(B) Division (A) of this section applies regarding any public or private residential premises, including, but not limited to, a private residence, a multi-unit residential facility, a halfway house, a homeless shelter, or any other type of residential premises. Division (A) of this section does not apply regarding an offender's registration, provision of notice of a change in, or verification of a school, institution of higher education, or place of employment address pursuant to section 2950.04, 2950.041, 2950.05, or 2950.06 of the Revised Code.

(C) A sheriff or designee of a sheriff may attempt to confirm that an offender or delinquent child who registers a residence address, provides notice of a change of any residence address, or verifies a current residence address as described in division (A) of this section currently resides at the address in question in manners other than the manner provided in this section. A sheriff or designee of a sheriff is not limited in the number of requests that may be made under this section regarding any registration, provision of notice, or verification, or in the number of times that the sheriff or designee may attempt to confirm, in manners other than the manner provided in this section, that an offender or delinquent child currently resides at the address in question.

(2003 S 5, eff. 7–31–03)

2950.12 Immunity from civil liability

(A) Except as provided in division (B) of this section, any of the following persons shall be immune from liability in a civil action to recover damages for injury, death, or loss to person or property allegedly caused by an act or omission in connection with a power, duty, responsibility, or authorization under this chapter or under rules adopted under authority of this chapter:

(1) An officer or employee of the bureau of criminal identification and investigation;

(2) The attorney general, a chief of police, marshal, or other chief law enforcement officer of a municipal corporation, a sheriff, a constable or chief of police of a township police department or police district police force, and a deputy, officer, or employee of the office of the attorney general, the law enforcement agency served by the marshal or the municipal or township chief, the office of the sheriff, or the constable;

(3) A prosecutor and an officer or employee of the office of a prosecutor;

(4) A supervising officer and an officer or employee of the adult parole authority of the department of rehabilitation and correction;

(5) A supervising officer and an officer or employee of the department of youth services;

(6) A supervisor and a caseworker or employee of a public children services agency acting pursuant to section 5153.16 of the Revised Code;

(7) A managing officer of a state correctional institution and an officer or employee of the department of rehabilitation and correction;

(8) A person identified in division (A)(2), (3), (4), (5), (6), or (7) of section 2950.11 of the Revised Code or the agent of that person;

(9) A person identified in division (A)(2) of section 2950.111 of the Revised Code, regarding the person's provision of information pursuant to that division to a sheriff or a designee of a sheriff.

(B) The immunity described in division (A) of this section does not apply to a person described in divisions (A)(1) to (8) of this section if, in relation to the act or omission in question, any of the following applies:

(1) The act or omission was manifestly outside the scope of the person's employment or official responsibilities.

(2) The act or omission was with malicious purpose, in bad faith, or in a wanton or reckless manner.

(3) Liability for the act or omission is expressly imposed by a section of the Revised Code.

(2003 S 5, eff. 7–31–03; 2002 S 175, eff. 5–7–02; 2001 S 3, eff. 1–1–02; 1996 H 180, eff. 7–1–97)

2950.13 Duties of attorney general

(A) The attorney general shall do all of the following:

(1) No later than July 1, 1997, establish and maintain a state registry of sex offenders and child-victim offenders that is housed at the bureau of criminal identification and investigation and that contains all of the registration, change of residence, school, institution of higher education, or place of employment address, and verification information the bureau receives pursuant to sections 2950.04, 2950.041, 2950.05, and 2950.06 of the Revised Code regarding a person who is convicted of or pleads guilty to, or has been convicted of or pleaded guilty to, either a sexually oriented offense that is not a registration-exempt sexually oriented offense or a child-victim oriented offense or a person who is adjudicated a delinquent child for committing either a sexually oriented offense that is not a registration-exempt sexually oriented offense or a child-victim oriented offense and is classified a juvenile offender registrant or is an out-of-state juvenile offender registrant based on that adjudication, and all of the information the bureau receives pursuant to section 2950.14 of the Revised Code . For a person who was convicted of or pleaded guilty to the sexually oriented offense or child-victim related offense, the registry also shall indicate whether the person was convicted of or pleaded guilty to the offense in a criminal prosecution or in a serious youthful offender case.

(2) In consultation with local law enforcement representatives and no later than July 1, 1997, adopt rules that contain guidelines necessary for the implementation of this chapter;

(3) In consultation with local law enforcement representatives, adopt rules for the implementation and administration of the provisions contained in section 2950.11 of the Revised Code that pertain to the notification of neighbors of an offender or a delinquent child who has committed a sexually oriented offense that is not a registration-exempt sexually oriented offense and has been adjudicated a sexual predator or determined to be a habitual sex offender, an offender who has committed an aggravated sexually oriented offense, or an offender or delinquent child who has committed a child-victim oriented offense and has been

adjudicated a child-victim predator or determined to be a habitual child-victim offender, and rules that prescribe a manner in which victims of either a sexually oriented offense that is not a registration-exempt sexually oriented offense or a child-victim oriented offense committed by an offender or a delinquent child who has been adjudicated a sexual predator or determined to be a habitual sex offender, an offender who has committed an aggravated sexually oriented offense, or an offender or delinquent child who has committed a child-victim oriented offense and has been adjudicated a child-victim predator or determined to be a habitual child-victim offender may make a request that specifies that the victim would like to be provided the notices described in divisions (A)(1) and (2) of section 2950.10 of the Revised Code;

(4) In consultation with local law enforcement representatives and through the bureau of criminal identification and investigation, prescribe the forms to be used by judges and officials pursuant to section 2950.03 of the Revised Code to advise offenders and delinquent children of their duties of filing a notice of intent to reside, registration, notification of a change of residence, school, institution of higher education, or place of employment address and registration of the new, school, institution of higher education, or place of employment address, as applicable, and address verification under sections 2950.04, 2950.041, 2950.05, and 2950.06 of the Revised Code, and prescribe the forms to be used by sheriffs relative to those duties of filing a notice of intent to reside, registration, change of residence, school, institution of higher education, or place of employment address notification, and address verification;

(5) Make copies of the forms prescribed under division (A)(4) of this section available to judges, officials, and sheriffs;

(6) Through the bureau of criminal identification and investigation, provide the notifications, the information, and the documents that the bureau is required to provide to appropriate law enforcement officials and to the federal bureau of investigation pursuant to sections 2950.04, 2950.041, 2950.05, and 2950.06 of the Revised Code;

(7) Through the bureau of criminal identification and investigation, maintain the verification forms returned under the address verification mechanism set forth in section 2950.06 of the Revised Code;

(8) In consultation with representatives of the officials, judges, and sheriffs, adopt procedures for officials, judges, and sheriffs to use to forward information, photographs, and fingerprints to the bureau of criminal identification and investigation pursuant to the requirements of sections 2950.03, 2950.04, 2950.041, 2950.05, and 2950.06 of the Revised Code;

(9) In consultation with the director of education, the director of job and family services, and the director of rehabilitation and correction, adopt rules that contain guidelines to be followed by boards of education of a school district, chartered nonpublic schools or other schools not operated by a board of education, preschool programs, child day-care centers, type A family day-care homes, certified type B family day-care homes, and institutions of higher education regarding the proper use and administration of information received pursuant to section 2950.11 of the Revised Code relative to an offender or delinquent child who has been adjudicated a sexual predator or child-victim predator or determined to be a habitual sex offender or habitual child-victim offender, or an offender who has committed an aggravated sexually oriented offense;

(10) In consultation with local law enforcement representatives and no later than July 1, 1997, adopt rules that designate a geographic area or areas within which the notice described in division (B) of section 2950.11 of the Revised Code must be given to the persons identified in divisions (A)(2) to (8) of that section;

(11) Through the bureau of criminal identification and investigation, not later than January 1, 2004, establish and operate on the internet a sex offender and child-victim offender database that contains information for every offender who has committed either a sexually oriented offense that is not a registration-exempt sexually oriented offense or a child-victim oriented offense and who registers in any county in this state pursuant to section 2950.04 or 2950.041 of the Revised Code. The bureau shall determine the information to be provided on the database for each offender and shall obtain that information from the information contained in the state registry of sex offenders and child-victim offenders described in division (A)(1) of this section, which information, while in the possession of the sheriff who provided it, is a public record open for inspection as described in section 2950.081 of the Revised Code. The information provided for each offender shall include at least the information set forth in division (B) of section 2950.11 of the Revised Code. The database is a public record open for inspection under section 149.43 of the Revised Code, and it shall be searchable by offender name, by county, by zip code, and by school district. The database shall provide a link to the web site of each sheriff who has established and operates on the internet a sex offender and child-victim offender database that contains information for offenders who register in that county pursuant to section 2950.04 or 2950.041 of the Revised Code, with the link being a direct link to the sex offender and child-victim offender database for the sheriff.

(12) Upon the request of any sheriff, provide technical guidance to the requesting sheriff in establishing on the internet a sex offender and child-victim offender database for the public dissemination of some or all of the materials described in division (A) of section 2950.081 of the Revised Code that are public records under that division and that pertain to offenders who register in that county pursuant to section 2950.04 or 2950.041 of the Revised Code;

(13) Through the bureau of criminal identification and investigation, not later than January 1, 2004, establish and operate on the internet a database that enables local law enforcement representatives to remotely search by electronic means the state registry of sex offenders and child-victim offenders described in division (A)(1) of this section and any information the bureau receives pursuant to sections 2950.04, 2950.041, 2950. 05, 2950.06, and 2950.14 of the Revised Code. The database shall enable local law enforcement representatives to obtain detailed information regarding each offender and delinquent child who is included in the registry, including, but not limited to the offender's or delinquent child's name, residence address, place of employment if applicable, motor vehicle license plate number if applicable, victim preference if available, date of most recent release from confinement if applicable, fingerprints, and other identification parameters the bureau considers appropriate. The database is not a public record open for inspection under section 149.43 of the Revised Code and shall be available only to law enforcement representatives as described in this division. Information obtained by local law enforcement representatives through use of this database is not open to inspection by the public or by any person other than a person identified in division (A) of section 2950.08 of the Revised Code.

(B) The attorney general in consultation with local law enforcement representatives, may adopt rules that establish one or more categories of neighbors of an offender or delinquent child who, in addition to the occupants of residential premises and other persons specified in division (A)(1) of section 2950.11 of the Revised Code, must be given the notice described in division (B) of that section.

(C) No person, other than a local law enforcement representative, shall knowingly do any of the following:

(1) Gain or attempt to gain access to the database established and operated by the attorney general, through the bureau of criminal identification and investigation, pursuant to division (A)(13) of this section.

(2) Permit any person to inspect any information obtained through use of the database described in division (C)(1) of this section, other than as permitted under that division.

(D) As used in this section, "local law enforcement representatives" means representatives of the sheriffs of this state, representatives of the municipal chiefs of police and marshals of this state, and representatives of the township constables and chiefs of police of the township police departments or police district police forces of this state.

(2003 S 5, eff. 7–31–03; 2002 H 485, eff. 6–13–02; 2001 S 3, eff. 1–1–02; 1999 H 471, eff. 7–1–00; 1996 H 72, eff. 7–1–97; 1996 H 180, eff. 7–1–97)

2950.14 Release of offender; information to be entered in state registry of sexual offenders

(A) Prior to releasing an offender who is under the custody and control of the department of rehabilitation and correction and who has been convicted of or pleaded guilty to committing, either prior to, on, or after January 1, 1997, any sexually oriented offense that is not a registration-exempt sexually oriented offense or any child-victim oriented offense, the department of rehabilitation and correction shall provide all of the information described in division (B) of this section to the bureau of criminal identification and investigation regarding the offender. Prior to releasing a delinquent child who is in the custody of the department of youth services who has been adjudicated a delinquent child for committing on or after January 1, 2002, any sexually oriented offense that is not a registration-exempt sexually oriented offense or any child-victim oriented offense, and who has been classified a juvenile offender registrant based on that adjudication, the department of youth services shall provide all of the information described in division (B) of this section to the bureau of criminal identification and investigation regarding the delinquent child.

(B) The department of rehabilitation and correction and the department of youth services shall provide all of the following information to the bureau of criminal identification and investigation regarding an offender or delinquent child described in division (A) of this section:

(1) The offender's or delinquent child's name and any aliases used by the offender or delinquent child;

(2) All identifying factors concerning the offender or delinquent child;

(3) The offender's or delinquent child's anticipated future residence;

(4) The offense and delinquency history of the offender or delinquent child;

(5) Whether the offender or delinquent child was treated for a mental abnormality or personality disorder while under the custody and control of the department;

(6) Any other information that the bureau indicates is relevant and that the department possesses.

(C) Upon receipt of the information described in division (B) of this section regarding an offender or delinquent child, the bureau immediately shall enter the information into the state registry of sex offenders and child-victim offenders that the bureau maintains pursuant to section 2950.13 of the Revised Code and into the records that the bureau maintains pursuant to division (A) of section 109.57 of the Revised Code.

(2003 S 5, eff. 7–31–03; 2002 H 393, eff. 7–5–02; 2001 S 3, eff. 1–1–02; 1998 H 565, eff. 3–30–99; 1996 H 180, eff. 1–1–97)

2950.99 Penalties

Note: See also following version of this section, eff. 4–29–05.

(A)(1)(a) Except as otherwise provided in division (A)(1)(b) of this section, whoever violates a prohibition in section 2950.04, 2950.041, 2950.05, or 2950.06 of the Revised Code shall be punished as follows:

(i) If the most serious sexually oriented offense or child-victim oriented offense that was the basis of the registration, notice of intent to reside, change of address notification, or address verification requirement that was violated under the prohibition is aggravated murder, murder, or a felony of the first, second, or third degree if committed by an adult, the offender is guilty of a felony of the third degree.

(ii) If the most serious sexually oriented offense or child-victim oriented offense that was the basis of the registration, notice of intent to reside, change of address notification, or address verification requirement that was violated under the prohibition is a felony of the fourth or fifth degree if committed by an adult, or if the most serious sexually oriented offense or child-victim oriented offense that was the basis of the registration, notice of intent to reside, change of address notification, or address verification requirement that was violated under the prohibition is a misdemeanor if committed by an adult, the offender is guilty of a felony of the same degree or a misdemeanor of the same degree as the most serious sexually oriented offense or child-victim oriented offense that was the basis of the registration, notice of intent to reside, change of address, or address verification requirement that was violated under the prohibition.

(b) If the offender previously has been convicted of or pleaded guilty to, or previously has been adjudicated a delinquent child for committing, a violation of a prohibition in section 2950.04, 2950.041, 2950.05, or 2950.06 of the Revised Code, whoever violates a prohibition in section 2950.04, 2950. 041, 2950.05, or 2950.06 of the Revised Code shall be punished as follows:

(i) If the most serious sexually oriented offense or child-victim oriented offense that was the basis of the registration, notice of intent to reside, change of address notification, or address verification requirement that was violated under the prohibition is aggravated murder, murder, or a felony of the first, second, third, or fourth degree if committed by an adult, the offender is guilty of a felony of the third degree.

(ii) If the most serious sexually oriented offense or child-victim oriented offense that was the basis of the registration, notice of intent to reside, change of address notification, or address verification requirement that was violated under the prohibition is a felony of the fifth degree if committed by an adult, the offender is guilty of a felony of the fourth degree.

(iii) If the most serious sexually oriented offense or child-victim oriented offense that was the basis of the registration, notice of intent to reside, change of address notification, or address verification requirement that was violated under the prohibition is a misdemeanor of the first degree if committed by an adult, the offender is guilty of a felony of the fifth degree.

(iv) If the most serious sexually oriented offense or child-victim oriented offense that was the basis of the registration, notice of intent to reside, change of address notification, or address verification requirement that was violated under the prohibition is a misdemeanor other than a misdemeanor of the first degree if committed by an adult, the offender is guilty of a misdemeanor that is one degree higher than the most serious sexually oriented offense or child-victim oriented offense that was the basis of the registration, change of address, or address verification requirement that was violated under the prohibition.

(2) In addition to any penalty or sanction imposed under division (A)(1) of this section or any other provision of law for a violation of a prohibition in section 2950.04, 2950.041, 2950.05, or

2950.06 of the Revised Code, if the offender or delinquent child is subject to a community control sanction, is on parole, is subject to one or more post-release control sanctions, or is subject to any other type of supervised release at the time of the violation, the violation shall constitute a violation of the terms and conditions of the community control sanction, parole, post-release control sanction, or other type of supervised release.

(B) If a person violates a prohibition in section 2950.04, 2950.041, 2950.05, or 2950.06 of the Revised Code that applies to the person as a result of the person being adjudicated a delinquent child and being classified a juvenile offender registrant or as an out-of-state juvenile offender registrant, both of the following apply:

(1) If the violation occurs while the person is under eighteen years of age, the person is subject to proceedings under Chapter 2152. of the Revised Code based on the violation.

(2) If the violation occurs while the person is eighteen years of age or older, the person is subject to criminal prosecution based on the violation.

(C) Whoever violates division (C) of section 2950.13 of the Revised Code is guilty of a misdemeanor of the first degree.

(2003 S 5, § 3, eff. 1–1–04; 2003 S 5, § 1, eff. 7–31–03; 2002 H 490, eff. 1–1–04; 2001 S 3, eff. 1–1–02; 1996 H 180, eff. 7–1–97; 1995 S 2, eff. 7–1–96; 1972 H 511, eff. 1–1–74; 130 v S 160)

Note: See also following version of this section, eff. 4–29–05.

2950.99 Penalties (later effective date)

Note: See also preceding version of this section, in effect until 4–29–05.

(A)(1)(a) Except as otherwise provided in division (A)(1)(b) of this section, whoever violates a prohibition in section 2950.04, 2950.041, 2950.05, or 2950.06 of the Revised Code shall be punished as follows:

(i) If the most serious sexually oriented offense or child-victim oriented offense that was the basis of the registration, notice of intent to reside, change of address notification, or address verification requirement that was violated under the prohibition is aggravated murder, murder, or a felony of the first, second, or third degree if committed by an adult or a comparable category of offense committed in another jurisdiction, the offender is guilty of a felony of the third degree.

(ii) If the most serious sexually oriented offense or child-victim oriented offense that was the basis of the registration, notice of intent to reside, change of address notification, or address verification requirement that was violated under the prohibition is a felony of the fourth or fifth degree if committed by an adult or a comparable category of offense committed in another jurisdiction, or if the most serious sexually oriented offense or child-victim oriented offense that was the basis of the registration, notice of intent to reside, change of address notification, or address verification requirement that was violated under the prohibition is a misdemeanor if committed by an adult or a comparable category of offense committed in another jurisdiction, the offender is guilty of a felony of the same degree or a misdemeanor of the same degree as the most serious sexually oriented offense or child-victim oriented offense that was the basis of the registration, notice of intent to reside, change of address, or address verification requirement that was violated under the prohibition or, if the most serious sexually oriented offense or child-victim oriented offense that was the basis of the registration, notice of intent to reside, change of address, or address verification requirement that was violated under the prohibition was a comparable category of offense committed in another jurisdiction, the offender is guilty of a felony of the same degree or a misdemeanor of the same degree as that offense committed in the other jurisdiction would constitute or would have constituted if it had been committed in this state.

(b) If the offender previously has been convicted of or pleaded guilty to, or previously has been adjudicated a delinquent child for committing, a violation of a prohibition in section 2950.04, 2950.041, 2950.05, or 2950.06 of the Revised Code, whoever violates a prohibition in section 2950.04, 2950. 041, 2950.05, or 2950.06 of the Revised Code shall be punished as follows:

(i) If the most serious sexually oriented offense or child-victim oriented offense that was the basis of the registration, notice of intent to reside, change of address notification, or address verification requirement that was violated under the prohibition is aggravated murder, murder, or a felony of the first, second, third, or fourth degree if committed by an adult or a comparable category of offense committed in another jurisdiction, the offender is guilty of a felony of the third degree.

(ii) If the most serious sexually oriented offense or child-victim oriented offense that was the basis of the registration, notice of intent to reside, change of address notification, or address verification requirement that was violated under the prohibition is a felony of the fifth degree if committed by an adult or a comparable category of offense committed in another jurisdiction, the offender is guilty of a felony of the fourth degree.

(iii) If the most serious sexually oriented offense or child-victim oriented offense that was the basis of the registration, notice of intent to reside, change of address notification, or address verification requirement that was violated under the prohibition is a misdemeanor of the first degree if committed by an adult or a comparable category of offense committed in another jurisdiction, the offender is guilty of a felony of the fifth degree.

(iv) If the most serious sexually oriented offense or child-victim oriented offense that was the basis of the registration, notice of intent to reside, change of address notification, or address verification requirement that was violated under the prohibition is a misdemeanor other than a misdemeanor of the first degree if committed by an adult or a comparable category of offense committed in another jurisdiction, the offender is guilty of a misdemeanor that is one degree higher than the most serious sexually oriented offense or child-victim oriented offense that was the basis of the registration, change of address, or address verification requirement that was violated under the prohibition or, if the most serious sexually oriented offense or child-victim oriented offense that was the basis of the registration, notice of intent to reside, change of address, or address verification requirement that was violated under the prohibition was a comparable category of offense committed in another jurisdiction, the offender is guilty of a misdemeanor that is one degree higher than the most serious sexually oriented offense or child-victim oriented offense committed in the other jurisdiction would constitute or would have constituted if it had been committed in this state.

(2) In addition to any penalty or sanction imposed under division (A)(1) of this section or any other provision of law for a violation of a prohibition in section 2950.04, 2950.041, 2950.05, or 2950.06 of the Revised Code, if the offender or delinquent child is subject to a community control sanction, is on parole, is subject to one or more post-release control sanctions, or is subject to any other type of supervised release at the time of the violation, the violation shall constitute a violation of the terms and conditions of the community control sanction, parole, post-release control sanction, or other type of supervised release.

(3) As used in division (A)(1) of this section, "comparable category of offense committed in another jurisdiction" means a sexually oriented offense or child-victim oriented offense that was the basis of the registration, notice of intent to reside, change of address notification, or address verification requirement that was violated, that is a violation of an existing or former law of another state or the United States, an existing or former law applicable in

a military court or in an Indian tribal court, or an existing or former law of any nation other than the United States, and that, if it had been committed in this state, would constitute or would have constituted aggravated murder, murder, or a felony of the first, second, or third degree for purposes of division (A)(1)(a)(i) of this section, a felony of the fourth or fifth degree or a misdemeanor for purposes of division (A)(1)(a)(ii) of this section, aggravated murder, murder, or a felony of the first, second, third, or fourth degree for purposes of division (A)(1)(b)(i) of this section, a felony of the fifth degree for purposes of division (A)(1)(b)(ii) of this section, a misdemeanor of the first degree for purposes of division (A)(1)(b)(iii) of this section, or a misdemeanor other than a misdemeanor of the first degree for purposes of division (A)(1)(b)(iv) of this section.

(B) If a person violates a prohibition in section 2950.04, 2950.041, 2950. 05, or 2950.06 of the Revised Code that applies to the person as a result of the person being adjudicated a delinquent child and being classified a juvenile offender registrant or as an out-of-state juvenile offender registrant, both of the following apply:

(1) If the violation occurs while the person is under eighteen years of age, the person is subject to proceedings under Chapter 2152. of the Revised Code based on the violation.

(2) If the violation occurs while the person is eighteen years of age or older, the person is subject to criminal prosecution based on the violation.

(C) Whoever violates division (C) of section 2950.13 of the Revised Code is guilty of a misdemeanor of the first degree.

(2004 H 473, eff. 4–29–05; 2003 S 5, § 3, eff. 1–1–04; 2003 S 5, § 1, eff. 7–31–03; 2002 H 490, eff. 1–1–04; 2001 S 3, eff. 1–1–02; 1996 H 180, eff. 7–1–97; 1995 S 2, eff. 7–1–96; 1972 H 511, eff. 1–1–74; 130 v S 160)

Note: See also preceding version of this section, in effect until 4–29–05.

CHAPTER 2951

PROBATION

Section

2951.01 Definitions

As used in this chapter:

(A) "Magistrate" has the same meaning as in section 2931.01 of the Revised Code.

(B) "Community control sanction" has the same meaning as in section 2929.01 of the Revised Code.

(C) "Ignition interlock device" has the same meaning as in section 4511.83 of the Revised Code.

(D) "Multicounty department of probation" means a probation department established under section 2301.27 of the Revised Code to serve more than one county.

(E) "Probation agency" means a county department of probation, a multicounty department of probation, a municipal court department of probation established under section 1901.33 of the Revised Code, or the adult parole authority.

(F) "County–operated municipal court" and "legislative authority" have the same meanings as in section 1901.03 of the Revised Code.

(G) "Detention facility" has the same meaning as in section 2921.01 of the Revised Code.

(H) "Repeat offender" and "dangerous offender" have the same meanings as in section 2935.36 of the Revised Code.

(I) "Minor drug possession offense" has the same meaning as in section 2925.01 of the Revised Code.

(J) "Peace officer" has the same meaning as in section 2935.01 of the Revised Code.

(K) "Firearm," "deadly weapon," and "dangerous ordnance" have the same meanings as in section 2923.11 of the Revised Code.

(2002 H 490, eff. 1–1–04; 1953 H 1, eff. 10–1–53)

2951.011 Effect of amendments to chapter

(A)(1) Chapter 2951. of the Revised Code, as it existed prior to July 1, 1996, applies to a person upon whom a court imposed a term of imprisonment prior to July 1, 1996, and a person upon whom a court, on or after July 1, 1996, and in accordance with law existing prior to July 1, 1996, imposed a term of imprisonment for an offense that was committed prior to July 1, 1996.

(2) Chapter 2951. of the Revised Code as it exists on and after July 1, 1996, applies to a person upon whom a court imposed a stated prison term for an offense committed on or after July 1, 1996.

(B)(1) Except as provided in division (A)(1) of this section, Chapter 2951. of the Revised Code, as it existed prior to January 1, 2004, applies to a person upon whom a court imposed a sentence for a misdemeanor offense prior to January 1, 2004, and a person upon whom a court, on or after January 1, 2004, and in accordance with law existing prior to January 1, 2004, imposed a sentence for a misdemeanor offense that was committed prior to January 1, 2004.

(2) Except as provided in division (A)(2) of this section, Chapter 2951. of the Revised Code as it exists on and after January 1, 2004, applies to a person upon whom a court imposes a sentence for a misdemeanor offense committed on or after January 1, 2004.

(2003 S 57, eff. 1–1–04; 2002 H 490, eff. 1–1–04; 1995 S 2, eff. 7–1–96)

2951.02 Supervision of community control or nonresidential sanction; community service work; ignition interlock devices

(A) During the period of a misdemeanor offender's community control sanction or during the period of a felony offender's nonresidential sanction, authorized probation officers who are engaged within the scope of their supervisory duties or responsibilities may search, with or without a warrant, the person of the offender, the place of residence of the offender, and a motor vehicle, another item of tangible or intangible personal property, or other real property in which the offender has a right, title, or interest or for which the offender has the express or implied permission of a person with a right, title, or interest to use, occupy, or possess if the probation officers have reasonable grounds to believe that the offender is not abiding by the law or otherwise is not complying with the conditions of the misdemeanor offender's community control sanction or the conditions of the felony offender's nonresidential sanction. If a felony offender who is sentenced to a nonresidential sanction is under the general control and supervision of the adult parole authority, as described in division (A)(2)(a) of section 2929.15 of the Revised Code, adult parole authority field officers with supervisory responsibilities over the felony offender shall have the same search authority relative to the felony offender during the period of the sanction that is described under this division for probation officers. The court that places the misdemeanor offender under a community control sanction pursuant to section 2929.25 of the Revised Code or that sentences the felony offender to a nonresidential sanction pursuant to section 2929.17 of the Revised Code shall provide the offender with a written notice that informs the offender that authorized probation officers or adult parole authority field officers with supervisory responsibilities over the offender who are engaged within the scope of their supervisory duties or responsibilities may conduct those types of searches during the period of community control sanction or the nonresidential sanction if they have reasonable grounds to believe that the offender is not abiding by the law or otherwise is not complying with the conditions of the offender's community control sanction or nonresidential sanction.

(B) If an offender is convicted of or pleads guilty to a misdemeanor, the court may require the offender, as a condition of the offender's sentence of a community control sanction, to perform supervised community service work in accordance with this division. If an offender is convicted of or pleads guilty to a felony, the court, pursuant to sections 2929.15 and 2929.17 of the Revised Code, may impose a sanction that requires the offender to perform supervised community service work in accordance with this division. The supervised community service work shall be under the authority of health districts, park districts, counties, municipal corporations, townships, other political subdivisions of the state, or agencies of the state or any of its political subdivisions, or under the authority of charitable organizations that render services to the community or its citizens, in accordance with this division. The court may require an offender who is ordered to perform the work to pay to it a reasonable fee to cover the costs of the offender's participation in the work, including, but not limited to, the costs of procuring a policy or policies of liability insurance to cover the period during which the offender will perform the work.

A court may permit any offender convicted of a felony or a misdemeanor to satisfy the payment of a fine imposed for the offense pursuant to section 2929.18 or 2929.28 of the Revised Code by performing supervised community service work as described in this division if the offender requests an opportunity to satisfy the payment by this means and if the court determines that the offender is financially unable to pay the fine.

The supervised community service work that may be imposed under this division shall be subject to the following limitations:

(1) The court shall fix the period of the work and, if necessary, shall distribute it over weekends or over other appropriate times that will allow the offender to continue at the offender's occupation or to care for the offender's family. The period of the work as fixed by the court shall not exceed in the aggregate the number of hours of community service imposed by the court pursuant to section 2929.17 or 2929.27 of the Revised Code.

(2) An agency, political subdivision, or charitable organization must agree to accept the offender for the work before the court requires the offender to perform the work for the entity. A court shall not require an offender to perform supervised community service work for an agency, political subdivision, or charitable organization at a location that is an unreasonable distance from the offender's residence or domicile, unless the offender is provided with transportation to the location where the work is to be performed.

(3) A court may enter into an agreement with a county department of job and family services for the management, placement, and supervision of offenders eligible for community service work in work activities, developmental activities, and alternative work activities under sections 5107.40 to 5107.69 of the Revised Code. If a court and a county department of job and family services have entered into an agreement of that nature, the clerk of that court is authorized to pay directly to the county department all or a portion of the fees collected by the court pursuant to this division in accordance with the terms of its agreement.

(4) Community service work that a court requires under this division shall be supervised by an official of the agency, political subdivision, or charitable organization for which the work is performed or by a person designated by the agency, political subdivision, or charitable organization. The official or designated person shall be qualified for the supervision by education, training, or experience, and periodically shall report, in writing, to the court and to the offender's probation officer concerning the conduct of the offender in performing the work.

(5) The total of any period of supervised community service work imposed on an offender under division (B) of this section plus the period of all other sanctions imposed pursuant to sections 2929.15, 2929.16, 2929.17, and 2929.18 of the Revised Code for a felony, or pursuant to sections 2929.25, 2929.26, 2929.27, and 2929.28 of the Revised Code for a misdemeanor, shall not exceed five years.

(C)(1) If an offender is convicted of a violation of section 4511.19 of the Revised Code, a municipal ordinance relating to operating a vehicle while under the influence of alcohol, a drug of abuse, or alcohol and a drug of abuse, or a municipal ordinance relating to operating a vehicle with a prohibited concentration of alcohol in the blood, breath, or urine, the court may require, as a condition of a community control sanction, any suspension of a driver's or commercial driver's license or permit or nonresident operating privilege, and all other penalties provided by law or by ordinance, that the offender operate only a motor vehicle equipped with an ignition interlock device that is certified pursuant to section 4510.43 of the Revised Code.

(2) If a court requires an offender, as a condition of a community control sanction pursuant to division (C)(1) of this section, to operate only a motor vehicle equipped with an ignition interlock device that is certified pursuant to section 4510.43 of the Revised Code, the offender immediately shall surrender the offender's driver's or commercial driver's license or permit to the court. Upon the receipt of the offender's license or permit, the court shall issue an order authorizing the offender to operate a motor vehicle equipped with a certified ignition interlock device, deliver the offender's license or permit to the bureau of motor vehicles, and include in the abstract of the case forwarded to the bureau pursuant to section 4510.036 of the Revised Code the conditions of the community control sanction imposed pursuant to division (C)(1) of this section. The court shall give the offender a copy of its order, and that copy shall be used by the offender in lieu of a driver's or commercial driver's license or permit until the bureau issues a restricted license to the offender.

(3) Upon receipt of an offender's driver's or commercial driver's license or permit pursuant to division (C)(2) of this section, the bureau of motor vehicles shall issue a restricted license to the offender. The restricted license shall be identical to the surren-

dered license, except that it shall have printed on its face a statement that the offender is prohibited from operating a motor vehicle that is not equipped with an ignition interlock device that is certified pursuant to section 4510.43 of the Revised Code. The bureau shall deliver the offender's surrendered license or permit to the court upon receipt of a court order requiring it to do so, or reissue the offender's license or permit under section 4510.52 of the Revised Code if the registrar destroyed the offender's license or permit under that section. The offender shall surrender the restricted license to the court upon receipt of the offender's surrendered license or permit.

(4) If an offender violates a requirement of the court imposed under division (C)(1) of this section, the court may impose a class seven suspension of the offender's driver's or commercial driver's license or permit or nonresident operating privilege from the range specified in division (A)(7) of section 4510.02 of the Revised Code. On a second or subsequent violation, the court may impose a class four suspension of the offender's driver's or commercial driver's license or permit or nonresident operating privilege from the range specified in division (A)(4) of section 4510.02 of the Revised Code.

(2002 H 490, eff. 1–1–04; 2002 S 123, eff. 1–1–04; 2000 H 349, eff. 9–22–00; 1999 H 471, eff. 7–1–00; 1999 S 107, eff. 3–23–00; 1999 S 9, eff. 3–8–00; 1997 H 408, eff. 10–1–97; 1996 S 269, eff. 7–1–96; 1995 S 2, eff. 7–1–96; 1995 H 167, eff. 11–15–95; 1995 H 4, eff. 11–9–95; 1994 H 687, eff. 10–12–94; 1994 H 571, eff. 10–6–94; 1993 H 152, eff. 7–1–93; 1990 S 258; 1989 H 381; 1988 H 322, H 429; 1983 S 210; 1982 S 432; 1981 H 1; 1980 H 682, H 892; 1978 S 119; 1975 S 144; 1972 H 511)

2951.021 Supervision fees

(A) (1) If a court places a misdemeanor offender under a community control sanction under section 2929.26, 2929.27, or 2929.28 of the Revised Code or places a felony offender under a community control sanction under section 2929.16, 2929.17, or 2929.18 of the Revised Code and if the court places the offender under the control and supervision of a probation agency, the court may require the offender, as a condition of community control, to pay a monthly supervision fee of not more than fifty dollars for supervision services. If the court requires an offender to pay a monthly supervision fee and the offender will be under the control of a county department of probation, a multicounty department of probation, or a municipal court department of probation established under section 1901.33 of the Revised Code, the court shall specify whether the offender is to pay the fee to the probation agency that will have control over the offender or to the clerk of the court for which the supervision agency is established. If the court requires an offender to pay a monthly probation fee and the offender will be under the control of the adult parole authority, the court shall specify that the offender is to pay the fee to the clerk of the court of common pleas.

(2) No person shall be assessed, in any month, more than fifty dollars in supervision fees.

(3) The prosecuting attorney of the county or the chief legal officer of a municipal corporation in which is located the court that imposed sentence upon an offender may bring a civil action to recover unpaid monthly supervision fees that the offender was required to pay. Any amount recovered in the civil action shall be paid into the appropriate county or municipal probation services fund in accordance with division (B) of this section.

(4) The failure of an offender to comply with a condition of community control that requires the offender to pay a monthly supervision fee and that is imposed under division (A)(1) of this section shall not constitute the basis for the modification of the offender's community control sanctions pursuant to section 2929.15 or 2929.25 of the Revised Code but may be considered with any other factors that form the basis of a modification of a sanction for violating a community control sanction under those sections. If the court determines that a misdemeanor offender on community control failed to pay a monthly supervision fee imposed under division (A)(1) of this section and that no other factors warranting the modification of the offender's community control sanction are present, the court shall remand the offender to the custody of the probation agency and may impose any additional conditions of community control upon the offender, including a requirement that the offender perform community service, as the ends of justice require. Any requirement imposed pursuant to division (A)(4) of this section that the offender perform community service shall be in addition to and shall not limit or otherwise affect any order that the offender perform community service pursuant to division (B) of section 2951.02 of the Revised Code.

(B) Prior to the last day of the month in each month during the period of community control, an offender who is ordered to pay a monthly supervision fee under this section shall pay the fee to the probation agency that has control and supervision over the offender or to the clerk of the court for which the probation agency is established, as specified by the court, except that, if the probation agency is the adult parole authority, the offender shall pay the fee to the clerk of the court of common pleas. Each probation agency or clerk of a court that receives any monthly supervision fees shall keep a record of the monthly supervision fees that are paid to the agency or the clerk and shall give a written receipt to each person who pays a supervision fee to the agency or clerk.

(C) Subject to division (E) of this section, all monthly supervision fees collected under this section by a probation agency or the clerk of a court shall be disposed of in the following manner:

(1) For offenders who are under the control and supervision of a county department of probation or a municipal court department of probation in a county-operated municipal court, on or before the fifth business day of each month, the chief probation officer, the chief probation officer's designee, or the clerk of the court shall pay all monthly supervision fees collected in the previous month to the county treasurer of the county in which the county department of probation or municipal court department of probation is established for deposit into the county probation services fund established in the county treasury of that county pursuant to division (A)(1) section 321.44 of the Revised Code.

(2) For offenders who are under the control and supervision of a multicounty department of probation, on or before the fifth business day of each month, the chief probation officer, the chief probation officer's designee, or the clerk of the court shall pay all monthly supervision fees collected in the previous month to the county treasurer of the county in which is located the court of common pleas that placed the offender under a community control sanction under the control of the department for deposit into the county probation services fund established in the county treasury of that county pursuant to division (A)(1) of section 321.44 of the Revised Code and for subsequent appropriation and transfer in accordance with division (A)(2) of that section to the appropriate multicounty probation services fund established pursuant to division (B) of that section.

(3) For offenders who are under the control and supervision of a municipal court department of probation in a municipal court that is not a county-operated municipal court, on or before the fifth business day of each month, the chief probation officer, the chief probation officer's designee, or the clerk of the court shall pay all monthly supervision fees collected in the previous month to the treasurer of the municipal corporation for deposit into the municipal probation services fund established pursuant to section 737.41 of the Revised Code.

(4) For offenders who are under the control and supervision of the adult parole authority, the clerk of the court of common pleas, on or before the fifth business day of January, April, July, and October, shall pay all monthly supervision fees collected by the clerk in the previous three months to the treasurer of the

county in which is located the court of common pleas that placed the offender under a community control sanction under the control of the authority for deposit into the county probation services fund established in the county treasury of that county pursuant to division (A)(1) of section 321.44 of the Revised Code and for subsequent appropriation and transfer in accordance with division (A)(2) of that section to the adult parole authority probation services fund established pursuant to section 5149.06 of the Revised Code.

(D) Not later than the first day of December of each year, each probation agency shall prepare a report regarding its use of money from a county probation services fund, a multicounty probation services fund, a municipal probation services fund, or the adult parole authority probation services fund, whichever is applicable. The report shall specify the amount appropriated from the fund to the probation agency during the current calendar year, an estimate of the amount that the probation agency will expend by the end of the year, a summary of how the amount appropriated has been expended for probation services, and an estimate of the amount of supervision fees that the probation agency will collect and pay to the appropriate treasurer for deposit in the appropriate fund in the next calendar year. The report shall be filed with one of the following:

(1) If the probation agency is a county department of probation or a municipal court department of probation in a county-operated municipal court, with the board of county commissioners of that county;

(2) If the probation agency is a multicounty department of probation, with the board of county commissioners of the county whose treasurer, in accordance with section 2301.27 of the Revised Code, is designated as the treasurer to whom supervision fees collected under this section are to be appropriated and transferred under division (A)(2) of section 321.44 of the Revised Code;

(3) If the probation agency is a department of probation of a municipal court that is not a county-operated municipal court, with the legislative authority of the municipal corporation that operates the court;

(4) If the probation agency is the adult parole authority, with the chairpersons of the finance committees of the senate and the house of representatives, the directors of the office of budget and management and the legislative service commission, and the board of county commissioners in each county for which the adult parole authority provides probation services.

(E) If the clerk of a court of common pleas or the clerk of a municipal court collects any monthly supervision fees under this section, the clerk may retain up to two per cent of the fees so collected to cover any administrative costs experienced in complying with the clerk's duties under this section.

(2002 H 490, eff. 1–1–04; 1996 S 269, eff. 7–1–96; 1995 S 2, eff. 7–1–96; 1994 H 406, eff. 11–11–94)

2951.03 Presentence investigation reports; confidentiality

(A)(1) No person who has been convicted of or pleaded guilty to a felony shall be placed under a community control sanction until a written presentence investigation report has been considered by the court. If a court orders the preparation of a presentence investigation report pursuant to this section, section 2947.06 of the Revised Code, or Criminal Rule 32.2, the officer making the report shall inquire into the circumstances of the offense and the criminal record, social history, and present condition of the defendant, all information available regarding any prior adjudications of the defendant as a delinquent child and regarding the dispositions made relative to those adjudications, and any other matters specified in Criminal Rule 32.2. Whenever the officer considers it advisable, the officer's investigation may include a physical and mental examination of the defendant. A physical examination of the defendant may include a drug test consisting of a chemical analysis of a blood or urine specimen of the defendant to determine whether the defendant ingested or was injected with a drug of abuse. If, pursuant to section 2930.13 of the Revised Code, the victim of the offense of which the defendant has been convicted wishes to make a statement regarding the impact of the offense for the officer's use in preparing the presentence investigation report, the officer shall comply with the requirements of that section.

(2) If a defendant is committed to any institution, the presentence investigation report shall be sent to the institution with the entry of commitment. If a defendant is committed to any institution and a presentence investigation report is not prepared regarding that defendant pursuant to this section, section 2947.06 of the Revised Code, or Criminal Rule 32.2, the director of the department of rehabilitation and correction or the director's designee may order that an offender background investigation and report be conducted and prepared regarding the defendant pursuant to section 5120.16 of the Revised Code. An offender background investigation report prepared pursuant to this section shall be considered confidential information and is not a public record under section 149.43 of the Revised Code.

(3) The department of rehabilitation and correction may use any presentence investigation report and any offender background investigation report prepared pursuant to this section for penological and rehabilitative purposes. The department may disclose any presentence investigation report and any offender background investigation report to courts, law enforcement agencies, community-based correctional facilities, halfway houses, and medical, mental health, and substance abuse treatment providers. The department shall make the disclosure in a manner calculated to maintain the report's confidentiality. Any presentence investigation report or offender background investigation report that the department discloses to a community-based correctional facility, a halfway house, or a medical, mental health, or substance abuse treatment provider shall not include a victim impact section or information identifying a witness.

(B)(1) If a presentence investigation report is prepared pursuant to this section, section 2947.06 of the Revised Code, or Criminal Rule 32.2, the court, at a reasonable time before imposing sentence, shall permit the defendant or the defendant's counsel to read the report, except that the court shall not permit the defendant or the defendant's counsel to read any of the following:

(a) Any recommendation as to sentence;

(b) Any diagnostic opinions that, if disclosed, the court believes might seriously disrupt a program of rehabilitation for the defendant;

(c) Any sources of information obtained upon a promise of confidentiality;

(d) Any other information that, if disclosed, the court believes might result in physical harm or some other type of harm to the defendant or to any other person.

(2) Prior to sentencing, the court shall permit the defendant and the defendant's counsel to comment on the presentence investigation report and, in its discretion, may permit the defendant and the defendant's counsel to introduce testimony or other information that relates to any alleged factual inaccuracy contained in the report.

(3) If the court believes that any information in the presentence investigation report should not be disclosed pursuant to division (B)(1) of this section, the court, in lieu of making the report or any part of the report available, shall state orally or in writing a summary of the factual information contained in the report that will be relied upon in determining the defendant's sentence. The court shall permit the defendant and the defen-

dant's counsel to comment upon the oral or written summary of the report.

(4) Any material that is disclosed to the defendant or the defendant's counsel pursuant to this section shall be disclosed to the prosecutor who is handling the prosecution of the case against the defendant.

(5) If the comments of the defendant or the defendant's counsel, the testimony they introduce, or any of the other information they introduce alleges any factual inaccuracy in the presentence investigation report or the summary of the report, the court shall do either of the following with respect to each alleged factual inaccuracy:

(a) Make a finding as to the allegation;

(b) Make a determination that no finding is necessary with respect to the allegation, because the factual matter will not be taken into account in the sentencing of the defendant.

(C) A court's decision as to the content of a summary under division (B)(3) of this section or as to the withholding of information under division (B)(1)(a), (b), (c), or (d) of this section shall be considered to be within the discretion of the court. No appeal can be taken from either of those decisions, and neither of those decisions shall be the basis for a reversal of the sentence imposed.

(D)(1) The contents of a presentence investigation report prepared pursuant to this section, section 2947.06 of the Revised Code, or Criminal Rule 32.2 and the contents of any written or oral summary of a presentence investigation report or of a part of a presentence investigation report described in division (B)(3) of this section are confidential information and are not a public record. The court, an appellate court, authorized probation officers, investigators, and court personnel, the defendant, the defendant's counsel, the prosecutor who is handling the prosecution of the case against the defendant, and authorized personnel of an institution to which the defendant is committed may inspect, receive copies of, retain copies of, and use a presentence investigation report or a written or oral summary of a presentence investigation only for the purposes of or only as authorized by Criminal Rule 32.2 or this section, division (F)(1) of section 2953.08, section 2947.06, or another section of the Revised Code.

(2) Immediately following the imposition of sentence upon the defendant, the defendant or the defendant's counsel and the prosecutor shall return to the court all copies of a presentence investigation report and of any written summary of a presentence investigation report or part of a presentence investigation report that the court made available to the defendant or the defendant's counsel and to the prosecutor pursuant to this section. The defendant or the defendant's counsel and the prosecutor shall not make any copies of the presentence investigation report or of any written summary of a presentence investigation report or part of a presentence investigation report that the court made available to them pursuant to this section.

(3) Except when a presentence investigation report or a written or oral summary of a presentence investigation report is being used for the purposes of or as authorized by Criminal Rule 32.2 or this section, division (F)(1) of section 2953.08, section 2947.06, or another section of the Revised Code, the court or other authorized holder of the report or summary shall retain the report or summary under seal.

(E) In inquiring into the information available regarding any prior adjudications of the defendant as a delinquent child and regarding the dispositions made relative to those adjudications, the officer making the report shall consider all information that is relevant, including, but not limited to, the materials described in division (B) of section 2151.14, division (C)(3) of section 2152.18, division (D)(3) of section 2152.19, and division (E) of section 2152.71 of the Revised Code.

(F) As used in this section:

(1) "Prosecutor" has the same meaning as in section 2935.01 of the Revised Code.

(2) "Community control sanction" has the same meaning as in section 2929.01 of the Revised Code.

(3) "Public record" has the same meaning as in section 149.43 of the Revised Code.

(2002 H 510, eff. 3–31–03; 2002 H 247, eff. 5–30–02; 2000 H 349, eff. 9–22–00; 1996 S 269, eff. 7–1–96; 1995 S 2, eff. 7–1–96; 1994 S 186, eff. 10–12–94; 1994 H 571, eff. 10–6–94; 1990 S 258, eff. 11–20–90; 1987 H 73, § 1, 5; 130 v H 686; 1953 H 1; GC 13452–1a)

2951.041 Drug treatment in lieu of conviction

(A)(1) If an offender is charged with a criminal offense and the court has reason to believe that drug or alcohol usage by the offender was a factor leading to the offender's criminal behavior, the court may accept, prior to the entry of a guilty plea, the offender's request for intervention in lieu of conviction. The request shall include a waiver of the defendant's right to a speedy trial, the preliminary hearing, the time period within which the grand jury may consider an indictment against the offender, and arraignment, unless the hearing, indictment, or arraignment has already occurred. The court may reject an offender's request without a hearing. If the court elects to consider an offender's request, the court shall conduct a hearing to determine whether the offender is eligible under this section for intervention in lieu of conviction and shall stay all criminal proceedings pending the outcome of the hearing. If the court schedules a hearing, the court shall order an assessment of the offender for the purpose of determining the offender's eligibility for intervention in lieu of conviction and recommending an appropriate intervention plan.

(2) The victim notification provisions of division (C) of section 2930.08 of the Revised Code apply in relation to any hearing held under division (A)(1) of this section.

(B) An offender is eligible for intervention in lieu of conviction if the court finds all of the following:

(1) The offender previously has not been convicted of or pleaded guilty to a felony, previously has not been through intervention in lieu of conviction under this section or any similar regimen, and is charged with a felony for which the court, upon conviction, would impose sentence under division (B)(2)(b) of section 2929.13 of the Revised Code or with a misdemeanor.

(2) The offense is not a felony of the first, second, or third degree, is not an offense of violence, is not a violation of division (A)(1) or (2) of section 2903.06 of the Revised Code, is not a violation of division (A)(1) of section 2903.08 of the Revised Code, is not a violation of division (A) of section 4511.19 of the Revised Code or a municipal ordinance that is substantially similar to that division, and is not an offense for which a sentencing court is required to impose a mandatory prison term, a mandatory term of local incarceration, or a mandatory term of imprisonment in a jail.

(3) The offender is not charged with a violation of section 2925.02, 2925.03, 2925.04, or 2925.06 of the Revised Code and is not charged with a violation of section 2925.11 of the Revised Code that is a felony of the first, second, or third degree.

(4) The offender is not charged with a violation of section 2925.11 of the Revised Code that is a felony of the fourth degree, or the offender is charged with a violation of that section that is a felony of the fourth degree and the prosecutor in the case has recommended that the offender be classified as being eligible for intervention in lieu of conviction under this section.

(5) The offender has been assessed by an appropriately licensed provider, certified facility, or licensed and credentialed professional, including, but not limited to, a program licensed by the department of alcohol and drug addiction services pursuant

to section 3793.11 of the Revised Code, a program certified by that department pursuant to section 3793.06 of the Revised Code, a public or private hospital, the United States department of veterans affairs, another appropriate agency of the government of the United States, or a licensed physician, psychiatrist, psychologist, independent social worker, professional counselor, or chemical dependency counselor for the purpose of determining the offender's eligibility for intervention in lieu of conviction and recommending an appropriate intervention plan.

(6) The offender's drug or alcohol usage was a factor leading to the criminal offense with which the offender is charged, intervention in lieu of conviction would not demean the seriousness of the offense, and intervention would substantially reduce the likelihood of any future criminal activity.

(7) The alleged victim of the offense was not sixty-five years of age or older, permanently and totally disabled, under thirteen years of age, or a peace officer engaged in the officer's official duties at the time of the alleged offense.

(8) If the offender is charged with a violation of section 2925.24 of the Revised Code, the alleged violation did not result in physical harm to any person, and the offender previously has not been treated for drug abuse.

(9) The offender is willing to comply with all terms and conditions imposed by the court pursuant to division (D) of this section.

(C) At the conclusion of a hearing held pursuant to division (A) of this section, the court shall enter its determination as to whether the offender is eligible for intervention in lieu of conviction and as to whether to grant the offender's request. If the court finds under division (B) of this section that the offender is eligible for intervention in lieu of conviction and grants the offender's request, the court shall accept the offender's plea of guilty and waiver of the defendant's right to a speedy trial, the preliminary hearing, the time period within which the grand jury may consider an indictment against the offender, and arraignment, unless the hearing, indictment, or arraignment has already occurred. In addition, the court then may stay all criminal proceedings and order the offender to comply with all terms and conditions imposed by the court pursuant to division (D) of this section. If the court finds that the offender is not eligible or does not grant the offender's request, the criminal proceedings against the offender shall proceed as if the offender's request for intervention in lieu of conviction had not been made.

(D) If the court grants an offender's request for intervention in lieu of conviction, the court shall place the offender under the general control and supervision of the county probation department, the adult parole authority, or another appropriate local probation or court services agency, if one exists, as if the offender was subject to a community control sanction imposed under section 2929.15, 2929.18, or 2929.25 of the Revised Code. The court shall establish an intervention plan for the offender. The terms and conditions of the intervention plan shall require the offender, for at least one year from the date on which the court grants the order of intervention in lieu of conviction, to abstain from the use of illegal drugs and alcohol and to submit to regular random testing for drug and alcohol use and may include any other treatment terms and conditions, or terms and conditions similar to community control sanctions, that are ordered by the court.

(E) If the court grants an offender's request for intervention in lieu of conviction and the court finds that the offender has successfully completed the intervention plan for the offender, including the requirement that the offender abstain from using drugs and alcohol for a period of at least one year from the date on which the court granted the order of intervention in lieu of conviction and all other terms and conditions ordered by the court, the court shall dismiss the proceedings against the offender. Successful completion of the intervention plan and period of abstinence under this section shall be without adjudication of guilt and is not a criminal conviction for purposes of any disqualification or disability imposed by law and upon conviction of a crime, and the court may order the sealing of records related to the offense in question in the manner provided in sections 2953.31 to 2953.36 of the Revised Code.

(F) If the court grants an offender's request for intervention in lieu of conviction and the offender fails to comply with any term or condition imposed as part of the intervention plan for the offender, the supervising authority for the offender promptly shall advise the court of this failure, and the court shall hold a hearing to determine whether the offender failed to comply with any term or condition imposed as part of the plan. If the court determines that the offender has failed to comply with any of those terms and conditions, it shall enter a finding of guilty and shall impose an appropriate sanction under Chapter 2929. of the Revised Code.

(G) As used in this section:

(1) "Community control sanction" has the same meaning as in section 2929.01 of the Revised Code.

(2) "Intervention in lieu of conviction" means any court-supervised activity that complies with this section.

(3) "Peace officer" has the same meaning as in section 2935.01 of the Revised Code.

(2002 H 490, eff. 1–1–04; 2002 H 327, eff. 7–8–02; 1999 H 202, eff. 2–9–00; 1999 S 107, eff. 3–23–00; 1996 S 269, eff. 7–1–96; 1995 S 2, eff. 7–1–96; 1994 H 385, eff. 7–19–94; 1990 S 258, eff. 11–20–90; 1989 H 317; 1980 H 900; 1975 H 300)

2951.05 Control and supervision random drug testing

(A) (1) A county department of probation, a multicounty department of probation, or the adult parole authority that has general control and supervision of offenders who are required to submit to random drug testing under division (A)(1)(a) of section 2929.25 of the Revised Code or who are subject to a nonresidential sanction that includes random drug testing under section 2929.17 or 2929.27 of the Revised Code, may cause each offender to submit to random drug testing performed by a laboratory or entity that has entered into a contract with any of the governmental entities or officers authorized to enter into a contract with that laboratory or entity under section 341.26, 753.33, or 5120.63 of the Revised Code.

(2) If no laboratory or entity described in division (A)(1) of this section has entered into a contract as specified in that division, the county department of probation, the multicounty department of probation, or the adult parole authority, as appropriate, that has general control and supervision of offenders shall cause the offender to submit to random drug testing performed by a reputable public laboratory to determine whether the individual who is the subject of the drug test ingested or was injected with a drug of abuse.

(3) A laboratory or entity that has entered into a contract as specified in division (A)(1) of this section shall perform the random drug testing in accordance with the applicable standards that are included in the terms of that contract. A public laboratory shall perform the random drug tests in accordance with the standards set forth in the policies and procedures established by the department of rehabilitation and correction pursuant to section 5120.63 of the Revised Code. An offender who is subject to a nonresidential sanction that includes random drug testing under section 2929.17 or 2929.27 of the Revised Code shall pay the fee for the drug test if the test results indicate that the offender ingested or was injected with a drug of abuse and if the county department of probation, the multicounty department of probation, or the adult parole authority that has general control and supervision of the offender requires payment of a fee. A laboratory or entity that performs the random drug

testing on an offender shall transmit the results of the drug test to the appropriate county probation department, multicounty probation department, or adult parole authority that has general control and supervision of the offender.

(B) As used in this section:

(1) "Multicounty department of probation" means a probation department established under section 2301.27 of the Revised Code to serve more than one county.

(2) "Random drug testing" has the same meaning as in section 5120.63 of the Revised Code.

(2002 H 490, eff. 1–1–04; 2000 H 349, eff. 9–22–00; 1994 H 406, eff. 11–11–94; 130 v Pt 2, H 28, eff. 3–18–65; 129 v 481; 128 v 959; 125 v 823; 1953 H 1; GC 13452–3)

2951.06 Release from custody

Upon entry in the records of the judge or magistrate of the sentence of a community control sanction provided for in section 2929.15 or 2929.25 of the Revised Code, the defendant shall be released from custody as soon as the requirements and conditions required by the judge supervising the community control sanction have been met. The defendant shall continue under the control and supervision of the appropriate probation agency, to the extent required by law, the conditions of the community control sanction, and the rules and regulations governing the probation agency.

(2002 H 490, eff. 1–1–04; 130 v Pt 2, H 28, eff. 3–18–65; 129 v 481; 125 v 823; 1953 H 1; GC 13452–4)

2951.07 Duration of community control sanction

A community control sanction continues for the period that the judge or magistrate determines and, subject to the five-year limit specified in section 2929.15 or 2929.25 of the Revised Code, may be extended. If the offender under community control absconds or otherwise leaves the jurisdiction of the court without permission from the probation officer, the probation agency, or the court to do so, or if the offender is confined in any institution for the commission of any offense, the period of community control ceases to run until the time that the offender is brought before the court for its further action.

(2002 H 490, eff. 1–1–04; 1996 S 269, eff. 7–1–96; 1995 S 2, eff. 7–1–96; 1990 S 258, eff. 11–20–90; 1953 H 1; GC 13452–5)

2951.08 Arrest of person violating probation or community control sanction

(A) During a period of community control, any field officer or probation officer may arrest the person under a community control sanction without a warrant and bring the person before the judge or magistrate before whom the cause was pending. During a period of community control, any peace officer may arrest the person under a community control sanction without a warrant upon the written order of the chief probation officer of the probation agency if the person under a community control sanction is under the supervision of that probation agency or on the order of an officer of the adult parole authority created pursuant to section 5149.02 of the Revised Code if the person under a community control sanction is under the supervision of the authority. During a period of community control, any peace officer may arrest the person under a community control sanction on the warrant of the judge or magistrate before whom the cause was pending.

During a period of community control, any peace officer may arrest the person under a community control sanction without a warrant if the peace officer has reasonable ground to believe that the person has violated or is violating any of the following that is a condition of the person's community control sanction:

(1) A condition that prohibits ownership, possession, or use of a firearm, deadly weapon, ammunition, or dangerous ordnance;

(2) A condition that prohibits the person from being within a specified structure or geographic area;

(3) A condition that confines the person to a residence, facility, or other structure;

(4) A condition that prohibits the person from contacting or communicating with any specified individual;

(5) A condition that prohibits the person from associating with a specified individual;

(6) A condition as provided in division (A)(1)(a) of section 2929.25 of the Revised Code or in division (A)(1) of section 2929.15 or (A)(8) of section 2929.27 of the Revised Code that requires that the person not ingest or be injected with a drug of abuse and submit to random drug testing and requires that the results of the drug test indicate that the person did not ingest or was not injected with a drug of abuse.

(B) Upon making an arrest under this section, the arresting field officer, probation officer, or peace officer or the department or agency of the arresting officer promptly shall notify the chief probation officer or the chief probation officer's designee that the person has been arrested. Upon being notified that a peace officer has made an arrest under this section, the chief probation officer or designee, or another probation officer designated by the chief probation officer, promptly shall bring the person who was arrested before the judge or magistrate before whom the cause was pending.

(C) Nothing in this section limits the powers of arrest granted to certain law enforcement officers and citizens under sections 2935.03 and 2935.04 of the Revised Code.

(D) A probation officer shall receive the actual and necessary expenses incurred in the performance of the officer's duties.

(E) As used in this section, "random drug testing" has the same meaning as in section 5120.63 of the Revised Code.

(2002 H 490, eff. 1–1–04; 2000 H 349, eff. 9–22–00; 1996 S 269, eff. 7–1–96; 1994 H 406, eff. 11–11–94; 1992 S 49, eff. 7–21–92; 130 v Pt 2, H 28; 129 v 481; 125 v 823; 1953 H 1; GC 13452–6)

2951.10 Final order

An order suspending the imposition of a sentence for a misdemeanor under section 2929.25 of the Revised Code and placing the defendant under a community control sanction is a final order from which appeal may be prosecuted.

(2002 H 490, eff. 1–1–04; 1953 H 1, eff. 10–1–53; GC 13452–9)

2951.13 Attendance of prisoner at probation revocation hearing; transportation

A convict confined in a state correctional institution for a felony committed while the convict was under a community control sanction imposed for a former conviction may be removed from the institution for the purpose of attending a hearing on revocation of the community control sanction. When a copy of the journal entry ordering the revocation hearing is presented to the warden or superintendent of the institution where the convict is confined, the warden or superintendent shall deliver the convict to the sheriff of the county where the hearing is to be held, and the sheriff shall convey the convict to and from the hearing. The approval of the governor on the journal entry is not required.

(1995 S 2, eff. 7–1–96; 1994 H 571, eff. 10–6–94; 1983 H 291, eff. 7–1–83; 1970 H 1136)

CHAPTER 2953

APPEALS; OTHER POSTCONVICTION REMEDIES

GENERAL PROVISIONS

2953.01 Definition of magistrate

The definition of "magistrate" set forth in section 2931.01 of the Revised Code applies to Chapter 2953. of the Revised Code.

(1953 H 1, eff. 10–1–53)

2953.02 Review of judgments and final orders

In a capital case in which a sentence of death is imposed for an offense committed before January 1, 1995, and in any other criminal case, including a conviction for the violation of an ordinance of a municipal corporation, the judgment or final order of a court of record inferior to the court of appeals may be reviewed in the court of appeals. A final order of an administrative officer or agency may be reviewed in the court of common pleas. A judgment or final order of the court of appeals involving a question arising under the Constitution of the United States or of this state may be appealed to the supreme court as a matter of right. This right of appeal from judgments and final orders of the court of appeals shall extend to cases in which a sentence of death is imposed for an offense committed before January 1, 1995, and in which the death penalty has been affirmed, felony cases in which the supreme court has directed the court of appeals to certify its record, and in all other criminal cases of public or general interest wherein the supreme court has granted a motion to certify the record of the court of appeals. In a capital case in which a sentence of death is imposed for an offense committed on or after January 1, 1995, the judgment or final order may be appealed from the trial court directly to the supreme court as a matter of right. The supreme court in criminal cases shall not be required to determine as to the weight of the evidence, except that, in cases in which a sentence of death is imposed for an offense committed on or after January 1, 1995, and in which the question of the weight of the evidence to support the judgment has been raised on appeal, the supreme court shall determine as to the weight of the evidence to support the judgment and shall determine as to the weight of the evidence to support the sentence of death as provided in section 2929.05 of the Revised Code.

(1995 S 4, eff. 9–21–95; 1981 S 1, eff. 10–19–81; 1970 S 530; 128 v 141; 1953 H 1; GC 13459–1)

2953.03 Suspension of execution of sentence or judgment when new trial motion or notice of appeal filed; bail

(A) If a motion for a new trial is filed pursuant to Criminal Rule 33 by a defendant who is convicted of a misdemeanor under the Revised Code or an ordinance of a municipal corporation, and if that defendant was on bail at the time of the conviction of that offense, the trial judge or magistrate shall suspend execution of the sentence or judgment imposed pending the determination on the motion for a new trial and shall determine the amount and nature of any bail that is required of the defendant in accordance with Criminal Rule 46.

(B) If a notice of appeal is filed pursuant to the Rules of Appellate Procedure or Chapter 1905. of the Revised Code by a defendant who is convicted in a municipal, county, or mayor's court or a court of common pleas of a misdemeanor under the Revised Code or an ordinance of a municipal corporation, if that defendant was on bail at the time of the conviction of that offense, and if execution of the sentence or judgment imposed is suspended, the trial court or magistrate or the court in which the appeal is being prosecuted shall determine the amount and nature of any bail that is required of the defendant as follows:

(1) In the case of an appeal to a court of appeals by a defendant who is convicted in a municipal or county court or a court of common pleas, in accordance with Appellate Rule 8 and Criminal Rule 46;

(2) In the case of an appeal to a municipal or county court by a defendant who is convicted in a mayor's court, in accordance with Criminal Rule 46.

(1986 H 412, eff. 3–17–87)

2953.07 Judgments on appeal; capital cases

(A) Upon the hearing of an appeal other than an appeal from a mayor's court, the appellate court may affirm the judgment or reverse it, in whole or in part, or modify it, and order the accused to be discharged or grant a new trial. The appellate court may remand the accused for the sole purpose of correcting a sentence imposed contrary to law, provided that, on an appeal of a sentence imposed upon a person who is convicted of or pleads guilty to a felony that is brought under section 2953.08 of the Revised Code, division (G) of that section applies to the court. If the judgment is reversed, the appellant shall recover from the appellee all court costs incurred to secure the reversal, including the cost of transcripts. In capital cases, when the judgment is affirmed and the day fixed for the execution is passed, the appellate court shall appoint a day for it, and the clerk of the appellate court shall issue a warrant under the seal of the appellate court, to the sheriff of the proper county, or the warden of the appropriate state correctional institution, commanding the sheriff or warden to carry the sentence into execution on the day so appointed. The sheriff or warden shall execute and return the warrant as in other cases, and the clerk shall record the warrant and return.

(B) As used in this section, "appellate court" means, for a case in which a sentence of death is imposed for an offense committed before January 1, 1995, both the court of appeals and the supreme court, and for a case in which a sentence of death is imposed for an offense committed on or after January 1, 1995, the supreme court.

(1995 S 2, eff. 7–1–96; 1995 S 4, eff. 9–21–95; 1994 H 571, eff. 10–6–94; 1986 H 412, eff. 3–17–87; 1953 H 1; GC 13459–6)

SUPREME COURT

2953.08 Appeals based on felony sentencing guidelines

Note: See also following version of this section, eff. 4–29–05.

(A) In addition to any other right to appeal and except as provided in division (D) of this section, a defendant who is convicted of or pleads guilty to a felony may appeal as a matter of right the sentence imposed upon the defendant on one of the following grounds:

(1) The sentence consisted of or included the maximum prison term allowed for the offense by division (A) of section 2929.14 of the Revised Code, the sentence was not imposed pursuant to division (D)(3)(b) of section 2929.14 of the Revised Code, the maximum prison term was not required for the offense pursuant to Chapter 2925. or any other provision of the Revised Code, and the court imposed the sentence under one of the following circumstances:

(a) The sentence was imposed for only one offense.

(b) The sentence was imposed for two or more offenses arising out of a single incident, and the court imposed the maximum prison term for the offense of the highest degree.

(2) The sentence consisted of or included a prison term, the offense for which it was imposed is a felony of the fourth or fifth degree or is a felony drug offense that is a violation of a provision of Chapter 2925. of the Revised Code and that is specified as being subject to division (B) of section 2929.13 of the Revised Code for purposes of sentencing, and the court did not specify at sentencing that it found one or more factors specified in divisions (B)(1)(a) to (i) of section 2929.13 of the Revised Code to apply relative to the defendant. If the court specifies that it found one or more of those factors to apply relative to the defendant, the defendant is not entitled under this division to appeal as a matter of right the sentence imposed upon the offender.

(3) The person was convicted of or pleaded guilty to a sexually violent offense, was adjudicated as being a sexually violent predator, and was sentenced pursuant to division (A)(3) of section 2971.03 of the Revised Code, if the minimum term of the indefinite term imposed pursuant to division (A)(3) of section 2971.03 of the Revised Code is the longest term available for the offense from among the range of terms listed in section 2929.14 of the Revised Code. As used in this division, "sexually violent offense" and "sexually violent predator" have the same meanings as in section 2971.01 of the Revised Code.

(4) The sentence is contrary to law.

(5) The sentence consisted of an additional prison term of ten years imposed pursuant to division (D)(2)(b) of section 2929.14 of the Revised Code.

(6) The sentence consisted of an additional prison term of ten years imposed pursuant to division (D)(3)(b) of section 2929.14 of the Revised Code.

(B) In addition to any other right to appeal and except as provided in division (D) of this section, a prosecuting attorney, a city director of law, village solicitor, or similar chief legal officer of a municipal corporation, or the attorney general, if one of those persons prosecuted the case, may appeal as a matter of right a sentence imposed upon a defendant who is convicted of or pleads guilty to a felony or, in the circumstances described in division (B)(3) of this section the modification of a sentence imposed upon such a defendant, on any of the following grounds:

(1) The sentence did not include a prison term despite a presumption favoring a prison term for the offense for which it was imposed, as set forth in section 2929.13 or Chapter 2925. of the Revised Code.

(2) The sentence is contrary to law.

(3) The sentence is a modification under section 2929.20 of the Revised Code of a sentence that was imposed for a felony of the first or second degree.

(C) In addition to the right to appeal a sentence granted under division (A) or (B) of this section, a defendant who is convicted of or pleads guilty to a felony may seek leave to appeal a sentence imposed upon the defendant on the basis that the sentencing judge has imposed consecutive sentences under division (E)(3) or (4) of section 2929.14 of the Revised Code and that the consecutive sentences exceed the maximum prison term allowed by division (A) of that section for the most serious offense of which the defendant was convicted. Upon the filing of a motion under this division, the court of appeals may grant leave to appeal the sentence if the court determines that the allegation included as the basis of the motion is true.

(D) A sentence imposed upon a defendant is not subject to review under this section if the sentence is authorized by law, has been recommended jointly by the defendant and the prosecution in the case, and is imposed by a sentencing judge. A sentence imposed for aggravated murder or murder pursuant to sections 2929.02 to 2929.06 of the Revised Code is not subject to review under this section.

(E) A defendant, prosecuting attorney, city director of law, village solicitor, or chief municipal legal officer shall file an appeal of a sentence under this section to a court of appeals within the time limits specified in Rule 4(B) of the Rules of Appellate Procedure, provided that if the appeal is pursuant to division (B)(3) of this section, the time limits specified in that rule shall not commence running until the court grants the motion that makes the sentence modification in question. A sentence appeal under this section shall be consolidated with any other appeal in the case. If no other appeal is filed, the court of appeals may review only the portions of the trial record that pertain to sentencing.

(F) On the appeal of a sentence under this section, the record to be reviewed shall include all of the following, as applicable:

(1) Any presentence, psychiatric, or other investigative report that was submitted to the court in writing before the sentence was imposed. An appellate court that reviews a presentence investigation report prepared pursuant to section 2947.06 or 2951.03 of the Revised Code or Criminal Rule 32.2 in connection with the appeal of a sentence under this section shall comply with division (D)(3) of section 2951.03 of the Revised Code when the appellate court is not using the presentence investigation report, and the appellate court's use of a presentence investigation report of that nature in connection with the appeal of a sentence under this section does not affect the otherwise confidential character of the contents of that report as described in division (D)(1) of section 2951.03 of the Revised Code and does not cause that report to become a public record, as defined in section 149.43 of the Revised Code, following the appellate court's use of the report.

(2) The trial record in the case in which the sentence was imposed;

(3) Any oral or written statements made to or by the court at the sentencing hearing at which the sentence was imposed;

(4) Any written findings that the court was required to make in connection with the modification of the sentence pursuant to a judicial release under division (H) of section 2929.20 of the Revised Code.

(G)(1) If the sentencing court was required to make the findings required by division (B) or (D) of section 2929.13, division (E)(4) of section 2929.14, or division (H) of section 2929.20 of the Revised Code relative to the imposition or modification of the sentence, and if the sentencing court failed to state the required findings on the record, the court hearing an appeal under division (A), (B), or (C) of this section shall remand the case to the sentencing court and instruct the sentencing court to state, on the record, the required findings.

(2) The court hearing an appeal under division (A), (B), or (C) of this section shall review the record, including the findings underlying the sentence or modification given by the sentencing court.

The appellate court may increase, reduce, or otherwise modify a sentence that is appealed under this section or may vacate the sentence and remand the matter to the sentencing court for resentencing. The appellate court's standard for review is not whether the sentencing court abused its discretion. The appellate court may take any action authorized by this division if it clearly and convincingly finds either of the following:

(a) That the record does not support the sentencing court's findings under division (B) or (D) of section 2929.13, division (E)(4) of section 2929.14, or division (H) of section 2929.20 of the Revised Code, whichever, if any, is relevant;

(b) That the sentence is otherwise contrary to law.

(H) A judgment or final order of a court of appeals under this section may be appealed, by leave of court, to the supreme court.

(I)(1) There is hereby established the felony sentence appeal cost oversight committee, consisting of eight members. One member shall be the chief justice of the supreme court or a representative of the court designated by the chief justice, one member shall be a member of the senate appointed by the president of the senate, one member shall be a member of the house of representatives appointed by the speaker of the house of representatives, one member shall be the director of budget and management or a representative of the office of budget and management designated by the director, one member shall be a judge of a court of appeals, court of common pleas, municipal court, or county court appointed by the chief justice of the supreme court, one member shall be the state public defender or a representative of the office of the state public defender designated by the state public defender, one member shall be a prosecuting attorney appointed by the Ohio prosecuting attorneys association, and one member shall be a county commissioner appointed by the county commissioners association of Ohio. No more than three of the appointed members of the committee may be members of the same political party.

The president of the senate, the speaker of the house of representatives, the chief justice of the supreme court, the Ohio prosecuting attorneys association, and the county commissioners association of Ohio shall make the initial appointments to the committee of the appointed members no later than ninety days after July 1, 1996. Of those initial appointments to the committee, the members appointed by the speaker of the house of representatives and the Ohio prosecuting attorneys association shall serve a term ending two years after July 1, 1996, the member appointed by the chief justice of the supreme court shall serve a term ending three years after July 1, 1996, and the members appointed by the president of the senate and the county commissioners association of Ohio shall serve terms ending four years after July 1, 1996. Thereafter, terms of office of the appointed members shall be for four years, with each term ending on the same day of the same month as did the term that it succeeds. Members may be reappointed. Vacancies shall be filled in the same manner provided for original appointments. A member appointed to fill a vacancy occurring prior to the expiration of the term for which that member's predecessor was appointed shall hold office as a member for the remainder of the predecessor's term. An appointed member shall continue in office subsequent to the expiration date of that member's term until that member's successor takes office or until a period of sixty days has elapsed, whichever occurs first.

If the chief justice of the supreme court, the director of the office of budget and management, or the state public defender serves as a member of the committee, that person's term of office as a member shall continue for as long as that person holds office as chief justice, director of the office of budget and management, or state public defender. If the chief justice of the supreme court designates a representative of the court to serve as a member, the director of budget and management designates a representative of the office of budget and management to serve as a member, or the state public defender designates a representative of the office of the state public defender to serve as a member, the person so designated shall serve as a member of the commission for as long as the official who made the designation holds office as chief justice, director of the office of budget and management, or state public defender or until that official revokes the designation.

The chief justice of the supreme court or the representative of the supreme court appointed by the chief justice shall serve as chairperson of the committee. The committee shall meet within two weeks after all appointed members have been appointed and shall organize as necessary. Thereafter, the committee shall meet at least once every six months or more often upon the call of the chairperson or the written request of three or more members, provided that the committee shall not meet unless moneys have been appropriated to the judiciary budget administered by the supreme court specifically for the purpose of providing financial assistance to counties under division (I)(2) of this section and the moneys so appropriated then are available for that purpose.

The members of the committee shall serve without compensation, but, if moneys have been appropriated to the judiciary budget administered by the supreme court specifically for the purpose of providing financial assistance to counties under division (I)(2) of this section, each member shall be reimbursed out of the moneys so appropriated that then are available for actual and necessary expenses incurred in the performance of official duties as a committee member.

(2) The state criminal sentencing commission periodically shall provide to the felony sentence appeal cost oversight committee all data the commission collects pursuant to division (A)(5) of section 181.25 of the Revised Code. Upon receipt of the data from the state criminal sentencing commission, the felony sentence appeal cost oversight committee periodically shall review the data; determine whether any money has been appropriated to the judiciary budget administered by the supreme court specifically for the purpose of providing state financial assistance to counties in accordance with this division for the increase in expenses the counties experience as a result of the felony sentence appeal provisions set forth in this section or as a result of a postconviction relief proceeding brought under division (A)(2) of section 2953.21 of the Revised Code or an appeal of a judgment in that proceeding; if it determines that any money has been so appropriated, determine the total amount of moneys that have been so appropriated specifically for that purpose and that then are available for that purpose; and develop a recommended method of distributing those moneys to the counties. The committee shall send a copy of its recommendation to the supreme court. Upon receipt of the committee's recommendation, the supreme court shall distribute to the counties, based upon that recommendation, the moneys that have been so appropriated specifically for the purpose of providing state financial assistance to counties under this division and that then are available for that purpose.

(2000 H 331, eff. 10–10–00; 1999 S 107, eff. 3–23–00; 1997 H 151, eff. 9–16–97; 1996 H 180, eff. 1–1–97; 1996 S 269, eff. 7–1–96; 1995 S 2, eff. 7–1–96)

Note: See also following version of this section, eff. 4–29–05.

2953.08 Appeals based on felony sentencing guidelines (later effective date)

Note: See also preceding version of this section, in effect until 4–29–05.

(A) In addition to any other right to appeal and except as provided in division (D) of this section, a defendant who is convicted of or pleads guilty to a felony may appeal as a matter of right the sentence imposed upon the defendant on one of the following grounds:

(1) The sentence consisted of or included the maximum prison term allowed for the offense by division (A) of section 2929.14 of the Revised Code, the sentence was not imposed pursuant to division (D)(3)(b) of section 2929.14 of the Revised Code, the maximum prison term was not required for the offense pursuant to Chapter 2925. or any other provision of the Revised Code, and the court imposed the sentence under one of the following circumstances:

(a) The sentence was imposed for only one offense.

(b) The sentence was imposed for two or more offenses arising out of a single incident, and the court imposed the maximum prison term for the offense of the highest degree.

(2) The sentence consisted of or included a prison term, the offense for which it was imposed is a felony of the fourth or fifth degree or is a felony drug offense that is a violation of a provision of Chapter 2925. of the Revised Code and that is specified as being subject to division (B) of section 2929.13 of the Revised Code for purposes of sentencing, and the court did not specify at sentencing that it found one or more factors specified in divisions (B)(1)(a) to (i) of section 2929.13 of the Revised Code to apply relative to the defendant. If the court specifies that it found one or more of those factors to apply relative to the defendant, the defendant is not entitled under this division to appeal as a matter of right the sentence imposed upon the offender.

(3) The person was convicted of or pleaded guilty to a violent sex offense or a designated homicide, assault, or kidnapping offense, was adjudicated a sexually violent predator in relation to that offense, and was sentenced pursuant to division (A)(3) of section 2971.03 of the Revised Code, if the minimum term of the indefinite term imposed pursuant to division (A)(3) of section 2971.03 of the Revised Code is the longest term available for the offense from among the range of terms listed in section 2929.14 of the Revised Code. As used in this division, "designated homicide, assault, or kidnapping offense" and " violent sex offense" have the same meanings as in section 2971.01 of the Revised Code. As used in this division, "adjudicated a sexually violent predator" has the same meaning as in section 2929.01 of the Revised Code, and a person is "adjudicated a sexually violent predator" in the same manner and the same circumstances as are described in that section.

(4) The sentence is contrary to law.

(5) The sentence consisted of an additional prison term of ten years imposed pursuant to division (D)(2)(b) of section 2929.14 of the Revised Code.

(6) The sentence consisted of an additional prison term of ten years imposed pursuant to division (D)(3)(b) of section 2929.14 of the Revised Code.

(B) In addition to any other right to appeal and except as provided in division (D) of this section, a prosecuting attorney, a city director of law, village solicitor, or similar chief legal officer of a municipal corporation, or the attorney general, if one of those persons prosecuted the case, may appeal as a matter of right a sentence imposed upon a defendant who is convicted of or pleads guilty to a felony or, in the circumstances described in division (B)(3) of this section the modification of a sentence imposed upon such a defendant, on any of the following grounds:

(1) The sentence did not include a prison term despite a presumption favoring a prison term for the offense for which it was imposed, as set forth in section 2929.13 or Chapter 2925. of the Revised Code.

(2) The sentence is contrary to law.

(3) The sentence is a modification under section 2929.20 of the Revised Code of a sentence that was imposed for a felony of the first or second degree.

(C) In addition to the right to appeal a sentence granted under division (A) or (B) of this section, a defendant who is convicted of or pleads guilty to a felony may seek leave to appeal a sentence imposed upon the defendant on the basis that the sentencing judge has imposed consecutive sentences under division (E)(3) or (4) of section 2929.14 of the Revised Code and that the consecutive sentences exceed the maximum prison term allowed by division (A) of that section for the most serious offense of which the defendant was convicted. Upon the filing of a motion under this division, the court of appeals may grant leave to appeal the sentence if the court determines that the allegation included as the basis of the motion is true.

(D) A sentence imposed upon a defendant is not subject to review under this section if the sentence is authorized by law, has been recommended jointly by the defendant and the prosecution in the case, and is imposed by a sentencing judge. A sentence imposed for aggravated murder or murder pursuant to sections 2929.02 to 2929.06 of the Revised Code is not subject to review under this section.

(E) A defendant, prosecuting attorney, city director of law, village solicitor, or chief municipal legal officer shall file an appeal of a sentence under this section to a court of appeals within the time limits specified in Rule 4(B) of the Rules of Appellate Procedure, provided that if the appeal is pursuant to division (B)(3) of this section, the time limits specified in that rule shall not commence running until the court grants the motion that makes the sentence modification in question. A sentence appeal under this section shall be consolidated with any other appeal in the case. If no other appeal is filed, the court of appeals may review only the portions of the trial record that pertain to sentencing.

(F) On the appeal of a sentence under this section, the record to be reviewed shall include all of the following, as applicable:

(1) Any presentence, psychiatric, or other investigative report that was submitted to the court in writing before the sentence was imposed. An appellate court that reviews a presentence investigation report prepared pursuant to section 2947.06 or 2951.03 of the Revised Code or Criminal Rule 32.2 in connection with the appeal of a sentence under this section shall comply with division (D)(3) of section 2951.03 of the Revised Code when the appellate court is not using the presentence investigation report, and the appellate court's use of a presentence investigation report of that nature in connection with the appeal of a sentence under this section does not affect the otherwise confidential character of the contents of that report as described in division (D)(1) of section 2951.03 of the Revised Code and does not cause that report to become a public record, as defined in section 149.43 of the Revised Code, following the appellate court's use of the report.

(2) The trial record in the case in which the sentence was imposed;

(3) Any oral or written statements made to or by the court at the sentencing hearing at which the sentence was imposed;

(4) Any written findings that the court was required to make in connection with the modification of the sentence pursuant to a judicial release under division (H) of section 2929.20 of the Revised Code.

(G)(1) If the sentencing court was required to make the findings required by division (B) or (D) of section 2929.13, division (E)(4) of section 2929.14, or division (H) of section 2929.20 of the Revised Code relative to the imposition or modification of the sentence, and if the sentencing court failed to state the required findings on the record, the court hearing an appeal under division (A), (B), or (C) of this section shall remand the case to the sentencing court and instruct the sentencing court to state, on the record, the required findings.

(2) The court hearing an appeal under division (A), (B), or (C) of this section shall review the record, including the findings underlying the sentence or modification given by the sentencing court.

The appellate court may increase, reduce, or otherwise modify a sentence that is appealed under this section or may vacate the sentence and remand the matter to the sentencing court for resentencing. The appellate court's standard for review is not whether the sentencing court abused its discretion. The appellate court may take any action authorized by this division if it clearly and convincingly finds either of the following:

(a) That the record does not support the sentencing court's findings under division (B) or (D) of section 2929.13, division (E)(4) of section 2929.14, or division (H) of section 2929.20 of the Revised Code, whichever, if any, is relevant;

(b) That the sentence is otherwise contrary to law.

(H) A judgment or final order of a court of appeals under this section may be appealed, by leave of court, to the supreme court.

(I)(1) There is hereby established the felony sentence appeal cost oversight committee, consisting of eight members. One member shall be the chief justice of the supreme court or a representative of the court designated by the chief justice, one member shall be a member of the senate appointed by the president of the senate, one member shall be a member of the house of representatives appointed by the speaker of the house of representatives, one member shall be the director of budget and management or a representative of the office of budget and management designated by the director, one member shall be a judge of a court of appeals, court of common pleas, municipal court, or county court appointed by the chief justice of the supreme court, one member shall be the state public defender or a representative of the office of the state public defender designated by the state public defender, one member shall be a prosecuting attorney appointed by the Ohio prosecuting attorneys association, and one member shall be a county commissioner appointed by the county commissioners association of Ohio. No more than three of the appointed members of the committee may be members of the same political party.

The president of the senate, the speaker of the house of representatives, the chief justice of the supreme court, the Ohio prosecuting attorneys association, and the county commissioners association of Ohio shall make the initial appointments to the committee of the appointed members no later than ninety days after July 1, 1996. Of those initial appointments to the committee, the members appointed by the speaker of the house of representatives and the Ohio prosecuting attorneys association shall serve a term ending two years after July 1, 1996, the member appointed by the chief justice of the supreme court shall serve a term ending three years after July 1, 1996, and the members appointed by the president of the senate and the county commissioners association of Ohio shall serve terms ending four years after July 1, 1996. Thereafter, terms of office of the appointed members shall be for four years, with each term ending on the same day of the same month as did the term that it succeeds. Members may be reappointed. Vacancies shall be filled in the same manner provided for original appointments. A member appointed to fill a vacancy occurring prior to the expiration of the term for which that member's predecessor was appointed shall hold office as a member for the remainder of the predecessor's term. An appointed member shall continue in office subsequent to the expiration date of that member's term until that member's successor takes office or until a period of sixty days has elapsed, whichever occurs first.

If the chief justice of the supreme court, the director of the office of budget and management, or the state public defender serves as a member of the committee, that person's term of office as a member shall continue for as long as that person holds office as chief justice, director of the office of budget and management, or state public defender. If the chief justice of the supreme court designates a representative of the court to serve as a member, the director of budget and management designates a representative of the office of budget and management to serve as a member, or the state public defender designates a representative of the office of the state public defender to serve as a member, the person so designated shall serve as a member of the commission for as long as the official who made the designation holds office as chief justice, director of the office of budget and management, or state public defender or until that official revokes the designation.

The chief justice of the supreme court or the representative of the supreme court appointed by the chief justice shall serve as chairperson of the committee. The committee shall meet within two weeks after all appointed members have been appointed and shall organize as necessary. Thereafter, the committee shall meet at least once every six months or more often upon the call of the chairperson or the written request of three or more members, provided that the committee shall not meet unless moneys have been appropriated to the judiciary budget administered by the supreme court specifically for the purpose of providing financial assistance to counties under division (I)(2) of this section and the moneys so appropriated then are available for that purpose.

The members of the committee shall serve without compensation, but, if moneys have been appropriated to the judiciary budget administered by the supreme court specifically for the purpose of providing financial assistance to counties under division (I)(2) of this section, each member shall be reimbursed out of the moneys so appropriated that then are available for actual and necessary expenses incurred in the performance of official duties as a committee member.

(2) The state criminal sentencing commission periodically shall provide to the felony sentence appeal cost oversight committee all data the commission collects pursuant to division (A)(5) of section 181.25 of the Revised Code. Upon receipt of the data from the state criminal sentencing commission, the felony sentence appeal cost oversight committee periodically shall review the data; determine whether any money has been appropriated to the judiciary budget administered by the supreme court specifically for the purpose of providing state financial assistance to counties in accordance with this division for the increase in expenses the counties experience as a result of the felony sentence appeal provisions set forth in this section or as a result of a postconviction relief proceeding brought under division (A)(2) of section 2953.21 of the Revised Code or an appeal of a judgment in that proceeding; if it determines that any money has been so appropriated, determine the total amount of moneys that have been so appropriated specifically for that purpose and that then are available for that purpose; and develop a recommended method of distributing those moneys to the counties. The committee shall send a copy of its recommendation to the supreme court. Upon receipt of the committee's recommendation, the supreme court shall distribute to the counties, based upon that recommendation, the moneys that have been so appropriated specifically for the purpose of providing state financial assistance to counties under this division and that then are available for that purpose.

(2004 H 473, eff. 4–29–05; 2000 H 331, eff. 10–10–00; 1999 S 107, eff. 3–23–00; 1997 H 151, eff. 9–16–97; 1996 H 180, eff. 1–1–97; 1996 S 269, eff. 7–1–96; 1995 S 2, eff. 7–1–96)

Note: See also preceding version of this section, in effect until 4–29–05.

SUSPENSION OF SENTENCE

2953.09 Suspension of execution of sentence or judgment when appeal to supreme court filed; bail; exceptions

(A)(1) Upon filing an appeal in the supreme court, the execution of the sentence or judgment imposed in cases of felony is suspended.

(2)(a) If a notice of appeal is filed pursuant to the Rules of Appellate Procedure by a defendant who is convicted in a municipal or county court or a court of common pleas of a felony or misdemeanor under the Revised Code or an ordinance of a municipal corporation, the filing of the notice of appeal does not suspend execution of the sentence or judgment imposed. However, consistent with divisions (A)(2)(b), (B), and (C) of this section, Appellate Rule 8, and Criminal Rule 46, the municipal or county court, court of common pleas, or court of appeals may suspend execution of the sentence or judgment imposed during the pendency of the appeal and shall determine whether that defendant is entitled to bail and the amount and nature of any bail that is required. The bail shall at least be conditioned that the defendant will prosecute the appeal without delay and abide by the judgment and sentence of the court.

(b)(i) A court of common pleas or court of appeals may suspend the execution of a sentence of death imposed for an offense committed before January 1, 1995, only if no date for execution has been set by the supreme court, good cause is shown for the suspension, the defendant files a motion requesting the suspension, and notice has been given to the prosecuting attorney of the appropriate county.

(ii) A court of common pleas may suspend the execution of a sentence of death imposed for an offense committed on or after January 1, 1995, only if no date for execution has been set by the supreme court, good cause is shown, the defendant files a motion requesting the suspension, and notice has been given to the prosecuting attorney of the appropriate county.

(iii) A court of common pleas or court of appeals may suspend the execution of the sentence or judgment imposed for a felony in a capital case in which a sentence of death is not imposed only if no date for execution of the sentence has been set by the supreme court, good cause is shown for the suspension, the defendant files a motion requesting the suspension, and only after notice has been given to the prosecuting attorney of the appropriate county.

(B) Notwithstanding any provision of Criminal Rule 46 to the contrary, a trial judge of a court of common pleas shall not release on bail pursuant to division (A)(2)(a) of this section a defendant who is convicted of a bailable offense if the defendant is sentenced to imprisonment for life or if that offense is a violation of section 2903.01, 2903.02, 2903.03, 2903.04, 2903.11, 2905.01, 2905.02, 2905.11, 2907.02, 2909.02, 2911.01, 2911.02, or 2911.11 of the Revised Code or is felonious sexual penetration in violation of former section 2907.12 of the Revised Code.

(C) If a trial judge of a court of common pleas is prohibited by division (B) of this section from releasing on bail pursuant to division (A)(2)(a) of this section a defendant who is convicted of a bailable offense and not sentenced to imprisonment for life, the appropriate court of appeals or two judges of it, upon motion of the defendant and for good cause shown, may release the defendant on bail in accordance with division (A)(2) of this section.

(1996 H 445, eff. 9–3–96; 1995 S 4, eff. 9–21–95; 1986 H 412, eff. 3–17–87; 1982 H 269, § 4, S 199; 129 v 423; 1953 H 1; GC 13459–8)

2953.10 Supreme court's power to suspend sentence

When an appeal is taken from a court of appeals to the supreme court, the supreme court has the same power and authority to suspend the execution of sentence during the pendency of the appeal and admit the defendant to bail as does the court of appeals unless another section of the Revised Code or the Rules of Practice of the Supreme Court specify a distinct bail or suspension of sentence authority.

When an appeal in a case in which a sentence of death is imposed for an offense committed on or after January 1, 1995, is taken directly from the trial court to the supreme court, the supreme court has the same power and authority to suspend the execution of the sentence during the pendency of the appeal and admit the defendant to bail as does the court of appeals for cases in which a sentence of death is imposed for an offense committed before January 1, 1995, unless another section of the Revised

Code or the Rules of Practice of the Supreme Court specify a distinct bail or suspension of sentence authority.

(1995 S 4, eff. 9–21–95; 1986 H 412, eff. 3–17–87; 1953 H 1; GC 13459–8a)

2953.11 Custody of defendant under suspended sentence

In cases of conviction of felony, except for aggravated murder or murder, if the defendant has been committed to a state correctional institution and sentence is suspended, the clerk of the court in which the entry is made suspending the sentence under the seal of the court shall forthwith certify the suspension to the warden of the state correctional institution, who shall deliver the defendant to the sheriff of the county in which the defendant was convicted. The sheriff thereupon shall convey the defendant to the jail of the county in which the defendant was convicted and keep the defendant in custody unless admitted to bail pending the decision on the appeal or the termination of the suspension of sentence. If the judgment is affirmed or if the suspension of sentence is terminated, the sheriff shall convey the defendant to the state correctional institution to serve the balance of the defendant's term of sentence. The supreme court in the order allowing the filing of an appeal may provide that the defendant shall remain in the custody of the warden of the state correctional institution pending the decision of the court in such case.

(1995 S 2, eff. 7–1–96; 1994 H 571, eff. 10–6–94; 129 v 322, eff. 7–14–61; 1953 H 1; GC 13459–9)

REVERSAL

2953.13 Certification when judgment reversed

When a defendant has been committed to a state correctional institution and the judgment, by virtue of which the commitment was made, is reversed on appeal, and the defendant is entitled to his discharge or a new trial, the clerk of the court reversing the judgment, under the seal thereof, shall forthwith certify said reversal to the warden of the state correctional institution.

The warden, on receipt of the certificate, if a discharge of the defendant is ordered, shall forthwith discharge him from the state correctional institution.

If a new trial is ordered, the warden shall forthwith cause the defendant to be conveyed to the jail of the county in which he was convicted, and committed to the custody of the sheriff thereof.

(1994 H 571, eff. 10–6–94; 1953 H 1, eff. 10–1–53; GC 13459–11 to 13459–13)

APPEAL BY STATE

2953.14 Appeal by prosecuting authority

Whenever a court superior to the trial court renders judgment adverse to the state in a criminal action or proceeding, the state, through either the prosecuting attorney or the attorney general, may institute an appeal to reverse such judgment in the next higher court. If the conviction was for a violation of a municipal ordinance, such appeal may be brought by the village solicitor, city director of law, or other chief legal officer of the municipal corporation. Like proceedings shall be had in the higher court at the hearing of the appeal as in the review of other criminal actions or proceedings. The clerk of the court rendering the judgment sought to be reversed, on application of the prosecuting attorney, attorney general, solicitor, director of law, or other chief legal officer shall make a transcript of the docket and journal entries in the action or proceeding, and transmit it with all papers and files in the action or proceeding to the higher court.

(1986 H 412, eff. 3–17–87; 1977 H 219; 1953 H 1; GC 13459–14)

POSTCONVICTION REMEDIES

2953.21 Petition for postconviction relief

(A)(1)(a) Any person who has been convicted of a criminal offense or adjudicated a delinquent child and who claims that there was such a denial or infringement of the person's rights as to render the judgment void or voidable under the Ohio Constitution or the Constitution of the United States, and any person who has been convicted of a criminal offense that is a felony, who is an inmate, and for whom DNA testing that was performed under sections 2953.71 to 2953.81 of the Revised Code or under section 2953.82 of the Revised Code provided results that establish, by clear and convincing evidence, actual innocence of that felony offense or, if the person was sentenced to death, establish, by clear and convincing evidence, actual innocence of the aggravating circumstance or circumstances the person was found guilty of committing and that is or are the basis of that sentence of death, may file a petition in the court that imposed sentence, stating the grounds for relief relied upon, and asking the court to vacate or set aside the judgment or sentence or to grant other appropriate relief. The petitioner may file a supporting affidavit and other documentary evidence in support of the claim for relief.

(b) As used in division (A)(1)(a) of this section, "actual innocence" means that, had the results of the DNA testing conducted under sections 2953.71 to 2953.81 of the Revised Code or under section 2953.82 of the Revised Code been presented at trial, no reasonable factfinder would have found the petitioner guilty of the offense of which the petitioner was convicted, or, if the person was sentenced to death, no reasonable factfinder would have found the petitioner guilty of the aggravating circumstance or circumstances the petitioner was found guilty of committing and that is or are the basis of that sentence of death.

(2) Except as otherwise provided in section 2953.23 of the Revised Code, a petition under division (A)(1) of this section shall be filed no later than one hundred eighty days after the date on which the trial transcript is filed in the court of appeals in the direct appeal of the judgment of conviction or adjudication or, if the direct appeal involves a sentence of death, the date on which the trial transcript is filed in the supreme court. If no appeal is taken, except as otherwise provided in section 2953.23 of the Revised Code, the petition shall be filed no later than one hundred eighty days after the expiration of the time for filing the appeal.

(3) In a petition filed under division (A) of this section, a person who has been sentenced to death may ask the court to render void or voidable the judgment with respect to the conviction of aggravated murder or the specification of an aggravating circumstance or the sentence of death.

(4) A petitioner shall state in the original or amended petition filed under division (A) of this section all grounds for relief claimed by the petitioner. Except as provided in section 2953.23 of the Revised Code, any ground for relief that is not so stated in the petition is waived.

(5) If the petitioner in a petition filed under division (A) of this section was convicted of or pleaded guilty to a felony, the petition may include a claim that the petitioner was denied the equal protection of the laws in violation of the Ohio Constitution or the United States Constitution because the sentence imposed upon the petitioner for the felony was part of a consistent pattern of disparity in sentencing by the judge who imposed the sentence, with regard to the petitioner's race, gender, ethnic background, or religion. If the supreme court adopts a rule requiring a court of common pleas to maintain information with regard to an offend-

er's race, gender, ethnic background, or religion, the supporting evidence for the petition shall include, but shall not be limited to, a copy of that type of information relative to the petitioner's sentence and copies of that type of information relative to sentences that the same judge imposed upon other persons.

(B) The clerk of the court in which the petition is filed shall docket the petition and bring it promptly to the attention of the court. The clerk of the court in which the petition is filed immediately shall forward a copy of the petition to the prosecuting attorney of that county.

(C) The court shall consider a petition that is timely filed under division (A)(2) of this section even if a direct appeal of the judgment is pending. Before granting a hearing on a petition filed under division (A) of this section, the court shall determine whether there are substantive grounds for relief. In making such a determination, the court shall consider, in addition to the petition, the supporting affidavits, and the documentary evidence, all the files and records pertaining to the proceedings against the petitioner, including, but not limited to, the indictment, the court's journal entries, the journalized records of the clerk of the court, and the court reporter's transcript. The court reporter's transcript, if ordered and certified by the court, shall be taxed as court costs. If the court dismisses the petition, it shall make and file findings of fact and conclusions of law with respect to such dismissal.

(D) Within ten days after the docketing of the petition, or within any further time that the court may fix for good cause shown, the prosecuting attorney shall respond by answer or motion. Within twenty days from the date the issues are raised, either party may move for summary judgment. The right to summary judgment shall appear on the face of the record.

(E) Unless the petition and the files and records of the case show the petitioner is not entitled to relief, the court shall proceed to a prompt hearing on the issues even if a direct appeal of the case is pending. If the court notifies the parties that it has found grounds for granting relief, either party may request an appellate court in which a direct appeal of the judgment is pending to remand the pending case to the court.

(F) At any time before the answer or motion is filed, the petitioner may amend the petition with or without leave or prejudice to the proceedings. The petitioner may amend the petition with leave of court at any time thereafter.

(G) If the court does not find grounds for granting relief, it shall make and file findings of fact and conclusions of law and shall enter judgment denying relief on the petition. If no direct appeal of the case is pending and the court finds grounds for relief or if a pending direct appeal of the case has been remanded to the court pursuant to a request made pursuant to division (E) of this section and the court finds grounds for granting relief, it shall make and file findings of fact and conclusions of law and shall enter a judgment that vacates and sets aside the judgment in question, and, in the case of a petitioner who is a prisoner in custody, shall discharge or resentence the petitioner or grant a new trial as the court determines appropriate. The court also may make supplementary orders to the relief granted, concerning such matters as rearraignment, retrial, custody, and bail. If the trial court's order granting the petition is reversed on appeal and if the direct appeal of the case has been remanded from an appellate court pursuant to a request under division (E) of this section, the appellate court reversing the order granting the petition shall notify the appellate court in which the direct appeal of the case was pending at the time of the remand of the reversal and remand of the trial court's order. Upon the reversal and remand of the trial court's order granting the petition, regardless of whether notice is sent or received, the direct appeal of the case that was remanded is reinstated.

(H) Upon the filing of a petition pursuant to division (A) of this section by a person sentenced to death, only the supreme court may stay execution of the sentence of death.

(I)(1) If a person sentenced to death intends to file a petition under this section, the court shall appoint counsel to represent the person upon a finding that the person is indigent and that the person either accepts the appointment of counsel or is unable to make a competent decision whether to accept or reject the appointment of counsel. The court may decline to appoint counsel for the person only upon a finding, after a hearing if necessary, that the person rejects the appointment of counsel and understands the legal consequences of that decision or upon a finding that the person is not indigent.

(2) The court shall not appoint as counsel under division (I)(1) of this section an attorney who represented the petitioner at trial in the case to which the petition relates unless the person and the attorney expressly request the appointment. The court shall appoint as counsel under division (I)(1) of this section only an attorney who is certified under Rule 20 of the Rules of Superintendence for the Courts of Ohio to represent indigent defendants charged with or convicted of an offense for which the death penalty can be or has been imposed. The ineffectiveness or incompetence of counsel during proceedings under this section does not constitute grounds for relief in a proceeding under this section, in an appeal of any action under this section, or in an application to reopen a direct appeal.

(3) Division (I) of this section does not preclude attorneys who represent the state of Ohio from invoking the provisions of 28 U.S.C. 154 with respect to capital cases that were pending in federal habeas corpus proceedings prior to the effective date of this amendment insofar as the petitioners in those cases were represented in proceedings under this section by one or more counsel appointed by the court under this section or section 120.06, 120.16, 120.26, or 120.33 of the Revised Code and those appointed counsel meet the requirements of division (I)(2) of this section.

(J) Subject to the appeal of a sentence for a felony that is authorized by section 2953.08 of the Revised Code, the remedy set forth in this section is the exclusive remedy by which a person may bring a collateral challenge to the validity of a conviction or sentence in a criminal case or to the validity of an adjudication of a child as a delinquent child for the commission of an act that would be a criminal offense if committed by an adult or the validity of a related order of disposition.

(2003 S 11, eff. 10–29–03; 2001 H 94, eff. 9–5–01; 1996 S 258, eff. 10–16–96; 1996 S 269, eff. 7–1–96; 1995 S 2, eff. 7–1–96; 1995 S 4, eff. 9–21–95; 1994 H 571, eff. 10–6–94; 1986 H 412, eff. 3–17–87; 132 v H 742; 131 v S 383)

2953.22 Hearing

If a hearing is granted pursuant to section 2953.21 of the Revised Code, the petitioner shall be permitted to attend the hearing. Testimony of the prisoner or other witnesses may be offered by deposition.

If the petitioner is in a state correctional institution, he may be returned for the hearing upon the warrant of the court of common pleas of the county where the hearing is to be held. The approval of the governor on the warrant shall not be required. The warrant shall be directed to the sheriff of the county in which the hearing is to be held. When a copy of the warrant is presented to the warden or other head of a state correctional institution, he shall deliver the convict to the sheriff, who shall convey him to the county. For removing and returning the convict, the sheriff shall receive the fees allowed for conveying convicts to the correctional institution.

(1994 H 571, eff. 10–6–94; 132 v H 742, eff. 12–9–67)

2953.23 Second or successive petitions; order; appeal

(A) Whether a hearing is or is not held on a petition filed pursuant to section 2953.21 of the Revised Code, a court may not entertain a petition filed after the expiration of the period prescribed in division (A) of that section or a second petition or successive petitions for similar relief on behalf of a petitioner unless division (A)(1) or (2) of this section applies:

(1) Both of the following apply:

(a) Either the petitioner shows that the petitioner was unavoidably prevented from discovery of the facts upon which the petitioner must rely to present the claim for relief, or, subsequent to the period prescribed in division (A)(2) of section 2953.21 of the Revised Code or to the filing of an earlier petition, the United States Supreme Court recognized a new federal or state right that applies retroactively to persons in the petitioner's situation, and the petition asserts a claim based on that right.

(b) The petitioner shows by clear and convincing evidence that, but for constitutional error at trial, no reasonable factfinder would have found the petitioner guilty of the offense of which the petitioner was convicted or, if the claim challenges a sentence of death that, but for constitutional error at the sentencing hearing, no reasonable factfinder would have found the petitioner eligible for the death sentence.

(2) The petitioner was convicted of a felony, the petitioner is an inmate for whom DNA testing was performed under sections 2953.71 to 2953.81 of the Revised Code or under section 2953.82 of the Revised Code, and the results of the DNA testing establish, by clear and convincing evidence, actual innocence of that felony offense or, if the person was sentenced to death, establish, by clear and convincing evidence, actual innocence of the aggravating circumstance or circumstances the person was found guilty of committing and that is or are the basis of that sentence of death.

As used in this division, "actual innocence" has the same meaning as in division (A)(1)(b) of section 2953.21 of the Revised Code.

(B) An order awarding or denying relief sought in a petition filed pursuant to section 2953.21 of the Revised Code is a final judgment and may be appealed pursuant to Chapter 2953. of the Revised Code.

(2003 S 11, eff. 10–29–03; 1995 S 4, eff. 9–21–95; 132 v H 742, eff. 12–9–67)

SEALING OF RECORDS

2953.31 Definitions

As used in sections 2953.31 to 2953.36 of the Revised Code:

(A) "First offender" means anyone who has been convicted of an offense in this state or any other jurisdiction and who previously or subsequently has not been convicted of the same or a different offense in this state or any other jurisdiction. When two or more convictions result from or are connected with the same act or result from offenses committed at the same time, they shall be counted as one conviction. When two or three convictions result from the same indictment, information, or complaint, from the same plea of guilty, or from the same official proceeding, and result from related criminal acts that were committed within a three-month period but do not result from the same act or from offenses committed at the same time, they shall be counted as one conviction, provided that a court may decide as provided in division (C)(1)(a) of section 2953.32 of the Revised Code that it is not in the public interest for the two or three convictions to be counted as one conviction.

For purposes of, and except as otherwise provided in, this division, a conviction for a minor misdemeanor, for a violation of any section in Chapter 4507., 4510., 4511., 4513., or 4549. of the Revised Code, or for a violation of a municipal ordinance that is substantially similar to any section in those chapters is not a previous or subsequent conviction. However, a conviction for a violation of section 4511.19, 4511.251, 4549.02, 4549.021, 4549.03, 4549.042, or 4549.62 or sections 4549.41 to 4549.46 of the Revised Code, for a violation of section 4510.11 or 4510.14 of the Revised Code that is based upon the offender's operation of a vehicle during a suspension imposed under section 4511.191 or 4511.196 of the Revised Code, for a violation of a substantially equivalent municipal ordinance, for a felony violation of Title XLV of the Revised Code, or for a violation of a substantially equivalent former law of this state or former municipal ordinance shall be considered a previous or subsequent conviction.

(B) "Prosecutor" means the county prosecuting attorney, city director of law, village solicitor, or similar chief legal officer, who has the authority to prosecute a criminal case in the court in which the case is filed.

(C) "Bail forfeiture" means the forfeiture of bail by a defendant who is arrested for the commission of a misdemeanor, other than a defendant in a traffic case as defined in Traffic Rule 2, if the forfeiture is pursuant to an agreement with the court and prosecutor in the case.

(D) "Official records" has the same meaning as in division (D) of section 2953.51 of the Revised Code.

(E) "Official proceeding" has the same meaning as in section 2921.01 of the Revised Code.

(F) "Community control sanction" has the same meaning as in section 2929.01 of the Revised Code.

(G) "Post-release control" and "post-release control sanction" have the same meanings as in section 2967.01 of the Revised Code.

(2002 H 490, eff. 1–1–04; 2002 S 123, eff. 1–1–04; 1999 S 13, eff. 3–23–00; 1996 H 274, eff. 8–8–96; 1990 S 382, eff. 12–31–90; 1989 S 49; 1988 H 175; 1984 H 227; 1973 S 5)

2953.32 Sealing of record of first offense; application; hearing; fee; re-examination of sealed record

(A)(1) Except as provided in section 2953.61 of the Revised Code, a first offender may apply to the sentencing court if convicted in this state, or to a court of common pleas if convicted in another state or in a federal court, for the sealing of the conviction record. Application may be made at the expiration of three years after the offender's final discharge if convicted of a felony, or at the expiration of one year after the offender's final discharge if convicted of a misdemeanor.

(2) Any person who has been arrested for any misdemeanor offense and who has effected a bail forfeiture may apply to the court in which the misdemeanor criminal case was pending when bail was forfeited for the sealing of the record of the case. Except as provided in section 2953.61 of the Revised Code, the application may be filed at any time after the expiration of one year from the date on which the bail forfeiture was entered upon the minutes of the court or the journal, whichever entry occurs first.

(B) Upon the filing of an application under this section, the court shall set a date for a hearing and shall notify the prosecutor for the case of the hearing on the application. The prosecutor may object to the granting of the application by filing an objection with the court prior to the date set for the hearing. The prosecutor shall specify in the objection the reasons for believing a denial of the application is justified. The court shall direct its regular probation officer, a state probation officer, or the department of probation of the county in which the applicant resides to make inquiries and written reports as the court requires concerning the applicant.

(C)(1) The court shall do each of the following:

(a) Determine whether the applicant is a first offender or whether the forfeiture of bail was agreed to by the applicant and the prosecutor in the case. If the applicant applies as a first offender pursuant to division (A)(1) of this section and has two or three convictions that result from the same indictment, information, or complaint, from the same plea of guilty, or from the same official proceeding, and result from related criminal acts that were committed within a three-month period but do not result from the same act or from offenses committed at the same time, in making its determination under this division, the court initially shall determine whether it is not in the public interest for the two or three convictions to be counted as one conviction. If the court determines that it is not in the public interest for the two or three convictions to be counted as one conviction, the court shall determine that the applicant is not a first offender; if the court does not make that determination, the court shall determine that the offender is a first offender.

(b) Determine whether criminal proceedings are pending against the applicant;

(c) If the applicant is a first offender who applies pursuant to division (A)(1) of this section, determine whether the applicant has been rehabilitated to the satisfaction of the court;

(d) If the prosecutor has filed an objection in accordance with division (B) of this section, consider the reasons against granting the application specified by the prosecutor in the objection;

(e) Weigh the interests of the applicant in having the records pertaining to the applicant's conviction sealed against the legitimate needs, if any, of the government to maintain those records.

(2) If the court determines, after complying with division (C)(1) of this section, that the applicant is a first offender or the subject of a bail forfeiture, that no criminal proceeding is pending against the applicant, and that the interests of the applicant in having the records pertaining to the applicant's conviction or bail forfeiture sealed are not outweighed by any legitimate governmental needs to maintain those records, and that the rehabilitation of an applicant who is a first offender applying pursuant to division (A)(1) of this section has been attained to the satisfaction of the court, the court, except as provided in division (G) of this section, shall order all official records pertaining to the case sealed and, except as provided in division (F) of this section, all index references to the case deleted and, in the case of bail forfeitures, shall dismiss the charges in the case. The proceedings in the case shall be considered not to have occurred and the conviction or bail forfeiture of the person who is the subject of the proceedings shall be sealed, except that upon conviction of a subsequent offense, the sealed record of prior conviction or bail forfeiture may be considered by the court in determining the sentence or other appropriate disposition, including the relief provided for in sections 2953.31 to 2953.33 of the Revised Code.

(3) Upon the filing of an application under this section, the applicant, unless indigent, shall pay a fee of fifty dollars. The court shall pay thirty dollars of the fee into the state treasury. It shall pay twenty dollars of the fee into the county general revenue fund if the sealed conviction or bail forfeiture was pursuant to a state statute, or into the general revenue fund of the municipal corporation involved if the sealed conviction or bail forfeiture was pursuant to a municipal ordinance.

(D) Inspection of the sealed records included in the order may be made only by the following persons or for the following purposes:

(1) By a law enforcement officer or prosecutor, or the assistants of either, to determine whether the nature and character of the offense with which a person is to be charged would be affected by virtue of the person's previously having been convicted of a crime;

(2) By the parole or probation officer of the person who is the subject of the records, for the exclusive use of the officer in supervising the person while on parole or under a community control sanction or a post-release control sanction, and in making inquiries and written reports as requested by the court or adult parole authority;

(3) Upon application by the person who is the subject of the records, by the persons named in the application;

(4) By a law enforcement officer who was involved in the case, for use in the officer's defense of a civil action arising out of the officer's involvement in that case;

(5) By a prosecuting attorney or the prosecuting attorney's assistants, to determine a defendant's eligibility to enter a pre-trial diversion program established pursuant to section 2935.36 of the Revised Code;

(6) By any law enforcement agency or any authorized employee of a law enforcement agency or by the department of rehabilitation and correction as part of a background investigation of a person who applies for employment with the agency as a law enforcement officer or with the department as a corrections officer;

(7) By any law enforcement agency or any authorized employee of a law enforcement agency, for the purposes set forth in, and in the manner provided in, section 2953.321 of the Revised Code;

(8) By the bureau of criminal identification and investigation or any authorized employee of the bureau for the purpose of providing information to a board or person pursuant to division (F) or (G) of section 109.57 of the Revised Code;

(9) By the bureau of criminal identification and investigation or any authorized employee of the bureau for the purpose of performing a criminal history records check on a person to whom a certificate as prescribed in section 109.77 of the Revised Code is to be awarded;

(10) By the bureau of criminal identification and investigation, an authorized employee of the bureau, a sheriff, or an authorized employee of a sheriff in connection with a criminal records check described in section 311. 41 of the Revised Code.

When the nature and character of the offense with which a person is to be charged would be affected by the information, it may be used for the purpose of charging the person with an offense.

(E) In any criminal proceeding, proof of any otherwise admissible prior conviction may be introduced and proved, notwithstanding the fact that for any such prior conviction an order of sealing previously was issued pursuant to sections 2953.31 to 2953.36 of the Revised Code.

(F) The person or governmental agency, office, or department that maintains sealed records pertaining to convictions or bail forfeitures that have been sealed pursuant to this section may maintain a manual or computerized index to the sealed records. The index shall contain only the name of, and alphanumeric identifiers that relate to, the persons who are the subject of the sealed records, the word "sealed," and the name of the person, agency, office, or department that has custody of the sealed records, and shall not contain the name of the crime committed. The index shall be made available by the person who has custody of the sealed records only for the purposes set forth in divisions (C), (D), and (E) of this section.

(G) Notwithstanding any provision of this section or section 2953.33 of the Revised Code that requires otherwise, a board of education of a city, local, exempted village, or joint vocational school district that maintains records of an individual who has been permanently excluded under sections 3301.121 and 3313.662 of the Revised Code is permitted to maintain records regarding a conviction that was used as the basis for the individual's permanent exclusion, regardless of a court order to seal the record. An order issued under this section to seal the record of a conviction does not revoke the adjudication order of the superintendent of public instruction to permanently exclude the individual who is the subject of the sealing order. An order issued under this section to seal the record of a conviction of an individual may be presented to a district superintendent as evidence to support the contention that the superintendent should recommend that the permanent exclusion of the individual who is the subject of the sealing order be revoked. Except as otherwise authorized by this division and sections 3301.121 and 3313.662 of the Revised Code, any school employee in possession of or having access to the sealed conviction records of an individual that were the basis of a permanent exclusion of the individual is subject to section 2953.35 of the Revised Code.

(2004 H 12, § 3, eff. 4–8–04; 2004 H 12, § 1, eff. 4–8–04; 2002 H 490, eff. 1–1–04; 1999 S 13, eff. 3–23–00; 1996 S 160, eff. 1–27–97; 1996 H 566, eff. 10–16–96; 1994 H 571, eff. 10–6–94; 1992 H 154, eff. 7–31–92; 1989 S 140, 1988 H 175, 1987 H 8, 1984 H 227; 1979 H 105; 1977 H 219; 1973 S 5)

2953.321 Confidentiality of investigatory work product; violations; exceptions

(A) As used in this section, "investigatory work product" means any records or reports of a law enforcement officer or agency that are excepted from the definition of "official records" contained in section 2953.51 of the Revised Code and that pertain to a case the records of which have been ordered sealed pursuant to division (C)(2) of section 2953.32 of the Revised Code.

(B) Upon the issuance of an order by a court pursuant to division (C)(2) of section 2953.32 of the Revised Code directing that all official records pertaining to a case be sealed:

(1) Every law enforcement officer who possesses investigatory work product immediately shall deliver that work product to his employing law enforcement agency.

(2) Except as provided in division (B)(3) of this section, every law enforcement agency that possesses investigatory work product shall close that work product to all persons who are not directly employed by the law enforcement agency and shall treat that work product, in relation to all persons other than those who are directly employed by the law enforcement agency, as if it did not exist and never had existed.

(3) A law enforcement agency that possesses investigatory work product may permit another law enforcement agency to use that work product in the investigation of another offense if the facts incident to the offense being investigated by the other law enforcement agency and the facts incident to an offense that is the subject of the case are reasonably similar. The agency that permits the use of investigatory work product may provide the other agency with the name of the person who is the subject of the case if it believes that the name of the person is necessary to the conduct of the investigation by the other agency.

(C)(1) Except as provided in division (B)(3) of this section, no law enforcement officer or other person employed by a law enforcement agency shall knowingly release, disseminate, or otherwise make the investigatory work product or any information contained in that work product available to, or discuss any information contained in it with, any person not employed by the employing law enforcement agency.

(2) No law enforcement agency, or person employed by a law enforcement agency, that receives investigatory work product pursuant to division (B)(3) of this section shall use that work product for any purpose other than the investigation of the offense for which it was obtained from the other law enforcement agency, or disclose the name of the person who is the subject of the work product except when necessary for the conduct of the investigation of the offense, or the prosecution of the person for committing the offense, for which it was obtained from the other law enforcement agency.

(D) Whoever violates division (C)(1) or (2) of this section is guilty of divulging confidential investigatory work product, a misdemeanor of the fourth degree.

(1988 H 175, eff. 6–29–88)

2953.33 Restoration of rights upon sealing of record

(A) Except as provided in division (G) of section 2953.32 of the Revised Code, an order to seal the record of a person's conviction restores the person who is the subject of the order to all rights and privileges not otherwise restored by termination of the sentence or community control sanction or by final release on parole or post-release control.

(B) In any application for employment, license, or other right or privilege, any appearance as a witness, or any other inquiry, except as provided in division (E) of section 2953.32 of the Revised Code, a person may be questioned only with respect to convictions not sealed, bail forfeitures not expunged under section 2953.42 of the Revised Code as it existed prior to June 29, 1988, and bail forfeitures not sealed, unless the question bears a direct and substantial relationship to the position for which the person is being considered.

(2002 H 490, eff. 1–1–04; 1992 H 154, eff. 7–31–92; 1988 H 175; 1979 H 105; 1973 S 5)

2953.34 Other remedies not precluded

Nothing in sections 2953.31 to 2953.33 of the Revised Code precludes a first offender from taking an appeal or seeking any relief from his conviction or from relying on it in lieu of any subsequent prosecution for the same offense.

(1973 S 5, eff. 1–1–74)

2953.35 Divulging sealed records prohibited

(A) Except as authorized by divisions (D), (E), and (F) of section 2953.32 of the Revised Code or by Chapter 2950. of the Revised Code, any officer or employee of the state, or a political subdivision of the state, who releases or otherwise disseminates or makes available for any purpose involving employment, bonding, or licensing in connection with any business, trade, or profession to any person, or to any department, agency, or other instrumentality of the state, or any political subdivision of the state, any information or other data concerning any arrest, complaint, indictment, trial, hearing, adjudication, conviction, or correctional supervision the records with respect to which the officer or employee had knowledge of were sealed by an existing order issued pursuant to sections 2953.31 to 2953.36 of the Revised Code, or were expunged by an order issued pursuant to section 2953.42 of the Revised Code as it existed prior to the effective date of this amendment, is guilty of divulging confidential information, a misdemeanor of the fourth degree.

(B) Any person who, in violation of section 2953.32 of the Revised Code, uses, disseminates, or otherwise makes available any index prepared pursuant to division (F) of section 2953.32 of the Revised Code is guilty of a misdemeanor of the fourth degree.

(1996 H 180, eff. 7–1–97; 1988 H 175, eff. 6–29–88; 1979 H 105; 1975 H 1; 1973 S 5)

2953.36 Convictions precluding sealing

Sections 2953.31 to 2953.35 of the Revised Code do not apply to any of the following:

(A) Convictions when the offender is subject to a mandatory prison term;

(B) Convictions under section 2907.02, 2907.03, 2907.04, 2907.05, 2907.06, 2907.321, 2907.322, or 2907.323, former section 2907.12, or Chapter 4507., 4510., 4511., or 4549. of the Revised Code, or a conviction for a violation of a municipal ordinance that is substantially similar to any section contained in any of those chapters;

(C) convictions of an offense of violence when the offense is a misdemeanor of the first degree or a felony and when the offense is not a violation of section 2917.03 of the Revised Code and is not a violation of section 2903.13, 2917.01 or 2917.31 of the Revised Code that is a misdemeanor of the first degree;

(D) Convictions of an offense in circumstances in which the victim of the offense was under eighteen years of age when the offense is a misdemeanor of the first degree or a felony;

(E) Convictions of a felony of the first or second degree;

(F) Bail forfeitures in a traffic case as defined in Traffic Rule 2.

(2002 S 123, eff. 1-1-04; 1999 S 13, eff. 3-23-00; 1996 S 269, eff. 7-1-96; 1996 H 353, eff. 9-17-96; 1996 H 445, eff. 9-3-96; 1994 H 335, eff. 12-9-94; 1988 H 175, eff. 6-29-88; 1973 S 5)

SEALING OF RECORDS—FURTHER PROVISIONS

2953.51 Definitions

As used in sections 2953.51 to 2953.55 of the Revised Code:

(A) "No bill" means a report by the foreperson or deputy foreperson of a grand jury that an indictment is not found by the grand jury against a person who has been held to answer before the grand jury for the commission of an offense.

(B) "Prosecutor" has the same meaning as in section 2953.31 of the Revised Code.

(C) "Court" means the court in which a case is pending at the time a finding of not guilty in the case or a dismissal of the complaint, indictment, or information in the case is entered on the minutes or journal of the court, or the court to which the foreperson or deputy foreperson of a grand jury reports, pursuant to section 2939.23 of the Revised Code, that the grand jury has returned a no bill.

(D) "Official records" means all records that are possessed by any public office or agency that relate to a criminal case, including, but not limited to: the notation to the case in the criminal docket; all subpoenas issued in the case; all papers and documents filed by the defendant or the prosecutor in the case; all records of all testimony and evidence presented in all proceedings in the case; all court files, papers, documents, folders, entries, affidavits, or writs that pertain to the case; all computer, microfilm, microfiche, or microdot records, indices, or references to the case; all index references to the case; all fingerprints and photographs; all records and investigative reports pertaining to the case that are possessed by any law enforcement officer or agency, except that any records or reports that are the specific investigatory work product of a law enforcement officer or agency are not and shall not be considered to be official records when they are in the possession of that officer or agency; and all investigative records and reports other than those possessed by a law enforcement officer or agency pertaining to the case. "Official records" does not include records or reports maintained pursuant to section 2151.421 of the Revised Code by a public children services agency or the department of job and family services.

(1999 H 471, eff. 7-1-00; 1996 H 274, eff. 8-8-96; 1984 H 227, eff. 9-26-84)

2953.52 Application to have records sealed; grounds; order

(A)(1) Any person, who is found not guilty of an offense by a jury or a court or who is the defendant named in a dismissed complaint, indictment, or information, may apply to the court for an order to seal his official records in the case. Except as provided in section 2953.61 of the Revised Code, the application may be filed at any time after the finding of not guilty or the dismissal of the complaint, indictment, or information is entered upon the minutes of the court or the journal, whichever entry occurs first.

(2) Any person, against whom a no bill is entered by a grand jury, may apply to the court for an order to seal his official records in the case. Except as provided in section 2953.61 of the Revised Code, the application may be filed at any time after the expiration of two years after the date on which the foreman or deputy foreman of the grand jury reports to the court that the grand jury has reported a no bill.

(B)(1) Upon the filing of an application pursuant to division (A) of this section, the court shall set a date for a hearing and shall notify the prosecutor in the case of the hearing on the application. The prosecutor may object to the granting of the application by filing an objection with the court prior to the date set for the hearing. The prosecutor shall specify in the objection the reasons he believes justify a denial of the application.

(2) The court shall do each of the following:

(a) Determine whether the person was found not guilty in the case, or the complaint, indictment, or information in the case was dismissed, or a no bill was returned in the case and a period of two years or a longer period as required by section 2953.61 of the Revised Code has expired from the date of the report to the court of that no bill by the foreman or deputy foreman of the grand jury;

(b) Determine whether criminal proceedings are pending against the person;

(c) If the prosecutor has filed an objection in accordance with division (B)(1) of this section, consider the reasons against granting the application specified by the prosecutor in the objection;

(d) Weigh the interests of the person in having the official records pertaining to the case sealed against the legitimate needs, if any, of the government to maintain those records.

(3) If the court determines, after complying with division (B)(2) of this section, that the person was found not guilty in the case, that the complaint, indictment, or information in the case was dismissed, or that a no bill was returned in the case and that the appropriate period of time has expired from the date of the report to the court of the no bill by the foreman or deputy foreman of the grand jury; that no criminal proceedings are pending against the person; and the interests of the person in having the records pertaining to the case sealed are not outweighed by any legitimate governmental needs to maintain such records, or if division (E)(2)(b) of section 4301.69 of the Revised Code applies, the court shall issue an order directing that all official records pertaining to the case be sealed and that, except as provided in section 2953.53 of the Revised Code, the proceedings in the case be deemed not to have occurred.

(2002 H 17, eff. 10-11-02; 1988 H 175, eff. 6-29-88; 1984 H 227)

2953.53 Notices of order to seal; offices and agencies affected; examination of sealed record

(A) The court shall send notice of any order to seal official records issued pursuant to section 2953.52 of the Revised Code to any public office or agency that the court knows or has reason to believe may have any record of the case, whether or not it is an official record, that is the subject of the order. The notice shall be sent by certified mail, return receipt requested.

(B) A person whose official records have been sealed pursuant to an order issued pursuant to section 2953.52 of the Revised Code may present a copy of that order and a written request to comply with it, to a public office or agency that has a record of the case that is the subject of the order.

(C) An order to seal official records issued pursuant to section 2953.52 of the Revised Code applies to every public office or agency that has a record of the case that is the subject of the order, regardless of whether it receives notice of the hearing on the application for the order to seal the official records or receives a copy of the order to seal the official records pursuant to division (A) or (B) of this section.

(D) Upon receiving a copy of an order to seal official records pursuant to division (A) or (B) of this section or upon otherwise becoming aware of an applicable order to seal official records issued pursuant to section 2953.52 of the Revised Code, a public office or agency shall comply with the order and, if applicable, with the provisions of section 2953.54 of the Revised Code, except that it may maintain a record of the case that is the subject of the order if the record is maintained for the purpose of compiling statistical data only and does not contain any reference to the person who is the subject of the case and the order.

A public office or agency also may maintain an index of sealed official records, in a form similar to that for sealed records of conviction as set forth in division (F) of section 2953.32 of the Revised Code, access to which may not be afforded to any person other than the person who has custody of the sealed official records. The sealed official records to which such an index pertains shall not be available to any person, except that the official records of a case that have been sealed may be made available to the following persons for the following purposes:

(1) To the person who is the subject of the records upon written application, and to any other person named in the application, for any purpose;

(2) To a law enforcement officer who was involved in the case, for use in the officer's defense of a civil action arising out of the officer's involvement in that case;

(3) To a prosecuting attorney or the prosecuting attorney's assistants to determine a defendant's eligibility to enter a pre-trial diversion program established pursuant to section 2935.36 of the Revised Code;

(4) To a prosecuting attorney or the prosecuting attorney's assistants to determine a defendant's eligibility to enter a pre-trial diversion program under division (E)(2)(b) of section 4301.69 of the Revised Code.

(2002 H 17, eff. 10–11–02; 1988 H 175, eff. 6–29–88; 1987 H 8; 1984 H 227)

2953.54 Exceptions; offense of divulging confidential information

(A) Except as otherwise provided in Chapter 2950. of the Revised Code, upon the issuance of an order by a court under division (B) of section 2953.52 of the Revised Code directing that all official records pertaining to a case be sealed and that the proceedings in the case be deemed not to have occurred:

(1) Every law enforcement officer possessing records or reports pertaining to the case that are the officer's specific investigatory work product and that are excepted from the definition of "official records" contained in section 2953.51 of the Revised Code shall immediately deliver the records and reports to his employing law enforcement agency. Except as provided in division (A)(3) of this section, no such officer shall knowingly release, disseminate, or otherwise make the records and reports or any information contained in them available to, or discuss any information contained in them with, any person not employed by the officer's employing law enforcement agency.

(2) Every law enforcement agency that possesses records or reports pertaining to the case that are its specific investigatory work product and that are excepted from the definition of "official records" contained in section 2953.51 of the Revised Code, or that are the specific investigatory work product of a law enforcement officer it employs and that were delivered to it under division (A)(1) of this section shall, except as provided in division (A)(3) of this section, close the records and reports to all persons who are not directly employed by the law enforcement agency and shall, except as provided in division (A)(3) of this section, treat the records and reports, in relation to all persons other than those who are directly employed by the law enforcement agency, as if they did not exist and had never existed. Except as provided in division (A)(3) of this section, no person who is employed by the law enforcement agency shall knowingly release, disseminate, or otherwise make the records and reports in the possession of the employing law enforcement agency or any information contained in them available to, or discuss any information contained in them with, any person not employed by the employing law enforcement agency.

(3) A law enforcement agency that possesses records or reports pertaining to the case that are its specific investigatory work product and that are excepted from the definition of "official records" contained in division (D) of section 2953.51 of the Revised Code, or that are the specific investigatory work product of a law enforcement officer it employs and that were delivered to it under division (A)(1) of this section may permit another law enforcement agency to use the records or reports in the investigation of another offense, if the facts incident to the offense being investigated by the other law enforcement agency and the facts incident to an offense that is the subject of the case are reasonably similar. The agency that provides the records and reports may provide the other agency with the name of the person who is the subject of the case, if it believes that the name of the person is necessary to the conduct of the investigation by the other agency.

No law enforcement agency, or person employed by a law enforcement agency, that receives from another law enforcement agency records or reports pertaining to a case the records of which have been ordered sealed pursuant to division (B) of section 2953.52 of the Revised Code shall use the records and reports for any purpose other than the investigation of the offense for which they were obtained from the other law enforcement agency, or disclose the name of the person who is the subject of the records or reports except when necessary for the conduct of the investigation of the offense, or the prosecution of the person for committing the offense, for which they were obtained from the other law enforcement agency.

(B) Whoever violates division (A)(1), (2), or (3) of this section is guilty of divulging confidential information, a misdemeanor of the fourth degree.

(1996 H 180, eff. 7–1–97; 1984 H 227, eff. 9–26–84)

2953.55 Effects of order; offense

(A) In any application for employment, license, or any other right or privilege, any appearance as a witness, or any other inquiry, a person may not be questioned with respect to any record that has been sealed pursuant to section 2953.52 of the Revised Code. If an inquiry is made in violation of this section, the person whose official record was sealed may respond as if the arrest underlying the case to which the sealed official records pertain and all other proceedings in that case did not occur, and the person whose official record was sealed shall not be subject to any adverse action because of the arrest, the proceedings, or his response.

(B) An officer or employee of the state or any of its political subdivisions who knowingly releases, disseminates, or makes available for any purpose involving employment, bonding, licensing, or education to any person or to any department, agency, or other instrumentality of the state, or of any of its political subdivisions, any information or other data concerning any arrest, complaint, indictment, information, trial, adjudication, or correctional supervision, the records of which have been sealed pursuant to section 2953.52 of the Revised Code, is guilty of divulging confidential information, a misdemeanor of the fourth degree.

(1984 H 227, eff. 9–26–84)

2953.61 Effect of multiple offenses with different dispositions

When a person is charged with two or more offenses as a result of or in connection with the same act and at least one of the charges has a final disposition that is different than the final disposition of the other charges, the person may not apply to the court for the sealing of his record in any of the cases until such time as he would be able to apply to the court and have all of the records in all of the cases pertaining to those charges sealed pursuant to divisions (A)(1) and (2) of section 2953.32 and divisions (A)(1) and (2) of section 2953.52 of the Revised Code.

(1988 H 175, eff. 6–29–88)

DNA TESTING OF ELIGIBLE INMATES

2953.71 Definitions

As used in sections 2953.71 to 2953.83 of the Revised Code:

(A) "Application" or "application for DNA testing" means a request through postconviction relief for the state to do DNA testing on biological material from whichever of the following is applicable:

(1) The case in which the inmate was convicted of the offense for which the inmate is an eligible inmate and is requesting the DNA testing under sections 2953.71 to 2953.81 of the Revised Code;

(2) The case in which the inmate pleaded guilty or no contest to the offense for which the inmate is requesting the DNA testing under section 2953.82 of the Revised Code.

(B) "Biological material" means any product of a human body containing DNA.

(C) "Chain of custody" means a record or other evidence that tracks a subject sample of biological material from the time the biological material was first obtained until the time it currently exists in its place of storage and, in relation to a DNA sample, a record or other evidence that tracks the DNA sample from the time it was first obtained until it currently exists in its place of storage. For purposes of this division, examples of when biological material or a DNA sample is first obtained include, but are not limited to, obtaining the material or sample at the scene of a crime, from a victim, from an inmate, or in any other manner or time as is appropriate in the facts and circumstances present.

(D) "Custodial agency" means the group or entity that has the responsibility to maintain biological material in question.

(E) "Custodian" means the person who is the primary representative of a custodial agency.

(F) "Eligible inmate" means an inmate who is eligible under division (C) of section 2953.72 of the Revised Code to request DNA testing to be conducted under sections 2953.71 to 2953.81 of the Revised Code.

(G) "Exclusion" or "exclusion result" means a result of DNA testing that scientifically precludes or forecloses the subject inmate as a contributor of biological material recovered from the crime scene or victim in question, in relation to the offense for which the inmate is an eligible inmate and for which the sentence of death or prison term was imposed upon the inmate or, regarding a request for DNA testing made under section 2953.82 of the Revised Code, in relation to the offense for which the inmate made the request and for which the sentence of death or prison term was imposed upon the inmate.

(H) "Extracting personnel" means medically approved personnel who are employed to physically obtain an inmate DNA specimen for purposes of DNA testing under sections 2953.71 to 2953.81 or section 2953.82 of the Revised Code.

(I) "Inclusion" or "inclusion result" means a result of DNA testing that scientifically cannot exclude, or that holds accountable, the subject inmate as a contributor of biological material recovered from the crime scene or victim in question, in relation to the offense for which the inmate is an eligible inmate and for which the sentence of death or prison term was imposed upon the inmate or, regarding a request for DNA testing made under section 2953.82 of the Revised Code, in relation to the offense for which the inmate made the request and for which the sentence of death or prison term was imposed upon the inmate.

(J) "Inconclusive" or "inconclusive result" means a result of DNA testing that is rendered when a scientifically appropriate and definitive DNA analysis or result, or both, cannot be determined.

(K) "Inmate" means an inmate in a prison who was sentenced by a court, or by a jury and a court, of this state.

(L) "Outcome determinative" means that had the results of DNA testing been presented at the trial of the subject inmate requesting DNA testing and been found relevant and admissible with respect to the felony offense for which the inmate is an eligible inmate and is requesting the DNA testing or for which the inmate is requesting the DNA testing under section 2953.82 of the Revised Code, no reasonable factfinder would have found the inmate guilty of that offense or, if the inmate was sentenced to death relative to that offense, would have found the inmate guilty of the aggravating circumstance or circumstances the inmate was found guilty of committing and that is or are the basis of that sentence of death.

(M) "Parent sample" means the biological material first obtained from a crime scene or a victim of an offense for which an inmate is an eligible inmate or for which the inmate is requesting the DNA testing under section 2953.82 of the Revised Code, and from which a sample will be presently taken to do a DNA comparison to the DNA of the subject inmate under sections 2953.71 to 2953.81 or section 2953.82 of the Revised Code.

(N) "Prison" has the same meaning as in section 2929.01 of the Revised Code.

(O) "Prosecuting attorney" means the prosecuting attorney who, or whose office, prosecuted the case in which the subject inmate was convicted of the offense for which the inmate is an eligible inmate and is requesting the DNA testing or for which the inmate is requesting the DNA testing under section 2953.82 of the Revised Code.

(P) "Prosecuting authority" means the prosecuting attorney or the attorney general.

(Q) "Reasonable diligence" means a degree of diligence that is comparable to the diligence a reasonable person would employ in searching for information regarding an important matter in the person's own life.

(R) "Testing authority" means a laboratory at which DNA testing will be conducted under sections 2953.71 to 2953.81 or section 2953.82 of the Revised Code.

(2003 S 11, eff. 10–29–03)

2953.72 Application for postconviction testing

(A) Any eligible inmate who wishes to request DNA testing under sections 2953.71 to 2953.81 of the Revised Code shall submit an application for the testing to the court of common pleas specified in section 2953.73 of the Revised Code, on a form prescribed by the attorney general for this purpose. The eligible inmate shall submit the application within the period of time, and in accordance with the procedures, set forth in section 2953.73 of the Revised Code. The eligible inmate shall specify on the application the offense or offenses for which the inmate is an eligible inmate and is requesting the DNA testing. Along with the application, the eligible inmate shall submit an acknowledgment that is on a form prescribed by the attorney general for this purpose and that is signed by the inmate. The acknowledgment shall set forth all of the following:

(1) That sections 2953.71 to 2953.81 of the Revised Code contemplate applications for DNA testing of eligible inmates at a stage of a prosecution or case after the inmate has been sentenced to a prison term or a sentence of death, that any exclusion or inclusion result of DNA testing rendered pursuant to those sections may be used by a party in any proceeding as described in section 2953.81 of the Revised Code, and that all requests for any DNA testing made at trial will continue to be handled by the prosecuting attorney in the case;

(2) That the process of conducting postconviction DNA testing for an eligible inmate under sections 2953.71 to 2953.81 of the Revised Code begins when the inmate submits an application under section 2953.73 of the Revised Code and the acknowledgment described in this section;

(3) That the eligible inmate must submit the application and acknowledgment to the court of common pleas that heard the case in which the inmate was convicted of the offense for which the inmate is an eligible offender and is requesting the DNA testing;

(4) That the state has established a set of criteria set forth in section 2953.74 of the Revised Code by which eligible inmate applications for DNA testing will be screened and that a judge of a court of common pleas upon receipt of a properly filed application and accompanying acknowledgment will apply those criteria to determine whether to accept or reject the application;

(5) That the results of DNA testing conducted under sections 2953.71 to 2953.81 of the Revised Code will be provided as described in section 2953.81 of the Revised Code to all parties in the postconviction proceedings and will be reported to various courts;

(6) That, if DNA testing is conducted with respect to an inmate under sections 2953.71 to 2953.81 of the Revised Code, the state will not offer the inmate a retest if an inclusion result is achieved relative to the testing and that, if the state were to offer a retest after an inclusion result, the policy would create an atmosphere in which endless testing could occur and in which postconviction proceedings could be stalled for many years;

(7) That, if the court rejects an eligible inmate's application for DNA testing because the inmate does not satisfy the acceptance criteria described in division (A)(4) of this section, the court will not accept or consider subsequent applications;

(8) That the acknowledgment memorializes the provisions of sections 2953.71 to 2953.81 of the Revised Code with respect to the application of postconviction DNA testing to inmates, that those provisions do not give any inmate any additional constitutional right that the inmate did not have prior to the effective date of those provisions, that the court has no duty or obligation to provide postconviction DNA testing to inmates, that the court of common pleas has the sole discretion subject to an appeal as described in this division to determine whether an inmate is an eligible inmate and whether an eligible inmate's application for DNA testing satisfies the acceptance criteria described in division (A)(4) of this section and whether the application should be accepted or rejected, that if the court of common pleas rejects an eligible inmate's application, the inmate may seek leave of the supreme court to appeal the rejection to that court if the inmate was sentenced to death for the offense for which the inmate is requesting the DNA testing and, if the inmate was not sentenced to death for that offense, may appeal the rejection to the court of appeals, and that no determination otherwise made by the court of common pleas in the exercise of its discretion regarding the eligibility of an inmate or regarding postconviction DNA testing under those provisions is reviewable by or appealable to any court;

(9) That the manner in which sections 2953.71 to 2953.81 of the Revised Code with respect to the offering of postconviction DNA testing to inmates are carried out does not confer any constitutional right upon any inmate, that the state has established guidelines and procedures relative to those provisions to ensure that they are carried out with both justice and efficiency in mind, and that an inmate who participates in any phase of the mechanism contained in those provisions, including, but not limited to, applying for DNA testing and being rejected, having an application for DNA testing accepted and not receiving the test, or having DNA testing conducted and receiving unfavorable results, does not gain as a result of the participation any constitutional right to challenge, or, except as provided in division (A)(8) of this section, any right to any review or appeal of, the manner in which those provisions are carried out;

(10) That the most basic aspect of sections 2953.71 to 2953.81 of the Revised Code is that, in order for DNA testing to occur, there must be an inmate sample against which other evidence may be compared, that, if an eligible inmate's application is accepted but the inmate subsequently refuses to submit to the collection of the sample of biological material from the inmate or hinders the state from obtaining a sample of biological material from the inmate, the goal of those provisions will be frustrated, and that an inmate's refusal or hindrance shall cause the court to rescind its prior acceptance of the application for DNA testing for the inmate and deny the application;

(11) That, if the inmate is an inmate who pleaded guilty or no contest to a felony offense and who is using the application and acknowledgment to request DNA testing under section 2953.82 of the Revised Code, all references in the acknowledgment to an "eligible inmate" are considered to be references to, and apply to, the inmate and all references in the acknowledgment to "sections 2953.71 to 2953.81 of the Revised Code" are considered to be references to "section 2953.82 of the Revised Code".

(B) The attorney general shall prescribe a form to be used to make an application for DNA testing under division (A) of this section and section 2953.73 of the Revised Code and a form to be used to provide the acknowledgment described in division (A) of this section. The forms shall include all information described in division (A) of this section, spaces for an inmate to insert all information necessary to complete the forms, including, but not limited to, specifying the offense or offenses for which the inmate is an eligible inmate and is requesting the DNA testing or for which the inmate is requesting the DNA testing under section 2953.82 of the Revised Code, and any other information or material the attorney general determines is necessary or relevant. The forms also shall be used to make an application requesting DNA testing under section 2953.82 of the Revised Code, and the attorney general shall ensure that they are sufficient for that type of use, and that they include all information and spaces necessary for that type of use. The attorney general shall distribute copies of the prescribed forms to the department of rehabilitation and correction, the department shall ensure that each prison in which inmates are housed has a supply of copies of the forms, and the department shall ensure that copies of the forms are provided free of charge to any inmate who requests them.

(C)(1) An inmate is eligible to request DNA testing to be conducted under sections 2953.71 to 2953.81 of the Revised Code only if all of the following apply:

(a) The offense for which the inmate claims to be an eligible inmate is a felony that was committed prior to the effective date of this section, and the inmate was convicted by a judge or jury of that offense.

(b) The inmate was sentenced to a prison term or sentence of death for the felony described in division (C)(1)(a) of this section and, on the effective date of this section, is in prison serving that prison term or under that sentence of death.

(c) On the date on which the application is filed, the inmate has at least one year remaining on the prison term described in division (C)(1)(b) of this section, or the inmate is in prison under a sentence of death as described in that division.

(2) An inmate is not an eligible inmate under division (C)(1) of this section regarding any offense to which the inmate pleaded guilty or no contest.

(2003 S 11, eff. 10–29–03)

2953.73 Submission of application

Note: See also following version of this section, eff. 5–18–05.

(A) An eligible inmate who wishes to request DNA testing to be conducted under sections 2953.71 to 2953.81 of the Revised Code shall submit an application for DNA testing on a form prescribed by the attorney general for this purpose and shall submit the form to the court of common pleas that sentenced the inmate for the offense for which the inmate is an eligible inmate and is requesting DNA testing. The eligible inmate shall submit the application to that court of common pleas not later than one year after the effective date of this section. No court of common pleas shall accept an application under this section after the expiration of the period of time specified in this division.

(B) If an eligible inmate submits an application for DNA testing under division (A) of this section, upon the submission of the application, all of the following apply:

(1) The eligible inmate shall serve a copy of the application on the prosecuting attorney and the attorney general.

(2) The application shall be assigned to the judge of that court of common pleas who was the trial judge in the case in which the eligible inmate was convicted of the offense for which the inmate is requesting DNA testing, or, if that judge no longer is a judge of that court, it shall be assigned according to court rules. The judge to whom the application is assigned shall decide the application. The application shall become part of the file in the case.

(C) If an eligible inmate submits an application for DNA testing under division (A) of this section, regardless of whether the inmate has commenced any federal habeas corpus proceeding relative to the case in which the inmate was convicted of the offense for which the inmate is an eligible inmate and is requesting DNA testing, any response to the application by the prosecuting attorney or the attorney general shall be filed not later than forty-five days after the date on which the eligible inmate submits the application. The prosecuting attorney or the attorney general, or both, may, but are not required to, file a response to the application. If the prosecuting attorney or the attorney general files a response under this division, the prosecuting attorney or attorney general, whoever filed the response, shall serve a copy of the response on the eligible inmate.

(D) If an eligible inmate submits an application for DNA testing under division (A) of this section, the court shall make the determination as to whether the application should be accepted or rejected. The court shall expedite its review of the application. The court shall make the determination in accordance with the criteria and procedures set forth in sections 2953.74 to 2953.81 of the Revised Code and, in making the determination, shall consider the application, the supporting affidavits, and the documentary evidence and, in addition to those materials, shall consider all the files and records pertaining to the proceedings against the applicant, including, but not limited to, the indictment, the court's journal entries, the journalized records of the clerk of the court, and the court reporter's transcript and all responses to the application filed under division (C) of this section by a prosecuting attorney or the attorney general, unless the application and the files and records show the applicant is not entitled to DNA testing, in which case the application may be denied. The court is not required to conduct an evidentiary hearing in conducting its review of, and in making its determination as to whether to accept or reject, the application. Upon making its determination, the court shall enter a judgment and order that either accepts or rejects the application and that includes within the judgment and order the reasons for the acceptance or rejection as applied to the criteria and procedures set forth in sections 2953.71 to 2953.81 of the Revised Code. The court shall send a copy of the judgment and order to the eligible inmate who filed it, the prosecuting attorney, and the attorney general.

(E) A judgment and order of a court entered under division (D) of this section is appealable only as provided in this division. If an eligible inmate submits an application for DNA testing under section 2953.73 of the Revised Code and the court of common pleas rejects the application under division (D) of this section, one of the following applies:

(a) If the inmate was sentenced to death for the offense for which the inmate claims to be an eligible inmate and is requesting DNA testing, the inmate may seek leave of the supreme court to appeal the rejection to the supreme court. Courts of appeals do not have jurisdiction to review any rejection if the inmate was sentenced to death for the offense for which the inmate claims to be an eligible inmate and is requesting DNA testing.

(b) If the inmate was not sentenced to death for the offense for which the inmate claims to be an eligible inmate and is requesting DNA testing, the rejection is a final appealable order, and the inmate may appeal it to the court of appeals of the district in which is located that court of common pleas.

(F) Notwithstanding any provision of law regarding fees and costs, no filing fee shall be required of, and no court costs shall be assessed against, an eligible offender who is indigent and who submits an application under this section.

(G) If a court rejects an eligible inmate's application for DNA testing under division (D) of this section, unless the rejection is overturned on appeal, no court shall require the state to administer a DNA test under sections 2953.71 to 2953.81 of the Revised Code on the eligible inmate.

(2003 S 11, eff. 10–29–03)

Note: See also following version of this section, eff. 5–18–05.

2953.73 Submission of application (later effective date)

Note: See also preceding version of this section, in effect until 5–18–05.

(A) An eligible inmate who wishes to request DNA testing to be conducted under sections 2953.71 to 2953.81 of the Revised Code shall submit an application for DNA testing on a form prescribed by the attorney general for this purpose and shall submit the form to the court of common pleas that sentenced the inmate for the offense for which the inmate is an eligible inmate and is requesting DNA testing. The eligible inmate shall submit the application to that court of common pleas not later than two years after October 29, 2003. No court of common pleas shall accept an application under this section after the expiration of the period of time specified in this division.

(B) If an eligible inmate submits an application for DNA testing under division (A) of this section, upon the submission of the application, all of the following apply:

(1) The eligible inmate shall serve a copy of the application on the prosecuting attorney and the attorney general.

(2) The application shall be assigned to the judge of that court of common pleas who was the trial judge in the case in which the eligible inmate was convicted of the offense for which the inmate is requesting DNA testing, or, if that judge no longer is a judge of that court, it shall be assigned according to court rules. The judge to whom the application is assigned shall decide the application. The application shall become part of the file in the case.

(C) If an eligible inmate submits an application for DNA testing under division (A) of this section, regardless of whether the inmate has commenced any federal habeas corpus proceeding relative to the case in which the inmate was convicted of the offense for which the inmate is an eligible inmate and is requesting DNA testing, any response to the application by the prosecuting attorney or the attorney general shall be filed not later than forty-five days after the date on which the eligible inmate submits the application. The prosecuting attorney or the attorney general, or both, may, but are not required to, file a response to the application. If the prosecuting attorney or the attorney general files a response under this division, the prosecuting attorney or attorney general, whoever filed the response, shall serve a copy of the response on the eligible inmate.

(D) If an eligible inmate submits an application for DNA testing under division (A) of this section, the court shall make the determination as to whether the application should be accepted or rejected. The court shall expedite its review of the application. The court shall make the determination in accordance with the criteria and procedures set forth in sections 2953.74 to 2953.81 of the Revised Code and, in making the determination, shall consider the application, the supporting affidavits, and the documentary evidence and, in addition to those materials, shall consider all the files and records pertaining to the proceedings against the applicant, including, but not limited to, the indictment, the court's journal entries, the journalized records of the clerk of the court, and the court reporter's transcript and all responses to the application filed under division (C) of this section by a prosecuting attorney or the attorney general, unless the application and the files and records show the applicant is not entitled to DNA testing, in which case the application may be denied. The court is not required to conduct an evidentiary hearing in conducting its review of, and in making its determination as to whether to accept or reject, the application. Upon making its determination, the court shall enter a judgment and order that either accepts or rejects the application and that includes within the judgment and order the reasons for the acceptance or rejection as applied to the criteria and procedures set forth in sections 2953.71 to 2953.81 of the Revised Code. The court shall send a copy of the judgment and order to the eligible inmate who filed it, the prosecuting attorney, and the attorney general.

(E) A judgment and order of a court entered under division (D) of this section is appealable only as provided in this division. If an eligible inmate submits an application for DNA testing under section 2953.73 of the Revised Code and the court of common pleas rejects the application under division (D) of this section, one of the following applies:

(1) If the inmate was sentenced to death for the offense for which the inmate claims to be an eligible inmate and is requesting DNA testing, the inmate may seek leave of the supreme court to appeal the rejection to the supreme court. Courts of appeals do not have jurisdiction to review any rejection if the inmate was sentenced to death for the offense for which the inmate claims to be an eligible inmate and is requesting DNA testing.

(2) If the inmate was not sentenced to death for the offense for which the inmate claims to be an eligible inmate and is requesting DNA testing, the rejection is a final appealable order, and the inmate may appeal it to the court of appeals of the district in which is located that court of common pleas.

(F) Notwithstanding any provision of law regarding fees and costs, no filing fee shall be required of, and no court costs shall be assessed against, an eligible offender who is indigent and who submits an application under this section.

(G) If a court rejects an eligible inmate's application for DNA testing under division (D) of this section, unless the rejection is overturned on appeal, no court shall require the state to administer a DNA test under sections 2953.71 to 2953.81 of the Revised Code on the eligible inmate.

(2004 H 525, eff. 5–18–05; 2003 S 11, eff. 10–29–03)

Note: See also preceding version of this section, in effect until 5–18–05.

2953.74 Prior tests

(A) If an eligible inmate submits an application for DNA testing under section 2953.73 of the Revised Code and a prior definitive DNA test has been conducted regarding the same biological evidence that the inmate seeks to have tested, the court shall reject the inmate's application. If an eligible inmate files an application for DNA testing and a prior inconclusive DNA test has been conducted regarding the same biological evidence that the inmate seeks to have tested, the court shall review the application and has the discretion, on a case-by-case basis, to either accept or reject the application. The court may direct a testing authority to provide the court with information that the court may use in determining whether prior DNA test results were definitive or inconclusive and whether to accept or reject an application in relation to which there were prior inconclusive DNA test results.

(B) If an eligible inmate submits an application for DNA testing under section 2953.73 of the Revised Code, the court may accept the application only if one of the following applies:

(1) The inmate did not have a DNA test taken at the trial stage in the case in which the inmate was convicted of the offense for which the inmate is an eligible inmate and is requesting the DNA testing regarding the same biological evidence that the inmate seeks to have tested, the inmate shows that DNA exclusion would have been outcome determinative at that trial stage in that case, and, at the time of the trial stage in that case, DNA testing was not generally accepted, the results of DNA testing were not generally admissible in evidence, or DNA testing was not yet available.

(2) The inmate had a DNA test taken at the trial stage in the case in which the inmate was convicted of the offense for which the inmate is an eligible inmate and is requesting the DNA testing regarding the same biological evidence that the inmate seeks to have tested, the test was not a prior definitive DNA test that is subject to division (A) of this section, and the inmate shows that DNA exclusion would have been outcome determinative at the trial stage in that case.

(C) If an eligible inmate submits an application for DNA testing under section 2953.73 of the Revised Code, the court may accept the application only if all of the following apply:

(1) The court determines pursuant to section 2953.75 of the Revised Code that biological material was collected from the crime scene or the victim of the offense for which the inmate is an eligible inmate and is requesting the DNA testing and that the parent sample of that biological material against which a sample from the inmate can be compared still exists at that point in time.

(2) The testing authority determines all of the following pursuant to section 2953.76 of the Revised Code regarding the parent sample of the biological material described in division (C)(1) of this section:

(a) The parent sample of the biological material so collected contains scientifically sufficient material to extract a test sample.

(b) The parent sample of the biological material so collected is not so minute or fragile as to risk destruction of the parent sample by the extraction described in division (D)(2)(a) of this section; provided that the court may determine in its discretion, on a case-by-case basis, that, even if the parent sample of the biological material so collected is so minute or fragile as to risk destruction of the parent sample by the extraction, the application should not be rejected solely on the basis of that risk.

(c) The parent sample of the biological material so collected has not degraded or been contaminated to the extent that it has become scientifically unsuitable for testing, and the parent sample otherwise has been preserved, and remains, in a condition that is scientifically suitable for testing.

(3) The court determines that, at the trial stage in the case in which the inmate was convicted of the offense for which the inmate is an eligible inmate and is requesting the DNA testing, the identity of the person who committed the offense was an issue.

(4) The court determines that one or more of the defense theories asserted by the inmate at the trial stage in the case described in division (C)(3) of this section or in a retrial of that case in a court of this state was of such a nature that, if DNA testing is conducted and an exclusion result is obtained, the exclusion result will be outcome determinative.

(5) The court determines that, if DNA testing is conducted and an exclusion result is obtained, the results of the testing will be outcome determinative regarding that inmate.

(6) The court determines pursuant to section 2953.76 of the Revised Code from the chain of custody of the parent sample of the biological material to be tested and of any test sample extracted from the parent sample, and from the totality of circumstances involved, that the parent sample and the extracted test sample are the same sample as collected and that there is no reason to believe that they have been out of state custody or have been tampered with or contaminated since they were collected.

(2003 S 11, eff. 10–29–03)

2953.75 Comparison samples

(A) If an eligible inmate submits an application for DNA testing under section 2953.73 of the Revised Code, the court shall require the prosecuting attorney to use reasonable diligence to determine whether biological material was collected from the crime scene or victim of the offense for which the inmate is an eligible inmate and is requesting the DNA testing against which a sample from the inmate can be compared and whether the parent sample of that biological material still exists at that point in time. In using reasonable diligence to make those determinations, the prosecuting attorney shall rely upon all relevant sources, including, but not limited to, all of the following:

(1) All prosecuting authorities in the case in which the inmate was convicted of the offense for which the inmate is an eligible inmate and is requesting the DNA testing and in the appeals of, and postconviction proceedings related to, that case;

(2) All law enforcement authorities involved in the investigation of the offense for which the inmate is an eligible offender and is requesting the DNA testing;

(3) All custodial agencies involved at any time with the biological material in question;

(4) The custodian of all custodial agencies described in division (A)(3) of this section;

(5) All crime laboratories involved at any time with the biological material in question;

(6) All other reasonable sources.

(B) The prosecuting attorney shall prepare a report that contains the prosecuting attorney's determinations made under division (A) of this section and shall file a copy of the report with the court and provide a copy to the eligible inmate and the attorney general.

(2003 S 11, eff. 10–29–03)

2953.76 Quality and quantity of samples

If an eligible inmate submits an application for DNA testing under section 2953.73 of the Revised Code, the court shall require the prosecuting attorney to consult with the testing authority and to prepare findings regarding the quantity and quality of the parent sample of the biological material collected from the crime scene or victim of the offense for which the inmate is an eligible inmate and is requesting the DNA testing and that is to be tested, and of the chain of custody and reliability regarding that parent sample, as follows:

(A) The testing authority shall determine whether there is a scientifically sufficient quantity of the parent sample to test and whether the parent sample is so minute or fragile that there is a substantial risk that the parent sample could be destroyed in testing. The testing authority may determine that there is not a sufficient quantity to test in order to preserve the state's ability to present in the future the original evidence presented at trial, if another trial is required. Upon making its determination under this division, the testing authority shall prepare a written document that contains its determination and the reasoning and rationale for that determination and shall provide a copy to the court, the eligible inmate, the prosecuting attorney, and the attorney general. The court may determine in its discretion, on a case-by-case basis, that, even if the parent sample of the biological material so collected is so minute or fragile as to risk destruction of the parent sample by the extraction, the application should not be rejected solely on the basis of that risk.

(B) The testing authority shall determine whether the parent sample has degraded or been contaminated to the extent that it has become scientifically unsuitable for testing and whether the parent sample otherwise has been preserved, and remains, in a condition that is suitable for testing. Upon making its determination under this division, the testing authority shall prepare a written document that contains its determination and the reasoning and rationale for that determination and shall provide a copy to the court, the eligible inmate, the prosecuting attorney, and the attorney general.

(C) The court shall determine, from the chain of custody of the parent sample of the biological material to be tested and of any test sample extracted from the parent sample and from the totality of circumstances involved, whether the parent sample and the extracted test sample are the same sample as collected and whether there is any reason to believe that they have been out of state custody or have been tampered with or contaminated since they were collected. Upon making its determination under this division, the court shall prepare and retain a written document that contains its determination and the reasoning and rationale for that determination.

(2003 S 11, eff. 10–29–03)

2953.77 Chain of custody

(A) If an eligible inmate submits an application for DNA testing under section 2953.73 of the Revised Code and if the application is accepted and DNA testing is to be performed, the court shall require that the chain of custody remain intact and that all of the applicable following precautions are satisfied to ensure that the parent sample of the biological material collected from the crime scene or the victim of the offense for which the inmate is an eligible inmate and requested the DNA testing, and the test sample of the parent sample that is extracted and actually is to be tested, are not contaminated during transport or the testing process:

(1) The court shall require that the chain of custody be maintained and documented relative to the parent sample and the test sample actually to be tested between the time they are removed from their place of storage or the time of their extraction to the time at which the DNA testing will be performed.

(2) The court, the testing authority, and the law enforcement and prosecutorial personnel involved in the process, or any combination of those entities and persons, shall coordinate the transport of the parent sample and the test sample actually to be tested between their place of storage and the place where the DNA testing will be performed, and the court and testing authority shall document the transport procedures so used.

(3) The testing authority shall determine and document the custodian of the parent sample and the test sample actually to be tested after they are in the possession of the testing authority.

(4) The testing authority shall maintain and preserve the parent sample and the test sample actually to be tested after they are in the possession of the testing authority and shall document the maintenance and preservation procedures used.

(5) After the DNA testing, the court, the testing authority, and the original custodial agency of the parent sample, or any combination of those entities, shall coordinate the return of the remaining parent sample back to its place of storage with the original custodial agency or to any other place determined in accordance with this division and section 2953.81 of the Revised Code. The court shall determine, in consultation with the testing authority, the custodial agency to maintain any newly created, extracted, or collected DNA material resulting from the testing. The court and testing authority shall document the return procedures for original materials and for any newly created, extracted, or collected DNA material resulting from the testing, and also the custodial agency to which those materials should be taken.

(B) A court or testing authority shall provide the documentation required under division (A) of this section in writing and shall maintain that documentation.

(2003 S 11, eff. 10–29–03)

2953.78 Laboratory selection

(A) If an eligible inmate submits an application for DNA testing under section 2953.73 of the Revised Code and if the application is accepted and DNA testing is to be performed, the court shall select the testing authority to be used for the testing. A court shall not select or use a testing authority for DNA testing unless the attorney general approves or designates the testing authority pursuant to division (C) of this section and unless the testing authority satisfies the criteria set forth in section 2953.80 of the Revised Code.

(B) If a court selects a testing authority pursuant to division (A) of this section and the eligible inmate for whom the test is to be performed objects to the use of the selected testing authority, the court shall rescind its prior acceptance of the application for DNA testing for the inmate and deny the application. An objection as described in this division, and the resulting rescission and denial, do not preclude a court from accepting in the court's discretion, a subsequent application by the same eligible inmate requesting DNA testing.

(C) The attorney general shall approve or designate testing authorities that may be selected and used to conduct DNA testing, shall prepare a list of the approved or designated testing authorities, and shall provide copies of the list to all courts of common pleas. The attorney general shall update the list as appropriate to reflect changes in the approved or designated testing authorities and shall provide copies of the updated list to all courts of common pleas. The attorney general shall not approve or designate a testing authority under this division unless the testing authority satisfies the criteria set forth in section 2953.80 of the Revised Code.

(D) The attorney general's approval or designation of testing authorities under division (C) of this section, and the selection and use of any approved or designated testing authority, do not afford an inmate any right to subsequently challenge the approval, designation, selection, or use, and an inmate may not appeal to any court the approval, designation, selection, or use of a testing authority.

(2003 S 11, eff. 10–29–03)

2953.79 Inmate samples

(A) If an eligible inmate submits an application for DNA testing under section 2953.73 of the Revised Code and if the application is accepted and DNA testing is to be performed, a sample of biological material shall be obtained from the inmate in accordance with this section, to be compared with the parent sample of biological material collected from the crime scene or the victim of the offense for which the inmate is an eligible inmate and requested the DNA testing. The inmate's filing of the application constitutes the inmate's consent to the obtaining of the sample of biological material from the inmate. The testing authority shall obtain the sample of biological material from the inmate in accordance with medically accepted procedures.

(B) If DNA testing is to be performed for an inmate as described in division (A) of this section, the court shall require the state to coordinate with the department of rehabilitation and correction as to the time and place at which the sample of biological material will be obtained from the inmate. The sample of biological material shall be obtained from the inmate at the facility in which the inmate is housed, and the department shall make the inmate available at the specified time. The court shall require the state to provide notice to the inmate and to the inmate's counsel of the date on which, and the time and place at which, the sample will be so obtained.

The court also shall require the state to coordinate with the testing authority regarding the obtaining of the sample from the inmate.

(C)(1) If DNA testing is to be performed for an inmate as described in division (A) of this section, and the inmate refuses to submit to the collection of the sample of biological material from the inmate or hinders the state from obtaining a sample of biological material from the inmate, the court shall rescind its prior acceptance of the application for DNA testing for the inmate and deny the application.

(2) For purposes of division (C)(1) of this section:

(a) An inmate's "refusal to submit to the collection of a sample of biological material from the inmate" includes, but is not limited to, the inmate's rejection of the physical manner in which a sample of the inmate's biological material is to be taken.

(b) An inmate's "hindrance of the state in obtaining a sample of biological material from the inmate" includes, but is not limited to, the inmate being physically or verbally uncooperative or antagonistic in the taking of a sample of the inmate's biological material.

(D) The extracting personnel shall make the determination as to whether an eligible inmate for whom DNA testing is to be performed is refusing to submit to the collection of a sample of biological material from the inmate or is hindering the state from obtaining a sample of biological material from the inmate at the time and date of the scheduled collection of the sample. If the extracting personnel determine that an inmate is refusing to submit to the collection of a sample or is hindering the state from obtaining a sample, the extracting personnel shall document in writing the conditions that constitute the refusal or hindrance, maintain the documentation, and notify the court of the inmate's refusal or hindrance.

(2003 S 11, eff. 10–29–03)

2953.80 Qualification of laboratory

(A) The attorney general shall not approve or designate a testing authority for conducting DNA testing under section 2953.78 of the Revised Code, and a court shall not select or use a testing authority for DNA testing under that section, unless the testing authority satisfies all of the following criteria:

(1) It is in compliance with nationally accepted quality assurance standards for forensic DNA testing, as published in the quality assurance standards for forensic DNA testing laboratories issued by the director of the federal bureau of investigation.

(2) It undergoes an annual internal or external audit for quality assurance in conformity with the standards identified in division (A)(1) of this section.

(3) At least once in the preceding two-year period, and at least once each two-year period thereafter, it undergoes an external audit for quality assurance in conformity with the standards identified in division (A)(1) of this section.

(B) As used in division (A) of this section:

(1) "External audit" means a quality assurance review of a testing authority that is conducted by a forensic DNA testing agency outside of, and not affiliated with, the testing authority.

(2) "Internal audit" means an internal review of a testing authority that is conducted by the testing authority itself.

(2003 S 11, eff. 10–29–03)

2953.81 Results; preservation of samples

If an eligible inmate submits an application for DNA testing under section 2953.73 of the Revised Code and if DNA testing is performed based on that application, upon completion of the testing, all of the following apply:

(A) The court or a designee of the court shall require the state to maintain the results of the testing and to maintain and preserve both the parent sample of the biological material used and the inmate sample of the biological material used. The testing authority may be designated as the person to maintain the results of the testing or to maintain and preserve some or all of the samples, or both. The results of the testing remain state's evidence. The samples shall be preserved during the entire period of time for which the inmate is imprisoned relative to the prison term or sentence of death in question and, if that prison term expires or the inmate is executed under that sentence of death, for a reasonable period of time of not less than twenty-four months after the term expires or the inmate is executed. The court shall determine the period of time that is reasonable for purposes of this division, provided that the period shall not be less than twenty-four months after the term expires or the inmate is executed.

(B) The results of the testing are a public record.

(C) The court or the testing authority shall provide a copy of the results of the testing to the prosecuting attorney, the attorney general, and the subject inmate.

(D) If the postconviction proceeding in question is pending at that time in a court of this state, the court of common pleas that decided the DNA application or the testing authority shall provide a copy of the results of the testing to any court of this state, and, if it is pending in a federal court, the court of common pleas that decided the DNA application or the testing authority shall provide a copy of the results of the testing to that federal court.

(E) The testing authority shall provide a copy of the results of the testing to the court of common pleas that decided the DNA application.

(F) The inmate or the state may enter the results of the testing into any proceeding.

(2003 S 11, eff. 10–29–03)

2953.82 Testing for inmates who pleaded guilty or no contest

Note: See also following version of this section, eff. 5–18–05.

(A) An inmate who pleaded guilty or no contest to a felony offense that was committed prior to the effective date of this section may request DNA testing under this section regarding that offense if all of the following apply:

(1) The inmate was sentenced to a prison term or sentence of death for that felony and, on the effective date of this section, is in prison serving that prison term or under that sentence of death.

(2) On the date on which the inmate files the application requesting the testing with the court as described in division (B) of this section, the inmate has at least one year remaining on the prison term described in division (A)(1) of this section, or the inmate is in prison under a sentence of death as described in that division.

(B) An inmate who pleaded guilty or no contest to a felony offense that was committed prior to the effective date of this section, who satisfies the criteria set forth in division (A) of this section, and who wishes to request DNA testing under this section shall submit, in accordance with this division, an application for the testing to the court of common pleas and the prosecuting attorney. The inmate shall specify on the application the offense or offenses for which the inmate is requesting the DNA testing under this section. Along with the application, the inmate shall submit an acknowledgment that is signed by the inmate. The application and acknowledgment required under this division shall be the same application and acknowledgment as are used by eligible inmates who request DNA testing under sections 2953.71 to 2953.81 of the Revised Code.

The inmate shall file the application with the court of common pleas not later than one year after the effective date of this section. Upon filing the application, the inmate shall serve a copy on the prosecuting attorney.

(C) Within forty-five days after the filing of an application for DNA testing under division (B) of this section, the prosecuting attorney shall file a statement with the court that indicates whether the prosecuting attorney agrees or disagrees that the inmate should be permitted to obtain DNA testing under this section. If the prosecuting attorney agrees that the inmate should be permitted to obtain DNA testing under this section, all of the following apply:

(1) The application and the written statement shall be considered for all purposes as if they were an application for DNA testing filed under section 2953.73 of the Revised Code that the court accepted, and the court, the prosecuting attorney, the attorney general, the inmate, law enforcement personnel, and all other involved persons shall proceed regarding DNA testing for the inmate pursuant to sections 2953.77 to 2953.81 of the Revised Code, in the same manner as if the inmate was an eligible inmate for whom an application for DNA testing had been accepted.

(2) Upon completion of the DNA testing, section 2953.81 of the Revised Code applies.

(D) If the prosecuting attorney disagrees that the inmate should be permitted to obtain DNA testing under this section, the prosecuting attorney's disagreement is final and is not appealable by any person to any court, and no court shall have authority, without agreement of the prosecuting attorney, to order DNA testing regarding that inmate and the offense or offenses for which the inmate requested DNA testing in the application.

(E) If the prosecuting attorney fails to file a statement of agreement or disagreement within the time provided in division (C) of this section, the court may order the prosecuting attorney to file a statement of that nature within fifteen days of the date of the order.

(2003 S 11, eff. 10–29–03)

Note: See also following version of this section, eff. 5–18–05.

2953.82 Testing for inmates who pleaded guilty or no contest (later effective date)

Note: See also preceding version of this section, in effect until 5–18–05.

(A) An inmate who pleaded guilty or no contest to a felony offense that was committed prior to October 29, 2003 may request DNA testing under this section regarding that offense if all of the following apply:

(1) The inmate was sentenced to a prison term or sentence of death for that felony and, on October 29, 2003, is in prison serving that prison term or under that sentence of death.

(2) On the date on which the inmate files the application requesting the testing with the court as described in division (B) of this section, the inmate has at least one year remaining on the prison term described in division (A)(1) of this section, or the inmate is in prison under a sentence of death as described in that division.

(B) An inmate who pleaded guilty or no contest to a felony offense that was committed prior to October 29, 2003, who satisfies the criteria set forth in division (A) of this section, and who wishes to request DNA testing under this section shall submit, in accordance with this division, an application for the testing to the court of common pleas and the prosecuting attorney. The inmate shall specify on the application the offense or offenses for which the inmate is requesting the DNA testing under this section. Along with the application, the inmate shall submit an acknowledgment that is signed by the inmate. The application and acknowledgment required under this division shall be the same application and acknowledgment as are used by eligible inmates who request DNA testing under sections 2953.71 to 2953.81 of the Revised Code.

The inmate shall file the application with the court of common pleas not later than two years after October 29, 2003. Upon filing the application, the inmate shall serve a copy on the prosecuting attorney.

(C) Within forty-five days after the filing of an application for DNA testing under division (B) of this section, the prosecuting attorney shall file a statement with the court that indicates whether the prosecuting attorney agrees or disagrees that the inmate should be permitted to obtain DNA testing under this section. If the prosecuting attorney agrees that the inmate should be permitted to obtain DNA testing under this section, all of the following apply:

(1) The application and the written statement shall be considered for all purposes as if they were an application for DNA testing filed under section 2953.73 of the Revised Code that the court accepted, and the court, the prosecuting attorney, the attorney general, the inmate, law enforcement personnel, and all other involved persons shall proceed regarding DNA testing for the inmate pursuant to sections 2953.77 to 2953.81 of the Revised Code, in the same manner as if the inmate was an eligible inmate for whom an application for DNA testing had been accepted.

(2) Upon completion of the DNA testing, section 2953.81 of the Revised Code applies.

(D) If the prosecuting attorney disagrees that the inmate should be permitted to obtain DNA testing under this section, the prosecuting attorney's disagreement is final and is not appealable by any person to any court, and no court shall have authority, without agreement of the prosecuting attorney, to order DNA testing regarding that inmate and the offense or offenses for which the inmate requested DNA testing in the application.

(E) If the prosecuting attorney fails to file a statement of agreement or disagreement within the time provided in division (C) of this section, the court may order the prosecuting attorney to file a statement of that nature within fifteen days of the date of the order.

(2004 H 525, eff. 5–18–05; 2003 S 11, eff. 10–29–03)

Note: See also preceding version of this section, in effect until 5–18–05.

2953.83 Procedure

In any court proceeding under sections 2953.71 to 2953.82 of the Revised Code, the Rules of Criminal Procedure apply, except to the extent that sections 2953.71 to 2953.82 of the Revised Code provide a different procedure or to the extent that the Rules would by their nature be clearly inapplicable.

(2003 S 11, eff. 10–29–03)

CHAPTER 2961

DISFRANCHISED CONVICTS; HABITUAL CRIMINALS

Section

2961.01 Civil rights of convicted felons

(A) A person convicted of a felony under the laws of this or any other state or the United States, unless the conviction is reversed or annulled, is incompetent to be an elector or juror or to hold an office of honor, trust, or profit. When any person convicted of a felony under any law of that type is granted parole, judicial release, or a conditional pardon or is released under a non-jail community control sanction or a post-release control sanction, the person is competent to be an elector during the period of community control, parole, post-release control, or release or until the conditions of the pardon have been performed or have transpired and is competent to be an elector thereafter following final discharge. The full pardon of a convict restores the rights and privileges so forfeited under this section, but a pardon shall not release a convict from the costs of the convict's conviction in this state, unless so specified.

(B) As used in this section:

(1) "Community control sanction" has the same meaning as in section 2929.01 of the Revised Code.

(2) "Non-jail community control sanction" means a community control sanction that is neither a term in a community-based correctional facility nor a term in a jail.

(3) "Post-release control" and "post-release control sanction" have the same meanings as in section 2967.01 of the Revised Code.

(2002 H 490, eff. 1-1-04; 1997 S 111, eff. 3-17-98; 1972 H 511, eff. 1-1-74; 1953 H 1; GC 13458-1)

2961.02 Conviction of disqualifying offense

(A) As used in this section:

(1) "Disqualifying offense" means an offense that has both of the following characteristics:

(a) It is one of the following:

(i) A theft offense that is a felony;

(ii) A felony under the laws of this state, another state, or the United States, that is not covered by division (A)(1)(a)(i) of this section and that involves fraud, deceit, or theft.

(b) It is an offense for which the laws of this state, another state, or the United States do not otherwise contain a provision specifying permanent disqualification, or disqualification for a specified period, from holding a public office or position of public employment, or from serving as an unpaid volunteer, as a result of conviction of the offense, including, but not limited to, a provision such as that in division (C)(1) of section 2921.41 of the Revised Code.

(2) "Political subdivision" has the same meaning as in section 2744.01 of the Revised Code.

(3) "Private entity" includes an individual, corporation, limited liability company, business trust, estate, trust, partnership, or association that receives any funds from a state agency or political subdivision to perform an activity on behalf of the state agency or political subdivision.

(4) "State agency" has the same meaning as in section 1.60 of the Revised Code.

(5) "Theft offense" has the same meaning as in section 2913.01 of the Revised Code.

(6) "Volunteer" means a person who serves as a volunteer without compensation with a state agency or political subdivision or who serves as a volunteer without compensation with a private entity, including, but not limited to, an uncompensated auxiliary police officer, auxiliary deputy sheriff, or volunteer firefighter.

(B) Any person who is convicted of a disqualifying offense is incompetent to hold a public office or position of public employment or to serve as a volunteer, if holding the public office or position of public employment or serving as the volunteer involves substantial management or control over the property of a state agency, political subdivision, or private entity.

(C) Division (B) of this section does not apply if a conviction of a disqualifying offense is reversed, expunged, or annulled. The full pardon of a person convicted of a disqualifying offense restores the privileges forfeited under division (B) of this section, but the pardon does not release the person from the costs of the person's conviction in this state, unless so specified.

(2004 H 181, eff. 5-18-05)

2961.03 Revocation of license in certain cases

Whenever a person engaged in business as a secondhand dealer, junk dealer, transient dealer, peddler, itinerant vendor, or pawnbroker, under a license issued under any law of this state or under any ordinance of a municipal corporation, is convicted and sentenced for knowingly and fraudulently buying, receiving, or concealing goods or property which has been stolen, taken by robbers, embezzled, or obtained by false pretenses, such judgment of conviction, in addition to the other penalties provided by law for such offense, acts as a cancellation and revocation of such license to conduct such business, and the court in which such conviction was had shall forthwith certify to the authority which issued such license, the fact of such conviction. A person who has been so convicted and whose license has been canceled or revoked, shall not again be licensed to engage in such business, or any of the businesses enumerated in this section, unless such person is pardoned by the governor.

(1953 H 1, eff. 10-1-53; GC 13458-3)

CHAPTER 2963

EXTRADITION

DEFINITIONS

2963.01 Definitions

As used in sections 2963.01 to 2963.27 of the Revised Code:

(A) "Governor" includes any person performing the functions of governor by authority of the law of this state.

(B) "Executive authority" includes the governor, and any person performing the functions of governor in a state other than this state.

(C) "State," referring to a state other than this state, includes any state or territory, organized or unorganized, of the United States.

(D) "Community control sanction" has the same meaning as in section 2929.01 of the Revised Code.

(E) "Post-release control" and "post-release control sanction" have the same meanings as in section 2967.01 of the Revised Code.

(2002 H 490, eff. 1–1–04; 1953 H 1, eff. 10–1–53; GC 109–1)

FUGITIVES FROM OTHER STATES

2963.02 Governor to deliver fugitives from justice

Subject to sections 2963.01 to 2963.27, inclusive, of the Revised Code, the constitution of the United States and all acts of congress enacted in pursuance thereof, the governor shall have arrested and delivered to the executive authority of any other state of the United States, any person charged in that state with treason, felony, or other crime, who has fled from justice and is found in this state.

(1953 H 1, eff. 10–1–53; GC 109–2)

2963.03 Demand for extradition

No demand for the extradition of a person charged with crime in another state shall be recognized by the governor unless the demand is in writing alleging, except in cases arising under section 2963.06 of the Revised Code, that the accused was present in the demanding state at the time of the commission of the alleged crime, and that thereafter he fled from the state, and unless the demand is accompanied by:

(A) A copy of an indictment found or by information supported by affidavit in the state having jurisdiction of the crime, or by a copy of an affidavit made before a magistrate there, together with a copy of any warrant which was issued thereupon;

(B) A copy of a judgment of conviction or of a sentence imposed in execution thereof, together with a statement by the executive authority of the demanding state that the person claimed has escaped from confinement or has broken the terms of his bail, probation, or parole. The indictment, information, or affidavit made before the magistrate must substantially charge the person demanded with having committed a crime under the law of that state. The copy of indictment, information, affidavit, judgment of conviction, or sentence must be authenticated by the executive authority making the demand.

(1953 H 1, eff. 10–1–53; GC 109–3)

2963.04 Demand investigated by order of governor

When a demand is made upon the governor of this state by the executive authority of another state for the surrender of a person charged with crime, the governor may call upon the attorney general or any prosecuting officer in this state to investigate or assist in investigating the demand, and to report to him the situation and circumstances of the person so demanded, and whether such person ought to be surrendered.

(1953 H 1, eff. 10–1–53; GC 109–4)

2963.05 Extradition upon agreement to return prisoner

When it is desired to have returned to this state a person charged in this state with a crime, and such person is imprisoned or is held under criminal proceedings then pending against him in another state, the governor may agree with the executive authority of such other state for the extradition of such person before the conclusion of such proceedings or his term of sentence in such other state, upon condition that such person be returned to such other state at the expense of this state as soon as the prosecution in this state is terminated.

The governor may also surrender, on demand of the executive authority of any other state, any person in this state who is charged under section 2963.21 of the Revised Code with having violated the laws of the state whose executive authority is making the demand, even though such person left the demanding state involuntarily. This section shall be carried out by conforming to the procedure outlined in sections 2963.01 to 2963.27, inclusive, of the Revised Code.

(1953 H 1, eff. 10–1–53; GC 109–5)

2963.06 Governor may surrender anyone charged with crime against another state

The governor may surrender, on demand of the executive authority of any other state, any person in this state charged in such other state in the manner provided in section 2963.03 of the Revised Code with committing an act in this state, or in a third state, intentionally resulting in a crime in the state whose executive authority is making the demand, and sections 2963.01 to 2963.27, inclusive, of the Revised Code, apply to such cases, even though the accused was not in that state at the time of the commission of the crime, and has not fled therefrom.

(1953 H 1, eff. 10–1–53; GC 109–6)

2963.07 Warrant for arrest

If the governor decides that a demand for extradition should be complied with, he shall sign a warrant of arrest, which shall be sealed with the state seal and be directed to any peace officer or other person whom the governor finds fit to entrust with the execution thereof. The warrant must substantially recite the facts necessary to the validity of its issuance.

Such warrant shall authorize the peace officer or other person to whom directed to arrest the accused at any time and any place where he may be found within the state and to command the aid of all peace officers or other persons in the execution of the warrant, and to deliver the accused, subject to sections 2963.01 to 2963.27, inclusive, of the Revised Code, to the authorized agent of the demanding state.

(1953 H 1, eff. 10–1–53; GC 109–7, 109–8)

2963.08 Authority to arrest accused

Every peace officer or other person empowered to make an arrest under section 2963.07 of the Revised Code has the same authority, in arresting the accused, to command assistance therein as peace officers have in the execution of any criminal process directed to them, with like penalties against those who refuse their assistance.

(1953 H 1, eff. 10–1–53; GC 109–9)

2963.09 Mandatory hearing

No person arrested upon a warrant under section 2963.07 of the Revised Code shall be delivered to the agent whom the executive authority demanding him appointed to receive him unless such person is first taken forthwith before a judge of a court of record in this state, who shall inform him of the demand made for his surrender and of the crime with which he is charged, and that he has the right to demand and procure legal counsel. If the prisoner or his counsel desires to test the legality of his arrest, the judge shall fix a reasonable time to be allowed him within which to apply for a writ of habeas corpus. When such writ is applied for, notice thereof and of the time and place of hearing thereon, shall be given to the prosecuting officer of the county in which the arrest is made and in which the accused is in custody, and to the said agent of the demanding state.

Whoever violates this section by willfully delivering a person arrested upon the governor's warrant to an agent for extradition of the demanding state before a hearing, shall be fined not more than one thousand dollars or imprisoned not more than six months, or both.

(1953 H 1, eff. 10–1–53; GC 109–10)

2963.10 Prisoner may be confined while enroute

A peace officer or other person executing a warrant of arrest issued by the governor, or an agent of the demanding state to whom the prisoner has been delivered, may, when necessary, confine the prisoner in the jail of any county or city through which he may pass.

The officer or agent of a demanding state to whom a prisoner has been delivered following extradition proceedings in another state, or to whom a prisoner has been delivered after waiving extradition in such other state, and who is passing through this state with such a prisoner for the purpose of immediately returning such prisoner to the demanding state may, when necessary, confine the prisoner in the jail of any county or city through which he may pass. Such officer or agent shall produce and show to the keeper of such jail his warrant and other written evidence of the fact that he is actually transporting such prisoner to the demanding state after a requisition by the executive authority of such demanding state. Such prisoner may not demand a new requisition while in this state.

The keeper of such jail must receive and safely keep a prisoner delivered to him under this section, until the officer or agent having charge of him is ready to proceed on his route. Such officer or agent is chargeable with the expense of such keeping.

(1953 H 1, eff. 10–1–53; GC 109–12)

2963.11 Fugitive from justice

When, on the oath of a credible person before any judge or magistrate of this state, any person within this state is charged with the commission of any crime in any other state and with having fled from justice, or with having been convicted of a crime in that state and having escaped from confinement, or having broken the terms of the person's bail or parole or violated the conditions of a community control sanction or post-release control sanction, or whenever complaint has been made before any judge or magistrate in this state setting forth on the affidavit of any credible person in another state that a crime has been committed in the other state and that the accused has been charged in that state with the commission of the crime, and has fled from justice, or with having been convicted of a crime in that state and having escaped from confinement, or having broken the terms of bail, probation, or parole, and is believed to be in this state, the judge or magistrate shall issue a warrant directed to any peace officer, commanding the peace officer to apprehend the person named in the warrant, wherever the person may be found in this state, and to bring the person before the same or any other judge, magistrate, or court that may be available in or convenient of access to the place where the arrest may be made, to answer the charge or complaint and affidavit, and a certified copy of the sworn charge or complaint and upon which the warrant is issued shall be attached to the warrant.

This section does not apply to cases arising under section 2963.06 of the Revised Code.

(2002 H 490, eff. 1–1–04; 1995 S 2, eff. 7–1–96; 1953 H 1, eff. 10–1–53; GC 109–13)

2963.12 Arrest without warrant

An arrest may be made by any peace officer or a private person without a warrant upon reasonable information that the accused stands charged in the courts of any state with a crime punishable by death or imprisonment for a term exceeding one year. When so arrested the accused must be taken before a judge or magistrate with all practicable speed and complaint must be made against him under oath setting forth the ground for the arrest, as provided in section 2963.11 of the Revised Code. Thereafter his answer shall be heard as if he had been arrested on a warrant.

(1953 H 1, eff. 10–1–53; GC 109–14)

2963.13 Fugitive to be confined pending requisition

If from the examination before the judge or magistrate it appears that the person held under section 2963.11 or 2963.12 of the Revised Code is the person charged with having committed the crime alleged and that he has fled from justice, the judge or magistrate must, by a warrant reciting the accusation, commit him to the county jail for such a time, not to exceed thirty days and specified in the warrant, as will enable the arrest of the accused to be made under a warrant of the governor on a requisition of the executive authority of the state having jurisdiction of the offense, unless the accused furnishes bail or until he is legally discharged.

(1953 H 1, eff. 10–1–53; GC 109–15)

2963.14 Bail

Unless the offense with which the prisoner is charged under sections 2963.11 and 2963.12 of the Revised Code is shown to be an offense punishable by death or life imprisonment under the laws of the state in which it was committed, a judge or magistrate in this state may admit the person arrested to bail by bond, with sufficient sureties and in such sum as he deems proper, conditioned for his appearance before said judge or magistrate at a time specified in such bond, and for his surrender, to be arrested upon the warrant of the governor of this state.

(1953 H 1, eff. 10–1–53; GC 109–16)

2963.15 Release of accused

If the accused mentioned in section 2963.14 of the Revised Code is not arrested under warrant of the governor by the expiration of the time specified in the warrant or bond, a judge or magistrate may discharge him or may recommit him for a further period not to exceed sixty days, or a judge or magistrate may again take bail for his appearance and surrender, under said section, but within a period not to exceed sixty days after the date of such new bond.

(1953 H 1, eff. 10–1–53; GC 109–17)

2963.16 Forfeited recognizance

If a prisoner admitted to bail under section 2963.14 of the Revised Code fails to appear and surrender himself according to the conditions of his bond, the judge or magistrate, by proper order, shall declare the bond forfeited and order his immediate arrest without warrant if he is within this state. Recovery may be had on such bond in the name of the state as in the case of other bonds given by the accused in criminal proceedings.

(1953 H 1, eff. 10–1–53; GC 109–18)

2963.17 Governor may hold fugitive indicted in this state or surrender him

If a criminal prosecution has been instituted under the laws of this state against a person sought by another state under sections 2963.01 to 2963.27, inclusive, of the Revised Code, and is still pending, the governor may surrender him on demand of the executive authority of another state or hold him until he has been tried and discharged or convicted and punished in this state.

(1953 H 1, eff. 10–1–53; GC 109–19)

2963.18 Guilt not to be inquired into by governor or in extradition proceedings

The guilt or innocence of an accused as to the crime of which he is charged may not be inquired into by the governor or in any proceeding after a demand for extradition accompanied by a charge of crime under section 2963.03 of the Revised Code has been presented to the governor, except as it may be involved in identifying the person held as the person charged with the crime.

(1953 H 1, eff. 10–1–53; GC 109–20)

2963.19 Governor may recall warrant for arrest

The governor may recall his warrant of arrest issued under section 2963.07 of the Revised Code or may issue another warrant whenever he thinks is proper.

(1953 H 1, eff. 10–1–53; GC 109–21)

FUGITIVES FROM THIS STATE

2963.20 Governor to demand fugitive from this state

Whenever the governor demands a person charged with crime, with escaping from confinement, or with breaking the terms of the person's bail or parole in this state or violating the conditions of a community control sanction or post-release control sanction imposed in this state, from the executive authority of any other state, or from the chief justice or an associate justice of the supreme court of the District of Columbia authorized to receive that demand under the laws of the United States, the governor shall issue a warrant under the seal of this state, to an agent, commanding the agent to receive the person so charged and convey that person to the proper officer of the county in which the offense was committed.

(2002 H 490, eff. 1–1–04; 1953 H 1, eff. 10–1–53; GC 109–22)

2963.21 Application for requisition for return of fugitive

When the return to this state of a person charged with crime in this state is required, the prosecuting attorney shall present to the governor a written application for a requisition for the return of the person charged. The application shall state the name of the person charged, the crime charged against the person, the approximate time, place, and circumstances of its commission, the state in which the person charged is believed to be located, and the location of the person in that state at the time the application is made. The prosecuting attorney shall certify that in the prosecuting attorney's opinion the ends of justice require the arrest and return of the person charged to this state for trial and that the proceeding is not instituted to enforce a private claim.

When the return to this state is required of a person who has been convicted of a crime in this state and has escaped from confinement or broken the terms of the person's bail, parole, community control sanction, or post-release control sanction, the prosecuting attorney of the county in which the offense was committed, the adult parole authority, or the warden of the institution or sheriff of the county from which escape was made shall present to the governor a written application for a requisition for the return of the person. The application shall state the person's name, the crime of which the person was convicted, the circumstances of the person's escape from confinement or of the breach of the terms of the person's bail, parole, community control sanction, or post-release control sanction, the state in which the person is believed to be located, and the location of the person in that state at the time the application is made.

An application presented under this section shall be verified by affidavit, executed in duplicate, and accompanied by two certified copies of the indictment returned, of the information and affidavit filed, of the complaint made to the judge or magistrate, stating the offense with which the accused is charged, of the judgment of conviction, or of the sentence. The prosecuting attorney, adult parole authority, warden, or sheriff also may attach any other affidavits or documents in duplicate that the prosecuting attorney, adult parole authority, warden, or sheriff finds proper to be submitted with the application. One copy of the application, with the action of the governor indicated by indorsement on the application, and one of the certified copies of the indictment, complaint, information, and affidavits, of the judgment of conviction, or of the sentence shall be filed in the office of the secretary of state to remain of record in that office. The other copies of all papers shall be forwarded with the governor's requisition.

(2002 H 490, eff. 1–1–04; 1996 S 269, eff. 7–1–96; 1953 H 1, eff. 10–1–53; GC 109–23)

2963.22 Reimbursement of fees

The director of budget and management shall provide for reimbursement of the fees to the officers of the state on whose governor the requisition is made under section 2963.21 of the Revised Code, and all necessary travel in returning the prisoner at the rates governing travel that have been adopted pursuant to section 126.31 of the Revised Code, on the certificate of the governor of such state.

(1990 S 336, eff. 4–10–90; 1985 H 201; 1953 H 1; GC 109–24)

2963.23 Accused immune from civil suits until conviction or return home

A person brought into this state by, or after waiver of, extradition based on a criminal charge is not subject to service of personal process in any civil action in this state until he has been convicted in the criminal proceeding, or, if acquitted, until he has had reasonable opportunity to return to the state from which he was extradited.

(1953 H 1, eff. 10–1–53; GC 109–25)

2963.24 Extradition hearing waived

Any person arrested in this state charged with having committed any crime in another state or alleged to have escaped from confinement, or broken the terms of his bail, probation, or parole may waive the issuance and service of the warrant provided for in section 2963.07 of the Revised Code and all other procedure incidental to extradition proceedings, by executing or subscribing in the presence of a judge of any court of record within this state, a writing which states that he consents to return to the demanding state. Before such waiver is executed or subscribed by such person the judge in open court shall inform such person of his rights to the issuance and service of a warrant of extradition and to obtain a writ of habeas corpus as provided for in section 2963.09 of the Revised Code.

When such consent has been executed it shall forthwith be forwarded to the office of the governor and filed therein. The judge shall direct the officer having such person in custody to deliver forthwith such person to the accredited agent of the demanding state, and shall deliver to such agent a copy of such consent. This section does not limit the rights of the accused person to return voluntarily and without formality to the demanding state before any such demand has been made, nor is this waiver procedure an exclusive procedure or a limitation on the powers, rights, or duties of the officers of the demanding state or of this state.

(1953 H 1, eff. 10–1–53; GC 109–26)

2963.25 Right to punish or regain custody by this state not waived

Sections 2963.01 to 2963.27, inclusive, of the Revised Code do not constitute a waiver by this state of its right, power, or privilege to try such demanded person for crime committed within this state, or of its right, power, or privilege to regain custody of such person by extradition proceedings or otherwise for the purpose of trial, sentence, or punishment for any crime committed within this state, nor are any proceedings had under such sections, which result in, or fail to result in, extradition, a waiver by this state of any of its rights, privileges, or jurisdiction.

(1953 H 1, eff. 10–1–53; GC 109–27)

2963.26 Extradited fugitive may be tried for other crimes committed in this state

A person returned to this state by, or after waiver of, extradition proceedings, may be tried in this state for other crimes which he may be charged with having committed here, as well as that specified in the requisition for his extradition.

(1953 H 1, eff. 10–1–53; GC 109–28)

2963.27 Uniform interpretation

Sections 2963.01 to 2963.26, inclusive, of the Revised Code shall be so interpreted and construed as to make the law of this state uniform with the law of those states which enact similar legislation.

(1953 H 1, eff. 10–1–53; GC 109–29)

2963.28 Request by governor for extradition of criminal

If it appears to the governor by sworn evidence in writing that a person has committed a crime within this state for which such person may be delivered to the United States or its authorities by a foreign government or its authorities, because of laws of the United States, or of a treaty between the United States and a foreign government, and that such person is a fugitive from justice of this state, and may be found within the territory of such foreign government, the governor, under the great seal of Ohio, shall request the president of the United States, or the secretary of state of the United States, to take any steps necessary for the extradition of such person and his delivery to any agent of this state appointed by the governor, or to the proper officer of the county within which he is charged with the commission of such crime.

(1953 H 1, eff. 10–1–53; GC 116)

2963.29 Governor must be satisfied by evidence of good faith

The governor shall not request the extradition of a person under section 2963.28 of the Revised Code unless he is satisfied by sworn evidence that extradition is sought in good faith for the punishment of the crime named and not for the purpose of collecting a debt or pecuniary mulct or of bringing the alleged fugitive within this state to serve him with civil process, or with criminal process other than for the crime for which his extradition is sought.

(1953 H 1, eff. 10–1–53; GC 117)

INTERSTATE AGREEMENT ON DETAINERS

2963.30 Interstate agreement on detainers

The Interstate Agreement on Detainers is hereby enacted into law and entered into by this state with all other jurisdictions legally joining therein, in the form substantially as follows:

THE INTERSTATE AGREEMENT ON DETAINERS

The contracting states solemnly agree that:

Article I

The party states find that charges outstanding against a prisoner, detainers based on untried indictments, informations or complaints, and difficulties in securing speedy trials of persons already incarcerated in other jurisdictions, produce uncertainties which obstruct programs of prisoner treatment and rehabilitation. Accordingly, it is the policy of the party states and the purpose of this agreement to encourage the expeditious and orderly disposition of such charges and determination of the proper status of any and all detainers based on untried indictments, informations or complaints. The party states also find that proceedings with reference to such charges and detainers, when emanating from another jurisdiction, cannot properly be had in the absence of cooperative procedures. It is the further purpose of this agreement to provide such cooperative procedures.

Article II

As used in this agreement:

(a) "State" shall mean a state of the United States: the United States of America: a territory or possession of the United States: the District of Columbia: the Commonwealth of Puerto Rico.

(b) "Sending state" shall mean a state in which a prisoner is incarcerated at the time that he initiates a request for final disposition pursuant to Article III hereof or at the time that a request for custody or availability is initiated pursuant to Article IV hereof.

(c) "Receiving state" shall mean the state in which trial is to be had on an indictment, information or complaint pursuant to Article III or Article IV hereof.

Article III

(a) Whenever a person has entered upon a term of imprisonment in a penal or correctional institution of a party state, and whenever during the continuance of the term of imprisonment there is pending in any other party state any untried indictment, information or complaint on the basis of which a detainer has been lodged against the prisoner, he shall be brought to trial within one hundred eighty days after he shall have caused to be delivered to the prosecuting officer and the appropriate court of the prosecuting officer's jurisdiction written notice of the place of his imprisonment and his request for a final disposition to be made of the indictment, information or complaint: provided that for good cause shown in open court, the prisoner or his counsel being present, the court having jurisdiction of the matter may grant any necessary or reasonable continuance. The request of the prisoner shall be accompanied by a certificate of the appropriate official having custody of the prisoner, stating the term of commitment under which the prisoner is being held, the time already served, the time remaining to be served on the sentence, the amount of good time earned, the time of parole eligibility of the prisoner, and any decisions of the state parole agency relating to the prisoner.

(b) The written notice and request for final disposition referred to in paragraph (a) hereof shall be given or sent by the prisoner to the warden, commissioner of corrections or other official having custody of him, who shall promptly forward it together with the certificate to the appropriate prosecuting official and court by registered or certified mail, return receipt requested.

(c) The warden, commissioner of corrections or other official having custody of the prisoner shall promptly inform him of the source and contents of any detainer lodged against him and shall also inform him of his right to make a request for final disposition of the indictment, information or complaint on which the detainer is based.

(d) Any request or final disposition made by a prisoner pursuant to paragraph (a) hereof shall operate as a request for final disposition of all untried indictments, informations or complaints on the basis of which detainers have been lodged against the prisoner from the state to whose prosecuting official the request for final disposition is specifically directed. The warden, commissioner of corrections or other officials having custody of the prisoner shall forthwith notify all appropriate prosecuting officers and courts in the several jurisdictions within the state to which the prisoner's request for final disposition is being sent of the proceeding being initiated by the prisoner. Any notification sent pursuant to this paragraph shall be accompanied by copies of the prisoner's written notice, request, and the certificate. If trial is not had on any indictment, information or complaint contemplated hereby prior to the return of the prisoner to the original place of imprisonment, such indictment, information or complaint shall not be of any further force or effect, and the court shall enter an order dismissing the same with prejudice.

(e) Any request for final disposition made by a prisoner pursuant to paragraph (a) hereof shall also be deemed to be a waiver of extradition with respect to any charge or proceeding contemplated thereby or included therein by reason of paragraph (d) hereof, and a waiver of extradition to the receiving state to serve any sentence there imposed upon him, after completion of his term of imprisonment in the sending state. The request for final disposition shall also constitute a consent by the prisoner to the production of his body in any court where his presence may be required in order to effectuate the purposes of this agreement and a further consent voluntarily to be returned to the original place of imprisonment in accordance with the provisions of this agreement. Nothing in this paragraph shall prevent the imposition of a concurrent sentence if otherwise permitted by law.

(f) Escape from custody by the prisoner subsequent to his execution of the request for final disposition referred to in paragraph (a) hereof shall void the request.

Article IV

(a) The appropriate officer of the jurisdiction in which an untried indictment, information or complaint is pending shall be entitled to have a prisoner against whom he has lodged a detainer and who is serving a term of imprisonment in any party state made available in accordance with Article V (a) hereof upon presentation of a written request for temporary custody or availability to the appropriate authorities of the state in which the prisoner is incarcerated: provided that the court having jurisdiction of such indictment, information or complaint shall have duly approved, recorded and transmitted the request: and provided further that there shall be a period of thirty days after receipt by the appropriate authorities before the request be honored, within which period the governor of the sending state may disapprove the request for temporary custody or availability, either upon his own motion or upon motion of the prisoner.

(b) Upon receipt of the officer's written request as provided in paragraph (a) hereof, the appropriate authorities having the prisoner in custody shall furnish the officer with a certificate stating the term of commitment under which the prisoner is being held, the time already served, the time remaining to be served on the sentence, the amount of good time earned, the time of parole eligibility of the prisoner, and any decisions of the state parole agency relating to the prisoner. Said authorities simultaneously shall furnish all other officers and appropriate courts in the receiving state who have lodged detainers against the prisoner with similar certificates and with notices informing them of the request for custody or availability and of the reasons therefor.

(c) In respect of any proceeding made possible by this Article, trial shall be commenced within one hundred twenty days of the arrival of the prisoner in the receiving state, but for good cause shown in open court, the prisoner or his counsel being present, the court having jurisdiction of the matter may grant any necessary or reasonable continuance.

(d) Nothing contained in this Article shall be construed to deprive any prisoner of any right which he may have to contest the legality of his delivery as provided in paragraph (a) hereof, but such delivery may not be opposed or denied on the ground that the executive authority of the sending state has not affirmatively consented to or ordered such delivery.

(e) If trial is not had on any indictment, information or complaint contemplated hereby prior to the prisoner's being returned to the original place of imprisonment pursuant to Article V (e) hereof, such indictment, information or complaint shall not be of any further force or effect, and the court shall enter an order dismissing the same with prejudice.

Article V

(a) In response to a request made under Article III or Article IV hereof, the appropriate authority in a sending state shall offer to deliver temporary custody of such prisoner to the appropriate authority in the state where such indictment, information or complaint is pending against such person in order that speedy and efficient prosecution may be had. If the request for final disposition is made by the prisoner, the offer of temporary custody shall accompany the written notice provided for in Article III of this agreement. In the case of a federal prisoner, the appropriate authority in the receiving state shall be entitled to temporary custody as provided by this agreement or to the prisoner's presence in federal custody at the place of trial, whichever custodial arrangement may be approved by the custodian.

(b) The officer or other representative of a state accepting an offer of temporary custody shall present the following upon demand:

(1) Proper identification and evidence of his authority to act for the state into whose temporary custody the prisoner is to be given.

(2) A duly certified copy of the indictment, information or complaint on the basis of which the detainer has been lodged and on the basis of which the request for temporary custody of the prisoner has been made.

(c) If the appropriate authority shall refuse or fail to accept temporary custody of said person, or in the event that an action on the indictment, information or complaint on the basis of which the detainer has been lodged is not brought to trial within the period provided in Article III or Article IV hereof, the appropriate court of the jurisdiction where the indictment, information or complaint has been pending shall enter an order dismissing the same with prejudice, and any detainer based thereon shall cease to be of any force or effect.

(d) The temporary custody referred to in this agreement shall be only for the purpose of permitting prosecution on the charge or charges contained in one or more untried indictments, informations or complaints which form the basis of the detainer or detainers or for prosecution on any other charge or charges arising out of the same transaction, except for his attendance at court and while being transported to or from any place at which his presence may be required, the prisoner shall be held in a suitable jail or other facility regularly used for persons awaiting prosecution.

(e) At the earliest practicable time consonant with the purposes of this agreement, the prisoner shall be returned to the sending state.

(f) During the continuance of temporary custody or while the prisoner is otherwise being made available for trial as required by this agreement, time being served on the sentence shall continue to run but good time shall be earned by the prisoner only if, and to the extent that, the law and practice of the jurisdiction which imposed the sentence may allow.

(g) For all purposes other than that for which temporary custody as provided in this agreement is exercised, the prisoner shall be deemed to remain in the custody of and subject to the jurisdiction of the sending state and any escape from temporary custody may be dealt with in the same manner as an escape from the original place of imprisonment or in any other manner permitted by law.

(h) From the time that a party state receives custody of a prisoner pursuant to this agreement until such prisoner is returned to the territory and custody of the sending state, the state in which the one or more untried indictments, informations or complaints are pending or in which trial is being had shall be responsible for the prisoner and shall also pay all costs of transporting, caring for, keeping and returning the prisoner, the provisions of this paragraph shall govern unless the states concerned shall have entered into a supplementary agreement providing for a different allocation of costs and responsibilities as between or among themselves. Nothing herein contained shall be construed to alter or affect any internal relationship among the departments, agencies and officers of and in the government of a party state, or between a party state and its subdivisions, as to the payment of costs, or responsibilities therefor.

Article VI

(a) In determining the duration and expiration dates of the time periods provided in Articles III and IV of this agreement, the running of said time periods shall be tolled whenever and for as long as the prisoner is unable to stand trial, as determined by the court having jurisdiction of the matter.

(b) No provision of this agreement, and no remedy made available by this agreement, shall apply to any person who is adjudged to be mentally ill, or who is under sentence of death.

Article VII

Each state party to this agreement shall designate an officer who, acting jointly with like officers of other party states, shall promulgate rules and regulations to carry out more effectively the terms and provisions of this agreement, and who shall provide, within and without the state, information necessary to the effective operation of this agreement.

Article VIII

This agreement shall enter into full force and effect as to a party state when such state has enacted the same into law. A state party to this agreement may withdraw herefrom by enacting a statute repealing the same. However, the withdrawal of any state shall not affect the status of any proceedings already initiated by inmates or by state officers at the time such withdrawal takes effect, nor shall it affect their rights in respect thereof.

Article IX

This agreement shall be liberally construed so as to effectuate its purposes. The provisions of this agreement shall be severable and if any phrase, clause, sentence or provision of this agreement is declared to be contrary to the constitution of any party state or of the United States or the applicability thereof to any government, agency, person or circumstance is held invalid, the validity of the remainder of this agreement and the applicability thereof to any agreement, agency, person or circumstance shall not be affected thereby. If this agreement shall be held contrary to the constitution of any state party hereto, the agreement shall remain in full force and effect as to the remaining states and in full force and effect as to the state affected as to all severable matters.

(1969 S 356, eff. 11–18–69)

2963.31 Definition of "appropriate court"

As used in section 2963.30 of the Revised Code, with reference to the courts of this state, "appropriate court" means the court of record having jurisdiction of the indictment, information, or complaint.

(1969 S 356, eff. 11–18–69)

2963.32 Duty to effectuate agreement

The courts, departments, agencies, and officers of this state and its political subdivisions shall do all things that are necessary to effectuate the agreement adopted pursuant to section 2963.30 of the Revised Code and that are appropriate within their respective jurisdictions and consistent with their duties and authority. The warden or other official in charge of a correctional institution in this state shall give over the person of any inmate of the institution when so required by the operation of the agreement.

(1994 H 571, eff. 10–6–94; 1969 S 356, eff. 11–18–69)

2963.34 Escape and aiding escape

A person, while in another state pursuant to the agreement, adopted pursuant to section 2963.30 of the Revised Code, is subject to the prohibitions and penalties provided by sections 2921.34 and 2921.35 of the Revised Code.

(1972 H 511, eff. 1–1–74; 1969 S 356)

2963.35 Powers and duties of administrator

The chief of the bureau of sentence computation or another individual specified by the director of rehabilitation and correction is designated as the administrator as required by Article VII of the agreement adopted pursuant to section 2963.30 of the Revised Code. The administrator, acting jointly with like officers of other party states, shall, in accordance with Chapter 119. of the Revised Code, promulgate rules and regulations to carry out the terms of the agreement. The administrator is authorized and empowered to cooperate with all departments, agencies, and officers of this state and its political subdivisions, in facilitating the proper administration of the agreement or of any supplementary agreement or agreements entered into by this state thereunder.

(1997 S 111, eff. 3–17–98; 1969 S 356, eff. 11–18–69)

CHAPTER 2967

PARDON; PAROLE; PROBATION

Section

2967.01 Definitions

As used in this chapter:

(A) "State correctional institution" includes any institution or facility that is operated by the department of rehabilitation and correction and that is used for the custody, care, or treatment of criminal, delinquent, or psychologically or psychiatrically disturbed offenders.

(B) "Pardon" means the remission of penalty by the governor in accordance with the power vested in the governor by the constitution.

(C) "Commutation" or "commutation of sentence" means the substitution by the governor of a lesser for a greater punishment. A stated prison term may be commuted without the consent of the convict, except when granted upon the acceptance and performance by the convict of conditions precedent. After commutation, the commuted prison term shall be the only one in existence. The commutation may be stated in terms of commuting from a named offense to a lesser included offense with a shorter prison term, in terms of commuting from a stated prison term in months and years to a shorter prison term in months and years, or in terms of commuting from any other stated prison term to a shorter prison term.

(D) "Reprieve" means the temporary suspension by the governor of the execution of a sentence or prison term. The governor may grant a reprieve without the consent of and against the will of the convict.

(E) "Parole" means, regarding a prisoner who is serving a prison term for aggravated murder or murder, who is serving a prison term of life imprisonment for rape or for felonious sexual penetration as it existed under section 2907.12 of the Revised Code prior to September 3, 1996, or who was sentenced prior to July 1, 1996, a release of the prisoner from confinement in any state correctional institution by the adult parole authority that is subject to the eligibility criteria specified in this chapter and that is under the terms and conditions, and for the period of time, prescribed by the authority in its published rules and official minutes or required by division (A) of section 2967.131 of the Revised Code or another provision of this chapter.

(F) "Head of a state correctional institution" or "head of the institution" means the resident head of the institution and the person immediately in charge of the institution, whether designated warden, superintendent, or any other name by which the head is known.

(G) "Convict" means a person who has been convicted of a felony under the laws of this state, whether or not actually confined in a state correctional institution, unless the person has been pardoned or has served the person's sentence or prison term.

(H) "Prisoner" means a person who is in actual confinement in a state correctional institution.

(I) "Parolee" means any inmate who has been released from confinement on parole by order of the adult parole authority or conditionally pardoned, who is under supervision of the adult parole authority and has not been granted a final release, and who has not been declared in violation of the inmate's parole by the authority or is performing the prescribed conditions of a conditional pardon.

(J) "Releasee" means an inmate who has been released from confinement pursuant to section 2967.28 of the Revised Code under a period of post-release control that includes one or more post-release control sanctions.

(K) "Final release" means a remission by the adult parole authority of the balance of the sentence or prison term of a parolee or prisoner or the termination by the authority of a term of post-release control of a releasee.

(L) "Parole violator" or "release violator" means any parolee or releasee who has been declared to be in violation of the condition of parole or post-release control specified in division (A) or (B) of section 2967.131 of the Revised Code or in violation of any other term, condition, or rule of the parolee's or releasee's parole or of the parolee's or releasee's post-release control sanctions, the determination of which has been made by the adult parole authority and recorded in its official minutes.

(M) "Administrative release" means a termination of jurisdiction over a particular sentence or prison term by the adult parole authority for administrative convenience.

(N) "Post–release control" means a period of supervision by the adult parole authority after a prisoner's release from imprisonment that includes one or more post-release control sanctions imposed under section 2967.28 of the Revised Code.

(O) "Post–release control sanction" means a sanction that is authorized under sections 2929.16 to 2929.18 of the Revised Code and that is imposed upon a prisoner upon the prisoner's release from a prison term.

(P) "Community control sanction," "prison term," "mandatory prison term," and "stated prison term" have the same meanings as in section 2929.01 of the Revised Code.

(Q) "Transitional control" means control of a prisoner under the transitional control program established by the department of rehabilitation and correction under section 2967.26 of the Revised Code, if the department establishes a program of that nature under that section.

(R) "Random drug testing" has the same meaning as in section 5120.63 of the Revised Code.

(2000 H 349, eff. 9–22–00; 1997 S 111, eff. 3–17–98; 1996 S 269, eff. 7–1–96; 1995 S 2, eff. 7–1–96; 1995 H 4, eff. 11–9–95; 1994 H 571, eff. 10–6–94; 1982 H 269, § 4, eff. 7–1–83; 1982 S 199; 1980 S 52; 1972 H 494; 131 v H 333; 130 v Pt 2, H 28)

2967.02 Administrative provisions

(A) The adult parole authority created by section 5149.02 of the Revised Code shall administer sections 2967.01 to 2967.28 of the Revised Code, and other sections of the Revised Code governing pardon, community control sanctions, post-release control, and parole.

(B) The governor may grant a pardon after conviction, may grant an absolute and entire pardon or a partial pardon, and may grant a pardon upon conditions precedent or subsequent.

(C) The adult parole authority shall supervise all parolees. The department of rehabilitation and correction has legal custody of a parolee until the authority grants the parolee a final release pursuant to section 2967.16 of the Revised Code.

(D) The department of rehabilitation and correction has legal custody of a releasee until the adult parole authority grants the releasee a final release pursuant to section 2967.16 of the Revised Code.

(2002 H 490, eff. 1–1–04; 1995 S 2, eff. 7–1–96; 130 v Pt 2, H 28, eff. 3–18–65)

2967.021 Effect of amendments to chapter

(A) Chapter 2967. of the Revised Code, as it existed prior to July 1, 1996, applies to a person upon whom a court imposed a term of imprisonment prior to July 1, 1996, and a person upon whom a court, on or after July 1, 1996, and in accordance with law existing prior to July 1, 1996, imposed a term of imprisonment for an offense that was committed prior to July 1, 1996.

(B) Chapter 2967. of the Revised Code, as it exists on and after July 1, 1996, applies to a person upon whom a court imposed a stated prison term for an offense committed on or after July 1, 1996.

(1995 S 2, eff. 7–1–96)

2967.03 Pardon, commutation, or reprieve

Note: See also following version of this section, eff. 4–29–05.

The adult parole authority may exercise its functions and duties in relation to the pardon, commutation of sentence, or reprieve of a convict upon direction of the governor or upon its own initiative. It may exercise its functions and duties in relation to the parole of a prisoner who is eligible for parole upon the initiative of the head of the institution in which the prisoner is confined or upon its own initiative. When a prisoner becomes eligible for parole, the head of the institution in which the prisoner is confined shall notify the authority in the manner prescribed by the authority. The authority may investigate and examine, or cause the investigation and examination of, prisoners confined in state correctional institutions concerning their conduct in the institutions, their mental and moral qualities and characteristics, their knowledge of a trade or profession, their former means of livelihood, their family relationships, and any other matters affecting their fitness to be at liberty without being a threat to society.

The authority may recommend to the governor the pardon, commutation of sentence, or reprieve of any convict or prisoner or grant a parole to any prisoner for whom parole is authorized, if in its judgment there is reasonable ground to believe that granting a pardon, commutation, or reprieve to the convict or paroling the prisoner would further the interests of justice and be consistent with the welfare and security of society. However, the authority shall not recommend a pardon or commutation of sentence of, or grant a parole to, any convict or prisoner until the authority has complied with the applicable notice requirements of sections 2930.16 and 2967.12 of the Revised Code and until it has considered any statement made by a victim or a victim's representative that is relevant to the convict's or prisoner's case and that was sent to the authority pursuant to section 2930.17 of the Revised Code and any other statement made by a victim or a victim's representative that is relevant to the convict's or prisoner's case and that was received by the authority after it provided notice of the pendency of the action under sections 2930.16 and 2967.12 of the Revised Code. If a victim or victim's representative appears at a full board hearing of the parole board and gives testimony as authorized by section 5149.101 of the Revised Code, the authority shall consider the testimony in determining whether to grant a parole. The trial judge and prosecuting attorney of the trial court in which a person was convicted shall furnish to the authority, at the request of the authority, a summarized statement of the facts proved at the trial and of all other facts having reference to the propriety of recommending a pardon or commutation, or granting a parole, together with a recommendation for or against a pardon, commutation, or parole, and the reasons for the recommendation. The trial judge of the court, and the prosecuting attorney in the trial, in which a prisoner was convicted may appear at a full board hearing of the parole board and give testimony in regard to the grant of a parole to the prisoner as authorized by section 5149.101 of the Revised Code. All state and local officials shall furnish information to the authority, when so requested by it in the performance of its duties.

The adult parole authority shall exercise its functions and duties in relation to the release of prisoners who are serving a stated prison term in accordance with section 2967.28 of the Revised Code.

(1995 S 2, eff. 7–1–96; 1994 S 186, eff. 10–12–94; 1994 H 571, eff. 10–6–94; 1987 S 6, § 1, eff. 6–10–87; 1987 S 6, § 3; 1984 S 172, § 1, 3; 130 v Pt 2, H 28)

Note: See also following version of this section, eff. 4–29–05.

2967.03 Pardon, commutation, or reprieve (later effective date)

Note: See also preceding version of this section, in effect until 4–29–05.

The adult parole authority may exercise its functions and duties in relation to the pardon, commutation of sentence, or reprieve of a convict upon direction of the governor or upon its own initiative. It may exercise its functions and duties in relation to the parole of a prisoner who is eligible for parole upon the initiative of the head of the institution in which the prisoner is confined or upon its own initiative. When a prisoner becomes eligible for parole, the head of the institution in which the prisoner is confined shall notify the authority in the manner prescribed by the authority. The authority may investigate and examine, or cause the investigation and examination of, prisoners confined in state correctional institutions concerning their conduct in the institutions, their mental and moral qualities and characteristics, their knowledge of a trade or profession, their former means of livelihood, their family relationships, and any other matters affecting their fitness to be at liberty without being a threat to society.

The authority may recommend to the governor the pardon, commutation of sentence, or reprieve of any convict or prisoner or grant a parole to any prisoner for whom parole is authorized, if in its judgment there is reasonable ground to believe that granting a pardon, commutation, or reprieve to the convict or paroling the prisoner would further the interests of justice and be consistent with the welfare and security of society. However, the authority shall not recommend a pardon or commutation of sentence of, or grant a parole to, any convict or prisoner until the authority has complied with the applicable notice requirements of sections 2930.16 and 2967.12 of the Revised Code and until it has considered any statement made by a victim or a victim's representative that is relevant to the convict's or prisoner's case and that was sent to the authority pursuant to section 2930.17 of the Revised Code and any other statement made by a victim or a victim's representative that is relevant to the convict's or prisoner's case and that was received by the authority after it provided notice of the pendency of the action under sections 2930.16 and 2967.12 of the Revised Code. If a victim , victim's representative, or the victim's spouse, parent, sibling, or child appears at a full board hearing of the parole board and gives testimony as authorized by section 5149.101 of the Revised Code, the authority shall consider the testimony in determining whether to grant a parole. The trial judge and prosecuting attorney of the trial court in which a person was convicted shall furnish to the authority, at the request of the authority, a summarized statement of the facts proved at the trial and of all other facts having reference to the propriety of recommending a pardon or commutation, or granting a parole, together with a recommendation for or against a pardon, commutation, or parole, and the reasons for the recommendation. The trial judge, the prosecuting attorney , specified law enforcement agency members, and a representative of the prisoner may appear at a full board hearing of the parole board and give testimony in regard to the grant of a parole to the prisoner as authorized by section 5149.101 of the Revised Code. All state and local officials shall furnish information to the authority, when so requested by it in the performance of its duties.

The adult parole authority shall exercise its functions and duties in relation to the release of prisoners who are serving a stated prison term in accordance with section 2967.28 of the Revised Code.

(2004 H 375, eff. 4–29–05; 1995 S 2, eff. 7–1–96; 1994 S 186, eff. 10–12–94; 1994 H 571, eff. 10–6–94; 1987 S 6, § 1, eff. 6–10–87; 1987 S 6, § 3; 1984 S 172, § 1, 3; 130 v Pt 2, H 28)

Note: See also preceding version of this section, in effect until 4–29–05.

2967.04 Pardons and commutations; conditions; effect

(A) A pardon or commutation may be granted upon such conditions precedent or subsequent as the governor may impose, which conditions shall be stated in the warrant. Such pardon or commutation shall not take effect until the conditions so imposed are accepted by the convict or prisoner so pardoned or having his sentence commuted, and his acceptance is indorsed upon the warrant, signed by him, and attested by one witness. Such witness shall go before the clerk of the court of common pleas in whose office the sentence is recorded and prove the signature of the convict. The clerk shall thereupon record the warrant, indorsement, and proof in the journal of the court, which record, or a duly certified transcript thereof, shall be evidence of such pardon or commutation, the conditions thereof, and the acceptance of the conditions.

(B) An unconditional pardon relieves the person to whom it is granted of all disabilities arising out of the conviction or convictions from which it is granted. For purposes of this section, "unconditional pardon" includes a conditional pardon with respect to which all conditions have been performed or have transpired.

(1972 H 511, eff. 1–1–74; 130 v Pt 2, H 28)

2967.05 Release of prisoner in imminent danger of death; return to institution from which released

Upon recommendation of the director of rehabilitation and correction, accompanied by a certificate of the attending physician that a prisoner or convict is in imminent danger of death, the governor may order his release as if on parole, reserving the right to return him to the institution pursuant to this section. If, subsequent to his release, his health improves so that he is no longer in imminent danger of death, he shall be returned, by order of the governor, to the institution from which he was released. If he violates any rules or conditions applicable to him, he may be returned to an institution under the control of the department of rehabilitation and correction.

(1994 H 571, eff. 10–6–94; 1982 H 269, § 4, eff. 7–1–83; 1982 S 199; 132 v S 394)

2967.06 Warrants of pardon and commutation

Warrants of pardon and commutation shall be issued in triplicate, one to be given to the convict, one to be filed with the clerk of the court of common pleas in whose office the sentence is recorded, and one to be filed with the head of the institution in which the convict was confined, in case he was confined.

All warrants of pardon, whether conditional or otherwise, shall be recorded by said clerk and the officer of the institution with whom such warrants and copies are filed, in a book provided for that purpose, which record shall include the indorsements on such warrants. A copy of such a warrant with all indorsements, certified by said clerk under seal, shall be received in evidence as proof of the facts set forth in such copy with indorsements.

(130 v Pt 2, H 28, eff. 3–18–65)

2967.07 Application for executive pardon, commutation, or reprieve

All applications for pardon, commutation of sentence, or reprieve shall be made in writing to the adult parole authority. Upon the filing of such application, or when directed by the governor in any case, a thorough investigation into the propriety of granting a pardon, commutation, or reprieve shall be made by the authority, which shall report in writing to the governor a brief statement of the facts in the case, together with the recommendation of the authority for or against the granting of a pardon, commutation, or reprieve, the grounds therefor and the records or minutes relating to the case.

(130 v Pt 2, H 28, eff. 3–18–65)

2967.08 Reprieve to a person under sentence of death

The governor may grant a reprieve for a definite time to a person under sentence of death, with or without notices or application.

(130 v Pt 2, H 28, eff. 3–18–65)

2967.09 Warrant of reprieve

On receiving a warrant of reprieve, the head of the institution, sheriff, or other officer having custody of the person reprieved, shall file it forthwith with the clerk of the court of common pleas in which the sentence is recorded, who shall thereupon record the warrant in the journal of the court.

(130 v Pt 2, H 28, eff. 3–18–65)

2967.10 Confinement of prisoner during reprieve

When the governor directs in a warrant of reprieve that the prisoner be confined in a state correctional institution for the time of the reprieve or any part thereof, the sheriff or other officer having the prisoner in custody shall convey him to the state correctional institution in the manner provided for the conveyance of convicts, and the warden shall receive the prisoner and warrant and proceed as the warrant directs. At the expiration of the time specified in the warrant for the confinement of the prisoner in the state correctional institution, the warden shall deal with him according to the sentence as originally imposed, or as modified by executive clemency as shown by a new warrant of pardon, commutation, or reprieve executed by the governor.

(1994 H 571, eff. 10–6–94; 130 v Pt 2, H 28, eff. 3–18–65)

2967.11 Administrative extension of prison term for offenses committed during term

(A) As used in this section, "violation" means an act that is a criminal offense under the law of this state or the United States, whether or not a person is prosecuted for the commission of the offense.

(B) As part of a prisoner's sentence, the parole board may punish a violation committed by the prisoner by extending the prisoner's stated prison term for a period of fifteen, thirty, sixty, or ninety days in accordance with this section. The parole board may not extend a prisoner's stated prison term for a period longer than one-half of the stated prison term's duration for all violations occurring during the course of the prisoner's stated prison term, including violations occurring while the offender is serving extended time under this section or serving a prison term imposed for a failure to meet the conditions of a post-release control sanction imposed under section 2967.28 of the Revised Code. If a prisoner's stated prison term is extended under this section, the time by which it is so extended shall be referred to as "bad time."

(C) The department of rehabilitation and correction shall establish a rules infraction board in each state correctional institution. When a prisoner in an institution is alleged by any person to have committed a violation, the institutional investigator or other appropriate official promptly shall investigate the alleged violation and promptly shall report the investigator's or other appropriate official's findings to the rules infraction board in that institution. The rules infraction board in that institution shall hold a hearing on the allegation to determine, for purposes of the parole board's possible extension of the prisoner's stated prison term under this section, whether there is evidence of a violation. At the hearing, the accused prisoner shall have the right to testify and be assisted by a member of the staff of the institution who is designated pursuant to rules adopted by the department to assist the prisoner in presenting a defense before the board in the hearing. The rules infraction board shall make an audio tape of the hearing. The board shall report its finding to the head of the institution within ten days after the date of the hearing. If the board finds any evidence of a violation, it also shall include with its finding a recommendation regarding a period of time, as specified in division (B) of this section, by which the prisoner's stated prison term should be extended as a result of the violation.

If the board does not so find, the board shall terminate the matter.

(D) Within ten days after receiving from the rules infraction board a finding and a recommendation that the prisoner's stated prison term be extended, the head of the institution shall review the finding and determine whether the prisoner committed a violation. If the head of the institution determines by clear and convincing evidence that the prisoner committed a violation and concludes that the prisoner's stated prison term should be extended as a result of the violation, the head of the institution shall report the determination in a finding to the parole board within ten days after making the determination and shall include with the finding a recommendation regarding the length of the extension of the stated prison term. If the head of the institution does not determine by clear and convincing evidence that the prisoner committed the violation or does not conclude that the prisoner's stated prison term should be extended, the head of the institution shall terminate the matter.

(E) Within thirty days after receiving a report from the head of an institution pursuant to division (D) of this section containing a finding and recommendation, the parole board shall review the findings of the rules infraction board and the head of the institution to determine whether there is clear and convincing evidence that the prisoner committed the violation and, if so, to determine whether the stated prison term should be extended and the length of time by which to extend it. If the parole board determines that there is clear and convincing evidence that the prisoner committed the violation and that the prisoner's stated prison term should be extended, the board shall consider the nature of the violation, other conduct of the prisoner while in prison, and any other evidence relevant to maintaining order in the institution. After considering these factors, the board shall extend the stated prison term by either fifteen, thirty, sixty, or ninety days for the violation, subject to the maximum extension authorized by division (B) of this section. The board shall act to extend a stated prison term no later than sixty days from the date of the finding by the rules infraction board pursuant to division (C) of this section.

(F) If an accusation of a violation is made within sixty days before the end of a prisoner's stated prison term, the rules infraction board, head of the institution, and parole board shall attempt to complete the procedures required by divisions (C) to (E) of this section before the prisoner's stated prison term ends. If necessary, the accused prisoner may be held in the institution for not more than ten days after the end of the prisoner's stated prison term pending review of the violation and a determination regarding an extension of the stated prison term.

(G) This section does not preclude the department of rehabilitation and correction from referring a criminal offense allegedly committed by a prisoner to the appropriate prosecuting authority or from disciplining a prisoner through the use of disciplinary processes other than the extension of the prisoner's stated prison term.

(H) Pursuant to section 111.15 of the Revised Code, the department of rehabilitation and correction shall adopt rules establishing standards and procedures for implementing the requirements of this section and for designating state correctional institution staff members to assist prisoners in hearings conducted under division (C) of this section.

(1996 S 269, eff. 7–1–96; 1995 S 2, eff. 7–1–96)

2967.12 Notice of pendency of pardon, commutation, parole, termination or transfer of control; rights of crime victim or representative

Note: See also following version of this section, eff. 4–29–05.

(A) Except as provided in division (G) of this section, at least three weeks before the adult parole authority recommends any pardon or commutation of sentence, or grants any parole, the authority shall send a notice of the pendency of the pardon, commutation, or parole, setting forth the name of the person on whose behalf it is made, the offense of which the person was convicted, the time of conviction, and the term of the person's sentence, to the prosecuting attorney and the judge of the court of common pleas of the county in which the indictment against the person was found. If there is more than one judge of that court of common pleas, the authority shall send the notice to the presiding judge.

(B) If a request for notification has been made pursuant to section 2930.16 of the Revised Code, the adult parole authority also shall give notice to the victim or the victim's representative prior to recommending any pardon or commutation of sentence for, or granting any parole to, the person. The authority shall provide the notice at the same time as the notice required by division (A) of this section and shall include in the notice the information required to be set forth in that notice. The notice also shall inform the victim or the victim's representative that the victim or representative may send a written statement relative to the victimization and the pending action to the adult parole authority and that, if the authority receives any written statement prior to recommending a pardon or commutation or granting a parole for a person, the authority will consider the statement before it recommends a pardon or commutation or grants a parole. If the person is being considered for parole, the notice shall inform the victim or the victim's representative that a full board hearing of the parole board may be held and that the victim or victim's representative may contact the office of victims' services for further information.

(C) When notice of the pendency of any pardon, commutation of sentence, or parole has been given as provided in division (A) of this section and a hearing on the pardon, commutation, or parole is continued to a date certain, the authority shall give notice by mail of the further consideration of the pardon, commutation, or parole to the proper judge and prosecuting attorney at least ten days before the further consideration. When notice of the pendency of any pardon, commutation, or parole has been given as provided in division (B) of this section and the hearing on it is continued to a date certain, the authority shall give notice of the further consideration to the victim or the victim's representative in accordance with section 2930.03 of the Revised Code.

(D) In case of an application for the pardon or commutation of sentence of a person sentenced to capital punishment, the governor may modify the requirements of notification and publication if there is not sufficient time for compliance with the requirements before the date fixed for the execution of sentence.

(E) If an offender is serving a prison term imposed under division (A)(3) of section 2971.03 of the Revised Code and if the parole board terminates its control over the offender's service of that term pursuant to section 2971.04 of the Revised Code, the parole board immediately shall provide written notice of its termination of control or the transfer of control to the entities and persons specified in section 2971.04 of the Revised Code.

(F) The failure of the adult parole authority to comply with the notice provisions of division (A), (B), or (C) of this section or the failure of the parole board to comply with the notice provisions of division (E) of this section do not give any rights or any grounds for appeal or post-conviction relief to the person serving the sentence.

(G) Divisions (A), (B), and (C) of this section do not apply to any release of a person that is of the type described in division (B)(2)(b) of section 5120.031 of the Revised Code.

(1996 H 180, eff. 1–1–97; 1995 S 2, eff. 7–1–96; 1994 S 186, eff. 10–12–94; 1990 S 258, eff. 11–20–90; 1987 S 6, § 3; 1984 S 172, § 1, 3; 130 v Pt 2, H 28)

Note: See also following version of this section, eff. 4–29–05.

2967.12 Notice of pendency of pardon, commutation, parole, termination or transfer of control; rights of crime victim or representative (later effective date)

Note: See also preceding version of this section, in effect until 4–29–05.

(A) Except as provided in division (G) of this section, at least three weeks before the adult parole authority recommends any pardon or commutation of sentence, or grants any parole, the authority shall send a notice of the pendency of the pardon, commutation, or parole, setting forth the name of the person on whose behalf it is made, the offense of which the person was convicted, the time of conviction, and the term of the person's sentence, to the prosecuting attorney and the judge of the court of common pleas of the county in which the indictment against the person was found. If there is more than one judge of that court of common pleas, the authority shall send the notice to the presiding judge.

(B) If a request for notification has been made pursuant to section 2930.16 of the Revised Code, the adult parole authority also shall give notice to the victim or the victim's representative prior to recommending any pardon or commutation of sentence for, or granting any parole to, the person. The authority shall provide the notice at the same time as the notice required by division (A) of this section and shall include in the notice the information required to be set forth in that notice. The notice also shall inform the victim or the victim's representative that the victim or representative may send a written statement relative to the victimization and the pending action to the adult parole authority and that, if the authority receives any written statement prior to recommending a pardon or commutation or granting a parole for a person, the authority will consider the statement before it recommends a pardon or commutation or grants a parole. If the person is being considered for parole, the notice shall inform the victim or the victim's representative that a full board hearing of the parole board may be held and that the victim or victim's representative may contact the office of victims' services for further information. If the person being considered for parole was convicted of or pleaded guilty to violating section 2903.01 or 2903.02 of the Revised Code, the notice shall inform the victim of that offense, the victim's representative, or a member of the victim's immediate family that the victim, the victim's representative, and the victim's immediate family have the right to give testimony at a full board hearing of the parole board and that the victim or victim's representative may contact the office of victims' services for further information. As used in this division, "the victim's immediate family" means the mother, father, spouse, sibling, or child of the victim.

(C) When notice of the pendency of any pardon, commutation of sentence, or parole has been given as provided in division (A) of this section and a hearing on the pardon, commutation, or parole is continued to a date certain, the authority shall give notice by mail of the further consideration of the pardon, commutation, or parole to the proper judge and prosecuting attorney at least ten days before the further consideration. When notice of the pendency of any pardon, commutation, or parole has been given as provided in division (B) of this section and the hearing on it is continued to a date certain, the authority shall give notice of the further consideration to the victim or the victim's representative in accordance with section 2930.03 of the Revised Code.

(D) In case of an application for the pardon or commutation of sentence of a person sentenced to capital punishment, the governor may modify the requirements of notification and publication if there is not sufficient time for compliance with the requirements before the date fixed for the execution of sentence.

(E) If an offender is serving a prison term imposed under division (A)(3) of section 2971.03 of the Revised Code and if the parole board terminates its control over the offender's service of that term pursuant to section 2971.04 of the Revised Code, the parole board immediately shall provide written notice of its termination of control or the transfer of control to the entities and persons specified in section 2971.04 of the Revised Code.

(F) The failure of the adult parole authority to comply with the notice provisions of division (A), (B), or (C) of this section or the failure of the parole board to comply with the notice provisions of division (E) of this section do not give any rights or any grounds for appeal or post-conviction relief to the person serving the sentence.

(G) Divisions (A), (B), and (C) of this section do not apply to any release of a person that is of the type described in division (B)(2)(b) of section 5120.031 of the Revised Code.

(2004 H 375, eff. 4–29–05; 1996 H 180, eff. 1–1–97; 1995 S 2, eff. 7–1–96; 1994 S 186, eff. 10–12–94; 1990 S 258, eff. 11–20–90; 1987 S 6, § 3; 1984 S 172, § 1, 3; 130 v Pt 2, H 28)

Note: See also preceding version of this section, in effect until 4–29–05.

2967.121 Notice to prosecuting attorney of pending release of certain prisoners

(A) Subject to division (C) of this section, at least two weeks before any convict who is serving a sentence for committing a felony of the first, second, or third degree is released from confinement in any state correctional institution pursuant to a pardon, commutation of sentence, parole, or completed prison term, the adult parole authority shall send notice of the release to the prosecuting attorney of the county in which the indictment of the convict was found.

(B) The notice required by division (A) of this section may be contained in a weekly list of all felons of the first, second, or third degree who are scheduled for release. The notice shall contain all of the following:

(1) The name of the convict being released;

(2) The date of the convict's release;

(3) The offense for the violation of which the convict was convicted and incarcerated;

(4) The date of the convict's conviction pursuant to which the convict was incarcerated;

(5) The sentence imposed for that conviction;

(6) The length of any supervision that the convict will be under;

(7) The name, business address, and business phone number of the convict's supervising officer;

(8) The address at which the convict will reside.

(C) Divisions (A) and (B) of this section do not apply to the release from confinement of an offender if the offender is serving a prison term imposed under division (A)(3) of section 2971.03 of the Revised Code, if the court pursuant to section 2971.05 of the Revised Code modifies the requirement that the offender serve that entire term in a state correctional institution, and if the release from confinement is pursuant to that modification. In a case of that type, the court that modifies the requirement promptly shall provide written notice of the modification and the order that modifies the requirement or revises the modification to the offender, the department of rehabilitation and correction, the prosecuting attorney, and any state agency or political subdivision that is affected by the order.

(1999 S 107, eff. 3–23–00; 1996 H 180, eff. 1–1–97; 1995 S 2, eff. 7–1–96; 1994 H 571, eff. 10–6–94; 1984 H 399, eff. 9–26–84)

2967.13 Parole eligibility

(A) Except as provided in division (G) of this section, a prisoner serving a sentence of imprisonment for life for an offense committed on or after July 1, 1996, is not entitled to any earned credit under section 2967.193 of the Revised Code and becomes eligible for parole as follows:

(1) If a sentence of imprisonment for life was imposed for the offense of murder, at the expiration of the prisoner's minimum term;

(2) If a sentence of imprisonment for life with parole eligibility after serving twenty years of imprisonment was imposed pursuant to section 2929.022 or 2929.03 of the Revised Code, after serving a term of twenty years;

(3) If a sentence of imprisonment for life with parole eligibility after serving twenty-five full years of imprisonment was imposed pursuant to section 2929.022 or 2929.03 of the Revised Code, after serving a term of twenty-five full years;

(4) If a sentence of imprisonment for life with parole eligibility after serving thirty full years of imprisonment was imposed pursuant to section 2929.022 or 2929.03 of the Revised Code, after serving a term of thirty full years;

(5) If a sentence of imprisonment for life was imposed for rape, after serving a term of ten full years' imprisonment;

(6) If a sentence of imprisonment for life with parole eligibility after serving fifteen years of imprisonment was imposed for a violation of section 2927.24 of the Revised Code, after serving a term of fifteen years.

(B) Except as provided in division (G) of this section, a prisoner serving a sentence of imprisonment for life with parole eligibility after serving twenty years of imprisonment or a sentence of imprisonment for life with parole eligibility after serving twenty-five full years or thirty full years of imprisonment imposed pursuant to section 2929.022 or 2929.03 of the Revised Code for an offense committed on or after July 1, 1996, consecutively to any other term of imprisonment, becomes eligible for parole after serving twenty years, twenty full years, or thirty full years, as applicable, as to each such sentence of life imprisonment, which shall not be reduced for earned credits under section 2967.193 of the Revised Code, plus the term or terms of the other sentences consecutively imposed or, if one of the other sentences is another type of life sentence with parole eligibility, the number of years before parole eligibility for that sentence.

(C) Except as provided in division (G) of this section, a prisoner serving consecutively two or more sentences in which an indefinite term of imprisonment is imposed becomes eligible for parole upon the expiration of the aggregate of the minimum terms of the sentences.

(D) Except as provided in division (G) of this section, a prisoner serving a term of imprisonment who is described in division (A) of section 2967.021 of the Revised Code becomes eligible for parole as described in that division or, if the prisoner is serving a definite term of imprisonment, shall be released as described in that division.

(E) A prisoner serving a sentence of life imprisonment without parole imposed pursuant to section 2907.02 or section 2929.03 or 2929.06 of the Revised Code is not eligible for parole and shall be imprisoned until death.

(F) A prisoner serving a stated prison term shall be released in accordance with section 2967.28 of the Revised Code.

(G) A prisoner serving a prison term or term of life imprisonment without parole imposed pursuant to section 2971.03 of the Revised Code never becomes eligible for parole during that term of imprisonment.

(2002 H 485, eff. 6–13–02; 1999 S 107, eff. 3–23–00; 1996 H 180, eff. 1–1–97; 1996 S 269, eff. 7–1–96; 1995 S 2, eff. 7–1–96; 1994 H 571, eff. 10–6–94; 1992 S 331, eff. 11–13–92; 1988 H 708; 1987 H 261, H 5; 1983 S 210; 1982 H 269, S 199; 1981 S 1; 1972 H 511)

2967.131 Released individuals to abide by firearms and drug laws; searches and random drug testing authorized

(A) In addition to any other terms and conditions of a conditional pardon or parole, of transitional control, or of another form of authorized release from confinement in a state correctional institution that is granted to an individual and that involves the placement of the individual under the supervision of the adult parole authority, and in addition to any other sanctions of post-release control of a felon imposed under section 2967.28 of the Revised Code, the authority or, in the case of a conditional pardon, the governor shall include in the terms and conditions of the conditional pardon, parole, transitional control, or other form of authorized release or shall include as conditions of the post-release control the conditions that the individual or felon not leave the state without permission of the court or the individual's or felon's parole or probation officer and that the individual or felon abide by the law during the period of the individual's or felon's conditional pardon, parole, transitional control, other form of authorized release, or post-release control.

(B)(1) The department of rehabilitation and correction, as a condition of parole or post-release control, may require that the individual or felon shall not ingest or be injected with a drug of abuse and shall submit to random drug testing as provided in divisions (B)(2), (3), and (4) of this section and that the results of the drug test indicate that the individual or felon did not ingest or was not injected with a drug of abuse.

(2) If the adult parole authority has general control and supervision of an individual or felon who is required to submit to random drug testing as a condition of parole or post-release control under division (B)(1) of this section, the authority may cause the individual or felon to submit to random drug testing performed by a laboratory or entity that has entered into a contract with any of the governmental entities or officers authorized to enter into a contract with that laboratory or entity under section 341.26, 753.33, or 5120.63 of the Revised Code.

(3) If no laboratory or entity described in division (B)(2) of this section has entered into a contract as specified in that division, the adult parole authority shall cause the individual or felon to submit to random drug testing performed by a reputable public laboratory to determine whether the individual or felon who is the subject of the drug test ingested or was injected with a drug of abuse.

(4) If a laboratory or entity has entered into a contract with a governmental entity or officer as specified in division (B)(2) of this section, the laboratory or entity shall perform the random drug testing under division (B)(2) of this section in accordance with the applicable standards that are included in the terms of that contract. A public laboratory shall perform the random drug tests under division (B)(3) of this section in accordance with the standards set forth in the policies and procedures established by the department of rehabilitation and correction pursuant to section 5120.63 of the Revised Code. An individual or felon who is required under division (B)(1) of this section to submit to random drug testing as a condition of parole or post-release control and whose test results indicate that the individual or felon ingested or was injected with a drug of abuse shall pay the fee for the drug test if the adult parole authority requires payment of a fee. A laboratory or entity that performs the random drug testing on a parolee or releasee under division (B)(2) or (3) of

this section shall transmit the results of the drug test to the adult parole authority.

(C) During the period of a conditional pardon or parole, of transitional control, or of another form of authorized release from confinement in a state correctional institution that is granted to an individual and that involves the placement of the individual under the supervision of the adult parole authority, and during a period of post-release control of a felon imposed under section 2967.28 of the Revised Code, authorized field officers of the authority who are engaged within the scope of their supervisory duties or responsibilities may search, with or without a warrant, the person of the individual or felon, the place of residence of the individual or felon, and a motor vehicle, another item of tangible or intangible personal property, or other real property in which the individual or felon has a right, title, or interest or for which the individual or felon has the express or implied permission of a person with a right, title, or interest to use, occupy, or possess, if the field officers have reasonable grounds to believe that the individual or felon has left the state, is not abiding by the law, or otherwise is not complying with the terms and conditions of the individual's or felon's conditional pardon, parole, transitional control, other form of authorized release, or post-release control. The authority shall provide each individual who is granted a conditional pardon or parole, transitional control, or another form of authorized release from confinement in a state correctional institution and each felon who is under post-release control with a written notice that informs the individual or felon that authorized field officers of the authority who are engaged within the scope of their supervisory duties or responsibilities may conduct those types of searches during the period of the conditional pardon, parole, transitional control, other form of authorized release, or post-release control if they have reasonable grounds to believe that the individual or felon has left the state, is not abiding by the law, or otherwise is not complying with the terms and conditions of the individual's or felon's conditional pardon, parole, transitional control, other form of authorized release, or post-release control.

(2000 H 349, eff. 9–22–00; 1999 S 107, eff. 3–23–00; 1997 S 111, eff. 3–17–98; 1996 S 269, eff. 7–1–96; 1995 H 4, eff. 11–9–95)

2967.14 Halfway house; requirement of residence; funding; licensing

(A) The adult parole authority may require a parolee or releasee to reside in a halfway house or other suitable community residential center that has been licensed by the division of parole and community services pursuant to division (C) of this section during a part or for the entire period of the parolee's conditional release or of the releasee's term of post-release control. The court of common pleas that placed an offender under a sanction consisting of a term in a halfway house or in an alternative residential sanction may require the offender to reside in a halfway house or other suitable community residential center that is designated by the court and that has been licensed by the division pursuant to division (C) of this section during a part or for the entire period of the offender's residential sanction.

(B) The division of parole and community services may negotiate and enter into agreements with any public or private agency or a department or political subdivision of the state that operates a halfway house or community residential center that has been licensed by the division pursuant to division (C) of this section. An agreement under this division shall provide for the purchase of beds, shall set limits of supervision and levels of occupancy, and shall determine the scope of services for all eligible offenders, including those subject to a residential sanction, as defined in rules adopted by the director of rehabilitation and correction in accordance with Chapter 119. of the Revised Code. The payments for beds and services shall be equal to the halfway house's or community residential center's average daily per capita costs with its facility at full occupancy. The payments for beds and services shall not exceed the total operating costs of the halfway house or community residential center during the term of an agreement. The director of rehabilitation and correction shall adopt rules in accordance with Chapter 119. of the Revised Code for determining includable and excludable costs and income to be used in computing the agency's average daily per capita costs with its facility at full occupancy.

The department of rehabilitation and correction may use no more than ten per cent of the amount appropriated to the department each fiscal year for the halfway house and community residential center program to pay for contracts for nonresidential services for offenders under the supervision of the adult parole authority. The nonresidential services may include, but are not limited to, treatment for substance abuse, mental health counseling, and counseling for sex offenders.

(C) The division of parole and community services may license a halfway house or community residential center as a suitable facility for the care and treatment of adult offenders, including offenders sentenced under section 2929.16 or 2929.26 of the Revised Code, only if the halfway house or community residential center complies with the standards that the division adopts in accordance with Chapter 119. of the Revised Code for the licensure of halfway houses and community residential centers. The division shall annually inspect each licensed halfway house and licensed community residential center to determine if it is in compliance with the licensure standards.

(2003 S 57, eff. 1–1–04; 2002 H 510, eff. 3–31–03; 1997 S 111, eff. 3–17–98; 1995 S 2, eff. 7–1–96; 1994 H 571, eff. 10–6–94; 1992 S 331, eff. 11–13–92; 1981 H 694; 1976 H 637)

2967.141 Violation sanction centers

(A) As used in this section, "alternative residential facility" has the same meaning as in section 2929.01 of the Revised Code.

(B) The department of rehabilitation and correction, through its division of parole and community services, may operate or contract for the operation of one or more violation sanction centers as an alternative residential facility. A violation sanction center operated under authority of this division is not a prison within the meaning of division (BB) of section 2929.01 of the Revised Code. A violation sanction center operated under authority of this division may be used for either of the following purposes:

(1) Service of the term of a more restrictive post-release control sanction that the parole board, subsequent to a hearing, imposes pursuant to division (F)(2) of section 2967.28 of the Revised Code upon a releasee who has violated a post-release control sanction imposed upon the releasee under that section;

(2) Service of a sanction that the adult parole authority or parole board imposes upon a parolee whom the authority determines to be a parole violator because of a violation of the terms and conditions of the parolee's parole or conditional pardon.

(C) If a violation sanction center is established under the authority of this section, notwithstanding the fact that the center is an alternative residential facility for the purposes described in division (B) of this section, the center shall be used only for the purposes described in that division. A violation sanction center established under the authority of this section is not an alternative residential facility for the purpose of imposing sentence on an offender who is convicted of or pleads guilty to a felony, and a court that is sentencing an offender for a felony pursuant to sections 2929.11 to 2929.19 of the Revised Code shall not sentence the offender to a community residential sanction that requires the offender to serve a term in the center.

(D) If a releasee is ordered to serve a sanction in a violation sanction center, as described in division (B)(1) of this section, all of the following apply:

(1) The releasee shall not be considered to be under a new prison term for a violation of post-release control.

(2) The time the releasee serves in the center shall not count toward, and shall not be considered in determining, the maximum cumulative prison term for all violations that is described in division (F)(3) of section 2967.28 of the Revised Code.

(3) The time the releasee serves in the center shall count as part of, and shall be credited toward, the remaining period of post-release control that is applicable to the releasee.

(1999 S 107, eff. 3–23–00; 1997 S 111, eff. 3–17–98)

2967.15 Violation of pardon, parole, or other supervised release

(A) If an adult parole authority field officer has reasonable cause to believe that a person who is a parolee or releasee, who is under transitional control, or who is under another form of authorized release and who is under the supervision of the adult parole authority has violated or is violating the condition of a conditional pardon, parole, other form of authorized release, transitional control, or post-release control specified in division (A) of section 2967.131 of the Revised Code or any other term or condition of the person's conditional pardon, parole, other form of authorized release, transitional control, or post-release control, the field officer may arrest the person without a warrant or order a peace officer to arrest the person without a warrant. A person so arrested shall be confined in the jail of the county in which the person is arrested or in another facility designated by the chief of the adult parole authority until a determination is made regarding the person's release status. Upon making an arrest under this section, the arresting or supervising adult parole authority field officer promptly shall notify the superintendent of parole supervision or the superintendent's designee, in writing, that the person has been arrested and is in custody and submit an appropriate report of the reason for the arrest.

(B) Except as otherwise provided in this division, prior to the revocation by the adult parole authority of a person's pardon, parole, transitional control, or other release and prior to the imposition by the parole board or adult parole authority of a new prison term as a post-release control sanction for a person, the adult parole authority shall grant the person a hearing in accordance with rules adopted by the department of rehabilitation and correction under Chapter 119. of the Revised Code. The adult parole authority is not required to grant the person a hearing if the person is convicted of or pleads guilty to an offense that the person committed while released on a pardon, on parole, transitional control, or another form of release, or on post-release control and upon which the revocation of the person's pardon, parole, transitional control, other release, or post-release control is based.

If a person who has been pardoned is found to be a violator of the conditions of the parolee's conditional pardon or commutation of sentence, the authority forthwith shall transmit to the governor its recommendation concerning that violation, and the violator shall be retained in custody until the governor issues an order concerning that violation.

If the authority fails to make a determination of the case of a parolee or releasee alleged to be a violator of the terms and conditions of the parolee's or releasee's conditional pardon, parole, other release, or post-release control sanctions within a reasonable time, the parolee or releasee shall be released from custody under the same terms and conditions of the parolee's or releasee's original conditional pardon, parole, other release, or post-release control sanctions.

(C)(1) If a person who is a parolee or releasee, who is under transitional control, or who is under another form of authorized release under the supervision of the adult parole authority absconds from supervision, the supervising adult parole authority field officer shall report that fact to the superintendent of parole supervision, in writing, and the authority shall declare that person to be a violator at large. Upon being advised of the apprehension and availability for return of a violator at large, the superintendent of parole supervision shall determine whether the violator at large should be restored to parole, transitional control, another form of authorized release, or post-release control.

The time between the date on which a person who is a parolee or other releasee is declared to be a violator or violator at large and the date on which that person is returned to custody in this state under the immediate control of the adult parole authority shall not be counted as time served under the sentence imposed on that person or as a part of the term of post-release control.

(2) A person who is under transitional control or who is under any form of authorized release under the supervision of the adult parole authority is considered to be in custody while under the transitional control or on release, and, if the person absconds from supervision, the person may be prosecuted for the offense of escape.

(D) A person who is a parolee or releasee, who is under transitional control, or who is under another form of authorized release under the supervision of the adult parole authority and who has violated a term or condition of the person's conditional pardon, parole, transitional control, other form of authorized release, or post-release control shall be declared to be a violator if the person is committed to a correctional institution outside the state to serve a sentence imposed upon the person by a federal court or a court of another state or if the person otherwise leaves the state.

(E) As used in this section, "peace officer" has the same meaning as in section 2935.01 of the Revised Code.

(1997 S 111, eff. 3–17–98; 1996 S 269, eff. 7–1–96; 1995 S 2, eff. 7–1–96; 1995 H 4, eff. 11–9–95; 1995 H 117, eff. 6–30–95; 1994 H 571, eff. 10–6–94; 1992 S 49, eff. 7–21–92; 130 v Pt 2, H 28)

2967.16 Final release of paroled prisoners

(A) Except as provided in division (D) of this section, when a paroled prisoner has faithfully performed the conditions and obligations of the paroled prisoner's parole and has obeyed the rules and regulations adopted by the adult parole authority that apply to the paroled prisoner, the authority upon the recommendation of the superintendent of parole supervision may enter upon its minutes a final release and thereupon shall issue to the paroled prisoner a certificate of final release, but the authority shall not grant a final release earlier than one year after the paroled prisoner is released from the institution on parole, and, in the case of a paroled prisoner whose minimum sentence is life imprisonment, the authority shall not grant a final release earlier than five years after the paroled prisoner is released from the institution on parole.

(B)(1) When a prisoner who has been released under a period of post-release control pursuant to section 2967.28 of the Revised Code has faithfully performed the conditions and obligations of the released prisoner's post-release control sanctions and has obeyed the rules and regulations adopted by the adult parole authority that apply to the released prisoner or has the period of post-release control terminated by a court pursuant to section 2929.141 of the Revised Code, the authority, upon the recommendation of the superintendent of parole supervision, may enter upon its minutes a final release and, upon the entry of the final release, shall issue to the released prisoner a certificate of final release. In the case of a prisoner who has been released under a period of post-release control pursuant to division (B) of section 2967.28 of the Revised Code, the authority shall not grant a final release earlier than one year after the released prisoner is released from the institution under a period of post-release control. The authority shall classify the termination of post-release control as favorable or unfavorable depending on the offender's conduct and compliance with the conditions of supervision. In the case of a released prisoner whose sentence is life imprisonment, the authority shall not grant a final release earlier than five years after the released prisoner is released from the institution under a period of post-release control.

(2) The department of rehabilitation and correction, no later than six months after the effective date of this section shall adopt a rule in accordance with Chapter 119. of the Revised Code that establishes the criteria for the classification of a post-release control termination as "favorable" or "unfavorable."

(C) The following prisoners or person shall be restored to the rights and privileges forfeited by a conviction:

(1) A prisoner who has served the entire prison term that comprises or is part of the prisoner's sentence and has not been placed under any post-release control sanctions;

(2) A prisoner who has been granted a final release by the adult parole authority pursuant to division (A) or (B) of this section;

(3) A person who has completed the period of a community control sanction or combination of community control sanctions, as defined in section 2929.01 of the Revised Code, that was imposed by the sentencing court.

(D) Division (A) of this section does not apply to a prisoner in the shock incarceration program established pursuant to section 5120.031 of the Revised Code.

(E) The adult parole authority shall record the final release of a parolee or prisoner in the official minutes of the authority.

(2002 H 327, eff. 7–8–02; 1999 S 107, eff. 3–23–00; 1996 S 269, eff. 7–1–96; 1995 S 2, eff. 7–1–96; 1994 H 314, eff. 9–29–94; 131 v H 848, eff. 11–1–65; 130 v Pt 2, H 28)

2967.17 Administrative release of parole violator

(A) The adult parole authority, in its discretion, may grant an administrative release to any of the following:

(1) A parole violator or release violator serving another felony sentence in a correctional institution within or without this state for the purpose of consolidation of the records or if justice would best be served;

(2) A parole violator at large or release violator at large whose case has been inactive for at least ten years following the date of declaration of the parole violation or the violation of a post-release control sanction;

(3) A parolee taken into custody by the immigration and naturalization service of the United States department of justice and deported from the United States.

(B) The adult parole authority shall not grant an administrative release except upon the concurrence of a majority of the parole board and approval of the chief of the adult parole authority. An administrative release does not restore for the person to whom it is granted the rights and privileges forfeited by conviction as provided in section 2961.01 of the Revised Code. Any person granted an administrative release under this section may subsequently apply for a commutation of sentence for the purpose of regaining the rights and privileges forfeited by conviction.

(1995 S 2, eff. 7–1–96; 1994 S 242, eff. 10–6–94; 1994 H 571, eff. 10–6–94; 131 v H 333, eff. 10–20–65)

2967.18 Reduction of sentences or advance of release dates when overcrowding emergency exists; when sentence reduction or advance of release date prohibited

(A) Whenever the director of rehabilitation and correction determines that the total population of the state correctional institutions for males and females, the total population of the state correctional institutions for males, or the total population of the state correctional institutions for females exceeds the capacity of those institutions and that an overcrowding emergency exists, the director shall notify the correctional institution inspection committee of the emergency and provide the committee with information in support of the director's determination. The director shall not notify the committee that an overcrowding emergency exists unless the director determines that no other reasonable method is available to resolve the overcrowding emergency.

(B) On receipt of the notice given pursuant to division (A) of this section, the correctional institution inspection committee promptly shall review the determination of the director of rehabilitation and correction. Notwithstanding any other provision of the Revised Code or the Administrative Code that governs the lengths of criminal sentences, sets forth the time within which a prisoner is eligible for parole or within which a prisoner may apply for release, or regulates the procedure for granting parole or release to prisoners confined in state correctional institutions, the committee may recommend to the governor that the prison terms of eligible male, female, or all prisoners, as determined under division (E) of this section, be reduced by thirty, sixty, or ninety days, in the manner prescribed in that division.

(C) If the correctional institution inspection committee disagrees with the determination of the director of rehabilitation and correction that an overcrowding emergency exists, if the committee finds that an overcrowding emergency exists but does not make a recommendation pursuant to division (B) of this section, or if the committee does not make a finding or a recommendation pursuant to that division within thirty days of receipt of the notice given pursuant to division (A) of this section, the director may recommend to the governor that the action set forth in division (B) of this section be taken.

(D) Upon receipt of a recommendation from the correctional institution inspection committee or the director of rehabilitation and correction made pursuant to this section, the governor may declare in writing that an overcrowding emergency exists in all of the institutions within the control of the department in which men are confined, in which women are confined, or both. The declaration shall state that the adult parole authority shall take the action set forth in division (B) of this section. After the governor makes the declaration, the director shall file a copy of it with the secretary of state, and the copy is a public record.

The department may begin to implement the declaration of the governor made pursuant to this section on the date that it is filed with the secretary of state. The department shall begin to implement the declaration within thirty days after the date of filing. The declaration shall be implemented in accordance with division (E) of this section.

(E)(1) No reduction of sentence pursuant to division (B) of this section shall be granted to any of the following:

(a) A person who is serving a term of imprisonment for aggravated murder, murder, voluntary manslaughter, involuntary manslaughter, felonious assault, kidnapping, rape, aggravated arson, aggravated robbery, or any other offense punishable by life imprisonment or by an indefinite term of a specified number of years to life, or for conspiracy in, complicity in, or attempt to commit any of those offenses;

(b) A person who is serving a term of imprisonment for any felony other than carrying a concealed weapon that was committed while the person had a firearm, as defined in section 2923.11 of the Revised Code, on or about the offender's person or under the offender's control;

(c) A person who is serving a term of imprisonment for a violation of section 2925.03 of the Revised Code;

(d) A person who is serving a term of imprisonment for engaging in a pattern of corrupt activity;

(e) A person who is serving a prison term or term of life imprisonment without parole imposed pursuant to section 2971.03 of the Revised Code;

(f) A person who was denied parole or release pursuant to section 2929.20 of the Revised Code during the term of imprisonment the person currently is serving.

(2) A declaration of the governor that requires the adult parole authority to take the action set forth in division (B) of this section shall be implemented only by reducing the prison terms of prisoners who are not in any of the categories set forth in division (E)(1) of this section, and only by granting reductions of prison terms in the following order:

(a) Under any such declaration, prison terms initially shall be reduced only for persons who are not in any of the categories set forth in division (E)(1) of this section and who are not serving a term of imprisonment for any of the following offenses:

(i) An offense of violence that is a felony of the first, second, or third degree or that, under the law in existence prior to the effective date of this amendment, was an aggravated felony of the first, second, or third degree or a felony of the first or second degree;

(ii) An offense set forth in Chapter 2925. of the Revised Code that is a felony of the first or second degree.

(b) If every person serving a term of imprisonment at the time of the implementation of any such declaration who is in the class of persons eligible for the initial reduction of prison terms, as described in division (E)(2)(a) of this section, has received a total of ninety days of term reduction for each three years of imprisonment actually served, then prison terms may be reduced for all other persons serving a term of imprisonment at that time who are not in any of the categories set forth in division (E)(1) of this section.

(F) An offender who is released from a state correctional institution pursuant to this section is subject to post-release control sanctions imposed by the adult parole authority as if the offender was a prisoner described in division (B) of section 2967.28 of the Revised Code who was being released from imprisonment.

(G) If more than one overcrowding emergency is declared while a prisoner is serving a prison term, the total term reduction for that prisoner as the result of multiple declarations shall not exceed ninety days for each three years of imprisonment actually served.

(1996 H 180, eff. 1–1–97; 1996 H 445, eff. 9–3–96; 1995 S 2, eff. 7–1–96; 1994 H 571, eff. 10–6–94; 1993 H 152, eff. 7–1–93; 1991 H 298; 1987 H 262; 1982 H 269, S 199)

2967.191 Credit for confinement awaiting trial and commitment

The department of rehabilitation and correction shall reduce the stated prison term of a prisoner or, if the prisoner is serving a term for which there is parole eligibility, the minimum and maximum term or the parole eligibility date of the prisoner by the total number of days that the prisoner was confined for any reason arising out of the offense for which the prisoner was convicted and sentenced, including confinement in lieu of bail while awaiting trial, confinement for examination to determine the prisoner's competence to stand trial or sanity, and confinement while awaiting transportation to the place where the prisoner is to serve the prisoner's prison term.

(1997 S 111, eff. 3–17–98; 1996 S 269, eff. 7–1–96; 1995 S 2, eff. 7–1–96; 1982 H 269, § 4, eff. 7–1–83; 1982 S 199; 1980 H 1000; 1978 H 565; 1972 H 511; 131 v S 133)

2967.193 Deduction from sentence for participation in certain programs; procedures

(A) Except as provided in division (C) of this section or in section 2929.13, 2929.14, or 2967.13 of the Revised Code, a person confined in a state correctional institution may earn one day of credit as a deduction from the person's stated prison term for each full month during which the person productively participates in an education program, vocational training, employment in prison industries, treatment for substance abuse, treatment as a sex offender, or any other constructive program developed by the department with specific standards for performance by prisoners. At the end of each calendar month in which a prisoner productively participates in a program or activity listed in this division, the department of rehabilitation and correction shall deduct one day from the date on which the prisoner's stated prison term will expire. If the prisoner violates prison rules, the department may deny the prisoner a credit that otherwise could have been awarded to the prisoner or may withdraw one or more credits previously earned by the prisoner.

If a prisoner is released before the expiration of the prisoner's stated prison term by reason of credit earned under this section, the department shall retain control of the prisoner by means of an appropriate post-release control sanction imposed by the parole board until the end of the stated prison term if the parole board imposes a post-release control sanction pursuant to section 2967.28 of the Revised Code. If the parole board is not required to impose a post-release control sanction under section 2967.28 of the Revised Code, the parole board may elect not to impose a post-release control sanction on the prisoner.

(B) The department of rehabilitation and correction shall adopt rules that specify the programs or activities for which credit may be earned under this section, the criteria for determining productive participation in the programs or activities and for awarding credit, and the criteria for denying or withdrawing previously earned credit as a result of a violation of prison rules.

(C) No person who is serving a sentence of life imprisonment without parole imposed pursuant to section 2929.03 or 2929.06 of the Revised Code or who is serving a prison term or a term of life imprisonment without parole imposed pursuant to section 2971.03 of the Revised Code shall be awarded any days of credit under division (A) of this section.

(1996 H 180, eff. 1–1–97; 1996 S 269, eff. 7–1–96; 1995 S 2, eff. 7–1–96; 1994 H 571, eff. 10–6–94; 1992 H 725, eff. 4–16–93; 1990 S 258; 1987 H 261)

2967.21 Effect of transfer on term of sentence

Any prisoner sentenced or committed to a state correctional institution may be transferred from that institution to another state correctional institution, but the prisoner shall continue to be subject to the same conditions as to the stated prison term, parole, and release as if the prisoner were confined in the institution to which the prisoner originally was sentenced or committed.

(1995 S 2, eff. 7–1–96; 1994 H 571, eff. 10–6–94; 130 v Pt 2, H 28, eff. 3–18–65)

2967.22 Parolee or person under community control sanction or supervised release appearing to be mentally ill; procedures; effects of escape and of return

Whenever it is brought to the attention of the adult parole authority or a department of probation that a parolee, person under a community control sanction, person under transitional control, or releasee appears to be a mentally ill person subject to hospitalization by court order, as defined in section 5122.01 of the Revised Code, or a mentally retarded person subject to institutionalization by court order, as defined in section 5123.01 of the Revised Code, the parole or probation officer, subject to the approval of the chief of the adult parole authority, the designee of the chief of the adult parole authority, or the chief probation officer, may file an affidavit under section 5122.11 or 5123.71 of the Revised Code. A parolee, person under a community control sanction, or releasee who is involuntarily detained under Chapter 5122. or 5123. of the Revised Code shall receive credit against the period of parole or community control or the term of post-release control for the period of involuntary detention.

If a parolee, person under a community control sanction, person under transitional control, or releasee escapes from an institution or facility within the department of mental health or the department of mental retardation and developmental disabilities, the superintendent of the institution immediately shall notify the chief of the adult parole authority or the chief probation officer. Notwithstanding the provisions of section 5122.26 of the Revised Code, the procedure for the apprehension, detention, and return of the parolee, person under a community control sanction, person under transitional control, or releasee is the same as that provided for the apprehension, detention, and return of persons who escape from institutions operated by the department of rehabilitation and correction. If the escaped parolee, person under transitional control, or releasee is not apprehended and returned to the custody of the department of mental health or the department of mental retardation and developmental disabilities within ninety days after the escape, the parolee, person under transitional control, or releasee shall be discharged from the custody of the department of mental health or the department of mental retardation and developmental disabilities and returned to the custody of the department of rehabilitation and correction. If the escaped person under a community control sanction is not apprehended and returned to the custody of the department of mental health or the department of mental retardation and developmental disabilities within ninety days after the escape, the person under a community control sanction shall be discharged from the custody of the department of mental health or the department of mental retardation and developmental disabilities and returned to the custody of the court that sentenced that person.

(2002 H 490, eff. 1–1–04; 1997 S 111, eff. 3–17–98; 1995 S 2, eff. 7–1–96; 1990 H 569, eff. 7–1–91; 1980 H 965, S 52; 1978 H 565; 1972 H 494; 130 v Pt 2, H 28)

2967.26 Transitional control program; fund

(A)(1) The department of rehabilitation and correction, by rule, may establish a transitional control program for the purpose of closely monitoring a prisoner's adjustment to community supervision during the final one hundred eighty days of the prisoner's confinement. If the department establishes a transitional control program under this division, the adult parole authority may transfer eligible prisoners to transitional control status under the program during the final one hundred eighty days of their confinement and under the terms and conditions established by the department, shall provide for the confinement as provided in this division of each eligible prisoner so transferred, and shall supervise each eligible prisoner so transferred in one or more community control sanctions. Each eligible prisoner who is transferred to transitional control status under the program shall be confined in a suitable facility that is licensed pursuant to division (C) of section 2967.14 of the Revised Code, or shall be confined in a residence the department has approved for this purpose and be monitored pursuant to an electronic monitoring device, as defined in section 2929.01 of the Revised Code. If the department establishes a transitional control program under this division, the rules establishing the program shall include criteria that define which prisoners are eligible for the program, criteria that must be satisfied to be approved as a residence that may be used for confinement under the program of a prisoner that is transferred to it and procedures for the department to approve residences that satisfy those criteria, and provisions of the type described in division (C) of this section. At a minimum, the criteria that define which prisoners are eligible for the program shall provide all of the following:

(a) That a prisoner is eligible for the program if the prisoner is serving a prison term or term of imprisonment for an offense committed prior to March 17, 1998, and if, at the time at which eligibility is being determined, the prisoner would have been eligible for a furlough under this section as it existed immediately prior to March 17, 1998, or would have been eligible for conditional release under former section 2967.23 of the Revised Code as that section existed immediately prior to March 17, 1998;

(b) That no prisoner who is serving a mandatory prison term is eligible for the program until after expiration of the mandatory term;

(c) That no prisoner who is serving a prison term or term of life imprisonment without parole imposed pursuant to section 2971.03 of the Revised Code is eligible for the program.

(2) At least three weeks prior to transferring to transitional control under this section a prisoner who is serving a term of imprisonment or prison term for an offense committed on or after July 1, 1996, the adult parole authority shall give notice of the pendency of the transfer to transitional control to the court of common pleas of the county in which the indictment against the prisoner was found and of the fact that the court may disapprove the transfer of the prisoner to transitional control and shall include a report prepared by the head of the state correctional institution in which the prisoner is confined. The head of the state correctional institution in which the prisoner is confined, upon the request of the adult parole authority, shall provide to the authority for inclusion in the notice sent to the court under this division a report on the prisoner's conduct in the institution and in any institution from which the prisoner may have been transferred. The report shall cover the prisoner's participation in school, vocational training, work, treatment, and other rehabilitative activities and any disciplinary action taken against the prisoner. If the court disapproves of the transfer of the prisoner to transitional control, the court shall notify the authority of the disapproval within thirty days after receipt of the notice. If the court timely disapproves the transfer of the prisoner to transitional control, the authority shall not proceed with the transfer. If the court does not timely disapprove the transfer of the prisoner to transitional control, the authority may transfer the prisoner to transitional control.

(3) If the victim of an offense for which a prisoner was sentenced to a prison term or term of imprisonment has requested notification under section 2930.16 of the Revised Code and has provided the department of rehabilitation and correction with the victim's name and address, the adult parole authority, at least three weeks prior to transferring the prisoner to transitional control pursuant to this section, shall notify the victim of the pendency of the transfer and of the victim's right to submit a statement to the authority regarding the impact of the transfer of the prisoner to transitional control. If the victim subsequently submits a statement of that nature to the authority, the authority shall consider the statement in deciding whether to transfer the prisoner to transitional control.

(B) Each prisoner transferred to transitional control under this section shall be confined in the manner described in division (A) of this section during any period of time that the prisoner is not actually working at the prisoner's approved employment, engaged in a vocational training or another educational program, engaged in another program designated by the director, or engaged in other activities approved by the department.

(C) The department of rehabilitation and correction shall adopt rules for transferring eligible prisoners to transitional control, supervising and confining prisoners so transferred, administering the transitional control program in accordance with this section, and using the moneys deposited into the transitional control fund established under division (E) of this section.

(D) The department of rehabilitation and correction may adopt rules for the issuance of passes for the limited purposes described in this division to prisoners who are transferred to transitional control under this section. If the department adopts rules of that nature, the rules shall govern the granting of the passes and shall provide for the supervision of prisoners who are temporarily released pursuant to one of those passes. Upon the adoption of rules under this division, the department may issue passes to prisoners who are transferred to transitional control status under this section in accordance with the rules and the provisions of this division. All passes issued under this division shall be for a maximum of forty-eight hours and may be issued only for the following purposes:

(1) To visit a relative in imminent danger of death;

(2) To have a private viewing of the body of a deceased relative;

(3) To visit with family;

(4) To otherwise aid in the rehabilitation of the prisoner.

(E) The adult parole authority may require a prisoner who is transferred to transitional control to pay to the division of parole and community services the reasonable expenses incurred by the division in supervising or confining the prisoner while under transitional control. Inability to pay those reasonable expenses shall not be grounds for refusing to transfer an otherwise eligible prisoner to transitional control. Amounts received by the division of parole and community services under this division shall be deposited into the transitional control fund, which is hereby created in the state treasury and which hereby replaces and succeeds the furlough services fund that formerly existed in the state treasury. All moneys that remain in the furlough services fund on March 17, 1998, shall be transferred on that date to the transitional control fund. The transitional control fund shall be used solely to pay costs related to the operation of the transitional control program established under this section. The director of rehabilitation and correction shall adopt rules in accordance with section 111.15 of the Revised Code for the use of the fund.

(F) A prisoner who violates any rule established by the department of rehabilitation and correction under division (A), (C), or (D) of this section may be transferred to a state correctional institution pursuant to rules adopted under division (A), (C), or (D) of this section, but the prisoner shall receive credit towards completing the prisoner's sentence for the time spent under transitional control.

If a prisoner is transferred to transitional control under this section, upon successful completion of the period of transitional control, the prisoner may be released on parole or under post-release control pursuant to section 2967.13 or 2967.28 of the Revised Code and rules adopted by the department of rehabilitation and correction. If the prisoner is released under post-release control, the duration of the post-release control, the type of post-release control sanctions that may be imposed, the enforcement of the sanctions, and the treatment of prisoners who violate any sanction applicable to the prisoner are governed by section 2967.28 of the Revised Code.

(2002 H 490, eff. 1–1–04; 2002 H 510, eff. 3–31–03; 1999 S 107, eff. 3–23–00; 1997 S 111, eff. 3–17–98; 1996 H 180, eff. 1–1–97; 1995 S 2, eff. 7–1–96; 1994 S 186, eff. 10–12–94; 1994 H 571, eff. 10–6–94; 1993 H 152, eff. 7–1–93; 1988 S 94; 1983 S 210; 1982 H 269, § 4, S 199; 1981 H 694, S 1; 1976 H 637; 1971 H 567)

2967.27 Escorted visits

(A)(1) The department of rehabilitation and correction may grant escorted visits to prisoners confined in any state correctional facility for the limited purpose of visiting a relative in imminent danger of death or having a private viewing of the body of a deceased relative.

(2) Prior to granting any prisoner an escorted visit for the limited purpose of visiting a relative in imminent danger of death or having a private viewing of the body of a deceased relative under this section, the department shall notify its office of victims' services so that the office may provide assistance to any victim or victims of the offense committed by the prisoner and to members of the family of the victim.

(B) The department of rehabilitation and correction shall adopt rules for the granting of escorted visits under this section and for supervising prisoners on an escorted visit.

(C) No prisoner shall be granted an escorted visit under this section if the prisoner is likely to pose a threat to the public safety or has a record of more than two felony commitments (including the present charge), not more than one of which may be for a crime of an assaultive nature.

(D) The procedure for granting an escorted visit under this section is separate from, and independent of, the transitional control program described in section 2967.26 of the Revised Code.

(2002 H 510, eff. 3–31–03; 1997 S 111, eff. 3–17–98; 1996 H 180, eff. 1–1–97; 1996 S 269, eff. 7–1–96; 1995 S 2, eff. 7–1–96; 1994 S 186, eff. 10–12–94; 1994 H 571, eff. 10–6–94; 1981 S 1, eff. 10–19–81; 1974 H 217)

2967.28 Post–release control

(A) As used in this section:

(1) "Monitored time" means the monitored time sanction specified in section 2929.17 of the Revised Code.

(2) "Deadly weapon" and "dangerous ordnance" have the same meanings as in section 2923.11 of the Revised Code.

(3) "Felony sex offense" means a violation of a section contained in Chapter 2907. of the Revised Code that is a felony.

(B) Each sentence to a prison term for a felony of the first degree, for a felony of the second degree, for a felony sex offense, or for a felony of the third degree that is not a felony sex offense and in the commission of which the offender caused or threatened to cause physical harm to a person shall include a requirement that the offender be subject to a period of post-release control imposed by the parole board after the offender's release from imprisonment. Unless reduced by the parole board pursuant to division (D) of this section when authorized under that division, a period of post-release control required by this division for an offender shall be of one of the following periods:

(1) For a felony of the first degree or for a felony sex offense, five years;

(2) For a felony of the second degree that is not a felony sex offense, three years;

(3) For a felony of the third degree that is not a felony sex offense and in the commission of which the offender caused or threatened physical harm to a person, three years.

(C) Any sentence to a prison term for a felony of the third, fourth, or fifth degree that is not subject to division (B)(1) or (3) of this section shall include a requirement that the offender be subject to a period of post-release control of up to three years after the offender's release from imprisonment, if the parole board, in accordance with division (D) of this section, determines that a period of post-release control is necessary for that offender.

(D)(1) Before the prisoner is released from imprisonment, the parole board shall impose upon a prisoner described in division (B) of this section, may impose upon a prisoner described in division (C) of this section, and shall impose upon a prisoner described in division (B)(2)(b) of section 5120.031 or in division (B)(1) of section 5120.032 of the Revised Code, one or more post-release control sanctions to apply during the prisoner's period of post-release control. Whenever the board imposes one or more post-release control sanctions upon a prisoner, the board, in addition to imposing the sanctions, also shall include as a condition of the post-release control that the individual or felon not leave the state without permission of the court or the individual's or felon's parole or probation officer and that the individual or felon abide by the law. The board may impose any other conditions of release under a post-release control sanction that the board considers appropriate, and the conditions of release may include any community residential sanction, community nonresidential sanction, or financial sanction that the sentencing court was authorized to impose pursuant to sections 2929.16, 2929.17, and 2929.18 of the Revised Code. Prior to the release of a prisoner for whom it will impose one or more post-release control sanctions under this division, the parole board shall review the prisoner's criminal history, all juvenile court adjudications finding the prisoner, while a juvenile, to be a delinquent child, and the record of the prisoner's conduct while imprisoned. The parole board shall consider any recommendation regarding post-release control sanctions for the prisoner made by the office of victims' services. After considering those materials, the board shall determine, for a prisoner described in division (B) of this section, division (B)(2)(b) of section 5120.031, or division (B)(1) of section 5120.032 of the Revised Code, which post-release control sanction or combination of post-release control sanctions is reasonable under the circumstances or, for a prisoner described in division (C) of this section, whether a post-release control sanction is necessary and, if so, which post-release control sanction or combination of post-release control sanctions is reasonable under the circumstances. In the case of a prisoner convicted of a felony of the fourth or fifth degree other than a felony sex offense, the board shall presume that monitored time is the appropriate post-release control sanction unless the board determines that a more restrictive sanction is warranted. A post-release control sanction imposed under this division takes effect upon the prisoner's release from imprisonment.

(2) At any time after a prisoner is released from imprisonment and during the period of post-release control applicable to the releasee, the adult parole authority may review the releasee's behavior under the post-release control sanctions imposed upon the releasee under this section. The authority may determine, based upon the review and in accordance with the standards established under division (E) of this section, that a more restrictive or a less restrictive sanction is appropriate and may impose a different sanction. Unless the period of post-release control was imposed for an offense described in division (B)(1) of this section, the authority also may recommend that the parole board reduce the duration of the period of post-release control imposed by the court. If the authority recommends that the board reduce the duration of control for an offense described in division (B)(2), (B)(3), or (C) of this section, the board shall review the releasee's behavior and may reduce the duration of the period of control imposed by the court. In no case shall the board reduce the duration of the period of control imposed by the court for an offense described in division (B)(1) of this section, and in no case shall the board permit the releasee to leave the state without permission of the court or the releasee's parole or probation officer.

(E) The department of rehabilitation and correction, in accordance with Chapter 119. of the Revised Code, shall adopt rules that do all of the following:

(1) Establish standards for the imposition by the parole board of post-release control sanctions under this section that are consistent with the overriding purposes and sentencing principles set forth in section 2929.11 of the Revised Code and that are appropriate to the needs of releasees;

(2) Establish standards by which the parole board can determine which prisoners described in division (C) of this section should be placed under a period of post-release control;

(3) Establish standards to be used by the parole board in reducing the duration of the period of post-release control imposed by the court when authorized under division (D) of this section, in imposing a more restrictive post-release control sanction than monitored time upon a prisoner convicted of a felony of the fourth or fifth degree other than a felony sex offense, or in imposing a less restrictive control sanction upon a releasee based on the releasee's activities including, but not limited to, remaining free from criminal activity and from the abuse of alcohol or other drugs, successfully participating in approved rehabilitation programs, maintaining employment, and paying restitution to the victim or meeting the terms of other financial sanctions;

(4) Establish standards to be used by the adult parole authority in modifying a releasee's post-release control sanctions pursuant to division (D)(2) of this section;

(5) Establish standards to be used by the adult parole authority or parole board in imposing further sanctions under division (F) of this section on releasees who violate post-release control sanctions, including standards that do the following:

(a) Classify violations according to the degree of seriousness;

(b) Define the circumstances under which formal action by the parole board is warranted;

(c) Govern the use of evidence at violation hearings;

(d) Ensure procedural due process to an alleged violator;

(e) Prescribe nonresidential community control sanctions for most misdemeanor and technical violations;

(f) Provide procedures for the return of a releasee to imprisonment for violations of post-release control.

(F)(1) If a post-release control sanction is imposed upon an offender under this section, the offender upon release from imprisonment shall be under the general jurisdiction of the adult parole authority and generally shall be supervised by the field services section through its staff of parole and field officers as described in section 5149.04 of the Revised Code, as if the offender had been placed on parole. If the offender upon release from imprisonment violates the post-release control sanction or any conditions described in division (A) of section 2967.131 of the Revised Code that are imposed on the offender, the public or private person or entity that operates or administers the sanction or the program or activity that comprises the sanction shall report the violation directly to the adult parole authority or to the officer of the authority who supervises the offender. The authority's officers may treat the offender as if the offender were on parole and in violation of the parole, and otherwise shall comply with this section.

(2) If the adult parole authority determines that a releasee has violated a post-release control sanction or any conditions described in division (A) of section 2967.131 of the Revised Code imposed upon the releasee and that a more restrictive sanction is appropriate, the authority may impose a more restrictive sanction upon the releasee, in accordance with the standards established under division (E) of this section, or may report the violation to the parole board for a hearing pursuant to division (F)(3) of this section. The authority may not, pursuant to this division, increase the duration of the releasee's post-release control or impose as a post-release control sanction a residential sanction that includes a prison term, but the authority may impose on the releasee any other residential sanction, nonresidential sanction, or financial sanction that the sentencing court was authorized to impose pursuant to sections 2929.16, 2929.17, and 2929.18 of the Revised Code.

(3) The parole board may hold a hearing on any alleged violation by a releasee of a post-release control sanction or any conditions described in division (A) of section 2967.131 of the Revised Code that are imposed upon the releasee. If after the hearing the board finds that the releasee violated the sanction or condition, the board may increase the duration of the releasee's post-release control up to the maximum duration authorized by division (B) or (C) of this section or impose a more restrictive post-release control sanction. When appropriate, the board may impose as a post-release control sanction a residential sanction that includes a prison term. The board shall consider a prison term as a post-release control sanction imposed for a violation of post-release control when the violation involves a deadly weapon or dangerous ordnance, physical harm or attempted serious physical harm to a person, or sexual misconduct, or when the releasee committed repeated violations of post-release control sanctions. The period of a prison term that is imposed as a post-release control sanction under this division shall not exceed nine months, and the maximum cumulative prison term for all violations under this division shall not exceed one half of the stated prison term originally imposed upon the offender as part of this sentence. The period of a prison term that is imposed as a post-release control sanction under this division shall not count as, or be credited toward, the remaining period of post-release control.

If an offender is imprisoned for a felony committed while under post-release control supervision and is again released on post-release control for a period of time determined by division (F)(4)(d) of this section, the maximum cumulative prison term for all violations under this division shall not exceed one-half of the total stated prison terms of the earlier felony, reduced by any prison term administratively imposed by the parole board, plus one-half of the total stated prison term of the new felony.

(4) Any period of post-release control shall commence upon an offender's actual release from prison. If an offender is serving an indefinite prison term or a life sentence in addition to a stated prison term, the offender shall serve the period of post-release control in the following manner:

(a) If a period of post-release control is imposed upon the offender and if the offender also is subject to a period of parole under a life sentence or an indefinite sentence, and if the period of post-release control ends prior to the period of parole, the offender shall be supervised on parole. The offender shall receive credit for post-release control supervision during the period of parole. The offender is not eligible for final release under section 2967.16 of the Revised Code until the post-release control period otherwise would have ended.

(b) If a period of post-release control is imposed upon the offender and if the offender also is subject to a period of parole under an indefinite sentence, and if the period of parole ends prior to the period of post-release control, the offender shall be supervised on post-release control. The requirements of parole supervision shall be satisfied during the post-release control period.

(c) If an offender is subject to more than one period of post-release control, the period of post-release control for all of the sentences shall be the period of post-release control that expires last, as determined by the parole board. Periods of post-release control shall be served concurrently and shall not be imposed consecutively to each other.

(d) The period of post-release control for a releasee who commits a felony while under post-release control for an earlier felony shall be the longer of the period of post-release control specified for the new felony under division (B) or (C) of this section or the time remaining under the period of post-release control imposed for the earlier felony as determined by the parole board.

(2002 H 510, eff. 3–31–03; 2002 H 327, eff. 7–8–02; 1999 S 107, eff. 3–23–00; 1997 S 111, eff. 3–17–98; 1996 S 269, eff. 7–1–96; 1995 S 2, eff. 7–1–96)

CHAPTER 2969

RECOVERY OF OFFENDER'S PROFITS; CRIME VICTIMS RECOVERY FUND; CIVIL ACTIONS OR APPEALS BY INMATE

RECOVERY OF OFFENDER'S PROFITS

RECOVERY OF OFFENDER'S PROFITS

2969.01 Definitions

As used in sections 2969.01 to 2969.06 of the Revised Code:

(A) "Offender" means a person who pleads guilty to, is convicted of, or is found not guilty by reason of insanity of an offense in this state or a person against whom a complaint or information has been filed or an indictment has been returned in this state.

(B) "Victim" means a person who suffers personal injury, death, or property loss as a result of any of the following, or the beneficiaries of an action for the wrongful death of any person killed as a result of any of the following:

(1) An offense;

(2) The good faith effort of a person to prevent an offense;

(3) The good faith effort of any person to apprehend a person suspected of engaging in an offense.

(C) "Member of the family of an offender" means an individual who is related by consanguinity or affinity to an offender.

(1995 S 91, eff. 11-15-95; 1984 S 172, eff. 9-26-84)

2969.02 Offender's contract to publish material related to his offense; money due to be paid to clerk of court of claims; liability

(A) Except as provided in section 2969.05 of the Revised Code, a person that enters into a contract with an offender, an agent, assignee, conspirator, or accomplice of an offender, a member of the family of an offender, or an agent or assignee of a member of the family of an offender shall pay the money, and the monetary value of the property other than money, due under the contract to the clerk of the court of claims for deposit in the recovery of offender's profits fund, if the terms of the contract provide for any of the following:

(1) The reenactment or description by the offender or by a member of the family of the offender in any of the following of an offense that the offender committed:

(a) A movie, book, magazine, newspaper, article, or other form of literary expression;

(b) A program on television, radio, or another broadcasting medium;

(c) A play, speech, or another form of live entertainment, instruction, or presentation.

(2) The expression or description of the thoughts, feelings, opinions, or emotions of the offender or of a member of the family of the offender regarding or experienced during the offense in a material, performance, or program described in division (A)(1)(a), (b), or (c) of this section;

(3) The life story or a part of the life story of the offender or of a member of the family of the offender or an interview or a part of an interview with the offender, an agent, assignee, conspirator, or accomplice of the offender, a member of the family of the offender, or an agent or assignee of a member of the family of an offender that is to be used in a material, performance, or program described in division (A)(1)(a), (b), or (c) of this section, if the publication value of the story or interview results in part from the notoriety brought by the commission of an offense.

(B) An offender, an agent, assignee, conspirator, or accomplice of an offender, a member of the family of an offender, or an agent or assignee of a member of the family of an offender who enters into a contract described in division (A) of this section or a person who receives money or property other than money pursuant to a contract of that nature shall pay the money or the monetary value of the property received pursuant to the contract to the clerk of the court of claims for deposit in the recovery of offender's profits fund. If a person receives money or property pursuant to a contract described in division (A) of this section and fails to pay it or its monetary value to the clerk of the court of claims for deposit in the fund as required by this division, the state has a lien upon the money or property and upon property that is purchased or otherwise obtained with the money or property. The attorney general shall enforce the lien in the same manner as a judgment lien may be enforced by a private individual.

(C)(1) A person who fails to pay money or the monetary value of property other than money to the clerk of the court of claims for deposit as required by this section is liable to the state for the money or the monetary value of the property.

(2) If a person who is required by this section to pay money or the monetary value of property other than money to the clerk of the court of claims for deposit in the recovery of offender's profits fund fails to do so, the attorney general shall bring an action to recover the money or the monetary value of the property against the person who has possession, custody, or control of the money or property or against the person who failed to pay the money or the monetary value of the property to the clerk for deposit in the fund as required by this section. The action shall be brought in the appropriate court. If the court determines in an action brought pursuant to this division that money or the monetary value of property is to be paid to the clerk for deposit in the fund, it shall order that the money be paid to the clerk for deposit in the fund and that the property be sold and the money received from the sale be paid to the clerk for deposit in the fund.

(1995 S 91, eff. 11-15-95; 1985 H 201, eff. 7-1-85; 1984 S 172)

2969.03 Any person may bring declaratory judgment action concerning such a contract

Any person may bring an action for a declaratory judgment to determine if section 2969.02 of the Revised Code applies to a particular contract. The action for a declaratory judgment shall be brought in the Franklin county court of common pleas.

(1984 S 172, eff. 9-26-84)

2969.04 Administration of recovery of offender's profits fund; separate accounts; procedures

(A) The clerk of the court of claims shall administer the recovery of offender's profits fund created by section 2969.06 of the Revised Code and shall maintain in the fund in the name of each offender a separate account for money received, or money received from the sale or other disposition of property, pursuant to section 2969.02 or 2969.03 of the Revised Code. The clerk shall distribute the money in each account in accordance with division (C) of this section.

If money is deposited in the fund and maintained in a separate account in the name of an offender and if the offender is found not guilty of all of the charges against the offender in this state, all of the charges against the offender in this state are dismissed, or the offender is found not guilty of some of the charges against the offender in this state and the remaining charges against the offender in this state are dismissed, the clerk shall return all of the money in the separate account plus the interest earned on the money to the persons from whom it was obtained.

(B) Notwithstanding a contrary provision of any section of the Revised Code that deals with the limitation of actions, a victim of an offense committed by an offender in whose name a separate account is maintained in the recovery of offender's profits fund may bring a civil action against the offender or the representatives of the offender, and, if money in the separate account was obtained from a member of the family of the offender or an agent or assignee of a member of the family of the offender, against the family member, agent, or assignee at any time within three years after the establishment of the separate account.

In order to recover from a separate account maintained in the fund in thc name of an offender, a victim of that offender shall do all of the following:

(1) Within the three-year period or, if the action was initiated before the separate account was established, within ninety days after the separate account is established, notify the clerk of the court of claims that a civil action has been brought against the offender or the representatives of the offender and, if money in the separate account was obtained from a member of the family of the offender or an agent or assignee of a member of the family of the offender, against the family member, agent, or assignee;

(2) Notify the clerk of the court of claims of the entry of any judgment in the civil action;

(3) Within ninety days after the judgment in the civil action is final or, if the judgment was obtained before the separate account

was established, within ninety days after the separate account is established, request the clerk of the court of claims to pay from the separate account the judgment that the victim is awarded in the civil action.

If a civil action is brought against an offender or the representatives of the offender and, if money in the separate account was obtained from a member of the family of the offender or an agent or assignee of a member of the family of the offender, against the family member, agent, or assignee and if the civil action is brought after the expiration of the statute of limitations that would apply to the civil action but for this division, the court shall state in a judgment in favor of the victim that the judgment may be enforced only against the separate account maintained in the name of that offender in the recovery of offender's profits fund.

(C) (1) The clerk of the court of claims shall not make a payment from the separate account maintained in the name of an offender in the recovery of offender's profits fund to a victim of the offender until the expiration of the later of the following periods:

(a) The expiration of three years after the establishment of the separate account, provided that no action of which the clerk was notified under division (B)(1) of this section is pending;

(b) If three years has elapsed since the establishment of the separate account and if one or more actions of which the clerk was notified under division (B)(1) of this section is pending at the expiration of that three-year period, the date of the final disposition of the last of those pending actions.

(2) Upon the expiration of the applicable period of time set forth in division (C)(1) of this section, the clerk of the court of claims shall make payments from the separate account maintained in the name of an offender in the recovery of offender's profits fund to any victim of the offender who has obtained a judgment against the offender or the representatives of the offender and, if money in the separate account was obtained from a member of the family of the offender or an agent or assignee of a member of the family of the offender, against the family member, agent, or assignee for damages resulting from an offense committed by the offender. The payments shall be made as provided in this division.

After an offender in whose name a separate account is maintained in the recovery of offender's profits fund is convicted of or found not guilty by reason of insanity of any offense in this state, the clerk of the court of claims shall determine on the second day of January and the first day of April, July, and October of each year the amount of money in that separate account. After the expiration of the applicable period of time set forth in division (C)(1) of this section, the clerk shall pay from that separate account any judgment for which a victim of that offender has requested payment pursuant to division (B)(3) of this section and has requested payment prior to the date of the most recent quarterly determination described in this division. If, at a time that payments would be made from that separate account, there are insufficient funds in that separate account to pay all of the applicable judgments against the offender or the representatives of the offender and, if money in the separate account was obtained from a member of the family of the offender or an agent or asignee [sic.] of a member of the family of the offender, against the family member, agent, or assignee, the clerk of the court of claims shall pay the judgments on a pro rata basis.

(1995 S 91, eff. 11–15–95; 1985 H 201, eff. 7–1–85; 1984 S 172)

2969.05 Distribution of moneys

If a separate account has been maintained in the recovery of offender's profits fund and if there is no further requirement to pay money or the monetary value of property into the fund pursuant to section 2969.02 of the Revised Code, unless otherwise ordered by a court of record in which a judgment has been rendered against the offender or the representatives of the offender and, if money in the separate account was obtained from a member of the family of the offender or an agent or assignee of a member of the family of the offender, against the family member, agent, or assignee, the clerk of the court of claims shall pay the money remaining in the separate account to the persons from whom the money was obtained, if all of the following apply:

(A) The applicable period of time that governs the making of payments from the separate account, as set forth in division (C)(1) of section 2969.04 of the Revised Code, has elapsed.

(B) None of the civil actions against the offender or the representatives of the offender and, if money in the separate account was obtained from a member of the family of the offender or an agent or assignee of a member of the family of the offender, against the family member, agent, or assignee of which the clerk of the court of claims has been notified pursuant to division (B)(1) of section 2969.04 of the Revised Code is pending.

(C) All judgments for which payment was requested pursuant to division (B)(3) of section 2969.04 of the Revised Code have been paid.

(1995 S 91, eff. 11–15–95; 1985 H 201, eff. 7–1–85; 1984 S 172)

2969.06 Recovery of offender's profits fund

All moneys collected pursuant to sections 2969.02 and 2969.03 of the Revised Code shall be credited by the treasurer of state to the recovery of offender's profits fund, which is hereby created in the state treasury. Except as provided in division (A) of section 2969.04 of the Revised Code, any interest earned on the money in the fund shall be credited to the fund.

(1985 H 201, eff. 7–1–85; 1984 S 172)

CRIME VICTIMS RECOVERY FUND

2969.11 Definitions

As used in sections 2969.11 to 2969.14 of the Revised Code:

(A) "Crime victims recovery fund" means the fund created by division (D) of section 2929.32 of the Revised Code.

(B) "Victim" means a person who suffers personal injury, death, or property loss as a result of any of the following, or the beneficiaries of an action for the wrongful death of any person killed as a result of any of the following:

(1) An offense committed by an offender in whose name a separate account is maintained in the crime victims recovery fund pursuant to section 2969.12 of the Revised Code;

(2) The good faith effort of a person to prevent an offense committed by an offender in whose name a separate account is maintained in the crime victims recovery fund pursuant to section 2969.12 of the Revised Code;

(3) The good faith effort of a person to apprehend a person suspected of engaging in an offense committed by an offender in whose name a separate account is maintained in the crime victims recovery fund pursuant to section 2969.12 of the Revised Code.

(2002 H 490, eff. 1–1–04; 1995 S 91, eff. 11–15–95)

2969.12 Administration of fund; separate accounts; civil actions; distribution of moneys

(A) The clerk of the court of claims shall administer the crime victims recovery fund and shall maintain in the fund in the name of each offender a separate account for money received, or money received from the sale or other disposition of property, pursuant to section 2929.32 of the Revised Code in connection with that offender. The clerk shall distribute the money in that separate account in accordance with division (C) of this section.

(B) Notwithstanding a contrary provision of any section of the Revised Code that deals with the limitation of actions, a victim of an offense committed by an offender in whose name a separate account is maintained in the crime victims recovery fund may bring a civil action against the offender or the representatives of the offender at any time within three years after the establishment of the separate account.

In order to recover from a separate account maintained in the fund in the name of an offender, a victim of that offender shall do all of the following:

(1) Within the three-year period or, if the action was initiated before the separate account was established, within ninety days after the separate account is established, notify the clerk of the court of claims that a civil action has been brought against the offender or the representatives of the offender;

(2) Notify the clerk of the court of claims of the entry of any judgment in the civil action;

(3) Within ninety days after the judgment in the civil action is final or, if the judgment was obtained before the separate account was established, within ninety days after the separate account is established, request the clerk of the court of claims to pay from the separate account the judgment that the victim is awarded in the civil action.

If a civil action is brought against an offender or the representatives of the offender after the expiration of the statute of limitations that would apply to the civil action but for this division, the court shall state in a judgment in favor of the victim that the judgment may be enforced only against the separate account maintained in the name of that offender in the crime victims recovery fund.

(C)(1) The clerk of the court of claims shall not make a payment from the separate account maintained in the name of an offender in the crime victims recovery fund to a victim of the offender until the expiration of the later of the following periods:

(a) The expiration of three years after the establishment of the separate account, provided that no action of which the clerk was notified under division (B)(1) of this section is pending;

(b) If three years has elapsed since the establishment of the separate account and if one or more actions of which the clerk was notified under division (B)(1) of this section is pending at the expiration of that three-year period, the date of the final disposition of the last of those pending actions.

(2) Upon the expiration of the applicable period of time set forth in division (C)(1) of this section, the clerk of the court of claims shall make payments from the separate account maintained in the name of the offender in the crime victims recovery fund to the victims of the offender who obtained a judgment against the offender or the representatives of the offender for damages resulting from the offense committed by the offender. The payments shall be made as provided in this division.

When a separate account is maintained in the name of an offender in the crime victims recovery fund, the clerk of the court of claims shall determine on the second day of January and the first day of April, July, and October of each year the amount of money in that separate account. After the expiration of the applicable period of time set forth in division (C)(1) of this section, the clerk shall pay from that separate account any judgment for which a victim of that offender has requested payment pursuant to division (B)(3) of this section and has requested payment prior to the date of the most recent quarterly determination described in this division. If at a time that payments would be made from that separate account there are insufficient funds in that separate account to pay all of the applicable judgments against the offender or the representatives of the offender, the clerk of the court of claims shall pay the judgments on a pro rata basis.

(2002 H 490, eff. 1-1-04; 1995 S 91, eff. 11-15-95)

2969.13 Moneys deposited in crime victims recovery fund

All moneys that are collected pursuant to section 2929.32 of the Revised Code and required to be deposited in the crime victims recovery fund shall be credited by the treasurer of state to the fund. Any interest earned on the money in the fund shall be credited to the fund.

(2002 H 490, eff. 1-1-04; 1995 S 91, eff. 11-15-95)

2969.14 Application of remainder of moneys to cover cost of incarceration

(A) If a separate account has been maintained in the name of an offender in the crime victims recovery fund and if there is no further requirement to pay into the fund money, or the monetary value of property, pursuant to section 2929.32 of the Revised Code, unless otherwise ordered by a court of record in which a judgment has been rendered against the offender or the representatives of the offender, the clerk of the court of claims shall pay the money remaining in the separate account in accordance with division (B) of this section, if all of the following apply:

(1) The applicable period of time that governs the making of payments from the separate account, as set forth in division (C)(1) of section 2969.12 of the Revised Code, has elapsed.

(2) None of the civil actions against the offender or the representatives of the offender of which the clerk of the court of claims has been notified pursuant to division (B)(1) of section 2969.12 of the Revised Code is pending.

(3) All judgments for which payment was requested pursuant to division (B)(3) of section 2969.12 of the Revised Code have been paid.

(B) If the clerk of the court of claims is required by division (A) of this section to pay the money remaining in the separate account established in the name of an offender in accordance with this division, the clerk shall pay the money as follows:

(1) If the offender was confined for a felony in a prison or other facility operated by the department of rehabilitation and correction under a sanction imposed pursuant to section 2929.14 or 2929.16 of the Revised Code, the clerk shall pay the money to the treasurer of state, in accordance with division (C)(1) of section 2929.18 of the Revised Code, to cover the costs of the confinement. If any money remains in the separate account after the payment of the costs of the confinement pursuant to this division, the clerk shall pay the remaining money in accordance with divisions (B)(2), (3), and (5) of this section.

(2) If the offender was confined for a felony in a facility operated by a county or a municipal corporation, after payment of any costs required to be paid under division (B)(1) of this section, the clerk shall pay the money to the treasurer of the county or of the municipal corporation that operated the facility, in accordance with division (C)(2) or (3) of section 2929.18 of the Revised Code, to cover the costs of the confinement. If more than one county or municipal corporation operated a facility in which the offender was confined, the clerk shall equitably apportion the money among each of those counties and municipal corporations. If any money remains in the separate account after the payment of the costs of the confinement pursuant to this division, the clerk shall pay the remaining money in accordance with divisions (B)(3) and (5) of this section.

(3) If the offender was sentenced for a felony to any community control sanction other than a sanction described in division

(B)(2) of this section, after payment of any costs required to be paid under division (B)(1) or (2) of this section, the clerk shall pay the money to the treasurer of the county or of the municipal corporation that incurred costs pursuant to the sanction, in accordance with division (C)(2) or (3) of section 2929.18 of the Revised Code, to cover the costs so incurred. If more than one county or municipal corporation incurred costs pursuant to the sanction, the clerk shall equitably apportion the money among each of those counties and municipal corporations. If any money remains in the separate account after the payment of the costs of the sanction pursuant to this division, the clerk shall pay the remaining money in accordance with division (B)(5) of this section.

(4) If the offender was imprisoned or incarcerated for a misdemeanor, to the treasurer of the political subdivision that operates the facility in which the offender was imprisoned or incarcerated, to cover the costs of the imprisonment or incarceration. If more than one political subdivision operated a facility in which the offender was confined, the clerk shall equitably apportion the money among each of those political subdivisions. If any money remains in the separate account after the payment of the costs of the imprisonment or incarceration under this division, the clerk shall pay the remaining money in accordance with division (B)(5) of this section.

(5) If any money remains in the separate account after payment of any costs required to be paid under division (B)(1), (2), (3), or (4) of this section, or if no provision of division (B)(1), (2), (3), or (4) of this section applies, the clerk shall distribute the amount of the money remaining in the separate account as otherwise provided by law for the distribution of money paid in satisfaction of a fine, as if that amount was a fine paid by the offender.

(2002 H 490, eff. 1–1–04; 1996 S 269, eff. 7–1–96; 1995 S 91, eff. 11–15–95)

CIVIL ACTIONS OR APPEALS BY INMATE

2969.21 Definitions

As used in sections 2969.21 to 2969.27 of the Revised Code:

(A) "Clerk" means the elected or appointed clerk of any court in this state, except the court of claims or the supreme court, in which an inmate has commenced a civil action against a government entity or employee or has filed an appeal of the judgment or order in a civil action of that nature.

(B)(1) "Civil action or appeal against a government entity or employee" means any of the following:

(a) A civil action that an inmate commences against the state, a political subdivision, or an employee of the state or a political subdivision in a court of common pleas, court of appeals, county court, or municipal court;

(b) An appeal of the judgment or order in a civil action of the type described in division (B)(1)(a) of this section that an inmate files in a court of appeals.

(2) "Civil action or appeal against a governmental entity or employee" does not include any civil action that an inmate commences against the state, a political subdivision, or an employee of the state or a political subdivision in the court of claims or the supreme court or an appeal of the judgment or order entered by the court of claims in a civil action of that nature, that an inmate files in a court of appeals or the supreme court.

(C) "Employee" means an officer or employee of the state or of a political subdivision who is acting under color of state law.

(D) "Inmate" means a person who is in actual confinement in a state correctional institution or in a county, multicounty, municipal, municipal-county, or multicounty-municipal jail or workhouse or a releasee who is serving a sanction in a violation sanction center.

(E) "Inmate account" means an account maintained by the department of rehabilitation and correction under rules adopted by the director of rehabilitation and correction pursuant to section 5120.01 of the Revised Code or a similar account maintained by a sheriff or any other administrator of a jail or workhouse or by the administrator of a violation sanction center.

(F) "Political subdivision" means a county, township, city, or village; the office of an elected officer of a county, township, city, or village; or a department, board, office, commission, agency, institution, or other instrumentality of a county, township, city, or village.

(G) "State" has the same meaning as in section 2743.01 of the Revised Code.

(H) "State correctional institution" has the same meaning as in section 2967.01 of the Revised Code.

(I) "Violation sanction center" means an alternative residential facility that houses releasees who have violated a post-release control sanction or the terms and conditions of parole or of a conditional pardon and that is operated pursuant to section 2967.141 of the Revised Code.

(2002 S 168, eff. 6–28–02; 1997 S 111, eff. 3–17–98; 1996 H 455, eff. 10–17–96)

2969.22 Procedures for payment of costs by inmate

(A)(1) Whenever an inmate commences a civil action or appeal against a government entity or employee on or after October 17, 1996, all of the following apply:

(a) The clerk of the court in which the civil action or appeal is filed shall notify the inmate and either the department of rehabilitation and correction, the sheriff or other administrator of the jail or workhouse, or the administrator of the violation sanction center, whichever has physical custody of the inmate, of the deductions and procedures required by divisions (A) to (D) of this section, and shall identify in the notice the civil action or appeal by case name, case number, name of each party, and the court in which the civil action or appeal was brought.

(b) The clerk of the court in which the civil action or appeal is filed shall charge to the inmate either the total payment of the requisite fees that are described in section 2303.20 of the Revised Code or that otherwise are applicable to actions or appeals filed in that court or, if the inmate has submitted an affidavit of indigency, all funds in the inmate account of that inmate in excess of ten dollars, and shall notify the inmate of the charge.

(c) Unless the amount charged under division (A)(1)(b) of this section constitutes the total amount of the requisite fees, all income in the inmate account of the inmate shall be forwarded to the clerk of the court during each calendar month following the month in which the inmate filed the civil action or appeal until the total payment of the requisite fees occurs. The first ten dollars in the inmate account of the inmate each month shall be excluded from that forwarding requirement. If multiple charges are assessed to an inmate account under this division, charges shall be calculated on the basis of the inmate's total income and shall be paid as described in this division until the charges exceed one hundred per cent of nonexcluded funds in the inmate account; thereafter, all unpaid fees shall be paid simultaneously from the inmate account of the inmate to the appropriate court or courts pro rata.

(d) Upon receipt of the notice of the requisite fees payable pursuant to divisions (A)(1)(a) to (c) of this section, the department, sheriff or other administrator of the jail or workhouse, or the administrator of the violation sanction center shall deduct from the inmate account of the inmate and transmit to the clerk of the appropriate court the appropriate amounts of the requisite fees as described in divisions (A)(1)(b) and (c) of this section.

(2) The procedures described in this section apply notwithstanding any contrary court rule or the filing of a poverty affidavit.

(3) This section does not limit the clerk of a court of common pleas, court of appeals, county court, or municipal court from considering any other inmate resources separate and apart from an inmate account of an inmate in evaluating the inmate's ability to pay court costs, fees, awards, or other amounts.

(B) An inmate who commences a civil action or appeal against a governmental entity or employee on or after October 17, 1996, shall be considered to have authorized payment as the plaintiff in the civil action or the appellant in the appeal of the requisite fees that are described in section 2303.20 of the Revised Code or that otherwise are applicable to actions or appeals filed in the court in which the action or appeal is filed, using the procedures set forth in this section, until total payment of the requisite fees.

(C)(1) If an inmate files a civil action or appeal against a government entity or employee on or after October 17, 1996, upon the termination of the civil action or appeal, the clerk of the court in which the action or appeal was filed shall notify the department of rehabilitation and correction, the sheriff or other administrator of the jail or workhouse, or the administrator of the violation sanction center of the outcome of the civil action or appeal and shall identify the civil action or appeal by case name, case number, name of each party, and the court in which the civil action or appeal was brought.

(2) The department of rehabilitation and correction, the sheriff or other administrator of a jail or workhouse, or the administrator of the violation sanction center shall keep in the inmate's file a record of the information supplied by the clerk of the appropriate court under division (C)(1) of this section.

(D) If an inmate is to be released from confinement prior to the total payment of the requisite fees as provided in divisions (A) and (B) of this section, the department of rehabilitation and correction, the sheriff or other administrator of the jail or workhouse, or the administrator of the violation sanction center, whichever has physical custody of the inmate, shall inform the clerk of the court of common pleas, court of appeals, county court, or municipal court of the release. The department, sheriff or other administrator of the jail or workhouse, or administrator of the violation sanction center shall deduct from the inmate account of the inmate in the month of the inmate's release from custody an amount sufficient to pay the remainder of the requisite fees owed and transmit that amount to the clerk. If there are insufficient funds in the inmate account of the inmate to totally pay the requisite fees, the department, sheriff or other administrator of the jail or workhouse, or administrator of the violation sanction center shall deduct the balance of the account and transmit that amount to the clerk. The clerk shall inform the court of the amount of the requisite fees still owed.

(2002 S 168, eff. 6–28–02; 1997 S 111, eff. 3–17–98; 1996 H 455, eff. 10–17–96)

2969.23 Collection of costs or fees

If an inmate files a civil action or appeal against a government entity or employee on or after the effective date of this section and if the inmate is ordered to pay court costs, an award of reasonable attorney's fees, or any other fees or expenses the clerk of the court in which the action or appeal is filed shall collect the court costs, reasonable attorney's fees, and other fees or expenses from the inmate using the procedures set forth in section 2969.22 of the Revised Code regarding the collection of fees.

(1996 H 455, eff. 10–17–96)

2969.24 Dismissal for false affidavit or for frivolous or malicious appeal

(A) If an inmate files a civil action or appeal against a government entity or employee, the court in which the action or appeal is filed, on its own motion or on the motion of a party, may dismiss the civil action or appeal at any stage in the proceedings if the court finds any of the following:

(1) The allegation of indigency in a poverty affidavit filed by the inmate is false.

(2) The claim that is the basis of the civil action or the issues of law that are the basis of the appeal are frivolous or malicious.

(3) The inmate filed an affidavit required by section 2969.25 or 2969.26 of the Revised Code that was materially false.

(B) For the purposes of this section, in determining whether a claim that is the basis of the civil action or the issues of law that are the basis of the appeal are frivolous or malicious, the court may consider whether any of the following applies:

(1) The claim fails to state a claim or the issues of law fail to state any issues of law.

(2) The claim has no arguable basis in law or fact or the issues of law have no arguable basis in law.

(3) It is clear that the inmate cannot prove material facts in support of the claim or in support of the issues of law.

(4) The claim that is the basis of the civil action is substantially similar to a claim in a previous civil action filed by the inmate or the issues of law that are the basis of the appeal are substantially similar to issues of law raised in a previous appeal filed by the inmate, in that the claim that is the basis of the current civil action or the issues of law that are the basis of the current appeal involve the same parties or arise from the same operative facts as the claim or issues of law in the previous civil action or appeal.

(C) If a party files a motion requesting the dismissal of a civil action or appeal under division (A) of this section, the court shall hold a hearing on the motion. If the court raises the issue of the dismissal of a civil action or appeal under division (A) of this section by its own motion, the court may hold a hearing on the motion. If practicable, the court may hold the hearing described in this division by telephone or, in the alternative, at the state correctional institution, jail, workhouse, or violation sanction center in which the inmate is confined.

(D) On the filing of a motion for dismissal of a civil action under division (A) of this section, the court may suspend discovery relating to the civil action pending the determination of the motion.

(E) Divisions (A) to (D) of this section do not limit the authority of the court in which the civil action or appeal is filed to otherwise dismiss the civil action or appeal.

(1997 S 111, eff. 3–17–98; 1996 H 455, eff. 10–17–96)

2969.25 Multiple actions or appeals filed by inmate; affidavit; review by attorney; fees

(A) At the time that an inmate commences a civil action or appeal against a government entity or employee, the inmate shall file with the court an affidavit that contains a description of each civil action or appeal of a civil action that the inmate has filed in the previous five years in any state or federal court. The affidavit shall include all of the following for each of those civil actions or appeals:

(1) A brief description of the nature of the civil action or appeal;

(2) The case name, case number, and the court in which the civil action or appeal was brought;

(3) The name of each party to the civil action or appeal;

(4) The outcome of the civil action or appeal, including whether the court dismissed the civil action or appeal as frivolous or malicious under state or federal law or rule of court, whether the court made an award against the inmate or the inmate's counsel of record for frivolous conduct under section 2323.51 of the Revised Code, another statute, or a rule of court, and, if the court so dismissed the action or appeal or made an award of that nature, the date of the final order affirming the dismissal or award.

(B) If an inmate who files a civil action in a court of common pleas, court of appeals, county court, or municipal court or an inmate who files an appeal from a judgment or order in a civil action in any of those courts has filed three or more civil actions or appeals of civil actions in a court of record in this state in the preceding twelve months or previously has been subject to the review procedure described in this division, the court may appoint a member of the bar to review the claim that is the basis of the civil action or the issues of law that are the basis of the appeal and to make a recommendation regarding whether the claim asserted in the action or the issues of law raised in the appeal are frivolous or malicious under section 2969.24 of the Revised Code, any other provision of law, or rule of court.

(C) If an inmate who files a civil action or appeal against a government entity or employee seeks a waiver of the prepayment of the full filing fees assessed by the court in which the action or appeal is filed, the inmate shall file with the complaint or notice of appeal an affidavit that the inmate is seeking a waiver of the prepayment of the court's full filing fees and an affidavit of indigency. The affidavit of waiver and the affidavit of indigency shall contain all of the following:

(1) A statement that sets forth the balance in the inmate account of the inmate for each of the preceding six months, as certified by the institutional cashier;

(2) A statement that sets forth all other cash and things of value owned by the inmate at that time.

(2002 S 168, eff. 6–28–02; 1996 H 455, eff. 10–17–96)

2969.26 Grievance system

(A) If an inmate commences a civil action or appeal against a government entity or employee and if the inmate's claim in the civil action or the inmate's claim in the civil action that is being appealed is subject to the grievance system for the state correctional institution, jail, workhouse, or violation sanction center in which the inmate is confined, the inmate shall file both of the following with the court:

(1) An affidavit stating that the grievance was filed and the date on which the inmate received the decision regarding the grievance.

(2) A copy of any written decision regarding the grievance from the grievance system.

(B) If the civil action or appeal is commenced before the grievance system process is complete, the court shall stay the civil action or appeal for a period not to exceed one hundred eighty days to permit the completion of the grievance system process.

(1997 S 111, eff. 3–17–98; 1996 H 455, eff. 10 17 96)

2969.27 Deductions from damages awarded inmate in civil action or appeal

If an inmate commences a civil action or appeal against a government entity or employee and is granted a judgment for damages in the civil action or appeal, the court shall order that the following be deducted and paid from the award on a pro rata basis before any payment is made to the inmate or the inmate's counsel:

(A) Any fine, court costs, or court-ordered restitution imposed upon the inmate for an offense for which the inmate is confined or for any previous offense committed by the inmate;

(B) The amount of an award of reparations made under sections 2743.51 to 2743.71 of the Revised Code to a victim of the inmate relative to the offense for which the inmate is confined or any previous offense committed by the inmate;

(C) Any other award ordered by a court against the inmate in any other criminal or civil action or proceeding in any court in this state.

(1996 H 455, eff. 10–17–96)

CHAPTER 2971

SEXUALLY VIOLENT PREDATORS

Section

Section

2971.01 Definitions

Note: See also following version of this section, eff. 4–29–05.

As used in this chapter:

(A) "Mandatory prison term" has the same meaning as in section 2929.01 of the Revised Code.

(B) "Designated homicide, assault, or kidnapping offense" means any of the following:

(1) A violation of section 2903.01, 2903.02, 2903.11, or 2905.01 of the Revised Code or a violation of division (A) of section 2903.04 of the Revised Code;

(2) An attempt to commit or complicity in committing a violation listed in division (B)(1) of this section, if the attempt or complicity is a felony.

(C) "Examiner" has the same meaning as in section 2945.371 of the Revised Code.

(D) "Peace officer" has the same meaning as in section 2935.01 of the Revised Code.

(E) "Prosecuting attorney" means the prosecuting attorney who prosecuted the case of the offender in question or the successor in office to that prosecuting attorney.

(F) "Sexually oriented offense" and "child- victim oriented offense" have the same meanings as in section 2950.01 of the Revised Code.

(G) "Sexually violent offense" means a violent sex offense, or a designated homicide, assault, or kidnapping offense for which the offender also was convicted of or pleaded guilty to a sexual motivation specification.

(H)(1) "Sexually violent predator" means a person who has been convicted of or pleaded guilty to committing, on or after January 1, 1997, a sexually violent offense and is likely to engage in the future in one or more sexually violent offenses.

(2) For purposes of division (H)(1) of this section, any of the following factors may be considered as evidence tending to indicate that there is a likelihood that the person will engage in the future in one or more sexually violent offenses:

(a) The person has been convicted two or more times, in separate criminal actions, of a sexually oriented offense or a child-victim oriented offense. For purposes of this division, convictions that result from or are connected with the same act or result from offenses committed at the same time are one conviction, and a conviction set aside pursuant to law is not a conviction.

(b) The person has a documented history from childhood, into the juvenile developmental years, that exhibits sexually deviant behavior.

(c) Available information or evidence suggests that the person chronically commits offenses with a sexual motivation.

(d) The person has committed one or more offenses in which the person has tortured or engaged in ritualistic acts with one or more victims.

(e) The person has committed one or more offenses in which one or more victims were physically harmed to the degree that the particular victim's life was in jeopardy.

(f) Any other relevant evidence.

(I) "Sexually violent predator specification" means a specification, as described in section 2941.148 of the Revised Code, charging a person with being a sexually violent predator.

(J) "Sexual motivation" means a purpose to gratify the sexual needs or desires of the offender.

(K) "Sexual motivation specification" means a specification, as described in section 2941.147 of the Revised Code, that charges that a person charged with a designated homicide, assault, or kidnapping offense committed the offense with a sexual motivation.

(L) "Violent sex offense" means any of the following:

(1) A violation of section 2907.02, 2907.03, or 2907.12 or of division (A)(4) of section 2907.05 of the Revised Code;

(2) A felony violation of a former law of this state that is substantially equivalent to a violation listed in division (L)(1) of this section or of an existing or former law of the United States or of another state that is substantially equivalent to a violation listed in division (L)(1) of this section;

(3) An attempt to commit or complicity in committing a violation listed in division (L)(1) or (2) of this section if the attempt or complicity is a felony.

(2003 S 5, eff. 7–31–03; 1996 H 180, eff. 1–1–97)

Note: See also following version of this section, eff. 4–29–05.

2971.01 Definitions (later effective date)

Note: See also preceding version of this section, in effect until 4–29–05.

As used in this chapter:

(A) "Mandatory prison term" has the same meaning as in section 2929.01 of the Revised Code.

(B) "Designated homicide, assault, or kidnapping offense" means any of the following:

(1) A violation of section 2903.01, 2903.02, 2903.11, or 2905.01 of the Revised Code or a violation of division (A) of section 2903.04 of the Revised Code;

(2) An attempt to commit or complicity in committing a violation listed in division (B)(1) of this section, if the attempt or complicity is a felony.

(C) "Examiner" has the same meaning as in section 2945.371 of the Revised Code.

(D) "Peace officer" has the same meaning as in section 2935.01 of the Revised Code.

(E) "Prosecuting attorney" means the prosecuting attorney who prosecuted the case of the offender in question or the successor in office to that prosecuting attorney.

(F) "Sexually oriented offense" and "child-victim oriented offense" have the same meanings as in section 2950.01 of the Revised Code.

(G) "Sexually violent offense" means any of the following:

(1) A violent sex offense;

(2) A designated homicide, assault, or kidnapping offense that the offender commits with a sexual motivation.

(H)(1) "Sexually violent predator" means a person who, on or after January 1, 1997, commits a sexually violent offense and is likely to engage in the future in one or more sexually violent offenses.

(2) For purposes of division (H)(1) of this section, any of the following factors may be considered as evidence tending to indicate that there is a likelihood that the person will engage in the future in one or more sexually violent offenses:

(a) The person has been convicted two or more times, in separate criminal actions, of a sexually oriented offense or a child-victim oriented offense. For purposes of this division, convictions that result from or are connected with the same act or result from offenses committed at the same time are one conviction, and a conviction set aside pursuant to law is not a conviction.

(b) The person has a documented history from childhood, into the juvenile developmental years, that exhibits sexually deviant behavior.

(c) Available information or evidence suggests that the person chronically commits offenses with a sexual motivation.

(d) The person has committed one or more offenses in which the person has tortured or engaged in ritualistic acts with one or more victims.

(e) The person has committed one or more offenses in which one or more victims were physically harmed to the degree that the particular victim's life was in jeopardy.

(f) Any other relevant evidence.

(I) "Sexually violent predator specification" means a specification, as described in section 2941.148 of the Revised Code, that charges that a person charged with a violent sex offense, or a person charged with a designated homicide, assault, or kidnapping offense and a sexual motivation specification, is a sexually violent predator.

(J) "Sexual motivation" means a purpose to gratify the sexual needs or desires of the offender.

(K) "Sexual motivation specification" means a specification, as described in section 2941.147 of the Revised Code, that charges that a person charged with a designated homicide, assault, or kidnapping offense committed the offense with a sexual motivation.

(L) "Violent sex offense" means any of the following:

(1) A violation of section 2907.02, 2907.03, or 2907.12 or of division (A)(4) of section 2907.05 of the Revised Code;

(2) A felony violation of a former law of this state that is substantially equivalent to a violation listed in division (L)(1) of this section or of an existing or former law of the United States or of another state that is substantially equivalent to a violation listed in division (L)(1) of this section;

(3) An attempt to commit or complicity in committing a violation listed in division (L)(1) or (2) of this section if the attempt or complicity is a felony.

(2004 H 473, eff. 4–29–05; 2003 S 5, eff. 7–31–03; 1996 H 180, eff. 1–1–97)

Note: See also preceding version of this section, in effect until 4–29–05.

2971.02 Procedure for determining sexually violent predator specification

Note: See also following version of this section, eff. 4–29–05.

In any case in which a sexually violent predator specification is included in the indictment, count in the indictment, or information charging a sexually violent offense and in which the defendant is tried by a jury, the defendant may elect to have the court instead of the jury determine the specification. If the defendant does not elect to have the court determine the specification, the defendant shall be tried before the jury on the charge of the offense, and, following a verdict of guilty on the charge of the offense, the defendant shall be tried before the jury on the sexually violent predator specification. If the defendant elects to have the court determine the specification, the defendant shall be tried on the charge of the offense before the jury, and, following a verdict of guilty on the charge of the offense, the court shall conduct a proceeding at which it shall determine the specification.

(1996 H 180, eff. 1–1–97)

Note: See also following version of this section, eff. 4–29–05.

2971.02 Procedure for determining sexually violent predator specification (later effective date)

Note: See also preceding version of this section, in effect until 4–29–05.

In any case in which a sexually violent predator specification is included in the indictment, count in the indictment, or information charging a violent sex offense or a designated homicide, assault, or kidnapping offense and in which the defendant is tried by a jury, the defendant may elect to have the court instead of the jury determine the sexually violent predator specification.

If the defendant does not elect to have the court determine the sexually violent predator specification, the defendant shall be tried before the jury on the charge of the offense and, if the offense is a designated homicide, assault, or kidnapping offense, on the sexual motivation specification that is included in the indictment, count in the indictment, or information charging the offense. Following a verdict of guilty on the charge of the offense and, if the offense is a designated homicide, assault, or kidnapping offense, on the related sexual motivation specification, the defendant shall be tried before the jury on the sexually violent predator specification.

If the defendant elects to have the court determine the sexually violent predator specification, the defendant shall be tried before the jury on the charge of the offense and, if the offense is a designated homicide, assault, or kidnapping offense, on the sexual motivation specification that is included in the indictment, count in the indictment, or information charging the offense. Following a verdict of guilty on the charge of the offense and, if the offense if a designated homicide, assault, or kidnapping offense, on the related sexual motivation specification, the court shall conduct a proceeding at which it shall determine the sexually violent predator specification.

(2004 H 473, eff. 4–29–05; 1996 H 180, eff. 1–1–97)

Note: See also preceding version of this section, in effect until 4–29–05.

2971.03 Sentence for offender convicted of sexually violent offense and sexually violent predator specification

Note: See also following version of this section, eff. 4–29–05.

(A) Notwithstanding divisions (A), (B), (C), and (F) of section 2929.14, section 2929.02, 2929.03, 2929.06, 2929.13, or another section of the Revised Code, other than divisions (D) and (E) of section 2929.14 of the Revised Code, that authorizes or requires a specified prison term or a mandatory prison term for a person who is convicted of or pleads guilty to a felony or that specifies the manner and place of service of a prison term or term of imprisonment, the court shall impose a sentence upon a person who is convicted of or pleads guilty to a sexually violent offense and who also is convicted of or pleads guilty to a sexually violent predator specification that was included in the indictment, count in the indictment, or information charging that offense as follows:

(1) If the offense is aggravated murder and if the court does not impose upon the offender a sentence of death, it shall impose upon the offender a term of life imprisonment without parole. If the court sentences the offender to death and the sentence of death is vacated, overturned, or otherwise set aside, the court shall impose upon the offender a term of life imprisonment without parole.

(2) If the offense is murder or an offense other than aggravated murder or murder for which a term of life imprisonment may be imposed, it shall impose upon the offender a term of life imprisonment without parole.

(3) Except as otherwise provided in division (A)(4) of this section, if the offense is an offense other than aggravated murder, murder, or an offense for which a term of life imprisonment may be imposed, it shall impose an indefinite prison term consisting of a minimum term fixed by the court from among the range of terms available as a definite term for the offense, but not less than two years, and a maximum term of life imprisonment.

(4) For any offense, if the offender previously has been convicted of or pleaded guilty to a sexually violent offense and also

to a sexually violent predator specification that was included in the indictment, count in the indictment, or information charging that offense, it shall impose upon the offender a term of life imprisonment without parole.

(B) If the offender is sentenced to a prison term pursuant to division (A)(3) of this section, the parole board shall have control over the offender's service of the term during the entire term unless the parole board terminates its control in accordance with section 2971.04 of the Revised Code.

(C)(1) Except as provided in division (C)(2) of this section, an offender sentenced to a prison term or term of life imprisonment without parole pursuant to division (A) of this section shall serve the entire prison term or term of life imprisonment in a state correctional institution. The offender is not eligible for judicial release under section 2929.20 of the Revised Code.

(2) For a prison term imposed pursuant to division (A)(3) of this section, the court, in accordance with section 2971.05 of the Revised Code, may terminate the prison term or modify the requirement that the offender serve the entire term in a state correctional institution if all of the following apply:

(a) The offender has served at least the minimum term imposed as part of that prison term.

(b) The parole board, pursuant to section 2971.04 of the Revised Code, has terminated its control over the offender's service of that prison term.

(c) The court has held a hearing and found, by clear and convincing evidence, one of the following:

(i) In the case of termination of the prison term, that the offender is unlikely to commit a sexually violent offense in the future;

(ii) In the case of modification of the requirement, that the offender does not represent a substantial risk of physical harm to others.

(3) An offender who has been sentenced to a term of life imprisonment without parole pursuant to division (A)(1), (2), or (4) of this section shall not be released from the term of life imprisonment or be permitted to serve a portion of it in a place other than a state correctional institution.

(D) If a court sentences an offender to a prison term or term of life imprisonment without parole pursuant to division (A) of this section and the court also imposes on the offender one or more additional prison terms pursuant to division (D) of section 2929.14 of the Revised Code, all of the additional prison terms shall be served consecutively with, and prior to, the prison term or term of life imprisonment without parole imposed upon the offender pursuant to division (A) of this section.

(E) If the offender is convicted of or pleads guilty to two or more offenses for which a prison term or term of life imprisonment without parole is required to be imposed pursuant to division (A) of this section, divisions (A) to (D) of this section shall be applied for each offense. All minimum terms imposed upon the offender pursuant to division (A)(3) of this section for those offenses shall be aggregated and served consecutively, as if they were a single minimum term imposed under that division.

(F) If an offender is convicted of or pleads guilty to a sexually violent offense and also is convicted of or pleads guilty to a sexually violent predator specification that was included in the indictment, count in the indictment, or information charging the sexually violent offense, the conviction of or plea of guilty to the specification automatically classifies the offender as a sexual predator for purposes of Chapter 2950. of the Revised Code. The classification of the offender as a sexual predator for purposes of that chapter is terminated only if the offender was sentenced to a prison term pursuant to division (A)(3) of section 2971.03 of the Revised Code and the court terminates the offender's prison term as provided in division (D) of section 2971.05 of the Revised Code, or as otherwise described in division (D)(2) of section 2950.09 of the Revised Code.

(1996 H 180, eff. 1–1–97)

Note: See also following version of this section, eff. 4–29–05.

2971.03 Sentence for offender convicted of violent sex offense and sexually violent predator specification; sentence for offender convicted of designated homicide, assault, or kidnapping offense and both a sexual motivation and sexually violent predator specification (later effective date)

Note: See also preceding version of this section, in effect until 4–29–05.

(A) Notwithstanding divisions (A), (B), (C), and (F) of section 2929.14, section 2929.02, 2929.03, 2929.06, 2929.13, or another section of the Revised Code, other than divisions (D) and (E) of section 2929.14 of the Revised Code, that authorizes or requires a specified prison term or a mandatory prison term for a person who is convicted of or pleads guilty to a felony or that specifies the manner and place of service of a prison term or term of imprisonment, the court shall impose a sentence upon a person who is convicted of or pleads guilty to a violent sex offense and who also is convicted of or pleads guilty to a sexually violent predator specification that was included in the indictment, count in the indictment, or information charging that offense, and upon a person who is convicted of or pleads guilty to a designated homicide, assault, or kidnapping offense and also is convicted of or pleads guilty to both a sexual motivation specification and a sexually violent predator specification that were included in the indictment, count in the indictment, or information charging that offense, as follows:

(1) If the offense for which the sentence is being imposed is aggravated murder and if the court does not impose upon the offender a sentence of death, it shall impose upon the offender a term of life imprisonment without parole. If the court sentences the offender to death and the sentence of death is vacated, overturned, or otherwise set aside, the court shall impose upon the offender a term of life imprisonment without parole.

(2) If the offense for which the sentence is being imposed is murder or an offense other than aggravated murder or murder for which a term of life imprisonment may be imposed, it shall impose upon the offender a term of life imprisonment without parole.

(3)(a) Except as otherwise provided in division (A)(3)(b), (c), or (d) or (A)(4) of this section, if the offense for which the sentence is being imposed is an offense other than aggravated murder, murder, or an offense for which a term of life imprisonment may be imposed, it shall impose an indefinite prison term consisting of a minimum term fixed by the court from among the range of terms available as a definite term for the offense, but not less than two years, and a maximum term of life imprisonment.

(b) Except as otherwise provided in division (A)(4) of this section, if the offense for which the sentence is being imposed is kidnapping that is a felony of the first degree, it shall impose an indefinite prison term consisting of a minimum term fixed by the court that is not less than ten years, and a maximum term of life imprisonment.

(c) Except as otherwise provided in division (A)(4) of this section, if the offense for which the sentence is being imposed is kidnapping that is a felony of the second degree, it shall impose an indefinite prison term consisting of a minimum term fixed by the court that is not less than eight years, and a maximum term of life imprisonment.

(d) Except as otherwise provided in division (A)(4) of this section, if the offense for which the sentence is being imposed is rape for which a term of life imprisonment is not imposed under section 2907.02 of the Revised Code or division (A)(2) of this section, it shall impose an indefinite prison term consisting of a minimum term fixed by the court that is not less than ten years, and a maximum term of life imprisonment.

(4) For any offense for which the sentence is being imposed, if the offender previously has been convicted of or pleaded guilty to a violent sex offense and also to a sexually violent predator specification that was included in the indictment, count in the indictment, or information charging that offense, or previously has been convicted of or pleaded guilty to a designated homicide, assault, or kidnapping offense and also to both a sexual motivation specification and a sexually violent predator specification that were included in the indictment, count in the indictment, or information charging that offense, it shall impose upon the offender a term of life imprisonment without parole.

(B) If the offender is sentenced to a prison term pursuant to division (A)(3) of this section, the parole board shall have control over the offender's service of the term during the entire term unless the parole board terminates its control in accordance with section 2971.04 of the Revised Code.

(C)(1) Except as provided in division (C)(2) of this section, an offender sentenced to a prison term or term of life imprisonment without parole pursuant to division (A) of this section shall serve the entire prison term or term of life imprisonment in a state correctional institution. The offender is not eligible for judicial release under section 2929.20 of the Revised Code.

(2) For a prison term imposed pursuant to division (A)(3) of this section, the court, in accordance with section 2971.05 of the Revised Code, may terminate the prison term or modify the requirement that the offender serve the entire term in a state correctional institution if all of the following apply:

(a) The offender has served at least the minimum term imposed as part of that prison term.

(b) The parole board, pursuant to section 2971.04 of the Revised Code, has terminated its control over the offender's service of that prison term.

(c) The court has held a hearing and found, by clear and convincing evidence, one of the following:

(i) In the case of termination of the prison term, that the offender is unlikely to commit a sexually violent offense in the future;

(ii) In the case of modification of the requirement, that the offender does not represent a substantial risk of physical harm to others.

(3) An offender who has been sentenced to a term of life imprisonment without parole pursuant to division (A)(1), (2), or (4) of this section shall not be released from the term of life imprisonment or be permitted to serve a portion of it in a place other than a state correctional institution.

(D) If a court sentences an offender to a prison term or term of life imprisonment without parole pursuant to division (A) of this section and the court also imposes on the offender one or more additional prison terms pursuant to division (D) of section 2929.14 of the Revised Code, all of the additional prison terms shall be served consecutively with, and prior to, the prison term or term of life imprisonment without parole imposed upon the offender pursuant to division (A) of this section.

(E) If the offender is convicted of or pleads guilty to two or more offenses for which a prison term or term of life imprisonment without parole is required to be imposed pursuant to division (A) of this section, divisions (A) to (D) of this section shall be applied for each offense. All minimum terms imposed upon the offender pursuant to division (A)(3) of this section for those offenses shall be aggregated and served consecutively, as if they were a single minimum term imposed under that division.

(F) If an offender is convicted of or pleads guilty to a violent sex offense and also is convicted of or pleads guilty to a sexually violent predator specification that was included in the indictment, count in the indictment, or information charging that offense, or is convicted of or pleads guilty to a designated homicide, assault, or kidnapping offense and also is convicted of or pleads guilty to both a sexual motivation specification and a sexually violent predator specification that were included in the indictment, count in the indictment, or information charging that offense, the conviction of or plea of guilty to the offense and the sexually violent predator specification automatically classifies the offender as a sexual predator for purposes of Chapter 2950. of the Revised Code. The classification of the offender as a sexual predator for purposes of that chapter is permanent and continues until the offender's death as described in division (D)(2) of section 2950.09 of the Revised Code.

(2004 H 473, eff 4–29–05; 1996 H 180, eff. 1–1–97)

Note: See also preceding version of this section, in effect until 4–29–05.

2971.04 Termination of parole board's control over offender's service of prison term; transfer of control to court

Note: See also following version of this section, eff. 4–29–05.

(A) If an offender is serving a prison term imposed under division (A)(3) of section 2971.03 of the Revised Code, at any time after the offender has served the minimum term imposed under that sentence, the parole board may terminate its control over the offender's service of the prison term. The parole board initially shall determine whether to terminate its control over the offender's service of the prison term upon the completion of the offender's service of the minimum term under the sentence and shall make subsequent determinations at least once every two years after that first determination. The parole board shall not terminate its control over the offender's service of the prison term unless it finds at a hearing that the offender does not represent a substantial risk of physical harm to others. Prior to determining whether to terminate its control over the offender's service of the prison term, the parole board shall request the department of rehabilitation and correction to prepare pursuant to section 5120.61 of the Revised Code an update of the most recent risk assessment and report relative to the offender. The offender has the right to be present at any hearing held under this section. At the hearing, the offender and the prosecuting attorney may make a statement and present evidence as to whether the parole board should terminate its control over the offender's service of the prison term. In making its determination as to whether to terminate its control over the offender's service of the prison term, the parole board may follow the standards and guidelines adopted by the department of rehabilitation and correction under section 5120.49 of the Revised Code and shall consider the updated risk assessment and report relating to the offender prepared by the department pursuant to section 5120.61 of the Revised Code in response to the request made under division (A)(1) of this section and any statements or evidence submitted by the offender or the prosecuting attorney. If the parole board terminates its control over an offender's service of a prison term imposed under division (A)(3) of section 2971.03 of the Revised Code, it shall recommend to the court modifications to the requirement that the offender serve the entire term in a state correctional institution. The court is not bound by the recommendations submitted by the parole board.

(B) If the parole board terminates its control over an offender's service of a prison term imposed pursuant to division (A)(3) of section 2971.03 of the Revised Code, the parole board immediately shall provide written notice of its termination of control to the department of rehabilitation and correction, the court, and the prosecuting attorney, and, after the board's termination of its control, the court shall have control over the offender's service of that prison term.

After the transfer, the court shall have control over the offender's service of that prison term for the offender's entire life, subject to the court's termination of the term pursuant to section 2971.05 of the Revised Code.

(C) If control over the offender's service of the prison term is transferred to the court, all of the following apply:

(1) The offender shall not be released solely as a result of the transfer of control over the service of that prison term.

(2) The offender shall not be permitted solely as a result of the transfer to serve a portion of that term in a place other than a state correctional institution.

(3) The offender shall continue serving that term in a state correctional institution, subject to the following:

(a) A release pursuant to a pardon, commutation, or reprieve;

(b) A modification or termination of the term by the court pursuant to this chapter.

(1996 H 180, eff. 1-1-97)

Note: See also following version of this section, eff. 4-29-05.

2971.04 Termination of parole board's control over offender's service of prison term; transfer of control to court (later effective date)

Note: See also preceding version of this section, in effect until 4-29-05.

(A) If an offender is serving a prison term imposed under division (A)(3) of section 2971.03 of the Revised Code, at any time after the offender has served the minimum term imposed under that sentence, the parole board may terminate its control over the offender's service of the prison term. The parole board initially shall determine whether to terminate its control over the offender's service of the prison term upon the completion of the offender's service of the minimum term under the sentence and shall make subsequent determinations at least once every two years after that first determination. The parole board shall not terminate its control over the offender's service of the prison term unless it finds at a hearing that the offender does not represent a substantial risk of physical harm to others. Prior to determining whether to terminate its control over the offender's service of the prison term, the parole board shall request the department of rehabilitation and correction to prepare pursuant to section 5120.61 of the Revised Code an update of the most recent risk assessment and report relative to the offender. The offender has the right to be present at any hearing held under this section. At the hearing, the offender and the prosecuting attorney may make a statement and present evidence as to whether the parole board should terminate its control over the offender's service of the prison term. In making its determination as to whether to terminate its control over the offender's service of the prison term, the parole board may follow the standards and guidelines adopted by the department of rehabilitation and correction under section 5120.49 of the Revised Code and shall consider the updated risk assessment and report relating to the offender prepared by the department pursuant to section 5120.61 of the Revised Code in response to the request made under this division and any statements or evidence submitted by the offender or the prosecuting attorney. If the parole board terminates its control over an offender's service of a prison term imposed under division (A)(3) of section 2971.03 of the Revised Code, it shall recommend to the court modifications to the requirement that the offender serve the entire term in a state correctional institution. The court is not bound by the recommendations submitted by the parole board.

(B) If the parole board terminates its control over an offender's service of a prison term imposed pursuant to division (A)(3) of section 2971.03 of the Revised Code, the parole board immediately shall provide written notice of its termination of control to the department of rehabilitation and correction, the court, and the prosecuting attorney, and, after the board's termination of its control, the court shall have control over the offender's service of that prison term.

After the transfer, the court shall have control over the offender's service of that prison term for the offender's entire life, subject to the court's termination of the term pursuant to section 2971.05 of the Revised Code.

(C) If control over the offender's service of the prison term is transferred to the court, all of the following apply:

(1) The offender shall not be released solely as a result of the transfer of control over the service of that prison term.

(2) The offender shall not be permitted solely as a result of the transfer to serve a portion of that term in a place other than a state correctional institution.

(3) The offender shall continue serving that term in a state correctional institution, subject to the following:

(a) A release pursuant to a pardon, commutation, or reprieve;

(b) A modification or termination of the term by the court pursuant to this chapter.

(2004 H 473, eff. 4-29-05; 1996 H 180, eff. 1-1-97)

Note: See also preceding version of this section, in effect until 4-29-05.

2971.05 Modification or termination of prison term; conditional release

Note: See also following version of this section, eff. 4-29-05.

(A)(1) After control over an offender's service of a prison term imposed pursuant to division (A)(3) of section 2971.03 of the Revised Code has been transferred pursuant to section 2971.04 of the Revised Code to the court, the court shall schedule, within thirty days of any of the following, a hearing on whether to modify in accordance with division (C) of this section the requirement that the offender serve the entire prison term in a state correctional institution or to terminate the prison term in accordance with division (D) of this section:

(a) Control over the offender's service of a prison term is transferred pursuant to section 2971.04 of the Revised Code to the court, and no hearing to modify the requirement has been held;

(b) Two years elapse after the most recent prior hearing held pursuant to division (A)(1) or (2) of this section;

(c) The prosecuting attorney, the department of rehabilitation and correction, or the adult parole authority requests the hearing, and recommends that the requirement be modified or that the offender's prison term be terminated.

(2) After control over the offender's service of a prison term has been transferred pursuant to section 2971.04 of the Revised Code to the court, the court, within thirty days of either of the following, shall conduct a hearing on whether to modify in accordance with division (C) of this section the requirement that the offender serve the entire prison term in a state correctional institution, whether to continue, revise, or revoke an existing

modification of that requirement, or whether to terminate the term in accordance with division (D) of this section:

(a) The requirement that the offender serve the entire prison term in a state correctional institution has been modified, and the offender is taken into custody for any reason.

(b) The department of rehabilitation and correction or the prosecuting attorney notifies the court pursuant to section 2971.06 of the Revised Code regarding a known or suspected violation of a term or condition of the modification or a belief that there is a substantial likelihood that the offender has committed or is about to commit a sexually violent offense.

(3) After control over the offender's service of a prison term has been transferred pursuant to section 2971.04 of the Revised Code to the court, the court, in any of the following circumstances, may conduct a hearing within thirty days to determine whether to modify in accordance with division (C) of this section the requirement that the offender serve the entire prison term in a state correctional institution, whether to continue, revise, or revoke an existing modification of that requirement, or whether to terminate the sentence in accordance with division (D) of this section:

(a) The offender requests the hearing;

(b) Upon the court's own motion;

(c) One or more examiners who have conducted a psychological examination and assessment of the offender file a statement that states that there no longer is a likelihood that the offender will engage in the future in a sexually violent offense.

(B)(1) Before a court holds a hearing pursuant to division (A) of this section, the court shall provide notice of the date, time, place, and purpose of the hearing to the offender, the prosecuting attorney, the department of rehabilitation and correction, and the adult parole authority and shall request the department to prepare pursuant to section 5120.61 of the Revised Code an update of the most recent risk assessment and report relative to the offender. The offender has the right to be present at any hearing held under this section. At the hearing, the offender and the prosecuting attorney may make a statement and present evidence as to whether the requirement should or should not be modified, whether the existing modification of the requirement should be continued, revised, or revoked, and whether the prison term should or should not be terminated.

(2) At a hearing held pursuant to division (A) of this section, the court may and, if the hearing is held pursuant to division (A)(1)(a), (1)(b), or (3)(c) of this section, shall determine by clear and convincing evidence whether the offender is unlikely to commit a sexually violent offense in the future.

(3) At the conclusion of the hearing held pursuant to division (A) of this section, the court may order that the requirement that the offender serve the entire prison term in a state correctional institution be continued, that the requirement be modified pursuant to division (C) of this section, that an existing modification be continued, revised, or revoked pursuant to division (C) of this section, or that the prison term be terminated pursuant to division (D) of this section.

(C)(1) If, at the conclusion of a hearing held pursuant to division (A) of this section, the court determines by clear and convincing evidence that the offender will not represent a substantial risk of physical harm to others, the court may modify the requirement that the offender serve the entire prison term in a state correctional institution in a manner that the court considers appropriate.

(2) The modification of the requirement does not terminate the prison term but serves only to suspend the requirement that the offender serve the entire term in a state correctional institution. The prison term shall remain in effect for the offender's entire life unless the court terminates the prison term pursuant to division (D) of this section. The offender shall remain under the jurisdiction of the court for the offender's entire life unless the court so terminates the prison term. The modification of the requirement does not terminate the classification of the offender, as described in division (F) of section 2971.03 of the Revised Code, as a sexual predator for purposes of Chapter 2950. of the Revised Code.

(3) If the court revokes the modification under consideration, the court shall order that the offender be returned to the custody of the department of rehabilitation and correction to continue serving the prison term to which the modification applied, and section 2971.06 of the Revised Code applies regarding the offender.

(D)(1) If, at the conclusion of a hearing held pursuant to division (A) of this section, the court determines by clear and convincing evidence that the offender is unlikely to commit a sexually violent offense in the future, the court may terminate the offender's prison term imposed under division (A)(3) of section 2971.03 of the Revised Code, subject to the offender satisfactorily completing the period of conditional release required by this division. If the court terminates the prison term, the court shall place the offender on conditional release for five years, notify the adult parole authority of its determination and of the termination of the prison term, and order the adult parole authority to supervise the offender during the five-year period of conditional release. Upon receipt of a notice from a court pursuant to this division, the adult parole authority shall supervise the offender who is the subject of the notice during the five-year period of conditional release, periodically notify the court of the offender's activities during that five-year period of conditional release, and file with the court no later than thirty days prior to the expiration of the five-year period of conditional release a written recommendation as to whether the termination of the offender's prison term should be finalized, whether the period of conditional release should be extended, or whether another type of action authorized pursuant to this chapter should be taken.

Upon receipt of a recommendation of the adult parole authority filed pursuant to this division, the court shall hold a hearing to determine whether to finalize the termination of the offender's prison term, to extend the period of conditional release, or to take another type of action authorized pursuant to this chapter. The court shall hold the hearing no later than the date on which the five-year period of conditional release terminates and shall provide notice of the date, time, place, and purpose of the hearing to the offender and to the prosecuting attorney. At the hearing, the offender, the prosecuting attorney, and the adult parole authority employee who supervised the offender during the period of conditional release may make a statement and present evidence.

(2) If the court determines to extend an offender's period of conditional release, it may do so for additional periods of one year in the same manner as the original period of conditional release, and except as otherwise described in this division, all procedures and requirements that applied to the original period of conditional release apply to the additional period of extended conditional release unless the court modifies a procedure or requirement. If an offender's period of conditional release is extended as described in this division, all references to a five-year period of conditional release that are contained in division (D)(1) of this section shall be construed, in applying the provisions of that division to the extension, as being references to the one-year period of the extension of the conditional release.

If the court determines to take another type of action authorized pursuant to this chapter, it may do so in the same manner as if the action had been taken at any other stage of the proceedings under this chapter. As used in this division, "another type of action" includes the revocation of the conditional release and the return of the offender to a state correctional institution to continue to serve the prison term.

If the court determines to finalize the termination of the offender's prison term, it shall notify the department of rehabilitation and correction, the department shall enter into its records a final release and issue to the offender a certificate of final release, and the prison term thereafter shall be considered completed and terminated in every way.

The termination of the offender's prison term pursuant to division (D)(1) or (2) of this section automatically terminates the classification of the offender, as described in division (F) of section 2971.03 of the Revised Code, as a sexual predator for purposes of Chapter 2950. of the Revised Code, and the court shall comply with division (D)(2) of section 2950.09 of the Revised Code.

(1996 H 180, eff. 1–1–97)

Note: See also following version of this section, eff. 4–29–05.

2971.05 Modification or termination of prison term; conditional release (later effective date)

Note: See also preceding version of this section, in effect until 4–29–05.

(A)(1) After control over an offender's service of a prison term imposed pursuant to division (A)(3) of section 2971.03 of the Revised Code has been transferred pursuant to section 2971.04 of the Revised Code to the court, the court shall schedule, within thirty days of any of the following, a hearing on whether to modify in accordance with division (C) of this section the requirement that the offender serve the entire prison term in a state correctional institution or to terminate the prison term in accordance with division (D) of this section:

(a) Control over the offender's service of a prison term is transferred pursuant to section 2971.04 of the Revised Code to the court, and no hearing to modify the requirement has been held;

(b) Two years elapse after the most recent prior hearing held pursuant to division (A)(1) or (2) of this section;

(c) The prosecuting attorney, the department of rehabilitation and correction, or the adult parole authority requests the hearing, and recommends that the requirement be modified or that the offender's prison term be terminated.

(2) After control over the offender's service of a prison term has been transferred pursuant to section 2971.04 of the Revised Code to the court, the court, within thirty days of either of the following, shall conduct a hearing on whether to modify in accordance with division (C) of this section the requirement that the offender serve the entire prison term in a state correctional institution, whether to continue, revise, or revoke an existing modification of that requirement, or whether to terminate the term in accordance with division (D) of this section:

(a) The requirement that the offender serve the entire prison term in a state correctional institution has been modified, and the offender is taken into custody for any reason.

(b) The department of rehabilitation and correction or the prosecuting attorney notifies the court pursuant to section 2971.06 of the Revised Code regarding a known or suspected violation of a term or condition of the modification or a belief that there is a substantial likelihood that the offender has committed or is about to commit a sexually violent offense.

(3) After control over the offender's service of a prison term has been transferred pursuant to section 2971.04 of the Revised Code to the court, the court, in any of the following circumstances, may conduct a hearing within thirty days to determine whether to modify in accordance with division (C) of this section the requirement that the offender serve the entire prison term in a state correctional institution, whether to continue, revise, or revoke an existing modification of that requirement, or whether to terminate the sentence in accordance with division (D) of this section:

(a) The offender requests the hearing;

(b) Upon the court's own motion;

(c) One or more examiners who have conducted a psychological examination and assessment of the offender file a statement that states that there no longer is a likelihood that the offender will engage in the future in a sexually violent offense.

(B)(1) Before a court holds a hearing pursuant to division (A) of this section, the court shall provide notice of the date, time, place, and purpose of the hearing to the offender, the prosecuting attorney, the department of rehabilitation and correction, and the adult parole authority and shall request the department to prepare pursuant to section 5120.61 of the Revised Code an update of the most recent risk assessment and report relative to the offender. The offender has the right to be present at any hearing held under this section. At the hearing, the offender and the prosecuting attorney may make a statement and present evidence as to whether the requirement should or should not be modified, whether the existing modification of the requirement should be continued, revised, or revoked, and whether the prison term should or should not be terminated.

(2) At a hearing held pursuant to division (A) of this section, the court may and, if the hearing is held pursuant to division (A)(1)(a), (1)(b), or (3)(c) of this section, shall determine by clear and convincing evidence whether the offender is unlikely to commit a sexually violent offense in the future.

(3) At the conclusion of the hearing held pursuant to division (A) of this section, the court may order that the requirement that the offender serve the entire prison term in a state correctional institution be continued, that the requirement be modified pursuant to division (C) of this section, that an existing modification be continued, revised, or revoked pursuant to division (C) of this section, or that the prison term be terminated pursuant to division (D) of this section.

(C)(1) If, at the conclusion of a hearing held pursuant to division (A) of this section, the court determines by clear and convincing evidence that the offender will not represent a substantial risk of physical harm to others, the court may modify the requirement that the offender serve the entire prison term in a state correctional institution in a manner that the court considers appropriate.

(2) The modification of the requirement does not terminate the prison term but serves only to suspend the requirement that the offender serve the entire term in a state correctional institution. The prison term shall remain in effect for the offender's entire life unless the court terminates the prison term pursuant to division (D) of this section. The offender shall remain under the jurisdiction of the court for the offender's entire life unless the court so terminates the prison term. The modification of the requirement does not terminate the classification of the offender, as described in division (F) of section 2971.03 of the Revised Code, as a sexual predator for purposes of Chapter 2950. of the Revised Code.

(3) If the court revokes the modification under consideration, the court shall order that the offender be returned to the custody of the department of rehabilitation and correction to continue serving the prison term to which the modification applied, and section 2971.06 of the Revised Code applies regarding the offender.

(D)(1) If, at the conclusion of a hearing held pursuant to division (A) of this section, the court determines by clear and convincing evidence that the offender is unlikely to commit a sexually violent offense in the future, the court may terminate the offender's prison term imposed under division (A)(3) of section 2971.03 of the Revised Code, subject to the offender satisfactorily completing the period of conditional release required by this division. If the court terminates the prison term, the court shall place the offender on conditional release for five years, notify the adult parole authority of its determination and of the termination of the prison term, and order the adult parole authority to supervise the offender during the five-year period of conditional release. Upon receipt of a notice from a court pursuant to this division, the adult parole authority shall supervise the offender who is the subject of the notice during the five-year period of conditional release, periodically notify the court of the offender's activities during that five-year period of conditional release, and file with the court no later than thirty days prior to the expiration of the five-year period of conditional release a written recommendation as to whether the termination of the offender's prison term should be finalized, whether the period of conditional release should be extended, or whether another type of action authorized pursuant to this chapter should be taken.

Upon receipt of a recommendation of the adult parole authority filed pursuant to this division, the court shall hold a hearing to determine whether to finalize the termination of the offender's prison term, to extend the period of conditional release, or to take another type of action authorized pursuant to this chapter. The court shall hold the hearing no later than the date on which the five-year period of conditional release terminates and shall provide notice of the date, time, place, and purpose of the hearing to the offender and to the prosecuting attorney. At the hearing, the offender, the prosecuting attorney, and the adult parole authority employee who supervised the offender during the period of conditional release may make a statement and present evidence.

(2) If the court determines to extend an offender's period of conditional release, it may do so for additional periods of one year in the same manner as the original period of conditional release, and except as otherwise described in this division, all procedures and requirements that applied to the original period of conditional release apply to the additional period of extended conditional release unless the court modifies a procedure or requirement. If an offender's period of conditional release is extended as described in this division, all references to a five-year period of conditional release that are contained in division (D)(1) of this section shall be construed, in applying the provisions of that division to the extension, as being references to the one-year period of the extension of the conditional release.

If the court determines to take another type of action authorized pursuant to this chapter, it may do so in the same manner as if the action had been taken at any other stage of the proceedings under this chapter. As used in this division, "another type of action" includes the revocation of the conditional release and the return of the offender to a state correctional institution to continue to serve the prison term.

If the court determines to finalize the termination of the offender's prison term, it shall notify the department of rehabilitation and correction, the department shall enter into its records a final release and issue to the offender a certificate of final release, and the prison term thereafter shall be considered completed and terminated in every way.

The termination of the offender's prison term pursuant to division (D)(1) or (2) of this section does not affect the classification of the offender, as described in division (F) of section 2971.03 of the Revised Code, as a sexual predator for purposes of Chapter 2950. of the Revised Code. The classification of the offender as a sexual predator is permanent and continues until the offender's death as described in division (D)(2) of section 2950.09 of the Revised Code.

(2004 H 473, eff. 4–29–05; 1996 H 180, eff. 1–1–97)

Note: See also preceding version of this section, in effect until 4–29–05.

2971.06 Violation of terms of prison term modification or conditional release; revision of modification

If, pursuant to section 2971.05 of the Revised Code, the court modifies the requirement that the offender serve the entire prison term in a state correctional institution or places the offender on conditional release and if, at any time after the offender has been released from serving the term in an institution, the department of rehabilitation and correction or the prosecuting attorney learns or obtains information indicating that the offender has violated a term or condition of the modification or conditional release or believes there is a substantial likelihood that the offender has committed or is about to commit a sexually violent offense, all of the following apply:

(A) The department or the prosecuting attorney may contact a peace officer, parole officer, or probation officer and request the officer to take the offender into custody. If the department contacts a peace officer, parole officer, or probation officer and requests that the offender be taken into custody, the department shall notify the prosecuting attorney that it made the request and shall provide the reasons for which it made the request. Upon receipt of a request that an offender be taken into custody, a peace officer, parole officer, or probation officer shall take the offender in question into custody and promptly shall notify the department and the prosecuting attorney, in writing, that the offender was taken into custody. After the offender has been taken into custody, the department or the prosecuting attorney shall notify the court of the violation or the belief that there is a substantial likelihood that the offender has committed or is about to commit a sexually violent offense, and the prosecuting attorney may request that the court, pursuant to section 2971.05 of the Revised Code, revise the modification. An offender may be held in custody under this provision for no longer than thirty days, pending a determination pursuant to section 2971.05 of the Revised Code of whether the modification of the requirement that the offender serve the entire prison term in a state correctional institution should be revised. If the court fails to make a determination under that section regarding the prosecuting attorney's request within thirty days after the offender was taken into custody, the offender shall be released from custody and shall be subject to the same terms and conditions as existed under the then-existing modification of the requirement that the offender serve the entire prison term in a state correctional institution, provided that if the act that resulted in the offender being taken into custody under this division is a criminal offense and if the offender is arrested for that act, the offender may be retained in custody in accordance with the applicable law.

(B) If the offender is not taken into custody pursuant to division (A) of this section, the department or the prosecuting attorney shall notify the court of the known or suspected violation or of the belief that there is a substantial likelihood that the offender has committed or is about to commit a sexually violent offense. If the department provides the notification to the court, it also shall notify the prosecuting attorney that it provided the notification and shall provide the reasons for which it provided the notification. The prosecuting attorney may request that the court, pursuant to section 2971.05 of the Revised Code, revise the modification.

(1996 H 180, eff. 1–1–97)

2971.07 Application of chapter; searches authorized

(A) This chapter does not apply to any offender unless the offender is convicted of or pleads guilty to a violent sex offense and also is convicted of or pleads guilty to a sexually violent predator specification that was included in the indictment, count in the indictment, or information charging that offense or unless the offender is convicted of or pleads guilty to a designated homicide, assault, or kidnapping offense and also is convicted of or pleads guilty to both a sexual motivation specification and a sexually violent predator specification that were included in the indictment, count in the indictment, or information charging that offense.

(B) This chapter does not limit or affect a court that sentences an offender who is convicted of or pleads guilty to a violent sex offense and also is convicted of or pleads guilty to a sexually violent predator specification or a court that sentences an offender who is convicted of or pleads guilty to a designated homicide, assault, or kidnapping offense and also is convicted of or pleads guilty to both a sexual motivation specification and a sexually violent predator specification in imposing upon the offender any financial sanction under section 2929.18 or any other section of the Revised Code, or, except as specifically provided in this chapter, any other sanction that is authorized or required for the offense by any other provision of law.

(C) If, pursuant to section 2971.05 of the Revised Code, the court modifies the requirement that the offender serve the entire prison term in a state correctional institution or places the offender on conditional release that involves the placement of the offender under the supervision of the adult parole authority, authorized field officers of the authority who are engaged within the scope of their supervisory duties or responsibilities may search, with or without a warrant, the person of the offender, the place of residence of the offender, and a motor vehicle, another item of tangible or intangible personal property, or any other real property in which the offender has the express or implied permission of a person with a right, title, or interest to use, occupy, or possess if the field officer has reasonable grounds to believe that the offender is not abiding by the law or otherwise is not complying with the terms and conditions of the offender's modification or release. The authority shall provide each offender with a written notice that informs the offender that authorized field officers of the authority who are engaged within the scope of their supervisory duties or responsibilities may conduct those types of searches during the period of the modification or release if they have reasonable grounds to believe that the offender is not abiding by the law or otherwise is not complying with the terms and conditions of the offender's modification or release.

(1996 H 180, eff. 1–1–97)

OHIO REVISED CODE
TITLES 31 TO 61
(Selected Provisions)

CHAPTER

3109 Children
3111 Parentage
3113 Neglect, Abandonment, or Domestic Violence
3121 Withholding or Deduction from Income
3123 Child Support—Default
3125 Child Support Enforcement
3301 Department of Education
3313 Boards of Education
3319 Schools—Superintendent; Teachers; Employees
3321 School Attendance
3345 State Universities—General Powers
3517 Campaigns; Political Parties
3599 Offenses and Penalties
3701 Department of Health
3716 Labeling of Hazardous Substances
3718 Household Sewage Treatment Systems and Small Flow On-Site Sewage Treatment Systems
3719 Controlled Substances
3737 Fire Marshal; Fire Safety; Petroleum Underground Storage
3743 Fireworks
3761 Unlawful Assemblies; Mobs
3767 Nuisances
3770 State Lottery
3773 Boxing; Discharging Firearms; Dueling
3793 Alcohol and Drug Addiction Services
3904 Insurance Transaction Information Standards
3905 Agents
3937 Casualty Insurance; Motor Vehicle Insurance
3999 Crimes relating to Insurance
4301 Liquor Control Law
4303 Liquor Permits
4399 Prohibitory Provisions and Crimes
4501 Motor Vehicles—Definitions; General Provisions
4503 Licensing of Motor Vehicles
4505 Certificate of Motor Vehicle Title Law
4506 Commercial Drivers' Licensing
4507 Driver's License Law
4509 Financial Responsibility
4510 Driver's License Suspension and Cancellation

CHAPTER

4511 Traffic Laws—Operation of Motor Vehicles
4513 Traffic Laws—Equipment; Loads
4549 Motor Vehicle Crimes
4561 Aeronautics
4582 Port Authorities
4729 Pharmacists; Dangerous Drugs
4731 Physicians; Limited Practitioners
4734 Chiropractors
4749 Private Investigators; Security Services
4752 Home Medical Equipment Services Providers
4762 Acupuncturists
4931 Companies—Telegraph; Telephone
4933 Companies—Gas; Electric; Water; Others
4953 Transportation Terminal Companies
4973 Employees; Policemen
4999 Crimes relating to Railroads
5101 Job and Family Services Department—General Provisions
5103 Placement of Children
5104 Child Day Care
5119 Department of Mental Health
5120 Department of Rehabilitation and Correction
5122 Hospitalization of Mentally ILL
5123 Department of Mental Retardation and Developmental Disabilities
5126 County Boards of Mental Retardation and Developmental Disabilities
5139 Youth Services
5145 State Correctional Institutions
5149 Adult Parole Authority
5153 County Children Services
5301 Conveyances; Encumbrances
5321 Landlords and Tenants
5502 Public Safety Department
5503 State Highway Patrol
5577 Load Limits on Highways
5589 Offenses relating to Highways
5743 Cigarette Tax
5907 Ohio Veterans' Home
6101 Conservancy Districts

CHAPTER 3109

CHILDREN

LIABILITY OF PARENTS

3109.09 Damages recoverable against parent of minor who willfully damages property or commits theft offense; community service

(A) As used in this section, "parent" means one of the following:

(1) Both parents unless division (A)(2) or (3) of this section applies;

(2) The parent designated the residential parent and legal custodian pursuant to an order issued under section 3109.04 of the Revised Code that is not a shared parenting order;

(3) The custodial parent of a child born out of wedlock with respect to whom no custody order has been issued.

(B) Any owner of property, including any board of education of a city, local, exempted village, or joint vocational school district, may maintain a civil action to recover compensatory damages not exceeding ten thousand dollars and court costs from the parent of a minor if the minor willfully damages property belonging to the owner or commits acts cognizable as a "theft offense," as defined in section 2913.01 of the Revised Code, involving the property of the owner. The action may be joined with an action under Chapter 2737. of the Revised Code against the minor, or the minor and the minor's parent, to recover the property regardless of value, but any additional damages recovered from the parent pursuant to this section shall be limited to compensatory damages not exceeding ten thousand dollars, as authorized by this section. A finding of willful destruction of property or of committing acts cognizable as a theft offense is not dependent upon a prior finding that the child is a delinquent child or upon the child's conviction of any criminal offense.

(C)(1) If a court renders a judgment in favor of a board of education of a city, local, exempted village, or joint vocational school district in an action brought pursuant to division (B) of this section, if the board of education agrees to the parent's performance of community service in lieu of full payment of the judgment, and if the parent who is responsible for the payment of the judgment agrees to voluntarily participate in the performance of community service in lieu of full payment of the judgment, the court may order the parent to perform community service in lieu of providing full payment of the judgment.

(2) If a court, pursuant to division (C)(1) of this section, orders a parent to perform community service in lieu of providing full payment of a judgment, the court shall specify in its order the amount of the judgment, if any, to be paid by the parent, the type and number of hours of community service to be performed by the parent, and any other conditions necessary to carry out the order.

(D) This section shall not apply to a parent of a minor if the minor was married at the time of the commission of the acts or violations that would otherwise give rise to a civil action commenced under this section.

(E) Any action brought pursuant to this section shall be commenced and heard as in other civil actions.

(F) The monetary limitation upon compensatory damages set forth in this section does not apply to a civil action brought pursuant to section 2307.70 of the Revised Code.

(1996 H 601, eff. 10–29–96; 1992 H 154, eff. 7–31–92; 1990 S 3; 1988 H 708; 1986 H 158, S 316; 1978 H 456; 1969 S 10; 132 v H 257; 131 v H 159)

3109.10 Liability of parents for assaults by their children

As used in this section, "parent" has the same meaning as in section 3109.09 of the Revised Code.

Any person is entitled to maintain an action to recover compensatory damages in a civil action, in an amount not to exceed ten thousand dollars and costs of suit in a court of competent jurisdiction, from the parent of a child under the age of eighteen if the child willfully and maliciously assaults the person by a means or force likely to produce great bodily harm. A finding of willful and malicious assault by a means or force likely to produce great bodily harm is not dependent upon a prior finding that the child is a delinquent child.

Any action brought pursuant to this section shall be commenced and heard as in other civil actions for damages.

The monetary limitation upon compensatory damages set forth in this section does not apply to a civil action brought pursuant to section 2307.70 of thc Revised Code.

(1996 H 601, eff. 10–29–96; 1995 H 18, eff. 11–24–95; 1990 S 3, eff. 4–11–91; 1986 S 316; 1969 S 11)

PARENT CONVICTED OF KILLING OTHER PARENT

3109.41 Definitions

As used in sections 3109.41 to 3109.48 of the Revised Code:

(A) A person is "convicted of killing" if the person has been convicted of or pleaded guilty to a violation of section 2903.01, 2903.02, or 2903.03 of the Revised Code.

(B) "Custody order" means an order designating a person as the residential parent and legal custodian of a child under section 3109.04 of the Revised Code or any order determining custody of a child under section 2151.23, 2151.33, 2151.353, 2151.354, 2151.415, 2151.417, 2152.16, 2152.17, 2152.19, 2152.21, or 3113.31 of the Revised Code.

(C) "Visitation order" means an order issued under division (B)(1)(c) of section 2151.33 or under section 2151.412, 3109.051, 3109.12, or 3113.31 of the Revised Code.

(2000 S 179, § 3, eff. 1–1–02; 1999 H 191, eff. 10–20–99)

3109.44 Notice of conviction

Upon receipt of notice that a visitation order is pending or has been issued granting a parent visitation rights with a child or a custody order is pending or has been issued designating a parent as the residential parent and legal custodian of a child or granting custody of a child to a parent prior to that parent being convicted of killing the other parent of the child, the court in which the parent is convicted of killing the other parent shall immediately notify the court that issued the visitation or custody order of the conviction.

(1999 H 191, eff. 10–20–99)

GRANDPARENT POWER OF ATTORNEY OR CARETAKER AUTHORIZATION AFFIDAVIT

3109.78 Creation of power of attorney or affidavit for participation in academic or interscholastic programs prohibited

(A) No person shall create a power of attorney under section 3109.52 of the Revised Code or execute a caretaker authorization affidavit under section 3109.67 of the Revised Code for the purpose of enrolling the child in a school or school district so that the child may participate in the academic or interscholastic athletic programs provided by the school or school district.

(B) A person who violates division (A) of this section is in violation of section 2921.13 of the Revised Code and is guilty of falsification, a misdemeanor of the first degree.

(C) A power of attorney created, or an affidavit executed, in violation of this section is void as of the date of its creation or execution.

(2004 H 130, eff. 7–20–04)

CHAPTER 3111

PARENTAGE

PRACTICE AND PROCEDURE

3111.19 Interference with parentage action

No person, by using physical harassment or threats of violence against another person, shall interfere with the other person's initiation or continuance of, or attempt to prevent the other person from initiating or continuing, an action under sections 3111.01 to 3111.18 of the Revised Code.

(2000 S 180, eff. 3–22–01)

ACKNOWLEDGMENT OF PATERNITY

3111.29 Complaint for child support

Once an acknowledgment of paternity becomes final under section 3111.25 of the Revised Code, the mother or other custodian or guardian of the child may file a complaint pursuant to section 2151.231 of the Revised Code in the juvenile court or other court with jurisdiction under section 2101.022 or 2301.03 of the Revised Code of the county in which the child or the guardian or legal custodian of the child resides requesting that the court order the father to pay an amount for the support of the child, may contact the child support enforcement agency for assistance in obtaining the order, or may request that an administrative officer of a child support enforcement agency issue an administrative order for the payment of child support pursuant to section 3111.81 of the Revised Code.

(2000 S 180, eff. 3–22–01)

3111.30 Department of health to receive notice of acknowledgment; preparation of new birth certificate consistent with acknowledgment

Once an acknowledgment of paternity becomes final, the office of child support shall notify the department of health of the acknowledgment. If the original birth record is inconsistent with the acknowledgment, on receipt of the notice, the department of health shall, in accordance with section 3705.09 of the Revised Code, prepare a new birth record consistent with the acknowledgment and substitute the new record for the original birth record.

(2000 S 180, eff. 3–22–01)

3111.31 Acknowledgment of paternity affidavit

The department of job and family services shall prepare an acknowledgment of paternity affidavit that includes in boldface type at the top of the affidavit the rights and responsibilities of and the due process safeguards afforded to a person who acknowledges that he is the natural father of a child, including that if an alleged father acknowledges a parent and child relationship he assumes the parental duty of support, that both signators waive any right to bring an action pursuant to sections 3111.01 to 3111.18 of the Revised Code or make a request pursuant to section 3111.38 of the Revised Code, other than for purposes of rescinding the acknowledgment pursuant to section 3111.27 of the Revised Code in order to ensure expediency in resolving the question of the existence of a parent and child relationship, that either parent may rescind the acknowledgment pursuant to section 3111.27 of the Revised Code, that an action may be brought pursuant to section 3111.28 of the Revised Code, or a motion may be filed pursuant to section 3119.961 of the Revised Code, to rescind the acknowledgment, and that the natural father has the right to petition a court pursuant to section 3109.12 of the Revised Code for an order granting him reasonable parenting time with respect to the child and to petition the court for custody of the child pursuant to section 2151.23 of the Revised Code. The affidavit shall include all of the following:

(A) Basic instructions for completing the form, including instructions that both the natural father and the mother of the child are required to sign the statement, that they may sign the statement without being in each other's presence, and that the signatures must be notarized;

(B) Blank spaces to enter the full name, social security number, date of birth and address of each parent;

(C) Blank spaces to enter the full name, date of birth, and the residence of the child;

(D) A blank space to enter the name of the hospital or department of health code number assigned to the hospital, for use in situations in which the hospital fills out the form pursuant to section 3727.17 of the Revised Code;

(E) An affirmation by the mother that the information she supplied is true to the best of her knowledge and belief and that she is the natural mother of the child named on the form and assumes the parental duty of support of the child;

(F) An affirmation by the father that the information he supplied is true to the best of his knowledge and belief, that he has received information regarding his legal rights and responsibilities, that he consents to the jurisdiction of the courts of this state, and that he is the natural father of the child named on the form and assumes the parental duty of support of the child;

(G) Signature lines for the mother of the child and the natural father;

(H) Signature lines for the notary public;

(I) An instruction to include or attach any other evidence necessary to complete the new birth record that is required by the department by rule.

(2000 S 180, eff. 3–22–01)

NON–SPOUSAL ARTIFICIAL INSEMINATION

3111.89 Sections applicable to non-spousal artificial insemination

Sections 3111.88 to 3111.96 of the Revised Code deal with non-spousal artificial insemination for the purpose of impregnating a woman so that she can bear a child that she intends to raise as her child. These sections do not deal with the artificial insemination of a wife with the semen of her husband or with surrogate motherhood.

(2000 S 180, eff. 3–22–01)

PENALTIES

3111.99 Penalties

Whoever violates section 3111.19 of the Revised Code is guilty of interfering with the establishment of paternity, a misdemeanor of the first degree.

(2000 S 180, eff. 3–22–01; 1999 H 471, eff. 7–1–00; 1997 H 352, eff. 1–1–98; 1996 H 710, § 7, eff. 6–11–96; 1995 H 167, eff. 6–11–96; 1995 S 2, eff. 7–1–96; 1992 S 10, eff. 7–15–92)

CHAPTER 3113

NEGLECT, ABANDONMENT, OR DOMESTIC VIOLENCE

FAILURE TO PAY SUPPORT; BOND

3113.04 Suspension of sentence on posting bond; contempt for failure to make support payments

(A) Sentence may be suspended if a person, after conviction under section 2919.21 of the Revised Code and before sentence under that section, appears before the court of common pleas in which the conviction took place and enters into bond to the state in a sum fixed by the court at not less than five hundred nor more than one thousand dollars, with sureties approved by the court, conditioned that the person will furnish the child or other dependent with necessary or proper home, care, food, and clothing, or will pay promptly each week for such purpose to the office of child support in the department of job and family services, a sum to be fixed by the agency. The child support enforcement agency shall comply with Chapter 3119. of the Revised Code when it fixes the sum to be paid to the division.

(B) If any person required to pay child support under an order made under this section on or after April 15, 1985, or modified on or after December 1, 1986, is found in contempt of court for failure to make support payments under the order, the court that makes the finding, in addition to any other penalty or remedy imposed, shall assess all court costs arising out of the contempt proceeding against the person and require the person to pay any reasonable attorney's fees of any adverse party, as determined by the court, that arose in relation to the act of contempt.

(2000 S 180, eff. 3–22–01; 1999 H 471, eff. 7–1–00; 1997 H 352, eff. 1–1–98; 1993 H 173, eff. 12–31–93; 1992 S 10; 1990 H 591; 1988 H 708; 1987 H 231; 1986 H 509; 1984 H 614; 1978 S 87; 1972 H 511; 1953 H 1; GC 13010)

3113.06 Failure to pay maintenance cost of child

No father, or mother when she is charged with the maintenance, of a child under eighteen years of age, or a mentally or physically handicapped child under age twenty-one, who is legally a ward of a public children services agency or is the recipient of aid pursuant to Chapter 5107. or 5115. of the Revised Code, shall neglect or refuse to pay such agency the reasonable cost of maintaining such child when such father or mother is able to do so by reason of property, labor, or earnings.

An offense under this section shall be held committed in the county in which the agency is located. The agency shall file charges against any parent who violates this section, unless the agency files charges under section 2919.21 of the Revised Code, or unless charges of nonsupport are filed by a relative or guardian of the child, or unless an action to enforce support is brought under Chapter 3115. of the Revised Code.

(1997 H 408, eff. 10–1–97; 1996 H 274, eff. 8–8–96; 1995 H 249, eff. 7–17–95; 1991 H 298, eff. 7–26–91; 1986 H 428; 1972 H 511; 1969 H 361, S 49; 132 v H 390; 1953 H 1; GC 13012, 13014)

3113.07 Suspension of sentence on entering into bond; payment of reasonable maintenance cost; requirement to provide for health care needs of child

As used in this section, "executive director" has the same meaning as in section 5153.01 of the Revised Code.

Sentence may be suspended, if a person, after conviction under section 3113.06 of the Revised Code and before sentence thereunder, appears before the court of common pleas in which such conviction took place and enters into bond to the state in a sum fixed by the court at not less than five hundred dollars, with sureties approved by such court, conditioned that such person will pay, so long as the child remains a ward of the public children services agency or a recipient of aid pursuant to Chapter 5107. or 5115. of the Revised Code, to the executive director thereof or to a trustee to be named by the court, for the benefit of such agency or if the child is a recipient of aid pursuant to Chapter 5107. or 5115. of the Revised Code, to the county department of job and family services, the reasonable cost of keeping such child. The amount of such costs and the time of payment shall be fixed by the court.

The court, in accordance with sections 3119.29 to 3119.56 of the Revised Code, shall include in each support order made under this section the requirement that one or both of the parents provide for the health care needs of the child to the satisfaction of the court.

(2002 H 657, eff. 12–13–02; 2000 S 180, eff. 3–22–01; 1999 H 471, eff. 7–1–00; 1997 H 352, eff. 1–1–98; 1997 H 408, eff. 10–1–97; 1995 H 249, eff. 7–17–95; 1991 H 298, eff. 7–26–91; 1991 H 82; 1986 H 428; 1969 S 49; 132 v H 390; 1953 H 1; GC 13013)

3113.08 Failure to give bond; arrest; sentence or modification of order

Upon failure of the father or mother of a child under eighteen years of age, or of a physically or mentally handicapped child under twenty-one years of age, or the husband of a pregnant woman to comply with any order and undertaking provided for in sections 3113.01 [1] to 3113.14, inclusive, of the Revised Code, such person may be arrested by the sheriff or other officer, on a warrant issued on the praecipe of the prosecuting attorney, and brought before the court of common pleas for sentence. Thereupon the court may pass sentence, or for good cause shown, may modify the order as to the time and amount of payments, or take a new undertaking and further suspend sentence, whichever is for the best interests of such child or pregnant woman and of the public.

(1996 H 274, eff. 8–8–96; 1953 H 1, eff. 10–1–53; GC 13015)

[1] Sections 3113.01 to 3113.03 were repealed by 1972 H 511, eff. 1–1–74; see now 2919.21 et seq. for provisions analogous to former 3113.01 to 3113.03.

TRUSTEE

3113.11 Amount credited convict paid to trustee

When a person is convicted, sentenced, and confined in a workhouse, under sections 3113.01 [1] to 3113.14, inclusive, of the Revised Code, the county from which he is so convicted, sentenced, and confined upon the warrant of the county auditor of such county, and out of the general revenue fund thereof, shall pay monthly fifty cents for each day he is so confined, to the trustee appointed by the court under such sections, to be expended by such trustee for the maintenance of the child under sixteen years of age.

(1953 H 1, eff. 10–1–53; GC 13018)

[1] Sections 3113.01 to 3113.03 were repealed by 1972 H 511, eff. 1–1–74; see now 2919.21 et seq. for provisions analogous to former 3113.01 to 3113.03.

DOMESTIC VIOLENCE

3113.31 Petitions; protection orders concerning domestic violence; support orders; sanctions for violations; notification of law enforcement agencies and courts

(A) As used in this section:

(1) "Domestic violence" means the occurrence of one or more of the following acts against a family or household member:

(a) Attempting to cause or recklessly causing bodily injury;

(b) Placing another person by the threat of force in fear of imminent serious physical harm or committing a violation of section 2903.211 or 2911.211 of the Revised Code;

(c) Committing any act with respect to a child that would result in the child being an abused child, as defined in section 2151.031 of the Revised Code.

(2) "Court" means the domestic relations division of the court of common pleas in counties that have a domestic relations division, and the court of common pleas in counties that do not have a domestic relations division.

(3) "Family or household member" means any of the following:

(a) Any of the following who is residing with or has resided with the respondent:

(i) A spouse, a person living as a spouse, or a former spouse of the respondent;

(ii) A parent or a child of the respondent, or another person related by consanguinity or affinity to the respondent;

(iii) A parent or a child of a spouse, person living as a spouse, or former spouse of the respondent, or another person related by consanguinity or affinity to a spouse, person living as a spouse, or former spouse of the respondent.

(b) The natural parent of any child of whom the respondent is the other natural parent or is the putative other natural parent.

(4) "Person living as a spouse" means a person who is living or has lived with the respondent in a common law marital relationship, who otherwise is cohabiting with the respondent, or who otherwise has cohabited with the respondent within five years prior to the date of the alleged occurrence of the act in question.

(5) "Victim advocate" means a person who provides support and assistance for a person who files a petition under this section.

(B) The court has jurisdiction over all proceedings under this section. The petitioner's right to relief under this section is not affected by the petitioner's leaving the residence or household to avoid further domestic violence.

(C) A person may seek relief under this section on the person's own behalf, or any parent or adult household member may seek relief under this section on behalf of any other family or household member, by filing a petition with the court. The petition shall contain or state:

(1) An allegation that the respondent engaged in domestic violence against a family or household member of the respondent, including a description of the nature and extent of the domestic violence;

(2) The relationship of the respondent to the petitioner, and to the victim if other than the petitioner;

(3) A request for relief under this section.

(D)(1) If a person who files a petition pursuant to this section requests an ex parte order, the court shall hold an ex parte hearing on the same day that the petition is filed. The court, for good cause shown at the ex parte hearing, may enter any temporary orders, with or without bond, including, but not limited to, an order described in division (E)(1)(a), (b), or (c) of this section, that the court finds necessary to protect the family or household member from domestic violence. Immediate and present danger of domestic violence to the family or household member constitutes good cause for purposes of this section. Immediate and present danger includes, but is not limited to, situations in which the respondent has threatened the family or household member with bodily harm or in which the respondent previously has been convicted of or pleaded guilty to an offense that constitutes domestic violence against the family or household member.

(2)(a) If the court, after an ex parte hearing, issues an order described in division (E)(1)(b) or (c) of this section, the court shall schedule a full hearing for a date that is within seven court days after the ex parte hearing. If any other type of protection order that is authorized under division (E) of this section is issued by the court after an ex parte hearing, the court shall schedule a full hearing for a date that is within ten court days after the ex parte hearing. The court shall give the respondent notice of, and an opportunity to be heard at, the full hearing. The court shall hold the full hearing on the date scheduled under this division unless the court grants a continuance of the hearing in accordance with this division. Under any of the following circumstances or for any of the following reasons, the court may grant a continuance of the full hearing to a reasonable time determined by the court:

(i) Prior to the date scheduled for the full hearing under this division, the respondent has not been served with the petition filed pursuant to this section and notice of the full hearing.

(ii) The parties consent to the continuance.

(iii) The continuance is needed to allow a party to obtain counsel.

(iv) The continuance is needed for other good cause.

(b) An ex parte order issued under this section does not expire because of a failure to serve notice of the full hearing upon the respondent before the date set for the full hearing under division (D)(2)(a) of this section or because the court grants a continuance under that division.

(3) If a person who files a petition pursuant to this section does not request an ex parte order, or if a person requests an ex parte order but the court does not issue an ex parte order after an ex parte hearing, the court shall proceed as in a normal civil action and grant a full hearing on the matter.

(E)(1) After an ex parte or full hearing, the court may grant any protection order, with or without bond, or approve any consent agreement to bring about a cessation of domestic violence against the family or household members. The order or agreement may:

(a) Direct the respondent to refrain from abusing the family or household members;

(b) Grant possession of the residence or household to the petitioner or other family or household member, to the exclusion of the respondent, by evicting the respondent, when the residence or household is owned or leased solely by the petitioner or other family or household member, or by ordering the respondent to vacate the premises, when the residence or household is jointly owned or leased by the respondent, and the petitioner or other family or household member;

(c) When the respondent has a duty to support the petitioner or other family or household member living in the residence or household and the respondent is the sole owner or lessee of the residence or household, grant possession of the residence or household to the petitioner or other family or household member, to the exclusion of the respondent, by ordering the respondent to vacate the premises, or, in the case of a consent agreement, allow the respondent to provide suitable, alternative housing;

(d) Temporarily allocate parental rights and responsibilities for the care of, or establish temporary parenting time rights with regard to, minor children, if no other court has determined, or is determining, the allocation of parental rights and responsibilities for the minor children or parenting time rights;

(e) Require the respondent to maintain support, if the respondent customarily provides for or contributes to the support of the family or household member, or if the respondent has a duty to support the petitioner or family or household member;

(f) Require the respondent, petitioner, victim of domestic violence, or any combination of those persons, to seek counseling;

(g) Require the respondent to refrain from entering the residence, school, business, or place of employment of the petitioner or family or household member;

(h) Grant other relief that the court considers equitable and fair, including, but not limited to, ordering the respondent to permit the use of a motor vehicle by the petitioner or other family or household member and the apportionment of household and family personal property.

(2) If a protection order has been issued pursuant to this section in a prior action involving the respondent and the petitioner or one or more of the family or household members, the court may include in a protection order that it issues a prohibition against the respondent returning to the residence or household. If it includes a prohibition against the respondent returning to the residence or household in the order, it also shall include in the order provisions of the type described in division (E)(7) of this section. This division does not preclude the court from including in a protection order or consent agreement, in circumstances other than those described in this division, a requirement that the respondent be evicted from or vacate the residence or household or refrain from entering the residence, school, business, or place of employment of the petitioner or a family or household member, and, if the court includes any requirement of that type in an order or agreement, the court also shall include in the order provisions of the type described in division (E)(7) of this section.

(3)(a) Any protection order issued or consent agreement approved under this section shall be valid until a date certain, but not later than five years from the date of its issuance or approval.

(b) Subject to the limitation on the duration of an order or agreement set forth in division (E)(3)(a) of this section, any order under division (E)(1)(d) of this section shall terminate on the date that a court in an action for divorce, dissolution of marriage, or legal separation brought by the petitioner or respondent issues an order allocating parental rights and responsibilities for the care of children or on the date that a juvenile court in an action brought by the petitioner or respondent issues an order awarding legal custody of minor children. Subject to the limitation on the duration of an order or agreement set forth in division (E)(3)(a) of this section, any order under division (E)(1)(e) of this section shall terminate on the date that a court in an action for divorce, dissolution of marriage, or legal separation brought by the petitioner or respondent issues a support order or on the date that a juvenile court in an action brought by the petitioner or respondent issues a support order.

(c) Any protection order issued or consent agreement approved pursuant to this section may be renewed in the same manner as the original order or agreement was issued or approved.

(4) A court may not issue a protection order that requires a petitioner to do or to refrain from doing an act that the court may require a respondent to do or to refrain from doing under division (E)(1)(a), (b), (c), (d), (e), (g), or (h) of this section unless all of the following apply:

(a) The respondent files a separate petition for a protection order in accordance with this section.

(b) The petitioner is served notice of the respondent's petition at least forty-eight hours before the court holds a hearing with respect to the respondent's petition, or the petitioner waives the right to receive this notice.

(c) If the petitioner has requested an ex parte order pursuant to division (D) of this section, the court does not delay any hearing required by that division beyond the time specified in that division in order to consolidate the hearing with a hearing on the petition filed by the respondent.

(d) After a full hearing at which the respondent presents evidence in support of the request for a protection order and the petitioner is afforded an opportunity to defend against that evidence, the court determines that the petitioner has committed an act of domestic violence or has violated a temporary protection order issued pursuant to section 2919.26 of the Revised Code, that both the petitioner and the respondent acted primarily as aggressors, and that neither the petitioner nor the respondent acted primarily in self-defense.

(5) No protection order issued or consent agreement approved under this section shall in any manner affect title to any real property.

(6)(a) If a petitioner, or the child of a petitioner, who obtains a protection order or consent agreement pursuant to division (E)(1) of this section or a temporary protection order pursuant to section 2919.26 of the Revised Code and is the subject of a parenting time order issued pursuant to section 3109.051 or 3109.12 of the Revised Code or a visitation or companionship order issued pursuant to section 3109.051, 3109.11, or 3109.12 of the Revised Code or division (E)(1)(d) of this section granting parenting time rights to the respondent, the court may require the public children services agency of the county in which the court is located to provide supervision of the respondent's exercise of parenting time or visitation or companionship rights with respect to the child for a period not to exceed nine months, if the court makes the following findings of fact:

(i) The child is in danger from the respondent;

(ii) No other person or agency is available to provide the supervision.

(b) A court that requires an agency to provide supervision pursuant to division (E)(6)(a) of this section shall order the respondent to reimburse the agency for the cost of providing the supervision, if it determines that the respondent has sufficient income or resources to pay that cost.

(7)(a) If a protection order issued or consent agreement approved under this section includes a requirement that the respondent be evicted from or vacate the residence or household or refrain from entering the residence, school, business, or place of employment of the petitioner or a family or household member, the order or agreement shall state clearly that the order or agreement cannot be waived or nullified by an invitation to the respondent from the petitioner or other family or household member to enter the residence, school, business, or place of employment or by the respondent's entry into one of those places otherwise upon the consent of the petitioner or other family or household member.

(b) Division (E)(7)(a) of this section does not limit any discretion of a court to determine that a respondent charged with a violation of section 2919.27 of the Revised Code, with a violation of a municipal ordinance substantially equivalent to that section, or with contempt of court, which charge is based on an alleged violation of a protection order issued or consent agreement approved under this section, did not commit the violation or was not in contempt of court.

(F)(1) A copy of any protection order, or consent agreement, that is issued or approved under this section shall be issued by the court to the petitioner, to the respondent, and to all law enforcement agencies that have jurisdiction to enforce the order or agreement. The court shall direct that a copy of an order be delivered to the respondent on the same day that the order is entered.

(2) All law enforcement agencies shall establish and maintain an index for the protection orders and the approved consent agreements delivered to the agencies pursuant to division (F)(1) of this section. With respect to each order and consent agreement delivered, each agency shall note on the index the date and time that it received the order or consent agreement.

(3) Regardless of whether the petitioner has registered the order or agreement in the county in which the officer's agency has jurisdiction pursuant to division (N) of this section, any officer of a law enforcement agency shall enforce a protection order issued or consent agreement approved by any court in this state in accordance with the provisions of the order or agreement, including removing the respondent from the premises, if appropriate.

(G) Any proceeding under this section shall be conducted in accordance with the Rules of Civil Procedure, except that an order under this section may be obtained with or without bond. An order issued under this section, other than an ex parte order, that grants a protection order or approves a consent agreement, or that refuses to grant a protection order or approve a consent agreement, is a final, appealable order. The remedies and procedures provided in this section are in addition to, and not in lieu of, any other available civil or criminal remedies.

(H) The filing of proceedings under this section does not excuse a person from filing any report or giving any notice required by section 2151.421 of the Revised Code or by any other law. When a petition under this section alleges domestic violence against minor children, the court shall report the fact, or cause reports to be made, to a county, township, or municipal peace officer under section 2151.421 of the Revised Code.

(I) Any law enforcement agency that investigates a domestic dispute shall provide information to the family or household members involved regarding the relief available under this section and section 2919.26 of the Revised Code.

(J) Notwithstanding any provision of law to the contrary and regardless of whether a protection order is issued or a consent agreement is approved by a court of another county or a court of another state, no court or unit of state or local government shall charge any fee, cost, deposit, or money in connection with the filing of a petition pursuant to this section or in connection with the filing, issuance, registration, or service of a protection order or consent agreement, or for obtaining a certified copy of a protection order or consent agreement.

(K)(1) The court shall comply with Chapters 3119., 3121., 3123., and 3125. of the Revised Code when it makes or modifies an order for child support under this section.

(2) If any person required to pay child support under an order made under this section on or after April 15, 1985, or modified under this section on or after December 31, 1986, is found in contempt of court for failure to make support payments under the order, the court that makes the finding, in addition to any other penalty or remedy imposed, shall assess all court costs arising out of the contempt proceeding against the person and require the person to pay any reasonable attorney's fees of any adverse party, as determined by the court, that arose in relation to the act of contempt.

(L)(1) A person who violates a protection order issued or a consent agreement approved under this section is subject to the following sanctions:

(a) Criminal prosecution for a violation of section 2919.27 of the Revised Code, if the violation of the protection order or consent agreement constitutes a violation of that section;

(b) Punishment for contempt of court.

(2) The punishment of a person for contempt of court for violation of a protection order issued or a consent agreement approved under this section does not bar criminal prosecution of the person for a violation of section 2919.27 of the Revised Code. However, a person punished for contempt of court is entitled to credit for the punishment imposed upon conviction of a violation of that section, and a person convicted of a violation of that section shall not subsequently be punished for contempt of court arising out of the same activity.

(M) In all stages of a proceeding under this section, a petitioner may be accompanied by a victim advocate.

(N)(1) A petitioner who obtains a protection order or consent agreement under this section or a temporary protection order under section 2919.26 of the Revised Code may provide notice of the issuance or approval of the order or agreement to the judicial and law enforcement officials in any county other than the county in which the order is issued or the agreement is approved by registering that order or agreement in the other county pursuant to division (N)(2) of this section and filing a copy of the registered order or registered agreement with a law enforcement agency in the other county in accordance with that division. A person who obtains a protection order issued by a court of another state may provide notice of the issuance of the order to the judicial and law enforcement officials in any county of this state by registering the order in that county pursuant to section 2919.272 of the Revised Code and filing a copy of the registered order with a law enforcement agency in that county.

(2) A petitioner may register a temporary protection order, protection order, or consent agreement in a county other than the county in which the court that issued the order or approved the agreement is located in the following manner:

(a) The petitioner shall obtain a certified copy of the order or agreement from the clerk of the court that issued the order or approved the agreement and present that certified copy to the clerk of the court of common pleas or the clerk of a municipal court or county court in the county in which the order or agreement is to be registered.

(b) Upon accepting the certified copy of the order or agreement for registration, the clerk of the court of common pleas, municipal court, or county court shall place an endorsement of registration on the order or agreement and give the petitioner a copy of the order or agreement that bears that proof of registration.

(3) The clerk of each court of common pleas, the clerk of each municipal court, and the clerk of each county court shall maintain a registry of certified copies of temporary protection orders, protection orders, or consent agreements that have been issued or approved by courts in other counties and that have been registered with the clerk.

(2002 H 548, eff. 3–31–03; 2000 S 180, eff. 3–22–01; 1997 H 352, eff. 1–1–98; 1997 S 1, eff. 10–21–97; 1996 H 438, eff. 7–1–97; 1996 H 274, eff. 8–8–96; 1994 H 335, eff. 12–9–94; 1993 H 173, eff. 12–31–93; 1992 H 536, S 10; 1990 S 3, H 591; 1988 H 172, H 708; 1987 H 231; 1986 H 428, H 509; 1984 H 113, H 614, H 587; 1980 H 920; 1978 H 835)

3113.32 Records of domestic disputes and violence; procedures

(A) The sheriff of a county, constable or chief of police of a township, and chief of police of a city or village shall keep a separate record of domestic dispute and domestic violence problems on a form prepared and distributed by the superintendent of the bureau of criminal identification and investigation. The forms shall contain spaces for the reporting of all information that the superintendent determines to be relevant to domestic dispute and domestic violence problems, including, but not limited to, the number of domestic dispute and domestic violence problems reported to the law enforcement agency for which the record is kept, the relationship of the complainant and the person allegedly the victim of the domestic violence, if different, to the alleged offender, and the relationship of all other persons involved in the domestic dispute or domestic violence problem, and the action taken by the law enforcement officers who handled the domestic dispute or domestic violence problem. A copy of the record shall be submitted to the bureau each month.

(B) The superintendent of the bureeau [sic.] of criminal identification and investigation shall receive copies of monthly records of domestic dispute and domestic violence problems kept by local law enforcement agencies and submitted to him under division (A) of this section. The superintendent shall compile the data and annually produce a statistical public report on the incidence of domestic disputes and violence in this state and its political subdivisions. The report shall be prepared in such a manner that there is no identifying data, including the names and addresses of the persons involved in the domestic dispute and domestic violence problems, that would enable any person to determine the identity of any of the persons involved.

(C) The attorney general shall oversee the statistical reporting required pursuant to this section to ensure that it is complete and accurate.

(1984 H 587, eff. 9–25–84)

PENALTIES

3113.99 Penalties

Whoever violates section 3113.06 of the Revised Code is guilty of a misdemeanor of the first degree. If the offender previously has been convicted of or pleaded guilty to a violation of section 3113.06 of the Revised Code or if the court finds that the offender has failed to pay the cost of child maintenance under section 3113.06 of the Revised Code for a total accumulated period of twenty-six weeks out of one hundred four consecutive weeks, whether or not the twenty-six weeks were consecutive, a violation of section 3113.06 of the Revised Code is a felony of the fifth degree.

(2000 S 180, eff. 3–22–01; 1999 H 471, eff. 7–1–00; 1997 H 352, eff. 1–1–98; 1996 H 710, § 7, eff. 6–11–96; 1995 H 167, eff. 6–11–96; 1995 S 2, eff. 7–1–96; 1972 H 511, eff. 1–1–74; 1953 H 1)

CHAPTER 3121

WITHHOLDING OR DEDUCTION FROM INCOME

3121.08 Distribution of prisoner's earnings for child support

(A) As used in this section, "prison," "prison term," and "jail" have the same meanings as in section 2929.01 of the Revised Code.

(B) Notwithstanding any other section of the Revised Code, including sections 5145.16 and 5147.30 of the Revised Code, twenty-five per cent of any money earned pursuant to section 5145.16 or 5147.30 of the Revised Code by a prisoner in a prison or jail who has a dependent child receiving assistance under Chapter 5107. of the Revised Code, shall be paid to the state department of job and family services.

(2000 S 180, eff. 3–22–01)

CHAPTER 3123

CHILD SUPPORT—DEFAULT

3123.16 Monthly payments; employment protected

Any order issued under section 3123.14 of the Revised Code shall be payable at least monthly.

(2000 S 180, eff. 3–22–01)

3123.20 Employer not to discharge employee because of support order

No employer shall discharge an employee for reason of any order issued under the Revised Code to collect support due from the employee under a support order.

(2000 S 180, eff. 3–22–01)

3123.99 Penalties

Whoever violates section 3123.20 of the Revised Code shall be fined not less than fifty nor more than two hundred dollars and imprisoned not less than ten nor more than thirty days.

(2000 S 180, eff. 3–22–01)

CHAPTER 3125

CHILD SUPPORT ENFORCEMENT

3125.17 Employment of attorneys; obtaining legal services

Without the authorization of the court of common pleas or the consent of the prosecuting attorney and without engaging in competitive bidding to obtain the legal services, any child support enforcement agency may employ, through its appointing authority, staff attorneys to advise, assist, and represent the agency in its performance of its functions pertaining to the enforcement of support orders. The option to employ the staff attorneys shall be in addition to any other options available to the agency to obtain necessary legal services in connection with its performance of its functions pertaining to the enforcement of support orders, including the use of legal services provided by the prosecuting attorney pursuant to contract or otherwise or the obtaining of legal services through a competitive bidding process.

(2000 S 180, eff. 3–22–01)

CHAPTER 3301

DEPARTMENT OF EDUCATION

3301.32 Criminal records check; disqualification from employment

(A)(1) The chief administrator of any head start agency shall request the superintendent of the bureau of criminal identification and investigation to conduct a criminal records check with respect to any applicant who has applied to the head start agency for employment as a person responsible for the care, custody, or control of a child. If the applicant does not present proof that the applicant has been a resident of this state for the five-year period immediately prior to the date upon which the criminal records check is requested or does not provide evidence that within that five-year period the superintendent has requested information about the applicant from the federal bureau of investigation in a criminal records check, the chief administrator shall request that the superintendent obtain information from the federal bureau of investigation as a part of the criminal records check for the applicant. If the applicant presents proof that the applicant has been a resident of this state for that five-year period, the chief administrator may request that the superintendent include information from the federal bureau of investigation in the criminal records check.

(2) Any person required by division (A)(1) of this section to request a criminal records check shall provide to each applicant a copy of the form prescribed pursuant to division (C)(1) of section 109.572 of the Revised Code, provide to each applicant a standard impression sheet to obtain fingerprint impressions prescribed pursuant to division (C)(2) of section 109.572 of the Revised Code, obtain the completed form and impression sheet from each applicant, and forward the completed form and impression sheet to the superintendent of the bureau of criminal identification and investigation at the time the chief administrator requests a criminal records check pursuant to division (A)(1) of this section.

(3) Any applicant who receives pursuant to division (A)(2) of this section a copy of the form prescribed pursuant to division (C)(1) of section 109.572 of the Revised Code and a copy of an impression sheet prescribed pursuant to division (C)(2) of that section and who is requested to complete the form and provide a set of fingerprint impressions shall complete the form or provide all the information necessary to complete the form and shall provide the impression sheets with the impressions of the applicant's fingerprints. If an applicant, upon request, fails to provide the information necessary to complete the form or fails to provide impressions of the applicant's fingerprints, the head start agency shall not employ that applicant for any position for which a criminal records check is required by division (A)(1) of this section.

(B)(1) Except as provided in rules adopted by the director of job and family services in accordance with division (E) of this section, no head start agency shall employ a person as a person responsible for the care, custody, or control of a child if the person previously has been convicted of or pleaded guilty to any of the following:

(a) A violation of section 2903.01, 2903.02, 2903.03, 2903.04, 2903.11, 2903.12, 2903.13, 2903.16, 2903.21, 2903.34, 2905.01, 2905.02, 2905.05, 2907.02, 2907.03, 2907.04, 2907.05, 2907.06, 2907.07, 2907.08, 2907.09, 2907.21, 2907.22, 2907.23, 2907.25, 2907.31, 2907.32, 2907.321, 2907.322, 2907.323, 2911.01, 2911.02, 2911.11, 2911.12, 2919.12, 2919.22, 2919.24, 2919.25, 2923.12, 2923.13, 2923.161, 2925.02, 2925.03, 2925.04, 2925.05, 2925.06, or 3716.11 of the Revised Code, a violation of section 2905.04 of the Revised Code as it existed prior to July 1, 1996, a violation of section 2919.23 of the Revised Code that would have been a violation of section 2905.04 of the Revised Code as it existed prior to July 1, 1996, had the violation occurred prior to that date, a violation of section 2925.11 of the Revised Code that is not a minor drug possession offense, or felonious sexual penetration in violation of former section 2907.12 of the Revised Code;

(b) A violation of an existing or former law of this state, any other state, or the United States that is substantially equivalent to any of the offenses or violations described in division (B)(1)(a) of this section.

(2) A head start agency may employ an applicant conditionally until the criminal records check required by this section is completed and the agency receives the results of the criminal records check. If the results of the criminal records check indicate that, pursuant to division (B)(1) of this section, the applicant does not qualify for employment, the agency shall release the applicant from employment.

(C)(1) Each head start agency shall pay to the bureau of criminal identification and investigation the fee prescribed pursuant to division (C)(3) of section 109.572 of the Revised Code for each criminal records check conducted in accordance with that section upon the request pursuant to division (A)(1) of this section of the chief administrator of the head start agency.

(2) A head start agency may charge an applicant a fee for the costs it incurs in obtaining a criminal records check under this section. A fee charged under this division shall not exceed the amount of fees the agency pays under division (C)(1) of this section. If a fee is charged under this division, the agency shall notify the applicant at the time of the applicant's initial application for employment of the amount of the fee and that, unless the fee is paid, the head start agency will not consider the applicant for employment.

(D) The report of any criminal records check conducted by the bureau of criminal identification and investigation in accordance with section 109.572 of the Revised Code and pursuant to a request made under division (A)(1) of this section is not a public record for the purposes of section 149.43 of the Revised Code and shall not be made available to any person other than the applicant who is the subject of the criminal records check or the applicant's representative, the head start agency requesting the criminal records check or its representative, and any court, hearing officer, or other necessary individual involved in a case dealing with the denial of employment to the applicant.

(E) The director of job and family services shall adopt rules pursuant to Chapter 119. of the Revised Code to implement this section, including rules specifying circumstances under which a head start agency may hire a person who has been convicted of an offense listed in division (B)(1) of this section but who meets standards in regard to rehabilitation set by the director.

(F) Any person required by division (A)(1) of this section to request a criminal records check shall inform each person, at the time of the person's initial application for employment, that the person is required to provide a set of impressions of the person's fingerprints and that a criminal records check is required to be conducted and satisfactorily completed in accordance with section 109.572 of the Revised Code if the person comes under final consideration for appointment or employment as a precondition to employment for that position.

(G) As used in this section:

(1) "Applicant" means a person who is under final consideration for appointment or employment in a position with a head start agency as a person responsible for the care, custody, or control of a child.

(2) "Head start agency" has the same meaning as in section 3301.31 of the Revised Code.

(3) "Criminal records check" has the same meaning as in section 109.572 of the Revised Code.

(4) "Minor drug possession offense" has the same meaning as in section 2925.01 of the Revised Code.

(1999 H 471, eff. 7–1–00; 1996 S 269, eff. 7–1–96; 1996 H 445, eff. 9–3–96; 1995 S 2, eff. 7–1–96; 1994 H 694, eff. 11–11–94; 1993 S 38, eff. 10–29–93)

3301.541 Criminal records check; disqualification from employment

(A)(1) The director, head teacher, elementary principal, or site administrator of a preschool program shall request the superintendent of the bureau of criminal identification and investigation to conduct a criminal records check with respect to any applicant who has applied to the preschool program for employment as a person responsible for the care, custody, or control of a child. If the applicant does not present proof that the applicant has been a resident of this state for the five-year period immediately prior to the date upon which the criminal records check is requested or does not provide evidence that within that five-year period the superintendent has requested information about the applicant from the federal bureau of investigation in a criminal records check, the director, head teacher, or elementary principal shall request that the superintendent obtain information from the federal bureau of investigation as a part of the criminal records check for the applicant. If the applicant presents proof that the applicant has been a resident of this state for that five-year period, the director, head teacher, or elementary principal may request that the superintendent include information from the federal bureau of investigation in the criminal records check.

(2) Any director, head teacher, elementary principal, or site administrator required by division (A)(1) of this section to request a criminal records check shall provide to each applicant a copy of the form prescribed pursuant to division (C)(1) of section 109.572 of the Revised Code, provide to each applicant a standard impression sheet to obtain fingerprint impressions prescribed pursuant to division (C)(2) of section 109.572 of the Revised Code, obtain the completed form and impression sheet from each applicant, and forward the completed form and impression sheet to the superintendent of the bureau of criminal identification and investigation at the time the person requests a criminal records check pursuant to division (A)(1) of this section.

(3) Any applicant who receives pursuant to division (A)(2) of this section a copy of the form prescribed pursuant to division (C)(1) of section 109.572 of the Revised Code and a copy of an impression sheet prescribed pursuant to division (C)(2) of that section and who is requested to complete the form and provide a set of fingerprint impressions shall complete the form or provide all the information necessary to complete the form and provide the impression sheet with the impressions of the applicant's fingerprints. If an applicant, upon request, fails to provide the information necessary to complete the form or fails to provide impressions of the applicant's fingerprints, the preschool program shall not employ that applicant for any position for which a criminal records check is required by division (A)(1) of this section.

(B)(1) Except as provided in rules adopted by the department of education in accordance with division (E) of this section, no preschool program shall employ a person as a person responsible for the care, custody, or control of a child if the person previously has been convicted of or pleaded guilty to any of the following:

(a) A violation of section 2903.01, 2903.02, 2903.03, 2903.04, 2903.11, 2903.12, 2903.13, 2903.16, 2903.21, 2903.34, 2905.01, 2905.02, 2905.05, 2907.02, 2907.03, 2907.04, 2907.05, 2907.06, 2907.07, 2907.08, 2907.09, 2907.21, 2907.22, 2907.23, 2907.25, 2907.31, 2907.32, 2907.321, 2907.322, 2907.323, 2911.01, 2911.02, 2911.11, 2911.12, 2919.12, 2919.22, 2919.24, 2919.25, 2923.12, 2923.13, 2923.161, 2925.02, 2925.03, 2925.04, 2925.05, 2925.06, or 3716.11 of the Revised Code, a violation of section 2905.04 of the Revised Code as it existed prior to July 1, 1996, a violation of section 2919.23 of the Revised Code that would have been a violation of section 2905.04 of the Revised Code as it existed prior to July 1, 1996, had the violation occurred prior to that date, a violation of section 2925.11 of the Revised Code that is not a minor drug possession offense, or felonious sexual penetration in violation of former section 2907.12 of the Revised Code;

(b) A violation of an existing or former law of this state, any other state, or the United States that is substantially equivalent to any of the offenses or violations described in division (B)(1)(a) of this section.

(2) A preschool program may employ an applicant conditionally until the criminal records check required by this section is completed and the preschool program receives the results of the criminal records check. If the results of the criminal records check indicate that, pursuant to division (B)(1) of this section, the applicant does not qualify for employment, the preschool program shall release the applicant from employment.

(C)(1) Each preschool program shall pay to the bureau of criminal identification and investigation the fee prescribed pursuant to division (C)(3) of section 109.572 of the Revised Code for each criminal records check conducted in accordance with that section upon the request pursuant to division (A)(1) of this section of the director, head teacher, elementary principal, or site administrator of the preschool program.

(2) A preschool program may charge an applicant a fee for the costs it incurs in obtaining a criminal records check under this section. A fee charged under this division shall not exceed the amount of fees the preschool program pays under division (C)(1) of this section. If a fee is charged under this division, the preschool program shall notify the applicant at the time of the applicant's initial application for employment of the amount of the fee and that, unless the fee is paid, the applicant will not be considered for employment.

(D) The report of any criminal records check conducted by the bureau of criminal identification and investigation in accordance with section 109.572 of the Revised Code and pursuant to a request under division (A)(1) of this section is not a public record for the purposes of section 149.43 of the Revised Code and shall not be made available to any person other than the applicant who is the subject of the criminal records check or the applicant's representative, the preschool program requesting the criminal records check or its representative, and any court, hearing officer, or other necessary individual in a case dealing with the denial of employment to the applicant.

(E) The department of education shall adopt rules pursuant to Chapter 119. of the Revised Code to implement this section, including rules specifying circumstances under which a preschool program may hire a person who has been convicted of an offense listed in division (B)(1) of this section but who meets standards in regard to rehabilitation set by the department.

(F) Any person required by division (A)(1) of this section to request a criminal records check shall inform each person, at the time of the person's initial application for employment, that the person is required to provide a set of impressions of the person's fingerprints and that a criminal records check is required to be conducted and satisfactorily completed in accordance with section 109.572 of the Revised Code if the person comes under final consideration for appointment or employment as a precondition to employment for that position.

(G) As used in this section:

(1) "Applicant" means a person who is under final consideration for appointment or employment in a position with a preschool program as a person responsible for the care, custody, or control of a child, except that "applicant" does not include a person already employed by a board of education or chartered nonpublic school in a position of care, custody, or control of a child who is under consideration for a different position with such board or school.

(2) "Criminal records check" has the same meaning as in section 109.572 of the Revised Code.

(3) "Minor drug possession offense" has the same meaning as in section 2925.01 of the Revised Code.

(H) If the board of education of a local school district adopts a resolution requesting the assistance of the educational service center in which the local district has territory in conducting criminal records checks of substitute teachers under this section, the appointing or hiring officer of such educational service center governing board shall serve for purposes of this section as the appointing or hiring officer of the local board in the case of hiring substitute teachers for employment in the local district.

(1997 H 396, eff. 1–30–98; 1996 S 269, eff. 7–1–96; 1996 H 445, eff. 9–3–96; 1995 S 2, eff. 7–1–96; 1995 H 117, eff. 9–29–95; 1994 H 694, eff. 11–11–94; 1993 S 38, eff. 10–29–93)

CHAPTER 3313

BOARDS OF EDUCATION

3313.20 Rules; persons entering premises; locker searches; employee attendance at professional meetings, expenses

(A) The board of education of a school district or the governing board of an educational service center shall make any rules that are necessary for its government and the government of its employees, pupils of its schools, and all other persons entering upon its school grounds or premises. Rules regarding entry of persons other than students, staff, and faculty upon school grounds or premises shall be posted conspicuously at or near the entrance to the school grounds or premises, or near the perimeter of the school grounds or premises, if there are no formal entrances, and at the main entrance to each school building.

(B)(1) The board of education of each city, local, exempted village, or joint vocational school district may adopt a written policy that authorizes principals of public schools within the district or their designees to do one or both of the following:

(a) Search any pupil's locker and the contents of the locker that is searched if the principal reasonably suspects that the locker or its contents contains evidence of a pupil's violation of a criminal statute or of a school rule;

(b) Search any pupil's locker and the contents of any pupil's locker at any time if the board of education posts in a conspicuous place in each school building that has lockers available for use by pupils a notice that the lockers are the property of the board of education and that the lockers and the contents of all the lockers are subject to random search at any time without regard to whether there is a reasonable suspicion that any locker or its contents contains evidence of a violation of a criminal statute or a school rule.

(2) A board of education's adoption of or failure to adopt a written policy pursuant to division (B)(1) of this section does not prevent the principal of any school from searching at any time the locker of any pupil and the contents of any locker of any pupil in the school if an emergency situation exists or appears to exist that immediately threatens the health or safety of any person, or threatens to damage or destroy any property, under the control of the board of education and if a search of lockers and the contents of the lockers is reasonably necessary to avert that threat or apparent threat.

(C) Any employee may receive compensation and expenses for days on which he is excused, in accordance with the policy statement of the board, by the superintendent of such board or by a responsible administrative official designated by the superintendent for the purpose of attending professional meetings as defined by the board policy, and the board may provide and pay the salary of a substitute for such days. The expenses thus incurred by an employee shall be paid by the board from the appropriate fund of the school district or the educational service center governing board fund provided that statements of expenses are furnished in accordance with the policy statement of the board.

(D) Each city, local, and exempted village school district shall adopt a written policy governing the attendance of employees at professional meetings.

(1995 H 117, eff. 9–29–95; 1993 S 29, eff. 9–1–94; 1992 H 154; 1984 S 385; 1974 S 436; 131 v S 21; 127 v 552; 125 v 903; 1953 H 1; GC 4834–5)

CHAPTER 3319

SCHOOLS—SUPERINTENDENT; TEACHERS; EMPLOYEES

3319.20 Prosecutor to notify board of education of certain convictions of board employees

Whenever an employee of a board of education, other than an employee who is a license holder to whom section 3319.52 of the Revised Code applies, is convicted of or pleads guilty to a felony, a violation of section 2907.04 or 2907.06 or of division (A) or (B) of section 2907.07 of the Revised Code, an offense of violence, theft offense, or drug abuse offense that is not a minor misdemeanor, or a violation of an ordinance of a municipal corporation that is substantively comparable to a felony or to a violation or offense of that nature, the prosecutor in the case, on forms prescribed and furnished by the state board of education, shall notify the employing board of education of the employee's name and residence address, the fact that the employee was convicted of or pleaded guilty to the specified offense, the section of the Revised Code or the municipal ordinance violated, and the sentence imposed by the court.

The prosecutor shall give the notification required by this section no earlier than the fifth day following the expiration of the period within which the employee may file a notice of appeal from the judgment of the trial court under Appellate Rule 4(B) and no later than the eighth day following the expiration of that period. The notification also shall indicate whether the employee appealed the conviction, and, if applicable, the court in which the appeal will be heard. If the employee is permitted, by leave of court pursuant to Appellate Rule 5, to appeal the judgment of the trial court subsequent to the expiration of the period for filing a notice of appeal under Appellate Rule 4(B), the prosecutor promptly shall notify the employing board of education of the appeal and the court in which the appeal will be heard.

As used in this section, "theft offense" has the same meaning as in section 2913.01 of the Revised Code, "drug abuse offense" has the same meaning as in section 2925.01 of the Revised Code, and "prosecutor" has the same meaning as in section 2935.01 of the Revised Code.

(2003 S 5, eff. 7–31–03; 1996 S 230, eff. 10–29–96; 1995 S 2, eff. 7–1–96; 1993 H 152, eff. 7–1–93; 1983 H 109)

3319.31 Refusal, limitation, suspension, or revocation of license

(A) As used in this section and sections 3123.41 to 3123.50 and 3319.311 of the Revised Code, "license" means a certificate, license, or permit described in division (B) of section 3301.071, in section 3301.074, 3319.088, 3319.29, 3319.302, or 3319.304, or in division (A) of section 3319.303 of the Revised Code.

(B) For any of the following reasons, the state board of education, in accordance with Chapter 119. and section 3319.311 of the Revised Code, may refuse to issue a license to an applicant, may limit a license it issues to an applicant, or may suspend, revoke, or limit a license that has been issued to any person:

(1) Engaging in an immoral act, incompetence, negligence, or conduct that is unbecoming to the applicant's or person's position;

(2) A plea of guilty to, a finding of guilt by a jury or court of, or a conviction of any of the following:

(a) A felony;

(b) A violation of section 2907.04 or 2907.06 or division (A) or (B) of section 2907.07 of the Revised Code;

(c) An offense of violence;

(d) A theft offense, as defined in section 2913.01 of the Revised Code;

(e) A drug abuse offense, as defined in section 2925.01 of the Revised Code, that is not a minor misdemeanor;

(f) A violation of an ordinance of a municipal corporation that is substantively comparable to an offense listed in divisions (B)(2)(a) to (e) of this section.

(C) The state board may take action under division (B) of this section on the basis of substantially comparable conduct occurring in a jurisdiction outside this state or occurring before a person applies for or receives any license.

(D) The state board may adopt rules in accordance with Chapter 119. of the Revised Code to carry out this section and section 3319.311 of the Revised Code.

(2004 H 106, eff. 9–16–04; 2004 S 2, eff. 6–9–04; 2003 S 5, eff. 7–31–03; 2001 H 196, eff. 11–20–01; 2000 S 180, eff. 3–22–01; 1996 S 230, § 3, eff. 11–15–96; 1996 S 230, § 1, eff. 10–29–96; 1995 H 167, eff. 11–15–96; 1995 S 2, eff. 7–1–96; 1993 H 152, eff. 7–1–93)

3319.311 Investigations; hearings; orders

(A) The state board of education, or the superintendent of public instruction on behalf of the board, may investigate any information received about a person that reasonably appears to be a basis for action under section 3319.31 of the Revised Code. The board shall contract with the office of the Ohio attorney general to conduct any investigation of that nature. The board shall pay for the costs of the contract only from moneys in the state board of education licensure fund established under division (B) of section 3319.51 of the Revised Code. All information obtained during an investigation is confidential and is not a public record under section 149.43 of the Revised Code. If an investigation is conducted under this division regarding information received about a person and no action is taken against the person under this section or section 3319.31 of the Revised Code within two years of the completion of the investigation, all records of the investigation shall be expunged.

(B) The superintendent of public instruction shall review the results of each investigation of a person conducted under division (A) of this section and shall determine, on behalf of the state board, whether the results warrant initiating action under section 3319.31 of the Revised Code. The superintendent shall advise the board of such determination at a meeting of the board. Within fourteen days of the next meeting of the board, any member of the board may ask that the question of initiating action under section 3319.31 of the Revised Code be placed on the board's agenda for that next meeting. Prior to initiating that action against any person, the person's name and any other personally identifiable information shall remain confidential.

(C) The board shall take no action against a person under section 3319.31 of the Revised Code without providing the person with written notice of the charges and with an opportunity for a hearing in accordance with Chapter 119. of the Revised Code.

(D) For purposes of an investigation under division (A) of this section or a hearing under division (C) of this section, the board, or the superintendent on behalf of the board, may administer oaths, order the taking of depositions, issue subpoenas, and compel the attendance of witnesses and the production of books, accounts, papers, records, documents, and testimony. The issuance of subpoenas under this division may be by certified mail or personal delivery to the person.

(E) The superintendent, on behalf of the board, may enter into a consent agreement with a person against whom action is being taken under section 3319.31 of the Revised Code. The board may adopt rules governing the superintendent's action under this division.

(F) The board automatically may suspend any license without a prior hearing if the license holder is convicted of or pleads guilty to one or more of the following offenses or a violation of an ordinance of a municipal corporation or a law of another state that is substantially comparable to one of the following offenses: aggravated murder; murder; aggravated arson; aggravated robbery; aggravated burglary; voluntary manslaughter; felonious assault; kidnapping; rape; sexual battery; gross sexual imposition; or unlawful sexual conduct with a minor. A suspension under this division is effective on the date of the conviction or guilty plea.

For a suspension under this division, the board, in accordance with section 119.07 of the Revised Code, shall issue a written order of suspension to the license holder by certified mail or in person and shall afford the person a hearing upon request. If the person does not request a hearing within the time limits established by that section, the board shall enter a final order revoking the person's license. An order of suspension under this division is not subject to suspension by a court during the pendency of an appeal filed under section 119.12 of the Revised Code.

An order of suspension under this division shall remain in effect, unless reversed on appeal, until the final order of the board, issued pursuant to this section and Chapter 119. of the Revised Code, becomes effective. The board shall issue a final order within sixty days of the date of an order of suspension under this division or a hearing on an order of suspension, whichever is later. If the board fails to issue a final order by that deadline, the order of suspension is dissolved. No dissolution of an order of suspension under this division shall invalidate a subsequent final order of the board.

(G) No surrender of a license shall be effective until the board takes action to accept the surrender unless the surrender is pursuant to a consent agreement entered into under division (E) of this section.

(2004 S 2, eff. 6–9–04; 2000 H 442, eff. 10–17–00; 1996 S 230, eff. 10–29–96; 1995 S 2, eff. 7–1–96; 1993 H 152, eff. 7–1–93)

3319.45 Reports of violations for which pupils subject to permanent exclusion

If a principal of a public school in a city, local, exempted village, or joint vocational school district, acting in his official or professional capacity, has knowledge of or has observed a pupil committing a violation listed in division (A) of section 3313.662 of the Revised Code, regardless of whether or not the pupil was sixteen years of age or older at the time of the commission of the act or violation, and the violation was committed on property owned and controlled by, or at any activity held under the auspices of, the board of education of the school district, both of the following apply:

(A) The principal, within one school day after obtaining his knowledge of or observing the act or violation, shall report the violation to the superintendent of the school district in which the school is located or to the designee of the superintendent.

(B) The principal, within a reasonable period of time after obtaining his knowledge of or observing the act or violation, may report the act or violation to a law enforcement officer of the jurisdiction in which the violation occurred or, if the pupil is a juvenile, report the violation to either a law enforcement officer of the jurisdiction in which the act occurred or in the jurisdiction in which the pupil resides.

(1992 H 154, eff. 7–31–92)

3319.52 Notification of convictions

(A) As used in this section:

(1) "License" has the same meaning as in section 3319.31 of the Revised Code.

(2) "Prosecutor" has the same meaning as in section 2935.01 of the Revised Code.

(B) If there is any judicial finding of guilt or any conviction against a license holder for any of the offenses listed in divisions (B)(2)(a) to (f) of section 3319.31 of the Revised Code, the prosecutor in the case, on forms that the state board of education shall prescribe and furnish, promptly shall notify the board and, if known, any school district or chartered nonpublic school employing the license holder of the license holder's name and residence address, and the fact that the license holder pleaded guilty to or was convicted of the offense.

(1996 S 230, eff. 10–29–96; 1995 S 2, eff. 7–1–96; 1993 H 152, eff. 7–1–93)

CHAPTER 3321

SCHOOL ATTENDANCE

ATTENDANCE OFFICERS

3321.14 Attendance officer; pupil–personnel workers

Notwithstanding division (D) of section 3311.19 and division (D) of section 3311.52 of the Revised Code, the provisions of this section and sections 3321.15 to 3321.21 of the Revised Code that apply to a city school district or its superintendent do not apply to any joint vocational or cooperative education school district or its superintendent unless otherwise specified.

The board of education of every city school district and of every exempted village school district shall employ an attendance officer, and may employ or appoint any assistants that the board deems advisable. In cities of one hundred thousand population or over, the board may appoint, subject to the nomination of the superintendent of schools, one or more pupil-personnel workers and make provision for the traveling expenses within the school district of those employees.

(2000 S 181, eff. 9–4–00; 1992 S 195, eff. 4–16–93; 1953 H 1; GC 4852)

3321.15 Educational service center attendance officer

Every governing board of an educational service center shall employ an educational service center attendance officer, and may employ or appoint such assistants as the board deems advisable. The compensation and necessary traveling expenses of such attendance officer and assistants shall be paid out of the educational service center governing board fund. With the consent and approval of the judge of the juvenile court, a probation officer of the court may be designated as the service center attendance officer or as an assistant. The compensation of the probation officers of the juvenile court so designated shall be fixed and paid in the same manner as salaries of other probation officers of the juvenile court; their traveling expenses as attendance officers which would not be incurred as probation officers shall be paid out of the educational service center governing board fund. In addition to the compensation provided in this section the board may pay such additional compensation as it deems advisable, to any probation officer designated as attendance officer and such additional amount shall be paid from the educational service center governing board fund. The attendance officer and assistants shall work under the direction of the educational service center superintendent. The authority of such attendance officer and assistants shall extend to all the local school districts served by the service center. This section does not confine their authority to investigate employment to that within the territory of the service center.

(1995 H 117, eff. 9–29–95; 1953 H 1, eff. 10–1–53; GC 4852–1)

3321.16 Investigation of nonattendance

An attendance officer or assistant provided for by section 3321.14 or 3321.15 of the Revised Code may investigate any case of nonattendance at school or part-time school of a child under eighteen years of age or supposed to be under eighteen years of age resident in the district for which such attendance officer or assistant is employed, or of any such child found in the district or enrolled in any school within the district and of any child above eighteen years of age if enrolled in any school within the district, and may take such action as the superintendent of schools directs or as such attendance officer or assistant deems proper in the absence of specific direction.

(126 v 392, eff. 3–17–55; 1953 H 1; GC 4852–2)

3321.17 Powers of officer and assistants

The attendance officer and assistants provided for by section 3321.14 or 3321.15 of the Revised Code shall be vested with police powers, may serve warrants, and may enter workshops, factories, stores, and all other places where children are employed and do whatever is necessary in the way of investigation or otherwise to enforce the laws relating to compulsory education and the employment of minors. The attendance officer or assistant may also take into custody any youth of compulsory school age not legally employed on an age and schooling certificate who is not attending school and shall conduct such youth to the school he has been attending or should rightfully attend.

(126 v 392, eff. 3–17–55; 1953 H 1; GC 4852–3)

ENFORCEMENT

3321.18 Enforcement proceedings

The attendance officer provided for by section 3321.14 or 3321.15 of the Revised Code shall institute proceedings against any officer, parent, guardian, or other person violating laws relating to compulsory education and the employment of minors, and otherwise discharge the duties described in sections 3321.14 to 3321.21 of the Revised Code, and perform any other service that the superintendent of schools or board of education of the district by which the attendance officer is employed considers necessary to preserve the morals and secure the good conduct of school children, and to enforce those laws.

The attendance officer shall be furnished with copies of the enumeration in each school district in which the attendance officer serves and of the lists of pupils enrolled in the schools and shall report to the superintendent discrepancies between these lists and the enumeration.

The attendance officer and assistants shall cooperate with the director of commerce in enforcing the laws relating to the employment of minors. The attendance officer shall furnish upon request any data that the attendance officer and the attendance officer's assistants have collected in their reports of children from six to eighteen years of age and also concerning employers to the director and upon request to the state board of education. The attendance officer shall keep a record of the attendance officer's transactions for the inspection and information of the superintendent of schools and the board of education; and shall make reports to the superintendent of schools as often as required by the superintendent. The state board of education may prescribe forms for the use of attendance officers in the performance of their duties. The blank forms and record books or indexes shall be furnished to the attendance officers by the boards of education by which they are employed.

(2000 S 181, eff. 9–4–00; 1999 H 471, eff. 7–1–00; 1995 S 162, eff. 10–29–95; 1978 H 811, eff. 8–21–78; 126 v 392, 655; 1953 H 1; GC 4852–4)

3321.19 Examination of cases of supposed truancy; notice to parent or guardian; educational program for parent or guardian; complaints

(A) As used in this section and section 3321.191 of the Revised Code:

(1) "Habitual truant" has the same meaning as in section 2151.011 of the Revised Code.

(2) "Chronic truant" has the same meaning as in section 2152.02 of the Revised Code.

(B) When a board of education of any city, exempted village, local, joint vocational, or cooperative education school district or the governing board of any educational service center determines that a student in its district has been truant and the parent, guardian, or other person having care of the child has failed to cause the student's attendance at school, the board may require the parent, guardian, or other person having care of the child pursuant to division (B) of this section to attend an educational program established pursuant to rules adopted by the state board of education for the purpose of encouraging parental involvement in compelling the attendance of the child at school.

No parent, guardian, or other person having care of a child shall fail without good cause to attend an educational program described in this division if the parent, guardian, or other person has been served notice pursuant to division (C) of this section.

(C) On the request of the superintendent of schools, the superintendent of any educational service center, the board of education of any city, exempted village, local, joint vocational, or cooperative education school district, or the governing board of any educational service center or when it otherwise comes to the notice of the attendance officer or other appropriate officer of the school district, the attendance officer or other appropriate officer shall examine into any case of supposed truancy within the district and shall warn the child, if found truant, and the child's parent, guardian, or other person having care of the child, in writing, of the legal consequences of being an habitual or chronic truant. When any child of compulsory school age, in violation of law, is not attending school, the attendance or other appropriate officer shall notify the parent, guardian, or other person having care of that child of the fact, and require the parent, guardian, or other person to cause the child to attend school immediately. The parent, guardian, or other person having care of the child shall cause the child's attendance at school. Upon the failure of the parent, guardian, or other person having care of the child to do so, the attendance officer or other appropriate officer, if so directed by the superintendent, the district board, or the educational service center governing board, shall send notice requiring the attendance of that parent, guardian, or other person at a parental education program established pursuant to division (B) of this section and, subject to divisions (D) and (E) of this section, may file a complaint against the parent, guardian, or other person having care of the child in any court of competent jurisdiction.

(D) Upon the failure of the parent, guardian, or other person having care of the child to cause the child's attendance at school, if the child is considered an habitual truant, the board of education of the school district or the governing board of the educational service center shall do either or both of the following:

(1) Take any appropriate action as an intervention strategy contained in the policy developed by the board pursuant to section 3321.191 of the Revised Code;

(2) File a complaint in the juvenile court of the county in which the child has a residence or legal settlement or in which the child is supposed to attend school jointly against the child and the parent, guardian, or other person having care of the child. A complaint filed in the juvenile court under this division shall allege that the child is an unruly child for being an habitual truant or is a delinquent child for being an habitual truant who previously has been adjudicated an unruly child for being an habitual truant and that the parent, guardian, or other person having care of the child has violated section 3321.38 of the Revised Code.

(E) Upon the failure of the parent, guardian, or other person having care of the child to cause the child's attendance at school, if the child is considered a chronic truant, the board of education of the school district or the governing board of the educational service center shall file a complaint in the juvenile court of the county in which the child has a residence or legal settlement or in which the child is supposed to attend school jointly against the child and the parent, guardian, or other person having care of the child. A complaint filed in the juvenile court under this division shall allege that the child is a delinquent child for being a chronic truant and that the parent, guardian, or other person having care of the child has violated section 3321.38 of the Revised Code.

(2000 S 179, § 3, eff. 1–1–02; 2000 S 181, eff. 9–4–00; 1989 S 140, eff. 10–2–89; 1953 H 1; GC 4852–5)

3321.191 Policy addressing attendance practice of habitual truant

(A) No later than August 31, 2000, the board of education of each city, exempted village, local, joint vocational, and cooperative education school district and the governing board of each educational service center shall adopt a policy to guide employees of the school district or service center in addressing and ameliorating the attendance practice of any pupil who is an habitual truant. In developing the policy, the appropriate board shall consult with the judge of the juvenile court of the county or counties in which the district or service center is located, with the parents, guardians, or other persons having care of the pupils attending school in the district, and with appropriate state and local agencies. The board shall incorporate into the policy as an intervention strategy the assignment of an habitual truant to an alternative school pursuant to section 3313.533 of the Revised Code if an alternative school has been established by the board under that section.

(B) The policy developed under division (A) of this section may include as an intervention strategy any of the following actions, if appropriate:

(1) Providing a truancy intervention program for an habitual truant;

(2) Providing counseling for an habitual truant;

(3) Requesting or requiring a parent, guardian, or other person having care of an habitual truant to attend parental involvement programs, including programs adopted under section 3313.472 or 3313.663 of the Revised Code;

(4) Requesting or requiring a parent, guardian, or other person having care of an habitual truant to attend truancy prevention mediation programs;

(5) Notification of the registrar of motor vehicles under section 3321.13 of the Revised Code;

(6) Taking legal action under section 2919.222, 3321.20, or 3321.38 of the Revised Code.

(C) Nothing in this section shall be construed to limit the duty or authority of a district board of education or governing body of an educational service center to develop other policies related to truancy or to limit the duty or authority of any employee of the school district or service center to respond to pupil truancy.

(2000 S 181, eff. 9–4–00)

3321.20 Warning to parent; complaint

When any child, in violation of section 3321.08 or 3321.09 of the Revised Code, is not attending a part-time school or class, the attendance officer shall warn the child and the child's parent, guardian, or other person in charge of the child in writing of the legal consequences of the child's failure to attend the part-time school or class. If the parent, guardian, or other person in charge of that child fails to cause the child's attendance at the part-time school or class, the attendance officer shall make complaint against the parent, guardian, or other person in charge of the child in the juvenile court of the county in which the child has a residence or legal settlement or in which the child is supposed to attend the part-time school or class.

(2000 S 181, eff. 9–4–00; 1953 H 1, eff. 10–1–53; GC 4852–6)

PROHIBITIONS AND PENALTIES

3321.38 Failure to send child to school

(A) No parent, guardian, or other person having care of a child of compulsory school age shall violate any provision of section 3321.01, 3321.03, 3321.04, 3321.07, 3321.10, 3321.19, 3321.20, or 3331.14 of the Revised Code. The juvenile court, which has exclusive original jurisdiction over any violation of this section pursuant to section 2151.23 of the Revised Code, may require a person convicted of violating this division to give bond in a sum of not more than five hundred dollars with sureties to the approval of the court, conditioned that the person will cause the child under the person's charge to attend upon instruction as provided by law, and remain as a pupil in the school or class during the term prescribed by law. If the juvenile court adjudicates the child as an unruly or delinquent child for being an habitual or chronic truant pursuant to section 2151.35 of the Revised Code, the court shall warn the parent, guardian, or other person having care of the child that any subsequent adjudication of that nature involving the child may result in a criminal charge against the parent, guardian, or other person having care of the child for a violation of division (C) of section 2919.21 or section 2919.24 of the Revised Code.

(B) This section does not relieve from prosecution and conviction any parent, guardian, or other person upon further violation of any provision in any of the sections specified in division (A) of this section, any provision of section 2919.222 or 2919.24 of the Revised Code, or division (C) of section 2919.21 of the Revised Code. A forfeiture of the bond shall not relieve that parent, guardian, or other person from prosecution and conviction upon further violation of any provision in any of those sections or that division.

(C) Section 4109.13 of the Revised Code applies to this section.

(D) No parent, guardian, or other person having care of a child of compulsary *[sic]* school age shall fail to give bond as required by division (A) of this section in the sum of one hundred dollars with sureties as required by the court.

(2002 H 490, eff. 1–1–04; 2000 S 181, eff. 9–4–00; 1995 S 2, eff. 7–1–96; 1989 S 140, eff. 10–2–89; 1978 H 883; 129 v 582; 126 v 655; 1953 H 1; GC 12974, 12975)

3321.99 Penalties

Whoever violates division (A) of section 3321.38 of the Revised Code may be fined not more than five hundred dollars or may be ordered to perform not more than seventy hours of community service work.

(2000 S 181, eff. 9–4–00; 1995 S 2, eff. 7–1–96; 132 v S 191, eff. 11–14–67; 1953 H 1)

CHAPTER 3345

STATE UNIVERSITIES—GENERAL POWERS

Section

3345.04 Appointment of state university law enforcement officers

(A) As used in this section, "felony" has the same meaning as in section 109.511 of the Revised Code.

(B) Subject to division (C) of this section, the board of trustees of a state university, the board of trustees of the medical college of Ohio at Toledo, the board of trustees of the northeastern Ohio universities college of medicine, the board of trustees of a state community college, and the board of trustees of a technical college or community college district operating a technical or a community college may designate one or more employees of the institution, as a state university law enforcement officer, in accordance with section 109.77 of the Revised Code, and, as state university law enforcement officers, those employees shall take an oath of office, wear the badge of office, serve as peace officers for the college or university, and give bond to the state for the proper and faithful discharge of their duties in the amount that the board of trustees requires.

(C)(1) The board of trustees of an institution listed in division (B) of this section shall not designate an employee of the institution as a state university law enforcement officer pursuant to that division on a permanent basis, on a temporary basis, for a probationary term, or on other than a permanent basis if the employee previously has been convicted of or has pleaded guilty to a felony.

(2)(a) The board of trustees shall terminate the employment as a state university law enforcement officer of an employee designated as a state university law enforcement officer under division (B) of this section if that employee does either of the following:

(i) Pleads guilty to a felony;

(ii) Pleads guilty to a misdemeanor pursuant to a negotiated plea agreement as provided in division (D) of section 2929.43 of the Revised Code in which the employee agrees to surrender the certificate awarded to the employee under section 109.77 of the Revised Code.

(b) The board of trustees shall suspend from employment as a state university law enforcement officer an employee designated as a state university law enforcement officer under division (B) of this section if that employee is convicted, after trial, of a felony. If the state university law enforcement officer files an appeal from that conviction and the conviction is upheld by the highest court to which the appeal is taken or if the state university law enforcement officer does not file a timely appeal, the board of trustees shall terminate the employment of that state university law enforcement officer. If the state university law enforcement officer files an appeal that results in that officer's acquittal of the felony or conviction of a misdemeanor, or in the dismissal of the felony charge against that officer, the board of trustees shall reinstate that state university law enforcement officer. A state university law enforcement officer who is reinstated under division (C)(2)(b) of this section shall not receive any back pay unless that officer's conviction of the felony was reversed on appeal, or the felony charge was dismissed, because the court found insufficient evidence to convict the officer of the felony.

(3) Division (C) of this section does not apply regarding an offense that was committed prior to January 1, 1997.

(4) The suspension from employment, or the termination of the employment, of a state university law enforcement officer under division (C)(2) of this section shall be in accordance with Chapter 119. of the Revised Code.

(2002 H 490, eff. 1–1–04; 1996 H 566, eff. 10–16–96; 1996 H 568, eff. 11–6–96; 1981 H 583, eff. 3–16–82; 1979 H 5; 1978 H 588; 1977 H 506; 1973 S 72; 132 v S 426, H 60, H 134; 131 v S 212, S 395; 130 v Pt 2, H 2, H 7; 1953 H 1; GC 4863–3, 4863–4)

3345.041 Counties, municipalities, townships, and park districts may use state university law enforcement officers

(A) The board of trustees of a state university or college may enter into an agreement with one or more townships, municipal corporations, counties, park districts created under section 1545.04 of the Revised Code, township park districts created under section 511.18 of the Revised Code, or other state universities or colleges and a township, municipal corporation, county, park district, or township park district may enter into an agreement with a state university or college upon such terms as are agreed to by them, to allow the use of state university law enforcement officers designated under section 3345.04 of the Revised Code to perform any police function, exercise any police power, or render any police service on behalf of the contracting political subdivision, or state university or college, that it may perform, exercise, or render.

(B) Chapter 2743. of the Revised Code applies to a state university or college when its law enforcement officers are serving outside the university or college pursuant to an agreement entered into pursuant to division (A) of this section. State university law enforcement officers acting outside the state university or college by which they are employed, pursuant to an agreement entered into pursuant to division (A) of this section, shall be entitled to participate in any indemnity fund established by their employer to the same extent as while acting within the employing state university or college and are entitled to all the rights and benefits of Chapter 4123. of the Revised Code. The state university law enforcement officers also retain their personal immunity from civil liability specified in section 9.86 of the Revised Code.

A township, municipal corporation, county, park district, or township park district that enters into an agreement pursuant to division (A) of this section is not subject to civil liability under Chapter 2744. of the Revised Code as the result of any action or omission of any state university law enforcement officer acting pursuant to the agreement.

(C) Agreements entered into pursuant to division (A) of this section may provide for the reimbursement of the state university or college providing police services under such agreement for the costs incurred by its law enforcement officers for the policing of the political subdivision, or of the state university or college to which such services are provided. Each contract may provide for the ascertainment of costs and shall be of a duration not in excess of four years. All payments pursuant to any agreement in reimbursement of the costs of policing shall be held and administered as provided by section 3345.05 of the Revised Code.

(D) An agreement entered into pursuant to division (A) of this section shall specify whether the political subdivision or the state university or college to which police services are provided under such agreement will or will not indemnify and hold harmless the state university or college providing police services under such agreement for any damages awarded by the court of claims in any civil action arising from any action or omission of any state university law enforcement officer acting pursuant to the agreement.

(E) As used in this section, "state university or college" means any state university or college identified in section 3345.04 of the Revised Code.

(1996 H 568, eff. 11–6–96; 1996 H 268, eff. 5–8–96; 1987 H 305, eff. 10–20–87)

3345.21 Authority to maintain law and order on campus

The board of trustees of any college or university which receives any state funds in support thereof, shall regulate the use of the grounds, buildings, equipment, and facilities of such college or university and the conduct of the students, staff, faculty, and visitors to the campus so that law and order are maintained and the college or university may pursue its educational objectives and programs in an orderly manner.

The board of trustees of each such college or university shall adopt rules for the conduct of the students, faculty, visitors, and staff, and may provide for the ejection from college or university property, suspension or expulsion of a person who violates such regulations [1]. All such rules shall be published in a manner reasonably designed to come to the attention of, and be available to, all faculty, staff, visitors, and students.

The board of trustees shall provide for the administration and enforcement of its rules and may authorize the use of state university law enforcement officers provided for in section 3345.04 of the Revised Code to assist in enforcing the rules and the law on the campus of the college or university. The board of trustees, or appropriate officials of such college or university when the authority to do so has been delegated by the board of trustees, may seek the assistance of other appropriate law enforcement officers to enforce the rules and to enforce laws for the preservation of good order on the campus, and to prevent the disruption of the educational functions of the college or university.

The rules of the board of trustees shall not restrict freedom of speech nor the right of persons on the campus to assemble peacefully.

(1978 H 588, eff. 6–19–78; 132 v S 468)

[1] The term "regulations" has been amended to read "rules" elsewhere in this section by 1978 H 588.

3345.22 College student or staff member arrested for certain offenses to be afforded hearing; suspension; appeal

(A) A student, faculty or staff member, or employee of a college or university that receives any state funds in support thereof, arrested for any offense covered by division (D) of section 3345.23 of the Revised Code shall be afforded a hearing, as provided in this section, to determine whether the person shall be immediately suspended from the college or university. The hearing shall be held within not more than five days after the person's arrest, subject to reasonable continuances for good cause shown, which continuances shall not exceed a total of ten days.

(B) The arresting authority shall immediately notify the president of the college or university of the arrest of a student, faculty or staff member, or employee of the college or university for any offense covered by division (D) of section 3345.23 of the Revised Code. The hearing to determine whether the person shall be immediately suspended shall be held in the county where the college or university is located, before a referee appointed by the president. The referee shall be an attorney admitted to the practice of law in Ohio, but the referee shall not be attorney for, or a faculty or staff member or employee of, any college or university. Immediate notice of the time and place of the hearing shall be given or sent to the person.

(C) The referee may administer oaths, issue subpoenas to compel the attendance of witnesses and the production of evidence, and enforce the subpoenas, as well as preserve the order and decorum of the proceedings over which the referee presides, by means of contempt proceedings in the court of common pleas as provided by law.

(D) The hearing shall be adversary in nature and shall be conducted fairly and impartially, but the formalities of the criminal process are not required. A person whose suspension is being considered has the right to be represented by counsel but counsel need not be furnished for the person. The person also has the right to cross-examine witnesses against the person, to testify, and to present the testimony of witnesses and other evidence in the person's behalf. In the absence of a waiver of the right against compulsory self-incrimination, the testimony of a person whose suspension is being considered, given at the hearing, shall not subsequently be used in any criminal proceeding against the person. The referee may require the separation of witnesses and may bar from the proceedings any person whose presence is not essential to the proceedings, except that members of the news media shall not be barred from the proceedings.

(E) Upon hearing, if the referee finds by a preponderance of the evidence that the person whose suspension is being considered committed any offense covered by division (D) of section 3345.23 of the Revised Code, the referee shall order the person suspended, except that when the good order and discipline of a college or university will not be prejudiced or compromised thereby, the referee may permit the person to return to the college or university on terms of strict disciplinary probation. Subsequent violation of the terms of the probation automatically effects a suspension. A person suspended under this section may be readmitted pursuant to division (A) of section 3345.23 of the Revised Code. A suspension under this section is in effect until the person is acquitted or convicted of the crime for which the person was arrested. If convicted, the person is dismissed pursuant to section 3345.23 of the Revised Code.

(F) Upon acquittal, or upon any final judicial determination not resulting in conviction, of the charges for which a person is suspended pursuant to this section, the suspension automatically terminates, and the person suspended shall be reinstated and the record of the suspension expunged from the person's college or university record.

(G) An order of a referee pursuant to this section may be appealed on questions of law and fact to the court of common pleas of the county in which the college or university is located, within twenty days after the date of the order. If the court to which an appeal is taken determines that the good order and discipline of a college or university will not be prejudiced thereby, it may permit the person suspended to return to the college or university on terms of strict disciplinary probation.

(H) A person afforded a hearing pursuant to this section who does not appear at the hearing shall be declared suspended by the hearing officer.

(1999 H 282, eff. 9–28–99; 1970 H 1219, eff. 9–16–70)

3345.23 Dismissal of student or faculty or staff member on conviction of certain offenses

(A) The conviction of a student, faculty or staff member, or employee of a college or university which receives any state funds in support thereof, of any offense covered by division (D) of this section, automatically effects the student's, faculty or staff member's, or employee's dismissal from such college or university, except as provided in division (E) of this section. A student dismissed pursuant to this section may be readmitted or admitted to any other college or university which receives state funds in support thereof, in the discretion of the board of trustees, but only upon the lapse of one calendar year following the student's dismissal, and only upon terms of strict disciplinary probation. The contract, if any, of a faculty or staff member or employee dismissed pursuant to this section is terminated thereby. A faculty or staff member or employee dismissed pursuant to this section may be re-employed by any such college or university, in the discretion of the board of trustees, but only upon the lapse of one calendar year following the faculty or staff member's or employee's dismissal.

(B) Upon conviction of a student, faculty or staff member, or employee of a college or university which receives any state funds in support thereof, of any offense covered by division (D) of this section, the court shall immediately notify the college or university of such conviction. The president, or other administrative official designated by the board of trustees, shall immediately notify such person of the person's dismissal. The notice shall be in writing and shall be mailed by certified mail to the person's address as shown in both the court and the university records. If such person has been suspended pursuant to section 3345.22 of the Revised Code, and not permitted to return to the college or university, the period of the person's dismissal shall run from the date of such suspension.

(C) No degrees or honors shall be conferred upon, no instructional credit or grades shall be given to, and no student assistance, scholarship funds, salaries, or wages shall be paid or credited to any student, faculty or staff member, or employee, in respect of the period such person is properly under dismissal pursuant to this section or under suspension pursuant to section 3345.22 of the Revised Code.

(D) Without limiting the grounds for dismissal, suspension, or other disciplinary action against a student, faculty or staff member, or employee of a college or university which receives any state funds in support thereof, the commission of an offense of violence as defined in division (A)(9)(a) of section 2901.01 of the Revised Code or a substantially equivalent offense under a municipal ordinance, which offense is committed on or affects persons or property on such college or university, or which offense is committed in the immediate vicinity of a college or university with respect to which an emergency has been declared and is in effect pursuant to section 3345.26 of the Revised Code, is cause for dismissal pursuant to this section or for suspension pursuant to section 3345.22 of the Revised Code. Criminal cases resulting from arrests for offenses covered by division (D) of this section shall take precedence over all civil matters and proceedings and over all other criminal cases.

(E) If a final judicial determination results in an acquittal, or if the conviction is reversed on appeal, the student, faculty or staff member, or employee shall be reinstated and the college or university shall expunge the record of the student's, faculty or staff member's, or employee's dismissal from the student's, faculty or staff member's, or employee's college or university records, and the dismissal shall be deemed never to have occurred.

(1996 S 239, eff. 9–6–96; 1972 H 511, eff. 1–1–74; 1970 H 1219)

3345.24 Duty of president or board of trustees not limited; classified civil service employees excepted

(A) Sections 3345.22 and 3345.23 of the Revised Code shall be applied and followed, notwithstanding any rule, regulation, or procedure of the college or university, but such sections shall not be construed to limit any duty or authority of the board of trustees, administrative officials, or faculty of such college or university to take appropriate disciplinary action, through such procedures as may be provided by rule, regulation, or custom of such college or university, against students, faculty or staff members, or employees, nor shall such sections be construed to modify, limit, or rescind any rule or regulation of the college or university not inconsistent therewith.

(B) Sections 3345.22 and 3345.23 of the Revised Code shall not be construed as modifying or limiting the duty or authority of the board of trustees or president of a college or university to summarily suspend a student, faculty or staff member, or employee, when necessary to preserve the good order and discipline of such college or university, provided that the person suspended is given notice of suspension and the reasons therefor, and is afforded a fair and impartial hearing within a reasonable time thereafter, under regular procedures of the college or university. The duty and authority of the board of trustees or president of a college or university to impose summary suspension shall not be abrogated or limited in any way by any rule or regulation.

(C) To the extent that sections 3345.22 and 3345.23 of the Revised Code conflict with civil service requirements and procedures, persons otherwise subject to disciplinary action pursuant to such sections, but who are employees in the classified civil service, shall be disciplined according to civil service requirements and procedures.

(1970 H 1219, eff. 9–16–70)

3345.25 Person suspended or dismissed prohibited from entering campus

No student, faculty or staff member, or employee under dismissal or suspension from a college or university pursuant to section 3345.22 or 3345.23 of the Revised Code, shall enter or remain upon the land or premises of the college or university from which he was suspended or dismissed, without the express permission of the board of trustees or the president.

(1970 H 1219, eff. 9–16–70)

3345.26 Powers of board of trustees or president to declare a state of emergency and impose certain restrictions

(A) The board of trustees or president of a college or university which receives any state funds in support thereof, may declare a state of emergency when there is a clear and present danger of disruption of the orderly conduct of lawful activities at such college or university through riot, mob action, or other substantial disorder, and may do any one or more of the following, as are necessary to preserve order and discipline at such college or university during such emergency:

(1) Limit access to university property and facilities by any person or persons;

(2) Impose a curfew;

(3) Restrict the right of assembly by groups of five or more persons;

(4) Provide reasonable measures to enforce limitations on access, a curfew, and restrictions on the right of assembly imposed pursuant to this section.

(B) Notice of action taken pursuant to division (A) of this section shall be posted or published in such manner as is reasonably calculated to reach all persons affected.

(C) Division (A)(1) and (A)(2) of this section shall not be construed to limit the authority of the board of trustees, president, or other proper official of a college or university to impose reasonable restrictions on use of and access to, and the hours of use of and access to university property and facilities, for purposes of regulating the proper operation of such university, and regardless whether any emergency exists.

(1970 H 1219, eff. 9–16–70)

3345.78 Concealing, withholding, or falsifying information or impeding work of appointed personnel

No current or former employee or current or former officer of a state university or college shall knowingly conceal any information from, withhold any information requested by, falsify any information to, or impede the work of any of the following:

(A) A conservator, governance authority, or executive director appointed for the institution under section 3345.74 or 3345.75 of the Revised Code;

(B) Any personnel appointed by the conservator or executive director under division (F) of section 3345.74 or division (B)(1) of section 3345.75 of the Revised Code.

(1997 S 6, eff. 6–20–97)

CHAPTER 3517

CAMPAIGNS; POLITICAL PARTIES

Section

3517.20 Political communications must be identified; penalty

(A)(1) As used in this section:

(a) "Political publication for or against a candidate" means a notice, placard, advertisement, sample ballot, brochure, flyer, direct mailer, or other form of general publication that is designed to promote the nomination, election, or defeat of a candidate.

(b) "Political publication for or against an issue" means a notice, placard, advertisement, sample ballot, brochure, flyer, direct mailer, or other form of general publication that is designed to promote the adoption or defeat of a ballot issue or question or to influence the voters in an election.

(c) "Public political advertising" means newspapers, magazines, outdoor advertising facilities, direct mailings, or other similar types of general public political advertising, or flyers, handbills, or other nonperiodical printed matter.

(d) "Statewide candidate" has the same meaning as in section 3517.102 of the Revised Code.

(e) "Legislative candidate" means a candidate for the office of member of the general assembly.

(f) "Local candidate" means a candidate for an elective office of a political subdivision of this state.

(g) "Legislative campaign fund" has the same meaning as in section 3517. 01 of the Revised Code.

(h) "Limited political action committee" means a political action committee of fewer than ten members.

(i) "Designated amount" means one hundred dollars in the case of a local candidate or a local ballot issue, two hundred fifty dollars in the case of a legislative candidate, or five hundred dollars in the case of a statewide candidate or a statewide ballot issue.

(j) "To issue" includes to print, post, distribute, reproduce for distribution, or cause to be issued, printed, posted, distributed, or reproduced for distribution.

(k) "Telephone bank" means more than five hundred telephone calls of an identical or substantially similar nature within any thirty-day period, whether those telephone calls are made by individual callers or by recording.

(2) No candidate, campaign committee, legislative campaign fund, political party, or other entity, except a political action committee, shall issue a form of political publication for or against a candidate, or shall make an expenditure for the purpose of financing political communications in support of or opposition to a candidate through public political advertising, unless the name and residence or business address of the candidate or the chairperson, treasurer, or secretary of the campaign committee, legislative campaign fund, political party, or other entity that issues or otherwise is responsible for that political publication or that makes an expenditure for that political communication appears in a conspicuous place on that political publication or is contained within that political communication.

(3) No limited political action committee shall do either of the following unless the name and residence or business address of the chairperson, treasurer, or secretary of the limited political action committee involved appears in a conspicuous place in the political publication for or against a candidate described in division (A)(3)(a) of this section or is contained within the political communication described in division (A)(3)(b) of this section:

(a) Issue a form of political publication for or against a candidate that costs in excess of the designated amount or that is issued in cooperation, consultation, or concert with, or at the request or suggestion of, a candidate, a campaign committee, a legislative campaign fund, a political party, a political action committee with ten or more members, or a limited political action committee that spends in excess of the designated amount on a related or the same or similar political publication for or against a candidate;

(b) Make an expenditure in excess of the designated amount in support of or opposition to a candidate or make an expenditure in cooperation, consultation, or concert with, or at the request or suggestion of, a candidate, a campaign committee, a legislative campaign fund, a political party, a political action committee with ten or more members, or a limited political action committee that spends in excess of the designated amount in support of or opposition to the same candidate, for the purpose of financing political communications in support of or opposition to that candidate through public political advertising.

(4) No political action committee with ten or more members shall issue a form of political publication for or against a candidate, or shall make an expenditure for the purpose of financing political communications in support of or opposition to a candidate through public political advertising, unless the name and residence or business address of the chairperson, treasurer, or secretary of the political action committee that issues or otherwise is responsible for that political publication or that makes an expenditure for that political communication through public political advertising appears in a conspicuous place in that political publication or is contained within that political communication.

(5) No corporation, labor organization, campaign committee, legislative campaign fund, political party, or other entity, except a political action committee, shall issue a form of political publication for or against an issue, or shall make an expenditure for the purpose of financing political communications in support of or opposition to a ballot issue or question through public political advertising, unless the name and residence or business address of the chairperson, treasurer, or secretary of the corporation, labor organization, campaign committee, legislative campaign fund, political party, or other entity that issues or otherwise is responsible for that political publication or that makes an expenditure for that political communication through public political advertising appears in a conspicuous place in that political publication or is contained within that political communication.

(6) No limited political action committee shall do either of the following unless the name and residence or business address of the chairperson, treasurer, or secretary of the limited political action committee involved appears in a conspicuous place in the political publication for or against a ballot issue described in division (A)(6)(a) of this section or is contained within the political communication described in division (A)(6)(b) of this section:

(a) Issue a form of political publication for or against a ballot issue that costs in excess of the designated amount or that is issued in cooperation, consultation, or concert with, or at the request or suggestion of, a candidate, a campaign committee, a legislative campaign fund, a political party, a political action committee with ten or more members, or a limited political action committee that spends in excess of the designated amount for a related or the same or similar political publication for or against an issue;

(b) Make an expenditure in excess of the designated amount in support of or opposition to a ballot issue or make an expenditure in cooperation, consultation, or concert with, or at the request or suggestion of, a candidate, a campaign committee, a legislative campaign fund, a political party, a political action committee with ten or more members, or a limited political action committee that spends in excess of the designated amount in support of or opposition to the same ballot issue, for the purpose of financing political communications in support of or opposition to that ballot issue through public political advertising.

(7) No political action committee with ten or more members shall issue a form of political publication for or against an issue, or shall make an expenditure for the purpose of financing political communications in support of or opposition to a ballot issue or question through public political advertising, unless the name and residence or business address of the chairperson, treasurer, or secretary of the political action committee that issues or otherwise is responsible for that political publication or that makes an expenditure for that political communication appears in a conspicuous place in that political publication or is contained within that political communication.

(8) The disclaimer "paid political advertisement" is not sufficient to meet the requirements of this section.

(9) If the political publication described in division (A) of this section is issued by the regularly constituted central or executive committee of a political party that is organized as provided in this chapter, it shall be sufficiently identified if it bears the name of the committee and its chairperson or treasurer.

(10) If more than one piece of printed matter or printed political communications are mailed as a single packet, the requirements of division (A) of this section are met if one of the pieces of printed matter or printed political communications in the packet contains the name and residence or business address of the chairperson, treasurer, or secretary of the organization or entity that issues or is responsible for the printed matter or other printed political communications.

(11) This section does not apply to the transmittal of personal correspondence that is not reproduced by machine for general distribution.

(12) The secretary of state, by rule, may exempt from the requirements of this section, printed matter and certain other kinds of printed communications such as campaign buttons, balloons, pencils, or similar items, the size or nature of which makes it unreasonable to add an identification or disclaimer.

(13) The disclaimer or identification described in division (A) of this section, when paid for by a campaign committee, shall be identified by the words "paid for by" followed by the name and address of the campaign committee and the appropriate officer of the committee, identified by name and title. The identification or disclaimer may use reasonable abbreviations for common terms such as "treasurer" or "committee".

(B)(1) No candidate, campaign committee, legislative campaign fund, political contributing entity, political party, political action committee, limited political action committee, or other entity shall utter or cause to be uttered, over the broadcasting facilities of any radio or television station within this state, any communication that is designed to promote the nomination, election, or defeat of a candidate, or the adoption or defeat of an issue or to influence the voters in an election, unless the speaker identifies the speaker with the speaker's name and residence address or unless the communication identifies the chairperson, treasurer, or secretary of the organization responsible for the communication with the name and residence or business address of that officer, except that communications by radio need not broadcast the residence or business address of the officer. However, a radio station, for a period of at least six months, shall keep the residence or business address on file and divulge it to any person upon request.

No person operating a broadcast station or an organ of printed media shall broadcast or print a paid political communication that does not contain the identification required by this section.

(2) Division (B) of this section does not apply to any communications made on behalf of a radio or television station or network by any employee of such radio or television station or network while acting in the course of the employee's employment.

(3) No candidate or entity described in division (B)(1) of this section shall use or cause to be used a false, fictitious, or

fraudulent name or address in the making or issuing of a publication or communication included within the provisions of this section.

(C) No candidate, campaign committee, legislative campaign fund, political party, political action committee, limited political action committee, or other person or entity shall conduct a telephone bank for the purpose of promoting the nomination, election, or defeat of a candidate or the adoption or defeat of an issue or to influence the voters in an election, unless the call includes a disclaimer that identifies the name of the candidate, campaign committee, legislative campaign fund, political party, political action committee, limited political action committee, or other person or entity paying for the telephone bank.

(D) Before a prosecution may commence under this section, a complaint shall be filed with the Ohio elections commission under section 3517.153 of the Revised Code. After the complaint is filed, the commission shall proceed in accordance with sections 3517.154 to 3517.157 of the Revised Code.

(2004 H 1 SS, eff. 3–31–05; 1998 S 134, eff. 7–13–98; 1995 H 99, eff. 8–22–95; 1995 S 9, eff. 8–24–95)

3517.21 Unfair political campaign activities

(A) No person, during the course of any campaign for nomination or election to public office or office of a political party, shall knowingly and with intent to affect the outcome of such campaign do any of the following:

(1) Serve, or place another person to serve, as an agent or employee in the election campaign organization of a candidate for the purpose of acting to impede the conduct of the candidate's campaign for nomination or election or of reporting information to the employee's employer or the agent's principal without the knowledge of the candidate or the candidate's organization;

(2) Promise, offer, or give any valuable thing or valuable benefit to any person who is employed by or is an agent of a candidate or a candidate's election campaign organization for the purpose of influencing the employee or agent with respect to the improper discharge of the employee's or agent's campaign duties or to obtain information about the candidate or the candidate's campaign organization.

(B) No person, during the course of any campaign for nomination or election to public office or office of a political party, by means of campaign materials, including sample ballots, an advertisement on radio or television or in a newspaper or periodical, a public speech, press release, or otherwise, shall knowingly and with intent to affect the outcome of such campaign do any of the following:

(1) Use the title of an office not currently held by a candidate in a manner that implies that the candidate does currently hold that office or use the term "re-elect" when the candidate has never been elected at a primary, general, or special election to the office for which he or she is a candidate;

(2) Make a false statement concerning the formal schooling or training completed or attempted by a candidate; a degree, diploma, certificate, scholarship, grant, award, prize, or honor received, earned, or held by a candidate; or the period of time during which a candidate attended any school, college, community technical school, or institution;

(3) Make a false statement concerning the professional, occupational, or vocational licenses held by a candidate, or concerning any position the candidate held for which the candidate received a salary or wages;

(4) Make a false statement that a candidate or public official has been indicted or convicted of a theft offense, extortion, or other crime involving financial corruption or moral turpitude;

(5) Make a statement that a candidate has been indicted for any crime or has been the subject of a finding by the Ohio elections commission without disclosing the outcome of any legal proceedings resulting from the indictment or finding;

(6) Make a false statement that a candidate or official has a record of treatment or confinement for mental disorder;

(7) Make a false statement that a candidate or official has been subjected to military discipline for criminal misconduct or dishonorably discharged from the armed services;

(8) Falsely identify the source of a statement, issue statements under the name of another person without authorization, or falsely state the endorsement of or opposition to a candidate by a person or publication;

(9) Make a false statement concerning the voting record of a candidate or public official;

(10) Post, publish, circulate, distribute, or otherwise disseminate a false statement concerning a candidate, either knowing the same to be false or with reckless disregard of whether it was false or not, if the statement is designed to promote the election, nomination, or defeat of the candidate.

As used in this section, "voting record" means the recorded "yes" or "no" vote on a bill, ordinance, resolution, motion, amendment, or confirmation.

(C) Before a prosecution may commence under this section, a complaint shall be filed with the Ohio elections commission under section 3517.153 of the Revised Code. After the complaint is filed, the commission shall proceed in accordance with sections 3517.154 to 3517.157 of the Revised Code.

(1995 S 9, eff. 8–24–95)

3517.22 Unfair activities in issue campaign

(A) No person during the course of any campaign in advocacy of or in opposition to the adoption of any proposition or issue submitted to the voters shall knowingly and with intent to affect the outcome of such campaign do any of the following:

(1) Serve, or place another person to serve, as an agent or employee in the election campaign organization of a committee which advocates or is in opposition to the adoption of any ballot proposition or issue for the purpose of acting to impede the conduct of the campaign on the proposition or issue or of reporting information to the employee's employer or the agent's principal without the knowledge of the committee;

(2) Promise, offer, or give any valuable thing or valuable benefit to any person who is employed by or is an agent of a committee in advocacy of or in opposition to the adoption of any ballot proposition or issue, for the purpose of influencing the employee or agent with respect to the improper discharge of the employee's or agent's campaign duties or to obtain information about the committee's campaign organization.

(B) No person, during the course of any campaign in advocacy of or in opposition to the adoption of any ballot proposition or issue, by means of campaign material, including sample ballots, an advertisement on radio or television or in a newspaper or periodical, a public speech, a press release, or otherwise, shall knowingly and with intent to affect the outcome of such campaign do any of the following:

(1) Falsely identify the source of a statement, issue statements under the name of another person without authorization, or falsely state the endorsement of or opposition to a ballot proposition or issue by a person or publication;

(2) Post, publish, circulate, distribute, or otherwise disseminate, a false statement, either knowing the same to be false or acting with reckless disregard of whether it was false or not, that is designed to promote the adoption or defeat of any ballot proposition or issue.

(C) Before a prosecution may commence under this section, a complaint shall be filed with the Ohio elections commission under section 3517.153 of the Revised Code. After the complaint is filed, the commission shall proceed in accordance with sections 3517.154 to 3517.157 of the Revised Code.

(1995 S 9, eff. 8–24–95)

CHAPTER 3599

OFFENSES AND PENALTIES

IMPROPER USE OF MONEY

3599.01 Bribery

(A) No person shall before, during, or after any primary, convention, or election:

(1) Give, lend, offer, or procure or promise to give, lend, offer, or procure any money, office, position, place or employment, influence, or any other valuable consideration to or for a delegate, elector, or other person;

(2) Attempt by intimidation, coercion, or other unlawful means to induce such delegate or elector to register or refrain from registering or to vote or refrain from voting at a primary, convention, or election for a particular person, question, or issue;

(3) Advance, pay, or cause to be paid or procure or offer to procure money or other valuable thing to or for the use of another, with the intent that it or part thereof shall be used to induce such person to vote or to refrain from voting.

(B) Whoever violates this section is guilty of bribery, a felony of the fourth degree; and if he is a candidate he shall forfeit the nomination he received, or if elected to any office he shall forfeit the office to which he was elected at the election with reference to which such offense was committed.

(1982 H 269, § 4, eff. 7–1–83; 1982 S 199; 126 v 575; 1953 H 1; GC 4785–190)

3599.02 Sale of vote by voter

No person shall before, during, or after any primary, general, or special election or convention solicit, request, demand, receive, or contract for any money, gift, loan, property, influence, position, employment, or other thing of value for that person or for another person for doing any of the following:

(A) Registering or refraining from registering to vote;

(B) Agreeing to register or to refrain from registering to vote;

(C) Agreeing to vote or to refrain from voting;

(D) Voting or refraining from voting at any primary, general, or special election or convention for a particular person, question, or issue;

(E) Registering or voting, or refraining from registering or voting, or voting or refraining from voting for a particular person, question, or issue.

Whoever violates this section is guilty of bribery, a felony of the fourth degree, and shall be disfranchised and excluded from holding any public office for five years immediately following such conviction.

(1997 S 116, eff. 12–9–97; 1953 H 1, eff. 10–1–53; GC 4785–191)

3599.03 Corporation or labor organization funds shall not be used to aid political organization; funds used to promote or oppose ballot issue; exemptions

(A)(1) Except to carry on activities specified in sections 3517.082 and 3517.1011, division (A)(2) of section 3517.1012, division (B) of section 3517.1013, and section 3599.031 of the Revised Code and except as provided in divisions (D), (E), and (F) of this section, no corporation, no nonprofit corporation, and no labor organization, directly or indirectly, shall pay or use, or offer, advise, consent, or agree to pay or use, the corporation's money or property, or the labor organization's money, including dues, initiation fees, or other assessments paid by members, or property, for or in aid of or opposition to a political party, a candidate for election or nomination to public office, a political action committee including a political action committee of the corporation or labor organization, a legislative campaign fund, or any organization that supports or opposes any such candidate, or for any partisan political purpose, shall violate any law requiring the filing of an affidavit or statement respecting such use of those funds, or shall pay or use the corporation's or labor organization's money for the expenses of a social fund-raising event for its political action committee if an employee's or labor organization member's right to attend such an event is predicated on the employee's or member's contribution to the corporation's or labor organization's political action committee.

(2) Whoever violates division (A)(1) of this section shall be fined not less than five hundred nor more than five thousand dollars.

(B)(1) No officer, stockholder, attorney, or agent of a corporation or nonprofit corporation, no member, including an officer, attorney, or agent, of a labor organization, and no candidate, political party official, or other individual shall knowingly aid, advise, solicit, or receive money or other property in violation of division (A)(1) of this section.

(2) Whoever violates division (B)(1) of this section shall be fined not more than one thousand dollars, or imprisoned not more than one year, or both.

(C) A corporation, a nonprofit corporation, or a labor organization may use its funds or property for or in aid of or opposition to a proposed or certified ballot issue. Such use of funds or property shall be reported on a form prescribed by the secretary of state. Reports of contributions in connection with statewide ballot issues shall be filed with the secretary of state. Reports of contributions in connection with local issues shall be filed with the board of elections of the most populous county of the district in which the issue is submitted or to be submitted to the electors. Reports made pursuant to this division shall be filed by the times specified in divisions (A)(1) and (2) of section 3517.10 of the Revised Code.

(D)(1) Any gift made pursuant to section 3517.101 of the Revised Code does not constitute a violation of this section or of any other section of the Revised Code.

(2) Any gift made pursuant to division (A)(2) of section 3517.1012 of the Revised Code does not constitute a violation of this section.

(3) Any gift made pursuant to division (B) of section 3517.1013 of the Revised Code does not constitute a violation of this section.

(E) Any compensation or fees paid by a financial institution to a state political party for services rendered pursuant to division (B) of section 3517.19 of the Revised Code do not constitute a violation of this section or of any other section of the Revised Code.

(F)(1) The use by a nonprofit corporation of its money or property for communicating information for a purpose specified in division (A) of this section is not a violation of that division if the stockholders, members, donors, trustees, or officers of the nonprofit corporation are the predominant recipients of the communication.

(2) The placement of a campaign sign on the property of a corporation, nonprofit corporation, or labor organization is not a use of property in violation of division (A) of this section by that corporation, nonprofit corporation, or labor organization.

(3) The use by a corporation or labor organization of its money or property for communicating information for a purpose specified in division (A) of this section is not a violation of that division if it is not a communication made by mass broadcast such as radio or television or made by advertising in a newspaper of general circulation but is a communication sent exclusively to members, employees, officers, or trustees of that labor organization or shareholders, employees, officers, or directors of that corporation or to members of the immediate families of any such individuals or if the communication intended to be so sent exclusively is unintentionally sent as well to a de minimis number of other individuals.

(G) In addition to the laws listed in division (A) of section 4117.10 of the Revised Code that prevail over conflicting agreements between employee organizations and public employers, this section prevails over any conflicting provisions of agreements between labor organizations and public employers that are entered into on or after the effective date of this section pursuant to Chapter 4117. of the Revised Code.

(H) As used in this section, "labor organization" has the same meaning as in section 3517.01 of the Revised Code.

(2004 H 1 SS, eff. 3–31–05)

3599.031 Deduction of political contribution from employee's wages; written authorization required

(A) Notwithstanding any provision of the Revised Code to the contrary and subject to division (C) of section 3517.09 of the Revised Code and division (B) of this section, any employer may deduct from the wages and salaries of its employees amounts for an account described in division (B) of this section, a separate segregated fund, a political action committee of the employer, a political action committee of a labor organization of the employer's employees, a political action committee of an association of which the employer is a member, a political party, a person making disbursements to pay the direct costs of producing or airing electioneering communications, or a ballot issue that the employee by written authorization may designate and shall transmit any amounts so deducted as a separate written authorization described in division (B) of this section shall direct. Any authorization authorizing a deduction from an employee's wages or salary may be on a form that is used to apply for or authorize membership in or authorize payment of dues or fees to any organization, but the authorization for a deduction shall be stated and signed separately from the application for membership or the authorization for the payment of dues or fees. The employer either may deduct from the amount to be so transmitted a uniform amount determined by the employer to be necessary to defray the actual cost of making such deduction and transmittal, or may utilize its own funds in an amount it determines is necessary to defray the actual administrative cost, including making the deduction and transmittal.

(B) If an employer establishes a separate account in the name of an employee for the purpose of depositing into the account amounts deducted from the wages and salary of the employee pursuant to division (A) of this section or amounts directly given by the employee to the employer for the support of a candidate, a separate segregated fund, a political action committee of the employer, a political action committee of a labor organization of the employer's employees, a political action committee of an association of which the employer is a member, a political party, a legislative campaign fund, a person making disbursements to pay the direct costs of producing or airing electioneering communications, or a ballot issue, the employee shall sign a written authorization designating the recipient of a disbursement from that account. The written authorization required under this division is separate and distinct from a written authorization required under division (A) of this section. The authorization required under this division shall clearly identify and designate the candidate, separate segregated fund, political action committee of the employer, political action committee of a labor organization of the employer's employees, political action committee of an association of which the employer is a member, political party, legislative campaign fund, person making disbursements to pay the direct costs of producing or airing electioneering communications, or ballot issue that is to receive any disbursement from the account established pursuant to this division. No person shall designate the recipient of a disbursement from the account except the employee from whose account the disbursement is made. No employer shall make a disbursement from the account of an employee established under this division unless the employer has received the written authorization required under this division.

(C) An employer shall furnish the recipient of any amount transmitted pursuant to this section with the employer's full name and the full name of the labor organization of which the employee whose amount is being transmitted is a member, if any. An employer shall keep and maintain the authorization forms of all its employees from whose wages and salaries any amounts were deducted pursuant to division (A) of this section and the authorizations of disbursements from accounts established under division (B) of this section for a period of at least six years after the year in which the deductions and disbursements were made.

(D) An employee who has made an authorization pursuant to division (A) or (B) of this section may revoke that authorization at any time. A revocation of the authorization does not affect any deduction already made from an employee's wages and salary or any amounts already transmitted or disbursed under this section.

(E) For purposes of this section and for the purpose of the information required to be filed under division (B)(4)(b)(iii) of section 3517.10 of the Revised Code:

(1) If an employer is a corporation, each subsidiary of a parent corporation shall be considered an entity separate and distinct from any other subsidiary and separate and distinct from the parent corporation.

(2) Each national, regional, state, and local affiliate of a labor organization shall be considered a distinct entity.

(F) Whoever violates division (B) of this section shall be fined not less than fifty nor more than five hundred dollars for each disbursement made in violation of that division.

(G) In addition to the laws listed in division (A) of section 4117.10 of the Revised Code that prevail over conflicting agreements between employee organizations and public employers, this section prevails over any conflicting provisions of agreements between labor organizations and public employers that are entered into on or after the effective date of this amendment pursuant to Chapter 4117. of the Revised Code.

(H) As used in this section:

(1) " Electioneering communication," "legislative campaign fund," "labor organization," "political action committee," and "separate segregated fund" have the same meanings as in section 3517.01 of the Revised Code.

(2) "Public employer" means an employer that is the state or a state agency, authority, commission, or board, a political subdivision of the state, a school district or state institution of higher learning, a public or special district, or any other public employer.

(3) "Employee" includes only an employee who is a resident of or is employed in this state.

(2004 H 1 SS, eff. 3–31–05; 1995 S 8, eff. 8–23–95; 1987 H 354, eff. 9–22–87; 1976 H 1379; 1974 S 46)

3599.04 Contributions for illegal purposes

No person shall, directly or indirectly, in connection with any election, pay, lend, or contribute or offer or promise to pay, lend, or contribute any money or other valuable consideration in the election or defeat of any candidate or the adoption or defeat of any question or issue for any purposes other than those enumerated in sections 3517.08 and 3517.12 of the Revised Code.

Whoever violates this section is guilty of corrupt practices and shall be fined not less than twenty-five nor more than five hundred dollars.

(1953 H 1, eff. 10–1–53; GC 4785–193)

EMPLOYERS AND EMPLOYEES

3599.05 Employer shall not influence political action of employee

No employer or his agent or a corporation shall print or authorize to be printed upon any pay envelopes any statements intended or calculated to influence the political action of his or its employees; or post or exhibit in the establishment or anywhere in or about the establishment any posters, placards, or hand bills containing any threat, notice, or information that if any particular candidate is elected or defeated work in the establishment will cease in whole or in part, or other threats expressed or implied, intended to influence the political opinions or votes of his or its employees.

Whoever violates this section is guilty of corrupt practices, and shall be punished by a fine of not less than five hundred nor more than one thousand dollars.

(1953 H 1, eff. 10–1–53; GC 4785–194)

3599.06 Employer shall not interfere with employee on election day

No employer, his officer or agent, shall discharge or threaten to discharge an elector for taking a reasonable amount of time to vote on election day; or require or order an elector to accompany him to a voting place upon such day; or refuse to permit such elector to serve as an election official on any registration or election day; or indirectly use any force or restraint or threaten to inflict any injury, harm, or loss; or in any other manner practice intimidation in order to induce or compel such person to vote or refrain from voting for or against any person or question or issue submitted to the voters.

Whoever violates this section shall be fined not less than fifty nor more than five hundred dollars.

(1953 H 1, eff. 10–1–53; GC 4785–195)

UNFAIR AND ILLEGAL CAMPAIGN ACTIVITIES

3599.08 Influencing candidates and voters by publications

No owner, editor, writer, or employee of any newspaper, magazine, or other publication of any description, whether published regularly or irregularly, shall use the columns of any such publication for the printing of any threats, direct or implied, in the columns of any such publication for the purpose of controlling or intimidating candidates for public office. Such person shall not directly or indirectly solicit, receive, or accept any payment, promise, or compensation for influencing or attempting to influence votes through any printing matter, except through matter inserted in such publication as "paid advertisement" and so designated.

Whoever violates this section is guilty of a corrupt practice and shall be fined not less than five hundred nor more than one thousand dollars.

(1953 H 1, eff. 10–1–53; GC 4785–197)

3599.09 Penalty

Whoever knowingly violates division (A) of section 3513.052 is guilty of seeking nomination or election to more than one prohibited office at the same election and shall be fined not more than five hundred dollars.

(2002 H 445, eff. 12–23–02)

CANDIDATE'S PLEDGE CONCERNING LEGISLATION

3599.10 Candidate for general assembly shall not be asked to pledge vote on legislation

No person, firm, or corporation shall demand of any candidate for the general assembly any pledge concerning his vote on any legislation, question, or proposition that may come before the general assembly; provided that this shall not be understood to prohibit a reasonable inquiry as to such candidate's views on such question or legislation.

Whoever violates this section is guilty of a corrupt practice and shall be fine not less than five hundred nor more than one thousand dollars.

(1953 H 1, eff. 10–1–53; GC 4785–200)

ELECTION PROCEDURE

3599.11 False registration; penalty; improper handling of forms

(A) No person shall knowingly register or make application or attempt to register in a precinct in which the person is not a qualified voter; or knowingly aid or abet any person to so register; or attempt to register or knowingly induce or attempt to induce any person to so register; or knowingly impersonate another or write or assume the name of another, real or fictitious, in registering or attempting to register; or by false statement or other unlawful means procure, aid, or attempt to procure the erasure or striking out on the register or duplicate list of the name of a qualified elector therein; or knowingly induce or attempt to induce a registrar or other election authority to refuse registration in a precinct to an elector thereof; or knowingly swear or affirm falsely upon a lawful examination by or before any registering officer; or make, print, or issue any false or counterfeit certificate of registration or knowingly alter any certificate of registration.

No person shall knowingly register under more than one name or knowingly induce any person to so register.

No person shall knowingly make any false statement on any form for registration or change of registration or upon any application or return envelope for an absent voter's ballot.

Whoever violates this division is guilty of a felony of the fifth degree.

(B) No person who helps another person register outside an official voter registration place shall knowingly destroy, or knowingly help another person to destroy, any completed registration form, or knowingly fail to return any registration form entrusted to that person to the board of elections on or before the thirtieth day before the election.

Whoever violates this division is guilty of a misdemeanor of the first degree.

(1997 S 116, eff. 12–9–97; 1995 S 2, eff. 7–1–96; 1978 H 1209, eff. 11–3–78; 1977 S 125; 1971 S 460; 1953 H 1; GC 4785–201)

3599.111 Certain forms of compensation prohibited

(A) As used in this section, "registering a voter" or "registering voters" includes any effort, for compensation, to provide voter registration forms or to assist persons in completing those forms or returning them to the board of elections, the office of the secretary of state, or other appropriate public office.

(B) No person shall receive compensation on a fee per signature or fee per volume basis for circulating any declaration of candidacy, nominating petition, declaration of intent to be a write-in candidate, initiative petition, referendum petition, recall petition, or any other election-related petition that is filed with or transmitted to a board of elections, the office of the secretary of state, or other appropriate public office.

(C) No person shall receive compensation on a fee per registration or fee per volume basis for registering a voter.

(D) Compensation for collecting signatures on election-related petitions and for registering voters shall be paid solely on the basis of time worked.

(E)(1) Whoever violates division (B) or (C) of this section is guilty of election falsification under section 3599.36 of the Revised Code.

(2) Whoever violates division (D) of this section is guilty of a felony of the fifth degree.

(2004 H 1 SS, eff. 3–31–05)

3599.12 Illegal voting

(A) No person shall do any of the following:

(1) Vote or attempt to vote in any primary, special, or general election in a precinct in which that person is not a legally qualified elector;

(2) Vote or attempt to vote more than once at the same election by any means, including voting or attempting to vote both by absent voter's ballots under division (B), (C), or (G) of section 3503.16 of the Revised Code and by regular ballot at the polls at the same election, or voting or attempting to vote both by absent voter's ballots under division (B), (C), or (G) of section 3503.16 of the Revised Code and by absent voter's ballots under Chapter 3509. or armed service absent voter's ballots under Chapter 3511. of the Revised Code at the same election;

(3) Impersonate or sign the name of another person, real or fictitious, living or dead, and vote or attempt to vote as that other person in any such election;

(4) Cast a ballot at any such election after objection has been made and sustained to that person's vote;

(5) Knowingly vote or attempt to vote a ballot other than the official ballot.

(B) Whoever violates division (A) of this section is guilty of a felony of the fourth degree.

(1997 S 116, eff. 12–9–97; 1982 H 269, § 4, eff. 7–1–83; 1982 S 199; 1953 H 1; GC 4785–202)

3599.13 Unqualified person signing petitions

No person shall sign an initiative, supplementary, referendum, recall, or nominating petition knowing that he is not at the time qualified to sign it; or knowingly sign such petition more than once; or sign a name other than his own; or accept anything of value for signing such petition; or seek by intimidation or threats to influence any person to sign or refrain from signing such petition, or from circulating or abstaining from circulating such petition; or sign a nominating petition for a candidate of a party with which he is not affiliated, as required by section 3513.05 of the Revised Code; or make a false affidavit or statement concerning the signatures on any such petition.

Whoever violates this section shall be fined not less than fifty nor more than five hundred dollars or imprisoned not less than three nor more than six months, or both.

(1980 H 1062, eff. 3–23–81; 1953 H 1; GC 4785–203)

3599.14 Prohibitions relating to petitions

(A) No person shall knowingly, directly or indirectly, do any of the following in connection with any declaration of candidacy, declaration of intent to be a write-in candidate, nominating petition, or other petition presented to or filed with the secretary of state, a board or [sic.] elections, or any other public office for the purpose of becoming a candidate for any elective office, including the office of a political party, for the purpose of submitting a question or issue to the electors at an election, or for the purpose of forming a political party:

(1) Misrepresent the contents, purpose, or effect of the petition or declaration for the purpose of persuading a person to sign or refrain from signing the petition or declaration;

(2) Pay or offer to pay anything of value for signing or refraining from signing the petition or declaration;

(3) Promise to assist any person to obtain appointment to an office or position as a consideration for obtaining or preventing signatures to the petition or declaration;

(4) Obtain or prevent signatures to the petition or declaration as a consideration for the assistance or promise of assistance of a person in securing appointment to an office or position;

(5) Circulate or cause to be circulated the petition or declaration knowing it to contain false, forged, or fictitious names;

(6) Add signatures or names except the person's own name on the petition or declaration;

(7) Make a false certification or statement concerning the petition or declaration;

(8) File with the election authorities the petition or declaration knowing it to contain false, forged, or fictitious names;

(9) Fail to fill out truthfully and file all itemized statements required by law in connection with the petition or declaration.

(B) Whoever violates division (A) of this section is guilty of a misdemeanor of the first degree.

(1997 S 116, eff. 12–9–97; 1995 S 2, eff. 7–1–96; 1990 H 405, eff. 4–11–91; 1980 H 1062; 1953 H 1; GC 4785–204)

3599.15 Sale, theft, destruction, or mutilation of petitions

No person shall purchase, steal, attempt to steal, sell, attempt to sell, or willfully destroy or mutilate any initiative, supplementary, referendum, recall, or nominating petition, or any part of a petition, that is being or has been lawfully circulated; provided that the words "purchase" and "sell" do not apply to persons paying or receiving pay for soliciting signatures to or circulating a petition or petition paper.

Whoever violates this section is guilty of a felony of the fifth degree.

(1995 S 2, eff. 7–1–96; 1982 H 269, § 4, eff. 7–1–83; 1982 S 199; 1953 H 1; GC 4785–205)

3599.16 Misconduct of members or employees of board of elections

No member, director, or employee of a board of elections shall:

(A) Willfully or negligently violate or neglect to perform any duty imposed upon him by law, or willfully perform or neglect to perform it in such a way as to hinder the objects of the law, or willfully disobey any law incumbent upon him so to do;

(B) Willfully or knowingly report as genuine a false or fraudulent signature on a petition or registration form, or willfully or knowingly report as false or fraudulent any such genuine signature;

(C) Willfully add to or subtract from the votes actually cast at an election in any official returns, or add to or take away or attempt to add to or take away any ballot from those legally polled at such election;

(D) Carry away, destroy, or mutilate any registration cards or forms, pollbooks, or other records of any election;

(E) Act as an election official in any capacity in an election, except as specifically authorized in his official capacity;

(F) In any other way willfully and knowingly or unlawfully violate or seek to prevent the enforcement of any other provisions of the election laws.

Whoever violates this section shall be dismissed from his position as a member or employee of the board and is guilty of a felony of the fourth degree.

(1982 H 269, § 4, eff. 7–1–83; 1982 S 199; 1980 H 1062; 1953 H 1; GC 4785–206)

3599.161 Access to records; denial prohibited

(A) The director of elections, deputy director of elections, or an employee of the board of elections designated by the director or deputy director shall be available during normal office hours to provide any person with access to the public records filed in the office of the board of elections.

(B) No director of elections, deputy director of elections, or employee of the board of elections designated by the director or deputy director shall knowingly prevent or prohibit any person from inspecting, under reasonable regulations established and posted by the board of elections, the public records filed in the office of the board of elections. Records relating to the declination of a person to register to vote and to the identity of a voter registration agency through which any particular person registered to vote are not public records for purposes of this section.

(C) Whoever violates division (B) of this section is guilty of prohibiting inspection of election records, a minor misdemeanor, and shall, upon conviction, be dismissed from his position as director of elections, deputy director of elections, or employee of the board of elections.

(1994 S 300, eff. 1–1–95; 1977 H 86, eff. 8–26–77)

3599.17 Failure of registrars, judges, and clerks to perform duties

(A) No elections official serving as a registrar, judge, or clerk of elections shall do any of the following:

(1) Fail to appear before the board of elections, or its representative, after notice has been served personally upon the official or left at the official's usual place of residence, for examination as to the official's qualifications;

(2) Fail to appear at the polling place to which the official is assigned at the hour and during the hours set for the registration or election;

(3) Fail to take the oath prescribed by section 3501.31 of the Revised Code, unless excused by such board;

(4) Refuse or sanction the refusal of another registrar or judge of elections to administer an oath required by law;

(5) Fail to send notice to the board of the appointment of a judge or clerk to fill a vacancy;

(6) Act as registrar, judge, or clerk without having been appointed and having received a certificate of appointment, except a judge or clerk appointed to fill a vacancy caused by absence or removal;

(7) Fail in any other way to perform any duty imposed by law.

(B) Whoever violates division (A) of this section is guilty of a misdemeanor of the first degree.

(1997 S 116, eff. 12–9–97; 1953 H 1, eff. 10–1–53; GC 4785–207)

3599.18 Misconduct of registrars and police officers

(A) No election official, person assisting in the registration of electors, or police officer shall knowingly do any of the following:

(1) Refuse, neglect, or unnecessarily delay, hinder, or prevent the registration of a qualified elector, who in a lawful manner applies for registration;

(2) Enter or consent to the entry of a fictitious name on a voter registration list;

(3) Alter the name on or remove or destroy the registration card or form of any qualified elector;

(4) Neglect, unlawfully execute, or fail to execute any duty enjoined upon that person as an election official, person assisting in the registration of electors, or police officer.

(B) Whoever violates division (A) of this section is guilty of a misdemeanor of the first degree.

(1997 S 116, eff. 12–9–97; 1975 H 1, eff. 6–13–75; 1953 H 1; GC 4785–208)

3599.19 Misconduct of judges and clerks of elections in polling place

(A) No judge or clerk of elections shall knowingly do any of the following:

(1) Unlawfully open or permit to be opened the sealed package containing registration lists, ballots, blanks, pollbooks, and other papers and material to be used in an election;

(2) Unlawfully misplace, carry away, negligently lose or permit to be taken from the judge or clerk, fail to deliver, or destroy any such packages, papers, or material;

(3) Receive or sanction the reception of a ballot from a person not a qualified elector or from a person who refused to answer a question in accordance with the election law;

(4) Refuse to receive or sanction the rejection of a ballot from a person, knowing that person to be a qualified elector;

(5) Permit a fraudulent ballot to be placed in the ballot box;

(6) Place or permit to be placed in any ballot box any ballot known by the judge or clerk to be improperly or falsely marked;

(7) Count or permit to be counted any illegal or fraudulent ballot;

(8) Mislead an elector who is physically unable to prepare the elector's ballot, mark a ballot for such elector otherwise than as directed by that elector, or disclose to any person, except when legally required to do so, how such elector voted;

(9) Alter or mark or permit any alteration or marking on any ballot when counting the ballots;

(10) Unlawfully count or tally or sanction the wrongful counting or tallying of votes;

(11) After the counting of votes commences, as required by law, postpone or sanction the postponement of the counting of votes, adjourn at any time or to any place, or remove the ballot box from the place of voting, or from the custody or presence of all the judges and clerks of such elections;

(12) Permit any ballot to remain or to be in the ballot box at the opening of the polls, or to be put in the box during the counting of the ballots, or to be left in the box without being counted;

(13) Admit or sanction the admission to the polling room at an election during the receiving, counting, and certifying of votes of any person not qualified by law to be so admitted;

(14) Refuse to admit or sanction the refusal to admit any person, upon lawful request for admission, who is legally qualified to be present;

(15) Permit or sanction the counting of the ballots contrary to the manner prescribed by law;

(16) Neglect or unlawfully execute any duty enjoined upon the judge or clerk by law.

(B) Whoever violates division (A) of this section is guilty of a misdemeanor of the first degree.

(1997 S 116, eff. 12–9–97; 1953 H 1, eff. 10–1–53; GC 4785–209)

3599.20 Secret ballot

No person shall attempt to induce an elector to show how the elector marked the elector's ballot at an election; or, being an elector, allow the elector's ballot to be seen by another, except as provided by section 3505.24 of the Revised Code, with the apparent intention of letting it be known how the elector is about to vote; or make a false statement as to the elector's ability to mark the ballot; or knowingly mark the ballot so it may be identified after it has been cast; or attempt to interfere with an elector in the voting booth when marking the elector's ballot; or knowingly destroy or mutilate a lawful ballot; or remove from the polling place or be found in unlawful possession of a lawful ballot outside the enclosure provided for voting; or knowingly hinder or delay the delivery of a lawful ballot to a person entitled to receive it; or give to an elector a ballot printed or written contrary to law; or forge or falsely make an official indorsement on a ballot.

Whoever violates this section is guilty of a felony of the fifth degree.

(1997 S 116, eff. 12–9–97; 1953 H 1, eff. 10–1–53; GC 4785–210)

3599.21 Absent voter's ballot

(A) No person shall knowingly do any of the following:

(1) Impersonate another, or make a false representation in order to obtain an absent voter's ballot;

(2) Aid or abet a person to vote an absent voter's ballot illegally;

(3) If the person is an election official, open, destroy, steal, mark, or mutilate any absent voter's ballot;

(4) Aid or abet another person to open, destroy, steal, mark, or mutilate any absent voter's ballot after the ballot has been voted;

(5) Delay the delivery of any such ballot with a view to preventing its arrival in time to be counted;

(6) Hinder or attempt to hinder the delivery or counting of such absent voter's ballot;

(7) Fail to forward to the appropriate election official an absent voter's ballot application entrusted to that person to so forward.

(B) Whoever violates division (A) of this section is guilty of a felony of the fourth degree.

(1997 S 116, eff. 12–9–97; 1982 H 269, § 4, eff. 7–1–83; 1982 S 199; 1953 H 1; GC 4785–211)

3599.22 Printing of ballots

(A) No person employed to print or engage in printing the official ballots shall knowingly do any of the following:

(1) Print or cause or permit to be printed an official ballot other than the official ballot furnished by the board of elections;

(2) Print or permit to be printed more ballots than are delivered to the board;

(3) Appropriate, give, deliver, or knowingly permit to be taken away any of such ballots by a person other than the person authorized by law to do so;

(4) Print such ballots on paper other than that provided in the contract with the board;

(5) Package or deliver to the board fewer ballots than the number the board directed to be printed.

(B) Whoever violates division (A) of this section is guilty of a misdemeanor of the first degree.

(1997 S 116, eff. 12–9–97; 1953 H 1, eff. 10–1–53; GC 4785–212)

3599.23 Custodian of ballots, papers, or marking devices, offenses and penalties

(A) No printer or other person entrusted with the printing, custody, or delivery of registration cards or forms, ballots, blanks, pollbooks, cards of instruction, or other required papers shall do any of the following:

(1) Knowingly and unlawfully open or permit to be opened a sealed package containing ballots or other printed forms;

(2) Knowingly give or deliver to another not lawfully entitled to them, or unlawfully misplace or carry away, or knowingly fail to deliver, or knowingly destroy any such forms or packages of ballots, or a ballot, pollbooks, cards of instruction, or other required papers;

(3) Negligently lose or permit to be taken from the printer or other entrusted person any of the materials described in division (A)(2) of this section.

(B) No person entrusted with the preparation, custody, or delivery of marking devices shall do either of the following:

(1) Unlawfully open or permit to be opened a sealed package containing marking devices, or give or deliver to another not lawfully entitled to them any such marking devices;

(2) Unlawfully or carelessly use or negligently lose or permit to be taken from the printer or other entrusted person and fail to deliver or destroy any such marking devices.

(C) Whoever violates division (A)(1) or (2) or (B) of this section is guilty of a misdemeanor of the first degree. Whoever violates division (A)(3) of this section is guilty of a misdemeanor of the second degree.

(1997 S 116, eff. 12–9–97; 129 v 1653, eff. 6–29–61; 1953 H 1; GC 4785–213)

3599.24 Interference with conduct of election

(A) No person shall do any of the following:

(1) By force, fraud, or other improper means, obtain or attempt to obtain possession of the ballots, ballot boxes, or pollbooks;

(2) Recklessly destroy any property used in the conduct of elections;

(3) Attempt to intimidate an election officer, or prevent an election official from performing the official's duties;

(4) Knowingly tear down, remove, or destroy any of the registration lists or sample ballots furnished by the board of elections at the polling place;

(5) Loiter in or about a registration or polling place during registration or the casting and counting of ballots so as to hinder, delay, or interfere with the conduct of the registration or election;

(6) Remove from the voting place the pencils, cards of instruction, supplies, or other conveniences furnished to enable the voter to mark the voter's ballot.

(B) Whoever violates division (A)(1) or (2) of this section is guilty of a felony of the fifth degree. Whoever violates division (A)(3) or (4) of this section is guilty of a misdemeanor of the first degree. Whoever violates division (A)(5) or (6) of this section is guilty of a minor misdemeanor.

(1995 S 2, eff. 7–1–96; 1980 H 1062, eff. 3–23–81; 1953 H 1; GC 4785–214)

3599.25 Inducing illegal voting

(A) No person shall knowingly do any of the following:

(1) Counsel or advise another to vote at an election, knowing that the person is not a qualified voter;

(2) Advise, aid, or assist another person to go or come into a precinct for the purpose of voting in it, knowing that such person is not qualified to vote in it;

(3) Counsel, advise, or attempt to induce an election officer to permit a person to vote, knowing such person is not a qualified elector.

(B) Whoever violates division (A) of this section is guilty of a felony of the fourth degree.

(1997 S 116, eff. 12–9–97; 1953 H 1, eff. 10–1–53; GC 4785–215)

3599.26 Tampering with ballots

No person shall fraudulently put a ballot or ticket into a ballot box; or knowingly and willfully vote a ballot other than an official ballot lawfully obtained by the person from the precinct election authorities; or fraudulently or deceitfully change a ballot of an elector, by which such elector is prevented from voting for such candidates or on an issue as the elector intends to do; or mark a ballot of an elector except as authorized by section 3505.24 of the Revised Code; or hand a marked ballot to an elector to vote, with intent to ascertain how the elector voted; or furnish a ballot to an elector who cannot read, knowingly informing the elector that it contains a name different from the one that is printed or written thereon, to induce the elector to vote contrary to the elector's intentions; or unduly delay or hinder an elector from applying for registration, registering, or from attempting to vote or voting; or knowingly print or distribute a ballot contrary to law.

Whoever violates this section is guilty of a felony of the fifth degree.

(1995 S 2, eff. 7–1–96; 1982 H 269, § 4, eff. 7–1–83; 1982 S 199; 1953 H 1; GC 4785–216)

3599.27 Possession of voting machine, tabulating equipment, or marking device prohibited; tampering; penalty

No unauthorized person shall have in the person's possession any voting machine that may be owned or leased by any county or any of the parts or the keys thereof. No person shall tamper or attempt to tamper with, deface, impair the use of, destroy, or otherwise injure in any manner any voting machine.

No unauthorized person shall have in the person's possession any marking device, automatic tabulating equipment, or any of the parts, appurtenances, or accessories thereof. No person shall tamper or attempt to tamper with, deface, impair the use of, destroy, or otherwise change or injure in any manner any marking device, automatic tabulating equipment, or any appurtenances or accessories thereof.

Whoever violates this section is guilty of a felony of the fifth degree.

(1995 S 2, eff. 7–1–96; 1982 H 269, § 4, eff. 7–1–83; 1982 S 199; 129 v 1653; 126 v 575; 1953 H 1; GC 4785–217)

3599.28 False signatures

No person, with intent to defraud or deceive, shall write or sign the name of another person to any document, petition, registration card, or other book or record authorized or required by Title XXXV of the Revised Code.

Whoever violates this section is guilty of a felony of the fifth degree.

(1995 S 2, eff. 7–1–96; 1982 H 269, § 4, eff. 7–1–83; 1982 S 199; 1953 H 1; GC 4785–219)

3599.29 Possession of false records

No person shall have in the person's possession a falsely made, altered, forged, or counterfeited registration card, form, or list, pollbook, tally sheet, or list of election returns of an election, knowing it to be such, with intent to hinder, defeat, or prevent a fair expression of the popular will at such election.

Whoever violates this section is guilty of a felony of the fifth degree.

(1995 S 2, eff. 7–1–96; 1982 H 269, § 4, eff. 7–1–83; 1982 S 199; 1953 H 1; GC 4785–220)

3599.31 Failure of officer of law to assist election officers

No officer of the law shall fail to obey forthwith an order of the presiding judge and aid in enforcing a lawful order of the presiding judges at an election, against persons unlawfully congregating or loitering within one hundred feet of a polling place, hindering or delaying an elector from reaching or leaving the polling place, soliciting or attempting, within one hundred feet of the polling place, to influence an elector in casting the elector's vote, or interfering with the registration of voters or casting and counting of the ballots.

Whoever violates this section is guilty of a misdemeanor of the first degree.

(1997 S 116, eff. 12–9–97; 1953 H 1, eff. 10–1–53; GC 4785–218)

3599.32 Failure of election official to enforce law

No official upon whom a duty is imposed by an election law for the violation of which no penalty is otherwise provided shall knowingly disobey such election law.

Whoever violates this section is guilty of a misdemeanor of the first degree.

(1997 S 116, eff. 12–9–97; 1953 H 1, eff. 10–1–53; GC 4785–222)

3599.33 Fraudulent writing on ballots or election records

No person, from the time ballots are cast or counted until the time has expired for using them as evidence in a recount or contest of election, shall willfully and with fraudulent intent make any mark or alteration on any ballot; or inscribe, write, or cause to be inscribed or written in or upon a registration form or list, pollbook, tally sheet, or list, lawfully made or kept at an election, or in or upon a book or paper purporting to be such, or upon an election return, or upon a book or paper containing such return the name of a person not entitled to vote at such election or not voting thereat, or a fictitious name, or, within such time, wrongfully change, alter, erase, or tamper with a name, word, or figure contained in such pollbook, tally sheet, list, book, or paper; or falsify, mark, or write thereon with intent to defeat, hinder, or prevent a fair expression of the will of the people at such election.

Whoever violates this section is guilty of a felony of the fifth degree.

(1995 S 2, eff. 7–1–96; 1982 H 269, § 4, eff. 7–1–83; 1982 S 199; 1953 H 1; GC 4785–223)

3599.34 Destruction of election records before expiration of time for contest

No person, from the time ballots are cast or voted until the time has expired for using them in a recount or as evidence in a contest of election, shall unlawfully destroy or attempt to destroy the ballots, or permit such ballots or a ballot box or pollbook used at an election to be destroyed; or destroy, falsify, mark, or write in a name on any such ballot that has been voted.

Whoever violates this section is guilty of a felony of the fifth degree.

(1995 S 2, eff. 7–1–96; 1982 H 269, § 4, eff. 7–1–83; 1982 S 199; 1953 H 1; GC 4785–224)

MISCELLANEOUS PROVISIONS

3599.35 Proxies shall not be given by party representatives; impersonation of representatives

No party committeeperson or party delegate or alternate chosen at an election, or a delegate or alternate appointed to a convention provided by law, shall give or issue a proxy or authority to another person to act or vote in that person's stead.

No person shall knowingly or fraudulently act or vote or attempt to impersonate, act, or vote in place of that committeeperson, delegate, or alternate.

Whoever violates this section is guilty of a misdemeanor of the first degree.

(1997 S 116, eff. 12–9–97; 1953 H 1, eff. 10–1–53; GC 4785–225)

3599.36 Perjury in matters relating to elections; election falsification

No person, either orally or in writing, on oath lawfully administered or in a statement made under penalty of election falsification, shall knowingly state a falsehood as to a material matter relating to an election in a proceeding before a court, tribunal, or election official, or in a matter in relation to which an oath or statement under penalty of election falsification is authorized by law, including a statement required for verifying or filing any declaration of candidacy, declaration of intent to be a write-in candidate, nominating petition, or other petition presented to or filed with the secretary of state, a board of elections, or any other public office for the purpose of becoming a candidate for any elective office, including the office of a political party, for the purpose of submitting a question or issue to the electors at an election, or for the purpose of forming a political party.

Whoever violates this section is guilty of election falsification, a felony of the fifth degree.

Every paper, card, or other document relating to any election matter that calls for a statement to be made under penalty of election falsification shall be accompanied by the following statement in bold face capital letters: "Whoever commits election falsification is guilty of a felony of the fifth degree."

(1997 S 116, eff. 12–9–97; 1980 H 1062, eff. 3–23–81; 1974 H 662, S 429; 128 v 255; 1953 H 1; GC 4785–226)

3599.37 Refusal to appear or testify concerning violation of election laws

(A) No person having been subpoenaed or ordered to appear before a grand jury, court, board, or officer in a proceeding or prosecution upon a complaint, information, affidavit, or indictment for an offense under an election law shall do either of the following:

(1) Fail to appear or, having appeared, refuse to answer a question pertinent to the matter under inquiry or investigation;

(2) Refuse to produce, upon reasonable notice, any material, books, papers, documents, or records in that person's possession or under that person's control.

(B) Whoever violates division (A) of this section, unless the violator claims the violator's constitutional rights, is guilty of a misdemeanor of the first degree.

(1997 S 116, eff. 12–9–97; 1953 H 1, eff. 10–1–53; GC 4785–227)

3599.38 Election officials shall not influence voters

(A) No election official, witness, challenger, deputy sheriff, special deputy sheriff, or police officer, while performing that person's duties related to the casting of votes, shall do either of the following:

(1) Wear any badge, sign, or other insignia or thing indicating that person's preference for any candidate or for any question submitted at an election;

(2) Influence or attempt to influence any voter to cast the voter's ballot for or against any candidate or issue submitted at an election.

(B) Whoever violates division (A) of this section is guilty of a misdemeanor of the first degree.

(1997 S 116, eff. 12–9–97; 1953 H 1, eff. 10–1–53; GC 4785–228)

3599.39 Second offense under election laws

Any person convicted of a violation of any provision of Title XXXV of the Revised Code, who is again convicted of a violation of any such provision, whether such conviction is for the same offense or not, is on such second conviction guilty of a felony of the fourth degree, and in addition, shall be disfranchised.

(1997 S 116, eff. 12–9–97; 126 v 575, eff. 10–6–55; 1953 H 1; GC 4785–230)

3599.40 General penalty

Except as otherwise provided in section 3599.39 of the Revised Code, whoever violates any provision of Title XXXV of the Revised Code, unless otherwise provided in such title, is guilty of a misdemeanor of the first degree.

(1997 S 116, eff. 12–9–97; 1972 H 511, eff. 1–1–74; 1953 H 1; GC 4785–232)

3599.41 Person violating election laws may testify against other violators

A person violating any provision of Title XXXV of the Revised Code is a competent witness against another person so offending, and may attend and testify at a trial, hearing, or investigation thereof.

(1953 H 1, eff. 10–1–53; GC 4785–229)

3599.42 Prima–facie case of fraud

A violation of any provision of Title XXXV of the Revised Code constitutes a prima-facie case of fraud within the purview of such title.

(1953 H 1, eff. 10–1–53; GC 4785–231)

3599.43 Communications purporting to be from boards of elections; penalty

No person, not authorized by a board of elections, shall send or transmit to any other person any written or oral communication which purports to be a communication from a board of elections, or which reasonably construed appears to be a communication from such a board and which was intended to be so construed.

Whoever violates this section shall be fined not less than one hundred nor more than one thousand dollars or imprisoned not more than six months or both.

(130 v H 709, eff. 9–16–63)

3599.45 Contributions from medicaid provider

(A) No candidate for the office of attorney general or county prosecutor or such a candidate's campaign committee shall knowingly accept any contribution from a provider of services or goods under contract with the department of job and family services pursuant to the medicaid program of Title XIX of the "Social Security Act," 49 Stat. 620 (1935), 42 U.S.C. 301, as amended, or from any person having an ownership interest in the provider.

As used in this section "candidate," "campaign committee," and "contribution" have the same meaning as in section 3517.01 of the Revised Code.

(B) Whoever violates this section is guilty of a misdemeanor of the first degree.

(1999 H 471, eff. 7–1–00; 1986 H 428, eff. 12–23–86; 1978 S 159)

CHAPTER 3701

DEPARTMENT OF HEALTH

3701.045 Rules

(A) The department of health, in consultation with the children's trust fund board established under section 3109.15 of the Revised Code and any bodies acting as child fatality review boards on the effective date of this section, shall adopt rules in accordance with Chapter 119. of the Revised Code that establish a procedure for child fatality review boards to follow in conducting a review of the death of a child. The rules shall do all of the following:

(1) Establish the format for the annual reports required by section 307.626 of the Revised Code;

(2) Establish guidelines for a child fatality review board to follow in compiling statistics for annual reports so that the reports do not contain any information that would permit any person's identity to be ascertained from a report;

(3) Establish guidelines for a child fatality review board to follow in creating and maintaining the comprehensive database of child deaths required by section 307.623 of the Revised Code, including provisions establishing uniform record-keeping procedures;

(4) Establish guidelines, materials, and training to help educate members of child fatality review boards about the purpose of the review process and the confidentiality of the information described in section 307.629 of the Revised Code and to make them aware that such information is not a public record under section 149.43 of the Revised Code.

(B) On or before the thirtieth day of September of each year, the department of health and the children's trust fund board jointly shall prepare and publish a report organizing and setting forth the data in all the reports provided by child fatality review boards in their annual reports for the previous calendar year and recommending any changes to law and policy that might prevent future deaths. The department and the children's trust fund board jointly shall provide a copy of the report to the governor, the speaker of the house of representatives, the president of the senate, the minority leaders of the house of representatives and the senate, each county or regional child fatality review board, and each county or regional family and children first council.

(2000 H 448, eff. 10–5–00)

3701.56 Enforcement of orders and rules

Boards of health of a general or city health district, health authorities and officials, officers of state institutions, police officers, sheriffs, constables, and other officers and employees of the state or any county, city, or township, shall enforce quarantine and isolation orders, and the rules the department of health adopts.

(2003 H 6, eff. 2–12–04; 1953 H 1, eff. 10–1–53; GC 1238)

3701.81 Spreading contagion

(A) No person, knowing or having reasonable cause to believe that he is suffering from a dangerous, contagious disease, shall knowingly fail to take reasonable measures to prevent exposing himself to other persons, except when seeking medical aid.

(B) No person, having charge or care of a person whom he knows or has reasonable cause to believe is suffering from a dangerous, contagious disease, shall recklessly fail to take reasonable measures to protect others from exposure to the contagion, and to inform health authorities of the existence of the contagion.

(C) No person, having charge of a public conveyance or place of public accommodation, amusement, resort, or trade, and knowing or having reasonable cause to believe that persons using such conveyance or place have been or are being exposed to a dangerous, contagious disease, shall negligently fail to take reasonable measures to protect the public from exposure to the contagion, and to inform health authorities of the existence of the contagion.

(1972 H 511, eff. 1–1–74)

3701.82 Venting of heaters and burners; unvented kerosene, natural gas, or liquid petroleum heaters

(A) A brazier, salamander, space heater, room heater, furnace, water heater, or other burner or heater using wood, coal, coke, fuel oil, kerosene, gasoline, natural gas, liquid petroleum gas, or similar fuel, and tending to give off carbon monoxide or other harmful gases:

(1) When used in living quarters, or in any enclosed building or space in which persons are usually present, shall be used with a flue or vent so designed, installed, and maintained as to vent the

products of combustion outdoors; except in storage, factory, or industrial buildings which are provided with sufficient ventilation to avoid the danger of carbon monoxide poisoning;

(2) When used as a portable or temporary burner or heater at a construction site, or in a warehouse, shed, or structure in which persons are temporarily present, shall be vented as provided in division (A)(1) of this section, or used with sufficient ventilation to avoid the danger of carbon monoxide poisoning.

(B) This section does not apply to domestic ranges, laundry stoves, gas logs installed in a fireplace with an adequate flue, or hot plates, unless the same are used as space or room heaters.

(C) No person shall negligently use, or, being the owner, person in charge, or occupant of premises, negligently permit the use of a burner or heater in violation of the standards for venting and ventilation provided in this section.

(D) Division (A) of this section does not apply to any kerosene-fired space or room heater that is equipped with an automatic extinguishing tip-over device, or to any natural gas-fired or liquid petroleum gas-fired space or room heater that is equipped with an oxygen depletion safety shutoff system, and that has its fuel piped from a source outside of the building in which it is located, that are approved by an authoritative source recognized by the state fire marshal in the state fire code adopted by him under section 3737.82 of the Revised Code.

(E) The state fire marshal may make rules to ensure the safe use of unvented kerosene, natural gas, or liquid petroleum gas heaters exempted from division (A) of this section when used in assembly buildings, business buildings, high hazard buildings, institutional buildings, mercantile buildings, and type R–1 and R–2 residential buildings, as these groups of buildings are defined in rules adopted by the board of building standards under section 3781.10 of the Revised Code. No person shall negligently use, or, being the owner, person in charge, or occupant of premises, negligently permit the use of a heater in violation of any rules adopted under this division.

(F) The state fire marshal may make rules prescribing standards for written instructions containing ventilation requirements and warning of any potential fire hazards that may occur in using a kerosene, natural gas, or liquid petroleum gas heater. No person shall sell or offer for sale any kerosene, natural gas, or liquid petroleum gas heater unless the manufacturer provides with the heater written instructions that comply with any rules adopted under this division.

(G) No product labeled as a fuel additive for kerosene heaters and having a flash point below one hundred degrees fahrenheit or thirty-seven and eight-tenths degrees centigrade shall be sold, offered for sale, or used in any kerosene space heater.

(H) No device that prohibits any safety feature on a kerosene, natural gas, or liquid petroleum gas space heater from operating shall be sold, offered for sale, or used in connection with any kerosene, natural gas, or liquid petroleum gas space heater.

(I) No person shall sell or offer for sale any kerosene-fired, natural gas, or liquid petroleum gas-fired heater that is not exempt from division (A) of this section unless it is marked conspicuously by the manufacturer on the container with the phrase "Not Approved For Home Use."

(J) No person shall use a cabinet-type, liquid petroleum gas-fired heater having a fuel source within the heater, inside any building, except as permitted by the state fire marshal in the state fire code adopted by him under section 3737.82 of the Revised Code.

(1985 S 184, eff. 3–13–86; 1981 H 382; 1979 H 815; 1972 H 511)

3701.881 Criminal records check; disqualification from employment

(A) As used in this section:

(1) "Applicant" means both of the following:

(a) A person who is under final consideration for appointment or employment with a home health agency in a position as a person responsible for the care, custody, or control of a child;

(b) A person who is under final consideration for employment with a home health agency in a full-time, part-time, or temporary position that involves providing direct care to an older adult. With regard to persons providing direct care to older adults, "applicant" does not include a person who provides direct care as a volunteer without receiving or expecting to receive any form of remuneration other than reimbursement for actual expenses.

(2) "Criminal records check" and "older adult" have the same meanings as in section 109.572 of the Revised Code.

(3) "Home health agency" means a person or government entity, other than a nursing home, residential care facility, or hospice care program, that has the primary function of providing any of the following services to a patient at a place of residence used as the patient's home:

(a) Skilled nursing care;

(b) Physical therapy;

(c) Speech–language pathology;

(d) Occupational therapy;

(e) Medical social services;

(f) Home health aide services.

(4) "Home health aide services" means any of the following services provided by an individual employed with or contracted for by a home health agency:

(a) Hands–on bathing or assistance with a tub bath or shower;

(b) Assistance with dressing, ambulation, and toileting;

(c) Catheter care but not insertion;

(d) Meal preparation and feeding.

(5) "Hospice care program" has the same meaning as in section 3712.01 of the Revised Code.

(6) "Medical social services" means services provided by a social worker under the direction of a patient's attending physician.

(7) "Minor drug possession offense" has the same meaning as in section 2925.01 of the Revised Code.

(8) "Nursing home," "residential care facility," and "skilled nursing care" have the same meanings as in section 3721.01 of the Revised Code.

(9) "Occupational therapy" has the same meaning as in section 4755.01 of the Revised Code.

(10) "Physical therapy" has the same meaning as in section 4755.40 of the Revised Code.

(11) "Social worker" means a person licensed under Chapter 4757. of the Revised Code to practice as a social worker or independent social worker.

(12) "Speech–language pathology" has the same meaning as in section 4753.01 of the Revised Code.

(B)(1) Except as provided in division (I) of this section, the chief administrator of a home health agency shall request the superintendent of the bureau of criminal identification and investigation to conduct a criminal records check with respect to each applicant. If the position may involve both responsibility for the care, custody, or control of a child and provision of direct care to an older adult, the chief administrator shall request that the superintendent conduct a single criminal records check for the applicant. If an applicant for whom a criminal records check request is required under this division does not present proof of having been a resident of this state for the five-year period immediately prior to the date upon which the criminal records check is requested or does not provide evidence that within that five-year period the superintendent has requested information about the applicant from the federal bureau of investigation in a criminal records check, the chief administrator shall request that the superintendent obtain information from the federal bureau of investigation as a part of the criminal records check for the applicant. Even if an applicant for whom a criminal records check request is required under this division presents proof that the applicant has been a resident of this state for that five-year period, the chief administrator may request that the superintendent include information from the federal bureau of investigation in the criminal records check.

(2) Any person required by division (B)(1) of this section to request a criminal records check shall provide to each applicant for whom a criminal records check request is required under that division a copy of the form prescribed pursuant to division (C)(1) of section 109.572 of the Revised Code and a standard impression sheet prescribed pursuant to division (C)(2) of section 109.572 of the Revised Code, obtain the completed form and impression sheet from each applicant, and forward the completed form and impression sheet to the superintendent of the bureau of criminal identification and investigation at the time the chief administrator requests a criminal records check pursuant to division (B)(1) of this section.

(3) An applicant who receives pursuant to division (B)(2) of this section a copy of the form prescribed pursuant to division (C)(1) of section 109.572 of the Revised Code and a copy of an impression sheet prescribed pursuant to division (C)(2) of that section and who is requested to complete the form and provide a set of fingerprint impressions shall complete the form or provide all the information necessary to complete the form and shall provide the impression sheets with the impressions of the applicant's fingerprints. If an applicant, upon request, fails to provide the information necessary to complete the form or fails to provide fingerprint impressions, the home health agency shall not employ that applicant for any position for which a criminal records check is required by division (B)(1) of this section.

(C)(1) Except as provided in rules adopted by the department of health in accordance with division (F) of this section and subject to division (C)(3) of this section, no home health agency shall employ a person as a person responsible for the care, custody, or control of a child if the person previously has been convicted of or pleaded guilty to any of the following:

(a) A violation of section 2903.01, 2903.02, 2903.03, 2903.04, 2903.11, 2903.12, 2903.13, 2903.16, 2903.21, 2903.34, 2905.01, 2905.02, 2905.05, 2907. 02, 2907.03, 2907.04, 2907.05, 2907.06, 2907.07, 2907.08, 2907.09, 2907.21, 2907.22, 2907.23, 2907.25, 2907.31, 2907.32, 2907.321, 2907.322, 2907.323, 2911.01, 2911.02, 2911.11, 2911.12, 2919.12, 2919.22, 2919.24, 2919.25, 2923. 12, 2923.13, 2923.161, 2925.02, 2925.03, 2925.04, 2925.05, 2925.06, or 3716.11 of the Revised Code, a violation of section 2905.04 of the Revised Code as it existed prior to July 1, 1996, a violation of section 2919.23 of the Revised Code that would have been a violation of section 2905.04 of the Revised Code as it existed prior to July 1, 1996, had the violation been committed prior to that date, a violation of section 2925.11 of the Revised Code that is not a minor drug possession offense, or felonious sexual penetration in violation of former section 2907.12 of the Revised Code;

(b) A violation of an existing or former law of this state, any other state, or the United States that is substantially equivalent to any of the offenses listed in division (C)(1)(a) of this section.

(2) Except as provided in rules adopted by the department of health in accordance with division (F) of this section and subject to division (C)(3) of this section, no home health agency shall employ a person in a position that involves providing direct care to an older adult if the person previously has been convicted of or pleaded guilty to any of the following:

(a) A violation of section 2903.01, 2903.02, 2903.03, 2903.04, 2903.11, 2903.12, 2903.13, 2903.16, 2903.21, 2903.34, 2905.01, 2905.02, 2905.11, 2905. 12, 2907.02, 2907.03, 2907.05, 2907.06, 2907.07, 2907.08, 2907.09, 2907.12, 2907.25, 2907.31, 2907.32, 2907.321, 2907.322, 2907.323, 2911.01, 2911.02, 2911.11, 2911.12, 2911.13, 2913.02, 2913.03, 2913.04, 2913.11, 2913.21, 2913. 31, 2913.40, 2913.43, 2913.47, 2913.51, 2919.25, 2921.36, 2923.12, 2923.13, 2923.161, 2925.02, 2925.03, 2925.11, 2925.13, 2925.22, 2925.23, or 3716.11 of the Revised Code.

(b) A violation of an existing or former law of this state, any other state, or the United States that is substantially equivalent to any of the offenses listed in division (C)(2)(a) of this section.

(3)(a) A home health agency may employ conditionally an applicant for whom a criminal records check request is required under division (B) of this section as a person responsible for the care, custody, or control of a child until the criminal records check regarding the applicant required by this section is completed and the agency receives the results of the criminal records check. If the results of the criminal records check indicate that, pursuant to division (C)(1) of this section, the applicant does not qualify for employment, the agency shall release the applicant from employment unless the agency chooses to employ the applicant pursuant to division (F) of this section.

(b)(i) A home health agency may employ conditionally an applicant for whom a criminal records check request is required under division (B) of this section in a position that involves providing direct care to an older adult or in a position that involves both responsibility for the care, custody, and control of a child and the provision of direct care to older adults prior to obtaining the results of a criminal records check regarding the individual, provided that the agency shall request a criminal records check regarding the individual in accordance with division (B)(1) of this section not later than five business days after the individual begins conditional employment. In the circumstances described in division (I)(2) of this section, a home health agency may employ conditionally in a position that involves providing direct care to an older adult an applicant who has been referred to the home health agency by an employment service that supplies full-time, part-time, or temporary staff for positions involving the direct care of older adults and for whom, pursuant to that division, a criminal records check is not required under division (B) of this section. In the circumstances described in division (I)(4) of this section, a home health agency may employ conditionally in a position that involves both responsibility for the care, custody, and control of a child and the provision of direct care to older adults an applicant who has been referred to the home health agency by an employment service that supplies full-time, part-time, or temporary staff for positions involving both responsibility for the care, custody, and control of a child and the provision of direct care to older adults and for whom, pursuant to that division, a criminal records check is not required under division (B) of this section.

(ii) A home health agency that employs an individual conditionally under authority of division (C)(3)(b)(i) of this section shall terminate the individual's employment if the results of the criminal records check requested under division (B)(1) of this section or described in division (I)(2) or (4) of this section, other than the results of any request for information from the federal bureau of investigation, are not obtained within the period ending thirty days after the date the request is made. Regardless of when the results of the criminal records check are obtained, if the individual was employed conditionally in a position that involves the provision of direct care to older adults and the results indicate that the individual has been convicted of or pleaded guilty to any of the offenses listed or described in division (C)(2) of this section, or if the individual was employed conditionally in a position that involves both responsibility for the care, custody, and control of a child and the provision of direct care to older adults and the results indicate that the individual has been convicted of or pleaded guilty to any of the offenses listed or described in division (C)(1) or (2) of this section, the agency shall terminate the individual's employment unless the agency chooses to employ the individual pursuant to division (F) of this section. Termination of employment under this division shall be considered just cause for discharge for purposes of division (D)(2) of section 4141.29 of the Revised Code if the individual makes any attempt to deceive the agency about the individual's criminal record.

(D)(1) Each home health agency shall pay to the bureau of criminal identification and investigation the fee prescribed pursuant to division (C)(3) of section 109.572 of the Revised Code for each criminal records check conducted in accordance with that section upon the request pursuant to division (B)(1) of this section of the chief administrator of the home health agency.

(2) A home health agency may charge an applicant a fee for the costs it incurs in obtaining a criminal records check under this section, unless the medical assistance program established under Chapter 5111. of the Revised Code reimburses the agency for the costs. A fee charged under division (D)(2) of this section shall not exceed the amount of fees the agency pays under division (D)(1) of this section. If a fee is charged under division (D)(2) of this section, the agency shall notify the applicant at the time of the applicant's initial application for employment of the amount of the fee and that, unless the fee is paid, the agency will not consider the applicant for employment.

(E) The report of any criminal records check conducted by the bureau of criminal identification and investigation in accordance with section 109.572 of the Revised Code and pursuant to a request made under division (B)(1) of this section is not a public record for the purposes of section 149.43 of the Revised Code and shall not be made available to any person other than the following:

(1) The individual who is the subject of the criminal records check or the individual's representative;

(2) The home health agency requesting the criminal records check or its representative;

(3) The administrator of any other facility, agency, or program that provides direct care to older adults that is owned or operated by the same entity that owns or operates the home health agency;

(4) Any court, hearing officer, or other necessary individual involved in a case dealing with a denial of employment of the applicant or dealing with employment or unemployment benefits of the applicant;

(5) Any person to whom the report is provided pursuant to, and in accordance with, division (I)(1), (2), (3), or (4) of this section.

(F) The department of health shall adopt rules in accordance with Chapter 119. of the Revised Code to implement this section. The rules shall specify circumstances under which the home health agency may employ a person who has been convicted of or pleaded guilty to an offense listed or described in division (C)(1) of this section but who meets standards in regard to rehabilitation set by the department or employ a person who has been convicted of or pleaded guilty to an offense listed or described in division (C)(2) of this section but meets personal character standards set by the department.

(G) Any person required by division (B)(1) of this section to request a criminal records check shall inform each person, at the time of initial application for employment that the person is required to provide a set of fingerprint impressions and that a criminal records check is required to be conducted and satisfactorily completed in accordance with section 109.572 of the Revised Code if the person comes under final consideration for appointment or employment as a precondition to employment for that position.

(H) In a tort or other civil action for damages that is brought as the result of an injury, death, or loss to person or property caused by an individual who a home health agency employs in a position that involves providing direct care to older adults, all of the following shall apply:

(1) If the agency employed the individual in good faith and reasonable reliance on the report of a criminal records check requested under this section, the agency shall not be found negligent solely because of its reliance on the report, even if the information in the report is determined later to have been incomplete or inaccurate;

(2) If the agency employed the individual in good faith on a conditional basis pursuant to division (C)(3)(b) of this section, the agency shall not be found negligent solely because it employed the individual prior to receiving the report of a criminal records check requested under this section;

(3) If the agency in good faith employed the individual according to the personal character standards established in rules adopted under division (F) of this section, the agency shall not be found negligent solely because the individual prior to being employed had been convicted of or pleaded guilty to an offense listed or described in division (C)(1) or (2) of this section.

(I)(1) The chief administrator of a home health agency is not required to request that the superintendent of the bureau of criminal identification and investigation conduct a criminal records check of an applicant for a position that involves the provision of direct care to older adults if the applicant has been referred to the agency by an employment service that supplies full-time, part-time, or temporary staff for positions involving the direct care of older adults and both of the following apply:

(a) The chief administrator receives from the employment service or the applicant a report of the results of a criminal records check regarding the applicant that has been conducted by the superintendent within the one-year period immediately preceding the applicant's referral;

(b) The report of the criminal records check demonstrates that the person has not been convicted of or pleaded guilty to an offense listed or described in division (C)(2) of this section, or the report demonstrates that the person has been convicted of or pleaded guilty to one or more of those offenses, but the home health agency chooses to employ the individual pursuant to division (F) of this section.

(2) The chief administrator of a home health agency is not required to request that the superintendent of the bureau of criminal identification and investigation conduct a criminal records check of an applicant for a position that involves providing direct care to older adults and may employ the applicant conditionally in a position of that nature as described in this division, if the applicant has been referred to the agency by an employment service that supplies full-time, part-time, or temporary staff for positions involving the direct care of older adults and if the chief administrator receives from the employment service or the applicant a letter from the employment service that is on the letterhead of the employment service, dated, and signed by a supervisor or another designated official of the employment service and that states that the employment service has requested the superintendent to conduct a criminal records check regarding the applicant, that the requested criminal records check will include a determination of whether the applicant has been convicted of or pleaded guilty to any offense listed or described in division (C)(2) of this section, that, as of the date set forth on the letter, the employment service had not received the results of the criminal records check, and that, when the employment service receives the results of the criminal records check, it promptly will send a copy of the results to the home health agency. If a home health agency employs an applicant conditionally in accordance with this division, the employment service, upon its receipt of the results of

the criminal records check, promptly shall send a copy of the results to the home health agency, and division (C)(3)(b) of this section applies regarding the conditional employment.

(3) The chief administrator of a home health agency is not required to request that the superintendent of the bureau of criminal identification and investigation conduct a criminal records check of an applicant for a position that involves both responsibility for the care, custody, and control of a child and the provision of direct care to older adults if the applicant has been referred to the agency by an employment service that supplies full-time, part-time, or temporary staff for positions involving both responsibility for the care, custody, and control of a child and the provision of direct care to older adults and both of the following apply:

(a) The chief administrator receives from the employment service or applicant a report of a criminal records check of the type described in division (I)(1)(a) of this section;

(b) The report of the criminal records check demonstrates that the person has not been convicted of or pleaded guilty to an offense listed or described in division (C)(1) or (2) of this section, or the report demonstrates that the person has been convicted of or pleaded guilty to one or more of those offenses, but the home health agency chooses to employ the individual pursuant to division (F) of this section.

(4) The chief administrator of a home health agency is not required to request that the superintendent of the bureau of criminal identification and investigation conduct a criminal records check of an applicant for a position that involves both responsibility for the care, custody, and control of a child and the provision of direct care to older adults and may employ the applicant conditionally in a position of that nature as described in this division, if the applicant has been referred to the agency by an employment service that supplies full-time, part-time, or temporary staff for positions involving both responsibility for the care, custody, and control of a child and the direct care of older adults and if the chief administrator receives from the employment service or the applicant a letter from the employment service that is on the letterhead of the employment service, dated, and signed by a supervisor or another designated official of the employment service and that states that the employment service has requested the superintendent to conduct a criminal records check regarding the applicant, that the requested criminal records check will include a determination of whether the applicant has been convicted of or pleaded guilty to any offense listed or described in division (C)(1) or (2) of this section, that, as of the date set forth on the letter, the employment service had not received the results of the criminal records check, and that, when the employment service receives the results of the criminal records check, it promptly will send a copy of the results to the home health agency. If a home health agency employs an applicant conditionally in accordance with this division, the employment service, upon its receipt of the results of the criminal records check, promptly shall send a copy of the results to the home health agency, and division (C)(3)(b) of this section applies regarding the conditional employment.

(2004 S 189, eff. 6–29–04; 2003 H 95, eff. 9–26–03; 1997 H 18, eff. 1–30–98; 1997 S 96, eff. 6–11–97; 1996 S 160, eff. 1–27–97; 1996 S 269, eff. 7–1–96; 1996 H 445, eff. 9–3–96; 1995 S 2, eff. 7–1–96; 1994 H 694, eff. 11–11–94; 1993 S 38, eff. 10–29–93)

3701.99 Penalties

(A) Whoever violates division (C) of section 3701.23, division (C) of section 3701.232, division (C) of section 3701.24, division (B) of section 3701.25, division (I) of section 3701.262, division (D) of section 3701.263, or sections 3701.46 to 3701. 55 of the Revised Code is guilty of a minor misdemeanor on a first offense; on each subsequent offense, the person is guilty of a misdemeanor of the fourth degree.

(B) Whoever violates section 3701.82 of the Revised Code is guilty of a misdemeanor of the first degree.

(C) Whoever violates section 3701.352 or 3701.81 of the Revised Code is guilty of a misdemeanor of the second degree.

(2003 H 6, eff. 2–12–04; 2003 H 95, eff. 9–26–03; 1995 S 19, eff. 9–8–95; 1992 S 130, eff. 8–19–92; 1991 H 213; 1989 H 257, § 3, S 145, S 2; 1984 H 29; 1983 H 157; 1982 S 251; 1972 H 511, S 397; 1970 S 460; 128 v 728; 1953 H 1)

CHAPTER 3716

LABELING OF HAZARDOUS SUBSTANCES

Section

3716.11 Adulteration of food

No person shall do either of the following, knowing or having reasonable cause to believe that any person may suffer physical harm or be seriously inconvenienced or annoyed thereby:

(A) Place a pin, needle, razor blade, glass, laxative, drug of abuse, or other harmful or hazardous object or substance in any food or confection;

(B) Furnish to any person any food or confection which has been adulterated in violation of division (A) of this section.

(1973 H 716, eff. 1–1–74)

3716.99 Penalties

(A) Whoever violates section 3716.02 of the Revised Code is guilty of a misdemeanor of the third degree on a first offense. On each subsequent offense such person is guilty of a misdemeanor of the second degree.

(B) No person is subject to prosecution for a violation of division (A) of section 3716.02 of the Revised Code with respect to any hazardous substance shipped or delivered for shipment for export to any foreign country, in a package marked for export and branded in accordance with the specifications of the foreign purchaser and in accordance with the laws of the foreign country.

(C) Whoever violates section 3716.11 of the Revised Code is guilty of a misdemeanor of the first degree.

(1973 H 716, eff. 1–1–74; 129 v 582; 128 v 484)

CHAPTER 3718

HOUSEHOLD SEWAGE TREATMENT SYSTEMS AND SMALL FLOW ON-SITE SEWAGE TREATMENT SYSTEMS

GENERAL PROVISIONS

3718.08 Prohibitions

No person shall violate this chapter, any rule adopted or order issued under it, or any condition of a registration or permit issued under rules adopted under it.

(2004 H 231, eff. 5–6–05)

3718.10 Injunction or other relief; civil penalty

(A) The prosecuting attorney of the county or the city director of law, village solicitor, or other chief legal officer of the municipal corporation where a violation has occurred or is occurring, upon complaint of the director of health or a board of health, shall prosecute to termination or bring an action for injunction or other appropriate relief against any person who is violating or has violated this chapter, any rule adopted or order issued under it, or any condition of a registration or permit issued under rules adopted under it. The court of common pleas or the municipal or county court in which an action for injunction is filed has jurisdiction to grant such relief upon a showing that the respondent named in the complaint is or was in violation of the chapter or rules, orders, or conditions.

Upon finding that a person intentionally has violated this chapter, a rule adopted or order issued under it, or any condition of a registration or permit issued under rules adopted under it, the court may assess a civil penalty of not more than one hundred dollars for each day of violation against the person. Seventy–five per cent of any penalties assessed by the court under this division shall be paid to the health district whose board of health brought the complaint, or to the state treasury to the credit of the general operations fund created in section 3701.83 of the Revised Code if the director of health is carrying out the duties of an unapproved health district in which the violation occurred in accordance with section 3718.07 of the Revised Code, and shall be used for the purposes of this chapter and the rules adopted under it. Twenty–five per cent of any penalties assessed by the court under this division shall be paid to the prosecuting attorney of the county or city director of law, village solicitor, or other chief legal officer of the municipal corporation that prosecuted or brought the action under this division to pay the expenses incurred in bringing the action.

(B) The remedies provided in this chapter are in addition to any other remedies available under law.

(2004 H 231, eff. 5–6–05)

PENALTIES

3718.99 Penalties

Whoever purposely violates section 3718.08 of the Revised Code shall be fined not more than one thousand dollars. Each day of violation is a separate offense. All money collected from fines under this section shall be used to administer and enforce this chapter and rules adopted under it and shall be deposited as follows:

(A) If the violation occurred within a health district that is approved under section 3718.07 of the Revised Code, the money shall be deposited to the credit of the district's special fund created under section 3718.06 of the Revised Code.

(B) If the violation occurred within a health district that is not approved under section 3718.07 of the Revised Code and a contracting district is carrying out the duties of the unapproved health district in accordance with that section, the money shall be deposited to the credit of the contracting district's special fund created under section 3718.06 of the Revised Code.

(C) If the violation occurred within an unapproved health district and the director of health is carrying out the duties of the unapproved health district in accordance with section 3718.07 of the Revised Code, the money shall be deposited in the state treasury to the credit of the general operations fund created in section 3701.83 of the Revised Code.

(2004 H 231, eff. 5–6–05)

CHAPTER 3719

CONTROLLED SUBSTANCES

Ed. Note: See RC Chapter 2925 for the drug offenses and penalties formerly carried in this chapter.

CONTROLLED SUBSTANCES

3719.01 Definitions

As used in this chapter:

(A) "Administer" means the direct application of a drug, whether by injection, inhalation, ingestion, or any other means to a person or an animal.

(B) "Drug enforcement administration" means the drug enforcement administration of the United States department of justice or its successor agency.

(C) "Controlled substance" means a drug, compound, mixture, preparation, or substance included in schedule I, II, III, IV, or V.

(D) "Dangerous drug" has the same meaning as in section 4729.01 of the Revised Code.

(E) "Dispense" means to sell, leave with, give away, dispose of, or deliver.

(F) "Distribute" means to deal in, ship, transport, or deliver but does not include administering or dispensing a drug.

(G) "Drug" has the same meaning as in section 4729.01 of the Revised Code.

(H) "Drug abuse offense," "felony drug abuse offense," "cocaine," and "hashish" have the same meanings as in section 2925.01 of the Revised Code.

(I) "Federal drug abuse control laws" means the "Comprehensive Drug Abuse Prevention and Control Act of 1970," 84 Stat. 1242, 21 U.S.C. 801, as amended.

(J) "Hospital" means an institution for the care and treatment of the sick and injured that is certified by the department of health and approved by the state board of pharmacy as proper to be entrusted with the custody of controlled substances and the professional use of controlled substances.

(K) "Hypodermic" means a hypodermic syringe or needle, or other instrument or device for the injection of medication.

(L) "Isomer," except as otherwise expressly stated, means the optical isomer.

(M) "Laboratory" means a laboratory approved by the state board of pharmacy as proper to be entrusted with the custody of controlled substances and the use of controlled substances for scientific and clinical purposes and for purposes of instruction.

(N) "Manufacturer" means a person who manufactures a controlled substance, as "manufacture" is defined in section 3715.01 of the Revised Code.

(O) "Marihuana" means all parts of a plant of the genus cannabis, whether growing or not; the seeds of a plant of that type; the resin extracted from a part of a plant of that type; and every compound, manufacture, salt, derivative, mixture, or preparation of a plant of that type or of its seeds or resin. "Marihuana" does not include the mature stalks of the plant, fiber produced from the stalks, oils or cake made from the seeds of the plant, or any other compound, manufacture, salt, derivative, mixture, or preparation of the mature stalks, except the resin extracted from the mature stalks, fiber, oil or cake, or the sterilized seed of the plant that is incapable of germination.

(P) "Narcotic drugs" means coca leaves, opium, isonipecaine, amidone, isoamidone, ketobemidone, as defined in this division, and every substance not chemically distinguished from them and every drug, other than cannabis, that may be included in the meaning of "narcotic drug" under the federal drug abuse control laws. As used in this division:

(1) "Coca leaves" includes cocaine and any compound, manufacture, salt, derivative, mixture, or preparation of coca leaves, except derivatives of coca leaves, that does not contain cocaine, ecgonine, or substances from which cocaine or ecgonine may be synthesized or made.

(2) "Isonipecaine" means any substance identified chemically as 1–methyl–4–phenyl–piperidine–4–carboxylic acid ethyl ester, or any salt thereof, by whatever trade name designated.

(3) "Amidone" means any substance identified chemically as 4–4–diphenyl–6–dimethylamino–heptanone–3, or any salt thereof, by whatever trade name designated.

(4) "Isoamidone" means any substance identified chemically as 4–4–diphenyl–5–methyl–6–dimethylaminohexanone–3, or any salt thereof, by whatever trade name designated.

(5) "Ketobemidone" means any substance identified chemically as 4–(3–hydroxyphenyl)–1–methyl–4–piperidyl ethyl ketone hydrochloride, or any salt thereof, by whatever trade name designated.

(Q) "Official written order" means an order written on a form provided for that purpose by the director of the United States drug enforcement administration, under any laws of the United States making provision for the order, if the order forms are authorized and required by federal law.

(R) "Opiate" means any substance having an addiction-forming or addiction-sustaining liability similar to morphine or being capable of conversion into a drug having addiction-forming or addiction-sustaining liability. "Opiate" does not include, unless specifically designated as controlled under section 3719.41 of the Revised Code, the dextrorotatory isomer of 3–methoxy–N–methylmorphinan and its salts (dextro–methorphan). "Opiate" does include its racemic and levoratory forms.

(S) "Opium poppy" means the plant of the species papaver somniferum L., except its seeds.

(T) "Person" means any individual, corporation, government, governmental subdivision or agency, business trust, estate, trust, partnership, association, or other legal entity.

(U) "Pharmacist" means a person licensed under Chapter 4729. of the Revised Code to engage in the practice of pharmacy.

(V) "Pharmacy" has the same meaning as in section 4729.01 of the Revised Code.

(W) "Poison" means any drug, chemical, or preparation likely to be deleterious or destructive to adult human life in quantities of four grams or less.

(X) "Poppy straw" means all parts, except the seeds, of the opium poppy, after mowing.

(Y) "Licensed health professional authorized to prescribe drugs," "prescriber," and "prescription" have the same meanings as in section 4729.01 of the Revised Code.

(Z) "Registry number" means the number assigned to each person registered under the federal drug abuse control laws.

(AA) "Sale" includes delivery, barter, exchange, transfer, or gift, or offer thereof, and each transaction of those natures made by any person, whether as principal, proprietor, agent, servant, or employee.

(BB) "Schedule I," "schedule II," "schedule III," "schedule IV," and "schedule V" mean controlled substance schedules I, II, III, IV, and V, respectively, established pursuant to section 3719.41 of the Revised Code, as amended pursuant to section 3719.43 or 3719.44 of the Revised Code.

(CC) "Wholesaler" means a person who, on official written orders other than prescriptions, supplies controlled substances that the person has not manufactured, produced, or prepared personally and includes a "wholesale distributor of dangerous drugs" as defined in section 4729.01 of the Revised Code.

(DD) "Animal shelter" means a facility operated by a humane society or any society organized under Chapter 1717. of the Revised Code or a dog pound operated pursuant to Chapter 955. of the Revised Code.

(EE) "Terminal distributor of dangerous drugs" has the same meaning as in section 4729.01 of the Revised Code.

(FF) "Category III license" means a license issued to a terminal distributor of dangerous drugs as set forth in section 4729.54 of the Revised Code.

(GG) "Prosecutor" has the same meaning as in section 2935.01 of the Revised Code.

(1998 S 66, eff. 7–22–98; 1996 H 162, eff. 1–1–97; 1996 S 269, eff. 7–1–96; 1995 S 2, eff. 7–1–96; 1994 H 391, eff. 7–21–94; 1994 H 88, eff. 6–29–94; 1977 H 1, eff. 8–26–77; 1976 S 414; 1975 H 300)

3719.011 Definitions of controlled substance, drug dependence

As used in the Revised Code:

(A) "Drug of abuse" means any controlled substance as defined in section 3719.01 of the Revised Code, any harmful intoxicant as defined in section 2925.01 of the Revised Code, and any dangerous drug as defined in section 4729.01 of the Revised Code.

(B) "Drug dependent person" means any person who, by reason of the use of any drug of abuse, is physically, psychologically, or physically and psychologically dependent upon the use of such drug, to the detriment of the person's health or welfare.

(C) "Person in danger of becoming a drug dependent person" means any person who, by reason of the person's habitual or incontinent use of any drug of abuse, is in imminent danger of becoming a drug dependent person.

(1998 S 66, eff. 7–22–98; 1975 H 300, eff. 7–1–76; 1971 S 141; 1970 H 874)

3719.012 Consent of minor to diagnosis and treatment of drug related conditions

(A) Notwithstanding any other provision of law, a minor may give consent for the diagnosis or treatment by a physician licensed to practice in this state of any condition which it is reasonable to believe is caused by a drug of abuse, beer, or intoxicating liquor. Such consent shall not be subject to disaffirmance because of minority.

(B) A physician licensed to practice in this state, or any person acting at his direction, who in good faith renders medical or surgical services to a minor giving consent under division (A) of this section, shall not be subject to any civil or criminal liability for assault, battery, or assault and battery.

(C) The parent or legal guardian of a minor giving consent under division (A) of this section is not liable for the payment of any charges made for medical or surgical services rendered such minor, unless the parent or legal guardian has also given consent for the diagnosis or treatment.

(1982 H 357, eff. 10–1–82; 1971 S 406)

3719.02 Manufacturer of controlled substances; license; fee

A person may cultivate, grow, or by other process produce or manufacture, and a person on land owned, occupied, or controlled by such person may knowingly allow to be cultivated, grown, or produced, any controlled substance if the person first obtains a license as a manufacturer of controlled substances from the state board of pharmacy.

All licenses issued pursuant to this section shall be for a period of one year from the last day of June and may be renewed for a like period annually according to the standard renewal procedure of sections 4745.01 to 4745.03 of the Revised Code.

The annual license fee shall be thirty-seven dollars and fifty cents and shall accompany each application for a license or renewal thereof. A license that has not been renewed by the first day of August in any year may be reinstated upon payment of the renewal fee and a penalty of fifty-five dollars.

The state board of pharmacy, subject to the approval of the controlling board, may establish a fee in excess of the amount provided in this section, provided that the fee does not exceed the amount established by this section by more than fifty per cent.

(1997 H 215, eff. 6–30–97; 1995 H 117, eff. 6–30–95; 1989 H 111, eff. 7–1–89; 1975 H 300; 1969 H 742; 132 v H 911; 126 v 178; 1953 H 1; GC 12672–2)

3719.021 Wholesaler of controlled substances; license; fee

Persons other than a licensed manufacturer, pharmacist, or owner of a pharmacy who possess for sale, sell, or dispense controlled substances at wholesale shall first obtain a license as a wholesaler of controlled substances from the state board of pharmacy.

All licenses issued pursuant to this section shall be for a period of one year from the thirtieth day of June and may be renewed for a like period annually according to the standard renewal procedure of sections 4745.01 to 4745.03 of the Revised Code.

The annual license fee shall be thirty-seven dollars and fifty cents and shall accompany each application for such license or renewal thereof. All such renewal fees shall be paid in advance by the renewal applicant to the treasurer of state, and entered by the treasurer of state on the records of the state board of pharmacy. A license that has not been renewed by the first day of August in any year may be reinstated upon payment of the renewal fee and a penalty of fifty-five dollars.

The state board of pharmacy, subject to the approval of the controlling board, may establish a fee in excess of the amount provided in this section, provided that the fee does not exceed the amount established by this section by more than fifty per cent.

(1997 H 215, eff. 6–30–97; 1995 H 117, eff. 6–30–95; 1989 H 111, eff. 7–1–89; 1975 H 300; 1969 H 742; 132 v H 911; 126 v 178)

3719.03 Qualifications of applicant; revocation

No license shall be issued under section 3719.02 or 3719.021 of the Revised Code unless and until the applicant therefor has furnished proof satisfactory to the state board of pharmacy:

(A) That the applicant is of good moral character or, if the applicant be an association or corporation, that the managing officers are of good moral character;

(B) That the applicant is equipped as to land, buildings, and paraphernalia properly to carry on the business described in his application;

(C) That the applicant's trade connections are such that there is a reasonable probability that he will apply all controlled substances grown, cultivated, processed, produced, or possessed by him to scientific, experimental, medicinal, or instructive purposes;

(D) That the applicant is in sufficiently good financial condition to carry out his obligation;

(E) That the applicant has satisfactorily shown that the granting of such license is in the public interest.

No license shall be granted to any person who has, within five years, been convicted of a drug abuse offense as defined in section 3719.01 of the Revised Code, or to any person who is a drug dependent person.

The board may suspend or revoke, for cause, any license issued under section 3719.02 or 3719.021 of the Revised Code.

(1975 H 300, eff. 7–1–76; 126 v 178; 1953 H 1; GC 12672–3)

3719.04 Regulations for sale by manufacturer or wholesaler; official written orders

(A) A licensed manufacturer or wholesaler of controlled substances may sell at wholesale controlled substances to any of the following persons and subject to the following conditions:

(1) To a licensed manufacturer or wholesaler of controlled substances, or a terminal distributor of dangerous drugs having a category III license;

(2) To a person in the employ of the United States government or of any state, territorial, district, county, municipal, or insular government, purchasing, receiving, possessing, or dispensing controlled substances by reason of his official duties;

(3) To a master of a ship or a person in charge of any aircraft upon which no physician is regularly employed, for the actual medical needs of persons on board the ship or aircraft, when not in port; provided such controlled substances shall be sold to the master of the ship or person in charge of the aircraft only in pursuance of a special official written order approved by a commissioned medical officer or acting assistant surgeon of the United States public health service;

(4) To a person in a foreign country, if the federal drug abuse control laws are complied with.

(B) An official written order for any schedule II controlled substances shall be signed in triplicate by the person giving the order or by his authorized agent. The original shall be presented to the person who sells or dispenses the schedule II controlled substances named in the order and, if that person accepts the order, each party to the transaction shall preserve his copy of the order for a period of two years in such a way as to be readily accessible for inspection by any public officer or employee engaged in the enforcement of Chapter 3719. of the Revised Code. Compliance with the federal drug abuse control laws, respecting the requirements governing the use of a special official written order constitutes compliance with this division.

(1994 H 88, eff. 6–29–94; 1977 H 1, eff. 8–26–77; 1971 H 924; 126 v 178; 1953 H 1; GC 12672–4)

3719.05 Rules for pharmacists

(A) A pharmacist may dispense controlled substances to any person upon a prescription issued in accordance with section 3719.06 of the Revised Code. When dispensing controlled substances, a pharmacist shall act in accordance with rules adopted by the state board of pharmacy and in accordance with the following:

(1) The prescription shall be retained on file by the owner of the pharmacy in which it is filled for a period of three years, so as to be readily accessible for inspection by any public officer or employee engaged in the enforcement of Chapter 2925., 3719., or 4729. of the Revised Code.

(2) Each oral prescription shall be recorded by the pharmacist and the record shall show the name and address of the patient for whom, or of the owner of the animal for which the controlled substance is dispensed, the full name, address, and registry number under the federal drug abuse control laws of the prescriber, the name of the controlled substance dispensed, the amount dispensed, and the date when dispensed. The record shall be retained on file by the owner of the pharmacy in which it is filled for a period of three years.

(3) A schedule II controlled substance shall be dispensed only upon a written prescription, except that it may be dispensed upon an oral prescription in emergency situations as provided in the federal drug abuse control laws.

(4) A prescription for a schedule II controlled substance shall not be refilled.

(5) Prescriptions for schedule III and IV controlled substances may be refilled not more than five times in a six-month period from the date the prescription is given by a prescriber.

(B) The legal owner of any stock of schedule II controlled substances in a pharmacy, upon discontinuance of dealing in those drugs, may sell the stock to a manufacturer, wholesaler, or owner of a pharmacy registered under the federal drug abuse control laws pursuant to an official written order.

(1998 S 66, eff. 7–22–98; 1994 H 391, eff. 7–21–94; 1975 H 300, eff. 7–1–76; 1971 H 924; 126 v 178; 1953 H 1; GC 12672–5)

3719.06 Rules for licensed health professionals; prescriptions

(A)(1) A licensed health professional authorized to prescribe drugs, if acting in the course of professional practice, in accordance with the laws regulating the professional's practice, and in accordance with rules adopted by the state board of pharmacy, may, except as provided in division (A)(2) of this section, do the following:

(a) Prescribe schedule II, III, IV, and V controlled substances;

(b) Administer or personally furnish to patients schedule II, III, IV, and V controlled substances;

(c) Cause schedule II, III, IV, and V controlled substances to be administered under the prescriber's direction and supervision.

(2) A licensed health professional authorized to prescribe drugs who is a clinical nurse specialist, certified nurse-midwife, or certified nurse practitioner is subject to both of the following:

(a) A schedule II controlled substance may be prescribed only for a patient with a terminal condition, as defined in section 2133.01 of the Revised Code, only if the nurse's collaborating physician initially prescribed the substance for the patient, and only in an amount that does not exceed the amount necessary for the patient's use in a single, twenty-four-hour period.

(b) No controlled substance shall be personally furnished to any patient.

(B) No licensed health professional authorized to prescribe drugs shall prescribe, administer, or personally furnish a schedule III anabolic steroid for the purpose of human muscle building or enhancing human athletic performance and no pharmacist shall dispense a schedule III anabolic steroid for either purpose, unless it has been approved for that purpose under the "Federal Food, Drug, and Cosmetic Act," 52 Stat. 1040 (1938), 21 U.S.C.A. 301, as amended.

(C) Each written prescription shall be properly executed, dated, and signed by the prescriber on the day when issued and shall bear the full name and address of the person for whom, or the owner of the animal for which, the controlled substance is prescribed and the full name, address, and registry number under the federal drug abuse control laws of the prescriber. If the prescription is for an animal, it shall state the species of the animal for which the controlled substance is prescribed.

(2000 H 241, eff. 5–17–00; 1998 S 66, eff. 7–22–98; 1994 H 391, eff. 7–21–94; 1991 H 62, eff. 5–21–91; 1975 H 300; 1971 H 924; 126 v 178; 1953 H 1; GC 12672–6)

3719.07 Records of controlled substances handled

(A) As used in this section, "description" means the dosage form, strength, and quantity, and the brand name, if any, or the generic name, of a drug or controlled substance.

(B)(1) Every licensed health professional authorized to prescribe drugs shall keep a record of all controlled substances received and a record of all controlled substances administered, dispensed, or used other than by prescription. Every other person, except a pharmacist, manufacturer, or wholesaler, who is authorized to purchase and use controlled substances shall keep a record of all controlled substances purchased and used other than by prescription. The records shall be kept in accordance with division (C)(1) of this section.

(2) Manufacturers and wholesalers shall keep records of all controlled substances compounded, mixed, cultivated, grown, or by any other process produced or prepared by them, and of all controlled substances received or sold by them. The records shall be kept in accordance with division (C)(2) of this section.

(3) Every category III terminal distributor of dangerous drugs shall keep records of all controlled substances received or sold. The records shall be kept in accordance with division (C)(3) of this section.

(4) Every person who sells or purchases for resale schedule V controlled substances exempted by section 3719.15 of the Revised Code shall keep a record showing the quantities and kinds thereof received or sold. The records shall be kept in accordance with divisions (C)(1), (2), and (3) of this section.

(C)(1) The records required by divisions (B)(1) and (4) of this section shall contain the following:

(a) The description of all controlled substances received, the name and address of the person from whom received, and the date of receipt;

(b) The description of controlled substances administered, dispensed, purchased, sold, or used; the date of administering, dispensing, purchasing, selling, or using; the name and address of the person to whom, or for whose use, or the owner and species of the animal for which the controlled substance was administered, dispensed, purchased, sold, or used.

(2) The records required by divisions (B)(2) and (4) of this section shall contain the following:

(a) The description of all controlled substances produced or prepared, the name and address of the person from whom received, and the date of receipt;

(b) The description of controlled substances sold, the name and address of each person to whom a controlled substance is sold, the amount of the controlled substance sold to each person, and the date it was sold.

(3) The records required by divisions (B)(3) and (4) of this section shall contain the following:

(a) The description of controlled substances received, the name and address of the person from whom controlled substances are received, and the date of receipt;

(b) The name and place of residence of each person to whom controlled substances, including those otherwise exempted by section 3719.15 of the Revised Code, are sold, the description of the controlled substances sold to each person, and the date the controlled substances are sold to each person.

(D) Every record required by this section shall be kept for a period of two years.

The keeping of a record required by or under the federal drug abuse control laws, containing substantially the same information as specified in this section, constitutes compliance with this section.

Every person who purchases for resale or who sells controlled substance preparations exempted by section 3719.15 of the Revised Code shall keep the record required by or under the federal drug abuse control laws.

(1998 S 66, eff. 7–22–98; 1994 H 88, eff. 6–29–94; 1984 H 208, eff. 9–20–84; 1975 H 300; 1971 H 924; 129 v 1796; 128 v 1044; 127 v 290; 126 v 178; 1953 H 1; GC 12672–8)

3719.08 Labeling

(A) Whenever a manufacturer sells a controlled substance, and whenever a wholesaler sells a controlled substance in a package the wholesaler has prepared, the manufacturer or wholesaler shall securely affix to each package in which the controlled substance is contained a label showing in legible English the name and address of the vendor and the quantity, kind, and form of controlled substance contained therein. No person, except a pharmacist for the purpose of dispensing a controlled substance upon a prescription shall alter, deface, or remove any label so affixed.

(B) Except as provided in division (C) of this section, when a pharmacist dispenses any controlled substance on a prescription for use by a patient, or supplies a controlled substance to a licensed health professional authorized to prescribe drugs for use by the professional in personally furnishing patients with controlled substances, the pharmacist shall affix to the container in which the controlled substance is dispensed or supplied a label showing the following:

(1) The name and address of the pharmacy dispensing or supplying the controlled substance;

(2) The name of the patient for whom the controlled substance is prescribed and, if the patient is an animal, the name of the owner and the species of the animal;

(3) The name of the prescriber;

(4) All directions for use stated on the prescription or provided by the prescriber;

(5) The date on which the controlled substance was dispensed or supplied;

(6) The name, quantity, and strength of the controlled substance and, if applicable, the name of the distributor or manufacturer.

(C) The requirements of division (B) of this section do not apply when a controlled substance is prescribed or supplied for administration to an ultimate user who is institutionalized.

(D) A licensed health professional authorized to prescribe drugs who personally furnishes a controlled substance to a patient shall comply with division (B) of section 4729.29 of the Revised Code with respect to labeling and packaging of the controlled substance.

(E) No person shall alter, deface, or remove any label affixed pursuant to this section as long as any of the original contents remain.

(F) Every label for a schedule II, III, or IV controlled substance shall contain the following warning:

"Caution: federal law prohibits the transfer of this drug to any person other than the patient for whom it was prescribed."

(1998 S 66, eff. 7–22–98; 1975 H 300, eff. 7–1–76; 1971 H 924; 126 v 178; 1953 H 1; GC 12672–9)

3719.09 Authorized possession of controlled substances

Possession or control of controlled substances is authorized in the following instances and subject to the following conditions:

(A) Possession of controlled substances in the course of business by a manufacturer, wholesaler, licensed health professional authorized to prescribe drugs, pharmacist, category III terminal distributor of dangerous drugs, or other person authorized to possess controlled substances under this chapter or Chapter 4729. of the Revised Code;

(B) Possession by any person of any schedule V narcotic drug exempted under section 3719.15 of the Revised Code, where the quantity of the drug does not exceed one hundred thirty milligrams of opium, thirty-two and five-tenths milligrams of morphine or any of its salts, two hundred sixty milligrams of codeine or any of its salts, one hundred thirty milligrams of dihydrocodeine or any of its salts, or thirty-two and five-tenths milligrams of ethylmorphine or any of its salts, or, in the case of any other schedule V controlled substance or any combination of narcotic drugs, where the quantity does not exceed in pharmacologic potency any one of the drugs named above in the quantity stated;

(C) Possession by any person of any controlled substance that the person obtained pursuant to a prescription issued by a licensed health professional authorized to prescribe drugs or that was obtained for the person pursuant to a prescription issued by a prescriber, when the drug is in a container regardless of whether the container is the original container in which the drug was dispensed to that person directly or indirectly by a pharmacist or personally furnished to that person by the prescriber;

(D) Possession in the course of business of combination drugs that contain pentobarbital and at least one noncontrolled substance active ingredient, in a manufactured dosage form, the only indication of which is for euthanizing animals, or other substance that the state veterinary medical licensing board and the state board of pharmacy both approve under division (A) of section 4729.532 of the Revised Code, by an agent or employee of an animal shelter who is authorized by the licensure of the animal shelter with the state board of pharmacy to purchase and possess the drug solely for use as specified in that section. As used in this division, "in the course of business" means possession or use at an establishment described in a license issued under section 4729.54 of the Revised Code, or outside that establishment when necessary because of a risk to the health or safety of any person, provided that the substance is in a quantity no greater than reasonably could be used to alleviate the risk, is in the original manufacturer's container, and is returned to the establishment as soon as possible after the risk has passed.

(1998 S 66, eff. 7–22–98; 1995 S 2, eff. 7–1–96; 1994 H 88, eff. 6–29–94; 1980 S 184, § 5, eff. 6–20–84)

3719.10 Nuisance abatement

Premises or real estate, including vacant land, on which a felony violation of Chapter 2925. or 3719. of the Revised Code occurs constitute a nuisance subject to abatement pursuant to Chapter 3767. of the Revised Code.

(1975 H 300, eff. 7–1–76)

3719.11 Controlled substances forfeited

All controlled substances, the lawful possession of which is not established or the title to which cannot be ascertained, that have come into the custody of a peace officer, shall be forfeited pursuant to sections 2923.44 to 2923.47, 2925.41 to 2925.45, 2933.41, or 2933.43 of the Revised Code, and, unless any such section provides for a different manner of disposition, shall be disposed of as follows:

(A) The court or magistrate having jurisdiction shall order the controlled substances forfeited and destroyed. The agency served by the peace officer who obtained or took custody of the controlled substances may destroy them or may send them to the bureau of criminal identification and investigation for destruction by it. A record of the place where the controlled substances were seized, of the kinds and quantities of controlled substances so destroyed, and of the time, place, and manner of destruction, shall be kept, and a return under oath, reporting the destruction, shall be made by the officer who destroys them to the court or magistrate and to the United States director, bureau of narcotics and dangerous drugs.

(B) Upon written application by the department of health, the court or magistrate that ordered the forfeiture of the controlled substances may order the delivery of any of them, except heroin and its salts and derivatives, to the department for distribution or destruction as provided in this section.

(C) Upon application by any hospital within this state that is not operated for private gain, the department of health may deliver any controlled substances that have come into its custody pursuant to this section to the applicant for medicinal use. The department may deliver excess stocks of the controlled substances to the United States director, bureau of narcotics and dangerous drugs, or may destroy the excess stocks.

(D) The department of health shall keep a complete record of all controlled substances received pursuant to this section and of all controlled substances disposed of pursuant to this section, showing all of the following:

(1) The exact kinds, quantities, and forms of the controlled substances;

(2) The persons from whom they were received and to whom they were delivered;

(3) By whose authority they were received, delivered, or destroyed;

(4) The dates of their receipt, delivery, or destruction.

(E) The record required by this section shall be open to inspection by all federal and state officers charged with the enforcement of federal and state narcotic and drug abuse control laws.

(1998 H 2, eff. 1–1–99; 1990 S 258, eff. 11–20–90; 1990 H 215; 1986 S 69; 1975 H 300; 1971 H 924; 1953 H 1; GC 12672–13)

3719.12 Procedure upon conviction; suspension or revocation of license or registration

Unless a report has been made pursuant to section 2929.42 of the Revised Code, on the conviction of a manufacturer, wholesaler, terminal distributor of dangerous drugs, pharmacist, pharmacy intern, dentist, chiropractor, physician, podiatrist, registered nurse, licensed practical nurse, physician assistant, optometrist, or veterinarian of the violation of this chapter or Chapter 2925. of the Revised Code, the prosecutor in the case promptly shall report the conviction to the board that licensed, certified, or registered the person to practice or to carry on business. The responsible board shall provide forms to the prosecutor. Within thirty days of the receipt of this information, the board shall initiate action in accordance with Chapter 119. of the Revised Code to determine whether to suspend or revoke the person's license, certificate, or registration.

(2002 H 490, eff. 1–1–04; 2000 H 506, eff. 4–10–01; 1998 S 66, eff. 7–22–98; 1995 S 143, § 5, eff. 7–1–96; 1995 S 2, eff. 7–1–96; 1995 S 143, § 1, eff. 3–5–96; 1990 H 615, eff. 3–27–91; 1975 H 300; 1971 H 924; 126 v 178; 1953 H 1; GC 12672–14)

3719.121 Suspension of licenses or registrations of addicts

(A) Except as otherwise provided in section 4723.28, 4723.35, 4730.25, 4731.22, 4734.39, or 4734.41 of the Revised Code, the license, certificate, or registration of any dentist, chiropractor, physician, podiatrist, registered nurse, licensed practical nurse, physician assistant, pharmacist, pharmacy intern, optometrist, or veterinarian who is or becomes addicted to the use of controlled substances shall be suspended by the board that authorized the person's license, certificate, or registration until the person offers satisfactory proof to the board that the person no longer is addicted to the use of controlled substances.

(B) If the board under which a person has been issued a license, certificate, or evidence of registration determines that there is clear and convincing evidence that continuation of the person's professional practice or method of prescribing or personally furnishing controlled substances presents a danger of immediate and serious harm to others, the board may suspend the person's license, certificate, or registration without a hearing. Except as otherwise provided in sections 4715.30, 4723.281, 4729.16, 4730.25, 4731.22, and 4734.36 of the Revised Code, the board shall follow the procedure for suspension without a prior hearing in section 119.07 of the Revised Code. The suspension shall remain in effect, unless removed by the board, until the board's final adjudication order becomes effective, except that if the board does not issue its final adjudication order within ninety days after the hearing, the suspension shall be void on the ninety-first day after the hearing.

(C) On receiving notification pursuant to section 2929.42 or 3719.12 of the Revised Code, the board under which a person has been issued a license, certificate, or evidence of registration immediately shall suspend the license, certificate, or registration of that person on a plea of guilty to, a finding by a jury or court of the person's guilt of, or conviction of a felony drug abuse offense; a finding by a court of the person's eligibility for intervention in lieu of conviction; a plea of guilty to, or a finding by a jury or court of the person's guilt of, or the person's conviction of an offense in another jurisdiction that is essentially the same as a felony drug abuse offense; or a finding by a court of the person's eligibility for treatment or intervention in lieu of conviction in another jurisdiction. The board shall notify the holder of the license, certificate, or registration of the suspension, which shall remain in effect until the board holds an adjudicatory hearing under Chapter 119. of the Revised Code.

(2002 H 490, eff. 1–1–04; 2000 H 506, eff. 4–10–01; 2000 S 172, eff. 2–12–01; 1999 S 107, eff. 3–23–00; 1998 S 66, eff. 7–22–98; 1995 S 143, § 5, eff. 7–1–96; 1995 S 2, eff. 7–1–96; 1995 S 143, § 1, eff. 3–5–96; 1990 H 615, eff. 3–27–91; 1975 H 300; 129 v 582; 126 v 178)

3719.13 Records of dangerous drugs and controlled substances

Prescriptions, orders, and records, required by Chapter 3719. of the Revised Code, and stocks of dangerous drugs and controlled substances, shall be open for inspection only to federal, state, county, and municipal officers, and employees of the state board of pharmacy whose duty it is to enforce the laws of this state or of the United States relating to controlled substances. Such prescriptions, orders, records, and stocks shall be open for inspection by employees of the state medical board for purposes of enforcing Chapter 4731. of the Revised Code and employees of the board of nursing for purposes of enforcing chapter 4723. of the Revised Code. No person having knowledge of any such prescription, order, or record shall divulge such knowledge, except in connection with a prosecution or proceeding in court or before a licensing or registration board or officer, to which prosecution or proceeding the person to whom such prescriptions, orders, or records relate is a party.

(2000 H 511, eff. 4–10–01; 1986 H 769, eff. 3–17–87; 1984 H 208; 1975 H 300; 1953 H 1; GC 12672–15)

3719.14 Exemptions

(A) A common carrier or warehouser while engaged in lawfully transporting or storing any controlled substance or an employee of a common carrier or warehouser of that nature who is acting within the scope of the employee's employment may control and possess any controlled substance.

(B) Any law enforcement official may purchase, collect, or possess any controlled substance or may offer to sell any controlled substance, or any counterfeit controlled substance as defined in section 2925.01 of the Revised Code, when the purchase, collection, possession, or offer to sell is necessary to do so in the performance of the official's official duties. This division does not permit a law enforcement official to sell any controlled substance in the performance of the official's official duties. A peace officer, as defined in section 3719.141 of the Revised Code, may sell a controlled substance in the performance of the officer's official duties only as provided in that section.

(C) Any employee or agent of a person who is entitled to possession of a controlled substance or whose possession of a controlled substance is for the purpose of aiding any law enforcement official in the official's official duties temporarily may possess any controlled substance.

(1996 H 125, eff. 7–1–96; 1990 H 215, eff. 4–11–90; 1975 H 300)

3719.141 Sale of controlled substances by peace officer in performance of official duties

(A) A peace officer may sell any controlled substance in the performance of the officer's official duties only if either of the following applies:

(1) A peace officer may sell any controlled substance in the performance of the officer's official duties if all of the following apply:

(a) Prior approval for the sale has been given by the prosecuting attorney of the county in which the sale takes place, in any manner described in division (B) of this section;

(b) The peace officer who makes the sale determines that the sale is necessary in the performance of the officer's official duties;

(c) Any of the following applies:

(i) The person to whom the sale is made or any other person who is involved in the sale does not know that the officer who makes the sale is a peace officer, and the peace officer who makes the sale determines that the sale is necessary to prevent the person from determining or suspecting that the officer who makes the sale is a peace officer.

(ii) The peace officer who makes the sale determines that the sale is necessary to preserve an identity that the peace officer who makes the sale has assumed in the performance of the officer's official duties.

(iii) The sale involves a controlled substance that, during the course of another sale, was intercepted by the peace officer who makes the sale or any other peace officer who serves the same agency served by the peace officer who makes the sale; the intended recipient of the controlled substance in the other sale does not know that the controlled substance has been so intercepted; the sale in question is made to the intended recipient of the controlled substance in the other sale and is undertaken with the intent of obtaining evidence of a drug abuse offense against the intended recipient of the controlled substance; and the sale in question does not involve the transfer of any money or other thing of value to the peace officer who makes the sale or any other peace officer who serves the same agency served by the peace officer who makes the sale in exchange for the controlled substance.

(d) If the sale is made under the circumstances described in division (A)(1)(c)(i) or (ii) of this section, no person is charged with any criminal offense or any delinquent act based upon the sale unless both of the following apply:

(i) The person also is charged with a criminal offense or a delinquent act that is based upon an act or omission that is independent of the sale but that either is connected together with the sale, or constitutes a part of a common scheme or plan with the sale, or is part of a course of criminal conduct involving the sale.

(ii) The criminal offense or delinquent act based upon the sale and the other criminal offense or delinquent act are charged in the same indictment, information, or complaint.

(e) The sale is not part of a continuing course of conduct involving the sale of controlled substances by the peace officer who makes the sale.

(f) The amount of the controlled substance sold and the scope of the sale of the controlled substance is as limited as possible under the circumstances.

(g) Prior to the sale, the law enforcement agency served by the peace officer who makes the sale has adopted a written internal control policy that does all of the following:

(i) Addresses the keeping of detailed records as to the amount of money or other things of value obtained in the sale in exchange for the controlled substance;

(ii) Addresses the delivery of all moneys or things of value so obtained to the prosecuting attorney pursuant to division (D) of this section;

(iii) Addresses the agency's use and disposition of all such moneys or things of value that are deposited in the law enforcement trust fund of the sheriff, municipal corporation, or township, pursuant to division (D) of this section, and that are used by the sheriff, are allocated to the police department of the municipal corporation by its legislative authority, or are allocated by the board of township trustees to the township police department, township police district police force, or office of the constable;

(iv) Provides for the keeping of detailed financial records of the receipts of the proceeds, the general types of expenditures made out of the proceeds received, and the specific amount of each general type of expenditure. The policy shall not provide for or permit the identification of any peace officer involved in the sale, any information that is or may be needed in an ongoing investigation, or any specific expenditure that is made in an ongoing investigation.

(2) A peace officer may sell any controlled substance in the performance of the officer's official duties if all of the following apply:

(a) Prior approval for the sale has been given by the prosecuting attorney of the county in which the sale takes place, in any manner described in division (B) of this section;

(b) Prior to the sale, the law enforcement agency served by the peace officer has adopted a written internal control policy that does the things listed in divisions (A)(1)(g)(i) to (iv) of this section;

(c) The purchaser of the controlled substance acquires possession of it in the presence of the peace officer who makes the sale.

(d) Upon the consummation of the sale, either of the following occurs:

(i) The peace officer arrests the purchaser of the controlled substance, recovers it and the proceeds of the sale, and secures it and the proceeds as evidence to be used in a subsequent prosecution.

(ii) The peace officer makes a reasonable, good faith effort to arrest the purchaser of the controlled substance and to recover the controlled substance and the proceeds of the sale, but the officer is unable to make the arrest and recover all of the controlled substance and proceeds for reasons beyond the officer's control, and the peace officer secures all of the controlled substance recovered and all of the proceeds recovered as evidence to be used in a subsequent prosecution.

(B) The approval of a prosecuting attorney required by division (A)(1)(a) or (2)(a) of this section may be in either of the following forms:

(1) A general approval that is given by the prosecuting attorney to the peace officer who makes the sale or to the law enforcement agency served by that peace officer, that grants approval only to that peace officer, and that grants approval for any such sale that may be necessary, after the approval has been granted, under the standards described in division (A)(1) or (2) of this section;

(2) A specific approval that is given by the prosecuting attorney to the peace officer who makes the sale or to the law enforcement agency served by that peace officer, and that grants approval only to that peace officer and only for the particular sale

in question, under the standards described in division (A)(1) or (2) of this section.

(C) If a peace officer sells a controlled substance in the performance of the officer's official duties under division (A)(1) or (2) of this section, the peace officer, within a reasonable time after the sale, shall provide the prosecuting attorney who granted approval for the sale with a written summary that identifies the amount and type of controlled substance sold, the circumstances of the sale, and the amount of any money or other thing of value obtained in the sale in exchange for the controlled substance. The summary shall not identify or enable the identification of any peace officer involved in the sale and shall not contain any information that is or may be needed in an ongoing investigation.

(D)(1) Except as provided in division (D)(2) of this section, if a peace officer sells a controlled substance in the performance of the officer's official duties under division (A)(1) or (2) of this section, the peace officer, as soon as possible after the sale, shall deliver all money or other things of value obtained in the sale in exchange for the controlled substance to the prosecuting attorney who granted approval for the sale. The prosecuting attorney shall safely keep all money and other things of value the prosecuting attorney receives under this division for use as evidence in any criminal action or delinquency proceeding based upon the sale. All money so received by a prosecuting attorney that no longer is needed as evidence in any criminal action or delinquency proceeding shall be deposited by the prosecuting attorney in the law enforcement trust fund of the sheriff if the peace officer who made the sale is the sheriff or a deputy sheriff or the law enforcement trust fund of a municipal corporation or township if it is served by the peace officer who made the sale, as established pursuant to section 2933.43 of the Revised Code, and upon deposit shall be expended only as provided in that section. All other things of value so received by a prosecuting attorney that no longer are needed as evidence in any criminal action or delinquency proceeding shall be disposed of, without appraisal, at a public auction to the highest bidder for cash; the proceeds of the sale shall be deposited by the prosecuting attorney in the law enforcement trust fund of the sheriff if the peace officer who made the sale is the sheriff or a deputy sheriff or the law enforcement trust fund of a municipal corporation or township if it is served by the peace officer who made the sale, as established pursuant to section 2933.43 of the Revised Code, and upon deposit shall be expended only as provided in that section. Each law enforcement agency that uses any money that was deposited in a law enforcement trust fund pursuant to this division shall comply with the written internal control policy adopted by the agency, as required by division (A)(1)(g) or (2)(b) of this section, in its use of the money.

(2) Division (D)(1) of this section does not apply in relation to a peace officer who sells a controlled substance in the performance of the officer's official duties under division (A)(1) of this section in any of the following circumstances:

(a) The person to whom the sale is made or any other person who is involved in the sale does not know that the officer is a peace officer, and, if the officer were to retain and deliver the money or other things of value to the prosecuting attorney, the person would determine or suspect that the officer is a peace officer.

(b) If the officer were to retain and deliver the money or other things of value to the prosecuting attorney, an identity that has been assumed in the performance of the officer's official duties would not be preserved.

(c) The sale is made under the circumstances described in division (A)(1)(c)(iii) of this section.

(3) If division (D)(1) of this section does not apply in relation to a peace officer who sells a controlled substance in the performance of the officer's official duties under division (A)(1) of this section due to the operation of division (D)(2) of this section, the peace officer, as soon as possible after the sale, shall deliver to the prosecuting attorney who granted approval for the sale a written summary that describes the circumstances of the sale and the reason for which division (D)(1) of this section does not apply. The summary shall not identify or enable the identification of any peace officer involved in the sale and shall not contain any information that is or may be needed in an ongoing investigation.

(E)(1) A written internal control policy adopted by a law enforcement agency that is served by a peace officer who sells a controlled substance under division (A)(1) or (2) of this section, as required by division (A)(1)(g) or (2)(b) of this section, is a public record open for inspection under section 149.43 of the Revised Code. Each law enforcement agency that adopts a written internal control policy of that nature shall comply with it in relation to any sale of a controlled substance under division (A)(1) or (2) of this section. All records as to the amount of money or things of value obtained in the sale of a controlled substance, in exchange for the controlled substance, and all financial records of the receipts of the proceeds, the general types of expenditures made out of the proceeds received, and the specific amounts of each general type of expenditure by a law enforcement agency in relation to any sale of a controlled substance under division (A)(1) or (2) of this section are public records open for inspection under section 149.43 of the Revised Code.

(2) A summary required by division (C) or (D)(3) of this section is a public record open for inspection under section 149.43 of the Revised Code.

(F)(1) Each prosecuting attorney who grants approval for a sale of controlled substances by a peace officer and who receives in any calendar year one or more summaries under division (C) of this section relative to the sale of a controlled substance by a peace officer shall prepare a report covering the calendar year that cumulates all of the information contained in each of the summaries so received in the calendar year and shall send the cumulative report, no later than the first day of March in the calendar year following the calendar year covered by the report, to the attorney general.

(2) Each prosecuting attorney who receives any money or any other thing of value under division (D)(1) of this section shall keep detailed financial records of the receipts and dispositions of all such moneys or things of value so received. No record of that nature shall identify, or enable the identification of, any person from whom money or another thing of value was received as a result of the sale of a controlled substance under division (A)(1) or (2) of this section or contain any information that is or may be needed in an ongoing investigation. Each record of that nature is a public record open for inspection under section 149.43 of the Revised Code and shall include, but is not limited to, all of the following information:

(a) The identity of each law enforcement agency that has so delivered any money or other thing of value to the prosecuting attorney;

(b) The total amount of money or other things of value so received from each law enforcement agency;

(c) The disposition made under this section of all money or other things of value so received.

(G) Divisions (A) to (F) of this section do not apply to any peace officer, or to any officer, agent, or employee of the United States, who is operating under the management and direction of the United States department of justice. Any peace officer, or any officer, agent, or employee of the United States, who is operating under the management and direction of the United States department of justice may sell a controlled substance in the performance of the officer's, agent's, or employee's official duties if the sale is made in accordance with federal statutes and regulations.

(H) As used in this section, "peace officer" has the same meaning as in section 2935.01 of the Revised Code and also includes a special agent of the bureau of criminal identification and investigation.

(1996 H 125, eff. 7–1–96; 1995 S 2, eff. 7–1–96; 1990 S 258, eff. 11–20–90; 1990 H 588, H 215)

3719.15 Substances excepted

This chapter and Chapter 2925. of the Revised Code shall not apply, except as specifically provided otherwise in those chapters, to the following cases:

(A) Where a licensed health professional authorized to prescribe drugs administers or personally furnishes, or where a pharmacist sells at retail, any medicinal preparation that contains in thirty milliliters, or if a solid or semisolid preparation, in thirty grams, of any of the following:

(1) Not more than one hundred thirty milligrams of opium;

(2) Not more than sixteen and twenty-five one hundreths milligrams of morphine or of any of its salts;

(3) Not more than sixty-five milligrams of codeine or of any of its salts;

(4) Not more than thirty-two and five-tenths milligrams of dihydrocodeine or any of its salts;

(5) Not more than sixteen and twenty-five one hundreths milligrams of ethylmorphine or any of its salts.

Each preparation specified in divisions (A)(1), (2), (3), (4), and (5) of this section shall in addition contain one or more non-narcotic active medicinal ingredients in sufficient proportion to confer upon the preparation valuable medicinal qualities other than those possessed by the narcotic drug alone.

(6) Pharmaceutical preparations in solid form containing not more than two and five-tenths milligrams diphenoxylate and not less than twenty-five micrograms atropine sulfate per dosage unit.

(B) Where a licensed health professional authorized to prescribe drugs administers or personally furnishes, or where a pharmacist sells at retail, liniments, ointments, and other preparations, that are susceptible of external use only and that contain narcotic drugs in a combination that prevents the drugs from being readily extracted from the liniments, ointments, or preparations, except that this chapter and Chapter 2925. of the Revised Code shall apply to all liniments, ointments, and other preparations that contain coca leaves in any quantity or combination.

The medicinal preparation, or the liniment, ointment, or other preparation susceptible of external use only, prescribed, personally furnished, administered, dispensed, or sold, shall contain, in addition to the narcotic drug in it, some drug or drugs conferring upon it medicinal qualities other than those possessed by the narcotic drug alone. The preparation shall be prescribed, personally furnished, administered, compounded, dispensed, and sold in good faith as a medicine, and not for the purpose of evading this chapter or Chapter 2925. of the Revised Code.

(1998 S 66, eff. 7–22–98; 1975 H 300, eff. 7–1–76; 1971 H 924; 129 v 1796; 126 v 178; 1953 H 1; GC 12672–7)

3719.16 Sale of exempted drugs

No person shall dispense or sell, under the exemptions of section 3719.15 of the Revised Code to any one person, or for the use of any one person or animal, any preparation included within such section, when he knows, or can by reasonable diligence ascertain, that such dispensing or selling will provide the person to whom or for whose use, or the owner of the animal for the use of which, such preparation is dispensed or sold, within any forty-eight consecutive hours, with more than two grains of opium, or more than one-half of a grain of morphine or any of its salts, or more than four grains of codeine or any of its salts, or more than two grains of dihydrocodeine or any of its salts, or more than one-half grain of ethylmorphine or any of its salts, or will provide such person or the owner of such animal, within forty-eight consecutive hours, with more than one preparation exempted by the provisions of section 3719.15 of the Revised Code.

No person shall obtain or attempt to obtain, under the exemptions of section 3719.15 of the Revised Code, more than one preparation exempted by the provisions of that section within forty-eight consecutive hours.

(1971 H 924, eff. 10–26–71; 129 v 1796; 128 v 1044; 127 v 290; 126 v 178; 1953 H 1; GC 12672–7)

3719.161 Prohibition against increasing concentration

No person shall alter any controlled substance from the original compounded form by evaporation or other means to increase the concentration of narcotic drug contained therein. Altered preparations having a greater concentration of schedule V narcotic drug content than specified under provisions of section 3719.15 of the Revised Code, shall be classified as a schedule III narcotic drug.

(1975 H 300, eff. 7–1–76; 1971 H 924; 128 v 1044)

GENERAL PROVISIONS

3719.172 Possession, sale, and disposal of hypodermics

(A) Possession of a hypodermic is authorized for the following:

(1) A manufacturer or distributor of, or dealer in, hypodermics or medication packaged in hypodermics, and any authorized agent or employee of that manufacturer, distributor, or dealer, in the regular course of business;

(2) A terminal distributor of dangerous drugs, in the regular course of business;

(3) A person authorized to administer injections, in the regular course of the person's profession or employment;

(4) A person, when the hypodermic was lawfully obtained and is kept and used for the purpose of self-administration of insulin or other drug prescribed for the treatment of disease by a licensed health professional authorized to prescribe drugs;

(5) A person whose use of a hypodermic is for legal research, clinical, educational, or medicinal purposes;

(6) A farmer, for the lawful administration of a drug to an animal;

(7) A person whose use of a hypodermic is for lawful professional, mechanical, trade, or craft purposes.

(B) No manufacturer or distributor of, or dealer in, hypodermics or medication packaged in hypodermics, or their authorized agents or employees, and no terminal distributor of dangerous drugs, shall display any hypodermic for sale. No person authorized to possess a hypodermic pursuant to division (A) of this section shall negligently fail to take reasonable precautions to prevent any hypodermic in the person's possession from theft or acquisition by any unauthorized person.

(C) No person other than one of the following shall sell or furnish a hypodermic to another person:

(1) A manufacturer or distributor of, or dealer in, hypodermics or medication packaged in hypodermics, or their authorized agents or employees;

(2) A terminal distributor of dangerous drugs;

(3) A person under the direct supervision of a pharmacist;

(4) A licensed health professional authorized to prescribe drugs, acting in the regular course of business and as permitted by law;

(5) An individual who holds a current license, certificate, or registration issued under Title 47 of the Revised Code and has been certified to conduct diabetes education by a national certifying body specified in rules adopted by the state board of pharmacy under section 4729.68 of the Revised Code, but only if diabetes education is within the individual's scope of practice under statutes and rules regulating the individual's profession.

(D) No person shall sell or furnish a hypodermic to another whom the person knows or has reasonable cause to believe is not authorized by division (A) of this section to possess a hypodermic.

(1998 S 66, eff. 7–22–98; 1996 S 246, eff. 11–6–96; 1975 H 300, eff. 7–1–76; 1972 H 521)

3719.18 Enforcement officers; cooperation with federal agencies

(A) The state board of pharmacy, its officers, agents, inspectors, and representatives, and all officers within the state, and all prosecuting attorneys, shall enforce Chapters 2925. and 3719. of the Revised Code, except those specifically delegated, and cooperate with all agencies charged with the enforcement of the laws of the United States, of this state, and of all other states, relating to controlled substances.

(B) Nothing in this chapter shall be construed to require the state board of pharmacy to enforce minor violations of Chapters 2925. and 3719. of the Revised Code if the board determines that the public interest is adequately served by a notice or warning to the alleged offender.

(1984 H 208, eff. 9–20–84; 1975 H 300; 1953 H 1; GC 12672–18)

3719.19 Persons not subject to prosecution

No person shall be prosecuted for a violation of this chapter if the person has been acquitted or convicted under the federal drug abuse control laws of the same act or omission which, it is alleged, constitutes a violation of this chapter.

(1998 S 66, eff. 7–22–98; 1975 H 300, eff. 7–1–76; 1953 H 1; GC 12672–20)

3719.21 Disposition of fines and forfeited bonds

Except as provided in division (C) of section 2923.42, division (B)(5) of section 2923.44, divisions (D)(1), (F), and (H) of section 2925.03, division (D)(1) of section 2925.02, 2925.04, or 2925.05, division (E)(1) of section 2925.11, division (F) of section 2925.13, division (F) of section 2925.36, division (D) of section 2925.22, division (H) of section 2925.23, division (M) of section 2925.37, division (B)(5) of section 2925.42, division (B) of section 2929.18, division (D) of section 3719.99, division (B)(1) of section 4729.65, and division (E)(3) of section 4729.99 of the Revised Code, the clerk of the court shall pay all fines or forfeited bail assessed and collected under prosecutions or prosecutions commenced for violations of this chapter, section 2923.42 of the Revised Code, or Chapter 2925. of the Revised Code, within thirty days, to the executive director of the state board of pharmacy, and the executive director shall deposit the fines into the state treasury to the credit of the occupational licensing and regulatory fund.

(2002 H 327, eff. 7–8–02; 1998 H 2, eff. 1–1–99; 1996 S 166, eff. 10–17–96; 1996 S 269, eff. 7–1–96; 1995 S 2, eff. 7–1–96; 1994 H 715, eff. 7–22–94; 1990 S 258, eff. 11–20–90; 1990 H 266; 1979 H 204; 1975 H 300; 1953 H 1; GC 12672–19)

3719.27 Inspection and checking of files and records

Persons required, by Chapter 3719. of the Revised Code, to keep files or records shall, upon the written request of an officer or employee designated by the state board of pharmacy, make such files or records available to such officer or employee, at all reasonable hours, for inspection and copying, and accord to such officer or employee full opportunity to check the correctness of such files or records, including opportunity to make inventory of all stocks of controlled substances on hand. No person shall fail to make such files or records available or to accord such opportunity to check their correctness.

(1975 H 300, eff. 7–1–76; 1969 H 90; 1953 H 1; GC 12673–4)

3719.28 Board to adopt rules

(A) The state board of pharmacy, pursuant to Chapter 119. of the Revised Code, shall adopt rules for administration and enforcement of Chapter 3719. of the Revised Code and prescribing the manner of keeping and the form and content of records to be kept by persons authorized to manufacture, distribute, dispense, conduct research in, prescribe, administer, or otherwise deal with controlled substances. Such rules shall be designed to:

(1) Facilitate surveillance of traffic in drugs, to prevent the improper acquisition or use of controlled substances or their diversion into illicit channels;

(2) Aid the state board of pharmacy and state, local, and federal law enforcement officers in enforcing the laws of this state and the federal government dealing with drug abuse and control of drug traffic.

(B) Rules adopted pursuant to this section shall not provide any less stringent requirements with respect to records than the requirements of the federal drug abuse control laws and regulations adopted thereunder. To the extent that records kept under the federal drug abuse control laws and regulations adopted thereunder fulfill requirements for similar records under rules adopted pursuant to this section, compliance with the federal law and regulations shall constitute compliance with the law and rules of this state with respect to such records.

(1975 H 300, eff. 7–1–76)

POISONS

3719.30 Prohibition against depositing dangerous drugs or poison on thoroughfares

No person shall leave or deposit dangerous drugs, poisons, or substances containing dangerous drugs or poisons in a common, street, alley, lane, or thoroughfare, or a yard or enclosure occupied by another.

Whoever violates this section shall be liable to the person injured for all damages sustained as a result of leaving or depositing the dangerous drugs, poisons, or other substances.

(1998 S 66, eff. 7–22–98; 1953 H 1, eff. 10–1–53; GC 12663)

3719.31 Prohibition against careless distribution of samples containing drug or poison

No person shall leave, throw, or deposit upon the doorstep or premises owned or occupied by another, or hand, give, or deliver to any person, except in a place where it is kept for sale, a patent or proprietary medicine, preparation, pill, tablet, powder, cosmetic, disinfectant, or antiseptic, or a drug or medicine that contains poison or any ingredient that is deleterious to health, as a sample or for the purpose of advertising.

As used in this section "drug," "medicine," "patent or proprietary medicine," "pill," "tablet," "powder," "cosmetic," "disinfectant," or "antiseptic" includes all remedies for internal or external use.

(1953 H 1, eff. 10–1–53; GC 12664, 12665)

3719.32 Regulating the sale of poisons

No person shall knowingly sell or deliver to any person otherwise than in the manner prescribed by laws, or sell or deliver to a minor under sixteen years of age in the manner prescribed by law but without the written order of an adult, any of the following substances or any poisonous compounds, combinations, or preparations thereof: the compounds and salts of antimony, arsenic, chromium, copper, lead, mercury, and zinc; the concentrated mineral acids; oxalic and hydrocyanic acids and their salts, and carbolic acid; yellow phosphorus; the essential oils of almonds, pennyroyal, tansy, and savin, croton oil, creosote, chloroform, chloral hydrate, and cantharides; aconite, belladonna, bitter almonds, colchicum, cotton root, cocculus indicus, conium, digitalis, hyoscyamus, ignatia, lobelia, nux vomica, opium, physostigma, phytolacca, strophanthus, stramonium, veratum viride, or any of the poisonous alkaloids or alkaloidal salts or other poisonous principles derived from such alkaloids, or other poisonous alkaloids or their salts; or other virulent poison.

(1975 H 300, eff. 7–1–76; 130 v Pt 2, H 5; 125 v 903; 1953 H 1; GC 12666)

3719.33 Labeling poisons

No person shall sell or deliver to another a substance named in section 3719.32 of the Revised Code without having first learned by due inquiry that such person is aware of the poisonous character of such substance and that it is desired for a lawful purpose; or without plainly labeling "poison," and the names of two or more antidotes therefor, upon the box, bottle, or package containing it; or deliver such substance without recording in a book kept for the purpose, the name thereof, the quantity delivered, the purpose for which it is alleged to be used, the date of its delivery, the name and address of the purchaser, and the name of the dispenser; or fail to preserve said book for five years and submit it at all times for inspection to proper officers of the law.

(1953 H 1, eff. 10–1–53; GC 12667)

3719.34 Poisons not labeled

Sections 3719.32 and 3719.33 of the Revised Code do not apply to substances sold or delivered upon the order or prescription of a person believed by the seller or deliverer to be a licensed health professional authorized to prescribe drugs.

(1998 S 66, eff. 7–22–98; 1953 H 1, eff. 10–1–53; GC 12668)

3719.35 Preparations not labeled poison

It is not necessary to place a poison label upon, nor record the delivery of, any of the following:

(A) Preparations containing substances named in section 3719.32 of the Revised Code when a single box, bottle, or other package of the bulk of fifteen milliliters or the weight of fifteen grams does not contain more than one adult medicinal dose of any of those substances;

(B) The sulphide of antimony, the oxide or carbonate of zinc, or colors ground in oil and intended for use as paints;

(C) Preparations recommended in good faith for diarrhea or cholera, when each bottle or package is accompanied by specific directions for use and a caution against the habitual use of the preparations;

(D) Liniments or ointments when plainly labeled "for external use only";

(E) Preparations put up and sold in the form of pills, tablets, or lozenges and intended for internal use, when the dose recommended does not contain more than one fourth of an adult medicinal dose of any of the substances named in section 3719.35 of the Revised Code.

(1998 S 66, eff. 7–22–98; 1953 H 1, eff. 10–1–53; GC 12669, 12670, 12671)

3719.36 Board of pharmacy shall enforce laws relating to poison; fines

The state board of pharmacy shall enforce sections 3719.30 to 3719.35 of the Revised Code. If the board has information that any of those sections has been violated, it shall investigate, and upon probable cause appearing, shall file a complaint and prosecute the offender.

Fines assessed and collected under prosecutions commenced by the board shall be paid to the executive director of the state board of pharmacy, and by the executive director paid into the state treasury to the credit of the board of pharmacy drug law enforcement fund created by section 4729.65 of the Revised Code.

(1998 S 66, eff. 7–22–98; 1994 H 715, eff. 7–22–94; 1953 H 1, eff. 10–1–53; GC 12671–1)

SCHEDULES OF CONTROLLED SUBSTANCES

3719.40 Names of controlled substances

The controlled substances included or to be included in the schedules in section 3719.41 of the Revised Code are included by whatever official, common, usual, chemical, or trade name designated.

(1975 H 300, eff. 7–1–76)

3719.41 Schedules of controlled substances

Publisher's Note: The following section is a compilation of controlled substances derived from three sources: the Ohio General Assembly, through direct enactment of the statute; the Attorney General of the United States in 21 CFR 1308.11 to 1308.15, under authority of the Comprehensive Drug Abuse Prevention and Control Act of 1970 (21 USC 801 to 966) (i.e., the federal government), per RC 3719.43; and the State Board of Pharmacy, per RC 3719.44. Pursuant to RC 3719.43, changes to the federal schedules of controlled substances automatically become part of the corresponding schedule or schedules in RC 3719.41. When this occurs, prior to conforming amendments by the General Assembly, the compilation of the section is prepared with the assistance of the Board to guide health professionals and law enforcement officials in determining (1) whether a drug or drug product is a controlled substance; (2) which schedule it has been placed in; (3) whether it was scheduled (a) by the state legislature through enactment of RC 3719.41, or (b) by either the federal government per RC 3719.43 or the State Board of Pharmacy per RC 3719.44; and (4), if added by the federal government or the State Board of Pharmacy, the date it was added or transferred from one schedule to another. If a date is in parentheses ( ), the substance was placed in the schedule by the federal government; if a date is in brackets [], the substance was added or transferred to the schedule by the State Board. Footnotes are used to provide additional information.

Controlled substance schedules I, II, III, IV, and V are hereby established, which schedules include the following, subject to amendment pursuant to section 3719.43 or 3719.44 of the Revised Code.

SCHEDULE I

(A) Narcotics–opiates

Any of the following opiates, including their isomers, esters, ethers, salts, and salts of isomers, esters, and ethers, unless specifically excepted under federal drug abuse control laws, whenever the existence of these isomers, esters, ethers, and salts is possible within the specific chemical designation:

(1) Acetyl–alpha–methylfentanyl (N- [1–(1–methyl–2–phenethyl)–4–piperidinyl]–N–phenylacetamide); (11–29–85)

(2) Acetylmethadol; (5–1–71)

(3) Allylprodine; (5–1–71)

(4) Alphacetylmethadol (except levo-alphacetylmethadol also known as levo-alpha-acetylmethadol, levomethadyl acetate, or LAAM); (5–1–71) (8–18–93) [1]

(5) Alphameprodine; (5 1 71)

(6) Alphamethadol; (5–1–71)

(7) Alpha–methylfentanyl (N- [1–(alpha–methyl–beta–phenyl)ethyl–4–piperidyl] propionanilide; 1–(1–methyl–2–phenylethyl)–4–(N–propanilido) piperidine); (9–22–81)

(8) Alpha–methylthiofentanyl (N- [1–methyl–2–(2–thienyl)ethyl–4–piperidinyl]–N–phenylpropanamide); (11–29–85)

(9) Benzethidine; (5–1–71)

(10) Betacetylmethadol; (5–1–71)

(11) Beta–hydroxyfentanyl (N- [1–(2–hydroxy–2–phenethyl–4–piperidinyl]–N–phenylpropanamide); (11–29–85)

(12) Beta–hydroxy–3–methylfentanyl (other name: N- [1–(2–hydroxy–2–phenethyl)–3–methyl–4–piperidinyl]–N–phenylpropanamide); (1–8–88)

(13) Betameprodine; (5–1–71)

(14) Betamethadol; (5–1–71)

(15) Betaprodine; (5–1–71)

(16) Clonitazene; (5–1–71)

(17) Dextromoramide; (5–1–71)

(18) Diampromide; (5–1–71)

(19) Diethylthiambutene; (5–1–71)

(20) Difenoxin; (6–1–75) [4–1–78]

(21) Dimenoxadol; (5–1–71)

(22) Dimepheptanol; (5–1–71)

(23) Dimethylthiambutene; (5–1–71)

(24) Dioxaphetyl butyrate; (5–1–71)

(25) Dipipanone; (5–1–71)

(26) Ethylmethylthiambutene; (5–1–71)

(27) Etonitazene; (5–1–71)

(28) Etoxeridine; (5–1–71)

(29) Furethidine; (5–1–71)

(30) Hydroxypethidine; (5–1–71)

(31) Ketobemidone; (5–1–71)

(32) Levomoramide; (5–1–71)

(33) Levophenacylmorphan; (5–1–71)

(34) 3–methylfentanyl (N- [3–methyl–1–(2–phenylethyl)–4–piperidyl]–N–phenylpropanamide); (4–25–85)

(35) 3–methylthiofentanyl (N- [3–methyl–1- [2–(thienyl)ethyl]–4–piperidinyl]–N–phenylpropanamide); (11–29–85)

(36) Morpheridine; (5–1–71)

(37) MPPP (1–methyl–4–phenyl–4–propionoxypiperidine); (8–12–85)

(38) Noracymethadol; (5–1–71)

(39) Norlevorphanol; (5–1–71)

(40) Normethadone; (5–1–71)

(41) Norpipanone; (5–1–71)

(42) Para–fluorofentanyl (N–(4–fluorophenyl)–N- [1–(2–phenethyl)–4–piperidinyl]propanamide; (3–10–86)

(43) PEPAP (1–(2–phenethyl)–4–phenyl–4–acetoxypiperidine; (8–12–85)

(44) Phenadoxone; (5–1–71)

(45) Phenampromide; (5–1–71)

(46) Phenomorphan; (5–1–71)

(47) Phenoperidine; (5–1–71)

(48) Piritramide; (5–1–71)

(49) Proheptazine; (5–1–71)

(50) Properidine; (5–1–71)

(51) Propiram; (2–28–72)

(52) Racemoramide; (5–1–71)

(53) Thiofentanyl (N–phenyl–N- [1–(2–thienyl)ethyl–4–piperidinyl]–propanamide; (11–29–85)

(54) Tilidine; (12 1 80)

(55) Trimeperidine. (5–1–71)

(B) Narcotics–opium derivatives

Any of the following opium derivatives, including their salts, isomers, and salts of isomers, unless specifically excepted under federal drug abuse control laws, whenever the existence of these salts, isomers, and salts of isomers is possible within the specific chemical designation:

(1) Acetorphine; (5–1–71)

(2) Acetyldihydrocodeine; (5–1–71)

(3) Benzylmorphine; (5–1–71)

(4) Codeine methylbromide; (5–1–71)

(5) Codeine–n–oxide; (5–1–71)

(6) Cyprenorphine; (5–1–71)

(7) Desomorphine; (5–1–71)

(8) Dihydromorphine; (5–1–71)

(9) Drotebanol; (8–6–73)

(10) Etorphine (except hydrochloride salt); (5–1–71)

(11) Heroin; (5–1–71)

(12) Hydromorphinol; (5–1–71)

(13) Methyldesorphine; (5–1–71)

(14) Methyldihydromorphine; (5–1–71)

(15) Morphine methylbromide; (5–1–71)

(16) Morphine methylsulfonate; (5–1–71)

(17) Morphine–n–oxide; (5–1–71)

(18) Myrophine; (5–1–71)

(19) Nicocodeine; (5–1–71)

(20) Nicomorphine; (5–1–71)

(21) Normorphine; (5–1–71)

(22) Pholcodine; (5–1–71)

(23) Thebacon. (5–1–71)

(C) Hallucinogens

Any material, compound, mixture, or preparation that contains any quantity of the following hallucinogenic substances, including their salts, isomers, and salts of isomers, unless specifically excepted under federal drug abuse control laws, whenever the existence of these salts, isomers, and salts of isomers is possible within the specific chemical designation. For the purposes of this division only, "isomer" includes the optical isomers, position isomers, and geometric isomers.

(1) Alpha–ethyltryptamine (some trade or other names: etryptamine; Monase; alpha–ethyl–1H–indole–3–ethanamine; 3–(2–aminobutyl) indole; alpha–ET; and AET); (9–12–94) [2]

(2) 4–bromo–2,5–dimethoxy–amphetamine (some trade or other names: 4–bromo–2,5–dimethoxy–alpha–methyphenethylamine; 4–bromo–2,5–DMA); (9–21–73)

(3) 4–bromo–2,5–dimethoxyphenethylamine (some trade or other names: 2–(4–bromo–2,5–dimethoxyphenyl)–1–aminoethane; alpha–desmethyl DOB; 2C–B, Nexus). (6–2–95) [3]

(4) 2,5–dimethoxyamphetamine (some trade or other names: 2,5–dimethoxy–alpha–methylphenethylamine; 2,5–DMA); (9–21–73)

(5) 2,5–dimethoxy–4–ethylamphetamine (some trade or other names: DOET); (2–16–93)

(6) 4–methoxyamphetamine (some trade or other names: 4–methoxy–alpha–methylphenethylamine; paramethoxyamphetamine; PMA); (9–21–73)

(7) 5–methoxy–3,4–methylenedioxy–amphetamine; (5–1–71)

(8) 4–methyl–2,5–dimethoxy–amphetamine (some trade or other names: 4–methyl–2,5–dimethoxy–alpha–methylphenethylamine; "DOM" and "STP"); (5–1–71)

(9) 3,4–methylenedioxy amphetamine; (5–1–71)

(10) 3,4–methylenedioxymethamphetamine (MDMA); (7–1–85)

(11) 3,4–methylenedioxy–N–ethylamphetamine (also known as N–ethyl–alpha–methyl–3,4(methylenedioxy)phenethylamine, N-ethyl MDA, MDE, MDEA); (10–15–87)

(12) N–hydroxy–3,4–methylenedioxyamphetamine (also known as N–hydroxy–alpha–methyl–3,4(methylenedioxy)phenethylamine and N-hydroxy MDA); (10–15–87)

(13) 3,4,5–trimethoxy amphetamine; (5–1–71)

(14) Bufotenine (some trade or other names: 3–(beta–dimethylaminoethyl)–5–hydroxyindole; 3–(2–dimethylaminoethyl)–5–indolol; N, N-dimethyl-serotonin; 5–hydroxy–N,N–dimethyltryptamine; mappine); (5–1–71)

(15) Diethyltryptamine (some trade or other names: N, N-diethyltryptamine; DET); (5–1–71)

(16) Dimethyltryptamine (some trade or other names: DMT); (5–1–71)

(17) Ibogaine (some trade or other names: 7–ethyl–6,6beta,7,8,9,10,12,13–octahydro–2–methoxy–6,9–methano–5H–pyrido [1',2':1,2] azepino [5,4–b] indole; tabernanthe iboga); (5–1–71)

(18) Lysergic acid diethylamide; (5–1–71)

(19) Marihuana; (5–1–71)

(20) Mescaline; (5–1–71)

(21) Parahexyl (some trade or other names: 3–hexyl–1–hydroxy–7,8,9,10–tetrahydro–6,6,9–trimethyl–6H–dibenzo [b,d] pyran; synhexyl); (12–22–82)

(22) Peyote (meaning all parts of the plant presently classified botanically as "Lophophora williamsii Lemaire," whether growing or not, the seeds of that plant, any extract from any part of that plant, and every compound, manufacture, salts, derivative, mixture, or preparation of that plant, its seeds, or its extracts); (5–1–71) (1–21–76) (10–1–76)

(23) N–ethyl–3–piperidyl benzilate; (5–1–71)

(24) N–methyl–3–piperidyl benzilate; (5–1–71)

(25) Psilocybin; (5–1–71)

(26) Psilocyn; (5–1–71)

(27) Tetrahydrocannabinols (synthetic equivalents of the substances contained in the plant, or in the resinous extractives of Cannabis, sp. and/or synthetic substances, derivatives, and their isomers with similar chemical structure and pharmacological activity such as the following: delta–1–cis or trans tetrahydrocannabinol, and their optical isomers; delta–6–cis or trans tetrahydrocannabinol, and their optical isomers; delta–3,4–cis or trans tetrahydrocannabinol, and its optical isomers. (Since nomenclature of these substances is not internationally standardized, compounds of these structures, regardless of numerical designation of atomic positions, are covered.)); (5–1–71)

(28) Ethylamine analog of phencyclidine (some trade or other names: N–ethyl–1–phenylcyclohexylamine; (1–phenylcyclohexyl)ethylamine; N–(1–phenylcyclohexyl)ethylamine; cyclohexamine; PCE); (10–25–78) [4]

(29) Pyrrolidine analog of phencyclidine (some trade or other names: 1–(1–phenylcyclohexyl)pyrrolidine; PCPy; PHP); (10–25–78) [5]

(30) Thiophene analog of phencyclidine (some trade or other names: 1- [1–(2–thienyl)–cyclohexyl]–piperidine; 2–thienyl analog of phencyclidine; TPCP; TCP); (8–11–75) [4–1–78]

(31) 1- [1–(2–thienyl)cyclohexyl]pyrrolidine; (7–6–89)

(32) Hashish.

(D) Depressants

Any material, compound, mixture, or preparation that contains any quantity of the following substances having a depressant effect on the central nervous system, including their salts, isomers, and salts of isomers, unless specifically excepted under federal drug abuse control laws, whenever the existence of these salts, isomers, and salts of isomers is possible within the specific chemical designation:

(1) Gamma–hydroxybutyric acid (some other names include GHB; gamma–hydroxybutyrate; 4–hydroxybutyrate; 4–hydroxybutanoic acid; sodium oxybate; sodium oxybutyrate); (3–13–00) [6]

(2) Mecloqualone; (7–10–75) [4–1–78]

(3) Methaqualone. (8–27–84) [7]

(E) Stimulants

Unless specifically excepted or unless listed in another schedule, any material, compound, mixture, or preparation that contains any quantity of the following substances having a stimulant effect on the central nervous system, including their salts, isomers, and salts of isomers:

(1) Aminorex (some other names: aminoxaphen; 2–amino–5–phenyl–2–oxazoline; or 4,5–dihydro–5–phenyl–2–oxazolamine); (3–18–94) [8]

(2) Cathinone (some trade or other names: 2–amino–1–phenyl–1–propanone, alpha-aminopropiophenone, 2–aminopropiophenone, and norephedrone); (2–16–93)

(3) Fenethylline; (8–20–81)

(4) Methcathinone (some other names: 2–(methylamino)propiophenone; alpha–(methylamino)propiophenone; 2–(methylamino)–1–phenylpropan–1–one; alpha–N–methylaminopropiophenone; monomethylpropion; ephedrone; N–methylcathinone; methylcathinone; AL–464; AL–422; AL–463 and UR1432), its salts, optical isomers, and salts of optical isomers; (10–15–93) [9]

(5) (+/–)cis–4–methylaminorex ((+/–)cis–4,5–dihydro–4–methyl–5–phenyl–2–oxazolamine); (10–15–87)

(6) N–ethylamphetamine; (1–7–82)

(7) N,N–dimethylamphetamine (also known as N,N-alpha-trimethyl-benzeneethanamine; N,N–alpha–trimethylphenethylamine). (8–3–88)

(F) Temporary Listing Of Substances Subject To Emergency Scheduling [10]

Any material, compound, mixture or preparation which contains any quantity of the following substances:

(1) N- [1–benzyl–4–piperidyl]–N–phenylpropanamide (benzylfentanyl), its optical isomers, salts and salts of isomers; (11–29–85) [11]

(2) N- [1–(2–thienyl)methyl–4–piperidyl]–N–phenylpropanamide (thenylfentanyl), its optical isomers, salts and salts of isomers. (11–29–85) [12]

SCHEDULE II

(A) Narcotics–opium and opium derivatives

Unless specifically excepted under federal drug abuse control laws or unless listed in another schedule, any of the following substances whether produced directly or indirectly by extraction from substances of vegetable origin, independently by means of chemical synthesis, or by a combination of extraction and chemical synthesis:

(1) Opium and opiate, and any salt, compound, derivative, or preparation of opium or opiate, excluding apomorphine (6–28–76) [4–1–78], thebaine-derived butorphanol (7–14–92), dextrorphan (10–1–76), nalbuphine (10–1–76) [4–1–78], nalmefene (11–4–85), naloxone, and naltrexone (3–6–75) [4–1–78], and their respective salts, but including the following:

(a) Raw opium; (5–1–71)

(b) Opium extracts; (5–1–71)

(c) Opium fluid extracts; (5–1–71)

(d) Powdered opium; (5–1–71)

(e) Granulated opium; (5–1–71)

(f) Tincture of opium; (5–1–71)

(g) Codeine; (5–1–71)

(h) Ethylmorphine; (5–1–71)

(i) Etorphine hydrochloride; (4–18–74)

(j) Hydrocodone; (5–1–71)

(k) Hydromorphone; (5–1–71)

(*l*) Metopon; (5–1–71)

(m) Morphine; (5–1–71)

(n) Oxycodone; (5–1–71)

(*o*) Oxymorphone; (5–1–71)

(p) Thebaine. (5–1–71)

(2) Any salt, compound, derivative, or preparation thereof that is chemically equivalent to or identical with any of the substances referred to in division (A)(1) of this schedule, except that these substances shall not include the isoquinoline alkaloids of opium; (5–1–71)

(3) Opium poppy and poppy straw; (5–1–71)

(4) Coca leaves and any salt, compound, derivative, or preparation of coca leaves (including cocaine and ecgonine, their salts, isomers, and derivatives, and salts of those isomers and derivatives), and any salt, compound, derivative, or preparation thereof that is chemically equivalent to or identical with any of these substances, except that the substances shall not include decocainized coca leaves or extraction of coca leaves, which extractions do not contain cocaine or ecgonine; (5–1–71) (4–23–86)

(5) Concentrate of poppy straw (the crude extract of poppy straw in either liquid, solid, or powder form that contains the phenanthrene alkaloids of the opium poppy) (2–14–75)

(B) Narcotics–opiates

Unless specifically excepted under federal drug abuse control laws or unless listed in another schedule, any of the following opiates, including their isomers, esters, ethers, salts, and salts of isomers, esters, and ethers, whenever the existence of these isomers, esters, ethers, and salts is possible within the specific chemical designation, but excluding dextrorphan and levopropoxyphene: (9–22–80)

(1) Alfentanil; (1–23–87) [13]

(2) Alphaprodine; (5–1–71)

(3) Anileridine; (5–1–71)

(4) Bezitramide; (5–1–71)

(5) Bulk dextropropoxyphene (non-dosage forms); (9–22–80) [14]

(6) Carfentanil; (10–28–88)

(7) Dihydrocodeine; (5–1–71)

(8) Diphenoxylate; (5–1–71)

(9) Fentanyl; (5–1–71)

(10) Isomethadone; (5–1–71)

(11) Levo–alphacetylmethadol (some other names: levo–alpha–acetylmethadol, levomethadyl acetate, LAAM); (8–18–93) [15]

(12) Levomethorphan; (5–1–71)

(13) Levorphanol; (5–1–71)

(14) Metazocine; (5–1–71)

(15) Methadone; (5–1–71)

(16) Methadone–intermediate, 4–cyano–2–dimethylamino–4,4–diphenyl butane; (5–1–71)

(17) Moramide–intermediate, 2–methyl–3–morpholino–1,1–diphenylpropane–carboxylic acid; (5–1–71)

(18) Pethidine (meperidine); (5–1–71)

(19) Pethidine–intermediate–A, 4–cyano–1–methyl–4–phenylpiperidine; (5–1–71)

(20) Pethidine–intermediate–B, ethyl–4–phenylpiperidine–4–carboxylate; (5–1–71)

(21) Pethidine–intermediate–C, 1–methyl–4–phenylpiperidine–4–carboxylic acid; (5–1–71)

(22) Phenazocine; (5–1–71)

(23) Piminodine; (5–1–71)

(24) Racemethorphan; (5–1–71)

(25) Racemorphan; (5–1–71)

(26) Remifentanil; (11–5–96)

(27) Sufentanil. (5–25–84) [16]

(C) Stimulants

Unless specifically excepted under federal drug abuse control laws or unless listed in another schedule, any material, compound, mixture, or preparation that contains any quantity of the following substances having a stimulant effect on the central nervous system: (7–7–71)

(1) Amphetamine, its salts, its optical isomers, and salts of its optical isomers; (7–7–71)

(2) Methamphetamine, its salts, its isomers, and salts of its isomers; (7–7–71)

(3) Methylphenidate; (10–28–71)

(4) Phenmetrazine and its salts. (10–28–71)

(D) Depressants

Unless specifically excepted under federal drug abuse control laws or unless listed in another schedule, any material, compound, mixture, or preparation that contains any quantity of the following substances having a depressant effect on the central nervous system, including their salts, isomers, and salts of isomers, whenever the existence of these salts, isomers, and salts of isomers is possible within the specific chemical designation:

(1) Amobarbital; (12–17–73)

(2) Glutethimide; (3–21–91) [17]

(3) Pentobarbital; (12–17–73)

(4) Phencyclidine (some trade or other names: 1–(1–phenylcyclohexyl)piperidine; PCP); (2–24–78) [7–1–78]

(5) Secobarbital; (12–17–73)

(6) 1–aminophenylcyclohexane and all N-mono-substituted and/or all N-N-disubstituted analogs, including, but not limited to, the following: [18]

(a) 1–phenylcyclohexylamine; [7–1–78]

(b) (1–phenylcyclohexyl) methylamine; [7–1–78]

(c) (1–phenylcyclohexyl) dimethylamine; [7–1–78]

(d) (1–phenylcyclohexyl) methylethylamine; [7–1–78]

(e) (1–phenylcyclohexyl) isopropylamine; [7–1–78]

(f) 1–(1–phenylcyclohexyl) morpholine. [7–1–78]

(E) Hallucinogenic substances [19]

(1) Nabilone (another name for nabilone: (+)–trans–3–(1,1–dimethylheptyl)–6,6a,7,8,10,10a–hexahydro–1–hydroxy–6,6–dimethyl-9H–dibenzo [b,d]pyran–9–one). (4–7–87)

(F) Immediate precursors

Unless specifically excepted under federal drug abuse control laws or unless listed in another schedule, any material, compound, mixture, or preparation that contains any quantity of the following substances:

(1) Immediate precursor to amphetamine and methamphetamine:

(a) Phenylacetone (some trade or other names: phenyl–2–propanone; P2P; benzyl methyl ketone; methyl benzyl ketone); (2–11–80)

(2) Immediate precursors to phencyclidine (PCP):

(a) 1–phenylcyclohexylamine; (6–16–78)

(b) 1–piperidinocyclohexanecarbonitrile (PCC). (6–16–78)

SCHEDULE III

(A) Stimulants

Unless specifically excepted under federal drug abuse control laws or unless listed in another schedule, any material, compound, mixture, or preparation that contains any quantity of the following substances having a stimulant effect on the central nervous system, including their salts, their optical isomers, position isomers, or geometric isomers, and salts of these isomers, whenever the existence of these salts, isomers, and salts of isomers is possible within the specific chemical designation:

(1) All stimulant compounds, mixtures, and preparations included in schedule III pursuant to the federal drug abuse control laws and regulations adopted under those laws; (6–15–73)

(2) Benzphetamine; (6–15–73)

(3) Chlorphentermine; (6–15–73)

(4) Clortermine; (6–15–73)

(5) Phendimetrazine. (6–15–73)

(B) Depressants

Unless specifically excepted under federal drug abuse control laws or unless listed in another schedule, any material, compound, mixture, or preparation that contains any quantity of the following substances having a depressant effect on the central nervous system: (11–8–73)

(1) Any compound, mixture, or preparation containing amobarbital, secobarbital, pentobarbital, or any salt of any of these drugs, and one or more other active medicinal ingredients that are not listed in any schedule; (11–8–73)

(2) Any suppository dosage form containing amobarbital, secobarbital, pentobarbital, or any salt of any of these drugs and approved by the food and drug administration for marketing only as a suppository; (11–8–73)

(3) Any substance that contains any quantity of a derivative of barbituric acid or any salt of a derivative of barbituric acid; (5–1–71)

(4) Chlorhexadol; (5–1–71)

(5) Any drug product containing gamma hydroxybutyric acid, including its salts, isomers, and salts of isomers, for which an application is approved under section 505 of the Federal Food, Drug, and Cosmetic Act; (3–13–00) [20]

(6) Ketamine, its salts, isomers, and salts of isomers (some other names for ketamine: (k)–2–(2–chlorophenyl)–2–(methylamino)–cyclohexanone); (8–12–99)

(7) Lysergic acid; (5–1–71)

(8) Lysergic acid amide; (5–1–71)

(9) Methyprylon; (5–1–71)

(10) Sulfondiethylmethane; (5–1–71)

(11) Sulfonethylmethane; (5–1–71)

(12) Sulfonmethane; (5–1–71)

(13) Tiletamine, zolazepam, or any salt of tiletamine or zolazepam (some trade or other names for a tiletamine-zolazepam combination product: Telazol); (some trade or other names for tiletamine: 2–(ethylamino)–2–(2–thienyl)–cyclohexanone); (some trade or other names for zolazepam: 4–(2–fluorophenyl)–6,8–dihydro–1,3,8–trimethylpyrazolo- [3,4–e] [1,4]–diazepin–7(1H)–one; flupyrazapon). (2–20–87)

(C) Narcotic antidotes

(1) Nalorphine. (5–1–71)

(D) Narcotics–narcotic preparations

Unless specifically excepted under federal drug abuse control laws or unless listed in another schedule, any material, compound, mixture, or preparation that contains any of the following narcotic drugs, or their salts calculated as the free anhydrous base or alkaloid, in limited quantities as set forth below: (7–26–79)

(1) Not more than 1.8 grams of codeine per 100 milliliters or not more than 90 milligrams per dosage unit, with an equal or greater quantity of an isoquinoline alkaloid of opium; (5–1–71)

(2) Not more than 1.8 grams of codeine per 100 milliliters or not more than 90 milligrams per dosage unit, with one or more active, nonnarcotic ingredients in recognized therapeutic amounts; (5–1–71)

(3) Not more than 300 milligrams of dihydrocodeinone per 100 milliliters or not more than 15 milligrams per dosage unit, with a fourfold or greater quantity of an isoquinoline alkaloid of opium; (5–1–71)

(4) Not more than 300 milligrams of dihydrocodeinone per 100 milliliters or not more than 15 milligrams per dosage unit, with one or more active, nonnarcotic ingredients in recognized therapeutic amounts; (5–1–71)

(5) Not more than 1.8 grams of dihydrocodeine per 100 milliliters or not more than 90 milligrams per dosage unit, with one or more active, nonnarcotic ingredients in recognized therapeutic amounts; (5–1–71)

(6) Not more than 300 milligrams of ethylmorphine per 100 milliliters or not more than 15 milligrams per dosage unit, with one or more active, nonnarcotic ingredients in recognized therapeutic amounts; (5–1–71)

(7) Not more than 500 milligrams of opium per 100 milliliters or per 100 grams or not more than 25 milligrams per dosage unit, with one or more active, nonnarcotic ingredients in recognized therapeutic amounts; (5–1–71)

(8) Not more than 50 milligrams of morphine per 100 milliliters or per 100 grams, with one or more active, nonnarcotic ingredients in recognized therapeutic amounts. (5–1–71)

(E) Anabolic steroids

Unless specifically excepted under federal drug abuse control laws or unless listed in another schedule, any material, compound, mixture, or preparation that contains any quantity of the following substances, including their salts, esters, isomers, and salts of esters and isomers, whenever the existence of these salts, esters, and isomers is possible within the specific chemical designation:

(1) Anabolic steroids. (2–27–91) [21] Except as otherwise provided in division (E)(1) of schedule III, "anabolic steroids" means any drug or hormonal substance that is chemically and pharmacologically related to testosterone (other than estrogens, progestins, and corticosteroids) and that promotes muscle growth. "Anabolic steroids" does not include an anabolic steroid that is expressly intended for administration through implants to cattle or other nonhuman species and that has been approved by the United States secretary of health and human services for that administration, unless a person prescribes, dispenses, or distributes this type of anabolic steroid for human use. "Anabolic steroid" includes, but is not limited to, the following:

(a) Boldenone;

(b) Chlorotestosterone (4–chlortestosterone);

(c) Clostebol;

(d) Dehydrochlormethyltestosterone;

(e) Dihydrotestosterone (4–dihydrotestosterone);

(f) Drostanolone;

(g) Ethylestrenol;

(h) Fluoxymesterone;

(i) Formebulone (formebolone);

(j) Mesterolone;

(k) Methandienone;

(*l*) Methandranone;

(m) Methandriol;

(n) Methandrostenolone;

(*o*) Methenolone;

(p) Methyltestosterone;

(q) Mibolerone;

(r) Nandrolone;

(s) Norethandrolone;

(t) Oxandrolone;

(u) Oxymesterone;

(v) Oxymetholone;

(w) Stanolone;

(x) Stanozolol;

(y) Testolactone;

(z) Testosterone;

(aa) Trenbolone;

(bb) Any salt, ester, isomer, or salt of an ester or isomer of a drug or hormonal substance described or listed in division (E)(1) of schedule III if the salt, ester, or isomer promotes muscle growth.

(F) Hallucinogenic substances

(1) Dronabinol (synthetic) in sesame oil and encapsulated in a soft gelatin capsule in a United States food and drug administration approved drug product (some other names for dronabinol: (6aR–trans)–6a,7,8,10a–tetrahydro–6,6,9–trimethyl–3–pentyl–6H–dibenzo [b,d]pyran–1–ol, or (–)–delta–9–(trans)–tetrahydrocannabinol); (7–2–99) [22]

SCHEDULE IV

(A) Narcotic drugs

Unless specifically excepted by federal drug abuse control laws or unless listed in another schedule, any material, compound, mixture, or preparation that contains any of the following narcotic drugs, or their salts calculated as the free anhydrous base or alkaloid, in limited quantities as set forth below: (7–26–79)

(1) Not more than one milligram of difenoxin and not less than 25 micrograms of atropine sulfate per dosage unit; (9–27–78)

(2) Dextropropoxyphene (alpha–(+)–4–dimethylamino–1,2–diphenyl–3–methyl–2–propionoxybutane) [final dosage forms]. (3–14–77) (7–24–80) [23]

(B) Depressants

Unless specifically excepted under federal drug abuse control laws or unless listed in another schedule, any material, compound, mixture, or preparation that contains any quantity of the following substances, including their salts, isomers, and salts of isomers, whenever the existence of these salts, isomers, and salts of isomers is possible within the specific chemical designation:

(1) Alprazolam; (11–12–81)

(2) Barbital; (5–1–71)

(3) Bromazepam; (11–5–84)

(4) Camazepam; (11–5–84)

(5) Chloral betaine; (5–1–71)

(6) Chloral hydrate; (5–1–71)

(7) Chlordiazepoxide; (7–2–75) [4–1–78]

(8) Clobazam; (11–5–84)

(9) Clonazepam; (7–2–75) [4–1–78]

(10) Clorazepate; (7–2–75) [4–1–78]

(11) Clotiazepam; (11–5–84)

(12) Cloxazolam; (11–5–84)

(13) Delorazepam; (11–5–84)

(14) Diazepam; (7–2–75) [4–1–78]

(15) Dichloralphenazone; (8–16–01)

(16) Estazolam; (11–5–84)

(17) Ethchlorvynol; (5–1–71)

(18) Ethinamate; (5–1–71)

(19) Ethyl loflazepate; (11–5–84)

(20) Fludiazepam; (11–5–84)

(21) Flunitrazepam; (11–5–84)

(22) Flurazepam; (7–2–75) [4–1–78]

(23) Halazepam; (10–29–81)

(24) Haloxazolam; (11–5–84)

(25) Ketazolam; (11–5–84)

(26) Loprazolam; (11–5–84)

(27) Lorazepam; (10–3–77)

(28) Lormetazepam; (11–5–84)

(29) Mebutamate; (1–30–75)

(30) Medazepam; (11–5–84)

(31) Meprobamate; (5–1–71)

(32) Methohexital; (5–1–71)

(33) Methylphenobarbital (mephobarbital); (5–1–71)

(34) Midazolam; (3–25–86)

(35) Nimetazepam; (11–5–84)

(36) Nitrazepam; (11–5–84)

(37) Nordiazepam; (11–5–84)

(38) Oxazepam; (7–2–75) [4–1–78]

(39) Oxazolam; (11–5–84)

(40) Paraldehyde; (5–1–71)

(41) Petrichloral; (5–1–71)

(42) Phenobarbital; (5–1–71)

(43) Pinazepam; (11–5–84)

(44) Prazepam; (12–17–86)

(45) Quazepam; (3–25–86)

(46) Temazepam; (4–7–81)

(47) Tetrazepam; (11–5–84)

(48) Triazolam; (12–28–82)

(49) Zaleplon; (9–15–99)

(50) Zolpidem. (2–5–93)

(C) Fenfluramine

Any material, compound, mixture, or preparation that contains any quantity of the following substances, including their salts, their optical isomers, position isomers, or geometric isomers, and salts of these isomers, whenever the existence of these salts, isomers, and salts of isomers is possible within the specific chemical designation:

(1) Fenfluramine. (6–15–73)

(D) Stimulants

Unless specifically excepted under federal drug abuse control laws or unless listed in another schedule, any material, compound, mixture, or preparation that contains any quantity of the following substances having a stimulant effect on the central nervous system, including their salts, their optical isomers, position isomers, or geometric isomers, and salts of these isomers, whenever the existence of these salts, isomers, and salts of isomers is possible within the specific chemical designation:

(1) Cathine ((+)–norpseudoephedrine); (6–16–88)

(2) Diethylpropion; (9–1–73)

(3) Fencamfamin; (6–16–88)

(4) Fenproporex; (6–16–88)

(5) Mazindol; (11–27–81) [24]

(6) Mefenorex; (6–16–88)

(7) Modafinil; (1–27–99)

(8) Pemoline (including organometallic complexes and chelates thereof); (1–28–75)

(9) Phentermine; (9–1–73)

(10) Pipradrol; (12–1–80)

(11) Sibutramine; (2–11–98)

(12) SPA [(–)–1–dimethylamino–1,2–diphenylethane]. (12–1–80)

(E) Other substances

Unless specifically excepted under federal drug abuse control laws or unless listed in another schedule, any material, compound, mixture or preparation that contains any quantity of the following substances, including their salts:

(1) Pentazocine; (2–9–79)

(2) Butorphanol (including its optical isomers). (10–31–97)

SCHEDULE V

(A) Narcotic drugs

Unless specifically excepted under federal drug abuse control laws or unless listed in another schedule, any material, compound, mixture, or preparation that contains any of the following narcotic drugs, and their salts, as set forth below:

(1) Buprenorphine. (4–1–85)

(B) Narcotics–narcotic preparations

Narcotic drugs containing nonnarcotic active medicinal ingredients. Any compound, mixture, or preparation that contains any of the following narcotic drugs, or their salts calculated as the free anhydrous base or alkaloid, in limited quantities as set forth below, and that includes one or more nonnarcotic active medicinal ingredients in sufficient proportion to confer upon the compound, mixture, or preparation valuable medicinal qualities other than those possessed by narcotic drugs alone: (7–26–79)

(1) Not more than 200 milligrams of codeine per 100 milliliters or per 100 grams; (5–1–71) (6–20–74)

(2) Not more than 100 milligrams of dihydrocodeine per 100 milliliters or per 100 grams; (5–1–71) (6–20–74)

(3) Not more than 100 milligrams of ethylmorphine per 100 milliliters or per 100 grams; (5–1–71) (6–20–74)

(4) Not more than 2.5 milligrams of diphenoxylate and not less than 25 micrograms of atropine sulfate per dosage unit; (5–1–71) (6–20–74)

(5) Not more than 100 milligrams of opium per 100 milliliters or per 100 grams; (5–1–71) (6–20–74)

(6) Not more than 0.5 milligram of difenoxin and not less than 25 micrograms of atropine sulfate per dosage unit. (9–27–78)

(C) Stimulants

Unless specifically exempted or excluded under federal drug abuse control laws or unless listed in another schedule, any material, compound, mixture, or preparation that contains any quantity of the following substances having a stimulant effect on the central nervous system, including their salts, isomers, and salts of isomers:

(1) Ephedrine, except as provided in division (K) of section 3719.44 of the Revised Code; [25]

(2) Pyrovalerone. (5–4–88)

(1999 H 428, eff. 5–17–00; 1996 S 269, eff. 7–1–96; 1994 H 391, eff. 7–21–94; 1993 H 156, eff. 5–19–93; 1991 H 62; 1975 H 300)

1 Levo-alphacetylmethadol was transferred to Schedule II by the Federal Government pursuant to Section 3719.43 of the Ohio Revised Code on August 18, 1993.

2 Originally placed in Schedule I on 3–12–93 under the Temporary Scheduling provisions of the Federal Government.

3 Originally placed in Schedule I on 1–6–94 under the Temporary Scheduling provisions of the Federal Government.

4 Placed in Schedule II by the Board of Pharmacy pursuant to Section 3719.44 of the Revised Code on July 1, 1978.

5 Placed in Schedule II by the Board of Pharmacy pursuant to Section 3719.44 of the Revised Code on July 1, 1978.

6 Placed in Schedule II by the Ohio Legislature pursuant to House Bill 428 to take effect May 17, 2000, but placement by the Federal Government into Schedule I takes precedence. [also see Schedule III, paragraph (B)(5)]

7 Methaqualone was previously placed by the Federal Government into Schedule II effective 10–4–73 and was moved, pursuant to Section 3719.43 of the Ohio Revised Code, to Schedule I effective 8–27–84.

8 Originally placed in Schedule I on 9–21–92 under the Temporary Scheduling provisions of the Federal Government.

9 Originally placed in Schedule I on 5–1–92 under the Temporary Scheduling provisions of the Federal Government.

10 **Temporary scheduling is under federal law only.** It is included here as a service and is not an actual part of Section 3719.41 of the Revised Code. All Schedule I restrictions and controls still apply to the substances listed until temporary placement expires or permanent placement occurs. Temporary placement will expire at the end of one year from the effective date but may be extended six months (noted by a second effective date). Emergency scheduling is intended to apply to "designer drugs".

11 Listed under Schedule I restrictions for a one-year period ending November 29, 1986.

12 Listed under Schedule I restrictions for a one-year period ending November 29, 1986.

13 Alfentanil was previously placed by the Federal Government, pursuant to Section 3719.43 of the Ohio Revised Code, into Schedule I effective 8–24–84, and was moved to Schedule II effective 1–23–87.

14 Dextropropoxyphene (final dosage forms) was reclassified in Schedule IV as a narcotic drug under federal drug abuse control laws on July 24, 1980. Bulk dextropropoxyphene (non–dosage forms) was placed in Schedule II on the same date.

15 Levo-alphacetylmethadol was previously placed by the Federal Government, pursuant to Section 3719.43 of the Ohio Revised Code, into Schedule I effective 5–1–71, and was moved to Schedule II effective 8–18–93.

16 Sufentanil was previously placed by the Federal Government, pursuant to Section 3719.43 of the Ohio Revised Code, into Schedule I effective 12–1–80, and was moved to Schedule II effective 5–25–84.

17 Glutethimide was placed in Schedule III by the Federal Government on 5–1–71 and was moved to Schedule II by the Federal Government, pursuant to Section 3719.43 of the Ohio Revised Code, effective 3–21–91.

18 (1–phenylcyclohexyl) ethylamine and 1–(1–phenylcyclohexyl) pyrrolidine were placed in Schedule II by the Board of Pharmacy on 7–1–78 and were moved to Schedule I by the Federal Government on 10–25–78.

19 Dronabinol (synthetic) in sesame oil and encapsulated in a soft gelatin capsule in a United States Food and Drug Administration approved drug product was placed in Schedule II by the Federal Government on 5–13–86 and was moved to Schedule III by the Federal Government on 7–2–99.

20 Even though this exception was included by the Federal Government, there are currently no drug products containing gamma hydroxybutyric acid approved under U.S.C. Section 505. [see Schedule I, paragraph (D)(1)]

21 Anabolic steroids was also added to Schedule III by the Ohio Legislature effective 5–21–91; a "cleanup" bill was passed by the Ohio Legislature on 5–19–93.

22 Dronabinol (synthetic) in sesame oil and encapsulated in a soft gelatin capsule in a United States Food and Drug Administration approved drug product was placed in Schedule II by the Federal Government on 5–13–86 and was moved to Schedule III by the Federal Government on 7–2–99.

23 Dextropropoxyphene (final dosage forms) was reclassified in Schedule IV as a narcotic drug under federal drug abuse control laws on 7–24–80. Bulk dextropropoxyphene (non–dosage forms) was placed in Schedule II on the same date.

24 Mazindol was previously placed by the Federal Government into Schedule III effective 6–15–73 and was moved, pursuant to Section 3719.43 of the Ohio Revised Code, to Schedule IV effective 11–27–81.

25 Ephedrine was added by the Ohio Legislature (Sub. H.B. 391) effective 7–21–94. Division (K) of Section 3719.44 of the Revised Code states:

(1) A drug product containing ephedrine that is known as one of the following and is in the form specified shall not be considered a schedule V controlled substance:

(a) Amesec capsules; *(effective 7–21–94)*
(b) Bronitin tablets; *(effective 7–21–94)*
(c) Bronkotabs; *(effective 7–21–94)*
(d) Bronkolixir; *(effective 7–21–94)*
(e) Bronkaid tablets; *(effective 7–21–94)*
(f) Efedron nasal jelly; *(effective 7–21–94)*
(g) Guiaphed elixir; *(effective 7–21–94)*
(h) Haysma; *(effective 7–21–94)*
(i) Pazo hemorrhoid ointment and suppositories; *(effective 7–21–94)*
(j) Primatene "M" formula tablets; *(effective 7–21–94)*
(k) Primatene "P" formula tablets; *(effective 7–21–94)*
(*l*) Tedrigen tablets; *(effective 7–21–94)*
(m) Tedral tablets, suspension, and elixir; *(effective 7–21–94)*
(n) T.E.P.; *(effective 7–21–94)*
(*o*) Vatronol nose drops. *(effective 7–21–94)*

(2)(a) A product containing ephedrine shall not be considered a controlled substance if the product is a food product or dietary supplement that meets all of the following criteria: *(effective 3–31–97)*

(i) It contains, per dosage unit or serving, not more than the lesser of twenty-five milligrams of ephedrine alkaloids or the maximum amount of ephedrine alkaloids provided in applicable regulations adopted by the United States food and drug administration, and no other controlled substance.

(ii) It contains no hydrochloride or sulfate salts of ephedrine alkaloids.

(iii) It is packaged with a prominent label securely affixed to each package that states all of the following: the amount in milligrams of ephedrine in a serving or dosage unit; the amount of the food product or dietary supplement that constitutes a serving or dosage unit; that the maximum recommended dosage of ephedrine for a healthy adult human is the lesser of one hundred milligrams in a twenty-four-hour period for not more than twelve weeks or the maximum recommended dosage or period of use provided in applicable regulations adopted by the United States food and drug administration; and that improper use of the product may be hazardous to a person's health.

(3) A drug product that contains the isomer pseudoephedrine, or any of its salts, optical isomers, or salts of optical isomers, shall not be considered a controlled substance if the drug product is labeled in a manner consistent with federal law or with the product's over the counter tentative final monograph or final monograph issued by the United States food and drug administration. *(effective 3–31–97)*

(4) At the request of any person, the board may except any product containing ephedrine not described in division (K)(1) or (2) of this section or any class of products containing ephedrine from being included as a schedule V controlled substance if it determines that the product or class of products does not contain any other controlled substance. The board shall make the determination in accordance with this section and by rule adopted in accordance with Chapter 119. of the Revised Code. *(effective 7–21–94 and 3–31–97)*

Board exceptions pursuant to Rule 4729–12–09 of the Administrative Code:

(A) All products that contain the isomer known as pseudoephedrine or its salts, but do not also contain any of the isomer known as ephedrine or its salts. (*excepted by emergency rule of the Board effective 8–24–94, and by permanent rule of the Board effective 12–15–94*)

(B) "Breathe Easy®" herb tea. (*exception effective 1–10–96*)
(C) "Bronkaid® Dual Action" caplets. (*exception effective 1–10–96*)
(D) "Hydrosal®" hemorrhoidal ointment. (*exception effective 1–10–96*)
(E) "Primatene® Dual Action Formula" tablets. (*exception effective 1–10–96*)
(F) "Primatene®" tablets. (*exception effective 1–10–96*)
(G) "SnoreStop ®" tablets. (*exception effective 7–1–97*)

Division (L) of Section 3719.44 of the Revised Code states: [effective 3–31–97]

"Food" means: *[Sec. 3715.01 of the Ohio Revised Code]*

(1) articles used for food or drink for humans or animals;
(2) chewing gum;
(3) articles used for components of any such articles.

"Dietary supplement" means: *[21 U.S.C.A. 321(ff)]*

(1) a product (other than tobacco) intended to supplement the diet that bears or contains one or more of the following dietary ingredients: (a) a vitamin; (b) a mineral; (c) an herb or other botanical; (d) an amino acid; (e) a dietary substance for use by man to supplement the diet by increasing the total dietary intake; or (f) a concentrate, metabolite, constituent, extract, or combination of any ingredient described in clause (a), (b), (c), (d), or (e);

(2) a product that (a) is intended for ingestion in a form described in section 350(c)(1)(B)(i) of this title; or complies with section 350(c)(1)(B)(ii) of this title; (b) is not represented for use as a conventional food or as a sole item of a meal or the diet; and (c) is labeled as a dietary supplement; and

(3) does:

(a) include an article that is approved as a new drug under section 355 of this title, certified as an antibiotic under section 357 of this title, or licensed as a biologic under section 262 Title 42, and was, prior to such approval, certification, or license, marketed as a dietary supplement or as a food unless the Secretary has issued a regulation, after notice and comment, finding that the article, when used as or in a dietary supplement under the conditions of use and dosages set forth in the labeling for such dietary supplement, is unlawful under section 342(f) of this title; and

(b) not include an article that is approved as a new drug under section 355 of this title, certified as an antibiotic under section 357 of this title, or licensed as a biologic under section 262 of Title 42, or an article authorized for investigation as a new drug, antibiotic, or biological for which substantial clinical investigations have been instituted and for which the existence of such investigations has been made public, which was not before such approval, certification, licensing, or authorization marketed as a dietary supplment [sic.] or as a food unless the Secretary, in the Secretary's discretion, has issued a regulation, after notice and comment, finding that the article would be lawful under this chapter.

"Ephedrine alkaloids" means: *[Sec. 3719.44(L) of the Ohio Revised Code]*

ephedrine, pseudoephedrine, norephedrine, norpseudoephedrine, methylephedrine, and methylpseudoephedrine.

3719.42 Board to meet regarding controlled substances

The state board of pharmacy shall meet in Columbus at least once each fiscal year for the purpose of carrying out its duties under this chapter.

(1998 S 66, eff. 7–22–98; 1975 H 300, eff. 7–1–76)

3719.43 Changes in federal schedules automatically adopted

When pursuant to the federal drug abuse control laws the attorney general of the United States adds a compound, mixture, preparation, or substance to a schedule of the laws, transfers any of the same between one schedule of the laws to another, or removes a compound, mixture, preparation, or substance from the schedules of the laws then such addition, transfer, or removal is automatically effected in the corresponding schedule or schedules in section 3719.41 of the Revised Code, subject to amendment pursuant to section 3719.44 of the Revised Code.

(1975 H 300, eff. 7–1–76)

Historical and Statutory Notes

Publisher's Note: See Publisher's Note at beginning of 3719.41.

3719.44 Board of pharmacy may change schedules

(A) Pursuant to this section, and by rule adopted in accordance with Chapter 119. of the Revised Code, the state board of pharmacy may do any of the following with respect to schedules I, II, III, IV, and V established in section 3719.41 of the Revised Code:

(1) Add a previously unscheduled compound, mixture, preparation, or substance to any schedule;

(2) Transfer a compound, mixture, preparation, or substance from one schedule to another, provided the transfer does not have the effect under this chapter of providing less stringent control of the compound, mixture, preparation, or substance than is provided under the federal drug abuse control laws;

(3) Remove a compound, mixture, preparation, or substance from the schedules where the board had previously added the compound, mixture, preparation, or substance to the schedules, provided that the removal shall not have the effect under this chapter of providing less stringent control of the compound, mixture, preparation, or substance than is provided under the federal drug abuse control laws.

(B) In making a determination to add, remove, or transfer pursuant to division (A) of this section, the board shall consider the following:

(1) The actual or relative potential for abuse;

(2) The scientific evidence of the pharmacological effect of the substance, if known;

(3) The state of current scientific knowledge regarding the substance;

(4) The history and current pattern of abuse;

(5) The scope, duration, and significance of abuse;

(6) The risk to the public health;

(7) The potential of the substance to produce psychic or physiological dependence liability;

(8) Whether the substance is an immediate precursor.

(C) The board may add or transfer a compound, mixture, preparation, or substance to schedule I when it appears that there is a high potential for abuse, that it has no accepted medical use in treatment in this state, or that it lacks accepted safety for use in treatment under medical supervision.

(D) The board may add or transfer a compound, mixture, preparation, or substance to schedule II when it appears that there is a high potential for abuse, that it has a currently accepted medical use in treatment in this state, or currently accepted medical use in treatment with severe restrictions, and that its abuse may lead to severe physical or severe psychological dependence.

(E) The board may add or transfer a compound, mixture, preparation, or substance to schedule III when it appears that there is a potential for abuse less than the substances included in schedules I and II, that it has a currently accepted medical use in treatment in this state, and that its abuse may lead to moderate or low physical or high psychological dependence.

(F) The board may add or transfer a compound, mixture, preparation, or substance to schedule IV when it appears that it has a low potential for abuse relative to substances included in schedule III, that it has a currently accepted medical use in treatment in this state, and that its abuse may lead to limited physical or psychological dependence relative to the substances included in schedule III.

(G) The board may add or transfer a compound, mixture, preparation, or substance to schedule V when it appears that it has lower potential for abuse than substances included in schedule IV, that it has currently accepted medical use in treatment in this state, and that its abuse may lead to limited physical or psychological dependence relative to substances included in schedule IV.

(H) Even though a compound, mixture, preparation, or substance does not otherwise meet the criteria in this section for adding or transferring it to a schedule, the board may nevertheless add or transfer it to a schedule as an immediate precursor when all of the following apply:

(1) It is the principal compound used, or produced primarily for use, in the manufacture of a controlled substance.

(2) It is an immediate chemical intermediary used or likely to be used in the manufacture of such a controlled substance.

(3) Its control is necessary to prevent, curtail, or limit the manufacture of the scheduled compound, mixture, preparation, or substance of which it is the immediate precursor.

(I) Authority to control under this section does not extend to distilled spirits, wine, or beer, as those terms are defined or used in Chapter 4301. of the Revised Code.

(J) Authority to control under this section does not extend to any nonnarcotic substance if the substance may, under the Federal Food, Drug, and Cosmetic Act and the laws of this state, be lawfully sold over the counter without a prescription. If a pattern of abuse develops for any nonnarcotic drug sold over the counter, the board may, by rule adopted in accordance with Chapter 119. of the Revised Code, after a public hearing and a documented study to determine that the substance actually meets the criteria listed in division (B) of this section, place the abused substance on a controlled substance schedule.

(K)(1) A drug product containing ephedrine that is known as one of the following and is in the form specified shall not be considered a schedule V controlled substance:

(a) Amesec capsules;

(b) Bronitin tablets;

(c) Bronkotabs;

(d) Bronkolixir;

(e) Bronkaid tablets;

(f) Efedron nasal jelly;

(g) Guiaphed elixir;

(h) Haysma;

(i) Pazo hemorrhoid ointment and suppositories;

(j) Primatene "M" formula tablets;

(k) Primatene "P" formula tablets;

(*l*) Tedrigen tablets;

(m) Tedral tablets, suspension and elixir;

(n) T.E.P.;

(*o*) Vatronol nose drops.

(2)(a) A product containing ephedrine shall not be considered a controlled substance if the product is a food product or dietary supplement that meets all of the following criteria:

(i) It contains, per dosage unit or serving, not more than the lesser of twenty-five milligrams of ephedrine alkaloids or the maximum amount of ephedrine alkaloids provided in applicable regulations adopted by the United States food and drug administration, and no other controlled substance.

(ii) It contains no hydrochloride or sulfate salts of ephedrine alkaloids.

(iii) It is packaged with a prominent label securely affixed to each package that states all of the following: the amount in milligrams of ephedrine in a serving or dosage unit; the amount of the food product or dietary supplement that constitutes a serving or dosage unit; that the maximum recommended dosage of ephedrine for a healthy adult human is the lesser of one hundred milligrams in a twenty-four-hour period for not more than twelve weeks or the maximum recommended dosage or period of use provided in applicable regulations adopted by the United States food and drug administration; and that improper use of the product may be hazardous to a person's health.

(b)(i) Subject to division (K)(2)(b)(ii) of this section, no person shall dispense, sell, or otherwise give a product described in division (K)(2)(a) of this section to any individual under eighteen years of age.

(ii) Division (K)(2)(b)(i) of this section does not apply to a physician or pharmacist who dispenses, sells, or otherwise gives a product described in division (K)(2)(a) of this section to an individual under eighteen years of age, to a parent or guardian of an individual under eighteen years of age who dispenses, sells, or otherwise gives a product of that nature to the individual under eighteen years of age, or to a person who, as authorized by the individual's parent or legal guardian, dispenses, sells, or otherwise gives a product of that nature to an individual under eighteen years of age.

(c) No person in the course of selling, offering for sale, or otherwise distributing a product described in division (K)(2)(a) of this section shall advertise or represent in any manner that the product causes euphoria, ecstasy, a "buzz" or "high," or an altered mental state; heightens sexual performance; or, because it contains ephedrine alkaloids, increased muscle mass.

(3) A drug product that contains the isomer pseudoephedrine, or any of its salts, optical isomers, or salts of optical isomers, shall not be considered a controlled substance if the drug product is labeled in a manner consistent with federal law or with the product's over-the-counter tentative final monograph or final monograph issued by the United States food and drug administration.

(4) At the request of any person, the board may except any product containing ephedrine not described in division (K)(1) or (2) of this section or any class of products containing ephedrine from being included as a schedule V controlled substance if it determines that the product or class of products does not contain any other controlled substance. The board shall make the determination in accordance with this section and by rule adopted in accordance with Chapter 119. of the Revised Code.

(L) As used in this section:

(1) "Food" has the same meaning as in section 3715.01 of the Revised Code.

(2) "Dietary supplement" has the same meaning as in the "Federal Food, Drug, and Cosmetic Act," 108 Stat. 4327 (1994), 21 U.S.C.A. 321 (ff), as amended.

(3) "Ephedrine alkaloids" means ephedrine, pseudoephedrine, norephedrine, norpseudoephedrine, methylephedrine, and methylpseudoephedrine.

(2002 H 371, eff. 10–11–02; 1998 S 66, eff. 7–22–98; 1996 H 523, eff. 3–31–97; 1994 H 391, eff. 7–21–94; 1975 H 300, eff. 7–1–76)

Historical and Statutory Notes

Publisher's Note: See Publisher's Note at beginning of 3719.41.

MISCELLANEOUS PROVISIONS

3719.61 Methadone treatment

Nothing in the laws dealing with drugs of abuse shall be construed to prohibit treatment of narcotic drug dependent persons by the continuing maintenance of their dependence through the administration of methadone in accordance with the rules adopted by the department of alcohol and drug addiction services under section 3793.11 of the Revised Code, when all of the following apply:

(A) The likelihood that any person undergoing maintenance treatment will be cured of dependence on narcotic drugs is remote, the treatment is prescribed for the purpose of alleviating or controlling the patient's drug dependence, and the patient's prognosis while undergoing treatment is at least a partial improvement in the patient's asocial or antisocial behavior patterns;

(B) In the case of an inpatient in a hospital or clinic, the amount of the maintenance drug dispensed at any one time does not exceed the quantity necessary for a single dose, and the dose is administered to the patient immediately;

(C) In the case of an outpatient, the amount of the maintenance drug dispensed at any one time shall be determined by the patient's treatment provider taking into account the patient's progress in the treatment program and the patient's needs for gainful employment, education, and responsible homemaking, except that in no event shall the dosage be greater than the amount permitted by federal law and rules adopted by the department pursuant to section 3793.11 of the Revised Code;

(D) The drug is not dispensed in any case to replace or supplement any part of a supply of the drug previously dispensed, or when there is reasonable cause to believe it will be used or disposed of unlawfully;

(E) The drug is dispensed through a program licensed and operated in accordance with section 3793.11 of the Revised Code.

(1998 S 66, eff. 7–22–98; 1994 H 385, eff. 7–19–94; 1989 H 317, eff. 10–10–89; 1980 H 900; 1975 H 300; 1972 H 521, H 494; 1970 H 874)

3719.70 Immunity; cooperation with law enforcement authorities

(A) When testimony, information, or other evidence in the possession of a person who uses, possesses, or trafficks in any drug of abuse appears necessary to an investigation by law enforcement authorities into illicit sources of any drug of abuse, or appears necessary to successfully institute, maintain, or conclude a prosecution for any drug abuse offense, as defined in section 2925.01 of the Revised Code, a judge of the court of common pleas may grant to that person immunity from prosecution for any offense based upon the testimony, information, or other evidence furnished by that person, other than a prosecution of that person for giving false testimony, information, or other evidence.

(B)(1) When a person is convicted of any misdemeanor drug abuse offense, the court, in determining whether to place the person under a community control sanction pursuant to section 2929.25 of the Revised Code, shall take into consideration whether the person truthfully has revealed all information within the person's knowledge concerning illicit traffic in or use of drugs of abuse and, when required, has testified as to that information in any proceeding to obtain a search or arrest warrant against another or to prosecute another for any offense involving a drug of abuse. The information shall include, but is not limited to, the identity and whereabouts of accomplices, accessories, aiders, and abettors, if any, of the person or persons from whom any drug of abuse was obtained or to whom any drug of abuse was distributed, and of persons known or believed to be drug dependent persons, together with the location of any place or places where and the manner in which any drug of abuse is illegally cultivated, manufactured, sold, possessed, or used. The information also shall include all facts and circumstances surrounding any illicit traffic in or use of drugs of abuse of that nature.

(2) If a person otherwise is eligible for intervention in lieu of conviction and being ordered to a period of rehabilitation under section 2951.041 of the Revised Code but the person has failed to cooperate with law enforcement authorities by providing them with the types of information described in division (B)(1) of this section, the person's lack of cooperation may be considered by the court under section 2951.041 of the Revised Code in determining whether to stay all criminal proceedings and order the person to a requested period of intervention.

(C) In the absence of a competent and voluntary waiver of the right against self-incrimination, no information or testimony furnished pursuant to division (B) of this section shall be used in a prosecution of the person furnishing it for any offense other than a prosecution of that person for giving false testimony, information, or other evidence.

(2002 H 490, eff. 1–1–04; 1999 S 107, eff. 3–23–00; 1996 S 269, eff. 7–1–96; 1995 S 2, eff. 7–1–96; 1975 H 300, eff. 7–1–76; 1970 H 874)

3719.81 Illegal use and distribution of drug samples; exceptions

(A) As used in this section, "sample drug" has the same meaning as in section 2925.01 of the Revised Code.

(B) A person may furnish another a sample drug, if all of the following apply:

(1) The sample drug is furnished free of charge by a manufacturer, manufacturer's representative, or wholesale dealer in pharmaceuticals to a licensed health professional authorized to prescribe drugs, or is furnished free of charge by such a professional to a patient for use as medication;

(2) The sample drug is in the original container in which it was placed by the manufacturer, and the container is plainly marked as a sample;

(3) Prior to its being furnished, the sample drug has been stored under the proper conditions to prevent its deterioration or contamination;

(4) If the sample drug is of a type which deteriorates with time, the sample container is plainly marked with the date beyond which the sample drug is unsafe to use, and the date has not expired on the sample furnished. Compliance with the labeling requirements of the "Federal Food, Drug, and Cosmetic Act," 52 Stat. 1040 (1938), 21 U.S.C.A. 301, as amended, shall be deemed compliance with this section.

(5) The sample drug is distributed, stored, or discarded in such a way that the sample drug may not be acquired or used by any unauthorized person, or by any person, including a child, for whom it may present a health or safety hazard.

(C) Division (B) of this section does not do any of the following:

(1) Apply to or restrict the furnishing of any sample of a nonnarcotic substance if the substance may, under the "Federal Food, Drug, and Cosmetic Act" and under the laws of this state, otherwise be lawfully sold over the counter without a prescription;

(2) Authorize a licensed health professional authorized to prescribe drugs who is a clinical nurse specialist, certified nurse-midwife, or certified nurse practitioner to furnish a sample drug that is not a drug the nurse is authorized to prescribe;

(3) Authorize an optometrist to furnish a sample drug that is not a drug the optometrist is authorized to prescribe.

(4) Prohibit a licensed health professional authorized to prescribe drugs, manufacturer of dangerous drugs, wholesale distributor of dangerous drugs, or representative of a manufacturer of dangerous drugs from furnishing a sample drug to a charitable pharmacy in accordance with section 3719.811 of the Revised Code.

(5) Prohibit a pharmacist working, whether or not for compensation, in a charitable pharmacy from dispensing a sample drug to a person in accordance with section 3719.811 of the Revised Code.

(D) The state board of pharmacy shall, in accordance with Chapter 119. of the Revised Code, adopt rules as necessary to give effect to this section.

(2004 H 454, eff. 4–15–05; 2004 S 80, eff. 4–7–05; 2000 H 241, eff. 5–17–00; 1998 S 66, eff. 7–22–98; 1975 H 300, eff. 7–1–76; 1972 H 521)

3719.811. Permissible distribution of drug samples; exceptions

(A) As used in this section:

(1) "Charitable pharmacy" means a pharmacy that meets all of the following requirements:

(a) Holds a terminal distributor of dangerous drugs license under section 4729.54 of the Revised Code.

(b) Is exempt from federal taxation pursuant to 26 U.S.C. 501(a) and (c)(3).

(c) Is not a hospital as defined in section 3727.01 of the Revised Code.

(2) "Prescription" has the same meaning as in section 4729.01 of the Revised Code.

(3) "Sample drug" has the same meaning as in section 2925.01 of the Revised Code.

(B) A manufacturer of dangerous drugs or wholesale distributor of dangerous drugs may furnish a sample drug to a charitable pharmacy if all of the following apply:

(1) The sample drug is in the original container in which it was placed by its manufacturer and the container is plainly marked as a sample.

(2) Prior to its being furnished, the sample drug has been stored under the proper conditions to prevent its deterioration or contamination.

(3) If the sample drug is of a type that deteriorates with time, the container in which the sample drug is stored is plainly marked with the date beyond which the sample drug is unsafe to use, and the date has not expired on the sample drug furnished. Compliance with the labeling requirements of the "Federal Food, Drug, and Cosmetic Act," 52 Stat. 1040 (1938), 21 U.S.C. 301, as amended, constitutes compliance with division (B) (3) of this section.

(4) The sample drug is distributed, stored, or discarded in such a way that the sample drug may not be acquired or used by any unauthorized person, or by any person, including a child, for whom it may present a health or safety hazard.

(5) The sample drug is furnished free of charge.

(6) The sample drug is not a controlled substance.

(C) A representative of a manufacturer of dangerous drugs or a licensed health professional authorized to prescribe drugs may furnish a sample drug to a charitable pharmacy if all of the following apply:

(1) The state board of pharmacy has adopted rules under division (F) of this section to permit such a representative or health professional to furnish a sample drug to a charitable pharmacy.

(2) The representative or health professional complies with standards and procedures established in rules adopted under division (F) of this section.

(3) The requirements in divisions (B)(1) to (6) of this section are satisfied.

(D) A pharmacist working, whether or not for compensation, in a charitable pharmacy may dispense a sample drug to a person if all of the following apply:

(1) The person to whom the sample drug is dispensed is eligible for the sample drug under standards established by the body responsible for the charitable pharmacy's general management.

(2) The person to whom the sample is dispensed presents to the pharmacist a valid prescription for the sample drug.

(3) The sample drug is dispensed free of charge.

(4) The requirements in divisions (B)(1) to (4) and (6) of this section are satisfied.

(E) Divisions (B), (C), and (D) of this section do not do either of the following:

(1) Apply to or restrict the furnishing of any sample of a nonnarcotic substance if the substance may, under the "Federal Food, Drug, and Cosmetic Act" and under the law of this state, otherwise be lawfully sold over the counter without a prescription.

(2) Authorize a pharmacist working, whether or not for compensation, in a charitable pharmacy to dispense a sample drug that the charitable pharmacy is unauthorized to possess, have custody or control of, or distribute.

(F) The state board of pharmacy shall, in accordance with Chapter 119. of the Revised Code, adopt rules as necessary to give effect to this section. The rules may permit representatives of manufacturers of dangerous drugs or licensed health professionals authorized to prescribe drugs to furnish sample drugs to charitable pharmacies under this section. If they do so, the rules shall establish standards and procedures for the representatives or health professionals to furnish the sample drugs.

(2004 H 454, eff. 4–15–05)

3719.812. Immunity relating to drug sample transactions

The state board of pharmacy; any person that donates a sample drug as permitted under section 3719.811 of the Revised Code; any charitable pharmacy or pharmacist working in a charitable pharmacy that accepts or dispenses sample drugs as permitted under section 3719.811 of the Revised Code; and any licensed health professional authorized to prescribe drugs who accepts delivery of a sample drug on behalf of a charitable pharmacy as permitted under section 3719.811 of the Revised Code shall not, in the absence of bad faith, be subject to any of the following for matters related to donating, accepting, or dispensing sample drugs under section 3719.811 of the Revised Code: criminal prosecution; liability in tort or other civil action for injury, death, or loss to person or property; or professional disciplinary action.

(2004 H 454, eff. 4–15–05)

3719.813 Immunity of drug manufacturer

A drug manufacturer shall not, in the absence of bad faith, be subject to criminal prosecution or liability in tort or other civil action for injury, death, or loss to person or property for matters related to the donation, acceptance, or dispensing of a drug manufactured by the drug manufacturer that is donated by any person as permitted under section 3719.811 of the Revised Code, including but not limited to liability for failure to transfer or communicate product or consumer information or the expiration date of the donated drug.

(2004 H 454, eff. 4–15–05)

PENALTIES

3719.99 Penalties

(A) Whoever violates section 3719.16 or 3719.161 of the Revised Code is guilty of a felony of the fifth degree. If the offender previously has been convicted of a violation of section 3719.16 or 3719.161 of the Revised Code or a drug abuse offense, a violation of section 3719.16 or 3719.161 of the Revised Code is a felony of the fourth degree. If the violation involves the sale, offer to sell, or possession of a schedule I or II controlled substance, with the exception of marihuana, and if the offender, as a result of the violation, is a major drug offender, division (D) of this section applies.

(B) Whoever violates division (C) or (D) of section 3719.172 of the Revised Code is guilty of a felony of the fifth degree. If the offender previously has been convicted of a violation of division (C) or (D) of section 3719.172 of the Revised Code or a drug abuse offense, a violation of division (C) or (D) of section 3719.172 of the Revised Code is a felony of the fourth degree. If the violation involves the sale, offer to sell, or possession of a schedule I or II controlled substance, with the exception of marihuana, and if the offender, as a result of the violation, is a major drug offender, division (D) of this section applies.

(C) Whoever violates section 3719.07 or 3719.08 of the Revised Code is guilty of a misdemeanor of the first degree. If the offender previously has been convicted of a violation of section 3719.07 or 3719.08 of the Revised Code or a drug abuse offense, a violation of section 3719.07 or 3719.08 of the Revised Code is a felony of the fifth degree. If the violation involves the sale, offer to sell, or possession of a schedule I or II controlled substance, with the exception of marihuana, and if the offender, as a result of the violation, is a major drug offender, division (D) of this section applies.

(D)(1) If an offender is convicted of or pleads guilty to a felony violation of section 3719.07, 3719.08, 3719.16, or 3719.161 or of division (C) or (D) of section 3719.172 of the Revised Code, if the violation involves the sale, offer to sell, or possession of a schedule I or II controlled substance, with the exception of marihuana, and if the court imposing sentence upon the offender finds that the offender as a result of the violation is a major drug offender and is guilty of a specification of the type described in section 2941.1410 of the Revised Code, the court, in lieu of the prison term authorized or required by division (A), (B), or (C) of this section and sections 2929.13 and 2929.14 of the Revised Code and in addition to any other sanction imposed for the offense under sections 2929.11 to 2929.18 of the Revised Code, shall impose upon the offender, in accordance with division (D)(3)(a) of section 2929.14 of the Revised Code, the mandatory prison term specified in that division and may impose an additional prison term under division (D)(3)(b) of that section.

(2) Notwithstanding any contrary provision of section 3719.21 of the Revised Code, the clerk of the court shall pay any fine imposed for a felony violation of section 3719.07, 3719.08, 3719.16, or 3719.161 or of division (C) or (D) of section 3719.172 of the Revised Code pursuant to division (A) of section 2929.18 of the Revised Code in accordance with and subject to the requirements of division (F) of section 2925.03 of the Revised Code. The agency that receives the fine shall use the fine as specified in division (F) of section 2925.03 of the Revised Code.

(E) Whoever violates section 3719.05, 3719.06, 3719.13, or 3719.31 or division (B) of section 3719.172 of the Revised Code is guilty of a misdemeanor of the third degree. If the offender previously has been convicted of a violation of section 3719.05, 3719.06, 3719.13, or 3719.31 or division (B) of section 3719.172 of the Revised Code or a drug abuse offense, a violation of section 3719.05, 3719.06, 3719.13, or 3719.31 or division (B) of section 3719.172 of the Revised Code is a misdemeanor of the first degree.

(F) Whoever violates section 3719.30 of the Revised Code is guilty of a misdemeanor of the fourth degree. If the offender previously has been convicted of a violation of section 3719.30 of the Revised Code or a drug abuse offense, a violation of section 3719.30 of the Revised Code is a misdemeanor of the third degree.

(G) Whoever violates section 3719.32 or 3719.33 of the Revised Code is guilty of a minor misdemeanor.

(H) Whoever violates division (K)(2)(b) of section 3719.44 of the Revised Code is guilty of a felony of the fifth degree.

(I) Whoever violates division (K)(2)(c) of section 3719.44 of the Revised Code is guilty of a misdemeanor of the second degree.

(J) As used in this section, "major drug offender" has the same meaning as in section 2929.01 of the Revised Code.

(1999 S 107, eff. 3–23–00; 1998 S 66, eff. 7–22–98; 1996 H 523, eff. 3–31–97; 1996 S 269, eff. 7–1–96; 1995 S 2, eff. 7–1–96; 1975 H 300, eff. 7–1–76)

CHAPTER 3737

FIRE MARSHAL; FIRE SAFETY; PETROLEUM UNDERGROUND STORAGE

POWERS, DUTIES, AND APPOINTMENT OF FIRE MARSHAL

3737.22 Duties of fire marshal; bureaus

Note: See also following version of this section, eff.5–18–05.

(A) The fire marshal shall do all of the following:

(1) Adopt the state fire code under sections 3737.82 to 3737.86 of the Revised Code;

(2) Enforce the state fire code;

(3) Appoint assistant fire marshals who are authorized to enforce the state fire code;

(4) Conduct investigations into the cause, origin, and circumstances of fires and explosions, and assist in the prosecution of persons believed to be guilty of arson or a similar crime;

(5) Compile statistics concerning loss due to fire and explosion as the fire marshal considers necessary, and consider the compatibility of the fire marshal's system of compilation with the systems of other state and federal agencies and fire marshals of other states;

(6) Engage in research on the cause and prevention of losses due to fire and explosion;

(7) Engage in public education and informational activities which will inform the public of fire safety information;

(8) Operate a fire training academy and forensic laboratory;

(9) Conduct other fire safety and fire fighting training activities for the public and groups as will further the cause of fire safety;

(10) Conduct licensing examinations, and issue permits, licenses, and certificates, as authorized by the Revised Code;

(11) Conduct tests of fire protection systems and devices, and firefighting equipment to determine compliance with the state fire code, unless a building is insured against the hazard of fire, in which case such tests may be performed by the company insuring the building;

(12) Establish and collect fees for conducting licensing examinations and for issuing permits, licenses, and certificates;

(13) Make available for the prosecuting attorney and an assistant prosecuting attorney from each county of this state, in accordance with section 3737.331 of the Revised Code, a seminar program, attendance at which is optional, that is designed to provide current information, data, training, and techniques relative to the prosecution of arson cases;

(14) Administer and enforce Chapter 3743. of the Revised Code;

(15) Develop a uniform standard for the reporting of information required to be filed under division (E)(4) of section 2921.22 of the Revised Code, and accept the reports of the information when they are filed.

(B) The fire marshal shall appoint a chief deputy fire marshal, and shall employ professional and clerical assistants as the fire marshal considers necessary. The chief deputy shall be a competent former or current member of a fire agency and possess five years of recent, progressively more responsible experience in fire inspection, fire code enforcement, and fire code management. The chief deputy, with the approval of the director of commerce, shall temporarily assume the duties of the fire marshal when the fire marshal is absent or temporarily unable to carry out the duties of the office. When there is a vacancy in the office of fire marshal, the chief deputy, with the approval of the director of commerce, shall temporarily assume the duties of the fire marshal until a new fire marshal is appointed under section 3737.21 of the Revised Code.

All employees, other than the fire marshal; the chief deputy fire marshal; the superintendent of the Ohio fire academy; the grants administrator; the fiscal officer; the executive secretary to the fire marshal; legal counsel; the pyrotechnics administrator, the chief of the forensic laboratory; the person appointed by the fire marshal to serve as administrator over functions concerning testing, license examinations, and the issuance of permits and certificates; and the chiefs of the bureaus of fire prevention, of fire and explosion investigation, of code enforcement, and of underground storage tanks shall be in the classified civil service. The fire marshal shall authorize the chief deputy and other employees under the fire marshal's supervision to exercise powers granted to the fire marshal by law as may be necessary to carry out the duties of the fire marshal's office.

(C) The fire marshal shall create, in and as a part of the office of fire marshal, a fire and explosion investigation bureau consisting of a chief of the bureau and additional assistant fire marshals as the fire marshal determines necessary for the efficient administration of the bureau. The chief shall be experienced in the investigation of the cause, origin, and circumstances of fires, and in administration, including the supervision of subordinates. The chief, among other duties delegated to the chief by the fire marshal, shall be responsible, under the direction of the fire marshal, for the investigation of the cause, origin, and circumstances of fires and explosions in the state, and for assistance in the prosecution of persons believed to be guilty of arson or a similar crime.

(D)(1) The fire marshal shall create, as part of the office of fire marshal, a bureau of code enforcement consisting of a chief of the bureau and additional assistant fire marshals as the fire marshal determines necessary for the efficient administration of the bureau. The chief shall be qualified, by education or experience, in fire inspection, fire code development, fire code enforcement, or any other similar field determined by the fire marshal, and in administration, including the supervision of subordinates. The chief is responsible, under the direction of the fire marshal, for fire inspection, fire code development, fire code enforcement, and any other duties delegated to the chief by the fire marshal.

(2) The fire marshal, the chief deputy fire marshal, the chief of the bureau of code enforcement, or any assistant fire marshal under the direction of the fire marshal, the chief deputy fire marshal, or the chief of the bureau of code enforcement may cause to be conducted the inspection of all buildings, structures, and other places, the condition of which may be dangerous from a fire safety standpoint to life or property, or to property adjacent to the buildings, structures, or other places.

(E) The fire marshal shall create, as a part of the office of fire marshal, a bureau of fire prevention consisting of a chief of the bureau and additional assistant fire marshals as the fire marshal determines necessary for the efficient administration of the bureau. The chief shall be qualified, by education or experience, to promote programs for rural and urban fire prevention and protection. The chief, among other duties delegated to the chief by the fire marshal, is responsible, under the direction of the fire marshal, for the promotion of rural and urban fire prevention and protection through public information and education programs.

(F) The fire marshal shall cooperate with the director of job and family services when the director adopts rules under section 5104.052 of the Revised Code regarding fire prevention and fire safety in certified type B family day-care homes, as defined in section 5104.01 of the Revised Code, recommend procedures for inspecting type B homes to determine whether they are in compliance with those rules, and provide training and technical assistance to the director and county directors of job and family services on the procedures for determining compliance with those rules.

(G) The fire marshal, upon request of a provider of child day-care in a type B home that is not certified by the county director of job and family services, as a precondition of approval by the state board of education under section 3313.813 of the Revised Code for receipt of United States department of agriculture child and adult care food program funds established under the "National School Lunch Act," 60 Stat. 230 (1946), 42 U.S.C. 1751, as amended, shall inspect the type B home to determine compliance with rules adopted under section 5104.052 of the Revised Code regarding fire prevention and fire safety in certified type B homes. In municipal corporations and in townships where there is a certified firesafety inspector, the inspections shall be made by that inspector under the supervision of the fire marshal, according to rules adopted under section 5104.052 of the Revised Code. In townships outside municipal corporations where there is no certified fire safety inspector, inspections shall be made by the fire marshal.

(2002 S 115, eff. 3–19–03; 1999 H 471, eff. 7–1–00; 1998 H 570, eff. 3–2–98; 1996 S 293, eff. 9–26–96 (See also Historical and Statutory Notes.); 1995 S 162, eff. 10–29–95; 1987 H 273, eff. 9–10–87; 1986 H 428, H 552, S 61; 1985 H 435; 1984 S 4; 1978 H 590)

Note: See also following version of this section, eff.5–18–05.

3737.22 Duties of fire marshal; bureaus (later effective date)

Note: See also preceding version of this section, in effect until 5–18–05.

(A) The fire marshal shall do all of the following:

(1) Adopt the state fire code under sections 3737.82 to 3737.86 of the Revised Code;

(2) Enforce the state fire code;

(3) Appoint assistant fire marshals who are authorized to enforce the state fire code;

(4) Conduct investigations into the cause, origin, and circumstances of fires and explosions, and assist in the prosecution of persons believed to be guilty of arson or a similar crime;

(5) Compile statistics concerning loss due to fire and explosion as the fire marshal considers necessary, and consider the compatibility of the fire marshal's system of compilation with the systems of other state and federal agencies and fire marshals of other states;

(6) Engage in research on the cause and prevention of losses due to fire and explosion;

(7) Engage in public education and informational activities which will inform the public of fire safety information;

(8) Operate a fire training academy and forensic laboratory;

(9) Conduct other fire safety and fire fighting training activities for the public and groups as will further the cause of fire safety;

(10) Conduct licensing examinations, and issue permits, licenses, and certificates, as authorized by the Revised Code;

(11) Conduct tests of fire protection systems and devices, and fire fighting equipment to determine compliance with the state fire code, unless a building is insured against the hazard of fire, in which case such tests may be performed by the company insuring the building;

(12) Establish and collect fees for conducting licensing examinations and for issuing permits, licenses, and certificates;

(13) Make available for the prosecuting attorney and an assistant prosecuting attorney from each county of this state, in accordance with section 3737.331 of the Revised Code, a seminar program, attendance at which is optional, that is designed to provide current information, data, training, and techniques relative to the prosecution of arson cases;

(14) Administer and enforce Chapter 3743. of the Revised Code;

(15) Develop a uniform standard for the reporting of information required to be filed under division (E)(4) of section 2921.22 of the Revised Code, and accept the reports of the information when they are filed.

(B) The fire marshal shall appoint a chief deputy fire marshal, and shall employ professional and clerical assistants as the fire marshal considers necessary. The chief deputy shall be a competent former or current member of a fire agency and possess five years of recent, progressively more responsible experience in fire inspection, fire code enforcement, and fire code management. The chief deputy, with the approval of the director of commerce, shall temporarily assume the duties of the fire marshal when the fire marshal is absent or temporarily unable to carry out the duties of the office. When there is a vacancy in the office of fire marshal, the chief deputy, with the approval of the director of commerce, shall temporarily assume the duties of the fire marshal until a new fire marshal is appointed under section 3737.21 of the Revised Code.

All employees, other than the fire marshal; the chief deputy fire marshal; the superintendent of the Ohio fire academy; the grants administrator; the fiscal officer; the executive secretary to the fire marshal; legal counsel; the pyrotechnics administrator, the chief of the forensic laboratory; the person appointed by the fire marshal to serve as administrator over functions concerning testing, license examinations, and the issuance of permits and certificates; and the chiefs of the bureaus of fire prevention, of fire and explosion investigation, of code enforcement, and of underground storage tanks shall be in the classified civil service. The fire marshal shall authorize the chief deputy and other employees under the fire marshal's supervision to exercise powers granted to the fire marshal by law as may be necessary to carry out the duties of the fire marshal's office.

(C) The fire marshal shall create, in and as a part of the office of fire marshal, a fire and explosion investigation bureau consisting of a chief of the bureau and additional assistant fire marshals as the fire marshal determines necessary for the efficient administration of the bureau. The chief shall be experienced in the investigation of the cause, origin, and circumstances of fires, and in administration, including the supervision of subordinates. The chief, among other duties delegated to the chief by the fire marshal, shall be responsible, under the direction of the fire marshal, for the investigation of the cause, origin, and circumstances of fires and explosions in the state, and for assistance in the prosecution of persons believed to be guilty of arson or a similar crime.

(D)(1) The fire marshal shall create, as part of the office of fire marshal, a bureau of code enforcement consisting of a chief of the bureau and additional assistant fire marshals as the fire marshal determines necessary for the efficient administration of the bureau. The chief shall be qualified, by education or experience, in fire inspection, fire code development, fire code enforcement, or any other similar field determined by the fire marshal, and in administration, including the supervision of subordinates. The chief is responsible, under the direction of the fire marshal, for fire inspection, fire code development, fire code enforcement, and any other duties delegated to the chief by the fire marshal.

(2) The fire marshal, the chief deputy fire marshal, the chief of the bureau of code enforcement, or any assistant fire marshal under the direction of the fire marshal, the chief deputy fire marshal, or the chief of the bureau of code enforcement may cause to be conducted the inspection of all buildings, structures, and other places, the condition of which may be dangerous from a fire safety standpoint to life or property, or to property adjacent to the buildings, structures, or other places.

(E) The fire marshal shall create, as a part of the office of fire marshal, a bureau of fire prevention consisting of a chief of the bureau and additional assistant fire marshals as the fire marshal determines necessary for the efficient administration of the bureau. The chief shall be qualified, by education or experience, to promote programs for rural and urban fire prevention and protection. The chief, among other duties delegated to the chief by the fire marshal, is responsible, under the direction of the fire marshal, for the promotion of rural and urban fire prevention and protection through public information and education programs.

(F) The fire marshal shall cooperate with the director of job and family services when the director adopts rules under section 5104.052 of the Revised Code regarding fire prevention and fire safety in certified type B family day-care homes, as defined in section 5104.01 of the Revised Code, recommend procedures for inspecting type B homes to determine whether they are in compliance with those rules, and provide training and technical assistance to the director and county directors of job and family services on the procedures for determining compliance with those rules.

(G) The fire marshal, upon request of a provider of child care in a type B home that is not certified by the county director of job and family services, as a precondition of approval by the state board of education under section 3313.813 of the Revised Code for receipt of United States department of agriculture child and adult care food program funds established under the "National School Lunch Act," 60 Stat. 230 (1946), 42 U.S.C. 1751, as amended, shall inspect the type B home to determine compliance with rules adopted under section 5104.052 of the Revised Code regarding fire prevention and fire safety in certified type B homes. In municipal corporations and in townships where there is a certified fire safety inspector, the inspections shall be made by that inspector under the supervision of the fire marshal, according to rules adopted under section 5104.052 of the Revised Code. In townships outside municipal corporations where there is no certified fire safety inspector, inspections shall be made by the fire marshal.

(2004 H 11, eff. 5–18–05; 2002 S 115, eff. 3–19–03; 1999 H 471, eff. 7–1–00; 1998 H 570, eff. 3–2–98; 1996 S 293, eff. 9–26–96 (See also Historical and Statutory Notes.); 1995 S 162, eff. 10–29–95; 1987 H 273, eff. 9–10–87; 1986 H 428, H 552, S 61; 1985 H 435; 1984 S 4; 1978 H 590)

Note: See also preceding version of this section, in effect until 5–18–05.

Historical and Statutory Notes

Ed. Note: 1996 S 293 Effective Date—The Secretary of State assigned a general effective date of 9–26–96 for 1996 S 293, along with notice that, in accordance with RC 1.471, the General Assembly has not determined which sections go into immediate effect, and that it appears that certain sections provide for appropriations for current expenses, and are immediately effective in accordance with RC 1.471 and O Const Art II, § 1d.

3737.221 Liability and immunity of fire marshal

(A) As used in this section, "motor vehicle" has the same meaning as in section 4511.01 of the Revised Code.

(B) The office of the fire marshal is liable for injury, death, or loss to person or property caused by the negligent operation of any motor vehicle by its employees upon the public roads, highways, or streets in the state when the employees are engaged within the scope of their employment and authority, without regard to the proximity of that operation to the office of the fire marshal. Notwithstanding division (A)(1) of section 2743.02 of the Revised Code, a full defense to that liability is that if the fire marshal, the chief deputy fire marshal, or an assistant fire marshal was operating the motor vehicle, the fire marshal, chief deputy fire marshal, or assistant fire marshal was acting within the scope of division (A)(2), (4), or (14) of section 3737.22, or section 3737.24 or 3737.26, of the Revised Code and the operation of the vehicle did not constitute willful or wanton misconduct.

(C) The fire marshal, the chief deputy fire marshal, and any assistant fire marshal is immune from liability for injury, death, or loss to person or property caused by the operation of any motor vehicle upon the public roads, highways, or streets in the state when acting within the scope of division (A)(2), (4), or (14) of section 3737.22, or section 3737.24 or 3737.26, of the Revised Code, without regard to the proximity of that operation to the office of the fire marshal, unless one of the following applies:

(1) The operation of the vehicle was manifestly outside the scope of the employee's employment or official responsibilities.

(2) The operation of the vehicle constituted willful or wanton misconduct.

(2002 S 115, eff. 3–19–03)

3737.23 Records

The fire marshal shall keep in his office a record of all fires occurring in the state, the origin of such fires, and all facts, statistics, and circumstances relating thereto which have been determined by investigations. Except for the testimony given upon an investigation, such record shall be a public record and such portions thereof, as the superintendent of insurance considers necessary, shall be transcribed and forwarded to the superintendent within fifteen days from the first day of January each year.

(1978 H 590, eff. 7–1–79)

3737.24 Investigation of major fires

The fire marshal and the chief of the fire department of each municipal corporation in which a fire department is established, the chief of the fire department in each township in which a fire department is established, the chief of the fire department of a joint fire district, or the fire prevention officer in each township or village where no fire department is established, shall investigate the cause, origin, and circumstances of each major fire, as determined by the rules of the fire marshal, occurring in such municipal corporation, joint fire district, or township by which property has been destroyed or damaged, and shall make an investigation to determine whether the fire was the result of carelessness or design. The investigation shall be commenced within two days, not including Sunday, if the fire occurred on that day. The marshal may superintend the investigation.

An officer making an investigation of a fire occurring in a municipal corporation, joint fire district, or township shall forthwith notify the marshal, and within one week of the occurrence of the fire shall furnish him a written statement of all facts relating to its cause and origin and such other information as is required by forms provided by the marshal.

In the performance of the duties imposed by Chapter 3737. of the Revised Code, the marshal and each of his subordinates, and any other officers mentioned in this section, at any time of day or night, may enter upon and examine any building or premises where a fire has occurred, and other buildings and premises adjoining or near thereto.

(1986 H 552, eff. 9–17–86; 1978 H 590)

3737.25 Taking testimony

If in the opinion of the fire marshal further investigation is necessary, he, or an assistant fire marshal, shall take or cause to be taken the testimony on oath of all persons supposed to be cognizant of any facts, or to have means of knowledge in relation to the matter concerning which an examination is required to be made, and cause such testimony to be reduced to writing.

(1978 H 590, eff. 7–1–79)

3737.26 Prosecutions

If the fire marshal or an assistant fire marshal determines that there is evidence sufficient to charge a person with arson or a similar crime, or with a violation of section 3737.62 of the Revised Code, the marshal or assistant marshal may arrest the person or cause the person to be arrested and charged with the offense. The fire marshal or assistant fire marshal shall provide the prosecuting attorney the evidence, the names of witnesses, and a copy of material testimony taken in the case.

(2002 S 115, eff. 3–19–03; 1978 H 590, eff. 7–1–79)

3737.27 Witnesses

The fire marshal or an assistant fire marshal may summon and compel the attendance of witnesses to testify in relation to any matter that is a proper subject of inquiry or investigation, and may require the production of any book, paper, document, or record, regardless of physical form or characteristic.

(2002 S 115, eff. 3–19–03; 1978 H 590, eff. 7–1–79)

3737.28 Oaths; duty to testify

The fire marshal or an assistant fire marshal may administer an oath to any person appearing as a witness before the fire marshal or assistant fire marshal. No witness shall refuse to be sworn, refuse to testify, disobey an order of the fire marshal or an assistant fire marshal, or fail or refuse to produce a book, paper, document, or record, regardless of physical form or characteristic, concerning a matter under examination, or be guilty of contemptuous conduct after being summoned by the fire marshal or an assistant fire marshal to appear before the fire marshal or assistant fire marshal to give testimony in relation to a matter or subject under investigation.

(2002 S 115, eff. 3–19–03; 1978 H 590, eff. 7–1–79)

3737.29 Private investigations

Investigation by or under the direction of the fire marshal may be private. The marshal may exclude from the place where such investigation is held all persons other than those required to be present, and witnesses may be kept separate from each other and not allowed to communicate with each other until they have been examined.

(1978 H 590, eff. 7–1–79)

3737.31 Superintendent of insurance may require reports

When required by the superintendent of insurance, the fire marshal shall report his proceedings, the progress made in all prosecutions for arson and similar crimes, and the result of all cases finally disposed of.

(1978 H 590, eff. 7–1–79)

3737.32 Investigation of bombing

The fire marshal shall, upon the request of any sheriff or mayor, investigate any bombing and shall work with local law enforcement officials in the apprehension of any person participating in any bombing.

(1978 H 590, eff. 7–1–79)

PROHIBITIONS

3737.51 Prohibitions; civil penalties

(A) No person shall knowingly violate any provision of the state fire code or any order made pursuant to it.

(B) Any person who has received a citation for a serious violation of the fire code or any order issued pursuant to it, shall be assessed a civil penalty of not more than one thousand dollars for each such violation.

(C) Any person who has received a citation for a violation of the fire code or any order issued pursuant to it, and such violation is specifically determined not to be of a serious nature, may be assessed a civil penalty of not more than one thousand dollars for each such violation.

(D) Any person who fails to correct a violation for which a citation has been issued within the period permitted for its correction, may be assessed a civil penalty of not more than one thousand dollars for each day during which such failure or violation continues.

(E) Any person who violates any of the posting requirements, as prescribed by division (C) of section 3737.42 of the Revised Code, shall be assessed a civil penalty of not more than one thousand dollars for each violation.

(F) Due consideration to the appropriateness of the penalty with respect to the gravity of the violation, the good faith of the person being charged, and the history of previous violations shall be given whenever a penalty is assessed under this chapter.

(G) For purposes of this section, a serious violation shall be considered to exist if there is a substantial probability that an occurrence causing death or serious physical harm to persons could result from a condition which exists or from one or more practices, means, methods, operations, or processes which have been adopted or are in use, unless the person did not and could not with the exercise of reasonable diligence, know of the presence of the violation.

(H) Civil penalties imposed by this chapter shall be paid to the fire marshal for deposit into the general revenue fund. Such penalties may be recovered in a civil action in the name of the state brought in the court of common pleas of the county where the violation is alleged to have occurred.

(1978 H 590, eff. 7–1–79)

3737.61 Posting notices in transient residential buildings

The owner, operator, or lessee of any transient residential building shall post the provisions of sections 2909.02 and 2909.03 of the Revised Code in a conspicuous place in each room occupied by guests in such building. The owner, operator, or lessee of any nontransient residential building, institution, school, or place of assembly shall post the provisions of such sections in conspicuous places upon such premises. No person shall fail to comply with this section.

(1978 H 590, eff. 7–1–79)

3737.62 Negligent burning

No person shall set, kindle, or cause to be set or kindled any fire, which through his negligence, spreads beyond its immediate confines to any structure, field, or wood lot.

(1978 H 590, eff. 7–1–79)

3737.63 Spreading alarm of unfriendly fire

(A) The owner, operator, or lessee, an employee of any owner, operator, or lessee, an occupant, and any person in direct control of any building regulated under the Ohio building code, upon the discovery of an unfriendly fire, or upon receiving information that there is an unfriendly fire on the premises, shall immediately, and with all reasonable dispatch and diligence, call or otherwise notify the fire department concerning the fire, and shall spread an alarm immediately to all occupants of the building.

(B) For the purposes of this section, "unfriendly fire" means a fire of a destructive nature as distinguished from a controlled fire intended for a beneficial purpose.

(C) No person shall fail to comply with this section.

(1978 H 590, eff. 7–1–79)

3737.64 Impersonating fire safety inspector

No person who is not a certified fire safety inspector shall act as such or hold himself out to be such, unless prior to commencing any inspection function, he discloses the purpose for which he is making such inspection and the fact that he is not employed by any state or local fire service or agency, and that he is not acting in an official capacity for any governmental subdivision or agency.

(1978 H 590, eff. 7–1–79)

3737.65 Standards for equipment; certificate and provisional certificate

(A) No person shall sell, offer for sale, or use any fire protection or fire fighting equipment that does not meet the minimum standards established by the fire marshal in the state fire code.

(B) Except for public and private mobile fire trucks, no person shall service, test, repair, or install for profit any fire protection or fire fighting equipment without a certificate or a provisional certificate issued by the fire marshal.

(C) The fire marshal shall not issue a provisional certificate pursuant to division (B) of this section to any individual who is not enrolled in a bona fide apprenticeship training program registered with the apprenticeship council pursuant to section 4139.05 of the Revised Code or with the bureau of apprenticeship and training of the United States department of labor. A provisional certificate issued pursuant to this section authorizes an individual to engage in the activities permitted under division (B) of this section only if the individual:

(1) Remains enrolled in such an apprenticeship training program; and

(2) Is directly supervised by an individual who possesses a valid and current certificate issued pursuant to division (B) of this section for the activities in which the individual issued the provisional certificate is engaged and the certified individual directly supervising the individual issued the provisional certificate only supervises one provisional certificate holder.

(1999 H 471, eff. 7–1–00; 1995 S 162, eff. 10–29–95; 1990 H 677, eff. 11–7–90; 1978 H 590)

MISCELLANEOUS PROVISIONS

3737.73 Safety measures in schools and other institutions housing children; precautions in case of tornado

(A) No principal or person in charge of a public or private school or educational institution having an average daily attendance of fifty or more pupils, and no person in charge of any children's home or orphanage housing twenty or more minor persons, shall willfully neglect to instruct and train such children by means of drills or rapid dismissals at least once a month while such school, institution, or children's home is in operation, so that such children in a sudden emergency may leave the building in the shortest possible time without confusion. In the case of schools, no such person shall willfully neglect to keep the doors and exits of such building unlocked during school hours. The fire marshal may order the immediate installation of necessary fire gongs or signals in such schools, institutions, or children's homes and enforce this section.

(B) In conjunction with the drills or rapid dismissals required by division (A) of this section, principals or persons in charge of public or private primary and secondary schools, or educational institutions, shall instruct pupils in safety precautions to be taken in case of a tornado alert or warning. Such principals or persons in charge of such schools or institutions shall designate, in accordance with standards prescribed by the fire marshal, appropriate locations to be used to shelter pupils in case of a tornado, tornado alert, or warning.

(C) The fire marshal or his designee shall annually inspect each school or institution subject to division (B) of this section to ascertain whether the locations comply with the prescribed standards. Nothing in this section shall require a school or institution to construct or improve a facility or location for use as a shelter area.

(D) The fire marshal or his designee shall issue a warning to any person found in violation of division (A) or (B) of this section. The warning shall indicate the specific violation and a date by which such violation shall be corrected. No person shall fail to correct violations by the date indicated on a warning issued under this division.

(1979 S 18, eff. 8–7–79; 1978 H 590)

PENALTIES

3737.99 Penalties

(A) Whoever violates section 3737.28 of the Revised Code may be summarily punished, by the officer concerned, by a fine of not more than one hundred dollars or commitment to the county jail until that person is willing to comply with the order of such officer.

(B) Except as a violation of section 2923.17 of the Revised Code involves subject matter covered by the state fire code and except as such a violation is covered by division (G) of this section, whoever violates division (A) of section 3737.51 of the Revised Code is guilty of a misdemeanor of the first degree.

(C) Whoever violates section 3737.61 of the Revised Code is guilty of a minor misdemeanor.

(D) Whoever violates section 3737.62 or 3737.64 of the Revised Code is guilty of a misdemeanor of the fourth degree.

(E) Whoever violates section 3737.63 or division (A) or (B) of section 3737.65 of the Revised Code is guilty of a misdemeanor of the third degree.

(F) Whoever violates division (D) of section 3737.73 of the Revised Code shall be fined not less than five nor more than twenty dollars.

(G) Whoever violates section 3737.66 of the Revised Code is guilty of a misdemeanor of the first degree.

(H) Whoever knowingly violates division (C) of section 3737.882 of the Revised Code is guilty of an unclassified felony and shall be fined not more than twenty-five thousand dollars or imprisoned for not more than fourteen months, or both. Whoever recklessly violates division (C) of section 3737.882 of the Revised Code is guilty of a misdemeanor of the first degree.

(I) Whoever knowingly violates division (F)(1), (2), or (3) of section 3737.881 or section 3737.93 of the Revised Code is guilty of a misdemeanor of the fourth degree.

(J) Whoever knowingly violates division (B) or (C) of section 3737.91 of the Revised Code is guilty of a misdemeanor of the second degree.

(1995 S 2, eff. 7–1–96; 1989 H 421, eff. 7–11–89; 1987 H 171; 1986 H 428, H 552, S 61; 1979 S 18; 1978 H 590)

CHAPTER 3743

FIREWORKS

DEFINITIONS

3743.01 Definitions

As used in this chapter:

(A) "Beer" and "intoxicating liquor" have the same meanings as in section 4301.01 of the Revised Code.

(B) "Booby trap" means a small tube that has a string protruding from both ends, that has a friction-sensitive composition, and that is ignited by pulling the ends of the string.

(C) "Cigarette load" means a small wooden peg that is coated with a small quantity of explosive composition and that is ignited in a cigarette.

(D)(1) "1.3G fireworks" means display fireworks consistent with regulations of the United States department of transportation as expressed using the designation "division 1.3" in Title 49, Code of Federal Regulations.

(2) "1.4G fireworks" means consumer fireworks consistent with regulations of the United States department of transportation as expressed using the designation "division 1.4" in Title 49, Code of Federal Regulations.

(E) "Controlled substance" has the same meaning as in section 3719.01 of the Revised Code.

(F) "Fireworks" means any composition or device prepared for the purpose of producing a visible or an audible effect by combustion, deflagration, or detonation, except ordinary matches and except as provided in section 3743.80 of the Revised Code.

(G) "Fireworks plant" means all buildings and other structures in which the manufacturing of fireworks, or the storage or sale of manufactured fireworks by a manufacturer, takes place.

(H) "Highway" means any public street, road, alley, way, lane, or other public thoroughfare.

(I) "Licensed exhibitor of fireworks" or "licensed exhibitor" means a person licensed pursuant to sections 3743.50 to 3743.55 of the Revised Code.

(J) "Licensed manufacturer of fireworks" or "licensed manufacturer" means a person licensed pursuant to sections 3743.02 to 3743.08 of the Revised Code.

(K) "Licensed wholesaler of fireworks" or "licensed wholesaler" means a person licensed pursuant to sections 3743.15 to 3743.21 of the Revised Code.

(L) "List of licensed exhibitors" means the list required by division (C) of section 3743.51 of the Revised Code.

(M) "List of licensed manufacturers" means the list required by division (C) of section 3743.03 of the Revised Code.

(N) "List of licensed wholesalers" means the list required by division (C) of section 3743.16 of the Revised Code.

(O) "Manufacturing of fireworks" means the making of fireworks from raw materials, none of which in and of themselves constitute a fireworks, or the processing of fireworks.

(P) "Navigable waters" means any body of water susceptible of being used in its ordinary condition as a highway of commerce over which trade and travel is or may be conducted in the customary modes, but does not include a body of water that is not capable of navigation by barges, tugboats, and other large vessels.

(Q) "Novelties and trick noisemakers" include the following items:

(1) Devices that produce a small report intended to surprise the user, including, but not limited to, booby traps, cigarette loads, party poppers, and snappers;

(2) Snakes or glow worms;

(3) Smoke devices;

(4) Trick matches.

(R) "Party popper" means a small plastic or paper item that contains not more than sixteen milligrams of friction-sensitive explosive composition, that is ignited by pulling a string protruding from the item, and from which paper streamers are expelled when the item is ignited.

(S) "Processing of fireworks" means the making of fireworks from materials all or part of which in and of themselves constitute a fireworks, but does not include the mere packaging or repackaging of fireworks.

(T) "Railroad" means any railway or railroad that carries freight or passengers for hire, but does not include auxiliary tracks, spurs, and sidings installed and primarily used in serving a mine, quarry, or plant.

(U) "Retail sale" or "sell at retail" means a sale of fireworks to a purchaser who intends to use the fireworks, and not resell them.

(V) "Smoke device" means a tube or sphere that contains pyrotechnic composition that, upon ignition, produces white or colored smoke as the primary effect.

(W) "Snake or glow worm" means a device that consists of a pressed pellet of pyrotechnic composition that produces a large, snake-like ash upon burning, which ash expands in length as the pellet burns.

(X) "Snapper" means a small, paper-wrapped item that contains a minute quantity of explosive composition coated on small bits of sand, and that, when dropped, implodes.

(Y) "Trick match" means a kitchen or book match that is coated with a small quantity of explosive composition and that, upon ignition, produces a small report or a shower of sparks.

(Z) "Wire sparkler" means a sparkler consisting of a wire or stick coated with a nonexplosive pyrotechnic mixture that produces a shower of sparks upon ignition and that contains no more than one hundred grams of this mixture.

(AA) "Wholesale sale" or "sell at wholesale" means a sale of fireworks to a purchaser who intends to resell the fireworks so purchased.

(BB) "Licensed premises" means the real estate upon which a licensed manufacturer or wholesaler of fireworks conducts business.

(CC) "Licensed building" means a building on the licensed premises of a licensed manufacturer or wholesaler of fireworks that is approved for occupancy by the building official having jurisdiction.

(DD) "Fireworks incident" means any action or omission that occurs at a fireworks exhibition, that results in injury or death, or a substantial risk of injury or death, to any person, and that involves either of the following:

(1) The handling or other use, or the results of the handling or other use, of fireworks or associated equipment or other materials;

(2) The failure of any person to comply with any applicable requirement imposed by this chapter or any applicable rule adopted under this chapter.

(EE) "Discharge site" means an area immediately surrounding the mortars used to fire aerial shells.

(FF) "Fireworks incident site" means a discharge site or other location at a fireworks exhibition where a fireworks incident occurs, a location where an injury or death associated with a fireworks incident occurs, or a location where evidence of a fireworks incident or an injury or death associated with a fireworks incident is found.

(2001 H 161, § 3, eff. 6–29–01; 2001 H 161, § 1, eff. 6–29–01; 1997 H 215, eff. 6–30–97; 1986 S 61, eff. 5–30–86)

WHOLESALERS

3743.25 Safety requirements for fireworks showroom structures

(A) A licensed manufacturer, wholesaler, or exhibitor shall bring fireworks showroom structures, to which the public may have any access and in which employees are required to work, on all licensed premises, into compliance with the following safety requirements:

(1) A fireworks showroom that is constructed or upon which expansion is undertaken on and after the effective date of this section, shall be equipped with interlinked fire detection, fire suppression, smoke exhaust, and smoke evacuation systems that are approved by the superintendent of the division of industrial compliance in the department of commerce.

(2) A fireworks showroom that first begins to operate on or after the effective date of this section and to which the public has access for retail purposes shall not exceed five thousand square feet in floor area.

(3) A fireworks showroom structure that exists on the effective date of this section but that, on or after the effective date of this section, is altered or added to in a manner requiring the submission of plans, drawings, specifications, or data pursuant to section 3791.04 of the Revised Code, shall comply with a graphic floor plan layout that is approved by the fire marshal and superintendent of the division of industrial compliance showing width of aisles, parallel arrangement of aisles to exits, number of exits per wall, maximum occupancy load, evacuation plan for occupants, height of storage or display of merchandise, and other information as may be required by the fire marshal and superintendent.

(4)(a) Except as provided in division (A)(4)(b) of this section, a fireworks showroom structure that exists on the effective date of this section shall be retrofitted on or before June 1, 1998, with interlinked fire detection, smoke exhaust, and smoke evacuation systems that are approved by the superintendent of the division of industrial compliance.

(b) If meeting the retrofitting requirements set forth in division (A)(4)(a) of this section would constitute an extreme financial hardship that would force a licensee to terminate business operations, the licensee shall conduct sales only on the basis of de-fused representative samples in closed and covered displays within the fireworks showroom.

(5) A fireworks showroom structure that exists on the effective date of this section shall be in compliance on or before June 1, 1998, with floor plans showing occupancy load limits and internal circulation and egress patterns that are approved by the fire marshal and superintendent of industrial compliance, and that are submitted under seal as required by section 3791.04 of the Revised Code.

(B) The safety requirements established in division (A) of this section are not subject to any variance, waiver, or exclusion pursuant to this chapter or any applicable building code.

(2001 H 161, eff. 6–29–01; 1997 H 215, eff. 6–30–97)

SHIPPERS

3743.40 Shipping permit; contents of application; fee; issuance; expiration

(A) Any person who resides in another state and who intends to ship fireworks into this state shall submit to the fire marshal an application for a shipping permit. As used in this section, "fireworks" includes only 1.3G and 1.4G fireworks. The application shall be submitted prior to shipping fireworks into this state, shall be on a form prescribed by the fire marshal, shall contain the information required by division (B) of this section and all information requested by the fire marshal, and shall be accompanied by the fee and the documentation described in division (C) of this section.

The fire marshal shall prescribe a form for applications for shipping permits and make a copy of the form available, upon request, to persons who seek such a permit.

(B) In an application for a shipping permit, the applicant shall specify the types of fireworks to be shipped into this state.

(C) An application for a shipping permit shall be accompanied by a fee of two thousand seven hundred fifty dollars.

An application for a shipping permit shall be accompanied by a certified copy of the applicant's license or permit issued in the applicant's state of residence and authorizing the applicant to engage in the manufacture, wholesale sale, or transportation of fireworks in that state, if that state issues such a license or permit, and by a statement by the applicant that the applicant understands and will abide by rules adopted by the fire marshal pursuant to section 3743.58 of the Revised Code for transporting fireworks.

(D) Except as otherwise provided in this division, and subject to section 3743.70 of the Revised Code, the fire marshal shall issue a shipping permit to an applicant only if the fire marshal determines that the applicant is a resident of another state and is the holder of a license or permit issued by that state authorizing it to engage in the manufacture, wholesale sale, or transportation of fireworks in that state, and the fire marshal is satisfied that the application and documentation are complete and in conformity with this section and that the applicant will transport fireworks into this state in accordance with rules adopted by the fire marshal pursuant to section 3743.58 of the Revised Code. The fire marshal shall issue a shipping permit to an applicant if the applicant meets all of the requirements of this section for the issuance of a shipping permit except that the applicant does not hold a license or permit issued by the state of residence authorizing the applicant to engage in the manufacture, wholesale sale, or transportation of fireworks in that state because that state does not issue such a license or permit.

(E) Each permit issued pursuant to this section shall contain a distinct number assigned to the particular permit holder, and contain the information described in division (B) of this section.

The fire marshal shall maintain a list of all persons issued shipping permits. In this list next to each person's name, the fire marshal shall insert the date upon which the permit was issued and the information described in division (B) of this section.

(F) A shipping permit is valid for one year from the date of issuance by the fire marshal and only if the permit holder ships the fireworks directly into this state to the holder of a license issued under section 3743.03 or 3743.16 of the Revised Code. The permit authorizes the permit holder to ship fireworks directly to the holder of a license issued under section 3743.03 or 3743.16 of the Revised Code, and to possess the fireworks in this state while the permit holder is in the course of shipping them directly into this state.

The holder of a shipping permit shall have the permit in the holder's possession in this state at all times while in the course of shipping the fireworks directly into this state. A shipping permit is not transferable or assignable.

(2001 H 161, eff. 6–29–01; 1997 H 215, eff. 6–30–97; 1992 H 508, eff. 12–14–92; 1986 S 61)

EXHIBITORS

3743.541 Notice of fireworks incident; supervision and coordination of investigation; dismantling, repositioning or removing of fireworks to prevent imminent fire or explosion

(A) The appropriate certified fire safety inspector, fire chief, or fire prevention officer or appropriate state or local law enforcement authority with jurisdiction over a fireworks incident site shall immediately notify the state fire marshal, the state fire marshal's designee, or a member of the state fire marshal's staff regarding the occurrence of the fireworks incident and the location of the fireworks incident site.

(B) At any time after a fireworks incident occurs, unless the fire marshal otherwise delegates the fire marshal's authority to the appropriate state or local law enforcement authority with jurisdiction over the fireworks incident site, the fire marshal, the fire marshal's designee, or a member of the fire marshal's staff shall supervise and coordinate the investigation of the fireworks incident and supervise any dismantling, repositioning, or other disturbance of fireworks, associated equipment or other materials, or other items within the fireworks incident site or of any evidence related to the fireworks incident.

(C) A state or local law enforcement officer, certified fire safety inspector, fire chief, or fire prevention officer, or any person authorized and supervised by a state or local law enforcement officer, certified fire safety inspector, fire chief, or fire prevention officer, prior to the arrival of the fire marshal, the fire marshal's designee, or a member of the fire marshal's staff at a fireworks incident site, may dismantle, reposition, or move any fireworks, any associated equipment or other materials, or any other items found within the site or any evidence related to the fireworks incident only as necessary to prevent an imminent fire, imminent explosion, or similar threat of additional injury or death to any member of the public at the site.

(2001 H 161, § 3, eff. 6–29–01)

3743.56 Registration of employees; records; fees

Each fireworks exhibitor licensed under section 3743.51 of the Revised Code shall register annually with the fire marshal all employees who assist the licensed exhibitor in conducting fireworks exhibitions. Once registered, such an employee may be employed by any other licensed fireworks exhibitor, without the need for that other licensed exhibitor to register the employee with the fire marshal. The fire marshal shall maintain a record of licensed exhibitors and registered employees and make it available, upon request, to any law enforcement agency.

The fire marshal shall adopt rules under Chapter 119. of the Revised Code that establish appropriate fees for the registration of employees of licensed exhibitors and otherwise implement this section.

In addition to the annual registration of employees required by this section, a licensed exhibitor shall file an application to register a new employee, unless the new employee is already registered under this section, not later than seven days after the date on which the employee is hired.

(2001 H 161, § 3, eff. 6–29–01; 2001 H 161, § 1, eff. 6–29–01; 1997 H 215, eff. 6–30–97)

PROHIBITIONS

3743.60 Manufacturing without license; prohibitions for manufacturers

(A) No person shall manufacture fireworks in this state unless it is a licensed manufacturer of fireworks, and no person shall operate a fireworks plant in this state unless it has been issued a license as a manufacturer of fireworks for the particular fireworks plant.

(B) No person shall operate a fireworks plant in this state after its license as a manufacturer of fireworks for the particular fireworks plant has expired, been denied renewal, or been revoked, unless a new license has been obtained.

(C) No licensed manufacturer of fireworks, during the effective period of its licensure, shall construct, locate, or relocate any buildings or other structures on the premises of its fireworks plant, make any structural change or renovation in any building or other structure on the premises of its fireworks plant, or change the nature of its manufacturing of fireworks so as to include the processing of fireworks without first obtaining a written authorization from the fire marshal pursuant to division (B) of section 3743.04 of the Revised Code.

(D) No licensed manufacturer of fireworks shall manufacture fireworks, possess fireworks for sale at wholesale or retail, or sell fireworks at wholesale or retail, in a manner not authorized by division (C) of section 3743.04 of the Revised Code.

(E) No licensed manufacturer of fireworks shall knowingly fail to comply with the rules adopted by the fire marshal pursuant to section 3743.05 of the Revised Code or the requirements of section 3743.06 of the Revised Code.

(F) No licensed manufacturer of fireworks shall fail to maintain complete inventory, wholesale sale, and retail records as required by section 3743.07 of the Revised Code, or to permit inspection of these records or the premises of a fireworks plant pursuant to section 3743.08 of the Revised Code.

(G) No licensed manufacturer of fireworks shall fail to comply with an order of the fire marshal issued pursuant to division (B)(1) of section 3743.08 of the Revised Code, within the specified period of time.

(H) No licensed manufacturer of fireworks shall fail to comply with an order of the fire marshal issued pursuant to division (B)(2) of section 3743.08 of the Revised Code until the nonconformities are eliminated, corrected, or otherwise remedied or the seventy-two hour period specified in that division has expired, whichever first occurs.

(I) No person shall smoke or shall carry a pipe, cigarette, or cigar, or a match, lighter, other flame-producing item, or open flame on, or shall carry a concealed source of ignition into, the premises of a fireworks plant, except as smoking is authorized in specified lunchrooms or restrooms by a manufacturer pursuant to division (C) of section 3743.06 of the Revised Code.

(J) No person shall have possession or control of, or be under the influence of, any intoxicating liquor, beer, or controlled substance, while on the premises of a fireworks plant.

(2001 H 161, eff. 6–29–01; 1997 H 215, eff. 6–30–97; 1986 S 61, eff. 5–30–86)

Notes of Decisions

Ed. Note: See notes of decisions at RC 4511.19 regarding construction of the term "under the influence."

3743.61 Wholesale sale without license; prohibitions for wholesalers

(A) No person, except a licensed manufacturer of fireworks engaging in the wholesale sale of fireworks as authorized by division (C)(2) of section 3743.04 of the Revised Code, shall operate as a wholesaler of fireworks in this state unless it is a licensed wholesaler of fireworks, or shall operate as a wholesaler of fireworks at any location in this state unless it has been issued a license as a wholesaler of fireworks for the particular location.

(B) No person shall operate as a wholesaler of fireworks at a particular location in this state after its license as a wholesaler of fireworks for the particular location has expired, been denied renewal, or been revoked, unless a new license has been obtained.

(C) No licensed wholesaler of fireworks, during the effective period of its licensure, shall perform any construction, or make any structural change or renovation, on the premises on which the fireworks are sold without first obtaining a written authorization from the fire marshal pursuant to division (B) of section 3743.17 of the Revised Code.

(D) No licensed wholesaler of fireworks shall possess fireworks for sale at wholesale or retail, or sell fireworks at wholesale or retail, in a manner not authorized by division (C) of section 3743.17 of the Revised Code.

(E) No licensed wholesaler of fireworks shall knowingly fail to comply with the rules adopted by the fire marshal pursuant to section 3743.18 or the requirements of section 3743.19 of the Revised Code.

(F) No licensed wholesaler of fireworks shall fail to maintain complete inventory, wholesale sale, and retail records as required by section 3743.20 of the Revised Code, or to permit inspection of these records or the premises of the wholesaler pursuant to section 3743.21 of the Revised Code.

(G) No licensed wholesaler of fireworks shall fail to comply with an order of the fire marshal issued pursuant to division (B)(1) of section 3743.21 of the Revised Code, within the specified period of time.

(H) No licensed wholesaler of fireworks shall fail to comply with an order of the fire marshal issued pursuant to division (B)(2) of section 3743.21 of the Revised Code until the nonconformities are eliminated, corrected, or otherwise remedied or the seventy-two hour period specified in that division has expired, whichever first occurs.

(I) No person shall smoke or shall carry a pipe, cigarette, or cigar, or a match, lighter, other flame-producing item, or open flame on, or shall carry a concealed source of ignition into, the premises of a wholesaler of fireworks, except as smoking is authorized in specified lunchrooms or restrooms by a wholesaler pursuant to division (D) of section 3743.19 of the Revised Code.

(J) No person shall have possession or control of, or be under the influence of, any intoxicating liquor, beer, or controlled substance, while on the premises of a wholesaler of fireworks.

(2001 H 161, eff. 6–29–01; 1997 H 215, eff. 6–30–97; 1986 S 61, eff. 5–30–86)

Notes of Decisions

Ed. Note: See notes of decisions at RC 4511.19 regarding construction of the term "under the influence."

3743.63 Purchasers to comply with laws; unauthorized purchases; failure to transport out of state

(A) No person who resides in another state and purchases fireworks in this state shall obtain possession of the fireworks in this state unless the person complies with section 3743.44 of the Revised Code, provided that knowingly making a false statement on the fireworks purchaser form is not a violation of this section but is a violation of section 2921.13 of the Revised Code.

(B) No person who resides in another state and who purchases fireworks in this state shall obtain possession of fireworks in this state other than from a licensed manufacturer or wholesaler, or fail, when transporting the fireworks, to transport them directly out of this state within seventy-two hours after the time of their purchase. No such person shall give or sell to any other person in this state fireworks that the person has acquired in this state.

(C) No person who resides in this state and purchases fireworks in this state shall obtain possession of the fireworks in this state unless the person complies with section 3743.45 of the Revised Code, provided that knowingly making a false statement on the fireworks purchaser form is not a violation of this section but is a violation of section 2921.13 of the Revised Code.

(D) No person who resides in this state and who purchases fireworks in this state under section 3743.45 of the Revised Code shall obtain possession of fireworks in this state other than from a licensed manufacturer or licensed wholesaler, or fail, when transporting the fireworks, to transport them directly out of this state within forty-eight hours after the time of their purchase. No such person shall give or sell to any other person in this state fireworks that the person has acquired in this state.

(1995 S 2, eff. 7–1–96; 1986 S 61, eff. 5–30–86)

3743.64 Exhibition without license; prohibitions for exhibitors

(A) No person shall conduct a fireworks exhibition in this state or act as an exhibitor of fireworks in this state unless the person is a licensed exhibitor of fireworks.

(B) No person shall conduct a fireworks exhibition in this state or act as an exhibitor of fireworks in this state after the person's license as an exhibitor of fireworks has expired, been denied renewal, or been revoked, unless a new license has been obtained.

(C) No licensed exhibitor of fireworks shall fail to comply with the applicable requirements of the rules adopted by the fire marshal pursuant to divisions (B) and (E) of section 3743.53 of the Revised Code or to comply with divisions (C) and (D) of that section.

(D) No licensed exhibitor of fireworks shall conduct a fireworks exhibition unless a permit has been secured for the exhibition pursuant to section 3743.54 of the Revised Code or if a permit so secured is revoked by a fire chief or fire prevention officer, in consultation with a police chief or other similar chief law enforcement officer of a municipal corporation, township, or township police district or with a designee of such a police chief or other similar chief law enforcement officer, pursuant to that section.

(E) No licensed exhibitor of fireworks shall acquire fireworks for use at a fireworks exhibition other than in accordance with sections 3743.54 and 3743.55 of the Revised Code.

(F) No licensed exhibitor of fireworks or other person associated with the conduct of a fireworks exhibition shall have possession or control of, or be under the influence of, any intoxicating liquor, beer, or controlled substance while on the premises on which the exhibition is being conducted.

(G) No licensed exhibitor of fireworks shall permit an employee to assist the licensed exhibitor in conducting fireworks exhibitions unless the employee is registered with the fire marshal under section 3743.56 of the Revised Code.

(H) Except as provided in division (C) of section 3743.541 of the Revised Code, no person shall knowingly, or knowingly permit another person to, dismantle, reposition, or otherwise disturb any fireworks, associated equipment or materials, or other items within a fireworks incident site, or any evidence related to a fireworks incident, at any time after that person has reason to believe a fireworks incident has occurred, before the state fire marshal, the state fire marshal's designee, a member of the state fire marshal's staff, or other appropriate state or local law enforcement authorities permit in accordance with section 3743.541 of the Revised Code the dismantling, repositioning, or other disturbance of the fireworks, equipment, materials, or items within the fireworks incident site or of any evidence related to the fireworks incident.

(2001 H 161, § 3, eff. 6–29–01; 2001 H 161, § 1, eff. 6–29–01; 2000 H 405, eff. 10–19–00; 1997 H 215, eff. 6–30–97; 1986 S 61, eff. 5–30–86)

Notes of Decisions

Ed. Note: See notes of decisions and opinions at RC 4511.19 regarding construction of the term "under the influence."

3743.65 Unauthorized possession, sale, or discharge of fireworks

(A) No person shall possess fireworks in this state or shall possess for sale or sell fireworks in this state, except a licensed manufacturer of fireworks as authorized by sections 3743.02 to 3743.08 of the Revised Code, a licensed wholesaler of fireworks as authorized by sections 3743.15 to 3743.21 of the Revised Code, a shipping permit holder as authorized by section 3743.40 of the Revised Code, an out-of-state resident as authorized by section 3743.44 of the Revised Code, a resident of this state as authorized by section 3743.45 of the Revised Code, or a licensed exhibitor of fireworks as authorized by sections 3743.50 to 3743.55 of the Revised Code, and except as provided in section 3743.80 of the Revised Code.

(B) Except as provided in section 3743.80 of the Revised Code and except for licensed exhibitors of fireworks authorized to conduct a fireworks exhibition pursuant to sections 3743.50 to 3743.55 of the Revised Code, no person shall discharge, ignite, or explode any fireworks in this state.

(C) No person shall use in a theater or public hall, what is technically known as fireworks showers, or a mixture containing potassium chlorate and sulphur.

(D) No person shall sell fireworks of any kind to a person under eighteen years of age.

(E) No person shall advertise 1.4G fireworks for sale. A sign located on a seller's premises identifying the seller as a seller of fireworks is not the advertising of fireworks for sale.

(F) No person, other than a licensed manufacturer, licensed wholesaler, licensed exhibitor, or shipping permit holder, shall possess 1.3G fireworks in this state.

(G) Except as otherwise provided in division (K) of section 3743.06 and division (L) of section 3743.19 of the Revised Code, no person shall knowingly disable a fire suppression system as defined in section 3781.108 of the Revised Code on the premises of a fireworks plant of a licensed manufacturer of fireworks or on the premises of the business operations of a licensed wholesaler of fireworks.

(2001 H 161, eff. 6–29–01; 1997 H 215, eff. 6–30–97; 1995 S 2, eff. 7–1–96; 1989 H 111, eff. 7–1–89; 1988 H 436; 1986 S 61)

3743.66 Unauthorized transporting or shipping of fireworks

(A) No person shall transport fireworks in this state except in accordance with rules adopted by the fire marshal pursuant to section 3743.58 of the Revised Code.

(B) As used in this division, "fireworks" includes only 1.3G and 1.4G fireworks. No person shall ship fireworks into this state by mail, parcel post, or common carrier unless the person possesses a valid shipping permit issued under section 3743.40 of the Revised Code, and the fireworks are shipped directly to the holder of a license issued under section 3743.03, 3743.16, or 3743.51 of the Revised Code.

No person shall ship fireworks within this state by mail, parcel post, or common carrier unless the fireworks are shipped directly to the holder of a license issued under section 3743.03, 3743.16, or 3743.51 of the Revised Code.

(2001 H 161, eff. 6–29–01; 1997 H 215, eff. 6–30–97; 1986 S 61, eff. 5–30–86)

ENFORCEMENT

3743.68 Arrest of violator; seizure and forfeiture of fireworks; distribution of fines

(A) The fire marshal, an assistant fire marshal, or a certified fire safety inspector may arrest, or may cause the arrest of, any person whom the fire marshal, assistant fire marshal, or certified fire safety inspector finds in the act of violating, or who the fire marshal, assistant fire marshal, or certified fire safety inspector has reasonable cause to believe has violated, sections 3743.60 to 3743.66 of the Revised Code. Any arrest shall be made in accordance with statutory and constitutional provisions governing arrests by law enforcement officers.

(B) If the fire marshal, an assistant fire marshal, or certified fire safety inspector has probable cause to believe that fireworks are being manufactured, sold, possessed, transported, or used in violation of this chapter, the fire marshal, assistant fire marshal, or certified fire safety inspector may seize the fireworks. Any seizure of fireworks shall be made in accordance with statutory and constitutional provisions governing searches and seizures by law enforcement officers. The fire marshal's or certified fire safety inspector's office shall impound at the site or safely keep seized fireworks pending the time they are no longer needed as evidence. A sample of the seized fireworks is sufficient for evidentiary purposes. The remainder of the seized fireworks may be disposed of pursuant to an order from a court of competent jurisdiction after notice and a hearing.

Fireworks manufactured, sold, possessed, transported, or used in violation of this chapter shall be forfeited by the violator. The fire marshal's or certified fire safety inspector's office shall dispose of seized fireworks pursuant to the procedures specified in section 2933.41 of the Revised Code for the disposal of forfeited property by law enforcement agencies, and the fire marshal or that office is not liable for claims for the loss of or damages to the seized fireworks.

(C) This section does not affect the authority of a peace officer, as defined in section 2935.01 of the Revised Code, to make arrests for violations of this chapter or to seize fireworks manufactured, sold, possessed, transported, or used in violation of this chapter.

(D) Any fines imposed for a violation of this chapter relating to the sale, purchase, possession, or discharge of fireworks shall be distributed in the following manner if a municipal corporation, county, or township either filed or enforced the complaint regarding the violation. One–half of the amount of the fine shall be distributed to the municipal corporation, county, or township which filed the complaint regarding the violation and one-half of the amount of the fine shall be distributed to the municipal corporation, county, or township which enforced the complaint. If the same municipal corporation, county, or township both filed the complaint regarding the violation and enforced the complaint, the entire amount of the fine shall be distributed to that municipal corporation, county, or township.

(2001 H 161, eff. 6–29–01; 1997 H 215, eff. 6–30–97; 1986 S 61, eff. 5–30–86)

3743.70 Felony convictions precluding licensure or permit

The fire marshal shall not issue an initial license or permit under this chapter on or after the effective date of this section if the applicant for the license or permit, or any individual holding, owning, or controlling a five per cent or greater beneficial or equity interest in the applicant for the license or permit, has been convicted of or pleaded guilty to a felony under the laws of this state, another state, or the United States. The fire marshal shall revoke or deny renewal of a license or permit first issued under this chapter on or after the effective date of this section if the holder of the license or permit, or any individual holding, owning, or controlling a five per cent or greater beneficial or equity interest in the holder of the license or permit, is convicted of or pleads guilty to a felony under the laws of this state, another state, or the United States.

(2001 H 161, eff. 6–29–01; 1997 H 215, eff. 6–30–97)

3743.75 Prohibitions on state fire marshal

(A) During the period beginning on June 29, 2001, and ending on December 15, 2008, the state fire marshal shall not do any of the following:

(1) Issue a license as a manufacturer of fireworks under sections 3743.02 and 3743.03 of the Revised Code to a person for a particular fireworks plant unless that person possessed such a license for that fireworks plant immediately prior to June 29, 2001;

(2) Issue a license as a wholesaler of fireworks under sections 3743.15 and 3743.16 of the Revised Code to a person for a particular location unless that person possessed such a license for that location immediately prior to June 29, 2001;

(3) Except as provided in division (B) of this section, approve the transfer of a license as a manufacturer or wholesaler of fireworks issued under this chapter to any location other than a location for which a license was issued under this chapter immediately prior to June 29, 2001.

(B) Division (A)(3) of this section does not apply to a transfer that the state fire marshal approves under division (D)(2) of section 3743.17 of the Revised Code. Section 3743.59 of the Revised Code does not apply to this section.

(2004 H 255, eff. 3–31–05; 2001 H 161, § 3, eff. 6–29–01; 1997 H 215, eff. 6–30–97)

APPLICABILITY

3743.80 Applicability of chapter

This chapter does not prohibit or apply to the following:

(A) The manufacture, sale, possession, transportation, storage, or use in emergency situations, of pyrotechnic signaling devices and distress signals for marine, aviation, or highway use;

(B) The manufacture, sale, possession, transportation, storage, or use of fusees, torpedoes, or other signals necessary for the safe operation of railroads;

(C) The manufacture, sale, possession, transportation, storage, or use of blank cartridges in connection with theaters or shows, or in connection with athletics as signals or for ceremonial purposes;

(D) The manufacture for, the transportation, storage, possession, or use by, or sale to the armed forces of the United States and the militia of this state of pyrotechnic devices;

(E) The manufacture, sale, possession, transportation, storage, or use of toy pistols, toy canes, toy guns, or other devices in which paper or plastic caps containing twenty-five hundredths grains or less of explosive material are used, provided that they are constructed so that a hand cannot come into contact with a cap when it is in place for explosion, or apply to the manufacture, sale, possession, transportation, storage, or use of those caps;

(F) The manufacture, sale, possession, transportation, storage, or use of novelties and trick noisemakers, auto burglar alarms, or model rockets and model rocket motors designed, sold, and used for the purpose of propelling recoverable aero models;

(G) The manufacture, sale, possession, transportation, storage, or use of wire sparklers.

(H) The conduct of radio-controlled special effect exhibitions that use an explosive black powder charge of not more than one-quarter pound per charge, and that are not connected in any manner to propellant charges, provided that the exhibition complies with all of following:

(1) No explosive aerial display is conducted in the exhibition;

(2) The exhibition is separated from spectators by not less than two hundred feet;

(3) The person conducting the exhibition complies with regulations of the bureau of alcohol, tobacco, and firearms of the United States department of the treasury and the United States department of transportation with respect to the storage and transport of the explosive black powder used in the exhibition.

(2001 H 161, eff. 6–29–01; 1997 H 215, eff. 6–30–97; 1986 S 61, eff. 5–30–86)

PENALTIES

3743.99 Penalties

(A) Whoever violates division (A) or (B) of section 3743.60 or division (H) of section 3743.64 of the Revised Code is guilty of a felony of the third degree.

(B) Whoever violates division (C) or (D) of section 3743.60, division (A), (B), (C), or (D) of section 3743.61, or division (A) or (B) of section 3743.64 of the Revised Code is guilty of a felony of the fourth degree.

(C) Whoever violates division (E), (F), (G), (H), (I), or (J) of section 3743.60, division (E), (F), (G), (H), (I), or (J) of section 3743.61, section 3743.63, division (D), (E), (F), or (G) of section 3743.64, division (A), (B), (C), (D), or (F) of section 3743.65, or section 3743.66 of the Revised Code is guilty of a misdemeanor of the first degree. If the offender previously has been convicted of or pleaded guilty to a violation of division (I) of section 3743.60 or 3743.61 of the Revised Code, a violation of either of these divisions is a felony of the fifth degree.

(D) Whoever violates division (C) of section 3743.64 of the Revised Code is guilty of a misdemeanor of the first degree. In addition to any other penalties that may be imposed on a licensed exhibitor of fireworks under this division and unless the third sentence of this division applies, the person's license as an exhibitor of fireworks or as an assistant exhibitor of fireworks shall be suspended, and the person is ineligible to apply for either type of license, for a period of five years. If the violation of division (C) of section 3743.64 of the Revised Code results in serious physical harm to persons or serious physical harm to property, the person's license as an exhibitor of fireworks or as an assistant exhibitor of fireworks shall be revoked, and that person is ineligible to apply for a license as or to be licensed as an exhibitor of fireworks or as an assistant exhibitor of fireworks in this state.

(E) Whoever violates division (G) of section 3743.65 of the Revised Code is guilty of a felony of the fifth degree.

(2001 H 161, § 3, eff. 6–29–01; 2001 H 161, § 1, eff. 6–29–01; 2000 H 405, eff. 10–19–00; 1997 H 215, eff. 6–30–97; 1995 S 2, eff. 7–1–96; 1988 H 436, eff. 6–14–88; 1986 S 61)

CHAPTER 3761

UNLAWFUL ASSEMBLIES; MOBS

MISCELLANEOUS PROVISIONS

3761.12 Prohibition against conspiracy while wearing disguise

No person shall unite with two or more others to commit a misdemeanor while wearing white caps, masks, or other disguise.

(1953 H 1, eff. 10–1–53; GC 12810)

3761.16 Cordoning off riot areas; prohibited sales of firearms, explosives, etc.

The chief administrative officer of a political subdivision with police powers, when engaged in suppressing a riot or when there is a clear and present danger of a riot, may cordon off any area or areas threatened by the riot and prohibit persons from entering the cordoned off area or areas except when carrying on necessary and legitimate pursuits and may prohibit the sale, offering for sale, dispensing, or transportation of firearms or other dangerous weapons, ammunition, dynamite, or other dangerous explosives in, to, or from the cordoned off areas.

(1995 S 2, eff. 7–1–96; 132 v H 753, eff. 9–8–67)

3761.99 Penalties

Whoever violates section 3761.12 of the Revised Code is guilty of a felony of the fourth degree.

(1995 S 2, eff. 7–1–96; 1982 H 269, § 4, eff. 7–1–83; 1982 S 199; 1975 H 1; 132 v H 996, H 753; 131 v S 405; 1953 H 1)

CHAPTER 3767

NUISANCES

DEFINITIONS

3767.01 Definitions

As used in all sections of the Revised Code relating to nuisances:

(A) "Place" includes any building, erection, or place or any separate part or portion thereof or the ground itself;

(B) "Person" includes any individual, corporation, association, partnership, trustee, lessee, agent, or assignee;

(C) "Nuisance" means any of the following:

(1) That which is defined and declared by statutes to be a nuisance;

(2) Any place in or upon which lewdness, assignation, or prostitution is conducted, permitted, continued, or exists, or any place, in or upon which lewd, indecent, lascivious, or obscene films or plate negatives, film or plate positives, films designed to be projected on a screen for exhibition films, or glass slides either in negative or positive form designed for exhibition by projection on a screen, are photographed, manufactured, developed, screened, exhibited, or otherwise prepared or shown, and the personal property and contents used in conducting and maintaining any such place for any such purpose. This chapter shall not affect any newspaper, magazine, or other publication entered as second class matter by the post-office department.

(3) Any room, house, building, boat, vehicle, structure, or place where beer or intoxicating liquor is manufactured, sold, bartered, possessed, or kept in violation of law and all property kept and used in maintaining the same, and all property designed for the unlawful manufacture of beer or intoxicating liquor and beer or intoxicating liquor contained in the room, house, building, boat, structure, or place, or the operation of such a room, house, building, boat, structure, or place as described in division (C)(3) of this section where the operation of that place substantially interferes with public decency, sobriety, peace, and good order. "Violation of law" includes, but is not limited to, sales to any person under the legal drinking age as prohibited in division (A) of section 4301.22 or division (A) of section 4301.69 of the Revised Code and any violation of section 2913.46 or 2925.03 of the Revised Code.

(1998 H 402, eff. 3–30–99; 129 v 1400, eff. 10–11–61; 1953 H 1; GC 6212–1)

INJUNCTIONS

3767.02 Nuisance

(A) Any person, who uses, occupies, establishes, or conducts a nuisance, or aids or abets in the use, occupancy, establishment, or conduct of a nuisance; the owner, agent, or lessee of an interest in any such nuisance; any person who is employed in that nuisance by that owner, agent, or lessee; and any person who is in control of that nuisance is guilty of maintaining a nuisance and shall be enjoined as provided in sections 3767.03 to 3767.11 of the Revised Code.

(B) A criminal gang that uses or occupies any building, premises, or real estate, including vacant land, on more than two occasions within a one-year period to engage in a pattern of criminal gang activity is guilty of maintaining a nuisance and shall be enjoined as provided in sections 3767.03 to 3767.11 of the Revised Code. As used in this division, "criminal gang" and "pattern of criminal gang activity" have the same meanings as in section 2923.41 of the Revised Code.

(1998 H 2, eff. 1–1–99; 1953 H 1, eff. 10–1–53; GC 6212–2)

3767.03 Abatement of nuisance; bond; notice

Whenever a nuisance exists, the attorney general; the village solicitor, city director of law, or other similar chief legal officer of the municipal corporation in which the nuisance exists; the prosecuting attorney of the county in which the nuisance exists; the law director of a township that has adopted a limited home rule government under Chapter 504. of the Revised Code; or any person who is a citizen of the county in which the nuisance exists may bring an action in equity in the name of the state, upon the relation of the attorney general; the village solicitor, city director of law, or other similar chief legal officer of the municipal corporation; the prosecuting attorney; the township law director; or the person, to abate the nuisance and to perpetually enjoin the person maintaining the nuisance from further maintaining it. If an action is instituted under this section by a person other than the prosecuting attorney; the village solicitor, city director of law, or other similar chief legal officer of the municipal corporation; the attorney general; or the township law director, the complainant shall execute a bond in the sum of not less than five hundred dollars, to the defendant, with good and sufficient surety to be approved by the court or clerk of the court, to secure to the defendant any damages the defendant may sustain and the reasonable attorney's fees the defendant may incur in defending the action if the action is wrongfully brought, not prosecuted to final judgment, is dismissed, or is not maintained, or if it is finally decided that an injunction should not have been granted. If it is finally decided that an injunction should not have been granted or if the action was wrongfully brought, not prosecuted to final judgment, dismissed, or not maintained, the defendant shall have recourse against the bond for all damages suffered, including damages to the defendant's property, person, or character, and for the reasonable attorney's fees incurred by the defendant in defending the action.

Any agency, officer, or other person bringing an action under this section against the holder of a liquor permit issued under Chapter 4303. of the Revised Code shall notify the division of liquor control, the liquor control commission, and the liquor enforcement division of the department of public safety regarding the action at the time of bringing the action.

(1999 H 187, eff. 9–20–99; 1998 H 402, eff. 3–30–99; 1996 H 501, eff. 11–6–96; 1992 H 343, eff. 6–1–92; 1953 H 1; GC 6212–3)

3767.04 Procedure in injunction action

(A) The civil action provided for in section 3767.03 of the Revised Code shall be commenced in the court of common pleas of the county in which the nuisance is located. At the commencement of the action, a complaint alleging the facts constituting the nuisance shall be filed in the office of the clerk of the court of common pleas.

(B)(1) After the filing of the complaint, an application for a temporary injunction may be filed with the court or a judge of the court. A hearing shall be held on the application within ten days after the filing.

(2) If an application for a temporary injunction is filed, the court or a judge of the court, on application of the complainant, may issue an ex parte restraining order restraining the defendant and all other persons from removing or in any manner interfering with the personal property and contents of the place where the nuisance is alleged to exist until the decision of the court or judge granting or refusing the requested temporary injunction and until the further order of the court. The restraining order may be served by handing it to and leaving a copy of it with any person who is in charge of the place where the nuisance is alleged to exist or who resides in that place, by posting a copy of it in a conspicuous place at or upon one or more of the principal doors or entrances to that place, or by both delivery and posting. The officer serving the restraining order forthwith shall make and return into court an inventory of the personal property and contents situated in and used in conducting or maintaining the nuisance. Any violation of the restraining order is a contempt of court, and, if the order is posted, its mutilation or removal while it remains in force is a contempt of court, provided the posted order contains a notice to that effect.

(3) A copy of the complaint, a copy of the application for the temporary injunction, and a notice of the time and place of the hearing on the application shall be served upon the defendant at least five days before the hearing. If the hearing then is continued on the motion of any defendant, the requested temporary injunction shall be granted as a matter of course. If, upon hearing, the allegations of the complaint are sustained to the satisfaction of the court or judge, the court or judge shall issue a temporary injunction without additional bond restraining the defendant and any other person from continuing the nuisance. Except as provided in division (C) of this section, if at the time of granting the temporary injunction it further appears that the person owning, in control, or in charge of the nuisance so enjoined had received five days' notice of the hearing and unless that person shows to the satisfaction of the court or judge that the nuisance complained of is abated or that he proceeded forthwith to enforce his rights under section 3767.10 of the Revised Code, the court or judge forthwith shall issue an order closing the place against its use for any purpose of lewdness, assignation, prostitution, or other prohibited conduct until a final decision is rendered on the complaint for the requested permanent injunction. Except as provided in division (C) of this section, the order closing the place also shall continue in effect for that further period any restraining order already issued under division (B)(2) of this section, or, if a restraining order was not so issued, the order closing the place shall include an order restraining for that further period the removal or interference with the personal property and contents located in the place. The order closing the place shall be served and an inventory of the personal property and contents situated in the place shall be made and filed as provided in division (B)(2) of this section for restraining orders.

(C) The owner of any real or personal property closed or restrained or to be closed or restrained may appear in the court of common pleas between the time of the filing of the complaint for the permanent injunction described in division (A) of this section and the hearing on the complaint, and, if all costs incurred are paid and if the owner of the real property files a bond with sureties approved by the clerk, in the full value of the real property as ascertained by the court or, in vacation, by the judge, and conditioned that the owner of the real property immediately will abate the nuisance and prevent it from being established or kept until the decision of the court or judge is rendered on the complaint for the permanent injunction, the court or judge in vacation, if satisfied of the good faith of the owner of the real property and of innocence on the part of any owner of the personal property of any knowledge of the use of the personal property as a nuisance and that, with reasonable care and diligence, the owner of the personal property could not have known of its use as a nuisance, shall deliver the real or personal property, or both, to the respective owners and discharge or refrain from issuing at the time of the hearing on the application for the temporary injunction any order closing the real property or restraining the removal or interference with the personal property. The release of any real or personal property under this division shall not release it from any judgment, lien, penalty, or liability to which it may be subjected.

(1992 H 343, eff. 6–1–92; 1953 H 1; GC 6212–4)

3767.05 Priority of action; evidence; costs; nuisances relating to liquor permit premises

(A) The civil action provided for in section 3767.03 of the Revised Code shall be set down for trial at the earliest possible time and shall have precedence over all other cases except those involving crimes, election contests, or injunctions regardless of the position of the proceedings on the calendar of the court. In the civil action, evidence of the general reputation of the place where the nuisance is alleged to exist or an admission or finding of guilt of any person under the criminal laws against prostitution, lewdness, assignation, or other prohibited conduct at the place is admissible for the purpose of proving the existence of the nuisance and is prima-facie evidence of the nuisance and of knowledge of and of acquiescence and participation in the nuisance on the part of the person charged with maintaining it.

(B) If the complaint for the permanent injunction is filed by a person who is a citizen of the county, it shall not be dismissed unless the complainant and the complainant's attorney submit a sworn statement setting forth the reasons why the civil action should be dismissed and the dismissal is approved by the prosecuting attorney in writing or in open court. If the person who files the complaint for the permanent injuction [sic] is a citizen of the county, if that person refuses or otherwise fails to prosecute the complaint to judgment, and if the civil action is not dismissed pursuant to this division, then, with the approval of the court, the attorney general, the prosecuting attorney of the county in which the nuisance exists, or the village solicitor, city director of law, or other similar chief legal officer of the municipal corporation in which the nuisance exists, may be substituted for the complainant and prosecute the civil action to judgment.

(C) If the civil action is commenced by a person who is a citizen of the county where the nuisance is alleged to exist and the court finds that there were no reasonable grounds or cause for the civil action, the costs may be taxed to that person.

(D) If the existence of the nuisance is established upon the trial of the civil action, a judgment shall be entered that perpetually enjoins the defendant and any other person from further maintaining the nuisance at the place complained of and the defendant from maintaining the nuisance elsewhere.

(E) If the court finds that a nuisance described in division (C)(3) of section 3767.01 of the Revised Code exists, the court shall order the nuisance to be abated, and, in entering judgment for nuisance, the court shall do all of the following:

(1) Specify that judgment is entered pursuant to division (E) of this section;

(2) Order that no beer or intoxicating liquor may be manufactured, sold, bartered, possessed, kept, or stored in the room, house, building, structure, place, boat, or vehicle or any part thereof. The court need not find that the property was being unlawfully used at the time of the hearing on the matter if the court finds there existed a nuisance as described in division (C)(3) of section 3767.01 of the Revised Code.

(3) Order that the room, house, building, boat, vehicle, structure, or place not be occupied or used for one year after the judgment is rendered. The court may permit the premises to be occupied by a person other than the defendant or a business affiliate of the defendant in the nuisance action, or an agent of, or entity owned in whole or part by, the defendant, if the person, lessee, tenant, or occupant of the location posts a bond with sufficient surety, to be approved by the court issuing the order, in the sum of not less than one thousand nor more than five thousand dollars, payable to the state of Ohio, on the condition that no beer or intoxicating liquor thereafter shall be manufactured, sold, bartered, possessed, kept, stored, transported, or otherwise disposed of on the premises, and the person agrees to pay all fines, costs, and damages that may be assessed for a violation. A reasonable sum shall be allowed an officer by the issuing court for the cost of closing and keeping closed the premises that is the subject of the nuisance action.

(4) Send notice of the judgment entered to the division of liquor control, the liquor control commission, and the liquor enforcement division of the department of public safety.

(F) A defendant found to have maintained a nuisance as described in division (C)(3) of section 3767.01 of the Revised Code also is subject to liability and penalties under sections 4301.74 and 4399.09 of the Revised Code. The abatement of a nuisance under section 4399.09 of the Revised Code is in addition to and does not prevent the abatement of a nuisance under division (D) or (E) of this section.

(G) If a court enters judgment pursuant to division (D) or (E) of this section finding that a nuisance exists at a liquor permit premises or as a result of the operation of a liquor permit premises, except in the case of a nuisance found as a result of a violation of a local zoning ordinance or resolution, the certified copy of the judgment required under division (A) of section 4301.331 of the Revised Code shall be filed with the board of elections in the county in which the nuisance exists, not later than four p.m. of the seventy-fifth day before the day of the next general or primary election. However, no election shall be conducted on sales at the liquor permit premises under section 4301.352 of the Revised Code until all appeals on the judgment are resolved. The court of appeals shall render a decision on any appeal of the judgment within six months after the date of the filing of the appeal of the judgment with the clerk of the court of appeals, and the supreme court shall render a decision on any appeal of the judgment within six months after the date of the filing of the appeal of the judgment with the clerk of the supreme court.

(1998 H 402, eff. 3–30–99; 1992 H 343, eff. 6–1–92; 1953 H 1; GC 6212–5)

3767.06 Content of judgment and order; attorney general nuisance abatement fund; proceeds from sale of property seized applied to costs of actions

(A) If the existence of a nuisance is admitted or established in the civil action provided for in section 3767.03 of the Revised Code or in a criminal action, an order of abatement shall be included in the judgment entry under division (D) of section 3767.05 of the Revised Code. The order shall direct the removal from the place where the nuisance is found to exist of all personal property and contents used in conducting or maintaining the nuisance and not already released under authority of the court as provided in division (C) of section 3767.04 of the Revised Code and shall direct that the personal property or contents that belong to the defendants notified or appearing be sold, without appraisal, at a public auction to the highest bidder for cash. The order also shall require the renewal for one year of any bond furnished by the owner of the real property under section 3767.04 of the Revised Code; if a bond was not so furnished, shall continue for one year any closing order issued at the time of granting the temporary injunction; or, if a closing order was not then issued, shall include an order directing the effectual closing of the place where the nuisance is found to exist against its use for any purpose and keeping it closed for a period of one year unless sooner released. The owner of any place closed and not released under bond may appear and obtain a release in the manner and upon fulfilling the requirements provided in section 3767.04 of the Revised Code. The release of property under this division shall not release it from any judgment, lien, penalty, or liability to which it may be subject.

(B) Owners of unsold personal property or contents seized pursuant to division (A) of this section shall appear and claim the personal property or contents within ten days after the order of abatement is issued and prove to the satisfaction of the court their lack of any actual knowledge of the use of the personal property or contents in the conduct or maintenance of the nuisance and that with reasonable care and diligence they could not have known of that use. Every defendant in the action shall be presumed to have had knowledge of the general reputation of the place where the nuisance is found to exist. If an owner establishes the lack of actual or constructive knowledge of the use of his personal property or contents in the conduct or maintenance of the nuisance, the unsold personal property and contents shall be delivered to the owner. If an owner does not so establish, the personal property or contents shall be sold or otherwise disposed of as provided in division (A) of this section. For removing and selling the personal property and contents, the officer involved shall be entitled to charge and receive the same fees as he would for levying upon and selling similar property on execution. For closing the place where the nuisance is found to exist and keeping it closed, a reasonable sum shall be allowed by the court.

(C) There is hereby established in the state treasury the attorney general nuisance abatement fund. Except as otherwise provided in sections 3767.07 to 3767.11 of the Revised Code, all proceeds from the sale of personal property or contents seized pursuant to a civil action commenced or otherwise prosecuted by the attorney general under sections 3767.03 to 3767.11 of the Revised Code shall be deposited into the state treasury and credited to the fund. The attorney general shall use the fund solely to defray expenses and costs associated with those types of civil actions.

(D) All proceeds from the sale of personal property or contents seized pursuant to a civil action commenced or otherwise prosecuted under sections 3767.03 to 3767.11 of the Revised Code by a village solicitor, city director of law, or other similar chief legal officer of a municipal corporation initially shall be applied to the payment of the costs incurred in the prosecution of the civil action and the costs associated with the abatement and sale ordered pursuant to division (A) of this section, including, but not limited to, court costs, reasonable attorney's fees, and other litigation expenses incurred by the complainant. Except as otherwise provided in sections 3767.07 to 3767.11 of the Revised Code, any proceeds remaining after that initial application shall be deposited into the city or village treasury and credited to the general fund.

(E) All proceeds from the sale of personal property or contents seized pursuant to a civil action commenced or otherwise prosecuted under sections 3767.03 to 3767.11 of the Revised Code by a prosecuting attorney initially shall be applied to the payment of the costs incurred in the prosecution of the civil action and the costs associated with the abatement and sale ordered pursuant to division (A) of this section, including, but not limited to, court costs, reasonable attorney's fees, and other litigation expenses incurred by the complainant. Except as otherwise provided in sections 3767.07 to 3767.11 of the Revised Code, any proceeds remaining after that initial application shall be deposited into the county treasury and credited to the general fund.

(F) All proceeds from the sale of personal property or contents seized pursuant to a civil action commenced under sections 3767.03 to 3767.11 of the Revised Code by a person who is a citizen of the county where the nuisance is found to exist initially shall be applied to the payment of the costs incurred in the prosecution of the civil action and the costs associated with the abatement and sale ordered pursuant to division (A) of this section, including, but not limited to, court costs, reasonable attorney's fees, and other litigation expenses incurred by the complainant. Except as otherwise provided in sections 3767.07 to 3767.11 of the Revised Code, any proceeds remaining after that initial application shall be deposited into the county treasury and credited to the general fund.

(1992 H 343, eff. 6–1–92; 1953 H 1; GC 6212–6)

3767.07 Court shall punish offender for violation of injunction or order

In case of the violation of any injunction or closing order, granted under sections 3767.01 to 3767.11, inclusive, of the Revised Code, or of a restraining order or the commission of any contempt of court in proceedings under such sections, the court or, in vacation, a judge thereof, may summarily try and punish the offender. The trial may be had upon affidavits or either party may demand the production and oral examination of the witnesses.

(1953 H 1, eff. 10–1–53; GC 6212–8)

TAXING OF NUISANCES

3767.08 Tax on nuisance

Whenever a permanent injunction issues against any person for maintaining a nuisance, there shall be imposed upon said nuisance and against the person maintaining the same a tax of three hundred dollars. Such tax may not be imposed upon the personal property or against the owner thereof who has proved innocence as provided in section 3767.06 of the Revised Code, or upon the real property or against the owner thereof who shows to the satisfaction of the court or judge thereof at the time of the granting of the permanent injunction, that he has, in good faith, permanently abated the nuisance complained of. The imposition of said tax shall be made by the court as a part of the proceeding and the clerk of said court shall make and certify a return of the imposition of said tax thereon to the county auditor, who shall enter the same as a tax upon the property and against the persons upon which or whom the lien was imposed as and when other taxes are entered, and the same shall be and remain a perpetual lien upon all property, both personal and real, used for the purpose of maintaining said nuisance except as excepted in this section until fully paid. Any such lien imposed while the tax books are in the hands of the auditor shall be immediately entered therein. The payment of said tax shall not relieve the persons or property from any other taxes. The provisions of the laws relating to the collection of taxes in this state, the delinquency thereof, and sale of property for taxes shall govern in the collection of the tax prescribed in this section in so far as the same are applicable, and the said tax collected shall be applied in payment of any deficiency in the costs of the action and abatement on behalf of the state to the extent of such deficiency after the application thereto of the proceeds of the sale of personal property.

(1972 H 511, eff. 1–1–74; 1953 H 1; GC 6212–9)

3767.09 Tax shall be imposed against owner of property

When a nuisance is found to exist in any proceeding under sections 3767.01 to 3767.11, inclusive, of the Revised Code, and the owner or agent of such place whereon the same has been found to exist was not a party to such proceeding, and did not appear therein, the tax of three hundred dollars, imposed under section 3767.08 of the Revised Code, shall, nevertheless, be imposed against the persons served or appearing and against the property as set forth in this section. Before such tax is enforced against such property, the owner or agent thereof shall have appeared therein or shall be served with summons therein, and existing laws, regarding the service of process, shall apply to service in proceedings under sections 3767.01 to 3767.11, inclusive, of the Revised Code. The person in whose name the real estate affected by the action stands on the books of the county auditor for purposes of taxation is presumed to be the owner thereof, and in case of unknown persons having or claiming any ownership, right, title, or interest in property affected by the action, such may be made parties to the action by designating them in the petition as "all other persons unknown claiming any ownership, right, title, or interest in the property affected by the action." Service thereon may be had by publication in the manner prescribed in sections 2703.14 to 2703.19, inclusive, of the Revised Code. Any person having or claiming such ownership, right, title, or interest, and any owner or agent in behalf of himself and such owner may make defense thereto and have trial of his rights in the premises by the court; and if said cause has already proceeded to trial or to findings and judgment, the court shall, by order, fix the time and place of such further trial and shall modify, add to, or confirm such findings and judgment. Other parties to said action shall not be affected thereby.

(1953 H 1, eff. 10–1–53; GC 6212–10)

EFFECT OF NUISANCES ON LEASES

3767.10 Lease void if building used for lewd purposes

If a tenant or occupant of a building or tenement, under a lawful title, uses such place for the purposes of lewdness, assignation, or prostitution, such use makes void the lease or other title under which he holds, at the option of the owner, and, without any act of the owner, causes the right of possession to revert and vest in such owner, who may without process of law make immediate entry upon the premises.

(1953 H 1, eff. 10–1–53; GC 6212–12)

CRIMINAL NUISANCES

3767.11 Procedure when nuisance established in criminal action

(A) If a nuisance is established in a criminal action, the prosecuting attorney, village solicitor, city director of law, or other similar chief legal officer shall proceed promptly under sections 3767.03 to 3767.11 of the Revised Code to enforce those sections. The finding of the defendant guilty in the criminal action, unless reversed or set aside, shall be conclusive against the defendant as to the existence of the nuisance in the civil action under those sections.

(B) Except for proceeds described in divisions (C) to (F) of section 3767.06 of the Revised Code, all moneys collected under sections 3767.03 to 3767.11 of the Revised Code shall be paid to the county treasurer.

(1992 H 343, eff. 6–1–92; 1953 H 1; GC 6212–7)

PROHIBITIONS—FINES

3767.12 Keeping a resort for thieves; prohibition

(A) As used in this section, "felonious conduct" means an offense that is a felony or a delinquent act that would be a felony if committed by an adult.

(B) A house or building used or occupied as a habitual resort for thieves, burglars, or robbers, or for persons who are conspiring or planning to commit, who are fleeing after having committed or after attempting to commit, or who are in hiding after having committed or after attempting to commit, felonious conduct is a public nuisance, and the court may order the public nuisance abated.

No person shall keep a house that is a habitual resort for thieves, burglars, or robbers, or for persons who are conspiring or planning to commit, who are fleeing after having committed or after attempting to commit, or who are in hiding after having committed or after attempting to commit, felonious conduct. No person shall let a house to be so kept, or knowingly permit a house that the person has let to be so kept.

(1999 S 107, eff. 3–23–00; 1953 H 1, eff. 10–1–53; GC 12453, 12454)

3767.13 Prohibitions; exemption

(A) No person shall erect, continue, use, or maintain a building, structure, or place for the exercise of a trade, employment, or business, or for the keeping or feeding of an animal which, by occasioning noxious exhalations or noisome or offensive smells, becomes injurious to the health, comfort, or property of individuals or of the public.

(B) No person shall cause or allow offal, filth, or noisome substances to be collected or remain in any place to the damage or prejudice of others or of the public.

(C) No person shall unlawfully obstruct or impede the passage of a navigable river, harbor, or collection of water, or corrupt or render unwholesome or impure, a watercourse, stream, or water, or unlawfully divert such watercourse from its natural course or state to the injury or prejudice of others.

(D) Persons who are engaged in agriculture-related activities, as "agriculture" is defined in section 519.01 of the Revised Code, and who are conducting those activities outside a municipal corporation, in accordance with generally accepted agricultural practices, and in such a manner so as not to have a substantial, adverse effect on the public health, safety, or welfare are exempt from divisions (A) and (B) of this section, from any similar ordinances, resolutions, rules, or other enactments of a state agency or political subdivision, and from any ordinances, resolutions, rules, or other enactments of a state agency or political subdivision that prohibit excessive noise.

(1982 S 78, eff. 6–29–82; 1953 H 1; GC 12646)

3767.14 Prohibition against throwing refuse, oil, or filth into lakes, streams, or drains

No person shall intentionally throw, deposit, or permit to be thrown or deposited, coal dirt, coal slack, coal screenings, or coal refuse from coal mines, refuse or filth from a coal oil refinery or gasworks, or whey or filthy drainage from a cheese factory, into a river, lake, pond, or stream, or a place from which it may wash therein. No person shall cause or permit petroleum, crude oil, refined oil, or a compound, mixture, residuum of oil or filth from an oil well, oil tank, oil vat, or place of deposit of crude or refined oil, to run into or be poured, emptied, or thrown into a river, ditch, drain, or watercourse, or into a place from which it may run or wash therein. Prosecution for a violation of this section must be brought in the county in which such coal mine, coal oil refinery gasworks, cheese factory, oil well, oil tank, oil vat, or place of deposit of crude or refined oil is situated.

(1953 H 1, eff. 10–1–53; GC 12647)

3767.15 Fine and costs are a lien

The fine and costs imposed in division (D) of section 3767.99 of the Revised Code shall be a lien on such oil well, oil tank, oil refinery, oil vat, or place of deposit and the contents thereof until paid, and such oil well, oil tank, oil refinery, oil vat, or place of deposit and the contents thereof, may be sold for the payment of such fine and costs upon execution issued for that purpose.

(1953 H 1, eff. 10–1–53; GC 12648)

3767.16 Prohibition against deposit of dead animals and offal upon land or water

No person shall put the carcass of a dead animal or the offal from a slaughterhouse, butcher's establishment, packing house, or fish house, or spoiled meat, spoiled fish, or other putrid substance or the contents of a privy vault, upon or into a lake, river, bay, creek, pond, canal, road, street, alley, lot, field, meadow, public ground, market place, or common. No owner or occupant of such place, shall knowingly permit such thing to remain therein to the annoyance of any citizen or neglect to remove or abate the nuisance occasioned thereby within twenty-four hours after knowledge of the existence thereof, or after notice thereof in writing from a township trustee or township highway superintendent, constable, or health commissioner of a city or general health district in which such nuisance exists or from a county commissioner of such county.

(1953 H 1, eff. 10–1–53; GC 12649)

3767.17 Prohibition against obstructing township or county ditch

No person shall willfully obstruct a ditch, drain, or watercourse constructed by order of a board of county commissioners or by a board of township trustees, or divert the water therefrom.

(1953 H 1, eff. 10–1–53; GC 12653)

3767.18 Prohibition against defiling spring or well

No person shall maliciously put a dead animal, carcass, or part thereof, or other putrid, nauseous, or offensive substance into, or befoul, a well, spring, brook, or branch of running water, or a reservoir of a water works, of which use is or may be made for domestic purposes.

(1953 H 1, eff. 10–1–53; GC 12654)

3767.19 Prohibition against nuisances when near state institutions

No person shall carry on the business of slaughtering, tallow chandlery, or the manufacturing of glue, soap, starch, or other article, the manufacture of which is productive of unwholesome or noxious odors in a building or place within one mile of a benevolent or correctional institution supported wholly or in part by the state. No person shall erect or operate, within one hundred twenty rods of such benevolent institution, a rolling mill, blast furnace, nail factory, copper-smelting works, petroleum oil refinery, or other works which may generate unwholesome or noxious odors or make loud noises, or which may annoy or endanger the health or prevent the recovery of the inmates of such institution. Each week such business is conducted, or works operated, constitutes a separate offense.

All property, real or personal, which is used with the knowledge of the owner thereof in violation of this section, shall be liable, without exemption, for the fines and costs assessed for such violation.

(1994 H 571, eff. 10–6–94; 125 v 903, eff. 10–1–53; 1953 H 1; GC 12655, 12656)

3767.201 Destruction or removal of barriers along limited access highways prohibited; vehicles to enter and leave limited access highways at designated intersections

No person, firm or corporation shall cut, injure, remove, or destroy any fence or other barrier designed and erected to prevent traffic from entering or leaving a limited access highway without the permission of the director of transportation, except in a case of emergency where life or property is in danger. No person, firm, or corporation shall cause a vehicle of any character to enter or leave a limited access highway at any point other than intersections designated by the director for such purpose, except in a case of emergency where life or property is in danger.

(1973 H 200, eff. 9–28–73; 128 v 1217)

MISCELLANEOUS PROVISIONS

3767.22 Exceptions

Section 3767.16 of the Revised Code does not prohibit the deposit of the contents of privy vaults and catch basins into trenches or pits not less than three feet deep excavated in a lot, field, or meadow, with the consent of the owner, outside of the limits of a municipal corporation and not less than thirty rods distant from a dwelling, well or spring of water, lake, bay, pond, canal, run, creek, brook or stream of water, public road or highway, provided that such contents so deposited are forthwith covered with at least twelve inches of dry earth; nor prohibit the deposit of such contents in furrows, as specified for such trenches or pits, to be forthwith covered with dry earth by plowing or otherwise, and with the consent of the owner or occupant of the land in which such furrows are plowed.

The board of health of a city or a general health district may allow the contents of privy vaults and catch basins to be deposited within corporate limits into such trenches, pits, or furrows.

(1953 H 1, eff. 10–1–53; GC 12650, 12651)

3767.23 Prosecution of corporations for nuisances; abatement

Corporations may be prosecuted by indictment for violation of sections 3767.13 to 3767.29, inclusive, of the Revised Code, and in every case of conviction under such sections, the court shall adjudge that the nuisance described in the indictment be abated or removed within a time fixed, and, if it is of a recurring character, the defendant shall keep such nuisance abated.

(126 v 374, eff. 8–1–55; 1953 H 1; GC 12657)

CONTEMPT PROCEEDINGS

3767.24 Contempt proceedings

If the defendant, convicted of a violation of sections 3767.13 to 3767.29, inclusive, of the Revised Code, fails, neglects, or refuses to abate the nuisance described in the indictment, as ordered by the court, or, if the nuisance is of a recurring character, and such defendant fails, neglects, or refuses to keep it abated, proceedings in contempt of court may be instituted against him and all others assisting in or conniving at the violation of such order, and the court may direct the sheriff to execute the order of abatement at the cost and expense of the defendant.

(126 v 374, eff. 8–1–55; 1953 H 1; GC 12658)

3767.25 Venue

An offense charged under sections 3767.13 to 3767.29, inclusive, of the Revised Code, shall be held to be committed in any county whose inhabitants are, or have been, aggrieved thereby. The continuance of such nuisance for five days after the prosecution thereof is begun is an additional offense.

(126 v 374, eff. 8–1–55; 1953 H 1; GC 12659)

3767.26 Judgment for fine and costs

A judgment for fine and costs rendered against a person or corporation for the violation of sections 3767.13 to 3767.29, inclusive, of the Revised Code, when the defendant has no property or has not a sufficient amount within the county upon which to levy to satisfy such judgment and costs, may be enforced and collected in the manner in which judgments are collected in civil cases.

(126 v 374, eff. 8–1–55; 1953 H 1; GC 12660)

NUISANCE INSPECTOR

3767.27 Inspector of nuisances

The board of county commissioners, whenever there is a violation of sections 3767.13 to 3767.29, inclusive, of the Revised Code, may employ and reasonably compensate one inspector of nuisances who shall be vested with police powers and authorized to examine all cases of violation of such sections.

(126 v 374, eff. 8–1–55; 1953 H 1; GC 12661)

3767.28 Powers and duties of inspector

For the purpose of examining cases of violations of sections 3767.13 to 3767.29, inclusive, of the Revised Code, and for obtaining evidence thereof, an inspector of nuisances may enter upon any premises in any county, and shall make a complaint, and institute prosecution, against any one violating such sections. The inspector shall not be required to give security for costs. The prosecuting attorney shall be the legal advisor of such inspector and the attorney in all such prosecutions.

(126 v 374, eff. 8–1–55; 1953 H 1; GC 12662)

ADDITIONAL PROHIBITIONS—PENALTIES

3767.29 Abandoned refrigerators

No person shall abandon, discard, or knowingly permit to remain on premises under his control, in a place accessible to children, any abandoned or discarded icebox, refrigerator, or other airtight or semi-airtight container which has a capacity of one and one-half cubic feet or more and an opening of fifty square inches or more and which has a door or lid equipped with hinge, latch or other fastening device capable of securing such door or lid, without rendering said equipment harmless to human life by removing such hinges, latches or other hardware which may cause a person to be confined therein. This section shall not apply to an icebox, refrigerator or other airtight or semi-airtight container located in that part of a building occupied by a dealer, warehouseman or repairman.

(126 v 374, eff. 8–1–55)

3767.30 Picketing during funeral or burial services

Every citizen may freely speak, write, and publish his sentiments on all subjects, being responsible for the abuse of the right, but no person shall picket, nor shall any association or corporation cause to be picketed, any residence, cemetery, funeral home, church, synagogue, or other establishment within one hour before and during the conducting of an actual funeral or burial service at such place. No person shall picket, nor shall any association or corporation cause to be picketed, any funeral procession.

(129 v 582, eff. 1–10–61; 127 v 242)

3767.32 Littering; unauthorized use of litter receptacle

(A) No person, regardless of intent, shall deposit litter or cause litter to be deposited on any public property, on private property not owned by him, or in or on waters of the state unless one of the following applies:

(1) The person is directed to do so by a public official as part of a litter collection drive;

(2) Except as provided in division (B) of this section, the person deposits the litter in a litter receptacle in a manner that prevents its being carried away by the elements;

(3) The person is issued a permit or license covering the litter pursuant to Chapter 3734. or 6111. of the Revised Code.

(B) No person, without privilege to do so, shall knowingly deposit litter, or cause it to be deposited, in a litter receptacle located on any public property or on any private property not owned by him unless one of the following applies:

(1) The litter was generated or located on the property on which the litter receptacle is located;

(2) The person is directed to do so by a public official as part of a litter collection drive;

(3) The person is directed to do so by a person whom he reasonably believes to have the privilege to use the litter receptacle;

(4) The litter consists of any of the following:

(a) The contents of a litter bag or container of a type and size customarily carried and used in a motor vehicle;

(b) The contents of an ash tray of a type customarily installed or carried and used in a motor vehicle;

(c) Beverage containers and food sacks, wrappings, and containers of a type and in an amount that reasonably may be expected to be generated during routine commuting or business or recreational travel by a motor vehicle;

(d) Beverage containers, food sacks, wrappings, containers, and other materials of a type and in an amount that reasonably may be expected to be generated during a routine day by a person and deposited in a litter receptacle by a casual passerby.

(C)(1) As used in division (B)(1) of this section, "public property" includes any private property open to the public for the conduct of business, the provision of a service, or upon the payment of a fee, but does not include any private property to which the public otherwise does not have a right of access.

(2) As used in division (B)(4) of this section, "casual passerby" means a person who does not have depositing litter in a litter receptacle as his primary reason for traveling to or by the property on which the litter receptacle is located.

(D) As used in this section:

(1) "Litter" means garbage, trash, waste, rubbish, ashes, cans, bottles, wire, paper, cartons, boxes, automobile parts, furniture, glass, or anything else of an unsightly or unsanitary nature.

(2) "Deposit" means to throw, drop, discard, or place.

(3) "Litter receptacle" means a dumpster, trash can, trash bin, garbage can, or similar container in which litter is deposited for removal.

(E) This section may be enforced by any sheriff, deputy sheriff, police officer of a municipal corporation, police constable or officer of a township or township police district, wildlife officer, park officer, forest officer, preserve officer, conservancy district police officer, inspector of nuisances of a county, or any other law enforcement officer within his jurisdiction.

(1994 S 182, eff. 10–20–94; 1993 H 114, eff. 9–27–93; 1987 H 333; 1980 H 361; 132 v H 152)

3767.33 Authorization for disposal of materials; injunction against disposal

No zoning commission, municipal corporation, or other governmental authority, except the director of environmental protection acting pursuant to the powers granted to him in sections 6111.01 to 6111.08 of the Revised Code, may authorize the placing or disposal of materials in or upon the banks of a ditch, stream, river, or other watercourse after January 1, 1968, where such placing or disposal would be prohibited under the provisions of section 3767.32 of the Revised Code. Such placing or disposal may be enjoined by the common pleas court in the county in which the placing or disposal occurs, upon application by the prosecuting attorney of the county, the director of environmental protection, the director of health, or the attorney general.

(1972 S 397, eff. 10–23–72; 132 v H 152)

3767.34 Rest rooms; certain free facilities required

(A) No person shall make available any rest room facility intended for multiple occupancy and which requires payment of money or any other thing of value for entry into the rest room facility, or for use of a toilet within, unless said person also makes available for use by the same sex, at the same location, an equal number of the same kind of rest room facilities, toilets, urinals, and washbowls free of charge.

(B) Rest room facilities having no more than one toilet and a washbowl, or having no more than one toilet, one urinal, and one washbowl, shall be exempt from the provisions of division (A) of this section if a key is made available immediately, or other means of access made available immediately, for any customer who requests use of the rest room facility or the toilet, urinal, or washbowl within.

(C) As used in divisions (A) and (B) of this section, "rest room facility" means any room or area containing one or more toilets, washbowls, or urinals; "multiple occupancy" means a rest room facility containing more than one toilet and one washbowl, or containing more than one toilet, one urinal, and one washbowl used for the purpose of eliminating human biological waste materials and commonly referred to as "lavatory," "toilet," "urinal," or "water closet."

(1976 S 71, eff. 8–18–76)

ABANDONED AND UNSAFE BUILDINGS

3767.41 Injunctive relief; appointment of receiver; rehabilitation plans; demolition

(A) As used in this section:

(1) "Building" means, except as otherwise provided in this division, any building or structure that is used or intended to be used for residential purposes. "Building" includes, but is not limited to, a building or structure in which any floor is used for retail stores, shops, salesrooms, markets, or similar commercial uses, or for offices, banks, civic administration activities, professional services, or similar business or civic uses, and in which the other floors are used, or designed and intended to be used, for residential purposes. "Building" does not include any building or structure that is occupied by its owner and that contains three or fewer residential units.

(2) "Public nuisance" means a building that is a menace to the public health, welfare, or safety; that is structurally unsafe, unsanitary, or not provided with adequate safe egress; that constitutes a fire hazard, is otherwise dangerous to human life, or is otherwise no longer fit and habitable; or that, in relation to its existing use, constitutes a hazard to the public health, welfare, or safety by reason of inadequate maintenance, dilapidation, obsolescence, or abandonment.

(3) "Abate" or "abatement" in connection with any building means the removal or correction of any conditions that constitute a public nuisance and the making of any other improvements that are needed to effect a rehabilitation of the building that is consistent with maintaining safe and habitable conditions over its remaining useful life. "Abatement" does not include the closing or boarding up of any building that is found to be a public nuisance.

(4) "Interested party" means any owner, mortgagee, lienholder, tenant, or person that possesses an interest of record in any property that becomes subject to the jurisdiction of a court pursuant to this section, and any applicant for the appointment of a receiver pursuant to this section.

(5) "Neighbor" means any owner of property, including, but not limited to, any person who is purchasing property by land installment contract or under a duly executed purchase contract, that is located within five hundred feet of any property that becomes subject to the jurisdiction of a court pursuant to this section, and any occupant of a building that is so located.

(6) "Tenant" has the same meaning as in section 5321.01 of the Revised Code.

(B)(1) In any civil action to enforce any local building, housing, air pollution, sanitation, health, fire, zoning, or safety code, ordinance, or regulation applicable to buildings, that is commenced in a court of common pleas, municipal court, housing or environmental division of a municipal court, or county court, or in any civil action for abatement commenced in a court of common pleas, municipal court, housing or environmental division of a municipal court, or county court, by a municipal corporation in which the building involved is located, by any neighbor, tenant, or by a nonprofit corporation that is duly organized and has as one of its goals the improvement of housing conditions in the county or municipal corporation in which the building involved is located, if a building is alleged to be a public nuisance, the municipal corporation, neighbor, tenant, or nonprofit corporation may apply in its complaint for an injunction or other order as described in division (C)(1) of this section, or for the relief described in division (C)(2) of this section, including, if necessary, the appointment of a receiver as described in divisions (C)(2) and (3) of this section, or for both such an injunction or other order and such relief. The municipal corporation, neighbor, tenant, or nonprofit corporation commencing the action is not liable for the costs, expenses, and fees of any receiver appointed pursuant to divisions (C)(2) and (3) of this section.

(2)(a) In a civil action described in division (B)(1) of this section, a copy of the complaint and a notice of the date and time of a hearing on the complaint shall be served upon the owner of the building and all other interested parties in accordance with the Rules of Civil Procedure. If certified mail service, personal service, or residence service of the complaint and notice is refused or certified mail service of the complaint and notice is not claimed, and if the municipal corporation, neighbor, tenant, or nonprofit corporation commencing the action makes a written request for ordinary mail service of the complaint and notice, or uses publication service, in accordance with the Rules of Civil Procedure, then a copy of the complaint and notice shall be posted in a conspicuous place on the building.

(b) The judge in a civil action described in division (B)(1) of this section shall conduct a hearing at least twenty-eight days after the owner of the building and the other interested parties have been served with a copy of the complaint and the notice of the date and time of the hearing in accordance with division (B)(2)(a) of this section.

(C)(1) If the judge in a civil action described in division (B)(1) of this section finds at the hearing required by division (B)(2) of this section that the building involved is a public nuisance, if the judge additionally determines that the owner of the building previously has not been afforded a reasonable opportunity to abate the public nuisance or has been afforded such an opportunity and has not refused or failed to abate the public nuisance, and if the complaint of the municipal corporation, neighbor, tenant, or nonprofit corporation commencing the action requested the issuance of an injunction as described in this division, then the judge may issue an injunction requiring the owner of the building to abate the public nuisance or issue any other order that the judge considers necessary or appropriate to cause the abatement of the public nuisance. If an injunction is issued pursuant to this division, the owner of the building involved shall be given no more than thirty days from the date of the entry of the judge's order to comply with the injunction, unless the judge, for good cause shown, extends the time for compliance.

(2) If the judge in a civil action described in division (B)(1) of this section finds at the hearing required by division (B)(2) of this section that the building involved is a public nuisance, if the judge additionally determines that the owner of the building previously has been afforded a reasonable opportunity to abate the public nuisance and has refused or failed to do so, and if the complaint of the municipal corporation, neighbor, tenant, or nonprofit corporation commencing the action requested relief as described in this division, then the judge shall offer any mortgagee, lienholder, or other interested party associated with the property on which the building is located, in the order of the priority of interest in title, the opportunity to undertake the work and to furnish the materials necessary to abate the public nuisance. Prior to selecting any interested party, the judge shall require the interested party to demonstrate the ability to promptly undertake the work and furnish the materials required, to provide the judge with a viable financial and construction plan for the rehabilitation of the building as described in division (D) of this section, and to

post security for the performance of the work and the furnishing of the materials.

If the judge determines, at the hearing, that no interested party is willing or able to undertake the work and to furnish the materials necessary to abate the public nuisance, or if the judge determines, at any time after the hearing, that any party who is undertaking corrective work pursuant to this division cannot or will not proceed, or has not proceeded with due diligence, the judge may appoint a receiver pursuant to division (C)(3) of this section to take possession and control of the building.

(3)(a) The judge in a civil action described in division (B)(1) of this section shall not appoint any person as a receiver unless the person first has provided the judge with a viable financial and construction plan for the rehabilitation of the building involved as described in division (D) of this section and has demonstrated the capacity and expertise to perform the required work and to furnish the required materials in a satisfactory manner. An appointed receiver may be a financial institution that possesses an interest of record in the building or the property on which it is located, a nonprofit corporation as described in divisions (B)(1) and (C)(3)(b) of this section, including, but not limited to, a nonprofit corporation that commenced the action described in division (B)(1) of this section, or any other qualified property manager.

(b) To be eligible for appointment as a receiver, no part of the net earnings of a nonprofit corporation shall inure to the benefit of any private shareholder or individual. Membership on the board of trustees of a nonprofit corporation appointed as a receiver does not constitute the holding of a public office or employment within the meaning of sections 731.02 and 731.12 or any other section of the Revised Code and does not constitute a direct or indirect interest in a contract or expenditure of money by any municipal corporation. A member of a board of trustees of a nonprofit corporation appointed as a receiver shall not be disqualified from holding any public office or employment, and shall not forfeit any public office or employment, by reason of his membership on the board of trustees, notwithstanding any law to the contrary.

(D) Prior to ordering any work to be undertaken, or the furnishing of any materials, to abate a public nuisance under this section, the judge in a civil action described in division (B)(1) of this section shall review the submitted financial and construction plan for the rehabilitation of the building involved and, if it specifies all of the following, shall approve that plan:

(1) The estimated cost of the labor, materials, and any other development costs that are required to abate the public nuisance;

(2) The estimated income and expenses of the building and the property on which it is located after the furnishing of the materials and the completion of the repairs and improvements;

(3) The terms, conditions, and availability of any financing that is necessary to perform the work and to furnish the materials;

(4) If repair and rehabilitation of the building are found not to be feasible, the cost of demolition of the building or of the portions of the building that constitute the public nuisance.

(E) Upon the written request of any of the interested parties to have a building, or portions of a building, that constitute a public nuisance demolished because repair and rehabilitation of the building are found not to be feasible, the judge may order the demolition. However, the demolition shall not be ordered unless the requesting interested parties have paid the costs of demolition and, if any, of the receivership, and, if any, all notes, certificates, mortgages, and fees of the receivership.

(F) Before proceeding with his duties, any receiver appointed by the judge in a civil action described in division (B)(1) of this section may be required by the judge to post a bond in an amount fixed by the judge, but not exceeding the value of the building involved as determined by the judge.

The judge may empower the receiver to do any or all of the following:

(1) Take possession and control of the building and the property on which it is located, operate and manage the building and the property, establish and collect rents and income, lease and rent the building and the property, and evict tenants;

(2) Pay all expenses of operating and conserving the building and the property, including, but not limited to, the cost of electricity, gas, water, sewerage, heating fuel, repairs and supplies, custodian services, taxes and assessments, and insurance premiums, and hire and pay reasonable compensation to a managing agent;

(3) Pay pre-receivership mortgages or installments of them and other liens;

(4) Perform or enter into contracts for the performance of all work and the furnishing of materials necessary to abate, and obtain financing for the abatement of, the public nuisance;

(5) Pursuant to court order, remove and dispose of any personal property abandoned, stored, or otherwise located in or on the building and the property that creates a dangerous or unsafe condition or that constitutes a violation of any local building, housing, air pollution, sanitation, health, fire, zoning, or safety code, ordinance, or regulation;

(6) Obtain mortgage insurance for any receiver's mortgage from any agency of the federal government;

(7) Enter into any agreement and do those things necessary to maintain and preserve the building and the property and comply with all local building, housing, air pollution, sanitation, health, fire, zoning, or safety codes, ordinances, and regulations;

(8) Give the custody of the building and the property, and the opportunity to abate the nuisance and operate the property, to its owner or any mortgagee or lienholder of record;

(9) Issue notes and secure them by a mortgage bearing interest, and upon terms and conditions, that the judge approves. When sold or transferred by the receiver in return for valuable consideration in money, material, labor, or services, the notes or certificates shall be freely transferable. Any mortgages granted by the receiver shall be superior to any claims of the receiver. Priority among the receiver's mortgages shall be determined by the order in which they are recorded.

(G) A receiver appointed pursuant to this section is not personally liable except for misfeasance, malfeasance, or nonfeasance in the performance of the functions of his office.

(H)(1) The judge in a civil action described in division (B)(1) of this section may assess as court costs, the expenses described in division (F)(2) of this section, and may approve receiver's fees to the extent that they are not covered by the income from the property. Subject to that limitation, a receiver appointed pursuant to divisions (C)(2) and (3) of this section is entitled to receive fees in the same manner and to the same extent as receivers appointed in actions to foreclose mortgages.

(2)(a) Pursuant to the police powers vested in the state, all expenditures of a mortgagee, lienholder, or other interested party that has been selected pursuant to division (C)(2) of this section to undertake the work and to furnish the materials necessary to abate a public nuisance, and any expenditures in connection with the foreclosure of the lien created by this division, is a first lien upon the building involved and the property on which it is located and is superior to all prior and subsequent liens or other encumbrances associated with the building or the property, including, but not limited to, those for taxes and assessments, upon the occurrence of both of the following:

(i) The prior approval of the expenditures by, and the entry of a judgment to that effect by, the judge in the civil action described in division (B)(1) of this section;

(ii) The recordation of a certified copy of the judgment entry and a sufficient description of the property on which the building is located with the county recorder in the county in which the property is located within sixty days after the date of the entry of the judgment.

(b) Pursuant to the police powers vested in the state, all expenses and other amounts paid in accordance with division (F) of this section by a receiver appointed pursuant to divisions (C)(2) and (3) of this section, the amounts of any notes issued by the receiver in accordance with division (F) of this section, all mortgages granted by the receiver in accordance with that division, the fees of the receiver approved pursuant to division (H)(1) of this section, and any amounts expended in connection with the foreclosure of a mortgage granted by the receiver in accordance with division (F) of this section or with the foreclosure of the lien created by this division, are a first lien upon the building involved and the property on which it is located and are superior to all prior and subsequent liens or other encumbrances associated with the building or the property, including, but not limited to, those for taxes and assessments, upon the occurrence of both of the following:

(i) The approval of the expenses, amounts, or fees by, and the entry of a judgment to that effect by, the judge in the civil action described in division (B)(1) of this section; or the approval of the mortgages in accordance with division (F)(9) of this section by, and the entry of a judgment to that effect by, that judge;

(ii) The recordation of a certified copy of the judgment entry and a sufficient description of the property on which the building is located, or, in the case of a mortgage, the recordation of the mortgage, a certified copy of the judgment entry, and such a description, with the county recorder of the county in which the property is located within sixty days after the date of the entry of the judgment.

(c) Priority among the liens described in divisions (H)(2)(a) and (b) of this section shall be determined as described in division (I) of this section. Additionally, the creation pursuant to this section of a mortgage lien that is prior to or superior to any mortgage of record at the time the mortgage lien is so created, does not disqualify the mortgage of record as a legal investment under Chapter 1107. or 1151. or any other chapter of the Revised Code.

(I)(1) If a receiver appointed pursuant to divisions (C)(2) and (3) of this section files with the judge in the civil action described in division (B)(1) of this section a report indicating that the public nuisance has been abated, if the judge confirms that the receiver has abated the public nuisance, and if the receiver or any interested party requests the judge to enter an order directing the receiver to sell the building and the property on which it is located, the judge may enter that order after holding a hearing as described in division (I)(2) of this section and otherwise complying with that division.

(2) The receiver or interested party requesting an order as described in division (I)(1) of this section shall cause a notice of the date and time of a hearing on the request to be served on the owner of the building involved and all other interested parties in accordance with division (B)(2)(a) of this section. The judge in the civil action described in division (B)(1) of this section shall conduct the scheduled hearing. At the hearing, if the owner or any interested party objects to the sale of the building and the property, the burden of proof shall be upon the objecting person to establish, by a preponderance of the evidence, that the benefits of not selling the building and the property outweigh the benefits of selling them. If the judge determines that there is no objecting person, or if the judge determines that there is one or more objecting persons but no objecting person has sustained the burden of proof specified in this division, the judge may enter an order directing the receiver to offer the building and the property for sale upon terms and conditions that the judge shall specify.

(3) If a sale of a building and the property on which it is located is ordered pursuant to divisions (I)(1) and (2) of this section and if the sale occurs in accordance with the terms and conditions specified by the judge in his order of sale, then the receiver shall distribute the proceeds of the sale and the balance of any funds that the receiver may possess, after the payment of the costs of the sale, in the following order of priority and in the described manner:

(a) First, in satisfaction of any notes issued by the receiver pursuant to division (F) of this section, in their order of priority;

(b) Second, any unreimbursed expenses and other amounts paid in accordance with division (F) of this section by the receiver, and the fees of the receiver approved pursuant to division (H)(1) of this section;

(c) Third, all expenditures of a mortgagee, lienholder, or other interested party that has been selected pursuant to division (C)(2) of this section to undertake the work and to furnish the materials necessary to abate a public nuisance, provided that the expenditures were approved as described in division (H)(2)(a) of this section and provided that, if any such interested party subsequently became the receiver, its expenditures shall be paid prior to the expenditures of any of the other interested parties so selected;

(d) Fourth, the amount due for delinquent taxes, assessments, charges, penalties, and interest owed to this state or a political subdivision of this state, provided that, if the amount available for distribution pursuant to division (I)(3)(d) of this section is insufficient to pay the entire amount of those taxes, assessments, charges, penalties, and interest, the proceeds and remaining funds shall be paid to each claimant in proportion to the amount of those taxes, assessments, charges, penalties, and interest that each is due.

(e) The amount of any pre-receivership mortgages, liens, or other encumbrances, in their order of priority.

(4) Following a distribution in accordance with division (I)(3) of this section, the receiver shall request the judge in the civil action described in division (B)(1) of this section to enter an order terminating the receivership. If the judge determines that the sale of the building and the property on which it is located occurred in accordance with the terms and conditions specified by the judge in his order of sale under division (I)(2) of this section and that the receiver distributed the proceeds of the sale and the balance of any funds that the receiver possessed, after the payment of the costs of the sale, in accordance with division (I)(3) of this section, and if the judge approves any final accounting required of the receiver, the judge may terminate the receivership.

(J)(1) A receiver appointed pursuant to divisions (C)(2) and (3) of this section may be discharged at any time in the discretion of the judge in the civil action described in division (B)(1) of this section. The receiver shall be discharged by the judge as provided in division (I)(4) of this section, or when all of the following have occurred:

(a) The public nuisance has been abated;

(b) All costs, expenses, and approved fees of the receivership have been paid;

(c) Either all receiver's notes issued and mortgages granted pursuant to this section have been paid, or all the holders of the notes and mortgages request that the receiver be discharged.

(2) If a judge in a civil action described in division (B)(1) of this section determines that, and enters of record a declaration that, a public nuisance has been abated by a receiver, and if, within three days after the entry of the declaration, all costs, expenses, and approved fees of the receivership have not been paid in full, then, in addition to the circumstances specified in division (I) of this section for the entry of such an order, the judge may enter an order directing the receiver to sell the

building involved and the property on which it is located. Any such order shall be entered, and the sale shall occur, only in compliance with division (I) of this section.

(K) The title in any building, and in the property on which it is located, that is sold at a sale ordered under division (I) or (J)(2) of this section shall be incontestable in the purchaser and shall be free and clear of all liens for delinquent taxes, assessments, charges, penalties, and interest owed to this state or any political subdivision of this state, that could not be satisfied from the proceeds of the sale and the remaining funds in the receiver's possession pursuant to the distribution under division (I)(3) of this section. All other liens and encumbrances with respect to the building and the property shall survive the sale, including, but not limited to, a federal tax lien notice properly filed in accordance with section 317.09 of the Revised Code prior to the time of the sale, and the easements and covenants of record running with the property that were created prior to the time of the sale.

(L)(1) Nothing in this section shall be construed as a limitation upon the powers granted to a court of common pleas, a municipal court or a housing or environmental division of a municipal court under Chapter 1901. of the Revised Code, or a county court under Chapter 1907. of the Revised Code.

(2) The monetary and other limitations specified in Chapters 1901. and 1907. of the Revised Code upon the jurisdiction of municipal and county courts, and of housing or environmental divisions of municipal courts, in civil actions do not operate as limitations upon any of the following:

(a) Expenditures of a mortgagee, lienholder, or other interested party that has been selected pursuant to division (C)(2) of this section to undertake the work and to furnish the materials necessary to abate a public nuisance;

(b) Any notes issued by a receiver pursuant to division (F) of this section;

(c) Any mortgage granted by a receiver in accordance with division (F) of this section;

(d) Expenditures in connection with the foreclosure of a mortgage granted by a receiver in accordance with division (F) of this section;

(e) The enforcement of an order of a judge entered pursuant to this section;

(f) The actions that may be taken pursuant to this section by a receiver or a mortgagee, lienholder, or other interested party that has been selected pursuant to division (C)(2) of this section to undertake the work and to furnish the materials necessary to abate a public nuisance.

(3) A judge in a civil action described in division (B)(1) of this section, or the judge's successor in office, has continuing jurisdiction to review the condition of any building that was determined to be a public nuisance pursuant to this section.

(1996 H 538, eff. 1–1–97; 1991 H 200, eff. 7–8–91; 1990 H 387; 1984 H 706)

PENALTIES

3767.99 Penalties

(A) Whoever is guilty of contempt under sections 3767.01 to 3767.11 or violates section 3767.14 of the Revised Code is guilty of a misdemeanor of the first degree.

(B) Whoever violates section 3767.12 or 3767.29, or, being an association, violates section 3767.30 of the Revised Code is guilty of a misdemeanor of the fourth degree.

(C) Whoever violates section 3767.13, 3767.19, or 3767.32 or, being a natural person, violates section 3767.30 of the Revised Code is guilty of a misdemeanor of the third degree. The sentencing court may, in addition to or in lieu of the penalty provided in this division, require a person who violates section 3767.32 of the Revised Code to remove litter from any public or private property, or in or on waters of the state.

(D) Whoever violates section 3767.16, 3767.17, 3767.18, 3767.201, or 3767.34 of the Revised Code is guilty of a minor misdemeanor.

(1980 H 361, eff. 7–14–80; 1976 S 71; 1970 S 460; 132 v H 152; 130 v H 1, H 602; 129 v 1075; 128 v 1217; 127 v 242; 126 v 374; 1953 H 1)

CHAPTER 3770

STATE LOTTERY

3770.08 Prohibitions

(A) No person shall sell a lottery ticket at a price greater than that fixed by rule of the state lottery commission.

(B) No person other than a licensed lottery sales agent shall sell lottery tickets, but nothing in this section shall be construed to prevent any person from giving lottery tickets to another as a gift. A transfer of lottery tickets by any person which is made in connection with a marketing, promotional, or advertising program shall be deemed to be a gift for the purposes of this chapter.

(C) No person shall sell a lottery ticket to any person under eighteen years of age, and no person under eighteen years of age shall attempt to purchase a lottery ticket.

(D) No person, directly or indirectly, on behalf of self, or another, nor any organization, shall invite, solicit, demand, offer, or accept any payment, contribution, favor, or other consideration to influence the award, renewal, or retention of a lottery sales agent license.

(E) Except as otherwise provided in this division, no person shall sell lottery tickets on any fairgrounds during any annual exhibition conducted in accordance with Chapter 991. or 1711. of the Revised Code. "Fairgrounds" includes any land or property under the control or management of any agricultural society or of the Ohio expositions commission. This division does not apply to the sale of lottery tickets by the commission at the state fairground during the state fair.

(1996 S 211, eff. 9–26–96; 1984 H 665, eff. 4–4–85; 1977 H 395; 1973 H 990)

3770.99 Penalties

(A) Whoever is prohibited from claiming a lottery prize award under division (E) of section 3770.07 of the Revised Code and attempts to claim or is paid a lottery prize award is guilty of a minor misdemeanor, and shall provide restitution to the state lottery commission of any moneys erroneously paid as a lottery prize award to that person.

(B) Whoever violates division (C) of section 3770.071 or section 3770.08 of the Revised Code is guilty of a misdemeanor of the third degree.

(2003 H 95, eff. 9–26–03; 1996 S 211, eff. 9–26–96; 1973 H 990, eff. 11–21–73)

CHAPTER 3773

BOXING; DISCHARGING FIREARMS; DUELING

PROHIBITIONS

3773.06 Hunting near township park

No person shall hunt, shoot, or kill game within one-half mile of a township park.

The board of township park commissioners may grant permission to kill game not desired within the limits prohibited by this section.

(1974 H 295, eff. 7–22–74; 1953 H 1; GC 12820)

3773.13 Suppression of prize fight

When a sheriff has reason to believe that a fight or contention is about to take place in his county, he shall forthwith summon sufficient citizens of the county, suppress such fight or contention, and arrest all persons found at such prize fight violating the law and take them before a judge of the court of common pleas or magistrate.

(1953 H 1, eff. 10–1–53; GC 13429–4)

OHIO ATHLETIC COMMISSION; LICENSES AND PERMITS

3773.32 Licenses required

No person shall promote, sponsor, or conduct a public boxing match or exhibition unless such person is licensed under section 3773.36, secures a permit to conduct the match or exhibition under section 3773.38, and otherwise complies with sections 3773.31 to 3773.57 of the Revised Code.

No person shall promote or conduct a professional wrestling match or exhibition unless such person is licensed under section 3773.36, secures a permit to conduct the match or exhibition under section 3773.38, and otherwise complies with applicable provisions of sections 3773.31 to 3773.57 of the Revised Code.

No person shall participate in a public boxing match or exhibition as a referee, judge, matchmaker, timekeeper, or contestant, or as a manager, trainer, or second of a contestant, unless such person is licensed under section 3773.41 of the Revised Code and otherwise complies with sections 3773.31 to 3773.57 of the Revised Code.

Sections 3773.31 to 3773.57 of the Revised Code do not apply to any boxing, karate, or wrestling match or exhibition conducted as part of an interscholastic or intercollegiate athletic program, or as part of an amateur athletic program sponsored by or under the supervision of the national amateur athletic union or the American olympic association in which all contestants are amateur boxers, amateur participants in a karate match or exhibition, or amateur wrestlers, or to any boxing, karate, or wrestling match or exhibition conducted under the supervision or control of the Ohio national guard, the state militia, or reserve officers' associations in which all contestants are members of the guard, militia, or officers' association.

(1996 S 240, eff. 9–3–96; 1983 H 291, eff. 7–1–83; 1981 S 60)

3773.33 Ohio athletic commission

(A) There is hereby created the Ohio athletic commission. The commission shall consist of five voting members appointed by the governor with the advice and consent of the senate, not more than three of whom shall be of the same political party, and two nonvoting members, one of whom shall be a member of the senate appointed by and to serve at the pleasure of the president of the senate and one of whom shall be a member of the house of representatives appointed by and to serve at the pleasure of the speaker of the house of representatives. To be eligible for appointment as a voting member, a person shall be a qualified elector and a resident of the state for not less than five years immediately preceding the person's appointment. Two voting members shall be knowledgeable in boxing, at least one voting member shall be knowledgeable and experienced in high school athletics, one voting member shall be knowledgeable and experienced in professional athletics, and at least one voting member shall be knowledgeable and experienced in collegiate athletics. One commission member shall hold the degree of doctor of medicine or doctor of osteopathy.

(B) No person shall be appointed to the commission or be an employee of the commission who is licensed, registered, or regulated by the commission. No member shall have any legal or beneficial interest, direct or indirect, pecuniary or otherwise, in any person who is licensed, registered, or regulated by the commission or who participates in prize fights or public boxing or wrestling matches or exhibitions. No member shall participate in any fight, match, or exhibition other than in the member's official capacity as a member of the commission, or as an inspector as authorized in section 3773.52 of the Revised Code.

(C) The governor shall appoint the voting members to the commission. Of the initial appointments, two shall be for terms ending one year after September 3, 1996, two shall be for terms ending two years after September 3, 1996, and one shall be for a term ending three years after September 3, 1996. Thereafter, terms of office shall be for three years, each term ending the same day of the same month of the year as did the term which it succeeds. Each member shall hold office from the date of the member's appointment until the end of the term for which the member was appointed. Any member appointed to fill a vacancy occurring prior to the expiration of the term for which the member's predecessor was appointed shall hold office for the remainder of the term. Any member shall continue in office subsequent to the expiration date of the member's term until the member's successor takes office, or until a period of sixty days has elapsed, whichever occurs first.

The governor shall name one voting member as chairperson of the commission at the time of making the appointment of any member for a full term. Three voting members shall constitute a quorum, and the affirmative vote of three voting members shall be necessary for any action taken by the commission. No vacancy on the commission impairs the authority of the remaining members to exercise all powers of the commission.

Voting members, when engaged in commission duties, shall receive a per diem compensation determined in accordance with division (J) of section 124.15 of the Revised Code, and all members shall receive their actual and necessary expenses incurred in the performance of their official duties.

Each voting member, before entering upon the discharge of the member's duties, shall file a surety bond payable to the treasurer of state in the sum of ten thousand dollars. Each surety bond shall be conditioned upon the faithful performance of the duties of the office, executed by a surety company authorized to transact business in this state, and filed in the office of the secretary of state.

The governor may remove any voting member for malfeasance, misfeasance, or nonfeasance in office after giving the member a copy of the charges against the member and affording the member an opportunity for a public hearing, at which the member may be represented by counsel, upon not less than ten days' notice. If the member is removed, the governor shall file a complete statement of all charges made against the member and the governor's finding on the charges in the office of the secretary of state, together with a complete report of the proceedings. The governor's decision shall be final.

(2003 H 95, eff. 9–26–03; 2000 H 107, eff. 3–22–01; 1996 S 240, eff. 9–3–96)

3773.37 Photographs for identification

The Ohio athletic commission shall cause a photograph with identification of any person signing the application for a license under section 3773.35 or 3773.41 of the Revised Code to be taken in duplicate and filed with the commission.. [sic.] For purposes of this section, the commission may allow a photograph with identification to be a photocopy of a valid commercial driver's license issued under Chapter 4506. or a driver's license issued under Chapter 4507. of the Revised Code.

(1996 S 240, eff. 9–3–96; 1981 S 60, eff. 7–27–81)

3773.40 Prohibitions; changes in conditions for match

No person who holds a promoter's license to conduct a public boxing match or exhibition under section 3773.36 of the Revised Code shall:

(A) Hold any match or exhibition at any time or place other than that stated on a permit issued under section 3773.38 of the Revised Code;

(B) Allow any contestant to participate in the match or exhibition unless the contestant is the licensed contestant named in the application for such permit or a licensed contestant authorized to compete as a substitute for such a contestant by the inspector assigned to the facility where the match or exhibition is held for that match or exhibition;

(C) Charge a higher admission price for a match or exhibition than that stated in the application;

(D) Pay a greater compensation or percentage of the gate receipts to any contestant than that stated in the application.

The Ohio athletic commission, upon application by a holder of a permit under section 3773.38 of the Revised Code, may allow the permit holder to hold the match or exhibition for which the permit was issued at an alternative site that is within the same municipal corporation or township and that offers substantially similar seating facilities, or allow the permit holder to substitute contestants or seconds, provided that the substitute contestants are evenly matched with their opponents in skill, experience, and weight.

(1996 S 240, eff. 9–3–96; 1981 S 60, eff. 7–27–81)

CONTESTANTS—PROMOTERS

3773.44 Insurance for contestants

No holder of a promoter's license under section 3773.36 of the Revised Code shall fail to insure each contestant in a public boxing match or exhibition the promoter conducts for hospital, nursing, and medication expenses and for physicians' and surgeons' services. The amount of such insurance shall not be less than five thousand dollars and shall be paid to or for the use of a contestant for any injuries sustained in a contest. No licensee shall fail to provide life insurance to each contestant. The amount of life insurance shall be not less than ten thousand dollars and shall be paid to the contestant's estate if the contestant dies as the result of participation in the match or exhibition.

(1996 S 240, eff. 9–3–96; 1981 S 60, eff. 7–27–81)

3773.45 Examinations by medical practitioner; reports; length of matches; officials; gloves

(A) Each contestant in a public boxing match or exhibition shall be examined not more than twenty-four hours before entering the ring by a licensed physician, a physician assistant, a clinical nurse specialist, a certified nurse practitioner, or a certified nurse-midwife. Each contestant who has had a previous match or exhibition on or after July 27, 1981, and was knocked out at that match or exhibition shall present to the examiner a record of the physical examination performed at the conclusion of that match or exhibition. If, after reviewing such record and performing a physical examination of the contestant, the examiner determines that the contestant is physically fit to compete, the physician shall certify that fact on the contestant's physical examination form. No physician, physician assistant, clinical nurse specialist, certified nurse practitioner, or certified nurse-midwife shall certify a contestant as physically fit to compete if the physician, physician assistant, clinical nurse specialist, certified nurse practitioner, or certified nurse-midwife determines that the contestant was knocked out in a contest that took place within the preceding thirty days. No contestant shall compete in a public boxing match or exhibition unless the contestant has been certified as physically fit in accordance with this section.

Immediately after the end of a match or exhibition, the examiner shall examine each contestant who was knocked out in the match or exhibition, and record the outcome of the match or exhibition and any physical injuries sustained by the contestant on the contestant's physical examination form.

Within twenty-four hours after the match or exhibition, the examiner shall mail one copy of the examination report to the Ohio athletic commission and one copy to the contestant. The commission shall furnish blank copies of the examination report to the examiner. The examiner shall answer all questions on the form. The person conducting the match or exhibition shall compensate the examiner. No person shall conduct such a match or exhibition unless an examiner appointed by the commission is in attendance.

(B) No holder of a promoter's license shall conduct a boxing match or exhibition that exceeds twelve rounds. Each round shall be not more than three minutes in length. A period of at least one minute, during which no boxing or sparring takes place, shall occur between rounds.

No holder of a promoter's license or a permit issued under section 3773.39 of the Revised Code shall allow a professional boxer to participate in more than twelve rounds of boxing within a period of seventy-two consecutive hours. For any match or exhibition or for a class of contestants, the commission may limit the number of rounds within the maximum of twelve rounds.

(C) No person shall conduct a boxing match or exhibition unless a licensed referee appointed by the commission and paid by the person is present. The referee shall direct and control the match or exhibition. Before each match or exhibition the referee shall obtain from each contestant the name of the contestant's chief second and shall hold the chief second responsible for the conduct of any assistant seconds during the match or exhibition. The referee may declare a prize, remuneration, or purse or any part thereof to which a contestant is otherwise entitled withheld if, in the referee's judgment, the contestant is not competing or did not compete honestly. A contestant may appeal the referee's decision in a hearing before the commission conducted in accordance with section 3773.52 of the Revised Code.

(D) No person shall hold or conduct a boxing match or exhibition unless three licensed judges appointed by the commission and paid by the person are present. Each judge shall render a decision at the end of each match or exhibition. The judges shall determine the outcome of the match or exhibition, and their decision shall be final.

(E) Each contestant in a boxing match or exhibition shall wear gloves weighing not less than six ounces during the boxing match or exhibition.

(2002 S 245, eff. 3–31–03; 1996 S 240, eff. 9–3–96; 1988 H 708, eff. 4–19–88; 1981 S 60)

3773.46 Age of contestants; gambling prohibited; fake matches

No person who sponsors, promotes, or conducts a public boxing or wrestling match or exhibition shall do any of the following:

(A) Knowingly permit a person less than eighteen years of age to participate in a public boxing or wrestling match or exhibition;

(B) Knowingly permit gambling, betting, or wagering on the result of a contingency in connection with the match or exhibition;

(C) Knowingly conduct or allow to be conducted a sham or fake match or exhibition unless the sport is professional wrestling.

(1996 S 240, eff. 9–3–96; 1981 S 60, eff. 7–27–81)

PROHIBITIONS

3773.47 Offenses by person other than promoter

No person shall do any of the following:

(A) Violate sections 3773.31 to 3773.57 of the Revised Code or any rule of the Ohio athletic commission;

(B) Gamble, bet, or wager on the result of a contingency connected with a public boxing or wrestling match or exhibition;

(C) Participate in a sham or fake public boxing match or exhibition that is conducted by a holder of a promoter's license issued under section 3773.36 of the Revised Code;

(D) Participate in a public boxing match or exhibition if the person is under eighteen years of age;

(E) Conduct a public boxing match or exhibition in violation of the official rules that govern the particular sport.

(1996 S 240, eff. 9–3–96; 1983 H 291, eff. 7–1–83; 1981 S 60)

BOXING MATCHES OR EXHIBITIONS

3773.48 Conflicting financial interests

No person shall have any financial interest in a boxer competing on premises owned or leased by the person or in which the person is otherwise financially interested.

(1981 S 60, eff. 7–27–81)

3773.49 Advertising to include price of admission

Each person who conducts a public boxing or wrestling match or exhibition shall cause to be inserted into each advertisement of the match or exhibition the price of admission.

Each ticket of admission to any such match or exhibition shall clearly bear the purchase price. No person shall sell such a ticket for a price greater than that printed on the ticket. No tickets shall be sold except from the box office on the premises in which the match or exhibition is held or such additional locations as the Ohio athletic commission has authorized in writing as locations from which tickets may be sold for a designated match or exhibition.

(1996 S 240, eff. 9–3–96; 1981 S 60, eff. 7–27–81)

3773.50 Sale of tickets in excess of capacity

No person licensed under section 3773.36 and issued a permit under section 3773.38 of the Revised Code shall sell and issue or cause to be sold or issued more tickets or invitations of admission to a public boxing or wrestling match or exhibition than, or admit to such match or exhibition a number of persons that exceeds, the authorized capacity of the facility or that part of the facility used for the match or exhibition. This limitation on the number of tickets extends to the issuance of complimentary tickets and free passes.

(1996 S 240, eff. 9–3–96; 1981 S 60, eff. 7–27–81)

PENALTIES

3773.99 Penalties

(A) Whoever violates section 3773.06 or 3773.50 of the Revised Code is guilty of a misdemeanor of the fourth degree.

(B) Whoever violates section 3773.32, 3773.40, 3773.44, 3773.45, 3773.46, or 3773.47, division (A) of section 3773.54, or division (B) of section 3773.33 of the Revised Code is guilty of a misdemeanor of the first degree.

(C) Whoever violates section 3773.48 or 3773.49 of the Revised Code is guilty of a minor misdemeanor.

(1999 S 107, eff. 3–23–00; 1996 S 240, eff. 9–3–96; 1983 H 133, eff. 9–27–83; 1981 S 60; 1975 H 1; 1974 H 1041; 1973 H 59; 1972 H 511; 129 v 1625; 128 v 862; 126 v 392; 1953 H 1)

CHAPTER 3793

ALCOHOL AND DRUG ADDICTION SERVICES

Section

3793.15 Program for addicted pregnant women

(A) The department of alcohol and drug addiction services, in accordance with division (B) of this section, shall give priority to developing, and promptly shall develop, with available public and private resources a program that does all of the following:

(1) Provides a manner of identifying the aggregate number of pregnant women in this state who are addicted to a drug of abuse;

(2) Provides for an effective means of intervention to eliminate the addiction of pregnant women to drugs of abuse prior to the birth of their children;

(3) Provides for the continued monitoring of women who were addicted to a drug of abuse during their pregnancies, after the birth of their children, and for the availability of treatment and rehabilitation for those women;

(4) Provides a manner of determining the aggregate number of children who are born in this state to women who are addicted, at the time of birth, to a drug of abuse, and of children who are born in this state with an addiction to or a dependency on a drug of abuse;

(5) Provides for the continued monitoring of children who are born in this state to women who are addicted, at the time of birth, to a drug of abuse, or who are born in this state with an addiction to or dependency on a drug of abuse, after their birth;

(6) Provides for the treatment and rehabilitation of any child who is born to a woman who is addicted, at the time of birth, to a drug of abuse, and of any child who is born with an addiction to or dependency on a drug of abuse.

(B) In developing the program described in division (A) of this section, the department may obtain information from the department of health and the department of job and family services, and those departments shall cooperate with the department of alcohol and drug addiction services in its development and implementation of the program.

(C) Immediately upon its development of the program described in division (A) of this section, the department shall implement the program.

(D) Any record or information that is obtained or maintained by the department in connection with the program described in division (A) of this section and could enable the identification of any woman or child described in division (A)(1) or (4) of this section is not a public record subject to inspection or copying under section 149.43 of the Revised Code.

(1999 H 471, eff. 7–1–00; 1990 S 258, eff. 8–22–90)

3793.16 Educational and training program for employees of correctional and youth services department institutions

(A) As used in this section, "state correctional institution" has the same meaning as in section 2967.01 of the Revised Code.

(B) The department of alcohol and drug addiction services shall develop a program that is designed to educate and train the employees of each state correctional institution, the employees of each department of youth services institution, and other persons associated by contract or otherwise with each state correctional institution or each department of youth services institution, who will be responsible for the conduct of, or otherwise providing treatment or rehabilitation services pursuant to, a substance abuse treatment or rehabilitation program offered in the institution to adult prisoners or juvenile offenders. Upon the development of the educational and training program, the department of alcohol and drug addiction services promptly shall commence its implementation. The department of alcohol and drug addiction services may charge to the department of rehabilitation and correction and to the department of youth services a reasonable annual fee that reflects the expenses incurred by it during the immediately preceding calendar year in preparing and offering the educational and training program during that year to the respective employees and other associated persons described in this division.

The director of rehabilitation and correction and the director of youth services shall require the respective employees and other associated persons described in this division to attend and successfully complete the educational and training program developed pursuant to this division as a condition of their continuing to have responsibility for the conduct of, or their continuing to provide treatment or rehabilitation services pursuant to, any treatment or rehabilitation program that is offered in a state correctional institution or in a department of youth services institution to adult prisoners or juvenile offenders. If the department of alcohol and drug addiction services charges a reasonable annual fee as described in this division, the director involved shall cause that fee to be paid from any available funds of the department of rehabilitation and correction or any available funds of the department of youth services.

(C) The department of rehabilitation and correction and the department of alcohol and drug addiction services jointly shall develop program specifications for the alcohol and drug addiction treatment programs offered in state correctional institutions.

(1995 H 117, eff. 9–29–95; 1994 H 571, eff. 10–6–94; 1990 S 258, eff. 8–22–90)

3793.18 Provision of information to courts

The department of alcohol and drug addiction services promptly shall develop and maintain a program that continually provides the courts of this state with relevant information pertaining to alcohol and drug addiction services and programs available both within their jurisdictions and statewide in order to facilitate the ability of the courts to utilize treatment and rehabilitation alternatives in addition to or in lieu of imposing sentences of imprisonment upon appropriate offenders.

(1990 S 258, eff. 8–22–90)

CHAPTER 3904

INSURANCE TRANSACTION INFORMATION STANDARDS

3904.14 Obtaining information under false pretenses

(A) No person shall knowingly obtain information under false pretenses about an individual from an insurance institution, agent, or insurance support organization.

(B) Whoever violates division (A) of this section is guilty of a felony of the fourth degree.

(1994 H 329, eff. 6–29–95)

CHAPTER 3905

AGENTS

LICENSING

3905.02 License required

No person shall sell, solicit, or negotiate insurance in this state unless the person is licensed for that line of authority in accordance with this chapter.

(2002 S 129, eff. 9–1–02)

LIFE INSURANCE AGENTS

3905.181 Acceptance of commission, service fee or brokerage fee by unlicensed person prohibited

A person shall not accept a commission, service fee, brokerage fee, or other type of consideration for selling, soliciting, or negotiating insurance in this state if that person is required to be licensed under this chapter and is not so licensed.

(2002 S 129, eff. 9–1–02)

3905.182 Life insurance agent not to sell stock of same company

No person licensed to sell life insurance under this chapter, although also licensed to sell securities under section 1707.32 of the Revised Code, shall sell, or receive any compensation in regard to the sale of, any shares of capital stock of any life insurance company or agency for which the person is appointed to sell life insurance, or of any issuer that owns or controls more than one fourth of the shares of any of such companies, or any rights or options to acquire any of such shares. This section does not prohibit the sale of shares of any investment company registered under the "Investment Company Act of 1940," 54 Stat. 789, 15 U.S.C.A. 80a–1, as amended, or any policies, annuities, or other contracts described in section 3907.15 of the Revised Code.

(2002 S 129, eff. 9–1–02)

3905.21 Termination of insurance agent

(A) An insurer or authorized representative of an insurer that terminates the appointment, employment, contract, or other insurance business relationship with an insurance agent shall notify the superintendent of insurance, in the manner prescribed by the superintendent, within thirty days after the effective date of the termination. The insurer shall provide any additional information, documents, records, or other data relating to the termination or activity of the insurance agent that the superintendent requests in writing.

(B) If the termination of an insurance agent is for any of the reasons set forth in division (B) of section 3905.14 of the Revised Code, the insurer or authorized representative of the insurer shall promptly notify the superintendent, in the manner prescribed by the superintendent, of any additional information the insurer discovers upon further review or investigation, which information would have been provided to the superintendent in accordance with division (A) of this section had the insurer known of its existence.

(C)(1) An insurer, within fifteen days after notifying the superintendent in accordance with division (A) or (B) of this section, shall mail a copy of the notification to the insurance agent at the agent's last known address. If the insurance agent was terminated for any of the reasons set forth in division (B) of section 3905.14 of the Revised Code, the notification shall be sent by certified mail, return receipt requested, postage prepaid, or by overnight delivery using a nationally recognized carrier.

(2) An insurance agent, within thirty days after receiving a copy of a notification pursuant to division (C)(1) of this section, may file written comments concerning the substance of the notification with the superintendent. If an insurance agent files such comments with the superintendent, the agent shall, at the same time, provide a copy of the comments to the insurer. Comments filed with the superintendent shall become part of the superintendent's file on the insurance agent and shall accompany every copy of any report distributed or disclosed for any reason about the agent.

(2002 S 129, eff. 9–1–02)

OTHER–THAN–LIFE INSURANCE AGENTS

3905.31 Prohibition against unauthorized business

No person not licensed under section 3905.30 of the Revised Code shall take or receive any application for such insurance upon property or persons in this state, or receive or collect a premium or any part thereof for any unauthorized insurance company, or attempt or assist in any such act, or perform any act in this state concerning any policy or contract of insurance of any unauthorized insurance company provided that any duly licensed property and casualty agent may place business with an agent licensed under section 3905.30 of the Revised Code and may accept compensation therefor, if such insurance is written in conformity with the insurance laws of this state. This section does not apply to those engaged in the act of adjusting claims or losses in connection with any policy of insurance written under the provisions of sections 3905.30 to 3905.35 of the Revised Code.

(2002 S 129, eff. 9–1–02; 129 v 582, eff. 1–10–61; 128 v 1200; 1953 H 1; GC 660)

3905.33 Eligibility of unauthorized insurers

(A) No person licensed under section 3905.30 of the Revised Code shall solicit, procure an application for, bind, issue, renew, or deliver a policy with any insurer that is not eligible to write insurance on a surplus line basis in this state.

To establish the eligibility of an unauthorized insurer, the superintendent of insurance may request copies of the insurer's most recent financial statements; instruments such as domestic trust agreements, powers of attorney, and investment management contracts; biographies of the owners and managers of the insurer; and any other information the superintendent believes may be helpful in determining an insurer's suitability. The suitability of each unauthorized insurer is subject to the continuous scrutiny and discretion of the superintendent.

(B)(1) No insurance agent or surplus line broker shall solicit, procure, place, or renew any insurance with an unauthorized insurer unless the agent or surplus line broker has complied with the due diligence requirements of this section and is unable to procure the requested insurance from an authorized insurer.

Due diligence requires the agent or surplus line broker to contact at least five of the authorized insurers the agent or surplus line broker represents, or as many insurers as the agent or surplus line broker represents, that customarily write the kind of insurance required by the insured. Due diligence is presumed if declinations are received from each authorized insurer contacted. If any authorized insurer fails to respond within ten days after the initial contact, the agent or surplus line broker may assume the insurer has declined to accept the risk.

(2) An insurance agent or surplus line broker is exempt from the due diligence requirements of this section if the agent or surplus line broker is procuring insurance from a risk purchasing group or risk retention group as provided in Chapter 3960. of the Revised Code.

(C) An insurance agent who procures or places insurance through a surplus line broker shall obtain an affidavit from the insured acknowledging that the insurance policy is to be placed with a company or insurer not authorized to do business in this state and acknowledging that, in the event of the insolvency of the insurer, the insured is not entitled to any benefits or proceeds from the Ohio insurance guaranty association. The affidavit must be on a form prescribed by the superintendent. The agent shall submit the original affidavit to the surplus line broker within thirty days after the effective date of the policy. If no other agent is involved, the surplus line broker shall obtain the affidavit from the insured.

The surplus line broker shall keep the original affidavit, and the originating agent shall keep a copy of the affidavit, for at least five years after the effective date of the policy to which the affidavit pertains. A copy of the affidavit shall be given to the insured at the time the insurance is bound or a policy is delivered.

(D) The superintendent may adopt rules in accordance with Chapter 119. of the Revised Code to carry out the purposes of sections 3905.30 to 3905.38 of the Revised Code.

(1997 H 215, eff. 6–30–97)

UNAUTHORIZED INSURANCE COMPANIES

3905.37 Prohibition

No person, company, association, or corporation shall fail to make the report required in section 3905.36 of the Revised Code and to furnish all the information that is required by the treasurer of state to determine the amount due under that section.

(1997 H 215, eff. 6–30–97; 1953 H 1, eff. 10–1–53; GC 664–2)

GENERAL PROVISIONS

3905.43 Advertising limitations

No person, firm, association, partnership, company, or corporation shall publish or distribute or receive and print for publication or distribution any advertising matter in which insurance business is solicited, unless such advertiser has complied with the laws of this state regulating the business of insurance, and a certificate of such compliance is issued by the superintendent of insurance.

(1953 H 1, eff. 10–1–53; GC 665)

SURETY BAIL BOND AGENTS

3905.84 License requirement

No person shall act in the capacity of a surety bail bond agent, or perform any of the functions, duties, or powers prescribed for surety bail bond agents under sections 3905.83 to 3905.95 of the Revised Code, unless that person i [sic.] qualified, licensed, and appointed as provided in those sections.

(2000 H 730, eff. 10–9–01)

3905.92 Collateral security or indemnity; forfeiture

(A) A surety bail bond agent that accepts collateral security or other indemnity shall comply with all of the following requirements:

(1) The collateral security or other indemnity shall be reasonable in relation to the amount of the bond.

(2) The collateral security or other indemnity shall not be used by the surety bail bond agent for personal benefit or gain and shall be returned in the same condition as received.

(3) Acceptable forms of collateral security or indemnity include cash or its equivalent, a promissory note, an indemnity agreement, a real property mortgage in the name of the surety, and any filing under Chapter 1309. of the Revised Code. If the surety bail bond agent accepts on a bond collateral security in excess of fifty thousand dollars in cash, the cash amount shall be made payable to the surety in the form of a cashier's check, United States postal money order, certificate of deposit, or wire transfer.

(4) The surety bail bond agent shall provide to the person giving the collateral security or other indemnity, a written, numbered receipt that describes in a detailed manner the collateral security or other indemnity received, along with copies of any documents rendered.

(5) The collateral security or other indemnity shall be received and held in the surety's name by the surety bail bond agent in a fiduciary capacity and, prior to any forfeiture of bail, shall be kept separate and apart from any other funds or assets of the surety bail bond agent. However, when collateral security in excess of fifty thousand dollars in cash or its equivalent is received on a bond, the surety bail bond agent promptly shall forward the entire amount to the surety or managing general agent.

(B) Collateral security may be placed in an interest-bearing account in a federally insured bank or savings and loan association in this state, to accrue to the benefit of the person giving the collateral security. The surety bail bond agent, surety, or managing general agent shall not make any pecuniary gain on the collateral security deposited.

(C)(1) The surety is liable for all collateral security or other indemnity accepted by a surety bail bond agent. If, upon final termination of liability on a bond, the surety bail bond agent or managing general agent fails to return the collateral security to the person that gave it, the surety shall return the actual collateral to that person or, in the event that the surety cannot locate the collateral, shall pay the person in accordance with this section.

(2) A surety's liability as described in division (C)(1) of this section survives the termination of the surety bail bond agent's appointment, with respect to those bonds that were executed by the surety bail bond agent prior to the termination of the appointment.

(D) If a forfeiture occurs, the surety bail bond agent or surety shall give the principal and the person that gave the collateral security ten days' written notice of intent to convert the collateral deposit into cash to satisfy the forfeiture. The notice shall be sent by certified mail, return receipt requested, to the last known address of the principal and the person that gave the collateral.

The surety bail bond agent or surety shall convert the collateral deposit into cash within a reasonable period of time and return that which is in excess of the face value of the bond minus the actual and reasonable expenses of converting the collateral into cash. In no event shall these expenses exceed ten per cent of the face value of the bond. However, upon motion and proof that the actual and reasonable expenses exceed ten per cent, the court may allow recovery of the full amount of the actual and reasonable expenses. If there is a remission of forfeiture that required the surety to pay the bond to the court, the surety shall pay to the person that gave the collateral the value of any collateral received for the bond minus the actual and reasonable expenses permitted to be recovered under this division.

(E) A surety bail bond agent or surety shall not solicit or accept a waiver of any of the provisions of this section, or enter into any agreement as to the value of the collateral.

(F) No person shall fail to comply with this section.

(2000 H 730, eff. 10–9–01)

3905.931 Furnishing supplies; liability of insurer

(A) No insurer, managing general agent, or surety bail bond agent shall furnish to any person any blank form, application, stationery, business card, or other supplies to be used in soliciting, negotiating, or effecting bail bonds unless the person is licensed to act as a surety bail bond agent and is appointed by an insurer. This division does not prohibit an unlicensed employee, under the direct supervision and control of a licensed and appointed surety bail bond agent, from possessing or executing in the surety bond office, any form, other than a power of attorney, bond form, or collateral receipt, while acting within the scope of the employee's employment.

(B) An insurer that furnishes any of the supplies mentioned in division (A) of this section to any surety bail bond agent or other person not appointed by an insurer and that accepts any bail bond business from or writes any bail bond business for that surety bail bond agent or other person is liable on the bond to the same extent and in the same manner as if the surety bail bond agent or other person had been appointed or authorized by an insurer to act in its behalf.

(2000 H 730, eff. 10–9–01)

PENALTIES

3905.99 Penalties

(A) Whoever violates section 3905.182 of the Revised Code shall be fined not less than twenty-five nor more than five hundred dollars or imprisoned not more than six months, or both.

(B) Whoever violates section 3905.31 or 3905.33 of the Revised Code shall be fined not less than twenty-five nor more than five hundred dollars or imprisoned not more than one year, or both.

(C) Whoever violates section 3905.37 or 3905.43 of the Revised Code shall be fined not less than one hundred nor more than five hundred dollars.

(D) Whoever violates section 3905.02, division (F) of section 3905.92, or division (A) of section 3905.931 of the Revised Code is guilty of a misdemeanor of the first degree.

(E) Whoever violates section 3905.84 of the Revised Code is guilty of a misdemeanor of the first degree on a first or second offense and of a felony of the third degree on each subsequent offense.

(2002 S 129, eff. 9–1–02; 2000 H 730, eff. 10–9–01; 1998 S 154, eff. 6–30–98; 1970 H 242, eff. 9–16 70; 128 v 1200; 1953 H 1)

CHAPTER 3937

MOTOR VEHICLE INSURANCE

3937.41 Emergency, police, and fire vehicle accidents not to have adverse effect on driver's private automobile insurance; exceptions

(A) As used in this section:

(1) "Ambulance" has the same meaning as in section 4765.01 of the Revised Code and also includes private ambulance companies under contract to a municipal corporation, township, or county.

(2) "Emergency vehicle" means any of the following:

(a) Any vehicle, as defined in section 4511.01 of the Revised Code, that is an emergency vehicle of a municipal, township, or county department or public utility corporation and that is identified as such as required by law, the director of public safety, or local authorities;

(b) Any motor vehicle, as defined in section 4511.01 of the Revised Code, when commandeered by a police officer;

(c) Any vehicle, as defined in section 4511.01 of the Revised Code, that is an emergency vehicle of a qualified nonprofit corporation police department established pursuant to section 1702.80 of the Revised Code and that is identified as an emergency vehicle;

(d) Any vehicle, as defined in section 4511.01 of the Revised Code, that is an emergency vehicle of a proprietary police department or security department of a hospital operated by a public hospital agency or a nonprofit hospital agency that employs police officers under section 4973.17 of the Revised Code, and that is identified as an emergency vehicle.

(3) "Firefighter" means any regular, paid, member of a lawfully constituted fire department of a municipal corporation or township.

(4) "Law enforcement officer" means a sheriff, deputy sheriff, constable, marshal, deputy marshal, municipal or township police officer, state highway patrol trooper, police officer employed by a qualified nonprofit police department pursuant to section 1702.80 of the Revised Code, or police officer employed by a proprietary police department or security department of a hospital operated by a public hospital agency or nonprofit hospital agency pursuant to section 4973.17 of the Revised Code.

(5) "Motor vehicle accident" means any accident involving a motor vehicle which results in bodily injury to any person, or damage to the property of any person.

(B) No insurer shall consider the circumstance that an applicant or policyholder has been involved in a motor vehicle accident while in the pursuit of the applicant's or policyholder's official duties as a law enforcement officer, firefighter, or operator of an emergency vehicle or ambulance, while operating a vehicle engaged in mowing or snow and ice removal as a county, township, or department of transportation employee, or while operating a vehicle while engaged in the pursuit of the applicant's or policyholder's official duties as a member of the motor carrier enforcement unit of the state highway patrol under section 5503.34 of the Revised Code, as a basis for doing either of the following:

(1) Refusing to issue or deliver a policy of insurance upon a private automobile, or increasing the rate to be charged for such a policy;

(2) Increasing the premium rate, canceling, or failing to renew an existing policy of insurance upon a private automobile.

(C) Any applicant or policyholder affected by an action of an insurer in violation of this section may appeal to the superintendent of insurance. After a hearing held upon not less than ten days' notice to the applicant or policyholder and to the insurer and if the superintendent determines that the insurer has violated this section, the superintendent may direct the issuance of a policy, decrease the premium rate on a policy, or reinstate insurance coverage.

(D) The employer of the law enforcement officer, firefighter, or operator of an emergency vehicle or ambulance, operator of a vehicle engaged in mowing or snow and ice removal, or operator of a vehicle who is a member of the motor carrier enforcement unit, except as otherwise provided in division (F) of this section, shall certify to the state highway patrol or law enforcement agency that investigates the accident whether the officer, firefighter, or operator of an emergency vehicle or ambulance, operator of a vehicle engaged in mowing or snow and ice removal, or operator of a vehicle who is a member of the motor carrier enforcement unit, was engaged in the performance of the person's official duties as such employee at the time of the accident. The employer shall designate an official authorized to make the certifications. The state highway patrol or law enforcement agency shall include the certification in any report of the accident forwarded to the department of public safety pursuant to sections 5502.11 and 5502.12 of the Revised Code and shall forward the certification to the department if received after the report of the accident has been forwarded to the department. The registrar of motor vehicles shall not include an accident in a certified abstract of information under division (A) of section 4509.05 of the Revised Code, if the person involved has been so certified as having been engaged in the performance of the person's official duties at the time of the accident.

(E) Division (B) of this section does not apply to an insurer whose policy covers the motor vehicle at the time the motor vehicle is involved in an accident described in division (B) of this section.

(F) Division (B) of this section does not apply if an applicant or policyholder, on the basis of the applicant's or policyholder's involvement in an accident described in that division, is convicted of or pleads guilty or no contest to a violation of section 4511.19 of the Revised Code; of a municipal ordinance relating to operating a vehicle while under the influence of alcohol, a drug of abuse, or alcohol and a drug of abuse; or of a municipal ordinance relating to operating a vehicle with a prohibited concentration of alcohol in the blood, breath, or urine, or other bodily substance.

(2004 H 230, eff. 9–16–04; 1998 S 213, eff. 7–29–98; 1996 S 121, eff. 11–19–96; 1992 H 508, eff. 12–14–92; 1992 S 98; 1991 S 144; 1990 H 110; 1989 H 381; 1980 H 990)

3937.42 Exchange of information with law enforcement and prosecuting agencies

(A) The chief or head law enforcement officer of any federal, state, or local law enforcement agency or a prosecuting attorney of any county may request any insurance company, or agent authorized by the company to act on its behalf, that has investigated or is investigating a claim involving motor vehicle insurance or vessel insurance to release any information in its possession relevant to the claim. The company or agent shall release the information that is requested in writing by the law enforcement officer.

(B) If an insurance company, or agent authorized by the company to act on its behalf, has reason to suspect that a loss involving a motor vehicle or vessel that is insured by the company is part of a fraudulent scheme to obtain control of insurance proceeds, the company or agent shall notify a law enforcement officer or a prosecuting attorney of any county having jurisdiction over the alleged fraud.

(C) An insurance company, or agent authorized by the company to act on its behalf, shall release any information requested in writing pursuant to division (A) of this section and cooperate with the officer or a prosecuting attorney of any county authorized to request the information. The company or agent shall take such action as may be reasonably requested of it by the officer or a prosecuting attorney of any county and shall permit any other person ordered by a court to inspect any information that is specifically requested by the court.

The information that may be requested pursuant to this section may include, but is not limited to, the following:

(1) Any insurance policy relevant to the claim under investigation and any application for such a policy;

(2) Policy premium payment records;

(3) History of previous claims involving a motor vehicle or vessel made by the insured;

(4) Material relating to the investigation of the claim, including statements of any person, proof of loss, and any other relevant evidence.

(D) If the law enforcement officer or a prosecuting attorney of any county mentioned in division (A) of this section has received information pursuant to this section from an insurance company, or agent authorized by the company to act on its behalf, the officer or a prosecuting attorney of any county may release to, and share with, the insurance company or agent any information in the officer's or prosecuting attorney's possession relative to the claim, upon the written request of the insurance company or agent.

(E) In the absence of fraud, recklessness, or malice, no insurance company, or agent authorized by the company to act on its behalf, is liable for damages in any civil action, including any action brought pursuant to section 1347.10 of the Revised Code for any oral or written statement made or any other action taken that is necessary to supply information required pursuant to this section.

(F) Except as otherwise provided in division (D) of this section, any officer or a prosecuting attorney of any county receiving any information furnished pursuant to this section shall hold the information in confidence and shall not disclose it to anyone except other law enforcement officers or agencies until its release is required pursuant to a criminal or civil proceeding.

(G) Any officer or a prosecuting attorney of any county referred to in division (A) of this section may testify as to any information in the officer's or prosecuting attorney's possession regarding the claim referred to in that division in any civil action in which any person seeks recovery under a policy against an insurance company.

(H) As used in this section:

(1) "Motor vehicle" has the same meaning as in section 4501.01 of the Revised Code.

(2) "Vessel" has the same meaning as in section 1547.01 of the Revised Code.

(I)(1) No person shall purposely refuse to release any information requested pursuant to this section by an officer or a prosecuting attorney of any county authorized by division (A) of this section to request the information.

(2) No person shall purposely refuse to notify an appropriate law enforcement officer or a prosecuting attorney of any county of a loss required to be reported pursuant to division (B) of this section.

(3) No person shall purposely fail to hold in confidence information required to be held in confidence by division (F) of this section.

(1998 S 187, eff. 3–18–99; 1984 S 2, eff. 9–26–84)

CHAPTER 3999

CRIMES RELATING TO INSURANCE

Section

3999.21 Insurance fraud warnings on forms

(A) As used in this section:

(1) "Deceptive," "insurer," "policy," and "statement" have the same meanings as in section 2913.47 of the Revised Code.

(2) "Defraud" has the same meaning as in section 2913.01 of the Revised Code.

(B) All applications for group or individual insurance issued by an insurer and all claim forms issued by an insurer, for use by persons in applying for insurance or submitting a claim for payment pursuant to a policy or a claim for any other benefit pursuant to a policy, shall clearly contain a warning substantially as follows: "Any person who, with intent to defraud or knowing that he is facilitating a fraud against an insurer, submits an application or files a claim containing a false or deceptive statement is guilty of insurance fraud."

(C) An insurer may comply with division (B) of this section by including the warning on an addendum to any application or claim form described in that division, if the addendum is attached to the form and satisfies the requirements set forth in that division.

(D) The absence of a warning as described in division (B) of this section does not constitute a defense in a prosecution for a violation of section 2913.47 or any other section of the Revised Code.

(1991 H 259, eff. 10–23–91; 1990 H 347)

3999.22 Kickbacks, bribes, and rebates prohibited

(A) As used in this section:

(1) "Claim" means any attempt to cause a health care insurer to make payment of a health care benefit.

(2) "Health care benefit" means the right under a contract or a certificate or policy of insurance to have a payment made by a health care insurer for a specified health care service.

(3) "Health care insurer" means any person that is authorized to do the business of sickness and accident insurance, any health insuring corporation, and any legal entity that is self-insured and provides health care benefits to its employees or members.

(B) No person shall knowingly solicit, offer, pay, or receive any kickback, bribe, or rebate, directly or indirectly, overtly or covertly, in cash or in kind, in return for referring an individual for the furnishing of health care services or goods for which whole or partial reimbursement is or may be made by a health care insurer, except as authorized by the health care or health insurance contract, policy, or plan. This division does not apply to any of the following:

(1) Deductibles, copayments, or similar amounts owed by the person covered by the health care or health insurance contract, policy, or plan;

(2) Discounts or similar reductions in prices;

(3) Any amount paid within a bona fide legal entity, or within legal entities under common ownership or control, including any amount paid to an employee in a bona fide employment relationship;

(4) Any amount paid as part of a bona fide lease, management, or other business contract.

(C) Nothing in this section shall be construed to apply to any of the following:

(1) A provider who provides goods or services requested by an individual that are not covered by the individual's health care or health insurance contract, policy, or plan;

(2) A provider who, in good faith, provides goods or services ordered by another health care provider;

(3) A provider who, in good faith, resubmits a claim previously submitted that has not been paid or denied within thirty days of the original submission, if the provider notifies the payor or returns any duplicate payment within sixty days after receipt of the duplicate payment;

(4) A provider who, in good faith, makes a diagnosis that differs from the interpretation of a diagnosis reached by a health care insurer in the payment of claims.

(D) Whoever violates this section is guilty of a felony of the fifth degree on a first offense and a felony of the fourth degree on each subsequent offense.

(1998 H 698, eff. 3–22–99; 1996 S 269, eff. 7–1–96)

CHAPTER 4301

LIQUOR CONTROL LAW

PRELIMINARY PROVISIONS

4301.01 Definitions

(A) As used in the Revised Code:

(1) "Intoxicating liquor" and "liquor" include all liquids and compounds, other than beer, containing one-half of one per cent or more of alcohol by volume which are fit to use for beverage purposes, from whatever source and by whatever process produced, by whatever name called, and whether they are medicated, proprietary, or patented. "Intoxicating liquor" and "liquor" include wine even if it contains less than four per cent of alcohol by volume, mixed beverages even if they contain less than four per cent of alcohol by volume, cider, alcohol, and all solids and confections which contain any alcohol.

(2) Except as used in sections 4301.01 to 4301.20, 4301.22 to 4301.52, 4301.56, 4301.70, 4301.72, and 4303.01 to 4303.36 of the Revised Code, "sale" and "sell" include exchange, barter, gift, offer for sale, sale, distribution and delivery of any kind, and the transfer of title or possession of beer and intoxicating liquor either by constructive or actual delivery by any means or devices whatever, including the sale of beer or intoxicating liquor by means of a controlled access alcohol and beverage cabinet pursuant to section 4301.21 of the Revised Code. "Sale" and "sell" do not include the mere solicitation of orders for beer or intoxicating liquor from the holders of permits issued by the division of liquor control authorizing the sale of the beer or intoxicating liquor, but no solicitor shall solicit any such orders until the solicitor has been registered with the division pursuant to section 4303.25 of the Revised Code.

(3) "Vehicle" includes all means of transportation by land, by water, or by air, and everything made use of in any way for such transportation.

(B) As used in this chapter:

(1) "Alcohol" means ethyl alcohol, whether rectified or diluted with water or not, whatever its origin may be, and includes synthetic ethyl alcohol. "Alcohol" does not include denatured alcohol and wood alcohol.

(2) "Beer" includes all beverages brewed or fermented wholly or in part from malt products and containing one-half of one per cent or more, but not more than twelve per cent, of alcohol by volume.

(3) "Wine" includes all liquids fit to use for beverage purposes containing not less than one-half of one per cent of alcohol by volume and not more than twenty-one per cent of alcohol by volume, which is made from the fermented juices of grapes, fruits, or other agricultural products, except that as used in sections 4301.13, 4301.421, 4301.422, 4301.432, and 4301.44 of the Revised Code, and, for purposes of determining the rate of the tax that applies, division (B) of section 4301.43 of the Revised Code, "wine" does not include cider.

(4) "Mixed beverages," such as bottled and prepared cordials, cocktails, and highballs, are products obtained by mixing any type of whiskey, neutral spirits, brandy, gin, or other distilled spirits with, or over, carbonated or plain water, pure juices from flowers and plants, and other flavoring materials. The completed product shall contain not less than one-half of one per cent of alcohol by volume and not more than twenty-one per cent of alcohol by volume.

(5) "Spirituous liquor" includes all intoxicating liquors containing more than twenty-one per cent of alcohol by volume.

(6) "Sealed container" means any container having a capacity of not more than one hundred twenty-eight fluid ounces, the opening of which is closed to prevent the entrance of air.

(7) "Person" includes firms and corporations.

(8) "Manufacture" includes all processes by which beer or intoxicating liquor is produced, whether by distillation, rectifying, fortifying, blending, fermentation, or brewing, or in any other manner.

(9) "Manufacturer" means any person engaged in the business of manufacturing beer or intoxicating liquor.

(10) "Wholesale distributor" and "distributor" means a person engaged in the business of selling to retail dealers for purposes of resale.

(11) "Hotel" has the same meaning as in section 3731.01 of the Revised Code, subject to the exceptions mentioned in section 3731.03 of the Revised Code.

(12) "Restaurant" means a place located in a permanent building provided with space and accommodations wherein, in consideration of the payment of money, hot meals are habitually prepared, sold, and served at noon and evening, as the principal business of the place. "Restaurant" does not include pharmacies, confectionery stores, lunch stands, night clubs, and filling stations.

(13) "Club" means a corporation or association of individuals organized in good faith for social, recreational, benevolent, charitable, fraternal, political, patriotic, or athletic purposes, which is the owner, lessor, or occupant of a permanent building or part of a permanent building operated solely for those purposes, membership in which entails the prepayment of regular dues, and includes the place so operated.

(14) "Night club" means a place operated for profit, where food is served for consumption on the premises and one or more forms of amusement are provided or permitted for a consideration that may be in the form of a cover charge or may be included in the price of the food and beverages, or both, purchased by patrons.

(15) "At retail" means for use or consumption by the purchaser and not for resale.

(16) "Pharmacy" means an establishment, as defined in section 4729.01 of the Revised Code, that is under the management or control of a licensed pharmacist in accordance with section 4729.27 of the Revised Code.

(17) "Enclosed shopping center" means a group of retail sales and service business establishments that face into an enclosed mall, share common ingress, egress, and parking facilities, and are situated on a tract of land that contains an area of not less than five hundred thousand square feet. "Enclosed shopping center" also includes not more than one business establishment that is located within a free-standing building on such a tract of land, so long as the sale of beer and intoxicating liquor on the tract of land was approved in an election held under former section 4301.353 of the Revised Code.

(18) "Controlled access alcohol and beverage cabinet" means a closed container, either refrigerated, in whole or in part, or nonrefrigerated, access to the interior of which is restricted by means of a device that requires the use of a key, magnetic card, or similar device and from which beer, intoxicating liquor, other beverages, or food may be sold.

(19) "Community facility" means either of the following:

(a) Any convention, sports, or entertainment facility or complex, or any combination of these, that is used by or accessible to the general public and that is owned or operated in whole or in part by the state, a state agency, or a political subdivision of the state or that is leased from, or located on property owned by or leased from, the state, a state agency, a political subdivision of the state, or a convention facilities authority created pursuant to section 351.02 of the Revised Code;

(b) An area designated as a community entertainment district pursuant to section 4301.80 of the Revised Code.

(20) "Low-alcohol beverage" means any brewed or fermented malt product, or any product made from the fermented juices of grapes, fruits, or other agricultural products, that contains either no alcohol or less than one-half of one per cent of alcohol by volume. The beverages described in division (B)(20) of this section do not include a soft drink such as root beer, birch beer, or ginger beer.

(21) "Cider" means all liquids fit to use for beverage purposes that contain one-half of one per cent of alcohol by volume, but not more than six per cent of alcohol by weight, and that are made through the normal alcoholic fermentation of the juice of sound, ripe apples, including, without limitation, flavored, sparkling, or carbonated cider and cider made from pure condensed apple must.

(22) "Sales area or territory" means an exclusive geographic area or territory that is assigned to a particular A or B permit holder and that either has one or more political subdivisions as its boundaries or consists of an area of land with readily identifiable geographic boundaries. "Sales area or territory" does not include, however, any particular retail location in an exclusive geographic area or territory that is assigned to another A or B permit holder.

(2002 H 371, eff. 10-11-02; 2000 S 262, eff. 4-9-01; 1998 H 402, eff. 3-30-99; 1998 S 66, eff. 7-22-98; 1997 H 390, eff. 7-19-97; 1995 S 162, eff. 7-1-97; 1995 H 239, eff. 11-24-95; 1995 S 149, eff. 11-21-95; 1994 S 167, eff. 11-1-94; 1994 S 209, eff. 11-9-94; 1992 H 340, eff. 4-24-92; 1990 H 405, S 131; 1989 H 481; 1988 H 562; 1987 H 419; 1986 H 39, H 428)

4301.02 Division of liquor control

The division of liquor control consists of the superintendent of liquor control appointed by the director of commerce and such deputies, chiefs, agents, and employees as the director of commerce shall appoint to administer the various functions of the division, including but not limited to, the operation of a beer and wine section and the issuance of permits. The deputies and chiefs shall serve in the unclassified civil service.

(1995 S 162, eff. 7-1-97; 1984 H 711, eff. 7-1-85; 130 v S 24; 1953 H 1; GC 6064-2)

4301.021 Powers and duties of superintendent of liquor control

The superintendent of liquor control shall exercise all powers and perform all duties created and enjoined by Chapters 4301. and 4303. of the Revised Code, except for the powers and duties vested in and enjoined upon the liquor control commission by section 4301.022 of the Revised Code and all chapters and sections of the Revised Code referred to in that section, and except for the powers and duties vested in the department of public safety under sections 5502.13 to 5502.19 of the Revised Code and all provisions of the Revised Code referred to in those sections that relate to liquor control enforcement.

(1999 H 163, eff. 6-30-99; 1996 S 293, eff. 9-26-96 (See also Historical and Statutory Notes.); 1995 S 162, eff. 10-29-95; 130 v S 24, eff. 4-17-63)

Historical and Statutory Notes

Ed. Note: 1996 S 293 Effective Date—The Secretary of State assigned a general effective date of 9-26-96 for 1996 S 293, along with notice that, in accordance with RC 1.471, the General Assembly has not determined which sections go into immediate effect, and that it appears that certain sections provide for appropriations for current expenses, and are immediately effective in accordance with RC 1.471 and O Const Art II, § 1d.

LIQUOR CONTROL COMMISSION

4301.022 Liquor control commission; appointment; terms; removal of member

The liquor control commission consists of three commissioners, not more than two of whom shall be of the same political party, who shall be appointed by the governor, with the advice and consent of the senate. Terms of office shall be for six years, commencing on the ninth day of February and ending on the eighth day of February, except that upon expiration of the term ending February 12, 1979, the new term which succeeds it shall commence on February 13, 1979 and end on February 8, 1985. Each member shall hold office from the date of his appointment until the end of the term for which he was appointed. Any member appointed to fill a vacancy occurring prior to the expiration of the term for which his predecessor was appointed shall hold office for the remainder of such term. Any member shall continue in office subsequent to the expiration date of his term until his successor takes office, or until a period of sixty days has elapsed, whichever occurs first.

A vacancy in the office of a member of the commission shall be filled pursuant to section 3.03 of the Revised Code.

The governor shall select a member of the commission to be its chairman and a second member of the commission to be its vice-chairman. The governor may remove a member of the commission at any time for misfeasance, nonfeasance, or malfeasance in office. The commission shall appoint an executive secretary and such other employees as it considers necessary to carry out its powers and duties.

The governor shall designate the chairman and vice-chairman at the time of making the original appointment of members of the commission, at the time thereafter of making an appointment of any member for a full term, and at the time of any vacancy in the office of chairman or vice-chairman.

(1986 H 428, eff. 12-23-86; 1984 H 711, H 37; 1973 S 131; 130 v Pt 2, H 5; 130 v S 24)

4301.03 Rules; procedure

The liquor control commission may adopt and promulgate, repeal, rescind, and amend, in the manner required by this section, rules, standards, requirements, and orders necessary to carry out this chapter and Chapter 4303. of the Revised Code, but all rules of the board of liquor control that were in effect immediately prior to April 17, 1963, shall remain in full force and effect as rules of the liquor control commission until and unless amended or repealed by the liquor control commission. The rules of the commission may include the following:

(A) Rules with reference to applications for and the issuance of permits for the manufacture, distribution, transportation, and sale of beer and intoxicating liquor, and the sale of alcohol; and rules governing the procedure of the division of liquor control in the suspension, revocation, and cancellation of those permits;

(B) Rules and orders providing in detail for the conduct of any retail business authorized under permits issued pursuant to this chapter and Chapter 4303. of the Revised Code, with a view to ensuring compliance with those chapters and laws relative to them, and the maintenance of public decency, sobriety, and good order in any place licensed under the permits. No rule or order shall prohibit the sale of lottery tickets issued pursuant to Chapter 3770. of the Revised Code by any retail business authorized under permits issued pursuant to that chapter.

No rule or order shall prohibit pari-mutuel wagering on simulcast horse races at a satellite facility that has been issued a D liquor permit under Chapter 4303. of the Revised Code. No rule or order shall prohibit a charitable organization that holds a D–4 permit from selling or serving beer or intoxicating liquor under its permit in a portion of its premises merely because that portion of its premises is used at other times for the conduct of a bingo game, as described in division (S) of section 2915.01 of the Revised Code. However, such an organization shall not sell or serve beer or intoxicating liquor or permit beer or intoxicating liquor to be consumed or seen in the same location in its premises where a bingo game, as described in division (S)(1) of section 2915. 01 of the Revised Code, is being conducted while the game is being conducted. As used in this division, "charitable organization" has the same meaning as in division (H) of section 2915.01 of the Revised Code. No rule or order pertaining to visibility into the premises of a permit holder after the legal hours of sale shall be adopted or maintained by the commission.

(C) Standards, not in conflict with those prescribed by any law of this state or the United States, to secure the use of proper ingredients and methods in the manufacture of beer, mixed beverages, and wine to be sold within this state;

(D) Rules determining the nature, form, and capacity of all packages and bottles to be used for containing beer or intoxicating liquor, except for spirituous liquor to be kept or sold, governing the form of all seals and labels to be used on those packages and bottles, and requiring the label on every package, bottle, and container to state the ingredients in the contents and, except on beer, the terms of weight, volume, or proof spirits, and whether the same is beer, wine, alcohol, or any intoxicating liquor except for spirituous liquor;

(E) Uniform rules governing all advertising with reference to the sale of beer and intoxicating liquor throughout the state and advertising upon and in the premises licensed for the sale of beer or intoxicating liquor;

(F) Rules restricting and placing conditions upon the transfer of permits;

(G) Rules and orders limiting the number of permits of any class within the state or within any political subdivision of the state; and, for that purpose, adopting reasonable classifications of persons or establishments to which any authorized class of permits may be issued within any political subdivision;

(H) Rules and orders with reference to sales of beer and intoxicating liquor on Sundays and holidays and with reference to the hours of the day during which and the persons to whom intoxicating liquor of any class may be sold, and rules with reference to the manner of sale;

(I) Rules requiring permit holders buying beer to pay and permit holders selling beer to collect minimum cash deposits for kegs, cases, bottles, or other returnable containers of the beer; requiring the repayment, or credit, of the minimum cash deposit charges upon the return of the empty containers; and requiring the posting of such form of indemnity or such other conditions with respect to the charging, collection, and repayment of minimum cash deposit charges for returnable containers of beer as are necessary to ensure the return of the empty containers or the repayment upon that return of the minimum cash deposits paid;

(J) Rules establishing the method by which alcohol products may be imported for sale by wholesale distributors and the method by which manufacturers and suppliers may sell alcohol products to wholesale distributors.

Every rule, standard, requirement, or order of the commission and every repeal, amendment, or rescission of them shall be posted for public inspection in the principal office of the commission and the principal office of the division of liquor control, and a certified copy of them shall be filed in the office of the secretary of state. An order applying only to persons named in it shall be served on the persons affected by personal delivery of a certified copy, or by mailing a certified copy to each person affected by it or, in the case of a corporation, to any officer or agent of the corporation upon whom a service of summons may be served in a civil action. The posting and filing required by this section constitutes sufficient notice to all persons affected by such rule or order which is not required to be served. General rules of the commission promulgated pursuant to this section shall be published in the manner the commission determines.

(2003 H 95, eff. 9–26–03; 2002 H 371, eff. 10–11–02; 1995 S 162, eff. 7–1–97; 1994 H 361, eff. 9–27–94; 1990 S 131, eff. 7–25–90; 1986 H 627; 1984 H 711; 1980 H 180; 1974 H 998; 130 v Pt 2, H 5; 130 v H 316, H 964, S 24; 128 v 1282; 1953 H 1; GC 6064–3)

4301.04 Powers of commission

The liquor control commission has the following powers which it may exercise by the vote of a majority of the commissioners:

(A) To suspend, revoke, and cancel permits. A majority of the commissioners constitutes a quorum for the transaction of any business, for the performance of any duty, or for the exercise of any power of the commission. No vacancy in the commission shall impair the right of the remaining commissioners to exercise all powers of the commission. The act of a majority of the commission, when in session, is the act of the commission. A finding, order, or decision of the commission to suspend a permit shall state and fix the effective date of the commencement and the period of duration of such suspension. Such finding, order, or decision of the commission to revoke or cancel a permit shall state and fix the effective date thereof.

(B) To consider, hear, and determine all appeals authorized by Chapters 4301. and 4303. of the Revised Code, to be taken from any decision, determination, or order of the division of liquor control, and all complaints for the revocation of permits. The liquor control commission shall accord a hearing to any person appealing or complained against, at which such person has the right to be present, to be represented by counsel, to offer evidence, and to require the attendance of witnesses.

(C) To adopt, repeal, and amend bylaws in relation to its meetings and the transaction of its business and regulating its procedure on appeal.

(D) To consider and make recommendations upon any matter which the superintendent of liquor control submits to it for recommendation and determine any matter which the superintendent submits to it for determination.

(E) To require of the superintendent and of any officer, department, board, or commission of the state of any county, township, or municipal officer in this state, information with respect to the social and economic effects of such chapters; and all such officers, departments, boards, and commissions shall furnish such information when requested in writing by the liquor control commission.

(F) To submit to the governor amendments to any laws affecting the sale of intoxicating liquor in this state when it deems desirable.

(G) For the purpose of any hearing or investigation which they are respectively authorized or required by such chapters to conduct, the liquor control commission or any member thereof, the superintendent, or any agent of the division designated in writing for that purpose, may administer oaths, take depositions, issue subpoenas, compel the attendance of witnesses and the production of books, accounts, papers, records, documents, and testimony. In case of disobedience of any person with respect to an order of the commission or a subpoena issued by the liquor control commission or any member thereof, the superintendent or such agent, or on the refusal of a witness to testify to any matter regarding which the witness may be lawfully interrogated, a judge of the court of common pleas of the county in which the person resides, on application of any member of the liquor control commission or the superintendent, shall compel obedience by attachment proceedings as for contempt, as in the case of disobedience with respect to the requirements of a subpoena issued from such court or a refusal to testify in such court. Each officer who serves such subpoena shall receive the same fees as a sheriff, and each witness who appears, in obedience to a subpoena, before the liquor control commission or any member thereof, or the superintendent, shall receive for attendance the fees and mileage provided for witnesses in civil cases in courts of common pleas, which shall be audited and paid upon presentation of proper vouchers approved by any two members of the commission. No witness subpoenaed at the instance of a party other than the liquor control commission or any member thereof, the superintendent, or such agent, is entitled to compensation unless the commission certifies that the testimony of the witness was material to the matter investigated.

(1995 S 162, eff. 7–1–97; 130 v S 24, eff. 4–17–63; 128 v 1282; 1953 H 1; GC 6064–3)

4301.041 Determination of sales mark-up

The liquor control commission may determine and fix by rule the minimum percentage mark-up for sales at retail of beer, whether in case lot or less.

To determine the retail price of beer, the minimum percentage mark-up may be applied to the wholesale price of the manufacturer or wholesale distributor charged to the retail permit holder. Such prices shall apply to sales made at retail by a permit holder for off-premise consumption only.

(2002 H 371, eff. 10 11 02; 130 v S 24, eff. 4–17–63; 128 v 687)

4301.042 Rules controlling pricing practices

The liquor control commission may adopt, repeal, and amend rules providing for and controlling pricing practices and the manner and frequency with which any person sets or changes prices at which beer is sold to or by the holders of B–1 permits, but the commission shall not set prices or markups between manufacturers or other suppliers and the holders of B–1 permits.

(2002 H 371, eff. 10–11–02; 1976 H 922, eff. 6–29–76)

4301.05 Limitation of powers of commission

Sections 4301.03, 4301.04, and 4301.041 of the Revised Code do not derogate from or prejudice any other power expressly or impliedly granted to the liquor control commission by Chapters 4301. and 4303. of the Revised Code; but except as expressly provided in sections 4301.03, 4301.04, and 4301.041 of the Revised Code, the commission shall not exercise executive or administrative duties or powers.

(130 v S 24, eff. 4–17–63; 1953 H 1; GC 6064–3)

4301.06 Information published; hearings; records

The division of liquor control shall compile and publish, in reasonable detail, information as to its financial and other operations; and the liquor control commission shall hold not less than four public hearings annually for the purpose of hearing general complaints as to its policies under Chapters 4301. and 4303. of the Revised Code, receiving suggestions with respect thereto, and for the dissemination of information to the public. All of the records of the proceedings of the division of liquor control shall be open to public inspection.

(1995 S 162, eff. 7–1–97; 130 v S 24, eff. 4–17–63; 1953 H 1; GC 6064–4)

4301.07 Full–time duties; salaries

Each member of the liquor control commission shall devote the member's entire time to the duties of office and shall hold no other public position of trust or profit. No member of the commission, nor the superintendent of liquor control, nor any of the employees of the commission or of the division of liquor control, shall have any direct financial interest in, or any interest otherwise prohibited by Chapter 102. or section 2921.42 or 2921.43 of the Revised Code in, the manufacture, distribution, or sale of beer or intoxicating liquor.

Each member of the commission and the chairperson shall receive a salary fixed pursuant to division (J) of section 124.15 of the Revised Code. In addition to that salary, each member shall receive actual and necessary travel expenses in connection with commission hearings and business. The chairperson shall be an attorney at law who has had five years of active law practice.

(2004 H 306, eff. 7–23–04; 1984 H 711, eff. 7–1–85; 1977 H 1; 132 v H 93; 130 v S 24; 128 v 1282; 127 v 382, 7; 125 v 289; 1953 H 1; GC 6064–5)

4301.08 Bond

Each member of the liquor control commission shall give bond to the state in the amount of ten thousand dollars, and the superintendent of liquor control shall give bond to the state in the amount of one hundred thousand dollars conditioned according to law with surety to the approval of the governor. Such bond shall be filed and kept in the office of the secretary of state. The commission may require any employee of the commission to give like bond in such amount as the commission prescribes, with surety to the satisfaction of the commission, which shall be filed and kept in the office of the commission. The director may require any employee of the division of liquor control to give like bond in such amount as the superintendent prescribes, with surety to the satisfaction of the superintendent, which shall be filed and kept in the office of the division. The premium on any bond required or authorized by this section may be paid from the moneys received for the use of the commission, in the case of bonds for commission employees, or the division, in the case of bonds for division employees, under Chapters 4301. and 4303. of the Revised Code or from appropriations made by the general assembly. Bonds authorized to be taken on employees may, in the discretion of the commission, in the case of bonds for commission employees, or the superintendent, in the case of bonds for division employees, be individual, schedule, or blanket bonds.

(1995 S 162, eff. 7–1–97; 1984 H 711, eff. 7–1–85; 130 v S 24; 127 v 907; 1953 H 1; GC 6064–6)

POWERS AND DUTIES OF DIVISION OF LIQUOR CONTROL

4301.10 Powers and duties of division of liquor control

(A) The division of liquor control shall do all of the following:

(1) Control the traffic in beer and intoxicating liquor in this state, including the manufacture, importation, and sale of beer and intoxicating liquor;

(2) Grant or refuse permits for the manufacture, distribution, transportation, and sale of beer and intoxicating liquor and the sale of alcohol, as authorized or required by this chapter and Chapter 4303. of the Revised Code. A certificate, signed by the superintendent of liquor control and to which is affixed the official seal of the division, stating that it appears from the records of the division that no permit has been issued to the person specified in the certificate, or that a permit, if issued, has been revoked, canceled, or suspended, shall be received as prima-facie evidence of the facts recited in the certificate in any court or before any officer of this state.

(3) Put into operation, manage, and control a system of state liquor stores for the sale of spirituous liquor at retail and to holders of permits authorizing the sale of spirituous liquor; however, the division shall not establish any drive-in state liquor stores; and by means of those types of stores, and any manufacturing plants, distributing and bottling plants, warehouses, and other facilities that it considers expedient, establish and maintain a state monopoly of the distribution of spirituous liquor and its sale in packages or containers; and for that purpose manufacture, buy, import, possess, and sell spirituous liquors as provided in this chapter and Chapter 4303. of the Revised Code, and in the rules promulgated by the superintendent of liquor control pursuant to those chapters; lease or in any manner acquire the use of any land or building required for any of those purposes; purchase any equipment that is required; and borrow money to carry on its business, and issue, sign, endorse, and accept notes, checks, and bills of exchange; but all obligations of the division created under authority of this division shall be a charge only upon the moneys received by the division from the sale of spirituous liquor and its other business transactions in connection with the sale of spirituous liquor, and shall not be general obligations of the state;

(4) Enforce the administrative provisions of this chapter and Chapter 4303. of the Revised Code, and the rules and orders of the liquor control commission and the superintendent relating to the manufacture, importation, transportation, distribution, and sale of beer and intoxicating liquors. The attorney general, any prosecuting attorney, and any prosecuting officer of a municipal corporation or a municipal court shall, at the request of the division of liquor control or the department of public safety, prosecute any person charged with the violation of any provision in those chapters or of any section of the Revised Code relating to the manufacture, importation, transportation, distribution, and sale of beer and intoxicating liquor.

(5) Determine the locations of all state liquor stores and manufacturing, distributing, and bottling plants required in connection with those stores, subject to this chapter and Chapter 4303. of the Revised Code;

(6) Conduct inspections of liquor permit premises to determine compliance with the administrative provisions of this chapter and Chapter 4303. of the Revised Code and the rules adopted under those provisions by the liquor control commission.

Except as otherwise provided in division (A)(6) of this section, those inspections may be conducted only during those hours in which the permit holder is open for business and only by authorized agents or employees of the division or by any peace officer, as defined in section 2935.01 of the Revised Code. Inspections may be conducted at other hours only to determine compliance with laws or commission rules that regulate the hours of sale of beer and intoxicating liquor and only if the investigator has reasonable cause to believe that those laws or rules are being violated. Any inspection conducted pursuant to division (A)(6) of this section is subject to all of the following requirements:

(a) The only property that may be confiscated is contraband, as defined in section 2901.01 of the Revised Code, or property that is otherwise necessary for evidentiary purposes.

(b) A complete inventory of all property confiscated from the premises shall be given to the permit holder or the permit holder's agent or employee by the confiscating agent or officer at the conclusion of the inspection. At that time, the inventory shall be signed by the confiscating agent or officer, and the agent or officer shall give the permit holder or the permit holder's agent or employee the opportunity to sign the inventory.

(c) Inspections conducted pursuant to division (A)(6) of this section shall be conducted in a reasonable manner. A finding by any court of competent jurisdiction that the inspection was not conducted in a reasonable manner in accordance with this section or any rules promulgated by the commission may be considered grounds for suppression of evidence. A finding by the liquor control commission that the inspection was not conducted in a reasonable manner in accordance with this section or any rules promulgated by the commission may be considered grounds for dismissal of the commission case.

If any court of competent jurisdiction finds that property confiscated as the result of an administrative inspection is not necessary for evidentiary purposes and is not contraband, as defined in section 2901.01 of the Revised Code, the court shall order the immediate return of the confiscated property, provided that property is not otherwise subject to forfeiture, to the permit holder. However, the return of this property is not grounds for dismissal of the case. The commission likewise may order the return of confiscated property if no criminal prosecution is pending or anticipated.

(7) Delegate to any of its agents or employees any power of investigation that the division possesses with respect to the enforcement of any of the administrative laws relating to beer and intoxicating liquor, provided that this division does not authorize the division to designate any agent or employee to serve as an enforcement agent. The employment and designation of enforcement agents shall be within the exclusive authority of the director of public safety pursuant to sections 5502.13 to 5502.19 of the Revised Code.

(8) Collect the following fees:

(a) A biennial fifty dollar registration fee for each agent, solicitor, or salesperson, registered pursuant to section 4303.25 of the Revised Code, of a beer or intoxicating liquor manufacturer, supplier, broker, or wholesale distributor doing business in this state;

(b) A fifty-dollar product registration fee for each new beer or intoxicating liquor product sold in this state. The product registration fee shall be accompanied by a copy of the federal label and product approval for the new product.

(c) An annual three-hundred-dollar supplier registration fee from each manufacturer or supplier that produces and ships into this state, or ships into this state, intoxicating liquor or beer, in addition to an initial application fee of one hundred dollars.

Each supplier, agent, solicitor, or salesperson registration issued under this division shall authorize the person named to carry on the activity specified in the registration. Each agent, solicitor, or salesperson registration is valid for two years or for the unexpired portion of a two-year registration period. Each supplier registration is valid for one year or for the unexpired portion of a one-year registration period. Registrations shall end on their respective uniform expiration date, which shall be designated by the division, and are subject to suspension, revocation, cancellation, or fine as authorized by this chapter and Chapter 4303. of the Revised Code.

(9) Establish a system of electronic data interchange within the division and regulate the electronic transfer of information and funds among persons and governmental entities engaged in the manufacture, distribution, and retail sale of alcoholic beverages;

(10) Exercise all other powers expressly or by necessary implication conferred upon the division by this chapter and Chapter 4303. of the Revised Code, and all powers necessary for the exercise or discharge of any power, duty, or function expressly conferred or imposed upon the division by those chapters.

(B) The division may do all of the following:

(1) Sue, but may be sued only in connection with the execution of leases of real estate and the purchases and contracts necessary for the operation of the state liquor stores that are made under this chapter and Chapter 4303. of the Revised Code;

(2) Enter into leases and contracts of all descriptions and acquire and transfer title to personal property with regard to the sale, distribution, and storage of spirituous liquor within the state;

(3) Terminate at will any lease entered into pursuant to division (B)(2) of this section upon first giving ninety days' notice in writing to the lessor of its intention to do so;

(4) Fix the wholesale and retail prices at which the various classes, varieties, and brands of spirituous liquor shall be sold by the division. Those retail prices shall be the same at all state liquor stores, except to the extent that a price differential is required to collect a county sales tax levied pursuant to section 5739.021 of the Revised Code and for which tax the tax commissioner has authorized prepayment pursuant to section 5739.05 of the Revised Code. In fixing selling prices, the division shall compute an anticipated gross profit at least sufficient to provide in each calendar year all costs and expenses of the division and also an adequate working capital reserve for the division. The gross profit shall not exceed forty per cent of the retail selling price based on costs of the division, and in addition the sum required by section 4301.12 of the Revised Code to be paid into the state treasury. An amount equal to one and one-half per cent of that gross profit shall be paid into the statewide treatment and prevention fund created by section 4301.30 of the Revised Code and be appropriated by the general assembly from the fund to the department of alcohol and drug addiction services as provided in section 4301.30 of the Revised Code.

On spirituous liquor manufactured in this state from the juice of grapes or fruits grown in this state, the division shall compute an anticipated gross profit of not to exceed ten per cent. The wholesale prices shall be at a discount of not less than twelve and one-half per cent of the retail selling prices as determined by the division in accordance with this section.

(C) The division may approve the expansion or diminution of a premises to which a liquor permit has been issued and may adopt standards governing such an expansion or diminution.

(2004 H 306, eff. 7–23–04; 1999 H 283, eff. 6–30–99; 1999 H 163, eff. 6–30–99; 1997 H 210, eff. 3–31–97; 1996 H 566, eff. 10–16–96; 1995 S 162, eff. 10–29–95; 1995 S 149, eff. 11–21–95; 1994 S 167, eff. 11–1–94; 1992 H 340, eff. 4–24–92; 1990 H 405; 1989 H 317; 1988 S 386; 1987 H 231; 1979 H 470; 1975 H 205; 132 v S 350; 130 v Pt 2, H 13; 130 v H 974; 129 v 1211; 128 v 1282; 1953 H 1; GC 6064–8)

4301.101 Superintendent may issue rules and regulations

The superintendent of liquor control may adopt and promulgate, repeal, rescind, and amend, in the manner required by this section, rules, standards, requirements, and orders necessary to carry out the following:

(A) Rules and regulations governing the management of the state liquor stores and the manner of conducting them;

(B) Standards, not in conflict with those prescribed by any law of this state or the United States, to secure the use of proper ingredients and methods in the manufacture of alcohol and spirituous liquor to be sold within this state;

(C) Rules and regulations determining the nature, form, and capacity of all packages and bottles to be used for containing spirituous liquor to be kept or sold, subject to the provisions of section 4301.19 of the Revised Code, governing the form of all seals and labels to be used thereon, prescribing that the stamps required by Chapters 4301. and 4303. of the Revised Code to be affixed to containers of such spirituous liquor shall bear the official seal of the division of liquor control, in addition to the official identification seal prescribed by the superintendent by rule to be affixed to all bottles of spirituous liquor, and requiring the label on every package, bottle, and container to state the ingredients in the contents and the terms of weight, volume, or proof spirits of the spirituous liquor.

(1995 S 162, eff. 7–1–97; 129 v 1211, eff. 10–7–61; 128 v 1282)

4301.102 Collection of county tax on spirituous liquor

(A) The superintendent of liquor control shall collect the tax levied under section 307.697 or 4301.424 of the Revised Code on sales of spirituous liquor sold to liquor permit holders for resale, and sold at retail by the division of liquor control, in the county in which the tax is levied, and shall deposit the tax into the state treasury to the credit of the liquor control fund created by section 4301.12 of the Revised Code. The superintendent shall provide for payment of the full amount of the tax collected to the county in which the tax is levied as follows:

(1) For each county in which a tax is levied under section 307.697 or 4301.424 of the Revised Code, the superintendent of liquor control shall, on or before the sixteenth day of each month:

(a) From the best information available to the superintendent, determine and certify to the director of budget and management and to the tax commissioner the full amount of the tax levied in the county and collected during the first fifteen days of the preceding month;

(b) On or before the last working day of each month, from the best information available to the superintendent, determine and certify to the director of budget and management and to the tax commissioner the full amount of the tax levied in the county and collected during the remainder of the preceding month.

(2) Upon receipt of such certification, the director of budget and management shall transfer from the liquor control fund to the permissive tax distribution fund created by division (B)(1) of section 4301.423 of the Revised Code the full amount certified to the director under division (A)(1) of this section.

(3) Within five working days after receiving the certification provided for in division (A)(1) of this section, the tax commissioner shall provide for payment to the county treasurer of each county that imposes a tax under section 307.697 or 4301.424 of the Revised Code the full amount certified to be paid to the county.

(B) The superintendent of liquor control may adopt any rules necessary for the administration, collection, and enforcement of taxes levied under section 307.697 or 4301.424 of the Revised Code.

(C) Notwithstanding any other provision of law to the contrary, no permit holder shall purchase liquor from the division of liquor control at wholesale from a store that is located outside of a county in which a tax is levied under section 307.697 or

4301.424 of the Revised Code if the liquor is to be resold in the county in which the tax is levied.

(1995 S 162, eff. 7–1–97; 1995 S 188, eff. 7–19–95; 1991 H 298, eff. 7–26–91; 1990 S 188; 1988 H 708)

4301.11 Contracts of lease for state liquor stores

All contracts of lease for a state liquor store entered into by the division of liquor control shall be made in writing with the lowest responsive and responsible bidder, in accordance with section 9.312 of the Revised Code, after an advertisement in a newspaper of general circulation in the community wherein it is proposed to establish such store. In determining the lowest responsive and responsible bid, the division shall consider the length of the lease, the location, size, character, and quality of the construction, and the general fitness for use as such store of the premises for which a bid is submitted.

The liquor control commission may prescribe the form of bid and shall prescribe rules pertaining to the receiving and advertisement of such bid; provided that before accepting a bid and before entering into any contract of lease of the premises for use as a state liquor store the division shall publish in a newspaper of general circulation in the community wherein such premises are located a synopsis of the terms of such proposed lease including the name of the lessor, the location of the premises, and the yearly rental.

The division may reject any or all bids. If the division rejects all bids it shall readvertise for bids for such leases and may continue to readvertise for such bids until bids satisfactory to it are received.

No member of the commission, or any officer or employee of the division, shall directly or indirectly have any interest in any contract of lease entered into by the division.

(1995 S 162, eff. 7–1–97; 1987 H 88, eff. 1–1–88; 1984 H 37; 1953 H 1; GC 6064–8)

4301.12 Custody, use, and deposit of moneys

The division of liquor control shall provide for the custody, safekeeping, and deposit of all moneys, checks, and drafts received by it or any of its employees or agents prior to paying them to the treasurer of state as provided by section 113.08 of the Revised Code.

A sum equal to three dollars and thirty-eight cents for each gallon of spirituous liquor sold by the division during the period covered by the payment shall be paid into the state treasury to the credit of the general revenue fund. All moneys received from permit fees shall be paid to the credit of the undivided liquor permit fund established by section 4301.30 of the Revised Code.

Except as otherwise provided by law, all moneys collected under Chapters 4301. and 4303. of the Revised Code shall be paid by the division into the state treasury to the credit of the liquor control fund, which is hereby created. Amounts in the liquor control fund may be used to pay the operating expenses of the liquor control commission.

Whenever, in the judgment of the director of budget and management, the amount in the liquor control fund is in excess of that needed to meet the maturing obligations of the division, as working capital for its further operations, to pay the operating expenses of the commission, and for the alcohol testing program under section 3701.143 of the Revised Code, the director shall transfer the excess to the credit of the general revenue fund.

(2001 H 94, eff. 9–5–01; 1997 H 215, eff. 6–30–97; 1997 H 210, eff. 6–30–97; 1995 S 162, eff. 7–1–97; 1992 H 904, eff. 1–1–93; 1991 H 298; 1985 H 201; 1979 H 204; 1977 S 221; 1973 S 174; 1969 H 531; 130 v Pt 2, H 13; 130 v H 974; 1953 H 1; GC 6064–10)

4301.13 Rules and regulations for sale of bottled wine; schedule of prices

The liquor control commission may adopt, promulgate, repeal, rescind, and amend rules to regulate the manner of dealing in and distributing and selling bottled wine within the state. The commission may require out-of-state producers, shippers, bottlers, and holders of federal importers' permits shipping bottled wine into Ohio and holders of A–2, B–5, B–3, and B–2 permits issued by the division of liquor control, engaged in distributing and selling bottled wine in Ohio, to file with the division a schedule of prices in which minimum prices are set forth for the sale of bottled wine at wholesale or retail, or both, in Ohio. Any amendments, additions, alterations, or revisions to the schedule of prices as originally filed with the division shall be filed in the same manner as the original schedule of prices required to be filed with the division.

The commission may determine and fix the minimum mark-ups at wholesale or retail, or both, for bottled wine, and fix the minimum prices at which the various classes of bottled wine shall be distributed and sold in Ohio either at wholesale or retail, or both.

(1995 S 162, eff. 7–1–97; 1984 H 37, eff. 6–22–84; 1953 H 1; GC 6064–3a)

4301.14 Rationing of liquor; purchase at retail by permit holder for resale prohibited

(A) When the supply of spirituous liquor in this state is insufficient to meet the demands of ordinary trade, due to causes beyond the control of the superintendent of liquor control, the superintendent may establish rules which will insure the equitable distribution of such supplies of spirituous liquor as are available. The superintendent may institute and terminate such rules as conditions demand, and also make changes and alterations therein in accordance with specific needs.

(B) No permit holder or his employee or agent shall purchase at retail any spirituous liquor for resale or in the permit premises possess such liquor. The permit of any person, firm, partnership, or corporation violating this section, or employing an employee, or authorizing an agent who violates this section shall be suspended or revoked.

(1995 S 162, eff. 7–1–97; 1974 H 496, eff. 9–30–74; 1953 H 1; GC 6064–8a)

4301.15 Violation of rationing prohibited

No person shall violate any rule issued by the superintendent of liquor control in pursuance of section 4301.14 of the Revised Code.

(1995 S 162, eff. 7–1–97; 1953 H 1, eff. 10–1–53; GC 6064–8a)

4301.16 Disposition of moneys received at state liquor stores; credit for breakage and loss

All moneys received from the sale of liquor at state liquor stores or otherwise, or arising in the administration of Chapters 4301. and 4303. of the Revised Code, other than from taxes, shall be paid to the division of liquor control and shall be accounted for and paid over by the division to the treasurer of state as custodian, as provided by section 4301.12 of the Revised Code.

Upon proof of accidental breakage or unintentional shortage of stock, which proof shall be subject to the final approval of the division, the division shall allow yearly credits to each state liquor store not to exceed one-fortieth of one per cent of each state liquor store's yearly gross sales, for the moneys required by this section to be paid by such state liquor store to the division.

(1995 S 162, eff. 7-1-97; 127 v 44, eff. 8-15-57; 1953 H 1; GC 6064-9)

4301.17 Allocation of state liquor stores and agency stores; notice to political subdivisions

(A)(1) Subject to local option as provided in sections 4301.32 to 4301.40 of the Revised Code, five state liquor stores or agencies may be established in each county. One additional store may be established in any county for each twenty-five thousand of population of that county or major fraction thereof in excess of the first forty thousand, according to the last preceding federal decennial census or according to the population estimates certified by the department of development between decennial censuses. A person engaged in a mercantile business may act as the agent for the division of liquor control for the sale of spirituous liquor in a municipal corporation, in the unincorporated area of a township, or in an area designated and approved as a resort area under section 4303.262 of the Revised Code. The division shall fix the compensation for such an agent in the manner it considers best, but the compensation shall not exceed seven per cent of the gross sales made by the agent in any one year.

(2) The division shall adopt rules in accordance with Chapter 119. of the Revised Code governing the allocation and equitable distribution of agency store contracts. The division shall comply with the rules when awarding a contract under division (A)(1) of this section.

(3) Except as otherwise provided in this section, no mercantile business that sells beer or intoxicating liquor for consumption on the premises under a permit issued by the division shall operate an agency store at the premises. An agency to which a D-1 permit has been issued may offer for sale tasting samples of beer, an agency to which a D-2 permit has been issued may offer for sale tasting samples of wine and mixed beverages, and an agency to which a D-5 permit has been issued may offer for sale tasting samples of beer, wine, and mixed beverages, but not spirituous liquor. A tasting sample shall not be sold for the purpose of general consumption. As used in this section, "tasting sample" means a small amount of beer, wine, or mixed beverages that is provided in not more than four servings of not more than two ounces each to an authorized purchaser and that allows the purchaser to determine, by tasting only, the quality and character of the beverage.

(B) When an agency contract is proposed or when an existing agency contract is assigned, before entering into any contract or consenting to any assignment, the division shall notify the legislative authority of the municipal corporation in which the agency store is to be located, or the board of county commissioners and the board of township trustees of the county and the township in which the agency store is to be located if the agency store is to be located outside the corporate limits of a municipal corporation, of the proposed contract or assignment, and an opportunity shall be provided officials or employees of the municipal corporation or county and township for a complete hearing upon the advisability of entering into the contract or consenting to the assignment. When the division sends notice to the legislative authority of the political subdivision, the division shall notify, by certified mail or by personal service, the chief peace officer of the political subdivision, who may appear and testify, either in person or through a representative, at any hearing held on the advisability of entering into the contract or consenting to the assignment.

If the proposed agency store would be located within five hundred feet of a school, church, library, public playground, or township park, the division shall not enter into an agency contract until it has provided notice of the proposed contract to the authorities in control of the school, church, library, public playground, or township park and has provided those authorities with an opportunity for a complete hearing upon the advisability of entering into the contract. If an agency store so located is operating under an agency contract, the division may consent to the assignment of that contract to operate an agency store at the same location, but the division shall not consent to an assignment until it has notified the authorities in control of the school, church, library, public playground, or township park and has provided those authorities with an opportunity for a complete hearing upon the advisability of consenting to the assignment.

Any hearing provided for in this division shall be held in the central office of the division, except that upon written request of the legislative authority of the municipal corporation, the board of county commissioners, the board of township trustees, or the authorities in control of the school, church, library, public playground, or township park, the hearing shall be held in the county seat of the county where the proposed agency store is to be located.

(C) All agency contracts entered into by the division pursuant to this section shall be in writing and shall contain a clause providing for the termination of the contract at will by the division upon its giving ninety days' notice in writing to the agent of its intention to do so. Any agency contract may include a clause requiring the agent to report to the appropriate law enforcement agency the name and address of any individual under twenty-one years of age who attempts to make an illegal purchase.

An agent may engage in the selling of beer, mixed beverages, and wine pursuant to permits issued to the agent under Chapter 4303. of the Revised Code.

The division shall issue a C-1 and C-2 permit to each agent who prior to November 1, 1994, had not been issued both of these permits, notwithstanding the population quota restrictions contained in section 4303.29 of the Revised Code or in any rule of the liquor control commission and notwithstanding the requirements of section 4303.31 of the Revised Code. The location of a C-1 or C-2 permit issued to such an agent shall not be transferred. The division shall revoke any C-1 or C-2 permit issued to an agent under this paragraph if the agent no longer operates an agency store.

The division may enter into agreements with the department of development to implement a minority loan program to provide low-interest loans to minority business enterprises, as defined in section 122.71 of the Revised Code, that are awarded liquor agency contracts or assignments.

(D) If the division closes a state liquor store and replaces that store with an agency store, any employees of the division employed at that state liquor store who lose their jobs at that store as a result shall be given preference by the agent who operates the agency store in filling any vacancies that occur among the agent's employees, if that preference does not conflict with the agent's obligations pursuant to a collective bargaining agreement.

If the division closes a state liquor store and replaces the store with an agency store, any employees of the division employed at the state liquor store who lose their jobs at that store as a result may displace other employees as provided in sections 124.321 to 124.328 of the Revised Code. If an employee cannot displace other employees and is laid off, the employee shall be reinstated in another job as provided in sections 124.321 to 124.328 of the Revised Code, except that the employee's rights of reinstatement in a job at a state liquor store shall continue for a period of two years after the date of the employee's layoff and shall apply to jobs at state liquor stores located in the employee's layoff jurisdiction and any layoff jurisdiction adjacent to the employee's layoff jurisdiction.

(E) The division shall require every agent to give bond with surety to the satisfaction of the division, in the amount the division fixes, conditioned for the faithful performance of the agent's duties as prescribed by the division.

(2002 H 330, eff. 10–11–02; 2001 H 94, eff. 9–5–01; 1997 H 215, § 10, eff. 3–4–98; 1997 H 215, § 1, eff. 6–30–97; 1995 H 60, eff. 3–4–98; 1995 S 162, eff. 7–1–97; 1995 S 149, eff. 11–21–95; 1995 H 57, eff. 7–20–95; 1994 S 167, eff. 11–1–94; 1994 H 715, eff. 7–22–94; 1993 H 152, eff. 7–1–93; 1990 H 405; 1988 H 562; 1986 H 328; 1983 H 291; 1953 H 1; GC 6064–11)

4301.18 Division may purchase, manufacture, blend, or bottle liquor

The division of liquor control may purchase spirituous liquor in barrels, casks, or other containers, and may establish plants for the manufacture of spirituous liquor or for the blending and bottling of such liquor. All spirituous liquors manufactured, blended, or bottled by the division shall be so labeled.

(1995 S 162, eff. 7–1–97; 1953 H 1, eff. 10–1–53; GC 6064–11)

REGULATIONS AND RESTRICTIONS

4301.19 Regulations for sale of spirituous liquor

The division of liquor control shall sell spirituous liquor only, whether from a warehouse or from a state liquor store or agency store. All sales shall be in sealed containers and for resale as authorized by this chapter and Chapter 4303. of the Revised Code or for consumption off the premises only. Except as otherwise provided in this section, sale of containers holding one-half pint or less of spirituous liquor by the division shall be made at retail only, and not for the purpose of resale by any purchaser, by special order placed with a state liquor store or agency store and subject to rules established by the superintendent of liquor control. The division may sell at wholesale spirituous liquor in fifty milliliter sealed containers to any holder of a permit issued under Chapter 4303. of the Revised Code that authorizes the sale of spirituous liquor for consumption on the premises where sold. A person appointed by the division to act as an agent for the sale of spirituous liquor pursuant to section 4301.17 of the Revised Code may provide and accept gift certificates and may accept credit cards and debit cards for the retail purchase of spirituous liquor. Deliveries shall be made in the manner the superintendent determines by rule.

If any person desires to purchase any variety or brand of spirituous liquor which is not in stock at the state liquor store or agency store where the variety or brand is ordered, the division shall immediately procure the variety or brand. The purchaser shall be immediately notified upon the arrival of the spirituous liquor at the store at which it was ordered. Unless the purchaser pays for the variety or brand and accepts delivery within five days after the giving of the notice, the division may place the spirituous liquor in stock for general sale.

(2004 H 306, eff. 7–23–04; 2003 H 95, eff. 9–26–03; 1997 H 215, eff. 6–30–97; 1995 S 162, eff. 7–1–97; 1988 H 562, eff. 6–29–88; 129 v 1211; 128 v 1282; 1953 H 1; GC 6064–12)

4301.20 Exemptions

This chapter and Chapter 4303. of the Revised Code do not prevent the following:

(A) The storage of intoxicating liquor in bonded warehouses, established in accordance with the acts of congress and under the regulation of the United States, located in this state, or the transportation of intoxicating liquor to or from bonded warehouses of the United States wherever located;

(B) A bona fide resident of this state who is the owner of a warehouse receipt from obtaining or transporting to the resident's residence for the resident's own consumption and not for resale spirituous liquor stored in a government bonded warehouse in this state or in another state prior to December 1933, subject to such terms as are prescribed by the division of liquor control;

(C) The manufacture of cider from fruit for the purpose of making vinegar, and nonintoxicating cider and fruit juices for use and sale;

(D) A licensed physician or dentist from administering or dispensing intoxicating liquor or alcohol to a patient in good faith in the actual course of the practice of the physician's or dentist's profession;

(E) The sale of alcohol to physicians, dentists, druggists, veterinary surgeons, manufacturers, hospitals, infirmaries, or medical or educational institutions using the alcohol for medicinal, mechanical, chemical, or scientific purposes;

(F) The sale, gift, or keeping for sale by druggists and others of any of the medicinal preparations manufactured in accordance with the formulas prescribed by the United States Pharmacopoeia and National Formulary, patent or proprietary preparations, and other bona fide medicinal and technical preparations, which contain no more alcohol than is necessary to hold the medicinal agents in solution and to preserve the same, which are manufactured and sold as medicine and not as beverages, are unfit for use for beverage purposes, and the sale of which does not require the payment of a United States liquor dealer's tax;

(G) The manufacture and sale of tinctures or of toilet, medicinal, and antiseptic preparations and solutions not intended for internal human use nor to be sold as beverages, and which are unfit for beverage purposes, if upon the outside of each bottle, box, or package of which there is printed in the English language, conspicuously and legibly, the quantity by volume of alcohol in the preparation or solution;

(H) The manufacture and keeping for sale of the food products known as flavoring extracts when manufactured and sold for cooking, culinary, or flavoring purposes, and which are unfit for use for beverage purposes;

(I) The lawful sale of wood alcohol or of ethyl alcohol for external use when combined with other substances as to make it unfit for internal use;

(J) The purchase and importation into this state of intoxicating liquor for use in manufacturing processes of nonbeverage food products under terms prescribed by the division, provided that the terms prescribed by the division shall not increase the cost of the intoxicating liquor to any person, firm, or corporation purchasing and importing it into this state for that use;

(K) Any resident of this state or any member of the armed forces of the United States, who has attained the age of twenty-one years, from bringing into this state, for personal use and not for resale, not more than one liter of spirituous liquor in any thirty-day period, and the same is free of any tax consent fee when the resident or member of the armed forces physically possesses and accompanies the spirituous liquor on returning from a foreign country, another state, or an insular possession of the United States;

(L) Persons, at least twenty-one years of age, who collect ceramic commemorative bottles containing spirituous liquor which have unbroken federal tax stamps on them from selling or trading the bottles to other collectors. The bottles must originally have been purchased at retail from the division, legally imported under division (K) of this section, or legally imported pursuant to a supplier registration issued by the division. The sales shall be for the purpose of exchanging a ceramic commemorative bottle between private collectors and shall not be for the purpose of selling the spirituous liquor for personal consumption. The sale or exchange authorized by this division shall not occur on the premises of any permit holder, shall not be made in connection with the business of any permit holder, and shall not be made in connection with any mercantile business.

(2004 H 306, eff. 7–23–04; 1995 S 162, eff. 7–1–97; 1995 S 149, eff. 11–21–95; 1980 H 669, eff. 10–22–80; 1969 H 637; 1953 H 1; GC 6064–13)

4301.21 Restrictions applicable to sale of beer or intoxicating liquor for consumption on the premises

The sale of beer or intoxicating liquor for consumption on the premises is subject to the following restrictions, in addition to those imposed by the rules and orders of the division of liquor control:

(A) Except as otherwise provided in this chapter, beer or intoxicating liquor may be served to a person not seated at a table unless there is reason to believe that the beer or intoxicating liquor so served will be consumed by a person under twenty-one years of age.

(B) Beer or intoxicating liquor may be served by a hotel in the room of a bona fide guest, and may be sold by a hotel holding a D–5a permit, or a hotel holding a D–3 or D–5 permit that otherwise meets all of the requirements for holding a D–5a permit, by means of a controlled access alcohol and beverage cabinet that shall be located only in the hotel room of a registered guest. A hotel may sell beer or intoxicating liquor as authorized by its permit to a registered guest by means of a controlled access alcohol and beverage cabinet in accordance with the following requirements:

(1) Only a person twenty-one years of age or older who is a guest registered to stay in a guestroom shall be provided a key, magnetic card, or other similar device necessary to obtain access to the contents of a controlled access alcohol and beverage cabinet in that guestroom.

(2) The hotel shall comply with section 4301.22 of the Revised Code in connection with the handling, restocking, and replenishing of the beer and intoxicating liquor in the controlled access alcohol and beverage cabinet.

(3) The hotel shall replenish or restock beer and intoxicating liquor in any controlled access alcohol and beverage cabinet only during the hours during which the hotel may serve or sell beer and intoxicating liquor.

(4) The registered guest shall verify in writing that the guest has read and understands the language that shall be posted on the controlled access alcohol and beverage cabinet as required by division (B)(5) of this section.

(5) A hotel authorized to sell beer and intoxicating liquor pursuant to division (B) of this section shall post on the controlled access alcohol and beverage cabinet, in conspicuous language, the following notice:

"The alcoholic beverages contained in this cabinet shall not be removed from the premises."

(6) The hotel shall maintain a record of each sale of beer or intoxicating liquor made by the hotel by means of a controlled access alcohol and beverage cabinet for any period in which the permit holder is authorized to hold the permit pursuant to sections 4303.26 and 4303.27 of the Revised Code and any additional period during which an applicant exercises its right to appeal a rejection by the department or division of liquor control to renew a permit pursuant to section 4303.271 of the Revised Code. The records maintained by the hotel shall comply with both of the following:

(a) Include the name, address, age, and signature of each hotel guest who is provided access by the hotel to a controlled access alcohol and beverage cabinet pursuant to division (B)(1) of this section;

(b) Be made available during business hours to authorized agents of the division of liquor control pursuant to division (A)(6) of section 4301.10 of the Revised Code or to enforcement agents of the department of public safety pursuant to sections 5502.13 to 5502.19 of the Revised Code.

(7) The hotel shall observe all other applicable rules adopted by the division of liquor control and the liquor control commission.

(C) Neither the seller nor the liquor control commission by its regulations shall require the purchase of food with the purchase of beer or intoxicating liquor; nor shall the seller of beer or intoxicating liquor give away food of any kind in connection with the sale of beer or intoxicating liquor, except as authorized by rule of the liquor control commission.

(D) The seller shall not permit the purchaser to remove beer or intoxicating liquor so sold from the premises.

(E) A hotel authorized to sell beer and intoxicating liquor pursuant to division (B) of this section shall provide a registered guest with the opportunity to refuse to accept a key, magnetic card, or other similar device necessary to obtain access to the contents of a controlled access alcohol and beverage cabinet in that guest room. If a registered guest refuses to accept such key, magnetic card, or other similar device, the hotel shall not assess any charges on the registered guest for use of the controlled access alcohol and beverage cabinet in that guest room.

(1999 H 163, eff. 6–30–99; 1995 S 162, eff. 10–29–95; 1988 H 562, eff. 6–29–88; 1987 H 419; 1982 H 357; 1973 H 294; 1969 H 558; 1953 H 1; GC 6064–21)

4301.22 Restrictions on sales of beer and liquor

Sales of beer and intoxicating liquor under all classes of permits and from state liquor stores are subject to the following restrictions, in addition to those imposed by the rules or orders of the division of liquor control:

(A)(1) Except as otherwise provided in this chapter, no beer or intoxicating liquor shall be sold to any person under twenty-one years of age.

(2) No low-alcohol beverage shall be sold to any person under eighteen years of age. No permit issued by the division shall be suspended, revoked, or canceled because of a violation of division (A)(2) of this section.

(3) No intoxicating liquor shall be handled by any person under twenty-one years of age, except that a person eighteen years of age or older employed by a permit holder may handle or sell beer or intoxicating liquor in sealed containers in connection with wholesale or retail sales, and any person nineteen years of age or older employed by a permit holder may handle intoxicating liquor in open containers when acting in the capacity of a server in a hotel, restaurant, club, or night club, as defined in division (B) of section 4301.01 of the Revised Code, or in the premises of a D–7 permit holder. This section does not authorize persons under twenty-one years of age to sell intoxicating liquor across a bar. Any person employed by a permit holder may handle beer or intoxicating liquor in sealed containers in connection with manufacturing, storage, warehousing, placement, stocking, bagging, loading, or unloading, and may handle beer or intoxicating liquor in open containers in connection with cleaning tables or handling empty bottles or glasses.

(B) No permit holder and no agent or employee of a permit holder shall sell or furnish beer or intoxicating liquor to an intoxicated person.

(C) No sales of intoxicating liquor shall be made after two-thirty a.m. on Sunday except under either of the following circumstances:

(1) Intoxicating liquor may be sold on Sunday under authority of a permit that authorizes Sunday sale.

(2) Spirituous liquor may be sold on Sunday by any person awarded an agency contract under section 4301.17 of the Revised Code if the sale of spirituous liquor is authorized in the applicable precinct as the result of an election on question (B)(1) or (2) of section 4301.351 of the Revised Code and if the agency contract authorizes the sale of spirituous liquor on Sunday.

This section does not prevent a municipal corporation from adopting a closing hour for the sale of intoxicating liquor earlier than two-thirty a.m. on Sunday or to provide that no intoxicating liquor may be sold prior to that hour on Sunday.

(D) No holder of a permit shall give away any beer or intoxicating liquor of any kind at any time in connection with the permit holder's business.

(E) Except as otherwise provided in this division, no retail permit holder shall display or permit the display on the outside of any licensed retail premises, or on any lot of ground on which the licensed premises are situated, or on the exterior of any building of which the licensed premises are a part, any sign, illustration, or advertisement bearing the name, brand name, trade name, trade-mark, designation, or other emblem of or indicating the manufacturer, producer, distributor, place of manufacture, production, or distribution of any beer or intoxicating liquor. Signs, illustrations, or advertisements bearing the name, brand name, trade name, trade-mark, designation, or other emblem of or indicating the manufacturer, producer, distributor, place of manufacture, production, or distribution of beer or intoxicating liquor may be displayed and permitted to be displayed on the interior or in the show windows of any licensed premises, if the particular brand or type of product so advertised is actually available for sale on the premises at the time of that display. The liquor control commission shall determine by rule the size and character of those signs, illustrations, or advertisements.

(F) No retail permit holder shall possess on the licensed premises any barrel or other container from which beer is drawn, unless there is attached to the spigot or other dispensing apparatus the name of the manufacturer of the product contained in the barrel or other container, provided that, if the beer is served at a bar, the manufacturer's name or brand shall appear in full view of the purchaser. The commission shall regulate the size and character of the devices provided for in this section.

(G) Except as otherwise provided in this division, no sale of any gift certificate shall be permitted whereby beer or intoxicating liquor of any kind is to be exchanged for the certificate, unless the gift certificate can be exchanged only for food, and beer or intoxicating liquor, for on-premises consumption and the value of the beer or intoxicating liquor for which the certificate can be exchanged does not exceed more than thirty per cent of the total value of the gift certificate. The sale of gift certificates for the purchase of beer, wine, or mixed beverages shall be permitted for the purchase of beer, wine, or mixed beverages for off-premises consumption. Limitations on the use of a gift certificate for the purchase of beer, wine, or mixed beverages for off-premises consumption may be expressed by clearly stamping or typing on the face of the certificate that the certificate may not be used for the purchase of beer, wine, or mixed beverages.

(2004 S 164, eff. 9–16–04; 2004 H 306, eff. 7–23–04; 1996 H 511, § 3, eff. 7–1–97; 1996 H 511, § 1, eff. 8–20–96; 1995 S 162, eff. 7–1–97; 1994 S 167, eff. 11–1–94; 1994 S 209, eff. 11–9–94; 1994 S 82, eff. 5–4–94; 1987 H 419, eff. 7–31–87; 1984 S 74; 1982 H 357; 1976 H 158; 1972 H 859; 1969 H 616; 129 v 1211; 128 v 1282; 1953 H 1; GC 6064–22)

CANCELLATION AND SUSPENSION OF PERMIT; APPEAL

4301.251 Suspension of beer and liquor sales during emergency

When so ordered by the governor, the director or, beginning on July 1, 1997, the superintendent of liquor control shall immediately and without a hearing suspend, for a period of not less than twenty-four hours nor more than seventy-two hours, any retail beer or liquor permit issued under Chapters 4301. and 4303. of the Revised Code and the retail sales of spirituous liquor by any state liquor store or agency for premises within any area where the director or superintendent designates that civil disorder, looting, or rioting exists.

Such order of emergency suspension shall contain an identifiable description of the area in which such retail permits and sales by stores and agencies are suspended and shall specify the calendar date and hour of the beginning and the calendar date and hour of the ending of such suspension period. A written copy of such order shall be served upon the owner, operator, manager, agent, bartender, or clerk of such beer or liquor permit premises, upon the manager or clerk of a state liquor store, or upon the agent, manager, or clerk of a state liquor agency by any law enforcement agency or officer designated by the director or superintendent.

The law enforcement officer, upon serving such emergency suspension order, shall forthwith fill in and sign a return of service form provided by the director or superintendent of liquor control, on which the officer shall write the name and address of the permit premises or the state liquor store or agency, the name and title of the person on whom such suspension order was served, and the day, hour, and address at which such service was made.

Upon receipt of such copy of the emergency suspension order by the owner, operator, manager, agent, bartender, or clerk of such retail beer or liquor permit premises or the state liquor store or agency, no beer, intoxicating liquor, or spirituous liquor shall be permitted to be consumed or sold at or upon such permit premises or the state liquor store or agency.

Upon completion of the return of service form, the law enforcement officer shall cause it to be transmitted immediately to the nearest district office of the department or, beginning on July 1, 1997, the division of liquor control, where it shall be filed, recorded, and reported forthwith by telephone or teletype to the central office of the department or division of liquor control.

Any subsequent order by the governor, to cancel or continue such order of emergency suspension or to diminish or expand the area of the last issued emergency suspension order, shall be processed and carried out in the same manner as that required for the issuance of the original order of emergency suspension.

(1995 H 60, eff. 3–4–98; 1995 S 162, eff. 10–29–95; 132 v H 345, eff. 7–20–67)

4301.252 Forfeiture in lieu of suspension

(A)(1) Except as provided in divisions (A)(2)(d), (B), and (C) of this section, when the liquor control commission determines that the permit of any permit holder is to be suspended under Title XLIII of the Revised Code or any rule of the commission, the commission may issue an order allowing a permit holder to elect to pay a forfeiture for each day of the suspension in accordance with division (A)(2) of this section, rather than to suspend operations under the permit holder's permit issued for the premises at which the violation occurred.

(2)(a) If the permit holder has not violated, at the premises for which the permit holder's permit was issued, any provision of Title XLIII of the Revised Code or rule of the commission during the preceding two years, the amount of the forfeiture for each day for the suspension shall be from one hundred to two hundred dollars.

(b) If the permit holder has violated, at the premises for which the permit holder's permit was issued, any provision of Title XLIII of the Revised Code or rule of the commission for which the permit holder has been disciplined by the commission not more than one other time during the preceding two years, the amount of the forfeiture for each day of the suspension shall be from two hundred to four hundred dollars.

(c) Except as provided under division (A)(2)(e) of this section, if the permit holder has violated, at the premises for which the permit holder's permit was issued, any provision of Title XLIII of the Revised Code or rule of the commission for which the permit holder has been disciplined by the commission more than once, but not more than twice, during the preceding two years, the commission shall establish the amount of the forfeiture for each day of the suspension, but the amount shall be not less than three hundred dollars for each day of suspension.

(d) If the permit holder has violated, at the premises for which the permit holder's permit was issued, any provision of Title XLIII of the Revised Code or rule of the commission for which the permit holder has been disciplined by the commission more than twice during the preceding two years, the commission may suspend or revoke the permit issued for the premises at which the violation occurred, or the commission shall establish the amount of the forfeiture for each day of a suspension, but the amount shall not be less than five hundred dollars for each day of suspension. The commission, and not the permit holder, shall determine whether the permit holder shall pay the forfeiture so established for a suspension instead of having the permit holder's permit suspended or revoked.

(e) If the permit holder has committed, at the premises for which the permit holder's permit was issued, a gambling offense as defined in section 2915.01, a drug abuse offense as defined in section 2925.01, or an offense described in section 2907.07, 2907.21, 2907.22, 2907.23, 2907.24, or 2907.25, division (A) or (B) of section 4301.22, or section 4301.69 of the Revised Code or a municipal ordinance substantially equivalent to any offense defined or described in a section or division listed in division (A)(2)(e) of this section for which the permit holder has been disciplined by the commission more than once, but not more than twice, during the preceding two years, the commission may suspend or revoke the permit issued for the premises at which the violation occurred. A person does not have to plead guilty to or be convicted of an offense defined or described in a section or division listed in division (A)(2)(e) of this section in order for this division to apply.

(3) When the commission issues an order allowing a permit holder the option of paying a forfeiture rather than suspending operations under the permit holder's permit issued for the premises at which the violation occurred, the order shall notify the permit holder of the option of paying a forfeiture. The order shall state the number of days for which the permit may be suspended, that the permit holder has twenty-one days after the date on which the order is sent to pay the full amount of the forfeiture by bank check, certified check, or money order, and that, if the permit holder does not do so, the permit holder's permit issued for the premises at which the violation occurred shall be suspended for the period stated in the order. If the permit holder fails to pay the full amount of the forfeiture by bank check, certified check, or money order within twenty-one days after the date on which the order is sent, the commission shall issue an order suspending the permit holder's permit issued for the premises at which the violation occurred for the period stated in the order allowing payment of a forfeiture. The suspension shall be effective on the twenty-eighth day after the date on which the order allowing the payment of a forfeiture is sent. Even a permit holder who pays a forfeiture may file an appeal under section 119.12 of the Revised Code. A permit holder shall be considered to have paid a forfeiture when the permit holder's bank check, certified check, or money order is received by the commission in Columbus. Upon receipt of a permit holder's bank check, certified check, or money order under this division, the commission shall promptly notify the division of liquor control of its receipt.

(B) No permit holder shall be permitted to pay a forfeiture instead of having the permit holder's permit issued for the premises at which the violation occurred suspended if the suspension is ordered for the reasons stated in division (A)(6) of section 4301.25 of the Revised Code.

(C) When the evidence and the nature of any violation of Title XLIII of the Revised Code show that continued operation of the permit premises presents a clear and present danger to public health and safety, or if the commission finds, upon reliable, probative, and substantial evidence, that the statutory elements of a felony committed in connection with the operation of the permit premises are present in the action for which the permit holder is being disciplined, the commission may suspend the permit issued for the premises at which the violation occurred and shall not allow the permit holder to pay a forfeiture instead of suspending the permit holder's permit operations.

(2003 S 23, eff. 4–7–04; 1998 H 402, eff. 3–30–99; 1995 S 162, eff. 7–1–97; 1995 S 2, eff. 7–1–96; 1992 H 340, eff. 4–24–92; 1983 H 67)

4301.253 Training program completion to be considered in suspension, revocation, or forfeiture decisions

In considering whether to suspend or revoke a permit issued under Chapter 4303. of the Revised Code or to issue an order allowing a permit holder to elect to pay a forfeiture under section 4301.252 of the Revised Code, the liquor control commission shall consider whether the permit holder and the permit holder's employees have successfully completed a training program that includes all of the following:

(A) Instruction on the statutes and rules that govern the sale of beer, wine, mixed beverages, and intoxicating liquor;

(B) Instruction on the prevention of the illegal serving of beer, wine, mixed beverages, and intoxicating liquor to persons under twenty-one years of age;

(C) Use of conflict management skills in alcohol-related situations;

(D) Instruction on methods to safely evacuate the premises of a permit holder in an emergency.

(2003 S 23, eff. 4–7–04)

OFFENSES, PROHIBITIONS, AND ENFORCEMENT

4301.45 Seizure and sale of conveyances transporting beer or intoxicating liquor illegally

When any law enforcement officer discovers any person in the act of transporting in violation of law beer or intoxicating liquors in any wagon, buggy, automobile, watercraft, aircraft, or other vehicle, he shall seize all beer or intoxicating liquors found therein being transported contrary to law. Whenever beer or intoxicating liquors transported or possessed illegally are seized by a law enforcement officer, the officer shall take possession of the vehicle and team, or automobile, boat, watercraft, aircraft, or any other conveyance, and shall arrest any person in charge thereof. The law enforcement officer shall at once proceed against the person arrested under Chapters 4301. and 4303. of the Revised Code, in any court having jurisdiction of offenses under those chapters, but the vehicle or conveyance shall be returned to the owner upon execution by him of a valid bond with sufficient sureties, in a sum equal to the value of the property, which bond shall be approved by the law enforcement officer and shall be conditioned to return said property to the custody of said officer on the day of trial to abide by the judgment of the court. The court, upon conviction of the person so arrested, shall order the beer or intoxicating liquor that was not illegally manufactured to be forfeited to the state and disposed of under section 2933.41 of the Revised Code, and unless good cause to the contrary is shown by the owner, shall order a sale at public auction of the property seized, and the officer making the sale, after deducting the expenses of keeping the property, the fee for the seizure, and the cost of the sale, shall pay all liens, according to their priorities, which are established, by intervention or otherwise at said hearing or in other proceeding brought for said purpose, as being bona fide and as having been created without the lienor having any notice that the carrying vehicle was being used or was to be used for illegal transportation of beer or intoxicating liquor, and shall distribute the balance as money arising from fines and forfeited bonds under such chapters is distributed. The court, upon conviction of the person so arrested, shall order the beer or intoxicating liquor that was illegally manufactured to be destroyed.

All liens against property sold under this section shall be transferred from the property to the proceeds of the sale of the property. If no claimant is found for the team, vehicle, watercraft, aircraft, automobile, or other conveyance, the taking of the same, with its description, shall be advertised in some newspaper published in the city or county where taken, or if there is no newspaper published in such city or county, in a newspaper having circulation in the county, once a week for four weeks and by handbills posted in three public places near the place of seizure, and if no claimant appears within ten days after the last publication of the advertisement, the property shall be sold and the proceeds after deducting the expense and costs shall be distributed as if there were a claimant for said vehicle or conveyance.

(1995 S 162, eff. 10–29–95; 1980 S 50, eff. 5–29–80; 1953 H 1; GC 6212–43)

4301.46 Moneys received and credited

Except as otherwise provided by law, moneys received into the state treasury from the taxes levied, penalties assessed, and sums recovered under Chapters 4301. and 4303. of the Revised Code shall be credited to the general revenue fund.

(1981 H 694, eff. 11–15–81; 1953 H 1; GC 6064–44)

4301.47 Records required

Every class A–1, A–2, and A–4 permit holder and each class B permit holder shall maintain and keep for a period of three years a record of the beer, wine, and mixed beverages purchased, distributed, or sold within this state by the permit holder, together with invoices, records, receipts, bills of lading, and other pertinent papers required by the tax commissioner and, upon demand by the tax commissioner, shall produce these records for a three-year period prior to the demand unless upon satisfactory proof it is shown that the nonproduction is due to causes beyond the permit holder's control.

(2002 H 371, eff. 10–11–02; 1987 H 231, eff. 10–5–87; 130 v H 964, H 316; 1953 H 1; GC 6064–45)

4301.48 False entry upon invoice or container prohibited

No person shall make any false entry upon an invoice or upon a container of beer, wine, or mixed beverages required to be made under this chapter and Chapters 4303. and 4307. of the Revised Code, or present any such false entry for the inspection of the tax commissioner.

(1990 S 188, eff. 3–20–90; 1982 H 357; 1953 H 1; GC 6064–46)

4301.49 Interference with inspection prohibited

No person shall prevent or hinder the tax commissioner from making a full inspection of any place where beer, wine, or mixed beverages subject to the tax imposed by section 4301.42, 4301.421, 4301.424, or 4301.43 of the Revised Code is manufactured, sold, or stored. No person shall prevent or hinder the full inspection of invoices, books, records, or papers required to be kept under this chapter and Chapters 4305. and 4307. of the Revised Code.

(1995 S 188, eff. 7–19–95; 1990 S 188, eff. 3–20–90; 1982 H 357; 1953 H 1; GC 6064–47)

4301.50 Sale of beverages without tax prohibited

No person, firm, or corporation or his or its employee or agent shall distribute or sell any beverage upon which the tax provided for by sections 4301.42, 4301.421, 4301.424, 4301.43, 4301.432, and 4305.01 of the Revised Code has not been paid. Any person, firm, or corporation or his or its employee or agent who violates this section or any rule of the tax commissioner shall be subject to all penalties provided in division (A) of section 4307.99 of the Revised Code.

(1995 S 188, eff. 7–19–95; 1990 S 188, eff. 3–20–90; 1982 H 357; 1981 H 694; 130 v H 964, H 316; 1953 H 1; GC 6064–48)

4301.52 Seizure and sale of wine or bulk beer by tax commissioner

Whenever the tax commissioner or any of his deputies or employees authorized by him for such purpose discover any wine, mixed beverage, or beer, subject to tax under this chapter or Chapter 4303. or 4305. of the Revised Code, and upon which the tax has not been paid, the commissioner or such deputy or employee may forthwith seize such wine, mixed beverage, or beer, which is thereby forfeited to the state. The commissioner may within a reasonable time thereafter by a notice posted upon the premises where such seizure is made, or by publication in some newspaper having circulation in the county wherein such seizure is made, at least five days before the date of sale, sell such forfeited wine, mixed beverage, or beer, and from the proceeds of such sale shall collect the tax due together with a forfeiture of fifty per cent thereof and the costs incurred in such proceedings and pay the balance to the person in whose possession such forfeited wine, mixed beverage, or beer was found, provided that such seizure and sale shall not relieve any person from fine or imprisonment provided for violation of this chapter and Chapters 4303. and 4305. of the Revised Code. Such sale shall be made in the county where most convenient and economical. All moneys collected under this section shall be paid into the state treasury to the credit of the general revenue fund.

(1990 S 188, eff. 3–20–90; 1982 H 357; 1953 H 1; GC 6064–51)

SEARCH WARRANTS

4301.53 Search warrants

The judge of a court of record may issue warrants to search a house, building, place, vehicle, watercraft, aircraft, or conveyance for beer, alcohol, or intoxicating liquor manufactured, possessed, stored, concealed, sold, furnished, given away, or transported in violation of Chapters 4301. and 4303. of the Revised Code, and the containers in which the same is found, or machinery, tools, implements, equipment, supplies, and materials used or kept for use in manufacturing beer or intoxicating liquor in violation of those chapters, and to seize any of that property and things found in it, together with the vehicle, watercraft, aircraft, or conveyance in which the same is found. The issuance of those warrants is subject in all respects to sections 2933.22 to 2933.27 of the Revised Code; except that any such vehicle, watercraft, aircraft, or other conveyance shall be returned to its owner upon execution by the owner of a bond with surety to the satisfaction of the enforcement agent of the department of public safety or other law enforcement officer making the seizure in an equal amount to its value, conditioned upon its return to the custody of such agent or officer on the day of trial to abide by the judgment of the court. Upon conviction of any violation of Chapters 4301. and 4303. of the Revised Code, any property found in the possession of the person convicted or the person's agent or employee shall be disposed of as provided in section 4301.45 of the Revised Code. If the accused is discharged by the judge or magistrate, such vehicle, watercraft, aircraft, or other conveyance shall be returned to its owner, and any bond given pursuant to this section shall be canceled. If the accused is the holder of a permit issued under Chapters 4301. and 4303. of the Revised Code, any beer, intoxicating liquor, or alcohol seized shall be disposed of as provided in section 4301.29 of the Revised Code, and any other property seized shall be returned to its owner by the officer having the custody or possession of such property. If the accused is not the holder of such a permit in force at the time, any beer, intoxicating liquor, or alcohol that was not illegally manufactured shall be forfeited to the state and shall forthwith be disposed of under section 2933.41 of the Revised Code. Illegally manufactured beer, intoxicating liquor, or alcohol, and other property, except as provided in this section, shall be destroyed, and any such beer, intoxicating liquor, or alcohol, or other property is hereby declared to be a public nuisance.

(1999 H 163, eff. 6–30–99; 1995 S 162, eff. 10–29–95; 1980 S 50, eff. 5–29–80; 1953 H 1; GC 6064–61)

4301.54 Retaliatory taxes, fees, and charges

If the laws of another state, territory, or nation, or the rules and regulations of an administrative body in another state, territory, or nation, provide for the levy and collection of taxes, fees, and charges upon the products of Ohio manufacturers of wine or manufacturers or brewers of beer when those products are sold in, delivered, or shipped into the other state, territory, or nation, in excess of the taxes, fees, and charges levied and collected on the products of manufacturers or brewers of those states, territories, or nations, whether those taxes, fees, and charges are in the nature of an excise, sales, or import tax, or by whatever name designated, the tax commissioner shall levy and collect additional taxes, fees, and charges on the products of manufacturers of wine or manufacturers and brewers of beer of that other state, territory, or nation when sold in, delivered, or shipped into this state.

The additional taxes, fees, and charges shall be in excess of those provided for in other sections of this chapter or Chapters 4303. and 4307. and section 4305.13 of the Revised Code, in the same proportion or in the same amount as taxes, fees, and charges levied and collected in the other state, territory, or nation upon the products of Ohio manufacturers of wine or manufacturers or brewers of beer are in excess of those levied and collected on the products of manufacturers and brewers of the other state, territory, or nation.

If the laws of another state, territory, or nation, or the rules and regulations of an administrative body in another state, territory, or nation, provide for the levy and collection of taxes, fees, or charges against Ohio manufacturers of wine or manufacturers or brewers of beer for the privilege of doing business in that state, territory, or nation, like amounts shall be levied and collected on manufacturers or brewers of that state, territory, or nation for the privilege of doing business in this state.

(2002 H 371, eff. 10–11–02; 1982 H 357, eff. 10–1–82; 132 v H 1; 1953 H 1; GC 6064–67)

4301.55 Retaliatory tax on sale of beer or wine manufactured in another state

If the laws of another state, territory, or nation, or the rules and regulations of any administrative body in another state, territory, or nation, authorize or impose any tax, fee, or charge upon the right to transport or import into that state, territory, or nation any beer or wine manufactured in this state; or authorize or impose any different warehousing requirements or higher warehousing or inspection fees upon any beer or wine manufactured in this state and imported into or sold in that state, territory, or nation than are imposed upon beer and wine manufactured in that state, territory, or nation; or impose any higher fee for the privilege of selling or handling beer or wine manufactured in this state than is imposed for the privilege of handling or selling the same kind of beverages manufactured within that state, territory, or nation or any other state, territory, or nation, the tax commissioner shall levy and collect similar taxes, fees, and charges from licensees or persons selling in this state beer and wine manufactured in that other state, territory, or nation. The taxes, fees, and charges shall be in addition to the taxes, fees, and charges assessed and collected by the commissioner under section 4301.54 of the Revised Code.

(2002 H 371, eff. 10–11–02; 1953 H 1, eff. 10–1–53; GC 6064–67a)

4301.56 List of holders of permits

The division of liquor control shall on the first day of each month certify to the tax commissioner a list of the names and addresses of all holders of permits issued by it during the preceding month and then in force, together with a list of eliminations from any prior list. The taxation provisions of Chapters 4301. and 4303. of the Revised Code are laws which the commissioner is required to administer within the meaning of sections 5703.19 to 5703.37 5703.39, and 5703.41 of the Revised Code.

(1995 S 162, eff. 7–1–97; 1953 H 1, eff. 10–1–53; GC 6064–52)

4301.57 Money from fines and forfeited bonds

Money from fines and forfeited bonds collected under any of the penal laws of this state relating to the manufacture, importation, transportation, distribution, or sale of beer or intoxicating liquor shall be paid as follows: one half to the credit of the general revenue fund and one half to the treasury of the county where the prosecution is held.

(1953 H 1, eff. 10–1–53; GC 6064–59)

4301.58 Activities prohibited without permit

(A) No person, by himself or herself or by the person's clerk, agent, or employee, who is not the holder of an A permit issued by the division of liquor control, in force at the time, and authorizing the manufacture of beer or intoxicating liquor, or who is not an agent or employee of the division authorized to manufacture such beer or intoxicating liquor, shall manufacture any beer or intoxicating liquor for sale, or shall manufacture spirituous liquor.

(B) No person, by himself or herself or by the person's clerk, agent, or employee, who is not the holder of a B, C, D, E, F, G, or I permit issued by the division, in force at the time, and authorizing the sale of beer, intoxicating liquor, or alcohol, or who is not an agent or employee of the division or the tax commissioner authorized to sell such beer, intoxicating liquor, or alcohol, shall sell, keep, or possess beer, intoxicating liquor, or alcohol for sale to any persons other than those authorized by Chapters 4301. and 4303. of the Revised Code to purchase any beer or intoxicating liquor, or sell any alcohol at retail. This division does not apply to or affect the sale or possession for sale of any low-alcohol beverage.

(C) No person, by himself or herself or by the person's clerk, agent, or employee, who is the holder of a permit issued by the division, shall sell, keep, or possess for sale any intoxicating liquor not purchased from the division or from the holder of a permit issued by the division authorizing the sale of such intoxicating liquor unless the same has been purchased with the special consent of the division. The division shall revoke the permit of any person convicted of a violation of division (C) of this section.

(1995 S 162, eff. 7–1–97; 1994 S 209, eff. 11–9–94; 1953 H 1, eff. 10–1–53; GC 6064–54)

4301.59 Fraudulent misrepresentation prohibited

No person, or his clerk, agent, or employee, shall make or issue any false or fraudulent statement, either orally or in writing, concerning the future value or use of any bonded warehouse receipt for spirituous liquor, or concerning the age, quality, quantity, ingredients, source, future value, or use of the spirituous liquor represented by such receipt for the purpose of promoting or inducing the sale or purchase of such receipt in this state.

(1953 H 1, eff. 10–1–53; GC 6064–54a)

4301.60 Illegal transportation prohibited

No person, who is not the holder of an H permit, shall transport beer, intoxicating liquor, or alcohol in this state. This section does not apply to the transportation and delivery of beer, alcohol, or intoxicating liquor purchased or to be purchased from the holder of a permit issued by the division of liquor control, in force at the time, and authorizing the sale and delivery of the beer, alcohol, or intoxicating liquor so transported, or to the transportation and delivery of beer, intoxicating liquor, or alcohol purchased from the division or the tax commissioner, or purchased by the holder of an A or B permit outside this state and transported within this state by them in their own trucks for the purpose of sale under their permits.

(1995 S 162, eff. 7–1–97; 1953 H 1, eff. 10–1–53; GC 6064–55)

4301.61 Liquor transaction scans

(A) As used in this section and section 4301.611 of the Revised Code:

(1) "Card holder" means any person who presents a driver's or commercial driver's license or an identification card to a permit holder, or an agent or employee of a permit holder, for either of the purposes listed in division (A)(4)(a) or (b) of this section.

(2) "Identification card" means an identification card issued under sections 4507.50 to 4507.52 of the Revised Code.

(3) "Permit holder" means the holder of a permit issued under Chapter 4303. of the Revised Code.

(4) "Transaction scan" means the process by which a permit holder or an agent or employee of a permit holder checks, by means of a transaction scan device, the validity of a driver's or commercial driver's license or an identification card that is presented as a condition for doing either of the following:

(a) Purchasing any beer, intoxicating liquor, or low-alcohol beverage;

(b) Gaining admission to a premises that has been issued a liquor permit authorizing the sale of beer or intoxicating liquor for consumption on the premises where sold, and where admission is restricted to persons twenty-one years of age or older.

(5) "Transaction scan device" means any commercial device or combination of devices used at a point of sale that is capable of deciphering in an electronically readable format the information encoded on the magnetic strip or bar code of a driver's or commercial driver's license or an identification card.

(B)(1) A permit holder or an agent or employee of a permit holder may perform a transaction scan by means of a transaction scan device to check the validity of a driver's or commercial driver's license or identification card presented by a card holder for either of the purposes listed in division (A)(4)(a) or (b) of this section.

(2) If the information deciphered by the transaction scan performed under division (B)(1) of this section fails to match the information printed on the driver's or commercial driver's license or identification card presented by the card holder, or if the transaction scan indicates that the information so printed is false or fraudulent, neither the permit holder nor any agent or employee of the permit holder shall sell any beer, intoxicating liquor, or low-alcohol beverage to the card holder.

(3) Division (B)(1) of this section does not preclude a permit holder or an agent or employee of a permit holder from using a transaction scan device to check the validity of a document other than a driver's or commercial driver's license or an identification card, if the document includes a bar code or magnetic strip that may be scanned by the device, as a condition of a sale of beer, intoxicating liquor, or a low-alcohol beverage or of granting admission to a premises described in division (A)(4) of this section.

(C) The registrar of motor vehicles, with the approval of the liquor control commission, shall adopt, and may amend or rescind, rules in accordance with Chapter 119. of the Revised Code that do both of the following:

(1) Govern the recording and maintenance of information described in divisions (D)(1)(a) and (b) of this section and divisions (D)(1)(a) and (b) of section 2927.021 of the Revised Code;

(2) Ensure quality control in the use of transaction scan devices under this section and sections 2927.021, 2927.022, and 4301.611 of the Revised Code.

(D)(1) No permit holder or agent or employee of a permit holder shall electronically or mechanically record or maintain any information derived from a transaction scan, except the following:

(a) The name and date of birth of the person listed on the driver's or commercial driver's license or identification card presented by a card holder;

(b) The expiration date and identification number of the driver's or commercial driver's license or identification card presented by a card holder.

(2) No permit holder or agent or employee of a permit holder shall use the information that is derived from a transaction scan or that is permitted to be recorded and maintained by division (D)(1) of this section, except for purposes of section 4301.611 of the Revised Code.

(3) No permit holder or agent or employee of a permit holder shall use a transaction scan device for a purpose other than a purpose listed in division (A)(4)(a) or (b) of this section.

(4) No permit holder or agent or employee of a permit holder shall sell or otherwise disseminate the information derived from a transaction scan to any third party, including, but not limited to, selling or otherwise disseminating that information for any mar-

keting, advertising, or promotional activities, but a permit holder or agent or employee of a permit holder may release that information pursuant to a court order or as specifically authorized by section 4301.611 or another section of the Revised Code.

(E) Nothing in this section or section 4301.611 of the Revised Code relieves a permit holder or an agent or employee of a permit holder of any responsibility to comply with any other applicable state or federal laws or rules governing the sale of beer, intoxicating liquor, or low-alcohol beverages.

(F) Whoever violates division (B)(2) or (D) of this section is guilty of an illegal liquor transaction scan, and the court may impose upon the offender a civil penalty of up to one thousand dollars for each violation. The clerk of the court shall pay each collected civil penalty to the county treasurer for deposit into the county treasury.

(2000 S 200, eff. 9–21–00)

4301.611 Affirmative defenses

(A) A permit holder or an agent or employee of a permit holder may not be found guilty of a charge of a violation of this chapter or any rule of the liquor control commission in which the age of a purchaser of any beer, intoxicating liquor, or low-alcohol beverage is an element of the alleged violation, if the permit holder, agent, or employee raises and proves as an affirmative defense that all of the following occurred:

(1) The card holder attempting to purchase any beer, intoxicating liquor, or low-alcohol beverage presented a driver's or commercial driver's license or an identification card.

(2) A transaction scan of the driver's or commercial driver's license or identification card that the card holder presented indicated that the license or card was valid.

(3) The beer, intoxicating liquor, or low-alcohol beverage was sold to the card holder in reasonable reliance upon the identification presented and the completed transaction scan.

(B) In determining whether a permit holder or an agent or employee of a permit holder has proven the affirmative defense provided by division (A) of this section, the liquor control commission or the trier of fact in a court of record shall consider any written policy that the permit holder has adopted and implemented and that is intended to prevent violations of division (A)(1) or (2) of section 4301.22 and of sections 4301.63 to 4301.636, 4301.69, and 4301.691 of the Revised Code. For purposes of division (A)(3) of this section, the commission or trier of fact shall consider that reasonable reliance upon the identification presented and the completed transaction scan may require a permit holder or an agent or employee of a permit holder to exercise reasonable diligence to determine, and that the use of a transaction scan device does not excuse a permit holder or an agent or employee of a permit holder from exercising reasonable diligence to determine, the following:

(1) Whether a person to whom the permit holder or agent or employee of a permit holder sells any beer or intoxicating liquor is twenty-one years of age or older or sells any low-alcohol beverage is eighteen years of age or older;

(2) Whether the description and picture appearing on the driver's or commercial driver's license or identification card presented by a card holder is that of the card holder.

(C) The affirmative defense provided by division (A) of this section is in addition to the defense provided by section 4301.639 of the Revised Code.

(D) In any hearing before the liquor control commission and in any criminal action in which the affirmative defense provided by division (A) of this section is raised, the registrar of motor vehicles or a deputy registrar who issued an identification card under sections 4507.50 to 4507.52 of the Revised Code shall be permitted to submit certified copies of the records of that issuance in lieu of the testimony of the personnel of or contractors with the bureau of motor vehicles in the hearing or action.

(2000 S 200, eff. 9–21–00)

4301.62 Open container prohibited; exceptions

(A) As used in this section:

(1) "Chauffeured limousine" means a vehicle registered under section 4503.24 of the Revised Code.

(2) "Street," "highway," and "motor vehicle" have the same meanings as in section 4511.01 of the Revised Code.

(B) No person shall have in the person's possession an opened container of beer or intoxicating liquor in any of the following circumstances:

(1) In a state liquor store;

(2) Except as provided in division (C) of this section, on the premises of the holder of any permit issued by the division of liquor control;

(3) In any other public place;

(4) Except as provided in division (D) of this section, while operating or being a passenger in or on a motor vehicle on any street, highway, or other public or private property open to the public for purposes of vehicular travel or parking;

(5) Except as provided in division (D) of this section, while being in or on a stationary motor vehicle on any street, highway, or other public or private property open to the public for purposes of vehicular travel or parking

(C)(1) A person may have in the person's possession an opened container of any of the following:

(a) Beer or intoxicating liquor that has been lawfully purchased for consumption on the premises where bought from the holder of an A–1–A, A–2, D–1, D–2, D–3, D–3a, D–4, D–4a, D–5, D–5a, D–5b, D–5c, D–5d, D–5e, D–5f, D–5g, D–5h, D–5i, D–5j, D–5k, D–7, D–8, E, F, F–2, or F–5 permit;

(b) Beer, wine, or mixed beverages served for consumption on the premises by the holder of an F–3 permit or wine served for consumption on the premises by the holder of an F–4 or F–6 permit;

(c) Beer or intoxicating liquor consumed on the premises of a convention facility as provided in section 4303.201 of the Revised Code;

(d) Beer or intoxicating liquor to be consumed during tastings and samplings approved by rule of the liquor control commission.

(2) A person may have in the person's possession on an F liquor permit premises an opened container of beer or intoxicating liquor that was not purchased from the holder of the F permit if the premises for which the F permit is issued is a music festival and the holder of the F permit grants permission for that possession on the premises during the period for which the F permit is issued. As used in this division, "music festival" means a series of outdoor live musical performances, extending for a period of at least three consecutive days and located on an area of land of at least forty acres.

(D) This section does not apply to a person who pays all or a portion of the fee imposed for the use of a chauffeured limousine pursuant to a prearranged contract, or the guest of the person, when all of the following apply:

(1) The person or guest is a passenger in the limousine.

(2) The person or guest is located in the limousine, but is not occupying a seat in the front compartment of the limousine where the operator of the limousine is located.

(3) The limousine is located on any street, highway, or other public or private property open to the public for purposes of vehicular travel or parking.

(2003 S 23, eff. 4–7–04; 2002 H 371, eff. 10–11–02; 2000 S 262, eff. 4–9–01; 2000 S 200, eff. 9–21–00; 1999 H 283, eff. 9–29–99; 1997 S 85, eff. 5–15–97; 1995 S 162, eff. 7–1–97; 1995 S 39, eff. 7–14–95; 1993 H 281, eff. 7–2–93)

PURCHASE BY PERSON UNDER TWENTY–ONE

4301.63 Minimum age for purchases

Except as otherwise provided in this chapter, no person under the age of twenty-one years shall purchase beer or intoxicating liquor.

(1987 H 419, eff. 7–31–87; 1982 H 357; 1975 H 315; 125 v 113; 1953 H 1; GC 6064–57a)

4301.631 Prohibition; minors under eighteen years; low alcohol beverages

(A) As used in this section, "underage person" means a person under eighteen years of age.

(B) No underage person shall purchase any low-alcohol beverage.

(C) No underage person shall order, pay for, share the cost of, or attempt to purchase any low-alcohol beverage.

(D) No person shall knowingly furnish any false information as to the name, age, or other identification of any underage person for the purpose of obtaining or with the intent to obtain any low-alcohol beverage for an underage person, by purchase or as a gift.

(E) No underage person shall knowingly show or give false information concerning the person's name, age, or other identification for the purpose of purchasing or otherwise obtaining any low-alcohol beverage in any place in this state.

(F) No person shall sell or furnish any low-alcohol beverage to, or buy any low-alcohol beverage for, an underage person, unless given by a physician in the regular line of his practice or given for established religious purposes, or unless the underage person is accompanied by a parent, spouse who is not an underage person, or legal guardian.

No permit issued by the division of liquor control shall be suspended, revoked, or canceled because of a violation of this division or division (G) of this section.

(G) No person who is the owner or occupant of any public or private place shall knowingly allow any underage person to remain in or on the place while possessing or consuming any low-alcohol beverage, unless the low-alcohol beverage is given to the person possessing or consuming it by that person's parent, spouse who is not an underage person, or legal guardian, and the parent, spouse who is not an underage person, or legal guardian is present when the person possesses or consumes the low-alcohol beverage.

An owner of a public or private place is not liable for acts or omissions in violation of this division that are committed by a lessee of that place, unless the owner authorizes or acquiesces in the lessee's acts or omissions.

(H) No underage person shall knowingly possess or consume any low-alcohol beverage in any public or private place, unless accompanied by a parent, spouse who is not an underage person, or legal guardian, or unless the low-alcohol beverage is given by a physician in the regular line of the physician's practice or given for established religious purposes.

(I) No parent, spouse who is not an underage person, or legal guardian of an underage person shall knowingly permit the underage person to violate this section.

(1995 S 162, eff. 7–1–97; 1994 S 209, eff. 11–9–94)

4301.633 Misrepresentation to obtain alcoholic beverage for a minor prohibited

Except as otherwise provided in this chapter, no person shall knowingly furnish any false information as to the name, age, or other identification of any person under twenty-one years of age for the purpose of obtaining or with the intent to obtain, beer or intoxicating liquor for a person under twenty-one years of age, by purchase, or as a gift.

(1987 H 419, eff. 7–31–87; 1982 H 357; 130 v H 325)

4301.634 Misrepresentation by a minor

Except as otherwise provided in this chapter, no person under the age of twenty-one years shall knowingly show or give false information concerning the person's name, age, or other identification for the purpose of purchasing or otherwise obtaining beer or intoxicating liquor in any place in this state where beer or intoxicating liquor is sold under a permit issued by the division of liquor control or sold by the division.

(1995 S 162, eff. 7–1–97; 1987 H 419, eff. 7–31–87; 1982 H 357; 130 v H 325)

4301.635 Compliance checks

(A) As used in this section:

(1) "Compliance check" means an attempt on behalf of a law enforcement agency or the division of liquor control to purchase any beer, wine, mixed beverages, or intoxicating liquor in the enforcement of any section of this chapter or any rule of the liquor control commission in which the age of the purchaser is an element of the offense.

(2) "Confidential informant" means a person who is under twenty-one years of age and who is engaged in conducting compliance checks.

(3) "Law enforcement agency" means an organization or unit made up of law enforcement officers authorized to enforce this chapter and also includes the investigative unit of the department of public safety described in section 5502.13 of the Revised Code.

(B) Within a reasonable period of time after the conduct of a compliance check, the law enforcement agency that conducted the compliance check, or the division of liquor control if the division conducted the compliance check, shall send written notification of it to the permit holder that was its subject. If the confidential informant who participated in the compliance check was able to purchase beer, wine, mixed beverages, or intoxicating liquor, the citation issued for the violation constitutes that notification. If the confidential informant who participated in the compliance check was unable to purchase beer, wine, mixed beverages, or intoxicating liquor, the notification shall indicate the date and time of the compliance check, the law enforcement agency that conducted the compliance check or, when applicable, that the division of liquor control conducted the compliance check, and the permit holder or a general description of the employee of the permit holder who refused to make the sale.

(2003 S 23, eff. 4–7–04)

4301.636 Identification cards

(A)(1) No person shall manufacture, transfer, or distribute in any manner any identification card issued for the purpose of establishing a person's age that displays the great seal of the state of Ohio, the word "Ohio," "state," or "official," or any other designation that represents the card as the official identification card of Ohio, except for those cards issued pursuant to section 4507.50 of the Revised Code.

(2) No person shall manufacture, sell, or distribute in any manner for any compensation any identification card issued for the purpose of establishing a person's age that displays the great seal of the state of Ohio, the word "Ohio," "state," or "official," or any other designation that represents the card as the official identification card of Ohio, except for those cards issued pursuant to section 4507.50 of the Revised Code.

(B)(1) No person, other than the registrar of motor vehicles or a deputy registrar, shall manufacture, transfer, or distribute in any manner any card that displays the great seal of the state of Ohio, the word "Ohio," "state," "official," "chauffeur," "chauffeur's," "commercial driver," "commercial driver's," "driver,""driver's," "operator," or "operator's," or any other designation that represents the card as the official driver's license of the state.

(2) No person, other than the registrar of motor vehicles or a deputy registrar, shall manufacture, sell, or distribute in any manner for any compensation any card that displays the great seal of the state of Ohio, the word "Ohio," "state," "official," "chauffeur," "chauffeur's," "commercial driver," "commercial driver's," "driver," "driver's," or any other designation that represents the card as the official driver's license of the state.

(1990 S 131, eff. 7-25-90; 1987 H 419)

4301.637 Printed warnings to be posted on licensed premises

(A) Except as otherwise provided in section 4301.691 of the Revised Code, every place in this state where beer, intoxicating liquor, or any low-alcohol beverage is sold for beverage purposes shall display at all times, in a prominent place on the premises thereof, a printed card, which shall be furnished by the division of liquor control and which shall read substantially as follows:

"WARNING TO PERSONS UNDER AGE

If you are under the age of 21

Under the statutes of the state of Ohio, if you order, pay for, share the cost of, or attempt to purchase, or possess or consume beer or intoxicating liquor in any public place, or furnish false information as to name, age, or other identification, you are subject to a fine of up to one thousand dollars, or imprisonment up to six months, or both.

If you are under the age of 18

Under the statutes of the state of Ohio, if you order, pay for, share the cost of, or attempt to purchase, or possess or consume, any type of beer or wine that contains either no alcohol or less than one-half of one per cent of alcohol by volume in any public place, or furnish false information as to name, age, or other identification, you are subject to a fine of up to two hundred fifty dollars or to imprisonment up to thirty days, or both."

No person shall be subject to any criminal prosecution or any proceedings before the division or the liquor control commission for failing to display this card. No permit issued by the division shall be suspended, revoked, or canceled because of the failure of the permit holder to display this card.

(B) Every place in this state for which a D permit has been issued under Chapter 4303. of the Revised Code shall be issued a printed card by the division that shall read substantially as follows:

"WARNING

If you are carrying a firearm

Under the statutes of Ohio, if you possess a firearm in any room in which liquor is being dispensed in premises for which a D permit has been issued under Chapter 4303. of the Revised Code, you may be guilty of a felony and may be subjected to a prison term of up to one year."

No person shall be subject to any criminal prosecution or any proceedings before the division or the liquor control commission for failing to display this card. No permit issued by the division shall be suspended, revoked, or canceled because of the failure of the permit holder to display this card.

(1995 S 162, eff. 7-1-97; 1995 S 2, eff. 7-1-96; 1994 S 209, eff. 11-9-94; 1987 H 419, eff. 7-31-87; 1986 H 39, H 51; 1982 H 357; 1977 S 49; 132 v H 1; 131 v S 388; 130 v H 325)

4301.638 No modification of other sections intended

Sections 4301.633 to 4301.637 of the Revised Code shall not be deemed to modify or affect division (A) of section 4301.22 or section 4301.69 of the Revised Code.

(2002 H 17, eff 10-11-02; 1987 H 419, eff 7-31-87; 130 v H 325)

4301.639 Immunity of permit holder, agent or employee

(A) No permit holder, agent or employee of a permit holder, or any other person may be found guilty of a violation of any section of this chapter or any rule of the liquor control commission in which age is an element of the offense, if the liquor control commission or any court of record finds all of the following:

(1) That the person buying, at the time of so doing, exhibited to the permit holder, the agent or employee of the permit holder, or the other person a driver's or commercial driver's license or an identification card issued under sections 4507.50 to 4507.52 of the Revised Code showing that the person buying was then at least twenty-one years of age if the person was buying beer as defined in section 4301.01 of the Revised Code or intoxicating liquor or that the person was then at least eighteen years of age if the person was buying any low-alcohol beverage;

(2) That the permit holder, the agent or employee of the permit holder, or the other person made a bona fide effort to ascertain the true age of the person buying by checking the identification presented, at the time of the purchase, to ascertain that the description on the identification compared with the appearance of the buyer and that the identification presented had not been altered in any way;

(3) That the permit holder, the agent or employee of the permit holder, or the other person had reason to believe that the person buying was of legal age.

(B) In any hearing before the liquor control commission and in any action or proceeding before a court of record in which a defense is raised under division (A) of this section, the registrar of motor vehicles or deputy registrar who issued an identification card under sections 4507.50 to 4507.52 of the Revised Code shall be permitted to submit certified copies of the records, in the registrar's or deputy's possession, of that issuance in lieu of the testimony of the personnel of or contractors with the bureau of motor vehicles at the hearing, action, or proceeding.

(C) The defense provided by division (A) of this section is in addition to the affirmative defense provided by section 4301.611 of the Revised Code.

(2000 S 200, eff. 9–21–00; 1994 S 209, eff. 11–9–94; 1989 H 381, eff. 7–1–89; 1977 H 90; 1972 H 453)

MISCELLANEOUS PROVISIONS

4301.64 Prohibition against consumption in motor vehicle

No person shall consume any beer or intoxicating liquor in a motor vehicle. This section does not apply to persons described in division (D) of section 4301.62 of the Revised Code.

(1995 S 39, eff. 7–14–95; 130 v H 88, eff. 7–11–63; 1953 H 1; GC 6064–58)

4301.66 Obstructing search of premises prohibited

No person shall hinder or obstruct any agent or employee of the division of liquor control, any enforcement agent of the department of public safety, or any officer of the law, from making inspection or search of any place, other than a bona fide private residence, where beer or intoxicating liquor is possessed, kept, sold, or given away.

(1999 H 163, eff. 6–30–99; 1995 S 162, eff. 10–29–95; 1982 H 357, eff. 10–1–82; 1953 H 1; GC 6064–63)

4301.67 Illegal possession of intoxicating liquor or beer prohibited

No person shall have that person's possession of [1] any spirituous liquor, in excess of one liter, in one or more containers, which was not purchased at wholesale or retail from the division of liquor control or otherwise lawfully acquired pursuant to Chapters 4301. and 4303. of the Revised Code, or any other intoxicating liquor or beer, in one or more containers, which was not lawfully acquired pursuant to Chapters 4301. and 4303. of the Revised Code.

(1995 S 162, eff. 7–1–97; 1995 S 149, eff. 11–21–95; 1982 H 357, eff. 10–1–82; 1969 H 638; 128 v 1282; 1953 H 1; GC 6064–64)

[1] Language appears as the result of the harmonization of 1995 S 162 and 1995 S 149.

4301.68 Prohibition against sale or possession of diluted liquor and refilled containers

No person shall sell, offer for sale, or possess intoxicating liquor in any original container which has been diluted, refilled, or partly refilled.

(1953 H 1, eff. 10–1–53; GC 6064–68)

4301.69 Sale to underage persons; restrictions relating to public and private places and accommodations

(A) Except as otherwise provided in this chapter, no person shall sell beer or intoxicating liquor to an underage person, shall buy beer or intoxicating liquor for an underage person, or shall furnish it to an underage person, unless given by a physician in the regular line of the physician's practice or given for established religious purposes or unless the underage person is accompanied by a parent, spouse who is not an underage person, or legal guardian.

In proceedings before the liquor control commission, no permit holder, or the employee or agent of a permit holder, charged with a violation of this division shall be charged, for the same offense, with a violation of division (A)(1) of section 4301.22 of the Revised Code.

(B) No person who is the owner or occupant of any public or private place shall knowingly allow any underage person to remain in or on the place while possessing or consuming beer or intoxicating liquor, unless the intoxicating liquor or beer is given to the person possessing or consuming it by that person's parent, spouse who is not an underage person, or legal guardian and the parent, spouse who is not an underage person, or legal guardian is present at the time of the person's possession or consumption of the beer or intoxicating liquor.

An owner of a public or private place is not liable for acts or omissions in violation of this division that are committed by a lessee of that place, unless the owner authorizes or acquiesces in the lessee's acts or omissions.

(C) No person shall engage or use accommodations at a hotel, inn, cabin, campground, or restaurant when the person knows or has reason to know either of the following:

(1) That beer or intoxicating liquor will be consumed by an underage person on the premises of the accommodations that the person engages or uses, unless the person engaging or using the accommodations is the spouse of the underage person and who is not an underage person, or is the parent or legal guardian of all of the underage persons, who consume beer or intoxicating liquor on the premises and that person is on the premises at all times when beer or intoxicating liquor is being consumed by an underage person;

(2) That a drug of abuse will be consumed on the premises of the accommodations by any person, except a person who obtained the drug of abuse pursuant to a prescription issued by a licensed health professional authorized to prescribe drugs and has the drug of abuse in the original container in which it was dispensed to the person.

(D)(1) No person is required to permit the engagement of accommodations at any hotel, inn, cabin, or campground by an underage person or for an underage person, if the person engaging the accommodations knows or has reason to know that the underage person is intoxicated, or that the underage person possesses any beer or intoxicating liquor and is not accompanied by a parent, spouse who is not an underage person, or legal guardian who is or will be present at all times when the beer or intoxicating liquor is being consumed by the underage person.

(2) No underage person shall knowingly engage or attempt to engage accommodations at any hotel, inn, cabin, or campground by presenting identification that falsely indicates that the underage person is twenty-one years of age or older for the purpose of violating this section.

(E)(1) No underage person shall knowingly order, pay for, share the cost of, attempt to purchase, possess, or consume any beer or intoxicating liquor in any public or private place. No underage person shall knowingly be under the influence of any beer or intoxicating liquor in any public place. The prohibitions set forth in division (E)(1) of this section against an underage person knowingly possessing, consuming, or being under the influence of any beer or intoxicating liquor shall not apply if the underage person is accompanied by a parent, spouse who is not an underage person, or legal guardian, or the beer or intoxicating liquor is given by a physician in the regular line of the physician's practice or given for established religious purposes.

(2)(a) If a person is charged with violating division (E)(1) of this section in a complaint filed under section 2151.27 of the

Revised Code, the court may order the child into a diversion program specified by the court and hold the complaint in abeyance pending successful completion of the diversion program. A child is ineligible to enter into a diversion program under division (E)(2)(a) of this section if the child previously has been diverted pursuant to division (E)(2)(a) of this section. If the child completes the diversion program to the satisfaction of the court, the court shall dismiss the complaint and order the child's record in the case sealed under division (D)(3) of section 2151.358 of the Revised Code. If the child fails to satisfactorily complete the diversion program, the court shall proceed with the complaint.

(b) If a person is charged in a criminal complaint with violating division (E)(1) of this section, section 2935.36 of the Revised Code shall apply to the offense, except that a person is ineligible for diversion under that section if the person previously has been diverted pursuant to division (E)(2)(a) or (b) of this section. If the person completes the diversion program to the satisfaction of the court, the court shall dismiss the complaint and order the record in the case sealed under section 2953.52 of the Revised Code. If the person fails to satisfactorily complete the diversion program, the court shall proceed with the complaint.

(F) No parent, spouse who is not an underage person, or legal guardian of a minor shall knowingly permit the minor to violate this section or section 4301.63, 4301.633, or 4301.634 of the Revised Code.

(G) The operator of any hotel, inn, cabin, or campground shall make the provisions of this section available in writing to any person engaging or using accommodations at the hotel, inn, cabin, or campground.

(H) As used in this section:

(1) "Drug of abuse" has the same meaning as in section 3719.011 of the Revised Code.

(2) "Hotel" has the same meaning as in section 3731.01 of the Revised Code.

(3) "Licensed health professional authorized to prescribe drugs" and "prescription" have the same meanings as in section 4729.01 of the Revised Code.

(4) "Minor" means a person under the age of eighteen years.

(5) "Underage person" means a person under the age of twenty-one years.

(2002 H 17, eff. 10–11–02; 1998 S 66, eff. 7–22–98; 1994 S 82, eff. 5–4–94; 1989 H 22, eff. 8–1–89; 1988 H 306; 1987 H 419; 1982 H 357; 1975 H 315; 132 v S 128; 1953 H 1; GC 12960)

4301.691 Changes to law if federal uniform drinking age is repealed or declared unconstitutional

If the United States congress repeals the mandate established by the "Surface Transportation Assistance Act of 1982" relating to a national uniform drinking age of twenty-one or if a court of competent jurisdiction declares the mandate to be unconstitutional or otherwise invalid, then upon the certification by the secretary of state that this mandate has been repealed or invalidated, the following shall apply:

(A) Beer or intoxicating liquor may be served to a person not seated at a table unless there is reason to believe that the beer will be consumed by a person under nineteen years of age or that the intoxicating liquor will be consumed by a person under twenty-one years of age.

(B) No person under the age of twenty-one years shall purchase intoxicating liquor, nor shall a person under the age of nineteen years purchase beer.

(C) No person under the age of nineteen years shall order, pay for, share the cost of, or attempt to purchase any beer or intoxicating liquor, or consume any beer or intoxicating liquor, either from a sealed or unsealed container or by the glass or by the drink, in any public or private place, except as provided in section 4301.69 of the Revised Code.

(D) No person under the age of twenty-one years shall order, pay for, share the cost of, or attempt to purchase any intoxicating liquor, or consume any intoxicating liquor, either from a sealed or unsealed container or by the glass or by the drink, except as provided in section 4301.69 of the Revised Code.

(E) No person shall knowingly furnish any false information as to the name, age, or other identification of any person under twenty-one years of age for the purpose of obtaining or with the intent to obtain, beer or intoxicating liquor for a person under nineteen years of age, or intoxicating liquor for a person under twenty-one years of age, by purchase, or as a gift.

(F) No person under the age of nineteen years shall knowingly show or give false information concerning the person's name, age, or other identification for the purpose of purchasing or otherwise obtaining beer or intoxicating liquor in any place in this state where beer or intoxicating liquor is sold under a permit issued by the division of liquor control or sold by the division.

(G) No person under the age of twenty-one years shall knowingly show or give false information concerning the person's name, age, or other identification for the purpose of purchasing or otherwise obtaining intoxicating liquor in any place in this state where intoxicating liquor is sold under a permit issued by the division or sold by the division.

(H) No person shall sell intoxicating liquor to a person under the age of twenty-one years or sell beer to a person under the age of nineteen, or buy intoxicating liquor for, or furnish it to, a person under the age of twenty-one years, or buy beer for or furnish it to a person under the age of nineteen, unless given by a physician in the regular line of his practice, or by a parent or legal guardian.

In proceedings before the liquor control commission, no permit holder or the permit holder's employee or agent charged with a violation of this section shall, for the same offense, be charged with a violation of division (A)(1) of section 4301.22 of the Revised Code.

(I) No person who is the owner or occupant of any public or private place shall knowingly allow any person under the age of twenty-one to remain in or on the place while possessing or consuming intoxicating liquor, or knowingly allow any person under the age of nineteen to remain in or on the place while possessing or consuming beer, unless the intoxicating liquor or beer is given to the person possessing or consuming it by that person's parent or legal guardian and the parent or legal guardian is present at the time of the person's possession or consumption of the intoxicating liquor or beer.

(J) The division shall revise the warning sign required by section 4301.637 of the Revised Code so that the sign conforms to this section.

(1995 S 162, eff. 7–1–97; 1994 S 82, eff. 5–4–94; 1989 H 22, eff. 8–1–89; 1988 H 306; 1987 H 419)

4301.70 Prohibition against violations not otherwise specified

Any person who is subject to Chapter 4301., 4303., or 4307. of the Revised Code, in the transportation, possession, or sale of wine or mixed beverage subject to the taxes imposed by sections 4301.43 and 4301.432 of the Revised Code, and who violates such chapters or any lawful rule promulgated by the tax commissioner under such chapters, for the violation of which no penalty is otherwise provided, shall be fined as provided in division (A) of section 4301.99 of the Revised Code.

(1982 H 357, eff. 10–1–82; 1981 H 694; 125 v 903; 1953 H 1; GC 6064–50)

4301.72 Taxes and fees a lien

The taxes imposed by sections 4301.42, 4301.43, 4301.432, and 4305.01 of the Revised Code and the permit fees imposed by Chapter 4303. of the Revised Code shall be a lien upon all property of the taxpayer or permit holder. If the surety on any bond required under Chapters 4301. and 4303. of the Revised Code makes payment of any sums due under any such bond, the surety shall be subrogated to any lien right on all property of the taxpayer or permit holder.

(1982 H 357, eff. 10–1–82; 1981 H 694; 1953 H 1; GC 6212–53)

4301.74 Procedure when injunction violated

Any person subject to an injunction, temporary or permanent, granted pursuant to division (D) or (E) of section 3767.05 of the Revised Code involving a condition described in division (C)(3) or (4) of section 3767.01 of the Revised Code shall obey such injunction. If such person violates such injunction, the court or in vacation a judge thereof, may summarily try and punish the violator. The proceedings for punishment for contempt shall be commenced by filing with the clerk of the court from which such injunction issued information under oath setting out the alleged facts constituting the violation, whereupon the court shall forthwith cause a warrant to issue under which the defendant shall be arrested. The trial may be had upon affidavits, or either party may demand the production and oral examination of the witnesses.

(1998 H 402, eff. 3–30–99; 1953 H 1, eff. 10–1–53; GC 13195–3)

4301.99 Penalties

(A) Whoever violates section 4301.47, 4301.48, 4301.49, 4301.62, or 4301.70 or division (B) of section 4301.691 of the Revised Code is guilty of a minor misdemeanor.

(B) Whoever violates section 4301.15, division (A)(2) or (C) of section 4301.22, division (C), (D), (E), (F), (G), (H), or (I) of section 4301.631, or section 4301.64 or 4301.67 of the Revised Code is guilty of a misdemeanor of the fourth degree.

If an offender who violates section 4301.64 of the Revised Code was under the age of eighteen years at the time of the offense, the court, in addition to any other penalties it imposes upon the offender, shall suspend the offender's temporary instruction permit, probationary driver's license, or driver's license for a period of not less than six months and not more than one year. If the offender is fifteen years and six months of age or older and has not been issued a temporary instruction permit or probationary driver's license, the offender shall not be eligible to be issued such a license or permit for a period of six months. If the offender has not attained the age of fifteen years and six months, the offender shall not be eligible to be issued a temporary instruction permit until the offender attains the age of sixteen years.

(C) Whoever violates division (D) of section 4301.21, section 4301.251, 4301.58, 4301.59, 4301.60, 4301.633, 4301.66, 4301.68, or 4301.74, division (B), (C), (D), (E)(1), or (F) of section 4301.69, or division (C), (D), (E), (F), (G), or (I) of section 4301.691 of the Revised Code is guilty of a misdemeanor of the first degree.

If an offender who violates division (E)(1) of section 4301.69 of the Revised Code was under the age of eighteen years at the time of the offense and the offense occurred while the offender was the operator of or a passenger in a motor vehicle, the court, in addition to any other penalties it imposes upon the offender, shall suspend the offender's temporary instruction permit or probationary driver's license for a period of not less than six months and not more than one year. If the offender is fifteen years and six months of age or older and has not been issued a temporary instruction permit or probationary driver's license, the offender shall not be eligible to be issued such a license or permit for a period of six months. If the offender has not attained the age of fifteen years and six months, the offender shall not be eligible to be issued a temporary instruction permit until the offender attains the age of sixteen years.

(D) Whoever violates division (B) of section 4301.14, or division (A)(1) or (3) or (B) of section 4301.22 of the Revised Code is guilty of a misdemeanor of the third degree.

(E) Whoever violates section 4301.63 or division (B) of section 4301.631 of the Revised Code shall be fined not less than twenty-five nor more than one hundred dollars. The court imposing a fine for a violation of section 4301.63 or division (B) of section 4301.631 of the Revised Code may order that the fine be paid by the performance of public work at a reasonable hourly rate established by the court. The court shall designate the time within which the public work shall be completed.

(F)(1) Whoever violates section 4301.634 of the Revised Code is guilty of a misdemeanor of the first degree. If, in committing a first violation of that section, the offender presented to the permit holder or the permit holder's employee or agent a false, fictitious, or altered identification card, a false or fictitious driver's license purportedly issued by any state, or a driver's license issued by any state that has been altered, the offender is guilty of a misdemeanor of the first degree and shall be fined not less than two hundred fifty and not more than one thousand dollars, and may be sentenced to a term of imprisonment of not more than six months.

(2) On a second violation in which, for the second time, the offender presented to the permit holder or the permit holder's employee or agent a false, fictitious, or altered identification card, a false or fictitious driver's license purportedly issued by any state, or a driver's license issued by any state that has been altered, the offender is guilty of a misdemeanor of the first degree and shall be fined not less than five hundred nor more than one thousand dollars, and may be sentenced to a term of imprisonment of not more than six months. The court also may impose a class seven suspension of the offender's driver's or commercial driver's license or permit or nonresident operating privilege from the range specified in division (A)(7) of section 4510.02 of the Revised Code.

(3) On a third or subsequent violation in which, for the third or subsequent time, the offender presented to the permit holder or the permit holder's employee or agent a false, fictitious, or altered identification card, a false or fictitious driver's license purportedly issued by any state, or a driver's license issued by any state that has been altered, the offender is guilty of a misdemeanor of the first degree and shall be fined not less than five hundred nor more than one thousand dollars, and may be sentenced to a term of imprisonment of not more than six months. The court also shall impose a class six suspension of the offender's driver's or commercial driver's license or permit or nonresident operating privilege from the range specified in division (A)(6) of section 4510.02 of the Revised Code, and the court may order that the suspension or denial remain in effect until the offender attains the age of twenty-one years. The court also may order the offender to perform a determinate number of hours of community service, with the court determining the actual number of hours and the nature of the community service the offender shall perform.

(G) Whoever violates section 4301.636 of the Revised Code is guilty of a felony of the fifth degree.

(H) Whoever violates division (A)(1) of section 4301.22 of the Revised Code is guilty of a misdemeanor, shall be fined not less than five hundred and not more than one thousand dollars, and, in addition to the fine, may be imprisoned for a definite term of not more than sixty days.

(I) Whoever violates division (A) of section 4301.69 or division (H) of section 4301.691 of the Revised Code is guilty of a misdemeanor, shall be fined not less than five hundred and not more than one thousand dollars, and, in addition to the fine, may be imprisoned for a definite term of not more than six months.

(2004 H 306, eff. 7-23-04; 2002 S 123, eff. 1-1-04; 2002 H 17, eff. 10-11-02; 1997 S 35, eff. 1-1-99; 1995 S 2, eff. 7-1-96; 1994 S 209, eff. 11-9-94; 1994 S 82, eff. 5-4-94; 1990 S 131, eff. 7-25-90; 1988 H 306, H 562; 1987 H 419; 1984 S 74; 1977 S 49; 1976 H 158; 1975 H 1; 1974 H 496, H 352)

4301.991 Liquor director to be notified of court decision

Upon the trial of a permit holder, the permit holder's employee, or the permit holder's agent for a violation of sections 4301.01 to 4301.74 of the Revised Code occurring on the premises for which a permit issued by the department or, beginning on July 1, 1997, the division of liquor control is held by the permit holder, the magistrate or the clerk of the municipal court or of the court of common pleas shall, if the permit holder, the permit holder's employee, or the permit holder's agent is found guilty, within seven days after the sentence has been imposed mail a certified copy of the record of such conviction to the director of public safety, who shall forward a copy of that certified copy to the director or, beginning on July 1, 1997, the superintendent of liquor control.

If the permit holder, the permit holder's employee, or the permit holder's agent is found to be not guilty after a trial on the merits, the magistrate or clerk of the municipal court or of the court of common pleas shall within seven days mail a certified copy of the journal entry to the director or superintendent of liquor control and the permit holder shall not be cited to the liquor control commission for any alleged violations of law or rules based upon specifications contained in the indictment, information, or affidavit in the case.

(1995 S 162, eff. 10-29-95; 1983 S 72, eff. 10-14-83; 126 v 324)

CHAPTER 4303

LIQUOR PERMITS

DEFINITIONS

4303.01 Definitions

As used in sections 4303.01 to 4303.37 of the Revised Code, "intoxicating liquor," "liquor," "sale," "sell," "vehicle," "alcohol," "beer," "wine," "mixed beverages," "spirituous liquor," "sealed container," "person," "manufacture," "manufacturer," "wholesale distributor," "distributor," "hotel," "restaurant," "club," "night club," "at retail," "pharmacy," and "enclosed shopping center" have the same meanings as in section 4301.01 of the Revised Code.

(2002 H 371, eff. 10-11-02; 1998 S 66, eff. 7-22-98; 1976 H 928, eff. 8-4-76; 1953 H 1)

CLASSIFICATION OF PERMITS

4303.02 A–1 permit

Permit A–1 may be issued to a manufacturer to manufacture beer and sell beer products in bottles or containers for home use and to retail and wholesale permit holders under rules promulgated by the division of liquor control. The fee for this permit is three thousand nine hundred six dollars for each plant during the year covered by the permit.

(2003 H 95, eff. 9–26–03; 2002 H 371, eff. 10–11–02; 1995 S 162, eff. 7–1–97; 1989 H 111, eff. 7–1–89; 1982 H 357; 1979 H 470; 1953 H 1; GC 6064–15)

4303.021 A–1–A permit

Permit A–1–A may be issued to the holder of an A–1 or A–2 permit to sell beer and any intoxicating liquor at retail, only by the individual drink in glass or from a container, provided such A–1–A permit premises are situated on the same parcel or tract of land as the related A–1 or A–2 manufacturing permit premises or are separated therefrom only by public streets or highways or by other lands owned by the holder of the A–1 or A–2 permit and used by the holder in connection with or in promotion of the holder's A–1 or A–2 permit business. The fee for this permit is three thousand nine hundred six dollars. The holder of an A–1–A permit may sell beer and any intoxicating liquor during the same hours as the holders of D–5 permits under this chapter or Chapter 4301. of the Revised Code or the rules of the liquor control commission and shall obtain a license as a retail food establishment or a food service operation pursuant to Chapter 3717. of the Revised Code and operate as a restaurant for purposes of this chapter.

Except as otherwise provided in this section, no new A–1–A permit shall be issued to the holder of an A–1 or A–2 permit unless the sale of beer and intoxicating liquor under class D permits is permitted in the precinct in which the A–1 or A–2 permit is located and, in the case of an A–2 permit, unless the holder of the A–2 permit manufactures or has a storage capacity of at least twenty-five thousand gallons of wine per year. The immediately preceding sentence does not prohibit the issuance of an A–1–A permit to an applicant for such a permit who is the holder of an A–1 permit and whose application was filed with the division of liquor control before June 1, 1994. The liquor control commission shall not restrict the number of A–1–A permits which may be located within a precinct.

(2003 H 95, eff. 9–26–03; 2001 S 136, eff. 11–21–01; 1999 H 223, eff. 11–3–99; 1998 H 402, eff. 3–30–99; 1995 S 162, eff. 7–1–97; 1994 S 167, eff. 11–1–94; 1989 H 111, eff. 7–1–89; 1979 H 470; 1975 S 108; 1969 H 558; 131 v S 377)

4303.03 A–2 permit

Permit A–2 may be issued to a manufacturer to manufacture wine from grapes or other fruits; to import and purchase wine in bond for blending purposes, the total amount of wine so imported during the year covered by the permit not to exceed forty per cent of all the wine manufactured and imported; to manufacture, purchase, and import brandy for fortifying purposes; and to sell those products either in glass or container for consumption on the premises where manufactured, for home use, and to retail and wholesale permit holders under the rules adopted by the division.

The fee for this permit is one hundred twenty-six dollars for each plant to which this permit is issued.

(2004 H 306, eff. 7–23–04; 2003 H 95, eff. 9–26–03; 1995 S 162, eff. 7–1–97; 1989 H 111, eff. 7–1–89; 1979 H 470; 1953 H 1; GC 6064–15)

4303.04 A–3 permit

Permit A–3 may be issued to a manufacturer to manufacture alcohol and spirituous liquor and sell such products to the division of liquor control or to the holders of a like permit or to the holders of A–4 permits for blending or manufacturing purposes; to import alcohol into this state upon such terms as are prescribed by the division; to sell alcohol to manufacturers, hospitals, infirmaries, medical or educational institutions using it for medicinal, mechanical, chemical, or scientific purposes, and to holders of I permits; to import into this state spirituous liquor and wine for blending or other manufacturing purposes; and to export spirituous liquor from this state for sale outside the state.

The fee for this permit is three thousand nine hundred six dollars for each plant; but, if a plant's production capacity is less than five hundred wine barrels of fifty gallons each annually, the fee is two dollars per barrel.

(2003 H 95, eff. 9–26–03; 1995 S 162, eff. 7–1–97; 1989 H 111, eff. 7–1–89; 1979 H 470; 1953 H 1; GC 6064–15)

4303.05 A–4 permit

Permit A–4 may be issued to a manufacturer to manufacture prepared highballs, cocktails, cordials, and other mixed drinks containing not less than four per cent of alcohol by volume and not more than twenty-one per cent of alcohol by volume, and to sell such products to wholesale and retail permit holders in sealed containers only under such rules as are adopted by the division of liquor control. The holder of such permit may import into the state spirituous liquor and wine only for blending or other manufacturing purposes under such rules as are prescribed by the division.

The holder of such permit may also purchase spirituous liquor for manufacturing and blending purposes from the holder of an A–3 permit issued by the division. The formulas and the beverages manufactured by the holder of an A–4 permit shall be submitted to the division for its analysis and approval before the beverages may be sold to or distributed in this state by holders of retail and wholesale permits. All labels and advertising matter used by the holders of A–4 permits shall be approved by the division before they may be used in this state. The fee for an A–4 permit is three thousand nine hundred six dollars for each plant.

(2003 H 95, eff. 9–26–03; 1995 S 162, eff. 7–1–97; 1990 S 131, eff. 7–25–90; 1989 H 111; 1986 H 428)

4303.06 B–1 permit

Permit B–1 may be issued to a wholesale distributor of beer to purchase from the holders of A–1 permits and to import and distribute or sell beer for home use and to retail permit holders under rules adopted by the division of liquor control. The fee for this permit is three thousand one hundred twenty-five dollars for each distributing plant or warehouse during the year covered by the permit.

(2003 H 95, eff. 9–26–03; 2002 H 371, eff. 10–11–02; 1995 S 162, eff. 7–1–97; 1989 H 111, eff. 7–1–89; 1982 H 357; 1979 H 470; 1953 H 1; GC 6064–15)

4303.07 B–2 permit

Permit B–2 may be issued to a wholesale distributor of wine to purchase from holders of A–2 and B–5 permits and distribute or sell that product, in the original container in which it was placed by the B–5 permit holder or manufacturer at the place where manufactured, to retail permit holders and for home use. The fee for this permit is five hundred dollars for each distributing plant or warehouse.

(2004 S 164, eff. 9–16–04; 2004 H 306, eff. 7–23–04; 2003 H 95, eff. 9–26–03; 2002 H 371, eff. 10–11–02; 1999 H 283, eff. 9–29–99; 1990 H 405, eff. 4–11–91; 1990 S 131; 1989 H 111; 1988 H 562; 1986 H 359; 1984 H 711; 1979 H 470; 1969 S 227; 1953 H 1; GC 6064–15)

4303.08 B–3 permit

Permit B–3 may be issued to a wholesale distributor of wine to bottle, distribute, or sell sacramental wine for religious rites upon an application signed, dated, and approved as required by section 4301.23 of the Revised Code. The fee for this permit is one hundred twenty-four dollars.

(2003 H 95, eff. 9–26–03; 1989 H 111, eff. 7–1–89; 1979 H 470; 1953 H 1; GC 6064–15)

4303.09 B–4 permit

Permit B–4 may be issued to a wholesale distributor to purchase from the holders of A–4 permits and to import, distribute, and sell prepared and bottled highballs, cocktails, cordials, and other mixed beverages containing not less than four per cent of alcohol by volume and not more than twenty-one per cent of alcohol by volume to retail permit holders, and for home use, under rules adopted by the division of liquor control. The formula and samples of all of those beverages to be handled by the permit holder shall be submitted to the division for its analysis and approval before those beverages may be sold and distributed in this state. All labels and advertising matter used by the holders of this permit shall be approved by the division before they may be used in this state. The fee for this permit is five hundred dollars for each distributing plant or warehouse.

(2004 H 306, eff. 7–23–04; 2003 H 95, eff. 9–26–03; 1995 S 162, eff. 7–1–97; 1990 S 131, eff. 7–25–90; 1989 H 111; 1986 H 428)

4303.10 B–5 permit

Permit B–5 may be issued to a wholesale distributor of wine to purchase wine from the holders of A–2 permits, to purchase and import wine in bond or otherwise, in bulk or in containers of any size, and to bottle wine for distribution and sale to holders of wholesale or retail permits and for home use in sealed containers. No wine shall be bottled by a B–5 permit holder in containers supplied by any person who intends the wine for home use. The fee for this permit is one thousand five hundred sixty-three dollars.

(2004 S 164, eff. 9–16–04; 2003 H 95, eff. 9–26–03; 2002 H 371, eff. 10–11–02; 1999 H 283, eff. 9–29–99; 1990 H 405, eff. 4–11–91; 1989 H 111; 1988 H 562; 1986 H 359; 1984 H 711; 1979 H 470; 1969 S 227; 1953 H 1; GC 6064–15)

4303.11 C–1 permit

Permit C–1 may be issued to the owner or operator of a retail store to sell beer in containers and not for consumption on the premises where sold in original containers having a capacity of not more than five and one-sixth gallons. The fee for this permit is two hundred fifty-two dollars for each location.

(2003 H 95, eff. 9–26–03; 1989 H 111, eff. 7–1–89; 1981 S 14; 1979 H 470; 130 v H 499; 1953 H 1; GC 6064–15)

4303.12 C–2 permit

Permit C–2 may be issued to the owner or operator of a retail store to sell wine in sealed containers only and not for consumption on the premises where sold in original containers. The holder of this permit may also sell and distribute in original packages and not for consumption on the premises where sold or for resale, prepared and bottled highballs, cocktails, cordials, and other mixed beverages manufactured and distributed by holders of A–4 and B–4 permits, and containing not less than four per cent of alcohol by volume, and not more than twenty-one per cent of alcohol by volume. The fee for this permit is three hundred seventy-six dollars for each location.

(2003 H 95, eff. 9–26–03; 1990 S 131, eff. 7–25–90; 1989 H 111; 1986 H 428)

4303.121 C–2x permit

Effective October 1, 1982, permit C–2x shall be issued to the holder of a C–2 permit who does not also hold a C–1 permit, to sell beer only not for consumption on the premises where sold, in original containers having a capacity of not more than five and one-sixth gallons. Applicants for a C–2 permit as of October 1, 1982 shall be issued a C–2x permit subject to the restrictions for the issuance of the C–2 permit. The fee for a C–2x permit is two hundred fifty-two dollars.

(2003 H 95, eff. 9–26–03; 1989 H 111, eff. 7–1–89; 1986 H 428; 1982 H 357)

4303.13 D–1 permit

Permit D–1 may be issued to the owner or operator of a hotel , of a retail food establishment or a food service operation licensed pursuant to Chapter 3717. of the Revised Code that operates as a restaurant for purposes of this chapter, or of a club, amusement park, drugstore, lunch stand, boat, or vessel, to sell beer at retail either in glass or container, for consumption on the premises where sold; and to sell beer at retail in other receptacles or in original containers having a capacity of not more than five and one-sixth gallons not for consumption on the premises where sold. The fee for this permit is three hundred seventy-six dollars for each location, boat, or vessel.

(2003 H 95, eff. 9–26–03; 2001 S 136, eff. 11–21–01; 1999 H 223, eff. 11–3–99; 1996 S 293, eff. 9–26–96 (See also Historical and Statutory Notes.); 1990 H 405, eff. 4–11–91; 1989 H 111; 1981 S 14; 1979 H 470; 132 v H 583; 130 v H 499; 125 v 200; 1953 H 1; GC 6064–15)

Historical and Statutory Notes

Ed. Note: 1996 S 293 Effective Date—The Secretary of State assigned a general effective date of 9–26–96 for 1996 S 293, along with notice that, in accordance with RC 1.471, the General Assembly has not determined which sections go into immediate effect, and that it appears that certain sections provide for appropriations for current expenses, and are immediately effective in accordance with RC 1.471 and O Const Art II, § 1d.

4303.14 D–2 permit

Permit D–2 may be issued to the owner or operator of a hotel , of a retail food establishment or a food service operation licensed pursuant to Chapter 3717. of the Revised Code that operates as a restaurant for purposes of this chapter, or of a club, boat, or vessel, to sell wine and prepared and bottled cocktails, cordials, and other mixed beverages manufactured and distributed by holders of A–4 and B–4 permits at retail, either in glass or container, for consumption on the premises where sold. The holder of this permit may also sell wine and prepared and bottled cocktails, cordials, and other mixed beverages in original packages and not for consumption on the premises where sold or for resale. The fee for this permit is five hundred sixty-four dollars for each location, boat, or vessel.

(2003 H 95, eff. 9–26–03; 2001 S 136, eff. 11–21–01; 1999 H 223, eff. 11–3–99; 1989 H 111, eff. 7–1–89; 1982 H 357; 1981 S 14; 1979 H 470; 1972 H 240; 1969 H 558; 132 v H 584; 131 v H 464; 130 v H 499; 125 v 200; 1953 H 1; GC 6064–15)

4303.141 D–2x permit

Effective October 1, 1982, permit D–2x shall be issued to the holder of a D–2 permit who does not also hold a D–1 permit, to sell beer at retail either in glass or container for consumption on the premises where sold and to sell beer at retail in other receptacles or original containers having a capacity of not more than five and one-sixth gallons not for consumption on the premises where sold. Applicants for a D–2 permit as of October 1, 1982, shall be issued a D–2x permit subject to the quota restrictions for the issuance of the D–2 permit. The fee for a D–2x permit is three hundred seventy-six dollars.

(2003 H 95, eff. 9–26–03; 1989 H 111, eff. 7–1–89; 1986 H 428; 1982 H 357)

4303.15 D–3 permit

Permit D–3 may be issued to the owner or operator of a hotel , of a retail food establishment or a food service operation licensed pursuant to Chapter 3717. of the Revised Code that operates as a restaurant for purposes of this chapter, or of a club, boat, or vessel, to sell spirituous liquor at retail, only by the individual drink in glass or from the container, for consumption on the premises where sold. No sales of intoxicating liquor shall be made by a holder of a D–3 permit after one a.m. The fee for this permit is seven hundred fifty dollars for each location, boat, or vessel.

(2003 H 95, eff. 9–26–03; 2001 S 136, eff. 11–21–01; 1999 H 223, eff. 11–3–99; 1989 H 111, eff. 7–1–89; 1982 H 357; 1979 H 470; 1969 H 558; 132 v H 585; 1953 H 1; GC 6064–15)

4303.151 D–3x permit

On October 1, 1982, permit D–3x shall be issued to the holder of a D–3 permit to sell wine by the individual drink in glass or from the container, for consumption on the premises where sold. Applications for a D–3 permit on October 1, 1982, may be issued a D–3x permit subject to the quota restrictions for the issuance of a D–3 permit. The fee for a D–3x permit is three hundred dollars.

(2003 H 95, eff. 9–26–03; 1989 H 111, eff. 7–1–89; 1982 H 357)

4303.16 D–3a permit

Permit D–3a may be issued to the holder of a D–3 permit whenever the holder's place of business is operated after one a.m. and spirituous liquor is sold or consumed after that hour. The holder of such permit may sell spirituous liquor during the same hours as the holders of D–5 permits under this chapter and Chapter 4301. of the Revised Code or the rules of the liquor control commission. The fee for a D–3a permit is nine hundred thirty-eight dollars in addition to the fee required for a D–3 permit.

If the holder of a D–3a permit is also the holder of a D–1 permit, the holder may sell beer after one a.m. and during the same hours as the holder of a D–5 permit. If the holder of a D–3a permit is also the holder of a D–2 permit, the holder may sell intoxicating liquor after one a.m. and during the same hours as the holder of a D–5 permit. The holder of a D–3a permit may furnish music and entertainment to the holder's patrons, subject to the same rules as govern D–5 permit holders.

(2003 H 95, eff. 9–26–03; 1989 H 111, eff. 7–1–89; 1979 H 470; 1953 H 1; GC 6064–15)

4303.17 D–4 permit; sale of beer or liquor at charitable bingo premises; transfer location of permit

(A)(1) Permit D–4 may be issued to a club that has been in existence for three years or more prior to the issuance of the permit to sell beer and any intoxicating liquor to its members only, in glass or container, for consumption on the premises where sold. The fee for this permit is four hundred sixty-nine dollars.

No D–4 permit shall be granted or retained until all elected officers of the organization controlling the club have filed with the division of liquor control a statement certifying that the club is operated in the interest of the membership of a reputable organization, which is maintained by a dues paying membership, setting forth the amount of initiation fee and yearly dues. All such matters shall be contained in a statement signed under oath and accompanied by a surety bond in the sum of one thousand dollars. The bond shall be declared forfeited in the full amount of the penal sum of the bond for any false statement contained in that statement, and the surety shall pay the amount of the bond to the division.

The roster of membership of a D–4 permit holder shall be submitted under oath on the request of the superintendent of liquor control. Any information acquired by the superintendent or the division with respect to that membership shall not be open to public inspection or examination and may be divulged by the superintendent and the division only in hearings before the liquor control commission or in a court action in which the division or the superintendent is named a party.

(2) The requirement that a club shall have been in existence for three years in order to qualify for a D–4 permit does not apply to units of organizations chartered by congress or to a subsidiary unit of a national fraternal organization if the parent organization has been in existence for three years or more at the time application for a permit is made by such unit.

(B) No rule or order of the division or commission shall prohibit a charitable organization that holds a D–4 permit from selling or serving beer or intoxicating liquor under its permit in a portion of its premises merely because that portion of its premises is used at other times for the conduct of a bingo game as described in division (S) of section 2915.01 of the Revised Code. However, such an organization shall not sell or serve beer or intoxicating liquor or permit beer or intoxicating liquor to be consumed or seen in the same location in its premises where a bingo game as described in division (S)(1) of section 2915.01 of the Revised Code is being conducted while the game is being conducted. As used in this division, "charitable organization" has the same meaning as in division (H) of section 2915.01 of the Revised Code.

(C) Notwithstanding any contrary provision of sections 4301.32 to 4301.41, division (C)(1) of section 4303.29, and section 4305.14 of the Revised Code, the holder of a D–4 permit may transfer the location of the permit and sell beer and wine at the new location if that location is in an election precinct in which the sale of beer and wine, but not spirituous liquor, otherwise is permitted by law.

(2004 S 164, eff. 6–17–04; 2003 H 95, eff. 9–26–03; 1995 S 162, eff. 7–1–97; 1989 H 111, eff. 7–1–89; 1986 H 627; 1979 H 470; 1953 H 1; GC 6064–15, 6064–15a)

4303.171 D–4a permit

Permit D–4a may be issued to an airline company that leases and operates a premises exclusively for the benefit of the members and their guests of a private club sponsored by the airline company, at a publicly owned airport, as defined in section 4563.01 of the Revised Code, at which commercial airline companies operate regularly scheduled flights on which space is available to the public, to sell beer and any intoxicating liquor to members of the private club and their guests, only by the individual drink in glass and from the container, for consumption on the premises where sold. In addition to the privileges authorized in this section, the holder of a D–4a permit may exercise the same privileges as a holder of a D–4 permit. The holder of a D–4a permit shall make no sales of beer or intoxicating liquor after two-thirty a.m.

A D–4a permit shall not be transferred to another location. No quota restriction shall be placed upon the number of such permits which may be issued.

The fee for this permit is seven hundred fifty dollars.

(2003 H 95, eff. 9–26–03; 1989 H 111, eff. 7–1–89; 1984 H 711)

4303.18 D–5 permit

Permit D–5 may be issued to the owner or operator of a retail food establishment or a food service operation licensed pursuant to Chapter 3717. of the Revised Code that operates as a restaurant or night club for purposes of this chapter, to sell beer and any intoxicating liquor at retail, only by the individual drink in glass and from the container, for consumption on the premises where sold, and to sell the same products in the same manner and amounts not for consumption on the premises as may be sold by holders of D–1 and D–2 permits. A person who is the holder of both a D–3 and D–3a permit need not obtain a D–5 permit. The fee for this permit is two thousand three hundred forty-four dollars.

(2003 H 95, eff. 9–26–03; 2001 S 136, eff. 11–21–01; 1996 S 293, eff. 9–26–96 (See also Historical and Statutory Notes.); 1990 H 405, eff. 4–11–91; 1989 H 111; 1979 H 470; 1969 H 558; 1953 H 1; GC 6064–15)

Historical and Statutory Notes

Ed. Note: 1996 S 293 Effective Date—The Secretary of State assigned a general effective date of 9–26–96 for 1996 S 293, along with notice that, in accordance with RC 1.471, the General Assembly has not determined which sections go into immediate effect, and that it appears that certain sections provide for appropriations for current expenses, and are immediately effective in accordance with RC 1.471 and O Const Art II, § 1d.

4303.181 Other D–5 permits

(A) Permit D–5a may be issued either to the owner or operator of a hotel or motel that is required to be licensed under section 3731.03 of the Revised Code, that contains at least fifty rooms for registered transient guests or is owned by a state institution of higher education as defined in section 3345.011 of the Revised Code or a private college or university, and that qualifies under the other requirements of this section, or to the owner or operator of a restaurant specified under this section, to sell beer and any intoxicating liquor at retail, only by the individual drink in glass and from the container, for consumption on the premises where sold, and to registered guests in their rooms, which may be sold by means of a controlled access alcohol and beverage cabinet in accordance with division (B) of section 4301.21 of the Revised Code; and to sell the same products in the same manner and amounts not for consumption on the premises as may be sold by holders of D–1 and D–2 permits. The premises of the hotel or motel shall include a retail food establishment or a food service operation licensed pursuant to Chapter 3717. of the Revised Code that operates as a restaurant for purposes of this chapter and that is affiliated with the hotel or motel and within or contiguous to the hotel or motel, and that serves food within the hotel or motel, but the principal business of the owner or operator of the hotel or motel shall be the accommodation of transient guests. In addition to the privileges authorized in this division, the holder of a D–5a permit may exercise the same privileges as the holder of a D–5 permit.

The owner or operator of a hotel, motel, or restaurant who qualified for and held a D–5a permit on August 4, 1976, may, if the owner or operator held another permit before holding a D–5a permit, either retain a D–5a permit or apply for the permit formerly held, and the division of liquor control shall issue the permit for which the owner or operator applies and formerly held, notwithstanding any quota.

A D–5a permit shall not be transferred to another location. No quota restriction shall be placed on the number of D–5a permits that may be issued.

The fee for this permit is two thousand three hundred forty-four dollars.

(B) Permit D–5b may be issued to the owner, operator, tenant, lessee, or occupant of an enclosed shopping center to sell beer and intoxicating liquor at retail, only by the individual drink in glass and from the container, for consumption on the premises where sold; and to sell the same products in the same manner and amount not for consumption on the premises as may be sold by holders of D–1 and D–2 permits. In addition to the privileges authorized in this division, the holder of a D–5b permit may exercise the same privileges as a holder of a D–5 permit.

A D–5b permit shall not be transferred to another location.

One D–5b permit may be issued at an enclosed shopping center containing at least two hundred twenty-five thousand, but less than four hundred thousand, square feet of floor area.

Two D–5b permits may be issued at an enclosed shopping center containing at least four hundred thousand square feet of floor area. No more than one D–5b permit may be issued at an enclosed shopping center for each additional two hundred thousand square feet of floor area or fraction of that floor area, up to a maximum of five D–5b permits for each enclosed shopping center. The number of D–5b permits that may be issued at an enclosed shopping center shall be determined by subtracting the number of D–3 and D–5 permits issued in the enclosed shopping center from the number of D–5b permits that otherwise may be issued at the enclosed shopping center under the formulas provided in this division. Except as provided in this section, no quota shall be placed on the number of D–5b permits that may be issued. Notwithstanding any quota provided in this section, the holder of any D–5b permit first issued in accordance with this section is entitled to its renewal in accordance with section 4303.271 of the Revised Code.

The holder of a D–5b permit issued before April 4, 1984, whose tenancy is terminated for a cause other than nonpayment of rent, may return the D–5b permit to the division of liquor control, and the division shall cancel that permit. Upon cancellation of that permit and upon the permit holder's payment of taxes, contributions, premiums, assessments, and other debts owing or accrued upon the date of cancellation to this state and its political subdivisions and a filing with the division of a certification of that payment, the division shall issue to that person either a D–5 permit, or a D–1, a D–2, and a D–3 permit, as that person requests. The division shall issue the D–5 permit, or the D–1, D–2, and D–3 permits, even if the number of D–1, D–2, D–3, or D–5 permits currently issued in the municipal corporation or in the unincorporated area of the township where that person's proposed premises is located equals or exceeds the maximum number of such permits that can be issued in that municipal corporation or in the unincorporated area of that township under the population quota restrictions contained in section 4303.29 of the Revised Code. Any D–1, D–2, D–3, or D–5 permit so issued shall not be transferred to another location. If a D–5b permit is canceled under the provisions of this paragraph, the number of D–5b permits that may be issued at the enclosed shopping center for which the D–5b permit was issued, under the formula provided in this division, shall be reduced by one if the enclosed shopping center was entitled to more than one D–5b permit under the formula.

The fee for this permit is two thousand three hundred forty-four dollars.

(C) Permit D–5c may be issued to the owner or operator of a retail food establishment or a food service operation licensed pursuant to Chapter 3717. of the Revised Code that operates as a restaurant for purposes of this chapter and that qualifies under the other requirements of this section to sell beer and any intoxicating liquor at retail, only by the individual drink in glass and from the container, for consumption on the premises where sold, and to sell the same products in the same manner and amounts not for consumption on the premises as may be sold by holders of D–1 and D–2 permits. In addition to the privileges authorized in this division, the holder of a D–5c permit may exercise the same privileges as the holder of a D–5 permit.

To qualify for a D–5c permit, the owner or operator of a retail food establishment or a food service operation licensed pursuant to Chapter 3717. of the Revised Code that operates as a restaurant for purposes of this chapter, shall have operated the restaurant at the proposed premises for not less than twenty-four consecutive months immediately preceding the filing of the application for the permit, have applied for a D–5 permit no later than December 31, 1988, and appear on the division's quota waiting list for not less than six months immediately preceding the filing of the application for the permit. In addition to these requirements, the proposed D–5c permit premises shall be located within a municipal corporation and further within an election precinct that, at the time of the application, has no more than twenty-five per cent of its total land area zoned for residential use.

A D–5c permit shall not be transferred to another location. No quota restriction shall be placed on the number of such permits that may be issued.

Any person who has held a D–5c permit for at least two years may apply for a D–5 permit, and the division of liquor control shall issue the D–5 permit notwithstanding the quota restrictions contained in section 4303.29 of the Revised Code or in any rule of the liquor control commission.

The fee for this permit is one thousand five hundred sixty-three dollars.

(D) Permit D–5d may be issued to the owner or operator of a retail food establishment or a food service operation licensed pursuant to Chapter 3717. of the Revised Code that operates as a restaurant for purposes of this chapter and that is located at an airport operated by a board of county commissioners pursuant to section 307.20 of the Revised Code, at an airport operated by a port authority pursuant to Chapter 4582. of the Revised Code, or at an airport operated by a regional airport authority pursuant to Chapter 308. of the Revised Code. The holder of a D–5d permit may sell beer and any intoxicating liquor at retail, only by the individual drink in glass and from the container, for consumption on the premises where sold, and may sell the same products in the same manner and amounts not for consumption on the premises where sold as may be sold by the holders of D–1 and D–2 permits. In addition to the privileges authorized in this division, the holder of a D–5d permit may exercise the same privileges as the holder of a D–5 permit.

A D–5d permit shall not be transferred to another location. No quota restrictions shall be placed on the number of such permits that may be issued.

The fee for this permit is two thousand three hundred forty-four dollars.

(E) Permit D–5e may be issued to any nonprofit organization that is exempt from federal income taxation under the "Internal Revenue Code of 1986," 100 Stat. 2085, 26 U.S.C.A. 501(c)(3), as amended, or that is a charitable organization under any chapter of the Revised Code, and that owns or operates a riverboat that meets all of the following:

(1) Is permanently docked at one location;

(2) Is designated as an historical riverboat by the Ohio historical society;

(3) Contains not less than fifteen hundred square feet of floor area;

(4) Has a seating capacity of fifty or more persons.

The holder of a D–5e permit may sell beer and intoxicating liquor at retail, only by the individual drink in glass and from the container, for consumption on the premises where sold.

A D–5e permit shall not be transferred to another location. No quota restriction shall be placed on the number of such permits that may be issued. The population quota restrictions contained in section 4303.29 of the Revised Code or in any rule of the liquor control commission shall not apply to this division, and the division shall issue a D–5e permit to any applicant who meets the requirements of this division. However, the division shall not issue a D–5e permit if the permit premises or proposed permit premises are located within an area in which the sale of spirituous liquor by the glass is prohibited.

The fee for this permit is one thousand two hundred nineteen dollars.

(F) Permit D–5f may be issued to the owner or operator of a retail food establishment or a food service operation licensed under Chapter 3717. of the Revised Code that operates as a restaurant for purposes of this chapter and that meets all of the following:

(1) It contains not less than twenty-five hundred square feet of floor area.

(2) It is located on or in, or immediately adjacent to, the shoreline of, a navigable river.

(3) It provides docking space for twenty-five boats.

(4) It provides entertainment and recreation, provided that not less than fifty per cent of the business on the permit premises shall be preparing and serving meals for a consideration.

In addition, each application for a D–5f permit shall be accompanied by a certification from the local legislative authority that the issuance of the D–5f permit is not inconsistent with that political subdivision's comprehensive development plan or other economic development goal as officially established by the local legislative authority.

The holder of a D–5f permit may sell beer and intoxicating liquor at retail, only by the individual drink in glass and from the container, for consumption on the premises where sold.

A D–5f permit shall not be transferred to another location.

The division of liquor control shall not issue a D–5f permit if the permit premises or proposed permit premises are located within an area in which the sale of spirituous liquor by the glass is prohibited.

A fee for this permit is two thousand three hundred forty-four dollars.

As used in this division, "navigable river" means a river that is also a "navigable water" as defined in the "Federal Power Act," 94 Stat. 770 (1980), 16 U.S.C. 796. [1]

(G) Permit D–5g may be issued to a nonprofit corporation that is either the owner or the operator of a national professional sports museum. The holder of a D–5g permit may sell beer and any intoxicating liquor at retail, only by the individual drink in glass and from the container, for consumption on the premises where sold. The holder of a D–5g permit shall sell no beer or intoxicating liquor for consumption on the premises where sold after one a.m. A D–5g permit shall not be transferred to another location. No quota restrictions shall be placed on the number of D–5g permits that may be issued. The fee for this permit is one thousand eight hundred seventy-five dollars.

(H) Permit D–5h may be issued to any nonprofit organization that is exempt from federal income taxation under the "Internal Revenue Code of 1986," 100 Stat. 2085, 26 U.S.C.A. 501(c)(3), as amended, that owns or operates a fine arts museum and has no less than five thousand bona fide members possessing full membership privileges. The holder of a D–5h permit may sell beer and any intoxicating liquor at retail, only by the individual drink in glass and from the container, for consumption on the premises where sold. The holder of a D–5h permit shall sell no beer or intoxicating liquor for consumption on the premises where sold after one a.m. A D–5h permit shall not be transferred to another location. No quota restrictions shall be placed on the number of D–5h permits that may be issued. The fee for this permit is one thousand eight hundred seventy-five dollars.

(I) Permit D–5i may be issued to the owner or operator of a retail food establishment or a food service operation licensed under Chapter 3717. of the Revised Code that operates as a restaurant for purposes of this chapter and that meets all of the following requirements:

(1) It is located in a municipal corporation or a township with a population of seventy-five thousand or less.

(2) It has inside seating capacity for at least one hundred forty persons.

(3) It has at least four thousand square feet of floor area.

(4) It offers full-course meals, appetizers, and sandwiches.

(5) Its receipts from beer and liquor sales do not exceed twenty-five per cent of its total gross receipts.

(6) It has at least one of the following characteristics:

(a) The value of its real and personal property exceeds seven hundred twenty-five thousand dollars.

(b) It is located on property that is owned or leased by the state or a state agency, and its owner or operator has authorization from the state or the state agency that owns or leases the property to obtain a D–5i permit.

The holder of a D–5i permit shall cause an independent audit to be performed at the end of one full year of operation following issuance of the permit in order to verify the requirements of division (I)(5) of this section. The results of the independent audit shall be transmitted to the division. Upon determining that the receipts of the holder from beer and liquor sales exceeded twenty-five per cent of its total gross receipts, the division shall suspend the permit of the permit holder under section 4301.25 of the Revised Code and may allow the permit holder to elect a forfeiture under section 4301.252 of the Revised Code.

The holder of a D–5i permit may sell beer and any intoxicating liquor at retail, only by the individual drink in glass and from the container, for consumption on the premises where sold, and may sell the same products in the same manner and amounts not for consumption on the premises where sold as may be sold by the holders of D–1 and D–2 permits. The holder of a D–5i permit shall sell no beer or intoxicating liquor for consumption on the premises where sold after two-thirty a.m. In addition to the privileges authorized in this division, the holder of a D–5i permit may exercise the same privileges as the holder of a D–5 permit.

A D–5i permit shall not be transferred to another location. The division of liquor control shall not renew a D–5i permit unless the retail food establishment or food service operation for which it is issued continues to meet the requirements described in divisions (I)(1) to (6) of this section. No quota restrictions shall be placed on the number of D–5i permits that may be issued. The fee for the D–5i permit is two thousand three hundred forty-four dollars.

(J)(1) Permit D–5j may be issued to the owner or the operator of a retail food establishment or a food service operation licensed under Chapter 3717. of the Revised Code to sell beer and intoxicating liquor at retail, only by the individual drink in glass and from the container, for consumption on the premises where sold and to sell beer and intoxicating liquor in the same manner and amounts not for consumption on the premises where sold as may be sold by the holders of D–1 and D–2 permits. The holder of a D–5j permit may exercise the same privileges, and shall observe the same hours of operation, as the holder of a D–5 permit.

(2) The D–5j permit shall be issued only within a community entertainment district that is designated under section 4301.80 of the Revised Code and that meets one of the following qualifications:

(a) It is located in a municipal corporation with a population of at least one hundred thousand.

(b) It is located in a municipal corporation with a population of at least twenty thousand, and either of the following applies:

(i) It contains an amusement park the rides of which have been issued a permit by the department of agriculture under Chapter 1711. of the Revised Code.

(ii) Not less than fifty million dollars will be invested in development and construction in the community entertainment district's area located in the municipal corporation.

(c) It is located in a township with a population of at least forty thousand.

(3) The location of a D–5j permit may be transferred only within the geographic boundaries of the community entertainment district in which it was issued and shall not be transferred outside the geographic boundaries of that district.

(4) Not more than one D–5j permit shall be issued within each community entertainment district for each five acres of land located within the district. Not more than fifteen D–5j permits may be issued within a single community entertainment district. Except as otherwise provided in division (J)(4) of this section, no quota restrictions shall be placed upon the number of D–5j permits that may be issued.

(5) The fee for a D–5j permit is two thousand three hundred forty-four dollars.

(K)(1) Permit D–5k may be issued to any nonprofit organization that is exempt from federal income taxation under the "Internal Revenue Code of 1986," 100 Stat. 2085, 26 U.S.C.A. 501(c)(3), as amended, that is the owner or operator of a botanical garden recognized by the American association of botanical gardens and arboreta, and that has not less than twenty-five hundred bona fide members.

(2) The holder of a D–5k permit may sell beer and any intoxicating liquor at retail, only by the individual drink in glass and from the container, on the premises where sold.

(3) The holder of a D–5k permit shall sell no beer or intoxicating liquor for consumption on the premises where sold after one a.m.

(4) A D–5k permit shall not be transferred to another location.

(5) No quota restrictions shall be placed on the number of D–5k permits that may be issued.

(6) The fee for the D–5k permit is one thousand eight hundred seventy-five dollars.

(2004 H 306, eff. 7–23–04; 2003 H 95, eff. 9–26–03; 2002 H 371, eff. 10–11–02; 2002 H 330, eff. 10–11–02; 2001 S 136, eff. 11–21–01; 2000 S 262, eff. 4–9–01; 1999 H 283, eff. 9–29–99; 1999 H 223, eff. 11–3–99; 1998 H 402, eff. 3–30–99; 1995 S 162, eff. 7–1–97; 1995 S 149, eff. 11–21–95; 1993 H 152, eff. 7–1–93; 1990 H 405; 1989 H 111; 1988 H 562; 1986 H 627, H 359; 1984 H 502; 1983 H 105; 1979 H 470; 1976 H 928; 1973 H 263; 1969 H 150)

[1] 16 U.S.C.A. § 796

4303.182 D–6 permit

(A) Except as otherwise provided in divisions (B) to (G) of this section, permit D–6 shall be issued to the holder of an A–1–A, A–2, C–2, D–2, D–3, D–4, D–4a, D–5, D–5a, D–5b, D–5c, D–5d, D–5e, D–5f, D–5h, D–5i, D–5j, D–5k, or D–7 permit to allow sale under that permit between the hours of ten a.m. and midnight, or between the hours of one p.m. and midnight, on Sunday, as applicable, if that sale has been authorized under section 4301.361, 4301.364, 4301.365, or 4301.366 of the Revised Code and under the restrictions of that authorization.

(B) Permit D–6 shall be issued to the holder of any permit, including a D–4a and D–5d permit, authorizing the sale of intoxicating liquor issued for a premises located at any publicly owned airport, as defined in section 4563. 01 of the Revised Code, at which commercial airline companies operate regularly scheduled flights on which space is available to the public, to allow sale under such permit between the hours of ten a.m. and midnight on Sunday, whether or not that sale has been authorized under section 4301.361, 4301.364, 4301.365, or 4301.366 of the Revised Code.

(C) Permit D–6 shall be issued to the holder of a D–5a permit, and to the holder of a D–3 or D–3a permit who is the owner or operator of a hotel or motel that is required to be licensed under section 3731.03 of the Revised Code, that contains at least fifty rooms for registered transient guests, and that has on its premises a retail food establishment or a food service operation licensed pursuant to Chapter 3717. of the Revised Code that operates as a restaurant for purposes of this chapter and is affiliated with the hotel or motel and within or contiguous to the hotel or motel and serving food within the hotel or motel, to allow sale under such permit between the hours of ten a.m. and midnight on Sunday, whether or not that sale has been authorized under section 4301.361, 4301.364, 4301.365, or 4301. 366 of the Revised Code.

(D) The holder of a D–6 permit that is issued to a sports facility may make sales under the permit between the hours of eleven a.m. and midnight on any Sunday on which a professional baseball, basketball, football, hockey, or soccer game is being played at the sports facility. As used in this division, "sports facility" means a stadium or arena that has a seating capacity of at least four thousand and that is owned or leased by a professional baseball, basketball, football, hockey, or soccer franchise or any combination of those franchises.

(E) Permit D–6 shall be issued to the holder of any permit that authorizes the sale of beer or intoxicating liquor and that is issued to a premises located in or at the Ohio historical society area or the state fairgrounds, as defined in division (B) of section 4301.40 of the Revised Code, to allow sale under that permit between the hours of ten a.m. and midnight on Sunday, whether or not that sale has been authorized under section 4301.361, 4301.364, 4301.365, or 4301.366 of the Revised Code.

(F) Permit D–6 shall be issued to the holder of any permit that authorizes the sale of intoxicating liquor and that is issued to an outdoor performing arts center to allow sale under that permit between the hours of one p.m. and midnight on Sunday, whether or not that sale has been authorized under section 4301.361 of the Revised Code. A D–6 permit issued under this division is subject to the results of an election, held after the D–6 permit is issued, on question (B)(4) as set forth in section 4301.351 of the Revised Code. Following the end of the period during which an election may be held on question (B)(4) as set forth in that section, sales of intoxicating liquor may continue at an outdoor performing arts center under a D–6 permit issued under this division, unless an election on that question is held during the permitted period and a majority of the voters voting in the precinct on that question vote "no."

As used in this division, "outdoor performing arts center" means an outdoor performing arts center that is located on not less than eight hundred acres of land and that is open for performances from the first day of April to the last day of October of each year.

(G) Permit D–6 shall be issued to the holder of any permit that authorizes the sale of beer or intoxicating liquor and that is issued to a golf course owned by the state, a conservancy district, a park district created under Chapter 1545. of the Revised Code, or another political subdivision to allow sale under that permit between the hours of ten a.m. and midnight on Sunday, whether or not that sale has been authorized under section 4301.361, 4301.364, 4301.365, or 4301.366 of the Revised Code.

(H) Permit D–6 shall be issued to the holder of a D–5g permit to allow sale under that permit between the hours of ten a.m. and midnight on Sunday, whether or not that sale has been authorized under section 4301.361, 4301.364, 4301.365, or 4301.366 of the Revised Code.

(I) If the restriction to licensed premises where the sale of food and other goods and services exceeds fifty per cent of the total gross receipts of the permit holder at the premises is applicable, the division of liquor control may accept an affidavit from the permit holder to show the proportion of the permit holder's gross receipts derived from the sale of food and other goods and services. If the liquor control commission determines that affidavit to have been false, it shall revoke the permits of the permit holder at the premises concerned.

(J) The fee for the D–6 permit is five hundred dollars when it is issued to the holder of an A–1–A, A–2, D–2, D–3, D–3a, D–4, D–4a, D–5, D–5a, D–5b, D–5c, D–5d, D–5e, D–5f, D–5g, D–5h, D–5i, D–5j, D–5k, or D–7 permit. The fee for the D–6 permit is four hundred dollars when it is issued to the holder of a C–2 permit.

(2003 H 95, eff. 9-26-03; 2002 H 371, eff. 10-11-02; 2001 S 136, eff. 11-21-01; 2000 S 262, eff. 4-9-01; 2000 S 200, eff. 9-21-00; 1999 H 283, eff. 9-29-99; 1999 H 223, eff. 11-3-99; 1995 S 162, eff. 7-1-97; 1990 H 405, eff. 4-11-91; 1989 H 111; 1988 H 562; 1986 H 359; 1984 H 711, H 502; 1983 H 291; 1979 H 470, H 324; 1977 H 123; 1976 H 856, H 928; 1970 H 947; 1969 H 616)

4303.183 D–7 permit

Permit D–7 may be issued to the holder of any D–2 permit issued by the division of liquor control, or if there is an insufficient number of D–2 permit holders to fill the resort quota, to the operator of a retail food establishment or a food service operation required to be licensed under Chapter 3717. of the Revised Code that operates as a restaurant for purposes of this chapter and which qualifies under the other requirements of this section, to sell beer and any intoxicating liquor at retail, only by the individual drink in glass and from the container, for consumption on the premises where sold. Not less than fifty per cent of the business on the permit premises shall be preparing and serving meals for a consideration in order to qualify for and continue to hold such D–7 permit. The permit premises shall be located in a resort area.

"Resort area" means a municipal corporation, township, county, or any combination thereof, which provides entertainment, recreation, and transient housing facilities specifically intended to provide leisure time activities for persons other than those whose permanent residence is within the "resort area" and who increase the population of the "resort area" on a seasonal basis, and which experiences seasonal peaks of employment and governmental services as a direct result of population increase generated by the transient, recreating public. A resort season shall begin on the first day of May and end on the last day of October. Notwithstanding section 4303.27 of the Revised Code, such permits may be issued for resort seasons without regard to the calendar year or permit year. Quota restrictions on the number of such permits shall take into consideration the transient population during the resort season, the custom and habits of visitors and tourists, and the promotion of the resort and tourist industry.

The fee for this permit is four hundred sixty-nine dollars per month.

Any suspension of a D–7 permit shall be satisfied during the resort season in which such suspension becomes final. If such suspension becomes final during the off-season, or if the period of the suspension extends beyond the last day of October, the suspension or remainder thereof shall be satisfied during the next resort season.

The ownership of a D–7 permit may be transferred from one permit holder to another. The holder of a D–7 permit may file an application to transfer such permit to a new location within the same resort area, provided that such permit holder shall be the owner or operator of a retail food establishment or a food service operation, required to be licensed under Chapter 3717. of the Revised Code, that operates as a restaurant for purposes of this chapter, at such new location.

(2003 H 95, eff. 9–26–03; 2001 S 136, eff. 11–21–01; 1999 H 223, eff. 11–3–99; 1995 S 162, eff. 7–1–97; 1989 H 111, eff. 7–1–89; 1988 H 562; 1979 H 470; 1975 H 1; 1974 H 416)

4303.184 D–8 permits

(A) Subject to division (B) of this section, a D–8 permit may be issued to the holder of a C–1, C–2, or C–2x permit issued to a retail store that has either of the following characteristics:

(1) The store has at least five thousand five hundred square feet of floor area, and it generates more than sixty per cent of its sales in general merchandise items and food for consumption off the premises where sold.

(2) Wine constitutes at least sixty per cent of the value of the store's inventory.

(B) A D–8 permit may be issued to the holder of a C–1, C–2, or C–2x permit only if the premises of the permit holder are located in a precinct, or at a particular location in a precinct, in which the sale of beer, wine, or mixed beverages is permitted for consumption off the premises where sold. Sales under a D–8 permit are not affected by whether sales for consumption on the premises where sold are permitted in the precinct or at the particular location where the D–8 premises are located.

(C) The holder of a D–8 permit may sell tasting samples of beer, wine, and mixed beverages, but not spirituous liquor, at retail, for consumption on the premises where sold in an amount not to exceed two ounces or another amount designated by rule of the liquor control commission. A tasting sample shall not be sold for general consumption. No D–8 permit holder shall allow any authorized purchaser to consume more than four tasting samples of beer, wine, or mixed beverages, or any combination of beer, wine, or mixed beverages, per day.

(D) The privileges authorized under a D–8 permit may only be exercised in conjunction with and during the hours of operation authorized by a C–1, C–2, C–2x, or D–6 permit.

(E) A D–8 permit shall not be transferred to another location.

(F) The fee for the D–8 permit is five hundred dollars.

(G) The holder of a D–8 permit shall cause an independent audit to be performed at the end of the first full year of operation following issuance of the permit, and at the end of each second year thereafter, in order to verify that the permit holder satisfies the applicable requirement of division (A)(1) or (2) of this section. The permit holder shall transmit the results of the independent audit to the division of liquor control. If the results of the audit indicate noncompliance with division (A) of this section, the division shall not renew the D–8 permit of the permit holder.

(2003 H 95, eff. 9–26–03; 2002 H 371, eff. 10–11–02; 2000 S 262, eff. 4–9–01)

4303.19 E permit

Permit E may be issued to the owner or operator of any railroad, a sleeping car company operating dining cars, buffet cars, club cars, lounge cars, or similar equipment, or an airline providing charter or regularly scheduled aircraft transportation service with dining, buffet, club, lounge, or similar facilities, to sell beer or any intoxicating liquor in any such car or aircraft to bona fide passengers at retail in glass and from the container for consumption in such car or aircraft, including sale on Sunday between the hours of one p.m. and midnight. The fee for this permit is five hundred dollars.

(2003, H 95, eff. 9–26–03; 1989 H 111, eff. 7–1–89; 1979 H 470; 1970 H 1140; 1969 H 616, H 147; 1953 H 1; GC 6064–15)

4303.20 F permit

Permit F may be issued to an association of ten or more persons, a labor union, or a charitable organization, or to an employer of ten or more persons sponsoring a function for the employer's employees, to purchase from the holders of A–1 and B–1 permits and to sell beer for a period lasting not to exceed five days. No more than two such permits may be issued to the same applicant in any thirty-day period.

The special function for which the permit is issued shall include a social, recreational, benevolent, charitable, fraternal, political, patriotic, or athletic purpose but shall not include any function the proceeds of which are for the profit or gain of any individual. The fee for this permit is forty dollars.

(2003 H 95, eff. 9–26–03; 1990 H 405, eff. 4–11–91; 1989 H 111; 1979 H 470; 126 v 336; 1953 H 1; GC 6064–15)

4303.201 F–1 permit

(A) As used in this section:

(1) "Convention facility" means any structure owned or leased by a municipal corporation or county which was expressly designed and constructed and is currently used for the purpose of presenting conventions, public meetings, and exhibitions.

(2) "Nonprofit organization" means any unincorporated association or nonprofit corporation that is not formed for the pecuniary gain or profit of, and whose net earnings or any part thereof is not distributable to, its members, trustees, officers, or other private persons; provided, that the payment of reasonable compensation for services rendered and the distribution of assets on dissolution shall not be considered pecuniary gain or profit or distribution of earnings in an association or corporation all of whose members are nonprofit corporations. Distribution of earnings to member organizations does not deprive it of the status of a nonprofit organization.

(B) An F–1 permit may be issued to any nonprofit organization to allow the nonprofit organization and its members and their guests to lawfully bring beer, wine, and intoxicating liquor in its original package, flasks, or other containers into a convention facility for consumption therein, if both of the following requirements are met:

(1) The superintendent of liquor control is satisfied the organization meets the definition of a nonprofit organization as set forth in division (A)(2) of this section, the nonprofit organization's membership includes persons residing in two or more states, and the organization's total membership is in excess of five hundred. The superintendent may accept a sworn statement by the president or other chief executive officer of the nonprofit organization as proof of the matters required in this division.

(2) The managing official or employee of the convention facility has given written consent to the use of the convention facility

and to the application for the F–1 permit, as shown in the nonprofit organization's application to the superintendent.

(C) The superintendent shall specify individually the effective period of each F–1 permit on the permit, which shall not exceed three days. The fee for an F–1 permit is two hundred fifty dollars. The superintendent shall prepare and make available application forms to request F–1 permits and may require applicants to furnish such information as the superintendent determines to be necessary for the administration of this section.

(D) No holder of an F–1 permit shall make a specific charge for beer, wine, or intoxicating liquor by the drink, or in its original package, flasks, or other containers in connection with its use of the convention facility under the permit.

(2003 H 95, eff. 9–26–03; 1995 S 162, eff. 7–1–97; 1989 H 111, eff. 7–1–89; 1979 H 470; 1975 H 613)

4303.202 F–2 permit

(A) The division of liquor control may issue an F–2 permit to an association or corporation, or to a recognized subordinate lodge, chapter, or other local unit of an association or corporation, to sell beer or intoxicating liquor by the individual drink at an event to be held on premises located in a political subdivision or part thereof where the sale of beer or intoxicating liquor on that day is otherwise permitted by law.

The division of liquor control may issue an F–2 permit to an association or corporation, or to a recognized subordinate lodge, chapter, or other local unit of an association or corporation, to sell beer, wine, and spirituous liquor by the individual drink at an event to be held on premises located in a political subdivision or part thereof where the sale of beer and wine, but not spirituous liquor, is otherwise permitted by law on that day.

Notwithstanding section 1711.09 of the Revised Code, this section applies to any association or corporation or a recognized subordinate lodge, chapter, or other local unit of an association or corporation.

In order to receive an F–2 permit, the association, corporation, or local unit shall be organized not for profit, shall be operated for a charitable, cultural, fraternal, or educational purpose, and shall not be affiliated with the holder of any class of liquor permit, other than a D–4 permit.

The premises on which the permit is to be used shall be clearly defined and sufficiently restricted to allow proper supervision of the permit use by state and local law enforcement personnel. An F–2 permit may be issued for the same premises for which another class of permit is issued.

No F–2 permit shall be effective for more than forty-eight consecutive hours, and sales shall be confined to the same hours permitted to the holder of a D–3 permit. The division shall not issue more than two F–2 permits in one calendar year to the same association, corporation, or local unit of an association or corporation. The fee for an F–2 permit is one hundred fifty dollars.

If an applicant wishes the holder of a D–3, D–4, or D–5 permit to conduct the sale of beer and intoxicating liquor at the event, the applicant may request that the F–2 permit be issued jointly to the association, corporation, or local unit and the D-permit holder. If a permit is issued jointly, the association, corporation, or local unit and the D-permit holder shall both be held responsible for any conduct that violates laws pertaining to the sale of alcoholic beverages, including sales by the D-permit holder; otherwise, the association, corporation, or local unit shall be held responsible. In addition to the permit fee paid by the association, corporation, or local unit, the D-permit holder shall pay a fee of ten dollars. A D-permit holder may receive an unlimited number of joint F–2 permits.

Any association, corporation, or local unit applying for an F–2 permit shall file with the application a statement of the organizational purpose of the association, corporation, or local unit, the location and purpose of the event, and a list of its officers. The application form shall contain a notice that a person who knowingly makes a false statement on the application or statement is guilty of the crime of falsification, a misdemeanor of the first degree. In ruling on an application, the division shall consider, among other things, the past activities of the association, corporation, or local unit and any D-permit holder while operating under other F–2 permits, the location of the event for which the current application is made, and any objections of local residents or law enforcement authorities. If the division approves the application, it shall send copies of the approved application to the proper law enforcement authorities prior to the scheduled event.

Using the procedures of Chapter 119. of the Revised Code, the liquor control commission may adopt such rules as are necessary to administer this section.

(B) No association, corporation, local unit of an association or corporation, or D-permit holder who holds an F–2 permit shall sell beer or intoxicating liquor beyond the hours of sale allowed by the permit. This division imposes strict liability on the holder of such permit and on any officer, agent, or employee of such permit holder.

(2003, H 95, eff. 9–26–03; 1998 H 402, eff. 3–30–99; 1995 S 162, eff. 7–1–97; 1990 H 405, eff. 4–11–91; 1989 H 111; 1979 H 470; 1976 H 1081)

4303.203 F–3 permit

(A) As used in this section:

(1) "Convention facility" and "nonprofit corporation" have the same meanings as in section 4303.201 of the Revised Code.

(2) "Hotel" means a hotel described in section 3731.01 of the Revised Code that has at least fifty rooms for registered transient guests and that is required to be licensed pursuant to section 3731.03 of the Revised Code.

(B) An F–3 permit may be issued to an organization whose primary purpose is to support, promote, and educate members of the beer, wine, or mixed beverage industries, to allow the organization to bring beer, wine, or mixed beverages in their original packages or containers into a convention facility or hotel for consumption in the facility or hotel, if all of the following requirements are met:

(1) The superintendent of liquor control is satisfied that the organization is a nonprofit organization and that the organization's membership is in excess of two hundred fifty persons.

(2) The general manager or the equivalent officer of the convention facility or hotel provides a written consent for the use of a portion of the facility or hotel by the organization and a written statement that the facility's or hotel's permit privileges will be suspended in the portion of the facility or hotel in which the F–3 permit is in force.

(3) The organization provides a written description that clearly sets forth the portion of the convention facility or hotel in which the F–3 permit will be used.

(4) The organization provides a written statement as to its primary purpose and the purpose of its event at the convention facility or hotel.

(5) Division (C) of this section does not apply.

(C) No F–3 permit shall be issued to any nonprofit organization that is created by or for a specific manufacturer, supplier, distributor, or retailer of beer, wine, or mixed beverages.

(D) Notwithstanding division (D) of section 4301.22 of the Revised Code, a holder of an F–3 permit may obtain by donation beer, wine, or mixed beverages from any manufacturer or producer of beer, wine, or mixed beverages.

(E) Nothing in this chapter prohibits the holder of an F–3 permit from bringing into the portion of the convention facility or hotel covered by the permit beer, wine, or mixed beverages otherwise not approved for sale in this state.

(F) Notwithstanding division (D) of section 4301.22 of the Revised Code, no holder of an F–3 permit shall make any charge for any beer, wine, or mixed beverage served by the drink, or in its original package or container, in connection with the use of the portion of the convention facility or hotel covered by the permit.

(G) The division of liquor control shall prepare and make available an F–3 permit application form and may require applicants for the permit to provide information, in addition to that required by this section, that is necessary for the administration of this section.

(H) An F–3 permit shall be effective for a period not to exceed five consecutive days. The division of liquor control shall not issue more than three F–3 permits per calendar year to the same nonprofit organization. The fee for an F–3 permit is three hundred dollars.

(2004 H 306, eff. 7–23–04; 2003 H 95, eff. 9–26–03; 2000 S 200, eff. 9–21–00)

4303.204 F–4 permits

(A) The division of liquor control may issue an F–4 permit to an association or corporation organized not-for-profit in this state to conduct an event that includes the introduction, showcasing, or promotion of Ohio wines, if the event has all of the following characteristics:

(1) It is coordinated by that association or corporation, and the association or corporation is responsible for the activities at it.

(2) It has as one of its purposes the intent to introduce, showcase, or promote Ohio wines to persons who attend it.

(3) It includes the sale of food for consumption on the premises where sold.

(4) It features at least three A–2 permit holders who sell Ohio wine at it.

(B) The holder of an F–4 permit may furnish, with or without charge, wine that it has obtained from the A–2 permit holders that are participating in the event for which the F–4 permit is issued, in two-ounce samples for consumption on the premises where furnished and may sell such wine by the glass for consumption on the premises where sold. The holder of an A–2 permit that is participating in the event for which the F–4 permit is issued may sell wine that it has manufactured, in sealed containers for consumption off the premises where sold. Wine may be furnished or sold on the premises of the event for which the F–4 permit is issued only where and when the sale of wine is otherwise permitted by law.

(C) The premises of the event for which the F–4 permit is issued shall be clearly defined and sufficiently restricted to allow proper enforcement of the permit by state and local law enforcement officers. If an F–4 permit is issued for all or a portion of the same premises for which another class of permit is issued, that permit holder's privileges will be suspended in that portion of the premises in which the F–4 permit is in effect.

(D) No F–4 permit shall be effective for more than seventy-two consecutive hours. No sales or furnishing of wine shall take place under an F–4 permit after one a.m.

(E) The division shall not issue more than six F–4 permits to the same not-for-profit association or corporation in any one calendar year.

(F) An applicant for an F–4 permit shall apply for the permit not later than thirty days prior to the first day of the event for which the permit is sought. The application for the permit shall list all of the A–2 permit holders that will participate in the event for which the F–4 permit is sought. The fee for the F–4 permit is sixty dollars per day.

The division shall prepare and make available an F–4 permit application form and may require applicants for and holders of the F–4 permit to provide information that is in addition to that required by this section and that is necessary for the administration of this section.

(G)(1) The holder of an F–4 permit is responsible for, and is subject to penalties for, any violations of this chapter or Chapter 4301. of the Revised Code or the rules adopted under this and that chapter.

(2) An F–4 permit holder shall not allow an A–2 permit holder to participate in the event for which the F–4 permit is issued if the A–2 or A–1–A permit of that A–2 permit holder is under suspension.

(3) The division may refuse to issue an F–4 permit to an applicant who has violated any provision of this chapter or Chapter 4301. of the Revised Code during the applicant's previous operation under an F–4 permit, for a period of up to two years after the date of the violation.

(H)(1) Notwithstanding division (D) of section 4301.22 of the Revised Code, an A–2 permit holder that participates in an event for which an F–4 permit is issued may donate wine that it has manufactured to the holder of that F–4 permit. The holder of an F–4 permit may return unused and sealed containers of wine to the A–2 permit holder that donated the wine at the conclusion of the event for which the F–4 permit was issued.

(2) The participation by an A–2 permit holder or its employees in an event for which an F–4 permit is issued does not violate section 4301.24 of the Revised Code.

(2004 H 306, eff. 7–23–04; 2003 H 95, eff. 9–26–03; 2002 H 371, eff. 10–11–02)

4303.205 F–5 permits

(A) As used in this section:

(1) "Festival" means an event organized by a nonprofit organization that includes food, music, and entertainment and the participation of at least five riverboats.

(2) "Nonprofit organization" has the same meaning as in section 4303.201 of the Revised Code.

(B) The division of liquor control may issue an F–5 permit to the owner or operator of a riverboat that has a capacity in excess of fifty-five persons, that is not regularly docked in this state, and whose owner or operator has entered into a written contract with a nonprofit organization for the riverboat to participate in a festival.

(C) The holder of an F–5 permit may sell beer and any intoxicating liquor, only by the individual drink in glass and from the container, for consumption on the premises where sold until one a.m., on any day of the week, including Sunday.

(D) The division shall prepare and make available an F–5 permit application form and may require applicants for the permit to provide information, in addition to that required by this section, that is necessary for the administration of this section.

(E) Sales under an F–5 permit are not affected by whether sales of beer or intoxicating liquor for consumption on the premises where sold are permitted to be made by persons holding another type of permit in the precinct or at the particular location where the riverboat is located.

(F) No F–5 permit shall be in effect for more than six consecutive days.

(G) The division shall not issue more than one F–5 permit in any one calendar year for the same riverboat.

(H) The fee for an F–5 permit is one hundred eighty dollars.

(2003 H 95, eff. 9–26–03)

4303.206 F-6 permits

(A) The division of liquor control may issue an F–6 permit to a nonprofit organization that is exempt from federal income taxation under the "Internal Revenue Code of 1986," 100 Stat. 2085, 26 U.S.C.A. 501(c)(3), as amended, to sell wine at an event organized and conducted by, and for the benefit of, the nonprofit organization.

(B) An F–6 permit may be issued to a nonprofit organization if the premises of the event for which the F–6 permit is sought is located in a precinct, or at a particular location in a precinct, in which the sale of wine is otherwise permitted by law. The premises of the event for which an F–6 permit is issued shall be clearly defined and sufficiently restricted to allow proper enforcement of the permit by state and local law enforcement officers. If an F–6 permit is issued for all or a portion of the same premises for which another class of permit is issued, that permit holder's privileges shall be suspended in that portion of the premises in which the F–6 permit is in effect.

(C) A holder of an F–6 permit may charge an admission price to attend the event for which the permit is issued, which price includes the consumption of wine or sale of wine by the individual drink.

(D) A holder of an F–6 permit may sell wine in its original sealed container by auction at the event for which the permit is issued.

(E) Nothing in this chapter or Chapter 4301. of the Revised Code or any rule adopted by the liquor control commission prevents the holder of an F–6 permit from obtaining wine by donation from a manufacturer, supplier, or wholesale distributor of wine or from any person who is not the holder of a permit issued by the division of liquor control.

(F) Notwithstanding any contrary provision of section 4301.24 of the Revised Code or of any rule adopted by the liquor control commission, employees of a manufacturer, supplier, or wholesale distributor may assist the holder of an F–6 permit in serving wine at the event for which the permit is issued.

(G) The division shall prepare and make available an F–6 permit application form and may require applicants for the permit to provide information necessary for the administration of this section.

(H) No F–6 permit shall be effective for more than seventy-two consecutive hours, and sales of wine under the permit shall be confined to the same hours permitted to the holder of a D–2 permit. The division shall not issue more than six F–6 permits per calendar year to the same nonprofit organization.

(I) The fee for an F–6 permit is fifty dollars.

(2003 S 23, eff. 4–7–04)

4303.21 G permit

Permit G may be issued to the owner of a pharmacy in charge of a licensed pharmacist to be named in the permit for the sale at retail of alcohol for medicinal purposes in quantities at each sale of not more than one gallon upon the written prescription of a physician or dentist who is lawfully and regularly engaged in the practice of the physician's or dentist's profession in this state, and for the sale of industrial alcohol for mechanical, chemical, or scientific purposes to a person known by the seller to be engaged in mechanical, chemical, or scientific pursuits; all subject to section 4303.34 of the Revised Code. The fee for this permit is one hundred dollars.

(2003 H 95, eff. 9–26–03; 1998 S 66, eff. 7–22–98; 1989 H 111, eff. 7–1–89; 1979 H 470; 1953 H 1; GC 6064–15)

4303.22 H permit

Permit H may be issued for a fee of three hundred dollars to a carrier by motor vehicle who also holds a license issued by the public utilities commission to transport beer, intoxicating liquor, and alcohol, or any of them, in this state for delivery or use in this state. This section does not prevent the division of liquor control from contracting with common or contract carriers for the delivery or transportation of liquor for the division, and any contract or common carrier so contracting with the division is eligible for an H permit. Manufacturers or wholesale distributors of beer or intoxicating liquor other than spirituous liquor who transport or deliver their own products to or from their premises licensed under this chapter and Chapter 4301. of the Revised Code by their own trucks as an incident to the purchase or sale of such beverages need not obtain an H permit. Carriers by rail shall receive an H permit upon application for it.

This section does not prevent the division from issuing, upon the payment of the permit fee, an H permit to any person, partnership, firm, or corporation licensed by any other state to engage in the business of manufacturing and brewing or producing beer, wine, and mixed beverages or any person, partnership, firm, or corporation licensed by the United States or any other state to engage in the business of importing beer, wine, and mixed beverages manufactured outside the United States. The manufacturer, brewer, or importer of products manufactured outside the United States, upon the issuance of an H permit, may transport, ship, and deliver only its own products to holders of B–1 or B–5 permits in Ohio in motor trucks and equipment owned and operated by such class H permit holder. No H permit shall be issued by the division to such applicant until the applicant files with the division a liability insurance certificate or policy satisfactory to the division, in a sum of not less than one thousand nor more than five thousand dollars for property damage and for not less than five thousand nor more than fifty thousand dollars for loss sustained by reason of injury or death and with such other terms as the division considers necessary to adequately protect the interest of the public, having due regard for the number of persons and amount of property affected. The certificate or policy shall insure the manufacturer, brewer, or importer of products manufactured outside the United States against loss sustained by reason of the death of or injury to persons, and for loss of or damage to property, from the negligence of such class H permit holder in the operation of its motor vehicles or equipment in this state.

(2003 H 95, eff. 9–26–03; 2002 H 371, eff. 10–11–02; 1995 S 162, eff. 7–1–97; 1989 H 111, eff. 7–1–89; 1979 H 470; 128 v 1041; 1953 H 1; GC 6064–15)

4303.23 I permit

Permit I may be issued to wholesale druggists to purchase alcohol from the holders of A–3 permits and to import alcohol into this state subject to terms imposed by the division of liquor control; to sell at wholesale to physicians, dentists, druggists, veterinary surgeons, manufacturers, hospitals, infirmaries, and medical or educational institutions using such alcohol for medicinal, mechanical, chemical, or scientific purposes, and to holders of G permits for nonbeverage purposes only; and to sell alcohol at retail in total quantities at each sale of not more than one quart, upon the written prescription of a physician or dentist who is lawfully and regularly engaged in the practice of the physician's or dentist's profession in this state. The sale of alcohol under this section is subject to section 4303.34 of the Revised Code. The fee for this permit is two hundred dollars.

"Wholesale druggists," as used in this, section includes all persons holding federal wholesale liquor dealers' licenses and who are engaged in the sale of medicinal drugs, proprietary medicines, and surgical and medical appliances and apparatus, at wholesale.

(2003 H 95, eff. 9–26–03; 1995 S 162, eff. 7–1–97; 1989 H 111, eff. 7–1–89; 1979 H 470; 1953 H 1; GC 6064–15)

4303.231 W permit

Permit W may be issued to a manufacturer or supplier of beer or intoxicating liquor to operate a warehouse for the storage of beer or intoxicating liquor within this state and to sell those products from the warehouse only to holders of B permits in this state and to other customers outside this state under rules adopted by the liquor control commission. Each holder of a B permit with a supplier registration on file with the division of liquor control may purchase beer or intoxicating liquor if designated by the permit to make those purchases, from the holder of a W permit. The fee for a W permit is one thousand five hundred sixty-three dollars for each warehouse during the year covered by the permit.

(2004 H 306, eff. 7–23–04; 2003 H 95, eff. 9–26–03; 1995 S 162, eff. 7–1–97; 1986 H 627, eff. 9–24–86)

ADMINISTRATIVE PROVISIONS

4303.25 Permit required

No person personally or by the person's clerk, agent, or employee shall manufacture, manufacture for sale, offer, keep, or possess for sale, furnish or sell, or solicit the purchase or sale of any beer or intoxicating liquor in this state, or transport, import, or cause to be transported or imported any beer, intoxicating liquor, or alcohol in or into this state for delivery, use, or sale, unless the person has fully complied with this chapter and Chapter 4301. of the Revised Code or is the holder of a permit issued by the division of liquor control and in force at the time.

The superintendent of liquor control may adopt rules requiring a person acting as an agent, solicitor, or salesperson for a manufacturer, supplier, broker, or wholesale distributor, who solicits permit holders authorized to deal in beer and intoxicating liquor, to be registered with the division and may cite the registrant to the liquor control commission for a violation of this chapter, Chapter 4301. of the Revised Code, or the rules adopted by the commission or superintendent.

(2004 H 306, eff. 7–23–04; 1995 S 162, eff. 7–1–97; 1984 H 37, eff. 6–22–84; 129 v 582; 128 v 1282; 1953 H 1; GC 6064–14)

APPLICATION FOR PERMITS

4303.28 Sale of services prohibited

No person shall sell or offer to sell services or shall solicit or receive anything of value in connection with the issuing of any permit under Chapters 4301. and 4303. of the Revised Code, except on appeal or rehearing. Such chapters do not prevent an applicant for a permit from employing an attorney at law to assist the applicant in making application for a permit, or prevent an attorney at law from accompanying any applicant for a permit, or permit holder, in reference to any matter pending before the superintendent or the division of liquor control.

(1995 S 162, eff. 7–1–97; 1953 H 1, eff. 10–1–53; GC 6064–20)

PROHIBITIONS AND PENALTIES

4303.36 Prohibition against violations not otherwise specified

Any person who is subject to Chapter 4301., 4303., or 4307. of the Revised Code, in the transportation, possession, or sale of wine or mixed beverages subject to the taxes imposed by section 4301.43 and, if applicable, section 4301.432 of the Revised Code, and who violates any provision of any of those chapters or any lawful rule promulgated by the tax commissioner under any provision of any of those chapters, for the violation of which no penalty is otherwise provided, shall be fined as provided in division (B) of section 4303.99 of the Revised Code.

(1996 S 293, eff. 9–26–96 (See also Historical and Statutory Notes.), 1996 S 269, eff. 7–1–96; 1995 S 2, eff. 7–1–96; 1995 H 239, eff. 11–24–95; 1982 H 357, eff. 10–1–82; 1981 H 694; 125 v 903; 1953 H 1; Source—GC 6064–50)

Historical and Statutory Notes

Ed. Note: The amendment of this section by 1996 S 293, eff. 9–26–96 (see also Historical and Statutory Notes), and 1996 S 269, eff. 7–1–96, was identical. See *Baldwin's Ohio Legislative Service*, 1996, pages 7/L–2211 and 6/L–1107, or the OH–LEGIS or OH–LEGIS–OLD database on WESTLAW, for original versions of these Acts.

Ed. Note: 1996 S 293 Effective Date—The Secretary of State assigned a general effective date of 9–26–96 for 1996 S 293, along with notice that, in accordance with RC 1.471, the General Assembly has not determined which sections go into immediate effect, and that it appears that certain sections provide for appropriations for current expenses, and are immediately effective in accordance with RC 1.471 and O Const Art II, § 1d.

4303.37 Prohibition against certain violations

No person shall violate sections 4303.01 to 4303.37, inclusive, of the Revised Code, for which no penalty is provided.

(126 v 324, eff. 10–4–55; 1953 H 1; Source—GC 6064–65)

4303.40 Notice of action to prohibit liquor business

Any party bringing an action to prohibit the operation of a business under a permit issued under this chapter shall, upon filing the complaint in the action, notify the division of liquor control of the filing of the complaint.

(1995 S 162, eff. 7–1–97; 1987 H 419, eff. 7–1–87)

4303.99 Penalties

(A) Whoever violates section 4303.28 of the Revised Code shall be fined not less than one thousand nor more than twenty-five hundred dollars or imprisoned not less than six months nor more than one year.

(B) Whoever violates section 4303.36 of the Revised Code shall be fined not less than twenty-five nor more than one hundred dollars.

(C) Whoever violates section 4303.37 of the Revised Code shall be fined not less than twenty-five nor more than fifty dollars.

(D) Whoever violates division (B) of section 4303.202 of the Revised Code is guilty of a misdemeanor of the fourth degree.

(1976 H 1081, eff. 8–31–76; 1953 H 1)

CHAPTER 4399

LIQUOR—PROHIBITORY PROVISIONS AND CRIMES

PROHIBITED PLACES OF SALE

4399.09 Keeping place where intoxicating liquors are sold in violation of law

(A) No person shall keep a place where beer or intoxicating liquors are sold, furnished, or given away in violation of law. The court, on conviction for a subsequent violation of this section, shall order the place where the beer or intoxicating liquor is sold, furnished, or given away to be abated as a nuisance or shall order the person so convicted to give bond payable to the state in the sum of one thousand dollars, with sureties to the acceptance of the court, that the person will not sell, furnish, or give away beer or intoxicating liquor in violation of law and will pay all fines, costs, and damages assessed against the person for that subsequent violation of this section. The giving away of beer or intoxicating liquors, or any other device to evade this division, constitutes unlawful selling.

As used in this division, "beer" has the same meaning as in section 4301.01 of the Revised Code.

(B) Division (A) of this section does not apply to any premises for which a permit has been issued under Chapter 4303. of the Revised Code while that permit is in effect.

(2002 H 371, eff. 10–11–02; 1984 S 74, eff. 7–4–84; 1953 H 1; GC 13195)

4399.10 Intoxicating liquors shall not be sold in brothels

No person shall sell, exchange, or give away intoxicating liquor in a brothel.

(1953 H 1, eff. 10–1–53; GC 13199)

4399.11 Selling intoxicating liquors at certain places prohibited

If a person is convicted of any violation of Title XLIII of the Revised Code that involves the sale of intoxicating liquors at or within twelve hundred yards of the administration or main central building of the Columbus state hospital, Dayton state hospital, Athens state hospital, or Toledo state hospital, within two miles of the place at which an agricultural fair is being held, or within one mile of a county children's home situated within one mile of a municipal corporation in which the sale of intoxicating liquors is prohibited by ordinance, the place in which the intoxicating liquors are sold shall be shut up and abated as a nuisance by order of the court upon conviction of its owner or keeper.

(1995 S 2, eff. 7–1–96; 1995 H 117, eff. 9–29–95; 1980 H 965, eff. 4–9–81; 1978 S 420; 1953 H 1; GC 13206)

4399.12 Permit holders excepted

No provision contained in Title XLIII of the Revised Code that prohibits the sale of intoxicating liquors in any of the circumstances described in section 4399.11 of the Revised Code extends to or prevents the holder of an A, B, C–2, D–2, D–3, D–3a, D–4, D–4a, D–5, D–5a, D–5b, D–5e, D–5f, D–5g, D–5h, D–5i, D–5j, D–5k, G, or I permit issued by the division of liquor control from distributing or selling intoxicating liquor at the place of business described in the permit of the holder.

(2002 H 371, eff. 10–11–02; 1999 H 283, eff. 9–29–99; 1995 S 162, eff. 7–1–97; 1995 S 2, eff. 7–1–96; 1990 H 405, eff. 4–11–91; 1988 H 562; 1984 H 711; 1953 H 1; GC 13207)

4399.14 Use of intoxicating liquor in a public dance hall prohibited; exceptions

No person who is the proprietor of any public dance hall, or who conducts, manages, or is in charge of any public dance hall, shall allow the use of any intoxicating liquor or the presence of intoxicated persons in such dance hall or on the premises on which such dance hall is located; but the prohibition against the use of any intoxicating liquor does not apply to establishments that are holders of a D–1, D–2, D–3, D–4, or D–5 permit whose principal business consists of conducting a hotel, a restaurant, a club, or a night club as defined by section 4301.01 of the Revised Code. No person who is the proprietor of any public dance hall, or who conducts, manages, or is in charge thereof, shall permit the presence at such public dance hall of any child younger than eighteen years of age, not accompanied by his father, mother, or legal guardian.

(1953 H 1, eff. 10–1–53; GC 13393–1)

MISCELLANEOUS PROVISIONS

4399.15 Poisonously adulterated liquors

No person, for the purpose of sale, shall adulterate spirituous liquor, alcoholic liquor, or beer used or intended for drink or medicinal or mechanical purposes, with cocculus indicus, vitriol, grains of paradise, opium, alum, capsicum, copperas, laurel water, logwood, Brazilwood, cochineal, sugar of lead, aloes, glucose, tannic acid, or any other substance that is poisonous or injurious to health, or with a substance not a necessary ingredient in the manufacture of the spirituous liquor, alcoholic liquor, or beer, or sell, offer, or keep for sale spirituous liquor, alcoholic liquor, or beer that is so adulterated.

In addition to the penalties provided in division (E) of section 4399.99 of the Revised Code, a person convicted of violating this section shall pay all necessary costs and expenses incurred in inspecting and analyzing spirituous liquor, alcoholic liquor, or beer that is so adulterated, sold, kept, or offered for sale.

(2002 H 371, eff. 10–11–02; 1995 S 2, eff. 7–1–96; 1953 H 1, eff. 10–1–53; GC 12676, 12677)

4399.16 Tavern keeper permitting rioting or drunkenness

No tavern keeper shall permit rioting, reveling, intoxication, or drunkenness in his house or on his premises.

(1953 H 1, eff. 10–1–53; GC 12813)

4399.17 Manufacturing or selling poisoned liquors

No person shall use an active poison in the manufacture or preparation of intoxicating liquor or sell intoxicating liquor so manufactured or prepared.

(1953 H 1, eff. 10–1–53; GC 12675)

4399.18 Action against liquor permit holder for sale of alcohol to intoxicated person

Notwithstanding division (A) of section 2307.60 of the Revised Code and except as otherwise provided in this section, no person, and no executor or administrator of the person, who suffers personal injury, death, or property damage as a result of the actions of an intoxicated person has a cause of action against any liquor permit holder or an employee of a liquor permit holder who sold beer or intoxicating liquor to the intoxicated person unless the personal injury, death, or property damage occurred on the permit holder's premises or in a parking lot under the control of the permit holder and was proximately caused by the negligence of the permit holder or an employee of the permit holder. A person has a cause of action against a permit holder or an employee of a permit holder for personal injury, death, or property damage caused by the negligent actions of an intoxicated person occurring off the premises or away from a parking lot under the permit holder's control only when both of the following can be shown by a preponderance of the evidence:

(A) The permit holder or an employee of the permit holder knowingly sold an intoxicating beverage to at least one of the following:

(1) A noticeably intoxicated person in violation of division (B) of section 4301.22 of the Revised Code;

(2) A person in violation of section 4301.69 of the Revised Code.

(B) The person's intoxication proximately caused the personal injury, death, or property damage.

Notwithstanding sections 4399.02 and 4399.05 of the Revised Code, no person, and no executor or administrator of the person, who suffers personal injury, death, or property damage as a result of the actions of an intoxicated person has a cause of action against the owner of a building or premises who rents or leases the building or premises to a liquor permit holder against whom a cause of action may be brought under this section, except when the owner and the permit holder are the same person.

(2004 H 306, eff. 7–23–04; 2002 S 107, eff. 6–28–02; 2001 S 108, § 2.01, eff. 7–6–01; 2001 S 108, § 2.02, eff. 7–6–01; 1996 H 350, eff. 1–27–97[1]*; 1986 H 759, eff. 7–21–86)*

[1] See Notes of Decisions, *State ex rel. Ohio Academy of Trial Lawyers v. Sheward* (Ohio 1999), 86 Ohio St.3d 451, 715 N.E.2d 1062.

Uncodified Law

2001 S 108, § 1, eff. 7–6–01, reads:

It is the intent of this act (1) to repeal the Tort Reform Act, Am. Sub. H.B. 350 of the 121st General Assembly, 146 Ohio Laws 3867, in conformity with the Supreme Court of Ohio's decision in *State, ex rel. Ohio Academy of Trial Lawyers, v. Sheward* (1999), 86 Ohio St.3d 451; (2) to clarify the status of the law; and (3) to revive the law as it existed prior to the Tort Reform Act.

Notes of Decisions

8. Constitutional issues

1996 H 350, which amended more than 100 statutes and a variety of rules relating to tort and other civil actions, and which was an attempt to reenact provisions of law previously held unconstitutional by the Supreme Court of Ohio, is an act of usurpation of judicial power in violation of the doctrine of separation of powers; for that reason, and because of violation of the one-subject rule of the Ohio Constitution, 1996 H 350 is unconstitutional. State ex rel. Ohio Academy of Trial Lawyers v. Sheward (Ohio, 08-16-1999) 86 Ohio St.3d 451, 715 N.E.2d 1062, 1999-Ohio-123, reconsideration denied 87 Ohio St.3d 1409, 716 N.E.2d 1170.

4399.99 Penalties

(A) Whoever violates section 4399.16 of the Revised Code shall be fined not less than five nor more than one hundred dollars.

(B) Whoever violates section 4399.09 of the Revised Code shall be fined not less than one hundred nor more than five hundred dollars on a first offense and shall be fined not less than two hundred nor more than five hundred dollars on each subsequent offense.

(C) Whoever violates section 4399.10 of the Revised Code shall be fined not less than one hundred nor more than five hundred dollars and imprisoned not less than one nor more than six months.

(D) Whoever violates section 4399.14 of the Revised Code shall be fined not less than twenty-five nor more than five hundred dollars, imprisoned not more than six months, or both.

(E) Whoever violates section 4399.15 of the Revised Code shall be fined not less than twenty nor more than one hundred dollars, imprisoned not less than twenty nor more than sixty days, or both.

(F) Whoever violates section 4399.17 of the Revised Code is guilty of a felony of the fourth degree.

(1995 S 2, eff. 7–1–96; 1982 H 269, § 4, eff. 7–1–83; 1982 S 199; 1970 H 876; 1953 H 1)

CHAPTER 4501

MOTOR VEHICLES—DEFINITIONS; GENERAL PROVISIONS

DEFINITIONS

4501.01 Definitions

As used in this chapter and Chapters 4503., 4505., 4507., 4509., 4510., 4511., 4513., 4515., and 4517. of the Revised Code, and in the penal laws, except as otherwise provided:

(A) "Vehicles" means everything on wheels or runners, including motorized bicycles, but does not mean electric personal assistive mobility devices, vehicles that are operated exclusively on rails or tracks or from overhead electric trolley wires, and vehicles that belong to any police department, municipal fire department, or volunteer fire department, or that are used by such a department in the discharge of its functions.

(B) "Motor vehicle" means any vehicle, including mobile homes and recreational vehicles, that is propelled or drawn by power other than muscular power or power collected from overhead electric trolley wires. "Motor vehicle" does not include motorized bicycles, road rollers, traction engines, power shovels, power cranes, and other equipment used in construction work and not designed for or employed in general highway transportation, well-drilling machinery, ditch-digging machinery, farm machinery, trailers that are used to transport agricultural produce or agricultural production materials between a local place of storage or supply and the farm when drawn or towed on a public road or highway at a speed of twenty-five miles per hour or less, threshing machinery, hay-baling machinery, corn sheller, hammermill and agricultural tractors, machinery used in the production of horticultural, agricultural, and vegetable products, and trailers that are designed and used exclusively to transport a boat between a place of storage and a marina, or in and around a marina, when drawn or towed on a public road or highway for a distance of no more than ten miles and at a speed of twenty-five miles per hour or less.

(C) "Agricultural tractor" and "traction engine" mean any self-propelling vehicle that is designed or used for drawing other vehicles or wheeled machinery, but has no provisions for carrying loads independently of such other vehicles, and that is used principally for agricultural purposes.

(D) "Commercial tractor," except as defined in division (C) of this section, means any motor vehicle that has motive power and either is designed or used for drawing other motor vehicles, or is designed or used for drawing another motor vehicle while carrying a portion of the other motor vehicle or its load, or both.

(E) "Passenger car" means any motor vehicle that is designed and used for carrying not more than nine persons and includes any motor vehicle that is designed and used for carrying not more than fifteen persons in a ridesharing arrangement.

(F) "Collector's vehicle" means any motor vehicle or agricultural tractor or traction engine that is of special interest, that has a fair market value of one hundred dollars or more, whether operable or not, and that is owned, operated, collected, preserved, restored, maintained, or used essentially as a collector's item, leisure pursuit, or investment, but not as the owner's principal means of transportation. "Licensed collector's vehicle" means a collector's vehicle, other than an agricultural tractor or traction engine, that displays current, valid license tags issued under section 4503.45 of the Revised Code, or a similar type of motor vehicle that displays current, valid license tags issued under substantially equivalent provisions in the laws of other states.

(G) "Historical motor vehicle" means any motor vehicle that is over twenty-five years old and is owned solely as a collector's item and for participation in club activities, exhibitions, tours, parades, and similar uses, but that in no event is used for general transportation.

(H) "Noncommercial motor vehicle" means any motor vehicle, including a farm truck as defined in section 4503.04 of the Revised Code, that is designed by the manufacturer to carry a load of no more than one ton and is used exclusively for purposes other than engaging in business for profit.

(I) "Bus" means any motor vehicle that has motor power and is designed and used for carrying more than nine passengers, except any motor vehicle that is designed and used for carrying not more than fifteen passengers in a ridesharing arrangement.

(J) "Commercial car" or "truck" means any motor vehicle that has motor power and is designed and used for carrying merchandise or freight, or that is used as a commercial tractor.

(K) "Bicycle" means every device, other than a tricycle that is designed solely for use as a play vehicle by a child, that is propelled solely by human power upon which any person may ride, and that has either two tandem wheels, or one wheel in front and two wheels in the rear, any of which is more than fourteen inches in diameter.

(L) "Motorized bicycle" means any vehicle that either has two tandem wheels or one wheel in the front and two wheels in the rear, that is capable of being pedaled, and that is equipped with a helper motor of not more than fifty cubic centimeters piston displacement that produces no more than one brake horsepower and is capable of propelling the vehicle at a speed of no greater than twenty miles per hour on a level surface.

(M) "Trailer" means any vehicle without motive power that is designed or used for carrying property or persons wholly on its own structure and for being drawn by a motor vehicle, and includes any such vehicle that is formed by or operated as a combination of a semitrailer and a vehicle of the dolly type such as that commonly known as a trailer dolly, a vehicle used to transport agricultural produce or agricultural production materials between a local place of storage or supply and the farm when drawn or towed on a public road or highway at a speed greater than twenty-five miles per hour, and a vehicle that is designed and used exclusively to transport a boat between a place of storage and a marina, or in and around a marina, when drawn or towed on a public road or highway for a distance of more than ten miles or at a speed of more than twenty-five miles per hour. "Trailer" does not include a manufactured home or travel trailer.

(N) "Noncommercial trailer" means any trailer, except a travel trailer or trailer that is used to transport a boat as described in division (B) of this section, but, where applicable, includes a vehicle that is used to transport a boat as described in division (M) of this section, that has a gross weight of no more than three thousand pounds, and that is used exclusively for purposes other than engaging in business for a profit.

(O) "Mobile home" means a building unit or assembly of closed construction that is fabricated in an off-site facility, is more than thirty-five body feet in length or, when erected on site, is three hundred twenty or more square feet, is built on a permanent chassis, is transportable in one or more sections, and does not qualify as a manufactured home as defined in division (C)(4) of section 3781.06 of the Revised Code or as an industrialized unit as defined in division (C)(3) of section 3781.06 of the Revised Code.

(P) "Semitrailer" means any vehicle of the trailer type that does not have motive power and is so designed or used with another and separate motor vehicle that in operation a part of its own weight or that of its load, or both, rests upon and is carried by the other vehicle furnishing the motive power for propelling itself and the vehicle referred to in this division, and includes, for the purpose only of registration and taxation under those chapters, any vehicle of the dolly type, such as a trailer dolly, that is designed or used for the conversion of a semitrailer into a trailer.

(Q) "Recreational vehicle" means a vehicular portable structure that meets all of the following conditions:

(1) It is designed for the sole purpose of recreational travel.

(2) It is not used for the purpose of engaging in business for profit.

(3) It is not used for the purpose of engaging in intrastate commerce.

(4) It is not used for the purpose of commerce as defined in 49 C.F.R. 383.5, as amended.

(5) It is not regulated by the public utilities commission pursuant to Chapter 4919., 4921., or 4923. of the Revised Code.

(6) It is classed as one of the following:

(a) "Travel trailer" means a nonself-propelled recreational vehicle that does not exceed an overall length of thirty-five feet, exclusive of bumper and tongue or coupling, and contains less than three hundred twenty square feet of space when erected on site. "Travel trailer" includes a tent-type fold-out camping trailer as defined in section 4517.01 of the Revised Code.

(b) "Motor home" means a self-propelled recreational vehicle that has no fifth wheel and is constructed with permanently installed facilities for cold storage, cooking and consuming of food, and for sleeping.

(c) "Truck camper" means a nonself-propelled recreational vehicle that does not have wheels for road use and is designed to be placed upon and attached to a motor vehicle. "Truck camper" does not include truck covers that consist of walls and a roof, but do not have floors and facilities enabling them to be used as a dwelling.

(d) "Fifth wheel trailer" means a vehicle that is of such size and weight as to be movable without a special highway permit, that has a gross trailer area of four hundred square feet or less, that is constructed with a raised forward section that allows a bi-level floor plan, and that is designed to be towed by a vehicle equipped with a fifth-wheel hitch ordinarily installed in the bed of a truck.

(e) "Park trailer" means a vehicle that is commonly known as a park model recreational vehicle, meets the American national standard institute standard A119.5 (1988) for park trailers, is built on a single chassis, has a gross trailer area of four hundred square feet or less when set up, is designed for seasonal or temporary living quarters, and may be connected to utilities necessary for the operation of installed features and appliances.

(R) "Pneumatic tires" means tires of rubber and fabric or tires of similar material, that are inflated with air.

(S) "Solid tires" means tires of rubber or similar elastic material that are not dependent upon confined air for support of the load.

(T) "Solid tire vehicle" means any vehicle that is equipped with two or more solid tires.

(U) "Farm machinery" means all machines and tools that are used in the production, harvesting, and care of farm products, and includes trailers that are used to transport agricultural produce or agricultural production materials between a local place of storage or supply and the farm when drawn or towed on a public road or highway at a speed of twenty-five miles per hour or less.

(V) "Owner" includes any person or firm, other than a manufacturer or dealer, that has title to a motor vehicle, except that, in sections 4505.01 to 4505.19 of the Revised Code, "owner" includes in addition manufacturers and dealers.

(W) "Manufacturer" and "dealer" include all persons and firms that are regularly engaged in the business of manufacturing, selling, displaying, offering for sale, or dealing in motor vehicles, at an established place of business that is used exclusively for the purpose of manufacturing, selling, displaying, offering for sale, or dealing in motor vehicles. A place of business that is used for manufacturing, selling, displaying, offering for sale, or dealing in motor vehicles shall be deemed to be used exclusively for those purposes even though snowmobiles or all-purpose vehicles are sold or displayed for sale thereat, even though farm machinery is sold or displayed for sale thereat, or even though repair, accessory, gasoline and oil, storage, parts, service, or paint departments are maintained thereat, or, in any county having a population of less than seventy-five thousand at the last federal census, even though a department in a place of business is used to dismantle, salvage, or rebuild motor vehicles by means of used parts, if such departments are operated for the purpose of furthering and assisting in the business of manufacturing, selling, displaying, offering for sale, or dealing in motor vehicles. Places of business or departments in a place of business used to dismantle, salvage, or rebuild motor vehicles by means of using used parts are not considered as being maintained for the purpose of assisting or furthering the manufacturing, selling, displaying, and offering for sale or dealing in motor vehicles.

(X) "Operator" includes any person who drives or operates a motor vehicle upon the public highways.

(Y) "Chauffeur" means any operator who operates a motor vehicle, other than a taxicab, as an employee for hire; or any operator whether or not the owner of a motor vehicle, other than a taxicab, who operates such vehicle for transporting, for gain, compensation, or profit, either persons or property owned by another. Any operator of a motor vehicle who is voluntarily involved in a ridesharing arrangement is not considered an employee for hire or operating such vehicle for gain, compensation, or profit.

(Z) "State" includes the territories and federal districts of the United States, and the provinces of Canada.

(AA) "Public roads and highways" for vehicles includes all public thoroughfares, bridges, and culverts.

(BB) "Manufacturer's number" means the manufacturer's original serial number that is affixed to or imprinted upon the chassis or other part of the motor vehicle.

(CC) "Motor number" means the manufacturer's original number that is affixed to or imprinted upon the engine or motor of the vehicle.

(DD) "Distributor" means any person who is authorized by a motor vehicle manufacturer to distribute new motor vehicles to licensed motor vehicle dealers at an established place of business that is used exclusively for the purpose of distributing new motor vehicles to licensed motor vehicle dealers, except when the distributor also is a new motor vehicle dealer, in which case the distributor may distribute at the location of the distributor's licensed dealership.

(EE) "Ridesharing arrangement" means the transportation of persons in a motor vehicle where the transportation is incidental to another purpose of a volunteer driver and includes ridesharing arrangements known as carpools, vanpools, and buspools.

(FF) "Apportionable vehicle" means any vehicle that is used or intended for use in two or more international registration plan member jurisdictions that allocate or proportionally register vehicles, that is used for the transportation of persons for hire or designed, used, or maintained primarily for the transportation of property, and that meets any of the following qualifications:

(1) Is a power unit having a gross vehicle weight in excess of twenty-six thousand pounds;

(2) Is a power unit having three or more axles, regardless of the gross vehicle weight;

(3) Is a combination vehicle with a gross vehicle weight in excess of twenty-six thousand pounds.

"Apportionable vehicle" does not include recreational vehicles, vehicles displaying restricted plates, city pick-up and delivery vehicles, buses used for the transportation of chartered parties, or vehicles owned and operated by the United States, this state, or any political subdivisions thereof.

(GG) "Chartered party" means a group of persons who contract as a group to acquire the exclusive use of a passenger-carrying motor vehicle at a fixed charge for the vehicle in accordance with the carrier's tariff, lawfully on file with the United States department of transportation, for the purpose of group travel to a specified destination or for a particular itinerary, either agreed upon in advance or modified by the chartered group after having left the place of origin.

(HH) "International registration plan" means a reciprocal agreement of member jurisdictions that is endorsed by the American association of motor vehicle administrators, and that promotes and encourages the fullest possible use of the highway system by authorizing apportioned registration of fleets of vehicles and recognizing registration of vehicles apportioned in member jurisdictions.

(II) "Restricted plate" means a license plate that has a restriction of time, geographic area, mileage, or commodity, and includes license plates issued to farm trucks under division (J) of section 4503.04 of the Revised Code.

(JJ) "Gross vehicle weight," with regard to any commercial car, trailer, semitrailer, or bus that is taxed at the rates established under section 4503.042 of the Revised Code, means the unladen weight of the vehicle fully equipped plus the maximum weight of the load to be carried on the vehicle.

(KK) "Combined gross vehicle weight" with regard to any combination of a commercial car, trailer, and semitrailer, that is taxed at the rates established under section 4503.042 of the Revised Code, means the total unladen weight of the combination of vehicles fully equipped plus the maximum weight of the load to be carried on that combination of vehicles.

(LL) "Chauffeured limousine" means a motor vehicle that is designed to carry nine or fewer passengers and is operated for hire on an hourly basis pursuant to a prearranged contract for the transportation of passengers on public roads and highways along a route under the control of the person hiring the vehicle and not over a defined and regular route. "Prearranged contract" means an agreement, made in advance of boarding, to provide transportation from a specific location in a chauffeured limousine at a fixed rate per hour or trip. "Chauffeured limousine" does not include any vehicle that is used exclusively in the business of funeral directing.

(MM) "Manufactured home" has the same meaning as in division (C)(4) of section 3781.06 of the Revised Code.

(NN) "Acquired situs," with respect to a manufactured home or a mobile home, means to become located in this state by the placement of the home on real property, but does not include the placement of a manufactured home or a mobile home in the inventory of a new motor vehicle dealer or the inventory of a manufacturer, remanufacturer, or distributor of manufactured or mobile homes.

(OO) "Electronic" includes electrical, digital, magnetic, optical, electromagnetic, or any other form of technology that entails capabilities similar to these technologies.

(PP) "Electronic record" means a record generated, communicated, received, or stored by electronic means for use in an information system or for transmission from one information system to another.

(QQ) "Electronic signature" means a signature in electronic form attached to or logically associated with an electronic record.

(RR) "Financial transaction device" has the same meaning as in division (A) of section 113.40 of the Revised Code.

(SS) "Electronic motor vehicle dealer" means a motor vehicle dealer licensed under Chapter 4517. of the Revised Code whom the registrar of motor vehicles determines meets the criteria designated in section 4503.035 of the Revised Code for electronic motor vehicle dealers and designates as an electronic motor vehicle dealer under that section.

(TT) "Electric personal assistive mobility device" means a self-balancing two non-tandem wheeled device that is designed to transport only one person, has an electric propulsion system of an average of seven hundred fifty watts, and when ridden on a paved level surface by an operator who weighs one hundred seventy pounds has a maximum speed of less than twenty miles per hour.

(UU) "Limited driving privileges" means the privilege to operate a motor vehicle that a court grants under section 4510.021 of the Revised Code to a person whose driver's or commercial driver's license or permit or nonresident operating privilege has been suspended.

(2004 H 230, eff. 9–16–04; 2002 S 123, eff. 1–1–04; 2002 S 231, eff. 10–24–02; 2001 S 59, eff. 10–31–01; 2000 H 672, eff. 4–9–01; 2000 H 600, eff. 9–1–00; 2000 S 242, eff. 9–14–00; 1998 H 611, eff. 7–1–99; 1998 S 142, eff. 3–30–99; 1997 S 60, eff. 10–21–97; 1997 H 210, eff. 3–31–97; 1994 S 191, eff. 10–20–94; 1992 H 485, eff. 10–7–92; 1992 H 282; 1990 H 422, H 831; 1984 S 231; 1981 H 53; 1980 H 1171; 1979 H 656, H 1; 1978 H 998, § 1; 1977 H 166, H 1, S 100, H 3; 1976 S 359, S 56; 1975 S 52; 1974 H 1161; 1973 S 108; 1969 S 410; 132 v H 684; 130 v H 479; 128 v 1170; 126 v 783; 125 v 268; 1953 H 1; GC 6290)

BUREAU AND REGISTRAR OF MOTOR VEHICLES

4501.022 Methods of notice

(A) The registrar of motor vehicles shall determine the necessary or appropriate method by which written notice of an order suspending a motor vehicle driver's or commercial driver's license or requiring the surrender of a certificate of registration and registration plates may be provided to the person holding the license or the certificate of registration and registration plates. Division (A) of this section does not apply if the registrar is required to provide notification by use of a method specified by law.

(B) Pursuant to rules adopted by the registrar, the bureau of motor vehicles shall implement proof of mailing procedures to provide verification that written notice of an order suspending a motor vehicle driver's or commercial driver's license or requiring the surrender of a certificate of registration and registration plates was sent to the person holding the license or the certificate of registration and registration plates.

(2002 S 123, eff. 1–1–04; 1992 S 331, eff. 11–13–92)

4501.024 Duties regarding anatomical gifts

The bureau of motor vehicles shall do both of the following:

(A) Develop and maintain a donor registry as required by section 2108.18 of the Revised Code;

(B) Maintain a toll-free telephone number as specified in section 2108.19 of the Revised Code.

(2000 S 188, eff. 12–13–00)

4501.025 Citizens advisory committee

(A) There is hereby created within the bureau of motor vehicles the citizens advisory committee consisting of nine appointed members and the registrar of motor vehicles, who shall serve as an ex officio nonvoting member. The governor, the president of the senate, and the speaker of the house of representatives each shall appoint three members to the committee. The president of the senate and the speaker of the house of representatives each shall appoint one member from their respective houses. Of the three members that the governor, the president of the senate, and the speaker of the house of representatives each appoint to the committee, no more than two shall be members of the same political party.

Of the initial appointments to the committee, the governor, the president of the senate, and the speaker of the house of representatives each shall appoint one member for one year, one member for two years, and one member for three years. Thereafter, terms of office shall be for three years, each term ending on the same day of the same month as did the term that it succeeds. Each member shall hold office from the date of appointment until the end of the term for which the member was appointed. Members may be reappointed. Vacancies shall be filled in the same manner as the original appointment. Any member appointed to fill a vacancy occurring prior to the expiration of the term for which the member's predecessor was appointed shall hold office for the remainder of that term. A member shall continue in office subsequent to the expiration date of the member's term until the member's successor takes office, or until a period of sixty days has elapsed, whichever occurs first.

The committee shall select from among its members a chairperson and a vice-chairperson. The committee shall meet at least twice each calendar year and at other times upon the call of the chair.

Voting members of the committee shall serve without compensation, but shall be reimbursed for travel and other necessary expenses incurred in the conduct of their official duties.

(B) The committee shall review and evaluate the client service practices of the bureau and advise the bureau on ways to improve its interaction with the public. The procedures that the committee shall review include, but are not limited to, the following:

(1) The form and processing of required applications and other documents;

(2) The administration of tests;

(3) The accessibility of bureau staff and the speed and accuracy with which questions are answered;

(4) Methods of notification for the suspension or revocation of a driver's license;

(5) Rules regarding proof of financial responsibility;

(6) The efficiency of service at the offices of deputy registrars.

The committee shall adopt recommendations by a majority vote of its members and shall present recommendations to the bureau for consideration. The committee shall provide copies of its recommendations to the governor, the president of the senate, the speaker of the house of representatives, and the director of public safety.

(C) The bureau shall establish a toll-free telephone number for the committee that citizens may call to register complaints, suggestions, or other comments about their interactions with the bureau. The bureau also shall establish an address at which citizens may contact the committee electronically via the internet. The committee periodically shall review all electronic communications and all calls placed to the toll-free number. The bureau shall cooperate with the committee in the committee's performance of its duties.

(D) The citizens advisory committee shall expire three years after the date of its creation unless the general assembly renews it pursuant to division (D) of section 101.83 of the Revised Code. A renewal of the committee shall be for a period of three years.

(2001 H 182, eff. 2–19–02)

GENERAL PROVISIONS

4501.05 Duty of garage keepers

Keepers of garages, parking lots, or other places where motor vehicles of any kind are stored or left for repair or for any other purpose, or any employee of any such person, who knows or becomes aware of the fact that any motor vehicle so stored or left has upon it, or in it, bullet marks, gunshot marks, blood stains, or marks or evidence of any crime, shall immediately report the facts to the police of a municipal corporation, a sheriff of the county, or a state highway patrol trooper.

Whoever violates this section shall forfeit not more than one hundred dollars, to be recovered on petition as in civil cases, filed by the prosecuting attorney, in the name of the state of Ohio, in the court of common pleas in the county in which such place is located.

(1991 S 144, eff. 8–8–91; 1953 H 1; GC 13431–2)

4501.271 Written request to prevent disclosure of peace officer's residence

(A)(1) A peace officer may file a written request with the bureau of motor vehicles to do either or both of the following:

(a) Prohibit disclosure of the peace officer's residence address as contained in motor vehicle records of the bureau;

(b) Provide a business address to be displayed on the peace officer's driver's license or certificate of registration, or both.

(2) The peace officer shall file the request on a form provided by the registrar of motor vehicles and shall provide any documentary evidence verifying the person's status as a peace officer and business address that the registrar requires pursuant to division (G) of this section.

(B)(1) Except as provided in division (C) of this section, if a peace officer has filed a request under division (A) of this section, neither the registrar nor an employee or contractor of the bureau of motor vehicles shall knowingly disclose the residence address of the peace officer that the bureau obtained in connection with a motor vehicle record.

(2) In accordance with section 149.43 of the Revised Code, the registrar or an employee or contractor of the bureau shall make available for inspection or copying a motor vehicle record of a peace officer who has filed a request under division (A) of this section if the record is a public record under that section, but shall obliterate the residence address of the peace officer from the record before making the record available for inspection or copying. The business address of the peace officer may be made available in response to a valid request under section 149.43 of the Revised Code.

(C) Notwithstanding division (B)(2) of section 4501.27 of the Revised Code, the registrar or an employee or contractor of the bureau may disclose the residence address of a peace officer who files a request under division (A) of this section only in accordance with division (B)(1) of section 4501.27 of the Revised Code or pursuant to a court order.

(D) If a peace officer files a request under division (A)(1)(b) of this section, the officer shall still provide a residence address in any application for a driver's license or license renewal and in any application for a motor vehicle registration or registration renewal. In accordance with sections 4503.101 and 4507.09 of the Revised Code, an officer shall notify the registrar of any change in the officer's residence within ten days after the change occurs.

(E) A certificate of registration issued to a peace officer who files a request under division (A)(1)(b) of this section shall display the business address of the officer. Notwithstanding section 4507.13 of the Revised Code, a driver's license issued to a peace officer who files a request under division (A)(1)(b) of this section shall display the business address of the officer.

(F) The registrar may utilize the residence address of a peace officer who files a request under division (A)(1)(b) of this section in carrying out the functions of the bureau of motor vehicles, including determining the district of registration for any applicable motor vehicle tax levied under Chapter 4504. of the Revised Code, determining whether tailpipe emissions inspections are required, and financial responsibility verification.

(G) The registrar shall adopt rules governing a request for confidentiality of a peace officer's residence address or use of a business address, including the documentary evidence required to verify the person's status as a peace officer, the length of time that the request will be valid, procedures for ensuring that the bureau of motor vehicles receives notice of any change in a person's status as a peace officer, and any other procedures the registrar considers necessary. The rules of the registrar may require a peace officer to surrender any certificate of registration and any driver's license bearing the business address of the officer and, upon payment of any applicable fees, to receive a certificate of registration and license bearing the officer's residence address, whenever the officer no longer is associated with that business address.

(H) As used in this section:

(1) "Motor vehicle record" has the same meaning as in section 4501.27 of the Revised Code.

(2) "Peace officer" means those persons described in division (A)(1), (2), (4), (5), (6), (9), (10), (12), or (13) of section 109.71 of the Revised Code, the house sergeant at arms appointed under division (B)(1) of section 101.311 of the Revised Code, and any assistant sergeant at arms appointed under division (C)(1) of section 101.311 of the Revised Code. "Peace officer" includes state highway patrol troopers but does not include the sheriff of a county or a supervisory employee who, in the absence of the sheriff, is authorized to stand in for, exercise the authority of, and perform the duties of the sheriff.

(2000 S 317, eff. 3–22–01; 2000 H 600, eff. 9–1–00)

4501.34 Records and proceedings of registrar

(A) The registrar of motor vehicles may adopt and publish rules to govern the registrar's proceedings. All proceedings of the registrar shall be open to the public, and all documents in the registrar's possession are public records. The registrar shall adopt a seal bearing the inscription: "Motor Vehicle Registrar of Ohio." The seal shall be affixed to all writs and authenticated copies of records, and, when it has been so attached, the copies shall be received in evidence with the same effect as other public records. All courts shall take judicial notice of the seal.

(B) Upon the request of any person accompanied by a nonrefundable fee of two dollars per name, the registrar may furnish lists of names and addresses as they appear upon the applications for driver's licenses, provided that any further information contained in the applications shall not be disclosed. The registrar shall pay all the fees collected into the state treasury to the credit of the state bureau of motor vehicles fund established in section 4501.25 of the Revised Code.

This division does not apply to the list of qualified driver licensees required to be compiled and filed pursuant to section 2313.06 of the Revised Code.

(2002 S 123, eff. 1–1–04)

Historical and Statutory Notes

Ed. Note: 4501.34 is former 4507.25, amended and recodified by 2002 S 123, eff. 1–1–04; 1995 H 107, eff. (See Historical and Statutory Notes); 1984 H 183, eff. 10–1–84; 1981 H 102; 129 v 381; 128 v 1176; 1953 H 1; GC 6296–31.

Ed. Note: 1995 H 107 Effective Date—The Secretary of State assigned a general effective date of 6–30–95 for 1995 H 107. Pursuant to O Const Art II § 1c and 1d, and RC 1.471, sections of 1995 H 107 that are, or depend for their implementation upon, current expense appropriations are effective 3–31–95; sections of 1995 H 107 that are not, and do not depend for their implementation upon, current expense appropriations are effective 6–30–95. See *Baldwin's Ohio Legislative Service*, 1995, page 3/L–98 for 1995 H 107, § 16.

4501.35 Film production reimbursement fund

There is hereby created in the state treasury the film production reimbursement fund. The fund shall be used by the department of public safety for the purpose of depositing moneys received from other agencies for services and supplies provided for the production of public service announcements, media materials, and training materials. Moneys in the fund shall be expended only for supplies and maintenance of equipment necessary to perform such services.

(2001 H 73, eff. 3–30–01)

4501.351 Order of registrar subject to reversal or modification

An order, except an order relating to a license as defined in section 119.01 of the Revised Code, made by the registrar of motor vehicles may be reversed, vacated, or modified by the court of common pleas of Franklin county, or by the court of common pleas in the county in which the party affected is a resident, or in which the matter complained of arose.

(2002 S 123, eff. 1–1–04)

Historical and Statutory Notes

Ed. Note: 4501.351 is former 4507.26, recodified by 2002 S 123, eff. 1–1–04; 1953 H 1, eff. 10–1–53; GC 6296–32.

4501.36 Reversal or modification of registrar's order by appeal

A proceeding to obtain the reversal, vacation, or modification of an order of the registrar of motor vehicles shall be by appeal. Any party to the proceedings before the registrar shall file notice of the appeal in the court of common pleas on or before the expiration of thirty days from date of entry of the order. The court shall set the appeal for hearing and take any testimony as is necessary to decide the matter. The court shall give the registrar at least ten days' notice of the time and place of the hearing.

(2002 S 123, eff. 1–1–04)

Historical and Statutory Notes

Ed. Note: 4501.36 is former 4507.27, amended and recodified by 2002 S 123, eff. 1–1–04; 1953 H 1, eff. 10–1–53; GC 6296–33.

4501.37 Restrictions against modification by court

No court may reverse, suspend, or delay any order made by the registrar of motor vehicles, or enjoin, restrain, or interfere with the registrar or a deputy registrar in the performance of official duties, except as provided in this chapter and Chapter 4507. or 4510. of the Revised Code.

(2002 S 123, eff. 1–1–04)

Historical and Statutory Notes

Ed. Note: 4501.37 is former 4507.28, amended and recodified by 2002 S 123, eff. 1–1–04; 1953 H 1, eff. 10–1–53; GC 6296–34.

4501.38 Prosecuting attorney to assist registrar

Upon the request of the registrar of motor vehicles, the prosecuting attorney of the county in which any proceedings are pending shall aid in any investigation, prosecution, hearing, or trial held under this chapter or Chapter 4506., 4507., 4510., or 4511. of the Revised Code and shall institute and prosecute any actions or proceedings for the enforcement of the sections contained in those chapters, and for the punishment of all violations of those sections, as the registrar directs.

(2002 S 123, eff. 1–1–04)

Historical and Statutory Notes

Ed. Note: 4501.38 is former 4507.29, amended and recodified by 2002 S 123, eff. 1–1–04; 1953 H 1, eff. 10–1–53; GC 6296–35.

4501.80 Written policy for notification of next of kin

(A) Every law enforcement agency whose law enforcement officers investigate motor vehicle accidents shall develop and adopt a written policy establishing reasonable procedures for determining and notifying the next of kin of any person who is found dead or is pronounced dead at the scene of a motor vehicle accident or who suffers a serious, life-threatening injury in a motor vehicle accident and who the investigating law enforcement officer reasonably determines in all probability will not be able to notify the person's next of kin within a reasonable time after the motor vehicle accident.

After a law enforcement agency adopts a written policy as required by this division, the law enforcement officers employed by that agency shall make a good faith effort to follow the procedures contained in the policy.

(B) The notification under this section of the next of kin of persons who are killed or injured in motor vehicle accidents is hereby deemed to be a governmental function for purposes of Chapter 2744. of the Revised Code.

(2000 S 244, eff. 10–5–00)

CHAPTER 4503

LICENSING OF MOTOR VEHICLES

GENERAL PROVISIONS

4503.01 Definition

"Motor vehicle" as defined in section 4505.01 of the Revised Code applies to sections 4503.02 to 4503.10, and 4503.12 to 4503.18 of the Revised Code. For the purposes of sections 4503.02 to 4503.04, 4503.10 to 4503.12, 4503.182, 4503.19, 4503.21, 4503.22, and 4503.25 of the Revised Code, the term "motor vehicle" also includes a motorized bicycle and a trailer or semitrailer whose weight is four thousand pounds or less.

As used in this chapter, "motor vehicle" does not include a concrete pump or a concrete conveyor.

(2004 H 230, eff. 9–16–04; 1984 S 169, eff. 1–1–85; 1953 H 1)

4503.034 Increased fees for deputy registrars to be based on achievement of certain statewide satisfaction rate

(A) Notwithstanding sections 4503.10, 4503.102, 4503.12, 4503.182, 4503. 24, 4505.061, 4506.08, 4507.24, 4507.50, 4507.52, 4519.03, 4519.05, 4519.10, 4519.56, and 4519.69 of the Revised Code:

(1) Each deputy registrar shall be allowed the increased fee otherwise allowed in those sections and commencing on January 1, 2003, for performing the services specified in those sections only if the deputy registrars achieve a statewide satisfaction rate of at least ninety per cent on the survey conducted by the registrar of motor vehicles under this section. If the deputy registrars fail to achieve a statewide satisfaction rate of at least ninety per cent on the survey, the fee for performing the services specified in those sections shall remain at the rate in effect for the immediately preceding year.

(2) Each deputy registrar shall be allowed the increased fee otherwise allowed in those sections and commencing on January 1, 2004, for performing the services specified in those sections only if the deputy registrars achieve a statewide satisfaction rate of at least ninety per cent on the survey conducted by the registrar under this section. If the deputy registrars fail to achieve a statewide satisfaction rate of at least ninety per cent on the survey, the fee for performing the services specified in those sections shall remain at the rate in effect for the immediately preceding year.

(B) The registrar shall develop and conduct a survey evaluating public satisfaction with the conduct of services by deputy registrars under sections 4503.10, 4503.102, 4503.12, 4503.182, 4503.24, 4505.061, 4506.08, 4507.24, 4507.50, 4507.52, 4519.03, 4519.05, 4519.10, 4519.56, and 4519.69 of the Revised Code. In developing the survey, the registrar also shall establish standards that shall enable a deputy registrar to achieve a ninety per cent satisfaction rating. The ninety per cent satisfaction rate required under divisions (A)(1) and (2) of this section as a condition to increasing the service fees shall be determined on a statewide basis and not on an individual basis. The registrar shall conduct the survey in 2002 to determine the satisfaction rating for purposes of division (A)(1) of this section and shall conduct the survey again in 2003 to determine the satisfaction rating for purposes of division (A)(2) of this section.

(2004 H 230, eff. 9–16–04; 2001 H 94, eff. 6–6–01)

4503.035 Electronic motor vehicle dealers

The registrar of motor vehicles shall designate as an electronic motor vehicle dealer a motor vehicle dealer who meets all of the following criteria:

(A) The dealer holds a current, valid dealer license issued under Chapter 4517. of the Revised Code.

(B) The dealer participates in the title defect recision fund created by section 1345.52 of the Revised Code.

(C) The dealer has the capability, via electronic means, to send motor vehicle title and registration information, as specified by the registrar, to the registrar and clerks of the courts of common pleas.

(D) The dealer meets other criteria for electronic motor vehicle dealers that the registrar may establish by rule adopted under Chapter 119. of the Revised Code.

(2001 S 59, eff. 10–31–01)

4503.036 Limited authority deputy registrars; powers and duties; contract terms

(A) Not later than January 1, 2005, the registrar of motor vehicles shall adopt rules for the appointment of limited authority deputy registrars. Notwithstanding section 4503.03 of the Revised Code, the registrar may appoint the clerk of a court or common pleas or an electronic motor vehicle dealer qualified under section 4503.035 of the Revised Code as a limited authority deputy registrar.

(B) A limited authority deputy registrar may conduct only initial and transfer motor vehicle transactions using electronic means, vehicle identification number inspections, and other associated transactions in a manner approved in the rules that the registrar adopts.

(C) A limited authority deputy registrar may collect and retain a fee of three dollars and fifty cents for each transaction or physical inspection that the limited authority deputy registrar conducts, and shall collect all fees and taxes that are required by law and related to the transaction or inspection in a manner approved by the registrar. A clerk of a court of common pleas shall pay all fees collected and retained under this section into the county treasury to the credit of the certificate of title administration fund created under section 325.33 of the Revised Code.

(D) The rules adopted by the registrar may establish reasonable eligibility standards for clerks and electronic motor vehicle dealers. The rules shall prescribe the terms and conditions of limited authority deputy registrar contracts and shall require each limited authority deputy registrar to sign a contract before assuming any duties as a limited authority deputy registrar. The rules may establish different eligibility standards and contract terms and conditions depending on whether the limited authority deputy registrar is a clerk or an electronic motor vehicle dealer. No contract shall be for a period of more than three years. The contract may contain any other provisions the registrar reasonably prescribes. Each contract shall terminate on a date specified by the registrar.

(E) Any eligible clerk or qualified electronic motor vehicle dealer may make an application to the registrar for appointment as a limited authority deputy registrar. With the approval of the director of public safety, the registrar shall make the appointments from the applications submitted, based upon the discretion of the registrar and director and not upon a competitive basis.

(F) A limited authority deputy registrar is not subject to the contribution limits of division (B) of section 4503.03 of the Revised Code or the filing requirement of division (A) of section 4503.033 of the Revised Code.

(2004 H 230, eff. 9–16–04)

4503.041 Registration of noncommercial trailer weighing four thousand pounds or less

(A) The original owner of any trailer weighing four thousand pounds or less and used exclusively for noncommercial purposes, upon application for initial registration, shall obtain and present such evidence of the trailer's weight as the registrar of motor vehicles may require. Whenever an application for registration other than an initial application by the original owner is made for a trailer to which this section applies, the application shall be accompanied by an affidavit, prescribed by the registrar and signed by the present owner, stating that the weight of the trailer is the same as that indicated by the evidence obtained and presented for initial registration by the original owner, and no other evidence of weight shall be required. This section does not apply to the owner of a boat trailer being registered in accordance with section 4503.173 of the Revised Code.

(B) The owner of a trailer described in division (A) of this section or the operator of a motor vehicle towing such a trailer may tow the trailer directly to and from a scale facility for the purpose of determining the trailer's weight prior to the registration of the trailer provided that at the time of such towing the owner or operator has in the owner's or operator's possession an official weight slip prescribed by the registrar and provided the trailer does not carry any load during such towing.

(2004 H 230, eff. 9–16–04; 1988 H 385, eff. 6–27–88; 1976 H 6; 1972 H 795)

4503.05 Improper use of noncommercial motor vehicle

(A) No person shall use a motor vehicle registered as a noncommercial motor vehicle for other than the purposes set forth in section 4501.01 of the Revised Code.

(B) Whoever violates this section is guilty of a misdemeanor of the fourth degree.

(2002 S 123, eff. 1–1–04; 1977 H 166, eff. 3–7–78)

4503.061 Manufactured or mobile homes; placement on tax list, registration, relocation notice

(A) All manufactured and mobile homes shall be listed on either the real property tax list or the manufactured home tax list of the county in which the home has situs. Each owner shall follow the procedures in this section to identify the home to the county auditor of the county containing the taxing district in which the home has situs so that the auditor may place the home on the appropriate tax list.

(B) When a manufactured or mobile home first acquires situs in this state and is subject to real property taxation pursuant to division (B)(1) or (2) of section 4503.06 of the Revised Code, the owner shall present to the auditor of the county containing the taxing district in which the home has its situs the certificate of title for the home, together with proof that all taxes due have been paid and proof that a relocation notice was obtained for the home if required under this section. Upon receiving the certificate of title and the required proofs, the auditor shall place the home on the real property tax list and proceed to treat the home as other properties on that list. After the auditor has placed the home on the tax list of real and public utility property, the auditor shall deliver the certificate of title to the clerk of the court of common pleas that issued it pursuant to section 4505.11 of the Revised Code, and the clerk shall inactivate the certificate of title.

(C)(1) When a manufactured or mobile home subject to a manufactured home tax is relocated to or first acquires situs in any county that has adopted a permanent manufactured home registration system, as provided in division (F) of this section, the owner, within thirty days after the home is relocated or first acquires situs under section 4503.06 of the Revised Code, shall register the home with the county auditor of the county containing the taxing district in which the home has its situs. For the first registration in each county of situs, the owner or vendee in possession shall present to the county auditor an Ohio certificate of title, certified copy of the certificate of title, or memorandum certificate of title as such are required by law, and proof, as required by the county auditor, that the home, if it has previously been occupied and is being relocated, has been previously registered, that all taxes due and required to be paid under division (H)(1) of this section before a relocation notice may be issued have been paid, and that a relocation notice was obtained for the home if required by division (H) of this section. If the owner or vendee does not possess the Ohio certificate of title, certified copy of the certificate of title, or memorandum certificate of title at the time the owner or vendee first registers the home in a county, the county auditor shall register the home without presentation of the document, but the owner or vendee shall present the certificate of title, certified copy of the certificate of title, or memorandum certificate of title to the county auditor within fourteen days after the owner or vendee obtains possession of the document.

(2) When a manufactured or mobile home is registered for the first time in a county and when the total tax due has been paid as required by division (F) of section 4503.06 of the Revised Code or divisions (E) and (H) of this section, the county treasurer shall note by writing or by a stamp on the certificate of title, certified copy of certificate of title, or memorandum certificate of title that the home has been registered and that the taxes due, if any, have been paid for the preceding five years and for the current year. The treasurer shall then issue a certificate evidencing registration and a decal to be displayed on the street side of the home. The certificate is valid in any county in this state during the year for which it is issued.

(3) For each year thereafter, the county treasurer shall issue a tax bill stating the amount of tax due under section 4503.06 of the Revised Code, as provided in division (D)(6) of that section. When the total tax due has been paid as required by division (F) of that section, the county treasurer shall issue a certificate evidencing registration that shall be valid in any county in this state during the year for which the certificate is issued.

(4) The permanent decal issued under this division is valid during the period of ownership, except that when a manufactured home is relocated in another county the owner shall apply for a new registration as required by this section and section 4503.06 of the Revised Code.

(D)(1) All owners of manufactured or mobile homes subject to the manufactured home tax being relocated to or having situs in a county that has not adopted a permanent registration system, as provided in division (F) of this section, shall register the home within thirty days after the home is relocated or first acquires situs under section 4503.06 of the Revised Code and thereafter shall annually register the home with the county auditor of the county containing the taxing district in which the home has its situs.

(2) Upon the annual registration, the county treasurer shall issue a tax bill stating the amount of annual manufactured home tax due under section 4503.06 of the Revised Code, as provided in division (D)(6) of that section. When a manufactured or mobile home is registered and when the tax for the current one-half year has been paid as required by division (F) of that section, the county treasurer shall issue a certificate evidencing registration and a decal. The certificate and decal are valid in any county in this state during the year for which they are issued. The decal shall be displayed on the street side of the home.

(3) For the first annual registration in each county of situs, the county auditor shall require the owner or vendee to present an Ohio certificate of title, certified copy of the certificate of title, or memorandum certificate of title as such are required by law, and proof, as required by the county auditor, that the manufactured or mobile home has been previously registered, if such registration was required, that all taxes due and required to be paid under division (H)(1) of this section before a relocation notice may be issued have been paid, and that a relocation notice was obtained for the home if required by division (H) of this section. If the owner or vendee does not possess the Ohio certificate of title, certified copy of the certificate of title, or memorandum certificate of title at the time the owner or vendee first registers the home in a county, the county auditor shall register the home without presentation of the document, but the owner or vendee shall present the certificate of title, certified copy of the certificate of title, or memorandum certificate of title to the county auditor within fourteen days after the owner or vendee obtains possession of the document. When the county treasurer receives the tax payment, the county treasurer shall note by writing or by a stamp on the certificate of title, certified copy of the certificate of title, or memorandum certificate of title that the home has been registered for the current year and that the manufactured home taxes due, if any, have been paid for the preceding five years and for the current year.

(4) For subsequent annual registrations, the auditor may require the owner or vendee in possession to present an Ohio certificate of title, certified copy of the certificate of title, or memorandum certificate of title to the county treasurer upon payment of the manufactured home tax that is due.

(E)(1) Upon the application to transfer ownership of a manufactured or mobile home for which manufactured home taxes are paid pursuant to division (C) of section 4503.06 of the Revised Code the clerk of the court of common pleas shall not issue any certificate of title that does not contain or have attached both of the following:

(a) An endorsement of the county treasurer stating that the home has been registered for each year of ownership and that all manufactured home taxes imposed pursuant to section 4503.06 of the Revised Code have been paid or that no tax is due;

(b) An endorsement of the county auditor that the manufactured home transfer tax imposed pursuant to section 322.06 of the Revised Code and any fees imposed under division (F) of section 319.54 of the Revised Code have been paid.

(2) If all the taxes have not been paid, the clerk shall notify the vendee to contact the county treasurer of the county containing the taxing district in which the home has its situs at the time of the proposed transfer. The county treasurer shall then collect all the taxes that are due for the year of the transfer and all previous years not exceeding a total of five years. The county treasurer shall distribute that part of the collection owed to the county treasurer of other counties if the home had its situs in another county during a particular year when the unpaid tax became due and payable. The burden to prove the situs of the home in the years that the taxes were not paid is on the transferor of the home. Upon payment of the taxes, the county auditor shall remove all remaining taxes from the manufactured home tax list and the delinquent manufactured home tax list, and the county treasurer shall release all liens for such taxes. The clerk of courts shall issue a certificate of title, free and clear of all liens for manufactured home taxes, to the transferee of the home.

(3) Once the transfer is complete and the certificate of title has been issued, the transferee shall register the manufactured or mobile home pursuant to division (C) or (D) of this section with the county auditor of the county containing the taxing district in which the home remains after the transfer or, if the home is relocated to another county, with the county auditor of the county to which the home is relocated. The transferee need not pay the annual tax for the year of acquisition if the original owner has already paid the annual tax for that year.

(F) The county auditor may adopt a permanent registration system and issue a permanent decal with the first registration as prescribed by the tax commissioner.

(G) When any manufactured or mobile home required to be registered by this section is not registered, the county auditor shall impose a penalty of one hundred dollars upon the owner and deposit the amount to the credit of the county real estate assessment fund to be used to pay the costs of administering this section and section 4503.06 of the Revised Code. If unpaid, the penalty shall constitute a lien on the home and shall be added by the county auditor to the manufactured home tax list for collection.

(H)(1) Except as otherwise provided in this division, before moving a manufactured or mobile home on public roads from one address within this state to another address within or outside this state, the owner of the home shall obtain a relocation notice, as provided by this section, from the auditor of the county in which the home is located if the home is currently subject to taxation pursuant to section 4503.06 of the Revised Code. The auditor shall charge five dollars for the notice, and deposit the amount to the credit of the county real estate assessment fund to be used to pay the costs of administering this section and section 4503.06 of the Revised Code. The auditor shall not issue a relocation notice unless all taxes owed on the home under section 4503.06 of the Revised Code that were first charged to the home during the period of ownership of the owner seeking the relocation notice have been paid. If the home is being moved by a new owner of the home or by a party taking repossession of the home, the auditor shall not issue a relocation notice unless all of the taxes due for the preceding five years and for the current year have been paid. A relocation notice issued by a county auditor is valid until the last day of December of the year in which it was issued.

If the home is being moved by a sheriff, police officer, constable, bailiff, or manufactured home park operator, as defined in section 3733.01 of the Revised Code, or any agent of any of these persons, for purposes of removal from a manufactured home park and storage, sale, or destruction under section 1923.14 of the Revised Code, the auditor shall issue a relocation notice without requiring payment of any taxes owed on the home under section 4503.06 of the Revised Code.

(2) If a manufactured or mobile home is not yet subject to taxation under section 4503.06 of the Revised Code, the owner of the home shall obtain a relocation notice from the dealer of the home. Within thirty days after the manufactured or mobile home is purchased, the dealer of the home shall provide the auditor of the county in which the home is to be located written notice of the name of the purchaser of the home, the registration number or vehicle identification number of the home, and the address or location to which the home is to be moved. The county auditor shall provide to each manufactured and mobile home dealer, without charge, a supply of relocation notices to be distributed to purchasers pursuant to this section.

(3) The notice shall be in the form of a one-foot square yellow sign with the words "manufactured home relocation notice" printed prominently on it. The name of the owner of the home, the home's registration number or vehicle identification number, the county and the address or location to which the home is being

moved, and the county in which the notice is issued shall also be entered on the notice.

(4) The relocation notice must be attached to the rear of the home when the home is being moved on a public road. Except as provided in divisions (H)(1) and (5) of this section, no person shall drive a motor vehicle moving a manufactured or mobile home on a public road from one address to another address within this state unless a relocation notice is attached to the rear of the home.

(5) If the county auditor determines that a manufactured or mobile home has been moved without a relocation notice as required under this division, the auditor shall impose a penalty of one hundred dollars upon the owner of the home and upon the person who moved the home and deposit the amount to the credit of the county real estate assessment fund to pay the costs of administering this section and section 4503.06 of the Revised Code. If the home was relocated from one county in this state to another county in this state and the county auditor of the county to which the home was relocated imposes the penalty, that county auditor, upon collection of the penalty, shall cause an amount equal to the penalty to be transmitted from the county real estate assessment fund to the county auditor of the county from which the home was relocated, who shall deposit the amount to the credit of the county real estate assessment fund. If the penalty on the owner is unpaid, the penalty shall constitute a lien on the home and the auditor shall add the penalty to the manufactured home tax list for collection. If the county auditor determines that a dealer that has sold a manufactured or mobile home has failed to timely provide the information required under this division, the auditor shall impose a penalty upon the dealer in the amount of one hundred dollars. The penalty shall be credited to the county real estate assessment fund and used to pay the costs of administering this section and section 4503.06 of the Revised Code.

(I) Whoever violates division (H)(4) of this section is guilty of a minor misdemeanor.

(2002 H 520, § 3, eff. 1-1-04; 2002 H 520, § 1, eff. 4-3-03; 2002 S 123, eff. 1-1-04; 2000 H 672, eff. 4-9-01; 1998 S 142, eff. 3-30-99; 1984 S 231, eff. 9-20-84; 1983 H 260; 1980 H 532; 1976 S 359; 131 v H 174; 129 v 284)

4503.062 Registers of manufactured home parks

(A) Every operator of a manufactured home court, or manufactured home park, as defined in section 3733.01 of the Revised Code, or when there is no operator, every owner of property used for such purposes on which three or more manufactured or mobile homes are located, shall keep a register of all manufactured and mobile homes that make use of the court, park, or property. The register shall contain all of the following:

(1) The name of the owner and all inhabitants of each home;

(2) The ages of all inhabitants of each home;

(3) The permanent and temporary post office addresses of all inhabitants of each home;

(4) The license number of each home;

(5) The state issuing each such license;

(6) The date of arrival and of departure of each home;

(7) The make and model of each home, if known and if either of the following applies:

(a) The home enters the court, park, or property on or after January 1, 2003.

(b) Ownership of the home in the court or park, or on the property, is transferred on or after January 1, 2003.

(B) The register shall be open to inspection by the county auditor, the county treasurer, agents of the auditor or treasurer, and all law enforcement agencies at all times.

(C) Any person who fails to comply with this section shall be fined not less than twenty-five nor more than one hundred dollars.

(2002 H 520, eff. 4-3-03; 1998 S 142, eff. 3-30-99; 1984 S 231, eff. 9-20-84; 130 v H 1; 129 v 284)

4503.0611 Tax refund, waiver, or deduction for destroyed or injured manufactured home

Whenever it is made to appear to the county auditor, by the oath of the owner or one of the owners of a manufactured home, or by the affidavit of two disinterested persons who are residents of the township or municipal corporation in which the manufactured home is or was situated, that the home is subject to taxation for the current year under section 4503.06 of the Revised Code and has been destroyed or injured after the first day of January of the current year, the county auditor shall investigate the matter, and shall refund or waive the payment of the current year's taxes on such home as prescribed by divisions (A) and (B) of this section. The oath or affidavit required by this section shall be filed with the county auditor not later than the thirty-first day of January of the year after the year in which the manufactured home was injured or destroyed.

(A) If the auditor determines the injury or destruction occurred during the first half of the calendar year, the auditor shall deduct from the taxes payable on the manufactured home for the current year an amount that, in the county auditor's judgment, bears the same ratio to those taxes as the extent of the injury or destruction bears to the cost or market value of the manufactured home. The auditor shall draw a warrant on the county treasurer to refund that amount. If the taxes have not been paid at the time of the auditor's determination, the auditor may waive the payment of the portion of the tax that would otherwise be refunded under this division.

(B) If the auditor determines the injury or destruction occurred during the second half of the calendar year, the auditor shall deduct from the taxes payable on the manufactured home for the current year one-half of the amount that, in the county auditor's judgment, bears the same ratio to those taxes as the extent of the injury or destruction bears to the cost or market value of the manufactured home. The auditor shall draw a warrant on the county treasurer to refund that amount. If the taxes have not been paid at the time of the auditor's determination, the auditor may waive the payment of the portion of the tax that would otherwise be refunded under this division.

(C) Taxes refunded under this section shall be paid from the county undivided general property tax fund.

(1997 S 123, eff. 10-22-97)

4503.10 Application or preprinted renewal notice for registration; fees and charges; false statements; inspections

(A) The owner of every snowmobile, off-highway motorcycle, and all-purpose vehicle required to be registered under section 4519.02 of the Revised Code shall file an application for registration under section 4519.03 of the Revised Code. The owner of a motor vehicle, other than a snowmobile, off-highway motorcycle, or all-purpose vehicle, that is not designed and constructed by the manufacturer for operation on a street or highway may not register it under this chapter except upon certification of inspection pursuant to section 4513.02 of the Revised Code by the sheriff, or the chief of police of the municipal corporation or township, with jurisdiction over the political subdivision in which the owner of the motor vehicle resides. Except as provided in section 4503.103 of the Revised Code, every owner of every other motor vehicle not previously described in this section and every person mentioned as owner in the last certificate of title of a motor vehicle that is operated or driven upon the public roads or highways shall cause to be filed each year, by mail or otherwise, in the office of the registrar of motor vehicles or a deputy registrar, a written or electronic application or a preprinted registration renewal notice issued under section 4503.102 of the Revised Code, the form of which shall be prescribed by the registrar, for registration for the following registration year, which shall begin on the first day of January of every calendar year and end on the thirty-first day of December in the same year. Applications for registration and registration renewal notices shall be filed at the times established by the registrar pursuant to section 4503.101 of the Revised Code. A motor vehicle owner also may elect to apply for or renew a motor vehicle registration by electronic means using electronic signature in accordance with rules adopted by the registrar. Except as provided in division (J) of this section, applications for registration shall be made on blanks furnished by the registrar for that purpose, containing the following information:

(1) A brief description of the motor vehicle to be registered, including the year, make, model, and vehicle identification number, and, in the case of commercial cars, the gross weight of the vehicle fully equipped computed in the manner prescribed in section 4503.08 of the Revised Code;

(2) The name and residence address of the owner, and the township and municipal corporation in which the owner resides;

(3) The district of registration, which shall be determined as follows:

(a) In case the motor vehicle to be registered is used for hire or principally in connection with any established business or branch business, conducted at a particular place, the district of registration is the municipal corporation in which that place is located or, if not located in any municipal corporation, the county and township in which that place is located.

(b) In case the vehicle is not so used, the district of registration is the municipal corporation or county in which the owner resides at the time of making the application.

(4) Whether the motor vehicle is a new or used motor vehicle;

(5) The date of purchase of the motor vehicle;

(6) Whether the fees required to be paid for the registration or transfer of the motor vehicle, during the preceding registration year and during the preceding period of the current registration year, have been paid. Each application for registration shall be signed by the owner, either manually or by electronic signature, or pursuant to obtaining a limited power of attorney authorized by the registrar for registration, or other document authorizing such signature. If the owner elects to apply for or renew the motor vehicle registration with the registrar by electronic means, the owner's manual signature is not required.

(7) The owner's social security number, if assigned, or, where a motor vehicle to be registered is used for hire or principally in connection with any established business, the owner's federal taxpayer identification number. The bureau of motor vehicles shall retain in its records all social security numbers provided under this section, but the bureau shall not place social security numbers on motor vehicle certificates of registration.

(B) Except as otherwise provided in this division, each time an applicant first registers a motor vehicle in the applicant's name, the applicant shall present for inspection a physical certificate of title or memorandum certificate showing title to the motor vehicle to be registered in the name of the applicant if a physical certificate of title or memorandum certificate has been issued by a clerk of a court of common pleas. If, under sections 4505.021, 4505.06, and 4505.08 of the Revised Code, a clerk instead has issued an electronic certificate of title for the applicant's motor vehicle, that certificate may be presented for inspection at the time of first registration in a manner prescribed by rules adopted by the registrar. An applicant is not required to present a certificate of title to an electronic motor vehicle dealer acting as a limited authority deputy registrar in accordance with rules adopted by the registrar. When a motor vehicle inspection and maintenance program is in effect under section 3704.14 of the Revised Code and rules adopted under it, each application for registration for a vehicle required to be inspected under that section and those rules shall be accompanied by an inspection certificate for the motor vehicle issued in accordance with that section. The application shall be refused if any of the following applies:

(1) The application is not in proper form.

(2) The application is prohibited from being accepted by division (D) of section 2935.27, division (A) of section 2937.221, division (A) of section 4503.13, division (B) of section 4510.22, or division (B)(1) of section 4521. 10 of the Revised Code.

(3) A certificate of title or memorandum certificate of title is required but does not accompany the application or, in the case of an electronic certificate of title, is required but is not presented in a manner prescribed by the registrar's rules.

(4) All registration and transfer fees for the motor vehicle, for the preceding year or the preceding period of the current registration year, have not been paid.

(5) The owner or lessee does not have an inspection certificate for the motor vehicle as provided in section 3704.14 of the Revised Code, and rules adopted under it, if that section is applicable.

This section does not require the payment of license or registration taxes on a motor vehicle for any preceding year, or for any preceding period of a year, if the motor vehicle was not taxable for that preceding year or period under sections 4503.02, 4503.04, 4503.11, 4503.12, and 4503.16 or Chapter 4504. of the Revised Code. When a certificate of registration is issued upon the first registration of a motor vehicle by or on behalf of the owner, the official issuing the certificate shall indicate the issuance with a stamp on the certificate of title or memorandum certificate or, in the case of an electronic certificate of title, an electronic stamp or other notation as specified in rules adopted by the registrar, and with a stamp on the inspection certificate for the motor vehicle, if any. The official also shall indicate, by a stamp or by other means the registrar prescribes, on the registration certificate issued upon the first registration of a motor vehicle by or on behalf of the owner the odometer reading of the motor vehicle as shown in the odometer statement included in or attached to the certificate of title. Upon each subsequent registration of the motor vehicle by or on behalf of the same owner, the official also shall so indicate the odometer reading of the motor vehicle as shown on the immediately preceding certificate of registration.

The registrar shall include in the permanent registration record of any vehicle required to be inspected under section 3704.14 of the Revised Code the inspection certificate number from the inspection certificate that is presented at the time of registration of the vehicle as required under this division.

(C)(1) Commencing with each registration renewal with an expiration date on or after October 1, 2003, and for each initial application for registration received on and after that date, the registrar and each deputy registrar shall collect an additional fee of eleven dollars for each application for registration and registration renewal received. The additional fee is for the purpose of defraying the department of public safety's costs associated with the administration and enforcement of the motor vehicle and traffic laws of Ohio. Each deputy registrar shall transmit the fees collected under division (C)(1) of this section in the time and manner provided in this section. The registrar shall deposit all moneys received under division (C)(1) of this section into the state highway safety fund established in section 4501.06 of the Revised Code.

(2) In addition, a charge of twenty-five cents shall be made for each reflectorized safety license plate issued, and a single charge of twenty-five cents shall be made for each county identification sticker or each set of county identification stickers issued, as the case may be, to cover the cost of producing the license plates and stickers, including material, manufacturing, and administrative costs. Those fees shall be in addition to the license tax. If the total cost of producing the plates is less than twenty-five cents per plate, or if the total cost of producing the stickers is less than twenty-five cents per sticker or per set issued, any excess moneys accruing from the fees shall be distributed in the same manner as provided by section 4501.04 of the Revised Code for the distribution of license tax moneys. If the total cost of producing the plates exceeds twenty-five cents per plate, or if the total cost of producing the stickers exceeds twenty-five cents per sticker or per set issued, the difference shall be paid from the license tax moneys collected pursuant to section 4503. 02 of the Revised Code.

(D) Each deputy registrar shall be allowed a fee of two dollars and seventy-five cents commencing on July 1, 2001, three dollars and twenty-five cents commencing on January 1, 2003, and three dollars and fifty cents commencing on January 1, 2004, for each application for registration and registration renewal notice the deputy registrar receives, which shall be for the purpose of compensating the deputy registrar for the deputy registrar's services, and such office and rental expenses, as may be necessary for the proper discharge of the deputy registrar's duties in the receiving of applications and renewal notices and the issuing of registrations.

(E) Upon the certification of the registrar, the county sheriff or local police officials shall recover license plates erroneously or fraudulently issued.

(F) Each deputy registrar, upon receipt of any application for registration or registration renewal notice, together with the license fee and any local motor vehicle license tax levied pursuant to Chapter 4504. of the Revised Code, shall transmit that fee and tax, if any, in the manner provided in this section, together with the original and duplicate copy of the application, to the registrar. The registrar, subject to the approval of the director of public safety, may deposit the funds collected by those deputies in a local bank or depository to the credit of the "state of Ohio, bureau of motor vehicles." Where a local bank or depository has been designated by the registrar, each deputy registrar shall deposit all moneys collected by the deputy registrar into that bank or depository not more than one business day after their collection and shall make reports to the registrar of the amounts so deposited, together with any other information, some of which may be prescribed by the treasurer of state, as the registrar may require and as prescribed by the registrar by rule. The registrar, within three days after receipt of notification of the deposit of funds by a deputy registrar in a local bank or depository, shall draw on that account in favor of the treasurer of state. The registrar, subject to the approval of the director and the treasurer of state, may make reasonable rules necessary for the prompt transmittal of fees and for safeguarding the interests of the state and of counties, townships, municipal corporations, and transportation improvement districts levying local motor vehicle license taxes. The registrar may pay service charges usually collected by banks and depositories for such service. If deputy registrars are located in communities where banking facilities are not available, they shall transmit the fees forthwith, by money order or otherwise, as the registrar, by rule approved by the director and the treasurer of state, may prescribe. The registrar may pay the usual and customary fees for such service.

(G) This section does not prevent any person from making an application for a motor vehicle license directly to the registrar by mail, by electronic means, or in person at any of the registrar's offices, upon payment of a service fee of two dollars and seventy-five cents commencing on July 1, 2001, three dollars and twenty-five cents commencing on January 1, 2003, and three dollars and fifty cents commencing on January 1, 2004, for each application.

(H) No person shall make a false statement as to the district of registration in an application required by division (A) of this section. Violation of this division is falsification under section 2921.13 of the Revised Code and punishable as specified in that section.

(I)(1) Where applicable, the requirements of division (B) of this section relating to the presentation of an inspection certificate issued under section 3704.14 of the Revised Code and rules adopted under it for a motor vehicle, the refusal of a license for failure to present an inspection certificate, and the stamping of the inspection certificate by the official issuing the certificate of registration apply to the registration of and issuance of license plates for a motor vehicle under sections 4503.102, 4503. 12, 4503.14, 4503.15, 4503.16, 4503.171, 4503.172, 4503.19, 4503.40, 4503.41, 4503.42, 4503.43, 4503.44, 4503.46, 4503.47, and 4503.51 of the Revised Code.

(2)(a) The registrar shall adopt rules ensuring that each owner registering a motor vehicle in a county where a motor vehicle inspection and maintenance program is in effect under section 3704.14 of the Revised Code and rules adopted under it receives information about the requirements established in that section and those rules and about the need in those counties to present an inspection certificate with an application for registration or preregistration.

(b) Upon request, the registrar shall provide the director of environmental protection, or any person that has been awarded a contract under division (D) of section 3704.14 of the Revised Code, an on-line computer data link to registration information for all passenger cars, noncommercial motor vehicles, and commercial cars that are subject to that section. The registrar also shall provide to the director of environmental protection a magnetic data tape containing registration information regarding passenger cars, noncommercial motor vehicles, and commercial cars for which a multi-year registration is in effect under section 4503.103 of the Revised Code or rules adopted under it, including, without limitation, the date of issuance of the multi-year registration, the registration deadline established under rules adopted under section 4503.101 of the Revised Code that was applicable in the year in which the multi-year registration was issued, and the registration deadline for renewal of the multi-year registration.

(J) Application for registration under the international registration plan, as set forth in sections 4503.60 to 4503.66 of the Revised Code, shall be made to the registrar on forms furnished by the registrar. In accordance with international registration plan guidelines and pursuant to rules adopted by the registrar, the forms shall include the following:

(1) A uniform mileage schedule;

(2) The gross vehicle weight of the vehicle or combined gross vehicle weight of the combination vehicle as declared by the registrant;

(3) Any other information the registrar requires by rule.

(2004 H 230, eff. 9–16–04; 2003 H 87, § 4, eff. 1–1–04; 2003 H 87, § 1, eff. 6–30–03; 2002 S 123, eff. 1–1–04; 2001 S 59, eff. 10–31–01; 2001 H 94, eff. 6–6–01; 2001 S 31, eff. 9–19–01; 2000 S 242, eff. 9–14–00; 1998 H 611, eff. 7–1–99; 1997 H 141, eff. 3–3–98; 1997 S 60, eff. 10–21–97; 1996 S 121, eff. 11–19–96; 1996 H 353, eff. 9–17–96; 1995 H 107, eff. (See Historical and Statutory Notes); 1993 H 154, eff. 6–30–93; 1993 S 18; 1992 S 98; 1990 H 831; 1989 H 381, § 1, 7, H 109, § 1, 3; 1988 S 1, § 1, 3, H 373, H 708; 1986 H 382, H 500; 1985 H 201; 1982 S 250, S 242; 1981 H 457; 1978 H 998; 1977 H 3; 1973 H 90; 1971 H 727; 1969 H 501, 594; 132 v S 451, H 919, S 146, S 162; 131 v S 359; 129 v 381; 128 v 117; 126 v 253; 125 v 127; 1953 H 1; GC 6294)

Historical and Statutory Notes

Ed. Note: 1995 H 107 Effective Date—The Secretary of State assigned a general effective date of 6–30–95 for 1995 H 107. Pursuant to O Const Art II § 1c and 1d, and RC 1.471, sections of 1995 H 107 that are, or depend for their implementation upon, current expense appropriations are effective 3–31–95; sections of 1995 H 107 that are not, and do not depend for their implementation upon, current expense appropriations are effective 6–30–95. See *Baldwin's Ohio Legislative Service*, 1995, page 3/L–98 for 1995 H 107, § 16.

4503.11 Application and tax payment required; tax prorated when less than full year

(A) Except as provided by sections 4503.103, 4503.173, 4503.41, 4503.43, and 4503.46 of the Revised Code, no person who is the owner or chauffeur of a motor vehicle operated or driven upon the public roads or highways shall fail to file annually the application for registration or to pay the tax therefor.

(B) Except as provided by sections 4503.12 and 4503.16 of the Revised Code, the taxes payable on all applications made under sections 4503.10 and 4503.102 of the Revised Code shall be the sum of the tax due under division (B)(1)(a) or (b) of this section plus the tax due under division (B)(2)(a) or (b) of this section:

(1)(a) If the application is made before the second month of the current registration period to which the motor vehicle is assigned as provided in section 4503.101 of the Revised Code, the tax due is the full amount of the tax provided in section 4503.04 of the Revised Code;

(b) If the application is made during or after the second month of the current registration period to which the motor vehicle is assigned as provided in section 4503.101 of the Revised Code, and prior to the beginning of the next such registration period, the amount of the tax provided in section 4503.04 of the Revised Code shall be reduced by one-twelfth of the amount of such tax, rounded upward to the nearest cent, multiplied by the number of full months that have elapsed in the current registration period. The resulting amount shall be rounded upward to the next highest dollar and shall be the amount of tax due.

(2)(a) If the application is made before the sixth month of the current registration period to which the motor vehicle is assigned as provided in section 4503.101 of the Revised Code, the amount of tax due is the full amount of local motor vehicle license taxes levied under Chapter 4504. of the Revised Code;

(b) If the application is made during or after the sixth month of the current registration period to which the motor vehicle is assigned as provided in section 4503.101 of the Revised Code and prior to the beginning of the next such registration period, the amount of tax due is one-half of the amount of local motor vehicle license taxes levied under Chapter 4504. of the Revised Code.

(C) The taxes payable on all applications made under division (A)(1)(b) of section 4503.103 of the Revised Code shall be the sum of the tax due under division (B)(1)(a) or (b) of this section plus the tax due under division (B)(2)(a) or (b) of this section for the first year plus the full amount of the tax provided in section 4503.04 of the Revised Code and the full amount of local motor vehicle license taxes levied under Chapter 4504. of the Revised Code for the second year.

(D) Whoever violates this section is guilty of a misdemeanor of the fourth degree.

(2003 H 87, § 4, eff. 1–1–04; 2003 H 87, § 1, eff. 6–30–03; 2002 S 123, eff. 1–1–04; 1990 S 178, § 5, eff. 6–28–90; 1990 H 197; 1988 S 1, H 385; 1984 H 37; 1978 H 998, § 1; 1977 H 3; 1971 H 136; 1953 H 1; GC 12620)

4503.12 Transfer of ownership and registration

(A) Upon the transfer of ownership of a motor vehicle, the registration of the motor vehicle expires, and the original owner immediately shall remove the license plates from the motor vehicle, except that:

(1) If a statutory merger or consolidation results in the transfer of ownership of a motor vehicle from a constituent corporation to the surviving corporation, or if the incorporation of a proprietorship or partnership results in the transfer of ownership of a motor vehicle from the proprietorship or partnership to the corporation, the registration shall be continued upon the filing by the surviving or new corporation, within thirty days of such transfer, of an application for an amended certificate of registration. Upon a proper filing, the registrar of motor vehicles shall issue an amended certificate of registration in the name of the new owner.

(2) If the death of the owner of a motor vehicle results in the transfer of ownership of the motor vehicle to the surviving spouse of the owner or if a motor vehicle is owned by two persons under joint ownership with right of survivorship established under section 2131.12 of the Revised Code and one of those persons dies, the registration shall be continued upon the filing by the survivor of an application for an amended certificate of registration. In relation to a motor vehicle that is owned by two persons under joint ownership with right of survivorship established under section 2131.12 of the Revised Code, the application shall be accompanied by a copy of the certificate of title that specifies that the vehicle is owned under joint ownership with right of survivorship. Upon a proper filing, the registrar shall issue an amended certificate of registration in the name of the survivor.

(3) If the death of the owner of a motor vehicle results in the transfer of ownership of the motor vehicle to a transfer-on-death beneficiary or beneficiaries designated under section 2131.13 of the Revised Code, the registration shall be continued upon the filing by the transfer-on-death beneficiary or beneficiaries of an application for an amended certificate of registration. The application shall be accompanied by a copy of the certificate of title that specifies that the owner of the motor vehicle has designated the motor vehicle in beneficiary form under section 2131.13 of the Revised Code. Upon a proper filing, the registrar shall issue an amended certificate of registration in the name of the transfer-on-death beneficiary or beneficiaries.

(4) If the original owner of a motor vehicle that has been transferred makes application for the registration of another motor vehicle at any time during the remainder of the registration period for which the transferred motor vehicle was registered, the owner may file an application for transfer of the registration and, where applicable, the license plates. The transfer of the registration and, where applicable, the license plates from the motor vehicle for which they originally were issued to a succeeding motor vehicle purchased by the same person in whose name the original registration and license plates were issued shall be done within a period not to exceed thirty days. During that thirty-day period, the license plates from the motor vehicle for which they originally were issued may be displayed on the succeeding motor vehicle, and the succeeding motor vehicle may be operated on the public roads and highways in this state.

At the time of application for transfer, the registrar shall compute and collect the amount of tax due on the succeeding motor vehicle, based upon the amount that would be due on a new registration as of the date on which the transfer is made less a credit for the unused portion of the original registration beginning on that date. If the credit exceeds the amount of tax due on the new registration, no refund shall be made. In computing the amount of tax due and credits to be allowed under this division, the provisions of division (B)(1)(a) and (b) of section 4503.11 of the Revised Code shall apply. As to passenger cars, noncommercial vehicles, motor homes, and motorcycles, transfers within or between these classes of motor vehicles only shall be allowed. If the succeeding motor vehicle is of a different class than the motor vehicle for which the registration originally was issued, new license plates also shall be issued upon the surrender of the license plates originally issued and payment of the fees provided in divisions (C) and (D) of section 4503.10 of the Revised Code.

(5) The owner of a commercial car having a gross vehicle weight or combined gross vehicle weight of more than ten thousand pounds may transfer the registration of that commercial car to another commercial car the owner owns without transferring ownership of the first commercial car. At any time during the remainder of the registration period for which the first commercial car was registered, the owner may file an application for the transfer of the registration and, where applicable, the license plates, accompanied by the certificate of registration of the first commercial car. The amount of any tax due or credit to be allowed for a transfer of registration under this division shall be computed in accordance with division (A)(4) of this section.

No commercial car to which a registration is transferred under this division shall be operated on a public road or highway in this state until after the transfer of registration is completed in accordance with this division.

(6) Upon application to the registrar or a deputy registrar, a person who owns or leases a motor vehicle may transfer special license plates assigned to that vehicle to any other vehicle that the person owns or leases or that is owned or leased by the person's spouse. As appropriate, the application also shall be accompanied by a power of attorney for the registration of a leased vehicle and a written statement releasing the special plates to the applicant. Upon a proper filing, the registrar or deputy registrar shall assign the special license plates to the motor vehicle owned or leased by the applicant and issue a new certificate of registration for that motor vehicle.

(7) If a corporation transfers the ownership of a motor vehicle to an affiliated corporation, the affiliated corporation may apply to the registrar for the transfer of the registration and any license plates. The registrar may require the applicant to submit documentation of the corporate relationship and shall determine whether the application for registration transfer is made in good faith and not for the purposes of circumventing the provisions of this chapter. Upon a proper filing, the registrar shall issue an amended certificate of registration in the name of the new owner.

(B) An application under division (A) of this section shall be accompanied by a service fee of two dollars and seventy-five cents commencing on July 1, 2001, three dollars and twenty-five cents commencing on January 1, 2003, and three dollars and fifty cents commencing on January 1, 2004, a transfer fee of one dollar, and the original certificate of registration, if applicable.

(C) Neither the registrar nor a deputy registrar shall transfer a registration under division (A) of this section if the registration is prohibited by division (D) of section 2935.27, division (A) of section 2937.221, division (A) of section 4503.13, division (D) of section 4503.234, division (B) of section 4510.22, or division (B)(1) of section 4521.10 of the Revised Code.

(D) Whoever violates division (A) of this section is guilty of a misdemeanor of the fourth degree.

(E) As used in division (A)(6) of this section, "special license plates" means either of the following:

(1) Any license plates for which the person to whom the license plates are issued must pay an additional fee in excess of the fees prescribed in section 4503.04 of the Revised Code, Chapter 4504. of the Revised Code, and the service fee prescribed in division (D) or (G) of section 4503.10 of the Revised Code;

(2) License plates issued under section 4503.44 of the Revised Code.

(2004 H 230, eff. 9–16–04; 2002 S 123, eff. 1–1–04; 2002 H 345, eff. 7–23–02; 2001 H 94, eff. 6–6–01; 1997 H 141, eff. 3–3–98; 1997 S 60, eff. 10–21–97; 1996 S 121, eff. 11–19–96; 1996 H 353, eff. 9–17–96; 1994 H 353, eff. 11–9–94; 1994 H 687, eff. 10–12–94; 1994 H 458, eff. 7–20–94; 1993 H 154, eff. 6–30–93; 1993 S 62, § 4; 1992 S 275; 1990 S 178; 1989 H 381; 1988 S 1, H 373; 1981 H 457; 1978 H 998, § 1; 1977 H 3; 1976 H 612; 1971 H 266, H 98; 1953 H 1; GC 6294–1)

4503.13 Certificates of registration for persons with outstanding arrest warrants

(A) A municipal court, county court, or mayor's court, at the court's discretion, may order the clerk of the court to send to the registrar of motor vehicles a report containing the name, address, and such other information as the registrar may require by rule, of any person for whom an arrest warrant has been issued by that court and is outstanding.

Upon receipt of such a report, the registrar shall enter the information contained in the report into the records of the bureau of motor vehicles. Neither the registrar nor any deputy registrar shall issue a certificate of registration for a motor vehicle owner or lessee, when a lessee is determinable under procedures established by the registrar under division (E) of this section, who is named in the report until the registrar receives notification from the municipal court, county court, or mayor's court that there are no outstanding arrest warrants in the name of the person. The registrar also shall send a notice to the person who is named in the report, via regular first class mail sent to the person's last known address as shown in the records of the bureau, informing the person that neither the registrar nor any deputy registrar is permitted to issue a certificate of registration for a motor vehicle in the name of the person until the registrar receives notification that there are no outstanding arrest warrants in the name of the person.

(B) A clerk who reports an outstanding arrest warrant in accordance with division (A) of this section immediately shall notify the registrar when the warrant has been executed and returned to the issuing court or has been canceled.

Upon receipt of such notification, the registrar shall charge and collect from the person named in the executed or canceled arrest warrant a processing fee of fifteen dollars to cover the costs of the bureau in administering this section. The registrar shall deposit all such processing fees into the state bureau of motor vehicles fund created by section 4501.25 of the Revised Code.

Upon payment of the processing fee, the registrar shall cause the report of that outstanding arrest warrant to be removed from the records of the bureau and, if there are no other outstanding arrest warrants issued by a municipal court, county court, or mayor's court in the name of the person and the person otherwise is eligible to be issued a certificate of registration for a motor vehicle, the registrar or a deputy registrar may issue a certificate of registration for a motor vehicle in the name of the person named in the executed or canceled arrest warrant.

(C) Neither the registrar, any employee of the bureau, a deputy registrar, nor any employee of a deputy registrar is personally liable for damages or injuries resulting from any error made by a clerk in entering information contained in a report submitted to the registrar under this section.

(D) Any information submitted to the registrar by a clerk under this section shall be transmitted by means of an electronic data transfer system.

(E) The registrar shall determine the procedures and information necessary to implement this section in regard to motor vehicle lessees. Division (A) of this section shall not apply to cases involving a motor vehicle lessee until such procedures are established.

(2004 H 230, eff. 9–16–04; 2002 H 490, eff. 1–1–04; 1997 H 141, eff. 3–3–98)

SPECIAL LICENSE PLATES

4503.16 State and federal vehicle registration; registration of federal vehicles loaned to state or subdivision

As used in this section, "original owner" includes, with respect to any motor vehicle owned by the federal government and loaned to the state or any of its political subdivisions for use in a federal program, the state or the political subdivision to which the motor vehicle has been loaned and in the name of which the vehicle is registered.

Title to motor vehicles acquired by the state or any of its political subdivisions, whether used for either governmental or proprietary functions, shall be registered. Motor vehicles owned by the federal government and loaned to the state or any of its political subdivisions for use in a federal program shall be registered in the name of the state or political subdivision without the presentation of a certificate of title or other evidence of ownership as required by section 4503.10 of the Revised Code, when the registrar is satisfied that the motor vehicles are on loan from the federal government and are being used exclusively in a federal program. Such vehicles that have been registered and that are used exclusively in the performance of the governmental or proprietary functions of the state or any political subdivision thereof shall not be subject to charge of any kind; but this provision does not exempt the operation of such vehicles from any other provision of Chapters 4501., 4503., 4505., 4507., 4509., 4511., 4515., and 4517. of the Revised Code, and the penal laws relating to them.

The registrar of motor vehicles shall accept any application to register a motor vehicle owned by the federal government that may be made by any officer, department, or agent of such government.

The registrar shall issue permanent license plates for motor vehicles acquired by the state or any of its political subdivisions, or loaned to the state or any of its political subdivisions by the federal government for use in a federal program, which have been registered and that are used exclusively in the performance of the governmental or proprietary functions of the state or any political subdivision thereof, or are used exclusively in a federal program. The registrar shall also issue permanent license plates for all motor vehicles owned and registered by the federal government. Such permanent license plates if lost, stolen, or destroyed, shall be replaced gratis with another permanent number.

Upon the transfer of ownership of a motor vehicle or termination by the federal government of any loan of a motor vehicle for which permanent license plates are issued, the registration of such motor vehicle shall expire and the original owner shall immediately remove such license plates from such motor vehicle. Should the original owner at any time make application for the registration of another motor vehicle, he may file an application for transfer of registration accompanied by the original certificate of registration, for which there shall be no transfer fee.

(1979 H 453, eff. 3–27–80; 1978 H 998, § 1; 1977 H 3; 1973 H 90; 131 v S 359; 128 v 1173; 1953 H 1; GC 6295)

4503.17 Plates and registration for school buses and postal vehicles

(A) No school bus as defined in division (F) of section 4511.01 of the Revised Code is required to pay the annual license tax provided for in section 4503.02 of the Revised Code or to apply for or display registration plates, provided: the school bus complies with the requirements of sections 4511.76 to 4511.77, inclusive, of the Revised Code.

(B) The owner of a school bus, other than a board of education, which is used as a school bus during the school year under a contract with a board of education may, upon proper application for registration and the payment of a license fee of twenty-five dollars, use such bus during summer vacation periods to transport children and their authorized supervisors to and from any camping function sponsored by a nonprofit, tax-exempt, charitable, or philanthropic organization. The application for registration of such bus shall be accompanied by:

(1) An affidavit, prescribed by the registrar of motor vehicles and signed by the owner of such bus, stating that such bus is to be used exclusively, during the summer months, to transport school children to and from any school function or to transport children and their authorized supervisors to and from any camping function sponsored by a nonprofit, tax-exempt, charitable, or philanthropic organization;

(2) A certificate from the state highway patrol stating that such bus is safe for operation in accordance with such standards as are prescribed by the state highway patrol.

The form of the license plate and the manner of its attachment to the vehicle shall be prescribed by the registrar of motor vehicles.

When the post-office department has the exclusive right and supervision of the use of a motor vehicle for a period of one year under contract by a United States civil service employee, the United States government shall be considered the owner of such vehicle and entitled to the registration thereof without charge.

(1971 H 1, eff. 3–26–71; 131 v S 112; 130 v H 1; 129 v 1273; 128 v 721; 1953 H 1; GC 6295–1)

4503.172 Volunteer rescue service organization vehicles exempt

(A) As used in this section, "volunteer rescue service organization" means any organization of volunteers organized to perform as an emergency medical service organization as defined in section 4765.01 of the Revised Code.

(B) A motor vehicle titled in the name of a volunteer rescue service organization and used solely in the transaction of the business of the organization may be registered without the payment of any registration fee and service fee required by sections 4503.02 and 4503.10 of the Revised Code, and without the payment of any applicable county or municipal motor vehicle tax levied under Chapter 4504. of the Revised Code. In applying for registration of such a motor vehicle, a member of a volunteer rescue service organization shall sign an affidavit, prescribed by the registrar of motor vehicles, stating that the vehicle is to be used solely in the transaction of the business of the organization, and shall present satisfactory evidence of certification of the rescue service organization by the department of public safety.

Upon receipt of such evidence, affidavit, and application for registration, the registrar shall issue the applicant permanent license plates.

(1995 S 150, eff. 11–24–95; 1992 S 98, eff. 11–12–92; 1989 H 381; 1977 H 34)

4503.18 Special license, fee; honorary license, fee

Upon application of any United States service organization chartered by congress the registrar of motor vehicles may issue a special license covering the operation for parade and exhibition purposes of especially equipped motor vehicles. Such license shall display the voiture or post number and shall authorize the operation of such motor vehicle for not more than twelve times per year. The annual fee for said license shall be two dollars.

Upon presentation of a paid valid current year registration, the president, commander, or adjutant of a United States service organization chartered by congress may apply for an honorary license designating the organization with which the applicant is affiliated. This honorary plate shall be displayed in lieu of the regular license plate. The original registration card shall be in the vehicle at all times and shall be submitted for inspection upon the demand of any police officer. The annual fee for such license shall be five dollars.

(1971 S 49, eff. 9–21–71; 1953 H 1; GC 6295–2)

4503.181 Historical motor vehicle license plates

(A) As used in this section, "historical motor vehicle" means any motor vehicle that is more than twenty-five years old and that is owned solely as a collector's item and for participation in club activities, exhibitions, tours, parades, and similar uses, but in no event is used for general transportation.

(B) In lieu of the annual license tax levied in sections 4503.02 and 4503.04 of the Revised Code, a license fee of ten dollars is levied on the operation of an historical motor vehicle.

(C) A person who owns an historical motor vehicle and applies for license plates under this section shall execute an affidavit that the vehicle for which plates are requested is owned and operated solely for the purposes enumerated in division (A) of this section, and also setting forth in the affidavit that the vehicle has been inspected and found safe to operate on the public roads and highways in the state. A person who owns an historical motor vehicle and desires to display model year license plates on the vehicle as permitted by this section shall execute at the time of registration an affidavit setting forth that the model year license plates the person desires to display on the person's historical motor vehicle are legible and serviceable license plates that originally were issued by this state. No registration issued pursuant to this section need specify the weight of the vehicle.

(D) A vehicle registered under this section may display historical vehicle license plates issued by the registrar of motor vehicles or model year license plates procured by the applicant. Historical vehicle license plates shall not bear a date, but shall bear the inscription "Historical Vehicle—Ohio" and the registration number, which shall be shown thereon. Model year license plates shall be legible and serviceable license plates issued by this state and inscribed with the date of the year corresponding to the model year when the vehicle was manufactured. Notwithstanding section 4503.21 of the Revised Code, only one model year license plate is required to be displayed on the rear of the historical motor vehicle at all times. The registration certificate and the historical vehicle license plates issued by the registrar shall be kept in the vehicle at all times the vehicle is operated on the public roads and highways in this state.

Notwithstanding section 4503.21 of the Revised Code, the owner of an historical motor vehicle that was manufactured for military purposes and that is registered under this section may display the assigned registration number of the vehicle by painting the number on the front and rear of the vehicle. The number shall be painted, in accordance with the size and style specifications established for numerals and letters shown on license plates in section 4503.22 of the Revised Code, in a color that contrasts clearly with the color of the vehicle, and shall be legible and visible at all times. Upon application for registration under this section and payment of the license fee prescribed in division (B) of this section, the owner of such an historical motor vehicle shall be issued historical vehicle license plates. The registration certificate and at least one such license plate shall be kept in the vehicle at all times the vehicle is operated on the public roads and highways in this state. If ownership of such a vehicle is transferred, the transferor shall surrender the historical vehicle license plates or transfer them to another historical motor vehicle the transferor owns, and remove or obliterate the registration numbers painted on the vehicle.

(E) Historical vehicle and model year license plates are valid without renewal as long as the vehicle for which they were issued or procured is in existence. Historical vehicle plates are issued for the owner's use only for such vehicle unless later transferred to another historical motor vehicle owned by that person. In order to effect such a transfer, the owner of the historical motor vehicle that originally displayed the historical vehicle plates shall comply with division (C) of this section. In the event of a transfer of title, the transferor shall surrender historical vehicle license plates or transfer them to another historical motor vehicle owned by the transferor, but model year license plates may be retained by the transferor. The registrar may revoke license plates issued under this section, for cause shown and after hearing, for failure of the applicant to comply with this section. Upon revocation, historical vehicle license plates shall be surrendered; model year license plates may be retained, but no longer are valid for display on the vehicle.

(F) The owner of an historical motor vehicle bearing historical vehicle license plates may replace them with model year license plates by surrendering the historical vehicle license plates and motor vehicle certificate of registration to the registrar. The owner, at the time of registration, shall execute an affidavit setting forth that the model year plates are legible and serviceable license plates that originally were issued by this state. Such an owner is required to pay the license fee prescribed by division (B) of this section, but the owner is not required to have the historical motor vehicle reinspected under division (C) of this section.

A person who owns an historical motor vehicle bearing model year license plates may replace them with historical vehicle license plates by surrendering the motor vehicle certificate of registration and applying for issuance of historical vehicle license plates. Such a person is required to pay the license fee prescribed by division (B) of this section, but the person is not required to have the historical motor vehicle reinspected under division (C) of this section.

(1998 S 213, eff. 7–29–98; 1996 H 353, eff. 9–17–96; 1991 H 165, eff. 12–17–91; 1973 S 204; 130 v H 195, H 1; 129 v 1087; 125 v 229)

4503.182 Temporary licenses; issuance by dealers

(A) A purchaser of a motor vehicle, upon application and proof of purchase of the vehicle, may be issued a temporary license placard or windshield sticker for the motor vehicle.

The purchaser of a vehicle applying for a temporary license placard or windshield sticker under this section shall execute an affidavit stating that the purchaser has not been issued previously during the current registration year a license plate that could legally be transferred to the vehicle.

Placards or windshield stickers shall be issued only for the applicant's use of the vehicle to enable the applicant to legally operate the motor vehicle while proper title, license plates, and a certificate of registration are being obtained, and shall be displayed on no other motor vehicle.

Placards or windshield stickers issued under this section are valid for a period of thirty days from date of issuance and are not transferable or renewable.

The fee for the placards or windshield stickers issued under this section is two dollars plus a service fee of two dollars and seventy-five cents commencing on July 1, 2001, three dollars and twenty-five cents commencing on January 1, 2003, and three dollars and fifty cents commencing on January 1, 2004.

(B)(1) The registrar of motor vehicles may issue to a motorized bicycle dealer or a licensed motor vehicle dealer temporary license placards to be issued to purchasers for use on vehicles sold by the dealer, in accordance with rules prescribed by the registrar. The dealer shall notify the registrar, within forty-eight hours, of the issuance of a placard by electronic means via computer equipment purchased and maintained by the dealer or in any other manner prescribed by the registrar.

(2) The fee for each placard issued by the registrar to a dealer is seven dollars, of which five dollars shall be deposited and used in accordance with division (D) of this section. The registrar shall charge an additional three dollars and fifty cents for each placard issued to a dealer who notifies the registrar of the issuance of the placards in a manner other than by approved electronic means.

(3) When a dealer issues a temporary license placard to a purchaser, the dealer shall collect and retain the fees established under divisions (A) and (D) of this section.

(C) The registrar of motor vehicles, at the registrar's discretion, may issue a temporary license placard. Such a placard may be issued in the case of extreme hardship encountered by a citizen from this state or another state who has attempted to comply with all registration laws, but for extreme circumstances is unable to properly register the citizen's vehicle.

(D) In addition to the fees charged under divisions (A) and (B) of this section, commencing on October 1, 2003, the registrar and each deputy registrar shall collect a fee of five dollars for each temporary license placard issued. The additional fee is for the purpose of defraying the department of public safety's costs associated with the administration and enforcement of the motor vehicle and traffic laws of Ohio. Each deputy registrar shall transmit the fees collected under this division in the same manner as provided for transmission of fees collected under division (A) of this section. The registrar shall deposit all moneys received under this division into the state highway safety fund established in section 4501.06 of the Revised Code.

(E) The registrar shall adopt rules, in accordance with division (B) of section 111.15 of the Revised Code, to specify the procedures for reporting the information from applications for temporary license placards and windshield stickers and for providing the information from these applications to law enforcement agencies.

(F) Temporary license placards issued under this section shall bear a distinctive combination of seven letters, numerals, or letters and numerals, and shall incorporate a security feature that, to the greatest degree possible, prevents tampering with any of the information that is entered upon a placard when it is issued.

(G) Whoever violates division (A) of this section is guilty of a misdemeanor of the fourth degree. Whoever violates division (B) of this section is guilty of a misdemeanor of the first degree.

(H) As used in this section, "motorized bicycle dealer" means any person engaged in the business of selling at retail, displaying, offering for sale, or dealing in motorized bicycles who is not subject to section 4503.09 of the Revised Code.

(2004 H 230, eff. 9–16–04; 2003 H 87, § 4, eff. 1–1–04; 2003 H 87, § 1, eff. 6–30–03; 2002 S 123, eff. 1–1–04; 2001 S 59, eff. 10–31–01; 2001 H 94, eff. 6–6–01; 2000 H 476, eff. 10–27–00; 1993 H 154, eff. 6–30–93; 1989 H 381; 1988 S 1; 1984 H 632, S 169; 1982 S 242; 1978 H 998, § 1; 1977 H 3; 1976 H 612; 1974 S 471; 1971 S 356; 1969 H 207; 127 v 256)

ISSUANCE OF DISPLAY LICENSE

4503.19 Issuance of certificates of registration and number plates; county identification stickers

(A) Upon the filing of an application for registration and the payment of the tax for registration, the registrar of motor vehicles or a deputy registrar shall determine whether the owner previously has been issued license plates for the motor vehicle described in the application. If no license plates previously have been issued to the owner for that motor vehicle, the registrar or deputy registrar shall assign to the motor vehicle a distinctive number and issue and deliver to the owner in the manner that the registrar may select a certificate of registration, in the form that the registrar shall prescribe, and, except as otherwise provided in this section, two license plates, duplicates of each other, and a validation sticker, or a validation sticker alone, to be attached to the number plates as provided in section 4503.191 of the Revised Code. The registrar or deputy registrar also shall charge the owner any fees required under division (C) of section 4503.10 of the Revised Code. Trailers, manufactured homes, mobile homes, semitrailers, the manufacturer thereof, the dealer, or in transit companies therein, shall be issued one license plate only and one validation sticker, or a validation sticker alone, and the license plate and validation sticker shall be displayed only on the rear of such vehicles. A commercial tractor that does not receive an apportioned license plate under the international registration plan shall be issued two license plates and one validation sticker, and the validation sticker shall be displayed on the front of the commercial tractor. An apportioned vehicle receiving an apportioned license plate under the international registration plan shall be issued one license plate only and one validation sticker, or a validation sticker alone; the license plate shall be displayed only on the front of a semitractor and on the rear of all other vehicles. School buses shall not be issued license plates but shall bear identifying numbers in the manner prescribed by section 4511.764 of the Revised Code. The certificate of registration and license plates and validation stickers, or validation stickers alone, shall be issued and delivered to the owner in person or by mail. Chauffeured limousines shall be issued license plates, a validation sticker, and a livery sticker as provided in section 4503.24 of the Revised Code. In the event of the loss, mutilation, or destruction of any certificate of registration, or of any license plates or validation stickers, or if the owner chooses to replace license plates previously issued for a motor vehicle, or if the registration certificate and license plates have been impounded as provided by division (B)(1) of section 4507.02 and section 4507.16 of the Revised Code, the owner of a motor vehicle, or manufacturer or dealer, may obtain from the registrar, or from a deputy registrar if authorized by the registrar, a duplicate thereof or new license plates bearing a different number, if the registrar considers it advisable, upon filing an application prescribed by the registrar, and upon paying a fee of one dollar for such certificate of registration, a fee of two dollars for each set of two license plates, or one dollar for each single license plate or validation sticker. In addition, each applicant for a replacement certificate of registration, license plate, or validation sticker shall pay the fees provided in divisions (C) and (D) of section 4503.10 of the Revised Code.

Additionally, the registrar and each deputy registrar who either issues license plates and a validation sticker for use on any vehicle other than a commercial tractor, semitrailer, or apportioned vehicle, or who issues a validation sticker alone for use on such a vehicle and the owner has changed the owner's county of residence since the owner last was issued county identification stickers, also shall issue and deliver to the owner either one or two county identification stickers, as appropriate, which shall be attached to the license plates in a manner prescribed by the director of public safety. The county identification stickers shall identify prominently by name or number the county in which the owner of the vehicle resides at the time of registration.

(B) Whoever violates this section is guilty of a minor misdemeanor.

(2002 S 123, eff. 1–1–04; 1999 S 107, eff. 3–23–00; 1999 H 163, eff. 6–30–99; 1998 S 142, eff. 3–30–99; 1997 H 143, eff. 12–18–97; 1997 S 60, eff. 10–21–97; 1996 H 353, eff. 9–17–96; 1995 H 107, eff. (See Historical and Statutory Notes); 1992 S 98, eff. 11–12–92; 1990 H 422, S 382, H 831; 1988 S 1; 1984 S 231; 1982 S 242; 1978 H 998, § 1; 1977 H 3; 1973 H 90; 131 v S 112; 125 v 230; 1953 H 1; GC 6298)

Historical and Statutory Notes

Ed. Note: 1995 H 107 Effective Date—The Secretary of State assigned a general effective date of 6–30–95 for 1995 H 107. Pursuant to O Const Art II § 1c and 1d, and RC 1.471, sections of 1995 H 107 that are, or depend for their implementation upon, current expense appropriations are effective 3–31–95; sections of 1995 H 107 that are not, and do not depend for their implementation upon, current expense appropriations are effective 6–30–95. See *Baldwin's Ohio Legislative Service*, 1995, page 3/L–98 for 1995 H 107, § 16.

4503.191 Multi–year license plates; validation and county identification stickers

(A) The identification license plate shall be issued for a multi-year period as determined by the director of public safety, and shall be accompanied by a validation sticker, to be attached to the license plate. The validation sticker shall indicate the expiration of the registration period to which the motor vehicle for which the license plate is issued is assigned, in accordance with rules adopted by the registrar of motor vehicles. During each succeeding year of the multi-year period following the issuance of the plate and validation sticker, upon the filing of an application for registration and the payment of the tax therefor, a validation sticker alone shall be issued. The validation stickers required under this section shall be of different colors or shades each year, the new colors or shades to be selected by the director.

(B) Identification license plates shall be produced by Ohio penal industries. Validation stickers and county identification stickers shall be produced by Ohio penal industries unless the registrar adopts rules that permit the registrar or deputy registrars to print or otherwise produce them in house.

(2001 H 73, eff. 6–29–01; 1997 H 210, eff. 6–30–97; 1992 S 98, eff. 11–12–92; 1988 S 1; 1978 H 998, § 1; 1977 H 3; 1973 H 90)

MISCELLANEOUS PROVISIONS

4503.20 Maintenance of proof of financial responsibility

(A) As used in this section:

(1) "Dealer engaged in the business of leasing motor vehicles" means any person engaged in the business of regularly making available, offering to make available, or arranging for another person to use a motor vehicle pursuant to a bailment, lease, or other contractual arrangement.

(2) "Motor vehicle" has the meaning set forth in section 4509.01 of the Revised Code.

(B) An application for the registration of a motor vehicle shall contain a statement, to be signed by the applicant either manually or by electronic signature, that does all of the following:

(1) States that the applicant maintains, or has maintained on the applicant's behalf, proof of financial responsibility at the time of application, and will not operate a motor vehicle in this state, unless the applicant maintains, with respect to that motor vehicle or the operation of such vehicle, proof of financial responsibility;

(2) Contains a brief summary of the purposes and operation of section 4509.101 of the Revised Code, the rights and duties of the applicant under that section, and the penalties for violation of that section;

(3) Warns the applicant that the financial responsibility law does not prevent the possibility that the applicant may be involved in an accident with an owner or operator of a motor vehicle who is without proof of financial responsibility.

(C)(1) A person who purchases any motor vehicle from a licensed motor vehicle dealer who agrees to make application for registration of the motor vehicle on behalf of the purchaser shall sign statements that comply with divisions (B) and (F) of this section. The dealer shall submit the statements to the deputy registrar where the dealer has agreed to make application for registration on behalf of the person.

(2) In the case of a person who leases any motor vehicle from a dealer engaged in the business of leasing motor vehicles who agrees to make application for registration of the motor vehicle on behalf of the lessee, the person shall sign a statement that complies with division (B) of this section, and the dealer shall do either of the following:

(a) Submit the statement signed by the person to the deputy registrar where the dealer has agreed to make application for registration on behalf of the person;

(b) Sign and submit a statement to the deputy registrar that certifies that a statement has been signed and filed with the dealer or incorporated into the lease.

The dealer shall submit to the registrar or deputy registrar to whom the dealer submits the application for registration a statement signed by the person that complies with division (F) of this section.

(D) The registrar of motor vehicles shall prescribe the form of the statements required under divisions (B), (C), and (F) of this section, and the manner or manners in which the statements required under divisions (B) and (F) of this section shall be presented to the applicant. Any statement that is required under divisions (B), (C), and (F) of this section shall be designed to enable the applicant to retain a copy of it.

(E) Nothing within this section shall be construed to excuse a violation of section 4509.101 of the Revised Code. A motor vehicle dealer who makes application for the registration of a motor vehicle on behalf of the purchaser or lessee of the motor vehicle is not liable in damages in any civil action on account of the act of making such application for registration or the content of any such application for registration.

(F) In addition to the statements required by divisions (B) and (C) of this section, a person who makes application for registration of a motor vehicle shall be furnished with a form that lists in plain language all the possible penalties to which a person could be subject for a violation of the financial responsibility law, including driver's license suspensions; all fees, including nonvoluntary compliance and reinstatement fees; and vehicle immobilization or impoundment. The person shall read the form and either manually or by electronic signature sign the form, which shall be submitted along with the application for registration as provided in this section. The form shall be retained by the registrar or deputy registrar who issues the motor vehicle registration or the registrar's or deputy registrar's successor for a period of two years from the date of issuance of the registration.

(G) Upon the registration of a motor vehicle, the owner of the motor vehicle is deemed to have agreed to the production of proof of financial responsibility by the owner or the operator of the motor vehicle, upon the request of a peace officer or state highway patrol trooper made in accordance with division (E)(2) of section 4509.101 of the Revised Code.

(H) The registrar shall adopt rules governing the renewal of motor vehicle registrations by electronic means and the completion and submission of statements that comply with divisions (B) and (F) of this section. The registrar shall adopt the rules prescribed by this division in accordance with Chapter 119. of the Revised Code.

(2000 S 242, eff. 9–14–00; 1994 S 20, eff. 4–20–95; 1984 H 767, eff. 8–1–84; 1982 S 250)

4503.21 Registration marks, placards, and stickers; display in plain view

(A) No person who is the owner or operator of a motor vehicle shall fail to display in plain view on the front and rear of the motor vehicle the distinctive number and registration mark, including any county identification sticker and any validation sticker issued under sections 4503.19 and 4503.191 of the Revised Code, furnished by the director of public safety, except that a manufacturer of motor vehicles or dealer therein, the holder of an in transit permit, and the owner or operator of a motorcycle, motorized bicycle, manufactured home, mobile home, trailer, or semitrailer shall display on the rear only. A motor vehicle that is issued two license plates shall display the validation sticker only on the rear license plate, except that a commercial tractor that does not receive an apportioned license plate under the international registration plan shall display the validation sticker on the front of the commercial tractor. An apportioned vehicle receiving an apportioned license plate under the international registration plan shall display the license plate only on the front of a commercial tractor and on the rear of all other vehicles. All license plates shall be securely fastened so as not to swing, and shall not be covered by any material that obstructs their visibility.

No person to whom a temporary license placard or windshield sticker has been issued for the use of a motor vehicle under section 4503.182 of the Revised Code, and no operator of that motor vehicle, shall fail to display the temporary license placard in plain view from the rear of the vehicle either in the rear window or on an external rear surface of the motor vehicle, or fail to display the windshield sticker in plain view on the rear window of the motor vehicle. No temporary license placard or windshield sticker shall be covered by any material that obstructs its visibility.

(B) Whoever violates this section is guilty of a minor misdemeanor.

(2002 S 123, eff. 1–1–04; 1998 S 142, eff. 3–30–99; 1997 H 143, eff. 12–18–97; 1997 S 60, eff. 10–21–97; 1992 S 98, eff. 11–12–92; 1990 S 382, H 831; 1987 H 158; 1986 H 428; 1984 H 632, S 231, S 169; 1973 H 90; 130 v H 1; 126 v 717; 125 v 230, 127; 1953 H 1; GC 12613)

4503.22 Specifications for license plates

The identification license plate shall consist of a placard upon the face of which shall appear the distinctive number assigned to the motor vehicle as provided in section 4503.19 of the Revised Code, in Arabic numerals or letters, or both. The dimensions of the numerals or letters and of each stroke shall be determined by the director of public safety. The license placard also shall contain the name of this state and the slogan "BIRTHPLACE OF AVIATION." The placard shall be made of steel and the background shall be treated with a reflective material that shall provide effective and dependable reflective brightness during the service period required of the placard. Specifications for the reflective and other materials and the design of the placard, the county identification stickers as provided by section 4503.19 of the Revised Code, and validation stickers as provided by section 4503.191 of the Revised Code, shall be adopted by the director as rules under sections 119.01 to 119.13 of the Revised Code. The identification license plate of motorized bicycles and of motor vehicles of the type commonly called "motorcycles" shall consist of a single placard, the size of which shall be prescribed by the director. The identification plate of a vehicle registered in accordance with the international registration plan shall contain the word "apportioned." The director may prescribe the type of placard, or means of fastening the placard, or both; the placard or means of fastening may be so designed and constructed as to render difficult the removal of the placard after it has been fastened to a motor vehicle.

(1996 S 289, eff. 9–27–96; 1994 H 687, eff. 10–12–94; 1993 H 154, eff. 6–30–93; 1992 S 98; 1990 H 831; 1984 S 169; 1982 S 242; 1978 H 998, § 1; 1977 H 1, H 3; 1975 H 1; 1973 H 90; 1971 H 727; 131 v S 79; 128 v 1173; 125 v 127; 1953 H 1; GC 6300)

4503.23 Special license plates for state owned motor vehicles

No motor vehicle designed to carry passengers, owned or leased by the state, or any of its departments, bureaus, commissions, or institutions supported in whole or in part by funds provided by the state, shall be operated or driven by any person unless it has displayed, in a prominent position on both the front and rear of the vehicle, identification plates which shall be the same size, shape, and treated for increased visibility in the same manner as those issued by the registrar of motor vehicles for private vehicles. Such identification plates shall be attached to the vehicle in the same manner as provided by statute for the illumination and attachment of license plates on private vehicles. The registrar shall designate the colors of the license tags which shall be used on state owned cars; such colors shall be other than those used on privately owned motor vehicles, and shall apply only to license plates used on state owned motor vehicles. Said plates shall bear a special serial number, and the words "Ohio State Car."

(1971 H 727, eff. 1–1–74; 128 v 1173; 1953 H 1; GC 6301–3; Source—GC 6301–5)

IMPOUNDMENT OF LICENSES; IMMOBILIZATION OR FORFEITURE OF VEHICLES

4503.231 Special plates for vehicles registered to persons whose registration certificates and license plates have been impounded

(A) No motor vehicle registered in the name of a person whose impounded as provided by division (B)(1) of section 4507.02 of the Revised Code, shall be operated on any highway in this state unless it displays restricted license plates that are a different color from those regularly issued and carry a special serial number that may be readily identified by law enforcement officers. The registrar of motor vehicles shall designate the color and serial number to be used on restricted license plates, which shall remain the same from year to year and shall not be displayed on any other motor vehicles.

The bureau of motor vehicles shall adopt rules providing for the decentralization of the issuance of restricted license plates under this section. The rules shall provide for the issuance of the restricted license plates by at least one agency in each county.

No person operating a motor vehicle displaying restricted license plates as described in this division shall knowingly disguise or obscure the color of the restricted plate.

(B) If a person has been granted limited driving privileges with a condition of the privileges being that the person must display on the vehicle that is driven under the privileges restricted license plates that are described in this section, the person may operate a motor vehicle that is owned by the person's employer only if the person is required to operate that motor vehicle in the course and scope of the person's employment. Such a person may operate that vehicle without displaying on that vehicle restricted license plates that are issued under this section if the employer has been notified that the person has limited driving privileges and of the nature of the restriction and if the person has proof of the employer's notification in the person's possession while operating the employer's vehicle for normal business duties. A motor vehicle owned by a business that is partly or entirely owned or controlled by the person with the limited driving privileges is not a motor vehicle owned by an employer, for purposes of this division.

(C) Whoever violates this section is guilty of a minor misdemeanor.

(2004 H 230, eff. 9–16–04; 2002 S 123, eff. 1–1–04; 1990 S 131, eff. 7–25–90; 1986 S 356; 1984 H 37; 132 v H 518)

4503.232 Destruction of suspended or impounded license plates

(A) Upon the receipt of identification license plates that have been suspended or impounded under any provision of law, and notwithstanding any other provision of law that requires the registrar of motor vehicles to retain the license plates, the registrar may destroy the license plates.

(B) If, as authorized by division (A) of this section, the registrar destroys license plates that have been suspended or impounded, he shall reissue or authorize the reissuance of new license plates to the person to whom the destroyed license plates originally were issued upon payment of a fee in the same amount as the fee specified in section 4503.19 of the Revised Code for replacement of a license plate that has been lost, mutilated, or destroyed and upon payment of a fee in the same amount as specified in division (D) of section 4503.10 of the Revised Code if issued by a deputy registrar or in division (G) of that section if issued by the registrar.

This division applies only if the identification license plates that were destroyed would have been valid at the time the person applies for the replacement license plates. License plates issued under this section shall expire on the same date as the license plates they replace.

(1994 H 687, eff. 10–12–94)

4503.233 Immobilization orders

(A)(1) If a court is required to order the immobilization of a vehicle for a specified period of time pursuant to section 4510.11, 4510.14, 4510.16, 4510.41, 4511.19, 4511.193, or 4511.203 of the Revised Code, the court shall issue an immobilization order in accordance with this division and for the period of time specified in the particular section, and the immobilization under the order shall be in accordance with this section. The court, at the time of sentencing the offender for the offense relative to which the immobilization order is issued or as soon thereafter as is practicable, shall give a copy of the order to the offender or the offender's counsel. The court promptly shall send a copy of the order to the registrar on a form prescribed by the registrar and to the person or agency it designates to execute the order.

The order shall indicate the date on which it is issued, shall identify the vehicle that is subject to the order, and shall specify all of the following:

(a) The period of the immobilization;

(b) The place at which the court determines that the immobilization shall be carried out, provided that the court shall not determine and shall not specify that the immobilization is to be carried out at any place other than a commercially operated private storage lot, a place owned by a law enforcement or other government agency, or a place to which one of the following applies:

(i) The place is leased by or otherwise under the control of a law enforcement or other government agency.

(ii) The place is owned by the offender, the offender's spouse, or a parent or child of the offender.

(iii) The place is owned by a private person or entity, and, prior to the issuance of the order, the private entity or person that owns the place, or the authorized agent of that private entity or person, has given express written consent for the immobilization to be carried out at that place.

(iv) The place is a public street or highway on which the vehicle is parked in accordance with the law.

(c) The person or agency designated by the court to execute the order, which shall be either the law enforcement agency that employs the law enforcement officer who seized the vehicle, a bailiff of the court, another person the court determines to be appropriate to execute the order, or the law enforcement agency with jurisdiction over the place of residence of the vehicle owner;

(d) That neither the registrar nor a deputy registrar will be permitted to accept an application for the license plate registration of any motor vehicle in the name of the vehicle owner until the immobilization fee is paid.

(2) The person or agency the court designates to immobilize the vehicle shall seize or retain that vehicle's license plates and forward them to the bureau of motor vehicles.

(3) In all cases, the offender shall be assessed an immobilization fee of one hundred dollars, and the immobilization fee shall be paid to the registrar before the vehicle may be released to the offender [1] Neither the registrar nor a deputy registrar shall accept an application for the registration of any motor vehicle in the name of the offender until the immobilization fee is paid.

(4) If the vehicle subject to the order is immobilized pursuant to the order and is found being operated upon any street or highway in this state during the immobilization period, it shall be seized, removed from the street or highway, and criminally forfeited and disposed of pursuant to section 4503.234 of the Revised Code.

(5) The registrar shall deposit the immobilization fee into the law enforcement reimbursement fund created by section 4501.19 of the Revised Code. Money in the fund shall be expended only as provided in division (A)(5) of this section. If the court designated in the order a court bailiff or another appropriate person other than a law enforcement officer to immobilize the vehicle, the amount of the fee deposited into the law enforcement reimbursement fund shall be paid out to the county treasury if the court that issued the order is a county court, to the treasury of the municipal corporation served by the court if the court that issued the order is a mayor's court, or to the city treasury of the legislative authority of the court, both as defined in section 1901.03 of the Revised Code, if the court that issued the order is a municipal court. If the court designated a law enforcement agency to immobilize the vehicle and if the law enforcement agency immobilizes the vehicle, the amount of the fee deposited into the law enforcement reimbursement fund shall be paid out to the law enforcement agency to reimburse the agency for the costs it incurs in obtaining immobilization equipment and, if required, in sending an officer or other person to search for and locate the vehicle specified in the immobilization order and to immobilize the vehicle.

In addition to the immobilization fee required to be paid under division (A)(3) of this section, the offender may be charged expenses or charges incurred in the removal and storage of the immobilized vehicle.

(B) If a court issues an immobilization order under division (A)(1) of this section, the person or agency designated by the court to execute the immobilization order promptly shall immobilize or continue the immobilization of the vehicle at the place specified by the court in the order. The registrar shall not authorize the release of the vehicle or authorize the issuance of new identification license plates for the vehicle at the end of the immobilization period until the immobilization fee has been paid.

(C) Upon receipt of the license plates for a vehicle under this section, the registrar shall destroy the license plates. At the end of the immobilization period and upon the payment of the immobilization fee that must be paid under this section, the registrar shall authorize the release of the vehicle and authorize the issuance, upon the payment of the same fee as is required for the replacement of lost, mutilated, or destroyed license plates and certificates of registration, of new license plates and, if necessary, a new certificate of registration to the offender for the vehicle in question.

(D)(1) If a court issues an immobilization order under division (A) of this section, the immobilization period commences on the day on which the vehicle in question is immobilized. If the vehicle in question had been seized under section 4510.41 or 4511.195 of the Revised Code, the time between the seizure and the beginning of the immobilization period shall be credited against the immobilization period specified in the immobilization order issued under division (A) of this section. No vehicle that is immobilized under this section is eligible to have restricted license plates under section 4503.231 of the Revised Code issued for that vehicle.

(2) If a court issues an immobilization order under division (A) of this section, if the vehicle subject to the order is immobilized under the order, and if the vehicle is found being operated upon any street or highway of this state during the immobilization period, it shall be seized, removed from the street or highway, and criminally forfeited, and disposed of pursuant to section 4503.234 of the Revised Code. No vehicle that is forfeited under this provision shall be considered contraband for purposes of section 2933.41, 2933.42, or 2933.43 of the Revised Code, but shall be held by the law enforcement agency that employs the officer who seized it for disposal in accordance with section 4503.234 of the Revised Code.

(3) If a court issues an immobilization order under division (A) of this section, and if the vehicle is not claimed within seven days after the end of the period of immobilization or if the offender has not paid the immobilization fee, the person or agency that immobilized the vehicle shall send a written notice to the offender at the offender's last known address informing the offender of the date on which the period of immobilization ended, that the offender has twenty days after the date of the notice to pay the immobilization fee and obtain the release of the vehicle, and that if the offender does not pay the fee and obtain the release of the vehicle within that twenty-day period, the vehicle will be forfeited under section 4503.234 of the Revised Code to the entity that is entitled to the immobilization fee.

(4) An offender whose motor vehicle is subject to an immobilization order issued under division (A) of this section shall not sell the motor vehicle without approval of the court that issued the order. If such an offender wishes to sell the motor vehicle during the immobilization period, the offender shall apply to the court that issued the immobilization order for permission to assign the title to the vehicle. If the court is satisfied that the sale will be in good faith and not for the purpose of circumventing the provisions of division (A)(1) of this section, it may certify its consent to the offender and to the registrar. Upon receipt of the court's consent, the registrar shall enter the court's notice in the offender's vehicle license plate registration record.

If, during a period of immobilization under an immobilization order issued under division (A) of this section, the title to the immobilized motor vehicle is transferred by the foreclosure of a chattel mortgage, a sale upon execution, the cancellation of a conditional sales contract, or an order of a court, the involved court shall notify the registrar of the action, and the registrar shall enter the court's notice in the offender's vehicle license plate registration record.

Nothing in this section shall be construed as requiring the registrar or the clerk of the court of common pleas to note upon the certificate of title records any prohibition regarding the sale of a motor vehicle.

(5) If the title to a motor vehicle that is subject to an immobilization order under division (A) of this section is assigned or transferred without court approval between the time of arrest of the offender who committed the offense for which such an order is to be issued and the time of the actual immobilization of the vehicle, the court shall order that, for a period of two years from the date of the order, neither the registrar nor any deputy registrar shall accept an application for the registration of any motor vehicle in the name of the offender whose vehicle was assigned or transferred without court approval. The court shall notify the registrar of the order on a form prescribed by the registrar for that purpose.

(E)(1) The court with jurisdiction over the case, after notice to all interested parties including lienholders, and after an opportunity for them to be heard, if the offender fails to appear in person, without good cause, or if the court finds that the offender does not intend to seek release of the vehicle at the end of the period of immobilization or that the offender is not or will not be able to pay the expenses and charges incurred in its removal and storage, may order that title to the vehicle be transferred, in order of priority, first into the name of the entity entitled to the immobilization fee under division (A)(5) of this section, next into the name of a lienholder, or lastly, into the name of the owner of the place of storage.

A lienholder that receives title under a court order shall do so on the condition that it pay any expenses or charges incurred in the vehicle's removal and storage. If the entity that receives title to the vehicle is the entity that is entitled to the immobilization fee under division (A)(5) of this section, it shall receive title on the condition that it pay any lien on the vehicle. The court shall not order that title be transferred to any person or entity other than the owner of the place of storage if the person or entity refuses to receive the title. Any person or entity that receives title may either keep title to the vehicle or may dispose of the vehicle in any legal manner that it considers appropriate, including assignment of the certificate of title to the motor vehicle to a salvage dealer or a scrap metal processing facility. The person or entity shall not transfer the vehicle to the person who is the vehicle's immediate previous owner.

If the person or entity assigns the motor vehicle to a salvage dealer or scrap metal processing facility, the person or entity shall send the assigned certificate of title to the motor vehicle to the clerk of the court of common pleas of the county in which the salvage dealer or scrap metal processing facility is located. The person or entity shall mark the face of the certificate of title with the words "FOR DESTRUCTION" and shall deliver a photocopy of the certificate of title to the salvage dealer or scrap metal processing facility for its records.

(2) Whenever a court issues an order under division (E)(1) of this section, the court also shall order removal of the license plates from the vehicle and cause them to be sent to the registrar if they have not already been sent to the registrar. Thereafter, no further proceedings shall take place under this section, but the offender remains liable for payment of the immobilization fee described in division (A)(3) of this section if an immobilization order previously had been issued by the court.

(3) Prior to initiating a proceeding under division (E)(1) of this section, and upon payment of the fee under division (B) of section 4505.14 of the Revised Code, any interested party may cause a search to be made of the public records of the bureau of motor vehicles or the clerk of the court of common pleas, to ascertain the identity of any lienholder of the vehicle. The initiating party shall furnish this information to the clerk of the court with jurisdiction over the case, and the clerk shall provide notice to the vehicle owner, the defendant, any lienholder, and any other interested parties listed by the initiating party, at the last known address supplied by the initiating party, by certified mail or, at the option of the initiating party, by personal service or ordinary mail.

As used in this section, "interested party" includes the offender, all lienholders, the owner of the place of storage, the person or entity that caused the vehicle to be removed, and the person or entity, if any, entitled to the immobilization fee under division (A)(5) of this section.

(2002 S 123, eff. 1–1–04; 2000 H 80, eff. 6–8–00; 1999 S 22, eff. 5–17–00; 1999 S 107, eff. 3–32–00; 1996 H 676, eff. 10–4–96; 1996 H 353, eff. 9–17–96; 1994 H 687, eff. 10–12–94; 1994 H 236, eff. 9–29–94; 1994 S 82, eff. 5–4–94; 1993 S 62, § 1, eff. 9–1–93; 1993 S 62, § 4; 1993 H 154; 1992 S 275)

[1] So in original; 2002 S 123.

4503.234 Criminal forfeiture orders

(A) If a court is required by section 4503.233, 4503.236, 4510.11, 4510.14, 4510.16, 4510.41, 4511.19, 4511.193, or 4511.203 of the Revised Code to order the criminal forfeiture of a vehicle, the order shall be issued and enforced in accordance with this division, subject to division (B) of this section. An order of criminal forfeiture issued under this division shall authorize an appropriate law enforcement agency to seize the vehicle ordered criminally forfeited upon the terms and conditions that the court determines proper. No vehicle ordered criminally forfeited pursuant to this division shall be considered contraband for purposes of section 2933.41, 2933.42, or 2933.43 of the Revised Code, but the law enforcement agency that employs the officer who seized it shall hold the vehicle for disposal in accordance with this section. A forfeiture order may be issued only after the offender has been provided with an opportunity to be heard. The prosecuting attorney shall give the offender written notice of the possibility of forfeiture by sending a copy of the relevant uniform traffic ticket or other written notice to the offender not less than seven days prior to the date of issuance of the forfeiture order. A vehicle is subject to an order of criminal forfeiture pursuant to this division upon the conviction of the offender of or plea of guilty by the offender to a violation of division (A) of section 4503.236, section 4510.11, 4510.14, 4510.16, or 4511.203, or division (A) of section 4511.19 of the Revised Code, or a municipal ordinance that is substantially equivalent to any of those sections or divisions.

(B)(1) Prior to the issuance of an order of criminal forfeiture pursuant to this section, the law enforcement agency that employs the law enforcement officer who seized the vehicle shall conduct or cause to be conducted a search of the appropriate public records that relate to the vehicle and shall make or cause to be made reasonably diligent inquiries to identify any lienholder or any person or entity with an ownership interest in the vehicle. The court that is to issue the forfeiture order also shall cause a notice of the potential order relative to the vehicle and of the expected manner of disposition of the vehicle after its forfeiture to be sent to any lienholder or person who is known to the court to have any right, title, or interest in the vehicle. The court shall give the notice by certified mail, return receipt requested, or by personal service.

(2) No order of criminal forfeiture shall be issued pursuant to this section if a lienholder or other person with an ownership interest in the vehicle establishes to the court, by a preponderance of the evidence after filing a motion with the court, that the lienholder or other person neither knew nor should have known after a reasonable inquiry that the vehicle would be used or involved, or likely would be used or involved, in the violation resulting in the issuance of the order of criminal forfeiture or the violation of the order of immobilization issued under section 4503.233 of the Revised Code, that the lienholder or other person did not expressly or impliedly consent to the use or involvement of the vehicle in that violation, and that the lien or ownership interest was perfected pursuant to law prior to the seizure of the vehicle under section 4503.236, 4510.41, 4511.195, or 4511.203 of the Revised Code. If the lienholder or holder of the ownership interest satisfies the court that these criteria have been met, the court shall preserve the lienholder's or other person's lien or interest, and the court either shall return the vehicle to the holder, or shall order that the proceeds of any sale held pursuant to division (C)(2) of this section be paid to the lienholder or holder of the interest less the costs of seizure, storage, and maintenance of the vehicle. The court shall not return a vehicle to a lienholder or a holder of an ownership interest unless the lienholder or holder submits an affidavit to the court that states that the lienholder or holder will not return the vehicle to the person from whom the vehicle was seized pursuant to the order of criminal forfeiture or to any member of that person's family and will not otherwise knowingly permit that person or any member of that person's family to obtain possession of the vehicle.

(3) No order of criminal forfeiture shall be issued pursuant to this section if a person with an interest in the vehicle establishes to the court, by a preponderance of the evidence after filing a motion with the court, that the person neither knew nor should have known after a reasonable inquiry that the vehicle had been used or was involved in the violation resulting in the issuance of the order of criminal forfeiture or the violation of the order of immobilization issued under section 4503.233 of the Revised Code, that the person did not expressly or impliedly consent to the use or involvement of the vehicle in that violation, that the interest was perfected in good faith and for value pursuant to law between the time of the arrest of the offender and the final disposition of the criminal charge in question, and that the vehicle was in the possession of the interest holder at the time of the perfection of the interest. If the court is satisfied that the interest holder has met these criteria, the court shall preserve the interest holder's interest, and the court either shall return the vehicle to the interest holder or order that the proceeds of any sale held pursuant to division (C) of this section be paid to the holder of the interest less the costs of seizure, storage, and maintenance of the vehicle. The court shall not return a vehicle to an interest holder unless the holder submits an affidavit to the court stating that the holder will not return the vehicle to the person from whom the holder acquired the holder's interest, nor to any member of that person's family, and the holder will not otherwise knowingly permit that person or any member of that person's family to obtain possession of the vehicle.

(C) A vehicle ordered criminally forfeited to the state pursuant to this section shall be disposed of as follows:

(1) It shall be given to the law enforcement agency that employs the law enforcement officer who seized the vehicle, if that agency desires to have it;

(2) If a vehicle is not disposed of pursuant to division (C)(1) of this section, the vehicle shall be sold, without appraisal, if the value of the vehicle is two thousand dollars or more as determined by publications of the national auto dealer's association, at a public auction to the highest bidder for cash. Prior to the sale, the prosecuting attorney in the case shall cause a notice of the proposed sale to be given in accordance with law. The court shall cause notice of the sale of the vehicle to be published in a newspaper of general circulation in the county in which the court is located at least seven days prior to the date of the sale. The proceeds of a sale under this division or division (F) of this section shall be applied in the following order:

(a) First, they shall be applied to the payment of the costs incurred in connection with the seizure, storage, and maintenance of, and provision of security for, the vehicle, any proceeding arising out of the forfeiture, and if any, the sale.

(b) Second, the remaining proceeds after compliance with division (C)(2)(a) of this section, shall be applied to the payment of the value of any lien or ownership interest in the vehicle preserved under division (B) of this section.

(c) Third, the remaining proceeds, after compliance with divisions (C)(2)(a) and (b) of this section, shall be applied to the appropriate funds in accordance with divisions (D)(1)(c) and (2) of section 2933.43 of the Revised Code, provided that the total of the amount so deposited under this division shall not exceed one thousand dollars. The remaining proceeds deposited under this division shall be used only for the purposes authorized by those divisions and division (D)(3)(a)(ii) of that section.

(d) Fourth, the remaining proceeds after compliance with divisions (C)(2)(a) and (b) of this section and after deposit of a total amount of one thousand dollars under division (C)(2)(c) of this section shall be applied so that fifty per cent of those remaining proceeds is paid into the reparation fund established by section 2743.191 of the Revised Code, twenty-five per cent is paid into the drug abuse resistance education programs fund created by division (F)(2)(e) of section 4511.191 of the Revised Code and shall be used only for the purposes authorized by division

(F)(2)(e) of that section, and twenty-five per cent is applied to the appropriate funds in accordance with division (D)(1)(c) of section 2933.43 of the Revised Code. The proceeds deposited into any fund described in section 2933.43 of the Revised Code shall be used only for the purposes authorized by division (D)(1)(c), (2), and (3)(a)(ii) of that section.

(D) Except as provided in division (E) of section 4511.203 of the Revised Code and notwithstanding any other provision of law, neither the registrar of motor vehicles nor any deputy registrar shall accept an application for the registration of any motor vehicle in the name of any person, or register any motor vehicle in the name of any person, if both of the following apply:

(1) Any vehicle registered in the person's name was criminally forfeited under this section and section 4503.233, 4503.236, 4510.10, 4510.11, 4510.14, 4510.16, 4510.161, 4510.41, 4511.19, 4511.193, or 4511.203 of the Revised Code;

(2) Less than five years have expired since the issuance of the most recent order of criminal forfeiture issued in relation to a vehicle registered in the person's name.

(E) If a court is required by section 4503.233, 4503.236, 4510.10, 4510.11, 4510.14, 4510.16, 4510.161, 4510.41, 4511.19, 4511.193, or 4511.203 of the Revised Code to order the criminal forfeiture to the state of a vehicle, and the title to the motor vehicle is assigned or transferred, and division (B)(2) or (3) of this section applies, in addition to or independent of any other penalty established by law, the court may fine the offender the value of the vehicle as determined by publications of the national auto dealer's association. The proceeds from any fine imposed under this division shall be distributed in accordance with division (C)(2) of this section.

(F) As used in this section and divisions (D)(1)(c), (D)(2), and (D)(3)(a)(ii) of section 2933.43 of the Revised Code in relation to proceeds of the sale of a vehicle under division (C) of this section, "prosecuting attorney" includes the prosecuting attorney, village solicitor, city director of law, or similar chief legal officer of a municipal corporation who prosecutes the case resulting in the conviction or guilty plea in question.

(G) If the vehicle to be forfeited has an average retail value of less than two thousand dollars as determined by publications of the national auto dealer's association, no public auction is required to be held. In such a case, the court may direct that the vehicle be disposed of in any manner that it considers appropriate, including assignment of the certificate of title to the motor vehicle to a salvage dealer or a scrap metal processing facility. The court shall not transfer the vehicle to the person who is the vehicle's immediate previous owner.

If the court assigns the motor vehicle to a salvage dealer or scrap metal processing facility and the court is in possession of the certificate of title to the motor vehicle, it shall send the assigned certificate of title to the motor vehicle to the clerk of the court of common pleas of the county in which the salvage dealer or scrap metal processing facility is located. The court shall mark the face of the certificate of title with the words "FOR DESTRUCTION" and shall deliver a photocopy of the certificate of title to the salvage dealer or scrap metal processing facility for its records.

If the court is not in possession of the certificate of title to the motor vehicle, the court shall issue an order transferring ownership of the motor vehicle to a salvage dealer or scrap metal processing facility, send the order to the clerk of the court of common pleas of the county in which the salvage dealer or scrap metal processing facility is located, and send a photocopy of the order to the salvage dealer or scrap metal processing facility for its records. The clerk shall make the proper notations or entries in the clerk's records concerning the disposition of the motor vehicle.

(2002 S 123, eff. 1–1–04; 1996 H 676, eff. 10–4–96; 1996 H 353, eff. 9–17–96; 1994 S 82, eff. 5–4–94; 1993 S 62, § 1, eff. 9–1–93; 1993 S 62, § 4; 1992 S 275)

4503.236 Operation of motor vehicle ordered immobilized; forfeiture

(A) No person shall operate a motor vehicle or permit the operation of a motor vehicle upon any public or private property used by the public for vehicular travel or parking knowing or having reasonable cause to believe that the motor vehicle has been ordered immobilized pursuant to an immobilization order issued under section 4503.233 of the Revised Code.

(B) A motor vehicle that is operated by a person during a violation of division (A) of this section shall be criminally forfeited to the state in accordance with the procedures contained in section 4503.234 of the Revised Code.

(C) Whoever violates division (A) of this section is guilty of a misdemeanor of the second degree.

(2002 S 123, eff. 1–1–04; 1996 H 353, eff. 9–17–96)

MANUFACTURERS AND DEALERS

4503.27 Registration requirements for manufacturers, dealers, and distributors

A manufacturer, dealer, or distributor shall make application for registration, for each place in this state at which the business of manufacturing, dealing, or distributing of motor vehicles is carried on. The application shall show the make of motor vehicles manufactured, dealt in, or distributed at such place and shall show the taxing district in which the place of business is located. Upon the filing of such application and the payment of the annual tax and postage therefor, the registrar of motor vehicles shall assign to the applicant a distinctive number which must be carried and displayed by each such motor vehicle in like manner as provided by law for other motor vehicles while it is operated on the public highway until it is sold or transferred. At the time the registrar assigns the distinctive number the registrar shall furnish one placard with the number thereon. Such manufacturer, dealer, or distributor may procure a reasonable number of certified copies of the registration certificate upon the payment for each of an annual fee of five dollars and the appropriate postage as required by the registrar. With each of the certified copies the registrar shall furnish one placard with the same numbering provided in the original registration certificate, and shall add thereto such special designation as necessary to distinguish one set of placards from another.

The registrar shall not assign any distinctive number and shall not furnish any placards to any dealer or distributor unless the dealer or distributor, at the time of making application for the placards, produces evidence to show that the dealer or distributor is the holder either of a motor vehicle dealer's license required by section 4517.04 or 4517.05 of the Revised Code or a distributor's license required by section 4517.08 of the Revised Code. Such evidence shall be presented in the manner prescribed by the registrar.

(1997 S 60, eff. 10–21–97; 1977 S 264, eff. 11–4–77; 1974 H 1161; 125 v 230; 1953 H 1; GC 6301)

4503.271 New motor vehicles being transported by railroad car; operation without license plate or placard

A new motor vehicle may be operated on the public roads or highways of this state without displaying a license plate or placard issued to a manufacturer, dealer, or distributor under section 4503.27 of the Revised Code or any other license plate specified in the Revised Code if all of the following apply to the new motor vehicle:

(A) The new motor vehicle was being transported on a railroad car;

(B) The railroad car or the train of which the railroad car was a part was involved in an accident that required the unloading of the new motor vehicle from the railroad car in order to preserve its condition or to facilitate the process of returning the accident site to its normal state;

(C) The operator of the new motor vehicle was instructed by a law enforcement officer at the accident site to drive the new motor vehicle from the accident site directly to another location for the purpose of removing the new motor vehicle from the accident site and storing the new motor vehicle;

(D) The operator of the new motor vehicle proceeds from the accident site to the storage location utilizing the most direct route.

(1996 H 353, eff. 9–17–96)

4503.28 Failure to register prohibited

(A) No person who is a manufacturer of, dealer in, or distributor of motor vehicles shall fail to file an application for registration and to pay the tax for the registration and to apply for and pay the legal fees for as many certified copies of the registration as the law requires.

(B) Whoever violates this section is guilty of a misdemeanor of the fourth degree.

(2002 S 123, eff. 1–1–04; 1974 H 1161, eff. 9–30–74; 1953 H 1; GC 12621)

4503.30 Display of placards issued to manufacturers or dealers

(A) Any placards issued by the registrar of motor vehicles and bearing the distinctive number assigned to a manufacturer, dealer, or distributor pursuant to section 4503.27 of the Revised Code may be displayed on any motor vehicle, other than commercial cars, or on any motorized bicycle owned by the manufacturer, dealer, or distributor, or lawfully in the possession or control of the manufacturer, or the agent or employee of the manufacturer, the dealer, or the agent or employee of the dealer, the distributor, or the agent or employee of the distributor, and shall be displayed on no other motor vehicle or motorized bicycle. A placard may be displayed on a motor vehicle, other than a commercial car, owned by a dealer when the vehicle is in transit from a dealer to a purchaser, when the vehicle is being demonstrated for sale or lease, or when the vehicle otherwise is being utilized by the dealer. A vehicle bearing a placard issued to a dealer under section 4503.27 of the Revised Code may be operated by the dealer, an agent or employee of the dealer, a prospective purchaser, or a third party operating the vehicle with the permission of the dealer.

Such placards may be displayed on commercial cars only when the cars are in transit from a manufacturer to a dealer, from a distributor to a dealer or distributor, or from a dealer to a purchaser, or when the cars are being demonstrated for sale or lease, and shall not be displayed when the cars are being used for delivery, hauling, transporting, or other commercial purpose.

(B) Whoever violates this section is guilty of a misdemeanor of the third degree.

(2002 S 123, eff. 1–1–04; 1996 S 182, eff. 12–3–96; 1984 S 169, eff. 1–1–85; 1974 H 1161; 1953 H 1; GC 6301–1a)

4503.301 Commercial car demonstration placard

(A) A manufacturer, dealer, or distributor of motor vehicles may apply for a reasonable number of commercial car demonstration placards. The application shall show the make of commercial cars, commercial tractors, trailers, and semitrailers manufactured, dealt, or distributed in and shall show the taxing district in which the applicant's place of business is located.

Upon the filing of such application and the payment of an annual fee of five hundred dollars and appropriate postage as required by the registrar of motor vehicles, the registrar shall assign to the applicant a distinctive placard and number. Such placards shall be known as "commercial car demonstration placards," and shall expire on a date prescribed by the registrar. Upon the first application by any person for such placards, the registrar shall prorate the annual fee in accordance with section 4503.11 of the Revised Code; for all renewals or replacements of such placards, the registrar shall collect the full amount of the annual fee.

Commercial car demonstration placards may be displayed on commercial cars, commercial tractors, trailers and semitrailers owned by the manufacturer, dealer, or distributor, when those vehicles are operated by or being demonstrated to a prospective purchaser. In addition to the purposes permitted by section 4503.30 of the Revised Code, the placards provided for in this section may be displayed on vehicles operated or used for delivery, hauling, transporting, or any other lawful purpose. When such placards are used, the placards provided for in section 4503.30 of the Revised Code need not be displayed.

The operator of any commercial car, commercial tractor, trailer, or semitrailer displaying the placards provided for in this section, at all times, shall carry with the operator a letter from the manufacturer, dealer, or distributor authorizing the use of such manufacturer's, dealer's, or distributor's commercial car demonstration placards.

When such placards are used on any commercial car or commercial tractor, such power unit shall be considered duly registered and licensed for the purposes of section 4503.38 of the Revised Code.

(B) No manufacturer, dealer, or distributor of motor vehicles shall use the commercial car demonstration placard for purposes other than those authorized by this section.

(C) Whoever violates division (B) of this section is guilty of a misdemeanor of the third degree.

(2002 S 123, eff. 1–1–04; 1997 S 60, eff. 10–21–97; 1974 H 1161, eff. 9–30–74; 132 v S 272)

PERSONS OTHER THAN MANUFACTURERS AND DEALERS

4503.31 Annual registration by persons other than manufacturers, dealers, and distributors; use of placards

As used in this section, "person" includes, but is not limited to, any person engaged in the business of manufacturing or distributing, or selling at retail, displaying, offering for sale, or dealing in, motorized bicycles who is not subject to section 4503.09 of the Revised Code, or an Ohio nonprofit corporation engaged in the business of testing of motor vehicles.

Persons other than manufacturers, dealers, or distributors may register annually with the registrar of motor vehicles and obtain placards to be displayed on motor vehicles as provided by this section. Applications for annual registration shall be made at the time provided for payment of the tax and postage imposed on manufacturers, dealers, or distributors and shall be in the manner to be prescribed by the registrar. The fee for such registration shall be twenty-five dollars and shall not be reduced when the registration is for a part of a year. Applicants may procure a reasonable number of certified copies of such registration upon the payment of a fee of five dollars and appropriate postage as required by the registrar for each copy.

Upon the filing of the application and the payment of the fee and postage prescribed by this section, the registrar shall issue to each applicant a certificate of registration and assign a distinctive number and furnish one placard with the number thereon. With each of the certified copies of the registration provided for in this section the registrar shall furnish one placard with the same numbering assigned in the original registration certificate and shall add thereto such special designation as necessary to distinguish one set of placards from another. All placards furnished by the registrar pursuant to this section shall be so marked as to be distinguishable from placards issued dealers, manufacturers, or distributors. Placards issued pursuant to this section may be used only on motor vehicles or motorized bicycles owned and being used in testing or being demonstrated for purposes of sale or lease; or on motor vehicles subject to the rights and remedies of a secured party being exercised under Chapter 1309. of the Revised Code; or on motor vehicles being held or transported by any insurance company for purposes of salvage disposition; or on motor vehicles being transported by any persons regularly engaged in salvage operations or scrap metal processing from the point of acquisition to their established place of business; or on motor vehicles owned by or in the lawful possession of an Ohio nonprofit corporation while being used in the testing of those motor vehicles.

Placards issued pursuant to this section also may be used by persons regularly engaged in the business of rustproofing, reconditioning, or installing equipment or trim on motor vehicles for motor vehicle dealers and shall be used exclusively when such motor vehicles are being transported to or from the motor vehicle dealer's place of business; and by persons engaged in manufacturing articles for attachment to motor vehicles when such motor vehicles are being transported to or from places where mechanical equipment is attached to the chassis of such new motor vehicles; or on motor vehicles being towed by any persons regularly and primarily engaged in the business of towing motor vehicles while such vehicle is being towed to a point of storage.

Placards issued pursuant to this section also may be used on trailers being transported by persons engaged in the business of selling tangible personal property other than motor vehicles.

No person required to register an apportionable vehicle under the international registration plan shall apply for or receive a placard for that vehicle under this section.

The fees collected by the registrar pursuant to this section shall be paid into the state bureau of motor vehicles fund established in section 4501.25 of the Revised Code and used for the purposes described in that section.

(2001 S 74, eff. 7–1–01; 1999 H 306, eff. 11–22–99; 1997 S 60, eff. 10–21–97; 1995 H 107, eff. (See Historical and Statutory Notes); 1990 H 831, eff. 7–17–90; 1988 S 321; 1984 S 169; 1978 H 857; 1974 H 1161; 1969 S 344; 132 v H 145; 130 v S 88; 129 v 381, 374; 125 v 230; 1953 H 1; GC 6301–2)

Historical and Statutory Notes

Ed. Note: 1995 H 107 Effective Date—The Secretary of State assigned a general effective date of 6–30–95 for 1995 H 107. Pursuant to O Const Art II § 1c and 1d, and RC 1.471, sections of 1995 H 107 that are, or depend for their implementation upon, current expense appropriations are effective 3–31–95; sections of 1995 H 107 that are not, and do not depend for their implementation upon, current expense appropriations are effective 6–30–95. See *Baldwin's Ohio Legislative Service*, 1995, page 3/L–98 for 1995 H 107, § 16.

4503.311 Dealer's plates for manufacturers or dealers in boat trailers

A manufacturer of or dealer in trailers for transporting watercraft may apply for registration with the registrar of motor vehicles for each place in this state where the manufacturer or dealer carries on the business of manufacturing or dealing in such trailers. Applications for annual registration shall be made at the time provided for payment of the tax imposed on manufacturers and dealers by section 4503.09 of the Revised Code and shall be in the manner to be prescribed by the registrar. The fee for such registration shall be twenty-five dollars and shall not be reduced when the registration is for a part of a year.

Upon the filing of such application and the payment of the fee and appropriate postage as required by the registrar of motor vehicles, the registrar shall assign to the applicant a distinctive number which shall be displayed on the rear of each trailer while it is operated on the public highway. Such trailer may be operated on the public highway while loaded, until it is sold or transferred. At the time the registrar assigns the distinctive number, the registrar shall furnish one placard with the number thereon. Such manufacturer or dealer may procure a reasonable number of certified copies of the registration certificate upon the payment of a fee of five dollars and postage. With each of such certified copies, the registrar shall furnish one placard with the same number provided in the original registration certificate, and shall add thereto such special designation as necessary to distinguish one set of placards from another. All placards furnished by the registrar pursuant to this section shall be so marked as to be distinguishable from placards issued to dealers in or manufacturers of motor vehicles.

The fees collected by the registrar pursuant to this section shall be paid into the state bureau of motor vehicles fund established in section 4501.25 of the Revised Code and used for the purposes described in that section.

(1997 S 60, eff. 10–21–97; 1995 H 107, eff. (See Historical and Statutory Notes); 1981 H 124, eff. 1–1–82; 132 v H 761)

Historical and Statutory Notes

Ed. Note: 1995 H 107 Effective Date—The Secretary of State assigned a general effective date of 6–30–95 for 1995 H 107. Pursuant to O Const Art II § 1c and 1d, and RC 1.471, sections of 1995 H 107 that are, or depend for their implementation upon, current expense appropriations are effective 3–31–95; sections of 1995 H 107 that are not, and do not depend for their implementation upon, current expense appropriations are effective 6–30–95. See *Baldwin's Ohio Legislative Service*, 1995, page 3/L–98 for 1995 H 107, § 16.

4503.312 Registration for manufacturer or distributor of certain trailers

As used in this section:

(A) "Utility trailer" means any trailer, except a travel trailer or trailer for transporting watercraft, having a gross weight of less than four thousand pounds.

(B) "Snowmobile" and "all-purpose vehicle" have the same meaning as in section 4519.01 of the Revised Code.

(C) "Distributor" means any person authorized by a manufacturer of utility trailers or trailers for transporting motorcycles, snowmobiles, or all-purpose vehicles to distribute new trailers to persons for purposes of resale.

A manufacturer or distributor of utility trailers or trailers for transporting motorcycles, snowmobiles, or all-purpose vehicles may apply for registration with the registrar of motor vehicles for each place in this state where the manufacturer or distributor carries on the business of manufacturing or distributing such trailers. Applications for annual registration shall be made at the time provided for payment of the tax imposed by section 4503.09

of the Revised Code; shall be in the manner to be prescribed by the registrar; and shall be accompanied by an affidavit certifying that the applicant is a manufacturer or distributor of utility trailers or trailers for transporting motorcycles, snowmobiles, or all-purpose vehicles. The fee for such registration shall be twenty five dollars and shall not be reduced when the registration is for a part of a year.

Upon the filing of the application and affidavit, and payment of the fee and appropriate postage as required by the registrar, the registrar shall assign to the applicant a distinctive number which shall be displayed on the rear of each trailer when it is operated on the public highway. Any trailer for transporting motorcycles, snowmobiles, or all-purpose vehicles that is not loaded may be operated on the public highway until it is sold or transferred; and any utility trailer that is not loaded, or that is being used to transport another utility trailer for purposes of demonstration or delivery, may be operated on the public highway until it is sold or transferred.

At the time the registrar assigns the distinctive number, the registrar shall furnish one placard with the number thereon. The manufacturer or distributor may procure a reasonable number of certified copies of the registration certificate upon the payment of a fee of five dollars and postage. With each of such certified copies, the registrar shall furnish one placard with the same number provided in the original registration certificate, and shall add thereto such special designation as necessary to distinguish one set of placards from another. All placards furnished by the registrar pursuant to this section shall be so marked as to be distinguishable from placards issued to dealers in or manufacturers of motor vehicles or trailers for transporting watercraft.

The fees collected by the registrar pursuant to this section shall be paid into the state bureau of motor vehicles fund established by section 4501.25 of the Revised Code and used for the purposes described in that section.

(1997 S 60, eff. 10–21–97; 1995 H 107, eff. (See Historical and Statutory Notes); 1981 H 124, eff. 1–1–82)

Historical and Statutory Notes

Ed. Note: 1995 H 107 Effective Date—The Secretary of State assigned a general effective date of 6–30–95 for 1995 H 107. Pursuant to O Const Art II § 1c and 1d, and RC 1.471, sections of 1995 H 107 that are, or depend for their implementation upon, current expense appropriations are effective 3–31–95; sections of 1995 H 107 that are not, and do not depend for their implementation upon, current expense appropriations are effective 6–30–95. See *Baldwin's Ohio Legislative Service*, 1995, page 3/L–98 for 1995 H 107, § 16.

4503.32 Special license plates

(A) No person shall use the license placards provided for in section 4503.31 of the Revised Code contrary to said section.

(B) Whoever violates this section is guilty of a misdemeanor of the third degree.

(2002 S 123, eff. 1–1–04; 1953 H 1, eff. 10–1–53; GC 12621–2)

4503.33 "In–transit" permits required

A person, firm, or corporation engaged in this state as a drive-away operator or trailer transporter or both in the business of transporting and delivering, by means of the full mount method, the saddle mount method, the tow bar method, tow-away method, or any combination thereof, or under their own power, new motor vehicles from the manufacturer or any other point of origin to any point of destination, or used motor vehicles from any individual, firm, or corporation to any point of destination, or both, shall make application to the registrar of motor vehicles for an "in transit" permit. This application shall be accompanied by a registration fee of fifty dollars, and shall show such information as is considered necessary by the registrar. Upon the filing of the application and the payment of the annual fee and appropriate postage as required by the registrar, the registrar shall issue to each permittee a certificate of registration bearing a distinctive number or designation of the registration and one placard bearing a corresponding number or designation, which placard must be carried and displayed by each such motor vehicle in like manner as provided by law for other motor vehicles while operated upon a public highway in transit from the manufacturer or any other point of origin to any point of destination.

A permittee may procure a reasonable number of certified copies of such registration certificate upon the payment of a fee of three dollars and postage. With each such certified copy the registrar shall furnish one placard with the same numbering or designation provided in the original registration certificate, and the registrar may add thereto such special designation as may be necessary to distinguish one placard from another.

No person required to register an apportionable vehicle under the international registration plan shall apply for or receive a placard for that vehicle under this section.

(1997 S 60, eff. 10–21–97; 1990 H 831, eff. 7–17–90; 126 v 727; 125 v 230; 1953 H 1; GC 6301–1)

4503.34 Drive–away operator required to file application

(A) No person who is a drive-away operator or trailer transporter, or both, engaged in the business of transporting and delivering new motor vehicles or used motor vehicles, or both, by means of the full mount method, the saddle mount method, the tow bar method, the tow-away method, or any combination thereof, or under their own power, shall fail to file an application as required by section 4503.33 of the Revised Code, and to pay the fees therefor and to apply for and pay the legal fees for as many certified copies thereof as said section requires.

(B) Whoever violates this section is guilty of a minor misdemeanor.

(2002 S 123, eff. 1–1–04; 126 v 727, eff. 3–31–55; 1953 H 1; GC 12621–1)

EXEMPTIONS

4503.35 Certain motor vehicles exempted

The motor vehicles furnished by the state for use by the elective state officials, and motor vehicles owned and operated by political subdivisions of the state, are exempt from section 4503.23 of the Revised Code.

The motor vehicles operated by troopers of the state highway patrol, and motor vehicles operated by or on behalf of any person whose responsibilities include involvement in authorized civil or criminal investigations requiring that the presence and identity of the vehicle occupants be undisclosed, are exempt from section 4503.23 of the Revised Code.

(1994 S 116, eff. 9–29–94; 1953 H 1, eff. 10–1–53; GC 6301–4)

4503.37 Reciprocity certificates

(A) A certificate of reciprocity issued under this section shall exempt the owner and the driver of every motor vehicle which is duly registered in the state, district, country, or sovereignty other than this state, to which the certificate is granted, from the laws of this state pertaining to registration and licensing and the penal statutes relating thereto, provided such owner or driver has complied with the law in regard to motor vehicles in the state, district, country, or sovereignty in which the motor vehicle is registered and complies with such law while operating and driving such motor vehicle upon the public roads of this state. Such certificate shall not, however, exempt such an owner from the requirements of sections 5728.01 to 5728.14 and 5728.99 of the Revised Code, from the provisions of section 2921.13 of the Revised Code in relation to the filing of a return, application, or permit under section 5728.02, 5728.03, or 5728.08 of the Revised Code, or from the payment of any other taxes which may be imposed on Ohio-owned motor vehicles.

(B) The registrar of motor vehicles shall issue a certificate of reciprocity to each state, district, country, or sovereignty other than this state:

(1) Which state, district, country, or sovereignty grants to the owners and drivers of Ohio-registered motor vehicles the same exemptions granted by a certificate of reciprocity to owners and drivers of motor vehicles not registered in Ohio;

(2) And in which state, district, country, or sovereignty, except for nominal charges for registration for identification purposes, all highway taxes, including use taxes, motor vehicle fuel taxes, flat fees, and public utility taxes, are levied impartially on all motor vehicles regardless of where the motor vehicles have been registered.

(C) The registrar of motor vehicles shall not issue a reciprocity certificate, and shall cancel any such certificate previously issued, if the state, district, country, or sovereignty concerned does not comply with divisions (B)(1) and (2) of this section, or charges registration flat fees of owners of Ohio-registered motor vehicles which fees are in no way governed by motor vehicle fuel consumption, or miles traveled, in that state, district, country, or sovereignty.

(D) Taxes and assessments levied impartially and collected directly on a per mile basis, or per gallon of motor vehicle fuel basis, shall not be construed to disqualify the state, district, country, or sovereignty levying the same from receiving a certificate of reciprocity; however, if a tax or assessment is imposed on vehicles registered in the state, district, country, or sovereignty levying the tax, or assessment, or not on similar vehicles registered in other jurisdictions, the registrar may refuse to grant a certificate of reciprocity, and if such a certificate has been previously granted, may cancel the certificate.

(E) The owner or operator of a motor vehicle duly registered under the international registration plan in this state or in any other jurisdiction for which this state has received an apportioned registration tax or fee, or which is otherwise operating in accordance with the provisions of the international registration plan, is not required by this section to obtain a certificate of registration under section 4503.10 of the Revised Code.

(1996 H 670, eff. 12–2–96; 1995 S 2, eff. 7–1–96; 1990 H 831, eff. 7–17–90; 1986 H 428; 130 v H 426)

4503.38 Exemption for foreign trailers

A trailer that is duly registered in any state, district, country, or sovereignty other than this state is exempt from the laws of this state pertaining to registration and licensing and the penal statutes relating thereto.

(1990 H 831, eff. 7–17–90; 129 v 582; 127 v 559)

RESERVED AND SPECIAL PLATES

4503.431 Silver star license plates

(A) Any person who has been awarded the silver star may apply to the registrar of motor vehicles for the registration of any passenger car, noncommercial motor vehicle, recreational vehicle, or other vehicle the person owns or leases of a class approved by the registrar. The application shall be accompanied by such documentary evidence in support of the award as the registrar shall require by rule. The application may be combined with a request for a special reserved license plate under section 4503.40 or 4503.42 of the Revised Code.

Upon receipt of an application for registration of a motor vehicle under this section; presentation of satisfactory evidence documenting that the applicant is a recipient of the silver star; payment of the regular license fee as prescribed under section 4503.04 of the Revised Code, any local motor vehicle license tax levied under Chapter 4504. of the Revised Code, and any applicable additional fee prescribed by section 4503.40 or 4503.42 of the Revised Code; and compliance with all other applicable laws relating to the registration of motor vehicles, the registrar shall issue to the applicant the appropriate motor vehicle registration and a set of license plates and a validation sticker, or a validation sticker alone when required by section 4503.191 of the Revised Code.

In addition to the letters and numbers ordinarily inscribed on the license plates, the license plates shall contain an illustration of the silver star and be inscribed with the words "combat veteran." The license plates shall bear county identification stickers that identify the county of registration by name or number.

(B) Sections 4503.77 and 4503.78 of the Revised Code do not apply to license plates issued under this section.

(C) No person who is not a recipient of the silver star shall willfully and falsely represent that the person is a recipient of the silver star for the purpose of obtaining license plates under this section. No person shall permit a motor vehicle owned or leased by such person to bear license plates issued under this section unless the person is eligible to be issued such license plates.

(2004 H 406, eff. 3–23–05)

4503.432 Bronze star medal license plates

(A) Any person who has been awarded the bronze star medal may apply to the registrar of motor vehicles for the registration of any passenger car, noncommercial motor vehicle, recreational vehicle, or other vehicle the person owns or leases of a class approved by the registrar. The application shall be accompanied by such documentary evidence in support of the award as the registrar shall require by rule. The application may be combined with a request for a special reserved license plate under section 4503.40 or 4503.42 of the Revised Code.

Upon receipt of an application for registration of a motor vehicle under this section; presentation of satisfactory evidence documenting that the applicant is a recipient of the bronze star medal; payment of the regular license fee as prescribed under section 4503.04 of the Revised Code, any local motor vehicle license tax levied under Chapter 4504. of the Revised Code, and any applicable additional fee prescribed by section 4503.40 or 4503.42 of the Revised Code; and compliance with all other applicable laws relating to the registration of motor vehicles, the registrar shall issue to the applicant the appropriate motor vehicle registration and a set of license plates and a validation sticker, or a validation sticker alone when required by section 4503.191 of the Revised Code.

In addition to the letters and numbers ordinarily inscribed on the license plates, the license plates shall contain an illustration of the bronze star medal and be inscribed with the words "combat veteran." The license plates shall bear county identification stickers that identify the county of registration by name or number.

(B) Sections 4503.77 and 4503.78 of the Revised Code do not apply to license plates issued under this section.

(C) No person who is not a recipient of the bronze star medal shall willfully and falsely represent that the person is a recipient of the bronze star medal for the purpose of obtaining license plates under this section. No person shall permit a motor vehicle owned or leased by such person to bear license plates issued under this section unless the person is eligible to be issued such license plates.

(2004 H 406, eff. 3–23–05)

4503.44 Registration of motor vehicle owned by or altered for use of disabled person; organization transporting disabled persons; removable windshield placard; fund; refueling service

(A) As used in this section and in section 4511.69 of the Revised Code:

(1) "Person with a disability that limits or impairs the ability to walk" means any person who, as determined by a physician or chiropractor, meets any of the following criteria:

(a) Cannot walk two hundred feet without stopping to rest;

(b) Cannot walk without the use of, or assistance from, a brace, cane, crutch, another person, prosthetic device, wheelchair, or other assistive device;

(c) Is restricted by a lung disease to such an extent that the person's forced (respiratory) expiratory volume for one second, when measured by spirometry, is less than one liter, or the arterial oxygen tension is less than sixty millimeters of mercury on room air at rest;

(d) Uses portable oxygen;

(e) Has a cardiac condition to the extent that the person's functional limitations are classified in severity as class III or class IV according to standards set by the American heart association;

(f) Is severely limited in the ability to walk due to an arthritic, neurological, or orthopedic condition;

(g) Is blind.

(2) "Organization" means any private organization or corporation, or any governmental board, agency, department, division, or office, that, as part of its business or program, transports persons with disabilities that limit or impair the ability to walk on a regular basis in a motor vehicle that has not been altered for the purpose of providing it with special equipment for use by handicapped persons. This definition does not apply to division (J) of this section.

(3) "Physician" means a person licensed to practice medicine or surgery or osteopathic medicine and surgery under Chapter 4731. of the Revised Code.

(4) "Chiropractor" means a person licensed to practice chiropractic under Chapter 4734. of the Revised Code.

(B) Any organization or person with a disability that limits or impairs the ability to walk may apply to the registrar of motor vehicles for a removable windshield placard or, if the person owns or leases a motor vehicle, the person may apply for the registration of any motor vehicle the person owns or leases. In addition to one or more sets of license plates or one placard, a person with a disability that limits or impairs the ability to walk is entitled to one additional placard, but only if the person applies separately for the additional placard, states the reasons why the additional placard is needed, and the registrar, in the registrar's discretion, determines that good and justifiable cause exists to approve the request for the additional placard. When a motor vehicle has been altered for the purpose of providing it with special equipment for a person with a disability that limits or impairs the ability to walk, but is owned or leased by someone other than such a person, the owner or lessee may apply to the registrar or a deputy registrar for registration under this section. The application for registration of a motor vehicle owned or leased by a person with a disability that limits or impairs the ability to walk shall be accompanied by a signed statement from the applicant's personal physician or chiropractor certifying that the applicant meets at least one of the criteria contained in division (A)(1) of this section and that the disability is expected to continue for more than six consecutive months. The application for a removable windshield placard made by a person with a disability that limits or impairs the ability to walk shall be accompanied by a prescription from the applicant's personal physician or chiropractor prescribing such a placard for the applicant, provided that the applicant meets at least one of the criteria contained in division (A)(1) of this section. The physician or chiropractor shall state on the prescription the length of time the physician or chiropractor expects the applicant to have the disability that limits or impairs the applicant's ability to walk. The application for a removable windshield placard made by an organization shall be accompanied by such documentary evidence of regular transport of persons with disabilities that limit or impair the ability to walk by the organization as the registrar may require by rule and shall be completed in accordance with procedures that the registrar may require by rule. The application for registration of a motor vehicle that has been altered for the purpose of providing it with special equipment for a person with a disability that limits or impairs the ability to walk but is owned by someone other than such a person shall be accompanied by such documentary evidence of vehicle alterations as the registrar may require by rule.

(C) When an organization, a person with a disability that limits or impairs the ability to walk, or a person who does not have a disability that limits or impairs the ability to walk but owns a motor vehicle that has been altered for the purpose of providing it with special equipment for a person with a disability that limits or impairs the ability to walk first submits an application for registration of a motor vehicle under this section and every fifth year thereafter, the organization or person shall submit a signed statement from the applicant's personal physician or chiropractor, a completed application, and any required documentary evidence of vehicle alterations as provided in division (B) of this section, and also a power of attorney from the owner of the motor vehicle if the applicant leases the vehicle. Upon submission of these items, the registrar or deputy registrar shall issue to the applicant appropriate vehicle registration and a set of license plates and validation stickers, or validation stickers alone when required by section 4503.191 of the Revised Code. In addition to the letters and numbers ordinarily inscribed thereon, the license plates shall be imprinted with the international symbol of access. The license plates and validation stickers shall be issued upon payment of the regular license fee as prescribed under section 4503.04 of the Revised Code and any motor vehicle tax levied under Chapter 4504. of the Revised Code, and the payment of a service fee equal to the amount specified in division (D) or (G) of section 4503.10 of the Revised Code.

(D)(1) Upon receipt of a completed and signed application for a removable windshield placard, a prescription as described in division (B) of this section, documentary evidence of regular transport of persons with disabilities that limit or impair the ability to walk, if required, and payment of a service fee equal to the amount specified in division (D) or (G) of section 4503.10 of the Revised Code, the registrar or deputy registrar shall issue to the applicant a removable windshield placard, which shall bear the date of expiration on both sides of the placard and shall be valid until expired, revoked, or surrendered. Every removable windshield placard expires as described in division (D)(2) of this section, but in no case shall a removable windshield placard be valid for a period of less than sixty days. Removable windshield placards shall be renewable upon application as provided in division (B) of this section, and a service fee equal to the amount specified in division (D) or (G) of section 4503.10 of the Revised Code shall be charged for the renewal of a removable windshield placard. The registrar shall provide the application form and shall determine the information to be included thereon. The registrar also shall determine the form and size of the removable windshield placard, the material of which it is to be made, and any other information to be included thereon, and shall adopt rules relating to the issuance, expiration, revocation, surrender, and proper display of such placards. Any placard issued after October 14, 1999, shall be manufactured in a manner that allows the expiration date of the placard to be indicated on it through the punching, drilling, boring, or creation by any other means of holes in the placard.

(2) At the time a removable windshield placard is issued to a person with a disability that limits or impairs the ability to walk, the registrar or deputy registrar shall enter into the records of the bureau of motor vehicles the last date on which the person will have that disability, as indicated on the accompanying prescription. Not less than thirty days prior to that date and all removable windshield placard renewal dates, the bureau shall send a renewal notice to that person at the person's last known address as shown in the records of the bureau, informing the person that the person's removable windshield placard will expire on the indicated date not to exceed five years from the date of issuance, and that the person is required to renew the placard by submitting to the registrar or a deputy registrar another prescription, as described in division (B) of this section, and by complying with the renewal provisions prescribed in division (D)(1) of this section. If such a prescription is not received by the registrar or a deputy registrar by that date, the placard issued to that person expires and no longer is valid, and this fact shall be recorded in the records of the bureau.

(3) At least once every year, on a date determined by the registrar, the bureau shall examine the records of the office of vital statistics, located within the department of health, that pertain to deceased persons, and also the bureau's records of all persons who have been issued removable windshield placards and temporary removable windshield placards. If the records of the office of vital statistics indicate that a person to whom a removable windshield placard or temporary removable windshield placard has been issued is deceased, the bureau shall cancel that placard, and note the cancellation in its records.

The office of vital statistics shall make available to the bureau all information necessary to enable the bureau to comply with division (D)(3) of this section.

(4) Nothing in this section shall be construed to require a person or organization to apply for a removable windshield placard or special license plates if the parking card or special license plates issued to the person or organization under prior law have not expired or been surrendered or revoked.

(E)(1)(a) Any person with a disability that limits or impairs the ability to walk may apply to the registrar or a deputy registrar for a temporary removable windshield placard. The application for a temporary removable windshield placard shall be accompanied by a prescription from the applicant's personal physician or chiropractor prescribing such a placard for the applicant, provided that the applicant meets at least one of the criteria contained in division (A)(1) of this section and that the disability is expected to continue for six consecutive months or less. The physician or chiropractor shall state on the prescription the length of time the physician or chiropractor expects the applicant to have the disability that limits or impairs the applicant's ability to walk, which cannot exceed six months from the date of the prescription. Upon receipt of an application for a temporary removable windshield placard, presentation of the prescription from the applicant's personal physician or chiropractor, and payment of a service fee equal to the amount specified in division (D) or (G) of section 4503.10 of the Revised Code, the registrar or deputy registrar shall issue to the applicant a temporary removable windshield placard.

(b) Any active-duty member of the armed forces of the United States, including the reserve components of the armed forces and the national guard, who has an illness or injury that limits or impairs the ability to walk may apply to the registrar or a deputy registrar for a temporary removable windshield placard. With the application, the person shall present evidence of the person's active-duty status and the illness or injury. Evidence of the illness or injury may include a current department of defense convalescent leave statement, any department of defense document indicating that the person currently has an ill or injured casualty status or has limited duties, or a prescription from any physician or chiropractor prescribing the placard for the applicant. Upon receipt of the application and the necessary evidence, the registrar or deputy registrar shall issue the applicant the temporary removable windshield placard without the payment of any service fee.

(2) The temporary removable windshield placard shall be of the same size and form as the removable windshield placard, shall be printed in white on a red-colored background, and shall bear the word "temporary" in letters of such size as the registrar shall prescribe. A temporary removable windshield placard also shall bear the date of expiration on the front and back of the placard, and shall be valid until expired, surrendered, or revoked, but in no case shall such a placard be valid for a period of less than sixty days. The registrar shall provide the application form and shall determine the information to be included on it, provided that the registrar shall not require a physician or chiropractor's prescription or certification for a person applying under division (E)(1)(b) of this section. The registrar also shall determine the material of which the temporary removable windshield placard is to be made and any other information to be included on the placard and shall adopt rules relating to the issuance, expiration, surrender, revocation, and proper display of those placards. Any temporary removable windshield placard issued after October 14, 1999, shall be manufactured in a manner that allows for the expiration date of the placard to be indicated on it through the punching, drilling, boring, or creation by any other means of holes in the placard.

(F) If an applicant for a removable windshield placard is a veteran of the armed forces of the United States whose disability, as defined in division (A)(1) of this section, is service-connected, the registrar or deputy registrar, upon receipt of the application, presentation of a signed statement from the applicant's personal physician or chiropractor certifying the applicant's disability, and presentation of such documentary evidence from the department of veterans affairs that the disability of the applicant meets at least one of the criteria identified in division (A)(1) of this section and is service-connected as the registrar may require by rule, but without the payment of any service fee, shall issue the applicant a removable windshield placard that is valid until expired, surrendered, or revoked.

(G) Upon a conviction of a violation of division (I), (J), or (K) of this section, the court shall report the conviction, and send the placard or parking card, if available, to the registrar, who thereupon shall revoke the privilege of using the placard or parking card and send notice in writing to the placardholder or cardholder at that holder's last known address as shown in the records of the bureau, and the placardholder or cardholder shall return the placard or card if not previously surrendered to the court, to the registrar within ten days following mailing of the notice.

Whenever a person to whom a removable windshield placard or parking card has been issued moves to another state, the person shall surrender the placard or card to the registrar; and whenever an organization to which a placard or card has been issued changes its place of operation to another state, the organization shall surrender the placard or card to the registrar.

(H) Subject to division (F) of section 4511.69 of the Revised Code, the operator of a motor vehicle displaying a removable windshield placard, temporary removable windshield placard, parking card, or the special license plates authorized by this section is entitled to park the motor vehicle in any special parking location reserved for persons with disabilities that limit or impair the ability to walk, also known as handicapped parking spaces or disability parking spaces.

(I) No person or organization that is not eligible under division (B) or (E) of this section shall willfully and falsely represent that the person or organization is so eligible.

No person or organization shall display license plates issued under this section unless the license plates have been issued for the vehicle on which they are displayed and are valid.

(J) No person or organization to which a removable windshield placard or temporary removable windshield placard is issued shall do either of the following:

(1) Display or permit the display of the placard on any motor vehicle when having reasonable cause to believe the motor vehicle is being used in connection with an activity that does not include providing transportation for persons with disabilities that limit or impair the ability to walk;

(2) Refuse to return or surrender the placard, when required.

(K)(1) No person or organization to which a parking card is issued shall do either of the following:

(a) Display or permit the display of the parking card on any motor vehicle when having reasonable cause to believe the motor vehicle is being used in connection with an activity that does not include providing transportation for a handicapped person;

(b) Refuse to return or surrender the parking card, when required.

(2) As used in division (K) of this section:

(a) "Handicapped person" means any person who has lost the use of one or both legs or one or both arms, who is blind, deaf, or so severely handicapped as to be unable to move about without the aid of crutches or a wheelchair, or whose mobility is restricted by a permanent cardiovascular, pulmonary, or other handicapping condition.

(b) "Organization" means any private organization or corporation, or any governmental board, agency, department, division, or office, that, as part of its business or program, transports handicapped persons on a regular basis in a motor vehicle that has not been altered for the purposes of providing it with special equipment for use by handicapped persons.

(L) If a removable windshield placard, temporary removable windshield placard, or parking card is lost, destroyed, or mutilated, the placardholder or cardholder may obtain a duplicate by doing both of the following:

(1) Furnishing suitable proof of the loss, destruction, or mutilation to the registrar;

(2) Paying a service fee equal to the amount specified in division (D) or (G) of section 4503.10 of the Revised Code.

Any placardholder or cardholder who loses a placard or card and, after obtaining a duplicate, finds the original, immediately shall surrender the original placard or card to the registrar.

(M) The registrar shall pay all fees received under this section for the issuance of removable windshield placards or temporary removable windshield placards or duplicate removable windshield placards or cards into the state treasury to the credit of the state bureau of motor vehicles fund created in section 4501.25 of the Revised Code.

(N) For purposes of enforcing this section, every peace officer is deemed to be an agent of the registrar. Any peace officer or any authorized employee of the bureau of motor vehicles who, in the performance of duties authorized by law, becomes aware of a person whose placard or parking card has been revoked pursuant to this section, may confiscate that placard or parking card and return it to the registrar. The registrar shall prescribe any forms used by law enforcement agencies in administering this section.

No peace officer, law enforcement agency employing a peace officer, or political subdivision or governmental agency employing a peace officer, and no employee of the bureau is liable in a civil action for damages or loss to persons arising out of the performance of any duty required or authorized by this section. As used in this division, "peace officer" has the same meaning as in division (B) of section 2935.01 of the Revised Code.

(O) All applications for registration of motor vehicles, removable windshield placards, and temporary removable windshield placards issued under this section, all renewal notices for such items, and all other publications issued by the bureau that relate to this section shall set forth the criminal penalties that may be imposed upon a person who violates any provision relating to special license plates issued under this section, the parking of vehicles displaying such license plates, and the issuance, procurement, use, and display of removable windshield placards and temporary removable windshield placards issued under this section.

(P) Whoever violates this section is guilty of a misdemeanor of the fourth degree.

(2004 H 230, eff. 9–16–04; 2002 S 123, eff. 1–1–04; 1999 S 22, eff. 5–17–00; 1999 H 148, eff. 10–14–99; 1996 H 353, eff. 9–17–96; 1995 S 2, eff. 7–1–96; 1995 H 107, eff. (See Historical and Statutory Notes); 1994 H 687, eff. 1–1–95; 1993 H 154, eff. 6–30–93; 1990 H 737; 1989 H 49; 1988 H 708; 1987 H 419, H 12; 1985 H 80, H 201; 1983 H 174; 1982 H 48; 1980 H 736)

Historical and Statutory Notes

Ed. Note: 1995 H 107 Effective Date—The Secretary of State assigned a general effective date of 6–30–95 for 1995 H 107. Pursuant to O Const Art II § 1c and 1d, and RC 1.471, sections of 1995 H 107 that are, or depend for their implementation upon, current expense appropriations are effective 3–31–95; sections of 1995 H 107 that are not, and do not depend for their implementation upon, current expense appropriations are effective 6–30–95. See *Baldwin's Ohio Legislative Service*, 1995, page 3/L–98 for 1995 H 107, § 16.

4503.541 National defense service medal license plates

(A) Any person who has been awarded the national defense service medal may apply to the registrar of motor vehicles for the registration of any passenger car, noncommercial motor vehicle, recreational vehicle, or other vehicle of a class approved by the registrar that the person owns or leases. The application shall be accompanied by such documentary evidence in support of the award as the registrar may require. The application may be combined with a request for a special reserved license plate under section 4503.40 or 4503.42 of the Revised Code.

Upon receipt of an application for registration of a motor vehicle under this section and the required taxes and fees, and upon presentation of the required supporting evidence of the award of the national defense service medal, the registrar shall issue to the applicant the appropriate motor vehicle registration and a set of license plates and a validation sticker, or a validation sticker alone when required by section 4503.191 of the Revised Code.

In addition to the letters and numbers ordinarily inscribed on license plates, the license plates shall be inscribed with the words "national defense" and bear a reproduction of the national defense service ribbon. The license plates shall bear county identification stickers that identify the county of registration by name or number.

The license plates and a validation sticker or, when applicable, a validation sticker alone shall be issued upon payment of the regular license tax required by section 4503.04 of the Revised Code, payment of any local motor vehicle license tax levied under Chapter 4504. of the Revised Code, payment of any applicable additional fee prescribed by section 4503.40 or 4503.42 of the Revised Code, and compliance with all other applicable laws relating to the registration of motor vehicles.

(B) No person who is not a recipient of the national defense service medal shall willfully and falsely represent that the person is a recipient of the national defense service medal for the purpose of obtaining license plates under this section. No person shall own a motor vehicle bearing license plates issued under this section unless the person is eligible to be issued those license plates.

(C) Sections 4503.77 and 4503.78 of the Revised Code do not apply to license plates issued under this section.

(2004 H 406, eff. 3–23–05)

4503.543 Armed forces expeditionary medal license plates

(A) Any person who has been awarded the armed forces expeditionary medal may apply to the registrar of motor vehicles for the registration of any passenger car, noncommercial motor vehicle, recreational vehicle, or other vehicle of a class approved by the registrar that the person owns or leases. The application shall be accompanied by such documentary evidence in support of the award as the registrar may require. The application may be combined with a request for a special reserved license plate under section 4503.40 or 4503.42 of the Revised Code.

Upon receipt of an application for registration of a motor vehicle under this section and the required taxes and fees, and upon presentation of the required supporting evidence of the award of the armed forces expeditionary medal, the registrar shall issue to the applicant the appropriate motor vehicle registration and a set of license plates and a validation sticker, or a validation sticker alone when required by section 4503.191 of the Revised Code.

In addition to the letters and numbers ordinarily inscribed on license plates, the license plates shall be inscribed with the words "expeditionary service" and bear a reproduction of the armed forces expeditionary service ribbon. The license plates shall bear county identification stickers that identify the county of registration by name or number.

The license plates and a validation sticker or, when applicable, a validation sticker alone shall be issued upon payment of the regular license tax required by section 4503.04 of the Revised Code, payment of any local motor vehicle license tax levied under Chapter 4504. of the Revised Code, payment of any applicable additional fee prescribed by section 4503.40 or 4503.42 of the Revised Code, and compliance with all other applicable laws relating to the registration of motor vehicles.

The registrar shall not issue license plates under this section unless the registrar first receives written permission from the United States department of defense allowing the registrar to place the image of the armed forces expeditionary service ribbon on the license plates.

(B) No person who is not a recipient of the armed forces expeditionary medal shall willfully and falsely represent that the person is a recipient of the armed forces expeditionary medal for the purpose of obtaining license plates under this section. No person shall own a motor vehicle bearing license plates issued under this section unless the person is eligible to be issued those license plates.

(C) Sections 4503.77 and 4503.78 of the Revised Code do not apply to license plates issued under this section.

(2004 H 406, eff. 3–23–05)

INTERNATIONAL REGISTRATION PLAN

4503.642 Performance registration and information systems management program; powers and duties of registrar; suspension, revocation or denial of privilege to operate commercial motor vehicle; hearing

(A) There is hereby created in the bureau of motor vehicles a performance registration and information systems management program for coordinating motor carrier safety information with federal and state agencies. The registrar of motor vehicles shall collect and maintain necessary motor carrier, commercial motor vehicle, and driver data in a manner that complies with the information systems established by the United States secretary of transportation under 49 U.S.C. 31106.

(B) The registrar shall refuse to issue a registration, license plate, permit, or certificate of title for any commercial motor vehicle that is assigned to a motor carrier that has been prohibited from operating by a federal agency. The registrar may allow a prohibited motor vehicle carrier to transfer title on a commercial motor vehicle if the prohibited carrier does not retain a direct or indirect interest in the vehicle.

(C) The registrar shall suspend, revoke, deny, or remove the registration, license plates, or any permit issued to any commercial motor vehicle that is assigned to a motor carrier who has been prohibited from operating by a federal agency. The suspension, revocation, denial, or removal shall remain in effect until the carrier is no longer prohibited from operating by the federal agency. The suspension, revocation, denial, or removal shall apply to all commercial motor vehicles under the carrier's control.

(D) A carrier or registrant whose privilege to operate a commercial motor vehicle has been suspended, revoked, denied, or removed under division (C) of this section may request a hearing in accordance with Chapter 119. of the Revised Code. The hearing shall be limited to whether the carrier or registrant has been correctly identified, whether the carrier or registrant has been prohibited from operating by the federal agency, and whether the federal agency subsequently has rescinded the prohibition.

(E) The registrar shall restore a motor carrier's or registrant's privilege to register, transfer a title, or operate a commercial motor vehicle only upon acceptable notification from the federal agency that the prohibition has been removed and upon payment of all applicable taxes and fees.

(F) The registrar shall take those steps necessary to implement this section, including the adoption of rules, procedures, and forms.

(2004 H 230, eff. 9–16–04)

CHAPTER 4505

CERTIFICATE OF MOTOR VEHICLE TITLE LAW

GENERAL PROVISIONS

GENERAL PROVISIONS

4505.01 Definitions

(A) As used in this chapter:

(1) "Lien" includes, unless the context requires a different meaning, a security interest in a motor vehicle.

(2) "Motor vehicle" includes manufactured homes, mobile homes, recreational vehicles, and trailers and semitrailers whose weight exceeds four thousand pounds.

(B) The various certificates, applications, and assignments necessary to provide certificates of title for manufactured homes, mobile homes, recreational vehicles, and trailers and semitrailers whose weight exceeds four thousand pounds, shall be made upon forms prescribed by the registrar of motor vehicles.

(1998 S 142, eff. 3–30–99; 1989 H 381, eff. 7–1–89; 1986 H 428; 1984 S 231, H 218; 1976 S 359; 1953 H 1; GC 6290–2a)

4505.021 Application for certificate of title

The owner of a motor vehicle shall apply for a certificate of title for the vehicle when required by this chapter, but, except as otherwise specifically required in this chapter, the owner may elect whether or not to have the clerk of the court of common pleas to whom the certificate of title application is submitted issue a physical certificate of title for the motor vehicle, as provided in section 4505.08 of the Revised Code.

Except as otherwise specifically provided in this chapter, any provision of this chapter relating to the cancellation, issuance, or surrender of a certificate of title, including, but not limited to, provisions that contain a phrase such as "when a certificate of title is issued," "the clerk shall issue a certificate of title," or "the person shall obtain a certificate of title to the motor vehicle," or another phrase of similar import, shall include those circumstances when a clerk enters certificate of title information into the automated title processing system, but does not take any further action relating to a physical certificate of title for the motor vehicle.

(2001 S 59, eff. 10–31–01)

4505.022 Electronic application by auction owners for certificate of title

The registrar of motor vehicles may adopt rules pursuant to Chapter 119. of the Revised Code to allow a motor vehicle auction owner licensed under section 4517.07 of the Revised Code to file an application for a certificate of title in an electronic manner approved by the registrar.

(2004 H 230, eff. 9–16–04)

4505.03 Certificate of title

No person, except as provided in sections 4505.032 and 4505.05 of the Revised Code, shall sell or otherwise dispose of a motor vehicle without delivering to the buyer or transferee of it a certificate of title with an assignment on it as is necessary to show title in the buyer or transferee; nor shall any person, except as provided in section 4505.032 or 4505.11 of the Revised Code, buy or otherwise acquire a motor vehicle without obtaining a certificate of title for it in the person's name in accordance with this chapter.

(2001 S 59, eff. 10–31–01; 1996 H 353, eff. 9–17–96; 1994 H 687, eff. 10–12–94; 132 v H 741, eff. 11–24–67; 1953 H 1; GC 6290–3)

4505.032 Sale of motor vehicle when physical certificate of title has not been issued and person not an electronic motor vehicle dealer

(A)(1) If a person who is not an electronic motor vehicle dealer owns a motor vehicle for which a physical certificate of title has not been issued by a clerk of a court of common pleas and the person sells the motor vehicle to a motor vehicle dealer licensed under Chapter 4517. of the Revised Code, the person is not required to obtain a physical certificate of title to the motor vehicle in order to transfer ownership to the dealer. The person shall present the dealer, in a manner approved by the registrar of motor vehicles, with sufficient proof of the person's identity and complete and sign a form prescribed by the registrar attesting to the person's identity and assigning the motor vehicle to the dealer. Except as otherwise provided in this section, the motor vehicle dealer shall present the assignment form to any clerk of a court of common pleas together with an application for a certificate of title and payment of the fees prescribed by section 4505.09 of the Revised Code.

In a case in which a person who is the owner of a motor vehicle for which a physical certificate of title has not been issued assigns the motor vehicle to an electronic motor vehicle dealer, the electronic motor vehicle dealer instead may inform a clerk of a court of common pleas via electronic means of the sale of the motor vehicle and assignment of ownership of the vehicle to the dealer. The clerk shall enter the information relating to the assignment, including, but not limited to, the odometer disclosure statement required by section 4505.06 of the Revised Code, into the automated title processing system, and ownership of the vehicle passes to the dealer when the clerk enters this information into the system. The dealer is not required to obtain a certificate of title to the vehicle in the dealer's name.

(2) A clerk shall charge and collect from a dealer a fee of five dollars for each motor vehicle assigned to the dealer under division (A)(1) of this section. The fee shall be distributed in accordance with section 4505.09 of the Revised Code.

(B) If a person who is not an electronic motor vehicle dealer owns a motor vehicle for which a physical certificate of title has not been issued by a clerk of a court of common pleas and the person sells the motor vehicle to a person who is not a motor vehicle dealer licensed under Chapter 4517. of the Revised Code, the person shall obtain a physical certificate of title to the motor vehicle in order to transfer ownership of the vehicle to that person.

(2004 H 230, eff. 9–16–04; 2001 S 59, eff. 10–31–01)

4505.04 Certificate of title as evidence of ownership; tort action by lessee

(A) No person acquiring a motor vehicle from its owner, whether the owner is a manufacturer, importer, dealer, or any other person, shall acquire any right, title, claim, or interest in or to the motor vehicle until there is issued to the person a certificate of title to the motor vehicle, or there is delivered to the person a manufacturer's or importer's certificate for it, or a certificate of title to it is assigned as authorized by section 4505.032 of the Revised Code; and no waiver or estoppel operates in favor of such person against a person having possession of the certificate of title to, or manufacturer's or importer's certificate for, the motor vehicle, for a valuable consideration.

(B) Subject to division (C) of this section, no court shall recognize the right, title, claim, or interest of any person in or to any motor vehicle sold or disposed of, or mortgaged or encumbered, unless evidenced:

(1) By a certificate of title, an assignment of a certificate of title made under section 4505.032 of the Revised Code, a manufacturer's or importer's certificate, or a certified receipt of title cancellation to an exported motor vehicle issued in accordance with sections 4505.01 to 4505.21 of the Revised Code;

(2) By admission in the pleadings or stipulation of the parties;

(3) In an action by a secured party to enforce a security interest perfected under Chapter 1309. of the Revised Code in accordance with division (A) of section 4505.13 of the Revised Code, by an instrument showing a valid security interest.

(C)(1) As used in division (C) of this section:

(a) "Harm" means damage or other loss.

(b) "Lease agreement" includes a sublease agreement as defined in division (C)(1)(d) of this section.

(c) "Lessee" includes a sublessee under a sublease agreement, but only if the sublessee is a motor vehicle leasing dealer licensed under Chapter 4517. of the Revised Code.

(d) "Sublease agreement" means a lease of a motor vehicle between a motor vehicle leasing dealer licensed under Chapter 4517. of the Revised Code and a second such duly licensed motor vehicle leasing dealer.

(e) "Tort action" means a civil action for damages for harm to a motor vehicle, other than a civil action for damages for a breach of contract or another agreement between persons.

(2) Notwithstanding divisions (A) and (B) of this section, if a motor vehicle that is the subject of a lease agreement sustains harm during the term of that agreement and if all of the following conditions are satisfied, the lessee may commence a tort action in the lessee's own name to recover damages for the harm from the person allegedly responsible for it:

(a) The lessee shall file with and attach to the complaint in the tort action a copy of the lease agreement pursuant to which the lessee is responsible for damage to the motor vehicle, for purposes of establishing the ownership of the motor vehicle and the interest of the lessee in it.

(b) The harm to the motor vehicle shall be such that, under the lease agreement, the lessee bringing the action is legally responsible for the repair of the harm.

(c) The lessee shall cause a copy of the complaint in the tort action to be served upon the owner of the motor vehicle and upon any other lessee of the vehicle in accordance with the Rules of Civil Procedure.

(2001 S 59, eff. 10–31–01; 2001 S 74, eff. 7–1–01; 1998 S 213, eff. 7–29–98; 1994 H 687, eff. 10–12–94; 1987 H 4, eff. 9–10–87; 1984 H 632, H 218; 125 v 117; 1953 H 1; GC 6290–4)

4505.05 Manufacturer's or importer's certificate

No manufacturer, importer, dealer, or other person shall sell or otherwise dispose of a new motor vehicle to a dealer to be used by the dealer for purposes of display and resale, without delivering to the dealer a manufacturer's or importer's certificate executed in accordance with this chapter, and with such assignments thereon as are necessary to show title in the buyer thereof. No dealer shall purchase or acquire a new motor vehicle without obtaining from the seller thereof a manufacturer's or importer's certificate as prescribed by the registrar of motor vehicles.

(1996 H 353, eff. 9–17–96; 1994 H 687, eff. 10–12–94; 1989 H 381, eff. 7–1–89; 1953 H 1; GC 6290–2)

OBTAINING A CERTIFICATE OF TITLE; SURRENDER AND CANCELLATION

4505.101 Certificate of title for abandoned vehicle

(A) The owner of any repair garage or place of storage in which a motor vehicle with a value of less than two thousand five hundred dollars has been left unclaimed for fifteen days or more following completion of the requested repair or the agreed term of storage may send by certified mail, return receipt requested, to the last known address of the owner a notice to remove the motor vehicle. If the motor vehicle remains unclaimed by the owner for fifteen days after the mailing of the notice, and the person on whose property the vehicle has been abandoned has received the signed receipt from the certified mail or has been notified that the delivery was not possible, the person shall obtain a certificate of title to the motor vehicle in the person's name in the manner provided in this section.

The owner of the repair garage or place of storage that mailed the notice shall execute an affidavit that all of the requirements of this section necessary to authorize the issuance of a certificate of title for the motor vehicle have been met. The affidavit shall set forth the value of the motor vehicle when unclaimed as determined in accordance with standards fixed by the registrar of motor vehicles; the length of time that the motor vehicle has remained unclaimed; the expenses incurred with the motor vehicle; that a notice to remove the vehicle has been mailed to the titled owner, if known, by certified mail, return receipt requested; and that a search of the records of the bureau of motor vehicles has been made for outstanding liens on the motor vehicle.

No affidavit shall be executed or filed under this section until after a search of the records of the bureau of motor vehicles has been made. If the research reveals any outstanding lien on the motor vehicle, the owner of the repair garage or place of storage of the motor vehicle shall notify the mortgagee or lienholder by certified mail, return receipt requested, stating where the motor vehicle is located and the value of the vehicle. Unless the mortgagee or lienholder claims the motor vehicle within fifteen days from the mailing of the notice, the mortgagee's mortgage or the lienholder's lien shall be invalid.

Upon presentation by the owner of the repair garage or place of storage of the affidavit, showing compliance with all requirements of this section to the clerk of courts of the county in which the repair garage or place of storage is located, the clerk of courts shall issue a certificate of title, free and clear of all liens and encumbrances, to the owner of the place of storage.

The value of the motor vehicle, as determined in accordance with standards fixed by the registrar of motor vehicles, less expenses incurred by the owner of such repair garage or place of storage, shall be paid to the clerk of courts for deposit into the county general fund upon receipt of the certificate of title.

(B) Whoever violates this section shall be fined not more than two hundred dollars, imprisoned not more than ninety days, or both.

(2002 S 123, eff. 1-1-04; 1996 S 182, § 4, eff. 12-3-96; 1996 S 182, § 1, eff. 12-3-96; 1995 S 2, eff. 7-1-96; 1987 S 10, eff. 8-13-87; 1979 S 118; 132 v H 555)

4505.102 Certificate of title for motor vehicle pledged for pawnbroker's loan

(A) If a pawnbroker licensed under Chapter 4727. of the Revised Code makes a loan that is secured by a motor vehicle, watercraft, or outboard motor and has taken possession of the motor vehicle, watercraft, or outboard motor and the certificate of title to the motor vehicle, watercraft, or outboard motor, and the owner of the motor vehicle, watercraft, or outboard motor fails to redeem or pay interest on the loan for which the motor vehicle, watercraft, or outboard motor was pledged within two months from the date of the loan or the date on which the last interest payment is due, and the pawnbroker notifies the owner by mail, with proof of mailing, as required by division (A) of section 4727.11 of the Revised Code, of the possible forfeiture of the motor vehicle, watercraft, or outboard motor, and the owner fails to redeem the motor vehicle, watercraft, or outboard motor within the thirty-day period required by that division to be specified in the notice, the pawnbroker shall proceed to obtain a certificate of title to the motor vehicle, watercraft, or outboard motor in the pawnbroker's name in the manner provided in this section.

(B) The pawnbroker shall execute an affidavit stating all of the following:

(1) That the pawnbroker is a pawnbroker licensed under Chapter 4727. of the Revised Code;

(2) That the pawnbroker has made a loan to the owner of a motor vehicle, watercraft, or outboard motor, and the security for the loan is the motor vehicle, watercraft, or outboard motor;

(3) That both the motor vehicle, watercraft, or outboard motor and the certificate of title to the motor vehicle, watercraft, or outboard motor are in the possession of the pawnbroker;

(4) That the owner of the motor vehicle, watercraft, or outboard motor has failed to redeem the pledged motor vehicle, watercraft, or outboard motor or pay interest on the loan for which the motor vehicle, watercraft, or outboard motor was pledged within two months from the date of the loan or the date on which the last interest payment was due;

(5) That the pawnbroker has notified the owner of the motor vehicle, watercraft, or outboard motor by mail, with proof of mailing, as required by division (A) of section 4727.11 of the Revised Code, and the owner has failed to redeem the motor vehicle, watercraft, or outboard motor within the thirty-day period required by that division to be specified in the notice.

Upon presentation by the pawnbroker of a copy of the affidavit, a copy of the pawn form, a copy of the proof of mailing, and the certificate of title to the motor vehicle, watercraft, or outboard motor, a clerk of a court of common pleas shall issue, if the record shows no lien or encumbrances exist, a certificate of title, free and clear of all liens and encumbrances, to the pawnbroker.

(C) No person shall execute or present the affidavit required by this section, knowing any entry on the affidavit to be false.

(D) Whoever violates this section shall be fined not more than two hundred dollars, imprisoned not more than ninety days, or both.

(2002 S 123, eff. 1-1-04; 2001 S 59, eff. 10-31-01; 1996 H 353, eff. 9-17-96)

4505.11 Surrender and cancellation of certificate; salvage certificate; rebuilt salvage certificate; manufactured or mobile homes

(A) Each owner of a motor vehicle and each person mentioned as owner in the last certificate of title, when the motor vehicle is dismantled, destroyed, or changed in such manner that it loses its character as a motor vehicle, or changed in such manner that it is not the motor vehicle described in the certificate of title, shall surrender the certificate of title to that motor vehicle to a clerk of a court of common pleas, and the clerk, with the consent of any holders of any liens noted on the certificate of title, then shall enter a cancellation upon the clerk's records and shall notify the registrar of motor vehicles of the cancellation.

Upon the cancellation of a certificate of title in the manner prescribed by this section, any clerk and the registrar of motor vehicles may cancel and destroy all certificates and all memorandum certificates in that chain of title.

(B) If an Ohio certificate of title or salvage certificate of title to a motor vehicle is assigned to a salvage dealer, the dealer is not required to obtain an Ohio certificate of title or a salvage certificate of title to the motor vehicle in the dealer's own name if the dealer dismantles or destroys the motor vehicle, indicates the number of the dealer's motor vehicle salvage dealer's license on it, marks "FOR DESTRUCTION" across the face of the certificate of title or salvage certificate of title, and surrenders the certificate of title or salvage certificate of title to a clerk of a court of common pleas as provided in division (A) of this section. If the salvage dealer retains the motor vehicle for resale, the dealer shall make application for a salvage certificate of title to the motor vehicle in the dealer's own name as provided in division (C)(1) of this section.

(C)(1) When an insurance company declares it economically impractical to repair such a motor vehicle and has paid an agreed price for the purchase of the motor vehicle to any insured or claimant owner, the insurance company shall receive the certificate of title and the motor vehicle and proceed as follows. Within thirty days, the insurance company shall deliver the certificate of title to a clerk of a court of common pleas and shall make application for a salvage certificate of title. The clerk shall issue the salvage certificate of title on a form, prescribed by the registrar, that shall be easily distinguishable from the original certificate of title and shall bear the same information as the original certificate of title except that it may bear a different number than that of the original certificate of title. Except as provided in division (C)(2) of this section, the salvage certificate of title shall be assigned by the insurance company to a salvage dealer or any other person for use as evidence of ownership upon the sale or other disposition of the motor vehicle, and the salvage certificate of title shall be transferrable to any other person. The clerk shall charge a fee of four dollars for the cost of processing each salvage certificate of title.

(2) If an insurance company considers a motor vehicle as described in division (C)(1) of this section to be impossible to restore for highway operation, the insurance company may assign the certificate of title to the motor vehicle to a salvage dealer or scrap metal processing facility and send the assigned certificate of title to the clerk of the court of common pleas of any county. The insurance company shall mark the face of the certificate of title "FOR DESTRUCTION" and shall deliver a photocopy of

the certificate of title to the salvage dealer or scrap metal processing facility for its records.

(3) If an insurance company declares it economically impractical to repair a motor vehicle, agrees to pay to the insured or claimant owner an amount in settlement of a claim against a policy of motor vehicle insurance covering the motor vehicle, and agrees to permit the insured or claimant owner to retain possession of the motor vehicle, the insurance company shall not pay the insured or claimant owner any amount in settlement of the insurance claim until the owner obtains a salvage certificate of title to the vehicle and furnishes a copy of the salvage certificate of title to the insurance company.

(D) When a self-insured organization, rental or leasing company, or secured creditor becomes the owner of a motor vehicle that is burned, damaged, or dismantled and is determined to be economically impractical to repair, the self-insured organization, rental or leasing company, or secured creditor shall do one of the following:

(1) Mark the face of the certificate of title to the motor vehicle "FOR DESTRUCTION" and surrender the certificate of title to a clerk of a court of common pleas for cancellation as described in division (A) of this section. The self-insured organization, rental or leasing company, or secured creditor then shall deliver the motor vehicle, together with a photocopy of the certificate of title, to a salvage dealer or scrap metal processing facility and shall cause the motor vehicle to be dismantled, flattened, crushed, or destroyed.

(2) Obtain a salvage certificate of title to the motor vehicle in the name of the self-insured organization, rental or leasing company, or secured creditor, as provided in division (C)(1) of this section, and then sell or otherwise dispose of the motor vehicle. If the motor vehicle is sold, the self-insured organization, rental or leasing company, or secured creditor shall obtain a salvage certificate of title to the motor vehicle in the name of the purchaser from a clerk of a court of common pleas.

(E) If a motor vehicle titled with a salvage certificate of title is restored for operation upon the highways, application shall be made to a clerk of a court of common pleas for a certificate of title. Upon inspection by the state highway patrol, which shall include establishing proof of ownership and an inspection of the motor number and vehicle identification number of the motor vehicle and of documentation or receipts for the materials used in restoration by the owner of the motor vehicle being inspected, which documentation or receipts shall be presented at the time of inspection, the clerk, upon surrender of the salvage certificate of title, shall issue a certificate of title for a fee prescribed by the registrar. The certificate of title shall be in the same form as the original certificate of title and shall bear the words "REBUILT SALVAGE" in black boldface letters on its face. Every subsequent certificate of title, memorandum certificate of title, or duplicate certificate of title issued for the motor vehicle also shall bear the words "REBUILT SALVAGE" in black boldface letters on its face. The exact location on the face of the certificate of title of the words "REBUILT SALVAGE" shall be determined by the registrar, who shall develop an automated procedure within the automated title processing system to comply with this division. The clerk shall use reasonable care in performing the duties imposed on the clerk by this division in issuing a certificate of title pursuant to this division, but the clerk is not liable for any of the clerk's errors or omissions or those of the clerk's deputies, or the automated title processing system in the performance of those duties. A fee of fifty dollars shall be assessed by the state highway patrol for each inspection made pursuant to this division and shall be deposited into the state highway safety fund established by section 4501.06 of the Revised Code.

(F) No person shall operate upon the highways in this state a motor vehicle, title to which is evidenced by a salvage certificate of title, except to deliver the motor vehicle pursuant to an appointment for an inspection under this section.

(G) No motor vehicle the certificate of title to which has been marked "FOR DESTRUCTION" and surrendered to a clerk of a court of common pleas shall be used for anything except parts and scrap metal.

(H)(1) Except as otherwise provided in this division, an owner of a manufactured or mobile home that will be taxed as real property pursuant to division (B) of section 4503.06 of the Revised Code shall surrender the certificate of title to the auditor of the county containing the taxing district in which the home is located. An owner whose home qualifies for real property taxation under divisions (B)(1)(a) and (b) of section 4503.06 of the Revised Code shall surrender the certificate within fifteen days after the home meets the conditions specified in those divisions. The auditor shall deliver the certificate of title to the clerk of the court of common pleas who issued it.

(2) If the certificate of title for a manufactured or mobile home that is to be taxed as real property is held by a lienholder, the lienholder shall surrender the certificate of title to the auditor of the county containing the taxing district in which the home is located, and the auditor shall deliver the certificate of title to the clerk of the court of common pleas who issued it. The lienholder shall surrender the certificate within thirty days after both of the following have occurred:

(a) The homeowner has provided written notice to the lienholder requesting that the certificate of title be surrendered to the auditor of the county containing the taxing district in which the home is located.

(b) The homeowner has either paid the lienholder the remaining balance owed to the lienholder, or, with the lienholder's consent, executed and delivered to the lienholder a mortgage on the home and land on which the home is sited in the amount of the remaining balance owed to the lienholder.

(3) Upon the delivery of a certificate of title by the county auditor to the clerk, the clerk shall inactivate it and maintain it in the automated title processing system for a period of thirty years.

(4) Upon application by the owner of a manufactured or mobile home that is taxed as real property pursuant to division (B) of section 4503.06 of the Revised Code and that no longer satisfies divisions (B)(1)(a) and (b) or divisions (B)(2)(a) and (b) of that section, the clerk shall reactivate the record of the certificate of title that was inactivated under division (H)(3) of this section and shall issue a new certificate of title, but only if the application contains or has attached to it all of the following:

(a) An endorsement of the county treasurer that all real property taxes charged against the home under Title LVII of the Revised Code and division (B) of section 4503.06 of the Revised Code for all preceding tax years have been paid;

(b) An endorsement of the county auditor that the home will be removed from the real property tax list;

(c) Proof that there are no outstanding mortgages or other liens on the home or, if there are such mortgages or other liens, that the mortgagee or lienholder has consented to the reactivation of the certificate of title.

(I)(1) Whoever violates division (F) of this section shall be fined not more than two thousand dollars, imprisoned not more than one year, or both.

(2) Whoever violates division (G) of this section shall be fined not more than one thousand dollars, imprisoned not more than six months, or both.

(2004 H 230, eff. 9–16–04; 2002 S 123, eff. 1–1–04; 2001 S 59, eff. 10–31–01; 2000 H 672, eff. 4–9–01; 1998 S 142, eff. 3–30–99; 1997 S 60, eff. 10–21–97; 1997 H 210, eff. 6–30–97; 1996 H 353, eff. 9–17–96; 1993 H 154, § 11, eff. 10–1–93; 1993 H 206; 1989 H 381; 1987 S 10; 1981 H 694; 1972 H 85; 132 v H 741; 1953 H 1; GC 6290–12)

4505.111 Restored motor vehicles; inspection

(A) Every motor vehicle, other than a motor vehicle as provided in divisions (C), (D), and (E) of section 4505.11 of the Revised Code, that is assembled from component parts by a person other than the manufacturer, shall be inspected by the state highway patrol prior to issuance of title to the motor vehicle. The inspection shall include establishing proof of ownership and an inspection of the motor number and vehicle identification number of the motor vehicle, and any items of equipment the director of public safety considers advisable and requires to be inspected by rule. A fee of forty dollars in fiscal year 1998 and fifty dollars in fiscal year 1999 and thereafter shall be assessed by the state highway patrol for each inspection made pursuant to this section, and shall be deposited in the state highway safety fund established by section 4501.06 of the Revised Code.

(B) Whoever violates this section shall be fined not more than two thousand dollars, imprisoned not more than one year, or both.

(2002 S 123, eff. 1–1–04; 1997 H 210, eff. 6–30–97; 1992 S 98, eff. 11–12–92; 1987 S 10; 1981 H 694, H 1, H 102)

PROHIBITIONS AND PENALTIES

4505.18 Operation or sale of motor vehicle without certificate of title

(A) No person shall do any of the following:

(1) Operate in this state a motor vehicle for which a certificate of title is required without having that certificate in accordance with this chapter or, if a physical certificate of title has not been issued for a motor vehicle, operate the motor vehicle in this state knowing that the ownership information relating to the vehicle has not been entered into the automated title processing system by a clerk of a court of common pleas;

(2) Display or display for sale or sell as a dealer or acting on behalf of a dealer, a motor vehicle without having obtained a manufacturer's or importer's certificate, a certificate of title, or an assignment of a certificate of title for it as provided in this chapter;

(3) Fail to surrender any certificate of title or any certificate of registration or license plates upon cancellation of the same by the registrar of motor vehicles and notice of the cancellation as prescribed in this chapter;

(4) Fail to surrender the certificate of title to a clerk of a court of common pleas as provided in this chapter in case of the destruction or dismantling or change of a motor vehicle in such respect that it is not the motor vehicle described in the certificate of title;

(5) Violate any rules adopted pursuant to this chapter;

(6) Except as otherwise provided in this chapter and Chapter 4517. of the Revised Code, sell at wholesale a motor vehicle the ownership of which is not evidenced by an Ohio certificate of title, or the current certificate of title issued for the motor vehicle, or the manufacturer's certificate of origin, and all title assignments that evidence the seller's ownership of the motor vehicle, and an odometer disclosure statement that complies with section 4505.06 of the Revised Code and subchapter IV of the "Motor Vehicle Information and Cost Savings Act," 86 Stat. 961 (1972), 15 U.S.C. 1981;

(7) Operate in this state a motor vehicle knowing that the certificate of title to the vehicle or ownership of the vehicle as otherwise reflected in the automated title processing system has been canceled.

(B) This section does not apply to persons engaged in the business of warehousing or transporting motor vehicles for the purpose of salvage disposition.

(C) Whoever violates this section shall be fined not more than two hundred dollars, imprisoned not more than ninety days, or both.

(2002 S 123, eff. 1–1–04; 2001 S 59, eff. 10–31–01; 1987 S 10, eff. 8–13–87; 1986 H 382; 130 v Pt 2, H 5; 130 v S 141, H 1; 129 v 1027; 1953 H 1; GC 6290–17)

4505.181 Motor vehicle dealer selling used vehicle without certificate of title; retail purchaser

(A) Notwithstanding divisions (A)(2), (5), and (6) of section 4505.18 of the Revised Code, a motor vehicle dealer or person acting on behalf of a motor vehicle dealer may display, offer for sale, or sell a used motor vehicle without having first obtained a certificate of title for the vehicle in the name of the dealer as required by this chapter if the dealer or person acting on behalf of the dealer complies with divisions (A)(1)(a) and (2) of this section, or divisions (A)(1)(b) and (2) of this section, as follows:

(1)(a) If the dealer has been licensed as a motor vehicle dealer for less than the three-year period prior to the date on which the dealer or person acting on behalf of the dealer displays, offers for sale, or sells the used motor vehicle for which the dealer has not obtained a certificate of title in the name of the dealer, or if the attorney general has paid a retail purchaser of the dealer under division (C) of this section within three years prior to such date, the dealer posts with the attorney general's office in favor of this state a bond of a surety company authorized to do business in this state, in an amount of not less than twenty-five thousand dollars, to be used solely for the purpose of compensating retail purchasers of motor vehicles who suffer damages due to failure of the dealer or person acting on behalf of the dealer to comply with this section. The dealer's surety shall notify the registrar and attorney general when a bond is canceled. Such notification of cancellation shall include the effective date of and reason for cancellation.

(b) If the dealer has been licensed as a motor vehicle dealer for longer than the three-year period prior to the date on which the dealer or person acting on behalf of the dealer displays, offers for sale, or sells the used motor vehicle for which the dealer has not obtained a certificate of title in the name of the dealer and the attorney general has not paid a retail purchaser of the dealer under division (C) of this section within three years prior to such date, the dealer pays one hundred fifty dollars to the attorney general for deposit into the title defect recision fund created by section 1345.52 of the Revised Code.

(2) The dealer or person acting on behalf of the dealer possesses a bill of sale for each motor vehicle proposed to be displayed, offered for sale, or sold under this section and a properly executed power of attorney or other related documents from the prior owner of the motor vehicle giving the dealer or person acting on behalf of the dealer authority to have a certificate of title to the motor vehicle issued in the name of the dealer, and retains copies of all such documents in the dealer's or person's files until such time as a certificate of title in the dealer's name is issued for each such motor vehicle by the clerk of the court of common pleas. Such documents shall be available for inspection by the bureau of motor vehicles during normal business hours.

(B) If a retail purchaser purchases a motor vehicle for which the dealer, pursuant to and in accordance with division (A) of this section, does not have a certificate of title issued in the name of the dealer at the time of the sale, the retail purchaser has an unconditional right to rescind the transaction and the dealer has an obligation to refund to the retail purchaser the full purchase price of the vehicle, if one of the following applies:

(1) The dealer fails, on or before the fortieth day following the date of the sale, to obtain a title in the name of the retail purchaser.

(2) The title for the vehicle indicates that it is a rebuilt salvage vehicle, and the fact that it is a rebuilt salvage vehicle was not disclosed to the retail purchaser in writing prior to the execution of the purchase agreement.

(3) The title for the vehicle indicates that the dealer has made an inaccurate odometer disclosure to the retail purchaser.

If any of the circumstances described in divisions (B)(1) to (3) of this section applies, a retail purchaser or the retail purchaser's representative shall notify the dealer and afford the dealer the opportunity to comply with the dealer's obligation to refund the full purchase price of the motor vehicle. Nothing in this division shall be construed as prohibiting the dealer and the retail purchaser or their representatives from negotiating a compromise resolution that is satisfactory to both parties.

(C) If a retail purchaser notifies a dealer of one or more of the circumstances listed in division (B) of this section and the dealer fails to refund to the retail purchaser the full purchase price of the vehicle or reach a satisfactory compromise with the retail purchaser within three business days of presentation of the retail purchaser's recision claim, the retail purchaser may apply to the attorney general for payment from the fund of the full purchase price to the retail purchaser.

(D) Upon application by a retail purchaser for payment from the fund, if the attorney general is satisfied that one or more of the circumstances contained in divisions (B)(1) to (3) of this section exist, the attorney general shall cause the full purchase price of the vehicle to be paid to the retail purchaser from the fund after delivery of the vehicle to the attorney general. The attorney general may sell or otherwise dispose of any vehicle that is delivered to the attorney general under this section, and may collect the proceeds of any bond posted under division (A) of this section by a dealer who has failed to comply with division (C) of this section. The proceeds from all such sales and collections shall be deposited into the title defect recision fund for use as specified in section 1345.52 of the Revised Code.

(E) Failure by a dealer to comply with division (A) or (B) of this section constitutes a deceptive act or practice in connection with a consumer transaction, and is a violation of section 1345.02 of the Revised Code.

(F) The remedy provided in this section to retail purchasers is in addition to any remedies otherwise available to the retail purchaser for the same conduct of the dealer or person acting on behalf of the dealer under federal law or the laws of this state or a political subdivision of this state.

(G) All motor vehicle dealers licensed under Chapter 4517. of the Revised Code shall pay to the attorney general for deposit into the title defect recision fund the amount described in division (A)(1)(b) of this section beginning with the calendar year during which this section becomes effective and each year subsequent to that year until the balance in the fund is not less than three hundred thousand dollars. All such dealers also shall pay to the attorney general for deposit into the fund that amount during any year and subsequent years during which the balance in the fund is less than three hundred thousand dollars until the balance in the fund reaches three hundred thousand dollars.

If a motor vehicle dealer fails to comply with this division, the attorney general may bring a civil action in a court of competent jurisdiction to collect the amount the dealer failed to pay to the attorney general for deposit into the fund.

(2001 S 59, eff. 10–31–01; 1996 S 182, eff. 12–3–96)

4505.19 Offenses

(A) No person shall do any of the following:

(1) Procure or attempt to procure a certificate of title or a salvage certificate of title to a motor vehicle, or pass or attempt to pass a certificate of title, a salvage certificate of title, or any assignment of a certificate of title or salvage certificate of title to a motor vehicle, or in any other manner gain or attempt to gain ownership to a motor vehicle, knowing or having reason to believe that the motor vehicle or any part of the motor vehicle has been acquired through commission of a theft offense as defined in section 2913.01 of the Revised Code;

(2) Purport to sell or transfer a motor vehicle without delivering to the purchaser or transferee of it a certificate of title, a salvage certificate of title, or a manufacturer's or importer's certificate to it, assigned to the purchaser as provided for in this chapter, except as otherwise provided in this chapter;

(3) With intent to defraud, possess, sell, offer to sell, counterfeit, or supply a blank, forged, fictitious, counterfeit, stolen, or fraudulently or unlawfully obtained certificate of title, registration, bill of sale, or other instruments of ownership of a motor vehicle, or conspire to do any of the foregoing;

(4) Knowingly obtain goods, services, credit, or money by means of an invalid, fictitious, forged, counterfeit, stolen, or unlawfully obtained original or duplicate certificate of title, registration, bill of sale, or other instrument of ownership of a motor vehicle;

(5) Knowingly obtain goods, services, credit, or money by means of a certificate of title to a motor vehicle, which is required to be surrendered to the registrar of motor vehicles or the clerk of the court of common pleas as provided in this chapter.

(B) Whoever violates this section shall be fined not more than five thousand dollars or imprisoned in the county jail or workhouse not less than six months nor more than one year, or both, or in a state correctional institution not less than one year nor more than five years.

(2002 S 123, eff. 1–1–04; 2001 S 59, eff. 10–31–01; 1996 H 353, eff. 9–17–96; 1994 H 687, eff. 10–12–94; 1984 H 632, eff. 3–28–85; 1972 H 511, H 85; 1971 H 84; 1953 H 1; GC 6290–16)

4505.20 Dealer may sell for secured party with written authorization but no transfer of title to dealer

(A) Notwithstanding division (A)(2) of section 4505.18 of the Revised Code or any other provision of this chapter or Chapter 4517. of the Revised Code, a secured party may designate any dealer to display, display for sale, or sell a manufactured or mobile home if the home has come into the possession of that secured party by a default in the terms of a security instrument and the certificate of title remains in the name and possession of the secured party.

(B) Notwithstanding division (A)(2) of section 4505.18 of the Revised Code or any other provision of this chapter or Chapter 4517. of the Revised Code, the owner of a recreational vehicle or a secured party of a recreational vehicle who has come into possession of the vehicle by a default in the terms of a security instrument, may designate any dealer to display, display for sale, or sell the vehicle while the certificate of title remains in the possession of the owner or secured party. No dealer may display or offer for sale more than five recreational vehicles at any time under this division. No dealer may display or offer for sale a recreational vehicle under this division unless the dealer maintains insurance or the bond of a surety company authorized to transact business within this state in an amount sufficient to satisfy the fair market value of the vehicle.

(C) The registrar of motor vehicles may adopt rules in accordance with Chapter 119. of the Revised Code prescribing the maximum number of manufactured or mobile homes that have come into the possession of a secured party by a default in the terms of a security instrument that any dealer may display or offer for sale at any time. The registrar may adopt other reasonable rules regarding the resale of such manufactured homes, mobile homes, and recreational vehicles that the registrar considers necessary.

(D) The secured party or owner shall provide the dealer with written authorization to display, display for sale, or sell the manufactured home, mobile home, or recreational vehicle. The dealer shall show and explain the written authorization to any prospective purchaser. The written authorization shall contain the vehicle identification number, make, model, year of manufacture, and physical description of the manufactured home, mobile home, or recreational vehicle that is provided to the dealer.

(E) As used in this section, "dealer" means a new motor vehicle dealer that is licensed under Chapter 4517. of the Revised Code.

(F) Whoever violates this section shall be fined not more than two hundred dollars, imprisoned not more than ninety days, or both.

(2002 S 123, eff. 1–1–04; 2001 S 59, eff. 10–31–01; 1998 S 142, eff. 3–30–99; 1996 H 353, eff. 9–17–96; 1994 S 191, eff. 10–20–94; 1994 H 687, eff. 10–12–94; 1984 S 231, eff. 9–20–84; 1978 S 332)

4505.21 Procedures in case of export

(A) As used in this section:

(1) "Certified receipt of title cancellation" means a form prescribed by the registrar of motor vehicles for use under this section that shall include all of the following:

(a) The name of the owner who surrenders a certificate of title to a vehicle intended to be exported;

(b) A description of the motor vehicle that shall include the year, make, model, style, vehicle identification number, color, license registration number, and the state of registration;

(c) The destination of the motor vehicle;

(d) Whether the purpose of the export is for sale, lease, personal use, or other specified use;

(e) Such other information as the registrar determines to be appropriate.

(2) A "declaration of temporary export" means a form prescribed by the registrar that includes all of the following:

(a) The items specified in divisions (A)(1)(a) to (c) of this section;

(b) A statement that the vehicle will not be permanently located outside of the United States and that the owner intends to return the vehicle to the United States;

(c) The period of time for which it is anticipated that the motor vehicle will be located outside of the United States.

(3) "Export" means the shipping or transportation of a motor vehicle from any point inside the United States to a point outside of the United States. "Export" does not include operating the motor vehicle by means of its own power or that of a motor vehicle drawing or towing it unless the purpose of the owner is to avoid compliance with division (B) or (C) of this section.

(4) "Owner" means the person named on a certificate of title issued by this state as the owner or assignee of the owner of the motor vehicle for which the certificate of title has been issued and includes any person who is lawfully entitled to the issuance of a new certificate of title to the motor vehicle naming the person as owner of the vehicle or who is lawfully entitled to surrender the certificate of title under this section. "Owner" includes a secured party who exports or permits the export of a motor vehicle in the exercise of the secured party's rights and powers under the security agreement.

(B) No owner of a motor vehicle who exports or permits the export of the motor vehicle for permanent location outside of the United States shall do any of the following:

(1) Fail to surrender the certificate of title to the motor vehicle to the registrar prior to the date that the motor vehicle is delivered to any person for export;

(2) Knowingly fail to surrender the certificate of title to the motor vehicle to the registrar prior to the date that the motor vehicle is delivered to any person for export.

(C) No owner of a motor vehicle who exports or permits the export of the motor vehicle for temporary location outside of the United States shall do any of the following:

(1) Fail to file a declaration of temporary export with the registrar prior to the date that the motor vehicle is delivered to any person for export;

(2) Purposely fail to file a declaration of temporary export with the registrar prior to the date that the motor vehicle is delivered to any person for export in order to facilitate the commission of a conspiracy, attempt, complicity, or theft offense related to the title of a motor vehicle or the proceeds of a motor vehicle insurance policy.

(D)(1) Proof that the defendant acted in good faith and surrendered the certificate of title to the registrar within a reasonable time after delivery of the motor vehicle for export is an affirmative defense to a prosecution under division (B)(1) of this section.

(2) Proof that the defendant acted in good faith and filed a declaration of temporary export with the registrar within a reasonable time after delivery of the motor vehicle for export is an affirmative defense to a prosecution under division (C)(1) of this section.

(E) The registrar shall prescribe forms to be signed by the owner who surrenders a certificate of title for cancellation under this section and by all secured parties whose uncanceled security interests are noted on the certificate. The form shall indicate the person to whom a certified receipt of title cancellation is to be delivered and any security interests that are to be noted on the certified receipt of title cancellation. The registrar shall inspect the title surrender form and the certificate of title to determine whether any uncanceled security interests have been noted on the title under section 4505.13 of the Revised Code and whether the person exporting the vehicle is the lawful owner. If the registrar determines that the certificate is in proper order and that all secured parties having uncanceled security interests noted on the certificate have consented to the surrender of the certificate, the registrar shall issue a certified receipt of title to the owner with such notation of security interests as shall be requested upon the title surrender form.

(F) The registrar shall record a declaration of temporary export filed under division (B)(2) of this section and retain it with the records of the certificate of title until the owner notifies the registrar, on a form prescribed by the registrar, that the motor vehicle has been returned to the United States.

(G)(1) Whoever violates division (B)(1) or (C)(1) of this section is guilty of a misdemeanor of the first degree.

(2) Whoever violates division (B)(2) or (C)(2) of this section is guilty of a felony of the fifth degree.

(2002 S 123, eff. 1–1–04; 1996 H 353, eff. 9–17–96; 1984 H 632, eff. 3–28–85)

4505.25 Use of money for implementation

The registrar of motor vehicles may use money from the automated title processing fund created in section 4505.09 of the Revised Code, in accordance with appropriations made by the general assembly, to pay expenses related to implementing Sub. S.B. 59 of the 124th general assembly.

(2001 S 59, eff. 10–31–01)

4505.99 Penalties

Whoever violates any provision of sections 4505.01 to 4505.21 of the Revised Code for which no penalty otherwise is provided in the section that contains the provision violated shall be fined not more than two hundred dollars, imprisoned not more than ninety days, or both.

(2002 S 123, eff. 1–1–04; 1995 S 2, eff. 7–1–96; 1994 H 571, eff. 10–6–94; 1987 S 10, eff. 8–13–87; 1984 H 632; 1981 H 671, H 275, H 102; 1972 H 85; 132 v H 555; 126 v 575; 1953 H 1)

CHAPTER 4506

COMMERCIAL DRIVERS' LICENSING

Section

4506.01 Definitions

As used in this chapter:

(A) "Alcohol concentration" means the concentration of alcohol in a person's blood, breath, or urine. When expressed as a percentage, it means grams of alcohol per the following:

(1) One hundred milliliters of whole blood, blood serum, or blood plasma;

(2) Two hundred ten liters of breath;

(3) One hundred milliliters of urine.

(B) "School bus" has the same meaning as in section 4511.01 of the Revised Code.

(C) "Commercial driver's license" means a license issued in accordance with this chapter that authorizes an individual to drive a commercial motor vehicle.

(D) "Commercial driver license information system" means the information system established pursuant to the requirements of the "Commercial Motor Vehicle Safety Act of 1986," 100 Stat. 3207–171, 49 U.S.C.A. App. 2701.

(E) Except when used in section 4506.25 of the Revised Code, "commercial motor vehicle" means any motor vehicle designed or used to transport persons or property that meets any of the following qualifications:

(1) Any combination of vehicles with a combined gross vehicle weight rating of twenty-six thousand one pounds or more, provided the gross vehicle weight rating of the vehicle or vehicles being towed is in excess of ten thousand pounds;

(2) Any single vehicle with a gross vehicle weight rating of twenty-six thousand one pounds or more, or any such vehicle towing a vehicle having a gross vehicle weight rating that is not in excess of ten thousand pounds;

(3) Any single vehicle or combination of vehicles that is not a class A or class B vehicle, but that either is designed to transport sixteen or more passengers including the driver, or is placarded for hazardous materials;

(4) Any school bus with a gross vehicle weight rating of less than twenty-six thousand one pounds that is designed to transport fewer than sixteen passengers including the driver;

(5) Is transporting hazardous materials for which placarding is required by regulations adopted under the "Hazardous Materials Transportation Act," 88 Stat. 2156 (1975), 49 U.S.C.A. 1801, as amended;

(6) Any single vehicle or combination of vehicles that is designed to be operated and to travel on a public street or highway and is considered by the federal highway administration to be a commercial motor vehicle, including, but not limited to, a motorized crane, a vehicle whose function is to pump cement, a rig for drilling wells, and a portable crane.

(F) "Controlled substance" means all of the following:

(1) Any substance classified as a controlled substance under the "Controlled Substances Act," 80 Stat. 1242 (1970), 21 U.S.C.A. 802(6), as amended;

(2) Any substance included in schedules I through V of 21 C.F.R. part 1308, as amended;

(3) Any drug of abuse.

(G) "Conviction" means an unvacated adjudication of guilt or a determination that a person has violated or failed to comply with the law in a court of original jurisdiction or an authorized administrative tribunal, an unvacated forfeiture of bail or collateral deposited to secure the person's appearance in court, the payment of a fine or court cost, or violation of a condition of release without bail, regardless of whether or not the penalty is rebated, suspended, or probated.

(H) "Disqualification" means withdrawal of the privilege to drive a commercial motor vehicle.

(I) "Drive" means to drive, operate, or be in physical control of a motor vehicle.

(J) "Driver" means any person who drives, operates, or is in physical control of a commercial motor vehicle or is required to have a commercial driver's license.

(K) "Driver's license" means a license issued by the bureau of motor vehicles that authorizes an individual to drive.

(L) "Drug of abuse" means any controlled substance, dangerous drug as defined in section 4729.01 of the Revised Code, or over-the-counter medication that, when taken in quantities exceeding the recommended dosage, can result in impairment of judgment or reflexes.

(M) "Employer" means any person, including the federal government, any state, and a political subdivision of any state, that owns or leases a commercial motor vehicle or assigns a person to drive such a motor vehicle.

(N) "Endorsement" means an authorization on a person's commercial driver's license that is required to permit the person to operate a specified type of commercial motor vehicle.

(O) "Felony" means any offense under federal or state law that is punishable by death or specifically classified as a felony under the law of this state, regardless of the penalty that may be imposed.

(P) "Foreign jurisdiction" means any jurisdiction other than a state.

(Q) "Gross vehicle weight rating" means the value specified by the manufacturer as the maximum loaded weight of a single or a combination vehicle. The gross vehicle weight rating of a combination vehicle is the gross vehicle weight rating of the power unit plus the gross vehicle weight rating of each towed unit.

(R) "Hazardous materials" means materials identified as such under regulations adopted under the "Hazardous Materials Transportation Act," 88 Stat. 2156 (1975), 49 U.S.C.A. 1801, as amended.

(S) "Motor vehicle" has the same meaning as in section 4511.01 of the Revised Code.

(T) Except when used in sections 4506.25 and 4506.26 of the Revised Code, "out-of-service order" means a temporary prohibition against driving a commercial motor vehicle issued under this chapter or a similar law of another state or of a foreign jurisdiction.

(U) "Residence" means any person's residence determined in accordance with standards prescribed in rules adopted by the registrar.

(V) "Temporary residence" means residence on a temporary basis as determined by the registrar in accordance with standards prescribed in rules adopted by the registrar.

(W) "Serious traffic violation" means a conviction arising from the operation of a commercial motor vehicle that involves any of the following:

(1) A single charge of any speed that is in excess of the posted speed limit by an amount specified by the United States secretary of transportation and that the director of public safety designates as such by rule;

(2) Violation of section 4511.20, 4511.201, or 4511.202 of the Revised Code or any similar ordinance or resolution, or of any similar law of another state or political subdivision of another state;

(3) Violation of a law of this state or an ordinance or resolution relating to traffic control, other than a parking violation, or of any similar law of another state or political subdivision of another state, that results in a fatal accident;

(4) Violation of any other law of this state or an ordinance or resolution relating to traffic control, other than a parking violation, that is determined to be a serious traffic violation by the United States secretary of transportation and the director designates as such by rule.

(X) "State" means a state of the United States and includes the District of Columbia.

(Y) "Tank vehicle" means any commercial motor vehicle that is designed to transport any liquid and has a maximum capacity greater than one hundred nineteen gallons or is designed to transport gaseous materials and has a water capacity greater than one thousand pounds within a tank that is either permanently or temporarily attached to the vehicle or its chassis. "Tank vehicle" does not include any of the following:

(1) Any portable tank having a rated capacity of less than one thousand gallons;

(2) Tanks used exclusively as a fuel tank for the motor vehicle to which it is attached;

(3) An empty storage container tank that is not designed for transportation and that is readily distinguishable from a transportation tank;

(4) Ready–mix concrete mixers.

(Z) "United States" means the fifty states and the District of Columbia.

(AA) "Vehicle" has the same meaning as in section 4511.01 of the Revised Code.

(BB) "Peace officer" has the same meaning as in section 2935.01 of the Revised Code.

(CC) "Portable tank" means a liquid or gaseous packaging designed primarily to be loaded on or temporarily attached to a vehicle and equipped with skids, mountings, or accessories to facilitate handling of the tank by mechanical means.

(2004 H 230, eff. 9–16–04; 2002 S 123, eff. 1–1–04; 2000 H 600, eff. 9–1–00; 2000 S 245, eff. 6–30–00; 1998 S 213, eff. 7–29–98; 1998 S 66, eff. 7–22–98; 1997 S 60, eff. 10–21–97; 1996 H 353, eff. 9–17–96; 1995 S 2, eff. 7–1–96; 1994 H 687, eff. 10–12–94; 1992 S 98, eff. 11–12–92; 1990 H 831, H 88; 1989 H 381)

4506.011 Use of actual gross weight of vehicle

For purposes of this chapter, the actual gross weight of a vehicle or combination of vehicles may be used in lieu of a gross vehicle weight rating to determine whether a vehicle or combination of vehicles qualifies as a commercial motor vehicle if the gross vehicle weight rating specified by the manufacturer for the vehicle or combination of vehicles is not determinable, or if the manufacturer of the vehicle has not specified a gross vehicle weight rating.

(2000 H 600, eff. 9–1–00)

4506.02 Exemptions

(A) Nothing in this chapter applies to any person when engaged in the operation of any of the following:

(1) A farm truck;

(2) Fire equipment for a fire department, volunteer or nonvolunteer fire company, fire district, or joint fire district;

(3) A public safety vehicle used to provide transportation or emergency medical service for ill or injured persons;

(4) A recreational vehicle;

(5) A commercial motor vehicle within the boundaries of an eligible unit of local government, if the person is employed by the eligible unit of local government and is operating the commercial motor vehicle for the purpose of removing snow or ice from a roadway by plowing, sanding, or salting, but only if either the employee who holds a commercial driver's license issued under this chapter and ordinarily operates a commercial motor vehicle for these purposes is unable to operate the vehicle, or the employing eligible unit of local government determines that a snow or ice emergency exists that requires additional assistance;

(6) A vehicle owned by the department of defense and operated by any member or uniformed employee of the armed forces of the United States or their reserve components, including the Ohio national guard. This exception does not apply to United States reserve technicians.

(7) A commercial motor vehicle that is operated for nonbusiness purposes. "Operated for nonbusiness purposes" means that the commercial motor vehicle is not used in commerce as "commerce" is defined in 49 C.F.R. 383.5, as amended, and is not regulated by the public utilities commission pursuant to Chapter 4919., 4921., or 4923. of the Revised Code.

(8) A motor vehicle that is designed primarily for the transportation of goods and not persons, while that motor vehicle is being used for the occasional transportation of personal property by individuals not for compensation and not in the furtherance of a commercial enterprise.

(B) Nothing contained in division (A)(5) of this section shall be construed as preempting or superseding any law, rule, or regulation of this state concerning the safe operation of commercial motor vehicles.

(C) As used in this section:

(1) "Eligible unit of local government" means a village, township, or county that has a population of not more than three thousand persons according to the most recent federal census.

(2) "Farm truck" means a truck controlled and operated by a farmer for use in the transportation to or from a farm, for a distance of no more than one hundred fifty miles, of products of the farm, including livestock and its products, poultry and its products, floricultural and horticultural products, and in the transportation to the farm, from a distance of no more than one hundred fifty miles, of supplies for the farm, including tile, fence, and every other thing or commodity used in agricultural, floricultural, horticultural, livestock, and poultry production, and livestock, poultry, and other animals and things used for breeding, feeding, or other purposes connected with the operation of the farm, when the truck is operated in accordance with this division and is not used in the operations of a motor transportation company or private motor carrier.

(3) "Public safety vehicle" has the same meaning as in divisions (E)(1) and (3) of section 4511.01 of the Revised Code.

(4) "Recreational vehicle" includes every vehicle that is defined as a recreational vehicle in section 4501.01 of the Revised Code and is used exclusively for purposes other than engaging in business for profit.

(2002 S 123, eff. 1–1–04; 1998 S 213, eff. 7–29–98; 1997 S 130, eff. 9–18–97; 1996 S 121, eff. 11–19–96; 1990 H 831, eff. 7–17–90; 1989 H 381)

4506.03 Prerequisites to operation of commercial motor vehicle on and after April 1, 1992

(A) On and after April 1, 1992, the following shall apply:

(1) No person shall drive a commercial motor vehicle on a highway in this state unless the person holds a valid commercial driver's license with proper endorsements for the motor vehicle being driven, issued by the registrar of motor vehicles, a valid examiner's commercial driving permit issued under section 4506.13 of the Revised Code, a valid restricted commercial driver's license and waiver for farm-related service industries issued under section 4506.24 of the Revised Code, or a valid commercial driver's license temporary instruction permit issued by the registrar and is accompanied by an authorized state driver's license examiner or tester or a person who has been issued and has in the person's immediate possession a current, valid commercial driver's license with proper endorsements for the motor vehicle being driven.

(2) No person shall be issued a commercial driver's license until the person surrenders to the registrar of motor vehicles all valid licenses issued to the person by another jurisdiction recognized by this state. All surrendered licenses shall be returned by the registrar to the issuing authority.

(3) No person who has been a resident of this state for thirty days or longer shall drive a commercial motor vehicle under the authority of a commercial driver's license issued by another jurisdiction.

(B) As used in this section and in section 4506.09 of the Revised Code, "tester" means a person or entity acting pursuant to a valid agreement entered into under division (B) of section 4506.09 of the Revised Code.

(C) Whoever violates this section is guilty of a misdemeanor of the first degree.

(2002 S 123, eff. 1–1–04; 1992 H 485, eff. 7–8–92; 1989 H 381)

4506.04 Prohibitions

(A) No person shall do any of the following:

(1) Drive a commercial motor vehicle while having in the person's possession or otherwise under the person's control more than one valid driver's license issued by this state, any other state, or by a foreign jurisdiction;

(2) Drive a commercial motor vehicle on a highway in this state in violation of an out-of-service order, while the person's driving privilege is suspended, revoked, or canceled, or while the person is subject to disqualification;

(3) Drive a motor vehicle on a highway in this state under authority of a commercial driver's license issued by another state or a foreign jurisdiction, after having been a resident of this state for thirty days or longer;

(4) Knowingly give false information in any application or certification required by section 4506.07 of the Revised Code.

(B) The department of public safety shall give every conviction occurring out of this state and notice of which is received after December 31, 1989, full faith and credit and treat it for sanctioning purposes under this chapter as though the conviction had occurred in this state.

(C)(1) Whoever violates division (A)(1), (2), or (3) of this section is guilty of a misdemeanor of the first degree.

(2) Whoever violates division (A)(4) of this section is guilty of falsification, a misdemeanor of the first degree. In addition, the provisions of section 4507.19 of the Revised Code apply.

(2002 S 123, eff. 1–1–04; 1992 S 98, eff. 11–12–92; 1989 H 381)

4506.05 Prerequisites to operation of commercial motor vehicle

(A) Notwithstanding any other provision of law, a person may drive a commercial motor vehicle on a highway in this state if all of the following conditions are met:

(1) The person has a valid commercial driver's license or commercial driver's license temporary instruction permit issued by any state in accordance with the minimum standards adopted by the federal highway administration under the "Commercial Motor Vehicle Safety Act of 1986," 100 Stat. 3207–171, 49 U.S.C.A. App. for [1] issuance of commercial drivers' licenses;

(2) The person's commercial driver's license or permit is not suspended, revoked, or canceled;

(3) The person is not disqualified from driving a commercial motor vehicle;

(4) The person is not subject to an out-of-service order.

(B) Whoever violates this section is guilty of a misdemeanor of the first degree.

(2002 S 123, eff. 1–1–04; 1989 H 381, eff. 7–1–89)

[1] Prior and current versions differ; although no amendment was indicated in 2002 S 123, "49 U.S.C.A. App. for" appeared as "49 U.S.C.A. App. 2701, for" in 1989 H 381.

4506.06 Commercial driver's temporary instruction permit

(A) The registrar of motor vehicles, upon receiving an application for a commercial driver's temporary instruction permit, may issue the permit to any person who is at least eighteen years of age and holds a valid driver's license, other than a restricted license, issued under Chapter 4507. of the Revised Code. A commercial driver's temporary instruction permit shall not be issued for a period exceeding six months and only one renewal of a permit shall be granted in a two-year period.

The holder of a commercial driver's temporary instruction permit, unless otherwise disqualified, may drive a commercial motor vehicle when having the permit in the holder's actual possession and accompanied by a person who holds a valid commercial driver's license valid for the type of vehicle being driven and who occupies a seat beside the permit holder for the purpose of giving instruction in driving the motor vehicle.

(B) Whoever violates this section is guilty of a misdemeanor of the first degree.

(2002 S 123, eff. 1–1–04; 1996 H 353, eff. 9–17–96; 1990 H 88, eff. 3–13–90; 1989 H 381)

4506.07 Applications; registration of voters

(A) Every application for a commercial driver's license, restricted commercial driver's license, or a commercial driver's temporary instruction permit, or a duplicate of such a license, shall be made upon a form approved and furnished by the registrar of motor vehicles. Except as provided in section 4506.24 of the Revised Code in regard to a restricted commercial driver's license, the application shall be signed by the applicant and shall contain the following information:

(1) The applicant's name, date of birth, social security account number, sex, general description including height, weight, and color of hair and eyes, current residence, duration of residence in this state, country of citizenship, and occupation;

(2) Whether the applicant previously has been licensed to operate a commercial motor vehicle or any other type of motor vehicle in another state or a foreign jurisdiction and, if so, when, by what state, and whether the license or driving privileges currently are suspended or revoked in any jurisdiction, or the applicant otherwise has been disqualified from operating a commercial motor vehicle, or is subject to an out-of-service order issued under this chapter or any similar law of another state or a foreign jurisdiction and, if so, the date of, locations involved, and reason for the suspension, revocation, disqualification, or out-of-service order;

(3) Whether the applicant is afflicted with or suffering from any physical or mental disability or disease that prevents the applicant from exercising reasonable and ordinary control over a motor vehicle while operating it upon a highway or is or has been subject to any condition resulting in episodic impairment of consciousness or loss of muscular control and, if so, the nature and extent of the disability, disease, or condition, and the names and addresses of the physicians attending the applicant;

(4) Whether the applicant has obtained a medical examiner's certificate as required by this chapter;

(5) Whether the applicant has pending a citation for violation of any motor vehicle law or ordinance except a parking violation and, if so, a description of the citation, the court having jurisdiction of the offense, and the date when the offense occurred;

(6) Whether the applicant wishes to certify willingness to make an anatomical donation under section 2108.04 of the Revised Code, which shall be given no consideration in the issuance of a license;

(7) On and after May 1, 1993, whether the applicant has executed a valid durable power of attorney for health care pursuant to sections 1337.11 to 1337.17 of the Revised Code or has executed a declaration governing the use or continuation, or the withholding or withdrawal, of life sustaining treatment pursuant to sections 2133.01 to 2133.15 of the Revised Code and, if the applicant has executed either type of instrument, whether the applicant wishes the license issued to indicate that the applicant has executed the instrument.

(B) Every applicant shall certify, on a form approved and furnished by the registrar, all of the following:

(1) That the motor vehicle in which the applicant intends to take the driving skills test is representative of the type of motor vehicle that the applicant expects to operate as a driver;

(2) That the applicant is not subject to any disqualification or out-of-service order, or license suspension, revocation, or cancellation, under the laws of this state, of another state, or of a foreign jurisdiction and does not have more than one driver's license issued by this or another state or a foreign jurisdiction;

(3) Any additional information, certification, or evidence that the registrar requires by rule in order to ensure that the issuance of a commercial driver's license to the applicant is in compliance with the law of this state and with federal law.

(C) Every applicant shall execute a form, approved and furnished by the registrar, under which the applicant consents to the release by the registrar of information from the applicant's driving record.

(D) The registrar or a deputy registrar, in accordance with section 3503.11 of the Revised Code, shall register as an elector any applicant for a commercial driver's license or for a renewal or duplicate of such a license under this chapter, if the applicant is eligible and wishes to be registered as an elector. The decision of an applicant whether to register as an elector shall be given no consideration in the decision of whether to issue the applicant a license or a renewal or duplicate.

(E) The registrar or a deputy registrar, in accordance with section 3503.11 of the Revised Code, shall offer the opportunity of completing a notice of change of residence or change of name to any applicant for a commercial driver's license or for a renewal or duplicate of such a license who is a resident of this state, if the applicant is a registered elector who has changed the applicant's residence or name and has not filed such a notice.

(1998 H 354, eff. 7–9–98; 1994 S 300, eff. 1–1–95; 1992 H 427, eff. 10–8–92; 1992 H 485; 1989 H 381)

4506.08 Fees

(A) Each application for a commercial driver's license temporary instruction permit shall be accompanied by a fee of ten dollars; except as provided in division (B) of this section, each application for a commercial driver's license, restricted commercial driver's license, or renewal of such a license shall be accompanied by a fee of twenty-five dollars; and each application for a duplicate commercial driver's license shall be accompanied by a fee of ten dollars. In addition, the registrar of motor vehicles or deputy registrar may collect and retain an additional fee of no more than two dollars and seventy-five cents commencing on July 1, 2001, three dollars and twenty-five cents commencing on January 1, 2003, and three dollars and fifty cents commencing on January 1, 2004, for each application for a commercial driver's license temporary instruction permit, commercial driver's license, renewal of a commercial driver's license, or duplicate commercial driver's license received by the registrar or deputy. No fee shall be charged for the annual issuance of a waiver for farm-related service industries pursuant to section 4506.24 of the Revised Code.

Each deputy registrar shall transmit the fees collected to the registrar at the time and in the manner prescribed by the registrar by rule. The registrar shall pay the fees into the state highway safety fund established in section 4501.06 of the Revised Code.

(B) In addition to the fees imposed under division (A) of this section, the registrar of motor vehicles or deputy registrar shall collect a fee of twelve dollars commencing on October 1, 2003, for each application for a commercial driver's license temporary instruction permit, commercial driver's license, or duplicate commercial driver's license and for each application for renewal of a commercial driver's license with an expiration date on or after that date received by the registrar or deputy registrar. The additional fee is for the purpose of defraying the department of public safety's costs associated with the administration and enforcement of the motor vehicle and traffic laws of Ohio. Each deputy registrar shall transmit the fees collected under division (B) of this section in the time and manner prescribed by the registrar. The registrar shall deposit all moneys received under division (B) of this section into the state highway safety fund established in section 4501.06 of the Revised Code.

(C) Information regarding the driving record of any person holding a commercial driver's license issued by this state shall be furnished by the registrar, upon request and payment of a fee of two dollars, to the employer or prospective employer of such a person and to any insurer.

(2004 H 230, eff. 9–16–04; 2003 H 87, eff. 6–30–03; 2001 H 94, eff. 6–6–01; 1997 S 60, eff. 10–21–97; 1995 H 107, eff. (See Historical and Statutory Notes); 1993 H 154, eff. 6–30–93; 1992 H 485; 1991 H 134; 1989 H 381)

Historical and Statutory Notes

Ed. Note: 1995 H 107 Effective Date—The Secretary of State assigned a general effective date of 6–30–95 for 1995 H 107. Pursuant to O Const Art II § 1c and 1d, and RC 1.471, sections of 1995 H 107 that are, or depend for their implementation upon, current expense appropriations are effective 3–31–95; sections of 1995 H 107 that are not, and do not depend for their implementation upon, current expense appropriations are effective 6–30–95. See *Baldwin's Ohio Legislative Service*, 1995, page 3/L–98 for 1995 H 107, § 16.

4506.081 Voluntary contributions to second chance trust fund

In addition to the fees collected under section 4506.08 of the Revised Code, the registrar or deputy registrar of motor vehicles shall ask each person applying for or renewing a commercial driver's license, restricted commercial driver's license, or duplicate whether the person wishes to make a one-dollar voluntary contribution to the second chance trust fund established under section 2108.15 of the Revised Code. The registrar or deputy registrar shall also make available to the person informational material provided by the department of health on the importance of organ, tissue, and eye donation.

All donations collected under this section during each month shall be forwarded by the registrar or deputy registrar not later than the fifth day of the immediately following month to the treasurer of state, who shall deposit them in the second chance trust fund.

(1996 S 300, eff. 7–1–97)

4506.09 Qualifications; skills test; fees

(A) The registrar of motor vehicles, subject to approval by the director of public safety, shall adopt rules conforming with applicable standards adopted by the federal motor carrier safety administration as regulations under Pub. L. No. 103–272, 108 Stat. 1014 to 1029 (1994), 49 U.S.C.A. 31301 to 31317. The rules shall establish requirements for the qualification and testing of persons applying for a commercial driver's license, which shall be in addition to other requirements established by this chapter. Except as provided in division (B) of this section, the highway patrol or any other employee of the department of public safety the registrar authorizes shall supervise and conduct the testing of persons applying for a commercial driver's license.

(B) The director may adopt rules, in accordance with Chapter 119. of the Revised Code and applicable requirements of the federal motor carrier safety administration, authorizing the skills test specified in this section to be administered by any person, by an agency of this or another state, or by an agency, department, or instrumentality of local government. Each party authorized under this division to administer the skills test may charge a maximum divisible fee of eighty-five dollars for each skills test given as part of a commercial driver's license examination. The fee shall consist of not more than twenty dollars for the pre-trip inspection portion of the test, not more than twenty dollars for the off-road maneuvering portion of the test, and not more than forty-five dollars for the on-road portion of the test. Each such party may require an appointment fee in the same manner provided in division (E)(2) of this section, except that the maximum amount such a party may require as an appointment fee is eighty-five dollars. The skills test administered by another party under this division shall be the same as otherwise would be administered by this state. The other party shall enter into an agreement with the director that, without limitation, does all of the following:

(1) Allows the director or the director's representative and the federal motor carrier safety administration or its representative to conduct random examinations, inspections, and audits of the other party without prior notice;

(2) Requires the director or the director's representative to conduct on-site inspections of the other party at least annually;

(3) Requires that all examiners of the other party meet the same qualification and training standards as examiners of the department of public safety, to the extent necessary to conduct skills tests in the manner required by 49 C.F.R. 383.110 through 383.135;

(4) Requires either that state employees take, at least annually and as though the employees were test applicants, the tests

actually administered by the other party, that the director test a sample of drivers who were examined by the other party to compare the test results, or that state employees accompany a test applicant during an actual test;

(5) Reserves to this state the right to take prompt and appropriate remedial action against testers of the other party if the other party fails to comply with standards of this state or federal standards for the testing program or with any other terms of the contract.

(C) The director shall enter into an agreement with the department of education authorizing the skills test specified in this section to be administered by the department at any location operated by the department for purposes of training and testing school bus drivers, provided that the agreement between the director and the department complies with the requirements of division (B) of this section. Skills tests administered by the department shall be limited to persons applying for a commercial driver's license with a school bus endorsement.

(D) The director shall adopt rules, in accordance with Chapter 119. of the Revised Code, authorizing waiver of the skills test specified in this section for any applicant for a commercial driver's license who meets all of the following requirements:

(1) Certifies that, during the two-year period immediately preceding application for a commercial driver's license, all of the following apply:

(a) The applicant has not had more than one license;

(b) The applicant has not had any license suspended, revoked, or canceled;

(c) The applicant has not had any convictions for any type of motor vehicle for the offenses for which disqualification is prescribed in section 4506.16 of the Revised Code;

(d) The applicant has not had any violation of a state or local law relating to motor vehicle traffic control other than a parking violation arising in connection with any traffic accident and has no record of an accident in which the applicant was at fault.

(2) Certifies and also provides evidence that the applicant is regularly employed in a job requiring operation of a commercial motor vehicle and that one of the following applies:

(a) The applicant has previously taken and passed a skills test given by a state with a classified licensing and testing system in which the test was behind-the-wheel in a representative vehicle for the applicant's commercial driver's license classification;

(b) The applicant has regularly operated, for at least two years immediately preceding application for a commercial driver's license, a vehicle representative of the commercial motor vehicle the applicant operates or expects to operate.

(E)(1) The department of public safety may charge and collect a divisible fee of fifty dollars for each skills test given as part of a commercial driver's license examination. The fee shall consist of ten dollars for the pre-trip inspection portion of the test, ten dollars for the off-road maneuvering portion of the test, and thirty dollars for the on-road portion of the test.

(2) The director may require an applicant for a commercial driver's license who schedules an appointment with the highway patrol or other authorized employee of the department of public safety to take all portions of the skills test, to pay an appointment fee of fifty dollars at the time of scheduling the appointment. If the applicant appears at the time and location specified for the appointment and takes all portions of the skills test during that appointment, the appointment fee shall serve as the skills test fee. If the applicant schedules an appointment to take all portions of the skills test and fails to appear at the time and location specified for the appointment, no portion of the appointment fee shall be refunded. If the applicant schedules an appointment to take all portions of the skills test and appears at the time and location specified for the appointment, but declines or is unable to take all portions of the skills test, the appointment fee shall serve as the skills test fee. If the applicant cancels a scheduled appointment forty-eight hours or more prior to the time of the appointment time, the applicant shall not forfeit the appointment fee.

An applicant for a commercial driver's license who schedules an appointment to take one or more, but not all, portions of the skills test shall not be required to pay any appointment fee when scheduling such an appointment.

(3) The department of public safety shall deposit all fees it collects under division (E) of this section in the state highway safety fund.

(F) As used in this section, "skills test" means a test of an applicant's ability to drive the type of commercial motor vehicle for which the applicant seeks a commercial driver's license by having the applicant drive such a motor vehicle while under the supervision of an authorized state driver's license examiner or tester.

(2004 H 230, eff. 9–16–04; 2000 H 600, eff. 9–1–00; 1994 H 687, eff. 10–12–94; 1992 S 98, eff. 11–12–92; 1990 H 88; 1989 H 381)

4506.10 Physical qualifications; medical examinations; suspension, cancellation, or restrictions on license

(A) No person who holds a valid commercial driver's license shall drive a commercial motor vehicle unless the person is physically qualified to do so. Each person who drives or expects to drive a commercial motor vehicle in interstate or foreign commerce or is otherwise subject to 49 C.F.R. 391, et seq., as amended, shall certify to the registrar of motor vehicles at the time of application for a commercial driver's license that the person is in compliance with these standards. Any person who is not subject to 49 C.F.R. 391, et seq., as amended, also shall certify at the time of application that the person is not subject to these standards.

(B) A person is qualified to drive a class B commercial motor vehicle with a school bus endorsement, if the person has been certified as medically qualified in accordance with rules adopted by the department of education.

(C)(1) Except as provided in division (C)(2) of this section, any medical examination required by this section shall be performed only by one of the following:

(a) A person licensed under Chapter 4731. of the Revised Code to practice medicine or surgery or osteopathic medicine and surgery in this state, or licensed under any similar law of another state;

(b) A physician assistant who is authorized by the supervising physician to perform such a medical examination;

(c) A certified nurse practitioner, a clinical nurse specialist, or a certified nurse-midwife.

(2) Any part of an examination required by this section that pertains to visual acuity, field of vision, and the ability to recognize colors may be performed by a person licensed under Chapter 4725. of the Revised Code to practice optometry in this state, or licensed under any similar law of another state.

(3) Any written documentation of a physical examination conducted pursuant to this section shall be completed by the individual who performed the examination.

(D) Whenever good cause appears, the registrar, upon issuing a commercial driver's license under this chapter, may impose restrictions suitable to the licensee's driving ability with respect to the type of motor vehicle or special mechanical control devices required on a motor vehicle that the licensee may operate, or such other restrictions applicable to the licensee as the registrar determines to be necessary.

The registrar may either issue a special restricted license or may set forth upon the usual license form the restrictions imposed.

The registrar, upon receiving satisfactory evidence of any violation of the restrictions of the license, may impose a class D license suspension of the license for the period of time specified in division (B)(4) of section 4510.02 of the Revised Code.

The registrar, upon receiving satisfactory evidence that an applicant or holder of a commercial driver's license has violated division (A)(4) of section 4506.04 of the Revised Code and knowingly given false information in any application or certification required by section 4506.07 of the Revised Code, shall cancel the commercial driver's license of the person or any pending application from the person for a commercial driver's license or class D driver's license for a period of at least sixty days, during which time no application for a commercial driver's license or class D driver's license shall be received from the person.

(E) Whoever violates this section is guilty of a misdemeanor of the first degree.

(2002 S 245, § 3, eff. 1–1–04; 2002 S 245, § 1, eff. 3–31–03; 2002 S 123, eff. 1–1–04; 2001 H 73, eff. 6–29–01; 1990 H 88, eff. 3–13–90; 1989 H 381)

4506.11 Form of license

(A) Every commercial driver's license shall be marked "commercial driver's license" or "CDL" and shall be of such material and so designed as to prevent its reproduction or alteration without ready detection, and, to this end, shall be laminated with a transparent plastic material. The commercial driver's license for licensees under twenty-one years of age shall have characteristics prescribed by the registrar of motor vehicles distinguishing it from that issued to a licensee who is twenty-one years of age or older. Every commercial driver's license shall display all of the following information:

(1) The name and residence address of the licensee;

(2) A color photograph of the licensee;

(3) A physical description of the licensee, including sex, height, weight, and color of eyes and hair;

(4) The licensee's date of birth;

(5) The licensee's social security number if the person has requested that the number be displayed in accordance with section 4501.31 of the Revised Code or if federal law requires the social security number to be displayed and any number or other identifier the director of public safety considers appropriate and establishes by rules adopted under Chapter 119. of the Revised Code and in compliance with federal law;

(6) The licensee's signature;

(7) The classes of commercial motor vehicles the licensee is authorized to drive and any endorsements or restrictions relating to the licensee's driving of those vehicles;

(8) The name of this state;

(9) The dates of issuance and of expiration of the license;

(10) If the licensee has certified willingness to make an anatomical donation under section 2108.04 of the Revised Code, any symbol chosen by the registrar of motor vehicles to indicate that the licensee has certified that willingness;

(11) If the licensee has executed a durable power of attorney for health care or a declaration governing the use or continuation, or the withholding or withdrawal, of life-sustaining treatment and has specified that the licensee wishes the license to indicate that the licensee has executed either type of instrument, any symbol chosen by the registrar to indicate that the licensee has executed either type of instrument;

(12) Any other information the registrar considers advisable and requires by rule.

(B) The registrar may establish and maintain a file of negatives of photographs taken for the purposes of this section.

(C) Neither the registrar nor any deputy registrar shall issue a commercial driver's license to anyone under twenty-one years of age that does not have the characteristics prescribed by the registrar distinguishing it from the commercial driver's license issued to persons who are twenty-one years of age or older.

(D) Whoever violates division (C) of this section is guilty of a minor misdemeanor.

(2004 H 230, eff. 9–16–04; 2002 S 123, eff. 1–1–04; 2001 H 46, eff. 2–1–02; 1998 S 213, eff. 7–29–98; 1994 H 580, eff. 12–9–94; 1992 S 98, eff. 11–12–92; 1992 H 427; 1991 H 134; 1990 S 131; 1989 H 381)

4506.12 Classes of licenses

(A) Commercial drivers' licenses shall be issued in the following classes and shall include any endorsements and restrictions that are applicable. Subject to any such endorsements and restrictions, the holder of a valid commercial driver's license may drive all commercial motor vehicles in the class for which that license is issued and all lesser classes of vehicles, except that the holder shall not operate a motorcycle unless the holder is licensed to do so under Chapter 4507. of the Revised Code.

(B) The classes of commercial drivers' licenses and the commercial motor vehicles that they authorize the operation of are as follows:

(1) Class A--any combination of vehicles with a combined gross vehicle weight rating of twenty-six thousand one pounds or more, if the gross vehicle weight rating of the vehicle or vehicles being towed is in excess of ten thousand pounds.

(2) Class B--any single vehicle with a gross vehicle weight rating of twenty-six thousand one pounds or more or any such vehicle towing a vehicle having a gross vehicle weight rating that is not in excess of ten thousand pounds.

(3) Class C--any single vehicle, or combination of vehicles, that is not a class A or class B vehicle, but that either is designed to transport sixteen or more passengers, including the driver, or is placarded for hazardous materials and any school bus with a gross vehicle weight rating of less than twenty-six thousand one pounds that is designed to transport fewer than sixteen passengers including the driver.

(C) The following endorsements and restrictions apply to commercial drivers' licenses:

(1) H—authorizes the driver to drive a vehicle transporting hazardous materials;

(2) K—restricts the driver to only intrastate operation;

(3) L—restricts the driver to vehicles not equipped with air brakes;

(4) T—authorizes the driver to drive double and triple trailers;

(5) P—authorizes the driver to drive vehicles carrying passengers;

(6) P1—authorizes the driver to drive class A vehicles with fewer than fifteen passengers and all lesser classes of vehicles without restriction as to the number of passengers;

(7) P2—authorizes the driver to drive class A or B vehicles with fewer than fifteen passengers and all lesser classes of vehicles without restriction as to the number of passengers;

(8) P3—restricts the driver to driving class B school buses;

(9) P4—Restricts the driver to driving class C school buses designed to transport fewer than sixteen passengers including the driver.

(10) N—authorizes the driver to drive tank vehicles;

(11) S—authorizes the driver to drive school buses;

(12) X—authorizes the driver to drive tank vehicles transporting hazardous materials;

(13) W—restricts the driver to the operation of commercial motor vehicles in accordance with a waiver for farm-related service industries issued under section 4506.24 of the Revised Code.

(D) In addition to any endorsement that otherwise may apply, a person who is engaged in the towing of a disabled or wrecked motor vehicle shall hold a commercial driver's license bearing any endorsement required to drive the towed vehicle except the driver is not required to have either of the following:

(1) A passenger endorsement to tow an unoccupied passenger vehicle;

(2) Any endorsement required for the wrecked or disabled vehicle when the driver initially removes a vehicle from the site of the emergency where the vehicle became wrecked or disabled to the nearest appropriate repair, disposal, or storage facility, as applicable.

(E) No person shall drive any commercial motor vehicle for which an endorsement is required under this section unless the proper endorsement appears on the person's commercial driver's license.

(F) Whoever violates this section is guilty of a misdemeanor of the first degree.

(2004 H 230, eff. 9–16–04; 2002 S 123, eff. 1–1–04; 1992 H 485, eff. 7–8–92; 1990 H 831, H 88; 1989 H 381)

4506.13 Examiner's commercial examinations passed form; information on applicant's driving record

(A) The registrar may authorize the highway patrol or any other employee of the department of public safety to issue an examiner's commercial examinations passed form to an applicant who has passed the required examinations. The examiner's commercial examinations passed form shall be used, once it has been validated, to indicate the examinations taken and passed by the commercial driver's license applicant.

(B) Before issuing a commercial driver's license, the registrar of motor vehicles shall obtain information about the applicant's driving record through the commercial driver license information system, when available, and the national driver register. If the record check reveals information that the applicant claims is outdated, contested, or invalid, the registrar shall deny the application until the applicant can resolve the conflict.

Within ten days after issuing a commercial driver's license, the registrar shall notify the commercial driver license information system, when available, of that fact and shall provide all information required to ensure identification of the licensee.

(2000 H 600, eff. 9–1–00; 1990 H 831, eff. 7–17–90; 1990 H 88; 1989 H 381)

4506.14 Expiration and renewal of license; waiver of examination for renewal

(A) Commercial driver's licenses shall expire as follows:

(1) Except as provided in division (A)(3) of this section, each such license issued to replace an operator's or chauffeur's license shall expire on the original expiration date of the operator's or chauffeur's license and, upon renewal, shall expire on the licensee's birthday in the fourth year after the date of issuance.

(2) Except as provided in division (A)(3) of this section, each such license issued as an original license to a person whose residence is in this state shall expire on the licensee's birthday in the fourth year after the date of issuance, and each such license issued to a person whose temporary residence is in this state shall expire in accordance with rules adopted by the registrar of motor vehicles. A license issued to a person with a temporary residence in this state is nonrenewable, but may be replaced with a new license within ninety days prior to its expiration upon the applicant's compliance with all applicable requirements.

(3) Each such license issued to replace the operator's or chauffeur's license of a person who is less than twenty-one years of age, and each such license issued as an original license to a person who is less than twenty-one years of age, shall expire on the licensee's twenty-first birthday.

(B) No commercial driver's license shall be issued for a period longer than four years and ninety days. Except as provided in section 4507.12 of the Revised Code, the registrar may waive the examination of any person applying for the renewal of a commercial driver's license issued under this chapter, provided that the applicant presents either an unexpired commercial driver's license or a commercial driver's license that has expired not more than six months prior to the date of application.

(C) Subject to the requirements of this chapter and except as provided in division (A)(2) of this section in regard to a person whose temporary residence is in this state, every commercial driver's license shall be renewable ninety days before its expiration upon payment of the fees required by section 4506.08 of the Revised Code. Each person applying for renewal of a commercial driver's license shall complete the application form prescribed by section 4506.07 of the Revised Code and shall provide all certifications required. If the person wishes to retain an endorsement authorizing the person to transport hazardous materials, the person shall take and successfully complete the written test for the endorsement and shall submit to any background check required by federal law.

(D) Each person licensed as a driver under this chapter shall notify the registrar of any change in the person's address within ten days following that change. The notification shall be in writing on a form provided by the registrar and shall include the full name, date of birth, license number, county of residence, social security number, and new address of the person.

(E) Whoever violates division (D) of this section is guilty of a minor misdemeanor.

(2003 H 95, § 3.13, eff. 1–1–04; 2003 H 95, § 1, eff. 9–26–03; 2002 S 123, eff. 1–1–04; 1997 S 60, eff. 10–21–97; 1994 H 687, eff. 10–12–94; 1992 S 98, eff. 11–12–92; 1991 H 134; 1990 S 382, H 88; 1989 H 381)

4506.15 Criminal offenses

(A) No person shall do any of the following:

(1) Drive a commercial motor vehicle while having a measurable or detectable amount of alcohol or of a controlled substance in the person's blood, breath, or urine;

(2) Drive a commercial motor vehicle while having an alcohol concentration of four-hundredths of one per cent or more;

(3) Drive a commercial motor vehicle while under the influence of a controlled substance;

(4) Knowingly leave the scene of an accident involving a commercial motor vehicle driven by the person;

(5) Use a commercial motor vehicle in the commission of a felony;

(6) Refuse to submit to a test under section 4506.17 of the Revised Code;

(7) Violate an out-of-service order issued under this chapter;

(8) Violate any prohibition described in divisions (A)(2) to (7) of this section while transporting hazardous materials;

(9) Use a commercial motor vehicle in the commission of a felony involving the manufacture, distribution, or dispensing of a controlled substance as defined in section 3719.01 of the Revised Code;

(10) Drive a commercial motor vehicle in violation of any provision of sections 4511.61 to 4511.63 of the Revised Code or any federal or local law or ordinance pertaining to railroad-highway grade crossings.

(B) Whoever violates this section is guilty of a misdemeanor of the first degree.

(2003 H 95, § 3.13, eff. 1–1–04; 2003 H 95, § 1, eff. 9–26–03; 2002 S 123, eff. 1–1–04; 1990 H 88, eff. 3–13–90; 1989 H 381)

4506.16 Criminal penalties

(A) Whoever violates division (A)(1) of section 4506.15 of the Revised Code or a similar law of another state or a foreign jurisdiction, immediately shall be placed out-of-service for twenty-four hours, in addition to any disqualification required by this section and any other penalty imposed by the Revised Code.

(B) The registrar of motor vehicles shall disqualify any person from operating a commercial motor vehicle as follows:

(1) Upon a first conviction for a violation of any provision of divisions (A)(2) to (7) of section 4506.15 of the Revised Code or a similar law of another state or a foreign jurisdiction, one year and upon a second conviction arising from two or more separate incidents, the person shall be disqualified for life or for any other period of time as determined by the United States secretary of transportation and designated by the director of public safety by rule;

(2) Upon a first conviction for a violation of division (A)(8) of section 4506.15 of the Revised Code or a similar law of another state or a foreign jurisdiction, three years;

(3) Upon conviction of a violation of division (A)(9) of section 4506.15 of the Revised Code or a similar law of another state or a foreign jurisdiction, the person shall be disqualified for life;

(4) Upon a first conviction for a violation of division (A)(10) of section 4506.15 of the Revised Code or a similar law of another state or a foreign jurisdiction, occurring in a three-year period, the person shall be disqualified for not less than sixty days, upon a second conviction occurring in the three-year period, the person shall be disqualified for not less than one hundred twenty days, and upon a subsequent conviction occurring within a three-year period, the person shall be disqualified for not less than one year;

(5) Upon conviction of two serious traffic violations involving the operation of a commercial motor vehicle by the person and arising from separate incidents occurring in a three-year period, the person shall be disqualified for sixty days;

(6) Upon conviction of three serious traffic violations involving the operation of a commercial motor vehicle by the person and arising from separate incidents occurring in a three-year period, the person shall be disqualified for one hundred twenty days.

(C) For the purposes of this section, conviction of a violation for which disqualification is required may be evidenced by any of the following:

(1) A judgment entry of a court of competent jurisdiction in this or any other state;

(2) An administrative order of a state agency of this or any other state having statutory jurisdiction over commercial drivers;

(3) A computer record obtained from or through the commercial driver's license information system;

(4) A computer record obtained from or through a state agency of this or any other state having statutory jurisdiction over commercial drivers or the records of commercial drivers.

(D) Any record described in division (C) of this section shall be deemed to be self-authenticating when it is received by the bureau of motor vehicles.

(E) When disqualifying a driver, the registrar shall cause the records of the bureau to be updated to reflect that action within ten days after it occurs.

(F) The registrar immediately shall notify a driver who is finally convicted of any offense described in section 4506.15 of the Revised Code or division (B)(3), (4), (5), or (6) of this section and thereby is subject to disqualification, of the offense or offenses involved, of the length of time for which disqualification is to be imposed, and that the driver may request a hearing within thirty days of the mailing of the notice to show cause why the driver should not be disqualified from operating a commercial motor vehicle. If a request for such a hearing is not made within thirty days of the mailing of the notice, the order of disqualification is final. The registrar may designate hearing examiners who, after affording all parties reasonable notice, shall conduct a hearing to determine whether the disqualification order is supported by reliable evidence. The registrar shall adopt rules to implement this division.

(G) Any person who is disqualified from operating a commercial motor vehicle under this section may apply to the registrar for a driver's license to operate a motor vehicle other than a commercial motor vehicle, provided the person's commercial driver's license is not otherwise suspended. A person whose commercial driver's license is suspended shall not apply to the registrar for or receive a driver's license under Chapter 4507. of the Revised Code during the period of suspension.

(H) The disqualifications imposed under this section are in addition to any other penalty imposed by the Revised Code.

(2003 H 95, § 3.13, eff. 1–1–04; 2003 H 95, § 1, eff. 9–26–03; 2002 S 123, eff. 1–1–04; 2000 H 600, eff. 9–1–00; 1997 S 60, eff. 10–21–97; 1993 S 62, § 4, eff. 9–1–93; 1992 S 275, S 98; 1989 H 381)

4506.17 Alcohol and controlled substance testing; disqualification of drivers

(A) Any person who drives a commercial motor vehicle within this state shall be deemed to have given consent to a test or tests of the person's whole blood, blood serum or plasma, breath, or urine for the purpose of determining the person's alcohol concentration or the presence of any controlled substance.

(B) A test or tests as provided in division (A) of this section may be administered at the direction of a peace officer having reasonable ground to stop or detain the person and, after investigating the circumstances surrounding the operation of the commercial motor vehicle, also having reasonable ground to believe the person was driving the commercial vehicle while having a measurable or detectable amount of alcohol or of a controlled substance in the person's whole blood, blood serum or plasma, breath, or urine. Any such test shall be given within two hours of the time of the alleged violation.

(C) A person requested to submit to a test under division (A) of this section shall be advised by the peace officer requesting the test that a refusal to submit to the test will result in the person immediately being placed out-of-service for a period of twenty-four hours and being disqualified from operating a commercial motor vehicle for a period of not less than one year, and that the person is required to surrender the person's commercial driver's license to the peace officer.

(D) If a person refuses to submit to a test after being warned as provided in division (C) of this section or submits to a test that discloses the presence of a controlled substance or an alcohol concentration of four-hundredths of one per cent or more, the person immediately shall surrender the person's commercial driver's license to the peace officer. The peace officer shall forward the license, together with a sworn report, to the registrar of motor vehicles certifying that the test was requested pursuant to division (A) of this section and that the person either refused to submit to testing or submitted to a test that disclosed the presence of a controlled substance or an alcohol concentration of four-hundredths of one per cent or more. The form and contents of the report required by this section shall be established by the registrar by rule, but shall contain the advice to be read to the driver and a statement to be signed by the driver acknowledging that the driver has been read the advice and that the form was shown to the driver.

(E) Upon receipt of a sworn report from a peace officer as provided in division (D) of this section, the registrar shall disqualify the person named in the report from driving a commercial motor vehicle for the period described below:

(1) Upon a first incident, one year;

(2) Upon an incident of refusal or of a prohibited concentration of alcohol after one or more previous incidents of either refusal or of a prohibited concentration of alcohol, the person shall be disqualified for life or such lesser period as prescribed by rule by the registrar.

(F) A test of a person's whole blood or a person's blood serum or plasma given under this section shall comply with the applicable provisions of division (D) of section 4511.19 of the Revised Code and any physician, registered nurse, or qualified technician, chemist, or phlebotomist who withdraws whole blood or blood serum or plasma from a person under this section, and any hospital, first-aid station, clinic, or other facility at which whole blood or blood serum or plasma is withdrawn from a person pursuant to this section, is immune from criminal liability, and from civil liability that is based upon a claim of assault and battery or based upon any other claim of malpractice, for any act performed in withdrawing whole blood or blood serum or plasma from the person.

(G) When a person submits to a test under this section, the results of the test, at the person's request, shall be made available to the person, the person's attorney, or the person's agent, immediately upon completion of the chemical test analysis. The person also may have an additional test administered by a physician, a registered nurse, or a qualified technician, chemist, or phlebotomist of the person's own choosing as provided in division (D) of section 4511.19 of the Revised Code for tests administered under that section, and the failure to obtain such a test has the same effect as in that division.

(H) No person shall refuse to immediately surrender the person's commercial driver's license to a peace officer when required to do so by this section.

(I) A peace officer issuing an out-of-service order or receiving a commercial driver's license surrendered under this section may remove or arrange for the removal of any commercial motor vehicle affected by the issuance of that order or the surrender of that license.

(J)(1) Except for civil actions arising out of the operation of a motor vehicle and civil actions in which the state is a plaintiff, no peace officer of any law enforcement agency within this state is liable in compensatory damages in any civil action that arises under the Revised Code or common law of this state for an injury, death, or loss to person or property caused in the performance of official duties under this section and rules adopted under this section, unless the officer's actions were manifestly outside the scope of the officer's employment or official responsibilities, or unless the officer acted with malicious purpose, in bad faith, or in a wanton or reckless manner.

(2) Except for civil actions that arise out of the operation of a motor vehicle and civil actions in which the state is a plaintiff, no peace officer of any law enforcement agency within this state is liable in punitive or exemplary damages in any civil action that arises under the Revised Code or common law of this state for any injury, death, or loss to person or property caused in the performance of official duties under this section of the Revised Code and rules adopted under this section, unless the officer's actions were manifestly outside the scope of the officer's employment or official responsibilities, or unless the officer acted with malicious purpose, in bad faith, or in a wanton or reckless manner.

(K) When disqualifying a driver, the registrar shall cause the records of the bureau of motor vehicles to be updated to reflect the disqualification within ten days after it occurs.

(L) The registrar immediately shall notify a driver who is subject to disqualification of the disqualification, of the length of the disqualification, and that the driver may request a hearing within thirty days of the mailing of the notice to show cause why the driver should not be disqualified from operating a commercial motor vehicle. If a request for such a hearing is not made within thirty days of the mailing of the notice, the order of disqualification is final. The registrar may designate hearing examiners who, after affording all parties reasonable notice, shall conduct a hearing to determine whether the disqualification order is supported by reliable evidence. The registrar shall adopt rules to implement this division.

(M) Any person who is disqualified from operating a commercial motor vehicle under this section may apply to the registrar for a driver's license to operate a motor vehicle other than a commercial motor vehicle, provided the person's commercial driver's license is not otherwise suspended. A person whose commercial driver's license is suspended shall not apply to the registrar for or receive a driver's license under Chapter 4507. of the Revised Code during the period of suspension.

(N) Whoever violates division (H) of this section is guilty of a misdemeanor of the first degree.

(2002 S 123, eff. 1–1–04; 1997 S 60, eff. 10–21–97; 1994 S 82, eff. 5–4–94; 1990 H 88, eff. 3–13–90; 1989 H 381)

4506.18 Notice of foreign convictions

(A) Any driver who holds a commercial driver's license issued by this state and is convicted in another state or a foreign jurisdiction of violating any law or ordinance relating to motor vehicle traffic control, other than a parking violation, shall provide written notice of that conviction within thirty days after the date of conviction to the bureau of motor vehicles and to the driver's employer in accordance with the provisions of 49 C.F.R. 383, subpart C, as amended.

(B) Whoever violates this section is guilty of a misdemeanor of the first degree.

(2002 S 123, eff. 1–1–04; 1989 H 381, eff. 7–1–89)

4506.19 Applicability of federal regulations

(A) The provisions of 49 C.F.R. 383, subpart C, as amended, shall apply to all commercial drivers or persons who apply for employment as commercial drivers. No person shall fail to make a report to the person's employer as required by this section.

(B) Whoever violates this section is guilty of a misdemeanor of the first degree.

(2002 S 123, eff. 1–1–04; 1989 H 381, eff. 7–1–89)

4506.20 Employment of drivers of commercial vehicles

(A) Each employer shall require every applicant for employment as a driver of a commercial motor vehicle to provide the information specified in section 4506.20 of the Revised Code.

(B) No employer shall knowingly permit or authorize any driver employed by the employer to drive a commercial motor vehicle during any period in which any of the following apply:

(1) The driver's commercial driver's license is suspended, revoked, or canceled by any state or a foreign jurisdiction;

(2) The driver has lost the privilege to drive, or currently is disqualified from driving, a commercial motor vehicle in any state or foreign jurisdiction;

(3) The driver is subject to an out-of-service order in any state or foreign jurisdiction;

(4) The driver has more than one driver's license.

(C) No employer shall knowingly permit or authorize a driver to operate a commercial motor vehicle in violation of section 4506.15 of the Revised Code.

(D)(1) Whoever violates division (A) or (B) of this section is guilty of a misdemeanor of the first degree.

(2) Whoever violates division (C) of this section may be assessed a fine not to exceed ten thousand dollars.

(2003 H 95, § 3.13, eff. 1–1–04; 2003 H 95, § 1, eff. 9–26–03; 2002 S 123, eff. 1–1–04; 1989 H 381, eff. 7–1–89)

4506.21 Notification of convictions of nonresident license holders

Within ten days after receiving a report of the conviction of any nonresident holder of a commercial driver's license for a violation of a state law or local ordinance or resolution relating to traffic control, other than parking violations, committed in a commercial motor vehicle, the registrar of motor vehicles shall notify the driver licensing authority in the state that issued the nonresident's commercial driver's license of the conviction.

(1989 H 381, eff. 7–1–89)

4506.22 Rulemaking powers; powers of public safety department

(A) The director of public safety and the registrar of motor vehicles, subject to approval by the director, may, in accordance with Chapter 119. of the Revised Code, adopt any rules necessary to carry out this chapter.

(B) The department of public safety may do all of the following:

(1) Enter into or make any agreements, arrangements, or declarations necessary to carry out this chapter;

(2) Charge a fee for all publications that is equal to the cost of printing the publications.

(C) Nothing in this chapter shall be construed to restrict the authority of the public utilities commission specified in Chapters 4921. and 4923. of the Revised Code regarding safety rules applicable to motor carriers.

(1995 S 162, eff. 10–29–95; 1992 S 98, eff. 11–12–92; 1989 H 381)

4506.23 Powers of peace officers

Within the jurisdictional limits of his appointing authority, any peace officer shall stop and detain any person found violating section 4506.15 of the Revised Code, without obtaining a warrant. When there is reasonable ground to believe that a violation of section 4506.15 of the Revised Code has been committed and a test or tests of the person's blood, breath, or urine is necessary, the peace officer shall take the person to an appropriate place for testing. If a person refuses to submit to a test after being warned as provided in division (C) of section 4506.17 of the Revised Code or submits to a test that discloses the presence of a controlled substance or an alcohol concentration of four-hundredths of one per cent or more, the peace officer shall require that the person immediately surrender his commercial driver's license to the peace officer.

As used in this section, "jurisdictional limits" means the limits within which a peace officer may arrest and detain a person without a warrant under section 2935.03 of the Revised Code, except that the superintendent and the troopers of the state highway patrol may stop and detain, without warrant, any person who, in the presence of the superintendent or any trooper, is engaged in the violation of this chapter.

(1991 S 144, eff. 8–8–91; 1990 H 88; 1989 H 381)

4506.24 Restricted commercial driver's license; waiver for farm-related service industries

(A) A restricted commercial driver's license and waiver for farm-related service industries may be issued by the registrar of motor vehicles to allow a person to operate a commercial motor vehicle during seasonal periods determined by the registrar and subject to the restrictions set forth in this section.

(B) Upon receiving an application for a restricted commercial driver's license under section 4506.07 of the Revised Code and payment of a fee as provided in section 4506.08 of the Revised Code, the registrar may issue such license to any person who meets all of the following requirements:

(1) Has at least one year of driving experience in any type of vehicle;

(2) Holds a valid driver's license, other than a restricted license, issued under Chapter 4507. of the Revised Code;

(3) Certifies that during the two-year period immediately preceding application, all of the following apply:

(a) The person has not had more than one license;

(b) The person has not had any license suspended, revoked, or canceled;

(c) The person has not had any convictions for any type of motor vehicle for the offenses for which disqualification is prescribed in section 4506.16 of the Revised Code;

(d) The person has not had any violation of a state or local law relating to motor vehicle traffic control other than a parking violation arising in connection with any traffic accident and has no record of an accident in which the person was at fault.

(4) Certifies and also provides evidence that the person is employed in one or more of the following farm-related service industries requiring the person to operate a commercial motor vehicle:

(a) Custom harvesters;

(b) Farm retail outlets and suppliers;

(c) Agri-chemical business;

(d) Livestock feeders.

(C) An annual waiver for farm-related service industries may be issued to authorize the holder of a restricted commercial driver's license to operate a commercial motor vehicle during seasonal periods designated by the registrar. The registrar shall determine the format of the waiver. The total number of days that a person may operate a commercial motor vehicle pursuant to a waiver for farm-related service industries shall not exceed one hundred eighty days in any twelve-month period. Each time the holder of a restricted commercial driver's license applies for a waiver for farm-related service industries, the registrar shall verify that the person meets all of the requirements set forth in division (B) of this section. The restricted commercial driver's license and waiver shall be carried at all times when a commercial motor vehicle is being operated by the holder of the license and waiver.

(D) The holder of a restricted commercial driver's license and valid waiver for farm-related service industries may operate a class B or C commercial motor vehicle subject to all of the following restrictions:

(1) The commercial motor vehicle is operated within a distance of no more than one hundred fifty miles of the employer's place of business or the farm currently being served;

(2) The operation of the commercial motor vehicle does not involve transporting hazardous materials for which placarding is required, except as follows:

(a) Diesel fuel in quantities of one thousand gallons or less;

(b) Liquid fertilizers in vehicles or implements of husbandry with total capacities of three thousand gallons or less;

(c) Solid fertilizers that are not transported with any organic substance.

(E) Except as otherwise provided in this section an applicant for or holder of a restricted commercial driver's license and waiver for farm-related service industries is subject to the provisions of this chapter. Divisions (A)(4) and (B)(1) of section 4506.07 and sections 4506.09 and 4506.10 of the Revised Code do not apply to an applicant for a restricted commercial driver's license and waiver.

(2003 H 95, eff. 9-26-03; 1997 H 210, eff. 3-31-97; 1992 H 485, eff. 7-8-92)

4506.25 "Out–of–service" orders

(A) As used in this section:

(1) "Commercial motor vehicle" means any self-propelled or towed vehicle used on public highways in intrastate or interstate commerce to transport passengers or property that meets any of the following specifications:

(a) The vehicle has a gross vehicle weight rating or gross combination weight rating of ten thousand one pounds or more.

(b) The vehicle is designed to transport sixteen or more passengers, including the driver.

(c) The vehicle is used in the transportation of hazardous materials in a quantity requiring placarding under the regulations issued by the United States secretary of transportation under the "Hazardous Materials Transportation Act," 88 Stat. 2156 (1975), 49 U.S.C.A. 1801, as amended.

(2) "Out–of–service order" means a declaration by an authorized enforcement officer of a federal, state, local, Canadian, or Mexican jurisdiction declaring that a driver, commercial motor vehicle, or commercial motor carrier operation is out of service pursuant to 49 C.F.R. 386.72, 392.5, 395.13, or 396.9, as amended, laws equivalent to those provisions, or the North American uniform out-of-service criteria.

(B) The registrar of motor vehicles shall disqualify any person from operating a commercial motor vehicle who receives a notice of a conviction for violation of an out-of-service order issued under rules of the public utilities commission adopted pursuant to section 4919.79, 4921.04, or 4923.20 of the Revised Code, or a conviction for a violation of the same or similar laws of another state or jurisdiction applicable to vehicles in regulated commerce.

(1998 S 213, eff. 7-29-98)

4506.26 Disqualification of commercial vehicle operators; period of disqualification

(A) As used in this section, "out–of–service order" has the same meaning as in division (A)(2) of section 4506.25 of the Revised Code.

(B) Any person who is found to have been convicted of a violation of an out-of-service order shall be disqualified by the registrar of motor vehicles as follows:

(1) If the person has not been convicted previously of a violation of an out-of-service order, the period of disqualification is ninety days.

(2) If, during any ten-year period, the driver is convicted of a second violation of an out-of-service order in an incident separate from the incident that resulted in the first violation, the period of disqualification is one year.

(3) If, during any ten-year period, the driver is convicted of a third or subsequent violation of an out-of-service order in an incident separate from the incidents that resulted in the previous violations during that ten-year period, the period of disqualification is three years.

(C)(1) A driver is disqualified for one hundred eighty days if the driver is convicted of a first violation of an out-of-service order while transporting hazardous materials required to be placarded under the "Hazardous Materials Transportation Act," 88 Stat. 2156 (1975), 49 U.S.C.A. 1801, as amended, or while operating a motor vehicle designed to transport sixteen or more passengers, including the driver.

(2) A driver is disqualified for a period of three years if, during any ten-year period, the driver is convicted of a second or subsequent violation, in an incident separate from the incident that resulted in a previous violation during that ten-year period, of an out-of-service order while transporting hazardous materials required to be placarded under that act, or while operating a motor vehicle designed to transport sixteen or more passengers, including the driver.

(1998 S 213, eff. 7-29-98)

4506.99 Penalties

Whoever violates any provision of sections 4506.03 to 4506.20 of the Revised Code for which no penalty otherwise is provided in the section that contains the provision violated is guilty of a misdemeanor of the first degree.

(2002 S 123, eff. 1-1-04; 1991 H 134, eff. 10-10-91; 1990 H 88; 1989 H 381)

CHAPTER 4507

DRIVER'S LICENSE LAW

GENERAL PROVISIONS

4507.01 Definitions; deputy registrars

(A) As used in this chapter, "motor vehicle," "motorized bicycle," "state," "owner," "operator," "chauffeur," and "highways" have the same meanings as in section 4501.01 of the Revised Code.

"Driver's license" means a class D license issued to any person to operate a motor vehicle or motor-driven cycle, other than a commercial motor vehicle, and includes "probationary license," "restricted license," and any operator's or chauffeur's license issued before January 1, 1990.

"Probationary license" means the license issued to any person between sixteen and eighteen years of age to operate a motor vehicle.

"Restricted license" means the license issued to any person to operate a motor vehicle subject to conditions or restrictions imposed by the registrar of motor vehicles.

"Commercial driver's license" means the license issued to a person under Chapter 4506. of the Revised Code to operate a commercial motor vehicle.

"Commercial motor vehicle" has the same meaning as in section 4506.01 of the Revised Code.

"Motorized bicycle license" means the license issued under section 4511.521 of the Revised Code to any person to operate a motorized bicycle including a "probationary motorized bicycle license."

"Probationary motorized bicycle license" means the license issued under section 4511.521 of the Revised Code to any person between fourteen and sixteen years of age to operate a motorized bicycle.

"Identification card" means a card issued under sections 4507.50 and 4507.51 of the Revised Code.

"Resident" means a person who, in accordance with standards prescribed in rules adopted by the registrar, resides in this state on a permanent basis.

"Temporary resident" means a person who, in accordance with standards prescribed in rules adopted by the registrar, resides in this state on a temporary basis.

(B) In the administration of this chapter and Chapter 4506. of the Revised Code, the registrar has the same authority as is conferred on the registrar by section 4501.02 of the Revised Code. Any act of an authorized deputy registrar of motor vehicles under direction of the registrar is deemed the act of the registrar.

To carry out this chapter, the registrar shall appoint such deputy registrars in each county as are necessary.

The registrar also shall provide at each place where an application for a driver's or commercial driver's license or identification card may be made the necessary equipment to take a color photograph of the applicant for such license or card as required under section 4506.11 or 4507.06 of the Revised Code, and to conduct the vision screenings required by section 4507.12 of the Revised Code, and equipment to laminate licenses, motorized bicycle licenses, and identification cards as required by sections 4507.13, 4507.52, and 4511.521 of the Revised Code.

The registrar shall assign one or more deputy registrars to any driver's license examining station operated under the supervision of the state highway patrol, whenever the registrar considers such assignment possible. Space shall be provided in the driver's license examining station for any such deputy registrar so assigned. The deputy registrars shall not exercise the powers conferred by such sections upon the registrar, unless they are specifically authorized to exercise such powers by such sections.

(C) No agent for any insurance company, writing automobile insurance, shall be appointed deputy registrar, and any such appointment is void. No deputy registrar shall in any manner solicit any form of automobile insurance, nor in any manner advise, suggest, or influence any licensee or applicant for license for or against any kind or type of automobile insurance, insurance company, or agent, nor have the deputy registrar's office directly connected with the office of any automobile insurance agent, nor impart any information furnished by any applicant for a license or identification card to any person, except the registrar. This division shall not apply to any nonprofit corporation appointed deputy registrar.

(D) The registrar shall immediately remove a deputy registrar who violates the requirements of this chapter.

(E) The registrar shall periodically solicit bids and enter into a contract for the provision of laminating equipment and laminating materials to the registrar and all deputy registrars. The registrar shall not consider any bid that does not provide for the supplying of both laminating equipment and laminating materials. The laminating materials selected shall contain a security feature so that any tampering with the laminating material covering a license or identification card is readily apparent. In soliciting bids and entering into a contract for the provision of laminating equipment and laminating materials, the registrar shall observe all procedures required by law.

(1997 S 60, eff. 10–21–97; 1990 S 131, eff. 7–25–90; 1989 H 381; 1988 S 1; 1986 H 428; 1984 S 169, H 58; 1977 S 100; 1976 S 435; 1974 S 313; 1973 S 1; 132 v S 43, H 380; 130 v H 772; 129 v 421; 127 v 839; 1953 H 1; GC 6296–2)

4507.011 Deputy registrar rental fees

(A) Each deputy registrar assigned to a driver's license examining station by the registrar of motor vehicles as provided in section 4507.01 of the Revised Code shall remit to the superintendent of the state highway patrol a rental fee equal to the percentage of space occupied by the deputy registrar in the driver's license examining station multiplied by the rental fee paid for the entire driver's license examining station plus a pro rata share of all utility costs. All such moneys received by the superintendent shall be deposited in the state treasury to the credit of the registrar rental fund, which is hereby created. The moneys in the fund shall be used by the state highway patrol only to pay the rent and expenses of the driver's license examining stations. All investment earnings of the fund shall be credited to the fund.

(B) Each deputy registrar assigned to a bureau of motor vehicles' location shall reimburse the registrar a monthly building rental fee, including applicable utility charges. All such moneys received by the registrar shall be deposited into the state bureau of motor vehicles fund created in section 4501.25 of the Revised Code.

(1999 H 163, eff. 6–30–99; 1993 H 154, eff. 6–30–93; 1985 S 269, H 201; 1984 H 58, § 1, 4)

4507.02 License required as driver or commercial driver on public or private property; surrender of out-of-state license; impounding license plates; restricted license plates

(A)(1) No person shall permit the operation of a motor vehicle upon any public or private property used by the public for purposes of vehicular travel or parking knowing the operator does not have a valid driver's license issued to the operator by the registrar of motor vehicles under this chapter or a valid commercial driver's license issued under Chapter 4506. of the Revised Code. Whoever violates this division is guilty of a misdemeanor of the first degree.

(2) No person shall receive a driver's license, or a motorcycle operator's endorsement of a driver's or commercial driver's license, unless and until the person surrenders to the registrar all valid licenses issued to the person by another jurisdiction recognized by this state. All surrendered licenses shall be returned by the registrar to the issuing authority, together with information that a license is now issued in this state. No person shall be permitted to have more than one valid license at any time.

(B)(1) If a person is convicted of a violation of section 4510.11, 4510.14, 4510.16, or 4510.21 of the Revised Code or if division (F) of section 4507.164 of the Revised Code applies, the trial judge of any court, in addition to or independent of, any other penalties provided by law or ordinance, shall impound the identification license plates of any motor vehicle registered in the name of the person. The court shall send the impounded license plates to the registrar, who may retain the license plates until the driver's or commercial driver's license of the owner has been reinstated or destroy them pursuant to section 4503.232 of the Revised Code.

If the license plates of a person convicted of a violation of any provision of those sections have been impounded in accordance with the provisions of this division, the court shall notify the registrar of that action. The notice shall contain the name and address of the driver, the serial number of the driver's driver's or commercial driver's license, the serial numbers of the license plates of the motor vehicle, and the length of time for which the license plates have been impounded. The registrar shall record the data in the notice as part of the driver's permanent record.

(2) Any motor vehicle owner who has had the license plates of a motor vehicle impounded pursuant to division (B)(1) of this

section may apply to the registrar, or to a deputy registrar, for restricted license plates that shall conform to the requirements of section 4503.231 of the Revised Code. The registrar or deputy registrar forthwith shall notify the court of the application and, upon approval of the court, shall issue restricted license plates to the applicant. Until the driver's or commercial driver's license of the owner is reinstated, any new license plates issued to the owner also shall conform to the requirements of section 4503.231 of the Revised Code.

The registrar or deputy registrar shall charge the owner of a vehicle the fees provided in section 4503.19 of the Revised Code for restricted license plates that are issued in accordance with this division, except upon renewal as specified in section 4503.10 of the Revised Code, when the regular fee as provided in section 4503.04 of the Revised Code shall be charged. The registrar or deputy registrar shall charge the owner of a vehicle the fees provided in section 4503.19 of the Revised Code whenever restricted license plates are exchanged, by reason of the reinstatement of the driver's or commercial driver's license of the owner, for those ordinarily issued.

(3) If an owner wishes to sell a motor vehicle during the time the restricted license plates provided under division (B)(2) of this section are in use, the owner may apply to the court that impounded the license plates of the motor vehicle for permission to transfer title to the motor vehicle. If the court is satisfied that the sale will be made in good faith and not for the purpose of circumventing the provisions of this section, it may certify its consent to the owner and to the registrar of motor vehicles who shall enter notice of the transfer of the title of the motor vehicle in the vehicle registration record.

If, during the time the restricted license plates provided under division (B)(2) of this section are in use, the title to a motor vehicle is transferred by the foreclosure of a chattel mortgage, a sale upon execution, the cancellation of a conditional sales contract, or by order of a court, the court shall notify the registrar of the action and the registrar shall enter notice of the transfer of the title to the motor vehicle in the vehicle registration record.

(C) This section is not intended to change or modify any provision of Chapter 4503. of the Revised Code with respect to the taxation of motor vehicles or the time within which the taxes on motor vehicles shall be paid.

(2004 H 163, eff. 9–23–04; 2002 S 123, eff. 1–1–04; 1999 H 163, eff. 6–30–99; 1997 S 60, eff. 10–21–97; 1994 S 20, eff. 4–20–95; 1994 H 687, eff. 10–12–94; 1993 S 62, § 1, eff. 9–1–93; 1993 S 62, § 4; 1992 S 275; 1990 S 131; 1989 H 381; 1987 H 419; 1986 S 262, S 356)

4507.023 Obtaining most recent address of holder of suspended or canceled license

The registrar of motor vehicles may furnish the name and social security number of any person whose driver's license or commercial driver's license has been suspended or canceled, or of any person whose certificate of registration and license plates are subject to impoundment, to the tax commissioner. The tax commissioner may return to the registrar the address of any such person as shown on the most recent return filed by that person under section 5747.08 of the Revised Code.

(2002 S 123, eff. 1–1–04; 1989 H 381, eff. 7–1–89)

4507.03 Exemptions

No person shall be required to obtain a driver's or commercial driver's license for the purpose of driving or operating a road roller, road machinery, or any farm tractor or implement of husbandry, temporarily drawn, moved, or propelled upon the highway.

Every person on active duty in the armed forces of the United States, when furnished with a driver's permit and when operating an official motor vehicle in connection with such duty, is exempt from the license requirements of Chapters 4506. and 4507. of the Revised Code.

Every person on active duty in the armed forces of the United States or in service with the peace corps, volunteers in service to America, or the foreign service of the United States is exempt from the license requirements of those chapters for the period of his active duty or service and for six months thereafter, provided the person was a licensee under those chapters at the time he commenced his active duty or service. The spouse or a dependent of any such person on active duty or in service also is exempt from the license requirements of those chapters for the period of the person's active duty or service and for six months thereafter, provided the spouse or dependent was a licensee under those chapters at the time the person commenced the active duty or service, and provided further that the person's active duty or service causes the spouse or dependent to relocate outside of this state during the period of the active duty or service.

This section does not prevent such a person or his spouse or dependent from making an application, as provided in division (C) of section 4507.10 of the Revised Code, for the renewal of a driver's license or motorcycle operator's endorsement or as provided in section 4506.14 of the Revised Code for the renewal of a commercial driver's license during the period of his active duty or service.

(1994 S 96, eff. 5–10–94; 1989 H 381, eff. 7–1–89; 1988 H 614; 1986 H 165; 1972 S 546; 132 v H 57; 1953 H 1; GC 6296–5)

4507.04 Nonresident exemption

Nonresidents, permitted to drive upon the highways of their own states, may operate any motor vehicle upon any highway in this state without examination or license under sections 4507.01 to 4507.39, inclusive, of the Revised Code, upon condition that such nonresidents may be required at any time or place to prove lawful possession, or their right to operate, such motor vehicle, and to establish proper identity.

(1953 H 1, eff. 10–1–53; GC 6296–6)

4507.05 Temporary instruction permit and identification card

(A) The registrar of motor vehicles, or a deputy registrar, upon receiving an application for a temporary instruction permit and a temporary instruction permit identification card for a driver's license from any person who is at least fifteen years and six months of age, may issue such a permit and identification card entitling the applicant to drive a motor vehicle, other than a commercial motor vehicle, upon the highways under the following conditions:

(1) If the permit is issued to a person who is at least fifteen years and six months of age, but less than sixteen years of age:

(a) The permit and identification card are in the holder's immediate possession;

(b) The holder is accompanied by an eligible adult who actually occupies the seat beside the permit holder and does not have a prohibited concentration of alcohol in the whole blood, blood serum or plasma, breath, or urine as provided in division (A) of section 4511.19 of the Revised Code;

(c) The total number of occupants of the vehicle does not exceed the total number of occupant restraining devices originally installed in the motor vehicle by its manufacturer, and each occupant of the vehicle is wearing all of the available elements of a properly adjusted occupant restraining device.

(2) If the permit is issued to a person who is at least sixteen years of age:

(a) The permit and identification card are in the holder's immediate possession;

(b) The holder is accompanied by a licensed operator who is at least twenty-one years of age, is actually occupying a seat beside the driver, and does not have a prohibited concentration of alcohol in the whole blood, blood serum or plasma, breath, or urine as provided in division (A) of section 4511.19 of the Revised Code;

(c) The total number of occupants of the vehicle does not exceed the total number of occupant restraining devices originally installed in the motor vehicle by its manufacturer, and each occupant of the vehicle is wearing all of the available elements of a properly adjusted occupant restraining device.

(B) The registrar or a deputy registrar, upon receiving from any person an application for a temporary instruction permit and temporary instruction permit identification card to operate a motorcycle or motorized bicycle, may issue such a permit and identification card entitling the applicant, while having the permit and identification card in the applicant's immediate possession, to drive a motorcycle or motorized bicycle under restrictions determined by the registrar. A temporary instruction permit and temporary instruction permit identification card to operate a motorized bicycle may be issued to a person fourteen or fifteen years old.

(C) Any permit and identification card issued under this section shall be issued in the same manner as a driver's license, upon a form to be furnished by the registrar. A temporary instruction permit to drive a motor vehicle other than a commercial motor vehicle shall be valid for a period of one year.

(D) Any person having in the person's possession a valid and current driver's license or motorcycle operator's license or endorsement issued to the person by another jurisdiction recognized by this state is exempt from obtaining a temporary instruction permit for a driver's license, but shall submit to the regular examination in obtaining a driver's license or motorcycle operator's endorsement in this state.

(E) The registrar may adopt rules governing the use of temporary instruction permits and temporary instruction permit identification cards.

(F)(1) No holder of a permit issued under division (A) of this section shall operate a motor vehicle upon a highway or any public or private property used by the public for purposes of vehicular travel or parking in violation of the conditions established under division (A) of this section.

(2) Except as provided in division (F)(2) of this section, no holder of a permit that is issued under division (A) of this section and that is issued on or after July 1, 1998, and who has not attained the age of seventeen years, shall operate a motor vehicle upon a highway or any public or private property used by the public for purposes of vehicular travel or parking between the hours of one a.m. and five a.m.

The holder of a permit issued under division (A) of this section on or after July 1, 1998, who has not attained the age of seventeen years, may operate a motor vehicle upon a highway or any public or private property used by the public for purposes of vehicular travel or parking between the hours of one a.m. and five a.m. if, at the time of such operation, the holder is accompanied by the holder's parent, guardian, or custodian, and the parent, guardian, or custodian holds a current valid driver's or commercial driver's license issued by this state , is actually occupying a seat beside the permit holder, and does not have a prohibited concentration of alcohol in the whole blood, blood serum or plasma, breath, or urine as provided in division (A) of section 4511.19 of the Revised Code.

(G)(1) Notwithstanding any other provision of law to the contrary, no law enforcement officer shall cause the operator of a motor vehicle being operated on any street or highway to stop the motor vehicle for the sole purpose of determining whether each occupant of the motor vehicle is wearing all of the available elements of a properly adjusted occupant restraining device as required by division (A) of this section, or for the sole purpose of issuing a ticket, citation, or summons if the requirement in that division has been or is being violated, or for causing the arrest of or commencing a prosecution of a person for a violation of that requirement.

(2) Notwithstanding any other provision of law to the contrary, no law enforcement officer shall cause the operator of a motor vehicle being operated on any street or highway to stop the motor vehicle for the sole purpose of determining whether a violation of division (F)(2) of this section has been or is being committed or for the sole purpose of issuing a ticket, citation, or summons for such a violation or for causing the arrest of or commencing a prosecution of a person for such violation.

(H) As used in this section:

(1) "Eligible adult" means any of the following:

(a) An instructor of a driver training course approved by the department of public safety;

(b) Any of the following persons who holds a current valid driver's or commercial driver's license issued by this state:

(i) A parent, guardian, or custodian of the permit holder;

(ii) A person twenty-one years of age or older who acts in loco parentis of the permit holder.

(2) "Occupant restraining device" has the same meaning as in section 4513.263 of the Revised Code.

(I) Whoever violates division (F)(1) or (2) of this section is guilty of a minor misdemeanor.

(2004 H 163, eff. 9–23–04; 2002 S 123, eff. 1–1–04; 2002 H 407, eff. 10–11–02; 1997 S 35, eff. 7 1 98; 1989 H 381, eff. 7–1–89; 1984 S 169; 1969 H 1; 132 v S 43, H 380; 131 v H 215; 129 v 1490; 128 v 1169; 1953 H 1; GC 6296–8)

4507.06 Form and contents of application for license; registration of voters

(A)(1) Every application for a driver's license or motorcycle operator's license or endorsement, or duplicate of any such license or endorsement, shall be made upon the approved form furnished by the registrar of motor vehicles and shall be signed by the applicant.

Every application shall state the following:

(a) The applicant's name, date of birth, social security number if such has been assigned, sex, general description, including height, weight, color of hair, and eyes, residence address, including county of residence, duration of residence in this state, and country of citizenship;

(b) Whether the applicant previously has been licensed as an operator, chauffeur, driver, commercial driver, or motorcycle operator and, if so, when, by what state, and whether such license is suspended or canceled at the present time and, if so, the date of and reason for the suspension or cancellation;

(c) Whether the applicant is now or ever has been afflicted with epilepsy, or whether the applicant now is suffering from any physical or mental disability or disease and, if so, the nature and extent of the disability or disease, giving the names and addresses of physicians then or previously in attendance upon the applicant;

(d) Whether an applicant for a duplicate driver's license, or duplicate license containing a motorcycle operator endorsement has pending a citation for violation of any motor vehicle law or ordinance, a description of any such citation pending, and the date of the citation;

(e) Whether the applicant wishes to certify willingness to make an anatomical gift under section 2108.04 of the Revised Code, which shall be given no consideration in the issuance of a license or endorsement;

(f) Whether the applicant has executed a valid durable power of attorney for health care pursuant to sections 1337.11 to 1337.17 of the Revised Code or has executed a declaration governing the use or continuation, or the withholding or withdrawal, of life-sustaining treatment pursuant to sections 2133.01 to 2133.15 of the Revised Code and, if the applicant has executed either type of instrument, whether the applicant wishes the applicant's license to indicate that the applicant has executed the instrument.

(2) Every applicant for a driver's license shall be photographed in color at the time the application for the license is made. The application shall state any additional information that the registrar requires.

(B) The registrar or a deputy registrar, in accordance with section 3503.11 of the Revised Code, shall register as an elector any person who applies for a driver's license or motorcycle operator's license or endorsement under division (A) of this section, or for a renewal or duplicate of the license or endorsement, if the applicant is eligible and wishes to be registered as an elector. The decision of an applicant whether to register as an elector shall be given no consideration in the decision of whether to issue the applicant a license or endorsement, or a renewal or duplicate.

(C) The registrar or a deputy registrar, in accordance with section 3503.11 of the Revised Code, shall offer the opportunity of completing a notice of change of residence or change of name to any applicant for a driver's license or endorsement under division (A) of this section, or for a renewal or duplicate of the license or endorsement, if the applicant is a registered elector who has changed the applicant's residence or name and has not filed such a notice.

(2002 S 123, eff. 1–1–04; 1998 H 354, eff. 7–9–98; 1996 H 353, eff. 9–17–96; 1994 S 300, eff. 1–1–95; 1992 H 427, eff. 10–8–92; 1990 H 21; 1989 H 381; 1986 H 428)

4507.062 Consent; forwarding of information to selective service system

(A) As used in this section, "license" includes a driver's license, commercial driver's license, temporary instruction permit, or identification card.

(B) Any person under twenty-six years of age who is required to register with the selective service system in accordance with the "Military Selective Service Act of 1967," 81 Stat. 100, 50 U.S.C. App. 451 et seq., as amended, upon submission of an application for issuance or renewal of a license is deemed to have given consent for the bureau of motor vehicles to forward to the selective service system the necessary information for such registration.

(C) Upon receipt of an application for issuance or renewal of a license from any person under twenty-six years of age who is required to register with the selective service system, the bureau shall forward to the selective service system in an electronic format the personal information necessary for such registration.

(D) Every application for a license shall state that submission of the application will serve as the applicant's consent to registration with the selective service system, if so required by federal law.

(E) The bureau may accept money from the selective service system to pay any costs that the bureau incurs in implementing this section.

(2001 H 46, eff. 8–1–02)

4507.07 Licenses of minors; signature by an adult; identification required; notice of liability; not imputed where proof of financial responsibility exists; exceptions to examination requirement

(A) The registrar of motor vehicles shall not grant the application of any minor under eighteen years of age for a probationary license, a restricted license, or a temporary instruction permit, unless the application is signed by one of the minor's parents, the minor's guardian, another person having custody of the applicant, or, if there is no parent or guardian, a responsible person who is willing to assume the obligation imposed under this section.

At the time a minor under eighteen years of age submits an application for a license or permit at a driver's license examining station, the adult who signs the application shall present identification establishing that the adult is the individual whose signature appears on the application. The registrar shall prescribe, by rule, the types of identification that are suitable for the purposes of this paragraph. If the adult who signs the application does not provide identification as required by this paragraph, the application shall not be accepted.

When a minor under eighteen years of age applies for a probationary license, a restricted license, or a temporary instruction permit, the registrar shall give the adult who signs the application notice of the potential liability that may be imputed to the adult pursuant to division (B) of this section and notice of how the adult may prevent any liability from being imputed to the adult pursuant to that division.

(B) Any negligence, or willful or wanton misconduct, that is committed by a minor under eighteen years of age when driving a motor vehicle upon a highway shall be imputed to the person who has signed the application of the minor for a probationary license, restricted license, or temporary instruction permit, which person shall be jointly and severally liable with the minor for any damages caused by the negligence or the willful or wanton misconduct. This joint and several liability is not subject to section 2307. 22 or 2315.36 of the Revised Code with respect to a tort claim that otherwise is subject to that section.

There shall be no imputed liability imposed under this division if a minor under eighteen years of age has proof of financial responsibility with respect to the operation of a motor vehicle owned by the minor or, if the minor is not the owner of a motor vehicle, with respect to the minor's operation of any motor vehicle, in the form and in the amounts required under Chapter 4509. of the Revised Code.

(C) Any person who has signed the application of a minor under eighteen years of age for a license or permit subsequently may surrender to the registrar the license or temporary instruction permit of the minor and request that the license or permit be canceled. The registrar then shall cancel the license or temporary instruction permit, and the person who signed the application of the minor shall be relieved from the liability imposed by division (B) of this section.

(D) Any minor under eighteen years of age whose probationary license, restricted license, or temporary instruction permit is surrendered to the registrar by the person who signed the application for the license or permit and whose license or temporary instruction permit subsequently is canceled by the registrar may obtain a new license or temporary instruction permit without having to undergo the examinations otherwise required by sections 4507.11 and 4507.12 of the Revised Code and without having to tender the fee for that license or temporary instruction permit, if the minor is able to produce another parent, guardian, other person having custody of the minor, or other adult, and that adult is willing to assume the liability imposed under division (B) of this section. That adult shall comply with the procedures contained in division (A) of this section.

(2004 S 80, eff. 4-7-05; 2002 S 120, eff. 4-9-03; 2001 S 108, § 2.01, eff. 7-6-01; 1997 S 35, eff. 1-1-99; 1996 H 350, eff. 1-27-97[1]*;1989 H 71, eff. 9-22-89; 1987 H 1; 1979 H 522; 132 v S 95; 130 v H 772; 127 v 839; 1953 H 1; GC 6296-10)*

[1] See Notes of Decisions, *State ex rel. Ohio Academy of Trial Lawyers v. Sheward* (Ohio 1999), 86 Ohio St.3d 451, 715 N.E.2d 1062.

Uncodified Law

2001 S 108, § 1, eff. 7-6-01, reads:

It is the intent of this act (1) to repeal the Tort Reform Act, Am. Sub. H.B. 350 of the 121st General Assembly, 146 Ohio Laws 3867, in conformity with the Supreme Court of Ohio's decision in *State, ex rel. Ohio Academy of Trial Lawyers, v. Sheward* (1999), 86 Ohio St.3d 451; (2) to clarify the status of the law; and (3) to revive the law as it existed prior to the Tort Reform Act.

Notes of Decisions

10. Constitutional issues

1996 H 350, which amended more than 100 statutes and a variety of rules relating to tort and other civil actions, and which was an attempt to reenact provisions of law previously held unconstitutional by the Supreme Court of Ohio, is an act of usurpation of judicial power in violation of the doctrine of separation of powers; for that reason, and because of violation of the one-subject rule of the Ohio Constitution, 1996 H 350 is unconstitutional. State ex rel. Ohio Academy of Trial Lawyers v. Sheward (Ohio, 08-16-1999) 86 Ohio St.3d 451, 715 N.E.2d 1062, 1999-Ohio-123, reconsideration denied 87 Ohio St.3d 1409, 716 N.E.2d 1170.

4507.071 Probationary licenses; restrictions

(A) No driver's license shall be issued to any person under eighteen years of age, except that a probationary license may be issued to a person who is at least sixteen years of age and has held a temporary instruction permit for a period of at least six months.

(B) No holder of a probationary driver's license issued on or after the effective date of this section who has not attained the age of seventeen years shall operate a motor vehicle upon a highway or any public or private property used by the public for purposes of vehicular travel or parking between the hours of one a.m. and five a.m. unless the holder is accompanied by the holder's parent or guardian.

(C) It is an affirmative defense to a violation of division (B) of this section if, at the time of the violation, the holder of the probationary driver's license was traveling to or from the holder's place of employment or an official function sponsored by the school the holder attends, or an emergency existed that required the holder to operate a motor vehicle in violation of division (B) of this section, or the holder was an emancipated minor.

(D) No holder of a probationary license shall operate a motor vehicle upon a highway or any public or private property used by the public for purposes of vehicular travel or parking unless the total number of occupants of the vehicle does not exceed the total number of occupant restraining devices originally installed in the motor vehicle by its manufacturer, and each occupant of the vehicle is wearing all of the available elements of a properly adjusted occupant restraining device.

(E) A restricted license may be issued to a person who is fourteen or fifteen years of age upon proof of hardship satisfactory to the registrar of motor vehicles.

(F) Notwithstanding any other provision of law to the contrary, no law enforcement officer shall cause the operator of a motor vehicle being operated on any street or highway to stop the motor vehicle for the sole purpose of determining whether each occupant of the motor vehicle is wearing all of the available elements of a properly adjusted occupant restraining device as required by division (D) of this section, or for the sole purpose of issuing a ticket, citation, or summons if the requirement in that division has been or is being violated, or for causing the arrest of or commencing a prosecution of a person for a violation of that requirement.

(G) Notwithstanding any other provision of law to the contrary, no law enforcement officer shall cause the operator of a motor vehicle being operated on any street or highway to stop the motor vehicle for the sole purpose of determining whether a violation of division (B) of this section has been or is being committed or for the sole purpose of issuing a ticket, citation, or summons for such a violation or for causing the arrest of or commencing a prosecution of a person for such violation.

(H) As used in this section, "occupant restraining device" has the same meaning as in section 4513.263 of the Revised Code.

(I) Whoever violates division (B) or (D) of this section is guilty of a minor misdemeanor.

(2002 S 123, eff. 1-1-04; 1997 S 35, eff. 1-1-99)

4507.08 Restrictions against issuance of license, probationary license, or temporary instruction permit

(A) No probationary license shall be issued to any person under the age of eighteen who has been adjudicated an unruly or delinquent child or a juvenile traffic offender for having committed any act that if committed by an adult would be a drug abuse offense, as defined in section 2925.01 of the Revised Code, a violation of division (B) of section 2917.11, or a violation of division (A) of section 4511.19 of the Revised Code, unless the person has been required by the court to attend a drug abuse or alcohol abuse education, intervention, or treatment program specified by the court and has satisfactorily completed the program.

(B) No temporary instruction permit or driver's license shall be issued to any person whose license has been suspended, during the period for which the license was suspended, nor to any person whose license has been canceled, under Chapter 4510. or any other provision of the Revised Code.

(C) No temporary instruction permit or driver's license shall be issued to any person whose commercial driver's license is suspended under Chapter 4510. or any other provision of the Revised Code during the period of the suspension.

No temporary instruction permit or driver's license shall be issued to any person when issuance is prohibited by division (A) of section 4507.091 of the Revised Code.

(D) No temporary instruction permit or driver's license shall be issued to, or retained by, any of the following persons:

(1) Any person who is an alcoholic, or is addicted to the use of controlled substances to the extent that the use constitutes an impairment to the person's ability to operate a motor vehicle with the required degree of safety;

(2) Any person who is under the age of eighteen and has been adjudicated an unruly or delinquent child or a juvenile traffic offender for having committed any act that if committed by an adult would be a drug abuse offense, as defined in section 2925.01 of the Revised Code, a violation of division (B) of section 2917.11, or a violation of division (A) of section 4511.19 of the Revised Code, unless the person has been required by the court to attend a drug abuse or alcohol abuse education, intervention, or treatment program specified by the court and has satisfactorily completed the program;

(3) Any person who, in the opinion of the registrar, is afflicted with or suffering from a physical or mental disability or disease that prevents the person from exercising reasonable and ordinary control over a motor vehicle while operating the vehicle upon the

highways, except that a restricted license effective for six months may be issued to any person otherwise qualified who is or has been subject to any condition resulting in episodic impairment of consciousness or loss of muscular control and whose condition, in the opinion of the registrar, is dormant or is sufficiently under medical control that the person is capable of exercising reasonable and ordinary control over a motor vehicle. A restricted license effective for six months shall be issued to any person who otherwise is qualified and who is subject to any condition that causes episodic impairment of consciousness or a loss of muscular control if the person presents a statement from a licensed physician that the person's condition is under effective medical control and the period of time for which the control has been continuously maintained, unless, thereafter, a medical examination is ordered and, pursuant thereto, cause for denial is found.

A person to whom a six-month restricted license has been issued shall give notice of the person's medical condition to the registrar on forms provided by the registrar and signed by the licensee's physician. The notice shall be sent to the registrar six months after the issuance of the license. Subsequent restricted licenses issued to the same individual shall be effective for six months.

(4) Any person who is unable to understand highway warnings or traffic signs or directions given in the English language;

(5) Any person making an application whose driver's license or driving privileges are under cancellation, revocation, or suspension in the jurisdiction where issued or any other jurisdiction, until the expiration of one year after the license was canceled or revoked or until the period of suspension ends. Any person whose application is denied under this division may file a petition in the municipal court or county court in whose jurisdiction the person resides agreeing to pay the cost of the proceedings and alleging that the conduct involved in the offense that resulted in suspension, cancellation, or revocation in the foreign jurisdiction would not have resulted in a suspension, cancellation, or revocation had the offense occurred in this state. If the petition is granted, the petitioner shall notify the registrar by a certified copy of the court's findings and a license shall not be denied under this division.

(6) Any person who is under a class one or two suspension imposed for a violation of section 2903.04, 2903.06, or 2903.08 of the Revised Code or whose driver's or commercial driver's license or permit was permanently revoked prior to the effective date of this amendment for a substantially equivalent violation pursuant to section 4507.16 of the Revised Code;

(7) Any person who is not a resident or temporary resident of this state.

(2002 S 123, eff. 1–1–04; 2000 S 180, eff. 3–22–01; 1997 S 35, eff. 1–1–99; 1997 H 141, eff. 3–3–98; 1997 S 60, eff. 10–21–97; 1995 H 167, eff. 5–15–97; 1994 S 82, eff. 5–4–94; 1993 S 62, § 1, eff. 9–1–93; 1993 S 62, § 4; 1992 S 275; 1989 H 381, H 330, H 329; 1988 H 643; 1986 S 262; 1980 H 965; 1979 H 328; 1977 H 71; 1975 H 300; 1974 S 313; 1973 S 1; 131 v H 183, H 274; 130 v H 758, H 772; 129 v 1448, 582; 128 v 539; 127 v 789, 839; 1953 H 1; GC 6296–7)

4507.081 Annual license for one with condition that is dormant or under effective medical control

(A) Upon the expiration of a restricted license issued under division (D)(3) of section 4507.08 of the Revised Code and submission of a statement as provided in division (C) of this section, the registrar of motor vehicles may issue a driver's license to the person to whom the restricted license was issued. A driver's license issued under this section, unless otherwise suspended or canceled, shall be effective for one year.

(B) A driver's license issued under this section may be renewed annually, for no more than three consecutive years, whenever the person to whom the license has been issued submits to the registrar, by certified mail and no sooner than thirty days prior to the expiration date of the license or renewal thereof, a statement as provided in division (C) of this section. A renewal of a driver's license, unless the license is otherwise suspended or canceled, shall be effective for one year following the expiration date of the license or renewal thereof, and shall be evidenced by a validation sticker. The renewal validation sticker shall be in a form prescribed by the registrar and shall be affixed to the license.

(C) No person may be issued a driver's license under this section, and no such driver's license may be renewed, unless the person presents a signed statement from a licensed physician that the person's condition either is dormant or is under effective medical control, that the control has been maintained continuously for at least one year prior to the date on which application for the license is made, and that, if continued medication is prescribed to control the condition, the person may be depended upon to take the medication.

The statement shall be made on a form provided by the registrar, shall be in not less than duplicate, and shall contain any other information the registrar considers necessary. The duplicate copy of the statement may be retained by the person requesting the license renewal and, when in the person's immediate possession and used in conjunction with the original license, shall entitle the person to operate a motor vehicle during a period of no more than thirty days following the date of submission of the statement to the registrar, except when the registrar denies the request for the license renewal and so notifies the person.

(D) Whenever the registrar receives a statement indicating that the condition of a person to whom a driver's license has been issued under this section no longer is dormant or under effective medical control, the registrar shall cancel the person's driver's license.

(E) Nothing in this section shall require a person submitting a signed statement from a licensed physician to obtain a medical examination prior to the submission of the statement.

(F) Any person whose driver's license has been canceled under this section may apply for a subsequent restricted license according to the provisions of section 4507.08 of the Revised Code.

(2002 S 123, eff. 1–1–04; 1997 S 35, eff. 1–1–99; 1989 H 381, eff. 7–1–89; 1989 H 329; 1988 H 643; 1984 H 37; 1979 H 328; 1977 H 71)

4507.09 Expiration and renewal dates for licenses; notice of expiration; notice of change of address; effect of outstanding arrest warrant

(A) Except as provided in division (B) of this section, every driver's license issued to a resident of this state expires on the birthday of the applicant in the fourth year after the date it is issued and every driver's license issued to a temporary resident expires in accordance with rules adopted by the registrar of motor vehicles. In no event shall any license be issued for a period longer than four years and ninety days.

Subject to the requirements of section 4507.12 of the Revised Code, every driver's license issued to a resident is renewable at any time prior to its expiration and any license of a temporary resident is nonrenewable. A nonrenewable license may be replaced with a new license within ninety days prior to its expiration in accordance with division (E) of this section. No refund shall be made or credit given for the unexpired portion of the driver's license that is renewed. The registrar of motor vehicles shall notify each person whose driver's license has expired within forty-five days after the date of expiration. Notification shall be made by regular mail sent to the person's last known address as shown in the records of the bureau of motor vehicles. Failure to provide such notification shall not be construed as a renewal or extension of any license. For the purposes of this section, the date of birth of any applicant born on the twenty-ninth day of February shall be deemed to be the first day of March in any year in which there is no twenty-ninth day of February.

(B) Every driver's license or renewal of a driver's license issued to an applicant who is sixteen years of age or older, but less than twenty-one years of age, expires on the twenty-first birthday of the applicant, except that an applicant who applies no more than thirty days before the applicant's twenty-first birthday shall be issued a license in accordance with division (A) of this section.

(C) Each person licensed as a driver under this chapter shall notify the registrar of any change in the person's address within ten days following that change. The notification shall be in writing on a form provided by the registrar and shall include the full name, date of birth, license number, county of residence, social security number, and new address of the person.

(D) No driver's license shall be renewed when renewal is prohibited by division (A) of section 4507.091 of the Revised Code.

(E) A nonrenewable license may be replaced with a new license within ninety days prior to its expiration upon the applicant's presentation of documentation verifying the applicant's legal presence in the United States. A nonrenewable license expires on the same date listed on the legal presence documentation, or on the same date in the fourth year after the date the nonrenewable license is issued, whichever comes first. A nonrenewable license is not transferable, and the applicant may not rely on it to obtain a driver's license in another state.

In accordance with Chapter 119. of the Revised Code, the registrar of motor vehicles shall adopt rules governing nonrenewable licenses for temporary residents. At a minimum, the rules shall include provisions specifying all of the following:

(1) That no nonrenewable license may extend beyond the duration of the applicant's temporary residence in this state;

(2) That no nonrenewable license may be replaced by a new license unless the applicant provides acceptable documentation of the person's identity and of the applicant's continued temporary residence in this state;

(3) That no nonrenewable license is valid to apply for a driver's license in any other state;

(4) That every nonrenewable license may contain any security features that the registrar prescribes.

(2002 S 184, eff. 5-15-02; 1997 H 141, eff. 3-3-98; 1997 S 60, eff. 10-21-97; 1996 H 353, eff. 9-17-96; 1994 S 96, eff. 5-10-94; 1991 H 134, eff. 10-10-91; 1990 H 88; 1989 H 381; 1984 H 58; 1978 H 215; 1976 H 1337; 1969 H 113; 1953 H 1; GC 6296-15)

4507.091 Issuance of licenses to persons with outstanding arrest warrants

(A) A municipal court, county court, or mayor's court, at the court's discretion, may order the clerk of the court to send to the registrar of motor vehicles a report containing the name, address, and such other information as the registrar may require by rule, of any person for whom an arrest warrant has been issued by that court and is outstanding.

Upon receipt of such a report, the registrar shall enter the information contained in the report into the records of the bureau of motor vehicles. Neither the registrar nor any deputy registrar shall issue a temporary instruction permit or driver's or commercial driver's license to the person named in the report, or renew the driver's or commercial driver's license of such person, until the registrar receives notification from the municipal court, county court, or mayor's court that there are no outstanding arrest warrants in the name of the person. The registrar also shall send a notice to the person who is named in the report, via regular first class mail sent to the person's last known address as shown in the records of the bureau, informing the person that neither the registrar nor any deputy registrar is permitted to issue a temporary instruction permit or driver's or commercial driver's license to the person, or renew the driver's or commercial driver's license of the person, until the registrar receives notification that there are no outstanding arrest warrants in the name of the person.

(B) A clerk who reports an outstanding arrest warrant in accordance with division (A) of this section immediately shall notify the registrar when the warrant has been executed and returned to the issuing court or has been canceled. The clerk shall charge and collect from the person named in the executed or canceled arrest warrant a processing fee of fifteen dollars to cover the costs of the bureau in administering this section. The clerk shall transmit monthly all such processing fees to the registrar for deposit into the state bureau of motor vehicles fund created by section 4501.25 of the Revised Code.

Upon receipt of such notification, the registrar shall cause the report of that outstanding arrest warrant to be removed from the records of the bureau and, if there are no other outstanding arrest warrants issued by a municipal court, county court, or mayor's court in the name of the person and the person otherwise is eligible to be issued a driver's or commercial driver's license or to have such a license renewed, the registrar or a deputy registrar may issue a driver's license or commercial driver's license to the person named in the executed or canceled arrest warrant, or renew the driver's or commercial driver's license of such person.

(C) Neither the registrar, any employee of the bureau, a deputy registrar, nor any employee of a deputy registrar is personally liable for damages or injuries resulting from any error made by a clerk in entering information contained in a report submitted to the registrar under this section.

(D) Any information submitted to the registrar by a clerk under this section shall be transmitted by means of an electronic data transfer system.

(2002 H 490, eff. 1-1-04; 1997 H 141, eff. 3-3-98)

4507.10 Examination for license, temporary instruction permit or motorcycle operator's endorsement; exceptions

(A) Except as provided in section 4507.11 of the Revised Code, the registrar of motor vehicles shall examine every applicant for a temporary instruction permit, driver's license, or motorcycle operator's endorsement before issuing any such permit, license, or endorsement.

(B) Except as provided in section 4507.12 of the Revised Code, the registrar may waive the examination of any person applying for the renewal of a driver's license or motorcycle operator's endorsement issued under this chapter, if the person presents and surrenders either an unexpired license or endorsement or a license or endorsement which has expired not more than six months prior to the date of application. Except as provided in section 4507.12 of the Revised Code, the registrar may waive the examination of any person applying for a driver's license if the person presents and surrenders a valid license issued by another state and the license is unexpired or expired not more than six months.

(C) The registrar may waive the examination of any person applying for the renewal of such a license or endorsement who is on active duty in the armed forces of the United States or in service with the peace corps, volunteers in service to America, or the foreign service of the United States if the applicant has no physical or mental disabilities that would affect the applicant's driving ability, had a valid Ohio driver's or commercial driver's license at the time the applicant commenced such active duty or service, and the applicant's license is not under suspension or revocation by this state or any other jurisdiction. The registrar also may waive the examination of the spouse or a dependent of any such person on active duty or in service if the applicant has no physical or mental disabilities that would affect the applicant's driving ability, was an Ohio licensee at the time the person commenced the active duty or service, and if the person's active duty caused the spouse or dependent to relocate outside of this state during the period of the active duty or service.

(D) Except as provided in section 4507.12 of the Revised Code, the registrar may waive the examination of any person applying for such a license or endorsement who meets any of the following sets of qualifications:

(1) Has been on active duty in the armed forces of the United States, presents an honorable discharge certificate showing that the applicant has no physical or mental disabilities that would affect the applicant's driving ability, had a valid Ohio driver's or commercial driver's license at the time the applicant commenced the applicant's active duty, is not under a license suspension or revocation by this state or any other jurisdiction, and makes the application not more than six months after the date of discharge or separation;

(2) Was in service with the peace corps, volunteers in service to America, or the foreign service of the United States; presents such evidence of the applicant's service as the registrar prescribes showing that the applicant has no physical or mental disabilities that would affect the applicant's driving ability; had a valid Ohio driver's or commercial driver's license at the time the applicant commenced the applicant's service, is not under a license suspension or revocation by this state or any other jurisdiction, and makes the application no more than six months after leaving the peace corps, volunteers, or foreign service.

(3) Is the spouse or a dependent of a person on active duty in the armed forces of the United States, or in service with the peace corps, volunteers in service to America, or the foreign service of the United States; presents such evidence as the registrar prescribes showing that the applicant has no physical or mental disabilities that would affect his driving ability; presents such evidence as the registrar prescribes showing that the applicant relocated outside of Ohio as a result of the person's active duty or service; was an Ohio licensee at the time of the relocation; and makes the application not more than six months after returning to Ohio.

(2000 S 271, eff. 1–1–01; 2000 H 600, eff. 9–1–00; 1997 S 35, eff. 1–1–99; 1997 S 60, eff. 10–21–97; 1994 S 96, eff. 5–10–94; 1989 H 381, eff. 7–1–89; 1988 H 614; 1984 H 58; 1972 S 546; 132 v H 380, H 57; 1953 H 1; GC 6296–11)

4507.101 Reciprocal arrangements with other countries

(A) The registrar of motor vehicles may enter into a reciprocal arrangement with another country for reciprocal recognition of driver's licenses if both of the following conditions are satisfied:

(1) The country grants the same or similar exemptions relating to drivers' licenses to persons holding valid driver's licenses issued by this state;

(2) The country charges only reasonable fees for driver's license applications, as determined by the registrar in the registrar's sole discretion, and the fees are charged impartially to all applicants.

(B) The registrar shall not enter into a reciprocal arrangement, and shall cancel any such arrangement previously entered into, if the country does not comply with divisions (A)(1) and (2) of this section.

(C) Except as provided in section 4507.12 of the Revised Code, the registrar may waive the examination of any person applying for a driver's license if the person presents a valid, unexpired license issued by a country with which the registrar has a reciprocal arrangement.

(D) The registrar may prescribe the conditions upon which a driver's license may be issued or retained under this section. The registrar shall not prohibit an applicant from retaining the foreign license after the registrar or deputy registrar issuing the Ohio license views and authenticates the foreign license.

(2000 H 600, eff. 9–1–00)

4507.11 Examination for license, temporary instruction permit or motorcycle operator's endorsement; examiner's permit; successful completion of basic instruction program provided by motorcycle safety and education program

(A) The registrar of motor vehicles shall conduct all necessary examinations of applicants for temporary instruction permits, drivers' licenses, or motorcycle operators' endorsements. The examination shall include a test of the applicant's knowledge of motor vehicle laws, including the laws on stopping for school buses, a test of the applicant's physical fitness to drive, and a test of the applicant's ability to understand highway traffic control devices. The examination may be conducted in such a manner that applicants who are illiterate or limited in their knowledge of the English language may be tested by methods that would indicate to the examining officer that the applicant has a reasonable knowledge of motor vehicle laws and understands highway traffic control devices. An applicant for a driver's license shall give an actual demonstration of the ability to exercise ordinary and reasonable control in the operation of a motor vehicle by driving the same under the supervision of an examining officer. Except as provided in division (B) of this section, an applicant for a motorcycle operator's endorsement or a restricted license that permits only the operation of a motorcycle shall give an actual demonstration of the ability to exercise ordinary and reasonable control in the operation of a motorcycle by driving the same under the supervision of an examining officer. Except as provided in section 4507.12 of the Revised Code, the registrar shall designate the highway patrol, any law enforcement body, or any other employee of the department of public safety to supervise and conduct examinations for temporary instruction permits, drivers' licenses, and motorcycle operators' endorsements and shall provide the necessary rules and forms to properly conduct the examinations. The records of the examinations, together with the application for a temporary instruction permit, driver's license, or motorcycle operator's endorsement, shall be forwarded to the registrar by the deputy registrar, and, if in the opinion of the registrar the applicant is qualified to operate a motor vehicle, the registrar shall issue the permit, license, or endorsement.

The registrar may authorize the highway patrol, other designated law enforcement body, or other designated employee of the department of public safety to issue an examiner's driving permit to an applicant who has passed the required examination, authorizing that applicant to operate a motor vehicle while the registrar is completing an investigation relative to that applicant's qualifications to receive a temporary instruction permit, driver's license, or motorcycle operator's endorsement. The examiner's driving permit shall be in the immediate possession of the applicant while operating a motor vehicle and shall be effective until final action and notification has been given by the registrar, but in no event longer than sixty days from its date of issuance.

(B)(1) An applicant for a motorcycle operator's endorsement or a restricted license that permits only the operation of a motorcycle who presents to the registrar of motor vehicles or a deputy registrar a form approved by the director of public safety attesting to the applicant's successful completion within the preceding sixty days of a course of basic instruction provided by the motorcycle safety and education program approved by the director pursuant to section 4508.08 of the Revised Code shall not be required to give an actual demonstration of the ability to operate a motorcycle by driving a motorcycle under the supervision of an examining officer, as described in division (A) of this section. Upon presentation of the form described in division (B)(1) of this section and compliance with all other requirements relating to the issuance of a motorcycle operator's endorsement or a restricted license that permits only the operation of a motorcycle, the registrar or deputy registrar shall issue to the applicant the endorsement or restricted license, as the case may be.

(2) A person who has not attained eighteen years of age and presents an application for a motorcycle operator's endorsement or a restricted license under division (B)(1) of this section also shall comply with the requirements of section 4507.21 of the Revised Code.

(2000 S 271, eff. 1–1–01; 2000 H 600, eff. 9–1–00; 1997 S 35, eff. 1–1–99; 1989 H 381, eff. 7–1–89; 1984 H 58; 1978 S 389; 1970 H 362; 132 v H 380; 129 v 1618; 1953 H 1; GC 6296–12)

4507.111 License or permit holders in default on child support orders

On receipt of a notice pursuant to section 3123.54 of the Revised Code, the registrar of motor vehicles shall comply with sections 3123.52 to 3123.614 of the Revised Code and any applicable rules adopted under section 3123.63 of the Revised Code with respect to any driver's or commercial license or permit, motorcycle operator's license or endorsement, or temporary instruction permit or commercial driver's temporary instruction permit issued by this state that is the subject of the notice.

(2002 S 123, eff. 1–1–04; 2000 S 180, eff. 3–22–01; 1995 H 167, eff. 5–15–97)

4507.12 Vision screening; further vision examination may be required; exemption of deputy registrar from certain liabilities

(A) Except as provided in division (C) of section 4507.10 of the Revised Code, each person applying for the renewal of a driver's license shall submit to a screening of the person's vision before the license may be renewed. The vision screening shall be conducted at the office of the deputy registrar receiving the application for license renewal.

(B) When the results of a vision screening given under division (A) of this section indicate that the vision of the person examined meets the standards required for licensing, the deputy registrar may renew the person's driver's license at that time.

(C) When the results of a vision screening given under division (A) of this section indicate that the vision of the person screened may not meet the standards required for licensing, the deputy registrar shall not renew the person's driver's license at that time but shall refer the person to a driver's license examiner appointed by the superintendent of the state highway patrol under section 5503.21 of the Revised Code for a further examination of the person's vision. When a person referred to a driver's license examiner by a deputy registrar does not meet the vision standards required for licensing, the driver's license examiner shall retain the person's operator's or chauffeur's license and shall immediately notify the registrar of motor vehicles of that fact. No driver's license shall be issued to any such person, until the person's vision is corrected to meet the standards required for licensing and the person passes the vision screening required by this section. Any person who operates a motor vehicle on a highway, or on any public or private property used by the public for purposes of vehicular travel or parking, during the time the person's driver's license is held by a driver's license examiner under this division, shall be deemed to be operating a motor vehicle in violation of division (A) of section 4510.12 of the Revised Code.

(D) The registrar shall adopt rules and shall provide any forms necessary to properly conduct vision screenings at the office of a deputy registrar.

(E) No person conducting vision screenings under this section shall be personally liable for damages for injury or loss to persons or property and for death caused by the operation of a motor vehicle by any person whose driver's license was renewed by the deputy registrar under division (B) of this section.

(2002 S 123, eff. 1–1–04; 1989 H 381, eff. 7–1–89; 1988 S 1; 1986 S 356; 1984 H 58)

4507.13 Contents of license; novice motorcycle operator

(A) The registrar of motor vehicles shall issue a driver's license to every person licensed as an operator of motor vehicles other than commercial motor vehicles. No person licensed as a commercial motor vehicle driver under Chapter 4506. of the Revised Code need procure a driver's license, but no person shall drive any commercial motor vehicle unless licensed as a commercial motor vehicle driver.

Every driver's license shall display on it the distinguishing number assigned to the licensee and shall display the licensee's name and date of birth; the licensee's residence address and county of residence; a color photograph of the licensee; a brief description of the licensee for the purpose of identification; a facsimile of the signature of the licensee as it appears on the application for the license; a notation, in a manner prescribed by the registrar, indicating any condition described in division (D)(3) of section 4507.08 of the Revised Code to which the licensee is subject; if the licensee has executed a durable power of attorney for health care or a declaration governing the use or continuation, or the withholding or withdrawal, of life-sustaining treatment and has specified that the licensee wishes the license to indicate that the licensee has executed either type of instrument, any symbol chosen by the registrar to indicate that the licensee has executed either type of instrument; and any additional information that the registrar requires by rule. No license shall display the licensee's social security number unless the licensee specifically requests that the licensee's social security number be displayed on the license. If federal law requires the licensee's social security number to be displayed on the license, the social security number shall be displayed on the license notwithstanding this section.

The driver's license for licensees under twenty-one years of age shall have characteristics prescribed by the registrar distinguishing it from that issued to a licensee who is twenty-one years of age or older, except that a driver's license issued to a person who applies no more than thirty days before the applicant's twenty-first birthday shall have the characteristics of a license issued to a person who is twenty-one years of age or older.

The driver's license issued to a temporary resident shall contain the word "nonrenewable" and shall have any additional characteristics prescribed by the registrar distinguishing it from a license issued to a resident.

Every driver's or commercial driver's license displaying a motorcycle operator's endorsement and every restricted license to operate a motor vehicle also shall display the designation "novice," if the endorsement or license is issued to a person who is eighteen years of age or older and previously has not been licensed to operate a motorcycle by this state or another jurisdiction recognized by this state. The "novice" designation shall be effective for one year after the date of issuance of the motorcycle operator's endorsement or license.

Each license issued under this section shall be of such material and so designed as to prevent its reproduction or alteration without ready detection and, to this end, shall be laminated with a transparent plastic material.

(B) Except in regard to a driver's license issued to a person who applies no more than thirty days before the applicant's twenty-first birthday, neither the registrar nor any deputy registrar shall issue a driver's license to anyone under twenty-one years of age that does not have the characteristics prescribed by the registrar distinguishing it from the driver's license issued to persons who are twenty-one years of age or older.

(C) Whoever violates division (B) of this section is guilty of a minor misdemeanor.

(2004 H 230, eff. 9–16–04; 2002 S 123, eff. 1–1–04; 2001 H 46, eff. 2–1–02; 1998 S 213, § 4, eff. 1–1–99; 1998 S 213, § 1, eff. 7–29–98; 1997 S 35, eff. 1–1–99; 1997 S 60, eff. 10–21–97; 1994 H 580, eff. 12–9–94; 1992 H 427, eff. 10–8–92; 1991 H 134; 1990 S 131; 1989 H 381, H 329; 1988 H 643; 1984 H 183; 1979 H 328; 1978 H 115; 1977 H 71; 1975 H 650; 132 v S 452, S 43, H 193; 131 v H 152; 1953 H 1; GC 6296–13)

4507.14 Restrictions on license by registrar

The registrar of motor vehicles upon issuing a driver's license, a motorcycle operator's endorsement, a driver's license renewal, or the renewal of any other license issued under this chapter, whenever good cause appears, may impose restrictions suitable to the licensee's driving ability with respect to the type of or special mechanical control devices required on a motor vehicle that the licensee may operate, or any other restrictions applicable to the licensee that the registrar determines to be necessary.

When issuing a license to a person with impaired hearing, the registrar shall require that a motor vehicle operated by the person be equipped with two outside rear vision mirrors, one on the left side and the other on the right side.

The registrar either may issue a special restricted license or may set forth any restrictions applicable to the license upon the usual license form.

The registrar, upon receiving satisfactory evidence of any violation of the restrictions of any license, after an opportunity for a hearing in accordance with Chapter 119. of the Revised Code, may impose upon the offender a class D suspension of the license from the range specified in division (B)(4) of section 4510.02 of the Revised Code.

(2002 S 123, eff. 1–1–04; 1997 S 60, eff. 10–21–97; 1989 H 381, eff. 7–1–89; 132 v H 380; 1953 H 1; GC 6296–14a)

4507.141 Identification cards for hearing-impaired persons

(A) Any hearing-impaired person may apply to the registrar of motor vehicles for an identification card identifying the person as hearing-impaired. The application for a hearing-impaired identification card shall be accompanied by a signed statement from the applicant's personal physician certifying that the applicant is hearing-impaired. Upon receipt of the application for the identification card and the signed statement from the applicant's personal physician, and upon presentation by the applicant of the applicant's driver's or commercial driver's license or motorcycle operator's license, the registrar shall issue the applicant an identification card. A hearing-impaired person may also apply for a hearing-impaired identification card at the time the person applies for a driver's or commercial driver's license or motorcycle operator's license or endorsement. Every hearing-impaired identification card shall expire on the same date that the cardholder's driver's or commercial driver's license or motorcycle operator's license expires.

(B) The hearing-impaired identification card shall be rectangular in shape, approximately the same size as an average motor vehicle sun visor, as determined by the registrar, to enable the identification card to be attached to a sun visor in a motor vehicle. The identification card shall contain the heading "Identification Card for the Hearing-impaired Driver" in boldface type, the name and signature of the hearing-impaired person to whom it is issued, an identifying number, and instructions on the actions the hearing-impaired person should take and the actions the person should refrain from taking in the event the person is stopped by a law enforcement officer while operating the motor vehicle. The registrar shall determine the preferred manner in which a hearing-impaired motorcycle operator should carry or display the hearing-impaired identification card, and the color and composition of, and any other information to be included on, the identification card.

(C) As used in this section, "hearing-impaired" means a hearing loss of forty decibels or more in one or both ears.

(2004 H 230, eff. 9–16–04; 1990 H 581, eff. 7–13–90)

4507.15 Courts of record; reports of convictions and forfeitures

For the purpose of enforcing this chapter and Chapter 4510. of the Revised Code, any court of record having criminal jurisdiction shall have county-wide jurisdiction within the county in which it is located to hear and finally determine cases arising under this chapter and Chapter 4510. of the Revised Code. An action arising under this section shall be commenced by the filing of an affidavit, and the right of trial by jury is preserved, but indictments are not required in misdemeanor cases arising under this chapter and Chapter 4510. of the Revised Code. The registrar shall prepare and furnish blanks for the use of the court in making reports of convictions and bond forfeitures arising under this chapter and Chapter 4510. of the Revised Code.

(2002 S 123, eff. 1–1–04; 127 v 525, eff. 6–22–57; 1953 H 1; GC 6296–16)

SUSPENSION AND REVOCATION OF LICENSE

4507.16 Suspension of licenses; registration or transfer of vehicle during suspension

(A) The trial judge of any court of record, in addition to or independent of all other penalties provided by law or by ordinance, shall impose upon any person who is convicted of or pleads guilty to perjury or the making of a false affidavit under this chapter, or any other law of this state requiring the registration of motor vehicles or regulating their operation on the highway, a class six suspension of the offender's driver's license, commercial driver's license, temporary instruction permit, probationary license, or nonresident operating privilege from the range specified in division (A)(6) of section 4510.02 of the Revised Code. No judge shall suspend the first three months of suspension of an offender's license, permit, or privilege required by this division.

(B) If the trial judge of any court of record suspends the driver's or commercial driver's license or permit or nonresident operating privilege of a person who is convicted of or pleads guilty to any offense for which a suspension of that type is provided by law or ordinance, in addition to all other penalties provided by law or ordinance, the judge may issue an order prohibiting the offender from registering, renewing, or transferring the registration of any vehicle during the period that the offender's license, permit, or privilege is suspended. The court promptly shall send a copy of the order to the registrar of motor vehicles.

Upon receipt of the order from the court, neither the registrar nor any deputy registrar shall accept any application for the registration, registration renewal, or transfer of registration of any motor vehicle owned or leased by the person named in the order during the period that the person's license, permit, or privilege is suspended, unless the registrar is properly notified by the court that the order of suspension has been canceled. When the period of suspension expires or the order is canceled, the registrar or deputy registrar shall accept the application for registration, registration renewal, or transfer of registration of the person named in the order.

(2002 S 123, eff. 1–1–04; 2003 H 50, eff. 10–21–03; 2001 H 7, eff. 8–7–01; 2000 S 180, eff. 3–22–01; 1999 S 107, eff. 3–23–00; 1997 S 60, eff. 10–21–97; 1996 S 166, § 6, eff. 5–15–97; 1996 S 166, § 1, eff. 10–17–96; 1996 H 676, § 3, eff. 5–15–97; 1996 H 676, § 1, eff. 10–4–96; 1996 S 269, § 8, eff. 5–15–97; 1996 S 269, § 1, eff. 7–1–96; 1996 H 353, § 4, eff. 5–15–97; 1996 H 353, § 1, eff. 9–17–96; 1995 H 167, eff. 5–15–97; 1995 S 2, eff. 7–1–96; 1995 H 107, eff. (See Historical and Statutory Notes); 1994 H 236, eff. 9–29–94; 1994 S 82, eff. 5–4–94; 1993 H 377, eff. 9–30–93, 1993 S 62, § 1, 4; 1992 S 275; 1990 S 258, H 837, S 131; 1989 H 381; 1988 H 429; 1987 H 303; 1986 S 262; 1982 S 432; 1978 H 469; 1977 S 141; 1975 H 300; 1969 H 1; 132 v H 380, S 37; 125 v 367; 1953 H 1; GC 6296–17)

Historical and Statutory Notes

Ed. Note: 1995 H 107 Effective Date—The Secretary of State assigned a general effective date of 6–30–95 for 1995 H 107. Pursuant to O Const Art II § 1c and 1d, and RC 1.471, sections of 1995 H 107 that are, or depend for their implementation upon, current expense appropriations are effective 3–31–95; sections of 1995 H 107 that are not, and do not depend for their implementation upon, current expense appropriations are effective 6–30–95. See *Baldwin's Ohio Legislative Service*, 1995, page 3/L–98 for 1995 H 107, § 16.

Notes of Decisions

Ed. Note: See notes of decisions and opinions at RC 4511.19 regarding construction of the term "under the influence."

4507.164 Impounding license plates when license suspended

(A) Except as provided in divisions (C) to (E) of this section, when the license of any person is suspended pursuant to any provision of the Revised Code other than division (G) of section 4511.19 of the Revised Code and other than section 4510.07 of the Revised Code for a violation of a municipal OVI ordinance, the trial judge may impound the identification license plates of any motor vehicle registered in the name of the person.

(B)(1) When the license of any person is suspended pursuant to division (G)(1)(a) of section 4511.19 of the Revised Code, or pursuant to section 4510.07 of the Revised Code for a municipal OVI offense when the suspension is equivalent in length to the suspension under division (G) of section 4511.19 of the Revised Code that is specified in this division, the trial judge of the court of record or the mayor of the mayor's court that suspended the license may impound the identification license plates of any motor vehicle registered in the name of the person.

(2) When the license of any person is suspended pursuant to division (G)(1)(b) of section 4511.19 of the Revised Code, or pursuant to section 4510.07 of the Revised Code for a municipal OVI offense when the suspension is equivalent in length to the suspension under division (G) of section 4511.19 of the Revised Code that is specified in this division, the trial judge of the court of record that suspended the license shall order the impoundment of the identification license plates of the motor vehicle the offender was operating at the time of the offense and the immobilization of that vehicle in accordance with section 4503.233 and division (G)(1)(b) of section 4511.19 or division (B)(2)(a) of section 4511.193 of the Revised Code and may impound the identification license plates of any other motor vehicle registered in the name of the person whose license is suspended.

(3) When the license of any person is suspended pursuant to division (G)(1)(c), (d), or (e) of section 4511.19 of the Revised Code, or pursuant to section 4510.07 of the Revised Code for a municipal OVI offense when the suspension is equivalent in length to the suspension under division (G) of section 4511.19 of the Revised Code that is specified in this division, the trial judge of the court of record that suspended the license shall order the criminal forfeiture to the state of the motor vehicle the offender was operating at the time of the offense in accordance with section 4503.234 and division (G)(1)(c), (d), or (e) of section 4511.19 or division (B)(2)(b) of section 4511.193 of the Revised Code and may impound the identification license plates of any other motor vehicle registered in the name of the person whose license is suspended.

(C)(1) When a person is convicted of or pleads guilty to a violation of section 4510.14 of the Revised Code or a substantially equivalent municipal ordinance and division (B)(1) or (2) of section 4510.14 or division (C)(1) or (2) of section 4510.161 of the Revised Code applies, the trial judge of the court of record or the mayor of the mayor's court that imposes sentence shall order the immobilization of the vehicle the person was operating at the time of the offense and the impoundment of its identification license plates in accordance with section 4503.233 and division (B)(1) or (2) of section 4510.14 or division (C)(1) or (2) of section 4510.161 of the Revised Code and may impound the identification license plates of any other vehicle registered in the name of that person.

(2) When a person is convicted of or pleads guilty to a violation of section 4510.14 of the Revised Code or a substantially equivalent municipal ordinance and division (B)(3) of section 4510.14 or division (C)(3) of section 4510.161 of the Revised Code applies, the trial judge of the court of record that imposes sentence shall order the criminal forfeiture to the state of the vehicle the person was operating at the time of the offense in accordance with section 4503.234 and division (B)(3) of section 4510.14 or division (C)(3) of section 4510.161 of the Revised Code and may impound the identification license plates of any other vehicle registered in the name of that person.

(D)(1) When a person is convicted of or pleads guilty to a violation of division (A) of section 4510.16 of the Revised Code or a substantially equivalent municipal ordinance and division (B)(2) or (3) of section 4510.16 or division (B)(1) or (2) of section 4510.161 of the Revised Code applies, the trial judge of the court of record or the mayor of the mayor's court that imposes sentence shall order the immobilization of the vehicle the person was operating at the time of the offense and the impoundment of its identification license plates in accordance with section 4503.233 and division (B)(2) or (3) of section 4510.16 or division (B)(1) or (2) of section 4510.161 of the Revised Code and may impound the identification license plates of any other vehicle registered in the name of that person.

(2) When a person is convicted of or pleads guilty to a violation of division (A) of section 4510.16 of the Revised Code or a substantially equivalent municipal ordinance and division (B)(4) of section 4510.16 or division (B)(3) of section 4510.161 of the Revised Code applies, the trial judge of the court of record that imposes sentence shall order the criminal forfeiture to the state of the vehicle the person was operating at the time of the offense in accordance with section 4503.234 and division (B)(4) of section 4510.16 or division (B)(3) of section 4510.161 of the Revised Code and may impound the identification license plates of any other vehicle registered in the name of that person.

(E)(1) When a person is convicted of or pleads guilty to a violation of section 4511.203 of the Revised Code and the person is sentenced pursuant to division (C)(1) or (2) of section 4511.203 of the Revised Code, the trial judge of the court of record or the mayor of the mayor's court that imposes sentence shall order the immobilization of the vehicle that was involved in the commission of the offense and the impoundment of its identification license plates in accordance with division (C)(1) or (2) of section 4511.203 and section 4503.233 of the Revised Code and may impound the identification license plates of any other vehicle registered in the name of that person.

(2) When a person is convicted of or pleads guilty to a violation of section 4511.203 of the Revised Code and the person is sentenced pursuant to division (C)(3) of section 4511.203 of the Revised Code, the trial judge of the court of record or the mayor of the mayor's court that imposes sentence shall order the criminal forfeiture to the state of the vehicle that was involved in the commission of the offense in accordance with division (C)(3) of section 4511.203 and section 4503.234 of the Revised Code and may impound the identification license plates of any other vehicle registered in the name of that person.

(F) Except as provided in section 4503.233 or 4503.234 of the Revised Code, when the certificate of registration, the identification license plates, or both have been impounded, division (B) of section 4507.02 of the Revised Code is applicable.

(G) As used in this section, "municipal OVI offense" has the same meaning as in section 4511.181 of the Revised Code.

(2002 S 123, eff. 1–1–04; 2000 H 80, eff. 6–8–00; 1999 S 22, eff. 5–17–00; 1999 S 107, eff. 3–23–00; 1993 S 62, § 1, eff. 9–1–93; 1993 S 62, § 4; 1992 S 275; 1987 H 303; 1986 S 356; 1984 H 37; 1974 S 313; 132 v H 518)

4507.1612 Reinstatement fee for licenses suspended in connection with illegal conveyance or possession of deadly weapons or dangerous ordnance on school premises

The registrar shall not restore any operating privileges or reissue a probationary driver's license, restricted license, driver's license, or probationary commercial driver's license suspended under section 2923.122 of the Revised Code until the person whose license was suspended pays a reinstatement fee of thirty dollars to the bureau of motor vehicles.

The bureau of motor vehicles shall pay all fees collected under this section into the state treasury to the credit of the state bureau of motor vehicles fund created by section 4501.25 of the Revised Code.

(1996 H 124, eff. 9–30–97)

4507.1614 Suspension of license; juvenile; effect of date of disposition of case

The registrar shall suspend the person's license or permit under division (A) of section 4507.162 of the Revised Code regardless of whether the disposition of the case in juvenile court occurred after the person's eighteenth birthday.

(2004 H 230, eff. 9–16–04)

4507.17 Effect of suspension or cancellation of license

Any person whose license is suspended or canceled is not entitled to apply for or receive a new license during the effective dates of the suspension or cancellation.

(2002 S 123, eff. 1–1–04; 125 v 367, eff. 10–15–53; 1953 H 1; GC 6296–21)

4507.19 Cancellation of license or identification card

The registrar of motor vehicles may cancel any driver's or commercial driver's license or identification card that was obtained fraudulently or unlawfully, was issued in error, or has been altered or willfully destroyed.

(2004 H 230, eff. 9–16–04; 2002 S 123, eff. 1–1–04; 1989 H 381, eff. 7–1–89; 130 v H 420; 1953 H 1; GC 6296–18a)

4507.20 Examination of licensee's competency; report

The registrar of motor vehicles, when the registrar has good cause to believe that the holder of a driver's or commercial driver's license is incompetent or otherwise not qualified to be licensed, shall send a written notice to the licensee's last known address, requiring the licensee to submit to a driver's license examination, a physical examination, or both, or a commercial driver's license examination within the time indicated on the notice. The physical examination may be conducted by any individual authorized by the Revised Code to do so, including a physician assistant, a clinical nurse specialist, a certified nurse practitioner, or a certified nurse-midwife. Any written documentation of the physical examination shall be completed by the individual who conducted the examination.

Upon the conclusion of the examination, the registrar may suspend the license of the person, may permit the licensee to retain the license, or may issue the licensee a restricted license. Refusal or neglect of the licensee to submit to the examination is ground for suspension of the licensee's license.

A physician licensed under Chapter 4731. of the Revised Code may submit a report to the registrar stating that in the physician's professional opinion the holder of a driver's or commercial driver's license may be incompetent or otherwise not qualified to operate safely a motor vehicle due to medical reasons. Any such report submitted to the registrar is confidential, is not a public record, and is not subject to disclosure under section 149.43 of the Revised Code.

(2004 H 230, eff. 9–16–04; 2002 S 245, § 3, eff. 1–1–04; 2002 S 245, § 1, eff. 3–31–03; 2002 S 123, eff. 1–1–04; 1992 S 331, eff. 11–13–92; 1989 H 381; 1986 S 356; 132 v H 135; 129 v 1493; 1953 H 1; GC 6296–18b)

APPLICATION AND ISSUANCE OF LICENSE; FEES

4507.21 Application for and issuance of license; registrar to maintain list for jury service; training, safety, and education programs

(A) Each applicant for a driver's license shall file an application in the office of the registrar of motor vehicles or of a deputy registrar.

(B)(1) Each person under eighteen years of age applying for a driver's license issued in this state shall present satisfactory evidence of having successfully completed any one of the following:

(a) A driver education course approved by the state department of education prior to December 31, 2003.

(b) A driver training course approved by the director of public safety.

(c) A driver training course comparable to a driver education or driver training course described in division (B)(1)(a) or (b) of this section and administered by a branch of the armed forces of the United States and completed by the applicant while residing outside this state for the purpose of being with or near any person serving in the armed forces of the United States.

(2) Each person under eighteen years of age applying for a driver's license also shall present, on a form prescribed by the registrar, an affidavit signed by an eligible adult attesting that the person has acquired at least fifty hours of actual driving experience, with at least ten of those hours being at night.

(C) If the registrar or deputy registrar determines that the applicant is entitled to the driver's license, it shall be issued. If the application shows that the applicant's license has been previously canceled or suspended, the deputy registrar shall forward the application to the registrar, who shall determine whether the license shall be granted.

(D) All applications shall be filed in duplicate, and the deputy registrar issuing the license shall immediately forward to the office of the registrar the original copy of the application, together with the duplicate copy of the certificate, if issued. The registrar shall prescribe rules as to the manner in which the deputy registrar files and maintains the applications and other records. The registrar shall file every application for a driver's or commercial driver's license and index them by name and number, and shall maintain a suitable record of all licenses issued, all convictions and bond forfeitures, all applications for licenses denied, and all licenses that have been suspended or canceled.

(E) For purposes of section 2313.06 of the Revised Code, the registrar shall maintain accurate and current lists of the residents of each county who are eighteen years of age or older, have been issued, on and after January 1, 1984, driver's or commercial driver's licenses that are valid and current, and would be electors if they were registered to vote, regardless of whether they actually are registered to vote. The lists shall contain the names, addresses, dates of birth, duration of residence in this state, citizenship status, and social security numbers, if the numbers are available, of the licensees, and may contain any other information that the registrar considers suitable.

(F) Each person under eighteen years of age applying for a motorcycle operator's endorsement or a restricted license enabling the applicant to operate a motorcycle shall present satisfactory evidence of having completed the courses of instruction in the motorcycle safety and education program described in section 4508.08 of the Revised Code or a comparable course of instruction administered by a branch of the armed forces of the United States and completed by the applicant while residing outside this state for the purpose of being with or near any person serving in the armed forces of the United States. If the registrar or deputy registrar then determines that the applicant is entitled to the endorsement or restricted license, it shall be issued.

(G) No person shall knowingly make a false statement in an affidavit presented in accordance with division (B)(2) of this section.

(H) As used in this section, "eligible adult" means any of the following persons:

(1) A parent, guardian, or custodian of the applicant;

(2) A person over the age of twenty-one who acts in loco parentis of the applicant and who maintains proof of financial responsibility with respect to the operation of a motor vehicle owned by the applicant or with respect to the applicant's operation of any motor vehicle.

(I) Whoever violates division (G) of this section is guilty of a minor misdemeanor and shall be fined one hundred dollars.

(2002 S 123, eff. 1–1–04; 2002 H 407, eff. 10–11–02; 1997 S 35, eff. 1–1–99; 1994 S 96, eff. 5–10–94; 1992 S 98, eff. 11–12–92; 1989 H 381; 1986 H 291; 1984 H 183; 1974 S 313; 132 v H 380; 1953 H 1; GC 6296–19)

4507.212 Statement of applicant; maintenance of proof of financial responsibility

(A) As used in this section, "motor vehicle" has the same meaning as in section 4509.01 of the Revised Code.

(B) An application for a driver's, commercial driver's, restricted, or probationary license, or renewal of such license shall contain a statement, to be signed by the applicant, that does all of the following:

(1) States that the applicant maintains, or has maintained on his behalf, proof of financial responsibility at the time of application, and will not operate a motor vehicle in this state, unless he maintains, or has maintained on his behalf, proof of financial responsibility;

(2) Contains a brief summary of the purposes and operation of section 4509.101 of the Revised Code, the rights and duties of the applicant under that section, and the penalties for violation of that section;

(3) Warns the applicant that the financial responsibility law does not prevent the possibility that the applicant may be involved in an accident with an owner or operator of a motor vehicle who is without proof of financial responsibility.

(C) The registrar of motor vehicles shall prescribe the form of the statement, and the manner in which the statement shall be presented to the applicant. The statement shall be designed to enable the applicant to retain a copy of it.

(D) Nothing within this section shall be construed to excuse a violation of section 4509.101 of the Revised Code.

(E) At the time a person submits an application for a driver's, commercial driver's, restricted, or probationary license, or renewal of such a license, the applicant also shall be furnished with a form that lists in plain language all the possible penalties to which the applicant could be subject for a violation of the financial responsibility law, including driver's license suspensions; all fees, including nonvoluntary compliance and reinstatement fees; and vehicle immobilization or impoundment. The applicant shall sign the form, which shall be submitted along with the application. The form shall be retained by the registrar or deputy registrar who issues the license or renewal or his successor for a period of two years from the date of issuance of the license or renewal. The registrar shall prescribe the manner in which the form shall be presented to the applicant, and the format of the form, which shall be such that the applicant can retain a copy of it.

(1994 S 20, eff. 10–20–94; 1989 H 381, eff. 7–1–89; 1984 H 767; 1982 S 250)

4507.22 Transmission of application with report of findings to registrar

If the deputy registrar finds that an applicant is not entitled to an identification card or a driver's license, he shall transmit to the registrar of motor vehicles the original of the application together with the written report of his findings and recommendations in connection with such application. Upon receipt thereof, the registrar shall review the findings and recommendations and determine whether the application shall be granted, and report his findings to the deputy registrar and the applicant. If the registrar determines the the [sic.] application should be granted, he shall thereupon notify the deputy registrar, who shall forthwith issue the license or card.

(1989 H 381, eff. 7–1–89; 1976 S 435; 1953 H 1; GC 6296–20)

4507.23 License fees; exemptions for disabled veterans

(A) Except as provided in division (I) of this section, each application for a temporary instruction permit and examination shall be accompanied by a fee of five dollars.

(B) Except as provided in division (I) of this section, each application for a driver's license made by a person who previously held such a license and whose license has expired not more than two years prior to the date of application, and who is required under this chapter to give an actual demonstration of the person's ability to drive, shall be accompanied by a fee of three dollars in addition to any other fees.

(C) Except as provided in divisions (E) and (I) of this section, each application for a driver's license, or motorcycle operator's endorsement, or renewal of a driver's license shall be accompanied by a fee of six dollars. Except as provided in division (I) of this section, each application for a duplicate driver's license shall be accompanied by a fee of two dollars and fifty cents. The duplicate driver's licenses issued under this section shall be distributed by the deputy registrar in accordance with rules adopted by the registrar of motor vehicles.

(D) Except as provided in division (I) of this section, each application for a motorized bicycle license or duplicate thereof shall be accompanied by a fee of two dollars and fifty cents.

(E) Except as provided in division (I) of this section, each application for a driver's license or renewal of a driver's license that will be issued to a person who is less than twenty-one years of age shall be accompanied by whichever of the following fees is applicable:

(1) If the person is sixteen years of age or older, but less than seventeen years of age, a fee of seven dollars and twenty-five cents;

(2) If the person is seventeen years of age or older, but less than eighteen years of age, a fee of six dollars;

(3) If the person is eighteen years of age or older, but less than nineteen years of age, a fee of four dollars and seventy-five cents;

(4) If the person is nineteen years of age or older, but less than twenty years of age, a fee of three dollars and fifty cents;

(5) If the person is twenty years of age or older, but less than twenty-one years of age, a fee of two dollars and twenty-five cents.

(F) Neither the registrar nor any deputy registrar shall charge a fee in excess of one dollar and fifty cents for laminating a driver's license, motorized bicycle license, or temporary instruction permit identification cards as required by sections 4507.13 and 4511.521 of the Revised Code. A deputy registrar laminating a driver's license, motorized bicycle license, or temporary instruction permit identification cards shall retain the entire amount of the fee charged for lamination, less the actual cost to the registrar of the laminating materials used for that lamination, as specified in the contract executed by the bureau for the laminating materials and laminating equipment. The deputy registrar shall forward the amount of the cost of the laminating materials to the registrar for deposit as provided in this section.

(G) Except as provided in division (I) of this section and except for the renewal of a driver's license, commencing on October 1, 2003, each transaction described in divisions (A), (B), (C), (D), and (E) of this section shall be accompanied by an additional fee of twelve dollars. A transaction involving the renewal of a driver's license with an expiration date on or after that date shall be accompanied by an additional fee of twelve dollars. The additional fee is for the purpose of defraying the department of public safety's costs associated with the administration and enforcement of the motor vehicle and traffic laws of Ohio.

(H) At the time and in the manner provided by section 4503.10 of the Revised Code, the deputy registrar shall transmit the fees collected under divisions (A), (B), (C), (D), and (E), those portions of the fees specified in and collected under division (F), and the additional fee under division (G) of this section to the registrar. The registrar shall pay two dollars and fifty cents of each fee collected under divisions (A), (B), (C), (D), and (E)(1) to (4) of this section, and the entire fee collected under division (E)(5) of this section, into the state highway safety fund established in section 4501.06 of the Revised Code, and such fees shall be used for the sole purpose of supporting driver licensing activities. The registrar also shall pay the entire fee collected under division (G) of this section into the state highway safety fund created in section 4501.06 of the Revised Code. The remaining fees collected by the registrar under this section shall be paid into the state bureau of motor vehicles fund established in section 4501.25 of the Revised Code.

(I) A disabled veteran who has a service-connected disability rated at one hundred per cent by the veterans' administration may apply to the registrar or a deputy registrar for the issuance to that veteran, without the payment of any fee prescribed in this section, of any of the following items:

(1) A temporary instruction permit and examination;

(2) A new, renewal, or duplicate driver's or commercial driver's license;

(3) A motorcycle operator's endorsement;

(4) A motorized bicycle license or duplicate thereof;

(5) Lamination of a driver's license, motorized bicycle license, or temporary instruction permit identification card as provided in division (F) of this section, if the circumstances specified in division (I)(5) of this section are met.

If the driver's license, motorized bicycle license, or temporary instruction permit identification card of a disabled veteran described in division (I) of this section is laminated by a deputy registrar who is acting as a deputy registrar pursuant to a contract with the registrar that is in effect on October 14, 1997, the disabled veteran shall be required to pay the deputy registrar the lamination fee provided in division (F) of this section. If the driver's license, motorized bicycle license, or temporary instruction permit identification card of such a disabled veteran is laminated by a deputy registrar who is acting as a deputy registrar pursuant to a contract with the registrar that is executed after October 14, 1997, the disabled veteran is not required to pay the deputy registrar the lamination fee provided in division (F) of this section.

A disabled veteran whose driver's license, motorized bicycle license, or temporary instruction permit identification card is laminated by the registrar is not required to pay the registrar any lamination fee.

An application made under division (I) of this section shall be accompanied by such documentary evidence of disability as the registrar may require by rule.

(2003 H 54, eff. 4–7–04; 2003 H 87, eff. 6–30–03; 2001 H 94, eff. 9–5–01; 1997 H 144, eff. 10–14–97; 1996 H 353, eff. 9–17–96; 1995 H 107, eff. (See Historical and Statutory Notes); 1993 H 154, eff. 6–30–93; 1991 H 134; 1990 S 131; 1989 H 381; 1988 S 1; 1987 H 171; 1983 H 373; 1979 H 204; 1978 H 215, S 393; 1977 S 100; 1969 H 113; 132 v H 380; 129 v 381; 125 v 1135; 1953 H 1; GC 6296–22)

Historical and Statutory Notes

Ed. Note: 1995 H 107 Effective Date—The Secretary of State assigned a general effective date of 6–30–95 for 1995 H 107. Pursuant to O Const Art II § 1c and 1d, and RC 1.471, sections of 1995 H 107 that are, or depend for their implementation upon, current expense appropriations are effective 3–31–95; sections of 1995 H 107 that are not, and do not depend for their implementation upon, current expense appropriations are effective 6–30–95. See *Baldwin's Ohio Legislative Service*, 1995, page 3/L–98 for 1995 H 107, § 16.

4507.231 Voluntary contributions to second chance trust fund

In addition to the fees collected under section 4507.23 of the Revised Code, the registrar or deputy registrar of motor vehicles shall ask each person applying for or renewing a driver's license, motorcycle operator's endorsement, or duplicate whether the person wishes to make a one-dollar voluntary contribution to the second chance trust fund established under section 2108.15 of the Revised Code. The registrar or deputy registrar shall also make available to the person informational material provided by the department of health on the importance of organ, tissue, and eye donation.

All donations collected under this section during each month shall be forwarded by the registrar or deputy registrar not later than the fifth day of the immediately following month to the treasurer of state, who shall deposit them in the second chance trust fund.

(1996 S 300, eff. 7–1–97)

4507.232 Student driver sticker or banner

When the registrar of motor vehicles or a deputy registrar issues a temporary instruction permit under this chapter, the registrar or deputy registrar also shall issue to the applicant a sticker or banner that reads "student driver." When the holder of the temporary instruction permit operates a motor vehicle, the sticker or banner may be displayed on the motor vehicle to inform other motor vehicle operators that the motor vehicle is being operated by a holder of a temporary instruction permit, but such display is not required.

The sticker or banner may be displayed on a side window or the rear window of the motor vehicle notwithstanding section 4513.24 and division (F) of section 4513.241 of the Revised Code or any rule adopted thereunder.

The registrar shall determine the size of the sticker or banner, which shall not exceed four inches in height by twelve inches in length, and the material and all other properties of the sticker or banner, but shall select a material so that the sticker or banner can be transferred readily from one motor vehicle to another.

(2003 H 54, eff. 4–7–04)

4507.24 Fees for deputy registrars; exemptions for disabled veterans

(A) Except as provided in division (B) of this section, each deputy registrar may collect a fee not to exceed the following:

(1) Three dollars and seventy-five cents commencing on July 1, 2001, four dollars and twenty-five cents commencing on January 1, 2003, and four dollars and fifty cents commencing on January 1, 2004, for each application for renewal of a driver's license received by the deputy registrar, when the applicant is required to submit to a screening of the applicant's vision under section 4507.12 of the Revised Code;

(2) Two dollars and seventy-five cents commencing on July 1, 2001, three dollars and twenty-five cents commencing on January 1, 2003, and three dollars and fifty cents commencing on January 1, 2004, for each application for a driver's license, or motorized bicycle license, or for renewal of such a license, received by the deputy registrar, when the applicant is not required to submit to a screening of the applicant's vision under section 4507.12 of the Revised Code.

(B) The fees prescribed by division (A) of this section shall be in addition to the fee for a temporary instruction permit and examination, a driver's license, a motorized bicycle license, or duplicates thereof, and shall compensate the deputy registrar for the deputy registrar's services, for office and rental expense, and for costs as provided in division (C) of this section, as are necessary for the proper discharge of the deputy registrar's duties under sections 4507.01 to 4507.39 of the Revised Code.

A disabled veteran who has a service-connected disability rated at one hundred per cent by the veterans' administration is required to pay the applicable fee prescribed in division (A) of this section if the disabled veteran submits an application for a driver's license or motorized bicycle license or a renewal of either of these licenses to a deputy registrar who is acting as a deputy registrar pursuant to a contract with the registrar that is in effect on the effective date of this amendment. The disabled veteran also is required to submit with the disabled veteran's application such documentary evidence of disability as the registrar may require by rule.

A disabled veteran who submits an application described in this division is not required to pay either of the fees prescribed in division (A) of this section if the disabled veteran submits the application to a deputy registrar who is acting as a deputy registrar pursuant to a contract with the registrar that is executed after the effective date of this amendment. The disabled veteran still is required to submit with the disabled veteran's application such documentary evidence of disability as the registrar may require by rule.

A disabled veteran who submits an application described in this division directly to the registrar is not required to pay either of the fees prescribed in division (A) of this section if the disabled veteran submits with the disabled veteran's application such documentary evidence of disability as the registrar may require by rule.

(C) Each deputy registrar shall transmit to the registrar of motor vehicles, at such time and in such manner as the registrar shall require by rule, an amount of each fee collected under division (A)(1) of this section as shall be determined by the registrar. The registrar shall pay all such moneys so received into the state bureau of motor vehicles fund created in section 4501.25 of the Revised Code.

(2001 H 94, eff. 6–6–01; 1997 H 144, eff. 10–14–97; 1995 H 107, eff. (See Historical and Statutory Notes); 1993 H 154, eff. 6–30–93; 1989 H 381; 1988 S 1; 1987 H 419; 1985 S 269, H 201; 1984 H 58; 1981 H 457; 1979 H 656; 1978 H 998, § 1, S 393; 1977 H 3; 132 v S 484; 1953 H 1; GC 6296–23)

Historical and Statutory Notes

Ed. Note: 1995 H 107 Effective Date—The Secretary of State assigned a general effective date of 6–30–95 for 1995 H 107. Pursuant to O Const Art II § 1c and 1d, and RC 1.471, sections of 1995 H 107 that are, or depend for their implementation upon, current expense appropriations are effective 3–31–95; sections of 1995 H 107 that are not, and do not depend for their implementation upon, current expense appropriations are effective 6–30–95. See *Baldwin's Ohio Legislative Service*, 1995, page 3/L–98 for 1995 H 107, § 16.

PROHIBITIONS AND RESTRICTIONS

4507.30 Certain acts prohibited

No person shall do any of the following:

(A) Display, or cause or permit to be displayed, or possess any identification card, driver's or commercial driver's license, temporary instruction permit, or commercial driver's license temporary instruction permit knowing the same to be fictitious, or to have been canceled, suspended, or altered;

(B) Lend to a person not entitled thereto, or knowingly permit a person not entitled thereto to use any identification card, driver's or commercial driver's license, temporary instruction permit, or commercial driver's license temporary instruction permit issued to the person so lending or permitting the use thereof;

(C) Display, or represent as one's own, any identification card, driver's or commercial driver's license, temporary instruction permit, or commercial driver's license temporary instruction permit not issued to the person so displaying the same;

(D) Fail to surrender to the registrar of motor vehicles, upon the registrar's demand, any identification card, driver's or commercial driver's license, temporary instruction permit, or commercial driver's license temporary instruction permit that has been suspended or canceled;

(E) In any application for an identification card, driver's or commercial driver's license, temporary instruction permit, or commercial driver's license temporary instruction permit, or any renewal or duplicate thereof, knowingly conceal a material fact, or present any physician's statement required under section 4507.08 or 4507.081 of the Revised Code when knowing the same to be false or fictitious.

(F) Whoever violates any division of this section is guilty of a misdemeanor of the first degree.

(2002 S 123, eff. 1–1–04; 1989 H 381, eff. 7–1–89; 1977 H 71; 1976 S 435; 129 v 1491; 1953 H 1; GC 6296–24)

4507.31 Prohibition against permitting minor to operate vehicle

(A) No person shall cause or knowingly permit any minor to drive a motor vehicle upon a highway as an operator, unless the minor has first obtained a license or permit to drive a motor vehicle under this chapter.

(B) Whoever violates this section is guilty of a misdemeanor of the first degree.

(2002 S 123, eff. 1–1–04; 1953 H 1, eff. 10–1–53; GC 6296–26)

4507.321 Employment of a minor to operate a taxicab prohibited

(A) Notwithstanding the definition of "chauffeur" in section 4501.01 of the Revised Code, no person shall employ any minor for the purpose of operating a taxicab.

(B) Whoever violates this section is guilty of a misdemeanor of the first degree.

(2002 S 123, eff. 1–1–04; 1984 H 37, eff. 6–22–84; 1969 S 410)

4507.35 Display of license

(A) The operator of a motor vehicle shall display the operator's driver's license, or furnish satisfactory proof that the operator has a driver's license, upon demand of any peace officer or of any person damaged or injured in any collision in which the licensee may be involved. When a demand is properly made and the operator has the operator's driver's license on or about the operator's person, the operator shall not refuse to display the license. A person's failure to furnish satisfactory evidence that the person is licensed under this chapter when the person does not have the person's license on or about the person's person shall be prima-facie evidence of the person's not having obtained a driver's license.

(B) Whoever violates this section is guilty of a misdemeanor of the first degree.

(2002 S 123, eff. 1–1–04; 1989 H 381, eff. 7–1–89; 1953 H 1; Source—GC 6296–14)

4507.36 Prohibition against false statements

(A) No person shall knowingly make a false statement to any matter or thing required by this chapter.

(B) Whoever violates this section is guilty of a misdemeanor of the first degree.

(2002 S 123, eff. 1–1–04; 126 v 253, eff. 9–13–55; 1953 H 1; GC 6296–25)

IDENTIFICATION CARDS FOR HANDICAPPED AND OLDER PERSONS

4507.50 Identification cards to be issued to persons not licensed to operate motor vehicle; fees; disabled veterans

(A) The registrar of motor vehicles or a deputy registrar, upon receipt of an application filed in compliance with section 4507.51 of the Revised Code by any person who is a resident or a temporary resident of this state and, except as otherwise provided in this section, is not licensed as an operator of a motor vehicle in this state or another licensing jurisdiction, and, except as provided in division (B) of this section, upon receipt of a fee of three dollars and fifty cents, shall issue an identification card to that person.

Any person who is a resident or temporary resident of this state whose Ohio driver's or commercial driver's license has been suspended or canceled, upon application in compliance with section 4507.51 of the Revised Code and, except as provided in division (B) of this section, payment of a fee of three dollars and fifty cents, may be issued a temporary identification card. The temporary identification card shall be identical to an identification card, except that it shall be printed on its face with a statement that the card is valid during the effective dates of the suspension or cancellation of the cardholder's license, or until the birthday of the cardholder in the fourth year after the date on which it is issued, whichever is shorter. The cardholder shall surrender the identification card to the registrar or any deputy registrar before the cardholder's driver's or commercial driver's license is restored or reissued.

Except as provided in division (B) of this section, the deputy registrar shall be allowed a fee of two dollars and seventy-five cents commencing on July 1, 2001, three dollars and twenty-five cents commencing on January 1, 2003, and three dollars and fifty cents commencing on January 1, 2004, for each identification card issued under this section. The fee allowed to the deputy registrar shall be in addition to the fee for issuing an identification card.

Neither the registrar nor any deputy registrar shall charge a fee in excess of one dollar and fifty cents for laminating an identification card or temporary identification card. A deputy registrar laminating such a card shall retain the entire amount of the fee charged for lamination, less the actual cost to the registrar of the laminating materials used for that lamination, as specified in the contract executed by the bureau for the laminating materials and laminating equipment. The deputy registrar shall forward the amount of the cost of the laminating materials to the registrar for deposit as provided in this section.

The fee collected for issuing an identification card under this section, except the fee allowed to the deputy registrar, shall be paid into the state treasury to the credit of the state bureau of motor vehicles fund created in section 4501.25 of the Revised Code.

(B) A disabled veteran who has a service-connected disability rated at one hundred per cent by the veterans' administration may apply to the registrar or a deputy registrar for the issuance to that veteran of an identification card or a temporary identification card under this section without payment of any fee prescribed in division (A) of this section, including any lamination fee.

An application made under division (B) of this section shall be accompanied by such documentary evidence of disability as the registrar may require by rule.

(2004 H 230, eff. 9–16–04; 2002 S 123, eff. 1–1–04; 2001 H 94, eff. 6–6–01; 1998 S 213, eff. 7–29–98; 1997 S 60, eff. 10–21–97; 1995 H 107, eff. (See Historical and Statutory Notes); 1993 H 154, eff. 6–30–93; 1990 S 131; 1989 H 381; 1988 S 1, H 165; 1987 H 419; 1986 H 165; 1985 S 269, H 201; 1981 H 457; 1979 H 656; 1978 H 998, § 1; 1977 H 90, S 221, H 3; 1976 S 435)

Historical and Statutory Notes

Ed. Note: 1995 H 107 Effective Date—The Secretary of State assigned a general effective date of 6–30–95 for 1995 H 107. Pursuant to O Const Art II § 1c and 1d, and RC 1.471, sections of 1995 H 107 that are, or depend for their implementation upon, current expense appropriations are effective 3–31–95; sections of 1995 H 107 that are not, and do not depend for their implementation upon, current expense appropriations are effective 6–30–95. See *Baldwin's Ohio Legislative Service*, 1995, page 3/L–98 for 1995 H 107, § 16.

4507.501 Voluntary contributions to second chance trust fund

In addition to the fees collected under section 4507.50 of the Revised Code, the registrar or deputy registrar of motor vehicles shall ask each applicant for an identification card or duplicate under section 4507.51 of the Revised Code whether the person wishes to make a one-dollar voluntary contribution to the second chance trust fund established under section 2108.15 of the Revised Code. The registrar or deputy registrar shall also make available to the person informational material provided by the department of health on the importance of organ, tissue, and eye donation.

All donations collected under this section during each month shall be forwarded by the registrar or deputy registrar not later than the fifth day of the immediately following month to the treasurer of state, who shall deposit them in the second chance trust fund.

(1996 S 300, eff. 7–1–97)

4507.51 Application; registration of voters; social security numbers

(A)(1) Every application for an identification card or duplicate shall be made on a form furnished by the registrar of motor vehicles, shall be signed by the applicant, and by the applicant's parent or guardian if the applicant is under eighteen years of age, and shall contain the following information pertaining to the applicant: name, date of birth, sex, general description including the applicant's height, weight, hair color, and eye color, address, and social security number. The application also shall state whether an applicant wishes to certify willingness to make an anatomical gift under section 2108.04 of the Revised Code and shall include information about the requirements of that section that apply to persons who are less than eighteen years of age. The statement regarding willingness to make such a donation shall be given no consideration in the decision of whether to issue an identification card. Each applicant shall be photographed in color at the time of making application.

(2) The application also shall state whether the applicant has executed a valid durable power of attorney for health care pursuant to sections 1337.11 to 1337.17 of the Revised Code or has executed a declaration governing the use or continuation, or the withholding or withdrawal, of life-sustaining treatment pursuant to sections 2133.01 to 2133.15 of the Revised Code and, if the applicant has executed either type of instrument, whether the applicant wishes the identification card issued to indicate that the applicant has executed the instrument.

(3) The registrar or deputy registrar, in accordance with section 3503.11 of the Revised Code, shall register as an elector any person who applies for an identification card or duplicate if the applicant is eligible and wishes to be registered as an elector. The decision of an applicant whether to register as an elector shall be given no consideration in the decision of whether to issue the applicant an identification card or duplicate.

(B) The application for an identification card or duplicate shall be filed in the office of the registrar or deputy registrar. Each applicant shall present documentary evidence as required by the registrar of the applicant's age and identity, and the applicant shall swear that all information given is true.

All applications for an identification card or duplicate shall be filed in duplicate, and if submitted to a deputy registrar, a copy shall be forwarded to the registrar. The registrar shall prescribe rules for the manner in which a deputy registrar is to file and maintain applications and other records. The registrar shall maintain a suitable, indexed record of all applications denied and cards issued or canceled.

(2004 H 230, eff. 9–16–04; 1998 S 213, eff. 7–29–98; 1998 H 354, eff. 7–9–98; 1994 S 300, eff. 1–1–95; 1992 H 427, eff. 10–8–92; 1990 H 21; 1989 H 529, H 381; 1988 H 165; 1984 S 302; 1977 H 90; 1976 S 435)

4507.52 Specifications; replacement; cancellation; uses; photographs

(A) Each identification card issued by the registrar of motor vehicles or a deputy registrar shall display a distinguishing number assigned to the cardholder, and shall display the following inscription:

"STATE OF OHIO IDENTIFICATION CARD

This card is not valid for the purpose of operating a motor vehicle. It is provided solely for the purpose of establishing the identity of the bearer described on the card, who currently is not licensed to operate a motor vehicle in the state of Ohio."

The identification card shall display substantially the same information as contained in the application and as described in division (A)(1) of section 4507.51 of the Revised Code, but shall not display the cardholder's social security number unless the cardholder specifically requests that the cardholder's social security number be displayed on the card. If federal law requires the cardholder's social security number to be displayed on the identification card, the social security number shall be displayed on the card notwithstanding this section. The identification card also shall display the color photograph of the cardholder. If the cardholder has executed a durable power of attorney for health care or a declaration governing the use or continuation, or the withholding or withdrawal, of life-sustaining treatment and has specified that the cardholder wishes the identification card to indicate that the cardholder has executed either type of instrument, the card also shall display any symbol chosen by the registrar to indicate that the cardholder has executed either type of instrument. The card shall be sealed in transparent plastic or similar material and shall be so designed as to prevent its reproduction or alteration without ready detection.

The identification card for persons under twenty-one years of age shall have characteristics prescribed by the registrar distinguishing it from that issued to a person who is twenty-one years of age or older, except that an identification card issued to a person who applies no more than thirty days before the applicant's twenty-first birthday shall have the characteristics of an identification card issued to a person who is twenty-one years of age or older.

Every identification card issued to a resident of this state shall expire, unless canceled or surrendered earlier, on the birthday of the cardholder in the fourth year after the date on which it is issued. Every identification card issued to a temporary resident shall expire in accordance with rules adopted by the registrar and is nonrenewable, but may be replaced with a new identification card upon the applicant's compliance with all applicable requirements. A cardholder may renew the cardholder's identification card within ninety days prior to the day on which it expires by filing an application and paying the prescribed fee in accordance with section 4507.50 of the Revised Code.

If a cardholder applies for a driver's or commercial driver's license in this state or another licensing jurisdiction, the cardholder shall surrender the cardholder's identification card to the registrar or any deputy registrar before the license is issued.

(B) If a card is lost, destroyed, or mutilated, the person to whom the card was issued may obtain a duplicate by doing both of the following:

(1) Furnishing suitable proof of the loss, destruction, or mutilation to the registrar or a deputy registrar;

(2) Filing an application and presenting documentary evidence under section 4507.51 of the Revised Code.

Any person who loses a card and, after obtaining a duplicate, finds the original, immediately shall surrender the original to the registrar or a deputy registrar.

A cardholder may obtain a replacement identification card that reflects any change of the cardholder's name by furnishing suitable proof of the change to the registrar or a deputy registrar and surrendering the cardholder's existing card.

When a cardholder applies for a duplicate or obtains a replacement identification card, the cardholder shall pay a fee of two dollars and fifty cents. A deputy registrar shall be allowed an additional fee of two dollars and seventy-five cents commencing on July 1, 2001, three dollars and twenty-five cents commencing on January 1, 2003, and three dollars and fifty cents commencing on January 1, 2004, for issuing a duplicate or replacement identification card. A disabled veteran who is a cardholder and has a service-connected disability rated at one hundred per cent by the veterans' administration may apply to the registrar or a deputy registrar for the issuance of a duplicate or replacement identification card without payment of any fee prescribed in this section, and without payment of any lamination fee if the disabled veteran would not be required to pay a lamination fee in connection with the issuance of an identification card or temporary identification card as provided in division (B) of section 4507.50 of the Revised Code.

A duplicate or replacement identification card shall expire on the same date as the card it replaces.

(C) The registrar shall cancel any card upon determining that the card was obtained unlawfully, issued in error, or was altered. The registrar also shall cancel any card that is surrendered to the registrar or to a deputy registrar after the holder has obtained a duplicate, replacement, or driver's or commercial driver's license.

(D)(1) No agent of the state or its political subdivisions shall condition the granting of any benefit, service, right, or privilege upon the possession by any person of an identification card. Nothing in this section shall preclude any publicly operated or franchised transit system from using an identification card for the purpose of granting benefits or services of the system.

(2) No person shall be required to apply for, carry, or possess an identification card.

(E) Except in regard to an identification card issued to a person who applies no more than thirty days before the applicant's twenty-first birthday, neither the registrar nor any deputy registrar shall issue an identification card to a person under twenty-one years of age that does not have the characteristics prescribed by the registrar distinguishing it from the identification card issued to persons who are twenty-one years of age or older.

(F) Whoever violates division (E) of this section is guilty of a minor misdemeanor.

(2002 S 123, eff. 1–1–04; 2001 H 46, eff. 2–1–02; 2001 H 299, eff. 6–29–01; 2001 H 94, eff. 6–6–01; 1998 S 213, eff. 7–29–98; 1997 S 60, eff. 10–21–97; 1996 H 353, eff. 9–17–96; 1994 H 580, eff. 12–9–94; 1992 H 427, eff. 10–8–92; 1991 H 134; 1990 S 131; 1989 H 381; 1988 H 165; 1977 H 90; 1976 S 435)

4507.53 Release of digitalized photographic records

Digitalized photographic records of the department of public safety may be released only to state, local, or federal governmental agencies for criminal justice purposes and to any court.

(2004 H 230, eff. 9–16–04; 1993 H 154, eff. 6–30–93)

PENALTIES

4507.99 Penalties

Unless another penalty is provided by the section that contains the provision violated or otherwise is provided by the laws of this state, whoever violates any provision of sections 4507.01 to 4507.081 or 4507.10 to 4507.37 of the Revised Code is guilty of a misdemeanor of the first degree.

(2004 H 230, eff. 9–16–04; 2002 S 123, eff. 1–1–04; 2000 S 180, eff. 3–22–01; 1997 S 35, eff. 7–1–98; 1996 H 438, eff. 7–1–97; 1996 H 676, § 6, eff. 5–15–97; 1996 H 676, § 1, eff. 10–4–96; 1995 H 167, eff. 5–15–97; 1995 S 2, eff. 7–1–96; 1994 S 20, eff. 10–20–94; 1994 S 82, eff. 5–4–94; 1993 S 62, § 1, eff. 9–1–93; 1993 S 62, § 4; 1992 S 275, H 725; 1991 H 134; 1990 H 837, S 131, H 88; 1989 H 381, S 102, H 329; 1988 H 643; 1986 S 356; 1984 H 252, H 767; 1982 S 432; 131 v H 435; 125 v 903; 1953 H 1)

CHAPTER 4509

FINANCIAL RESPONSIBILITY

ACCIDENT REPORTS

ACCIDENT REPORTS

4509.06 Reports relating to motor vehicle accidents regarding proof of financial responsibility

(A) The driver of any motor vehicle which is in any manner involved in a motor vehicle accident within six months of the accident may forward a written report of the accident to the registrar of motor vehicles on a form prescribed by the registrar alleging that a driver or owner of any other vehicle involved in the accident was uninsured at the time of the accident.

(B) Upon receipt of the accident report, the registrar shall send a notice by regular mail to the driver and owner alleged to be uninsured requiring the person to give evidence that the person had proof of financial responsibility in effect at the time of the accident.

(C) Within thirty days after the mailing of the notice by the registrar, the driver of the vehicle alleged to be uninsured shall forward a report together with acceptable proof of financial responsibility to the registrar in a form prescribed by the registrar. The forwarding of the report by the owner of the motor vehicle involved in the accident is deemed compliance with this section by the driver. This section does not change or modify the duties of the driver or operator of a motor vehicle as set forth in section 4549.02 of the Revised Code.

(D) In accordance with sections 4509.01 to 4509.78 of the Revised Code, the registrar shall suspend the license of any person who fails to give acceptable proof of financial responsibility as required in this section.

(1997 H 210, eff. 3–31–97; 1969 H 131, eff. 7–25–69; 1953 H 1; GC 6298–17)

4509.07 Contents of accident report

The report prescribed by the registrar of motor vehicles shall request only information sufficient to enable the registrar to administer and enforce the provisions of sections 4509.01 to 4509.78, inclusive, of the Revised Code.

The driver or owner of a motor vehicle involved in an accident shall furnish such additional relevant information as the registrar requires.

(125 v 383, eff. 10–15–53; 1953 H 1; GC 6298–18, 6298–19)

4509.08 Exception to report requirement

A driver involved in a motor vehicle accident is not subject to section 4509.06 of the Revised Code if, during the time provided in such section, the driver is physically incapable of making a report, but in such event, the owner, if he were not the driver of the motor vehicle involved in the accident, shall within thirty days after learning of the accident make the report.

(1969 H 131, eff. 7–25–69; 1953 H 1; GC 6298–20)

4509.10 Use of report

The accident reports submitted pursuant to sections 4509.01 to 4509.78 of the Revised Code, shall be without prejudice to the person reporting and shall be for the confidential use of the registrar of motor vehicles, except that the registrar shall furnish a copy of such report to any person claiming to have been injured or damaged in a motor vehicle accident, or to his attorney, upon the receipt of a fee of one dollar and fifty cents for each search or report.

Motor vehicle accident reports shall not be subject to subpoena or be used as evidence in any trial, civil or criminal, arising out of the accident, except that in order to prove compliance or failure to comply with the accident reporting requirement the registrar shall furnish, upon demand of a court or any person who claims to have made an accident report, a certificate stating that a specified accident report has or has not been made to the registrar.

(1981 H 102, eff. 7–1–81; 125 v 383; 1953 H 1; GC 6298–22)

OPERATION OF MOTOR VEHICLES

4509.101 Operation without proof of financial responsibility prohibited; civil penalties; procedures of courts and registrar; proof with accident reports; financial responsibility compliance fund; findings not binding on insurer; relief granted for certain reasons

(A)(1) No person shall operate, or permit the operation of, a motor vehicle in this state, unless proof of financial responsibility is maintained continuously throughout the registration period with respect to that vehicle, or, in the case of a driver who is not the owner, with respect to that driver's operation of that vehicle.

(2) Whoever violates division (A)(1) of this section shall be subject to the following civil penalties:

(a) Subject to divisions (A)(2)(b) and (c) of this section, a class E suspension of the person's driver's license, commercial driver's license, temporary instruction permit, probationary license, or nonresident operating privilege for the period of time specified in division (B)(5) of section 4510.02 of the Revised Code and impoundment of the person's license. The court may grant limited driving privileges to the person only if the person presents proof of financial responsibility and has complied with division (A)(5) of this section.

(b) If, within five years of the violation, the person's operating privileges are again suspended and the person's license again is impounded for a violation of division (A)(1) of this section, a class C suspension of the person's driver's license, commercial driver's license, temporary instruction permit, probationary license, or nonresident operating privilege for the period of time specified in division (B)(3) of section 4510.02 of the Revised Code. The court may grant limited driving privileges to the person only if the person presents proof of financial responsibility and has complied with division (A)(5) of this section, and no court may grant limited driving privileges for the first fifteen days of the suspension.

(c) If, within five years of the violation, the person's operating privileges are suspended and the person's license is impounded two or more times for a violation of division (A)(1) of this section, a class B suspension of the person's driver's license, commercial driver's license, temporary instruction permit, probationary license, or nonresident operating privilege for the period of time specified in division (B)(2) of section 4510.02 of the Revised Code. No court may grant limited driving privileges during the suspension.

(d) In addition to the suspension of an owner's license under division (A)(2)(a), (b), or (c) of this section, the suspension of the rights of the owner to register the motor vehicle and the impoundment of the owner's certificate of registration and license plates until the owner complies with division (A)(5) of this section.

(3) A person to whom this state has issued a certificate of registration for a motor vehicle or a license to operate a motor vehicle or who is determined to have operated any motor vehicle or permitted the operation in this state of a motor vehicle owned by the person shall be required to verify the existence of proof of financial responsibility covering the operation of the motor vehicle or the person's operation of the motor vehicle under any of the following circumstances:

(a) The person or a motor vehicle owned by the person is involved in a traffic accident that requires the filing of an accident report under section 4509.06 of the Revised Code.

(b) The person receives a traffic ticket indicating that proof of the maintenance of financial responsibility was not produced upon the request of a peace officer or state highway patrol trooper made in accordance with division (D)(2) of this section.

(c) Whenever, in accordance with rules adopted by the registrar, the person is randomly selected by the registrar and requested to provide such verification.

(4) An order of the registrar that suspends and impounds a license or registration, or both, shall state the date on or before which the person is required to surrender the person's license or certificate of registration and license plates. The person is deemed to have surrendered the license or certificate of registration and license plates, in compliance with the order, if the person does either of the following:

(a) On or before the date specified in the order, personally delivers the license or certificate of registration and license plates, or causes the delivery of the items, to the registrar;

(b) Mails the license or certificate of registration and license plates to the registrar in an envelope or container bearing a postmark showing a date no later than the date specified in the order.

(5) Except as provided in division (A)(6) or (L) of this section, the registrar shall not restore any operating privileges or registration rights suspended under this section, return any license, certificate of registration, or license plates impounded under this section, or reissue license plates under section 4503.232 of the Revised Code, if the registrar destroyed the impounded license plates under that section, or reissue a license under section 4510.52 of the Revised Code, if the registrar destroyed the suspended license under that section, unless the rights are not subject to suspension or revocation under any other law and unless the person, in addition to complying with all other conditions required by law for reinstatement of the operating privileges or registration rights, complies with all of the following:

(a) Pays a financial responsibility reinstatement fee of seventy-five dollars for the first violation of division (A)(1) of this section, two hundred fifty dollars for a second violation of that division, and five hundred dollars for a third or subsequent violation of that division;

(b) If the person has not voluntarily surrendered the license, certificate, or license plates in compliance with the order, pays a financial responsibility nonvoluntary compliance fee in an amount, not to exceed fifty dollars, determined by the registrar;

(c) Files and continuously maintains proof of financial responsibility under sections 4509.44 to 4509.65 of the Revised Code.

(6) If the registrar issues an order under division (A)(2) of this section resulting from the failure of a person to respond to a financial responsibility random verification request under division (A)(3)(c) of this section and the person successfully maintains an affirmative defense to a violation of section 4510.16 of the Revised Code or is determined by the registrar or a deputy registrar to have been in compliance with division (A)(1) of this section at the time of the initial financial responsibility random verification request, the registrar shall do both of the following:

(a) Terminate the order of suspension or impoundment;

(b) Restore the operating privileges and registration rights of the person without payment of the fees established in divisions (A)(5)(a) and (b) of this section and without a requirement to file proof of financial responsibility.

(B)(1) Every party required to file an accident report under section 4509. 06 of the Revised Code also shall include with the report a document described in division (G)(1) of this section.

If the registrar determines, within forty-five days after the report is filed, that an operator or owner has violated division (A)(1) of this section, the registrar shall do all of the following:

(a) Order the impoundment, with respect to the motor vehicle involved, required under division (A)(2)(d) of this section, of the certificate of registration and license plates of any owner who has violated division (A)(1) of this section;

(b) Order the suspension required under division (A)(2)(a), (b), or (c) of this section of the license of any operator or owner who has violated division (A)(1) of this section;

(c) Record the name and address of the person whose certificate of registration and license plates have been impounded or are under an order of impoundment, or whose license has been suspended or is under an order of suspension; the serial number of the person's license; the serial numbers of the person's certificate of registration and license plates; and the person's social security account number, if assigned, or, where the motor vehicle is used for hire or principally in connection with any established business, the person's federal taxpayer identification number. The information shall be recorded in such a manner that it becomes a part of the person's permanent record, and assists the registrar in monitoring compliance with the orders of suspension or impoundment.

(d) Send written notification to every person to whom the order pertains, at the person's last known address as shown on the records of the bureau. The person, within ten days after the date of the mailing of the notification, shall surrender to the registrar, in a manner set forth in division (A)(4) of this section, any certificate of registration and registration plates under an order of impoundment, or any license under an order of suspension.

(2) The registrar shall issue any order under division (B)(1) of this section without a hearing. Any person adversely affected by the order, within ten days after the issuance of the order, may request an administrative hearing before the registrar, who shall provide the person with an opportunity for a hearing in accordance with this paragraph. A request for a hearing does not operate as a suspension of the order. The scope of the hearing shall be limited to whether the person in fact demonstrated to the

registrar proof of financial responsibility in accordance with this section. The registrar shall determine the date, time, and place of any hearing, provided that the hearing shall be held, and an order issued or findings made, within thirty days after the registrar receives a request for a hearing. If requested by the person in writing, the registrar may designate as the place of hearing the county seat of the county in which the person resides or a place within fifty miles of the person's residence. The person shall pay the cost of the hearing before the registrar, if the registrar's order of suspension or impoundment is upheld.

(C) Any order of suspension or impoundment issued under this section or division (B) of section 4509.37 of the Revised Code may be terminated at any time if the registrar determines upon a showing of proof of financial responsibility that the operator or owner of the motor vehicle was in compliance with division (A)(1) of this section at the time of the traffic offense, motor vehicle inspection, or accident that resulted in the order against the person. A determination may be made without a hearing. This division does not apply unless the person shows good cause for the person's failure to present satisfactory proof of financial responsibility to the registrar prior to the issuance of the order.

(D)(1) For the purpose of enforcing this section, every peace officer is deemed an agent of the registrar.

(a) Except as provided in division (D)(1)(b) of this section, any peace officer who, in the performance of the peace officer's duties as authorized by law, becomes aware of a person whose license is under an order of suspension, or whose certificate of registration and license plates are under an order of impoundment, pursuant to this section, may confiscate the license, certificate of registration, and license plates, and return them to the registrar.

(b) Any peace officer who, in the performance of the peace officer's duties as authorized by law, becomes aware of a person whose license is under an order of suspension, or whose certificate of registration and license plates are under an order of impoundment resulting from failure to respond to a financial responsibility random verification, shall not, for that reason, arrest the owner or operator or seize the vehicle or license plates. Instead, the peace officer shall issue a citation for a violation of section 4510.16 of the Revised Code specifying the circumstances as failure to respond to a financial responsibility random verification.

(2) A peace officer shall request the owner or operator of a motor vehicle to produce proof of financial responsibility in a manner described in division (G) of this section at the time the peace officer acts to enforce the traffic laws of this state and during motor vehicle inspections conducted pursuant to section 4513.02 of the Revised Code.

(3) A peace officer shall indicate on every traffic ticket whether the person receiving the traffic ticket produced proof of the maintenance of financial responsibility in response to the officer's request under division (D)(2) of this section. The peace officer shall inform every person who receives a traffic ticket and who has failed to produce proof of the maintenance of financial responsibility that the person must submit proof to the traffic violations bureau with any payment of a fine and costs for the ticketed violation or, if the person is to appear in court for the violation, the person must submit proof to the court.

(4)(a) If a person who has failed to produce proof of the maintenance of financial responsibility appears in court for a ticketed violation, the court may permit the defendant to present evidence of proof of financial responsibility to the court at such time and in such manner as the court determines to be necessary or appropriate. In a manner prescribed by the registrar, the clerk of courts shall provide the registrar with the identity of any person who fails to submit proof of the maintenance of financial responsibility pursuant to division (D)(3) of this section.

(b) If a person who has failed to produce proof of the maintenance of financial responsibility also fails to submit that proof to the traffic violations bureau with payment of a fine and costs for the ticketed violation, the traffic violations bureau, in a manner prescribed by the registrar, shall notify the registrar of the identity of that person.

(5)(a) Upon receiving notice from a clerk of courts or traffic violations bureau pursuant to division (D)(4) of this section, the registrar shall order the suspension of the license of the person required under division (A)(2)(a), (b), or (c) of this section and the impoundment of the person's certificate of registration and license plates required under division (A)(2)(d) of this section, effective thirty days after the date of the mailing of notification. The registrar also shall notify the person that the person must present the registrar with proof of financial responsibility in accordance with this section, surrender to the registrar the person's certificate of registration, license plates, and license, or submit a statement subject to section 2921.13 of the Revised Code that the person did not operate or permit the operation of the motor vehicle at the time of the offense. Notification shall be in writing and shall be sent to the person at the person's last known address as shown on the records of the bureau of motor vehicles. The person, within fifteen days after the date of the mailing of notification, shall present proof of financial responsibility, surrender the certificate of registration, license plates, and license to the registrar in a manner set forth in division (A)(4) of this section, or submit the statement required under this section together with other information the person considers appropriate.

If the registrar does not receive proof or the person does not surrender the certificate of registration, license plates, and license, in accordance with this division, the registrar shall permit the order for the suspension of the license of the person and the impoundment of the person's certificate of registration and license plates to take effect.

(b) In the case of a person who presents, within the fifteen-day period, documents to show proof of financial responsibility, the registrar shall terminate the order of suspension and the impoundment of the registration and license plates required under division (A)(2)(d) of this section and shall send written notification to the person, at the person's last known address as shown on the records of the bureau.

(c) Any person adversely affected by the order of the registrar under division (D)(5)(a) or (b) of this section, within ten days after the issuance of the order, may request an administrative hearing before the registrar, who shall provide the person with an opportunity for a hearing in accordance with this paragraph. A request for a hearing does not operate as a suspension of the order. The scope of the hearing shall be limited to whether, at the time of the hearing, the person presents proof of financial responsibility covering the vehicle and whether the person is eligible for an exemption in accordance with this section or any rule adopted under it. The registrar shall determine the date, time, and place of any hearing; provided, that the hearing shall be held, and an order issued or findings made, within thirty days after the registrar receives a request for a hearing. If requested by the person in writing, the registrar may designate as the place of hearing the county seat of the county in which the person resides or a place within fifty miles of the person's residence. Such person shall pay the cost of the hearing before the registrar, if the registrar's order of suspension or impoundment under division (D)(5)(a) or (b) of this section is upheld.

(6) A peace officer may charge an owner or operator of a motor vehicle with a violation of section 4510.16 of the Revised Code when the owner or operator fails to show proof of the maintenance of financial responsibility pursuant to a peace officer's request under division (D)(2) of this section, if a check of the owner or operator's driving record indicates that the owner or operator, at the time of the operation of the motor vehicle, is required to file and maintain proof of financial responsibility

under section 4509.45 of the Revised Code for a previous violation of this chapter.

(7) Any forms used by law enforcement agencies in administering this section shall be prescribed, supplied, and paid for by the registrar.

(8) No peace officer, law enforcement agency employing a peace officer, or political subdivision or governmental agency that employs a peace officer shall be liable in a civil action for damages or loss to persons arising out of the performance of any duty required or authorized by this section.

(9) As used in this division and divisions (E) and (G) of this section, "peace officer" has the meaning set forth in section 2935.01 of the Revised Code.

(E) All fees, except court costs, collected under this section shall be paid into the state treasury to the credit of the financial responsibility compliance fund. The financial responsibility compliance fund shall be used exclusively to cover costs incurred by the bureau in the administration of this section and sections 4503.20, 4507.212, and 4509.81 of the Revised Code, and by any law enforcement agency employing any peace officer who returns any license, certificate of registration, and license plates to the registrar pursuant to division (C) of this section, except that the director of budget and management may transfer excess money from the financial responsibility compliance fund to the state bureau of motor vehicles fund if the registrar determines that the amount of money in the financial responsibility compliance fund exceeds the amount required to cover such costs incurred by the bureau or a law enforcement agency and requests the director to make the transfer.

All investment earnings of the financial responsibility compliance fund shall be credited to the fund.

(F) Chapter 119. of the Revised Code applies to this section only to the extent that any provision in that chapter is not clearly inconsistent with this section.

(G)(1) The registrar, court, traffic violations bureau, or peace officer may require proof of financial responsibility to be demonstrated by use of a standard form prescribed by the registrar. If the use of a standard form is not required, a person may demonstrate proof of financial responsibility under this section by presenting to the traffic violations bureau, court, registrar, or peace officer any of the following documents or a copy of the documents:

(a) A financial responsibility identification card as provided in section 4509.103 of the Revised Code;

(b) A certificate of proof of financial responsibility on a form provided and approved by the registrar for the filing of an accident report required to be filed under section 4509.06 of the Revised Code;

(c) A policy of liability insurance, a declaration page of a policy of liability insurance, or liability bond, if the policy or bond complies with section 4509.20 or sections 4509.49 to 4509.61 of the Revised Code;

(d) A bond or certification of the issuance of a bond as provided in section 4509.59 of the Revised Code;

(e) A certificate of deposit of money or securities as provided in section 4509.62 of the Revised Code;

(f) A certificate of self-insurance as provided in section 4509.72 of the Revised Code.

(2) If a person fails to demonstrate proof of financial responsibility in a manner described in division (G)(1) of this section, the person may demonstrate proof of financial responsibility under this section by any other method that the court or the bureau, by reason of circumstances in a particular case, may consider appropriate.

(3) A motor carrier certificated by the interstate commerce commission or by the public utilities commission may demonstrate proof of financial responsibility by providing a statement designating the motor carrier's operating authority and averring that the insurance coverage required by the certificating authority is in full force and effect.

(4)(a) A finding by the registrar or court that a person is covered by proof of financial responsibility in the form of an insurance policy or surety bond is not binding upon the named insurer or surety or any of its officers, employees, agents, or representatives and has no legal effect except for the purpose of administering this section.

(b) The preparation and delivery of a financial responsibility identification card or any other document authorized to be used as proof of financial responsibility under this division does not do any of the following:

(i) Create any liability or estoppel against an insurer or surety, or any of its officers, employees, agents, or representatives;

(ii) Constitute an admission of the existence of, or of any liability or coverage under, any policy or bond;

(iii) Waive any defenses or counterclaims available to an insurer, surety, agent, employee, or representative in an action commenced by an insured or third-party claimant upon a cause of action alleged to have arisen under an insurance policy or surety bond or by reason of the preparation and delivery of a document for use as proof of financial responsibility.

(c) Whenever it is determined by a final judgment in a judicial proceeding that an insurer or surety, which has been named on a document accepted by a court or the registrar as proof of financial responsibility covering the operation of a motor vehicle at the time of an accident or offense, is not liable to pay a judgment for injuries or damages resulting from such operation, the registrar, notwithstanding any previous contrary finding, shall forthwith suspend the operating privileges and registration rights of the person against whom the judgment was rendered as provided in division (A)(2) of this section.

(H) In order for any document described in division (G)(1)(b) of this section to be used for the demonstration of proof of financial responsibility under this section, the document shall state the name of the insured or obligor, the name of the insurer or surety company, and the effective and expiration dates of the financial responsibility, and designate by explicit description or by appropriate reference all motor vehicles covered which may include a reference to fleet insurance coverage.

(I) For purposes of this section, "owner" does not include a licensed motor vehicle leasing dealer as defined in section 4517.01 of the Revised Code, but does include a motor vehicle renting dealer as defined in section 4549.65 of the Revised Code. Nothing in this section or in section 4509.51 of the Revised Code shall be construed to prohibit a motor vehicle renting dealer from entering into a contractual agreement with a person whereby the person renting the motor vehicle agrees to be solely responsible for maintaining proof of financial responsibility, in accordance with this section, with respect to the operation, maintenance, or use of the motor vehicle during the period of the motor vehicle's rental.

(J) The purpose of this section is to require the maintenance of proof of financial responsibility with respect to the operation of motor vehicles on the highways of this state, so as to minimize those situations in which persons are not compensated for injuries and damages sustained in motor vehicle accidents. The general assembly finds that this section contains reasonable civil penalties and procedures for achieving this purpose.

(K) Nothing in this section shall be construed to be subject to section 4509.78 of the Revised Code.

(L)(1) The registrar may terminate any suspension imposed under this section and not require the owner to comply with divisions (A)(5)(a), (b), and (c) of this section if the registrar with or without a hearing determines that the owner of the vehicle has established by clear and convincing evidence that all of the following apply:

(a) The owner customarily maintains proof of financial responsibility.

(b) Proof of financial responsibility was not in effect for the vehicle on the date in question for one of the following reasons:

(i) The vehicle was inoperable.

(ii) The vehicle is operated only seasonally, and the date in question was outside the season of operation.

(iii) A person other than the vehicle owner or driver was at fault for the lapse of proof of financial responsibility through no fault of the owner or driver.

(iv) The lapse of proof of financial responsibility was caused by excusable neglect under circumstances that are not likely to recur and do not suggest a purpose to evade the requirements of this chapter.

(2) The registrar may grant an owner or driver relief for a reason specified in division (L)(1)(b)(i) or (ii) of this section whenever the owner or driver is randomly selected to verify the existence of proof of financial responsibility for such a vehicle. However, the registrar may grant an owner or driver relief for a reason specified in division (L)(1)(b)(iii) or (iv) of this section only if the owner or driver has not previously been granted relief under division (L)(1)(b)(iii) or (iv) of this section.

(M) The registrar shall adopt rules in accordance with Chapter 119. of the Revised Code that are necessary to administer and enforce this section. The rules shall include procedures for the surrender of license plates upon failure to maintain proof of financial responsibility and provisions relating to reinstatement of registration rights, acceptable forms of proof of financial responsibility, and verification of the existence of financial responsibility during the period of registration.

(2004 H 230, eff. 9–16–04; 2002 S 123, eff. 1–1–04; 1999 H 163, eff. 6–30–99; 1997 H 215, eff. 6–30–97; 1997 H 261, eff. 9–3–97; 1996 H 438, eff 7–1–97; 1996 H 353, eff. 9–17–96; 1995 H 107, eff. (See Historical and Statutory Notes); 1994 S 20, eff. 4–20–95; 1994 H 687, eff. 10–12–94; 1993 S 62, § 4, eff. 9–1–93; 1992 S 275, S 331; 1990 H 422; 1987 H 419; 1985 S 269, H 201; 1984 H 767; 1982 S 250)

Historical and Statutory Notes

Ed. Note: 1995 H 107 Effective Date—The Secretary of State assigned a general effective date of 6–30–95 for 1995 H 107. Pursuant to O Const Art II § 1c and 1d, and RC 1.471, sections of 1995 H 107 that are, or depend for their implementation upon, current expense appropriations are effective 3–31–95; sections of 1995 H 107 that are not, and do not depend for their implementation upon, current expense appropriations are effective 6–30–95. See *Baldwin's Ohio Legislative Service*, 1995, page 3/L–98 for 1995 H 107, § 16.

4509.102 Misleading peace officer as falsification

No person who has knowingly failed to maintain proof of financial responsibility in accordance with section 4509.101 of the Revised Code shall produce any document with the purpose to mislead a peace officer upon the request of a peace officer for proof of financial responsibility made in accordance with division (D)(2) of section 4509.101 of the Revised Code. Any person who violates this division is guilty of falsification under section 2921.13 of the Revised Code.

(1996 H 438, eff. 7–1–97; 1994 S 20, eff. 4–20–95)

4509.103 Financial responsibility identification cards

(A) Each insurer writing motor vehicle liability insurance in this state shall provide financial responsibility identification cards to every policyholder in this state to whom it has delivered or issued for delivery a motor vehicle liability insurance policy. A minimum of one financial responsibility identification card shall be issued for every motor vehicle insured under a motor vehicle liability insurance policy.

(B) A financial responsibility identification card shall be valid only for the policy period. The card shall be in a form prescribed by the registrar of motor vehicles. It shall disclose the policy period and shall contain such other information as required by the registrar.

(1995 H 248, § 1, eff. 10–20–95; 1994 S 20, eff. 10–20–95)

4509.104 Warning stating that insurance policy does not constitute proof of financial responsibility

Any automobile insurance policy that does not provide liability coverage at the time of issuance of at least the minimum amounts provided under division (K) of section 4509.01 of the Revised Code for proof of financial responsibility shall contain a clear and conspicuous warning on the face of the policy stating the policy does not constitute proof of financial responsibility as required for the operation of a motor vehicle under division (A)(1) of section 4509.101 of the Revised Code.

(1994 S 20, eff. 4–20–95)

ACCIDENT REPORT INADMISSIBLE

4509.30 Accident report and findings of registrar prohibited at trial

The report required following a motor vehicle accident, the action taken by the registrar of motor vehicles pursuant to sections 4509.11 to 4509.291, inclusive, of the Revised Code, the findings of the registrar upon which such action is based, and the security filed as provided in such sections, shall not be referred to in any way and shall not be evidence of the negligence or due care of either party at the trial of any action to recover damages.

(128 v 1221, eff. 7–1–60; 1953 H 1; GC 6298–41)

PROOF OF FINANCIAL RESPONSIBILITY

4509.44 Proof of financial responsibility required for registration

No motor vehicle shall be or continue to be registered in the name of any person required to file proof of financial responsibility unless such proof is furnished and maintained in accordance with section 4509.45 of the Revised Code.

(131 v S 52, eff. 10–30–65; 1953 H 1; GC 6298–58)

4509.45 Proof of financial responsibility

(A) Proof of financial responsibility when required under section 4509.101, 4509.33, 4509.34, 4509.38, 4509.40, 4509.42, 4509.44, or 4510.038 of the Revised Code may be given by filing any of the following:

(1) A financial responsibility identification card as provided in section 4509.104 of the Revised Code;

(2) A certificate of insurance as provided in section 4509.46 or 4509.47 of the Revised Code;

(3) A bond as provided in section 4509.59 of the Revised Code;

(4) A certificate of deposit of money or securities as provided in section 4509.62 of the Revised Code;

(5) A certificate of self-insurance, as provided in section 4509.72 of the Revised Code, supplemented by an agreement by the self-insurer that, with respect to accidents occurring while the certificate is in force, the self-insurer will pay the same amounts that an insurer would have been obligated to pay under an owner's motor vehicle liability policy if it had issued such a policy to the self-insurer.

(B) Proof under division (A) of this section shall be filed and maintained for five years from the date of the registrar's imposition of a class A, B, or C suspension of operating privileges and shall be filed and maintained for three years from the date of the registrar's imposition of a class D, E, or F suspension of operating privileges.

(2002 S 123, eff. 1–1–04; 1994 S 20, eff. 4–20–95; 1986 S 356, eff. 9–24–86; 1982 S 250; 131 v S 52; 1953 H 1; GC 6298–59)

PROHIBITIONS

4509.74 Prohibition against failure to report accident

(A) No person shall fail to report a motor vehicle accident as required under the laws of this state.

(B) Whoever violates this section is guilty of a minor misdemeanor.

(2002 S 123, eff. 1–1–04; 1953 H 1, eff. 10–1–53; GC 6298–85)

4509.77 Prohibition against failure to return license

(A) No person shall willfully fail to return a license or registration as required in section 4509.69 of the Revised Code.

(B) Whoever violates this section shall be fined not more than five hundred dollars, imprisoned for not more than thirty days, or both.

(2002 S 123, eff. 1–1–04; 1953 H 1, eff. 10–1–53; GC 6298–88)

4509.78 General prohibition

(A) No person shall violate section [1] 4509.01 to 4509.78 of the Revised Code for which no penalty is otherwise provided.

(B) Whoever violates this section shall be fined not more than five hundred dollars, imprisoned not more than ninety days, or both.

(2002 S 123, eff. 1–1–04; 1953 H 1, eff. 10–1–53; GC 6298–89)

[1] Prior and current versions differ; although no amendment was indicated in 2002 S 123, "section" appeared as "sections" in 1953 H 1.

4509.79 Ridesharing arrangement; liability insurance

(A) As used in this section, "ridesharing arrangement" means the transportation of persons in a motor vehicle where such transportation is incidental to another purpose of a volunteer driver and includes ridesharing arrangements known as carpools, vanpools, and buspools.

(B) Every owner registering as a passenger car a motor vehicle designed and used for carrying more than nine but not more than fifteen passengers or registering a bus under division (G) of section 4503.04 of the Revised Code shall have in effect, whenever the motor vehicle is used in a ridesharing arrangement, a policy of liability insurance with respect to the motor vehicle in amounts and coverage no less than:

(1) One hundred thousand dollars because of bodily injury to or death of one person in any one accident;

(2) Three hundred thousand dollars because of bodily injury to or death of two or more persons in any one accident;

(3) Fifty thousand dollars because of injury to property of others in any one accident.

(C) Whoever violates this section shall be fined not more than five thousand dollars.

(2004 H 230, eff. 9–16–04; 2002 S 123, eff. 1–1–04; 1982 S 331, eff. 5–21–82; 1981 H 53)

CHAPTER 4510

DRIVER'S LICENSE SUSPENSION AND CANCELLATION

Section

Section

4510.01 Definitions

As used in this title and in Title XXIX of the Revised Code:

(A) "Cancel" or "cancellation" means the annulment or termination by the bureau of motor vehicles of a driver's license, commercial driver's license, temporary instruction permit, probationary license, or nonresident operating privilege because it was obtained unlawfully, issued in error, altered, or willfully destroyed, or because the holder no longer is entitled to the license, permit, or privilege.

(B) "Drug abuse offense" has the same meaning as in section 2925.01 of the Revised Code.

(C) "Ignition interlock device" means a device approved by the director of public safety that connects a breath analyzer to a motor vehicle's ignition system, that is constantly available to monitor the concentration by weight of alcohol in the breath of any person attempting to start that motor vehicle by using its ignition system, and that deters starting the motor vehicle by use of its ignition system unless the person attempting to start the vehicle provides an appropriate breath sample for the device and the device determines that the concentration by weight of alcohol in the person's breath is below a preset level.

(D) "Immobilizing or disabling device" means a device approved by the director of public safety that may be ordered by a court to be used by an offender as a condition of limited driving privileges. "Immobilizing or disabling device" includes an ignition interlock device, and any prototype device that is used according to protocols designed to ensure efficient and effective monitoring of limited driving privileges granted by a court to an offender.

(E) "Moving violation" means any violation of any statute or ordinance that regulates the operation of vehicles, streetcars, or trackless trolleys on the highways or streets. "Moving violation" does not include a violation of section 4513.263 of the Revised Code or a substantially equivalent municipal ordinance, a violation of any statute or ordinance regulating pedestrians or the parking of vehicles, vehicle size or load limitations, vehicle fitness requirements, or vehicle registration.

(F) "Municipal OVI ordinance" and "municipal OVI offense" have the same meanings as in section 4511.181 of the Revised Code.

(G) "Prototype device" means any testing device to monitor limited driving privileges that has not yet been approved or disapproved by the director of public safety.

(H) "Suspend" or "suspension" means the permanent or temporary withdrawal, by action of a court or the bureau of motor vehicles, of a driver's license, commercial driver's license, temporary instruction permit, probationary license, or nonresident operating privilege for the period of the suspension or the permanent or temporary withdrawal of the privilege to obtain a license, permit, or privilege of that type for the period of the suspension.

(2002 S 123, eff. 1–1–04)

4510.02 Classification of suspensions

(A) When a court elects or is required to suspend the driver's license, commercial driver's license, temporary instruction permit, probationary license, or nonresident operating privilege of any offender from a specified suspension class, for each of the following suspension classes, the court shall impose a definite period of suspension from the range specified for the suspension class:

(1) For a class one suspension, a definite period for the life of the person subject to the suspension;

(2) For a class two suspension, a definite period of three years to life;

(3) For a class three suspension, a definite period of two to ten years;

(4) For a class four suspension, a definite period of one to five years;

(5) For a class five suspension, a definite period of six months to three years;

(6) For a class six suspension, a definite period of three months to two years;

(7) For a class seven suspension, a definite period not to exceed one year.

(B) When the bureau of motor vehicles elects or is required to suspend the driver's license, commercial driver's license, temporary instruction permit, probationary license, or nonresident operating privilege of any person from a specified suspension class, for each of the following suspension classes, the period of suspension shall be as follows:

(1) For a class A suspension, three years;

(2) For a class B suspension, two years;

(3) For a class C suspension, one year;

(4) For a class D suspension, six months;

(5) For a class E suspension, three months;

(6) For a class F suspension, until conditions are met.

(C) The court may require a person to successfully complete a remedial driving course as a condition for the return of full driving privileges after a suspension period imposed from any range in division (A) of this section or otherwise imposed by the court pursuant to any other provision of law ends.

(D) When a court or the bureau suspends the driver's license, commercial driver's license, temporary instruction permit, probationary license, or nonresident operating privilege of any offender or person pursuant to any provision of law that does not provide for the suspension to be from a class set forth in division (A) or (B) of this section, except as otherwise provided in the provision that authorizes or requires the suspension, the suspension shall be subject to and governed by this chapter.

(2002 S 123, eff. 1–1–04)

4510.021 Limited driving privileges

(A) Unless expressly prohibited by section 2919.22, section 4510.13, or any other section of the Revised Code, a court may grant limited driving privileges for any purpose described in division (A)(1), (2), or (3) of this section during any suspension imposed by the court. In granting the privileges, the court shall specify the purposes, times, and places of the privileges and may impose any other reasonable conditions on the person's driving of a motor vehicle. The privileges shall be for any of the following limited purposes:

(1) Occupational, educational, vocational, or medical purposes;

(2) Taking the driver's or commercial driver's license examination;

(3) Attending court-ordered treatment.

(B) Unless expressly authorized by a section of the Revised Code, a court may not grant limited driving privileges during any suspension imposed by the bureau of motor vehicles. To obtain limited driving privileges during a suspension imposed by the bureau, the person under suspension may file a petition in a court of record in the county in which the person resides. A person who is not a resident of this state shall file any petition for privileges either in the Franklin county municipal court or in the municipal or county court located in the county where the offense occurred. If the person who is not a resident of this state is a minor, the person may file the petition either in the Franklin county juvenile court or in the juvenile court with jurisdiction over the offense. If a court grants limited driving privileges as described in this division, the privileges shall be for any of the limited purposes identified in division (A) of this section.

(C) When the use of an immobilizing or disabling device is not otherwise required by law, the court, as a condition of granting limited driving privileges, may require that the person's vehicle be equipped with an immobilizing or disabling device, except as provided in division (C) of section 4510.43 of the Revised Code. When the use of restricted license plates issued under section 4503.231 of the Revised Code is not otherwise required by law, the court, as a condition of granting limited driving privileges, may require that the person's vehicle be equipped with restricted license plates of that nature, except as provided in division (B) of that section.

(D) When the court grants limited driving privileges under section 4510.31 of the Revised Code or any other provision of law during the suspension of the temporary instruction permit or probationary driver's license of a person who is under eighteen years of age, the court may include as a purpose of the privilege the person's practicing of driving with the person's parent, guardian, or other custodian during the period of the suspension. If the court grants limited driving privileges for this purpose, the court, in addition to all other conditions it imposes, shall impose as a condition that the person exercise the privilege only when a parent, guardian, or custodian of the person who holds a current valid driver's or commercial driver's license issued by this state actually occupies the seat beside the person in the vehicle the person is operating.

(E) Before granting limited driving privileges under this section, the court shall require the offender to provide proof of financial responsibility pursuant to section 4509.45 of the Revised Code.

(2004 H 52, eff. 6–1–04; 2002 S 123, eff. 1–1–04)

4510.03 Abstract of conviction or bail forfeiture

(A) Every county court judge, mayor of a mayor's court, and clerk of a court of record shall keep a full record of every case in which a person is charged with any violation of any provision of sections 4511.01 to 4511.771 or 4513.01 to 4513.36 of the Revised Code or of any other law or ordinance regulating the operation of vehicles, streetcars, and trackless trolleys on highways or streets.

(B) If a person is convicted of or forfeits bail in relation to a violation of any section listed in division (A) of this section or a violation of any other law or ordinance regulating the operation of vehicles, streetcars, and trackless trolleys on highways or streets, the county court judge, mayor of a mayor's court, or clerk, within ten days after the conviction or bail forfeiture, shall prepare and immediately forward to the bureau of motor vehicles an abstract, certified by the preparer to be true and correct, of the court record covering the case in which the person was convicted or forfeited bail. Every court of record also shall forward to the bureau of motor vehicles an abstract of the court record as described in division (C) of this section upon the conviction of any person of aggravated vehicular homicide or vehicular homicide or of a felony in the commission of which a vehicle was used.

(C) Each abstract required by this section shall be made upon a form approved and furnished by the bureau and shall include the name and address of the person charged, the number of the person's driver's or commercial driver's license, probationary driver's license, or temporary instruction permit, the registration number of the vehicle involved, the nature of the offense, the date of the offense, the date of hearing, the plea, the judgment, or whether bail was forfeited, and the amount of the fine or forfeiture.

(2002 S 123, eff. 1–1–04)

4510.031 U.S. district court jurisdiction

(A) A United States district court that has jurisdiction within this state may utilize the provisions of section 4510.03 of the Revised Code in regard to any case in which a person is charged with any violation of any provision of sections 4511.01 to 4511.771 or 4513.01 to 4513.36 of the Revised Code or of any other law or ordinance regulating the operation of vehicles, streetcars, and trackless trolleys on highways or streets located on federal property within this state. The court also may forward to the bureau an abstract upon the conviction of any person of aggravated vehicular homicide or vehicular homicide or of a felony in the commission of which a vehicle was used.

(B) If a United States district court acts under this section, it shall follow the procedures established in section 4510.03 of the Revised Code.

(C) The bureau of motor vehicles shall accept and process an abstract received from a United States district court under this section in the same manner as it accepts and processes an abstract received from a county court judge, mayor of a mayor's court, or clerk of a court of record.

(2002 S 123, eff. 1–1–04)

4510.032 Inclusion of dismissal, reduced charges or juvenile adjudications in abstract

(A) If a person is charged with a violation of section 4511.19 of the Revised Code or a violation of any municipal OVI ordinance; if that charge is dismissed or reduced; if the person is convicted of or forfeits bail in relation to a violation of any other section of the Revised Code or of any ordinance that regulates the operation of vehicles, streetcars, and trackless trolleys on highways and streets but that does not relate to operating a vehicle while under the influence of alcohol, a drug of abuse, or a combination of them or to operating a vehicle with a prohibited concentration of alcohol in the whole blood, blood serum or plasma, breath, or urine; and if the violation of which the person was convicted or in relation to which the person forfeited bail arose out of the same facts and circumstances and the same act as did the charge that was dismissed or reduced, the abstract prepared under section 4510.03 of the Revised Code also shall set forth the charge that was dismissed or reduced, indicate that it was dismissed or reduced, and indicate that the violation resulting in the conviction or bail forfeiture arose out of the same facts and circumstances and the same act as did the charge that was dismissed or reduced.

(B) If a charge against a person of a violation of division (A) of section 4510.11, division (A) of section 4510.14, or division (A) of section 4510.16 of the Revised Code or any municipal ordinance that is substantially equivalent to any of those divisions is dismissed or reduced and if the person is convicted of or forfeits bail in relation to a violation of any other section of the Revised Code or any other ordinance that regulates the operation of vehicles, streetcars, and trackless trolleys on highways and streets that arose out of the same facts and circumstances as did the charge that was dismissed or reduced, the abstract also shall set forth the charge that was dismissed or reduced, indicate that it was dismissed or reduced, and indicate that the violation resulting in the conviction or bail forfeiture arose out of the same facts and circumstances and the same act as did the charge that was dismissed or reduced.

(C)(1) If a child has been adjudicated an unruly or delinquent child or a juvenile traffic offender for having committed any act that if committed by an adult would be a drug abuse offense or any violation of division (B) of section 2917.11 or of section 4511.19 of the Revised Code, the court shall notify the bureau, by means of an abstract of the court record as described in divisions (B) and (C) of section 4510.03 of the Revised Code, within ten days after the adjudication.

(2) If a court requires a child to attend a drug abuse or alcohol abuse education, intervention, or treatment program, the abstract required by division (C)(1) of this section and forwarded to the bureau also shall include the name and address of the operator of the program and the date that the child entered the program. If the child satisfactorily completes the program, the court, immediately upon receipt of the information, shall send to the bureau an updated abstract that also shall contain the date on which the child satisfactorily completed the program.

(2002 S 123, eff. 1-1-04)

4510.034 Abstract to include prohibition of vehicle registration

(A) Division (B) of this section applies in relation to persons who are convicted of or plead guilty to any of the following:

(1) A violation of division (A) of section 4510.11, division (A) of section 4510.14, or division (A) of section 4510.16 of the Revised Code;

(2) A violation of a municipal ordinance substantially equivalent to any division set forth in division (A)(1) of this section;

(3) A violation of division (A) of section 4511.19 of the Revised Code or a violation of section 4511.203 of the Revised Code;

(4) A violation of a municipal OVI ordinance.

(B) If a person is convicted of or pleads guilty to any violation set forth in division (A) of this section and if division (D) of section 4503.234 of the Revised Code prohibits the registrar of motor vehicles and all deputy registrars from accepting an application for the registration of, or registering, any motor vehicle in the name of that person, the abstract prepared pursuant to section 4510.03, 4510.031, or 4510.032 of the Revised Code shall specifically set forth these facts and clearly indicate the date on which the order of criminal forfeiture was issued or would have been issued but for the operation of section 4503.234 of the Revised Code. If the registrar receives an abstract containing this information relating to a person, the registrar, in accordance with sections 4503.12 and 4503.234 of the Revised Code, shall take all necessary measures to prevent the registrar's office or any deputy registrar from accepting from the person, for the period of time ending five years after the date on which the order was issued or would have been issued and as described in section 4503.234 of the Revised Code, any new application for the registration of any motor vehicle in the name of the person.

(2002 S 123, eff. 1-1-04)

4510.035 Failure to comply with abstract reporting provisions

The purposeful failure or refusal of any person to comply with any provision of section 4510.03, 4510.032, 4510.034, 4510.036, or 4510.037 of the Revised Code constitutes misconduct in office and is a ground for removal of the person from the office.

(2002 S 123, eff. 1-1-04)

4510.036 Record of abstracts; point system for motor vehicle violations

(A) The bureau of motor vehicles shall record within ten days, after receipt, and shall keep at its main office, all abstracts received under this section or section 4510.03, 4510.031, 4510.032, or 4510.034 of the Revised Code and shall maintain records of convictions and bond forfeitures for any violation of a state law or a municipal ordinance regulating the operation of vehicles, streetcars, and trackless trolleys on highways and streets, except a violation related to parking a motor vehicle.

(B) Every court of record or mayor's court before which a person is charged with a violation for which points are chargeable by this section shall assess and transcribe to the abstract of conviction that is furnished by the bureau to the court the number of points chargeable by this section in the correct space assigned on the reporting form. A United States district court that has jurisdiction within this state and before which a person is charged with a violation for which points are chargeable by this section may assess and transcribe to the abstract of conviction report that is furnished by the bureau the number of points chargeable by this section in the correct space assigned on the reporting form. If the federal court so assesses and transcribes the points chargeable for the offense and furnishes the report to the bureau, the bureau shall record the points in the same manner as those assessed and transcribed by a court of record or mayor's court.

(C) A court shall assess the following points for an offense based on the following formula:

(1) Aggravated vehicular homicide, vehicular homicide, vehicular manslaughter, aggravated vehicular assault, or vehicular assault when the offense involves the operation of a vehicle, streetcar, or trackless trolley on a highway or street . 6 points

(2) A violation of section 2921.331 of the Revised Code or any ordinance prohibiting the willful fleeing or eluding of a law enforcement officer . . . . 6 points

(3) A violation of section 4549.02 or 4549.021 of the Revised Code or any ordinance requiring the driver of a vehicle to stop and disclose identity at the scene of an accident . 6 points

(4) A violation of section 4511.251 of the Revised Code or any ordinance prohibiting street racing . . . . 6 points

(5) A violation of section 4510.11, 4510.14, 4510.16, or 4510.21 of the Revised Code or any ordinance prohibiting the operation of a motor vehicle while the driver's or commercial driver's license is under suspension .... 6 points

(6) A violation of division (A) of section 4511.19 of the Revised Code, any ordinance prohibiting the operation of a vehicle while under the influence of alcohol, a drug of abuse, or a combination of them, or any ordinance substantially equivalent to division (A) of section 4511.19 of the Revised Code prohibiting the operation of a vehicle with a prohibited concentration of alcohol in the whole blood, blood serum or plasma, breath, or urine .... 6 points

(7) A violation of section 2913.03 of the Revised Code that does not involve an aircraft or motorboat or any ordinance prohibiting the operation of a vehicle without the consent of the owner .... 6 points

(8) Any offense under the motor vehicle laws of this state that is a felony, or any other felony in the commission of which a motor vehicle was used .... 6 points

(9) A violation of division (B) of section 4511.19 of the Revised Code or any ordinance substantially equivalent to that division prohibiting the operation of a vehicle with a prohibited concentration of alcohol in the whole blood, blood serum or plasma, breath, or urine .... 4 points

(10) A violation of section 4511.20 of the Revised Code or any ordinance prohibiting the operation of a motor vehicle in willful or wanton disregard of the safety of persons or property . 4 points

(11) A violation of any law or ordinance pertaining to speed:

(a) Notwithstanding divisions (C)(11)(b) and (c) of this section, when the speed exceeds the lawful speed limit by thirty miles per hour or more .... 4 points

(b) When the speed exceeds the lawful speed limit of fifty-five miles per hour or more by more than ten miles per hour . 2 points

(c) When the speed exceeds the lawful speed limit of less than fifty-five miles per hour by more than five miles per hour . 2 points

(d) When the speed does not exceed the amounts set forth in divisions (C)(11)(a), (b), or (c) of this section .... 0 points

(12) Operating a motor vehicle in violation of a restriction imposed by the registrar.......................... 2 points

(13) All other moving violations reported under this section .... 2 points

(D) Upon receiving notification from the proper court, including a United States district court that has jurisdiction within this state, the bureau shall delete any points entered for a bond forfeiture if the driver is acquitted of the offense for which bond was posted.

(E) If a person is convicted of or forfeits bail for two or more offenses arising out of the same facts and points are chargeable for each of the offenses, points shall be charged for only the conviction or bond forfeiture for which the greater number of points is chargeable, and, if the number of points chargeable for each offense is equal, only one offense shall be recorded, and points shall be charged only for that offense.

(2002 S 123, eff. 1–1–04)

4510.037 Repeat traffic offender; point system suspension

(A) When the registrar of motor vehicles determines that the total points charged against any person under section 4510.036 of the Revised Code exceed five, the registrar shall send a warning letter to the person at the person's last known address by regular mail. The warning letter shall list the reported violations that are the basis of the points charged, list the number of points charged for each violation, and outline the suspension provisions of this section.

(B) When the registrar determines that the total points charged against any person under section 4510.036 of the Revised Code within any two-year period beginning on the date of the first conviction within the two-year period is equal to twelve or more, the registrar shall send a written notice to the person at the person's last known address by regular mail. The notice shall list the reported violations that are the basis of the points charged, list the number of points charged for each violation, and state that, because the total number of points charged against the person within the applicable two-year period is equal to twelve or more, the registrar is imposing a class D suspension of the person's driver's or commercial driver's license or permit or nonresident operating privileges for the period of time specified in division (B)(4) of section 4510.02 of the Revised Code. The notice also shall state that the suspension is effective on the twentieth day after the mailing of the notice, unless the person files a petition appealing the determination and suspension in the municipal court, county court, or, if the person is under the age of eighteen, the juvenile division of the court of common pleas in whose jurisdiction the person resides or, if the person is not a resident of this state, in the Franklin county municipal court or juvenile division of the Franklin county court of common pleas. By filing the appeal of the determination and suspension, the person agrees to pay the cost of the proceedings in the appeal of the determination and suspension and alleges that the person can show cause why the person's driver's or commercial driver's license or permit or nonresident operating privileges should not be suspended.

(C)(1) Any person against whom at least two but less than twelve points have been charged under section 4510.036 of the Revised Code may enroll in a course of remedial driving instruction that is approved by the director of public safety. Upon the person's completion of an approved course of remedial driving instruction, the person may apply to the registrar on a form prescribed by the registrar for a credit of two points on the person's driving record. Upon receipt of the application and proof of completion of the approved remedial driving course, the registrar shall approve the two-point credit. The registrar shall not approve any credits for a person who completes an approved course of remedial driving instruction pursuant to a judge's order under section 4510.02 of the Revised Code.

(2) In any three-year period, the registrar shall approve only one two-point credit on a person's driving record under division (C)(1) of this section. The registrar shall approve not more than five two-point credits on a person's driving record under division (C)(1) of this section during that person's lifetime.

(D) When a judge of a court of record suspends a person's driver's or commercial driver's license or permit or nonresident operating privilege and charges points against the person under section 4510.036 of the Revised Code for the offense that resulted in the suspension, the registrar shall credit that period of suspension against the time of any subsequent suspension imposed under this section for which those points were used to impose the subsequent suspension. When a United States district court that has jurisdiction within this state suspends a person's driver's or commercial driver's license or permit or nonresident operating privileges pursuant to the "Assimilative Crimes Act," 102 Stat. 4381 (1988), 18 U.S.C.A. 13, as amended, the district court prepares an abstract pursuant to section 4510.031 of the Revised Code, and the district court charges points against the person under section 4510.036 of the Revised Code for the offense that resulted in the suspension, the registrar shall credit the period of suspension imposed by the district court against the time of any subsequent suspension imposed under this section for which the points were used to impose the subsequent suspension.

(E) The registrar, upon the written request of a licensee who files a petition under division (B) of this section, shall furnish the licensee a certified copy of the registrar's record of the convictions and bond forfeitures of the person. This record shall include the name, address, and date of birth of the licensee; the name of the court in which each conviction or bail forfeiture took place; the nature of the offense that was the basis of the conviction or bond forfeiture; and any other information that the registrar considers necessary. If the record indicates that twelve points or more have been charged against the person within a two-year period, it is prima-facie evidence that the person is a repeat traffic offender, and the registrar shall suspend the person's driver's or commercial driver's license or permit or nonresident operating privilege pursuant to division (B) of this section.

In hearing the petition and determining whether the person filing the petition has shown cause why the person's driver's or commercial driver's license or permit or nonresident operating privilege should not be suspended, the court shall decide the issue on the record certified by the registrar and any additional relevant, competent, and material evidence that either the registrar or the person whose license is sought to be suspended submits.

(F) If a petition is filed under division (B) of this section in a county court, the prosecuting attorney of the county in which the case is pending shall represent the registrar in the proceedings, except that, if the petitioner resides in a municipal corporation within the jurisdiction of the county court, the city director of law, village solicitor, or other chief legal officer of the municipal corporation shall represent the registrar in the proceedings. If a petition is filed under division (B) of this section in a municipal court, the registrar shall be represented in the resulting proceedings as provided in section 1901.34 of the Revised Code.

(G) If the court determines from the evidence submitted that a person who filed a petition under division (B) of this section has failed to show cause why the person's driver's or commercial driver's license or permit or nonresident operating privileges should not be suspended, the court shall assess against the person the cost of the proceedings in the appeal of the determination and suspension and shall impose the applicable suspension under this section or suspend all or a portion of the suspension and impose any conditions upon the person that the court considers proper or impose upon the person a community control sanction pursuant to section 2929.15 or 2929.25 of the Revised Code. If the court determines from the evidence submitted that a person who filed a petition under division (B) of this section has shown cause why the person's driver's or commercial driver's license or permit or nonresident operating privileges should not be suspended, the costs of the appeal proceeding shall be paid out of the county treasury of the county in which the proceedings were held.

(H) Any person whose driver's or commercial driver's license or permit or nonresident operating privileges are suspended under this section is not entitled to apply for or receive a new driver's or commercial driver's license or permit or to request or be granted nonresident operating privileges during the effective period of the suspension.

(I) Upon the termination of any suspension or other penalty imposed under this section involving the surrender of license or permit and upon the request of the person whose license or permit was suspended or surrendered, the registrar shall return the license or permit to the person upon determining that the person has complied with all provisions of section 4510.038 of the Revised Code or, if the registrar destroyed the license or permit pursuant to section 4510.52 of the Revised Code, shall reissue the person's license or permit.

(J) Any person whose driver's or commercial driver's license or permit or nonresident operating privileges are suspended as a repeat traffic offender under this section and who, during the suspension, operates any motor vehicle upon any public roads and highways is guilty of a misdemeanor of the first degree, and the court shall sentence the offender to a minimum term of three days in jail. No court shall suspend the first three days of jail time imposed pursuant to this division.

(K) The registrar, in accordance with specific statutory authority, may suspend the privilege of driving a motor vehicle on the public roads and highways of this state that is granted to nonresidents by section 4507.04 of the Revised Code.

(2002 H 490, eff. 1–1–04; 2002 S 123, eff. 1–1–04)

4510.038 Conditions for return of full driving privileges

Any person whose driver's or commercial driver's license or permit is suspended or who is granted limited driving privileges under section 4510.037, under division (H) of section 4511.19, or under section 4510.07 of the Revised Code for a violation of a municipal ordinance that is substantially equivalent to division (B) of section 4511.19 of the Revised Code is not eligible to retain the license, or to have the driving privileges reinstated, until each of the following has occurred:

(A) The person successfully completes a course of remedial driving instruction approved by the director of public safety. A minimum of twenty-five per cent of the number of hours of instruction included in the course shall be devoted to instruction on driver attitude.

The course also shall devote a number of hours to instruction in the area of alcohol and drugs and the operation of vehicles. The instruction shall include, but not be limited to, a review of the laws governing the operation of a vehicle while under the influence of alcohol, drugs, or a combination of them, the dangers of operating a vehicle while under the influence of alcohol, drugs, or a combination of them, and other information relating to the operation of vehicles and the consumption of alcoholic beverages and use of drugs. The director, in consultation with the director of alcohol and drug addiction services, shall prescribe the content of the instruction. The number of hours devoted to the area of alcohol and drugs and the operation of vehicles shall comprise a minimum of twenty five per cent of the number of hours of instruction included in the course.

(B) The person is examined in the manner provided for in section 4507.20 of the Revised Code, and found by the registrar of motor vehicles to be qualified to operate a motor vehicle;

(C) The person gives and maintains proof of financial responsibility, in accordance with section 4509.45 of the Revised Code.

(2002 S 123, eff. 1–1–04)

Historical and Statutory Notes

Ed. Note: 4510.038 is former 4507.022, amended and recodified by 2002 S 123, eff. 1–1–04; 1997 S 60, eff. 10–21–97; 1996 H 353, eff. 9–17–96; 1994 S 82, eff. 5–4–94

4510.04 Affirmative defenses

It is an affirmative defense to any prosecution brought under section 4510.11, 4510.14, 4510.16, or 4510.21 of the Revised Code or under any substantially equivalent municipal ordinance that the alleged offender drove under suspension, without a valid permit or driver's or commercial driver's license, or in violation of a restriction because of a substantial emergency, and because no other person was reasonably available to drive in response to the emergency.

It is an affirmative defense to any prosecution brought under section 4510.16 of the Revised Code that the order of suspension resulted from the failure of the alleged offender to respond to a financial responsibility random verification request under division (A)(3)(c) of section 4509.101 of the Revised Code and that, at the time of the initial financial responsibility random verification request, the alleged offender was in compliance with division

(A)(1) of section 4509.101 of the Revised Code as shown by proof of financial responsibility that was in effect at the time of that request.

(2002 S 123, eff. 1–1–04)

4510.05 Violation of municipal ordinance

Except as otherwise provided in section 4510.07 or in any other provision of the Revised Code, whenever an offender is convicted of or pleads guilty to a violation of a municipal ordinance that is substantially similar to a provision of the Revised Code, and a court is permitted or required to suspend a person's driver's or commercial driver's license or permit for a violation of that provision, a court, in addition to any other penalties authorized by law, may suspend the offender's driver's or commercial driver's license or permit or nonresident operating privileges for the period of time the court determines appropriate, but the period of suspension imposed for the violation of the municipal ordinance shall not exceed the period of suspension that is permitted or required to be imposed for the violation of the provision of the Revised Code to which the municipal ordinance is substantially similar.

(2002 S 123, eff. 1–1–04)

Historical and Statutory Notes

Ed. Note: 4510.05 is former 4507.1611, amended and recodified by 2002 S 123, eff. 1–1–04; 1996 H 510, eff. 9–19–96.

4510.06 Suspension or cancellation of license under Assimilative Crimes Act

If a United States district court whose jurisdiction lies within this state suspends or cancels the driver's or commercial driver's license, permit, or nonresident operating privileges of any person pursuant to the "Assimilative Crimes Act," 102 Stat. 4381 (1988), 18 U.S.C.A. 13, as amended, that suspension or cancellation is deemed to have the same effect throughout this state as if it were imposed under the laws of this state. In that type of case, if the United States district court observes the procedures prescribed by the Revised Code and utilizes the forms prescribed by the registrar of motor vehicles, the bureau of motor vehicles shall make the appropriate notation or record and shall take any other action that is prescribed or permitted by the Revised Code.

(2002 S 123, eff. 1–1–04)

Historical and Statutory Notes

Ed. Note: 4510.06 is former 4507.1610, amended and recodified by 2002 S 123, eff. 1–1–04; 1996 H 353, eff. 9–17–96.

4510.07 Violation of municipal ordinance substantially equivalent to vehicular homicide or solicitation

The court imposing a sentence upon an offender for any violation of a municipal ordinance that is substantially equivalent to a violation of section 2903.06 or 2907.24 of the Revised Code or for any violation of a municipal OVI ordinance also shall impose a suspension of the offender's driver's license, commercial driver's license, temporary instruction permit, probationary license, or nonresident operating privilege from the range specified in division (B) of section 4510.02 of the Revised Code that is equivalent in length to the suspension required for a violation of section 2903.06 or 2907.24 or division (A) or (B) of section 4511.19 of the Revised Code under similar circumstances.

(2002 S 123, eff. 1–1–04)

Historical and Statutory Notes

Ed. Note: 4510.07 is former 4507.1613, amended and recodified by 2002 S 123, eff. 1–1–04; 1999 S 107, eff. 3–23–00.

4510.10 Extension of time or installment plan for payment of reinstatement fees

(A) As used in this section, "reinstatement fees" means the fees that are required under section 4507.1612, 4507.45, 4509.101, 4509.81, 4511.191, 4511.951, or any other provision of the Revised Code, or under a schedule established by the bureau of motor vehicles, in order to reinstate a driver's or commercial driver's license or permit or nonresident operating privilege of an offender under a suspension.

(B) Reinstatement fees are those fees that compensate the bureau of motor vehicles for suspensions, cancellations, or disqualifications of a person's driving privileges and to compensate the bureau and other agencies in their administration of programs intended to reduce and eliminate threats to public safety through education, treatment, and other activities. The registrar of motor vehicles shall not reinstate a driver's or commercial driver's license or permit or nonresident operating privilege of a person until the person has paid all reinstatement fees and has complied with all conditions for each suspension, cancellation, or disqualification incurred by that person.

(C) When a municipal court or county court determines in a pending case involving an offender that the offender cannot reasonably pay reinstatement fees due and owing by the offender relative to a suspension that has been or that will be imposed in the case, then the court, by order, may undertake either of the following, in order of preference:

(1) Establish a reasonable payment plan of not less than fifty dollars per month, to be paid by the offender to the bureau of motor vehicles in all succeeding months until all reinstatement fees required of the offender are paid in full;

(2) If the offender, but for the payment of the reinstatement fees, otherwise would be entitled to operate a vehicle in this state or to obtain reinstatement of the offender's operating privileges, permit the offender to operate a motor vehicle, as authorized by the court, until a future date upon which date all reinstatement fees must be paid in full. A payment extension granted under this division shall not exceed one hundred eighty days, and any operating privileges granted under this division shall be solely for the purpose of permitting the offender occupational or "family necessity" privileges in order to enable the offender to reasonably acquire the delinquent reinstatement fees due and owing.

(D) If a municipal court or county court, by order, undertakes either activity described in division (C)(1) or (2) of this section, the court, at any time after the issuance of the order, may determine that a change of circumstances has occurred and may amend the order as justice requires, provided that the amended order also shall be an order that is permitted under division (C)(1) or (2) of this section.

(E) If a court enters an order of the type described in division (C)(1), (C)(2), or (D) of this section, during the pendency of the order, the offender in relation to whom it applies is not subject to prosecution for failing to pay the reinstatement fees covered by the order.

(F) Reinstatement fees are debts that may be discharged in bankruptcy.

(2004 H 230, eff. 9–16–04; 2002 S 123, eff. 1–1–04)

4510.11 Driving under suspension or in violation of license restriction

(A) No person whose driver's or commercial driver's license or permit or nonresident operating privilege has been suspended under any provision of the Revised Code, other than Chapter 4509. of the Revised Code, or under any applicable law in any other jurisdiction in which the person's license or permit was issued shall operate any motor vehicle upon the public roads and highways or upon any public or private property used by the public for purposes of vehicular travel or parking within this state during the period of suspension unless the person is granted limited driving privileges and is operating the vehicle in accordance with the terms of the limited driving privileges.

(B) No person shall operate any motor vehicle upon a highway or any public or private property used by the public for purposes of vehicular travel or parking in this state in violation of any restriction of the person's driver's or commercial driver's license or permit imposed under division (D) of section 4506.10 or under section 4507.14 of the Revised Code.

(C)(1) Whoever violates this section is guilty of driving under suspension or in violation of a license restriction, a misdemeanor of the first degree. The court shall impose upon the offender a class seven suspension of the offender's driver's license, commercial driver's license, temporary instruction permit, probationary license, or nonresident operating privilege from the range specified in division (A)(7) of section 4510.02 of the Revised Code.

(2) Except as provided in division (C)(3) or (4) of this section, the court, in addition to any other penalty that it imposes on the offender and if the vehicle is registered in the offender's name, shall order the immobilization of the vehicle involved in the offense for thirty days in accordance with section 4503.233 of the Revised Code and the impoundment of that vehicle's license plates for thirty days.

(3) If the offender previously has been convicted of or pleaded guilty to one violation of this section or of a substantially similar municipal ordinance, the court, in addition to any other sentence that it imposes on the offender and if the vehicle is registered in the offender's name, shall order the immobilization of the vehicle involved in the offense for sixty days in accordance with section 4503.233 of the Revised Code and the impoundment of that vehicle's license plates for sixty days.

(4) If the offender previously has been convicted of or pleaded guilty to two or more violations of this section or of a substantially similar municipal ordinance, the court, in addition to any other sentence that it imposes on the offender and if the vehicle is registered in the offender's name, shall order the criminal forfeiture of the vehicle involved in the offense to the state.

(D) Any order for immobilization and impoundment under this section shall be issued and enforced under section 4503.233 of the Revised Code. The court shall not release a vehicle from immobilization ordered under this section unless the court is presented with current proof of financial responsibility with respect to that vehicle.

(E) Any order of criminal forfeiture under this section shall be issued and enforced under section 4503.234 of the Revised Code. Upon receipt of the copy of the order from the court, neither the registrar of motor vehicles nor a deputy registrar shall accept any application for the registration or transfer of registration of any motor vehicle owned or leased by the person named in the declaration of forfeiture. The period of registration denial shall be five years after the date of the order, unless, during that period, the court having jurisdiction of the offense that led to the order terminates the forfeiture and notifies the registrar of the termination. The registrar then shall take necessary measures to permit the person to register a vehicle owned or leased by the person or to transfer registration of the vehicle.

(2002 S 123, eff. 1–1–04)

4510.12 Operating a motor vehicle without a valid license

(A)(1) No person, except those expressly exempted under sections 4507.03, 4507.04, and 4507.05 of the Revised Code, shall operate any motor vehicle upon a public road or highway or any public or private property used by the public for purposes of vehicular travel or parking in this state unless the person has a valid driver's license issued under Chapter 4507. of the Revised Code or a commercial driver's license issued under Chapter 4506. of the Revised Code.

(2) No person, except a person expressly exempted under sections 4507.03, 4507.04, and 4507.05 of the Revised Code, shall operate any motorcycle upon a public road or highway or any public or private property used by the public for purposes of vehicular travel or parking in this state unless the person has a valid license as a motorcycle operator that was issued upon application by the registrar of motor vehicles under Chapter 4507. of the Revised Code. The license shall be in the form of an endorsement, as determined by the registrar, upon a driver's or commercial driver's license, if the person has a valid license to operate a motor vehicle or commercial motor vehicle, or in the form of a restricted license as provided in section 4507.14 of the Revised Code, if the person does not have a valid license to operate a motor vehicle or commercial motor vehicle.

(B) Whoever violates this section is guilty of operating a motor vehicle without a valid license and shall be punished as follows:

(1) If the trier of fact finds that the offender never has held a valid driver's or commercial driver's license issued by this state or any other jurisdiction, the offense is a misdemeanor of the first degree.

(2)(a) Subject to division (B)(2)(b) of this section, if the offender's driver's or commercial driver's license or permit was expired at the time of the offense for no more than six months, the offense is a minor misdemeanor and if the offender's driver's or commercial driver's license or permit was expired at the time of the offense for more than six months, the offense is a misdemeanor of the fourth degree.

(b)(i) If the offender previously was convicted of or pleaded guilty to one violation of this section or a substantially equivalent municipal ordinance within the past three years, the offense is a misdemeanor of the third degree.

(ii) If the offender previously was convicted of or pleaded guilty to two violations of this section or a substantially equivalent municipal ordinance within the past three years, the offense is a misdemeanor of the second degree.

(iii) If the offender previously was convicted of or pleaded guilty to three or more violations of this section or a substantially equivalent municipal ordinance within the past three years, the offense is a misdemeanor of the first degree.

(C) The court shall not impose a license suspension for a first violation of this section or if more than three years have passed since the offender's last violation of this section or a substantially equivalent municipal ordinance.

(D) If the offender was convicted of or pleaded guilty to one or more violations of this section or a substantially equivalent municipal ordinance within the past three years, and if the offender's license was expired for more than six months at the time of the offense, the court shall impose a class seven suspension of the offender's driver license, commercial driver's license, temporary instruction permit, probationary license, or nonresident operating privilege from the range specified in division (A)(7) of section 4510.02 of the Revised Code.

(2004 H 52, eff. 6–1–04; 2002 S 123, eff. 1–1–04)

4510.13 Mandatory suspension periods; immobilizing or disabling device; restricted license

(A)(1) Divisions (A)(2) to (7) of this section apply to a judge or mayor regarding the suspension of, or the grant of limited driving privileges during a suspension of, an offender's driver's or commercial driver's license or permit or nonresident operating privilege imposed under division (G) or (H) of section 4511.19 of the Revised Code, under division (B) or (C) of section 4511.191 of the Revised Code, or under section 4510.07 of the Revised Code for a conviction of a violation of a municipal OVI ordinance.

(2) No judge or mayor shall suspend the following portions of the suspension of an offender's driver's or commercial driver's license or permit or nonresident operating privilege imposed under division (G) or (H) of section 4511.19 of the Revised Code or under section 4510.07 of the Revised Code for a conviction of a violation of a municipal OVI ordinance, provided that division (A)(2) of this section does not limit a court or mayor in crediting any period of suspension imposed pursuant to division (B) or (C) of section 4511.191 of the Revised Code against any time of judicial suspension imposed pursuant to section 4511.19 or 4510.07 of the Revised Code, as described in divisions (B)(2) and (C)(2) of section 4511.191 of the Revised Code:

(a) The first six months of a suspension imposed under division (G)(1)(a) of section 4511.19 of the Revised Code or of a comparable length suspension imposed under section 4510.07 of the Revised Code;

(b) The first year of a suspension imposed under division (G)(1)(b) or (c) of section 4511.19 of the Revised Code or of a comparable length suspension imposed under section 4510.07 of the Revised Code;

(c) The first three years of a suspension imposed under division (G)(1)(d) or (e) of section 4511.19 of the Revised Code or of a comparable length suspension imposed under section 4510.07 of the Revised Code;

(d) The first sixty days of a suspension imposed under division (H) of section 4511.19 of the Revised Code or of a comparable length suspension imposed under section 4510.07 of the Revised Code.

(3) No judge or mayor shall grant limited driving privileges to an offender whose driver's or commercial driver's license or permit or nonresident operating privilege has been suspended under division (G) or (H) of section 4511.19 of the Revised Code, under division (C) of section 4511.191 of the Revised Code, or under section 4510.07 of the Revised Code for a municipal OVI conviction if the offender, within the preceding six years, has been convicted of or pleaded guilty to three or more violations of one or more of the Revised Code sections, municipal ordinances, statutes of the United States or another state, or municipal ordinances of a municipal corporation of another state that are identified in divisions (G)(2)(b) to (h) of section 2919.22 of the Revised Code.

Additionally, no judge or mayor shall grant limited driving privileges to an offender whose driver's or commercial driver's license or permit or nonresident operating privilege has been suspended under division (B) of section 4511.191 of the Revised Code if the offender, within the preceding six years, has refused three previous requests to consent to a chemical test of the person's whole blood, blood serum or plasma, breath, or urine to determine its alcohol content.

(4) No judge or mayor shall grant limited driving privileges for employment as a driver of commercial motor vehicles to an offender whose driver's or commercial driver's license or permit or nonresident operating privilege has been suspended under division (G) or (H) of section 4511.19 of the Revised Code, under division (B) or (C) of section 4511.191 of the Revised Code, or under section 4510.07 of the Revised Code for a municipal OVI conviction if the offender is disqualified from operating a commercial motor vehicle, or whose license or permit has been suspended, under section 3123.58 or 4506.16 of the Revised Code.

(5) No judge or mayor shall grant limited driving privileges to an offender whose driver's or commercial driver's license or permit or nonresident operating privilege has been suspended under division (G) or (H) of section 4511.19 of the Revised Code, under division (C) of section 4511.191 of the Revised Code, or under section 4510.07 of the Revised Code for a conviction of a violation of a municipal OVI ordinance during any of the following periods of time:

(a) The first fifteen days of a suspension imposed under division (G)(1)(a) of section 4511.19 of the Revised Code or a comparable length suspension imposed under section 4510.07 of the Revised Code, or of a suspension imposed under division (C)(1)(a) of section 4511.191 of the Revised Code. On or after the sixteenth day of the suspension, the court may grant limited driving privileges, but the court may require that the offender shall not exercise the privileges unless the vehicles the offender operates are equipped with immobilizing or disabling devices that monitor the offender's alcohol consumption or any other type of immobilizing or disabling devices, except as provided in division (C) of section 4510.43 of the Revised Code.

(b) The first thirty days of a suspension imposed under division (G)(1)(b) of section 4511.19 of the Revised Code or a comparable length suspension imposed under section 4510.07 of the Revised Code, or of a suspension imposed under division (C)(1)(b) of section 4511.191 of the Revised Code. On or after the thirty-first day of suspension, the court may grant limited driving privileges, but the court may require that the offender shall not exercise the privileges unless the vehicles the offender operates are equipped with immobilizing or disabling devices that monitor the offender's alcohol consumption or any other type of immobilizing or disabling devices, except as provided in division (C) of section 4510.43 of the Revised Code.

(c) The first sixty days of a suspension imposed under division (H) of section 4511.19 of the Revised Code or a comparable length suspension imposed under section 4510.07 of the Revised Code.

(d) The first one hundred eighty days of a suspension imposed under division (G)(1)(c) of section 4511.19 of the Revised Code or a comparable length suspension imposed under section 4510.07 of the Revised Code, or of a suspension imposed under division (C)(1)(c) of section 4511.191 of the Revised Code. The judge may grant limited driving privileges on or after the one hundred eighty-first day of the suspension only if the judge, at the time of granting the privileges, also issues an order prohibiting the offender, while exercising the privileges during the period commencing with the one hundred eighty-first day of suspension and ending with the first year of suspension, from operating any motor vehicle unless it is equipped with an immobilizing or disabling device that monitors the offender's alcohol consumption. After the first year of the suspension, the court may authorize the offender to continue exercising the privileges in vehicles that are not equipped with immobilizing or disabling devices that monitor the offender's alcohol consumption, except as provided in division (C) of section 4510.43 of the Revised Code. If the offender does not petition for limited driving privileges until after the first year of suspension, the judge may grant limited driving privileges without requiring the use of an immobilizing or disabling device that monitors the offender's alcohol consumption.

(e) The first three years of a suspension imposed under division (G)(1)(d) or (e) of section 4511.19 of the Revised Code or a comparable length suspension imposed under section 4510.07 of the Revised Code, or of a suspension imposed under division (C)(1)(d) of section 4511.191 of the Revised Code. The judge may grant limited driving privileges after the first three years of suspension only if the judge, at the time of granting the privileges, also issues an order prohibiting the offender from operating any motor vehicle, for the period of suspension following the first three years of suspension, unless the motor vehicle is equipped with an immobilizing or disabling device that monitors the offender's alcohol consumption, except as provided in division (C) of section 4510.43 of the Revised Code.

(6) No judge or mayor shall grant limited driving privileges to an offender whose driver's or commercial driver's license or permit or nonresident operating privilege has been suspended under division (B) of section 4511.191 of the Revised Code during any of the following periods of time:

(a) The first thirty days of suspension imposed under division (B)(1)(a) of section 4511.191 of the Revised Code;

(b) The first ninety days of suspension imposed under division (B)(1)(b) of section 4511.191 of the Revised Code;

(c) The first year of suspension imposed under division (B)(1)(c) of section 4511.191 of the Revised Code;

(d) The first three years of suspension imposed under division (B)(1)(d) of section 4511.191 of the Revised Code.

(7) In any case in which a judge or mayor grants limited driving privileges to an offender whose driver's or commercial driver's license or permit or nonresident operating privilege has been suspended under division (G)(1)(b), (c), (d), or (e) of section 4511.19 of the Revised Code, under division (G)(1)(a) of section 4511.19 of the Revised Code for a violation of division (A)(1)(f), (g), (h), or (i) of that section, or under section 4510.07 of the Revised Code for a municipal OVI conviction for which sentence would have been imposed under division (G)(1)(a)(ii) or (G)(1)(b), (c), (d), or (e) of section 4511.19 of the Revised Code had the offender been charged with and convicted of a violation of section 4511.19 of the Revised Code instead of a violation of the municipal OVI ordinance, the judge or mayor shall impose as a condition of the privileges that the offender must display on the vehicle that is driven subject to the privileges restricted license plates that are issued under section 4503.231 of the Revised Code, except as provided in division (B) of that section.

(B) Any person whose driver's or commercial driver's license or permit or nonresident operating privilege has been suspended pursuant to section 4511.19 or 4511.191 of the Revised Code or under section 4510.07 of the Revised Code for a violation of a municipal OVI ordinance may file a petition for limited driving privileges during the suspension. The person shall file the petition in the court that has jurisdiction over the place of arrest. Subject to division (A) of this section, the court may grant the person limited driving privileges during the period during which the suspension otherwise would be imposed. However, the court shall not grant the privileges for employment as a driver of a commercial motor vehicle to any person who is disqualified from operating a commercial motor vehicle under section 4506.16 of the Revised Code or during any of the periods prescribed by division (A) of this section.

(C)(1) After a driver's or commercial driver's license or permit or nonresident operating privilege has been suspended pursuant to section 2903.06, 2903.08, 2907.24, 2921.331, 4511.19, 4511.251, 4549.02, 4549.021, or 5743.99 of the Revised Code, any provision of Chapter 2925. of the Revised Code, or section 4510.07 of the Revised Code for a violation of a municipal OVI ordinance, the judge of the court or mayor of the mayor's court that suspended the license, permit, or privilege shall cause the offender to deliver to the court the license or permit. The judge, mayor, or clerk of the court or mayor's court shall forward to the registrar the license or permit together with notice of the action of the court.

(2) A suspension of a commercial driver's license under any section or chapter identified in division (C)(1) of this section shall be concurrent with any period of suspension or disqualification under section 3123.58 or 4506.16 of the Revised Code. No person who is disqualified for life from holding a commercial driver's license under section 4506.16 of the Revised Code shall be issued a driver's license under this chapter during the period for which the commercial driver's license was suspended under this section, and no person whose commercial driver's license is suspended under any section or chapter identified in division (C)(1) of this section shall be issued a driver's license under Chapter 4507. of the Revised Code during the period of the suspension.

(3) No judge or mayor shall suspend any class one suspension, or any portion of any class one suspension, required by section 2903.04 or 2903.06 of the Revised Code. No judge or mayor shall suspend the first thirty days of any class two, class three, class four, class five, or class six suspension imposed under section 2903.06 or 2903.08 of the Revised Code.

(D) The judge of the court or mayor of the mayor's court shall credit any time during which an offender was subject to an administrative suspension of the offender's driver's or commercial driver's license or permit or nonresident operating privilege imposed pursuant to section 4511.191 or 4511. 192 of the Revised Code or a suspension imposed by a judge, referee, or mayor pursuant to division (B)(1) or (2) of section 4511.196 of the Revised Code against the time to be served under a related suspension imposed pursuant to any section or chapter identified in division (C)(1) of this chapter.

(E) The judge or mayor shall notify the bureau of motor vehicles of any determinations made pursuant to this section and of any suspension imposed pursuant to any section or chapter identified in division (C)(1) of this section.

(F)(1) If a court issues an immobilizing or disabling device order under section 4510.43 of the Revised Code, the order shall authorize the offender during the specified period to operate a motor vehicle only if it is equipped with an immobilizing or disabling device, except as provided in division (C) of that section. The court shall provide the offender with a copy of an immobilizing or disabling device order issued under section 4510.43 of the Revised Code, and the offender shall use the copy of the order in lieu of an Ohio driver's or commercial driver's license or permit until the registrar or a deputy registrar issues the offender a restricted license.

An order issued under section 4510.43 of the Revised Code does not authorize or permit the offender to whom it has been issued to operate a vehicle during any time that the offender's driver's or commercial driver's license or permit is suspended under any other provision of law.

(2) An offender may present an immobilizing or disabling device order to the registrar or to a deputy registrar. Upon presentation of the order to the registrar or a deputy registrar, the registrar or deputy registrar shall issue the offender a restricted license. A restricted license issued under this division shall be identical to an Ohio driver's license, except that it shall have printed on its face a statement that the offender is prohibited during the period specified in the court order from operating any motor vehicle that is not equipped with an immobilizing or disabling device. The date of commencement and the date of termination of the period of suspension shall be indicated conspicuously upon the face of the license.

(2004 H 163, eff. 9–23–04; 2002 S 123, eff. 1–1–04)

4510.14 Driving under OVI suspension

(A) No person whose driver's or commercial driver's license or permit or nonresident operating privilege has been suspended under section 4511.19, 4511.191, or 4511.196 of the Revised Code or under section 4510.07 of the Revised Code for a conviction of a violation of a municipal OVI ordinance shall operate any motor vehicle upon the public roads or highways within this state during the period of the suspension.

(B) Whoever violates this section is guilty of driving under OVI suspension. The court shall sentence the offender under Chapter 2929. of the Revised Code, subject to the differences authorized or required by this section.

(1) Except as otherwise provided in division (B)(2) or (3) of this section, driving under OVI suspension is a misdemeanor of the first degree. The court shall sentence the offender to all of the following:

(a) A mandatory jail term of three consecutive days. The three-day term shall be imposed, unless, subject to division (C) of this section, the court instead imposes a sentence of not less than thirty consecutive days of house arrest with electronic monitoring. A period of house arrest with electronic monitoring imposed under this division shall not exceed six months. If the court imposes a mandatory three-day jail term under this division, the court may impose a jail term in addition to that term, provided that in no case shall the cumulative jail term imposed for the offense exceed six months.

(b) A fine of not less than two hundred fifty and not more than one thousand dollars;

(c) A license suspension under division (E) of this section;

(d) If the vehicle the offender was operating at the time of the offense is registered in the offender's name, immobilization for thirty days of the offender's vehicle and impoundment for thirty days of the identification license plates of that vehicle. The order for immobilization and impoundment shall be issued and enforced in accordance with section 4503.233 of the Revised Code.

(2) If, within six years of the offense, the offender previously has been convicted of or pleaded guilty to one violation of this section or one equivalent offense, driving under OVI suspension is a misdemeanor of the first degree. The court shall sentence the offender to all of the following:

(a) A mandatory jail term of ten consecutive days. Notwithstanding the jail terms provided in sections 2929.21 to 2929.28 of the Revised Code, the court may sentence the offender to a longer jail term of not more than one year. The ten-day mandatory jail term shall be imposed unless, subject to division (C) of this section, the court instead imposes a sentence of not less than ninety consecutive days of house arrest with electronic monitoring. The period of house arrest with electronic monitoring shall not exceed one year.

(b) Notwithstanding the fines provided for in Chapter 2929. of the Revised Code, a fine of not less than five hundred and not more than two thousand five hundred dollars;

(c) A license suspension under division (E) of this section;

(d) If the vehicle the offender was operating at the time of the offense is registered in the offender's name, immobilization of the offender's vehicle for sixty days and the impoundment for sixty days of the identification license plates of that vehicle. The order for immobilization and impoundment shall be issued and enforced in accordance with section 4503.233 of the Revised Code.

(3) If, within six years of the offense, the offender previously has been convicted of or pleaded guilty to two or more violations of this section or two or more equivalent offenses, driving under OVI suspension is a misdemeanor. The court shall sentence the offender to all of the following:

(a) A mandatory jail term of thirty consecutive days. Notwithstanding the jail terms provided in sections 2929.21 to 2929.28 of the Revised Code, the court may sentence the offender to a longer jail term of not more than one year. The court shall not sentence the offender to a term of house arrest with electronic monitoring in lieu of the mandatory portion of the jail term.

(b) Notwithstanding the fines set forth in Chapter 2929. of the Revised Code, a fine of not less than five hundred and not more than two thousand five hundred dollars;

(c) A license suspension under division (E) of this section;

(d) If the vehicle the offender was operating at the time of the offense is registered in the offender's name, criminal forfeiture to the state of the offender's vehicle. The order of criminal forfeiture shall be issued and enforced in accordance with section 4503.234 of the Revised Code. If title to a motor vehicle that is subject to an order for criminal forfeiture under this division is assigned or transferred and division (B)(2) or (3) of section 4503.234 of the Revised Code applies, the court may fine the offender the value of the vehicle as determined by publications of the national auto dealer's association. The proceeds from any fine so imposed shall be distributed in accordance with division (C)(2) of section 4503.234 of the Revised Code.

(C) No court shall impose an alternative sentence of house arrest with electronic monitoring under division (B)(1) or (2) of this section unless, within sixty days of the date of sentencing, the court issues a written finding on the record that, due to the unavailability of space at the jail where the offender is required to serve the jail term imposed, the offender will not be able to begin serving that term within the sixty-day period following the date of sentencing.

An offender sentenced under this section to a period of house arrest with electronic monitoring shall be permitted work release during that period.

(D) Fifty per cent of any fine imposed by a court under division (B)(1), (2), or (3) of this section shall be deposited into the county indigent drivers alcohol treatment fund or municipal indigent drivers alcohol treatment fund under the control of that court, as created by the county or municipal corporation pursuant to division (H) of section 4511.191 of the Revised Code.

(E) In addition to or independent of all other penalties provided by law or ordinance, the trial judge of any court of record or the mayor of a mayor's court shall impose on an offender who is convicted of or pleads guilty to a violation of this section a class seven suspension of the offender's driver's or commercial driver's license or permit or nonresident operating privilege from the range specified in division (A)(7) of section 4510.02 of the Revised Code.

When permitted as specified in section 4510.021 of the Revised Code, if the court grants limited driving privileges during a suspension imposed under this section, the privileges shall be granted on the additional condition that the offender must display restricted license plates, issued under section 4503.231 of the Revised Code, on the vehicle driven subject to the privileges, except as provided in division (B) of that section.

A suspension of a commercial driver's license under this section shall be concurrent with any period of suspension or disqualification under section 3123.58 or 4506.16 of the Revised Code. No person who is disqualified for life from holding a commercial driver's license under section 4506.16 of the Revised Code shall be issued a driver's license under Chapter 4507. of the Revised Code during the period for which the commercial driver's license was suspended under this section, and no person whose commercial driver's license is suspended under this section shall be issued a driver's license under Chapter 4507. of the Revised Code during the period of the suspension.

(F) As used in this section:

(1) "Electronic monitoring" has the same meaning as in section 2929.01 of the Revised Code.

(2) "Equivalent offense" means any of the following:

(a) A violation of a municipal ordinance, law of another state, or law of the United States that is substantially equivalent to division (A) of this section;

(b) A violation of a former law of this state that was substantially equivalent to division (A) of this section.

(3) "Jail" has the same meaning as in section 2929.01 of the Revised Code.

(4) "Mandatory jail term" means the mandatory term in jail of three, ten, or thirty consecutive days that must be imposed under division (B)(1), (2), or (3) of this section upon an offender convicted of a violation of division (A) of this section and in relation to which all of the following apply:

(a) Except as specifically authorized under this section, the term must be served in a jail.

(b) Except as specifically authorized under this section, the term cannot be suspended, reduced, or otherwise modified pursuant to any provision of the Revised Code.

(2002 H 490, eff. 1–1–04; 2002 S 123, eff. 1–1–04)

4510.15 License suspension for reckless operation

Whenever a person is found guilty under the laws of this state, or under any ordinance of any political subdivision of this state, of operating a motor vehicle in violation of any such law or ordinance relating to reckless operation, the trial court of any court of record, in addition to or independent of all other penalties provided by law, may impose a class five suspension of the offender's driver's or commercial driver's license or permit or nonresident operating privilege from the range specified in division (A)(5) of section 4510.02 of the Revised Code.

Suspension of a commercial driver's license under this section shall be concurrent with any period of suspension disqualification under section 3123. 58 or 4506.16 of the Revised Code. No person who is disqualified for life from holding a commercial driver's license under section 4506.16 of the Revised Code shall be issued a driver's license under Chapter 4507. of the Revised Code during the period for which the commercial driver's license was suspended under this section, and no person whose commercial driver's license is suspended under this section shall be issued a driver's license under Chapter 4507. of the Revised Code during the period of the suspension.

(2004 H 52, eff. 6–1–04; 2002 S 123, eff. 1–1–04)

Historical and Statutory Notes

Ed. Note: 4510.15 is former 4507.34, amended and recodified by 2002 S 123, eff. 1–1–04, 2000 S 180, eff. 3–22–01; 1995 H 167, eff. 5–15–97; 1993 S 62, § 4, eff. 9–1–93; 1992 S 275; 1989 H 381; 1953 H 1; GC 6296–30.

4510.16 Driving under financial responsibility law suspension or cancellation

(A) No person, whose driver's or commercial driver's license or temporary instruction permit or nonresident's operating privilege has been suspended or canceled pursuant to Chapter 4509. of the Revised Code, shall operate any motor vehicle within this state, or knowingly permit any motor vehicle owned by the person to be operated by another person in the state, during the period of the suspension or cancellation, except as specifically authorized by Chapter 4509. of the Revised Code. No person shall operate a motor vehicle within this state, or knowingly permit any motor vehicle owned by the person to be operated by another person in the state, during the period in which the person is required by section 4509.45 of the Revised Code to file and maintain proof of financial responsibility for a violation of section 4509.101 of the Revised Code, unless proof of financial responsibility is maintained with respect to that vehicle.

(B)(1) Whoever violates this section is guilty of driving under financial responsibility law suspension or cancellation, a misdemeanor of the first degree. The court shall impose a class seven suspension of the offender's driver's or commercial driver's license or permit or nonresident operating privilege for the period of time specified in division (A)(7) of section 4510.02 of the Revised Code.

(2) If the vehicle is registered in the offender's name, the court, in addition to or independent of any other sentence that it imposes upon the offender, shall do one of the following:

(a) Except as otherwise provided in division (B)(2)(b) or (c) of this section, order the immobilization for thirty days of the vehicle involved in the offense and the impoundment for thirty days of the license plates of that vehicle;

(b) If, within five years of the offense, the offender has been convicted of or pleaded guilty to one violation of this section or a substantially similar municipal ordinance, order the immobilization for sixty days of the vehicle involved in the offense and impoundment for sixty days of the license plates of that vehicle;

(c) If, within five years of the offense, the offender has been convicted of or pleaded guilty to two or more violations of this section or a substantially similar municipal ordinance, order the criminal forfeiture to the state of the vehicle involved in the offense. If title to a motor vehicle that is subject to an order for criminal forfeiture under this division is assigned or transferred and division (B)(2) or (3) of section 4503.234 of the Revised Code applies, in addition to or independent of any other penalty established by law, the court may fine the offender the value of the vehicle as determined by publications of the national auto dealers association. The proceeds from any fine so imposed shall be distributed in accordance with division (C)(2) of that section.

(C) Any order for immobilization and impoundment under this section shall be issued and enforced in accordance with sections 4503.233 and 4507.02 of the Revised Code, as applicable. Any order of criminal forfeiture shall be issued and enforced in accordance with section 4503.234 of the Revised Code. The court shall not release a vehicle from immobilization orders under this section unless the court is presented with current proof of financial responsibility with respect to that vehicle.

(2004 H 52, eff. 6–1–04; 2002 S 123, eff. 1–1–04)

4510.161 Immobilization of vehicle; impoundment of license plates; criminal forfeiture of vehicle

(A) The requirements and sanctions imposed by divisions (B) and (C) of this section are an adjunct to and derive from the state's exclusive authority over the registration and titling of motor vehicles and do not comprise a part of the criminal sentence to be imposed upon a person who violates a municipal ordinance that is substantially equivalent to section 4510.14 or to division (A) of section 4510.16 of the Revised Code.

(B) If a person is convicted of or pleads guilty to a municipal ordinance that is substantially equivalent to division (A) of section 4510.16 of the Revised Code, the court, in addition to and independent of any sentence that it imposes upon the offender for the offense, if the vehicle the offender was operating at the time of the offense is registered in the offender's name, shall do whichever of the following is applicable:

(1) If, within five years of the current offense, the offender has not been convicted of or pleaded guilty to a violation of division (A) of section 4510.16 or former division (B)(1) of section 4507.02 of the Revised Code or a municipal ordinance that is substantially equivalent to either division, the court shall order the immobilization for thirty days of the vehicle the offender was operating at the time of the offense and the impoundment for thirty days of the identification license plates of that vehicle.

(2) If, within five years of the current offense, the offender has been convicted of or pleaded guilty to one violation of division

(A) of section 4510.16 or former division (B)(1) of section 4507.02 of the Revised Code or a municipal ordinance that is substantially equivalent to either division, the court shall order the immobilization for sixty days of the vehicle the offender was operating at the time of the offense and the impoundment for sixty days of the identification license plates of that vehicle.

(3) If, within five years of the current offense, the offender has been convicted of or pleaded guilty to two or more violations of division (A) of section 4510.16 or former division (B)(1) of section 4507.02 of the Revised Code or a municipal ordinance that is substantially equivalent to either division, the court shall order the criminal forfeiture to the state of the vehicle the offender was operating at the time of the offense. The order of criminal forfeiture shall be issued and enforced in accordance with section 4503.234 of the Revised Code.

(C) If a person is convicted of or pleads guilty to a municipal ordinance that is substantially equivalent to section 4510.14 of the Revised Code, the court, in addition to and independent of any sentence that it imposes upon the offender for the offense, if the vehicle the offender was operating at the time of the offense is registered in the offender's name, shall do whichever of the following is applicable:

(1) If, within five years of the current offense, the offender has not been convicted of or pleaded guilty to a violation of section 4510.14 or former division (D)(2) of section 4507.02 of the Revised Code or a municipal ordinance that is substantially equivalent to that section or former division, the court shall order the immobilization for thirty days of the vehicle the offender was operating at the time of the offense and the impoundment for thirty days of the identification license plates of that vehicle.

(2) If, within five years of the current offense, the offender has been convicted of or pleaded guilty to one violation of section 4510.14 or former division (D)(2) of section 4507.02 of the Revised Code or a municipal ordinance that is substantially equivalent to that section or former division, the court shall order the immobilization for sixty days of the vehicle the offender was operating at the time of the offense and the impoundment for sixty days of the identification license plates of that vehicle.

(3) If, within five years of the current offense, the offender has been convicted of or pleaded guilty to two or more violations of section 4510.14 or former division (D)(2) of section 4507.02 of the Revised Code or a municipal ordinance that is substantially equivalent to that section or former division, the court shall order the criminal forfeiture to the state of the vehicle the offender was operating at the time of the offense.

(D) An order of criminal forfeiture issued pursuant to this section shall be issued and enforced in accordance with section 4503.234 of the Revised Code. An order for the immobilization and impoundment of a vehicle that issued pursuant to this section shall be issued and enforced in accordance with section 4503.233 of the Revised Code.

(2002 S 123, eff. 1–1–04)

Historical and Statutory Notes

Ed. Note: 4510.161 is former 4507.361, amended and recodified by 2002 S 123, eff. 1–1–04; 1993 S 62, eff. 9–1–93.

4510.17 Drug offense convictions

(A) The registrar of motor vehicles shall impose a class D suspension of the person's driver's license, commercial driver's license, temporary instruction permit, probationary license, or nonresident operating privilege for the period of time specified in division (B)(4) of section 4510.02 of the Revised Code on any person who is a resident of this state and is convicted of or pleads guilty to a violation of a statute of any other state or any federal statute that is substantially similar to section 2925.02, 2925.03, 2925.04, 2925.041, 2925.05, 2925.06, 2925.11, 2925.12, 2925.13, 2925.14, 2925.22, 2925.23, 2925.31, 2925.32, 2925.36, or 2925.37 of the Revised Code. Upon receipt of a report from a court, court clerk, or other official of any other state or from any federal authority that a resident of this state was convicted of or pleaded guilty to an offense described in this division, the registrar shall send a notice by regular first class mail to the person, at the person's last known address as shown in the records of the bureau of motor vehicles, informing the person of the suspension, that the suspension will take effect twenty-one days from the date of the notice, and that, if the person wishes to appeal the suspension or denial, the person must file a notice of appeal within twenty-one days of the date of the notice requesting a hearing on the matter. If the person requests a hearing, the registrar shall hold the hearing not more than forty days after receipt by the registrar of the notice of appeal. The filing of a notice of appeal does not stay the operation of the suspension that must be imposed pursuant to this division. The scope of the hearing shall be limited to whether the person actually was convicted of or pleaded guilty to the offense for which the suspension is to be imposed.

The suspension the registrar is required to impose under this division shall end either on the last day of the class D suspension period or of the suspension of the person's nonresident operating privilege imposed by the state or federal court, whichever is earlier.

The registrar shall subscribe to or otherwise participate in any information system or register, or enter into reciprocal and mutual agreements with other states and federal authorities, in order to facilitate the exchange of information with other states and the United States government regarding persons who plead guilty to or are convicted of offenses described in this division and therefore are subject to the suspension or denial described in this division.

(B) The registrar shall impose a class D suspension of the person's driver's license, commercial driver's license, temporary instruction permit, probationary license, or nonresident operating privilege for the period of time specified in division (B)(4) of section 4510.02 of the Revised Code on any person who is a resident of this state and is convicted of or pleads guilty to a violation of a statute of any other state or a municipal ordinance of a municipal corporation located in any other state that is substantially similar to section 4511.19 of the Revised Code. Upon receipt of a report from another state made pursuant to section 4510.61 of the Revised Code indicating that a resident of this state was convicted of or pleaded guilty to an offense described in this division, the registrar shall send a notice by regular first class mail to the person, at the person's last known address as shown in the records of the bureau of motor vehicles, informing the person of the suspension, that the suspension or denial will take effect twenty-one days from the date of the notice, and that, if the person wishes to appeal the suspension, the person must file a notice of appeal within twenty-one days of the date of the notice requesting a hearing on the matter. If the person requests a hearing, the registrar shall hold the hearing not more than forty days after receipt by the registrar of the notice of appeal. The filing of a notice of appeal does not stay the operation of the suspension that must be imposed pursuant to this division. The scope of the hearing shall be limited to whether the person actually was convicted of or pleaded guilty to the offense for which the suspension is to be imposed.

The suspension the registrar is required to impose under this division shall end either on the last day of the class D suspension period or of the suspension of the person's nonresident operating privilege imposed by the state or federal court, whichever is earlier.

(C) The registrar shall impose a class D suspension of the child's driver's license, commercial driver's license, temporary instruction permit, or nonresident operating privilege for the period of time specified in division (B)(4) of section 4510.02 of the Revised Code on any child who is a resident of this state and is convicted of or pleads guilty to a violation of a statute of any other state or any federal statute that is substantially similar to section 2925.02, 2925.03, 2925.04, 2925.041, 2925.05, 2925.06, 2925.11, 2925.12, 2925.13, 2925.14, 2925.22, 2925.23, 2925.31, 2925.32, 2925. 36, or 2925.37 of the Revised Code. Upon receipt of a report from a court, court clerk, or other official of any other state or from any federal authority that a child who is a resident of this state was convicted of or pleaded guilty to an offense described in this division, the registrar shall send a notice by regular first class mail to the child, at the child's last known address as shown in the records of the bureau of motor vehicles, informing the child of the suspension, that the suspension or denial will take effect twenty-one days from the date of the notice, and that, if the child wishes to appeal the suspension, the child must file a notice of appeal within twenty-one days of the date of the notice requesting a hearing on the matter. If the child requests a hearing, the registrar shall hold the hearing not more than forty days after receipt by the registrar of the notice of appeal. The filing of a notice of appeal does not stay the operation of the suspension that must be imposed pursuant to this division. The scope of the hearing shall be limited to whether the child actually was convicted of or pleaded guilty to the offense for which the suspension is to be imposed.

The suspension the registrar is required to impose under this division shall end either on the last day of the class D suspension period or of the suspension of the child's nonresident operating privilege imposed by the state or federal court, whichever is earlier. If the child is a resident of this state who is sixteen years of age or older and does not have a current, valid Ohio driver's or commercial driver's license or permit, the notice shall inform the child that the child will be denied issuance of a driver's or commercial driver's license or permit for six months beginning on the date of the notice. If the child has not attained the age of sixteen years on the date of the notice, the notice shall inform the child that the period of denial of six months shall commence on the date the child attains the age of sixteen years.

The registrar shall subscribe to or otherwise participate in any information system or register, or enter into reciprocal and mutual agreements with other states and federal authorities, in order to facilitate the exchange of information with other states and the United States government regarding children who are residents of this state and plead guilty to or are convicted of offenses described in this division and therefore are subject to the suspension or denial described in this division.

(D) The registrar shall impose a class D suspension of the child's driver's license, commercial driver's license, temporary instruction permit, probationary license, or nonresident operating privilege for the period of time specified in division (B)(4) of section 4510.02 of the Revised Code on any child who is a resident of this state and is convicted of or pleads guilty to a violation of a statute of any other state or a municipal ordinance of a municipal corporation located in any other state that is substantially similar to section 4511.19 of the Revised Code. Upon receipt of a report from another state made pursuant to section 4510.61 of the Revised Code indicating that a child who is a resident of this state was convicted of or pleaded guilty to an offense described in this division, the registrar shall send a notice by regular first class mail to the child, at the child's last known address as shown in the records of the bureau of motor vehicles, informing the child of the suspension, that the suspension will take effect twenty-one days from the date of the notice, and that, if the child wishes to appeal the suspension, the child must file a notice of appeal within twenty-one days of the date of the notice requesting a hearing on the matter. If the child requests a hearing, the registrar shall hold the hearing not more than forty days after receipt by the registrar of the notice of appeal. The filing of a notice of appeal does not stay the operation of the suspension that must be imposed pursuant to this division. The scope of the hearing shall be limited to whether the child actually was convicted of or pleaded guilty to the offense for which the suspension is to be imposed.

The suspension the registrar is required to impose under this division shall end either on the last day of the class D suspension period or of the suspension of the child's nonresident operating privilege imposed by the state or federal court, whichever is earlier. If the child is a resident of this state who is sixteen years of age or older and does not have a current, valid Ohio driver's or commercial driver's license or permit, the notice shall inform the child that the child will be denied issuance of a driver's or commercial driver's license or permit for six months beginning on the date of the notice. If the child has not attained the age of sixteen years on the date of the notice, the notice shall inform the child that the period of denial of six months shall commence on the date the child attains the age of sixteen years.

(E) Any person whose license or permit has been suspended pursuant to this section may file a petition in the municipal or county court, or in case the person is under eighteen years of age, the juvenile court, in whose jurisdiction the person resides, agreeing to pay the cost of the proceedings and alleging that the suspension would seriously affect the person's ability to continue the person's employment. Upon satisfactory proof that there is reasonable cause to believe that the suspension would seriously affect the person's ability to continue the person's employment, the judge may grant the person limited driving privileges during the period during which the suspension otherwise would be imposed, except that the judge shall not grant limited driving privileges for employment as a driver of a commercial motor vehicle to any person who would be disqualified from operating a commercial motor vehicle under section 4506.16 of the Revised Code if the violation had occurred in this state, or during any of the following periods of time:

(1) The first fifteen days of a suspension under division (B) or (D) of this section, if the person has not been convicted within six years of the date of the offense giving rise to the suspension under this section of a violation of any of the following:

(a) Section 4511.19 of the Revised Code, or a municipal ordinance relating to operating a vehicle while under the influence of alcohol, a drug of abuse, or alcohol and a drug of abuse;

(b) A municipal ordinance relating to operating a motor vehicle with a prohibited concentration of alcohol in the blood, breath, or urine;

(c) Section 2903.04 of the Revised Code in a case in which the person was subject to the sanctions described in division (D) of that section;

(d) Division (A)(1) of section 2903.06 or division (A)(1) of section 2903. 08 of the Revised Code or a municipal ordinance that is substantially similar to either of those divisions;

(e) Division (A)(2), (3), or (4) of section 2903.06, division (A)(2) of section 2903.08, or as it existed prior to March 23, 2000, section 2903.07 of the Revised Code, or a municipal ordinance that is substantially similar to any of those divisions or that former section, in a case in which the jury or judge found that the person was under the influence of alcohol, a drug of abuse, or alcohol and a drug of abuse.

(2) The first thirty days of a suspension under division (B) or (D) of this section, if the person has been convicted one time within six years of the date of the offense giving rise to the suspension under this section of any violation identified in division (E)(1) of this section.

(3) The first one hundred eighty days of a suspension under division (B) or (D) of this section, if the person has been convicted two times within six years of the date of the offense giving rise to the suspension under this section of any violation identified in division (E)(1) of this section.

(4) No limited driving privileges may be granted if the person has been convicted three or more times within five years of the date of the offense giving rise to a suspension under division (B) or (D) of this section of any violation identified in division (E)(1) of this section.

If a person petitions for limited driving privileges under division (E) of this section, the registrar shall be represented by the county prosecutor of the county in which the person resides if the petition is filed in a juvenile court or county court, except that if the person resides within a city or village that is located within the jurisdiction of the county in which the petition is filed, the city director of law or village solicitor of that city or village shall represent the registrar. If the petition is filed in a municipal court, the registrar shall be represented as provided in section 1901.34 of the Revised Code.

In granting limited driving privileges under division (E) of this section, the court may impose any condition it considers reasonable and necessary to limit the use of a vehicle by the person. The court shall deliver to the person a permit card, in a form to be prescribed by the court, setting forth the time, place, and other conditions limiting the person's use of a motor vehicle. The grant of limited driving privileges shall be conditioned upon the person's having the permit in the person's possession at all times during which the person is operating a vehicle.

A person granted limited driving privileges who operates a vehicle for other than limited purposes, in violation of any condition imposed by the court or without having the permit in the person's possession, is guilty of a violation of section 4510.11 of the Revised Code.

(F) As used in divisions (C) and (D) of this section:

(1) "Child" means a person who is under the age of eighteen years, except that any person who violates a statute or ordinance described in division (C) or (D) of this section prior to attaining eighteen years of age shall be deemed a "child" irrespective of the person's age at the time the complaint or other equivalent document is filed in the other state or a hearing, trial, or other proceeding is held in the other state on the complaint or other equivalent document, and irrespective of the person's age when the period of license suspension or denial prescribed in division (C) or (D) of this section is imposed.

(2) "Is convicted of or pleads guilty to" means, as it relates to a child who is a resident of this state, that in a proceeding conducted in a state or federal court located in another state for a violation of a statute or ordinance described in division (C) or (D) of this section, the result of the proceeding is any of the following:

(a) Under the laws that govern the proceedings of the court, the child is adjudicated to be or admits to being a delinquent child or a juvenile traffic offender for a violation described in division (C) or (D) of this section that would be a crime if committed by an adult;

(b) Under the laws that govern the proceedings of the court, the child is convicted of or pleads guilty to a violation described in division (C) or (D) of this section;

(c) Under the laws that govern the proceedings of the court, irrespective of the terminology utilized in those laws, the result of the court's proceedings is the functional equivalent of division (F)(2)(a) or (b) of this section.

(2004 H 163, eff. 9–23–04; 2002 S 123, eff. 1–1–04)

Historical and Statutory Notes

Ed. Note: RC 4510.17 is former RC 4507.169, amended and recodified by 2002 S 123, eff. 1–1–04; 2001 H 7, eff. 8–7–01; 1999 S 107, eff. 3–23–00; 1997 S 60, eff. 10–21–97; 1996 H 353, eff. 9–17–96; 1995 S 2, eff. 7–1–96; 1993 H 377, eff. 9–30–93.

4510.21 Failure to reinstate a license

(A) No person whose driver's license, commercial driver's license, temporary instruction permit, or nonresident's operating privilege has been suspended shall operate any motor vehicle upon a public road or highway or any public or private property after the suspension has expired unless the person has complied with all license reinstatement requirements imposed by the court, the bureau of motor vehicles, or another provision of the Revised Code.

(B) Whoever violates this section is guilty of failure to reinstate a license, a misdemeanor of the first degree. The court may impose upon the offender a class seven suspension of the offender's driver's license, commercial driver's license, temporary instruction permit, probationary driver's license, or nonresident operating privilege from the range specified in division (A)(7) of section 4510.02 of the Revised Code.

(2002 S 123, eff. 1–1–04)

4510.22 Forfeiture upon failure to appear in court or to pay fines

(A) If a person who has a current valid Ohio driver's, commercial driver's license, or temporary instruction permit is charged with a violation of any provision in sections 4511.01 to 4511.76, 4511.84, 4513.01 to 4513.65, or 4549.01 to 4549.65 of the Revised Code that is classified as a misdemeanor of the first, second, third, or fourth degree or with a violation of any substantially equivalent municipal ordinance and if the person either fails to appear in court at the required time and place to answer the charge or pleads guilty to or is found guilty of the violation and fails within the time allowed by the court to pay the fine imposed by the court, the court shall declare the forfeiture of the person's license. Thirty days after the declaration of forfeiture, the court shall inform the registrar of motor vehicles of the forfeiture by entering information relative to the of forfeiture on a form approved and furnished by the registrar and sending the form to the registrar. The court also shall forward the person's license, if it is in the possession of the court, to the registrar.

The registrar shall impose a class F suspension of the person's driver's or commercial driver's license, or temporary instruction permit for the period of time specified in division (B)(6) of section 4510.02 of the Revised Code on any person who is named in a declaration received by the registrar under this section. The registrar shall send written notification of the suspension to the person at the person's last known address and, if the person is in possession of the license, order the person to surrender the person's license or permit to the registrar within forty-eight hours.

No valid driver's or commercial driver's license shall be granted to the person after the suspension, unless the court having jurisdiction of the offense that led to the suspension orders that the forfeiture be terminated. The court shall order the termination of the forfeiture if the person thereafter appears to answer the charge and pays any fine imposed by the court or pays the fine originally imposed by the court. The court shall inform the registrar of the termination of the forfeiture by entering information relative to the termination on a form approved and furnished by the registrar and sending the form to the registrar. The person shall pay to the bureau of motor vehicles a fifteen-dollar reinstatement fee to cover the costs of the bureau in administering this section. The registrar shall deposit the fee into the state bureau of motor vehicles fund created by section 4501.25 of the Revised Code.

(B) In addition to suspending the driver's or commercial driver's license or permit of the person named in a declaration of forfeiture, the registrar, upon receipt from the court of the copy of the declaration of forfeiture, shall take any measures that may be necessary to ensure that neither the registrar nor any deputy registrar accepts any application for the registration or transfer of registration of any motor vehicle owned or leased by the person named in the declaration of forfeiture. However, for a motor vehicle leased by a person named in a declaration of forfeiture, the registrar shall not implement the preceding sentence until the registrar adopts procedures for that implementation under section 4503.39 of the Revised Code. The period of denial of registration or transfer shall continue until such time as the court having jurisdiction of the offense that led to the suspension orders the forfeiture be terminated. Upon receipt by the registrar of an order terminating the forfeiture, the registrar also shall take any measures that may be necessary to permit the person to register a motor vehicle owned or leased by the person or to transfer the registration of such a motor vehicle, if the person later makes application to take such action and otherwise is eligible to register the motor vehicle or to transfer its registration.

The registrar shall not be required to give effect to any declaration of forfeiture or order terminating a forfeiture provided by a court under this section unless the information contained in the declaration or order is transmitted to the registrar by means of an electronic transfer system. The registrar shall not restore the person's driving or vehicle registration privileges until the person pays the reinstatement fee as provided in this section.

The period of denial relating to the issuance or transfer of a certificate of registration for a motor vehicle imposed pursuant to this division remains in effect until the person pays any fine imposed by the court relative to the offense.

(2004 H 230, eff. 9–16–04; 2002 S 123, eff. 1–1–04)

Historical and Statutory Notes

Ed. Note: RC 4510.22 is former RC 4507.168, amended and recodified by 2002 S 123, eff. 1–1–04; 1997 S 85, eff. 5–15–97; 1996 S 121, eff. 11–19–96; 1996 H 353, eff. 9–17–96; 1994 H 687, eff. 10–12–94; 1993 S 62, § 4, eff. 9–1–93; 1992 S 275, S 331; 1990 S 285, S 338.

4510.23 Suspension upon adjudication of incompetence

When any person having a driver's or commercial driver's license is adjudicated incompetent for the purpose of holding the license, as provided in section 5122.301 of the Revised Code, the probate judge shall order the license of the person delivered to the court. The court shall forward the license with notice of the adjudication to the registrar of motor vehicles. The registrar shall impose a class F suspension of the person's driver's or commercial driver's license for the period of time specified in division (B)(6) of section 4510.02 of the Revised Code. The suspension shall remain in effect until receipt of written notice by the head of the hospital, or other agency which has or had custody of such person, that such person's mental illness is not an impairment to such person's ability to operate a motor vehicle, or upon receipt of notice from the adjudicating court that such person has been restored to competency by court decree.

(2002 S 123, eff. 1–1–04)

Historical and Statutory Notes

Ed. Note: 4510.23 is former 4507.161, amended and recodified by 2002 S 123, eff. 1–1–04; 1989 H 381, eff. 7–1–89; 1977 H 725; 130 v H 758; 129 v 1448; 126 v 600.

4510.31 Suspension upon adjudication in juvenile court

(A)(1) Except as provided in division (C) of this section, the registrar of motor vehicles shall suspend the probationary driver's license, restricted license, or temporary instruction permit issued to any person when the person has been convicted of, pleaded guilty to, or been adjudicated in juvenile court of having committed, prior to the person's eighteenth birthday, any of the following:

(a) Three separate violations of section 2903.06, 2903.08, 2921.331, 4511. 12, 4511.13, 4511.15, 4511.191, 4511.20, 4511.201, 4511.202, 4511.21, 4511.22, 4511.23, 4511.25 to 4511.48, 4511.57 to 4511.65, 4511.75, 4549.02, 4549.021, or 4549.03 of the Revised Code, section 4510.14 of the Revised Code involving a suspension imposed under section 4511.191 or 4511.196 of the Revised Code, section 2903.04 of the Revised Code in a case in which the person would have been subject to the sanctions described in division (D) of that section had the person been convicted of the violation of that section, former section 2903.07 of the Revised Code, or any municipal ordinances similarly relating to the offenses referred to in those sections;

(b) One violation of section 4511.19 of the Revised Code or a substantially similar municipal ordinance;

(c) Two separate violations of any of the Revised Code sections referred to in division (A)(1)(a) of this section, or any municipal ordinance that is substantially similar to any of those sections.

(2) Any person whose license or permit is suspended under division (A)(1)(a), (b), or (c) of this section shall mail or deliver the person's probationary driver's license, restricted license, or temporary instruction permit to the registrar within fourteen days of notification of the suspension. The registrar shall retain the license or permit during the period of the suspension. A suspension pursuant to division (A)(1)(a) of this section shall be a class C suspension, a suspension pursuant to division (A)(1)(b) of this section shall be a class D suspension, and a suspension pursuant to division (A)(1)(c) of this section shall be a class E suspension, all for the periods of time specified in division (B) of section 4510.02 of the Revised Code. If the person's probationary driver's license, restricted license, or temporary instruction permit is under suspension on the date the court imposes sentence upon the person for a violation described in division (A)(1)(b) of this section, the suspension shall take effect on the next day immediately following the end of that period of suspension. If the person is sixteen years of age or older and pleads guilty to or is convicted of a violation described in division (A)(1)(b) of this section and the person does not have a current, valid probationary driver's license, restricted license, or temporary instruction permit, the registrar shall deny the issuance to the person of a probationary driver's license, restricted license, driver's license, commercial driver's license, or temporary instruction permit, as the case may be, for six months beginning on the date the court imposes sentence upon the person for the violation. If the person has not attained the age of sixteen years on the date the court imposes sentence upon the person for the violation, the period of denial shall commence on the date the person attains the age of sixteen years.

(3) The registrar shall suspend the person's license or permit under division (A) of this section regardless of whether the disposition of the case in juvenile court occurred after the person's eighteenth birthday.

(B) The registrar also shall impose a class D suspension for the period of time specified in division (B)(4) of section 4510.02 of the Revised Code of the temporary instruction permit or probationary driver's license of any person under the age of eighteen who has been adjudicated an unruly child, delinquent child, or juvenile traffic offender for having committed any act that if committed by an adult would be a drug abuse offense or a violation of division (B) of section 2917.11 of the Revised Code. The registrar, in the registrar's discretion, may terminate the suspension if the child, at the discretion of the court, attends and satisfactorily completes a drug abuse or alcohol abuse education, intervention, or treatment program specified by the court. Any person whose temporary instruction permit or probationary driver's license is suspended under this division shall mail or deliver the person's permit or license to the registrar within fourteen days of notification of the suspension. The registrar shall retain the permit or license during the period of the suspension.

(C)(1) Except as provided in division (C)(3) of this section, for any person who is convicted of, pleads guilty to, or is adjudicated in juvenile court of having committed a second or third violation of section 4511.12, 4511.13, 4511.15, 4511.20 to 4511.23, 4511.25,

4511.26 to 4511.48, 4511.57 to 4511.65, or 4511.75 of the Revised Code or any similar municipal ordinances and whose license or permit is suspended under division (A)(1)(a) or (c) of this section, the court in which the second or third conviction, finding, plea, or adjudication resulting in the suspension was made, upon petition of the person, may grant the person limited driving privileges during the period during which the suspension otherwise would be imposed under division (A)(1)(a) or (c) of this section if the court finds reasonable cause to believe that the suspension will seriously affect the person's ability to continue in employment, educational training, vocational training, or treatment. In granting the limited driving privileges, the court shall specify the purposes, times, and places of the privileges and may impose any other conditions upon the person's driving a motor vehicle that the court considers reasonable and necessary.

A court that grants limited driving privileges to a person under this division shall retain the person's probationary driver's license, restricted license, or temporary instruction permit during the period the license or permit is suspended and also during the period for which limited driving privileges are granted, and shall deliver to the person a permit card, in a form to be prescribed by the court, setting forth the date on which the limited driving privileges will become effective, the purposes for which the person may drive, the times and places at which the person may drive, and any other conditions imposed upon the person's use of a motor vehicle.

The court immediately shall notify the registrar, in writing, of a grant of limited driving privileges under this division. The notification shall specify the date on which the limited driving privileges will become effective, the purposes for which the person may drive, the times and places at which the person may drive, and any other conditions imposed upon the person's use of a motor vehicle. The registrar shall not suspend the probationary driver's license, restricted license, or temporary instruction permit of any person pursuant to division (A) of this section during any period for which the person has been granted limited driving privileges as provided in this division, if the registrar has received the notification described in this division from the court.

(2) Except as provided in division (C)(3) of this section, in any case in which the temporary instruction permit or probationary driver's license of a person under eighteen years of age has been suspended under division (A) or (B) of this section or any other provision of law, the court may grant the person limited driving privileges for the purpose of the person's practicing of driving with the person's parent, guardian, or other custodian during the period of the suspension. Any grant of limited driving privileges under this division shall comply with division (D) of section 4510.021 of the Revised Code.

(3) A court shall not grant limited driving privileges to a person identified in division (C)(1) or (2) of this section if the person, within the preceding six years, has been convicted of, pleaded guilty to, or adjudicated in juvenile court of having committed three or more violations of one or more of the divisions or sections set forth in divisions (G)(2)(b) to (g) of section 2919.22 of the Revised Code.

(D) If a person who has been granted limited driving privileges under division (C) of this section is convicted of, pleads guilty to, or is adjudicated in juvenile court of having committed, a violation of Chapter 4510. of the Revised Code, or a subsequent violation of any of the sections of the Revised Code listed in division (A)(1)(a) of this section or any similar municipal ordinance during the period for which the person was granted limited driving privileges, the court that granted the limited driving privileges shall suspend the person's permit card. The court or the clerk of the court immediately shall forward the person's probationary driver's license, restricted license, or temporary instruction permit together with written notification of the court's action to the registrar. Upon receipt of the license or permit and notification, the registrar shall impose a class C suspension of the person's probationary driver's license, restricted license, or temporary instruction permit for the period of time specified in division (B)(3) of section 4510.02 of the Revised Code. The registrar shall retain the license or permit during the period of suspension, and no further limited driving privileges shall be granted during that period.

(E) No application for a driver's or commercial driver's license shall be received from any person whose probationary driver's license, restricted license, or temporary instruction permit has been suspended under this section until each of the following has occurred:

(1) The suspension period has expired;

(2) A temporary instruction permit or commercial driver's license temporary instruction permit has been issued;

(3) The person successfully completes a juvenile driver improvement program approved by the registrar under section 4510.311 of the Revised Code;

(4) The applicant has submitted to the examination for a driver's license as provided for in section 4507.11 or a commercial driver's license as provided in Chapter 4506. of the Revised Code.

(2004 H 230, eff. 9–16–04; 2002 S 123, eff. 1–1–04)

Historical and Statutory Notes

Ed. Note: RC 4510.31 is former RC 4507.162, amended and recodified by 2002 S 123, eff. 1–1–04; 2002 H 490, eff. 4–3–03; 1999 S 107, eff. 3–23–00; 1997 S 35, eff. 1–1–99; 1997 S 60, eff. 10–21–97; 1994 H 236, eff. 9–29–94; 1993 H 377, eff. 9–30–93; 1993 S 62, § 4; 1992 S 275; 1990 S 131; 1989 S 49, H 381, H 330, H 329; 1988 H 643; 1984 H 252; 1973 S 1; 132 v H 380; 130 v H 772; 129 v 1599; 128 v 539; 127 v 839.

4510.311 Juvenile driver improvement programs

The registrar of motor vehicles shall establish standards for juvenile driver improvement programs and shall approve any programs that meet the established standards. The standards established by the registrar shall require a minimum of five hours of classroom instruction, with at least three hours devoted to driver skill requirements and two hours devoted to juvenile driver information related to the driving records of drivers under eighteen years of age, driver perceptions, and the value of the traffic laws. The standards also shall require a person whose probationary driver's license was suspended under section 4510.31 of the Revised Code to undertake and pass, as successful completion of an approved juvenile driver improvement program, the driver's license examination that a person who holds a temporary instruction permit is required to undertake and pass in order to be issued a probationary driver's license. The person shall pay the applicable fee that is required to accompany an application for a driver's license as prescribed in division (E) of section 4507.23 of the Revised Code. The registrar shall prescribe the requirements for the curriculum to be provided as well as other program directives. Only those programs approved by the registrar shall be acceptable for reinstatement of the driving privileges of a person whose probationary driver's license was suspended under section 4510.31 of the Revised Code.

(2002 S 123, eff. 1–1–04)

4510.32 Suspension of truant, suspended or expelled school pupils; notice; petition to juvenile court

(A) The registrar of motor vehicles shall record within ten days of receipt and keep at the main office of the bureau of motor vehicles all information provided to the registrar by the superintendent of a school district in accordance with division (B) of section 3321.13 of the Revised Code.

(B) Whenever the registrar receives a notice under division (B) of section 3321.13 of the Revised Code, the registrar shall impose a class F suspension of the temporary instruction permit or driver's license of the person who is the subject of the notice for the period of time specified in division (B)(6) of section 4510.02 of the Revised Code, or, if the person has not been issued a temporary instruction permit or driver's license, the registrar shall deny to the person the issuance of a permit or license. The requirements of the second paragraph of section 119.06 of the Revised Code do not apply to a suspension of a person's temporary instruction permit or driver's license or a denial of a person's opportunity to obtain a temporary instruction permit or driver's license by the registrar under this division.

(C) Upon suspending the temporary instruction permit or driver's license of any person or denying any person the opportunity to be issued such a license or permit as provided in division (B) of this section, the registrar immediately shall notify the person in writing of the suspension or denial and inform the person that the person may petition for a hearing as provided in division (E) of this section.

(D) Any person whose permit or license is suspended under this section shall mail or deliver the person's permit or license to the registrar of motor vehicles within twenty days of notification of the suspension; however, the person's permit or license and the person's driving privileges shall be suspended immediately upon receipt of the notification. The registrar may retain the permit or license during the period of the suspension or the registrar may destroy it under section 4510.52 of the Revised Code.

(E) Any person whose temporary instruction permit or driver's license has been suspended, or whose opportunity to obtain such a permit or license has been denied pursuant to this section, may file a petition in the juvenile court in whose jurisdiction the person resides alleging error in the action taken by the registrar under division (B) of this section or alleging one or more of the matters within the scope of the hearing, as described in this division, or both. The petitioner shall notify the registrar and the superintendent of the school district who gave the notice to the registrar and juvenile judge under division (B) of section 3321.13 of the Revised Code of the filing of the petition and send them copies of the petition. The scope of the hearing is limited to the issues of whether the notice given by the superintendent to the registrar was in error and whether the suspension or denial of driving privileges will result in substantial hardship to the petitioner.

The registrar shall furnish the court a copy of the record created in accordance with division (A) of this section. The registrar and the superintendent shall furnish the court with any other relevant information required by the court.

In hearing the matter and determining whether the petitioner has shown that the petitioner's temporary instruction permit or driver's license should not be suspended or that the petitioner's opportunity to obtain such a permit or license should not be denied, the court shall decide the issue upon the information furnished by the registrar and the superintendent and any such additional evidence that the registrar, the superintendent, or the petitioner submits.

If the court finds from the evidence submitted that the petitioner has failed to show error in the action taken by the registrar under division (B) of this section and has failed to prove any of the matters within the scope of the hearing, then the court may assess the cost of the proceeding against the petitioner and shall uphold the suspension of the petitioner's permit or license or the denial of the petitioner's opportunity to obtain a permit or license. If the court finds that the petitioner has shown error in the action taken by the registrar under division (B) of this section or has proved one or more of the matters within the scope of the hearing, or both, the cost of the proceeding shall be paid out of the county treasury of the county in which the proceedings were held, and the suspension of the petitioner's permit or license or the denial of the person's opportunity to obtain a permit or license shall be terminated.

(F) The registrar shall cancel the record created under this section of any person who is the subject of a notice given under division (B) of section 3321.13 of the Revised Code and shall terminate the suspension of the person's permit or license or the denial of the person's opportunity to obtain a permit or license, if any of the following applies:

(1) The person is at least eighteen years of age.

(2) The person provides evidence, as the registrar shall require by rule, of receipt of a high school diploma or a general educational development certificate of high school equivalence.

(3) The superintendent of a school district informs the registrar that the notification of withdrawal, habitual absence without legitimate excuse, suspension, or expulsion concerning the person was in error.

(4) The suspension or denial was imposed subsequent to a notification given under division (B)(3) or (4) of section 3321.13 of the Revised Code, and the superintendent of a school district informs the registrar that the person in question has satisfied any terms or conditions established by the school as necessary to terminate the suspension or denial of driving privileges.

(5) The suspension or denial was imposed subsequent to a notification given under division (B)(1) of section 3321.13 of the Revised Code, and the superintendent of a school district informs the registrar that the person in question is now attending school or enrolled in and attending an approved program to obtain a diploma or its equivalent to the satisfaction of the school superintendent.

(6) The suspension or denial was imposed subsequent to a notification given under division (B)(2) of section 3321.13 of the Revised Code, the person has completed at least one semester or term of school after the one in which the notification was given, the person requests the superintendent of the school district to notify the registrar that the person no longer is habitually absent without legitimate excuse, the superintendent determines that the person has not been absent from school without legitimate excuse in the current semester or term, as determined under that division, for more than ten consecutive school days or for more than fifteen total school days, and the superintendent informs the registrar of that fact. If a person described in division (F)(6) of this section requests the superintendent of the school district to notify the registrar that the person no longer is habitually absent without legitimate excuse and the superintendent makes the determination described in this division, the superintendent shall provide the information described in division (F)(6) of this section to the registrar within five days after receiving the request.

(7) The suspension or denial was imposed subsequent to a notification given under division (B)(2) of section 3321.13 of the Revised Code, and the superintendent of a school district informs the registrar that the person in question has received an age and schooling certificate in accordance with section 3331.01 of the Revised Code.

(8) The person filed a petition in court under division (E) of this section and the court found that the person showed error in the action taken by the registrar under division (B) of this section or proved one or more of the matters within the scope of the hearing on the petition, as set forth in division (E) of this section, or both.

At the end of the suspension period under this section and upon the request of the person whose temporary instruction permit or driver's license was suspended, the registrar shall return the driver's license or permit to the person or reissue the person's license or permit under section 4510.52 of the Revised Code, if the registrar destroyed the suspended license or permit under that section.

(2002 S 123, eff. 1–1–04)

Historical and Statutory Notes

Ed. Note: 4510.32 is former 4507.061, amended and recodified by 2002 S 123, eff. 1–1–04; 1999 S 1, eff. 8–6–99; 1994 H 687, eff. 10–12–94; 1990 H 204, eff. 5–2–90.

4510.33 Use of license to violate liquor laws; suspension; procedures

(A) No person of insufficient age to purchase intoxicating liquor or beer, contrary to division (A) or (C) of section 4507.30 of the Revised Code, shall display as proof that the person is of sufficient age to purchase intoxicating liquor or beer, a driver's or commercial driver's license, knowing the same to be fictitious, altered, or not the person's own. The registrar of motor vehicles shall impose a class C suspension of the person's driver's license, probationary driver's license, commercial driver's license, temporary instruction permit, or commercial driver's license temporary instruction permit for the period of time specified in division (B)(3) of section 4510.02 of the Revised Code upon the offender and shall not issue or reissue a license or permit of that type to the offender during the suspension period.

(B) In any prosecution, or in any proceeding before the liquor control commission, in which the defense authorized by section 4301.639 of the Revised Code is sustained, the clerk of the court in which the prosecution was had, or the clerk of the liquor control commission, shall certify to the registrar the facts ascertainable from the clerk's records evidencing violation of division (A) or (C) of section 4507.30 of the Revised Code by a person of insufficient age to purchase intoxicating liquor or beer, including in the certification the person's name and residence address.

(C) The registrar, upon receipt of the certification, shall suspend the person's license or permit to drive subject to review as provided in this section, and shall mail to the person, at the person's last known address, a notice of the suspension and of the hearing provided in division (D) of this section.

(D) Any person whose license or permit to drive has been suspended under this section, within twenty days of the mailing of the notice provided above, may file a petition in the municipal court or county court, or in case the person is under the age of eighteen years, in the juvenile court, in whose jurisdiction the person resides, agreeing to pay the cost of the proceedings, and alleging error by the registrar in the suspension of the license or permit to drive, or in one or more of the matters within the scope of the hearing as provided in this section, or both. The petitioner shall notify the registrar of the filing of the petition and send the registrar a copy thereof. The scope of the hearing shall be limited to whether a court of record did in fact find that the petitioner displayed, or, if the original proceedings were before the liquor control commission, whether the petitioner did in fact display, as proof that the person was of sufficient age to purchase intoxicating liquor or beer, a driver's or commercial driver's license knowing the same to be fictitious, altered, or not the person's own, and whether the person was at that time of insufficient age legally to make a purchase of intoxicating liquor or beer.

(E) In any hearing authorized by this section, the registrar shall be represented by the prosecuting attorney of the county where the petitioner resides.

(F) If the court finds from the evidence submitted that the person has failed to show error in the action by the registrar or in one or more of the matters within the scope of the hearing as limited in division (D) of this section, or both, the court shall assess the cost of the proceeding against the person and shall impose the suspension provided in divisions (A) and (C) of this section. If the court finds that the person has shown error in the action taken by the registrar, or in one or more of the matters within the scope of the hearing as limited in division (B) of this section, or both, the cost of the proceeding shall be paid out of the county treasury of the county in which the proceedings were held, and the suspension provided in divisions (A) and (C) of this section shall not be imposed. The court shall inform the registrar in writing of the action taken.

(2002 S 123, eff. 1–1–04)

Historical and Statutory Notes

Ed. Note: 4510.33 is former 4507.163, amended and recodified by 2002 S 123, eff. 1–1–04; 1997 S 60, eff. 10–21–97; 1989 H 381, eff. 7–1–89; 1972 H 453.

4510.34 Suspension of probationary motorized bicycle license

(A) The registrar of motor vehicles shall impose a class F suspension for the period of time specified in division (B)(6) of section 4510.02 of the Revised Code of the probationary motorized bicycle license issued to any person when the person has been convicted of or has been adjudicated in juvenile court of having committed, a violation of division (A) or (D) of section 4511.521 of the Revised Code, or of any other section of the Revised Code or similar municipal ordinance for which points are chargeable under section 4510.036 of the Revised Code.

(B) Any person whose license is suspended under this section shall mail or deliver the person's probationary motorized bicycle license to the registrar within fourteen days of notification of the suspension. The registrar shall retain the license during the period of suspension.

(C) No application for a motorized bicycle license or probationary motorized bicycle license shall be received from any person whose probationary motorized bicycle license has been suspended under this section until the person reaches sixteen years of age.

(2002 S 123, eff. 1–1–04)

Historical and Statutory Notes

Ed. Note: 4510.34 is former 4507.167, amended and recodified by 2002 S 123, eff. 1–1–04; 1986 S 356, eff. 9–24–86.

4510.41 Seizure of vehicle upon arrest

(A) As used in this section:

(1) "Arrested person" means a person who is arrested for a violation of section 4510.14, 4510.16, or 4511.203 of the Revised Code, or a municipal ordinance that is substantially equivalent to any of those sections, and whose arrest results in a vehicle being seized under division (B) of this section.

(2) "Vehicle owner" means either of the following:

(a) The person in whose name is registered, at the time of the seizure, a vehicle that is seized under division (B) of this section;

(b) A person to whom the certificate of title to a vehicle that is seized under division (B) of this section has been assigned and who has not obtained a certificate of title to the vehicle in that person's name, but who is deemed by the court as being the owner of the vehicle at the time the vehicle was seized under division (B) of this section.

(3) "Interested party" includes the owner of a vehicle seized under this section, all lienholders, the arrested person, the owner of the place of storage at which a vehicle seized under this section is stored, and the person or entity that caused the vehicle to be removed.

(B)(1) If a person is arrested for a violation of section 4510.14, 4510.16, or 4511.203 of the Revised Code, or a municipal ordinance that is substantially equivalent to any of those sections, the arresting officer or another officer of the law enforcement agency that employs the arresting officer, in addition to any action that the arresting officer is required or authorized to take by any other provision of law, shall seize the vehicle that the person was operating at the time of, or that was involved in, the alleged offense if the vehicle is registered in the arrested person's name and its license plates. A law enforcement agency that employs a law enforcement officer who makes an arrest of a type that is described in this division and that involves a rented or leased vehicle that is being rented or leased for a period of thirty days or less shall notify, within twenty-four hours after the officer makes the arrest, the lessor or owner of the vehicle regarding the circumstances of the arrest and the location at which the vehicle may be picked up. At the time of the seizure of the vehicle, the law enforcement officer who made the arrest shall give the arrested person written notice that the vehicle and its license plates have been seized; that the vehicle either will be kept by the officer's law enforcement agency or will be immobilized at least until the person's initial appearance on the charge of the offense for which the arrest was made; that, at the initial appearance, the court in certain circumstances may order that the vehicle and license plates be released to the arrested person until the disposition of that charge; that, if the arrested person is convicted of that charge, the court generally must order the immobilization of the vehicle and the impoundment of its license plates or the forfeiture of the vehicle; and that the arrested person may be charged expenses or charges incurred under this section and section 4503.233 of the Revised Code for the removal and storage of the vehicle.

(2) The arresting officer or a law enforcement officer of the agency that employs the arresting officer shall give written notice of the seizure to the court that will conduct the initial appearance of the arrested person on the charges arising out of the arrest. Upon receipt of the notice, the court promptly shall determine whether the arrested person is the vehicle owner. If the court determines that the arrested person is not the vehicle owner, it promptly shall send by regular mail written notice of the seizure to the vehicle's registered owner. The written notice shall contain all of the information required by division (B)(1) of this section to be in a notice to be given to the arrested person and also shall specify the date, time, and place of the arrested person's initial appearance. The notice also shall inform the vehicle owner that if title to a motor vehicle that is subject to an order for criminal forfeiture under this section is assigned or transferred and division (B)(2) or (3) of section 4503.234 of the Revised Code applies, the court may fine the arrested person the value of the vehicle. The notice also shall state that if the vehicle is immobilized under division (A) of section 4503.233 of the Revised Code, seven days after the end of the period of immobilization a law enforcement agency will send the vehicle owner a notice, informing the owner that if the release of the vehicle is not obtained in accordance with division (D)(3) of section 4503.233 of the Revised Code, the vehicle shall be forfeited. The notice also shall inform the vehicle owner that the owner may be charged expenses or charges incurred under this section and section 4503.233 of the Revised Code for the removal and storage of the vehicle.

The written notice that is given to the arrested person also shall state that if the person is convicted of or pleads guilty to the offense and the court issues an immobilization and impoundment order relative to that vehicle, division (D)(4) of section 4503.233 of the Revised Code prohibits the vehicle from being sold during the period of immobilization without the prior approval of the court.

(3) At or before the initial appearance, the vehicle owner may file a motion requesting the court to order that the vehicle and its license plates be released to the vehicle owner. Except as provided in this division and subject to the payment of expenses or charges incurred in the removal and storage of the vehicle, the court, in its discretion, then may issue an order releasing the vehicle and its license plates to the vehicle owner. Such an order may be conditioned upon such terms as the court determines appropriate, including the posting of a bond in an amount determined by the court. If the arrested person is not the vehicle owner and if the vehicle owner is not present at the arrested person's initial appearance, and if the court believes that the vehicle owner was not provided with adequate notice of the initial appearance, the court, in its discretion, may allow the vehicle owner to file a motion within seven days of the initial appearance. If the court allows the vehicle owner to file such a motion after the initial appearance, the extension of time granted by the court does not extend the time within which the initial appearance is to be conducted. If the court issues an order for the release of the vehicle and its license plates, a copy of the order shall be made available to the vehicle owner. If the vehicle owner presents a copy of the order to the law enforcement agency that employs the law enforcement officer who arrested the arrested person, the law enforcement agency promptly shall release the vehicle and its license plates to the vehicle owner upon payment by the vehicle owner of any expenses or charges incurred in the removal or storage of the vehicle.

(4) A vehicle seized under division (B)(1) of this section either shall be towed to a place specified by the law enforcement agency that employs the arresting officer to be safely kept by the agency at that place for the time and in the manner specified in this section or shall be otherwise immobilized for the time and in the manner specified in this section. A law enforcement officer of that agency shall remove the identification license plates of the vehicle, and they shall be safely kept by the agency for the time and in the manner specified in this section. No vehicle that is seized and either towed or immobilized pursuant to this division shall be considered contraband for purposes of section 2933.41, 2933.42, or 2933.43 of the Revised Code. The vehicle shall not be immobilized at any place other than a commercially operated private storage lot, a place owned by a law enforcement or other government agency, or a place to which one of the following applies:

(a) The place is leased by or otherwise under the control of a law enforcement or other government agency.

(b) The place is owned by the arrested person, the arrested person's spouse, or a parent or child of the arrested person.

(c) The place is owned by a private person or entity, and, prior to the immobilization, the private entity or person that owns the place, or the authorized agent of that private entity or person, has given express written consent for the immobilization to be carried out at that place.

(d) The place is a public street or highway on which the vehicle is parked in accordance with the law.

(C)(1) A vehicle seized under division (B) of this section shall be safely kept at the place to which it is towed or otherwise moved by the law enforcement agency that employs the arresting officer until the initial appearance of the arrested person relative to the charge in question. The license plates of the vehicle that are removed pursuant to division (B) of this section shall be safely kept by the law enforcement agency that employs the arresting officer until at least the initial appearance of the arrested person relative to the charge in question.

(2)(a) At the initial appearance or not less than seven days prior to the date of final disposition, the court shall notify the arrested person that, if title to a motor vehicle that is subject to an order for criminal forfeiture under this section is assigned or transferred and division (B)(2) or (3) of section 4503.234 of the Revised Code applies, the court may fine the arrested person the value of the vehicle. If, at the initial appearance, the arrested person pleads guilty to the violation of section 4510.14, 4510.16, or 4511.203 of the Revised Code, or a municipal ordinance that is substantially equivalent to any of those sections or pleads no contest to and is convicted of the violation, the court shall impose sentence upon the person as provided by law or ordinance; the court shall order the immobilization of the vehicle the arrested person was operating at the time of, or that was involved in, the offense if registered in the arrested person's name and the impoundment of its license plates under section 4503.233 and section 4510.14, 4510.16, 4510.161, or 4511.203 of the Revised Code or the criminal forfeiture to the state of the vehicle if registered in the arrested person's name under section 4503.234 and section 4510.14, 4510.16, 4510.161, or 4511.203 of the Revised Code, whichever is applicable; and the vehicle and its license plates shall not be returned or released to the arrested person.

(b) If, at any time, the charge that the arrested person violated section 4510.14, 4510.16, or 4511.203 of the Revised Code, or a municipal ordinance that is substantially equivalent to any of those sections is dismissed for any reason, the court shall order that the vehicle seized at the time of the arrest and its license plates immediately be released to the person.

(D) If a vehicle and its license plates are seized under division (B) of this section and are not returned or released to the arrested person pursuant to division (C) of this section, the vehicle and its license plates shall be retained until the final disposition of the charge in question. Upon the final disposition of that charge, the court shall do whichever of the following is applicable:

(1) If the arrested person is convicted of or pleads guilty to the violation of section 4510.14, 4510.16, or 4511.203 of the Revised Code, or a municipal ordinance that is substantially equivalent to any of those sections, the court shall impose sentence upon the person as provided by law or ordinance and shall order the immobilization of the vehicle the person was operating at the time of, or that was involved in, the offense if it is registered in the arrested person's name and the impoundment of its license plates under section 4503.233 and section 4510.14, 4510.16, 4510.161, or 4511.203 of the Revised Code or the criminal forfeiture of the vehicle if it is registered in the arrested person's name under section 4503.234 and section 4510.14, 4510.16, 4510.161, or 4511.203 of the Revised Code, whichever is applicable.

(2) If the arrested person is found not guilty of the violation of section 4510.14, 4510.16, or 4511.203 of the Revised Code, or a municipal ordinance that is substantially equivalent to any of those sections, the court shall order that the vehicle and its license plates immediately be released to the arrested person.

(3) If the charge that the arrested person violated section 4510.14, 4510.16, or 4511.203 of the Revised Code, or a municipal ordinance that is substantially equivalent to any of those sections is dismissed for any reason, the court shall order that the vehicle and its license plates immediately be released to the arrested person.

(4) If the impoundment of the vehicle was not authorized under this section, the court shall order that the vehicle and its license plates be returned immediately to the arrested person or, if the arrested person is not the vehicle owner, to the vehicle owner and shall order that the state or political subdivision of the law enforcement agency served by the law enforcement officer who seized the vehicle pay all expenses and charges incurred in its removal and storage.

(E) If a vehicle is seized under division (B) of this section, the time between the seizure of the vehicle and either its release to the arrested person pursuant to division (C) of this section or the issuance of an order of immobilization of the vehicle under section 4503.233 of the Revised Code shall be credited against the period of immobilization ordered by the court.

(F)(1) Except as provided in division (D)(4) of this section, the arrested person may be charged expenses or charges incurred in the removal and storage of the immobilized vehicle. The court with jurisdiction over the case, after notice to all interested parties, including lienholders, and after an opportunity for them to be heard, if the court finds that the arrested person does not intend to seek release of the vehicle at the end of the period of immobilization under section 4503.233 of the Revised Code or that the arrested person is not or will not be able to pay the expenses and charges incurred in its removal and storage, may order that title to the vehicle be transferred, in order of priority, first into the name of the person or entity that removed it, next into the name of a lienholder, or lastly into the name of the owner of the place of storage.

Any lienholder that receives title under a court order shall do so on the condition that it pay any expenses or charges incurred in the vehicle's removal and storage. If the person or entity that receives title to the vehicle is the person or entity that removed it, the person or entity shall receive title on the condition that it pay any lien on the vehicle. The court shall not order that title be transferred to any person or entity other than the owner of the place of storage if the person or entity refuses to receive the title. Any person or entity that receives title either may keep title to the vehicle or may dispose of the vehicle in any legal manner that it considers appropriate, including assignment of the certificate of title to the motor vehicle to a salvage dealer or a scrap metal processing facility. The person or entity shall not transfer the vehicle to the person who is the vehicle's immediate previous owner.

If the person or entity that receives title assigns the motor vehicle to a salvage dealer or scrap metal processing facility, the person or entity shall send the assigned certificate of title to the motor vehicle to the clerk of the court of common pleas of the county in which the salvage dealer or scrap metal processing facility is located. The person or entity shall mark the face of the certificate of title with the words "FOR DESTRUCTION" and shall deliver a photocopy of the certificate of title to the salvage dealer or scrap metal processing facility for its records.

(2) Whenever a court issues an order under division (F)(1) of this section, the court also shall order removal of the license plates from the vehicle and cause them to be sent to the registrar if they have not already been sent to the registrar. Thereafter, no further proceedings shall take place under this section or under section 4503.233 of the Revised Code.

(3) Prior to initiating a proceeding under division (F)(1) of this section, and upon payment of the fee under division (B) of section 4505.14, any interested party may cause a search to be made of the public records of the bureau of motor vehicles or the clerk of the court of common pleas, to ascertain the identity of any lienholder of the vehicle. The initiating party shall furnish this information to the clerk of the court with jurisdiction over the case, and the clerk shall provide notice to the arrested person, any lienholder, and any other interested parties listed by the initiating party, at the last known address supplied by the initiating party, by certified mail, or, at the option of the initiating party, by personal service or ordinary mail.

(2002 S 123, eff. 1–1–04)

Historical and Statutory Notes

Ed. Note: 4510.41 is former 4507.38, amended and recodified by 2002 S 123, eff. 1–1–04; 1996 H 676, eff. 10–4–96; 1996 H 353, eff. 9–17–96; 1994 H 687, eff. 10–12–94; 1994 H 236, eff. 9–29–94; 1993 S 62, § 1, eff. 9–1–93; 1993 S 62, § 4; 1992 S 275.

4510.43 Immobilizing and disabling devices

(A)(1) The director of public safety, upon consultation with the director of health and in accordance with Chapter 119. of the Revised Code, shall certify immobilizing and disabling devices and shall publish and make available to the courts, without charge, a list of approved devices together with information about the manufacturers of the devices and where they may be obtained. The manufacturer of an immobilizing or disabling device shall pay the cost of obtaining the certification of the device to the director of public safety, and the director shall deposit the payment in the drivers' treatment and intervention fund established by sections 4511.19 and 4511.191 of the Revised Code.

(2) The director of public safety, in accordance with Chapter 119. of the Revised Code, shall adopt and publish rules setting forth the requirements for obtaining the certification of an immobilizing or disabling device. The director of public safety shall not certify an immobilizing or disabling device under this section unless it meets the requirements specified and published by the director in the rules adopted pursuant to this division. A certified device may consist of an ignition interlock device, an ignition blocking device initiated by time or magnetic or electronic encoding, an activity monitor, or any other device that reasonably assures compliance with an order granting limited driving privileges.

The requirements for an immobilizing or disabling device that is an ignition interlock device shall include provisions for setting a minimum and maximum calibration range and shall include, but shall not be limited to, specifications that the device complies with all of the following:

(a) It does not impede the safe operation of the vehicle.

(b) It has features that make circumvention difficult and that do not interfere with the normal use of the vehicle.

(c) It correlates well with established measures of alcohol impairment.

(d) It works accurately and reliably in an unsupervised environment.

(e) It is resistant to tampering and shows evidence of tampering if tampering is attempted.

(f) It is difficult to circumvent and requires premeditation to do so.

(g) It minimizes inconvenience to a sober user.

(h) It requires a proper, deep-lung breath sample or other accurate measure of the concentration by weight of alcohol in the breath.

(i) It operates reliably over the range of automobile environments.

(j) It is made by a manufacturer who is covered by product liability insurance.

(3) The director of public safety may adopt, in whole or in part, the guidelines, rules, regulations, studies, or independent laboratory tests performed and relied upon by other states, or their agencies or commissions, in the certification or approval of immobilizing or disabling devices.

(4) The director of public safety shall adopt rules in accordance with Chapter 119. of the Revised Code for the design of a warning label that shall be affixed to each immobilizing or disabling device upon installation. The label shall contain a warning that any person tampering, circumventing, or otherwise misusing the device is subject to a fine, imprisonment, or both and may be subject to civil liability.

(B) A court considering the use of a prototype device in a pilot program shall advise the director of public safety, thirty days before the use, of the prototype device and its protocol, methodology, manufacturer, and licensor, lessor, other agent, or owner, and the length of the court's pilot program. A prototype device shall not be used for a violation of section 4510.14 or 4511.19 of the Revised Code, a violation of a municipal OVI ordinance, or in relation to a suspension imposed under section 4511.191 of the Revised Code. A court that uses a prototype device in a pilot program, periodically during the existence of the program and within fourteen days after termination of the program, shall report in writing to the director of public safety regarding the effectiveness of the prototype device and the program.

(C) If a person has been granted limited driving privileges with a condition of the privileges being that the motor vehicle that is operated under the privileges must be equipped with an immobilizing or disabling device, the person may operate a motor vehicle that is owned by the person's employer only if the person is required to operate that motor vehicle in the course and scope of the offender's employment. Such a person may operate that vehicle without the installation of an immobilizing or disabling device, provided that the employer has been notified that the person has limited driving privileges and of the nature of the restriction and further provided that the person has proof of the employer's notification in the person's possession while operating the employer's vehicle for normal business duties. A motor vehicle owned by a business that is partly or entirely owned or controlled by a person with limited driving privileges is not a motor vehicle owned by an employer, for purposes of this division.

(2004 H 230, eff. 9–16–04; 2002 S 123, eff. 1–1–04)

4510.44 Immobilizing or disabling device, prohibitions

(A)(1) No offender with limited driving privileges, during any period that the offender is required to operate only a motor vehicle equipped with an immobilizing or disabling device, shall request or permit any other person to breathe into the device if it is an ignition interlock device or another type of device that monitors the concentration of alcohol in a person's breath or to otherwise start the motor vehicle equipped with the device, for the purpose of providing the offender with an operable motor vehicle.

(2)(a) Except as provided in division (A)(2)(b) of this section, no person shall breathe into an immobilizing or disabling device that is an ignition interlock device or another type of device that monitors the concentration of alcohol in a person's breath or otherwise start a motor vehicle equipped with an immobilizing or disabling device, for the purpose of providing an operable motor vehicle to an offender with limited driving privileges who is permitted to operate only a motor vehicle equipped with an immobilizing or disabling device.

(b) Division (A)(2)(a) of this section does not apply to a person in the following circumstances:

(i) The person is an offender with limited driving privileges.

(ii) The person breathes into an immobilizing or disabling device that is an ignition interlock device or another type of device that monitors the concentration of alcohol in a person's breath or otherwise starts a motor vehicle equipped with an immobilizing or disabling device.

(iii) The person breathes into the device or starts the vehicle for the purpose of providing the person with an operable motor vehicle.

(3) No unauthorized person shall tamper with or circumvent the operation of an immobilizing or disabling device.

(B) Whoever violates this section is guilty of an immobilizing or disabling device violation, a misdemeanor of the first degree.

(2002 S 123, eff. 1–1–04)

4510.52 Reissuance of license for fee

(A) Upon the receipt of any driver's license or commercial driver's license or permit that has been suspended or canceled under any provision of law, and notwithstanding any other provision of law that requires the registrar of motor vehicles to retain the license or permit, the registrar may destroy the license or permit.

(B) If, as authorized by division (A) of this section, the registrar destroys a license or permit that has been suspended or canceled, the registrar shall reissue or authorize the reissuance of a new license or permit to the person to whom the destroyed license or permit originally was issued upon payment of a fee in the same amount as the fee specified in division (C) of section 4507.23 of the Revised Code for a duplicate license or permit and upon payment of a service fee in the same amount as specified in division (D) of section 4503.10 of the Revised Code if issued by a deputy registrar or in division (G) of that section if issued by the registrar.

This division applies only if the driver's license or commercial driver's license or permit that was destroyed would have been valid at the time the person applies for the duplicate license or permit. A duplicate driver's license or commercial driver's license or permit issued under this section shall bear the same expiration date that appeared on the license or permit it replaces.

(2002 S 123, eff. 1–1–04)

Historical and Statutory Notes

Ed. Note: 4510.52 is former 4507.54, amended and recodified by 2002 S 123, eff. 1–1–04; 1994 H 687, eff. 10–12–94.

4510.53 Reissuance of license following suspension for operating under the influence

(A) Upon receipt of any driver's or commercial driver's license or permit that has been suspended under section 4511.19 or 4511.191 of the Revised Code, the registrar of motor vehicles, notwithstanding any other provision of law that purports to require the registrar to retain the license or permit, may destroy the license or permit.

(B)(1) Subject to division (B)(2) of this section, if a driver's or commercial driver's license or permit that has been suspended under section 4511.19 or 4511.191 of the Revised Code is delivered to the registrar and if the registrar destroys the license or permit under authority of division (A) of this section, the registrar shall reissue or authorize the reissuance of a driver's or commercial driver's license to the person, free of payment of any type of fee or charge, if either of the following applies:

(a) The person appeals the suspension of the license or permit at or within thirty days of the person's initial appearance, pursuant to section 4511.197 of the Revised Code, the judge of the court of record or the mayor of the mayor's court who conducts the initial appearance terminates the suspension, and the judge or mayor does not suspend the license or permit under section 4511.196 of the Revised Code;

(b) The person appeals the suspension of the license or permit at or within thirty days of the person's initial appearance, pursuant to section 4511.197 of the Revised Code, the judge of the court of record or the mayor of the mayor's court who conducts the initial appearance does not terminate the suspension, the person appeals the judge's or mayor's decision not to terminate the suspension that is made at the initial appearance, and upon appeal of the decision, the suspension is terminated.

(2) Division (B)(1) of this section applies only if the driver's or commercial driver's license that was destroyed would have been valid at the time in question, if it had not been destroyed as permitted by division (A) of this section.

(C) A driver's or commercial driver's license or permit issued to a person pursuant to division (B)(1) of this section shall bear the same expiration date as the expiration date that appeared on the license it replaces.

(2002 S 123, eff. 1–1–04)

Historical and Statutory Notes

Ed. Note: 4510.53 is former 4507.55, amended and recodified by 2002 S 123, eff. 1–1–04; 1994 H 687, eff. 10–12–94.

4510.54 Modification or termination of suspension of fifteen years or longer

(A) A person whose driver's or commercial driver's license has been suspended for life under a class one suspension or as otherwise provided by law or has been suspended for a period in excess of fifteen years under a class two suspension may file a motion with the sentencing court for modification or termination of the suspension. The person filing the motion shall demonstrate all of the following:

(1) At least fifteen years have elapsed since the suspension began.

(2) For the past fifteen years, the person has not been found guilty of any felony, any offense involving a moving violation under federal law, the law of this state, or the law of any of its political subdivisions, or any violation of a suspension under this chapter or a substantially equivalent municipal ordinance.

(3) The person has proof of financial responsibility, a policy of liability insurance in effect that meets the minimum standard set forth in section 4509.51 of the Revised Code, or proof, to the satisfaction of the registrar of motor vehicles, that the person is able to respond in damages in an amount at least equal to the minimum amounts specified in that section.

(4) If the suspension was imposed because the person was under the influence of alcohol, a drug of abuse, or combination of them at the time of the offense or because at the time of the offense the person's whole blood, blood serum or plasma, breath, or urine contained at least the concentration of alcohol specified in division (A) (1)(b), (c), (d), or (e) of section 4511.19 of the Revised Code, the person also shall demonstrate all of the following:

(a) The person successfully completed an alcohol, drug, or alcohol and drug treatment program.

(b) The person has not abused alcohol or other drugs for a period satisfactory to the court.

(c) For the past fifteen years, the person has not been found guilty of any alcohol-related or drug-related offense.

(B) Upon receipt of a motion for modification or termination of the suspension under this section, the court may schedule a hearing on the motion. The court may deny the motion without a hearing but shall not grant the motion without a hearing. If the court denies a motion without a hearing, the court may consider a subsequent motion filed under this section by that person. If a court denies the motion after a hearing, the court shall not consider a subsequent motion for that person. The court shall hear only one motion filed by a person under this section. If scheduled, the hearing shall be conducted in open court within ninety days after the date on which the motion is filed.

(C) The court shall notify the person whose license was suspended and the prosecuting attorney of the date, time, and location of the hearing. Upon receipt of the notice from the court, the prosecuting attorney shall notify the victim or the victim's representative of the date, time, and location of the hearing.

(D) At any hearing under this section, the person who seeks modification or termination of the suspension has the burden to demonstrate, under oath, that the person meets the requirements of division (A) of this section. At the hearing, the court shall afford the offender or the offender's counsel an opportunity to present oral or written information relevant to the motion. The court shall afford a similar opportunity to provide relevant information to the prosecuting attorney and the victim or victim's representative.

Before ruling on the motion, the court shall take into account the person's driving record, the nature of the offense that led to the suspension, and the impact of the offense on any victim. In addition, if the offender is eligible for modification or termination of the suspension under division (A)(2) of this section, the court shall consider whether the person committed any other offense while under suspension and determine whether the offense is relevant to a determination under this section. The court may modify or terminate the suspension subject to any considerations it considers proper if it finds that allowing the person to drive is not likely to present a danger to the public. After the court makes a ruling on a motion filed under this section, the prosecuting attorney shall notify the victim or the victim's representative of the court's ruling.

(E) If a court modifies a person's license suspension under this section and the person subsequently is found guilty of any moving violation or of any substantially equivalent municipal ordinance that carries as a possible penalty the suspension of a person's driver's or commercial driver's license, the court may reimpose the class one or other lifetime suspension, or the class two suspension, whichever is applicable.

(2004 H 163, eff. 9–23–04; 2004 H 52, eff. 6–1–04; 2002 S 123, eff. 1–1–04)

4510.61 Policy; definitions; reports and effect of conviction; application for new license

The driver license compact is hereby enacted into law and entered into with all other jurisdictions legally joining therein in the form substantially as follows:

ARTICLE I
Findings and Declaration of Policy

(a) The party states find that:

(1) The safety of their streets and highways is materially affected by the degree of compliance with state and local ordinances relating to the operation of motor vehicles.

(2) Violation of such a law or ordinance is evidence that the violator engages in conduct which is likely to endanger the safety of persons and property.

(3) The continuance in force of a license to drive is predicated upon compliance with laws and ordinances relating to the operation of motor vehicles, in whichever jurisdiction the vehicle is operated.

(b) It is the policy of each of the party states to:

(1) Promote compliance with the laws, ordinances, and administrative rules and regulations relating to the operation of motor vehicles by their operators in each of the jurisdictions where such operators drive motor vehicles.

(2) Make the reciprocal recognition of licenses to drive and eligibility therefor more just and equitable by considering the over-all compliance with motor vehicle laws, ordinances, and administrative rules and regulations as a condition precedent to the continuance or issuance of any license by reason of which the licensee is authorized or permitted to operate a motor vehicle in any of the party states.

ARTICLE II
Definitions

As used in this compact:

(a) "State" means a state, territory, or possession of the United States, the District of Columbia, or the Commonwealth of Puerto Rico.

(b) "Home state" means the state that has issued and has the power to suspend or revoke the use of the license or permit to operate a motor vehicle.

(c) "Conviction" means a conviction of any offense related to the use or operation of a motor vehicle that is prohibited by state law, municipal ordinance, or administrative rule or regulation; or a forfeiture of bail, bond, or other security deposited to secure appearance by a person charged with having committed any such offense, and which conviction or forfeiture is required to be reported to the licensing authority.

ARTICLE III
Reports of Conviction

The licensing authority of a party state shall report each conviction of a person from another party state occurring within its jurisdiction to the licensing authority of the home state of the licensee. Such report shall clearly identify the person convicted; describe the violation specifying the section of the statute, code, or ordinance violated; identify the court in which action was taken; indicate whether a plea of guilty or not guilty was entered, or the security; and shall include any special findings made in connection therewith.

ARTICLE IV
Effect of Conviction

(a) The licensing authority in the home state, for the purpose of suspension, revocation, or limitation of the license to operate a motor vehicle, shall give the same effect to the conduct reported, pursuant to Article III of this compact, as it would if such conduct had occurred in the home state, in the case of convictions for:

(1) Manslaughter or negligent homicide resulting from the operation of a motor vehicle;

(2) Driving a motor vehicle while under the influence of intoxicating liquor or a narcotic drug, or under the influence of any other drug to a degree that renders the driver incapable of safely driving a motor vehicle;

(3) Any felony in the commission of which a motor vehicle is used;

(4) Failure to stop and render aid in the event of a motor vehicle accident resulting in the death or personal injury of another.

(b) As to other convictions, reported pursuant to Article III, the licensing authority in the home state shall give such effect to conduct as is provided by the laws of the home state.

(c) If the laws of a party state do not provide for offenses or violations denominated or described in precisely the words employed in subdivision (a) of this Article, such party state shall construe the denominations and descriptions appearing in subdivision (a) hereof as being applicable to and identifying those offenses or violations of a substantially similar nature, and the laws of such party state shall contain such provisions as may be necessary to ensure that full force and effect is given to this Article.

ARTICLE V
Applications for New Licenses

Upon application for a license to drive, the licensing authority in a party state shall ascertain whether the applicant has ever held, or is the holder of, a license to drive issued by any other party state. The licensing authority in the state where application is made shall not issue a license to drive to the applicant if:

(1) The applicant has held such a license, but the same has been suspended by reason, in whole or in part, of a violation and if such suspension period has not terminated.

(2) The applicant has held such a license, but the same has been revoked by reason, in whole or in part, of a violation; and if such revocation has not terminated, except that after the expiration of one year from the date the license was revoked, such person may make application for a new license if permitted by law. The licensing authority may refuse to issue a license to any such applicant if, after investigation, the licensing authority determines that it will not be safe to grant to such person the privilege of driving a motor vehicle on the public highways.

(3) The applicant is the holder of a license to drive issued by another party state and currently in force unless the applicant surrenders such license.

ARTICLE VI
Applicability of Other Laws

Except as expressly required by provisions of this compact, nothing contained herein shall be construed to affect the right of any party state to apply any of its other laws relating to licenses to drive to any person or circumstance, nor to invalidate or prevent any driver license agreement or other cooperative arrangement between a party state and a nonparty state.

ARTICLE VII
Compact Administrator and Interchange of Information

(a) The head of the licensing authority of each party state shall be the administrator of this compact for his state. The administrators, acting jointly, shall have the power to formulate all necessary and proper procedures for the exchange of information under this compact.

(b) The administrator of each party state shall furnish to the administrator of each other party state any information or documents reasonably necessary to facilitate the administration of this compact.

ARTICLE VIII
Entry Into Force and Withdrawal

(a) This compact shall enter into force and become effective as to any state when it has enacted the same into law.

(b) Any party state may withdraw from this compact by enacting a statute repealing the same, but no such withdrawal shall take effect until six months after the executive head of the withdrawing state has given notice of the withdrawal to the executive heads of all other party states. No withdrawal shall affect the validity or applicability by the licensing authorities of states remaining party to the compact of any report of conviction occurring prior to the withdrawal.

ARTICLE IX
Construction and Severability

This compact shall be liberally construed so as to effectuate the purposes thereof. The provisions of this compact shall be severable; and if any phrase, clause, sentence, or provision of this compact is declared to be contrary to the constitution of any party state or of the United States or the applicability thereof to any government, agency, person, or circumstance is held invalid, the validity of the remainder of this compact and the applicability thereof to any government, agency, person, or circumstance shall not be affected thereby. If this compact shall be held contrary to the constitution of any state party thereto, the compact shall remain in full force and effect as to the remaining states and in full force and effect as to the state affected as to all severable matters.

(2002 S 123, eff. 1–1–04)

Historical and Statutory Notes

Ed. Note: 4510.61 is former 4507.60, recodified by 2002 S 123, eff. 1–1–04; 1987 H 419, eff. 7–1–87.

Notes of Decisions

Ed. Note: See notes of decisions at RC 4511.19 regarding construction of the term "under the influence."

4510.62 Governor as executive head; bureau of motor vehicles as licensing authority

(A) "Executive head" as used in article VIII (b) of the compact set forth in section 4510.61 of the Revised Code with reference to this state means the governor.

(B) "Licensing authority" as used in Articles III, IV, V, and VII of the compact set forth in section 4510.61 of the Revised Code with reference to this state means the bureau of motor vehicles within the department of public safety.

(2002 S 123, eff. 1–1–04)

Historical and Statutory Notes

Ed. Note: 4510.62 is former 4507.61, amended and recodified by 2002 S 123, eff. 1–1–04; 1992 S 98, eff. 11–12–92; 1987 H 419, eff. 7–1–87.

4510.63 Information and documents to be furnished to foreign state

Pursuant to Article VII of the compact set forth in section 4510.61 of the Revised Code the bureau of motor vehicles shall furnish to the appropriate authorities of any other party state any information or documents reasonably necessary to facilitate the administration of Articles III, IV, and V of the compact set forth in section 4510.61 of the Revised Code.

(2002 S 123, eff. 1–1–04)

Historical and Statutory Notes

Ed. Note: 4510.63 is former 4507.62, amended and recodified by 2002 S 123, eff. 1–1–04; 1987 H 419, eff. 7–1–87.

4510.64 Reimbursement of expenses for compact administrator

The compact administrator provided for in Article VII of the compact set forth in section 4510.61 of the Revised Code is not entitled to any additional compensation for serving as administrator of the compact, but shall be reimbursed for travel and other necessary expenses incurred in the performance of official duties thereunder as provided by law for other state officers.

(2002 S 123, eff. 1–1–04)

Historical and Statutory Notes

Ed. Note: 4510.64 is former 4507.63, amended and recodified by 2002 S 123, eff. 1–1–04; 1987 H 419, eff. 7–1–87.

4510.71 Nonresident violator compact

The nonresident violator compact, hereinafter called "the compact," is hereby enacted into law and entered into with all other jurisdictions legally joining therein in the form substantially as follows:

"NONRESIDENT VIOLATOR COMPACT

Article I
Findings, Declaration of Policy and Purpose

(A) The party jurisdictions find that:

(1) In most instances, a motorist who is cited for a traffic violation in a jurisdiction other than his home jurisdiction:

(a) Must post collateral or bond to secure appearance for trial at a later date; or

(b) If unable to post collateral or bond, is taken into custody until the collateral or bond is posted; or

(c) Is taken directly to court for his trial to be held.

(2) In some instances, the motorist's driver's license may be deposited as collateral to be returned after he has complied with the terms of the citation.

(3) The purpose of the practices described in divisions (A)(1) and (2) of this article is to ensure compliance with the terms of a traffic citation by the motorist who, if permitted to continue on his way after receiving the traffic citation, could return to his home jurisdiction and disregard his duty under the terms of the traffic citation.

(4) A motorist receiving a traffic citation in his home jurisdiction is permitted, except for certain violations, to accept the citation from the officer at the scene of the violation and to immediately continue on his way after promising or being instructed to comply with the terms of the citation.

(5) The practice described in division (A)(1) of this article causes unnecessary inconvenience and, at times, a hardship for the motorist who is unable at the time to post collateral, furnish a bond, stand trial, or pay the fine, and thus is compelled to remain in custody until some arrangement can be made.

(6) The deposit of a driver's license as a bail bond, as described in division (A)(2) of this article, is viewed with disfavor.

(7) The practices described herein consume an undue amount of law enforcement time.

(B) It is the policy of the party jurisdictions to:

(1) Seek compliance with the laws, ordinances, and administrative rules and regulations relating to the operation of motor vehicles in each of the jurisdictions;

(2) Allow motorists to accept a traffic citation for certain violations and proceed on their way without delay whether or not the motorist is a resident of the jurisdiction in which the citation was issued;

(3) Extend cooperation to its fullest extent among the jurisdictions for obtaining compliance with the terms of a traffic citation issued in one jurisdiction to a resident of another jurisdiction;

(4) Maximize effective utilization of law enforcement personnel and assist court systems in the efficient disposition of traffic violations.

(C) The purpose of this compact is to:

(1) Provide a means through which the party jurisdictions may participate in a reciprocal program to effectuate the policies enumerated in division (B) of this article in a uniform and orderly manner;

(2) Provide for the fair and impartial treatment of traffic violators operating within party jurisdictions in recognition of the motorist's right of due process and the sovereign status of a party jurisdiction.

Article II
Definitions

(A) In the nonresident violator compact, the following words have the meaning indicated, unless the context requires otherwise.

(B)(1) "Citation" means any summons, ticket, or other official document issued by a police officer for a traffic violation containing an order which requires the motorist to respond.

(2) "Collateral" means any cash or other security deposited to secure an appearance for trial, following the issuance by a police officer of a citation for a traffic violation.

(3) "Court" means a court of law or traffic tribunal.

(4) "Driver's license" means any license or privilege to operate a motor vehicle issued under the laws of the home jurisdiction.

(5) "Home jurisdiction" means the jurisdiction that issued the driver's license of the traffic violator.

(6) "Issuing jurisdiction" means the jurisdiction in which the traffic citation was issued to the motorist.

(7) "Jurisdiction" means a state, territory, or possession of the United States, the District of Columbia, or the Commonwealth of Puerto Rico.

(8) "Motorist" means a driver of a motor vehicle operating in a party jurisdiction other than the home jurisdiction.

(9) "Personal recognizance" means an agreement by a motorist made at the time of issuance of the traffic citation that he will comply with the terms of that traffic citation.

(10) "Police officer" means any individual authorized by the party jurisdiction to issue a citation for a traffic violation.

(11) "Terms of the citation" means those options expressly stated upon the citation.

Article III
Procedure for Issuing Jurisdiction

(A) When issuing a citation for a traffic violation, a police officer shall issue the citation to a motorist who possesses a driver's license issued by a party jurisdiction and shall not, subject to the exceptions noted in division (B) of this article, require the motorist to post collateral to secure appearance, if the officer receives the motorist's signed, personal recognizance that he or she will comply with the terms of the citation.

(B) Personal recognizance is acceptable only if not prohibited by law. If mandatory appearance is required, it must take place immediately following issuance of the citation.

(C) Upon failure of a motorist to comply with the terms of a traffic citation, the appropriate official shall report the failure to comply to the licensing authority of the jurisdiction in which the traffic citation was issued. The report shall be made in accordance with procedures specified by the issuing jurisdiction and shall contain information as specified in the compact manual as minimum requirements for effective processing by the home jurisdiction.

(D) Upon receipt of the report, the licensing authority of the issuing jurisdiction shall transmit to the licensing authority in the home jurisdiction of the motorist the information in a form and content as contained in the compact manual.

(E) The licensing authority of the issuing jurisdiction may not suspend the privilege of a motorist for whom a report has been transmitted.

(F) The licensing authority of the issuing jurisdiction shall not transmit a report on any violation if the date of transmission is more than six months after the date on which the traffic citation was issued.

(G) The licensing authority of the issuing jurisdiction shall not transmit a report on any violation where the date of issuance of the citation predates the most recent of the effective dates of entry for the two jurisdictions affected.

Article IV
Procedures for Home Jurisdiction

(A) Upon receipt of a report of a failure to comply from the licensing authority of the issuing jurisdiction, the licensing authority of the home jurisdiction shall notify the motorist and initiate a suspension action, in accordance with the home jurisdiction's procedures, to suspend the motorist's driver's license until satisfactory evidence of compliance with the terms of the traffic citation has been furnished to the home jurisdiction licensing authority. Due process safeguards will be accorded.

(B) The licensing authority of the home jurisdiction shall maintain a record of actions taken and make reports to issuing jurisdictions as provided in the compact manual.

Article V
Applicability of Other Laws

Except as expressly required by provisions of this compact, nothing contained herein shall be construed to affect the right of any party jurisdiction to apply any of its other laws relating to licenses to drive to any person or circumstance, or to invalidate or prevent any driver license agreement or other cooperative arrangement between a party jurisdiction and nonparty jurisdiction.

Article VI
Compact Administrator Procedures

(A) For the purpose of administering the provisions of this compact and to serve as a governing body for the resolution of all matters relating to the operation of this compact, a board of compact administrators is established. The board shall be composed of one representative from each party jurisdiction to be known as the compact administrator. The compact administrator shall be appointed by the jurisdiction executive and will serve and be subject to removal in accordance with the laws of the jurisdiction he represents. A compact administrator may provide for the discharge of his duties and the performance of his functions as a board member by an alternate. An alternate may not be entitled to serve unless written notification of his identity has been given to the board.

(B) Each member of the board of compact administrators shall be entitled to one vote. No action of the board shall be binding unless taken at a meeting at which a majority of the total number of votes on the board are cast in favor. Action by the board shall be only at a meeting at which a majority of the party jurisdictions are represented.

(C) The board shall elect annually, from its membership, a chairman and a vice chairman.

(D) The board shall adopt bylaws, not inconsistent with the provisions of this compact or the laws of a party jurisdiction, for the conduct of its business and shall have the power to amend and rescind its bylaws.

(E) The board may accept for any of its purposes and functions under this compact any and all donations, and grants of money, equipment, supplies, materials, and services, conditional or otherwise, from any jurisdiction, the United States, or any other governmental agency, and may receive, utilize, and dispose of the same.

(F) The board may contract with, or accept services or personnel from, any governmental or intergovernmental agency, person, firm, or corporation, or any private nonprofit organization or institution.

(G) The board shall formulate all necessary procedures and develop uniform forms and documents for administering the provisions of this compact. All procedures and forms adopted pursuant to board action shall be contained in the compact manual.

Article VII
Entry into Compact and Withdrawal

(A) This compact shall become effective when it has been adopted by at least two jurisdictions.

(B)(1) Entry into the compact shall be made by a resolution of ratification executed by the authorized officials of the applying jurisdiction and submitted to the chairman of the board.

(2) The resolution shall be in a form and content as provided in the compact manual and shall include statements that in substance are as follows:

(a) A citation of the authority by which the jurisdiction is empowered to become a party to this compact;

(b) Agreement to comply with the terms and provisions of the compact;

(c) That compact entry is with all jurisdictions then party to the compact and with any jurisdiction that legally becomes a party to the compact.

(3) The effective date of entry shall be specified by the applying jurisdiction, but it shall not be less than sixty days after notice has been given by the chairman of the board of compact administrators or by the secretariat of the board to each party jurisdiction that the resolution from the applying jurisdiction has been received.

(C) A party jurisdiction may withdraw from this compact by official written notice to the other party jurisdictions, but a withdrawal shall not take effect until ninety days after notice of withdrawal is given. The notice shall be directed to the compact administrator of each member jurisdiction. No withdrawal shall affect the validity of this compact as to the remaining party jurisdictions.

Article VIII
Exceptions

The provisions of this compact shall not apply to parking or standing violations, highway weight limit violations, and violations of law governing the transportation of hazardous materials.

Article IX
Amendments to the Compact

(A) This compact may be amended from time to time. Amendments shall be presented in resolution form to the chairman of the board of compact administrators and may be initiated by one or more party jurisdictions.

(B) Adoption of an amendment shall require endorsement of all party jurisdictions and shall become effective thirty days after the date of the last endorsement.

(C) Failure of a party jurisdiction to respond to the compact chairman within one hundred twenty days after receipt of the proposed amendment shall constitute endorsement.

Article X
Construction and Severability

This compact shall be liberally construed so as to effectuate the purposes stated herein. The provisions of this compact shall be severable and if any phrase, clause, sentence, or provision of this compact is declared to be contrary to the constitution of any party jurisdiction or of the United States or the applicability thereof to any government, agency, person, or circumstance, the compact shall not be affected thereby. If this compact shall be held contrary to the constitution of any jurisdiction party thereto, the compact shall remain in full force and effect as to the remaining jurisdictions and in full force and effect as to the jurisdiction affected as to all severable matters.

Article XI
Title

This compact shall be known as the Nonresident Violator Compact of 1977."

(2002 S 123, eff. 1–1–04)

Historical and Statutory Notes

Ed. Note: 4510.71 is former 4511.95, recodified by 2002 S 123, eff. 1–1–04; 1986 S 356, § 5, eff. 9–24–86; 1984 S 40, § 1, 4.

4510.72 Fee for reinstatement of suspended license; director of public safety as administrator of compact

(A) A fee of thirty dollars shall be charged by the registrar of motor vehicles for the reinstatement of any driver's license suspended pursuant to division (A) of Article IV of the compact enacted in section 4510.71 of the Revised Code.

(B) Pursuant to division (A) of Article VI of the nonresident violator compact of 1977 enacted in section 4510.71 of the Revised Code, the director of public safety shall serve as the compact administrator for Ohio.

(2002 S 123, eff. 1–1–04)

Historical and Statutory Notes

Ed. Note: 4510.72 is former 4511.951, amended and recodified by 2002 S 123, eff. 1–1–04; 1997 H 210, eff. 3–31–97; 1992 S 98, eff. 11–12–92; 1986 S 356, § 5; 1984 S 40, § 1, 4.

CHAPTER 4511

TRAFFIC LAWS—OPERATION OF MOTOR VEHICLES

PRELIMINARY PROVISIONS

4511.01 Definitions

As used in this chapter and in Chapter 4513. of the Revised Code:

(A) "Vehicle" means every device, including a motorized bicycle, in, upon, or by which any person or property may be transported or drawn upon a highway, except that "vehicle" does not include any motorized wheelchair, any electric personal assistive mobility device, any device that is moved by power collected from overhead electric trolley wires or that is used exclusively upon stationary rails or tracks, or any device, other than a bicycle, that is moved by human power.

(B) "Motor vehicle" means every vehicle propelled or drawn by power other than muscular power or power collected from overhead electric trolley wires, except motorized bicycles, road rollers, traction engines, power shovels, power cranes, and other equipment used in construction work and not designed for or employed in general highway transportation, hole-digging machinery, well-drilling machinery, ditch-digging machinery, farm machinery, trailers used to transport agricultural produce or agricultural production materials between a local place of storage or supply and the farm when drawn or towed on a street or highway at a speed of twenty-five miles per hour or less, threshing machinery, hay-baling machinery, agricultural tractors and machinery used in the production of horticultural, floricultural, agricultural, and vegetable products, and trailers designed and used exclusively to transport a boat between a place of storage and a marina, or in and around a marina, when drawn or towed on a street or highway for a distance of no more than ten miles and at a speed of twenty-five miles per hour or less.

(C) "Motorcycle" means every motor vehicle, other than a tractor, having a saddle for the use of the operator and designed to travel on not more than three wheels in contact with the ground, including, but not limited to, motor vehicles known as "motor-driven cycle," "motor scooter," or "motorcycle" without regard to weight or brake horsepower.

(D) "Emergency vehicle" means emergency vehicles of municipal, township, or county departments or public utility corporations when identified as such as required by law, the director of public safety, or local authorities, and motor vehicles when commandeered by a police officer.

(E) "Public safety vehicle" means any of the following:

(1) Ambulances, including private ambulance companies under contract to a municipal corporation, township, or county, and private ambulances and nontransport vehicles bearing license plates issued under section 4503.49 of the Revised Code;

(2) Motor vehicles used by public law enforcement officers or other persons sworn to enforce the criminal and traffic laws of the state;

(3) Any motor vehicle when properly identified as required by the director of public safety, when used in response to fire emergency calls or to provide emergency medical service to ill or injured persons, and when operated by a duly qualified person who is a member of a volunteer rescue service or a volunteer fire department, and who is on duty pursuant to the rules or directives of that service. The state fire marshal shall be designated by the director of public safety as the certifying agency for all public safety vehicles described in division (E)(3) of this section.

(4) Vehicles used by fire departments, including motor vehicles when used by volunteer fire fighters responding to emergency calls in the fire department service when identified as required by the director of public safety.

Any vehicle used to transport or provide emergency medical service to an ill or injured person, when certified as a public safety vehicle, shall be considered a public safety vehicle when transporting an ill or injured person to a hospital regardless of whether such vehicle has already passed a hospital.

(5) Vehicles used by the motor carrier enforcement unit for the enforcement of orders and rules of the public utilities commission as specified in section 5503.34 of the Revised Code.

(F) "School bus" means every bus designed for carrying more than nine passengers that is owned by a public, private, or governmental agency or institution of learning and operated for the transportation of children to or from a school session or a school function, or owned by a private person and operated for compensation for the transportation of children to or from a school session or a school function, provided "school bus" does not include a bus operated by a municipally owned transportation system, a mass transit company operating exclusively within the territorial limits of a municipal corporation, or within such limits and the territorial limits of municipal corporations immediately contiguous to such municipal corporation, nor a common passenger carrier certified by the public utilities commission unless such bus is devoted exclusively to the transportation of children to and from a school session or a school function, and "school bus" does not include a van or bus used by a licensed child day-care center or type A family day-care home to transport children from the child day-care center or type A family day-care home to a school if the van or bus does not have more than fifteen children in the van or bus at any time.

(G) "Bicycle" means every device, other than a tricycle designed solely for use as a play vehicle by a child, propelled solely by human power upon which any person may ride having either two tandem wheels, or one wheel in the front and two wheels in the rear, any of which is more than fourteen inches in diameter.

(H) "Motorized bicycle" means any vehicle having either two tandem wheels or one wheel in the front and two wheels in the rear, that is capable of being pedaled and is equipped with a helper motor of not more than fifty cubic centimeters piston displacement that produces no more than one brake horsepower and is capable of propelling the vehicle at a speed of no greater than twenty miles per hour on a level surface.

(I) "Commercial tractor" means every motor vehicle having motive power designed or used for drawing other vehicles and not so constructed as to carry any load thereon, or designed or used for drawing other vehicles while carrying a portion of such other vehicles, or load thereon, or both.

(J) "Agricultural tractor" means every self-propelling vehicle designed or used for drawing other vehicles or wheeled machinery but having no provision for carrying loads independently of such other vehicles, and used principally for agricultural purposes.

(K) "Truck" means every motor vehicle, except trailers and semitrailers, designed and used to carry property.

(L) "Bus" means every motor vehicle designed for carrying more than nine passengers and used for the transportation of persons other than in a ridesharing arrangement, and every motor vehicle, automobile for hire, or funeral car, other than a taxicab or motor vehicle used in a ridesharing arrangement, designed and used for the transportation of persons for compensation.

(M) "Trailer" means every vehicle designed or used for carrying persons or property wholly on its own structure and for being drawn by a motor vehicle, including any such vehicle when formed by or operated as a combination of a "semitrailer" and a vehicle of the dolly type, such as that commonly known as a "trailer dolly," a vehicle used to transport agricultural produce or agricultural production materials between a local place of storage or supply and the farm when drawn or towed on a street or highway at a speed greater than twenty-five miles per hour, and a vehicle designed and used exclusively to transport a boat between a place of storage and a marina, or in and around a marina, when drawn or towed on a street or highway for a distance of more than ten miles or at a speed of more than twenty-five miles per hour.

(N) "Semitrailer" means every vehicle designed or used for carrying persons or property with another and separate motor vehicle so that in operation a part of its own weight or that of its load, or both, rests upon and is carried by another vehicle.

(O) "Pole trailer" means every trailer or semitrailer attached to the towing vehicle by means of a reach, pole, or by being boomed or otherwise secured to the towing vehicle, and ordinarily used for transporting long or irregular shaped loads such as poles, pipes, or structural members capable, generally, of sustaining themselves as beams between the supporting connections.

(P) "Railroad" means a carrier of persons or property operating upon rails placed principally on a private right-of-way.

(Q) "Railroad train" means a steam engine or an electric or other motor, with or without cars coupled thereto, operated by a railroad.

(R) "Streetcar" means a car, other than a railroad train, for transporting persons or property, operated upon rails principally within a street or highway.

(S) "Trackless trolley" means every car that collects its power from overhead electric trolley wires and that is not operated upon rails or tracks.

(T) "Explosives" means any chemical compound or mechanical mixture that is intended for the purpose of producing an explosion that contains any oxidizing and combustible units or other ingredients in such proportions, quantities, or packing that an ignition by fire, by friction, by concussion, by percussion, or by a detonator of any part of the compound or mixture may cause such a sudden generation of highly heated gases that the resultant gaseous pressures are capable of producing destructive effects on contiguous objects, or of destroying life or limb. Manufactured articles shall not be held to be explosives when the individual units contain explosives in such limited quantities, of such nature, or in such packing, that it is impossible to procure a simultaneous or a destructive explosion of such units, to the injury of life, limb, or property by fire, by friction, by concussion, by percussion, or by a detonator, such as fixed ammunition for small arms, firecrackers, or safety fuse matches.

(U) "Flammable liquid" means any liquid that has a flash point of seventy degrees Fahrenheit, or less, as determined by a tagliabue or equivalent closed cup test device.

(V) "Gross weight" means the weight of a vehicle plus the weight of any load thereon.

(W) "Person" means every natural person, firm, co-partnership, association, or corporation.

(X) "Pedestrian" means any natural person afoot.

(Y) "Driver or operator" means every person who drives or is in actual physical control of a vehicle, trackless trolley, or streetcar.

(Z) "Police officer" means every officer authorized to direct or regulate traffic, or to make arrests for violations of traffic regulations.

(AA) "Local authorities" means every county, municipal, and other local board or body having authority to adopt police regulations under the constitution and laws of this state.

(BB) "Street" or "highway" means the entire width between the boundary lines of every way open to the use of the public as a thoroughfare for purposes of vehicular travel.

(CC) "Controlled–access highway" means every street or highway in respect to which owners or occupants of abutting lands and other persons have no legal right of access to or from the same except at such points only and in such manner as may be determined by the public authority having jurisdiction over such street or highway.

(DD) "Private road or driveway" means every way or place in private ownership used for vehicular travel by the owner and those having express or implied permission from the owner but not by other persons.

(EE) "Roadway" means that portion of a highway improved, designed, or ordinarily used for vehicular travel, except the berm or shoulder. If a highway includes two or more separate roadways the term "roadway" means any such roadway separately but not all such roadways collectively.

(FF) "Sidewalk" means that portion of a street between the curb lines, or the lateral lines of a roadway, and the adjacent property lines, intended for the use of pedestrians.

(GG) "Laned highway" means a highway the roadway of which is divided into two or more clearly marked lanes for vehicular traffic.

(HH) "Through highway" means every street or highway as provided in section 4511.65 of the Revised Code.

(II) "State highway" means a highway under the jurisdiction of the department of transportation, outside the limits of municipal corporations, provided that the authority conferred upon the director of transportation in section 5511.01 of the Revised Code to erect state highway route markers and signs directing traffic shall not be modified by sections 4511.01 to 4511.79 and 4511.99 of the Revised Code.

(JJ) "State route" means every highway that is designated with an official state route number and so marked.

(KK) "Intersection" means:

(1) The area embraced within the prolongation or connection of the lateral curb lines, or, if none, then the lateral boundary lines of the roadways of two highways which join one another at, or approximately at, right angles, or the area within which vehicles traveling upon different highways joining at any other angle may come in conflict.

(2) Where a highway includes two roadways thirty feet or more apart, then every crossing of each roadway of such divided highway by an intersecting highway shall be regarded as a separate intersection. If an intersecting highway also includes two roadways thirty feet or more apart, then every crossing of two roadways of such highways shall be regarded as a separate intersection.

(3) The junction of an alley with a street or highway, or with another alley, shall not constitute an intersection.

(LL) "Crosswalk" means:

(1) That part of a roadway at intersections ordinarily included within the real or projected prolongation of property lines and curb lines or, in the absence of curbs, the edges of the traversable roadway;

(2) Any portion of a roadway at an intersection or elsewhere, distinctly indicated for pedestrian crossing by lines or other markings on the surface;

(3) Notwithstanding divisions (LL)(1) and (2) of this section, there shall not be a crosswalk where local authorities have placed signs indicating no crossing.

(MM) "Safety zone" means the area or space officially set apart within a roadway for the exclusive use of pedestrians and protected or marked or indicated by adequate signs as to be plainly visible at all times.

(NN) "Business district" means the territory fronting upon a street or highway, including the street or highway, between successive intersections within municipal corporations where fifty per cent or more of the frontage between such successive intersections is occupied by buildings in use for business, or within or outside municipal corporations where fifty per cent or more of the frontage for a distance of three hundred feet or more is occupied by buildings in use for business, and the character of such territory is indicated by official traffic control devices.

(OO) "Residence district" means the territory, not comprising a business district, fronting on a street or highway, including the street or highway, where, for a distance of three hundred feet or more, the frontage is improved with residences or residences and buildings in use for business.

(PP) "Urban district" means the territory contiguous to and including any street or highway which is built up with structures devoted to business, industry, or dwelling houses situated at intervals of less than one hundred feet for a distance of a quarter of a mile or more, and the character of such territory is indicated by official traffic control devices.

(QQ) "Traffic control devices" means all flaggers, signs, signals, markings, and devices placed or erected by authority of a public body or official having jurisdiction, for the purpose of regulating, warning, or guiding traffic, including signs denoting names of streets and highways.

(RR) "Traffic control signal" means any device, whether manually, electrically, or mechanically operated, by which traffic is alternately directed to stop, to proceed, to change direction, or not to change direction.

(SS) "Railroad sign or signal" means any sign, signal, or device erected by authority of a public body or official or by a railroad and intended to give notice of the presence of railroad tracks or the approach of a railroad train.

(TT) "Traffic" means pedestrians, ridden or herded animals, vehicles, streetcars, trackless trolleys, and other devices, either singly or together, while using any highway for purposes of travel.

(UU) "Right–of–way" means either of the following, as the context requires:

(1) The right of a vehicle, streetcar, trackless trolley, or pedestrian to proceed uninterruptedly in a lawful manner in the direction in which it or the individual is moving in preference to another vehicle, streetcar, trackless trolley, or pedestrian approaching from a different direction into its or the individual's path;

(2) A general term denoting land, property, or the interest therein, usually in the configuration of a strip, acquired for or devoted to transportation purposes. When used in this context, right-of-way includes the roadway, shoulders or berm, ditch, and slopes extending to the right-of-way limits under the control of the state or local authority.

(VV) "Rural mail delivery vehicle" means every vehicle used to deliver United States mail on a rural mail delivery route.

(WW) "Funeral escort vehicle" means any motor vehicle, including a funeral hearse, while used to facilitate the movement of a funeral procession.

(XX) "Alley" means a street or highway intended to provide access to the rear or side of lots or buildings in urban districts and not intended for the purpose of through vehicular traffic, and includes any street or highway that has been declared an "alley" by the legislative authority of the municipal corporation in which such street or highway is located.

(YY) "Freeway" means a divided multi-lane highway for through traffic with all crossroads separated in grade and with full control of access.

(ZZ) "Expressway" means a divided arterial highway for through traffic with full or partial control of access with an excess of fifty per cent of all crossroads separated in grade.

(AAA) "Thruway" means a through highway whose entire roadway is reserved for through traffic and on which roadway parking is prohibited.

(BBB) "Stop intersection" means any intersection at one or more entrances of which stop signs are erected.

(CCC) "Arterial street" means any United States or state numbered route, controlled access highway, or other major radial or circumferential street or highway designated by local authorities within their respective jurisdictions as part of a major arterial system of streets or highways.

(DDD) "Ridesharing arrangement" means the transportation of persons in a motor vehicle where such transportation is incidental to another purpose of a volunteer driver and includes ridesharing arrangements known as carpools, vanpools, and buspools.

(EEE) "Motorized wheelchair" means any self-propelled vehicle designed for, and used by, a handicapped person and that is incapable of a speed in excess of eight miles per hour.

(FFF) "Child day-care center" and "type A family day- care home" have the same meanings as in section 5104.01 of the Revised Code.

(GGG) "Multi–wheel agricultural tractor" means a type of agricultural tractor that has two or more wheels or tires on each side of one axle at the rear of the tractor, is designed or used for drawing other vehicles or wheeled machinery, has no provision for carrying loads independently of the drawn vehicles or machinery, and is used principally for agricultural purposes.

(HHH) "Operate" means to cause or have caused movement of a vehicle, streetcar, or trackless trolley.

(III) "Predicate motor vehicle or traffic offense" means any of the following:

(1) A violation of section 4511.03, 4511.051, 4511.12, 4511.132, 4511.16, 4511.20, 4511.201, 4511.21, 4511.211, 4511.213, 4511.22, 4511.23, 4511.25, 4511.26, 4511.27, 4511.28, 4511.29, 4511.30, 4511.31, 4511.32, 4511.33, 4511.34, 4511.35, 4511.36, 4511.37, 4511.38, 4511.39, 4511.40, 4511.41, 4511.42, 4511.43, 4511.431, 4511.432, 4511.44, 4511.441, 4511.451, 4511.452, 4511.46, 4511.47, 4511.48, 4511.481, 4511.49, 4511.50, 4511.511, 4511.53, 4511.54, 4511.55, 4511.56, 4511.57, 4511.58, 4511.59, 4511.60, 4511.61, 4511.64, 4511.66, 4511.661, 4511.68, 4511.70, 4511.701, 4511.71, 4511.711, 4511.712, 4511.713, 4511.72, 4511.73, 4511.763, 4511.771, 4511.78, or 4511.84 of the Revised Code;

(2) A violation of division (A)(2) of section 4511.17, divisions (A) to (D) of section 4511.51, or division (A) of section 4511.74 of the Revised Code;

(3) A violation of any provision of sections 4511.01 to 4511.76 of the Revised Code for which no penalty otherwise is provided in the section that contains the provision violated;

(4) A violation of a municipal ordinance that is substantially similar to any section or provision set forth or described in division (III)(1), (2), or (3) of this section.

(2004 H 230, eff. 9–16–04; 2004 H 52, eff. 6–1–04; 2002 S 123, eff. 1–1–04; 2002 S 231, eff. 10–24–02; 2000 H 484, eff. 10–5–00; 1996 S 293, eff. 9–26–96 (See also Historical and Statutory Notes.); 1992 H 356, eff. 12–31–92; 1992 S 98, H 485; 1990 S 382, S 272, H 319; 1989 H 258; 1981 H 53; 1979 S 9; 1977 S 100; 1976 H 235, S 56; 1975 H 338; 1974 H 995; 1973 S 108, H 200; 132 v S 451, H 878, H 380, H 684; 131 v S 78; 130 v H 391, S 70; 129 v 1273; 128 v 1270; 127 v 54; 126 v 1165, 790, 115, 392; 1953 H 1; GC 6307–2)

Historical and Statutory Notes

Ed. Note: 1996 S 293 Effective Date—The Secretary of State assigned a general effective date of 9–26–96 for 1996 S 293, along with notice that, in accordance with RC 1.471, the General Assembly has not determined which sections go into immediate effect, and that it appears that certain sections provide for appropriations for current expenses, and are immediately effective in accordance with RC 1.471 and O Const Art II, § 1d.

4511.011 Designation of freeway, expressway, and thruway

The director of transportation, the board of county commissioners of a county, and the legislative authority of a municipality may, for highways under their jurisdiction, designate an existing highway in whole or in part as or included in a "freeway," "expressway," or "thruway."

(1973 H 200, eff. 9–28–73; 130 v S 70)

4511.03 Emergency or public safety vehicles to proceed cautiously past red or stop signal

(A) The driver of any emergency vehicle or public safety vehicle, when responding to an emergency call, upon approaching a red or stop signal or any stop sign shall slow down as necessary for safety to traffic, but may proceed cautiously past such red or stop sign or signal with due regard for the safety of all persons using the street or highway.

(B) Except as otherwise provided in this division, whoever violates this section is guilty of a minor misdemeanor. If, within one year of the offense, the offender previously has been convicted of or pleaded guilty to one predicate motor vehicle or traffic offense, whoever violates this section is guilty of a misdemeanor of the fourth degree. If, within one year of the offense, the offender previously has been convicted of two or more predicate motor vehicle or traffic offenses, whoever violates this section is guilty of a misdemeanor of the third degree.

(2002 S 123, eff. 1–1–04; 132 v H 878, eff. 12–14–67; 1953 H 1; GC 6307–4)

4511.031 Possessing portable preemption device; penalty

(A)(1) No person shall possess a portable signal preemption device.

(2) No person shall use a portable signal preemption device to affect the operation of the traffic control signal.

(B) Division (A)(1) of this section does not apply to any of the following persons and division (A)(2) of this section does not apply to any of the following persons when responding to an emergency call:

(1) A peace officer, as defined in division (A)(1), (12), (14), or (19) of section 109.71 of the Revised Code;

(2) A state highway patrol trooper;

(3) A person while occupying a public safety vehicle as defined in division (E)(1), (3), or (4) of section 4511.01 of the Revised Code.

(C) Whoever violates division (A)(1) of this section is guilty of a misdemeanor of the fourth degree. Whoever violates division (A)(2) of this section is guilty of a misdemeanor of the first degree.

(D) As used in this section, "portable signal preemption device" means a device that, if activated by a person, is capable of changing a traffic control signal to green out of sequence.

(2004 H 406, eff. 3–23–05)

4511.04 Exemptions

(A) Sections 4511.01 to 4511.18, 4511.20 to 4511.78, 4511.99, and 4513.01 to 4513.37 of the Revised Code do not apply to persons, teams, motor vehicles, and other equipment while actually engaged in work upon the surface of a highway within an area designated by traffic control devices, but apply to such persons and vehicles when traveling to or from such work.

(B) The driver of a highway maintenance vehicle owned by this state or any political subdivision of this state, while the driver is engaged in the performance of official duties upon a street or highway, provided the highway maintenance vehicle is equipped with flashing lights and such other markings as are required by law and such lights are in operation when the driver and vehicle are so engaged, shall be exempt from criminal prosecution for violations of sections 4511.22, 4511.25, 4511.26, 4511.27, 4511.28, 4511.30, 4511.31, 4511.33, 4511.35, 4511.66, 4513.02, and 5577.01 to 5577.09 of the Revised Code.

(C)(1) This section does not exempt a driver of a highway maintenance vehicle from civil liability arising from a violation of section 4511.22, 4511.25, 4511.26, 4511.27, 4511.28, 4511.30, 4511.31, 4511.33, 4511.35, 4511.66, or 4513.02 or sections 5577.01 to 5577.09 of the Revised Code.

(2) This section does not exempt the driver of a vehicle that is engaged in the transport of highway maintenance equipment from criminal liability for a violation of sections 5577.01 to 5577.09 of the Revised Code.

(D) As used in this section, "highway maintenance vehicle" means a vehicle used in snow and ice removal or road surface maintenance, including a snow plow, traffic line striper, road sweeper, mowing machine, asphalt distributing vehicle, or other such vehicle designed for use in specific highway maintenance activities.

(2003 H 87, eff. 6–30–03; 1969 S 77, eff. 11–17–69; 1953 H 1; GC 6307–4)

4511.041 Emergency vehicles or public safety vehicles exempt

Sections 4511.12, 4511.13, 4511.131, 4511.132, 4511.14, 4511.15, 4511.202, 4511.21, 4511.211, 4511.22, 4511.23, 4511.25, 4511.26, 4511.27, 4511.28, 4511.29, 4511.30, 4511.31, 4511.32, 4511.33, 4511.34, 4511.35, 4511.36, 4511.37, 4511.38, 4511.39, 4511.40, 4511.41, 4511.42, 4511.43, 4511.431, 4511.432, 4511.44, 4511.441, 4511.57, 4511.58, 4511.59, 4511.60, 4511.61, 4511.62, 4511.66, 4511.68, 4511.681, and 4511.69 of the Revised Code do not apply to the driver of an emergency vehicle or public safety vehicle if the emergency vehicle or public safety vehicle is responding to an emergency call, is equipped with and displaying at least one flashing, rotating, or oscillating light visible under normal atmospheric conditions from a distance of five hundred feet to the front of the vehicle and if the driver of the vehicle is giving an audible signal by siren, exhaust whistle, or bell. This section does not relieve the driver of an emergency vehicle or public safety vehicle from the duty to drive with due regard for the safety of all persons and property upon the highway.

(1993 H 149, eff. 5–20–93)

4511.042 Coroners' vehicles exempt

Sections 4511.25, 4511.26, 4511.27, 4511.28, 4511.29, 4511.30, 4511.31, 4511.32, 4511.33, 4511.35, 4511.36, 4511.37, 4511.38, and 4511.66 of the Revised Code do not apply to a coroner, deputy coroner, or coroner's investigator operating a motor vehicle in accordance with section 4513.171 of the Revised Code. This section does not relieve a coroner, deputy coroner, or coroner's investigator operating a motor vehicle from the duty to drive with due regard for the safety of all persons and property upon the highway.

(1997 H 282, eff. 11–12–97)

4511.05 Persons riding or driving animals upon roadways

Every person riding, driving, or leading an animal upon a roadway is subject to sections 4511.01 to 4511.78, inclusive, 4511.99, and 4513.01 to 4513.37, inclusive, of the Revised Code, applicable to the driver of a vehicle, except those provisions of such sections which by their nature are inapplicable.

(1953 H 1, eff. 10–1–53; GC 6307–5)

4511.051 Prohibition against pedestrians and slow-moving vehicles on freeways

(A) No person, unless otherwise directed by a police officer, shall:

(1) As a pedestrian, occupy any space within the limits of the right-of-way of a freeway, except: in a rest area; on a facility that is separated from the roadway and shoulders of the freeway and is designed and appropriately marked for pedestrian use; in the performance of public works or official duties; as a result of an emergency caused by an accident or breakdown of a motor vehicle; or to obtain assistance;

(2) Occupy any space within the limits of the right-of-way of a freeway, with: an animal-drawn vehicle; a ridden or led animal; herded animals; a pushcart; a bicycle, except on a facility that is separated from the roadway and shoulders of the freeway and is designed and appropriately marked for bicycle use; a bicycle with motor attached; a motor driven cycle with a motor which produces not to exceed five brake horsepower; an agricultural tractor; farm machinery; except in the performance of public works or official duties.

(B) Except as otherwise provided in this division, whoever violates this section is guilty of a minor misdemeanor. If, within one year of the offense, the offender previously has been convicted of or pleaded guilty to one predicate motor vehicle or traffic offense, whoever violates this section is guilty of a misdemeanor of the fourth degree. If, within one year of the offense, the offender previously has been convicted of two or more predicate motor vehicle or traffic offenses, whoever violates this section is guilty of a misdemeanor of the third degree.

(2002 S 123, eff. 1–1–04; 1989 H 258, eff. 11–2–89; 132 v H 1; 131 v H 101)

4511.06 Uniform application and precedence of traffic law

Sections 4511.01 to 4511.78, 4511.99, and 4513.01 to 4513.37 of the Revised Code shall be applicable and uniform throughout this state and in all political subdivisions and municipal corporations of this state. No local authority shall enact or enforce any rule in conflict with such sections, except that this section does not prevent local authorities from exercising the rights granted them by Chapter 4521. of the Revised Code and does not limit the effect or application of the provisions of that chapter.

(1982 H 707, eff. 1–1–83; 1953 H 1; GC 6307–6)

4511.07 Local traffic regulations

Sections 4511.01 to 4511.78, 4511.99, and 4513.01 to 4513.37 of the Revised Code do not prevent local authorities from carrying out the following activities with respect to streets and highways under their jurisdiction and within the reasonable exercise of the police power:

(A) Regulating the stopping, standing, or parking of vehicles, trackless trolleys, and streetcars;

(B) Regulating traffic by means of police officers or traffic control devices;

(C) Regulating or prohibiting processions or assemblages on the highways;

(D) Designating particular highways as one-way highways and requiring that all vehicles, trackless trolleys, and streetcars on the one-way highways be moved in one specific direction;

(E) Regulating the speed of vehicles, streetcars, and trackless trolleys in public parks;

(F) Designating any highway as a through highway and requiring that all vehicles, trackless trolleys, and streetcars stop before entering or crossing a through highway, or designating any intersection as a stop intersection and requiring all vehicles, trackless trolleys, and streetcars to stop at one or more entrances to the intersection;

(G) Regulating or prohibiting vehicles and trackless trolleys from passing to the left of safety zones;

(H) Regulating the operation of bicycles and requiring the registration and licensing of bicycles, including the requirement of a registration fee;

(I) Regulating the use of certain streets by vehicles, streetcars, or trackless trolleys.

No ordinance or regulation enacted under division (D), (E), (F), (G), or (I) of this section shall be effective until signs giving notice of the local traffic regulations are posted upon or at the entrance to the highway or part of the highway affected, as may be most appropriate.

Every ordinance, resolution, or regulation enacted under division (A) of this section shall be enforced in compliance with section 4511.071 of the Revised Code, unless the local authority that enacted it also enacted an ordinance, resolution, or regulation pursuant to division (A) of section 4521.02 of the Revised Code that specifies that a violation of it shall not be considered a criminal offense, in which case the ordinance, resolution, or regulation shall be enforced in compliance with Chapter 4521. of the Revised Code.

(1982 H 707, eff. 1–1–83; 1980 S 257; 1974 H 995; 1970 S 452; 129 v 1037; 1953 H 1; GC 6307–7)

4511.071 Owner may establish nonliability for local traffic offenses by proof of lease of vehicle; exception

(A) Except as provided in division (C) of this section, the owner of a vehicle shall be entitled to establish nonliability for prosecution for violation of an ordinance, resolution, or regulation enacted under division (A) of section 4511.07 of the Revised Code by proving the vehicle was in the care, custody, or control of a person other than the owner at the time of the violation pursuant to a written rental or lease agreement or affidavit providing that except for such agreement, no other business relationship with respect to the vehicle in question exists between the operator and owner.

(B) Proof that the vehicle was in the care, custody, or control of a person other than the owner shall be established by sending a copy of such written rental or lease agreement or affidavit to the prosecuting authority within thirty days from the date of receipt by the owner of the notice of violation. The furnishing of a copy of a written rental or lease agreement or affidavit shall be prima-facie evidence that a vehicle was in the care, custody, or control of a person other than the owner.

(C) This section does not apply to a violation of an ordinance, resolution, or regulation enacted under division (A) of section 4511.07 of the Revised Code if the ordinance, resolution, or regulation is one that is required to be enforced in compliance with Chapter 4521. of the Revised Code.

(1982 H 707, eff. 1–1–83; 1980 S 257)

4511.08 Use of private property for vehicular travel

Sections 4511.01 to 4511.78, inclusive, 4511.99, and 4513.01 to 4513.37, inclusive, of the Revised Code do not prevent the owner of real property, used by the public for purposes of vehicular travel by permission of the owner and not as a matter of right, from prohibiting such use or from requiring additional conditions to those specified in such sections, or otherwise regulating such use as may seem best to such owner.

(1953 H 1, eff. 10–1–53; GC 6307–8)

TRAFFIC CONTROL DEVICES AND SIGNS

4511.09 Uniform system of traffic control devices

The department of transportation shall adopt a manual and specifications for a uniform system of traffic control devices, including signs denoting names of streets and highways, for use upon highways within this state. Such uniform system shall correlate with, and so far as possible conform to, the system approved by the American Association of State Highway Officials.

(1973 H 200, eff. 9–28–73; 1953 H 1; GC 6307–9)

4511.091 Arrest pending warrant when radar, electrical, or mechanical timing device used

(A) The driver of any motor vehicle that has been checked by radar, or by any electrical or mechanical timing device to determine the speed of the motor vehicle over a measured distance of a highway or a measured distance of a private road or driveway, and found to be in violation of any of the provisions of section 4511.21 or 4511.211 of the Revised Code, may be arrested until a warrant can be obtained, provided the arresting officer has observed the recording of the speed of the motor vehicle by the radio microwaves, electrical or mechanical timing device, or has received a radio message from the officer who observed the speed of the motor vehicle recorded by the radio microwaves, electrical or mechanical timing device; provided, in case of an arrest based on such a message, the radio message has been dispatched immediately after the speed of the motor vehicle was recorded and the arresting officer is furnished a description of the motor vehicle for proper identification and the recorded speed.

(B) If the driver of a motor vehicle being driven on a public street or highway of this state is observed violating any provision of this chapter other than section 4511.21 or 4511.211 of the Revised Code by a law enforcement officer situated at any location, including in any type of airborne aircraft or airship, that law enforcement officer may send a radio message to another law enforcement officer, and the other law enforcement officer may arrest the driver of the motor vehicle until a warrant can be obtained or may issue the driver a citation for the violation; provided, if an arrest or citation is based on such a message, the radio message is dispatched immediately after the violation is observed and the law enforcement officer who observes the violation furnishes to the law enforcement officer who makes the arrest or issues the citation a description of the alleged violation and the motor vehicle for proper identification.

(1998 S 213, eff. 7–29–98; 1990 H 171, eff. 5–31–90; 132 v H 380; 130 v H 324; 129 v 582; 125 v 396)

4511.10 Placing and maintaining traffic control devices on state highways

The department of transportation may place and maintain traffic control devices, conforming to its manual and specifications, upon all state highways as are necessary to indicate and to carry out sections 4511.01 to 4511.78 and 4511.99 of the Revised Code, or to regulate, warn, or guide traffic.

No local authority shall place or maintain any traffic control device upon any highway under the jurisdiction of the department except by permission of the director of transportation.

(1973 H 200, eff. 9–28–73; 1953 H 1; GC 6307–10)

4511.101 Business logo sign program

(A) The director of transportation, in accordance with 23 U.S.C.A. 109(d), 131(f), and 315, as amended, shall establish a program for the placement of business logos for identification purposes on state directional signs within the rights-of-way of divided, multi-lane, limited access highways in both rural and urban areas.

(B) All direct and indirect costs of the business logo sign program established pursuant to this section shall be fully paid by the businesses applying for participation in the program. At any interchange where a business logo sign is erected, such costs shall be divided equally among the participating businesses. The direct and indirect costs of the program shall include, but not be limited to, the cost of capital, directional signs, blanks, posts, logos, installation, repair, engineering, design, insurance, removal, replacement, and administration. Nothing in this chapter shall be construed to prohibit the director from establishing such a program.

(C) The director, in accordance with rules adopted pursuant to Chapter 119. of the Revised Code, may contract with any private person to operate, maintain, and market the business logo sign program. The rules shall describe the terms of the contract, and shall allow for a reasonable profit to be earned by the successful applicant. In awarding the contract, the director shall consider the skill, expertise, prior experience, and other qualifications of each applicant.

(D) As used in this section, "urban area" means an area having a population of fifty thousand or more according to the most recent federal census and designated as such on urban maps prepared by the department.

(E) Neither the department nor the director shall do either of the following:

(1) Limit the right of any person to erect, maintain, repair, remove, or utilize any off-premises or on-premises advertising device;

(2) Make participation in the business logo sign program conditional upon a business agreeing to limit, discontinue, withdraw, modify, alter, or change any advertising or sign.

(1998 H 462, eff. 3–18–99; 1997 H 210, eff. 6–30–97; 1996 H 670, eff. 12–2–96; 1996 H 353, eff. 9–17–96; 1995 H 107, eff. (See Historical and Statutory Notes); 1993 H 154, eff. 6–30–93; 1990 H 737; 1989 H 356)

Historical and Statutory Notes

Ed. Note: 1995 H 107 Effective Date—The Secretary of State assigned a general effective date of 6–30–95 for 1995 H 107. Pursuant to O Const Art II § 1c and 1d, and RC 1.471, sections of 1995 H 107 that are, or depend for their implementation upon, current expense appropriations are effective 3–31–95; sections of 1995 H 107 that are not, and do not depend for their implementation upon, current expense appropriations are effective 6–30–95. See *Baldwin's Ohio Legislative Service*, 1995, page 3/L–98 for 1995 H 107, § 16.

4511.102 Definitions relating to tourist-oriented directional sign program

As used in sections 4511.102 to 4511.106 of the Revised Code:

(A) "Tourist–oriented activity" includes any lawful cultural, historical, recreational, educational, or commercial activity a major portion of whose income or visitors are derived during the normal business season from motorists not residing in the immediate area of the activity and attendance at which is no less than two thousand visitors in any consecutive twelve-month period.

(B) "Eligible attraction" means any tourist-oriented activity that meets all of the following criteria:

(1) Is not eligible for inclusion in the business logo sign program established under section 4511.101 of the Revised Code;

(2) If currently advertised by signs adjacent to a highway on the interstate system or state system, those signs are consistent with Chapter 5516. of the Revised Code and the "National Highway Beautification Act of 1965," 79 Stat. 1028, 23 U.S.C. 131, and the national standards, criteria, and rules adopted pursuant to that act;

(3) Is within ten miles of the highway for which signing is sought under sections 4511.102 to 4511.105 of the Revised Code;

(4) Meets any additional criteria developed by the director of transportation and adopted by the director as rules in accordance with Chapter 119. of the Revised Code.

(C) "Interstate system" has the same meaning as in section 5516.01 of the Revised Code.

(D) "Commercial activity" means a farm market, winery, bed and breakfast, lodging that is not a franchise or part of a national chain, antiques shop, craft store, or gift store.

(1997 H 215, eff. 6–30–97; 1997 H 210, eff. 6–30–97; 1995 H 217, eff. 11–1–95; 1994 H 687, eff. 10–12–94)

4511.103 Tourist–oriented directional sign program

(A) The director of transportation, in accordance with 23 U.S.C. 109(d) and 315, with the provisions of the federal manual of uniform traffic control devices relating to tourist-oriented directional signs and trailblazer markers, and with Chapter 119. of the Revised Code, shall adopt rules to carry out a program for the placement of tourist-oriented directional signs and trailblazer markers within the rights-of-way of those portions of rural state highways that are not on the interstate system. The rules shall prohibit the placement of tourist-oriented directional signs and trailblazer markers at interchanges on state system expressways and freeways. The rules shall include, but need not be limited to, all of the following:

(1) The form of the application to participate in the program. The form shall include such necessary information as the director requires to ensure that a tourist-oriented activity for which signing is sought is an eligible attraction.

(2) Provisions for covering or otherwise obscuring signs during off-seasons for eligible attractions that operate on a seasonal basis;

(3) A determination as to the circumstances that justify including on a sign the hours of operation of an eligible attraction;

(4) Criteria for use of the signs at at-grade intersections on expressways.

(B) The program established pursuant to division (A) of this section may be operated, maintained, and marketed either by the department of transportation or by any private person with whom the director, in accordance with rules adopted by the director pursuant to Chapter 119. of the Revised Code, contracts for the operation, maintenance, and marketing. The rules shall describe the terms of the contract and shall allow for a reasonable profit to be made by the successful applicant. In awarding the contract, the director shall consider the skill, expertise, prior experience, and other qualifications of each applicant.

(C) All direct and indirect costs of the program shall be fully paid by the eligible attractions that participate in the program. The director shall develop a fee schedule for participation in the program, and shall charge each program participant the appropriate fee. Direct and indirect costs include, but are not limited to, the cost of all of the following:

(1) Capital;

(2) Insurance;

(3) Directional signs, sign blanks, and posts, and the design, engineering, installation, repair, replacement, and removal of directional signs and posts;

(4) Program administration.

(1995 H 217, eff. 11–1–95; 1994 H 687, eff. 10–12–94)

4511.104 Participation in tourist-oriented directional sign program; permits

(A) The operator of any tourist-oriented activity who wishes to participate in the tourist-oriented directional sign program established under sections 4511.102 to 4511.105 of the Revised Code shall forward a completed application, as provided in section 4511.103 of the Revised Code, to the director of transportation or person holding a contract under division (B) of section 4511.103 of the Revised Code. If the director or person finds the application to be complete and determines that the activity constitutes an eligible attraction, the director or person shall so notify the applicant in writing. Upon receipt of the notice, the applicant shall forward to the director or person, in a manner determined by the director, the amount of the fee due and thereupon shall execute an advertising agreement in a form prescribed by the director.

(B) The operator of any eligible attraction for which an advertising agreement is in effect under this section immediately shall forward the advertising agreement to the director or person holding a contract under division (B) of section 4511.103 of the Revised Code for cancellation if the eligible attraction ceases to be such an attraction.

(C) The director, when having reasonable cause to believe that an eligible attraction for which an advertising agreement is in effect has ceased to be such an attraction, immediately and without conducting an adjudication shall issue an order canceling the advertising agreement and forward notice of the cancellation in writing to the operator of the attraction together with information that the cancellation may be appealed in accordance with section 119.12 of the Revised Code. If no appeal is entered within the period specified in that section or if an appeal is entered but cancellation of the advertising agreement subsequently is affirmed, the director shall order the removal of the signs relating to the former eligible attraction.

(D) Any person holding a contract under division (B) of section 4511.103 of the Revised Code, when having reasonable cause to believe that an eligible attraction for which an advertising agreement is in effect has ceased to be such an attraction, immediately shall notify the director in writing of that fact. Upon receipt of the notice, the director shall proceed in accordance with division (C) of this section.

(1995 H 217, eff. 11–1–95; 1994 H 687, eff. 10–12–94)

4511.105 Specifications for tourist-oriented directional signs

Tourist-oriented directional signs shall conform to the specifications contained in the federal manual of uniform traffic control devices.

If more than one eligible attraction requires a sign at the same location, multiple signs may be combined on the same panel in accordance with the federal manual of uniform traffic control devices.

Advance signing may be installed in those situations where sight distance, intersection vehicle maneuvers, or other vehicle operating characteristics require advance notice of an eligible attraction in order to reduce vehicle conflicts and improve highway safety.

The design, arrangement, size, and location of tourist-oriented directional signs, including advance signs and trailblazer markers, authorized under sections 4511.102 to 4511.105 of the Revised Code shall conform to the applicable specifications contained in the federal manual of uniform traffic control devices.

(1995 H 217, eff. 11–1–95; 1994 H 687, eff. 10–12–94)

4511.106 County or township establishing tourist-oriented directional sign program

The legislative authority of a local authority may adopt a resolution establishing a program for the placement of tourist-oriented directional signs and trailblazer markers within the rights-of-way of streets and highways under its jurisdiction. Any program established under this section shall conform to the rules and specifications contained in the program established by the director of transportation pursuant to sections 4511.102 to 4511.105 of the Revised Code and the applicable provisions of the federal manual of uniform traffic control devices. If a local authority establishes a program under this section, the local authority may request guidance from the department of transportation in structuring, implementing, and administering its program, but the local authority is solely responsible for the structure and actual implementation and administration of its program, including, but not limited to, the evaluation and review of applications to participate in the local program and the execution of advertising agreements with eligible attractions.

(1995 H 217, eff. 11–1–95; 1994 H 687, eff. 10–12–94)

4511.107 Purchase approval for outdoor advertising devices

The department of transportation shall not enter into any program to purchase or acquire any outdoor advertising device for which a valid permit has been issued by this state, except in cases of eminent domain involving an appropriation pursuant to Chapter 163. of the Revised Code, unless the purchase or acquisition program is first approved by the general assembly.

(1994 H 687, eff. 10–12–94)

4511.11 Local authorities' traffic control device placement and maintenance

(A) Local authorities in their respective jurisdictions shall place and maintain traffic control devices in accordance with the department of transportation manual and specifications for a uniform system of traffic control devices, adopted under section 4511.09 of the Revised Code, upon highways under their jurisdiction as are necessary to indicate and to carry out sections 4511.01 to 4511.76 and 4511.99 of the Revised Code, local traffic ordinances, or to regulate, warn, or guide traffic.

(B) The director of transportation may require to be removed any traffic control device that does not conform to the manual and specifications for a uniform system of traffic control devices on the extensions of the state highway system within municipal corporations.

(C) No village shall place or maintain any traffic control signal upon an extension of the state highway system within the village without first obtaining the permission of the director. The director may revoke the permission and may require to be removed any traffic control signal that has been erected without the director's permission on an extension of a state highway within a village, or that, if erected under a permit granted by the director, does not conform to the state manual and specifications, or that is not operated in accordance with the terms of the permit.

(D) All traffic control devices erected on a public road, street, or alley, shall conform to the state manual and specifications.

(E) No person, firm, or corporation shall sell or offer for sale to local authorities any traffic control device that does not conform to the state manual and specifications, except by permission of the director.

(F) No local authority shall purchase or manufacture any traffic control device that does not conform to the state manual and specifications, except by permission of the director.

(G) Whoever violates division (E) of this section is guilty of a misdemeanor of the third degree.

(2002 S 123, eff. 1–1–04; 1990 H 162, eff. 6–28–90; 1989 H 258; 1973 H 200; 131 v H 119; 130 v Pt 2, H 5; 130 v H 881; 1953 H 1; GC 6307–11)

4511.12 Obeying traffic control devices

(A) No pedestrian, driver of a vehicle, or operator of a streetcar or trackless trolley shall disobey the instructions of any traffic control device placed in accordance with this chapter, unless at the time otherwise directed by a police officer.

No provision of this chapter for which signs are required shall be enforced against an alleged violator if at the time and place of the alleged violation an official sign is not in proper position and sufficiently legible to be seen by an ordinarily observant person. Whenever a particular section of this chapter does not state that signs are required, that section shall be effective even though no signs are erected or in place.

(B) Except as otherwise provided in this division, whoever violates this section is guilty of a minor misdemeanor. If, within one year of the offense, the offender previously has been convicted of or pleaded guilty to one predicate motor vehicle or traffic offense, whoever violates this section is guilty of a misdemeanor of the fourth degree. If, within one year of the offense, the offender previously has been convicted of two or more predicate motor vehicle or traffic offenses, whoever violates this section is guilty of a misdemeanor of the third degree.

(2002 S 123, eff. 1–1–04; 1989 H 258, eff. 11–2–89; 1953 H 1; GC 6307–12)

4511.121 Obeying traffic control devices or peace officer orders at weigh scale locations; bypass of scale locations; penalties

(A)(1) Except as provided in division (B) of this section, any operator of a commercial motor vehicle, upon approaching a scale location established for the purpose of determining the weight of the vehicle and its load, shall comply with any traffic control device or the order of a peace officer directing the vehicle to proceed to be weighed or otherwise inspected.

(2) Any operator of a commercial motor vehicle, upon bypassing a scale location in accordance with division (B) of this section, shall comply with an order of a peace officer to stop the vehicle to verify the use and operation of an electronic clearance device.

(B) Any operator of a commercial motor vehicle that is equipped with an electronic clearance device authorized by the superintendent of the state highway patrol under section 4549.081 of the Revised Code may bypass a scale location, regardless of the instruction of a traffic control device to enter the scale facility, if either of the following apply:

(1) The in-cab transponder displays a green light or other affirmative visual signal and also sounds an affirmative audible signal;

(2) Any other criterion established by the superintendent by rule is met.

(C) Any peace officer may order the operator of a commercial motor vehicle that bypasses a scale location to stop the vehicle to verify the use and operation of an electronic clearance device.

(D) Whoever violates division (A) of this section is guilty of a minor misdemeanor. If, within one year of the offense, the offender previously has been convicted of or pleaded guilty to a violation of division (A) of this section, whoever violates that division is guilty of a misdemeanor of the fourth degree. If, within one year of the offense, the offender previously has been convicted of or pleaded guilty to two or more violations of division (A) of this section, whoever violates division (A) is guilty of a misdemeanor of the third degree.

(E) As used in this section and in section 4549.081 of the Revised Code, "commercial motor vehicle" means any combination of vehicles with a gross vehicle weight rating or an actual gross vehicle weight of more than ten thousand pounds if the vehicle is used in interstate or intrastate commerce to transport property and also means any vehicle that is transporting hazardous materials for which placarding is required pursuant to 49 C.F.R. Parts 100 to 180.

(2004 H 230, eff. 9–16–04)

4511.13 Signal lights

Whenever traffic is controlled by traffic control signals exhibiting different colored lights, or colored lighted arrows, successively one at a time or in combination, only the colors green, red, and yellow shall be used, except for special pedestrian signals carrying words or symbols, and said lights shall indicate and apply to drivers of vehicles, streetcars, and trackless trolleys and to pedestrians as follows:

(A) Green indication:

(1) Vehicular traffic, streetcars, and trackless trolleys, facing a circular green signal may proceed straight through or turn right or left unless a sign at such place prohibits either such turn. But vehicular traffic, streetcars, and trackless trolleys, including vehicles, streetcars, and trackless trolleys turning right or left, shall yield the right-of-way to other vehicles, streetcars, trackless trolleys, and pedestrians lawfully within the intersection or an adjacent crosswalk at the time such signal is exhibited.

(2) Vehicular traffic, streetcars, and trackless trolleys facing a green arrow signal, shown alone or in combination with another indication, may cautiously enter the intersection only to make the movement indicated by such arrow, or such other movement as is permitted by other indications shown at the same time. Such vehicular traffic, streetcars, and trackless trolleys shall yield the right-of-way to pedestrians lawfully within an adjacent crosswalk and to other traffic lawfully using the intersection.

(3) Unless otherwise directed by a pedestrian-control signal, as provided in section 4511.14 of the Revised Code, pedestrians facing any green signal, except when the sole green signal is a turn arrow, may proceed across the roadway within any marked or unmarked crosswalk.

(B) Steady yellow indication:

(1) Vehicular traffic, streetcars, and trackless trolleys facing a steady circular yellow or yellow arrow signal are thereby warned that the related green movement is being terminated or that a red indication will be exhibited immediately thereafter when vehicular traffic, streetcars and trackless trolleys shall not enter the intersection.

(2) Pedestrians facing a steady circular yellow or yellow arrow signal, unless otherwise directed by a pedestrian-control signal as provided in section 4511.14 of the Revised Code, are thereby advised that there is insufficient time to cross the roadway before a red indication is shown and no pedestrian shall then start to cross the roadway.

(C) Steady red indication:

(1) Vehicular traffic, streetcars, and trackless trolleys facing a steady red signal alone shall stop at a clearly marked stop line, but if none, before entering the crosswalk on the near side of the intersection, or if none, then before entering the intersection and shall remain standing until an indication to proceed is shown except as provided in divisions (C)(2) and (3) of this section.

(2) Unless a sign is in place prohibiting a right turn as provided in division (C)(5) of this section, vehicular traffic, streetcars, and trackless trolleys facing a steady red signal may cautiously enter the intersection to make a right turn after stopping as required by division (C)(1) of this section. Such vehicular traffic, streetcars, and trackless trolleys shall yield the right-of-way to pedestrians lawfully within an adjacent crosswalk and to other traffic lawfully using the intersection.

(3) Unless a sign is in place prohibiting a left turn as provided in division (C)(5) of this section, vehicular traffic, streetcars, and trackless trolleys facing a steady red signal on a one-way street that intersects another one-way street on which traffic moves to the left may cautiously enter the intersection to make a left turn into the one-way street after stopping as required by division (C)(1) of this section, and yielding the right-of-way to pedestrians lawfully within an adjacent crosswalk and to other traffic lawfully using the intersection.

(4) Unless otherwise directed by a pedestrian-control signal as provided in section 4511.14 of the Revised Code, pedestrians facing a steady red signal alone shall not enter the roadway.

(5) Local authorities may by ordinance, or the director of transportation on state highways may, prohibit a right or a left turn against a steady red signal at any intersection, which shall be effective when signs giving notice thereof are posted at the intersection.

(D) In the event an official traffic-control signal is erected and maintained at a place other than an intersection, the provisions of this section shall be applicable except as to those provisions which by their nature can have no application. Any stop required shall be made at a sign or marking on the pavement indicating where the stop shall be made, but in the absence of any such sign or marking the stop shall be made at the signal.

(1984 H 703, eff. 3–28–85; 1977 H 171; 1974 H 99, S 263; 130 v S 71; 1953 H 1; GC 6307–13)

4511.131 Signals over reversible lanes

When lane-use control signals are placed over individual lanes of a street or highway, said signals shall indicate and apply to drivers of vehicles and trackless trolleys as follows:

(A) A steady downward green arrow:

Vehicular traffic and trackless trolleys may travel in any lane over which a green arrow signal is shown.

(B) A steady yellow "X":

Vehicular traffic and trackless trolleys are warned to vacate in a safe manner any lane over which such signal is shown to avoid occupying that lane when a steady red "X" signal is shown.

(C) A flashing yellow "X":

Vehicular traffic and trackless trolleys may use with proper caution any lane over which such signal is shown for only the purpose of making a left turn.

(D) A steady red "X".

Vehicular traffic and trackless trolleys shall not enter or travel in any lane over which such signal is shown.

(1974 S 263, eff. 7–3–74; 130 v S 71)

4511.132 Driver's duties upon approaching intersection with ambiguous or non-working traffic signal

(A) The driver of a vehicle, streetcar, or trackless trolley who approaches an intersection where traffic is controlled by traffic control signals shall do all of the following, if the signal facing the driver either exhibits no colored lights or colored lighted arrows or exhibits a combination of such lights or arrows that fails to clearly indicate the assignment of right–of–way:

(1) Stop at a clearly marked stop line, but if none, stop before entering the crosswalk on the near side of the intersection, or, if none, stop before entering the intersection;

(2) Yield the right-of-way to all vehicles, streetcars, or trackless trolleys in the intersection or approaching on an intersecting road, if the vehicles, streetcars, or trackless trolleys will constitute an immediate hazard during the time the driver is moving across or within the intersection or junction of roadways;

(3) Exercise ordinary care while proceeding through the intersection.

(B) Except as otherwise provided in this division, whoever violates this section is guilty of a minor misdemeanor. If, within one year of the offense, the offender previously has been convicted of or pleaded guilty to one predicate motor vehicle or traffic offense, whoever violates this section is guilty of a misdemeanor of the fourth degree. If, within one year of the offense, the offender previously has been convicted of two or more predicate motor vehicle or traffic offenses, whoever violates this section is guilty of a misdemeanor of the third degree.

(2002 S 123, eff. 1–1–04; 1989 S 44, eff. 7–25–89)

4511.14 Pedestrian control signals

Whenever special pedestrian control signals exhibiting the words "walk" or "don't walk," or the symbol of a walking person or an upraised palm are in place, such signals shall indicate the following instructions:

(A) "Walk" or the symbol of a walking person: Pedestrians facing such signal may proceed across the roadway in the direction of the signal and shall be given the right of way by the operators of all vehicles, streetcars, and trackless trolleys.

(B) "Don't walk" or the symbol of an upraised palm: No pedestrian shall start to cross the roadway in the direction of the signal.

(C) Nothing in this section shall be construed to invalidate the continued use of pedestrian control signals utilizing the word "wait" if those signals were installed prior to the effective date of this act.

(1984 H 703, eff. 3–28–85; 1953 H 1; GC 6307–14)

4511.15 Flashing traffic signals

Whenever an illuminated flashing red or yellow traffic signal is used in a traffic signal or with a traffic sign it shall require obedience as follows:

(A) Flashing red stop signal: Operators of vehicles, trackless trolleys, and streetcars shall stop at a clearly marked stop line, but if none, before entering the crosswalk on the near side of the intersection, or if none, then at the point nearest the intersecting roadway where the driver has a view of approaching traffic on the intersecting roadway before entering it, and the right to proceed shall be subject to the rules applicable after making a stop at a stop sign.

(B) Flashing yellow caution signal: Operators of vehicles, trackless trolleys, and streetcars may proceed through the intersection or past such signal only with caution.

This section shall not apply at railroad grade crossings. Conduct of drivers of vehicles, trackless trolleys, and streetcars approaching railroad grade crossings shall be governed by sections 4511.61 and 4511.62 of the Revised Code.

(1974 H 995, eff. 1–1–75; 1953 H 1; GC 6307–15)

4511.16 Prohibition against unauthorized signs and signals

(A) No person shall place, maintain, or display upon or in view of any highway any unauthorized sign, signal, marking, or device which purports to be, is an imitation of, or resembles a traffic control device or railroad sign or signal, or which attempts to direct the movement of traffic or hides from view or interferes with the effectiveness of any traffic control device or any railroad sign or signal, and no person shall place or maintain, nor shall any public authority permit, upon any highway any traffic sign or signal bearing thereon any commercial advertising. This section does not prohibit either the erection upon private property adjacent to highways of signs giving useful directional information and of a type that cannot be mistaken for traffic control devices or the erection upon private property of traffic control devices by the owner of real property in accordance with sections 4511.211 and 4511.432 of the Revised Code.

Every such prohibited sign, signal, marking, or device is a public nuisance, and the authority having jurisdiction over the highway may remove it or cause it to be removed.

(B) Except as otherwise provided in this division, whoever violates this section is guilty of a minor misdemeanor. If, within one year of the offense, the offender previously has been convicted of or pleaded guilty to one predicate motor vehicle or traffic offense, whoever violates this section is guilty of a misdemeanor of the fourth degree. If, within one year of the offense, the offender previously has been convicted of two or more predicate motor vehicle or traffic offenses, whoever violates this section is guilty of a misdemeanor of the third degree.

(2002 S 123, eff. 1–1–04; 1990 H 171, eff. 5–31–90; 1953 H 1; GC 6307–16)

4511.17 Tampering with traffic control devices prohibited

(A) No person, without lawful authority, shall do any of the following:

(1) Knowingly move, deface, damage, destroy, or otherwise improperly tamper with any traffic control device, any railroad sign or signal, or any inscription, shield, or insignia on the device, sign, or signal, or any part of the device, sign, or signal;

(2) Knowingly drive upon or over any freshly applied pavement marking material on the surface of a roadway while the

marking materiel [1] is in an undried condition and is marked by flags, markers, signs, or other devices intended to protect it;

(3) Knowingly move, damage, destroy, or otherwise improperly tamper with a manhole cover.

(B)(1) Except as otherwise provided in this division, whoever violates division (A)(1) or (3) of this section is guilty of a misdemeanor of the third degree. If a violation of division (A)(1) or (3) of this section creates a risk of physical harm to any person, the offender is guilty of a misdemeanor of the first degree. If a violation of division (A)(1) or (3) of this section causes serious physical harm to property that is owned, leased, or controlled by a state or local authority, the offender is guilty of a felony of the fifth degree.

(2) Except as otherwise provided in this division, whoever violates division (A)(2) of this section is guilty of a minor misdemeanor. If, within one year of the offense, the offender previously has been convicted of or pleaded guilty to one predicate motor vehicle or traffic offense, whoever violates division (A)(2) of this section is guilty of a misdemeanor of the fourth degree. If, within one year of the offense, the offender previously has been convicted of two or more predicate motor vehicle or traffic offenses, whoever violates division (A)(2) of this section is guilty of a misdemeanor of the third degree.

(2002 S 123, eff. 1–1–04; 1990 H 162, eff. 6–28–90; 1953 H 1; GC 6307–17)

[1] So in original; 2002 S 123.

4511.18 Possession or sale of traffic control device prohibited

(A) As used in this section, "traffic control device" means any sign, traffic control signal, or other device conforming to and placed or erected in accordance with the manual adopted under section 4511.09 of the Revised Code by authority of a public body or official having jurisdiction, for the purpose of regulating, warning, or guiding traffic, including signs denoting the names of streets and highways, but does not mean any pavement marking.

(B) No individual shall buy or otherwise possess, or sell, a traffic control device, except when one of the following applies:

(1) In the course of the individual's employment by the state or a local authority for the express or implied purpose of manufacturing, providing, erecting, moving, or removing such a traffic control device;

(2) In the course of the individual's employment by any manufacturer of traffic control devices other than a state or local authority;

(3) For the purpose of demonstrating the design and function of a traffic control device to state or local officials;

(4) When the traffic control device has been purchased from the state or a local authority at a sale of property that is no longer needed or is unfit for use;

(5) The traffic control device has been properly purchased from a manufacturer for use on private property and the person possessing the device has a sales receipt for the device or other acknowledgment of sale issued by the manufacturer.

(C) This section does not preclude, and shall not be construed as precluding, prosecution for theft in violation of section 2913.02 of the Revised Code or a municipal ordinance relating to theft, or for receiving stolen property in violation of section 2913.51 of the Revised Code or a municipal ordinance relating to receiving stolen property.

(D) Whoever violates this section is guilty of a misdemeanor of the third degree.

(2002 S 123, eff. 1–1–04; 1990 H 162, eff. 6–28–90)

4511.181 Definitions

As used in sections 4511.181 to 4511.197 of the Revised Code:

(A) "Equivalent offense" means any of the following:

(1) A violation of division (A) or (B) of section 4511.19 of the Revised Code;

(2) A violation of a municipal OVI ordinance;

(3) A violation of section 2903.04 of the Revised Code in a case in which the offender was subject to the sanctions described in division (D) of that section;

(4) A violation of division (A)(1) of section 2903.06 or 2903.08 of the Revised Code or a municipal ordinance that is substantially equivalent to either of those divisions;

(5) A violation of division (A)(2), (3), or (4) of section 2903.06, division (A)(2) of section 2903.08, or former section 2903.07 of the Revised Code, or a municipal ordinance that is substantially equivalent to any of those divisions or that former section, in a case in which a judge or jury as the trier of fact found that the offender was under the influence of alcohol, a drug of abuse, or a combination of them;

(6) A violation of an existing or former municipal ordinance, law of another state, or law of the United States that is substantially equivalent to division (A) or (B) of section 4511.19 of the Revised Code;

(7) A violation of a former law of this state that was substantially equivalent to division (A) or (B) of section 4511.19 of the Revised Code.

(B) "Mandatory jail term" means the mandatory term in jail of three, six, ten, twenty, thirty, or sixty days that must be imposed under division (G)(1)(a), (b), or (c) of section 4511.19 of the Revised Code upon an offender convicted of a violation of division (A) of that section and in relation to which all of the following apply:

(1) Except as specifically authorized under section 4511.19 of the Revised Code, the term must be served in a jail.

(2) Except as specifically authorized under section 4511.19 of the Revised Code, the term cannot be suspended, reduced, or otherwise modified pursuant to sections 2929.21 to 2929.28 or any other provision of the Revised Code.

(C) "Municipal OVI ordinance" and "municipal OVI offense" mean any municipal ordinance prohibiting a person from operating a vehicle while under the influence of alcohol, a drug of abuse, or a combination of them or prohibiting a person from operating a vehicle with a prohibited concentration of alcohol in the whole blood, blood serum or plasma, breath, or urine.

(D) "Community residential sanction," "jail," "mandatory prison term," "mandatory term of local incarceration," "sanction," and "prison term" have the same meanings as in section 2929.01 of the Revised Code.

(2002 H 490, eff. 1–1–04; 2002 S 123, eff. 1–1–04)

OPERATION OF MOTOR VEHICLE WHILE INTOXICATED

4511.19 Driving while under the influence of alcohol or drugs; tests; presumptions; penalties; immunity for those withdrawing blood

(A)(1) No person shall operate any vehicle, streetcar, or trackless trolley within this state, if, at the time of the operation, any of the following apply:

(a) The person is under the influence of alcohol, a drug of abuse, or a combination of them.

(b) The person has a concentration of eight-hundredths of one per cent or more but less than seventeen-hundredths of one per cent by weight per unit volume of alcohol in the person's whole blood.

(c) The person has a concentration of ninety-six-thousandths of one per cent or more but less than two hundred four-thousandths of one per cent by weight per unit volume of alcohol in the person's blood serum or plasma.

(d) The person has a concentration of eight-hundredths of one gram or more but less than seventeen-hundredths of one gram by weight of alcohol per two hundred ten liters of the person's breath.

(e) The person has a concentration of eleven-hundredths of one gram or more but less than two hundred thirty-eight-thousandths of one gram by weight of alcohol per one hundred milliliters of the person's urine.

(f) The person has a concentration of seventeen-hundredths of one per cent or more by weight per unit volume of alcohol in the person's whole blood.

(g) The person has a concentration of two hundred four-thousandths of one per cent or more by weight per unit volume of alcohol in the person's blood serum or plasma.

(h) The person has a concentration of seventeen-hundredths of one gram or more by weight of alcohol per two hundred ten liters of the person's breath.

(i) The person has a concentration of two hundred thirty-eight-thousandths of one gram or more by weight of alcohol per one hundred milliliters of the person's urine.

(2) No person who, within twenty years of the conduct described in division (A)(2)(a) of this section, previously has been convicted of or pleaded guilty to a violation of this division, division (A)(1) or (B) of this section, or a municipal OVI offense shall do both of the following:

(a) Operate any vehicle, streetcar, or trackless trolley within this state while under the influence of alcohol, a drug of abuse, or a combination of them;

(b) Subsequent to being arrested for operating the vehicle, streetcar, or trackless trolley as described in division (A)(2)(a) of this section, being asked by a law enforcement officer to submit to a chemical test or tests under section 4511.191 of the Revised Code, and being advised by the officer in accordance with section 4511.192 of the Revised Code of the consequences of the person's refusal or submission to the test or tests, refuse to submit to the test or tests.

(B) No person under twenty-one years of age shall operate any vehicle, streetcar, or trackless trolley within this state, if, at the time of the operation, any of the following apply:

(1) The person has a concentration of at least two-hundredths of one per cent but less than eight-hundredths of one per cent by weight per unit volume of alcohol in the person's whole blood.

(2) The person has a concentration of at least three-hundredths of one per cent but less than ninety-six-thousandths of one per cent by weight per unit volume of alcohol in the person's blood serum or plasma.

(3) The person has a concentration of at least two-hundredths of one gram but less than eight-hundredths of one gram by weight of alcohol per two hundred ten liters of the person's breath.

(4) The person has a concentration of at least twenty-eight one-thousandths of one gram but less than eleven-hundredths of one gram by weight of alcohol per one hundred milliliters of the person's urine.

(C) In any proceeding arising out of one incident, a person may be charged with a violation of division (A)(1)(a) or (A)(2) and a violation of division (B)(1), (2), or (3) of this section, but the person may not be convicted of more than one violation of these divisions.

(D)(1) In any criminal prosecution or juvenile court proceeding for a violation of division (A) or (B) of this section or for an equivalent offense, the court may admit evidence on the concentration of alcohol, drugs of abuse, or a combination of them in the defendant's whole blood, blood serum or plasma, breath, urine, or other bodily substance at the time of the alleged violation as shown by chemical analysis of the substance withdrawn within two hours of the time of the alleged violation.

When a person submits to a blood test at the request of a law enforcement officer under section 4511.191 of the Revised Code, only a physician, a registered nurse, or a qualified technician, chemist, or phlebotomist shall withdraw blood for the purpose of determining the alcohol, drug, or alcohol and drug content of the whole blood, blood serum, or blood plasma. This limitation does not apply to the taking of breath or urine specimens. A person authorized to withdraw blood under this division may refuse to withdraw blood under this division, if in that person's opinion, the physical welfare of the person would be endangered by the withdrawing of blood.

The bodily substance withdrawn shall be analyzed in accordance with methods approved by the director of health by an individual possessing a valid permit issued by the director pursuant to section 3701.143 of the Revised Code.

(2) In a criminal prosecution or juvenile court proceeding for a violation of division (A) of this section or for an equivalent offense, if there was at the time the bodily substance was withdrawn a concentration of less than the applicable concentration of alcohol specified in divisions (A) (1)(b), (c), (d), and (e) of this section, that fact may be considered with other competent evidence in determining the guilt or innocence of the defendant. This division does not limit or affect a criminal prosecution or juvenile court proceeding for a violation of division (B) of this section or for an equivalent offense that is substantially equivalent to that division.

(3) Upon the request of the person who was tested, the results of the chemical test shall be made available to the person or the person's attorney, immediately upon the completion of the chemical test analysis.

The person tested may have a physician, a registered nurse, or a qualified technician, chemist, or phlebotomist of the person's own choosing administer a chemical test or tests, at the person's expense, in addition to any administered at the request of a law enforcement officer. The form to be read to the person to be tested, as required under section 4511.192 of the Revised Code, shall state that the person may have an independent test performed at the person's expense. The failure or inability to obtain an additional chemical test by a person shall not preclude the admission of evidence relating to the chemical test or tests taken at the request of a law enforcement officer.

(4)(a) As used in divisions (D)(4)(b) and (c) of this section, "national highway traffic safety administration" means the national highway traffic safety administration established as an administration of the United States department of transportation under 96 Stat. 2415 (1983), 49 U.S.C.A. 105.

(b) In any criminal prosecution or juvenile court proceeding for a violation of division (A) or (B) of this section, of a municipal ordinance relating to operating a vehicle while under the influence of alcohol, a drug of abuse, or alcohol and a drug of abuse, or of a municipal ordinance relating to operating a vehicle with a prohibited concentration of alcohol in the blood, breath, or urine, if a law enforcement officer has administered a field sobriety test to the operator of the vehicle involved in the violation and if it is shown by clear and convincing evidence that the officer administered the test in substantial compliance with the testing standards for any reliable, credible, and generally accepted field sobriety tests that were in effect at the time the tests were administered, including, but not limited to, any testing standards then in effect that were set by the national highway traffic safety administration, all of the following apply:

(i) The officer may testify concerning the results of the field sobriety test so administered.

(ii) The prosecution may introduce the results of the field sobriety test so administered as evidence in any proceedings in the criminal prosecution or juvenile court proceeding.

(iii) If testimony is presented or evidence is introduced under division (D)(4)(b)(i) or (ii) of this section and if the testimony or evidence is admissible under the Rules of Evidence, the court shall admit the testimony or evidence and the trier of fact shall give it whatever weight the trier of fact considers to be appropriate.

(c) Division (D)(4)(b) of this section does not limit or preclude a court, in its determination of whether the arrest of a person was supported by probable cause or its determination of any other matter in a criminal prosecution or juvenile court proceeding of a type described in that division, from considering evidence or testimony that is not otherwise disallowed by division (D)(4)(b) of this section.

(E)(1) Subject to division (E)(3) of this section, in any criminal prosecution or juvenile court proceeding for a violation of division (A) (1)(b), (c), (d), (e), (f), (g), (h), or (i) or (B)(1), (2), (3), or (4) of this section or for an equivalent offense that is substantially equivalent to any of those divisions, a laboratory report from any forensic laboratory certified by the department of health that contains an analysis of the whole blood, blood serum or plasma, breath, urine, or other bodily substance tested and that contains all of the information specified in this division shall be admitted as prima-facie evidence of the information and statements that the report contains. The laboratory report shall contain all of the following:

(a) The signature, under oath, of any person who performed the analysis;

(b) Any findings as to the identity and quantity of alcohol, a drug of abuse, or a combination of them that was found;

(c) A copy of a notarized statement by the laboratory director or a designee of the director that contains the name of each certified analyst or test performer involved with the report, the analyst's or test performer's employment relationship with the laboratory that issued the report, and a notation that performing an analysis of the type involved is part of the analyst's or test performer's regular duties;

(d) An outline of the analyst's or test performer's education, training, and experience in performing the type of analysis involved and a certification that the laboratory satisfies appropriate quality control standards in general and, in this particular analysis, under rules of the department of health.

(2) Notwithstanding any other provision of law regarding the admission of evidence, a report of the type described in division (E)(1) of this section is not admissible against the defendant to whom it pertains in any proceeding, other than a preliminary hearing or a grand jury proceeding, unless the prosecutor has served a copy of the report on the defendant's attorney or, if the defendant has no attorney, on the defendant.

(3) A report of the type described in division (E)(1) of this section shall not be prima-facie evidence of the contents, identity, or amount of any substance if, within seven days after the defendant to whom the report pertains or the defendant's attorney receives a copy of the report, the defendant or the defendant's attorney demands the testimony of the person who signed the report. The judge in the case may extend the seven-day time limit in the interest of justice.

(F) Except as otherwise provided in this division, any physician, registered nurse, or qualified technician, chemist, or phlebotomist who withdraws blood from a person pursuant to this section, and any hospital, first-aid station, or clinic at which blood is withdrawn from a person pursuant to this section, is immune from criminal liability and civil liability based upon a claim of assault and battery or any other claim that is not a claim of malpractice, for any act performed in withdrawing blood from the person. The immunity provided in this division is not available to a person who withdraws blood if the person engages in willful or wanton misconduct.

(G)(1) Whoever violates any provision of divisions (A)(1)(a) to (i) or (A)(2) of this section is guilty of operating a vehicle under the influence of alcohol, a drug of abuse, or a combination of them. The court shall sentence the offender under Chapter 2929. of the Revised Code, except as otherwise authorized or required by divisions (G)(1)(a) to (e) of this section:

(a) Except as otherwise provided in division (G)(1)(b), (c), (d), or (e) of this section, the offender is guilty of a misdemeanor of the first degree, and the court shall sentence the offender to all of the following:

(i) If the sentence is being imposed for a violation of division (A)(1) (a), (b), (c), (d), or (e) of this section, a mandatory jail term of three consecutive days. As used in this division, three consecutive days means seventy-two consecutive hours. The court may sentence an offender to both an intervention program and a jail term. The court may impose a jail term in addition to the three-day mandatory jail term or intervention program. However, in no case shall the cumulative jail term imposed for the offense exceed six months.

The court may suspend the execution of the three-day jail term under this division if the court, in lieu of that suspended term, places the offender under a community control sanction pursuant to section 2929.25 of the Revised Code and requires the offender to attend, for three consecutive days, a drivers' intervention program certified under section 3793.10 of the Revised Code. The court also may suspend the execution of any part of the three-day jail term under this division if it places the offender under a community control sanction pursuant to section 2929.25 of the Revised Code for part of the three days, requires the offender to attend for the suspended part of the term a drivers' intervention program so certified, and sentences the offender to a jail term equal to the remainder of the three consecutive days that the offender does not spend attending the program. The court may require the offender, as a condition of community control and in addition to the required attendance at a drivers' intervention program, to attend and satisfactorily complete any treatment or education programs that comply with the minimum standards adopted pursuant to Chapter 3793. of the Revised Code by the director of alcohol and drug addiction services that the operators of the drivers' intervention program determine that the offender should attend and to report periodically to the court on the offender's progress in the programs. The court also may impose on the offender any other conditions of community control that it considers necessary.

(ii) If the sentence is being imposed for a violation of division (A) (1)(f), (g), (h), or (i) or division (A)(2) of this section, except as otherwise provided in this division, a mandatory jail term of at least three consecutive days and a requirement that the offender attend, for three consecutive days, a drivers' intervention program that is certified pursuant to section 3793.10 of the Revised Code. As used in this division, three consecutive days means seventy-two consecutive hours. If the court determines that the offender is not conducive to treatment in a drivers' intervention program, if the offender refuses to attend a drivers' intervention program, or if the jail at which the offender is to serve the jail term imposed can provide a driver's intervention program, the court shall sentence the offender to a mandatory jail term of at least six consecutive days.

The court may require the offender, under a community control sanction imposed under section 2929.25 of the Revised Code, to attend and satisfactorily complete any treatment or education programs that comply with the minimum standards adopted pursuant to Chapter 3793. of the Revised Code by the director of alcohol and drug addiction services, in addition to the required attendance at drivers' intervention program, that the operators of the drivers' intervention program determine that the offender should attend and to report periodically to the court on the offender's progress in the programs. The court also may impose any other conditions of community control on the offender that it considers necessary.

(iii) In all cases, a fine of not less than two hundred fifty and not more than one thousand dollars;

(iv) In all cases, a class five license suspension of the offender's driver's or commercial driver's license or permit or nonresident operating privilege from the range specified in division (A)(5) of section 4510.02 of the Revised Code. The court may grant limited driving privileges relative to the suspension under sections 4510.021 and 4510.13 of the Revised Code.

(b) Except as otherwise provided in division (G)(1)(e) of this section, an offender who, within six years of the offense, previously has been convicted of or pleaded guilty to one violation of division (A) or (B) of this section or one other equivalent offense is guilty of a misdemeanor of the first degree. The court shall sentence the offender to all of the following:

(i) If the sentence is being imposed for a violation of division (A)(1) (a), (b), (c), (d), or (e) of this section, a mandatory jail term of ten consecutive days. The court shall impose the ten-day mandatory jail term under this division unless, subject to division (G)(3) of this section, it instead imposes a sentence under that division consisting of both a jail term and a term of house arrest with electronic monitoring, with continuous alcohol monitoring, or with both electronic monitoring and continuous alcohol monitoring. The court may impose a jail term in addition to the ten-day mandatory jail term. The cumulative jail term imposed for the offense shall not exceed six months.

In addition to the jail term or the term of house arrest with electronic monitoring or continuous alcohol monitoring or both types of monitoring and jail term, the court may require the offender to attend a drivers' intervention program that is certified pursuant to section 3793.10 of the Revised Code. If the operator of the program determines that the offender is alcohol dependent, the program shall notify the court, and, subject to division (I) of this section, the court shall order the offender to obtain treatment through an alcohol and drug addiction program authorized by section 3793.02 of the Revised Code.

(ii) If the sentence is being imposed for a violation of division (A) (1)(f), (g), (h), or (i) or division (A)(2) of this section, except as otherwise provided in this division, a mandatory jail term of twenty consecutive days. The court shall impose the twenty-day mandatory jail term under this division unless, subject to division (G)(3) of this section, it instead imposes a sentence under that division consisting of both a jail term and a term of house arrest with electronic monitoring, with continuous alcohol monitoring, or with both electronic monitoring and continuous alcohol monitoring. The court may impose a jail term in addition to the twenty-day mandatory jail term. The cumulative jail term imposed for the offense shall not exceed six months.

In addition to the jail term or the term of house arrest with electronic monitoring or continuous alcohol monitoring or both types of monitoring and jail term, the court may require the offender to attend a driver's intervention program that is certified pursuant to section 3793.10 of the Revised Code. If the operator of the program determines that the offender is alcohol dependent, the program shall notify the court, and, subject to division (I) of this section, the court shall order the offender to obtain treatment through an alcohol and drug addiction program authorized by section 3793.02 of the Revised Code.

(iii) In all cases, notwithstanding the fines set forth in Chapter 2929. of the Revised Code, a fine of not less than three hundred fifty and not more than one thousand five hundred dollars;

(iv) In all cases, a class four license suspension of the offender's driver's license, commercial driver's license, temporary instruction permit, probationary license, or nonresident operating privilege from the range specified in division (A)(4) of section 4510.02 of the Revised Code. The court may grant limited driving privileges relative to the suspension under sections 4510.021 and 4510.13 of the Revised Code.

(v) In all cases, if the vehicle is registered in the offender's name, immobilization of the vehicle involved in the offense for ninety days in accordance with section 4503.233 of the Revised Code and impoundment of the license plates of that vehicle for ninety days.

(c) Except as otherwise provided in division (G)(1)(e) of this section, an offender who, within six years of the offense, previously has been convicted of or pleaded guilty to two violations of division (A) or (B) of this section or other equivalent offenses is guilty of a misdemeanor. The court shall sentence the offender to all of the following:

(i) If the sentence is being imposed for a violation of division (A)(1) (a), (b), (c), (d), or (e) of this section, a mandatory jail term of thirty consecutive days. The court shall impose the thirty-day mandatory jail term under this division unless, subject to division (G)(3) of this section, it instead imposes a sentence under that division consisting of both a jail term and a term of house arrest with electronic monitoring, with continuous alcohol monitoring, or with both electronic monitoring and continuous alcohol monitoring. The court may impose a jail term in addition to the thirty-day mandatory jail term. Notwithstanding the jail terms set forth in sections 2929.21 to 2929.28 of the Revised Code, the additional jail term shall not exceed one year, and the cumulative jail term imposed for the offense shall not exceed one year.

(ii) If the sentence is being imposed for a violation of division (A) (1)(f), (g), (h), or (i) or division (A)(2) of this section, a mandatory jail term of sixty consecutive days. The court shall impose the sixty-day mandatory jail term under this division unless, subject to division (G)(3) of this section, it instead imposes a sentence under that division consisting of both a jail term and a term of house arrest with electronic monitoring, with continuous alcohol monitoring, or with both electronic monitoring and continuous alcohol monitoring. The court may impose a jail term in addition to the sixty-day mandatory jail term. Notwithstanding the jail terms set forth in sections 2929.21 to 2929.28 of the Revised Code, the additional jail term shall not exceed one year, and the cumulative jail term imposed for the offense shall not exceed one year.

(iii) In all cases, notwithstanding the fines set forth in Chapter 2929. of the Revised Code, a fine of not less than five hundred fifty and not more than two thousand five hundred dollars;

(iv) In all cases, a class three license suspension of the offender's driver's license, commercial driver's license, temporary instruction permit, probationary license, or nonresident operating privilege from the range specified in division (A)(3) of section 4510.02 of the Revised Code. The court may grant limited driving privileges relative to the suspension under sections 4510.021 and 4510.13 of the Revised Code.

(v) In all cases, if the vehicle is registered in the offender's name, criminal forfeiture of the vehicle involved in the offense in accordance with section 4503.234 of the Revised Code. Division (G)(6) of this section applies regarding any vehicle that is subject to an order of criminal forfeiture under this division.

(vi) In all cases, participation in an alcohol and drug addiction program authorized by section 3793.02 of the Revised Code, subject to division (I) of this section.

(d) Except as otherwise provided in division (G)(1)(e) of this section, an offender who, within six years of the offense, previously has been convicted of or pleaded guilty to three or four violations of division (A) or (B) of this section or other equivalent offenses or an offender who, within twenty years of the offense, previously has been convicted of or pleaded guilty to five or more violations of that nature is guilty of a felony of the fourth degree. The court shall sentence the offender to all of the following:

(i) If the sentence is being imposed for a violation of division (A)(1) (a), (b), (c), (d), or (e) of this section, a mandatory prison term of one, two, three, four, or five years as required by and in accordance with division (G)(2) of section 2929.13 of the Revised Code if the offender also is convicted of or also pleads guilty to a specification of the type described in section 2941.1413 of the Revised Code or, in the discretion of the court, either a mandatory term of local incarceration of sixty consecutive days in accordance with division (G)(1) of section 2929.13 of the Revised Code or a mandatory prison term of sixty consecutive days in accordance with division (G)(2) of that section if the offender is not convicted of and does not plead guilty to a specification of that type. If the court imposes a mandatory term of local incarceration, it may impose a jail term in addition to the sixty-day mandatory term, the cumulative total of the mandatory term and the jail term for the offense shall not exceed one year, and, except as provided in division (A)(1) of section 2929.13 of the Revised Code, no prison term is authorized for the offense. If the court imposes a mandatory prison term, notwithstanding division (A)(4) of section 2929.14 of the Revised Code, it also may sentence the offender to a definite prison term that shall be not less than six months and not more than thirty months and the prison terms shall be imposed as described in division (G)(2) of section 2929.13 of the Revised Code. If the court imposes a mandatory prison term or mandatory prison term and additional prison term, in addition to the term or terms so imposed, the court also may sentence the offender to a community control sanction for the offense, but the offender shall serve all of the prison terms so imposed prior to serving the community control sanction.

(ii) If the sentence is being imposed for a violation of division (A) (1)(f), (g), (h), or (i) or division (A)(2) of this section, a mandatory prison term of one, two, three, four, or five years as required by and in accordance with division (G)(2) of section 2929.13 of the Revised Code if the offender also is convicted of or also pleads guilty to a specification of the type described in section 2941.1413 of the Revised Code or, in the discretion of the court, either a mandatory term of local incarceration of one hundred twenty consecutive days in accordance with division (G)(1) of section 2929.13 of the Revised Code or a mandatory prison term of one hundred twenty consecutive days in accordance with division (G)(2) of that section if the offender is not convicted of and does not plead guilty to a specification of that type. If the court imposes a mandatory term of local incarceration, it may impose a jail term in addition to the one hundred twenty-day mandatory term, the cumulative total of the mandatory term and the jail term for the offense shall not exceed one year, and, except as provided in division (A)(1) of section 2929.13 of the Revised Code, no prison term is authorized for the offense. If the court imposes a mandatory prison term, notwithstanding division (A)(4) of section 2929.14 of the Revised Code, it also may sentence the offender to a definite prison term that shall be not less than six months and not more than thirty months and the prison terms shall be imposed as described in division (G)(2) of section 2929.13 of the Revised Code. If the court imposes a mandatory prison term or mandatory prison term and additional prison term, in addition to the term or terms so imposed, the court also may sentence the offender to a community control sanction for the offense, but the offender shall serve all of the prison terms so imposed prior to serving the community control sanction.

(iii) In all cases, notwithstanding section 2929.18 of the Revised Code, a fine of not less than eight hundred nor more than ten thousand dollars;

(iv) In all cases, a class two license suspension of the offender's driver's license, commercial driver's license, temporary instruction permit, probationary license, or nonresident operating privilege from the range specified in division (A)(2) of section 4510.02 of the Revised Code. The court may grant limited driving privileges relative to the suspension under sections 4510.021 and 4510.13 of the Revised Code.

(v) In all cases, if the vehicle is registered in the offender's name, criminal forfeiture of the vehicle involved in the offense in accordance with section 4503.234 of the Revised Code. Division (G)(6) of this section applies regarding any vehicle that is subject to an order of criminal forfeiture under this division.

(vi) In all cases, participation in an alcohol and drug addiction program authorized by section 3793.02 of the Revised Code, subject to division (I) of this section.

(vii) In all cases, if the court sentences the offender to a mandatory term of local incarceration, in addition to the mandatory term, the court, pursuant to section 2929.17 of the Revised Code, may impose a term of house arrest with electronic monitoring. The term shall not commence until after the offender has served the mandatory term of local incarceration.

(e) An offender who previously has been convicted of or pleaded guilty to a violation of division (A) of this section that was a felony, regardless of when the violation and the conviction or guilty plea occurred, is guilty of a felony of the third degree. The court shall sentence the offender to all of the following:

(i) If the offender is being sentenced for a violation of division (A)(1) (a), (b), (c), (d), or (e) of this section, a mandatory prison term of one, two, three, four, or five years as required by and in accordance with division (G)(2) of section 2929.13 of the Revised Code if the offender also is convicted of or also pleads guilty to a specification of the type described in section 2941.1413 of the Revised Code or a mandatory prison term of sixty consecutive days in accordance with division (G)(2) of section 2929.13 of the Revised Code if the offender is not convicted of and does not plead guilty to a specification of that type. The court may impose a prison term in addition to the mandatory prison term. The cumulative total of a sixty-day mandatory prison term and the additional prison term for the offense shall not exceed five years. In addition to the mandatory prison term or mandatory prison term and additional prison term the court imposes, the court also may sentence the offender to a community control sanction for the offense, but the offender shall serve all of the prison terms so imposed prior to serving the community control sanction.

(ii) If the sentence is being imposed for a violation of division (A) (1)(f), (g), (h), or (i) or division (A)(2) of this section, a mandatory prison term of one, two, three, four, or five years as required by and in accordance with division (G)(2) of section 2929.13 of the Revised Code if the offender also is convicted of or also pleads guilty to a specification of the type described in section 2941.1413 of the Revised Code or a mandatory prison term of one hundred twenty consecutive days in accordance with division (G)(2) of section 2929.13 of the Revised Code if the offender is not convicted of and does not plead guilty to a specification of that type. The court may impose a prison term in addition to the mandatory prison term. The cumulative total of a one hundred twenty-day mandatory prison term and the additional prison term for the offense shall not exceed five years. In addition to the mandatory prison term or mandatory prison term and additional prison term the court imposes, the court also may sentence the offender to a community control sanction for the offense, but the offender shall serve all of the prison terms so imposed prior to serving the community control sanction.

(iii) In all cases, notwithstanding section 2929.18 of the Revised Code, a fine of not less than eight hundred nor more than ten thousand dollars;

(iv) In all cases, a class two license suspension of the offender's driver's license, commercial driver's license, temporary instruction permit, probationary license, or nonresident operating privilege from the range specified in division (A)(2) of section 4510.02 of the Revised Code. The court may grant limited driving privileges relative to the suspension under sections 4510.021 and 4510.13 of the Revised Code.

(v) In all cases, if the vehicle is registered in the offender's name, criminal forfeiture of the vehicle involved in the offense in accordance with section 4503.234 of the Revised Code. Division (G)(6) of this section applies regarding any vehicle that is subject to an order of criminal forfeiture under this division.

(vi) In all cases, participation in an alcohol and drug addiction program authorized by section 3793.02 of the Revised Code, subject to division (I) of this section.

(2) An offender who is convicted of or pleads guilty to a violation of division (A) of this section and who subsequently seeks reinstatement of the driver's or occupational driver's license or permit or nonresident operating privilege suspended under this section as a result of the conviction or guilty plea shall pay a reinstatement fee as provided in division (F)(2) of section 4511.191 of the Revised Code.

(3) If an offender is sentenced to a jail term under division (G)(1)(b)(i) or (ii) or (G)(1)(c)(i) or (ii) of this section and if, within sixty days of sentencing of the offender, the court issues a written finding on the record that, due to the unavailability of space at the jail where the offender is required to serve the term, the offender will not be able to begin serving that term within the sixty-day period following the date of sentencing, the court may impose an alternative sentence under this division that includes a term of house arrest with electronic monitoring, with continuous alcohol monitoring, or with both electronic monitoring and continuous alcohol monitoring.

As an alternative to a mandatory jail term of ten consecutive days required by division (G)(1)(b)(i) of this section, the court, under this division, may sentence the offender to five consecutive days in jail and not less than eighteen consecutive days of house arrest with electronic monitoring, with continuous alcohol monitoring, or with both electronic monitoring and continuous alcohol monitoring. The cumulative total of the five consecutive days in jail and the period of house arrest with electronic monitoring, continuous alcohol monitoring, or both types of monitoring shall not exceed six months. The five consecutive days in jail do not have to be served prior to or consecutively to the period of house arrest.

As an alternative to the mandatory jail term of twenty consecutive days required by division (G)(1)(b)(ii) of this section, the court, under this division, may sentence the offender to ten consecutive days in jail and not less than thirty-six consecutive days of house arrest with electronic monitoring, with continuous alcohol monitoring, or with both electronic monitoring and continuous alcohol monitoring. The cumulative total of the ten consecutive days in jail and the period of house arrest with electronic monitoring, continuous alcohol monitoring, or both types of monitoring shall not exceed six months. The ten consecutive days in jail do not have to be served prior to or consecutively to the period of house arrest.

As an alternative to a mandatory jail term of thirty consecutive days required by division (G)(1)(c)(i) of this section, the court, under this division, may sentence the offender to fifteen consecutive days in jail and not less than fifty-five consecutive days of house arrest with electronic monitoring, with continuous alcohol monitoring, or with both electronic monitoring and continuous alcohol monitoring. The cumulative total of the fifteen consecutive days in jail and the period of house arrest with electronic monitoring, continuous alcohol monitoring, or both types of monitoring shall not exceed one year. The fifteen consecutive days in jail do not have to be served prior to or consecutively to the period of house arrest.

As an alternative to the mandatory jail term of sixty consecutive days required by division (G)(1)(c)(ii) of this section, the court, under this division, may sentence the offender to thirty consecutive days in jail and not less than one hundred ten consecutive days of house arrest with electronic monitoring, with continuous elcohol [1] monitoring, or with both electronic monitoring and continuous alcohol monitoring. The cumulative total of the thirty consecutive days in jail and the period of house arrest with electronic monitoring, continuous alcohol monitoring, or both types of monitoring shall not exceed one year. The thirty consecutive days in jail do not have to be served prior to or consecutively to the period of house arrest.

(4) If an offender's driver's or occupational driver's license or permit or nonresident operating privilege is suspended under division (G) of this section and if section 4510.13 of the Revised Code permits the court to grant limited driving privileges, the court may grant the limited driving privileges in accordance with that section. If division (A)(7) of that section requires that the court impose as a condition of the privileges that the offender must display on the vehicle that is driven subject to the privileges restricted license plates that are issued under section 4503.231 of the Revised Code, except as provided in division (B) of that section, the court shall impose that condition as one of the conditions of the limited driving privileges granted to the offender, except as provided in division (B) of section 4503.231 of the Revised Code.

(5) Fines imposed under this section for a violation of division (A) of this section shall be distributed as follows:

(a) Twenty–five dollars of the fine imposed under division (G)(1)(a)(iii), thirty-five dollars of the fine imposed under division (G)(1)(b)(iii), one hundred twenty-three dollars of the fine imposed under division (G)(1)(c)(iii), and two hundred ten dollars of the fine imposed under division (G)(1)(d)(iii) or (e)(iii) of this section shall be paid to an enforcement and education fund established by the legislative authority of the law enforcement agency in this state that primarily was responsible for the arrest of the offender, as determined by the court that imposes the fine. The agency shall use this share to pay only those costs it incurs in enforcing this section or a municipal OVI ordinance and in informing the public of the laws governing the operation of a vehicle while under the influence of alcohol, the dangers of the operation of a vehicle under the influence of alcohol, and other information relating to the operation of a vehicle under the influence of alcohol and the consumption of alcoholic beverages.

(b) Fifty dollars of the fine imposed under division (G)(1)(a)(iii) of this section shall be paid to the political subdivision that pays the cost of housing the offender during the offender's term of incarceration. If the offender is being sentenced for a violation of division (A)(1) (a), (b), (c), (d), or (e) of this section and was confined as a result of the offense prior to being sentenced for the offense but is not sentenced to a term of incarceration, the fifty dollars shall be paid to the political subdivision that paid the cost of housing the offender during that period of confinement. The political subdivision shall use the share under this division to pay or reimburse incarceration or treatment costs it incurs in housing or providing drug and alcohol treatment to persons who violate this section or a municipal OVI ordinance, costs of any immobilizing or disabling device used on the offender's vehicle, and costs of electronic house arrest equipment needed for persons who violate this section.

(c) Twenty–five dollars of the fine imposed under division (G)(1)(a)(iii) and fifty dollars of the fine imposed under division (G)(1)(b)(iii) of this section shall be deposited into the county or municipal indigent drivers' alcohol treatment fund under the control of that court, as created by the county or municipal corporation under division (N) of section 4511.191 of the Revised Code.

(d) One hundred fifteen dollars of the fine imposed under division (G)(1)(b)(iii), two hundred seventy-seven dollars of the fine imposed under division (G)(1)(c)(iii), and four hundred forty dollars of the fine imposed under division (G)(1)(d)(iii) or (e)(iii) of this section shall be paid to the political subdivision that pays the cost of housing the offender during the offender's term of incarceration. The political subdivision shall use this share to pay or reimburse incarceration or treatment costs it incurs in housing or providing drug and alcohol treatment to persons who violate this section or a municipal OVI ordinance, costs for any immobilizing or disabling device used on the offender's vehicle, and costs of electronic house arrest equipment needed for persons who violate this section.

(e) The balance of the fine imposed under division (G)(1)(a)(iii), (b)(iii), (c)(iii), (d)(iii), or (e)(iii) of this section shall be disbursed as otherwise provided by law.

(6) If title to a motor vehicle that is subject to an order of criminal forfeiture under division (G)(1)(c), (d), or (e) of this section is assigned or transferred and division (B)(2) or (3) of section 4503.234 of the Revised Code applies, in addition to or independent of any other penalty established by law, the court may fine the offender the value of the vehicle as determined by publications of the national auto dealers association. The proceeds of any fine so imposed shall be distributed in accordance with division (C)(2) of that section.

(7) As used in division (G) of this section, "electronic monitoring," "mandatory prison term," and "mandatory term of local incarceration" have the same meanings as in section 2929.01 of the Revised Code.

(H) Whoever violates division (B) of this section is guilty of operating a vehicle after underage alcohol consumption and shall be punished as follows:

(1) Except as otherwise provided in division (H)(2) of this section, the offender is guilty of a misdemeanor of the fourth degree. In addition to any other sanction imposed for the offense, the court shall impose a class six suspension of the offender's driver's license, commercial driver's license, temporary instruction permit, probationary license, or nonresident operating privilege from the range specified in division (A)(6) of section 4510.02 of the Revised Code.

(2) If, within one year of the offense, the offender previously has been convicted of or pleaded guilty to one or more violations of division (A) or (B) of this section or other equivalent offense, the offender is guilty of a misdemeanor of the third degree. In addition to any other sanction imposed for the offense, the court shall impose a class four suspension of the offender's driver's license, commercial driver's license, temporary instruction permit, probationary license, or nonresident operating privilege from the range specified in division (A)(4) of section 4510.02 of the Revised Code.

(3) If the offender also is convicted of or also pleads guilty to a specification of the type described in section 2941.1414 [2] of the Revised Code and if the court imposes a jail term for the violation of division (B) of this section, the court shall impose upon the offender an additional definite jail term pursuant to division (E) of section 2929.24 of the Revised Code.

(I)(1) No court shall sentence an offender to an alcohol treatment program under this section unless the treatment program complies with the minimum standards for alcohol treatment programs adopted under Chapter 3793. of the Revised Code by the director of alcohol and drug addiction services.

(2) An offender who stays in a drivers' intervention program or in an alcohol treatment program under an order issued under this section shall pay the cost of the stay in the program. However, if the court determines that an offender who stays in an alcohol treatment program under an order issued under this section is unable to pay the cost of the stay in the program, the court may order that the cost be paid from the court's indigent drivers' alcohol treatment fund.

(J) If a person whose driver's or commercial driver's license or permit or nonresident operating privilege is suspended under this section files an appeal regarding any aspect of the person's trial or sentence, the appeal itself does not stay the operation of the suspension.

(K) All terms defined in section 4510.01 of the Revised Code apply to this section. If the meaning of a term defined in section 4510.01 of the Revised Code conflicts with the meaning of the same term as defined in section 4501.01 or 4511.01 of the Revised Code, the term as defined in section 4510.01 of the Revised Code applies to this section.

(L)(1) The Ohio Traffic Rules in effect on January 1, 2004, as adopted by the supreme court under authority of section 2937.46 of the Revised Code, do not apply to felony violations of this section. Subject to division (L)(2) of this section, the Rules of Criminal Procedure apply to felony violations of this section.

(2) If, on or after January 1, 2004, the supreme court modifies the Ohio Traffic Rules to provide procedures to govern felony violations of this section, the modified rules shall apply to felony violations of this section.

(2004 H 163, eff. 9–23–04; 2003 H 87, § 4, eff 1–1–04; 2003 H 87, § 1, eff. 6–30–03; 2002 S 163, § 3, eff. 1–1–04; 2002 S 163, § 1, eff 4–9–03; 2002 H 490, eff. 1–1–04; 2002 S 123, eff. 1–1–04; 1999 S 22, eff. 5–17–00; 1994 S 82, eff. 5–4–94; 1990 H 837, eff. 7–25–90; 1990 S 131; 1986 S 262; 1982 S 432; 1974 H 995; 1971 S 14; 1970 H 874; 132 v H 380; 130 v S 41; 125 v 461; 1953 H 1; GC 6307–19)

1 So in original; 2004 H 163.

2 Section renumbered to RC 2941.1416 by the Legislative Service Commission.

Notes of Decisions

5. Under the influence, intoxicating liquor, defined

Evidence was sufficient to support defendant's conviction for driving under the influence (DUI); defendant parked his car so that it impeded the flow of traffic, was observed driving through alleys without using turn signals, chugged a beer in the presence of a police officer, stated "that'll mess up your test," had bloodshot eyes, emitted strong odor of alcohol, and had several empty beer cans behind the driver's seat of his vehicle. State v. Clark (Ohio App. 2 Dist., Darke, 04-04-2003) No. 1590, 2003-Ohio-1759, 2003 WL 1795559, Unreported. Automobiles ⚖ 355(6)

Evidence that defendant driving at a high rate of speed, weaving within his lane and straddling both lanes, along with evidence that after he was stopped his movements were lethargic, he had difficulty exiting his vehicle, his speech was slurred, and he was unsteady on his feet, was sufficient to support conviction for operating a motor vehicle while under the influence (OMVI). State v. Apple (Ohio App. 5 Dist., Fairfield, 12-02-2002) No. 02CA36, 2002-Ohio-6731, 2002 WL 31750208, Unreported. Automobiles ⚖ 355(6)

"Lacquer," as inhaled by defendant charged with operating a motor vehicle while under the influence (OMVI), was a harmful intoxicant as defined by drug offense definition statute. State v. Apple (Ohio App. 5 Dist., Fairfield, 12-02-2002) No. 02CA36, 2002-Ohio-6731, 2002 WL 31750208, Unreported. Automobiles ⚖ 332; Controlled Substances ⚖ 9

Defendant's impairment, even if involuntarily caused by inhalation of lacquer fumes, constituted operating a motor vehicle while under the influence (OMVI), because statute imposed strict criminal liability. State v. Apple (Ohio App. 5 Dist., Fairfield, 12-02-2002) No. 02CA36, 2002-Ohio-6731, 2002 WL 31750208, Unreported. Automobiles ⚖ 332

In trial of case where defendant is charged with operating vehicle while under influence of alcohol, it is prejudicial for court to charge jury that: "Now further in connection with the charge against the defendant, I believe that it is only proper that the court define to you what is meant by being under the influence of alcohol, the language of the statute that I read to you. In that connection, let me say the expression "under the influence of alcohol" means exactly what it says and that is that some alcohol must have been drunk by the person, the amount being immaterial, but the effect of which caused some influence on that person at the time and place alleged in the affidavit. That is a very short definition, but very expressive and very definite." State v. Hardy (Ohio 1971) 28 Ohio St.2d 89, 276 N.E.2d 247, 57 O.O.2d 284. Criminal Law ⚖ 1172.1(3)

Where a jury instruction concerning meaning of "under the influence of alcohol," as those words appear in RC 4511.19, contains both erroneous and nonerroneous statements of meaning of such words, total charge must be reviewed to determine whether jury has been instructed so as to reasonably afford a basis to apply the law to facts of the case without prejudice to the parties; however, where language used highlights the erroneous statement to such an extent that it appears to be specific and controlling, and the nonerroneous statement appears to be general, the whole instruction is misleading to jury and therefore prejudicial to a defendant. State v. Hardy (Ohio 1971) 28 Ohio St.2d 89, 276 N.E.2d 247, 57 O.O.2d 284. Criminal Law ⚷ 1172.1(5)

Evidence that driver crossed over center line into passing lane on at least three separate occasions and that at time he was pulled over by highway patrol officer his breath smelled strongly of alcohol, his eyes were red and his speech was slurred, was sufficient to support conviction on charge of driving under the influence (DUI). State v. Applegarth (Ohio App. 7 Dist., 10-23-1996) 114 Ohio App.3d 666, 683 N.E.2d 869. Automobiles ⚷ 355(6)

In prosecution for violation of municipal ordinance prohibiting driving under the influence of alcohol, it is behavior of driver which is at issue; therefore, even though results of breath alcohol content (BAC) verifier test were inadmissible, driver's conviction for driving while under influence of alcohol could stand based on other evidence. Mentor v. Kennell (Lake 1992) 83 Ohio App.3d 637, 615 N.E.2d 658. Automobiles ⚷ 355(6)

Court of Appeals would take judicial notice of fact that Betadine did not contain alcohol, for purposes of prosecution of defendant for driving under influence of alcohol where the defendant allegedly used Betadine as an antiseptic. State v. Mays (Pike 1992) 83 Ohio App.3d 610, 615 N.E.2d 641. Criminal Law ⚷ 304(1)

Evidence that a motorist smelled strongly of alcohol, staggered when leaving his vehicle, and had five empty beer cans plus one partially full can in his car is sufficient to support a conviction of operating a motor vehicle under the influence of alcohol. State v. Lowman (Warren 1992) 82 Ohio App.3d 831, 613 N.E.2d 692, motion overruled 66 Ohio St.3d 1423, 607 N.E.2d 845. Automobiles ⚷ 355(6)

Under RC 4511.19(A)(1) the prosecution need not establish a threshold level of alcohol concentration but it must prove that the defendant operated a motor vehicle with his faculties appreciably impaired by alcohol consumption; the fact troopers do not explicitly state that they believed a motorist to be intoxicated does not invalidate a conviction, however, where there was evidence of behavior and appearance from which the court could infer intoxication. State v. Lowman (Warren 1992) 82 Ohio App.3d 831, 613 N.E.2d 692, motion overruled 66 Ohio St.3d 1423, 607 N.E.2d 845.

A urinalysis indicating a positive test for marijuana, coupled with speeding, crossing the center line, failure of field sobriety tests, and the presence of marijuana cigarettes in the defendant's vehicle, is sufficient to support a conviction for driving under the influence of marijuana pursuant to RC 4511.19(A)(1); no threshold level of concentration of controlled substances is required under this section. State v. McLemore (Crawford 1992) 82 Ohio App.3d 541, 612 N.E.2d 795.

To determine if reasonable grounds existed to believe a person was operating a motor vehicle under the influence of alcohol, a court must apply a totality-of-the-circumstances test. State v. McCaig (Wood 1988) 51 Ohio App.3d 94, 554 N.E.2d 925. Automobiles ⚷ 349(6)

Where the evidence in a prosecution for driving under the influence of alcohol under RC 4511.19(A)(1) establishes the following: (1) defendant's vehicle struck the vehicle ahead with such force that it was damaged to the extent that it was necessary for that vehicle to be towed away, (2) a police officer at the scene thought defendant was more nervous and shaken up than anything else, (3) defendant's speech improved as time passed, and (4) defendant was very excited throughout the whole ordeal, it is as reasonable to conclude that defendant's condition was a result of the accident as it was the result of alcohol and a conviction for driving under the influence of alcohol is against the manifest weight of the evidence. State v. Murphy (Warren 1986) 30 Ohio App.3d 255, 507 N.E.2d 409, 30 O.B.R. 414.

The fact that results of an intoxilyzer test are insufficient to sustain a charge of driving with a proscribed breath alcohol concentration under RC 4511.19(A)(3) does not preclude a conviction on the charge of driving under the influence of alcohol under RC 4511.19(A)(1). State v. Bakst (Hamilton 1986) 30 Ohio App.3d 141, 506 N.E.2d 1208, 30 O.B.R. 259.

Evidence that defendant was seen consuming beer at lounge a few minutes before car accident occurred and testimony by three police officers that defendant was under influence of alcohol when he arrived at city police department after the accident sustained finding that defendant operated car while intoxicated. City of Xenia v. Manker (Greene 1984) 18 Ohio App.3d 9, 480 N.E.2d 94, 18 O.B.R. 33. Automobiles ⚷ 355(6)

Jury instruction which charges jury to find defendant guilty if ordinance is violated, but omits requirement that jury find beyond reasonable doubt that defendant violated such ordinance prohibiting driving motor vehicle while under the influence of intoxicating liquor, is erroneous. City of Toledo v. Starks (Lucas 1971) 25 Ohio App.2d 162, 267 N.E.2d 824, 54 O.O.2d 339.

Proof of factual circumstances concerning defendant's conduct and activity preceding and following driving of vehicle he is charged to have driven while under the influence of intoxicating liquor is relevant to ultimate issue for jury determination and is admissible, thereby making jury instruction on circumstantial evidence proper. City of Toledo v. Starks (Lucas 1971) 25 Ohio App.2d 162, 267 N.E.2d 824, 54 O.O.2d 339. Automobiles ⚷ 354

Jury instruction is incorrect which defines "under the influence of intoxicating liquor" as follows: "Under the influence of intoxicating liquor means exactly what it says, and that is that some alcohol must have been drunk by the person, the amount being immaterial, but the effect of which caused some influence on that person at the time and place alleged in the affidavit"; the correct definition thereof is as follows: "The condition in which a person finds himself after having consumed some intoxicating beverage in such quantity that its effect on him adversely affects his actions, reactions, conduct, movement or mental processes or impairs his reactions to an appreciable degree, thereby lessening his ability to operate a motor vehicle." City of Toledo v. Starks (Lucas 1971) 25 Ohio App.2d 162, 267 N.E.2d 824, 54 O.O.2d 339.

Where jury instruction embodies incorrect definition of "under the influence of intoxicating liquor," giving of correct definition whether such precedes or follows instruction does not cure error. City of Toledo v. Starks (Lucas 1971) 25 Ohio App.2d 162, 267 N.E.2d 824, 54 O.O.2d 339.

Where it is reasonably foreseeable that the taking of medication before driving an automobile may render one incapable of safe operation thereof, the operator bears the same responsibility as in case of voluntary intoxication. Mikula v. Balogh (Montgomery 1965) 9 Ohio App.2d 250, 224 N.E.2d 148, 38 O.O.2d 311.

A charge to the jury that, "under the influence of intoxicating liquor means exactly what it says, and that some intoxicating liquor must have been drunk by the person, the amount being immaterial, but the effect of which causes some influence on that person," is incomplete and prejudicially erroneous. State v. Jennings (Wyandot 1959) 112 Ohio App. 455, 176 N.E.2d 304, 16 O.O.2d 346.

In a criminal action, evidence by arresting officers that defendant's eyes were glassy and bloodshot, that his breath smelled strongly of some intoxicant, that his speech was slurred, that his eyes did not seem to focus, that his walk was unsteady and uncertain, that he admitted having had "a couple of beers," and that he stated he was not ill, is sufficient to support a finding of the trial court that defendant was "under the influence" of intoxicating liquor. State v. Neff (Hancock 1957) 104 Ohio App. 289, 148 N.E.2d 236, 4 O.O.2d 423.

A motorist can be under the influence of a drug of abuse even when taking a prescription medication for a back injury if the medication impairs the person's ability to operate the motor vehicle. State v. Smith (Ohio App. 6 Dist., Ottawa, 02-27-1998) No. OT-97-037, 1998 WL 102143, Unreported.

A defendant found asleep in the driver's seat with truck keys in his right hand is under the influence of alcohol at the time of his arrest where (1) the truck had not been viewed in that exact location just ten minutes before the police approached the vehicle, (2) the defendant smells of alcoholic beverage and has partially urinated on himself, and (3) there is circumstantial and direct evidence coupled with the defendant's testimony, not credible, that the reason he was found in the driver's seat was because he had to urinate but couldn't open the passenger's side door because it was broken so that he slid over to the driver's side, turned sideways, cracked the door open and urinated, fell asleep, and was later awakened by the police officers; the testimony conflicts with an inventory search that reveals the passenger's side door was not broken, so that combined direct and circumstantial evidence is sufficient to conclude the defendant operated the truck while under the influence of alcohol. State v. Riley (Ohio App. 10 Dist., Franklin, 01-20-1994) No. 93AP-518, No. 93AP-537, 1994 WL 14782, Unreported.

A trial court's instruction that carbon monoxide is a drug of abuse is prejudicial in a prosecution for driving under the influence of a drug of abuse where a defendant testifies at trial his condition at the time of arrest resulted from carbon monoxide poisoning due to a faulty muffler, because if the jury believes the defendant was overcome by carbon monoxide, the jury is required to find the defendant guilty without any evidence the defendant knowingly used carbon monoxide. State v McDonald, No. 93CA-C-01-005, 1993 WL 289906 (5th Dist Ct App, Delaware, 7-27-93).

A person may be convicted for driving under the influence of a drug of abuse where her ingestion of valium impairs her ability to drive, even though she had a prescription for the valium and took only the prescribed dosage. State v BoCook, No. 1813 (4th Dist Ct App, Ross, 10–6–92).

The taking of a "drug of abuse" pursuant to a prescription issued by a licensed medical professional is not a defense to a charge of driving under the influence of the "drug of abuse" if that drug impairs the person's ability to operate a motor vehicle. S. Euclid v. Heil (Ohio Mun. 1991) 62 Ohio Misc.2d 540, 604 N.E.2d 1388.

In order to apply the statutory presumption of RC 4511.19 that the defendant was under the influence of alcohol, the results of the intoxilyzer test, when taken together with its margin of error, must equal or exceed the statutory level. State v. Prestier (Ohio Mun. 1982) 7 Ohio Misc.2d 36, 455 N.E.2d 24, 7 O.B.R. 250. Automobiles ⚷ 353

The definition of intoxicating liquor set forth in RC 4301.01 is intended to apply to all sections of the code. City of Cincinnati v. McBrayer (Ohio Mun. 1962) 182 N.E.2d 646, 88 Ohio Law Abs. 395, 19 O.O.2d 254.

In a drunken driving prosecution a charge that the jury should convict if convinced that the defendant's ability to drive an auto was impaired in even the slightest degree by his use of intoxicating beverages at the times and places stated in the affidavit was improper. City of Lyndhurst v. Beaumont (Ohio Com.Pl. 1959) 170 N.E.2d 291, 84 Ohio Law Abs. 103.

Persons whose driving ability has been affected through the imbibing of beverages whose alcoholic content is less than 3.2 per cent by weight, regardless of the extent of such effect, may not be considered to be under the influence of intoxicating liquors and thus are immune from convictions under RC 4511.19. State v. Mikola (Ohio Co. 1959) 163 N.E.2d 82, 82 Ohio Law Abs. 517, 12 O.O.2d 25.

A charge that in general it may be said that a person who has a concentration of fifteen one-hundredths of one per cent or more alcohol in his bloodstream is under the influence of alcohol is not erroneous. State v. Titak (Columbiana 1955) 144 N.E.2d 255, 75 Ohio Law Abs. 430.

The definition of "intoxicating liquor" as found in RC 4301.01 is restricted to the Liquor Control Act and has no reference to or application to any other section of the code, civil or penal. State v. Hale (Miami 1955) 140 N.E.2d 55, 74 Ohio Law Abs. 274, appeal dismissed 165 Ohio St. 104, 133 N.E.2d 104, 59 O.O. 104. Automobiles ⚷ 332

Operating motor vehicle with proscribed level of alcohol content in blood, breath, or urine is per se offense, which represents the point the legislature has determined an individual cannot drive without posing substantial danger, not only to himself, but to others. In re Howard (Bkrtcy.S.D.Ohio, 03-19-1996) 193 B.R. 835. Automobiles ⚷ 332

Driving "under the influence" of alcohol within the meaning of RC 4511.19(A) is legal intoxication for purposes of 11 USC 523(a)(9), which prevents the discharge in a motorist's bankruptcy proceedings of any debt arising from driving in such a state; congress meant to protect victims of drunk drivers in the bankruptcy code and used the term "legally intoxicated" to encompass the various degrees of drunkenness defined by the laws of the several states. In re Humphrey (Bkrtcy.S.D.Ohio 1989) 102 B.R. 629.

Under Ohio law, an individual who drinks beer for four hours in an undetermined amount, collides with two separate automobiles in the space of a few minutes, speaks with a slur, cannot stand straight, and fails a field sobriety test may be found to be "under the influence of alcohol," for purposes of RC 4511.19(A), by a federal court. In re Humphrey (Bkrtcy. S.D.Ohio 1989) 102 B.R. 629.

Driving a motor vehicle after drinking liquor is not, in and of itself, an unlawful act in Ohio, and evidence that a motorist drank half a pitcher of beer in three hours, drove erratically, and then crossed the center line does not warrant a summary judgment that the motorist was "under the influence of alcohol" for purposes of 11 USC 523, which renders debts arising from any "willful and malicious" injury inflicted by the debtor nondischargeable in bankruptcy. In re Ustaszewski (Bkrtcy.N.D.Ohio 1987) 71 B.R. 282.

Proof that a motorist drank five servings of beer during the course of eight hours is insufficient to support a finding that he was under the influence of alcohol. In re Coupe (Bkrtcy.N.D.Ohio 1985) 51 B.R. 939.

4511.191 Chemical tests for determining alcoholic content of blood; effect of refusal to submit to test; seizure of license; indigent drivers alcohol treatment funds; procedures (first version)

Note: See also following version of this section, and Publisher's Note.

(A) Any person who operates a vehicle upon a highway or any public or private property used by the public for vehicular travel or parking within this state shall be deemed to have given consent to a chemical test or tests of the person's blood, breath, or urine for the purpose of determining the alcohol, drug, or alcohol and drug content of the person's blood, breath, or urine if arrested for operating a vehicle while under the influence of alcohol, a drug of abuse, or alcohol and a drug of abuse or for operating a vehicle with a prohibited concentration of alcohol in the blood, breath, or urine. The chemical test or tests shall be administered at the request of a police officer having reasonable grounds to believe the person to have been operating a vehicle upon a highway or any public or private property used by the public for vehicular travel or parking in this state while under the influence of alcohol, a drug of abuse, or alcohol and a drug of abuse or with a prohibited concentration of alcohol in the blood, breath, or urine. The law enforcement agency by which the officer is employed shall designate which of the tests shall be administered.

(B) Any person who is dead or unconscious, or who is otherwise in a condition rendering the person incapable of refusal, shall be deemed not to have withdrawn consent as provided by division (A) of this section and the test or tests may be administered, subject to sections 313.12 to 313.16 of the Revised Code.

(C)(1) Any person under arrest for operating a vehicle while under the influence of alcohol, a drug of abuse, or alcohol and a drug of abuse or for operating a vehicle with a prohibited concentration of alcohol in the blood, breath, or urine shall be advised at a police station, or at a hospital, first-aid station, or clinic to which the person has been taken for first-aid or medical treatment, of both of the following:

(a) The consequences, as specified in division (E) of this section, of the person's refusal to submit upon request to a chemical test designated by the law enforcement agency as provided in division (A) of this section;

(b) The consequences, as specified in division (F) of this section, of the person's submission to the designated chemical test if the person is found to have a prohibited concentration of alcohol in the blood, breath, or urine.

(2)(a) The advice given pursuant to division (C)(1) of this section shall be in a written form containing the information described in division (C)(2)(b) of this section and shall be read to the person. The form shall contain a statement that the form was shown to the person under arrest and read to the person in the presence of the arresting officer and either another police officer, a civilian police employee, or an employee of a hospital, first-aid station, or clinic, if any, to which the person has been taken for first-aid or medical treatment. The witnesses shall certify to this fact by signing the form.

(b) The form required by division (C)(2)(a) of this section shall read as follows:

"You now are under arrest for operating a vehicle while under the influence of alcohol, a drug of abuse, or both alcohol and a drug of abuse and will be requested by a police officer to submit to a chemical test to determine the concentration of alcohol, drugs of abuse, or alcohol and drugs of abuse in your blood, breath, or urine.

If you refuse to submit to the requested test or if you submit to the requested test and are found to have a prohibited concentration of alcohol in your blood, breath, or urine, your driver's or commercial driver's license or permit or nonresident operating privilege immediately will be suspended for the period of time specified by law by the officer, on behalf of the registrar of motor vehicles. You may appeal this suspension at your initial appearance before the court that hears the charges against you resulting from the arrest, and your initial appearance will be conducted no later than five days after the arrest. This suspension is independent of the penalties for the offense, and you may be subject to other penalties upon conviction."

(D)(1) If a person under arrest as described in division (C)(1) of this section is not asked by a police officer to submit to a chemical test designated as provided in division (A) of this section, the arresting officer shall seize the Ohio or out-of-state driver's or commercial driver's license or permit of the person and immediately forward the seized license or permit to the court in which the arrested person is to appear on the charge for which the person was arrested. If the arrested person does not have the person's driver's or commercial driver's license or permit on the person's self or in the person's vehicle, the arresting officer shall order the arrested person to surrender it to the law enforcement agency that employs the officer within twenty-four hours after the arrest, and, upon the surrender, the officer's employing agency immediately shall forward the license or permit to the court in which the arrested person is to appear on the charge for which the person was arrested. Upon receipt of the license or permit, the court shall retain it pending the initial appearance of the arrested person and any action taken under section 4511.196 of the Revised Code.

If a person under arrest as described in division (C)(1) of this section is asked by a police officer to submit to a chemical test designated as provided in division (A) of this section and is advised of the consequences of the person's refusal or submission as provided in division (C) of this section and if the person either refuses to submit to the designated chemical test or the person submits to the designated chemical test and the test results indicate that the person's blood contained a concentration of eight-hundredths of one per cent or more by weight of alcohol, the person's breath contained a concentration of eight-hundredths of one gram or more by weight of alcohol per two hundred ten liters of the person's breath, or the person's urine contained a concentration of eleven-hundredths of one gram or more by weight of alcohol per one hundred milliliters of the person's urine at the time of the alleged offense, the arresting officer shall do all of the following:

(a) On behalf of the registrar, serve a notice of suspension upon the person that advises the person that, independent of any penalties or sanctions imposed upon the person pursuant to any other section of the Revised Code or any other municipal ordinance, the person's driver's or commercial driver's license or permit or nonresident operating privilege is suspended, that the suspension takes effect immediately, that the suspension will last at least until the person's initial appearance on the charge that will be held within five days after the date of the person's arrest or the issuance of a citation to the person, and that the person may appeal the suspension at the initial appearance; seize the Ohio or out-of-state driver's or commercial driver's license or permit of the person; and immediately forward the seized license or permit to the registrar. If the arrested person does not have the person's driver's or commercial driver's license or permit on the person's self or in the person's vehicle, the arresting officer shall order the person to surrender it to the law enforcement agency that employs the officer within twenty-four hours after the service of the notice of suspension, and, upon the surrender, the officer's employing agency immediately shall forward the license or permit to the registrar.

(b) Verify the current residence of the person and, if it differs from that on the person's driver's or commercial driver's license or permit, notify the registrar of the change;

(c) In addition to forwarding the arrested person's driver's or commercial driver's license or permit to the registrar, send to the registrar, within forty-eight hours after the arrest of the person, a sworn report that includes all of the following statements:

(i) That the officer had reasonable grounds to believe that, at the time of the arrest, the arrested person was operating a vehicle upon a highway or public or private property used by the public for vehicular travel or parking within this state while under the influence of alcohol, a drug of abuse, or alcohol and a drug of abuse or with a prohibited concentration of alcohol in the blood, breath, or urine;

(ii) That the person was arrested and charged with operating a vehicle while under the influence of alcohol, a drug of abuse, or alcohol and a drug of abuse or with operating a vehicle with a prohibited concentration of alcohol in the blood, breath, or urine;

(iii) That the officer asked the person to take the designated chemical test, advised the person of the consequences of submitting to the chemical test or refusing to take the chemical test, and gave the person the form described in division (C)(2) of this section;

(iv) That the person refused to submit to the chemical test or that the person submitted to the chemical test and the test results indicate that the person's blood contained a concentration of eight-hundredths of one per cent or more by weight of alcohol, the person's breath contained a concentration of eight-hundredths of one gram or more by weight of alcohol per two hundred ten liters of the person's breath, or the person's urine contained a concentration of eleven-hundredths of one gram or more by weight of alcohol per one hundred milliliters of the person's urine at the time of the alleged offense;

(v) That the officer served a notice of suspension upon the person as described in division (D)(1)(a) of this section.

(2) The sworn report of an arresting officer completed under division (D)(1)(c) of this section shall be given by the officer to the arrested person at the time of the arrest or sent to the person by regular first class mail by the registrar as soon thereafter as possible, but no later than fourteen days after receipt of the report. An arresting officer may give an unsworn report to the arrested person at the time of the arrest provided the report is complete when given to the arrested person and subsequently is sworn to by the arresting officer. As soon as possible, but no later than forty-eight hours after the arrest of the person, the arresting officer shall send a copy of the sworn report to the court in which the arrested person is to appear on the charge for which the person was arrested.

(3) The sworn report of an arresting officer completed and sent to the registrar and the court under divisions (D)(1)(c) and (D)(2) of this section is prima-facie proof of the information and statements that it contains and shall be admitted and considered as prima-facie proof of the information and statements that it contains in any appeal under division (H) of this section relative to any suspension of a person's driver's or commercial driver's license or permit or nonresident operating privilege that results from the arrest covered by the report.

(E)(1) Upon receipt of the sworn report of an arresting officer completed and sent to the registrar and a court pursuant to divisions (D)(1)(c) and (D)(2) of this section in regard to a person who refused to take the designated chemical test, the registrar shall enter into the registrar's records the fact that the person's driver's or commercial driver's license or permit or nonresident operating privilege was suspended by the arresting officer under division (D)(1)(a) of this section and the period of the suspension, as determined under divisions (E)(1)(a) to (d) of this section. The suspension shall be subject to appeal as provided in this section and shall be for whichever of the following periods applies:

(a) If the arrested person, within five years of the date on which the person refused the request to consent to the chemical test, had not refused a previous request to consent to a chemical test of the person's blood, breath, or urine to determine its alcohol content, the period of suspension shall be one year. If the person is a resident without a license or permit to operate a vehicle within this state, the registrar shall deny to the person the issuance of a driver's or commercial driver's license or permit for a period of one year after the date of the alleged violation.

(b) If the arrested person, within five years of the date on which the person refused the request to consent to the chemical test, had refused one previous request to consent to a chemical test of the person's blood, breath, or urine to determine its alcohol content, the period of suspension or denial shall be two years.

(c) If the arrested person, within five years of the date on which the person refused the request to consent to the chemical test, had refused two previous requests to consent to a chemical test of the person's blood, breath, or urine to determine its alcohol content, the period of suspension or denial shall be three years.

(d) If the arrested person, within five years of the date on which the person refused the request to consent to the chemical test, had refused three or more previous requests to consent to a chemical test of the person's blood, breath, or urine to determine its alcohol content, the period of suspension or denial shall be five years.

(2) The suspension or denial imposed under division (E)(1) of this section shall continue for the entire one-year, two-year, three-year, or five-year period, subject to appeal as provided in this section and subject to termination as provided in division (K) of this section.

(F) Upon receipt of the sworn report of an arresting officer completed and sent to the registrar and a court pursuant to divisions (D)(1)(c) and (D)(2) of this section in regard to a person whose test results indicate that the person's blood contained a concentration of eight-hundredths of one per cent or more by weight of alcohol, the person's breath contained a concentration of eight-hundredths of one gram or more by weight of alcohol per two hundred ten liters of the person's breath, or the person's urine contained a concentration of eleven-hundredths of one gram or more by weight of alcohol per one hundred milliliters of the person's urine at the time of the alleged offense, the registrar shall enter into the registrar's records the fact that the person's driver's or commercial driver's license or permit or nonresident operating privilege was suspended by the arresting officer under division (D)(1)(a) of this section and the period of the suspension, as determined under divisions (F)(1) to (4) of this section. The suspension shall be subject to appeal as provided in this section and shall be for whichever of the following periods that applies:

(1) Except when division (F)(2), (3), or (4) of this section applies and specifies a different period of suspension or denial, the period of the suspension or denial shall be ninety days.

(2) The period of suspension or denial shall be one year if the person has been convicted, within six years of the date the test was conducted, of a violation of one of the following:

(a) Division (A) or (B) of section 4511.19 of the Revised Code;

(b) A municipal ordinance relating to operating a vehicle while under the influence of alcohol, a drug of abuse, or alcohol and a drug of abuse;

(c) A municipal ordinance relating to operating a vehicle with a prohibited concentration of alcohol in the blood, breath, or urine;

(d) Section 2903.04 of the Revised Code in a case in which the offender was subject to the sanctions described in division (D) of that section;

(e) Division (A)(1) of section 2903.06 or division (A)(1) of section 2903. 08 of the Revised Code or a municipal ordinance that is substantially similar to either of those divisions;

(f) Division (A)(2), (3), or (4) of section 2903.06, division (A)(2) of section 2903.08, or former section 2903.07 of the Revised Code, or a municipal ordinance that is substantially similar to any of those divisions or that former section, in a case in which the jury or judge found that at the time of the commission of the offense the offender was under the influence of alcohol, a drug of abuse, or alcohol and a drug of abuse;

(g) A statute of the United States or of any other state or a municipal ordinance of a municipal corporation located in any other state that is substantially similar to division (A) or (B) of section 4511.19 of the Revised Code.

(3) If the person has been convicted, within six years of the date the test was conducted, of two violations of a statute or ordinance described in division (F)(2) of this section, the period of the suspension or denial shall be two years.

(4) If the person has been convicted, within six years of the date the test was conducted, of more than two violations of a statute or ordinance described in division (F)(2) of this section, the period of the suspension or denial shall be three years.

(G)(1) A suspension of a person's driver's or commercial driver's license or permit or nonresident operating privilege under division (D)(1)(a) of this section for the period of time described in division (E) or (F) of this section is effective immediately from the time at which the arresting officer serves the notice of suspension upon the arrested person. Any subsequent finding that the person is not guilty of the charge that resulted in the person being requested to take, or in the person taking, the chemical test or tests under division (A) of this section affects the suspension only as described in division (H)(2) of this section.

(2) If a person is arrested for operating a vehicle while under the influence of alcohol, a drug of abuse, or alcohol and a drug of abuse or for operating a vehicle with a prohibited concentration of alcohol in the blood, breath, or urine and regardless of whether the person's driver's or commercial driver's license or permit or nonresident operating privilege is or is not suspended under division (E) or (F) of this section, the person's initial appearance on the charge resulting from the arrest shall be held within five days of the person's arrest or the issuance of the citation to the person, subject to any continuance granted by the court pursuant to division (H)(1) of this section regarding the issues specified in that division.

(H)(1) If a person is arrested for operating a vehicle while under the influence of alcohol, a drug of abuse, or alcohol and a drug of abuse or for operating a vehicle with a prohibited concentration of alcohol in the blood, breath, or urine and if the person's driver's or commercial driver's license or permit or nonresident operating privilege is suspended under division (E) or (F) of this section, the person may appeal the suspension at the person's initial appearance on the charge resulting from the arrest in the court in which the person will appear on that charge. If the person appeals the suspension at the person's initial appearance, the appeal does not stay the operation of the suspension. Subject to division (H)(2) of this section, no court has jurisdiction to grant a stay of a suspension imposed under division (E) or (F) of this section, and any order issued by any court that purports to grant a stay of any suspension imposed under either of those divisions shall not be given administrative effect.

If the person appeals the suspension at the person's initial appearance, either the person or the registrar may request a continuance of the appeal. Either the person or the registrar shall make the request for a continuance of the appeal at the same time as the making of the appeal. If either the person or the registrar requests a continuance of the appeal, the court may grant the continuance. The court also may continue the appeal on its own motion. The granting of a continuance applies only to the conduct of the appeal of the suspension and does not extend the time within which the initial appearance must be conducted, and the court shall proceed with all other aspects of the initial appearance in accordance with its normal procedures. Neither the request for nor the granting of a continuance stays the operation of the suspension that is the subject of the appeal.

If the person appeals the suspension at the person's initial appearance, the scope of the appeal is limited to determining whether one or more of the following conditions have not been met:

(a) Whether the law enforcement officer had reasonable ground to believe the arrested person was operating a vehicle upon a highway or public or private property used by the public for vehicular travel or parking within this state while under the influence of alcohol, a drug of abuse, or alcohol and a drug of abuse or with a prohibited concentration of alcohol in the blood, breath, or urine and whether the arrested person was in fact placed under arrest;

(b) Whether the law enforcement officer requested the arrested person to submit to the chemical test designated pursuant to division (A) of this section;

(c) Whether the arresting officer informed the arrested person of the consequences of refusing to be tested or of submitting to the test;

(d) Whichever of the following is applicable:

(i) Whether the arrested person refused to submit to the chemical test requested by the officer;

(ii) Whether the chemical test results indicate that the arrested person's blood contained a concentration of eight- hundredths of one per cent or more by weight of alcohol, the person's breath contained a concentration of eight-hundredths of one gram or more by weight of alcohol per two hundred ten liters of the person's breath, or the person's urine contained a concentration of eleven-hundredths of one gram or more by weight of alcohol per one hundred milliliters of the person's urine at the time of the alleged offense.

(2) If the person appeals the suspension at the initial appearance, the judge or referee of the court or the mayor of the mayor's court shall determine whether one or more of the conditions specified in divisions (H)(1)(a) to (d) of this section have not been met. The person who appeals the suspension has the burden of proving, by a preponderance of the evidence, that one or more of the specified conditions has not been met. If during the appeal at the initial appearance the judge or referee of the court or the mayor of the mayor's court determines that all of those conditions have been met, the judge, referee, or mayor shall uphold the suspension, shall continue the suspension, and shall notify the registrar of the decision on a form approved by the registrar. Except as otherwise provided in division (H)(2) of this section, if the suspension is upheld or if the person does not appeal the suspension at the person's initial appearance under division (H)(1) of this section, the suspension shall continue until the complaint alleging the violation for which the person was arrested and in relation to which the suspension was imposed is adjudicated on the merits by the judge or referee of the trial court or by the mayor of the mayor's court. If the suspension was imposed under division (E) of this section and it is continued under this division, any subsequent finding that the person is not guilty of the charge that resulted in the person being requested to take the chemical test or tests under division (A) of this section does not terminate or otherwise affect the suspension. If the suspension was imposed under division (F) of this section and it is continued under this division, the suspension shall terminate if, for any reason, the person subsequently is found not guilty of the charge that resulted in the person taking the chemical test or tests under division (A) of this section.

If, during the appeal at the initial appearance, the judge or referee of the trial court or the mayor of the mayor's court determines that one or more of the conditions specified in divisions (H)(1)(a) to (d) of this section have not been met, the judge, referee, or mayor shall terminate the suspension, subject to the imposition of a new suspension under division (B) of section 4511.196 of the Revised Code; shall notify the registrar of the decision on a form approved by the registrar; and, except as provided in division (B) of section 4511.196 of the Revised Code, shall order the registrar to return the driver's or commercial driver's license or permit to the person or to take such measures as may be necessary, if the license or permit was destroyed under section 4507.55 of the Revised Code, to permit the person to obtain a replacement driver's or commercial driver's license or permit from the registrar or a deputy registrar in accordance with that section. The court also shall issue to the person a court order, valid for not more than ten days from the date of issuance, granting the person operating privileges for that period of time.

If the person appeals the suspension at the initial appearance, the registrar shall be represented by the prosecuting attorney of the county in which the arrest occurred if the initial appearance is conducted in a juvenile court or county court, except that if the arrest occurred within a city or village within the jurisdiction of the county court in which the appeal is conducted, the city director of law or village solicitor of that city or village shall represent the registrar. If the appeal is conducted in a municipal court, the registrar shall be represented as provided in section 1901.34 of the Revised Code. If the appeal is conducted in a mayor's court, the registrar shall be represented by the city director of law, village solicitor, or other chief legal officer of the municipal corporation that operates that mayor's court.

(I)(1)(a) A person is not entitled to request, and a court shall not grant to the person, occupational driving privileges under division (I)(1) of this section if a person's driver's or commercial driver's license or permit or nonresident operating privilege has been suspended pursuant to division (E) of this section, and the person, within the preceding seven years, has refused three previous requests to consent to a chemical test of the person's blood, breath, or urine to determine its alcohol content or has been convicted of or pleaded guilty to three or more violations of one or more of the following:

(i) Division (A) or (B) of section 4511.19 of the Revised Code;

(ii) A municipal ordinance relating to operating a vehicle while under the influence of alcohol, a drug of abuse, or alcohol and a drug of abuse;

(iii) A municipal ordinance relating to operating a vehicle with a prohibited concentration of alcohol in the blood, breath, or urine;

(iv) Section 2903.04 of the Revised Code in a case in which the person was subject to the sanctions described in division (D) of that section;

(v) Division (A)(1) of section 2903.06 or division (A)(1) of section 2903. 08 of the Revised Code or a municipal ordinance that is substantially similar to either of those divisions;

(vi) Division (A)(2), (3), or (4) of section 2903.06, division (A)(2) of section 2903.08, or former section 2903.07 of the Revised Code, or a municipal ordinance that is substantially similar to any of those divisions or that former section, in a case in which the jury or judge found that the person was under the influence of alcohol, a drug of abuse, or alcohol and a drug of abuse;

(vii) A statute of the United States or of any other state or a municipal ordinance of a municipal corporation located in any other state that is substantially similar to division (A) or (B) of section 4511.19 of the Revised Code.

(b) Any other person who is not described in division (I)(1)(a) of this section and whose driver's or commercial driver's license or nonresident operating privilege has been suspended pursuant to division (E) of this section may file a petition requesting occupational driving privileges in the common pleas court, municipal court, county court, mayor's court, or, if the person is a minor, juvenile court with jurisdiction over the related criminal or delinquency case. The petition may be filed at any time subsequent to the date on which the notice of suspension is served upon the arrested person. The person shall pay the costs of the proceeding, notify the registrar of the filing of the petition, and send the registrar a copy of the petition.

In the proceedings, the registrar shall be represented by the prosecuting attorney of the county in which the arrest occurred if the petition is filed in the juvenile court, county court, or common pleas court, except that, if the arrest occurred within a city or village within the jurisdiction of the county court in which the petition is filed, the city director of law or village solicitor of that city or village shall represent the registrar. If the petition is filed in the municipal court, the registrar shall be represented as provided in section 1901.34 of the Revised Code. If the petition is filed in a mayor's court, the registrar shall be represented by the city director of law, village solicitor, or other chief legal officer of the municipal corporation that operates the mayor's court.

The court, if it finds reasonable cause to believe that suspension would seriously affect the person's ability to continue in the person's employment, may grant the person occupational driving privileges during the period of suspension imposed pursuant to division (E) of this section, subject to the limitations contained in this division and division (I)(2) of this section. The court may grant the occupational driving privileges, subject to the limitations contained in this division and division (I)(2) of this section, regardless of whether the person appeals the suspension at the person's initial appearance under division (H)(1) of this section or appeals the decision of the court made pursuant to the appeal conducted at the initial appearance, and, if the person has appealed the suspension or decision, regardless of whether the matter at issue has been heard or decided by the court. The court shall not grant occupational driving privileges for employment as a driver of commercial motor vehicles to any person who is disqualified from operating a commercial motor vehicle under section 3123.611 or 4506.16 of the Revised Code or whose commercial driver's license or commercial driver's temporary instruction permit has been suspended under section 3123.58 of the Revised Code.

(2)(a) In granting occupational driving privileges under division (I)(1) of this section, the court may impose any condition it considers reasonable and necessary to limit the use of a vehicle by the person. The court shall deliver to the person a permit card, in a form to be prescribed by the court, setting forth the time, place, and other conditions limiting the defendant's use of a vehicle. The grant of occupational driving privileges shall be conditioned upon the person's having the permit in the person's possession at all times during which the person is operating a vehicle.

A person granted occupational driving privileges who operates a vehicle for other than occupational purposes, in violation of any condition imposed by the court, or without having the permit in the person's possession, is guilty of a violation of section 4507.02 of the Revised Code.

(b) The court may not grant a person occupational driving privileges under division (I)(1) of this section when prohibited by a limitation contained in that division or during any of the following periods of time:

(i) The first thirty days of suspension imposed upon a person who, within five years of the date on which the person refused the request to consent to a chemical test of the person's blood, breath, or urine to determine its alcohol content and for which refusal the suspension was imposed, had not refused a previous request to consent to a chemical test of the person's blood, breath, or urine to determine its alcohol content;

(ii) The first ninety days of suspension imposed upon a person who, within five years of the date on which the person refused the request to consent to a chemical test of the person's blood, breath, or urine to determine its alcohol content and for which refusal the suspension was imposed, had refused one previous request to consent to a chemical test of the person's blood, breath, or urine to determine its alcohol content;

(iii) The first year of suspension imposed upon a person who, within five years of the date on which the person refused the request to consent to a chemical test of the person's blood, breath, or urine to determine its alcohol content and for which refusal the suspension was imposed, had refused two previous requests to consent to a chemical test of the person's blood, breath, or urine to determine its alcohol content;

(iv) The first three years of suspension imposed upon a person who, within five years of the date on which the person refused the request to consent to a chemical test of the person's blood, breath, or urine to determine its alcohol content and for which refusal the suspension was imposed, had refused three or more previous requests to consent to a chemical test of the person's blood, breath, or urine to determine its alcohol content.

(3) The court shall give information in writing of any action taken under this section to the registrar.

(4) If a person's driver's or commercial driver's license or permit or nonresident operating privilege has been suspended pursuant to division (F) of this section, and the person, within the preceding seven years, has been convicted of or pleaded guilty to three or more violations of division (A) or (B) of section 4511.19 of the Revised Code, a municipal ordinance relating to operating a vehicle while under the influence of alcohol, a drug of abuse, or alcohol and a drug of abuse, a municipal ordinance relating to operating a vehicle with a prohibited concentration of alcohol in the blood, breath, or urine, section 2903.04 of the Revised Code in a case in which the person was subject to the sanctions described in division (D) of that section, or section 2903.06 or 2903.08 or former section 2903.07 of the Revised Code or a municipal ordinance that is substantially similar to former section 2903.07 of the Revised Code in a case in which the jury or judge found that the person was under the influence of alcohol, a drug of abuse, or alcohol and a drug of abuse, or a statute of the United States or of any other state or a municipal ordinance of a municipal corporation located in any other state that is substantially similar to division (A) or (B) of section 4511.19 of the Revised Code, the person is not entitled to request, and the court shall not grant to the person, occupational driving privileges under this division. Any other person whose driver's or commercial driver's license or nonresident operating privilege has been suspended pursuant to division (F) of this section may file in the court specified in division (I)(1)(b) of this section a petition requesting occupational driving privileges in accordance with section 4507.16 of the Revised Code. The petition may be filed at any time subsequent to the date on which the arresting officer serves the notice of suspension upon the arrested person. Upon the making of the request, occupational driving privileges may be granted in accordance with section 4507.16 of the Revised Code. The court may grant the occupational driving privileges, subject to the limitations contained in section 4507.16 of the Revised Code, regardless of whether the person appeals the suspension at the person's initial appearance under division (H)(1) of this section or appeals the decision of the court made pursuant to the appeal conducted at the initial appearance, and, if the person has appealed the suspension or decision, regardless of whether the matter at issue has been heard or decided by the court.

(J) When it finally has been determined under the procedures of this section that a nonresident's privilege to operate a vehicle within this state has been suspended, the registrar shall give information in writing of the action taken to the motor vehicle administrator of the state of the person's residence and of any state in which the person has a license.

(K) A suspension of the driver's or commercial driver's license or permit of a resident, a suspension of the operating privilege of a nonresident, or a denial of a driver's or commercial driver's license or permit pursuant to division (E) or (F) of this section shall be terminated by the registrar upon receipt of notice of the person's entering a plea of guilty to, or of the person's conviction of, operating a vehicle while under the influence of alcohol, a drug of abuse, or alcohol and a drug of abuse or with a prohibited concentration of alcohol in the blood, breath, or urine, if the offense for which the plea is entered or that resulted in the conviction arose from the same incident that led to the suspension or denial.

The registrar shall credit against any judicial suspension of a person's driver's or commercial driver's license or permit or nonresident operating privilege imposed pursuant to division (B) or (E) of section 4507.16 of the Revised Code any time during which the person serves a related suspension imposed pursuant to division (E) or (F) of this section.

(L) At the end of a suspension period under this section, section 4511.196, or division (B) of section 4507.16 of the Revised Code and upon the request of the person whose driver's or commercial driver's license or permit was suspended and who is not otherwise subject to suspension, revocation, or disqualification, the registrar shall return the driver's or commercial driver's license or permit to the person upon the person's compliance with all of the conditions specified in divisions (L)(1) and (2) of this section:

(1) A showing by the person that the person has proof of financial responsibility, a policy of liability insurance in effect that meets the minimum standards set forth in section 4509.51 of the Revised Code, or proof, to the satisfaction of the registrar, that the person is able to respond in damages in an amount at least equal to the minimum amounts specified in section 4509.51 of the Revised Code.

(2) Subject to the limitation contained in division (L)(3) of this section, payment by the person of a license reinstatement fee of four hundred twenty-five dollars to the bureau of motor vehicles, which fee shall be deposited in the state treasury and credited as follows:

(a) One hundred twelve dollars and fifty cents shall be credited to the statewide treatment and prevention fund created by section 4301.30 of the Revised Code. The fund shall be used to pay the costs of driver treatment and intervention programs operated pursuant to sections 3793.02 and 3793.10 of the Revised Code. The director of alcohol and drug addiction services shall determine the share of the fund that is to be allocated to alcohol and drug addiction programs authorized by section 3793.02 of the Revised Code, and the share of the fund that is to be allocated to drivers' intervention programs authorized by section 3793.10 of the Revised Code.

(b) Seventy–five dollars shall be credited to the reparations fund created by section 2743.191 of the Revised Code.

(c) Thirty–seven dollars and fifty cents shall be credited to the indigent drivers alcohol treatment fund, which is hereby established. Except as otherwise provided in division (L)(2)(c) of this section, moneys in the fund shall be distributed by the department of alcohol and drug addiction services to the county indigent drivers alcohol treatment funds, the county juvenile indigent drivers alcohol treatment funds, and the municipal indigent drivers alcohol treatment funds that are required to be established by counties and municipal corporations pursuant to division (N) of this section, and shall be used only to pay the cost of an alcohol and drug addiction treatment program attended by an offender or juvenile traffic offender who is ordered to attend an alcohol and drug addiction treatment program by a county, juvenile, or municipal court judge and who is determined by the county, juvenile, or municipal court judge not to have the means to pay for attendance at the program or to pay the costs specified in division (N)(4) of this section in accordance with that division. Moneys in the fund that are not distributed to a county indigent drivers alcohol treatment fund, a county juvenile indigent drivers alcohol treatment fund, or a municipal indigent drivers alcohol treatment fund under division (N) of this section because the director of alcohol and drug addiction services does not have the information necessary to identify the county or municipal corporation where the offender or juvenile offender was arrested may be transferred by the director of budget and management to the statewide treatment and prevention fund created by section 4301.30 of the Revised Code, upon certification of the amount by the director of alcohol and drug addiction services.

(d) Seventy–five dollars shall be credited to the Ohio rehabilitation services commission established by section 3304.12 of the Revised Code, to the services for rehabilitation fund, which is hereby established. The fund shall be used to match available federal matching funds where appropriate, and for any other purpose or program of the commission to rehabilitate people with disabilities to help them become employed and independent.

(e) Seventy–five dollars shall be deposited into the state treasury and credited to the drug abuse resistance education programs fund, which is hereby established, to be used by the attorney general for the purposes specified in division (L)(4) of this section.

(f) Thirty dollars shall be credited to the state bureau of motor vehicles fund created by section 4501.25 of the Revised Code.

(g) Twenty dollars shall be credited to the trauma and emergency medical services grants fund created by section 4513.263 of the Revised Code.

(3) If a person's driver's or commercial driver's license or permit is suspended under division (E) or (F) of this section, section 4511.196, or division (B) of section 4507.16 of the Revised Code, or any combination of the suspensions described in division (L)(3) of this section, and if the suspensions arise from a single incident or a single set of facts and circumstances, the person is liable for payment of, and shall be required to pay to the bureau, only one reinstatement fee of four hundred five dollars. The reinstatement fee shall be distributed by the bureau in accordance with division (L)(2) of this section.

(4) The attorney general shall use amounts in the drug abuse resistance education programs fund to award grants to law enforcement agencies to establish and implement drug abuse resistance education programs in public schools. Grants awarded to a law enforcement agency under division (L)(4) of this section shall be used by the agency to pay for not more than fifty per cent of the amount of the salaries of law enforcement officers who conduct drug abuse resistance education programs in public schools. The attorney general shall not use more than six per cent of the amounts the attorney general's office receives under division (L)(2)(e) of this section to pay the costs it incurs in administering the grant program established by division (L)(4) of this section and in providing training and materials relating to drug abuse resistance education programs.

The attorney general shall report to the governor and the general assembly each fiscal year on the progress made in establishing and implementing drug abuse resistance education programs. These reports shall include an evaluation of the effectiveness of these programs.

(M) Suspension of a commercial driver's license under division (E) or (F) of this section shall be concurrent with any period of disqualification under section 3123.611 or 4506.16 of the Revised Code or any period of suspension under section 3123.58 of the Revised Code. No person who is disqualified for life from holding a commercial driver's license under section 4506.16 of the Revised Code shall be issued a driver's license under Chapter 4507. of the Revised Code during the period for which the commercial driver's license was suspended under division (E) or (F) of this section, and no person whose commercial driver's license is suspended under division (E) or (F) of this section shall be issued a driver's license under that chapter during the period of the suspension.

(N)(1) Each county shall establish an indigent drivers alcohol treatment fund, each county shall establish a juvenile indigent drivers alcohol treatment fund, and each municipal corporation in which there is a municipal court shall establish an indigent drivers alcohol treatment fund. All revenue that the general assembly appropriates to the indigent drivers alcohol treatment fund for transfer to a county indigent drivers alcohol treatment fund, a county juvenile indigent drivers alcohol treatment fund, or a municipal indigent drivers alcohol treatment fund, all portions of fees that are paid under division (L) of this section and that are credited under that division to the indigent drivers alcohol treatment fund in the state treasury for a county indigent drivers alcohol treatment fund, a county juvenile indigent drivers alcohol treatment fund, or a municipal indigent drivers alcohol treatment fund, and all portions of fines that are specified for deposit into a county or municipal indigent drivers alcohol treatment fund by section 4511.193 of the Revised Code shall be deposited into that county indigent drivers alcohol treatment fund, county juvenile indigent drivers alcohol treatment fund, or municipal indigent drivers alcohol treatment fund in accordance with division (N)(2) of this section. Additionally, all portions of fines that are paid for a violation of section 4511.19 of the Revised Code or division (B)(2) of section 4507.02 of the Revised Code, and that are required under division (A)(1), (2), (5), or (6) of section 4511.99 or division (B)(5) of section 4507.99 of the Revised Code to be deposited into a county indigent drivers alcohol treatment fund or municipal indigent drivers alcohol treatment fund shall be deposited into the appropriate fund in accordance with the applicable division.

(2) That portion of the license reinstatement fee that is paid under division (L) of this section and that is credited under that division to the indigent drivers alcohol treatment fund shall be deposited into a county indigent drivers alcohol treatment fund, a county juvenile indigent drivers alcohol treatment fund, or a municipal indigent drivers alcohol treatment fund as follows:

(a) If the suspension in question was imposed under this section, that portion of the fee shall be deposited as follows:

(i) If the fee is paid by a person who was charged in a county court with the violation that resulted in the suspension, the portion shall be deposited into the county indigent drivers alcohol treatment fund under the control of that court;

(ii) If the fee is paid by a person who was charged in a juvenile court with the violation that resulted in the suspension, the portion shall be deposited into the county juvenile indigent drivers alcohol treatment fund established in the county served by the court;

(iii) If the fee is paid by a person who was charged in a municipal court with the violation that resulted in the suspension, the portion shall be deposited into the municipal indigent drivers alcohol treatment fund under the control of that court.

(b) If the suspension in question was imposed under division (B) of section 4507.16 of the Revised Code, that portion of the fee shall be deposited as follows:

(i) If the fee is paid by a person whose license or permit was suspended by a county court, the portion shall be deposited into the county indigent drivers alcohol treatment fund under the control of that court;

(ii) If the fee is paid by a person whose license or permit was suspended by a municipal court, the portion shall be deposited into the municipal indigent drivers alcohol treatment fund under the control of that court.

(3) Expenditures from a county indigent drivers alcohol treatment fund, a county juvenile indigent drivers alcohol treatment fund, or a municipal indigent drivers alcohol treatment fund shall be made only upon the order of a county, juvenile, or municipal court judge and only for payment of the cost of the attendance at an alcohol and drug addiction treatment program of a person who is convicted of, or found to be a juvenile traffic offender by reason of, a violation of division (A) of section 4511.19 of the Revised Code or a substantially similar municipal ordinance, who is ordered by the court to attend the alcohol and drug addiction treatment program, and who is determined by the court to be unable to pay the cost of attendance at the treatment program or for payment of the costs specified in division (N)(4) of this section in accordance with that division. The alcohol and drug addiction services board or the board of alcohol, drug addiction, and mental health services established pursuant to section 340.02 or 340.021 of the Revised Code and serving the alcohol, drug addiction, and mental health service district in which the court is located shall administer the indigent drivers alcohol treatment program of the court. When a court orders an offender or juvenile traffic offender to attend an alcohol and drug addiction treatment program, the board shall determine which program is suitable to meet the needs of the offender or juvenile traffic offender, and when a suitable program is located and space is available at the program, the offender or juvenile traffic offender shall attend the program designated by the board. A reasonable amount not to exceed five per cent of the amounts credited to and deposited into the county indigent drivers alcohol treatment fund, the county juvenile indigent drivers alcohol treatment fund, or the municipal indigent drivers alcohol treatment fund serving every court whose program is administered by that board shall be paid to the board to cover the costs it incurs in administering those indigent drivers alcohol treatment programs.

(4) If a county, juvenile, or municipal court determines, in consultation with the alcohol and drug addiction services board or the board of alcohol, drug addiction, and mental health services established pursuant to section 340.02 or 340.021 of the Revised Code and serving the alcohol, drug addiction, and mental health district in which the court is located, that the funds in the county indigent drivers alcohol treatment fund, the county juvenile indigent drivers alcohol treatment fund, or the municipal indigent drivers alcohol treatment fund under the control of the court are more than sufficient to satisfy the purpose for which the fund was established, as specified in divisions (N)(1) to (3) of this section, the court may declare a surplus in the fund. If the court declares a surplus in the fund, the court may expend the amount of the surplus in the fund for alcohol and drug abuse assessment and treatment of persons who are charged in the court with committing a criminal offense or with being a delinquent child or juvenile traffic offender and in relation to whom both of the following apply:

(a) The court determines that substance abuse was a contributing factor leading to the criminal or delinquent activity or the juvenile traffic offense with which the person is charged.

(b) The court determines that the person is unable to pay the cost of the alcohol and drug abuse assessment and treatment for which the surplus money will be used.

(2003 H 87, eff. 6–30–03; 2000 S 180, eff. 3–22–01; 2000 H 138, eff. 11–3–00; 1999 S 22, eff. 5–17–00; 1999 S 107, eff. 3–23–00; 1999 H 283, eff. 6–30–99; 1998 S 80, eff. 9–16–98; 1997 S 60, eff. 10–21–97; 1997 S 85, eff. 5–15–97; 1997 H 210, eff. 6–30–97; 1996 S 166, § 6, eff. 5–15–97; 1996 S 166, § 1, eff. 10–17–96; 1996 H 353, § 4, eff. 5–15–97; 1996 H 353, § 1, eff. 9–17–96; 1995 H 167, eff. 5–15–97; 1995 S 2, eff. 7–1–96; 1995 H 117, eff. 6–30–95; 1994 H 687, eff. 10–12–94; 1994 H 236, eff. 9–29–94; 1994 S 82, eff. 5–4–94; 1993 H 152, eff. 7–1–93; 1993 S 62, § 1, 4; 1992 S 275; 1990 H 837, S 131; 1989 H 317, H 381, H 329; 1988 H 643, S 308; 1987 H 303; 1986 S 262; 1985 H 201; 1982 S 432; 1978 H 469; 1977 H 219; 1976 H 451; 1975 H 1; 1971 H 792; 1969 H 1; 132 v S 512, H 380)

Note: See also following version of this section, and Publisher's Note.

4511.191 Chemical tests for determining alcoholic content of blood; effect of refusal to submit to test; seizure of license; indigent drivers alcohol treatment funds; procedures (second version)

Note: See also preceding version of this section, and Publisher's Note.

(A)(1) "Physical control" has the same meaning as in section 4511.194 of the Revised Code.

(2) Any person who operates a vehicle, streetcar, or trackless trolley upon a highway or any public or private property used by

the public for vehicular travel or parking within this state or who is in physical control of a vehicle, streetcar, or trackless trolley shall be deemed to have given consent to a chemical test or tests of the person's whole blood, blood serum or plasma, breath, or urine to determine the alcohol, drug, or alcohol and drug content of the person's whole blood, blood serum or plasma, breath, or urine if arrested for a violation of division (A) or (B) of section 4511.19 of the Revised Code, section 4511.194 of the Revised Code or a substantially equivalent municipal ordinance, or a municipal OVI ordinance.

(3) The chemical test or tests under division (A)(2) of this section shall be administered at the request of a law enforcement officer having reasonable grounds to believe the person was operating or in physical control of a vehicle, streetcar, or trackless trolley in violation of a division, section, or ordinance identified in division (A)(2) of this section. The law enforcement agency by which the officer is employed shall designate which of the tests shall be administered.

(4) Any person who is dead or unconscious, or who otherwise is in a condition rendering the person incapable of refusal, shall be deemed to have consented as provided in division (A)(2) of this section, and the test or tests may be administered, subject to sections 313.12 to 313.16 of the Revised Code.

(B)(1) Upon receipt of the sworn report of a law enforcement officer who arrested a person for a violation of division (A) or (B) of section 4511.19 of the Revised Code, section 4511.194 of the Revised Code or a substantially equivalent municipal ordinance, or a municipal OVI ordinance that was completed and sent to the registrar and a court pursuant to section 4511.192 of the Revised Code in regard to a person who refused to take the designated chemical test, the registrar shall enter into the registrar's records the fact that the person's driver's or commercial driver's license or permit or nonresident operating privilege was suspended by the arresting officer under this division and that section and the period of the suspension, as determined under this section. The suspension shall be subject to appeal as provided in section 4511.197 of the Revised Code. The suspension shall be for whichever of the following periods applies:

(a) Except when division (B)(1)(b), (c), or (d) of this section applies and specifies a different class or length of suspension, the suspension shall be a class C suspension for the period of time specified in division (B)(3) of section 4510.02 of the Revised Code.

(b) If the arrested person, within six years of the date on which the person refused the request to consent to the chemical test, had refused one previous request to consent to a chemical test, the suspension shall be a class B suspension imposed for the period of time specified in division (B)(2) of section 4510.02 of the Revised Code.

(c) If the arrested person, within six years of the date on which the person refused the request to consent to the chemical test, had refused two previous requests to consent to a chemical test, the suspension shall be a class A suspension imposed for the period of time specified in division (B)(1) of section 4510.02 of the Revised Code.

(d) If the arrested person, within six years of the date on which the person refused the request to consent to the chemical test, had refused three or more previous requests to consent to a chemical test, the suspension shall be for five years.

(2) The registrar shall terminate a suspension of the driver's or commercial driver's license or permit of a resident or of the operating privilege of a nonresident, or a denial of a driver's or commercial driver's license or permit, imposed pursuant to division (B)(1) of this section upon receipt of notice that the person has entered a plea of guilty to, or that the person has been convicted after entering a plea of no contest to, operating a vehicle in violation of section 4511.19 of the Revised Code or in violation of a municipal OVI ordinance, if the offense for which the conviction is had or the plea is entered arose from the same incident that led to the suspension or denial.

The registrar shall credit against any judicial suspension of a person's driver's or commercial driver's license or permit or nonresident operating privilege imposed pursuant to section 4511.19 of the Revised Code, or pursuant to section 4510.07 of the Revised Code for a violation of a municipal OVI ordinance, any time during which the person serves a related suspension imposed pursuant to division (B)(1) of this section.

(C)(1) Upon receipt of the sworn report of the law enforcement officer who arrested a person for a violation of division (A) or (B) of section 4511.19 of the Revised Code or a municipal OVI ordinance that was completed and sent to the registrar and a court pursuant to section 4511.192 of the Revised Code in regard to a person whose test results indicate that the person's whole blood, blood serum or plasma, breath, or urine contained at least the concentration of alcohol specified in division (A) (1)(b), (c), (d), or (e) of section 4511.19 of the Revised Code, the registrar shall enter into the registrar's records the fact that the person's driver's or commercial driver's license or permit or nonresident operating privilege was suspended by the arresting officer under this division and section 4511.192 of the Revised Code and the period of the suspension, as determined under divisions (F)(1) to (4) of this section. The suspension shall be subject to appeal as provided in section 4511.197 of the Revised Code. The suspension described in this division does not apply to, and shall not be imposed upon, a person arrested for a violation of section 4511.194 of the Revised Code or a substantially equivalent municipal ordinance who submits to a designated chemical test. The suspension shall be for whichever of the following periods applies:

(a) Except when division (C)(1)(b), (c), or (d) of this section applies and specifies a different period, the suspension shall be a class E suspension imposed for the period of time specified in division (B)(5) of section 4510.02 of the Revised Code.

(b) The suspension shall be a class C suspension for the period of time specified in division (B)(3) of section 4510.02 of the Revised Code if the person has been convicted of or pleaded guilty to, within six years of the date the test was conducted, one violation of division (A) or (B) of section 4511.19 of the Revised Code or one other equivalent offense.

(c) If, within six years of the date the test was conducted, the person has been convicted of or pleaded guilty to two violations of a statute or ordinance described in division (C)(1)(b) of this section, the suspension shall be a class B suspension imposed for the period of time specified in division (B)(2) of section 4510.02 of the Revised Code.

(d) If, within six years of the date the test was conducted, the person has been convicted of or pleaded guilty to more than two violations of a statute or ordinance described in division (C)(1)(b) of this section, the suspension shall be a class A suspension imposed for the period of time specified in division (B)(1) of section 4510.02 of the Revised Code.

(2) The registrar shall terminate a suspension of the driver's or commercial driver's license or permit of a resident or of the operating privilege of a nonresident, or a denial of a driver's or commercial driver's license or permit, imposed pursuant to division (C)(1) of this section upon receipt of notice that the person has entered a plea of guilty to, or that the person has been convicted after entering a plea of no contest to, operating a vehicle in violation of section 4511.19 of the Revised Code or in violation of a municipal OVI ordinance, if the offense for which the conviction is had or the plea is entered arose from the same incident that led to the suspension or denial.

The registrar shall credit against any judicial suspension of a person's driver's or commercial driver's license or permit or nonresident operating privilege imposed pursuant to section 4511.19 of the Revised Code, or pursuant to section 4510.07 of the Revised Code for a violation of a municipal OVI ordinance, any time during which the person serves a related suspension imposed pursuant to division (C)(1) of this section.

(D)(1) A suspension of a person's driver's or commercial driver's license or permit or nonresident operating privilege under this section for the time described in division (B) or (C) of this section is effective immediately from the time at which the arresting officer serves the notice of suspension upon the arrested person. Any subsequent finding that the person is not guilty of the charge that resulted in the person being requested to take the chemical test or tests under division (A) of this section does not affect the suspension.

(2) If a person is arrested for operating a vehicle, streetcar, or trackless trolley in violation of division (A) or (B) of section 4511.19 of the Revised Code or a municipal OVI ordinance, or for being in physical control of a vehicle, streetcar, or trackless trolley in violation of section 4511.194 of the Revised Code or a substantially equivalent municipal ordinance, regardless of whether the person's driver's or commercial driver's license or permit or nonresident operating privilege is or is not suspended under division (B) or (C) of this section or Chapter 4510. of the Revised Code, the person's initial appearance on the charge resulting from the arrest shall be held within five days of the person's arrest or the issuance of the citation to the person, subject to any continuance granted by the court pursuant to section 4511.197 of the Revised Code regarding the issues specified in that division.

(E) When it finally has been determined under the procedures of this section and sections 4511.192 through 4511.197 of the Revised Code that a nonresident's privilege to operate a vehicle within this state has been suspended, the registrar shall give information in writing of the action taken to the motor vehicle administrator of the state of the person's residence and of any state in which the person has a license.

(F) At the end of a suspension period under this section, under section 4511.194, section 4511.196, or division (G) of section 4511.19 of the Revised Code, or under section 4510.07 of the Revised Code for a violation of a municipal OVI ordinance and upon the request of the person whose driver's or commercial driver's license or permit was suspended and who is not otherwise subject to suspension, cancellation, or disqualification, the registrar shall return the driver's or commercial driver's license or permit to the person upon the occurrence of all of the conditions specified in divisions (F)(1) and (2) of this section:

(1) A showing that the person has proof of financial responsibility, a policy of liability insurance in effect that meets the minimum standards set forth in section 4509.51 of the Revised Code, or proof, to the satisfaction of the registrar, that the person is able to respond in damages in an amount at least equal to the minimum amounts specified in section 4509.51 of the Revised Code.

(2) Subject to the limitation contained in division (F)(3) of this section, payment by the person to the bureau of motor vehicles of a license reinstatement fee of four hundred twenty-five dollars, which fee shall be deposited in the state treasury and credited as follows:

(a) One hundred twelve dollars and fifty cents shall be credited to the statewide treatment and prevention fund created by section 4301.30 of the Revised Code. The fund shall be used to pay the costs of driver treatment and intervention programs operated pursuant to sections 3793.02 and 3793.10 of the Revised Code. The director of alcohol and drug addiction services shall determine the share of the fund that is to be allocated to alcohol and drug addiction programs authorized by section 3793.02 of the Revised Code, and the share of the fund that is to be allocated to drivers' intervention programs authorized by section 3793.10 of the Revised Code.

(b) Seventy–five dollars shall be credited to the reparations fund created by section 2743.191 of the Revised Code.

(c) Thirty–seven dollars and fifty cents shall be credited to the indigent drivers alcohol treatment fund, which is hereby established. Except as otherwise provided in division (F)(2)(c) of this section, moneys in the fund shall be distributed by the department of alcohol and drug addiction services to the county indigent drivers alcohol treatment funds, the county juvenile indigent drivers alcohol treatment funds, and the municipal indigent drivers alcohol treatment funds that are required to be established by counties and municipal corporations pursuant to this section, and shall be used only to pay the cost of an alcohol and drug addiction treatment program attended by an offender or juvenile traffic offender who is ordered to attend an alcohol and drug addiction treatment program by a county, juvenile, or municipal court judge and who is determined by the county, juvenile, or municipal court judge not to have the means to pay for the person's attendance at the program or to pay the costs specified in division (H)(4) of this section in accordance with that division. Moneys in the fund that are not distributed to a county indigent drivers alcohol treatment fund, a county juvenile indigent drivers alcohol treatment fund, or a municipal indigent drivers alcohol treatment fund under division (H) of this section because the director of alcohol and drug addiction services does not have the information necessary to identify the county or municipal corporation where the offender or juvenile offender was arrested may be transferred by the director of budget and management to the statewide treatment and prevention fund created by section 4301.30 of the Revised Code, upon certification of the amount by the director of alcohol and drug addiction services.

(d) Seventy–five dollars shall be credited to the Ohio rehabilitation services commission established by section 3304.12 of the Revised Code, to the services for rehabilitation fund, which is hereby established. The fund shall be used to match available federal matching funds where appropriate, and for any other purpose or program of the commission to rehabilitate people with disabilities to help them become employed and independent.

(e) Seventy–five dollars shall be deposited into the state treasury and credited to the drug abuse resistance education programs fund, which is hereby established, to be used by the attorney general for the purposes specified in division (L)(4) of this section.

(f) Thirty dollars shall be credited to the state bureau of motor vehicles fund created by section 4501.25 of the Revised Code.

(g) Twenty dollars shall be credited to the trauma and emergency medical services grants fund created by section 4513.263 of the Revised Code.

(3) If a person's driver's or commercial driver's license or permit is suspended under this section, under section 4511.196 or division (G) of section 4511.19 of the Revised Code, under section 4510.07 of the Revised Code for a violation of a municipal OVI ordinance or under any combination of the suspensions described in division (F)(3) of this section, and if the suspensions arise from a single incident or a single set of facts and circumstances, the person is liable for payment of, and shall be required to pay to the bureau, only one reinstatement fee of four hundred twenty-five dollars. The reinstatement fee shall be distributed by the bureau in accordance with division (F)(2) of this section.

(4) The attorney general shall use amounts in the drug abuse resistance education programs fund to award grants to law enforcement agencies to establish and implement drug abuse resistance education programs in public schools. Grants awarded to a law enforcement agency under this section shall be used by the agency to pay for not more than fifty per cent of the amount of the salaries of law enforcement officers who conduct drug abuse resistance education programs in public schools. The attorney general shall not use more than six per cent of the amounts the attorney general's office receives under division (F)(2)(e) of this section to pay the costs it incurs in administering the grant program established by division (F)(2)(e) of this section and in

providing training and materials relating to drug abuse resistance education programs.

The attorney general shall report to the governor and the general assembly each fiscal year on the progress made in establishing and implementing drug abuse resistance education programs. These reports shall include an evaluation of the effectiveness of these programs.

(G) Suspension of a commercial driver's license under division (B) or (C) of this section shall be concurrent with any period of disqualification under section 3123.611 or 4506.16 of the Revised Code or any period of suspension under section 3123.58 of the Revised Code. No person who is disqualified for life from holding a commercial driver's license under section 4506.16 of the Revised Code shall be issued a driver's license under Chapter 4507. of the Revised Code during the period for which the commercial driver's license was suspended under division (B) or (C) of this section. No person whose commercial driver's license is suspended under division (B) or (C) of this section shall be issued a driver's license under Chapter 4507. of the Revised Code during the period of the suspension.

(H)(1) Each county shall establish an indigent drivers alcohol treatment fund, each county shall establish a juvenile indigent drivers alcohol treatment fund, and each municipal corporation in which there is a municipal court shall establish an indigent drivers alcohol treatment fund. All revenue that the general assembly appropriates to the indigent drivers alcohol treatment fund for transfer to a county indigent drivers alcohol treatment fund, a county juvenile indigent drivers alcohol treatment fund, or a municipal indigent drivers alcohol treatment fund, all portions of fees that are paid under division (L) [1] of this section and that are credited under that division to the indigent drivers alcohol treatment fund in the state treasury for a county indigent drivers alcohol treatment fund, a county juvenile indigent drivers alcohol treatment fund, or a municipal indigent drivers alcohol treatment fund, and all portions of fines that are specified for deposit into a county or municipal indigent drivers alcohol treatment fund by section 4511.193 of the Revised Code shall be deposited into that county indigent drivers alcohol treatment fund, county juvenile indigent drivers alcohol treatment fund, or municipal indigent drivers alcohol treatment fund in accordance with division (H)(2) of this section. Additionally, all portions of fines that are paid for a violation of section 4511.19 of the Revised Code or of any prohibition contained in Chapter 4510. of the Revised Code, and that are required under section 4511.19 or any provision of Chapter 4510. of the Revised Code to be deposited into a county indigent drivers alcohol treatment fund or municipal indigent drivers alcohol treatment fund shall be deposited into the appropriate fund in accordance with the applicable division.

(2) That portion of the license reinstatement fee that is paid under division (F) of this section and that is credited under that division to the indigent drivers alcohol treatment fund shall be deposited into a county indigent drivers alcohol treatment fund, a county juvenile indigent drivers alcohol treatment fund, or a municipal indigent drivers alcohol treatment fund as follows:

(a) If the suspension in question was imposed under this section, that portion of the fee shall be deposited as follows:

(i) If the fee is paid by a person who was charged in a county court with the violation that resulted in the suspension, the portion shall be deposited into the county indigent drivers alcohol treatment fund under the control of that court;

(ii) If the fee is paid by a person who was charged in a juvenile court with the violation that resulted in the suspension, the portion shall be deposited into the county juvenile indigent drivers alcohol treatment fund established in the county served by the court;

(iii) If the fee is paid by a person who was charged in a municipal court with the violation that resulted in the suspension, the portion shall be deposited into the municipal indigent drivers alcohol treatment fund under the control of that court.

(b) If the suspension in question was imposed under section 4511.19 of the Revised Code or under section 4510.07 of the Revised Code for a violation of a municipal OVI ordinance, that portion of the fee shall be deposited as follows:

(i) If the fee is paid by a person whose license or permit was suspended by a county court, the portion shall be deposited into the county indigent drivers alcohol treatment fund under the control of that court;

(ii) If the fee is paid by a person whose license or permit was suspended by a municipal court, the portion shall be deposited into the municipal indigent drivers alcohol treatment fund under the control of that court.

(3) Expenditures from a county indigent drivers alcohol treatment fund, a county juvenile indigent drivers alcohol treatment fund, or a municipal indigent drivers alcohol treatment fund shall be made only upon the order of a county, juvenile, or municipal court judge and only for payment of the cost of the attendance at an alcohol and drug addiction treatment program of a person who is convicted of, or found to be a juvenile traffic offender by reason of, a violation of division (A) of section 4511.19 of the Revised Code or a substantially similar municipal ordinance, who is ordered by the court to attend the alcohol and drug addiction treatment program, and who is determined by the court to be unable to pay the cost of attendance at the treatment program or for payment of the costs specified in division (H)(4) of this section in accordance with that division. The alcohol and drug addiction services board or the board of alcohol, drug addiction, and mental health services established pursuant to section 340.02 or 340.021 of the Revised Code and serving the alcohol, drug addiction, and mental health service district in which the court is located shall administer the indigent drivers alcohol treatment program of the court. When a court orders an offender or juvenile traffic offender to attend an alcohol and drug addiction treatment program, the board shall determine which program is suitable to meet the needs of the offender or juvenile traffic offender, and when a suitable program is located and space is available at the program, the offender or juvenile traffic offender shall attend the program designated by the board. A reasonable amount not to exceed five per cent of the amounts credited to and deposited into the county indigent drivers alcohol treatment fund, the county juvenile indigent drivers alcohol treatment fund, or the municipal indigent drivers alcohol treatment fund serving every court whose program is administered by that board shall be paid to the board to cover the costs it incurs in administering those indigent drivers alcohol treatment programs.

(4) If a county, juvenile, or municipal court determines, in consultation with the alcohol and drug addiction services board or the board of alcohol, drug addiction, and mental health services established pursuant to section 340.02 or 340.021 of the Revised Code and serving the alcohol, drug addiction, and mental health district in which the court is located, that the funds in the county indigent drivers alcohol treatment fund, the county juvenile indigent drivers alcohol treatment fund, or the municipal indigent drivers alcohol treatment fund under the control of the court are more than sufficient to satisfy the purpose for which the fund was established, as specified in divisions (H)(1) to (3) of this section, the court may declare a surplus in the fund. If the court declares a surplus in the fund, the court may expend the amount of the surplus in the fund for alcohol and drug abuse assessment and treatment of persons who are charged in the court with committing a criminal offense or with being a delinquent child or juvenile traffic offender and in relation to whom both of the following apply:

(a) The court determines that substance abuse was a contributing factor leading to the criminal or delinquent activity or the juvenile traffic offense with which the person is charged.

(b) The court determines that the person is unable to pay the cost of the alcohol and drug abuse assessment and treatment for which the surplus money will be used.

(2004 H 163, eff. 9–23–04; 2002 S 123, eff. 1–1–04; 2000 S 180, eff. 3–22–01; 2000 H 138, eff. 11–3–00; 1999 S 22, eff. 5–17–00; 1999 S 107, eff. 3–23–00; 1999 H 283, eff. 6–30–99; 1998 S 80, eff. 9–16–98; 1997 S 60, eff. 10–21–97; 1997 S 85, eff. 5–15–97; 1997 H 210, eff. 6–30–97; 1996 S 166, § 6, eff. 5–15–97; 1996 S 166, § 1, eff. 10–17–96; 1996 H 353, § 4, eff. 5–15–97; 1996 H 353, § 1, eff. 9–17–96; 1995 H 167, eff. 5–15–97; 1995 S 2, eff. 7–1–96; 1995 H 117, eff. 6–30–95; 1994 H 687, eff. 10–12–94; 1994 H 236, eff. 9–29–94; 1994 S 82, eff. 5–4–94; 1993 H 152, eff. 7–1–93; 1993 S 62, § 1, 4; 1992 S 275; 1990 H 837, S 131; 1989 H 317, H 381, H 329; 1988 H 643, S 308; 1987 H 303; 1986 S 262; 1985 H 201; 1982 S 432; 1978 H 469; 1977 H 219; 1976 H 451; 1975 H 1; 1971 H 792; 1969 H 1; 132 v S 512, H 380)

1 So in original; 2002 S 123 redesignated former division (L) as division (F).

Note: See also preceding version of this section, and Publisher's Note.

Historical and Statutory Notes

Publisher's Note: 4511.191 was amended by 2004 H 163, eff. 9–23–04, 2002 S 123, eff. 1–1–04, and 2003 H 87, eff. 6–30–03. Harmonization pursuant to section 1.52 of the Revised Code is in question. See *Baldwin's Ohio Legislative Service Annotated*, 2004, page 5/L–1347, 2002, page 7/L–1716, and 2003, page 2/L–83, or the OH-LEGIS or OH-LEGIS-OLD database on Westlaw, for original versions of these Acts.

Ed. Note: The effective date of the amendment of this section by 1992 S 275 was changed from 7–1–93 to 9–1–93 by 1993 S 62, § 4, eff. 6–30–93.

4511.192 Written notice of effect of refusal; seizure of license

(A) The arresting law enforcement officer shall give advice in accordance with this section to any person under arrest for a violation of division (A) or (B) of section 4511.19 of the Revised Code, section 4511.194 of the Revised Code or a substantially equivalent municipal ordinance, or a municipal OVI ordinance. The officer shall give that advice in a written form that contains the information described in division (B) of this section and shall read the advice to the person. The form shall contain a statement that the form was shown to the person under arrest and read to the person by the arresting officer. One or more persons shall witness the arresting officer's reading of the form, and the witnesses shall certify to this fact by signing the form.

(B) If a person is under arrest as described in division (A) of this section, before the person may be requested to submit to a chemical test or tests to determine the alcohol and drug content of the person's blood, breath, or urine, the arresting officer shall read the following form to the person:

"You now are under arrest for (specifically state the offense under state law or a substantially equivalent municipal ordinance for which the person was arrested—operating a vehicle under the influence of alcohol, a drug, or a combination of them; operating a vehicle after underage alcohol consumption; or having physical control of a vehicle while under the influence).

If you refuse to take any chemical test required by law, your Ohio driving privileges will be suspended immediately, and you will have to pay a fee to have the privileges reinstated. If you have a prior OVI or OVUAC conviction under state or municipal law within the preceding twenty years, you now are under arrest for state OVI, and, if you refuse to take a chemical test, you will face increased penalties if you subsequently are convicted of the state OVI.

(Read this part unless the person is under arrest for solely having physical control of a vehicle while under the influence.) If you take any chemical test required by law and are found to be at or over the prohibited amount of alcohol in your blood, breath, or urine as set by law, your Ohio driving privileges will be suspended immediately, and you will have to pay a fee to have the privileges reinstated.

If you take a chemical test, you may have an independent chemical test taken at your own expense."

(C) If the arresting law enforcement officer does not ask a person under arrest as described in division (A) of this section to submit to a chemical test or tests under section 4511.191 of the Revised Code, the arresting officer shall seize the Ohio or out-of-state driver's or commercial driver's license or permit of the person and immediately forward it to the court in which the arrested person is to appear on the charge. If the arrested person is not in possession of the person's license or permit or it is not in the person's vehicle, the officer shall order the person to surrender it to the law enforcement agency that employs the officer within twenty-four hours after the arrest, and, upon the surrender, the agency immediately shall forward the license or permit to the court in which the person is to appear on the charge. Upon receipt of the license or permit, the court shall retain it pending the arrested person's initial appearance and any action taken under section 4511.196 of the Revised Code.

(D)(1) If a law enforcement officer asks a person under arrest as described in division (A) of this section to submit to a chemical test or tests under section 4511.191 of the Revised Code, if the officer advises the person in accordance with this section of the consequences of the person's refusal or submission, and if either the person refuses to submit to the test or tests or, unless the arrest was for a violation of section 4511.194 of the Revised Code or a substantially equivalent municipal ordinance, the person submits to the test or tests and the test results indicate a prohibited concentration of alcohol in the person's whole blood, blood serum or plasma, breath, or urine at the time of the alleged offense, the arresting officer shall do all of the following:

(a) On behalf of the registrar of motor vehicles, notify the person that, independent of any penalties or sanctions imposed upon the person, the person's Ohio driver's or commercial driver's license or permit or nonresident operating privilege is suspended immediately, that the suspension will last at least until the person's initial appearance on the charge, which will be held within five days after the date of the person's arrest or the issuance of a citation to the person, and that the person may appeal the suspension at the initial appearance or during the period of time ending thirty days after that initial appearance;

(b) Seize the driver's or commercial driver's license or permit of the person and immediately forward it to the registrar. If the arrested person is not in possession of the person's license or permit or it is not in the person's vehicle, the officer shall order the person to surrender it to the law enforcement agency that employs the officer within twenty-four hours after the person is given notice of the suspension, and, upon the surrender, the officer's employing agency immediately shall forward the license or permit to the registrar.

(c) Verify the person's current residence and, if it differs from that on the person's driver's or commercial driver's license or permit, notify the registrar of the change;

(d) Send to the registrar, within forty-eight hours after the arrest of the person, a sworn report that includes all of the following statements:

(i) That the officer had reasonable grounds to believe that, at the time of the arrest, the arrested person was operating a vehicle, streetcar, or trackless trolley in violation of division (A) or (B) of section 4511.19 of the Revised Code or a municipal OVI ordinance or for being in physical control of a stationary vehicle, streetcar, or trackless trolley in violation of section 4511.194 of the Revised Code or a substantially equivalent municipal ordinance;

(ii) That the person was arrested and charged with a violation of division (A) or (B) of section 4511.19 of the Revised Code, section 4511.194 of the Revised Code or a substantially equivalent municipal ordinance, or a municipal OVI ordinance;

(iii) That the officer asked the person to take the designated chemical test or tests, advised the person in accordance with this section of the consequences of submitting to, or refusing to take, the test or tests, and gave the person the form described in division (B) of this section;

(iv) That either the person refused to submit to the chemical test or tests or, unless the arrest was for a violation of section 4511.194 of the Revised Code or a substantially equivalent municipal ordinance, the person submitted to the chemical test or tests and the test results indicate a prohibited concentration of alcohol in the person's whole blood, blood serum or plasma, breath, or urine at the time of the alleged offense.

(2) Division (D)(1) of this section does not apply to a person who is arrested for a violation of section 4511.194 of the Revised Code or a substantially equivalent municipal ordinance, who is asked by a law enforcement officer to submit to a chemical test or tests under section 4511. 191 of the Revised Code, and who submits to the test or tests, regardless of the amount of alcohol that the test results indicate is present in the person's whole blood, blood serum or plasma, breath, or urine.

(E) The arresting officer shall give the officer's sworn report that is completed under this section to the arrested person at the time of the arrest, or the registrar of motor vehicles shall send the report to the person by regular first class mail as soon as possible after receipt of the report, but not later than fourteen days after receipt of it. An arresting officer may give an unsworn report to the arrested person at the time of the arrest provided the report is complete when given to the arrested person and subsequently is sworn to by the arresting officer. As soon as possible, but not later than forty-eight hours after the arrest of the person, the arresting officer shall send a copy of the sworn report to the court in which the arrested person is to appear on the charge for which the person was arrested.

(F) The sworn report of an arresting officer completed under this section is prima-facie proof of the information and statements that it contains. It shall be admitted and considered as prima-facie proof of the information and statements that it contains in any appeal under section 4511.197 of the Revised Code relative to any suspension of a person's driver's or commercial driver's license or permit or nonresident operating privilege that results from the arrest covered by the report.

(2004 H 163, eff. 9–23–04; 2002 S 123, eff. 1–1–04; 1993 S 62, eff. 9–1–93; 1989 H 381; 1986 S 262; 1982 S 432; 1978 S 381)

4511.193 Disposition of fines; immobilization of vehicle; impoundment of license plates; criminal forfeiture of vehicle

(A) Twenty–five dollars of any fine imposed for a violation of a municipal OVI ordinance shall be deposited into the municipal or county indigent drivers alcohol treatment fund created pursuant to division (H) of section 4511.191 of the Revised Code in accordance with this section and section 733.40, divisions (A) and (B) of section 1901.024, division (F) of section 1901.31, or division (C) of section 1907.20 of the Revised Code. Regardless of whether the fine is imposed by a municipal court, a mayor's court, or a juvenile court, if the fine was imposed for a violation of an ordinance of a municipal corporation that is within the jurisdiction of a municipal court, the twenty-five dollars that is subject to this section shall be deposited into the indigent drivers alcohol treatment fund of the municipal corporation in which is located the municipal court that has jurisdiction over that municipal corporation. Regardless of whether the fine is imposed by a county court, a mayor's court, or a juvenile court, if the fine was imposed for a violation of an ordinance of a municipal corporation that is within the jurisdiction of a county court, the twenty-five dollars that is subject to this section shall be deposited into the indigent drivers alcohol treatment fund of the county in which is located the county court that has jurisdiction over that municipal corporation. The deposit shall be made in accordance with section 733.40, divisions (A) and (B) of section 1901.024, division (F) of section 1901.31, or division (C) of section 1907.20 of the Revised Code.

(B)(1) The requirements and sanctions imposed by divisions (B)(1) and (2) of this section are an adjunct to and derive from the state's exclusive authority over the registration and titling of motor vehicles and do not comprise a part of the criminal sentence to be imposed upon a person who violates a municipal OVI ordinance.

(2) If a person is convicted of or pleads guilty to a violation of a municipal OVI ordinance, if the vehicle the offender was operating at the time of the offense is registered in the offender's name, and if, within six years of the current offense, the offender has been convicted of or pleaded guilty to one or more violations of division (A) or (B) of section 4511.19 of the Revised Code or one or more other equivalent offenses, the court, in addition to and independent of any sentence that it imposes upon the offender for the offense, shall do whichever of the following is applicable:

(a) Except as otherwise provided in division (B)(2)(b) of this section, if, within six years of the current offense, the offender has been convicted of or pleaded guilty to one violation described in division (B)(2) of this section, the court shall order the immobilization for ninety days of that vehicle and the impoundment for ninety days of the license plates of that vehicle. The order for the immobilization and impoundment shall be issued and enforced in accordance with section 4503.233 of the Revised Code.

(b) If, within six years of the current offense, the offender has been convicted of or pleaded guilty to two or more violations described in division (B)(2) of this section, or if the offender previously has been convicted of or pleaded guilty to a violation of division (A) of section 4511.19 of the Revised Code under circumstances in which the violation was a felony and regardless of when the violation and the conviction or guilty plea occurred, the court shall order the criminal forfeiture to the state of that vehicle The [1] order of criminal forfeiture shall be issued and enforced in accordance with section 4503.234 of the Revised Code.

(2002 S 123, eff. 1–1–04; 2000 H 80, eff. 6–8–00; 1999 S 107, eff. 3–30–00; 1997 S 60, eff. 10–21–97; 1996 S 166, eff. 10–17–96; 1996 H 353, eff. 9–17–96; 1993 S 62, § 1, eff. 9–1–93)

[1] So in original; 2002 S 123.

4511.194 Physical control of vehicle while under the influence; testimony and evidence regarding field sobriety test

(A) As used in this section:

(1) "National highway traffic safety administration" has the same meaning as in section 4511.19 of the Revised Code.

(2) "Physical control" means being in the driver's position of the front seat of a vehicle or in the driver's position of a streetcar or trackless trolley and having possession of the vehicle's, streetcar's, or trackless trolley's ignition key or other ignition device.

(B) No person shall be in physical control of a vehicle, streetcar, or trackless trolley while under the influence of alcohol, a drug of abuse, or a combination of them or while the person's whole blood, blood serum or plasma, breath, or urine contains at least the concentration of alcohol specified in division (A) (1)(b), (c), (d), or (e) of section 4511.19 of the Revised Code.

(C)(1) In any criminal prosecution or juvenile court proceeding for a violation of this section or a substantially equivalent municipal ordinance, if a law enforcement officer has administered a field sobriety test to the person in physical control of the vehicle involved in the violation and if it is shown by clear and convincing evidence that the officer administered the test in substantial compliance with the testing standards for any reliable, credible, and generally accepted field sobriety tests that were in effect at the time the tests were administered, including, but not limited to, any testing standards then in effect that were set by the national highway traffic safety administration, all of the following apply:

(a) The officer may testify concerning the results of the field sobriety test so administered.

(b) The prosecution may introduce the results of the field sobriety test so administered as evidence in any proceedings in the criminal prosecution or juvenile court proceeding.

(c) If testimony is presented or evidence is introduced under division (C)(1)(a) or (b) of this section and if the testimony or evidence is admissible under the Rules of Evidence, the court shall admit the testimony or evidence, and the trier of fact shall give it whatever weight the trier of fact considers to be appropriate.

(2) Division (C)(1) of this section does not limit or preclude a court, in its determination of whether the arrest of a person was supported by probable cause or its determination of any other matter in a criminal prosecution or juvenile court proceeding of a type described in that division, from considering evidence or testimony that is not otherwise disallowed by division (C)(1) of this section.

(D) Whoever violates this section is guilty of having physical control of a vehicle while under the influence, a misdemeanor of the first degree. In addition to other sanctions imposed, the court may impose on the offender a class seven suspension of the offender's driver's license, commercial driver's license, temporary instruction permit, probationary license, or nonresident operating privilege from the range specified in division (A)(7) of section 4510.02 of the Revised Code.

(2004 H 163, eff. 9–23–04; 2002 S 163, eff. 1–1–04; 2002 S 123, eff. 1–1–04)

4511.195 Seizure of vehicles upon arrest

(A) As used in this section:

(1) "Arrested person" means a person who is arrested for a violation of division (A) of section 4511.19 of the Revised Code or a municipal OVI ordinance and whose arrest results in a vehicle being seized under division (B) of this section.

(2) "Vehicle owner" means either of the following:

(a) The person in whose name is registered, at the time of the seizure, a vehicle that is seized under division (B) of this section;

(b) A person to whom the certificate of title to a vehicle that is seized under division (B) of this section has been assigned and who has not obtained a certificate of title to the vehicle in that person's name, but who is deemed by the court as being the owner of the vehicle at the time the vehicle was seized under division (B) of this section.

(3) "Interested party" includes the owner of a vehicle seized under this section, all lienholders, the arrested person, the owner of the place of storage at which a vehicle seized under this section is stored, and the person or entity that caused the vehicle to be removed.

(B)(1) The arresting officer or another officer of the law enforcement agency that employs the arresting officer, in addition to any action that the arresting officer is required or authorized to take by section 4511.19 or 4511.191 of the Revised Code or by any other provision of law, shall seize the vehicle that a person was operating at the time of the alleged offense and its license plates if the vehicle is registered in the arrested person's name and if either of the following applies:

(a) The person is arrested for a violation of division (A) of section 4511.19 of the Revised Code or of a municipal OVI ordinance and, within six years of the alleged violation, the person previously has been convicted of or pleaded guilty to one or more violations of division (A) or (B) of section 4511.19 of the Revised Code or one or more other equivalent offenses.

(b) The person is arrested for a violation of division (A) of section 4511.19 of the Revised Code or of a municipal OVI ordinance and the person previously has been convicted of or pleaded guilty to a violation of division (A) of section 4511.19 of the Revised Code under circumstances in which the violation was a felony, regardless of when the prior felony violation of division (A) of section 4511.19 of the Revised Code and the conviction or guilty plea occurred.

(2) A law enforcement agency that employs a law enforcement officer who makes an arrest of a type that is described in division (B)(1) of this section and that involves a rented or leased vehicle that is being rented or leased for a period of thirty days or less shall notify, within twenty-four hours after the officer makes the arrest, the lessor or owner of the vehicle regarding the circumstances of the arrest and the location at which the vehicle may be picked up. At the time of the seizure of the vehicle, the law enforcement officer who made the arrest shall give the arrested person written notice that the vehicle and its license plates have been seized; that the vehicle either will be kept by the officer's law enforcement agency or will be immobilized at least until the operator's initial appearance on the charge of the offense for which the arrest was made; that, at the initial appearance, the court in certain circumstances may order that the vehicle and license plates be released to the arrested person until the disposition of that charge; and that, if the arrested person is convicted of that charge, the court generally must order the immobilization of the vehicle and the impoundment of its license plates, or the forfeiture of the vehicle.

(3) The arresting officer or a law enforcement officer of the agency that employs the arresting officer shall give written notice of the seizure to the court that will conduct the initial appearance of the arrested person on the charges arising out of the arrest. Upon receipt of the notice, the court promptly shall determine whether the arrested person is the vehicle owner. If the court determines that the arrested person is not the vehicle owner, it promptly shall send by regular mail written notice of the seizure to the vehicle's registered owner. The written notice shall contain all of the information required by division (B)(2) of this section to be in a notice to be given to the arrested person and also shall specify the date, time, and place of the arrested person's initial appearance. The notice also shall inform the vehicle owner that if title to a motor vehicle that is subject to an order for criminal forfeiture under this section is assigned or transferred and division (B)(2) or (3) of section 4503.234 of the Revised Code applies, the court may fine the arrested person the value of the vehicle. The notice also shall state that if the vehicle is immobilized under division (A) of section 4503.233 of the Revised Code, seven days after the end of the period of immobilization a law enforcement agency will send the vehicle owner a notice, informing the owner that if the release of the vehicle is not obtained in accordance with division (D)(3) of section 4503.233 of the Revised Code, the vehicle shall be forfeited. The notice also shall inform the vehicle owner that the vehicle owner may be charged expenses or charges incurred under this section and section 4503.233 of the Revised Code for the removal and storage of the vehicle.

The written notice that is given to the arrested person also shall state that if the person is convicted of or pleads guilty to the offense and the court issues an immobilization and impoundment order relative to that vehicle, division (D)(4) of section 4503.233

of the Revised Code prohibits the vehicle from being sold during the period of immobilization without the prior approval of the court.

(4) At or before the initial appearance, the vehicle owner may file a motion requesting the court to order that the vehicle and its license plates be released to the vehicle owner. Except as provided in this division and subject to the payment of expenses or charges incurred in the removal and storage of the vehicle, the court, in its discretion, then may issue an order releasing the vehicle and its license plates to the vehicle owner. Such an order may be conditioned upon such terms as the court determines appropriate, including the posting of a bond in an amount determined by the court. If the arrested person is not the vehicle owner and if the vehicle owner is not present at the arrested person's initial appearance, and if the court believes that the vehicle owner was not provided with adequate notice of the initial appearance, the court, in its discretion, may allow the vehicle owner to file a motion within seven days of the initial appearance. If the court allows the vehicle owner to file such a motion after the initial appearance, the extension of time granted by the court does not extend the time within which the initial appearance is to be conducted. If the court issues an order for the release of the vehicle and its license plates, a copy of the order shall be made available to the vehicle owner. If the vehicle owner presents a copy of the order to the law enforcement agency that employs the law enforcement officer who arrested the arrested person, the law enforcement agency promptly shall release the vehicle and its license plates to the vehicle owner upon payment by the vehicle owner of any expenses or charges incurred in the removal and storage of the vehicle.

(5) A vehicle seized under division (B)(1) of this section either shall be towed to a place specified by the law enforcement agency that employs the arresting officer to be safely kept by the agency at that place for the time and in the manner specified in this section or shall be otherwise immobilized for the time and in the manner specified in this section. A law enforcement officer of that agency shall remove the identification license plates of the vehicle, and they shall be safely kept by the agency for the time and in the manner specified in this section. No vehicle that is seized and either towed or immobilized pursuant to this division shall be considered contraband for purposes of section 2933.41, 2933.42, or 2933.43 of the Revised Code. The vehicle shall not be immobilized at any place other than a commercially operated private storage lot, a place owned by a law enforcement agency or other government agency, or a place to which one of the following applies:

(a) The place is leased by or otherwise under the control of a law enforcement agency or other government agency.

(b) The place is owned by the vehicle operator, the vehicle operator's spouse, or a parent or child of the vehicle operator.

(c) The place is owned by a private person or entity, and, prior to the immobilization, the private entity or person that owns the place, or the authorized agent of that private entity or person, has given express written consent for the immobilization to be carried out at that place.

(d) The place is a street or highway on which the vehicle is parked in accordance with the law.

(C)(1) A vehicle seized under division (B) of this section shall be safely kept at the place to which it is towed or otherwise moved by the law enforcement agency that employs the arresting officer until the initial appearance of the arrested person relative to the charge in question. The license plates of the vehicle that are removed pursuant to division (B) of this section shall be safely kept by the law enforcement agency that employs the arresting officer until the initial appearance of the arrested person relative to the charge in question.

(2)(a) At the initial appearance or not less than seven days prior to the date of final disposition, the court shall notify the arrested person that, if title to a motor vehicle that is subject to an order for criminal forfeiture under this section is assigned or transferred and division (B)(2) or (3) of section 4503.234 of the Revised Code applies, the court may fine the arrested person the value of the vehicle. If, at the initial appearance, the arrested person pleads guilty to the violation of division (A) of section 4511.19 of the Revised Code or of the municipal OVI ordinance or pleads no contest to and is convicted of the violation, the court shall impose sentence upon the person as provided by law or ordinance; the court shall order the immobilization of the vehicle the arrested person was operating at the time of the offense if registered in the arrested person's name and the impoundment of its license plates under section 4503.233 and section 4511.19 or 4511.193 of the Revised Code or the criminal forfeiture to the state of the vehicle if registered in the arrested person's name under section 4503.234 and section 4511.19 or 4511.193 of the Revised Code, whichever is applicable; and the vehicle and its license plates shall not be returned or released to the arrested person.

(b) If, at any time, the charge that the arrested person violated division (A) of section 4511.19 of the Revised Code or the municipal OVI ordinance is dismissed for any reason, the court shall order that the vehicle seized at the time of the arrest and its license plates immediately be released to the person.

(D) If a vehicle and its license plates are seized under division (B) of this section and are not returned or released to the arrested person pursuant to division (C) of this section, the vehicle and its license plates shall be retained until the final disposition of the charge in question. Upon the final disposition of that charge, the court shall do whichever of the following is applicable:

(1) If the arrested person is convicted of or pleads guilty to the violation of division (A) of section 4511.19 of the Revised Code or of the municipal OVI ordinance, the court shall impose sentence upon the person as provided by law or ordinance and shall order the immobilization of the vehicle the person was operating at the time of the offense if it is registered in the arrested person's name and the impoundment of its license plates under section 4503.233 and section 4511.19 or 4511.193 of the Revised Code, or the criminal forfeiture of the vehicle if it is registered in the arrested person's name under section 4503.234 and section 4511.19 or 4511.193 of the Revised Code, whichever is applicable.

(2) If the arrested person is found not guilty of the violation of division (A) of section 4511.19 of the Revised Code or of the municipal OVI ordinance, the court shall order that the vehicle and its license plates immediately be released to the arrested person.

(3) If the charge that the arrested person violated division (A) of section 4511.19 of the Revised Code or the municipal OVI ordinance is dismissed for any reason, the court shall order that the vehicle and its license plates immediately be released to the arrested person.

(4) If the impoundment of the vehicle was not authorized under this section, the court shall order that the vehicle and its license plates be returned immediately to the arrested person or, if the arrested person is not the vehicle owner, to the vehicle owner, and shall order that the state or political subdivision of the law enforcement agency served by the law enforcement officer who seized the vehicle pay all expenses and charges incurred in its removal and storage.

(E) If a vehicle is seized under division (B) of this section, the time between the seizure of the vehicle and either its release to the arrested person under division (C) of this section or the issuance of an order of immobilization of the vehicle under section 4503.233 of the Revised Code shall be credited against the period of immobilization ordered by the court.

(F)(1) Except as provided in division (D)(4) of this section, the arrested person may be charged expenses or charges incurred in the removal and storage of the immobilized vehicle. The court with jurisdiction over the case, after notice to all interested parties, including lienholders, and after an opportunity for them to be heard, if the court finds that the arrested person does not intend to seek release of the vehicle at the end of the period of immobilization under section 4503.233 of the Revised Code or that the arrested person is not or will not be able to pay the expenses and charges incurred in its removal and storage, may order that title to the vehicle be transferred, in order of priority, first into the name of the person or entity that removed it, next into the name of a lienholder, or lastly into the name of the owner of the place of storage.

Any lienholder that receives title under a court order shall do so on the condition that it pay any expenses or charges incurred in the vehicle's removal and storage. If the person or entity that receives title to the vehicle is the person or entity that removed it, the person or entity shall receive title on the condition that it pay any lien on the vehicle. The court shall not order that title be transferred to any person or entity other than the owner of the place of storage if the person or entity refuses to receive the title. Any person or entity that receives title either may keep title to the vehicle or may dispose of the vehicle in any legal manner that it considers appropriate, including assignment of the certificate of title to the motor vehicle to a salvage dealer or a scrap metal processing facility. The person or entity shall not transfer the vehicle to the person who is the vehicle's immediate previous owner.

If the person or entity that receives title assigns the motor vehicle to a salvage dealer or scrap metal processing facility, the person or entity shall send the assigned certificate of title to the motor vehicle to the clerk of the court of common pleas of the county in which the salvage dealer or scrap metal processing facility is located. The person or entity shall mark the face of the certificate of title with the words "FOR DESTRUCTION" and shall deliver a photocopy of the certificate of title to the salvage dealer or scrap metal processing facility for its records.

(2) Whenever a court issues an order under division (F)(1) of this section, the court also shall order removal of the license plates from the vehicle and cause them to be sent to the registrar of motor vehicles if they have not already been sent to the registrar. Thereafter, no further proceedings shall take place under this section or under section 4503.233 of the Revised Code.

(3) Prior to initiating a proceeding under division (F)(1) of this section, and upon payment of the fee under division (B) of section 4505.14 of the Revised Code, any interested party may cause a search to be made of the public records of the bureau of motor vehicles or the clerk of the court of common pleas, to ascertain the identity of any lienholder of the vehicle. The initiating party shall furnish this information to the clerk of the court with jurisdiction over the case, and the clerk shall provide notice to the arrested person, any lienholder, and any other interested parties listed by the initiating party, at the last known address supplied by the initiating party, by certified mail or, at the option of the initiating party, by personal service or ordinary mail.

(2002 S 123, eff. 1–1–04; 1999 S 107, eff. 3–23–00; 1998 S 213, eff. 7–29–98; 1997 S 60, eff. 10–21–97; 1996 S 166, eff. 10–17–96; 1996 H 676, eff. 10–4–96; 1996 H 353, eff. 9–17–96; 1994 H 687, eff. 10–12–94; 1994 H 236, eff. 9–29–94; 1994 S 82, eff. 5–4–94; 1993 S 62, § 1, eff. 9–1–93; 1993 S 62, § 4; 1992 S 275)

4511.196 Initial appearance, suspension of driver's or commercial driver's license

(A) If a person is arrested for being in physical control of a vehicle, streetcar, or trackless trolley in violation of section 4511.194 of the Revised Code or a substantially equivalent municipal ordinance, or for operating a vehicle, streetcar, or trackless trolley in violation of division (A) or (B) of section 4511.19 of the Revised Code or a municipal OVI ordinance, regardless of whether the person's driver's or commercial driver's license or permit or nonresident operating privilege is or is not suspended under section 4511.191 of the Revised Code, the person's initial appearance on the charge resulting from the arrest shall be held within five days of the person's arrest or the issuance of the citation to the person.

(B)(1) If a person is arrested as described in division (A) of this section, if the person's driver's or commercial driver's license or permit or nonresident operating privilege has been suspended under section 4511.191 of the Revised Code in relation to that arrest, if the person appeals the suspension in accordance with section 4511.197 of the Revised Code, and if the judge, magistrate, or mayor terminates the suspension in accordance with that section, the judge, magistrate, or mayor, at any time prior to adjudication on the merits of the charge resulting from the arrest, may impose a new suspension of the person's license, permit, or nonresident operating privilege, notwithstanding the termination, if the judge, magistrate, or mayor determines that the person's continued driving will be a threat to public safety.

(2) If a person is arrested as described in division (A) of this section and if the person's driver's or commercial driver's license or permit or nonresident operating privilege has not been suspended under section 4511.191 of the Revised Code in relation to that arrest, the judge, magistrate, or mayor, at any time prior to the adjudication on the merits of the charge resulting from the arrest, may impose a suspension of the person's license, permit, or nonresident operating privilege if the judge, magistrate, or mayor determines that the person's continued driving will be a threat to public safety.

(C) A suspension under division (B)(1) or (2) of this section shall continue until the complaint on the charge resulting from the arrest is adjudicated on the merits. A court that imposes a suspension under division (B)(2) of this section shall send the person's driver's license or permit to the registrar of motor vehicles. If the court possesses the license or permit of a person in the category described in division (B)(2) of this section and the court does not impose a suspension under that division, the court shall return the license or permit to the person if the license or permit has not otherwise been suspended or cancelled.

Any time during which the person serves a suspension of the person's license, permit, or privilege that is imposed pursuant to division (B)(1) or (2) of this section shall be credited against any period of judicial suspension of the person's license, permit, or privilege that is imposed under division (G) of section 4511.19 of the Revised Code or under section 4510.07 of the Revised Code for a violation of a municipal ordinance substantially equivalent to division (A) of section 4511.19 of the Revised Code.

(D) If a person is arrested and charged with a violation of section 2903.08 of the Revised Code or a violation of section 2903.06 of the Revised Code that is a felony offense, the judge at the person's initial appearance, preliminary hearing, or arraignment may suspend the person's driver's or commercial driver's license or permit or nonresident operating privilege if the judge determines at any of those proceedings that the person's continued driving will be a threat to public safety.

A suspension imposed under this division shall continue until the indictment or information alleging the violation specified in this division is adjudicated on the merits. A court that imposes a suspension under this division shall send the person's driver's or commercial driver's license or permit to the registrar.

(2004 H 163, eff. 9–23–04; 2002 S 123, eff. 1–1–04; 1999 S 107, eff. 3–23–00; 1999 H 61, eff. 8–25–99; 1997 S 60, eff. 10–21–97; 1993 S 62, eff. 9–1–93)

4511.197 Appeal of suspension

(A) If a person is arrested for operating a vehicle, streetcar, or trackless trolley in violation of division (A) or (B) of section 4511.19 of the Revised Code or a municipal OVI ordinance or for being in physical control of a vehicle, streetcar, or trackless trolley in violation of section 4511.194 of the Revised Code or a substantially equivalent municipal ordinance and if the person's driver's or commercial driver's license or permit or nonresident operating privilege is suspended under section 4511.191 of the Revised Code, the person may appeal the suspension at the person's initial appearance on the charge resulting from the arrest or within the period ending thirty days after the person's initial appearance on that charge, in the court in which the person will appear on that charge. If the person appeals the suspension, the appeal itself does not stay the operation of the suspension. If the person appeals the suspension, either the person or the registrar of motor vehicles may request a continuance of the appeal, and the court may grant the continuance. The court also may continue the appeal on its own motion. Neither the request for, nor the granting of, a continuance stays the suspension that is the subject of the appeal, unless the court specifically grants a stay.

(B) A person shall file an appeal under division (A) of this section in the municipal court, county court, juvenile court, mayor's court, or court of common pleas that has jurisdiction over the charge in relation to which the person was arrested.

(C) If a person appeals a suspension under division (A) of this section, the scope of the appeal is limited to determining whether one or more of the following conditions have not been met:

(1) Whether the arresting law enforcement officer had reasonable ground to believe the arrested person was operating a vehicle, streetcar, or trackless trolley in violation of division (A) or (B) of section 4511.19 of the Revised Code or a municipal OVI ordinance or was in physical control of a vehicle, streetcar, or trackless trolley in violation of section 4511.194 of the Revised Code or a substantially equivalent municipal ordinance and whether the arrested person was in fact placed under arrest;

(2) Whether the law enforcement officer requested the arrested person to submit to the chemical test or tests designated pursuant to division (A) of section 4511.191 of the Revised Code;

(3) Whether the arresting officer informed the arrested person of the consequences of refusing to be tested or of submitting to the test or tests;

(4) Whichever of the following is applicable:

(a) Whether the arrested person refused to submit to the chemical test or tests requested by the officer;

(b) Whether the arrest was for a violation of division (A) or (B) of section 4511.19 of the Revised Code or a municipal OVI ordinance and, if it was, whether the chemical test results indicate that the arrested person's whole blood contained a concentration of eight-hundredths of one per cent or more by weight of alcohol, the person's blood serum or plasma contained a concentration of ninety-six-thousandths of one per cent or more by weight of alcohol, the person's breath contained a concentration of eight-hundredths of one gram or more by weight of alcohol per two hundred ten liters of the person's breath, or the person's urine contained a concentration of eleven-hundredths of one gram or more by weight of alcohol per one hundred milliliters of the person's urine at the time of the alleged offense.

(D) A person who appeals a suspension under division (A) of this section has the burden of proving, by a preponderance of the evidence, that one or more of the conditions specified in division (C) of this section has not been met. If, during the appeal, the judge or magistrate of the court or the mayor of the mayor's court determines that all of those conditions have been met, the judge, magistrate, or mayor shall uphold the suspension, continue the suspension, and notify the registrar of motor vehicles of the decision on a form approved by the registrar.

Except as otherwise provided in this section, if a suspension imposed under section 4511.191 of the Revised Code is upheld on appeal or if the subject person does not appeal the suspension under division (A) of this section, the suspension shall continue until the complaint alleging the violation for which the person was arrested and in relation to which the suspension was imposed is adjudicated on the merits or terminated pursuant to law. If the suspension was imposed under division (B)(1) of section 4511. 191 of the Revised Code and it is continued under this section, any subsequent finding that the person is not guilty of the charge that resulted in the person being requested to take the chemical test or tests under division (A) of section 4511.191 of the Revised Code does not terminate or otherwise affect the suspension. If the suspension was imposed under division (C) of section 4511.191 of the Revised Code in relation to an alleged misdemeanor violation of division (A) or (B) of section 4511.19 of the Revised Code or of a municipal OVI ordinance and it is continued under this section, the suspension shall terminate if, for any reason, the person subsequently is found not guilty of the charge that resulted in the person taking the chemical test or tests.

If, during the appeal, the judge or magistrate of the trial court or the mayor of the mayor's court determines that one or more of the conditions specified in division (C) of this section have not been met, the judge, magistrate, or mayor shall terminate the suspension, subject to the imposition of a new suspension under division (B) of section 4511.196 of the Revised Code; shall notify the registrar of motor vehicles of the decision on a form approved by the registrar; and, except as provided in division (B) of section 4511.196 of the Revised Code, shall order the registrar to return the driver's or commercial driver's license or permit to the person or to take any other measures that may be necessary, if the license or permit was destroyed under section 4510.53 of the Revised Code, to permit the person to obtain a replacement driver's or commercial driver's license or permit from the registrar or a deputy registrar in accordance with that section. The court also shall issue to the person a court order, valid for not more than ten days from the date of issuance, granting the person operating privileges for that period.

(E) Any person whose driver's or commercial driver's license or permit or nonresident operating privilege has been suspended pursuant to section 4511.191 of the Revised Code may file a petition requesting limited driving privileges in the common pleas court, municipal court, county court, mayor's court, or juvenile court with jurisdiction over the related criminal or delinquency case. The petition may be filed at any time subsequent to the date on which the arresting law enforcement officer serves the notice of suspension upon the arrested person but no later than thirty days after the arrested person's initial appearance or arraignment. Upon the making of the request, limited driving privileges may be granted under sections 4510.021 and 4510.13 of the Revised Code, regardless of whether the person appeals the suspension under this section or appeals the decision of the court on the appeal, and, if the person has so appealed the suspension or decision, regardless of whether the matter has been heard or decided by the court. The person shall pay the costs of the proceeding, notify the registrar of the filing of the petition, and send the registrar a copy of the petition.

The court may not grant the person limited driving privileges when prohibited by section 4510.13 or 4511.191 of the Revised Code.

(F) Any person whose driver's or commercial driver's license or permit has been suspended under section 4511.19 of the Revised Code or under section 4510.07 of the Revised Code for a conviction of a municipal OVI offense and who desires to retain the license or permit during the pendency of an appeal, at the time sentence is pronounced, shall notify the court of record or mayor's court that suspended the license or permit of the person's intention to appeal. If the person so notifies the court, the court, mayor, or clerk of the court shall retain the license or permit until the appeal is perfected, and, if execution of sentence is stayed, the license or permit shall be returned to the person to be held by the person during the pendency of the appeal. If the appeal is not perfected or is dismissed or terminated in an affirmance of the conviction, then the license or permit shall be taken up by the court, mayor, or clerk, at the time of putting the sentence into execution, and the court shall proceed in the same manner as if no appeal was taken.

(G) Except as otherwise provided in this division, if a person whose driver's or commercial driver's license or permit or nonresident operating privilege was suspended under section 4511.191 of the Revised Code appeals the suspension under division (A) of this section, the prosecuting attorney of the county in which the arrest occurred shall represent the registrar of motor vehicles in the appeal. If the arrest occurred within a municipal corporation within the jurisdiction of the court in which the appeal is conducted, the city director of law, village solicitor, or other chief legal officer of that municipal corporation shall represent the registrar. If the appeal is conducted in a municipal court, the registrar shall be represented as provided in section 1901.34 of the Revised Code. If the appeal is conducted in a mayor's court, the city director of law, village solicitor, or other chief legal officer of the municipal corporation that operates that mayor's court shall represent the registrar.

(H) The court shall give information in writing of any action taken under this section to the registrar of motor vehicles.

(I) When it finally has been determined under the procedures of this section that a nonresident's privilege to operate a vehicle within this state has been suspended, the registrar of motor vehicles shall give information in writing of the action taken to the motor vehicle administrator of the state of the nonresident's residence and of any state in which the nonresident has a license.

(2004 H 163, eff. 9–23–04; 2003 H 87, eff. 1–1–04; 2002 S 123, eff. 1–1–04)

OFFENSES

4511.20 Willful or wanton disregard of safety on highways

(A) No person shall operate a vehicle, trackless trolley, or streetcar on any street or highway in willful or wanton disregard of the safety of persons or property.

(B) Except as otherwise provided in this division, whoever violates this section is guilty of a minor misdemeanor. If, within one year of the offense, the offender previously has been convicted of or pleaded guilty to one predicate motor vehicle or traffic offense, whoever violates this section is guilty of a misdemeanor of the fourth degree. If, within one year of the offense, the offender previously has been convicted of two or more predicate motor vehicle or traffic offenses, whoever violates this section is guilty of a misdemeanor of the third degree.

(2002 S 123, eff. 1–1–04; 1982 S 432, eff. 3–16–83; 132 v S 179; 1953 H 1; GC 6307–20)

4511.201 Willful or wanton disregard of safety elsewhere; exception

(A) No person shall operate a vehicle, trackless trolley, or streetcar on any public or private property other than streets or highways, in willful or wanton disregard of the safety of persons or property.

This section does not apply to the competitive operation of vehicles on public or private property when the owner of such property knowingly permits such operation thereon.

(B) Except as otherwise provided in this division, whoever violates this section is guilty of a minor misdemeanor. If, within one year of the offense, the offender previously has been convicted of or pleaded guilty to one predicate motor vehicle or traffic offense, whoever violates this section is guilty of a misdemeanor of the fourth degree. If, within one year of the offense, the offender previously has been convicted of two or more predicate motor vehicle or traffic offenses, whoever violates this section is guilty of a misdemeanor of the third degree.

(2002 S 123, eff. 1–1–04; 1982 S 432, eff. 3–16–83; 132 v S 179; 129 v 1637)

4511.202 Operation without reasonable control

(A) No person shall operate a motor vehicle, trackless trolley, or streetcar on any street, highway, or property open to the public for vehicular traffic without being in reasonable control of the vehicle, trolley, or streetcar.

(B) Whoever violates this section is guilty of operating a motor vehicle without being in control of it, a minor misdemeanor.

(2002 S 123, eff. 1–1–04; 1982 S 432, eff. 3–16–83)

4511.203 Wrongful entrustment of a motor vehicle

(A) No person shall permit a motor vehicle owned by the person or under the person's control to be driven by another if any of the following apply:

(1) The offender knows or has reasonable cause to believe that the other person does not have a valid driver's or commercial driver's license or permit or valid nonresident driving privileges.

(2) The offender knows or has reasonable cause to believe that the other person's driver's or commercial driver's license or permit or nonresident operating privileges have been suspended or canceled under Chapter 4510. or any other provision of the Revised Code.

(3) The offender knows or has reasonable cause to believe that the other person's act of driving the motor vehicle would violate any prohibition contained in Chapter 4509. of the Revised Code.

(4) The offender knows or has reasonable cause to believe that the other person's act of driving would violate section 4511.19 of the Revised Code or any substantially equivalent municipal ordinance.

(B) Without limiting or precluding the consideration of any other evidence in determining whether a violation of division (A)(1), (2), (3), or (4) of this section has occurred, it shall be prima-facie evidence that the offender knows or has reasonable cause to believe that the operator of the motor vehicle owned by the offender or under the offender's control is in a category described in division (A)(1), (2), (3), or (4) of this section if any of the following applies:

(1) Regarding an operator allegedly in the category described in division (A)(1) or (3) of this section, the offender and the operator of the motor vehicle reside in the same household and are related by consanguinity or affinity.

(2) Regarding an operator allegedly in the category described in division (A)(2) of this section, the offender and the operator of the motor vehicle reside in the same household, and the offender knows or has reasonable cause to believe that the operator has been charged with or convicted of any violation of law or ordinance, or has committed any other act or omission, that would or could result in the suspension or cancellation of the operator's license, permit, or privilege.

(3) Regarding an operator allegedly in the category described in division (A)(4) of this section, the offender and the operator of the motor vehicle occupied the motor vehicle together at the time of the offense.

(C) Whoever violates this section is guilty of wrongful entrustment of a motor vehicle, a misdemeanor of the first degree. In addition to the penalties imposed under Chapter 2929. of the Revised Code, the court shall impose a class seven suspension of the offender's driver's license, commercial driver's license, temporary instruction permit, probationary license, or nonresident operating privilege from the range specified in division (A)(7) of section 4510.02 of the Revised Code, and, if the vehicle involved in the offense is registered in the name of the offender, the court shall order one of the following:

(1) Except as otherwise provided in division (C)(2) or (3) of this section, the court shall order, for thirty days, the immobilization of the vehicle involved in the offense and the impoundment of that vehicle's license plates. The order shall be issued and enforced under section 4503.233 of the Revised Code.

(2) If the offender previously has been convicted of or pleaded guilty to one violation of this section or a substantially equivalent municipal ordinance, the court shall order, for sixty days, the immobilization of the vehicle involved in the offense and the impoundment of that vehicle's license plates. The order shall be issued and enforced under section 4503.233 of the Revised Code.

(3) If the offender previously has been convicted of or pleaded guilty to two or more violations of this section or a substantially equivalent municipal ordinance, the court shall order the criminal forfeiture to the state of the vehicle involved in the offense. The order shall be issued and enforced under section 4503.234 of the Revised Code.

If title to a motor vehicle that is subject to an order for criminal forfeiture under this division is assigned or transferred and division (B)(2) or (3) of section 4503.234 of the Revised Code applies, in addition to or independent of any other penalty established by law, the court may fine the offender the value of the vehicle as determined by publications of the national auto dealer's association. The proceeds from any fine imposed under this division shall be distributed in accordance with division (C)(2) of section 4503.234 of the Revised Code.

(D) If a court orders the immobilization of a vehicle under division (C) of this section, the court shall not release the vehicle from the immobilization before the termination of the period of immobilization ordered unless the court is presented with current proof of financial responsibility with respect to that vehicle.

(E) If a court orders the criminal forfeiture of a vehicle under division (C) of this section, upon receipt of the order from the court, neither the registrar of motor vehicles nor any deputy registrar shall accept any application for the registration or transfer of registration of any motor vehicle owned or leased by the person named in the order. The period of denial shall be five years after the date the order is issued, unless, during that five-year period, the court with jurisdiction of the offense that resulted in the order terminates the forfeiture and notifies the registrar of the termination. If the court terminates the forfeiture and notifies the registrar, the registrar shall take all necessary measures to permit the person to register a vehicle owned or leased by the person or to transfer the registration of the vehicle.

(F) This section does not apply to motor vehicle rental dealers or motor vehicle leasing dealers, as defined in section 4549.65 of the Revised Code.

(G) Evidence of a conviction of, plea of guilty to, or adjudication as a delinquent child for a violation of this section or a substantially similar municipal ordinance shall not be admissible as evidence in any civil action that involves the offender or delinquent child who is the subject of the conviction, plea, or adjudication and that arises from the wrongful entrustment of a motor vehicle.

(H) As used in this section, a vehicle is owned by a person if, at the time of a violation of this section, the vehicle is registered in the person's name.

(2002 S 123, eff. 1–1–04)

Historical and Statutory Notes

Ed. Note: 4511.203 is former 4507.33, amended and recodified by 2002 S 123, eff. 1–1–04; 1993 S 62, § 4, eff. 9–1–93; 1992 S 275; 1953 H 1; GC 6296–28.

SPEED LIMITS

4511.21 Speed limits; school zones; modifications

(A) No person shall operate a motor vehicle, trackless trolley, or streetcar at a speed greater or less than is reasonable or proper, having due regard to the traffic, surface, and width of the street or highway and any other conditions, and no person shall drive any motor vehicle, trackless trolley, or streetcar in and upon any street or highway at a greater speed than will permit the person to bring it to a stop within the assured clear distance ahead.

(B) It is prima-facie lawful, in the absence of a lower limit declared pursuant to this section by the director of transportation or local authorities, for the operator of a motor vehicle, trackless trolley, or streetcar to operate the same at a speed not exceeding the following:

(1)(a) Twenty miles per hour in school zones during school recess and while children are going to or leaving school during the opening or closing hours, and when twenty miles per hour school speed limit signs are erected; except that, on controlled-access highways and expressways, if the right-of-way line fence has been erected without pedestrian opening, the speed shall be governed by division (B)(4) of this section and on freeways, if the right-of-way line fence has been erected without pedestrian opening, the speed shall be governed by divisions (B)(8) and (9) of this section. The end of every school zone may be marked by a sign indicating the end of the zone. Nothing in this section or in the manual and specifications for a uniform system of traffic control devices shall be construed to require school zones to be indicated by signs equipped with flashing or other lights, or giving other special notice of the hours in which the school zone speed limit is in effect.

(b) As used in this section and in section 4511.212 of the Revised Code, "school" means any school chartered under section 3301.16 of the Revised Code and any nonchartered school that during the preceding year filed with the department of education in compliance with rule 3301–35–08 of the Ohio Administrative Code, a copy of the school's report for the parents of the school's pupils certifying that the school meets Ohio minimum standards for nonchartered, nontax-supported schools and presents evidence of this filing to the jurisdiction from which it is requesting the establishment of a school zone.

(c) As used in this section, "school zone" means that portion of a street or highway passing a school fronting upon the street or highway that is encompassed by projecting the school property lines to the fronting street or highway, and also includes that portion of a state highway. Upon request from local authorities for streets and highways under their jurisdiction and that portion of a state highway under the jurisdiction of the director of transportation, the director may extend the traditional school zone boundaries. The distances in divisions (B)(1)(c)(i), (ii), and (iii) of this section shall not exceed three hundred feet per approach per direction and are bounded by whichever of the following distances or combinations thereof the director approves as most appropriate:

(i) The distance encompassed by projecting the school building lines normal to the fronting highway and extending a distance of three hundred feet on each approach direction;

(ii) The distance encompassed by projecting the school property lines intersecting the fronting highway and extending a distance of three hundred feet on each approach direction;

(iii) The distance encompassed by the special marking of the pavement for a principal school pupil crosswalk plus a distance of three hundred feet on each approach direction of the highway.

Nothing in this section shall be construed to invalidate the director's initial action on August 9, 1976, establishing all school zones at the traditional school zone boundaries defined by projecting school property lines, except when those boundaries are extended as provided in divisions (B)(1)(a) and (c) of this section.

(d) As used in this division, "crosswalk" has the meaning given that term in division (LL)(2) of section 4511.01 of the Revised Code.

The director may, upon request by resolution of the legislative authority of a municipal corporation, the board of trustees of a township, or a county board of mental retardation and developmental disabilities created pursuant to Chapter 5126. of the Revised Code, and upon submission by the municipal corporation, township, or county board of such engineering, traffic, and other information as the director considers necessary, designate a school zone on any portion of a state route lying within the municipal corporation, lying within the unincorporated territory of the township, or lying adjacent to the property of a school that is operated by such county board, that includes a crosswalk customarily used by children going to or leaving a school during recess and opening and closing hours, whenever the distance, as measured in a straight line, from the school property line nearest the crosswalk to the nearest point of the crosswalk is no more than one thousand three hundred twenty feet. Such a school zone shall include the distance encompassed by the crosswalk and extending three hundred feet on each approach direction of the state route.

(2) Twenty–five miles per hour in all other portions of a municipal corporation, except on state routes outside business districts, through highways outside business districts, and alleys;

(3) Thirty–five miles per hour on all state routes or through highways within municipal corporations outside business districts, except as provided in divisions (B)(4) and (6) of this section;

(4) Fifty miles per hour on controlled-access highways and expressways within municipal corporations;

(5) Fifty–five miles per hour on highways outside of municipal corporations, other than freeways as provided in division (B)(12) of this section;

(6) Fifty miles per hour on state routes within municipal corporations outside urban districts unless a lower prima-facie speed is established as further provided in this section;

(7) Fifteen miles per hour on all alleys within the municipal corporation;

(8) Fifty–five miles per hour at all times on freeways with paved shoulders inside municipal corporations, other than freeways as provided in division (B)(12) of this section;

(9) Fifty–five miles per hour at all times on freeways outside municipal corporations, other than freeways as provided in division (B)(12) of this section;

(10) Fifty–five miles per hour at all times on all portions of freeways that are part of the interstate system and on all portions of freeways that are not part of the interstate system, but are built to the standards and specifications that are applicable to freeways that are part of the interstate system for operators of any motor vehicle weighing in excess of eight thousand pounds empty weight and any noncommercial bus;

(11) Fifty–five miles per hour for operators of any motor vehicle weighing eight thousand pounds or less empty weight and any commercial bus at all times on all portions of freeways that are part of the interstate system and that had such a speed limit established prior to October 1, 1995, and freeways that are not part of the interstate system, but are built to the standards and specifications that are applicable to freeways that are part of the interstate system and that had such a speed limit established prior to October 1, 1995, unless a higher speed limit is established under division (L) of this section;

(12) Sixty–five miles per hour for operators of any motor vehicle weighing eight thousand pounds or less empty weight and any commercial bus at all times on all portions of the following:

(a) Freeways that are part of the interstate system and that had such a speed limit established prior to October 1, 1995, and freeways that are not part of the interstate system, but are built to the standards and specifications that are applicable to freeways that are part of the interstate system and that had such a speed limit established prior to October 1, 1995;

(b) Freeways that are part of the interstate system and freeways that are not part of the interstate system but are built to the standards and specifications that are applicable to freeways that are part of the interstate system, and that had such a speed limit established under division (L) of this section;

(c) Rural, divided, multi-lane highways that are designated as part of the national highway system under the "National Highway System Designation Act of 1995," 109 Stat. 568, 23 U.S.C.A. 103, and that had such a speed limit established under division (M) of this section.

(C) It is prima-facie unlawful for any person to exceed any of the speed limitations in divisions (B)(1)(a), (2), (3), (4), (6), and (7) of this section, or any declared pursuant to this section by the director or local authorities and it is unlawful for any person to exceed any of the speed limitations in division (D) of this section. No person shall be convicted of more than one violation of this section for the same conduct, although violations of more than one provision of this section may be charged in the alternative in a single affidavit.

(D) No person shall operate a motor vehicle, trackless trolley, or streetcar upon a street or highway as follows:

(1) At a speed exceeding fifty-five miles per hour, except upon a freeway as provided in division (B)(12) of this section;

(2) At a speed exceeding sixty-five miles per hour upon a freeway as provided in division (B)(12) of this section except as otherwise provided in division (D)(3) of this section;

(3) If a motor vehicle weighing in excess of eight thousand pounds empty weight or a noncommercial bus as prescribed in division (B)(10) of this section, at a speed exceeding fifty-five miles per hour upon a freeway as provided in that division;

(4) At a speed exceeding the posted speed limit upon a freeway for which the director has determined and declared a speed limit of not more than sixty-five miles per hour pursuant to division (L)(2) or (M) of this section;

(5) At a speed exceeding sixty-five miles per hour upon a freeway for which such a speed limit has been established through the operation of division (L)(3) of this section;

(6) At a speed exceeding the posted speed limit upon a freeway for which the director has determined and declared a speed limit pursuant to division (I)(2) of this section.

(E) In every charge of violation of this section the affidavit and warrant shall specify the time, place, and speed at which the defendant is alleged to have driven, and in charges made in reliance upon division (C) of this section also the speed which division (B)(1)(a), (2), (3), (4), (6), or (7) of, or a limit declared pursuant to, this section declares is prima-facie lawful at the time and place of such alleged violation, except that in affidavits where a person is alleged to have driven at a greater speed than will permit the person to bring the vehicle to a stop within the assured clear distance ahead the affidavit and warrant need not specify the speed at which the defendant is alleged to have driven.

(F) When a speed in excess of both a prima-facie limitation and a limitation in division (D)(1), (2), (3), (4), (5), or (6) of this section is alleged, the defendant shall be charged in a single affidavit, alleging a single act, with a violation indicated of both division (B)(1)(a), (2), (3), (4), (6), or (7) of this section, or of a limit declared pursuant to this section by the director or local authorities, and of the limitation in division (D)(1), (2), (3), (4), (5), or (6) of this section. If the court finds a violation of division (B)(1)(a), (2), (3), (4), (6), or (7) of, or a limit declared pursuant to, this section has occurred, it shall enter a judgment of conviction under such division and dismiss the charge under division (D)(1), (2), (3), (4), (5), or (6) of this section. If it finds no violation of division (B)(1)(a), (2), (3), (4), (6), or (7) of, or a limit declared pursuant to, this section, it shall then consider whether the evidence supports a conviction under division (D)(1), (2), (3), (4), (5), or (6) of this section.

(G) Points shall be assessed for violation of a limitation under division (D) of this section in accordance with section 4510.036 of the Revised Code.

(H) Whenever the director determines upon the basis of a geometric and traffic characteristic study that any speed limit set forth in divisions (B)(1)(a) to (D) of this section is greater or less than is reasonable or safe under the conditions found to exist at any portion of a street or highway under the jurisdiction of the director, the director shall determine and declare a reasonable and safe prima-facie speed limit, which shall be effective when appropriate signs giving notice of it are erected at the location.

(I)(1) Except as provided in divisions (I)(2) and (K) of this section, whenever local authorities determine upon the basis of an engineering and traffic investigation that the speed permitted by divisions (B)(1)(a) to (D) of this section, on any part of a highway under their jurisdiction, is greater than is reasonable and safe under the conditions found to exist at such location, the local authorities may by resolution request the director to determine and declare a reasonable and safe prima-facie speed limit. Upon receipt of such request the director may determine and declare a reasonable and safe prima-facie speed limit at such location, and if the director does so, then such declared speed limit shall become effective only when appropriate signs giving notice thereof are erected at such location by the local authorities. The director may withdraw the declaration of a prima-facie speed limit whenever in the director's opinion the altered prima-facie speed becomes unreasonable. Upon such withdrawal, the declared prima-facie speed shall become ineffective and the signs relating thereto shall be immediately removed by the local authorities.

(2) A local authority may determine on the basis of a geometric and traffic characteristic study that the speed limit of sixty-five miles per hour on a portion of a freeway under its jurisdiction that was established through the operation of division (L)(3) of this section is greater than is reasonable or safe under the conditions found to exist at that portion of the freeway. If the local authority makes such a determination, the local authority by resolution may request the director to determine and declare a reasonable and safe speed limit of not less than fifty-five miles per hour for that portion of the freeway. If the director takes such action, the declared speed limit becomes effective only when appropriate signs giving notice of it are erected at such location by the local authority.

(J) Local authorities in their respective jurisdictions may authorize by ordinance higher prima-facie speeds than those stated in this section upon through highways, or upon highways or portions thereof where there are no intersections, or between widely spaced intersections, provided signs are erected giving notice of the authorized speed, but local authorities shall not modify or alter the basic rule set forth in division (A) of this section or in any event authorize by ordinance a speed in excess of fifty miles per hour.

Alteration of prima-facie limits on state routes by local authorities shall not be effective until the alteration has been approved by the director. The director may withdraw approval of any altered prima-facie speed limits whenever in the director's opinion any altered prima-facie speed becomes unreasonable, and upon such withdrawal, the altered prima-facie speed shall become ineffective and the signs relating thereto shall be immediately removed by the local authorities.

(K)(1) As used in divisions (K)(1), (2), (3), and (4) of this section, "unimproved highway" means a highway consisting of any of the following:

(a) Unimproved earth;

(b) Unimproved graded and drained earth;

(c) Gravel.

(2) Except as otherwise provided in divisions (K)(4) and (5) of this section, whenever a board of township trustees determines upon the basis of an engineering and traffic investigation that the speed permitted by division (B)(5) of this section on any part of an unimproved highway under its jurisdiction and in the unincorporated territory of the township is greater than is reasonable or safe under the conditions found to exist at the location, the board may by resolution declare a reasonable and safe prima-facie speed limit of fifty-five but not less than twenty-five miles per hour. An altered speed limit adopted by a board of township trustees under this division becomes effective when appropriate traffic control devices, as prescribed in section 4511.11 of the Revised Code, giving notice thereof are erected at the location, which shall be no sooner than sixty days after adoption of the resolution.

(3)(a) Whenever, in the opinion of a board of township trustees, any altered prima-facie speed limit established by the board under this division becomes unreasonable, the board may adopt a resolution withdrawing the altered prima-facie speed limit. Upon the adoption of such a resolution, the altered prima-facie speed limit becomes ineffective and the traffic control devices relating thereto shall be immediately removed.

(b) Whenever a highway ceases to be an unimproved highway and the board has adopted an altered prima-facie speed limit pursuant to division (K)(2) of this section, the board shall, by resolution, withdraw the altered prima-facie speed limit as soon as the highway ceases to be unimproved. Upon the adoption of such a resolution, the altered prima-facie speed limit becomes ineffective and the traffic control devices relating thereto shall be immediately removed.

(4)(a) If the boundary of two townships rests on the centerline of an unimproved highway in unincorporated territory and both townships have jurisdiction over the highway, neither of the boards of township trustees of such townships may declare an altered prima-facie speed limit pursuant to division (K)(2) of this section on the part of the highway under their joint jurisdiction unless the boards of township trustees of both of the townships determine, upon the basis of an engineering and traffic investigation, that the speed permitted by division (B)(5) of this section is greater than is reasonable or safe under the conditions found to exist at the location and both boards agree upon a reasonable and safe prima-facie speed limit of less than fifty-five but not less than twenty-five miles per hour for that location. If both boards so agree, each shall follow the procedure specified in division (K)(2) of this section for altering the prima-facie speed limit on the highway. Except as otherwise provided in division (K)(4)(b) of this section, no speed limit altered pursuant to division (K)(4)(a) of this section may be withdrawn unless the boards of township trustees of both townships determine that the altered prima-facie speed limit previously adopted becomes unreasonable and each board adopts a resolution withdrawing the altered prima-facie speed limit pursuant to the procedure specified in division (K)(3)(a) of this section.

(b) Whenever a highway described in division (K)(4)(a) of this section ceases to be an unimproved highway and two boards of township trustees have adopted an altered prima-facie speed limit pursuant to division (K)(4)(a) of this section, both boards shall, by resolution, withdraw the altered prima-facie speed limit as soon as the highway ceases to be unimproved. Upon the adoption of the resolution, the altered prima-facie speed limit becomes ineffective and the traffic control devices relating thereto shall be immediately removed.

(5) As used in division (K)(5) of this section:

(a) "Commercial subdivision" means any platted territory outside the limits of a municipal corporation and fronting a highway where, for a distance of three hundred feet or more, the frontage is improved with buildings in use for commercial purposes, or where the entire length of the highway is less than three hundred feet long and the frontage is improved with buildings in use for commercial purposes.

(b) "Residential subdivision" means any platted territory outside the limits of a municipal corporation and fronting a highway, where, for a distance of three hundred feet or more, the frontage is improved with residences or residences and buildings in use for business, or where the entire length of the highway is less than three hundred feet long and the frontage is improved with residences or residences and buildings in use for business.

Whenever a board of township trustees finds upon the basis of an engineering and traffic investigation that the prima-facie speed permitted by division (B)(5) of this section on any part of a highway under its jurisdiction that is located in a commercial or residential subdivision, except on highways or portions thereof at the entrances to which vehicular traffic from the majority of intersecting highways is required to yield the right-of-way to vehicles on such highways in obedience to stop or yield signs or traffic control signals, is greater than is reasonable and safe under the conditions found to exist at the location, the board may by resolution declare a reasonable and safe prima-facie speed limit of less than fifty-five but not less than twenty-five miles per hour at the location. An altered speed limit adopted by a board of township trustees under this division shall become effective when appropriate signs giving notice thereof are erected at the location by the township. Whenever, in the opinion of a board of township trustees, any altered prima-facie speed limit established by it under this division becomes unreasonable, it may adopt a resolution withdrawing the altered prima-facie speed, and upon such withdrawal, the altered prima-facie speed shall become ineffective, and the signs relating thereto shall be immediately removed by the township.

(L)(1) Within one hundred twenty days of February 29, 1996, the director of transportation, based upon a geometric and traffic characteristic study of a freeway that is part of the interstate system or that is not part of the interstate system, but is built to the standards and specifications that are applicable to freeways that are part of the interstate system, in consultation with the director of public safety and, if applicable, the local authority having jurisdiction over a portion of such freeway, may determine and declare that the speed limit of less than sixty-five miles per hour established on such freeway or portion of freeway either is reasonable and safe or is less than that which is reasonable and safe.

(2) If the established speed limit for such a freeway or portion of freeway is determined to be less than that which is reasonable and safe, the director of transportation, in consultation with the director of public safety and, if applicable, the local authority having jurisdiction over the portion of freeway, shall determine and declare a reasonable and safe speed limit of not more than sixty-five miles per hour for that freeway or portion of freeway.

The director of transportation or local authority having jurisdiction over the freeway or portion of freeway shall erect appropriate signs giving notice of the speed limit at such location within one hundred fifty days of February 29, 1996. Such speed limit becomes effective only when such signs are erected at the location.

(3) If, within one hundred twenty days of February 29, 1996, the director of transportation does not make a determination and declaration of a reasonable and safe speed limit for a freeway or portion of freeway that is part of the interstate system or that is not part of the interstate system, but is built to the standards and specifications that are applicable to freeways that are part of the interstate system and that has a speed limit of less than sixty-five miles per hour, the speed limit on that freeway or portion of a freeway shall be sixty-five miles per hour. The director of transportation or local authority having jurisdiction over the freeway or portion of the freeway shall erect appropriate signs giving notice of the speed limit of sixty-five miles per hour at such location within one hundred fifty days of February 29, 1996. Such speed limit becomes effective only when such signs are erected at the location. A speed limit established through the operation of division (L)(3) of this section is subject to reduction under division (I)(2) of this section.

(M) Within three hundred sixty days after February 29, 1996, the director of transportation, based upon a geometric and traffic characteristic study of a rural, divided, multi-lane highway that has been designated as part of the national highway system under the "National Highway System Designation Act of 1995," 109 Stat. 568, 23 U.S.C.A. 103, in consultation with the director of public safety and, if applicable, the local authority having jurisdiction over a portion of the highway, may determine and declare that the speed limit of less than sixty-five miles per hour established on the highway or portion of highway either is reasonable and safe or is less than that which is reasonable and safe.

If the established speed limit for the highway or portion of highway is determined to be less than that which is reasonable and safe, the director of transportation, in consultation with the director of public safety and, if applicable, the local authority having jurisdiction over the portion of highway, shall determine and declare a reasonable and safe speed limit of not more than sixty-five miles per hour for that highway or portion of highway. The director of transportation or local authority having jurisdiction over the highway or portion of highway shall erect appropriate signs giving notice of the speed limit at such location within three hundred ninety days after February 29, 1996. The speed limit becomes effective only when such signs are erected at the location.

(N) As used in this section:

(1) "Interstate system" has the same meaning as in 23 U.S.C.A. 101.

(2) "Commercial bus" means a motor vehicle designed for carrying more than nine passengers and used for the transportation of persons for compensation.

(3) "Noncommercial bus" includes but is not limited to a school bus or a motor vehicle operated solely for the transportation of persons associated with a charitable or nonprofit organization.

(O)(1) A violation of any provision of this section is one of the following:

(a) Except as otherwise provided in divisions (O)(1)(b), (1)(c), (2), and (3) of this section, a minor misdemeanor;

(b) If, within one year of the offense, the offender previously has been convicted of or pleaded guilty to two violations of any provision of this section or of any provision of a municipal ordinance that is substantially similar to any provision of this section, a misdemeanor of the fourth degree;

(c) If, within one year of the offense, the offender previously has been convicted of or pleaded guilty to three or more violations of any provision of this section or of any provision of a municipal ordinance that is substantially similar to any provision of this section, a misdemeanor of the third degree.

(2) If the offender has not previously been convicted of or pleaded guilty to a violation of any provision of this section or of any provision of a municipal ordinance that is substantially similar to this section and operated a motor vehicle faster than

thirty-five miles an hour in a business district of a municipal corporation, faster than fifty miles an hour in other portions of a municipal corporation, or faster than thirty-five miles an hour in a school zone during recess or while children are going to or leaving school during the school's opening or closing hours, a misdemeanor of the fourth degree.

(3) Notwithstanding division (O)(1) of this section, if the offender operated a motor vehicle in a construction zone where a sign was then posted in accordance with section 4511.98 of the Revised Code, the court, in addition to all other penalties provided by law, shall impose upon the offender a fine of two times the usual amount imposed for the violation. No court shall impose a fine of two times the usual amount imposed for the violation upon an offender if the offender alleges, in an affidavit filed with the court prior to the offender's sentencing, that the offender is indigent and is unable to pay the fine imposed pursuant to this division and if the court determines that the offender is an indigent person and unable to pay the fine.

(2002 S 123, eff. 1–1–04; 1996 H 565, eff. 2–29–96; 1992 S 301, eff. 3–15–93; 1992 S 201; 1991 H 96; 1989 H 381; 1987 H 493, H 43; 1986 H 666, H 428, S 356, H 795; 1983 S 37; 1979 S 14, H 20, H 32; 1977 H 587; 1976 H 1166; 1975 H 632; 1973 H 200; 132 v H 1; 131 v H 315; 130 v Pt 2, H 5; 130 v H 509; 128 v 1270; 127 v 931; 126 v 115; 1953 H 1; GC 6307–21)

4511.211 Speed limits for private roads and driveways

(A) The owner of a private road or driveway located in a private residential area containing twenty or more dwelling units may establish a speed limit on the road or driveway by complying with all of the following requirements:

(1) The speed limit is not less than twenty-five miles per hour and is indicated by a sign that is in a proper position, is sufficiently legible to be seen by an ordinarily observant person, and meets the specifications for the basic speed limit sign included in the manual adopted by the department of transportation pursuant to section 4511.09 of the Revised Code;

(2) The owner has posted a sign at the entrance of the private road or driveway that is in plain view and clearly informs persons entering the road or driveway that they are entering private property, a speed limit has been established for the road or driveway, and the speed limit is enforceable by law enforcement officers under state law.

(B) No person shall operate a vehicle upon a private road or driveway as provided in division (A) of this section at a speed exceeding any speed limit established and posted pursuant to that division.

(C) When a speed limit is established and posted in accordance with division (A) of this section, any law enforcement officer may apprehend a person violating the speed limit of the residential area by utilizing any of the means described in section 4511.091 of the Revised Code or by any other accepted method of determining the speed of a motor vehicle and may stop and charge the person with exceeding the speed limit.

(D) Points shall be assessed for violation of a speed limit established and posted in accordance with division (A) of this section in accordance with section 4510.036 of the Revised Code.

(E) As used in this section:

(1) "Owner" includes but is not limited to a person who holds title to the real property in fee simple, a condominium owners' association, a property owner's association, the board of directors or trustees of a private community, and a nonprofit corporation governing a private community.

(2) "Private residential area containing twenty or more dwelling units" does not include a Chautauqua assembly as defined in section 4511.90 of the Revised Code.

(F) A violation of division (B) of this section is one of the following:

(1) Except as otherwise provided in divisions (F)(2) and (3) of this section, a minor misdemeanor;

(2) If, within one year of the offense, the offender previously has been convicted of or pleaded guilty to two violations of division (B) of this section or of any municipal ordinance that is substantially similar to division (B) of this section, a misdemeanor of the fourth degree;

(3) If, within one year of the offense, the offender previously has been convicted of or pleaded guilty to three or more violations of division (B) of this section or of any municipal ordinance that is substantially similar to division (B) of this section, a misdemeanor of the third degree.

(2002 S 123, eff. 1–1–04; 1990 H 171, eff. 5–31–90)

4511.212 Orders directing local authorities to comply with laws regarding school zones

(A) As used in this section, "Local authority" means the legislative authority of a municipal corporation, the board of trustees of a township, or the board of county commissioners of a county.

(B) The board of education or the chief administrative officer operating or in charge of any school may submit a written complaint to the director of transportation alleging that a local authority is not complying with section 4511.11 or divisions (B)(1)(a) to (d) of section 4511.21 of the Revised Code with regard to school zones. Upon receipt of such a complaint, the director shall review or investigate the facts of the complaint and discuss the complaint with the local authority and the board of education or chief administrative officer submitting the complaint. If the director finds that the local authority is not complying with section 4511.11 or divisions (B)(1)(a) to (d) of section 4511.21 of the Revised Code with regard to school zones, the director shall issue a written order requiring the local authority to comply by a specified date and the local authority shall comply with the order. If the local authority fails to comply with the order, the director shall implement the order and charge the local authority for the cost of the implementation. Any local authority being so charged shall pay to the state the amount charged. Any amounts received under this section shall be deposited into the state treasury to the credit of the highway operating fund created by section 5735.291 of the Revised Code.

(1992 S 201, eff. 8–19–92)

4511.213 Approaching stationary public safety vehicle with caution

(A) The driver of a motor vehicle, upon approaching a stationary public safety vehicle that is displaying a flashing red light, flashing combination red and white light, oscillating or rotating red light, oscillating or rotating combination red and white light, flashing blue light, flashing combination blue and white light, oscillating or rotating blue light, or oscillating or rotating combination blue and white light, shall do either of the following:

(1) If the driver of the motor vehicle is traveling on a highway that consists of at least two lanes that carry traffic in the same direction of travel as that of the driver's motor vehicle, the driver shall proceed with due caution and, if possible and with due regard to the road, weather, and traffic conditions, shall change lanes into a lane that is not adjacent to that of the stationary public safety vehicle.

(2) If the driver is not traveling on a highway of a type described in division (A)(1) of this section, or if the driver is traveling on a highway of that type but it is not possible to change lanes or if to do so would be unsafe, the driver shall proceed with

due caution, reduce the speed of the motor vehicle, and maintain a safe speed for the road, weather, and traffic conditions.

(B) This section does not relieve the driver of a public safety vehicle from the duty to drive with due regard for the safety of all persons and property upon the highway.

(C) No person shall fail to drive a motor vehicle in compliance with division (A)(1) or (2) of this section when so required by division (A) of this section.

(D)(1) Except as otherwise provided in this division, whoever violates this section is guilty of a minor misdemeanor. If, within one year of the offense, the offender previously has been convicted of or pleaded guilty to one predicate motor vehicle or traffic offense, whoever violates this section is guilty of a misdemeanor of the fourth degree. If, within one year of the offense, the offender previously has been convicted of two or more predicate motor vehicle or traffic offenses, whoever violates this section is guilty of a misdemeanor of the third degree.

(2) Notwithstanding section 2929.28 of the Revised Code, upon a finding that a person operated a motor vehicle in violation of division (C) of this section, the court, in addition to all other penalties provided by law, shall impose a fine of two times the usual amount imposed for the violation.

(E) As used in this section, "public safety vehicle" has the same meaning as in section 4511.01 of the Revised Code.

(2002 H 490, eff. 1–1–04; 2002 S 123, eff. 1–1–04; 1999 H 86, eff. 9–28–99)

4511.22 Stopping or slow speed

(A) No person shall stop or operate a vehicle, trackless trolley, or street car at such a slow speed as to impede or block the normal and reasonable movement of traffic, except when stopping or reduced speed is necessary for safe operation or to comply with law.

(B) Whenever the director of transportation or local authorities determine on the basis of an engineering and traffic investigation that slow speeds on any part of a controlled-access highway, expressway, or freeway consistently impede the normal and reasonable movement of traffic, the director or such local authority may declare a minimum speed limit below which no person shall operate a motor vehicle, trackless trolley, or street car except when necessary for safe operation or in compliance with law. No minimum speed limit established hereunder shall be less than thirty miles per hour, greater than fifty miles per hour, nor effective until the provisions of section 4511.21 of the Revised Code, relating to appropriate signs, have been fulfilled and local authorities have obtained the approval of the director.

(C) Except as otherwise provided in this division, whoever violates this section is guilty of a minor misdemeanor. If, within one year of the offense, the offender previously has been convicted of or pleaded guilty to one predicate motor vehicle or traffic offense, whoever violates this section is guilty of a misdemeanor of the fourth degree. If, within one year of the offense, the offender previously has been convicted of two or more predicate motor vehicle or traffic offenses, whoever violates this section is guilty of a misdemeanor of the third degree.

(2002 S 123, eff. 1–1–04; 1991 H 96, eff. 6–18–91; 1975 H 632; 1973 H 200; 127 v 51; 1953 H 1; GC 6307–22)

4511.23 Speed regulations on bridges

(A) No person shall operate a vehicle, trackless trolley, or streetcar over any bridge or other elevated structure constituting a part of a highway at a speed which is greater than the maximum speed that can be maintained with safety to such bridge or structure, when such structure is posted with signs as provided in this section.

The department of transportation upon request from any local authority shall, or upon its own initiative may, conduct an investigation of any bridge or other elevated structure constituting a part of a highway, and if it finds that such structure cannot with safety withstand traffic traveling at the speed otherwise permissible under sections 4511.01 to 4511.85 and 4511.98 of the Revised Code, the department shall determine and declare the maximum speed of traffic which such structure can withstand, and shall cause or permit suitable signs stating such maximum speed to be erected and maintained at a distance of at least one hundred feet before each end of such structure.

Upon the trial of any person charged with a violation of this section, proof of said determination of the maximum speed by the department and the existence of said signs shall constitute prima-facie evidence of the maximum speed which can be maintained with safety to such bridge or structure.

(B) Except as otherwise provided in this division, whoever violates this section is guilty of a minor misdemeanor. If, within one year of the offense, the offender previously has been convicted of or pleaded guilty to one predicate motor vehicle or traffic offense, whoever violates this section is guilty of a misdemeanor of the fourth degree. If, within one year of the offense, the offender previously has been convicted of two or more predicate motor vehicle or traffic offenses, whoever violates this section is guilty of a misdemeanor of the third degree.

(2002 S 123, eff. 1–1–04; 1973 H 200, eff. 9–28–73; 1953 H 1; GC 6307–23)

4511.24 Emergency and public safety vehicles excepted; conditions

The prima-facie speed limitations set forth in section 4511.21 of the Revised Code do not apply to emergency vehicles or public safety vehicles when they are responding to emergency calls and are equipped with and displaying at least one flashing, rotating, or oscillating light visible under normal atmospheric conditions from a distance of five hundred feet to the front of the vehicle and when the drivers thereof sound audible signals by bell, siren, or exhaust whistle. This section does not relieve the driver of an emergency vehicle or public safety vehicle from the duty to drive with due regard for the safety of all persons using the street or highway.

(1974 H 995, eff. 1–1–75; 132 v H 878; 1953 H 1; GC 6307–24)

OPERATION OF MOTOR VEHICLES

4511.25 Lanes of travel upon roadways

(A) Upon all roadways of sufficient width, a vehicle or trackless trolley shall be driven upon the right half of the roadway, except as follows:

(1) When overtaking and passing another vehicle proceeding in the same direction, or when making a left turn under the rules governing such movements;

(2) When an obstruction exists making it necessary to drive to the left of the center of the highway; provided, any person so doing shall yield the right of way to all vehicles traveling in the proper direction upon the unobstructed portion of the highway within such distance as to constitute an immediate hazard;

(3) When driving upon a roadway divided into three or more marked lanes for traffic under the rules applicable thereon;

(4) When driving upon a roadway designated and posted with signs for one-way traffic;

(5) When otherwise directed by a police officer or traffic control device.

(B) Upon all roadways any vehicle or trackless trolley proceeding at less than the normal speed of traffic at the time and place and under the conditions then existing shall be driven in the right-hand lane then available for traffic, or as close as practicable to the right-hand curb or edge of the roadway, except when overtaking and passing another vehicle or trackless trolley proceeding in the same direction or when preparing for a left turn.

(C) Upon any roadway having four or more lanes for moving traffic and providing for two-way movement of traffic, no vehicle or trackless trolley shall be driven to the left of the center line of the roadway, except when authorized by official traffic control devices designating certain lanes to the left of the center of the roadway for use by traffic not otherwise permitted to use the lanes, or except as permitted under division (A)(2) of this section.

This division shall not be construed as prohibiting the crossing of the center line in making a left turn into or from an alley, private road, or driveway.

(D) Except as otherwise provided in this division, whoever violates this section is guilty of a minor misdemeanor. If, within one year of the offense, the offender previously has been convicted of or pleaded guilty to one predicate motor vehicle or traffic offense, whoever violates this section is guilty of a misdemeanor of the fourth degree. If, within one year of the offense, the offender previously has been convicted of two or more predicate motor vehicle or traffic offenses, whoever violates this section is guilty of a misdemeanor of the third degree.

(2002 S 123, eff. 1–1–04; 1974 H 995, eff. 1–1–75; 130 v H 404; 129 v 1032; 1953 H 1; GC 6307–25)

4511.251 Street racing; prohibition

(A) As used in this section and section 4510.036 of the Revised Code, "street racing" means the operation of two or more vehicles from a point side by side at accelerating speeds in a competitive attempt to out-distance each other or the operation of one or more vehicles over a common selected course, from the same point to the same point, wherein timing is made of the participating vehicles involving competitive accelerations or speeds. Persons rendering assistance in any manner to such competitive use of vehicles shall be equally charged as the participants. The operation of two or more vehicles side by side either at speeds in excess of prima-facie lawful speeds established by divisions (B)(1)(a) to (B)(7) of section 4511.21 of the Revised Code or rapidly accelerating from a common starting point to a speed in excess of such prima-facie lawful speeds shall be prima-facie evidence of street racing.

(B) No person shall participate in street racing upon any public road, street, or highway in this state.

(C) Whoever violates this section is guilty of street racing, a misdemeanor of the first degree. In addition to any other sanctions, the court shall suspend the offender's driver's license, commercial driver's license, temporary instruction permit, probationary license, or nonresident operating privilege for not less than thirty days or more than three years. No judge shall suspend the first thirty days of any suspension of an offender's license, permit, or privilege imposed under this division.

(2004 H 52, eff. 6–1–04; 2002 S 123, eff. 1–1–04; 1995 H 107, eff. (See Historical and Statutory Notes); 1979 S 14, eff. 10–25–79; 128 v 469)

Historical and Statutory Notes

Ed. Note: 1995 H 107 Effective Date—The Secretary of State assigned a general effective date of 6–30–95 for 1995 H 107. Pursuant to O Const Art II § 1c and 1d, and RC 1.471, sections of 1995 H 107 that are, or depend for their implementation upon, current expense appropriations are effective 3–31–95; sections of 1995 H 107 that are not, and do not depend for their implementation upon, current expense appropriations are effective 6–30–95. See *Baldwin's Ohio Legislative Service*, 1995, page 3/L–98 for 1995 H 107, § 16.

4511.252 Closing of public roads for competitive racing

In townships in this state composed entirely of islands, the legislative authority of a municipal corporation, the county commissioners of the county wherein such township is located, and the trustees of such township may, by joint consent, cause any road, street, or highway in said township, whether within or without the limits of a municipal corporation, excepting state highways, to be closed to public travel, except in cases of emergency, for periods of not to exceed twenty-four hours, and during such period such roads, streets, or highways so closed may be used for supervised sports car racing;

(A) Any competitive racing event to be held upon a public road, street, or highway shall be sponsored by a recognized responsible organization.

(B) Any race held pursuant to division (A) of this section shall be conducted under the rules and regulations of the Sports Car Clubs of America.

(C) Adequate barricades shall be maintained at all hazardous sections of the racing course, hazardous corners shall be provided with barricades in the form of bales of hay or similar material sufficient to check accidental deviations from the course, and spectators shall be prohibited from entering a designated zone within two hundred feet from such corner extending two hundred feet along the exit outside section of such corner.

(D) The sponsoring organization under division (A) of this section shall furnish public liability insurance in the amount of two hundred fifty thousand dollars because of bodily injury to or death of one person resulting from any one accident, in the amount of one million dollars because of bodily injury to or death of two or more persons in any one accident, and in the amount of fifty thousand dollars because of injury to property of others in any one accident.

(130 v H 450, eff. 5–1–63)

4511.26 Vehicles traveling in opposite directions

(A) Operators of vehicles and trackless trolleys proceeding in opposite directions shall pass each other to the right, and upon roadways having width for not more than one line of traffic in each direction, each operator shall give to the other one-half of the main traveled portion of the roadway or as nearly one-half as is reasonable possible [1].

(B) Except as otherwise provided in this division, whoever violates this section is guilty of a minor misdemeanor. If, within one year of the offense, the offender previously has been convicted of or pleaded guilty to one predicate motor vehicle or traffic offense, whoever violates this section is guilty of a misdemeanor of the fourth degree. If, within one year of the offense, the offender previously has been convicted of two or more predicate motor vehicle or traffic offenses, whoever violates this section is guilty of a misdemeanor of the third degree.

(2002 S 123, eff. 1–1–04; 1953 H 1, eff. 10–1–53; GC 6307–26)

1 Prior and current versions differ; although no amendment was indicated in 2002 S 123, "reasonable possible" appeared as "reasonably possible" in 1953 H 1.

4511.27 Rules governing overtaking and passing of vehicles

(A) The following rules govern the overtaking and passing of vehicles or trackless trolleys proceeding in the same direction:

(1) The operator of a vehicle or trackless trolley overtaking another vehicle or trackless trolley proceeding in the same direction shall, except as provided in division (A)(3) of this section, signal to the vehicle or trackless trolley to be overtaken, shall pass to the left thereof at a safe distance, and shall not again drive to the right side of the roadway until safely clear of the overtaken vehicle or trackless trolley.

(2) Except when overtaking and passing on the right is permitted, the operator of an overtaken vehicle shall give way to the right in favor of the overtaking vehicle at the latter's audible signal, and the operator shall not increase the speed of the operator's vehicle until completely passed by the overtaking vehicle.

(3) The operator of a vehicle or trackless trolley overtaking and passing another vehicle or trackless trolley proceeding in the same direction on a divided highway as defined in section 4511.35 of the Revised Code, a limited access highway as defined in section 5511.02 of the Revised Code, or a highway with four or more traffic lanes, is not required to signal audibly to the vehicle or trackless trolley being overtaken and passed.

(B) Except as otherwise provided in this division, whoever violates this section is guilty of a minor misdemeanor. If, within one year of the offense, the offender previously has been convicted of or pleaded guilty to one predicate motor vehicle or traffic offense, whoever violates this section is guilty of a misdemeanor of the fourth degree. If, within one year of the offense, the offender previously has been convicted of two or more predicate motor vehicle or traffic offenses, whoever violates this section is guilty of a misdemeanor of the third degree.

(2002 S 123, eff. 1–1–04; 1969 S 289, eff. 11–6–69; 1953 H 1; GC 6307–27)

4511.28 Overtaking and passing on the right

(A) The driver of a vehicle or trackless trolley may overtake and pass upon the right of another vehicle or trackless trolley only under the following conditions:

(1) When the vehicle or trackless trolley overtaken is making or about to make a left turn;

(2) Upon a roadway with unobstructed pavement of sufficient width for two or more lines of vehicles moving lawfully in the direction being traveled by the overtaking vehicle.

(B) The driver of a vehicle or trackless trolley may overtake and pass another vehicle or trackless trolley only under conditions permitting such movement in safety. The movement shall not be made by driving off the roadway.

(C) Except as otherwise provided in this division, whoever violates this section is guilty of a minor misdemeanor. If, within one year of the offense, the offender previously has been convicted of or pleaded guilty to one predicate motor vehicle or traffic offense, whoever violates this section is guilty of a misdemeanor of the fourth degree. If, within one year of the offense, the offender previously has been convicted of two or more predicate motor vehicle or traffic offenses, whoever violates this section is guilty of a misdemeanor of the third degree.

(2002 S 123, eff. 1–1–04; 1974 H 995, eff. 1–1–75; 1953 H 1; GC 6307–28)

4511.29 Driving left of center in passing

(A) No vehicle or trackless trolley shall be driven to the left of the center of the roadway in overtaking and passing traffic proceeding in the same direction, unless such left side is clearly visible and is free of oncoming traffic for a sufficient distance ahead to permit such overtaking and passing to be completely made, without interfering with the safe operation of any traffic approaching from the opposite direction or any traffic overtaken. In every event the overtaking vehicle or trackless trolley must return to an authorized lane of travel as soon as practicable and in the event the passing movement involves the use of a lane authorized for traffic approaching from the opposite direction, before coming within two hundred feet of any approaching vehicle.

(B) Except as otherwise provided in this division, whoever violates this section is guilty of a minor misdemeanor. If, within one year of the offense, the offender previously has been convicted of or pleaded guilty to one predicate motor vehicle or traffic offense, whoever violates this section is guilty of a misdemeanor of the fourth degree. If, within one year of the offense, the offender previously has been convicted of two or more predicate motor vehicle or traffic offenses, whoever violates this section is guilty of a misdemeanor of the third degree.

(2002 S 123, eff. 1–1–04; 1974 H 995, eff. 1–1–75; 1953 H 1; GC 6307–29)

4511.30 Prohibition against driving to left of center line

(A) No vehicle or trackless trolley shall be driven upon the left side of the roadway under the following conditions:

(1) When approaching the crest of a grade or upon a curve in the highway, where the operator's view is obstructed within such a distance as to create a hazard in the event traffic might approach from the opposite direction;

(2) When the view is obstructed upon approaching within one hundred feet of any bridge, viaduct, or tunnel;

(3) When approaching within one hundred feet of or traversing any intersection or railroad grade crossing.

(B) This section does not apply to vehicles or trackless trolleys upon a one-way roadway, upon a roadway where traffic is lawfully directed to be driven to the left side, or under the conditions described in division (A)(2) of section 4511.25 of the Revised Code.

(C) Except as otherwise provided in this division, whoever violates this section is guilty of a minor misdemeanor. If, within one year of the offense, the offender previously has been convicted of or pleaded guilty to one predicate motor vehicle or traffic offense, whoever violates this section is guilty of a misdemeanor of the fourth degree. If, within one year of the offense, the offender previously has been convicted of two or more predicate motor vehicle or traffic offenses, whoever violates this section is guilty of a misdemeanor of the third degree.

(2002 S 123, eff. 1–1–04; 1974 H 995, eff. 1–1–75; 1953 H 1; GC 6307–30)

4511.31 Hazardous passing zones

(A) The department of transportation may determine those portions of any state highway where overtaking and passing other traffic or driving to the left of the center or center line of the roadway would be especially hazardous and may, by appropriate signs or markings on the highway, indicate the beginning and end of such zones. When such signs or markings are in place and clearly visible, every operator of a vehicle or trackless trolley shall obey the directions of the signs or markings, notwithstanding the distances set out in section 4511.30 of the Revised Code.

(B) Except as otherwise provided in this division, whoever violates this section is guilty of a minor misdemeanor. If, within one year of the offense, the offender previously has been convicted of or pleaded guilty to one predicate motor vehicle or traffic offense, whoever violates this section is guilty of a misdemeanor of the fourth degree. If, within one year of the offense, the offender previously has been convicted of two or more predicate

motor vehicle or traffic offenses, whoever violates this section is guilty of a misdemeanor of the third degree.

(2002 S 123, eff. 1–1–04; 1973 H 200, eff. 9–28–73; 1953 H 1; GC 6307–31)

4511.32 One–way highways and rotary traffic islands

(A) The department of transportation may designate any highway or any separate roadway under its jurisdiction for one-way traffic and shall erect appropriate signs giving notice thereof.

Upon a roadway designated and posted with signs for one-way traffic a vehicle shall be driven only in the direction designated.

A vehicle passing around a rotary traffic island shall be driven only to the right of the rotary traffic island.

(B) Except as otherwise provided in this division, whoever violates this section is guilty of a minor misdemeanor. If, within one year of the offense, the offender previously has been convicted of or pleaded guilty to one predicate motor vehicle or traffic offense, whoever violates this section is guilty of a misdemeanor of the fourth degree. If, within one year of the offense, the offender previously has been convicted of two or more predicate motor vehicle or traffic offenses, whoever violates this section is guilty of a misdemeanor of the third degree.

(2002 S 123, eff. 1–1–04; 1973 H 200, eff. 9–28–73; 1953 H 1; GC 6307–32)

4511.33 Rules for driving in marked lanes

(A) Whenever any roadway has been divided into two or more clearly marked lanes for traffic, or wherever within municipal corporations traffic is lawfully moving in two or more substantially continuous lines in the same direction, the following rules apply:

(1) A vehicle or trackless trolley shall be driven, as nearly as is practicable, entirely within a single lane or line of traffic and shall not be moved from such lane or line until the driver has first ascertained that such movement can be made with safety.

(2) Upon a roadway which is divided into three lanes and provides for two-way movement of traffic, a vehicle or trackless trolley shall not be driven in the center lane except when overtaking and passing another vehicle or trackless trolley where the roadway is clearly visible and such center lane is clear of traffic within a safe distance, or when preparing for a left turn, or where such center lane is at the time allocated exclusively to traffic moving in the direction the vehicle or trackless trolley is proceeding and is posted with signs to give notice of such allocation.

(3) Official signs may be erected directing specified traffic to use a designated lane or designating those lanes to be used by traffic moving in a particular direction regardless of the center of the roadway, or restricting the use of a particular lane to only buses during certain hours or during all hours, and drivers of vehicles and trackless trolleys shall obey the directions of such signs.

(4) Official traffic control devices may be installed prohibiting the changing of lanes on sections of roadway and drivers of vehicles shall obey the directions of every such device.

(B) Except as otherwise provided in this division, whoever violates this section is guilty of a minor misdemeanor. If, within one year of the offense, the offender previously has been convicted of or pleaded guilty to one predicate motor vehicle or traffic offense, whoever violates this section is guilty of a misdemeanor of the fourth degree. If, within one year of the offense, the offender previously has been convicted of two or more predicate motor vehicle or traffic offenses, whoever violates this section is guilty of a misdemeanor of the third degree.

(2003 H 95, § 3.13, eff. 1–1–04; 2003 H 95, § 1, eff. 9–26–03; 2002 S 123, eff. 1–1–04; 1974 H 995, eff. 1–1–75; 1953 H 1; GC 6307–33)

4511.34 Space between moving vehicles

(A) The operator of a motor vehicle, streetcar, or trackless trolley shall not follow another vehicle, streetcar, or trackless trolley more closely than is reasonable and prudent, having due regard for the speed of such vehicle, streetcar, or trackless trolley, and the traffic upon and the condition of the highway.

The driver of any truck, or motor vehicle drawing another vehicle, when traveling upon a roadway outside a business or residence district shall maintain a sufficient space, whenever conditions permit, between such vehicle and another vehicle ahead so an overtaking motor vehicle may enter and occupy such space without danger. This paragraph does not prevent overtaking and passing nor does it apply to any lane specially designated for use by trucks.

Outside a municipal corporation, the driver of any truck, or motor vehicle when drawing another vehicle, while ascending to the crest of a grade beyond which the driver's view of a roadway [1] is obstructed, shall not follow within three hundred feet of another truck, or motor vehicle drawing another vehicle. This paragraph shall not apply to any lane specially designated for use by trucks.

Motor vehicles being driven upon any roadway outside of a business or residence district in a caravan or motorcade, shall maintain a sufficient space between such vehicles so an overtaking vehicle may enter and occupy such space without danger. This paragraph shall not apply to funeral processions.

(B) Except as otherwise provided in this division, whoever violates this section is guilty of a minor misdemeanor. If, within one year of the offense, the offender previously has been convicted of or pleaded guilty to one predicate motor vehicle or traffic offense, whoever violates this section is guilty of a misdemeanor of the fourth degree. If, within one year of the offense, the offender previously has been convicted of two or more predicate motor vehicle or traffic offenses, whoever violates this section is guilty of a misdemeanor of the third degree.

(2002 S 123, eff. 1–1–04; 126 v 113, eff. 9–30–55; 1953 H 1; GC 6307–34)

[1] Prior and current versions differ; although no amendment was indicated in 2002 S 123, "view of a roadway" appeared as "view of the roadway" in 126 v 113.

4511.35 Divided roadways

(A) Whenever any highway has been divided into two roadways by an intervening space, or by a physical barrier, or clearly indicated dividing section so constructed as to impede vehicular traffic, every vehicle shall be driven only upon the right-hand roadway, and no vehicle shall be driven over, across, or within any such dividing space, barrier, or section, except through an opening, crossover, or intersection established by public authority. This section does not prohibit the occupancy of such dividing space, barrier, or section for the purpose of an emergency stop or in compliance with an order of a police officer.

(B) Except as otherwise provided in this division, whoever violates this section is guilty of a minor misdemeanor. If, within one year of the offense, the offender previously has been convicted of or pleaded guilty to one predicate motor vehicle or traffic offense, whoever violates this section is guilty of a misdemeanor of the fourth degree. If, within one year of the offense, the offender previously has been convicted of two or more predicate

motor vehicle or traffic offenses, whoever violates this section is guilty of a misdemeanor of the third degree.

(2002 S 123, eff. 1–1–04; 1953 H 1, eff. 10–1–53; GC 6307–34a)

4511.36 Rules for turns at intersections

(A) The driver of a vehicle intending to turn at an intersection shall be governed by the following rules:

(1) Approach for a right turn and a right turn shall be made as close as practicable to the right-hand curb or edge of the roadway.

(2) At any intersection where traffic is permitted to move in both directions on each roadway entering the intersection, an approach for a left turn shall be made in that portion of the right half of the roadway nearest the center line thereof and by passing to the right of such center line where it enters the intersection and after entering the intersection the left turn shall be made so as to leave the intersection to the right of the center line of the roadway being entered. Whenever practicable the left turn shall be made in that portion of the intersection to the left of the center of the intersection.

(3) At any intersection where traffic is restricted to one direction on one or more of the roadways, the driver of a vehicle intending to turn left at any such intersection shall approach the intersection in the extreme left-hand lane lawfully available to traffic moving in the direction of travel of such vehicle, and after entering the intersection the left turn shall be made so as to leave the intersection, as nearly as practicable, in the left-hand lane of the roadway being entered lawfully available to traffic moving in that lane.

(B) The operator of a trackless trolley shall comply with divisions (A)(1), (2), and (3) of this section wherever practicable.

(C) The department of transportation and local authorities in their respective jurisdictions may cause markers, buttons, or signs to be placed within or adjacent to intersections and thereby require and direct that a different course from that specified in this section be traveled by vehicles, streetcars, or trackless trolleys, turning at an intersection, and when markers, buttons, or signs are so placed, no operator of a vehicle, streetcar, or trackless trolley shall turn such vehicle, streetcar, or trackless trolley at an intersection other than as directed and required by such markers, buttons, or signs.

(D) Except as otherwise provided in this division, whoever violates this section is guilty of a minor misdemeanor. If, within one year of the offense, the offender previously has been convicted of or pleaded guilty to one predicate motor vehicle or traffic offense, whoever violates this section is guilty of a misdemeanor of the fourth degree. If, within one year of the offense, the offender previously has been convicted of two or more predicate motor vehicle or traffic offenses, whoever violates this section is guilty of a misdemeanor of the third degree.

(2002 S 123, eff. 1–1–04; 1973 H 200, eff. 9–28–73; 1953 H 1; GC 6307–35)

4511.37 Turning in roadway prohibited; exception

(A) Except as provided in division (B) of this section, no vehicle shall be turned so as to proceed in the opposite direction upon any curve, or upon the approach to or near the crest of a grade, if the vehicle cannot be seen within five hundred feet by the driver of any other vehicle approaching from either direction.

(B) The driver of an emergency vehicle or public safety vehicle, when responding to an emergency call, may turn the vehicle so as to proceed in the opposite direction. This division applies only when the emergency vehicle or public safety vehicle is responding to an emergency call, is equipped with and displaying at least one flashing, rotating, or oscillating light visible under normal atmospheric conditions from a distance of five hundred feet to the front of the vehicle, and when the driver of the vehicle is giving an audible signal by siren, exhaust whistle, or bell. This division does not relieve the driver of an emergency vehicle or public safety vehicle from the duty to drive with due regard for the safety of all persons and property upon the highway.

(C) Except as otherwise provided in this division, whoever violates this section is guilty of a minor misdemeanor. If, within one year of the offense, the offender previously has been convicted of or pleaded guilty to one predicate motor vehicle or traffic offense, whoever violates this section is guilty of a misdemeanor of the fourth degree. If, within one year of the offense, the offender previously has been convicted of two or more predicate motor vehicle or traffic offenses, whoever violates this section is guilty of a misdemeanor of the third degree.

(2002 S 123, eff. 1–1–04; 1993 H 149, eff. 5–20–93; 1953 H 1; GC 6307–36)

4511.38 Care to be exercised in starting or backing vehicles

(A) No person shall start a vehicle, streetcar, or trackless trolley which is stopped, standing, or parked until such movement can be made with reasonable safety.

Before backing, operators of vehicle [1], streetcars, or trackless trolleys shall give ample warning, and while backing they shall exercise vigilance not to injure person or property on the street or highway.

No person shall back a motor vehicle on a freeway, except: in a rest area; in the performance of public works or official duties; as a result of an emergency caused by an accident or breakdown of a motor vehicle.

(B) Except as otherwise provided in this division, whoever violates this section is guilty of a minor misdemeanor. If, within one year of the offense, the offender previously has been convicted of or pleaded guilty to one predicate motor vehicle or traffic offense, whoever violates this section is guilty of a misdemeanor of the fourth degree. If, within one year of the offense, the offender previously has been convicted of two or more predicate motor vehicle or traffic offenses, whoever violates this section is guilty of a misdemeanor of the third degree.

(2002 S 123, eff. 1–1–04; 131 v H 102, eff. 11–4–65; 1953 H 1; GC 6307–37)

1 Prior and current versions differ; although no amendment was indicated in 2002 S 123, "operators of vehicle" appeared as "operators of vehicles" in 131 v H 102.

4511.39 Use of signals for stopping, turning, decreasing speed, moving left or right; limitations

(A) No person shall turn a vehicle or trackless trolley or move right or left upon a highway unless and until such person has exercised due care to ascertain that the movement can be made with reasonable safety nor without giving an appropriate signal in the manner hereinafter provided.

When required, a signal of intention to turn or move right or left shall be given continuously during not less than the last one hundred feet traveled by the vehicle or trackless trolley before turning.

No person shall stop or suddenly decrease the speed of a vehicle or trackless trolley without first giving an appropriate signal in the manner provided herein to the driver of any vehicle or trackless trolley immediately to the rear when there is opportunity to give a signal.

Any stop or turn signal required by this section shall be given either by means of the hand and arm, or by signal lights that clearly indicate to both approaching and following traffic intention to turn or move right or left, except that any motor vehicle in use on a highway shall be equipped with, and the required signal shall be given by, signal lights when the distance from the center of the top of the steering post to the left outside limit of the body, cab, or load of such motor vehicle exceeds twenty-four inches, or when the distance from the center of the top of the steering post to the rear limit of the body or load thereof exceeds fourteen feet, whether a single vehicle or a combination of vehicles.

The signal lights required by this section shall not be flashed on one side only on a disabled vehicle or trackless trolley, flashed as a courtesy or "do pass" signal to operators of other vehicles or trackless trolleys approaching from the rear, nor be flashed on one side only of a parked vehicle or trackless trolley except as may be necessary for compliance with this section.

(B) Except as otherwise provided in this division, whoever violates this section is guilty of a minor misdemeanor. If, within one year of the offense, the offender previously has been convicted of or pleaded guilty to one predicate motor vehicle or traffic offense, whoever violates this section is guilty of a misdemeanor of the fourth degree. If, within one year of the offense, the offender previously has been convicted of two or more predicate motor vehicle or traffic offenses, whoever violates this section is guilty of a misdemeanor of the third degree.

(2002 S 123, eff. 1–1–04; 1974 H 995, eff. 1–1–75; 125 v 460; 1953 H 1; GC 6307–38)

4511.40 Hand and arm signals

(A) Except as provided in division (B) of this section, all signals required by sections 4511.01 to 4511.78 of the Revised Code, when given by hand and arm, shall be given from the left side of the vehicle in the following manner, and such signals shall indicate as follows:

(1) Left turn, hand and arm extended horizontally;

(2) Right turn, hand and arm extended upward;

(3) Stop or decrease speed, hand and arm extended downward.

(B) As an alternative to division (A)(2) of this section, a person operating a bicycle may give a right turn signal by extending the right hand and arm horizontally and to the right side of the bicycle.

(C) Except as otherwise provided in this division, whoever violates this section is guilty of a minor misdemeanor. If, within one year of the offense, the offender previously has been convicted of or pleaded guilty to one predicate motor vehicle or traffic offense, whoever violates this section is guilty of a misdemeanor of the fourth degree. If, within one year of the offense, the offender previously has been convicted of two or more predicate motor vehicle or traffic offenses, whoever violates this section is guilty of a misdemeanor of the third degree.

(2002 S 123, eff. 1–1–04; 1996 H 461, eff. 9–10–96; 1953 H 1, eff. 10–1–53; GC 6307–39)

RIGHT OF WAY

4511.41 Right–of–way at intersections

(A) When two vehicles, including any trackless trolley or streetcar, approach or enter an intersection from different streets or highways at approximately the same time, the driver of the vehicle on the left shall yield the right-of-way to the vehicle on the right.

(B) The right-of-way rule declared in division (A) of this section is modified at through highways and otherwise as stated in Chapter 4511. of the Revised Code.

(C) Except as otherwise provided in this division, whoever violates this section is guilty of a minor misdemeanor. If, within one year of the offense, the offender previously has been convicted of or pleaded guilty to one predicate motor vehicle or traffic offense, whoever violates this section is guilty of a misdemeanor of the fourth degree. If, within one year of the offense, the offender previously has been convicted of two or more predicate motor vehicle or traffic offenses, whoever violates this section is guilty of a misdemeanor of the third degree.

(2002 S 123, eff. 1–1–04; 1975 H 1, eff. 6–13–75; 1974 H 995)

4511.42 Right of way when turning left

(A) The operator of a vehicle, streetcar, or trackless trolley intending to turn to the left within an intersection or into an alley, private road, or driveway shall yield the right of way to any vehicle, streetcar, or trackless trolley approaching from the opposite direction, whenever the approaching vehicle, streetcar, or trackless trolley is within the intersection or so close to the intersection, alley, private road, or driveway as to constitute an immediate hazard.

(B) Except as otherwise provided in this division, whoever violates this section is guilty of a minor misdemeanor. If, within one year of the offense, the offender previously has been convicted of or pleaded guilty to one predicate motor vehicle or traffic offense, whoever violates this section is guilty of a misdemeanor of the fourth degree. If, within one year of the offense, the offender previously has been convicted of two or more predicate motor vehicle or traffic offenses, whoever violates this section is guilty of a misdemeanor of the third degree.

(2002 S 123, eff. 1–1–04; 1977 S 62, eff. 7–8–77; 1974 H 995; 130 v H 14; 1953 H 1; GC 6307–41)

4511.43 Driving in response to stop or yield sign

(A) Except when directed to proceed by a law enforcement officer, every driver of a vehicle or trackless trolley approaching a stop sign shall stop at a clearly marked stop line, but if none, before entering the crosswalk on the near side of the intersection, or, if none, then at the point nearest the intersecting roadway where the driver has a view of approaching traffic on the intersecting roadway before entering it. After having stopped, the driver shall yield the right-of-way to any vehicle in the intersection or approaching on another roadway so closely as to constitute an immediate hazard during the time the driver is moving across or within the intersection or junction of roadways.

(B) The driver of a vehicle or trackless trolley approaching a yield sign shall slow down to a speed reasonable for the existing conditions and, if required for safety to stop, shall stop at a clearly marked stop line, but if none, before entering the crosswalk on the near side of the intersection, or, if none, then at the point nearest the intersecting roadway where the driver has a view of approaching traffic on the intersecting roadway before entering it. After slowing or stopping, the driver shall yield the right-of-way to any vehicle or trackless trolley in the intersection or approaching on another roadway so closely as to constitute an immediate hazard during the time the driver is moving across or within the intersection or junction of roadways. Whenever a driver is involved in a collision with a vehicle or trackless trolley in the intersection or junction of roadways, after driving past a yield sign without stopping, the collision shall be prima-facie evidence of the driver's failure to yield the right-of-way.

(C) Except as otherwise provided in this division, whoever violates this section is guilty of a minor misdemeanor. If, within one year of the offense, the offender previously has been convicted of or pleaded guilty to one predicate motor vehicle or traffic offense, whoever violates this section is guilty of a misdemeanor of the fourth degree. If, within one year of the offense, the offender previously has been convicted of two or more predicate motor vehicle or traffic offenses, whoever violates this section is guilty of a misdemeanor of the third degree.

(2002 S 123, eff. 1-1-04; 1974 H 995, eff. 1-1-75)

4511.431 Stopping prior to driving onto or across sidewalk

(A) The driver of a vehicle or trackless trolley emerging from an alley, building, private road, or driveway within a business or residence district shall stop the vehicle or trackless trolley immediately prior to driving onto a sidewalk or onto the sidewalk area extending across the alley, building entrance, road, or driveway, or in the event there is no sidewalk area, shall stop at the point nearest the street to be entered where the driver has a view of approaching traffic thereon.

(B) Except as otherwise provided in this division, whoever violates this section is guilty of a minor misdemeanor. If, within one year of the offense, the offender previously has been convicted of or pleaded guilty to one predicate motor vehicle or traffic offense, whoever violates this section is guilty of a misdemeanor of the fourth degree. If, within one year of the offense, the offender previously has been convicted of two or more predicate motor vehicle or traffic offenses, whoever violates this section is guilty of a misdemeanor of the third degree.

(2002 S 123, eff. 1-1-04; 1974 H 995, eff. 1-1-75)

4511.432 Stop signs on private roads and driveways

(A) The owner of a private road or driveway located in a private residential area containing twenty or more dwelling units may erect stop signs at places where the road or driveway intersects with another private road or driveway in the residential area, in compliance with all of the following requirements:

(1) The stop sign is sufficiently legible to be seen by an ordinarily observant person and meets the specifications of and is placed in accordance with the manual adopted by the department of transportation pursuant to section 4511.09 of the Revised Code.

(2) The owner has posted a sign at the entrance of the private road or driveway that is in plain view and clearly informs persons entering the road or driveway that they are entering private property, stop signs have been posted and must be obeyed, and the signs are enforceable by law enforcement officers under state law. The sign required by division (A)(2) of this section, where appropriate, may be incorporated with the sign required by division (A)(2) of section 4511.211 of the Revised Code.

(B) Division (A) of section 4511.43 and section 4511.46 of the Revised Code shall be deemed to apply to the driver of a vehicle on a private road or driveway where a stop sign is placed in accordance with division (A) of this section and to a pedestrian crossing such a road or driveway at an intersection where a stop sign is in place.

(C) When a stop sign is placed in accordance with division (A) of this section, any law enforcement officer may apprehend a person found violating the stop sign and may stop and charge the person with violating the stop sign.

(D) Except as otherwise provided in this division, whoever violates this section is guilty of a minor misdemeanor. If, within one year of the offense, the offender previously has been convicted of or pleaded guilty to one predicate motor vehicle or traffic offense, whoever violates this section is guilty of a misdemeanor of the fourth degree. If, within one year of the offense, the offender previously has been convicted of two or more predicate motor vehicle or traffic offenses, whoever violates this section is guilty of a misdemeanor of the third degree.

(E) As used in this section, and for the purpose of applying division (A) of section 4511.43 and section 4511.46 of the Revised Code to conduct under this section:

(1) "Intersection" means:

(a) The area embraced within the prolongation or connection of the lateral curb lines, or, if none, then the lateral boundary lines of the roadways of two private roads or driveways which join one another at, or approximately at, right angles, or the area within which vehicles traveling upon different private roads or driveways joining at any other angle may come in conflict.

(b) Where a private road or driveway includes two roadways thirty feet or more apart, then every crossing of two roadways of such private roads or driveways shall be regarded as a separate intersection.

(2) "Roadway" means that portion of a private road or driveway improved, designed, or ordinarily used for vehicular travel, except the berm or shoulder. If a private road or driveway includes two or more separate roadways, the term "roadway" means any such roadway separately but not all such roadways collectively.

(3) "Owner" and "private residential area containing twenty or more dwelling units" have the same meanings as in section 4511.211 of the Revised Code.

(2002 S 123, eff. 1-1-04; 1990 H 171, eff. 5-31-90)

4511.44 Entering roadway from any place other than another roadway; duty to yield

(A) The operator of a vehicle, streetcar, or trackless trolley about to enter or cross a highway from any place other than another roadway shall yield the right of way to all traffic approaching on the roadway to be entered or crossed.

(B) Except as otherwise provided in this division, whoever violates this section is guilty of a minor misdemeanor. If, within one year of the offense, the offender previously has been convicted of or pleaded guilty to one predicate motor vehicle or traffic offense, whoever violates this section is guilty of a misdemeanor of the fourth degree. If, within one year of the offense, the offender previously has been convicted of two or more predicate motor vehicle or traffic offenses, whoever violates this section is guilty of a misdemeanor of the third degree.

(2002 S 123, eff. 1-1-04; 1974 H 995, eff. 1-1-75; 1953 H 1; GC 6307-43)

4511.441 Right-of-way of pedestrian on sidewalk

(A) The driver of a vehicle shall yield the right-of-way to any pedestrian on a sidewalk.

(B) Except as otherwise provided in this division, whoever violates this section is guilty of a minor misdemeanor. If, within one year of the offense, the offender previously has been convicted of or pleaded guilty to one predicate motor vehicle or traffic offense, whoever violates this section is guilty of a misdemeanor of the fourth degree. If, within one year of the offense, the offender previously has been convicted of two or more predicate motor vehicle or traffic offenses, whoever violates this section is guilty of a misdemeanor of the third degree.

(2002 S 123, eff. 1-1-04; 1974 H 995, eff. 1-1-75)

4511.45 Right–of–way of public safety vehicles

(A)(1) Upon the approach of a public safety vehicle or coroner's vehicle, equipped with at least one flashing, rotating or oscillating light visible under normal atmospheric conditions from a distance of five hundred feet to the front of the vehicle and the driver is giving an audible signal by siren, exhaust whistle, or bell, no driver of any other vehicle shall fail to yield the right-of-way, immediately drive if practical to a position parallel to, and as close as possible to, the right edge or curb of the highway clear of any intersection, and stop and remain in that position until the public safety vehicle or coroner's vehicle has passed, except when otherwise directed by a police officer.

(2) Upon the approach of a public safety vehicle or coroner's vehicle, as stated in division (A)(1) of this section, no operator of any streetcar or trackless trolley shall fail to immediately stop the streetcar or trackless trolley clear of any intersection and keep it in that position until the public safety vehicle or coroner's vehicle has passed, except when otherwise directed by a police officer.

(B) This section does not relieve the driver of a public safety vehicle or coroner's vehicle from the duty to drive with due regard for the safety of all persons and property upon the highway.

(C) This section applies to a coroner's vehicle only when the vehicle is operated in accordance with section 4513.171 of the Revised Code. As used in this section, "coroner's vehicle" means a vehicle used by a coroner, deputy coroner, or coroner's investigator that is equipped with a flashing, oscillating, or rotating red or blue light and a siren, exhaust whistle, or bell capable of giving an audible signal.

(D) Except as otherwise provided in this division, whoever violates division (A)(1) or (2) of this section is guilty of a misdemeanor of the fourth degree on a first offense. On a second offense within one year after the first offense, the person is guilty of a misdemeanor of the third degree, and, on each subsequent offense within one year after the first offense, the person is guilty of a misdemeanor of the second degree.

(2002 S 123, eff. 1–1–04; 1997 H 282, eff. 11–12–97; 1993 H 149, eff. 5–20–93; 132 v S 451, H 878; 1953 H 1; GC 6307–44)

4511.451 Funeral procession has right of way

(A) As used in this section, "funeral procession" means two or more vehicles accompanying the cremated remains or the body of a deceased person in the daytime when each of the vehicles has its headlights lighted and is displaying a purple and white or orange and white pennant attached to each vehicle in such a manner as to be clearly visible to traffic approaching from any direction.

(B) Excepting public safety vehicles proceeding in accordance with section 4511.45 of the Revised Code or when directed otherwise by a police officer, pedestrians and the operators of all vehicles, street cars, and trackless trolleys shall yield the right of way to each vehicle that is a part of a funeral procession. Whenever the lead vehicle in a funeral procession lawfully enters an intersection, the remainder of the vehicles in the procession may continue to follow the lead vehicle through the intersection notwithstanding any traffic control devices or right of way provisions of the Revised Code, provided that the operator of each vehicle exercises due care to avoid colliding with any other vehicle or pedestrian.

(C) [1] No person shall operate any vehicle as a part of a funeral procession without having the headlights of the vehicle lighted and without displaying a purple and white or an orange and white pennant in such a manner as to be clearly visible to traffic approaching from any direction.

(C) Except as otherwise provided in this division, whoever violates this section is guilty of a minor misdemeanor. If, within one year of the offense, the offender previously has been convicted of or pleaded guilty to one predicate motor vehicle or traffic offense, whoever violates this section is guilty of a misdemeanor of the fourth degree. If, within one year of the offense, the offender previously has been convicted of two or more predicate motor vehicle or traffic offenses, whoever violates this section is guilty of a misdemeanor of the third degree.

(2002 H 322, eff. 4–7–03; 2002 S 123, eff. 1–1–04; 132 v H 878, eff. 12–14–67; 126 v 632)

[1] So in original; 2002 H 322.

4511.452 Pedestrian to yield to public safety vehicle; care of driver

(A) Upon the immediate approach of a public safety vehicle, as stated in section 4511.45 of the Revised Code, every pedestrian shall yield the right-of-way to the public safety vehicle.

(B) This section shall not relieve the driver of a public safety vehicle from the duty to exercise due care to avoid colliding with any pedestrian.

(C) Except as otherwise provided in this division, whoever violates this section is guilty of a minor misdemeanor. If, within one year of the offense, the offender previously has been convicted of or pleaded guilty to one predicate motor vehicle or traffic offense, whoever violates this section is guilty of a misdemeanor of the fourth degree. If, within one year of the offense, the offender previously has been convicted of two or more predicate motor vehicle or traffic offenses, whoever violates this section is guilty of a misdemeanor of the third degree.

(2002 S 123, eff. 1–1–04; 1974 H 995, eff. 1–1–75)

4511.46 Right–of–way of pedestrian in crosswalk; limitations

(A) When traffic control signals are not in place, not in operation, or are not clearly assigning the right-of-way, the driver of a vehicle, trackless trolley, or streetcar shall yield the right of way, slowing down or stopping if need be to so yield or if required by section 4511.132 of the Revised Code, to a pedestrian crossing the roadway within a crosswalk when the pedestrian is upon the half of the roadway upon which the vehicle is traveling, or when the pedestrian is approaching so closely from the opposite half of the roadway as to be in danger.

(B) No pedestrian shall suddenly leave a curb or other place of safety and walk or run into the path of a vehicle, trackless trolley, or streetcar which is so close as to constitute an immediate hazard.

(C) Division (A) of this section does not apply under the conditions stated in division (B) of section 4511.48 of the Revised Code.

(D) Whenever any vehicle, trackless trolley, or streetcar is stopped at a marked crosswalk or at any unmarked crosswalk at an intersection to permit a pedestrian to cross the roadway, the driver of any other vehicle, trackless trolley, or streetcar approaching from the rear shall not overtake and pass the stopped vehicle.

(E) Except as otherwise provided in this division, whoever violates this section is guilty of a minor misdemeanor. If, within one year of the offense, the offender previously has been convicted of or pleaded guilty to one predicate motor vehicle or traffic offense, whoever violates this section is guilty of a misdemeanor of the fourth degree. If, within one year of the offense, the offender previously has been convicted of two or more predicate

motor vehicle or traffic offenses, whoever violates this section is guilty of a misdemeanor of the third degree.

(2002 S 123, eff. 1-1-04; 1989 S 44, eff. 7-25-89; 1974 H 995)

4511.47 Right of way yielded to blind person; prohibition against use of white or metallic cane by others

(A) As used in this section "blind person" or "blind pedestrian" means a person having not more than 20/200 visual acuity in the better eye with correcting lenses or visual acuity greater than 20/200 but with a limitation in the fields of vision such that the widest diameter of the visual field subtends an angle no greater than twenty degrees.

The driver of every vehicle shall yield the right of way to every blind pedestrian guided by a guide dog, or carrying a cane which is predominantly white or metallic in color, with or without a red tip.

(B) No person, other than a blind person, while on any public highway, street, alley, or other public thoroughfare shall carry a white or metallic cane with or without a red tip.

(C) Except as otherwise provided in this division, whoever violates this section is guilty of a minor misdemeanor. If, within one year of the offense, the offender previously has been convicted of or pleaded guilty to one predicate motor vehicle or traffic offense, whoever violates this section is guilty of a misdemeanor of the fourth degree. If, within one year of the offense, the offender previously has been convicted of two or more predicate motor vehicle or traffic offenses, whoever violates this section is guilty of a misdemeanor of the third degree.

(2002 S 123, eff. 1-1-04; 1970 S 514, eff. 7-16-70; 1953 H 1; GC 6307-45a to 6307-45c)

4511.48 Pedestrian crossing roadway outside crosswalk

(A) Every pedestrian crossing a roadway at any point other than within a marked crosswalk or within an unmarked crosswalk at an intersection shall yield the right of way to all vehicles, trackless trolleys, or streetcars upon the roadway.

(B) Any pedestrian crossing a roadway at a point where a pedestrian tunnel or overhead pedestrian crossing has been provided shall yield the right of way to all traffic upon the roadway.

(C) Between adjacent intersections at which traffic control signals are in operation, pedestrians shall not cross at any place except in a marked crosswalk.

(D) No pedestrian shall cross a roadway intersection diagonally unless authorized by official traffic control devices; and, when authorized to cross diagonally, pedestrians shall cross only in accordance with the official traffic control devices pertaining to such crossing movements.

(E) This section does not relieve the operator of a vehicle, streetcar, or trackless trolley from exercising due care to avoid colliding with any pedestrian upon any roadway.

(F) Except as otherwise provided in this division, whoever violates this section is guilty of a minor misdemeanor. If, within one year of the offense, the offender previously has been convicted of or pleaded guilty to one predicate motor vehicle or traffic offense, whoever violates this section is guilty of a misdemeanor of the fourth degree. If, within one year of the offense, the offender previously has been convicted of two or more predicate motor vehicle or traffic offenses, whoever violates this section is guilty of a misdemeanor of the third degree.

(2002 S 123, eff. 1-1-04; 1974 H 995, eff. 1-1-75; 1953 H 1; GC 6307-46)

PEDESTRIANS

4511.481 Intoxicated pedestrian on public highway

(A) A pedestrian who is under the influence of alcohol, any drug of abuse, or any combination of them to a degree that renders the pedestrian a hazard shall not walk or be upon a highway.

(B) Except as otherwise provided in this division, whoever violates this section is guilty of a minor misdemeanor. If, within one year of the offense, the offender previously has been convicted of or pleaded guilty to one predicate motor vehicle or traffic offense, whoever violates this section is guilty of a misdemeanor of the fourth degree. If, within one year of the offense, the offender previously has been convicted of two or more predicate motor vehicle or traffic offenses, whoever violates this section is guilty of a misdemeanor of the third degree.

(2002 S 123, eff. 1-1-04; 1974 H 995, eff. 1-1-75)

Notes of Decisions

Ed. Note: See notes of decisions at RC 4511.19 regarding construction of the term "under the influence."

4511.49 Pedestrian movement in crosswalk

(A) Pedestrians shall move, whenever practicable, upon the right half of crosswalks.

(B) Except as otherwise provided in this division, whoever violates this section is guilty of a minor misdemeanor. If, within one year of the offense, the offender previously has been convicted of or pleaded guilty to one predicate motor vehicle or traffic offense, whoever violates this section is guilty of a misdemeanor of the fourth degree. If, within one year of the offense, the offender previously has been convicted of two or more predicate motor vehicle or traffic offenses, whoever violates this section is guilty of a misdemeanor of the third degree.

(2002 S 123, eff. 1-1-04; 1974 H 995, eff. 1-1-75; 1953 H 1; GC 6307-47)

4511.491 Persons operating motorized wheelchairs

Every person operating a motorized wheelchair shall have all of the rights and duties applicable to a pedestrian that are contained in this chapter, except those provisions which by their nature can have no application.

(1990 S 272, eff. 11-28-90)

4511.50 Pedestrians walking along highways

(A) Where a sidewalk is provided and its use is practicable, it shall be unlawful for any pedestrian to walk along and upon an adjacent roadway.

(B) Where a sidewalk is not available, any pedestrian walking along and upon a highway shall walk only on a shoulder, as far as practicable from the edge of the roadway.

(C) Where neither a sidewalk nor a shoulder is available, any pedestrian walking along and upon a highway shall walk as near as practicable to an outside edge of the roadway, and, if on a two-way roadway, shall walk only on the left side of the roadway.

(D) Except as otherwise provided in sections 4511.13 and 4511.46 of the Revised Code, any pedestrian upon a roadway shall yield the right-of-way to all vehicles, trackless trolleys, or streetcars upon the roadway.

(E) Except as otherwise provided in this division, whoever violates this section is guilty of a minor misdemeanor. If, within one year of the offense, the offender previously has been convicted of or pleaded guilty to one predicate motor vehicle or traffic offense, whoever violates this section is guilty of a misdemeanor of the fourth degree. If, within one year of the offense, the offender previously has been convicted of two or more predicate motor vehicle or traffic offenses, whoever violates this section is guilty of a misdemeanor of the third degree.

(2002 S 123, eff. 1–1–04; 1974 H 995, eff. 1–1–75)

4511.51 Use of highway for soliciting; riding in cargo storage area, on tailgate or on outside of vehicle

(A) No person while on a roadway outside a safety zone shall solicit a ride from the driver of any vehicle.

(B)(1) Except as provided in division (B)(2) of this section, no person shall stand on a highway for the purpose of soliciting employment, business, or contributions from the occupant of any vehicle.

(2) The legislative authority of a municipal corporation, by ordinance, may authorize the issuance of a permit to a charitable organization to allow a person acting on behalf of the organization to solicit charitable contributions from the occupant of a vehicle by standing on a highway, other than a freeway as provided in division (A)(1) of section 4511.051 of the Revised Code, that is under the jurisdiction of the municipal corporation. The permit shall be valid for only one period of time, which shall be specified in the permit, in any calendar year. The legislative authority also may specify the locations where contributions may be solicited and may impose any other restrictions on or requirements regarding the manner in which the solicitations are to be conducted that the legislative authority considers advisable.

(3) As used in division (B)(2) of this section, "charitable organization" means an organization that has received from the internal revenue service a currently valid ruling or determination letter recognizing the tax-exempt status of the organization pursuant to section 501(c)(3) of the "Internal Revenue Code."

(C) No person shall hang onto or ride on the outside of any motor vehicle, streetcar, or trackless trolley while it is moving upon a roadway, except mechanics or test engineers making repairs or adjustments, or workers performing specialized highway or street maintenance or construction under authority of a public agency.

(D) No operator shall knowingly permit any person to hang onto, or ride on the outside of, any motor vehicle, streetcar, or trackless trolley while it is moving upon a roadway, except mechanics or test engineers making repairs or adjustments, or workers performing specialized highway or street maintenance or construction under authority of a public agency.

(E) No driver of a truck, trailer, or semitrailer shall knowingly permit any person who has not attained the age of sixteen years to ride in the unenclosed or unroofed cargo storage area of the driver's vehicle if the vehicle is traveling faster than twenty-five miles per hour, unless either of the following applies:

(1) The cargo storage area of the vehicle is equipped with a properly secured seat to which is attached a seat safety belt that is in compliance with federal standards for an occupant restraining device as defined in division (A)(2) of section 4513.263 of the Revised Code, the seat and seat safety belt were installed at the time the vehicle was originally assembled, and the person riding in the cargo storage area is in the seat and is wearing the seat safety belt;

(2) An emergency exists that threatens the life of the driver or the person being transported in the cargo storage area of the truck, trailer, or semitrailer.

(F) No driver of a truck, trailer, or semitrailer shall permit any person, except for those workers performing specialized highway or street maintenance or construction under authority of a public agency, to ride in the cargo storage area or on a tailgate of the driver's vehicle while the tailgate is unlatched.

(G)(1) Except as otherwise provided in this division, whoever violates any provision of divisions (A) to (D) of this section is guilty of a minor misdemeanor. If, within one year of the offense, the offender previously has been convicted of or pleaded guilty to one predicate motor vehicle or traffic offense, whoever violates any provision of divisions (A) to (D) of this section is guilty of a misdemeanor of the fourth degree. If, within one year of the offense, the offender previously has been convicted of two or more predicate motor vehicle or traffic offenses, whoever violates any provision of divisions (A) to (D) of this section is guilty of a misdemeanor of the third degree.

(2) Whoever violates division (E) or (F) of this section is guilty of a minor misdemeanor.

(2002 S 123, eff. 1–1–04; 1993 H 331, eff. 7–2–93; 1989 H 8; 1974 H 995; 1953 H 1; GC 6307–49)

4511.511 Pedestrians on bridges or railroad crossings

(A) No pedestrian shall enter or remain upon any bridge or approach thereto beyond the bridge signal, gate, or barrier after a bridge operation signal indication has been given.

(B) No pedestrian shall pass through, around, over, or under any crossing gate or barrier at a railroad grade crossing or bridge while the gate or barrier is closed or is being opened or closed.

(C) Except as otherwise provided in this division, whoever violates this section is guilty of a minor misdemeanor. If, within one year of the offense, the offender previously has been convicted of or pleaded guilty to one predicate motor vehicle or traffic offense, whoever violates this section is guilty of a misdemeanor of the fourth degree. If, within one year of the offense, the offender previously has been convicted of two or more predicate motor vehicle or traffic offenses, whoever violates this section is guilty of a misdemeanor of the third degree.

(2002 S 123, eff. 1–1–04; 1974 H 995, eff. 1–1–75)

ELECTRIC PERSONAL ASSISTIVE MOBILITY DEVICES

4511.512 Operation of electric personal assistive mobility devices

(A)(1) Electric personal assistive mobility devices may be operated on the public streets, highways, sidewalks, and paths and portions of roadways set aside for the exclusive use of bicycles in accordance with this section.

(2) Except as otherwise provided in this section, those sections of this chapter that by their nature are applicable to an electric personal assistive mobility device apply to the device and the person operating it whenever it is operated upon any public street, highway, sidewalk, or path or upon any portion of a roadway set aside for the exclusive use of bicycles.

(3) A local authority may regulate or prohibit the operation of electric personal assistive mobility devices on public streets, highways, sidewalks, and paths, and portions of roadways set aside for the exclusive use of bicycles, under its jurisdiction.

(B) No operator of an electric personal assistive mobility device shall do any of the following:

(1) Fail to yield the right-of-way to all pedestrians and human-powered vehicles at all times;

(2) Fail to give an audible signal before overtaking and passing a pedestrian;

(3) Operate the device at night unless the device or its operator is equipped with or wearing both of the following:

(a) A lamp pointing to the front that emits a white light visible from a distance of not less than five hundred feet;

(b) A red reflector facing the rear that is visible from all distances from one hundred feet to six hundred feet when directly in front of lawful lower beams of head lamps on a motor vehicle.

(4) Operate the device on any portion of a street or highway that has an established speed limit of fifty-five miles per hour or more;

(5) Operate the device upon any path set aside for the exclusive use of pedestrians or other specialized use when an appropriate sign giving notice of the specialized use is posted on the path;

(6) If under eighteen years of age, operate the device unless wearing a protective helmet on the person's head with the chin strap properly fastened;

(7) If under sixteen years of age, operate the device unless, during the operation, the person is under the direct visual and audible supervision of another person who is eighteen years of age or older and is responsible for the immediate care of the person under sixteen years of age.

(C) No person who is under fourteen years of age shall operate an electric personal assistive mobility device.

(D) No person shall distribute or sell an electric personal assistive mobility device unless the device is accompanied by a written statement that is substantially equivalent to the following: "WARNING: TO REDUCE THE RISK OF SERIOUS INJURY, USE ONLY WHILE WEARING FULL PROTECTIVE EQUIPMENT—HELMET, WRIST GUARDS, ELBOW PADS, AND KNEE PADS."

(E) Nothing in this section affects or shall be construed to affect any rule of the director of natural resources or a board of park district commissioners governing the operation of vehicles on lands under the control of the director or board, as applicable.

(F)(1) Whoever violates division (B) or (C) of this section is guilty of a minor misdemeanor and shall be punished as follows:

(a) The offender shall be fined ten dollars.

(b) If the offender previously has been convicted of or pleaded guilty to a violation of division (B) or (C) of this section or a substantially similar municipal ordinance, the court, in addition to imposing the fine required under division (F)(1) of this section, shall do one of the following:

(i) Order the impoundment for not less than one day but not more than thirty days of the electric personal assistive mobility device that was involved in the current violation of that division. The court shall order the device to be impounded at a safe indoor location designated by the court and may assess storage fees of not more than five dollars per day, provided the total storage, processing, and release fees assessed against the offender or the device in connection with the device's impoundment or subsequent release shall not exceed fifty dollars.

(ii) If the court does not issue an impoundment order pursuant to division (F)(1)(b)(i) of this section, issue an order prohibiting the offender from operating any electric personal assistive mobility device on the public streets, highways, sidewalks, and paths and portions of roadways set aside for the exclusive use of bicycles for not less than one day but not more than thirty days.

(2) Whoever violates division (D) of this section is guilty of a minor misdemeanor.

(2002 H 490, eff. 1–1–04; 2002 S 231, eff. 10–24–02)

BICYCLES

4511.52 Bicycles

Sections 4511.01 to 4511.78, inclusive, 4511.99, and 4513.01 to 4513.37, inclusive, of the Revised Code which are applicable to bicycles apply whenever a bicycle is operated upon any highway or upon any path set aside for the exclusive use of bicycles.

(1953 H 1, eff. 10–1–53; GC 6307–50)

4511.521 Operators of motorized bicycles to be licensed; rules concerning equipment

(A) No person shall operate a motorized bicycle upon a highway or any public or private property used by the public for purposes of vehicular travel or parking, unless all of the following conditions are met:

(1) The person is fourteen or fifteen years of age and holds a valid probationary motorized bicycle license issued after the person has passed the test provided for in this section, or the person is sixteen years of age or older and holds either a valid commercial driver's license issued under Chapter 4506. or a driver's license issued under Chapter 4507. of the Revised Code or a valid motorized bicycle license issued after the person has passed the test provided for in this section, except that if a person is sixteen years of age, has a valid probationary motorized bicycle license and desires a motorized bicycle license, the person is not required to comply with the testing requirements provided for in this section;

(2) The motorized bicycle is equipped in accordance with the rules adopted under division (B) of this section and is in proper working order;

(3) The person, if under eighteen years of age, is wearing a protective helmet on the person's head with the chin strap properly fastened and the motorized bicycle is equipped with a rear-view mirror.

(4) The person operates the motorized bicycle when practicable within three feet of the right edge of the roadway obeying all traffic rules applicable to vehicles.

(B) The director of public safety, subject to sections 119.01 to 119.13 of the Revised Code, shall adopt and promulgate rules concerning protective helmets, the equipment of motorized bicycles, and the testing and qualifications of persons who do not hold a valid driver's or commercial driver's license. The test shall be as near as practicable to the examination required for a motorcycle operator's endorsement under section 4507.11 of the Revised Code. The test shall also require the operator to give an actual demonstration of the operator's ability to operate and control a motorized bicycle by driving one under the supervision of an examining officer.

(C) Every motorized bicycle license expires on the birthday of the applicant in the fourth year after the date it is issued, but in no event shall any motorized bicycle license be issued for a period longer than four years.

(D) No person operating a motorized bicycle shall carry another person upon the motorized bicycle.

(E) The protective helmet and rear-view mirror required by division (A)(3) of this section shall, on and after January 1, 1985, conform with rules adopted by the director under division (B) of this section.

(F) Each probationary motorized bicycle license or motorized bicycle license shall be laminated with a transparent plastic material.

(G) Whoever violates division (A), (D), or (E) of this section is guilty of a minor misdemeanor.

(2002 S 123, eff. 1–1–04; 1992 S 98, eff. 11–12–92; 1990 S 131; 1989 H 381; 1984 S 169; 1978 S 393; 1977 S 100)

4511.53 Rules for bicycles, motorcycles and snowmobiles

(A) For purposes of this section, "snowmobile" has the same meaning as given that term in section 4519.01 of the Revised Code.

(B) A person operating a bicycle or motorcycle shall not ride other than upon the permanent and regular seat attached thereto, nor carry any other person upon such bicycle or motorcycle other than upon a firmly attached and regular seat thereon, nor shall any person ride upon a bicycle or motorcycle other than upon such a firmly attached and regular seat.

A person shall ride upon a motorcycle only while sitting astride the seat, facing forward, with one leg on each side of the motorcycle.

No person operating a bicycle shall carry any package, bundle, or article that prevents the driver from keeping at least one hand upon the handle bars.

No bicycle or motorcycle shall be used to carry more persons at one time than the number for which it is designed and equipped, nor shall any motorcycle be operated on a highway when the handle bars or grips are more than fifteen inches higher than the seat or saddle for the operator.

No person shall operate or be a passenger on a snowmobile or motorcycle without using safety glasses or other protective eye device. No person who is under the age of eighteen years, or who holds a motorcycle operator's endorsement or license bearing a "novice" designation that is currently in effect as provided in section 4507.13 of the Revised Code, shall operate a motorcycle on a highway, or be a passenger on a motorcycle, unless wearing a protective helmet on the person's head, and no other person shall be a passenger on a motorcycle operated by such a person unless similarly wearing a protective helmet. The helmet, safety glasses, or other protective eye device shall conform with regulations prescribed and promulgated by the director of public safety. The provisions of this paragraph or a violation thereof shall not be used in the trial of any civil action.

(C) Except as otherwise provided in this division, whoever violates this section is guilty of a minor misdemeanor. If, within one year of the offense, the offender previously has been convicted of or pleaded guilty to one predicate motor vehicle or traffic offense, whoever violates this section is guilty of a misdemeanor of the fourth degree. If, within one year of the offense, the offender previously has been convicted of two or more predicate motor vehicle or traffic offenses, whoever violates this section is guilty of a misdemeanor of the third degree.

(2002 S 123, eff. 1–1–04; 1992 S 98, eff. 11–12–92; 1978 H 115; 1974 H 995; 1971 H 214; 132 v H 380; 1953 H 1; GC 6307–51)

4511.54 Prohibition against attaching bicycles and sleds to vehicles

(A) No person riding upon any bicycle, coaster, roller skates, sled, or toy vehicle shall attach the same or self to any streetcar, trackless trolley, or vehicle upon a roadway.

No operator shall knowingly permit any person riding upon any bicycle, coaster, roller skates, sled, or toy vehicle to attach the same or self to any streetcar, trackless trolley, or vehicle while it is moving upon a roadway.

This section does not apply to the towing of a disabled vehicle.

(B) Except as otherwise provided in this division, whoever violates this section is guilty of a minor misdemeanor. If, within one year of the offense, the offender previously has been convicted of or pleaded guilty to one predicate motor vehicle or traffic offense, whoever violates this section is guilty of a misdemeanor of the fourth degree. If, within one year of the offense, the offender previously has been convicted of two or more predicate motor vehicle or traffic offenses, whoever violates this section is guilty of a misdemeanor of the third degree.

(2002 S 123, eff. 1–1–04; 1953 H 1, eff. 10–1–53; GC 6307–52)

4511.55 Place and manner of operating bicycles; riding bicycles and motorcycles abreast

(A) Every person operating a bicycle upon a roadway shall ride as near to the right side of the roadway as practicable obeying all traffic rules applicable to vehicles and exercising due care when passing a standing vehicle or one proceeding in the same direction.

(B) Persons riding bicycles or motorcycles upon a roadway shall ride not more than two abreast in a single lane, except on paths or parts of roadways set aside for the exclusive use of bicycles or motorcycles.

(C) Except as otherwise provided in this division, whoever violates this section is guilty of a minor misdemeanor. If, within one year of the offense, the offender previously has been convicted of or pleaded guilty to one predicate motor vehicle or traffic offense, whoever violates this section is guilty of a misdemeanor of the fourth degree. If, within one year of the offense, the offender previously has been convicted of two or more predicate motor vehicle or traffic offenses, whoever violates this section is guilty of a misdemeanor of the third degree.

(2002 S 123, eff. 1–1–04; 1974 H 995, eff. 1–1–75; 1953 H 1; GC 6307–53)

4511.56 Equipment of bicycles

(A) Every bicycle when in use at the times specified in section 4513.03 of the Revised Code, shall be equipped with the following:

(1) A lamp on the front that shall emit a white light visible from a distance of at least five hundred feet to the front;

(2) A red reflector on the rear of a type approved by the director of public safety that shall be visible from all distances from one hundred feet to six hundred feet to the rear when directly in front of lawful lower beams of head lamps on a motor vehicle;

(3) A lamp emitting a red light visible from a distance of five hundred feet to the rear shall be used in addition to the red reflector;

(4) An essentially colorless reflector on the front of a type approved by the director;

(5) Either with tires with retroreflective sidewalls or with an essentially colorless or amber reflector mounted on the spokes of the front wheel and an essentially colorless or red reflector mounted on the spokes of the rear wheel. Each reflector shall be visible on each side of the wheel from a distance of six hundred feet when directly in front of lawful lower beams of head lamps on a motor vehicle. Retroreflective tires or reflectors shall be of a type approved by the director.

(B) No person shall operate a bicycle unless it is equipped with a bell or other device capable of giving a signal audible for a distance of at least one hundred feet, except that a bicycle shall not be equipped with nor shall any person use upon a bicycle any siren or whistle.

(C) Every bicycle shall be equipped with an adequate brake when used on a street or highway.

(D) Except as otherwise provided in this division, whoever violates this section is guilty of a minor misdemeanor. If, within one year of the offense, the offender previously has been convicted of or pleaded guilty to one predicate motor vehicle or traffic offense, whoever violates this section is guilty of a misdemeanor of the fourth degree. If, within one year of the offense, the offender previously has been convicted of two or more predicate motor vehicle or traffic offenses, whoever violates this section is guilty of a misdemeanor of the third degree.

(2002 S 123, eff. 1–1–04; 1992 S 98, eff. 11–12–92; 1988 H 412; 1974 H 995)

4511.57 Passing on left side of streetcar

(A) The driver of a vehicle shall not overtake and pass upon the left nor drive upon the left side of any streetcar proceeding in the same direction, whether such streetcar is in motion or at rest, except:

(1) When so directed by a police officer or traffic control device;

(2) When upon a one-way street;

(3) When upon a street where the tracks are so located as to prevent compliance with this section;

(4) When authorized by local authorities.

(B) The driver of any vehicle when permitted to overtake and pass upon the left of a streetcar which has stopped for the purpose of receiving or discharging any passenger shall accord pedestrians the right of way.

(C) Except as otherwise provided in this division, whoever violates this section is guilty of a minor misdemeanor. If, within one year of the offense, the offender previously has been convicted of or pleaded guilty to one predicate motor vehicle or traffic offense, whoever violates this section is guilty of a misdemeanor of the fourth degree. If, within one year of the offense, the offender previously has been convicted of two or more predicate motor vehicle or traffic offenses, whoever violates this section is guilty of a misdemeanor of the third degree.

(2002 S 123, eff. 1–1–04; 1953 H 1, eff. 10–1–53; GC 6307–55)

4511.58 Vehicle shall not pass streetcar discharging passengers; exception

(A) The driver of a vehicle overtaking upon the right any streetcar stopped for the purpose of receiving or discharging any passenger shall stop such vehicle at least five feet to the rear of the nearest running board or door of such streetcar and remain standing until all passengers have boarded such streetcar, or upon alighting therefrom have reached a place of safety, except that where a safety zone has been established, a vehicle need not be brought to a stop before passing any such streetcar or any trackless trolley, but may proceed past such streetcar or trackless trolley at a speed not greater than is reasonable and proper considering the safety of pedestrians.

(B) Except as otherwise provided in this division, whoever violates this section is guilty of a minor misdemeanor. If, within one year of the offense, the offender previously has been convicted of or pleaded guilty to one predicate motor vehicle or traffic offense, whoever violates this section is guilty of a misdemeanor of the fourth degree. If, within one year of the offense, the offender previously has been convicted of two or more predicate motor vehicle or traffic offenses, whoever violates this section is guilty of a misdemeanor of the third degree.

(2002 S 123, eff. 1–1–04; 1953 H 1, eff. 10–1–53; GC 6307–56)

4511.59 Driving and turning in front of streetcars

(A) The driver of any vehicle proceeding upon any streetcar tracks in front of a streetcar shall remove such vehicle from the track as soon as practicable after signal from the operator of said streetcar.

The driver of a vehicle upon overtaking and passing a streetcar shall not turn in front of such streetcar unless such movement can be made in safety.

(B) Except as otherwise provided in this division, whoever violates this section is guilty of a minor misdemeanor. If, within one year of the offense, the offender previously has been convicted of or pleaded guilty to one predicate motor vehicle or traffic offense, whoever violates this section is guilty of a misdemeanor of the fourth degree. If, within one year of the offense, the offender previously has been convicted of two or more predicate motor vehicle or traffic offenses, whoever violates this section is guilty of a misdemeanor of the third degree.

(2002 S 123, eff. 1–1–04; 1953 H 1, eff. 10–1–53; GC 6307–57)

4511.60 Driving through safety zone

(A) No vehicle shall at any time be driven through or within a safety zone.

(B) Except as otherwise provided in this division, whoever violates this section is guilty of a minor misdemeanor. If, within one year of the offense, the offender previously has been convicted of or pleaded guilty to one predicate motor vehicle or traffic offense, whoever violates this section is guilty of a misdemeanor of the fourth degree. If, within one year of the offense, the offender previously has been convicted of two or more predicate motor vehicle or traffic offenses, whoever violates this section is guilty of a misdemeanor of the third degree.

(2002 S 123, eff. 1–1–04; 1953 H 1, eff. 10–1–53; GC 6307–58)

RAILROAD CROSSINGS

4511.61 Stop signs at grade crossings

(A) The department of transportation and local authorities in their respective jurisdictions, with the approval of the department, may designate dangerous highway crossings over railroad tracks whether on state, county, or township highways or on streets or ways within municipal corporations, and erect stop signs thereat. When such stop signs are erected, the operator of any vehicle, streetcar, or trackless trolley shall stop within fifty, but not less than fifteen, feet from the nearest rail of the railroad tracks and shall exercise due care before proceeding across such grade crossing.

(B) Except as otherwise provided in this division, whoever violates this section is guilty of a minor misdemeanor. If, within one year of the offense, the offender previously has been convicted of or pleaded guilty to one predicate motor vehicle or traffic offense, whoever violates this section is guilty of a misdemeanor of the fourth degree. If, within one year of the offense, the offender previously has been convicted of two or more predicate motor vehicle or traffic offenses, whoever violates this section is guilty of a misdemeanor of the third degree.

(2002 S 123, eff. 1–1–04; 1973 S 171, eff. 10–31–73; 1973 H 200; 127 v 887; 1953 H 1; GC 6307–59)

4511.62 Driving across railroad grade crossings

(A)(1) Whenever any person driving a vehicle or trackless trolley approaches a railroad grade crossing, the person shall stop within fifty feet, but not less than fifteen feet from the nearest rail of the railroad if any of the following circumstances exist at the crossing:

(a) A clearly visible electric or mechanical signal device gives warning of the immediate approach of a train.

(b) A crossing gate is lowered.

(c) A flagperson gives or continues to give a signal of the approach or passage of a train.

(d) There is insufficient space on the other side of the railroad grade crossing to accommodate the vehicle or trackless trolley the person is operating without obstructing the passage of other vehicles, trackless trolleys, pedestrians, or railroad trains, notwithstanding any traffic control signal indication to proceed.

(e) An approaching train is emitting an audible signal or is plainly visible and is in hazardous proximity to the crossing.

(f) There is insufficient undercarriage clearance to safely negotiate the crossing.

(2) A person who is driving a vehicle or trackless trolley and who approaches a railroad grade crossing shall not proceed as long as any of the circumstances described in divisions (A)(1)(a) to (f) of this section exist at the crossing.

(B) No person shall drive any vehicle through, around, or under any crossing gate or barrier at a railroad crossing while the gate or barrier is closed or is being opened or closed unless the person is signaled by a law enforcement officer or flagperson that it is permissible to do so.

(C) Whoever violates this section is guilty of a misdemeanor of the fourth degree.

(2003 H 95, § 3.13, eff. 1–1–04; 2003 H 95, § 1, eff. 9–26–03; 2002 S 123, eff. 1–1–04; 1997 S 60, eff. 10–21–97; 1974 H 995, eff. 1–1–75; 1953 H 1; GC 6307–60)

4511.63 Vehicles required to stop at grade crossings

Note: See also following version of this section, eff. 5–18–05.

(A) The operator of any bus, any vehicle described in division (C) of this section, or any vehicle transporting a material or materials required to be placarded under 49 C.F.R. Parts 100–185, before crossing at grade any track of a railroad, shall stop the vehicle and, while so stopped, shall listen through an open door or open window and look in both directions along the track for any approaching train, and for signals indicating the approach of a train, and shall proceed only upon exercising due care after stopping, looking, and listening as required by this section. Upon proceeding, the operator of such a vehicle shall cross only in a gear that will ensure there will be no necessity for changing gears while traversing the crossing and shall not shift gears while crossing the tracks.

(B) This section does not apply at any street railway grade crossings within a municipal corporation, or to abandoned tracks, spur tracks, side tracks, and industrial tracks when the public utilities commission has authorized and approved the crossing of the tracks without making the stop required by this section.

(C) This section applies to any vehicle used for the transportation of pupils to and from a school or school-related function if the vehicle is owned or operated by, or operated under contract with, a public or nonpublic school.

(D) For purposes of this section, "bus" means any vehicle originally designed by its manufacturer to transport sixteen or more passengers, including the driver, or carries sixteen or more passengers, including the driver.

(E) Except as otherwise provided in this division, whoever violates this section is guilty of a minor misdemeanor. If the offender previously has been convicted of or pleaded guilty to one or more violations of this section or section 4511.76, 4511.761, 4511.762, 4511.764, 4511.77, or 4511.79 of the Revised Code or a municipal ordinance that is substantially similar to any of those sections, whoever violates this section is guilty of a misdemeanor of the fourth degree.

(2003 H 95, § 3.13, eff. 1–1–04; 2003 H 95, § 1, eff. 9–26–03; 2002 S 123, eff. 1–1–04; 1993 H 154, eff. 6–30–93; 125 v 903; 1953 H 1; GC 6307–61)

Note: See also following version of this section, eff. 5–18–05.

4511.63 Vehicles required to stop at grade crossings; application for exempt crossing; rescission of exempt crossing designation (later effective date)

Note: See also preceding version of this section, in effect until 5–18–05.

(A) Except as provided in division (B) of this section, the operator of any bus, any school vehicle, or any vehicle transporting a material or materials required to be placarded under 49 C.F.R. Parts 100–185, before crossing at grade any track of a railroad, shall stop the vehicle and, while so stopped, shall listen through an open door or open window and look in both directions along the track for any approaching train, and for signals indicating the approach of a train, and shall proceed only upon exercising due care after stopping, looking, and listening as required by this section. Upon proceeding, the operator of such a vehicle shall cross only in a gear that will ensure there will be no necessity for changing gears while traversing the crossing and shall not shift gears while crossing the tracks.

(B) This section does not apply at grade crossings when the public utilities commission has authorized and approved an exempt crossing as provided in this division.

(1) Any local authority may file an application with the commission requesting the approval of an exempt crossing. Upon receipt of such a request, the commission shall authorize a limited period for the filing of comments by any party regarding the application and then shall conduct a public hearing in the community seeking the exempt crossing designation. The commission shall provide appropriate prior public notice of the comment period and the public hearing. By registered mail, the commission shall notify each railroad operating over the crossing of the comment period.

(2) After considering any comments or other information received, the commission may approve or reject the application. By order, the commission may establish conditions for the exempt crossing designation, including compliance with division (b) of 49 C.F.R. Part 392.10, when applicable. An exempt crossing designation becomes effective only when appropriate signs giving notice of the exempt designation are erected at the crossing as ordered by the commission and any other conditions ordered by the commission are satisfied.

(3) By order, the commission may rescind any exempt crossing designation made under this section if the commission finds that a condition at the exempt crossing has changed to such an extent that the continuation of the exempt crossing designation compromises public safety. The commission may conduct a public hearing to investigate and determine whether to rescind the exempt crossing designation. If the commission rescinds the designation, it shall order the removal of any exempt crossing signs and may make any other necessary order.

(C) As used in this section:

(1) "School vehicle" means any vehicle used for the transportation of pupils to and from a school or school-related function if

the vehicle is owned or operated by, or operated under contract with, a public or nonpublic school.

(2) "Bus" means any vehicle originally designed by its manufacturer to transport sixteen or more passengers, including the driver, or carries sixteen or more passengers, including the driver.

(3) "Exempt crossing" means a highway rail grade crossing authorized and approved by the public utilities commission under division (B) of this section at which vehicles may cross without making the stop otherwise required by this section.

(D) Except as otherwise provided in this division, whoever violates this section is guilty of a minor misdemeanor. If the offender previously has been convicted of or pleaded guilty to one or more violations of this section or section 4511.76, 4511.761, 4511.762, 4511.764, 4511.77, or 4511.79 of the Revised Code or a municipal ordinance that is substantially similar to any of those sections, whoever violates this section is guilty of a misdemeanor of the fourth degree.

(2004 S 156, eff. 5–18–05; 2003 H 95, § 3.13, eff. 1–1–04; 2003 H 95, § 1, eff. 9–26–03; 2002 S 123, eff. 1–1–04; 1993 H 154, eff. 6–30–93; 125 v 903; 1953 H 1; GC 6307–61)

Note: See also preceding version of this section, in effect until 5–18–05.

4511.64 Slow-moving vehicles or equipment crossing railroad tracks

(A) No person shall operate or move any crawler-type tractor, steam shovel, derrick, roller, or any equipment or structure having a normal operating speed of six or less miles per hour or a vertical body or load clearance of less than nine inches above the level surface of a roadway, upon or across any tracks at a railroad grade crossing without first complying with divisions (A)(1) and (2) of this section.

(1) Before making any such crossing, the person operating or moving any such vehicle or equipment shall first stop the same, and while stopped the person shall listen and look in both directions along such track for any approaching train and for signals indicating the approach of a train, and shall proceed only upon exercising due care.

(2) No such crossing shall be made when warning is given by automatic signal or crossing gates or a flagperson or otherwise of the immediate approach of a railroad train or car.

(B) If the normal sustained speed of such vehicle, equipment, or structure is not more than three miles per hour, the person owning, operating, or moving the same shall also give notice of such intended crossing to a station agent or superintendent of the railroad, and a reasonable time shall be given to such railroad to provide proper protection for such crossing. Where such vehicles or equipment are being used in constructing or repairing a section of highway lying on both sides of a railroad grade crossing, and in such construction or repair it is necessary to repeatedly move such vehicles or equipment over such crossing, one daily notice specifying when such work will start and stating the hours during which it will be prosecuted is sufficient.

(C) Except as otherwise provided in this division, whoever violates this section is guilty of a minor misdemeanor. If, within one year of the offense, the offender previously has been convicted of or pleaded guilty to one predicate motor vehicle or traffic offense, whoever violates this section is guilty of a misdemeanor of the fourth degree. If, within one year of the offense, the offender previously has been convicted of two or more predicate motor vehicle or traffic offenses, whoever violates this section is guilty of a misdemeanor of the third degree.

(2002 S 123, eff. 1–1–04; 1953 H 1, eff. 10–1–53; GC 6307–62)

HIGHWAYS

4511.65 Through highways; manner of designation

(A) All state routes are hereby designated as through highways, provided that stop signs, yield signs, or traffic control signals shall be erected at all intersections with such through highways by the department of transportation as to highways under its jurisdiction and by local authorities as to highways under their jurisdiction, except as otherwise provided in this section. Where two or more state routes that are through highways intersect and no traffic control signal is in operation, stop signs or yield signs shall be erected at one or more entrances thereto by the department, except as otherwise provided in this section.

Whenever the director of transportation determines on the basis of an engineering and traffic investigation that stop signs are necessary to stop traffic on a through highway for safe and efficient operation, nothing in this section shall be construed to prevent such installations. When circumstances warrant, the director also may omit stop signs on roadways intersecting through highways under his jurisdiction. Before the director either installs or removes a stop sign under this division, he shall give notice, in writing, of that proposed action to the affected local authority at least thirty days before installing or removing the stop sign.

(B) Other streets or highways, or portions thereof, are hereby designated through highways if they are within a municipal corporation, if they have a continuous length of more than one mile between the limits of said street or highway or portion thereof, and if they have "stop" or "yield" signs or traffic control signals at the entrances of the majority of intersecting streets or highways. For purposes of this section, the limits of said street or highway or portion thereof shall be a municipal corporation line, the physical terminus of the street or highway, or any point on said street or highway at which vehicular traffic thereon is required by regulatory signs to stop or yield to traffic on the intersecting street, provided that in residence districts a municipal corporation may by ordinance designate said street or highway, or portion thereof, not to be a through highway and thereafter the affected residence district shall be indicated by official traffic control devices. Where two or more through highways designated under this division intersect and no traffic control signal is in operation, stop signs or yield signs shall be erected at one or more entrances thereto by the department or by local authorities having jurisdiction, except as otherwise provided in this section.

(C) The department or local authorities having jurisdiction need not erect stop signs at intersections they find to be so constructed as to permit traffic to safely enter a through highway without coming to a stop. Signs shall be erected at such intersections indicating that the operator of a vehicle shall yield the right-of-way to or merge with all traffic proceeding on the through highway.

(D) Local authorities with reference to highways under their jurisdiction may designate additional through highways and shall erect stop signs, yield signs, or traffic control signals at all streets and highways intersecting such through highways, or may designate any intersection as a stop or yield intersection and shall erect like signs at one or more entrances to such intersection.

(1989 H 258, eff. 11–2–89; 1979 H 290; 1975 H 21; 1973 H 200; 131 v S 78; 128 v 1270; 1953 H 1; GC 6307–63)

PARKING

4511.66 Prohibition against parking on highways

(A) Upon any highway outside a business or residence district, no person shall stop, park, or leave standing any vehicle, whether attended or unattended, upon the paved or main traveled part of the highway if it is practicable to stop, park, or so leave such vehicle off the paved or main traveled part of said highway. In every event a clear and unobstructed portion of the highway opposite such standing vehicle shall be left for the free passage of other vehicles, and a clear view of such stopped vehicle shall be available from a distance of two hundred feet in each direction upon such highway.

This section does not apply to the driver of any vehicle which is disabled while on the paved or improved or main traveled portion of a highway in such manner and to such extent that it is impossible to avoid stopping and temporarily leaving the disabled vehicle in such position.

(B) Except as otherwise provided in this division, whoever violates this section is guilty of a minor misdemeanor. If, within one year of the offense, the offender previously has been convicted of or pleaded guilty to one predicate motor vehicle or traffic offense, whoever violates this section is guilty of a misdemeanor of the fourth degree. If, within one year of the offense, the offender previously has been convicted of two or more predicate motor vehicle or traffic offenses, whoever violates this section is guilty of a misdemeanor of the third degree.

(2002 S 123, eff. 1–1–04; 1953 H 1, eff. 10–1–53; GC 6307–64)

4511.661 Requirements when leaving motor vehicle unattended; exceptions

(A) No person driving or in charge of a motor vehicle shall permit it to stand unattended without first stopping the engine, locking the ignition, removing the key from the ignition, effectively setting the parking brake, and, when the motor vehicle is standing upon any grade, turning the front wheels to the curb or side of the highway.

The requirements of this section relating to the stopping of the engine, locking of the ignition, and removing the key from the ignition of a motor vehicle shall not apply to an emergency vehicle or a public safety vehicle.

(B) Except as otherwise provided in this division, whoever violates this section is guilty of a minor misdemeanor. If, within one year of the offense, the offender previously has been convicted of or pleaded guilty to one predicate motor vehicle or traffic offense, whoever violates this section is guilty of a misdemeanor of the fourth degree. If, within one year of the offense, the offender previously has been convicted of two or more predicate motor vehicle or traffic offenses, whoever violates this section is guilty of a misdemeanor of the third degree.

(2002 S 123, eff. 1–1–04; 1976 H 763, eff. 8–6–76; 1974 H 995)

4511.67 Police may remove illegally parked vehicle

Whenever any police officer finds a vehicle standing upon a highway in violation of section 4511.66 of the Revised Code, such officer may move such vehicle, or require the driver or other person in charge of the vehicle to move the same, to a position off the paved or improved or main traveled part of such highway.

Whenever any police officer finds a vehicle unattended upon any highway, bridge, or causeway, or in any tunnel, where such vehicle constitutes an obstruction to traffic, such officer may provide for the removal of such vehicle to the nearest garage or other place of safety.

(1953 H 1, eff. 10–1–53; GC 6307–65)

4511.68 Parking prohibitions

(A) No person shall stand or park a trackless trolley or vehicle, except when necessary to avoid conflict with other traffic or to comply with sections 4511.01 to 4511.78, 4511.99, and 4513.01 to 4513.37 of the Revised Code, or while obeying the directions of a police officer or a traffic control device, in any of the following places:

(1) On a sidewalk, except a bicycle;

(2) In front of a public or private driveway;

(3) Within an intersection;

(4) Within ten feet of a fire hydrant;

(5) On a crosswalk;

(6) Within twenty feet of a crosswalk at an intersection;

(7) Within thirty feet of, and upon the approach to, any flashing beacon, stop sign, or traffic control device;

(8) Between a safety zone and the adjacent curb or within thirty feet of points on the curb immediately opposite the ends of a safety zone, unless a different length is indicated by a traffic control device;

(9) Within fifty feet of the nearest rail of a railroad crossing;

(10) Within twenty feet of a driveway entrance to any fire station and, on the side of the street opposite the entrance to any fire station, within seventy-five feet of the entrance when it is properly posted with signs;

(11) Alongside or opposite any street excavation or obstruction when such standing or parking would obstruct traffic;

(12) Alongside any vehicle stopped or parked at the edge or curb of a street;

(13) Upon any bridge or elevated structure upon a highway, or within a highway tunnel;

(14) At any place where signs prohibit stopping;

(15) Within one foot of another parked vehicle;

(16) On the roadway portion of a freeway, expressway, or thruway.

(B) Except as otherwise provided in this division, whoever violates this section is guilty of a minor misdemeanor. If, within one year of the offense, the offender previously has been convicted of or pleaded guilty to one predicate motor vehicle or traffic offense, whoever violates this section is guilty of a misdemeanor of the fourth degree. If, within one year of the offense, the offender previously has been convicted of two or more predicate motor vehicle or traffic offenses, whoever violates this section is guilty of a misdemeanor of the third degree.

(2002 S 123, eff. 1–1–04; 130 v S 70, eff. 8–5–63; 1953 H 1; GC 6307–66)

4511.681 Parking on private property in violation of posted prohibition or restriction

(A) If an owner of private property posts on the property, in a conspicuous manner, a prohibition against parking on the property or conditions and regulations under which parking is permitted, no person shall do either of the following:

(1) Park a vehicle on the property without the owner's consent;

(2) Park a vehicle on the property in violation of any condition or regulation posted by the owner.

(B) Whoever violates this section is guilty of a minor misdemeanor.

(2002 S 123, eff. 1–1–04; 1984 H 112, eff. 10–4–84; 1982 H 707)

4511.69 Parking near curb; privileges of vehicle registered to handicapped person; privately owned lots; special parking locations for handicapped to be marked

(A) Every vehicle stopped or parked upon a roadway where there is an adjacent curb shall be stopped or parked with the right-hand wheels of the vehicle parallel with and not more than twelve inches from the right-hand curb, unless it is impossible to approach so close to the curb; in such case the stop shall be made as close to the curb as possible and only for the time necessary to discharge and receive passengers or to load or unload merchandise. Local authorities by ordinance may permit angle parking on any roadway under their jurisdiction, except that angle parking shall not be permitted on a state route within a municipal corporation unless an unoccupied roadway width of not less than twenty-five feet is available for free-moving traffic.

(B) Local authorities by ordinance may permit parking of vehicles with the left-hand wheels adjacent to and within twelve inches of the left-hand curb of a one-way roadway.

(C) No vehicle or trackless trolley shall be stopped or parked on a road or highway with the vehicle or trackless trolley facing in a direction other than the direction of travel on that side of the road or highway.

(D) Notwithstanding any statute or any rule, resolution, or ordinance adopted by any local authority, air compressors, tractors, trucks, and other equipment, while being used in the construction, reconstruction, installation, repair, or removal of facilities near, on, over, or under a street or highway, may stop, stand, or park where necessary in order to perform such work, provided a flagperson is on duty or warning signs or lights are displayed as may be prescribed by the director of transportation.

(E) Special parking locations and privileges for persons with disabilities that limit or impair the ability to walk, also known as handicapped parking spaces or disability parking spaces, shall be provided and designated by all political subdivisions and by the state and all agencies and instrumentalities thereof at all offices and facilities, where parking is provided, whether owned, rented, or leased, and at all publicly owned parking garages. The locations shall be designated through the posting of an elevated sign, whether permanently affixed or movable, imprinted with the international symbol of access and shall be reasonably close to exits, entrances, elevators, and ramps. All elevated signs posted in accordance with this division and division (C) of section 3781.111 of the Revised Code shall be mounted on a fixed or movable post, and the distance from the ground to the top edge of the sign shall measure five feet. If a new sign or a replacement sign designating a special parking location is posted on or after October 14, 1999, there also shall be affixed upon the surface of that sign or affixed next to the designating sign a notice that states the fine applicable for the offense of parking a motor vehicle in the special designated parking location if the motor vehicle is not legally entitled to be parked in that location.

(F)(1) No person shall stop, stand, or park any motor vehicle at special parking locations provided under division (E) of this section or at special clearly marked parking locations provided in or on privately owned parking lots, parking garages, or other parking areas and designated in accordance with that division, unless one of the following applies:

(a) The motor vehicle is being operated by or for the transport of a person with a disability that limits or impairs the ability to walk and is displaying a valid removable windshield placard or special license plates;

(b) The motor vehicle is being operated by or for the transport of a handicapped person and is displaying a parking card or special handicapped license plates.

(2) Any motor vehicle that is parked in a special marked parking location in violation of division (F)(1)(a) or (b) of this section may be towed or otherwise removed from the parking location by the law enforcement agency of the political subdivision in which the parking location is located. A motor vehicle that is so towed or removed shall not be released to its owner until the owner presents proof of ownership of the motor vehicle and pays all towing and storage fees normally imposed by that political subdivision for towing and storing motor vehicles. If the motor vehicle is a leased vehicle, it shall not be released to the lessee until the lessee presents proof that that person is the lessee of the motor vehicle and pays all towing and storage fees normally imposed by that political subdivision for towing and storing motor vehicles.

(3) If a person is charged with a violation of division (F)(1)(a) or (b) of this section, it is an affirmative defense to the charge that the person suffered an injury not more than seventy-two hours prior to the time the person was issued the ticket or citation and that, because of the injury, the person meets at least one of the criteria contained in division (A)(1) of section 4503.44 of the Revised Code.

(G) When a motor vehicle is being operated by or for the transport of a person with a disability that limits or impairs the ability to walk and is displaying a removable windshield placard or a temporary removable windshield placard or special license plates, or when a motor vehicle is being operated by or for the transport of a handicapped person and is displaying a parking card or special handicapped license plates, the motor vehicle is permitted to park for a period of two hours in excess of the legal parking period permitted by local authorities, except where local ordinances or police rules provide otherwise or where the vehicle is parked in such a manner as to be clearly a traffic hazard.

(H) No owner of an office, facility, or parking garage where special parking locations are required to be designated in accordance with division (E) of this section shall fail to properly mark the special parking locations in accordance with that division or fail to maintain the markings of the special locations, including the erection and maintenance of the fixed or movable signs.

(I) Nothing in this section shall be construed to require a person or organization to apply for a removable windshield placard or special license plates if the parking card or special license plates issued to the person or organization under prior law have not expired or been surrendered or revoked.

(J)(1) Whoever violates division (A) or (C) of this section is guilty of a minor misdemeanor.

(2)(a) Whoever violates division (F)(1)(a) or (b) of this section is guilty of a misdemeanor and shall be punished as provided in division (J)(2)(a) and (b) of this section. Except as otherwise provided in division (J)(2)(a) of this section, an offender who violates division (F)(1)(a) or (b) of this section shall be fined not less than two hundred fifty nor more than five hundred dollars. An offender who violates division (F)(1)(a) or (b) of this section shall be fined not more than one hundred dollars if the offender, prior to sentencing, proves either of the following to the satisfaction of the court:

(i) At the time of the violation of division (F)(1)(a) of this section, the offender or the person for whose transport the motor vehicle was being operated had been issued a removable windshield placard that then was valid or special license plates that then were valid but the offender or the person neglected to display the placard or license plates as described in division (F)(1)(a) of this section.

(ii) At the time of the violation of division (F)(1)(b) of this section, the offender or the person for whose transport the motor vehicle was being operated had been issued a parking card that then was valid or special handicapped license plates that then were valid but the offender or the person neglected to display the card or license plates as described in division (F)(1)(b) of this section.

(b) In no case shall an offender who violates division (F)(1)(a) or (b) of this section be sentenced to any term of imprisonment.

An arrest or conviction for a violation of division (F)(1)(a) or (b) of this section does not constitute a criminal record and need not be reported by the person so arrested or convicted in response to any inquiries contained in any application for employment, license, or other right or privilege, or made in connection with the person's appearance as a witness.

The clerk of the court shall pay every fine collected under division (J)(2) of this section to the political subdivision in which the violation occurred. Except as provided in division (J)(2) of this section, the political subdivision shall use the fine moneys it receives under division (J)(2) of this section to pay the expenses it incurs in complying with the signage and notice requirements contained in division (E) of this section. The political subdivision may use up to fifty per cent of each fine it receives under division (J)(2) of this section to pay the costs of educational, advocacy, support, and assistive technology programs for persons with disabilities, and for public improvements within the political subdivision that benefit or assist persons with disabilities, if governmental agencies or nonprofit organizations offer the programs.

(3) Whoever violates division (H) of this section shall be punished as follows:

(a) Except as otherwise provided in division (J)(3) of this section, the offender shall be issued a warning.

(b) If the offender previously has been convicted of or pleaded guilty to a violation of division (H) of this section or of a municipal ordinance that is substantially similar to that division, the offender shall not be issued a warning but shall be fined not more than twenty-five dollars for each parking location that is not properly marked or whose markings are not properly maintained.

(K) As used in this section:

(1) "Handicapped person" means any person who has lost the use of one or both legs or one or both arms, who is blind, deaf, or so severely handicapped as to be unable to move without the aid of crutches or a wheelchair, or whose mobility is restricted by a permanent cardiovascular, pulmonary, or other handicapping condition.

(2) "Person with a disability that limits or impairs the ability to walk" has the same meaning as in section 4503.44 of the Revised Code.

(3) "Special license plates" and "removable windshield placard" mean any license plates or removable windshield placard or temporary removable windshield placard issued under section 4503.41 or 4503.44 of the Revised Code, and also mean any substantially similar license plates or removable windshield placard or temporary removable windshield placard issued by a state, district, country, or sovereignty.

(2002 H 490, eff. 1–1–04; 2002 S 123, eff. 1–1–04; 1999 H 148, eff. 10–14–99; 1994 H 687, eff. 1–1–95; 1992 S 98, eff. 11–12–92; 1991 H 73; 1988 H 111; 1983 H 174; 1982 H 116, H 48; 1981 H 1; 1977 H 652; 1976 S 162; 1973 H 200; 1953 H 1; GC 6307–67)

PROHIBITIONS

4511.70 Obstruction and interference affecting view and control of driver; opening door on traffic side

(A) No person shall drive a vehicle or trackless trolley when it is so loaded, or when there are in the front seat such number of persons, as to obstruct the view of the driver to the front or sides of the vehicle or to interfere with the driver's control over the driving mechanism of the vehicle.

(B) No passenger in a vehicle or trackless trolley shall ride in such position as to interfere with the driver's view ahead or to the sides, or to interfere with the driver's control over the driving mechanism of the vehicle.

(C) No person shall open the door of a vehicle on the side available to moving traffic unless and until it is reasonably safe to do so, and can be done without interfering with the movement of other traffic, nor shall any person leave a door open on the side of a vehicle available to moving traffic for a period of time longer than necessary to load or unload passengers.

(D) Except as otherwise provided in this division, whoever violates this section is guilty of a minor misdemeanor. If, within one year of the offense, the offender previously has been convicted of or pleaded guilty to one predicate motor vehicle or traffic offense, whoever violates this section is guilty of a misdemeanor of the fourth degree. If, within one year of the offense, the offender previously has been convicted of two or more predicate motor vehicle or traffic offenses, whoever violates this section is guilty of a misdemeanor of the third degree.

(2002 S 123, eff. 1–1–04; 1974 H 995, eff. 1–1–75; 1953 H 1; GC 6307–68)

4511.701 Prohibition against occupancy of trailer or manufactured or mobile home while in motion

(A) No person shall occupy any travel trailer or manufactured or mobile home while it is being used as a conveyance upon a street or highway.

(B) Except as otherwise provided in this division, whoever violates this section is guilty of a minor misdemeanor. If, within one year of the offense, the offender previously has been convicted of or pleaded guilty to one predicate motor vehicle or traffic offense, whoever violates this section is guilty of a misdemeanor of the fourth degree. If, within one year of the offense, the offender previously has been convicted of two or more predicate motor vehicle or traffic offenses, whoever violates this section is guilty of a misdemeanor of the third degree.

(2002 S 123, eff. 1–1–04; 1998 S 142, eff. 3–30–99; 1984 S 231, eff. 9–20–84; 1973 S 205)

4511.71 Prohibition against driving upon closed highway

(A) No person shall drive upon, along, or across a street or highway, or any part of a street or highway that has been closed in the process of its construction, reconstruction, or repair, and posted with appropriate signs by the authority having jurisdiction to close such highway.

(B) Except as otherwise provided in this division, whoever violates this section is guilty of a minor misdemeanor. If, within one year of the offense, the offender previously has been convicted of or pleaded guilty to one predicate motor vehicle or traffic offense, whoever violates this section is guilty of a misdemeanor of the fourth degree. If, within one year of the offense, the offender previously has been convicted of two or more predicate motor vehicle or traffic offenses, whoever violates this section is guilty of a misdemeanor of the third degree.

(2002 S 123, eff. 1–1–04; 1953 H 1, eff. 10–1–53; GC 6307–69)

4511.711 Driving upon sidewalks

(A) No person shall drive any vehicle, other than a bicycle, upon a sidewalk or sidewalk area except upon a permanent or duly authorized temporary driveway.

Nothing in this section shall be construed as prohibiting local authorities from regulating the operation of bicycles within their respective jurisdictions.

(B) Except as otherwise provided in this division, whoever violates this section is guilty of a minor misdemeanor. If, within one year of the offense, the offender previously has been convicted of or pleaded guilty to one predicate motor vehicle or traffic offense, whoever violates this section is guilty of a misdemeanor of the fourth degree. If, within one year of the offense, the offender previously has been convicted of two or more predicate motor vehicle or traffic offenses, whoever violates this section is guilty of a misdemeanor of the third degree.

(2002 S 123, eff. 1–1–04; 1976 S 56, eff. 5–25–76; 1974 H 995)

4511.712 Obstructing intersection, crosswalk, grade crossing

(A) No driver shall enter an intersection or marked crosswalk or drive onto any railroad grade crossing unless there is sufficient space on the other side of the intersection, crosswalk, or grade crossing to accommodate the vehicle, streetcar, or trackless trolley the driver is operating without obstructing the passage of other vehicles, streetcars, trackless trolleys, pedestrians, or railroad trains, notwithstanding any traffic control signal indication to proceed.

(B) Except as otherwise provided in this division, whoever violates this section is guilty of a minor misdemeanor. If, within one year of the offense, the offender previously has been convicted of or pleaded guilty to one predicate motor vehicle or traffic offense, whoever violates this section is guilty of a misdemeanor of the fourth degree. If, within one year of the offense, the offender previously has been convicted of two or more predicate motor vehicle or traffic offenses, whoever violates this section is guilty of a misdemeanor of the third degree.

(2002 S 123, eff. 1–1–04; 1974 H 995, eff. 1–1–75)

4511.713 Prohibition against operation of motor vehicles on bicycle paths

(A) No person shall operate a motor vehicle, snowmobile, or all-purpose vehicle upon any path set aside for the exclusive use of bicycles, when an appropriate sign giving notice of such use is posted on the path.

Nothing in this section shall be construed to affect any rule of the director of natural resources governing the operation of motor vehicles, snowmobiles, all-purpose vehicles, and bicycles on lands under the director's jurisdiction.

(B) Except as otherwise provided in this division, whoever violates this section is guilty of a minor misdemeanor. If, within one year of the offense, the offender previously has been convicted of or pleaded guilty to one predicate motor vehicle or traffic offense, whoever violates this section is guilty of a misdemeanor of the fourth degree. If, within one year of the offense, the offender previously has been convicted of two or more predicate motor vehicle or traffic offenses, whoever violates this section is guilty of a misdemeanor of the third degree.

(2002 S 123, eff. 1–1–04; 1986 H 311, eff. 3–11–87)

4511.72 Following an emergency vehicle or a public safety vehicle prohibited

(A) The driver of any vehicle, other than an emergency vehicle or public safety vehicle on official business, shall not follow any emergency vehicle or public safety vehicle traveling in response to an alarm closer than five hundred feet, or drive into or park such vehicle within the block where fire apparatus has stopped in answer to a fire alarm, unless directed to do so by a police officer or a firefighter.

(B) Except as otherwise provided in this division, whoever violates this section is guilty of a minor misdemeanor. If, within one year of the offense, the offender previously has been convicted of or pleaded guilty to one predicate motor vehicle or traffic offense, whoever violates this section is guilty of a misdemeanor of the fourth degree. If, within one year of the offense, the offender previously has been convicted of two or more predicate motor vehicle or traffic offenses, whoever violates this section is guilty of a misdemeanor of the third degree.

(2002 S 123, eff. 1–1–04; 132 v H 878, eff. 12–14–67; 1953 H 1; GC 6307–70)

4511.73 Driving over unprotected fire hose

(A) No streetcar, trackless trolley, or vehicle shall, without the consent of the fire department official in command, be driven over any unprotected hose of a fire department that is laid down on any street, private driveway, or streetcar track to be used at any fire or alarm of fire.

(B) Except as otherwise provided in this division, whoever violates this section is guilty of a minor misdemeanor. If, within one year of the offense, the offender previously has been convicted of or pleaded guilty to one predicate motor vehicle or traffic offense, whoever violates this section is guilty of a misdemeanor of the fourth degree. If, within one year of the offense, the offender previously has been convicted of two or more predicate motor vehicle or traffic offenses, whoever violates this section is guilty of a misdemeanor of the third degree.

(2002 S 123, eff. 1–1–04; 1953 H 1, eff. 10–1–53; GC 6307–71)

4511.74 Prohibition against placing injurious material on highway

(A) No person shall place or knowingly drop upon any part of a highway, lane, road, street, or alley any tacks, bottles, wire, glass, nails, or other articles which may damage or injure any person, vehicle, streetcar, trackless trolley, or animal traveling along or upon such highway, except such substances that may be placed upon the roadway by proper authority for the repair or construction thereof.

Any person who drops or permits to be dropped or thrown upon any highway any destructive or injurious material shall immediately remove the same.

Any person authorized to remove a wrecked or damaged vehicle, streetcar, or trackless trolley from a highway shall remove any glass or other injurious substance dropped upon the highway from such vehicle, streetcar, or trackless trolley.

No person shall place any obstruction in or upon a highway without proper authority.

(B) No person, with intent to cause physical harm to a person or a vehicle, shall place or knowingly drop upon any part of a highway, lane, road, street, or alley any tacks, bottles, wire, glass, nails, or other articles which may damage or injure any person, vehicle, streetcar, trackless trolley, or animal traveling along or upon such highway, except such substances that may be placed upon the roadway by proper authority for the repair or construction thereof.

(C)(1) Except as otherwise provided in this division, whoever violates division (A) of this section is guilty of a minor misdemeanor. If, within one year of the offense, the offender previously has been convicted of or pleaded guilty to one predicate motor vehicle or traffic offense, whoever violates division (A) of this section is guilty of a misdemeanor of the fourth degree. If, within one year of the offense, the offender previously has been convicted of two or more predicate motor vehicle or traffic offenses, whoever violates division (A) of this section is guilty of a misdemeanor of the third degree.

(2) Whoever violates division (B) of this section is guilty of a misdemeanor of the first degree.

(2002 S 123, eff. 1–1–04; 1983 H 133, eff. 9–27–83; 1953 H 1; GC 6307–72)

TRANSPORTATION OF SCHOOL CHILDREN

4511.75 Stopping for school bus; signals on bus

(A) The driver of a vehicle, streetcar, or trackless trolley upon meeting or overtaking from either direction any school bus stopped for the purpose of receiving or discharging any school child, person attending programs offered by community boards of mental health and county boards of mental retardation and developmental disabilities, or child attending a program offered by a head start agency, shall stop at least ten feet from the front or rear of the school bus and shall not proceed until such school bus resumes motion, or until signaled by the school bus driver to proceed.

It is no defense to a charge under this division that the school bus involved failed to display or be equipped with an automatically extended stop warning sign as required by division (B) of this section.

(B) Every school bus shall be equipped with amber and red visual signals meeting the requirements of section 4511.771 of the Revised Code, and an automatically extended stop warning sign of a type approved by the state board of education, which shall be actuated by the driver of the bus whenever but only whenever the bus is stopped or stopping on the roadway for the purpose of receiving or discharging school children, persons attending programs offered by community boards of mental health and county boards of mental retardation and developmental disabilities, or children attending programs offered by head start agencies. A school bus driver shall not actuate the visual signals or the stop warning sign in designated school bus loading areas where the bus is entirely off the roadway or at school buildings when children or persons attending programs offered by community boards of mental health and county boards of mental retardation and developmental disabilities are loading or unloading at curbside or at buildings when children attending programs offered by head start agencies are loading or unloading at curbside. The visual signals and stop warning sign shall be synchronized or otherwise operated as required by rule of the board.

(C) Where a highway has been divided into four or more traffic lanes, a driver of a vehicle, streetcar, or trackless trolley need not stop for a school bus approaching from the opposite direction which has stopped for the purpose of receiving or discharging any school child, persons attending programs offered by community boards of mental health and county boards of mental retardation and developmental disabilities, or children attending programs offered by head start agencies. The driver of any vehicle, streetcar, or trackless trolley overtaking the school bus shall comply with division (A) of this section.

(D) School buses operating on divided highways or on highways with four or more traffic lanes shall receive and discharge all school children, persons attending programs offered by community boards of mental health and county boards of mental retardation and developmental disabilities, and children attending programs offered by head start agencies on their residence side of the highway.

(E) No school bus driver shall start the driver's bus until after any child, person attending programs offered by community boards of mental health and county boards of mental retardation and developmental disabilities, or child attending a program offered by a head start agency who may have alighted therefrom has reached a place of safety on the child's or person's residence side of the road.

(F)(1) Whoever violates division (A) of this section may be fined an amount not to exceed five hundred dollars. A person who is issued a citation for a violation of division (A) of this section is not permitted to enter a written plea of guilty and waive the person's right to contest the citation in a trial but instead must appear in person in the proper court to answer the charge.

(2) In addition to and independent of any other penalty provided by law, the court or mayor may impose upon an offender who violates this section a class seven suspension of the offender's driver's license, commercial driver's license, temporary instruction permit, probationary license, or nonresident operating privilege from the range specified in division (A)(7) of section 4510.02 of the Revised Code. When a license is suspended under this section, the court or mayor shall cause the offender to deliver the license to the court, and the court or clerk of the court immediately shall forward the license to the registrar of motor vehicles, together with notice of the court's action.

(G) As used in this section:

(1) "Head start agency" has the same meaning as in section 3301.31 of the Revised Code.

(2) "School bus," as used in relation to children who attend a program offered by a head start agency, means a bus that is owned and operated by a head start agency, is equipped with an automatically extended stop warning sign of a type approved by the state board of education, is painted the color and displays the markings described in section 4511.77 of the Revised Code, and is equipped with amber and red visual signals meeting the requirements of section 4511.771 of the Revised Code, irrespective of whether or not the bus has fifteen or more children aboard at any time. "School bus" does not include a van owned and operated by a head start agency, irrespective of its color, lights, or markings.

(2003 H 95, § 3.13, eff. 7–1–04; 2002 S 123, eff. 1–1–04; 1998 H 618, eff. 3–22–99; 1984 H 478, eff. 3–28–85; 1980 S 160; 1978 S 389; 1975 H 369; 1974 H 995; 125 v 167; 1953 H 1; GC 6307–73)

4511.751 Failure–to–stop violations; reporting license plate number; procedures for prosecution or warning

As used in this section, "license plate" includes, but is not limited to, any temporary license placard issued under section 4503.182 of the Revised Code or similar law of another jurisdiction.

When the operator of a school bus believes that a motorist has violated division (A) of section 4511.75 of the Revised Code, the operator shall report the license plate number and a general description of the vehicle and of the operator of the vehicle to the law enforcement agency exercising jurisdiction over the area where the alleged violation occurred. The information contained in the report relating to the license plate number and to the general description of the vehicle and the operator of the vehicle at the time of the alleged violation may be supplied by any person with first-hand knowledge of the information. Information of which the operator of the school bus has first-hand knowledge also may be corroborated by any other person.

Upon receipt of the report of the alleged violation of division (A) of section 4511.75 of the Revised Code, the law enforcement agency shall conduct an investigation to attempt to determine or confirm the identity of the operator of the vehicle at the time of the alleged violation. If the identity of the operator at the time of the alleged violation is established, the reporting of the license plate number of the vehicle shall establish probable cause for the law enforcement agency to issue a citation for the violation of division (A) of section 4511.75 of the Revised Code. However, if the identity of the operator of the vehicle at the time of the alleged violation cannot be established, the law enforcement agency shall issue a warning to the owner of the vehicle at the time of the alleged violation, except in the case of a leased or rented vehicle when the warning shall be issued to the lessee at the time of the alleged violation.

The registrar of motor vehicles and deputy registrars shall, at the time of issuing license plates to any person, include with the license plate a summary of the requirements of division (A) of section 4511.75 of the Revised Code and the procedures of, and penalty in, division (F) of section 4511.75 of the Revised Code.

(2002 S 123, eff. 1–1–04; 1991 H 130, eff. 10–10–91; 1978 S 389)

4511.76 School bus regulation by education and public safety departments

(A) The department of public safety, by and with the advice of the superintendent of public instruction, shall adopt and enforce rules relating to the construction, design, and equipment, including lighting equipment required by section 4511.771 of the Revised Code, of all school buses both publicly and privately owned and operated in this state.

(B) The department of education, by and with the advice of the director of public safety, shall adopt and enforce rules relating to the operation of all vehicles used for pupil transportation.

(C) No person shall operate a vehicle used for pupil transportation within this state in violation of the rules of the department of education or the department of public safety. No person, being the owner thereof or having the supervisory responsibility therefor, shall permit the operation of a vehicle used for pupil transportation within this state in violation of the rules of the department of education or the department of public safety.

(D) The department of public safety shall adopt and enforce rules relating to the issuance of a license under section 4511.763 of the Revised Code. The rules may relate to the moral character of the applicant; the condition of the equipment to be operated; the liability and property damage insurance carried by the applicant; the posting of satisfactory and sufficient bond; and such other rules as the director of public safety determines reasonably necessary for the safety of the pupils to be transported.

(E) As used in this section, "vehicle used for pupil transportation" means any vehicle that is identified as such by the department of education by rule and that is subject to Chapter 3301–83 of the Administrative Code.

(F) Except as otherwise provided in this division, whoever violates this section is guilty of a minor misdemeanor. If the offender previously has been convicted of or pleaded guilty to one or more violations of this section or section 4511.63, 4511.761, 4511.762, 4511.764, 4511.77, or 4511.79 of the Revised Code or a municipal ordinance that is substantially similar to any of those sections, whoever violates this section is guilty of a misdemeanor of the fourth degree.

(2002 S 123, eff. 1–1–04; 2001 H 73, eff. 6–29–01; 1997 S 60, eff. 10–21–97; 1992 S 98, eff. 11–12–92; 1974 H 995; 132 v H 1; 131 v H 435; 129 v 1273; 126 v 392; 1953 H 1; GC 6307–74)

4511.761 School bus inspection

(A) The state highway patrol shall inspect every school bus to ascertain whether its construction, design, and equipment comply with the regulations adopted pursuant to section 4511.76 of the Revised Code and all other provisions of law.

The superintendent of the state highway patrol shall adopt a distinctive inspection decal not less than twelve inches in size, and bearing the date of the inspection, which shall be affixed to the outside surface of each side of each school bus which upon such inspection is found to comply with the regulations adopted pursuant to section 4511.76 of the Revised Code. The appearance of said decal shall be changed from year to year as to shape and color in order to provide easy visual inspection.

No person shall operate, nor shall any person being the owner thereof or having supervisory responsibility therefor permit the operation of, a school bus within this state unless there are displayed thereon the decals issued by the state highway patrol bearing the proper date of inspection for the calendar year for which the inspection decals were issued.

(B) Except as otherwise provided in this division, whoever violates this section is guilty of a minor misdemeanor. If the offender previously has been convicted of or pleaded guilty to one or more violations of this section or section 4511.63, 4511.76, 4511.762, 4511.764, 4511.77, or 4511.79 of the Revised Code or a municipal ordinance that is substantially similar to any of those sections, whoever violates this section is guilty of a misdemeanor of the fourth degree.

(C) Whenever a person is found guilty in a court of record of a violation of this section, the trial judge, in addition to or independent of all other penalties provided by law, may suspend for any period of time not exceeding three years, or cancel the license of any person, partnership, association, or corporation, issued under section 4511.763 of the Revised Code.

(2002 S 123, eff. 1–1–04; 1994 H 687, eff. 10–12–94; 1992 S 98, eff. 11–12–92; 131 v H 435; 129 v 1273)

4511.762 School bus not used for school purposes

(A) Except as provided in division (B) of this section, no person who is the owner of a bus that previously was registered as a school bus that is used or is to be used exclusively for purposes other than the transportation of children, shall operate the bus or permit it to be operated within this state unless the bus has been painted a color different from that prescribed for school buses by section 4511.77 of the Revised Code and painted in such a way that the words "stop" and "school bus" are obliterated.

(B) Any church bus that previously was registered as a school bus and is registered under section 4503.07 of the Revised Code may retain the paint color prescribed for school buses by section 4511.77 of the Revised Code if the bus complies with all of the following:

(1) The words "school bus" required by section 4511.77 of the Revised Code are covered or obliterated and the bus is marked on the front and rear with the words "church bus" painted in black lettering not less than ten inches in height;

(2) The automatically extended stop warning sign required by section 4511.75 of the Revised Code is removed and the word "stop" required by section 4511.77 of the Revised Code is covered or obliterated;

(3) The flashing red and amber lights required by section 4511.771 of the Revised Code are covered or removed;

(4) The inspection decal required by section 4511.761 of the Revised Code is covered or removed;

(5) The identification number assigned under section 4511.764 of the Revised Code and marked in black lettering on the front and rear of the bus is covered or obliterated.

(C) Except as otherwise provided in this division, whoever violates this section is guilty of a minor misdemeanor. If the offender previously has been convicted of or pleaded guilty to one or more violations of this section or section 4511.63, 4511.76,

4511.761, 4511.764, 4511.77, or 4511.79 of the Revised Code or a municipal ordinance that is substantially similar to any of those sections, whoever violates this section is guilty of a misdemeanor of the fourth degree.

(D) Whenever a person is found guilty in a court of record of a violation of this section, the trial judge, in addition to or independent of all other penalties provided by law, may suspend for any period of time not exceeding three years, or cancel the license of any person, partnership, association, or corporation, issued under section 4511.763 of the Revised Code.

(2002 S 123, eff. 1–1–04; 1997 S 85, eff. 5–15–97; 129 v 1273, eff. 10–26–61)

4511.763 License from public safety department

(A) No person, partnership, association, or corporation shall transport pupils to or from school on a school bus or enter into a contract with a board of education of any school district for the transportation of pupils on a school bus, without being licensed by the department of public safety.

(B) Except as otherwise provided in this division, whoever violates this section is guilty of a minor misdemeanor. If, within one year of the offense, the offender previously has been convicted of or pleaded guilty to one predicate motor vehicle or traffic offense, whoever violates this section is guilty of a misdemeanor of the fourth degree. If, within one year of the offense, the offender previously has been convicted of two or more predicate motor vehicle or traffic offenses, whoever violates this section is guilty of a misdemeanor of the third degree.

(2002 S 123, eff. 1–1–04; 1994 H 687, eff. 10–12–94; 1992 S 98, eff. 11–12–92; 131 v H 435)

4511.764 Registration of school buses

(A) The superintendent of the state highway patrol shall require school buses to be registered, in the name of the owner, with the state highway patrol on forms and in accordance with regulations as the superintendent may adopt.

When the superintendent is satisfied that the registration has been completed, the superintendent shall assign an identifying number to each school bus registered in accordance with this section. The number so assigned shall be marked on the front and rear of the vehicle in black lettering not less than six inches in height and will remain unchanged as long as the ownership of that vehicle remains the same.

No person shall operate, nor shall any person, being the owner thereof or having supervisory responsibility therefor, permit the operation of a school bus within this state unless there is displayed thereon an identifying number in accordance with this section.

(B) Except as otherwise provided in this division, whoever violates this section is guilty of a minor misdemeanor. If the offender previously has been convicted of or pleaded guilty to one or more violations of section 4511.63, 4511.76, 4511.761, 4511.762, 4511.77, or 4511.79 of the Revised Code or a municipal ordinance that is substantially similar to any of those sections, whoever violates this section is guilty of a misdemeanor of the fourth degree.

(2002 S 123, eff. 1–1–04; 1975 H 1, eff. 6–13–75; 131 v S 112)

4511.77 School bus marking

(A) No person shall operate, nor shall any person being the owner thereof or having supervisory responsibility therefor permit the operation of, a school bus within this state unless it is painted national school bus yellow and is marked on both front and rear with the words "school bus" in black lettering not less than eight inches in height and on the rear of the bus with the word "stop" in black lettering not less than ten inches in height.

(B) Except as otherwise provided in this division, whoever violates this section is guilty of a minor misdemeanor. If the offender previously has been convicted of or pleaded guilty to one or more violations of this section or section 4511.63, 4511.76, 4511.761, 4511.762, 4511.764, or 4511.79 of the Revised Code or a municipal ordinance that is substantially similar to any of those sections, whoever violates this section is guilty of a misdemeanor of the fourth degree.

(C) Whenever a person is found guilty in a court of record of a violation of this section, the trial judge, in addition to or independent of all other penalties provided by law, may suspend for any period of time not exceeding three years, or cancel the license of any person, partnership, association, or corporation, issued under section 4511.763 of the Revised Code.

(2002 S 123, eff. 1–1–04; 2000 H 600, eff. 9–1–00; 129 v 1273, eff. 10–26–61)

4511.771 School bus to be equipped with flashing red and amber lights

(A) Every school bus shall, in addition to any other equipment and distinctive markings required pursuant to sections 4511.76, 4511.761, 4511.764, and 4511.77 of the Revised Code, be equipped with signal lamps mounted as high as practicable, which shall display to the front two alternately flashing red lights and two alternately flashing amber lights located at the same level and to the rear two alternately flashing red lights and two alternately flashing amber lights located at the same level, and these lights shall be visible at five hundred feet in normal sunlight. The alternately flashing red lights shall be spaced as widely as practicable, and the alternately flashing amber lights shall be located next to them.

(B) Except as otherwise provided in this division, whoever violates this section is guilty of a minor misdemeanor. If, within one year of the offense, the offender previously has been convicted of or pleaded guilty to one predicate motor vehicle or traffic offense, whoever violates this section is guilty of a misdemeanor of the fourth degree. If, within one year of the offense, the offender previously has been convicted of two or more predicate motor vehicle or traffic offenses, whoever violates this section is guilty of a misdemeanor of the third degree.

(2002 S 123, eff. 1–1–04; 1978 S 389, eff. 3–15–79; 1974 H 995)

4511.772 Seat belt for school bus driver

(A) On and after May 6, 1986, no person, school board, or governmental entity shall purchase, lease, or rent a new school bus unless the school bus has an occupant restraining device, as defined in section 4513.263 of the Revised Code, installed for use in its operator's seat.

(B) Whoever violates this section is guilty of a minor misdemeanor.

(2002 S 123, eff. 1–1–04; 1986 S 54, eff. 5–6–86)

4511.78 Safety standards for transportation of school children by mass transit system

(A) As used in this section:

(1) "Mass transit system" means any county transit system, regional transit authority, regional transit commission, municipally owned transportation system, mass transit company operating exclusively within the territorial limits of a municipal corporation, or within such limits and the territorial limits of municipal

corporations immediately contiguous to such municipal corporation, and any common passenger carrier certified by the public utilities commission, that provides transportation for children to or from a school session or a school function.

(2) "Bus" means every motor vehicle designed for carrying more than nine passengers and used for the transportation of persons, but does not mean any school bus as defined in section 4511.01 of the Revised Code.

(B) Whenever a mass transit system transports children to or from a school session or school function, the mass transit system shall provide for:

(1) Periodic safety inspections of all buses used to provide transportation service. The inspections shall be based on rules adopted by the public utilities commission under Chapters 4921. and 4923. of the Revised Code to ensure the safety of operation of motor transportation companies and private motor carriers.

(2) The safety training of all drivers operating buses used to provide transportation service;

(3) The equipping of every bus with outside rear-view mirrors meeting the motor carrier regulations for bus equipment adopted by the federal highway administration. No exclusions from this requirement granted under the federal regulations shall be considered exclusions for the purposes of this division.

(C) Except as otherwise provided in this division, whoever violates this section is guilty of a minor misdemeanor. If, within one year of the offense, the offender previously has been convicted of or pleaded guilty to one predicate motor vehicle or traffic offense, whoever violates this section is guilty of a misdemeanor of the fourth degree. If, within one year of the offense, the offender previously has been convicted of two or more predicate motor vehicle or traffic offenses, whoever violates this section is guilty of a misdemeanor of the third degree.

(2002 S 123, eff. 1–1–04; 1976 H 234, eff. 8–25–76)

MISCELLANEOUS PROVISIONS

4511.79 Driving with impaired alertness or ability; use of drugs

(A) No person shall drive a "commercial motor vehicle" as defined in section 4506.01 of the Revised Code, or a "commercial car" or "commercial tractor," as defined in section 4501.01 of the Revised Code, while the person's ability or alertness is so impaired by fatigue, illness, or other causes that it is unsafe for the person to drive such vehicle. No driver shall use any drug which would adversely affect the driver's ability or alertness.

(B) No owner, as defined in section 4501.01 of the Revised Code, of a "commercial motor vehicle," "commercial car," or "commercial tractor," or a person employing or otherwise directing the driver of such vehicle, shall require or knowingly permit a driver in any such condition described in division (A) of this section to drive such vehicle upon any street or highway.

(C) Except as otherwise provided in this division, whoever violates this section is guilty of a minor misdemeanor. If the offender previously has been convicted of or pleaded guilty to one or more violations of this section or section 4511.63, 4511.76, 4511.761, 4511.762, 4511.764, or 4511.77 of the Revised Code or a municipal ordinance that is substantially similar to any of those sections, whoever violates this section is guilty of a misdemeanor of the fourth degree.

(2002 S 123, eff. 1–1–04; 1989 H 381, eff. 7–1–89; 130 v H 391)

4511.81 Certain children to be secured in child restraint system; exceptions; child highway safety fund

(A) When any child who is in either or both of the following categories is being transported in a motor vehicle, other than a taxicab or public safety vehicle as defined in section 4511.01 of the Revised Code, that is registered in this state and is required by the United States department of transportation to be equipped with seat belts at the time of manufacture or assembly, the operator of the motor vehicle shall have the child properly secured in accordance with the manufacturer's instructions in a child restraint system that meets federal motor vehicle safety standards:

(1) A child who is less than four years of age;

(2) A child who weighs less than forty pounds.

(B) When any child who is in either or both of the following categories is being transported in a motor vehicle, other than a taxicab, that is registered in this state and is owned, leased, or otherwise under the control of a nursery school, kindergarten, or day-care center, the operator of the motor vehicle shall have the child properly secured in accordance with the manufacturer's instructions in a child restraint system that meets federal motor vehicle safety standards:

(1) A child who is less than four years of age;

(2) A child who weighs less than forty pounds.

(C) The director of public safety shall adopt such rules as are necessary to carry out this section.

(D) The failure of an operator of a motor vehicle to secure a child in a child restraint system as required by this section is not negligence imputable to the child, is not admissible as evidence in any civil action involving the rights of the child against any other person allegedly liable for injuries to the child, is not to be used as a basis for a criminal prosecution of the operator of the motor vehicle other than a prosecution for a violation of this section, and is not admissible as evidence in any criminal action involving the operator of the motor vehicle other than a prosecution for a violation of this section.

(E) This section does not apply when an emergency exists that threatens the life of any person operating a motor vehicle and to whom this section otherwise would apply or the life of any child who otherwise would be required to be restrained under this section.

(F) If a person who is not a resident of this state is charged with a violation of division (A) or (B) of this section and does not prove to the court, by a preponderance of the evidence, that the person's use or nonuse of a child restraint system was in accordance with the law of the state of which the person is a resident, the court shall impose the fine levied by division (H)(2) of this section.

(G) There is hereby created in the state treasury the "child highway safety fund," consisting of fines imposed pursuant to divisions (H)(1) and (2) of this section for violations of divisions (A) and (B) of this section. The money in the fund shall be used by the department of health only to defray the cost of designating hospitals as pediatric trauma centers under section 3727.081 of the Revised Code and to establish and administer a child highway safety program. The purpose of the program shall be to educate the public about child restraint systems generally and the importance of their proper use. The program also shall include a process for providing child restraint systems to persons who meet the eligibility criteria established by the department, and a toll-free telephone number the public may utilize to obtain information about child restraint systems and their proper use.

The director of health, in accordance with Chapter 119. of the Revised Code, shall adopt any rules necessary to carry out this section, including rules establishing the criteria a person must meet in order to receive a child restraint system under the department's child restraint system program; provided that rules relating to the verification of pediatric trauma centers shall not be adopted under this section.

(H)(1) Whoever is a resident of this state and violates division (A) or (B) of this section shall be punished as follows:

(a) Except as otherwise provided in division (H)(1)(b) of this section, the offender is guilty of a minor misdemeanor.

(b) If the offender previously has been convicted of or pleaded guilty to a violation of division (A) or (B) of this section or of a municipal ordinance that is substantially similar to either of those divisions, the offender is guilty of a misdemeanor of the fourth degree.

(2) Whoever is not a resident of this state, violates division (A) or (B) of this section, and fails to prove by a preponderance of the evidence that the offender's use or nonuse of a child restraint system was in accordance with the law of the state of which the offender is a resident is guilty of a minor misdemeanor on a first offense; on a second or subsequent offense, that person is guilty of a misdemeanor of the fourth degree.

(3) All fines imposed pursuant to division (H)(1) or (2) of this section shall be forwarded to the treasurer of state for deposit in the "child highway safety fund" created by division (G) of this section.

(2002 S 123, eff. 1–1–04; 2001 H 94, eff. 6–6–01; 2000 H 138, eff. 11–3–00; 1994 H 381, eff. 6–23–94; 1992 S 98, eff. 11–12–92; 1987 S 53; 1986 H 428, S 54; 1982 H 605)

4511.82 Littering by operators of motor vehicles prohibited

(A) No operator or occupant of a motor vehicle shall, regardless of intent, throw, drop, discard, or deposit litter from any motor vehicle in operation upon any street, road, or highway, except into a litter receptacle in a manner that prevents its being carried away or deposited by the elements.

(B) No operator of a motor vehicle in operation upon any street, road, or highway shall allow litter to be thrown, dropped, discarded, or deposited from the motor vehicle, except into a litter receptacle in a manner that prevents its being carried away or deposited by the elements.

(C) Whoever violates division (A) or (B) of this section is guilty of a minor misdemeanor.

(D) As used in this section, "litter" means garbage, trash, waste, rubbish, ashes, cans, bottles, wire, paper, cartons, boxes, automobile parts, furniture, glass, or anything else of an unsightly or unsanitary nature.

(2002 S 123, eff. 1–1–04; 1987 H 333, eff. 10–20–87)

4511.84 Prohibition against driving while wearing earphones or earplugs

(A) No person shall operate a motor vehicle while wearing earphones over, or earplugs in, both ears. As used in this section, "earphones" means any headset, radio, tape player, or other similar device that provides the listener with radio programs, music, or other recorded information through a device attached to the head and that covers all or a portion of both ears. "Earphones" does not include speakers or other listening devices that are built into protective headgear.

(B) This section does not apply to:

(1) Any person wearing a hearing aid;

(2) Law enforcement personnel while on duty;

(3) Fire department personnel and emergency medical service personnel while on duty;

(4) Any person engaged in the operation of equipment for use in the maintenance or repair of any highway;

(5) Any person engaged in the operation of refuse collection equipment.

(C) Except as otherwise provided in this division, whoever violates this section is guilty of a minor misdemeanor. If, within one year of the offense, the offender previously has been convicted of or pleaded guilty to one predicate motor vehicle or traffic offense, whoever violates this section is guilty of a misdemeanor of the fourth degree. If, within one year of the offense, the offender previously has been convicted of two or more predicate motor vehicle or traffic offenses, whoever violates this section is guilty of a misdemeanor of the third degree.

(2002 S 123, eff. 1–1–04; 1989 S 86, eff. 10–30–89)

4511.85 Chauffeured limousines and livery services; prohibitions

(A) The operator of a chauffeured limousine shall accept passengers only on the basis of prearranged contracts, as defined in division (LL) of section 4501.01 of the Revised Code, and shall not cruise in search of patronage unless the limousine is in compliance with any statute or ordinance governing the operation of taxicabs or other similar vehicles for hire.

(B) No person shall advertise or hold self out as doing business as a limousine service or livery service or other similar designation unless each vehicle used by the person to provide the service is registered in accordance with section 4503.24 of the Revised Code and is in compliance with section 4509.80 of the Revised Code.

(C) Whoever violates this section is guilty of a misdemeanor of the first degree.

(2002 S 123, eff. 1–1–04; 1998 H 611, eff. 7–1–99; 1990 H 422, eff. 7–1–91)

4511.90 Chautauqua assemblies; traffic code applicable on streets

As used in this section, "Chautauqua assembly" means a corporation that is organized in this state for the purpose of holding Chautauqua assemblies or encouraging religion, art, science, literature, or the general dissemination of knowledge, or two or more of such purposes, and that occupies grounds and holds meetings or entertainments on the grounds for the purposes for which it is organized.

Chapters 4511. and 4513. of the Revised Code are applicable to streets within a Chautauqua assembly. A Chautauqua assembly is a local authority for the purposes of section 4511.07 of the Revised Code.

(1980 H 948, eff. 5–22–80; 1979 H 316)

PENALTIES

4511.98 Signs regarding increased penalties in construction zones

The director of transportation, board of county commissioners, or board of township trustees shall cause signs to be erected advising motorists that increased penalties apply for certain traffic violations occurring on streets or highways in a construction zone. The increased penalties shall be effective only when signs are erected in accordance with the guidelines and design specifications established by the director under section 5501.27 of the

Revised Code, and when a violation occurs during hours of actual work within the construction zone.

(2004 H 52, eff. 6 1 04; 1994 H 247, eff. 5 1 95)

4511.99 Penalties not otherwise specified

Whoever violates any provision of sections 4511.01 to 4511.76 of the Revised Code for which no penalty otherwise is provided in the section violated is guilty of one of the following:

(A) Except as otherwise provided in division (B) or (C) of this section, a minor misdemeanor;

(B) If, within one year of the offense, the offender previously has been convicted of or pleaded guilty to one predicate motor vehicle or traffic offense, a misdemeanor of the fourth degree;

(C) If, within one year of the offense, the offender previously has been convicted of or pleaded guilty to two or more predicate motor vehicle or traffic offenses, a misdemeanor of the third degree.. [sic.]

(2002 H 490, eff. 1–1–04; 2002 S 123, eff. 1–1–04; 2002 S 231, eff. 10–24–02; 2000 H 138, eff. 11–3–00; 2000 H 80, eff. 6–8–00; 1999 S 22, eff. 5–17–00; 1999 S 107, eff. 3–23–00; 1999 H 148, eff. 10–14–99; 1999 H 86, eff. 9–28–99; 1997 S 60, eff. 10–21–97; 1996 H 72, eff. 3–18–97; 1996 S 166, eff. 10–17–96; 1996 H 676, eff. 10–4–96; 1996 H 353, eff. 9–17–96; 1995 S 2, eff. 7–1–96; 1994 H 247, eff. 5–1–95; 1994 H 381, eff. 6–23–94; 1994 S 82, eff. 5–4–94; 1993 S 62, § 1, eff. 9–1–93; 1993 S 62, § 4, H 149; 1992 S 275, H 725; 1991 H 130, H 73; 1990 H 422, S 382, H 837, S 131, H 162; 1989 H 317, S 49, H 381, S 86, H 8; 1988 H 708, H 429; 1987 S 53, H 333; 1986 S 262, S 54; 1984 H 460, H 112, S 169, § 1, 3; 1983 H 133; 1982 S 432, H 605, H 707; 1978 S 389, S 381; 1977 H 652; 1972 H 511; 132 v H 380, S 37, H 1; 131 v S 112, H 435; 130 v H 391; 129 v 1273; 128 v 469; 125 v 461; 1953 H 1)

CHAPTER 4513

TRAFFIC LAWS—EQUIPMENT; LOADS

PRELIMINARY PROVISIONS

4513.01 Definitions

As provided in section 4511.01 of the Revised Code, the definitions set forth in that section apply to this chapter.

(2002 H 520, eff. 4–3–03; 2000 H 672, eff. 4–9–01; 1953 H 1, eff. 10–1–53)

4513.02 Prohibition against operating unsafe vehicles; inspection of vehicles; exemptions; official inspection stations

(A) No person shall drive or move, or cause or knowingly permit to be driven or moved, on any highway any vehicle or combination of vehicles which is in such unsafe condition as to endanger any person.

(B) When directed by any state highway patrol trooper, the operator of any motor vehicle shall stop and submit such motor vehicle to an inspection under division (B)(1) or (2) of this section, as appropriate, and such tests as are necessary.

(1) Any motor vehicle not subject to inspection by the public utilities commission shall be inspected and tested to determine whether it is unsafe or not equipped as required by law, or that its equipment is not in proper adjustment or repair, or in violation of the equipment provisions of Chapter 4513. of the Revised Code.

Such inspection shall be made with respect to the brakes, lights, turn signals, steering, horns and warning devices, glass, mirrors, exhaust system, windshield wipers, tires, and such other items of equipment as designated by the superintendent of the state highway patrol by rule or regulation adopted pursuant to sections 119.01 to 119.13 of the Revised Code.

Upon determining that a motor vehicle is in safe operating condition and its equipment in conformity with Chapter 4513. of the Revised Code, the inspecting officer shall issue to the operator an official inspection sticker, which shall be in such form as the superintendent prescribes except that its color shall vary from year to year.

(2) Any motor vehicle subject to inspection by the public utilities commission shall be inspected and tested in accordance with rules adopted by the commission. Upon determining that the vehicle and operator are in compliance with rules adopted by the commission, the inspecting officer shall issue to the operator an appropriate official inspection sticker.

(C) The superintendent of the state highway patrol, pursuant to sections 119.01 to 119.13 of the Revised Code, shall determine and promulgate standards for any inspection program conducted by a political subdivision of this state. These standards shall exempt licensed collector's vehicles and historical motor vehicles from inspection. Any motor vehicle bearing a valid certificate of inspection issued by another state or a political subdivision of this state whose inspection program conforms to the superintendent's standards, and any licensed collector's vehicle or historical motor vehicle which is not in a condition which endangers the safety of persons or property, shall be exempt from the tests provided in division (B) of this section.

(D) Every person, firm, association, or corporation that, in the conduct of its business, owns and operates not less than fifteen motor vehicles in this state that are not subject to regulation by the public utilities commission and that, for the purpose of storing, repairing, maintaining, and servicing such motor vehicles, equips and operates one or more service departments within this state, may file with the superintendent of the state highway patrol applications for permits for such service departments as official inspection stations for its own motor vehicles. Upon receiving an application for each such service department, and after determining that it is properly equipped and has competent personnel to perform the inspections referred to in this section, the superintendent shall issue the necessary inspection stickers and permit to operate as an official inspection station. Any such person who has had one or more service departments so designated as official inspection stations may have motor vehicles that are owned and operated by the person and that are not subject to regulation by the public utilities commission, excepting private passenger cars owned by the person or the person's employees, inspected at such service department; and any motor vehicle bearing a valid certificate of inspection issued by such service department shall be exempt from the tests provided in division (B) of this section.

No permit for an official inspection station shall be assigned or transferred or used at any location other than therein designated, and every such permit shall be posted in a conspicuous place at the location designated.

If a person, firm, association, or corporation owns and operates fifteen or more motor vehicles in the conduct of business and is subject to regulation by the public utilities commission, that person, firm, association, or corporation is not eligible to apply to the superintendent for permits to enable any of its service departments to serve as official inspection stations for its own motor vehicles.

(E) When any motor vehicle is found to be unsafe for operation, the inspecting officer may order it removed from the highway and not operated, except for purposes of removal and repair, until it has been repaired pursuant to a repair order as provided in division (F) of this section.

(F) When any motor vehicle is found to be defective or in violation of Chapter 4513. of the Revised Code, the inspecting officer may issue a repair order, in such form and containing such information as the superintendent shall prescribe, to the owner or operator of the motor vehicle. The owner or operator shall thereupon obtain such repairs as are required and shall, as directed by the inspecting officer, return the repair order together with proof of compliance with its provisions. When any motor vehicle or operator subject to rules of the public utilities commission fails the inspection, the inspecting officer shall issue an appropriate order to obtain compliance with such rules.

(G) Sections 4513.01 to 4513.37 of the Revised Code, with respect to equipment on vehicles, do not apply to implements of husbandry, road machinery, road rollers, or agricultural tractors except as made applicable to such articles of machinery.

(H) Except as otherwise provided in this division, whoever violates this section is guilty of a minor misdemeanor. If the offender previously has been convicted of a violation of this section, whoever violates this section is guilty of a misdemeanor of the third degree.

(2002 S 123, eff. 1–1–04; 1999 H 86, eff. 6–29–99; 1992 S 301, eff. 3–15–93; 1992 S 351; 1991 S 144; 1975 S 52; 132 v H 380; 1953 H 1; GC 6307–75)

4513.021 Motor vehicle bumper regulations

(A) As used in this section:

(1) "Passenger car" means any motor vehicle with motive power, designed for carrying ten persons or less, except a multipurpose passenger vehicle or motorcycle.

(2) "Multipurpose passenger vehicle" means a motor vehicle with motive power, except a motorcycle, designed to carry ten persons or less, that is constructed either on a truck chassis or with special features for occasional off-road operation.

(3) "Truck" means every motor vehicle, except trailers and semitrailers, designed and used to carry property and having a gross vehicle weight rating of ten thousand pounds or less.

(4) "Manufacturer" has the same meaning as in section 4501.01 of the Revised Code.

(5) "Gross vehicle weight rating" means the manufacturer's gross vehicle weight rating established for that vehicle.

(B) The director of public safety, in accordance with Chapter 119. of the Revised Code, shall adopt rules in conformance with standards of the vehicle equipment safety commission, that shall govern the maximum bumper height or, in the absence of bumpers and in cases where bumper heights have been lowered or modified, the maximum height to the bottom of the frame rail, of any passenger car, multipurpose passenger vehicle, or truck.

(C) No person shall operate upon a street or highway any passenger car, multipurpose passenger vehicle, or truck registered in this state that does not conform to the requirements of this section or to any applicable rule adopted pursuant to this section.

(D) No person shall modify any motor vehicle registered in this state in such a manner as to cause the vehicle body or chassis to come in contact with the ground, expose the fuel tank to damage from collision, or cause the wheels to come in contact with the body under normal operation, and no person shall disconnect any part of the original suspension system of the vehicle to defeat the safe operation of that system.

(E) Nothing contained in this section or in the rules adopted pursuant to this section shall be construed to prohibit either of the following:

(1) The installation upon a passenger car, multipurpose passenger vehicle, or truck registered in this state of heavy duty equipment, including shock absorbers and overload springs;

(2) The operation on a street or highway of a passenger car, multipurpose passenger vehicle, or truck registered in this state with normal wear to the suspension system if the normal wear does not adversely affect the control of the vehicle.

(F) This section and the rules adopted pursuant to it do not apply to any specially designed or modified passenger car, multipurpose passenger vehicle, or truck when operated off a street or highway in races and similar events.

(G) Except as otherwise provided in this division, whoever violates this section is guilty of a minor misdemeanor. If the offender previously has been convicted of a violation of this section, whoever violates this section is guilty of a misdemeanor of the third degree.

(2002 S 123, eff. 1–1–04; 1992 S 98, eff. 11–12–92; 1988 H 447)

4513.022 Request to produce proof of financial responsibility

(A) As part of the motor vehicle inspection conducted pursuant to section 4513.02 of the Revised Code, the state highway patrol trooper shall request that the owner or operator of the motor vehicle produce proof that the owner maintains or has maintained on the owner's behalf, proof of financial responsibility as required by section 4509.101 of the Revised Code.

(B) A state highway patrol trooper shall indicate on every traffic ticket issued pursuant to a motor vehicle inspection whether the person receiving the traffic ticket produced proof of the maintenance of financial responsibility in response to the state highway patrol trooper's request. The state highway patrol trooper shall inform every person who receives a traffic ticket and who has failed to produce proof of the maintenance of financial responsibility at the time of the motor vehicle inspection that the person must submit proof to the traffic violations bureau with any payment of a fine and costs for the ticketed violation or, if the person is to appear in court for the violation, the person must submit proof to the court.

(C)(1) If a person who has failed to produce proof of the maintenance of financial responsibility appears in court for a ticketed violation, the court may permit the defendant to present evidence of proof of financial responsibility to the court at such time and in such manner as the court determines to be necessary or appropriate. The clerk of courts shall provide the registrar with the identity of any person who fails to submit proof of the maintenance of financial responsibility pursuant to division (B) of this section.

(2) If a person who has failed to present proof of the maintenance of financial responsibility also fails to submit that proof to the traffic violations bureau, the traffic violations bureau shall notify the registrar of the identity of that person.

(3) Upon receiving notice from a clerk of courts or a traffic violation bureau pursuant to division (C) of this section, the registrar shall proceed against these persons under division (D) of section 4509.101 of the Revised Code in the same manner as the registrar proceeds against persons identified by the clerk of courts under division (D)(4) of section 4509.101 of the Revised Code.

(D) A state highway patrol trooper may charge an owner or operator of a motor vehicle with a violation of section 4510.16 of the Revised Code when the operator fails to produce proof of the maintenance of financial responsibility upon the state highway patrol trooper's request under division (A) of this section, if a check of the owner or operator's driving record indicates that the owner or operator, at the time of the motor vehicle inspection, is required to file and maintain proof of financial responsibility under section 4509.45 of the Revised Code for a previous violation of Chapter 4509. of the Revised Code.

(2002 S 123, eff. 1–1–04; 1996 H 438, eff. 7–1–97; 1995 H 248, § 1, eff. 10–20–95; 1994 S 20, eff. 10–20–95)

LIGHTS

4513.03 Lighted lights required

(A) Every vehicle upon a street or highway within this state during the time from sunset to sunrise, and at any other time when there are unfavorable atmospheric conditions or when there is not sufficient natural light to render discernible persons, vehicles, and substantial objects on the highway at a distance of one thousand feet ahead, shall display lighted lights and illuminating devices as required by sections 4513.04 to 4513.37 of the Revised Code, for different classes of vehicles; except that every motorized bicycle shall display at such times lighted lights meeting the rules adopted by the director of public safety under section 4511.521 of the Revised Code. No motor vehicle, during such times, shall be operated upon a street or highway within this state using only parking lights as illumination.

Whenever in such sections a requirement is declared as to the distance from which certain lamps and devices shall render objects visible, or within which such lamps or devices shall be visible, such distance shall be measured upon a straight level unlighted highway under normal atmospheric conditions unless a different condition is expressly stated.

Whenever in such sections a requirement is declared as to the mounted height of lights or devices, it shall mean from the center of such light or device to the level ground upon which the vehicle stands.

(B) Whoever violates this section shall be punished as provided in section 4513.99 of the Revised Code.

(2002 S 123, eff. 1–1–04; 2000 H 484, eff. 10–5–00; 1992 S 98, eff. 11–12–92; 1977 S 100; 1973 H 272; 129 v 232; 1953 H 1; GC 6307–76)

4513.04 Headlights

(A) Every motor vehicle, other than a motorcycle, and every trackless trolley shall be equipped with at least two headlights with at least one near each side of the front of the motor vehicle or trackless trolley.

Every motorcycle shall be equipped with at least one and not more than two headlights.

(B) Whoever violates this section shall be punished as provided in section 4513.99 of the Revised Code.

(2002 S 123, eff. 1–1–04; 1953 H 1, eff. 10–1–53; GC 6307–77)

4513.05 Tail lights and illumination of rear license plate

(A) Every motor vehicle, trackless trolley, trailer, semitrailer, pole trailer, or vehicle which is being drawn at the end of a train of vehicles shall be equipped with at least one tail light mounted on the rear which, when lighted, shall emit a red light visible from a distance of five hundred feet to the rear, provided that in the case of a train of vehicles only the tail light on the rearmost vehicle need be visible from the distance specified.

Either a tail light or a separate light shall be so constructed and placed as to illuminate with a white light the rear registration plate, when such registration plate is required, and render it legible from a distance of fifty feet to the rear. Any tail light, together with any separate light for illuminating the rear registration plate, shall be so wired as to be lighted whenever the headlights or auxiliary driving lights are lighted, except where separate lighting systems are provided for trailers for the purpose of illuminating such registration plate.

(B) Whoever violates this section shall be punished as provided in section 4513.99 of the Revised Code.

(2002 S 123, eff. 1–1–04; 1953 H 1, eff. 10–1–53; GC 6307–78)

4513.06 Red reflectors required

(A) Every new motor vehicle sold after September 6, 1941, and operated on a highway, other than a commercial tractor, to which a trailer or semitrailer is attached shall carry at the rear, either as a part of the tail lamps or separately, two red reflectors meeting the requirements of this section, except that vehicles of the type mentioned in section 4513.07 of the Revised Code shall be equipped with reflectors as required by the regulations provided for in said section.

Every such reflector shall be of such size and characteristics and so maintained as to be visible at night from all distances within three hundred feet to fifty feet from such vehicle.

(B) Whoever violates this section shall be punished as provided in section 4513.99 of the Revised Code.

(2002 S 123, eff. 1–1–04; 1953 H 1, eff. 10–1–53; GC 6307–79)

4513.07 Safety lighting of commercial vehicles

(A) The director of public safety shall prescribe and promulgate regulations relating to clearance lights, marker lights, reflectors, and stop lights on buses, trackless trolleys, trucks, commercial tractors, trailers, semitrailers, and pole trailers, when operated upon any highway, and such vehicles shall be equipped as required by such regulations, and such equipment shall be lighted at all times mentioned in section 4513.03 of the Revised Code, except that clearance lights and side marker lights need not be lighted on any such vehicle when it is operated within a municipal corporation where there is sufficient light to reveal any person or substantial object on the highway at a distance of five hundred feet.

Such equipment shall be in addition to all other lights specifically required by sections 4513.03 to 4513.16 of the Revised Code.

Vehicles operated under the jurisdiction of the public utilities commission are not subject to this section.

(B) Whoever violates this section shall be punished as provided in section 4513.99 of the Revised Code.

(2002 S 123, eff. 1–1–04; 1992 S 98, eff. 11–12–92; 128 v 1180; 1953 H 1; GC 6307–80)

4513.071 Stop lights required

(A) Every motor vehicle, trailer, semitrailer, and pole trailer when operated upon a highway shall be equipped with two or more stop lights, except that passenger cars manufactured or assembled prior to January 1, 1967, motorcycles, and motor-driven cycles shall be equipped with at least one stop light. Stop lights shall be mounted on the rear of the vehicle, actuated upon application of the service brake, and may be incorporated with other rear lights. Such stop lights when actuated shall emit a red light visible from a distance of five hundred feet to the rear, provided that in the case of a train of vehicles only the stop lights on the rear-most vehicle need be visible from the distance specified.

Such stop lights when actuated shall give a steady warning light to the rear of a vehicle or train of vehicles to indicate the intention of the operator to diminish the speed of or stop a vehicle or train of vehicles.

When stop lights are used as required by this section, they shall be constructed or installed so as to provide adequate and reliable illumination and shall conform to the appropriate rules and regulations established under section 4513.19 of the Revised Code.

Historical motor vehicles as defined in section 4503.181 of the Revised Code, not originally manufactured with stop lights, are not subject to this section.

(B) Whoever violates this section shall be punished as provided in section 4513.99 of the Revised Code.

(2002 S 123, eff. 1–1–04; 2000 H 600, eff. 9–1–00; 1971 S 227, eff. 12–17–71)

4513.08 Obscured lights on vehicles

Whenever motor and other vehicles are operated in combination during the time that lights are required, any light, except tail lights, which by reason of its location on a vehicle of the combination would be obscured by another vehicle of the combination need not be lighted, but this section does not affect the requirement that lighted clearance lights be displayed on the front of the foremost vehicle required to have clearance lights or that all lights required on the rear of the rearmost vehicle of any combination shall be lighted.

(1953 H 1, eff. 10–1–53; GC 6307–81)

4513.09 Red light or flag required

(A) Whenever the load upon any vehicle extends to the rear four feet or more beyond the bed or body of such vehicle, there shall be displayed at the extreme rear end of the load, at the times specified in section 4513.03 of the Revised Code, a red light or lantern plainly visible from a distance of at least five hundred feet to the sides and rear. The red light or lantern required by this section is in addition to the red rear light required upon every vehicle. At any other time there shall be displayed at the extreme rear end of such load a red flag or cloth not less than sixteen inches square.

(B) Whoever violates this section shall be punished as provided in section 4513.99 of the Revised Code.

(2002 S 123, eff. 1–1–04; 1953 H 1, eff. 10–1–53; GC 6307–82)

4513.10 Lights on parked vehicles

(A) Except in case of an emergency, whenever a vehicle is parked or stopped upon a roadway open to traffic or a shoulder adjacent thereto, whether attended or unattended, during the times mentioned in section 4513.03 of the Revised Code, such vehicle shall be equipped with one or more lights which shall exhibit a white or amber light on the roadway side visible from a distance of five hundred feet to the front of such vehicle, and a red light visible from a distance of five hundred feet to the rear. No lights need be displayed upon any such vehicle when it is stopped or parked within a municipal corporation where there is sufficient light to reveal any person or substantial object within a distance of five hundred feet upon such highway. Any lighted headlights upon a parked vehicle shall be depressed or dimmed.

(B) Whoever violates this section shall be punished as provided in section 4513.99 of the Revised Code.

(2002 S 123, eff. 1–1–04; 128 v 1167, eff. 10–19–59; 1953 H 1; GC 6307–83)

4513.11 Lights on slow-moving vehicles; emblem; animal–drawn vehicle

(A) All vehicles other than bicycles, including animal-drawn vehicles and vehicles referred to in division (G) of section 4513.02 of the Revised Code, not specifically required to be equipped with lamps or other lighting devices by sections 4513.03 to 4513.10 of the Revised Code, shall, at the times specified in section 4513.03 of the Revised Code, be equipped with at least one lamp displaying a white light visible from a distance of not less than one thousand feet to the front of the vehicle, and also shall be equipped with two lamps displaying red light visible from a distance of not less than one thousand feet to the rear of the vehicle, or as an alternative, one lamp displaying a red light visible from a distance of not less than one thousand feet to the rear and two red reflectors visible from all distances of six hundred feet to one hundred feet to the rear when illuminated by the lawful lower beams of headlamps.

Lamps and reflectors required or authorized by this section shall meet standards adopted by the director of public safety.

(B) All boat trailers, farm machinery, and other machinery, including all road construction machinery, upon a street or highway, except when being used in actual construction and maintenance work in an area guarded by a flagperson, or where flares are used, or when operating or traveling within the limits of a construction area designated by the director of transportation, a city engineer, or the county engineer of the several counties, when such construction area is marked in accordance with requirements of the director and the manual of uniform traffic control devices, as set forth in section 4511.09 of the Revised Code, which is designed for operation at a speed of twenty-five miles per hour or less shall be operated at a speed not exceeding twenty-five miles per hour, and shall display a triangular slow-moving vehicle emblem (SMV). The emblem shall be mounted so as to be visible from a distance of not less than five hundred feet to the rear. The director of public safety shall adopt standards and specifications for the design and position of mounting the SMV emblem. The standards and specifications for SMV emblems referred to in this section shall correlate with and, so far as possible, conform with those approved by the American society of agricultural engineers.

As used in this division, "machinery" does not include any vehicle designed to be drawn by an animal.

(C) The use of the SMV emblem shall be restricted to animal-drawn vehicles, and to the slow-moving vehicles specified in division (B) of this section operating or traveling within the limits of the highway. Its use on slow-moving vehicles being transported upon other types of vehicles or on any other type of vehicle or stationary object on the highway is prohibited.

(D) No person shall sell, lease, rent, or operate any boat trailer, farm machinery, or other machinery defined as a slow-moving vehicle in division (B) of this section, except those units designed to be completely mounted on a primary power unit, which is manufactured or assembled on or after April 1, 1966, unless the vehicle is equipped with a slow-moving vehicle emblem mounting device as specified in division (B) of this section.

(E) Any boat trailer, farm machinery, or other machinery defined as a slow-moving vehicle in division (B) of this section, in addition to the use of the slow-moving vehicle emblem, may be equipped with a red flashing light that shall be visible from a distance of not less than one thousand feet to the rear at all times specified in section 4513.03 of the Revised Code. When a double-faced light is used, it shall display amber light to the front and red light to the rear.

In addition to the lights described in this division, farm machinery and motor vehicles escorting farm machinery may display a flashing, oscillating, or rotating amber light, as permitted by section 4513.17 of the Revised Code, and also may display simultaneously flashing turn signals or warning lights, as permitted by that section.

(F) Every animal-drawn vehicle upon a street or highway shall at all times be equipped in one of the following ways:

(1) With a slow-moving vehicle emblem complying with division (B) of this section;

(2) With alternate reflective material complying with rules adopted under this division;

(3) With both a slow-moving vehicle emblem and alternate reflective material as specified in this division.

The director of public safety, subject to Chapter 119. of the Revised Code, shall adopt rules establishing standards and specifications for the position of mounting of the alternate reflective material authorized by this division. The rules shall permit, as a minimum, the alternate reflective material to be black, gray, or silver in color. The alternate reflective material shall be mounted on the animal-drawn vehicle so as to be visible, at all times specified in section 4513.03 of the Revised Code, from a distance of not less than five hundred feet to the rear when illuminated by the lawful lower beams of headlamps.

(G) Whoever violates this section shall be punished as provided in section 4513.99 of the Revised Code.

(H) As used in this section, "boat trailer" means any vehicle designed and used exclusively to transport a boat between a place of storage and a marina, or in and around a marina, when drawn or towed on a street or highway for a distance of no more than ten miles and at a speed of twenty-five miles per hour or less.

(2002 S 123, eff. 1–1–04; 1997 H 282, eff. 11–12–97; 1996 S 121, eff. 11–19–96; 1992 S 98, eff. 11–12–92; 1992 H 485; 1988 H 708; 1987 H 52; 1975 H 1; 1974 H 995, H 472; 1973 H 200; 132 v H 172; 131 v H 147; 128 v 591; 1953 H 1; GC 6307–84)

4513.111 Light and reflector requirements for multi-wheel agricultural tractors or farm machinery

(A)(1) Every multi-wheel agricultural tractor whose model year was 2001 or earlier, when being operated or traveling on a street or highway at the times specified in section 4513.03 of the Revised Code, at a minimum shall be equipped with and display reflectors and illuminated amber lamps so that the extreme left and right projections of the tractor are indicated by flashing lamps displaying amber light, visible to the front and the rear, by amber reflectors, all visible to the front, and by red reflectors, all visible to the rear.

(2) The lamps displaying amber light need not flash simultaneously and need not flash in conjunction with any directional signals of the tractor.

(3) The lamps and reflectors required by division (A)(1) of this section and their placement shall meet standards and specifications contained in rules adopted by the director of public safety in accordance with Chapter 119. of the Revised Code. The rules governing the amber lamps, amber reflectors, and red reflectors and their placement shall correlate with and, as far as possible, conform with paragraphs 4.1.4.1, 4.1.7.1, and 4.1.7.2 respectively of the American society of agricultural engineers standard ANSI/ ASAE S279.10 OCT98, lighting and marking of agricultural equipment on highways.

(B) Every unit of farm machinery whose model year was 2002 or later, when being operated or traveling on a street or highway at the times specified in section 4513.03 of the Revised Code, shall be equipped with and display markings and illuminated lamps that meet or exceed the lighting, illumination, and marking standards and specifications that are applicable to that type of farm machinery for the unit's model year specified in the American society of agricultural engineers standard ANSI/ASAE S279.11 APR01, lighting and marking of agricultural equipment on highways, or any subsequent revisions of that standard.

(C) The lights and reflectors required by division (A) of this section are in addition to the slow-moving vehicle emblem and lights required or permitted by section 4513.11 or 4513.17 of the Revised Code to be displayed on farm machinery being operated or traveling on a street or highway.

(D) No person shall operate any unit of farm machinery on a street or highway or cause any unit of farm machinery to travel on a street or highway in violation of division (A) or (B) of this section.

(E) Whoever violates this section shall be punished as provided in section 4513.99 of the Revised Code.

(2003 H 87, § 4, eff. 1–1–04; 2003 H 87, § 1, eff. 6–30–03; 2002 S 123, eff. 1–1–04; 2000 H 484, eff. 10–5–00)

4513.12 Spotlight and auxiliary driving lights

(A) Any motor vehicle may be equipped with not more than one spotlight and every lighted spotlight shall be so aimed and used upon approaching another vehicle that no part of the high-intensity portion of the beam will be directed to the left of the prolongation of the extreme left side of the vehicle, nor more than one hundred feet ahead of the vehicle.

Any motor vehicle may be equipped with not more than three auxiliary driving lights mounted on the front of the vehicle. The director of public safety shall prescribe specifications for auxiliary driving lights and regulations for their use, and any such lights which do not conform to said specifications and regulations shall not be used.

(B) Whoever violates this section shall be punished as provided in section 4513.99 of the Revised Code.

(2002 S 123, eff. 1–1–04; 1992 S 98, eff. 11–12–92; 128 v 1180; 1953 H 1; GC 6307–85)

4513.13 Cowl, fender, and back-up lights

(A) Any motor vehicle may be equipped with side cowl or fender lights which shall emit a white or amber light without glare.

Any motor vehicle may be equipped with lights on each side thereof which shall emit a white or amber light without glare.

Any motor vehicle may equipped [1] with back-up lights, either separately or in combination with another light. No back-up lights shall be continuously lighted when the motor vehicle is in forward motion.

(B) Whoever violates this section shall be punished as provided in section 4513.99 of the Revised Code.

(2002 S 123, eff. 1–1–04; 1953 H 1, eff. 10–1–53; GC 6307–86)

[1] Prior and current versions differ; although no amendment was indicated in 2002 S 123, "may equipped" appeared as "may be equipped" in 1953 H 1.

4513.14 Two lights displayed

(A) At all times mentioned in section 4513.03 of the Revised Code at least two lighted lights shall be displayed, one near each side of the front of every motor vehicle and trackless trolley, except when such vehicle or trackless trolley is parked subject to the regulations governing lights on parked vehicles and trackless trolleys.

The director of public safety shall prescribe and promulgate regulations relating to the design and use of such lights and such regulations shall be in accordance with currently recognized standards.

(B) Whoever violates this section shall be punished as provided in section 4513.99 of the Revised Code.

(2002 S 123, eff. 1–1–04; 1992 S 98, eff. 11–12–92; 128 v 1180; 1953 H 1; GC 6307–87)

4513.15 Headlights required

(A) Whenever a motor vehicle is being operated on a roadway or shoulder adjacent thereto during the times specified in section 4513.03 of the Revised Code, the driver shall use a distribution of light, or composite beam, directed high enough and of sufficient intensity to reveal persons, vehicles, and substantial objects at a safe distance in advance of the vehicle, subject to the following requirements;

(1) Whenever the driver of a vehicle approaches an oncoming vehicle, such driver shall use a distribution of light, or composite beam, so aimed that the glaring rays are not projected into the eyes of the oncoming driver.

(2) Every new motor vehicle registered in this state, which has multiple-beam road lighting equipment shall be equipped with a beam indicator, which shall be lighted whenever the uppermost distribution of light from the headlights is in use, and shall not otherwise be lighted. Said indicator shall be so designed and

located that, when lighted, it will be readily visible without glare to the driver of the vehicle.

(B) Whoever violates this section shall be punished as provided in section 4513.99 of the Revised Code.

(2002 S 123, eff. 1–1–04; 1953 H 1, eff. 10–1–53; GC 6307–88)

4513.16 Lights of less intensity

(A) Any motor vehicle may be operated under the conditions specified in section 4513.03 of the Revised Code when it is equipped with two lighted lights upon the front thereof capable of revealing persons and substantial objects seventy-five feet ahead, in lieu of lights required in section 4513.14 of the Revised Code, provided that such vehicle shall not be operated at a speed in excess of twenty miles per hour.

(B) Whoever violates this section shall be punished as provided in section 4513.99 of the Revised Code.

(2002 S 123, eff. 1–1–04; 1953 H 1, eff. 10–1–53; GC 6307–89)

4513.17 Number of lights permitted; limitations on red and flashing lights

(A) Whenever a motor vehicle equipped with headlights also is equipped with any auxiliary lights or spotlight or any other light on the front thereof projecting a beam of an intensity greater than three hundred candle power, not more than a total of five of any such lights on the front of a vehicle shall be lighted at any one time when the vehicle is upon a highway.

(B) Any lighted light or illuminating device upon a motor vehicle, other than headlights, spotlights, signal lights, or auxiliary driving lights, that projects a beam of light of an intensity greater than three hundred candle power, shall be so directed that no part of the beam will strike the level of the roadway on which the vehicle stands at a distance of more than seventy-five feet from the vehicle.

(C)(1) Flashing lights are prohibited on motor vehicles, except as a means for indicating a right or a left turn, or in the presence of a vehicular traffic hazard requiring unusual care in approaching, or overtaking or passing. This prohibition does not apply to emergency vehicles, road service vehicles servicing or towing a disabled vehicle, traffic line stripers, snow plows, rural mail delivery vehicles, vehicles as provided in section 4513.182 of the Revised Code, department of transportation maintenance vehicles, funeral hearses, funeral escort vehicles, and similar equipment operated by the department or local authorities, which shall be equipped with and display, when used on a street or highway for the special purpose necessitating such lights, a flashing, oscillating, or rotating amber light, but shall not display a flashing, oscillating, or rotating light of any other color, nor to vehicles or machinery permitted by section 4513.11 of the Revised Code to have a flashing red light.

(2) When used on a street or highway, farm machinery and vehicles escorting farm machinery may be equipped with and display a flashing, oscillating, or rotating amber light, and the prohibition contained in division (C)(1) of this section does not apply to such machinery or vehicles. Farm machinery also may display the lights described in section 4513.11 of the Revised Code.

(D) Except a person operating a public safety vehicle, as defined in division (E) of section 4511.01 of the Revised Code, or a school bus, no person shall operate, move, or park upon, or permit to stand within the right-of-way of any public street or highway any vehicle or equipment that is equipped with and displaying a flashing red or a flashing combination red and white light, or an oscillating or rotating red light, or a combination red and white oscillating or rotating light; and except a public law enforcement officer, or other person sworn to enforce the criminal and traffic laws of the state, operating a public safety vehicle when on duty, no person shall operate, move, or park upon, or permit to stand within the right-of-way of any street or highway any vehicle or equipment that is equipped with, or upon which is mounted, and displaying a flashing blue or a flashing combination blue and white light, or an oscillating or rotating blue light, or a combination blue and white oscillating or rotating light.

(E) This section does not prohibit the use of warning lights required by law or the simultaneous flashing of turn signals on disabled vehicles or on vehicles being operated in unfavorable atmospheric conditions in order to enhance their visibility. This section also does not prohibit the simultaneous flashing of turn signals or warning lights either on farm machinery or vehicles escorting farm machinery, when used on a street or highway.

(F) Whoever violates this section shall be punished as provided in section 4513.99 of the Revised Code.

(2002 S 123, eff. 1–1–04; 1997 H 282, eff. 11–12–97; 1996 S 121, eff. 11–19–96; 1975 H 272, eff. 1–1–76; 1974 H 956; 132 v H 878; 131 v S 247, H 147; 128 v 591; 127 v 54; 126 v 790; 1953 H 1; GC 6307–90)

4513.171 Lights and sirens on coroners' vehicles

(A) Notwithstanding any other provision of law, a motor vehicle operated by a coroner, deputy coroner, or coroner's investigator may be equipped with a flashing, oscillating, or rotating red or blue light and a siren, whistle, or bell capable of emitting sound audible under normal conditions from a distance of not less than five hundred feet. Such a vehicle may display the flashing, oscillating, or rotating red or blue light and may give the audible signal of the siren, exhaust whistle, or bell only when responding to a fatality or a fatal motor vehicle accident on a street or highway and only at those locations where the stoppage of traffic impedes the ability of the coroner, deputy coroner, or coroner's investigator to arrive at the site of the fatality.

This section does not relieve a coroner, deputy coroner, or coroner's investigator operating a motor vehicle from the duty to drive with due regard for the safety of all persons and property upon the highway.

(B) Whoever violates this section shall be punished as provided in section 4513.99 of the Revised Code.

(2002 S 123, eff. 1–1–04; 1997 H 282, eff. 11–12–97)

4513.18 Standards for lights on snow removal equipment

(A) The director of transportation shall adopt standards and specifications applicable to headlights, clearance lights, identification, and other lights, on snow removal equipment when operated on the highways, and on vehicles operating under special permits pursuant to section 4513.34 of the Revised Code, in lieu of the lights otherwise required on motor vehicles. Such standards and specifications may permit the use of flashing lights for purposes of identification on snow removal equipment, and oversize vehicles when in service upon the highways. The standards and specifications for lights referred to in this section shall correlate with and, so far as possible, conform with those approved by the American association of state highway officials.

It is unlawful to operate snow removal equipment on a highway unless the lights thereon comply with and are lighted when and as required[1] by the standards and specifications adopted as provided in this section.

(B) Whoever violates this section shall be punished as provided in section 4513.99 of the Revised Code.

(2002 S 123, eff. 1–1–04; 1973 H 200, eff. 9–28–73; 132 v H 1; 131 v S 247; 1953 H 1; GC 6307–90a)

1 Prior and current versions differ; although no amendment was indicated in 2002 S 123, "when and as required" appeared as "when as required" in 1973 H 200.

4513.181 Standards and specifications for certain types of vehicles

The director of public safety subject to the provisions of sections 119.01 to 119.13 of the Revised Code shall adopt standards and specifications applicable to rural mail delivery vehicles, state highway survey vehicles, and funeral escort vehicles. Such standards and specifications shall permit rural mail delivery vehicles, state highway survey vehicles, and funeral escort vehicles the use of flashing lights.

(1992 S 98, eff. 11–12–92; 127 v 54; 126 v 790)

4513.182 Lights and sign on vehicle transporting preschool children

(A) No person shall operate any motor vehicle owned, leased, or hired by a nursery school, kindergarten, or day-care center, while transporting preschool children to or from such an institution unless the motor vehicle is equipped with and displaying two amber flashing lights mounted on a bar attached to the top of the vehicle, and a sign bearing the designation "caution—children," which shall be attached to the bar carrying the amber flashing lights in such a manner as to be legible to persons both in front of and behind the vehicle. The lights and sign shall meet standards and specifications adopted by the director of public safety. The director, subject to Chapter 119. of the Revised Code, shall adopt standards and specifications for the lights and sign, which shall include, but are not limited to, requirements for the color and size of lettering to be used on the sign, the type of material to be used for the sign, and the method of mounting the lights and sign so that they can be removed from a motor vehicle being used for purposes other than those specified in this section.

(B) No person shall operate a motor vehicle displaying the lights and sign required by this section for any purpose other than the transportation of preschool children as provided in this section.

(C) Whoever violates this section shall be punished as provided in section 4513.99 of the Revised Code.

(2002 S 123, eff. 1–1–04; 1992 S 98, eff. 11–12–92; 1975 H 272)

4513.19 Focus and aim of headlights

(A) No person shall use any lights mentioned in sections 4513.03 to 4513.18 of the Revised Code upon any motor vehicle, trailer, or semitrailer unless said lights are equipped, mounted, and adjusted as to focus and aim in accordance with regulations which are prescribed by the director of public safety.

(B) Whoever violates this section shall be punished as provided in section 4513.99 of the Revised Code.

(2002 S 123, eff. 1–1–04; 1992 S 98, eff. 11–12–92; 128 v 1180; 1953 H 1; GC 6307–91)

OTHER EQUIPMENT REQUIREMENTS

4513.20 Brake equipment

(A) The following requirements govern as to brake equipment on vehicles:

(1) Every trackless trolley and motor vehicle, other than a motorcycle, when operated upon a highway shall be equipped with brakes adequate to control the movement of and to stop and hold such trackless trolley or motor vehicle, including two separate means of applying the brakes, each of which means shall be effective to apply the brakes to at least two wheels. If these two separate means of applying the brakes are connected in any way, then on such trackless trolleys or motor vehicles manufactured or assembled after January 1, 1942, they shall be so constructed that failure of any one part of the operating mechanism shall not leave the trackless trolley or motor vehicle without brakes on at least two wheels.

(2) Every motorcycle, when operated upon a highway shall be equipped with at least one adequate brake, which may be operated by hand or by foot.

(3) Every motorized bicycle shall be equipped with brakes meeting the rules adopted by the director of public safety under section 4511.521 of the Revised Code.

(4) When operated upon the highways of this state, the following vehicles shall be equipped with brakes adequate to control the movement of and to stop and to hold the vehicle, designed to be applied by the driver of the towing motor vehicle from its cab, and also designed and connected so that, in case of a breakaway of the towed vehicle, the brakes shall be automatically applied:

(a) Every trailer or semitrailer, except a pole trailer, with an empty weight of two thousand pounds or more, manufactured or assembled on or after January 1, 1942;

(b) Every manufactured home or travel trailer with an empty weight of two thousand pounds or more, manufactured or assembled on or after January 1, 2001.

(5) In any combination of motor-drawn trailers or semitrailers equipped with brakes, means shall be provided for applying the rearmost brakes in approximate synchronism with the brakes on the towing vehicle, and developing the required braking effort on the rearmost wheels at the fastest rate; or means shall be provided for applying braking effort first on the rearmost brakes; or both of the above means, capable of being used alternatively, may be employed.

(6) Every vehicle and combination of vehicles, except motorcycles and motorized bicycles, and except trailers and semitrailers of a gross weight of less than two thousand pounds, and pole trailers, shall be equipped with parking brakes adequate to hold the vehicle on any grade on which it is operated, under all conditions of loading, on a surface free from snow, ice, or loose material. The parking brakes shall be capable of being applied in conformance with the foregoing requirements by the driver's muscular effort or by spring action or by equivalent means. Their operation may be assisted by the service brakes or other source of power provided that failure of the service brake actuation system or other power assisting mechanism will not prevent the parking brakes from being applied in conformance with the foregoing requirements. The parking brakes shall be so designed that when once applied they shall remain applied with the required effectiveness despite exhaustion of any source of energy or leakage of any kind.

(7) The same brake drums, brake shoes and lining assemblies, brake shoe anchors, and mechanical brake shoe actuation mechanism normally associated with the wheel brake assemblies may be used for both the service brakes and the parking brakes. If the means of applying the parking brakes and the service brakes are connected in any way, they shall be so constructed that failure of any one part shall not leave the vehicle without operative brakes.

(8) Every trackless trolley, motor vehicle, or combination of motor-drawn vehicles shall be capable at all times and under all conditions of loading of being stopped on a dry, smooth, level road free from loose material, upon application of the service or foot brake, within the following specified distances, or shall be capable of being decelerated at a sustained rate corresponding to these distances:

(a) Trackless trolleys, vehicles, or combinations of vehicles having brakes on all wheels shall come to a stop in thirty feet or less from a speed of twenty miles per hour.

(b) Vehicles or combinations of vehicles not having brakes on all wheels shall come to a stop in forty feet or less from a speed of twenty miles per hour.

(9) All brakes shall be maintained in good working order and shall be so adjusted as to operate as equally as practicable with respect to the wheels on opposite sides of the trackless trolley or vehicle.

(B) Whoever violates this section shall be punished as provided in section 4513.99 of the Revised Code.

(2002 S 123, eff. 1–1–04; 2000 H 600, eff. 9–1–00; 1992 S 98, eff. 11–12–92; 1980 H 736; 1977 S 100; 132 v H 1; 131 v H 611; 130 v S 54; 1953 H 1; GC 6307–92)

4513.201 Brake fluid

(A) No hydraulic brake fluid for use in motor vehicles shall be sold in this state if the brake fluid is below the minimum standard of specifications for heavy duty type brake fluid established by the society of automotive engineers and the standard of specifications established by 49 C.F.R. 571.116, as amended.

(B) All manufacturers, packers, or distributors of brake fluid selling such fluid in this state shall state on the containers that the brake fluid therein meets or exceeds the applicable minimum SAE standard of specifications and the standard of specifications established in 49 C.F.R. 571.116, as amended.

(C) Whoever violates this section shall be punished as provided in section 4513.99 of the Revised Code.

(2002 S 123, eff. 1–1–04; 1997 S 60, eff. 10–21–97; 1992 S 98, eff. 11–12–92; 129 v 1374)

4513.202 Standards for repair and replacement of brake linings

(A) No brake lining, brake lining material, or brake lining assemblies for use as repair and replacement parts in motor vehicles shall be sold in this state if these items do not meet or exceed the minimum standard of specifications established by the society of automotive engineers and the standard of specifications established in 49 C.F.R. 571.105, as amended, and 49 C.F.R. 571.135, as amended.

(B) All manufacturers or distributors of brake lining, brake lining material, or brake lining assemblies selling these items for use as repair and replacement parts in motor vehicles shall state that the items meet or exceed the applicable minimum standard of specifications.

(C) Whoever violates this section shall be punished as provided in section 4513.99 of the Revised Code.

(D) As used in this section, "minimum standard of specifications" means a minimum standard for brake system or brake component performance that meets the need for motor vehicle safety and complies with the applicable SAE standards and recommended practices, and the federal motor vehicle safety standards that cover the same aspect of performance for any brake lining, brake lining material, or brake lining assemblies.

(2002 S 123, eff. 1–1–04; 1997 S 60, eff. 10–21–97; 1992 S 98, eff. 11–12–92; 1971 H 150)

4513.21 Horns, sirens, and warning devices

(A) Every motor vehicle or trackless trolley when operated upon a highway shall be equipped with a horn which is in good working order and capable of emitting sound audible, under normal conditions, from a distance of not less than two hundred feet.

No motor vehicle or trackless trolley shall be equipped with, nor shall any person use upon a vehicle, any siren, whistle, or bell. Any vehicle may be equipped with a theft alarm signal device which shall be so arranged that it cannot be used as an ordinary warning signal. Every emergency vehicle shall be equipped with a siren, whistle, or bell, capable of emitting sound audible under normal conditions from a distance of not less than five hundred feet and of a type approved by the director of public safety. Such equipment shall not be used except when such vehicle is operated in response to an emergency call or is in the immediate pursuit of an actual or suspected violator of the law, in which case the driver of the emergency vehicle shall sound such equipment when it is necessary to warn pedestrians and other drivers of the approach thereof.

(B) Whoever violates this section shall be punished as provided in section 4513.99 of the Revised Code.

(2002 S 123, eff. 1–1–04; 1992 S 98, eff. 11–12–92; 1973 H 200; 1953 H 1; GC 6307–93)

4513.22 Mufflers; excessive smoke or gas

(A) Every motor vehicle and motorcycle with an internal combustion engine shall at all times be equipped with a muffler which is in good working order and in constant operation to prevent excessive or unusual noise, and no person shall use a muffler cutout, by-pass, or similar device upon a motor vehicle on a highway. Every motorcycle muffler shall be equipped with baffle plates.

No person shall own, operate, or have in the person's possession any motor vehicle or motorcycle equipped with a device for producing excessive smoke or gas, or so equipped as to permit oil or any other chemical to flow into or upon the exhaust pipe or muffler of such vehicle, or equipped in any other way to produce or emit smoke or dangerous or annoying gases from any portion of such vehicle, other than the ordinary gases emitted by the exhaust of an internal combustion engine under normal operation.

(B) Whoever violates this section shall be punished as provided in section 4513.99 of the Revised Code.

(2002 S 123, eff. 1–1–04; 1978 H 115, eff. 7–10–78; 132 v H 380; 1953 H 1; GC 6307–94)

4513.221 Noise control

(A) The board of county commissioners of any county, and the board of township trustees of any township subject to section 505.17 of the Revised Code, may regulate passenger car and motorcycle noise on streets and highways under their jurisdiction. Such regulations shall include maximum permissible noise limits measured in decibels, subject to the requirements of this section.

(B) Regulations establishing maximum permissible noise limits measured in decibels shall prohibit the operation, within the speed limits specified herein, of a passenger car or motorcycle of a type subject to registration at any time or under any condition of load, acceleration, or deceleration in such manner as to exceed the following maximum noise limits, based on a distance of not less than fifty feet from the center of the line of travel:

(1) For passenger cars:

(a) When operated at a speed of thirty-five miles per hour or less, a maximum noise limit of seventy decibels;

(b) When operated at a speed of more than thirty-five miles per hour, a maximum noise limit of seventy-nine decibels.

(2) For motorcycles:

(a) When operated at a speed of thirty-five miles per hour or less, a maximum noise limit of eighty-two decibels;

(b) When operated at a speed of more than thirty-five miles per hour, a maximum noise limit of eighty-six decibels.

(C) Maximum noise limits established pursuant to division (B) of this section shall be measured on the "A" scale of a standard sound level meter meeting the applicable requirements for a type 2 sound level meter as defined in American national standards institute standard S1.4—1983, or the most recent revision thereof. Measurement practices shall be in substantial conformity with standards and recommended practice established by the society of automotive engineers, including SAE standard J 986 A NOV81, SAE standard J 366 MAR85, SAE standard J 331 A, and such other standards and practices as may be approved by the federal government.

(D) No regulation enacted under division (B) of this section shall be effective until signs giving notice of the regulation are posted upon or at the entrance to the highway or part thereof affected, as may be most appropriate.

(E) A board of county commissioners of any county may regulate noise from passenger cars, motorcycles, or other devices using internal combustion engines in the unincorporated area of the county, and a board of township trustees may regulate such noise in the unincorporated area of the township, in any of the following ways:

(1) By prohibiting operating or causing to be operated any motor vehicle, agricultural tractor, motorcycle, all-purpose vehicle, or snowmobile not equipped with a factory-installed muffler or equivalent muffler in good working order and in constant operation;

(2) By prohibiting the removing or rendering inoperative, or causing to be removed or rendered inoperative, other than for purposes of maintenance, repair, or replacement, of any muffler;

(3) By prohibiting the discharge into the open air of exhaust of any stationary or portable internal combustion engine except through a factory-installed muffler or equivalent muffler in good working order and in constant operation;

(4) By prohibiting racing the motor of any vehicle described in division (E)(1) of this section in such a manner that the exhaust system emits a loud, cracking, or chattering noise unusual to its normal operation.

(F) Whoever violates any maximum noise limit established as provided in division (B) of this section or any of the prohibitions authorized in division (E) of this section is guilty of a minor misdemeanor. Fines collected under this section by the county shall be paid into the county general fund, and such fines collected by the township shall be paid into the township general fund.

No regulation adopted under this section shall apply to commercial racetrack operations.

(1986 H 131, eff. 6–26–86)

4513.23 Rear view mirrors

(A) Every motor vehicle, motorcycle, and trackless trolley shall be equipped with a mirror so located as to reflect to the operator a view of the highway to the rear of such vehicle, motorcycle, or trackless trolley. Operators of vehicles, motorcycles, streetcars, and trackless trolleys shall have a clear and unobstructed view to the front and to both sides of their vehicles, motorcycles, streetcars, or trackless trolleys and shall have a clear view to the rear of their vehicles, motorcycles, streetcars, or trackless trolleys by mirror.

(B) Whoever violates this section shall be punished as provided in section 4513.99 of the Revised Code.

(2002 S 123, eff. 1–1–04; 132 v H 380, eff. 1–1–68; 1953 H 1; GC 6307–95)

4513.24 Windshields and wipers

(A) No person shall drive any motor vehicle on a street or highway in this state, other than a motorcycle or motorized bicycle, that is not equipped with a windshield.

(B) No person shall drive any motor vehicle, other than a bus, with any sign, poster, or other nontransparent material upon the front windshield, sidewings, side, or rear windows of such vehicle other than a certificate or other paper required to be displayed by law, except that there may be in the lower left-hand or right-hand corner of the windshield a sign, poster, or decal not to exceed four inches in height by six inches in width. No sign, poster, or decal shall be displayed in the front windshield in such a manner as to conceal the vehicle identification number for the motor vehicle when, in accordance with federal law, that number is located inside the vehicle passenger compartment and so placed as to be readable through the vehicle glazing without moving any part of the vehicle.

(C) The windshield on every motor vehicle, streetcar, and trackless trolley shall be equipped with a device for cleaning rain, snow, or other moisture from the windshield. The device shall be maintained in good working order and so constructed as to be controlled or operated by the operator of the vehicle, streetcar, or trackless trolley.

(D) Whoever violates this section shall be punished as provided in section 4513.99 of the Revised Code.

(2002 S 123, eff. 1–1–04; 1996 H 353, eff. 9–17–96; 1989 S 117, eff. 10–26–89; 1953 H 1; GC 6307–96)

4513.241 Rules governing materials used in windshields and windows; exceptions

(A) The director of public safety, in accordance with Chapter 119. of the Revised Code, shall adopt rules governing the use of tinted glass, and the use of transparent, nontransparent, translucent, and reflectorized materials in or on motor vehicle windshields, side windows, sidewings, and rear windows that prevent a person of normal vision looking into the motor vehicle from seeing or identifying persons or objects inside the motor vehicle.

(B) The rules adopted under this section may provide for persons who meet either of the following qualifications:

(1) On November 11, 1994, or the effective date of any rule adopted under this section, own a motor vehicle that does not conform to the requirements of this section or of any rule adopted under this section;

(2) Establish residency in this state and are required to register a motor vehicle that does not conform to the requirements of this section or of any rule adopted under this section.

(C) No person shall operate, on any highway or other public or private property open to the public for vehicular travel or parking, lease, or rent any motor vehicle that is registered in this state unless the motor vehicle conforms to the requirements of this section and of any applicable rule adopted under this section.

(D) No person shall install in or on any motor vehicle, any glass or other material that fails to conform to the requirements of this section or of any rule adopted under this section.

(E) No used motor vehicle dealer or new motor vehicle dealer, as defined in section 4517.01 of the Revised Code, shall sell any motor vehicle that fails to conform to the requirements of this section or of any rule adopted under this section.

(F) No reflectorized materials shall be permitted upon or in any front windshield, side windows, sidewings, or rear window.

(G) This section does not apply to the manufacturer's tinting or glazing of motor vehicle windows or windshields that is otherwise in compliance with or permitted by federal motor vehicle safety standard number two hundred five.

(H) With regard to any side window behind a driver's seat or any rear window other than any window on an emergency door, this section does not apply to any school bus used to transport a handicapped child pursuant to a special education program under Chapter 3323. of the Revised Code, whom it is impossible or impractical to transport by regular school bus in the course of regular route transportation provided by a school district. As used in this division, "handicapped child" and "special education program" have the same meanings as in section 3323.01 of the Revised Code.

(I) This section does not apply to any school bus that is to be sold and operated outside this state.

(J) Whoever violates division (C), (D), (E), or (F) of this section is guilty of a minor misdemeanor.

(2002 S 123, eff. 1–1–04; 1994 S 234, eff. 11–11–94; 1992 S 98, eff. 11–12–92; 1986 H 291)

4513.242 Decals on side windows or sidewings

(A) Notwithstanding section 4513.24 and division (F) of section 4513.241 of the Revised Code or any rule adopted thereunder, a decal, whether reflectorized or not, may be displayed upon any side window or sidewing of a motor vehicle if all of the following are met:

(1) The decal is necessary for public or private security arrangements to which the motor vehicle periodically is subjected;

(2) The decal is no larger than is necessary to accomplish the security arrangements;

(3) The decal does not obscure the vision of the motor vehicle operator or prevent a person looking into the motor vehicle from seeing or identifying persons or objects inside the motor vehicle.

(B) Whoever violates this section shall be punished as provided in section 4513.99 of the Revised Code.

(2002 S 123, eff. 1–1–04; 1997 H 210, eff. 3–31–97)

4513.25 Solid tire requirements

(A) Every solid tire, as defined in section 4501.01 of the Revised Code, on a vehicle shall have rubber or other resilient material on its entire traction surface at least one inch thick above the edge of the flange of the entire periphery.

(B) Whoever violates this section shall be punished as provided in section 4513.99 of the Revised Code.

(2002 S 123, eff. 1–1–04; 1953 H 1, eff. 10–1–53; GC 6307–97)

4513.26 Requirements for safety glass in motor vehicles

(A) No person shall sell any new motor vehicle nor shall any new motor vehicle be registered, and no person shall operate any motor vehicle, which is registered in this state and which has been manufactured or assembled on or after January 1, 1936, unless the motor vehicle is equipped with safety glass wherever glass is used in the windshields, doors, partitions, rear windows, and windows on each side immediately adjacent to the rear window.

"Safety glass" means any product composed of glass so manufactured, fabricated, or treated as substantially to prevent shattering and flying of the glass when it is struck or broken, or such other or similar product as may be approved by the registrar of motor vehicles.

Glass other than safety glass shall not be offered for sale, or sold for use in, or installed in any door, window, partition, or windshield that is required by this section to be equipped with safety glass.

(B) Whoever violates this section shall be punished as provided in section 4513.99 of the Revised Code.

(2002 S 123, eff. 1–1–04; 1996 H 353, eff. 9–17–96; 1953 H 1, eff. 10–1–53; GC 6307–98)

4513.261 Directional signals

(A)(1) No person shall operate any motor vehicle manufactured or assembled on or after January 1, 1954, unless the vehicle is equipped with electrical or mechanical directional signals.

(2) No person shall operate any motorcycle or motor-driven cycle manufactured or assembled on or after January 1, 1968, unless the vehicle is equipped with electrical or mechanical directional signals.

(B) "Directional signals" means an electrical or mechanical signal device capable of clearly indicating an intention to turn either to the right or to the left and which shall be visible from both the front and rear.

(C) All mechanical signal devices shall be self-illuminating devices when in use at the times mentioned in section 4513.03 of the Revised Code.

(D) Whoever violates this section is guilty of a minor misdemeanor.

(2002 S 123, eff. 1–1–04; 2000 H 600, eff. 9–1–00; 125 v 456, eff. 10–19–53)

4513.262 Installation of anchorage units for safety belts; specifications

(A) As used in this section and in section 4513.263 of the Revised Code, the component parts of a "seat safety belt" include a belt, anchor attachment assembly, and a buckle or closing device.

(B) No person shall sell, lease, rent, or operate any passenger car, as defined in division (E) of section 4501.01 of the Revised Code, that is registered or to be registered in this state and that is manufactured or assembled on or after January 1, 1962, unless the passenger car is equipped with sufficient anchorage units at the attachment points for attaching at least two sets of seat safety belts to its front seat. Such anchorage units at the attachment points shall be of such construction, design, and strength to support a loop load pull of not less than four thousand pounds for each belt.

(C) No person shall sell, lease, or rent any passenger car, as defined in division (E) of section 4501.01 of the Revised Code, that is registered or to be registered in this state and that is manufactured or assembled on or after January 1, 1966, unless the passenger car has installed in its front seat at least two seat safety belt assemblies.

(D) After January 1, 1966, neither any seat safety belt for use in a motor vehicle nor any component part of any such seat safety belt shall be sold in this state unless the seat safety belt or the component part satisfies the minimum standard of specifications established by the society of automotive engineers for automotive seat belts and unless the seat safety belt or component part is labeled so as to indicate that it meets those minimum standard specifications.

(E) Each sale, lease, or rental in violation of this section constitutes a separate offense.

(F) Whoever violates this section is guilty of a minor misdemeanor.

(2002 S 123, eff. 1–1–04; 1986 S 54, eff. 5–6–86; 131 v S 7; 129 v 1567)

4513.263 Seat belt requirements; exceptions; fines

(A) As used in this section and in section 4513.99 of the Revised Code:

(1) "Automobile" means any commercial tractor, passenger car, commercial car, or truck that is required to be factory-equipped with an occupant restraining device for the operator or any passenger by regulations adopted by the United States secretary of transportation pursuant to the "National Traffic and Motor Vehicle Safety Act of 1966," 80 Stat. 719, 15 U.S.C.A. 1392.

(2) "Occupant restraining device" means a seat safety belt, shoulder belt, harness, or other safety device for restraining a person who is an operator of or passenger in an automobile and that satisfies the minimum federal vehicle safety standards established by the United States department of transportation.

(3) "Passenger" means any person in an automobile, other than its operator, who is occupying a seating position for which an occupant restraining device is provided.

(4) "Commercial tractor," "passenger car," and "commercial car" have the same meanings as in section 4501.01 of the Revised Code.

(5) "Vehicle" and "motor vehicle," as used in the definitions of the terms set forth in division (A)(4) of this section, have the same meanings as in section 4511.01 of the Revised Code.

(6) "Tort action" means a civil action for damages for injury, death, or loss to person or property. "Tort action" includes a product liability claim, as defined in section 2307.71 of the Revised Code, and an asbestos claim, as defined in section 2307.91 of the Revised Code, but does not include a civil action for damages for breach of contract or another agreement between persons.

(B) No person shall do any of the following:

(1) Operate an automobile on any street or highway unless that person is wearing all of the available elements of a properly adjusted occupant restraining device, or operate a school bus that has an occupant restraining device installed for use in its operator's seat unless that person is wearing all of the available elements of the device, as properly adjusted;

(2) Operate an automobile on any street or highway unless each passenger in the automobile who is subject to the requirement set forth in division (B)(3) of this section is wearing all of the available elements of a properly adjusted occupant restraining device;

(3) Occupy, as a passenger, a seating position on the front seat of an automobile being operated on any street or highway unless that person is wearing all of the available elements of a properly adjusted occupant restraining device;

(4) Operate a taxicab on any street or highway unless all factory-equipped occupant restraining devices in the taxicab are maintained in usable form.

(C) Division (B)(3) of this section does not apply to a person who is required by section 4511.81 of the Revised Code to be secured in a child restraint device. Division (B)(1) of this section does not apply to a person who is an employee of the United States postal service or of a newspaper home delivery service, during any period in which the person is engaged in the operation of an automobile to deliver mail or newspapers to addressees. Divisions (B)(1) and (3) of this section do not apply to a person who has an affidavit signed by a physician licensed to practice in this state under Chapter 4731. of the Revised Code or a chiropractor licensed to practice in this state under Chapter 4734. of the Revised Code that states that the person has a physical impairment that makes use of an occupant restraining device impossible or impractical.

(D) Notwithstanding any provision of law to the contrary, no law enforcement officer shall cause an operator of an automobile being operated on any street or highway to stop the automobile for the sole purpose of determining whether a violation of division (B) of this section has been or is being committed or for the sole purpose of issuing a ticket, citation, or summons for a violation of that nature or causing the arrest of or commencing a prosecution of a person for a violation of that nature, and no law enforcement officer shall view the interior or visually inspect any automobile being operated on any street or highway for the sole purpose of determining whether a violation of that nature has been or is being committed.

(E) All fines collected for violations of division (B) of this section, or for violations of any ordinance or resolution of a political subdivision that is substantively comparable to that division, shall be forwarded to the treasurer of state for deposit as follows:

(1) Eight per cent shall be deposited into the seat belt education fund, which is hereby created in the state treasury, and shall be used by the department of public safety to establish a seat belt education program.

(2) Eight per cent shall be deposited into the elementary school program fund, which is hereby created in the state treasury, and shall be used by the department of public safety to establish and administer elementary school programs that encourage seat safety belt use.

(3) Two per cent shall be deposited into the Ohio medical transportation trust fund created by section 4766.05 of the Revised Code.

(4) Twenty–eight per cent shall be deposited into the trauma and emergency medical services fund, which is hereby created in the state treasury, and shall be used by the department of public safety for the administration of the division of emergency medical services and the state board of emergency medical services.

(5) Fifty–four per cent shall be deposited into the trauma and emergency medical services grants fund, which is hereby created in the state treasury, and shall be used by the state board of emergency medical services to make grants, in accordance with section 4765.07 of the Revised Code and rules the board adopts under section 4765.11 of the Revised Code.

(F)(1) Subject to division (F)(2) of this section, the failure of a person to wear all of the available elements of a properly adjusted occupant restraining device in violation of division (B)(1) or (3) of this section or the failure of a person to ensure that each minor who is a passenger of an automobile being operated by that person is wearing all of the available elements of a properly adjusted occupant restraining device in violation of division (B)(2) of this section shall not be considered or used by the trier of fact in a tort action as evidence of negligence or contributory negligence. But, the trier of fact may determine based on evidence admitted consistent with the Ohio rules of evidence that the failure contributed to the harm alleged in the tort action and may diminish a recovery of compensatory damages that represents noneconomic loss, as defined in section 2307.011 of the Revised Code, in a tort action that could have been recovered but for the plaintiff's failure to wear all of the available elements of a properly adjusted occupant restraining device. Evidence of that failure shall not be used as a basis for a criminal prosecution of the person other than a prosecution for a violation of this section; and shall not be admissible as evidence in a criminal action involving the person other than a prosecution for a violation of this section.

(2) If, at the time of an accident involving a passenger car equipped with occupant restraining devices, any occupant of the passenger car who sustained injury or death was not wearing an available occupant restraining device, was not wearing all of the available elements of such a device, or was not wearing such a device as properly adjusted, then, consistent with the Rules of Evidence, the fact that the occupant was not wearing the avail-

able occupant restraining device, was not wearing all of the available elements of such a device, or was not wearing such a device as properly adjusted is admissible in evidence in relation to any claim for relief in a tort action to the extent that the claim for relief satisfies all of the following:

(a) It seeks to recover damages for injury or death to the occupant.

(b) The defendant in question is the manufacturer, designer, distributor, or seller of the passenger car.

(c) The claim for relief against the defendant in question is that the injury or death sustained by the occupant was enhanced or aggravated by some design defect in the passenger car or that the passenger car was not crashworthy.

(G)(1) Whoever violates division (B)(1) of this section shall be fined thirty dollars.

(2) Whoever violates division (B)(3) of this section shall be fined twenty dollars.

(3) Except as otherwise provided in this division, whoever violates division (B)(4) of this section is guilty of a minor misdemeanor. If the offender previously has been convicted of or pleaded guilty to a violation of division (B)(4) of this section, whoever violates division (B)(4) of this section is guilty of a misdemeanor of the third degree.

(2004 S 80, eff. 4–7–05; 2003 H 85, § 3, eff. 1–1–04[1]*; 2003 H 85, § 1, eff. 3 9 04; 2002 S 123, eff. 1–1–04; 2001 S 108, § 2.01, eff. 7–6–01; 2000 H 138, eff. 11–3–00; 1997 H 215, eff. 6–30–97; 1996 H 350, eff. 1–27–97*[2]*; 1993 H 154, eff. 6–30–93; 1992 S 98; 1992 S 105, H 118; 1987 H 1; 1986 H 428, S 262, S 54)*

[1] O Const Art II, # 1c and 1d, and RC 1.471, state that sections of law are subject to the referendum unless providing for tax levies, state appropriations, or are emergency in nature. Since this Act is apparently not an exception, and 1–1–04 is within the ninety-day period, the effective date should probably be 3 9 04.

[2] See Notes of Decisions and Opinions, *State ex rel. Ohio Academy of Trial Lawyers v. Sheward* (Ohio 1999), 86 Ohio St.3d 451, 715 N.E.2d 1062.

Uncodified Law

2001 S 108, § 1, eff. 7–6–01, reads:

It is the intent of this act (1) to repeal the Tort Reform Act, Am. Sub. H.B. 350 of the 121st General Assembly, 146 Ohio Laws 3867, in conformity with the Supreme Court of Ohio's decision in *State, ex rel. Ohio Academy of Trial Lawyers, v. Sheward* (1999), 86 Ohio St.3d 451; (2) to clarify the status of the law; and (3) to revive the law as it existed prior to the Tort Reform Act.

Notes of Decisions

1. Constitutional issues

1996 H 350, which amended more than 100 statutes and a variety of rules relating to tort and other civil actions, and which was an attempt to reenact provisions of law previously held unconstitutional by the Supreme Court of Ohio, is an act of usurpation of judicial power in violation of the doctrine of separation of powers; for that reason, and because of violation of the one-subject rule of the Ohio Constitution, 1996 H 350 is unconstitutional. State ex rel. Ohio Academy of Trial Lawyers v. Sheward (Ohio, 08-16-1999) 86 Ohio St.3d 451, 715 N.E.2d 1062, 1999-Ohio-123, reconsideration denied 87 Ohio St.3d 1409, 716 N.E.2d 1170.

SPECIAL REQUIREMENTS

4513.27 Disabled vehicle, extra signal equipment; exemptions

(A) No person shall operate any motor truck, trackless trolley, bus, or commercial tractor upon any highway outside the corporate limits of municipalities at any time from sunset to sunrise unless there is carried in such vehicle and trackless trolley, except as provided in division (B) of this section, the following equipment which shall be of the types approved by the director of transportation:

(1) At least three flares or three red reflectors or three red electric lanterns, each of which is capable of being seen and distinguished at a distance of five hundred feet under normal atmospheric conditions at night time;

(2) At least three red-burning fusees, unless red reflectors or red electric lanterns are carried;

(3) At least two red cloth flags, not less than twelve inches square, with standards to support them;

(4) The type of red reflectors shall comply with such standards and specifications in effect on September 16, 1963 or later established by the interstate commerce commission and must be certified as meeting such standards by underwriter's laboratories.

(B) No person shall operate at the time and under the conditions stated in this section any motor vehicle used in transporting flammable liquids in bulk, or in transporting compressed flammable gases, unless there is carried in such vehicle three red electric lanterns or three red reflectors meeting the requirements stated in division (A) of this section. There shall not be carried in any such vehicle any flare, fusee, or signal produced by a flame.

(C) This section does not apply to any person who operates any motor vehicle in a work area designated by protection equipment devices that are displayed and used in accordance with the manual adopted by the department of transportation under section 4511.09 of the Revised Code.

(D) Whoever violates this section shall be punished as provided in section 4513.99 of the Revised Code.

(2002 S 123, eff. 1–1–04; 2000 H 484, eff. 10–5–00; 1989 H 258, eff. 11–2–89; 1973 H 200; 130 v Pt 2, H 5; 130 v H 603, 1953 H 1; GC 6307–99)

4513.28 Display of warning devices on disabled vehicles; exemptions

(A) Whenever any motor truck, trackless trolley, bus, commercial tractor, trailer, semi-trailer, or pole trailer is disabled upon the traveled portion of any highway or the shoulder thereof outside of any municipality, or upon any freeway, expressway, thruway and connecting, entering or exiting ramps within a municipality, at any time when lighted lamps are required on vehicles and trackless trolleys, the operator of such vehicle or trackless trolley shall display the following warning devices upon the highway during the time the vehicle or trackless trolley is so disabled on the highway except as provided in division (B) of this section:

(1) A lighted fusee shall be immediately placed on the roadway at the traffic side of such vehicle or trackless trolley, unless red electric lanterns or red reflectors are displayed.

(2) Within the burning period of the fusee and as promptly as possible, three lighted flares or pot torches, or three red reflectors or three red electric lanterns shall be placed on the roadway as follows:

(a) One at a distance of forty paces or approximately one hundred feet in advance of the vehicle;

(b) One at a distance of forty paces or approximately one hundred feet to the rear of the vehicle or trackless trolley except as provided in this section, each in the center of the lane of traffic occupied by the disabled vehicle or trackless trolley;

(c) One at the traffic side of the vehicle or trackless trolley.

(B) Whenever any vehicle used in transporting flammable liquids in bulk, or in transporting compressed flammable gases, is disabled upon a highway at any time or place mentioned in division (A) of this section, the driver of such vehicle shall display upon the roadway the following warning devices:

(1) One red electric lantern or one red reflector shall be immediately placed on the roadway at the traffic side of the vehicle;

(2) Two other red electric lanterns or two other red reflectors shall be placed to the front and rear of the vehicle in the same manner prescribed for flares in division (A) of this section.

(C) When a vehicle of a type specified in division (B) of this section is disabled, the use of flares, fusees, or any signal produced by flame as warning signals is prohibited.

(D) Whenever any vehicle or trackless trolley of a type referred to in this section is disabled upon the traveled portion of a highway or the shoulder thereof, outside of any municipality, or upon any freeway, expressway, thruway and connecting, entering or exiting ramps within a municipality, at any time when the display of fusees, flares, red reflectors, or electric lanterns is not required, the operator of such vehicle or trackless trolley shall display two red flags upon the roadway in the lane of traffic occupied by the disabled vehicle or trackless trolley, one at a distance of forty paces or approximately one hundred feet in advance of the vehicle or trackless trolley, and one at a distance of forty paces or approximately one hundred feet to the rear of the vehicle or trackless trolley, except as provided in this section.

(E) The flares, fusees, lanterns, red reflectors, and flags to be displayed as required in this section shall conform with the requirements of section 4513.27 of the Revised Code applicable thereto.

(F) In the event the vehicle or trackless trolley is disabled near a curve, crest of a hill, or other obstruction of view, the flare, flag, reflector, or lantern in that direction shall be placed as to afford ample warning to other users of the highway, but in no case shall it be placed less than forty paces or approximately one hundred feet nor more than one hundred twenty paces or approximately three hundred feet from the disabled vehicle or trackless trolley.

(G) This section does not apply to the operator of any vehicle in a work area designated by protection equipment devices that are displayed and used in accordance with the manual adopted by the department of transportation under section 4511.09 of the Revised Code.

(H) Whoever violates this section shall be punished as provided in section 4513.99 of the Revised Code.

(2002 S 123, eff. 1–1–04; 1989 H 258, eff. 11–2–89; 130 v H 603; 1953 H 1; GC 6307–100)

4513.29 Requirements for vehicles transporting explosives

(A) Any person operating any vehicle transporting explosives upon a highway shall at all times comply with the following requirements:

(1) Said vehicle shall be marked or placarded on each side and on the rear with the word "explosives" in letters not less than eight inches high, or there shall be displayed on the rear of such vehicle a red flag not less than twenty-four inches square marked with the word "danger" in white letters six inches high, or shall be marked or placarded in accordance with section 177.823 of the United States department of transportation regulations.

(2) Said vehicle shall be equipped with not less than two fire extinguishers, filled and ready for immediate use, and placed at convenient points on such vehicle.

(3) The director of transportation may promulgate such regulations governing the transportation of explosives and other dangerous articles by vehicles upon the highway as are reasonably necessary to enforce sections 4513.01 to 4513.37 of the Revised Code.

(B) Whoever violates this section shall be punished as provided in section 4513.99 of the Revised Code.

(2002 S 123, eff. 1–1–04; 1973 H 200, eff. 9–28–73; 1969 H 460; 1953 H 1; GC 6307–101)

LOAD LIMITATIONS

4513.30 Limitation of load extension on left side of vehicle

(A) No passenger-type vehicle shall be operated on a highway with any load carried on such vehicle which extends more than six inches beyond the line of the fenders on the vehicle's left side.

(B) Whoever violates this section shall be punished as provided in section 4513.99 of the Revised Code.

(2002 S 123, eff. 1–1–04; 1953 H 1, eff. 10–1–53; GC 6307–102)

4513.31 Securing of loads

(A) No vehicle shall be driven or moved on any highway unless the vehicle is so constructed, loaded, or covered as to prevent any of its load from dropping, sifting, leaking, or otherwise escaping therefrom, except that sand or other substance may be dropped for the purpose of securing traction, or water or other substance may be sprinkled on a roadway in cleaning or maintaining the roadway.

(B) Except for a farm vehicle used to transport agricultural produce or agricultural production materials or a rubbish vehicle in the process of acquiring its load, no vehicle loaded with garbage, swill, cans, bottles, waste paper, ashes, refuse, trash, rubbish, waste, wire, paper, cartons, boxes, glass, solid waste, or any other material of an unsanitary nature that is susceptible to blowing or bouncing from a moving vehicle shall be driven or moved on any highway unless the load is covered with a sufficient cover to prevent the load or any part of the load from spilling onto the highway.

(C) Whoever violates this section shall be punished as provided in section 4513.99 of the Revised Code.

(2002 S 123, eff. 1–1–04; 1988 H 514, eff. 2–11–88; 1953 H 1; GC 6307–103)

4513.32 Towing requirements; exception

(A) When one vehicle is towing another vehicle, the drawbar or other connection shall be of sufficient strength to pull all the weight towed thereby, and the drawbar or other connection shall not exceed fifteen feet from one vehicle to the other, except the connection between any two vehicles transporting poles, pipe, machinery, or other objects of structural nature which cannot readily be dismembered.

When one vehicle is towing another and the connection consists only of a chain, rope, or cable, there shall be displayed upon such connection a white flag or cloth not less than twelve inches square.

In addition to such drawbar or other connection, each trailer and each semitrailer which is not connected to a commercial tractor by means of a fifth wheel shall be coupled with stay chains or cables to the vehicle by which it is being drawn. The chains or cables shall be of sufficient size and strength to prevent the towed vehicle's parting from the drawing vehicle in case the drawbar or other connection should break or become disengaged. In case of a loaded pole trailer, the connecting pole to the drawing vehicle shall be coupled to the drawing vehicle with stay chains or cables of sufficient size and strength to prevent the towed vehicle's parting from the drawing vehicle.

Every trailer or semitrailer, except pole and cable trailers and pole and cable dollies operated by a public utility as defined in section 5727.01 of the Revised Code, shall be equipped with a coupling device, which shall be so designed and constructed that the trailer will follow substantially in the path of the vehicle drawing it, without whipping or swerving from side to side. Vehicles used to transport agricultural produce or agricultural production materials between a local place of storage and supply and the farm, when drawn or towed on a street or highway at a speed of twenty-five miles per hour or less, and vehicles designed and used exclusively to transport a boat between a place of storage and a marina, or in and around a marina, when drawn or towed on a street or highway for a distance of no more than ten miles and at a speed of twenty-five miles per hour or less, shall have a drawbar or other connection, including the hitch mounted on the towing vehicle, which shall be of sufficient strength to pull all the weight towed thereby. Only one such vehicle used to transport agricultural produce or agricultural production materials as provided in this section may be towed or drawn at one time, except as follows:

(1) An agricultural tractor may tow or draw more than one such vehicle;

(2) A pickup truck or straight truck designed by the manufacturer to carry a load of not less than one-half ton and not more than two tons may tow or draw not more than two such vehicles that are being used to transport agricultural produce from the farm to a local place of storage. No vehicle being so towed by such a pickup truck or straight truck shall be considered to be a motor vehicle.

(B) Whoever violates this section shall be punished as provided in section 4513.99 of the Revised Code.

(2002 S 123, eff. 1–1–04; 1998 H 425, eff. 7–29–98; 1992 H 485, eff. 10–7–92; 1979 H 1; 132 v H 1002, H 684; 1953 H 1; GC 6307–104)

4513.33 Weighing vehicle; scales to be used; removal of excess load; alteration of weight limits

Any police officer having reason to believe that the weight of a vehicle and its load is unlawful may require the driver of said vehicle to stop and submit to a weighing of it by means of a compact, self-contained, portable, sealed scale specially adapted to determining the wheel loads of vehicles on highways; a sealed scale permanently installed in a fixed location, having a load-receiving element specially adapted to determining the wheel loads of highway vehicles; a sealed scale, permanently installed in a fixed location, having a load-receiving element specially adapted to determining the combined load of all wheels on a single axle or on successive axles of a highway vehicle, or a sealed scale adapted to weighing highway vehicles, loaded or unloaded. The driver of such vehicle shall, if necessary, be directed to proceed to the nearest available of such sealed scales to accomplish the weighing, provided such scales are within three miles of the point where such vehicle is stopped. Any vehicle stopped in accordance with this section may be held by the police officer for a reasonable time only to accomplish the weighing as prescribed by this section. All scales used in determining the lawful weight of a vehicle and its load shall be annually compared by a municipal, county, or state sealer with the state standards or standards approved by the state and such scales shall not be sealed if they do not conform to the state standards or standards approved by the state.

At each end of a permanently installed scale, there shall be a straight approach in the same plane as the platform, of sufficient length and width to insure the level positioning of vehicles during weight determinations.

During determination of weight by compact, self-contained, portable, sealed scales, specially adapted to determining the wheel loads of vehicles on highways, they shall always be used on terrain of sufficient length and width to accommodate the entire vehicle being weighed. Such terrain shall be level, or if not level, it shall be of such elevation that the difference in elevation between the wheels on any one axle does not exceed two inches and the difference in elevation between axles being weighed does not exceed one-fourth inch per foot of the distance between said axles.

In all determination of all weights, except gross weight, by compact, self-contained, portable, sealed scales, specially adapted to determining the wheel loads of vehicles on highways, all successive axles, twelve feet or less apart, shall be weighed simultaneously by placing one such scale under the outside wheel of each such axle. In determinations of gross weight by the use of compact, self-contained, portable, sealed scales, specially adapted to determining the wheel loads of vehicles on highways, all axles shall be weighed simultaneously by placing one such scale under the outside wheel of each axle.

Whenever such officer upon weighing a vehicle and load determines that the weight is unlawful, he may require the driver to stop the vehicle in a suitable place and remain standing until such portion of the load is removed as is necessary to reduce the weight of such vehicle to the limit permitted under sections 5577.01 to 5577.14 of the Revised Code.

Whenever local authorities determine upon the basis of an engineering and traffic investigation that the weight limits permitted under sections 5577.01 to 5577.14 of the Revised Code, or the weight limits permitted when compact, self-contained, portable, sealed scales, specially adapted to determining the wheel loads of vehicles on highways, are used on any part of a state route under their jurisdiction is greater than is reasonable under the conditions found to exist at such location, the local authorities may, by resolution, request the director of transportation to determine and declare reasonable weight limits. Upon receipt of such request the director may determine and declare reasonable weight limits at such location, and if the director alters the weight limits set by sections 5577.01 to 5577.14 and this section of the Revised Code, then such altered weight limits shall become effective only when appropriate signs giving notice thereof are erected at such location by local authorities.

The director may withdraw his approval of any altered weight limit whenever, in his opinion, any altered weight limit becomes unreasonable, and upon such withdrawal the altered weight limit shall become ineffective, and the signs relating thereto shall be immediately removed by local authorities. Alteration of weight limits on state routes by local authorities is not effective until alteration has been approved by the director.

This section does not derogate or limit the power and authority conferred upon the director or boards of county commissioners by section 5577.07 of the Revised Code.

(1975 H 624, eff. 11–26–75; 1973 H 200; 132 v H 1; 131 v H 338; 130 v H 23; 1953 H 1; GC 6307–105)

4513.34 Special permit for vehicles; fees

(A) The director of transportation with respect to all highways that are a part of the state highway system and local authorities with respect to highways under their jurisdiction, upon application in writing and for good cause shown, may issue a special permit in writing authorizing the applicant to operate or move a vehicle or combination of vehicles of a size or weight of vehicle or load exceeding the maximum specified in sections 5577.01 to 5577.09 of the Revised Code, or otherwise not in conformity with sections 4513.01 to 4513.37 of the Revised Code, upon any highway under the jurisdiction of the authority granting the permit.

For purposes of this section, the director may designate certain state highways or portions of state highways as special economic development highways. If an application submitted to the director under this section involves travel of a nonconforming vehicle or combination of vehicles upon a special economic development highway, the director, in determining whether good cause has been shown that issuance of a permit is justified, shall consider the effect the travel of the vehicle or combination of vehicles will have on the economic development in the area in which the designated highway or portion of highway is located.

(B) Notwithstanding sections 715.22 and 723.01 of the Revised Code, the holder of a special permit issued by the director under this section may move the vehicle or combination of vehicles described in the special permit on any highway that is a part of the state highway system when the movement is partly within and partly without the corporate limits of a municipal corporation. No local authority shall require any other permit or license or charge any license fee or other charge against the holder of a permit for the movement of a vehicle or combination of vehicles on any highway that is a part of the state highway system. The director shall not require the holder of a permit issued by a local authority to obtain a special permit for the movement of vehicles or combination of vehicles on highways within the jurisdiction of the local authority. Permits may be issued for any period of time not to exceed one year, as the director in the director's discretion or a local authority in its discretion determines advisable, or for the duration of any public construction project.

(C) The application for a permit shall be in the form that the director or local authority prescribes. The director or local authority may prescribe a permit fee to be imposed and collected when any permit described in this section is issued. The permit fee may be in an amount sufficient to reimburse the director or local authority for the administrative costs incurred in issuing the permit, and also to cover the cost of the normal and expected damage caused to the roadway or a street or highway structure as the result of the operation of the nonconforming vehicle or combination of vehicles. The director, in accordance with Chapter 119. of the Revised Code, shall establish a schedule of fees for permits issued by the director under this section.

For the purposes of this section and of rules adopted by the director under this section, milk transported in bulk by vehicle is deemed a nondivisible load.

(D) The director or local authority may issue or withhold a permit. If a permit is to be issued, the director or local authority may limit or prescribe conditions of operation for the vehicle and may require the posting of a bond or other security conditioned upon the sufficiency of the permit fee to compensate for damage caused to the roadway or a street or highway structure. In addition, a local authority, as a condition of issuance of an overweight permit, may require the applicant to develop and enter into a mutual agreement with the local authority to compensate for or to repair excess damage caused to the roadway by travel under the permit.

For a permit that will allow travel of a nonconforming vehicle or combination of vehicles on a special economic development highway, the director, as a condition of issuance, may require the applicant to agree to make periodic payments to the department to compensate for damage caused to the roadway by travel under the permit.

(E) Every permit shall be carried in the vehicle or combination of vehicles to which it refers and shall be open to inspection by any police officer or authorized agent of any authority granting the permit. No person shall violate any of the terms of a permit.

(F) Whoever violates this section shall be punished as provided in section 4513.99 of the Revised Code.

(2002 S 123, eff. 1–1–04; 2001 H 73, eff. 6–29–01; 1991 S 223, eff. 9–30–92; 1988 H 712; 1973 H 200; 131 v S 44; 1953 H 1; GC 6307–106)

ADMINISTRATION AND ENFORCEMENT

4513.35 Disposition of moneys collected

(A) All fines collected under sections 4511.01 to 4511.78, 4511.99, and 4513.01 to 4513.37 of the Revised Code shall be paid into the county treasury and, with the exception of that portion distributed under section 3375.53 of the Revised Code, shall be placed to the credit of the fund for the maintenance and repair of the highways within that county, except that:

(1) All fines for violations of division (B) of section 4513.263 shall be delivered to the treasurer of state as provided in division (E) of section 4513.263 of the Revised Code.

(2) All fines collected from, or moneys arising from bonds forfeited by, persons apprehended or arrested by state highway patrolmen shall be distributed as provided in section 5503.04 of the Revised Code.

(3)(a) Subject to division (E) of section 4513.263 of the Revised Code and except as otherwise provided in division (A)(3)(b) of this section, one-half of all fines collected from, and one-half of all moneys arising from bonds forfeited by, persons apprehended or arrested by a township constable or other township police officer shall be paid to the township treasury to be placed to the credit of the general fund.

(b) All fines collected from, and all moneys arising from bonds forfeited by, persons apprehended or arrested by a township constable or other township police officer pursuant to division (B)(2) of section 4513.39 of the Revised Code for a violation of section 4511.21 of the Revised Code or any other law, ordinance, or regulation pertaining to speed that occurred on a highway included as part of the interstate system, as defined in section 5516.01 of the Revised Code, shall be paid into the county treasury and be credited as provided in the first paragraph of this section.

(B) Notwithstanding any other provision of this section or of any other section of the Revised Code:

(1) All fines collected from, and all moneys arising from bonds forfeited by, persons arrested under division (E)(1) or (2) of section 2935.03 of the Revised Code are deemed to be collected, and to arise, from arrests made within the jurisdiction in which the arresting officer is appointed, elected, or employed, for violations of one of the sections or chapters of the Revised Code listed in division (E)(1) of that section and shall be distributed accordingly.

(2) All fines collected from, and all moneys arising from bonds forfeited by, persons arrested under division (E)(3) of section 2935.03 of the Revised Code are deemed to be collected, and to arise, from arrests made within the jurisdiction in which the arresting officer is appointed, elected, or employed, for violations of municipal ordinances that are substantially equivalent to one of the sections or one of the provisions of one of the chapters of the Revised Code listed in division (E)(1) of that section and shall be distributed accordingly.

(1994 H 687, eff. 10–12–94; 1990 H 669, eff. 1–10–91; 1990 H 171; 1986 S 54; 132 v H 24; 126 v 773; 1953 H 1; GC 6307–108)

4513.36 Prohibition against resisting officer

(A) No person shall resist, hinder, obstruct, or abuse any sheriff, constable, or other official while that official is attempting to arrest offenders under any provision of sections 4511.01 to 4511.78, 4511.99, and 4513.01 to 4513.37 of the Revised Code. No person shall interfere with any person charged under any provision of any of those sections with the enforcement of the law relative to public highways.

(B) Whoever violates this section is guilty of a minor misdemeanor.

(2002 S 123, eff. 1–1–04; 1953 H 1, eff. 10–1–53; GC 6307–109)

4513.361 Presenting false name or information to law enforcement officer

(A) No person shall knowingly present, display, or orally communicate a false name, social security number, or date of birth to a law enforcement officer who is in the process of issuing to the person a traffic ticket or complaint.

(B) Whoever violates this section is guilty of a misdemeanor of the first degree.

(2002 S 123, eff. 1–1–04; 1991 H 96, eff. 6–18–91)

4513.37 Record of violations

Every county court judge, mayor, and clerk of a court of record shall keep a full record of every case in which a person is charged with any violation of sections 4511.01 to 4511.78, section 4511.99, and sections 4513.01 to 4513.37 of the Revised Code, or of any other law or ordinance regulating the operation of vehicles, streetcars, and trackless trolleys on highways.

Within ten days after the conviction or forfeiture of bail of a person upon a charge of violating any of such sections or other law or ordinance regulating the operation of vehicles, streetcars, and trackless trolleys on highways, said judge, mayor, or clerk shall prepare and immediately forward to the department of public safety an abstract of the court record covering the case in which said person was convicted or forfeited bail, which abstract must be certified by the person required to prepare the same to be true and correct.

Said abstract shall be made upon a form approved and furnished by the department and shall include the name and address of the party charged, the number of his driver's or commercial driver's license, the registration number of the vehicle involved, the nature of the offense, the date of hearing, the plea, the judgment, or whether bail forfeited, and the amount of the fine or forfeiture.

Every court of record shall also forward a like report to the department upon the conviction of any person of manslaughter or other felony in the commission of which a vehicle was used.

The failure, refusal, or neglect of such officer to comply with this section constitutes misconduct in office and is ground for removal therefrom.

The department shall keep all abstracts received under this section at its main office.

(1992 S 98, eff. 11–12–92; 1989 H 381; 127 v 1039)

4513.38 Exemption of collector's or historical vehicles from equipment standards

No person shall be prohibited from owning or operating a licensed collector's vehicle or historical motor vehicle that is equipped with a feature of design, type of material, or article of equipment that was not in violation of any motor vehicle equipment law of this state or of its political subdivisions in effect during the calendar year the vehicle was manufactured, and no licensed collector's vehicle or historical motor vehicle shall be prohibited from displaying or using any such feature of design, type of material, or article of equipment.

No person shall be prohibited from owning or operating a licensed collector's vehicle or historical motor vehicle for failing to comply with an equipment provision contained in Chapter 4513. of the Revised Code or in any state rule that was enacted or adopted in a year subsequent to that in which the vehicle was manufactured, and no licensed collector's vehicle or historical motor vehicle shall be required to comply with an equipment provision enacted into Chapter 4513. of the Revised Code or adopted by state rule subsequent to the calendar year in which it was manufactured. No political subdivision shall require an owner of a licensed collector's vehicle or historical motor vehicle to comply with equipment provisions contained in laws or rules that were enacted or adopted subsequent to the calendar year in which the vehicle was manufactured, and no political subdivision shall prohibit the operation of a licensed collector's vehicle or historical motor vehicle for failure to comply with any such equipment laws or rules.

(1975 S 52, eff. 9–15–75)

4513.39 Power of arrest for violations on state highways

(A) The state highway patrol and sheriffs or their deputies shall exercise, to the exclusion of all other peace officers except within municipal corporations and except as specified in division (B) of this section and division (E) of section 2935.03 of the Revised Code, the power to make arrests for violations on all state highways, of sections 4503.11, 4503.21, 4511.14 to 4511.16, 4511.20 to 4511.23, 4511.26 to 4511.40, 4511.42 to 4511.48, 4511.58, 4511.59, 4511.62 to 4511.71, 4513.03 to 4513.13, 4513.15 to 4513.22, 4513.24 to 4513.34, 4549.01, 4549.08 to 4549.12, and 4549.62 of the Revised Code.

(B) A member of the police force of a township police district created under section 505.48 of the Revised Code, and a township constable appointed pursuant to section 509.01 of the Revised Code, who has received a certificate from the Ohio peace officer training commission under section 109.75 of the Revised Code, shall exercise the power to make arrests for violations of those sections listed in division (A) of this section, other than sections 4513.33 and 4513.34 of the Revised Code, as follows:

(1) If the population of the township that created the township police district served by the member's police force or the township that is served by the township constable is fifty thousand or less, the member or constable shall exercise that power on those portions of all state highways, except those highways included as part of the interstate system, as defined in section 5516.01 of the Revised Code, that are located within the township police district, in the case of a member of a township police district police force, or within the unincorporated territory of the township, in the case of a township constable;

(2) If the population of the township that created the township police district served by the member's police force or the township that is served by the township constable is greater than fifty thousand, the member or constable shall exercise that power on those portions of all state highways and highways included as part of the interstate highway system, as defined in section 5516.01 of the Revised Code, that are located within the township police district, in the case of a member of a township police district police force, or within the unincorporated territory of the township, in the case of a township constable.

(2004 H 163, eff. 9–23–04; 1996 H 670, eff. 12–2–96; 1994 H 687, eff. 10–12–94; 1990 H 669, eff. 1–10–91; 1990 H 171; 1984 H 632; 1982 H 738; 1980 H 207; 1953 H 1; GC 6297)

4513.40 Warning sign before safety device at street crossing

When a safety device has been installed in the traveled portion of a street at a railroad grade crossing for the protection of the traveling public, the municipal corporation shall place a warning sign not less than two hundred feet from the crossing. The driver of any vehicle shall place his vehicle under control at the location of said warning signs so as to be able to bring said vehicle to a complete stop at said safety device. Colliding with such safety device at the crossing is prima-facie evidence that the driver is a reckless driver.

(125 v 903, eff. 10–1–53; 1953 H 1; GC 591–1)

4513.41 Exemption of certain vehicles from emission, noise control, or fuel usage standards

(A) No owner of a licensed collector's vehicle, a historical motor vehicle, or a collector's vehicle that is an agricultural tractor or traction engine shall be required to comply with an emission, noise control, or fuel usage provision contained in a law or rule of this state or its political subdivisions that was enacted or adopted subsequent to the calendar year in which the vehicle was manufactured.

(B) No person shall be prohibited from operating a licensed collector's vehicle, a historical motor vehicle, or a collector's vehicle that is an agricultural tractor or traction engine for failing to comply with an emission, noise control, or fuel usage law or rule of this state or its political subdivisions that was enacted or adopted subsequent to the calendar year in which his vehicle was manufactured.

(C) Except as provided in section 4505.061 of the Revised Code, no person shall be required to submit his collector's vehicle to a physical inspection prior to or in connection with an issuance of title to, or the sale or transfer of ownership of such vehicle, except that a police officer may inspect it to determine ownership.

In accordance with section 1.51 of the Revised Code, this section shall, without exception, prevail over any special or local provision of the Revised Code that requires owners or operators of collector's vehicles to comply with standards of emission, noise, fuel usage, or physical condition in connection with an issuance of title to, or the sale or transfer of ownership of such vehicle or part thereof.

(1975 S 52, eff. 9–15–75)

4513.50 Definitions

As used in sections 4513.50 to 4513.53 of the Revised Code:

(A)(1) "Bus" means any vehicle used for the transportation of passengers that meets at least one of the following:

(a) Was originally designed by the manufacturer to transport more than fifteen passengers, including the driver;

(b) Either the gross vehicle weight rating or the gross vehicle weight exceeds ten thousand pounds.

(2) "Bus" does not include a church bus as defined in section 4503.07 of the Revised Code or a school bus unless the church bus or school bus is used in the transportation of passengers for hire by a motor transportation company or a common carrier by motor vehicle or by a private motor carrier or contract carrier by motor vehicle.

(3) "Bus" also does not include any of the following:

(a) Any vehicle operated exclusively on a rail or rails;

(b) A trolley bus operated by electric power derived from a fixed overhead wire furnishing local passenger transportation similar to street-railway service;

(c) Vehicles owned or leased by government agencies or political subdivisions.

(B)(1) "Motor transportation company" and "common carrier by motor vehicle" have the same meanings as in section 4921.02 of the Revised Code.

(2) "Private motor carrier" and "contract carrier by motor vehicle" have the same meanings as in section 4923.02 of the Revised Code.

(2000 H 600, eff. 9–1–00)

VEHICLE EQUIPMENT SAFETY COMPACT

4513.51 Safety inspection decals

(A) Except as provided in division (B) of this section, on and after July 1, 2001, no person shall operate a bus, nor shall any person being the owner of a bus or having supervisory responsibility for a bus permit the operation of any bus, unless the bus displays a valid, current safety inspection decal issued by the state highway patrol under section 4513.52 of the Revised Code.

(B) For the purpose of complying with the requirements of this section and section 4513.52 of the Revised Code, the owner or other operator of a bus may drive the bus directly to an inspection site conducted by the state highway patrol and directly back to the person's place of business without a valid registration and without displaying a safety inspection decal, provided that no passengers may occupy the bus during such operation.

(C) The registrar of motor vehicles shall not accept an application for registration of a bus unless the bus owner presents a valid safety inspection report for the applicable registration year.

(D) Whoever violates division (A) of this section is guilty of a misdemeanor of the first degree.

(2002 S 123, eff. 1–1–04; 2000 H 600, eff. 9–1–00)

4513.52 Rules relating to inspection of buses

(A) The department of public safety, with the advice of the public utilities commission, shall adopt and enforce rules relating to the inspection of buses to determine whether a bus is safe and lawful, including whether its equipment is in proper adjustment or repair.

(B) The rules shall determine the safety features, items of equipment, and other safety-related conditions subject to inspection. The rules may authorize the state highway patrol to operate safety inspection sites, or to enter in or upon the property of any bus operator to conduct the safety inspections, or both. The rules also shall establish a fee, not to exceed two hundred dollars, for each bus inspected.

(C) The state highway patrol shall conduct the bus safety inspections at least on an annual basis. An inspection conducted under this section is valid for twelve months unless, prior to that time, the bus fails a subsequent inspection or ownership of the bus is transferred.

(D) The state highway patrol shall collect a fee for each bus inspected.

(E) Upon determining that a bus is in safe operating condition, that its equipment is in proper adjustment and repair, and that it is otherwise lawful, the inspecting officer shall do both of the following:

(1) Affix an official safety inspection decal to the outside surface of each side of the bus;

(2) Issue the owner or operator of the bus a safety inspection report, to be presented to the registrar or a deputy registrar upon application for registration of the bus.

(2003 H 87, eff. 6–30–03; 2000 H 600, eff. 9–1–00)

4513.53 Inspection staff; safety inspection decals; fees

(A) The superintendent of the state highway patrol, with approval of the director of public safety, may appoint and maintain necessary staff to carry out the inspection of buses.

(B) The superintendent of the state highway patrol shall adopt a distinctive annual safety inspection decal bearing the date of inspection. The state highway patrol may remove any decal from a bus that fails any inspection.

(C) Fees collected by the state highway patrol shall be paid into the state treasury to the credit of the general revenue fund. Annually by the first day of June, the director of public safety shall determine the amount of fees collected under section 4513.52 of the Revised Code and shall certify the amount to the director of budget and management for reimbursement. The director of budget and management then may transfer cash up to the amount certified from the general revenue fund to the state highway safety fund.

(2003 H 87, eff. 6–30–03; 2000 H 600, eff. 6–1–00)

ABANDONED AND UNCLAIMED MOTOR VEHICLES

4513.60 Impounding motor vehicle left on private residential or agricultural property; posting tow-away zone on other private property; removal of motor vehicle by owner of posted property; reclaiming of vehicle by its owner; notice by those removing vehicles to police authorities; improper removal prohibited

(A)(1) The sheriff of a county or chief of police of a municipal corporation, township, or township police district, within the sheriff's or chief's respective territorial jurisdiction, upon complaint of any person adversely affected, may order into storage any motor vehicle, other than an abandoned junk motor vehicle as defined in section 4513.63 of the Revised Code, that has been left on private residential or private agricultural property for at least four hours without the permission of the person having the right to the possession of the property. The sheriff or chief of police, upon complaint of the owner of a repair garage or place of storage, may order into storage any motor vehicle, other than an abandoned junk motor vehicle, that has been left at the garage or place of storage for a longer period than that agreed upon. The place of storage shall be designated by the sheriff or chief of police. When ordering a motor vehicle into storage pursuant to this division, a sheriff or chief of police, whenever possible, shall arrange for the removal of the motor vehicle by a private tow truck operator or towing company. Subject to division (C) of this section, the owner of a motor vehicle that has been removed pursuant to this division may recover the vehicle only in accordance with division (E) of this section.

(2) Divisions (A)(1) to (3) of this section do not apply to any private residential or private agricultural property that is established as a private tow-away zone in accordance with division (B) of this section.

(3) As used in divisions (A)(1) and (2) of this section, "private residential property" means private property on which is located one or more structures that are used as a home, residence, or sleeping place by one or more persons, if no more than three separate households are maintained in the structure or structures. "Private residential property" does not include any private property on which is located one or more structures that are used as a home, residence, or sleeping place by two or more persons, if more than three separate households are maintained in the structure or structures.

(B)(1) The owner of private property may establish a private tow-away zone only if all of the following conditions are satisfied:

(a) The owner posts on the owner's property a sign, that is at least eighteen inches by twenty-four inches in size, that is visible from all entrances to the property, and that contains at least all of the following information:

(i) A notice that the property is a private tow-away zone and that vehicles not authorized to park on the property will be towed away;

(ii) The telephone number of the person from whom a towed-away vehicle can be recovered, and the address of the place to which the vehicle will be taken and the place from which it may be recovered;

(iii) A statement that the vehicle may be recovered at any time during the day or night upon the submission of proof of ownership and the payment of a towing charge, in an amount not to exceed ninety dollars, and a storage charge, in an amount not to exceed twelve dollars per twenty-four-hour period; except that the charge for towing shall not exceed one hundred fifty dollars, and the storage charge shall not exceed twenty dollars per twenty-four-hour period, if the vehicle has a manufacturer's gross vehicle weight rating in excess of ten thousand pounds and is a truck, bus, or a combination of a commercial tractor and trailer or semitrailer.

(b) The place to which the towed vehicle is taken and from which it may be recovered is conveniently located, is well lighted, and is on or within a reasonable distance of a regularly scheduled route of one or more modes of public transportation, if any public transportation is available in the municipal corporation or township in which the private tow-away zone is located.

(2) If a vehicle is parked on private property that is established as a private tow-away zone in accordance with division (B)(1) of this section, without the consent of the owner of the property or in violation of any posted parking condition or regulation, the owner or the owner's agent may remove, or cause the removal of, the vehicle, the owner and the operator of the vehicle shall be deemed to have consented to the removal and storage of the vehicle and to the payment of the towing and storage charges specified in division (B)(1)(a)(iii) of this section, and the owner, subject to division (C) of this section, may recover a vehicle that has been so removed only in accordance with division (E) of this section.

(3) If a municipal corporation requires tow trucks and tow truck operators to be licensed, no owner of private property located within the municipal corporation shall remove, or shall cause the removal and storage of, any vehicle pursuant to division (B)(2) of this section by an unlicensed tow truck or unlicensed tow truck operator.

(4) Divisions (B)(1) to (3) of this section do not affect or limit the operation of division (A) of this section or sections 4513.61 to 4513.65 of the Revised Code as they relate to property other than private property that is established as a private tow-away zone under division (B)(1) of this section.

(C) If the owner or operator of a motor vehicle that has been ordered into storage pursuant to division (A)(1) of this section or of a vehicle that is being removed under authority of division (B)(2) of this section arrives after the motor vehicle or vehicle has been prepared for removal, but prior to its actual removal from the property, the owner or operator shall be given the opportunity to pay a fee of not more than one-half of the charge for the removal of motor vehicles under division (A)(1) of this section or of vehicles under division (B)(2) of this section, whichever is applicable, that normally is assessed by the person who has prepared the motor vehicle or vehicle for removal, in order to obtain release of the motor vehicle or vehicle. Upon payment of that fee, the motor vehicle or vehicle shall be released to the owner or operator, and upon its release, the owner or operator immediately shall move it so that:

(1) If the motor vehicle was ordered into storage pursuant to division (A)(1) of this section, it is not on the private residential or private agricultural property without the permission of the person having the right to possession of the property, or is not at the garage or place of storage without the permission of the owner, whichever is applicable.

(2) If the vehicle was being removed under authority of division (B)(2) of this section, it is not parked on the private property established as a private tow-away zone without the consent of the owner or in violation of any posted parking condition or regulation.

(D)(1) If an owner of private property that is established as a private tow-away zone in accordance with division (B)(1) of this section or the authorized agent of such an owner removes or causes the removal of a vehicle from that property under authority of division (B)(2) of this section, the owner or agent promptly shall notify the police department of the municipal corporation, township, or township police district in which the property is located, of the removal, the vehicle's license number, make, model, and color, the location from which it was removed, the date and time of its removal, the telephone number of the person from whom it may be recovered, and the address of the place to which it has been taken and from which it may be recovered.

(2) Each county sheriff and each chief of police of a municipal corporation, township, or township police district shall maintain a record of motor vehicles that the sheriff or chief orders into storage pursuant to division (A)(1) of this section and of vehicles removed from private property in the sheriff's or chief's jurisdiction that is established as a private tow-away zone of which the sheriff or chief has received notice under division (D)(1) of this section. The record shall include an entry for each such motor vehicle or vehicle that identifies the motor vehicle's or vehicle's license number, make, model, and color, the location from which it was removed, the date and time of its removal, the telephone number of the person from whom it may be recovered, and the address of the place to which it has been taken and from which it may be recovered. Any information in the record that pertains to a particular motor vehicle or vehicle shall be provided to any person who, either in person or pursuant to a telephone call, identifies self as the owner or operator of the motor vehicle or vehicle and requests information pertaining to its location.

(3) Any person who registers a complaint that is the basis of a sheriff's or police chief's order for the removal and storage of a motor vehicle under division (A)(1) of this section shall provide the identity of the law enforcement agency with which the complaint was registered to any person who identifies self as the owner or operator of the motor vehicle and requests information pertaining to its location.

(E) The owner of a motor vehicle that is ordered into storage pursuant to division (A)(1) of this section or of a vehicle that is removed under authority of division (B)(2) of this section may reclaim it upon payment of any expenses or charges incurred in its removal, in an amount not to exceed ninety dollars, and storage, in an amount not to exceed twelve dollars per twenty-four-hour period; except that the charge for towing shall not exceed one hundred fifty dollars, and the storage charge shall not exceed twenty dollars per twenty-four-hour period, if the vehicle has a manufacturer's gross vehicle weight rating in excess of ten thousand pounds and is a truck, bus, or a combination of a commercial tractor and trailer or semitrailer. Presentation of proof of ownership, which may be evidenced by a certificate of title to the motor vehicle or vehicle also shall be required for reclamation of the vehicle. If a motor vehicle that is ordered into storage pursuant to division (A)(1) of this section remains unclaimed by the owner for thirty days, the procedures established by sections 4513.61 and 4513.62 of the Revised Code shall apply.

(F) No person shall remove, or cause the removal of, any vehicle from private property that is established as a private tow-away zone under division (B)(1) of this section other than in accordance with division (B)(2) of this section, and no person shall remove, or cause the removal of, any motor vehicle from any other private property other than in accordance with division (A)(1) of this section or sections 4513.61 to 4513.65 of the Revised Code.

(G)(1) Whoever violates division (B)(3) of this section is guilty of a minor misdemeanor.

(2) Except as otherwise provided in this division, whoever violates division (F) of this section is guilty of a minor misdemeanor. If the offender previously has been convicted of or pleaded guilty to a violation of division (F) of this section, whoever violates division (F) of this section is guilty of a misdemeanor of the third degree.

(2002 S 123, eff. 1–1–04; 2000 H 600, eff. 9–1–00; 1990 S 285, eff. 4–10–91; 1984 H 112; 1980 S 257; 1974 H 650; 1971 H 24)

4513.61 Impounding abandoned motor vehicle; notice to owner; disposition of vehicle

The sheriff of a county or chief of police of a municipal corporation, township, or township police district, within the sheriff's or chief's respective territorial jurisdiction, or a state highway patrol trooper, upon notification to the sheriff or chief of police of such action and of the location of the place of storage, may order into storage any motor vehicle, including an abandoned junk motor vehicle as defined in section 4513.63 of the Revised Code, that has come into the possession of the sheriff, chief of police, or state highway patrol trooper as a result of the performance of the sheriff's, chief's, or trooper's duties or that has been left on a public street or other property open to the public for purposes of vehicular travel, or upon or within the right-of-way of any road or highway, for forty-eight hours or longer without notification to the sheriff or chief of police of the reasons for leaving the motor vehicle in such place, except that when such a motor vehicle constitutes an obstruction to traffic it may be ordered into storage immediately. The sheriff or chief of police shall designate the place of storage of any motor vehicle so ordered removed.

The sheriff or chief of police immediately shall cause a search to be made of the records of the bureau of motor vehicles to ascertain the owner and any lienholder of a motor vehicle ordered into storage by the sheriff or chief of police, or by a state highway patrol trooper, and, if known, shall send or cause to be sent notice to the owner or lienholder at the owner's or lienholder's last known address by certified mail with return receipt requested, that the motor vehicle will be declared a nuisance and disposed of if not claimed within ten days of the date of mailing of the notice. The owner or lienholder of the motor vehicle may reclaim it upon payment of any expenses or charges incurred in its removal and storage, and presentation of proof of ownership, which may be evidenced by a certificate of title or memorandum certificate of title to the motor vehicle. If the owner or lienholder of the motor vehicle reclaims it after a search of the records of the bureau has been conducted and after notice has been sent to the owner or lienholder as described in this section, and the search was conducted by the owner of the place of storage or the owner's employee, and the notice was sent to the motor vehicle owner by the owner of the place of storage or the owner's employee, the owner or lienholder shall pay to the place of storage a processing fee of twenty-five dollars, in addition to any expenses or charges incurred in the removal and storage of the vehicle.

If the owner or lienholder makes no claim to the motor vehicle within ten days of the date of mailing of the notice, and if the vehicle is to be disposed of at public auction as provided in section 4513.62 of the Revised Code, the sheriff or chief of police shall file with the clerk of courts of the county in which the place of storage is located an affidavit showing compliance with the requirements of this section. Upon presentation of the affidavit, the clerk, without charge, shall issue a salvage certificate of title, free and clear of all liens and encumbrances, to the sheriff or chief of police. If the vehicle is to be disposed of to a motor vehicle salvage dealer or other facility as provided in section 4513.62 of the Revised Code, the sheriff or chief of police shall execute in triplicate an affidavit, as prescribed by the registrar of motor vehicles, describing the motor vehicle and the manner in which it was disposed of, and that all requirements of this section have been complied with. The sheriff or chief of police shall retain the original of the affidavit for the sheriff's or chief's records, and shall furnish two copies to the motor vehicle salvage dealer or other facility. Upon presentation of a copy of the affidavit by the motor vehicle salvage dealer, the clerk of courts, within thirty days of the presentation, shall issue to such owner a salvage certificate of title, free and clear of all liens and encumbrances.

Whenever a motor vehicle salvage dealer or other facility receives an affidavit for the disposal of a motor vehicle as provided in this section, the dealer or facility shall not be required to obtain an Ohio certificate of title to the motor vehicle in the dealer's or facility's own name if the vehicle is dismantled or destroyed and both copies of the affidavit are delivered to the clerk of courts.

(2004 H 230, eff. 9–16–04; 1997 S 60, eff. 10–21–97; 1996 S 121, eff. 11–19–96; 1991 S 144, eff. 8–8–91; 1988 H 373; 1987 S 10; 1986 H 428; 1980 S 257; 1974 H 650; 1971 H 24)

4513.62 Disposition of vehicle ordered into storage

Unclaimed motor vehicles ordered into storage pursuant to division (A)(1) of section 4513.60 or section 4513.61 of the Revised Code shall be disposed of at the order of the sheriff of the county or the chief of police of the municipal corporation, township, or township police district to a motor vehicle salvage dealer or scrap metal processing facility as defined in section 4737.05 of the Revised Code, or to any other facility owned by or under contract with the county, municipal corporation, or township, for the disposal of such motor vehicles, or shall be sold by the sheriff, chief of police, or licensed auctioneer at public auction, after giving notice thereof by advertisement, published once a week for two successive weeks in a newspaper of general circulation in the county. Any moneys accruing from the disposition of an unclaimed motor vehicle that are in excess of the expenses resulting from the removal and storage of the vehicle shall be credited to the general fund of the county, the municipal corporation, or the township, as the case may be.

(1988 H 373, eff. 10–9–89; 1987 S 10; 1984 H 112; 1980 S 257; 1971 H 24)

4513.63 Disposition of abandoned junk motor vehicles

"Abandoned junk motor vehicle" means any motor vehicle meeting all of the following requirements:

(A) Left on private property for forty-eight hours or longer without the permission of the person having the right to the possession of the property, on a public street or other property open to the public for purposes of vehicular travel or parking, or upon or within the right-of-way of any road or highway, for forty-eight hours or longer;

(B) Three years old, or older;

(C) Extensively damaged, such damage including but not limited to any of the following: missing wheels, tires, motor, or transmission;

(D) Apparently inoperable;

(E) Having a fair market value of one thousand five hundred dollars or less.

The sheriff of a county or chief of police of a municipal corporation, township, or township police district, within the sheriff's or chief's respective territorial jurisdiction, or a state highway patrol trooper, upon notification to the sheriff or chief of police of such action, shall order any abandoned junk motor vehicle to be photographed by a law enforcement officer. The officer shall record the make of motor vehicle, the serial number when available, and shall also detail the damage or missing equipment to substantiate the value of one thousand five hundred dollars or less. The sheriff or chief of police shall thereupon immediately dispose of the abandoned junk motor vehicle to a motor vehicle salvage dealer as defined in section 4738.01 of the Revised Code or a scrap metal processing facility as defined in section 4737.05 of the Revised Code which is under contract to the county, township, or municipal corporation, or to any other facility owned by or under contract with the county, township, or municipal corporation for the destruction of such motor vehicles. The records and photograph relating to the abandoned junk motor vehicle shall be retained by the law enforcement agency ordering the disposition of such vehicle for a period of at least two years. The law enforcement agency shall execute in quadruplicate an affidavit, as prescribed by the registrar of motor vehicles, describing the motor vehicle and the manner in which it was disposed of, and that all requirements of this section have been complied with, and, within thirty days of disposing of the vehicle, shall sign and file the affidavit with the clerk of courts of the county in which the motor vehicle was abandoned. The clerk of courts shall retain the original of the affidavit for the clerk's files, shall furnish one copy thereof to the registrar, one copy to the motor vehicle salvage dealer or other facility handling the disposal of the vehicle, and one copy to the law enforcement agency ordering the disposal, who shall file such copy with the records and photograph relating to the disposal. Any moneys arising from the disposal of an abandoned junk motor vehicle shall be deposited in the general fund of the county, township, or the municipal corporation, as the case may be.

Notwithstanding section 4513.61 of the Revised Code, any motor vehicle meeting the requirements of divisions (C), (D), and (E) of this section which has remained unclaimed by the owner or lienholder for a period of ten days or longer following notification as provided in section 4513.61 of the Revised Code may be disposed of as provided in this section.

(2004 H 230, eff. 9–16–04; 1997 S 60, eff. 10–21–97; 1992 S 125, eff. 4–16–93; 1991 S 144; 1980 S 257; 1978 H 865; 1975 S 52; 1974 H 650; 1971 H 24)

4513.64 Prohibition against abandonment of junk motor vehicle

(A) No person shall willfully leave an abandoned junk motor vehicle as defined in section 4513.63 of the Revised Code on private property for more than seventy-two hours without the permission of the person having the right to the possession of the property, or on a public street or other property open to the public for purposes of vehicular travel or parking, or upon or within the right-of-way of any road or highway, for forty-eight hours or longer without notification to the sheriff of the county or chief of police of the municipal corporation, township, or township police district of the reasons for leaving the motor vehicle in such place.

For purposes of this section, the fact that a motor vehicle has been so left without permission or notification is prima-facie evidence of abandonment.

Nothing contained in sections 4513.60, 4513.61, and 4513.63 of the Revised Code shall invalidate the provisions of municipal ordinances or township resolutions regulating or prohibiting the abandonment of motor vehicles on streets, highways, public property, or private property within municipal corporations or townships.

(B) Whoever violates this section is guilty of a minor misdemeanor and shall also be assessed any costs incurred by the county, township, or municipal corporation in disposing of the abandoned junk motor vehicle that is the basis of the violation, less any money accruing to the county, to the township, or to the municipal corporation from this disposal of the vehicle.

(2002 S 123, eff. 1–1–04; 1991 H 77, eff. 9–17–91; 1980 S 257; 1971 H 24)

4513.65 Junk motor vehicle; order to cover or remove; notice; exception

(A) For purposes of this section, "junk motor vehicle" means any motor vehicle meeting the requirements of divisions (B), (C), (D), and (E) of section 4513.63 of the Revised Code that is left uncovered in the open on private property for more than seventy-two hours with the permission of the person having the right to the possession of the property, except if the person is operating a junk yard or scrap metal processing facility licensed under authority of sections 4737.05 to 4737.12 of the Revised Code, or regulated under authority of a political subdivision; or if the property on which the motor vehicle is left is not subject to licensure or regulation by any governmental authority, unless the person having the right to the possession of the property can establish that the motor vehicle is part of a bona fide commercial operation; or if the motor vehicle is a collector's vehicle.

No political subdivision shall prevent a person from storing or keeping, or restrict a person in the method of storing or keeping, any collector's vehicle on private property with the permission of the person having the right to the possession of the property; except that a political subdivision may require a person having such permission to conceal, by means of buildings, fences, vegetation, terrain, or other suitable obstruction, any unlicensed collector's vehicle stored in the open.

The sheriff of a county, or chief of police of a municipal corporation, within the sheriff's or chief's respective territorial jurisdiction, a state highway patrol trooper, a board of township trustees, the legislative authority of a municipal corporation, or the zoning authority of a township or a municipal corporation, may send notice, by certified mail with return receipt requested, to the person having the right to the possession of the property on which a junk motor vehicle is left, that within ten days of receipt of the notice, the junk motor vehicle either shall be covered by being housed in a garage or other suitable structure, or shall be removed from the property.

No person shall willfully leave a junk motor vehicle uncovered in the open for more than ten days after receipt of a notice as provided in this section. The fact that a junk motor vehicle is so left is prima-facie evidence of willful failure to comply with the notice, and each subsequent period of thirty days that a junk motor vehicle continues to be so left constitutes a separate offense.

(B) Except as otherwise provided in this division, whoever violates this section is guilty of a minor misdemeanor on a first offense. If the offender previously has been convicted of or pleaded guilty to one violation of this section, whoever violates this section is guilty of a misdemeanor of the fourth degree. If the offender previously has been convicted of or pleaded guilty to two or more violations of this section, whoever violates this section is guilty of a misdemeanor of the third degree.

(2002 S 123, eff. 1–1–04; 1991 S 144, eff. 8–8–91; 1975 S 52; 1974 H 635)

PENALTIES

4513.99 Penalties

(A) Any violation of section 4513.03, 4513.04, 4513.05, 4513.06, 4513.07, 4513.071, 4513.09, 4513.10, 4513.11, 4513.111, 4513.12, 4513.13, 4513.14, 4513.15, 4513.16, 4513.17, 4513.171, 4513.18, 4513.182, 4513.19, 4513.20, 4513.201, 4513.202, 4513.21, 4513.22, 4513.23, 4513.24, 4513.242, 4513.25, 4513.26, 4513.27, 4513.28, 4513.29, 4513.30, 4513.31, 4513.32, or 4513.34 of the Revised Code shall be punished under division (B) of this section.

(B) Whoever violates the sections of this chapter that are specifically required to be punished under this division, or any provision of sections 4513.03 to 4513.262 or 4513.27 to 4513.37 of the Revised Code for which violation no penalty is otherwise provided, is guilty of a minor misdemeanor on a first offense; on a second offense within one year after the first offense, the person is guilty of a misdemeanor of the fourth degree; on each subsequent offense within one year after the first offense, the person is guilty of a misdemeanor of the third degree.

([1]

(2002 S 123, eff. 1–1–04; 2000 H 138, eff. 11–3–00; 2000 H 600, eff. 9–1–00; 1992 S 98, eff. 11–12–92; 1992 H 118; 1991 H 96; 1986 H 291, S 54; 1984 H 112; 1980 S 257; 1974 H 635; 1973 H 173, § 1, 3; 1971 H 24; 132; v H 380; 129 v 1567; 125 v 903, 456; 1953 H 1)

[1] So in original; 2002 S 123.

CHAPTER 4549

MOTOR VEHICLE CRIMES

STOPPING MOTOR VEHICLE

4549.01 Stopping motor vehicle when signalled

(A) No person while operating a motor vehicle shall fail to slow down and stop the vehicle when signalled to do so upon meeting or overtaking a horse-drawn vehicle or person on horseback and to remain stationary until the vehicle or person has passed, provided the signal to stop is given in good faith, under circumstances of necessity, and only as often and for that length of time as is required for the vehicle or person to pass, whether it is approaching from the front or rear.

(B) Whoever violates this section is guilty of a minor misdemeanor on a first offense and a misdemeanor of the fourth degree on each subsequent offense.

(2002 S 123, eff. 1–1–04; 1953 H 1, eff. 10–1–53; GC 12605)

4549.02 Stopping after accident; exchange of identity and vehicle registration

(A) In case of accident to or collision with persons or property upon any of the public roads or highways, due to the driving or operation thereon of any motor vehicle, the person driving or operating the motor vehicle, having knowledge of the accident or collision, immediately shall stop the driver's or operator's motor vehicle at the scene of the accident or collision and shall remain at the scene of the accident or collision until the driver or operator has given the driver's or operator's name and address and, if the driver or operator is not the owner, the name and address of the owner of that motor vehicle, together with the registered number of that motor vehicle, to any person injured in the accident or collision or to the operator, occupant, owner, or attendant of any motor vehicle damaged in the accident or collision, or to any police officer at the scene of the accident or collision.

In the event the injured person is unable to comprehend and record the information required to be given by this section, the other driver involved in the accident or collision forthwith shall notify the nearest police authority concerning the location of the accident or collision, and the driver's name, address, and the registered number of the motor vehicle the driver was operating, and then remain at the scene of the accident or collision until a police officer arrives, unless removed from the scene by an emergency vehicle operated by a political subdivision or an ambulance.

If the accident or collision is with an unoccupied or unattended motor vehicle, the operator who collides with the motor vehicle shall securely attach the information required to be given in this section, in writing, to a conspicuous place in or on the unoccupied or unattended motor vehicle.

(B) Whoever violates division (A) of this section is guilty of failure to stop after an accident, a misdemeanor of the first degree. If the violation results in serious physical harm to a person, failure to stop after an accident is a felony of the fifth degree. If the violation results in the death of a person, failure to stop after an accident is a felony of the third degree. The court, in addition to any other penalties provided by law, shall impose upon the offender a class five suspension of the offender's driver's license, commercial driver's license, temporary instruction permit, probationary license, or nonresident operating privilege from the range specified in division (A)(5) of section 4510.02 of the Revised Code. No judge shall suspend the first six months of suspension of an offender's license, permit, or privilege required by this division.

(2003 H 50, § 4, eff. 1–1–04; 2002 S 123, eff. 1–1–04; 130 v H 180, eff. 8–19–63; 1953 H 1; GC 12606)

4549.021 Duty to stop after accident occurring on property other than public highways

(A) In case of accident or collision resulting in injury or damage to persons or property upon any public or private property other than public roads or highways, due to the driving or operation thereon of any motor vehicle, the person driving or operating the motor vehicle, having knowledge of the accident or collision, shall stop, and, upon request of the person injured or damaged, or any other person, shall give that person the driver's or operator's name and address, and, if the driver or operator is not the owner, the name and address of the owner of that motor vehicle, together with the registered number of that motor vehicle, and, if available, exhibit the driver's or operator's driver's or commercial driver's license.

If the owner or person in charge of the damaged property is not furnished such information, the driver of the motor vehicle involved in the accident or collision, within twenty-four hours after the accident or collision, shall forward to the police department of the city or village in which the accident or collision occurred or if it occurred outside the corporate limits of a city or village to the sheriff of the county in which the accident or collision occurred the same information required to be given to the owner or person in control of the damaged property and give the date, time, and location of the accident or collision.

If the accident or collision is with an unoccupied or unattended motor vehicle, the operator who collides with the motor vehicle shall securely attach the information required to be given in this section, in writing, to a conspicuous place in or on the unoccupied or unattended motor vehicle.

(B) Whoever violates division (A) of this section is guilty of failure to stop after a nonpublic road accident, a misdemeanor of the first degree. If the violation results in serious physical harm to a person, failure to stop after a nonpublic road accident is a felony of the fifth degree. If the violation results in the death of a person, failure to stop after a nonpublic road accident is a felony of the third degree. The court, in addition to any other penalties provided by law, shall impose upon the offender a class five suspension of the offender's driver's license, commercial driver's license, temporary instruction permit, probationary license, or nonresident operating privilege from the range specified in division (A)(5) of section 4510.02 of the Revised Code. No judge shall suspend the first six months of suspension of an offender's license, permit, or privilege required by this division.

(2003 H 50, § 4, eff. 1–1–04; 2002 S 123, eff. 1–1–04; 1989 H 381, eff. 7–1–89; 131 v H 207; 130 v S 312)

4549.03 Motor vehicle accident resulting in damage to realty

(A) The driver of any vehicle involved in an accident resulting in damage to real property, or personal property attached to real property, legally upon or adjacent to a public road or highway immediately shall stop and take reasonable steps to locate and notify the owner or person in charge of the property of that fact, of the driver's name and address, and of the registration number of the vehicle the driver is driving and, upon request and if available, shall exhibit the driver's driver's or commercial driver's license.

If the owner or person in charge of the property cannot be located after reasonable search, the driver of the vehicle involved in the accident resulting in damage to the property, within twenty-four hours after the accident, shall forward to the police department of the city or village in which the accident or collision occurred, or if it occurred outside the corporate limits of a city or village to the sheriff of the county in which the accident or collision occurred, the same information required to be given to the owner or person in control of the property and give the location of the accident and a description of the damage insofar as it is known.

(B) Whoever violates division (A) of this section is guilty of failure to stop after an accident involving the property of others, a misdemeanor of the first degree.

(2002 S 123, eff. 1–1–04; 1989 H 381, eff. 7–1–89; 131 v H 207; 1953 H 1; GC 12606–1)

CAR KEYS

4549.042 Sale or possession of master car keys for illegal purposes

(A)(1) No person shall sell or otherwise dispose of a master key designed to fit more than one motor vehicle, knowing or having reasonable cause to believe the key will be used to commit a crime.

(2) No person shall buy, receive, or have in the person's possession a master key designed to fit more than one motor vehicle, for the purpose of using the key to commit a crime.

(B) Whoever violates division (A)(1) or (2) of this section is guilty of a motor vehicle master key violation, a felony of the fifth degree on a first offense and a felony of the fourth degree on each subsequent offense.

(2002 S 123, eff. 1–1–04; 132 v H 591, eff. 12–14–67)

4549.05 Officer may remove ignition key

A law enforcement officer may remove the ignition key left in the ignition switch of an unlocked and unattended motor vehicle parked on a street or highway. The officer removing said key shall place notification upon the vehicle detailing his name and badge number, the place where said key may be reclaimed, and the procedure for reclaiming said key. The key shall be returned to the owner of the motor vehicle upon presentation of proof of ownership.

(1972 H 511, eff. 1–1–74; 1969 H 386; 1953 H 1; GC 12619–1)

IMPROPER LICENSE PLATES AND IDENTIFICATION

4549.08 Use of unauthorized plates

(A) No person shall operate or drive a motor vehicle upon the public roads and highways in this state if it displays a license plate or a distinctive number or identification mark that meets any of the following criteria:

(1) Is fictitious;

(2) Is a counterfeit or an unlawfully made copy of any distinctive number or identification mark;

(3) Belongs to another motor vehicle, provided that this section does not apply to a motor vehicle that is operated on the public roads and highways in this state when the motor vehicle displays license plates that originally were issued for a motor vehicle that previously was owned by the same person who owns the motor vehicle that is operated on the public roads and highways in this state, during the thirty-day period described in division (A)(4) of section 4503.12 of the Revised Code.

(B) A person who fails to comply with the transfer of registration provisions of section 4503.12 of the Revised Code and is charged with a violation of that section shall not be charged with a violation of this section.

(C) Whoever violates division (A)(1), (2), or (3) of this section is guilty of operating a motor vehicle bearing an invalid license plate or identification mark, a misdemeanor of the fourth degree on a first offense and a misdemeanor of the third degree on each subsequent offense.

(2002 S 123, eff. 1–1–04; 2002 H 345, eff. 7–23–02; 1996 H 353, eff. 9–17–96; 130 v H 1, eff. 1–23–63; 129 v 1030; 1953 H 1; GC 12618)

4549.081 Electronic clearance device to bypass scale location; penalties

(A) The superintendent of the state highway patrol shall adopt rules governing the use of an electronic clearance device that enables an operator of a commercial motor vehicle, in accordance with division (B) of section 4511.121 of the Revised Code, to bypass a scale location established for the purpose of determining the weight of the vehicle and its load. The superintendent shall establish the acceptable types and features of such devices. The rules of the superintendent also shall establish a method for a peace officer to determine that the device and its use are in compliance with this section and the rules of the superintendent.

(B) No person shall use an electronic clearance device if the device or its use is not in compliance with rules of the superintendent.

(C) Whoever violates division (B) of this section is guilty of a misdemeanor of the fourth degree on a first offense and a misdemeanor of the third degree on each subsequent offense.

(2004 H 230, eff. 9–16–04)

4549.10 Operating without license plates

(A) No person shall operate or cause to be operated upon a public road or highway a motor vehicle of a manufacturer or dealer unless the vehicle carries and displays two placards, except as provided in section 4503.21 of the Revised Code, issued by the director of public safety that bear the registration number of its manufacturer or dealer.

(B) Whoever violates division (A) of this section is guilty of illegal operation of a manufacturer's or dealer's motor vehicle, a minor misdemeanor on a first offense and a misdemeanor of the fourth degree on each subsequent offense.

(2002 S 123, eff. 1–1–04; 1992 S 98, eff. 11–12–92; 129 v 1492; 1953 H 1; GC 12622)

4549.11 Operating with number of former owner

(A) No person shall operate or drive upon the highways of this state a motor vehicle acquired from a former owner who has registered the motor vehicle, while the motor vehicle displays the distinctive number or identification mark assigned to it upon its original registration.

(B) Whoever violates division (A) of this section is guilty of operation of a motor vehicle bearing license plates or an identification mark issued to another, a minor misdemeanor on a first offense and a misdemeanor of the fourth degree on each subsequent offense.

(2002 S 123, eff. 1–1–04; 1953 H 1, eff. 10–1–53; GC 12618–1)

4549.12 Resident operating with number issued by foreign state

(A) No person who is the owner of a motor vehicle and a resident of this state shall operate or drive the motor vehicle upon the highways of this state, while it displays a distinctive number or identification mark issued by or under the authority of another state, without complying with the laws of this state relating to the registration and identification of motor vehicles.

(B) Whoever violates division (A) of this section is guilty of illegal operation by a resident of this state of a motor vehicle bearing the distinctive number or identification mark issued by a foreign jurisdiction, a minor misdemeanor on a first offense and a misdemeanor of the fourth degree on each subsequent offense.

(2002 S 123, eff. 1–1–04; 1953 H 1, eff. 10–1–53; GC 12618–3)

TRAFFIC OFFICERS

4549.13 Motor vehicles used by traffic officers

Any motor vehicle used by a member of the state highway patrol or by any other peace officer, while said officer is on duty for the exclusive or main purpose of enforcing the motor vehicle or traffic laws of this state, provided the offense is punishable as a misdemeanor, shall be marked in some distinctive manner or color and shall be equipped with, but need not necessarily have in operation at all times, at least one flashing, oscillating, or rotating colored light mounted outside on top of the vehicle. The superintendent of the state highway patrol shall specify what constitutes such a distinctive marking or color for the state highway patrol.

(1979 S 141, eff. 10–25–79; 1969 H 625; 1953 H 1; GC 12616)

4549.14 Incompetency of officer as witness

Any officer arresting, or participating or assisting in the arrest of, a person charged with violating the motor vehicle or traffic laws of this state, provided the offense is punishable as a misdemeanor, such officer being on duty exclusively or for the main purpose of enforcing such laws, is incompetent to testify as a witness in any prosecution against such arrested person if such officer at the time of the arrest was using a motor vehicle not marked in accordance with section 4549.13 of the Revised Code.

(1953 H 1, eff. 10–1–53; GC 12616–1)

4549.15 Uniform for traffic officers

Every member of the state highway patrol and every other peace officer, while such officer is on duty for the exclusive or main purpose of enforcing motor vehicle or traffic laws of this state, provided the offense is punishable as a misdemeanor, shall wear a distinctive uniform. The superintendent of the patrol shall specify what constitutes such a distinctive uniform for the state highway patrol.

(1979 S 141, eff. 10–25–79, 1969 H 625, 1953 H 1, GC 12616–2)

4549.16 Arresting officer as witness

Any officer arresting, or participating or assisting in the arrest of, a person charged with violating the motor vehicle or traffic laws of this state, provided the offense is punishable as a misdemeanor, such officer being on duty exclusively or for the main purpose of enforcing such laws is incompetent to testify as a witness in any prosecution against such arrested person if such officer at the time of the arrest was not wearing a distinctive uniform in accordance with section 4549.15 of the Revised Code.

(1953 H 1, eff. 10–1–53; GC 12616–3)

4549.17 Limitation on speeding and vehicle weight citations on interstates with less than one-half mile in officer's jurisdiction

(A) No law enforcement officer employed by a law enforcement agency of a municipal corporation, township, or joint township police district shall issue any citation, summons, or ticket for a violation of section 4511.21 of the Revised Code or a substantially similar municipal ordinance or for a violation of section 5577.04 of the Revised Code or a substantially similar municipal ordinance, if all of the following apply:

(1) The citation, summons, or ticket would be issued for a violation described in division (A) of this section that occurs on a freeway that is part of the interstate system;

(2) The municipal corporation, township, or joint township police district that employs the law enforcement officer has less than eight hundred eighty yards of the freeway that is part of the interstate system within its jurisdiction;

(3) The law enforcement officer must travel outside the boundaries of the municipal corporation, township, or joint township police district that employs him in order to enter onto the freeway;

(4) The law enforcement officer travels onto the freeway for the primary purpose of issuing citations, summonses, or tickets for violations of section 4511.21 of the Revised Code or a substantially similar municipal ordinance or for violations of section 5577.04 of the Revised Code or a substantially similar municipal ordinance.

(B) As used in this section, "interstate system" has the same meaning as in section 5516.01 of the Revised Code.

(1994 H 687, eff. 10–12–94)

4549.18 Display of certificates of registration

(A) The operator of a "commercial car," as defined in section 4501.01 of the Revised Code, when the commercial car is required to be registered under the Revised Code, shall, when operating the commercial car, trailer, or semitrailer on the streets, roads, or highways of this state, display inside or on the vehicle the certificate of registration for the commercial car, trailer, or semitrailer provided for in section 4503.19 of the Revised Code, or shall carry the certificate on the operator's person and display it upon the demand of any state highway patrol trooper or other peace officer.

Every person operating a commercial car, trailer, or semitrailer required to be registered under the Revised Code shall permit the inspection of the certificate of registration upon demand of the superintendent or any member of the state highway patrol or other peace officer of this state.

(B) Whoever violates division (A) of this section is guilty of a commercial car certificate of registration violation, a minor misdemeanor.

(2002 S 123, eff. 1–1–04; 1991 S 144, eff. 8–8–91; 1990 H 831; 1971 H 1; 1953 H 1; GC 12630–1, 12630–2)

ENFORCEMENT

4549.19 Enforcement of proceedings against violators

Proceedings to enforce section 4549.18 of the Revised Code shall be brought in any court of record situated in the county in which the violation occurred, and all municipal courts shall have county-wide jurisdiction over such violations. Such actions shall be governed by section 4507.15 of the Revised Code. Commercial cars which are registered under the laws of another state, the owners of which are not residents of this state and which are operated in compliance with the laws of the state of their owner's residence, are not subject to this section and section 4549.18 of the Revised Code.

(1953 H 1, eff. 10–1–53; GC 12630–3)

AIRBAGS

4549.20 Installation of nonconforming airbag; penalty

(A) As used in this section, "air bag" has the same meaning as in 49 C.F.R. 579.4, as amended.

(B) No person shall install or reinstall in any motor vehicle any object to fulfill the function of an air bag, including an air bag, other than an air bag that was designed in conformance with or that is regulated by federal motor vehicle safety standard number 208 for the make, model, and model year of the vehicle, knowing that the object is not in accordance with that standard.

(C) Whoever violates division (B) of this section is guilty of improper replacement of a motor vehicle air bag, a misdemeanor of the first degree on a first offense. On each subsequent offense, the person is guilty of a felony of the fifth degree.

(2004 H 219, eff. 9–16–04)

VENUE

4549.31 Venue of auto theft offenses

(A) Any person who as a part of a continuing course of criminal conduct commits auto theft offenses in more than one county may be indicted and tried for all such offenses in any county where one such offense was committed. It is prima-facie evidence of a continuing course of criminal conduct if an offender commits two or more auto theft offenses within a period of six months.

(B) As used in this section "auto theft offense" means any of the following:

(1) A violation of section 4505.19, 4549.05, 4549.08, or 4549.62 of the Revised Code;

(2) A violation of a law of another state or the United States substantially equivalent to any offense listed in division (B)(1) of this section;

(3) A violation of a law of this or any other state, or of the United States, of which an element is forging or altering a motor vehicle title or registration, or obtaining a motor vehicle or motor vehicle parts or accessories by theft or fraud, or wrongful conversion of a motor vehicle, or taking, operating, or keeping a motor vehicle without the consent of the owner, or receiving or disposing of a motor vehicle or motor vehicle parts or accessories knowing the same to have been unlawfully obtained.

(1984 H 632, eff. 3–28–85; 1976 H 837; 1971 H 101)

ODOMETER ROLLBACK AND DISCLOSURE ACT

4549.41 Definitions

As used in sections 4549.41 to 4549.51 of the Revised Code:

(A) "Person" includes an individual, corporation, government, governmental subdivision or agency, business trust, estate, trust, partnership, association, or cooperative or any other legal entity, whether acting individually or by their agents, officers, employees, or representatives.

(B) "Motor vehicle" means any vehicle driven or drawn by mechanical power for use on the public streets, roads, or highways.

(C) "Odometer" means an instrument for measuring and recording the total distance that a motor vehicle travels while in operation, including any cable, line, or other part necessary to make the instrument function properly. Odometer does not include any auxiliary odometer designed to be reset by the operator of a motor vehicle for the purpose of recording mileage on trips.

(D) "Transfer" means to change ownership of a motor vehicle by purchase, by gift, or, except as otherwise provided in this division, by any other means. A "transfer" does not include a change of ownership as a result of a bequest, under the laws of intestate succession, as a result of a surviving spouse's actions pursuant to section 2106.18 or 4505.10 of the Revised Code, as a result of the operation of section 2131.12 or 2131.13 of the Revised Code, or in connection with the creation of a security interest.

(E) "Transferor" means the person involved in a transfer, who transfers ownership of a motor vehicle.

(F) "Transferee" means the person involved in a transfer, to whom the ownership of a motor vehicle is transferred.

(G) "Service" means to repair or replace an odometer that is not properly functioning.

(2002 H 345, eff. 7–23–02; 1994 H 458, eff. 7–20–94; 1990 H 346, eff. 5–31–90; 1986 H 382; 1983 S 115; 1977 S 78)

4549.42 Tampering with odometer; repairs

(A) No person shall adjust, alter, change, tamper with, advance, set back, disconnect, or fail to connect, an odometer of a motor vehicle, or cause any of the foregoing to occur to an odometer of a motor vehicle with the intent to alter the number of miles registered on the odometer.

(B) Division (A) of this section does not apply to the disconnection of an odometer used for registering the mileage of any new motor vehicle being tested by the manufacturer prior to delivery to a franchise dealer.

(C) Nothing in this section prevents the service of an odometer, provided that after the service a completed form, captioned "notice of odometer repair," shall be attached to the left door frame of the motor vehicle by the person performing the repairs. The notice shall contain, in bold-face type, the following information and statements:

"Notice of Odometer Repair

The odometer of this motor vehicle was repaired or replaced on ________ (date of service).

The mileage registered on the odometer of this motor vehicle before repair was ________ (mileage).

The mileage registered on the odometer of this motor vehicle after repair is ________ (mileage).

____

(Repairer's signature)"

(D) No person shall intentionally remove or alter the notice required by division (C) of this section.

(E) If after the service of an odometer, the odometer can be set at the same mileage as before the service, the odometer shall be adjusted to reflect that mileage registered on the odometer of the motor vehicle before the service. If the odometer cannot be set at the same mileage as before the service, the odometer of the motor vehicle shall be adjusted to read "zero."

(F) Except as otherwise provided in this division, whoever violates this section is guilty of tampering with an odometer, a felony of the fifth degree. If the offender previously has been convicted of or pleaded guilty to a violation of this section or of any provision of sections 4549.43 to 4549.46 of the Revised Code, tampering with an odometer is a felony of the fourth degree.

(2002 S 123, eff. 1-1-04; 1977 S 78, eff. 9-6-77)

4549.43 Sale of device to affect odometer

(A) No person, with intent to defraud, shall advertise for sale, sell, use, or install on any part of any motor vehicle or an odometer in any motor vehicle any device that causes the odometer to register any mileage other than the actual mileage driven by the motor vehicle. For the purpose of this section, the actual mileage driven is that mileage driven by the motor vehicle as registered by an odometer within the manufacturer's designed tolerance.

(B) Except as otherwise provided in this division, whoever violates this section is guilty of selling or installing an odometer tampering device, a felony of the fourth degree. If the offender previously has been convicted of or pleaded guilty to a violation of this section, section 4549.42, or any provision of sections 4549.44 to 4549.46 of the Revised Code, selling or installing an odometer tampering device is a felony of the third degree.

(2002 S 123, eff. 1-1-04; 1977 S 78, eff. 9-6-77)

4549.44 Operation of vehicle with odometer disconnected

(A) No person, with intent to defraud, shall operate a motor vehicle on any public street, road, or highway of this state knowing that the odometer of the vehicle is disconnected or nonfunctional.

A person's intent to defraud under this section may be inferred from evidence of the circumstances of the vehicle's operation, including facts pertaining to the length of time or number of miles of operation with a nonfunctioning or disconnected odometer, and the fact that the person subsequently transferred the vehicle without disclosing the inoperative odometer to the transferee in violation of section 4549.45 of the Revised Code.

(B) Except as otherwise provided in this division, whoever violates this section is guilty of fraudulent driving without a functional odometer, a felony of the fourth degree. If the offender previously has been convicted of or pleaded guilty to a violation of this section, section 4549.42 or 4549.43, or any provision of sections 4549.45 to 4549.46 of the Revised Code, fraudulent driving without a functional odometer is a felony of the third degree.

(2002 S 123, eff. 1-1-04; 1986 H 382, eff. 3-19-87; 1977 S 78)

4549.45 Sale of vehicle with tampered odometer

(A) No person shall transfer a motor vehicle if the person knows or recklessly disregards facts indicating that the odometer of the motor vehicle has been changed, tampered with, or disconnected, or has been in any other manner nonfunctional, to reflect a lesser mileage or use, unless that person gives clear and unequivocal notice of the tampering or nonfunction or of the person's reasonable belief of tampering or nonfunction, to the transferee in writing prior to the transfer. In a prosecution for violation of this section, evidence that a transferor or the transferor's agent has changed, tampered with, disconnected, or failed to connect the odometer of the motor vehicle constitutes prima-facie evidence of knowledge of the odometer's altered condition.

(B) Except as otherwise provided in this division, whoever violates this section is guilty of transferring a motor vehicle that has a tampered or nonfunctional odometer, a felony of the fourth degree. If the offender previously has been convicted of or pleaded guilty to a violation of this section, any provision of sections 4549.42 to 4549.44, or any provision of section 4549.451 or 4549.46 of the Revised Code, transferring a motor vehicle that has a tampered or nonfunctional odometer is a felony of the third degree.

(2002 S 123, eff. 1-1-04; 1986 H 382, eff. 3-19-87; 1977 S 78)

4549.451 Auctioneers to disclose odometer discrepancies

(A) No auctioneer licensed under Chapter 4707. of the Revised Code shall advertise for sale by means of any written advertisement, brochure, flyer, or other writing, any motor vehicle the auctioneer knows or has reason to believe has an odometer that has been changed, tampered with, or disconnected, or in any other manner has been nonfunctional, unless the listing or description of the vehicle contained in the written advertisement, brochure, flyer, or other writing contains one of the two following statements:

(1) "This motor vehicle has an odometer that has been changed, tampered with, or disconnected, or otherwise has been nonfunctional."

(2) "Nonactual odometer reading: warning—odometer discrepancy."

(B) The statement selected by the auctioneer shall be printed in type identical in size to the other type used in the listing or description, and shall be located within the listing or description and not located as a footnote to the listing or description.

(C) Except as otherwise provided in this division, whoever violates this section is guilty of a felony of the fourth degree. If the offender previously has been convicted of or pleaded guilty to a violation of this section, any provision of sections 4549.42 to

4549.45, or section 4549.46 of the Revised Code, whoever violates this section is guilty of a felony of the third degree.

(2002 S 123, eff. 1–1–04; 1997 S 60, eff. 10–21–97)

4549.46 Odometer disclosures

(A) No transferor shall fail to provide the true and complete odometer disclosures required by section 4505.06 of the Revised Code. The transferor of a motor vehicle is not in violation of this division requiring a true odometer reading if the odometer reading is incorrect due to a previous owner's violation of any of the provisions contained in sections 4549.42 to 4549.46 of the Revised Code, unless the transferor knows of or recklessly disregards facts indicating the violation.

(B) No dealer or wholesaler who acquires ownership of a motor vehicle shall accept any written odometer disclosure statement unless the statement is completed as required by section 4505.06 of the Revised Code.

(C) A motor vehicle leasing dealer may obtain a written odometer disclosure statement completed as required by section 4505.06 of the Revised Code from a motor vehicle lessee that can be used as prima-facie evidence in any legal action arising under sections 4549.41 to 4549.46 of the Revised Code.

(D) Except as otherwise provided in this division, whoever violates division (A) or (B) of this section is guilty of an odometer disclosure violation, a felony of the fourth degree. If the offender previously has been convicted of or pleaded guilty to a violation of this section or any provision of sections 4549.42 to 4549.451 of the Revised Code, a violation of this section is a felony of the third degree.

(2002 S 123, eff. 1–1–04; 1986 H 382, eff. 3–19–87; 1983 S 115; 1977 S 78)

4549.47 Powers of attorney general

(A) If by his own inquiries or as a result of complaints, the attorney general has reason to believe that a person has engaged, is engaging, or is preparing to engage, in a violation of sections 4549.41 to 4549.46 of the Revised Code, he may investigate.

(B) For this purpose the attorney general may administer oaths, subpoena witnesses, adduce evidence, and require the production of relevant matter.

If the matter that the attorney general requires to be produced is located outside the state, he may designate representatives, including officials of the state in which the matter is located, to inspect the matter on his behalf, and he may respond to similar requests from officials of other states. The person subpoenaed may make the matter available to the attorney general at a convenient location within the state or pay the reasonable and necessary expenses for the attorney general or his representative to examine the matter at the place where it is located, provided that expenses shall not be charged to a party not subsequently found to have engaged in a violation of sections 4549.41 to 4549.46 of the Revised Code.

(C) At any time before the return day specified in the subpoena, or within twenty days after the subpoena has been served, whichever period is shorter, a petition to extend the return day, or to modify or quash the subpoena, stating good cause, may be filed in the court of common pleas in Franklin county or in the county where the person served resides or has his principal place of business.

(D) A person subpoenaed under this section shall comply with the terms of the subpoena unless otherwise provided by court order entered prior to the day for return contained in the subpoena or as extended by the court. If a person fails without lawful excuse to obey a subpoena or to produce relevant matter, the attorney general may apply to a court of common pleas and obtain an order doing any of the following:

(1) Adjudging the person in contempt of court;

(2) Granting injunctive relief to restrain the person from engaging in any conduct that violates sections 4549.41 to 4549.46 of the Revised Code;

(3) Granting injunctive relief to preserve or restore the status quo;

(4) Granting such other relief as may be required until the person obeys the subpoena.

If a person violates any order entered by a court under this section, the violation shall be punished as a violation of an injunction issued under division (A) of section 4549.48 of the Revised Code.

(E) The attorney general may request that an individual who refuses to testify or to produce relevant matter on the ground that the testimony or matter may incriminate him be ordered by the court to provide the testimony or matter. With the exception of a prosecution for perjury and an action for damages under section 4549.49 of the Revised Code, an individual who complies with a court order to provide testimony or matter, after asserting a privilege against self-incrimination to which he is entitled by law, shall not be subjected to a criminal proceeding on the basis of the testimony or matter required to be disclosed or testimony or matter discovered through that testimony or matter.

(1977 S 78, eff. 9–6–77)

4549.48 Action for injunction; civil penalties

(A) Whenever it appears that a person has violated, is violating, or is about to violate any provision of sections 4549.41 to 4549.46 of the Revised Code, the attorney general may bring an action in the court of common pleas to enjoin the violation. Upon a showing of a violation of sections 4549.41 to 4549.46 of the Revised Code, a temporary restraining order, preliminary injunction, or permanent injunction shall be granted without bond. The court may impose a penalty of not more than five thousand dollars for each day of violation of a temporary restraining order, preliminary injunction, or permanent injunction issued under this section. The court may issue an order requiring the reimbursement of a consumer for any loss that results from a violation of sections 4549.41 to 4549.46 of the Revised Code, for the recovery of any amounts for which a violator is liable pursuant to division (A) of section 4549.49 of the Revised Code, for the appointment of a referee or receiver, for the sequestration of assets, for the rescission of transfers of motor vehicles, or granting any other appropriate relief. The court may award the attorney general all costs together with all expenses of his investigation and reasonable attorneys' fees incurred in the prosecution of the action, which shall be deposited in the consumer protection enforcement fund created by section 1345.51 of the Revised Code.

(B) In addition to the remedies otherwise provided by this section, the attorney general may request and the court shall impose a civil penalty of not less than one thousand nor more than two thousand dollars for each violation. A violation of any provision of sections 4549.41 to 4549.46 of the Revised Code shall, for purposes of this section, constitute a separate violation with respect to each motor vehicle or unlawful device involved, except that the maximum civil penalty shall not exceed one hundred thousand dollars for any related series of violations by a person. Civil penalties ordered pursuant to this division shall be paid as follows: one–fourth of the amount to the treasurer of the county in which the action is brought; three–fourths to the consumer protection enforcement fund created by section 1345.51 of the Revised Code.

(C) The remedies prescribed by this section are cumulative and concurrent with any other remedy, and the existence or exercise of one remedy does not prevent the exercise of any other remedy.

(1986 H 382, eff. 3–19–87; 1977 S 78)

4549.49 Liability for damages; limitation of action

(A) Any person who violates any requirement imposed by sections 4549.41 to 4549.46 of the Revised Code is liable to any transferee of the motor vehicle subsequent to the violation, in an amount equal to:

(1) Three times the amount of actual damages sustained or fifteen hundred dollars, whichever is greater; and

(2) In the case of any successful action to enforce the foregoing liability, the costs of the action together with reasonable attorneys' fees as determined by the court.

(B) An action to enforce any liability created under sections 4549.41 to 4549.46 of the Revised Code may be brought in a court of common pleas without regard to the amount in controversy, or in any other court of competent jurisdiction, within two years from the date on which the liability arises. For the purpose of this section, liability arises when the transferee discovers, or with due diligence should have discovered, the violation.

(1977 S 78, eff. 9–6–77)

4549.50 Presumption of fraud; revocation or suspension of license or permit; bond

Violation of sections 4549.41 to 4549.46 of the Revised Code by any person licensed or granted a permit by this state as a dealer, wholesaler, distributor, salesman, or auction owner under Chapter 4517. of the Revised Code, is prima-facie evidence of intent to defraud and constitutes cause for the revocation or denial of the license of such person to sell any motor vehicle in this state.

Any person who violates sections 4549.41 to 4549.46 of the Revised Code, upon receiving notice from the registrar of motor vehicles or motor vehicle dealers board of the intent to revoke or suspend a license or permit, shall immediately post a surety bond with the registrar in favor of the state in the amount of twenty-five thousand dollars and shall maintain the bond while the license or permit is in effect. The bond shall be for the use, benefit, and protection of any transferee damaged by the licensee's or permitee's violation of sections 4549.41 to 4549.46 of the Revised Code or for the payment of civil penalties or costs resulting from enforcement actions. Any transferee claiming against the bond or the attorney general may maintain an action against the transferor or the surety, except that the surety is liable only for actual damages. The aggregate liability of the surety shall not exceed twenty-five thousand dollars. Any money unclaimed by transferees after two years from the date of the conviction of or judgment against the transferor shall be deposited in the consumer protection enforcement fund created by section 1345.51 of the Revised Code. The surety bond shall remain in effect until the license or permit is revoked or suspended by the motor vehicle dealers board pursuant to section 4517.33 of the Revised Code. Upon reinstatement of a license or permit that has been suspended, or upon reissuance of a license or permit after the period of revocation, the licensee or permitee shall post an additional surety bond in accordance with this section. The surety bond shall remain in effect during the period in which the licensee or permitee engages in business in the state.

(1986 H 382, eff. 3–19–87; 1977 S 78)

4549.51 Remedies additional

The remedies under sections 4549.41 to 4549.51 of the Revised Code are in addition to remedies otherwise available for the same conduct under federal, state, or local law.

(1977 S 78, eff. 9–6–77)

4549.52 Enforcement

The prosecuting attorney of the county in which a violation of any provision of sections 4549.41 to 4549.51 of the Revised Code occurs, or the attorney general, may bring a criminal action to enforce the provisions of sections 4549.41 to 4549.51 of the Revised Code. The attorney general and the prosecuting attorney of the county in which a person licensed or granted a permit under Chapter 4517. of the Revised Code is convicted of or pleads guilty to a violation of any provision of sections 4549.41 to 4549.46 of the Revised Code shall report the conviction or guilty plea to the registrar of motor vehicles within five business days of the conviction or plea.

(2002 S 123, eff. 1–1–04)

CRIMES INVOLVING VEHICLE IDENTIFICATION NUMBERS

4549.61 Definition

As used in sections 4549.61 to 4549.63 of the Revised Code, "vehicle identification number or derivative thereof" means any number or derivative of such a number that is embossed, engraved, etched, or otherwise marked on any vehicle or vehicle part by the manufacturer. "Vehicle identification number" also includes a duplicate vehicle identification number replaced upon a vehicle under the authority of the registrar of motor vehicles.

(1984 H 632, eff. 3–28–85)

4549.62 Fraudulent actions concerning vehicle identification number

(A) No person, with purpose to conceal or destroy the identity of a vehicle or vehicle part, shall remove, deface, cover, alter, or destroy any vehicle identification number or derivative of a vehicle identification number on a vehicle or vehicle part.

(B) No person, with purpose to conceal or destroy the identity of a vehicle or a vehicle part, shall remove, deface, cover, alter, or destroy any identifying number that has been lawfully placed upon a vehicle or vehicle part by an owner of the vehicle or vehicle part, other than the manufacturer, for the purpose of deterring its theft and facilitating its recovery if stolen.

(C) No person, with purpose to conceal or destroy the identity of a vehicle or vehicle part, shall place a counterfeit vehicle identification number or derivative of a vehicle identification number upon the vehicle or vehicle part.

(D)(1) No person shall buy, offer to buy, sell, offer to sell, receive, dispose of, conceal, or, except as provided in division (D)(4) of this section, possess any vehicle or vehicle part with knowledge that the vehicle identification number or a derivative of the vehicle identification number has been removed, defaced, covered, altered, or destroyed in such a manner that the identity of the vehicle or part cannot be determined by a visual examination of the number at the site where the manufacturer placed the number.

(2)(a) A vehicle or vehicle part from which the vehicle identification number or a derivative of the vehicle identification number has been so removed, defaced, covered, altered, or destroyed shall be seized and forfeited under section 2933.41 of the Revised Code unless division (D)(3) or (4) of this section applies to the vehicle or part. If a derivative of the vehicle identification number has been removed, defaced, covered, altered, or destroyed in such a manner that the identity of the part cannot be determined, the entire vehicle is subject to seizure pending a determination of the original identity and ownership of the vehicle and parts of the vehicle, and the rights of innocent owners to reclaim the remainder or any part of the vehicle.

(b) The lawful owners of parts upon a vehicle that has been seized under this section and that is subject to forfeiture under section 2933.41 of the Revised Code are entitled to reclaim their respective parts upon satisfactory proof of all of the following:

(i) That the part is not needed for evidence in pending proceedings involving the vehicle or part and is not subject to forfeiture under section 2933.41 of the Revised Code;

(ii) That the original identity and ownership of the part can be determined and that the claimant is the lawful owner of the part;

(iii) That no vehicle identification number or derivative of a vehicle identification number on the part has been destroyed or concealed in such a manner that the identity of the part cannot be determined from that number;

(iv) Payment of all costs of removing the part.

(3) Divisions (A), (B), and (D)(1) and (2) of this section do not apply to the good faith acquisition and disposition of vehicles and vehicle parts as junk or scrap in the ordinary course of business by a scrap metal processing facility as defined in division (D) of section 4737.05 of the Revised Code or by a motor vehicle salvage dealer licensed under Chapter 4738. of the Revised Code. This division does not create an element of an offense or an affirmative defense, or affect the burden of proceeding with the evidence or burden of proof in a criminal proceeding.

(4)(a) Divisions (D)(1) and (2) of this section do not apply to the possession of an owner, or the owner's insurer, who provides satisfactory evidence of all of the following:

(i) That the vehicle identification number or derivative thereof on the vehicle or part has been removed, defaced, covered, altered, or destroyed, after the owner acquired such possession, by another person without the consent of the owner, by accident or other casualty not due to the owner's purpose to conceal or destroy the identity of the vehicle or vehicle part, or by ordinary wear and tear;

(ii) That the person is the owner of the vehicle as shown on a valid certificate of title issued by this state or certificate of title or other lawful evidence of title issued in another state, in a clear chain of title beginning with the manufacturer;

(iii) That the original identity of the vehicle can be established in a manner that excludes any reasonable probability that the vehicle has been stolen from another person.

(b) The registrar of motor vehicles shall adopt rules under Chapter 119. of the Revised Code to permit an owner described in division (D)(4)(a) of this section, upon application and submission of satisfactory evidence to the registrar, to obtain authority to replace the vehicle identification number under the supervision of a peace officer, trooper of the state highway patrol, or representative of the registrar. The rules shall be designed to restore the identification of the vehicle in a manner that will deter its theft and facilitate its marketability. Until such rules are adopted, the registrar shall follow the existing procedure for the replacement of vehicle identification numbers that have been established by the registrar, with such modifications as the registrar determines to be necessary or appropriate for the administration of the laws the registrar is required to administer.

The registrar may issue a temporary permit to an owner of a motor vehicle who is described in division (D)(4)(a) of this section to authorize the owner to retain possession of the motor vehicle and to transfer title to the motor vehicle with the consent of the registrar.

(c) No owner described in division (D)(4)(a) of this section shall fail knowingly to apply to the registrar for authority to replace the vehicle identification number, within thirty days after the later of the following dates:

(i) The date of receipt by the applicant of actual knowledge of the concealment or destruction;

(ii) If the property has been stolen, the date thereafter upon which the applicant obtains possession of the vehicle or has been notified by a law enforcement agency that the vehicle has been recovered.

The requirement of division (D)(4)(c) of this section may be excused by the registrar for good cause shown.

(E) Whoever violates division (A), (B), (C), or (D)(1) of this section is guilty of a felony of the fifth degree on a first offense and a felony of the fourth degree on each subsequent offense.

(F) Whoever violates division (D)(4)(c) of this section is guilty of a minor misdemeanor.

(2002 S 123, eff. 1–1–04; 1991 S 144, eff. 8–8–91; 1984 H 632)

4549.63 Seizure of vehicle by police

(A) A law enforcement officer may seize and take possession of a vehicle or vehicle part if the officer has probable cause to believe that any vehicle identification number or derivative thereof on the vehicle or part has been removed, defaced, covered, altered, or destroyed in such a manner that the identity of the vehicle or part cannot be determined by visual examination of the number at the site where the manufacturer placed the number. The seizure shall be pursuant to a warrant, unless the circumstances are within one of the exceptions to the warrant requirement that have been established by the supreme court of the United States or of the supreme court of this state.

(B) A vehicle or vehicle part seized under division (A) of this section shall be held in custody pursuant to section 2933.41 of the Revised Code or any applicable municipal ordinance.

(C) A law enforcement officer who acts in good faith in the belief that the seizure of a vehicle or vehicle part is justified under division (A) of this section is immune from any civil or criminal liability for such seizure.

(D) The lawful owner of a vehicle or vehicle part seized under this section that is not needed as evidence and is not subject to forfeiture under division (D)(2) of section 4549.62 of the Revised Code may reclaim the property by submitting satisfactory proof of ownership to the law enforcement agency or court holding the property.

(1984 H 632, eff. 3–28–85)

LIABILITY OF MOTOR VEHICLE LEASING AND RENTING DEALERS

4549.65 Immunity for leasing dealer who reports vehicle as converted or stolen

(A) As used in this section:

(1) "Motor vehicle leasing dealer" has the meaning set forth in division (M) of section 4517.01 of the Revised Code.

(2) "Motor vehicle renting dealer" means any person engaged in the business of regularly making available, offering to make available, or arranging for another person to use a motor vehicle pursuant to a bailment, rental agreement, or other contractual arrangement for a period of less than thirty days under which a charge is made for its use at a periodic rate and the title to the motor vehicle is in a person other than the user, but does not mean a manufacturer or its affiliate renting to its employees or to dealers.

(B) A motor vehicle leasing dealer or a motor vehicle renting dealer and its officers, employees, agents, and representatives are not liable to a lessee or renter for damages or injuries sustained as a result of the lessee's or renter's being stopped, detained, arrested, or charged in connection with a theft offense involving the leased or rented motor vehicle if such dealer, its officers, employees, agents, or representatives act in good faith upon a reasonable belief that the motor vehicle was or is being converted or stolen or if both of the following apply:

(1) The lessee or renter did not return the motor vehicle at the time and place specified in the lease or rental contract;

(2) The lessee or renter failed to return the motor vehicle within twenty-four hours after the dealer, or an officer, employee, agent, or representative of the dealer has served a written notice upon the lessee or renter, requesting the return of the motor vehicle, at the lessee's or renter's address set forth in the lease or rental contract. Service may be by certified mail, return receipt requested, or by personal or residence service.

(1984 H 632, eff. 3–28–85)

CHAPTER 4561

AERONAUTICS

DEFINITIONS

4561.01 Definitions

As used in sections 4561.01 to 4561.151 of the Revised Code:

(A) "Aviation" means transportation by aircraft; operation of aircraft; the establishment, operation, maintenance, repair, and improvement of airports, landing fields, and other air navigation facilities; and all other activities connected therewith or incidental thereto.

(B) "Aircraft" means any contrivance used or designed for navigation or flight in the air, excepting a parachute or other contrivance for such navigation used primarily as safety equipment.

(C) "Airport" means any location either on land or water which is used for the landing and taking off of aircraft.

(D) "Landing field" means any location either on land or water of such size and nature as to permit the landing or taking off of aircraft with safety, and used for that purpose but not equipped to provide for the shelter, supply, or care of aircraft.

(E) "Air navigation facility" means any facility used, available for use, or designed for use in aid of navigation of aircraft, including airports, landing fields, facilities for the servicing of aircraft or for the comfort and accommodation of air travelers, and any structures, mechanisms, lights, beacons, marks, communicating systems, or other instrumentalities or devices used or useful as an aid to the safe taking off, navigation, and landing of aircraft, or to the safe and efficient operation or maintenance of an airport or landing field, and any combination of such facilities.

(F) "Air navigation hazard" means any structure, object of natural growth, or use of land, that obstructs the air space required for the flight of aircraft in landing or taking off at any airport or landing field, or that otherwise is hazardous to such landing or taking off.

(G) "Air navigation," "navigation of aircraft," or "navigate aircraft" means the operation of aircraft in the air space over this state.

(H) "Airman" means any individual who, as the person in command, or as pilot, mechanic, or member of the crew, engages in the navigation of aircraft.

(I) "Airway" means a route in the air space over and above the lands or waters of this state, designated by the Ohio aviation board as a route suitable for the navigation of aircraft.

(J) "Person" means any individual, firm, partnership, corporation, company, association, joint stock association, or body politic, and includes any trustee, receiver, assignee, or other similar representative thereof.

(1995 S 2, eff. 7–1–96; 1953 H 1, eff. 10–1–53; GC 6310–38)

AIRPORTS, AIRCRAFT AND PILOTS' LICENSES

4561.15 Unsafe operation of aircraft

(A) No person shall commit any of the following acts:

(1) Carry passengers in an aircraft unless the person piloting the aircraft is a holder of a valid airperson's certificate of competency in the grade of private pilot or higher issued by the United States; this division of this section is inapplicable to the operation of military aircraft of the United States, aircraft of a state, territory, or possession of the United States, or aircraft licensed by a foreign country with which the United States has a reciprocal agreement covering the operation of such aircraft;

(2) Operate an aircraft on the land or water or in the air space over this state in a careless or reckless manner that endangers any person or property, or with willful or wanton disregard for the rights or safety of others;

(3) Operate an aircraft on the land or water or in the air space over this state while under the influence of intoxicating liquor, controlled substances, or other habit-forming drugs;

(4) Tamper with, alter, destroy, remove, carry away, or cause to be carried away any object used for the marking of airports, landing fields, or other aeronautical facilities in this state, or in any way change the position or location of such markings, except by the direction of the proper authorities charged with the maintenance and operation of such facilities, or illegally possess any object used for such markings.

(B) Jurisdiction over any proceedings charging a violation of this section is limited to courts of record.

(C) Whoever violates this section shall be fined not more than five hundred dollars, imprisoned not more than six months, or both.

(2002 S 123, eff. 1–1–04; 1995 S 2, eff. 7–1–96; 1975 H 300, eff. 7–1–76; 1953 H 1; GC 6310–50a)

Notes of Decisions

Ed. Note: See notes of decisions and opinions at RC 4511.19 regarding construction of the term "under the influence."

GENERAL PROVISIONS

4561.24 Operation of motor vehicles on airport runways

(A) No person shall operate a motor vehicle upon any runway of an airport without prior approval of the person in charge of the airport when the airport has been certified as a commercial airport by the office of aviation.

Any person lending assistance to the operator or operation of a vehicle engaged in such activity shall be equally charged as the participants.

(B) Except as otherwise provided in this division, whoever violates this section shall be fined not less than one hundred nor more than five hundred dollars, imprisoned for not more than six months, or both. If the offender previously has committed a violation of this section, whoever violates this section shall be fined not less than two hundred nor more than one thousand dollars, imprisoned for not more than one year, or both.

(C) As used in this section, "motor vehicle" has the same meaning as in section 4501.01 of the Revised Code.

(D) Airport vehicles and emergency and maintenance equipment are exempted from this section.

(2002 S 123, eff. 1-1-04; 1996 H 572, eff. 9-17-96; 1969 H 266, eff. 8-28-69)

PENALTIES

4561.99 Penalties

Whoever violates any provision of sections 4561.021 to 4561.13 of the Revised Code for which no penalty otherwise is provided in the section that contains the provision violated shall be fined not more than five hundred dollars, imprisoned not more than ninety days, or both.

(2002 S 123, eff. 1-1-04; 1995 S 2, eff. 7-1-96; 1994 H 571, eff. 10-6-94; 1991 H 15, eff. 10-15-91; 1969 H 266; 1953 H 1)

CHAPTER 4582

PORT AUTHORITIES

4582.28 Employees; special police officers

(A) A port authority created in accordance with section 4582.22 of the Revised Code shall employ and fix the qualifications, duties, and compensation of any employees and enter into contracts for any professional services it may require to conduct the business of the port authority and may appoint an advisory board, which shall serve without compensation. Any employee may be suspended or dismissed, and any contract for professional services may be terminated at any time by the port authority.

(B) A port authority may provide for the administration and enforcement of the laws of the state by employing special police officers, and may seek the assistance of other appropriate law enforcement officers to enforce its rules and maintain order.

(C) Special police officers employed by a port authority shall serve as a police force with respect to the property, grounds, buildings, equipment, and facilities under the control of the port authority, to prevent hijacking of aircraft or watercraft, protect the property of the authority and the property of others located thereon, suppress nuisances and disturbances and breaches of the peace, and enforce laws and the rules of the port authority for the preservation of good order. In performing their duties, special police officers are vested with the same powers of arrest as police officers under section 2935.03 of the Revised Code.

Any person employed as a special police officer by a port authority is a "public employee" as defined in section 145.01 of the Revised Code and is not a "member of a police department" as defined in section 742.01 of the Revised Code.

(2000 S 137, eff. 5-17-00; 1982 H 439, eff. 7-9-82)

CHAPTER 4729

PHARMACISTS; DANGEROUS DRUGS

STATE BOARD OF PHARMACY

4729.01 Definitions

As used in this chapter:

(A) "Pharmacy," except when used in a context that refers to the practice of pharmacy, means any area, room, rooms, place of business, department, or portion of any of the foregoing where the practice of pharmacy is conducted.

(B) "Practice of pharmacy" means providing pharmacist care requiring specialized knowledge, judgment, and skill derived from the principles of biological, chemical, behavioral, social, pharmaceutical, and clinical sciences. As used in this division, "pharmacist care" includes the following:

(1) Interpreting prescriptions;

(2) Compounding or dispensing drugs and dispensing drug therapy related devices;

(3) Counseling individuals with regard to their drug therapy, recommending drug therapy related devices, and assisting in the selection of drugs and appliances for treatment of common diseases and injuries and providing instruction in the proper use of the drugs and appliances;

(4) Performing drug regimen reviews with individuals by discussing all of the drugs that the individual is taking and explaining the interactions of the drugs;

(5) Performing drug utilization reviews with licensed health professionals authorized to prescribe drugs when the pharmacist determines that an individual with a prescription has a drug regimen that warrants additional discussion with the prescriber;

(6) Advising an individual and the health care professionals treating an individual with regard to the individual's drug therapy;

(7) Acting pursuant to a consult agreement with a physician authorized under Chapter 4731. of the Revised Code to practice medicine and surgery or osteopathic medicine and surgery, if an agreement has been established with the physician;

(8) Administering the adult immunizations specified in section 4729.41 of the Revised Code, if the pharmacist has met the requirements of that section.

(C) "Compounding" means the preparation, mixing, assembling, packaging, and labeling of one or more drugs in any of the following circumstances:

(1) Pursuant to a prescription issued by a licensed health professional authorized to prescribe drugs;

(2) Pursuant to the modification of a prescription made in accordance with a consult agreement;

(3) As an incident to research, teaching activities, or chemical analysis;

(4) In anticipation of prescription drug orders based on routine, regularly observed dispensing patterns.

(D) "Consult agreement" means an agreement to manage an individual's drug therapy that has been entered into by a pharmacist and a physician authorized under Chapter 4731. of the Revised Code to practice medicine and surgery or osteopathic medicine and surgery.

(E) "Drug" means:

(1) Any article recognized in the United States pharmacopoeia and national formulary, or any supplement to them, intended for use in the diagnosis, cure, mitigation, treatment, or prevention of disease in humans or animals;

(2) Any other article intended for use in the diagnosis, cure, mitigation, treatment, or prevention of disease in humans or animals;

(3) Any article, other than food, intended to affect the structure or any function of the body of humans or animals;

(4) Any article intended for use as a component of any article specified in division (E)(1), (2), or (3) of this section; but does not include devices or their components, parts, or accessories.

(F) "Dangerous drug" means any of the following:

(1) Any drug to which either of the following applies:

(a) Under the "Federal Food, Drug, and Cosmetic Act," 52 Stat. 1040 (1938), 21 U.S.C.A. 301, as amended, the drug is required to bear a label containing the legend "Caution: Federal law prohibits dispensing without prescription" or "Caution: Federal law restricts this drug to use by or on the order of a licensed veterinarian" or any similar restrictive statement, or the drug may be dispensed only upon a prescription;

(b) Under Chapter 3715. or 3719. of the Revised Code, the drug may be dispensed only upon a prescription.

(2) Any drug that contains a schedule V controlled substance and that is exempt from Chapter 3719. of the Revised Code or to which that chapter does not apply;

(3) Any drug intended for administration by injection into the human body other than through a natural orifice of the human body.

(G) "Federal drug abuse control laws" has the same meaning as in section 3719.01 of the Revised Code.

(H) "Prescription" means a written, electronic, or oral order for drugs or combinations or mixtures of drugs to be used by a particular individual or for treating a particular animal, issued by a licensed health professional authorized to prescribe drugs.

(I) "Licensed health professional authorized to prescribe drugs" or "prescriber" means an individual who is authorized by law to prescribe drugs or dangerous drugs or drug therapy related devices in the course of the individual's professional practice, including only the following:

(1) A dentist licensed under Chapter 4715. of the Revised Code;

(2) A clinical nurse specialist, certified nurse-midwife, or certified nurse practitioner who holds a certificate to prescribe issued under section 4723.48 of the Revised Code;

(3) An optometrist licensed under Chapter 4725. of the Revised Code to practice optometry under a therapeutic pharmaceutical agents certificate;

(4) A physician authorized under Chapter 4731. of the Revised Code to practice medicine and surgery, osteopathic medicine and surgery, or podiatry;

(5) A veterinarian licensed under Chapter 4741. of the Revised Code.

(J) "Sale" and "sell" include delivery, transfer, barter, exchange, or gift, or offer therefor, and each such transaction made by any person, whether as principal proprietor, agent, or employee.

(K) "Wholesale sale" and "sale at wholesale" mean any sale in which the purpose of the purchaser is to resell the article purchased or received by the purchaser.

(L) "Retail sale" and "sale at retail" mean any sale other than a wholesale sale or sale at wholesale.

(M) "Retail seller" means any person that sells any dangerous drug to consumers without assuming control over and responsibility for its administration. Mere advice or instructions regarding administration do not constitute control or establish responsibility.

(N) "Price information" means the price charged for a prescription for a particular drug product and, in an easily understandable manner, all of the following:

(1) The proprietary name of the drug product;

(2) The established (generic) name of the drug product;

(3) The strength of the drug product if the product contains a single active ingredient or if the drug product contains more than one active ingredient and a relevant strength can be associated with the product without indicating each active ingredient. The established name and quantity of each active ingredient are required if such a relevant strength cannot be so associated with a drug product containing more than one ingredient.

(4) The dosage form;

(5) The price charged for a specific quantity of the drug product. The stated price shall include all charges to the consumer, including, but not limited to, the cost of the drug product, professional fees, handling fees, if any, and a statement identifying professional services routinely furnished by the pharmacy. Any mailing fees and delivery fees may be stated separately without repetition. The information shall not be false or misleading.

(O) "Wholesale distributor of dangerous drugs" means a person engaged in the sale of dangerous drugs at wholesale and includes any agent or employee of such a person authorized by the person to engage in the sale of dangerous drugs at wholesale.

(P) "Manufacturer of dangerous drugs" means a person, other than a pharmacist, who manufactures dangerous drugs and who is engaged in the sale of those dangerous drugs within this state.

(Q) "Terminal distributor of dangerous drugs" means a person who is engaged in the sale of dangerous drugs at retail, or any person, other than a wholesale distributor or a pharmacist, who has possession, custody, or control of dangerous drugs for any purpose other than for that person's own use and consumption, and includes pharmacies, hospitals, nursing homes, and laboratories and all other persons who procure dangerous drugs for sale or other distribution by or under the supervision of a pharmacist or licensed health professional authorized to prescribe drugs.

(R) "Promote to the public" means disseminating a representation to the public in any manner or by any means, other than by labeling, for the purpose of inducing, or that is likely to induce, directly or indirectly, the purchase of a dangerous drug at retail.

(S) "Person" includes any individual, partnership, association, limited liability company, or corporation, the state, any political subdivision of the state, and any district, department, or agency of the state or its political subdivisions.

(T) "Finished dosage form" has the same meaning as in section 3715.01 of the Revised Code.

(U) "Generically equivalent drug" has the same meaning as in section 3715.01 of the Revised Code.

(V) "Animal shelter" means a facility operated by a humane society or any society organized under Chapter 1717. of the Revised Code or a dog pound operated pursuant to Chapter 955. of the Revised Code.

(W) "Food" has the same meaning as in section 3715.01 of the Revised Code.

(2004 S 80, eff. 4–7–05; 2003 H 95, eff. 6–26–03; 2000 S 248, eff. 3–12–01; 2000 H 241, eff. 5–17–00; 1998 S 66, eff. 7–22–98)

4729.02 State board of pharmacy

There shall be a state board of pharmacy, consisting of nine members, eight of whom shall be pharmacists licensed under this chapter, representing to the extent practicable various phases of the practice of pharmacy, and one of whom shall be a public member at least sixty years of age. Members shall be appointed by the governor with the advice and consent of the senate. Terms of office shall be for four years, commencing on the first day of July and ending on the thirtieth day of June. The Ohio pharmacists association may annually submit to the governor the names of not less than five pharmacists licensed under this chapter, and from the names submitted or from others, at the governor's discretion, the governor each year shall make appointments to the board. Each member shall hold office from the date of appointment until the end of the term for which the member was appointed. Any member appointed to fill a vacancy occurring prior to the expiration of the term for which the predecessor was appointed shall hold office for the remainder of such term. Any member shall continue in office subsequent to the expiration date of the member's term until a successor takes office, or until a period of sixty days has elapsed, whichever occurs first.

No member of the board shall be reappointed to the board more than once.

(1998 S 66, eff. 7–22–98)

4729.03 Organization

The state board of pharmacy shall organize by electing a president and a vice-president who are members of the board. The president shall preside over the meetings of the board, but shall not vote upon matters determined by the board, except in the event of a tie vote, in which case the president shall vote. The board shall also employ an executive director who is a licensed pharmacist in good standing in the practice of pharmacy in this state. The person employed shall not be a member of the board. Each of the officers elected shall serve for a term of one year. The members of the board shall receive an amount fixed pursuant to division (J) of section 124.15 of the Revised Code for each day employed in the discharge of their official duties and their necessary expenses while engaged therein.

(1998 S 66, eff. 7–22–98; 1977 H 1, eff. 8–26–77; 1971 S 141; 132 v H 93; 1953 H 1; GC 1297)

4729.04 Executive director; functions; bond

(A) The executive director of the state board of pharmacy is the chief administrative officer of the board.

(B) The executive director is an appointing authority, as defined in section 124.01 of the Revised Code, and may appoint employees necessary to carry out the board's functions.

(1) The executive director, with the board's approval, may prescribe rules for the conduct of board employees, the performance of its business, and the custody, use, and preservation of its records, papers, books, documents, and property.

(2) The executive director shall carry out his duties as an appointing authority subject to internal management rules adopted by the board.

(3) The executive director shall give a blanket bond to the state covering all employees of the agency in the sum of twenty-five thousand dollars, conditioned for the faithful discharge of the duties of their offices.

(1984 H 208, eff. 9–20–84; 1971 S 141; 1953 H 1; GC 1298)

4729.05 Quorum; meetings

Five of the voting members of the state board of pharmacy shall constitute a quorum. The board shall meet at least once during each quarter of the fiscal year and at such other times and places as the board may direct. The board shall have a seal and prescribe such rules for its own government as it deems proper.

(1990 H 623, eff. 7–24–90; 1984 H 208; 1977 S 221; 1971 S 141; 130 v S 173; 1953 H 1; GC 1299)

4729.06 Records; court evidence

The state board of pharmacy shall keep a record of its proceedings and a register of all persons to whom identification cards and licenses have been granted as pharmacists or pharmacy interns, together with each renewal and suspension or revocation of an identification card and license. The books and registers of the board shall be prima-facie evidence of the matters therein recorded. The president and executive director of the board may administer oaths.

A statement signed by the executive director to which is affixed the official seal of the board to the effect that it appears from the records of the board that the board has not issued an identification card and license to practice pharmacy, or any of its branches, to the person specified in the statement, or that an identification card and license, if issued, has been revoked or suspended, shall be received as prima-facie evidence of the record of the board in any court or before any officer of this state.

(1998 S 66, eff. 7 22 98; 1971 S 141, eff. 12 31 71; 130 v S 173; 1953 H 1; GC 1300)

REGISTRATION OF PHARMACISTS

4729.07 Application for licensure; examination

An individual desiring to be licensed as a pharmacist shall file with the executive director of the state board of pharmacy a verified application giving such information as the board requires. An application filed under this section may not be withdrawn without the approval of the board.

Each applicant shall take an examination to determine fitness to practice pharmacy. Examinations of those applying for licensure as pharmacists shall be held at such times, during each year, and at such places as the board determines. The board may use all or any part of the licensure examination of the national association of boards of pharmacy or any other national standardized pharmacy examination that it considers appropriate. The board may require applicants to purchase the examination and any related materials from the organization providing it.

(2000 S 172, eff. 2 12 01; 1998 S 66, eff. 7 22 98; 1981 H 694, eff. 11–15–81; 1971 S 141; 128 v 867; 1953 H 1; GC 1301)

4729.08 Qualifications

Every applicant for examination and licensure as a pharmacist shall:

(A) Be at least eighteen years of age;

(B) Be of good moral character and habits;

(C) Have obtained a degree in pharmacy from a program that has been recognized and approved by the state board of pharmacy, except that graduates of schools or colleges of pharmacy that are located outside the United States and have not demonstrated that the standards of their programs are at least equivalent to programs recognized and approved by the board shall be required to pass an equivalency examination recognized and approved by the board and to establish written and oral proficiency in English.

(D) Have satisfactorily completed at least the minimum requirements for pharmacy internship as outlined by the board.

If the board is satisfied that the applicant meets the foregoing requirements and if the applicant passes the examination required under section 4729.07 of the Revised Code, the board shall issue to the applicant a license and an identification card authorizing the individual to practice pharmacy.

(1998 S 66, eff. 7–22–98; 1984 H 208, eff. 9–20–84; 1973 S 1; 1971 S 141; 128 v 867; 127 v 162; 1953 H 1; GC 1302)

4729.09 Reciprocal licensure

The state board of pharmacy may license an individual as a pharmacist without examination and issue an identification card to the pharmacist if the individual:

(A) Holds a license in good standing to practice pharmacy under the laws of another state, has successfully completed an examination for licensure in the other state, and in the opinion of the board, the examination was at least as thorough as that required by the board at the time the individual took the examination;

(B) Is of good moral character and habit;

(C) Has filed with the licensing body of the other state at least the credentials or the equivalent that were required by this state at the time the individual was licensed a pharmacist.

The board shall not issue any identification card or license to an individual licensed in another state if the state in which the individual is licensed does not reciprocate by granting licenses to practice pharmacy to persons holding valid licenses received through examination by the state board of pharmacy.

(1998 S 66, eff. 7–22–98; 1971 S 141, eff. 12–31–71)

4729.11 Pharmacy internship program; registration; director; duties

The state board of pharmacy shall establish a pharmacy internship program for the purpose of providing the practical experience necessary to practice as a pharmacist. Any individual who desires to become a pharmacy intern shall apply for licensure to the board. An application filed under this section may not be withdrawn without the approval of the board.

Each applicant shall be issued an identification card and license as a pharmacy intern if in the opinion of the board the applicant is actively pursuing an educational program in preparation for licensure as a pharmacist and meets the other requirements as determined by the board. An identification card and license shall be valid until the next annual renewal date and shall be renewed only if the intern is meeting the requirements and rules of the board.

The state board of pharmacy may appoint a director of pharmacy internship who is a licensed pharmacist and who is not directly or indirectly connected with a school or college of pharmacy or department of pharmacy of a university. The director of pharmacy internship shall be responsible to the board for the operation and direction of the pharmacy internship program established by the board under this section, and for such other duties as the board may assign.

(2000 S 172, eff. 2–12–01; 1998 S 66, eff. 7–22–98; 1971 S 141, eff. 12–31–71; 128 v 867; 1953 H 1; GC 1303–3)

4729.12 Identification card; display of license; renewal; renewal after lapse

An identification card issued by the state board of pharmacy under section 4729.08 of the Revised Code entitles the individual to whom it is issued to practice as a pharmacist or as a pharmacy intern in this state until the next annual renewal date.

Identification cards shall be renewed annually on the fifteenth day of September, according to the standard renewal procedure of Chapter 4745. of the Revised Code.

Each pharmacist and pharmacy intern shall carry the identification card or renewal identification card while engaged in the practice of pharmacy. The license shall be conspicuously exposed at the principal place where the pharmacist or pharmacy intern practices pharmacy.

A pharmacist or pharmacy intern who desires to continue in the practice of pharmacy shall file with the board an application in such form and containing such data as the board may require for renewal of an identification card. An application filed under this section may not be withdrawn without the approval of the board. If the board finds that the applicant's card has not been revoked or placed under suspension and that the applicant has paid the renewal fee, has continued pharmacy education in accordance with the rules of the board, and is entitled to continue in the practice of pharmacy, the board shall issue a renewal identification card to the applicant.

When an identification card has lapsed for more than sixty days but application is made within three years after the expiration of the card, the applicant shall be issued a renewal identification card without further examination if the applicant meets the requirements of this section and pays the fee designated under division (E) of section 4729.15 of the Revised Code.

(2000 S 172, eff. 2–12–01; 1998 S 66, eff. 7–22–98; 1986 H 428, eff. 12–23–86; 1982 S 550; 1971 S 141)

4729.13 Renewal of identification card after three year lapse

A pharmacist who fails to make application to the state board of pharmacy for a renewal identification card within a period of three years from the expiration of the identification card must pass an examination for registration; except that a pharmacist whose registration has expired, but who has continually practiced pharmacy in another state under a license issued by the authority of that state, may obtain a renewal identification card upon payment to the executive director of the board the fee designated under division (F) of section 4729.15 of the Revised Code.

(1998 S 66, eff. 7–22–98; 1982 S 550, eff. 11–26–82; 1971 S 141)

4729.14 Replacement license or identification card

A replacement license or identification card may be issued a person registered with the state board of pharmacy as a pharmacist or as a pharmacy intern whose license or identification card has been lost or destroyed, upon condition that the applicant by affidavit sets forth the facts concerning the loss or destruction of the previously issued license or identification card.

(1998 S 66, eff. 7–22–98; 1971 S 141, eff. 12–31–71)

4729.15 Fees

The state board of pharmacy shall charge the following fees:

(A) For applying for a license to practice as a pharmacist, an amount adequate to cover all rentals, compensation for proctors, and other expenses of the board related to examination except the expenses of procuring and grading the examination, which fee shall not be returned if the applicant fails to pass the examination;

(B) For the examination of an applicant for licensure as a pharmacist, an amount adequate to cover any expenses to the board of procuring and grading the examination or any part thereof, which fee shall not be returned if the applicant fails to pass the examination;

(C) For issuing a license and an identification card to an individual who passes the examination described in section 4729.07 of the Revised Code, an amount that is adequate to cover the expense;

(D) For a pharmacist applying for renewal of an identification card within sixty days after the expiration date, ninety-seven dollars and fifty cents, which fee shall not be returned if the applicant fails to qualify for renewal;

(E) For a pharmacist applying for renewal of an identification card that has lapsed for more than sixty days, but for less than three years, one hundred thirty-five dollars, which fee shall not be returned if the applicant fails to qualify for renewal;

(F) For a pharmacist applying for renewal of an identification card that has lapsed for more than three years, three hundred thirty-seven dollars and fifty cents, which fee shall not be returned if the applicant fails to qualify for renewal;

(G) For a pharmacist applying for a license and identification card, on presentation of a pharmacist license granted by another state, three hundred thirty-seven dollars and fifty cents, which fee shall not be returned if the applicant fails to qualify for licensure.

(H) For a license and identification card to practice as a pharmacy intern, twenty-two dollars and fifty cents, which fee shall not be returned if the applicant fails to qualify for licensure;

(I) For the renewal of a pharmacy intern identification card, twenty-two dollars and fifty cents, which fee shall not be returned if the applicant fails to qualify for renewal;

(J) For issuing a replacement license to a pharmacist, twenty-two dollars and fifty cents;

(K) For issuing a replacement license to a pharmacy intern, seven dollars and fifty cents;

(L) For issuing a replacement identification card to a pharmacist, thirty-seven dollars and fifty cents, or pharmacy intern, seven dollars and fifty cents;

(M) For certifying licensure and grades for reciprocal licensure, ten dollars;

(N) For making copies of any application, affidavit, or other document filed in the state board of pharmacy office, an amount fixed by the board that is adequate to cover the expense, except that for copies required by federal or state agencies or law enforcement officers for official purposes, no charge need be made;

(O) For certifying and affixing the seal of the board, an amount fixed by the board that is adequate to cover the expense, except that for certifying and affixing the seal of the board to a document required by federal or state agencies or law enforcement officers for official purposes, no charge need be made;

(P) For each copy of a book or pamphlet that includes laws administered by the state board of pharmacy, rules adopted by the board, and chapters of the Revised Code with which the board is required to comply, an amount fixed by the board that is adequate to cover the expense of publishing and furnishing the book or pamphlet.

(1998 S 66, eff. 7–22–98; 1997 H 215, eff. 6–30–97; 1995 H 117, eff. 6–30–95; 1989 H 111, eff. 7–1–89; 1981 H 694; 1971 S 141)

4729.16 Revoke, suspend, place on probation, or refuse to grant or renew identification card; hearing, notice; penalty; return of card

(A) The state board of pharmacy, after notice and hearing in accordance with Chapter 119. of the Revised Code, may revoke, suspend, limit, place on probation, or refuse to grant or renew an identification card, or may impose a monetary penalty or forfeiture not to exceed in severity any fine designated under the Revised Code for a similar offense, or in the case of a violation of a section of the Revised Code that does not bear a penalty, a monetary penalty or forfeiture of not more than five hundred dollars, if the board finds a pharmacist or pharmacy intern:

(1) Guilty of a felony or gross immorality;

(2) Guilty of dishonesty or unprofessional conduct in the practice of pharmacy;

(3) Addicted to or abusing liquor or drugs or impaired physically or mentally to such a degree as to render the pharmacist or pharmacy intern unfit to practice pharmacy;

(4) Has been convicted of a misdemeanor related to, or committed in, the practice of pharmacy;

(5) Guilty of willfully violating, conspiring to violate, attempting to violate, or aiding and abetting the violation of any of the provisions of this chapter, sections 3715.52 to 3715.72 of the Revised Code, Chapter 2925. or 3719. of the Revised Code, or any rule adopted by the board under those provisions;

(6) Guilty of permitting anyone other than a pharmacist or pharmacy intern to practice pharmacy;

(7) Guilty of knowingly lending the pharmacist's or pharmacy intern's name to an illegal practitioner of pharmacy or having professional connection with an illegal practitioner of pharmacy;

(8) Guilty of dividing or agreeing to divide remuneration made in the practice of pharmacy with any other individual, including, but not limited to, any licensed health professional authorized to prescribe drugs or any owner, manager, or employee of a health care facility, residential care facility, or nursing home;

(9) Has violated the terms of a consult agreement entered into pursuant to section 4729.39 of the Revised Code;

(10) Has committed fraud, misrepresentation, or deception in applying for or securing a license or identification card issued by the board under this chapter or under Chapter 3715. or 3719. of the Revised Code.

(B) Any individual whose identification card is revoked, suspended, or refused, shall return the identification card and license to the offices of the state board of pharmacy within ten days after receipt of notice of such action.

(C) As used in this section:

"Unprofessional conduct in the practice of pharmacy" includes any of the following:

(1) Advertising or displaying signs that promote dangerous drugs to the public in a manner that is false or misleading;

(2) Except as provided in section 4729.281 of the Revised Code, the sale of any drug for which a prescription is required, without having received a prescription for the drug;

(3) Knowingly dispensing medication pursuant to false or forged prescriptions;

(4) Knowingly failing to maintain complete and accurate records of all dangerous drugs received or dispensed in compliance with federal laws and regulations and state laws and rules;

(5) Obtaining any remuneration by fraud, misrepresentation, or deception.

(D) The board may suspend a license or identification card under division (B) of section 3719.121 of the Revised Code by utilizing a telephone conference call to review the allegations and take a vote.

(E) If, pursuant to an adjudication under Chapter 119. of the Revised Code, the board has reasonable cause to believe that a pharmacist or pharmacy intern is physically or mentally impaired, the board may require the pharmacist or pharmacy intern to submit to a physical or mental examination, or both.

(2000 S 172, eff. 2–12–01; 1998 S 66, eff. 7–22–98; 1995 H 117, eff. 9–29–95; 1994 S 279, eff. 10–20–94; 1984 H 208, eff. 9–20–84; 1975 H 300; 1971 S 141; 1969 H 1; 132 v S 70; 129 v 582; 128 v 867; 127 v 162; 1953 H 1; GC 1307)

4729.161 Practice through corporation, limited liability company, partnership or professional association permitted

(A) An individual registered with the state board of pharmacy to engage in the practice of pharmacy may render the professional services of a pharmacist within this state through a corporation formed under division (B) of section 1701.03 of the Revised Code, a limited liability company formed under Chapter 1705. of the Revised Code, a partnership, or a professional association formed under Chapter 1785. of the Revised Code. This division does not preclude an individual of that nature from rendering professional services as a pharmacist through another form of business entity, including, but not limited to, a nonprofit corporation or foundation, or in another manner that is authorized by or in accordance with this chapter, another chapter of the Revised Code, or rules of the state board of pharmacy adopted pursuant to this chapter.

(B) A corporation, limited liability company, partnership, or professional association described in division (A) of this section may be formed for the purpose of providing a combination of the professional services of the following individuals who are licensed, certificated, or otherwise legally authorized to practice their respective professions:

(1) Optometrists who are authorized to practice optometry under Chapter 4725. of the Revised Code;

(2) Chiropractors who are authorized to practice chiropractic under Chapter 4734. of the Revised Code;

(3) Psychologists who are authorized to practice psychology under Chapter 4732. of the Revised Code;

(4) Registered or licensed practical nurses who are authorized to practice nursing as registered nurses or as licensed practical nurses under Chapter 4723. of the Revised Code;

(5) Pharmacists who are authorized to practice pharmacy under Chapter 4729. of the Revised Code;

(6) Physical therapists who are authorized to practice physical therapy under sections 4755.40 to 4755.53 of the Revised Code;

(7) Mechanotherapists who are authorized to practice mechanotherapy under section 4731.151 of the Revised Code;

(8) Doctors of medicine and surgery, osteopathic medicine and surgery, or podiatric medicine and surgery who are authorized for their respective practices under Chapter 4731. of the Revised Code.

This division shall apply notwithstanding a provision of a code of ethics applicable to a pharmacist that prohibits a pharmacist from engaging in the practice of pharmacy in combination with a person who is licensed, certificated, or otherwise legally authorized to practice optometry, chiropractic, psychology, nursing, physical therapy, mechanotherapy, medicine and surgery, osteopathic medicine and surgery, or podiatric medicine and surgery, but who is not also licensed, certificated, or otherwise legally authorized to engage in the practice of pharmacy.

(1998 H 698, eff. 3–22–99; 1997 S 31, eff. 4–10–98)

4729.17 Hearing before board

Any investigation, inquiry, or hearing, which the state board of pharmacy is empowered to hold or undertake may be held or undertaken by or before any member or members of the board and the finding or order of such member or members shall be deemed to be the order of said board when approved and confirmed by a majority of the board.

(1971 S 141, eff. 12–31–71; 1953 H 1; GC 1307–2)

4729.18 Treatment providers for pharmacists with substance abuse problems

The state board of pharmacy shall adopt rules in accordance with Chapter 119. of the Revised Code establishing standards for approving and designating physicians and facilities as treatment providers for pharmacists with substance abuse problems and shall approve and designate treatment providers in accordance with the rules. The rules shall include standards for both inpatient and outpatient treatment. The rules shall provide that to be approved, a treatment provider must be capable of making an initial examination to determine the type of treatment required for a pharmacist with substance abuse problems. Subject to the rules, the board shall review and approve treatment providers on a regular basis and may, at its discretion, withdraw or deny approval.

An approved treatment provider shall:

(A) Report to the board the name of any pharmacist suffering or showing evidence of suffering impairment by reason of being addicted to or abusing liquor or drugs as described in division (A)(3) of section 4729.16 of the Revised Code who fails to comply within one week with a referral for examination;

(B) Report to the board the name of any impaired pharmacist who fails to enter treatment within forty-eight hours following the provider's determination that the pharmacist needs treatment;

(C) Require every pharmacist who enters treatment to agree to a treatment contract establishing the terms of treatment and aftercare, including any required supervision or restrictions of practice during treatment or aftercare;

(D) Require a pharmacist to suspend practice on entering any required inpatient treatment;

(E) Report to the board any failure by an impaired pharmacist to comply with the terms of the treatment contract during inpatient or outpatient treatment or aftercare;

(F) Report to the board the resumption of practice of any impaired pharmacist before the treatment provider has made a clear determination that the pharmacist is capable of practicing according to acceptable and prevailing standards;

(G) Require a pharmacist who resumes practice after completion of treatment to comply with an aftercare contract that meets the requirements of rules adopted by the board for approval of treatment providers;

(H) Report to the board any pharmacist who suffers a relapse at any time during or following aftercare.

Any pharmacist who enters into treatment by an approved treatment provider shall be deemed to have waived any confidentiality requirements that would otherwise prevent the treatment provider from making reports required under this section.

In the absence of fraud or bad faith, no professional association of pharmacists licensed under this chapter that sponsors a committee or program to provide peer assistance to pharmacists with substance abuse problems, no representative or agent of such a committee or program, and no member of the state board of pharmacy shall be liable to any person for damages in a civil action by reason of actions taken to refer a pharmacist to a treatment provider designated by the board or actions or omissions of the provider in treating a pharmacist.

In the absence of fraud or bad faith, no person who reports to the board a pharmacist with a suspected substance abuse problem shall be liable to any person for damages in a civil action as a result of the report.

(1990 H 615, eff. 3–27–91)

4729.19 Cooperation with investigations

Notwithstanding division (B)(4) of section 2317.02 of the Revised Code, a pharmacist shall cooperate with federal, state, and local government investigations and shall divulge all relevant information when requested by a government agency.

(2000 S 172, eff. 2–12–01)

ENFORCEMENT

4729.25 Enforcement; investigation

Note: See also following version of this section, eff. 5–18–05.

(A) The state board of pharmacy shall enforce, or cause to be enforced, this chapter. If it has information that any provision of this chapter has been violated, it shall investigate the matter, and take such action as it considers appropriate in accordance with its rules adopted under section 4729.26 of the Revised Code. With regard to violations of sections 4729.51 to 4729.62 of the Revised Code, the board's actions also shall be taken in accordance with section 4729.63 of the Revised Code.

(B) Nothing in this chapter shall be construed to require the state board of pharmacy to enforce minor violations of this chapter if the board determines that the public interest is adequately served by a notice or warning to the alleged offender.

(1998 S 66, eff. 7–22–98; 1984 H 208, eff. 9–20–84; 1971 S 141; 130 v H 948; 1953 H 1; GC 1313)

Note: See also following version of this section, eff. 5–18–05.

4729.25 Enforcement; investigation (later effective date)

Note: See also preceding version of this section, in effect until 5–18–05.

(A) The state board of pharmacy shall enforce, or cause to be enforced, this chapter. If it has information that any provision of this chapter has been violated, it shall investigate the matter, and take such action as it considers appropriate.

(B) Nothing in this chapter shall be construed to require the state board of pharmacy to enforce minor violations of this chapter if the board determines that the public interest is adequately served by a notice or warning to the alleged offender.

(2004 H 377, eff. 5–18–05; 1998 S 66, eff. 7–22–98; 1984 H 208, eff. 9–20–84; 1971 S 141; 130 v H 948; 1953 H 1; GC 1313)

Note: See also preceding version of this section, in effect until 5–18–05.

4729.26 Rules for enforcement

Note: See also following version of this section, eff. 5–18–05.

The state board of pharmacy may adopt rules in accordance with Chapter 119. of the Revised Code, not inconsistent with the law, as may be necessary to carry out the purposes of and to enforce the provisions of this chapter pertaining to the practice of pharmacy. The rules shall be published and made available by the board to each pharmacist licensed under this chapter.

(1998 S 66, eff. 7–22–98; 1971 S 141, eff. 12–31–71; 1953 H 1; GC 12705–1)

Note: See also following version of this section, eff. 5–18–05.

4729.26 Rules for enforcement (later effective date)

Note: See also preceding version of this section, in effect until 5–18–05.

The state board of pharmacy may adopt rules in accordance with Chapter 119. of the Revised Code, not inconsistent with the law, as may be necessary to carry out the purposes of and to enforce the provisions of this chapter. The rules shall be published and made available by the board to each pharmacist licensed under this chapter.

(2004 H 377, eff. 5–18–05; 1998 S 66, eff. 7–22–98; 1971 S 141, eff. 12–31–71; 1953 H 1; GC 12705–1)

Note: See also preceding version of this section, in effect until 5–18–05.

4729.27 Pharmacy must be conducted by legally licensed pharmacist

A person not a pharmacist, who owns, manages, or conducts a pharmacy, shall employ a pharmacist to be in full and actual charge of such pharmacy. Any pharmacist who owns, manages, or conducts a pharmacy shall be personally in full and actual charge of the pharmacy, or shall employ another pharmacist to be in full and actual charge of the pharmacy.

(1998 S 66, eff. 7–22–98; 1971 S 141, eff. 12–31–71; 1953 H 1; GC 12705)

SALE OF DRUGS AND WOOD ALCOHOL

4729.28 Unlawful selling of drugs or practice of pharmacy

No person who is not a pharmacist or a pharmacy intern under the personal supervision of a pharmacist shall compound, dispense, or sell dangerous drugs or otherwise engage in the practice of pharmacy.

(1998 S 66, eff. 7–22–98; 1971 S 141, eff. 12–31–71; 1953 H 1; GC 12706)

4729.281 Dispensing of drug without written or oral prescription

(A) A pharmacist may dispense or sell a dangerous drug, other than a schedule II controlled substance as defined in section 3719.01 of the Revised Code, without a written or oral prescription from a licensed health professional authorized to prescribe drugs if all of the following conditions are met:

(1) The pharmacy at which the pharmacist works has a record of a prescription for the drug in the name of the patient who is requesting it, but the prescription does not provide for a refill or the time permitted by rules adopted by the state board of pharmacy for providing refills has elapsed.

(2) The pharmacist is unable to obtain authorization to refill the prescription from the health care professional who issued the prescription or another health professional responsible for the patient's care.

(3) In the exercise of the pharmacist's professional judgment:

(a) The drug is essential to sustain the life of the patient or continue therapy for a chronic condition of the patient.

(b) Failure to dispense or sell the drug to the patient could result in harm to the health of the patient.

(4) The amount of the drug that is dispensed or sold under this section does not exceed a seventy-two hour supply as provided in the prescription.

(B) A pharmacist who dispenses or sells a drug under this section shall do all of the following:

(1) For one year after the date of dispensing or sale, maintain a record in accordance with this chapter of the drug dispensed or sold, including the name and address of the patient and the individual receiving the drug, if the individual receiving the drug is not the patient, the amount dispensed or sold, and the original prescription number;

(2) Notify the health professional who issued the prescription described in division (A)(1) of this section or another health professional responsible for the patient's care not later than seventy-two hours after the drug is sold or dispensed;

(3) If applicable, obtain authorization for additional dispensing from one of the health professionals described in division (B)(2) of this section.

(C) A pharmacist who dispenses or sells a drug under this section may do so once for each prescription described in division (A)(1) of this section.

(1998 S 66, eff. 7–22–98)

4729.29 Exceptions to certain provisions

(A) Divisions (A) and (B) of section 4729.01 and section 4729.28 of the Revised Code do not do either of the following:

(1) Apply to a licensed health professional authorized to prescribe drugs or prevent a prescriber from personally furnishing the prescriber's patients with drugs, within the prescriber's scope of professional practice, that seem proper to the prescriber.

(2) Apply to the sale of oxygen, peritoneal dialysis solutions, or the sale of drugs that are not dangerous drugs by a retail dealer, in original packages when labeled as required by the "Federal Food, Drug, and Cosmetic Act," 52 Stat. 1040 (1938), 21 U.S.C.A. 301, as amended.

(B) When a prescriber personally furnishes drugs to a patient pursuant to division (A)(1) of this section, the prescriber shall ensure that the drugs are labeled and packaged in accordance with state and federal drug laws and any rules and regulations adopted pursuant to those laws. Records of purchase and disposition of all drugs personally furnished to patients shall be maintained by the prescriber in accordance with state and federal drug statutes and any rules adopted pursuant to those statutes.

When personally furnishing to a patient RU–486 (mifepristone), a prescriber is subject to section 2919.123 of the Revised Code. A prescription for RU–486 (mifepristone) shall be in writing and in accordance with section 2919.123 of the Revised Code.

(2004 H 126, eff. 9–23–04; 1998 H 553, eff. 3–9–99; 1998 S 66, eff. 7–22–98; 1997 H 215, eff. 6–30–97; 1996 H 595, eff. 10–16–96; 1994 H 391, eff. 7–21–94; 1984 S 187, eff. 6–14–84; 1971 S 141; 1953 H 1; GC 12707)

4729.30 Sale of Paris green not prohibited

Sections 4729.27 and 4729.28 of the Revised Code shall not prohibit a person from selling Paris green and other materials or compounds used exclusively for spraying and disinfecting when put up in bottles or boxes, bearing the name of a licensed pharmacist or wholesale dealer, and labeled as required by section 3719.33 of the Revised Code or apply to or interfere with the exclusively wholesale business of a dealer.

(1998 S 66, eff. 7–22–98; 1953 H 1, eff. 10–1–53; GC 12708)

4729.31 Exceptions

Sections 4729.27 and 4729.28 of the Revised Code shall not apply to, interfere with, or prohibit any person, firm, or corporation from selling completely denatured alcohol or wood alcohol.

(1953 H 1, eff. 10–1–53; GC 12708–1)

4729.32 Requirements for sale of denatured or wood alcohol in five gallon lots or more

No person shall have in his possession, or dispense or sell packages or containers of completely denatured alcohol or wood alcohol containing five wine gallons or more without having marked or stenciled thereon the name and address of the seller, the degree of proof of such alcohol, the formula number, and, in letters of not less than one inch in height, the words, "Completely Denatured Alcohol" or "Wood Alcohol," as the case may be, and the names of two or more antidotes for the same. This section, and sections 4729.33 and 3719.33 of the Revised Code shall not interfere with the transfer of such alcohol from storage tanks to other packages or containers, nor require the placing of such mark or stencil upon transportation tanks, nor the registration or placing of mark or stencil upon fuel tanks, automobile radiators, or similar containers for the final use or consumption of such alcohol and from which no further distribution thereof is made.

(1953 H 1, eff. 10–1–53; GC 12708–2)

4729.33 Requirements for sale of denatured or wood alcohol in less than five gallon lots

No person shall dispense or sell completely denatured alcohol or wood alcohol in packages containing less than five wine gallons without having affixed thereto a label on which is printed or stenciled in plain, legible, red letters of equal prominence on a white background the words, "Completely Denatured Alcohol" or "Wood Alcohol," as the case may be, and in addition on the same label in red ink, under the skull and crossbones symbol, the word "POISON" together with the following statement: "Completely denatured alcohol, or wood alcohol is a violent poison. It cannot be applied externally to human or animal tissue without serious injurious results. It cannot be taken internally without inducing blindness and general physical decay ultimately resulting in death," and without having stamped, stenciled, or printed upon such label the name and address of the seller, the degree of proof, and the formula number thereof. Neither the word "pure" nor the single word "alcohol" alone shall appear on any label of completely denatured alcohol or wood alcohol.

(1953 H 1, eff. 10–1–53; GC 12708–3)

GENERAL PROVISIONS

4729.34 Advertising

No person shall dispense, sell, or offer for sale completely denatured alcohol or wood alcohol, or shall display a sign or use a label or advertise such alcohol having the word "pure" or the single word "alcohol" alone thereon, or shall fail to state the degree of proof of such alcohol, or to have the letters displaying or advertising "Completely Denatured Alcohol" or "Wood Alcohol" plain, legible, and of equal prominence.

(1953 H 1, eff. 10–1–53; GC 12708–4)

4729.35 Unlawful distribution of drugs of abuse; prosecution

The violation by a pharmacist or other person of any laws of Ohio or of the United States of America or of any rule of the board of pharmacy controlling the distribution of a drug of abuse as defined in section 3719.011 of the Revised Code or the commission of any act set forth in division (A) of section 4729.16 of the Revised Code, is hereby declared to be inimical, harmful, and adverse to the public welfare of the citizens of Ohio and to constitute a public nuisance. The attorney general, the prosecuting attorney of any county in which the offense was committed or in which the person committing the offense resides, or the state board of pharmacy may maintain an action in the name of the state to enjoin such person from engaging in such violation. Any action under this section shall be brought in the common pleas court of the county where the offense occurred or the county where the alleged offender resides.

(1984 H 208, eff. 9–20–84; 1973 H 716)

4729.36 Advertising prohibitions

(A) No place except a pharmacy licensed as a terminal distributor of dangerous drugs and no person except a licensed pharmacist shall display any sign or advertise in any fashion, using the words "pharmacy," "drugs," "drug store," "drug store supplies," "pharmacist," "druggist," "pharmaceutical chemist," "apothecary," "drug sundries," "medicine," or any of these words or their equivalent, in any manner.

(B) A pharmacy making retail sales may advertise by name or therapeutic class the availability for sale or dispensing of any dangerous drug provided that the advertising includes the price information specified in the definition of that term in section 4729.01 of the Revised Code.

(1998 S 66, eff. 7–22–98; 1984 H 208, eff. 9–20–84; 1977 H 1; 1976 H 912; 1971 S 141; 130 v S 173)

4729.361 Disclosure of price information

(A) A retail seller of dangerous drugs shall disclose price information regarding dangerous drugs to any person requesting such information.

(B) Pursuant to division (A) of this section, a retail seller of dangerous drugs shall disclose price information in the following ways:

(1) By means of verbal disclosure on the premises of the retail seller to all persons requesting such information;

(2) By means of telephone to any person having a valid prescription, who identifies himself and requests such information.

(C) Price disclosure shall not be required for those schedule II controlled substances where lives or property could be endangered by such disclosure.

(1976 H 912, eff. 10–1–76)

4729.37 Filling prescriptions; records

A copy of an original prescription may only be filled in accordance with the rules and regulations adopted by the state board of pharmacy.

Prescriptions received electronically or by word of mouth, telephone, telegraph, or other means of communication shall be recorded in writing by the pharmacist and the record so made by the pharmacist shall constitute the original prescription to be filled by the pharmacist. All prescriptions shall be preserved on file at the pharmacy for a period of three years, subject to inspection by the proper officers of the law.

(1998 S 66, eff. 7–22–98; 1971 S 141, eff. 12–31–71; 130 v S 173)

4729.38 Substitution of generically equivalent drug; conditions

(A) Unless instructed otherwise by the person receiving the drug pursuant to the prescription, a pharmacist filling a prescription for a drug prescribed by its brand name may select a generically equivalent drug, as defined in section 3715.01 of the Revised Code, subject to the following conditions:

(1) The pharmacist shall not select a generically equivalent drug if the prescriber handwrites "dispense as written," or "D.A.W.," on the written prescription, or, when ordering a prescription electronically or orally, the prescriber specifies that the prescribed drug is medically necessary. These designations shall not be preprinted or stamped on the prescription. Division (A)(1) of this section does not preclude a reminder of the procedure required to prohibit the selection of a generically equivalent drug from being preprinted on the prescription.

(2) The pharmacist shall not select a generically equivalent drug unless its price to the patient is less than or equal to the price of the prescribed drug.

(3) The pharmacist, or the pharmacist's agent, assistant, or employee shall inform the patient or the patient's agent if a generically equivalent drug is available at a lower or equal cost, and of the person's right to refuse the drug selected. Division (A)(3) of this section does not apply to any:

(a) Prescription that is billed to any agency, division, or department of this state which will reimburse the pharmacy;

(b) Prescriptions for patients of a hospital, nursing home, or similar patient care facility.

(B) Unless the prescriber instructs otherwise, the label for every drug dispensed shall include the drug's brand name, if any, or its generic name and the name of the distributor, using abbreviations if necessary. When dispensing at retail a generically equivalent drug for the brand name drug prescribed, the pharmacist shall indicate on the drug's label or container that a generic substitution was made. The labeling requirements established by this division are in addition to all other labeling requirements of Chapter 3715. of the Revised Code.

(C) A pharmacist who selects a generically equivalent drug pursuant to this section assumes no greater liability for selecting the dispensed drug than would be incurred in filling a prescription for a drug prescribed by its brand name.

(D) The failure of a prescriber to restrict a prescription by specifying "dispense as written," or "D.A.W.," pursuant to division (A)(1) of this section shall not constitute evidence of the prescriber's negligence unless the prescriber had reasonable cause to believe that the health condition of the patient for whom the drug was intended warranted the prescription of a specific brand name drug and no other. No prescriber shall be liable for civil damages or in any criminal prosecution arising from the interchange of a generically equivalent drug for a prescribed brand name drug by a pharmacist, unless the prescribed brand name drug would have reasonably caused the same loss, damage, injury, or death.

(1998 S 66, eff. 7–22–98; 1981 H 694, eff. 11–15–81)

4729.381 Exemption from liability for dispensing drug based upon formulary of certain organizations

No licensed pharmacist shall be liable for civil damages or in any criminal prosecution arising from the dispensing of a drug based upon a formulary established by a hospital, a health insuring corporation, a long-term care facility, or the department of rehabilitation and corrections and requiring the pharmacist to dispense the particular drug.

(1998 S 66, eff. 7–22–98; 1997 S 67, eff. 6–4–97; 1984 H 208, eff. 9–20–84)

4729.39 Consult agreements

(A) A pharmacist may enter into a consult agreement with a physician authorized under Chapter 4731. of the Revised Code to practice medicine and surgery or osteopathic medicine and surgery. Under a consult agreement, a pharmacist is authorized to manage an individual's drug therapy, but only to the extent specified in the agreement, this section, and the rules adopted under this section.

(B) All of the following apply to a consult agreement that authorizes a pharmacist to manage the drug therapy of an individual who is not a patient of a hospital, as defined in section 3727.01 of the Revised Code, or a resident in a long-term care facility, as defined in section 3729.01 of the Revised Code:

(1) A separate consult agreement must be entered into for each individual whose drug therapy is to be managed by a pharmacist. A consult agreement applies only to the particular diagnosis for which a physician prescribed an individual's drug therapy. If a different diagnosis is made for the individual, the pharmacist and physician must enter into a new or additional consult agreement.

(2) Management of an individual's drug therapy by a pharmacist under a consult agreement may include monitoring and modifying a prescription that has been issued for the individual. Except as provided in section 4729.38 of the Revised Code for the selection of generically equivalent drugs, management of an individual's drug therapy by a pharmacist under a consult agreement shall not include dispensing a drug that has not been prescribed by the physician.

(3) Each consult agreement shall be in writing, except that a consult agreement may be entered into verbally if it is immediately reduced to writing.

(4) A physician entering into a consult agreement shall specify in the agreement the extent to which the pharmacist is authorized to manage the drug therapy of the individual specified in the agreement.

(5) A physician entering into a consult agreement may specify one other physician who has agreed to serve as an alternate physician in the event that the primary physician is unavailable to consult directly with the pharmacist. The pharmacist may specify one other pharmacist who has agreed to serve as an alternate pharmacist in the event that the primary pharmacist is unavailable to consult directly with the physician.

(6) A consult agreement may not be implemented until it has been signed by the primary pharmacist, the primary physician, and the individual whose drug therapy will be managed or another person who has the authority to provide consent to treatment on behalf of the individual. Once the agreement is signed by all required parties, the physician shall include in the individual's medical record the fact that a consult agreement has been entered into with a pharmacist.

(7) Prior to commencing any action to manage an individual's drug therapy under a consult agreement, the pharmacist shall make reasonable attempts to contact and confer with the physician who entered into the consult agreement with the pharmacist. A pharmacist may commence an action to manage an individual's drug therapy prior to conferring with the physician or the physician's alternate, but shall immediately cease the action that was commenced if the pharmacist has not conferred with either physician within forty-eight hours.

A pharmacist acting under a consult agreement shall maintain a record of each action taken to manage an individual's drug therapy. The pharmacist shall send to the individual's physician a written report of all actions taken to manage the individual's drug therapy at intervals the physician shall specify when entering into the agreement. The physician shall include the pharmacist's report in the medical records the physician maintains for the individual.

(8) A consult agreement may be terminated by either the pharmacist or physician who entered into the agreement. By withdrawing consent, the individual whose drug therapy is being managed or the individual who consented to the treatment on behalf of the individual may terminate a consult agreement. The pharmacist or physician who receives the individual's withdrawal of consent shall provide written notice to the opposite party. A pharmacist or physician who terminates a consult agreement shall provide written notice to the opposite party and to the individual who consented to treatment under the agreement. The termination of a consult agreement shall be recorded by the pharmacist and physician in the records they maintain on the individual being treated.

(9) Except as described in division (B)(5) of this section, the authority of a pharmacist to manage an individual's drug therapy under a consult agreement does not permit the pharmacist to manage drug therapy prescribed by any other physician.

(C) All of the following apply to a consult agreement that authorizes a pharmacist to manage the drug therapy of an individual who is a patient of a hospital, as defined in section 3727.01 of the Revised Code, or a resident in a long-term care facility, as defined in section 3729.01 of the Revised Code:

(1) Before a consult agreement may be entered into and implemented, a hospital or long-term care facility shall adopt a policy for consult agreements. For any period of time during which a pharmacist or physician acting under a consult agreement is not physically present and available at the hospital or facility, the policy shall require that another pharmacist and physician be available at the hospital or facility.

(2) The consult agreement shall be made in writing and shall comply with the hospital's or facility's policy on consult agreements.

(3) The content of the consult agreement shall be communicated to the individual whose drug therapy will be managed in a manner consistent with the hospital's or facility's policy on consult agreements.

(4) A pharmacist acting under a consult agreement shall maintain in the individual's medical record a record of each action taken under the agreement.

(5) Communication between a pharmacist and physician acting under the consult agreement shall take place at regular intervals specified by the primary physician acting under the agreement.

(6) A consult agreement may be terminated by the individual, a person authorized to act on behalf of the individual, the primary physician acting under the agreement, or the primary pharmacist acting under the agreement. When a consult agreement is terminated, all parties to the agreement shall be notified and the termination shall be recorded in the individual's medical record.

(7) The authority of a pharmacist acting under a consult agreement does not permit the pharmacist to act under the agreement in a hospital long-term care facility at which the pharmacist is not authorized to practice.

(D) The state board of pharmacy, in consultation with the state medical board, shall adopt rules to be followed by pharmacists, and the state medical board, in consultation with the state board of pharmacy, shall adopt rules to be followed by physicians, that establish standards and procedures for entering into a consult agreement and managing an individual's drug therapy under a consult agreement. The boards shall specify in the rules any categories of drugs or types of diseases for which a consult agreement may not be established. Either board may adopt any other rules it considers necessary for the implementation and administration of this section. All rules adopted under this division shall be adopted in accordance with Chapter 119. of the Revised Code.

(2000 S 172, eff. 2–12–01; 1998 S 66, eff. 7–22–98)

4729.41 Administration of adult immunizations

(A) A pharmacist licensed under this chapter who meets the requirements of division (B) of this section may administer adult immunizations for any of the following:

(1) Influenza;

(2) Pneumonia;

(3) Tetanus;

(4) Hepatitis A;

(5) Hepatitis B.

(B) To be authorized to administer the adult immunizations specified in division (A) of this section, a pharmacist shall do all of the following:

(1) Successfully complete a course in the administration of adult immunizations that has been approved by the state board of pharmacy as meeting the standards established for such courses by the centers for disease control and prevention in the public health service of the United States department of health and human services;

(2) Receive and maintain certification to perform basic life-support procedures by successfully completing a basic life-support training course certified by the American red cross or American heart association;

(3) Practice in accordance with a definitive set of treatment guidelines specified in a protocol established by a physician and approved by the state board of pharmacy. The protocol shall include provisions requiring that the pharmacist do both of the following:

(a) Observe an individual who has been immunized by the pharmacist to determine whether the individual has an adverse reaction to the immunization. The length of time and location of the observation shall be specified in rules adopted by the state board of pharmacy under division (D) of this section.

(b) Not later than thirty days after administering an adult immunization to an individual, notify the individual's family physician or, if the individual has no family physician, the board of health of the health district in which the individual resides.

(C) No pharmacist shall do either of the following:

(1) Engage in the administration of adult immunizations by injection unless the requirements of division (B) of this section have been met;

(2) Delegate to any person the pharmacist's authority to administer adult immunizations.

(D) The state board of pharmacy shall adopt rules to implement this section, including rules for approval of courses in administration of adult immunizations and approval of protocols to be followed by pharmacists in administering adult immunizations. Prior to adopting the rules regarding approval of protocols, the state board of pharmacy shall consult with the state medical board and the board of nursing. The rules shall be adopted in accordance with Chapter 119. of the Revised Code.

(2003 H 95, eff. 6–26–03; 2000 S 248, eff. 3–12–01)

DANGEROUS DRUGS, WHOLESALE AND TERMINAL DISTRIBUTORS

4729.51 Persons who may sell, deliver, distribute and possess dangerous drugs

(A) No person other than a registered wholesale distributor of dangerous drugs shall possess for sale, sell, distribute, or deliver, at wholesale, dangerous drugs, except as follows:

(1) A pharmacist who is a licensed terminal distributor of dangerous drugs or who is employed by a licensed terminal distributor of dangerous drugs may make occasional sales of dangerous drugs at wholesale;

(2) A licensed terminal distributor of dangerous drugs having more than one establishment or place may transfer or deliver dangerous drugs from one establishment or place for which a license has been issued to the terminal distributor to another establishment or place for which a license has been issued to the terminal distributor if the license issued for each establishment or place is in effect at the time of the transfer or delivery.

(B)(1) No registered wholesale distributor of dangerous drugs shall possess for sale, or sell, at wholesale, dangerous drugs to any person other than the following:

(a) A licensed health professional authorized to prescribe drugs;

(b) An optometrist licensed under Chapter 4725. of the Revised Code who holds a topical ocular pharmaceutical agents certificate;

(c) A registered wholesale distributor of dangerous drugs;

(d) A manufacturer of dangerous drugs;

(e) A licensed terminal distributor of dangerous drugs, subject to division (B)(2) of this section;

(f) Carriers or warehousers for the purpose of carriage or storage;

(g) Terminal or wholesale distributors of dangerous drugs who are not engaged in the sale of dangerous drugs within this state;

(h) An individual who holds a current license, certificate, or registration issued under Title 47 of the Revised Code and has been certified to conduct diabetes education by a national certifying body specified in rules adopted by the state board of pharmacy under section 4729. 68 of the Revised Code, but only with respect to insulin that will be used for the purpose of diabetes education and only if diabetes education is within the individual's scope of practice under statutes and rules regulating the individual's profession;

(i) An individual who holds a valid certificate issued by a nationally recognized S.C.U.B.A. diving certifying organization approved by the pharmacy board in rule, but only with respect to medical oxygen that will be used for the purpose of emergency care or treatment at the scene of a diving emergency.

(2) No registered wholesale distributor of dangerous drugs shall possess dangerous drugs for sale at wholesale, or sell such drugs at wholesale, to a licensed terminal distributor of dangerous drugs, except to:

(a) A terminal distributor who has a category I license, only dangerous drugs described in category I, as defined in division (A)(1) of section 4729. 54 of the Revised Code;

(b) A terminal distributor who has a category II license, only dangerous drugs described in category I and category II, as defined in divisions (A)(1) and (2) of section 4729.54 of the Revised Code;

(c) A terminal distributor who has a category III license, dangerous drugs described in category I, category II, and category

III, as defined in divisions (A)(1), (2), and (3) of section 4729.54 of the Revised Code;

(d) A terminal distributor who has a limited category I, II, or III license, only the dangerous drugs specified in the certificate furnished by the terminal distributor in accordance with section 4729.60 of the Revised Code.

(C)(1) Except as provided in division (C)(4) of this section, no person shall sell, at retail, dangerous drugs.

(2) Except as provided in division (C)(4) of this section, no person shall possess for sale, at retail, dangerous drugs.

(3) Except as provided in division (C)(4) of this section, no person shall possess dangerous drugs.

(4) Divisions (C)(1), (2), and (3) of this section do not apply to a registered wholesale distributor of dangerous drugs, a licensed terminal distributor of dangerous drugs, or a person who possesses, or possesses for sale or sells, at retail, a dangerous drug in accordance with Chapters 3719., 4715., 4723., 4725., 4729., 4731., and 4741. of the Revised Code.

Divisions (C)(1), (2), and (3) of this section do not apply to an individual who holds a current license, certificate, or registration issued under Title XLVII of the Revised Code and has been certified to conduct diabetes education by a national certifying body specified in rules adopted by the state board of pharmacy under section 4729.68 of the Revised Code, but only to the extent that the individual possesses insulin or personally supplies insulin solely for the purpose of diabetes education and only if diabetes education is within the individual's scope of practice under statutes and rules regulating the individual's profession.

Divisions (C)(1), (2), and (3) of this section do not apply to an individual who holds a valid certificate issued by a nationally recognized S. C.U.B.A. diving certifying organization approved by the pharmacy board in rule, but only to the extent that the individual possesses medical oxygen or personally supplies medical oxygen for the purpose of emergency care or treatment at the scene of a diving emergency.

(D) No licensed terminal distributor of dangerous drugs shall purchase for the purpose of resale dangerous drugs from any person other than a registered wholesale distributor of dangerous drugs, except as follows:

(1) A licensed terminal distributor of dangerous drugs may make occasional purchases of dangerous drugs for resale from a pharmacist who is a licensed terminal distributor of dangerous drugs or who is employed by a licensed terminal distributor of dangerous drugs;

(2) A licensed terminal distributor of dangerous drugs having more than one establishment or place may transfer or receive dangerous drugs from one establishment or place for which a license has been issued to the terminal distributor to another establishment or place for which a license has been issued to the terminal distributor if the license issued for each establishment or place is in effect at the time of the transfer or receipt.

(E) No licensed terminal distributor of dangerous drugs shall engage in the sale or other distribution of dangerous drugs at retail or maintain possession, custody, or control of dangerous drugs for any purpose other than the distributor's personal use or consumption, at any establishment or place other than that or those described in the license issued by the board of pharmacy to such terminal distributor.

(F) Nothing in this section shall be construed to interfere with the performance of official duties by any law enforcement official authorized by municipal, county, state, or federal law to collect samples of any drug, regardless of its nature or in whose possession it may be.

(2004 H 64, eff. 5–4–04; 2000 H 241, eff. 5–17–00; 1998 H 553, eff. 3–9–99; 1998 S 66, eff. 7–22–98; 1997 H 215, eff. 6–30–97; 1996 S 246, eff. 11–6–96; 1994 H 391, eff. 7–21–94; 1984 S 187, eff. 6–14–84; 1982 S 4; 1969 H 90; 129 v 1376)

4729.52 Registration as wholesale distributor; fees

(A) A person desiring to be registered as a wholesale distributor of dangerous drugs shall file with the executive director of the state board of pharmacy a verified application containing such information as the board requires of the applicant relative to the qualifications to be registered as a wholesale distributor of dangerous drugs set forth in section 4729.53 of the Revised Code and the rules adopted under that section. The board shall register as a wholesale distributor of dangerous drugs each applicant who has paid the required registration fee, if the board determines that the applicant meets the qualifications to be registered as a wholesale distributor of dangerous drugs set forth in section 4729.53 of the Revised Code and the rules adopted under that section.

(B) The board may register and issue to a person who does not reside in this state a registration certificate as a wholesale distributor of dangerous drugs if the person possesses a current and valid wholesale distributor of dangerous drugs registration certificate or license issued by another state that has qualifications for licensure or registration comparable to the registration requirements in this state and pays the required registration fee.

(C) All registration certificates issued pursuant to this section are effective for a period of twelve months from the first day of July of each year. A registration certificate shall be renewed annually by the board for a like period, pursuant to this section and the standard renewal procedure of Chapter 4745. of the Revised Code. A person desiring to renew a registration certificate shall submit an application for renewal and pay the required renewal fee before the first day of July each year.

(D) Each registration certificate and its application shall describe not more than one establishment or place where the registrant or applicant may engage in the sale of dangerous drugs at wholesale. No registration certificate shall authorize or permit the wholesale distributor of dangerous drugs named therein to engage in the sale of drugs at wholesale or to maintain possession, custody, or control of dangerous drugs for any purpose other than for the registrant's own use and consumption at any establishment or place other than that described in the certificate.

(E)(1) The registration fee is one hundred fifty dollars and shall accompany each application for registration. The registration renewal fee is one hundred fifty dollars and shall accompany each renewal application.

A registration certificate that has not been renewed in any year by the first day of August may be reinstated upon payment of the renewal fee and a penalty of fifty-five dollars.

(2) Renewal fees and penalties assessed under division (E)(1) of this section shall not be returned if the applicant fails to qualify for renewal.

(F) The registration of any person as a wholesale distributor of dangerous drugs subjects the person and the person's agents and employees to the jurisdiction of the board and to the laws of this state for the purpose of the enforcement of this chapter and the rules of the board. However, the filing of an application for registration as a wholesale distributor of dangerous drugs by, or on behalf of, any person or the registration of any person as a wholesale distributor of dangerous drugs shall not, of itself, constitute evidence that the person is doing business within this state.

(1998 S 66, eff. 7–22–98; 1997 H 215, eff. 6–30–97; 1995 H 117, eff. 6–30–95; 1992 S 193, eff. 7–1–92; 1991 H 298; 1981 H 694; 1969 H 742; 132 v H 911, S 70; 129 v 1376)

4729.53 Qualifications of wholesale distributor

(A) The board of pharmacy shall not register any person as a wholesale distributor of dangerous drugs unless the applicant for registration furnishes satisfactory proof to the board of pharmacy that he meets all of the following:

(1) That if the applicant has been convicted of a violation of any federal, state, or local law relating to drug samples, wholesale or retail drug distribution, or distribution of controlled substances or of a felony, or if a federal, state, or local governmental entity has suspended or revoked any current or prior license or registration of the applicant for the manufacture or sale of any dangerous drugs, including controlled substances, the applicant, to the satisfaction of the board, assures that he has in place adequate safeguards to prevent the recurrence of any such violations;

(2) The applicant's past experience in the manufacture or distribution of dangerous drugs, including controlled substances, is acceptable to the board.

(3) The applicant is equipped as to land, buildings, equipment, and personnel to properly carry on the business of a wholesale distributor of dangerous drugs, including providing adequate security for and proper storage conditions and handling for dangerous drugs, and is complying with the requirements under this chapter and the rules adopted pursuant thereto for maintaining and making available records to properly identified board officials and federal, state, and local law enforcement agencies.

(4) Personnel employed by the applicant have the appropriate education or experience, as determined by the board, to assume responsibility for positions related to compliance with this chapter and the rules adopted pursuant thereto.

(5) The applicant has designated the name and address of a person to whom communications from the board may be directed and upon whom the notices and citations provided for in section 4729.56 of the Revised Code may be served.

(6) Adequate safeguards are assured to prevent the sale of dangerous drugs to any person other than those named in division (B) of section 4729.51 of the Revised Code.

(7) Any other requirement or qualification the board, by rule adopted in accordance with Chapter 119. of the Revised Code, considers relevant to and consistent with the public safety and health.

(B) The board may refuse to register or renew the registration certificate of any person if the board determines that the granting of the registration certificate or its renewal is not in the public interest.

(1992 S 193, eff. 7–1–92; 1975 H 300; 129 v 1376)

4729.531 License for euthanasia of animals by use of drugs

(A) The state board of pharmacy may issue a limited license to animal shelters solely for the purpose of purchasing, possessing, and administering combination drugs that contain pentobarbital and at least one noncontrolled substance ingredient, in a manufactured dosage form, whose only indication is for euthanizing animals, or other substances described in section 4729.532 of the Revised Code. No such license shall authorize or permit the distribution of these drugs to any person other than the originating wholesale distributor of the drugs. An application for licensure shall include the information the board requires by rule under this section. If the application meets the requirements of the rules adopted under this section, the board shall issue the license.

(B) The board, in accordance with Chapter 119. of the Revised Code, shall adopt any rules necessary to administer and enforce this section. The rules shall do all of the following:

(1) Require as a condition of licensure of the facility that an agent or employee of an animal shelter, other than a registered veterinary technician as defined in section 4741.01 of the Revised Code, has successfully completed a euthanasia technician certification course described in section 4729.532 of the Revised Code;

(2) Specify the information the animal shelter must provide the board for issuance or renewal of a license;

(3) Establish criteria for the board to use in determining whether to refuse to issue or renew, suspend, or revoke a license issued under this section;

(4) Address any other matters the board considers necessary or appropriate for the administration and enforcement of this section.

(1994 H 88, eff. 6–29–94)

4729.532 Method and requirements for euthanasia of animals by use of drugs

(A) No agent or employee of an animal shelter shall perform euthanasia by means of lethal injection on an animal by use of any substance other than combination drugs that contain pentobarbital and at least one noncontrolled substance active ingredient, in a manufactured dosage form, whose only indication is for euthanizing animals, or other substance that the state veterinary medical licensing board and the state board of pharmacy both approve by rule adopted in accordance with Chapter 119. of the Revised Code.

The agent or employee of an animal shelter when using a lethal solution to perform euthanasia on an animal shall use such solution in accordance with the following methods and in the following order of preference:

(1) Intravenous injection by hypodermic needle;

(2) Intraperitoneal injection by hypodermic needle;

(3) Intracardial injection by hypodermic needle, but only on a sedated or unconscious animal;

(4) Solution or powder added to food.

(B) Except as provided in division (D) of this section, no agent or employee of an animal shelter, other than a registered veterinary technician as defined in section 4741.01 of the Revised Code, shall perform euthanasia by means of lethal injection on an animal unless he has received certification after successfully completing a euthanasia technician certification course as described in this division.

The curriculum for a euthanasia technician certification course shall be one that has been approved by the state veterinary medical licensing board, shall be at least sixteen hours in length, and shall include information in at least all of the following areas:

(1) The pharmacology, proper administration, and storage of euthanasia solutions;

(2) Federal and state laws regulating the storage and accountability of euthanasia solutions;

(3) Euthanasia technician stress management;

(4) Proper disposal of euthanized animals.

(C)(1) Except as provided in division (D) of this section, no agent or employee of an animal shelter shall perform euthanasia by means of lethal injection on animals under this section unless the facility in which he works or is employed is licensed with the state board of pharmacy under section 4729.531 of the Revised Code.

(2) Any agent or employee of an animal shelter performing euthanasia by means of lethal injection shall do so only in a humane and proficient manner that is in conformity with the methods described in division (A) of this section and not in violation of Chapter 959. of the Revised Code.

(D) An agent or employee of an animal shelter who is performing euthanasia by means of lethal injection on animals on or before the effective date of this section may continue to perform such euthanasia and is not required to be certified in compliance with division (B) of this section until ninety days after the effective date of the rules adopted in compliance with Section 3 of House Bill No. 88 of the 120th general assembly.

(1994 H 88, eff. 6–29–94)

4729.54 Categories of licenses of terminal distributors of dangerous drugs; applications; authority; fees; requirements upon licensees

(A) As used in this section:

(1) Category I means single-dose injections of intravenous fluids, including saline, Ringer's lactate, five per cent dextrose and distilled water, and other intravenous fluids or parenteral solutions included in this category by rule of the board of pharmacy, that have a volume of one hundred milliliters or more and that contain no added substances, or single-dose injections of epinephrine to be administered pursuant to sections 4765.38 and 4765.39 of the Revised Code.

(2) Category II means any dangerous drug that is not included in category I or III.

(3) Category III means any controlled substance that is contained in schedule I, II, III, IV, or V.

(4) Emergency medical service organization has the same meaning as in section 4765.01 of the Revised Code.

(5) Person includes an emergency medical service organization.

(6) Schedule I, schedule II, schedule III, schedule IV, and schedule V mean controlled substance schedules I, II, III, IV, and V, respectively, as established pursuant to section 3719.41 of the Revised Code and as amended.

(B) A person who desires to be licensed as a terminal distributor of dangerous drugs shall file with the executive director of the board of pharmacy a verified application that contains the following:

(1) Information that the board requires relative to the qualifications of a terminal distributor of dangerous drugs set forth in section 4729.55 of the Revised Code;

(2) A statement that the person wishes to be licensed as a category I, category II, category III, limited category I, limited category II, or limited category III terminal distributor of dangerous drugs;

(3) If the person wishes to be licensed as a limited category I, limited category II, or limited category III terminal distributor of dangerous drugs, a notarized list of the dangerous drugs that the person wishes to possess, have custody or control of, and distribute, which list shall also specify the purpose for which those drugs will be used and their source;

(4) If the person is an emergency medical service organization, the information that is specified in division (C)(1) of this section;

(5) Except for an emergency medical service organization, the identity of the one establishment or place at which the person intends to engage in the sale or other distribution of dangerous drugs at retail, and maintain possession, custody, or control of dangerous drugs for purposes other than the person's own use or consumption.

(C)(1) An emergency medical service organization that wishes to be licensed as a terminal distributor of dangerous drugs shall list in its application for licensure the following additional information:

(a) The units under its control that the organization determines will possess dangerous drugs for the purpose of administering emergency medical services in accordance with Chapter 4765. of the Revised Code;

(b) With respect to each such unit, whether the dangerous drugs that the organization determines the unit will possess are in category I, II, or III.

(2) An emergency medical service organization that is licensed as a terminal distributor of dangerous drugs shall file a new application for such licensure if there is any change in the number, or location of, any of its units or any change in the category of the dangerous drugs that any unit will possess.

(3) A unit listed in an application for licensure pursuant to division (C)(1) of this section may obtain the dangerous drugs it is authorized to possess from its emergency medical service organization or, on a replacement basis, from a hospital pharmacy. If units will obtain dangerous drugs from a hospital pharmacy, the organization shall file, and maintain in current form, the following items with the pharmacist who is responsible for the hospital's terminal distributor of dangerous drugs license:

(a) A copy of its standing orders or protocol;

(b) A list of the personnel employed or used by the organization to provide emergency medical services in accordance with Chapter 4765. of the Revised Code, who are authorized to possess the drugs, which list also shall indicate the personnel who are authorized to administer the drugs.

(D) Each emergency medical service organization that applies for a terminal distributor of dangerous drugs license shall submit with its application the following:

(1) A notarized copy of its standing orders or protocol, which orders or protocol shall be signed by a physician and specify the dangerous drugs that its units may carry, expressed in standard dose units;

(2) A list of the personnel employed or used by the organization to provide emergency medical services in accordance with Chapter 4765. of the Revised Code.

An emergency medical service organization that is licensed as a terminal distributor shall notify the board immediately of any changes in its standing orders or protocol.

(E) There shall be six categories of terminal distributor of dangerous drugs licenses, which categories shall be as follows:

(1) Category I license. A person who obtains this license may possess, have custody or control of, and distribute only the dangerous drugs described in category I.

(2) Limited category I license. A person who obtains this license may possess, have custody or control of, and distribute only the dangerous drugs described in category I that were listed in the application for licensure.

(3) Category II license. A person who obtains this license may possess, have custody or control of, and distribute only the dangerous drugs described in category I and category II.

(4) Limited category II license. A person who obtains this license may possess, have custody or control of, and distribute only the dangerous drugs described in category I or category II that were listed in the application for licensure.

(5) Category III license. A person who obtains this license may possess, have custody or control of, and distribute the dangerous drugs described in category I, category II, and category III.

(6) Limited category III license. A person who obtains this license may possess, have custody or control of, and distribute only the dangerous drugs described in category I, category II, or category III that were listed in the application for licensure.

(F) Except for an application made on behalf of an animal shelter, if an applicant for licensure as a limited category I, II, or III terminal distributor of dangerous drugs intends to administer dangerous drugs to a person or animal, the applicant shall submit, with the application, a notarized copy of its protocol or standing orders, which protocol or orders shall be signed by a licensed health professional authorized to prescribe drugs, specify the dangerous drugs to be administered, and list personnel who are authorized to administer the dangerous drugs in accordance with federal law or the law of this state. An application made on behalf of an animal shelter shall include a notarized list of the dangerous drugs to be administered to animals and the personnel who are authorized to administer the drugs to animals in accordance with section 4729.532 of the Revised Code. After obtaining a terminal distributor license, a licensee shall notify the board immediately of any changes in its protocol or standing orders, or in such personnel.

(G)(1) Except as provided in division (G)(2) of this section, each applicant for licensure as a terminal distributor of dangerous drugs shall submit, with the application, a license fee determined as follows:

(a) For a category I or limited category I license, forty-five dollars;

(b) For a category II or limited category II license, one hundred twelve dollars and fifty cents;

(c) For a category III or limited category III license, one hundred fifty dollars.

(2) For a professional association, corporation, partnership, or limited liability company organized for the purpose of practicing veterinary medicine, the fee shall be forty dollars.

Fees assessed under divisions (G)(1) and (2) of this section shall not be returned if the applicant fails to qualify for registration.

(H)(1) The board shall issue a terminal distributor of dangerous drugs license to each person who submits an application for such licensure in accordance with this section, pays the required license fee, is determined by the board to meet the requirements set forth in section 4729.55 of the Revised Code, and satisfies any other applicable requirements of this section.

(2) The license of a person other than an emergency medical service organization shall describe the one establishment or place at which the licensee may engage in the sale or other distribution of dangerous drugs at retail and maintain possession, custody, or control of dangerous drugs for purposes other than the licensee's own use or consumption. The one establishment or place shall be that which is described in the application for licensure.

No such license shall authorize or permit the terminal distributor of dangerous drugs named in it to engage in the sale or other distribution of dangerous drugs at retail or to maintain possession, custody, or control of dangerous drugs for any purpose other than the distributor's own use or consumption, at any establishment or place other than that described in the license, except that an agent or employee of an animal shelter may possess and use dangerous drugs in the course of business as provided in division (D) of section 4729.532 of the Revised Code.

(3) The license of an emergency medical service organization shall cover and describe all the units of the organization listed in its application for licensure.

(4) The license of every terminal distributor of dangerous drugs shall indicate, on its face, the category of licensure. If the license is a limited category I, II, or III license, it shall specify, and shall authorize the licensee to possess, have custody or control of, and distribute only, the dangerous drugs that were listed in the application for licensure.

(I) All licenses issued pursuant to this section shall be effective for a period of twelve months from the first day of January of each year. A license shall be renewed by the board for a like period, annually, according to the provisions of this section, and the standard renewal procedure of Chapter 4745. of the Revised Code. A person who desires to renew a license shall submit an application for renewal and pay the required fee on or before the thirty-first day of December each year. The fee required for the renewal of a license shall be the same as the fee paid for the license being renewed, and shall accompany the application for renewal.

A license that has not been renewed during December in any year and by the first day of February of the following year may be reinstated only upon payment of the required renewal fee and a penalty fee of fifty-five dollars.

(J)(1) No emergency medical service organization that is licensed as a terminal distributor of dangerous drugs shall fail to comply with division (C)(2) or (3) of this section.

(2) No emergency medical service organization that is licensed as a terminal distributor of dangerous drugs shall fail to comply with division (D) of this section.

(3) No licensed terminal distributor of dangerous drugs shall possess, have custody or control of, or distribute dangerous drugs that the terminal distributor is not entitled to possess, have custody or control of, or distribute by virtue of its category of licensure.

(4) No licensee that is required by division (F) of this section to notify the board of changes in its protocol or standing orders, or in personnel, shall fail to comply with that division.

(1999 H 283, eff. 6–30–99; 1998 S 66, eff. 7–22–98; 1997 H 215, eff. 6–30–97; 1995 H 117, eff. 6–30–95; 1994 H 88, eff. 6–29–94; 1992 S 98, eff. 11–12–92; 1991 H 298; 1984 S 19; 1982 S 4; 1981 H 694; 1969 H 742; 132 v H 911, S 70; 129 v 1376)

4729.55 Qualifications of terminal distributor

No license shall be issued to an applicant for licensure as a terminal distributor of dangerous drugs unless the applicant has furnished satisfactory proof to the state board of pharmacy that:

(A) The applicant is equipped as to land, buildings, and equipment to properly carry on the business of a terminal distributor of dangerous drugs within the category of licensure approved by the board.

(B) A pharmacist, licensed health professional authorized to prescribe drugs, animal shelter licensed with the state board of pharmacy under section 4729.531 of the Revised Code, or a laboratory as defined in section 3719.01 of the Revised Code will maintain supervision and control over the possession and custody of dangerous drugs that may be acquired by or on behalf of the applicant.

(C) Adequate safeguards are assured to prevent the sale or other distribution of dangerous drugs by any person other than a pharmacist or licensed health professional authorized to prescribe drugs.

(D) Adequate safeguards are assured that the applicant will carry on the business of a terminal distributor of dangerous drugs in a manner that allows pharmacists and pharmacy interns employed by the terminal distributor to practice pharmacy in a safe and effective manner.

(E) If the applicant, or any agent or employee of the applicant, has been found guilty of violating section 4729.51 of the Revised Code, the "Federal Food, Drug, and Cosmetic Act," 52 Stat. 1040 (1938), 21 U.S.C.A. 301, the federal drug abuse control laws, Chapter 2925., 3715., 3719., or 4729. of the Revised Code, or any rule of the board, adequate safeguards are assured to prevent the recurrence of the violation.

(F) In the case of an applicant who is a food processor or retail seller of food, the applicant will maintain supervision and control over the possession and custody of nitrous oxide.

(G) In the case of an applicant who is a retail seller of oxygen in original packages labeled as required by the "Federal Food, Drug, and Cosmetic Act," the applicant will maintain supervision and control over the possession, custody, and retail sale of the oxygen.

(H) If the application is made on behalf of an animal shelter, at least one of the agents or employees of the animal shelter is certified in compliance with section 4729.532 of the Revised Code.

(I) In the case of an applicant who is a retail seller of peritoneal dialysis solutions in original packages labeled as required by the "Federal Food, Drug, and Cosmetic Act," 52 Stat. 1040 (1938), 21 U.S.C.A. 301, the applicant will maintain supervision and control over the possession, custody, and retail sale of the peritoneal dialysis solutions.

(2000 S 172, eff. 2-12-01; 1998 S 66, eff. 7-22-98; 1997 H 215, eff. 6-30-97; 1996 H 595, eff. 10-16-96; 1994 H 391, eff. 7-21-94; 1994 H 88, eff. 6-29-94; 1982 S 4, eff. 10-1-82; 1975 H 300; 129 v 1376)

4729.551 Licensing of terminal distributor; investigations and information exchange

Each person, whether located within or outside this state, who sells dangerous drugs at retail for delivery or distribution to persons residing in this state, shall be licensed as a terminal distributor of dangerous drugs pursuant to sections 4729.54 and 4729.55 of the Revised Code.

The board of pharmacy may enter into agreements with other states, federal agencies, and other entities to exchange information concerning the licensing and inspection of terminal distributors of dangerous drugs who are located within or outside this state and to investigate any alleged violations of the laws and rules governing the legal distribution of drugs by such persons.

(1994 H 391, eff. 7-21-94)

4729.56 Suspension, revocation, or refusal of renewal of registration certificate of wholesale distributor; monetary penalty; placing under seal dangerous drugs

(A) In accordance with Chapter 119. of the Revised Code, the board of pharmacy may suspend, revoke, or refuse to renew any registration certificate issued to a wholesale distributor of dangerous drugs pursuant to section 4729.52 of the Revised Code or may impose a monetary penalty or forfeiture not to exceed in severity any fine designated under the Revised Code for a similar offense or one thousand dollars if the acts committed are not classified as an offense by the Revised Code for any of the following causes:

(1) Making any false material statements in an application for registration as a wholesale distributor of dangerous drugs;

(2) Violating any federal, state, or local drug law; any provision of this chapter or Chapter 2925., 3715., or 3719. of the Revised Code; or any rule of the board;

(3) A conviction of a felony;

(4) Ceasing to satisfy the qualifications for registration under section 4729.53 of the Revised Code or the rules of the board.

(B) Upon the suspension or revocation of the registration certificate of any wholesale distributor of dangerous drugs, the distributor shall immediately surrender his registration certificate to the board.

(C) If the board suspends, revokes, or refuses to renew any registration certificate issued to a wholesale distributor of dangerous drugs and determines that there is clear and convincing evidence of a danger of immediate and serious harm to any person, the board may place under seal all dangerous drugs owned by or in the possession, custody, or control of the affected wholesale distributor of dangerous drugs. Except as provided in this division, the board shall not dispose of the dangerous drugs sealed under this division until the wholesale distributor of dangerous drugs exhausts all of his appeal rights under Chapter 119. of the Revised Code. The court involved in such an appeal may order the board, during the pendency of the appeal, to sell sealed dangerous drugs that are perishable. The board shall deposit the proceeds of the sale with the court.

(1992 S 193, eff. 7-1-92; 1981 H 135; 129 v 1376)

4729.57 Revocation of license of terminal distributor; monetary penalty; sealing dangerous drugs of suspended licensee

(A) The state board of pharmacy may suspend, revoke, or refuse to renew any license issued to a terminal distributor of dangerous drugs pursuant to section 4729.54 of the Revised Code, or may impose a monetary penalty or forfeiture not to exceed in severity any fine designated under the Revised Code for a similar offense or one thousand dollars if the acts committed have not been classified as an offense by the Revised Code, for any of the following causes:

(1) Making any false material statements in an application for a license as a terminal distributor of dangerous drugs;

(2) Violating any rule of the board;

(3) Violating any provision of this chapter;

(4) Violating any provision of the "Federal Food, Drug, and Cosmetic Act," 52 Stat. 1040 (1938), 21 U.S.C.A. 301, or Chapter 3715. of the Revised Code;

(5) Violating any provision of the federal drug abuse control laws or Chapter 2925. or 3719. of the Revised Code;

(6) Falsely or fraudulently promoting to the public a dangerous drug, except that nothing in this division prohibits a terminal distributor of dangerous drugs from furnishing information concerning a dangerous drug to a health care provider or another licensed terminal distributor;

(7) Ceasing to satisfy the qualifications of a terminal distributor of dangerous drugs set forth in section 4729.55 of the Revised Code;

(8) Except as provided in division (B) of this section:

(a) Waiving the payment of all or any part of a deductible or copayment that an individual, pursuant to a health insurance or health care policy, contract, or plan that covers the services provided by a terminal distributor of dangerous drugs, would otherwise be required to pay for the services if the waiver is used as an enticement to a patient or group of patients to receive pharmacy services from that terminal distributor;

(b) Advertising that the terminal distributor will waive the payment of all or any part of a deductible or copayment that an individual, pursuant to a health insurance or health care policy, contract, or plan that covers the pharmaceutical services, would otherwise be required to pay for the services.

(B) Sanctions shall not be imposed under division (A)(8) of this section against any terminal distributor of dangerous drugs that waives deductibles and copayments as follows:

(1) In compliance with a health benefit plan that expressly allows such a practice. Waiver of the deductibles or copayments shall be made only with the full knowledge and consent of the plan purchaser, payer, and third-party administrator. Documentation of the consent shall be made available to the board on request.

(2) For professional services rendered to any other person licensed pursuant to this chapter to the extent allowed by this chapter and the rules of the board.

(C)(1) Upon the suspension or revocation of a license issued to a terminal distributor of dangerous drugs or the refusal by the board to renew such a license, the distributor shall immediately surrender the license to the board.

(2) The board may place under seal all dangerous drugs that are owned by or in the possession, custody, or control of a terminal distributor at the time the license is suspended or revoked or at the time the board refuses to renew the license. Except as otherwise provided in this division, dangerous drugs so sealed shall not be disposed of until appeal rights under Chapter 119. of the Revised Code have expired or an appeal filed pursuant to that chapter has been determined.

The court involved in an appeal filed pursuant to Chapter 119. of the Revised Code may order the board, during the pendency of the appeal, to sell sealed dangerous drugs that are perishable. The proceeds of such a sale shall be deposited with that court.

(1998 S 66, eff. 7–22–98; 1982 S 4, eff. 10–1–82; 1981 H 135; 1975 H 300; 1971 S 141; 130 v H 1; 129 v 1376)

4729.58 Issuance or renewal of license or registration certificate

The board of pharmacy, within thirty days after receipt of an application filed in the form and manner set forth in section 4729.52 or 4729.54 of the Revised Code for the issuance of a new license or registration certificate or the renewal of a license or registration certificate previously issued, shall notify the applicant therefor whether or not such license or registration certificate will be issued or renewed. If the board determines that such license or registration certificate will not be issued or renewed, such notice to the applicant shall set forth the reason or reasons that such license or registration certificate will not be issued or renewed.

(129 v 1376, eff. 1–1–62)

4729.59 Registration of distributors; roster; evidence of distributor being licensed

The executive director of the state board of pharmacy shall maintain a register of the names, addresses, and the date of registration of those persons to whom a registration certificate has been issued pursuant to section 4729.52 of the Revised Code and those persons to whom a license has been issued pursuant to section 4729.54 of the Revised Code. The register shall be the property of the board and shall be open for public examination and inspection at all reasonable times, as the board may direct.

The board shall publish or make available to registered wholesale distributors and licensed terminal distributors of dangerous drugs, annually, and at such other times and in such manner as the board shall prescribe, a roster setting forth the names and addresses of those persons who have been registered by the board pursuant to section 4729.52 of the Revised Code and those persons who have been licensed pursuant to section 4729.54 of the Revised Code, those persons whose licenses or registration certificates have been suspended, revoked, or surrendered, and those persons whose licenses or registration certificates have not been renewed.

A written statement signed and verified by the executive director of the board in which it is stated that after diligent search of the register no record or entry of the issuance of a license or registration certificate to a person is found is admissible in evidence and constitutes presumptive evidence of the fact that the person is not a licensed terminal distributor or is not a registered wholesale distributor of dangerous drugs.

(1998 S 66, eff. 7–22–98; 129 v 1376, eff. 1–1–62)

4729.60 Certificate required by wholesale distributor

(A) Before a registered wholesale distributor of dangerous drugs may sell dangerous drugs at wholesale to any person, other than the persons specified in divisions (B)(1)(a) to (d) and (B)(1)(f) to (h) of section 4729.51 of the Revised Code, such wholesale distributor shall obtain from the purchaser and the purchaser shall furnish to the wholesale distributor a certificate indicating that the purchaser is a licensed terminal distributor of dangerous drugs. The certificate shall be in the form that the state board of pharmacy shall prescribe, and shall set forth the name of the licensee, the number of the license, a description of the place or establishment or each place or establishment for which the license was issued, the category of licensure, and, if the license is a limited category I, II, or III license, the dangerous drugs that the licensee is authorized to possess, have custody or control of, and distribute.

If no certificate is obtained or furnished before a sale is made, it shall be presumed that the sale of dangerous drugs by the wholesale distributor is in violation of division (B) of section 4729.51 of the Revised Code and the purchase of dangerous drugs by the purchaser is in violation of division (C) of section 4729.51 of the Revised Code. If a registered wholesale distributor of dangerous drugs obtains or is furnished a certificate from a terminal distributor of dangerous drugs and relies on the certificate in selling dangerous drugs at wholesale to the terminal distributor of dangerous drugs, the wholesale distributor of dangerous drugs shall be deemed not to have violated division (B) of section 4729.51 of the Revised Code in making the sale.

(B) Before a licensed terminal distributor of dangerous drugs may purchase dangerous drugs at wholesale, the terminal distributor shall obtain from the seller and the seller shall furnish to the terminal distributor the number of the seller's registration certificate to engage in the sale of dangerous drugs at wholesale.

If no registration number is obtained or furnished before a purchase is made, it shall be presumed that the purchase of dangerous drugs by the terminal distributor is in violation of division (D) of section 4729.51 of the Revised Code and the sale of dangerous drugs by the seller is in violation of division (A) of section 4729.51 of the Revised Code. If a licensed terminal distributor of dangerous drugs obtains or is furnished a registration number from a wholesale distributor of dangerous drugs and relies on the registration number in purchasing dangerous drugs at wholesale from the wholesale distributor of dangerous drugs, the terminal distributor shall be deemed not to have violated division (D) of section 4729.51 of the Revised Code in making the purchase.

(1998 H 553, eff. 3–9–99; 1998 S 66, eff. 7–22–98; 1982 S 4, eff. 10–1–82; 129 v 1376)

4729.61 False registration certificate

(A) No person shall make or cause to be made, or furnish or cause to be furnished to a wholesale distributor of dangerous drugs, a false certificate required to be furnished to a wholesale distributor of dangerous drugs by section 4729.60 of the Revised Code for the purchase of dangerous drugs at wholesale.

(B) No person shall make or cause to be made a false registration certificate of a wholesale distributor of dangerous drugs or a false or fraudulent license of a terminal distributor of dangerous drugs.

(1995 S 2, eff. 7–1–96; 1975 H 300, eff. 7–1–76; 129 v 1376)

4729.62 Surrender of license or certificate

If a wholesale distributor of dangerous drugs who has been registered ceases to engage in the sale of dangerous drugs at wholesale, or if a terminal distributor of dangerous drugs to whom a license has been issued ceases to engage in the sale of dangerous drugs at retail, such terminal or wholesale distributor of dangerous drugs shall notify the board of pharmacy of such fact and shall surrender such license or registration certificate to the board; provided, that on dissolution of a partnership by death, the surviving partner may operate under a license or registration certificate issued to the partnership until expiration, revocation, or suspension of such license or registration certificate, and the heirs or legal representatives of deceased persons, and receivers and trustees in bankruptcy appointed by any competent authority, may operate under the license or registration certificate issued to the persons succeeded in possession by such heir, representative, receiver, or trustee in bankruptcy until expiration, revocation, or suspension of such license or registration certificate.

(129 v 1376, eff. 1–1–62)

4729.63 Enforcement by board of pharmacy

Note: Repealed by 2004 H 377, eff. 5–18–05.

If the state board of pharmacy has information that sections 4729.51 to 4729.62 of the Revised Code have been violated, it shall investigate the matter and upon probable cause appearing file a complaint in an appropriate court for prosecution of the offender. The attorney general, prosecuting attorney, or city director of law to whom the board reports any violation of sections 4729.51 to 4729.62 of the Revised Code shall cause appropriate proceedings to be instituted in the proper court without delay and to be prosecuted in the manner provided by law.

(2004 H 377, eff. 5–18–05; 1998 S 66, eff. 7–22–98; 1984 H 208, eff. 9–20–84; 1977 H 219; 129 v 1376)

4729.64 Injunctive proceedings

In addition to the remedies provided and irrespective of whether or not there exists an adequate remedy at law, the board of pharmacy may apply to the court of common pleas in the county where any of the provisions of sections 4729.51 to 4729.62 of the Revised Code are being violated or where any violation described in section 4729.35 of the Revised Code is occurring for a temporary or permanent injunction restraining any person from such violation.

(1984 H 206, eff. 3–14–85; 129 v 1376)

MISCELLANEOUS PROVISIONS

4729.65 Disposition of fees; board of pharmacy drug law enforcement fund

(A) Except as provided in division (B) of this section, all receipts of the state board of pharmacy, from any source, shall be deposited into the state treasury to the credit of the occupational licensing and regulatory fund. All vouchers of the board shall be approved by the president or executive director of the board, or both, as authorized by the board. All initial issuance fees and renewal fees required by sections 4729.01 to 4729.54 of the Revised Code shall be payable by the applicant at the time of making application.

(B)(1) There is hereby created in the state treasury the board of pharmacy drug law enforcement fund. All moneys that are derived from any fines, mandatory fines, or forfeited bail to which the board may be entitled under Chapter 2925., division (C)(1) of section 2923.42, or division (B)(5) of section 2925.42 of the Revised Code and all moneys that are derived from forfeitures of property to which the board may be entitled pursuant to Chapter 2925. of the Revised Code, section 2923.32, 2923.35, 2923.44, 2923.45, 2923.46, or 2933.43 of the Revised Code, any other section of the Revised Code, or federal law shall be deposited into the fund. Subject to division (B)(2) of this section, division (D)(2)(c) of section 2923.35, division (B)(5) of section 2923.44, division (B)(7)(c) of section 2923.46, and divisions (D)(1)(c) and (3) of section 2933.43 of the Revised Code, the moneys in the fund shall be used solely to subsidize the drug law enforcement efforts of the board.

(2) Notwithstanding any contrary provision in the Revised Code, moneys that are derived from forfeitures of property pursuant to federal law and that are deposited into the board of pharmacy drug law enforcement fund in accordance with division (B)(1) of this section shall be used and accounted for in accordance with the applicable federal law, and the board otherwise shall comply with that law in connection with the moneys.

(C) All fines and forfeited bonds assessed and collected under prosecution or prosecution commenced in the enforcement of this chapter shall be paid to the executive director of the board within thirty days and by the executive director paid into the state treasury to the credit of the occupational licensing and regulatory fund. The board, subject to the approval of the controlling board and except for fees required to be established by the board at amounts "adequate" to cover designated expenses, may establish fees in excess of the amounts provided by this chapter, provided that such fees do not exceed the amounts permitted by this chapter by more than fifty per cent.

(1998 H 2, eff. 1–1–99; 1997 H 215, eff. 9–29–97; 1994 H 715, eff. 7–22–94; 1991 S 218, eff. 10–11–91; 1990 S 258, H 266; 1988 S 386; 1985 H 201; 1981 H 694; 1979 H 204; 1975 H 300; 1971 S 141; 132 v H 911; 130 v H 948; 129 v 1376)

4729.66 Rulemaking powers of board of pharmacy

Note: Repealed by 2004 H 377, eff. 5–18–05.

In addition to the rules it adopts for the practice of pharmacy under section 4729.26 of the Revised Code, the state board of pharmacy may adopt rules in accordance with Chapter 119. of the Revised Code, not inconsistent with the law, as may be necessary to carry out the purposes of and to enforce the provisions of this chapter pertaining to the purchase for resale, possession for sale, sale, and other distribution of dangerous drugs.

(2004 H 377, eff. 5–18–05; 1998 S 66, eff. 7–22–98; 129 v 1376, eff. 1–1–62)

4729.68 Specification of national bodies that certify persons who complete diabetes education programs

The state board of pharmacy shall adopt rules pursuant to Chapter 119. of the Revised Code specifying for the purposes of sections 3719.172 and 4729.51 of the Revised Code the national bodies recognized by the board that certify persons who successfully complete diabetes education programs.

(1996 S 246, eff. 11–6–96)

4729.99 Penalties

(A) Whoever violates section 4729.16, division (A) or (B) of section 4729.38, or section 4729.57 of the Revised Code is guilty of a minor misdemeanor. Each day's violation constitutes a separate offense.

(B) Whoever violates section 4729.27, 4729.28, or 4729.36 of the Revised Code is guilty of a misdemeanor of the third degree. Each day's violation constitutes a separate offense. If the offender previously has been convicted of or pleaded guilty to a violation of this chapter, that person is guilty of a misdemeanor of the second degree.

(C) Whoever violates section 4729.32, 4729.33, or 4729.34 of the Revised Code is guilty of a misdemeanor.

(D) Whoever violates division (A), (B), (D), or (E) of section 4729.51 of the Revised Code is guilty of a misdemeanor of the first degree.

(E)(1) Whoever violates section 4729.37, division (C)(2) of section 4729.51, division (J) of section 4729.54, or section 4729.61 of the Revised Code is guilty of a felony of the fifth degree. If the offender previously has been convicted of or pleaded guilty to a violation of this chapter or a violation of Chapter 2925. or 3719. of the Revised Code, that person is guilty of a felony of the fourth degree.

(2) If an offender is convicted of or pleads guilty to a violation of section 4729.37, division (C) of section 4729.51, division (J) of section 4729.54, or section 4729.61 of the Revised Code, if the violation involves the sale, offer to sell, or possession of a schedule I or II controlled substance, with the exception of marihuana, and if the court imposing sentence upon the offender finds that the offender as a result of the violation is a major drug offender, as defined in section 2929.01 of the Revised Code, and is guilty of a specification of the type described in section 2941.1410 of the Revised Code, the court, in lieu of the prison term authorized or required by division (E)(1) of this section and sections 2929.13 and 2929.14 of the Revised Code and in addition to any other sanction imposed for the offense under sections 2929.11 to 2929.18 of the Revised Code, shall impose upon the offender, in accordance with division (D)(3)(a) of section 2929.14 of the Revised Code, the mandatory prison term specified in that division and may impose an additional prison term under division (D)(3)(b) of that section.

(3) Notwithstanding any contrary provision of section 3719.21 of the Revised Code, the clerk of court shall pay any fine imposed for a violation of section 4729.37, division (C) of section 4729.51, division (J) of section 4729.54, or section 4729.61 of the Revised Code pursuant to division (A) of section 2929.18 of the Revised Code in accordance with and subject to the requirements of division (F) of section 2925.03 of the Revised Code. The agency that receives the fine shall use the fine as specified in division (F) of section 2925.03 of the Revised Code.

(F) Whoever violates section 4729.531 of the Revised Code or any rule adopted thereunder or section 4729.532 of the Revised Code is guilty of a misdemeanor of the first degree.

(G) Whoever violates division (C)(1) of section 4729.51 of the Revised Code is guilty of a felony of the fourth degree. If the offender has previously been convicted of or pleaded guilty to a violation of this chapter, or of a violation of Chapter 2925. or 3719. of the Revised Code, that person is guilty of a felony of the third degree.

(H) Whoever violates division (C)(3) of section 4729.51 of the Revised Code is guilty of a misdemeanor of the first degree. If the offender has previously been convicted of or pleaded guilty to a violation of this chapter, or of a violation of Chapter 2925. or 3719. of the Revised Code, that person is guilty of a felony of the fifth degree.

(1999 S 107, eff. 3–23–00; 1996 S 269, eff. 7–1–96; 1995 S 2, eff. 7–1–96; 1994 H 391, eff. 7–21–94; 1994 H 88, eff. 6–29–94; 1984 H 208, eff. 9–20–84; 1982 S 4; 1981 H 694; 1977 S 45; 1975 H 1, H 300; 1971 S 141; 1970 H 874; 130 v H 967; 129 v 1376; 127 v 162; 1953 H 1)

CHAPTER 4731

PHYSICIANS; LIMITED PRACTITIONERS

CERTIFICATES

CERTIFICATES

4731.223 Prosecutor to notify state medical board of conviction of physician

(A) As used in this section, "prosecutor" has the same meaning as in section 2935.01 of the Revised Code.

(B) Whenever any person holding a valid certificate issued pursuant to this chapter pleads guilty to, is subject to a judicial finding of guilt of, or is subject to a judicial finding of eligibility for intervention in lieu of conviction for a violation of Chapter 2907., 2925., or 3719. of the Revised Code or of any substantively comparable ordinance of a municipal corporation in connection with the person's practice, or for a second or subsequent time pleads guilty to, or is subject to a judicial finding of guilt of, a violation of section 2919.123 of the Revised Code, the prosecutor in the case, on forms prescribed and provided by the state medical board, shall promptly notify the board of the conviction or guilty plea. Within thirty days of receipt of that information, the board shall initiate action in accordance with Chapter 119. of the Revised Code to determine whether to suspend or revoke the certificate under section 4731.22 of the Revised Code.

(C) The prosecutor in any case against any person holding a valid certificate issued pursuant to this chapter, on forms prescribed and provided by the state medical board, shall notify the board of any of the following:

(1) A plea of guilty to, a finding of guilt by a jury or court of, or judicial finding of eligibility for intervention in lieu of conviction for a felony, or a case in which the trial court issues an order of dismissal upon technical or procedural grounds of a felony charge;

(2) A plea of guilty to, a finding of guilt by a jury or court of, or judicial finding of eligibility for intervention in lieu of conviction for a misdemeanor committed in the course of practice, or a case in which the trial court issues an order of dismissal upon technical or procedural grounds of a charge of a misdemeanor, if the alleged act was committed in the course of practice;

(3) A plea of guilty to, a finding of guilt by a jury or court of, or judicial finding of eligibility for intervention in lieu of conviction for a misdemeanor involving moral turpitude, or a case in which the trial court issues an order of dismissal upon technical or procedural grounds of a charge of a misdemeanor involving moral turpitude.

The report shall include the name and address of the certificate holder, the nature of the offense for which the action was taken, and the certified court documents recording the action.

(2004 H 126, eff. 9–23–04; 2000 H 341, eff. 8–10–00; 1998 H 606, eff. 3–9–99; 1995 S 2, eff. 7–1–96; 1986 H 769, eff. 3–17–87)

CHAPTER 4734

CHIROPRACTORS

DISCIPLINARY PROCEEDINGS; ENFORCEMENT

Section

DISCIPLINARY PROCEEDINGS; ENFORCEMENT

4734.31 Disciplinary proceedings

(A) The state chiropractic board may take any of the actions specified in division (B) of this section against an individual who has applied for or holds a license to practice chiropractic in this state if any of the reasons specified in division (C) of this section for taking action against an individual are applicable. Except as provided in division (D) of this section, actions taken against an individual shall be taken in accordance with Chapter 119. of the Revised Code. The board may specify that any action it takes is a permanent action. The board's authority to take action against an individual is not removed or limited by the individual's failure to renew a license.

(B) In its imposition of sanctions against an individual, the board may do any of the following:

(1) Refuse to issue, renew, restore, or reinstate a license to practice chiropractic;

(2) Reprimand or censure a license holder;

(3) Place limits, restrictions, or probationary conditions on a license holder's practice;

(4) Impose a civil fine of not more than five thousand dollars according to a schedule of fines specified in rules that the board shall adopt in accordance with chapter 119. of the Revised Code;

(5) Suspend a license for a limited or indefinite period;

(6) Revoke a license.

(C) The board may take the actions specified in division (B) of this section for any of the following reasons:

(1) A plea of guilty to, a judicial finding of guilt of, or a judicial finding of eligibility for intervention in lieu of conviction for, a felony in any jurisdiction, in which case a certified copy of the court record shall be conclusive evidence of the conviction;

(2) Commission of an act that constitutes a felony in this state, regardless of the jurisdiction in which the act was committed;

(3) A plea of guilty to, a judicial finding of guilt of, or a judicial finding of eligibility for intervention in lieu of conviction for, a misdemeanor involving moral turpitude, as determined by the board, in which case a certified copy of the court record shall be conclusive evidence of the matter;

(4) Commission of an act involving moral turpitude that constitutes a misdemeanor in this state, regardless of the jurisdiction in which the act was committed;

(5) A plea of guilty to, a judicial finding of guilt of, or a judicial finding of eligibility for intervention in lieu of conviction for, a misdemeanor committed in the course of practice, in which case a certified copy of the court record shall be conclusive evidence of the matter;

(6) Commission of an act in the course of practice that constitutes a misdemeanor in this state, regardless of the jurisdiction in which the act was committed;

(7) A violation or attempted violation of this chapter or the rules adopted under it governing the practice of chiropractic;

(8) Failure to cooperate in an investigation conducted by the board, including failure to comply with a subpoena or order issued by the board or failure to answer truthfully a question presented by the board at a deposition or in written interrogatories, except that failure to cooperate with an investigation shall not constitute grounds for discipline under this section if the board or a court of competent jurisdiction has issued an order that either quashes a subpoena or permits the individual to withhold the testimony or evidence in issue;

(9) Engaging in an ongoing professional relationship with a person or entity that violates any provision of this chapter or the rules adopted under it, unless the chiropractor makes a good faith effort to have the person or entity comply with the provisions;

(10) Retaliating against a chiropractor for the chiropractor's reporting to the board or any other agency with jurisdiction any violation of the law or for cooperating with the board of another agency in the investigation of any violation of the law;

(11) Aiding, abetting, assisting, counseling, or conspiring with any person in that person's violation of any provision of this chapter or the rules adopted under it, including the practice of chiropractic without a license, or aiding, abetting, assisting, counseling, or conspiring with any person in that person's unlicensed practice of any other health care profession that has licensing requirements;

(12) With respect to a report or record that is made, filed, or signed in connection with the practice of chiropractic, knowingly making or filing a report or record that is false, intentionally or negligently failing to file a report or record required by federal, state, or local law or willfully impeding or obstructing the required filing, or inducing another person to engage in any such acts;

(13) Making a false, fraudulent, or deceitful statement to the board or any agent of the board during any investigation or other official proceeding conducted by the board under this chapter or in any filing that must be submitted to the board;

(14) Attempting to secure a license or to corrupt the outcome of an official board proceeding through bribery or any other improper means;

(15) Willfully obstructing or hindering the board or any agent of the board in the discharge of the board's duties;

(16) Habitually using drugs or intoxicants to the extent that the person is rendered unfit for the practice of chiropractic;

(17) Inability to practice chiropractic according to acceptable and prevailing standards of care by reason of chemical dependency, mental illness, or physical illness, including conditions in which physical deterioration has adversely affected the person's cognitive, motor, or perceptive skills and conditions in which a chiropractor's continued practice may pose a danger to the chiropractor or the public;

(18) Any act constituting gross immorality relative to the person's practice of chiropractic, including acts involving sexual abuse, sexual misconduct, or sexual exploitation;

(19) Exploiting a patient for personal or financial gain;

(20) Failing to maintain proper, accurate, and legible records in the English language documenting each patient's care, including, as appropriate, records of the following: dates of treatment, services rendered, examinations, tests, x-ray reports, referrals, and the diagnosis or clinical impression and clinical treatment plan provided to the patient;

(21) Except as otherwise required by the board or by law, disclosing patient information gained during the chiropractor's professional relationship with a patient without obtaining the patient's authorization for the disclosure;

(22) Commission of willful or gross malpractice, or willful or gross neglect, in the practice of chiropractic;

(23) Failing to perform or negligently performing an act recognized by the board as a general duty or the exercise of due care in the practice of chiropractic, regardless of whether injury results to a patient from the failure to perform or negligent performance of the act;

(24) Engaging in any conduct or practice that impairs or may impair the ability to practice chiropractic safely and skillfully;

(25) Practicing, or claiming to be capable of practicing, beyond the scope of the practice of chiropractic as established under this chapter and the rules adopted under this chapter;

(26) Accepting and performing professional responsibilities as a chiropractor when not qualified to perform those responsibilities, if the person knew or had reason to know that the person was not qualified to perform them;

(27) Delegating any of the professional responsibilities of a chiropractor to an employee or other individual when the delegating chiropractor knows or had reason to know that the employee or other individual is not qualified by training, experience, or professional licensure to perform the responsibilities;

(28) Delegating any of the professional responsibilities of a chiropractor to an employee or other individual in a negligent manner or failing to provide proper supervision of the employee or other individual to whom the responsibilities are delegated;

(29) Failing to refer a patient to another health care practitioner for consultation or treatment when the chiropractor knows or has reason to know that the referral is in the best interest of the patient;

(30) Obtaining or attempting to obtain any fee or other advantage by fraud or misrepresentation;

(31) Making misleading, deceptive, false, or fraudulent representations in the practice of chiropractic;

(32) Being guilty of false, fraudulent, deceptive, or misleading advertising or other solicitations for patients or knowingly having professional connection with any person that advertises or solicits for patients in such a manner;

(33) Violation of a provision of any code of ethics established or adopted by the board under section 4734.16 of the Revised Code;

(34) Failing to meet the examination requirements for receipt of a license specified under section 4734.20 of the Revised Code;

(35) Actions taken for any reason, other than nonpayment of fees, by the chiropractic licensing authority of another state or country;

(36) Failing to maintain clean and sanitary conditions at the clinic, office, or other place in which chiropractic services are provided;

(37) Except as provided in division (G) of this section:

(a) Waiving the payment of all or any part of a deductible or copayment that a patient, pursuant to a health insurance or health care policy, contract, or plan that covers the chiropractor's services, otherwise would be required to pay if the waiver is used as an enticement to a patient or group of patients to receive health care services from that chiropractor;

(b) Advertising that the chiropractor will waive the payment of all or any part of a deductible or copayment that a patient, pursuant to a health insurance or health care policy, contract, or plan that covers the chiropractor's services, otherwise would be required to pay.

(D) The adjudication requirements of Chapter 119. of the Revised Code apply to the board when taking actions against an individual under this section, except as follows:

(1) An applicant is not entitled to an adjudication for failing to meet the conditions specified under section 4734.20 of the Revised Code for receipt of a license that involve the board's examination on jurisprudence or the examinations of the national board of chiropractic examiners.

(2) A person is not entitled to an adjudication if the person fails to make a timely request for a hearing, in accordance with Chapter 119. of the Revised Code.

(3) In lieu of an adjudication, the board may accept the surrender of a license from a chiropractor.

(4) In lieu of an adjudication, the board may enter into a consent agreement with an individual to resolve an allegation of a violation of this chapter or any rule adopted under it. A consent agreement, when ratified by the board, shall constitute the findings and order of the board with respect to the matter addressed in the agreement. If the board refuses to ratify a consent agreement, the admissions and findings contained in the consent agreement shall be of no force or effect.

(E) This section does not require the board to hire, contract with, or retain the services of an expert witness when the board takes action against a chiropractor concerning compliance with acceptable and prevailing standards of care. As part of an action taken concerning compliance with acceptable and prevailing standards of care, the board may rely on the knowledge of its members for purposes of making a determination of compliance, notwithstanding any expert testimony presented by the chiropractor that contradicts the knowledge and opinions of the members of the board.

(F) The sealing of conviction records by a court shall have no effect on a prior board order entered under this section or on the board's jurisdiction to take action under this section if, based on a plea of guilty, a judicial finding of guilt, or a judicial finding of eligibility for intervention in lieu of conviction, the board issued a notice of opportunity for a hearing prior to the court's order to seal the records. The board shall not be required to seal, destroy, redact, or otherwise modify its records to reflect the court's sealing of conviction records.

(G) Actions shall not be taken pursuant to division (C)(37) of this section against any chiropractor who waives deductibles and copayments as follows:

(1) In compliance with the health benefit plan that expressly allows a practice of that nature. Waiver of the deductibles or copayments shall be made only with the full knowledge and consent of the plan purchaser, payer, and third-party administra-

tor. Documentation of the consent shall be made available to the board upon request.

(2) For professional services rendered to any other person licensed pursuant to this chapter, to the extent allowed by this chapter and the rules of the board.

(2000 H 506, eff. 4–10–01)

4734.32 Reports of disciplinary actions

(A)(1) Except as provided in division (A)(2) of this section, if formal disciplinary action is taken against a chiropractor by any health care facility, including a clinic, hospital, or similar facility, the chief administrator or executive officer of the facility shall file a report with the state chiropractic board not later than sixty days after the disciplinary action is imposed. The report shall include the name of the individual, the action taken by the facility, and a summary of the underlying facts leading to the action taken. On request, the board shall be provided certified copies of the patient records that were the basis for the facility's action. Prior to release to the board, the summary shall be approved by the peer review committee that reviewed the case or by the governing board of the facility.

The filing of a report with the board, a decision not to file a report with the board, an investigation by the board, or any disciplinary action taken by the board, does not preclude a health care facility from taking disciplinary action against a chiropractor.

In the absence of fraud or bad faith, no individual or entity that provides patient records to the board shall be liable in damages to any person as a result of providing the records.

(2) Disciplinary action taken against a chiropractor by a chiropractic clinic need not be reported to the board in either of the following circumstances:

(a) The clinic takes the disciplinary action for reasons that do not involve clinical or patient care issues.

(b) The clinic employs fewer than five chiropractors and the disciplinary action taken does not rise above the level of a written reprimand.

(B) A chiropractor or professional association or society of chiropractors that believes a violation of any provision of this chapter or rule of the board has occurred shall report to the board the information upon which the belief is based. This division does not require any treatment provider approved by the board under section 4734.40 of the Revised Code or any employee, agent, or representative of such a provider to make reports with respect to a chiropractor participating in treatment or aftercare for substance abuse as long as the chiropractor maintains participation in accordance with the requirements of section 4734.40 of the Revised Code and the treatment provider or employee, agent, or representative of the provider has no reason to believe that the chiropractor has violated any provision of this chapter or rule adopted under it, other than being impaired by alcohol, drugs, or other substances. This division does not require reporting by any member of an impaired practitioner committee established by a health care facility or by any representative or agent of a committee or program sponsored by a professional association or society of chiropractors to provide peer assistance to chiropractors with substance abuse problems with respect to a chiropractor who has been referred for examination to a treatment program approved by the board under section 4734.40 of the Revised Code if the chiropractor cooperates with the referral for examination and with any determination that the chiropractor should enter treatment and as long as the committee member, representative, or agent has no reason to believe that the chiropractor has ceased to participate in the treatment program in accordance with section 4734.40 of the Revised Code or has violated any provision of this chapter or rule adopted under it, other than being impaired by alcohol, drugs, or other substances.

(C) Any professional association or society composed primarily of chiropractors that suspends or revokes an individual's membership for violations of professional ethics, or for reasons of professional incompetence or professional malpractice, within sixty days after a final decision, shall report to the board, on forms prescribed and provided by the board, the name of the individual, the action taken by the professional organization, and a summary of the underlying facts leading to the action taken.

The filing of a report with the board, a decision not to file a report with the board, an investigation by the board, or any disciplinary action taken by the board, shall not preclude a professional organization from taking disciplinary action against a chiropractor.

(D) Any insurer providing professional liability insurance to any person holding a valid license as a chiropractor or any other entity that seeks to indemnify the professional liability of a chiropractor shall notify the board within thirty days after the final disposition of any written claim for damages where such disposition results in a payment exceeding ten thousand dollars. The notice shall contain the following information:

(1) The name and address of the person submitting the notification;

(2) The name and address of the insured who is the subject of the claim;

(3) The name of the person filing the written claim;

(4) The date of final disposition;

(5) If applicable, the identity of the court in which the final disposition of the claim took place.

(E) The board may investigate possible violations of this chapter or the rules adopted under it that are brought to its attention as a result of the reporting requirements of this section, except that the board shall conduct an investigation if a possible violation involves repeated malpractice. As used in this division, "repeated malpractice" means three or more claims for malpractice within the previous five-year period, each resulting in a judgment or settlement in excess of ten thousand dollars in favor of the claimant, and each involving tortious conduct by the chiropractor.

(F) All summaries, reports, and records received and maintained by the board pursuant to this section shall be held in confidence and shall not be subject to discovery or introduction in evidence in any federal or state civil action involving a chiropractor or health care facility arising out of matters that are the subject of the reporting required by this section. The board may use the information obtained only as the basis for an investigation, as evidence in a disciplinary hearing against a chiropractor, or in any subsequent trial or appeal of a board action or order.

The board may disclose the summaries and reports it receives under this section only to health care facility committees within or outside this state that are involved in credentialing or recredentialing a chiropractor or reviewing the chiropractor's privilege to practice within a particular facility. The board shall indicate whether or not the information has been verified. Information transmitted by the board shall be subject to the same confidentiality provisions as when maintained by the board.

(G) Except for reports filed by an individual pursuant to division (B) of this section, the board shall send a copy of any reports or summaries it receives pursuant to this section to the chiropractor. The chiropractor shall have the right to file a statement with the board concerning the correctness or relevance of the information. The statement shall at all times accompany that part of the record in contention.

(H) An individual or entity that reports to the board or refers an impaired chiropractor to a treatment provider approved by the board under section 4734.40 of the Revised Code shall not be subject to suit for civil damages as a result of the report, referral, or provision of the information.

(I) In the absence of fraud or bad faith, a professional association or society of chiropractors that sponsors a committee or program to provide peer assistance to a chiropractor with substance abuse problems, a representative or agent of such a committee or program, and a member of the state chiropractic board shall not be held liable in damages to any person by reason of actions taken to refer a chiropractor to a treatment provider approved under section 4734.40 of the Revised Code for examination or treatment.

(2000 H 506, eff. 4–10–01)

4734.34 Restoration of license following disciplinary action

An individual subject to an action taken under section 4734.31 of the Revised Code, other than permanent revocation of a license, may apply to the state chiropractic board to have the individual's license restored to good standing. The board shall consider the moral character and the activities of the applicant since the board's action was taken, in accordance with the standards for issuance of a license established under section 4734.20 of the Revised Code. The board may impose terms and conditions on restoration of the license by doing any of the following:

(A) Requiring the applicant to obtain training, which may include requiring the applicant to pass an examination upon completion of the training;

(B) Requiring the applicant to pass an oral or written examination, or both, to determine fitness to resume practice;

(C) Restricting or limiting the extent, scope, or type of practice of the applicant.

(2000 H 506, eff. 4–10–01)

4734.35 Reports of convictions and guilty pleas

(A) As used in this section, "prosecutor" has the same meaning as in section 2935.01 of the Revised Code.

(B) The prosecutor in any case against any chiropractor holding a valid license issued under this chapter shall promptly notify the state chiropractic board of any of the following:

(1) A plea of guilty to, or a finding of guilt by a jury or court of, a felony, or a case in which the trial court issues an order of dismissal upon technical or procedural grounds of a felony charge;

(2) A plea of guilty to, or a finding of guilt by a jury or court of, a misdemeanor committed in the course of practice, or a case in which the trial court issues an order of dismissal upon technical or procedural grounds of a charge of a misdemeanor, if the alleged act was committed in the course of practice;

(3) A plea of guilty to, or a finding of guilt by a jury or court of, a misdemeanor involving moral turpitude, or a case in which the trial court issues an order of dismissal upon technical or procedural grounds of a charge of a misdemeanor involving moral turpitude.

(C) The report shall include the name and address of the chiropractor, the nature of the offense for which the action was taken, and the certified court documents recording the action. The board may prescribe and provide forms for prosecutors to make reports under this section. The form may be the same as the form required to be provided under section 2929.42 of the Revised Code.

(2002 H 490, eff. 1–1–04; 2000 H 506, eff. 4–10–01)

4734.36 Automatic suspension upon certain convictions

A chiropractor who in this state pleads guilty to or is convicted of aggravated murder, murder, voluntary manslaughter, felonious assault, kidnapping, rape, sexual battery, gross sexual imposition, aggravated arson, aggravated robbery, or aggravated burglary, or who in another jurisdiction pleads guilty to or is convicted of any substantially equivalent criminal offense, is automatically suspended from practice in this state and the license issued under this chapter is automatically suspended as of the date of the guilty plea or conviction. Continued practice after suspension under this section shall be considered practicing chiropractic without a license. On receiving notice or otherwise becoming aware of the conviction, the state chiropractic board shall notify the individual of the suspension under this section by certified mail or in person in accordance with section 119.07 of the Revised Code. If an individual whose license is suspended under this section fails to make a timely request for an adjudication, the board shall enter a final order revoking the individual's license.

(2000 H 506, eff. 4–10–01)

4734.37 Summary suspension of license

If the state chiropractic board determines that there is clear and convincing evidence that a person who has been granted a license under this chapter has committed an act that subjects the person's license to board action under section 4734.31 of the Revised Code and that the person's continued practice presents a danger of immediate and serious harm to the public, the board may suspend the license without a prior hearing. A telephone conference call may be utilized for reviewing the matter and taking the vote.

The board shall issue a written order of suspension by certified mail or in person in accordance with section 119.07 of the Revised Code. The order is not subject to suspension by the court during pendency of any appeal filed under section 119.12 of the Revised Code. If the person subject to the suspension requests an adjudication by the board, the date set for the adjudication shall be within twenty days, but not earlier than seven days, after the request, unless otherwise agreed to by both the board and the person subject to the suspension.

Any summary suspension imposed under this section shall remain in effect, unless reversed on appeal, until a final adjudicative order issued by the board pursuant to section 4734.31 and Chapter 119. of the Revised Code becomes effective. The board shall issue its final adjudicative order within sixty days after completion of its adjudication. A failure to issue the order within sixty days shall result in dissolution of the summary suspension order but shall not invalidate any subsequent, final adjudicative order.

(2000 H 506, eff. 4–10–01)

CHAPTER 4749

PRIVATE INVESTIGATORS; SECURITY SERVICES

4749.01 Definitions

As used in this chapter:

(A) "Private investigator" means any person who engages in the business of private investigation.

(B) "Business of private investigation" means, except when performed by one excluded under division (H) of this section, the conducting, for hire, in person or through a partner or employees, of any investigation relevant to any crime or wrong done or threatened, or to obtain information on the identity, habits, conduct, movements, whereabouts, affiliations, transactions, reputation, credibility, or character of any person, or to locate and recover lost or stolen property, or to determine the cause of or responsibility for any libel or slander, or any fire, accident, or damage to property, or to secure evidence for use in any legislative, administrative, or judicial investigation or proceeding.

(C) "Security guard provider" means any person who engages in the business of security services.

(D) "Business of security services" means either of the following:

(1) Furnishing, for hire, watchpersons, guards, private patrol officers, or other persons whose primary duties are to protect persons or property;

(2) Furnishing, for hire, guard dogs, or armored motor vehicle security services, in connection with the protection of persons or property.

(E) "Class A license" means a license issued under section 4749.03 of the Revised Code that qualifies the person issued the license to engage in the business of private investigation and the business of security services.

(F) "Class B license" means a license issued under section 4749.03 of the Revised Code that qualifies the person issued the license to engage only in the business of private investigation.

(G) "Class C license" means a license issued under section 4749.03 of the Revised Code that qualifies the person issued the license to engage only in the business of security services.

(H) "Private investigator," "business of private investigation," "security guard provider," and "business of security services" do not include:

(1) Public officers and employees whose official duties require them to engage in investigatory activities;

(2) Attorneys at law or any expert hired by an attorney at law for consultation or litigation purposes;

(3) A consumer reporting agency, as defined in the "Fair Credit Reporting Act," 84 Stat. 1128, 15 U.S.C.A. 1681a, as amended, provided that the consumer reporting agency is in compliance with the requirements of that act and that the agency's activities are confined to any of the following:

(a) The issuance of consumer credit reports;

(b) The conducting of limited background investigations that pertain only to a client's prospective tenant and that are engaged in with the prior written consent of the prospective tenant;

(c) The business of pre-employment background investigation. As used in division (H)(3)(c) of this section, "business of pre-employment background investigation" means, and is limited to, furnishing for hire, in person or through a partner or employees, the conducting of limited background investigations, in-person interviews, telephone interviews, or written inquiries that pertain only to a client's prospective employee and the employee's employment and that are engaged in with the prior written consent of the prospective employee.

(4) Certified public insurance adjusters that hold a certificate of authority issued pursuant to sections 3951.01 to 3951.09 of the Revised Code, while the adjuster is investigating the cause of or responsibility for a fire, accident, or other damage to property with respect to a claim or claims for loss or damage under a policy of insurance covering real or personal property;

(5) Personnel placement services and persons who act as employees of such entities engaged in investigating matters related to personnel placement activities;

(6) An employee in the regular course of the employee's employment, engaged in investigating matters pertinent to the business of the employee's employer or protecting property in the possession of the employee's employer, provided the employer is deducting all applicable state and federal employment taxes on behalf of the employee and neither the employer nor the employee is employed by, associated with, or acting for or on behalf of any private investigator or security guard provider;

(7) Any better business bureau or similar organization or any of its employees while engaged in the maintenance of the quality of business activities relating to consumer sales and services;

(8) An accountant who is registered or certified under Chapter 4701. of the Revised Code or any of the accountant's employees while engaged in activities for which the accountant is certified or registered;

(9) Any person who, for hire or otherwise, conducts genealogical research in this state.

As used in division (H)(9) of this section, "genealogical research" means the determination of the origins and descent of families, including the identification of individuals, their family relationships, and the biographical details of their lives. "Genealogical research" does not include furnishing for hire services for locating missing persons or natural or birth parents or children.

(10) Any person residing in this state who conducts research for the purpose of locating the last known owner of unclaimed funds, provided that the person is in compliance with Chapter 169. of the Revised Code and rules adopted thereunder. The

exemption set forth in division (H)(10) of this section applies only to the extent that the person is conducting research for the purpose of locating the last known owner of unclaimed funds.

As used in division (H)(10) of this section, "owner" and "unclaimed funds" have the same meanings as in section 169.01 of the Revised Code.

(11) A professional engineer who is registered under Chapter 4733. of the Revised Code or any of his employees.

As used in division (H)(11) of this section and notwithstanding division (I) of this section, "employee" has the same meaning as in section 4101.01 of the Revised Code.

(12) Any person residing in this state who, for hire or otherwise, conducts research for the purpose of locating persons to whom the state of Ohio owes money in the form of warrants, as defined in division (S) of section 131.01 of the Revised Code, that the state voided but subsequently reissues.

(13) An independent insurance adjuster who, as an individual, an independent contractor, an employee of an independent contractor, adjustment bureau association, corporation, insurer, partnership, local recording agent, managing general agent, or self-insurer, engages in the business of independent insurance adjustment, or any person who supervises the handling of claims except while acting as an employee of an insurer licensed in this state while handling claims pertaining to specific policies written by that insurer.

As used in division (H)(13) of this section, "independent insurance adjustment" means conducting investigations to determine the cause of or circumstances concerning a fire, accident, bodily injury, or damage to real or personal property; determining the extent of damage of that fire, accident, injury, or property damage; securing evidence for use in a legislative, administrative, or judicial investigation or proceeding, adjusting losses; and adjusting or settling claims, including the investigation, adjustment, denial, establishment of damages, negotiation, settlement, or payment of claims in connection with insurance contractors, self-insured programs, or other similar insurance programs. "Independent adjuster" does not include either of the following:

(a) An attorney who adjusts insurance losses incidental to the practice of law and who does not advertise or represent that the attorney is an independent insurance adjuster;

(b) A licensed agent or general agent of an insurer licensed in this state who processes undisputed or uncontested losses for insurers under policies issued by that agent or general agent.

(14) Except for a commissioned peace officer who engages in the business of private investigation or compensates others who engage in the business of private investigation or the business of security services or both, any commissioned peace officer as defined in division (B) of section 2935.01 of the Revised Code.

(I) "Employee" means every person who may be required or directed by any employer, in consideration of direct or indirect gain or profit, to engage in any employment, or to go, or work, or be at any time in any place of employment, provided that the employer of the employee deducts all applicable state and federal employment taxes on behalf of the employee.

(2002 H 188, eff. 3–24–03; 1995 H 229, eff. 3–11–96; 1995 S 162, eff. 10–29–95; 1994 H 383, eff. 10–12–94; 1985 H 402, eff. 11–27–85; 1969 H 341)

4749.02 Administration of chapter; appointment of employees

The director of public safety shall administer this chapter, and for that purpose, may appoint employees and adopt rules that the director considers necessary.

(2004 H 230, eff. 7–1–04; 1997 H 215, eff. 6–30–97; 1996 S 293, eff. 9–26–96 (See also Historical and Statutory Notes.))

Historical and Statutory Notes

Ed. Note: 1996 S 293 Effective Date—The Secretary of State assigned a general effective date of 9–26–96 for 1996 S 293, along with notice that, in accordance with RC 1.471, the General Assembly has not determined which sections go into immediate effect, and that it appears that certain sections provide for appropriations for current expenses, and are immediately effective in accordance with RC 1.471 and O Const Art II, § 1d.

4749.021 Private investigation and security services commission

(A) There is hereby created the Ohio private investigation and security services commission, consisting of the director of public safety or the director's designee, who shall be a nonvoting member; the superintendent of the highway patrol or the superintendent's designee, who shall be a voting member; and twelve members appointed by the governor with the advice and consent of the senate, as follows:

(1) Three members shall be owners or operators of a business that maintains a class A license and shall have at least five years' experience in this state in the business of private investigation or security services.

(2) One member shall be an owner or operator of a business that maintains a class B license and shall have at least five years' experience in this state in the business of private investigation or security services.

(3) One member shall be an owner or operator of a business that maintains a class C license and shall have at least five years' experience in this state in the business of private investigation or security services.

(4) Two members shall be owners or operators of a business that maintains a class A, B, or C license and shall have at least five years' experience in this state in the business of private investigation or security services.

(5) One member shall be an incumbent chief of police.

(6) One member shall be an active law enforcement officer, not above the rank of lieutenant.

(7) One member shall be an incumbent sheriff.

(8) Two members shall be representatives of the general public who have never had a direct employment relationship with any class A, B, or C licensee.

(B)(1) The governor shall make initial appointments to the commission by January 1, 2005, and the commission shall hold its first meeting, at the call of the director of public safety, in January 2005. Of the initial appointments made to the commission, three shall be for a term ending December 31, 2005, three shall be for a term ending December 31, 2006, three shall be for a term ending December 31, 2007, and three shall be for a term ending December 31, 2008. Thereafter, terms of office shall be for five years, with each term ending on the same day of the same month as did the term that it succeeds. Each member shall hold office from the date of appointment until the end of the term for which the member was appointed. Members may be reappointed, but may serve not more than two complete consecutive five-year terms. Vacancies shall be filled in the manner provided for original appointments. Any member appointed to fill a vacancy occurring before the expiration date of the term for which the member's predecessor was appointed shall hold office as a member for the remainder of that term. A member shall continue in office subsequent to the expiration of the member's term until the member's successor takes office or until a period of sixty days has elapsed, whichever occurs first. The governor, after notice and the opportunity for a hearing, may remove any appointed member for misfeasance, malfeasance, or nonfeasance.

(2) Ninety days before the expiration of a member's term, or in the event of a vacancy, the Ohio association of security and

investigation services may submit names to the governor for consideration of appointment to the commission.

(C) The commission shall advise the director of public safety on all matters related to the regulation of private investigation and the business of security services and on all matters related to this chapter. The commission shall advise the director on the format, content, and all other aspects of all private investigation and security services licensure examinations.

(D) In accordance with Chapter 119. of the Revised Code, the department may establish rules on behalf of the commission.

(E) The commission shall meet not less than four times each year. It also shall meet upon the call of the chairperson, upon the request of five members, or at the request of the director of public safety or the director's designee.

(F) At the first regular meeting of each year, which shall be called by the chairperson, the members shall elect a chairperson and a vice-chairperson by a majority vote, and also shall establish its meeting schedule for the remainder of the year. The chairperson and vice-chairperson shall serve until their successors are elected. No member may serve as chairperson more than three times during a five-year term. The chairperson shall preside over the commission's meetings, shall set the meeting agenda, and shall serve as the commission's chief spokesperson and liaison to the department of public safety. The chairperson or vice-chairperson shall approve all vouchers of the commission. Subject to the commission's approval, the chairperson may appoint committees to assist the commission. Committee members may be members of the commission. The vice-chairperson shall exercise the duties of the chairperson when the chairperson is not available.

(G) A quorum of seven appointed members is necessary for a meeting to convene or continue. All actions of the commission shall be by a majority of the members present. Members may not participate or vote by proxy. In accordance with Chapter 121. of the Revised Code, at least fourteen days before a regular meeting and twenty-four hours before a special meeting, the chairperson shall notify all members of the commission in writing of the agenda. Upon a timely request, any member of the commission may have an item added to the commission's agenda.

(H) Each member of the commission shall receive the member's necessary expenses incurred in the performance of official duties, including travel, hotel, and other necessary expenses. Members of any special committee, which may be appointed by the commission to assist it, who are not members of the commission also may receive necessary expenses.

(I) The department of public safety shall provide the commission with suitable office and meeting space and necessary technical, clerical, and administrative support. The department shall serve as the official repository of the commission's records. Expenses of the commission shall be paid from the private investigator and security guard provider fund created in section 4749.07 of the Revised Code.

(J) In the absence of fraud or bad faith, the commission, a current or former commission member, or an agent, representative, or employee of the commission is not liable in damages to any person because of any act, omission, proceeding, or decision related to official duties.

(2004 H 230, eff. 9–16–04)

4749.03 License requirements; application; fees; duplicate license; corporate licenses

(A)(1) Any individual, including a partner in a partnership, may be licensed as a private investigator under a class B license, or as a security guard provider under a class C license, or as a private investigator and a security guard provider under a class A license, if the individual meets all of the following requirements:

(a) Has a good reputation for integrity, has not been convicted of a felony within the last twenty years or any offense involving moral turpitude, and has not been adjudicated incompetent for the purpose of holding the license, as provided in section 5122.301 of the Revised Code, without having been restored to legal capacity for that purpose.

(b) Depending upon the class of license for which application is made, for a continuous period of at least two years immediately preceding application for a license, has been engaged in investigatory or security services work for a law enforcement or other public agency engaged in investigatory activities, or for a private investigator or security guard provider, or engaged in the practice of law, or has acquired equivalent experience as determined by rule of the director of public safety.

(c) Demonstrates competency as a private investigator or security guard provider by passing an examination devised for this purpose by the director, except that any individually licensed person who qualifies a corporation for licensure shall not be required to be reexamined if the person qualifies the corporation in the same capacity that the person was individually licensed.

(d) Submits evidence of comprehensive general liability insurance coverage, or other equivalent guarantee approved by the director in such form and in principal amounts satisfactory to the director, but not less than one hundred thousand dollars for each person and three hundred thousand dollars for each occurrence for bodily injury liability, and one hundred thousand dollars for property damage liability.

(e) Pays the requisite examination and license fees.

(2) A corporation may be licensed as a private investigator under a class B license, or as a security guard provider under a class C license, or as a private investigator and a security guard provider under a class A license, if an application for licensure is filed by an officer of the corporation and the officer, another officer, or the qualifying agent of the corporation satisfies the requirements of divisions (A)(1) and (F)(1) of this section. Officers and the statutory agent of a corporation shall be determined in accordance with Chapter 1701. of the Revised Code.

(3) At least one partner in a partnership shall be licensed as a private investigator, or as a security guard provider, or as a private investigator and a security guard provider. Partners in a partnership shall be determined as provided for in Chapter 1775. of the Revised Code.

(B) Application for a class A, B, or C license shall be in writing, under oath, to the director. In the case of an individual, the application shall state the applicant's name, birth date, citizenship, physical description, current residence, residences for the preceding ten years, current employment, employment for the preceding seven years, experience qualifications, the location of each of the applicant's offices in this state, and any other information that is necessary in order for the director to comply with the requirements of this chapter. In the case of a corporation, the application shall state the name of the officer or qualifying agent filing the application; the state in which the corporation is incorporated and the date of incorporation; the states in which the corporation is authorized to transact business; the name of its qualifying agent; the name of the officer or qualifying agent of the corporation who satisfies the requirements of divisions (A)(1) and (F)(1) of this section and the birth date, citizenship, physical description, current residence, residences for the preceding ten years, current employment, employment for the preceding seven years, and experience qualifications of that officer or qualifying agent; and other information that the director requires. A corporation may specify in its application information relative to one or more individuals who satisfy the requirements of divisions (A)(1) and (F)(1) of this section.

The application described in this division shall be accompanied by all of the following:

(1) One recent full-face photograph of the applicant or, in the case of a corporation, of each officer or qualifying agent specified in the application as satisfying the requirements of divisions (A)(1) and (F)(1) of this section;

(2) One complete set of the applicant's fingerprints or, in the case of a corporation, of the fingerprints of each officer or qualifying agent specified in the application as satisfying the requirements of divisions (A)(1) and (F)(1) of this section;

(3) Character references from at least five reputable citizens for the applicant or, in the case of a corporation, for each officer or qualifying agent specified in the application as satisfying the requirements of divisions (A)(1) and (F)(1) of this section, each of whom has known the applicant, officer, or qualifying agent for at least five years preceding the application, and none of whom are connected with the applicant, officer, or qualifying agent by blood or marriage;

(4) An examination fee of twenty-five dollars for the applicant or, in the case of a corporation, for each officer or qualifying agent specified in the application as satisfying the requirements of divisions (A)(1) and (F)(1) of this section, and a license fee of two hundred fifty dollars. The license fee shall be refunded if a license is not issued.

(C) Upon receipt of the application and accompanying matter described in division (B) of this section, the director shall forward to the bureau of criminal identification and investigation a request that it make an investigation of the applicant or, in the case of a corporation, each officer or qualifying agent specified in the application as satisfying the requirements of divisions (A)(1) and (F)(1) of this section, to determine whether the applicant, officer, or qualifying agent meets the requirements of division (A)(1)(a) of this section. If the director determines that the applicant, officer, or qualifying agent meets the requirements of divisions (A)(1)(a), (b), and (d) of this section and that an officer or qualifying agent meets the requirement of division (F)(1) of this section, the director shall notify the applicant, officer, or agent of the time and place for the examination. If the director determines that an applicant does not meet the requirements of divisions (A)(1)(a), (b), and (d) of this section, the director shall notify the applicant that the applicant's application is refused and refund the license fee. If the director determines that none of the individuals specified in the application of a corporation as satisfying the requirements of divisions (A)(1) and (F)(1) of this section meet the requirements of divisions (A)(1)(a), (b), and (d) and (F)(1) of this section, the director shall notify the corporation that its application is refused and refund the license fee. If the director requests an investigation of any applicant, officer, or qualifying agent and if the bureau assesses the director a fee for the investigation, the director, in addition to any other fee assessed pursuant to this chapter, may assess the applicant, officer, or qualifying agent, as appropriate, a fee that is equal to the fee assessed by the bureau.

(D) If upon application, investigation, and examination, the director finds that the applicant or, in the case of a corporation, any officer or qualifying agent specified in the application as satisfying the requirements of divisions (A)(1) and (F)(1) of this section, meets the applicable requirements, the director shall issue the applicant or the corporation a class A, B, or C license. The director also shall issue an identification card to an applicant, but not an officer or qualifying agent of a corporation, who meets the applicable requirements. The license and identification card shall state the licensee's name, the classification of the license, the location of the licensee's principal place of business in this state, and the expiration date of the license, and, in the case of a corporation, it also shall state the name of each officer or qualifying agent who satisfied the requirements of divisions (A)(1) and (F)(1) of this section.

Licenses expire on the first day of March following the date of initial issue, and on the first day of March of each year thereafter. Renewals shall be according to the standard renewal procedures contained in Chapter 4745. of the Revised Code, upon payment of a renewal fee of two hundred fifty dollars. No license shall be renewed if the licensee or, in the case of a corporation, each officer or qualifying agent who qualified the corporation for licensure no longer meets the applicable requirements of this section. No license shall be renewed unless the licensee provides evidence of workers' compensation risk coverage and unemployment compensation insurance coverage, other than for clerical employees and excepting sole proprietors who are exempted therefrom, as provided for in Chapters 4123. and 4141. of the Revised Code, respectively, as well as the licensee's state tax identification number. No reexamination shall be required for renewal of a current license.

For purposes of this chapter, a class A, B, or C license issued to a corporation shall be considered as also having licensed the individuals who qualified the corporation for licensure, for as long as they are associated with the corporation.

For purposes of this division, "sole proprietor" means an individual licensed under this chapter who does not employ any other individual.

(E) The director may issue a duplicate copy of a license issued under this section for the purpose of replacement of a lost, spoliated, or destroyed license, upon payment of a fee fixed by the director, not exceeding twenty-five dollars. Any change in license classification requires new application and application fees.

(F)(1) In order to qualify a corporation for a class A, B, or C license, an officer or qualifying agent may qualify another corporation for similar licensure, provided that the officer or qualifying agent is actively engaged in the business of both corporations.

(2) Each officer or qualifying agent who qualifies a corporation for class A, B, or C licensure shall surrender any personal license of a similar nature that the officer or qualifying agent possesses.

(3) Upon written notification to the director, completion of an application similar to that for original licensure, surrender of the corporation's current license, and payment of a twenty-five dollar fee, a corporation's class A, B, or C license may be transferred to another corporation.

(4) Upon written notification to the director, completion of an application similar to that for an individual seeking class A, B, or C licensure, payment of a twenty-five dollar fee, and, if the individual was the only individual that qualified a corporation for licensure, surrender of the corporation's license, any officer or qualifying agent who qualified a corporation for licensure under this chapter may obtain a similar license in the individual's own name without reexamination. A request by an officer or qualifying agent for an individual license shall not affect a corporation's license unless the individual is the only individual that qualified the corporation for licensure or all the other individuals who qualified the corporation for licensure submit such requests.

(G) If a corporation is for any reason no longer associated with an individual who qualified it for licensure under this chapter, an officer of the corporation shall notify the director of that fact by certified mail, return receipt requested, within ten days after the association terminates. If the notification is so given, the individual was the only individual that qualified the corporation for licensure, and the corporation submits the name of another officer or qualifying agent to qualify the corporation for the license within thirty days after the association terminates, the corporation may continue to operate in the business of private investigation, the business of security services, or both businesses in this state under that license for ninety days after the association terminates. If the officer or qualifying agent whose name is submitted satisfies the requirements of divisions (A)(1) and (F)(1) of this section, the director shall issue a new license to the corporation within that ninety-day period. The names of more than one individual may be submitted.

(2004 H 230, eff. 7-1-04; 1996 H 245, eff. 9-17-96; 1991 H 298, eff. 7-26-91; 1986 H 428; 1985 H 402; 1977 H 725; 1976 S 447; 1974 H 1241; 1970 H 1146; 1969 H 341)

4749.04 Grounds for revocation, suspension, or refusal to renew license; appeal

(A) The director of public safety may revoke, suspend, or refuse to renew, when a renewal form has been submitted, the license of any private investigator or security guard provider, or the registration of any employee of a private investigator or security guard provider, for any of the following:

(1) Violation of any of the provisions of division (B) or (C) of section 4749.13 of the Revised Code;

(2) Conviction of a felony or a crime involving moral turpitude;

(3) Violation of any rule of the director governing private investigators, the business of private investigation, security guard providers, or the business of security services;

(4) Testifying falsely under oath, or suborning perjury, in any judicial proceeding;

(5) Failure to satisfy the requirements specified in division (D) of section 4749.03 of the Revised Code.

Any person whose license or registration is revoked, suspended, or not renewed when a renewal form is submitted may appeal in accordance with Chapter 119. of the Revised Code.

(B) In lieu of suspending, revoking, or refusing to renew the class A, B, or C license, or of suspending, revoking, or refusing to renew the registration of an employee of a class A, B, or C licensee, the director may impose a civil penalty of not more than one hundred dollars for each calendar day of a violation of any of the provisions of this section or of division (B) or (C) of section 4749.13 of the Revised Code or of a violation of any rule of the director governing private investigators, the business of private investigation, security guard providers, or the business of security services.

(2004 H 230, eff. 7-1-04; 2002 H 188, eff. 3-24-03; 1985 H 402, eff. 11-27-85; 1969 H 341)

4749.05 Branch offices; notification of change of location; report to sheriff and police chief before engaging in investigation

(A) Each class A, B, or C licensee shall report the location of branch offices to the department of public safety, and to the sheriff of the county and the police chief of any municipal corporation in which the office is located, and shall post a branch office license conspicuously in that office. Application for a branch office license shall be made on a form prescribed by the director of public safety, and a license shall be issued upon receipt of the form and payment of a fee fixed by the director, not exceeding one hundred dollars. If a licensee moves an office, the licensee shall notify, in writing, the department of public safety and any affected sheriff and chief of police within forty-eight hours of the change.

This division does not apply to a licensed private investigator who is engaging in the business of private investigation as a registered employee of a licensed private investigator.

(B) Pursuant to Chapter 119. of the Revised Code, the director of public safety shall adopt rules regarding when a class A, B, or C licensee, or any of such a licensee's employees, is required to report the licensee's or employee's presence and length of stay to the sheriff and police chief of any county or municipal corporation in which the licensee or employee operates. The rules shall include reporting requirements for licenses or employees conducting fraud investigations or physical surveillance.

(2004 H 230, eff. 7-1-04; 1985 H 402, eff. 11-27-85; 1976 S 447; 1969 H 341)

4749.06 Registration of private investigator or security guard employees; identification card required; firearms basic training program

(A) Each class A, B, or C licensee shall register the licensee's investigator or security guard employees, with the department of public safety, which shall maintain a record of each licensee and registered employee and make it available, upon request, to any law enforcement agency. The class A, B, or C licensee shall file an application to register a new employee no sooner than three days nor later than seven calendar days after the date on which the employee is hired.

(B)(1) Each employee's registration application shall be accompanied by one complete set of the employee's fingerprints, one recent photograph of the employee, the employee's physical description, and an eighteen-dollar registration fee.

(2) If the director of public safety requests the bureau of criminal identification and investigation to conduct an investigation of a licensee's employee and if the bureau assesses the director a fee for the investigation, the director, in addition to any other fee assessed pursuant to this chapter, may assess the licensee a fee that is equal to the fee assessed by the bureau. If, after investigation, the bureau finds that the employee has not been convicted of a felony within the last twenty years, the director shall issue to the employee an identification card bearing the license number and signature of the licensee, which in the case of a corporation shall be the signature of its president or its qualifying agent, and containing the employee's name, address, age, physical description, and right thumb print or other identifying mark as the director prescribes, a recent photograph of the employee, and the employee's signature. The director may issue a duplicate of a lost, spoliated, or destroyed identification card issued under this section, upon payment of a fee fixed by the director, not exceeding five dollars.

(C) Except as provided in division (E) of this section, no class A, B, or C licensee shall permit an employee, other than an individual who qualified a corporation for licensure, to engage in the business of private investigation, the business of security services, or both businesses until the employee receives an identification card from the department, except that pending the issuance of an identification card, a class A, B, or C licensee may offer for hire security guard or investigator employees provided the licensee obtains a waiver from the person who receives, for hire, security guard or investigative services, acknowledging that the person is aware the employees have not completed their registration and agreeing to their employment.

(D) If a class A, B, or C licensee, or a registered employee of a class A, B, or C licensee, intends to carry a firearm, as defined in section 2923.11 of the Revised Code, in the course of engaging in the business or employment, the licensee or registered employee shall satisfactorily complete a firearms basic training program that includes twenty hours of handgun training and five hours of training in the use of other firearms, if any other firearm is to be used, or equivalency training, if authorized, or shall be a former peace officer who previously had successfully completed a firearms training course, shall receive a certificate of satisfactory completion of that program or written evidence of approval of the equivalency training, shall file an application for registration, shall receive a firearm-bearer notation on the licensee's or registered employee's identification card, and shall annually requalify on a firearms range, all as described in division (A) of section 4749.10 of the Revised Code. A private investigator, security guard provider, or employee is authorized to carry a firearm only in accordance with that division.

(E) This section does not apply to commissioned peace officers, as defined in division (B) of section 2935.01 of the Revised Code, working for, either as an employee or independent contractor, a class A, B, or C licensee. For purposes of this chapter, a commissioned peace officer is an employee exempt from registration.

(2004 H 230, eff. 7–1–04; 2002 H 188, eff. 3–24–03; 1991 H 298, eff. 7–26–91; 1986 H 428; 1985 H 402; 1976 S 447; 1970 H 1146; 1969 H 341)

4749.07 Disposition of fines

(A) After refund of any license fees as required by section 4749.03 of the Revised Code, the department of public safety shall pay all fees received pursuant to this chapter to the treasurer of state, to be credited to the private investigator and security guard provider fund, which is hereby created.

(B) Moneys received in payment of fines levied pursuant to section 4749.99 of the Revised Code shall be distributed as follows:

(1) One–third to the general fund of the municipal corporation or township in which the prosecution occurs;

(2) One–third to the general fund of the county in which the prosecution occurs;

(3) One–third to the private investigator and security guard provider fund.

(2004 H 230, eff. 7–1–04; 1996 S 293, eff. 9–26–96 (See also Historical and Statutory Notes.); 1985 H 402, eff. 11–27–85; 1985 H 201; 1981 H 694; 1980 H 1237, H 736; 1976 S 447; 1970 H 1146; 1969 H 341)

Historical and Statutory Notes

Ed. Note: 1996 S 293 Effective Date—The Secretary of State assigned a general effective date of 9–26–96 for 1996 S 293, along with notice that, in accordance with RC 1.471, the General Assembly has not determined which sections go into immediate effect, and that it appears that certain sections provide for appropriations for current expenses, and are immediately effective in accordance with RC 1.471 and O Const Art II, § 1d.

4749.08 Private investigators and security guards not considered law enforcement officers

(A) No class A, B, or C licensee, or registered employee of a class A, B, or C licensee shall be considered, because of licensure or registration under this chapter, a law enforcement officer for any purpose. Nothing in this chapter shall be construed as granting the right to carry a concealed weapon.

(B) The rules of the department of public safety adopted for the administration of this chapter shall include provisions to assure that any uniform or identification card shall be so designed as to avoid confusion of a private investigator, security guard provider, or registered employee with any law enforcement officer in this state.

(2004 H 230, eff. 7–1–04; 1985 H 402, eff. 11–27–85; 1969 H 341)

4749.09 Compliance with municipal ordinances not in conflict; limitation on fees

Any class A, B, or C licensee, or registered employee of a class A, B, or C licensee, who operates in a municipal corporation that provides by ordinance for the licensing, registering, or regulation of private investigators, security guard providers, or their employees shall conform to those ordinances insofar as they do not conflict with this chapter. No license or registration fees shall be charged by the state or any of its subdivisions for conducting the business of private investigation, the business of security services, or both businesses other than as provided in this chapter.

(1985 H 402, eff. 11–27–85; 1969 H 341)

4749.10 Basic firearm training program; application to carry firearm

(A) No class A, B, or C licensee and no registered employee of a class A, B, or C licensee shall carry a firearm, as defined in section 2923.11 of the Revised Code, in the course of engaging in the business of private investigation, the business of security services, or both businesses, unless all of the following apply:

(1) The licensee or employee either has successfully completed a basic firearm training program at a training school approved by the Ohio peace officer training commission, which program includes twenty hours of training in handgun use and, if any firearm other than a handgun is to be used, five hours of training in the use of other firearms, and has received a certificate of satisfactory completion of that program from the executive director of the commission; the licensee or employee has, within three years prior to November 27, 1985, satisfactorily completed firearms training that has been approved by the commission as being equivalent to such a program and has received written evidence of approval of that training from the executive director of the commission; or the licensee or employee is a former peace officer, as defined in section 109.71 of the Revised Code, who previously had successfully completed a firearms training course at a training school approved by the Ohio peace officer training commission and has received a certificate or other evidence of satisfactory completion of that course from the executive director of the commission.

(2) The licensee or employee submits an application to the director of public safety, on a form prescribed by the director, in which the licensee or employee requests registration as a class A, B, or C licensee or employee who may carry a firearm. The application shall be accompanied by a copy of the certificate or the written evidence or other evidence described in division (A)(1) of this section, the identification card issued pursuant to section 4749.03 or 4749.06 of the Revised Code if one has previously been issued, a statement of the duties that will be performed while the licensee or employee is armed, and a fee of ten dollars. In the case of a registered employee, the statement shall be prepared by the employing class A, B, or C licensee.

(3) The licensee or employee receives a notation on the licensee's or employee's identification card that the licensee or employee is a firearm-bearer and carries the identification card whenever the licensee or employee carries a firearm in the course of engaging in the business of private investigation, the business of security services, or both businesses.

(4) At any time within the immediately preceding twelve-month period, the licensee or employee has requalified in firearms use on a firearms training range at a firearms requalification program certified by the Ohio peace officer training commission or on a firearms training range under the supervision of an instructor certified by the commission and has received a certificate of satisfactory requalification from the certified program or certified instructor, provided that this division does not apply to any licensee or employee prior to the expiration of eighteen months after the licensee's or employee's completion of the program described in division (A)(1) of this section. A certificate of satisfactory requalification is valid and remains in effect for twelve months from the date of the requalification.

(5) If division (A)(4) of this section applies to the licensee or employee, the licensee or employee carries the certificate of satisfactory requalification that then is in effect or any other evidence of requalification issued or provided by the director.

(B)(1) The director of public safety shall register an applicant under division (A) of this section who satisfies divisions (A)(1) and (2) of this section, and place a notation on the applicant's identification card indicating that the applicant is a firearm-bearer and the date on which the applicant completed the program described in division (A)(1) of this section.

(2) A firearms requalification training program or instructor certified by the commission for the annual requalification of class A, B, or C licensees or employees who are authorized to carry a firearm under section 4749.10 of the Revised Code shall award a certificate of satisfactory requalification to each class A, B, or C licensee or registered employee of a class A, B, or C licensee who satisfactorily requalifies in firearms training. The certificate shall identify the licensee or employee and indicate the date of the requalification. A licensee or employee who receives such a certificate shall submit a copy of it to the director of public safety. A licensee shall submit the copy of the requalification certificate at the same time that the licensee makes application for renewal of the licensee's class A, B, or C license. The director shall keep a record of all copies of requalification certificates the director receives under this division and shall establish a procedure for the updating of identification cards to provide evidence of compliance with the annual requalification requirement. The procedure for the updating of identification cards may provide for the issuance of a new card containing the evidence, the entry of a new notation containing the evidence on the existing card, the issuance of a separate card or paper containing the evidence, or any other procedure determined by the director to be reasonable. Each person who is issued a requalification certificate under this division promptly shall pay to the Ohio peace officer training commission established by section 109.71 of the Revised Code a fee of five dollars, which fee shall be transmitted to the treasurer of state for deposit in the peace officer private security fund established by section 109.78 of the Revised Code.

(C) Nothing in this section prohibits a private investigator or a security guard provider from carrying a concealed handgun if the private investigator or security guard provider complies with sections 2923.124 to 2923.1213 of the Revised Code.

(2004 H 230, eff. 7–1–04; 2004 H 12, eff. 4–8–04; 1996 H 670, eff. 12–2–96; 1986 H 428, eff. 12–23–86; 1985 H 402)

4749.11 Investigation of applicants; complaints; actions

(A) The director of public safety may investigate any applicant for a class A, B, or C license, any principal officer or qualifying agent of a corporation who is specified in an application for licensure as satisfying the requirements of divisions (A)(1) and (F)(1) of section 4749.03 of the Revised Code, and any employee of a class A, B, or C licensee who seeks to be registered under section 4749.06 of the Revised Code to determine whether the individual satisfies the applicable requirements for licensure or registration.

(B) The director may investigate, on the director's own initiative, the actions or proposed actions of a class A, B, or C licensee, or registered employee of a class A, B, or C licensee to determine whether the person is, has been, or will be in violation of section 4749.13 of the Revised Code. The director shall investigate any of these persons if a verified written complaint is filed indicating that a person has violated, or is or will be violating, section 4749.13 of the Revised Code; the complaint is supported by evidence submitted with it; and the director determines that a prima-facie case exists that a violation of that section is being, has been, or will be committed by the person.

(C) The director may investigate, on the director's own initiative, the actions or proposed actions of a person who is not licensed or registered under this chapter and who appears to be acting as a class A, B, or C licensee, or employee of a class A, B, or C licensee. The director shall investigate such a person if a verified written complaint is filed indicating that a person was, is, or will be acting as a class A, B, or C licensee or employee of a class A, B, or C licensee but is not licensed or registered as such under this chapter; the complaint is supported by evidence that is submitted with it; and the director determines that a prima-facie case exists that the person was, is, or will be acting in the alleged manner.

(D) In connection with investigations under divisions (B) and (C) of this section, the director may file an action with the court of common pleas of Franklin county or the court of common pleas of the county in which the person who is the subject of the investigation resides, is engaging in actions, or proposing to engage in actions, to obtain an injunction, restraining order, or other appropriate relief.

(E) The director may compel by subpoena witnesses to appear and testify in relation to investigations under this chapter and may require by subpoena duces tecum the production of any book, paper, or document pertaining to an investigation. If a person does not comply with a subpoena or subpoena duces tecum, the director may apply to the court of common pleas of Franklin county for an order compelling the person to comply with the subpoena or subpoena duces tecum or, for failure to do so, to be held in contempt of court.

(F) If, in an investigation under division (C) of this section, the director determines that a person is not a class A, B, or C licensee, or a registered employee of a class A, B, or C licensee, and that the person was, is, or will be acting in the alleged manner, the director may issue an order to the person to show cause why the person should not be subject to licensing or registration under this chapter. The director shall hold a hearing on the order, and if following the hearing the director determines that the person has engaged, or is or will be engaging, in activities requiring licensure or registration under this chapter, the director may issue a cease and desist order that shall describe the person and the activities that are the subject of it. The cease and desist order is enforceable in and may be appealed to a court of common pleas pursuant to Chapter 119. of the Revised Code.

(G) In any proceeding or action brought under this chapter, the burden of proving an exemption from the licensure requirements of this chapter is on the person claiming the benefit of the exemption.

(2004 H 230, eff. 7–1–04; 1994 H 383, eff. 10–12–94; 1986 H 428, eff. 12–23–86; 1985 H 402)

4749.12 Nonresident licensees

(A) A person who is a resident of another state; is licensed as a private investigator, security guard provider, or as a private investigator and a security guard provider in another state; and wishes to engage in the business of private investigation, the business of security services, or both businesses in this state, shall be licensed pursuant to section 4749.03 of the Revised Code, but the director of public safety may waive the examination requirement of that section and issue a license to a nonresident under the circumstances described in division (B) of this section.

(B) If a nonresident private investigator, security guard provider, or private investigator and security guard provider seeking licensure under this chapter submits with the application and accompanying matter specified in section 4749.03 of the Revised Code proof of licensure in another state, and if the requirements of divisions (A)(1)(a), (b), and (d) and, if applicable, (F)(1) of section 4749.03 of the Revised Code are satisfied and the nonresident meets all current requirements of the laws of the other state regulating the business of private investigation, the business of security services, or both businesses, the director may waive the examination requirement and fee of that section. This waiver authority may be exercised only if the director determines that the other state has a law similar to this division and extends to residents of this state a similar waiver of examination privilege.

(2004 H 230, eff. 7–1–04; 1985 H 402, eff. 11–27–85)

4749.13 Prohibitions

(A) No person shall engage in the business of private investigation, the business of security services, or both businesses in this state unless the person is licensed pursuant to this chapter. Each day of continuing violation constitutes a separate offense. Nothing in this chapter shall be construed to require any employee of a class A, B, or C licensee to obtain a class A, B, or C license, provided that an employee shall be registered by a licensee when required by section 4749.06 of the Revised Code. Nothing in this chapter shall be construed to require a partner to be a class A, B, or C licensee except as provided in division (A)(3) of section 4749.03 of the Revised Code. Nothing in this chapter shall be construed to require a director, officer, or qualifying agent of a corporation to individually be a class A, B, or C licensee if the corporation is licensed pursuant to this chapter.

(B) No class A, B, or C licensee, or registered employee of a class A, B, or C licensee shall:

(1) Knowingly violate any provision of this chapter or any rule of the director of public safety adopted for the administration of this chapter;

(2) Knowingly make a false report with respect to any matter with which the licensee or registered employee is employed;

(3) Divulge any information acquired from or for a client to persons other than the client or the client's authorized agent without express authorization to do so or unless required by law;

(4) Knowingly accept employment which includes obtaining information intended for illegal purposes.

(C) No person shall knowingly authorize or permit another person to violate any provision of this chapter or any rule of the director adopted for the administration of this chapter.

(D) No person who is not licensed as a class A, B, or C licensee shall advertise that the person is or otherwise hold self out as a class A, B, or C licensee. This division does not prohibit registered employees from indicating in the course of authorized employment for a class A, B, or C licensee that they are authorized to engage in investigatory, security services activities, or both activities.

(2004 H 230, eff. 7–1–04; 1985 H 402, eff. 11–27–85)

4749.99 Penalty

(A) Except as otherwise provided in this division, whoever violates division (A) of section 4749.13 of the Revised Code is guilty of a misdemeanor of the first degree. Whoever violates division (A) of section 4749.13 of the Revised Code and previously has been convicted of one or more violations of division (A) of that section is guilty of a felony of the fifth degree. If the offender previously has been convicted of two or more violations of division (A) of that section, the offender shall be fined ten thousand dollars and also may be imprisoned not more than one year.

(B) Whoever violates division (B), (C), or (D) of section 4749.13 of the Revised Code shall be fined not less than one hundred or more than one thousand dollars, imprisoned not more than one year, or both.

(1995 S 2, eff. 7–1–96; 1992 H 536, eff. 11–5–92; 1985 H 402; 1969 H 341)

CHAPTER 4752

HOME MEDICAL EQUIPMENT SERVICES PROVIDERS

DEFINITIONS

4752.01 Definitions

As used in this chapter:

(A) "Authorized health care professional" means a person authorized under Chapter 4731. of the Revised Code to practice medicine and surgery or osteopathic medicine and surgery or otherwise authorized under Ohio law to prescribe the use of home medical equipment by a patient.

(B) "Home medical equipment" means equipment that can stand repeated use, is primarily and customarily used to serve a medical purpose, is not useful to a person in the absence of illness or injury, is appropriate for use in the home, and is one or more of the following:

(1) Life-sustaining equipment prescribed by an authorized health care professional that mechanically sustains, restores, or supplants a vital bodily function, such as breathing;

(2) Technologically sophisticated medical equipment prescribed by an authorized health care professional that requires individualized adjustment or regular maintenance by a home medical equipment services provider to maintain a patient's health care condition or the effectiveness of the equipment;

(3) An item specified by the Ohio respiratory care board in rules adopted under division (B) of section 4752.17 of the Revised Code.

(C) "Home medical equipment services" means the sale, delivery, installation, maintenance, replacement, or demonstration of home medical equipment.

(D) "Home medical equipment services provider" means a person engaged in offering home medical equipment services to the public.

(E) "Hospital" has the same meaning as in section 3727.01 of the Revised Code.

(F) "Sell or rent" means to transfer ownership or the right to use property, whether in person or through an agent, employee, or other person, in return for compensation.

(2004 H 105, eff. 9–16–04)

LICENSE OR CERTIFICATE OF REGISTRATION

4752.02 License or certificate of registration required

Note: Effective 9–16–05.

(A) Except as provided in division (B) of this section, no person shall provide home medical equipment services or claim to the public to be a home medical equipment services provider unless either of the following is the case:

(1) The person holds a valid license issued under this chapter;

(2) The person holds a valid certificate of registration issued under this chapter.

(B) Division (A) of this section does not apply to any of the following:

(1) A health care practitioner, as defined in section 4769.01 of the Revised Code, who does not sell or rent home medical equipment;

(2) A hospital that provides home medical equipment services only as an integral part of patient care and does not provide the services through a separate entity that has its own medicare or medicaid provider number;

(3) A manufacturer or wholesale distributor of home medical equipment that does not sell directly to the public;

(4) A hospice care program, as defined by section 3712.01 of the Revised Code, that does not sell or rent home medical equipment;

(5) A home, as defined by section 3721.01 of the Revised Code;

(6) A home health agency that is certified under Title XVIII of the "Social Security Act," 79 Stat. 286 (1965), 42 U.S.C. 1395, as a provider of home health services and does not sell or rent home medical equipment;

(7) An individual who holds a current, valid license issued under Chapter 4741. of the Revised Code to practice veterinary medicine;

(8) An individual who holds a current, valid license issued under Chapter 4779. of the Revised Code to practice orthotics, prosthetics, or pedorthics;

(9) A pharmacy licensed under Chapter 4729. of the Revised Code that either does not sell or rent home medical equipment or receives total payments of less than ten thousand dollars per year from selling or renting home medical equipment;

(10) A home dialysis equipment provider regulated by federal law.

(2004 H 105, eff. 9–16–05)

LICENSES

4752.09 Suspension or revocation of license; fines

(A) The Ohio respiratory care board may, in accordance with Chapter 119. of the Revised Code, suspend or revoke a license issued under this chapter or discipline a license holder by imposing a fine of not more than five thousand dollars or taking other disciplinary action on any of the following grounds:

(1) Violation of any provision of this chapter or an order or rule of the board, as those provisions, orders, or rules are applicable to persons licensed under this chapter;

(2) A plea of guilty to or a judicial finding of guilt of a felony or a misdemeanor that involves dishonesty or is directly related to the provision of home medical equipment services;

(3) Making a material misstatement in furnishing information to the board;

(4) Professional incompetence;

(5) Being guilty of negligence or gross misconduct in providing home medical equipment services;

(6) Aiding, assisting, or willfully permitting another person to violate any provision of this chapter or an order or rule of the board, as those provisions, orders, or rules are applicable to persons licensed under this chapter;

(7) Failing, within sixty days, to provide information in response to a written request by the board;

(8) Engaging in conduct likely to deceive, defraud, or harm the public;

(9) Denial, revocation, suspension, or restriction of a license to provide home medical equipment services, for any reason other than failure to renew, in another state or jurisdiction;

(10) Directly or indirectly giving to or receiving from any person a fee, commission, rebate, or other form of compensation for services not rendered;

(11) Knowingly making or filing false records, reports, or billings in the course of providing home medical equipment services, including false records, reports, or billings prepared for or submitted to state and federal agencies or departments;

(12) Failing to comply with federal rules issued pursuant to the medicare program established under Title XVIII of the "Social Security Act," 49 Stat. 620(1935), 42 U.S.C. 1395, as amended, relating to operations, financial transactions, and general business practices of home medical services providers.

(B) The respiratory care board immediately may suspend a license without a hearing if it determines that there is evidence that the license holder is subject to actions under this section and that there is clear and convincing evidence that continued operation by the license holder presents an immediate and serious harm to the public. The president and executive director of the board shall make a preliminary determination and describe, by telephone conference or any other method of communication, the evidence on which they made their determination to the other members of the board. The board may by resolution designate another board member to act in place of the president of the board or another employee to act in the place of the executive director, in the event that the board president or executive director is unavailable or unable to act. On review of the evidence, the board may by a vote of not less than seven of its members, suspend a license without a prior hearing. The board may vote on the suspension by way of a telephone conference call.

Immediately following the decision to suspend a license under this division, the board shall issue a written order of suspension and cause it to be delivered in accordance with section 119.07 of the Revised Code. The order shall not be subject to suspension by the court during the pendency of any appeal filed under section 119.12 of the Revised Code. If the license holder requests an adjudication hearing, the date set for the hearing shall be within fifteen days but not earlier than seven days after the license holder requests the hearing, unless another date is agreed to by the license holder and the board. The suspension shall remain in effect, unless reversed by the board, until a final adjudication order issued by the board pursuant to this section and Chapter 119. of the Revised Code becomes effective. The board shall issue its final adjudication order not later than ninety days after completion of the hearing. The board's failure to issue the order by that day shall cause the summary suspension to end, but shall not affect the validity of any subsequent final adjudication order.

(2004 H 105, eff. 9–16–04)

CERTIFICATES OF REGISTRATION

4752.11 Application for certificate of registration; fee

(A) A person seeking a certificate of registration to provide home medical equipment services shall apply to the Ohio respiratory care board on a form the board shall prescribe and provide. The application must be accompanied by the registration fee established in rules adopted under section 4752.17 of the Revised Code.

(B) The applicant shall specify in the application all of the following:

(1) The name of the facility from which services will be provided;

(2) The facility's address;

(3) The facility's telephone number;

(4) A person who may be contacted with regard to the facility;

(5) The name of the national accrediting body that issued the accreditation on which the application is based;

(6) The applicant's accreditation number and the expiration date of the accreditation;

(7) A telephone number that may be used twenty-four hours a day, seven days a week, to obtain information related to the facility's provision of home medical equipment services.

(2004 H 105, eff. 9–16–04)

4752.15 Suspension or revocation of certificate of registration; notice of status changes

(A) The Ohio respiratory care board shall, in accordance with Chapter 119. of the Revised Code, suspend or revoke a certificate of registration issued under this chapter if it learns from any source that the accreditation on which the certificate of registration was issued has been revoked or suspended or is otherwise no longer valid.

(B) If the status of the accreditation on which a certificate of registration is issued under this chapter changes for any reason, the holder of the certificate shall notify the board. On receipt of the notice, the board shall take action under division (A) of this section, if appropriate.

(2004 H 105, eff. 9–16–04)

PENALTIES

4752.99 Penalties

Whoever violates division (A) of section 4752.02 of the Revised Code is guilty of a minor misdemeanor on the first offense. On the second offense, the person is guilty of a misdemeanor of the fourth degree. On each subsequent offense, the person is guilty of a misdemeanor of the first degree.

(2004 H 105, eff. 9–16–04)

CHAPTER 4762

ACUPUNCTURISTS

4762.02 Certificate of registration; exemptions

(A) Except as provided in division (B) of this section, no person shall engage in the practice of acupuncture unless the person holds a valid certificate of registration as an acupuncturist issued by the state medical board under this chapter.

(B) Division (A) of this section does not apply to a physician or to a person who performs acupuncture as part of a training program in acupuncture operated by an educational institution that holds an effective certificate of authorization issued by the Ohio board of regents under section 1713.02 of the Revised Code or a school that holds an effective certificate of registration issued by the state board of career colleges and schools under section 3332.05 of the Revised Code.

(2002 S 266, eff. 4–3–03; 2000 H 341, eff. 8–10–00)

4762.16 Disciplinary action by health care facility; reports to state medical board; malpractice suits

(A) Within sixty days after the imposition of any formal disciplinary action taken by any health care facility, including a hospital, health care facility operated by an insuring corporation, ambulatory surgical center, or similar facility, against any individual holding a valid certificate of registration as an acupuncturist, the chief administrator or executive officer of the facility shall report to the state medical board the name of the individual, the action taken by the facility, and a summary of the underlying facts leading to the action taken. Upon request, the board shall be provided certified copies of the patient records that were the basis for the facility's action. Prior to release to the board, the summary shall be approved by the peer review committee that reviewed the case or by the governing board of the facility.

The filing of a report with the board or decision not to file a report, investigation by the board, or any disciplinary action taken by the board, does not preclude a health care facility from taking disciplinary action against an acupuncturist.

In the absence of fraud or bad faith, no individual or entity that provides patient records to the board shall be liable in damages to any person as a result of providing the records.

(B) An acupuncturist, professional association or society of acupuncturists, physician, or professional association or society of physicians that believes a violation of any provision of this chapter, Chapter 4731. of the Revised Code, or rule of the board has occurred shall report to the board the information upon which the belief is based. This division does not require any treatment provider approved by the board under section 4731.25 of the Revised Code or any employee, agent, or representative of such a provider to make reports with respect to an acupuncturist participating in treatment or aftercare for substance abuse as long as the acupuncturist maintains participation in accordance with the requirements of section 4731.25 of the Revised Code and the treatment provider or employee, agent, or representative of the provider has no reason to believe that the acupuncturist has violated any provision of this chapter or rule adopted under it, other than being impaired by alcohol, drugs, or other substances. This division does not require reporting by any member of an impaired practitioner committee established by a health care facility or by any representative or agent of a committee or program sponsored by a professional association or society of acupuncturists to provide peer assistance to acupuncturists with substance abuse problems with respect to an acupuncturist who has been referred for examination to a treatment program approved by the board under section 4731.25 of the Revised Code if the acupuncturist cooperates with the referral for examination and with any determination that the acupuncturist should enter treatment and as long as the committee member, representative, or agent has no reason to believe that the acupuncturist has ceased to participate in the treatment program in accordance with section 4731.25 of the Revised Code or has violated any provision of this chapter or rule adopted under it, other than being impaired by alcohol, drugs, or other substances.

(C) Any professional association or society composed primarily of acupuncturists that suspends or revokes an individual's membership for violations of professional ethics, or for reasons of professional incompetence or professional malpractice, within sixty days after a final decision, shall report to the board, on forms prescribed and provided by the board, the name of the individual, the action taken by the professional organization, and a summary of the underlying facts leading to the action taken.

The filing of a report with the board or decision not to file a report, investigation by the board, or any disciplinary action taken by the board, does not preclude a professional organization from taking disciplinary action against an acupuncturist.

(D) Any insurer providing professional liability insurance to any person holding a valid certificate of registration as an acupuncturist or any other entity that seeks to indemnify the professional liability of an acupuncturist shall notify the board within thirty days after the final disposition of any written claim for damages where such disposition results in a payment exceeding twenty-five thousand dollars. The notice shall contain the following information:

(1) The name and address of the person submitting the notification;

(2) The name and address of the insured who is the subject of the claim;

(3) The name of the person filing the written claim;

(4) The date of final disposition;

(5) If applicable, the identity of the court in which the final disposition of the claim took place.

(E) The board may investigate possible violations of this chapter or the rules adopted under it that are brought to its attention as a result of the reporting requirements of this section, except that the board shall conduct an investigation if a possible violation involves repeated malpractice. As used in this division, "repeated malpractice" means three or more claims for malpractice within the previous five-year period, each resulting in a judgment or settlement in excess of twenty-five thousand dollars in favor of the claimant, and each involving negligent conduct by the acupuncturist.

(F) All summaries, reports, and records received and maintained by the board pursuant to this section shall be held in confidence and shall not be subject to discovery or introduction in evidence in any federal or state civil action involving an acupuncturist, supervising physician, or health care facility arising out of matters that are the subject of the reporting required by this section. The board may use the information obtained only as the basis for an investigation, as evidence in a disciplinary hearing against an acupuncturist or supervising physician, or in any subsequent trial or appeal of a board action or order.

The board may disclose the summaries and reports it receives under this section only to health care facility committees within or outside this state that are involved in credentialing or recredentialing an acupuncturist or supervising physician or reviewing their privilege to practice within a particular facility. The board shall indicate whether or not the information has been verified. Information transmitted by the board shall be subject to the same confidentiality provisions as when maintained by the board.

(G) Except for reports filed by an individual pursuant to division (B) of this section, the board shall send a copy of any reports or summaries it receives pursuant to this section to the acupuncturist. The acupuncturist shall have the right to file a statement with the board concerning the correctness or relevance of the information. The statement shall at all times accompany that part of the record in contention.

(H) An individual or entity that reports to the board or refers an impaired acupuncturist to a treatment provider approved by the board under section 4731.25 of the Revised Code shall not be subject to suit for civil damages as a result of the report, referral, or provision of the information.

(I) In the absence of fraud or bad faith, a professional association or society of acupuncturists that sponsors a committee or program to provide peer assistance to an acupuncturist with substance abuse problems, a representative or agent of such a committee or program, and a member of the state medical board shall not be held liable in damages to any person by reason of actions taken to refer an acupuncturist to a treatment provider approved under section 4731.25 of the Revised Code for examination or treatment.

(2000 H 341, eff. 8–10–00)

4762.99 Penalties

(A) Whoever violates section 4762.02 of the Revised Code is guilty of a misdemeanor of the first degree on a first offense; on each subsequent offense, the person is guilty of a felony of the fourth degree.

(B) Whoever violates division (A), (B), (C), or (D) of section 4762.16 of the Revised Code is guilty of a minor misdemeanor on a first offense; on each subsequent offense the person is guilty of a misdemeanor of the fourth degree, except that an individual guilty of a subsequent offense shall not be subject to imprisonment, but to a fine alone of up to one thousand dollars for each offense.

(2000 H 341, eff. 8–10–00)

CHAPTER 4931

COMPANIES—TELEGRAPH; TELEPHONE

DISPATCHES

4931.25 Injuring or destroying property of telegraph companies

No person shall intentionally injure, molest, or destroy a line, post, abutment, or any material or property of a telephone or telegraph company. Prosecution under this section shall be by indictment.

(1953 H 1, eff. 10–1–53; GC 12511)

4931.26 Divulging telegraph message

No person connected with a telegraph or messenger company, incorporated or unincorporated, operating a telegraph line or engaged in the business of receiving and delivering messages, shall willfully divulge the contents or the nature of the contents of a private communication entrusted to him for transmission or delivery, willfully refuse or neglect to transmit or deliver it, willfully delay its transmission or delivery, or willfully forge the name of the intended receiver to a receipt for such message, communication, or article of value entrusted to him by said company, with intent to injure, deceive, or defraud the sender or intended receiver thereof or such telegraph or messenger company, or to benefit himself or any other person.

(1953 H 1, eff. 10–1–53; GC 13388)

4931.27 Delaying telegraph message

No telegraph operator of a railroad or telegraph company shall fail, on tender of the usual charge at regular commercial offices, to accept a telegram for transmission from any passenger delayed by an accident, or to send it forthwith to the person and point designated, without alteration, revision, or approval. If a violation of this section arises from obeying an order or rule of the employer of the telegraph operator, such employer shall repay him any fine imposed under division (B) of section 4931.99 of the Revised Code and costs.

(1992 S 343, eff. 3–24–93; 1953 H 1; GC 13389)

TELEPHONE AND TELEGRAPH PROVISIONS

4931.28 Interfering with telegraph or telephone messages

Except as authorized pursuant to sections 2933.51 to 2933.66 of the Revised Code, no person shall willfully and maliciously cut, break, tap, or make connection with a telegraph or telephone wire or read or copy in an unauthorized manner, a telegraphic message or communication from or upon a telegraph or telephone line, wire, or cable, so cut or tapped, or make unauthorized use thereof, or willfully and maliciously prevent, obstruct, or delay the sending, conveyance, or delivery of an authorized telegraphic message or communication by or through a line, cable, or wire, under the control of a telegraph or telephone company.

(1986 S 222, eff. 3–25–87; 1953 H 1; GC 13402)

4931.29 Divulging telephone communication

No person connected with a telephone company, incorporated or unincorporated, operating a telephone line or engaged in the business of transmitting to, from, through, or in this state, telephone messages, in any capacity, shall willfully divulge a private telephone message or the nature of such message, or a private conversation between persons communicating over the wires of such company, or willfully delay the transmission of a telephonic message or communication, with intent to injure, deceive, or defraud the sender or receiver thereof or any other person, or any such telephone company, or to benefit himself or any other person.

(1953 H 1, eff. 10–1–53; GC 13419)

4931.30 Party lines to be yielded in emergencies

No person shall willfully refuse immediately to yield or relinquish the use of a party line to another person for the purpose of permitting such other person to report a fire or summon law enforcement agencies, ambulance service, medical, or other aid in case of emergency.

No person shall ask for or request the use of a party line on the pretext that an emergency exists, knowing that no emergency exists.

Every telephone directory distributed after June 30, 1955, to the members of the general public in this state or in any portion thereof which lists the calling numbers of telephones of any telephone exchange located in this state shall contain a notice which explains the offenses provided for in this section, such notice to be printed in type which is not smaller than any other type on the same page and to be preceded by the word "warning" printed in type with at least equal prominence as other regulations or information on the same page; provided, that the provisions of this section do not apply to those directories distributed solely for business advertising purposes, commonly known as classified directories, nor to any telephone directory distributed or for which copy has been sent to the printer or is in the process of printing or distribution to the general public prior to June 30, 1955. Any person, firm, or corporation providing telephone service which distributes or causes to be distributed in this state one or more copies of a telephone directory which is subject to the provisions of this section and which willfully omits such notice is guilty of a violation of this section.

As used in this section:

(A) "Party line" means a subscribers' line telephone circuit, to which two or more main telephone stations are connected, each station having a distinctive ring or telephone number.

(B) "Emergency" means a situation in which property or human life is in jeopardy and in which prompt summoning of aid is essential.

(129 v 582, eff. 1–10–61; 126 v 74)

4931.31 Threat or harassment in telephone communication prohibited; directory notice

No person shall, while communicating with any other person over a telephone, threaten to do bodily harm or use or address to such other person any words or language of a lewd, lascivious, or indecent character, nature, or connotation for the sole purpose of annoying such other person; nor shall any person telephone any other person repeatedly or cause any person to be telephoned repeatedly for the sole purpose of harassing or molesting such other person or his family.

Any use, communication, or act prohibited by this section may be deemed to have occurred or to have been committed at either the place at which the telephone call was made or was received.

Every telephone directory distributed to the general public in this state which lists the calling numbers of telephones of any telephone exchange located in this state shall contain a notice which explains the offenses provided for in this section, such notice to be printed in type which is not smaller than the general body of the other type on the same page and to be preceded by the word "warning" printed in type with at least equal prominence as the headings of other regulations or information on the same page; provided, that the provisions of this section shall not apply to those directories distributed solely for business advertising purposes, commonly known as classified directories, nor to any telephone directory distributed or for which copy has been sent to the printer or is in the process of printing or distribution to the general public prior to August 14, 1959.

Any person, firm, or corporation providing telephone service which distributes or causes to be distributed in this state one or more copies of a telephone directory which is subject to the provisions of this section and which willfully omits such notice is guilty of a violation of this section.

(129 v 582, eff. 1–10–61; 128 v 692)

UNIFORM EMERGENCY TELEPHONE NUMBER SYSTEM

4931.49 Liability; improper use of system; disclosure

Note: See also following version of this section, eff. 5–6–05.

(A) The state, the state highway patrol, or a subdivision participating in a 9–1–1 system and any officer, agent, or employee of the state, state highway patrol, or a participating subdivision is not liable in damages in a civil action for injuries, death, or loss to persons or property arising from any act or omission, except willful or wanton misconduct, in connection with developing, adopting, or approving any final plan or any agreement made under section 4931.48 of the Revised Code or otherwise bringing into operation a 9–1–1 system pursuant to those provisions.

(B) Except as otherwise provided in sections 701.02 and 4765.49 of the Revised Code, an individual who gives emergency instructions through a 9–1–1 system established under sections 4931.40 to 4931.54 of the Revised Code, and the principals for whom the person acts, including both employers and independent contractors, public and private, and an individual who follows emergency instructions and the principals for whom that person acts, including both employers and independent contractors, public and private, are not liable in damages in a civil action for injuries, death, or loss to persons or property arising from the issuance or following of emergency instructions, except where the issuance or following of the instructions constitutes willful or wanton misconduct.

(C) A telephone company, and any other installer, maintainer, or provider, through the sale or otherwise, of customer premises equipment, and their respective officers, directors, employees, agents, and suppliers are not liable in damages in a civil action for injuries, death, or loss to persons or property incurred by any person resulting from such an entity's or its officers', directors', employees', agents', or suppliers' participation in or acts or omissions in connection with that participation in a 9–1–1 system whether that system is established pursuant to sections 4931.40 to 4931.54 of the Revised Code or otherwise in accordance with the telephone company's schedules regarding 9–1–1 systems filed with the public utilities commission pursuant to section 4905.30 of the Revised Code.

(D) No person shall knowingly use the telephone number of the 9–1–1 system to report an emergency if the person knows that no emergency exists.

(E) No person shall disclose or use, for any purpose other than for the 9–1–1 system, any information concerning telephone numbers, addresses, or names obtained from the data base that serves the public safety answering point of a 9–1–1 system established under sections 4931.40 to 4931.54 of the Revised Code, except that a telephone company may disclose or use such information to assist a public utility or municipal utility in handling customer calls in times of public emergency or service outages. The charge, terms, and conditions for the disclosure or use of such information by the telephone company shall be subject to the jurisdiction of the public utilities commission. In no event shall such information be disclosed or used for any purpose not permitted by this division.

(2000 H 152, eff. 9–21–00; 1994 H 344, eff. 6–1–94; 1992 S 98, eff. 11–12–92; 1992 S 131; 1991 H 418; 1988 H 131; 1985 H 491)

Note: See also following version of this section, eff. 5–6–05.

FACSIMILE TRANSMISSIONS

4931.55 Transmission of advertisements to facsimile devices

Note: See also following repeal of this section, eff. 5–6–05. See now RC 4931.75.

(A) As used in this section:

(1) "Advertisement" means a message or material intended to cause the sale of realty, goods, or services.

(2) "Facsimile device" means a device that electronically or telephonically receives and copies onto paper reasonable reproductions or facsimiles of documents and photographs through connection with a telephone network.

(3) "Pre–existing business relationship" does not include transmitting an advertisement to the owner's or lessee's facsimile device.

(B) No person shall transmit an advertisement to a facsimile device unless the person has received prior permission from the owner or, if the device is leased, from the lessee of the device to which the message is to be sent to transmit the advertisement; or the person has a pre-existing business relationship with such owner or lessee.

(C) When requested by the owner or lessee, the transmission shall occur between seven p.m. and five a.m.

This section applies to all such advertisements intended to be so transmitted within this state.

(1991 H 233, eff. 1–10–92)

Note: See also following repeal of this section, eff. 5–6–05. See now RC 4931.75.

4931.55 Transmission of advertisements to facsimile devices—Repealed

Note: See also preceding version of this section, in effect until 5–6–05, and RC 4931.75.

(2004 H 361, eff. 5–6–05; 1991 H 233, eff. 1–10–92)

Note: See also preceding version of this section, in effect until 5–6–05, and RC 4931.75.

Historical and Statutory Notes

Ed. Note: Former RC 4931.55 amended and recodified as RC 4931.75 by2004 H 361, eff. 5–6–05.

4931.75 Transmission of advertisements to certain facsimile devices

(A) As used in this section:

(1) "Advertisement" means a message or material intended to cause the sale of realty, goods, or services.

(2) "Facsimile device" means a device that electronically or telephonically receives and copies onto paper reasonable reproductions or facsimiles of documents and photographs through connection with a telephone network.

(3) "Pre–existing business relationship" does not include transmitting an advertisement to the owner's or lessee's facsimile device.

(B)(1) No person shall transmit an advertisement to a facsimile device unless the person has received prior permission from the owner or, if the device is leased, from the lessee of the device to which the message is to be sent to transmit the advertisement; or the person has a pre-existing business relationship with such owner or lessee. Division (B)(1) of this section does not apply to a person who transmits an advertisement to a facsimile device located on residential premises.

(2) No person shall transmit an advertisement to a facsimile device located on residential premises unless the person has received prior written permission from the owner or, if the device is leased, from the lessee of the device to which the message is to be sent to transmit the advertisement. In addition to any other penalties or remedies, a recipient of an advertisement transmitted in violation of division (B)(2) of this section may bring a civil action against the person who transmitted that advertisement or caused it to be transmitted. In that action, the recipient may recover one thousand dollars for each violation.

(C) When requested by the owner or lessee, the transmission shall occur between seven p.m. and five a.m.

This section applies to all such advertisements intended to be so transmitted within this state.

(2004 H 361, eff. 5–6–05)

Historical and Statutory Notes

Ed. Note: RC 4931.75 is former RC 4931.55, amended and recodifiedby 2004 H 361, eff. 5–6–05; 1991 H 233, eff. 1–10–92.

PENALTY

4931.99 Penalties

Note: See also following version of this section, eff. 5–6–05.

(A) Whoever violates section 4931.49 of the Revised Code is guilty of a misdemeanor of the fourth degree.

(B) Whoever violates section 4931.25, 4931.26, 4931.27, 4931.30, or 4931.31 of the Revised Code is guilty of a misdemeanor of the third degree.

(C) Whoever violates section 4931.28 of the Revised Code is guilty of a felony of the fourth degree.

(D) Whoever violates section 4931.29 or division (B) of section 4931.35 of the Revised Code is guilty of a misdemeanor in the first degree.

(E) Whoever violates division (E) of section 4931.49 of the Revised Code is guilty of a misdemeanor of the fourth degree on a first offense and a felony of the fifth degree on each subsequent offense.

(F) Whoever violates section 4931.55 of the Revised Code is guilty of a minor misdemeanor for a first offense and a misdemeanor of the first degree on each subsequent offense.

(1999 H 283, eff. 9–29–99; 1995 S 2, eff. 7–1–96; 1992 S 343, eff. 3–24–93; 1991 H 233; 1985 H 491; 1982 H 269, S 199; 131 v S 110, S 109; 129 v 1306; 128 v 692; 126 v 74; 1953 H 1)

Note: See also following version of this section, eff. 5–6–05.

4931.99 Penalties (later effective date)

Note: See also preceding version of this section, in effect until 5–6–05.

(A) Whoever violates division (D) of section 4931.49 of the Revised Code is guilty of a misdemeanor of the fourth degree.

(B) Whoever violates section 4931.25, 4931.26, 4931.27, 4931.30, or 4931.31 of the Revised Code is guilty of a misdemeanor of the third degree.

(C) Whoever violates section 4931.28 of the Revised Code is guilty of a felony of the fourth degree.

(D) Whoever violates section 4931.29 or division (B) of section 4931.35 of the Revised Code is guilty of a misdemeanor in the first degree.

(E) Whoever violates division (E) or (F) of section 4931.49 or division (B)(2) of section 4931.66 of the Revised Code is guilty of a misdemeanor of the fourth degree on a first offense and a felony of the fifth degree on each subsequent offense.

(F) Whoever violates section 4931.75 of the Revised Code is guilty of a minor misdemeanor for a first offense and a misdemeanor of the first degree on each subsequent offense.

(2004 H 361, eff. 5–6–05; 1999 H 283, eff. 9–29–99; 1995 S 2, eff. 7–1–96; 1992 S 343, eff. 3–24–93; 1991 H 233; 1985 H 491; 1982 H 269, S 199; 131 v S 110, S 109; 129 v 1306; 128 v 692; 126 v 74; 1953 H 1)

Note: See also preceding version of this section, in effect until 5–6–05.

CHAPTER 4933

COMPANIES—GAS; ELECTRIC; WATER; OTHERS

GENERAL PROVISIONS

GENERAL PROVISIONS

4933.16 Municipal control of electricity

No person or company shall place, string, construct, or maintain a line, wire, fixture, or appliance of any kind to conduct electricity for lighting, heating, or power purposes through a street, alley, lane, square, place, or land of a municipal corporation without the consent of such municipal corporation.

This prohibition extends to all levels above or below the surface of such public ways, grounds, or places, as well as along their surfaces, but not to rights received through and exercised under proceedings of a probate court prior to February 26, 1910.

The penalty provided by section 4933.99 of the Revised Code for a violation of this section is cumulative to other means of enforcing this section open to the municipal corporation, by way of injunction or otherwise, and is not exclusive.

(1953 H 1, eff. 10–1–53; GC 9193, 9194)

TAMPERING AND INTERFERENCE WITH FACILITIES

4933.18 Tampering with utility equipment

(A) In a prosecution for a theft offense, as defined in section 2913.01 of the Revised Code, that involves alleged tampering with a gas, electric, steam, or water meter, conduit, or attachment of a utility that has been disconnected by the utility, proof that a meter, conduit, or attachment of a utility has been tampered with is prima-facie evidence that the person who is obligated to pay for the service rendered through the meter, conduit, or attachment and is in possession or control of the meter, conduit, or attachment at the time the tampering occurred has caused the tampering with intent to commit a theft offense.

In a prosecution for a theft offense, as defined in section 2913.01 of the Revised Code, that involves the alleged reconnection of a gas, electric, steam, or water meter, conduit, or attachment of a utility that has been disconnected by the utility, proof that a meter, conduit, or attachment disconnected by a utility has been reconnected without the consent of the utility is prima-facie evidence that the person in possession or control of the meter, conduit, or attachment at the time of the reconnection has reconnected the meter, conduit, or attachment with intent to commit a theft offense.

(B) As used in this section:

(1) "Utility" means any electric light company, gas company, natural gas company, pipe-line company, water-works company, or heating or cooling company, as defined by division (A)(4), (5), (6), (7), (8), or (9) of section 4905.03 of the Revised Code, its lessees, trustees, or receivers, or any similar utility owned or operated by a political subdivision.

(2) "Tamper" means to interfere with, damage, or by-pass a utility meter, conduit, or attachment with the intent to impede the correct registration of a meter or the proper functions of a conduit or attachment so as to reduce the amount of utility service that is registered on the meter.

(1995 S 2, eff. 7–1–96; 1978 H 605, eff. 8–18–78)

4933.19 Notice regarding theft of utility service

Each electric light company, gas company, natural gas company, pipe-line company, water-works company, or heating or cooling company, as defined by division (A)(4), (5), (6), (7), (8), or (9) of section 4905.03 of the Revised Code, or its lessees, trustees, or receivers, and each similar utility owned or operated by a political subdivision shall notify its customers, on an annual basis, that tampering with or bypassing a meter constitutes a theft offense that could result in the imposition of criminal sanctions.

(1995 S 2, eff. 7–1–96; 1978 H 605, eff. 8–18–78)

4933.20 Tampering with gas pipes and apparatus

No person shall maliciously open, close, adjust, or interfere with a valve, regulator, gauge, gate, disc, curb cock, stopcock, meter, or other regulating, operating, or measuring device or appliance in or attached to the wells, tanks, conduits, pipelines, mains, service pipes, house pipes, display pipes, or other pipes of a gas company or manufacturer or furnisher of gas with intent to cause the escape of gas or to injure or destroy such property. No person shall maliciously enlarge or alter a mixer furnished or approved by a gas company or manufacturer or furnisher of gas to or for a consumer of gas, or maliciously remove from its connection a mixer so furnished or approved. No person shall without express permission, consume for fuel the gas of a gas company or manufacturer or furnisher of gas without the use of a mixer so furnished or approved by such gas company or manufacturer or furnisher of gas, or tap, sever, or open a main or pipe used or intended for the transmission of gas, or connect with such main or pipe any other main or pipe. This section does not apply to an agent or employee, for that purpose, of the owner, manufacturer, or operator of the devices or appliances referred to in this section.

As used in this section, "gas" includes natural and artificial gas used for heating and illuminating purposes.

(1978 H 605, eff. 8–18–78)

4933.21 Interfering with electric wires

No person shall willfully or maliciously injure, destroy, or intentionally permit to be injured or destroyed, disconnect, displace, cut, break, tap, ground, or make a connection with, or willfully or maliciously interfere with any pole, pier, cable, tower, or wire, legally erected, put, or strung, or electrical apparatus, appliance, or machinery used in the construction or operation of an electrical railway, electric light plant, or plant used in generating or transmitting electricity, or any meter, pipe, conduit, wire, line, post, lamp, burner, heater, machine, motor, or other appliance or apparatus used in the construction or operation of any such electrical railway or electrical plant. No person shall willfully or maliciously prevent any electric meter used in the construction or operation of any such electrical railway or electrical plant, from registering the quantity of electricity supplied, interfere with the proper action or just registration by such meter, alter the index in such meter, or, without the consent of the owner of such electrical railway or electrical plant, willfully or maliciously divert electric current from any such wire or otherwise willfully or maliciously use or cause to be used, without the consent of the owner of such electrical railway or electrical plant, electricity manufactured or distributed by any such electrical railway or electrical plant.

(1953 H 1, eff. 10–1–53; GC 12507)

4933.22 Tampering with hydrant, pipe, or meter

No person shall maliciously open, close, adjust, or interfere with a fire hydrant, valve, regulator, gauge, gate, disc, curb cock, stopcock, meter, or other regulator, operating or measuring device, or appliance in or attached to the wells, tanks, reservoirs, conduits, pipes, mains, service pipes, house pipes, or other pipes or apparatus of a water company or furnisher of water, with intent to cause the escape of water or to injure or destroy such property. No person shall tap, sever, open, or make unauthorized connections with a main or pipe used or intended for the transmission of water. This section does not apply to the agent or employee for that purpose, of the owner or operator of the appliances referred to in this section, and does not apply to anything done by or under authority of any regularly constituted fire department.

(1953 H 1, eff. 10–1–53; GC 12512–1)

4933.23 Interfering with pipes and meters

No person shall willfully or maliciously injure or destroy, or intentionally permit to be injured or destroyed, cut, break, adjust, or interfere with any pipe, valve, regulator, gauge, gate, stopcock, trap, meter, or other regulating or measuring device or appliance used in the construction or operation of any plant furnishing or distributing hot water or steam for heating purposes. No person shall willfully or maliciously prevent any meter or other measuring device or appliance used in any such heating plant from duly registering the quantity of hot water or steam supplied. No person shall, without the consent of the owner of such heating plant, willfully or maliciously divert any hot water or steam from any pipe or other part of such heating plant or otherwise willfully or maliciously use or cause to be used, without the consent of the owner of such heating plant, hot water or steam supplied by any such heating plant.

(1953 H 1, eff. 10–1–53; GC 12512–2)

4933.24 Interference with flow or transmission of sewage

No person shall maliciously open, close, adjust, or interfere with a valve, regulator, gauge, gate, disc, curb cock, stopcock, meter, or other regulator, operating or measuring device, or appliance in or attached to the tanks, conduits, pipes, mains, service pipes, house pipes, or other pipes or apparatus of a sewage disposal company, with intent to interfere with the flow of sewage, or to injure or destroy such property. No person shall tap, sever, open, or make unauthorized connections with a main or pipe used or intended for the transmission of sewage.

(129 v 501, eff. 9–19–61)

SEWAGE DISPOSAL SYSTEM AND WATERWORKS

4933.25 Sewage disposal system companies and water-works companies to obtain certificates of public convenience and necessity

No sewage disposal system company established after September 19, 1961, or expanding after October 2, 1969, or water-works company established or expanding after October 2, 1969, shall construct, install, or operate sewage disposal system facilities or water distribution facilities until it has been issued a certificate of public convenience and necessity by the public utilities commission. The commission shall adopt rules prescribing requirements and the manner and form in which sewage disposal system companies and water-works companies shall apply for such a certificate.

Before the commission issues a certificate of public convenience and necessity, it may hold a public hearing concerning the issuance of the certificate. Notice of the hearing shall be given to the board of county commissioners of any county and the chief executive authority of any municipal corporation to be served by a sewage disposal system company or water-works company.

As used in this section, "sewage disposal system company" and "water–works company" have the same meanings as in section 4905.03 of the Revised Code and include only "public utilities" as defined in section 4905.02 of the Revised Code.

(1998 H 26, eff. 5–6–98; 1971 H 1, eff. 3–26–71; 1969 S 58; 130 v H 1; 129 v 501)

PENALTIES

4933.99 Penalties

(A) Whoever violates section 4933.16 of the Revised Code is guilty of a misdemeanor of the third degree.

(B) Whoever violates section 4933.20, 4933.22, 4933.24, or 4933.25 of the Revised Code is guilty of a misdemeanor of the fourth degree.

(C) Whoever violates section 4933.21 or 4933.23 of the Revised Code is guilty of a misdemeanor of the first degree.

(D) Whoever violates division (E) of section 4933.28 of the Revised Code is guilty of a misdemeanor of the fourth degree. Each day of a violation of that division constitutes a separate offense.

(1995 S 2, eff. 7–1–96; 1984 S 183, eff. 9–26–84; 1982 H 269, § 4, S 199; 1978 H 1111, H 605; 1977 H 271; 129 v 501)

CHAPTER 4953

TRANSPORTATION TERMINAL COMPANIES

Section

4953.11 Authority to detain

(A) An officer or agent of a union terminal company who has probable cause to believe that a person is a pickpocket, is a thief, has violated the public peace, has violated any rule or regulation posted as provided by section 4953.07 of the Revised Code, or has committed any crime or misdemeanor on the depot grounds may detain the person in a reasonable manner and for a reasonable length of time within the property of the union terminal company, for the purpose of recovering any property involved in the violation, causing an arrest to be made by a peace officer, or obtaining a warrant of arrest.

(B) An officer or agent of a union terminal company acting under division (A) of this section shall not search the person detained, search or seize any property belonging to the person detained without the person's consent, or use undue restraint upon the person detained.

(C) Any peace officer, as defined in section 2935.01 of the Revised Code, may arrest without a warrant any person who the officer has probable cause to believe is a pickpocket, is a thief, has violated any rule or regulation provided by section 4953.07 of the Revised Code that also is a violation of law, or has committed any crime or misdemeanor on the depot grounds and shall make the arrest within a reasonable time after the commission of the act or violation that is the basis of the arrest.

(1999 S 107, eff. 3–23–00; 1953 H 1, eff. 10–1–53; GC 9166)

CHAPTER 4973

EMPLOYEES; POLICEMEN

SPECIAL POLICE OFFICERS

4973.17 Commissions for special police officer; term of office; hospital police officers

(A) Upon the application of any bank, building and loan association, or association of banks or building and loan associations in this state, the secretary of state may appoint and commission any persons that the bank, building and loan association, or association of banks or building and loan associations designates, or as many of those persons as the secretary of state considers proper, to act as police officers for and on the premises of that bank, building and loan association, or association of banks or building and loan associations, or elsewhere, when directly in the discharge of their duties. Police officers so appointed shall be citizens of this state and of good character. They shall hold office for three years, unless, for good cause shown, their commission is revoked by the secretary of state, or by the bank, building and loan association, or association of banks or building and loan associations, as provided by law.

(B) Upon the application of a company owning or using a railroad in this state and subject to section 4973.171 of the Revised Code, the secretary of state may appoint and commission any persons that the railroad company designates, or as many of those persons as the secretary of state considers proper, to act as police officers for and on the premises of the railroad company, its affiliates or subsidiaries, or elsewhere, when directly in the discharge of their duties. Police officers so appointed, within the time set by the Ohio peace officer training commission, shall successfully complete a commission approved training program and be certified by the commission. They shall hold office for three years, unless, for good cause shown, their commission is revoked by the secretary of state, or railroad company, as provided by law.

Any person holding a similar commission in another state may be commissioned and may hold office in this state without completing the approved training program required by this division provided that the person has completed a substantially equivalent training program in the other state. The Ohio peace officer training commission shall determine whether a training program in another state meets the requirements of this division.

(C) Upon the application of any company under contract with the United States atomic energy commission for the construction or operation of a plant at a site owned by the commission, the secretary of state may appoint and commission persons the company designates, not to exceed one hundred fifty, to act as police officers for the company at the plant or site owned by the commission. Police officers so appointed shall be citizens of this state and of good character. They shall hold office for three years, unless, for good cause shown, their commission is revoked by the secretary of state or by the company, as provided by law.

(D)(1) Upon the application of any hospital that is operated by a public hospital agency or a nonprofit hospital agency and that employs and maintains its own proprietary police department or security department and subject to section 4973.171 of the Revised Code, the secretary of state may appoint and commission any persons that the hospital designates, or as many of those persons as the secretary of state considers proper, to act as police officers for the hospital. No person who is appointed as a police officer under this division shall engage in any duties or activities as a police officer for the hospital or any affiliate or subsidiary of the hospital unless all of the following apply:

(a) The chief of police of the municipal corporation in which the hospital is located or, if the hospital is located in the unincorporated area of a county, the sheriff of that county has granted approval to the hospital to permit persons appointed as police officers under this division to engage in those duties and activities. The approval required by this division is general in nature and is intended to cover in the aggregate all persons appointed as police officers for the hospital under this division; a separate approval is not required for each appointee on an individual basis.

(b) Subsequent to the grant of approval described in division (D)(1)(a) of this section, the hospital has entered into a written agreement with the chief of police of the municipal corporation in which the hospital is located or, if the hospital is located in the unincorporated area of a county, with the sheriff of that county, that sets forth the standards and criteria to govern the interaction and cooperation between persons appointed as police officers for the hospital under this division and law enforcement officers serving the agency represented by the chief of police or sheriff who signed the agreement in areas of their concurrent jurisdiction. The written agreement shall be signed by the appointing authority of the hospital and by the chief of police or sheriff. The standards and criteria may include, but are not limited to, provisions governing the reporting of offenses discovered by hospital police officers to the agency represented by the chief of police or sheriff, provisions governing investigatory responsibilities relative to offenses committed on hospital property, and provisions governing the processing and confinement of persons arrested for offenses committed on hospital property. The agreement required by this division is intended to apply in the aggregate to all persons appointed as police officers for the hospital under this division; a separate agreement is not required for each appointee on an individual basis.

(c) The person has successfully completed a training program approved by the Ohio peace officer training commission and has been certified by the commission. A person appointed as a police officer under this division may attend a training program approved by the commission and be certified by the commission regardless of whether the appropriate chief of police or sheriff has granted the approval described in division (D)(1)(a) of this section and regardless of whether the hospital has entered into the written agreement described in division (D)(1)(b) of this section with the appropriate chief of police or sheriff.

(2)(a) A person who is appointed as a police officer under division (D)(1) of this section is entitled, upon the grant of approval described in division (D)(1)(a) of this section and upon the person's and the hospital's compliance with the requirements of divisions (D)(1)(b) and (c) of this section, to act as a police officer for the hospital on the premises of the hospital and of its affiliates and subsidiaries that are within the territory of the municipal corporation served by the chief of police or the unincorporated area of the county served by the sheriff who signed the written agreement described in division (D)(1)(b) of this section, whichever is applicable, and anywhere else within the territory of that municipal corporation or within the unincorporated area of that county. The authority to act as a police officer as described in this division is granted only if the person, when engaging in that activity, is directly in the discharge of the person's duties as a police officer for the hospital. The authority to act as a police officer as described in this division shall be exercised in accordance with the standards and criteria set forth in the written agreement described in division (D)(1)(b) of this section.

(b) Additionally, a person appointed as a police officer under division (D)(1) of this section is entitled, upon the grant of approval described in division (D)(1)(a) of this section and upon the person's and the hospital's compliance with the requirements of divisions (D)(1)(b) and (c) of this section, to act as a police officer elsewhere, within the territory of a municipal corporation or within the unincorporated area of a county, if the chief of police of that municipal corporation or the sheriff of that county, respectively, has granted approval for that activity to the hospital, police department, or security department served by the person as a police officer and if the person, when engaging in that activity, is directly in the discharge of the person's duties as a police officer for the hospital. The approval described in this division may be general in nature or may be limited in scope, duration, or applicability, as determined by the chief of police or sheriff granting the approval.

(3) Police officers appointed under division (D)(1) of this section shall hold office for three years, unless, for good cause shown, their commission is revoked by the secretary of state or by the hospital, as provided by law. As used in divisions (D)(1) to (3) of this section, "public hospital agency" and "nonprofit hospital agency" have the same meanings as in section 140.01 of the Revised Code.

(E) A fee of fifteen dollars for each commission applied for under this section shall be paid at the time the application is made, and this amount shall be returned if for any reason a commission is not issued.

(2003 H 95, eff. 9–26–03; 1996 H 670, eff. 12–2–96; 1996 H 566, eff. 10–16–96; 1986 S 364, eff. 3–17–87; 1980 H 746; 125 v 437; 1953 H 1; GC 9150)

4973.171 Offenses affecting employment eligibility of police officer for railroad company or hospital

(A) As used in this section, "felony" has the same meaning as in section 109.511 of the Revised Code.

(B)(1) The governor shall not appoint or commission a person as a police officer for a railroad company under division (B) of section 4973.17 of the Revised Code and shall not appoint or commission a person as a police officer for a hospital under division (D) of section 4973.17 of the Revised Code on a permanent basis, on a temporary basis, for a probationary term, or on other than a permanent basis if the person previously has been convicted of or has pleaded guilty to a felony.

(2)(a) The governor shall revoke the appointment or commission of a person appointed or commissioned as a police officer for a railroad company or as a police officer for a hospital under division (B) or (D) of section 4973.17 of the Revised Code if that person does either of the following:

(i) Pleads guilty to a felony;

(ii) Pleads guilty to a misdemeanor pursuant to a negotiated plea agreement as provided in division (D) of section 2929.43 of the Revised Code in which the person agrees to surrender the certificate awarded to that person under section 109.77 of the Revised Code.

(b) The governor shall suspend the appointment or commission of a person appointed or commissioned as a police officer for a railroad company or as a police officer for a hospital under division (B) or (D) of section 4973.17 of the Revised Code if that person is convicted, after trial, of a felony. If the person files an appeal from that conviction and the conviction is upheld by the highest court to which the appeal is taken or if the person does not file a timely appeal, the governor shall revoke the appointment or commission of that person as a police officer for a railroad company or as a police officer for a hospital. If the person files an appeal that results in that person's acquittal of the felony or conviction of a misdemeanor, or in the dismissal of the felony charge against that person, the governor shall reinstate the appointment or commission of that person as a police officer for a railroad company or as a police officer for a hospital. A person whose appointment or commission is reinstated under division (B)(2)(b) of this section shall not receive any back pay unless that person's conviction of the felony was reversed on appeal, or the felony charge was dismissed, because the court found insufficient evidence to convict the person of the felony.

(3) Division (B) of this section does not apply regarding an offense that was committed prior to January 1, 1997.

(4) The suspension or revocation of the appointment or commission of a person as a police officer for a railroad company or as a police officer for a hospital under division (B)(2) of this section shall be in accordance with Chapter 119. of the Revised Code.

(2002 H 490, eff. 1–1–04; 1996 H 566, eff. 10–16–96)

4973.18 Oath of office and commission; powers; liabilities

Before entering upon the duties of his office, each policeman appointed under section 4973.17 of the Revised Code shall take and subscribe an oath of office which shall be indorsed on his commission, and said commission with the oath shall be recorded in the office of the secretary of state who shall charge and collect a fee of one dollar for such recording. Policemen so appointed and commissioned shall severally possess and exercise the powers of, and be subject to the liabilities of, municipal policemen while discharging the duties for which they are appointed.

(1953 H 1, eff. 10–1–53; GC 9151)

4973.19 Power of police to enforce regulations and make arrests

A company which avails itself of sections 4973.17 and 4973.18 of the Revised Code may make needful regulations to promote the public convenience and safety in and about its depots, stations, and grounds, not inconsistent with law, and print and post such regulations conspicuously upon its depots or station buildings. Policemen appointed under such sections shall enforce and compel obedience to such regulations. The keeper of jails, lockups, or station houses in each county shall receive persons arrested for the commission of an offense against such regulations or the laws of the state upon or along the railroad or premises of such company.

(1953 H 1, eff. 10–1–53; GC 9152)

4973.20 When police to wear badges

Except while acting in the discharge of duty as a detective for the railroad, every policeman appointed under section 4973.17 of the Revised Code shall, when on duty, wear in plain view a metallic shield with the word "police" and the name of the railroad for which he is appointed inscribed on it.

(1953 H 1, eff. 10–1–53; GC 9153)

4973.21 Compensation

The compensation of policemen appointed or commissioned as provided in section 4973.17 of the Revised Code shall be paid by the company for which they respectively are appointed, and at such rates as are agreed upon by the parties.

(1953 H 1, eff. 10–1–53; GC 9154)

4973.22 Notice terminating services filed with secretary of state

When a company no longer requires the services of a policeman appointed as provided in section 4973.17 of the Revised Code, it may file in the office of the secretary of state a notice to that effect signed by its authorized officer, which notice shall be noted by the secretary of state upon the margin of the record where the commission is recorded, and thereupon the power of such policeman shall cease. No charge shall be made by the secretary of state for the filing of such notice.

(1953 H 1, eff. 10–1–53; GC 9155)

4973.23 When conductor and ticket agent may detain person

(A) A conductor of any train carrying passengers or of the cars of any interurban railroad carrying passengers, and a ticket agent employed in or about a railroad or interurban railroad station, while on duty on the train or cars, or in or about the station, who has probable cause to believe that a person has committed an offense may detain the person in a reasonable manner and for a reasonable length of time within the train, the cars, or the station, for the purpose of recovering any property involved in the offense, causing an arrest to be made by a peace officer, or obtaining a warrant of arrest.

(B) A conductor or ticket agent acting under division (A) of this section shall not search the person detained, search or seize any property belonging to the person detained without the person's consent, or use undue restraint upon the person detained.

(C) Any peace officer, as defined in section 2935.01 of the Revised Code, may arrest without a warrant any person who the officer has probable cause to believe has committed any violation of law and shall make the arrest within a reasonable time after the commission of the violation of law.

(1999 S 107, eff. 3–23–00; 1953 H 1, eff. 10–1–53; GC 9156)

4973.24 Conductor may eject passenger

When a passenger is guilty of disorderly conduct, uses obscene language, or plays a game of cards or chance for money or other thing of value on a passenger train or the cars of an interurban railroad carrying passengers, the conductor of such train or cars shall stop his train or cars at the place where such offense is committed, or at the next stopping place for such train or cars and eject such passenger from the train or cars, using only such force as is necessary. The conductor may command the assistance of employees of the company, person, or firm owning or operating such railroad or interurban railroad and of the passengers on such train or cars, to assist in such removal. Before removing such passenger, the conductor shall tender to the passenger such proportion of the fare he paid as the distance he then is from the place to which he paid fare bears to the whole distance for which his fare is paid.

(1953 H 1, eff. 10–1–53; GC 9157)

4973.25 Liability for damages caused by conductor's conduct

In no case shall the liability of a railroad company for damages caused by the conduct of its conductor be affected by section 4973.23 or 4973.24 of the Revised Code.

(1999 S 107, eff. 3–23–00; 1953 H 1, eff. 10–1–53; GC 9158)

4973.26 Negligence of official duty prohibited

No conductor having charge of a passenger train or of the cars of any interurban railroad carrying passengers within this state shall willfully neglect his duty as required by sections 4973.24 and 4973.25 of the Revised Code, or fail to use all the means in his power to carry out such sections. Whoever violates this section is guilty of negligence of official duty.

(1953 H 1, eff. 10–1–53; GC 9159)

PENALTIES

4973.99 Penalties

(A) Whoever violates section 4973.12 of the Revised Code shall be fined not less than fifty nor more than one hundred dollars or imprisoned not less than ten nor more than thirty days.

(B) Whoever violates section 4973.26 of the Revised Code shall be fined not less than five nor more than twenty-five dollars.

(1953 H 1, eff. 10–1–53)

CHAPTER 4999

CRIMES RELATING TO RAILROADS

GENERAL VIOLATIONS

GENERAL VIOLATIONS

4999.01 Drawing, driving, or moving vehicle on railroad track

No person shall draw, drive, or cause to be moved any vehicle on or between the rails or tracks or on or along the graded roadway of a railroad without the knowledge and consent of the owner or controller of such railroad, unless compelled by necessity to do so. Whoever violates this section is guilty of a minor misdemeanor.

(1992 H 667, eff. 3–15–93; 1953 H 1; GC 12542)

4999.02 Climbing upon railroad cars

No person shall climb, jump, step, or stand upon, or cling or attach himself to, a locomotive, engine, or car upon the track of a railroad, unless in compliance with law or by permission under the rules of the corporation managing such railroad. Whoever violates this section is guilty of a minor misdemeanor.

(1992 H 667, eff. 3–15–93; 1953 H 1; GC 12543)

4999.03 Riding or driving into enclosures of railroads

No person shall, at a place other than a private crossing or for a purpose other than crossing a railroad, ride or drive a horse or other domestic animal into an enclosure of a railroad or knowingly permit such animal to go into or remain in such enclosure, or place feed, salt, or other thing within such enclosure to induce such animal to enter into it or upon the track of such railroad, or, while constructing a private crossing or crossing a railroad at a private crossing, permit a fence to remain down or open for a longer time than is necessary to construct or use such crossing. Whoever violates this section shall be fined not more than ten dollars or imprisoned for not less than ten nor more than thirty days.

Each ten hours such animal is knowingly permitted to remain in such enclosure or upon such track is an additional offense. Such animal is not exempt from execution for a fine or costs imposed under this section.

(1953 H 1, eff. 10–1–53; GC 12544, 12545)

4999.04 Duties of engineer

(A) No person in charge of a locomotive shall do the following:

(1) Fail to bring the locomotive to a full stop at least two hundred feet before arriving at a crossing with another track, or proceed through the crossing before signaled to do so or before the way is clear;

(2) When approaching a grade crossing, fail to sound the locomotive whistle at frequent intervals, beginning not less than thirteen hundred twenty feet from such crossing and continuing until the locomotive has passed the crossing.

(B) Whoever violates this section is guilty of a misdemeanor of the fourth degree. If violation of this section causes physical harm to any person, whoever violates this section is guilty of a misdemeanor of the third degree.

(1977 S 167, eff. 8–26–77; 1972 H 511)

CHAPTER 5101

JOB AND FAMILY SERVICES DEPARTMENT—GENERAL PROVISIONS

PROTECTIVE SERVICES FOR ADULTS

PROTECTIVE SERVICES FOR ADULTS

5101.61 Duty to report suspected abuse of adult

(A) As used in this section:

(1) "Senior service provider" means any person who provides care or services to a person who is an adult as defined in division (B) of section 5101.60 of the Revised Code.

(2) "Ambulatory health facility" means a nonprofit, public or proprietary freestanding organization or a unit of such an agency or organization that:

(a) Provides preventive, diagnostic, therapeutic, rehabilitative, or palliative items or services furnished to an outpatient or ambulatory patient, by or under the direction of a physician or dentist in a facility which is not a part of a hospital, but which is organized and operated to provide medical care to outpatients;

(b) Has health and medical care policies which are developed with the advice of, and with the provision of review of such policies, an advisory committee of professional personnel, including one or more physicians, one or more dentists, if dental care is provided, and one or more registered nurses;

(c) Has a medical director, a dental director, if dental care is provided, and a nursing director responsible for the execution of such policies, and has physicians, dentists, nursing, and ancillary staff appropriate to the scope of services provided;

(d) Requires that the health care and medical care of every patient be under the supervision of a physician, provides for medical care in a case of emergency, has in effect a written agreement with one or more hospitals and other centers or clinics, and has an established patient referral system to other resources, and a utilization review plan and program;

(e) Maintains clinical records on all patients;

(f) Provides nursing services and other therapeutic services in accordance with programs and policies, with such services supervised by a registered professional nurse, and has a registered professional nurse on duty at all times of clinical operations;

(g) Provides approved methods and procedures for the dispensing and administration of drugs and biologicals;

(h) Has established an accounting and record keeping system to determine reasonable and allowable costs;

(i) "Ambulatory health facilities" also includes an alcoholism treatment facility approved by the joint commission on accreditation of healthcare organizations as an alcoholism treatment facility or certified by the department of alcohol and drug addiction services, and such facility shall comply with other provisions of this division not inconsistent with such accreditation or certification.

(3) "Community mental health facility" means a facility which provides community mental health services and is included in the comprehensive mental health plan for the alcohol, drug addiction, and mental health service district in which it is located.

(4) "Community mental health service" means services, other than inpatient services, provided by a community mental health facility.

(5) "Home health agency" means an institution or a distinct part of an institution operated in this state which:

(a) Is primarily engaged in providing home health services;

(b) Has home health policies which are established by a group of professional personnel, including one or more duly licensed doctors of medicine or osteopathy and one or more registered professional nurses, to govern the home health services it provides and which includes a requirement that every patient must be under the care of a duly licensed doctor of medicine or osteopathy;

(c) Is under the supervision of a duly licensed doctor of medicine or doctor of osteopathy or a registered professional nurse who is responsible for the execution of such home health policies;

(d) Maintains comprehensive records on all patients;

(e) Is operated by the state, a political subdivision, or an agency of either, or is operated not for profit in this state and is licensed or registered, if required, pursuant to law by the appropriate department of the state, county, or municipality in which it furnishes services; or is operated for profit in this state, meets all the requirements specified in divisions (A)(5)(a) to (d) of this section, and is certified under Title XVIII of the "Social Security Act," 49 Stat. 620 (1935), 42 U.S.C. 301, as amended.

(6) "Home health service" means the following items and services, provided, except as provided in division (A)(6)(g) of this section, on a visiting basis in a place of residence used as the patient's home:

(a) Nursing care provided by or under the supervision of a registered professional nurse;

(b) Physical, occupational, or speech therapy ordered by the patient's attending physician;

(c) Medical social services performed by or under the supervision of a qualified medical or psychiatric social worker and under the direction of the patient's attending physician;

(d) Personal health care of the patient performed by aides in accordance with the orders of a doctor of medicine or osteopathy and under the supervision of a registered professional nurse;

(e) Medical supplies and the use of medical appliances;

(f) Medical services of interns and residents-in-training under an approved teaching program of a nonprofit hospital and under the direction and supervision of the patient's attending physician;

(g) Any of the foregoing items and services which:

(i) Are provided on an outpatient basis under arrangements made by the home health agency at a hospital or skilled nursing facility;

(ii) Involve the use of equipment of such a nature that the items and services cannot readily be made available to the patient in the patient's place of residence, or which are furnished at the hospital or skilled nursing facility while the patient [sic.] there to receive any item or service involving the use of such equipment.

Any attorney, physician, osteopath, podiatrist, chiropractor, dentist, psychologist, any employee of a hospital as defined in section 3701.01 of the Revised Code, any nurse licensed under Chapter 4723. of the Revised Code, any employee of an ambulatory health facility, any employee of a home health agency, any employee of an adult care facility as defined in section 3722.01 of the Revised Code, any employee of a community alternative home as defined in section 3724.01 of the Revised Code, any employee of a nursing home, residential care facility, or home for the aging, as defined in section 3721.01 of the Revised Code, any senior service provider, any peace officer, coroner, clergyman, any employee of a community mental health facility, and any person engaged in social work or counseling having reasonable cause to believe that an adult is being abused, neglected, or exploited, or is in a condition which is the result of abuse, neglect, or exploitation shall immediately report such belief to the county department of job and family services. This section does not apply to employees of any hospital or public hospital as defined in section 5122.01 of the Revised Code.

(B) Any person having reasonable cause to believe that an adult has suffered abuse, neglect, or exploitation may report, or cause reports to be made of such belief to the department.

(C) The reports made under this section shall be made orally or in writing except that oral reports shall be followed by a written report if a written report is requested by the department. Written reports shall include:

(1) The name, address, and approximate age of the adult who is the subject of the report;

(2) The name and address of the individual responsible for the adult's care, if any individual is, and if the individual is known;

(3) The nature and extent of the alleged abuse, neglect, or exploitation of the adult;

(4) The basis of the reporter's belief that the adult has been abused, neglected, or exploited.

(D) Any person with reasonable cause to believe that an adult is suffering abuse, neglect, or exploitation who makes a report pursuant to this section or who testifies in any administrative or judicial proceeding arising from such a report, or any employee of the state or any of its subdivisions who is discharging responsibilities under section 5101.62 of the Revised Code shall be immune from civil or criminal liability on account of such investigation, report, or testimony, except liability for perjury, unless the person has acted in bad faith or with malicious purpose.

(E) No employer or any other person with the authority to do so shall discharge, demote, transfer, prepare a negative work performance evaluation, or reduce benefits, pay, or work privileges, or take any other action detrimental to an employee or in any way retaliate against an employee as a result of the employee's having filed a report under this section.

(F) Neither the written or oral report provided for in this section nor the investigatory report provided for in section 5101.62 of the Revised Code shall be considered a public record as defined in section 149.43 of the Revised Code. Information contained in the report shall upon request be made available to the adult who is the subject of the report, to agencies authorized by the department to receive information contained in the report, and to legal counsel for the adult.

(1999 H 471, eff. 7–1–00; 1995 H 117, eff. 9–29–95; 1989 H 317, eff. 10–10–89; 1989 H 253, S 2; 1987 S 124; 1985 H 66; 1981 H 694)

5101.611 Referral of cases involving mentally retarded or developmentally disabled persons

If a county department of job and family services knows or has reasonable cause to believe that the subject of a report made under section 5101.61 or of an investigation conducted under sections 5101.62 to 5101.64 or on the initiative of the department is mentally retarded or developmentally disabled as defined in section 5126.01 of the Revised Code, the department shall refer the case to the county board of mental retardation and developmental disabilities of that county for review pursuant to section 5126.31 of the Revised Code.

If a county board of mental retardation and developmental disabilities refers a case to the county department of job and family services in accordance with section 5126.31, the department shall proceed with the case in accordance with sections 5101.60 to 5101.71 of the Revised Code.

(1999 H 471, eff. 7–1–00; 1988 H 403, eff. 3–16–89)

5101.62 County department of job and family services to investigate

The county department of job and family services shall be responsible for the investigation of all reports provided for in section 5101.61 and all cases referred to it under section 5126.31 of the Revised Code and for evaluating the need for and, to the extent of available funds, providing or arranging for the provision of protective services. The department may designate another agency to perform the department's duties under this section.

Investigation of the report provided for in section 5101.61 or a case referred to the department under section 5126.31 of the Revised Code shall be initiated within twenty-four hours after the department receives the report or case if any emergency exists; otherwise investigation shall be initiated within three working days.

Investigation of the need for protective services shall include a face-to-face visit with the adult who is the subject of the report, preferably in the adult's residence, and consultation with the person who made the report, if feasible, and agencies or persons who have information about the adult's alleged abuse, neglect, or exploitation.

The department shall give written notice of the intent of the investigation and an explanation of the notice in language reasonably understandable to the adult who is the subject of the investigation, at the time of the initial interview with that person.

Upon completion of the investigation, the department shall determine from its findings whether or not the adult who is the subject of the report is in need of protective services. No adult shall be determined to be abused, neglected, or in need of protective services for the sole reason that, in lieu of medical treatment, the adult relies on or is being furnished spiritual treatment through prayer alone in accordance with the tenets and practices of a church or religious denomination of which the adult is a member or adherent. The department shall write a report which confirms or denies the need for protective services and states why it reached this conclusion.

(1999 H 471, eff. 7–1–00; 1988 H 403, eff. 3–16–89; 1986 H 428; 1981 H 694)

5101.63 Court may restrain interference

If, during the course of an investigation conducted under section 5101.62 of the Revised Code, any person, including the adult who is the subject of the investigation, denies or obstructs access to the residence of the adult, the county department of job and family services may file a petition in court for a temporary restraining order to prevent the interference or obstruction. The court shall issue a temporary restraining order to prevent the interference or obstruction if it finds there is reasonable cause to believe that the adult is being or has been abused, neglected, or exploited and access to the person's residence has been denied or obstructed. Such a finding is prima-facie evidence that immediate and irreparable injury, loss, or damage will result, so that notice is not required. After obtaining an order restraining the obstruction of or interference with the access of the protective services representative, the representative may be accompanied to the residence by a peace officer.

(1999 H 471, eff. 7–1–00; 1988 H 403, eff. 3–16–89; 1986 H 428; 1981 H 694)

5101.64 Protective services

Any person who requests or consents to receive protective services shall receive such services only after an investigation and determination of a need for protective services, which investigation shall be performed in the same manner as the investigation of a report pursuant to sections 5101.62 and 5101.63 of the Revised Code. If the person withdraws consent, the protective services shall be terminated.

(1981 H 694, eff. 11–15–81)

5101.65 Department may petition court

If the county department of job and family services determines that an adult is in need of protective services and is an incapacitated person, the department may petition the court for an order authorizing the provision of protective services. The petition shall state the specific facts alleging the abuse, neglect, or exploitation and shall include a proposed protective service plan. Any plan for protective services shall be specified in the petition.

(1999 H 471, eff. 7–1–00; 1986 H 428, eff. 12–23–86; 1981 H 694)

5101.66 Procedures

Notice of a petition for the provision of court-ordered protective services as provided for in section 5101.65 of the Revised Code shall be personally served upon the adult who is the subject of the petition at least five working days prior to the date set for the hearing as provided in section 5101.67 of the Revised Code. Notice shall be given orally and in writing in language reasonably understandable to the adult. The notice shall include the names of all petitioners, the basis of the belief that protective services are needed, the rights of the adult in the court proceedings, and the consequences of a court order for protective services. The adult shall be informed of his right to counsel and his right to appointed counsel if he is indigent and if appointed counsel is requested. Written notice by certified mail shall also be given to the adult's guardian, legal counsel, caretaker, and spouse, if any, or if he has none of these, to his adult children or next of kin, if any, or to any other person as the court may require. The adult who is the subject of the petition may not waive notice as provided in this section.

(1981 H 694, eff. 11–15–81)

5101.67 Hearing; order; placement; renewal or modification

(A) The court shall hold a hearing on the petition as provided in section 5101.65 of the Revised Code within fourteen days after its filing. The adult who is the subject of the petition shall have the right to be present at the hearing, present evidence, and examine and cross-examine witnesses. The adult shall be represented by counsel unless the right to counsel is knowingly waived. If the adult is indigent, the court shall appoint counsel to represent the adult. If the court determines that the adult lacks the capacity to waive the right to counsel, the court shall appoint counsel to represent the adult's interests.

(B) If the court finds, on the basis of clear and convincing evidence, that the adult has been abused, neglected, or exploited, is in need of protective services, and is incapacitated, and no person authorized by law or by court order is available to give consent, it shall issue an order requiring the provision of protective services only if they are available locally.

(C) If the court orders placement under this section it shall give consideration to the choice of residence of the adult. The court may order placement in settings which have been approved by the department of job and family services as meeting at least minimum community standards for safety, security, and the requirements of daily living. The court shall not order an institutional placement unless it has made a specific finding entered in the record that no less restrictive alternative can be found to meet the needs of the individual. No individual may be committed to a hospital or public hospital as defined in section 5122.01 of the Revised Code pursuant to this section.

(D) The placement of an adult pursuant to court order as provided in this section shall not be changed unless the court authorized the transfer of placement after finding compelling reasons to justify the transfer. Unless the court finds that an emergency exists, the court shall notify the adult of a transfer at least thirty days prior to the actual transfer.

(E) A court order provided for in this section shall remain in effect for no longer than six months. Thereafter, the county department of job and family services shall review the adult's need for continued services and, if the department determines that there is a continued need, it shall apply for a renewal of the order for additional periods of no longer than one year each. The adult who is the subject of the court-ordered services may petition for modification of the order at any time.

(1999 H 471, eff. 7–1–00; 1986 H 428, eff. 12–23–86; 1981 H 694)

5101.68 Interference by another; procedures

(A) If an adult has consented to the provision of protective services but any other person refuses to allow such provision, the county department of human services may petition the court for a temporary restraining order to restrain the person from interfering with the provision of protective services for the adult.

(B) The petition shall state specific facts sufficient to demonstrate the need for protective services, the consent of the adult, and the refusal of some other person to allow the provision of these services.

(C) Notice of the petition shall be given in language reasonably understandable to the person alleged to be interfering with the provision of services;

(D) The court shall hold a hearing on the petition within fourteen days after its filing. If the court finds that the protective services are necessary, that the adult has consented to the provisions of such services, and that the person who is the subject of the petition has prevented such provision, the court shall issue a temporary restraining order to restrain the person from interfering with the provision of protective services to the adult.

(1986 H 428, eff. 12–23–86; 1981 H 694)

5101.69 Emergency provision for protective services

(A) Upon petition by the county department of human services, the court may issue an order authorizing the provision of protective services on an emergency basis to an adult. The petition for any emergency order shall include:

(1) The name, age, and address of the adult in need of protective services;

(2) The nature of the emergency;

(3) The proposed protective services;

(4) The petitioner's reasonable belief, together with facts supportive thereof, as to the existence of the circumstances described in divisions (D)(1) to (3) of this section;

(5) Facts showing the petitioner's attempts to obtain the adult's consent to the protective services.

(B) Notice of the filing and contents of the petition provided for in division (a) of this section, the rights of the person in the hearing provided for in division (C) of this section, and the possible consequences of a court order, shall be given to the adult. Notice shall also be given to the spouse of the adult or, if he has none, to his adult children or next of kin, and his guardian, if any, if his whereabouts are known. The notice shall be given in language reasonably understandable to its recipients at least twenty-four hours prior to the hearing provided for in this section. The court may waive the twenty-four hour notice requirement upon a showing that:

(1) Immediate and irreparable physical harm to the adult or others will result from the twenty-four hour delay; and

(2) Reasonable attempts have been made to notify the adult, his spouse, or, if he has none, his adult children or next of kin, if any, and his guardian, if any, if his whereabouts are known.

Notice of the court's determination shall be given to all persons receiving notice of the filing of the petition provided for in this division.

(C) Upon receipt of a petition for an order for emergency services, the court shall hold a hearing no sooner than twenty-four and no later than seventy-two hours after the notice provided for in division (B) of this section has been given, unless the court has waived the notice. The adult who is the subject of the petition shall have the right to be present at the hearing, present, evidence, and examine and cross-examine witnesses.

(D) The court shall issue an order authorizing the provision of protective services on an emergency basis if it finds, on the basis of clear and convincing evidence, that:

(1) The adult is an incapacitated person;

(2) An emergency exists;

(3) No person authorized by law or court order to give consent for the adult is available or willing to consent to emergency services.

(E) In issuing an emergency order, the court shall adhere to the following limitations:

(1) The court shall order only such protective services as are necessary and available locally to remove the conditions creating the emergency, and the court shall specifically designate those protective services the adult shall receive;

(2) The court shall not order any change of residence under this section unless the court specifically finds that a change of residence is necessary;

(3) The court may order emergency services only for fourteen days. The department may petition the court for a renewal of the order for a fourteen-day period upon a showing that continuation of the order is necessary to remove the emergency.

(4) In its order the court shall authorize the director of the department or his designee to give consent for the person for the approved emergency services until the expiration of the order;

(5) The court shall not order a person to a hospital or public hospital as defined in section 5122.01 of the Revised Code.

(F) If the department determines that the adult continues to need protective services after the order provided for in division (D) of this section has expired, the department may petition the court for an order to continue protective services, pursuant to section 5101.65 of the Revised Code. After the filing of the petition, the department may continue to provide protective services pending a hearing by the court.

(1986 H 428, eff. 12–23–86; 1981 H 694)

5101.70 Determination of ability to pay

(A) If it appears that an adult in need of protective services has the financial means sufficient to pay for such services, the county department of job and family services shall make an evaluation regarding such means. If the evaluation establishes that the adult has such financial means, the department shall initiate procedures for reimbursement pursuant to rules promulgated by the department. If the evaluation establishes that the adult does not have such financial means, the services shall be provided in accordance with the policies and procedures established by the department of job and family services for the provision of welfare assistance. An adult shall not be required to pay for court-ordered protective services unless the court determines upon a showing by the department that the adult is financially able to pay and the court orders the adult to pay.

(B) Whenever the department has petitioned the court to authorize the provision of protective services and the adult who is the subject of the petition is indigent, the court shall appoint legal counsel.

(1999 H 471, eff. 7–1–00; 1986 H 428, eff. 12–23–86; 1981 H 694)

5101.71 County to implement; training

(A) The county departments of job and family services shall implement sections 5101.60 to 5101.71 of the Revised Code. The department of job and family services may provide a program of ongoing, comprehensive, formal training to county departments and other agencies authorized to implement sections 5101.60 to 5101.71 of the Revised Code. Training shall not be limited to the procedures for implementing section 5101.62 of the Revised Code.

(B) The director of job and family services may adopt rules in accordance with section 111.15 of the Revised Code governing the county departments' implementation of sections 5101.60 to 5101.71 of the Revised Code. The rules adopted pursuant to this division may include a requirement that the county departments provide on forms prescribed by the rules a plan of proposed expenditures, and a report of actual expenditures, of funds necessary to implement sections 5101.60 to 5101.71 of the Revised Code.

(1999 H 471, eff. 7–1–00; 1991 H 298, eff. 7–26–91; 1989 H 111; 1986 H 428; 1981 H 694)

5101.72 Reimbursement for costs of implementation

The department of job and family services, to the extent of available funds, may reimburse county departments of job and family services for all or part of the costs they incur in implementing sections 5101.60 to 5101.71 of the Revised Code. The director of job and family services shall adopt, and may amend or rescind, rules under section 111.15 of the Revised Code that provide for reimbursement of county departments of job and family services under this section.

(1999 H 471, eff. 7–1–00; 1989 H 111, eff. 7–1–89)

KINSHIP CARE SERVICES

5101.85 Kinship caregiver defined

As used in sections 5101.851 to 5101.853 of the Revised Code, "kinship caregiver" means any of the following who is eighteen years of age or older and is caring for a child in place of the child's parents:

(A) The following individuals related by blood or adoption to the child:

(1) Grandparents, including grandparents with the prefix "great," "great-great," or "great-great-great";

(2) Siblings;

(3) Aunts, uncles, nephews, and nieces, including such relatives with the prefix "great," "great-great," "grand," or "great-grand";

(4) First cousins and first cousins once removed.

(B) Stepparents and stepsiblings of the child;

(C) Spouses and former spouses of individuals named in divisions (A) and (B) of this section;

(D) A legal guardian of the child;

(E) A legal custodian of the child.

(2001 H 94, eff. 6–6–01; 1999 H 283, eff. 9–29–99)

5101.851 Statewide program of kinship care navigators to assist kinship caregivers

Note: See also following version of this section, eff. 5–18–05.

The department of job and family services may establish a statewide program of kinship care navigators to assist kinship caregivers who are seeking information regarding, or assistance obtaining, services and benefits available at the state and local level that address the needs of those caregivers residing in each county. The program shall provide to kinship caregivers information and referral services and assistance obtaining support services including the following:

(A) Publicly funded child day-care;

(B) Respite care;

(C) Training related to caring for special needs children;

(D) A toll-free telephone number that may be called to obtain basic information about the rights of, and services available to, kinship caregivers;

(E) Legal services.

(2001 H 94, eff. 6–6–01)

Note: See also following version of this section, eff. 5–18–05.

5101.851 Statewide program of kinship care navigators to assist kinship caregivers (later effective date)

Note: See also preceding version of this section, in effect until 5–18–05.

The department of job and family services may establish a statewide program of kinship care navigators to assist kinship caregivers who are seeking information regarding, or assistance obtaining, services and benefits available at the state and local level that address the needs of those caregivers residing in each county. The program shall provide to kinship caregivers information and referral services and assistance obtaining support services including the following:

(A) Publicly funded child care;

(B) Respite care;

(C) Training related to caring for special needs children;

(D) A toll-free telephone number that may be called to obtain basic information about the rights of, and services available to, kinship caregivers;

(E) Legal services.

(2004 H 11, eff. 5–18–05; 2001 H 94, eff. 6–6–01)

Note: See also preceding version of this section, in effect until 5–18–05.

5101.852 Kinship care navigator information and referral services

Within available funds, the department of job and family services shall make payments to public children services agencies for the purpose of permitting the agencies to provide kinship care navigator information and referral services and assistance obtaining support services to kinship caregivers pursuant to the kinship care navigator program. The department may provide training and technical assistance concerning the needs of kinship caregivers to employees of public children services agencies and to persons or entities that serve kinship caregivers or perform the duties of a kinship care navigator and are under contract with an agency.

(2001 H 94, eff. 6–6–01)

5101.853 Rules

The department of job and family services may adopt rules to implement the kinship care navigators program. The rules shall be adopted under Chapter 119. of the Revised Code, except that rules governing fiscal and administrative matters related to implementation of the navigators program are internal management rules and shall be adopted under section 111.15 of the Revised Code.

(2001 H 94, eff. 6–6–01)

PENALTIES

5101.99 Penalties

(A) Whoever violates division (A) or (B) of section 5101.61 of the Revised Code shall be fined not more than five hundred dollars.

(B) Whoever violates division (A) of section 5101.27 of the Revised Code is guilty of a misdemeanor of the first degree.

(2000 S 180, eff. 3–22–01; 1997 H 352, eff. 1–1–98; 1997 H 408, eff. 10–1–97; 1995 H 167, eff. 11–15–95; 1995 H 249, eff. 7–17–95; 1991 H 298, eff. 10–1–91; 1987 H 231; 1984 H 37; 1982 S 550, § 38, S 530; 1981 H 694)

CHAPTER 5103

PLACEMENT OF CHILDREN

5103.0318 Foster homes considered residential property use

Any certified foster home shall be considered to be a residential use of property for purposes of municipal, county, and township zoning and shall be a permitted use in all zoning districts in which residential uses are permitted. No municipal, county, or township zoning regulation shall require a conditional permit or any other special exception certification for any certified foster home.

(2000 H 332, eff. 1–1–01)

CHAPTER 5104

CHILD DAY CARE

5104.012 Criminal records check; disqualification from employment

(A)(1) The administrator of a child day-care center or a type A family day-care home and the provider of a certified type B family day-care home shall request the superintendent of the bureau of criminal identification and investigation to conduct a criminal records check with respect to any applicant who has applied to the center, type A home, or certified type B home for employment as a person responsible for the care, custody, or control of a child. If the applicant does not present proof that the applicant has been a resident of this state for the five-year period immediately prior to the date upon which the criminal records check is requested or does not provide evidence that within that five-year period the superintendent has requested information about the applicant from the federal bureau of investigation in a criminal records check, the administrator or provider shall request that the superintendent obtain information from the federal bureau of investigation as a part of the criminal records check for the applicant. If the applicant presents proof that the applicant has been a resident of this state for that five-year period, the administrator or provider may request that the superintendent include information from the federal bureau of investigation in the criminal records check.

(2) A person required by division (A)(1) of this section to request a criminal records check shall provide to each applicant a copy of the form prescribed pursuant to division (C)(1) of section 109.572 of the Revised Code, provide to each applicant a standard impression sheet to obtain fingerprint impressions prescribed pursuant to division (C)(2) of section 109.572 of the Revised Code, obtain the completed form and impression sheet from each applicant, and forward the completed form and impression sheet to the superintendent of the bureau of criminal identification and investigation at the time the person requests a criminal records check pursuant to division (A)(1) of this section.

(3) An applicant who receives pursuant to division (A)(2) of this section a copy of the form prescribed pursuant to division (C)(1) of section 109.572 of the Revised Code and a copy of an impression sheet prescribed pursuant to division (C)(2) of that section and who is requested to complete the form and provide a set of fingerprint impressions shall complete the form or provide all the information necessary to complete the form and shall provide the impression sheet with the impressions of the applicant's fingerprints. If an applicant, upon request, fails to provide the information necessary to complete the form or fails to provide impressions of the applicant's fingerprints, the center, type A home, or type B home shall not employ that applicant for any position for which a criminal records check is required by division (A)(1) of this section.

(B)(1) Except as provided in rules adopted under division (E) of this section, no child day-care center, type A family day-care home, or certified type B family day-care home shall employ or contract with another entity for the services of a person as a person responsible for the care, custody, or control of a child if the person previously has been convicted of or pleaded guilty to any of the following:

(a) A violation of section 2903.01, 2903.02, 2903.03, 2903.04, 2903.11, 2903.12, 2903.13, 2903.16, 2903.21, 2903.34, 2905.01, 2905.02, 2905.05, 2907.02, 2907.03, 2907.04, 2907.05, 2907.06, 2907.07, 2907.08, 2907.09, 2907.21, 2907.22, 2907.23, 2907.25, 2907.31, 2907.32, 2907.321, 2907.322, 2907.323, 2911.01, 2911.02, 2911.11, 2911.12, 2919.12, 2919.22, 2919.24, 2919.25, 2923.12, 2923.13, 2923.161, 2925.02, 2925.03, 2925.04, 2925.05, 2925.06, or 3716.11 of the Revised Code, a violation of section 2905.04 of the Revised Code as it existed prior to July 1, 1996, a violation of section 2919.23 of the Revised Code that would have been a violation of section 2905.04 of the Revised Code as it existed prior to July 1, 1996, had the violation occurred prior to that date, a violation of section 2925.11 of the Revised Code that is not a minor drug possession offense, or felonious sexual penetration in violation of former section 2907.12 of the Revised Code;

(b) A violation of an existing or former law of this state, any other state, or the United States that is substantially equivalent to any of the offenses or violations described in division (B)(1)(a) of this section.

(2) A child day-care center, type A family day-care home, or certified type B family day-care home may employ an applicant conditionally until the criminal records check required by this section is completed and the center or home receives the results of the criminal records check. If the results of the criminal records check indicate that, pursuant to division (B)(1) of this section, the applicant does not qualify for employment, the center or home shall release the applicant from employment.

(C)(1) Each child day-care center, type A family day-care home, and certified type B family day-care home shall pay to the bureau of criminal identification and investigation the fee prescribed pursuant to division (C)(3) of section 109.572 of the Revised Code for each criminal records check conducted in accordance with that section upon the request pursuant to division (A)(1) of this section of the administrator or provider of the center or home.

(2) A child day-care center, type A family day-care home, and certified type B family day-care home may charge an applicant a fee for the costs it incurs in obtaining a criminal records check under this section. A fee charged under this division shall not exceed the amount of fees the center or home pays under division (C)(1) of this section. If a fee is charged under this division, the center or home shall notify the applicant at the time of the applicant's initial application for employment of the amount of the fee and that, unless the fee is paid, the center, type A home, or type B home will not consider the applicant for employment.

(D) The report of any criminal records check conducted by the bureau of criminal identification and investigation in accordance with section 109.572 of the Revised Code and pursuant to a request under division (A)(1) of this section is not a public record for the purposes of section 149.43 of the Revised Code and shall not be made available to any person other than the applicant who is the subject of the criminal records check or the applicant's representative; the center, type A home, or certified type B home requesting the criminal records check or its representative; the department of job and family services or a county department of job and family services; and any court, hearing officer, or other necessary individual involved in a case dealing with the denial of employment to the applicant.

(E) The director of job and family services shall adopt rules pursuant to Chapter 119. of the Revised Code to implement this section, including rules specifying circumstances under which a center or home may hire a person who has been convicted of an offense listed in division (B)(1) of this section but who meets standards in regard to rehabilitation set by the department.

(F) Any person required by division (A)(1) of this section to request a criminal records check shall inform each person, at the time of the person's initial application for employment, that the person is required to provide a set of impressions of the person's fingerprints and that a criminal records check is required to be conducted and satisfactorily completed in accordance with section 109.572 of the Revised Code if the person comes under final consideration for appointment or employment as a precondition to employment for that position.

(G) As used in this section:

(1) "Applicant" means a person who is under final consideration for appointment to or employment in a position with a child day-care center, a type A family day-care home, or a certified type B family day-care home as a person responsible for the care, custody, or control of a child; an in-home aide certified pursuant to section 5104.12 of the Revised Code; or any person who would serve in any position with a child day-care center, a type A family day-care home, or a certified type B family day-care home as a person responsible for the care, custody, or control of a child pursuant to a contract with another entity.

(2) "Criminal records check" has the same meaning as in section 109.572 of the Revised Code.

(3) "Minor drug possession offense" has the same meaning as in section 2925.01 of the Revised Code.

(1999 H 471, eff. 7–1–00; 1996 S 269, eff. 7–1–96; 1996 H 445, eff. 9–3–96; 1995 S 2, eff. 7–1–96; 1994 H 694, eff. 11–11–94; 1993 S 38, eff. 10–29–93)

5104.013 Criminal records check; disqualification from licensure

Note: See also following version of this section, eff. 5–18–05.

(A)(1) The director of job and family services, as part of the process of licensure of child day-care centers and type A family day-care homes, shall request the superintendent of the bureau of criminal identification and investigation to conduct a criminal records check with respect to the following persons:

(a) Any owner, licensee, or administrator of a child day-care center;

(b) Any owner, licensee, or administrator of a type A family day-care home and any person eighteen years of age or older who resides in a type A family day-care home.

(2) The director of a county department of job and family services, as part of the process of certification of type B family day-care homes, shall request the superintendent of the bureau of criminal identification and investigation to conduct a criminal records check with respect to any authorized provider of a certified type B family day-care home and any person eighteen years of age or older who resides in a certified type B family day-care home.

(B) The director of job and family services or the director of a county department of job and family services shall provide to each person for whom a criminal records check is required under this section a copy of the form prescribed pursuant to division (C)(1) of section 109.572 of the Revised Code and a standard impression sheet to obtain fingerprint impressions prescribed pursuant to division (C)(2) of that section, obtain the completed form and impression sheet from that person, and forward the completed form and impression sheet to the superintendent of the bureau of criminal identification and investigation.

(C) A person who receives pursuant to division (B) of this section a copy of the form and standard impression sheet described in that division and who is requested to complete the form and provide a set of fingerprint impressions shall complete the form or provide all the information necessary to complete the form and shall provide the impression sheet with the impressions of the person's fingerprints. If the person, upon request, fails to provide the information necessary to complete the form or fails to provide impressions of the person's fingerprints, the director may consider the failure as a reason to deny licensure or certification.

(D) Except as provided in rules adopted under division (G) of this section, the director of job and family services shall not grant a license to a child day-care center or type A family day-care home and a county director of job and family services shall not certify a type B family day-care home if a person for whom a criminal records check was required in connection with the center or home previously has been convicted of or pleaded guilty to any of the following:

(1) A violation of section 2903.01, 2903.02, 2903.03, 2903.04, 2903.11, 2903.12, 2903.13, 2903.16, 2903.21, 2903.34, 2905.01, 2905.02, 2905.05, 2907.02, 2907.03, 2907.04, 2907.05, 2907.06, 2907.07, 2907.08, 2907.09, 2907.21, 2907.22, 2907.23, 2907.25, 2907.31, 2907.32, 2907.321, 2907.322, 2907.323, 2911.01, 2911.02, 2911.11, 2911.12, 2919.12, 2919.22, 2919.24, 2919.25, 2923.12, 2923.13, 2923.161, 2925.02, 2925.03, 2925.04, 2925.05, 2925.06, or 3716.11 of the Revised Code, a violation of section 2905.04 as it existed prior to July 1, 1996, a violation of section 2919.23 of the Revised Code that would have been a violation of section 2905.04 of the Revised Code as it existed prior to July 1, 1996, had the violation been committed prior to that date, a violation of section 2925.11 of the Revised Code that is not a minor drug possession offense, or felonious sexual penetration in violation of former section 2907.12 of the Revised Code;

(2) A violation of an existing or former law of this state, any other state, or the United States that is substantially equivalent to any of the offenses or violations described in division (D)(1) of this section.

(E) Each child day-care center, type A family day-care home, and type B family day-care home shall pay to the bureau of criminal identification and investigation the fee prescribed pursuant to division (C)(3) of section 109.572 of the Revised Code for each criminal records check conducted in accordance with that section upon a request made pursuant to division (A) of this section.

(F) The report of any criminal records check conducted by the bureau of criminal identification and investigation in accordance with section 109.572 of the Revised Code and pursuant to a request made under division (A) of this section is not a public record for the purposes of section 149.43 of the Revised Code and shall not be made available to any person other than the person who is the subject of the criminal records check or the person's representative, the director of job and family services, the director of a county department of job and family services, the center, type A home, or type B home involved, and any court, hearing officer, or other necessary individual involved in a case dealing with a denial of licensure or certification related to the criminal records check.

(G) The director of job and family services shall adopt rules pursuant to Chapter 119. of the Revised Code to implement this section, including rules specifying exceptions to the prohibition in division (D) of this section for persons who have been convicted of an offense listed in that division but who meet standards in regard to rehabilitation set by the department.

(H) As used in this section:

(1) "Criminal records check" has the same meaning as in section 109.572 of the Revised Code.

(2) "Minor drug possession offense" has the same meaning as in section 2925.01 of the Revised Code.

(1999 H 471, eff. 7–1–00; 1996 S 269, eff. 7–1–96; 1996 H 445, eff. 9–3–96; 1995 S 2, eff. 7–1–96; 1994 H 694, eff. 11–11–94; 1993 S 38, eff. 10–29–93)

Note: See also following version of this section, eff. 5–18–05.

5104.013 Criminal records check; disqualification from licensure (later effective date)

Note: See also preceding version of this section, in effect until 5–18–05.

(A)(1) The director of job and family services, as part of the process of licensure of child day-care centers and type A family day-care homes, shall request the superintendent of the bureau of criminal identification and investigation to conduct a criminal records check with respect to the following persons:

(a) Any owner, licensee, or administrator of a child day-care center;

(b) Any owner, licensee, or administrator of a type A family day-care home and any person eighteen years of age or older who resides in a type A family day-care home.

(2) The director of a county department of job and family services, as part of the process of certification of type B family day-care homes, shall request the superintendent of the bureau of criminal identification and investigation to conduct a criminal records check with respect to any authorized provider of a certified type B family day-care home and any person eighteen years of age or older who resides in a certified type B family day-care home.

(3) If the owner, licensee, administrator, or person eighteen years of age or older who is the subject of a criminal records check pursuant to division (A)(1) of this section, or the authorized provider or person eighteen years of age or older who is the subject of a criminal records check pursuant to division (A)(2) of this section, does not present proof that the owner, licensee, administrator, authorized provider, or person has been a resident of this state for the five-year period immediately prior to the date upon which the criminal records check is requested or does not provide evidence that within that five-year period the superintendent of the bureau of criminal identification and investigation has requested information about the owner, licensee, administrator, authorized provider, or person from the federal bureau of investigation in a criminal records check, the director shall request that the superintendent obtain information from the federal bureau of investigation as a part of the criminal records check for the applicant. If the owner, licensee, administrator, authorized provider, or person presents proof that the owner, licensee, administrator, authorized provider, or person has been a resident of this state for that five-year period, the director may request that the superintendent include information from the federal bureau of investigation in the criminal records check.

(B) The director of job and family services or the director of a county department of job and family services shall provide to each person for whom a criminal records check is required under this section a copy of the form prescribed pursuant to division (C)(1) of section 109.572 of the Revised Code and a standard impression sheet to obtain fingerprint impressions prescribed pursuant to division (C)(2) of that section, obtain the completed form and impression sheet from that person, and forward the completed form and impression sheet to the superintendent of the bureau of criminal identification and investigation.

(C) A person who receives pursuant to division (B) of this section a copy of the form and standard impression sheet described in that division and who is requested to complete the form and provide a set of fingerprint impressions shall complete the form or provide all the information necessary to complete the form and shall provide the impression sheet with the impressions of the person's fingerprints. If the person, upon request, fails to provide the information necessary to complete the form or fails to provide impressions of the person's fingerprints, the director may consider the failure as a reason to deny licensure or certification.

(D)(1) Except as provided in rules adopted under division (G) of this section, the director of job and family services shall not grant a license to a child day-care center or type A family day-care home and a county director of job and family services shall not certify a type B family day-care home if a person for whom a criminal records check was required in connection with the center or home previously has been convicted of or pleaded guilty to any of the following:

(a) A violation of section 2903.01, 2903.02, 2903.03, 2903.04, 2903.11, 2903.12, 2903.13, 2903.16, 2903.21, 2903.34, 2905.01, 2905. 02, 2905.05, 2907.02, 2907.03, 2907.04, 2907.05, 2907.06, 2907.07, 2907.08, 2907.09, 2907.21, 2907.22, 2907.23, 2907.25, 2907.31, 2907.32, 2907.321, 2907.322, 2907.323, 2911.01, 2911.02, 2911.11, 2911.12, 2919.12, 2919.22, 2919.24, 2919.25, 2923.12, 2923.13, 2923.161, 2925.02, 2925.03, 2925.04, 2925.05, 2925.06, or 3716.11 of the Revised Code, a violation of section 2905.04 as it existed prior to July 1, 1996, a violation of section 2919.23 of the Revised Code that would have been a violation of section 2905.04 of the Revised Code as it existed prior to July 1, 1996, had the violation been committed prior to that date, a violation of section 2925.11 of the Revised Code that is not a minor drug possession offense, or felonious sexual penetration in violation of former section 2907.12 of the Revised Code;

(b) A violation of an existing or former law of this state, any other state, or the United States that is substantially equivalent to any of the offenses or violations described in division (D)(1)(a) of this section.

(2) In addition to the prohibition described in division (D)(1) of this section, and except as provided in rules adopted under division (G) of this section, the director shall not grant a license to a child day-care center or type A family day-care home and a county director shall not certify a type B family day-care home if an owner, licensee, or administrator of a child day-care center or type A family day-care home or an authorized provider of a certified type B family day-care home previously has been convicted of or pleaded guilty to any of the following:

(a) A violation of section 2913.02, 2913.03, 2913.04, 2913.041, 2913.05, 2913.06, 2913.11, 2913.21, 2913.31, 2913.32, 2913.33, 2913.34, 2913. 40, 2913.41, 2913.42, 2913.43, 2913.44, 2913.441, 2913.45, 2913.46, 2913.47, 2913.48, 2913.49, 2921.11, 2921.13, or 2923.01 of the Revised Code, a violation of section 2923.02 or 2923.03 of the Revised Code that relates to a crime specified in this division or division (D)(1) of this section, or a second violation of section 4511.19 of the Revised Code within five years of the date of application for licensure or certification.

(b) A violation of an existing or former law of this state, any other state, or the United States that is substantially equivalent to any of the offenses or violations described in division (D)(2)(a) of this section.

(E) Each child day-care center, type A family day-care home, and type B family day-care home shall pay to the bureau of criminal identification and investigation the fee prescribed pursuant to division (C)(3) of section 109.572 of the Revised Code for each criminal records check conducted in accordance with that section upon a request made pursuant to division (A) of this section.

(F) The report of any criminal records check conducted by the bureau of criminal identification and investigation in accordance with section 109.572 of the Revised Code and pursuant to a request made under division (A) of this section is not a public record for the purposes of section 149.43 of the Revised Code and shall not be made available to any person other than the person who is the subject of the criminal records check or the person's representative, the director of job and family services, the director of a county department of job and family services, the center, type A home, or type B home involved, and any court, hearing officer, or other necessary individual involved in a case dealing with a denial of licensure or certification related to the criminal records check.

(G) The director of job and family services shall adopt rules pursuant to Chapter 119. of the Revised Code to implement this section, including rules specifying exceptions to the prohibition in division (D) of this section for persons who have been convicted of an offense listed in that division but who meet standards in regard to rehabilitation set by the department.

(H) As used in this section:

(1) "Criminal records check" has the same meaning as in section 109.572 of the Revised Code.

(2) "Minor drug possession offense" has the same meaning as in section 2925.01 of the Revised Code.

(2004 H 11, eff. 5–18–05; 1999 H 471, eff. 7–1–00; 1996 S 269, eff. 7–1–96; 1996 H 445, eff. 9–3–96; 1995 S 2, eff. 7–1–96; 1994 H 694, eff. 11–11–94; 1993 S 38, eff. 10–29–93)

Note: See also preceding version of this section, in effect until 5–18–05.

5104.09 Persons prohibited from employment; statements

Note: See also following version of this section, eff. 5–18–05.

(A)(1) No individual who has been convicted of or pleaded guilty to a violation of section 2903.01, 2903.02, 2903.03, 2903.04, 2903.11, 2903.12, 2903.13, 2903.16, 2903.21, 2903.22, 2903.34, 2905.01, 2905.02, 2905.04, 2905.05, 2905.11, 2907.02, 2907.03, 2907.04, 2907.05, 2907.06, 2907.07, 2907.08, 2907.09, 2907.21, 2907.22, 2907.23, 2907.25, 2907.31, 2907.32, 2907.321, 2907.322, 2907.323, 2909.02, 2909.03, 2909.04, 2909.05, 2911.01, 2911.02, 2911.11, 2911.12, 2917.01, 2917.02, 2917.03, 2917.31, 2919.12, 2919.24, 2919.25, 2921.03, 2921.34, 2921.35, 2923.12, 2923.13, 2923.161, 2919.22, 2925.02, 2925.03, 2925.04, 2925.05, 2925.06, or 3716.11 of the Revised Code, a violation of section 2925.11 of the Revised Code that is not a minor drug possession offense, as defined in section 2925.01 of the Revised Code, felonious sexual penetration in violation of former section 2907.12 of the Revised Code, or a violation of an existing or former law or ordinance of any municipal corporation, this state, any other state, or the United States that is substantially equivalent to any of those violations shall be certified as an in-home aide or be employed in any capacity in or own or operate a child day-care center, type A family day-care home, type B family day-care home, or certified type B family day-care home.

(2) Each employee of a child day-care center and type A home and every person eighteen years of age or older residing in a type A home shall sign a statement on forms prescribed by the director of job and family services attesting to the fact that the employee or resident person has not been convicted of or pleaded guilty to any offense set forth in division (A)(1) of this section and that no child has been removed from the employee's or resident person's home pursuant to section 2151.353 of the Revised Code. Each licensee of a type A home shall sign a statement on a form prescribed by the director attesting to the fact that no person who resides at the type A home and who is under the age of eighteen has been adjudicated a delinquent child for committing a violation of any section listed in division (A)(1) of this section. The statements shall be kept on file at the center or type A home.

(3) Each in-home aide, each authorized provider, and every person eighteen years of age or older residing in a certified type B home shall sign a statement on forms prescribed by the director of job and family services attesting that the aide, provider, or resident person has not been convicted of or pleaded guilty to any offense set forth in division (A)(1) of this section and that no child has been removed from the aide's, provider's, or resident person's home pursuant to section 2151.353 of the Revised Code. Each authorized provider shall sign a statement on a form prescribed by the director attesting to the fact that no person who resides at the certified type B home and who is under the age of eighteen has been adjudicated a delinquent child for committing a violation of any section listed in division (A)(1) of this section. The statements shall be kept on file at the county department of job and family services.

(4) Each administrator and licensee of a center or type A home shall sign a statement on a form prescribed by the director of job and family services attesting that the administrator or licensee has not been convicted of or pleaded guilty to any offense set forth in division (A)(1) of this section and that no child has been removed from the administrator's or licensee's home pursuant to section 2151.353 of the Revised Code. The statement shall be kept on file at the center or type A home.

(B) No in-home aide, no administrator, licensee, authorized provider, or employee of a center, type A home, or certified type B home, and no person eighteen years of age or older residing in a type A home or certified type B home shall withhold information from, or falsify information on, any statement required pursuant to division (A)(2), (3), or (4) of this section.

(C) No administrator, licensee, or child-care staff member shall discriminate in the enrollment of children in a child day-care center upon the basis of race, color, religion, sex, or national origin.

(1999 H 471, eff. 7–1–00; 1996 H 445, eff. 9–3–96; 1995 S 2, eff. 7–1–96; 1993 S 38, eff. 10–29–93; 1985 H 435)

Note: See also following version of this section, eff. 5–18–05.

5104.09 Persons prohibited from employment; statements (later effective date)

Note: See also preceding version of this section, in effect until 5–18–05.

(A)(1) Except as provided in rules adopted pursuant to division (D) of this section:

(a) No individual who has been convicted of or pleaded guilty to a violation of section 2903.01, 2903.02, 2903.03, 2903.04, 2903.11, 2903.12, 2903.13, 2903.16, 2903.21, 2903.22, 2903.34, 2905.01, 2905.02, 2905.04, 2905. 05, 2905.11, 2907.02, 2907.03, 2907.04, 2907.05, 2907.06, 2907.07, 2907.08, 2907.09, 2907.21, 2907.22, 2907.23, 2907.25, 2907.31, 2907.32, 2907.321, 2907.322, 2907.323, 2909.02, 2909.03, 2909.04, 2909.05, 2911.01, 2911.02, 2911.11, 2911.12, 2917.01, 2917.02, 2917.03, 2917.31, 2919.12, 2919.24, 2919. 25, 2921.03, 2921.34, 2921.35, 2923.12, 2923.13, 2923.161, 2919.22, 2925.02, 2925.03, 2925.04, 2925.05, 2925.06, or 3716.11 of the Revised Code, a violation of section 2925.11 of the Revised Code that is not a minor drug possession offense, as defined in section 2925.01 of the Revised Code, felonious sexual penetration in violation of former section 2907.12 of the Revised Code, or a violation of an existing or former law or ordinance of any municipal corporation, this state, any other state, or the United States that is substantially equivalent to any of those violations shall be certified as an in-home aide or be employed in any capacity in or own or operate a child day-care center, type A family day-care home, type B family day-care home, or certified type B family day-care home.

(b) No individual who has been convicted of or pleaded guilty to a violation of section 2913.02, 2913.03, 2913.04, 2913.041, 2913.05, 2913.06, 2913.11, 2913.21, 2913.31, 2913.32, 2913.33, 2913.34, 2913.40, 2913.41, 2913. 42, 2913.43, 2913.44, 2913.441, 2913.45, 2913.46, 2913.47, 2913.48, 2913.49, 2921.11, 2921.13, or 2923.01 of the Revised Code, a violation of section 2923.02 or 2923.03 of the Revised Code that relates to a crime specified in this division or division (A)(1)(a) of this section, a second violation of section 4511.19 of the Revised Code within five years of the date of operation of the child day-care center or family day-care home, or two violations of section 4511.19 of the Revised Code during operation of the center or home, or a violation of an existing or former law of this state, any other state, or the United States that is substantially equivalent to any of those violations shall own or operate a child day-care center, type A family day-care home, type B family day-care home, or certified type B family day-care home.

(2) Each employee of a child day-care center and type A home and every person eighteen years of age or older residing in a type A home shall sign a statement on forms prescribed by the director of job and family services attesting to the fact that the employee or resident person has not been convicted of or pleaded guilty to any offense set forth in division (A)(1)(a) of this section and that no child has been removed from the employee's or resident person's home pursuant to section 2151.353 of the Revised Code. Each licensee of a type A home shall sign a statement on a form prescribed by the director attesting to the fact that no person who resides at the type A home and who is under the age of eighteen has been adjudicated a delinquent child for committing a violation of any section listed in division (A)(1)(a) of this section. The statements shall be kept on file at the center or type A home.

(3) Each in-home aide and every person eighteen years of age or older residing in a certified type B home shall sign a statement on forms prescribed by the director of job and family services attesting that the aide or resident person has not been convicted of or pleaded guilty to any offense set forth in division (A)(1)(a) of this section and that no child has been removed from the aide's or resident person's home pursuant to section 2151.353 of the Revised Code. Each authorized provider shall sign a statement on forms prescribed by the director attesting that the provider has not been convicted of or pleaded guilty to any offense set forth in division (A)(1)(a) or (b) of this section and that no child has been removed from the provider's home pursuant to section 2151.353 of the Revised Code. Each authorized provider shall sign a statement on a form prescribed by the director attesting to the fact that no person who resides at the certified type B home and who is under the age of eighteen has been adjudicated a delinquent child for committing a violation of any section listed in division (A)(1)(a) of this section. The statements shall be kept on file at the county department of job and family services.

(4) Each administrator and licensee of a center or type A home shall sign a statement on a form prescribed by the director of job and family services attesting that the administrator or licensee has not been convicted of or pleaded guilty to any offense set forth in division (A)(1)(a) or (b) of this section and that no child has been removed from the administrator's or licensee's home pursuant to section 2151.353 of the Revised Code. The statement shall be kept on file at the center or type A home.

(B) No in-home aide, no administrator, licensee, authorized provider, or employee of a center, type A home, or certified type B home, and no person eighteen years of age or older residing in a type A home or certified type B home shall withhold information from, or falsify information on, any statement required pursuant to division (A)(2), (3), or (4) of this section.

(C) No administrator, licensee, or child-care staff member shall discriminate in the enrollment of children in a child day-care center upon the basis of race, color, religion, sex, or national origin.

(D) The director of job and family services shall adopt rules pursuant to Chapter 119. of the Revised Code to implement this section, including rules specifying exceptions to the prohibition in division (A)(1) of this section for persons who have been convicted of an offense listed in that division but meet rehabilitation standards set by the department.

(2004 H 11, eff. 5–18–05; 1999 H 471, eff. 7–1–00; 1996 H 445, eff. 9–3–96; 1995 S 2, eff. 7–1–96; 1993 S 38, eff. 10–29–93; 1985 H 435)

Note. See also preceding version of this section, in effect until 5–18–05.

CHAPTER 5119

DEPARTMENT OF MENTAL HEALTH

5119.14 Appointment and qualification of special police

(A) As used in this section, "felony" has the same meaning as in section 109.511 of the Revised Code.

(B)(1) Subject to division (C) of this section, upon the recommendation of the director of mental health, the managing officer of an institution under the jurisdiction of the department of mental health may designate one or more employees to be special police officers of the department. The special police officers shall take an oath of office, wear the badge of office, and give bond for the proper and faithful discharge of their duties in an amount that the director requires.

(2) In accordance with section 109.77 of the Revised Code, the special police officers shall be required to complete successfully a peace officer basic training program approved by the Ohio peace officer training commission and to be certified by the commission. The cost of the training shall be paid by the department of mental health.

(3) Special police officers, on the premises of institutions under the jurisdiction of the department of mental health and subject to the rules of the department, shall protect the property of the institutions and the persons and property of patients in the institutions, suppress riots, disturbances, and breaches of the peace, and enforce the laws of the state and the rules of the department for the preservation of good order. They may arrest any person without a warrant and detain the person until a warrant can be obtained under the circumstances described in division (F) of section 2935.03 of the Revised Code.

(C)(1) The managing officer of an institution under the jurisdiction of the department of mental health shall not designate an employee as a special police officer of the department pursuant to division (B)(1) of this section on a permanent basis, on a temporary basis, for a probationary term, or on other than a permanent basis if the employee previously has been convicted of or has pleaded guilty to a felony.

(2)(a) The managing officer of an institution under the jurisdiction of the department of mental health shall terminate the employment as a special police officer of the department of an employee designated as a special police officer under division (B)(1) of this section if that employee does either of the following:

(i) Pleads guilty to a felony;

(ii) Pleads guilty to a misdemeanor pursuant to a negotiated plea agreement as provided in division (D) of section 2929.43 of the Revised Code in which the employee agrees to surrender the certificate awarded to that employee under section 109.77 of the Revised Code.

(b) The managing officer shall suspend from employment as a special police officer of the department an employee designated as a special police officer under division (B)(1) of this section if that employee is convicted, after trial, of a felony. If the special police officer files an appeal from that conviction and the conviction is upheld by the highest court to which the appeal is taken or if the special police officer does not file a timely appeal, the managing officer shall terminate the employment of that special police officer. If the special police officer files an appeal that results in that special police officer's acquittal of the felony or conviction of a misdemeanor, or in the dismissal of the felony charge against that special police officer, the managing officer shall reinstate that special police officer. A special police officer of the department who is reinstated under division (C)(2)(b) of this section shall not receive any back pay unless that special police officer's conviction of the felony was reversed on appeal, or the felony charge was dismissed, because the court found insufficient evidence to convict the special police officer of the felony.

(3) Division (C) of this section does not apply regarding an offense that was committed prior to January 1, 1997.

(4) The suspension from employment, or the termination of the employment, of a special police officer under division (C)(2) of this section shall be in accordance with Chapter 119. of the Revised Code.

(2002 H 490, eff. 1–1–04; 1996 H 670, eff. 12–2–96; 1996 H 566, eff. 10–16–96; 1993 H 42, eff. 2–9–94; 1992 S 49; 1988 S 156; 1980 H 900, eff. 7–1–80)

CHAPTER 5120

DEPARTMENT OF REHABILITATION AND CORRECTION

ADMINISTRATIVE PROVISIONS

5120.01 Director is executive head of department; powers and duties

The director of rehabilitation and correction is the executive head of the department of rehabilitation and correction. All duties conferred on the various divisions and institutions of the department by law or by order of the director shall be performed under the rules and regulations that the director prescribes and shall be under the director's control. Inmates committed to the department of rehabilitation and correction shall be under the legal custody of the director or the director's designee, and the director or the director's designee shall have power to control transfers of inmates between the several state institutions included under section 5120.05 of the Revised Code.

(2002 H 510, eff. 3–31–03; 1972 H 494, eff. 7–1–72)

5120.011 Rules and sanctions governing frivolous actions or appeals filed by inmate

(A) As used in this section, "civil action or appeal against a government entity or employee," "inmate," "political subdivision," and "employee" have the same meanings as in section 2969.21 of the Revised Code.

(B) The director of rehabilitation and correction may adopt rules under section 5120.01 of the Revised Code to implement the procedures described in sections 2323.51, 2969.22, and 2969.23 of the Revised Code.

(C) The director of rehabilitation and correction shall adopt rules that provide that, if an inmate files a civil action or appeal against a government entity or employee or files a civil action against the state, a political subdivision, or an employee in a federal court and if the court in which the action or appeal is filed dismisses the action or appeal pursuant to section 2969.24 of the Revised Code or the federal court finds the action to be frivolous under 28 U.S.C. 1915(d), the inmate shall be subject to one or more of the following sanctions:

(1) Extra work duty, without compensation, for not more than sixty days;

(2) The loss of commissary privileges for not more than sixty days;

(3) The loss of sundry-package privileges for one time in any calendar year;

(4) The loss of television privileges for not more than sixty days;

(5) The loss of radio privileges for not more than sixty days;

(6) The loss of recreational activity privileges for not more than sixty days.

(1996 H 455, eff. 10–17–96)

5120.02 Assistant director; powers and duties

The assistant director of the department of rehabilitation and correction is hereby excepted from section 121.05 of the Revised Code. The assistant director shall exercise the powers and perform the duties which the director of correction may order and shall act as director in the absence or disability of the director, or in case of a vacancy in the position of director.

(1972 H 494, eff. 7–1–72)

5120.021 Effect of amendments to chapter

Note: See also following version of this section, eff. 5–18–05.

(A) Chapter 5120. of the Revised Code, as it existed prior to July 1, 1996, applies to a person upon whom a court imposed a term of imprisonment prior to July 1, 1996, and a person upon whom a court, on or after July 1, 1996, and in accordance with law existing prior to July 1, 1996, imposed a term of imprisonment for an offense that was committed prior to July 1, 1996.

(B) Chapter 5120. of the Revised Code, as it exists on and after the effective date of this section, applies to a person upon whom a court imposed a stated prison term for an offense committed on or after the effective date of this section.

(1995 S 2, eff. 7–1–96)

Note: See also following version of this section, eff. 5–18–05.

5120.021 Effect of amendments to chapter (later effective date)

Note: See also preceding version of this section, in effect until 5–18–05.

(A) The provisions of Chapter 5120. of the Revised Code, as they existed prior to July 1, 1996, and that address the duration or potential duration of incarceration or parole or other forms of supervised release, apply to all persons upon whom a court imposed a term of imprisonment prior to July 1, 1996, and all persons upon whom a court, on or after July 1, 1996, and in accordance with law existing prior to July 1, 1996, imposed a term of imprisonment for an offense that was committed prior to July 1, 1996.

(B) The provisions of Chapter 5120. of the Revised Code, as they exist on or after July 1, 1996, and that address the duration or potential duration of incarceration or supervised release, apply to all persons upon whom a court imposed a stated prison term for an offense committed on or after July 1, 1996.

(C) Nothing in this section limits or affects the applicability of any provision in Chapter 5120. of the Revised Code, as amended or enacted on or after July 1, 1996, that pertains to an issue other than the duration or potential duration of incarceration or supervised release, to persons in custody or under the supervision of the department of rehabilitation and correction.

(2004 H 525, eff. 5–18–05; 1995 S 2, eff. 7–1–96)

Note: See also preceding version of this section, in effect until 5–18–05.

5120.03 Change of purpose or use of institution or place; elimination of distinction between penal and reformatory institutions; privatization of facility

(A) The director of rehabilitation and correction, by executive order and with the approval of the governor, may change the purpose for which any institution or place under the control of the department of rehabilitation and correction, is being used. The director may designate a new or another use for such institution, if the change of use and new designation has for its objective, improvement in the classification, segregation, care, education, cure, or rehabilitation of persons subject to the control of the department.

(B) The director of rehabilitation and correction, by executive order, issued on or before December 31, 1988, shall eliminate the distinction between penal institutions and reformatory institutions. Notwithstanding any provision of the Revised Code or the Administrative Code to the contrary, upon the issuance of the executive order, any distinction made between the types of prisoners sentenced to or otherwise assigned to the institutions under the control of the department shall be discontinued.

(C) The director may contract under section 9.06 of the Revised Code for the private operation and management of a facility under the control of the department. All inmates assigned to a facility operated and managed by a private contractor remain inmates in the care and custody of the department. The statutes, rules, and policies of the department may apply to the private contractor and any inmate assigned to a facility operated and managed by a private contractor as agreed to in the contract entered into under section 9.06 of the Revised Code.

(1997 H 215, eff. 9–29–97; 1987 H 261, eff. 11–1–87; 1972 H 494)

5120.031 Pilot program of shock incarceration

(A) As used in this section:

(1) "Certificate of high school equivalence" means a statement that is issued by the state board of education or an equivalent agency of another state and that indicates that its holder has achieved the equivalent of a high school education as measured by scores obtained on the tests of general educational development published by the American council on education.

(2) "Certificate of adult basic education" means a statement that is issued by the department of rehabilitation and correction through the Ohio central school system approved by the state board of education and that indicates that its holder has achieved a 6.0 grade level, or higher, as measured by scores of nationally standardized or recognized tests.

(3) "Deadly weapon" and "firearm" have the same meanings as in section 2923.11 of the Revised Code.

(4) "Eligible offender" means a person, other than one who is ineligible to participate in an intensive program prison under the criteria specified in section 5120.032 of the Revised Code, who has been convicted of or pleaded guilty to, and has been sentenced for, a felony.

(5) "Shock incarceration" means the program of incarceration that is established pursuant to the rules of the department of rehabilitation and correction adopted under this section.

(B)(1) The director of rehabilitation and correction, by rules adopted under Chapter 119. of the Revised Code, shall establish a pilot program of shock incarceration that may be used for offenders who are sentenced to serve a term of imprisonment under the custody of the department of rehabilitation and correction, whom the department determines to be eligible offenders, and whom the department, subject to the approval of the sentencing judge, may permit to serve their sentence as a sentence of shock incarceration in accordance with this section.

(2) The rules for the pilot program shall require that the program be established at an appropriate state correctional institution designated by the director and that the program consist of both of the following for each eligible offender whom the department, with the approval of the sentencing judge, permits to serve the eligible offender's sentence as a sentence of shock incarceration:

(a) A period of imprisonment at that institution of ninety days that shall consist of a military style combination of discipline, physical training, and hard labor and substance abuse education, employment skills training, social skills training, and psychological treatment. During the ninety-day period, the department may permit an eligible offender to participate in a self-help program. Additionally, during the ninety-day period, an eligible offender who holds a high school diploma or a certificate of high school equivalence may be permitted to tutor other eligible offenders in the shock incarceration program. If an eligible offender does not hold a high school diploma or certificate of high school equivalence, the eligible offender may elect to participate in an education program that is designed to award a certificate of adult basic education or an education program that is designed to award a certificate of high school equivalence to those eligible offenders who successfully complete the education program, whether the completion occurs during or subsequent to the ninety-day period. To the extent possible, the department shall use as teachers in the education program persons who have been issued a license pursuant to sections 3319.22 to 3319.31 of the Revised Code, who have volunteered their services to the education program, and who satisfy any other criteria specified in the rules for the pilot project.

(b) Immediately following the ninety-day period of imprisonment, and notwithstanding any other provision governing the early release of a prisoner from imprisonment or the transfer of a prisoner to transitional control, one of the following, as determined by the director:

(i) An intermediate, transitional type of detention for the period of time determined by the director and, immediately following the intermediate, transitional type of detention, a release under a post-release control sanction imposed in accordance with section 2967.28 of the Revised Code. The period of intermediate, transitional type of detention imposed by the director under this division may be in a halfway house, in a community-based correctional facility and program or district community-based correctional facility and program established under sections 2301.51 to 2301.56 of the Revised Code, or in any other facility approved by the director that provides for detention to serve as a transition between imprisonment in a state correctional institution and release from imprisonment.

(ii) A release under a post-release control sanction imposed in accordance with section 2967.28 of the Revised Code.

(3) The rules for the pilot program also shall include, but are not limited to, all of the following:

(a) Rules identifying the locations within the state correctional institution designated by the director that will be used for eligible offenders serving a sentence of shock incarceration;

(b) Rules establishing specific schedules of discipline, physical training, and hard labor for eligible offenders serving a sentence of shock incarceration, based upon the offender's physical condition and needs;

(c) Rules establishing standards and criteria for the department to use in determining which eligible offenders the department will permit to serve their sentence of imprisonment as a sentence of shock incarceration;

(d) Rules establishing guidelines for the selection of post-release control sanctions for eligible offenders;

(e) Rules establishing procedures for notifying sentencing courts of the performance of eligible offenders serving their sentences of imprisonment as a sentence of shock incarceration;

(f) Any other rules that are necessary for the proper conduct of the pilot program.

(C)(1) If an offender is sentenced to a term of imprisonment under the custody of the department, if the sentencing court either recommends the offender for placement in a program of shock incarceration under this section or makes no recommendation on placement of the offender, and if the department determines that the offender is an eligible offender for placement in a program of shock incarceration under this section, the department may permit the eligible offender to serve the sentence in a program of shock incarceration, in accordance with division (K) of section 2929.14 of the Revised Code, with this section, and with the rules adopted under this section. If the sentencing court disapproves placement of the offender in a program of shock incarceration, the department shall not place the offender in any program of shock incarceration.

If the sentencing court recommends the offender for placement in a program of shock incarceration and if the department subsequently places the offender in the recommended program, the department shall notify the court of the offender's placement in the recommended program and shall include with the notice a brief description of the placement.

If the sentencing court recommends placement of the offender in a program of shock incarceration and the department for any reason does not subsequently place the offender in the recommended program, the department shall send a notice to the court indicating why the offender was not placed in the recommended program.

If the sentencing court does not make a recommendation on the placement of an offender in a program of shock incarceration and if the department determines that the offender is an eligible offender for placement in a program of that nature, the department shall screen the offender and determine if the offender is suited for the program of shock incarceration. If the offender is suited for the program of shock incarceration, at least three weeks prior to permitting an eligible offender to serve the sentence in a program of shock incarceration, the department shall notify the sentencing court of the proposed placement of the offender in the program and shall include with the notice a brief description of the placement. The court shall have ten days from receipt of the notice to disapprove the placement. If the sentencing court disapproves of the placement, the department shall not permit the eligible offender to serve the sentence in a program of shock incarceration. If the judge does not timely disapprove of placement of the offender in the program of shock incarceration, the department may proceed with plans for placement of the offender.

If the department determines that the offender is not eligible for placement in a program of shock incarceration, the department shall not place the offender in any program of shock incarceration.

(2) If the department permits an eligible offender to serve the eligible offender's sentence of imprisonment as a sentence of shock incarceration and the eligible offender does not satisfactorily complete the entire period of imprisonment described in division (B)(2)(a) of this section, the offender shall be removed from the pilot program for shock incarceration and shall be required to serve the remainder of the offender's sentence of imprisonment imposed by the sentencing court as a regular term of imprisonment. If the eligible offender commences a period of post-release control described in division (B)(2)(b) of this section and violates the conditions of that post-release control, the eligible offender shall be subject to the provisions of sections 2929.141, 2967.15, and 2967.28 of the Revised Code regarding violation of post-release control sanctions.

(3) If an eligible offender's stated prison term expires at any time during the eligible offender's participation in the shock incarceration program, the adult parole authority shall terminate the eligible offender's participation in the program and shall issue to the eligible offender a certificate of expiration of the stated prison term.

(D) The director shall keep sentencing courts informed of the performance of eligible offenders serving their sentences of imprisonment as a sentence of shock incarceration, including, but not limited to, notice of eligible offenders who fail to satisfactorily complete their entire sentence of shock incarceration or who satisfactorily complete their entire sentence of shock incarceration.

(E) Within a reasonable period of time after November 20, 1990, the director shall appoint a committee to search for one or more suitable sites at which one or more programs of shock incarceration, in addition to the pilot program required by division (B)(1) of this section, may be established. The search committee shall consist of the director or the director's designee, as chairperson; employees of the department of rehabilitation and correction appointed by the director; and any other persons that the director, in the director's discretion, appoints. In searching for such sites, the search committee shall give preference to any site owned by the state or any other governmental entity and to any existing structure that reasonably could be renovated, enlarged, converted, or remodeled for purposes of establishing such a program. The search committee shall prepare a report concerning its activities and, on the earlier of the day that is twelve months after the first day on which an eligible offender began serving a sentence of shock incarceration under the pilot program or January 1, 1992, shall file the report with the president and the minority leader of the senate, the speaker and the minority leader of the house of representatives, the members of the senate who were members of the senate judiciary committee in the 118th general assembly or their successors, and the members of the house of representatives who were members of the select committee to hear drug legislation that was established in the 118th general assembly or their successors. Upon the filing of the report, the search committee shall terminate. The report required by this division shall contain all of the following:

(1) A summary of the process used by the search committee in performing its duties under this division;

(2) A summary of all of the sites reviewed by the search committee in performing its duties under this division, and the benefits and disadvantages it found relative to the establishment of a program of shock incarceration at each such site;

(3) The findings and recommendations of the search committee as to the suitable site or sites, if any, at which a program of shock incarceration, in addition to the pilot program required by division (B)(1) of this section, may be established.

(F) The director periodically shall review the pilot program for shock incarceration required to be established by division (B)(1) of this section. The director shall prepare a report relative to the pilot program and, on the earlier of the day that is twelve months after the first day on which an eligible offender began serving a sentence of shock incarceration under the pilot program or January 1, 1992, shall file the report with the president and the minority leader of the senate, the speaker and the minority leader of the house of representatives, the members of the senate who were members of the senate judiciary committee in the 118th general assembly or their successors, and the members of the house of representatives who were members of the select committee to hear drug legislation that was established in the 118th general assembly or their successors. The pilot program shall not terminate at the time of the filing of the report, but shall continue in operation in accordance with this section. The report required by this division shall include all of the following:

(1) A summary of the pilot program as initially established, a summary of all changes in the pilot program made during the period covered by the report and the reasons for the changes, and a summary of the pilot program as it exists on the date of preparation of the report;

(2) A summary of the effectiveness of the pilot program, in the opinion of the director and employees of the department involved in its operation;

(3) An analysis of the total cost of the pilot program, of its cost per inmate who was permitted to serve a sentence of shock incarceration and who served the entire sentence of shock incarceration, and of its cost per inmate who was permitted to serve a sentence of shock incarceration;

(4) A summary of the standards and criteria used by the department in determining which eligible offenders were permitted to serve their sentence of imprisonment as a sentence of shock incarceration;

(5) A summary of the characteristics of the eligible offenders who were permitted to serve their sentence of imprisonment as a sentence of shock incarceration, which summary shall include, but not be limited to, a listing of every offense of which any such eligible offender was convicted or to which any such eligible offender pleaded guilty and in relation to which the eligible offender served a sentence of shock incarceration, and the total number of such eligible offenders who were convicted of or pleaded guilty to each such offense;

(6) A listing of the number of eligible offenders who were permitted to serve a sentence of shock incarceration and who did not serve the entire sentence of shock incarceration, and, to the extent possible, a summary of the length of the terms of imprisonment served by such eligible offenders after they were removed from the pilot program;

(7) A summary of the effect of the pilot program on overcrowding at state correctional institutions;

(8) To the extent possible, an analysis of the rate of recidivism of eligible offenders who were permitted to serve a sentence of shock incarceration and who served the entire sentence of shock incarceration;

(9) Recommendations as to legislative changes to the pilot program that would assist in its operation or that could further alleviate overcrowding at state correctional institutions, and recommendations as to whether the pilot program should be expanded.

(2002 H 327, eff. 7–8–02; 1999 S 107, eff. 3–23–00; 1997 S 111, eff. 3–17–98; 1996 S 230, eff. 10–29–96; 1996 S 269, eff. 7–1–96; 1995 S 2, eff. 7–1–96; 1994 H 571, eff. 10–6–94; 1994 H 314, eff. 9–29–94; 1990 S 258, eff. 11–20–90)

5120.032 Intensive program prisons

(A) No later than January 1, 1998, the department of rehabilitation and correction shall develop and implement intensive program prisons for male and female prisoners other than prisoners described in division (B)(2) of this section. The intensive program prisons shall include institutions at which imprisonment of the type described in division (B)(2)(a) of section 5120.031 of the Revised Code is provided and prisons that focus on educational achievement, vocational training, alcohol and other drug abuse treatment, community service and conservation work, and other intensive regimens or combinations of intensive regimens.

(B)(1)(a) Except as provided in division (B)(2) of this section, if an offender is sentenced to a term of imprisonment under the custody of the department, if the sentencing court either recommends the prisoner for placement in the intensive program prison under this section or makes no recommendation on placement of the prisoner, and if the department determines that the prisoner is eligible for placement in an intensive program prison under this section, the department may place the prisoner in an intensive program prison established pursuant to division (A) of this section. If the sentencing court disapproves placement of the prisoner in an intensive program prison, the department shall not place the prisoner in any intensive program prison.

If the sentencing court recommends a prisoner for placement in an intensive program prison and if the department subsequently places the prisoner in the recommended prison, the department shall notify the court of the prisoner's placement in the recommended intensive program prison and shall include with the notice a brief description of the placement.

If the sentencing court recommends placement of a prisoner in an intensive program prison and the department for any reason does not subsequently place the prisoner in the recommended prison, the department shall send a notice to the court indicating why the prisoner was not placed in the recommended prison.

If the sentencing court does not make a recommendation on the placement of a prisoner in an intensive program prison and if the department determines that the prisoner is eligible for placement in a prison of that nature, the department shall screen the prisoner and determine if the prisoner is suited for the prison. If the prisoner is suited for the intensive program prison, at least three weeks prior to placing the prisoner in the prison, the department shall notify the sentencing court of the proposed placement of the prisoner in the intensive program prison and shall include with the notice a brief description of the placement. The court shall have ten days from receipt of the notice to disapprove the placement. If the sentencing court disapproves the placement, the department shall not proceed with it. If the sentencing court does not timely disapprove of the placement, the department may proceed with plans for it.

If the department determines that a prisoner is not eligible for placement in an intensive program prison, the department shall not place the prisoner in any intensive program prison.

(b) The department may reduce the stated prison term of a prisoner upon the prisoner's successful completion of a ninety-day period in an intensive program prison. A prisoner whose term has been so reduced shall be required to serve an intermediate, transitional type of detention followed by a release under post-release control sanctions or, in the alternative, shall be placed under post-release control sanctions, as described in division (B)(2)(b)(ii) of section 5120.031 of the Revised Code. In either case, the placement under post-release control sanctions shall be under terms set by the parole board in accordance with section 2967.28 of the Revised Code and shall be subject to the provisions of that section and section 2929.141 of the Revised Code with respect to a violation of any post-release control sanction.

(2) A prisoner who is in any of the following categories is not eligible to participate in an intensive program prison established pursuant to division (A) of this section:

(a) The prisoner is serving a prison term for aggravated murder, murder, or a felony of the first or second degree or a comparable offense under the law in effect prior to July 1, 1996, or the prisoner previously has been imprisoned for aggravated murder, murder, or a felony of the first or second degree or a comparable offense under the law in effect prior to July 1, 1996.

(b) The prisoner is serving a mandatory prison term, as defined in section 2929.01 of the Revised Code.

(c) The prisoner is serving a prison term for a felony of the third, fourth, or fifth degree that either is a sex offense, an offense betraying public trust, or an offense in which the prisoner caused or attempted to cause actual physical harm to a person, the prisoner is serving a prison term for a comparable offense under the law in effect prior to July 1, 1996, or the prisoner previously has been imprisoned for an offense of that type or a comparable offense under the law in effect prior to July 1, 1996.

(d) The prisoner is serving a mandatory prison term in prison for a third or fourth degree felony OVI offense, as defined in section 2929.01 of the Revised Code, that was imposed pursuant to division (G)(2) of section 2929.13 of the Revised Code.

(C) Upon the implementation of intensive program prisons pursuant to division (A) of this section, the department at all times shall maintain intensive program prisons sufficient in number to reduce the prison terms of at least three hundred fifty prisoners who are eligible for reduction of their stated prison terms as a result of their completion of a regimen in an intensive program prison under this section.

(2002 S 123, eff. 1-1-04; 2002 H 327, eff. 7-8-02; 1999 S 22, eff. 5-17-00; 1999 S 107, eff. 3-23-00; 1996 S 166, eff. 10-17-96; 1996 S 269, eff. 7-1-96; 1995 S 2, eff. 7-1-96)

5120.033 Intensive program prisons for fourth degree felony OVI offenders

(A) As used in this section, "third degree felony OVI offense" and "fourth degree felony OVI offense" have the same meanings as in section 2929.01 of the Revised Code.

(B) Within eighteen months after October 17, 1996, the department of rehabilitation and correction shall develop and implement intensive program prisons for male and female prisoners who are sentenced pursuant to division (G)(2) of section 2929.13 of the Revised Code to a mandatory prison term for a third or fourth degree felony OVI offense. The department shall contract pursuant to section 9.06 of the Revised Code for the private operation and management of the initial intensive program prison established under this section and may contract pursuant to that section for the private operation and management of any other intensive program prison established under this section. The intensive program prisons established under this section shall include prisons that focus on educational achievement, vocational training, alcohol and other drug abuse treatment, community service and conservation work, and other intensive regimens or combinations of intensive regimens.

(C) Except as provided in division (D) of this section, the department may place a prisoner who is sentenced to a mandatory prison term for a third or fourth degree felony OVI offense in an intensive program prison established pursuant to division (B) of this section if the sentencing judge, upon notification by the department of its intent to place the prisoner in an intensive program prison, does not notify the department that the judge disapproves the placement. If the stated prison term imposed on a prisoner who is so placed is longer than the mandatory prison term that is required to be imposed on the prisoner, the department may reduce the stated prison term upon the prisoner's successful completion of the prisoner's mandatory prison term in an intensive program prison. A prisoner whose term has been so reduced shall be required to serve an intermediate, transitional type of detention followed by a release under post-release control sanctions or, in the alternative, shall be placed under post-release control sanctions, as described in division (B)(2)(b)(ii) of section 5120.031 of the Revised Code. In either case, the placement under post-release control sanctions shall be under terms set by the parole board in accordance with section 2967.28 of the Revised Code and shall be subject to the provisions of that section and section 2929.141 of the Revised Code with respect to a violation of any post-release control sanction. Upon the establishment of the initial intensive program prison pursuant to division (B) of this section that is privately operated and managed by a contractor pursuant to a contract entered into under section 9.06 of the Revised Code, the department shall comply with divisions (G)(2)(a) and (b) of section 2929.13 of the Revised Code in placing prisoners in intensive program prisons under this section.

(D) A prisoner who is sentenced to a mandatory prison term for a third or fourth degree felony OVI offense is not eligible to participate in an intensive program prison established under division (B) of this section if any of the following applies regarding the prisoner:

(1) In addition to the mandatory prison term for the third or fourth degree felony OVI offense, the prisoner also is serving a prison term of a type described in division (B)(2)(a), (b), or (c) of section 5120.032 of the Revised Code.

(2) The prisoner previously has been imprisoned for an offense of a type described in division (B)(2)(a) or (c) of section 5120.032 of the Revised Code or a comparable offense under the law in effect prior to July 1, 1996.

(E) Intensive program prisons established under division (B) of this section are not subject to section 5120.032 of the Revised Code.

(2002 S 123, eff. 1–1–04; 2002 H 327, eff. 7–8–02; 1999 S 22, eff. 5–17–00; 1998 H 293, eff. 3–17–98; 1996 S 166, eff. 10–17–96)

5120.04 Assignment of labor to public works

The department of rehabilitation and correction, with the approval of the governor and in accordance with rules adopted pursuant to division (B) of section 5145.03 of the Revised Code, may assign prisoners who are committed or transferred to institutions under the administration of the department to perform labor on any public work of the state.

(1980 H 654, eff. 4–9–82; 1972 H 494)

5120.05 Maintenance of institutions; naming institutions; transfer of children from youth services department

The department of rehabilitation and correction may maintain, operate, manage, and govern all state institutions for the custody, control, training, and rehabilitation of persons convicted of crime and sentenced to correctional institutions.

The department may designate correctional institutions by appropriate respective names.

The department may receive from the department of youth services any children in the custody of the department of youth services, committed to the department of rehabilitation and correction by the department of youth services, upon the terms and conditions that are agreed upon by the departments.

(1997 S 111, eff. 3–17–98; 1994 H 571, eff. 10–6–94; 1981 H 440, eff. 11–23–81; 1972 H 494)

5120.051 Care of mentally ill and mentally retarded offenders

The department of rehabilitation and correction shall provide for the needs of mentally ill and mentally retarded persons who are incarcerated in state correctional institutions. The department may designate an institution or a unit within an institution for the custody, care, special training, treatment, and rehabilitation of mentally ill or mentally retarded persons.

(1996 S 310, eff. 6–20–96; 1994 H 571, eff. 10–6–94)

5120.06 Divisions of rehabilitation and correction department

(A) The following divisions are hereby established in the department of rehabilitation and correction:

(1) The division of business administration;

(2) The division of parole and community services.

(B) The director of rehabilitation and correction may establish offices, divisions in addition to those specified in division (A) of this section, bureaus, and other administrative units within the department of rehabilitation and correction and prescribe their powers and duties.

(1997 S 111, eff. 3–17–98; 1972 H 494, eff. 7–1–72)

MISCELLANEOUS PROVISIONS

5120.08 Bond of employees

The department of rehabilitation and correction shall require any of its employees and each officer and employee of every institution under its control who may be charged with custody or control of any money or property belonging to the state or who is required to give bond, to give a surety company bond, properly conditioned, in a sum to be fixed by the department which when approved by the department, shall be filed in the office of the secretary of state. The cost of such bonds, when approved by the department, shall be paid from funds available for the department. The bonds required or authorized by this section may, in the discretion of the director of rehabilitation and correction, be individual, schedule, or blanket bonds.

(1972 H 494, eff. 7–1–72)

5120.09 Duties of division of business administration

Under the supervision and control of the director of rehabilitation and correction, the division of business administration shall do all of the following:

(A) Submit the budgets for the several divisions of the department of rehabilitation and correction, as prepared by the respective chiefs of those divisions, to the director. The director, with the assistance of the chief of the division of business administration, shall compile a departmental budget that contains all proposals submitted by the chiefs of the divisions and shall forward the departmental budget to the governor with comments and recommendations that the director considers necessary.

(B) Maintain accounts and records and compile statistics that the director prescribes;

(C) Under the control of the director, coordinate and make the necessary purchases and requisitions for the department and its divisions, except as provided under section 5119.16 of the Revised Code;

(D) Administer within this state federal criminal justice acts that the governor requires the department to administer. In order to improve the criminal justice system of this state, the division of business administration shall apply for, allocate, disburse, and account for grants that are made available pursuant to those federal criminal justice acts and grants that are made available from other federal government sources, state government sources, or private sources. As used in this division, "criminal justice system" and "federal criminal justice acts" have the same meanings as in section 181.51 of the Revised Code.

(E) Audit the activities of governmental entities, persons as defined in section 1.59 of the Revised Code, and other types of nongovernmental entities that are financed in whole or in part by funds that the department allocates or disburses and that are derived from grants described in division (D) of this section;

(F) Enter into contracts, including contracts with federal, state, or local governmental entities, persons as defined in section 1.59 of the Revised Code, foundations, and other types of nongovernmental entities, that are necessary for the department to carry out its duties and that neither the director nor another section of the Revised Code authorizes another division of the department to enter;

(G) Exercise other powers and perform other duties that the director may assign to the division of business administration.

(1997 H 215, eff. 9–29–97; 1983 H 291, eff. 7–1–83; 1981 H 1; 1972 H 494)

5120.091 Education services fund

There is hereby created in the state treasury the education services fund. The department of rehabilitation and correction shall deposit into the fund all state revenues it receives from the Ohio department of education. Any money in the fund shall solely be used to pay educational expenses incurred by the department.

(1994 H 715, eff. 7–22–94)

5120.10 Minimum standards for jails; parole and community services division

(A)(1) The director of rehabilitation and correction, by rule, shall promulgate minimum standards for jails in Ohio, including minimum security jails dedicated under section 341.34 or 753.21 of the Revised Code. Whenever the director files a rule or an amendment to a rule in final form with both the secretary of state and the director of the legislative service commission pursuant to section 111.15 of the Revised Code, the director of rehabilitation and correction promptly shall send a copy of the rule or amendment, if the rule or amendment pertains to minimum jail standards, by ordinary mail to the political subdivisions or affiliations of political subdivisions that operate jails to which the standards apply.

(2) The rules promulgated in accordance with division (A)(1) of this section shall serve as criteria for the investigative and supervisory powers and duties vested by division (D) of this section in the division of parole and community services of the department of rehabilitation and correction or in another division of the department to which those powers and duties are assigned.

(B) The director may initiate an action in the court of common pleas of the county in which a facility that is subject to the rules promulgated under division (A)(1) of this section is situated to enjoin compliance with the minimum standards for jails or with the minimum standards and minimum renovation, modification, and construction criteria for minimum security jails.

(C) Upon the request of an administrator of a jail facility, the chief executive of a municipal corporation, or a board of county commissioners, the director of rehabilitation and correction or the director's designee shall grant a variance from the minimum standards for jails in Ohio for a facility that is subject to one of those minimum standards when the director determines that strict compliance with the minimum standards would cause unusual, practical difficulties or financial hardship, that existing or alternative practices meet the intent of the minimum standards, and that granting a variance would not seriously affect the security of the facility, the supervision of the inmates, or the safe, healthful operation of the facility. If the director or the director's designee denies a variance, the applicant may appeal the denial pursuant to section 119.12 of the Revised Code.

(D) The following powers and duties shall be exercised by the division of parole and community services unless assigned to another division by the director:

(1) The investigation and supervision of county and municipal jails, workhouses, minimum security jails, and other correctional institutions and agencies;

(2) The review and approval of plans submitted to the department of rehabilitation and correction pursuant to division (E) of this section;

(3) The management and supervision of the adult parole authority created by section 5149.02 of the Revised Code;

(4) The review and approval of proposals for community-based correctional facilities and programs and district community-based correctional facilities and programs that are submitted pursuant to division (B) of section 2301.51 of the Revised Code;

(5) The distribution of funds made available to the division for purposes of assisting in the renovation, maintenance, and operation of community-based correctional facilities and programs and district community-based correctional facilities and programs in accordance with section 5120.112 of the Revised Code;

(6) The performance of the duty imposed upon the department of rehabilitation and correction in section 5149.31 of the Revised Code to establish and administer a program of subsidies to eligible municipal corporations, counties, and groups of contiguous counties for the development, implementation, and operation of community-based corrections programs;

(7) Licensing halfway houses and community residential centers for the care and treatment of adult offenders in accordance with section 2967.14 of the Revised Code;

(8) Contracting with a public or private agency or a department or political subdivision of the state that operates a licensed halfway house or community residential center for the provision of housing, supervision, and other services to parolees, releasees, persons placed under a residential sanction, persons under transitional control, and other eligible offenders in accordance with section 2967.14 of the Revised Code.

Other powers and duties may be assigned by the director of rehabilitation and correction to the division of parole and community services. This section does not apply to the department of youth services or its institutions or employees.

(E) No plan for any new jail, workhouse, or lockup, and no plan for a substantial addition or alteration to an existing jail, workhouse, or lockup, shall be adopted unless the officials responsible for adopting the plan have submitted the plan to the department of rehabilitation and correction for approval, and the department has approved the plan as provided in division (D)(2) of this section.

(2002 H 490, eff. 1–1–04; 2001 H 269, eff. 7–24–02; 1996 H 480, eff. 10–16–96; 1994 H 571, eff. 10–6–94; 1992 S 351, eff. 7–1–92; 1990 S 131; 1982 S 23; 1981 H 440; 1972 H 494)

HALFWAY HOUSE FACILITIES

5120.102 Definitions

As used in sections 5120.102 to 5120.105 of the Revised Code:

(A) "Private, nonprofit organization" means a private association, organization, corporation, or other entity that is exempt from federal income taxation under section 501(a) and is described in section 501(c) of the "Internal Revenue Code of 1986," 100 Stat. 2085, 26 U.S.C.A. 501, as amended.

(B) "Governmental agency" means a state agency; a municipal corporation, county, township, other political subdivision or special district in this state established by or pursuant to law, or a combination of those political subdivisions or special districts; the United States or a department, division, or agency of the United States; or an agency, commission, or authority established pursuant to an interstate compact or agreement.

(C) "State agency" means the state or one of its branches, offices, boards, commissions, authorities, departments, divisions, or other units or agencies of the state.

(D) "Halfway house organization" means a private, nonprofit organization or a governmental agency that provides programs or activities in areas directly concerned with housing and monitoring offenders who are under the community supervision of the department of rehabilitation and correction or whom a court places in a halfway house pursuant to section 2929.16 or 2929.26 of the Revised Code.

(E) "Halfway house facility" means a capital facility in this state to which all of the following apply:

(1) The construction of the capital facility is authorized or funded by the general assembly pursuant to division (C) of section 5120.105 of the Revised Code.

(2) The state owns or has a sufficient real property interest in the capital facility or in the site of the capital facility for a period of not less than the greater of the useful life of the capital facility, as determined by the director of budget and management using the guidelines for maximum maturities as provided under divisions (B), (C), and (E) of section 133.20 of the Revised Code and certified to the department of rehabilitation and correction and the Ohio building authority, or the final maturity of obligations issued by the Ohio building authority to finance the capital facility.

(3) The capital facility is managed directly by, or by contract with, the department of rehabilitation and correction and is used for housing offenders who are under the community supervision of the department of rehabilitation and correction or whom a court places in a halfway house pursuant to section 2929.16 or 2929.26 of the Revised Code.

(F) "Construction" includes acquisition, demolition, reconstruction, alteration, renovation, remodeling, enlargement, improvement, site improvements, and related equipping and furnishing.

(G) "General building services" means general building services for a halfway house facility that include, but are not limited to, general custodial care, security, maintenance, repair, painting, decoration, cleaning, utilities, fire safety, grounds and site maintenance and upkeep, and plumbing.

(H) "Manage," "operate," or "management" means the provision of, or the exercise of control over the provision of, activities that relate to the housing of offenders in correctional facilities, including, but not limited to, providing for release services for offenders who are under the community supervision of the department of rehabilitation and correction or are placed by a court in a halfway house pursuant to section 2929.16 or 2929.26 of the Revised Code, and who reside in halfway house facilities.

(2002 H 490, eff. 1–1–04; 1997 S 111, eff. 3–17–98; 1996 S 269, eff. 7–1–96; 1995 H 117, eff. 6–30–95)

5120.103 Application for construction

(A) To the extent that funds are available, the department of rehabilitation and correction, in accordance with this section and sections 5120.104 and 5120.105 of the Revised Code, may construct or provide for the construction of halfway house facilities for offenders whom a court places in a halfway house pursuant to section 2929.16 or 2929.26 of the Revised Code or who are eligible for community supervision by the department of rehabilitation and correction.

(B) A halfway house organization that seeks to assist in the program planning of a halfway house facility described in division (A) of this section shall file an application with the director of rehabilitation and correction as set forth in a request for proposal. Upon the submission of an application, the division of parole and community services shall review it and, if the division believes it is appropriate, shall submit a recommendation for its approval to the director. When the division submits a recommendation for approval of an application, the director may approve the application. The director shall not take action or fail to take action, or permit the taking of action or the failure to take action, with respect to halfway house facilities that would adversely affect the exclusion of interest on public obligations or on fractionalized interests in public obligations from gross income for federal income tax purposes, or the classification or qualification of the public obligations or the interest on or fractionalized interests in public obligations for, or their exemption from, other treatment under the Internal Revenue Code.

(C) The director of rehabilitation and correction and the halfway house organization may enter into an agreement establishing terms for the program planning of the halfway house facility. Any terms so established shall conform to the terms of any covenant or agreement pertaining to an obligation from which the funds used for the construction of the halfway house facility are derived.

(D) The director of rehabilitation and correction, in accordance with Chapter 119. of the Revised Code, shall adopt rules that specify procedures by which a halfway house organization may apply for a contract for program planning of a halfway house facility constructed under this section, procedures for the department to follow in considering an application, criteria for granting approval of an application, and any other rules that are necessary for the selection of program planners of a halfway house facility.

(2002 H 490, eff. 1–1–04; 1997 S 111, eff. 3–17–98; 1996 S 269, eff. 7–1–96; 1995 S 2, eff. 7–1–96; 1995 H 117, eff. 9–29–95; 1992 H 904, eff. 12–22–92)

5120.104 Acquisition of capital facilities or sites

(A) It is hereby declared to be a public purpose and an essential governmental function of the state that the department of rehabilitation and correction, in the name of the state and for the use and benefit of the department, purchase, acquire, construct, own, lease, or sublease capital facilities or sites for capital facilities for use as halfway house facilities.

(B) The director of rehabilitation and correction may lease or sublease capital facilities or sites for capital facilities under division (A) of this section to or from, and may make any other agreement with respect to the purchase, construction, management, or operation of those capital facilities with, a halfway house organization or the Ohio building authority. The director may make any lease, sublease, or other agreement under this division without the necessity for advertisement, auction, competitive bidding, court order, or other action or formality otherwise required by law. Notwithstanding any other provision of the Revised Code, the director shall make each lease or sublease to or from the Ohio building authority in accordance with division (D) of section 152.24 of the Revised Code.

(C) The director, by a sale, lease, sublease, release, or other agreement, may dispose of real or personal property or a lesser interest in real or personal property that is held or owned by the state for the use and benefit of the department, if the department does not need the property or interest for its purposes. The department shall make a sale, lease, sublease, release, or other agreement under this division upon the terms that it determines, subject to the approval by the governor in the case of a sale, lease, sublease, release, or other agreement regarding real property or an interest in real property. The director may make a lease, sublease, or other grant of use of property or an interest in property under this division without the necessity for advertisement, auction, competitive bidding, court order, or other action or formality otherwise required by law.

(D) The director may grant an easement or other interest in real property held by the state for the use and benefit of the department if that easement or interest will not interfere with the use of the property as a halfway house facility.

(E) All property purchased, acquired, constructed, owned, leased, or subleased by the department in the exercise of its powers and duties are public property used exclusively for a public purpose, and that property and the income derived by the department from the property are exempt from all taxation within this state, including without limitation, ad valorem and excise taxes.

(1997 S 111, eff. 3–17–98; 1995 H 117, eff. 9–29–95)

5120.105 Construction services

(A) The department of administrative services shall provide for the construction of a halfway house facility in conformity with Chapter 153. of the Revised Code, except that construction services may be provided by the department of rehabilitation and correction.

(B) The director of rehabilitation and correction may enter into an agreement with a halfway house organization for the management of a halfway house facility. The halfway house organization that occupies, will occupy, or is responsible for the management of a halfway house facility shall pay the costs of management of and general building services for the halfway house facility as provided in an agreement between the department of rehabilitation and correction and the halfway house organization.

(C) No state funds, including state bond proceeds, shall be spent on the construction of a halfway house facility under sections 5120.102 to 5120.105 of the Revised Code, unless the general assembly has specifically authorized the spending of money on, or has made an appropriation to the department of rehabilitation and correction for, the construction of the halfway house facility or rental payments relating to the financing of the construction of that facility. An authorization to spend money or an appropriation for planning a halfway house facility does not constitute an authorization to spend money on, or an appropriation for, the construction of that facility. Capital funds for the construction of halfway house facilities under sections 5120.102 to 5120.105 of the Revised Code shall be paid from the adult correctional building fund created by the general assembly in the custody of the state treasurer.

(1997 S 111, eff. 3–17–98; 1995 H 117, eff. 9–29–95)

GENERAL PROVISIONS

5120.11 Bureau of examination and classification; duties

Within the department of rehabilitation and correction, there shall be established and maintained a bureau of examination and classification. The bureau shall conduct or provide for sociological, psychological, and psychiatric examination of each inmate of the correctional institutions. The examination shall be made as soon as possible after each inmate is admitted to any of the institutions, and further examinations may be made, if it is advisable. If the inmate is determined to be a mentally retarded or developmentally disabled person, as defined in section 5123.01 of the Revised Code, the bureau shall notify the sentencing court in writing of its determination within forty-five days after sentencing.

The bureau shall collect such social and other information as will aid in the interpretation of its examinations.

Subject to division (C) of section 5120.21 of the Revised Code, the bureau shall keep a record of the health, activities, and behavior of each inmate while the inmate is in the custody of the state. The records, including the findings and recommendations of the bureau, shall be made available to the adult parole authority for use in imposing post-release control sanctions under section 2967.28 of the Revised Code or any other section of the Revised Code, in granting parole, and in making parole, post-release, and rehabilitation plans for the inmate when the inmate leaves the institution, and to the department for its use in approving transfers of inmates from one institution to another.

(1996 S 269, eff. 7–1–96; 1995 S 2, eff. 7–1–96; 1994 H 571, eff. 10–6–94; 1990 H 569, eff. 7–1–91; 1988 S 94; 1980 H 965, S 297; 1978 H 565; 1972 H 494)

5120.111 Duties to community based correctional programs

With respect to community based correctional facilities and programs and district community based correctional facilities and programs authorized under section 2301.51 of the Revised Code, the department of rehabilitation and correction shall do all of the following:

(A) Adopt rules, under Chapter 119. of the Revised Code, that serve as criteria for the operation of community-based correctional facilities and programs and district community-based correctional facilities and programs approved in accordance with sections 2301.51 and 5120.10 of the Revised Code;

(B) Adopt rules, under Chapter 119. of the Revised Code, prescribing the minimum educational and experience requirements that must be satisfied by persons who staff and operate the facilities and programs;

(C) Adopt rules, under Chapter 119. of the Revised Code, governing the procedures for the submission of proposals for the establishment of community-based correctional facilities and programs and district community-based correctional facilities and programs to the division of parole and community services under division (B) of section 2301.51 of the Revised Code;

(D) Prescribe forms that are to be used by judicial corrections boards of community-based correctional facilities and programs and district community-based correctional facilities and programs in making application for state financial assistance under section 2301.56 of the Revised Code and that include a requirement that the applicant estimate the number of offenders that will be committed or referred to a facility and program and that the facility and program will serve in the year of application;

(E) Adopt rules, under Chapter 119. of the Revised Code, that prescribe the standards of operation and the training and qualifications of persons who staff and operate the facilities and programs and that must be satisfied for the facilities and programs to be eligible for state financial assistance. The standards prescribed shall include, but shall not be limited to, the minimum requirements that each proposal submitted for approval to the division of parole and community services, as contained in section 2301.52 of the Revised Code, must satisfy for approval.

(F) Through the division of parole and community services, accept and review proposals for the establishment of the facilities and programs and approve those proposals that satisfy the minimum requirements contained in section 2301.52 of the Revised Code; and administer the program for state financial assistance to the facilities and programs in accordance with section 5120.112 of the Revised Code.

(1994 H 571, eff. 10–6–94; 1980 H 1000, eff. 4–9–81)

5120.112 Financial assistance to community-based programs; agreement required

(A) The division of parole and community services shall accept applications for state financial assistance for the renovation, maintenance, and operation of proposed and approved community-based correctional facilities and programs and district community-based correctional facilities and programs that are filed in accordance with section 2301.56 of the Revised Code. The division, upon receipt of an application for a particular facility and program, shall determine whether the application is in proper form, whether the applicant satisfies the standards of operation and training and qualifications of personnel that are prescribed by the department of rehabilitation and correction under section 5120.111 of the Revised Code, whether the applicant has established the facility and program, and, if the applicant has not at that time established the facility and program, whether the proposal of the applicant sufficiently indicates that the standards will be satisfied upon the establishment of the facility and program.

If the division determines that the application is in proper form and that the applicant has satisfied or will satisfy the standards of the department, the division shall notify the applicant that it is qualified to receive state financial assistance for the facility and program under this section from moneys made available to the division for purposes of providing assistance to community-based correctional facilities and programs and district community-based correctional facilities and programs.

(B) The amount of state financial assistance that is granted to a qualified applicant under this section shall be determined by the division of parole and community services in accordance with this division. The division shall adopt a formula to determine the allocation of state financial assistance to qualified applicants. The formula shall provide for funding that is based upon a set fee to be paid to an applicant per person committed or referred in the year of application. In no case shall the set fee be greater than the average yearly cost of incarceration per inmate in all state correctional institutions, as defined in section 2967.01 of the Revised Code, as determined by the department of rehabilitation and correction.

The times and manner of distribution of state financial assistance to be granted to a qualified applicant under this section shall be determined by the division of parole and community services.

(C) No state financial assistance shall be distributed to a qualified applicant until an agreement concerning the assistance has been entered into by the director of rehabilitation and correction and the deputy director of the division of parole and community services on the part of the state, and by the chairman of the judicial corrections board of the community-based correctional facility and program or district community-based correctional facility and program to receive the financial assistance, whichever is applicable. The agreement shall be effective for a period of one year from the date of the agreement and shall specify all terms and conditions that are applicable to the granting of the assistance, including, but not limited to:

(1) The total amount of assistance to be granted for each community-based correctional facility and program or district community-based correctional facility and program, and the times and manner of the payment of the assistance;

(2) How persons who will staff and operate the facility and program are to be utilized during the period for which the assistance is to be granted, including descriptions of their positions and duties, their salaries and fringe benefits, and their job qualifications and classifications;

(3) A statement that none of the persons who will staff and operate the facility and program, including those who are receiving some or all of their salaries out of funds received by the facility and program as state financial assistance, are employees or are to be considered as being employees of the department of rehabilitation and correction, and a statement that the employees who will staff and operate that facility and program are employees of the facility and program;

(4) A list of the type of expenses, other than salaries of persons who will staff and operate the facility and program, for which the state financial assistance can be used, and a requirement that purchases made with funds received as state financial assistance be made through the use of competitive bidding;

(5) The accounting procedures that are to be used by the facility and program in relation to the state financial assistance;

(6) A requirement that the facility and program file quarterly reports, during the period that it receives state financial assistance, with the division of parole and community services, which reports shall be statistical in nature and shall contain that information required under a research design agreed upon by all parties to the agreement, for purposes of evaluating the facility and program;

(7) A requirement that the facility and program comply with all of the standards of operation and training and qualifications of personnel prescribed by the department under section 5120.111 of the Revised Code, and with all information submitted on its application;

(8) A statement that the facility and program will attempt to accept and treat at least fifteen per cent of the eligible adult felony offenders sentenced in the county or counties it serves during the period that it receives state financial assistance;

(9) A statement that the facility and program will make a reasonable effort to augment the funding received from the state.

(D)(1) No state financial assistance shall be distributed to a qualified applicant until its proposal for a community-based correctional facility and program or district community-based correctional facility and program has been approved by the division of parole and community services.

(2) State financial assistance may be denied to any applicant if it fails to comply with the terms of any agreement entered into pursuant to division (C) of this section.

(1994 H 335, eff. 12–9–94; 1994 H 571, eff. 10–6–94)

5120.12 Lease of real estate for oil or gas

The director of rehabilitation and correction may lease, for oil and gas, any real estate owned by the state and placed under the supervision of the department of rehabilitation and correction, to any person, upon such terms and for such number of years, not more than forty, as will be for the best interest of the state. No such lease shall be agreed upon or entered into before the proposal to lease the property has been advertised once each week for four weeks in a newspaper of general circulation in the city where the central office of the department is located. Such lease shall be made with the person offering the best terms to the state.

The director, in such lease, may grant to such lessee the right to use so much of the surface of such land as may be reasonably necessary to carry on the work of prospecting for, extracting, piping, storing, and removing all oil or gas, and for depositing waste material and maintaining such buildings and constructions as are reasonably necessary for exploring or prospecting for such oil and gas.

All leases made under this section shall be prepared by the attorney general and approved by the governor. All moneys received from any such leases shall be paid into the state treasury to the credit of the general revenue fund.

(1995 H 60, eff. 3–4–98; 1986 S 312, eff. 9–24–86; 1972 H 494)

5120.13 Acceptance of devise, grant, or bequest by department; trust funds for inmates

(A) The department of rehabilitation and correction shall accept and hold on behalf of the state, if it is for the public interest, any grant, gift, devise, or bequest of money or property made to or for the use or benefit of any institution described in section 5120.05 of the Revised Code. The department shall keep such gift, grant, devise, or bequest as a distinct property or fund, and shall invest the same, if in money, in the manner provided by law. The department may deposit in a proper trust company or savings bank any fund left in trust during a specified life or lives, and shall adopt rules governing the deposit, transfer, withdrawal, or investment of such funds and the income thereof. Upon the expiration of any trust according to its terms, the department shall dispose of the funds or property held thereunder in the manner provided in the instrument creating the trust; except that, if the instrument creating the trust failed to make any terms of disposition, or if no trust was in evidence, then the decedent patient's, pupil's, or inmate's moneys, savings or commercial deposits, dividends or distributions, bonds, or any other interest bearing debt certificate or stamp issued by the United States government shall escheat to the state. All such unclaimed intangible personal property of a former inmate shall be retained by the managing officer in such institution for the period of one year during which time every possible effort shall be made to find that former inmate or that former inmate's legal representative. If, after a period of one year from the time such inmate has left such institution or has died, the managing officer is unable to locate the inmate or the inmate's legal representative, upon proper notice of such fact, the director of rehabilitation and correction shall at that time formulate in writing a method of disposition on the minutes of the department authorizing the managing officer of the institution to convert the same to cash to be paid into the treasury of the state to the credit of the general revenue fund. The department shall include in the annual report a statement of all such funds and property and the terms and conditions relating thereto.

Moneys or property deposited with managing officers of institutions by relatives, guardians, conservators, and friends for the special benefit of any inmate shall remain in the hands of such officers for use accordingly. Such funds shall be deposited in a personal deposit fund. Each such managing officer shall keep an itemized book account of the receipt and disposition thereof, which book shall be open at all times to the inspection of the department. The department shall adopt rules governing the deposit, transfer, withdrawal, or investment of such funds and the income thereof.

(B) Whenever an inmate confined in any state institution subject to the jurisdiction of the department dies, escapes, is discharged or paroled from the institution, or is placed on a term of post-release control under any section of the Revised Code and personal funds of the person remain in the hands of the managing officer of the institution and no demand is made upon the managing officer by the owner of the funds or the owner's legally appointed representative, the managing officer shall hold the funds in the personal deposit fund for a period of at least one year during which time the managing officer shall make every effort possible to locate the owner or the owner's legally appointed representative.

If, at the end of this period, no demand has been made for the funds, the managing officer shall dispose of the funds as follows:

(1) All moneys in a personal deposit fund in excess of ten dollars due for the support of an inmate shall be paid into the state's general revenue fund.

(2) All moneys in a personal deposit fund in excess of ten dollars not due for the support of an inmate shall be placed to the credit of the institution's local account designated as "industrial and entertainment" fund.

(3) All moneys less than ten dollars to the credit of an inmate shall be placed to the credit of the institution's local account designated as "industrial and entertainment" fund.

(C) Whenever an inmate in any state institution subject to the jurisdiction of the department dies, escapes, is discharged or paroled from the institution or is placed on a term of post-release control, and personal effects of the person remain in the hands of the managing officer of the institution, and no demand is made upon the managing officer by the owner of the property or the owner's legally appointed representative, the managing officer shall hold and dispose of such property as follows:

All the miscellaneous personal effects shall be held for a period of at least one year, during which time the managing officer shall make every effort possible to locate the owner or the owner's legal representative. If at the end of this period no demand has been made by the owner of the property or the owner's legal representative, the managing officer shall file with the county recorder of the county of commitment of the owner, all deeds, wills, contract mortgages, or assignments. The balance of the personal effects shall be sold at public auction after being duly advertised, and the funds turned over to the treasurer of state for credit to the general revenue fund. If any of the property is not of a type to be filed with the county recorder and is not salable at public auction, then the managing officer of the institution shall destroy the property.

(1995 S 2, eff. 7–1–96; 1984 H 250, eff. 7–30–84; 1977 S 221; 1972 H 494)

5120.131 Industrial and entertainment fund; commissary fund

Each managing officer of an institution under the jurisdiction of the department of rehabilitation and correction as described in section 5120.05 of the Revised Code, with the approval of the director of the department of rehabilitation and correction, may establish local institution funds designated as follows:

(A) Industrial and entertainment fund created and maintained for the entertainment and welfare of the inmates of the institutions under the jurisdiction of the department. The director shall establish rules and regulations for the operation of the industrial and entertainment fund.

(B) Commissary fund created and maintained for the benefit of inmates in the institutions under the jurisdiction of the department.

Commissary revenue over and above operating costs and reserve shall be considered profits. All profits from the commissary fund operations shall be paid into the industrial and entertainment fund and used only for the entertainment and welfare of inmates. The director shall establish rules and regulations for the operation of the commissary fund.

(1972 H 494, eff. 7–1–72)

5120.132 Prisoner programs fund

(A) There is hereby created in the state treasury the prisoner programs fund. The director of rehabilitation and correction shall deposit in the fund all moneys received by the department from commissions on telephone systems established for the use of prisoners. The money in the fund shall be used only to pay for the costs of the following:

(1) The purchase of material, supplies, and equipment used in any library program, educational program, religious program, recreational program, or pre-release program operated by the department for the benefit of prisoners;

(2) The construction, alteration, repair, or reconstruction of buildings and structures owned by the department for use in any library program, educational program, religious program, recreational program, or pre-release program operated by the department for the benefit of prisoners;

(3) The payment of salary, wages, and other compensation to employees of the department who are employed in any library program, educational program, religious program, recreational program, or pre-release program operated by the department for the benefit of prisoners;

(4) The compensation to vendors that contract with the department for the provision of services for the benefit of prisoners in any library program, educational program, religious program, recreational program, or pre-release program operated by the department;

(5) The payment of prisoner release payments in an appropriate amount as determined pursuant to rule;

(6) The purchase of other goods and the payment of other services that are determined, in the discretion of the director, to be goods and services that may provide additional benefit to prisoners.

(B) The director shall establish rules for the operation of the prisoner programs fund.

(1992 S 351, eff. 7–1–92)

5120.133 Payment of obligations from prisoners' accounts

(A) The department of rehabilitation and correction, upon receipt of a certified copy of the judgment of a court of record in an action in which a prisoner was a party that orders a prisoner to pay a stated obligation, may apply toward payment of the obligation money that belongs to a prisoner and that is in the account kept for the prisoner by the department. The department may transmit the prisoner's funds directly to the court for disbursement or may make payment in another manner as directed by the court. Except as provided in rules adopted under this section, when an amount is received for the prisoner's account, the department shall use it for the payment of the obligation and shall continue using amounts received for the account until the full amount of the obligation has been paid. No proceedings in aid of execution are necessary for the department to take the action required by this section.

(B) The department may adopt rules specifying a portion of an inmate's earnings or other receipts that the inmate is allowed to retain to make purchases from the commissary and that may not be used to satisfy an obligation pursuant to division (A) of this section. The rules shall not permit the application or disbursement of funds belonging to an inmate if those funds are exempt from execution, garnishment, attachment, or sale to satisfy a judgment or order pursuant to section 2329.66 of the Revised Code or to any other provision of law.

(1994 H 571, eff. 10–6–94)

5120.134 Vending commission funds

Each managing officer of an institution under the jurisdiction of the department of rehabilitation and correction, based upon a recommendation of the institution's joint labor management committee, may establish a local institution fund that shall be designated the vending commission fund and that shall be created and maintained for the benefit and welfare of the employees of that institution. The fund shall receive the profits from vending commission areas that are designated solely for use by department of rehabilitation and correction employees. The director of rehabilitation and correction shall establish rules for the operation of employee vending commission funds.

(1995 H 117, eff. 6–30–95)

5120.135 Laboratory services

(A) As used in this section, "laboratory services" includes the performance of medical laboratory analysis; professional laboratory and pathologist consultation; the procurement, storage, and distribution of laboratory supplies; and the performance of phlebotomy services.

(B) The department of rehabilitation and correction shall provide laboratory services to the departments of mental health, mental retardation and developmental disabilities, youth services, and rehabilitation and correction. The department of rehabilitation and correction may also provide laboratory services to other state, county, or municipal agencies and to private persons that request laboratory services if the department of rehabilitation and correction determines that the provision of laboratory services is in the public interest and considers it advisable to provide such services. The department of rehabilitation and correction may also provide laboratory services to agencies operated by the United States government and to public and private entities funded in whole or in part by the state if the director of rehabilitation and correction designates them as eligible to receive such services.

The department of rehabilitation and correction shall provide laboratory services from a laboratory that complies with the standards for certification set by the United States department of health and human services under the "Clinical Laboratory Improvement Amendments of 1988," 102 Stat. 293, 42 U.S.C.A. 263a. In addition, the laboratory shall maintain accreditation or certification with an appropriate accrediting or certifying organization as considered necessary by the recipients of its laboratory services and as authorized by the director of rehabilitation and correction.

(C) The cost of administering this section shall be determined by the department of rehabilitation and correction and shall be paid by entities that receive laboratory services to the department for deposit in the state treasury to the credit of the laboratory services fund, which is hereby created. The fund shall be used to pay the costs the department incurs in administering this section.

(D) If the department of rehabilitation and correction does not provide laboratory services under this section in a satisfactory manner to the department of mental retardation and developmental disabilities, youth services, or mental health, the director of mental retardation and developmental disabilities, youth services, or mental health shall attempt to resolve the matter of the unsatisfactory provision of services with the director of rehabilitation and correction. If, after this attempt, the provision of laboratory services continues to be unsatisfactory, the director of mental retardation and developmental disabilities, youth services, or mental health shall notify the director of rehabilitation and correction regarding the continued unsatisfactory provision of laboratory services. If, within thirty days after the director receives this notice, the department of rehabilitation and correction does not provide the specified laboratory services in a satisfactory manner, the director of mental retardation and developmental disabilities, youth services, or mental health shall notify the director of rehabilitation and correction of the notifying director's intent to cease obtaining laboratory services from the department of rehabilitation and correction. Following the end of a cancellation period of sixty days that begins on the date of the notice, the department that sent the notice may obtain laboratory services from a provider other than the department of rehabilitation and correction, if the department that sent the notice certifies to the department of administrative services that the requirements of this division have been met.

(E) Whenever a state agency fails to make a payment for laboratory services provided to it by the department of rehabilitation and correction under this section within thirty-one days after the date the payment was due, the office of budget and management may transfer moneys from that state agency to the department of rehabilitation and correction for deposit to the credit of the laboratory services fund. The amount transferred shall not exceed the amount of the overdue payments. Prior to making a transfer under this division, the office shall apply any credits the state agency has accumulated in payment for laboratory services provided under this section.

(1998 H 850, eff. 3–18–99)

5120.14 Department to notify law enforcement agencies, prosecutor, and newspaper when criminal escapes

(A) If a person who was convicted of or pleaded guilty to an offense escapes from a correctional institution in this state under the control of the department of rehabilitation and correction or otherwise escapes from the custody of the department, the department immediately after the escape shall report the escape, by telephone and in writing, to all local law enforcement agencies with jurisdiction in the county in which the institution from which the escape was made or to which the person was sentenced is located, to all local law enforcement agencies with jurisdiction in the county in which the person was convicted or pleaded guilty to the offense for which the escaped person was sentenced, to the state highway patrol, to the prosecuting attorney of the county in which the institution from which the escape was made or to which the person was sentenced is located, to the prosecuting attorney of the county in which the person was convicted or pleaded guilty to the offense for which the escaped person was sentenced, to a newspaper of general circulation in the county in which the institution from which the escape was made or to which the person was sentenced is located, and to a newspaper of general circulation in each county in which the escaped person was indicted for an offense for which, at the time of the escape, the escaped person had been sentenced to that institution. The written notice may be by either facsimile transmission or mail. A failure to comply with this requirement is a violation of section 2921.22 of the Revised Code.

(B) Upon the apprehension of the escaped person, the department shall give notice of the apprehension by telephone and in writing to the persons who were given notice of the escape under division (A) of this section.

(1999 H 283, eff. 6–30–99; 1994 H 571, eff. 10–6–94; 1987 H 207, eff. 9–24–87)

5120.15 Admission and discharge

The department of rehabilitation and correction shall regulate the admission and discharge of inmates in the institutions described in section 5120.05 of the Revised Code.

(1972 H 494, eff. 7–1–72)

5120.16 Examination, observation, and classification; assignment to institutions; transfer; delinquent children; AIDS policy

(A) Persons sentenced to any institution, division, or place under the control of the department of rehabilitation and correction are committed to the control, care, and custody of the department. Subject to division (B) of this section, the director of rehabilitation and correction or the director's designee may direct that persons sentenced to the department, or to any institution or place within the department, shall be conveyed initially to an appropriate facility established and maintained by the department for reception, examination, observation, and classification of the persons so sentenced. If a presentence investigation report was not prepared pursuant to section 2947.06 or 2951.03 of the Revised Code or Criminal Rule 32.2 regarding any person sentenced to the department or to any institution or place within the department, the director or the director's designee may order the department's field staff to conduct an offender background investigation and prepare an offender background investigation report regarding the person. The investigation and report shall be conducted in accordance with division (A) of section 2951.03 of the Revised Code and the report shall contain the same information as a presentence investigation report prepared pursuant to that section.

When the examination, observation, and classification of the person have been completed by the facility and a written report of the examination, observation, and classification is filed with the commitment papers, the director or the director's designee, subject to division (B) of this section, shall assign the person to a suitable state institution or place maintained by the state within the director's department or shall designate that the person is to be housed in a county, multicounty, municipal, municipal-county, or multicounty-municipal jail or workhouse, if authorized by section 5120.161 of the Revised Code, there to be confined, cared for, treated, trained, and rehabilitated until paroled, released in accordance with section 2929.20, 2967.26, or 2967.28 of the Revised Code, or otherwise released under the order of the court that imposed the person's sentence. No person committed by a probate court, a trial court pursuant to section 2945.40, 2945.401, or 2945.402 of the Revised Code subsequent to a finding of not guilty by reason of insanity, or a juvenile court shall be assigned to a state correctional institution.

If a person is sentenced, committed, or assigned for the commission of a felony to any one of the institutions or places maintained by the department or to a county, multicounty, municipal, municipal-county, or multicounty-municipal jail or workhouse, the department, by order duly recorded and subject to division (B) of this section, may transfer the person to any other institution, or, if authorized by section 5120.161 of the Revised Code, to a county, multicounty, municipal, municipal-county, or multicounty-municipal jail or workhouse.

(B) If the case of a child who is alleged to be a delinquent child is transferred for criminal prosecution to the appropriate court having jurisdiction of the offense pursuant to section 2152.12 of the Revised Code, if the child is convicted of or pleads guilty to a felony in that case, if the child is sentenced to a prison term, as defined in section 2901.01 of the Revised Code, and if the child is under eighteen years of age when delivered to the custody of the department of rehabilitation and correction, all of the following apply regarding the housing of the child:

(1) Until the child attains eighteen years of age, subject to divisions (B)(2), (3), and (4) of this section, the department shall house the child in a housing unit in a state correctional institution separate from inmates who are eighteen years of age or older.

(2) The department is not required to house the child in the manner described in division (B)(1) of this section if the child does not observe the rules and regulations of the institution or the child otherwise creates a security risk by being housed separately.

(3) If the department receives too few inmates who are under eighteen years of age to fill a housing unit in a state correctional institution separate from inmates who are eighteen years of age or older, as described in division (B)(1) of this section, the department may house the child in a housing unit in a state correctional institution that includes both inmates who are under eighteen years of age and inmates who are eighteen years of age or older and under twenty-one years of age.

(4) Upon the child's attainment of eighteen years of age, the department may house the child with the adult population of the state correctional institution.

(C) The director or the director's designee shall develop a policy for dealing with problems related to infection with the human immunodeficiency virus. The policy shall include methods of identifying individuals committed to the custody of the department who are at high risk of infection with the virus and counseling those individuals.

Arrangements for housing individuals diagnosed as having AIDS or an AIDS-related condition shall be made by the department based on security and medical considerations and in accordance with division (B) of this section, if applicable.

(2000 S 179, § 3, eff. 1–1–02; 1997 S 111, eff. 3–17–98; 1997 H 215, eff. 9–29–97; 1996 S 285, eff. 7–1–97; 1996 H 124, eff. 3–31–97; 1996 S 310, eff. 6–20–96; 1995 S 2, eff. 7–1–96; 1994 H 571, eff. 10–6–94; 1992 S 331, eff. 11–13–92; 1989 S 2; 1987 H 455; 1982 H 269, § 4, S 199; 1980 H 965, H 900, S 297; 1978 H 565; 1972 H 494)

5120.161 Agreement with local authority for housing prisoners; procedures; compliance with minimum standards

(A) Except as provided in division (C) of this section, the department of rehabilitation and correction may enter into an agreement with any local authority operating a county, multicounty, municipal, municipal-county, or multicounty-municipal jail or workhouse, as described in section 307.93, 341.21, or 753.16 of the Revised Code, for the housing in the jail or workhouse operated by the local authority of persons who are convicted of or plead guilty to a felony of the fourth or fifth degree if the person previously has not been convicted of or pleaded guilty to a felony and if the felony is not an offense of violence. The agreement shall specify a per diem fee that the department shall pay the local authority for each such person housed in the jail or workhouse pursuant to the agreement, shall set forth any other terms and conditions for the housing of such persons in the jail or workhouse, and shall indicate that the department, subject to the relevant terms and conditions set forth, may designate those persons to be housed at the jail or workhouse.

(B) A person designated by the department to be housed in a county, multicounty, municipal, municipal-county, or multicounty-municipal jail or workhouse that is the subject of an agreement entered into under division (A) of this section shall be conveyed by the department to that jail or workhouse and shall be kept at the jail or workhouse until the person's term of imprisonment expires, the person is pardoned, paroled, or placed under a post-release control sanction, or the person is transferred under the laws permitting the transfer of prisoners. The department shall pay the local authority that operates the jail or workhouse the per diem fee specified in the agreement for each such person housed in the jail or workhouse. Each such person housed in the jail or workhouse shall be under the direct supervision and control of the keeper, superintendent, or other person in charge of the jail or workhouse, but shall be considered for all other purposes to be within the custody of the department of rehabilitation and correction. Section 2967.193 of the Revised Code and all other provisions of the Revised Code that pertain to persons within the custody of the department that would not by their nature clearly be inapplicable apply to persons housed pursuant to this section.

(C) The department of rehabilitation and correction shall not enter into an agreement pursuant to division (A) of this section with any local authority unless the jail or workhouse operated by the authority complies with the Minimum Standards for Jails in Ohio.

(D) A court that sentences a person for a felony may include as the sentence or part of the sentence, in accordance with division (A) of section 2929.16 of the Revised Code and regardless of whether the jail or workhouse is the subject of an agreement entered into under division (A) of this section, a sanction that consists of a term of up to six months in a jail or workhouse or, if the offense is a fourth degree felony OVI offense and the offender is sentenced under division (G)(1) of section 2929.13 of the Revised Code, a sanction that consists of a term of up to one year in jail less the mandatory term of local incarceration of sixty or one hundred twenty consecutive days imposed pursuant to division (G)(1) of section 2929.13 of the Revised Code.

(E) "Fourth degree felony OVI offense" and "mandatory term of local incarceration" have the same meanings as in section 2929.01 of the Revised Code.

(2002 S 123, eff. 1–1–04; 1999 S 22, eff. 5–17–00; 1996 H 72, eff. 3–18–97; 1996 S 269, eff. 7–1–96; 1995 S 2, eff. 7–1–96; 1987 H 455, eff. 7–20–87; 1982 H 269, S 199)

5120.162 Transfer of children to correctional medical center

(A) The department of rehabilitation and correction may enter into an agreement with the department of youth services pursuant to which the department of youth services may transfer to a correctional medical center established by the department of rehabilitation and correction children who are within its custody, who have an illness, physical condition, or other medical problem, and who apparently would benefit from diagnosis or treatment at the center for that illness, condition, or problem. Notwithstanding the fact that portions of the center may be used for the benefit of children in the custody of the department of youth services, the center shall be considered a facility of the department of rehabilitation and correction and shall be controlled and operated in accordance with the agreement and the provisions of this section. A child who is in the custody of the department of youth services and who is transferred to the center shall be considered as remaining in the custody of the department of youth services during the period of his diagnosis, treatment, or housing for diagnosis or treatment in the center.

During the development or renovation of a correctional medical center that is the subject of an agreement under this section, the department of rehabilitation and correction shall confer with the department of youth services to ensure that the center is planned and constructed or renovated to facilitate its use for the diagnosis or treatment of both prisoners in the custody of the department of rehabilitation and correction and children in the custody of the department of youth services who may be transferred to the center.

(B) All children who are in the custody of the department of youth services and who are transferred to a correctional medical center pursuant to an agreement under this section shall be housed in areas of the center that are totally separate and removed by sight and sound from all prisoners who are in the custody of the department of rehabilitation and correction and who are being diagnosed, treated, or housed for diagnosis or treatment in the center or who otherwise are in the center. For purposes of this division, children who are being diagnosed, treated, or housed for diagnosis or treatment in a building or wing of a building in which no prisoners in the custody of the department of rehabilitation and correction are being diagnosed, treated, or housed for diagnosis or treatment or otherwise are present are being housed totally separate from any prisoners who are in the custody of the department of rehabilitation and correction.

(1992 S 331, eff. 11–13–92)

5120.163 Testing for contagious diseases

At the time of reception and at other times the director determines to be appropriate, the department of rehabilitation and correction may examine and test a prisoner for tuberculosis, HIV infection, hepatitis, including but not limited to hepatitis A, B, and C, and other contagious diseases. The department may test and treat involuntarily a prisoner in a state correctional institution who refuses to be tested or treated for tuberculosis, HIV infection, hepatitis, including but not limited to hepatitis A, B, and C, or another contagious disease.

(1997 S 111, eff. 3–17–98)

5120.17 Transfer of mentally ill or mentally retarded prisoners to psychiatric hospitals; emergency transfers; uncontested transfers

(A) As used in this section:

(1) "Mental illness" means a substantial disorder of thought, mood, perception, orientation, or memory that grossly impairs judgment, behavior, capacity to recognize reality, or ability to meet the ordinary demands of life.

(2) "Mentally ill person subject to hospitalization" means a mentally ill person to whom any of the following applies because of the person's mental illness:

(a) The person represents a substantial risk of physical harm to the person as manifested by evidence of threats of, or attempts at, suicide or serious self-inflicted bodily harm.

(b) The person represents a substantial risk of physical harm to others as manifested by evidence of recent homicidal or other violent behavior, evidence of recent threats that place another in reasonable fear of violent behavior and serious physical harm, or other evidence of present dangerousness.

(c) The person represents a substantial and immediate risk of serious physical impairment or injury to the person as manifested by evidence that the person is unable to provide for and is not providing for the person's basic physical needs because of the person's mental illness and that appropriate provision for those needs cannot be made immediately available in the correctional institution in which the inmate is currently housed.

(d) The person would benefit from treatment in a hospital for the person's mental illness and is in need of treatment in a hospital as manifested by evidence of behavior that creates a grave and imminent risk to substantial rights of others or the person.

(3) "Psychiatric hospital" means a facility that is operated by the department of rehabilitation and correction, is designated as a psychiatric hospital, is licensed by the department of mental health pursuant to section 5119.20 of the Revised Code, and is in substantial compliance with the standards set by the joint commission on accreditation of healthcare organizations.

(4) "Inmate patient" means an inmate who is admitted to a psychiatric hospital.

(5) "Admitted" to a psychiatric hospital means being accepted for and staying at least one night at the psychiatric hospital.

(6) "Treatment plan" means a written statement of reasonable objectives and goals for an inmate patient that is based on the needs of the inmate patient and that is established by the treatment team, with the active participation of the inmate patient and with documentation of that participation. "Treatment plan" includes all of the following:

(a) The specific criteria to be used in evaluating progress toward achieving the objectives and goals;

(b) The services to be provided to the inmate patient during the inmate patient's hospitalization;

(c) The services to be provided to the inmate patient after discharge from the hospital, including, but not limited to, housing and mental health services provided at the state correctional institution to which the inmate patient returns after discharge or community mental health services.

(7) "Mentally retarded person subject to institutionalization by court order" has the same meaning as in section 5123.01 of the Revised Code.

(8) "Emergency transfer" means the transfer of a mentally ill inmate to a psychiatric hospital when the inmate presents an immediate danger to self or others and requires hospital-level care.

(9) "Uncontested transfer" means the transfer of a mentally ill inmate to a psychiatric hospital when the inmate has the mental capacity to, and has waived, the hearing required by division (B) of this section.

(10)(a) "Independent decision–maker" means a person who is employed or retained by the department of rehabilitation and correction and is appointed by the chief or chief clinical officer of mental health services as a hospitalization hearing officer to conduct due process hearings.

(b) An independent decision-maker who presides over any hearing or issues any order pursuant to this section shall be a psychiatrist, psychologist, or attorney, shall not be specifically associated with the institution in which the inmate who is the subject of the hearing or order resides at the time of the hearing or order, and previously shall not have had any treatment relationship with nor have represented in any legal proceeding the inmate who is the subject of the order.

(B)(1) Except as provided in division (C) of this section, if the warden of a state correctional institution or the warden's designee believes that an inmate should be transferred from the institution to a psychiatric hospital, the department shall hold a hearing to determine whether the inmate is a mentally ill person subject to hospitalization. The department shall conduct the hearing at the state correctional institution in which the inmate is confined, and the department shall provide qualified independent assistance to the inmate for the hearing. An independent decision-maker provided by the department shall preside at the hearing and determine whether the inmate is a mentally ill person subject to hospitalization.

(2) Except as provided in division (C) of this section, prior to the hearing held pursuant to division (B)(1) of this section, the warden or the warden's designee shall give written notice to the inmate that the department is considering transferring the inmate to a psychiatric hospital, that it will hold a hearing on the proposed transfer at which the inmate may be present, that at the hearing the inmate has the rights described in division (B)(3) of this section, and that the department will provide qualified independent assistance to the inmate with respect to the hearing. The department shall not hold the hearing until the inmate has received written notice of the proposed transfer and has had sufficient time to consult with the person appointed by the department to provide assistance to the inmate and to prepare for a presentation at the hearing.

(3) At the hearing held pursuant to division (B)(1) of this section, the department shall disclose to the inmate the evidence that it relies upon for the transfer and shall give the inmate an opportunity to be heard. Unless the independent decision-maker finds good cause for not permitting it, the inmate may present documentary evidence and the testimony of witnesses at the hearing and may confront and cross-examine witnesses called by the department.

(4) If the independent decision-maker does not find clear and convincing evidence that the inmate is a mentally ill person subject to hospitalization, the department shall not transfer the inmate to a psychiatric hospital but shall continue to confine the inmate in the same state correctional institution or in another state correctional institution that the department considers appropriate. If the independent decision-maker finds clear and convincing evidence that the inmate is a mentally ill person subject to hospitalization, the decision-maker shall order that the inmate be transported to a psychiatric hospital for observation and treatment for a period of not longer than thirty days. After the hearing, the independent decision-maker shall submit to the department a written decision that states one of the findings described in division (B)(4) of this section, the evidence that the decision-maker relied on in reaching that conclusion, and, if the decision is that the inmate should be transferred, the reasons for the transfer.

(C)(1) The department may transfer an inmate to a psychiatric hospital under an emergency transfer order if the chief clinical officer of mental health services of the department or that officer's designee and either a psychiatrist employed or retained by the department or, in the absence of a psychiatrist, a psychologist employed or retained by the department determines that the inmate is mentally ill, presents an immediate danger to self or others, and requires hospital-level care.

(2) The department may transfer an inmate to a psychiatric hospital under an uncontested transfer order if both of the following apply:

(a) A psychiatrist employed or retained by the department determines all of the following apply:

(i) The inmate has a mental illness or is a mentally ill person subject to hospitalization.

(ii) The inmate requires hospital care to address the mental illness.

(iii) The inmate has the mental capacity to make a reasoned choice regarding the inmate's transfer to a hospital.

(b) The inmate agrees to a transfer to a hospital.

(3) The written notice and the hearing required under divisions (B)(1) and (2) of this section are not required for an emergency transfer or uncontested transfer under division (C)(1) or (2) of this section.

(4) After an emergency transfer under division (C)(1) of this section, the department shall hold a hearing for continued hospitalization within five working days after admission of the transferred inmate to the psychiatric hospital. The department shall hold subsequent hearings pursuant to division (F) of this section at the same intervals as required for inmate patients who are transported to a psychiatric hospital under division (B)(4) of this section.

(5) After an uncontested transfer under division (C)(2) of this section, the inmate may withdraw consent to the transfer in writing at any time. Upon the inmate's withdrawal of consent, the hospital shall discharge the inmate, or, within five working days, the department shall hold a hearing for continued hospitalization. The department shall hold subsequent hearings pursuant to division (F) of this section at the same time intervals as required for inmate patients who are transported to a psychiatric hospital under division (B)(4) of this section.

(D)(1) If an independent decision-maker, pursuant to division (B)(4) of this section, orders an inmate transported to a psychiatric hospital or if an inmate is transferred pursuant to division (C)(1) or (2) of this section, the staff of the psychiatric hospital shall examine the inmate patient when admitted to the psychiatric hospital as soon as practicable after the inmate patient arrives at the hospital and no later than twenty-four hours after the time of arrival. The attending physician responsible for the inmate patient's care shall give the inmate patient all information necessary to enable the patient to give a fully informed, intelligent, and knowing consent to the treatment the inmate patient will receive in the hospital. The attending physician shall tell the inmate patient the expected physical and medical consequences of any proposed treatment and shall give the inmate patient the opportunity to consult with another psychiatrist at the hospital and with the inmate advisor.

(2) No inmate patient who is transported or transferred to a psychiatric hospital pursuant to division (B)(4) or (C)(1) or (2) of this section and who is in the physical custody of the department of rehabilitation and correction shall be subjected to any of the following procedures:

(a) Convulsive therapy;

(b) Major aversive interventions;

(c) Any unusually hazardous treatment procedures;

(d) Psychosurgery.

(E) The warden of the psychiatric hospital or the warden's designee shall ensure that an inmate patient hospitalized pursuant to this section receives or has all of the following:

(1) Receives sufficient professional care within twenty days of admission to ensure that an evaluation of the inmate patient's current status, differential diagnosis, probable prognosis, and description of the current treatment plan have been formulated and are stated on the inmate patient's official chart;

(2) Has a written treatment plan consistent with the evaluation, diagnosis, prognosis, and goals of treatment;

(3) Receives treatment consistent with the treatment plan;

(4) Receives periodic reevaluations of the treatment plan by the professional staff at intervals not to exceed thirty days;

(5) Is provided with adequate medical treatment for physical disease or injury;

(6) Receives humane care and treatment, including, without being limited to, the following:

(a) Access to the facilities and personnel required by the treatment plan;

(b) A humane psychological and physical environment;

(c) The right to obtain current information concerning the treatment program, the expected outcomes of treatment, and the expectations for the inmate patient's participation in the treatment program in terms that the inmate patient reasonably can understand;

(d) Opportunity for participation in programs designed to help the inmate patient acquire the skills needed to work toward discharge from the psychiatric hospital;

(e) The right to be free from unnecessary or excessive medication and from unnecessary restraints or isolation;

(f) All other rights afforded inmates in the custody of the department consistent with rules, policy, and procedure of the department.

(F) The department shall hold a hearing for the continued hospitalization of an inmate patient who is transported or transferred to a psychiatric hospital pursuant to division (B)(4) or (C)(1) of this section prior to the expiration of the initial thirty-day period of hospitalization. The department shall hold any subsequent hearings, if necessary, not later than ninety days after the first thirty-day hearing and then not later than each one hundred and eighty days after the immediately prior hearing. An independent decision-maker shall conduct the hearings at the psychiatric hospital in which the inmate patient is confined. The inmate patient shall be afforded all of the rights set forth in this section for the hearing prior to transfer to the psychiatric hospital. The department may not waive a hearing for continued commitment. A hearing for continued commitment is mandatory for an inmate patient transported or transferred to a psychiatric hospital pursuant to division (B)(4) or (C)(1) of this section unless the inmate patient has the capacity to make a reasoned choice to execute a waiver and waives the hearing in writing. An inmate patient who is transferred to a psychiatric hospital pursuant to an uncontested transfer under division (C)(2) of this section and who has scheduled hearings after withdrawal of consent for hospitalization may waive any of the scheduled hearings if the inmate has the capacity to make a reasoned choice and executes a written waiver of the hearing.

If upon completion of the hearing the independent decision-maker does not find by clear and convincing evidence that the inmate patient is a mentally ill person subject to hospitalization, the independent decision-maker shall order the inmate patient's discharge from the psychiatric hospital. If the independent decision-maker finds by clear and convincing evidence that the inmate patient is a mentally ill person subject to hospitalization, the independent decision-maker shall order that the inmate patient remain at the psychiatric hospital for continued hospitalization until the next required hearing.

If at any time prior to the next required hearing for continued hospitalization, the medical director of the hospital or the attending physician determines that the treatment needs of the inmate patient could be met equally well in an available and appropriate less restrictive state correctional institution or unit, the medical director or attending physician may discharge the inmate to that facility.

(G) An inmate patient is entitled to the credits toward the reduction of the inmate patient's stated prison term pursuant to Chapters 2967. and 5120. of the Revised Code under the same terms and conditions as if the inmate patient were in any other institution of the department of rehabilitation and correction.

(H) The adult parole authority may place an inmate patient on parole or under post-release control directly from a psychiatric hospital.

(I) If an inmate patient who is a mentally ill person subject to hospitalization is to be released from a psychiatric hospital because of the expiration of the inmate patient's stated prison term, the warden of the psychiatric hospital, at least fourteen days before the expiration date, may file an affidavit under section 5122.11 or 5123.71 of the Revised Code with the probate court in the county where the psychiatric hospital is located or the probate court in the county where the inmate will reside, alleging that the inmate patient is a mentally ill person subject to hospitalization by court order or a mentally retarded person subject to institutionalization by court order, whichever is applicable. The proceedings in the probate court shall be conducted pursuant to Chapter 5122. or 5123. of the Revised Code except as modified by this division.

Upon the request of the inmate patient, the probate court shall grant the inmate patient an initial hearing under section 5122.141 of the Revised Code or a probable cause hearing under section 5123.75 of the Revised Code before the expiration of the stated prison term. After holding a full hearing, the probate court shall make a disposition authorized by section 5122.15 or 5123.76 of the Revised Code before the date of the expiration of the stated prison term. No inmate patient shall be held in the custody of the department of rehabilitation and correction past the date of the expiration of the inmate patient's stated prison term.

(J) The department of rehabilitation and correction shall set standards for treatment provided to inmate patients, consistent where applicable with the standards set by the joint commission on accreditation of healthcare organizations.

(K) A certificate, application, record, or report that is made in compliance with this section and that directly or indirectly identifies an inmate or former inmate whose hospitalization has been sought under this section is confidential. No person shall disclose the contents of any certificate, application, record, or report of that nature or any other psychiatric or medical record or report regarding a mentally ill inmate unless one of the following applies:

(1) The person identified, or the person's legal guardian, if any, consents to disclosure, and the chief clinical officer or designee of mental health services of the department of rehabilitation and correction determines that disclosure is in the best interests of the person.

(2) Disclosure is required by a court order signed by a judge.

(3) An inmate patient seeks access to the inmate patient's own psychiatric and medical records, unless access is specifically restricted in the treatment plan for clear treatment reasons.

(4) Hospitals and other institutions and facilities within the department of rehabilitation and correction may exchange psychiatric records and other pertinent information with other hospitals, institutions, and facilities of the department, but the information that may be released about an inmate patient is limited to medication history, physical health status and history, summary of course of treatment in the hospital, summary of treatment needs, and a discharge summary, if any.

(5) An inmate patient's family member who is involved in planning, providing, and monitoring services to the inmate patient may receive medication information, a summary of the inmate patient's diagnosis and prognosis, and a list of the services and personnel available to assist the inmate patient and family if the attending physician determines that disclosure would be in the best interest of the inmate patient. No disclosure shall be made under this division unless the inmate patient is notified of the possible disclosure, receives the information to be disclosed, and does not object to the disclosure.

(6) The department of rehabilitation and correction may exchange psychiatric hospitalization records, other mental health treatment records, and other pertinent information with county sheriffs' offices, hospitals, institutions, and facilities of the department of mental health and with community mental health agencies and boards of alcohol, drug addiction, and mental health services with which the department of mental health has a current agreement for patient care or services to ensure continuity of care. Disclosure under this division is limited to records regarding a mentally ill inmate's medication history, physical health status and history, summary of course of treatment, summary of treatment needs, and a discharge summary, if any. No office, department, agency, or board shall disclose the records and other information unless one of the following applies:

(a) The mentally ill inmate is notified of the possible disclosure and consents to the disclosure.

(b) The mentally ill inmate is notified of the possible disclosure, an attempt to gain the consent of the inmate is made, and the office, department, agency, or board documents the attempt to gain consent, the inmate's objections, if any, and the reasons for disclosure in spite of the inmate's objections.

(7) Information may be disclosed to staff members designated by the director of rehabilitation and correction for the purpose of evaluating the quality, effectiveness, and efficiency of services and determining if the services meet minimum standards.

The name of an inmate patient shall not be retained with the information obtained during the evaluations.

(L) The director of rehabilitation and correction may adopt rules setting forth guidelines for the procedures required under divisions (B), (C)(1), and (C)(2) of this section.

(2002 H 355, eff. 7–23–02; 1997 S 52, eff. 9–3–97; 1996 S 310, eff. 6–20–96)

5120.171 Care and treatment of seriously mentally ill inmates

(A) The department of rehabilitation and correction shall have exclusive direction and control of the care and treatment of seriously mentally ill inmates who are in the department's custody. The department shall enter into any arrangements it considers desirable on such matters, including but not limited to both of the following:

(1) The monitoring of such services by another state agency or agencies;

(2) Adopting joint standards for the provision and monitoring of mental health services with the department of mental health and other state agencies.

(B) In order to implement its duties imposed by division (A) of this section, the department of rehabilitation and correction may enter into a contract for the provision of the mental health services described in that division.

(1995 H 117, eff. 6–30–95)

5120.172 Imprisoned minors deemed emancipated for purpose of consent to medical treatment

A minor whose case is transferred for criminal prosecution pursuant to section 2152.12 of the Revised Code, who is prosecuted as an adult and is convicted of or pleads guilty to one or more offenses in that case, and who is sentenced to a prison term or term of imprisonment in a state correctional institution for one or more of those offenses shall be considered emancipated for the purpose of consenting to medical treatment while confined in the state correctional institution.

(2000 S 179, § 3, eff. 1–1–02; 1997 S 111, eff. 3–17–98)

5120.173 Abuse or neglect of minor inmate to be reported to state highway patrol

Any person who is required to report suspected abuse or neglect of a child under eighteen years of age pursuant to division (A) of section 2151.421 of the Revised Code, any person who is permitted to report or cause a report to be made of suspected abuse or neglect of a child under eighteen years of age pursuant to division (B) of that section, any person who is required to report suspected abuse or neglect of a person with mental retardation or a developmental disability pursuant to division (C) of section 5123.61 of the Revised Code, and any person who is permitted to report suspected abuse or neglect of a person with mental retardation or a developmental disability pursuant to division (F) of that section and who makes or causes the report to be made, shall direct that report to the state highway patrol if the child or the person with mental retardation or a developmental disability is an inmate in the custody of a state correctional institution. If the state highway patrol determines after receipt of the report that it is probable that abuse or neglect of the inmate occurred, the patrol shall report its findings to the department of rehabilitation and correction, to the court that sentenced the inmate for the offense for which the inmate is in the custody of the department, and to the chairman and vice-chairman of the correctional institution inspection committee established by section 103.71 of the Revised Code.

(2004 S 178, eff. 1–30–04; 2002 H 510, eff. 3–31–03)

5120.18 Department shall classify buildings and determine designs and patterns for articles

The department of rehabilitation and correction shall, with the advice and consent of the department of administrative services, classify public buildings, offices, and institutions and determine the kinds, patterns, designs, and qualities of articles to be manufactured for use therein, which shall be uniform for each class, so far as practicable.

Whenever the department of rehabilitation and correction gives written notice to the superintendent of purchases and printing, or other official having authority to purchase articles, that the department is prepared to supply such articles from any institution under its control, the superintendent or other official shall make any needed purchases of said articles from such institution, unless the chief officer thereof, or the department, having been requested to furnish such articles, gives notice in writing within thirty days from the date of the request, that such articles cannot be furnished.

If the superintendent requires such articles within thirty days from the day of making such request and so states upon the face of such request, the chief officer of such institution or the department of rehabilitation and correction shall forthwith advise the superintendent whether it will be able to furnish such articles within such time, the superintendent may purchase such articles in the open market as in other cases. This section does not apply to any officer, board, or agent of any municipal corporation which maintains an institution that produces or manufactures articles of the kind desired.

(1977 H 1, eff. 8–26–77; 1972 H 494)

5120.19 Use of lands belonging to institutions; purchase of supplies; accounting system; payment of prisoners

(A) The department of rehabilitation and correction, in accordance with rules adopted pursuant to division (B) of section 5145.03 of the Revised Code, shall determine and direct what lands belonging to institutions under its control shall be cultivated, the crops to be raised, and the use to be made of the land and crops, and may distribute the products among the different institutions. If the crops are distributed to institutions under the control of the department, the department shall keep records of the distributions and of the fair market value of the crops distributed. The department may sell any crops that are not necessary for the institutions under its control to any person. The money received from the sale of the crops shall be deposited in the services and agricultural fund created pursuant to section 5120.29 of the Revised Code.

The department may require institutions under its control, when they have proper lands and labor, to undertake intensive agriculture, may rent lands for the production of supplies for any of the institutions that have surplus labor, and may rent lands for the production of crops for sale, when it can be done to advantage.

The department shall pay and assign the prisoners who perform any labor pursuant to this division in accordance with the rules adopted pursuant to division (B) of section 5145.03 of the Revised Code.

(B) The department may direct the purchase of any materials, supplies, or other articles for any institution under its control from any other institution under its control at the reasonable market value, which value shall be fixed by the department. Payments for the articles shall be made as between institutions in the manner provided for payment for supplies.

(1987 H 171, eff. 7–1–87; 1985 H 201; 1980 H 654; 1972 H 494)

5120.20 Cooperation of department and institutions in making tests

The department of agriculture, department of health, and Ohio state university shall cooperate with the department of rehabilitation and correction in making such cooperative tests as are necessary to determine the quality, strength, and purity of supplies, the value and use of farm lands, or conditions and needs of mechanical equipment.

(1975 H 1, eff. 6–13–75; 1972 H 494)

5120.21 Records; report on accident or injury or peculiar death

(A) The department of rehabilitation and correction shall keep in its office, accessible only to its employees, except by the consent of the department or the order of the judge of a court of record, and except as provided in division (C) of this section, a record showing the name, residence, sex, age, nativity, occupation, condition, and date of entrance or commitment of every inmate in the several institutions governed by it. The record also shall include the date, cause, and terms of discharge and the condition of such person at the time of leaving, a record of all transfers from one institution to another, and, if such inmate is dead, the date and cause of death. These and other facts that the department requires shall be furnished by the managing officer of each institution within ten days after the commitment, entrance, death, or discharge of an inmate.

(B) In case of an accident or injury or peculiar death of an inmate, the managing officer shall make a special report to the department within twenty-four hours thereafter, giving the circumstances as fully as possible.

(C)(1) As used in this division, "medical record" means any document or combination of documents that pertains to the medical history, diagnosis, prognosis, or medical condition of a patient and that is generated and maintained in the process of medical treatment.

(2) A separate medical record of every inmate in an institution governed by the department shall be compiled, maintained, and kept apart from and independently of any other record pertaining

to the inmate. Upon the signed written request of the inmate to whom the record pertains together with the written request of either a licensed attorney at law or a licensed physician designated by the inmate, the department shall make the inmate's medical record available to the designated attorney or physician. The record may be inspected or copied by the inmate's designated attorney or physician. The department may establish a reasonable fee for the copying of any medical record. If a physician concludes that presentation of all or any part of the medical record directly to the inmate will result in serious medical harm to the inmate, the physician shall so indicate on the medical record. An inmate's medical record shall be made available to a physician or to an attorney designated in writing by the inmate not more than once every twelve months.

(D) Except as otherwise provided by a law of this state or the United States, the department and the officers of its institutions shall keep confidential and accessible only to its employees, except by the consent of the department or the order of a judge of a court of record, all of the following:

(1) Architectural, engineering, or construction diagrams, drawings, or plans of a correctional institution;

(2) Plans for hostage negotiation, for disturbance control, for the control and location of keys, and for dealing with escapes;

(3) Statements made by inmate informants;

(4) Records that are maintained by the department of youth services, that pertain to children in its custody, and that are released to the department of rehabilitation and correction by the department of youth services pursuant to section 5139.05 of the Revised Code;

(5) Victim impact statements and information provided by victims of crimes that the department considers when determining the security level assignment, program participation, and release eligibility of inmates;

(6) Information and data of any kind or medium pertaining to groups that pose a security threat;

(7) Conversations recorded from the monitored inmate telephones that involve nonprivileged communications.

(E) Except as otherwise provided by a law of this state or the United States, the department of rehabilitation and correction may release inmate records to the department of youth services or a court of record, and the department of youth services or the court of record may use those records for the limited purpose of carrying out the duties of the department of youth services or the court of record. Inmate records released by the department of rehabilitation and correction to the department of youth services or a court of record shall remain confidential and shall not be considered public records as defined in section 149.43 of the Revised Code.

(F) Except as otherwise provided in division (C) of this section, records of inmates committed to the department of rehabilitation and correction as well as records of persons under the supervision of the adult parole authority shall not be considered public records as defined in section 149.43 of the Revised Code.

(2002 H 510, eff. 3–31–03; 1996 S 269, eff. 7–1–96; 1994 H 571, eff. 10–6–94; 1988 S 94, eff. 7–20–88; 1972 H 494)

5120.211 Confidentiality of quality assurance records

(A) As used in this section:

(1) "Quality assurance committee" means a committee that is appointed in the central office of the department of rehabilitation and correction by the director of rehabilitation and correction, a committee appointed at a state correctional institution by the managing officer of the institution, or a duly authorized subcommittee of a committee of that nature and that is designated to carry out quality assurance program activities.

(2) "Quality assurance program" means a comprehensive program within the department of rehabilitation and correction to systematically review and improve the quality of medical and mental health services within the department and its institutions, the safety and security of persons receiving medical and mental health services within the department and its institutions, and the efficiency and effectiveness of the utilization of staff and resources in the delivery of medical and mental health services within the department and its institutions.

(3) "Quality assurance program activities" includes the activities of the institutional and central office quality assurance committees, of persons who provide, collect, or compile information and reports required by quality assurance committees, and of persons who receive, review, or implement the recommendations made by quality assurance committees. "Quality assurance program activities" includes credentialing, infection control, utilization review including access to patient care, patient care assessments, medical and mental health records, medical and mental health resource management, mortality and morbidity review, and identification and prevention of medical or mental health incidents and risks, whether performed by a quality assurance committee or by persons who are directed by a quality assurance committee.

(4) "Quality assurance records" means the proceedings, records, minutes, and reports that emanate from quality assurance program activities. "Quality assurance records" does not include aggregate statistical information that does not disclose the identity of persons receiving or providing medical or mental health services in state correctional institutions.

(B)(1) Except as provided in division (E) of this section, quality assurance records are confidential and are not public records under section 149.43 of the Revised Code, and shall be used only in the course of the proper functions of a quality assurance program.

(2) Except as provided in division (E) of this section, no person who possesses or has access to quality assurance records and who knows that the records are quality assurance records shall wilfully disclose the contents of the records to any person or entity.

(C)(1) Except as provided in division (E) of this section, no quality assurance record shall be subject to discovery, and is not admissible in evidence, in any judicial or administrative proceeding.

(2) Except as provided in division (E) of this section, no member of a quality assurance committee or a person who is performing a function that is part of a quality assurance program shall be permitted or required to testify in a judicial or administrative proceeding with respect to quality assurance records or with respect to any finding, recommendation, evaluation, opinion, or other action taken by the committee, member, or person.

(3) Information, documents, or records otherwise available from original sources are not to be construed as being unavailable for discovery or admission in evidence in a judicial or administrative proceeding merely because they were presented to a quality assurance committee. No person testifying before a quality assurance committee or person who is a member of a quality assurance committee shall be prevented from testifying as to matters within the person's knowledge, but the witness cannot be asked about the witness' testimony before the quality assurance committee or about an opinion formed by the person as a result of the quality assurance committee proceedings.

(D)(1) A person who, without malice and in the reasonable belief that the information is warranted by the facts known to the person, provides information to a person engaged in quality assurance program activities is not liable for damages in a civil action for injury, death, or loss to person or property to any person as a result of providing the information.

(2) A member of a quality assurance committee, a person engaged in quality assurance program activities, and an employee of the department of rehabilitation and correction shall not be liable in damages in a civil action for injury, death, or loss to person or property to any person for any acts, omissions, decisions, or other conduct within the scope of the functions of the quality assurance program.

(3) Nothing in this section shall relieve any institution or individual from liability arising from the treatment of a patient.

(E) Quality assurance records may be disclosed, and testimony may be provided concerning quality assurance records, only to the following persons or entities or in the following circumstances:

(1) Persons who are employed or retained by the department of rehabilitation and correction and who have authority to evaluate or implement the recommendations of an institutional or central office quality assurance committee;

(2) Public or private agencies or organizations if needed to perform a licensing or accreditation function related to state correctional institutions or to perform monitoring of state correctional institutions as required by law;

(3) A governmental board or agency, a professional health care society or organization, or a professional standards review organization, if the records or testimony are needed to perform licensing, credentialing, or monitoring of professional standards with respect to medical or mental health professionals employed or retained by the department;

(4) A criminal or civil law enforcement agency or public health agency charged by law with the protection of public health or safety, if a qualified representative of the agency makes a written request stating that the records or testimony is necessary for a purpose authorized by law;

(5) In a judicial or administrative proceeding commenced by an entity described in division (E)(3) or (4) of this section and for a purpose described in that division, but only with respect to the subject of the proceedings.

(F) A disclosure of quality assurance records pursuant to division (E) of this section does not otherwise waive the confidential and privileged status of the disclosed quality assurance records. The names and other identifying information regarding individual patients, employees, or members of a quality assurance committee contained in a quality assurance record shall be deleted from the record prior to the disclosure of the record unless the identity of an individual is necessary to the purpose for which disclosure is being made and does not constitute a clearly unwarranted invasion of personal privacy.

(1997 S 111, eff. 3–17–98)

5120.22 Examination to be made by division of business administration; rules; property receipts fund

The division of business administration shall examine the conditions of all buildings, grounds, and other property connected with the institutions under the control of the department of rehabilitation and correction, the methods of bookkeeping and storekeeping, and all matters relating to the management of such property. The division shall study and become familiar with the advantages and disadvantages of each as to location, freight rates, and efficiency of farm and equipment, for the purpose of aiding in the determination of the local and general requirements both for maintenance and improvements.

The division, with respect to the various types of state-owned housing under jurisdiction of the department, shall adopt, in accordance with section 111.15 of the Revised Code, rules governing maintenance of the housing and its usage by department personnel. The rules shall include a procedure for determining charges for rent and utilities, which the division shall assess against and collect from department personnel using the housing. All money collected for rent and utilities pursuant to the rules shall be deposited into the property receipts fund, which is hereby created in the state treasury. Money in the fund shall be used for any expenses necessary to provide housing of department employees, including but not limited to expenses for the acquisition, construction, operation, maintenance, repair, reconstruction, or demolition of land and buildings.

(1995 H 117, eff. 6–30–95; 1993 H 152, eff. 7–1–93; 1972 H 494)

5120.23 Agencies to estimate needs for supplies produced by prisoners; disposition of proceeds

(A) The department of rehabilitation and correction shall require proper officials of the state and its political subdivisions and of the institutions of the state and its political subdivisions, to report estimates for the ensuing year of the amount of supplies required by them, of the kinds that are produced by the state correctional and penal institutions. It may make rules for the reports and provide the manner in which the estimates shall be made.

(B) Any money that is received by the department of rehabiliation [sic.] and correction from the state and its political subdivisions, any other state and its political subdivisions, the United States, or private persons for products and services produced by the state correctional and penal institutions shall be deposited in the services and agricultural fund or the Ohio penal industries manufacturing fund created pursuant to section 5120.29 of the Revised Code and shall be used and accounted for as provided in that section.

(1987 H 171, eff. 7–1–87; 1980 H 654; 1972 H 494)

5120.24 Competitive bidding; exception

The department of administrative services shall purchase all supplies needed for the proper support and maintenance of the institutions under the control of the department of rehabilitation and correction in accordance with the competitive selection procedures of Chapter 125. of the Revised Code and such rules as the department of administrative services adopts. All bids shall be publicly opened on the day and hour and at the place specified in the advertisement.

Preference shall be given to bidders in localities wherein the institution is located if the price is fair and reasonable and not greater than the usual price. Bids not meeting the specifications shall be rejected.

The department of administrative services may require such security as it considers proper to accompany the bids and shall fix the security to be given by the contractor.

The department of administrative services may reject any or all bids and secure new bids, if for any reason it is considered to be in the best interest of the state to do so, and it may authorize the managing officer of any institution to purchase perishable goods and supplies for use in cases of emergency, in which cases such managing officer shall certify such fact in writing and the department of administrative services shall record the reasons for such purchase.

(1993 H 152, eff. 7–1–93; 1987 H 88; 1976 S 430; 1972 H 494)

5120.25 Books and accounts; department to prescribe form and method; audit

The department of correction shall keep in its office a proper and complete set of books and accounts with each institution, which shall clearly show the nature and amount of every expenditure authorized and made at such institution, and which shall contain an account of all appropriations made by the general assembly and of all other funds, together with the disposition of such funds.

The department shall prescribe the form of vouchers, records, and methods of keeping accounts at each of the institutions, which shall be as nearly uniform as possible. The department may examine the records of each institution, at any time.

The department may authorize any of its bookkeepers, accountants, or employees to examine and check the records, accounts, and vouchers or take an inventory of the property of any institution, or do whatever is necessary, and pay the actual and reasonable expenses incurred in such service when an itemized account is filed and approved.

(1972 H 494, eff. 7–1–72)

5120.26 Use, custody, and insurance of funds

(A) The treasurer of state shall have charge of all funds under the jurisdiction of the department of rehabilitation and correction and shall pay out the funds only in accordance with this chapter.

(B) The department shall cause to be furnished a contract of indemnity to cover all moneys and funds received by it or by its managing officers, employees, or agents while the moneys or funds are in the possession of the managing officers, employees, or agents. The funds are designated as follows:

(1) Funds that are due and payable to the treasurer of state as provided by Chapter 131. of the Revised Code;

(2) Funds that are held in trust by the managing officers, employees, or agents of the institution as local funds or accounts under the jurisdiction of the department.

The contract of indemnity shall be made payable to the state and the premium for the contract of indemnity may be paid from any of the moneys received for the use of the department under this chapter and Chapters 5121., 5123., and 5125. of the Revised Code.

(C) Moneys collected from various sources, such as the sale of goods, farm products, services, and all miscellaneous articles, shall be transmitted on or before Monday of each week to the treasurer of state and a detailed statement of the collections shall be made to the division of business administration by each managing officer. The receipts from manufacturing and service industries and agricultural products shall be used and accounted for as provided in section 5120.29 of the Revised Code.

(1980 H 654, eff. 4–9–82; 1977 S 221; 1972 H 494)

5120.27 Industries to be carried on

The department of rehabilitation and correction may assign, among the correctional and penal institutions under its control and in accordance with the rules adopted pursuant to division (B) of section 5145.03 of the Revised Code, the industries to be carried on by the institutions, having due regard to the location and convenience of the industries, other institutions to be supplied, to the machinery in the institutions, and to the number and character of prisoners employed in the industries.

(1980 H 654, eff. 4–9–82; 1972 H 494)

5120.28 Department shall set prices of labor and articles manufactured; accounting

(A) The department of rehabilitation and correction, subject to the approval of the office of budget and management, shall fix the prices at which all labor and services performed, all agricultural products produced, and all articles manufactured in correctional and penal institutions shall be furnished to the state, the political subdivisions of the state, and the public institutions of the state and the political subdivisions, and to private persons. The prices shall be uniform to all and not higher than the usual market price for like labor, products, services, and articles.

(B) Any money received by the department of rehabilitation and correction for labor and services performed and agricultural products produced shall be deposited into the services and agricultural fund created pursuant to division (A) of section 5120.29 of the Revised Code and shall be used and accounted for as provided in that section and division (B) of section 5145.03 of the Revised Code.

(C) Any money received by the department of rehabilitation and correction for articles manufactured in penal and correctional institutions shall be deposited into the Ohio penal industries manufacturing fund created pursuant to division (B) of section 5120.29 of the Revised Code and shall be used and accounted for as provided in that section and division (B) of section 5145.03 of the Revised Code.

(1987 H 171, eff. 7–1–87; 1980 H 654; 1977 H 1; 1972 H 494)

5120.29 Services and agricultural fund; Ohio penal industries manufacturing fund

(A) There is hereby created, in the state treasury, the services and agricultural fund, which shall be used for the:

(1) Purchase of material, supplies, and equipment and the erection and extension of buildings used in service industries and agriculture;

(2) Purchase of lands and buildings necessary to carry on or extend the service industries and agriculture, upon the approval of the governor;

(3) Payment of compensation to employees necessary to carry on the service industries and agriculture;

(4) Payment of prisoners confined in state correctional institutions a portion of their earnings in accordance with rules adopted pursuant to section 5145.03 of the Revised Code.

(B) There is hereby created, in the state treasury, the Ohio penal industries manufacturing fund, which shall be used for the:

(1) Purchase of material, supplies, and equipment and the erection and extension of buildings used in manufacturing industries;

(2) Purchase of lands and buildings necessary to carry on or extend the manufacturing industries upon the approval of the governor;

(3) Payment of compensation to employees necessary to carry on the manufacturing industries;

(4) Payment of prisoners confined in state correctional institutions a portion of their earnings in accordance with rules adopted pursuant to section 5145.03 of the Revised Code.

(C) The department of rehabilitation and correction shall, in accordance with rules adopted pursuant to section 5145.03 of the Revised Code and subject to any pledge made as provided in division (D) of this section, place to the credit of each prisoner his earnings and pay the earnings so credited to the prisoner or his family.

(D) Receipts credited to the funds created in divisions (A) and (B) of this section constitute available receipts as defined in section 152.09 of the Revised Code, and may be pledged to the payment of bond service charges on obligations issued by the Ohio building authority pursuant to Chapter 152. of the Revised Code to construct, reconstruct, or otherwise improve capital facilities useful to the department. The authority may, with the consent of the department, provide in the bond proceedings for a pledge of all or such portion of receipts credited to the funds as the authority determines. The authority may provide in the bond proceedings for the transfer of receipts credited to the funds to the appropriate bond service fund or bond service reserve fund as required to pay the bond service charges when due, and any such provision for the transfer of receipts shall be controlling notwithstanding any other provision of law pertaining to such receipts.

All receipts received by the treasurer of state on account of the department and required by the applicable bond proceedings to be deposited, transferred, or credited to the bond service fund or bond service reserve fund established by such bond proceedings shall be transferred by the treasurer of state to such fund, whether or not such fund is in the custody of the treasurer of state, without necessity for further appropriation, upon receipt of notice from the Ohio building authority as prescribed in the bond proceedings. The authority may covenant in the bond proceedings that so long as any obligations are outstanding to which receipts credited to the fund are pledged, the state and the department shall neither reduce the prices charged pursuant to section 5120.28 of the Revised Code nor the level of manpower collectively devoted to the production of goods and services for which prices are set pursuant to section 5120.28 of the Revised Code, which covenant shall be controlling notwithstanding any other provision of law; provided, that no covenant shall require the general assembly to appropriate money derived from the levying of excises or taxes to purchase such goods and services or to pay rent or bond service charges.

(1994 H 571, eff. 10–6–94; 1987 H 171, eff. 7–1–87; 1985 H 201; 1982 H 530, § 1, 3; 1980 H 654; 1972 H 494)

5120.30 Investigations; director to have powers of county court judge; stenographic report; witness fees; attendance of witnesses, etc.

The department of rehabilitation and correction may make any investigations that are necessary in the performance of its duties, and to that end the director of rehabilitation and correction shall have the same power as a judge of a county court to administer oaths and to enforce the attendance and testimony of witnesses and the production of books or papers.

The department shall keep a record of the investigations pursuant to the record retention schedule approved by the department of administrative services.

The fees of witnesses for attendance and travel shall be the same as in the court of common pleas, but no officer or employee of the institution under investigation is entitled to such fees.

Any judge of the probate court or of the court of common pleas, upon application of the department, may compel the attendance of witnesses, the production of books or papers, and the giving of testimony before the department, by a judgment for contempt or otherwise, in the same manner as in cases before courts of common pleas.

(2002 H 510, eff. 3–31–03; 1976 H 390, eff. 8–6–76; 1972 H 494)

5120.31 Appointment of competent agency or person; contents of credentials

The department of rehabilitation and correction may appoint and commission any competent agency or person, to serve without compensation, as a special agent, investigator, or representative to perform a designated duty for and in behalf of the department. Specific credentials shall be given by the department to each person so designated, and each credential shall state:

(A) The name;

(B) Agency with which such person is connected;

(C) Purpose of appointment;

(D) Date of expiration of appointment;

(E) Such information as the department considers proper.

(1972 H 494, eff. 7–1–72)

5120.32 Annual report; financial statement

In its annual report, the department of rehabilitation and correction shall include a complete financial statement of the various institutions under its control. The report shall state, as to each such institution, whether:

(A) The moneys appropriated have been economically and judiciously expended;

(B) The objects of the several institutions have been accomplished;

(C) The laws in relation to such institutions have been fully complied with;

(D) All parts of the state are equally benefited by said institutions.

Such annual report shall be accompanied by the reports of the managing officers and such other information and recommendations as the department considers proper.

(1972 H 494, eff. 7–1–72)

5120.33 Contents of annual report

The annual report of the department of rehabilitation and correction shall include a list of the officers and agents employed, and the condition of the state institutions under its control. Such report may include statistics and information in regard to correctional institutions of this or other states.

(1972 H 494, eff. 7–1–72)

5120.331 Annual report to contain statistics on prisoners

(A) Not later than the first day of April of each year, the department of rehabilitation and correction shall prepare an annual report covering the preceding calendar year that does all of the following:

(1) Indicates the total number of persons sentenced to any institution, division, or place under its control and management who are delivered within that calendar year to its custody and control;

(2) Indicates the total number of persons who, during that calendar year, were released from a prison term on any of the following bases:

(a) On judicial release under section 2929.20 of the Revised Code;

(b) On transitional control under section 2967.26 of the Revised Code;

(c) On parole;

(d) Due to the expiration of the stated prison term imposed;

(e) On any basis not described in divisions (A)(2)(a) to (d) of this section.

(3) Lists each offense, by Revised Code section number and, if applicable, by designated name, for which at least one person who was released from a prison term in that calendar year was serving a prison term at the time of release;

(4) For each offense included in the list described in division (A)(3) of this section, indicates all of the following:

(a) The total number of persons released from a prison term in that calendar year who were serving a prison term for that offense at the time of release;

(b) The shortest, longest, and average prison term that had been imposed for that offense upon the persons described in division (A)(4)(a) of this section and that they were serving at the time of release;

(c) The shortest, longest, and average period of imprisonment actually served by the persons described in division (A)(4)(a) of this section under a prison term that had been imposed for that offense upon them and that they were serving at the time of release;

(d) The total number of persons released from a prison term in that calendar year under each of the bases for release set forth in division (A)(2) of this section who were serving a prison term for that offense at the time of release;

(e) The shortest, longest, and average prison term that had been imposed for that offense upon the persons in each category described in division (A)(4)(d) of this section and that they were serving at the time of release;

(f) The shortest, longest, and average period of imprisonment actually served by the persons in each category described in division (A)(4)(d) of this section under a prison term that had been imposed for that offense upon them and that they were serving at the time of release.

(B) No report prepared under division (A) of this section shall identify or enable the identification of any person released from a prison term in the preceding calendar year.

(C) Each annual report prepared under division (A) of this section shall be distributed to each member of the general assembly.

(D) As used in this section, "prison term" and "stated prison term" have the same meanings as in section 2929.01 of the Revised Code.

(1997 S 111, eff. 3–17–98; 1995 S 2, eff. 7–1–96; 1987 H 261, eff. 11–1–87)

5120.34 Internal management

The department of rehabilitation and correction shall make rules for the nonpartisan management of the institutions under its control. Any officer or employee of the department or any officer or employee of any institution under its control, who, by solicitation or otherwise, exerts his influence, directly or indirectly, to induce any other officer or employee of any such institutions to adopt his political views or to favor any particular person, issue, or candidate for office shall be removed from his office or position, by the department in case of an officer or employee and by the governor in case of the director of rehabilitation and correction.

(1975 H 617, eff. 11–7–75; 1972 H 494)

5120.35 Suggestions of department in annual report

In its annual report, the department of rehabilitation and correction shall make any suggestions or recommendations it considers wise for the more effectual accomplishment of the general purpose of Chapter 5120. of the Revised Code.

(1972 H 494, eff. 7–1–72)

5120.36 Additional powers of department

The department of rehabilitation and correction, in addition to the powers expressly conferred, shall have all power and authority necessary for the full and efficient exercise of the executive, administrative, and fiscal supervision over the state institutions described in section 5120.05 of the Revised Code.

(1972 H 494, eff. 7–1–72)

5120.37 Agreements with job and family services department to share information

The department of rehabilitation and correction shall enter into an agreement with the department of job and family services to exchange or share information monthly concerning persons under the control or supervision of the department of rehabilitation and correction.

(1999 H 471, eff. 7–1–00; 1997 S 52, eff. 9–3–97)

5120.38 Managing officer; duties

Subject to the rules of the department of rehabilitation and correction, each institution under the department's jurisdiction other than an institution operated pursuant to a contract entered into under section 9.06 of the Revised Code shall be under the control of a managing officer known as a warden or other appropriate title. The managing officer shall be appointed by the director of the department of rehabilitation and correction and shall be in the unclassified service and serve at the pleasure of the director. Appointment to the position of managing officer shall be made from persons who have criminal justice experience.

A person who is appointed to the position of managing officer from a position in the classified service shall retain the right to resume the status that the person held in the classified service immediately prior to the appointment. Upon being relieved of the person's duties as managing officer, the person shall be reinstated to the position in the classified service that the person held immediately prior to the appointment to the position of managing officer or to another position that the director, with approval of the state department of administrative services, certifies as being substantially equal to that prior position. Service as a managing officer shall be counted as service in the position in the classified service held by the person immediately preceding the person's appointment as managing officer. A person who is reinstated to a position in the classified service, as provided in this section, shall be entitled to all rights and emoluments accruing to the position during the time of the person's service as managing officer.

The managing officer, under the director, shall have entire executive charge of the institution for which the managing officer is appointed. Subject to civil service rules and regulations, the managing officer shall appoint the necessary employees and the managing officer or the director may remove such employees for cause. A report of all appointments, resignations, and discharges shall be filed with the director at the close of each month.

(2002 H 510, eff. 3–31–03; 1997 S 111, eff. 3–17–98; 1997 H 215, eff. 9–29–97; 1972 H 494, eff. 7–1–72)

5120.381 Deputy wardens

Subject to the rules of the department of rehabilitation and correction, the director of rehabilitation and correction may appoint a deputy warden for each institution under the jurisdiction of the department. A deputy warden shall be in the unclassified service and serve at the pleasure of the director. The director shall make an appointment to the position of deputy warden from persons having criminal justice experience. A person who is appointed to a position as deputy warden from a position in the classified service shall retain the right to resume the position and status that the person held in the classified service immediately prior to the appointment. If the person is relieved of the person's duties as deputy warden, the director shall reinstate the person to the position in the classified service that the person held immediately prior to the appointment as deputy warden or to another position that is certified by the director, with approval of the department of administrative services, as being substantially equal to that prior position. Service as deputy warden shall be counted as service in the position in the classified service that the person held immediately preceding the appointment as deputy warden. A person who is reinstated to a position in the classified service as provided in this section is entitled to all rights and emoluments accruing to the position during the time of the person's service as deputy warden.

(1997 S 111, eff. 3–17–98)

5120.382 Appointment of employees

Except as otherwise provided in this chapter for appointments by division chiefs and managing officers, the director of rehabilitation and correction shall appoint employees who are necessary for the efficient conduct of the department of rehabilitation and correction and prescribe their titles and duties. A person who is appointed to an unclassified position from a position in the classified service shall serve at the pleasure of the director and retain the right to resume the position and status that the person held in the classified service immediately prior to the appointment. If the person is relieved of the person's duties for the unclassified position, the director shall reinstate the person to the position in the classified service that the person held immediately prior to the appointment or to another position that is certified by the director, with approval of the department of administrative services, as being substantially equal to that prior classified position. Service in the unclassified service pursuant to the appointment shall be counted as service in the position in the classified service that the person held immediately preceding the appointment. A person who is reinstated to a position in the classified service as provided in this section is entitled to all rights and emoluments accruing to the position during the time of the person's unclassified service.

(1997 S 111, eff. 3–17–98)

5120.39 Qualifications of superintendent; duties

Each superintendent of an institution under the control of the department of rehabilitation and correction shall be of good moral character and have skill, ability, and experience in his profession. He shall have control of the institution, and be responsible for the management thereof and for the service of all its employees. He shall appoint necessary teachers, attendants, nurses, servants, and other persons, assign their places and duties, and may discharge them, keeping a record thereof and reasons therefor.

(1972 H 494, eff. 7–1–72)

5120.40 Teachers in institutions, qualifications

All teachers employed in any institution under the jurisdiction of the department of rehabilitation and correction shall possess educator licenses or have the qualifications and approval that the superintendent of the Ohio central school system, after conference with the officers in charge of the several institutions, prescribes for the various particular types of service or service in the particular institutions.

(1996 S 230, eff. 10–29–96; 1994 H 571, eff. 10–6–94; 1980 H 900, eff. 7–1–80; 1972 H 494)

5120.41 Approval of courses of study by superintendent of public instruction

The courses of study for the instruction and training of all persons in the correctional institutions under the control of the department of rehabilitation and correction shall be subject to the approval of the superintendent of public instruction.

(1994 H 571, eff. 10–6–94; 1972 H 494, eff. 7–1–72)

5120.42 Rules; estimates

The department of rehabilitation and correction shall make rules for the proper execution of its powers and may require the performance of additional duties by the officers of the several institutions, so as to fully meet the requirements, intents, and purposes of Chapter 5120. of the Revised Code, and particularly those relating to making estimates and furnishing proper proof of the use made of all articles furnished or produced in such institutions. In case of an apparent conflict between the powers conferred upon any managing officer and those conferred by such sections upon the department, the presumption shall be conclusive in favor of the department.

(1972 H 494, eff. 7–1–72)

5120.421 Searches of visitors to institutions

(A) As used in this section:

(1) "Body cavity search" means an inspection of the anal or vaginal cavity of a person that is conducted visually, manually, by means of any instrument, apparatus, or object, or in any other manner.

(2) "Deadly weapon" and "dangerous ordnance" have the same meanings as in section 2923.11 of the Revised Code.

(3) "Drug of abuse" has the same meaning as in section 3719.011 of the Revised Code.

(4) "Intoxicating liquor" has the same meaning as in section 4301.01 of the Revised Code.

(5) "Strip search" means an inspection of the genitalia, buttocks, breasts, or undergarments of a person that is preceded by the removal or rearrangement of some or all of the person's clothing that directly covers the person's genitalia, buttocks, breasts, or undergarments and that is conducted visually, manually, by means of any instrument, apparatus, or object, or in any other manner.

(B) For purposes of determining whether visitors to an institution under the control of the department of rehabilitation and correction are knowingly conveying, or attempting to convey, onto the grounds of the institution any deadly weapon, dangerous ordnance, drug of abuse, intoxicating liquor, or electronic communications device in violation of section 2921.36 of the Revised Code, the department may adopt rules, pursuant to Chapter 119. of the Revised Code, that are consistent with this section.

(C) For the purposes described in division (B) of this section, visitors who are entering or have entered an institution under the control of the department of rehabilitation and correction may be searched by the use of a magnetometer or similar device, by a pat-down of the visitor's person that is conducted by a person of the same sex as that of the visitor, and by an examination of the contents of pockets, bags, purses, packages, and other containers proposed to be conveyed or already conveyed onto the grounds of the institution. Searches of visitors authorized by this division may be conducted without cause, but shall be conducted uniformly or by automatic random selection. Discriminatory or arbitrary selection searches of visitors are prohibited under this division.

(D) For the purposes described in division (B) of this section, visitors who are entering or have entered an institution under the control of the department of rehabilitation and correction may be searched by a strip or body cavity search, but only under the circumstances described in this division. In order for a strip or body cavity search to be conducted of a visitor, the highest officer present in the institution shall expressly authorize the search on the basis of a reasonable suspicion, based on specific objective facts and reasonable inferences drawn from those facts in the light of experience, that a visitor proposed to be so searched possesses, and intends to convey or already has conveyed, a deadly weapon, dangerous ordnance, drug of abuse, intoxicating liquor, or electronic communications device onto the grounds of the institution in violation of section 2921.36 of the Revised Code.

Except as otherwise provided in this division, prior to the conduct of the strip or body cavity search, the highest officer present in the institution shall cause the visitor to be provided with a written statement that sets forth the specific objective facts upon which the proposed search is based. In the case of an emergency under which time constraints make it impossible to prepare the written statement before the conduct of the proposed search, the highest officer in the institution instead shall cause the visitor to be orally informed of the specific objective facts upon which the proposed search is based prior to its conduct, and shall cause the preparation of the written statement and its provision to the visitor within twenty four hours after the conduct of the search. Both the highest officer present in the institution and the visitor shall retain a copy of a written statement provided in accordance with this division.

Any strip or body cavity search conducted pursuant to this division shall be conducted in a private setting by a person of the same sex as that of the visitor. Any body cavity search conducted under this division additionally shall be conducted by medical personnel.

This division does not preclude, and shall not be construed as precluding, a less intrusive search as authorized by division (C) of this section when reasonable suspicion as described in this division exists for a strip or body cavity search.

(2002 H 510, eff. 3–31–03; 1990 S 258, eff. 8–22–90)

5120.422 Rules governing site selection for proposed correctional institutions

The department of rehabilitation and correction shall prescribe rules, in accordance with Chapter 119. of the Revised Code, that govern the department's actions whenever it has the authority to select a site for a proposed state correctional institution. The rules shall include at least procedures under which the department shall receive, review, and select proposals from persons and political subdivisions for the establishment of a proposed state correctional institution at a particular geographic location.

(1995 H 117, eff. 9–29–95)

5120.423 Designation of devices and programs to increase muscle mass and physical strength or improve fighting skills

The department of rehabilitation and correction shall adopt rules in accordance with Chapter 119. of the Revised Code that designate devices and programs that, in addition to free weight exercise equipment as defined in sections 341.41, 753.31, and 5145.30 of the Revised Code and in addition to boxing, wrestling, and martial arts programs, would enable a person who uses a designated device or participates in a designated program to increase muscle mass and physical strength or to improve fighting skills.

(1996 H 152, eff. 10–4–96)

5120.424 Purchase of fixed weight exercise equipment prohibited

On and after the effective date of this act, no moneys in the treasury of the state, or moneys coming lawfully into the possession or custody of the Treasurer of State, except moneys donated by gift, devise, or bequest specifically for this purpose, shall be used to purchase any fixed weight exercise equipment authorized by the act, and no moneys in the treasury of any subdivision of the state, or moneys coming lawfully into the possession or custody of the treasurer of any subdivision, shall be used to purchase any fixed weight exercise equipment for use at any facility described in Section 5 of this act.

(1996 H 152, § 6, eff. 10–4–96)

REGULATION OF INFLAMMATORY MATERIALS

5120.425 Definitions

As used in sections 5120.425 to 5120.428 of the Revised Code:

(A) "Head of a state correctional institution," "prisoner," and "state correctional institution" have the same meanings as in section 2967.01 of the Revised Code.

(B) "Material" means a prerecorded magnetic audio or video tape, book, drawing, magazine, newspaper, pamphlet, poster, print, photograph, or other similar printed, written, recorded, or otherwise produced item.

(C) "Prohibited inflammatory material" means a material that, in the determination of the warden or the warden's designee, is detrimental to, or poses a threat to, the rehabilitation of the inmates or the security, good order, or discipline within or on the grounds of the institution for any reason, including, but not limited to, that it is material with a sexually explicit nature.

(D) "Publication review committee" means the committee created by the director of rehabilitation and correction pursuant to division (C) of section 5120.426 of the Revised Code.

(E) "Warden" means the head of a state correctional institution.

(F) "Warden's designee" means a person or a panel of persons designated by a warden to perform a responsibility that sections 5120.425 to 5120.428 of the Revised Code generally otherwise impose upon the warden.

(1999 H 62, eff. 11–3–99)

5120.426 Regulation of materials received by prisoners; determination of inflammatory materials; publication review committee

(A) The director of rehabilitation and correction shall adopt rules, and each warden shall adopt regulations that govern the form, medium, and quantity of materials that each prisoner confined in the warden's institution is permitted to receive and retain. Those rules and regulations shall be consistent with sections 5120.425 to 5120.428 of the Revised Code. The regulations adopted by the warden shall be consistent with the rules that the director of rehabilitation and correction adopts pursuant to this division.

(B) The director of rehabilitation and correction shall adopt a rule establishing a standard for determining whether material is a prohibited inflammatory material. In establishing the standard for determining whether material is a prohibited inflammatory material, the director shall consider all relevant information, including, but not limited to, the standard established for material that is harmful to juveniles in section 2907.01 of the Revised Code; in establishing the standard under this division, the director shall not be governed or limited by the standard established by section 2907.01 of the Revised Code.

(C) The director of rehabilitation and correction shall appoint a publication review committee of one or more persons. The member or members of the committee shall review withholding determinations pursuant to section 5120.428 of the Revised Code.

(1999 H 62, eff. 11–3–99)

5120.427 Receipt of materials by prisoners; security inspections; withholding of inflammatory materials; requests for review of withholding decisions

(A) Each prisoner confined in a state correctional institution may receive a reasonable number of materials directly from the publishers or other distributors of those materials. With the prior approval of the warden of the state correctional institution in which a prisoner is confined, each prisoner also may receive a reasonable number of materials from a source other than the publisher or other distributor of those materials.

A prisoner's receipt and retention of materials is subject to security inspections conducted by the institution in which the prisoner is confined and to the rules and regulations adopted pursuant to section 5120.426 of the Revised Code. Subject to a contrary decision with respect to a material's nature by the publication review committee following a review pursuant to section 5120.428 of the Revised Code, a prisoner is not entitled to receive or retain any material that a warden or the warden's designee determines during the course of a security inspection to be a prohibited inflammatory material.

(B)(1) For each state correctional institution, the warden or the warden's designee shall inspect each incoming material to determine whether the material is a prohibited inflammatory material or another type of material. The warden or the warden's designee shall not determine a material to be a prohibited inflammatory material solely on the basis of its appeal to a particular ethnic, racial, or religious audience.

(2) If the warden or the warden's designee determines that an incoming material is not a prohibited inflammatory material, the warden or the warden's designee shall cause the material to be promptly forwarded to the prisoner who is its intended recipient. If the warden or the warden's designee determines that an incoming material is a prohibited inflammatory material, the warden or the warden's designee shall cause the material to be withheld from the prisoner who is its intended recipient and promptly shall provide that prisoner with a written withholding notice containing all of the following:

(a) A general description of the withheld material;

(b) The reason why the material has not been forwarded to the prisoner;

(c) A statement of the prisoner's right under division (A) of section 5120.428 of the Revised Code to have the publication review committee review the withholding decision of the warden or the warden's designee.

(3) Within five working days after a prisoner's receipt of the withholding notice described in division (B)(2) of this section, the prisoner may submit to the warden a written request for a review of the withholding decision. If the prisoner fails to submit a timely written request for a review of that nature, the failure shall constitute the prisoner's acceptance of the withholding decision, and the warden or the warden's designee shall cause the material to be disposed of in the manner that the warden or the warden's designee considered to be most appropriate under the circumstances.

(1999 H 62, eff. 11–3–99)

5120.428 Review of materials by publication review committee

(A) If a prisoner confined in a state correctional institution submits a timely written review request under division (B)(3) of section 5120.427 of the Revised Code, the warden of the state correctional institution in which the prisoner is confined or the warden's designee promptly shall forward the withheld material to the publication review committee. As soon as is practicable after receipt of the withheld material, the publication review committee shall review the material to determine whether it is a prohibited inflammatory material or another type of material.

(B) If the publication review committee determines that the withheld material is not a prohibited inflammatory material, the committee shall cause the withheld material to be promptly forwarded to the prisoner who requested the review.

(C) If the publication review committee determines that the withheld material is a prohibited inflammatory material, the committee shall forward the material to the warden or the warden's designee for disposal in the manner considered to be most appropriate under the circumstances.

(1999 H 62, eff. 11–3–99)

GENERAL PROVISIONS

5120.44 Purpose of chapter

Chapter 5120. of the Revised Code attempts:

(A) To provide humane and scientific treatment and care and the highest attainable degree of individual development for the dependent wards of the state;

(B) To provide for the delinquent, conditions of modern education and training that will restore the largest possible portion of them to useful citizenship;

(C) To promote the study of the causes of dependency and delinquency, and of mental, moral, and physical defects, with a view to cure and ultimate prevention;

(D) To secure by uniform and systematic management the highest attainable degree of economy in the administration of the state institutions.

Such sections shall be liberally construed to attain such purposes.

(1972 H 494, eff. 7–1–72)

5120.45 Expenses of burial of inmates

The state shall bear the expense of the burial or cremation of an inmate who dies in a state correctional institution, if the body is not claimed for interment or cremation at the expense of friends or relatives, or is not delivered for anatomical purposes or for the study of embalming in accordance with section 1713.34 of the Revised Code. When the expense is borne by the state, interment of the person or the person's cremated remains shall be in the institution cemetery or other place provided by the state. The managing officer of the institution shall provide at the grave of the person or, if the person's cremated remains are buried, at the grave of the person's cremated remains, a metal, stone, or concrete marker on which shall be inscribed the name and age of the person and the date of death.

(1998 S 117, eff. 8–5–98; 1994 H 571, eff. 10–6–94; 1980 H 900, eff. 7–1–80)

5120.46 Appropriation of real property

When it is necessary for a state correctional institution to acquire any real estate, right-of-way, or easement in real estate in order to accomplish the purposes for which it was organized or is being conducted, and the department of rehabilitation and correction is unable to agree with the owner of the property upon the price to be paid therefor, the property may be appropriated in the manner provided for the appropriation of property for other state purposes.

Any instrument by which real property is acquired pursuant to this section shall identify the agency of the state that has the use and benefit of the real property as specified in section 5301.012 of the Revised Code.

(1999 H 19, eff. 10–26–99; 1994 H 571, eff. 10–6–94; 1980 H 900, eff. 7–1–80)

5120.47 Agreements for facilities with Ohio building authority

The department of rehabilitation and correction shall lease capital facilities constructed, reconstructed, otherwise improved, or financed by the Ohio building authority pursuant to Chapter 152. of the Revised Code for the use of the department, and may enter into any other agreements with the authority ancillary to the construction, reconstruction, improvement, financing, leasing, or operation of such capital facilities, including, but not limited to, any agreements required by the applicable bond proceedings authorized by Chapter 152. of the Revised Code. Such agreements shall not be subject to section 5120.24 of the Revised Code. Any lease of capital facilities authorized by this section shall be governed by division (D) of section 152.24 of the Revised Code.

(1982 H 530, eff. 5–28–82)

5120.48 Assignment and deployment of staff to apprehend escaped or erroneously released prisoners

(A) If a prisoner escapes from a state correctional institution, the managing officer of the institution, after consultation with and upon the advice of appropriate law enforcement officials, shall assign and deploy into the community appropriate staff persons necessary to apprehend the prisoner. Correctional officers and officials may carry firearms when required in the discharge of their duties in apprehending, taking into custody, or transporting to a place of confinement a prisoner who has escaped from a state correctional institution.

(B) If a prisoner is released from a state correctional institution prior to the lawful end of the person's prison term or term of imprisonment, whether by error, inadvertence, fraud, or any other cause except a lawful parole or judicial release granted pursuant to section 2929.20 of the Revised Code, the managing officer of the institution, after consulting with the bureau of sentence computation, shall notify the chief of the adult parole authority, the office of victim services of the division of parole and community services, and the sentencing court of the mistaken release. Upon the direction of the chief, or the chief's designee, field officers of the authority may arrest the prisoner without a warrant and return the prisoner to the state correctional institution to complete the balance of the prisoner's sentence. The chief of the adult parole authority, or the chief's designee, may require the assistance of any peace officer or law enforcement officer in the apprehension of a prisoner of that nature.

(2002 H 510, eff. 3–31–03; 1994 H 571, eff. 10–6–94)

5120.49 Parole board standards and guidelines for termination of control over sexually violent offender's service of prison term

Note: See also following version of this section, eff. 4–29–05.

The department of rehabilitation and correction, by rule adopted under Chapter 119. of the Revised Code, shall prescribe standards and guidelines to be used by the parole board in determining, pursuant to section 2971.04 of the Revised Code, whether it should terminate its control over an offender's service of a prison term imposed upon the offender for a sexually violent offense under division (A)(3) of section 2971.03 of the Revised Code. The rules shall include provisions that specify that the parole board may not terminate its control over an offender's service of a prison term imposed upon the offender under that division until after the offender has served the minimum term imposed as part of that prison term and until the parole board has determined that the offender does not represent a substantial risk of physical harm to others.

(1996 H 180, eff. 1–1–97)

Note: See also following version of this section, eff. 4–29–05.

5120.49 Parole board standards and guidelines for termination of control over violent sex offender's service of prison term (later effective date)

Note: See also preceding version of this section, in effect until 4–29–05.

The department of rehabilitation and correction, by rule adopted under Chapter 119. of the Revised Code, shall prescribe standards and guidelines to be used by the parole board in determining, pursuant to section 2971.04 of the Revised Code, whether it should terminate its control over an offender's service of a prison term imposed upon the offender under division (A)(3) of section 2971.03 of the Revised Code for conviction of a violent sex offense and a sexually violent predator specification or for conviction of a designated homicide, assault, or kidnapping offense and both a sexual motivation specification and a sexually violent predator specification. The rules shall include provisions that specify that the parole board may not terminate its control over an offender's service of a prison term imposed upon the offender under that division until after the offender has served the minimum term imposed as part of that prison term and until the parole board has determined that the offender does not represent a substantial risk of physical harm to others.

(2004 H 473, eff. 4–29–05; 1996 H 180, eff. 1–1–97)

Note: See also preceding version of this section, in effect until 4–29–05.

5120.50 Interstate correction compact

(A) The party states, desiring by common action to fully utilize and improve their programs for the confinement, treatment, and rehabilitation of various types of offenders, declare that it is the policy of each of the party states to provide institutional facilities and such programs on a basis of cooperation with one another, thereby serving the best interest of such offenders and of society and effecting economies in capital expenditures and operational costs. The purpose of this compact is to provide for the mutual development and execution of such programs of cooperation for the confinement, treatment, and rehabilitation of offenders with the most economical use of human and material resources.

(B) DEFINITIONS

As used in this compact, unless the context clearly requires otherwise:

(1) "State" means a state of the United States; the United States; a territory or possession of the United States; the District of Columbia; the Commonwealth of Puerto Rico.

(2) "Sending state" means a state party to this compact in which conviction or court commitment was had.

(3) "Receiving state" means a state party to this compact to which an inmate is sent for confinement other than a state in which conviction or court commitment was had.

(4) "Inmate" means a male or female offender who is committed, under sentence to or confined in a state penal or state reformatory institution.

(5) "Institution" means any state penal or state reformatory facility, including but not limited to a facility for the mentally ill or mentally defective, in which inmates as defined in division (B)(4) of this section may lawfully be confined.

(C) CONTRACTS

(1) Each party state may make one or more contracts with any one or more of the other party states for the confinement of inmates on behalf of a sending state in institutions situated within receiving states. Any such contract shall provide for:

(a) Its duration;

(b) Payments to be made to the receiving state by the sending state for inmate maintenance, extraordinary medical and dental expenses, and any participation in or receipt by inmates of rehabilitative or correctional services, facilities, programs, or treatment not reasonably included as part of normal maintenance;

(c) Participation in programs of inmate employment, if any; the disposition or crediting of any payments received by inmates on account thereof; and the crediting of proceeds from or disposal of any products resulting therefrom;

(d) Delivery and retaking of inmates;

(e) Such other matters as may be necessary and appropriate to fix the obligations, responsibilities, and rights of the sending and receiving states.

(2) The terms and provisions of this compact shall be a part of any contract entered into by the authority of or pursuant thereto, and nothing in any such contract shall be inconsistent therewith.

(D) PROCEDURES AND RIGHTS

(1) Whenever the duly constituted authorities in a state party to this compact, and which has entered into a contract pursuant to division (C) of this section, shall decide that confinement in, or transfer of an inmate to, an institution within the territory of another party state is necessary or desirable in order to provide adequate quarters and care, or an appropriate program of rehabilitation or treatment, said officials may direct that the confinement be within an institution within the territory of said other party state, the receiving state to act in that regard solely as agent for the sending state.

(2) No transfer shall take place pursuant to this compact unless one of the following has occurred: (a) the inmate has given his written consent to such transfer; (b) in the event the inmate does not consent to such transfer, a hearing shall be held and a record made indicating the reasons for said transfer.

(3) The appropriate officials of any state party to this compact shall have access, at all reasonable times, to any institution in which it has a contractural [sic.] right to confine inmates for the purpose of inspecting the facilities thereof and visiting such of its inmates as may be confined in the institution.

(4) Inmates confined in an institution pursuant to the terms of this compact shall at all times be subject to the jurisdiction of the sending state and may at any time be removed therefrom for transfer to a prison or other institution within the sending state, for transfer to another institution in which the sending state may have a contractual or other right to confine inmates, for release on probation or parole, for discharge, or for any other purpose permitted by the laws of the sending state; provided that the sending state shall continue to be obligated to such payments as may be required pursuant to the terms of any contract entered into under the terms of division (C) of this section.

(5) Each receiving state shall provide regular reports, no less than semiannually, to each sending state on the inmates of that sending state in institutions pursuant to this compact, including a conduct record of each inmate and certify said record to the official designated by the sending state, in order that each inmate may have official review of his or her record in determining and altering the disposition of said inmate in accordance with the law which may obtain in the sending state and in order that the same may be a source of information for the sending state.

(6) All inmates who may be confined in an institution pursuant to the provisions of this compact shall be treated in a reasonable and humane manner and shall be treated equally with such similar inmates of the receiving state as may be confined in the same institution. The fact of confinement in a receiving state shall not deprive any inmate so confined of any legal rights which said inmate would have had if confined in an appropriate institution of the sending state.

(7) Any hearing or hearings to which an inmate confined pursuant to this compact may be entitled by the laws of the sending state may be had before the appropriate authorities of the sending state, or of the receiving state if authorized by the sending state. The receiving state shall provide adequate facilities for such hearings as may be conducted by the appropriate officials of a sending state. In the event such hearing or hearings are had before officials of the receiving state, the governing law shall be that of the sending state and a record of the hearing or hearings as prescribed by the sending state shall be made. Said record together with any recommendations of the hearing officials shall be transmitted forthwith to the official or officials before whom the hearing would have been had if it had taken place in the sending state. In any and all proceedings had pursuant to the provisions of this division, the officials of the receiving state shall act solely as agents of the sending state and no final determination shall be made in any matter except by the appropriate officials of the sending state.

(8) Any inmate confined pursuant to this compact shall be released within the territory of the sending state unless the inmate, and the sending and receiving states, shall agree upon release in some other place. The sending state shall bear the cost of such return to its territory.

(9) Any inmate confined pursuant to the terms of this compact shall have any and all rights to participate in and derive any benefits, or incur or be relieved of any obligations, or have such obligations modified or his status changed on account of any action or proceeding in which he could have participated if confined in any appropriate institution of the sending state located within such state.

(10) The parent, guardian, trustee, or other person or persons entitled under the laws of the sending state to act for, advise, or otherwise function with respect to any inmate shall not be deprived of or restricted in his exercise of any power in respect of any inmate confined pursuant to the terms of this compact.

(E) ACTS NOT REVIEWABLE IN RECEIVING STATE: EXTRADITION

(1) Any decision of the sending state in respect of any matter over which it retains jurisdiction pursuant to this compact shall be conclusive upon and not reviewable within the receiving state, but if at the time the sending state seeks to remove an inmate from an institution in the receiving state there is pending against the inmate within such state any criminal charge or if the inmate is formally accused of having committed within such state a criminal offense, the inmate shall not be returned without the consent of the receiving state until discharged from prosecution or other form of proceeding, imprisonment or detention for such offense. The duly accredited officers of the sending state shall be permitted to transport inmates pursuant to this compact through any and all states party to this compact without interference.

(2) An inmate who escapes from an institution in which he is confined pursuant to this compact shall be deemed a fugitive from the sending state and from the state in which the institution is situated. In the case of an escape to a jurisdiction other than the sending or receiving state, the responsibility for institution of extradition or rendition proceedings shall be that of the sending state, but nothing contained herein shall be construed to prevent or affect the activities of officers and agencies of any jurisdiction directed toward the apprehension and return of an escapee.

(F) FEDERAL AID

Any state party to this compact may accept federal aid for use in connection with any institution or program, the use of which is or may be affected by this compact or any contract pursuant hereto. Any inmate in a receiving state pursuant to this compact may participate in any such federally aided program or activity for which the sending and receiving states have made contractual provision, provided that if such program or activity is not part of the customary correctional regimen, the express consent of the appropriate official of the sending state shall be required therefor.

(G) ENTRY INTO FORCE

This compact shall enter into force and become effective and binding upon the states so acting when it has been enacted into law by any two states. Thereafter, this compact shall enter into force and become effective and binding as to any other of said states upon similar action by such state.

(H) WITHDRAWAL AND TERMINATION

This compact shall continue in force and remain binding upon a party state until it shall have enacted a statute repealing the same and providing for the sending of formal written notice of withdrawal from the compact to the appropriate officials of all other party states. An actual withdrawal shall not take effect until one year after the notices provided in said statute have been sent. Such withdrawal shall not relieve the withdrawing state from its obligations assumed hereunder prior to the effective date of withdrawal. Before the effective date of withdrawal, a withdrawing state shall remove to its territory, at its own expense, such inmates as it may have confined pursuant to the provisions of this compact.

(I) OTHER ARRANGEMENTS UNAFFECTED

Nothing contained in this compact shall be construed to abrogate or impair any agreement or other arrangement which a party state may have with a nonparty state for the confinement, rehabilitation, or treatment of inmates nor to repeal any oher [sic.] laws of a party state authorizing the making of cooperative institutional arrangements.

(J) CONSTRUCTION AND SEVERABILITY

The provisions of this compact shall be liberally construed and shall be severable. If any phrase, clause, sentence, or provision of this compact is declared to be contrary to the constitution of any participating state or of the United States, or the applicability thereof to any government, agency, person, or circumstance is held invalid, the validity of the remainder of this compact and the applicability thereof to any government, agency, person, or circumstance shall not be affected thereby. If this compact shall be held contrary to the constitution of any state participating therein, the compact shall remain in full force and effect as to the remaining states and in full force and effect as to the state affected as to all severable matters.

(K) POWERS

The director of the department of rehabilitation and correction is hereby authorized and directed to do all things necessary or incidental to the carrying out of the compact in every particular and he may in his discretion delegate this authority to the deputy director of the department of rehabilitation and correction.

(1976 H 47, eff. 12–28–76)

5120.51 Population and cost impact statements with respect to bills in general assembly

(A)(1) If the director of rehabilitation and correction determines that a bill introduced in the general assembly is likely to have a significant impact on the population of, or the cost of operating, any or all state correctional institutions under the administration of the department of rehabilitation and correction, the department shall prepare a population and cost impact statement for the bill, in accordance with division (A)(2) of this section.

(2) A population and cost impact statement required for a bill nshall [sic.] estimate the increase or decrease in the correctional institution population that likely would result if the bill were enacted, shall estimate, in dollars, the amount by which revenues or expenditures likely would increase or decrease if the bill were enacted, and briefly shall explain each of the estimates.

A population and cost impact statement required for a bill initially shall be prepared after the bill is referred to a committee of the general assembly in the house of origination but before the meeting of the committee at which the committee is scheduled to vote on whether to recommend the bill for passage. A copy of the statement shall be distributed to each member of the committee that is considering the bill and to the member of the general assembly who introduced it. If the bill is recommended for passage by the committee, the department shall update the statement before the bill is taken up for final consideration by the house of origination. A copy of the updated statement shall be distributed to each member of that house and to the member of the general assembly who introduced the bill. If the bill is passed by the house of origination and is introduced in the second house, the provisions of this division concerning the preparation, updating, and distribution of the statement in the house of origination also apply in the second house.

(B) The governor or any member of the general assembly, at any time, may request the department to prepare a population and cost impact statement for any bill introduced in the general assembly. Upon receipt of a request, the department promptly shall prepare a statement that includes the estimates and explanations described in division (A)(2) of this section and present a copy of it to the governor or member who made the request.

(C) In the preparation of a population and cost impact statement required by division (A) or (B) of this section, the department shall use a technologically sophisticated system capable of estimating future state correctional institution populations. The system shall have the capability to adjust its estimates based on actual and proposed changes in sentencing laws and trends, sentence durations, parole rates, crime rates, and any other data that affect state correctional institution populations. The department, in conjunction with the advisory committee appointed under division (E) of this section, shall review and update the data used in the system, not less than once every six months, to improve the accuracy of the system.

(D) At least once every six months, the department shall provide to the correctional institution inspection committee a copy of the estimates of state correctional institution populations obtained through use of the system described in division (C) of this section and a description of the assumptions regarding sentencing laws and trends, sentence durations, parole rates, crime rates, and other relevant data that were made by the department to obtain the estimates. Additionally, a copy of the estimates and a description of the assumptions made to obtain them shall be provided, upon reasonable request, to other legislative staff, including the staff of the legislative service commission and the legislative budget office of the legislative service commission, to the office of budget and management, and to the office of criminal justice services.

(E) The correctional institution inspection committee shall appoint an advisory committee to review the operation of the system for estimating future state correctional institution populations that is used by the department in the preparation of population cost impact statements pursuant to this section and to join with the department in its reviews and updating of the data used in the system under division (C) of this section. The advisory committee shall be comprised of at least one prosecuting attorney, at least one common pleas court judge, at least one public defender, at least one person who is a member or staff employee of the committee, and at least one representative of the office of criminal justice services.

(1994 H 571, eff. 10–6–94; 1993 H 152, eff. 7–1–93; 1991 H 298; 1988 S 94)

5120.52 Contract for correctional institution to provide sewage treatment services to political subdivision

The department of rehabilitation and correction may enter into a contract with a political subdivision in which a state correctional institution is located under which the institution will provide sewage treatment services for the political subdivision if the institution has a sewage treatment facility with sufficient excess capacity to provide the services.

Any such contract shall include all of the following:

(A) Limitations on the quantity of sewage that the facility will accept that are compatible with the needs of the state correctional institution;

(B) The bases for calculating reasonable rates to be charged the political subdivision for sewage treatment services and for adjusting the rates;

(C) All other provisions the department considers necessary or proper to protect the interests of the state in the facility and the purpose for which it was constructed.

All amounts due the department under the contract shall be paid to the department by the political subdivision at the times specified in the contract. The department shall deposit all such amounts in the state treasury to the credit of the correctional institutions sewage treatment facility services fund, which is hereby created. The fund shall be used by the department to pay costs associated with operating and maintaining the sewage treatment facility.

(1994 H 571, eff. 10–6–94; 1990 S 330, eff. 7–18–90)

5120.53 Transfer or exchange of convicted offender to foreign country

(A) If a treaty between the United States and a foreign country provides for the transfer or exchange, from one of the signatory countries to the other signatory country, of convicted offenders who are citizens or nationals of the other signatory country, the governor, subject to and in accordance with the terms of the treaty, may authorize the director of rehabilitation and correction to allow the transfer or exchange of convicted offenders and to take any action necessary to initiate participation in the treaty. If the governor grants the director the authority described in this division, the director may take the necessary action to initiate participation in the treaty and, subject to and in accordance with division (B) of this section and the terms of the treaty, may allow the transfer or exchange to a foreign country that has signed the treaty of any convicted offender who is a citizen or national of that signatory country.

(B)(1) No convicted offender who is serving a term of imprisonment in this state for aggravated murder, murder, or a felony of the first or second degree, who is serving a mandatory prison term imposed under section 2925.03 or 2925.11 of the Revised Code in circumstances in which the court was required to impose as the mandatory prison term the maximum prison term authorized for the degree of offense committed, who is serving a term of imprisonment in this state imposed for an offense committed prior to the effective date of this amendment that was an aggravated felony of the first or second degree or that was aggravated trafficking in violation of division (A)(9) or (10) of section 2925.03 of the Revised Code, or who has been sentenced to death in this state shall be transferred or exchanged to another country pursuant to a treaty of the type described in division (A) of this section.

(2) If a convicted offender is serving a term of imprisonment in this state and the offender is a citizen or national of a foreign country that has signed a treaty of the type described in division (A) of this section, if the governor has granted the director of rehabilitation and correction the authority described in that division, and if the transfer or exchange of the offender is not barred by division (B)(1) of this section, the director or the director's designee may approve the offender for transfer or exchange pursuant to the treaty if the director or the designee, after consideration of the factors set forth in the rules adopted by the department under division (D) of this section and all other relevant factors, determines that the transfer or exchange of the offender is appropriate.

(C) Notwithstanding any provision of the Revised Code regarding the parole eligibility of, or the duration or calculation of a sentence of imprisonment imposed upon, an offender, if a convicted offender is serving a term of imprisonment in this state and the offender is a citizen or national of a foreign country that has signed a treaty of the type described in division (A) of this section, if the offender is serving an indefinite term of imprisonment, if the offender is barred from being transferred or exchanged pursuant to the treaty due to the indefinite nature of the offender's term of imprisonment, and if in accordance with division (B)(2) of this section the director of rehabilitation and correction or the director's designee approves the offender for transfer or exchange pursuant to the treaty, the parole board, pursuant to rules adopted by the director, shall set a date certain for the release of the offender. To the extent possible, the date certain that is set shall be reasonably proportionate to the indefinite term of imprisonment that the offender is serving. The date certain that is set for the release of the offender shall be considered only for purposes of facilitating the international transfer or exchange of the offender, shall not be viable or actionable for any other purpose, and shall not create any expectation or guarantee of release. If an offender for whom a date certain for release is set under this division is not transferred to or exchanged with the foreign country pursuant to the treaty, the date certain is null and void, and the offender's release shall be determined pursuant to the laws and rules of this state pertaining to parole eligibility and the duration and calculation of an indefinite sentence of imprisonment.

(D) If the governor, pursuant to division (A) of this section, authorizes the director of rehabilitation and correction to allow any transfer or exchange of convicted offenders as described in that division, the director shall adopt rules under Chapter 119. of the Revised Code to implement the provisions of this section.

The rules shall include a rule that requires the director or the director's designee, in determining whether to approve a convicted offender who is serving a term of imprisonment in this state for transfer or exchange pursuant to a treaty of the type described in division (A) of this section, to consider all of the following factors:

(1) The nature of the offense for which the offender is serving the term of imprisonment in this state;

(2) The likelihood that, if the offender is transferred or exchanged to a foreign country pursuant to the treaty, the offender will serve a shorter period of time in imprisonment in the foreign country than the offender would serve if the offender is not transferred or exchanged to the foreign country pursuant to the treaty;

(3) The likelihood that, if the offender is transferred or exchanged to a foreign country pursuant to the treaty, the offender will return or attempt to return to this state after the offender has been released from imprisonment in the foreign country;

(4) The degree of any shock to the conscience of justice and society that will be experienced in this state if the offender is transferred or exchanged to a foreign country pursuant to the treaty;

(5) All other factors that the department determines are relevant to the determination.

(1995 S 2, eff. 7–1–96; 1994 S 242, eff. 10–6–94)

5120.55 Physician recruitment program

(A) As used in this section, "physician" means an individual who is authorized under Chapter 4731. of the Revised Code to practice medicine and surgery, osteopathic medicine and surgery, or podiatry.

(B) The department of rehabilitation and correction may establish a physician recruitment program under which the department, by means of a contract entered into under division (C) of this section, agrees to repay all or part of the principal and interest of a government or other educational loan incurred by a physician who agrees to provide services to inmates of correctional institutions under the department's administration. To be eligible to participate in the program, a physician must have attended a school that was, during the time of attendance, a medical school or osteopathic medical school in this country accredited by the liaison committee on medical education or the American osteopathic association, a college of podiatry in this country recognized as being in good standing under section 4731.53 of the Revised Code, or a medical school, osteopathic medical school, or college of podiatry located outside this country that was acknowledged by the world health organization and verified by a member state of that organization as operating within that state's jurisdiction.

(C) The department shall enter into a contract with each physician it recruits under this section. Each contract shall include at least the following terms:

(1) The physician agrees to provide a specified scope of medical, osteopathic medical, or podiatric services to inmates of one or more specified state correctional institutions for a specified number of hours per week for a specified number of years.

(2) The department agrees to repay all or a specified portion of the principal and interest of a government or other educational loan taken by the physician for the following expenses to attend, for up to a maximum of four years, a school that qualifies the physician to participate in the program:

(a) Tuition;

(b) Other educational expenses for specific purposes, including fees, books, and laboratory expenses, in amounts determined to be reasonable in accordance with rules adopted under division (D) of this section;

(c) Room and board, in an amount determined to be reasonable in accordance with rules adopted under division (D) of this section.

(3) The physician agrees to pay the department a specified amount, which shall be no less than the amount already paid by the department pursuant to its agreement, as damages if the physician fails to complete the service obligation agreed to or fails to comply with other specified terms of the contract. The contract may vary the amount of damages based on the portion of the physician's service obligation that remains uncompleted.

(4) Other terms agreed upon by the parties.

The physician's lending institution or the Ohio board of regents may be a party to the contract. The contract may include an assignment to the department of the physician's duty to repay the principal and interest of the loan.

(D) If the department elects to implement the physician recruitment program, it shall adopt rules in accordance with Chapter 119. of the Revised Code that establish all of the following:

(1) Criteria for designating institutions for which physicians will be recruited;

(2) Criteria for selecting physicians for participation in the program;

(3) Criteria for determining the portion of a physician's loan which the department will agree to repay;

(4) Criteria for determining reasonable amounts of the expenses described in divisions (C)(2)(b) and (c) of this section;

(5) Procedures for monitoring compliance by physicians with the terms of their contracts;

(6) Any other criteria or procedures necessary to implement the program.

(1996 H 627, eff. 12–2–96; 1995 S 143, eff. 3–5–96; 1994 H 571, eff. 10–6–94; 1992 H 478, eff. 1–14–93)

5120.56 Recovery of cost debts from offenders in custody; offender financial responsibility fund

(A) As used in sections 5120.56 to 5120.58 of the Revised Code:

(1) "Ancillary services" means services provided to an offender as necessary for the particular circumstances of the offender's personal supervision, including, but not limited to, specialized counseling, testing, or other services not included in the calculation of residential or supervision costs.

(2) "Cost debt" means a cost of incarceration or supervision that may be assessed against and collected from an offender as a debt to the state as described in division (D) of this section.

(3) "Detention facility" means any place used for the confinement of a person charged with or convicted of any crime.

(4) "Offender" means any inmate, parolee, person placed under a community control sanction, releasee, or other person who has been convicted of or pleaded guilty to any felony or misdemeanor and is sentenced to any of the following:

(a) A term of imprisonment, a prison term, a jail term, or another type of confinement in a detention facility;

(b) Participation in another correctional program in lieu of incarceration.

(5) "Community control sanction," "prison term," and "jail term" have the same meanings as in section 2929.01 of the Revised Code.

(6) "Parolee" and "releasee" have the same meanings as in section 2967.01 of the Revised Code.

(B) The department of rehabilitation and correction may recover from an offender who is in its custody or under its supervision any cost debt described in division (D) of this section. To satisfy a cost debt described in that division that relates to an offender, the department may apply directly assets that are in the department's possession and that are being held for that offender without further proceedings in aid of execution, and, if assets belonging to or subject to the direction of that offender are in the possession of a third party, the department may request the attorney general to initiate proceedings to collect the assets from the third party to satisfy the cost debt.

(C) Except as otherwise provided in division (E) or (G) of this section, all of the following assets of an offender shall be subject to attachment, collection, or application toward the cost debts described in division (D) of this section that are to be recovered under division (B) of this section:

(1) Subject to division (E) of this section, any pay the offender receives from the state;

(2) Subject to division (E) of this section, any funds the offender receives from persons on an approved visitor list;

(3) Any liquid assets belonging to the offender and in the custody of the department;

(4) Any assets the offender acquires or any other income the offender earns subsequent to the offender's commitment.

(D) Costs of incarceration or supervision that may be assessed against and collected from an offender under division (B) of this section as a debt to the state shall include, but are not limited to, all of the following costs that accrue while the offender is in the custody or under the supervision of the department:

(1) Any user fee or copayment for services at a detention facility or housing facility, including, but not limited to, a fee or copayment for sick call visits;

(2) Assessment for damage to or destruction of property in a detention facility subsequent to commitment;

(3) Restitution to an offender or to a staff member of a state correctional institution for theft, loss, or damage to the personal property of the offender or staff member;

(4) The cost of housing and feeding the offender in a detention facility;

(5) The cost of supervision of the offender;

(6) The cost of any ancillary services provided to the offender;

(7) The cost of any medical care provided to the offender.

(E) The cost of housing and feeding an offender in a state correctional institution shall not be collected from a payment made to the offender for performing an activity at a state job or assignment that pays less than the minimum wage or from money the offender receives from visitors, unless the combined assets in the offender's institution personal account exceed, at any time, one hundred dollars. If the combined assets in that account exceed one hundred dollars, the cost of housing and feeding the offender may be collected from the amount in excess of one hundred dollars.

(F)(1) The department shall adopt rules pursuant to section 111.15 of the Revised Code to implement the requirements of this section.

(2) The rules adopted under division (F)(1) of this section shall include, but are not limited to, rules that establish or contain all of the following:

(a) A process for ascertaining the items of cost to be assessed against an offender;

(b) Subject to division (F)(3) of this section, a process by which the offender shall have the opportunity to respond to the assessment of costs under division (B) of this section and to contest any item of cost in the department's calculation or as it applies to the offender;

(c) A requirement that the offender be notified, in writing, of a final decision to collect or apply the offender's assets under division (B) of this section and that the notification be provided after the offender has had an opportunity to contest the application or collection;

(d) Criteria for evaluating an offender's ongoing, permanent injury and evaluating the ability of that type of offender to provide for the offender after incarceration.

(3) The rules adopted under division (F)(1) of this section may allow the collection of a cost debt as a flat fee or over time in installments. If the cost debt is to be collected over time in installments, the rules are not required to permit the offender an opportunity to contest the assessment of each installment. The rules may establish a standard fee to apply to all offenders who receive a particular service.

(G) The department shall not collect cost debts or apply offender assets toward a cost debt under division (B) of this section if, due to an ongoing, permanent injury, the collection or application would unjustly limit the offender's ability to provide for the offender after incarceration.

(H) If an offender acquires assets after the offender is convicted of or pleads guilty to an offense and if the transferor knows of the offender's status as an offender, the transferor shall notify the department in advance of the transfer.

(I) There is hereby created in the state treasury the offender financial responsibility fund. All moneys collected by or on behalf of the department under this section, and all moneys currently in the department's custody that are applied to satisfy an allowable cost debt under this section, shall be deposited into the fund. The department may expend moneys in the fund for goods and services of the same type as those for which offenders are assessed pursuant to this section.

(2002 H 490, eff. 1–1–04; 2002 H 170, eff. 9–6–02; 1997 S 111, eff. 3–17–98)

5120.57 Offenders covered under sickness, health or accident insurance

(A) For each offender who is in the custody or under the supervision of the department of rehabilitation and correction, the department may make a determination as to whether the offender is covered under an individual or group sickness and accident insurance policy or an individual or group health insuring corporation policy, contract, or agreement. If the offender has coverage of that type, the department shall familiarize itself with the terms and conditions to receive benefits under the policy, contract, or agreement.

(B) If, pursuant to division (A) of this section, it is determined that the offender is covered under an individual or group sickness and accident insurance policy or an individual or group health insuring corporation policy, contract, or agreement and if, while that coverage is in force, the department renders or arranges for the rendering of health care services to the person in accordance with the terms and conditions of the policy, contract, or agreement, the department or provider of the health care services, as appropriate under the terms and conditions of the policy, contract, or agreement, may submit a claim for payment for the health care services to the appropriate third-party payer. If the policy holder is the offender, the offender shall be required to assign payment of benefits directly to the provider or department, as appropriate. If the policy holder is not the offender, the policy holder shall be asked to voluntarily provide policy information and assign payments directly to the provider or department, as appropriate. The department shall provide the third-party payer with a copy of the assignment of benefits by the policy holder. The policy holder and the third-party payer shall make all arrangements necessary to ensure that payment of any amount due on the claim is made to the provider or department as specified in the assignment. The department shall remain ultimately responsible for payment of all health care services provided to an offender in the custody or under the supervision of the department but shall be the payer of last resort. If the department pays a provider for health care services rendered to an offender and payment subsequently is made for the same services by a third-party payer, the provider shall refund the duplicate payment to the department and, the department shall deposit the refunded payment into the offender financial responsibility fund as described in division (E) of this section.

(C) If, pursuant to division (A) of this section, it is determined that the offender is covered under an individual or group sickness and accident insurance policy or an individual or group health insuring corporation policy, contract, or agreement, the department shall make a determination, after considering security, public safety, and transportation issues, whether or not to render or arrange for the rendering of health care services in accordance with the terms and conditions of the policy, contract, or agreement. The department, based on security, public safety, or transportation concerns or any combination of those concerns, may arrange for the rendering of health care services for the offender at a health care facility, by a provider, or at a health care facility and by a provider not covered by the policy, contract, or agreement and pay the costs of the health care services for the offender.

(D) If the department renders or arranges for the rendering of health care services to an offender and pays for the services, the department reserves the right to seek reimbursement from a third-party payer for the services if it subsequently is determined that the offender was covered under an individual or group sickness and accident insurance policy or an individual or group health insuring corporation policy, contract, or agreement. The department shall submit a claim for reimbursement of the type described in this division within the time frames applicable to claims submitted by a policy holder in accordance with the terms and conditions of the policy, contract, or agreement.

(E) Any payment made to the department pursuant to division (B) of this section shall be deposited into the offender financial responsibility fund created in section 5120.56 of the Revised Code.

(F) If, at the time the department arranges for health care services for an offender and a provider renders those services, the department determines pursuant to division (A) of this section that the offender is covered, or potentially is covered, under an individual or group sickness and accident insurance policy or an individual or group health insuring corporation policy, contract, or agreement, then all of the following apply:

(1) The department is responsible for any cost-sharing, copayments, or deductibles required under the policy, contract, or agreement.

(2) If the insurer or potential insurer denies the claim for payment, the department remains liable for payment to the provider of services.

(3) If an insurer covers a service, but the amount the insurer pays to the provider is less than the amount negotiated and established by contract then in effect between the department and the provider, the department is liable for reimbursing the difference to the provider.

(G) Nothing in this section requires a third-party payer to reimburse any provider or the department for health care services not covered under the terms or conditions of an individual or group sickness and accident insurance policy, an individual or group health insuring corporation policy, contract, or agreement, or any other policy, contract, or agreement.

(2002 H 170, eff. 9–6–02)

5120.58 Rehabilitation and correction department to adopt rules

The department of rehabilitation and correction shall adopt rules under section 111.15 of the Revised Code to do both of the following:

(A) Establish a schedule of health care benefits that are available to offenders who are in the custody or under the supervision of the department;

(B) Establish a program to encourage the utilization of preventive health care services by offenders.

(2002 H 170, eff. 9–6–02)

5120.60 Office of victims' services

(A) There is hereby created in the division of parole and community services the office of victims' services.

(B) The office shall provide assistance to victims of crime, victims' representatives designated under section 2930.02 of the Revised Code, and members of the victim's family. The assistance shall include, but not be limited to, providing information about the policies and procedures of the department of rehabilitation and correction and the status of offenders under the department's jurisdiction.

(C) The office shall also make available publications that will assist victims in contacting staff of the department about problems with offenders under the supervision of the adult parole authority or confined in state correctional institutions under the department's jurisdiction.

(D) The office shall employ a victims coordinator who shall administer the office's functions. The victims coordinator shall be in the unclassified civil service and report directly to the chief of the division.

(E) The office shall also employ at least three persons in the unclassified civil service whose primary duties shall be to help parole board hearing officers identify victims' issues and to make recommendations to the parole board in accordance with rules adopted by the department. The member of the parole board appointed pursuant to division (B) of section 5149.10 of the Revised Code shall approve the hiring of the employees of the office.

(F) The office shall coordinate its activities with the member of the parole board appointed pursuant to division (B) of section 5149.10 of the Revised Code. The victims coordinator and other employees of the office shall have full access to records of prisoners under the department's jurisdiction.

(G) Information provided to the office of victim services by victims of crime or a victim representative designated under section 2930.02 of the Revised Code for the purpose of program participation, of receiving services, or to communicate acts of an inmate or person under the supervision of the adult parole authority that threaten the safety and security of the victim shall be confidential and is not a public record under section 149.43 of the Revised Code.

(H) As used in this section, "crime," "member of the victim's family," and "victim" have the meanings given in section 2930.01 of the Revised Code.

(2002 H 510, eff. 3–31–03; 1995 S 2, eff. 7–1–96)

5120.61 Standards for assessing offender convicted of sexually violent offense and sexually violent predator specification; risk assessment report

Note: See also following version of this section, eff. 4–29–05.

(A)(1) Not later than ninety days after the effective date of this section, the department of rehabilitation and correction shall adopt standards that it will use under this section to assess a criminal offender who is convicted of or pleads guilty to a sexually violent offense and also is convicted of or pleads guilty to a sexually violent predator specification that was included in the indictment, count in the indictment, or information charging that offense. The department may periodically revise the standards.

(2) When the department is requested by the parole board or the court to provide a risk assessment report of the offender under section 2971.04 or 2971.05 of the Revised Code, it shall assess the offender and complete the assessment as soon as possible after the offender has commenced serving the prison term or term of life imprisonment without parole imposed under division (A) of section 2971.03 of the Revised Code. Thereafter, the department shall update a risk assessment report pertaining to an offender as follows:

(a) Periodically, in the discretion of the department, provided that each report shall be updated no later than two years after its initial preparation or most recent update;

(b) Upon the request of the parole board for use in determining pursuant to section 2971.04 of the Revised Code whether it should terminate its control over an offender's service of a prison term imposed upon the offender under division (A)(3) of section 2971.03 of the Revised Code;

(c) Upon the request of the court.

(3) After the department of rehabilitation and correction assesses an offender pursuant to division (A)(2) of this section, it shall prepare a report that contains its risk assessment for the offender or, if a risk assessment report previously has been prepared, it shall update the risk assessment report.

(4) The department of rehabilitation and correction shall provide each risk assessment report that it prepares or updates pursuant to this section regarding an offender to all of the following:

(a) The parole board for its use in determining pursuant to section 2971.04 of the Revised Code whether it should terminate its control over an offender's service of a prison term imposed upon the offender under division (A)(3) of section 2971.03 of the Revised Code, if the parole board has not terminated its control over the offender;

(b) The court for use in determining, pursuant to section 2971.05 of the Revised Code, whether to modify the requirement that the offender serve the entire prison term imposed upon the offender under division (A)(3) of section 2971.03 of the Revised Code in a state correctional institution, whether to revise any modification previously made, or whether to terminate the prison term;

(c) The prosecuting attorney who prosecuted the case, or the successor in office to that prosecuting attorney;

(d) The offender.

(B) When the department of rehabilitation and correction provides a risk assessment report regarding an offender to the parole board or court pursuant to division (A)(4)(a) or (b) of this section, the department, prior to the parole board's or court's hearing, also shall provide to the offender or to the offender's attorney of record a copy of the report and a copy of any other relevant documents the department possesses regarding the offender that the department does not consider to be confidential.

(C) As used in this section, "sexually violent offense" and "sexually violent predator specification" have the same meanings as in section 2971.01 of the Revised Code.

(1996 H 180, eff. 1-1-97)

Note: See also following version of this section, eff. 4–29–05.

5120.61 Standards for assessing offender convicted of violent sex offense or designated homicide, assault, or kidnapping offense and adjudicated a sexually violent predator; risk assessment report (later effective date)

Note: See also preceding version of this section, in effect until 4–29–05.

(A)(1) Not later than ninety days after the effective date of this section, the department of rehabilitation and correction shall adopt standards that it will use under this section to assess a criminal offender who is convicted of or pleads guilty to a violent sex offense or designated homicide, assault, or kidnapping offense and is adjudicated a sexually violent predator in relation to that offense. The department may periodically revise the standards.

(2) When the department is requested by the parole board or the court to provide a risk assessment report of the offender under section 2971.04 or 2971.05 of the Revised Code, it shall assess the offender and complete the assessment as soon as possible after the offender has commenced serving the prison term or term of life imprisonment without parole imposed under division (A) of section 2971.03 of the Revised Code. Thereafter, the department shall update a risk assessment report pertaining to an offender as follows:

(a) Periodically, in the discretion of the department, provided that each report shall be updated no later than two years after its initial preparation or most recent update;

(b) Upon the request of the parole board for use in determining pursuant to section 2971.04 of the Revised Code whether it should terminate its control over an offender's service of a prison term imposed upon the offender under division (A)(3) of section 2971.03 of the Revised Code;

(c) Upon the request of the court.

(3) After the department of rehabilitation and correction assesses an offender pursuant to division (A)(2) of this section, it shall prepare a report that contains its risk assessment for the offender or, if a risk assessment report previously has been prepared, it shall update the risk assessment report.

(4) The department of rehabilitation and correction shall provide each risk assessment report that it prepares or updates pursuant to this section regarding an offender to all of the following:

(a) The parole board for its use in determining pursuant to section 2971.04 of the Revised Code whether it should terminate its control over an offender's service of a prison term imposed upon the offender under division (A)(3) of section 2971.03 of the Revised Code, if the parole board has not terminated its control over the offender;

(b) The court for use in determining, pursuant to section 2971.05 of the Revised Code, whether to modify the requirement that the offender serve the entire prison term imposed upon the offender under division (A)(3) of section 2971.03 of the Revised Code in a state correctional institution, whether to revise any modification previously made, or whether to terminate the prison term;

(c) The prosecuting attorney who prosecuted the case, or the successor in office to that prosecuting attorney;

(d) The offender.

(B) When the department of rehabilitation and correction provides a risk assessment report regarding an offender to the parole board or court pursuant to division (A)(4)(a) or (b) of this section, the department, prior to the parole board's or court's hearing, also shall provide to the offender or to the offender's attorney of record a copy of the report and a copy of any other relevant documents the department possesses regarding the offender that the department does not consider to be confidential.

(C) As used in this section:

(1) "Adjudicated a sexually violent predator" has the same meaning as in section 2929.01 of the Revised Code, and a person is " adjudicated a sexually violent predator" in the same manner and the same circumstances as are described in that section.

(2) "Designated homicide, assault, or kidnapping offense" and " violent sex offense" have the same meanings as in section 2971.01 of the Revised Code.

(2004 H 473, eff. 4–29–05; 1996 H 180, eff. 1–1–97)

Note: See also preceding version of this section, in effect until 4–29–05.

5120.62 Internet access for prisoners

The director of rehabilitation and correction shall adopt rules under Chapter 119. of the Revised Code that govern the establishment and operation of a system that provides access to the internet for prisoners who are participating in an approved educational program with direct supervision that requires the use of the internet for training or research purposes. The rules shall include all of the following:

(A) Criteria by which inmates may be screened and approved for access or training involving the internet;

(B) Designation of the authority to approve internet sites for authorized use;

(C) A requirement that only pre-approved sites will be accessible on the computers used by prisoners in the educational program;

(D) A process for the periodic review of the operation of the system, including users of the system and the sites accessed by the system;

(E) Sanctions that must be imposed against prisoners and staff members who violate the department rules governing prisoner access to the internet.

(2000 S 12, eff. 6–8–00)

5120.63 Random drug testing program

(A) As used in this section:

(1) "Random drug testing" means a procedure in which blood or urine specimens are collected from individuals chosen by automatic, random selection and without prearrangement or planning, for the purpose of scientifically analyzing the specimens to determine whether the individual ingested or was injected with a drug of abuse.

(2) "State correctional institution" has the same meaning as in section 2967.01 of the Revised Code.

(3) "Stated prison term" has the same meaning as in section 2929.01 of the Revised Code.

(B) The department of rehabilitation and correction shall establish and administer a statewide random drug testing program in which all persons who were convicted of or pleaded guilty to a felony offense and are serving a stated prison term in a state correctional institution shall submit to random drug testing. The department may enter into contracts with laboratories or entities in the state that are accredited by the national institute on drug abuse to perform blood or urine specimen collection, documentation, maintenance, transportation, preservation, storage, and analyses and other duties required under this section in the performance of random drug testing of prisoners in those correctional institutions. The terms of any contract entered into under this division shall include a requirement that the laboratory or entity and its employees, the superintendents, managing officers, and employees of state correctional institutions, all employees of the department, and all other persons comply with the standards for the performance of random drug testing as specified in the policies and procedures established by the department under division (D) of this section. If no laboratory or entity has entered into a contract as specified in this division, the department shall cause a prisoner to submit to random drug testing performed by a reputable public laboratory to determine whether the prisoner ingested or was injected with a drug of abuse.

(C) A prisoner who is subjected to random drug testing under this section and whose test indicates that the prisoner ingested or was injected with a drug of abuse shall pay the fee for that positive test and other subsequent test fees as a sanction specified by the department of rehabilitation and correction pursuant to division (D)(6) of this section.

(D) The department of rehabilitation and correction shall establish policies and procedures to implement the random drug testing program established under this section. The policies and procedures shall include, but are not limited to, provisions that do the following:

(1) Establish standards for the performance of random drug testing that include, but are not limited to, standards governing the following:

(a) The collection by the laboratory or entity described in division (B) of this section of blood or urine specimens of individuals in a scientifically or medically approved manner and under reasonable and sanitary conditions;

(b) The collection and testing by the laboratory or entity described in division (B) of this section of blood or urine specimens with due regard for the privacy of the individual being tested and in a manner reasonably calculated to prevent substitutions or interference with the collection and testing of the specimens;

(c) The documentation of blood or urine specimens collected by the laboratory or entity described in division (B) of this section and documentation procedures that reasonably preclude the possibility of erroneous identification of test results and that provide the individual being tested an opportunity to furnish information identifying any prescription or nonprescription drugs used by the individual in connection with a medical condition;

(d) The collection, maintenance, storage, and transportation by the laboratory or entity described in division (B) of this section of blood or urine specimens in a manner that reasonably precludes the possibility of contamination or adulteration of the specimens;

(e) The testing by the laboratory or entity described in division (B) of this section of blood or urine specimen of an individual to determine whether the individual ingested or was injected with a drug of abuse, in a manner that conforms to scientifically accepted analytical methods and procedures and that may include verification or confirmation of any positive test result by a reliable analytical method;

(f) The analysis of an individual's blood or urine specimen by an employee of the laboratory or entity described in division (B) of this section who is qualified by education, training, and experience to perform that analysis and whose regular duties include the analysis of blood or urine specimens to determine the presence of a drug of abuse and whether the individual who is the subject of the test ingested or was injected with a drug of abuse.

(2) Specify the frequency of performing random drug testing of prisoners in a state correctional institution;

(3) Prescribe procedures for the automatic, random selection of prisoners in a state correctional institution to submit to random drug testing under this section;

(4) Provide for reasonable safeguards for the transmittal from the laboratory or entity described in division (B) of this section to the department of the results of the random drug testing of

prisoners in state correctional institutions pursuant to division (F) of this section;

(5) Establish a reasonable fee to cover the costs associated with random drug testing and analyses performed by a laboratory or entity under this section and establish procedures for the collection of those fees from the prisoners subjected to the drug test;

(6) Establish guidelines for imposing sanctions upon a prisoner whose test results indicate that the prisoner ingested or was injected with a drug of abuse.

(E) The warden of each correctional institution, pursuant to the contract entered into under division (B) of this section or, if no contract was entered into under that division, pursuant to the policies and procedures established by the department of rehabilitation and correction under division (D) of this section, shall facilitate the collection, documentation, maintenance, and transportation by the laboratory or entity described in division (B) of this section, of the blood or urine specimens of the prisoners in the state correctional institution who are subject to random drug testing.

(F) A laboratory or entity that performs random drug testing of prisoners and analyses of blood or urine specimens under this section shall transmit the results of each drug test to the department of rehabilitation and correction. The department shall file for record the results of the drug tests that indicate whether or not each prisoner in the state correctional institution who was subjected to the drug test ingested or was injected with a drug of abuse. The department shall send a copy of the results of the drug tests to the warden of the state correctional institution in which the prisoner who was subjected to the drug test is confined. The warden shall give appropriate notice of the drug test results to each prisoner who was subjected to the drug test and whose drug test results indicate that the prisoner ingested or was injected with a drug of abuse. In accordance with institutional disciplinary procedures, the warden shall afford that prisoner an opportunity to be heard regarding the results of the drug test and to present contrary evidence at a hearing held before the warden within thirty days after notification to the prisoner under this division. After the hearing, if a hearing is held, the warden shall make a determination regarding any evidence presented by the prisoner. If the warden rejects the evidence presented by the prisoner at the hearing or if no hearing is held under this division, the warden may subject the prisoner to sanctions that include payment of the fee for the test.

(G) If a prisoner has been subjected to two or more drug tests pursuant to this section and if the results of two of those tests indicate that the prisoner ingested or was injected with a drug of abuse, the parole board may extend the stated prison term of the prisoner pursuant to the bad time provisions in section 2967.11 of the Revised Code if by ingesting or being injected with the drug of abuse the prisoner committed a violation as defined in that section.

(H) All fees for random drug tests collected from prisoners under this section or collected by the adult parole authority under section 2929.15, 2951.05, or 2967.131 of the Revised Code shall be forwarded to the treasurer of state for deposit in the offender financial responsibility fund created in division (I) of section 5120.56 of the Revised Code.

(2000 H 349, eff. 9–22–00)

5120.64 Rules regarding return of prisoners from outside of state

(A) As used in this section:

(1) "Ohio prisoner" means a person who is charged with or convicted of a crime in this state or who is alleged or found to be a delinquent child in this state.

(2) "Out–of–state prisoner" and "private contractor" have the same meanings as in section 9.07 of the Revised Code.

(B) Not later than nine months after the effective date of this section, the department of rehabilitation and correction, in consultation with the attorney general, the county commissioners association of Ohio, and the buckeye state sheriffs association, shall adopt rules under Chapter 119. of the Revised Code regarding the return of Ohio prisoners from outside of this state into this state by a private person or entity pursuant to a contract entered into with a sheriff under authority of division (e) of section 311.29 of the Revised Code or the adult parole authority under authority of division (b) of section 5149.03 of the Revised Code. The rules shall establish all of the following:

(1) Standards that specify required training of officers and employees of the private person or entity that actually engage in the return of the prisoners, including standards related to the length and nature of the training;

(2) Physical standards for vehicles used in the return of the prisoners;

(3) Standards that govern the responsibility of the private person or entity to do one or more of the following:

(a) Provide an adequate policy of liability insurance to cover all injuries, death, or loss to person or property that arise from or is related to its return of the prisoners;

(b) Indemnify and hold harmless the sheriff, the county, and all county officers and employees regarding a contract for the return of prisoners entered into under division (E) of section 311.29 of the Revised Code or the department of rehabilitation and correction and all state officers and employees regarding a contract for the return of prisoners entered into under division (B) of section 5149.03 of the Revised Code;

(c) File a performance bond or other surety to guarantee performance.

(4) Standards requiring the private person or entity to have criminal records checks and pre-employment drug testing performed for officers and employees of the private person or entity that actually engage in the return of the prisoners and to have a random drug-screening policy and be able to document compliance with the policy;

(5) Standards requiring the private person or entity to have twenty-four-hour operations staff to constantly monitor activities in the field and to have on-board, constant communication ability with vehicles in the field;

(6) Standards requiring the officers and employees of the private person or entity that actually engage in the return of the prisoners to be CPR and first-aid certified.

(C) Upon the effective date of the rules adopted under division (B) of this section, in no case shall a private person or entity return Ohio prisoners from outside of this state into this state for a sheriff or for the adult parole authority unless the private person or entity complies with all applicable standards that are contained in the rules.

(D) This section does not apply regarding any out-of-state prisoner who is brought into this state to be housed pursuant to section 9.07 of the Revised Code in a correctional facility in this state that is managed and operated by a private contractor.

(2000 H 661, eff. 3–15–01)

PRISON NURSERY PROGRAM

5120.65 Establishment; definitions

(A) The department of rehabilitation and correction may establish in one or more of the institutions for women operated by the department a prison nursery program under which eligible inmates and children born to them while in the custody of the department may reside together in the institution. If the department establishes a prison nursery program in one or more institutions under this section, sections 5120.651 to 5120.657 of the Revised Code apply regarding the program. If the department establishes a prison nursery program and an inmate participates in the program, neither the inmate's participation in the program nor any provision of sections 5120.65 to 5120.657 of the Revised Code affects, modifies, or interferes with the inmate's custodial rights of the child or establishes legal custody of the child with the department.

(B) As used in sections 5120.651 to 5120.657 of the Revised Code:

(1) "Prison nursery program" means the prison nursery program established by the department of rehabilitation and correction under this section, if one is so established.

(2) "Public assistance" has the same meaning as in section 5101.58 of the Revised Code.

(3) "Support" means amounts to be paid under a support order.

(4) "Support order" has the same meaning as in section 3119.01 of the Revised Code.

(2004 H 117, eff. 9–3–04; 2000 H 661, eff. 3–15–01)

5120.651 Eligibility

An inmate is eligible to participate in the prison nursery program if she is pregnant at the time she is delivered into the custody of the department of rehabilitation and correction, she gives birth on or after the date the program is implemented, she is subject to a sentence of imprisonment of not more than eighteen months, and she and the child meet any other criteria established by the department.

(2000 H 661, eff. 3–15–01)

5120.652 Written agreements; assignment of rights to support; placement of children specified

To participate in the prison nursery program, each eligible inmate selected by the department shall do all the following:

(A) Agree in writing to do all the following:

(1) Comply with any program, educational, counseling, and other requirements established for the program by the department of rehabilitation and correction;

(2) If eligible, have the child participate in the medicaid program or a health insurance program;

(3) Accept the normal risks of childrearing;

(4) Abide by any court decisions regarding the allocation of parental rights and responsibilities with respect to the child.

(B) Assign to the department any rights to support from any other person, excluding support assigned pursuant to section 5107.20 of the Revised Code and medical support assigned pursuant to section 5101.59 of the Revised Code;

(C) Specify with whom the child is to be placed in the event the inmate's participation in the program is terminated for a reason other than release from imprisonment.

(2000 H 661, eff. 3–15–01)

5120.653 Termination of participation

An inmate's participation in the prison nursery program may be terminated by the department of rehabilitation and correction if one of the following occurs:

(A) The inmate fails to comply with the agreement entered into under division (A) of section 5120.652 of the Revised Code.

(B) The inmate's child becomes seriously ill, cannot meet medical criteria established by the department of rehabilitation and correction for the program, or otherwise cannot safely participate in the program.

(C) A court issues an order that designates a person other than the inmate as the child's residential parent and legal custodian.

(D) A juvenile court, in an action brought pursuant to division (A)(2) of section 2151.23 of the Revised Code, grants custody of the child to a person other than the inmate.

(E) An order is issued pursuant to section 3109.04 of the Revised Code granting shared parenting of the child.

(F) An order of disposition regarding the child is issued pursuant to division (A)(2), (3), or (4) of section 2151.353 of the Revised Code granting temporary, permanent, or legal custody of the child to a person, other than the inmate, or to a public children services agency or private child placing agency.

(G) The inmate is released from imprisonment.

(2000 H 661, eff. 3–15–01)

5120.654 Collection of support payments upon assignment of rights to support

(A) The rights to support assigned by an inmate pursuant to section 5120.652 of the Revised Code constitute an obligation of the person who is responsible for providing the support to the department of rehabilitation and correction for the support provided the inmate and child pursuant to the prison nursery program. The division of child support in the department of job and family services shall collect support payments made pursuant to the assignment and forward them to the department of rehabilitation and correction.

(B) The department of rehabilitation and correction may receive the following:

(1) Money that is assigned or donated on behalf of, and public assistance provided to, a specific inmate or child participating in the prison nursery program;

(2) Money assigned or donated to establish and maintain the prison nursery program.

(C) The amounts described in division (B)(1) of this section shall be placed in the individual nursery account created and maintained under section 5120.655 of the Revised Code for the inmate and child for whom the money was received. The money described in division (B)(2) of this section shall be deposited in the appropriate prison nursery program fund.

(2000 H 661, eff. 3–15–01)

5120.655 Funds and accounts

The managing officer of each institution in which a prison nursery program is established pursuant to section 5120.65 of the Revised Code shall do the following:

(A) Create and maintain a prison nursery program fund to pay expenses associated with the prison nursery program;

(B) Create and maintain an individual nursery account for each inmate participating in the prison nursery program at the institution to help pay for the support provided to the inmate and child pursuant to the program.

(2000 H 661, eff. 3–15–01)

5120.656 Regulatory power of job and family services department

Notwithstanding any other provision of the Revised Code, neither the prison nursery program nor the department of rehabilitation and correction, with respect to the program, is subject to any regulation, licensing, or oversight by the department of job and family services unless the departments agree to voluntary regulation, licensing, or oversight by the department of job and family services.

(2000 H 661, eff. 3–15–01)

5120.657 Rulemaking powers

If the department of rehabilitation and correction establishes the prison nursery program, it shall, in accordance with Chapter 119. of the Revised Code, adopt rules that establish requirements necessary and appropriate to the establishment, implementation, and operation of the program. The department shall adopt the rules prior to implementing the program.

(2000 H 661, eff. 3–15–01)

PENALTIES

5120.99 Penalties

A person who violates division (B)(2) of section 5120.211 of the Revised Code shall be fined not more than two thousand five hundred dollars on a first offense and not more than twenty thousand dollars on a subsequent offense.

(1997 S 111, eff. 3–17–98)

CHAPTER 5122

HOSPITALIZATION OF MENTALLY ILL

Section

5122.011 Applicability of provisions; conflicts

The provisions of this chapter regarding hospitalization apply to a person who is found incompetent to stand trial or not guilty by reason of insanity and is committed pursuant to section 2945.39, 2945.40, 2945.401, or 2945.402 of the Revised Code to the extent that the provisions are not in conflict with any provision of sections 2945.37 to 2945.402 of the Revised Code. If a provision of this chapter is in conflict with a provision in sections 2945.37 to 2945.402 of the Revised Code regarding a person who has been so committed, the provision in sections 2945.37 to 2945.402 of the Revised Code shall control regarding that person.

(1996 S 285, eff. 7–1–97)

5122.10 Emergency hospitalization; examination; disposition

Any psychiatrist, licensed clinical psychologist, licensed physician, health officer, parole officer, police officer, or sheriff may take a person into custody, or the chief of the adult parole authority or a parole or probation officer with the approval of the chief of the authority may take a parolee, an offender under a community control sanction or a post-release control sanction, or an offender under transitional control into custody and may immediately transport the parolee, offender on community control or post-release control, or offender under transitional control to a hospital or, notwithstanding section 5119.20 of the Revised Code, to a general hospital not licensed by the department of mental health where the parolee, offender on community control or post-release control, or offender under transitional control may be held for the period prescribed in this section, if the psychiatrist, licensed clinical psychologist, licensed physician, health officer, parole officer, police officer, or sheriff has reason to believe that the person is a mentally ill person subject to hospitalization by court order under division (B) of section 5122.01 of the Revised Code, and represents a substantial risk of physical harm to self or others if allowed to remain at liberty pending examination.

A written statement shall be given to such hospital by the transporting psychiatrist, licensed clinical psychologist, licensed physician, health officer, parole officer, police officer, chief of the adult parole authority, parole or probation officer, or sheriff stating the circumstances under which such person was taken into custody and the reasons for the psychiatrist's, licensed clinical psychologist's, licensed physician's, health officer's, parole officer's, police officer's, chief of the adult parole authority's, parole or probation officer's, or sheriff's belief. This statement shall be made available to the respondent or the respondent's attorney upon request of either.

Every reasonable and appropriate effort shall be made to take persons into custody in the least conspicuous manner possible. A person taking the respondent into custody pursuant to this section shall explain to the respondent: the name, professional designation, and agency affiliation of the person taking the respondent into custody; that the custody-taking is not a criminal arrest; and that the person is being taken for examination by mental health professionals at a specified mental health facility identified by name.

If a person taken into custody under this section is transported to a general hospital, the general hospital may admit the person, or provide care and treatment for the person, or both, notwithstanding section 5119.20 of the Revised Code, but by the end of twenty-four hours after arrival at the general hospital, the person shall be transferred to a hospital as defined in section 5122.01 of the Revised Code.

A person transported or transferred to a hospital or community mental health agency under this section shall be examined by the staff of the hospital or agency within twenty-four hours after arrival at the hospital or agency. If to conduct the examination requires that the person remain overnight, the hospital or agency shall admit the person in an unclassified status until making a disposition under this section. After the examination, if the chief clinical officer of the hospital or agency believes that the person is not a mentally ill person subject to hospitalization by court order, the chief clinical officer shall release or discharge the person immediately unless a court has issued a temporary order of detention applicable to the person under section 5122.11 of the Revised Code. After the examination, if the chief clinical officer believes that the person is a mentally ill person subject to hospitalization by court order, the chief clinical officer may detain the person for not more than three court days following the day of the examination and during such period admit the person as a voluntary patient under section 5122.02 of the Revised Code or file an affidavit under section 5122.11 of the Revised Code. If neither action is taken and a court has not otherwise issued a temporary order of detention applicable to the person under section 5122.11 of the Revised Code, the chief clinical officer shall discharge the person at the end of the three-day period unless the person has been sentenced to the department of rehabilitation and correction and has not been released from the person's sentence, in which case the person shall be returned to that department.

(2002 H 490, eff. 1–1–04; 1997 S 111, eff. 3–17–98; 1988 S 156, eff. 7–1–89; 1981 H 1; 1980 H 965, S 52, S 297, H 900; 1977 H 725; 1976 H 244; 1972 H 494; 130 v H 758; 129 v 1448)

5122.311 Notification of identity of mentally ill person subject to hospitalization by court order or person becoming involuntary patient; compilation and maintenance of notices

(A) Notwithstanding any provision of the Revised Code to the contrary, if, on or after the effective date of this section, an individual is found by a court to be a mentally ill person subject to hospitalization by court order or becomes an involuntary patient other than one who is a patient only for purposes of observation, the probate judge who made the adjudication or the chief clinical officer of the hospital, agency, or facility in which the person is an involuntary patient shall notify the bureau of criminal identification and investigation, on the form described in division (C) of this section, of the identity of the individual. The notification shall be transmitted by the judge or the chief clinical officer not later than seven days after the adjudication or commitment.

(B) The bureau of criminal identification and investigation shall compile and maintain the notices it receives under division (A) of this section and shall use them for the purpose of conducting incompetency records checks pursuant to section 311.41 of the Revised Code. The notices and the information they contain are confidential, except as provided in this division, and are not public records.

(C) The attorney general, by rule adopted under Chapter 119. of the Revised Code, shall prescribe and make available to all probate judges and all chief clinical officers a form to be used by them for the purpose of making the notifications required by division (A) of this section.

(2004 H 12, eff. 4–8–04)

5122.32 Confidentiality of quality assurance records

(A) As used in this section:

(1) "Quality assurance committee" means a committee that is appointed in the central office of the department of mental health by the director of mental health, a committee of a hospital or community setting program, a committee established pursuant to section 5119.47 of the Revised Code of the department of mental health appointed by the managing officer of the hospital or program, or a duly authorized subcommittee of a committee of that nature and that is designated to carry out quality assurance program activities.

(2) "Quality assurance program" means a comprehensive program within the department of mental health to systematically review and improve the quality of medical and mental health services within the department and its hospitals and community setting programs, the safety and security of persons receiving medical and mental health services within the department and its hospitals and community setting programs, and the efficiency and effectiveness of the utilization of staff and resources in the delivery of medical and mental health services within the department and its hospitals and community setting programs. "Quality assurance program" includes the central office quality assurance committees, morbidity and mortality review committees, quality assurance programs of community setting programs, quality assurance committees of hospitals operated by the department of mental health, and the office of licensure and certification of the department.

(3) "Quality assurance program activities" include collecting or compiling information and reports required by a quality assurance committee, receiving, reviewing, or implementing the recommendations made by a quality assurance committee, and credentialing, privileging, infection control, tissue review, peer review, utilization review including access to patient care records, patient care assessment records, and medical and mental health records, medical and mental health resource management, mortality and morbidity review, and identification and prevention of medical or mental health incidents and risks, whether performed by a quality assurance committee or by persons who are directed by a quality assurance committee.

(4) "Quality assurance records" means the proceedings, discussion, records, findings, recommendations, evaluations, opinions, minutes, reports, and other documents or actions that emanate from quality assurance committees, quality assurance programs, or quality assurance program activities. "Quality assurance records" does not include aggregate statistical information that does not disclose the identity of persons receiving or providing medical or mental health services in department of mental health institutions.

(B)(1) Except as provided in division (E) of this section, quality assurance records are confidential and are not public records under section 149.43 of the Revised Code, and shall be used only in the course of the proper functions of a quality assurance program.

(2) Except as provided in division (E) of this section, no person who possesses or has access to quality assurance records and who knows that the records are quality assurance records shall willfully disclose the contents of the records to any person or entity.

(C)(1) Except as provided in division (E) of this section, no quality assurance record shall be subject to discovery in, and is not admissible in evidence, in any judicial or administrative proceeding.

(2) Except as provided in division (E) of this section, no member of a quality assurance committee or a person who is performing a function that is part of a quality assurance program shall be permitted or required to testify in a judicial or administrative proceeding with respect to quality assurance records or with respect to any finding, recommendation, evaluation, opinion, or other action taken by the committee, member, or person.

(3) Information, documents, or records otherwise available from original sources are not to be construed as being unavailable for discovery or admission in evidence in a judicial or administrative proceeding merely because they were presented to a quality assurance committee. No person testifying before a quality assurance committee or person who is a member of a quality assurance committee shall be prevented from testifying as to matters within the person's knowledge, but the witness cannot be asked about the witness' testimony before the quality assurance committee or about an opinion formed by the person as a result of the quality assurance committee proceedings.

(D)(1) A person who, without malice and in the reasonable belief that the information is warranted by the facts known to the person, provides information to a person engaged in quality assurance program activities is not liable for damages in a civil action for injury, death, or loss to person or property to any person as a result of providing the information.

(2) A member of a quality assurance committee, a person engaged in quality assurance program activities, and an employee of the department of mental health shall not be liable in damages in a civil action for injury, death, or loss to person or property to any person for any acts, omissions, decisions, or other conduct within the scope of the functions of the quality assurance program.

(3) Nothing in this section shall relieve any institution or individual from liability arising from the treatment of a patient.

(E) Quality assurance records may be disclosed, and testimony may be provided concerning quality assurance records, only to the following persons or entities:

(1) Persons who are employed or retained by the department of mental health and who have authority to evaluate or implement the recommendations of a state-operated hospital, community setting program, or central office quality assurance committee;

(2) Public or private agencies or organizations if needed to perform a licensing or accreditation function related to department of mental health hospitals or community setting programs, or to perform monitoring of a hospital or program of that nature as required by law.

(F) A disclosure of quality assurance records pursuant to division (E) of this section does not otherwise waive the confidential and privileged status of the disclosed quality assurance records.

(G) Nothing in this section shall limit the access of the legal rights service to records or personnel as set forth in sections 5123.60 to 5123.604 of the Revised Code. Nothing in this section shall limit the admissibility of documentary or testimonial evidence in an action brought by the legal rights service in its own name or on behalf of a client.

(1997 S 111, eff. 3–17–98)

5122.99 Penalties

A person who violates division (B)(2) of section 5122.32 of the Revised Code shall be fined not more than two thousand five hundred dollars on a first offense and not more than twenty thousand dollars on a subsequent offense.

(1997 S 111, eff. 3–17–98)

CHAPTER 5123

DEPARTMENT OF MENTAL RETARDATION AND DEVELOPMENTAL DISABILITIES

DEFINITIONS; GENERAL PROVISIONS

5123.011 Director to adopt rules establishing definitions (first version)

Note: See also following version of this section, and Publisher's Note.

The director of mental retardation and developmental disabilities shall adopt rules in accordance with Chapter 119. of the Revised Code that establish definitions of "substantial functional limitation," "developmental delay," "established risk," "biological risk," and "environmental risk."

(1992 S 156, eff. 1–10–92; 1990 H 569)

Note: See also following version of this section, and Publisher's Note.

5123.011 Applicability of provisions; conflicts (second version)

Note: See also preceding version of this section, and Publisher's Note.

The provisions of this chapter regarding institutionalization apply to a person who is found incompetent to stand trial or not guilty by reason of insanity and is committed pursuant to section 2945.39, 2945.40, 2945.401, or 2945.402 of the Revised Code to the extent that the provisions are not in conflict with any provision of sections 2945.37 to 2945.402 of the Revised Code. If a provision of this chapter is in conflict with a provision in sections 2945.37 to 2945.402 of the Revised Code regarding a person who has been so committed, the provision in sections 2945.37 to 2945.402 of the Revised Code shall control regarding that person.

(1996 S 285, eff. 7–1–97)

Note: See also preceding version of this section, and Publisher's Note.

Historical and Statutory Notes

Publisher's Note: 5123.011 was enacted by 1996 S 285, eff. 7–1–97. However, a separate statute, as enacted by 1990 H 569, eff. 11–11–90, and amended by 1992 S 156, eff. 1–10–92, also exists at that number. See *Baldwin's Ohio Legislative Service*, 1992, page 5–1, and 1996, page 12/L–3563, or the OH–LEGIS or OH–LEGIS–OLD database on WESTLAW, for original versions of these Acts.

PERSONNEL; GENERAL PROVISIONS

5123.081 Criminal records check; form and standard impression sheet; violations preventing employment; fee; confidentiality of reports; conditional employment

(A) As used in this section:

(1) "Applicant" means a person who is under final consideration for appointment to or employment with the department of mental retardation and developmental disabilities, including, but not limited to, a person who is being transferred to the department and an employee who is being recalled or reemployed after a layoff.

(2) "Criminal records check" has the same meaning as in section 109.572 of the Revised Code.

(3) "Minor drug possession offense" has the same meaning as in section 2925.01 of the Revised Code.

(B) The director of mental retardation and developmental disabilities shall request the superintendent of the bureau of criminal identification and investigation to conduct a criminal records check with respect to each applicant, except that the director is not required to request a criminal records check for an employee of the department who is being considered for a different position or is returning after a leave of absence or seasonal break in employment, as long as the director has no reason to believe that the employee has committed any of the offenses listed or described in division (E) of this section.

If the applicant does not present proof that the applicant has been a resident of this state for the five-year period immediately prior to the date upon which the criminal records check is requested, the director shall request that the superintendent of the bureau obtain information from the federal bureau of investigation as a part of the criminal records check for the applicant. If the applicant presents proof that the applicant has been a resident of this state for that five-year period, the director may request that the superintendent of the bureau include information from the federal bureau of investigation in the criminal records check. For purposes of this division, an applicant may provide proof of residency in this state by presenting, with a notarized statement asserting that the applicant has been a resident of this state for that five-year period, a valid driver's license, notification of registration as an elector, a copy of an officially filed federal or state tax form identifying the applicant's permanent residence, or any other document the director considers acceptable.

(C) The director shall provide to each applicant a copy of the form prescribed pursuant to division (C)(1) of section 109.572 of the Revised Code, provide to each applicant a standard impression sheet to obtain fingerprint impressions prescribed pursuant to division (C)(2) of section 109.572 of the Revised Code, obtain the completed form and impression sheet from each applicant, and forward the completed form and impression sheet to the superintendent of the bureau of criminal identification and investigation at the time the criminal records check is requested.

Any applicant who receives pursuant to this division a copy of the form prescribed pursuant to division (C)(1) of section 109.572 of the Revised Code and a copy of an impression sheet prescribed pursuant to division (C)(2) of that section and who is requested to complete the form and provide a set of fingerprint impressions shall complete the form or provide all the information necessary to complete the form and shall provide the material with the impressions of the applicant's fingerprints. If an applicant, upon request, fails to provide the information necessary to complete the form or fails to provide impressions of the applicant's fingerprints, the director shall not employ the applicant.

(D) The director may request any other state or federal agency to supply the director with a written report regarding the criminal record of each applicant. With regard to an applicant who becomes a department employee, if the employee holds an occupational or professional license or other credentials, the director may request that the state or federal agency that regulates the employee's occupation or profession supply the director with a written report of any information pertaining to the employee's criminal record that the agency obtains in the course of conducting an investigation or in the process of renewing the employee's license or other credentials.

(E) Except as provided in division (K)(2) of this section and in rules adopted by the director in accordance with division (M) of this section, the director shall not employ a person to fill a position with the department who has been convicted of or pleaded guilty to any of the following:

(1) A violation of section 2903.01, 2903.02, 2903.03, 2903.04, 2903.11, 2903.12, 2903.13, 2903.16, 2903.21, 2903.34, 2903.341, 2905.01, 2905.02, 2905.05, 2907.02, 2907.03, 2907.04, 2907.05, 2907.06, 2907.07, 2907.08, 2907.09, 2907.21, 2907.22, 2907.23, 2907.25, 2907.31, 2907.32, 2907.321, 2907.322, 2907.323, 2911.01, 2911.02, 2911.11, 2911.12, 2919.12, 2919.22, 2919.24, 2919.25, 2923.12, 2923.13, 2923.161, 2925.02, 2925.03, 2925.04, 2925.05, 2925.06, or 3716.11 of the Revised Code, a violation of section 2905.04 of the Revised Code as it existed prior to July 1, 1996, a violation of section 2919.23 of the Revised Code that would have been a violation of section 2905.04 of the Revised Code as it existed prior to July 1, 1996, had the violation occurred prior to that date, a violation of section 2925.11 of the Revised Code that is not a minor drug possession offense, or felonious sexual penetration in violation of former section 2907.12 of the Revised Code;

(2) A felony contained in the Revised Code that is not listed in this division, if the felony bears a direct and substantial relationship to the duties and responsibilities of the position being filled;

(3) Any offense contained in the Revised Code constituting a misdemeanor of the first degree on the first offense and a felony on a subsequent offense, if the offense bears a direct and substantial relationship to the position being filled and the nature of the services being provided by the department;

(4) A violation of an existing or former municipal ordinance or law of this state, any other state, or the United States, if the offense is substantially equivalent to any of the offenses listed or described in division (E)(1), (2), or (3) of this section.

(F) Prior to employing an applicant, the director shall require the applicant to submit a statement with the applicant's signature attesting that the applicant has not been convicted of or pleaded guilty to any of the offenses listed or described in division (E) of this section. The director also shall require the applicant to sign an agreement under which the applicant agrees to notify the director within fourteen calendar days if, while employed with the department, the applicant is ever formally charged with, convicted of, or pleads guilty to any of the offenses listed or described in division (E) of this section. The agreement shall inform the applicant that failure to report formal charges, a conviction, or a guilty plea may result in being dismissed from employment.

(G) The director shall pay to the bureau of criminal identification and investigation the fee prescribed pursuant to division (C)(3) of section 109.572 of the Revised Code for each criminal records check requested and conducted pursuant to this section.

(H)(1) Any report obtained pursuant to this section is not a public record for purposes of section 149.43 of the Revised Code and shall not be made available to any person, other than the applicant who is the subject of the records check or criminal records check or the applicant's representative, the department or its representative, a county board of mental retardation and developmental disabilities, and any court, hearing officer, or other necessary individual involved in a case dealing with the denial of employment to the applicant or the denial, suspension, or revocation of a certificate or evidence of registration under section 5123.082 of the Revised Code.

(2) An individual for whom the director has obtained reports under this section may submit a written request to the director to have copies of the reports sent to any state agency, entity of local government, or private entity. The individual shall specify in the request the agencies or entities to which the copies are to be sent. On receiving the request, the director shall send copies of the reports to the agencies or entities specified.

The director may request that a state agency, entity of local government, or private entity send copies to the director of any report regarding a records check or criminal records check that the agency or entity possesses, if the director obtains the written consent of the individual who is the subject of the report.

(I) The director shall request the registrar of motor vehicles to supply the director with a certified abstract regarding the record of convictions for violations of motor vehicle laws of each applicant who will be required by the applicant's employment to transport individuals with mental retardation or a developmental disability or to operate the department's vehicles for any other purpose. For each abstract provided under this section, the director shall pay the amount specified in section 4509.05 of the Revised Code.

(J) The director shall provide each applicant with a copy of any report or abstract obtained about the applicant under this section.

(K)(1) The director shall inform each person, at the time of the person's initial application for employment, that the person is required to provide a set of impressions of the person's fingerprints and that a criminal records check is required to be conducted and satisfactorily completed in accordance with section 109.572 of the Revised Code if the person comes under final consideration for employment as a precondition to employment in a position.

(2) The director may employ an applicant pending receipt of reports requested under this section. The director shall terminate employment of any such applicant if it is determined from the reports that the applicant failed to inform the director that the applicant had been convicted of or pleaded guilty to any of the offenses listed or described in division (E) of this section.

(L) The director may charge an applicant a fee for costs the director incurs in obtaining reports, abstracts, or fingerprint impressions under this section. A fee charged under this division shall not exceed the amount of the fees the director pays under divisions (G) and (I) of this section. If a fee is charged under this division, the director shall notify the applicant of the amount of the fee at the time of the applicant's initial application for employment and that, unless the fee is paid, the director will not consider the applicant for employment.

(M) The director shall adopt rules in accordance with Chapter 119. of the Revised Code to implement this section, including rules specifying circumstances under which the director may employ a person who has been convicted of or pleaded guilty to an offense listed or described in division (E) of this section but who meets standards in regard to rehabilitation set by the director.

(2004 S 178, eff. 1–30–04; 2000 H 538, eff. 9–22–00)

MISCELLANEOUS POWERS AND DUTIES OF DEPARTMENT AND DIRECTOR

5123.13 Special police

(A) As used in this section, "felony" has the same meaning as in section 109.511 of the Revised Code.

(B)(1) Subject to division (C) of this section, upon the recommendation of the director of mental retardation and developmental disabilities, the managing officer of an institution under the jurisdiction of the department of mental retardation and developmental disabilities may designate one or more employees to be special police officers of the department. The special police officers shall take an oath of office, wear the badge of office, and give bond for the proper and faithful discharge of their duties in an amount that the director requires.

(2) In accordance with section 109.77 of the Revised Code, the special police officers shall be required to complete successfully a peace officer basic training program approved by the Ohio peace officer training commission and to be certified by the commission. The cost of the training shall be paid by the department of mental retardation and developmental disabilities.

(3) Special police officers, on the premises of institutions under the jurisdiction of the department of mental retardation and developmental disabilities and subject to the rules of the department, shall protect the property of the institutions and the persons and property of patients in the institutions, suppress riots, disturbances, and breaches of the peace, and enforce the laws of the state and the rules of the department for the preservation of good order. They may arrest any person without a warrant and detain the person until a warrant can be obtained under the circumstances described in division (F) of section 2935.03 of the Revised Code.

(C)(1) The managing officer of an institution under the jurisdiction of the department of mental retardation and developmental disabilities shall not designate an employee as a special police officer of the department pursuant to division (B)(1) of this section on a permanent basis, on a temporary basis, for a probationary term, or on other than a permanent basis if the employee previously has been convicted of or has pleaded guilty to a felony.

(2)(a) The managing officer of an institution under the jurisdiction of the department of mental retardation and developmental disabilities shall terminate the employment as a special police officer of the department of an employee designated as a special police officer under division (B)(1) of this section if that employee does either of the following:

(i) Pleads guilty to a felony;

(ii) Pleads guilty to a misdemeanor pursuant to a negotiated plea agreement as provided in division (D) of section 2929.43 of the Revised Code in which the employee agrees to surrender the certificate awarded to that employee under section 109.77 of the Revised Code.

(b) The managing officer shall suspend from employment as a special police officer of the department an employee designated as a special police officer under division (B)(1) of this section if that employee is convicted, after trial, of a felony. If the special police officer files an appeal from that conviction and the conviction is upheld by the highest court to which the appeal is taken or if the special police officer does not file a timely appeal, the managing officer shall terminate the employment of that special police officer. If the special police officer files an appeal that results in that special police officer's acquittal of the felony or conviction of a misdemeanor, or in the dismissal of the felony charge against that special police officer, the managing officer shall reinstate that special police officer. A special police officer of the department who is reinstated under division (C)(2)(b) of this section shall not receive any back pay unless that special police officer's conviction of the felony was reversed on appeal, or the felony charge was dismissed, because the court found insufficient evidence to convict the special police officer of the felony.

(3) Division (C) of this section does not apply regarding an offense that was committed prior to January 1, 1997.

(4) The suspension from employment, or the termination of the employment, of a special police officer under division (C)(2)

of this section shall be in accordance with Chapter 119. of the Revised Code.

(2002 H 490, eff. 1–1–04; 1996 H 670, eff. 12–2–96; 1996 H 566, eff. 10–16–96; 1993 H 42, eff. 2–9–94; 1992 S 49; 1981 H 694; 1980 H 900)

5123.14 Powers to investigate

The department of mental retardation and developmental disabilities may make such investigations as are necessary in the performance of its duties and to that end the director of mental retardation and developmental disabilities shall have the same power as a judge of a county court to administer oaths and to enforce the attendance and testimony of witnesses and the production of books or papers.

The department shall keep a record of such investigations stating the time, place, charges or subject, witnesses summoned and examined, and its conclusions.

In matters involving the conduct of an officer, a stenographic report of the evidence shall be taken and a copy of such report, with all documents introduced, kept on file at the office of the department.

The fees of witnesses for attendance and travel shall be the same as in the court of common pleas, but no officer or employee of the institution under investigation is entitled to such fees.

Any judge of the probate court or of the court of common pleas, upon application of the department, may compel the attendance of witnesses, the production of books or papers, and the giving of testimony before the department, by a judgment for contempt or otherwise, in the same manner as in cases before said courts.

(1980 H 900, eff. 7–1–80)

REGISTRY OF ABUSIVE OR NEGLECTFUL EMPLOYEES

5123.50 Definitions

As used in this section and sections 5123.51, 5123.52, and 5123.541 of the Revised Code:

(A) "Abuse" means all of the following:

(1) The use of physical force that can reasonably be expected to result in physical harm or serious physical harm;

(2) Sexual abuse;

(3) Verbal abuse.

(B) "Misappropriation" means depriving, defrauding, or otherwise obtaining the real or personal property of an individual by any means prohibited by the Revised Code, including violations of Chapter 2911. or 2913. of the Revised Code.

(C) "MR/DD employee" means all of the following:

(1) An employee of the department of mental retardation and developmental disabilities;

(2) An employee of a county board of mental retardation and developmental disabilities;

(3) An employee in a position that includes providing specialized services to an individual with mental retardation or another developmental disability.

(D) "Neglect" means, when there is a duty to do so, failing to provide an individual with any treatment, care, goods, or services that are necessary to maintain the health and safety of the individual.

(E) "Physical harm" and "serious physical harm" have the same meanings as in section 2901.01 of the Revised Code.

(F) "Sexual abuse" means unlawful sexual conduct or sexual contact.

(G) "Specialized services" means any program or service designed and operated to serve primarily individuals with mental retardation or a developmental disability, including a program or service provided by an entity licensed or certified by the department of mental retardation and developmental disabilities. A program or service available to the general public is not a specialized service.

(H) "Verbal abuse" means purposely using words to threaten, coerce, intimidate, harass, or humiliate an individual.

(I) "Sexual conduct," "sexual contact," and "spouse" have the same meanings as in section 2907.01 of the Revised Code.

(2004 S 178, eff. 1–30–04; 2002 S 191, eff. 12–31–03; 2000 S 171, eff. 11–22–00)

5123.51 Review of reports of abuse or neglect; investigations; hearings; inclusion of employee in registry; notice

(A) In addition to any other action required by sections 5123.61 and 5126. 31 of the Revised Code, the department of mental retardation and developmental disabilities shall review each report the department receives of abuse or neglect of an individual with mental retardation or a developmental disability or misappropriation of an individual's property that includes an allegation that an MR/DD employee committed or was responsible for the abuse, neglect, or misappropriation. The department shall review a report it receives from a public children services agency only after the agency completes its investigation pursuant to section 2151.421 of the Revised Code. On receipt of a notice under section 2930.061 or 5123.541 of the Revised Code, the department shall review the notice.

(B) The department shall do both of the following:

(1) Investigate the allegation or adopt the findings of an investigation or review of the allegation conducted by another person or government entity and determine whether there is a reasonable basis for the allegation;

(2) If the department determines that there is a reasonable basis for the allegation, conduct an adjudication pursuant to Chapter 119. of the Revised Code.

(C)(1) The department shall appoint an independent hearing officer to conduct any hearing conducted pursuant to division (B)(2) of this section, except that, if the hearing is regarding an employee of the department who is represented by a union, the department and a representative of the union shall jointly select the hearing officer.

(2)(a) Except as provided in division (C)(2)(b) of this section, no hearing shall be conducted under division (B)(2) of this section until any criminal proceeding or collective bargaining arbitration concerning the same allegation has concluded.

(b) The department may conduct a hearing pursuant to division (B)(2) of this section before a criminal proceeding concerning the same allegation is concluded if both of the following are the case:

(i) The department notifies the prosecutor responsible for the criminal proceeding that the department proposes to conduct a hearing.

(ii) The prosecutor consents to the hearing.

(3) In conducting a hearing pursuant to division (B)(2) of this section, the hearing officer shall do all of the following:

(a) Determine whether there is clear and convincing evidence that the MR/DD employee has done any of the following:

(i) Misappropriated property of one or more individuals with mental retardation or a developmental disability that has a value, either separately or taken together, of one hundred dollars or more;

(ii) Misappropriated property of an individual with mental retardation or a developmental disability that is designed to be used as a check, draft, negotiable instrument, credit card, charge card, or device for initiating an electronic fund transfer at a point of sale terminal, automated teller machine, or cash dispensing machine;

(iii) Knowingly abused such an individual;

(iv) Recklessly abused or neglected such an individual, with resulting physical harm;

(v) Negligently abused or neglected such an individual, with resulting serious physical harm;

(vi) Recklessly neglected such an individual, creating a substantial risk of serious physical harm;

(vii) Engaged in sexual conduct or had sexual contact with an individual with mental retardation or another developmental disability who was not the MR/DD employee's spouse and for whom the MR/DD employee was employed or under a contract to provide care;

(viii) Unreasonably failed to make a report pursuant to division (C) of section 5123.61 of the Revised Code when the employee knew or should have known that the failure would result in a substantial risk of harm to an individual with mental retardation or a developmental disability.

(b) Give weight to the decision in any collective bargaining arbitration regarding the same allegation;

(c) Give weight to any relevant facts presented at the hearing.

(D)(1) Unless the director of mental retardation and developmental disabilities determines that there are extenuating circumstances and except as provided in division (E) of this section, if the director, after considering all of the factors listed in division (C)(3) of this section, finds that there is clear and convincing evidence that an MR/DD employee has done one or more of the things described in division (C)(3)(a) of this section the director shall include the name of the employee in the registry established under section 5123.52 of the Revised Code.

(2) Extenuating circumstances the director must consider include the use of physical force by an MR/DD employee that was necessary as self-defense.

(3) If the director includes an MR/DD employee in the registry established under section 5123.52 of the Revised Code, the director shall notify the employee, the person or government entity that employs or contracts with the employee, the individual with mental retardation or a developmental disability who was the subject of the report and that individual's legal guardian, if any, the attorney general, and the prosecuting attorney or other law enforcement agency. If the MR/DD employee holds a license, certificate, registration, or other authorization to engage in a profession issued pursuant to Title XLVII of the Revised Code, the director shall notify the appropriate agency, board, department, or other entity responsible for regulating the employee's professional practice.

(4) If an individual whose name appears on the registry is involved in a court proceeding or arbitration arising from the same facts as the allegation resulting in the individual's placement on the registry, the disposition of the proceeding or arbitration shall be noted in the registry next to the individual's name.

(E) In the case of an allegation concerning an employee of the department, after the hearing conducted pursuant to division (B)(2) of this section, the director of health or that director's designee shall review the decision of the hearing officer to determine whether the standard described in division (C)(3) of this section has been met. If the director or designee determines that the standard has been met and that no extenuating circumstances exist, the director or designee shall notify the director of mental retardation and developmental disabilities that the MR/DD employee is to be included in the registry established under section 5123.52 of the Revised Code. If the director of mental retardation and developmental disabilities receives such notification, the director shall include the MR/DD employee in the registry and shall provide the notification described in division (D)(3) of this section.

(F) If the department is required by Chapter 119. of the Revised Code to give notice of an opportunity for a hearing and the MR/DD employee subject to the notice does not timely request a hearing in accordance with section 119.07 of the Revised Code, the department is not required to hold a hearing.

(G) Files and records of investigations conducted pursuant to this section are not public records as defined in section 149.43 of the Revised Code, but, on request, the department shall provide copies of those files and records to the attorney general, a prosecuting attorney, or a law enforcement agency.

(2004 S 178, eff. 1–30–04; 2000 S 171, eff. 11–22–00)

5123.52 Registry of abusive or neglectful employees

(A) The department of mental retardation and developmental disabilities shall establish a registry of MR/DD employees consisting of the names of MR/DD employees included in the registry pursuant to section 5123.51 of the Revised Code.

(B) Before a person or government entity hires, contracts with, or employs an individual as an MR/DD employee, the person or government entity shall inquire whether the individual is included in the registry.

(C) When it receives an inquiry regarding whether an individual is included in the registry, the department shall inform the person making the inquiry whether the individual is included in the registry.

(D)(1) Except as otherwise provided in a collective bargaining agreement entered into under Chapter 4117. of the Revised Code that is in effect on the effective date of this section, no person or government entity shall hire, contract with, or employ as an MR/DD employee an individual who is included in the registry. Notwithstanding sections 4117.08 and 4117.10 of the Revised Code, no agreement entered into under Chapter 4117. of the Revised Code after the effective date of this section may contain any provision that in any way limits the effect or operation of this section.

(2) Neither the department nor any county board of mental retardation and developmental disabilities may enter into a new contract or renew a contract with a person or government entity that fails to comply with division (D)(1) of this section until the department or board is satisfied that the person or government entity will comply.

(3) A person or government entity that fails to hire or retain as an MR/DD employee a person because the person is included in the registry shall not be liable in damages in a civil action brought by the employee or applicant for employment. Termination of employment pursuant to division (D)(1) of this section constitutes a discharge for just cause for the purposes of section 4141.29 of the Revised Code.

(E) Information contained in the registry is a public record for the purposes of section 149.43 of the Revised Code and is subject to inspection and copying under section 1347.08 of the Revised Code.

(2000 S 171, eff. 11–22–00)

5123.53 Removal of individuals from registry

An individual who is included in the registry may petition the director of mental retardation and developmental disabilities for removal from the registry. If the director determines that good cause exists, the director shall remove the individual from the registry and may properly reply to an inquiry that the individual is not included in the registry. Good cause includes meeting rehabilitation standards established in rules adopted under section 5123.54 of the Revised Code.

(2000 S 171, eff. 11–22–00)

LEGAL RIGHTS SERVICE; OMBUDSMAN SECTION; ABUSE OF MENTALLY RETARDED ADULT

5123.61 Duty of certain persons to report believed abuse of mentally retarded or developmentally disabled adult; registry office; immunity

(A) As used in this section:

(1) "Law enforcement agency" means the state highway patrol, the police department of a municipal corporation, or a county sheriff.

(2) "Abuse" has the same meaning as in section 5123.50 of the Revised Code, except that it includes a misappropriation, as defined in that section.

(3) "Neglect" has the same meaning as in section 5123.50 of the Revised Code.

(B) The department of mental retardation and developmental disabilities shall establish a registry office for the purpose of maintaining reports of abuse, neglect, and other major unusual incidents made to the department under this section and reports received from county boards of mental retardation and developmental disabilities under section 5126.31 of the Revised Code. The department shall establish committees to review reports of abuse, neglect, and other major unusual incidents.

(C)(1) Any person listed in division (C)(2) of this section, having reason to believe that a person with mental retardation or a developmental disability has suffered or faces a substantial risk of suffering any wound, injury, disability, or condition of such a nature as to reasonably indicate abuse or neglect of that person, shall immediately report or cause reports to be made of such information to the entity specified in this division. Except as provided in section 5120.173 of the Revised Code or as otherwise provided in this division, the person making the report shall make it to a law enforcement agency or to the county board of mental retardation and developmental disabilities. If the report concerns a resident of a facility operated by the department of mental retardation and developmental disabilities the report shall be made either to a law enforcement agency or to the department. If the report concerns any act or omission of an employee of a county board of mental retardation and developmental disabilities, the report immediately shall be made to the department and to the county board.

(2) All of the following persons are required to make a report under division (C)(1) of this section:

(a) Any physician, including a hospital intern or resident, any dentist, podiatrist, chiropractor, practitioner of a limited branch of medicine as specified in section 4731.15 of the Revised Code, hospital administrator or employee of a hospital, nurse licensed under Chapter 4723. of the Revised Code, employee of an ambulatory health facility as defined in section 5101.61 of the Revised Code, employee of a home health agency, employee of an adult care facility licensed under Chapter 3722. of the Revised Code, or employee of a community mental health facility;

(b) Any school teacher or school authority, social worker, psychologist, attorney, peace officer, coroner, or residents' rights advocate as defined in section 3721.10 of the Revised Code;

(c) A superintendent, board member, or employee of a county board of mental retardation and developmental disabilities; an administrator, board member, or employee of a residential facility licensed under section 5123.19 of the Revised Code; an administrator, board member, or employee of any other public or private provider of services to a person with mental retardation or a developmental disability, or any MR/DD employee, as defined in section 5123.50 of the Revised Code;

(d) A member of a citizen's advisory council established at an institution or branch institution of the department of mental retardation and developmental disabilities under section 5123.092 of the Revised Code;

(e) A clergyman who is employed in a position that includes providing specialized services to an individual with mental retardation or another developmental disability, while acting in an official or professional capacity in that position, or a person who is employed in a position that includes providing specialized services to an individual with mental retardation or another developmental disability and who, while acting in an official or professional capacity, renders spiritual treatment through prayer in accordance with the tenets of an organized religion.

(3)(a) The reporting requirements of this division do not apply to members of the legal rights service commission or to employees of the legal rights service.

(b) An attorney or physician is not required to make a report pursuant to division (C)(1) of this section concerning any communication the attorney or physician receives from a client or patient in an attorney-client or physician-patient relationship, if, in accordance with division (A) or (B) of section 2317.02 of the Revised Code, the attorney or physician could not testify with respect to that communication in a civil or criminal proceeding, except that the client or patient is deemed to have waived any testimonial privilege under division (A) or (B) of section 2317.02 of the Revised Code with respect to that communication and the attorney or physician shall make a report pursuant to division (C)(1) of this section, if both of the following apply:

(i) The client or patient, at the time of the communication, is a person with mental retardation or a developmental disability.

(ii) The attorney or physician knows or suspects, as a result of the communication or any observations made during that communication, that the client or patient has suffered or faces a substantial risk of suffering any wound, injury, disability, or condition of a nature that reasonably indicates abuse or neglect of the client or patient.

(4) Any person who fails to make a report required under division (C) of this section and who is an MR/DD employee, as defined in section 5123.50 of the Revised Code, shall be eligible to be included in the registry regarding misappropriation, abuse, neglect, or other specified misconduct by MR/DD employees established under section 5123.52 of the Revised Code.

(D) The reports required under division (C) of this section shall be made forthwith by telephone or in person and shall be followed by a written report. The reports shall contain the following:

(1) The names and addresses of the person with mental retardation or a developmental disability and the person's custodian, if known;

(2) The age of the person with mental retardation or a developmental disability;

(3) Any other information that would assist in the investigation of the report.

(E) When a physician performing services as a member of the staff of a hospital or similar institution has reason to believe that a person with mental retardation or a developmental disability has suffered injury, abuse, or physical neglect, the physician shall notify the person in charge of the institution or that person's designated delegate, who shall make the necessary reports.

(F) Any person having reasonable cause to believe that a person with mental retardation or a developmental disability has suffered or faces a substantial risk of suffering abuse or neglect may report or cause a report to be made of that belief to the entity specified in this division. Except as provided in section 5120.173 of the Revised Code or as otherwise provided in this division, the person making the report shall make it to a law enforcement agency or the county board of mental retardation and developmental disabilities. If the person is a resident of a facility operated by the department of mental retardation and developmental disabilities, the report shall be made to a law enforcement agency or to the department. If the report concerns any act or omission of an employee of a county board of mental retardation and developmental disabilities, the report immediately shall be made to the department and to the county board.

(G)(1) Upon the receipt of a report concerning the possible abuse or neglect of a person with mental retardation or a developmental disability, the law enforcement agency shall inform the county board of mental retardation and developmental disabilities or, if the person is a resident of a facility operated by the department of mental retardation and developmental disabilities, the director of the department or the director's designee.

(2) On receipt of a report under this section that includes an allegation of action or inaction that may constitute a crime under federal law or the law of this state, the department of mental retardation and developmental disabilities shall notify the law enforcement agency.

(3) When a county board of mental retardation and developmental disabilities receives a report under this section that includes an allegation of action or inaction that may constitute a crime under federal law or the law of this state, the superintendent of the board or an individual the superintendent designates under division (H) of this section shall notify the law enforcement agency. The superintendent or individual shall notify the department of mental retardation and developmental disabilities when it receives any report under this section.

(4) When a county board of mental retardation and developmental disabilities receives a report under this section and believes that the degree of risk to the person is such that the report is an emergency, the superintendent of the board or an employee of the board the superintendent designates shall attempt a face-to-face contact with the person with mental retardation or a developmental disability who allegedly is the victim within one hour of the board's receipt of the report.

(H) The superintendent of the board may designate an individual to be responsible for notifying the law enforcement agency and the department when the county board receives a report under this section.

(I) An adult with mental retardation or a developmental disability about whom a report is made may be removed from the adult's place of residence only by law enforcement officers who consider that the adult's immediate removal is essential to protect the adult from further injury or abuse or in accordance with the order of a court made pursuant to section 5126.33 of the Revised Code.

(J) A law enforcement agency shall investigate each report of abuse or neglect it receives under this section. In addition, the department, in cooperation with law enforcement officials, shall investigate each report regarding a resident of a facility operated by the department to determine the circumstances surrounding the injury, the cause of the injury, and the person responsible. The investigation shall be in accordance with the memorandum of understanding prepared under section 5126.058 of the Revised Code. The department shall determine, with the registry office which shall be maintained by the department, whether prior reports have been made concerning an adult with mental retardation or a developmental disability or other principals in the case. If the department finds that the report involves action or inaction that may constitute a crime under federal law or the law of this state, it shall submit a report of its investigation, in writing, to the law enforcement agency. If the person with mental retardation or a developmental disability is an adult, with the consent of the adult, the department shall provide such protective services as are necessary to protect the adult. The law enforcement agency shall make a written report of its findings to the department.

If the person is an adult and is not a resident of a facility operated by the department, the county board of mental retardation and developmental disabilities shall review the report of abuse or neglect in accordance with sections 5126.30 to 5126.33 of the Revised Code and the law enforcement agency shall make the written report of its findings to the county board.

(K) Any person or any hospital, institution, school, health department, or agency participating in the making of reports pursuant to this section, any person participating as a witness in an administrative or judicial proceeding resulting from the reports, or any person or governmental entity that discharges responsibilities under sections 5126.31 to 5126.33 of the Revised Code shall be immune from any civil or criminal liability that might otherwise be incurred or imposed as a result of such actions except liability for perjury, unless the person or governmental entity has acted in bad faith or with malicious purpose.

(L) No employer or any person with the authority to do so shall discharge, demote, transfer, prepare a negative work performance evaluation, reduce pay or benefits, terminate work privileges, or take any other action detrimental to an employee or retaliate against an employee as a result of the employee's having made a report under this section. This division does not preclude an employer or person with authority from taking action with regard to an employee who has made a report under this section if there is another reasonable basis for the action.

(M) Reports made under this section are not public records as defined in section 149.43 of the Revised Code. Information contained in the reports on request shall be made available to the person who is the subject of the report, to the person's legal counsel, and to agencies authorized to receive information in the report by the department or by a county board of mental retardation and developmental disabilities.

(N) Notwithstanding section 4731.22 of the Revised Code, the physician-patient privilege shall not be a ground for excluding evidence regarding the injuries or physical neglect of a person with mental retardation or a developmental disability or the cause thereof in any judicial proceeding resulting from a report submitted pursuant to this section.

(2004 S 178, eff. 1–30–04; 2000 S 171, eff. 11–22–00; 1998 H 606, eff. 3–9–99; 1996 H 670, eff. 12–2–96; 1993 S 21, eff. 10–29–93; 1990 H 569; 1988 H 403; 1985 H 66; 1980 H 900)

5123.611 Report of findings following review of report of abuse, neglect, or major unusual incident

(A) As used in this section, "MR/DD employee" means all of the following:

(1) An employee of the department of mental retardation and developmental disabilities;

(2) An employee of a county board of mental retardation and developmental disabilities;

(3) An employee in a position that includes providing specialized services, as defined in section 5123.50 of the Revised Code, to an individual with mental retardation or a developmental disability.

(B) At the conclusion of a review of a report of abuse, neglect, or a major unusual incident that is conducted by a review committee established pursuant to section 5123.61 of the Revised Code, the committee shall issue recommendations to the department. The department shall review the committee's recommendations and issue a report of its findings. The department shall make the report available to all of the following:

(1) The individual with mental retardation or a developmental disability who is the subject of the report;

(2) That individual's guardian or legal counsel;

(3) The licensee, as defined in section 5123.19 of the Revised Code, of a residential facility in which the individual resides;

(4) The employer of any MR/DD employee who allegedly committed or was responsible for the abuse, neglect, or major unusual incident.

(C) Except as provided in this section, the department shall not disclose its report to any person or government entity that is not authorized to investigate reports of abuse, neglect, or other major unusual incidents, unless the individual with mental retardation or a developmental disability who is the subject of the report or the individual's guardian gives the department written consent.

(2002 S 191, eff. 12–31–03; 2000 H 538, eff. 9–22–00)

5123.612 Rules regarding reporting of incidents

The director of mental retardation and developmental disabilities shall adopt rules in accordance with Chapter 119. of the Revised Code regarding the reporting of major unusual incidents and unusual incidents concerning persons with mental retardation or a developmental disability. The rules shall specify what constitutes a major unusual incident or an unusual incident.

(2000 H 538, eff. 9–22–00)

5123.613 Reports

(A) When a person who is the subject of a report under section 5123.61 of the Revised Code dies, the department of mental retardation and developmental disabilities or the county board of mental retardation and developmental disabilities, whichever is applicable, shall, on written request, provide to both of the following persons the report and any records relating to the report:

(1) If the report or records are necessary to administer the estate of the person who is the subject of the report, to the executor or administrator of the person's estate;

(2) To the guardian of the person who is the subject of the report or, if the individual had no guardian at the time of death, to a person in the first applicable of the following categories:

(a) The person's spouse;

(b) The person's children;

(c) The person's parents;

(d) The person's brothers or sisters;

(e) The person's uncles or aunts;

(f) The person's closest relative by blood or adoption;

(g) The person's closest relative by marriage.

(B) The department or county board shall provide the report and related records as required by this section not later than thirty days after receipt of the request." [1]

(2000 H 538, eff. 9–22–00)

[1] So in original.

5123.614 Reports; independent review or investigation

(A) Subject to division (B) of this section, on receipt of a report of a major unusual incident made pursuant to section 5123.61 or 5126.31 of the Revised Code or rules adopted under section 5123.612 of the Revised Code, the department of mental retardation and developmental disabilities may do either of the following:

(1) Conduct an independent review or investigation of the incident;

(2) Request that an independent review or investigation of the incident be conducted by a county board of mental retardation and developmental disabilities that is not implicated in the report, a regional council of government, or any other entity authorized to conduct such investigations.

(B) If a report described in division (A) of this section concerning the health or safety of a person with mental retardation or a developmental disability involves an allegation that an employee of a county board of mental retardation and developmental disabilities has created a substantial risk of serious physical harm to a person with mental retardation or a developmental disability, the department shall do one of the following:

(1) Conduct an independent investigation regarding the incident;

(2) Request that an independent review or investigation of the incident be conducted by a county board of mental retardation and developmental disabilities that is not implicated in the report, a regional council of government, or any other entity authorized to conduct such investigations.

(2004 S 178, eff. 1–30–04)

CHAPTER 5126

COUNTY BOARDS OF MENTAL RETARDATION AND DEVELOPMENTAL DISABILITIES

Section

5126.058 Memorandum of understanding to outline normal operating procedure

(A) Each county board of mental retardation and developmental disabilities shall prepare a memorandum of understanding that is developed by all of the following and that is signed by the persons identified in divisions (A)(3) to (8) of this section:

(1) If there is only one probate judge in the county, the probate judge of the county or the probate judge's representative;

(2) If there is more than one probate judge in the county, a probate judge or the probate judge's representative selected by the probate judges or, if they are unable to do so for any reason, the probate judge who is senior in point of service or the senior probate judge's representative;

(3) The county peace officer;

(4) All chief municipal peace officers within the county;

(5) Other law enforcement officers handling abuse, neglect, and exploitation of mentally retarded and developmentally disabled persons in the county;

(6) The prosecuting attorney of the county;

(7) The public children services agency;

(8) The coroner of the county.

(B) A memorandum of understanding shall set forth the normal operating procedure to be employed by all concerned officials in the execution of their respective responsibilities under this section and sections 313.12, 2151.421, 2903.16, 5126.31, and 5126.33 of the Revised Code and shall have as its primary goal the elimination of all unnecessary interviews of persons who are the subject of reports made pursuant to this section. A failure to follow the procedure set forth in the memorandum by the concerned officials is not grounds for, and shall not result in, the dismissal of any charge or complaint arising from any reported case of abuse, neglect, or exploitation or the suppression of any evidence obtained as a result of any reported abuse, neglect, or exploitation and does not give any rights or grounds for appeal or post-conviction relief to any person.

(C) A memorandum of understanding shall include, but is not limited to, all of the following:

(1) The roles and responsibilities for handling emergency and nonemergency cases of abuse, neglect, or exploitation;

(2) The roles and responsibilities for handling and coordinating investigations of reported cases of abuse, neglect, or exploitation and methods to be used in interviewing the person who is the subject of the report and who allegedly was abused, neglected, or exploited;

(3) The roles and responsibilities for addressing the categories of persons who may interview the person who is the subject of the report and who allegedly was abused, neglected, or exploited;

(4) The roles and responsibilities for providing victim services to mentally retarded and developmentally disabled persons pursuant to Chapter 2930. of the Revised Code;

(5) The roles and responsibilities for the filing of criminal charges against persons alleged to have abused, neglected, or exploited mentally retarded or developmentally disabled persons.

(D) A memorandum of understanding may be signed by victim advocates, municipal court judges, municipal prosecutors, and any other person whose participation furthers the goals of a memorandum of understanding, as set forth in this section.

(2004 S 178, eff. 1–30–04)

5126.28 Criminal records check; disqualification from employment

(A) As used in this section:

(1) "Applicant" means a person who is under final consideration for appointment or employment in a position with a county board of mental retardation and developmental disabilities, including, but not limited to, a person who is being transferred to the county board and an employee who is being recalled or reemployed after a layoff.

(2) "Criminal records check" has the same meaning as in section 109.572 of the Revised Code.

(3) "Minor drug possession offense" has the same meaning as in section 2925.01 of the Revised Code.

(B) The superintendent of a county board of mental retardation and developmental disabilities shall request the superintendent of the bureau of criminal identification and investigation to conduct a criminal records check with respect to any applicant who has applied to the board for employment in any position, except that a county board superintendent is not required to request a criminal records check for an employee of the board who is being considered for a different position or is returning after a leave of absence or seasonal break in employment, as long as the superintendent has no reason to believe that the employee has committed any of the offenses listed or described in division (E) of this section.

If the applicant does not present proof that the applicant has been a resident of this state for the five-year period immediately prior to the date upon which the criminal records check is requested, the county board superintendent shall request that the superintendent of the bureau obtain information from the federal bureau of investigation as a part of the criminal records check for the applicant. If the applicant presents proof that the applicant has been a resident of this state for that five-year period, the county board superintendent may request that the superintendent of the bureau include information from the federal bureau of investigation in the criminal records check. For purposes of this division, an applicant may provide proof of residency in this state by presenting, with a notarized statement asserting that the applicant has been a resident of this state for that five-year period, a valid driver's license, notification of registration as an elector, a copy of an officially filed federal or state tax form identifying the applicant's permanent residence, or any other document the superintendent considers acceptable.

(C) The county board superintendent shall provide to each applicant a copy of the form prescribed pursuant to division (C)(1) of section 109.572 of the Revised Code, provide to each applicant a standard impression sheet to obtain fingerprint impressions prescribed pursuant to division (C)(2) of section 109.572 of the Revised Code, obtain the completed form and impression sheet from each applicant, and forward the completed form and impression sheet to the superintendent of the bureau of criminal identification and investigation at the time the criminal records check is requested.

Any applicant who receives pursuant to this division a copy of the form prescribed pursuant to division (C)(1) of section 109.572 of the Revised Code and a copy of an impression sheet prescribed pursuant to division (C)(2) of that section and who is requested to complete the form and provide a set of fingerprint impressions shall complete the form or provide all the information necessary to complete the form and shall provide the impression sheet with the impressions of the applicant's fingerprints. If an applicant, upon request, fails to provide the information necessary to complete the form or fails to provide impressions of the applicant's fingerprints, the county board superintendent shall not employ that applicant.

(D) A county board superintendent may request any other state or federal agency to supply the board with a written report regarding the criminal record of each applicant. With regard to an applicant who becomes a board employee, if the employee holds an occupational or professional license or other credentials, the superintendent may request that the state or federal agency that regulates the employee's occupation or profession supply the board with a written report of any information pertaining to the employee's criminal record that the agency obtains in the course of conducting an investigation or in the process of renewing the employee's license or other credentials.

(E) Except as provided in division (K)(2) of this section and in rules adopted by the department of mental retardation and developmental disabilities in accordance with division (M) of this section, no county board of mental retardation and developmental disabilities shall employ a person to fill a position with the board who has been convicted of or pleaded guilty to any of the following:

(1) A violation of section 2903.01, 2903.02, 2903.03, 2903.04, 2903.11, 2903.12, 2903.13, 2903.16, 2903.21, 2903.34, 2903.341, 2905.01, 2905.02, 2905.05, 2907.02, 2907.03, 2907.04, 2907.05, 2907.06, 2907.07, 2907.08, 2907. 09, 2907.21, 2907.22, 2907.23, 2907.25, 2907.31, 2907.32, 2907.321, 2907.322, 2907.323, 2911.01, 2911.02, 2911.11, 2911.12, 2919.12, 2919.22, 2919.24, 2919.25, 2923.12, 2923.13, 2923.161, 2925.02, 2925.03, 2925.04, 2925.05, 2925.06, or 3716.11 of the Revised Code, a violation of section 2905.04 of the Revised Code as it existed prior to July 1, 1996, a violation of section 2919.23 of the Revised Code that would have been a violation of section 2905.04 of the Revised Code as it existed prior to July 1, 1996, had the violation occurred prior to that date, a violation of section 2925.11 of the Revised Code that is not a minor drug possession offense, or felonious sexual penetration in violation of former section 2907.12 of the Revised Code;

(2) A felony contained in the Revised Code that is not listed in this division, if the felony bears a direct and substantial relationship to the duties and responsibilities of the position being filled;

(3) Any offense contained in the Revised Code constituting a misdemeanor of the first degree on the first offense and a felony on a subsequent offense, if the offense bears a direct and substantial relationship to the position being filled and the nature of the services being provided by the county board;

(4) A violation of an existing or former municipal ordinance or law of this state, any other state, or the United States, if the offense is substantially equivalent to any of the offenses listed or described in division (E)(1), (2), or (3) of this section.

(F) Prior to employing an applicant, the county board superintendent shall require the applicant to submit a statement with the applicant's signature attesting that the applicant has not been convicted of or pleaded guilty to any of the offenses listed or described in division (E) of this section. The superintendent also shall require the applicant to sign an agreement under which the applicant agrees to notify the superintendent within fourteen calendar days if, while employed by the board, the applicant is ever formally charged with, convicted of, or pleads guilty to any of the offenses listed or described in division (E) of this section. The agreement shall inform the applicant that failure to report formal charges, a conviction, or a guilty plea may result in being dismissed from employment.

(G) A county board of mental retardation and developmental disabilities shall pay to the bureau of criminal identification and investigation the fee prescribed pursuant to division (C)(3) of section 109.572 of the Revised Code for each criminal records check requested and conducted pursuant to this section.

(H)(1) Any report obtained pursuant to this section is not a public record for purposes of section 149.43 of the Revised Code and shall not be made available to any person, other than the applicant who is the subject of the records check or criminal records check or the applicant's representative, the board requesting the records check or criminal records check or its representative, the department of mental retardation and developmental disabilities, and any court, hearing officer, or other necessary individual involved in a case dealing with the denial of employment to the applicant or the denial, suspension, or revocation of a certificate or evidence of registration under section 5126.25 of the Revised Code.

(2) An individual for whom a county board superintendent has obtained reports under this section may submit a written request to the county board to have copies of the reports sent to any state agency, entity of local government, or private entity. The individual shall specify in the request the agencies or entities to which the copies are to be sent. On receiving the request, the county board shall send copies of the reports to the agencies or entities specified.

A county board may request that a state agency, entity of local government, or private entity send copies to the board of any report regarding a records check or criminal records check that the agency or entity possesses, if the county board obtains the written consent of the individual who is the subject of the report.

(I) Each county board superintendent shall request the registrar of motor vehicles to supply the superintendent with a certified abstract regarding the record of convictions for violations of motor vehicle laws of each applicant who will be required by the applicant's employment to transport individuals with mental retardation or developmental disabilities or to operate the board's vehicles for any other purpose. For each abstract provided under this section, the board shall pay the amount specified in section 4509.05 of the Revised Code.

(J) The county board superintendent shall provide each applicant with a copy of any report or abstract obtained about the applicant under this section. At the request of the director of mental retardation and developmental disabilities, the superintendent also shall provide the director with a copy of a report or abstract obtained under this section.

(K)(1) The county board superintendent shall inform each person, at the time of the person's initial application for employment, that the person is required to provide a set of impressions of the person's fingerprints and that a criminal records check is required to be conducted and satisfactorily completed in accordance with section 109.572 of the Revised Code if the person comes under final consideration for appointment or employment as a precondition to employment in a position.

(2) A board may employ an applicant pending receipt of reports requested under this section. The board shall terminate employment of any such applicant if it is determined from the reports that the applicant failed to inform the county board that the applicant had been convicted of or pleaded guilty to any of the offenses listed or described in division (E) of this section.

(L) The board may charge an applicant a fee for costs it incurs in obtaining reports, abstracts, or fingerprint impressions under this section. A fee charged under this division shall not exceed the amount of the fees the board pays under divisions (G) and (I) of this section. If a fee is charged under this division, the board shall notify the applicant of the amount of the fee at the time of the applicant's initial application for employment and that, unless the fee is paid, the board will not consider the applicant for employment.

(M) The department of mental retardation and developmental disabilities shall adopt rules pursuant to Chapter 119. of the Revised Code to implement this section and section 5126.281 of the Revised Code, including rules specifying circumstances under which a county board or contracting entity may hire a person who has been convicted of or pleaded guilty to an offense listed or described in division (E) of this section but who meets standards in regard to rehabilitation set by the department. The rules may not authorize a county board or contracting entity to hire an individual who is included in the registry established under section 5123.52 of the Revised Code.

(2004 S 178, eff. 1–30–04; 2000 S 171, eff. 11–22–00; 2000 H 538, eff. 9–22–00; 1996 H 629, eff. 3–13–97; 1996 S 269, eff. 7–1–96; 1996 H 445, eff. 9–3–96; 1995 S 2, eff. 7–1–96; 1994 H 694, eff. 11–11–94; 1993 S 38, eff. 10–29–93; 1992 H 387)

5126.281 Contracting entities to conduct background investigations

(A) As used in this section:

(1) "Contracting entity" means an entity under contract with a county board of mental retardation and developmental disabilities for the provision of specialized services to individuals with mental retardation or a developmental disability.

(2) "Direct services position" means an employment position in which the employee has physical contact with, the opportunity to be alone with, or exercises supervision or control over one or more individuals with mental retardation or a developmental disability.

(3) "Specialized services" means any program or service designed and operated to serve primarily individuals with mental retardation or a developmental disability, including a program or service provided by an entity licensed or certified by the department of mental retardation and developmental disabilities. If there is a question as to whether a contracting entity is providing specialized services, the contracting entity may request that the director of mental retardation and developmental disabilities make a determination. The director's determination is final.

(B)(1) Except as provided in division (B)(2) of this section, each contracting entity shall conduct background investigations in the same manner county boards conduct investigations under section 5126.28 of the Revised Code of all persons under final consideration for employment with the contracting entity in a direct services position. On request, the county board shall assist a contracting entity in obtaining reports from the bureau of criminal identification and investigation or any other state or federal agency and in obtaining abstracts from the registrar of motor vehicles.

(2) A contracting entity is not required to request a criminal records check for either of the following:

(a) An employee of the entity who is in a direct services position and being considered for a different direct services position or is returning after a leave of absence or seasonal break in employment, as long as the contracting entity has no reason to believe that the employee has committed any of the offenses listed or described in division (E) of section 5126.28 of the Revised Code;

(b) A person who will provide only respite care under a family support services program established under section 5126.11 of the Revised Code, if the person is selected by a family member of the individual with mental retardation or a developmental disability who is to receive the respite care.

(C) No contracting entity shall place a person in a direct services position if the person has been convicted of or pleaded guilty to any offense listed or described in division (E) of section 5126.28 of the Revised Code, unless the person meets the standards for rehabilitation established by rules adopted under section 5126.28 of the Revised Code.

(D) A contracting entity may place a person in a direct services position pending receipt of information concerning the person's background investigation from the bureau of criminal identification and investigation, the registrar of motor vehicles, or any other state or federal agency if the person submits to the contracting entity a statement with the person's signature that the person has not been convicted of or pleaded guilty to any of the offenses listed or described in division (E) of section 5126.28 of the Revised Code. No contracting entity shall fail to terminate the placement of such person if the contracting entity is informed that the person has been convicted of or pleaded guilty to any of the offenses listed or described in division (E) of section 5126.28 of the Revised Code.

(E) Prior to employing a person in a direct services position, the contracting entity shall require the person to submit a statement with the applicant's signature attesting that the applicant has not been convicted of or pleaded guilty to any of the offenses listed or described in division (E) of section 5126.28 of the Revised Code. The contracting entity also shall require the person to sign an agreement to notify the contracting entity within fourteen calendar days if, while employed by the entity, the person is ever formally charged with, convicted of, or pleads guilty to any of the offenses listed or described in division (E) of section 5126.28 of the Revised Code. The agreement shall inform the person that failure to report formal charges, a conviction, or a guilty plea may result in being dismissed from employment.

(F) A county board may take appropriate action against a contracting entity that violates this section, including terminating the contracting entity's contract with the board.

(2000 H 538, eff. 9–22–00; 1996 H 629, eff. 3–13–97; 1994 H 694, eff. 11–11–94)

5126.311 Review of reports of abuse or neglect by other governmental entity

(A) Notwithstanding the requirement of section 5126.31 of the Revised Code that a county board of mental retardation and developmental disabilities review reports of abuse and neglect, one of the following government entities, at the request of the county board or the department of mental retardation and developmental disabilities, shall review the report instead of the county board if circumstances specified in rules adopted under division (B) of this section exist:

(1) Another county board of mental retardation and developmental disabilities;

(2) The department;

(3) A regional council of government established pursuant to Chapter 167. of the Revised Code;

(4) Any other government entity authorized to investigate reports of abuse and neglect.

(B) The director of mental retardation and developmental disabilities shall adopt rules in accordance with Chapter 119. of the Revised Code specifying circumstances under which it is inappropriate for a county board to review reports of abuse and neglect.

(2001 H 94, eff. 6–6–01; 2000 H 538, eff. 9–22–00)

CHAPTER 5139

YOUTH SERVICES

DEPARTMENT OF YOUTH SERVICES POWERS AND DUTIES

GENERAL PROVISIONS

DEPARTMENT OF YOUTH SERVICES POWERS AND DUTIES

5139.05 Order of commitment to department of youth services; release; records; parental rights

(A) The juvenile court may commit any child to the department of youth services as authorized in Chapter 2152. of the Revised Code, provided that any child so committed shall be at least ten years of age at the time of the child's delinquent act, and, if the child is ten or eleven years of age, the delinquent act is a violation of section 2909.03 of the Revised Code or would be aggravated murder, murder, or a first or second degree felony offense of violence if committed by an adult. Any order to commit a child to an institution under the control and management of the department shall have the effect of ordering that the child be committed to the department and assigned to an institution as follows:

(1) For an indefinite term consisting of the prescribed minimum period specified by the court under division (A)(1) of section 2152.16 of the Revised Code and a maximum period not to exceed the child's attainment of twenty-one years of age, if the child was committed pursuant to section 2152. 16 of the Revised Code;

(2) Until the child's attainment of twenty-one years of age, if the child was committed for aggravated murder or murder pursuant to section 2152.16 of the Revised Code;

(3) For a period of commitment that shall be in addition to, and shall be served consecutively with and prior to, a period of commitment described in division (A)(1) or (2) of this section, if the child was committed pursuant to section 2152.17 of the Revised Code;

(4) If the child is ten or eleven years of age, to an institution, a residential care facility, a residential facility, or a facility licensed by the department of job and family services that the department of youth services considers best designated for the training and rehabilitation of the child and protection of the public. The child shall be housed separately from children who are twelve years of age or older until the child is released or discharged or until the child attains twelve years of age, whichever occurs first. Upon the child's attainment of twelve years of age, if the child has not been released or discharged, the department is not required to house the child separately.

(B)(1) Except as otherwise provided in section 5139.54 of the Revised Code, the release authority of the department of youth services, in accordance with section 5139.51 of the Revised Code and at any time after the end of the minimum period specified under division (A)(1) of section 2152.16 of the Revised Code, may grant the release from custody of any child committed to the department.

The order committing a child to the department of youth services shall state that the child has been adjudicated a delinquent child and state the minimum period. The jurisdiction of the court terminates at the end of the minimum period except as follows:

(a) In relation to judicial release procedures, supervision, and violations;

(b) With respect to functions of the court related to the revocation of supervised release that are specified in sections 5139.51 and 5139.52 of the Revised Code;

(c) In relation to its duties relating to serious youthful offender dispositional sentences under sections 2152.13 and 2152.14 of the Revised Code.

(2) When a child has been committed to the department under section 2152.16 of the Revised Code, the department shall retain legal custody of the child until one of the following:

(a) The department discharges the child to the exclusive management, control, and custody of the child's parent or the guardian of the child's person or, if the child is eighteen years of age or older, discharges the child.

(b) The committing court, upon its own motion, upon petition of the parent, guardian of the person, or next friend of a child, or upon petition of the department, terminates the department's legal custody of the child.

(c) The committing court grants the child a judicial release to court supervision under section 2152.22 of the Revised Code.

(d) The department's legal custody of the child is terminated automatically by the child attaining twenty-one years of age.

(e) If the child is subject to a serious youthful offender dispositional sentence, the adult portion of that dispositional sentence is imposed under section 2152.14 of the Revised Code.

(C) When a child is committed to the department of youth services, the department may assign the child to a hospital for mental, physical, and other examination, inquiry, or treatment for the period of time that is necessary. The department may remove any child in its custody to a hospital for observation, and a complete report of every observation at the hospital shall be made in writing and shall include a record of observation, treatment, and medical history and a recommendation for future treatment, custody, and maintenance. The department shall thereupon order the placement and treatment that it determines to be most conducive to the purposes of Chapters 2151. and 5139. of the Revised Code. The committing court and all public authorities shall make available to the department all pertinent data in their possession with respect to the case.

(D) Records maintained by the department of youth services pertaining to the children in its custody shall be accessible only to department employees, except by consent of the department, upon the order of the judge of a court of record, or as provided in divisions (D)(1) and (2) of this section. These records shall not be considered "public records," as defined in section 149.43 of the Revised Code.

(1) Except as otherwise provided by a law of this state or the United States, the department of youth services may release records that are maintained by the department of youth services and that pertain to children in its custody to the department of rehabilitation and correction regarding persons who are under the jurisdiction of the department of rehabilitation and correction and who have previously been committed to the department of youth services. The department of rehabilitation and correction may use those records for the limited purpose of carrying out the duties of the department of rehabilitation and correction. Records released by the department of youth services to the department of rehabilitation and correction shall remain confidential and shall not be considered public records as defined in section 149.43 of the Revised Code.

(2) The department of youth services shall provide to the superintendent of the school district in which a child discharged or released from the custody of the department is entitled to attend school under section 3313.64 or 3313.65 of the Revised Code the records described in divisions (D)(4)(a) to (d) of section 2152.18 of the Revised Code. Subject to the provisions of section 3319.321 of the Revised Code and the Family Educational Rights and Privacy Act, 20 U.S.C. 1232g, as amended, the records released to the superintendent shall remain confidential and shall not be considered public records as defined in section 149.43 of the Revised Code.

(E)(1) When a child is committed to the department of youth services, the department, orally or in writing, shall notify the parent, guardian, or custodian of a child that the parent, guardian, or custodian may request at any time from the superintendent of the institution in which the child is located any of the information described in divisions (E)(1)(a), (b), (c), and (d) of this section. The parent, guardian, or custodian may provide the department with the name, address, and telephone number of the parent, guardian, or custodian, and, until the department is notified of a change of name, address, or telephone number, the department shall use the name, address, and telephone number provided by the parent, guardian, or custodian to provide notices or answer inquiries concerning the following information:

(a) When the department of youth services makes a permanent assignment of the child to a facility, the department, orally or in writing and on or before the third business day after the day the permanent assignment is made, shall notify the parent, guardian, or custodian of the child of the name of the facility to which the child has been permanently assigned.

If a parent, guardian, or custodian of a child who is committed to the department of youth services requests, orally or in writing, the department to provide the parent, guardian, or custodian with the name of the facility in which the child is currently located, the department, orally or in writing and on or before the next business day after the day on which the request is made, shall provide the name of that facility to the parent, guardian, or custodian.

(b) If a parent, guardian, or custodian of a child who is committed to the department of youth services, orally or in writing, asks the superintendent of the institution in which the child is located whether the child is being disciplined by the personnel of the institution, what disciplinary measure the personnel of the institution are using for the child, or why the child is being disciplined, the superintendent or the superintendent's designee, on or before the next business day after the day on which the request is made, shall provide the parent, guardian, or custodian with written or oral responses to the questions.

(c) If a parent, guardian, or custodian of a child who is committed to the department of youth services, orally or in writing, asks the superintendent of the institution in which the child is held whether the child is receiving any medication from personnel of the institution, what type of medication the child is receiving, or what condition of the child the medication is intended to treat, the superintendent or the superintendent's designee, on or before the next business day after the day on which the request is made, shall provide the parent, guardian, or custodian with oral or written responses to the questions.

(d) When a major incident occurs with respect to a child who is committed to the department of youth services, the department, as soon as reasonably possible after the major incident occurs, shall notify the parent, guardian, or custodian of the child that a major incident has occurred with respect to the child and of all the details of that incident that the department has ascertained.

(2) The failure of the department of youth services to provide any notification required by or answer any requests made pursuant to division (E) of this section does not create a cause of action against the state.

(F) The department of youth services, as a means of punishment while the child is in its custody, shall not prohibit a child who is committed to the department from seeing that child's parent, guardian, or custodian during standard visitation periods allowed by the department of youth services unless the superintendent of the institution in which the child is held determines that permitting that child to visit with the child's parent, guardian, or custodian would create a safety risk to that child, that child's parents, guardian, or custodian, the personnel of the institution, or other children held in that institution.

(G) As used in this section:

(1) "Permanent assignment" means the assignment or transfer for an extended period of time of a child who is committed to the department of youth services to a facility in which the child will receive training or participate in activities that are directed toward the child's successful rehabilitation. "Permanent assignment" does not include the transfer of a child to a facility for judicial release hearings pursuant to section 2152.22 of the Revised Code or for any other temporary assignment or transfer to a facility.

(2) "Major incident" means the escape or attempted escape of a child who has been committed to the department of youth services from the facility to which the child is assigned; the return to the custody of the department of a child who has escaped or otherwise fled the custody and control of the department without authorization; the allegation of any sexual activity with a child committed to the department; physical injury to a child committed to the department as a result of alleged abuse by department staff; an accident resulting in injury to a child committed to the department that requires medical care or treatment outside the institution in which the child is located; the discovery of a controlled substance upon the person or in the property of a child committed to the department; a suicide attempt by a child committed to the department; a suicide attempt by a child committed to the department that results in injury to the child requiring emergency medical services outside the institution in which the child is located; the death of a child committed to the department; an injury to a visitor at an institution under the control of the department that is caused by a child committed to the department; and the commission or suspected commission of an act by a child committed to the department that would be an offense if committed by an adult.

(3) "Sexual activity" has the same meaning as in section 2907.01 of the Revised Code.

(4) "Controlled substance" has the same meaning as in section 3719.01 of the Revised Code.

(5) "Residential care facility" and "residential facility" have the same meanings as in section 2151.011 of the Revised Code.

(2004 H 106, eff. 9–16–04; 2002 H 393, eff. 7–5–02; 2000 S 179, § 3, eff. 1–1–02; 1998 H 526, eff. 9–1–98; 1997 H 1, eff. 7–1–98; 1996 S 269, eff. 7–1–96; 1995 H 1, eff. 1–1–96; 1993 H 152, eff. 7–1–93; 1993 S 28, eff. 6–23–93; 1983 S 210; 1981 H 440; 1977 H 1; 1975 H 85, H 839; 132 v H 1; 130 v H 968, H 299)

5139.06 Disposition of child committed to department; limits; procedures

(A) When a child has been committed to the department of youth services, the department shall do both of the following:

(1) Place the child in an appropriate institution under the condition that it considers best designed for the training and rehabilitation of the child and the protection of the public, provided that the institutional placement shall be consistent with the order committing the child to its custody;

(2) Maintain the child in institutional care or institutional care in a secure facility for the required period of institutionalization in a manner consistent with division (A)(1) of section 2152.16 and divisions (A) to (F) of section 2152.17 of the Revised Code, whichever are applicable, and with section 5139.38 or division (B) or (C) of section 2152.22 of the Revised Code.

(B) When a child has been committed to the department of youth services and has not been institutionalized or institutionalized in a secure facility for the prescribed minimum period of time, including, but not limited to, a prescribed period of time under division (A)(1)(a) of section 2152.16 of the Revised Code, the department, the child, or the child's parent may request the court that committed the child to order a judicial release to court supervision or a judicial release to department of youth services supervision in accordance with division (B) or (C) of section 2152.22 of the Revised Code, and the child may be released from institutionalization or institutionalization in a secure facility in accordance with the applicable division. A child in those circumstances shall not be released from institutionalization or institutionalization in a secure facility except in accordance with section 2152.22 or 5139.38 of the Revised Code. When a child is released pursuant to a judicial release to court supervision under division (B) of section 2152.22 of the Revised Code, the department shall comply with division (B)(3) of that section and, if the court requests, shall send the committing court a report on the child's progress in the institution and recommendations for conditions of supervision by the court after release. When a child is released pursuant to a judicial release to department of youth services supervision under division (C) of section 2152.22 of the Revised Code, the department shall comply with division (C)(3) of that section relative to the child and shall send the committing court and the juvenile court of the county in which the child is placed a copy of the treatment and rehabilitation plan described in that division and the conditions that it fixed. The court of the county in which the child is placed may adopt the conditions as an order of the court and may add any additional consistent conditions it considers appropriate, provided that the court may not add any condition that decreases the level or degree of supervision specified by the department in its plan, that substantially increases the financial burden of supervision that will be experienced by the department, or that alters the placement specified by the department in its plan. Any violations of the conditions of the child's judicial release or early release shall be handled pursuant to division (D) of section 2152.22 of the Revised Code.

(C) When a child has been committed to the department of youth services, the department may do any of the following:

(1) Notwithstanding the provisions of this chapter, Chapter 2151., or Chapter 2152. of the Revised Code that prescribe required periods of institutionalization, transfer the child to any other state institution, whenever it appears that the child by reason of mental illness, mental retardation, or other developmental disability ought to be in another state institution. Before transferring a child to any other state institution, the department shall include in the minutes a record of the order of transfer and the reason for the transfer and, at least seven days prior to the transfer, shall send a certified copy of the order to the person shown by its record to have had the care or custody of the child immediately prior to the child's commitment. Except as provided in division (C)(2) of this section, no person shall be transferred from a benevolent institution to a correctional institution or to a facility or institution operated by the department of youth services.

(2) Notwithstanding the provisions of this chapter, Chapter 2151., or Chapter 2152. of the Revised Code that prescribe required periods of institutionalization, transfer the child under section 5120.162 of the Revised Code to a correctional medical center established by the department of rehabilitation and correction, whenever the child has an illness, physical condition, or other medical problem and it appears that the child would benefit from diagnosis or treatment at the center for that illness, condition, or problem. Before transferring a child to a center, the department of youth services shall include in the minutes a record of the order of transfer and the reason for the transfer and, except in emergency situations, at least seven days prior to the transfer, shall send a certified copy of the order to the person shown by its records to have had the care or custody of the child immediately prior to the child's commitment. If the transfer of the child occurs in an emergency situation, as soon as possible after the decision is made to make the transfer, the department of youth services shall send a certified copy of the order to the person shown by its records to have had the care or custody of the child immediately prior to the child's commitment. A transfer under this division shall be in accordance with the terms of the agreement the department of youth services enters into with the department of rehabilitation and correction under section 5120.162 of the Revised Code and shall continue only as long as the child reasonably appears to receive benefit from diagnosis or treatment at the center for an illness, physical condition, or other medical problem.

(3) Revoke or modify any order of the department except an order of discharge as often as conditions indicate it to be desirable;

(4) If the child was committed pursuant to division (A)(1)(b), (c), (d), or (e) of section 2152.16 of the Revised Code and has been institutionalized or institutionalized in a secure facility for the prescribed minimum periods of time under those divisions, assign the child to a family home, a group care facility, or other place maintained under public or private auspices, within or without this state, for necessary treatment and rehabilitation, the costs of which may be paid by the department, provided that the department shall notify the committing court, in writing, of the place and terms of the assignment at least fifteen days prior to the scheduled date of the assignment;

(5) Release the child from an institution in accordance with sections 5139.51 to 5139.54 of the Revised Code in the circumstances described in those sections.

(D) The department of youth services shall notify the committing court of any order transferring the physical location of any child committed to it in accordance with section 5139.35 of the Revised Code. Upon the discharge from its custody and control, the department may petition the court for an order terminating its custody and control.

(2002 H 393, eff. 7–5–02; 2000 S 179, § 3, eff. 1–1–02; 1997 H 1, eff. 7–1–98; 1995 H 1, eff. 1–1–96; 1994 H 571, eff. 10–6–94; 1993 H 152, eff. 7–1–93; 1992 S 331; 1983 H 291; 1981 H 440; 1975 H 155; 130 v H 299)

5139.07 Rehabilitation of child committed to youth services

(A)(1)(a) As a means of correcting the socially harmful tendencies of a child committed to it, the department of youth services may require a child to participate in vocational, physical, and corrective training and activities, and the conduct and modes of life that seem best adapted to rehabilitate the child and fit the child for return to full liberty without danger to the public welfare.

(b) Except as otherwise provided, the department shall require any child committed to it who has not attained a diploma or certificate of high school equivalence, to participate in courses leading toward a high school diploma or an Ohio certificate of high school equivalence. This requirement does not apply to a child in an assessment program or treatment intervention program prescribed by the department.

(c) The department may monetarily compensate the child for the activities described in this section by transferring the wages of the child for those activities to the appropriate youth benefit fund created under section 5139.86 of the Revised Code.

(d) This section does not permit the department to release a child committed to it from institutional care or institutional care in a secure facility, whichever is applicable, other than in accordance with sections 2152.22, 5139.06, 5139.38, and 5139.50 to 5139.54 of the Revised Code.

(2) The failure of the department of youth services to provide, pursuant to division (A)(1) of this section, an opportunity for any child committed to it to participate in courses that lead to a high school diploma or an Ohio certificate of high school equivalence, does not give rise to a claim for damages against the department.

(B) The department may require a child committed to it to return to the child's home or to be placed in a foster care placement if it is authorized to make a placement of that nature under sections 2152.22, 5139.06, 5139.38, and 5139.50 to 5139.54 of the Revised Code. Any placement of that nature shall be made in accordance with those sections. The legal residence of a child so placed by the department is the place in which the child is residing in accordance with a department order of placement. The school district responsible for payment of tuition on behalf of the child so placed shall be determined pursuant to section 3313.64 or 3313.65 of the Revised Code.

(2000 S 179, § 3, eff. 1–1–02; 2000 S 115, eff. 3–22–01; 1997 H 1, eff. 7–1–98; 1997 H 215, eff. 9–29–97; 1993 H 152, eff. 7–1–93; 1983 H 210; 1981 H 440, S 140; 1969 H 22; 130 v H 299)

5139.08 Agreement with other agencies

The department of youth services may enter into an agreement with the director of rehabilitation and correction pursuant to which the department of youth services, in accordance with division (C)(2) of section 5139.06 and section 5120.162 of the Revised Code, may transfer to a correctional medical center established by the department of rehabilitation and correction, children who are within its custody for diagnosis or treatment of an illness, physical condition, or other medical problem. The department of youth services may enter into any other agreements with the director of job and family services, the director of mental health, the director of mental retardation and developmental disabilities, the director of rehabilitation and correction, with the courts having probation officers or other public officials, and with private agencies or institutions for separate care or special treatment of children subject to the control of the department of youth services. The department of youth services may, upon the request of a juvenile court not having a regular probation officer, provide probation services for such court.

Upon request by the department of youth services, any public agency or group care facility established or administered by the state for the care and treatment of children and youth shall, consistent with its functions, accept and care for any child whose custody is vested in the department in the same manner as it would be required to do if custody had been vested by a court in such agency or group care facility. If the department has reasonable grounds to believe that any child or youth whose custody is vested in it is mentally ill or mentally retarded, the department may file an affidavit under section 5122.11 or 5123.76 of the Revised Code. The department's affidavit for admission of a child or youth to such institution shall be filed with the probate court of the county from which the child was committed to the department. Such court may request the probate court of the county in which the child is held to conduct the hearing on the application, in which case the court making such request shall bear the expenses of the proceeding. If the department files such an affidavit, the child or youth may be kept in such institution until a final decision on the affidavit is made by the appropriate court.

(1999 H 471, eff. 7–1–00; 1997 H 1, eff. 7–1–98; 1992 S 331, eff. 11–13–92; 1988 S 156; 1986 H 428; 1983 H 291; 1981 H 440; 1980 H 900; 1977 H 725; 1972 H 494; 1969 H 688; 130 v H 299, H 968)

5139.09 Reexamination of children

The department of youth services shall make periodic reexamination of all children under its control for the purpose of determining whether existing orders in individual cases should be modified or continued in force. These examinations shall be made with respect to every child at least once annually.

(1981 H 440, eff. 11–23–81; 130 v H 299)

5139.10 Discharge; control period

Unless the child has already received a final discharge, the control by the department of youth services of a child committed as a delinquent shall cease when the child reaches the age of twenty-one years.

(1981 H 440, eff. 11–23–81; 130 v H 299)

5139.11 Reduction and control of juvenile delinquency

The department of youth services shall do all of the following:

(A) Through a program of education, promotion, and organization, form groups of local citizens and assist these groups in conducting activities aimed at the prevention and control of juvenile delinquency, making use of local people and resources for the following purposes:

(1) Combatting local conditions known to contribute to juvenile delinquency;

(2) Developing recreational and other programs for youth work;

(3) Providing adult sponsors for delinquent children cases;

(4) Dealing with other related problems of the locality.

(B) Advise local, state, and federal officials, public and private agencies, and lay groups on the needs for and possible methods of the reduction and prevention of juvenile delinquency and the treatment of delinquent children;

(C) Consult with the schools and courts of this state on the development of programs for the reduction and prevention of delinquency and the treatment of delinquents;

(D) Cooperate with other agencies whose services deal with the care and treatment of delinquent children to the end that delinquent children who are state wards may be assisted whenever possible to a successful adjustment outside of institutional care;

(E) Cooperate with other agencies in surveying, developing, and utilizing the recreational resources of a community as a means of combatting the problem of juvenile delinquency and effectuating rehabilitation;

(F) Hold district and state conferences from time to time in order to acquaint the public with current problems of juvenile delinquency and develop a sense of civic responsibility toward the prevention of juvenile delinquency;

(G) Assemble and distribute information relating to juvenile delinquency and report on studies relating to community conditions that affect the problem of juvenile delinquency;

(H) Assist any community within the state by conducting a comprehensive survey of the community's available public and private resources, and recommend methods of establishing a community program for combatting juvenile delinquency and crime, but no survey of that type shall be conducted unless local individuals and groups request it through their local authorities, and no request of that type shall be interpreted as binding the community to following the recommendations made as a result of the request;

(I) Evaluate the rehabilitation of children committed to the department and prepare and submit periodic reports to the committing court for the following purposes:

(1) Evaluating the effectiveness of institutional treatment;

(2) Making recommendations for judicial release under section 2152.22 of the Revised Code if appropriate and recommending conditions for judicial release;

(3) Reviewing the placement of children and recommending alternative placements where appropriate.

(J) Coordinate dates for hearings to be conducted under section 2152.22 of the Revised Code and assist in the transfer and release of children from institutionalization to the custody of the committing court;

(K)(1) Coordinate and assist juvenile justice systems by doing the following:

(a) Performing juvenile justice system planning in the state, including any planning that is required by any federal law;

(b) Collecting, analyzing, and correlating information and data concerning the juvenile justice system in the state;

(c) Cooperating with and providing technical assistance to state departments, administrative planning districts, metropolitan county criminal justice services agencies, criminal justice coordinating councils, and agencies, offices, and departments of the juvenile justice system in the state, and other appropriate organizations and persons;

(d) Encouraging and assisting agencies, offices, and departments of the juvenile justice system in the state and other appropriate organizations and persons to solve problems that relate to the duties of the department;

(e) Administering within the state any juvenile justice acts and programs that the governor requires the department to administer;

(f) Implementing the state comprehensive plans;

(g) Auditing grant activities of agencies, offices, organizations, and persons that are financed in whole or in part by funds granted through the department;

(h) Monitoring or evaluating the performance of juvenile justice system projects and programs in the state that are financed in whole or in part by funds granted through the department;

(i) Applying for, allocating, disbursing, and accounting for grants that are made available pursuant to federal juvenile justice acts, or made available from other federal, state, or private sources, to improve the criminal and juvenile justice systems in the state. All money from federal juvenile justice act grants shall, if the terms under which the money is received require that the money be deposited into an interest bearing fund or account, be deposited in the state treasury to the credit of the federal juvenile justice program purposes fund, which is hereby created. All investment earnings shall be credited to the fund.

(j) Contracting with federal, state, and local agencies, foundations, corporations, businesses, and persons when necessary to carry out the duties of the department;

(k) Overseeing the activities of metropolitan county criminal justice services agencies, administrative planning districts, and juvenile justice coordinating councils in the state;

(*l*) Advising the general assembly and governor on legislation and other significant matters that pertain to the improvement and reform of the juvenile justice system in the state;

(m) Preparing and recommending legislation to the general assembly and governor for the improvement of the juvenile justice system in the state;

(n) Assisting, advising, and making any reports that are required by the governor, attorney general, or general assembly;

(*o*) Adopting rules pursuant to Chapter 119. of the Revised Code.

(2) Division (K)(1) of this section does not limit the discretion or authority of the attorney general with respect to crime victim assistance and criminal and juvenile justice programs.

(3) Nothing in division (K)(1) of this section is intended to diminish or alter the status of the office of the attorney general as a criminal justice services agency.

(4) The governor may appoint any advisory committees to assist the department that the governor considers appropriate or that are required under any state or federal law.

(2001 H 94, § 6, eff. 1–1–02; 2001 H 94, § 1, eff. 6–6–01; 2000 S 179, § 3, eff. 1–1–02; 1993 H 152, eff. 7–1–93; 1983 H 291; 1981 H 440; 1973 H 760; 132 v S 235; 130 v H 299)

GENERAL PROVISIONS

5139.18 Placement of released children

(A) Except with respect to children who are granted a judicial release to court supervision pursuant to division (B) of section 2152.22 of the Revised Code, the department of youth services is responsible for locating homes or jobs for children released from its institutions, for supervision of children released from its institutions, and for providing or arranging for the provision to those children of appropriate services that are required to facilitate their satisfactory community adjustment.

(B) The department of youth services shall exercise general supervision over all children who have been released on placement from any of its institutions other than children who are granted a judicial release to court supervision pursuant to division (B) of section 2152.22 of the Revised Code. The director of youth services, with the consent and approval of the board of county commissioners of any county, may contract with the public children services agency of that county, the department of probation of that county established pursuant to section 2301.27 of the Revised Code, or the probation department or service established pursuant to sections 2151.01 to 2151.54 of the Revised Code for the provision of direct supervision and control over and the provision of supportive assistance to all children who have been released on placement into that county from any of its institutions, or, with the consent of the juvenile judge or the administrative judge of the juvenile court of any county, contract with any other public agency, institution, or organization that is qualified to provide the care and supervision that is required under the terms and conditions of the child's treatment plan for the provision of direct supervision and control over and the provision of supportive assistance to all children who have been released on placement into that county from any of its institutions.

(C) Whenever any placement official has reasonable cause to believe that any child released by a court pursuant to section 2152.22 of the Revised Code has violated the conditions of the child's placement, the official may request, in writing, from the committing court or transferee court a custodial order, and, upon reasonable and probable cause, the court may order any sheriff, deputy sheriff, constable, or police officer to apprehend the child. A child so apprehended may be confined in the detention facility of the county in which the child is apprehended until further order of the court. If a child who was released on supervised release by the release authority of the department of youth services or a child who was granted a judicial release to department of youth services supervision violates the conditions of the supervised release or judicial release, section 5139.52 of the Revised Code applies with respect to that child.

(2000 S 179, § 3, eff. 1–1–02; 1998 H 526, eff. 9–1–98; 1997 H 1, eff. 7–1–98; 1997 H 408, eff. 10–1–97; 1993 H 152, eff. 7–1–93; 1986 H 428; 1983 H 291; 1981 H 440; 1973 H 760; 132 v H 367; 130 v H 968, H 299)

5139.191 Apprehension and return of escapees from youth commission institutions

Any sheriff, deputy sheriff, constable, officer of state or local police, or employee of the department of youth services shall apprehend any child who has escaped from an institution under the jurisdiction of the department and return the child. The written request of the superintendent of the institution from which the child has escaped shall be sufficient cause to authorize the apprehension and return of the child to the institution. Such request shall state the name and description of the child, that the child is under the jurisdiction of the department of youth services, and that the superintendent has personal knowledge that the child has escaped. A child so apprehended may be confined in the detention facility of the county in which the child is apprehended until removed to the proper institution.

(2000 S 179, § 3, eff. 1–1–02; 1981 H 440, eff. 11–23–81; 1969 S 84)

5139.21 Influencing child under jurisdiction of department of youth services

No person shall influence or attempt to influence any child under supervision of the department of youth services, to leave the institution or home in which he was placed, his home, or place of employment or to violate any of the conditions upon which he was released under supervision.

(1981 H 440, eff. 11–23–81; 132 v H 491; 130 v H 299)

5139.251 Searches of visitors to institutions

(A) As used in this section:

(1) "Body cavity search" and "strip search" have the same meanings as in section 5120.421 of the Revised Code.

(2) "Deadly weapon" and "dangerous ordnance" have the same meanings as in section 2923.11 of the Revised Code.

(3) "Drug of abuse" has the same meaning as in section 3719.011 of the Revised Code.

(4) "Intoxicating liquor" has the same meaning as in section 4301.01 of the Revised Code.

(B) For purposes of determining whether visitors to an institution under the control of the department of youth services are knowingly conveying, or attempting to convey, onto the grounds of the institution any deadly weapon, dangerous ordnance, drug of abuse, intoxicating liquor, or electronic communications device in violation of section 2921.36 of the Revised Code, the department may adopt rules, pursuant to Chapter 119. of the Revised Code, that are consistent with this section.

(C) For the purposes described in division (B) of this section, visitors who are entering or have entered an institution under the control of the department of youth services may be searched by the use of a magnetometer or similar device, by a pat-down of the visitor's person that is conducted by a person of the same sex as that of the visitor, and by an examination of the contents of pockets, bags, purses, packages, and other containers proposed to be conveyed or already conveyed onto the grounds of the institution. Searches of visitors authorized by this division may be conducted without cause, but shall be conducted uniformly or by automatic random selection. Discriminatory or arbitrary selection searches of visitors are prohibited under this division.

(D) For the purposes described in division (B) of this section, visitors who are entering or have entered an institution under the control of the department of youth services may be searched by a strip or body cavity search, but only under the circumstances described in this division. In order for a strip or body cavity search to be conducted of a visitor, the highest officer present in the institution shall expressly authorize the search on the basis of a reasonable suspicion, based on specific objective facts and reasonable inferences drawn from those facts in the light of experience, that a visitor proposed to be so searched possesses, and intends to convey or already has conveyed, a deadly weapon, dangerous ordnance, drug of abuse, intoxicating liquor, or electronic communication device onto the grounds of the institution in violation of section 2921.36 of the Revised Code.

Except as otherwise provided in this division, prior to the conduct of the strip or body cavity search, the highest officer present in the institution shall cause the visitor to be provided with a written statement that sets forth the specific objective facts upon which the proposed search is based. In the case of an emergency under which time constraints make it impossible to prepare the written statement before the conduct of the proposed search, the highest officer in the institution instead shall cause the visitor to be orally informed of the specific objective facts upon which the proposed search is based prior to its conduct, and shall cause the preparation of the written statement and its provision to the visitor within twenty-four hours after the conduct of the search. Both the highest officer present in the institution and the visitor shall retain a copy of a written statement provided in accordance with this division.

Any strip or body cavity search conducted pursuant to this division shall be conducted in a private setting by a person of the same sex as that of the visitor. Any body cavity search conducted under this division additionally shall be conducted by medical personnel.

This division does not preclude, and shall not be construed as precluding, a less intrusive search as authorized by division (C) of this section when reasonable suspicion as described in this division exists for a strip or body cavity search.

(2002 H 510, eff. 3–31–03; 1990 S 258, eff. 8–22–90)

REHABILITATION FACILITIES

5139.30 Transfer of child committed to facility

The department of youth services may, by mutual agreement with the governing board of a school, forestry camp, or other facility established under section 2151.65 of the Revised Code, transfer to such school, forestry camp, or other facility any child committed to the department.

(1981 H 440, eff. 11–23–81; 131 v H 943)

MISCELLANEOUS PROVISIONS

5139.32 Return of child to committing court

(A) Whenever a child committed to the department of youth services is unable to benefit from the programs conducted by the department, as found under division (B) of this section, the department forthwith shall release or discharge such child from its jurisdiction and either return the child to the committing court, provided that such court so consents or directs, or otherwise secure for the child an environment more beneficial to the child's future development.

(B) The determination that a child is unable to benefit from the programs conducted by the department shall be made by the committing court on its own motion or upon application by the department or by a parent or the guardian of the person of the child, or, if the child has been institutionalized or institutionalized in a secure facility, whichever is applicable, for the prescribed minimum period set forth in Chapter 2152. of the Revised Code and the child's commitment order, by the department itself.

(2000 S 179, § 3, eff. 1–1–02; 1981 H 440, eff. 11–23–81; 131 v H 943)

5139.33 Grants for community-based programs and services for delinquent children

(A) The department of youth services shall make grants in accordance with this section to encourage counties to use community-based programs and services for juveniles who are adjudicated delinquent children for the commission of acts that would be felonies if committed by an adult.

(B) Each county seeking a grant under this section shall file an application with the department of youth services. The application shall be filed at the time and in accordance with procedures established by the department in rules adopted under this section. Each application shall be accompanied by a plan designed to reduce the county's commitment percentage, or to enable it to maintain or attain a commitment percentage that is equal to or below the statewide average commitment percentage. A county's commitment percentage is the percentage determined by dividing the number of juveniles the county committed to the department during the year by the number of juveniles who were eligible to be committed. The statewide average commitment percentage is the percentage determined by dividing the number of juveniles in the state committed to the department during the year by the number of juveniles who were eligible to be committed. These percentages shall be determined by the department using the most reliable data available to it.

Each plan shall include a method of ensuring equal access for minority youth to the programs and services for which the grant will be used.

The department shall review each application and plan to ensure that the requirements of this division are satisfied. Any county applying for a grant under this section that received a grant under this section during the preceding year and that failed to meet its commitment goals for that year shall make the changes in its plan that the department requires in order to continue to be eligible for grants under this section.

(C) Subject to division (E) of this section, the amounts appropriated for the purpose of making grants under this section shall be distributed annually on a per capita basis among the counties that have complied with division (B) of this section.

(D) The department shall adopt rules to implement this section. The rules shall include, but are not limited to, procedures and schedules for submitting applications and plans under this section, including procedures allowing joint-county applications and plans; and procedures for monitoring and evaluating the effectiveness of the programs and services financed with grant money, the enhancement of the use of local facilities and services, and the adequacy of the supervision and treatment provided to juveniles by those programs and services.

(E)(1) Three months prior to the implementation of the felony delinquent care and custody program described in section 5139.43 of the Revised Code, each county that is entitled to a grant under this section shall receive its grant money for the fiscal year or the remainder of its grant money for the fiscal year, other than any grant money to which it is entitled and that is set aside by the department of youth services for purposes of division (E)(2) of this section. The grant money so distributed shall be paid in a lump sum.

(2) During the first twelve months that the felony delinquent care and custody program described in section 5139.43 of the Revised Code is implemented in a county, any grant or the remainder of any grant to which a county is entitled and that is payable from the appropriation made to the department of youth services for community sanctions shall be distributed as follows:

(a) In the first quarter of the twelve-month period, the county shall receive one hundred per cent of the quarterly distribution.

(b) In the second quarter of the twelve-month period, the county shall receive seventy-five per cent of the quarterly distribution.

(c) In the third quarter of the twelve-month period, the county shall receive fifty per cent of the quarterly distribution.

(d) In the fourth quarter of the twelve-month period, the county shall receive twenty-five per cent of the quarterly distribution.

(3) Grant moneys received pursuant to divisions (E)(1) and (2) of this section shall be transmitted by the juvenile court of the recipient county to the county treasurer, shall be deposited by the county treasurer into the felony delinquent care and custody fund created pursuant to division (B)(1) of section 5139.43 of the Revised Code, and shall be used by the juvenile court in accordance with division (B)(2) of that section. The grant moneys shall be in addition to, and shall not be used to reduce, any usual annual increase in county funding that the juvenile court is eligible to receive or the current level of county funding of the juvenile court and of any programs or services for delinquent children, unruly children, or juvenile traffic offenders.

(4) One year after the commencement of its operation of the felony delinquent care and custody program described in section 5139.43 of the Revised Code, the department shall not make any further grants under this section.

(2003 H 95, eff. 9–26–03; 1994 H 715, eff. 7–22–94; 1993 H 152, eff. 7–1–93; 1990 S 268)

5139.34 Subsidies to counties

(A) Funds may be appropriated to the department of youth services for the purpose of granting state subsidies to counties. A county or the juvenile court that serves a county shall use state subsidies granted to the county pursuant to this section only in accordance with divisions (B)(2)(a) and (3)(a) of section 5139.43 of the Revised Code and the rules pertaining to the state subsidy funds that the department adopts pursuant to division (D) of section 5139.04 of the Revised Code. The department shall not grant financial assistance pursuant to this section for the provision of care and services for children in a placement facility unless the facility has been certified, licensed, or approved by a state or national agency with certification, licensure, or approval authority, including, but not limited to, the department of job and family services, department of education, department of mental health, department of mental retardation and developmental disabilities, or American Correctional Association. For the purposes of this section, placement facilities do not include a state institution or a county or district children's home.

The department also shall not grant financial assistance pursuant to this section for the provision of care and services for children, including, but not limited to, care and services in a detention facility, in another facility, or in out-of-home placement, unless the minimum standards applicable to the care and services that the department prescribes in rules adopted pursuant to division (D) of section 5139.04 of the Revised Code have been satisfied.

(B) The department of youth services shall apply the following formula to determine the amount of the annual grant that each county is to receive pursuant to division (A) of this section, subject to the appropriation for this purpose to the department made by the general assembly:

(1) Each county shall receive a basic annual grant of fifty thousand dollars.

(2) The sum of the basic annual grants provided under division (B)(1) of this section shall be subtracted from the total amount of funds appropriated to the department of youth services for the purpose of making grants pursuant to division (A) of this section to determine the remaining portion of the funds appropriated. The remaining portion of the funds appropriated shall be distributed on a per capita basis to each county that has a population of more than twenty-five thousand for that portion of the population of the county that exceeds twenty-five thousand.

(C)(1) Prior to a county's receipt of an annual grant pursuant to this section, the juvenile court that serves the county shall prepare, submit, and file in accordance with division (B)(3)(a) of section 5139.43 of the Revised Code an annual grant agreement and application for funding that is for the combined purposes of, and that satisfies the requirements of, this section and section 5139.43 of the Revised Code. In addition to the subject matters described in division (B)(3)(a) of section 5139.43 of the Revised Code or in the rules that the department adopts to implement that division, the annual grant agreement and application for funding shall address fiscal accountability and performance matters pertaining to the programs, care, and services that are specified in the agreement and application and for which state subsidy funds granted pursuant to this section will be used.

(2) The county treasurer of each county that receives an annual grant pursuant to this section shall deposit the state subsidy funds so received into the county's felony delinquent care and custody fund created pursuant to division (B)(1) of section 5139.43 of the Revised Code. Subject to exceptions prescribed in section 5139.43 of the Revised Code that may apply to the disbursement, the department shall disburse the state subsidy funds to which a county is entitled in a lump sum payment that shall be made in July of each calendar year.

(3) Upon an order of the juvenile court that serves a county and subject to appropriation by the board of county commissioners of that county, a county treasurer shall disburse from the county's felony delinquent care and custody fund the state subsidy funds granted to the county pursuant to this section for use only in accordance with this section, the applicable provisions of section 5139.43 of the Revised Code, and the county's approved annual grant agreement and application for funding.

(4) The moneys in a county's felony delinquent care and custody fund that represent state subsidy funds granted pursuant to this section are subject to appropriation by the board of county commissioners of the county; shall be disbursed by the county treasurer as required by division (C)(3) of this section; shall be used in the manners referred to in division (C)(3) of this section; shall not revert to the county general fund at the end of any fiscal year; shall carry over in the felony delinquent care and custody fund from the end of any fiscal year to the next fiscal year; shall be in addition to, and shall not be used to reduce, any usual annual increase in county funding that the juvenile court is eligible to receive or the current level of county funding of the juvenile court and of any programs, care, or services for alleged or adjudicated delinquent children, unruly children, or juvenile traffic offenders or for children who are at risk of becoming delinquent children, unruly children, or juvenile traffic offenders; and shall not be used to pay for the care and custody of felony deliquents[1] who are in the care and custody of an institution pursuant to a commitment, recommitment, or revocation of a release on parole by the juvenile court of that county or who are in the care and custody of a community corrections facility pursuant to a placement by the department with the consent of the juvenile court as described in division (E) of section 5139.36 of the Revised Code.

(5) As a condition of the continued receipt of state subsidy funds pursuant to this section, each county and the juvenile court that serves each county that receives an annual grant pursuant to this section shall comply with divisions (B)(3)(b), (c), and (d) of section 5139.43 of the Revised Code.

(2003 H 95, eff. 9–26–03; 1999 H 471, eff. 7–1–00; 1997 H 215, eff. 6–30–97; 1993 H 152, eff. 7–1–93; 1986 H 428; 1983 H 291; 1981 H 440)

[1] So in original. 1997 H 215.

5139.35 Placement in less restrictive setting; court approval required

(A) Except as provided in division (C) of this section and division (C)(2) of section 5139.06 of the Revised Code, the department of youth services shall not place a child committed to it pursuant to section 2152.16 or divisions (A) and (B) of section 2152.17 of the Revised Code who has not been institutionalized or institutionalized in a secure facility for the prescribed minimum period of institutionalization in an institution with a less restrictive setting than that in which the child was originally placed, other than an institution under the management and control of the department, without first obtaining the prior consent of the committing court.

(B) Except as provided in division (C) of this section, the department of youth services shall notify the committing court, in writing, of any placement of a child committed to it pursuant to division (A)(1)(b), (c), (d), or (e) of section 2152.16 or divisions (A) and (B) of section 2152.17 of the Revised Code who has been institutionalized or institutionalized in a secure facility for the prescribed minimum period of institutionalization under those divisions in an institution with a less restrictive setting than that in which the child was originally placed, other than an institution under the management and control of the department, at least fifteen days before the scheduled date of placement.

(C) If, pursuant to division (C)(2) of section 5139.06 of the Revised Code, the department of youth services transfers a child committed to it pursuant to division (A)(1)(b), (c), (d), or (e) of section 2152.16 or divisions (A) and (B) of section 2152.17 of the Revised Code to a correctional medical center established by the department of rehabilitation and correction, the department of youth services shall send the committing court a certified copy of the transfer order.

(2000 S 179, § 3, eff. 1–1–02; 1997 H 1, eff. 7–1–98; 1995 H 1, eff. 1–1–96; 1992 S 331, eff. 11–13–92; 1983 H 291; 1981 H 440)

FOSTER CARE FACILITIES

5139.38 Transfer of felony delinquent to community facility

Within ninety days prior to the expiration of the prescribed minimum period of institutionalization of a felony delinquent committed to the department of youth services and with prior notification to the committing court, the department may transfer the felony delinquent to a community facility for a period of supervised treatment prior to ordering a release of the felony delinquent on supervised release or prior to the release and placement of the felony delinquent as described in section 5139.18 of the Revised Code. For purposes of transfers under this section, both of the following apply:

(A) The community facility may be a community corrections facility that has received a grant pursuant to section 5139.36 of the Revised Code, a community residential program with which the department has contracted for purposes of this section, or another private entity with which the department has contracted for purposes of this section. Division (E) of section 5139.36 of the Revised Code does not apply in connection with a transfer of a felony delinquent that is made to a community corrections facility pursuant to this section.

(B) During the period in which the felony delinquent is in the community facility, the felony delinquent shall remain in the custody of the department.

(1997 H 1, eff. 7–1–98; 1994 H 715, eff. 7–22–94; 1993 H 152, eff. 7–1–93)

5139.39 Transfer of child to foster care facility

The department of youth services, in the manner provided in this chapter and Chapter 2151. of the Revised Code, may transfer to a foster care facility certified by the department of job and family services under section 5103.03 of the Revised Code, any child committed to it and, in the event of a transfer of that nature, unless otherwise mutually agreed, the department of youth services shall bear the cost of care and services provided for the child in the foster care facility. A juvenile court may transfer to any foster facility certified by the department of job and family services any child between twelve and eighteen years of age, other than a psychotic or mentally retarded child, who has been designated a delinquent child and placed on probation by order of the juvenile court as a result of having violated any law of this state or the United States or any ordinance of a political subdivision of this state.

(1999 H 471, eff. 7–1–00; 1993 H 152, eff. 7–1–93; 1981 H 440; 132 v S 278)

FELONY DELINQUENTS

5139.41 Appropriations for care and custody of felony delinquents

The appropriation made to the department of youth services for care and custody of felony delinquents shall be expended in accordance with the following procedure that the department shall use for each year of a biennium. The procedure shall be consistent with sections 5139.41 to 5139.43 of the Revised Code and shall be developed in accordance with the following guidelines:

(A) The line item appropriation for the care and custody of felony delinquents shall provide funding for operational costs for the following:

(1) Institutions and the diagnosis, care, or treatment of felony delinquents at facilities pursuant to contracts entered into under section 5139.08 of the Revised Code;

(2) Community corrections facilities constructed, reconstructed, improved, or financed as described in section 5139.36 of the Revised Code for the purpose of providing alternative placement and services for felony delinquents who have been diverted from care and custody in institutions;

(3) County juvenile courts that administer programs and services for prevention, early intervention, diversion, treatment, and rehabilitation services and programs that are provided for alleged or adjudicated unruly or delinquent children or for children who are at risk of becoming unruly or delinquent children;

(4) Administrative expenses the department incurs in connection with the felony delinquent care and custody programs described in section 5139.43 of the Revised Code.

(B) From the appropriated line item for the care and custody of felony delinquents, the department, with the advice of the RECLAIM advisory committee established under section 5139.44 of the Revised Code, shall allocate annual operational funds for county juvenile programs, institutional care and custody, community corrections facilities care and custody, and administrative expenses incurred by the department associated with felony delinquent care and custody programs. The department, with the advice of the RECLAIM advisory committee, shall adjust these allocations, when modifications to this line item are made by legislative or executive action.

(C) The department shall divide county juvenile program allocations among county juvenile courts that administer programs and services for prevention, early intervention, diversion, treatment, and rehabilitation that are provided for alleged or adjudicated unruly or delinquent children or for children who are at risk of becoming unruly or delinquent children. The department shall base funding on the county's previous year's ratio of the department's institutional and community correctional facilities commitments to that county's four year average of felony adjudications, divided by statewide ratios of commitments to felony adjudications, as specified in the following formula:

(1) The department shall give to each county a proportional allocation of commitment credits. The proportional allocation of commitment credits shall be calculated by the following procedures:

(a) The department shall determine for each county and for the state a four year average of felony adjudications.

(b) The department shall determine for each county and for the state the number of charged bed days, for both the department and community correctional facilities, from the previous year.

(c) The department shall divide the statewide total number of charged bed days by the statewide total number of felony adjudications, which quotient shall then be multiplied by a factor determined by the department.

(d) The department shall calculate the county's allocation of credits by multiplying the number of adjudications for each court by the result determined pursuant to division (C)(1)(c) of this section.

(2) The department shall subtract from the allocation determined pursuant to division (C)(1) of this section a credit for every chargeable bed day a youth stays in a department institution and two-thirds of credit for every chargeable bed day a youth stays in a community correctional facility. At the end of the year, the department shall divide the amount of remaining credits of that county's allocation by the total number of remaining credits to all counties, to determine the county's percentage, which shall then be applied to the total county allocation to determine the county's payment for the fiscal year.

(3) The department shall pay counties three times during the fiscal year to allow for credit reporting and audit adjustments, and modifications to the appropriated line item for the care and custody of felony delinquents, as described in this section. The department shall pay fifty per cent of the payment by the fifteenth of July of each fiscal year, twenty-five per cent by the fifteenth of January of that fiscal year, and twenty-five per cent of the payment by the fifteenth of June of that fiscal year.

(D) In fiscal year 2004, the payment of county juvenile programs shall be based on the following procedure:

(1) The department shall divide the funding earned by each court in fiscal year 2003 by the aggregate funding of all courts, resulting in a percentage.

(2) The department shall apply the percentage determined under division (D)(1) of this section to the total county juvenile program allocation for fiscal year 2004 to determine each court's total payment.

(3) The department shall make payments in accordance with the schedule established in division (C)(3) of this section.

(2003 H 95, eff. 9–26–03; 2003 H 40, eff. 3–7–03; 2000 S 179, § 3, eff. 1–1–02; 1996 H 670, eff. 12–2–96; 1995 H 117, eff. 6–30–95; 1994 H 715, eff. 7–22–94; 1993 H 152, eff. 7–1–93)

5139.43 Felony delinquent care and custody program

(A) The department of youth services shall operate a felony delinquent care and custody program that shall be operated in accordance with the formula developed pursuant to section 5139.41 of the Revised Code, subject to the conditions specified in this section.

(B)(1) Each juvenile court shall use the moneys disbursed to it by the department of youth services pursuant to division (B) of section 5139.41 of the Revised Code in accordance with the applicable provisions of division (B)(2) of this section and shall transmit the moneys to the county treasurer for deposit in accordance with this division. The county treasurer shall create in the county treasury a fund that shall be known as the felony delinquent care and custody fund and shall deposit in that fund the moneys disbursed to the juvenile court pursuant to division (B) of section 5139.41 of the Revised Code. The county treasurer also shall deposit into that fund the state subsidy funds granted to the county pursuant to section 5139.34 of the Revised Code. The moneys disbursed to the juvenile court pursuant to division (B) of section 5139.41 of the Revised Code and deposited pursuant to this division in the felony delinquent care and custody fund shall not be commingled with any other county funds except state subsidy funds granted to the county pursuant to section 5139.34 of the Revised Code; shall not be used for any capital construction projects; upon an order of the juvenile court and subject to appropriation by the board of county commissioners, shall be disbursed to the juvenile court for use in accordance with the applicable provisions of division (B)(2) of this section; shall not revert to the county general fund at the end of any fiscal year; and shall carry over in the felony delinquent care and custody fund from the end of any fiscal year to the next fiscal year. The moneys disbursed to the juvenile court pursuant to division (B) of section 5139.41 of the Revised Code and deposited pursuant to this division in the felony delinquent care and custody fund shall be in addition to, and shall not be used to reduce, any usual annual increase in county funding that the juvenile court is eligible to receive or the current level of county funding of the juvenile court and of any programs or services for delinquent children, unruly children, or juvenile traffic offenders.

(2)(a) A county and the juvenile court that serves the county shall use the moneys in its felony delinquent care and custody fund in accordance with rules that the department of youth services adopts pursuant to division (D) of section 5139.04 of the Revised Code and as follows:

(i) The moneys in the fund that represent state subsidy funds granted to the county pursuant to section 5139.34 of the Revised Code shall be used to aid in the support of prevention, early intervention, diversion, treatment, and rehabilitation programs that are provided for alleged or adjudicated unruly children or delinquent children or for children who are at risk of becoming unruly children or delinquent children. The county shall not use for capital improvements more than fifteen per cent of the moneys in the fund that represent the applicable annual grant of those state subsidy funds.

(ii) The moneys in the fund that were disbursed to the juvenile court pursuant to division (B) of section 5139.41 of the Revised Code and deposited pursuant to division (B)(1) of this section in the fund shall be used to provide programs and services for the training, treatment, or rehabilitation of felony delinquents that are alternatives to their commitment to the department, including, but not limited to, community residential programs, day treatment centers, services within the home, and electronic monitoring, and shall be used in connection with training, treatment, rehabilitation, early intervention, or other programs or services for any delinquent child, unruly child, or juvenile traffic offender who is under the jurisdiction of the juvenile court.

The fund also may be used for prevention, early intervention, diversion, treatment, and rehabilitation programs that are provided for alleged or adjudicated unruly children, delinquent children, or juvenile traffic offenders or for children who are at risk of becoming unruly children, delinquent children, or juvenile traffic offenders. Consistent with division (B)(1) of this section, a county and the juvenile court of a county shall not use any of those moneys for capital construction projects.

(iii) The county and the juvenile court that serves the county may not use moneys in the fund for the provision of care and services for children, including, but not limited to, care and services in a detention facility, in another facility, or in out-of-home placement, unless the minimum standards that apply to the care and services and that the department prescribes in rules adopted pursuant to division (D) of section 5139.04 of the Revised Code have been satisfied.

(b) Each juvenile court shall comply with division (B)(3)(d) of this section as implemented by the department.

(3) In accordance with rules adopted by the department pursuant to division (D) of section 5139.04 of the Revised Code, each juvenile court and the county served by that juvenile court shall do all of the following that apply:

(a) The juvenile court shall prepare an annual grant agreement and application for funding that satisfies the requirements of this section and section 5139.34 of the Revised Code and that pertains to the use, upon an order of the juvenile court and subject to appropriation by the board of county commissioners, of the moneys in its felony delinquent care and custody fund for specified programs, care, and services as described in division (B)(2)(a) of this section, shall submit that agreement and application to the county family and children first council, the regional family and children first council, or the local intersystem services to children cluster as described in sections 121.37 and 121.38 of the Revised Code, whichever is applicable, and shall file that agreement and application with the department for its approval. The annual grant agreement and application for funding shall include a method of ensuring equal access for minority youth to the programs, care, and services specified in it.

The department may approve an annual grant agreement and application for funding only if the juvenile court involved has complied with the preparation, submission, and filing requirements described in division (B)(3)(a) of this section. If the juvenile court complies with those requirements and the department approves that agreement and application, the juvenile court and the county served by the juvenile court may expend the state subsidy funds granted to the county pursuant to section 5139.34 of the Revised Code only in accordance with division (B)(2)(a) of this section, the rules pertaining to state subsidy funds that the department adopts pursuant to division (D) of section 5139.04 of the Revised Code, and the approved agreement and application.

(b) By the thirty-first day of August of each year, the juvenile court shall file with the department a report that contains all of the statistical and other information for each month of the prior state fiscal year. If the juvenile court fails to file the report required by division (B)(3)(b) of this section by the thirty-first day of August of any year, the department shall not disburse any payment of state subsidy funds to which the county otherwise is entitled pursuant to section 5139.34 of the Revised Code and shall not disburse pursuant to division (B) of section 5139.41 of the Revised Code the applicable allocation until the juvenile court fully complies with division (B)(3)(b) of this section.

(c) If the department requires the juvenile court to prepare monthly statistical reports and to submit the reports on forms provided by the department, the juvenile court shall file those reports with the department on the forms so provided. If the juvenile court fails to prepare and submit those monthly statistical reports within the department's timelines, the department shall not disburse any payment of state subsidy funds to which the county otherwise is entitled pursuant to section 5139.34 of the Revised Code and shall not disburse pursuant to division (B) of section 5139.41 of the Revised Code the applicable allocation until the juvenile court fully complies with division (B)(3)(c) of this section. If the juvenile court fails to prepare and submit those monthly statistical reports within one hundred eighty days of the date the department establishes for their submission, the department shall not disburse any payment of state subsidy funds to which the county otherwise is entitled pursuant to section 5139.34 of the Revised Code and shall not disburse pursuant to division (B) of section 5139.41 of the Revised Code the applicable allocation, and the state subsidy funds and the remainder of the applicable allocation shall revert to the department. If a juvenile court states in a monthly statistical report that the juvenile court adjudicated within a state fiscal year five hundred or more children to be delinquent children for committing acts that would be felonies if committed by adults and if the department determines that the data in the report may be inaccurate, the juvenile court shall have an independent auditor or other qualified entity certify the accuracy of the data on a date determined by the department.

(d) If the department requires the juvenile court and the county to participate in a fiscal monitoring program or another monitoring program that is conducted by the department to ensure compliance by the juvenile court and the county with division (B) of this section, the juvenile court and the county shall participate in the program and fully comply with any guidelines for the performance of audits adopted by the department pursuant to that program and all requests made by the department pursuant to that program for information necessary to reconcile fiscal accounting. If an audit that is performed pursuant to a fiscal monitoring program or another monitoring program described in this division determines that the juvenile court or the county used moneys in the county's felony delinquent care and custody fund for expenses that are not authorized under division (B) of this section, within forty-five days after the department notifies the county of the unauthorized expenditures, the county either shall repay the amount of the unauthorized expenditures from the county general revenue fund to the state's general revenue fund or shall file a written appeal with the department. If an appeal is timely filed, the director of the department shall render a decision on the appeal and shall notify the appellant county or its juvenile court of that decision within forty-five days after the date that the appeal is filed. If the director denies an appeal, the county's fiscal agent shall repay the amount of the unauthorized expenditures from the county general revenue fund to the state's general revenue fund within thirty days after receiving the director's notification of the appeal decision. If the county fails to make the repayment within that thirty-day period and if the unauthorized expenditures pertain to moneys allocated under sections 5139.41 to 5139.43 of the Revised Code, the department shall deduct the amount of the unauthorized expenditures from the next allocation of those moneys to the county in accordance with this section or from the allocations that otherwise would be made under those sections to the county during the next state fiscal year in accordance with this section and shall return that deducted amount to the state's general revenue fund. If the county fails to make the repayment within that thirty-day period and if the unauthorized expenditures pertain to moneys granted pursuant to section 5139. 34 of the Revised Code, the department shall deduct the amount of the unauthorized expenditures from the next annual grant to the county pursuant to that section and shall return that deducted amount to the state's general revenue fund.

(C) The determination of which county a reduction of the care and custody allocation will be charged against for a particular youth shall be made as outlined below for all youths who do not qualify as public safety beds. The determination of which county a reduction of the care and custody allocation will be charged against shall be made as follows until each youth is released:

(1) In the event of a commitment, the reduction shall be charged against the committing county.

(2) In the event of a recommitment, the reduction shall be charged against the original committing county until the expiration of the minimum period of institutionalization under the original order of commitment or until the date on which the youth is admitted to the department of youth services pursuant to the order of recommitment, whichever is later. Reductions of the allocation shall be charged against the county that recommitted the youth after the minimum expiration date of the original commitment.

(3) In the event of a revocation of a release on parole, the reduction shall be charged against the county that revokes the youth's parole.

(D) A juvenile court is not precluded by its allocation amount for the care and custody of felony delinquents from committing a felony delinquent to the department of youth services for care and custody in an institution or a community corrections facility when the juvenile court determines that the commitment is appropriate.

(2003 H 95, eff. 9–26–03; 1999 H 283, eff. 6–30–99; 1997 H 1, eff. 7–1–98; 1997 H 215, eff. 6–30–97 (See Uncodified Law); 1995 H 117, eff. 6–30–95; 1994 H 715, eff. 7–22–94; 1993 H 152, eff. 7–1–93)

Uncodified Law

1997 H 215, § 236, eff. 6–30–97, reads:

(A) The amendments by this act to section 5139.43 of the Revised Code, except for the amendments to division (B)(2)(a)(ii) of the section, constitute items of law that are not subject to the referendum. Therefore, under Ohio Constitution, Article II, Section 1d and section 1.471 of the Revised Code, these items of law go into immediate effect when this act becomes law.

(B) The amendment by this act to the first and second paragraphs of division (B)(2)(a)(ii) of section 5139.43 of the Revised Code constitute separate items of law that are each subject to the referendum. Therefore, under Ohio Constitution, Article II, Section 1c and section 1.471 of the Revised Code, these items of law take effect on the ninety-first day after this act is filed with the Secretary of State. If, however, a referendum petition is filed against any such item of law, the item of law, unless rejected at the referendum, takes effect at the earliest time permitted by law.

5139.44 RECLAIM advisory committee

(A)(1) There is hereby created the RECLAIM advisory committee that shall be composed of the following nine members:

(a) Two members shall be juvenile court judges appointed by the Ohio association of juvenile and family court judges.

(b) One member shall be the director of youth services or the director's designee.

(c) One member shall be the director of budget and management or the director's designee.

(d) One member shall be a member of a senate committee dealing with finance or criminal justice issues appointed by the president of the senate.

(e) One member shall be a member of a committee of the house of representatives dealing with finance or criminal justice issues appointed by the speaker of the house of representatives.

(f) One member shall be a member of a board of county commissioners appointed by the county commissioners association of Ohio.

(g) Two members shall be juvenile court administrators appointed by the Ohio association of juvenile and family court judges.

(2) The members of the committee shall be appointed or designated within thirty days after the effective date of this section, and the director of youth services shall be notified of the names of the members.

(3) Members described in divisions (A)(1)(a), (f), and (g) of this section shall serve for terms of two years and shall hold office from the date of the member's appointment until the end of the term for which the member was appointed. Members described in divisions (A)(1)(b) and (c) of this section shall serve as long as they hold the office described in that division. Members described in divisions (A)(1)(d) and (e) of this section shall serve for the duration of the session of the general assembly during which they were appointed, provided they continue to hold the office described in that division. The members described in divisions (A)(1)(a), (d), (e), (f), and (g) may be reappointed. Vacancies shall be filled in the manner provided for original appointments. Any member appointed to fill a vacancy occurring prior to the expiration date of the term for which the member's predecessor was appointed shall hold office as a member for the remainder of that term. A member shall continue in office subsequent to the expiration date of the member's term until the member's successor takes office or until a period of sixty days has elapsed, whichever occurs first.

(4) Membership on the committee does not constitute the holding of an incompatible public office or employment in violation of any statutory or common law prohibition pertaining to the simultaneous holding of more than one public office or employment. Members of the committee are not disqualified from holding by reason of that membership and do not forfeit because of that membership their public office or employment that qualifies them for membership on the committee notwithstanding any contrary disqualification or forfeiture requirement under existing Revised Code sections.

(B) The director of youth services shall serve as an interim chair of the RECLAIM advisory committee until the first meeting of the committee. Upon receipt of the names of the members of the committee, the director shall schedule the initial meeting of the committee that shall take place at an appropriate location in Columbus and occur not later than sixty days after the effective date of this section. The director shall notify the members of the committee of the time, date, and place of the meeting. At the initial meeting, the committee shall organize itself by selecting from among its members a chair, vice-chair, and secretary. The committee shall meet at least once each quarter of the calendar year but may meet more frequently at the call of the chair.

(C) In addition to its functions with respect to the RECLAIM program described in section 5139.41 of the Revised Code, the RECLAIM advisory committee periodically shall do all of the following:

(1) Evaluate the operation of the RECLAIM program by the department of youth services, evaluate the implementation of the RECLAIM program by the counties, and evaluate the efficiency of the formula described in section 5139.41 of the Revised Code. In conducting these evaluations, the committee shall consider the public policy that RECLAIM funds are to be expended to provide the most appropriate programs and services for felony delinquents and other youthful offenders.

(2) Advise the department of youth services, the office of budget and management, and the general assembly on the following changes that the committee believes should be made:

(a) Changes to sections of the Revised Code that pertain to the RECLAIM program, specifically the formula specified in section 5139.41 of the Revised Code;

(b) Changes in the funding level for the RECLAIM program, specifically the amounts distributed under the formula for county allocations, community correctional facilities, and juvenile correctional facility budgets.

(2003 H 95, eff. 9–26–03)

RELEASE AUTHORITY

5139.50 Release authority; membership; powers and duties

(A) The release authority of the department of youth services is hereby created as a bureau in the department. The release authority shall consist of five members who are appointed by the director of youth services and who have the qualifications specified in division (B) of this section. The members of the release authority shall devote their full time to the duties of the release authority and shall neither seek nor hold other public office. The members shall be in the unclassified civil service.

(B) A person appointed as a member of the release authority shall have a bachelor's degree from an accredited college or university or equivalent relevant experience and shall have the skills, training, or experience necessary to analyze issues of law, administration, and public policy. The membership of the release authority shall represent, insofar as practicable, the diversity found in the children in the legal custody of the department of youth services.

In appointing the five members, the director shall ensure that the appointments include all of the following:

(1) At least four members who have five or more years of experience in criminal justice, juvenile justice, or an equivalent relevant profession;

(2) At least one member who has experience in victim services or advocacy or who has been a victim of a crime or is a family member of a victim;

(3) At least one member who has experience in direct care services to delinquent children;

(4) At least one member who holds a juris doctor degree from an accredited college or university.

(C) The initial appointments of members of the release authority shall be for a term of six years for the chairperson and one member, a term of four years for two members, and a term of two years for one member. Thereafter, members shall be appointed for six-year terms. At the conclusion of a term, a member shall hold office until the appointment and qualification of the member's successor. The director shall fill a vacancy occurring before the expiration of a term for the remainder of that term and, if a member is on extended leave or disability status for more than thirty work days, may appoint an interim member to fulfill the duties of that member. A member may be reappointed, but a member may serve no more than two consecutive terms regardless of the length of the member's initial term. A member may be removed for good cause by the director.

(D) The director of youth services shall designate as chairperson of the release authority one of the members who has experience in criminal justice, juvenile justice, or an equivalent relevant profession. The chairperson shall be a managing officer of the department, shall supervise the members of the board and the other staff in the bureau, and shall perform all duties and functions necessary to ensure that the release authority discharges its responsibilities. The chairperson shall serve as the official spokesperson for the release authority.

(E) The release authority shall do all of the following:

(1) Serve as the final and sole authority for making decisions, in the interests of public safety and the children involved, regarding the release and discharge of all children committed to the legal custody of the department of youth services, except children placed by a juvenile court on judicial release to court supervision or on judicial release to department of youth services supervision, children who have not completed a prescribed minimum period of time or prescribed period of time in a secure facility, or children who are required to remain in a secure facility until they attain twenty-one years of age;

(2) Establish written policies and procedures for conducting reviews of the status for all youth in the custody of the department, setting or modifying dates of release and discharge, specifying the duration, terms, and conditions of release to be carried out in supervised release subject to the addition of additional consistent terms and conditions by a court in accordance with section 5139.51 of the Revised Code, and giving a child notice of all reviews;

(3) Maintain records of its official actions, decisions, orders, and hearing summaries and make the records accessible in accordance with division (D) of section 5139.05 of the Revised Code;

(4) Cooperate with public and private agencies, communities, private groups, and individuals for the development and improvement of its services;

(5) Collect, develop, and maintain statistical information regarding its services and decisions;

(6) Submit to the director an annual report that includes a description of the operations of the release authority, an evaluation of its effectiveness, recommendations for statutory, budgetary, or other changes necessary to improve its effectiveness, and any other information required by the director.

(F) The release authority may do any of the following:

(1) Conduct inquiries, investigations, and reviews and hold hearings and other proceedings necessary to properly discharge its responsibilities;

(2) Issue subpoenas, enforceable in a court of law, to compel a person to appear, give testimony, or produce documentary information or other tangible items relating to a matter under inquiry, investigation, review, or hearing;

(3) Administer oaths and receive testimony of persons under oath;

(4) Request assistance, services, and information from a public agency to enable the authority to discharge its responsibilities and receive the assistance, services, and information from the public agency in a reasonable period of time;

(5) Request from a public agency or any other entity that provides or has provided services to a child committed to the department's legal custody information to enable the release authority to properly discharge its responsibilities with respect to that child and receive the information from the public agency or other entity in a reasonable period of time.

(G) The release authority may delegate responsibilities to hearing officers or other designated staff under the release authority's auspices. However, the release authority shall not delegate its authority to make final decisions regarding policy or the release of a child.

The release authority shall adopt a written policy and procedures governing appeals of its release and discharge decisions.

(H) The legal staff of the department of youth services shall provide assistance to the release authority in the formulation of policy and in its handling of individual cases.

(2002 H 393, eff. 7–5–02; 2000 S 179, § 3, eff. 1–1–02; 1999 H 283, eff. 9–29–99; 1998 H 526, eff. 9–1–98; 1997 H 1, eff. 1–1–98)

5139.51 Procedures for release; supervised release or discharge plan

(A) The release authority of the department of youth services shall not release a child who is in the custody of the department of youth services from institutional care or institutional care in a secure facility and shall not discharge the child or order the child's release on supervised release prior to the expiration of the prescribed minimum period of institutionalization or institutionalization in a secure facility or prior to the child's attainment of twenty-one years of age, whichever is applicable under the order of commitment, other than as is provided in section 2152.22 of the Revised Code. The release authority may conduct periodic reviews of the case of each child who is in the custody of the department and who is eligible for supervised release or discharge after completing the minimum period of time or period of time in an institution prescribed by the committing court. At least thirty days prior to conducting a periodic review of the case of a child who was committed to the department regarding the possibility of supervised release or discharge and at least thirty days prior to conducting a release review, a release hearing, or a discharge review under division (E) of this section, the release authority shall give notice of the review or hearing to the court that committed the child, to the prosecuting attorney in the case, and to the victim of the delinquent act for which the child was committed or the victim's representative. If a child is on supervised release and has had the child's parole revoked, and if, upon release, there is insufficient time to provide the notices otherwise required by this division, the release authority, at least ten days prior to the child's release, shall provide reasonable notice of the child's release to the court that committed the child, to the prosecuting attorney in the case, and to the victim of the delinquent act for which the child was committed or the victim's representative. The court or prosecuting attorney may submit to the release authority written comments regarding, or written objections to, the supervised release or discharge of that child. Additionally, if the child was committed for an act that is a category one or category two offense, the court or prosecuting attorney orally may communicate to a representative of the release authority comments regarding, or objections to, the supervised release or discharge of the child or, if a hearing is held regarding the possible release or discharge of the child, may communicate those comments at the hearing. In conducting the review of the child's case regarding the possibility of supervised release or discharge, the release authority shall consider any comments and objections so submitted or communicated by the court or prosecutor and any statements or comments submitted or communicated under section 5139.56 of the Revised Code by a victim of an act for which the child was committed to the legal custody of the department or by the victim's representative of a victim of an act of that type.

The release authority shall determine the date on which a child may be placed on supervised release or discharged. If the release authority believes that a child should be placed on supervised release, it shall comply with division (B) of this section. If the release authority believes that a child should be discharged, it shall comply with division (C) or (E) of this section. If the release authority denies the supervised release or discharge of a child, it shall provide the child with a written record of the reasons for the decision.

(B)(1) When the release authority decides to place a child on supervised release, consistent with division (D) of this section, the department shall prepare a written supervised release plan that specifies the terms and conditions upon which the child is to be released from an institution on supervised release and, at least thirty days prior to the release of the child on the supervised release, shall send to the committing court and the juvenile court of the county in which the child will be placed a copy of the supervised release plan and the terms and conditions of release. The juvenile court of the county in which the child will be placed, within fifteen days after its receipt of the copy of the supervised release plan, may add to the supervised release plan any additional consistent terms and conditions it considers appropriate, provided that the court may not add any term or condition that decreases the level or degree of supervision specified by the release authority in the plan, that substantially increases the financial burden of supervision that will be experienced by the department of youth services, or that alters the placement specified by the plan.

If, within fifteen days after its receipt of the copy of the supervised release plan, the juvenile court of the county in which the child will be placed does not add to the supervised release plan any additional terms and conditions, the court shall enter the supervised release plan in its journal within that fifteen-day period and, within that fifteen-day period, shall send to the release authority a copy of the journal entry of the supervised release plan. The journalized plan shall apply regarding the child's supervised release.

If, within fifteen days after its receipt of the copy of the supervised release plan, the juvenile court of the county in which the child will be placed adds to the supervised release plan any additional terms and conditions, the court shall enter the supervised release plan and the additional terms and conditions in its journal and, within that fifteen-day period, shall send to the release authority a copy of the journal entry of the supervised release plan and additional terms and conditions. The journalized supervised release plan and additional terms and conditions added by the court that satisfy the criteria described in this division shall apply regarding the child's supervised release.

If, within fifteen days after its receipt of the copy of the supervised release plan, the juvenile court of the county in which the child will be placed neither enters in its journal the supervised release plan nor enters in its journal the supervised release plan plus additional terms and conditions added by the court, the court and the department of youth services may attempt to resolve any differences regarding the plan within three days. If a resolution is not reached within that three-day period, thereafter, the supervised release plan shall be enforceable to the same extent as if the court actually had entered the supervised release plan in its journal.

(2) When the release authority receives from the court a copy of the journalized supervised release plan and, if applicable, a copy of the journalized additional terms and conditions added by the court, the release authority shall keep the original copy or copies in the child's file and shall provide a copy of each document to the child, the employee of the department who is assigned to supervise and assist the child while on release, and the committing court.

(C) If a child who is in the custody of the department of youth services was committed pursuant to division (A)(1)(b), (c), (d), or (e) of section 2152.16 of the Revised Code and has been institutionalized or institutionalized in a secure facility for the prescribed minimum periods of time under those divisions and if the release authority is satisfied that the discharge of the child without the child being placed on supervised release would be consistent with the welfare of the child and protection of the public, the release authority, without approval of the court that committed the child, may discharge the child from the department's custody and control without placing the child on supervised release. Additionally, the release authority may discharge a child in the department's custody without the child being placed on supervised release if the child is removed from the jurisdiction of this state by a court order of a court of this state, another state, or the United States, or by any agency of this state, another state, or the United States, if the child is convicted of or pleads guilty to any criminal offense, or as otherwise provided by law. At least fifteen days before the scheduled date of discharge of the child without the child being placed on supervised release, the department shall notify the committing court, in writing, that it is going to discharge the child and of the reason for the discharge. Upon discharge of the child without the child being placed on supervised release, the department immediately shall certify the discharge in writing and shall transmit the certificate of discharge to the committing court.

(D) In addition to requirements that are reasonably related to the child's prior pattern of criminal or delinquent behavior and the prevention of further criminal or delinquent behavior, the release authority shall specify the following requirements for each child whom it releases:

(1) The child shall observe the law.

(2) The child shall maintain appropriate contact, as specified in the written supervised release plan for that child.

(3) The child shall not change residence unless the child seeks prior approval for the change from the employee of the department assigned to supervise and assist the child, provides that employee, at the time the child seeks the prior approval for the change, with appropriate information regarding the new residence address at which the child wishes to reside, and obtains the prior approval of that employee for the change.

(E) The period of a child's supervised release may extend from the date of release from an institution until the child attains twenty-one years of age. If the period of supervised release extends beyond one year after the date of release, the child may request in writing that the release authority conduct a discharge review after the expiration of the one-year period or the minimum period or period. If the child so requests, the release authority shall conduct a discharge review and give the child its decision in writing. The release authority shall not grant a discharge prior to the discharge date if it finds good cause for retaining the child in the custody of the department until the discharge date. A child may request an additional discharge review six months after the date of a previous discharge review decision, but not more than once during any six-month period after the date of a previous discharge review decision.

(F) At least two weeks before the release authority places on supervised release or discharge a child who was committed to the legal custody of the department, the release authority shall provide notice of the release or discharge as follows:

(1) In relation to the placement on supervised release or discharge of a child who was committed to the department for committing an act that is a category one or category two offense, the release authority shall notify, by the specified deadline, all of the following of the release or discharge:

(a) The prosecuting attorney of the county in which the child was adjudicated a delinquent child and committed to the custody of the department;

(b) Whichever of the following is applicable:

(i) If upon the supervised release or discharge the child will reside in a municipal corporation, the chief of police or other chief law enforcement officer of that municipal corporation;

(ii) If upon the supervised release or discharge the child will reside in an unincorporated area of a county, the sheriff of that county.

(2) In relation to the placement on supervised release or discharge of a child who was committed to the department for committing any act, the release authority shall notify, by the specified deadline, each victim of the act for which the child was committed to the legal custody of the department who, pursuant to section 5139.56 of the Revised Code, has requested to be notified of the placement of the child on supervised release or the discharge of the child, provided that, if any victim has designated a person pursuant to that section to act on the victim's behalf as a victim's representative, the notification required by this division shall be provided to that victim's representative.

(2000 S 179, § 3, eff. 1–1–02; 1999 H 283, eff. 9–29–99; 1998 H 526, eff. 9–1–98; 1997 H 1, eff. 7–1–98)

5139.52 Violation of supervised release

(A) At any time during a child's supervised release or during the period of a child's judicial release to department of youth services supervision, if the regional administrator or the employee of the department assigned to supervise and assist the child has reasonable grounds to believe that the child has violated a term or condition of the supervised release or judicial release, the administrator or employee may request a court to issue a summons that requires the child to appear for a hearing to answer charges of the alleged violation. The summons shall contain a brief statement of the alleged violation, including the date and place of the violation, and shall require the child to appear for a hearing before the court at a specific date, time, and place.

(B)(1) At any time while a child is on supervised release or during the period of a child's judicial release to department of youth services supervision, a regional administrator or a designee of a regional administrator, upon application of the employee of the department assigned to supervise and assist the child as described in this division, may issue, or cause to be issued, an order of apprehension for the arrest of the child for the alleged violation of a term or condition of the child's supervised release or judicial release. An application requesting an order of apprehension shall set forth that, in the good faith judgment of the employee of the department assigned to supervise and assist the child making the application, there is reasonable cause to believe that the child who is on supervised release or judicial release to department of youth services supervision has violated or is violating a term or condition of the child's supervised release or judicial release, shall state the basis for that belief, and shall request that the child be taken to an appropriate place of secure detention pending a probable cause determination. As an alternative to an order of apprehension for the child, a regional administrator or the employee of the department assigned to supervise and assist the child may request a court to issue a warrant for the arrest of the child.

Subject to the provision of prior notice required by division (D)(1) of this section, if a regional administrator or a designee of a regional administrator issues, in writing, an order of apprehension for the arrest of a child, a staff member of the department of youth services who has been designated pursuant to division (A)(1) of section 5139.53 of the Revised Code as being authorized to arrest and who has received the training described in division (B)(1) of that section, or a peace officer, as defined in section 2935.01 of the Revised Code, may arrest the child, without a warrant, and place the child in secure detention in accordance with this section.

If a child is on supervised release or judicial release to department of youth services supervision, any peace officer, as defined in section 2935.01 of the Revised Code, may arrest the child without a warrant or order of apprehension if the peace officer has reasonable grounds to believe that the child has violated or is violating any of the following that has been prescribed by the release authority or department of youth services relative to the child:

(a) A condition that prohibits the child's ownership, possession, or use of a firearm, deadly weapon, ammunition, or dangerous ordnance, all as defined in section 2923.11 of the Revised Code;

(b) A condition that prohibits the child from being within a specified structure or geographic area;

(c) A condition that confines the child to a residence, facility, or other structure;

(d) A condition that prohibits the child from contacting or communicating with any specified individual;

(e) A condition that prohibits the child from associating with a specified individual;

(f) Any other rule, term, or condition governing the conduct of the child that has been prescribed by the release authority.

(2) Subject to the provision of prior notice required by division (D)(1) of this section, a staff member of the department of youth services who is designated by the director pursuant to division (A)(1) of section 5139.53 of the Revised Code and who has received the training described in division (B)(1) of that section, a peace officer, as defined in section 2935.01 of the Revised Code, or any other officer with the power to arrest may execute a warrant or order of apprehension issued under division (B)(1) of this section and take the child into secure custody.

(C) A staff member of the department of youth services who is designated by the director of youth services pursuant to division (A)(1) of section 5139.53 of the Revised Code and who has received the training described in division (B)(1) of that section, a peace officer, as defined in section 2935.01 of the Revised Code, or any other officer with the power to arrest may arrest without a warrant or order of apprehension and take into secure custody a child in the legal custody of the department, if the staff member, peace officer, or other officer has reasonable cause to believe that the child who is on supervised release or judicial release to department of youth services supervision has violated or is violating a term or condition of the supervised release or judicial release in any of the following manners:

(1) The child committed or is committing an offense or delinquent act in the presence of the staff member, peace officer, or other officer.

(2) There is probable cause to believe that the child violated a term or condition of supervised release or judicial release and that the child is leaving or is about to leave the state.

(3) The child failed to appear before the release authority pursuant to a summons for a modification or failed to appear for a scheduled court hearing.

(4) The arrest of the child is necessary to prevent physical harm to another person or to the child.

(D)(1) Except as otherwise provided in this division, prior to arresting a child under this section, either in relation to an order of apprehension or a warrant for arrest or in any other manner authorized by this section, a staff member or employee of the department of youth services shall provide notice of the anticipated arrest to each county, municipal, or township law enforcement agency with jurisdiction over the place at which the staff member or employee anticipates making the arrest. A staff member or employee is not required to provide the notice described in this division prior to making an arrest in any emergency situation or circumstance described under division (C) of this section.

(2) If a child is arrested under this section and if it is known that the child is on supervised release or judicial release to department of youth services supervision, a juvenile court, local juvenile detention facility, or jail shall notify the appropriate department of youth services regional office that the child has been arrested and shall provide to the regional office or to an employee of the department of youth services a copy of the arrest information pertaining to the arrest.

(3) Nothing in this section limits the power to make an arrest that is granted to specified peace officers under section 2935.03 of the Revised Code, to any person under section 2935.04 of the Revised Code, or to any other specified category of persons by any other provision of the Revised Code, or the power to take a child into custody that is granted pursuant to section 2151.31 of the Revised Code.

(E) If a child who is on supervised release or who is under a period of judicial release to department of youth services supervision is arrested under an order of apprehension, under a warrant, or without a warrant as described in division (B)(1), (B)(2), or (C) of this section and taken into secure custody, all of the following apply:

(1) If no motion to revoke the child's supervised release or judicial release has been filed within seventy-two hours after the child is taken into secure custody, the juvenile court, in making its determinations at a detention hearing as to whether to hold the child in secure custody up to seventy-two hours so that a motion to revoke the child's supervised release or judicial release may be filed, may consider, in addition to all other evidence and information considered, the circumstances of the child's arrest and, if the arrest was pursuant to an order of apprehension, the order and the application for the order.

(2) If no motion to revoke the child's supervised release or judicial release has been filed within seventy-two hours after the child is taken into secure custody and if the child has not otherwise been released prior to the expiration of that seventy-two-hour period, the child shall be released upon the expiration of that seventy-two-hour period.

(3) If the person is eighteen, nineteen, or twenty years of age, the person may be confined in secure detention in the jail of the county in which the person is taken into custody. If the person is under eighteen years of age, the person may be confined in secure detention in the nearest juvenile detention facility.

(4) If a motion to revoke the child's supervised release or judicial release is filed after the child has been taken into secure custody and the court decides at the detention hearing to release the child from secure custody, the court may release the child on the same terms and conditions that are currently in effect regarding the child's supervised release or judicial release, pending revocation or subsequent modification.

(F) If a child who is on supervised release is arrested under an order of apprehension, under a warrant, or without a warrant as described in division (B)(1), (B)(2), or (C) of this section and taken into secure custody, and if a motion to revoke the child's supervised release is filed, the juvenile court of the county in which the child is placed promptly shall schedule a time for a hearing on whether the child violated any of the terms and conditions of the supervised release. If a child is released on supervised release and the juvenile court of the county in which the child is placed otherwise has reason to believe that the child has not complied with the terms and conditions of the supervised release, the court of the county in which the child is placed, in its discretion, may schedule a time for a hearing on whether the child violated any of the terms and conditions of the supervised release. If the court of the county in which the child is placed on supervised release conducts a hearing and determines at the hearing that the child did not violate any term or condition of the child's supervised release, the child shall be released from custody, if the child is in custody at that time, and shall continue on supervised release under the terms and conditions that were in effect at the time of the child's arrest, subject to subsequent revocation or modification. If the court of the county in which the child is placed on supervised release conducts a hearing and determines at the hearing that the child violated one or more of the terms and conditions of the child's supervised release, the court, if it determines that the violation was a serious violation, may revoke the child's supervised release and order the child to be returned to the department of youth services for institutionalization or, in any case, may make any other disposition of the child authorized by law that the court considers proper. If the court orders the child to be returned to a department of youth services institution, the child shall remain institutionalized for a minimum period of thirty days, the department shall not reduce the minimum thirty-day period of institutionalization for any time that the child was held in secure custody subsequent to the child's arrest and pending the revocation hearing and the child's return to the department, the release authority, in its discretion, may require the child to remain in institutionalization for longer than the minimum thirty-day period, and the child is not eligible for judicial release or early release during the minimum thirty-day period of institutionalization or any period of institutionalization in excess of the minimum thirty-day period.

This division does not apply regarding a child who is under a period of judicial release to department of youth services supervision. Division (D) of section 2152.22 of the Revised Code applies in relation to a child who is under a period of judicial release to department of youth services supervision.

(2000 S 179, § 3, eff. 1–1–02; 1998 H 526, eff. 9–1–98; 1997 H 1, eff. 7–1–98)

5139.53 Personnel authorized to execute apprehension orders or arrest warrants; training; deadly force; firearms; bond

(A)(1) The director of youth services shall designate certain employees of the department of youth services, including regional administrators, as persons who are authorized, in accordance with section 5139.52 of the Revised Code, to execute an order of apprehension or a warrant for, or otherwise to arrest, children in the custody of the department who are violating or are alleged to have violated the terms and conditions of supervised release or judicial release to department of youth services supervision.

(2) The director of youth services may designate some of the employees designated under division (A)(1) of this section as employees authorized to carry a firearm issued by the department while on duty for their protection in carrying out official duties.

(B)(1) An employee of the department designated by the director pursuant to division (A)(1) of this section as having the authority to execute orders of apprehension or warrants and to arrest children as described in that division shall not undertake an arrest until the employee has successfully completed training courses regarding the making of arrests by employees of that nature that are developed in cooperation with and approved by the executive director of the Ohio peace officer training commission. The courses shall include, but shall not be limited to, training in arrest tactics, defensive tactics, the use of force, and response tactics.

(2) The director of youth services shall develop, and shall submit to the governor for the governor's approval, a deadly force policy for the department. The deadly force policy shall require each employee who is designated under division (A)(2) of this section to carry a firearm in the discharge of official duties to receive training in the use of deadly force, shall specify the number of hours and the general content of the training in the use of deadly force that each of the designated employees must receive, and shall specify the procedures that must be followed after the use of deadly force by any of the designated employees. Upon receipt of the policy developed by the director under this division, the governor, in writing, promptly shall approve or disapprove the policy. If the governor, in writing, disapproves the policy, the director shall develop and resubmit a new policy under this division, and no employee shall be trained under the disapproved policy. If the governor, in writing, approves the policy, the director shall adopt it as a department policy and shall distribute it to each employee designated under (A)(2) of this section to carry a firearm in the discharge of official duties. An employee designated by the director pursuant to division (A)(2) of this section to carry a firearm in the discharge of official duties shall not carry a firearm until the employee has successfully completed both of the following:

(a) Training in the use of deadly force that comports with the policy approved by the governor and developed and adopted by the director under division (B)(2) of this section. The training required by this division shall be conducted at a training school approved by the Ohio peace officer training commission and shall be in addition to the training described in divisions (B)(1) and (2)(b) of this section that the employee must complete prior to undertaking an arrest and separate from and independent of the training required by division (B)(2)(b) of this section.

(b) A basic firearm training program that is conducted at a training school approved by the Ohio peace officer training commission and that is substantially similar to the basic firearm training program for peace officers conducted at the Ohio peace officer training academy and has received a certificate of satisfactory completion of that program from the executive director of the Ohio peace officer training commission. The training described in this division that an employee must complete prior to carrying a firearm shall be in addition to the training described in division (B)(1) of this section that the employee must complete prior to undertaking an arrest.

(C) After receipt of a certificate of satisfactory completion of a basic firearm training program, to maintain the right to carry a firearm in the discharge of official duties, an employee authorized under this section to carry a firearm shall successfully complete a firearms requalification program in accordance with section 109.801 of the Revised Code.

(D) Each employee authorized to carry a firearm shall give bond to the state to be approved by the clerk of the court of common pleas in the county of that employee's residence. The bond shall be in the sum of one thousand dollars, conditioned to save the public harmless by reason of the unlawful use of a firearm. A person injured or the family of a person killed by the employee's improper use of a firearm may have recourse on the bond.

(E) In addition to the deadly force policy adopted under division (B)(2) of this section, the director of youth services shall establish policies for the carrying and use of firearms by the employees that the director designates under this section.

(2002 H 393, eff. 7-5-02; 2000 S 179, § 3, eff. 1-1-02; 1998 H 526, eff. 9-1-98; 1997 H 1, eff. 7-1-98)

5139.54 Discharge from custody due to medical condition

(A) Notwithstanding any other provision for determining when a child shall be released or discharged from the legal custody of the department of youth services, including jurisdictional provisions in section 2152.22 of the Revised Code, the release authority, for medical reasons, may release a child upon supervised release or discharge the child from the custody of the department when any of the following applies:

(1) The child is terminally ill or otherwise in imminent danger of death.

(2) The child is incapacitated due to injury, disease, illness, or other medical condition and is no longer a threat to public safety.

(3) The child appears to be a mentally ill person subject to hospitalization by court order, as defined in section 5122.01 of the Revised Code, or a mentally retarded person subject to institutionalization by court order, as defined in section 5123.01 of the Revised Code.

(B) When considering whether to release or discharge a child under this section for medical reasons, the release authority may request additional medical information about the child or may ask the department to conduct additional medical examinations.

(C) The release authority shall determine the appropriate level of supervised release for a child released under this section. The terms and conditions of the release may require periodic medical reevaluations as appropriate. Upon granting a release or discharge under this section, the release authority shall give notice of the release and its terms and conditions or of the discharge to the court that committed the child to the custody of the department.

(D) The release authority shall submit annually to the director of youth services a report that includes all of the following information for the previous calendar year:

(1) The number of children the release authority considered for medical release or discharge;

(2) The nature of the injury, disease, illness, or other medical condition of each child considered for medical release or discharge;

(3) The decision made by the release authority for each child, including the reasons for denying medical release or discharge or for granting it;

(4) The number of children on medical release who were returned to a secure facility or whose supervised release was revoked.

(2000 S 179, § 3, eff. 1-1-02; 1997 H 1, eff. 7-1-98)

5139.55 Office of victims' services; duties; victims coordinator; employees

(A)(1) The office of victims' services is hereby created within the release authority of the department of youth services. The office of victims' services shall provide assistance to victims, victims' representatives, and members of a victim's family. The assistance shall include, but shall not be limited to, all of the following:

(a) If the court has provided the name and address of the victims of the child's acts to the department of youth services, notification that the child has been committed to the department, notification of the right of the victim or another authorized person to designate a person as a victim's representative under section 5139.56 of the Revised Code and of the actions that must be taken to make that designation, and notification of the right to be notified of release reviews, pending release hearings, revocation reviews, and discharge reviews related to that child and of the right to participate in release proceedings under that section and of the actions that must be taken to exercise those rights;

(b) The provision of information about the policies and procedures of the department of youth services and the status of children in the legal custody of the department.

(2) The office shall make available information to assist victims of delinquent children on supervised release or in a secure facility.

(B) The office of victims' services shall employ a victims administrator who shall administer the duties of the office. The victims administrator shall be in the unclassified civil service and a managing officer of the department. The office shall employ other staff members to assist the members of the release authority and hearing representatives in identifying victims' issues, ensure that the release authority upholds the provisions of section 5139.56 of the Revised Code, and make recommendations to the release authority in accordance with policies adopted by the department.

(C) The office of victims' services shall coordinate its activities with the chairperson of the release authority. The victims administrator and other employees of the office shall have full access to the records of children in the legal custody of the department in accordance with division (D) of section 5139.05 of the Revised Code.

(2000 S 179, § 3, eff. 1-1-02; 1999 H 283, eff. 9-29-99; 1997 H 1, eff. 7-1-98)

5139.56 Notification of victims regarding possible release or discharge of child; hearings

(A) The victim of an act for which a child has been committed to the legal custody of the department of youth services may submit a written request to the release authority to notify the victim of all release reviews, pending release hearings, supervised release revocation hearings, and discharge reviews relating to the child, of the placement of the child on supervised release, and of the discharge of the child. If the victim is a minor, is incapacitated, incompetent, or chooses to be represented by another person, the victim may designate in writing a person to act on the victim's behalf as a victim's representative and to request and receive the notices. If the victim is deceased, the executor or administrator of the victim's estate or, if there is no executor or administrator of the victim's estate, a member of the victim's family may designate in writing a person to act on the victim's behalf as a victim's representative and to request and receive the notices. If more than one person seeks to act as the representative of the victim, the release authority shall designate one person to act as the victim's representative. If the victim chooses not to have a representative, the victim shall be the sole person accorded rights under this section. The release authority may give notice by any means reasonably calculated to provide prompt actual notice.

If a victim, an executor or administrator, or a member of a victim's family designates a person in writing pursuant to this division to act on the victim's behalf as a victim's representative, the victim, executor, administrator, or family member, or the victim's representative, shall notify the release authority that the victim's representative is to act for the victim. A victim, executor, administrator, or member of a victim's family who has designated a person in writing pursuant to this division to act on the victim's behalf as a victim's representative may revoke the authority of that person to act as the victim's representative. Upon the revocation, the victim, executor, administrator, or member of the victim's family shall notify the release authority in writing that the authority of the person to so act has been revoked. At any time after the revocation, the victim, executor, administrator, or member of the victim's family may designate in writing a different person to act on the victim's behalf as a victim's representative.

The victim or victim's representative shall provide the release authority an address or telephone number at which notice may be given and shall notify the release authority in writing of any changes in that information. If at any time the victim or victim's representative elects to waive notice and other rights afforded by this section, the victim or victim's representative may do so in a written statement to the release authority.

(B) If a victim or victim's representative has requested notice of release reviews, pending release hearings, supervised release revocation hearings, and discharge reviews related to a child, of the placement of the child on supervised release, and of the discharge of the child, the release authority shall give that person notice of a release review, release hearing, or discharge review at least thirty days prior to the date of the review or hearing. The notice shall specify the date, time, and place of the review or hearing, the right of the victim or victim's representative to make an oral or written statement addressing the impact of the offense or delinquent act upon the victim or oral or written comments regarding the possible release or discharge, and, if the notice pertains to a hearing, the right to attend, and make the statements or comments at the hearing. Upon receiving notice that a release hearing is scheduled, a victim or victim's representative who intends to attend the release hearing, at least two days prior to the hearing, shall notify the release authority of the victim's or representative's intention to be present at the release hearing so that the release authority may ensure appropriate accommodations and security. If the child is placed on supervised release or is discharged, the release authority shall provide notice of the release or discharge to the victim or victim's representative in accordance with division (F) of section 5139.51 of the Revised Code. If the child is on supervised release, if a court has scheduled a hearing pursuant to division (F) of section 5139.52 of the Revised Code to consider the revocation of the supervised release, and if the release authority has been informed of the hearing, the release authority promptly shall notify the victim or victim's representative of the date, time, and place of the hearing.

(C) If a victim or victim's representative has requested notice of release reviews, pending release hearings, supervised release revocation hearings, and discharge reviews related to a child, of the placement of the child on supervised release, and of the discharge of the child, and if a release review, release hearing, or discharge review is scheduled or pending, the release authority shall give that person an opportunity to provide a written statement or communicate orally with a representative of the release authority regarding the possible release or discharge or to make oral or written comments regarding the possible release or discharge to a representative of the release authority, regardless of whether the victim or victim's representative is present at a hearing on the matter. If a victim or victim's representative is present at a release hearing, the authority shall give that person an opportunity to make the oral or written statement or comments at the hearing. The oral or written statement and comments may address the impact of the offense or delinquent act upon the victim, including the nature and extent of any harm suffered, the extent of any property damage or economic loss, any restitution ordered by the committing court and the progress the child has made toward fulfillment of that obligation, and the victim's recommendation for the outcome of the release hearing. A written statement or written comments submitted by a victim or a victim's representative under this section are confidential, are not a public record, and shall be returned to the release authority at the end of a release hearing by any person who receives a copy of them.

At a release hearing before the release authority, a victim or victim's representative may be accompanied by another person for support, but that person shall not act as a victim's representative. The release authority and other employees of the department of youth services shall make reasonable efforts to minimize contact between the child and the victim, victim's representative, or support person before, during, and after the hearing. The release authority shall use a separate waiting area for the victim, victim's representative, and support person if a separate area is available.

(D) At no time shall a victim or victim's representative be compelled to disclose the victim's address, place of employment, or similar identifying information to the child or the child's parent or legal guardian. Upon request of a victim or a victim's representative, the release authority shall keep in its files only the address or telephone number to which it shall send notice of a release review, pending release hearing, supervised release revocation hearing, discharge review, grant of supervised release, or discharge.

(E) No employer shall discharge, discipline, or otherwise retaliate against a victim or victim's representative for participating in a hearing before the release authority. This division generally does not require an employer to compensate an employee for time lost as a result of attendance at a hearing before the release authority.

(F) The release authority shall make reasonable, good faith efforts to comply with the provisions of this section. Failure of the release authority to comply with this section does not give rise to a claim for damages against the release authority and does not require modification of a final decision by the release authority.

(G) If a victim is in the legal custody of the department of youth services and resides in a secure facility or in another secure residential program, including a community corrections facility, or is incarcerated, the release authority may modify the victim's rights under this section to prevent a security risk, hardship, or undue burden upon a public official or agency with a duty under this section. If the victim resides in another state under similar circumstances, the release authority may make similar modifications of the victim's rights.

(1998 H 526, eff. 9–1–98; 1997 H 1, eff. 7–1–98)

PENALTY

5139.99 Penalty

Whoever violates section 5139.21 of the Revised Code shall be fined not less than ten nor more than five hundred dollars or imprisoned not more than one year, or both.

(130 v H 299, eff. 10–7–63)

CHAPTER 5145

STATE CORRECTIONAL INSTITUTIONS

5145.01 Duration of sentences

Courts shall impose sentences to a state correctional institution for felonies pursuant to sections 2929.13 and 2929.14 of the Revised Code. All prison terms may be ended in the manner provided by law, but no prison term shall exceed the maximum term provided for the felony of which the prisoner was convicted as extended pursuant to section 2929.141, 2967.11, or 2967.28 of the Revised Code.

If a prisoner is sentenced for two or more separate felonies, the prisoner's term of imprisonment shall run as a concurrent sentence, except if the consecutive sentence provisions of sections 2929.14 and 2929.41 of the Revised Code apply. If sentenced consecutively, for the purposes of sections 5145.01 to 5145.27 of the Revised Code, the prisoner shall be held to be serving one continuous term of imprisonment.

If a court imposes a sentence to a state correctional institution for a felony of the fourth or fifth degree, the department of rehabilitation and correction, notwithstanding the court's designation of a state correctional institution as the place of service of the sentence, may designate that the person sentenced is to be housed in a county, multicounty, municipal, municipal-county, or multicounty-municipal jail or workhouse if authorized pursuant to section 5120.161 of the Revised Code.

If, through oversight or otherwise, a person is sentenced to a state correctional institution under a definite term for an offense for which a definite term of imprisonment is not provided by statute, the sentence shall not thereby become void, but the person shall be subject to the liabilities of such sections and receive the benefits thereof, as if the person had been sentenced in the manner required by this section.

As used in this section, "prison term" has the same meaning as in section 2929.01 of the Revised Code.

(2002 H 327, eff. 7–8–02; 1995 S 2, eff. 7–1–96; 1994 H 571, eff. 10–6–94; 1987 H 455, eff. 7–20–87; 1983 S 210; 1982 H 269, § 4, S 199; 129 v 1193; 1953 H 1; GC 2166)

5145.21 Escaped convicts to be arrested and returned (first version)

Note: See also following version of this section, and Publisher's Note.

The warden of a state correctional institution shall arrest and again commit to the institution a convict who escapes from the institution and is found at large, whether the term for which he was sentenced to imprisonment has expired.

(1994 H 571, § 1, eff. 10–6–94; 1953 H 1, eff. 10–1–53; GC 2186)

Note: See also following version of this section, and Publisher's Note.

5145.21 Escaped convicts to be arrested and returned—Repealed (second version)

Note: See also preceding version of this section, and Publisher's Note.

(1994 H 571, § 2, eff. 10–6–94; 1953 H 1, eff. 10–1–53, GC 2186)

Note: See also preceding version of this section, and Publisher's Note.

Historical and Statutory Notes

Publisher's Note: 5145.21 was simultaneously amended and repealed by 1994 H 571, eff. 10–6–94. The legal effect of these actions is in question. See *Baldwin's Ohio Legislative Service*, 1994 Laws of Ohio, pages 5–1191 and 5–1196, for original versions of these Acts.

5145.24 Administrative release for certain elderly escapees

(A) The director of rehabilitation and correction may grant an administrative release, as defined in section 2967.01 of the Revised Code, to a prisoner who escaped from a state correctional institution and whose whereabouts are unknown when both of the following apply:

(1) The ninetieth anniversary of the prisoner's birth has passed;

(2) A period of at least twenty years has passed since the date of the prisoner's escape.

(B) The director shall adopt rules pursuant to section 111.15 of the Revised Code for the granting of an administrative release under this section.

(C) An administrative release granted under this section does not operate to restore the rights and privileges forfeited by conviction as provided in section 2961.01 of the Revised Code.

(D) The authority to grant an administrative release that is contained in this section is independent of the administrative release provisions contained in section 2967.17 of the Revised Code.

(1997 S 111, eff. 3–17–98)

5145.31 Internet access for prisoners; improper internet access

(A) As used in this section, "computer," "computer network," "computer system," "computer services," "telecommunications service," and "information service" have the same meanings as in section 2913.01 of the Revised Code.

(B) No officer or employee of a correctional institution under the control or supervision of the department of rehabilitation and correction shall provide a prisoner access to or permit a prisoner to have access to the internet through the use of a computer, computer network, computer system, computer services, telecommunications service, or information service unless both of the following apply:

(1) The prisoner is participating in an approved educational program with direct supervision that requires the use of the internet for training or research purposes.

(2) The provision of and access to the internet is in accordance with rules promulgated by the department of rehabilitation and correction pursuant to section 5120.62 of the Revised Code.

(C)(1) No prisoner in a correctional institution under the control or supervision of the department of rehabilitation and correction shall access the internet through the use of a computer, computer network, computer system, computer services, telecommunications service, or information service unless both of the following apply:

(a) The prisoner is participating in an approved educational program with direct supervision that requires the use of the internet for training or research purposes.

(b) The provision of and access to the internet is in accordance with rules promulgated by the department of rehabilitation and correction pursuant to section 5120.62 of the Revised Code.

(2) Whoever violates division (C)(1) of this section is guilty of improper internet access, a misdemeanor of the first degree.

(2004 H 204, eff. 11–5–04; 2000 S 12, eff. 6–8–00)

5145.32 Prohibition on smoking and tobacco usage

(A) As used in this section:

(1) "Smoke" means to burn any substance containing tobacco, including, but not limited to, a lighted cigarette, cigar, or pipe.

(2) "State correctional institution" has the same meaning as in section 2967.01 of the Revised Code and includes a prison that is privately operated and managed pursuant to a contract the department of rehabilitation and correction enters into under section 9.06 of the Revised Code.

(3) "Use tobacco" means to chew or maintain any substance containing tobacco, including smokeless tobacco, in the mouth to derive the effects of tobacco.

(B) No person shall smoke, use, or possess tobacco or have tobacco under the person's control on any property under the control of the corrections medical center in Columbus or the Ohio state penitentiary in Youngstown.

(C) No person shall smoke or use tobacco in a building of the north coast correctional treatment facility in Grafton, Lake Erie correctional institution, Toledo correctional institution, Hocking correctional facility, Oakwood correctional facility, northeast pre-release center, Franklin pre-release center, or Montgomery education pre-release center.

(D)(1) The director of rehabilitation and correction shall designate at least one tobacco-free housing area within each state correctional institution that is not identified in division (B) or (C) of this section.

(2) No person shall smoke or use tobacco in an area designated by the director under division (D)(1) of this section.

(E) A violation of division (B), (C), or (D)(2) of this section is not a criminal offense. The department of rehabilitation and correction shall adopt rules that establish procedures for the enforcement of those divisions and that establish disciplinary measures for a violation of those divisions.

(F) The department may designate locations at which it is permissible to smoke or use tobacco outside of a building of an institution identified in division (C) of this section.

(G) The department shall provide smoking and tobacco usage cessation programs for prisoners at all state correctional institutions, subject to available funding.

(H) The director shall review the practicality of eliminating access to smoking or tobacco usage in specialized units to which this section's prohibitions do not otherwise apply.

(2000 S 192, eff. 6–2–00)

CHAPTER 5149

ADULT PAROLE AUTHORITY

ADMINISTRATIVE PROVISIONS

Section

ADMINISTRATIVE PROVISIONS

5149.01 Definitions

As used in Chapter 5149. of the Revised Code:

(A) "Authority" means the adult parole authority created by section 5149.02 of the Revised Code.

(B) "State correctional institution," "pardon," "commutation," "reprieve," "parole," "head of a state correctional institution," "convict," "prisoner," "parolee," "final release," and "parole violator" have the same meanings as in section 2967.01 of the Revised Code.

(C) "Full board hearing" means a parole board hearing conducted by a minimum of seven parole board members as described in section 5149.101 of the Revised Code.

(1995 S 2, eff. 7–1–96; 1994 H 571, eff. 10–6–94; 130 v Pt 2, H 28, eff. 3–18–65)

5149.05 Firearms for employees

The chief of the adult parole authority may grant an employee permission to carry a firearm in the discharge of the employee's official duties if the employee has successfully completed a basic firearm training program that is approved by the executive director of the Ohio peace officer training commission. In order to continue to carry a firearm in the discharge of the employee's official duties, the employee annually shall successfully complete a firearms requalification program in accordance with section 109.801 of the Revised Code.

(2002 H 510, eff. 3–31–03; 1997 S 111, eff. 3–17–98; 1996 H 670, eff. 12–2–96; 1994 H 406, eff. 11–11–94; 1994 H 571, eff. 10–6–94; 130 v Pt 2, H 28, eff. 3–18–65)

5149.06 Probation development and supervision section; adult parole authority probation services fund

(A) One of the primary duties of the field services section is to assist the counties in developing their own probation services on either a single-county or multiple-county basis. The section, within limits of available personnel and funds, may supervise selected probationers from local courts.

(B) The adult parole authority probation services fund shall be created in the state treasury. The fund shall consist of all moneys that are paid to the treasurer of any county under section 2951.021 of the Revised Code for deposit into the county's probation services fund established under division (A)(1) of section 321.44 of the Revised Code and that subsequently are appropriated and transferred to the adult parole authority probation services fund under division (A)(2) of that section. The chief of the adult parole authority, with the approval of the director of the department of rehabilitation and correction, shall use the money contained in the adult parole authority probation services fund for probation-related expenses in the counties for which the authority provides probation services. Probation–related expenses may include specialized staff, purchase of equipment, purchase of services, reconciliation programs for victims and offenders, other treatment programs, including alcohol and drug addiction programs certified under section 3793.06 of the Revised Code, determined to be appropriate by the chief of the authority, and other similar probation-related expenses.

(2002 H 510, eff. 3–31–03; 1994 H 406, eff. 11–11–94; 1994 H 571, eff. 10–6–94; 1980 H 1000, eff. 4–9–81; 130 v Pt 2, H 28)

5149.101 Full board hearing of parole board on proposed parole of prisoner

Note: See also following version of this section, eff. 4–29–05.

(A) A board hearing officer, a board member, or the office of victims' services may petition the board for a full board hearing that relates to the proposed parole of a prisoner. At a meeting of the board at which at least seven board members are present, a majority of those present shall determine whether a full board hearing shall be held.

(B) At a full board hearing that relates to the proposed parole of a prisoner and that has been petitioned for in accordance with division (A) of this section, the parole board shall permit the following persons to appear and to give testimony or to submit written statements:

(1) The prosecuting attorney of the county in which the indictment against the prisoner was found and members of any law enforcement agency that assisted in the prosecution of the offense;

(2) The judge of the court of common pleas who imposed the sentence of incarceration upon the prisoner, or the judge's successor;

(3) The victim of the offense for which the prisoner is serving the sentence or the victim's representative designated pursuant to section 2930.02 of the Revised Code.

(C) Except as otherwise provided in this division, a full board hearing of the parole board is not subject to section 121.22 of the Revised Code. The persons who may attend a full board hearing are the persons described in divisions (B)(1) to (3) of this section, and representatives of the press, radio and television stations, and broadcasting networks who are members of a generally recognized professional media organization.

At the request of a person described in division (B)(3) of this section, representatives of the news media described in this division shall be excluded from the hearing while that person is giving testimony at the hearing. The prisoner being considered for parole has no right to be present at the hearing, but may be represented by counsel or some other person designated by the prisoner.

If there is an objection at a full board hearing to a recommendation for the parole of a prisoner, the board may approve or disapprove the recommendation or defer its decision until a subsequent full board hearing. The board may permit interested persons other than those listed in this division and division (B) of this section to attend full board hearings pursuant to rules adopted by the adult parole authority.

(D) The adult parole authority shall adopt rules for the implementation of this section. The rules shall specify reasonable restrictions on the number of media representatives that may attend a hearing, based on considerations of space, and other procedures designed to accomplish an effective, orderly process for full board hearings.

(1995 S 2, eff. 7–1–96)

Note: See also following version of this section, eff. 4–29–05.

5149.101 Full board hearing of parole board on parole or re-parole of prisoner (later effective date)

Note: See also preceding version of this section, in effect until 4–29–05.

(A)(1) A board hearing officer, a board member, or the office of victims' services may petition the board for a full board hearing that relates to the proposed parole or re-parole of a prisoner. At a meeting of the board at which a majority of board members are present, the majority of those present shall determine whether a full board hearing shall be held.

(2) A victim of a violation of section 2903.01 or 2903.02 of the Revised Code, the victim's representative, or any person described in division (B)(5) of this section may request the board hold a full board hearing that relates to the proposed parole or re-parole of the person that committed the violation. If a victim, victim's representative, or other person requests a full board hearing pursuant to this division, the board shall hold a full board hearing.

(B) At a full board hearing that relates to the proposed parole or re-parole of a prisoner and that has been petitioned for or requested in accordance with division (A) of this section, the parole board shall permit the following persons to appear and to give testimony or to submit written statements:

(1) The prosecuting attorney of the county in which the original indictment against the prisoner was found and members of any law enforcement agency that assisted in the prosecution of the original offense;

(2) The judge of the court of common pleas who imposed the original sentence of incarceration upon the prisoner, or the judge's successor;

(3) The victim of the original offense for which the prisoner is serving the sentence or the victim's representative designated pursuant to section 2930.02 of the Revised Code:

(4) The victim of any behavior that resulted in parole being revoked;

(5) With respect to a full board hearing held pursuant to division (A)(2) of this section, all of the following:

(a) The spouse of the victim of the original offense;

(b) The parent or parents of the victim of the original offense;

(c) The sibling of the victim of the original offense;

(d) The child or children of the victim of the original offense.

(6) Counsel or some other person designated by the prisoner as a representative, as described in division (C) of this section.

(C) Except as otherwise provided in this division, a full board hearing of the parole board is not subject to section 121.22 of the Revised Code. The persons who may attend a full board hearing are the persons described in divisions (B)(1) to (6) of this section, and representatives of the press, radio and television stations, and broadcasting networks who are members of a generally recognized professional media organization.

At the request of a person described in division (B)(3) of this section, representatives of the news media described in this division shall be excluded from the hearing while that person is giving testimony at the hearing. The prisoner being considered for parole has no right to be present at the hearing, but may be represented by counsel or some other person designated by the prisoner.

If there is an objection at a full board hearing to a recommendation for the parole of a prisoner, the board may approve or disapprove the recommendation or defer its decision until a subsequent full board hearing. The board may permit interested persons other than those listed in this division and division (B) of this section to attend full board hearings pursuant to rules adopted by the adult parole authority.

(D) The adult parole authority shall adopt rules for the implementation of this section. The rules shall specify reasonable restrictions on the number of media representatives that may attend a hearing, based on considerations of space, and other procedures designed to accomplish an effective, orderly process for full board hearings.

(2004 H 375, eff. 4–29–05; 1995 S 2, eff. 7–1–96)

Note: See also preceding version of this section, in effect until 4–29–05.

5149.12 General duties

The adult parole authority shall exercise general supervision over the work of all probation and parole officers throughout the state, excluding those appointed in county probation departments and those appointed by municipal judges.

(2002 H 510, eff. 3–31–03; 1975 H 205, eff. 1–1–76; 130 v Pt 2, H 28)

INTERSTATE COMPACTS

5149.21 Interstate compact for adult offender supervision

The "interstate compact for adult offender supervision" is hereby enacted into law and entered into with all other jurisdictions legally joining in that compact in the form substantially as follows:

"INTERSTATE COMPACT FOR ADULT OFFENDER SUPERVISION

ARTICLE I
PURPOSE

The compacting states to this interstate compact recognize that each state is responsible for the supervision of adult offenders in the community who are authorized pursuant to the bylaws and rules of this compact to travel across state lines both to and from each compacting state in such a manner as to track the location of offenders, transfer supervision authority in an orderly and efficient manner, and when necessary return offenders to the originating jurisdictions. The compacting states also recognize that Congress, by enacting the "Crime Control Act," 4 U.S.C. Section 112 (1965), has authorized and encouraged compacts for cooperative efforts and mutual assistance in the prevention of crime.

It is the purpose of this compact and the interstate commission created under this compact, through means of joint and cooperative action among the compacting states: to provide the framework for the promotion of public safety and protect the rights of victims through the control and regulation of the interstate movement of offenders in the community; to provide for the effective tracking, supervision, and rehabilitation of these offenders by the sending and receiving states; and to equitably distribute the costs, benefits, and obligations of the compact among the compacting states.

In addition, this compact will: create an interstate commission that will establish uniform procedures to manage the movement between states of adults placed under community supervision and released to the community under the jurisdiction of courts, paroling authorities, corrections, or other criminal justice agencies that will promulgate rules to achieve the purpose of this compact; ensure an opportunity for input and timely notice to victims and to jurisdictions where defined offenders are authorized to travel or to relocate across state lines; establish a system of uniform data collection, access to information on active cases by authorized criminal justice officials, and regular reporting of compact activities to heads of state councils, state executive, judicial, and legislative branches and criminal justice administrators; monitor compliance with rules governing interstate movement of offenders and initiate interventions to address and correct noncompliance; and coordinate training and education regarding regulations of interstate movement of offenders for officials involved in such activity.

The compacting states recognize that there is no "right" of any offender to live in another state and that duly accredited officers of a sending state may at all times enter a receiving state and in that state apprehend and retake any offender under supervision subject to the provisions of this compact and bylaws and rules promulgated under this compact. It is the policy of the compacting states that the activities conducted by the interstate commission created in this compact are the formation of public policies and are therefore public business.

ARTICLE II
DEFINITIONS

As used in this compact, unless the context clearly requires a different construction:

(A) "Adult" means both individuals legally classified as adults and juveniles treated as adults by court order, statute, or operation of law.

(B) "Bylaws" means those bylaws established by the interstate commission for its governance, or for directing or controlling the interstate commission's actions or conduct.

(C) "Compact administrator" means the individual in each compacting state who is appointed pursuant to the terms of this compact and who is responsible for the administration and management of the state's supervision and transfer of offenders subject to the terms of this compact, the rules adopted by the interstate commission, and policies adopted by the state council under this compact.

(D) "Compacting state" means any state that has enacted the enabling legislation for this compact.

(E) "Commissioner" means the voting representative of each compacting state appointed pursuant to Article III of this compact.

(F) "Interstate commission" means the interstate commission for adult offender supervision established by this compact.

(G) "Member" means the commissioner of a compacting state or designee, who is a person officially connected with the commissioner.

(H) "Noncompacting state" means any state that has not enacted the enabling legislation for this compact.

(I) "Offender" means an adult placed under, or subject, to supervision as the result of the commission of a criminal offense and released to the community under the jurisdiction of courts, paroling authorities, corrections, or other criminal justice agencies.

(J) "Person" means any individual, corporation, business enterprise, or other legal entity, either public or private.

(K) "Rules" means acts of the interstate commission, duly promulgated pursuant to Article VIII of this compact, substantially affecting interested parties in addition to the interstate commission.

The rules shall have the force and effect of law in the compacting states.

(L) "State" means a state of the United States, the District of Columbia, and any other territorial possessions of the United States.

(M) "State council" means the resident members of the state council for interstate adult offender supervision created by each state under Article III of this compact.

ARTICLE III
THE COMPACT COMMISSION

The compacting states hereby create the "interstate commission for adult offender supervision." The interstate commission shall be a body corporate and joint agency of the compacting states. The interstate commission shall have all the responsibilities, powers, and duties set forth in this compact, including the power to sue and be sued, and any additional powers that may be conferred upon it by subsequent action of the respective legislatures of the compacting states in accordance with the terms of this compact.

The interstate commission shall consist of commissioners selected and appointed by resident members of a state council for interstate adult offender supervision for each state.

In addition to the commissioners who are the voting representatives of each state, the interstate commission shall include individuals who are not commissioners but who are members of interested organizations. The non-commissioner members must include a member of the national organizations of governors, legislators, state chief justices, attorneys general, and crime victims. All non-commissioner members of the interstate commission shall be ex-officio (nonvoting) members. The interstate commission may provide in its bylaws for any additional, ex-officio, nonvoting members that it deems necessary.

Each compacting state represented at any meeting of the interstate commission is entitled to one vote. A majority of the compacting states shall constitute a quorum for the transaction of business, unless a larger quorum is required by the bylaws of the interstate commission. The interstate commission shall meet at least once each calendar year. The chairperson may call additional meetings and, upon the request of twenty-seven or more compacting states, shall call additional meetings. Public notice shall be given of all meetings, and meetings shall be open to the public.

The interstate commission shall establish an executive committee, which shall include commission officers, members, and others as shall be determined by the bylaws. The executive committee shall have the power to act on behalf of the interstate commission during periods when the interstate commission is not in session, with the exception of rulemaking or amendment to the compact. The executive committee oversees the day-to-day activities managed by the executive director and interstate commission staff; administers enforcement and compliance with the provisions of the compact, its bylaws, and as directed by the interstate commission; and performs other duties as directed by commission or set forth in the bylaws.

ARTICLE IV
THE STATE COUNCIL

Each member state shall create a state council for interstate adult offender supervision. The compact administrator or the administrator's designee shall be the commissioner of the state council to serve on the interstate commission. While each member state may determine the membership of its own state council, its membership must include at least one representative from the legislative, judicial, and executive branches of government, victims groups, and compact administrators. Each compacting state retains the right to determine the qualifications of the compact administrator who shall be appointed by the governor. In addition to appointment of its commissioner to the national interstate commission, each state council shall exercise oversight and advocacy concerning its participation in interstate commission activities and other duties as may be determined by each member state, including, but not limited to, development of policy concerning operations and procedures of the compact within that state.

ARTICLE V
POWERS AND DUTIES OF THE INTERSTATE COMMISSION

The interstate commission shall have the following powers:

(A) To adopt a seal and suitable bylaws governing the management and operation of the interstate commission;

(B) To promulgate rules that have the force and effect of statutory law and are binding in the compacting states to the extent and in the manner provided in this compact;

(C) To oversee, supervise, and coordinate the interstate movement of offenders subject to the terms of this compact and any bylaws adopted and rules promulgated by the compact commission;

(D) To enforce compliance with compact provisions, interstate commission rules, and bylaws, using all necessary and proper means, including, but not limited to, the use of judicial process;

(E) To establish and maintain offices;

(F) To purchase and maintain insurance and bonds;

(G) To borrow, accept, or contract for services of personnel, including, but not limited to, members and their staffs;

(H) To establish and appoint committees and hire staff that it considers necessary for the carrying out of its functions, including, but not limited to, an executive committee as required by Article III of this compact. The committees shall have the power to act on behalf of the interstate commission in carrying out its powers and duties under this compact.

(I) To elect or appoint any officers, attorneys, employees, agents, or consultants, and to fix their compensation, define their duties, and determine their qualifications; and to establish the interstate commission's personnel policies and programs relating to, among other things, conflicts of interest, rates of compensation, and qualifications of personnel;

(J) To accept any and all donations and grants of money, equipment, supplies, materials, and services, and to receive, utilize, and dispose of those donations and grants;

(K) To lease, purchase, accept contributions or donations of, or otherwise to own, hold, improve, or use any property, real, personal, or mixed;

(L) To sell, convey, mortgage, pledge, lease, exchange, abandon, or otherwise dispose of any property, real, personal, or mixed;

(M) To establish a budget and make expenditures and levy dues as provided in Article X of this compact;

(N) To sue and be sued;

(O) To provide for dispute resolution among compacting states;

(P) To perform any functions that may be necessary or appropriate to achieve the purposes of this compact;

(Q) To report annually to the legislatures, governors, judiciary, and state councils of the compacting states concerning the activities of the interstate commission during the preceding year. The reports shall also include any recommendations that may have been adopted by the interstate commission.

(R) To coordinate education, training, and public awareness regarding the interstate movement of offenders for officials involved in such activity;

(S) To establish uniform standards for the reporting, collecting, and exchanging of data.

ARTICLE VI
ORGANIZATION AND OPERATION OF THE INTERSTATE COMMISSION

(A) Bylaws

The interstate commission shall, by a majority of the members, within twelve months of the first interstate commission meeting, adopt bylaws to govern its conduct as may be necessary or appropriate to carry out the purposes of the compact, including, but, not limited to all of the following:

(1) Establishing the fiscal year of the interstate commission;

(2) Establishing an executive committee and any other committees that may be necessary;

(3) Providing reasonable standards and procedures:

(a) For the establishment of committees;

(b) Governing any general or specific delegation of any authority or function of the interstate commission.

(4) Providing reasonable procedures for calling and conducting meetings of the interstate commission, and ensuring reasonable notice of each meeting;

(5) Establishing the titles and responsibilities of the officers of the interstate commission;

(6) Providing reasonable standards and procedures for the establishment of the personnel policies and programs of the interstate commission. Notwithstanding any civil service or other similar laws of any compacting state, the bylaws shall exclusively govern the personnel policies and programs of the interstate commission.

(7) Providing a mechanism for winding up the operations of the interstate commission and the equitable return of any surplus funds that may exist upon the termination of the compact after the payment or reserving of all of its debts and obligations;

(8) Providing transition rules for "start up" administration of the compact;

(9) Establishing standards and procedures for compliance and technical assistance in carrying out the compact.

(B) Officers and staff

The interstate commission shall, by a majority of the members, elect from among its members a chairperson and a vice chairperson, each of whom shall have the authorities and duties as may be specified in the bylaws. The chairperson or, in his or her absence or disability, the vice chairperson, shall preside at all meetings of the interstate commission. The officers so elected shall serve without compensation or remuneration from the interstate commission; provided that, subject to the availability of budgeted funds, the officers shall be reimbursed for any actual and necessary costs and expenses incurred by them in the performance of their duties and responsibilities as officers of the interstate commission.

The interstate commission shall, through its executive committee, appoint or retain an executive director for the period, upon the terms and conditions, and for the compensation that the interstate commission considers appropriate. The executive director shall serve as secretary to the interstate commission, and hire and supervise the other staff that may be authorized by the interstate commission, but shall not be a member.

(C) Corporate records of the interstate commission

The interstate commission shall maintain its corporate books and records in accordance with the bylaws.

(D) Qualified immunity, defense and indemnification

The members, officers, executive director, and employees of the interstate commission shall be immune from suit and liability, either personally or in their official capacity, for any claim for damage to or loss of property or personal injury or other civil liability caused or arising out of any actual or alleged act, error or omission that occurred within the scope of interstate commission employment, duties, or responsibilities; provided that nothing in this paragraph shall be construed to protect any such person from suit or liability for any damage, loss, injury, or liability caused by the intentional or willful and wanton misconduct of any such person.

Upon the request of the attorney general, the interstate commission shall assist in the defense of the commissioner of a compacting state, or the commissioner's representatives or employees, or the interstate commission's representatives or employees, in any civil action seeking to impose liability, arising out of any actual or alleged act, error, or omission that occurred within the scope of interstate commission employment, duties, or responsibilities, or that the defendant had a reasonable basis for believing occurred within the scope of interstate commission employment, duties, or responsibilities; provided, that the actual or alleged act, error, or omission did not result from intentional wrongdoing on the part of the person.

The interstate commission shall indemnify and hold the commissioner of a compacting state, the appointed designee, or employees, or the interstate commission's representatives or employees, harmless in the amount of any settlement or judgment obtained against such persons arising out of any actual or alleged act, error, or omission that occurred within the scope of interstate commission employment, duties, or responsibilities, or that such persons had a reasonable basis for believing occurred within the scope of interstate commission employment, duties, or responsibilities, provided that the actual or alleged act, error, or omission did not result from gross negligence or intentional wrongdoing on the part of the person.

ARTICLE VII
ACTIVITIES OF THE INTERSTATE COMMISSION

(A) The interstate commission shall meet and take any actions that are consistent with the provisions of this compact.

Except as otherwise provided in this compact and unless a greater percentage is required by the bylaws, in order to constitute an act of the interstate commission, the act shall have been taken at a meeting of the interstate commission and shall have received an affirmative vote of a majority of the members present.

Each member of the interstate commission shall have the right and power to cast a vote to which that compacting state is entitled and to participate in the business and affairs of the interstate commission. A member shall vote in person on behalf of the state and shall not delegate a vote to another member state. However, a state council shall appoint another authorized representative, in the absence of the commissioner from that state, to cast a vote on behalf of the member state at a specified meeting. The bylaws may provide for members' participation in meetings by telephone or other means of telecommunication or electronic communication. Any voting conducted by telephone or other means of telecommunication or electronic communication shall be subject to the same quorum requirements of meetings where members are present in person.

The interstate commission shall meet at least once during each calendar year. The chairperson of the interstate commission may call additional meetings at any time and, upon the request of a majority of the members, shall call additional meetings.

The interstate commission's bylaws shall establish conditions and procedures under which the interstate commission shall make its information and official records available to the public for inspection or copying. The interstate commission may exempt from disclosure any information or official records to the extent they would adversely affect personal privacy rights or proprietary interests. In promulgating those rules, the interstate commission may make available to law enforcement agencies records and information otherwise exempt from disclosure and may enter into agreements with law enforcement agencies to receive or exchange information or records subject to nondisclosure and confidentiality provisions.

Public notice shall be given of all meetings, and all meetings shall be open to the public, except as set forth in the rules or as otherwise provided in the compact. The interstate commission shall promulgate rules consistent with the principles contained in the "Government in Sunshine Act," 5 U.S.C. Section 552(b), as amended. The interstate commission and any of its committees may close a meeting to the public if it determines by two-thirds vote that an open meeting would be likely to do any of the following:

(1) Relate solely to the interstate commission's internal personnel practices and procedures;

(2) Disclose matters specifically exempted from disclosure by statute;

(3) Disclose trade secrets or commercial or financial information that is privileged or confidential;

(4) Involve accusing any person of a crime or formally censuring any person;

(5) Disclose information of a personal nature if disclosure would constitute a clearly unwarranted invasion of personal privacy;

(6) Disclose investigatory records compiled for law enforcement purposes;

(7) Disclose information contained in or related to examination, operating, or condition reports prepared by, on behalf of, or for the use of the interstate commission with respect to a regulated entity for the purpose of regulation or supervision of the regulated entity;

(8) Disclose information, the premature disclosure of which would significantly endanger the life of a person or the stability of a regulated entity;

(9) Specifically relate to the interstate commission's issuance of a subpoena or its participation in a civil action or proceeding.

(B) For every meeting closed pursuant to this provision, the interstate commission's chief legal officer shall publicly certify that, in the legal officer's opinion, the meeting may be closed to the public, and shall reference each relevant exemptive provision. The interstate commission shall keep minutes, and the minutes shall fully and clearly describe all matters discussed in any meeting and shall provide a full and accurate summary of any actions taken, and the reasons for the actions, including a description of each of the views expressed on any item and the record of any roll call vote (reflected in the vote of each member on the question). All documents considered in connection with any action shall be identified in the minutes.

The interstate commission shall collect standardized data concerning the interstate movement of offenders as directed through its bylaws and rules. The bylaws and rules shall specify the data to be collected, the means of collection and data exchange, and reporting requirements.

ARTICLE VIII
RULEMAKING FUNCTIONS OF THE INTERSTATE COMMISSION

(A) The interstate commission shall promulgate rules in order to effectively and efficiently achieve the purposes of the compact including transition rules governing administration of the compact during the period in which it is being considered and enacted by the states.

Rulemaking shall occur pursuant to the criteria set forth in this article and the bylaws and rules adopted pursuant to this article. The rulemaking shall substantially conform to the principles of the "Federal Administrative Procedure Act," 5 U.S.C.S. section 551 et seq., and the "Federal Advisory Committee Act," 5 U.S.C.S. app. 2, section 1 et seq., as amended (hereinafter "APA"). All rules and amendments shall become binding as of the date specified in each rule or amendment.

If a majority of the legislatures of the compacting states rejects a rule, by enactment of a statute or resolution in the same manner used to adopt the compact, then the rule shall have no further force and effect in any compacting state.

When promulgating a rule, the interstate commission shall do all of the following:

(1) Publish the proposed rule stating with particularity the text of the rule that is proposed and the reason for the proposed rule;

(2) Allow persons to submit written data, facts, opinions and arguments, which information shall be publicly available;

(3) Provide an opportunity for an informal hearing;

(4) Promulgate a final rule and its effective date, if appropriate, based on the rulemaking record.

(B) Not later than sixty days after a rule is promulgated, any interested person may file a petition in the United States district court for the District of Columbia or in the federal district court where the interstate commission's principal office is located for judicial review of the rule. If the court finds that the interstate commission's action is not supported by substantial evidence, as defined in the APA, in the rulemaking record, the court shall hold the rule unlawful and set it aside.

Subjects to be addressed within twelve months after the first meeting shall at a minimum include all of the following:

(1) Notice to victims and an opportunity to be heard;

(2) Offender registration and compliance;

(3) Violations and returns;

(4) Transfer procedures and forms;

(5) Eligibility for transfer;

(6) Collection of restitution and fees from offenders;

(7) Data collection and reporting;

(8) The level of supervision to be provided by the receiving state;

(9) Transition rules governing the operation of the compact and the interstate commission during all or part of the period between the effective date of the compact and the date on which the last eligible state adopts the compact;

(10) Mediation, arbitration, and dispute resolution.

(C) The existing rules governing the operation of the previous compact superseded by this act shall be null and void twelve months after the first meeting of the interstate commission created under this compact.

Upon determination by the interstate commission that an emergency exists, it may promulgate an emergency rule, and the emergency rule shall become effective immediately upon adoption, provided that the usual rulemaking procedures provided under this compact shall be retroactively applied to the rule as soon as reasonably possible, in no event later than ninety days after the effective date of the rule.

ARTICLE IX
OVERSIGHT, ENFORCEMENT, AND DISPUTE RESOLUTION BY THE INTERSTATE COMMISSION

(A) Oversight

The interstate commission shall oversee the interstate movement of adult offenders in the compacting states and shall monitor such activities being administered in noncompacting states that may significantly affect compacting states.

The courts and executive agencies in each compacting state shall enforce this compact and shall take all actions necessary and appropriate to effectuate the compact's purposes and intent. In any judicial or administrative proceeding in a compacting state pertaining to the subject matter of this compact that may affect the powers, responsibilities, or actions of the interstate commission, the interstate commission shall be entitled to receive all service of process in any such proceeding and shall have standing to intervene in the proceeding for all purposes.

(B) Dispute Resolution

The compacting states shall report to the interstate commission on issues or activities of concern to them and cooperate with and support the interstate commission in the discharge of its duties and responsibilities.

The interstate commission shall attempt to resolve any disputes or other issues that are subject to the compact and that may arise among compacting states and noncompacting states.

The interstate commission shall enact a bylaw or promulgate a rule providing for both mediation and binding dispute resolution for disputes among the compacting states.

(C) Enforcement

The interstate commission, in the reasonable exercise of its discretion, shall enforce the provisions of this compact using any or all means set forth in Article XII, division B, of this compact.

ARTICLE X
FINANCE

The interstate commission shall pay or provide for the payment of the reasonable expenses of its establishment, organization, and ongoing activities.

The interstate commission shall levy on and collect an annual assessment from each compacting state to cover the cost of the internal operations and activities of the interstate commission and its staff. The annual assessment shall be in a total amount sufficient to cover the interstate commission's annual budget as approved each year. The aggregate annual assessment amount shall be allocated based upon a formula to be determined by the interstate commission, taking into consideration the population of the state and the volume of interstate movement of offenders in each compacting state, and shall promulgate a rule that is binding upon all compacting states and governs the assessment.

The interstate commission shall not incur any obligations of any kind prior to securing the funds adequate to meet the obligation, and the interstate commission shall not pledge the credit of any of the compacting states, except by and with the authority of the compacting state.

The interstate commission shall keep accurate accounts of all receipts and disbursements. The receipts and disbursements of the interstate commission shall be subject to the audit and accounting procedures established under its bylaws. However, all receipts and disbursements of funds handled by the interstate commission shall be audited yearly by a certified or licensed public accountant, and the report of the audit shall be included in and become part of the annual report of the interstate commission.

ARTICLE XI
COMPACTING STATES, EFFECTIVE DATE AND AMENDMENT

Any state, as defined in Article II of this compact, is eligible to become a compacting state. The compact shall become effective and binding upon legislative enactment of the compact into law by no less than thirty-five of the states. The initial effective date shall be the later of July 1, 2001, or upon enactment into law by the thirty-fifth jurisdiction. After the initial effective date, it shall become effective and binding, as to any other compacting state, upon enactment of the compact into law by that state. The governors of nonmember states or their designees shall be invited to participate in interstate commission activities on a nonvoting basis prior to adoption of the compact by all states and territories of the United States.

Amendments to the compact may be proposed by the interstate commission for enactment by the compacting states. No amendment shall become effective and binding upon the interstate commission and the compacting states unless and until it is enacted into law by unanimous consent of the compacting states.

ARTICLE XII
WITHDRAWAL, DEFAULT, TERMINATION, AND JUDICIAL ENFORCEMENT

(A) Withdrawal

Once effective, the compact shall continue in force and remain binding upon each and every compacting state; provided that a compacting state may withdraw from the compact ("withdrawing state") by enacting a statute specifically repealing the statute that enacted the compact into law.

The effective date of withdrawal is the effective date of the repeal.

The withdrawing state shall immediately notify the chairperson of the interstate commission in writing upon the introduction of legislation repealing this compact in the withdrawing state.

The interstate commission shall notify the other compacting states of the withdrawing state's intent to withdraw within sixty days of its receipt of the notice from the withdrawing state.

The withdrawing state is responsible for all assessments, obligations, and liabilities incurred through the effective date of withdrawal, including any obligations, the performance of which extend beyond the effective date of withdrawal.

Reinstatement following withdrawal of any compacting state shall occur upon the withdrawing state reenacting the compact or upon any later date as determined by the interstate commission.

(B) Default

(1) If the interstate commission determines that any compacting state has at any time defaulted ("defaulting state") in the performance of any of its obligations or responsibilities under this compact, the bylaws, or any duly promulgated rules, the interstate commission may impose any or all of the following penalties:

(a) Fines, fees, and costs in any amounts that are determined to be reasonable as fixed by the interstate commission;

(b) Remedial training and technical assistance as directed by the interstate commission;

(c) Suspension and termination of membership in the compact. Suspension shall be imposed only after all other reasonable means of securing compliance under the bylaws and rules have been exhausted. Immediate notice of suspension shall be given by the interstate commission to the governor, the chief justice or chief judicial officer of the state, the majority and minority leaders of the defaulting state's legislature, and the state council.

(2) The grounds for default include, but are not limited to, failure of a compacting state to perform the obligations or responsibilities imposed upon it by this compact, interstate commission bylaws, or duly promulgated rules. The interstate commission shall immediately notify the defaulting state in writing of the penalty imposed by the interstate commission on the defaulting state pending a cure of the default. The interstate commission shall stipulate the conditions and the time period within which the defaulting state must cure its default. If the defaulting state fails to cure the default within the time period specified by the interstate commission, in addition to any other penalties imposed in this compact, the defaulting state may be terminated from the compact upon an affirmative vote of a majority of the compacting states and all rights, privileges, and benefits conferred by this compact shall be terminated from the effective date of suspension. Within sixty days of the effective date of termination of a defaulting state, the interstate commission shall notify the governor, the chief justice or chief judicial officer, the majority and minority leaders of the defaulting state's legislature, and the state council of the termination.

The defaulting state is responsible for all assessments, obligations and liabilities incurred through the effective date of termination including any obligations, the performance of which extends beyond the effective date of termination.

The interstate commission shall not bear any costs relating to the defaulting state unless otherwise mutually agreed upon between the interstate commission and the defaulting state. Reinstatement following termination of any compacting state requires both a reenactment of the compact by the defaulting state and the approval of the interstate commission pursuant to the rules.

(C) Judicial enforcement

The interstate commission may, by majority vote of the members, initiate legal action in the United States district court for the District of Columbia or, at the discretion of the interstate commission, in the federal district where the interstate commission has its offices to enforce compliance with the provisions of the compact, its duly promulgated rules, and bylaws, against any compacting state in default. In the event judicial enforcement is necessary, the prevailing party shall be awarded all costs of the litigation including reasonable attorneys fees.

(D) Dissolution of compact

The compact dissolves effective upon the date of the withdrawal or default of the compacting state that reduces membership in the compact to one compacting state.

Upon the dissolution of this compact, the compact becomes null and void and shall be of no further force or effect, and the business and affairs of the interstate commission shall be wound up, and any surplus funds shall be distributed in accordance with the bylaws.

ARTICLE XIII
SEVERABILITY AND CONSTRUCTION

The provisions of this compact shall be severable, and, if any phrase, clause, sentence, or provision is deemed unenforceable, the remaining provisions of the compact shall be enforceable.

The provisions of this compact shall be liberally constructed to effectuate its purposes.

ARTICLE XIV
BINDING EFFECT OF COMPACT AND OTHER LAWS

(A) Other laws

Nothing in this compact prevents the enforcement of any other law of a compacting state that is not inconsistent with this compact.

All compacting states' laws conflicting with this compact are superseded to the extent of the conflict.

(B) Binding effect of the compact

All lawful actions of the interstate commission, including all rules and bylaws promulgated by the interstate commission, are binding upon the compacting states.

All agreements between the interstate commission and the compacting states are binding in accordance with their terms.

Upon the request of a party to a conflict over meaning or interpretation of interstate commission actions, and upon a majority vote of the compacting states, the interstate commission may issue advisory opinions regarding such meaning or interpretation.

If any provision of this compact exceeds the constitutional limits imposed on the legislature of any compacting state, the obligations, duties, powers, or jurisdiction sought to be conferred by that provision upon the interstate commission shall be ineffective and the obligations, duties, powers, or jurisdiction shall remain in the compacting state and shall be exercised by the agency of that state to which the obligations, duties, powers, or jurisdiction are delegated by law in effect at the time this compact becomes effective."

(2001 H 269, eff. 7–24–02)

5149.22 Ohio council for interstate adult offender supervision

There is hereby established the Ohio council for interstate adult offender supervision pursuant to Article IV of the interstate compact for adult offender supervision. The council shall be comprised of seven members. One member shall be the compact administrator for this state for the interstate compact for adult offender supervision, or the administrator's designee. The speaker of the house of representatives shall appoint one member, who shall be a member of the house of representatives. The president of the senate shall appoint one member, who shall be a member of the senate. The chief justice of the supreme court shall appoint one member, who shall be a member of the judiciary. The governor shall appoint three members, one of whom shall be a representative of a crime victim's organization, and one of whom shall be from the executive branch. The Ohio council for interstate adult offender supervision is not subject to section 101.84 of the Revised Code.

Each appointee to the state council shall be appointed in consultation with the department of rehabilitation and correction and shall serve at the pleasure of the appointing authority. The members of the council shall serve without compensation, but each member shall be reimbursed for the member's actual and necessary expenses incurred in the performance of the member's official duties on the council.

The compact administrator for this state for the interstate compact for adult offender supervision, or the administrator's designee shall serve as commissioner of the state council and as this state's representative to the interstate commission established under Article III of that compact.

(2002 H 327, eff. 7–24–02; 2001 H 269, eff. 7–24–02)

5149.24 Prohibitions on release on bond or final release from supervision

(A) When a sending state places a hold warrant or a detainer warrant on an offender supervised under the interstate compact for adult offender supervision who is in custody in this state and that warrant does not provide that the offender may be released on bond pending return to the sending state, no court of record in this state has authority to release the offender on bond until the sending state withdraws the warrant.

(B) A receiving state has no authority to grant a final release from supervision to any offender supervised under the interstate compact for adult offender supervision unless and until the final release has been approved by the supervising authority of the sending state. The sending state shall not unreasonably withhold such a final release and shall promptly communicate the release to the supervising authorities of the receiving state.

(2001 H 269, eff. 7–24–02)

CHAPTER 5153

COUNTY CHILDREN SERVICES

Section

5153.111 Criminal records check; disqualification from employment

(A)(1) The executive director of a public children services agency shall request the superintendent of the bureau of criminal identification and investigation to conduct a criminal records check with respect to any applicant who has applied to the agency for employment as a person responsible for the care, custody, or control of a child. If the applicant does not present proof that the applicant has been a resident of this state for the five-year period immediately prior to the date upon which the criminal records check is requested or does not provide evidence that within that five-year period the superintendent has requested information about the applicant from the federal bureau of investigation in a criminal records check, the executive director shall request that the superintendent obtain information from the federal bureau of investigation as a part of the criminal records check for the applicant. If the applicant presents proof that the applicant has been a resident of this state for that five-year period, the executive director may request that the superintendent include information from the federal bureau of investigation in the criminal records check.

(2) Any person required by division (A)(1) of this section to request a criminal records check shall provide to each applicant a copy of the form prescribed pursuant to division (C)(1) of section 109.572 of the Revised Code, provide to each applicant a standard impression sheet to obtain fingerprint impressions prescribed pursuant to division (C)(2) of section 109.572 of the Revised Code, obtain the completed form and impression sheet from each applicant, and forward the completed form and impression sheet to the superintendent of the bureau of criminal identification and investigation at the time the person requests a criminal records check pursuant to division (A)(1) of this section.

(3) Any applicant who receives pursuant to division (A)(2) of this section a copy of the form prescribed pursuant to division (C)(1) of section 109.572 of the Revised Code and a copy of an impression sheet prescribed pursuant to division (C)(2) of that section and who is requested to complete the form and provide a set of fingerprint impressions shall complete the form or provide all the information necessary to complete the form and shall provide the impression sheet with the impressions of the applicant's fingerprints. If an applicant, upon request, fails to provide the information necessary to complete the form or fails to provide impressions of the applicant's fingerprints, that agency shall not employ that applicant for any position for which a criminal records check is required by division (A)(1) of this section.

(B)(1) Except as provided in rules adopted by the director of job and family services in accordance with division (E) of this section, no public children services agency shall employ a person as a person responsible for the care, custody, or control of a child if the person previously has been convicted of or pleaded guilty to any of the following:

(a) A violation of section 2903.01, 2903.02, 2903.03, 2903.04, 2903.11, 2903.12, 2903.13, 2903.16, 2903.21, 2903.34, 2905.01, 2905.02, 2905.05, 2907.02, 2907.03, 2907.04, 2907.05, 2907.06, 2907.07, 2907.08, 2907.09, 2907.21, 2907.22, 2907.23, 2907.25, 2907.31, 2907.32, 2907.321, 2907.322, 2907.323, 2911.01, 2911.02, 2911.11, 2911.12, 2919.12, 2919.22, 2919.24, 2919.25, 2923.12, 2923.13, 2923.161, 2925.02, 2925.03, 2925.04, 2925.05, 2925.06, or 3716.11 of the Revised Code, a violation of section 2905.04 of the Revised Code as it existed prior to July 1, 1996, a violation of section 2919.23 of the Revised Code that would have been a violation of section 2905.04 of the Revised Code as it existed prior to July 1, 1996, had the violation occurred prior to that date, a violation of section 2925.11 of the Revised Code that is not a minor drug possession offense, or felonious sexual penetration in violation of former section 2907.12 of the Revised Code;

(b) A violation of an existing or former law of this state, any other state, or the United States that is substantially equivalent to any of the offenses or violations described in division (B)(1)(a) of this section.

(2) A public children services agency may employ an applicant conditionally until the criminal records check required by this section is completed and the agency receives the results of the criminal records check. If the results of the criminal records check indicate that, pursuant to division (B)(1) of this section, the applicant does not qualify for employment, the agency shall release the applicant from employment.

(C)(1) Each public children services agency shall pay to the bureau of criminal identification and investigation the fee prescribed pursuant to division (C)(3) of section 109.572 of the Revised Code for each criminal records check conducted in accordance with that section upon the request pursuant to division (A)(1) of this section of the executive director of the agency.

(2) A public children services agency may charge an applicant a fee for the costs it incurs in obtaining a criminal records check under this section. A fee charged under this division shall not exceed the amount of fees the agency pays under division (C)(1) of this section. If a fee is charged under this division, the agency shall notify the applicant at the time of the applicant's initial application for employment of the amount of the fee and that, unless the fee is paid, the agency will not consider the applicant for employment.

(D) The report of any criminal records check conducted by the bureau of criminal identification and investigation in accordance with section 109.572 of the Revised Code and pursuant to a request under division (A)(1) of this section is not a public record for the purposes of section 149.43 of the Revised Code and shall not be made available to any person other than the applicant who is the subject of the criminal records check or the applicant's representative, the public children services agency requesting the criminal records check or its representative, and any court, hearing officer, or other necessary individual involved in a case dealing with the denial of employment to the applicant.

(E) The director of job and family services shall adopt rules pursuant to Chapter 119. of the Revised Code to implement this section, including rules specifying circumstances under which a public children services agency may hire a person who has been convicted of an offense listed in division (B)(1) of this section but who meets standards in regard to rehabilitation set by the department.

(F) Any person required by division (A)(1) of this section to request a criminal records check shall inform each person, at the time of the person's initial application for employment, that the person is required to provide a set of impressions of the person's fingerprints and that a criminal records check is required to be conducted and satisfactorily completed in accordance with section 109.572 of the Revised Code if the person comes under final consideration for appointment or employment as a precondition to employment for that position.

(G) As used in this section:

(1) "Applicant" means a person who is under final consideration for appointment or employment in a position with the agency as a person responsible for the care, custody, or control of a child.

(2) "Criminal records check" has the same meaning as in section 109.572 of the Revised Code.

(3) "Minor drug possession offense" has the same meaning as in section 2925.01 of the Revised Code.

(1999 H 471, eff. 7–1–00; 1997 H 408, eff. 10–1–97; 1996 S 269, eff. 7–1–96; 1996 H 445, eff. 9–3–96; 1995 S 2, eff. 7–1–96; 1994 H 694, eff. 11–11–94; 1993 S 38, eff. 10–29–93)

5153.171 Death of child under eighteen; duties of public children services agency director

(A) On receipt by a public children services agency of a request for the release of information about a child under eighteen years of age who was a resident of the county served by the agency at the time of death and whose death may have been caused by abuse, neglect, or other criminal conduct, the director of the agency immediately shall confer with the prosecuting attorney of that county. After the executive director confers with the prosecuting attorney, the following apply:

(1) If the prosecuting attorney intends to prosecute a person for causing the child's death, the prosecuting attorney shall determine the information described in division (A) of section 5153.172 of the Revised Code that may be released, if any, and notify the director of the intent to prosecute and the determination of what information may be released. Except as provided in section 5153.173 of the Revised Code, on receipt of the notice, the director shall release the information the prosecutor determines may be released and no other information.

(2) If the prosecuting attorney does not intend to prosecute a person for causing the death of the child, the prosecuting attorney shall notify the director that no prosecution is intended. Except as provided in section 5153.173 of the Revised Code, on receipt of the notice, the director shall release the information described in division (A) of section 5153.172 of the Revised Code.

(B) A public children services agency director who releases information in accordance with this section in good faith shall not be subject to civil or criminal liability for injury, death, or loss to person or property incurred or imposed as a result of provision of the information.

(2000 H 448, eff. 10–5–00)

5153.172 Disclosure of information

(A) Notwithstanding sections 2151.421, 3701.243, 5153.17, and any other section of the Revised Code pertaining to confidentiality and unless precluded by section 5153.173 of the Revised Code, the director shall disclose the following information concerning a deceased child in accordance with section 5153.171 of the Revised Code:

(1) The child's name;

(2) A summary report of the chronology of abuse or neglect reports made pursuant to section 2151.421 of the Revised Code of which the child is the subject and the final disposition of the investigations of the reports or, if investigations have not been completed, the status of any investigations;

(3) Services provided to or purchased for the child or to which the child was referred by a public children services agency;

(4) Actions taken by a public children services agency in response to any report of abuse or neglect of which the child was the subject.

(B) No person may release, pursuant to a request made under this section concerning a deceased child, the name of any person or entity that made a report or participated in making a report of child abuse or neglect of which the child was the subject; the names of the parents or siblings of the child; the contents of any psychological, psychiatric, therapeutic, clinical, or medical reports or evaluations regarding the child; witness statements; police or other investigative reports; or any other information other than the information that may be released in accordance with this section.

(2000 H 448, eff. 10–5–00)

5153.173 Disclosure of information; exceptions

The director shall not disclose any information pursuant to section 5153.172 of the Revised Code if a judge of the common pleas court of the county the deceased child resided in at the time of death determines, on motion of the public children services agency, that disclosing the information would not be in the best interest of a sibling of the deceased child or another child residing in the household the child resided in at the time of death.

(2000 H 448, eff. 10–5–00)

5153.175 Disclosure of information relevant to evaluation of fitness of applicant for type A family day-care home or type B family day-care home

(A) Notwithstanding sections 2151.421 and 5153.17 and any other section of the Revised Code pertaining to confidentiality, a public children services agency shall promptly provide to the department of job and family services or to a county department of job and family services any information the public children services agency determines to be relevant for the purpose of evaluating the fitness of a person who has applied for licensure or renewal of licensure as a type A family day-care home or certification or renewal of certification as a type B family day-care home, including, but not limited to, both of the following:

(1) A summary report of the chronology of abuse and neglect reports made pursuant to section 2151.421 of the Revised Code of which the person is the subject and the final disposition of the investigation of the reports or, if the investigations have not been completed, the status of the investigations;

(2) Any underlying documentation concerning those reports.

(B) The agency shall not include in the information provided to the department or county department under division (A) of this section the name of the person or entity that made the report or participated in the making of the report of child abuse or neglect.

(2004 H 11, eff. 5–18–05)

CHAPTER 5301

CONVEYANCES; ENCUMBRANCES

MORTGAGED REALTY, REMOVAL OF IMPROVEMENTS

5301.61 Improper removal of improvements from mortgaged realty

No person having an interest in real property, buyer, lessee, tenant, or occupant of real property, knowing that such real property is mortgaged or the subject of a land contract, shall remove, or cause or permit the removal of any improvement or fixture from such real property without the consent of the mortgagee, vendor under the land contract, or other person authorized to give such consent.

(1972 H 511, eff. 1–1–74)

5301.99 Penalties

(A) Any individual, corporation, or other business entity that violates section 5301.254 of the Revised Code shall be fined not less than five thousand dollars nor more than an amount equal to twenty-five per cent of the market value of the real property or mineral or mining rights about which information must be filed with the secretary of state pursuant to section 5301.254 of the Revised Code.

(B) Whoever violates section 5301.61 of the Revised Code is guilty of a misdemeanor of the first degree.

(1978 S 508, eff. 3–19–79; 1972 H 511; 1953 H 1)

CHAPTER 5321

LANDLORDS AND TENANTS

PRELIMINARY PROVISIONS

5321.01 Definitions

As used in this chapter:

(A) "Tenant" means a person entitled under a rental agreement to the use and occupancy of residential premises to the exclusion of others.

(B) "Landlord" means the owner, lessor, or sublessor of residential premises, the agent of the owner, lessor, or sublessor, or any person authorized by the owner, lessor, or sublessor to manage the premises or to receive rent from a tenant under a rental agreement.

(C) "Residential premises" means a dwelling unit for residential use and occupancy and the structure of which it is a part, the facilities and appurtenances in it, and the grounds, areas, and facilities for the use of tenants generally or the use of which is promised the tenant. "Residential premises" includes a dwelling unit that is owned or operated by a college or university. "Residential premises" does not include any of the following:

(1) Prisons, jails, workhouses, and other places of incarceration or correction, including, but not limited to, halfway houses or residential arrangements that are used or occupied as a requirement of a community control sanction, a post-release control sanction, or parole;

(2) Hospitals and similar institutions with the primary purpose of providing medical services, and homes licensed pursuant to Chapter 3721. of the Revised Code;

(3) Tourist homes, hotels, motels, recreational vehicle parks, recreation camps, combined park-camps, temporary park-camps, and other similar facilities where circumstances indicate a transient occupancy;

(4) Elementary and secondary boarding schools, where the cost of room and board is included as part of the cost of tuition;

(5) Orphanages and similar institutions;

(6) Farm residences furnished in connection with the rental of land of a minimum of two acres for production of agricultural products by one or more of the occupants;

(7) Dwelling units subject to sections 3733.41 to 3733.49 of the Revised Code;

(8) Occupancy by an owner of a condominium unit;

(9) Occupancy in a facility licensed as an SRO facility pursuant to Chapter 3731. of the Revised Code, if the facility is owned or operated by an organization that is exempt from taxation under section 501(c)(3) of the "Internal Revenue Code of 1986," 100 Stat. 2085, 26 U.S.C.A. 501, as amended, or by an entity or group of entities in which such an organization has a controlling interest, and if either of the following applies:

(a) The occupancy is for a period of less than sixty days.

(b) The occupancy is for participation in a program operated by the facility, or by a public entity or private charitable organization pursuant to a contract with the facility, to provide either of the following:

(i) Services licensed, certified, registered, or approved by a governmental agency or private accrediting organization for the rehabilitation of mentally ill persons, developmentally disabled persons, adults or juveniles convicted of criminal offenses, or persons suffering from substance abuse;

(ii) Shelter for juvenile runaways, victims of domestic violence, or homeless persons.

(10) Emergency shelters operated by organizations exempt from federal income taxation under section 501(c)(3) of the "Internal Revenue Code of 1986," 100 Stat. 2085, 26 U.S.C.A. 501, as amended, for persons whose circumstances indicate a transient occupancy, including homeless people, victims of domestic violence, and juvenile runaways.

(D) "Rental agreement" means any agreement or lease, written or oral, which establishes or modifies the terms, conditions, rules, or any other provisions concerning the use and occupancy of residential premises by one of the parties.

(E) "Security deposit" means any deposit of money or property to secure performance by the tenant under a rental agreement.

(F) "Dwelling unit" means a structure or the part of a structure that is used as a home, residence, or sleeping place by one person who maintains a household or by two or more persons who maintain a common household.

(G) "Controlled substance" has the same meaning as in section 3719.01 of the Revised Code.

(H) "Student tenant" means a person who occupies a dwelling unit owned or operated by the college or university at which the person is a student, and who has a rental agreement that is contingent upon the person's status as a student.

(I) "Recreational vehicle park," "recreation camp," "combined park-camp," and "temporary park- camp" have the same meanings as in section 3729.01 of the Revised Code.

(J) "Community control sanction" has the same meaning as in section 2929.01 of the Revised Code.

(K) "Post-release control sanction" has the same meaning as in section 2967.01 of the Revised Code.

(L) "School premises" has the same meaning as in section 2925.01 of the Revised Code.

(M) "Sexually oriented offense" and "child-victim oriented offense" have the same meanings as in section 2950.01 of the Revised Code.

(2004 H 368, eff. 10–13–04; 2003 S 5, § 3, eff. 1–1–04; 2003 S 5, § 1, eff. 7–31–03; 2002 H 490, eff. 1–1–04; 2002 H 520, eff. 4–3–03; 1996 H 347, eff. 10–16–96; 1994 H 438, eff. 10–12–94; 1990 S 258, eff. 8–22–90; 1983 S 244; 1974 S 103)

LANDLORD—TENANT RIGHTS AND OBLIGATIONS

5321.04 Obligations of landlord

(A) A landlord who is a party to a rental agreement shall do all of the following:

(1) Comply with the requirements of all applicable building, housing, health, and safety codes that materially affect health and safety;

(2) Make all repairs and do whatever is reasonably necessary to put and keep the premises in a fit and habitable condition;

(3) Keep all common areas of the premises in a safe and sanitary condition;

(4) Maintain in good and safe working order and condition all electrical, plumbing, sanitary, heating, ventilating, and air conditioning fixtures and appliances, and elevators, supplied or required to be supplied by him;

(5) When he is a party to any rental agreements that cover four or more dwelling units in the same structure, provide and maintain appropriate receptacles for the removal of ashes, garbage, rubbish, and other waste incidental to the occupancy of a dwelling unit, and arrange for their removal;

(6) Supply running water, reasonable amounts of hot water, and reasonable heat at all times, except where the building that includes the dwelling unit is not required by law to be equipped for that purpose, or the dwelling unit is so constructed that heat or hot water is generated by an installation within the exclusive control of the tenant and supplied by a direct public utility connection;

(7) Not abuse the right of access conferred by division (B) of section 5321.05 of the Revised Code;

(8) Except in the case of emergency or if it is impracticable to do so, give the tenant reasonable notice of his intent to enter and enter only at reasonable times. Twenty–four hours is presumed

to be a reasonable notice in the absence of evidence to the contrary.

(9) Promptly commence an action under Chapter 1923. of the Revised Code, after complying with division (C) of section 5321.17 of the Revised Code, to remove a tenant from particular residential premises, if the tenant fails to vacate the premises within three days after the giving of the notice required by that division and if the landlord has actual knowledge of or has reasonable cause to believe that the tenant, any person in the tenant's household, or any person on the premises with the consent of the tenant previously has or presently is engaged in a violation as described in division (A)(6)(a)(i) of section 1923.02 of the Revised Code, whether or not the tenant or other person has been charged with, has pleaded guilty to or been convicted of, or has been determined to be a delinquent child for an act that, if committed by an adult, would be a violation as described in that division. Such actual knowledge or reasonable cause to believe shall be determined in accordance with that division.

(B) If the landlord makes an entry in violation of division (A)(8) of this section, makes a lawful entry in an unreasonable manner, or makes repeated demands for entry otherwise lawful that have the effect of harassing the tenant, the tenant may recover actual damages resulting from the entry or demands, obtain injunctive relief to prevent the recurrence of the conduct, and obtain a judgment for reasonable attorney's fees, or may terminate the rental agreement.

(1990 S 258, eff. 8–22–90; 1974 S 103)

5321.05 Obligations of tenant

(A) A tenant who is a party to a rental agreement shall do all of the following:

(1) Keep that part of the premises that he occupies and uses safe and sanitary;

(2) Dispose of all rubbish, garbage, and other waste in a clean, safe, and sanitary manner;

(3) Keep all plumbing fixtures in the dwelling unit or used by him as clean as their condition permits;

(4) Use and operate all electrical and plumbing fixtures properly;

(5) Comply with the requirements imposed on tenants by all applicable state and local housing, health, and safety codes;

(6) Personally refrain and forbid any other person who is on the premises with his permission from intentionally or negligently destroying, defacing, damaging, or removing any fixture, appliance, or other part of the premises;

(7) Maintain in good working order and condition any range, regrigerator [sic.], washer, dryer, dishwasher, or other appliances supplied by the landlord and required to be maintained by the tenant under the terms and conditions of a written rental agreement;

(8) Conduct himself and require other persons on the premises with his consent to conduct themselves in a manner that will not disturb his neighbors' peaceful enjoyment of the premises;

(9) Conduct himself, and require persons in his household and persons on the premises with his consent to conduct themselves, in connection with the premises so as not to violate the prohibitions contained in Chapters 2925. and 3719. of the Revised Code, or in municipal ordinances that are substantially similar to any section in either of those chapters, which relate to controlled substances.

(B) The tenant shall not unreasonably withhold consent for the landlord to enter into the dwelling unit in order to inspect the premises, make ordinary, necessary, or agreed repairs, decorations, alterations, or improvements, deliver parcels that are too large for the tenant's mail facilities, supply necessary or agreed services, or exhibit the dwelling unit to prospective or actual purchasers, mortgagees, tenants, workmen, or contractors.

(C)(1) If the tenant violates any provision of this section, other than division (A)(9) of this section, the landlord may recover any actual damages that result from the violation together with reasonable attorney's fees. This remedy is in addition to any right of the landlord to terminate the rental agreement, to maintain an action for the possession of the premises, or to obtain injunctive relief to compel access under division (B) of this section.

(2) If the tenant violates division (A)(9) of this section and if the landlord has actual knowledge of or has reasonable cause to believe that the tenant, any person in the tenant's household, or any person on the premises with the consent of the tenant previously has or presently is engaged in a violation as described in division (A)(6)(a)(i) of section 1923.02 of the Revised Code, whether or not the tenant or other person has been charged with, has pleaded guilty to or been convicted of, or has been determined to be a delinquent child for an act that, if committed by an adult, would be a violation as described in that division, then the landlord promptly shall give the notice required by division (C) of section 5321.17 of the Revised Code. If the tenant fails to vacate the premises within three days after the giving of that notice, then the landlord promptly shall comply with division (A)(9) of section 5321.04 of the Revised Code. For purposes of this division, actual knowledge or reasonable cause to believe as described in this division shall be determined in accordance with division (A)(6)(a)(i) of section 1923.02 of the Revised Code.

(1990 S 258, eff. 8–22–90; 1974 S 103)

5321.051 Residential premises near a school; obligation of tenant regarding sex offender

(A)(1) No tenant of any residential premises located within one thousand feet of any school premises shall allow any person to occupy those residential premises if both of the following apply regarding the person:

(a) The person's name appears on the state registry of sex offenders and child-victim offenders maintained under section 2950.13 of the Revised Code.

(b) The state registry of sex offenders and child-victim offenders indicates that the person was convicted of or pleaded guilty to either a sexually oriented offense that is not a registration-exempt sexually oriented offense or a child-victim oriented offense in a criminal prosecution and was not sentenced to a serious youthful offender dispositional sentence for that offense.

(2) If a tenant allows occupancy in violation of this section or a person establishes a residence or occupies residential premises in violation of section 2950.031 of the Revised Code, the landlord for the residential premises that are the subject of the rental agreement or other tenancy may terminate the rental agreement or other tenancy of the tenant and all other occupants.

(B) If a landlord is authorized to terminate a rental agreement or other tenancy pursuant to division (A) of this section but does not so terminate the rental agreement or other tenancy, the landlord is not liable in a tort or other civil action in damages for any injury, death, or loss to person or property that allegedly results from that decision.

(2003 S 5, eff. 7–31–03)

RENT WITHHOLDING AND OTHER REMEDIES

5321.07 Notice to remedy conditions; rent withholding; other remedies; exceptions

(A) If a landlord fails to fulfill any obligation imposed upon him by section 5321.04 of the Revised Code, other than the obligation specified in division (A)(9) of that section, or any obligation imposed upon him by the rental agreement, if the conditions of the residential premises are such that the tenant reasonably believes that a landlord has failed to fulfill any such obligations, or if a governmental agency has found that the premises are not in compliance with building, housing, health, or safety codes that apply to any condition of the premises that could materially affect the health and safety of an occupant, the tenant may give notice in writing to the landlord, specifying the acts, omissions, or code violations that constitute noncompliance. The notice shall be sent to the person or place where rent is normally paid.

(B) If a landlord receives the notice described in division (A) of this section and after receipt of the notice fails to remedy the condition within a reasonable time considering the severity of the condition and the time necessary to remedy it, or within thirty days, whichever is sooner, and if the tenant is current in rent payments due under the rental agreement, the tenant may do one of the following:

(1) Deposit all rent that is due and thereafter becomes due the landlord with the clerk of the municipal or county court having jurisdiction in the territory in which the residential premises are located;

(2) Apply to the court for an order directing the landlord to remedy the condition. As part of the application, the tenant may deposit rent pursuant to division (B)(1) of this section, may apply for an order reducing the periodic rent due the landlord until the landlord remedies the condition, and may apply for an order to use the rent deposited to remedy the condition. In any order issued pursuant to this division, the court may require the tenant to deposit rent with the clerk of court as provided in division (B)(1) of this section.

(3) Terminate the rental agreement.

(C) This section does not apply to any landlord who is a party to rental agreements that cover three or fewer dwelling units and who provides notice of that fact in a written rental agreement or, in the case of an oral tenancy, delivers written notice of that fact to the tenant at the time of initial occupancy by the tenant.

(D) This section does not apply to a dwelling unit occupied by a student tenant.

(1994 H 438, eff. 10–12–94; 1990 S 258, eff. 8–22–90; 1974 S 103)

5321.09 Defensive actions of landlord

(A) A landlord who receives notice that rent due him has been deposited with a clerk of a municipal or county court pursuant to section 5321.07 of the Revised Code, may do any of the following:

(1) Apply to the clerk of the court for release of the rent on the ground that the condition contained in the notice given pursuant to division (A) of section 5321.07 of the Revised Code has been remedied. The clerk shall forthwith release the rent, less costs, to the landlord if the tenant gives written notice to the clerk that the condition has been remedied.

(2) Apply to the court for release of the rent on the ground that the tenant did not comply with the notice requirement of division (A) of section 5321.07 of the Revised Code, or that the tenant was not current in rent payments due under the rental agreement at the time the tenant initiated rent deposits with the clerk of the court under division (B)(1) of section 5321.07 of the Revised Code.

(3) Apply to the court for release of the rent on the ground that there was no violation of any obligation imposed upon the landlord by section 5321.04 of the Revised Code, other than the obligation specified in division (A)(9) of that section, any obligation imposed upon him by the rental agreement, or any obligation imposed upon him by any building, housing, health, or safety code, or that the condition contained in the notice given pursuant to division (A) of section 5321.07 of the Revised Code has been remedied.

(B) The tenant shall be named as a party to any action filed by the landlord under this section, and shall have the right to file an answer and counterclaim, as in other civil actions. A trial shall be held within sixty days of the date of the filing of the landlord's complaint, unless, for good cause shown, the court continues the period for trial.

(C) If the court finds that there was no violation of any obligation imposed upon the landlord by section 5321.04 of the Revised Code, other than the obligation specified in division (A)(9) of that section, any obligation imposed upon him by the rental agreement, or any obligation imposed upon him by any building, housing, health, or safety code, that the condition contained in the notice given pursuant to division (A) of section 5321.07 of the Revised Code has been remedied, that the tenant did not comply with the notice requirement of division (A) of section 5321.07 of the Revised Code, or that the tenant was not current in rent payments at the time the tenant initiated rent deposits with the clerk of court under division (B)(1) of section 5321.07 of the Revised Code, the court shall order the release to the landlord of rent on deposit with the clerk, less costs.

(D) If the court finds that the condition contained in the notice given pursuant to division (A) of section 5321.07 of the Revised Code was the result of an act or omission of the tenant, or that the tenant intentionally acted in bad faith in proceeding under section 5321.07 of the Revised Code, the tenant shall be liable for damages caused to the landlord and costs, together with reasonable attorney's fees if the tenant intentionally acted in bad faith.

(1990 S 258, eff. 8–22–90; 1974 S 103)

5321.11 Termination of agreement for noncompliance by tenant

If the tenant fails to fulfill any obligation imposed upon him by section 5321.05 of the Revised Code that materially affects health and safety, other than the obligation described in division (A)(9) of that section, the landlord may deliver a written notice of this fact to the tenant specifying the act or omission that constitutes noncompliance with the pertinent obligations and specifying that the rental agreement will terminate upon a date specified in the notice, not less than thirty days after receipt of the notice. If the tenant fails to remedy the condition specified in the notice, the rental agreement shall terminate as provided in the notice.

(1990 S 258, eff. 8–22–90; 1974 S 103)

CONTRACTUAL PROVISIONS

5321.13 Terms barred from rental agreements

(A) No provision of this chapter may be modified or waived by any oral or written agreement except as provided in division (F) of this section.

(B) No warrant of attorney to confess judgment shall be recognized in any rental agreement or in any other agreement between a landlord and tenant for the recovery of rent or damages to the residential premises.

(C) No agreement to pay the landlord's or tenant's attorney's fees shall be recognized in any rental agreement for residential premises or in any other agreement between a landlord and tenant.

(D) No agreement by a tenant to the exculpation or limitation of any liability of the landlord arising under law or to indemnify the landlord for that liability or its related costs shall be recognized in any rental agreement or in any other agreement between a landlord and tenant.

(E) A rental agreement, or the assignment, conveyance, trust deed, or security instrument of the landlord's interest in the rental agreement may not permit the receipt of rent free of the obligation to comply with section 5321.04 of the Revised Code.

(F) The landlord may agree to assume responsibility for fulfilling any duty or obligation imposed on a tenant by section 5321.05 of the Revised Code, other than the obligation specified in division (A)(9) of that section.

(1990 S 258, eff. 8–22–90; 1974 S 103)

MISCELLANEOUS PROVISIONS

5321.17 Termination of periodic tenancies; inapplicability where termination based on breach of condition or duty

(A) Except as provided in division (C) of this section, the landlord or the tenant may terminate or fail to renew a week-to-week tenancy by notice given the other at least seven days prior to the termination date specified in the notice.

(B) Except as provided in division (C) of this section, the landlord or the tenant may terminate or fail to renew a month-to-month tenancy by notice given the other at least thirty days prior to the periodic rental date.

(C) If a tenant violates division (A)(9) of section 5321.05 of the Revised Code and if the landlord has actual knowledge of or has reasonable cause to believe that the tenant, any person in the tenant's household, or any person on the residential premises with the consent of the tenant previously has or presently is engaged in a violation as described in division (A)(6)(a)(i) of section 1923.02 of the Revised Code, the landlord shall terminate the week-to-week tenancy, month-to-month tenancy, or other rental agreement with the tenant by giving a notice of termination to the tenant in accordance with this division. The notice shall specify that the tenancy or other rental agreement is terminated three days after the giving of the notice, and the landlord may give the notice whether or not the tenant or other person has been charged with, has pleaded guilty to or been convicted of, or has been determined to be a delinquent child for an act that, if committed by an adult, would be a violation as described in division (A)(6)(a)(i) of section 1923.02 of the Revised Code. If the tenant fails to vacate the premises within three days after the giving of that notice, then the landlord promptly shall comply with division (A)(9) of section 5321.04 of the Revised Code. For purposes of this division, actual knowledge or reasonable cause to believe as described in this division shall be determined in accordance with division (A)(6)(a)(i) of section 1923.02 of the Revised Code.

(D) This section does not apply to a termination based on the breach of a condition of a rental agreement or the breach of a duty and obligation imposed by law, except that it does apply to a breach of the obligation imposed upon a tenant by division (A)(9) of section 5321.05 of the Revised Code.

(1990 S 258, eff. 8–22–90; 1974 S 103)

5321.19 Conflicting ordinances and resolutions prohibited

No municipal corporation may adopt or continue in existence any ordinance and no township may adopt or continue in existence any resolution that is in conflict with this chapter, or that regulates the rights and obligations of parties to a rental agreement that are regulated by this chapter. This chapter does not preempt any housing, building, health, or safety code, or any ordinance as described in division (A)(9) of section 5321.04 of the Revised Code, of any municipal corporation or township.

(1991 H 77, eff. 9–17–91; 1990 S 258; 1974 S 103)

CHAPTER 5502

PUBLIC SAFETY DEPARTMENT

5502.14 Enforcement agents; powers

(A) As used in this section, "felony" has the same meaning as in section 109.511 of the Revised Code.

(B)(1) Any person who is employed by the department of public safety and designated by the director of public safety to enforce Title XLIII of the Revised Code, the rules adopted under it, and the laws and rules regulating the use of food stamps shall be known as an enforcement agent. The employment by the department of public safety and the designation by the director of public safety of a person as an enforcement agent shall be subject to division (D) of this section. An enforcement agent has the authority vested in peace officers pursuant to section 2935.03 of the Revised Code to keep the peace, to enforce all applicable laws and rules on any retail liquor permit premises, or on any other premises of public or private property, where a violation of Title XLIII of the Revised Code or any rule adopted under it is occurring, and to enforce all laws and rules governing the use of food stamp coupons, women, infants, and children's coupons, electronically transferred benefits, or any other access device that is used alone or in conjunction with another access device to obtain payments, allotments, benefits, money, goods, or other things of value, or that can be used to initiate a transfer of funds, pursuant to the food stamp program established under the "Food Stamp Act of 1977," 91 Stat. 958, 7 U.S.C.A. 2011, as amended, or any supplemental food program administered by any department of this state pursuant to the "Child Nutrition Act of 1966," 80 Stat. 885, 42 U.S.C.A. 1786. Enforcement agents, in enforcing compliance with the laws and rules described in this division, may keep the peace and make arrests for violations of those laws and rules.

(2) In addition to the authority conferred by division (B)(1) of this section, an enforcement agent also may execute search warrants and seize and take into custody any contraband, as defined in section 2901.01 of the Revised Code, or any property that is otherwise necessary for evidentiary purposes related to any violations of the laws or rules described in division (B)(1) of this section. An enforcement agent may enter public or private premises where activity alleged to violate the laws or rules described in division (B)(1) of this section is occurring.

(3) Enforcement agents who are on, immediately adjacent to, or across from retail liquor permit premises and who are performing investigative duties relating to that premises, enforcement agents who are on premises that are not liquor permit premises but on which a violation of Title XLIII of the Revised Code or any rule adopted under it allegedly is occurring, and enforcement agents who view a suspected violation of Title XLIII

of the Revised Code, of a rule adopted under it, or of another law or rule described in division (B)(1) of this section have the authority to enforce the laws and rules described in division (B)(1) of this section, authority to enforce any section in Title XXIX of the Revised Code or any other section of the Revised Code listed in section 5502.13 of the Revised Code if they witness a violation of the section under any of the circumstances described in this division, and authority to make arrests for violations of the laws and rules described in division (B)(1) of this section and violations of any of those sections.

(4) The jurisdiction of an enforcement agent under division (B) of this section shall be concurrent with that of the peace officers of the county, township, or municipal corporation in which the violation occurs.

(C) Enforcement agents of the department of public safety who are engaged in the enforcement of the laws and rules described in division (B)(1) of this section may carry concealed weapons when conducting undercover investigations pursuant to their authority as law enforcement officers and while acting within the scope of their authority pursuant to this chapter.

(D)(1) The department of public safety shall not employ, and the director of public safety shall not designate, a person as an enforcement agent on a permanent basis, on a temporary basis, for a probationary term, or on other than a permanent basis if the person previously has been convicted of or has pleaded guilty to a felony.

(2)(a) The department of public safety shall terminate the employment of a person who is designated as an enforcement agent and who does either of the following:

(i) Pleads guilty to a felony;

(ii) Pleads guilty to a misdemeanor pursuant to a negotiated plea agreement as provided in division (D) of section 2929.43 of the Revised Code in which the enforcement agent agrees to surrender the certificate awarded to that agent under section 109.77 of the Revised Code.

(b) The department shall suspend the employment of a person who is designated as an enforcement agent if the person is convicted, after trial, of a felony. If the enforcement agent files an appeal from that conviction and the conviction is upheld by the highest court to which the appeal is taken or if no timely appeal is filed, the department shall terminate the employment of that agent. If the enforcement agent files an appeal that results in that agent's acquittal of the felony or conviction of a misdemeanor, or in the dismissal of the felony charge against the agent, the department shall reinstate the agent. An enforcement agent who is reinstated under division (D)(2)(b) of this section shall not receive any back pay unless the conviction of that agent of the felony was reversed on appeal, or the felony charge was dismissed, because the court found insufficient evidence to convict the agent of the felony.

(3) Division (D) of this section does not apply regarding an offense that was committed prior to January 1, 1997.

(4) The suspension or termination of the employment of a person designated as an enforcement agent under division (D)(2) of this section shall be in accordance with Chapter 119. of the Revised Code.

(2002 H 490, eff. 1–1–04; 1999 H 163, eff. 6–30–99; 1996 H 566, eff. 10–16–96; 1995 S 162, eff. 10–29–95)

5502.18 Enforcement agents assisting law enforcement officers

Enforcement agents of the department of public safety may render assistance to a state or local law enforcement officer at the request of that officer or may render assistance to a state or local law enforcement officer in the event of an emergency. An enforcement agent who serves outside the department under this section shall be considered as performing services within the agent's regular employment for purposes of compensation, indemnity fund rights, workers' compensation, and any other rights and benefits to which the agent may be entitled as incidents of the agent's regular employment. Such an enforcement agent retains personal immunity from civil liability under section 9.86 of the Revised Code and shall not be considered an employee of a political subdivision for purposes of Chapter 2744. of the Revised Code.

A political subdivision that receives the assistance of an enforcement agent under this section is not subject to civil liability under Chapter 2744. of the Revised Code as a result of any action or omission of the agent.

(1999 H 163, eff. 6–30–99; 1995 S 162, eff. 10–29–95)

CHAPTER 5503

STATE HIGHWAY PATROL

ADMINISTRATIVE PROVISIONS

5503.01 State highway patrol division; superintendent

There is hereby created in the department of public safety a division of state highway patrol which shall be administered by a superintendent of the state highway patrol.

The superintendent shall be appointed by the director of public safety, and shall serve at the director's pleasure. The superintendent shall give bond for the faithful performance of the superintendent's official duties in such amount and with such security as the director approves.

The superintendent, with the approval of the director, may appoint any number of state highway patrol troopers and radio operators as are necessary to carry out sections 5503.01 to 5503.06 of the Revised Code, but the number of troopers shall not be less than eight hundred eighty. The number of radio operators shall not exceed eighty in number. Except as provided in this section, at the time of appointment, troopers shall be not less than twenty-one years of age, nor have reached thirty-five years of age. A person who is attending a training school for prospective state highway patrol troopers established under section 5503.05 of the Revised Code and attains the age of thirty-five years during the person's period of attendance at that training school shall not be disqualified as over age and shall be permitted to continue to attend the training school as long as the person otherwise is eligible to do so. Such a person also remains eligible to be appointed a trooper. Any other person who attains or will attain the age of thirty-five years prior to the time of appointment shall be disqualified as over age.

At the time of appointment, troopers shall have been legal residents of Ohio for at least one year, except that this residence requirement may be waived by the superintendent.

If any state highway patrol troopers become disabled through accident or illness, the superintendent, with the approval of the director, shall fill any vacancies through the appointment of other troopers from a qualified list to serve during the period of the disability.

The superintendent and state highway patrol troopers shall be vested with the authority of peace officers for the purpose of enforcing the laws of the state that it is the duty of the patrol to enforce and may arrest, without warrant, any person who, in the presence of the superintendent or any trooper, is engaged in the violation of any such laws. The state highway patrol troopers shall never be used as peace officers in connection with any strike or labor dispute.

Each state highway patrol trooper and radio operator, upon appointment and before entering upon official duties, shall take an oath of office for faithful performance of the trooper's or radio operator's official duties and execute a bond in the sum of twenty-five hundred dollars, payable to the state and for the use and benefit of any aggrieved party who may have a cause of action against any trooper or radio operator for misconduct while in the performance of official duties. In no event shall the bond include any claim arising out of negligent operation of a motorcycle or motor vehicle used by a trooper or radio operator in the performance of official duties.

The superintendent shall prescribe a distinguishing uniform and badge which shall be worn by each state highway patrol trooper and radio operator while on duty, unless otherwise designated by the superintendent. No person shall wear the distinguishing uniform of the state highway patrol or the badge or any distinctive part of that uniform, except on order of the superintendent.

The superintendent, with the approval of the director, may appoint necessary clerks, stenographers, and employees.

(1997 S 22, eff. 4–22–97; 1992 S 98, eff. 11–12–92; 1991 S 144; 1979 H 165; 132 v H 658, H 1; 131 v H 20; 129 v 1671; 126 v 621; 125 v 127; 1953 H 1; GC 1183)

5503.02 Duties and powers of state highway patrol

(A) The state highway patrol shall enforce the laws of the state relating to the titling, registration, and licensing of motor vehicles; enforce on all roads and highways, notwithstanding section 4513.39 of the Revised Code, the laws relating to the operation and use of vehicles on the highways; enforce and prevent the violation of the laws relating to the size, weight, and speed of commercial motor vehicles and all laws designed for the protection of the highway pavements and structures on the highways; investigate and enforce rules and laws of the public utilities commission governing the transportation of persons and property by motor carriers and report violations of such rules and laws to the commission; enforce against any motor transportation company as defined in section 4921.02 of the Revised Code, any contract carrier by motor vehicle as defined in section 4923.02 of the Revised Code, any private motor carrier as defined in section 4923.20 of the Revised Code, and any motor carrier as defined in section 4919.75 of the Revised Code those rules and laws that, if violated, may result in a forfeiture as provided in section 4905.83, 4919.99, 4921.99, or 4923.99 of the Revised Code; investigate and report violations of all laws relating to the collection of excise taxes on motor vehicle fuels; and regulate the movement of traffic on the roads and highways of the state, notwithstanding section 4513.39 of the Revised Code.

The patrol, whenever possible, shall determine the identity of the persons who are causing or who are responsible for the breaking, damaging, or destruction of any improved surfaced roadway, structure, sign, marker, guardrail, or other appurtenance constructed or maintained by the department of transportation and shall arrest the persons who are responsible for the breaking, damaging, or destruction and bring them before the proper officials for prosecution.

State highway patrol troopers shall investigate and report all motor vehicle accidents on all roads and highways outside of municipal corporations. The superintendent of the patrol or any state highway patrol trooper may arrest, without a warrant, any person, who is the driver of or a passenger in any vehicle operated or standing on a state highway, whom the superintendent or trooper has reasonable cause to believe is guilty of a felony, under the same circumstances and with the same power that any peace officer may make such an arrest.

The superintendent or any state highway patrol trooper may enforce the criminal laws on all state properties and state institutions, owned or leased by the state, and, when so ordered by the governor in the event of riot, civil disorder, or insurrection, may, pursuant to sections 2935.03 to 2935.05 of the Revised Code, arrest offenders against the criminal laws wherever they may be found within the state if the violations occurred upon, or resulted in injury to person or property on, state properties or state institutions, or under the conditions described in division (B) of this section.

(B) In the event of riot, civil disorder, or insurrection, or the reasonable threat of riot, civil disorder, or insurrection, and upon request, as provided in this section, of the sheriff of a county or the mayor or other chief executive of a municipal corporation, the governor may order the state highway patrol to enforce the criminal laws within the area threatened by riot, civil disorder, or insurrection, as designated by the governor, upon finding that law enforcement agencies within the counties involved will not be reasonably capable of controlling the riot, civil disorder, or insurrection and that additional assistance is necessary. In cities in which the sheriff is under contract to provide exclusive police services pursuant to section 311.29 of the Revised Code, in villages, and in the unincorporated areas of the county, the sheriff has exclusive authority to request the use of the patrol. In cities in which the sheriff does not exclusively provide police services, the mayor, or other chief executive performing the duties of mayor, has exclusive authority to request the use of the patrol.

The superintendent or any state highway patrol trooper may enforce the criminal laws within the area designated by the governor during the emergency arising out of the riot, civil disorder, or insurrection until released by the governor upon consultation with the requesting authority. State highway patrol troopers shall never be used as peace officers in connection with any strike or labor dispute.

When a request for the use of the patrol is made pursuant to this division, the requesting authority shall notify the law enforcement authorities in contiguous communities and the sheriff of each county within which the threatened area, or any part of the threatened area, lies of the request, but the failure to notify the authorities or a sheriff shall not affect the validity of the request.

(C) Any person who is arrested by the superintendent or a state highway patrol trooper shall be taken before any court or magistrate having jurisdiction of the offense with which the person is charged. Any person who is arrested or apprehended within the limits of a municipal corporation shall be brought before the municipal court or other tribunal of the municipal corporation.

(D)(1) State highway patrol troopers have the same right and power of search and seizure as other peace officers.

No state official shall command, order, or direct any state highway patrol trooper to perform any duty or service that is not authorized by law. The powers and duties conferred on the patrol are supplementary to, and in no way a limitation on, the powers and duties of sheriffs or other peace officers of the state.

(2)(a) A state highway patrol trooper, pursuant to the policy established by the superintendent of the state highway patrol under division (D)(2)(b) of this section, may render emergency assistance to any other peace officer who has arrest authority under section 2935.03 of the Revised Code, if both of the following apply:

(i) There is a threat of imminent physical danger to the peace officer, a threat of physical harm to another person, or any other serious emergency situation;

(ii) Either the peace officer requests emergency assistance or it appears that the peace officer is unable to request emergency assistance and the circumstances observed by the state highway patrol trooper reasonably indicate that emergency assistance is appropriate.

(b) The superintendent of the state highway patrol shall establish, within sixty days of August 8, 1991, a policy that sets forth the manner and procedures by which a state highway patrol trooper may render emergency assistance to any other peace officer under division (D)(2)(a) of this section. The policy shall include a provision that a state highway patrol trooper never be used as a peace officer in connection with any strike or labor dispute.

(3)(a) A state highway patrol trooper who renders emergency assistance to any other peace officer under the policy established by the superintendent pursuant to division (D)(2)(b) of this section shall be considered to be performing regular employment for the purposes of compensation, pension, indemnity fund rights, workers' compensation, and other rights or benefits to which the trooper may be entitled as incident to regular employment.

(b) A state highway patrol trooper who renders emergency assistance to any other peace officer under the policy established by the superintendent pursuant to division (D)(2)(b) of this section retains personal immunity from liability as specified in section 9.86 of the Revised Code.

(c) A state highway patrol trooper who renders emergency assistance under the policy established by the superintendent pursuant to division (D)(2)(b) of this section has the same authority as the peace officer for or with whom the state highway patrol trooper is providing emergency assistance.

(E)(1) Subject to the availability of funds specifically appropriated by the general assembly for security detail purposes, the state highway patrol shall provide security as follows:

(a) For the governor;

(b) At the direction of the governor, for other officials of the state government of this state; officials of the state governments of other states who are visiting this state; officials of the United States government who are visiting this state; officials of the governments of foreign countries or their political subdivisions who are visiting this state; or other officials or dignitaries who are visiting this state, including, but not limited to, members of trade missions;

(c) For the capitol square, as defined in section 105.41 of the Revised Code;

(d) For other state property.

(2) To carry out the security responsibilities of the patrol listed in division (E)(1) of this section, the superintendent may assign state highway patrol troopers to a separate unit that is responsible for security details. The number of troopers assigned to particular security details shall be determined by the superintendent.

(3) The superintendent and any state highway patrol trooper, when providing security pursuant to division (E)(1)(a) or (b) of this section, have the same arrest powers as other peace officers to apprehend offenders against the criminal laws who endanger or threaten the security of any person being protected, no matter where the offense occurs.

The superintendent, any state highway patrol trooper, and any special police officer designated under section 5503.09 of the Revised Code, when providing security pursuant to division (E)(1)(c) of this section, shall enforce any rules governing capitol square adopted by the capitol square review and advisory board.

(F) The governor may order the state highway patrol to undertake major criminal investigations that involve state property interests. If an investigation undertaken pursuant to this division results in either the issuance of a no bill or the filing of an indictment, the superintendent shall file a complete and accurate report of the investigation with the president of the senate, the speaker of the house of representatives, the minority leader of the senate, and the minority leader of the house of representatives within fifteen days after the issuance of the no bill or the filing of an indictment. If the investigation does not have as its result any prosecutorial action, the superintendent shall, upon reporting this fact to the governor, file a complete and accurate report of the investigation with the president of the senate, the speaker of the house of representatives, the minority leader of the senate, and the minority leader of the house of representatives.

(G) The superintendent may purchase or lease real property and buildings needed by the patrol, negotiate the sale of real property owned by the patrol, rent or lease real property owned or leased by the patrol, and make or cause to be made repairs to all property owned or under the control of the patrol. Any instrument by which real property is acquired pursuant to this division shall identify the agency of the state that has the use and benefit of the real property as specified in section 5301.012 of the Revised Code.

Sections 123.01 and 125.02 of the Revised Code do not limit the powers granted to the superintendent by this division.

(1999 H 19, eff. 10–26–99; 1995 S 34, eff. 10–25–95; 1995 H 117, eff. 9–29–95; 1994 H 687, eff. 10–12–94; 1992 S 381, eff. 1–15–93; 1992 S 351; 1991 S 144; 1988 H 428; 1981 H 694; 1980 H 837; 1977 S 221; 1973 H 323, H 200; 1971 H 600; 132 v H 996; 1953 H 1; GC 1183–2)

5503.03 Equipment; rules; promotions

The state highway patrol and the superintendent of the state highway patrol shall be furnished by the state with such vehicles, equipment, and supplies as the director of public safety deems necessary, all of which shall remain the property of the state and be strictly accounted for by each member of the patrol.

The patrol may be equipped with standardized and tested devices for weighing vehicles, and may stop and weigh any vehicle which appears to weigh in excess of the amounts permitted by sections 5577.01 to 5577.14 of the Revised Code.

The superintendent, with the approval of the director, shall prescribe rules for instruction and discipline, make all administrative rules, and fix the hours of duty for patrol officers. He shall divide the state into districts and assign members of the patrol to such districts in a manner that he deems proper. He may transfer members of the patrol from one district to another, and classify and rank members of the patrol. All promotions to a higher grade shall be made from the next lower grade. When a patrol officer is promoted by the superintendent, the officer's salary shall be increased to that of the lowest step in the pay range for the new grade which shall increase the officer's salary or wage by at least nine per cent of the base pay wherever possible.

(1992 S 98, eff. 11–12–92; 1981 H 694; 125 v 127; 1953 H 1; GC 1183–3)

5503.04 Disposition of moneys collected by state patrol troopers

Forty-five per cent of the fines collected from or moneys arising from bail forfeited by persons apprehended or arrested by state highway patrol troopers shall be paid into the state treasury to be credited to the general revenue fund, five per cent shall be paid into the state treasury to be credited to the trauma and emergency medical services grants fund created by division (E) of section 4513.263 of the Revised Code, and fifty per cent shall be paid into the treasury of the municipal corporation where the case is prosecuted, if in a mayor's court. If the prosecution is in a trial court outside a municipal corporation, or outside the territorial jurisdiction of a municipal court, the fifty per cent of the fines and moneys that is not paid into the state treasury shall be paid into the treasury of the county where the case is prosecuted. The fines and moneys paid into a county treasury and the fines and moneys paid into the treasury of a municipal corporation shall be deposited one-half to the same fund and expended in the same manner as is the revenue received from the registration of motor vehicles, and one-half to the general fund of such county or municipal corporation.

If the prosecution is in a municipal court, forty-five per cent of the fines and moneys shall be paid into the state treasury to be credited to the general revenue fund, five per cent shall be paid into the state treasury to be credited to the trauma and emergency medical services grants fund created by division (E) of section 4513.263 of the Revised Code, ten per cent shall be paid into the county treasury to be credited to the general fund of the county, and forty per cent shall be paid into the municipal treasury to be credited to the general fund of the municipal corporation. In the Auglaize county, Clermont county, Crawford county, Hocking county, Jackson county, Lawrence county, Madison county, Miami county, Ottawa county, Portage county, and Wayne county municipal courts, that portion of money otherwise paid into the municipal treasury shall be paid into the county treasury.

The trial court shall make remittance of the fines and moneys as prescribed in this section, and at the same time as the remittance is made of the state's portion to the state treasury, the trial court shall notify the superintendent of the state highway patrol of the case and the amount covered by the remittance.

This section does not apply to fines for violations of division (B) of section 4513.263 of the Revised Code, or for violations of any municipal ordinance that is substantively comparable to that division, all of which shall be delivered to the treasurer of state as provided in division (E) of section 4513.263 of the Revised Code.

(2000 H 138, eff. 11–3–00; 1994 H 21, eff. 2–4–94; 1991 S 144, eff. 8–8–91; 1991 H 200; 1987 H 171; 1986 S 54; 1980 H 961; 1979 H 1; 1977 S 221, H 312; 1975 H 205; 132 v H 361; 129 v 1011; 126 v 773; 1953 H 1; GC 1183–4)

5503.05 Training schools for patrol troopers

The superintendent of the state highway patrol, with the approval of the director of public safety, may conduct training schools for prospective state highway patrol troopers. The prospective troopers, during the period of their training and as members of the state patrol school, shall be paid a reasonable salary out of highway funds. The superintendent may furnish the necessary supplies and equipment for the use of the prospective troopers during the training period.

The superintendent may establish rules governing the qualifications for admission to training schools for prospective troopers and provide for competitive examinations to determine the fitness of the students and prospective troopers, not inconsistent with the rules of the director of administrative services.

(1992 S 98, eff. 11–12–92; 1991 S 144; 1977 H 1; 125 v 127; 1953 H 1; GC 1183–6)

5503.06 Regulation of motor transportation by public utilities commission not affected; motor vehicle inspections

Sections 5503.01 to 5503.05 of the Revised Code do not supersede, limit, or suspend any law relative to the regulation of motor transportation upon the public highways of the state by the public utilities commission.

In addition to the powers and duties of the state highway patrol set forth in section 5503.02 of the Revised Code, a state highway patrol trooper or other authorized employee may conduct inspections of any motor vehicle subject to inspection by the commission. Such inspections shall be conducted in accordance with rules adopted by the commission and for the purpose of ensuring compliance with such rules.

(1992 S 351, eff. 7–1–92; 1953 H 1; GC 1183–5)

5503.07 Control and use of rest areas and roadside parks on interstate and state highways

In addition to the powers and duties of the state highway patrol set forth in section 5503.02 of the Revised Code and subject to the limitations of section 5503.01 of the Revised Code, a state highway patrol trooper shall arrest any person found committing a misdemeanor within the bounds of rest areas or roadside parks within the limits of the right-of-way of interstate highways and other state highways, or in violation of section 5515.07 of the Revised Code in other areas within the limits of the right-of-way of interstate highways.

(1991 S 144, eff. 8–8–91; 130 v H 639)

5503.08 Occupational injury leave

Each state highway patrol officer shall, in addition to the sick leave benefits provided in section 124.38 of the Revised Code, be entitled to occupational injury leave. Occupational injury leave of one thousand five hundred hours with pay may, with the approval of the superintendent of the state highway patrol, be used for absence resulting from each independent injury incurred in the line of duty, except that occupational injury leave is not available for injuries incurred during those times when the patrol officer is actually engaged in administrative or clerical duties at a patrol facility, when a patrol officer is on a meal or rest period, or when the patrol officer is engaged in any personal business. The superintendent of the state highway patrol shall, by rule, define those administrative and clerical duties and those situations where the occurrence of an injury does not entitle the patrol officer to occupational injury leave. Each injury incurred in the line of duty which aggravates a previously existing injury, whether the previously existing injury was so incurred or not, shall be considered an independent injury. When its use is authorized under this section, all occupational injury leave shall be exhausted before any credit is deducted from unused sick leave accumulated under section 124.38 of the Revised Code, except that, unless otherwise provided by the superintendent of the state highway patrol, occupational injury leave shall not be used for absence occurring within seven calendar days of the injury. During that seven calendar day period, unused sick leave may be used for such an absence.

When occupational injury leave is used, it shall be deducted from the unused balance of the patrol officer's occupational injury leave for that injury on the basis of one hour for every one hour of absence from previously scheduled work.

Before a patrol officer may use occupational injury leave, the patrol officer shall:

(A) Apply to the superintendent for permission to use occupational injury leave on a form that requires the patrol officer to explain the nature of the patrol officer's independent injury and the circumstances under which it occurred; and

(B) Submit to a medical examination. The individual who conducts the examination shall report to the superintendent the results of the examination and whether or not the independent injury prevents the patrol officer from attending work.

The superintendent shall, by rule, provide for periodic medical examinations of patrol officers who are using occupational injury leave. The individual selected to conduct the medical examinations shall report to the superintendent the results of each such examination, including a description of the progress made by the patrol officer in recovering from the independent injury, and whether or not the independent injury continues to prevent the patrol officer from attending work.

The superintendent shall appoint to conduct medical examinations under this division individuals authorized by the Revised Code to do so, including any physician assistant, clinical nurse specialist, certified nurse practitioner, or certified nurse-midwife.

A patrol officer is not entitled to use or continue to use occupational injury leave after refusing to submit to a medical examination or if the individual examining the patrol officer reports that the independent injury does not prevent the patrol officer from attending work.

A patrol officer who falsifies an application for permission to use occupational injury leave or a medical examination report is subject to disciplinary action, including dismissal.

The superintendent shall, by rule, prescribe forms for the application and medical examination report.

Occupational injury leave pay made according to this section is in lieu of such workers' compensation benefits as would have been payable directly to a patrol officer pursuant to sections 4123.56 and 4123.58 of the Revised Code, but all other compensation and benefits pursuant to Chapter 4123. of the Revised Code are payable as in any other case. If at the close of the period, the patrol officer remains disabled, the patrol officer is entitled to all compensation and benefits, without a waiting period pursuant to section 4123.55 of the Revised Code based upon the injury received, for which the patrol officer qualifies pursuant to Chapter 4123. of the Revised Code. Compensation shall be paid from the date that the patrol officer ceases to receive the patrol officer's regular rate of pay pursuant to this section.

Occupational injury leave shall not be credited to or, upon use, deducted from, a patrol officer's sick leave.

(2002 S 245, eff. 3–31–03; 1987 H 178, eff. 6–24–87; 1978 H 839)

5503.09 Special police officers; training; oath; bond

The superintendent of the state highway patrol, with the approval of the director of public safety, may designate one or more persons to be special police officers to preserve the peace and enforce the laws of this state with respect to persons and property under their jurisdiction and control. The officers are vested with the same powers of arrest as police officers under section 2935.03 of the Revised Code when exercising their responsibilities on lands owned by the Ohio expositions commission and on those state properties and institutions owned or leased by the state where the officers are assigned by the superintendent.

Special police officers shall be required to complete peace officer basic training for the position to which they have been appointed as required by the Ohio peace officer training commission as authorized in section 109.73 of the Revised Code. They also shall take an oath of office, wear the badge of office, and provide bond to the state in the amount of twenty-five hundred dollars for the proper performance of their duties.

(1997 S 60, eff. 10–21–97; 1996 H 670, eff. 12–2–96; 1992 S 98, eff. 11–12–92; 1987 H 419)

5503.11 Auxiliary unit

(A) The superintendent of the state highway patrol, with the approval of the director of public safety, may establish an auxiliary unit within the state highway patrol, and provide for the regulation of the auxiliary officers. The superintendent shall be the head of the auxiliary unit, and shall have the sole authority to make all appointments to and dismissals from the auxiliary unit. The superintendent shall prescribe rules for the organization, administration, and control of the auxiliary unit, and the eligibility requirements, training, and conduct of the auxiliary officers. The superintendent also shall have the authority to expend any funds appropriated to the state highway patrol to pay any expenses the state highway patrol incurs in administering the auxiliary unit. Members of the auxiliary unit may be required to pay any portion of their expenses, as determined by the superintendent.

No member of the auxiliary unit shall have any power to arrest any person or to enforce any law of this state.

(B) Each member of the auxiliary unit, in the performance of the member's official duties as determined by the superintendent, possesses personal immunity from civil liability for damages for injury, death, or loss to person or property as specified in section 9.86 of the Revised Code, and is entitled to indemnification and representation as an officer or employee of this state to the extent described in and in accordance with sections 109.361 to 109.366 of the Revised Code.

(1998 H 599, eff. 6–1–98)

DRIVER'S LICENSE EXAMINATION

5503.21 Driver's license examination section

There is hereby created in the department of public safety, division of state highway patrol, a driver's license examination section to be administered by the superintendent of the state highway patrol.

The superintendent, with the approval of the director of public safety, may appoint necessary driver's license examiners and clerical personnel necessary to carry out the duties assigned under this section. The examiners shall be citizens of the United

States and residents of the state and shall have such additional qualifications as the superintendent, with the approval of the director, prescribes.

The salaries and classifications of examiners and personnel shall be fixed in accordance with section 124.15 or 124.152 of the Revised Code.

(1992 S 98, eff. 11–12–92; 1986 H 831; 1984 H 58; 1977 H 1; 132 v H 380; 131 v H 78; 129 v 582; 127 v 575; 125 v 127; 1953 H 1; GC 1184)

5503.22 Duty of examiners

Driver's license examiners assigned to the driver's license examination section shall conduct all examinations for driver's licenses as required by sections 4507.01 to 4507.36 of the Revised Code, subject to the regulations issued by the registrar of motor vehicles.

(2002 S 123, eff. 1–1–04; 1953 H 1, eff. 10–1–53; GC 1184–1)

5503.23 Training schools for examiners

The superintendent of the state highway patrol, with the approval of the director of public safety, may conduct training schools for prospective driver's license examiners. The superintendent may establish rules governing the qualifications for admission to such schools and provide for competitive examinations to determine the fitness of such students for prospective examiners, not inconsistent with the rules of the director of administrative services.

(1992 S 98, eff. 11–12–92; 1977 H 1; 125 v 127; 1953 H 1; GC 1184–2)

TURNPIKES

5503.31 Authority on turnpike projects

The state highway patrol shall have the same authority as is conferred upon it by section 5503.02 of the Revised Code with respect to the enforcement of state laws on other roads and highways and on other state properties, to enforce on all turnpike projects the laws of the state and the bylaws, rules, and regulations of the Ohio turnpike commission. The patrol, the superintendent of the patrol, and all state highway patrol troopers shall have the same authority to make arrests on all turnpike projects for violations of state laws and of bylaws, rules, and regulations of the Ohio turnpike commission as is conferred upon them by section 5503.02 of the Revised Code to make arrests on, and in connection with offenses committed on, other roads and highways and on other state properties.

(1991 S 144, eff. 8–8–91; 126 v 1036)

5503.32 Turnpike policing contracts; reimbursement of costs incurred

The director of public safety may from time to time enter into contracts with the Ohio turnpike commission with respect to the policing of turnpike projects by the state highway patrol. The contracts shall provide for the reimbursement of the state by the commission for the costs incurred by the patrol in policing turnpike projects, including, but not limited to, the salaries of employees of the patrol assigned to the policing, the current costs of funding retirement pensions for the employees of the patrol and of providing workers' compensation for them, the cost of training state highway patrol troopers and radio operators assigned to turnpike projects, and the cost of equipment and supplies used by the patrol in such policing, and of housing for such troopers and radio operators, to the extent that the equipment, supplies, and housing are not directly furnished by the commission. Each contract may provide for the ascertainment of such costs, and shall be of any duration, not in excess of five years, and may contain any other terms, that the director and the commission may agree upon. The patrol shall not be obligated to furnish policing services on any turnpike project beyond the extent required by the contract. All payments pursuant to any contract in reimbursement of the costs of the policing shall be deposited in the state treasury to the credit of the turnpike policing fund, which is hereby created. All investment earnings of the fund shall be credited to the fund.

(1992 S 98, eff. 11–12–92; 1991 S 144; 1985 S 269, H 201; 1977 S 221; 1976 S 545; 126 v 1036)

5503.33 Patrol troopers and radio operators assigned

The superintendent of the state highway patrol shall assign any number of state highway patrol troopers and radio operators to each turnpike project that may be provided for in any contract or contracts made pursuant to section 5503.32 of the Revised Code. The number of troopers and radio operators from time to time regularly assigned to policing turnpike projects shall be in addition to, and an enlargement of, the authorized complement of the patrol as provided in any other law or laws; provided, however, that nothing in this section shall preclude the superintendent from temporarily increasing or decreasing the troopers or radio operators so assigned, as emergencies indicate a need for shifting assignments, to the extent provided by any contracts made pursuant to section 5503.32 of the Revised Code. All such troopers and radio operators shall have the same qualifications and be appointed and paid, and receive the same benefits and provisions, as all other troopers and radio operators.

(1991 S 144, eff. 8–8–91; 126 v 1036)

COMMERCIAL MOTOR VEHICLE SAFETY ENFORCEMENT

5503.34 Motor carrier enforcement unit

There is hereby created in the department of public safety, division of state highway patrol, a motor carrier enforcement unit, to be administered by the superintendent of the state highway patrol. This unit shall be responsible for enforcement of commercial motor vehicle transportation safety, economic, and hazardous materials requirements.

The superintendent, with the approval of the director of public safety, may appoint and maintain necessary staff to carry out the duties assigned under this section.

Employees of the motor carrier enforcement unit shall cooperate with the public utilities commission to enforce compliance with orders and rules of the commission, applicable laws under Chapters 4919., 4921., and 4923. of the Revised Code, and any other applicable laws or rules.

Uniformed employees of the motor carrier enforcement unit may stop commercial motor vehicles for the exclusive purpose of inspecting such vehicles to enforce compliance with orders and rules of the public utilities commission as required by division (F) of section 5502.01 of the Revised Code.

(2004 H 230, eff. 9–16–04; 1996 S 293, eff. 9–26–96 (See also Historical and Statutory Notes.); 1995 S 162, eff. 10–29–95)

Historical and Statutory Notes

Ed. Note: 1996 S 293 Effective Date—The Secretary of State assigned a general effective date of 9–26–96 for 1996 S 293, along with notice that, in accordance with RC 1.471, the General Assembly has not determined which sections go into immediate effect, and that it appears that certain sections provide for appropriations for current expenses, and are immediately effective in accordance with RC 1.471 and O Const Art II, § 1d.

CHAPTER 5577

LOAD LIMITS ON HIGHWAYS

PRELIMINARY PROVISIONS

5577.01 Definitions

(A) As used in sections 5577.01 to 5577.14 of the Revised Code:

(1) "Axle" means one or more load-carrying wheels mounted in a single transverse vertical plane.

(2) "Spacing between axles" means the distance between any two successive such planes.

(3) "Maximum axle load" means the gross weight of vehicle and load imposed by any axle upon the road surface.

(4) "Maximum wheel load" means the proportionate gross weight of vehicle and load imposed by any wheel upon the road surface.

(5) "Automobile transporter" means any vehicle combination designed and used expressly for the transport of assembled motor vehicles.

(6) "Stinger–steered automobile transporter" means any automobile transporter configured as a semitrailer combination in which the fifth wheel is located on a drop frame located behind and below the rearmost axle of the power unit.

(7) "Boat transporter" means any vehicle combination, including a straight truck towing a trailer typically using a ball and socket connection, designed and used specifically for the transport of boat hulls and boats, whether the hulls or boats are assembled or partially disassembled to facilitate transportation.

(8) "Stinger–steered boat transporter" means a boat transporter configured as a semitrailer combination in which the fifth wheel is located on a drop frame located behind and below the rearmost axle of the power unit.

(9) "Assembled" means, in regard to motor vehicles, capable of being driven.

(10) "B–train assembly" means any rigid frame extension that is attached to the rear frame of one semitrailer and provides a fifth wheel connection point for a second semitrailer.

(11) "Saddlemount vehicle transporter combination" means any combination of vehicles in which a straight truck or commercial tractor tows one or more straight trucks or commercial tractors, each connected by a saddle to the frame or fifth wheel of the straight truck or commercial tractor in front of it. Such a combination may include a fullmount, in which a smaller vehicle is mounted completely on the frame of either the first or last straight truck or commercial tractor in the saddlemount combination.

(B) "Vehicle," as used in section 5577.04 of the Revised Code, means any single vehicle when not in combination, or any combination of vehicles, as defined in section 4501.01 of the Revised Code.

(1993 H 154, eff. 6–30–93; 1989 H 258; 1988 H 357; 125 v 545; 1953 H 1; GC 7246; Source—GC 7248–1)

5577.02 Operation of vehicle on highways in excess of prescribed weights forbidden

No trackless trolley, traction engine, steam roller, or other vehicle, load, object, or structure, whether propelled by muscular or motor power, not including vehicles run upon stationery rails or tracks, fire engines, fire trucks, or other vehicles or apparatus belonging to or used by any municipal or volunteer fire department in the discharge of its functions, shall be operated or moved over or upon the improved public streets, highways, bridges, or culverts in this state, upon wheels, rollers, or otherwise, weighing in excess of the weights prescribed in sections 5577.01 to 5577.14, inclusive, of the Revised Code, including the weight of vehicle, object, structure, or contrivance and load, except upon special permission, granted as provided by section 4513.34 of the Revised Code.

(1953 H 1, eff. 10–1–53; GC 7246)

WEIGHT AND SIZE REQUIREMENTS

5577.03 Weight of load; width of tire

No person, firm, or corporation shall transport over the improved public streets, alleys, intercounty highways, state highways, bridges, or culverts, in any vehicle propelled by muscular, motor, or other power, any burden, including weight of vehicle and load, greater than the following:

(A) (1) In vehicles having metal tires three inches or less in width, a load of five hundred pounds for each inch of the total width of tire on all wheels;

(2) When the tires on such vehicles exceed three inches in width, an additional load of eight hundred pounds shall be permitted for each inch by which the total width of the tires on all wheels exceeds twelve inches.

(B) In vehicles having tires of rubber or other similar substances, for each inch of the total width of tires on all wheels, as follows:

(1) For tires three inches in width, a load of four hundred fifty pounds;

(2) For tires three and one-half inches in width, a load of four hundred fifty pounds;

(3) For tires four inches in width, a load of five hundred pounds;

(4) For tires five inches in width, a load of six hundred pounds;

(5) For tires six inches and over in width, a load of six hundred fifty pounds.

The total width of tires on all wheels shall be, in case of solid tires of rubber or other similar substance, the actual width in inches of all such tires between the flanges at the base of the tires, but in no event shall that portion of the tire coming in contact with the road surface be less than two thirds the width so measured between the flanges.

In the case of pneumatic tires, of rubber or other similar substance, the total width of tires on all wheels shall be the actual width of all such tires, measured at the widest portion thereof when inflated and not bearing a load.

In no event shall the load, including the proportionate weight of vehicle that can be concentrated on any wheel, exceed six hundred fifty pounds to each inch in width of the tread as defined in this section for solid tires, or each inch in the actual diameter of pneumatic tires measured when inflated and not bearing a load.

(1953 H 1, eff. 10–1–53; GC 7248)

5577.04 Vehicles with pneumatic tires; load limits

(A) The maximum wheel load of any one wheel of any vehicle, trackless trolley, load, object, or structure operated or moved upon improved public highways, streets, bridges, or culverts shall not exceed six hundred fifty pounds per inch width of pneumatic tire, measured as prescribed by section 5577.03 of the Revised Code.

(B) The weight of vehicle and load imposed upon a road surface that is part of the interstate system by vehicles with pneumatic tires shall not exceed any of the following weight limitations:

(1) On any one axle, twenty thousand pounds;

(2) On any tandem axle, thirty-four thousand pounds;

(3) On any two or more consecutive axles, the maximum weight as determined by application of the formula provided in division (C) of this section.

(C) For purposes of division (B)(3) of this section, the maximum gross weight on any two or more consecutive axles shall be determined by application of the following formula:

W = 500((LN/N–1) + 12N +36).

In this formula, W equals the overall gross weight on any group of two or more consecutive axles to the nearest five hundred pounds, L equals the distance in rounded whole feet between the extreme of any group of two or more consecutive axles, and N equals the number of axles in the group under consideration. However, two consecutive sets of tandem axles may carry a gross load of thirty-four thousand pounds each, provided the overall distance between the first and last axles of such consecutive sets of tandem axles is thirty-six feet or more.

(D) Except as provided in division (I) of this section, the weight of vehicle and load imposed upon a road surface that is not part of the interstate system by vehicles with pneumatic tires shall not exceed any of the following weight limitations:

(1) On any one axle, twenty thousand pounds;

(2) On any two successive axles:

(a) Spaced four feet or less apart, and weighed simultaneously, twenty-four thousand pounds;

(b) Spaced more than four feet apart, and weighed simultaneously, thirty-four thousand pounds, plus one thousand pounds per foot or fraction thereof, over four feet, not to exceed forty thousand pounds.

(3) On any three successive load-bearing axles designed to equalize the load between such axles and spaced so that each such axle of the three-axle group is more than four feet from the next axle in the three-axle group and so that the spacing between the first axle and the third axle of the three-axle group is no more than nine feet, and with such load-bearing three-axle group weighed simultaneously as a unit:

(a) Forty–eight thousand pounds, with the total weight of vehicle and load not exceeding thirty-eight thousand pounds plus an additional nine hundred pounds for each foot of spacing between the front axle and the rearmost axle of the vehicle;

(b) As an alternative to division (D)(3)(a) of this section, forty-two thousand five hundred pounds, if part of a six-axle vehicle combination with at least twenty feet of spacing between the front axle and rearmost axle, with the total weight of vehicle and load not exceeding fifty-four thousand pounds plus an additional six hundred pounds for each foot of spacing between the front axle and the rearmost axle of the vehicle.

(4) The total weight of vehicle and load utilizing any combination of axles, other than as provided for three-axle groups in division (D) of this section, shall not exceed thirty-eight thousand pounds plus an additional nine hundred pounds for each foot of spacing between the front axle and rearmost axle of the vehicle.

(E) Notwithstanding divisions (B) and (D) of this section, the maximum overall gross weight of vehicle and load imposed upon the road surface shall not exceed eighty thousand pounds.

(F) Notwithstanding any other provision of law, when a vehicle is towing another vehicle, such drawbar or other connection shall be of a length such as will limit the spacing between nearest axles of the respective vehicles to a distance not in excess of twelve feet and six inches.

(G) As used in division (B) of this section, "tandem axle" means two or more consecutive axles whose centers may be included between parallel transverse vertical planes spaced more than forty inches but not more than ninety-six inches apart, extending across the full width of the vehicle.

(H) This section does not apply to passenger bus type vehicles operated by a regional transit authority pursuant to sections 306.30 to 306.54 of the Revised Code.

(I) Either division (B) or (D) of this section applies to the weight of a vehicle and its load imposed upon any road surface that is not a part of the interstate system by vehicles with pneumatic tires. As between divisions (B) and (D) of this section, only the division that yields the highest total gross vehicle weight limit shall be applied to any such vehicle. Once that division is determined, only the limits contained in the subdivisions of that division shall apply to that vehicle.

(2001 H 73, eff. 6–29–01; 1994 S 96, eff. 5–10–94; 1993 H 154, eff. 6–30–93; 1991 S 223; 1980 S 272; 1978 S 421; 1975 H 624; 132 v H 679; 131 v S 171; 128 v 292; 1953 H 1; GC 7248–1)

5577.041 Maximum axle load, wheel load, gross weights and towing connection length for solid rubber tires

No vehicle, trackless trolley, load, object, or structure having a maximum axle load greater than sixteen thousand pounds when such vehicle is equipped with solid rubber tires shall be operated or moved upon the improved public highways, streets, bridges, or culverts. The maximum wheel load of any one wheel of any such vehicle shall not exceed six hundred fifty pounds per inch width of tire, measured as prescribed by section 5577.03 of the Revised Code, nor shall any solid tire of rubber or other resilient material, on any wheel of any such vehicle, be less than one inch thick when measured from the top of the flanges of the tire channel.

The weight of vehicle and load imposed upon the road surface by any two successive axles, spaced four feet or less apart, shall not exceed nineteen thousand pounds for solid tires; or by any two successive axles spaced more than four feet but less than eight feet apart shall not exceed twenty-four thousand pounds for solid tires; or by any two successive axles, spaced eight feet or more apart, shall not exceed twenty-eight thousand pounds for solid tires; nor shall the total weight of vehicle and load exceed, for solid rubber tires, twenty-eight thousand pounds plus an additional six hundred pounds for each foot or fraction thereof of spacing between the front axle and the rearmost axle of the vehicle; nor shall the weight of vehicle and load imposed upon the road surface by any vehicle equipped with solid rubber tires, exceed eighty per cent of the permissible weight of vehicle and load as provided for pneumatic tires.

Notwithstanding any other provision of law, when a vehicle is towing another vehicle, such drawbar or other connection shall be of a length such as will limit the spacing between nearest axles of the respective vehicles to a distance not in excess of twelve feet and six inches. If the provisions of this section are held to exceed the weight limitations or other provisions set forth in the "Federal-Aid Highway Act of 1958," 72 Stat. 902, 23 U.S.C. 127, this section shall become null and void to the extent of such inconsistency.

(132 v H 679, eff. 11–21–67)

5577.042 Exceptions for coal trucks, farm trucks, farm machinery, log trucks, and solid waste haul vehicles

(A) As used in this section:

(1) "Farm machinery" has the same meaning as in section 4501.01 of the Revised Code.

(2) "Farm commodities" includes livestock, bulk milk, corn, soybeans, tobacco, and wheat.

(3) "Farm truck" means a truck used in the transportation from a farm of farm commodities when the truck is operated in accordance with this section.

(4) "Log truck" means a truck used in the transportation of timber from the site of its cutting when the truck is operated in accordance with this section.

(5) "Coal truck" means a truck transporting coal from the site where it is mined when the truck is operated in accordance with this section.

(6) "Solid waste" has the same meaning as in section 3734.01 of the Revised Code.

(7) "Solid waste haul vehicle" means a vehicle hauling solid waste for which a bill of lading has not been issued.

(B) Notwithstanding sections 5577.02 and 5577.04 of the Revised Code, a coal truck transporting coal, a farm truck or farm machinery transporting farm commodities, a log truck transporting timber, or a solid waste haul vehicle hauling solid waste, from the place of production to the first point of delivery where the commodities are weighed and title to the commodities, coal, or timber is transferred, or, in the case of solid waste, from the place of production to the first point of delivery where the solid waste is disposed of or title to the solid waste is transferred, may exceed by no more than seven and one-half per cent the weight provisions of sections 5577.01 to 5577.09 of the Revised Code and no penalty prescribed in section 5577.99 of the Revised Code shall be imposed. If a coal truck so transporting coal, a farm truck or farm machinery so transporting farm commodities, a timber truck so transporting timber, or a solid waste haul vehicle hauling solid waste, exceeds by more than seven and one-half per cent the weight provisions of those sections, both of the following apply without regard to the seven and one-half per cent allowance provided by this division:

(1) The applicable penalty prescribed in section 5577.99 of the Revised Code;

(2) The civil liability imposed by section 5577.12 of the Revised Code.

(C)(1) Division (B) of this section does not apply to the operation of a farm truck, log truck, or farm machinery transporting farm commodities during the months of February and March.

(2) Regardless of when the operation occurs, division (B) of this section does not apply to the operation of a coal truck, a farm truck, a log truck, a solid waste haul vehicle, or farm machinery transporting farm commodities on either of the following:

(a) A highway that is part of the Interstate system;

(b) A highway, road, or bridge that is subject to reduced maximum weights under section 4513.33, 5577.07, 5577.071, 5577.08, 5577.09, or 5591.42 of the Revised Code.

(2004 H 230, eff. 9–16–04; 2003 H 87, eff. 6–30–03; 1998 H 425, eff. 7–29–98)

5577.05 Maximum width, height, and length

(A) No vehicle shall be operated upon the public highways, streets, bridges, and culverts within the state, whose dimensions exceed those specified in this section.

(B) No such vehicle shall have a width in excess of:

(1) One hundred four inches for passenger bus type vehicles operated exclusively within municipal corporations;

(2) One hundred two inches, excluding such safety devices as are required by law, for passenger bus type vehicles operated over freeways, and such other state roads with minimum pavement widths of twenty-two feet, except those roads or portions thereof over which operation of one hundred two-inch buses is prohibited by order of the director of transportation;

(3) One hundred thirty-two inches for traction engines;

(4) One hundred two inches for recreational vehicles, excluding safety devices and retracted awnings and other appurtenances of six inches or less in width and except that the director may prohibit the operation of one hundred two inch recreational vehicles on designated state highways or portions of highways;

(5) One hundred two inches, including load, for all other vehicles, except that the director may prohibit the operation of

one hundred two-inch vehicles on such state highways or portions thereof as the director designates.

(C) No such vehicle shall have a length in excess of:

(1) Sixty-six feet for passenger bus type vehicles and articulated passenger bus type vehicles operated by a regional transit authority pursuant to sections 306.30 to 306.54 of the Revised Code;

(2) Forty-five feet for all other passenger bus type vehicles;

(3) Fifty–three feet for any semitrailer when operated in a commercial tractor-semitrailer combination, with or without load, except that the director may prohibit the operation of any such commercial tractor-semitrailer combination on such state highways or portions thereof as the director designates.

(4) Twenty–eight and one-half feet for any semitrailer or trailer when operated in a commercial tractor-semitrailer-trailer or commercial tractor-semitrailer-semitrailer combination, except that the director may prohibit the operation of any such commercial tractor-semitrailer-trailer or commercial tractor-semitrailer-semitrailer combination on such state highways or portions thereof as the director designates;

(5) Seventy–five feet for drive-away saddlemount vehicle transporter combinations and drive-away saddlemount with fullmount vehicle transporter combinations, not to exceed three saddle-mounted vehicles, but which may include one fullmount.

(6) Sixty–five feet for any other combination of vehicles coupled together, with or without load, except as provided in divisions (C)(3) and (4), and in division (E) of this section;

(7) Forty–five feet for recreational vehicles;

(8) Forty feet for all other vehicles except trailers and semitrailers, with or without load.

(D) No such vehicle shall have a height in excess of thirteen feet six inches, with or without load.

(E) An automobile transporter or boat transporter shall be allowed a length of sixty-five feet and a stinger-steered automobile transporter or stinger-steered boat transporter shall be allowed a length of seventy-five feet, except that the load thereon may extend no more than four feet beyond the rear of such vehicles and may extend no more than three feet beyond the front of such vehicles, and except further that the director may prohibit the operation of a stinger-steered automobile transporter, stinger-steered boat transporter, or a B-train assembly on any state highway or portion thereof that the director designates.

(F) The widths prescribed in division (B) of this section shall not include side mirrors, turn signal lamps, marker lamps, handholds for cab entry and egress, flexible fender extensions, mud flaps, splash and spray suppressant devices, and load-induced tire bulge.

The width prescribed in division (B)(5) of this section shall not include automatic covering devices, tarp and tarp hardware, and tiedown assemblies, provided these safety devices do not extend more than three inches from each side of the vehicle.

The lengths prescribed in divisions (C)(2) to (7) of this section shall not include safety devices, bumpers attached to the front or rear of such bus or combination, B-train assembly used between the first and second semitrailer of a commercial tractor-semitrailer-semitrailer combination, energy conservation devices as provided in any regulations adopted by the secretary of the United States department of transportation, or any noncargo-carrying refrigeration equipment attached to the front of trailers and semitrailers. In special cases, vehicles whose dimensions exceed those prescribed by this section may operate in accordance with rules adopted by the director.

(G) This section does not apply to fire engines, fire trucks, or other vehicles or apparatus belonging to any municipal corporation or to the volunteer fire department of any municipal corporation or used by such department in the discharge of its functions. This section does not apply to vehicles and pole trailers used in the transportation of wooden and metal poles, nor to the transportation of pipes or well-drilling equipment, nor to farm machinery and equipment. The owner or operator of any vehicle, machinery, or equipment not specifically enumerated in this section but the dimensions of which exceed the dimensions provided by this section, when operating the same on the highways and streets of this state, shall comply with the rules of the director governing such movement, which the director may adopt. Sections 119.01 to 119.13 of the Revised Code apply to any rules the director adopts under this section, or the amendment or rescission thereof, and any person adversely affected shall have the same right of appeal as provided in those sections.

This section does not require the state, a municipal corporation, county, township, or any railroad or other private corporation to provide sufficient vertical clearance to permit the operation of such vehicle, or to make any changes in or about existing structures now crossing streets, roads, and other public thoroughfares in this state.

(H) As used in this section, "recreational vehicle" has the same meaning as in section 4501.01 of the Revised Code.

(2004 H 230, eff. 9–16–04; 2000 H 600, eff. 9–1–00; 1996 H 572, eff. 9–17–96; 1993 H 154, eff. 6–30–93; 1989 H 258; 1988 H 357; 1985 H 167; 1984 H 281; 1983 H 448; 1982 S 436; 1979 S 22; 1977 H 1, S 207; 1975 H 624; 1973 H 200; 132 v S 112; 131 v H 587; 130 v H 523; 127 v 735; 126 v 797; 1953 H 1; GC 7248–2)

5577.06 Prohibition against violation

No person shall violate any rule or regulation promulgated by the director of transportation in accordance with section 5577.05 of the Revised Code.

(1973 H 200, eff. 9–28–73; 1953 H 1; Source—GC 7248–2)

5577.07 Reduction of weight and speed during times of thaws and moisture

When thaws or excessive moisture render the improved highways of this state or any sections of them insufficient to bear the traffic thereon, or when such highways would be damaged or destroyed by heavy traffic during the period of thawing or excessive moisture, the maximum weight of vehicle and load, or the maximum speed, or both, for motor vehicles, as prescribed by law shall be reduced in the following manner:

(A) On state highways, the director of transportation shall prescribe such reduction which shall not be more than twenty-five per cent;

(B) On improved highways and all other roads in the county, other than state highways, the board of county commissioners shall prescribe such reduction as the condition of the road or highway justifies, but in no case shall the reduction be more than fifty per cent.

The schedule of the reduction of maximum weights and speeds shall be filed, for the information of the public, in the office of the board of each county in which the schedule is operative and in the office of the director. The director or board, at least one day before such reduction becomes effective, shall cause to be placed and retained on such highways, at both ends and at the points of intersections by principal roads, during the period of such reduced limitation of weight, speed, or both, signs, of substantial construction, which will conspicuously indicate the limitations of weight and speed, which are allowed on the highways and the date on which such limitations shall go into effect. No person shall operate upon any such highway, a motor vehicle whose maximum weight or speed is in excess of the limitations prescribed. The expense of the purchase and erection of signs, provided for in this section, shall be paid from funds for the maintenance and repair of roads.

(1973 H 200, eff. 9–28–73; 1953 H 1; GC 7250)

5577.071 Reduced load limits and speeds on county bridges

(A) When deterioration renders any bridge or section of a bridge in a county insufficient to bear the traffic thereon, or when the bridge or section of a bridge would be damaged or destroyed by heavy traffic, the board of county commissioners may reduce the maximum weight of vehicle and load, or the maximum speed, or both, for motor vehicles, as prescribed by law, and prescribe whatever reduction the condition of the bridge or section of the bridge justifies. This section does not apply to bridges on state highways.

(B) A schedule of any reductions made pursuant to division (A) of this section shall be filed, for the information of the public, in the office of the board of county commissioners in each county in which the schedule is operative. A board of county commissioners that makes a reduction pursuant to division (A) of this section shall, at least one day before a reduction becomes effective, cause to be placed and retained on any bridge on which a reduction is made, at both ends of the bridge, during the period of a reduced limitation of weight, speed, or both, signs of substantial construction conspicuously indicating the limitations of weight or speed or both which are permitted on the bridge and the date on which these limitations go into effect. No person shall operate upon any such bridge a motor vehicle whose maximum weight or speed is in excess of the limitations prescribed. The cost of purchasing and erecting the signs provided for in this division shall be paid from any fund for the maintenance and repair of bridges and culverts.

(C) Except as otherwise provided in this division, no reduction shall be made pursuant to division (A) of this section on a joint bridge as provided in section 5591.25 of the Revised Code unless the board of county commissioners of every county sharing the joint bridge agrees to the reduction, the amount of the reduction, and how the cost of purchasing and erecting signs indicating the limitations of weight and speed is to be borne. A board of county commissioners may make a reduction pursuant to division (A) of this section on a section of a joint bridge, without the agreement any other county sharing the bridge, if the section of the bridge on which the reduction is to be made is located solely in that county.

(1988 H 409, eff. 5–31–88)

GENERAL PROVISIONS

5577.08 Classification of roads by board of county commissioners

The board of county commissioners may classify the county and township roads and bridges and all other roads and bridges within their respective counties, except state highways and bridges on state highways, with reference to the maximum weights and speeds permitted on such roads and bridges.

The classifications made by the board under this section shall not apply to vehicles of a weight of five tons or less for vehicle and load.

In making the classifications, the board shall take into consideration the nature of the roadbed, construction, and any other factors which are material in the proper classification of such roads and bridges.

The board shall make rules governing the weight of vehicle and load and the speed permitted on the several classes of roads and bridges.

(1988 H 409, eff. 5–31–88; 1953 H 1; GC 7249–2)

5577.09 Rules

All rules as provided by section 5577.08 of the Revised Code shall be made by the board of county commissioners, at regular meetings, by a majority vote. Such rules shall be kept on file in the office of the board and open for inspection by the public.

At least two days before such rules become effective the board shall cause to be placed and retained on county and township highways classified under section 5577.08 of the Revised Code or sections thereof, and on any bridge classified under section 5577.08 of the Revised Code, at both ends and at any points of intersection, signs, of substantial construction, which will conspicuously indicate the limitations of weight of vehicle and load or speed which will be allowed on such highways or bridges.

It shall be unlawful to operate upon such highway or bridge a vehicle whose maximum weight or speed is in excess of the limitations prescribed. The expense of the purchase and erection of signs provided for in this section shall be paid from the county funds for the maintenance and repair of highways, bridges, and culverts.

(1988 H 409, eff. 5–31–88; 1953 H 1; GC 7249–3)

5577.10 Statement of gross vehicle weight

No person shall issue or aid in issuing any bill of lading or other document of like nature in lieu thereof, which bill or document is to accompany a shipment of goods or property by truck, trailer, semitrailer, commercial tractor, or any other commercial vehicle used for the transportation of property, the gross weight of which, with load, exceeds three tons, with intent to defraud by misrepresenting thereon the weight of such goods or property to be so transported.

Any driver or operator of a commercial car, trailer, or semitrailer may obtain from any person, firm, partnership, corporation, or association, including the owner, lessee, or operator of such commercial car, trailer, or semitrailer, owning and operating sealed scales in this state, a written "statement of gross vehicle weight" showing the gross weight of the vehicle including the cargo on the vehicle, the name and address of the person issuing the statement, and the date and place where the vehicle and its cargo were weighed. The driver or operator of the commercial car, trailer, or semitrailer shall retain such statement of gross vehicle weight on his person, and any law enforcement officer of this state may request that such driver or operator exhibit it to him. If, upon examining the statement of gross vehicle weight, the law enforcement officer has reason to believe that the information contained therein is correct in every respect, he shall indorse it with his name and the date and place where it was exhibited to him. The law enforcement officer may then permit such driver or operator to proceed without weighing by a law enforcement officer of this state. No person shall willfully issue a written statement of gross vehicle weight and knowingly give any false information in such statement.

(1953 H 1, eff. 10–1–53; GC 7250–2)

5577.11 Protectors or flaps

No person shall drive or operate, or cause to be driven or operated, any commercial car, trailer, or semitrailer, used for the transportation of goods or property, the gross weight of which, with load, exceeds three tons, upon the public highways, streets, bridges, and culverts within this state, unless such vehicle is equipped with suitable metal protectors or substantial flexible flaps on the rearmost wheels of such vehicle or combination of vehicles to prevent, as far as practicable, the wheels from throwing dirt, water, or other materials on the windshields of following vehicles. Such protectors or flaps shall have a ground clearance of not more than one third of the distance from the center of the rearmost axle to the center of the flaps under any conditions of loading of the vehicle, and they shall be at least as wide as the tires they are protecting. If the vehicle is so designed and constructed that such requirements are accomplished by means of fenders, body construction, or other means of enclosure, then no such protectors or flaps are required. Rear wheels not covered at the top by fenders, bodies, or other parts of the vehicle shall be covered at the top by protective means extending at least to the center line of the rearmost axle.

(2000 H 600, eff. 9–1–00; 1953 H 1, eff. 10–1–53; GC 7250–3)

ENFORCEMENT

5577.12 Liability for damages; prosecution; application of moneys

Any person violating any law relating to or regulating the use of the improved public roads shall be liable for all damage resulting to any such street, highway, bridge, or culvert by reason of such violation. In case of any injury to such a street, highway, bridge, or culvert, such damages shall be collected by civil action, brought in the name of the state, on the relation of the director of transportation with respect to highways under his jurisdiction, and the attorney general or prosecuting attorney of any county shall institute such action, when requested by the director and prosecute it to final judgment. In case of any injury to an improved public road, bridge, or culvert of a county, by reason of the violations of any of the rules or regulations made by the board of county commissioners, the damages shall be recovered by a civil action prosecuted by the board; in case of an injury to an improved public street, highway, bridge, or culvert of a municipal corporation, it shall be the duty of the proper authorities of such municipal corporation to institute an action for the recovery of such damages; and in the case of an injury to an improved public street, road, bridge, or culvert of a township, the damages shall be recovered by a civil action prosecuted by the board of township trustees. All damages collected under this section shall be paid into the treasury of the state or proper political subdivision, and credited to any fund for the repair of streets, highways, roads, bridges, or culverts.

(1973 H 200, eff. 9–28–73; 125 v 311; 1953 H 1; GC 7251)

5577.13 Enforcement by deputies

In those counties having forty miles or more of improved intercounty or state highways, the sheriff of each such county shall, and in all other counties may, detail one or more deputies for the work of enforcing sections 5577.01 to 5577.14, inclusive, of the Revised Code. The board of county commissioners shall appropriate such amount of money annually, from the road fund of the county, as is necessary to equip and compensate such deputy. The patrolmen of the county highways may be deputized by the sheriffs of the counties in which they are employed, as deputy sheriffs, but shall receive no extra compensation.

(1953 H 1, eff. 10–1–53; GC 7251–1)

5577.14 Notice of arrest

Whenever the driver or operator of any truck, trailer, semitrailer, commercial tractor, or any other commercial vehicle used for the transportation of goods or property, the gross weight of which, with load, exceeds three tons, has been arrested for a violation of any provision of sections 4511.01 to 4511.76, inclusive, and 4513.01 to 4513.40, inclusive, or sections 5577.01 to 5577.09, inclusive, of the Revised Code, the officer making such arrest shall immediately notify, in writing, the person, firm, association, or corporation holding the certificate of public convenience and necessity or permit under which such vehicle is being driven or operated, and in whose name the vehicle is registered with and licensed by the bureau of motor vehicles, of the fact of such arrest. Such notification shall describe the vehicle involved, the name of the driver or operator thereof, and the time, place, and nature of the offense committed. Copies of such notification shall be immediately transmitted by the arresting officer to the public utilities commission and to the superintendent of the state highway patrol.

(129 v 582, eff. 1–10–61; 1953 H 1; GC 7250–4)

5577.15 Exception for initial towing or removal of certain vehicles from site of emergency

(A) The size and weight provisions of this chapter do not apply to a person who is engaged in the initial towing or removal of a wrecked or disabled motor vehicle from the site of an emergency on a public highway where the vehicle became wrecked or disabled to the nearest site where the vehicle can be brought into conformance with the requirements of this chapter or to the nearest qualified repair facility.

(B) Any subsequent towing of a wrecked or disabled vehicle shall comply with the size and weight provisions of this chapter.

(C) No court shall impose any penalty prescribed in section 5577.99 of the Revised Code or the civil liability established in section 5577.12 of the Revised Code upon a person towing or removing a vehicle in the manner described in division (A) of this section.

(2004 H 230, eff. 9–16–04)

PENALTIES

5577.99 Penalties

(A) Whoever violates the weight provisions of sections 5577.01 to 5577.07 or the weight provisions in regard to highways under section 5577.04[1] of the Revised Code shall be fined eighty dollars for the first two thousand pounds, or fraction thereof, of overload; for overloads in excess of two thousand pounds, but not in excess of five thousand pounds, such person shall be fined one hundred dollars, and in addition thereto one dollar per one hundred pounds of overload; for overloads in excess of five thousand pounds, but not in excess of ten thousand pounds, such person shall be fined one hundred thirty dollars and in addition thereto two dollars per one hundred pounds of overload, or imprisoned not more than thirty days, or both. For all overloads in excess of ten thousand pounds such person shall be fined one hundred sixty dollars, and in addition thereto three dollars per one hundred pounds of overload, or imprisoned not more than thirty days, or both. Whoever violates the weight provisions of vehicle and load relating to gross load limits shall be fined not less than one hundred dollars. No penalty prescribed in this division shall be imposed on any vehicle combination if the overload on any axle does not exceed one thousand pounds, and if the immediately preceding or following axle, excepting the front axle of the vehicle combination, is underloaded by the same or a greater amount. For purposes of this division, two axles on one vehicle less than eight feet apart, shall be considered as one axle.

(B) Whoever violates the weight provisions of section 5571.071[2] or 5577.08 or the weight provisions in regard to bridges under section 5577.09, and whoever exceeds the carrying capacity specified under section 5591.42 of the Revised Code, shall be fined eighty dollars for the first two thousand pounds, or fraction thereof, of overload; for overloads in excess of two thousand pounds, but not in excess of five thousand pounds, the person shall be fined one hundred dollars, and in addition thereto one dollar per one hundred pounds of overload; for overloads in excess of five thousand pounds, but not in excess of ten thousand pounds, the person shall be fined one hundred thirty dollars, and in addition thereto two dollars per one hundred pounds of overload, or imprisoned not more than thirty days, or both. For all overloads in excess of ten thousand pounds, the person shall be fined one hundred sixty dollars, and in addition thereto three dollars per one hundred pounds of overload, or imprisoned not more than thirty days, or both.

Notwithstanding any other provision of the Revised Code that specifies a procedure for the distribution of fines, all fines collected pursuant to this section shall be paid into the treasury of the county and credited to any fund for the maintenance and repair of roads, highways, bridges, or culverts.

(C) Whoever violates any other provision of sections 5577.01 to 5577.09 of the Revised Code is guilty of a minor misdemeanor on a first offense; on a second or subsequent offense, such person is guilty of a misdemeanor of the fourth degree.

(D) Whoever violates section 5577.10 of the Revised Code shall be fined not more than five thousand dollars or imprisoned for not less than thirty days nor more than six months, or both.

(E) Whoever violates section 5577.11 of the Revised Code shall be fined not more than twenty-five dollars.

(2004 H 230, eff. 9–16–04; 1988 H 409, eff. 5–31–88; 126 v 795; 125 v 268; 1953 H 1; GC 7250–1)

1 Prior and current versions differ; although no amendment to this language was indicated in 1988 H 409, "5577.04" appeared as "5577.09" in 126 v 795.

2 So in original; should this read: "5577.071"?

CHAPTER 5589

OFFENSES RELATING TO HIGHWAYS

GENERAL OFFENSES

5589.01 Obstructing public grounds, highway, street, or alley

No person shall obstruct or encumber by fences, buildings, structures, or otherwise, a public ground, highway, street, or alley of a municipal corporation.

(1953 H 1, eff. 10–1–53; GC 13421)

5589.02 Altering or injuring marker or monument

No person shall alter, deface, injure, or destroy any marker or monument placed along, upon, or near a public highway, by the proper authorities, to mark the boundaries thereof, or for any other purpose.

(1953 H 1, eff. 10–1–53; GC 13421–4)

5589.03 Refusal or neglect of officials to perform duty

No county engineer, township trustee, or township highway superintendent shall willfully neglect, fail, or refuse to perform the duties of his office. Conviction for such neglect, failure, or refusal shall operate as a removal from office.

(1953 H 1, eff. 10–1–53; GC 13421–5)

5589.05 Interfering with drawbridge on Muskingum improvement

No person, except a commissioner, engineer, superintendent, lock tender, bridge tender, or collector and without express direction or permission from one of them, shall open or interfere with a drawbridge on the Muskingum improvement.

(1953 H 1, eff. 10–1–53; GC 12640)

5589.06 Obstructing ditch, drain, or watercourse; duty of superintendent

No person shall wrongfully obstruct any ditch, drain, or watercourse along, upon, or across a public highway, or divert any water from adjacent lands to or upon a public highway. Whenever the township highway superintendent learns of any obstruction of any ditch, drain, or watercourse along, upon, or across a public highway, or diversion of any water from adjacent lands to or upon a public highway, he shall notify the board of township trustees, which shall cause written notice thereof to be personally served upon the person, firm, or corporation, or upon any agent in charge of the property of the person, firm, or corporation causing such obstruction or diversion. Notice may be served by a constable of the proper township or any person authorized and deputed therefor by the board of township trustees, and shall describe and locate said obstruction or diversion and direct its immediate removal. If the person, company, or corporation does not within five days from the receipt of written notice proceed to remove such obstruction and complete the removal within a reasonable time, the township highway superintendent, upon the order of the board of township trustees, shall remove the obstruction. The expense incurred shall be paid in the first instance out of any money levied, collected, and available for highway purposes and shall then be collected from the person, company, or corporation by civil action by the board of township trustees, and paid into the highway fund of the township.

(1953 H 1, eff. 10–1–53; GC 13421–7)

5589.07 Failure to make levy or furnish estimates

No person charged with the duty of making any levy or furnishing any estimates or budgets requesting any levy or allowance for the construction, improvement, maintenance, or repair of any public highway, bridge, or culvert shall fail to make such levy or allowance, or furnish such estimate, budget, or request.

(1953 H 1, eff. 10–1–53; GC 13421–8)

5589.08 Operating traction engines upon improved highways

No person shall drive over the improved highways of the state, or any political subdivision thereof, a traction engine or tractor with tires or wheels equipped with ice picks, spuds, spikes, chains, or other projections of any kind extending beyond the cleats, or no person shall tow or in any way pull another vehicle over the improved highways of the state, or any political subdivision thereof, which towed or pulled vehicle has tires or wheels equipped with ice picks, spuds, spikes, chains or other projections of any kind. "Traction engine" or "tractor," as used in this section, applies to all self-propelling engines equipped with metal-tired wheels operated or propelled by any form of engine, motor, or mechanical power.

No municipal corporation, county, or township shall adopt, enforce, or maintain any ordinance, rule, or regulation contrary to or inconsistent with this section, or require of any person any license tax upon or registration fee for any traction engine, tractor, or trailer, or any permit or license to operate. Operators of traction engines or tractors shall have the same rights upon the public streets and highways as the drivers of any other vehicles, unless some other safe and convenient way is provided, and no public road open to traffic shall be closed to traction engines or tractors.

(125 v 401, eff. 10–16–53; 1953 H 1; GC 13421–12)

5589.081 Studded tire defined; seasonal use permitted

(A) For purposes of this section, "studded tire" means any tire designed for use on a vehicle and equipped with metal studs or studs of wear-resisting material that project beyond the tread of the traction surface of the tire; and "motor vehicle," "street or highway," "public safety vehicle," and "school bus" have the same meaning as given those terms in section 4511.01 of the Revised Code.

(B) No person shall operate any motor vehicle, other than a public safety vehicle or school bus, that is equipped with studded tires on any street or highway in this state, except during the period extending from the first day of November of each year through the fifteenth day of April of the succeeding year.

(C) This section does not apply to the use of tire chains when there is snow or ice on the streets or highways where such chains are being used, or the immediate vicinity thereof.

(1975 S 40, eff. 3–12–75; 1973 H 398)

5589.09 Failure or neglect to drag road

No person, charged with the duty of causing any unimproved or gravel road or part thereof to be dragged, shall willfully fail, neglect, or refuse to cause the same to be done, in such manner and within the time fixed by the sections of the Revised Code applicable thereto, or by the proper authority.

(1953 H 1, eff. 10–1–53; GC 13421–13)

5589.10 Digging, excavating, piling earth, or building fence on highway

No person shall dig up, remove, excavate, or place any earth or mud upon any portion of any public highway or build a fence upon the same without authority to do so. Each day that such person continues to dig up, remove, or excavate any portion of the public highway constitutes a separate offense.

(1953 H 1, eff. 10–1–53; GC 13421–14)

5589.11 Failure or neglect to cut weeds, briers, or bushes

No person, charged with the duty of cutting, destroying, or removing any weeds, briers, or bushes upon or along a public highway shall willfully fail, neglect, or refuse to cut, destroy, or remove such weeds, briers, or bushes as required in sections 5579.04 and 5579.08 of the Revised Code or on the order of the proper officials.

(1984 S 108, eff. 7–4–84; 1953 H 1; GC 13421–15)

5589.12 Possession of tools belonging to state or county

No person shall, without being authorized, have in his control or possession any equipment, tools, implements, or other property belonging to the state, county, or township.

(1953 H 1, eff. 10–1–53; GC 13421–18)

5589.13 Fines credited to maintenance and repair fund

All fines collected for violations of sections 5589.02 to 5589.14, inclusive, of the Revised Code, shall be paid into the county treasury and placed to the credit of the fund for the maintenance and repair of the highways within such county.

(1953 H 1, eff. 10–1–53; GC 13421–20)

5589.14 Prosecution of offenses

The prosecuting attorney shall prosecute all offenders under sections 5589.02 to 5589.13, inclusive, of the Revised Code, upon application of any official or individual filing any affidavit before any magistrate of the county charging an offense under such sections. This section shall not prevent the prosecuting attorney or any other official from prosecuting offenders under such sections upon his own initiative.

(1953 H 1, eff. 10–1–53; GC 13421–22)

OFFENSES BY RAILROADS

5589.21 Obstruction of public roads by railroad companies

(A) No railroad company shall obstruct, or permit or cause to be obstructed a public street, road, or highway, by permitting a railroad car, locomotive, or other obstruction to remain upon or across it for longer than five minutes, to the hindrance or inconvenience of travelers or a person passing along or upon such street, road, or highway.

(B) At the end of each five minute period of obstruction of a public street, road, or highway, each railroad company shall cause such railroad car, locomotive, or other obstruction to be removed for sufficient time, not less than three minutes, to allow the passage of persons and vehicles waiting to cross.

(C) This section does not apply to obstruction of a public street, road, or highway by a continuously moving through train or caused by circumstances wholly beyond the control of the railroad company, but does apply to other obstructions, including without limitation those caused by stopped trains and trains engaged in switching, loading, or unloading operations.

(D) If a railroad car, locomotive, or other obstruction is obstructing a public street, road, or highway in violation of division (A) of this section and the violation occurs in the unincorporated area of one or more counties, or in one or more municipal corporations, the officers and employees of each affected county or municipal corporation may charge the railroad company with only one violation of the law arising from the same facts and circumstances and the same act.

(E) Upon the filing of an affidavit or complaint for violation of division (A) of this section, summons shall be issued to the railroad company pursuant to division (B) of section 2935.10 of the Revised Code, which summons shall be served on the regular ticket or freight agent of the company in the county where the offense occurred.

(2000 S 207, eff. 10–27–00; 1969 S 5, eff. 9–4–69; 1953 H 1; GC 7472)

5589.211 Obstruction of public roads by railroad companies; abandonment of locomotive

No railroad company shall obstruct, or permit or cause to be obstructed, a public street, road, or highway, by permitting any part of a train whose crew has abandoned the locomotive to remain across it for longer than five minutes to the hindrance or inconvenience of travelers or a person passing along or upon the street, road, or highway, unless the safety of the train crew requires them to abandon the locomotive.

Upon the filing of an affidavit or complaint for violation of this section, summons shall be issued to the railroad company pursuant to division (B) of section 2935.10 of the Revised Code, which summons shall be served on the regular ticket or freight agent of the company in the county where the offense occurred.

(2000 S 207, eff. 10–27–00)

5589.22 Damages

A corporation or person shall be liable for all damages arising to a person from an obstruction or injury to a road or highway as provided by section 5589.21 of the Revised Code, which damage shall be recovered by an action at the suit of the board of township trustees of the township in which the offense is committed, or of any person suing therefor before a judge of a county court or judge of a municipal court having jurisdiction where the offense is committed, or by indictment in the court of common pleas in the proper county. Each twenty-four hours the person or corporation, after being notified, permits such obstruction to remain, shall be an additional offense against such section.

(129 v 582, eff. 1–10–61; 1953 H 1; GC 7473)

5589.23 Company liable for fines against employees

A railroad company or other corporation, the servant, agent, or employee of which, in any manner, obstructs a public road or highway, shall pay all penalties which may be assessed against such servant, agent, or employee for obstructing it. The penalties may be enforced by execution issued against such corporation on the judgment rendered against the servant, agent, or employee.

(1953 H 1, eff. 10–1–53; GC 7475)

5589.24 Moneys collected

(A) All fines collected for a violation of division (A) of section 5589.21 or 5589.211 of the Revised Code shall be paid as follows:

(1) To the railroad grade crossing improvement fund of the county if the violation occurred in an unincorporated area of the county;

(2) To the railroad grade crossing improvement fund of the municipal corporation in which the violation occurred if the violation occurred in a municipal corporation.

(B) The board of county commissioners of each county and the legislative authority of each municipal corporation shall establish a railroad grade crossing improvement fund. The fund shall consist of fines paid to the county or municipal corporation under division (A) of this section and any other moneys allocated to the fund by the county or municipal corporation. Except as otherwise provided in this division, a county or municipal corporation shall use its railroad grade crossing improvement fund to pay any part of the cost assigned by the public utilities commission to the county or municipal corporation under section 4907.471 of the Revised Code. The county or municipal corporation also may use its railroad grade crossing improvement fund for other improvements to railroad grade crossings, including signs, signals, gates, or other protective devices, as the board of county commissioners or legislative authority of a municipal corporation determines to be appropriate.

If, during any fiscal year, the fines a county collects for violations of division (A) of section 5589.21 and section 5589.211 of the Revised Code equal three thousand dollars or less, during the subsequent fiscal year the county may use that amount of money in its railroad grade crossing improvement fund for any purpose that the board of county commissioners determines to be appropriate.

If, during any fiscal year, the fines a county collects for violations of division (A) of section 5589.21 and section 5589.211 of the Revised Code exceed three thousand dollars, during the subsequent two fiscal years the county shall use all the money in its railroad grade crossing improvement fund only for those purposes described in this division. In such a case, the amount of money the county collects for violations of division (A) of section 5589.21 and section 5589.211 of the Revised Code during the fiscal year immediately following the second of those two fiscal years shall determine the disposition under this division of the money the county collects during that fiscal year.

(2000 S 207, eff. 10–27–00; 1953 H 1, eff. 10–1–53; GC 7474)

MISCELLANEOUS PROVISIONS

5589.31 Construction of walk or ditch across highway

No person, firm, or corporation shall construct a walk or dig a ditch across a public highway outside any municipal corporation without the consent of the director of transportation in the case of an intercounty or a state highway, county engineer in the case of a county road, or board of township trustees in the case of a township road.

(1973 H 200, eff. 9–28–73; 1953 H 1; GC 7202)

5589.32 Erection of advertising signs resembling those required of railroad companies

No person, firm, or corporation shall erect, display, or maintain an advertising or other sign on, along, or near any public highway, in any county of this state, which resembles the highway crossing signs which steam and interurban railroads have erected, in compliance with section 4955.33 of the Revised Code, at the crossings of public roads and railroads.

The public utilities commission shall enforce this section, prosecute any violations thereof, and order the removal of any such prohibited sign.

The attorney general and the prosecuting attorney of any county shall carry into effect the orders of the commission made under this section and shall prosecute any violations of such orders.

Each day that any violation of this section continues constitutes a separate offense. The erection, display, or maintenance of each advertising or other sign referred to in this section, except as provided in section 4955.33 of the Revised Code, constitutes a separate offense.

(1953 H 1, eff. 10–1–53; GC 7204–1, 7204–2, 7204–3)

5589.33 Advertising on public highway

Except as provided in this section and in section 5515.04 of the Revised Code, no person shall place within the limits of the right-of-way or affix any sign, poster, or advertisement to any tree or utility pole within the right-of-way of any public highway outside of municipal corporations. No person, organization, corporation, or group shall place within the limits of the right-of-way any object as determined by the department of transportation to obscure sight distance.

Nothing in this section shall be construed to prohibit the erection and maintaining of notices of the existence and location of public utility facilities under or upon the highway and warnings against disturbing such facilities, or of notices that emergency or other public telephones are available for users of the highway at specified locations upon or near the highway.

(1973 H 200, eff. 9–28–73; 130 v H 1; 129 v 995)

5589.99 Penalties

(A) Whoever violates section 5589.01 of the Revised Code is guilty of a misdemeanor of the third degree.

(B) Whoever violates section 5589.02, 5589.03, 5589.05, 5589.06, 5589.08, 5589.081, 5589.09, 5589.11, 5589.12, 5589.32, or 5589.33 of the Revised Code is guilty of a minor misdemeanor.

(C) Whoever violates section 5589.07 or 5589.10 of the Revised Code is guilty of a misdemeanor of the fourth degree.

(D) Whoever violates division (A) of section 5589.21 of the Revised Code is guilty of a misdemeanor of the first degree and shall be fined one thousand dollars.

(E) Whoever violates section 5589.211 of the Revised Code is guilty of a misdemeanor of the first degree and shall be fined five thousand dollars.

(2000 S 207, eff. 10–27–00; 1995 S 2, eff. 7–1–96; 1973 H 398, eff. 1–1–74; 1969 S 5; 129 v 995; 1953 H 1)

CHAPTER 5743

CIGARETTE TAX

5743.45 Enforcement agents; powers

(A) As used in this section, "felony" has the same meaning as in section 109.511 of the Revised Code.

(B) For purposes of enforcing this chapter and Chapters 5728., 5735., 5739., 5741., and 5747. of the Revised Code and subject to division (C) of this section, the tax commissioner, by journal entry, may delegate any investigation powers of the commissioner to an employee of the department of taxation who has been certified by the Ohio peace officer training commission and who is engaged in the enforcement of those chapters. A separate journal entry shall be entered for each employee to whom that power is delegated. Each journal entry shall be a matter of public record and shall be maintained in an administrative portion of the journal as provided for in division (L) of section 5703.05 of the Revised Code. When that journal entry is completed, the employee to whom it pertains, while engaged within the scope of the employee's duties in enforcing the provisions of this chapter or Chapter 5728., 5735., 5739., 5741., or 5747. of the Revised Code, has the power of a police officer to carry concealed weapons, make arrests, and obtain warrants for violations of any provision in those chapters. The commissioner, at any time, may suspend or revoke the commissioner's delegation by journal entry. No employee of the department shall divulge any information acquired as a result of an investigation pursuant to this chapter or Chapter 5728., 5735., 5739., 5741., or 5747. of the Revised Code, except as may be required by the commissioner or a court.

(C)(1) The tax commissioner shall not delegate any investigation powers to an employee of the department of taxation pursuant to division (B) of this section on a permanent basis, on a temporary basis, for a probationary term, or on other than a permanent basis if the employee previously has been convicted of or has pleaded guilty to a felony.

(2)(a) The tax commissioner shall revoke the delegation of investigation powers to an employee to whom the delegation was made pursuant to division (B) of this section if that employee does either of the following:

(i) Pleads guilty to a felony;

(ii) Pleads guilty to a misdemeanor pursuant to a negotiated plea agreement as provided in division (D) of section 2929.43 of the Revised Code in which the employee agrees to surrender the certificate awarded to that employee under section 109.77 of the Revised Code.

(b) The tax commissioner shall suspend the delegation of investigation powers to an employee to whom the delegation was made pursuant to division (B) of this section if that employee is convicted, after trial, of a felony. If the employee files an appeal from that conviction and the conviction is upheld by the highest court to which the appeal is taken or if the employee does not file a timely appeal, the commissioner shall revoke the delegation of investigation powers to that employee. If the employee files an appeal that results in that employee's acquittal of the felony or conviction of a misdemeanor, or in the dismissal of the felony charge against that employee, the commissioner shall reinstate the delegation of investigation powers to that employee. The suspension, revocation, and reinstatement of the delegation of investigation powers to an employee under division (C)(2) of this section shall be made by journal entry pursuant to division (B) of this section. An employee to whom the delegation of investigation powers is reinstated under division (C)(2)(b) of this section shall not receive any back pay for the exercise of those investigation powers unless that employee's conviction of the felony was reversed on appeal, or the felony charge was dismissed, because the court found insufficient evidence to convict the employee of the felony.

(3) Division (C) of this section does not apply regarding an offense that was committed prior to January 1, 1997.

(4) The suspension or revocation of the delegation of investigation powers to an employee under division (C)(2) of this section shall be in accordance with Chapter 119. of the Revised Code.

(2003 H 95, eff. § 3.23, eff. 1–1–04; 2003 H 95, § 1, eff. 9–26–03; 2002 H 490, eff. 1–1–04; 1996 H 670, eff. 12–2–96; 1996 H 566, eff. 10–16–96; 1990 S 223, eff. 4–10–91; 1977 S 141)

CHAPTER 5907

OHIO VETERANS' HOME

5907.02 Board of trustees; terms; duties; superintendent; veterans' home policemen; annual report

The board of trustees of the Ohio veterans' home agency, which is hereby created, shall consist of seven members who shall govern the agency and have charge and custody of the agency's facilities. The members shall be the director of administrative services or that director's designee, the director of aging or that director's designee, and five members who shall be appointed by the governor with the advice and consent of the senate. All the members of the board appointed by the governor shall be veterans of wars in which the United States has participated, and not more than three of the members shall be of the same political party. The trustees shall serve without compensation, but they shall be allowed their actual expenses incurred in the discharge of their duties. Each year, the governor shall appoint one trustee. The term of office for each member of the board shall be for five years, commencing on the first day of July and ending on the thirtieth day of June. Each member shall hold office from the date of that member's appointment until the end of the term for which the member was appointed. Any member appointed to fill a vacancy occurring prior to the expiration of the term for which that member's predecessor was appointed shall hold office for the remainder of that term. Any member shall continue in office subsequent to the expiration date of that member's term until the member's successor takes office, or until a period of sixty days has elapsed, whichever occurs first. The board shall govern, conduct, and care for veterans' homes, the property of the homes, and the veterans residing in the home.

Four members of the board constitute a quorum, but any three may approve the payment of current expenses, salaries, and open contracts previously entered into by the board.

All supplies for the agency shall be purchased as provided in sections 125.04 to 125.15 of the Revised Code.

The board shall appoint a superintendent of the Ohio veterans' home agency upon any terms that are proper, and the superintendent, with the advice and consent of the board, shall employ aides, assistants, and employees, and perform other duties that may be assigned to the superintendent by the board or become necessary in the carrying out of the superintendent's duties. The superintendent shall be responsible directly to the board.

Subject to section 5907.021 of the Revised Code, the superintendent may appoint one or more employees at each veterans' home as veterans' home police officers authorized to act on the grounds of that home. The superintendent shall provide to those employees a copy of the rules that apply to their appointment. The rules shall specify whether or not the police officers may carry a firearm.

Subject to section 5907.021 of the Revised Code, the superintendent shall appoint a chief of police of the Ohio veterans' home agency, determine the number of officers and other personnel required by each veterans' home, and establish salary schedules and other conditions of employment for veterans' homes police officers. The chief of police shall serve at the pleasure of the superintendent and shall appoint officers and other personnel as the veterans' homes may require, subject to the rules and limits that the superintendent establishes regarding qualifications, salary ranges, and the number of personnel. The superintendent, with the approval of the board, may purchase or otherwise acquire any police apparatus, equipment, or materials, including a police communication system and vehicles, that the veterans' homes police officers may require. The superintendent may send one or more of the officers or employees nominated by the police chief to a school of instruction designed to provide additional training or skills related to their work assignment at their veterans' home. The superintendent may send those officers or employees to the Ohio peace officer training academy that the superintendent considers appropriate.

The board shall make an annual report to the governor as to all expenditures and as to the management of the Ohio veterans' home agency.

(2002 H 675, eff. 3–14–03; 1996 H 566, eff. 10–16–96; 1987 H 231, eff. 10–5–87; 1984 H 660; 1981 H 694; 1979 H 38; 1977 H 1; 1973 S 131; 129 v 582; 1953 H 1; GC 1905–1)

CHAPTER 6101

CONSERVANCY DISTRICTS

6101.75 Law enforcement; offenses affecting employment eligibility

(A) As used in this section, "felony" has the same meaning as in section 109.511 of the Revised Code.

(B) The board of directors of a conservancy district may police the works of the district and, in times of great emergency, may compel assistance in the protection of those works. The board may prevent persons, vehicles, or livestock from passing over the property or works of the district at any places or in any manner that would result in damage to the property or works or in the opinion of the board would endanger the property or works or the safety of persons lawfully on the property or works.

The employees that the board designates for that purpose have all the powers of police officers within and adjacent to the properties owned or controlled by the district. Before entering upon the exercise of those powers, each employee shall take an oath and give a bond to the state, in the amount that the board prescribes, for the proper exercise of those powers. The cost of the bond shall be borne by the district. This division is subject to division (C) of this section.

(C)(1) The board of directors shall not designate an employee as provided in division (B) of this section on a permanent basis, on a temporary basis, for a probationary term, or on other than a permanent basis if the employee previously has been convicted of or has pleaded guilty to a felony.

(2)(a) The board of directors shall terminate the employment of an employee designated as provided in division (B) of this section if that employee does either of the following:

(i) Pleads guilty to a felony;

(ii) Pleads guilty to a misdemeanor pursuant to a negotiated plea agreement as provided in division (D) of section 2929.43 of the Revised Code in which the employee agrees to surrender the certificate awarded to that employee under section 109.77 of the Revised Code.

(b) The board of directors shall suspend from employment an employee designated as provided in division (B) of this section if that employee is convicted, after trial, of a felony. If the employee files an appeal from that conviction and the conviction is upheld by the highest court to which the appeal is taken or if the employee does not file a timely appeal, the board shall terminate the employment of that employee. If the employee files an appeal that results in that employee's acquittal of the felony or conviction of a misdemeanor, or in the dismissal of the felony charge against that employee, the board shall reinstate that employee. An employee who is reinstated under division (C)(2)(b) of this section shall not receive any back pay unless that employee's conviction of the felony was reversed on appeal, or the felony charge was dismissed, because the court found insufficient evidence to convict the employee of the felony.

(3) Division (C) of this section does not apply regarding an offense that was committed prior to January 1, 1997.

(4) The suspension from employment, or the termination of the employment, of an employee under division (C)(2) of this section shall be in accordance with Chapter 119. of the Revised Code.

(2002 H 490, eff. 1–1–04; 1996 H 566, eff. 10–16–96; 128 v 967, eff. 10–12–59; 1953 H 1; GC 6828–65)

RULES OF CRIMINAL PROCEDURE

Publisher's Note: Until 1968, when the Modern Courts Amendment to the Ohio Constitution was adopted, Ohio court procedure was governed entirely by statute and caselaw. The Modern Courts Amendment required the Supreme Court of Ohio, subject to the approval of the General Assembly, to "prescribe rules governing practice and procedure in all courts of the state." Rules of practice and procedure are the Civil, Criminal, Appellate, and Juvenile Rules, Rules of the Court of Claims, and the Ohio Rules of Evidence. Pursuant to Ohio Constitution Article IV, Section 5(B), such rules "shall not abridge, enlarge, or modify any substantive right," and "all laws in conflict with such rules shall be of no further force or effect."

Crim R 1 Scope of rules: applicability; construction; exceptions

(A) Applicability

These rules prescribe the procedure to be followed in all courts of this state in the exercise of criminal jurisdiction, with the exceptions stated in division (C) of this rule.

(B) Purpose and construction

These rules are intended to provide for the just determination of every criminal proceeding. They shall be construed and applied to secure the fair, impartial, speedy, and sure administration of justice, simplicity in procedure, and the elimination of unjustifiable expense and delay.

(C) Exceptions

These rules, to the extent that specific procedure is provided by other rules of the Supreme Court or to the extent that they would by their nature be clearly inapplicable, shall not apply to procedure (1) upon appeal to review any judgment, order or ruling, (2) upon extradition and rendition of fugitives, (3) in cases covered by the Uniform Traffic Rules, (4) upon the application and enforcement of peace bonds, (5) in juvenile proceedings against a child as defined in Rule 2(D) of the Rules of Juvenile Procedure, (6) upon forfeiture of property for violation of a statute of this state, or (7) upon the collection of fines and penalties. Where any statute or rule provides for procedure by a general or specific reference to the statutes governing procedure in criminal actions, the procedure shall be in accordance with these rules.

(Adopted eff. 7–1–73; amended eff. 7–1–75, 7–1–96)

Crim R 2 Definitions

As used in these rules:

(A) "Felony" means an offense defined by law as a felony.

(B) "Misdemeanor" means an offense defined by law as a misdemeanor.

(C) "Serious offense" means any felony, and any misdemeanor for which the penalty prescribed by law includes confinement for more than six months.

(D) "Petty offense" means a misdemeanor other than serious offense.

(E) "Judge" means judge of the court of common pleas, juvenile court, municipal court, or county court, or the mayor or mayor's court magistrate of a municipal corporation having a mayor's court.

(F) "Magistrate" means any person appointed by a court pursuant to Crim. R. 19. "Magistrate" does not include an official included within the definition of magistrate contained in section 2931.01 of the Revised Code, or a mayor's court magistrate appointed pursuant to section 1905.05 of the Revised Code.

(G) "Prosecuting attorney" means the attorney general of this state, the prosecuting attorney of a county, the law director, city solicitor, or other officer who prosecutes a criminal case on behalf of the state or a city, village, township, or other political subdivision, and the assistant or assistants of any of them. As used in Crim. R. 6, "prosecuting attorney" means the attorney general of this state, the prosecuting attorney of a county, and the assistant or assistants of either of them.

(H) "State" means this state, a county, city, village, township, other political subdivision, or any other entity of this state that may prosecute a criminal action.

(I) "Clerk of court" means the duly elected or appointed clerk of any court of record or the deputy clerk, and the mayor or mayor's court magistrate of a municipal corporation having a mayor's court.

(J) "Law enforcement officer" means a sheriff, deputy sheriff, constable, municipal police officer, marshal, deputy marshal, or state highway patrolman, and also means any officer, agent, or employee of the state or of any of its agencies, instrumentalities, or political subdivisions, upon whom, by statute, the authority to arrest violators is conferred, when the officer, agent, or employee is acting within the limits of statutory authority. The definition of "law enforcement officer" contained in this rule shall not be construed to limit, modify, or expand any statutory definition, to the extent the statutory definition applies to matters not covered by the Rules of Criminal Procedure.

(Adopted eff. 7–1–73; amended eff. 7–1–76, 7–1–90)

Crim R 3 Complaint

The complaint is a written statement of the essential facts constituting the offense charged. It shall also state the numerical designation of the applicable statute or ordinance. It shall be made upon oath before any person authorized by law to administer oaths.

(Adopted eff. 7–1–73)

Crim R 4 Warrant or summons; arrest

(A) Issuance

(1) Upon complaint. If it appears from the complaint, or from an affidavit or affidavits filed with the complaint, that there is probable cause to believe that an offense has been committed, and that the defendant has committed it, a warrant for the arrest of the defendant, or a summons in lieu of a warrant, shall be issued by a judge, magistrate, clerk of court, or officer of the court designated by the judge, to any law enforcement officer authorized by law to execute or serve it.

The finding of probable cause may be based upon hearsay in whole or in part, provided there is a substantial basis for believing the source of the hearsay to be credible and for believing that there is a factual basis for the information furnished. Before ruling on a request for a warrant, the issuing authority may require the complainant to appear personally and may examine under oath the complainant and any witnesses. The testimony shall be admissible at a hearing on a motion to suppress, if it was taken down by a court reporter or recording equipment.

The issuing authority shall issue a summons instead of a warrant upon the request of the prosecuting attorney, or when issuance of a summons appears reasonably calculated to ensure the defendant's appearance.

(2) By law enforcement officer with warrant. In misdemeanor cases where a warrant has been issued to a law enforcement officer, the officer, unless the issuing authority includes a prohibition against it in the warrant, may issue a summons in lieu of executing the warrant by arrest, when issuance of a summons appears reasonably calculated to ensure the defendant's appearance. The officer issuing the summons shall note on the warrant and the return that the warrant was executed by issuing summons, and shall also note the time and place the defendant shall appear. No alias warrant shall be issued unless the defendant fails to appear in response to the summons, or unless subsequent to the issuance of summons it appears improbable that the defendant will appear in response to the summons.

(3) By law enforcement officer without a warrant. In misdemeanor cases where a law enforcement officer is empowered to arrest without a warrant, the officer may issue a summons in lieu of making an arrest, when issuance of a summons appears reasonably calculated to ensure the defendant's appearance. The officer issuing the summons shall file, or cause to be filed, a complaint describing the offense. No warrant shall be issued unless the defendant fails to appear in response to the summons, or unless subsequent to the issuance of summons it appears improbable that the defendant will appear in response to the summons.

(B) Multiple issuance; sanction

More than one warrant or summons may issue on the same complaint. If the defendant fails to appear in response to summons, a warrant or alias warrant shall issue.

(C) Warrant and summons: form

(1) Warrant. The warrant shall contain the name of the defendant or, if that is unknown, any name or description by which the defendant can be identified with reasonable certainty, a description of the offense charged in the complaint, whether the warrant is being issued before the defendant has appeared or was scheduled to appear, and the numerical designation of the applicable statute or ordinance. A copy of the complaint shall be attached to the warrant.

(a) If the warrant is issued after the defendant has made an initial appearance or has failed to appear at an initial appearance, the warrant shall command that the defendant be arrested and either of the following:

(i) That the defendant shall be required to post a sum of cash or secured bail bond with the condition that the defendant appear before the issuing court at a time and date certain;

(ii) That the defendant shall be held without bail until brought before the issuing court without unnecessary delay.

(b) If the warrant is issued before the defendant has appeared or is scheduled to appear, the warrant shall so indicate and the bail provisions of Crim. R. 46 shall apply.

(2) Summons. The summons shall be in the same form as the warrant, except that it shall not command that the defendant be arrested, but shall order the defendant to appear at a stated time and place and inform the defendant that he or she may be arrested if he or she fails to appear at the time and place stated in the summons. A copy of the complaint shall be attached to the summons, except where an officer issues summons in lieu of making an arrest without a warrant, or where an officer issues summons after arrest without a warrant.

(D) Warrant and summons: execution or service; return

(1) By whom. Warrants shall be executed and summons served by any officer authorized by law.

(2) Territorial limits. Warrants may be executed or summons may be served at any place within this state.

(3) Manner. Except as provided in division (A)(2) of this rule, warrants shall be executed by the arrest of the defendant. The officer need not have the warrant in the officer's possession at the time of the arrest. In such case, the officer shall inform the defendant of the offense charged and of the fact that the warrant has been issued. A copy of the warrant shall be given to the defendant as soon as possible.

Summons may be served upon a defendant by delivering a copy to the defendant personally, or by leaving it at the defendant's usual place of residence with some person of suitable age and discretion then residing therein, or, except when the summons is issued in lieu of executing a warrant by arrest, by mailing it to the defendant's last known address by certified mail with a return receipt requested. When service of summons is made by certified mail it shall be served by the clerk in the manner prescribed by Civil Rule 4.1(1). A summons to a corporation shall be served in the manner provided for service upon corporations in Civil Rules 4 through 4.2 and 4.6(A) and (B), except that the waiver provisions of Civil Rule 4(D) shall not apply. Summons issued under division (A)(2) of this rule in lieu of executing a warrant by arrest shall be served by personal or residence service. Summons issued under division (A)(3) of this rule in lieu of arrest and summons issued after arrest under division (F) of this rule shall be served by personal service only.

(4) Return. The officer executing a warrant shall make return of the warrant to the issuing court before whom the defendant is brought pursuant to Crim. R. 5. At the request of the prosecuting attorney, any unexecuted warrant shall be returned to the issuing court and cancelled by a judge of that court.

When the copy of the summons has been served, the person serving summons shall endorse that fact on the summons and return it to the clerk, who shall make the appropriate entry on the appearance docket.

When the person serving summons is unable to serve a copy of the summons within twenty-eight days of the date of issuance, the person serving summons shall endorse that fact and the reasons for the failure of service on the summons and return the summons and copies to the clerk, who shall make the appropriate entry on the appearance docket.

At the request of the prosecuting attorney, made while the complaint is pending, a warrant returned unexecuted and not cancelled, or a summons returned unserved, or a copy of either, may be delivered by the court to an authorized officer for execution or service.

(E) Arrest

(1) Arrest upon warrant.

(a) Where a person is arrested upon a warrant that states it was issued before a scheduled initial appearance, or the warrant is silent as to when it was issued, the judicial officer before whom the person is brought shall apply Crim. R. 46.

(b) Where a person is arrested upon a warrant that states it was issued after an initial appearance or the failure to appear at an initial appearance and the arrest occurs either in the county from which the warrant issued or in an adjoining county, the arresting officer shall, except as provided in division (F) of this rule, where the warrant provides for the posting of bail, permit the arrested person to post a sum of cash or secured bail bond as contained in the warrant with the requirement that the arrested person appear before the warrant issuing court at a time and date certain, or bring the arrested person without unnecessary delay before the court that issued the warrant.

(c) Where a person is arrested upon a warrant that states it was issued after an initial appearance or the failure to appear at an initial appearance and the arrest occurs in any county other than the county from which the warrant was issued or in an adjoining county, the following sequence of procedures shall be followed:

(i) Where the warrant provides for the posting of bail, the arrested person shall be permitted to post a sum of cash or secured bail bond as contained in the warrant with the requirement that the arrested person appear before the warrant issuing court at a time and date certain.

(ii) The arrested person may in writing waive the procedures in division (E)(1)(c)(iii) of this rule after having been informed in writing and orally by a law enforcement officer of those procedures, and consenting to being removed to the warrant issuing court without further delay. This waiver shall contain a representation by a law enforcement officer that the waiver was read to the arrested person and that the arrested person signed the waiver in the officer's presence.

(iii) Where the warrant is silent as to the posting of bail, requires that the arrested person be held without bail, the arrested person chooses not to post bail, or the arrested person chooses not to waive the procedures contained in division (E)(1) of this rule, the arrested person shall, except as provided in division (F) of this rule, be brought without unnecessary delay before a court of record therein, having jurisdiction over such an offense, and the arrested person shall not be removed from that county until the arrested person has been given a reasonable opportunity to consult with an attorney, or individual of the arrested person's choice, and to post bail to be determined by the judge or magistrate of that court not inconsistent with the directions of the issuing court as contained in the warrant or after consultation with the issuing court. If the warrant is silent as to the posting of bail or holding the arrested person without bail, the court may permit the arrested person to post bail, hold the arrested person without bail, or consult with the warrant issuing court on the issue of bail.

(d) If the arrested person is not released, the arrested person shall then be removed from the county and brought before the court issuing the warrant, without unnecessary delay. If the arrested person is released, the release shall be on condition that the arrested person appear in the issuing court at a time and date certain.

(2) Arrest without warrant. Where a person is arrested without a warrant the arresting officer shall, except as provided in division (F), bring the arrested person without unnecessary delay before a court having jurisdiction of the offense, and shall file or cause to be filed a complaint describing the offense for which the person was arrested. Thereafter the court shall proceed in accordance with Crim. R. 5.

(F) Release after arrest

In misdemeanor cases where a person has been arrested with or without a warrant, the arresting officer, the officer in charge of the detention facility to which the person is brought or the superior of either officer, without unnecessary delay, may release the arrested person by issuing a summons when issuance of a summons appears reasonably calculated to assure the person's appearance. The officer issuing such summons shall note on the summons the time and place the person must appear and, if the person was arrested without a warrant, shall file or cause to be filed a complaint describing the offense. No warrant or alias warrant shall be issued unless the person fails to appear in response to the summons.

(Adopted eff. 7–1–73; amended eff. 7–1–75, 7–1–90, 7–1–98)

Crim R 4.1 Optional procedure in minor misdemeanor cases

(A) Procedure in minor misdemeanor cases

Notwithstanding Rule 3, Rule 5(A), Rule 10, Rule 11(A), Rule 11(E), Rule 22, Rule 43(A), and Rule 44, a court may establish the following procedure for all or particular minor misdemeanors other than offenses covered by the Uniform Traffic Rules.

(B) Definition of minor misdemeanor

A minor misdemeanor is an offense for which the potential penalty does not exceed a fine of one hundred fifty dollars. With respect to offenses committed prior to January 1, 2004, a minor misdemeanor is an offense for which the potential penalty does not exceed a fine of one hundred dollars.

(C) Form of citation

In minor misdemeanor cases a law enforcement officer may issue a citation. The citation shall: contain the name and address of the defendant; describe the offense charged; give the numerical designation of the applicable statute or ordinance; state the name of the law enforcement officer who issued the citation; and order the defendant to appear at a stated time and place.

The citation shall inform the defendant that, in lieu of appearing at the time and place stated, he may, within that stated time, appear personally at the office of the clerk of court and upon signing a plea of guilty and a waiver of trial pay a stated fine and stated costs, if any. The citation shall inform the defendant that, in lieu of appearing at the time and place stated, he may, within a stated time, sign the guilty plea and waiver of trial provision of the citation, and mail the citation and a check or money order for the total amount of the fine and costs to the violations bureau. The citation shall inform the defendant that he may be arrested if he fails to appear either at the clerk's office or at the time and place stated in the citation.

(D) Duty of law enforcement officer

A law enforcement officer who issues a citation shall complete and sign the citation form, serve a copy of the completed form upon the defendant and, without unnecessary delay, swear to and file the original with the court.

(E) Fine schedule

The court shall establish a fine schedule which shall list the fine for each minor misdemeanor, and state the court costs. The fine schedule shall be prominently posted in the place where violation fines are paid.

(F) Procedure upon failure to appear

When a defendant fails to appear, the court may issue a supplemental citation, or a summons or warrant under Rule 4. Supplemental citations shall be in the form prescribed by division (C) of this rule, but shall be issued and signed by the clerk and served in the same manner as a summons under Rule 4.

(G) Procedure where defendant does not enter a waiver

Where a defendant appears but does not sign a guilty plea and waiver of trial, the court shall proceed in accordance with Rule 5.

(Adopted eff. 7–1–73; amended eff. 7–1–78, 7–1–04)

Crim R 5 Initial appearance, preliminary hearing

(A) Procedure upon initial appearance

When a defendant first appears before a judge or magistrate, the judge or magistrate shall permit the accused or his counsel to read the complaint or a copy thereof, and shall inform the defendant:

(1) Of the nature of the charge against him;

(2) That he has a right to counsel and the right to a reasonable continuance in the proceedings to secure counsel, and, pursuant to Crim. R. 44, the right to have counsel assigned without cost to himself if he is unable to employ counsel;

(3) That he need make no statement and any statement made may be used against him;

(4) Of his right to a preliminary hearing in a felony case, when his initial appearance is not pursuant to indictment;

(5) Of his right, where appropriate, to jury trial and the necessity to make demand therefor in petty offense cases.

In addition, if the defendant has not been admitted to bail for a bailable offense, the judge or magistrate shall admit the defendant to bail as provided in these rules.

In felony cases the defendant shall not be called upon to plead either at the initial appearance or at a preliminary hearing.

In misdemeanor cases the defendant may be called upon to plead at the initial appearance. Where the defendant enters a plea the procedure established by Crim. R. 10 and Crim. R. 11 applies.

(B) Preliminary hearing in felony cases; procedure

(1) In felony cases a defendant is entitled to a preliminary hearing unless waived in writing. If the defendant waives preliminary hearing, the judge or magistrate shall forthwith order the defendant bound over to the court of common pleas. If the defendant does not waive the preliminary hearing, the judge or magistrate shall schedule a preliminary hearing within a reasonable time, but in any event no later than ten consecutive days following arrest or service of summons if the defendant is in custody and not later than fifteen consecutive days following arrest or service of summons if he is not in custody. The preliminary hearing shall not be held, however, if the defendant is indicted. With the consent of the defendant and upon a showing of good cause, taking into account the public interest in the prompt disposition of criminal cases, time limits specified in this division may be extended. In the absence of such consent by the defendant, time limits may be extended only as required by law, or upon a showing that extraordinary circumstances exist and that delay is indispensable to the interest of justice.

(2) At the preliminary hearing the prosecuting attorney may state orally the case for the state, and shall then proceed to examine witnesses and introduce exhibits for the state. The defendant and the judge or magistrate have full right of cross-examination, and the defendant has the right of inspection of exhibits prior to their introduction. The hearing shall be conducted under the rules of evidence prevailing in criminal trial generally.

(3) At the conclusion of the presentation of the state's case, defendant may move for discharge for failure of proof, and may offer evidence on his own behalf. If the defendant is not represented by counsel, the court shall advise him, prior to the offering of evidence on behalf of the defendant:

(a) That any such evidence, if unfavorable to him in any particular, may be used against him at later trial.

(b) That he may make a statement, not under oath, regarding the charge, for the purpose of explaining the facts in evidence.

(c) That he may refuse to make any statement, and such refusal may not be used against him at trial.

(d) That any statement he makes may be used against him at trial.

(4) Upon conclusion of all the evidence and the statement, if any, of the accused, the court shall do one of the following:

(a) Find that there is probable cause to believe the crime alleged or another felony has been committed and that the defendant committed it, and bind the defendant over to the court of common pleas of the county or any other county in which venue appears.

(b) Find that there is probable cause to believe that a misdemeanor was committed and that the defendant committed it, and retain the case for trial or order the defendant to appear for trial before an appropriate court.

(c) Order the accused discharged.

(5) Any finding requiring the accused to stand trial on any charge shall be based solely on the presence of substantial credible evidence thereof. No appeal shall lie from such decision and the discharge of defendant shall not be a bar to further prosecution.

(6) In any case in which the defendant is ordered to appear for trial for any offense other than the one charged the court shall cause a complaint charging such offense to be filed.

(7) Upon the conclusion of the hearing and finding, the court or the clerk of such court, shall, within seven days, complete all notations of appearance, motions, pleas, and findings on the criminal docket of the court, and shall transmit a transcript of the appearance docket entries, together with a copy of the original complaint and affidavits, if any, filed with the complaint, the journal or docket entry of reason for changes in the charge, if any, together with the order setting bail and the bail including any bail deposit, if any, filed, to the clerk of the court in which defendant is to appear. Such transcript shall contain an itemized account of the costs accrued.

(Adopted eff. 7–1–73; amended eff. 7–1–75, 7–1–76, 7–1–82, 7–1–90)

Crim R 6 The grand jury

(A) Summoning grand juries

The judge of the court of common pleas for each county, or the administrative judge of the general division in a multi-judge court of common pleas or a judge designated by him, shall order one or more grand juries to be summoned at such times as the public interest requires. The grand jury shall consist of nine members, including the foreman, plus not more than five alternates.

(B) Objections to grand jury and to grand jurors

(1) Challenges. The prosecuting attorney, or the attorney for a defendant who has been held to answer in the court of common pleas, may challenge the array of jurors or an individual juror on the ground that the grand jury or individual juror was not selected, drawn, or summoned in accordance with the statutes of this state. Challenges shall be made before the administration of the oath to the jurors and shall be tried by the court.

(2) Motion to dismiss. A motion to dismiss the indictment may be based on objections to the array or on the lack of legal qualification of an individual juror, if not previously determined upon challenge. An indictment shall not be dismissed on the ground that one or more members of the grand jury were not legally qualified, if it appears from the record kept pursuant to subdivision (C) that seven or more jurors, after deducting the number not legally qualified, concurred in finding the indictment.

(C) Foreman and deputy foreman

The court may appoint any qualified elector or one of the jurors to be foreman and one of the jurors to be deputy foreman. The foreman shall have power to administer oaths and affirmations and shall sign all indictments. He or another juror designated by him shall keep a record of the number of jurors concurring in the finding of every indictment and shall upon the return of the indictment file the record with the clerk of court, but the record shall not be made public except on order of the court. During the absence or disqualification of the foreman, the deputy foreman shall act as foreman.

(D) Who may be present

The prosecuting attorney, the witness under examination, interpreters when needed and, for the purpose of taking the evidence, a stenographer or operator of a recording device may be present while the grand jury is in session, but no person other than the jurors may be present while the grand jury is deliberating or voting.

(E) Secrecy of proceedings and disclosure

Deliberations of the grand jury and the vote of any grand juror shall not be disclosed. Disclosure of other matters occurring before the grand jury may be made to the prosecuting attorney for use in the performance of his duties. A grand juror, prosecuting attorney, interpreter, stenographer, operator of a recording device, or typist who transcribes recorded testimony, may disclose matters occurring before the grand jury, other than the deliberations of a grand jury or the vote of a grand juror, but may disclose such matters only when so directed by the court preliminary to or in connection with a judicial proceeding, or when permitted by the court at the request of the defendant upon a showing that grounds may exist for a motion to dismiss the indictment because of matters occurring before the grand jury. No grand juror, officer of the court, or other person shall disclose that an indictment has been found against a person before such indictment is filed and the case docketed. The court may direct that an indictment shall be kept secret until the defendant is in custody or has been released pursuant to Rule 46. In that event the clerk shall seal the indictment, the indictment shall not be docketed by name until after the apprehension of the accused, and no person shall disclose the finding of the indictment except when necessary for the issuance of a warrant or summons. No obligation of secrecy may be imposed upon any person except in accordance with this rule.

(F) Finding and return of indictment

An indictment may be found only upon the concurrence of seven or more jurors. When so found the foreman or deputy foreman shall sign the indictment as foreman or deputy foreman. The indictment shall be returned by the foreman or deputy foreman to a judge of the court of common pleas and filed with the clerk who shall endorse thereon the date of filing and enter each case upon the appearance and trial dockets. If the defendant is in custody or has been released pursuant to Rule 46 and seven jurors do not concur in finding an indictment, the foreman shall so report to the court forthwith.

(G) Discharge and excuse

A grand jury shall serve until discharged by the court. A grand jury may serve for four months, but the court upon a showing of good cause by the prosecuting attorney may order a grand jury to serve more than four months but not more than nine months. The tenure and powers of a grand jury are not affected by the beginning or expiration of a term of court. At any time for cause shown the court may excuse a juror either temporarily or permanently, and in the latter event the court may impanel another eligible person in place of the juror excused.

(H) Alternate grand jurors

The court may order that not more than five grand jurors, in addition to the regular grand jury, be called, impanelled and sit as alternate grand jurors. Alternate grand jurors, in the order in which they are called, shall replace grand jurors who, prior to the time the grand jury votes on an indictment, are found to be unable or disqualified to perform their duties. Alternate grand jurors shall be drawn in the same manner, shall have the same qualifications, shall be subjected to the same examination and challenges, shall take the same oath, and shall have the same functions, powers, facilities, and privileges as the regular grand jurors. Alternate grand jurors may sit with the regular grand jury, but shall not be present when the grand jury deliberates and votes.

(Adopted eff. 7–1–73)

Crim R 7 The indictment and the information

(A) Use of indictment or information

A felony that may be punished by death or life imprisonment shall be prosecuted by indictment. All other felonies shall be prosecuted by indictment, except that after a defendant has been advised by the court of the nature of the charge against the defendant and of the defendant's right to indictment, the defendant may waive that right in writing and in open court.

Where an indictment is waived, the offense may be prosecuted by information, unless an indictment is filed within fourteen days after the date of waiver. If an information or indictment is not filed within fourteen days after the date of waiver, the defendant shall be discharged and the complaint dismissed. This division shall not prevent subsequent prosecution by information or indictment for the same offense.

A misdemeanor may be prosecuted by indictment or information in the court of common pleas, or by complaint in the juvenile court, as defined in the Rules of Juvenile Procedure, and in courts inferior to the court of common pleas. An information may be filed without leave of court.

(B) Nature and contents

The indictment shall be signed in accordance with Crim.R. 6(C) and (F) and contain a statement that the defendant has committed a public offense specified in the indictment. The information shall be signed by the prosecuting attorney or in the name of the prosecuting attorney by an assistant prosecuting attorney and shall contain a statement that the defendant has committed a public offense specified in the information. The statement may be made in ordinary and concise language without technical averments or allegations not essential to be proved. The statement may be in the words of the applicable section of the statute, provided the words of that statute charge an offense, or in words sufficient to give the defendant notice of all the elements of the offense with which the defendant is charged. It may be alleged in a single count that the means by which the defendant committed the offense are unknown or that the defendant committed it by one or more specified means. Each count of the indictment or information shall state the numerical designation of the statute that the defendant is alleged to have violated. Error in the numerical designation or omission of the numerical designation shall not be ground for dismissal of the indictment or information, or for reversal of a conviction, if the error or omission did not prejudicially mislead the defendant.

(C) Surplusage

The court on motion of the defendant or the prosecuting attorney may strike surplusage from the indictment or information.

(D) Amendment of indictment, information, or complaint

The court may at any time before, during, or after a trial amend the indictment, information, complaint, or bill of particulars, in respect to any defect, imperfection, or omission in form or substance, or of any variance with the evidence, provided no change is made in the name or identity of the crime charged. If any amendment is made to the substance of the indictment, information, or complaint, or to cure a variance between the indictment, information, or complaint and the proof, the defendant is entitled to a discharge of the jury on the defendant's motion, if a jury has been impanelled, and to a reasonable continuance, unless it clearly appears from the whole proceedings that the defendant has not been misled or prejudiced by the defect or variance in respect to which the amendment is made, or that the defendant's rights will be fully protected by proceeding with the trial, or by a postponement thereof to a later day with the same or another jury. Where a jury is discharged under this division, jeopardy shall not attach to the offense charged in the amended indictment, information, or complaint. No action of the court in refusing a continuance or postponement under this division is reviewable except after motion to grant a new trial therefor is refused by the trial court, and no appeal based upon such action of the court shall be sustained nor reversal had unless, from consideration of the whole proceedings, the reviewing court finds that a failure of justice resulted.

(E) Bill of particulars

When the defendant makes a written request within twenty-one days after arraignment but not later than seven days before trial, or upon court order, the prosecuting attorney shall furnish the defendant with a bill of particulars setting up specifically the nature of the offense charge and of the conduct of the defendant alleged to constitute the offense. A bill of particulars may be amended at any time subject to such conditions as justice requires.

(Adopted eff. 7–1–73; amended eff. 7–1–93, 7–1–00)

Crim R 8 Joinder of offenses and defendants

(A) Joinder of offenses

Two or more offenses may be charged in the same indictment, information or complaint in a separate count for each offense if the offenses charged, whether felonies or misdemeanors or both, are of the same or similar character, or are based on the same act or transaction, or are based on two or more acts or transactions connected together or constituting parts of a common scheme or plan, or are part of a course of criminal conduct.

(B) Joinder of defendants

Two or more defendants may be charged in the same indictment, information or complaint if they are alleged to have participated in the same act or transaction or in the same series of acts or transactions constituting an offense or offenses, or in the same course of criminal conduct. Such defendants may be charged in one or more counts together or separately, and all of the defendants need not be charged in each count.

(Adopted eff. 7–1–73)

Crim R 9 Warrant or summons upon indictment or information

(A) Issuance

Upon the request of the prosecuting attorney the clerk shall forthwith issue a warrant for each defendant named in the indictment or in the information. The clerk shall issue a summons instead of a warrant where the defendant has been released pursuant to Rule 46 and is indicted for the same offense for which he was bound over pursuant to Rule 5. In addition, the clerk shall issue a summons instead of a warrant upon the request of the prosecuting attorney or by direction of the court.

Upon like request or direction, the clerk shall issue more than one warrant or summons for the same defendant. He shall deliver the warrant or summons to any officer authorized by law to execute or serve it. If a defendant fails to appear in response to summons, a warrant shall issue.

(B) Form of warrant and summons

(1) Warrant. The form of the warrant shall be as provided in Rule 4(C)(1) except that it shall be signed by the court or clerk. It shall describe the offense charged in the indictment or information. A copy of the indictment or information shall be attached to the warrant which shall command that the defendant be arrested and brought before the court issuing the warrant without unnecessary delay.

(2) Summons. The summons shall be in the same form as the warrant, except that it shall not command that the defendant be arrested, but shall order the defendant to appear before the court at a stated time and place and inform him that he may be arrested if he fails to appear at the time and place stated in the summons. A copy of the indictment or information shall be attached to the summons.

(C) Execution or service; return

(1) Execution or service. Warrants shall be executed or summons served as provided in Rule 4(D) and the arrested person shall be treated in accordance with Rule 4(E)(1).

(2) Return. The officer executing a warrant shall make return thereof to the court.

When the person serving summons is unable to serve a copy of the summons within twenty-eight days of the date of issuance, he shall endorse that fact and the reasons therefor on the summons and return the summons, and copies to the clerk, who shall make the appropriate entry on the appearance docket.

At the request of the prosecuting attorney made at any time while the indictment or information is pending, a warrant returned unexecuted and not cancelled, or a summons returned unserved, or a copy thereof, may be delivered by the clerk to the sheriff or other authorized person for execution or service.

(Adopted eff. 7–1–73; amended eff. 7–1–75)

Crim R 10 Arraignment

(A) Arraignment procedure

Arraignment shall be conducted in open court, and shall consist of reading the indictment, information or complaint to the defendant, or stating to him the substance of the charge, and calling on him to plead thereto. The defendant may in open court waive the reading of the indictment, information, or complaint. The defendant shall be given a copy of the indictment, information, or complaint, or shall acknowledge receipt thereof, before being called upon to plead.

(B) Presence of defendant

The defendant must be present, except that the court, with the written consent of the defendant and the approval of the prosecuting attorney, may permit arraignment without the presence of the defendant, if a plea of not guilty is entered.

(C) Explanation of rights

When a defendant not represented by counsel is brought before a court and called upon to plead, the judge or magistrate shall cause him to be informed and shall determine that he understands all of the following:

(1) He has a right to retain counsel even if he intends to plead guilty, and has a right to a reasonable continuance in the proceedings to secure counsel.

(2) He has a right to counsel, and the right to a reasonable continuance in the proceeding to secure counsel, and, pursuant to Crim. R. 44, the right to have counsel assigned without cost to himself if he is unable to employ counsel.

(3) He has a right to bail, if the offense is bailable.

(4) He need make no statement at any point in the proceeding, but any statement made can and may be used against him.

(D) Joint arraignment

If there are multiple defendants to be arraigned, the judge or magistrate may by general announcement advise them of their rights as prescribed in this rule.

(Adopted eff. 7–1–73; amended eff. 7–1–90)

Crim R 11 Pleas, rights upon plea

(A) Pleas

A defendant may plead not guilty, not guilty by reason of insanity, guilty or, with the consent of the court, no contest. A plea of not guilty by reason of insanity shall be made in writing by either the defendant or the defendant's attorney. All other pleas may be made orally. The pleas of not guilty and not guilty by reason of insanity may be joined. If a defendant refuses to plead, the court shall enter a plea of not guilty on behalf of the defendant.

(B) Effect of guilty or no contest pleas

With reference to the offense or offenses to which the plea is entered:

(1) The plea of guilty is a complete admission of the defendant's guilt.

(2) The plea of no contest is not an admission of defendant's guilt, but is an admission of the truth of the facts alleged in the indictment, information, or complaint, and the plea or admission shall not be used against the defendant in any subsequent civil or criminal proceeding.

(3) When a plea of guilty or no contest is accepted pursuant to this rule, the court, except as provided in divisions (C)(3) and (4) of this rule, shall proceed with sentencing under Crim. R. 32.

(C) Pleas of guilty and no contest in felony cases

(1) Where in a felony case the defendant is unrepresented by counsel the court shall not accept a plea of guilty or no contest unless the defendant, after being readvised that he or she has the right to be represented by retained counsel, or pursuant to Crim. R. 44 by appointed counsel, waives this right.

(2) In felony cases the court may refuse to accept a plea of guilty or a plea of no contest, and shall not accept a plea of guilty or no contest without first addressing the defendant personally and doing all of the following:

(a) Determining that the defendant is making the plea voluntarily, with understanding of the nature of the charges and of the maximum penalty involved, and, if applicable, that the defendant is not eligible for probation or for the imposition of community control sanctions at the sentencing hearing.

(b) Informing the defendant of and determining that the defendant understands the effect of the plea of guilty or no contest, and that the court, upon acceptance of the plea, may proceed with judgment and sentence.

(c) Informing the defendant and determining that the defendant understands that by the plea the defendant is waiving the rights to jury trial, to confront witnesses against him or her, to have compulsory process for obtaining witnesses in the defendant's favor, and to require the state to prove the defendant's guilt beyond a reasonable doubt at a trial at which the defendant cannot be compelled to testify against himself or herself.

(3) With respect to aggravated murder committed on and after January 1, 1974, the defendant shall plead separately to the charge and to each specification, if any. A plea of guilty or no contest to the charge waives the defendant's right to a jury trial, and before accepting a plea of guilty or no contest the court shall so advise the defendant and determine that the defendant understands the consequences of the plea.

If the indictment contains no specification, and a plea of guilty or no contest to the charge is accepted, the court shall impose the sentence provided by law.

If the indictment contains one or more specifications, and a plea of guilty or no contest to the charge is accepted, the court may dismiss the specifications and impose sentence accordingly, in the interests of justice.

If the indictment contains one or more specifications that are not dismissed upon acceptance of a plea of guilty or no contest to the charge, or if pleas of guilty or no contest to both the charge and one or more specifications are accepted, a court composed of three judges shall: (a) determine whether the offense was aggravated murder or a lesser offense; and (b) if the offense is determined to have been a lesser offense, impose sentence accordingly; or (c) if the offense is determined to have been aggravated murder, proceed as provided by law to determine the presence or absence of the specified aggravating circumstances and of mitigating circumstances, and impose sentence accordingly.

(4) With respect to all other cases the court need not take testimony upon a plea of guilty or no contest.

(D) Misdemeanor cases involving serious offenses

In misdemeanor cases involving serious offenses the court may refuse to accept a plea of guilty or no contest, and shall not accept such plea without first addressing the defendant personally and informing the defendant of the effect of the pleas of guilty, no contest, and not guilty and determining that the defendant is making the plea voluntarily. Where the defendant is unrepresented by counsel the court shall not accept a plea of guilty or no contest unless the defendant, after being readvised that he or she has the right to be represented by retained counsel, or pursuant to Crim. R. 44 by appointed counsel, waives this right.

(E) Misdemeanor cases involving petty offenses

In misdemeanor cases involving petty offenses the court may refuse to accept a plea of guilty or no contest, and shall not accept such pleas without first informing the defendant of the effect of the plea of guilty, no contest, and not guilty.

The counsel provisions of Crim. R. 44(B) and (C) apply to division (E) of this rule.

(F) Negotiated plea in felony cases

When, in felony cases, a negotiated plea of guilty or no contest to one or more offenses charged or to one or more other or lesser offenses is offered, the underlying agreement upon which the plea is based shall be stated on the record in open court.

(G) Refusal of court to accept plea

If the court refuses to accept a plea of guilty or no contest, the court shall enter a plea of not guilty on behalf of the defendant. In such cases neither plea shall be admissible in evidence nor be the subject of comment by the prosecuting attorney or court.

(H) Defense of insanity

The defense of not guilty by reason of insanity must be pleaded at the time of arraignment, except that the court for good cause shown shall permit such a plea to be entered at any time before trial.

(Adopted eff. 7–1–73; amended eff. 7–1–76, 7–1–80, 7–1–98)

Crim R 12 Pleadings and motions before trial: defenses and objections

(A) Pleadings and motions

Pleadings in criminal proceedings shall be the complaint, and the indictment or information, and the pleas of not guilty, not guilty by reason of insanity, guilty, and no contest. All other pleas, demurrers, and motions to quash, are abolished. Defenses and objections raised before trial which heretofore could have been raised by one or more of them shall be raised only by motion to dismiss or to grant appropriate relief, as provided in these rules.

(B) Filing with the court defined

The filing of documents with the court, as required by these rules, shall be made by filing them with the clerk of court, except that the judge may permit the documents to be filed with the judge, in which event the judge shall note the filing date on the documents and transmit them to the clerk. A court may provide, by local rules adopted pursuant to the Rules of Superintendence, for the filing of documents by electronic means. If the court adopts such local rules, they shall include all of the following:

(1) The complaint, if permitted by local rules to be filed electronically, shall comply with Crim. R. 3.

(2) Any signature on electronically transmitted documents shall be considered that of the attorney or party it purports to be for all purposes. If it is established that the documents were transmitted without authority, the court shall order the filing stricken.

(3) A provision shall specify the days and hours during which electronically transmitted documents will be received by the court, and a provision shall specify when documents received electronically will be considered to have been filed.

(4) Any document filed electronically that requires a filing fee may be rejected by the clerk of court unless the filer has complied with the mechanism established by the court for the payment of filing fees.

(C) Pretrial motions

Prior to trial, any party may raise by motion any defense, objection, evidentiary issue, or request that is capable of determination without the trial of the general issue. The following must be raised before trial:

(1) Defenses and objections based on defects in the institution of the prosecution;

(2) Defenses and objections based on defects in the indictment, information, or complaint (other than failure to show jurisdiction in the court or to charge an offense, which objections shall be noticed by the court at any time during the pendency of the proceeding);

(3) Motions to suppress evidence, including but not limited to statements and identification testimony, on the ground that it was illegally obtained. Such motions shall be filed in the trial court only.

(4) Requests for discovery under Crim. R. 16;

(5) Requests for severance of charges or defendants under Crim. R. 14.

(D) Motion date

All pretrial motions except as provided in Crim. R. 7(E) and 16(F) shall be made within thirty-five days after arraignment or seven days before trial, whichever is earlier. The court in the interest of justice may extend the time for making pretrial motions.

(E) Notice by the prosecuting attorney of the intention to use evidence

(1) At the discretion of the prosecuting attorney. At the arraignment or as soon thereafter as is practicable, the prosecuting attorney may give notice to the defendant of the prosecuting attorney's intention to use specified evidence at trial, in order to afford the defendant an opportunity to raise objections to such evidence prior to trial under division (C)(3) of this rule.

(2) At the request of the defendant. At the arraignment or as soon thereafter as is practicable, the defendant, in order to raise objections prior to trial under division (C)(3) of this rule, may request notice of the prosecuting attorney's intention to use evidence in chief at trial, which evidence the defendant is entitled to discover under Crim. R. 16.

(F) Ruling on motion

The court may adjudicate a motion based upon briefs, affidavits, the proffer of testimony and exhibits, a hearing, or other appropriate means.

A motion made pursuant to divisions (C)(1) to (C)(5) of this rule shall be determined before trial. Any other motion made pursuant to division (C) of this rule shall be determined before trial whenever possible. Where the court defers ruling on any motion made by the prosecuting attorney before trial and makes a ruling adverse to the prosecuting attorney after the commencement of trial, and the ruling is appealed pursuant to law with the certification required by division (K) of this rule, the court shall stay the proceedings without discharging the jury or dismissing the charges.

Where factual issues are involved in determining a motion, the court shall state its essential findings on the record.

(G) Return of tangible evidence

Where a motion to suppress tangible evidence is granted, the court upon request of the defendant shall order the property returned to the defendant if the defendant is entitled to possession of the property. The order shall be stayed pending appeal by the state pursuant to division (K) of this rule.

(H) Effect of failure to raise defenses or objections

Failure by the defendant to raise defenses or objections or to make requests that must be made prior to trial, at the time set by the court pursuant to division (D) of this rule, or prior to any extension of time made by the court, shall constitute waiver of the defenses or objections, but the court for good cause shown may grant relief from the waiver.

(I) Effect of plea of no contest

The plea of no contest does not preclude a defendant from asserting upon appeal that the trial court prejudicially erred in ruling on a pretrial motion, including a pretrial motion to suppress evidence.

(J) Effect of determination

If the court grants a motion to dismiss based on a defect in the institution of the prosecution or in the indictment, information, or complaint, it may also order that the defendant be held in custody or that the defendant's bail be continued for a specified time not exceeding fourteen days, pending the filing of a new indictment, information, or complaint. Nothing in this rule shall affect any statute relating to periods of limitations. Nothing in this rule shall affect the state's right to appeal an adverse ruling on a motion under divisions (C)(1) or (2) of this rule, when the motion raises issues that were formerly raised pursuant to a motion to quash, a plea in abatement, a demurrer, or a motion in arrest of judgment.

(K) Appeal by state

When the state takes an appeal as provided by law from an order suppressing or excluding evidence, the prosecuting attorney shall certify that both of the following apply:

(1) the appeal is not taken for the purpose of delay;

(2) the ruling on the motion or motions has rendered the state's proof with respect to the pending charge so weak in its entirety that any reasonable possibility of effective prosecution has been destroyed.

The appeal from an order suppressing or excluding evidence shall not be allowed unless the notice of appeal and the certification by the prosecuting attorney are filed with the clerk of the trial court within seven days after the date of the entry of the judgment or order granting the motion. Any appeal taken under this rule shall be prosecuted diligently.

If the defendant previously has not been released, the defendant shall, except in capital cases, be released from custody on his or her own recognizance pending appeal when the prosecuting attorney files the notice of appeal and certification.

This appeal shall take precedence over all other appeals.

If an appeal pursuant to this division results in an affirmance of the trial court, the state shall be barred from prosecuting the defendant for the same offense or offenses except upon a showing of newly discovered evidence that the state could not, with reasonable diligence, have discovered before filing of the notice of appeal.

(Adopted eff. 7–1–73; amended eff. 7–1–75, 7–1–80, 7–1–95, 7–1–98, 7–1–01)

Crim R 12.1 Notice of alibi

Whenever a defendant in a criminal case proposes to offer testimony to establish an alibi on his behalf, he shall, not less than seven days before trial, file and serve upon the prosecuting attorney a notice in writing of his intention to claim alibi. The notice shall include specific information as to the place at which the defendant claims to have been at the time of the alleged offense. If the defendant fails to file such written notice, the court may exclude evidence offered by the defendant for the purpose of proving such alibi, unless the court determines that in the interest of justice such evidence should be admitted.

(Adopted eff. 7–1–73)

Crim R 13 Trial together of indictments or informations or complaints

The court may order two or more indictments or informations or both to be tried together, if the offenses or the defendants could have been joined in a single indictment or information. The procedure shall be the same as if the prosecution were under such single indictment or information.

The court may order two or more complaints to be tried together, if the offenses or the defendants could have been joined in a single complaint. The procedure shall be the same as if the prosecution were under such single complaint.

(Adopted eff. 7–1–73)

Crim R 14 Relief from prejudicial joinder

If it appears that a defendant or the state is prejudiced by a joinder of offenses or of defendants in an indictment, information, or complaint, or by such joinder for trial together of indictments, informations or complaints, the court shall order an election or separate trial of counts, grant a severance of defendants, or provide such other relief as justice requires. In ruling on a motion by a defendant for severance, the court shall order the prosecuting attorney to deliver to the court for inspection pursuant to Rule 16(B)(1)(a) any statements or confessions made by the defendants which the state intends to introduce in evidence at the trial.

When two or more persons are jointly indicted for a capital offense, each of such persons shall be tried separately, unless the court orders the defendants to be tried jointly, upon application by the prosecuting attorney or one or more of the defendants, and for good cause shown.

(Adopted eff. 7–1–73)

Crim R 15 Deposition

(A) When taken

If it appears probable that a prospective witness will be unable to attend or will be prevented from attending a trial or hearing, and if it further appears that his testimony is material and that it is necessary to take his deposition in order to prevent a failure of justice, the court at any time after the filing of an indictment, information, or complaint shall upon motion of the defense attorney or the prosecuting attorney and notice to all the parties, order that his testimony be taken by deposition and that any designated books, papers, documents or tangible objects, not privileged, be produced at the same time and place.

If a witness is committed for failure to give bail or to appear to testify at a trial or hearing, the court on written motion of the witness and notice to the parties, may direct that his deposition be taken. After the deposition is completed, the court may discharge the witness.

(B) Notice of taking

The party at whose instance a deposition is to be taken shall give to every other party reasonable written notice of the time and place for taking the deposition. The notice shall state the name and address of each person to be examined. On motion of a party upon whom the notice is served, the court for cause shown may extend or shorten the time or fix the place of deposition.

(C) Attendance of defendants

The defendant shall have the right to attend the deposition. If he is confined the person having custody of the defendant shall be ordered by the court to take him to the deposition. The defendant may waive his right to attend the deposition, provided he does so in writing and in open court, is represented by counsel, and is fully advised of his right to attend by the court at a recorded proceeding.

(D) Counsel

Where a defendant is without counsel the court shall advise him of his right to counsel and assign counsel to represent him unless the defendant waives counsel or is able to obtain counsel. If it appears that a defendant at whose instance a deposition is to be taken cannot bear the expense thereof, the court may direct that all deposition expenses, including but not limited to travel and subsistence of the defendant's attorney for attendance at such examination together with a reasonable attorney fee, in addition to the compensation allowed for defending the defendant, and the expenses of the prosecuting attorney in the taking of such deposition, shall be paid out of public funds upon the certificate of the court making such order. Waiver of counsel shall be as prescribed in Rule 44(C).

(E) How taken

Depositions shall be taken in the manner provided in civil cases. The prosecution and defense shall have the right, as at trial, to full examination of witnesses. A deposition taken under this rule shall be filed in the court in which the action is pending.

(F) Use

At the trial or upon any hearing, a part or all of a deposition, so far as otherwise admissible under the rules of evidence, may be used if it appears: that the witness is dead; or, that the witness is out of the state, unless it appears that the absence of the witness was procured by the party offering the deposition; or that the witness is unable to attend or testify because of sickness or infirmity; or that the party offering the deposition has been unable to procure the attendance of the witness by subpoena. Any deposition may also be used by any party for the purpose of refreshing the recollection, or contradicting or impeaching the testimony of the deponent as a witness. If only a part of a deposition is offered in evidence by a party, any party may offer other parts.

(G) Objections to admissibility

Objections to receiving in evidence a deposition or a part thereof shall be made as provided in civil actions.

(Adopted eff. 7–1–73)

Crim R 16 Discovery and inspection

(A) Demand for discovery

Upon written request each party shall forthwith provide the discovery herein allowed. Motions for discovery shall certify that demand for discovery has been made and the discovery has not been provided.

(B) Disclosure of evidence by the prosecuting attorney

(1) Information subject to disclosure.

(a) Statement of defendant or co-defendant. Upon motion of the defendant, the court shall order the prosecuting attorney to permit the defendant to inspect and copy or photograph any of the following which are available to, or within the possession, custody, or control of the state, the existence of which is known or by the exercise of due diligence may become known to the prosecuting attorney:

(i) Relevant written or recorded statements made by the defendant or co-defendant, or copies thereof;

(ii) Written summaries of any oral statement, or copies thereof, made by the defendant or co-defendant to a prosecuting attorney or any law enforcement officer;

(iii) Recorded testimony of the defendant or co-defendant before a grand jury.

(b) Defendant's prior record. Upon motion of the defendant the court shall order the prosecuting attorney to furnish defendant a copy of defendant's prior criminal record, which is available to or within the possession, custody or control of the state.

(c) Documents and tangible objects. Upon motion of the defendant the court shall order the prosecuting attorney to permit the defendant to inspect and copy or photograph books, papers, documents, photographs, tangible objects, buildings or places, or copies or portions thereof, available to or within the possession, custody or control of the state, and which are material to the preparation of his defense, or are intended for use by the prosecuting attorney as evidence at the trial, or were obtained from or belong to the defendant.

(d) Reports of examination and tests. Upon motion of the defendant the court shall order the prosecuting attorney to permit the defendant to inspect and copy or photograph any results or reports of physical or mental examinations, and of scientific tests or experiments, made in connection with the particular case, or copies thereof, available to or within the possession, custody or control of the state, the existence of which is known or by the exercise of due diligence may become known to the prosecuting attorney.

(e) Witness names and addresses; record. Upon motion of the defendant, the court shall order the prosecuting attorney to furnish to the defendant a written list of the names and addresses of all witnesses whom the prosecuting attorney intends to call at trial, together with any record of prior felony convictions of any such witness, which record is within the knowledge of the prosecuting attorney. Names and addresses of witnesses shall not be subject to disclosure if the prosecuting attorney certifies to the court that to do so may subject the witness or others to physical or substantial economic harm or coercion. Where a motion for discovery of the names and addresses of witnesses has been made by a defendant, the prosecuting attorney may move the court to perpetuate the testimony of such witnesses in a hearing before the court, in which hearing the defendant shall have the right of cross-examination. A record of the witness' testimony shall be made and shall be admissible at trial as part of the state's case in chief, in the event the witness has become unavailable through no fault of the state.

(f) Disclosure of evidence favorable to defendant. Upon motion of the defendant before trial the court shall order the prosecuting attorney to disclose to counsel for the defendant all evidence, known or which may become known to the prosecuting attorney, favorable to the defendant and material either to guilt or punishment. The certification and the perpetuation provisions of subsection (B)(1)(e) apply to this subsection.

(g) In camera inspection of witness' statement. Upon completion of a witness' direct examination at trial, the court on motion of the defendant shall conduct an in camera inspection of the witness' written or recorded statement with the defense attorney and prosecuting attorney present and participating, to determine the existence of inconsistencies, if any, between the testimony of such witness and the prior statement.

If the court determines that inconsistencies exist, the statement shall be given to the defense attorney for use in cross-examination of the witness as to the inconsistencies.

If the court determines that inconsistencies do not exist the statement shall not be given to the defense attorney and he shall not be permitted to cross-examine or comment thereon.

Whenever the defense attorney is not given the entire statement, it shall be preserved in the records of the court to be made available to the appellate court in the event of an appeal.

(2) Information not subject to disclosure. Except as provided in subsections (B)(1)(a), (b), (d), (f), and (g), this rule does not authorize the discovery or inspection of reports, memoranda, or other internal documents made by the prosecuting attorney or his agents in connection with the investigation or prosecution of the case, or of statements made by witnesses or prospective witnesses to state agents.

(3) Grand jury transcripts. The discovery or inspection of recorded proceedings of a grand jury shall be governed by Rule 6(E) and subsection (B)(1)(a) of this rule.

(4) Witness list; no comment. The fact that a witness' name is on a list furnished under subsections (B)(1)(b) and (f), and that such witness is not called shall not be commented upon at the trial.

(C) Disclosure of evidence by the defendant

(1) Information subject to disclosure.

(a) Documents and tangible objects. If on request or motion the defendant obtains discovery under subsection (B)(1)(c), the court shall, upon motion of the prosecuting attorney order the defendant to permit the prosecuting attorney to inspect and copy or photograph books, papers, documents, photographs, tangible objects, or copies or portions thereof, available to or within the possession, custody or control of the defendant and which the defendant intends to introduce in evidence at the trial.

(b) Reports of examinations and tests. If on request or motion the defendant obtains discovery under subsection (B)(1)(d), the court shall, upon motion of the prosecuting attorney, order the defendant to permit the prosecuting attorney to inspect and copy or photograph any results or reports of physical or mental examinations and of scientific tests or experiments made in connection with the particular case, or copies thereof, available to or within the possession or control of the defendant, and which the defendant intends to introduce in evidence at the trial, or which were prepared by a witness whom the defendant intends to call at the trial, when such results or reports relate to his testimony.

(c) Witness names and addresses. If on request or motion the defendant obtains discovery under subsection (B)(1)(e), the court shall, upon motion of the prosecuting attorney, order the defendant to furnish the prosecuting attorney a list of the names and addresses of the witnesses he intends to call at the trial. Where a motion for discovery of the names and addresses of witnesses has been made by the prosecuting attorney, the defendant may move the court to perpetuate the testimony of such witnesses in a hearing before the court in which hearing the prosecuting attorney shall have the right of cross-examination. A record of the witness' testimony shall be made and shall be admissible at trial as part of the defendant's case in chief in the event the witness has become unavailable through no fault of the defendant.

(d) In camera inspection of witness' statement. Upon completion of the direct examination, at trial, of a witness other than the defendant, the court on motion of the prosecuting attorney shall conduct an in camera inspection of the witness' written or recorded statement obtained by the defense attorney or his agents with the defense attorney and prosecuting attorney present and participating, to determine the existence of inconsistencies, if any, between the testimony of such witness and the prior statement.

If the court determines that inconsistencies exist the statement shall be given to the prosecuting attorney for use in cross-examination of the witness as to the inconsistencies.

If the court determines that inconsistencies do not exist the statement shall not be given to the prosecuting attorney, and he shall not be permitted to cross-examine or comment thereon.

Whenever the prosecuting attorney is not given the entire statement it shall be preserved in the records of the court to be made available to the appellate court in the event of an appeal.

(2) Information not subject to disclosure. Except as provided in subsections (C)(1)(b) and (d), this rule does not authorize the discovery or inspection of reports, memoranda, or other internal documents made by the defense attorney or his agents in connection with the investigation or defense of the case, or of statements made by witnesses or prospective witnesses to the defense attorney or his agents.

(3) Witness list; no comment. The fact that a witness' name is on a list furnished under subsection (C)(1)(c), and that the witness is not called shall not be commented upon at the trial.

(D) Continuing duty to disclose

If, subsequent to compliance with a request or order pursuant to this rule, and prior to or during trial, a party discovers additional matter which would have been subject to discovery or inspection under the original request or order, he shall promptly make such matter available for discovery or inspection, or notify the other party or his attorney or the court of the existence of the additional matter, in order to allow the court to modify its previous order, or to allow the other party to make an appropriate request for additional discovery or inspection.

(E) Regulation of discovery

(1) Protective orders. Upon a sufficient showing the court may at any time order that the discovery or inspection be denied, restricted or deferred, or make such other order as is appropriate. Upon motion by a party the court may permit a party to make such showing, or part of such showing, in the form of a written statement to be inspected by the judge alone. If the court enters an order granting relief following such a showing, the entire text of the party's statement shall be sealed and preserved in the records of the court to be made available to the appellate court in the event of an appeal.

(2) Time, place and manner of discovery and inspection. An order of the court granting relief under this rule shall specify the time, place and manner of making the discovery and inspection permitted, and may prescribe such terms and conditions as are just.

(3) Failure to comply. If at any time during the course of the proceedings it is brought to the attention of the court that a party has failed to comply with this rule or with an order issued pursuant to this rule, the court may order such party to permit the discovery or inspection, grant a continuance, or prohibit the party from introducing in evidence the material not disclosed, or it may make such other order as it deems just under the circumstances.

(F) Time of motions

A defendant shall make his motion for discovery within twenty-one days after arraignment or seven days before the date of trial, whichever is earlier, or at such reasonable time later as the court may permit. The prosecuting attorney shall make his motion for discovery within seven days after defendant obtains discovery or three days before trial, whichever is earlier. The motion shall include all relief sought under this rule. A subsequent motion may be made only upon showing of cause why such motion would be in the interest of justice.

(Adopted eff. 7–1–73)

Crim R 17 Subpoena

(A) For attendance of witnesses; form; issuance

Every subpoena issued by the clerk shall be under the seal of the court, shall state the name of the court and the title of the action, and shall command each person to whom it is directed to attend and give testimony at a time and place therein specified. The clerk shall issue a subpoena, or a subpoena for the production of documentary evidence, signed and sealed but otherwise in blank, to a party requesting it, who shall fill it in and file a copy thereof with the clerk before service.

(B) Defendants unable to pay

The court shall order at any time that a subpoena be issued for service on a named witness upon an ex parte application of a defendant upon a satisfactory showing that the presence of the witness is necessary to an adequate defense and that the defendant is financially unable to pay the witness fees required by subdivision (D). If the court orders the subpoena to be issued the costs incurred by the process and the fees of the witness so subpoenaed shall be taxed as costs.

(C) For production of documentary evidence

A subpoena may also command the person to whom it is directed to produce the books, papers, documents or other objects designated therein; but the court, upon motion made promptly and in any event made at or before the time specified in the subpoena for compliance therewith, may quash or modify the subpoena if compliance would be unreasonable or oppressive. The court may direct that the books, papers, documents or other objects designated in the subpoena be produced before the court at a time prior to the trial or prior to the time they are offered in evidence, and may, upon their production, permit them or portions thereof to be inspected by the parties or their attorneys.

(D) Service

A subpoena may be served by a sheriff, bailiff, coroner, clerk of court, constable, marshal, or a deputy of any, by a municipal or township policeman, by an attorney at law or by any person designated by order of the court who is not a party and is not less than eighteen years of age. Service of a subpoena upon a person named therein shall be made by delivering a copy thereof to such person or by reading it to him in person or by leaving it at his usual place of residence, and by tendering to him upon demand the fees for one day's attendance and the mileage allowed by law. The person serving the subpoena shall file a return thereof with the clerk. If the witness being subpoenaed resides outside the county in which the court is located, the fees for one day's attendance and mileage shall be tendered without demand. The return may be forwarded through the postal service, or otherwise.

(E) Subpoena for taking depositions; place of examination

When the attendance of a witness before an official authorized to take depositions is required, the subpoena shall be issued by such person and shall command the person to whom it is directed to attend and give testimony at a time and place specified therein. The subpoena may command the person to whom it is directed to produce designated books, papers, documents, or tangible objects which constitute or contain evidence relating to any of the matters within the scope of the examination permitted by Rule 16.

A person whose deposition is to be taken may be required to attend an examination in the county wherein he resides or is employed or transacts his business in person, or at such other convenient place as is fixed by an order of court.

(F) Subpoena for a hearing or trial

At the request of any party, subpoenas for attendance at a hearing or trial shall be issued by the clerk of the court in which the hearing or trial is held. A subpoena requiring the attendance of a witness at a hearing or trial may be served at any place within this state.

(G) Contempt

Failure by any person without adequate excuse to obey a subpoena served upon him may be deemed a contempt of the court or officer issuing the subpoena.

(Adopted eff. 7–1–73; amended eff. 7–1–78)

Crim R 17.1 Pretrial conference

At any time after the filing of an indictment, information or complaint the court may, upon its own motion or the motion of any party, order one or more conferences to consider such matters as will promote a fair and expeditious trial. At the conclusion of a conference the court shall prepare and file a memorandum of the matters agreed upon. No admissions made by the defendant or defendant's counsel at the conference shall be used against the defendant unless the admissions are reduced to writing and signed by the defendant and defendant's counsel. The court shall not conduct pretrial conferences in any case in which a term of imprisonment is a possible penalty unless the defendant is represented by counsel or counsel has been waived pursuant to Crim. R. 44. In any case in which the defendant is not represented by counsel, any pretrial conference shall be conducted in open court and shall be recorded as provided in Crim. R. 22.

(Adopted eff. 7–1–73; amended eff. 7–1–00)

Crim R 18 Venue and change of venue

(A) General venue provisions

The venue of a criminal case shall be as provided by law.

(B) Change of venue; procedure upon change of venue

Upon the motion of any party or upon its own motion the court may transfer an action to any court having jurisdiction of the subject matter outside the county in which trial would otherwise be held, when it appears that a fair and impartial trial cannot be held in the court in which the action is pending.

(1) Time of motion. A motion under this rule shall be made within thirty-five days after arraignment or seven days before trial, whichever is earlier, or at such reasonable time later as the court may permit.

(2) Clerk's obligations upon change of venue. Where a change of venue is ordered the clerk of the court in which the cause is pending shall make copies of all of the papers in the action which, with the original complaint, indictment, or information, he shall transmit to the clerk of the court to which the action is sent for trial, and the trial and all subsequent proceedings shall be conducted as if the action had originated in the latter court.

(3) Additional counsel for prosecuting attorney. The prosecuting attorney of the political subdivision in which the action originated shall take charge of and try the case. The court to which the action is sent may on application appoint one or more attorneys to assist the prosecuting attorney in the trial, and allow the appointed attorneys reasonable compensation.

(4) Appearance of defendant, witnesses. Where a change of venue is ordered and the defendant is in custody, a warrant shall

be issued by the clerk of the court in which the action originated, directed to the person having custody of the defendant commanding him to bring the defendant to the jail of the county to which the action is transferred, there to be kept until discharged. If the defendant on the date of the order changing venue is not in custody, the court in the order changing venue shall continue the conditions of release and direct the defendant to appear in the court to which the venue is changed. The court shall recognize the witnesses to appear before the court in which the accused is to be tried.

(5) Expenses. The reasonable expenses of the prosecuting attorney incurred in consequence of a change of venue, compensation of counsel appointed pursuant to Rule 44, the fees of the clerk of the court to which the venue is changed, the sheriff or bailiff, and of the jury shall be allowed and paid out of the treasury of the political subdivision in which the action originated.

(Adopted eff. 7–1–73)

Crim R 19 Magistrates

(A) Appointment

A court other than a mayor's court may appoint one or more magistrates. A magistrate shall be an attorney admitted to practice in Ohio. A magistrate may serve in more than one county or in two or more courts of the same criminal jurisdiction within the same county.

(B) Compensation

The compensation for the services of a magistrate shall be fixed by the court, and no part of the compensation shall be taxed as costs.

(C) Reference and powers

(1) Order of reference. A court of record may by order refer any of the following to a magistrate:

(a) Initial appearances and preliminary hearings conducted pursuant to Crim. R. 5.

(b) Arraignments conducted pursuant to Crim. R. 10.

(c) Proceedings at which a plea may be entered in accordance with Crim. R. 11, only as follows:

(i) A magistrate may accept and enter not guilty pleas in felony and misdemeanor cases;

(ii) In misdemeanor cases, a magistrate may accept and enter guilty and no contest pleas, determine guilt or innocence, receive statements in explanation and in mitigation of sentence, and recommend a penalty to be imposed. If the offense charged is an offense for which imprisonment is a possible penalty, the matter may be referred only with the unanimous consent of the parties, in writing or on the record in open court.

(d) Pretrial conferences conducted pursuant to Crim. R. 17.1.

(e) Proceedings to establish bail pursuant to Crim. R. 46.

(f) Motions. A magistrate may hear and decide motions in referred cases as follows:

(i) Any pretrial or post-judgment motion in any misdemeanor case for which imprisonment is not a possible penalty.

(ii) Upon the unanimous consent of the parties in writing or on the record in open court, any pretrial or post-judgment motion in any misdemeanor case for which imprisonment is a possible penalty.

(g) Proceedings for the issuance of a temporary protection order as authorized by law.

(h) The trial of any misdemeanor case that will not be tried to a jury. If the offense charged is an offense for which imprisonment is a possible penalty, the matter may be referred only with unanimous consent of the parties in writing or on the record in open court.

(2) Except as is otherwise provided in this rule, an order of reference may be specific to a particular case or may refer categories of motions or cases.

(3) The order of reference to a magistrate may do all of the following:

(a) Specify or limit the magistrate's powers;

(b) Direct the magistrate to report only upon particular issues, do or perform particular acts, or receive and report evidence only;

(c) Fix the time and place for beginning and closing the hearings and for the filing of the magistrate's decision.

(4) General powers. Subject to the specifications and limitations stated in the order of reference, the magistrate shall regulate all proceedings in every hearing as if by the court and do all acts and take all measures necessary or proper for the efficient performance of the magistrate's duties under the order. The magistrate may do all of the following:

(a) Issue subpoenas for the attendance of witnesses and the production of evidence;

(b) Rule upon the admissibility of evidence in misdemeanor cases in accordance with division (C)(1)(f) of this rule;

(c) Put witnesses under oath and examine them;

(d) In cases involving direct or indirect contempt of court, and when necessary to obtain the alleged contemnor's presence for hearing, issue an attachment for the alleged contemnor and set bail to secure the alleged contemnor's appearance, considering the conditions of release prescribed in Crim. R. 46.

(5) Power to enter orders.

(a) Orders. Unless otherwise specified in the order of reference, the magistrate may enter pretrial orders without judicial approval which are necessary to regulate the proceedings and are not dispositive of a claim or a defense of a party.

(b) Appeal of orders. Any party may appeal to the court from any order of a magistrate entered under division (C)(5)(a) of this rule by filing a motion to set the order aside, stating the party's objections with particularity. The motion shall be filed no later than fourteen days after the magistrate's order is entered. The pendency of a motion to set aside does not stay the effectiveness of the magistrate's order unless the magistrate or the court grants a stay. A party's failure to appeal pursuant to division (C)(5)(b) of this rule does not preclude review of the order on objection to the magistrate's decision pursuant to division (E) of this rule.

(c) Contempt in the magistrate's presence. In cases of contempt in the presence of the magistrate, the magistrate may impose an appropriate civil or criminal contempt sanction. Contempt sanctions under division (C)(5)(c) of this rule may be imposed only by a written order that recites the facts and certifies that the magistrate saw or heard the conduct constituting contempt. The contempt order shall be filed and a copy provided by the clerk to the appropriate judge of the court forthwith. The contemnor may by motion obtain immediate review of the magistrate's contempt order by a judge, or the judge or magistrate may set bail pending judicial review.

(d) Powers conveyed by statute. Unless prohibited by the order of reference, a magistrate shall continue to be authorized to enter orders when authority is specifically conveyed by statute to magistrates.

(e) Form of magistrate's orders. All orders of a magistrate shall be in writing, signed by the magistrate, identified as a magistrate's order in the caption, and filed with the clerk, who shall serve copies on all parties or their attorneys.

(D) Proceedings

(1) All proceedings before the magistrate shall be in accordance with these rules and any applicable statutes, as if before the court.

(2) Except as otherwise provided by law, all proceedings before the magistrate shall be recorded in accordance with procedures established by the court.

(E) Decisions in referred matters

Unless specifically required by the order of reference, a magistrate is not required to prepare any report other than the magistrate's decision. All matters referred to magistrates shall be decided as follows:

(1) Magistrate's decision. The magistrate promptly shall conduct all proceedings necessary for decision of referred matters. All decisions of a magistrate shall be in writing, signed by the magistrate, identified as a magistrate's decision in the caption, and filed with the clerk, who shall serve copies on all parties or their attorneys.

(2) Objections.

(a) Time for filing. Within fourteen days after the filing of a magistrate's decision, a party may file written objections to the magistrate's decision. If any party timely files objections, any other party may also file objections no later than seven days after the first objections are filed.

(b) Form of objections. Objections shall be specific and state with particularity the grounds for the objections. A party shall not assign as error on appeal the court's adoption of the decision of the magistrate unless the party has timely objected to the magistrate's decision.

(3) Court's action on magistrate's decision.

(a) When effective. The magistrate's decision shall become effective when adopted by the court. The court may adopt the magistrate's decision and enter judgment if no written objections are filed or the parties have waived the filing of objections in writing or on the record in open court, unless the court determines that there is an error of law or other defect on the face of the magistrate's decision. No sentence recommended by a magistrate shall be enforced until the court has entered judgment.

(b) Disposition of objections. The court shall rule on any objections. The court may adopt, reject, or modify the magistrate's decision, hear additional evidence, recommit the matter to the magistrate with instructions, or hear the matter. The court may refuse to consider additional evidence proffered upon objections unless the objecting party demonstrates that with reasonable diligence the party could not have produced that evidence for the magistrate's consideration.

(Adopted eff. 7–1–90; amended eff. 7–1–95, 7–1–00)

Crim R 20 [Reserved]

Crim R 21 Transfer from common pleas court for trial

(A) When permitted

Where an indictment or information charging only misdemeanors is filed in the court of common pleas, the court may retain the case for trial or the administrative judge, within fourteen days after the indictment or information is filed with the clerk of the court of common pleas, may transfer it to the court from which the bind over to the grand jury was made or to the court of record of the jurisdiction in which venue appears.

(B) Proceedings on transfer

When a transfer is ordered, the clerk of the court of common pleas, within three days, shall transmit to the clerk of the court to which the case is transferred, certified copies of the indictment, information, and all other papers in the case, and any bail taken, and the prosecution shall continue in that court.

(Adopted eff. 7–1–73; amended eff. 7–1–04)

Crim R 22 Recording of proceedings

In serious offense cases all proceedings shall be recorded.

In petty offense cases all waivers of counsel required by Rule 44(B) shall be recorded, and if requested by any party all proceedings shall be recorded.

Proceedings may be recorded in shorthand, or stenotype, or by any other adequate mechanical, electronic or video recording device.

(Adopted eff. 7–1–73)

Crim R 23 Trial by jury or by the court

(A) Trial by jury

In serious offense cases the defendant before commencement of the trial may knowingly, intelligently and voluntarily waive in writing his right to trial by jury. Such waiver may also be made during trial with the approval of the court and the consent of the prosecuting attorney. In petty offense cases, where there is a right of jury trial, the defendant shall be tried by the court unless he demands a jury trial. Such demand must be in writing and filed with the clerk of court not less than ten days prior to the date set for trial, or on or before the third day following receipt of notice of the date set for trial, whichever is later. Failure to demand a jury trial as provided in this subdivision is a complete waiver of the right thereto.

(B) Number of jurors

In felony cases juries shall consist of twelve.

In misdemeanor cases juries shall consist of eight.

If a defendant is charged with a felony and with a misdemeanor or, if a felony and a misdemeanor involving different defendants are joined for trial, the jury shall consist of twelve.

(C) Trial without a jury

In a case tried without a jury the court shall make a general finding.

(Adopted eff. 7–1–73; amended eff. 7–1–80)

Crim R 24 Trial jurors

(A) Examination of jurors

Any person called as a juror for the trial of any cause shall be examined under oath or upon affirmation as to the juror's qualifications. The court may permit the attorney for the defendant, or the defendant if appearing *pro se*, and the attorney for the state to conduct the examination of the prospective jurors or may itself conduct the examination. In the latter event, the court shall permit the state and defense to supplement the examination by further inquiry.

(B) Challenge for cause

A person called as a juror may be challenged for the following causes:

(1) That the juror has been convicted of a crime which by law renders the juror disqualified to serve on a jury.

(2) That the juror is a chronic alcoholic, or drug dependent person.

(3) That the juror was a member of the grand jury which found the indictment in the case.

(4) That the juror served on a petit jury drawn in the same cause against the same defendant, and the petit jury was discharged after hearing the evidence or rendering a verdict on the evidence that was set aside.

(5) That the juror served as a juror in a civil case brought against the defendant for the same act.

(6) That the juror has an action pending between him or her and the State of Ohio or the defendant.

(7) That the juror or the juror's spouse is a party to another action then pending in any court in which an attorney in the cause then on trial is an attorney, either for or against the juror.

(8) That the juror has been subpoenaed in good faith as a witness in the case.

(9) That the juror is possessed of a state of mind evincing enmity or bias toward the defendant or the state; but no person summoned as a juror shall be disqualified by reason of a previously formed or expressed opinion with reference to the guilt or innocence of the accused, if the court is satisfied, from the examination of the juror or from other evidence, that the juror will render an impartial verdict according to the law and the evidence submitted to the jury at the trial.

(10) That the juror is related by consanguinity or affinity within the fifth degree to the person alleged to be injured or attempted to be injured by the offense charged, or to the person on whose complaint the prosecution was instituted; or to the defendant.

(11) That the juror is the person alleged to be injured or attempted to be injured by the offense charged, or the person on whose complaint the prosecution was instituted, or the defendant.

(12) That the juror is the employer or employee, or the spouse, parent, son, or daughter of the employer or employee, or the counselor, agent, or attorney, of any person included in division (B)(11) of this rule.

(13) That English is not the juror's native language, and the juror's knowledge of English is insufficient to permit the juror to understand the facts and the law in the case.

(14) That the juror is otherwise unsuitable for any other cause to serve as a juror.

The validity of each challenge listed in division (B) of this rule shall be determined by the court.

(C) Peremptory challenges

In addition to challenges provided in division (B) of this rule, if there is one defendant, each party peremptorily may challenge three jurors in misdemeanor cases, four jurors in felony cases other than capital cases, and six jurors in capital cases. If there is more than one defendant, each defendant peremptorily may challenge the same number of jurors as if the defendant was the sole defendant.

In any case where there are multiple defendants, the prosecuting attorney peremptorily may challenge a number of jurors equal to the total peremptory challenges allowed all defendants. In case of the consolidation of any indictments, informations or complaints for trial, such consolidated cases shall be considered, for purposes of exercising peremptory challenges, as though the defendants or offenses had been joined in the same indictment, information or complaint.

(D) Manner of exercising peremptory challenges

Peremptory challenges may be exercised after the minimum number of jurors allowed by the Rules of Criminal Procedure has been passed for cause and seated on the panel. Peremptory challenges shall be exercised alternately, with the first challenge exercised by the state. The failure of a party to exercise a peremptory challenge constitutes a waiver of that challenge. If all parties, alternately and in sequence, fail to exercise a peremptory challenge, the joint failure constitutes a waiver of all peremptory challenges.

A prospective juror peremptorily challenged by either party shall be excused and another juror shall be called who shall take the place of the juror excused and be sworn and examined as other jurors. The other party, if that party has peremptory challenges remaining, shall be entitled to challenge any juror then seated on the panel.

(E) Challenge to array

The prosecuting attorney or the attorney for the defendant may challenge the array of petit jurors on the ground that it was not selected, drawn or summoned in accordance with law. A challenge to the array shall be made before the examination of the jurors pursuant to division (A) of this rule and shall be tried by the court.

No array of petit jurors shall be set aside, nor shall any verdict in any case be set aside because the jury commissioners have returned such jury or any juror in any informal or irregular manner, if in the opinion of the court the irregularity is unimportant and insufficient to vitiate the return.

(F) Alternate jurors

(1) Non–capital cases. The court may direct that not more than six jurors in addition to the regular jury be called and impaneled to sit as alternate jurors. Alternate jurors in the order in which they are called shall replace jurors who, prior to the time the jury retires to consider its verdict, become or are found to be unable or disqualified to perform their duties. Alternate jurors shall be drawn in the same manner, have the same qualifications, be subject to the same examination and challenges, take the same oath, and have the same functions, powers, facilities, and privileges as the regular jurors. Except in capital cases, an alternate juror who does not replace a regular juror shall be discharged after the jury retires to consider its verdict. Each party is entitled to one peremptory challenge in addition to those otherwise allowed if one or two alternate jurors are to be impaneled, two peremptory challenges if three or four alternate jurors are to be impaneled, and three peremptory challenges if five or six alternative jurors are to be impaneled. The additional peremptory challenges may be used against an alternate juror only, and the other peremptory challenges allowed by this rule may not be used against an alternate juror.

(2) Capital cases. The procedure designated in division (F)(1) of this rule shall be the same in capital cases, except that any alternate juror shall continue to serve if more than one deliberation is required. If an alternate juror replaces a regular juror after a guilty verdict, the court shall instruct the alternate juror that the juror is bound by that verdict. No alternate juror shall be substituted during any deliberation. Any alternate juror shall be discharged after the trial jury retires to consider the penalty.

(G) Control of juries

(1) Before submission of case to jury. Before submission of a case to the jury, the court, upon its own motion or the motion of a party, may restrict the separation of jurors or may sequester the jury.

(2) After submission of case to jury. (a) Misdemeanor cases. After submission of a misdemeanor case to the jury, the court, after giving cautionary instructions, may permit the separation of jurors.

(b) Non–capital felony cases. After submission of a non-capital felony case to the jury, the court, after giving cautionary instructions, may permit the separation of jurors during any period of court adjournment or may require the jury to remain under the supervision of an officer of the court.

(c) Capital cases. After submission of a capital case to the jury, the jury shall remain under the supervision of an officer of the court until a verdict is rendered or the jury is discharged by the court.

(3) Separation in emergency. Where the jury is sequestered or after a capital case is submitted to the jury, the court may, in an emergency and upon giving cautionary instructions, allow temporary separation of jurors.

(4) Duties of supervising officer. Where jurors are required to remain under the supervision of an officer of the court, the court shall make arrangements for their care, maintenance and comfort.

When the jury is in the care of an officer of the court and until the jury is discharged by the court, the officer may inquire whether the jury has reached a verdict, but shall not:

(a) Communicate any matter concerning jury conduct to anyone except the judge or;

(b) Communicate with the jurors or permit communications with jurors, except as allowed by court order.

(Adopted eff. 7–1–73; amended eff. 7–1–75, 7–1–02)

Crim R 25 Disability of a judge

(A) During trial

If for any reason the judge before whom a jury trial has commenced is unable to proceed with the trial, another judge designated by the administrative judge, or, in the case of a single-judge division, by the Chief Justice of the Supreme Court of Ohio, may proceed with and finish the trial, upon certifying in the record that he has familiarized himself with the record of the trial. If such other judge is satisfied that he cannot adequately familiarize himself with the record, he may in his discretion grant a new trial.

(B) After verdict or finding of guilt

If for any reason the judge before whom the defendant has been tried is unable to perform the duties of the court after a verdict or finding of guilt, another judge designated by the administrative judge, or, in the case of a single-judge division, by the Chief Justice of the Supreme Court of Ohio, may perform those duties. If such other judge is satisfied that he cannot perform those duties because he did not preside at the trial, he may in his discretion grant a new trial.

(Adopted eff. 7–1–73)

Crim R 26 Substitution of photographs for physical evidence

Physical property, other than contraband, as defined by statute, under the control of a prosecuting attorney for use as evidence in a hearing or trial should be returned to the owner at the earliest possible time. To facilitate the early return of such property, where appropriate, and by court order, photographs, as defined in Evid. R. 1001(2), may be taken of the property and introduced as evidence in the hearing or trial. The admission of such photographs is subject to the relevancy requirements of Evid. R. 401, Evid. R. 402, Evid. R. 403, the authentication requirements of Evid. R. 901, and the best evidence requirements of Evid. R. 1002.

(Adopted eff. 7–1–81)

Crim R 27 Proof of official record; judicial notice: determination of foreign law

The proof of official records provisions of Civil Rule 44, and the judicial notice and determination of foreign law provisions of Civil Rule 44.1 apply in criminal cases.

(Adopted eff. 7–1–73)

Crim R 28 [Reserved]

Crim R 29 Motion for acquittal

(A) Motion for judgment of acquittal

The court on motion of a defendant or on its own motion, after the evidence on either side is closed, shall order the entry of a judgment of acquittal of one or more offenses charged in the indictment, information, or complaint, if the evidence is insufficient to sustain a conviction of such offense or offenses. The court may not reserve ruling on a motion for judgment of acquittal made at the close of the state's case.

(B) Reservation of decision on motion

If a motion for a judgment of acquittal is made at the close of all the evidence, the court may reserve decision on the motion, submit the case to the jury and decide the motion either before the jury returns a verdict, or after it returns a verdict of guilty, or after it is discharged without having returned a verdict.

(C) Motion after verdict or discharge of jury

If a jury returns a verdict of guilty or is discharged without having returned a verdict, a motion for judgment of acquittal may be made or renewed within fourteen days after the jury is discharged or within such further time as the court may fix during the fourteen day period. If a verdict of guilty is returned, the court may on such motion set aside the verdict and enter judgment of acquittal. If no verdict is returned, the court may enter judgment of acquittal. It shall not be a prerequisite to the making of such motion that a similar motion has been made prior to the submission of the case to the jury.

(Adopted eff. 7–1–73)

Crim R 30 Instructions

(A) Instructions; error; record

At the close of the evidence or at such earlier time during the trial as the court reasonably directs, any party may file written requests that the court instruct the jury on the law as set forth in the requests. Copies shall be furnished to all other parties at the time of making the requests. The court shall inform counsel of its proposed action on the requests prior to counsel's arguments to the jury and shall give the jury complete instructions after the arguments are completed. The court also may give some or all of its instructions to the jury prior to counsel's arguments. The court need not reduce its instructions to writing.

On appeal, a party may not assign as error the giving or the failure to give any instructions unless the party objects before the jury retires to consider its verdict, stating specifically the matter objected to and the grounds of the objection. Opportunity shall be given to make the objection out of the hearing of the jury.

(B) Cautionary instructions

At the commencement and during the course of the trial, the court may give the jury cautionary and other instructions of law relating to trial procedure, credibility and weight of the evidence, and the duty and function of the jury and may acquaint the jury generally with the nature of the case.

(Adopted eff. 7–1–73; amended eff. 7–1–75, 7–1–82, 7–1–92)

Crim R 31 Verdict

(A) Return

The verdict shall be unanimous. It shall be in writing, signed by all jurors concurring therein, and returned by the jury to the judge in open court.

(B) Several defendants

If there are two or more defendants the jury at any time during its deliberations may return a verdict or verdicts with respect to a defendant or defendants as to whom it has agreed. If the jury cannot agree with respect to all, the defendant or defendants as to whom it does not agree may be tried again.

(C) Conviction of lesser offense

The defendant may be found not guilty of the offense charged but guilty of an attempt to commit it if such an attempt is an offense at law. When the indictment, information, or complaint charges an offense including degrees, or if lesser offenses are included within the offense charged, the defendant may be found not guilty of the degree charged but guilty of an inferior degree thereof, or of a lesser included offense.

(D) Poll of jury

When a verdict is returned and before it is accepted the jury shall be polled at the request of any party or upon the court's own motion. If upon the poll there is not unanimous concurrence, the jury may be directed to retire for further deliberation or may be discharged.

(Adopted eff. 7–1–73)

Crim R 32 Sentence

(A) Imposition of sentence

Sentence shall be imposed without unnecessary delay. Pending sentence, the court may commit the defendant or continue or alter the bail. At the time of imposing sentence, the court shall do all of the following:

(1) Afford counsel an opportunity to speak on behalf of the defendant and address the defendant personally and ask if he or she wishes to make a statement in his or her own behalf or present any information in mitigation of punishment.

(2) Afford the prosecuting attorney an opportunity to speak;

(3) Afford the victim the rights provided by law;

(4) In serious offenses, state its statutory findings and give reasons supporting those findings, if appropriate.

(B) Notification of right to appeal

(1) After imposing sentence in a serious offense that has gone to trial, the court shall advise the defendant that the defendant has a right to appeal the conviction.

(2) After imposing sentence in a serious offense, the court shall advise the defendant of the defendant's right, where applicable, to appeal or to seek leave to appeal the sentence imposed.

(3) If a right to appeal or a right to seek leave to appeal applies under division (B)(1) or (B)(2) of this rule, the court also shall advise the defendant of all of the following:

(a) That if the defendant is unable to pay the cost of an appeal, the defendant has the right to appeal without payment;

(b) That if the defendant is unable to obtain counsel for an appeal, counsel will be appointed without cost;

(c) That if the defendant is unable to pay the costs of documents necessary to an appeal, the documents will be provided without cost;

(d) That the defendant has a right to have a notice of appeal timely filed on his or her behalf.

Upon defendant's request, the court shall forthwith appoint counsel for appeal.

(C) Judgment

A judgment of conviction shall set forth the plea, the verdict or findings, and the sentence. If the defendant is found not guilty or for any other reason is entitled to be discharged, the court shall render judgment accordingly. The judge shall sign the judgment and the clerk shall enter it on the journal. A judgment is effective only when entered on the journal by the clerk.

(Adopted eff. 7–1–73; amended eff. 7–1–92, 7–1–98, 7–1–04)

Crim R 32.1 Withdrawal of guilty plea

A motion to withdraw a plea of guilty or no contest may be made only before sentence is imposed; but to correct manifest injustice the court after sentence may set aside the judgment of conviction and permit the defendant to withdraw his or her plea.

(Adopted eff. 7–1–73; amended eff. 7–1–98)

Crim R 32.2 Presentence investigation

In felony cases the court shall, and in misdemeanor cases the court may, order a presentence investigation and report before imposing community control sanctions or granting probation.

(Adopted eff. 7–1–73; amended eff. 7–1–76, 7–1–98)

Crim R 32.3 Revocation of community release

(A) Hearing

The court shall not impose a prison term for violation of the conditions of a community control sanction or revoke probation except after a hearing at which the defendant shall be present and apprised of the grounds on which action is proposed. The defendant may be admitted to bail pending hearing.

(B) Counsel

The defendant shall have the right to be represented by retained counsel and shall be so advised. Where a defendant convicted of a serious offense is unable to obtain counsel, counsel shall be assigned to represent the defendant, unless the defendant after being fully advised of his or her right to assigned counsel, knowingly, intelligently, and voluntarily waives the right to counsel. Where a defendant convicted of a petty offense is unable to obtain counsel, the court may assign counsel to represent the defendant.

(C) Confinement in petty offense cases

If confinement after conviction was precluded by Crim. R. 44(B), revocation of probation shall not result in confinement.

If confinement after conviction was not precluded by Crim. R. 44(B), revocation of probation shall not result in confinement unless, at the revocation hearing, there is compliance with Crim. R. 44(B).

(D) Waiver of counsel

Waiver of counsel shall be as prescribed in Crim. R. 44(C).

(Adopted eff. 7–1–73; amended eff. 7–1–98)

Crim R 33 New trial

(A) Grounds

A new trial may be granted on motion of the defendant for any of the following causes affecting materially his substantial rights:

(1) Irregularity in the proceedings, or in any order or ruling of the court, or abuse of discretion by the court, because of which the defendant was prevented from having a fair trial;

(2) Misconduct of the jury, prosecuting attorney, or the witnesses for the state;

(3) Accident or surprise which ordinary prudence could not have guarded against;

(4) That the verdict is not sustained by sufficient evidence or is contrary to law. If the evidence shows the defendant is not guilty

of the degree of crime for which he was convicted, but guilty of a lesser degree thereof, or of a lesser crime included therein, the court may modify the verdict or finding accordingly, without granting or ordering a new trial, and shall pass sentence on such verdict or finding as modified;

(5) Error of law occurring at the trial;

(6) When new evidence material to the defense is discovered which the defendant could not with reasonable diligence have discovered and produced at the trial. When a motion for a new trial is made upon the ground of newly discovered evidence, the defendant must produce at the hearing on the motion, in support thereof, the affidavits of the witnesses by whom such evidence is expected to be given, and if time is required by the defendant to procure such affidavits, the court may postpone the hearing of the motion for such length of time as is reasonable under all the circumstances of the case. The prosecuting attorney may produce affidavits or other evidence to impeach the affidavits of such witnesses.

(B) Motion for new trial; form, time

Application for a new trial shall be made by motion which, except for the cause of newly discovered evidence, shall be filed within fourteen days after the verdict was rendered, or the decision of the court where a trial by jury has been waived, unless it is made to appear by clear and convincing proof that the defendant was unavoidably prevented from filing his motion for a new trial, in which case the motion shall be filed within seven days from the order of the court finding that the defendant was unavoidably prevented from filing such motion within the time provided herein.

Motions for new trial on account of newly discovered evidence shall be filed within one hundred twenty days after the day upon which the verdict was rendered, or the decision of the court where trial by jury has been waived. If it is made to appear by clear and convincing proof that the defendant was unavoidably prevented from the discovery of the evidence upon which he must rely, such motion shall be filed within seven days from an order of the court finding that he was unavoidably prevented from discovering the evidence within the one hundred twenty day period.

(C) Affidavits required

The causes enumerated in subsection (A)(2) and (3) must be sustained by affidavit showing their truth, and may be controverted by affidavit.

(D) Procedure when new trial granted

When a new trial is granted by the trial court, or when a new trial is awarded on appeal, the accused shall stand trial upon the charge or charges of which he was convicted.

(E) Invalid grounds for new trial

No motion for a new trial shall be granted or verdict set aside, nor shall any judgment of conviction be reversed in any court because of:

(1) An inaccuracy or imperfection in the indictment, information, or complaint, provided that the charge is sufficient to fairly and reasonably inform the defendant of all the essential elements of the charge against him.

(2) A variance between the allegations and the proof thereof, unless the defendant is misled or prejudiced thereby;

(3) The admission or rejection of any evidence offered against or for the defendant, unless the defendant was or may have been prejudiced thereby;

(4) A misdirection of the jury, unless the defendant was or may have been prejudiced thereby;

(5) Any other cause, unless it affirmatively appears from the record that the defendant was prejudiced thereby or was prevented from having a fair trial.

(F) Motion for new trial not a condition for appellate review

A motion for a new trial is not a prerequisite to obtain appellate review.

(Adopted eff. 7–1–73)

Crim R 34 Arrest of judgment

The court on motion of the defendant shall arrest judgment if the indictment, information, or complaint does not charge an offense or if the court was without jurisdiction of the offense charged. The motion shall be made within fourteen days after verdict, or finding of guilty, or after plea of guilty or no contest, or within such further time as the court may fix during the fourteen day period.

When the judgment is arrested, the defendant shall be discharged, and his position with respect to the prosecution is as if the indictment, information, or complaint had not been returned or filed.

(Adopted eff. 7–1–73)

Crim R 35 Post–conviction petition

(A) A petition for post-conviction relief pursuant to section 2953.21 of the Revised Code shall contain a case history, statement of facts, and separately identified grounds for relief. Each ground for relief shall not exceed three pages in length. (See recommended Form XV in Appendix of Forms.) A petition may be accompanied by an attachment of exhibits or other supporting materials. A trial court may extend the page limits provided in this rule, request further briefing on any ground for relief presented, or direct the petitioner to file a supplemental petition in the recommended form.

(B) The clerk of court immediately shall send a copy of the petition to the prosecuting attorney. Upon order of the trial court, the clerk of court shall duplicate all or any part of the record that the trial court requires.

(C) The trial court shall file its ruling upon a petition for post-conviction relief, including findings of fact and conclusions of law if required by law, not later than one hundred eighty days after the petition is filed.

(Reserved eff. 7–1–73; amended eff. 7–1–97)

Crim R 36 Clerical mistakes

Clerical mistakes in judgments, orders, or other parts of the record, and errors in the record arising from oversight or omission, may be corrected by the court at any time.

(Adopted eff. 7–1–73)

Crim R 37 [Reserved]

Crim R 38 [Reserved]

Crim R 39 [Reserved]

Crim R 40 [Reserved]

Crim R 41 Search and seizure

(A) Authority to issue warrant

A search warrant authorized by this rule may be issued by a judge of a court of record to search and seize property located within the court's territorial jurisdiction, upon the request of a prosecuting attorney or a law enforcement officer.

(B) Property which may be seized with a warrant

A warrant may be issued under this rule to search for and seize any: (1) evidence of the commission of a criminal offense; or (2) contraband, the fruits of crime, or things otherwise criminally possessed; or (3) weapons or other things by means of which a crime has been committed or reasonably appears about to be committed.

(C) Issuance and contents

A warrant shall issue under this rule only on an affidavit or affidavits sworn to before a judge of a court of record and establishing the grounds for issuing the warrant. The affidavit shall name or describe the person to be searched or particularly describe the place to be searched, name or describe the property to be searched for and seized, state substantially the offense in relation thereto, and state the factual basis for the affiant's belief that such property is there located. If the judge is satisfied that probable cause for the search exists, he shall issue a warrant identifying the property and naming or describing the person or place to be searched. The finding of probable cause may be based upon hearsay in whole or in part, provided there is a substantial basis for believing the source of the hearsay to be credible and for believing that there is a factual basis for the information furnished. Before ruling on a request for a warrant, the judge may require the affiant to appear personally, and may examine under oath the affiant and any witnesses he may produce. Such testimony shall be admissible at a hearing on a motion to suppress if taken down by a court reporter or recording equipment, transcribed and made part of the affidavit. The warrant shall be directed to a law enforcement officer. It shall command the officer to search, within three days, the person or place named for the property specified. The warrant shall be served in the daytime, unless the issuing court, by appropriate provision in the warrant, and for reasonable cause shown, authorizes its execution at times other than daytime. The warrant shall designate a judge to whom it shall be returned.

(D) Execution and return with inventory

The officer taking property under the warrant shall give to the person from whom or from whose premises the property was taken a copy of the warrant and a receipt for the property taken, or shall leave the copy and receipt at the place from which the property was taken. The return shall be made promptly and shall be accompanied by a written inventory of any property taken. The inventory shall be made in the presence of the applicant for the warrant and the person from whose possession or premises the property was taken, if they are present, or in the presence of at least one credible person other than the applicant for the warrant or the person from whose possession or premises the property was taken, and shall be verified by the officer. The judge shall upon request deliver a copy of the inventory to the person from whom or from whose premises the property was taken and to the applicant for the warrant. Property seized under a warrant shall be kept for use as evidence by the court which issued the warrant or by the law enforcement agency which executed the warrant.

(E) Return of papers to clerk

The judge before whom the warrant is returned shall attach to the warrant a copy of the return, inventory, and all other papers in connection therewith and shall file them with the clerk.

(F) Definition of property and daytime

The term "property" is used in this rule to include documents, books, papers and any other tangible objects. The term "daytime" is used in this rule to mean the hours from 7:00 a.m. to 8:00 p.m.

(Adopted eff. 7–1–73)

Crim R 42 [Reserved]

Crim R 43 Presence of the defendant

(A) Defendant's presence

The defendant shall be present at the arraignment and every stage of the trial, including the impaneling of the jury, the return of the verdict, and the imposition of sentence, except as otherwise provided by these rules. In all prosecutions, the defendant's voluntary absence after the trial has been commenced in his presence shall not prevent continuing the trial to and including the verdict. A corporation may appear by counsel for all purposes.

(B) Defendant excluded because of disruptive conduct

Where a defendant's conduct in the courtroom is so disruptive that the hearing or trial cannot reasonably be conducted with his continued presence, the hearing or trial may proceed in his absence, and judgment and sentence may be pronounced as if he were present. Where the court determines that it may be essential to the preservation of the constitutional rights of the defendant, it may take such steps as are required for the communication of the courtroom proceedings to the defendant.

(Adopted eff. 7–1–73)

Crim R 44 Assignment of counsel

(A) Counsel in serious offenses

Where a defendant charged with a serious offense is unable to obtain counsel, counsel shall be assigned to represent him at every stage of the proceedings from his initial appearance before a court through appeal as of right, unless the defendant, after being fully advised of his right to assigned counsel, knowingly, intelligently, and voluntarily waives his right to counsel.

(B) Counsel in petty offenses

Where a defendant charged with a petty offense is unable to obtain counsel, the court may assign counsel to represent him. When a defendant charged with a petty offense is unable to obtain counsel, no sentence of confinement may be imposed upon him, unless after being fully advised by the court, he knowingly, intelligently, and voluntarily waives assignment of counsel.

(C) Waiver of counsel

Waiver of counsel shall be in open court and the advice and waiver shall be recorded as provided in Rule 22. In addition, in serious offense cases the waiver shall be in writing.

(D) Assignment procedure

The determination of whether a defendant is able or unable to obtain counsel shall be made in a recorded proceeding in open court.

(Adopted eff. 7–1–73)

Crim R 45 Time

(A) Time: computation

In computing any period of time prescribed or allowed by these rules, by the local rules of any court, by order of court, or by any applicable statute, the date of the act or event from which the designated period of time begins to run shall not be included. The last day of the period so computed shall be included, unless it is a Saturday, Sunday, or legal holiday, in which event the period runs until the end of the next day which is not Saturday, Sunday, or legal holiday. When the period of time prescribed or allowed is less than seven days, intermediate Saturdays, Sundays, and legal holidays shall be excluded in computation.

(B) Time: enlargement

When an act is required or allowed to be performed at or within a specified time, the court for cause shown may at any time in its discretion (1) with or without motion or notice, order the period enlarged if application therefor is made before expiration of the period originally prescribed or as extended by a previous order; or (2) upon motion permit the act to be done after expiration of the specified period, if the failure to act on time was the result of excusable neglect or would result in injustice to the defendant. The court may not extend the time for taking any action under Rule 23, Rule 29, Rule 33, and Rule 34 except to the extent and under the conditions stated in them.

(C) Time: unaffected by expiration of term

The period of time provided for the doing of any act or the taking of any proceeding is not affected or limited by the expiration of a term of court. The expiration of a term of court in no way affects the power of a court to do any act in a criminal proceeding.

(D) Time: for motions; affidavits

A written motion, other than one which may be heard ex parte, and notice of the hearing thereof, shall be served not later than seven days before the time specified for the hearing unless a different period is fixed by rule or order of the court. For cause shown such an order may be made on ex parte application. When a motion is supported by affidavit, the affidavit shall be served with the motion. Opposing affidavits may be served not less than one day before the hearing, unless the court permits them to be served at a later time.

(E) Time: additional time after service by mail

Whenever a party has the right or is required to do an act within a prescribed period after the service of a notice or other paper upon him, and the notice or other paper is served upon him by mail, three days shall be added to the prescribed period. This subdivision does not apply to responses to service of summons under Rule 4 and Rule 9.

(Adopted eff. 7–1–73)

Crim R 46 Bail

(A) Types and amounts of bail

Any person who is entitled to release shall be released upon one or more of the following types of bail in the amount set by the courts:

(1) The personal recognizance of the accused or an unsecured bail bond;

(2) A bail bond secured by the deposit of ten percent of the amount of the bond in cash. Ninety percent of the deposit shall be returned upon compliance with all conditions of the bond;

(3) A surety bond, a bond secured by real estate or securities as allowed by law, or the deposit of cash, at the option of the defendant.

(B) Conditions of bail

The court may impose any of the following conditions of bail:

(1) Place the person in the custody of a designated person or organization agreeing to supervise the person;

(2) Place restrictions on the travel, association, or place of abode of the person during the period of release;

(3) Place the person under a house arrest or work release program;

(4) Regulate or prohibit the person's contact with the victim;

(5) Regulate the person's contact with witnesses or others associated with the case upon proof of the likelihood that the person will threaten, harass, cause injury, or seek to intimidate those persons;

(6) Require a person who is charged with an offense that is alcohol or drug related, and who appears to need treatment, to attend treatment while on bail;

(7) Any other constitutional condition considered reasonably necessary to ensure appearance or public safety.

(C) Factors

In determining the types, amounts, and conditions of bail, the court shall consider all relevant information, including but not limited to:

(1) The nature and circumstances of the crime charged;

(2) The weight of the evidence against the defendant;

(3) The confirmation of the defendant's identity;

(4) The defendant's family ties, employment, financial resources, character, mental condition, length of residence in the community, jurisdiction of residence, record of convictions, record of appearance at court proceedings or of flight to avoid prosecution;

(5) Whether the defendant is on probation, a community control sanction, parole, post-release control, or bail.

(D) Appearance pursuant to summons

When summons has been issued and the defendant has appeared pursuant to the summons, absent good cause, a recognizance bond shall be the preferred type of bail.

(E) Amendments

A court, at any time, may order additional or different types, amounts, or conditions of bail.

(F) Information need not be admissible

Information stated in or offered in connection with any order entered pursuant to this rule need not conform to the rules pertaining to the admissibility of evidence in a court of law. Statements or admissions of the defendant made at a bail proceeding shall not be received as substantive evidence in the trial of the case.

(G) Bond schedule

Each court shall establish a bail bond schedule covering all misdemeanors including traffic offenses, either specifically, by type, by potential penalty, or by some other reasonable method of classification. Each municipal or county court shall, by rule, establish a method whereby a person may make bail by use of a credit card. No credit card transaction shall be permitted when a service charge is made against the court or clerk unless allowed by law.

(H) Continuation of bonds

Unless otherwise ordered by the court pursuant to division (E) of this rule, or if application is made by the surety for discharge, the same bond shall continue until the return of a verdict or the acceptance of a guilty plea. In the discretion of the court, the same bond may also continue pending sentence or disposition of the case on review. Any provision of a bond or similar instrument that is contrary to this rule is void.

(I) Failure to appear; breach of conditions

Any person who fails to appear before any court as required is subject to the punishment provided by the law, and any bail given for the person's release may be forfeited. If there is a breach of condition of bail, the court may amend the bail.

(J) Justification of sureties

Every surety, except a corporate surety licensed as provided by law, shall justify by affidavit, and may be required to describe in the affidavit, the property that the surety proposes as security and the encumbrances on it, the number and amount of other bonds and undertakings for bail entered into by the surety and remaining undischarged, and all of the surety's other liabilities. The surety shall provide other evidence of financial responsibility as the court or clerk may require. No bail bond shall be approved unless the surety or sureties appear, in the opinion of the court or clerk, to be financially responsible in at least the amount of the bond. No licensed attorney at law shall be a surety.

(Adopted eff. 7–1–73; amended eff. 7–1–90, 7–1–94, 7–1–98)

Crim R 47 Motions

An application to the court for an order shall be by motion. A motion, other than one made during trial or hearing, shall be in writing unless the court permits it to be made orally. It shall state with particularity the grounds upon which it is made and shall set forth the relief or order sought. It shall be supported by a memorandum containing citations of authority, and may also be supported by an affidavit.

To expedite its business, the court may make provision by rule or order for the submission and determination of motions without oral hearing upon brief written statements of reasons in support and opposition.

(Adopted eff. 7–1–73)

Crim R 48 Dismissal

(A) Dismissal by the state

The state may by leave of court and in open court file an entry of dismissal of an indictment, information, or complaint and the prosecution shall thereupon terminate.

(B) Dismissal by the court

If the court over objection of the state dismisses an indictment, information, or complaint, it shall state on the record its findings of fact and reasons for the dismissal.

(Adopted eff. 7–1–73)

Crim R 49 Service and filing of papers

(A) Service: when required

Written notices, requests for discovery, designation of record on appeal, written motions other than those heard ex parte, and similar papers, shall be served upon each of the parties.

(B) Service: how made

Whenever under these rules or by court order service is required or permitted to be made upon a party represented by an attorney, the service shall be made upon the attorney unless service upon the party himself is ordered by the court. Service upon the attorney or upon the party shall be made in the manner provided in Civil Rule 5(B).

(C) Filing

All papers required to be served upon a party shall be filed simultaneously with or immediately after service. Papers filed with the court shall not be considered until proof of service is endorsed thereon or separately filed. The proof of service shall state the date and the manner of service and shall be signed and filed in the manner provided in Civil Rule 5(D).

(Adopted eff. 7–1–73)

Crim R 50 Calendars

Criminal cases shall be given precedence over civil matters and proceedings.

(Adopted eff. 7–1–73)

Crim R 51 Exceptions unnecessary

An exception, at any stage or step of the case or matter, is unnecessary to lay a foundation for review, whenever a matter has been called to the attention of the court by objection, motion, or otherwise, and the court has ruled thereon.

(Adopted eff. 7–1–73)

Crim R 52 Harmless error and plain error

(A) Harmless error

Any error, defect, irregularity, or variance which does not affect substantial rights shall be disregarded.

(B) Plain error

Plain errors or defects affecting substantial rights may be noticed although they were not brought to the attention of the court.

(Adopted eff. 7–1–73)

Crim R 53 [Reserved]

Crim R 54 Amendment of incorporated civil rules

An amendment to or recision of any provision of the Ohio Rules of Civil Procedure which has been incorporated by reference in these rules, shall, without the necessity of further action, be incorporated by reference in these rules unless the amendment or recision specifies otherwise, effective on the effective date of the amendment or recision.

(Adopted eff. 7–1–73)

Crim R 55 Records

(A) Criminal appearance docket

The clerk shall keep a criminal appearance docket. Upon the commencement of a criminal action the clerk shall assign each action a number. This number shall be placed on the first page, and every continuation page, of the appearance docket which concerns the particular action. In addition this number and the names of the parties shall be placed on the case file and every paper filed in the action.

At the time the action is commenced the clerk shall enter in the appearance docket the names, except as provided in Rule 6(E), of the parties in full, the names of counsel and index the action by the name of each defendant. Thereafter the clerk shall chronologically note in the appearance docket all: process issued and returns, pleas and motions, papers filed in the action, orders, verdicts and judgments. The notations shall be brief but shall show the date of filing and the substance of each order, verdict and judgment.

An action is commenced for purposes of this rule by the earlier of, (a) the filing of a complaint, uniform traffic ticket, citation, indictment, or information with the clerk, or (b) the receipt by the clerk of the court of common pleas of a bind over order under Rule 5(B)(4)(a).

(B) Files

All papers filed in a case shall be filed in a separate file folder and on or after July 1, 1986 shall not exceed 8 1/2 inches x 11 inches in size and without backing or cover.

(C) Other books and records

The clerk shall keep such other books and records as required by law and as the supreme court or other court may from time to time require.

(D) Applicability to courts not of record

In courts not of record the notations required by subdivision (A) shall be placed on a separate sheet or card kept in the file folder.

(Adopted eff. 7–1–73; amended eff. 7–1–85)

Crim R 56 [Reserved]

Crim R 57 Rule of court; procedure not otherwise specified

(A) Rule of court

(1) The expression "rule of court" as used in these rules means a rule promulgated by the Supreme Court or a rule concerning local practice adopted by another court that is not inconsistent with the rules promulgated by the Supreme Court and is filed with the Supreme Court.

(2) Local rules shall be adopted only after the court gives appropriate notice and an opportunity for comment. If the court determines that there is an immediate need for a rule, the court may adopt the rule without prior notice and opportunity for comment, but promptly shall afford notice and opportunity for comment.

(B) Procedure not otherwise specified

If no procedure is specifically prescribed by rule, the court may proceed in any lawful manner not inconsistent with these rules of criminal procedure, and shall look to the rules of civil procedure and to the applicable law if no rule of criminal procedure exists.

(Adopted eff. 7–1–73; amended eff. 7–1–94)

Crim R 58 Forms

The forms contained in the Appendix of Forms which the supreme court from time to time may approve are illustrative and not mandatory.

(Adopted eff. 7–1–73)

Crim R 59 Effective date

(A) Effective date of rules

These rules shall take effect on July 1, 1973, except for rules or portions of rules for which a later date is specified, which shall take effect on such later date. They govern all proceedings in actions brought after they take effect, and also all further proceedings in actions then pending, except to the extent that their application in a particular action pending when the rules take effect would not be feasible or would work injustice, in which event the former procedure applies.

(B) Effective date of amendments

The amendments submitted by the supreme court to the general assembly on January 10, 1975, shall take effect on July 1, 1975. They govern all proceedings in actions brought after they take effect and also all further proceedings in actions then pending, except to the extent that their application in a particular action pending when the amendments take effect would not be feasible or would work injustice, in which event the former procedure applies.

(C) Effective date of amendments

The amendments submitted by the supreme court to the general assembly on January 9, 1976 shall take effect on July 1, 1976. They govern all proceedings in actions brought after they take effect and also all further proceedings in actions then pending, except to the extent that their application in a particular action pending when the amendments take effect would not be feasible or would work injustice, in which event the former procedure applies.

(D) Effective date of amendments

The amendments submitted by the Supreme Court to the General Assembly on January 12, 1978 and on April 28, 1978, shall take effect on July 1, 1978. They govern all proceedings in actions brought after they take effect and also all further proceedings in actions then pending, except to the extent that their application in a particular action pending when the amendments take effect would not be feasible or would work injustice, in which event the former procedure applies.

(E) Effective date of amendments

The amendments submitted by the Supreme Court to the General Assembly on January 14, 1980, shall take effect on July 1, 1980. They govern all proceedings in actions brought after they take effect and also all further proceedings in actions then pending, except to the extent that their application in a particular action pending when the amendments take effect would not be feasible or would work injustice, in which event the former procedure applies.

(F) Effective date of amendments

The amendments submitted by the Supreme Court to the general assembly on January 14, 1981, and on April 29, 1981, shall take effect on July 1, 1981. They govern all proceedings in actions brought after they take effect and also all further proceedings in actions then pending, except to the extent that their application in a particular action pending when the amendments take effect would not be feasible or would work injustice, in which event the former procedure applies.

(G) Effective date of amendments

The amendments submitted by the Supreme Court to the General Assembly on January 14, 1982 shall take effect on July 1, 1982. They govern all proceedings in actions brought after they take effect and also all further proceedings in actions then pending, except to the extent that their application in a particular action pending when the amendments take effect would not be feasible or would work injustice, in which event the former procedure applies.

(H) Effective date of amendments

The amendments submitted by the Supreme Court to the General Assembly on December 24, 1984 and January 8, 1985 shall take effect on July 1, 1985. They govern all proceedings in actions brought after they take effect and also all further proceedings in actions then pending, except to the extent that their application in a particular action pending when the amendments take effect would not be feasible or would work injustice, in which event the former procedure applies.

(I) Effective date of amendments

The amendments submitted by the Supreme Court to the General Assembly on January 12, 1990 and further revised and submitted on April 16, 1990, shall take effect on July 1, 1990. They govern all proceedings in actions brought after they take effect and also all further proceedings in actions then pending, except to the extent that their application in a particular action pending when the amendments take effect would not be feasible or would work injustice, in which event the former procedure applies.

(J) Effective date of amendments

The amendments filed by the Supreme Court with the General Assembly on January 14, 1992 and further revised and filed on April 30, 1992, shall take effect on July 1, 1992. They govern all proceedings in actions brought after they take effect and also all further proceedings in actions then pending, except to the extent that their application in a particular action pending when the amendments take effect would not be feasible or would work injustice, in which event the former procedure applies.

(K) Effective date of amendments

The amendments submitted by the Supreme Court to the General Assembly on January 8, 1993 and further filed on April 30, 1993 shall take effect on July 1, 1993. They govern all proceedings in actions brought after they take effect and also all further proceedings in actions then pending, except to the extent that their application in a particular action pending when the amendments take effect would not be feasible or would work injustice, in which event the former procedure applies.

(L) Effective date of amendments

The amendments submitted by the Supreme Court to the General Assembly on January 14, 1994 and further filed on April 29, 1994 shall take effect on July 1, 1994. They govern all proceedings in actions brought after they take effect and also all further proceedings in actions then pending, except to the extent that their application in a particular action pending when the amendments take effect would not be feasible or would work injustice, in which event the former procedure applies.

(M) Effective date of amendments

The amendments to rules 12 and 19 filed by the Supreme Court with the General Assembly on January 11, 1995, and refiled on April 25, 1995 shall take effect on July 1, 1995. They govern all proceedings in actions brought after they take effect and also all further proceedings in actions then pending, except to the extent that their application in a particular action pending when the amendments take effect would not be feasible or would work injustice, in which event the former procedure applies.

(N) Effective date of amendments

The amendments to Rule 1 filed by the Supreme Court with the General Assembly on January 5, 1996 and refiled on April 26, 1996 shall take effect on July 1, 1996. They govern all proceedings in actions brought after they take effect and also all further proceedings in actions then pending, except to the extent that their application in a particular action pending when the amendments take effect would not be feasible or would work injustice, in which event the former procedure applies.

(O) Effective date of amendments

The amendments to Rule 35 filed by the Supreme Court with the General Assembly on January 10, 1997 and refiled on April 24, 1997 shall take effect on July 1, 1997. They govern all proceedings in actions brought after they take effect and also all further proceedings in actions then pending, except to the extent that their application in a particular action pending when the amendments take effect would not be feasible or would work injustice, in which event the former procedure applies.

(P) Effective date of amendments

The amendments to Rules 4, 11, 12, 32, 32.1, 32.2, 32.3, and 46 filed by the Supreme Court with the General Assembly on January 15, 1998 and further revised and refiled on April 30, 1998 shall take effect on July 1, 1998. They govern all proceedings in actions brought after they take effect and also all further proceedings in actions then pending, except to the extent that their application in a particular action pending when the amendments take effect would not be feasible or would work injustice, in which event the former procedure applies.

(Q) Effective date of amendments

The amendments to Criminal Rules 7, 17.1, and 19 filed by the Supreme Court with the General Assembly on January 13, 2000 and refiled on April 27, 2000 shall take effect on July 1, 2000. They govern all proceedings in actions brought after they take effect and also all further proceedings in actions then pending, except to the extent that their application in a particular action pending when the amendments take effect would not be feasible or would work injustice, in which event the former procedure applies.

(R) Effective date of amendments

The amendments to Criminal Rule 12 filed by the Supreme Court with the General Assembly on January 12, 2001, and refiled on April 26, 2001, shall take effect on July 1, 2001. They govern all proceedings in actions brought after they take effect and also all further proceedings in actions then pending, except to the extent that their application in a particular action pending when the amendments take effect would not be feasible or would work injustice, in which event the former procedure applies.

(S) Effective date of amendments

The amendments to Criminal Rule 24 filed by the Supreme Court with the General Assembly on January 11, 2002, and refiled on April 18, 2002, shall take effect on July 1, 2002. They govern all proceedings in actions brought after they take effect and also all further proceedings in actions then pending, except to the extent that their application in a particular action pending when the amendments take effect would not be feasible or would work injustice, in which event the former procedure applies.

(T) Effective date of amendments

The amendments to Criminal Rules 4. 1, 21, and 32, filed by the Supreme Court with the General Assembly on January 7, 2004 and refiled on April 28, 2004 shall take effect on July 1, 2004. They govern all proceedings in actions brought after they take effect and also all further proceedings in actions then pending, except to the extent that their application in a particular action pending when the amendments take effect would not be feasible or would work injustice, in which event the former procedure applies.

(Adopted eff. 7–1–73; amended eff. 7–1–75, 7–1–76, 7–1–78, 7–1–80, 7–1–81, 7–1–82, 7–1–85, 7–1–90, 7–1–92, 7–1–93, 7–1–94, 7–1–95, 7–1–96, 7–1–97, 7–1–98, 7–1–00, 7–1–01, 7–1–02, 7–1–04)

Crim R 60 Title

These rules shall be known as the Ohio Rules of Criminal Procedure and may be cited as "Criminal Rules" or "Crim. R. ___."

(Adopted eff. 7–1–73)

APPENDIX OF FORMS

Form I Complaint

(Crim R 4)

FRANKLIN COUNTY MUNICIPAL COURT
FRANKLIN COUNTY, OHIO

State of Ohio
/City of Columbus/
v.
__[*name*]__
__[*address*]__

No. ________

COMPLAINT
(Rule 4)

Complainant being duly sworn states that C.D. [*defendant*] at __[*place*]__, County, Ohio on or about ________, 19___, __[*state the essential facts*]__ in violation of __[*state the numerical designation of the applicable statute or ordinance*]__.

A.B. ________________________________
Complainant

Sworn to and subscribed before me by ________________ on ________, 19___.

____
/Judge/Clerk/Deputy Clerk/
Franklin County Municipal Court
[*or*]

____
Notary Public,
My Commission expires ________, 19___
/Franklin County/State of Ohio/

Form II Complaint by prosecuting attorney upon affidavit

(Crim R 4)

FRANKLIN COUNTY MUNICIPAL COURT
FRANKLIN COUNTY, OHIO

State of Ohio
/City of Columbus/
v.
__[*name*]__
__[*address*]__

NO. ________

COMPLAINT BY PROSECUTING ATTORNEY UPON AFFIDAVIT
(Rule 4)

Complainant prosecuting attorney being duly sworn states that __[*name of affiant*]__, has filed an affidavit, a copy of which is attached hereto, stating that C.D. at __[*place*]__, County, Ohio on or about ________, 19__, __[*state the essential facts*]__.

Upon this affidavit complainant states that C.D. __[*defendant*]__ on or about the above date and at the above place did violate __[*state the numerical designation of the applicable statute or ordinance*]__.

A.B. ______________________
Complainant, Title

Sworn to and subscribed before me by A.B. on ________, 19__.

____
/Judge/Clerk/Deputy Clerk/
Franklin County Municipal Court

[*or*]

____
Notary Public,
My Commission expires ________, 19__
/Franklin County/State of Ohio/

Form III Direction to issue summons

(Crim R 4, 9)

/FRANKLIN COUNTY MUNICIPAL COURT/
/COURT OF COMMON PLEAS/
FRANKLIN COUNTY, OHIO

State of Ohio
/City of Columbus/
v.
__[*name*]__
__[*address*]__

NO. ________

DIRECTION TO ISSUE SUMMONS

(Rules 4 and 9)

TO /Clerk/Deputy Clerk/:

Issue summons to an appropriate officer and direct him to make /personal service/residence service/certified mail service/ upon C.D. [*defendant*] at /the address stated in the caption of this direction. /__[*fill in address if different from caption*]__./

Special instructions for server:______________________
____
____

____
/Judge/Officer Designated by Judge(s)/
Franklin County Municipal Court

[*or*]

____
Judge
Court of Common Pleas
Franklin County, Ohio

Form IV Clerk's memorandum of determination to issue summons upon complaint

(Crim R 4)

FRANKLIN COUNTY MUNICIPAL COURT
FRANKLIN COUNTY, OHIO

State of Ohio
/City of Columbus/
v.
__[*name*]__
__[*address*]__

NO. ________

CLERK'S MEMORANDUM
OF DETERMINATION TO
ISSUE SUMMONS UPON
COMPLAINT
(Rule 4)

It appearing that summons will reasonably assure the appearance of C.D. [*defendant*] summons shall issue:
/to an appropriate officer and such officer shall be directed to make/personal service/residence service/.
/by certified mail/.
Service shall be at /the address stated in the caption of this notice/__[*fill in address if different from caption*]__.
Special instructions for server:____

____

____

/Clerk/Deputy Clerk/
Franklin County Municipal Court

Form V Prosecuting attorney's request for issuance of summons upon complaint

(Crim R 4)

FRANKLIN COUNTY MUNICIPAL COURT
FRANKLIN COUNTY, OHIO

State of Ohio
/City of Columbus/
v.
__[*name*]__
__[*address*]__

NO. ________

PROSECUTING ATTORNEY'S
REQUEST FOR ISSUANCE OF
SUMMONS UPON COMPLAINT
(Rule 4)

TO /Clerk/Deputy Clerk/:
A complaint has been filed against C.D. [*defendant*]
Issue summons to an appropriate officer and direct him to make /personal service/residence service/certified mail service/ upon defendant at /the address stated in the caption of this request. /__[*fill in address if different from caption*]__/.
Special instructions for server:____

____

____

Prosecuting Attorney, Title

Form VI Summons upon complaint, indictment, or information

(Crim R 4, 9)

/FRANKLIN COUNTY MUNICIPAL COURT/
/COURT OF COMMON PLEAS/
FRANKLIN COUNTY, OHIO

State of Ohio
/City of Columbus/
v.
__[*name*]__
__[*address*]__

NO. __________

SUMMONS UPON/COMPLAINT/
/INDICTMENT/INFORMATION/

(Rules 4 and 9)

TO C.D. __[*defendant*]__:

A /complaint/indictment/information/, a copy of which is attached hereto, has been filed in the /Franklin County Municipal Court, 120 West Gay Street, Columbus, Ohio 43215,/Franklin County Court of Common Pleas, 410 South High Street, Columbus, Ohio 43215,/ charging that you: __[*describe the offense and state the numerical designation of the applicable statute or ordinance*]__.

You are hereby summoned and ordered to appear at __[*time, day, date, room*]__, /Franklin County Municipal Court, 120 West Gay Street, Columbus, Ohio 43215. /Franklin County Municipal Court of Common Pleas, 410 South High Street, Columbus, Ohio 43215./

If you fail to appear at the time and place stated above you may be arrested.

____
/Judge/Officer Designated by Judge(s)/
Clerk/Deputy Clerk/
Franklin County Municipal Court
[*or*]
____
Judge/Clerk/Deputy Clerk/
Court of Common Pleas
Franklin County, Ohio

NOTICE TO DEFENDANT: For information regarding your duty to appear call __[*fill in phone number(s)*]__.

CLERK'S INSTRUCTIONS TO SERVING OFFICER FOR PERSONAL OR RESIDENCE SERVICE

TO __[*officer other than clerk authorized to serve summons*]__:

Make /personal service/residence service/ upon [*defendant*] at /the address stated in the caption of the summons./__[*fill in address for service if different from caption of summons*]__./

Special instructions for server:____
____.

____
/Clerk/Deputy Clerk/

CLERK'S INSTRUCTIONS FOR CERTIFIED MAIL SERVICE

TO __[*clerk*]__:

Make certified mail service upon __[*defendant*]__ at /the address stated in the caption of the summons. /__[*fill in address for service if different from caption of summons*]__./

Special instructions for server:____
____
____

____
/Clerk/Deputy Clerk/

RECEIPT OF SUMMONS BY SERVING AUTHORITY

First Receipt

Received this summons on ________, 19___, at ___o'clock ___m.

____
Officer

By ________________________
Title

Subsequent Receipt

Received this summons on ________, 19___, at ___o'clock ___m.

____
Officer

By ________________________
Title

RETURN OF SERVICE OF SUMMONS (PERSONAL)

Fees	
Mileage	$_____
	_____
	_____
	_____
	_____
Total	$_____

I received this summons on ________, 19___, at ___o'clock ___.m., and made personal service of it upon __[*fill in name*]__ by locating /him/her/ and tendering a copy of the summons, a copy of the /complaint/indictment/information/ and accompanying documents on ________, 19___.

____
Serving Officer, Title

Date return made: ________, 19___

RETURN OF SERVICE OF SUMMONS (RESIDENCE)

Fees	
Mileage	$_____
	_____
	_____
	_____
	_____
Total	$_____

I received this summons on ________, 19___, at ___o'clock ___.m., and made residence service of it upon __[*fill in name*]__ by leaving, at /his/her/ usual place of residence with __[*fill in name*]__ a person of suitable age and discretion then residing therein, a copy of the summons, a copy of the /complaint/indictment/information/ and accompanying documents, on ________, 19___.

____
Serving Officer, Title

Date return made: ________, 19___

RETURN OF SERVICE OF SUMMONS (FAILURE OF SERVICE)

Fees	
Mileage	$_____
	_____
	_____
	_____
	_____
Total	$_____

I received this summons on __________, 19___, at ___o'clock ___.m., with instructions to make /personal service/residence service/ upon [*fill in name*]__ and I was unable to serve a copy of the summons upon /him/ her/ for the following reasons: ________________________

____

____

____

____

Serving Officer, Title

Date return made: __________, 19___

Form VII Warrant on complaint

(Crim R 4)

FRANKLIN COUNTY MUNICIPAL COURT
FRANKLIN COUNTY, OHIO

State of Ohio
/City of Columbus/
v.
__[*name*]__
__[*address*]__

NO. __________

WARRANT ON COMPLAINT
(Rule 4)

TO __[*officer authorized to execute a warrant*]__:

A complaint, a copy of which is attached hereto, has been filed in this court charging __[*describe the offense and state the numerical designation of the applicable statute or ordinance*]__.

You are ordered to arrest C.D. [*defendant*] and bring /him/her/ before this court without unnecessary delay.

You /may/may not/ issue summons in lieu of arrest under Rule 4(A)(2) or issue summons after arrest under Rule 4(F) because __[*state specific reason if issuance of summons restricted*]__.

Special instructions to executing officer: ____

____

____

____
Judge/Officer designated by Judge(s)/
Clerk/Deputy Clerk/
Franklin County Municipal Court

SUMMONS ENDORSEMENT
See NOTE: Use only in appropriate case

This warrant was executed/by arrest and/by issuing the following summons:

TO C.D. [*defendant*]

You are hereby summoned and ordered to appear at __[*time, day, date, room*]__, Franklin County Municipal Court, 120 West Gay Street, Columbus, Ohio 43215.

If you fail to appear at the time and place stated above you may be arrested.

____
Issuing Officer, Title
See Rule 4(A)(2), Rule 4(F) and Return Forms

NOTICE TO DEFENDANT: For information regarding your duty to appear call __[*fill in telephone number(s)*]__.

RECEIPT OF WARRANT BY EXECUTING AUTHORITY

First Receipt

Received this warrant on __________, 19___, at ___o'clock ___.m.

____
Officer
By ____________________________
Title

Subsequent Receipt

Received this/alias/warrant on __________, 19___, at ___o'clock ___.m.

____
Officer
By ____________________________
Title

RETURN OF EXECUTED WARRANT

Fees	
Mileage	$______
	______
	______
	______
	______
Total	$______

1. Execution by Arrest

I received this warrant on __________, 19___, at ___o'clock ___.m. On __________, 19___, I arrested C.D. and gave /him/her/ a copy of this warrant with complaint attached and brought /him/her/ to __[*state the place*]__.

____
Arresting Officer, Title

Fees	
Mileage	$______
	______
	______
	______
	______
Total	$______

2. Execution By Issuance Of Summons Under Rule 4(A)(2) By Executing Officer

I received this warrant on __________, 19___, at ___o'clock ___.m. On __________, 19___, I executed this warrant by issuing C.D. a summons by /personal service/residence service/ which ordered /him/her/ to appear at __[*time, day, date, room*]__, Franklin County Municipal Court, 120 West Gay Street, Columbus, Ohio 43215. The summons was endorsed upon the warrant and accompanied by a copy of the complaint.

____
Issuing Officer, Title

Fees	
Mileage	$______
	______
	______
	______
	______
Total	$______

3. Execution By Arrest And Issuance Of Summons Under Rule 4(F) By Arresting Officer

I received this warrant on __________, 19___, at ___o'clock ___.m. On __________, 19___, I arrested C.D. and after arrest I issued C.D. a summons by personal service which ordered /him/her/ to appear at __________, Franklin County Municipal Court, 120 West Gay Street, Columbus, Ohio 43215. The summons was endorsed upon the warrant and accompanied by a copy of the complaint.

____
Arresting–Issuing Officer, Title

Fees	
Mileage	$______
	______
	______
	______
	______
Total	$______

4. Execution By Arrest And Issuance Of Summons Under Rule 4(F) By Superior Of Arresting Officer

On __________, 19___, C.D. was arrested by __[*name of arresting officer*]__ and I issued C.D. a summons by personal service which ordered /him/her/ to appear at __[*time, day, date, room*]__, Franklin County Municipal Court, 120 West Gay Street, Columbus, Ohio 43215. The summons was endorsed upon the warrant and accompanied by a copy of the complaint.

____
Issuing Officer, Title

RETURN OF UNEXECUTED WARRANT

Fees		
Mileage	$____	I received this warrant on ______, 19__, at __o'clock __.m. On ______, 19__, I attempted to execute this warrant but was unable to do so because __[*state specific reason or reasons and additional information regarding defendant's whereabouts*]__.
	____	
	____	
	____	
	____	________________
Total	$____	Executing Officer, Title

Form VIII Clerk's memorandum of determination to issue summons upon indictment

(Crim R 9)

COURT OF COMMON PLEAS
FRANKLIN COUNTY, OHIO

State of Ohio v. __[*name*]__ __[*address*]__	NO. ______ CLERK'S MEMORANDUM OF DETERMINATION TO ISSUE SUMMONS UPON INDICTMENT (Rule 9)

It appearing that defendant __[*name*]__ was released pursuant to Rule 46 by the __[*bind-over court*]__ on the same offense for which /he/she/ was indicted in this court, summons shall issue: /to an appropriate officer and such officer shall be directed to make /personal service/residence service/.

/by certified mail/.

Service shall be at /the address stated in the caption of this notice/__[*fill in address if different from caption*]__.

Special instructions for server:________________________________
____
____

____
/Clerk/Deputy Clerk/
Court of Common Pleas
Franklin County, Ohio

Form IX Prosecuting attorney's request for issuance of summons upon indictment or information

(Crim R 9)

COURT OF COMMON PLEAS
FRANKLIN COUNTY, OHIO

State of Ohio v. __[*name*]__ __[*address*]__	NO. __________ PROSECUTING ATTORNEY'S REQUEST FOR ISSUANCE OF SUMMONS UPON /INDICTMENT/ INFORMATION (Rule 9)

To /Clerk/Deputy Clerk/:

C.D. [*defendant*] has been named a defendant in an /indictment returned by the grand jury/information filed by the prosecuting attorney./ Issue summons to an appropriate officer and direct him to make /personal service/residence service/certified mail service/ upon defendant at /the address stated in the caption of this request. / __[*fill in address if different from caption*]__./

Special instructions for server:____

____

____

____
Prosecuting Attorney, Title

Form X Prosecuting attorney's request for issuance of warrant upon indictment or information

(Crim R 9)

COURT OF COMMON PLEAS
FRANKLIN COUNTY, OHIO

State of Ohio v. __[*name*]__ __[*address*]__	NO. __________ PROSECUTING ATTORNEY'S REQUEST FOR ISSUANCE OF WARRANT UPON /INDICTMENT/ INFORMATION/ (Rule 9)

TO /Clerk/Deputy Clerk/:

C.D. [*defendant*] has been named a defendant in an /indictment returned by the grand jury/information filed by the prosecuting attorney./

Issue a warrant to an appropriate officer and direct him to execute it upon C.D. [*defendant*] at the address stated in the caption of this request. /__[*fill in address if different from caption*]__./

Special instructions for executing officer:______________________________________

____

____

____
Prosecuting Attorney, Title

Form XI Warrant upon indictment or information

(Crim R 9)

COURT OF COMMON PLEAS
FRANKLIN COUNTY, OHIO

State of Ohio v. __[*name*]__ __[*address*]__	NO. ______ WARRANT UPON /INDICTMENT/INFORMATION/ (Rule 9)

TO __[*officer authorized to execute a warrant*]__:

An /indictment/information/, a copy of which is attached hereto has been filed in the Franklin County Court of Common Pleas, 410 South High Street, Columbus, Ohio 43215, charging C.D. [*defendant*] with: __[*describe the offense and state the numerical designation of the applicable statute*]

You are ordered to arrest C.D. [*defendant*] and bring him before this court without unnecessary delay.

Special instructions to executing officer: ______________________________
____
____

____
/Judge/Clerk/Deputy Clerk/
Court of Common Pleas
Franklin County, Ohio

RECEIPT OF WARRANT BY EXECUTING AUTHORITY

First Receipt

Received this warrant on ________, 19___, at ___o'clock ___.m.

____
Officer

By ______________________________
Title

Subsequent Receipt

Received this warrant on ________, 19___, at ___o'clock ___.m.

____
Officer

By ______________________________
Title

RETURN OF EXECUTED WARRANT

Fees	
Mileage	$______
	______
	______
	______
	______
Total	$______

I received this warrant on ________, 19___, at ___o'clock ___.m. On ________, 19___, I arrested C.D. and gave /him/her/ a copy of this warrant with /indictment/information/ attached and brought /him/her/to __[*state the place*]__.

____
Arresting Officer, Title

RETURN OF UNEXECUTED WARRANT

Fees	
Mileage	$____
	____
	____
	____
	____
Total	$____

I received this warrant on ________, 19___, at ___o'clock ___.m. On ________, 19___, I attempted to execute this warrant but was unable to do so because __*[state specific reason or reasons and additional information regarding defendant's whereabouts]*__.

____
Executing Officer, Title

Form XII Summons in lieu of arrest without warrant, and complaint upon such summons

(Crim R 4(A)(3))

FRANKLIN COUNTY MUNICIPAL COURT
FRANKLIN COUNTY, OHIO

State of Ohio
/City of Columbus/
v.
__*[name of defendant]*__
__*[address]*__
__*[age]*__

SUMMONS NO. ________
CASE NO. ________
SUMMONS IN LIEU OF ARREST WITHOUT WARRANT, AND COMPLAINT UPON SUCH SUMMONS
(Rule 4(A)(3))

TO DEFENDANT:

SUMMONS

In lieu of immediate arrest upon a misdemeanor you are summoned and ordered to appear /at __*[time, day, date, room]*__, Franklin County Municipal Court, 120 West Gay Street, Columbus, Ohio 43215./ before the Franklin County Juvenile Court, 50 East Mound Street, Columbus, Ohio 43215 at the time and place ordered by that court./ If you fail to appear at this time and place you may be arrested.

This summons served personally on the defendant on ________, 19___.

COMPLAINT

On ________, 19___, at __*[place]*__, you __*[describe the offense charged and state the numerical designation of the applicable statute or ordinance]*__.

____
Signature of Issuing–Charging
Law Enforcement Officer

Being duly sworn the issuing-charging law enforcement officer states that he has read the above complaint and that it is true.

____
Issuing–Charging Law Enforcement Officer

Sworn to and subscribed before me by _______________________________ on ________, 19___.

____
/Judge/Clerk/Deputy Clerk/
Franklin County Municipal Court

[*or*]

____
Notary Public,
My Commission expires ________, 19___
/Franklin County/State of Ohio/

NOTICE TO DEFENDANT: The officer is not required to swear to the complaint upon your copy of the summons and complaint. He swears to the complaint on the copy he files with the court. You may obtain a copy of the sworn complaint before hearing time. You will be given a copy of the sworn complaint before or at the hearing. For information regarding your duty to appear call __[*fill in telephone number(s)*]__.

NOTICE TO DEFENDANT UNDER EIGHTEEN YEARS OF AGE: You must appear before the Franklin County Juvenile Court, 50 East Mound Street, Columbus, Ohio 43215, at the time and place determined by that Court. The Juvenile Court will notify you when and where to appear. This Summons and Complaint will be filed with the Juvenile Court. The Complaint may be used as a juvenile complaint. You may obtain a copy of the sworn complaint from the Juvenile Court before the Juvenile Court hearing. You will be given a copy of the sworn complaint before or at the Juvenile Court hearing. For information regarding your duty to appear at Juvenile Court call __[*fill in telephone number(s)*]__.

Form XIII Summons after arrest without warrant, and complaint upon such summons

(Crim R 4(F))

FRANKLIN COUNTY MUNICIPAL COURT
FRANKLIN COUNTY, OHIO

State of Ohio
/City of Columbus/
v.
__[*name of defendant*]__
__[*address*]__
__[*age*]__

SUMMONS NO. ________

CASE NO. ________

SUMMONS AFTER ARREST WITHOUT WARRANT, AND COMPLAINT UPON SUCH SUMMONS
(Rule 4(F))

TO DEFENDANT:

SUMMONS

In lieu of continued custody upon a misdemeanor you are summoned and ordered to appear /at __[*time, day, date, room*]__, Franklin County Municipal Court, 120 West Gay Street, Columbus, Ohio 43215./ before the Franklin County Juvenile Court, 50 East Mound Street, Columbus, Ohio 43215 at the time and place ordered by that court./ If you fail to appear at this time and place you may be rearrested.

This summons served personally on the defendant on ________, 19___.

COMPLAINT

On ________, 19___, at __[*place*]__, you __[*describe the offense charged and state the numerical designation of the applicable statute or ordinance*]__.

____
Signature of Issuing–Charging
Law Enforcement Officer

Being duly sworn the issuing-charging law enforcement officer states that he has read the above complaint and that it is true.

____
Issuing–Charging Law
Enforcement Officer

Sworn to and subscribed before me by ____
on _________, 19___.

____
/Judge/Clerk/Deputy Clerk/
Franklin County Municipal Court
[*or*]

____
Notary Public,
My Commission expires _________, 19___
/Franklin County/State of Ohio/

NOTICE TO DEFENDANT: The officer is not required to swear to the complaint upon your copy of the summons and complaint. He swears to the complaint on the copy he files with the court. You may obtain a copy of the sworn complaint before hearing time. You will be given a copy of the sworn complaint before or at the hearing. For information regarding your duty to appear call __[*fill in telephone number(s)*]__.

NOTICE TO DEFENDANT UNDER EIGHTEEN YEARS OF AGE: You must appear before the Franklin County Juvenile Court, 50 East Mound Street, Columbus, Ohio 43215, at the time and place determined by that Court. The Juvenile Court will notify you when and where to appear. This Summons and Complaint will be filed with the Juvenile Court. The Complaint may be used as a juvenile complaint. You may obtain a copy of the sworn complaint from the Juvenile Court before the Juvenile Court hearing. You will be given a copy of the sworn complaint before or at the Juvenile Court hearing. For information regarding your duty to appear at Juvenile Court call __[*fill in telephone number(s)*]__.

Form XIV Minor misdemeanor citation

(Crim R 4.1)

FRANKLIN COUNTY MUNICIPAL COURT
FRANKLIN COUNTY, OHIO

State of Ohio /City of Columbus/ v. __[*name of defendant*]__ __[*address*]__ __[*age*]__	Citation No. ________ Case No. ________ MINOR MISDEMEANOR CITATION (Rule 4.1)

TO DEFENDANT.

On __[*date*]__, 19___, at __[*place*]__.

You __[*describe the offense charged and state the numerical designation of the applicable statute or ordinance*]__.

You are ordered to appear at __[*time, day, date, room*]__, Franklin County Municipal Court, 120 West Gay Street, Columbus, Ohio 43215./before the Franklin County Juvenile Court, 50 East Mound Street, Columbus, Ohio 43215, at the time and place ordered by that court./

If you wish to contest this matter you must appear at the above time and place. In lieu of appearing at the above time and place you may, within the time stated above, appear personally at 120 West Gay Street, Columbus, Ohio 43215, Room 120, sign the guilty plea and waiver of trial which appear in this form, and pay a fine of $_____ and court costs of $_____.

If you fail to appear at the time and place stated above you may be arrested.

This citation was served personally on the defendant.

____
Signature of Issuing Law
Enforcement Officer

Being duly sworn the issuing law enforcement officer states that he has read the citation and that it is true.

____
Issuing Officer

Sworn to and subscribed before me by ______________________________
on ________, 19___.

____
/Judge/Clerk/Deputy Clerk/
[*or*]

____
Notary Public,
My Commission expires __________, 19___
/Franklin County/State of Ohio/

NOTICE TO DEFENDANT: The officer is not required to swear to your copy of the citation and complaint. He swears to the citation in the copy he files with the court. You may obtain a copy of the sworn citation before hearing time. You will be given a copy of the sworn citation before or at the hearing. For information regarding your duty to appear call __[*fill in telephone number(s)*]__.

NOTICE TO DEFENDANT UNDER EIGHTEEN YEARS OF AGE: The appearance, guilty plea, waiver and payment provisions of this form do not apply to you. You must appear before the Franklin County Juvenile Court, 50 East Mound Street, Columbus, Ohio 43215, at the time and place determined by that Court. The Juvenile Court will notify you when and where to appear. This citation will be filed with the Juvenile Court. The citation may be used as a juvenile complaint. You may obtain a copy of the sworn citation from the Juvenile Court before the Juvenile Court hearing. You will be given a copy of the sworn citation before or at the Juvenile Court hearing. For information regarding your duty to appear at Juvenile Court call __[*fill in telephone number(s)*]__.

GUILTY PLEA WAIVER OF TRIAL, PAYMENT OF FINE AND COSTS

I, the undersigned defendant, do hereby enter my written plea of guilty to the offense charged in this citation. I realize that by signing this guilty plea I admit my guilt of the offense charged and waive my right to contest the offense in a trial before the court. I plead guilty to the offense charged in the citation.

FINE ____________________
COST ____________________
TOTAL ____________________

RECEIPT NO. ____________________

____
Signature of Defendant

____
Address

____
Signature And Title Of Person Taking Guilty Plea, Waiver And Payment

Form XV Uniform Petition Form

(Crim R 35)

IN THE COURT OF COMMON PLEAS
________________ COUNTY, OHIO

CASE NOS.: ________________
____
JUDGE: ________________

STATE OF OHIO
Plaintiff–Respondent
-vs-
____
Defendant–Petitioner

POST–CONVICTION PETITION

I. CASE HISTORY

TRIAL:

Charge (include specifications)	Disposition
________________	________________
________________	________________

Date Sentenced: ________________
Name of Attorney: ________________

Was this conviction the result of a (circle one): **Guilty Plea No Contest Plea Trial**
If the conviction resulted in a trial, what was the length of the trial? ________________

Appeal to Court of Appeals
Number or citation ________________
Disposition ________________
Name of Attorney ________________

Appeal to Supreme Court of Ohio
Number or citation ________________
Disposition ________________
Name of Attorney ________________

HAS A POST–CONVICTION PETITION BEEN FILED BEFORE IN THIS CASE?
YES NO
If YES, attach a copy of the Petition and the Judgment Entry showing how it was disposed.

IF THIS IS NOT THE FIRST POST–CONVICTION PETITION, OR IT IS FILED OUTSIDE THE TIME LIMITS PROVIDED BY LAW, STATE THE REASONS WHY THE COURT SHOULD CONSIDER THIS PETITION: ________

OTHER RELEVANT CASE HISTORY: ________

II. STATEMENT OF FACTS

III. GROUNDS FOR RELIEF
(each ground not to exceed three pages)

Ground for relief 1: ________

Attached exhibit numbers which support ground for relief: ________

Legal authority (constitutional provisions, statutes, cases, rules, etc.) in support of ground for relief: ________

(name)

RULES OF APPELLATE PROCEDURE

Publisher's Note: Until 1968, when the Modern Courts Amendment to the Ohio Constitution was adopted, Ohio court procedure was governed entirely by statute and caselaw. The Modern Courts Amendment required the Supreme Court of Ohio, subject to the approval of the General Assembly, to prescribe rules governing practice and procedure in all courts of the state." Rules of practice and procedure are the Civil, Criminal, Appellate, and Juvenile Rules, Rules of the Court of Claims, and the Ohio Rules of Evidence. Pursuant to Ohio Constitution Article IV, Section 5(B), such rules shall not abridge, enlarge, or modify any substantive right," and all laws in conflict with such rules shall be of no further force or effect."

TITLE

Title I

APPLICABILITY OF RULES

Rule

App R 1 Scope of rules

(A) These rules govern procedure in appeals to courts of appeals from the trial courts of record in Ohio.

(B) Procedure in appeals to courts of appeals from the board of tax appeals shall be as provided by law, except that App. R. 13 to 33 shall be applicable to those appeals.

(C) Procedures in appeals to courts of appeals from juvenile courts pursuant to section 2505.073 of the Revised Code shall be as provided by that section, except that these rules govern to the extent that the rules do not conflict with that section.

(Adopted eff. 7–1–71; amended eff. 7–1–94)

App R 2 Law and fact appeals abolished

Appeals on questions of law and fact are abolished.

(Adopted eff. 7–1–71)

Title II

APPEALS FROM JUDGMENTS AND ORDERS OF COURT OF RECORD

Rule

App R 3 Appeal as of right—how taken

(A) Filing the notice of appeal

An appeal as of right shall be taken by filing a notice of appeal with the clerk of the trial court within the time allowed by Rule 4. Failure of an appellant to take any step other than the timely filing of a notice of appeal does not affect the validity of the appeal, but is ground only for such action as the court of appeals deems appropriate, which may include dismissal of the appeal. Appeals by leave of court shall be taken in the manner prescribed by Rule 5.

(B) Joint or consolidated appeals

If two or more persons are entitled to appeal from a judgment or order of a trial court and their interests are such as to make joinder practicable, they may file a joint notice of appeal, or may join in appeal after filing separate timely notices of appeal, and they may thereafter proceed on appeal as a single appellant. Appeals may be consolidated by order of the court of appeals upon its own motion or upon motion of a party, or by stipulation of the parties to the several appeals.

(C) Cross appeal

(1) Cross appeal required. A person who intends to defend a judgment or order against an appeal taken by an appellant and who also seeks to change the judgment or order or, in the event the judgment or order may be reversed or modified, an interlocutory ruling merged into the judgment or order, shall file a notice of cross appeal within the time allowed by App.R. 4.

(2) Cross appeal not required. A person who intends to defend a judgment or order appealed by an appellant on a ground other than that relied on by the trial court but who does not seek to change the judgment or order is not required to file a notice of cross appeal.

(D) Content of the notice of appeal

The notice of appeal shall specify the party or parties taking the appeal; shall designate the judgment, order or part thereof appealed from; and shall name the court to which the appeal is taken. The title of the case shall be the same as in the trial court with the designation of the appellant added, as appropriate. Form 1 in the Appendix of Forms is a suggested form of a notice of appeal.

(E) Service of the notice of appeal

The clerk of the trial court shall serve notice of the filing of a notice of appeal and, where required by local rule, a docketing statement, by mailing, or by facsimile transmission, a copy to counsel of record of each party other than the appellant, or, if a party is not represented by counsel, to the party at the party's last known address. The clerk shall mail or otherwise forward a copy of the notice of appeal and of the docket entries, together with a copy of all filings by appellant pursuant to App. R. 9(B), to the clerk of the court of appeals named in the notice. The clerk shall note on each copy served the date on which the notice of appeal was filed. Failure of the clerk to serve notice shall not affect the validity of the appeal. Service shall be sufficient notwithstanding the death of a party or a party's counsel. The clerk shall note in the docket the names of the parties served, the date served, and the means of service.

(F) Amendment of the notice of appeal

The court of appeals within its discretion and upon such terms as are just may allow the amendment of a timely filed notice of appeal.

(G) Docketing statement

If a court of appeals has adopted an accelerated calendar by local rule pursuant to Rule 11.1, a docketing statement shall be filed with the clerk of the trial court with the notice of appeal. (See Form 2, Appendix of Forms.)

The purpose of the docketing statement is to determine whether an appeal will be assigned to the accelerated or the regular calendar.

A case may be assigned to the accelerated calendar if any of the following apply:

(1) No transcript is required (e.g. summary judgment or judgment on the pleadings);

(2) The length of the transcript is such that its preparation time will not be a source of delay;

(3) An agreed statement is submitted in lieu of the record;

(4) The record was made in an administrative hearing and filed with the trial court;

(5) All parties to the appeal approve an assignment of the appeal to the accelerated calendar; or

(6) The case has been designated by local rule for the accelerated calendar.

The court of appeals by local rule may assign a case to the accelerated calendar at any stage of the proceeding. The court of appeals may provide by local rule for an oral hearing before a full panel in order to assist it in determining whether the appeal should be assigned to the accelerated calendar.

Upon motion of appellant or appellee for a procedural order pursuant to App. R. 15(B) filed within seven days after the notice of appeal is filed with the clerk of the trial court, a case may be removed for good cause from the accelerated calendar and assigned to the regular calendar. Demonstration of a unique issue of law which will be of substantial precedential value in the determination of similar cases will ordinarily be good cause for transfer to the regular calendar.

(Adopted eff. 7–1–71; amended eff. 7–1–72, 7–1–77, 7–1–82, 7–1–91, 7–1–92, 7–1–94)

App R 4 Appeal as of right—when taken

(A) Time for appeal

A party shall file the notice of appeal required by App.R. 3 within thirty days of the later of entry of the judgment or order appealed or, in a civil case, service of the notice of judgment and its entry if service is not made on the party within the three day period in Rule 58(B) of the Ohio Rules of Civil Procedure.

(B) Exceptions

The following are exceptions to the appeal time period in division (A) of this rule:

(1) *Multiple or cross appeals.* If a notice of appeal is timely filed by a party, another party may file a notice of appeal within the appeal time period otherwise prescribed by this rule or within ten days of the filing of the first notice of appeal.

(2) *Civil or juvenile post-judgment motion.* In a civil case or juvenile proceeding, if a party files a timely motion for judgment under Civ.R. 50(B), a new trial under Civ.R. 59(B), vacating or modifying a judgment by an objection to a magistrate's decision under Civ.R. 53(E)(4)(c) or Rule 40(E)(4)(c) of the Ohio Rules of Juvenile Procedure, or findings of fact and conclusions of law under Civ.R. 52, the time for filing a notice of appeal begins to run as to all parties when the order disposing of the motion is entered.

(3) *Criminal post-judgment motion.* In a criminal case, if a party timely files a motion for arrest of judgment or a new trial for a reason other than newly discovered evidence, the time for filing a notice of appeal begins to run when the order denying the motion is entered. A motion for a new trial on the ground of newly discovered evidence made within the time for filing a motion for a new trial on other grounds extends the time for filing a notice of appeal from a judgment of conviction in the same manner as a motion on other grounds. If made after the expiration of the time for filing a motion on other grounds, the motion on the ground of newly discovered evidence does not extend the time for filing a notice of appeal.

(4) *Appeal by prosecution.* In an appeal by the prosecution under Crim. R. 12(K) or Juv. R. 22(F), the prosecution shall file a notice of appeal within seven days of entry of the judgment or order appealed.

(5) *Partial final judgment or order.* If an appeal is permitted from a judgment or order entered in a case in which the trial court has not disposed of all claims as to all parties, other than a judgment or order entered under Civ.R. 54(B), a party may file a notice of appeal within thirty days of entry of the judgment or order appealed or the judgment or order that disposes of the remaining claims. Division (A) of this rule applies to a judgment or order entered under Civ.R. 54(B).

(C) Premature notice of appeal

A notice of appeal filed after the announcement of a decision, order, or sentence but before entry of the judgment or order that begins the running of the appeal time period is treated as filed immediately after the entry.

(D) Definition of "entry" or "entered"

As used in this rule, "entry" or "entered" means when a judgment or order is entered under Civ.R. 58(A) or Crim.R. 32(C).

(Adopted eff. 7–1–71; amended eff. 7–1–72, 7–1–85, 7–1–89, 7–1–92, 7–1–96, 7–1–02)

App R 5 Appeals by leave of court

(A) Motion by defendant for delayed appeal.

(1) After the expiration of the thirty day period provided by App. R. 4(A) for the filing of a notice of appeal as of right, an

appeal may be taken by a defendant with leave of the court to which the appeal is taken in the following classes of cases:

(a) Criminal proceedings;

(b) Delinquency proceedings; and

(c) Serious youthful offender proceedings.

(2) A motion for leave to appeal shall be filed with the court of appeals and shall set forth the reasons for the failure of the appellant to perfect an appeal as of right. Concurrently with the filing of the motion, the movant shall file with the clerk of the trial court a notice of appeal in the form prescribed by App. R. 3 and shall file a copy of the notice of the appeal in the court of appeals. The movant also shall furnish an additional copy of the notice of appeal and a copy of the motion for leave to appeal to the clerk of the court of appeals who shall serve the notice of appeal and the motions upon the prosecuting attorney.

(B) Motion to reopen appellate proceedings.

If a federal court grants a conditional writ of habeas corpus upon a claim that a defendant's constitutional rights were violated during state appellate proceedings terminated by a final judgment, a motion filed by the defendant or on behalf of the state to reopen the appellate proceedings may be granted by leave of the court of appeals that entered the judgment. The motion shall be filed with the clerk of the court of appeals within forty-five days after the conditional writ is granted. A certified copy of the conditional writ and any supporting opinion shall be filed with the motion. The clerk shall serve a copy of a defendant's motion on the prosecuting attorney.

(C) Motion by prosecution for leave to appeal

When leave is sought by the prosecution from the court of appeals to appeal a judgment or order of the trial court, a motion for leave to appeal shall be filed with the court of appeals within thirty days from the entry of the judgment and order sought to be appealed and shall set forth the errors that the movant claims occurred in the proceedings of the trial court. The motion shall be accompanied by affidavits, or by the parts of the record upon which the movant relies, to show the probability that the errors claimed did in fact occur, and by a brief or memorandum of law in support of the movant's claims. Concurrently with the filing of the motion, the movant shall file with the clerk of the trial court a notice of appeal in the form prescribed by App. R. 3 and file a copy of the notice of appeal in the court of appeals. The movant also shall furnish a copy of the motion and a copy of the notice of appeal to the clerk of the court of appeals who shall serve the notice of appeal and a copy of the motion for leave to appeal upon the attorney for the defendant who, within thirty days from the filing of the motion, may file affidavits, parts of the record, and brief or memorandum of law to refute the claims of the movant.

(D)(1) Motion by defendant for leave to appeal consecutive sentences pursuant to R.C. 2953.08(C)

When leave is sought from the court of appeals for leave to appeal consecutive sentences pursuant to R.C. 2953.08(C), a motion for leave to appeal shall be filed with the court of appeals within thirty days from the entry of the judgment and order sought to be appealed and shall set forth the reason why the consecutive sentences exceed the maximum prison term allowed. The motion shall be accompanied by a copy of the judgment and order stating the sentences imposed and stating the offense of which movant was found guilty or to which movant pled guilty. Concurrently with the filing of the motion, the movant shall file with the clerk of the trial court a notice of appeal in the form prescribed by App. R. 3 and file a copy of the notice of appeal in the court of appeals. The movant also shall furnish a copy of the notice of appeal and a copy of the motion to the clerk of the court of appeals who shall serve the notice of appeal and the motion upon the prosecuting attorney.

(D)(2) Leave to appeal consecutive sentences incorporated into appeal as of right

When a criminal defendant has filed a notice of appeal pursuant to App. R. 4, the defendant may elect to incorporate in defendant's initial appellate brief an assignment of error pursuant to R.C. 2953.08(C), and this assignment of error shall be deemed to constitute a timely motion for leave to appeal pursuant to R.C. 2953.08(C).

(E) Determination of the motion

Except when required by the court the motion shall be determined by the court of appeals on the documents filed without formal hearing or oral argument.

(F) Order and procedure following determination

Upon determination of the motion, the court shall journalize its order and the order shall be filed with the clerk of the court of appeals, who shall certify a copy of the order and mail or otherwise forward the copy to the clerk of the trial court. If the motion for leave to appeal is overruled, except as to motions for leave to appeal filed by the prosecution, the clerk of the trial court shall collect the costs pertaining to the motion, in both the court of appeals and the trial court, from the movant. If the motion is sustained and leave to appeal is granted, the further procedure shall be the same as for appeals as of right in criminal cases, except as otherwise specifically provided in these rules.

(Adopted eff. 7–1–71; amended eff. 7–1–88, 7–1–92, 7–1–94, 7–1–96, 7–1–03)

App R 6 Concurrent jurisdiction in criminal actions

(A) Whenever a trial court and an appellate court are exercising concurrent jurisdiction to review a judgment of conviction, and the trial court files a written determination that grounds exist for granting a petition for post-conviction relief, the trial court shall notify the parties and the appellate court of that determination. On such notification, or pursuant to a party's motion in the court of appeals, the appellate court may remand the case to the trial court.

(B) When an appellate court reverses, vacates, or modifies a judgment of conviction on direct appeal, the trial court may dismiss a petition for post-conviction relief to the extent that it is moot. The petition shall be reinstated pursuant to motion if the appellate court's judgment on direct appeal is reversed, vacated, or modified in such a manner that the petition is no longer moot.

(C) Whenever a trial court's grant of post-conviction relief is reversed, vacated, or modified in such a manner that the direct appeal is no longer moot, the direct appeal shall be reinstated pursuant to statute. Upon knowledge that a statutory reinstatement of the appeal has occurred, the court of appeals shall enter an order journalizing the reinstatement and providing for resumption of the appellate process.

(D) Whenever a direct appeal is pending concurrently with a petition for post-conviction relief or a review of the petition in any court, each party shall include, in any brief, memorandum, or motion filed, a list of case numbers of all actions and appeals, and the court in which they are pending, regarding the same judgment of conviction.

(Reserved eff. 7–1–71; amended eff. 7–1–97)

App R 7 Stay or injunction pending appeal—civil and juvenile actions

(A) Stay must ordinarily be sought in the first instance in trial court; motion for stay in court of appeals.

Application for a stay of the judgment or order of a trial court pending appeal, or for the determination of the amount of and the approval of a supersedeas bond, must ordinarily be made in the first instance in the trial court. A motion for such relief or for an order suspending, modifying, restoring or granting an injunction during the pendency of an appeal may be made to the court of appeals or to a judge thereof, but, except in cases of injunction pending appeal, the motion shall show that application to the trial court for the relief sought is not practicable, or that the trial court has, by journal entry, denied an application or failed to afford the relief which the applicant requested. The motion shall also show the reasons for the relief requested and the facts relied upon, and if the facts are subject to dispute the motion shall be supported by affidavits or other sworn statements or copies thereof. With the motion shall be filed such parts of the record as are relevant and as are reasonably available at the time the motion is filed. Reasonable notice of the motion and the intention to apply to the court shall be given by the movant to all parties. The motion shall be filed with the clerk of the court of appeals and normally will be considered by at least two judges of the court, but in exceptional cases where the attendance of two judges of the court would be impracticable due to the requirements of time, the application may be made to and considered by a single judge of the court on reasonable notice to the adverse party, provided, however, that when an injunction is appealed from it shall be suspended only by order of at least two of the judges of the court of appeals, on reasonable notice to the adverse party.

(B) Stay may be conditioned upon giving of bond; proceedings against sureties

Relief available in the court of appeals under this rule may be conditioned upon the filing of a bond or other appropriate security in the trial court. If security is given in the form of a bond or stipulation or other undertaking with one or more sureties, each surety submits himself or herself to the jurisdiction of the trial court and irrevocably appoints the clerk of the trial court as the surety's agent upon whom any process affecting the surety's liability on the bond or undertaking may be served. Subject to the limits of its monetary jurisdiction, this liability may be enforced on motion in the trial court without the necessity of an independent action. The motion and such notice of the motion as the trial court prescribes may be served on the clerk of the trial court, who shall forthwith mail copies to the sureties if their addresses are known.

(C) Stay in juvenile actions

No order, judgment, or decree of a juvenile court, concerning a dependent, neglected, unruly, or delinquent child, shall be stayed upon appeal, unless suitable provision is made for the maintenance, care, and custody of the dependent, neglected, unruly, or delinquent child pending the appeal.

(Adopted eff. 7–1–71; amended eff. 7–1–73, 7–1–01)

App R 8 Bail and suspension of execution of sentence in criminal cases

(A) Discretionary right of court to release pending appeal

The discretionary right of the trial court or the court of appeals to admit a defendant in a criminal action to bail and to suspend the execution of his sentence during the pendency of his appeal is as prescribed by law.

(B) Release on bail and suspension of execution of sentence pending appeal from a judgment of conviction

Application for release on bail and for suspension of execution of sentence after a judgment of conviction shall be made in the first instance in the trial court. Thereafter, if such application is denied, a motion for bail and suspension of execution of sentence pending review may be made to the court of appeals or to two judges thereof. The motion shall be determined promptly upon such papers, affidavits, and portions of the record as the parties shall present and after reasonable notice to the appellee.

(Adopted eff. 7–1–71; amended eff. 7–1–75)

App R 9 The record on appeal

(A) Composition of the record on appeal

The original papers and exhibits thereto filed in the trial court, the transcript of proceedings, if any, including exhibits, and a certified copy of the docket and journal entries prepared by the clerk of the trial court shall constitute the record on appeal in all cases. A videotape recording of the proceedings constitutes the transcript of proceedings other than hereinafter provided, and, for purposes of filing, need not be transcribed into written form. Proceedings recorded by means other than videotape must be transcribed into written form. When the written form is certified by the reporter in accordance with App. R. 9(B), such written form shall then constitute the transcript of proceedings. When the transcript of proceedings is in the videotape medium, counsel shall type or print those portions of such transcript necessary for the court to determine the questions presented, certify their accuracy, and append such copy of the portions of the transcripts to their briefs.

In all capital cases the trial proceedings shall include a written transcript of the record made during the trial by stenographic means.

(B) The transcript of proceedings; duty of appellant to order; notice to appellee if partial transcript is ordered

At the time of filing the notice of appeal the appellant, in writing, shall order from the reporter a complete transcript or a transcript of the parts of the proceedings not already on file as the appellant considers necessary for inclusion in the record and file a copy of the order with the clerk. The reporter is the person appointed by the court to transcribe the proceedings for the trial court whether by stenographic, phonogramic, or photographic means, by the use of audio electronic recording devices, or by the use of video recording systems. If there is no officially appointed reporter, App.R. 9(C) or 9(D) may be utilized. If the appellant intends to urge on appeal that a finding or conclusion is unsupported by the evidence or is contrary to the weight of the evidence, the appellant shall include in the record a transcript of all evidence relevant to the findings or conclusion.

Unless the entire transcript is to be included, the appellant, with the notice of appeal, shall file with the clerk of the trial court and serve on the appellee a description of the parts of the transcript that the appellant intends to include in the record, a statement that no transcript is necessary, or a statement that a statement pursuant to either App.R. 9(C) or 9(D) will be submitted, and a statement of the assignments of error the appellant intends to present on the appeal. If the appellee considers a transcript of other parts of the proceedings necessary, the appellee, within ten days after the service of the statement of the appellant, shall file and serve on the appellant a designation of additional parts to be included. The clerk of the trial court shall forward a copy of this designation to the clerk of the court of appeals.

If the appellant refuses or fails, within ten days after service on the appellant of appellee's designation, to order the additional parts, the appellee, within five days thereafter, shall either order the parts in writing from the reporter or apply to the court of appeals for an order requiring the appellant to do so. At the time of ordering, the party ordering the transcript shall arrange for the payment to the reporter of the cost of the transcript.

A transcript prepared by a reporter under this rule shall be in the following form:

(1) The transcript shall include a front and back cover; the front cover shall bear the title and number of the case and the name of the court in which the proceedings occurred;

(2) The transcript shall be firmly bound on the left side;

(3) The first page inside the front cover shall set forth the nature of the proceedings, the date or dates of the proceedings, and the judge or judges who presided;

(4) The transcript shall be prepared on white paper eight and one-half inches by eleven inches in size with the lines of each page numbered and the pages sequentially numbered;

(5) An index of witnesses shall be included in the front of the transcript and shall contain page and line references to direct, cross, re-direct, and re-cross examination;

(6) An index to exhibits, whether admitted or rejected, briefly identifying each exhibit, shall be included following the index to witnesses reflecting the page and line references where the exhibit was identified and offered into evidence, was admitted or rejected, and if any objection was interposed;

(7) Exhibits such as papers, maps, photographs, and similar items that were admitted shall be firmly attached, either directly or in an envelope to the inside rear cover, except as to exhibits whose size or bulk makes attachment impractical; documentary exhibits offered at trial whose admission was denied shall be included in a separate envelope with a notation that they were not admitted and also attached to the inside rear cover unless attachment is impractical;

(8) No volume of a transcript shall exceed two hundred and fifty pages in length, except it may be enlarged to three hundred pages, if necessary, to complete a part of the voir dire, opening statements, closing arguments, or jury instructions; when it is necessary to prepare more than one volume, each volume shall contain the number and name of the case and be sequentially numbered, and the separate volumes shall be approximately equal in length.

The reporter shall certify the transcript as correct, whether in written or videotape form, and state whether it is a complete or partial transcript, and, if partial, indicate the parts included and the parts excluded.

If the proceedings were recorded in part by videotape and in part by other media, the appellant shall order the respective parts from the proper reporter. The record is complete for the purposes of appeal when the last part of the record is filed with the clerk of the trial court.

(C) Statement of the evidence or proceedings when no report was made or when the transcript is unavailable

If no report of the evidence or proceedings at a hearing or trial was made, or if a transcript is unavailable, the appellant may prepare a statement of the evidence or proceedings from the best available means, including the appellant's recollection. The statement shall be served on the appellee no later than twenty days prior to the time for transmission of the record pursuant to App.R. 10, who may serve objections or propose amendments to the statement within ten days after service. The statement and any objections or proposed amendments shall be forthwith submitted to the trial court for settlement and approval. The trial court shall act prior to the time for transmission of the record pursuant to App.R. 10, and, as settled and approved, the statement shall be included by the clerk of the trial court in the record on appeal.

(D) Agreed statement as the record on appeal

In lieu of the record on appeal as defined in division (A) of this rule, the parties, no later than ten days prior to the time for transmission of the record pursuant to App.R. 10, may prepare and sign a statement of the case showing how the issues presented by the appeal arose and were decided in the trial court and setting forth only so many of the facts averred and proved or sought to be proved as are essential to a decision of the issues presented. If the statement conforms to the truth, it, together with additions as the trial court may consider necessary to present fully the issues raised by the appeal, shall be approved by the trial court prior to the time for transmission of the record pursuant to App.R. 10 and shall then be certified to the court of appeals as the record on appeal and transmitted to the court of appeals by the clerk of the trial court within the time provided by App.R. 10.

(E) Correction or modification of the record

If any difference arises as to whether the record truly discloses what occurred in the trial court, the difference shall be submitted to and settled by that court and the record made to conform to the truth. If anything material to either party is omitted from the record by error or accident or is misstated therein, the parties by stipulation, or the trial court, either before or after the record is transmitted to the court of appeals, or the court of appeals, on proper suggestion or of its own initiative, may direct that the omission or misstatement be corrected, and if necessary that a supplemental record be certified and transmitted. All other questions as to the form and content of the record shall be presented to the court of appeals.

(Adopted eff. 7–1–71; amended eff. 7–1–77, 7–1–78, 7–1–88, 7–1–92)

App R 10 Transmission of the record

(A) Time for transmission; duty of appellant

The record on appeal, including the transcript and exhibits necessary for the determination of the appeal, shall be transmitted to the clerk of the court of appeals when the record is complete for the purposes of appeal, or when forty days, which is reduced to twenty days for an accelerated calendar case, have elapsed after the filing of the notice of appeal and no order extending time has been granted under subdivision (C). After filing the notice of appeal the appellant shall comply with the provisions of Rule 9(B) and shall take any other action necessary to enable the clerk to assemble and transmit the record. If more than one appeal is taken, each appellant shall comply with the provisions of Rule 9(B) and this subdivision, and a single record shall be transmitted when forty days have elapsed after the filing of the final notice of appeal.

(B) Duty of clerk to transmit the record

The clerk of the trial court shall prepare the certified copy of the docket and journal entries, assemble the original papers, (or in the instance of an agreed statement of the case pursuant to Rule 9(D), the agreed statement of the case), and transmit the record upon appeal to the clerk of the court of appeals within the time stated in subdivision (A). The clerk of the trial court shall number the documents comprising the record and shall transmit with the record a list of the documents correspondingly numbered and identified with reasonable definiteness. Documents of unusual bulk or weight and physical exhibits other than documents shall not be transmitted by the clerk unless he is directed to do so by a party or by the clerk of the court of appeals. A party must make advance arrangements with the clerks for the transportation and receipt of exhibits of unusual bulk or weight.

Transmission of the record is effected when the clerk of the trial court mails or otherwise forwards the record to the clerk of the court of appeals. The clerk of the trial court shall indicate, by endorsement on the face of the record or otherwise, the date upon which it is transmitted to the court of appeals and shall note the transmission on the appearance docket.

The record shall be deemed to be complete for the purposes of appeal under the following circumstances:

(1) When the transcript of proceedings is filed with the clerk of the trial court.

(2) When a statement of the evidence or proceedings, pursuant to Rule 9(C), is settled and approved by the trial court, and filed with the clerk of the trial court.

(3) When an agreed statement in lieu of the record, pursuant to Rule 9(D), is approved by the trial court, and filed with the clerk of the trial court.

(4) Where appellant, pursuant to Rule 9(B), designates that no part of the transcript of proceedings is to be included in the record or that no transcript is necessary for appeal, after the

expiration of ten days following service of such designation upon appellee, unless appellee has within such time filed a designation of additional parts of the transcript to be included in the record.

(5) When forty days have elapsed after filing of the last notice of appeal, and there is no extension of time for transmission of the record.

(6) When twenty days have elapsed after filing of the last notice of appeal in an accelerated calendar case, and there is no extension of time for transmission of the record.

(7) Where the appellant fails to file either the docketing statement or the statement required by App. R. 9(B), ten days after filing the notice of appeal.

(C) Extension of time for transmission of the record; reduction of time

Except as may be otherwise provided by local rule adopted by the court of appeals pursuant to Rule 30, the trial court for cause shown set forth in the order may extend the time for transmitting the record. The clerk shall certify the order of extension to the court of appeals. A request for extension to the trial court and a ruling by the trial court must be made within the time originally prescribed or within an extension previously granted. If the trial court is without authority to grant the relief sought, by operation of this rule or local rule, or has denied a request therefor, the court of appeals may on motion for cause shown extend the time for transmitting the record or may permit the record to be transmitted and filed after the expiration of the time allowed or fixed. If a request for an extension of time for transmitting the record has been previously denied, the motion shall set forth the denial and shall state the reasons therefor, if any were given. The court of appeals may require the record to be transmitted and the appeal to be docketed at any time within the time otherwise fixed or allowed therefor.

(D) Retention of the record in the trial court by order of court

If the record or any part thereof is required in the trial court for use there pending the appeal, the trial court may make an order to that effect, and the clerk of the trial court shall retain the record or parts thereof subject to the request of the court of appeals, and shall transmit a copy of the order and of the docket and journal entries together with such parts of the original record as the trial court shall allow and copies of such parts as the parties may designate.

(E) Stipulation of parties that parts of the record be retained in the trial court

The parties may agree by written stipulation filed in the trial court that designated parts of the record shall be retained in the trial court unless thereafter the court of appeals shall order or any party shall request their transmittal. The parts thus designated shall nevertheless be a part of the record on appeal for all purposes.

(F) Record for preliminary hearing in the court of appeals

If prior to the time the record is transmitted a party desires to make in the court of appeals a motion for dismissal, for release, for a stay pending appeal, for additional security on the bond on appeal or on a supersedeas bond, or for any intermediate order, the clerk of the trial court at the request of any party shall transmit to the court of appeals such parts of the original record as any party shall designate.

(G) Transmission of the record when leave to appeal obtained

In all cases where leave to appeal must first be obtained all time limits for the preparation and transmission of the record hereinbefore set forth shall run from the filing of the journal entry of the court of appeals granting such leave rather than from the filing of the notice of appeal.

(Adopted eff. 7–1–71; amended eff. 7–1–72, 7–1–73, 7–1–75, 7–1–76, 7–1–77, 7–1–82)

App R 11 Docketing the appeal; filing of the record

(A) Docketing the appeal

Upon receiving a copy of the notice of appeal, as provided in App.R. 3(D) and App.R. 5, the clerk of the court of appeals shall enter the appeal upon the docket. An appeal shall be docketed under the title given to the action in the trial court, with the appellant identified as such, but if the title does not contain the name of the appellant, the appellant's name, identified as appellant, shall be added parenthetically to the title.

(B) Filing of the record

Upon receipt of the record, the clerk shall file the record, and shall immediately give notice to all parties of the date on which the record was filed. When a trial court is exercising concurrent jurisdiction to review a judgment of conviction pursuant to a petition for post-conviction relief, the clerk shall either make a duplicate record and send it to the clerk of the trial court or arrange for each court to have access to the original record.

(C) Dismissal for failure of appellant to cause timely transmission of record

If the appellant fails to cause timely transmission of the record, any appellee may file a motion in the court of appeals to dismiss the appeal. The motion shall be supported by a certificate of the clerk of the trial court showing the date and substance of the judgment or order from which the appeal was taken, the date on which the notice of appeal was filed, the expiration date of any order extending the time for transmitting the record, and by proof of service. The appellant may respond within ten days of such service.

(D) Leave to appeal

In all cases where leave to appeal must first be obtained the docketing of the appeal by the clerk of the court of appeals upon receiving a copy of the notice of appeal filed in the trial court shall be deemed conditional and subject to such leave being granted.

(Adopted eff. 7–1–71; amended eff. 7–1–75, 7–1–97)

App R 11.1 Accelerated calendar

(A) Applicability

If a court of appeals has adopted an accelerated calendar by local rule, cases designated by its rule shall be placed on an accelerated calendar. The Ohio Rules of Appellate Procedure shall apply with the modifications or exceptions set forth in this rule.

The accelerated calendar is designed to provide a means to eliminate delay and unnecessary expense in effecting a just decision on appeal by the recognition that some cases do not require as extensive or time consuming procedure as others.

(B) Record

The record on appeal, including the transcripts and the exhibits necessary for the determination of the appeal, shall be transmitted to the clerk of the court of appeals as provided by App. R. 10.

(C) Briefs

Briefs shall be in the form specified by App. R. 16. Appellant shall serve and file his brief within fifteen days after the date on which the record is filed. The appellee shall serve and file his brief within fifteen days after service of the brief of the appellant. Reply briefs shall not be filed unless ordered by the court.

(D) Oral argument

Oral argument will apply as provided by App. R. 21. If oral argument is waived, the case will be submitted to the court for disposition upon filing of appellee's brief.

(E) Determination and judgment on appeal

The appeal will be determined as provided by App. R. 11.1. It shall be sufficient compliance with App. R. 12(A) for the statement of the reason for the court's decision as to each error to be in brief and conclusionary form.

The decision may be by judgment entry in which case it will not be published in any form. (See Form 3, Appendix of Forms.)

(Adopted eff. 7–1–82)

App R 11.2 Expedited appeals

(A) Applicability

Appeals in actions described in this rule shall be expedited and given calendar priority over all other cases, including criminal and administrative appeals. The Ohio Rules of Appellate Procedure shall apply with the modifications or exceptions set forth in this rule.

(B) Abortion without parental consent appeals

(1) Applicability. App. R. 11.2(B) shall govern appeals pursuant to sections 2151.85, 2505.073, and 2919.121 of the Revised Code.

(2) General rule of expedition. If an appellant files her notice of appeal on the same day as the dismissal of her complaint or petition by the juvenile court, the entire court process, including the juvenile court hearing, appeal, and decision, shall be completed in sixteen calendar days from the time the original complaint or petition was filed.

(3) Processing appeal.

(a) Immediately after the notice of appeal has been filed by the appellant, the clerk of the juvenile court shall notify the court of appeals. Within four days after the notice of appeal is filed in juvenile court, the clerk of the juvenile court shall deliver a copy of the notice of appeal and the record, except page two of the complaint or petition, to the clerk of the court of appeals who immediately shall place the appeal on the docket of the court of appeals.

(b) Record of all testimony and other oral proceedings in actions pursuant to sections 2151.85 or 2919.121 of the Revised Code may be made by audio recording. If the testimony is on audio tape and a transcript cannot be prepared timely, the court of appeals shall accept the audio tape as the transcript in this case without prior transcription. The juvenile court shall ensure that the court of appeals has the necessary equipment to listen to the audio tape.

(c) The appellant under division (B) of this rule shall file her brief within four days after the appeal is docketed. Unless waived, the oral argument shall be within five days after docketing. Oral arguments must be closed to the public and exclude all persons except the appellant, her attorney, her guardian *ad litem*, and essential court personnel.

(d) Under division (B) of this rule, "days" means calendar days and includes any intervening Saturday, Sunday, or legal holiday. To provide full effect to the expedition provision of the statute, if the last day on which a judgment is required to be entered falls on a Saturday, Sunday, or legal holiday, the computation of days shall not be extended and judgment shall be made either on the last business day before the Saturday, Sunday, or legal holiday, or on the Saturday, Sunday, or legal holiday.

(4) Confidentiality. All proceedings in appeals governed by App. R. 11.2(B) shall be conducted in a manner that will preserve the anonymity of the appellant. Except as set forth in App. R. 11.2(B)(6) and (7), all papers and records that pertain to the appeal shall be kept confidential.

(5) Judgment entry. The court shall enter judgment immediately after conclusion of oral argument or, if oral argument is waived, within five days after the appeal is docketed.

(6) Release of records. The public is entitled to secure all of the following from the records pertaining to appeals governed by App. R. 11.2(B):

(a) the docket number;

(b) the name of the judge;

(c) the judgment entry and, if appropriate, a properly redacted opinion.

Opinions shall set forth the reasoning in support of the decision in a way that does not directly or indirectly compromise the anonymity of the appellant. Opinions written in compliance with this requirement shall be considered public records available upon request. If, in the judgment of the court, it is impossible to release an opinion without compromising the anonymity of the appellant, the entry that journalizes the outcome of the case shall include a specific finding that no opinion can be written without disclosing the identity of the appellant. Such finding shall be a matter of public record. It is the obligation of the court to remove any and all information in its opinion that would directly or indirectly disclose the identity of the appellant.

(7) Notice and hearing before release of opinion. After an opinion is written and before it is available for release to the public, the appellant must be notified and be given the option to appear and argue at a hearing if she believes the opinion may disclose her identity. Notice may be provided by including the following language in the opinion:

If appellant believes that this opinion may disclose her identity, appellant has the right to appear and argue at a hearing before this court. Appellant may perfect this right to a hearing by filing a motion for a hearing within fourteen days of the date of this opinion.

The clerk is instructed that this opinion is not to be made available for release until either of the following:

(a) Twenty–one days have passed since the date of the opinion and appellant has not filed a motion;

(b) If appellant has filed a motion, after this court has ruled on the motion.

Notice shall be provided by mailing a copy of the opinion to the attorney for the appellant or, if she is not represented, to the address provided by appellant for receipt of notice.

(8) Form 25–A. Upon request of the appellant or her attorney, the clerk shall verify on Form 25–A, as provided in the Rules of Superintendence, the date the appeal was docketed and whether a judgment has been entered within five days of that date. The completed form shall include the case number from the juvenile court and the court of appeals, and shall be filed and included as part of the record. A date-stamped copy shall be provided to the appellant or her attorney.

(C) Adoption and parental rights appeals

(1) Applicability. Appeals from orders granting or denying adoption of a minor child or from orders granting or denying termination of parental rights shall be given priority over all cases except those governed by App. R. 11.2(B).

(2) Record. Preparation of the record, including the transcripts and exhibits necessary for determination of the appeal, shall be given priority over the preparation and transmission of the records in all cases other than those governed by App. R. 11.2(B).

(3) Briefs. Extensions of time for filing briefs shall not be granted except in the most unusual circumstances and only for the most compelling reasons in the interest of justice.

(4) Oral argument. After briefs have been filed, the case shall be considered submitted for immediate decision unless oral argument is requested or ordered. Any oral argument shall be heard within thirty days after the briefs have been filed.

(5) Entry of judgment. The court shall enter judgment within thirty days of submission of the briefs, or of the oral argument,

whichever is later, unless compelling reasons in the interest of justice require a longer time.

(D) Dependent, abused, neglected, unruly, or delinquent child appeals

Appeals concerning a dependent, abused, neglected, unruly, or delinquent child shall be expedited and given calendar priority over all cases other than those governed by App. R. 11.2(B) and (C).

(Adopted eff. 7–1–00; amended eff. 7–1–01)

App R 12 Determination and judgment on appeal

(A) Determination

(1) On an undismissed appeal from a trial court, a court of appeals shall do all of the following:

(a) Review and affirm, modify, or reverse the judgment or final order appealed;

(b) Determine the appeal on its merits on the assignments of error set forth in the briefs under App.R. 16, the record on appeal under App.R. 9, and, unless waived, the oral argument under App.R. 21;

(c) Unless an assignment of error is made moot by a ruling on another assignment of error, decide each assignment of error and give reasons in writing for its decision.

(2) The court may disregard an assignment of error presented for review if the party raising it fails to identify in the record the error on which the assignment of error is based or fails to argue the assignment separately in the brief, as required under App.R. 16(A).

(B) Judgment as a matter of law

When the court of appeals determines that the trial court committed no error prejudicial to the appellant in any of the particulars assigned and argued in the appellant's brief and that the appellee is entitled to have the judgment or final order of the trial court affirmed as a matter of law, the court of appeals shall enter judgment accordingly. When the court of appeals determines that the trial court committed error prejudicial to the appellant and that the appellant is entitled to have judgment or final order rendered in his favor as a matter of law, the court of appeals shall reverse the judgment or final order of the trial court and render the judgment or final order that the trial court should have rendered, or remand the cause to the court with instructions to render such judgment or final order. In all other cases where the court of appeals determines that the judgment or final order of the trial court should be modified as a matter of law it shall enter its judgment accordingly.

(C) Judgment in civil action or proceeding when sole prejudicial error found is that judgment of trial court is against the manifest weight of the evidence

In any civil action or proceeding which was tried to the trial court without the intervention of a jury, and when upon appeal a majority of the judges hearing the appeal find that the judgment or final order rendered by the trial court is against the manifest weight of the evidence and do not find any other prejudicial error of the trial court in any of the particulars assigned and argued in the appellant's brief, and do not find that the appellee is entitled to judgment or final order as a matter of law, the court of appeals shall reverse the judgment or final order of the trial court and either weigh the evidence in the record and render the judgment or final order that the trial court should have rendered on that evidence or remand the case to the trial court for further proceedings; provided further that a judgment shall be reversed only once on the manifest weight of the evidence.

(D) All other cases

In all other cases where the court of appeals finds error prejudicial to the appellant, the judgment or final order of the trial court shall be reversed and the cause shall be remanded to the trial court for further proceedings.

(Adopted eff. 7–1–71; amended eff. 7–1–73, 7–1–92)

Title III

GENERAL PROVISIONS

App R 13 Filing and service

(A) Filing

Documents required or permitted to be filed in a court of appeals shall be filed with the clerk. Filing may be accomplished by mail addressed to the clerk, but filing shall not be timely unless the documents are received by the clerk within the time fixed for filing, except that briefs shall be deemed filed on the day of mailing. If a motion requests relief which may be granted by a single judge, the judge may permit the motion to be filed with the judge, in which event the judge shall note the filing date on the motion and transmit it to the clerk. A court may provide, by local rules adopted pursuant to the Rules of Superintendence, for the filing of documents by electronic means. If the court adopts such local rules, they shall include all of the following:

(1) Any signature on electronically transmitted documents shall be considered that of the attorney or party it purports to be for all purposes. If it is established that the documents were

transmitted without authority, the court shall order the filing stricken.

(2) A provision shall specify the days and hours during which electronically transmitted documents will be received by the court, and a provision shall specify when documents received electronically will be considered to have been filed.

(3) Any document filed electronically that requires a filing fee may be rejected by the clerk of court unless the filer has complied with the mechanism established by the court for the payment of filing fees.

(B) Service of all documents required

Copies of all documents filed by any party and not required by these rules to be served by the clerk shall, at or before the time of filing, be served by a party or person acting for the party on all other parties to the appeal. Service on a party represented by counsel shall be made on counsel.

(C) Manner of service

Service may be personal or by mail. Personal service includes delivery of the copy to a clerk or other responsible person at the office of counsel. Service by mail is complete on mailing.

(D) Proof of service

Documents presented for filing shall contain an acknowledgment of service by the person served or proof of service in the form of a statement of the date and manner of service and of the names of the persons served, certified by the person who made service. Documents filed with the court shall not be considered until proof of service is endorsed on the documents or separately filed.

(Adopted eff. 7–1–71; amended eff. 7–1–01)

App R 14 Computation and extension of time

(A) Computation of time

In computing any period of time prescribed or allowed by these rules, by the local rules of any court, by an order of court or by any applicable statute, the day of the act, event or default from which the designated period of time begins to run shall not be included. The last day of the period so computed shall be included, unless it is a Saturday, Sunday or a legal holiday, in which event the period runs until the end of the next day which is not a Saturday, Sunday or a legal holiday. When the period of time prescribed or allowed is less than seven days, intermediate Saturdays, Sundays and legal holidays shall be excluded in the computation.

(B) Enlargement or reduction of time

For good cause shown, the court, upon motion, may enlarge or reduce the time prescribed by these rules or by its order for doing any act, or may permit an act to be done after the expiration of the prescribed time. The court may not enlarge or reduce the time for filing a notice of appeal or a motion to certify pursuant to App. R. 25. Enlargement of time to file an application to reconsider pursuant to App. R. 26(A) shall not be granted except on a showing of extraordinary circumstances.

(C) Additional time after service by mail

Whenever a party is required or permitted to do an act within a prescribed period after service of a paper upon him and the paper is served by mail, three days shall be added to the prescribed period.

(Adopted eff. 7–1–71; amended eff. 7–1–94)

App R 15 Motions

(A) Content of motions; response; reply

Unless another form is prescribed by these rules, an application for an order or other relief shall be made by motion with proof of service on all other parties. The motion shall contain or be accompanied by any matter required by a specific provision of these rules governing such a motion, shall state with particularity the grounds on which it is based and shall set forth the order or relief sought. If a motion is supported by briefs, affidavits or other papers, they shall be served and filed with the motion. Any party may file a response in opposition to a motion other than one for a procedural order [for which see subdivision (B)] within ten days after service of the motion, but motions authorized by Rule 7, Rule 8 and Rule 27 may be acted upon after reasonable notice, and the court may shorten or extend the time for responding to any motion.

(B) Determination of motions for procedural orders

Motions for procedural orders, including any motion under Rule 14(B) may be acted upon at any time, without awaiting a response thereto. Any party adversely affected by such action may request reconsideration, vacation or modification of such action.

(C) Power of a single judge to entertain motions

In addition to the authority expressly conferred by these rules or by law, and unless otherwise provided by rule or law, a single judge of a court of appeals may entertain and may grant or deny any request for relief, which under these rules may properly be sought by motion, except that a single judge may not dismiss or otherwise determine an appeal or other proceeding, and except that a court of appeals may provide by order or rule that any motion or class of motions must be acted upon by the court. The action of a single judge may be reviewed by the court.

(D) Number of copies

Three copies of all papers relating to motions shall be filed with the original, but the court may require that additional copies be furnished.

(Adopted eff. 7–1–71)

App R 16 Briefs

(A) Brief of the appellant

The appellant shall include in its brief, under the headings and in the order indicated, all of the following:

(1) A table of contents, with page references.

(2) A table of cases alphabetically arranged, statutes, and other authorities cited, with references to the pages of the brief where cited.

(3) A statement of the assignments of error presented for review, with reference to the place in the record where each error is reflected.

(4) A statement of the issues presented for review, with references to the assignments of error to which each issue relates.

(5) A statement of the case briefly describing the nature of the case, the course of proceedings, and the disposition in the court below.

(6) A statement of facts relevant to the assignments of error presented for review, with appropriate references to the record in accordance with division (D) of this rule.

(7) An argument containing the contentions of the appellant with respect to each assignment of error presented for review and the reasons in support of the contentions, with citations to the authorities, statutes, and parts of the record on which appellant relies. The argument may be preceded by a summary.

(8) A conclusion briefly stating the precise relief sought.

(B) Brief of the appellee

The brief of the appellee shall conform to the requirements of divisions (A)(1) to (A)(8) of this rule, except that a statement of the case or of the facts relevant to the assignments of error need not be made unless the appellee is dissatisfied with the statement of the appellant.

(C) Reply brief

The appellant may file a brief in reply to the brief of the appellee, and, if the appellee has cross-appealed, the appellee may file a brief in reply to the response of the appellant to the assignments of errors presented by the cross-appeal. No further briefs may be filed except with leave of court.

(D) References in briefs to the record

References in the briefs to parts of the record shall be to the pages of the parts of the record involved; e.g., Answer p. 7, Motion for Judgment p. 2, Transcript p. 231. Intelligible abbreviations may be used. If reference is made to evidence, the admissibility of which is in controversy, reference shall be made to the pages of the transcript at which the evidence was identified, offered, and received or rejected.

(E) Reproduction of statutes, rules, regulations

If determination of the assignments of error presented requires the consideration of provisions of constitutions, statutes, ordinances, rules, or regulations, the relevant parts shall be reproduced in the brief or in an addendum at the end or may be supplied to the court in pamphlet form.

(Adopted eff. 7–1–71; amended eff. 7–1–72, 7–1–92)

App R 17 Brief of an amicus curiae

A brief of an amicus curiae may be filed only if accompanied by written consent of all parties, or by leave of court granted on motion or at the request of the court. The brief may be conditionally filed with the motion for leave. A motion for leave shall identify the interest of the applicant and shall state the reasons why a brief of an amicus curiae is desirable. Unless all parties otherwise consent, any amicus curiae shall file its brief within the time allowed the party whose position as to affirmance or reversal the amicus brief will support unless the court for cause shown shall grant leave for later filing, in which event it shall specify within what period an opposing party may answer. A motion of an amicus curiae to participate in the oral argument will be granted only for extraordinary reasons.

(Adopted eff. 7–1–71)

App R 18 Filing and service of briefs

(A) Time for serving and filing briefs

Except as provided in App. R. 14(C), the appellant shall serve and file the appellant's brief within twenty days after the date on which the clerk has mailed the notice required by App. R. 11(B). The appellee shall serve and file the appellee's brief within twenty days after service of the brief of the appellant. The appellant may serve and file a reply brief within ten days after service of the brief of the appellee.

(B) Number of copies to be filed and served

Four copies of each brief shall be filed with the clerk, unless the court by order in a particular case shall direct a different number, and one copy shall be served on counsel for each party separately represented. If the court by local rule adopted pursuant to App. R. 13 permits electronic filing of court documents, then the requirement for filing of copies with the clerk required in this division may be waived or modified by the local rule so adopted.

(C) Consequence of failure to file briefs

If an appellant fails to file the appellant's brief within the time provided by this rule, or within the time as extended, the court may dismiss the appeal. If an appellee fails to file the appellee's brief within the time provided by this rule, or within the time as extended, the appellee will not be heard at oral argument except by permission of the court upon a showing of good cause submitted in writing prior to argument; and in determining the appeal, the court may accept the appellant's statement of the facts and issues as correct and reverse the judgment if appellant's brief reasonably appears to sustain such action.

(Adopted eff. 7–1–71; amended eff. 7–1–82, 7–1–01)

App R 19 Form of briefs and other papers

(A) Form of briefs

Briefs may be typewritten or be produced by standard typographic printing or by any duplicating or copying process which produces a clear black image on white paper. Carbon copies of briefs may not be submitted without permission of the court, except in behalf of parties allowed to proceed in forma pauperis. All printed matter must appear in at least a twelve point type on opaque, unglazed paper. Briefs produced by standard typographic process shall be bound in volumes having pages 6 1/8 by 9 1/4 inches and type matter 4 1/6 by 7 1/6 inches. Those produced by any other process shall be bound in volumes having pages not exceeding 8 1/2 by 11 inches and type matter not exceeding 6 1/2 by 9 1/2 inches, with double spacing between each line of text except quoted matter which shall be single spaced. Where necessary, briefs may be of such size as required to utilize copies of pertinent documents.

Without prior leave of court, no initial brief of appellant or cross-appellant and no answer brief of appellee or cross-appellee shall exceed thirty-five pages in length, and no reply brief shall exceed fifteen pages in length, exclusive of the table of contents, table of cases, statutes and other authorities cited, and appendices, if any. A court of appeals, by local rule, may adopt shorter or longer page limitations.

The front covers of the briefs, if separately bound, shall contain: (1) the name of the court and the number of the case; (2) the title of the case [see App. R. 11(A)]; (3) the nature of the proceeding in the court (e.g., Appeal) and the name of the court below; (4) the title of the document (e.g., Brief for Appellant); and (5) the names and addresses of counsel representing the party on whose behalf the document is filed.

(B) Form of other papers

Applications for reconsideration shall be produced in a manner prescribed by subdivision (A). Motions and other papers may be produced in a like manner, or they may be typewritten upon opaque, unglazed paper 8 1/2 by 11 inches in size. Lines of typewritten text shall be double spaced except quoted matter which shall be single spaced. Consecutive sheets shall be attached at the left margin. Carbon copies may be used for filing and service if they are legible.

A motion or other paper addressed to the court shall contain a caption setting forth the name of the court, the title of the case, the case number and a brief descriptive title indicating the purpose of the paper.

(Adopted eff. 7–1–71; amended eff. 7–1–72, 7–1–97)

App R 20 Prehearing conference

The court may direct the attorneys for the parties to appear before the court or a judge thereof for a prehearing conference to consider the simplification of the issues and such other matters as may aid in the disposition of the proceeding by the court. The court or judge shall make an order which recites the action taken at the conference and the agreements made by the parties as to any of the matters considered and which limits the issues to those not disposed of by admissions or agreements of counsel, and such order when entered controls the subsequent course of the proceeding, unless modified to prevent manifest injustice.

(Adopted eff. 7–1–71)

App R 21 Oral argument

(A) Notice of argument

The court shall advise all parties of the time and place at which oral argument will be heard.

(B) Time allowed for argument

Unless otherwise ordered, each side will be allowed thirty minutes for argument. A party is not obliged to use all of the time allowed, and the court may terminate the argument whenever in its judgment further argument is unnecessary.

(C) Order and content of argument

The appellant is entitled to open and conclude the argument. The opening argument shall include a fair statement of the case. Counsel will not be permitted to read at length from briefs, records or authorities.

(D) Cross and separate appeals

A cross-appeal or separate appeal shall be argued with the initial appeal at a single argument, unless the court otherwise directs. If separate appellants support the same argument, they shall share the thirty minutes allowed to their side for argument unless pursuant to timely request the court grants additional time.

(E) Nonappearance of parties

If the appellee fails to appear to present argument, the court will hear argument on behalf of the appellant, if present. If the appellant fails to appear, the court may hear argument on behalf of the appellee, if his counsel is present. If neither party appears, the case will be decided on the briefs unless the court shall otherwise order.

(F) Submission on briefs

By agreement of the parties, a case may be submitted for decision on the briefs, but the court may direct that the case be argued.

(G) Motions

Oral argument will not be heard upon motions unless ordered by the court.

(H) Authorities in briefs

If counsel on oral argument intends to present authorities not cited in his brief, he shall, prior to oral argument, present in writing such authorities to the court and to opposing counsel.

(Adopted eff. 7–1–71; amended eff. 7–1–72, 7–1–76)

App R 22 Entry of judgment

(A) Form

All judgments shall be in the form of a journal entry signed by a judge of the court and filed with the clerk.

(B) Notice

When a decision is announced, the clerk shall give notice thereof by mail to counsel of record in the case.

(C) Time

Unless further time is allowed by the court or a judge thereof, counsel for the party in whose favor an order, decree or judgment is announced shall, within five days, prepare the proper journal entry and submit the entry to counsel for the opposite party. Counsel for the opposite party shall within five days after receipt of the entry (1) approve or reject the entry and (2) forward the entry to counsel for the prevailing party for immediate submission to the court.

(D) Objections

All objections to proposed journal entries shall be in writing, and may be answered in writing. Such entry as the court may deem proper shall be approved by the court, in writing, and filed with the clerk of the court for journalization. The provisions of this rule shall not be deemed to preclude the court from sua sponte preparing and filing with the clerk for journalization its own entry. No oral arguments will be heard in the settlement of journal entries.

(E) Filing

The filing of a journal entry of judgment by the court with the clerk for journalization constitutes entry of the judgment.

(Adopted eff. 7–1–71; amended eff. 7–1–72)

App R 23 Damages for delay

If a court of appeals shall determine that an appeal is frivolous, it may require the appellant to pay reasonable expenses of the appellee including attorney fees and costs.

(Adopted eff. 7–1–71)

App R 24 Costs

(A) Except as otherwise provided by law or as the court may order, the party liable for costs is as follows:

(1) If an appeal is dismissed, the appellant or as agreed by the parties.

(2) If the judgment appealed is affirmed, the appellant.

(3) If the judgment appealed is reversed, the appellee.

(4) If the judgment appealed is affirmed or reversed in part or is vacated, as ordered by the court.

(B) As used in this rule, "costs" means an expense incurred in preparation of the record including the transcript of proceedings, fees allowed by law, and the fee for filing the appeal. It does not mean the expense of printing or copying a brief or an appendix.

(Adopted eff. 7–1–71; amended eff. 7–1–92)

App R 25 Motion to certify a conflict

(A) A motion to certify a conflict under Article IV, Section 3(B)(4) of the Ohio Constitution shall be made in writing before the judgment or order of the court has been approved by the court and filed by the court with the clerk for journalization or within ten days after the announcement of the court's decision, whichever is the later. The filing of a motion to certify a conflict does not extend the time for filing a notice of appeal. A motion under this rule shall specify the issue proposed for certification and shall cite the judgment or judgments alleged to be in conflict with the judgment of the court in which the motion is filed.

(B) Parties opposing the motion must answer in writing within ten days after the filing of the motion. Copies of the motion, brief, and opposing briefs shall be served as prescribed for the service and filing of briefs in the initial action. Oral argument of a motion to certify a conflict shall not be permitted except at the request of the court.

(C) The court of appeals shall rule upon a motion to certify within sixty days of its filing.

(Adopted eff. 7–1–94)

App R 26 Application for reconsideration; application for reopening

(A) Application for reconsideration

Application for reconsideration of any cause or motion submitted on appeal shall be made in writing before the judgment or order of the court has been approved by the court and filed by the court with the clerk for journalization or within ten days after the announcement of the court's decision, whichever is the later. The filing of an application for reconsideration shall not extend the time for filing a notice of appeal in the Supreme Court.

Parties opposing the application shall answer in writing within ten days after the filing of the application. Copies of the application, brief, and opposing briefs shall be served in the manner prescribed for the service and filing of briefs in the initial action. Oral argument of an application for reconsideration shall not be permitted except at the request of the court.

(B) Application for reopening

(1) A defendant in a criminal case may apply for reopening of the appeal from the judgment of conviction and sentence, based on a claim of ineffective assistance of appellate counsel. An application for reopening shall be filed in the court of appeals where the appeal was decided within ninety days from journalization of the appellate judgment unless the applicant shows good cause for filing at a later time.

(2) An application for reopening shall contain all of the following:

(a) The appellate case number in which reopening is sought and the trial court case number or numbers from which the appeal was taken;

(b) A showing of good cause for untimely filing if the application is filed more than ninety days after journalization of the appellate judgment.

(c) One or more assignments of error or arguments in support of assignments of error that previously were not considered on the merits in the case by any appellate court or that were considered on an incomplete record because of appellate counsel's deficient representation;

(d) A sworn statement of the basis for the claim that appellate counsel's representation was deficient with respect to the assignments of error or arguments raised pursuant to division (B)(2)(c) of this rule and the manner in which the deficiency prejudicially affected the outcome of the appeal, which may include citations to applicable authorities and references to the record;

(e) Any parts of the record available to the applicant and all supplemental affidavits upon which the applicant relies.

(3) The applicant shall furnish an additional copy of the application to the clerk of the court of appeals who shall serve it on the attorney for the prosecution. The attorney for the prosecution, within thirty days from the filing of the application, may file and serve affidavits, parts of the record, and a memorandum of law in opposition to the application.

(4) An application for reopening and an opposing memorandum shall not exceed ten pages, exclusive of affidavits and parts of the record. Oral argument of an application for reopening shall not be permitted except at the request of the court.

(5) An application for reopening shall be granted if there is a genuine issue as to whether the applicant was deprived of the effective assistance of counsel on appeal.

(6) If the court denies the application, it shall state in the entry the reasons for denial. If the court grants the application, it shall do both of the following:

(a) appoint counsel to represent the applicant if the applicant is indigent and not currently represented;

(b) impose conditions, if any, necessary to preserve the status quo during pendency of the reopened appeal.

The clerk shall serve notice of journalization of the entry on the parties and, if the application is granted, on the clerk of the trial court.

(7) If the application is granted, the case shall proceed as on an initial appeal in accordance with these rules except that the court may limit its review to those assignments of error and arguments not previously considered. The time limits for preparation and transmission of the record pursuant to App.R. 9 and 10 shall run from journalization of the entry granting the application. The parties shall address in their briefs the claim that representation by prior appellate counsel was deficient and that the applicant was prejudiced by that deficiency.

(8) If the court of appeals determines that an evidentiary hearing is necessary, the evidentiary hearing may be conducted by the court or referred to a magistrate.

(9) If the court finds that the performance of appellate counsel was deficient and the applicant was prejudiced by that deficiency, the court shall vacate its prior judgment and enter the appropriate judgment. If the court does not so find, the court shall issue an order confirming its prior judgment.

(C) If an application for reconsideration under division (A) of this rule is filed with the court of appeals, the application shall be ruled upon within forty-five days of its filing.

(Adopted eff. 7–1–71; amended eff. 7–1–75, 7–1–93, 7–1–94, 7–1–97)

App R 27 Execution, mandate

A court of appeals may remand its final decrees, judgments, or orders, in cases brought before it on appeal, to the court or agency below for specific or general execution thereof, or to the court below for further proceedings therein.

A certified copy of the judgment shall constitute the mandate. A stay of execution of the judgment mandate pending appeal may be granted upon motion, and a bond or other security may be required as a condition to the grant or continuance of the stay.

(Adopted eff. 7–1–71)

App R 28 Voluntary dismissal

If the parties to an appeal or other proceeding shall sign and file with the clerk of the court of appeals an agreement that the proceedings be dismissed and shall pay whatever costs are due, the court shall order the case dismissed.

An appeal may be dismissed on motion of the appellant upon such terms as may be fixed by the court.

(Adopted eff. 7–1–71)

App R 29 Substitution of parties

(A) Death of a party

If a party dies after a notice of appeal is filed or while a proceeding is otherwise pending in the court of appeals, the personal representative of the deceased party may be substituted as a party on motion filed by the representative, or by any party, with the clerk of the court of appeals. The motion of a party shall be served upon the representative in accordance with the provisions of Rule 13. If the deceased party has no representative, any party may suggest the death on the record and proceedings shall then be had as the court of appeals may direct. If a party against whom an appeal may be taken dies after entry of a judgment or order in the trial court but before a notice of appeal is filed, an appellant may proceed as if death had not occurred.

After the notice of appeal is filed substitution shall be effected in the court of appeals in accordance with this subdivision. If a party entitled to appeal shall die before filing a notice of appeal, the notice of appeal may be filed by his personal representative, or, if he has no personal representative, by his attorney of record within the time prescribed by these rules. After the notice of appeal is filed, substitution shall be effected in the court of appeals in accordance with this subdivision.

(B) Substitution for other causes

If substitution of a party in the court of appeals is necessary for any reason other than death, substitution shall be effected in accordance with the procedure prescribed in subdivision (A).

(C) Public officers; death or separation from office

(1) When a public officer is a party to an appeal or other proceeding in the court of appeals in his official capacity and during its pendency dies, resigns or otherwise ceases to hold office, the action does not abate and his successor is automatically substituted as a party. Proceedings following the substitution shall be in the name of the substituted party, but any misnomer not affecting the substantial rights of the parties shall be disregarded. An order of substitution may be entered at any time, but the omission to enter such an order shall not affect the substitution.

(2) When a public officer is a party to an appeal or other proceeding in his official capacity, he may be described as a party by his official title rather than by name, but the court may require his name to be added.

(Adopted eff. 7–1–71)

App R 30 Duties of clerks

(A) Notice of orders or judgments

Immediately upon the entry of an order or judgment, the clerk shall serve by mail a notice of entry upon each party to the proceeding and shall make a note in the docket of the mailing. Service on a party represented by counsel shall be made on counsel.

(B) Custody of records and papers

The clerk shall have custody of the records and papers of the court. Papers transmitted as the record on appeal or review shall upon disposition of the case be returned to the court or agency from which they were received. The clerk shall preserve copies of briefs and other filings.

(Adopted eff. 7–1–71; amended eff. 7–1–72)

App R 31 [Reserved]

(Reserved eff. 7–1–97)

App R 32 [Reserved]

(Reserved eff. 7–1–97)

App R 33 [Reserved]

(Reserved eff. 7–1–97)

App R 34 Appointment of magistrates

(A) Original actions

Original actions in the court of appeals may be referred to a magistrate pursuant to Civ. R. 53.

(B) Appeals

When the court orders an evidentiary hearing in an appeal, the court may appoint a magistrate pursuant to Civ. R. 53 to conduct the hearing.

(C) Reference to magistrates

In any matter referred to a magistrate, all proceedings shall be governed by Civ. R. 53 and the order of reference, except that the word "judge" in Civ. R. 53 shall mean the court of appeals. An order of reference shall be signed by at least two judges of the court. Where the court has entered a general order referring a category of actions, appeals, or motions to magistrates generally, a subsequent order referring a particular action, appeal, or motion to a specific magistrate pursuant to the general order may be signed by one judge.

(Adopted eff. 7–1–97)

App R 41 Rules of courts of appeals

(A) The courts of appeals may adopt rules concerning local practice in their respective courts that are not inconsistent with the rules promulgated by the Supreme Court. Local rules shall be filed with the Supreme Court.

(B) Local rules shall be adopted only after the court gives appropriate notice and an opportunity for comment. If the court determines that there is an immediate need for a rule, the court may adopt the rule without prior notice and opportunity for comment, but promptly shall afford notice and opportunity for comment.

(Adopted eff. 7–1–97)

App R 42 Title

These rules shall be known as the Ohio Rules of Appellate Procedure and may be cited as "Appellate Rules" or "App. R ——."

(Adopted eff. 7–1–97)

App R 43 Effective date

(A) Effective date of rules

These rules shall take effect on the first day of July, 1971. They govern all proceedings in actions brought after they take effect and also all further proceedings in actions then pending, except to the extent that in the opinion of the court their application in a particular action pending when the rules take effect would not be feasible or would work injustice in which event the former procedure applies.

(B) Effective date of amendments

The amendments submitted by the supreme court to the general assembly on January 15, 1972, shall take effect on the first day of July, 1972. They govern all proceedings in actions brought after they take effect and also all further proceedings in actions then pending, except to the extent that their application in a particular action pending when the rules take effect would not be feasible or would work injustice, in which event the former procedure applies.

(C) Effective date of amendments

The amendments submitted by the supreme court to the general assembly on January 12, 1973, and on April 30, 1973, shall take effect on July 1, 1973. They govern all proceedings in actions brought after they take effect and also all further proceedings in actions then pending, except to the extent that their application in a particular action pending when the amendments take effect would not be feasible or would work injustice, in which event the former procedure applies.

(D) Effective date of amendments

The amendments submitted by the supreme court to the general assembly on January 10, 1975, and on April 29, 1975, shall take effect on July 1, 1975. They govern all proceedings in actions brought after they take effect and also all further proceedings in actions then pending, except to the extent that their application in a particular action pending when the amendments take effect would not be feasible or would work injustice, in which event the former procedure applies.

(E) Effective date of amendments

The amendments submitted by the supreme court to the general assembly on January 9, 1976, shall take effect on July 1, 1976. They govern all proceedings in actions brought after they take effect and also all further proceedings in actions then pending, except to the extent that their application in a particular action pending when the amendments take effect would not be feasible or would work injustice, in which event the former procedure applies.

(F) Effective date of amendments

The amendments submitted by the Supreme Court to the General Assembly on January 12, 1978 shall take effect on July 1, 1978. They govern all proceedings in actions brought after they take effect and also all further proceedings in actions then pending, except to the extent that their application in a particular action pending when the amendments take effect would not be feasible or would work injustice, in which event the former procedure applies.

(G) Effective date of amendments

The amendments submitted by the Supreme court to the General Assembly on January 14, 1982 shall take effect on July 1, 1982. They govern all proceedings in actions brought after they take effect and also all further proceedings in actions then pending, except to the extent that their application in a particular action pending when the amendments take effect would not be feasible or would work injustice, in which event the former procedure applies.

(H) Effective date of amendments

The amendments submitted by the Supreme Court to the General Assembly on December 24, 1984 and January 8, 1985 shall take effect on July 1, 1985. They govern all proceedings in actions brought after they take effect and also all further proceedings in actions then pending, except to the extent that their application in a particular action pending when the amendments take effect would not be feasible or would work injustice, in which event the former procedure applies.

(I) Effective date of amendments

The amendments submitted by the Supreme Court to the General Assembly on January 14, 1988, as amended, shall take effect on July 1, 1988. They govern all proceedings in actions brought after they take effect and also all further proceedings in actions then pending, except to the extent that their application in a particular action pending when the amendments take effect would not be feasible or would work injustice, in which event the former procedure applies.

(J) Effective date of amendments

The amendments submitted by the Supreme Court to the General Assembly on January 6, 1989, shall take effect on July 1, 1989. They govern all proceedings in actions brought after they take effect and also all further proceedings in actions then pending, except to the extent that their application in a particular action pending when the amendments take effect would not be feasible or would work injustice, in which event the former procedure applies.

(K) Effective date of amendments

The amendments submitted by the Supreme Court to the General Assembly on January 10, 1991 shall take effect on July 1, 1991. They govern all proceedings in actions brought after they take effect and also all further proceedings in actions then pending, except to the extent that their application in a particular action pending when the amendments take effect would not be feasible or would work injustice, in which event the former procedure applies.

(L) Effective date of amendments

The amendments filed by the Supreme Court with the General Assembly on January 14, 1992 and further filed on April 30, 1992, shall take effect on July 1, 1992. They govern all proceedings in actions brought after they take effect and also all future proceedings in actions then pending, except to the extent that their application in a particular action pending when the amendments take effect would not be feasible or would work injustice, in which event the former procedure applies.

(M) Effective date of amendments

The amendments submitted by the Supreme Court to the General Assembly on January 8, 1993 and further revised and filed on April 30, 1993 shall take effect on July 1, 1993. They govern all proceedings in actions brought after they take effect and also all further proceedings in actions then pending, except to the extent that their application in a particular action pending when the amendments take effect would not be feasible or would work injustice, in which event the former procedure applies.

(N) Effective date of amendments

The amendments submitted by the Supreme Court to the General Assembly on January 14, 1994 and further revised and filed on April 29, 1994 shall take effect on July 1, 1994. They govern all proceedings in actions brought after they take effect and also all further proceedings in actions then pending, except to the extent that their application in a particular action pending when the amendments take effect would not be feasible or would work injustice, in which event the former procedure applies.

(O) Effective date of amendments

The amendments to Rules 4 and 5 filed by the Supreme Court with the General Assembly on January 5, 1996 and further revised and filed on April 26, 1996 shall take effect on July 1, 1996. They govern all proceedings in actions brought after they take effect and also all further proceedings in actions then pending, except to the extent that their application in a particular action pending when the amendments take effect would not be feasible or would work injustice, in which event the former procedure applies.

(P) Effective date of amendments

The amendments to Rules 6, 11, 19, 26, 31, 32, 33, 34, 41, 42, and 43 filed by the Supreme Court with the General Assembly on January 10, 1997 and further revised and refiled on April 24, 1997 shall take effect on July 1, 1997. They govern all proceedings in actions brought after they take effect and also all further proceedings in actions then pending, except to the extent that their application in a particular action pending when the amendments take effect would not be feasible or would work injustice, in which event the former procedure applies.

(Q) Effective date of amendments

The amendments to Appellate Rule 11.2 filed by the Supreme Court with the General Assembly on January 13, 2000 and refiled on April 27, 2000 shall take effect on July 1, 2000. They govern all proceedings in actions brought after they take effect and also all further proceedings in actions then pending, except to the extent that their application in a particular action pending when the amendments take effect would not be feasible or would work injustice, in which event the former procedure applies.

(R) Effective date of amendments

The amendments to Appellate Rules 7, 11.2, 13, and 18 filed by the Supreme Court with the General Assembly on January 12, 2001, and revised and refiled on April 26, 2001, shall take effect on July 1, 2001. They govern all proceedings in actions brought after they take effect and also all further proceedings in actions then pending, except to the extent that their application in a particular action pending when the amendments take effect would not be feasible or would work injustice, in which event the former procedure applies.

(S) Effective date of amendments

The amendments to Appellate Rule 4 filed by the Supreme Court with the General Assembly on January 11, 2002, and revised and refiled on April 18, 2002 shall take effect on July 1, 2002. They govern all proceedings in actions brought after they take effect and also all further proceedings in actions then pending, except to the extent that their application in a particular action pending when the amendments take effect would not be feasible or would work injustice, in which event the former procedure applies.

(S)[1] Effective date of amendments.

The amendments to Appellate Rule 5 filed by the Supreme Court with the General Assembly on January 9, 2003 and refiled on April 28, 2003, shall take effect on July 1, 2003. They govern all proceedings in actions brought after they take effect and also all further proceedings in actions then pending, except to the extent that their application in a particular action pending when the amendments take effect would not be feasible or would work injustice, in which event the former procedure applies.

(Adopted eff. 7–1–97; amended eff. 7–1–00, 7–1–01, 7–1–02, 7–1–03)

[1] So in original.

APPENDIX OF FORMS

App R Form 1

FORM 1

NOTICE OF APPEAL TO A COURT OF APPEALS FROM A JUDGMENT OR APPEALABLE ORDER

COURT OF COMMON PLEAS
FRANKLIN COUNTY, OHIO

A.B. 221 E. West Street Columbus, Ohio 43215 Plaintiff v. C.D. 122 W. East Street Columbus, Ohio 43214 Defendant–Appellant	)))))))))))	NO. ____________________ NOTICE OF APPEAL

Notice is hereby given that C.D., defendant, hereby appeals to the Court of Appeals of Franklin County, Ohio, Tenth Appellate District (from the final judgment), from the order (describing it) entered in this action on the _____ day of _________, 19___.

____
(Attorney for Defendant)

____
(Address)

Note: The above form is designed for use in Courts of Common Pleas. Appropriate changes in the designation of the court are required when the form is used for other courts.

App R Form 2

FORM 2

DOCKETING STATEMENT

COURT OF COMMON PLEAS
FRANKLIN COUNTY, OHIO

A.B., 221 East West Street, Columbus, Ohio, Plaintiff,	:	
v.	:	No. CV–1981–453
C.D., 122 West East Street, Columbus, Ohio, Defendant.	:	

DOCKETING STATEMENT

(Insert one of the following statements, as applicable):

(1) No transcript is required.
(2) The approximate number of pages of transcript ordered is ______.
(3) An agreed statement will be submitted in lieu of the record.
(4) The record was made in an administrative hearing and filed with the trial court.
(5) All parties to the appeal as shown by the attached statement approve assignment of the appeal to the accelerated calendar.
(6) The case is of a category designated for the accelerated calendar by local rule. (Specify category.)

____
Attorney for Appellant

Note: App R 3(D) requires the clerk of the trial court to file a docketing statement with the notice of the filing of a notice of appeal, for any case assigned to an accelerated calendar. The contents of the docketing statement are described in App R 3(F). Form 2, above, is an example of the docketing statement referred to in App R 3(F). The above form is designed for use in Courts of Common Pleas. Appropriate changes to the caption are required when the form is used for other courts.

App R Form 3

FORM 3

JUDGMENT ENTRY—ACCELERATED CALENDAR

TENTH DISTRICT COURT OF APPEALS
FRANKLIN COUNTY

A.B., 221 East West Street, Columbus, Ohio, Plaintiff, v. C.D., 122 West East Street, Columbus, Ohio, Defendant.	))))))))))	No. CV–1981–453

JUDGMENT ENTRY

Assignment of error number one is overruled for the reason that the trial court's instruction on the burden of proof was correct. See *Jones v. State* (1980), 64 Ohio St.2d 173.

Assignment of error number two is overruled as there was sufficient evidence presented (see testimony of Smith, R. 22) to support a factual finding of agency.

The judgment of the trial court is affirmed.

____
Judge, Presiding Judge

____
Judge

____
Judge

Note: App R 11.1 sets forth the procedure to be followed in a case assigned to an accelerated calendar. The rule states that the decision of a case may be by judgment entry. Form 3, above, is an example of a judgment entry, as referred to in App R 11.1(E). The above form is designed for use in the Courts of Appeals. Appropriate changes to the caption are required when the form is used for other courts.

RULES OF JUVENILE PROCEDURE

Publisher's Note: Until 1968, when the Modern Courts Amendment to the Ohio Constitution was adopted, Ohio court procedure was governed entirely by statute and case law. The Modern Courts Amendment required the Supreme Court of Ohio, subject to the approval of the General Assembly, to "prescribe rules governing practice and procedure in all courts of the state." Rules of practice and procedure are the Civil, Criminal, Appellate, and Juvenile Rules, Rules of the Court of Claims, and the Ohio Rules of Evidence. Pursuant to Ohio Constitution Article IV, Section 5(B), such rules "shall not abridge, enlarge, or modify any substantive right," and " [a]ll laws in conflict with such rules shall be of no further force or effect."

Juv R 1 Scope of rules: applicability; construction; exceptions

(A) Applicability

These rules prescribe the procedure to be followed in all juvenile courts of this state in all proceedings coming within the jurisdiction of such courts, with the exceptions stated in subdivision (C).

(B) Construction

These rules shall be liberally interpreted and construed so as to effectuate the following purposes:

(1) to effect the just determination of every juvenile court proceeding by ensuring the parties a fair hearing and the recognition and enforcement of their constitutional and other legal rights;

(2) to secure simplicity and uniformity in procedure, fairness in administration, and the elimination of unjustifiable expense and delay;

(3) to provide for the care, protection, and mental and physical development of children subject to the jurisdiction of the juvenile court, and to protect the welfare of the community; and

(4) to protect the public interest by treating children as persons in need of supervision, care and rehabilitation.

(C) Exceptions

These rules shall not apply to procedure (1) Upon appeal to review any judgment, order, or ruling; (2) Upon the trial of criminal actions; (3) Upon the trial of actions for divorce, annulment, legal separation, and related proceedings; (4) In proceedings to determine parent-child relationships, provided, however that appointment of counsel shall be in accordance with Rule 4(A) of the Rules of Juvenile Procedure; (5) In the commitment of the mentally ill and mentally retarded; (6) In proceedings under section 2151.85 of the Revised Code to the extent that there is a conflict between these rules and section 2151.85 of the Revised Code.

When any statute provides for procedure by general or specific reference to the statutes governing procedure in juvenile court actions, procedure shall be in accordance with these rules.

(Adopted eff. 7–1–72; amended eff. 7–1–91, 7–1–94, 7–1–95)

Juv R 2 Definitions

As used in these rules:

(A) "Abused child" has the same meaning as in section 2151.031 of the Revised Code.

(B) "Adjudicatory hearing" means a hearing to determine whether a child is a juvenile traffic offender, delinquent, unruly, abused, neglected, or dependent or otherwise within the jurisdiction of the court.

(C) "Agreement for temporary custody" means a voluntary agreement that is authorized by section 5103.15 of the Revised

Code and transfers the temporary custody of a child to a public children services agency or a private child placing agency.

(D) "Child" has the same meaning as in sections 2151.011 and 2152.02 of the Revised Code.

(E) "Chronic truant" has the same meaning as in section 2151.011 of the Revised Code.

(F) "Complaint" means the legal document that sets forth the allegations that form the basis for juvenile court jurisdiction.

(G) "Court proceeding" means all action taken by a court from the earlier of (1) the time a complaint is filed and (2) the time a person first appears before an officer of a juvenile court until the court relinquishes jurisdiction over such child.

(H) "Custodian" means a person who has legal custody of a child or a public children's services agency or private child-placing agency that has permanent, temporary, or legal custody of a child.

(I) "Delinquent child" has the same meaning as in section 2152.02 of the Revised Code.

(J) "Dependent child" has the same meaning as in section 2151.04 of the Revised Code.

(K) "Detention" means the temporary care of children in restricted facilities pending court adjudication or disposition.

(L) "Detention hearing" means a hearing to determine whether a child shall be held in detention or shelter care prior to or pending execution of a final dispositional order.

(M) "Dispositional hearing" means a hearing to determine what action shall be taken concerning a child who is within the jurisdiction of the court.

(N) "Guardian" means a person, association, or corporation that is granted authority by a probate court pursuant to Chapter 2111 of the Revised Code to exercise parental rights over a child to the extent provided in the court's order and subject to the residual parental rights of the child's parents.

(O) "Guardian ad litem" means a person appointed to protect the interests of a party in a juvenile court proceeding.

(P) "Habitual truant" has the same meaning as in section 2151.011 of the Revised Code.

(Q) "Hearing" means any portion of a juvenile court proceeding before the court, whether summary in nature or by examination of witnesses.

(R) "Indigent person" means a person who, at the time need is determined, is unable by reason of lack of property or income to provide for full payment of legal counsel and all other necessary expenses of representation.

(S) "Juvenile court" means a division of the court of common pleas, or a juvenile court separately and independently created, that has jurisdiction under Chapters 2151 and 2152 of the Revised Code.

(T) "Juvenile judge" means a judge of a court having jurisdiction under Chapters 2151 and 2152 of the Revised Code.

(U) "Juvenile traffic offender" has the same meaning as in section 2151.021 of the Revised Code.

(V) "Legal custody" means a legal status that vests in the custodian the right to have physical care and control of the child and to determine where and with whom the child shall live, and the right and duty to protect, train, and discipline the child and provide the child with food, shelter, education, and medical care, all subject to any residual parental rights, privileges, and responsibilities. An individual granted legal custody shall exercise the rights and responsibilities personally unless otherwise authorized by any section of the Revised Code or by the court.

(W) "Mental examination" means an examination by a psychiatrist or psychologist.

(X) "Neglected child" has the same meaning as in section 2151.03 of the Revised Code.

(Y) "Party" means a child who is the subject of a juvenile court proceeding, the child's spouse, if any, the child's parent or parents, or if the parent of a child is a child, the parent of that parent, in appropriate cases, the child's custodian, guardian, or guardian ad litem, the state, and any other person specifically designated by the court.

(Z) "Permanent custody" means a legal status that vests in a public children's services agency or a private child-placing agency, all parental rights, duties, and obligations, including the right to consent to adoption, and divests the natural parents or adoptive parents of any and all parental rights, privileges, and obligations, including all residual rights and obligations.

(AA) "Permanent surrender" means the act of the parents or, if a child has only one parent, of the parent of a child, by a voluntary agreement authorized by section 5103.15 of the Revised Code, to transfer the permanent custody of the child to a public children's services agency or a private child-placing agency.

(BB) "Person" includes an individual, association, corporation, or partnership and the state or any of its political subdivisions, departments, or agencies.

(CC) "Physical examination" means an examination by a physician.

(DD) "Planned permanent living arrangement" means an order of a juvenile court pursuant to which both of the following apply:

(1) The court gives legal custody of a child to a public children's services agency or a private child-placing agency without the termination of parental rights;

(2) The order permits the agency to make an appropriate placement of the child and to enter into a written planned permanent living arrangement agreement with a foster care provider or with another person or agency with whom the child is placed.

(EE) "Private child-placing agency" means any association, as defined in section 5103.02 of the Revised Code that is certified pursuant to sections 5103.03 to 5103.05 of the Revised Code to accept temporary, permanent, or legal custody of children and place the children for either foster care or adoption.

(FF) "Public children's services agency" means a children's services board or a county department of human services that has assumed the administration of the children's services function prescribed by Chapter 5153 of the Revised Code.

(GG) "Removal action" means a statutory action filed by the superintendent of a school district for the removal of a child in an out-of-county foster home placement.

(HH) "Residence or legal settlement" means a location as defined by section 2151.06 of the Revised Code.

(II) "Residual parental rights, privileges, and responsibilities" means those rights, privileges, and responsibilities remaining with the natural parent after the transfer of legal custody of the child, including but not limited to the privilege of reasonable visitation, consent to adoption, the privilege to determine the child's religious affiliation, and the responsibility for support.

(JJ) "Rule of court" means a rule promulgated by the Supreme Court or a rule concerning local practice adopted by another court that is not inconsistent with the rules promulgated by the Supreme Court and that is filed with the Supreme Court.

(KK) "Serious youthful offender" means a child eligible for sentencing as described in sections 2152.11 and 2152.13 of the Revised Code.

(LL) "Serious youthful offender proceedings" means proceedings after a probable cause determination that a child is eligible for sentencing as described in sections 2152.11 and 2152.13 of the

Revised Code. Serious youthful offender proceedings cease to be serious youthful offender proceedings once a child has been determined by the trier of fact not to be a serious youthful offender or the juvenile judge has determined not to impose a serious youthful offender disposition on a child eligible for discretionary serious youthful offender sentencing.

(MM) "Shelter care" means the temporary care of children in physically unrestricted facilities, pending court adjudication or disposition.

(NN) "Social history" means the personal and family history of a child or any other party to a juvenile proceeding and may include the prior record of the person with the juvenile court or any other court.

(OO) "Temporary custody" means legal custody of a child who is removed from the child's home, which custody may be terminated at any time at the discretion of the court or, if the legal custody is granted in an agreement for temporary custody, by the person or persons who executed the agreement.

(PP) "Unruly child" has the same meaning as in section 2151.022 of the Revised Code.

(QQ) "Ward of court" means a child over whom the court assumes continuing jurisdiction.

(Adopted eff. 7–1–72; amended eff. 7–1–94, 7–1–98, 7–1–01, 7–1–02)

Juv R 3 Waiver of rights

A child's right to be represented by counsel at a hearing conducted pursuant to Juv. R. 30 may not be waived. Other rights of a child may be waived with the permission of the court.

(Adopted eff. 7–1–72; amended eff. 7–1–94)

Juv R 4 Assistance of counsel; guardian ad litem

(A) Assistance of counsel

Every party shall have the right to be represented by counsel and every child, parent, custodian, or other person in loco parentis the right to appointed counsel if indigent. These rights shall arise when a person becomes a party to a juvenile court proceeding. When the complaint alleges that a child is an abused child, the court must appoint an attorney to represent the interests of the child. This rule shall not be construed to provide for a right to appointed counsel in cases in which that right is not otherwise provided for by constitution or statute.

(B) Guardian ad litem; when appointed

The court shall appoint a guardian *ad litem* to protect the interests of a child or incompetent adult in a juvenile court proceeding when:

(1) The child has no parents, guardian, or legal custodian;

(2) The interests of the child and the interests of the parent may conflict;

(3) The parent is under eighteen years of age or appears to be mentally incompetent;

(4) The court believes that the parent of the child is not capable of representing the best interest of the child.

(5) Any proceeding involves allegations of abuse or neglect, voluntary surrender of permanent custody, or termination of parental rights as soon as possible after the commencement of such proceeding.

(6) There is an agreement for the voluntary surrender of temporary custody that is made in accordance with section 5103.15 of the Revised Code, and thereafter there is a request for extension of the voluntary agreement.

(7) The proceeding is a removal action.

(8) Appointment is otherwise necessary to meet the requirements of a fair hearing.

(C) Guardian ad litem as counsel

(1) When the guardian ad litem is an attorney admitted to practice in this state, the guardian may also serve as counsel to the ward providing no conflict between the roles exist.

(2) If a person is serving as guardian ad litem and as attorney for a ward and either that person or the court finds a conflict between the responsibilities of the role of attorney and that of guardian ad litem, the court shall appoint another person as guardian ad litem for the ward.

(3) If a court appoints a person who is not an attorney admitted to practice in this state to be a guardian ad litem, the court may appoint an attorney admitted to pracice [sic.] in this state to serve as attorney for the guardian ad litem.

(D) Appearance of attorneys

An attorney shall enter appearance by filing a written notice with the court or by appearing personally at a court hearing and informing the court of said representation.

(E) Notice to guardian ad litem

The guardian ad litem shall be given notice of all proceedings in the same manner as notice is given to other parties to the action.

(F) Withdrawal of counsel or guardian ad litem

An attorney or guardian ad litem may withdraw only with the consent of the court upon good cause shown.

(G) Costs

The court may fix compensation for the services of appointed counsel and guardians ad litem, tax the same as part of the costs and assess them against the child, the child's parents, custodian, or other person in loco parentis of such child.

(Adopted eff. 7–1–72; amended eff. 7–1–76, 7–1–94, 7–1–95, 7–1–98)

Juv R 5 [Reserved]

Juv R 6 Taking into custody

(A) A child may be taken into custody:

(1) pursuant to an order of the court;

(2) pursuant to the law of arrest;

(3) by a law enforcement officer or duly authorized officer of the court when any of the following conditions exist:

(a) There are reasonable grounds to believe that the child is suffering from illness or injury and is not receiving proper care, and the child's removal is necessary to prevent immediate or threatened physical or emotional harm;

(b) There are reasonable grounds to believe that the child is in immediate danger from the child's surroundings and that the child's removal is necessary to prevent immediate or threatened physical or emotional harm;

(c) There are reasonable grounds to believe that a parent, guardian, custodian, or other household member of the child has abused or neglected another child in the household, and that the child is in danger of immediate or threatened physical or emotional harm;

(d) There are reasonable grounds to believe that the child has run away from the child's parents, guardian, or other custodian;

(e) There are reasonable grounds to believe that the conduct, conditions, or surroundings of the child are endangering the health, welfare, or safety of the child;

(f) During the pendency of court proceedings, there are reasonable grounds to believe that the child may abscond or be removed from the jurisdiction of the court or will not be brought to the court;

(g) A juvenile judge or designated magistrate has found that there is probable cause to believe any of the conditions set forth in division (A)(3)(a), (b), or (c) of this rule are present, has found that reasonable efforts have been made to notify the child's parents, guardian ad litem or custodian that the child may be placed into shelter care, except where notification would jeopardize the physical or emotional safety of the child or result in the child's removal from the court's jurisdiction, and has ordered ex parte, by telephone or otherwise, the taking of the child into custody.

(4) By the judge or designated magistrate ex parte pending the outcome of the adjudicatory and dispositional hearing in an abuse, neglect, or dependency proceeding, where it appears to the court that the best interest and welfare of the child require the immediate issuance of a shelter care order.

(B) Probable cause hearing

When a child is taken into custody pursuant to an ex parte emergency order pursuant to division (A)(3)(g) or (A)(4) of this rule, a probable cause hearing shall be held before the end of the next business day after the day on which the order is issued but not later than seventy-two hours after the issuance of the emergency order.

(Adopted eff. 7–1–72; amended eff. 7–1–94, 7–1–96)

Juv R 7 Detention and shelter care

(A) Detention: standards

A child taken into custody shall not be placed in detention or shelter care prior to final disposition unless any of the following apply:

(1) Detention or shelter care is required:

(a) to protect the child from immediate or threatened physical or emotional harm; or

(b) to protect the person or property of others from immediate or threatened physical or emotional harm.

(2) The child may abscond or be removed from the jurisdiction of the court;

(3) The child has no parent, guardian, custodian or other person able to provide supervision and care for the child and return the child to the court when required;

(4) An order for placement of the child in detention or shelter care has been made by the court;

(5) Confinement is authorized by statute.

(B) Priorities in placement prior to hearing

A person taking a child into custody shall, with all reasonable speed, do either of the following:

(1) Release the child to a parent, guardian, or other custodian;

(2) Where detention or shelter care appears to be required under the standards of division (A) of this rule, bring the child to the court or deliver the child to a place of detention or shelter care designated by the court.

(C) Initial procedure upon detention

Any person who delivers a child to a shelter or detention facility shall give the admissions officer at the facility a signed report stating why the child was taken into custody and why the child was not released to a parent, guardian or custodian, and shall assist the admissions officer, if necessary, in notifying the parent pursuant to division (E)(3) of this rule.

(D) Admission

The admissions officer in a shelter or detention facility, upon receipt of a child, shall review the report submitted pursuant to division (C) of this rule, make such further investigation as is feasible and do either of the following:

(1) Release the child to the care of a parent, guardian or custodian;

(2) Where detention or shelter care is required under the standards of division (A) of this rule, admit the child to the facility or place the child in some appropriate facility.

(E) Procedure after admission

When a child has been admitted to detention or shelter care the admissions officer shall do all of the following:

(1) Prepare a report stating the time the child was brought to the facility and the reasons the child was admitted;

(2) Advise the child of the right to telephone parents and counsel immediately and at reasonable times thereafter and the time, place, and purpose of the detention hearing;

(3) Use reasonable diligence to contact the child's parent, guardian, or custodian and advise that person of all of the following:

(a) The place of and reasons for detention;

(b) The time the child may be visited;

(c) The time, place, and purpose of the detention hearing;

(d) The right to counsel and appointed counsel in the case of indigency.

(F) Detention hearing

(1) Hearing: time; notice. When a child has been admitted to detention or shelter care, a detention hearing shall be held promptly, not later than seventy-two hours after the child is placed in detention or shelter care or the next court day, whichever is earlier, to determine whether detention or shelter care is required. Reasonable oral or written notice of the time, place, and purpose of the detention hearing shall be given to the child and the parents, guardian, or other custodian, if that person or those persons can be found.

(2) Hearing: advisement of rights. Prior to the hearing, the court shall inform the parties of the right to counsel and to appointed counsel if indigent and the child's right to remain silent with respect to any allegation of a juvenile traffic offense, delinquency, or unruliness.

(3) Hearing procedure. The court may consider any evidence, including the reports filed by the person who brought the child to the facility and the admissions officer, without regard to formal rules of evidence. Unless it appears from the hearing that the child's detention or shelter care is required under division (A) of this rule, the court shall order the child's release to a parent, guardian, or custodian. Whenever abuse, neglect, or dependency is alleged, the court shall determine whether there are any appropriate relatives of the child who are willing to be temporary custodians and, if so, appoint an appropriate relative as the temporary custodian of the child. The court shall make a reasonable efforts determination in accordance with Juv. R. 27(B)(1).

(G) Rehearing

If a parent, guardian, or custodian did not receive notice of the initial hearing and did not appear or waive appearance at the hearing, the court shall rehear the matter promptly. After a child is placed in shelter care or detention care, any party and the guardian ad litem of the child may file a motion with the court requesting that the child be released from detention or shelter care. Upon the filing of the motion, the court shall hold a hearing within seventy-two hours.

(H) Separation from adults

No child shall be placed in or committed to any prison, jail, lockup, or any other place where the child can come in contact or communication with any adult convicted of crime, under arrest, or charged with crime.

(I) Physical examination

The supervisor of a shelter or detention facility may provide for a physical examination of a child placed in the shelter or facility.

(J) Telephone and visitation rights

A child may telephone the child's parents and attorney immediately after being admitted to a shelter or detention facility and at reasonable times thereafter.

The child may be visited at reasonable visiting hours by the child's parents and adult members of the family, the child's pastor, and the child's teachers. The child may be visited by the child's attorney at any time.

(Adopted eff. 7-1-72; amended eff. 7-1-94, 7-1-01)

Juv R 8 Filing by electronic means

A court may provide, by local rules adopted pursuant to the Rules of Superintendence, for the filing of documents by electronic means. If the court adopts such local rules, they shall include all of the following:

(A) Any signature on electronically transmitted documents shall be considered that of the attorney or party it purports to be for all purposes. If it is established that the documents were transmitted without authority, the court shall order the filing stricken.

(B) A provision shall specify the days and hours during which electronically transmitted documents will be received by the court, and a provision shall specify when documents received electronically will be considered to have been filed.

(C) Any document filed electronically that requires a filing fee may be rejected by the clerk of court unless the filer has complied with the mechanism established by the court for the payment of filing fees.

(Adopted eff. 7-1-94, amended eff. 7-1-96, 7-1-01)

Juv R 9 Intake

(A) Court action to be avoided

In all appropriate cases formal court action should be avoided and other community resources utilized to ameliorate situations brought to the attention of the court.

(B) Screening; referral

Information that a child is within the court's jurisdiction may be informally screened prior to the filing of a complaint to determine whether the filing of a complaint is in the best interest of the child and the public.

(Adopted eff. 7-1-72)

Juv R 10 Complaint

(A) Filing

Any person having knowledge of a child who appears to be a juvenile traffic offender, delinquent, unruly, neglected, dependent, or abused may file a complaint with respect to the child in the juvenile court of the county in which the child has a residence or legal settlement, or in which the traffic offense, delinquency, unruliness, neglect, dependency, or abuse occurred.

Persons filing complaints that a child appears to be an unruly or delinquent child for being an habitual or chronic truant and the parent, guardian, or other person having care of the child has failed to cause the child to attend school may also file the complaint in the county in which the child is supposed to attend public school.

Any person may file a complaint to have determined the custody of a child not a ward of another court of this state, and any person entitled to the custody of a child and unlawfully deprived of such custody may file a complaint requesting a writ of habeas corpus. Complaints concerning custody shall be filed in the county where the child is found or was last known to be.

Any person with standing may file a complaint for the determination of any other matter over which the juvenile court is given jurisdiction by the Revised Code. The complaint shall be filed in the county in which the child who is the subject of the complaint is found or was last known to be. In a removal action, the complaint shall be filed in the county where the foster home is located.

When a case concerning a child is transferred or certified from another court, the certification from the transferring court shall be considered the complaint. The juvenile court may order the certification supplemented upon its own motion or that of a party.

(B) Complaint: general form

The complaint, which may be upon information and belief, shall satisfy all of the following requirements:

(1) State in ordinary and concise language the essential facts that bring the proceeding within the jurisdiction of the court, and in juvenile traffic offense and delinquency proceedings, shall contain the numerical designation of the statute or ordinance alleged to have been violated;

(2) Contain the name and address of the parent, guardian, or custodian of the child or state that the name or address is unknown;

(3) Be made under oath.

(C) Complaint: juvenile traffic offense

A Uniform Traffic Ticket shall be used as a complaint in juvenile traffic offense proceedings.

(D) Complaint: permanent custody

A complaint seeking permanent custody of a child shall state that permanent custody is sought.

(E) Complaint: temporary custody

A complaint seeking temporary custody of a child shall state that temporary custody is sought.

(F) Complaint: planned permanent living arrangement

A complaint seeking the placement of a child into a planned permanent living arrangement shall state that placement into a planned permanent living arrangement is sought.

(G) Complaint: habeas corpus

Where a complaint for a writ of habeas corpus involving the custody of a child is based on the existence of a lawful court order, a certified copy of the order shall be attached to the complaint.

(Adopted eff. 7-1-72; amended eff. 7-1-75, 7-1-76, 7-1-94, 7-1-98, 7-1-01, 7-1-02)

Juv R 11 Transfer to another county

(A) Residence in another county; transfer optional

If the child resides in a county of this state and the proceeding is commenced in a court of another county, that court, on its own motion or a motion of a party, may transfer the proceeding to the county of the child's residence upon the filing of the complaint or after the adjudicatory or dispositional hearing for such further proceeding as required. The court of the child's residence shall then proceed as if the original complaint had been filed in that court. Transfer may also be made if the residence of the child changes.

(B) Proceedings in another county; transfer required

The proceedings, other than a removal action, shall be so transferred if other proceedings involving the child are pending in the juvenile court of the county of the child's residence.

(C) Adjudicatory hearing in county where complaint filed

Where either the transferring or receiving court finds that the interests of justice and the convenience of the parties so require, the adjudicatory hearing shall be held in the county wherein the complaint was filed. Thereafter the proceeding may be transferred to the county of the child's residence for disposition.

(D) Transfer of records

Certified copies of all legal and social records pertaining to the proceeding shall accompany the transfer.

(Adopted eff. 7–1–72; amended eff. 7–1–94, 7–1–98)

Juv R 12 [Reserved]

Juv R 13 Temporary disposition; temporary orders; emergency medical and surgical treatment

(A) Temporary disposition

Pending hearing on a complaint, the court may make such temporary orders concerning the custody or care of a child who is the subject of the complaint as the child's interest and welfare may require.

(B) Temporary orders

(1) Pending hearing on a complaint, the judge or magistrate may issue temporary orders with respect to the relations and conduct of other persons toward a child who is the subject of the complaint as the child's interest and welfare may require.

(2) Upon the filing of an abuse, neglect, or dependency complaint, any party may by motion request that the court issue any of the following temporary orders to protect the best interest of the child:

(a) An order granting temporary custody of the child to a particular party;

(b) An order for the taking of the child into custody pending the outcome of the adjudicatory and dispositional hearings;

(c) An order granting, limiting, or eliminating visitation rights with respect to the child;

(d) An order for the payment of child support and continued maintenance of any medical, surgical, or hospital policies of insurance for the child that existed at the time of the filing of the complaint, petition, writ, or other document;

(e) An order requiring a party to vacate a residence that will be lawfully occupied by the child;

(f) An order requiring a party to attend an appropriate counseling program that is reasonably available to that party;

(g) Any other order that restrains or otherwise controls the conduct of any party which conduct would not be in the best interest of the child.

(3) The orders permitted by division (B)(2) of this rule may be granted ex parte if it appears that the best interest and welfare of the child require immediate issuance. If the court issues the requested ex parte order, the court shall hold a hearing to review the order within seventy-two hours after it is issued or before the end of the next court day after the day on which it is issued, whichever occurs first. The court shall appoint a guardian ad litem for the child prior to the hearing. The court shall give written notice of the hearing by means reasonably likely to result in the party's receiving actual notice and include all of the following:

(a) The date, time, and location of the hearing;

(b) The issues to be addressed at the hearing;

(c) A statement that every party to the hearing has a right to counsel and to court appointed counsel, if the party is indigent;

(d) The name, telephone number, and address of the person requesting the order;

(e) A copy of the order, except when it is not possible to obtain it because of the exigent circumstances in the case.

(4) The court may review any order under this rule at any time upon motion of any party for good cause shown or upon the motion of the court.

(5) If the court does not grant an ex parte order, the court shall hold a shelter care hearing on the motion within ten days after the motion is filed.

(C) Emergency medical and surgical treatment

Upon the certification of one or more reputable practicing physicians, the court may order such emergency medical and surgical treatment as appears to be immediately necessary for any child concerning whom a complaint has been filed.

(D) Ex parte proceedings

In addition to the ex parte proceeding described in division (B) of this rule, the court may proceed summarily and without notice under division (A), (B), or (C) of this rule, where it appears to the court that the interest and welfare of the child require that action be taken immediately.

(E) Hearing; notice

In addition to the procedures specified in division (B) of this rule and wherever possible, the court shall provide an opportunity for hearing before proceeding under division (D) of this rule. Where the court has proceeded without notice under division (D) of this rule, it shall give notice of the action it has taken to the parties and any other affected person and provide them an opportunity for a hearing concerning the continuing effects of the action.

(F) Probable cause finding

Upon the finding of probable cause at a shelter care hearing that a child is an abused child, the court may do any of the following:

(1) Upon motion by the court or of any party, issue reasonable protective orders with respect to the interviewing or deposition of the child;

(2) Order that the child's testimony be videotaped for preservation of the testimony for possible use in any other proceedings in the case;

(3) Set any additional conditions with respect to the child or the case involving the child that are in the best interest of the child.

(G) Payment

The court may order the parent, guardian, or custodian, if able, to pay for any emergency medical or surgical treatment provided pursuant to division (C) of this rule. The order of payment may be enforced by judgment, upon which execution may issue, and a failure to pay as ordered may be punished as contempt of court.

(Adopted eff. 7–1–72; amended eff. 7–1–94, 7–1–96)

Juv R 14 Termination, extension or modification of temporary custody orders

(A) Termination

Any temporary custody order issued shall terminate one year after the earlier of the date on which the complaint in the case was filed or the child was first placed into shelter care. A temporary custody order shall extend beyond a year and until the court issues another dispositional order, where any public or private agency with temporary custody, not later than thirty days prior to the earlier of the date for the termination of the custody order or the date set at the dispositional hearing for the hearing to be held pursuant to division (A) of section 2151.415 of the Revised Code, files a motion requesting that any of the following orders of disposition be issued:

(1) An order that the child be returned home with custody to the child's parents, guardian, or custodian without any restrictions;

(2) An order for protective supervision;

(3) An order that the child be placed in the legal custody of a relative or other interested individual;

(4) An order terminating parental rights;

(5) An order for long term foster care;

(6) An order for the extension of temporary custody.

(B) Extension

Upon the filing of an agency's motion for the extension of temporary custody, the court shall schedule a hearing and give notice to all parties in accordance with these rules. The agency shall include in the motion an explanation of the progress on the case plan and of its expectations of reunifying the child with the child's family, or placing the child in a permanent placement, within the extension period. The court may extend the temporary custody order for a period of up to six months. Prior to the end of the extension period, the agency may request one additional extension of up to six months. The court shall grant either extension upon finding that it is in the best interest of the child, that there has been significant progress on the case plan, and that there is reasonable cause to believe that the child will be reunited with one of the child's parents or otherwise permanently placed within the period of extension. Prior to the end of either extension, the agency that received the extension shall file a motion and the court shall issue one of the orders of disposition set forth in division (A) of this rule. Upon the agency's motion or upon its own motion, the court shall conduct a hearing and issue an appropriate order of disposition.

(C) Modification

The court, upon its own motion or that of any party, shall conduct a hearing with notice to all parties to determine whether any order issued should be modified or terminated, or whether any other dispositional order set forth in division (A) should be issued. The court shall so modify or terminate any order in accordance with the best interest of the child.

(Adopted eff. 7–1–94)

Juv R 15 Process: issuance, form

(A) Summons: issuance

After the complaint has been filed, the court shall cause the issuance of a summons directed to the child, the parents, guardian, custodian, and any other persons who appear to the court to be proper or necessary parties. The summons shall require the parties to appear before the court at the time fixed to answer the allegations of the complaint. A child alleged to be abused, neglected, or dependent shall not be summoned unless the court so directs.

A summons issued for a child under fourteen years of age alleged to be delinquent, unruly, or a juvenile traffic offender shall be made by serving either the child's parents, guardian, custodian, or other person with whom the child lives or resides. If the person who has physical custody of the child or with whom the child resides is other than the parent or guardian, then the parents and guardian also shall be summoned. A copy of the complaint shall accompany the summons.

(B) Summons: form

The summons shall contain:

(1) The name of the party or person with whom the child may be or, if unknown, any name or description by which the party or person can be identified with reasonable certainty.

(2) A summary statement of the complaint and in juvenile traffic offense and delinquency proceedings the numerical designation of the applicable statute or ordinance.

(3) A statement that any party is entitled to be represented by an attorney and that upon request the court will appoint an attorney for an indigent party entitled to appointed counsel under Juv. R. 4(A).

(4) An order to the party or person to appear at a stated time and place with a warning that the party or person may lose valuable rights or be subject to court sanction if the party or person fails to appear at the time and place stated in the summons.

(5) An order to the parent, guardian, or other person having care of a child alleged to be an unruly or delinquent child for being an habitual or chronic truant, to appear personally at the hearing and all proceedings, and an order directing the person having the physical custody or control of the child to bring the child to the hearing, with a warning that if the child fails to appear, the parent, guardian, or other person having care of the child may be subject to court sanction, including a finding of contempt.

(6) A statement that if a child is adjudicated abused, neglected, or dependent and the complaint seeks an order of permanent custody, an order of permanent custody would cause the parents, guardian, or legal custodian to be divested permanently of all parental rights and privileges.

(7) A statement that if a child is adjudicated abused, neglected, or dependent and the complaint seeks an order of temporary custody, an order of temporary custody will cause the removal of the child from the legal custody of the parents, guardian, or other custodian until the court terminates the order of temporary custody or permanently divests the parents of their parental rights

(8) A statement that if the child is adjudicated abused, neglected, or dependent and the complaint seeks an order for a planned permanent living arrangement, an order for a planned permanent living arrangement will cause the removal of the child from the legal custody of the parent, guardian, or other custodian.

(9) A statement, in a removal action, of the specific disposition sought.

(10) The name and telephone number of the court employee designated by the court to arrange for the prompt appointment of counsel for indigent persons.

(C) Summons: endorsement

The court may endorse upon the summons an order directed to the parents, guardian, or other person with whom the child may be, to appear personally and bring the child to the hearing.

(D) Warrant: issuance

If it appears that the summons will be ineffectual or the welfare of the child requires that the child be brought forthwith to the court, a warrant may be issued against the child. A copy of the complaint shall accompany the warrant.

(E) Warrant: form

The warrant shall contain the name of the child or, if that is unknown, any name or description by which the child can be identified with reasonable certainty. It shall contain a summary statement of the complaint and in juvenile traffic offense and delinquency proceedings the numerical designation of the applicable statute or ordinance. A copy of the complaint shall be attached to the warrant. The warrant shall command that the child be taken into custody and be brought before the court that issued the warrant without unnecessary delay.

(Adopted eff. 7–1–72; amended eff. 7–1–94, 7–1–98, 7–1–01, 7–1–02)

Juv R 16 Process: service

(A) Summons: service, return

Except as otherwise provided in these rules, summons shall be served as provided in Civil Rules 4(A), (C) and (D), 4.1, 4.2, 4.3, 4.5 and 4.6. The summons shall direct the party served to appear at a stated time and place. Where service is by certified mail, the time shall not be less than seven days after the date of mailing.

Except as otherwise provided in this rule, when the residence of a party is unknown and cannot be ascertained with reasonable diligence, service shall be made by publication. Service by publication upon a non-custodial parent is not required in delinquent child or unruly child cases when the person alleged to have legal custody of the child has been served with summons pursuant to this rule, but the court may not enter any order or judgment against any person who has not been served with process or served by publication unless that person appears. Before service by publication can be made, an affidavit of a party or party's counsel shall be filed with the court. The affidavit shall aver that service of summons cannot be made because the residence of the person is unknown to the affiant and cannot be ascertained with reasonable diligence and shall set forth the last known address of the party to be served.

Service by publication shall be made by newspaper publication, by posting and mail, or by a combination of these methods. The court, by local rule, shall determine which method or methods of publication shall be used. If service by publication is made by newspaper publication, upon the filing of the affidavit, the clerk shall serve notice by publication in a newspaper of general circulation in the county in which the complaint is filed. If no newspaper is published in that county, then publication shall be in a newspaper published in an adjoining county. The publication shall contain the name and address of the court, the case number, the name of the first party on each side, and the name and last known address, if any, of the person or persons whose residence is unknown. The publication shall also contain a summary statement of the object of the complaint and shall notify the person to be served that the person is required to appear at the time and place stated. The time stated shall not be less than seven days after the date of publication. The publication shall be published once and service shall be complete on the date of publication.

After the publication, the publisher or the publisher's agent shall file with the court an affidavit showing the fact of publication together with a copy of the notice of publication. The affidavit and copy of the notice shall constitute proof of service.

If service by publication is made by posting and mail, upon the filing of the affidavit, the clerk shall cause service of notice to be made by posting in a conspicuous place in the courthouse in which the division of the common pleas court exercising jurisdiction over the complaint is located and in additional public places in the county that have been designated by local rule for the posting of notices pursuant to this rule. The number of additional public places to be designated shall be either two places or the number of state representative districts that are contained wholly or partly in the county in which the courthouse is located, whichever is greater. The notice shall contain the same information required to be contained in a newspaper publication. The notice shall be posted in the required locations for seven consecutive days. The clerk also shall cause the summons and accompanying pleadings to be mailed by ordinary mail, address correction requested, to the last known address of the party to be served. The clerk shall obtain a certificate of mailing from the United States Postal Service. If the clerk is notified of a corrected or forwarding address of the party to be served within the seven day period that notice is posted pursuant to this rule, the clerk shall cause the summons and accompanying pleadings to be mailed to the corrected or forwarding address. The clerk shall note the name, address, and date of each mailing in the docket.

After the seven days of posting, the clerk shall note on the docket where and when notice was posted. Service shall be complete upon the entry of posting.

(B) Warrant: execution; return

(1) By whom. The warrant shall be executed by any officer authorized by law.

(2) Territorial limits. The warrant may be executed at any place within this state.

(3) Manner. The warrant shall be executed by taking the party against whom it is issued into custody. The officer is not required to have possession of the warrant at the time it is executed, but in such case the officer shall inform the party of the complaint made and the fact that the warrant has been issued. A copy of the warrant shall be given to the person named in the warrant as soon as possible.

(4) Return. The officer executing a warrant shall make return thereof to the issuing court. Unexecuted warrants shall upon request of the issuing court be returned to that court.

A warrant returned unexecuted and not cancelled or a copy thereof may, while the complaint is pending, be delivered by the court to an authorized officer for execution.

An officer executing a warrant shall take the person named therein without unnecessary delay before the court which issued the warrant.

(Adopted eff. 7–1–72; amended eff. 7–1–94, 7–1–98)

Juv R 17 Subpoena

(A) Form; issuance

(1) Every subpoena shall do all of the following:

(a) State the name of the court from which it is issued, the title of the action, and the case number;

(b) Command each person to whom it is directed, at a time and place specified in the subpoena, to do one or more of the following:

(i) Attend and give testimony at a trial, hearing, proceeding, or deposition;

(ii) Produce documents or tangible things at a trial, hearing, proceeding, or deposition;

(iii) Produce and permit inspection and copying of any designated documents that are in the possession, custody, or control of the person;

(iv) Produce and permit inspection and copying, testing, or sampling of any tangible things that are in the possession, custody, or control of the person.

(c) Set forth the text of divisions (D) and (E) of this rule.

A command to produce and permit inspection may be joined with a command to attend and give testimony, or may be issued separately.

(2) The clerk shall issue a subpoena, signed but otherwise in blank, to a party requesting it, who shall complete it before service. An attorney who has filed an appearance on behalf of a party in an action also may sign and issue a subpoena on behalf of the court in which the action is pending.

(3) If the issuing attorney modifies the subpoena in any way, the issuing attorney shall give prompt notice of the modifications to all other parties.

(B) Parties unable to pay

The court shall order at any time that a subpoena be issued for service on a named witness upon an ex parte application of a party and upon a satisfactory showing that the presence of the witness is necessary and that the party is financially unable to pay the witness fees required by division (C) of this rule. If the court orders the subpoena to be issued, the costs incurred by the process and the fees of the witness so subpoenaed shall be paid in the same manner that similar costs and fees are paid in case of a witness subpoenaed in behalf of the state in a criminal prosecution.

(C) Service

A subpoena may be served by a sheriff, bailiff, coroner, clerk of court, constable, probation officer, or a deputy of any, by an attorney or the attorney's agent, or by any person designated by order of the court who is not a party and is not less than eighteen years of age. Service of a subpoena upon a person named in the subpoena shall be made by delivering a copy of the subpoena to the person, by reading it to him or her in person, or by leaving it at the person's usual place of residence, and by tendering to the person upon demand the fees for one day's attendance and the mileage allowed by law. The person serving the subpoena shall file a return of the subpoena with the clerk. If the witness being subpoenaed resides outside the county in which the court is located, the fees for one day's attendance and mileage shall be tendered without demand. The return may be forwarded through the postal service or otherwise.

(D) Protection of persons subject to subpoenas

(1) A party or an attorney responsible for the issuance and service of a subpoena shall take reasonable steps to avoid imposing undue burden or expense on a person subject to that subpoena.

(2) (a) A person commanded to produce under division (A)(1)(b)(ii), (iii), or (iv) of this rule is not required to appear in person at the place of production or inspection unless commanded to attend and give testimony at a trial, hearing, proceeding, or deposition.

(b) Subject to division (E)(2) of this rule, a person commanded to produce under division (A)(1)(b)(ii), (iii), or (iv) of this rule may serve upon the party or attorney designated in the subpoena written objections to production. The objections must be served within fourteen days after service of the subpoena or before the time specified for compliance if that time is less than fourteen days after service. If objection is made, the party serving the subpoena shall not be entitled to production except pursuant to an order of the court that issued the subpoena. If objection has been made, the party serving the subpoena, upon notice to the person commanded to produce, may move at any time for an order to compel the production. An order to compel production shall protect any person who is not a party or an officer of a party from significant expense resulting from the production commanded.

(3) On timely motion, the court from which the subpoena was issued shall quash or modify the subpoena, or order appearance or production only under specified conditions, if the subpoena does any of the following:

(a) Fails to allow reasonable time to comply;

(b) Requires disclosure of privileged or otherwise protected matter and no exception or waiver applies;

(c) Requires disclosure of a fact known or opinion held by an expert not retained or specially employed by any party in anticipation of litigation or preparation for trial if the fact or opinion does not describe specific events or occurrences in dispute and results from study by that expert that was not made at the request of any party;

(d) Subjects a person to undue burden.

(4) Before filing a motion pursuant to division (D)(3)(d) of this rule, a person resisting discovery under this rule shall attempt to resolve any claim of undue burden through discussions with the issuing attorney. A motion filed pursuant to division (D)(3)(d) of this rule shall be supported by an affidavit of the subpoenaed person or a certificate of that person's attorney of the efforts made to resolve any claim of undue burden.

(5) If a motion is made under division (D)(3)(c) or (D)(3)(d) of this rule, the court shall quash or modify the subpoena unless the party in whose behalf the subpoena is issued shows a substantial need for the testimony or material that cannot be otherwise met without undue hardship and assures that the person to whom the subpoena is addressed will be reasonably compensated.

(E) Duties in responding to subpoena

(1) A person responding to a subpoena to produce documents shall, at the person's option, produce the documents as they are kept in the usual course of business or organized and labeled to correspond with the categories in the subpoena. A person producing documents pursuant to a subpoena for them shall permit their inspection and copying by all parties present at the time and place set in the subpoena for inspection and copying.

(2) When information subject to a subpoena is withheld on a claim that it is privileged or subject to protection as trial preparation materials, the claim shall be made expressly and shall be supported by a description of the nature of the documents, communications, or things not produced that is sufficient to enable the demanding party to contest the claim.

(F) Sanctions

Failure by any person without adequate excuse to obey a subpoena served upon that person may be a contempt of the court from which the subpoena issued. A subpoenaed person or that person's attorney who frivolously resists discovery under this rule may be required by the court to pay the reasonable expenses, including reasonable attorney's fees, of the party seeking the discovery. The court from which a subpoena was issued may impose upon a party or attorney in breach of the duty imposed by division (D)(1) of this rule an appropriate sanction, that may include, but is not limited to, lost earnings and reasonable attorney's fees.

(G) Privileges

Nothing in this rule shall be construed to authorize a party to obtain information protected by any privilege recognized by law or to authorize any person to disclose such information.

(H) Time

Nothing in this rule shall be construed to expand any other time limits imposed by rule or statute. All issues concerning subpoenas shall be resolved prior to the time otherwise set for hearing or trial.

(Adopted eff. 7–1–72; amended eff. 7–1–94)

Juv R 18 Time

(A) Time: computation

In computing any period of time prescribed or allowed by these rules, by the local rules of any court, by order of court, or by any applicable statute, the date of the act or event from which the designated period of time begins to run shall not be included. The last day of the period so computed shall be included, unless it is a Saturday, a Sunday, or a legal holiday, in which event the period runs until the end of the next day that is not a Saturday, a Sunday or a legal holiday. Such extension of time includes, but is not limited to, probable cause, shelter care, and detention hearings.

Except in the case of probable cause, shelter care, and detention hearings when the period of time prescribed or allowed is less than seven days, intermediate Saturdays, Sundays, and legal holidays shall be excluded in computation.

(B) Time: enlargement

When an act is required or allowed to be performed at or within a specified time, the court for cause shown may at any time in its discretion (1) with or without motion or notice, order the period enlarged if application therefor is made before expiration of the period originally prescribed or of that period as extended by a previous order, or (2) upon motion permit the act to be done after expiration of the specified period if the failure to act on time was the result of excusable neglect or would result in injustice to a party, but the court may not extend the time for taking any action under Rule 7(F)(1), Rule 22(F), Rule 29(A) and Rule 29(F)(2)(b), except to the extent and under the conditions stated in them.

(C) Time: unaffected by expiration of term

The period of time provided for the doing of any act or the taking of any proceeding is not affected or limited by the expiration of a term of court. The expiration of a term of court in no way affects the power of a court to do any act in a juvenile proceeding.

(D) Time: for motions; affidavits

A written motion, other than one which may be heard ex parte, and notice of the hearing thereof, shall be served not later than seven days before the time specified for the hearing unless a different period is fixed by rule or order of the court. For cause shown such an order may be made on ex parte application. When a motion is supported by affidavit, the affidavit shall be served with the motion, and opposing affidavits may be served not less than one day before the hearing unless the court permits them to be served at a later time.

(E) Time: additional time after service by mail

Whenever a party has the right or is required to do an act within a prescribed period after the service of a notice or other paper upon the person and the notice or other paper is served upon the person by mail, three days shall be added to the prescribed period. This division does not apply to service of summons.

(Adopted eff. 7–1–72; amended eff. 7–1–94)

Juv R 19 Motions

An application to the court for an order shall be by motion. A motion other than one made during trial or hearing shall be in writing unless the court permits it to be made orally. It shall state with particularity the grounds upon which it is made and shall set forth the relief or order sought. It shall be supported by a memorandum containing citations of authority and may be supported by an affidavit.

To expedite its business, unless otherwise provided by statute or rule, the court may make provision by rule or order for the submission and determination of motions without oral hearing upon brief written statements of reasons in support and opposition.

(Adopted eff. 7–1–72; amended eff. 7–1–94)

Juv R 20 Service and filing of papers when required subsequent to filing of complaint

(A) Service: when required

Written notices, requests for discovery, designation of record on appeal and written motions, other than those which are heard ex parte, and similar papers shall be served upon each of the parties.

(B) Service: how made

Whenever under these rules or by an order of the court service is required or permitted to be made upon a party represented by an attorney, the service shall be made upon the attorney unless service is ordered by the court upon the party. Service upon the attorney or upon the party shall be made in the manner provided in Civ. R. 5(B).

(C) Filing

All papers required to be served upon a party shall be filed simultaneously with or immediately after service. Papers filed with the court shall not be considered until proof of service is endorsed thereon or separately filed. The proof of service shall state the date and the manner of service and shall be signed and filed in the manner provided in Civil Rule 5(D).

(Adopted eff. 7–1–72; amended eff. 7–1–94)

Juv R 21 Preliminary conferences

At any time after the filing of a complaint, the court upon motion of any party or upon its own motion may order one or more conferences to consider such matters as will promote a fair and expeditious proceeding.

(Adopted eff. 7–1–72)

Juv R 22 Pleadings and motions; defenses and objections

(A) Pleadings and motions

Pleadings in juvenile proceedings shall be the complaint and the answer, if any, filed by a party. A party may move to dismiss the complaint or for other appropriate relief.

(B) Amendment of pleadings

Any pleading may be amended at any time prior to the adjudicatory hearing. After the commencement of the adjudicatory hearing, a pleading may be amended upon agreement of the parties or, if the interests of justice require, upon order of the court. A complaint charging an act of delinquency may not be amended unless agreed by the parties, if the proposed amendment would change the name or identity of the specific violation of law so that it would be considered a change of the crime charged if committed by an adult. Where requested, a court order shall grant a party reasonable time in which to respond to an amendment.

(C) Answer

No answer shall be necessary. A party may file an answer to the complaint, which, if filed, shall contain specific and concise admissions or denials of each material allegation of the complaint.

(D) Prehearing motions

Any defense, objection or request which is capable of determination without hearing on the allegations of the complaint may be raised before the adjudicatory hearing by motion. The following must be heard before the adjudicatory hearing, though not necessarily on a separate date:

(1) Defenses or objections based on defects in the institution of the proceeding;

(2) Defenses or objections based on defects in the complaint (other than failure to show jurisdiction in the court or to charge an offense which objections shall be noticed by the court at any time during the pendency of the proceeding);

(3) Motions to suppress evidence on the ground that it was illegally obtained;

(4) Motions for discovery;

(5) Motions to determine whether the child is eligible to receive a sentence as a serious youthful offender.

(E) Motion time

Except for motions filed under division (D)(5) of this rule, all prehearing motions shall be filed by the earlier of:

(1) seven days prior to the hearing, or

(2) ten days after the appearance of counsel.

Rule 22(D)(5) motions shall be filed by the later of:

(1) twenty days after the date of the child's initial appearance in juvenile court; or

(2) twenty days after denial of a motion to transfer.

The filing of the Rule 22(D)(5) motion shall constitute notice of intent to pursue a serious youthful offender disposition.

The court in the interest of justice may extend the time for making prehearing motions.

The court for good cause shown may permit a motion to suppress evidence under division (D)(3) of this rule to be made at the time the evidence is offered.

(F) State's right to appeal upon granting a motion to suppress

In delinquency proceedings the state may take an appeal as of right from the granting of a motion to suppress evidence if, in addition to filing a notice of appeal, the prosecuting attorney certifies that (1) the appeal is not taken for the purpose of delay and (2) the granting of the motion has rendered proof available to the state so weak in its entirety that any reasonable possibility of proving the complaint's allegations has been destroyed.

Such appeal shall not be allowed unless the notice of appeal and the certification by the prosecuting attorney are filed with the clerk of the juvenile court within seven days after the date of the entry of the judgment or order granting the motion. Any appeal which may be taken under this rule shall be diligently prosecuted.

A child in detention or shelter care may be released pending this appeal when the state files the notice of appeal and certification.

This appeal shall take precedence over all other appeals.

(Adopted eff. 7–1–72; amended eff. 7–1–77, 7–1–94, 7–1–01)

Juv R 23 Continuance

Continuances shall be granted only when imperative to secure fair treatment for the parties.

(Adopted eff. 7–1–72)

Juv R 24 Discovery

(A) Request for discovery

Upon written request, each party of whom discovery is requested shall, to the extent not privileged, produce promptly for inspection, copying, or photographing the following information, documents, and material in that party's custody, control, or possession:

(1) The names and last known addresses of each witness to the occurrence that forms the basis of the charge or defense;

(2) Copies of any written statements made by any party or witness;

(3) Transcriptions, recordings, and summaries of any oral statements of any party or witness, except the work product of counsel;

(4) Any scientific or other reports that a party intends to introduce at the hearing or that pertain to physical evidence that a party intends to introduce;

(5) Photographs and any physical evidence which a party intends to introduce at the hearing;

(6) Except in delinquency and unruly child proceedings, other evidence favorable to the requesting party and relevant to the subject matter involved in the pending action. In delinquency and unruly child proceedings, the prosecuting attorney shall disclose to respondent's counsel all evidence, known or that may become known to the prosecuting attorney, favorable to the respondent and material either to guilt or punishment.

(B) Order granting discovery: limitations; sanctions

If a request for discovery is refused, application may be made to the court for a written order granting the discovery. Motions for discovery shall certify that a request for discovery has been made and refused. An order granting discovery may make such discovery reciprocal for all parties to the proceeding, including the party requesting discovery. Notwithstanding the provisions of subdivision (A), the court may deny, in whole or part, or otherwise limit or set conditions on the discovery authorized by such subdivision, upon its own motion, or upon a showing by a party upon whom a request for discovery is made that granting discovery may jeopardize the safety of a party, witness, or confidential informant, result in the production of perjured testimony or evidence, endanger the existence of physical evidence, violate a privileged communication, or impede the criminal prosecution of a minor as an adult or of an adult charged with an offense arising from the same transaction or occurrence.

(C) Failure to comply

If at any time during the course of the proceedings it is brought to the attention of the court that a person has failed to comply with an order issued pursuant to this rule, the court may grant a continuance, prohibit the person from introducing in evidence the material not disclosed, or enter such other order as it deems just under the circumstances.

(Adopted eff. 7–1–72; amended eff. 7–1–94)

Juv R 25 Depositions

The court upon good cause shown may grant authority to take the deposition of a party or other person upon such terms and conditions and in such manner as the court may fix.

(Adopted eff. 7–1–72)

Juv R 26 [Reserved]

Juv R 27 Hearings: general

(A) General provisions

Unless otherwise stated in this rule, the juvenile court may conduct its hearings in an informal manner and may adjourn its hearings from time to time.

The court may excuse the attendance of the child at the hearing in neglect, dependency, or abuse cases.

(1) Public access to hearings. In serious youthful offender proceedings, hearings shall be open to the public. In all other proceedings, the court may exclude the general public from any hearing, but may not exclude either of the following:

(a) persons with a direct interest in the case;

(b) persons who demonstrate, at a hearing, a countervailing right to be present.

(2) Separation of juvenile and adult cases. Cases involving children shall be heard separate and apart from the trial of cases against adults, except for cases involving chronic or habitual truancy.

(3) Jury trials. The court shall hear and determine all cases of children without a jury, except for the adjudication of a serious youthful offender complaint, indictment, or information in which trial by jury has not been waived.

Unless otherwise stated in this rule, the juvenile court may conduct its hearings in an informal manner and may adjourn its hearings from time to time.

The court may excuse the attendance of the child at the hearing in neglect, dependency, or abuse cases.

(B) Special provisions for abuse, neglect, and dependency proceedings

(1) In any proceeding involving abuse, neglect, or dependency at which the court removes a child from the child's home or continues the removal of a child from the child's home, or in a proceeding where the court orders detention, the court shall determine whether the person who filed the complaint in the case and removed the child from the child's home has custody of the child or will be given custody and has made reasonable efforts to do any of the following:

(a) Prevent the removal of the child from the child's home;

(b) Eliminate the continued removal of the child from the child's home;

(c) Make it possible for the child to return home.

(2) In a proceeding involving abuse, neglect, or dependency, the examination made by the court to determine whether a child is a competent witness shall comply with all of the following:

(a) Occur in an area other than a courtroom or hearing room;

(b) Be conducted in the presence of only those individuals considered necessary by the court for the conduct of the examination or the well being of the child;

(c) Be recorded in accordance with Juv. R. 37 or Juv. R. 40. The court may allow the prosecutor, guardian ad litem, or attorney for any party to submit questions for use by the court in determining whether the child is a competent witness.

(3) In a proceeding where a child is alleged to be an abused child, the court may order that the testimony of the child be taken by deposition in the presence of a judge or a magistrate. On motion of the prosecuting attorney, guardian ad litem, or a party, or in its own discretion, the court may order that the deposition be videotaped. All or part of the deposition is admissible in evidence where all of the following apply:

(a) It is filed with the clerk;

(b) Counsel for all parties had an opportunity and similar motive at the time of the taking of the deposition to develop the testimony by direct, cross, or redirect examination;

(c) The judge or magistrate determines there is reasonable cause to believe that if the child were to testify in person at the hearing, the child would experience emotional trauma as a result of the child's participation at the hearing.

(Adopted eff. 7–1–72; amended eff. 7–1–76, 7–1–94, 7–1–96, 7–1–01)

Juv R 28 [Reserved]

Juv R 29 Adjudicatory hearing

(A) Scheduling the hearing

The date for the adjudicatory hearing shall be set when the complaint is filed or as soon thereafter as is practicable. If the child is the subject of a complaint alleging a violation of a section of the Revised Code that may be violated by an adult and that does not request a serious youthful offender sentence, and if the child is in detention or shelter care, the hearing shall be held not later than fifteen days after the filing of the complaint. Upon a showing of good cause, the adjudicatory hearing may be continued and detention or shelter care extended.

The prosecuting attorney's filing of either a notice of intent to pursue or a statement of an interest in pursuing a serious youthful offender sentence shall constitute good cause for continuing the adjudicatory hearing date and extending detention or shelter care.

The hearing of a removal action shall be scheduled in accordance with Juv. R. 39(B).

If the complaint alleges abuse, neglect, or dependency, the hearing shall be held no later than thirty days after the complaint is filed. For good cause shown, the adjudicatory hearing may extend beyond thirty days either for an additional ten days to allow any party to obtain counsel or for a reasonable time beyond thirty days to obtain service on all parties or complete any necessary evaluations. However, the adjudicatory hearing shall be held no later than sixty days after the complaint is filed.

The failure of the court to hold an adjudicatory hearing within any time period set forth in this rule does not affect the ability of the court to issue any order otherwise provided for in statute or rule and does not provide any basis for contesting the jurisdiction of the court or the validity of any order of the court.

(B) Advisement and findings at the commencement of the hearing

At the beginning of the hearing, the court shall do all of the following:

(1) Ascertain whether notice requirements have been complied with and, if not, whether the affected parties waive compliance;

(2) Inform the parties of the substance of the complaint, the purpose of the hearing, and possible consequences of the hearing, including the possibility that the cause may be transferred to the appropriate adult court under Juv. R. 30 where the complaint alleges that a child fourteen years of age or over is delinquent by conduct that would constitute a felony if committed by an adult;

(3) Inform unrepresented parties of their right to counsel and determine if those parties are waiving their right to counsel;

(4) Appoint counsel for any unrepresented party under Juv. R. 4(A) who does not waive the right to counsel;

(5) Inform any unrepresented party who waives the right to counsel of the right: to obtain counsel at any stage of the proceedings, to remain silent, to offer evidence, to cross-examine witnesses, and, upon request, to have a record of all proceedings made, at public expense if indigent.

(C) Entry of admission or denial

The court shall request each party against whom allegations are being made in the complaint to admit or deny the allegations. A failure or refusal to admit the allegations shall be deemed a denial, except in cases where the court consents to entry of a plea of no contest.

(D) Initial procedure upon entry of an admission

The court may refuse to accept an admission and shall not accept an admission without addressing the party personally and determining both of the following:

(1) The party is making the admission voluntarily with understanding of the nature of the allegations and the consequences of the admission;

(2) The party understands that by entering an admission the party is waiving the right to challenge the witnesses and evidence against the party, to remain silent, and to introduce evidence at the adjudicatory hearing.

The court may hear testimony, review documents, or make further inquiry, as it considers appropriate, or it may proceed directly to the action required by division (F) of this rule.

(E) Initial procedure upon entry of a denial

If a party denies the allegations the court shall:

(1) Direct the prosecuting attorney or another attorney-at-law to assist the court by presenting evidence in support of the allegations of a complaint;

(2) Order the separation of witnesses, upon request of any party;

(3) Take all testimony under oath or affirmation in either question-answer or narrative form; and

(4) Determine the issues by proof beyond a reasonable doubt in juvenile traffic offense, delinquency, and unruly proceedings; by clear and convincing evidence in dependency, neglect, and abuse cases, and in a removal action; and by a preponderance of the evidence in all other cases.

(F) Procedure upon determination of the issues

Upon the determination of the issues, the court shall do one of the following:

(1) If the allegations of the complaint, indictment, or information were not proven, dismiss the complaint;

(2) If the allegations of the complaint, indictment, or information are admitted or proven, do any one of the following, unless precluded by statute:

(a) Enter an adjudication and proceed forthwith to disposition;

(b) Enter an adjudication and continue the matter for disposition for not more than six months and may make appropriate temporary orders;

(c) Postpone entry of adjudication for not more than six months;

(d) Dismiss the complaint if dismissal is in the best interest of the child and the community.

(3) Upon request make written findings of fact and conclusions of law pursuant to Civ. R. 52.

(4) Ascertain whether the child should remain or be placed in shelter care until the dispositional hearing in an abuse, neglect, or dependency proceeding. In making a shelter care determination, the court shall make written finding of facts with respect to reasonable efforts in accordance with the provisions in Juv. R. 27(B)(1) and to relative placement in accordance with Juv. R. 7(F)(3).

(Adopted eff. 7–1–72; amended eff. 7–1–76, 7–1–94, 7–1–98, 7–1–01, 7–1–04)

Juv R 30 Relinquishment of jurisdiction for purposes of criminal prosecution

(A) Preliminary hearing

In any proceeding where the court considers the transfer of a case for criminal prosecution, the court shall hold a preliminary hearing to determine if there is probable cause to believe that the child committed the act alleged and that the act would be an offense if committed by an adult. The hearing may be upon motion of the court, the prosecuting attorney, or the child.

(B) Mandatory transfer

In any proceeding in which transfer of a case for criminal prosecution is required by statute upon a finding of probable cause, the order of transfer shall be entered upon a finding of probable cause.

(C) Discretionary transfer

In any proceeding in which transfer of a case for criminal prosecution is permitted, but not required, by statute, and in which probable cause is found at the preliminary hearing, the court shall continue the proceeding for full investigation. The investigation shall include a mental examination of the child by a public or private agency or by a person qualified to make the examination. When the investigation is completed, an amenability hearing shall be held to determine whether to transfer jurisdiction. The criteria for transfer shall be as provided by statute.

(D) Notice

Notice in writing of the time, place, and purpose of any hearing held pursuant to this rule shall be given to the state, the child's parents, guardian, or other custodian and the child's counsel at least three days prior to the hearing, unless written notice has been waived on the record.

(E) Retention of jurisdiction

If the court retains jurisdiction, it shall set the proceedings for hearing on the merits.

(F) Waiver of mental examination

The child may waive the mental examination required under division (C) of this rule. Refusal by the child to submit to a mental examination or any part of the examination shall constitute a waiver of the examination.

(G) Order of transfer

The order of transfer shall state the reasons for transfer.

(H) Release of child

With respect to the transferred case, the juvenile court shall set the terms and conditions for release of the child in accordance with Crim. R. 46.

(Adopted eff. 7–1–72; amended eff. 7–1–76, 7–1–94, 7–1–97)

Juv R 31 [Reserved]

Juv R 32 Social history; physical examination; mental examination; investigation involving the allocation of parental rights and responsibilities for the care of children

(A) Social history and physical or mental examination: availability before adjudication

The court may order and utilize a social history or physical or mental examination at any time after the filing of a complaint under any of the following circumstances:

(1) Upon the request of the party concerning whom the history or examination is to be made;

(2) Where transfer of a child for adult prosecution is an issue in the proceeding;

(3) Where a material allegation of a neglect, dependency, or abused child complaint relates to matters that a history or examination may clarify;

(4) Where a party's legal responsibility for the party's acts or the party's competence to participate in the proceedings is an issue;

(5) Where a physical or mental examination is required to determine the need for emergency medical care under Juv. R. 13; or

(6) Where authorized under Juv. R. 7(I).

(B) Limitations on preparation and use

Until there has been an admission or adjudication that the child who is the subject of the proceedings is a juvenile traffic offender, delinquent, unruly, neglected, dependent, or abused, no social history, physical examination or mental examination shall be ordered except as authorized under subdivision (A) and any social history, physical examination or mental examination ordered pursuant to subdivision (A) shall be utilized only for the limited purposes therein specified. The person preparing a social history or making a physical or mental examination shall not testify about the history or examination or information received in its preparation in any juvenile traffic offender, delinquency, or unruly child adjudicatory hearing, except as may be required in a hearing to determine whether a child should be transferred to an adult court for criminal prosecution.

(C) Availability of social history or investigation report

A reasonable time before the dispositional hearing, or any other hearing at which a social history or physical or mental examination is to be utilized, counsel shall be permitted to inspect any social history or report of a mental or physical examination. The court may, for good cause shown, deny such inspection or limit its scope to specified portions of the history or report. The court may order that the contents of the history or report, in whole or part, not be disclosed to specified persons. If inspection or disclosure is denied or limited, the court shall state its reasons for such denial or limitation to counsel.

(D) Investigation: allocation of parental rights and responsibilities for the care of children; habeas corpus

On the filing of a complaint for the allocation of parental rights and responsibilities for the care of children or for a writ of habeas corpus to determine the allocation of parental rights and responsibilities for the care of a child, or on the filing of a motion for change in the allocation of parental rights and responsibilities for the care of children, the court may cause an investigation to be made as to the character, health, family relations, past conduct, present living conditions, earning ability, and financial worth of the parties to the action. The report of the investigation shall be confidential, but shall be made available to the parties or their counsel upon written request not less than three days before hearing. The court may tax as costs all or any part of the expenses of each investigation.

(Adopted eff. 7–1–72; amended eff. 7–1–73, 7–1–76, 7–1–91, 7–1–94)

Juv R 33 [Reserved]

Juv R 34 Dispositional hearing

(A) Scheduling the hearing

Where a child has been adjudicated as an abused, neglected, or dependent child, the court shall not issue a dispositional order until after it holds a separate dispositional hearing. The dispositional hearing for an adjudicated abused, neglected, or dependent child shall be held at least one day but not more than thirty days after the adjudicatory hearing is held. The dispositional hearing may be held immediately after the adjudicatory hearing if all parties were served prior to the adjudicatory hearing with all documents required for the dispositional hearing and all parties consent to the dispositional hearing being held immediately after the adjudicatory hearing. Upon the request of any party or the guardian ad litem of the child, the court may continue a dispositional hearing for a reasonable time not to exceed the time limit set forth in this division to enable a party to obtain or consult counsel. The dispositional hearing shall not be held more than ninety days after the date on which the complaint in the case was filed. If the dispositional hearing is not held within this ninety day period of time, the court, on its own motion or the motion of any party or the guardian ad litem of the child, shall dismiss the complaint without prejudice.

In all other juvenile proceedings, the dispositional hearing shall be held pursuant to Juv. R. 29(F)(2)(a) through (d) and the ninety day requirement shall not apply. Where the dispositional hearing is to be held immediately following the adjudicatory hearing, the court, upon the request of any party, shall continue the hearing for a reasonable time to enable the party to obtain or consult counsel.

(B) Hearing procedure

The hearing shall be conducted in the following manner:

(1) The judge or magistrate who presided at the adjudicatory hearing shall, if possible, preside;

(2) Except as provided in division (I) of this rule, the court may admit evidence that is material and relevant, including, but not limited to, hearsay, opinion, and documentary evidence;

(3) Medical examiners and each investigator who prepared a social history shall not be cross-examined, except upon consent of all parties, for good cause shown, or as the court in its discretion may direct. Any party may offer evidence supplementing, explaining, or disputing any information contained in the social history or other reports that may be used by the court in determining disposition.

(C) Judgment

After the conclusion of the hearing, the court shall enter an appropriate judgment within seven days. A copy of the judgment shall be given to any party requesting a copy. In all cases where a child is placed on probation, the child shall receive a written statement of the conditions of probation. If the judgment is conditional, the order shall state the conditions. If the child is not returned to the child's home, the court shall determine the school district that shall bear the cost of the child's education and may fix an amount of support to be paid by the responsible parent or from public funds.

(D) Dispositional Orders

Where a child is adjudicated an abused, neglected, or dependent child, the court may make any of the following orders of disposition:

(1) Place the child in protective supervision;

(2) Commit the child to the temporary custody of a public or private agency, either parent, a relative residing within or outside the state, or a probation officer for placement in a certified foster home or approved foster care;

(3) Award legal custody of the child to either parent or to any other person who, prior to the dispositional hearing, files a motion requesting legal custody;

(4) Commit the child to the permanent custody of a public or private agency, if the court determines that the child cannot be placed with one of the child's parents within a reasonable time or should not be placed with either parent and determines that the permanent commitment is in the best interest of the child;

(5) Place the child in a planned permanent living arrangement with a public or private agency if the agency requests the court for placement, if the court finds that a planned permanent living arrangement is in the best interest of the child, and if the court finds that one of the following exists:

(a) The child because of physical, mental, or psychological problems or needs is unable to function in a family-like setting;

(b) The parents of the child have significant physical, mental or psychological problems and are unable to care for the child, adoption is not in the best interest of the child and the child retains a significant and positive relationship with a parent or relative;

(c) The child is sixteen years of age or older, has been counseled, is unwilling to accept or unable to adapt to a permanent placement and is in an agency program preparing the child for independent living.

(E) Protective supervision

If the court issues an order for protective supervision, the court may place any reasonable restrictions upon the child, the child's parents, guardian, or any other person including, but not limited to, any of the following:

(1) Ordering a party within forty-eight hours to vacate the child's home indefinitely or for a fixed period of time;

(2) Ordering a party, parent, or custodian to prevent any particular person from having contact with the child;

(3) Issuing a restraining order to control the conduct of any party.

(F) Case plan

As part of its dispositional order, the court shall journalize a case plan for the child. The agency required to maintain a case plan shall file the case plan with the court prior to the child's adjudicatory hearing but not later than thirty days after the earlier of the date on which the complaint in the case was filed or the child was first placed in shelter care. The plan shall specify what additional information, if any, is necessary to complete the plan and how the information will be obtained. All parts of the case plan shall be completed by the earlier of thirty days after the adjudicatory hearing or the date of the dispositional hearing for the child. If all parties agree to the content of the case plan and the court approves it, the court shall journalize the plan as part of its dispositional order. If no agreement is reached, the court, based upon the evidence presented at the dispositional hearing and the best interest of the child, shall determine the contents of the case plan and journalize it as part of the dispositional order for the child.

(G) Modification of temporary order

The department of human services or any other public or private agency or any party, other than a parent whose parental rights have been terminated, may at any time file a motion requesting that the court modify or terminate any order of disposition. The court shall hold a hearing upon the motion as if the hearing were the original dispositional hearing and shall give all parties and the guardian ad litem notice of the hearing pursuant to these rules. The court, on its own motion and upon proper notice to all parties and any interested agency, may modify or terminate any order of disposition.

(H) Restraining orders

In any proceeding where a child is made a ward of the court, the court may grant a restraining order controlling the conduct of any party if the court finds that the order is necessary to control any conduct or relationship that may be detrimental or harmful to the child and tend to defeat the execution of a dispositional order.

(I) Bifurcation; Rules of Evidence

Hearings to determine whether temporary orders regarding custody should be modified to orders for permanent custody shall be considered dispositional hearings and need not be bifurcated. The Rules of Evidence shall apply in hearings on motions for permanent custody.

(J) Advisement of rights after hearing

At the conclusion of the hearing, the court shall advise the child of the child's right to record expungement and, where any part of the proceeding was contested, advise the parties of their right to appeal.

(Adopted eff. 7–1–72; amended eff. 7–1–94, 7–1–96, 7 1 02)

Juv R 35 Proceedings after judgment

(A) Continuing jurisdiction; invoked by motion

The continuing jurisdiction of the court shall be invoked by motion filed in the original proceeding, notice of which shall be served in the manner provided for the service of process.

(B) Revocation of probation

The court shall not revoke probation except after a hearing at which the child shall be present and apprised of the grounds on which revocation is proposed. The parties shall have the right to counsel and the right to appointed counsel where entitled pursuant to Juv. R. 4(A). Probation shall not be revoked except upon a finding that the child has violated a condition of probation of which the child had, pursuant to Juv. R. 34(C), been notified.

(C) Detention

During the pendency of proceedings under this rule, a child may be placed in detention in accordance with the provisions of Rule 7.

(Adopted eff. 7–1–72; amended eff. 7–1–94)

Juv R 36 Dispositional review

(A) Court review

A court that issues a dispositional order in an abuse, neglect, or dependency case may review the child's placement or custody arrangement, the case plan, and the actions of the public or private agency implementing that plan at any time. A court that issues a dispositional order shall hold a review hearing one year after the earlier of the date on which the complaint in the case was filed or the child was first placed into shelter care. The court shall schedule the review hearing at the time that it holds the dispositional hearing. The court shall hold a similar review hearing no later than every twelve months after the initial review hearing until the child is adopted, returned to the child's parents, or the court otherwise terminates the child's placement or custody arrangement. A hearing pursuant to section 2151.415 of the Revised Code shall take the place of the first review hearing. The court shall schedule each subsequent review hearing at the conclusion of the review hearing immediately preceding the review hearing to be scheduled. Review hearings may be conducted by a judge or magistrate.

(B) Citizens' review board

The court may appoint a citizens' review board to conduct review hearings, subject to the review and approval by the court.

(C) Agency review

Each agency required to prepare a case plan for a child shall complete a semiannual administrative review of the case plan no later than six months after the earlier of the date on which the complaint in the case was filed or the child was first placed in shelter care. After the first administrative review, the agency shall complete semiannual administrative reviews no later than every six months. The agency shall prepare and file a written summary of the semiannual administrative review that shall include an updated case plan. If the agency, parents, guardian, or custodian of the child and guardian ad litem stipulate to the revised case plan, the plan shall be signed by all parties and filed with the written summary of the administrative review no later than seven days after the completion of the administrative review. If the court does not object to the revised case plan, it shall journalize the case plan within fourteen days after it is filed with the court. If the court does not approve of the revised case plan or if the agency, parties, guardian ad litem, and the attorney of the child do not agree to the need for changes to the case plan and to all of the proposed changes, the agency shall file its written summary and request a hearing. The court shall schedule a review hearing to be held no later than thirty days after the filing of the case plan or written summary or both, if required. The court shall give notice of the date, time, and location of the hearing to all interested parties and the guardian ad litem of the child. The court shall take one of the following actions:

(1) Approve or modify the case plan based upon the evidence presented;

(2) Return the child home with or without protective supervision and terminate temporary custody or determine which agency shall have custody;

(3) If the child is in permanent custody determine what actions would facilitate adoption;

(4) Journalize the terms of the updated case plan.

(Adopted eff. 7–1–94; amended eff. 7–1–96)

Juv R 37 Recording of proceedings

(A) Record of proceedings

The juvenile court shall make a record of adjudicatory and dispositional proceedings in abuse, neglect, dependent, unruly, and delinquent cases; permanent custody cases; and proceedings before magistrates. In all other proceedings governed by these rules, a record shall be made upon request of a party or upon motion of the court. The record shall be taken in shorthand, stenotype, or by any other adequate mechanical, electronic, or video recording device.

(B) Restrictions on use of recording or transcript

No public use shall be made by any person, including a party, of any juvenile court record, including the recording or a transcript of any juvenile court hearing, except in the course of an appeal or as authorized by order of the court or by statute.

(Adopted eff. 7–1–72; amended eff. 7–1–96, 7–1–01)

Juv R 38 Voluntary surrender of custody

(A) Temporary custody

(1) A person with custody of a child may enter into an agreement with any public or private children services agency giving the agency temporary custody for a period of up to thirty days without the approval of the juvenile court. The agency may request the court to grant a thirty day extension of the original agreement. The court may grant the original extension if it determines the extension to be in the best interest of the child. A case plan shall be filed at the same time the request for extension is filed. At the expiration of the original thirty day extension period, the agency may request the court to grant an additional thirty day extension. The court may grant the additional extension if it determines the extension is in the child's best interest. The agency shall file an updated case plan at the same time it files the request for additional extension. At the expiration of the additional thirty day extension period, or at the expiration of the original thirty day extension period if no additional thirty day extension was requested, the agency shall either return the child to the custodian or file a complaint requesting temporary or permanent custody and a case plan.

(2) Notwithstanding division (A)(1) of this rule, the agreement may be for a period of sixty days if executed solely for the purpose of obtaining the adoption of a child less than six months of age. The agency may request the court to extend the temporary custody agreement for thirty days. A case plan shall be filed at the same time the request for extension is filed. At the expiration of the thirty day extension, the agency shall either return the child to the child's custodian or file a complaint with the court requesting temporary or permanent custody and a case plan.

(B) Permanent custody

(1) A person with custody of a child may make an agreement with court approval surrendering the child into the permanent custody of a public children service agency or private child placing agency. A public children service agency shall request and a private child placing agency may request the juvenile court of the county in which the child had residence or legal settlement to approve the permanent surrender agreement. The court may approve the agreement if it determines it to be in the best interest of the child. The agency requesting the approval shall file a case plan at the same time it files its request for approval of the permanent surrender agreement.

(2) An agreement for the surrender of permanent custody of a child to a private service agency is not required to be approved by the court if the agreement is executed solely for the purpose of obtaining an adoption of a child who is less than six months of age on the date of the execution of the agreement.

One year after the agreement is entered and every subsequent twelve months after that date, the court shall schedule a review hearing if a final decree of adoption has not been entered for a child who is the subject of an agreement for the surrender of permanent custody.

(Adopted eff. 7–1–94)

Juv R 39 Out of county removal hearings

(A) Notice of removal hearing

Upon the filing of a removal action, the court in which the complaint is filed shall immediately contact the court that issued the original dispositional order for information necessary for service of summons and issuance of notice of the removal hearing. The court that issued the original dispositional order shall respond within five days after receiving the request.

Summons shall issue pursuant to Juv. R. 15 and 16.

Notice of the removal hearing shall be sent by first class mail, as evidenced by a certificate of mailing filed with the clerk of court, to the following, not otherwise summoned, at least five days before the hearing:

(1) The court issuing the dispositional order;

(2) The guardian *ad litem* for the child;

(3) Counsel for the child;

(4) The placing entity;

(5) The custodial entity;

(6) The complainant;

(7) The guardian *ad litem* and counsel presently representing the child in the court that issued the original dispositional order;

(8) Any other persons the court determines to be appropriate.

(B) Removal hearing

The removal hearing shall be held not later than thirty days after service of summons is obtained. If, after the removal hearing, the court grants relief in favor of the complainant, the court shall send written notice of such relief to the juvenile court that issued the original dispositional order.

(Adopted eff. 7–1–98)

Juv R 40 Magistrates

(A) Appointment

The court may appoint one or more magistrates. Magistrates first appointed on or after the effective date of this amendment shall be attorneys admitted to practice in Ohio. A magistrate appointed under this rule also may serve as a magistrate under Crim.R. 19. The court shall not appoint as a magistrate any person who has contemporaneous responsibility for working with, or supervising the behavior of, children who are subject to dispositional orders of the appointing court or any other juvenile court.

(B) Compensation

The compensation of the magistrate shall be fixed by the court and no part of the compensation shall be taxed as costs.

(C) Reference and powers

(1) Order of reference.

(a) The court by order may refer any of the following to a magistrate:

(i) pretrial or post-judgment motion or proceeding in any case, except a case involving the determination of a child's status as a serious youthful offender;

(ii) the trial of any case not to be tried to a jury, except the adjudication of a case against an alleged serious youthful offender;

(iii) upon the unanimous written consent of the parties, the trial of any case to be tried to a jury, except the adjudication of a case against an alleged serious youthful offender.

Except as provided in division (C)(1)(a)(iii) of this rule, the effect of a magistrate's order or decision is the same regardless of whether the parties have consented to the order of reference.

(b) An order of reference may be specific to a particular case or proceeding or may refer categories of motions, cases, or proceedings.

(c) The order of reference to a magistrate may do all of the following:

(i) Specify the magistrate's powers;

(ii) Direct the magistrate to report only upon particular issues, perform particular acts, or receive and report evidence only;

(iii) Fix the time and place for beginning and closing the hearings and for the filing of the magistrate's decision or order.

(2) General powers

Subject to the specifications stated in the order of reference, the magistrate shall regulate all proceedings in every hearing as if by the court and do all acts and take all measures necessary or property for the efficient performance of the magistrate's duties under the order. The magistrate may do all of the following:

(a) Issue subpoenas for the attendance of witnesses and the production of evidence;

(b) Rule upon the admissibility of evidence, unless otherwise directed by the order of reference;

(c) Put witnesses under oath and examine them;

(d) Call the parties to the action and examine them under oath.

(e) In cases involving direct or indirect contempt of court, when necessary to obtain the alleged contemnor's presence for hearing, issue an attachment for the alleged contemnor and set bail to secure the alleged contemnor's appearance. In determining bail, the magistrate shall consider the conditions of release prescribed in Crim.R. 46.

(3) Power to enter orders

(a) Pretrial orders. Unless otherwise specified in the order of reference, the magistrate may enter orders effective without judicial approval in pretrial proceedings under Civ.R. 16, in discovery proceedings under Civ.R. 26 to 37, Juv.R. 24 and 25, and in the following situations:

(i) Appointment of an attorney or guardian ad litem pursuant to Juv.R. 4 and 29(B)(4);

(ii) Taking a child into custody pursuant to Juv.R. 6;

(iii) Detention hearings pursuant to Juv.R. 7;

(iv) Temporary orders pursuant to Juv.R. 13;

(v) Extension of temporary orders pursuant to Juv.R. 14;

(vi) Summons and warrants pursuant to Juv.R. 15;

(vii) Preliminary conferences pursuant to Juv.R. 21;

(viii) Continuances pursuant to Juv.R. 23;

(ix) Deposition orders pursuant to Juv.R. 27(B)(3);

(x) Orders for social histories, physical and mental examinations pursuant to Juv.R. 32;

(xi) Other orders as necessary to regulate the proceedings.

(b) Appeal of pretrial orders. Any person may appeal to the court from any order of a magistrate entered under division (C)(3)(a) of this rule by filing a motion to set the order aside, stating the party's objections with particularity. The motion shall be filed no later than ten days after the magistrate's order is entered. The pendency of a motion to set aside does not stay the effectiveness of the magistrate's order unless the magistrate or the court grants a stay.

(c) Contempt in the magistrate's presence. In cases of contempt in the presence of the magistrate, the magistrate may impose an appropriate civil or criminal contempt sanction. Contempt sanctions under division (C)(3)(c) of this rule may be imposed only by a written order that recites the facts and certifies that the magistrate saw or heard the conduct constituting contempt. The contempt order shall be filed and a copy provided by the clerk to the appropriate judge of the court forthwith. The contemnor may by motion obtain immediate review of the magistrate's contempt order by a judge, or the judge or magistrate may set bail pending judicial review.

(d) Other orders. Unless prohibited by the order of reference, magistrates shall continue to be authorized to enter orders when authority to enter orders is specifically conveyed by statute or rule to magistrates or referees.

(e) Form of magistrate's orders. All orders of a magistrate shall be in writing, signed by the magistrate, identified as a magistrate's order in the caption, filed with the clerk, and served on all parties or their attorneys.

(D) Proceedings

(1) All proceedings before the magistrate shall be in accordance with these rules and any applicable statutes, as if before the court.

(2) Except as otherwise provided by law and notwithstanding the provisions of Juv.R. 37, all proceedings before magistrates shall be recorded in accordance with procedures established by the court.

(E) Decisions in referred matters.

Unless specifically required by the order of reference, a magistrate is not required to prepare any report other than the magistrate's decision. Except as to matters on which magistrates are permitted by division (C)(3) of this rule to enter orders without judicial approval, all matters referred to magistrates shall be decided as follows:

(1) *Magistrate's decision.* The magistrate promptly shall conduct all proceedings necessary for decision of referred matters. The magistrate shall then prepare, sign, and file a magistrate's decision of the referred matter with the clerk, who shall serve copies on all parties or their attorneys.

(2) *Findings of fact and conclusions of law.* If any party makes a request for findings of fact and conclusions of law under Civ. R. 52 or if findings and conclusions are otherwise required by law or

by the order of reference, the magistrate's decision shall include findings of fact and conclusions of law. If the request under Civ. R. 52 is made after the magistrate's decision is filed, the magistrate shall include the findings of fact and conclusions of law in an amended magistrate's decision. A magistrate's findings of fact and conclusions of law shall indicate conspicuously that a party shall not assign as error on appeal the court's adoption of any finding of fact or conclusion of law unless the party timely and specifically objects to that finding or conclusion as required by Juv. R. 40(E)(3).

(3) *Objections.*

(a) Time for filing. A party may file written objections to a magistrate's decision within fourteen days of the filing of the decision, regardless of whether the court has adopted the decision pursuant to Juv. R. 40(E)(4)(c). If any party timely files objections, any other party also may file objections not later than ten days after the first objections are filed. If a party makes a request for findings of fact and conclusions of law under Civ. R. 52, the time for filing objections begins to run when the magistrate files a decision including findings of fact and conclusions of law.

(b) Form of objections. Objections shall be specific and state with particularity the grounds of objection.

(c) Objections to magistrate's findings of fact. If the parties stipulate in writing that the magistrate's findings of fact shall be final, they may only object to errors of law in the magistrate's decision. Any objection to a finding of fact shall be supported by a transcript of all the evidence submitted to the magistrate relevant to that fact or an affidavit of the evidence if a transcript is not available.

(d) Waiver of right to assign adoption by court as error on appeal. A party shall not assign as error on appeal the court's adoption of any finding of fact or conclusion of law unless the party has objected to that finding or conclusion under this rule.

(4) *Court's action on magistrate's decision.*

(a) When effective. The magistrate's decision shall be effective when adopted by the court as noted in the journal record. The court may adopt the magistrate's decision if no written objections are filed unless it determines that there is an error of law or other defect on the face of the magistrate's decision.

(b) Disposition of objections. The court shall rule on any objections. The court may adopt, reject, or modify the magistrate's decision, hear additional evidence, recommit the matter to the magistrate with instructions, or hear the matter itself. In delinquency, unruly, or juvenile traffic offender cases, the court may hear additional evidence or hear the matter itself only with the consent of the child. The court may refuse to consider additional evidence proffered upon objections unless the objecting party demonstrates that with reasonable diligence the party could not have produced that evidence for the magistrate's consideration.

(c) Permanent and interim orders. The court may adopt a magistrate's decision and enter judgment without waiting for timely objections by the parties, but the filing of timely written objections shall operate as an automatic stay of execution of that judgment until the court disposes of those objections and vacates, modifies, or adheres to the judgment previously entered. The court may make an interim order on the basis of a magistrate's decision without waiting for or ruling on timely objections by the parties where immediate relief is justified. An interim order shall not be subject to the automatic stay caused by the filing of timely objections. An interim order shall not extend more than twenty-eight days from the date of its entry unless, within that time and for good cause shown, the court extends the interim order for an additional twenty-eight days.

(Adopted eff. 7-1-72; amended eff. 7-1-75, 7-1-85, 7-1-92, 7-1-95, 7-1-98, 7-1-01, 7-1-03)

Juv R 41 [Reserved]

Juv R 42 Consent to marry

(A) Application where parental consent not required

When a minor desires to contract matrimony and has no parent, guardian, or custodian whose consent to the marriage is required by law, the minor shall file an application under oath in the county where the female resides requesting that the judge of the juvenile court give consent and approbation in the probate court for such marriage.

(B) Contents of application

The application required by division (A) of this rule shall contain all of the following:

(1) The name and address of the person for whom consent is sought;

(2) The age of the person for whom consent is sought;

(3) The reason why consent of a parent is not required;

(4) The name and address, if known, of the parent, where the minor alleges that parental consent is unnecessary because the parent has neglected or abandoned the child for at least one year immediately preceding the application.

(C) Application where female pregnant or delivered of child born out of wedlock

Where a female is pregnant or delivered of a child born out of wedlock and the parents of such child seek to marry even though one or both of them is under the minimum age prescribed by law for persons who may contract marriage, such persons shall file an application under oath in the county where the female resides requesting that the judge of the juvenile court give consent in the probate court to such marriage.

(D) Contents of application

The application required by subdivision (C) shall contain:

(1) The name and address of the person or persons for whom consent is sought;

(2) The age of such person;

(3) An indication of whether the female is pregnant or has already been delivered;

(4) An indication of whether or not any applicant under eighteen years of age is already a ward of the court; and

(5) Any other facts which may assist the court in determining whether to consent to such marriage.

If pregnancy is asserted, a certificate from a physician verifying pregnancy shall be attached to the application. If an illegitimate child has been delivered, the birth certificate of such child shall be attached.

The consent to the granting of the application by each parent whose consent to the marriage is required by law shall be indorsed on the application.

(E) Investigation

Upon receipt of an application under subdivision (C), the court shall set a date and time for hearing thereon at its earliest convenience and shall direct that an inquiry be made as to the circumstances surrounding the applicants.

(F) Notice

If neglect or abandonment is alleged in an application under subdivision (A) and the address of the parent is known, the court shall cause notice of the date and time of hearing to be served upon such parent.

(G) Judgment

If the court finds that the allegations stated in the application are true, and that the granting of the application is in the best interest of the applicants, the court shall grant the consent and shall make the applicant referred to in subdivision (C) a ward of the court.

(H) Certified copy

A certified copy of the judgment entry shall be transmitted to the probate court.

(Adopted eff. 7–1–72; amended eff. 7–1–80, 7–1–94)

Juv R 43 Reference to Ohio Revised Code

A reference in these rules to a section of the Revised Code shall mean the section as amended from time to time including the enactment of additional sections, the numbers of which are subsequent to the section referred to in the rules.

(Adopted eff. 7–1–94)

Juv R 44 Jurisdiction unaffected

These rules shall not be construed to extend or limit the jurisdiction of the juvenile court.

(Adopted eff. 7–1–72)

Juv R 45 Rules by juvenile courts; procedure not otherwise specified

(A) Local rules

The juvenile court may adopt rules concerning local practice that are not inconsistent with these rules. Local rules shall be adopted only after the court gives appropriate notice and an opportunity for comment. If the court determines that there is an immediate need for a rule, the court may adopt the rule without prior notice and opportunity for comment but promptly shall afford notice and opportunity for comment. Local rules shall be filed with the Supreme Court.

(B) Procedure not otherwise specified

If no procedure is specifically prescribed by these rules or local rule, the court shall proceed in any lawful manner not inconsistent with these rules or local rule.

(Adopted eff. 7–1–72; amended eff. 7–1–94)

Juv R 46 Forms

The forms contained in the Appendix of Forms which the supreme court from time to time may approve are illustrative and not mandatory.

(Adopted eff. 7–1–72)

Juv R 47 Effective date

(A) Effective date of rules

These rules shall take effect on the first day of July, 1972. They govern all proceedings in actions brought after they take effect and also all further proceedings in actions then pending, except to the extent that their application in a particular action pending when the rules take effect would not be feasible or would work injustice, in which event the former procedure applies.

(B) Effective date of amendments

The amendments submitted by the Supreme Court to the general assembly on January 12, 1973, shall take effect on the first day of July, 1973. They govern all proceedings in actions brought after they take effect and also all further proceedings in actions then pending, except to the extent that their application in a particular action pending when the amendments take effect would not be feasible or would work injustice, in which event the former procedure applies.

(C) Effective date of amendments

The amendments submitted by the Supreme Court to the General Assembly on January 10, 1975, and on April 29, 1975, shall take effect on July 1, 1975. They govern all proceedings in actions brought after they take effect and also all further proceedings in actions then pending, except to the extent that their application in a particular action pending when the amendments take effect would not be feasible or would work injustice, in which event the former procedure applies.

(D) Effective date of amendments

The amendments submitted by the Supreme Court to the General Assembly on January 9, 1976 shall take effect on July 1, 1976. They govern all proceedings in actions brought after they take effect and also all further proceedings in actions then pending, except to the extent that their application in a particular action pending when the amendments take effect would not be feasible or would work injustice, in which event the former procedure applies.

(E) Effective date of amendments

The amendments submitted by the Supreme Court to the General Assembly on January 14, 1980, shall take effect on July 1, 1980. They govern all proceedings in actions brought after they take effect and also all further proceedings in actions then pending, except to the extent that their application in a particular action pending when the amendments take effect would not be feasible or would work injustice, in which event the former procedure applies.

(F) Effective date of amendments.

The amendments submitted by the Supreme Court to the General Assembly on December 24, 1984 and January 8, 1985 shall take effect on July 1, 1985. They govern all proceedings in actions brought after they take effect and also all further proceedings in actions then pending, except to the extent that their application in a particular action pending when the amendments take effect would not be feasible or would work injustice, in which event the former procedure applies.

(G) Effective date of amendments

The amendments submitted by the Supreme Court to the General Assembly on January 10, 1991 shall take effect on July 1, 1991. They govern all proceedings in actions brought after they take effect and also all further proceedings in actions then pending, except to the extent that their application in a particular action pending when the amendments take effect would not be feasible or would work injustice, in which event the former procedure applies.

(H) Effective date of amendments

The amendments filed by the Supreme Court with the General Assembly on January 14, 1992 and further filed on April 30, 1992, shall take effect on July 1, 1992. They govern all proceedings in actions brought after they take effect and also all future proceedings in actions then pending, except to the extent that their application in a particular action pending when the amendments take effect would not be feasible or would work injustice, in which event the former procedure applies.

(I) Effective date of amendments

The amendments filed by the Supreme Court with the General Assembly on January 14, 1994 and further revised and filed on April 29, 1994 shall take effect on July 1, 1994. They govern all proceedings in actions brought after they take effect and also all future proceedings in actions then pending, except to the extent that their application in a particular action pending when the amendments take effect would not be feasible or would work injustice, in which event the former procedure applies.

(J) Effective date of amendments

The amendments to Rules 1, 4, and 40 filed by the Supreme court [sic] with the General Assembly on January 11, 1995 and further revised and filed on April 25, 1995 shall take effect on July 1, 1995. They govern all proceedings in actions brought after they take effect and also all further proceedings in actions then pending, except to the extent that their application in a particular action pending when the amendments take effect would not be feasible or would work injustice, in which event the former procedure applies.

(K) Effective date of amendments

The amendments to Rules 6, 8, 13, 27, 34, 36, and 37 filed by the Supreme Court with the General Assembly on January 5, 1996 and refiled on April 26, 1996 shall take effect on July 1, 1996. They govern all proceedings in actions brought after they take effect and also all further proceedings in actions then pending, except to the extent that their application in a particular action pending when the amendments take effect would not be feasible or would work injustice, in which event the former procedure applies.

(L) Effective date of amendments

The amendments to Rule 30 filed by the Supreme Court with the General Assembly on January 10, 1997 and refiled on April 24, 1997 shall take effect on July 1, 1997. They govern all proceedings in actions brought after they take effect and also all further proceedings in actions then pending, except to the extent that their application in a particular action pending when the amendments take effect would not be feasible or would work injustice, in which event the former procedure applies.

(M) Effective date of amendments

The amendments to rules 2, 4, 10, 11, 15, 16, 29, 39, and 40 filed by the Supreme Court with the General Assembly on January 15, 1998 and further revised and refiled on April 30, 1998 shall take effect on July 1, 1998. They govern all proceedings in actions brought after they take effect and also all further proceedings in actions then pending, except to the extent that their application in a particular action pending when the amendments take effect would not be feasible or would work injustice, in which event the former procedure applies.

(N) Effective date of amendments

The amendments to Juvenile Rules 2, 7, 8, 10, 15, 22, 27, 29, 37, and 40 filed by the Supreme Court with the General Assembly on January 12, 2001, and revised and refiled on April 26, 2001, shall take effect on July 1, 2001. They govern all proceedings in actions brought after they take effect and also all further proceedings in actions then pending, except to the extent that their application in a particular action pending when the amendments take effect would not be feasible or would work injustice, in which event the former procedure applies.

(O) Effective date of amendments

The amendments to Juvenile Rules 2, 10, 15, and 34 filed by the Supreme Court with the General Assembly on January 11, 2002, and refiled on April 18, 2002 shall take effect on July 1, 2002. They govern all proceedings in actions brought after they take effect and also all further proceedings in actions then pending, except to the extent that their application in a particular action pending when the amendments take effect would not be feasible or would work injustice, in which event the former procedure applies.

(P) Effective date of amendments.

The amendments to Juvenile Rule 40 filed by the Supreme Court with the General Assembly on January 9, 2003 and refiled on April 28, 2003, shall take effect on July 1, 2003. They govern all proceedings in actions brought after they take effect and also all further proceedings in actions then pending, except to the extent that their application in a particular action pending when the amendments take effect would not be feasible or would work injustice, in which event the former procedure applies.

(Q) Effective date of amendments

The amendments to Juvenile Rule 29 filed by the Supreme Court with the General Assembly on January 7, 2004 and refiled on April 28, 2004 shall take effect on July 1, 2004. They govern all proceedings in actions brought after they take effect and also all further proceedings in actions then pending, except to the extent that their application in a particular action pending when the amendments take effect would not be feasible or would work injustice, in which event the former procedure applies.

(Adopted eff. 7-1-72; amended eff. 7-1-73, 7-1-75, 7-1-76, 7-1-80, 7-1-85, 7-1-91, 7-1-92, 7-1-94, 7-1-95, 7-1-96, 7-1-97, 7-1-98, 7-1-01, 7-1-02, 7-1-03, 7-1-04)

Juv R 48 Title

These rules shall be known as the Ohio Rules of Juvenile Procedure and may be cited as "Juvenile Rules" or "Juv. R. ___."

(Adopted eff. 7-1-72)

OHIO RULES OF EVIDENCE

Publisher's Note: Until 1968, when the Modern Courts Amendment to the Ohio Constitution was adopted, Ohio court procedure was governed entirely by statute and case law. The Modern Courts Amendment required the Supreme Court of Ohio, subject to the approval of the General Assembly, to "prescribe rules governing practice and procedure in all courts of the state." Rules of practice and procedure are the Civil, Criminal, Appellate, and Juvenile Rules, Rules of the Court of Claims, and the Ohio Rules of Evidence. Pursuant to Ohio Constitution Article IV, Section 5(B), such rules "shall not abridge, enlarge, or modify any substantive right," and " [a]ll laws in conflict with such rules shall be of no further force or effect."

ARTICLE

Article I

GENERAL PROVISIONS

Rule

Evid R 101 Scope of rules: applicability; privileges; exceptions

(A) Applicability

These rules govern proceedings in the courts of this state, subject to the exceptions stated in division (C) of this rule.

(B) Privileges

The rule with respect to privileges applies at all stages of all actions, cases, and proceedings conducted under these rules.

(C) Exceptions

These rules (other than with respect to privileges) do not apply in the following situations:

(1) Admissibility determinations. Determinations prerequisite to rulings on the admissibility of evidence when the issue is to be determined by the court under Evid. R. 104.

(2) Grand jury. Proceedings before grand juries.

(3) Miscellaneous criminal proceedings. Proceedings for extradition or rendition of fugitives; sentencing; granting or revoking probation; proceedings with respect to community control sanctions; issuance of warrants for arrest; criminal summonses and search warrants; and proceedings with respect to release on bail or otherwise.

(4) Contempt. Contempt proceedings in which the court may act summarily.

(5) Arbitration. Proceedings for those mandatory arbitrations of civil cases authorized by the rules of superintendence and governed by local rules of court.

(6) Other rules. Proceedings in which other rules prescribed by the Supreme Court govern matters relating to evidence.

(7) Special non-adversary statutory proceedings. Special statutory proceedings of a non-adversary nature in which these rules would by their nature be clearly inapplicable.

(8) Small claims division. Proceedings in the small claims division of a county or municipal court.

(Adopted eff. 7–1–80; amended eff. 7–1–90, 7–1–96, 7–1–99)

Evid R 102 Purpose and construction; supplementary principles

The purpose of these rules is to provide procedures for the adjudication of causes to the end that the truth may be ascertained and proceedings justly determined. The principles of the common law of Ohio shall supplement the provisions of these rules, and the rules shall be construed to state the principles of the common law of Ohio unless the rule clearly indicates that a change is intended. These rules shall not supersede substantive statutory provisions.

(Adopted eff. 7–1–80; amended eff. 7–1–96)

Evid R 103 Rulings on evidence

(A) Effect of erroneous ruling

Error may not be predicated upon a ruling which admits or excludes evidence unless a substantial right of the party is affected, and

(1) Objection. In case the ruling is one admitting evidence, a timely objection or motion to strike appears of record stating the specific ground of objection, if the specific ground was not apparent from the context; or

(2) Offer of proof. In case the ruling is one excluding evidence, the substance of the evidence was made known to the court by offer or was apparent from the context within which questions were asked. Offer of proof is not necessary if evidence is excluded during cross-examination.

(B) Record of offer and ruling

At the time of making the ruling, the court may add any other or further statement which shows the character of the evidence, the form in which it was offered, the objection made, and the ruling thereon. It may direct the making of an offer in question and answer form.

(C) Hearing of jury

In jury cases, proceedings shall be conducted, to the extent practicable, so as to prevent inadmissible evidence from being suggested to the jury by any means, such as making statements or offers of proof or asking questions in the hearing of the jury.

(D) Plain error

Nothing in this rule precludes taking notice of plain errors affecting substantial rights although they were not brought to the attention of the court.

(Adopted eff. 7–1–80)

Evid R 104 Preliminary questions

(A) Questions of admissibility generally

Preliminary questions concerning the qualification of a person to be a witness, the existence of a privilege, or the admissibility of evidence shall be determined by the court, subject to the provisions of subdivision (B). In making its determination it is not bound by the rules of evidence except those with respect to privileges.

(B) Relevancy conditioned on fact

When the relevancy of evidence depends upon the fulfillment of a condition of fact, the court shall admit it upon, or subject to, the introduction of evidence sufficient to support a finding of the fulfillment of the condition.

(C) Hearing of jury

Hearings on the admissibility of confessions shall in all cases be conducted out of the hearing of the jury. Hearings on other preliminary matters shall also be conducted out of the hearing of the jury when the interests of justice require.

(D) Testimony by accused

The accused does not, by testifying upon a preliminary matter, subject himself to cross-examination as to other issues in the case.

(E) Weight and credibility

This rule does not limit the right of a party to introduce before the jury evidence relevant to weight or credibility.

(Adopted eff. 7–1–80)

Evid R 105 Limited admissibility

When evidence which is admissible as to one party or for one purpose but not admissible as to another party of [1] for another purpose is admitted, the court, upon request of a party, shall restrict the evidence to its proper scope and instruct the jury accordingly.

(Adopted eff. 7–1–80)

1 So in 62 OS(2d) xxxiv; federal rule reads "or."

Evid R 106 Remainder of or related writings or recorded statements

When a writing or recorded statement or part thereof is introduced by a party, an adverse party may require him at that time to introduce any other part or any other writing or recorded statement which is otherwise admissible and which ought in fairness to be considered contemporaneously with it.

(Adopted eff. 7–1–80)

Article II

JUDICIAL NOTICE

Rule

Evid R 201 Judicial notice of adjudicative facts

(A) Scope of rule

This rule governs only judicial notice of adjudicative facts; i.e., the facts of the case.

(B) Kinds of facts

A judicially noticed fact must be one not subject to reasonable dispute in that it is either (1) generally known within the territorial jurisdiction of the trial court or (2) capable of accurate and ready determination by resort to sources whose accuracy cannot reasonable [1] be questioned.

(C) When discretionary

A court may take judicial notice, whether requested or not.

(D) When mandatory

A court shall take judicial notice if requested by a party and supplied with the necessary information.

(E) Opportunity to be heard

A party is entitled upon timely request to an opportunity to be heard as to the propriety of taking judicial notice and the tenor of the matter noticed. In the absence of prior notification, the request may be made after judicial notice has been taken.

(F) Time of taking notice

Judicial notice may be taken at any stage of the proceeding.

(G) Instructing jury

In a civil action or proceeding, the court shall instruct the jury to accept as conclusive any fact judicially noticed. In a criminal case, the court shall instruct the jury that it may, but is not required to, accept as conclusive any fact judicially noticed.

(Adopted eff. 7–1–80)

1 So in 62 OS(2d) xxxv; federal rule reads "reasonably."

Article III

PRESUMPTIONS

Evid R 301 Presumptions in general in civil actions and proceedings

In all civil actions and proceedings not otherwise provided for by statute enacted by the General Assembly or by these rules, a presumption imposes on the party against whom it is directed the burden of going forward with evidence to rebut or meet the presumption, but does not shift to such party the burden of proof in the sense of the risk of non-persuasion, which remains throughout the trial upon the party on whom it was originally cast.

(Adopted eff. 7–1–80)

Evid R 302 [Reserved]

Article IV

RELEVANCY AND ITS LIMITS

Evid R 401 Definition of "relevant evidence"

"Relevant evidence" means evidence having any tendency to make the existence of any fact that is of consequence to the determination of the action more probable or less probable than it would be without the evidence.

(Adopted eff. 7–1–80)

Evid R 402 Relevant evidence generally admissible; irrelevant evidence inadmissible

All relevant evidence is admissible, except as otherwise provided by the Constitution of the United States, by the Constitution of the State of Ohio, by statute enacted by the General Assembly not in conflict with a rule of the Supreme Court of Ohio, by these rules, or by other rules prescribed by the Supreme Court of Ohio. Evidence which is not relevant is not admissible.

(Adopted eff. 7–1–80)

Evid R 403 Exclusion of relevant evidence on grounds of prejudice, confusion, or undue delay

(A) Exclusion mandatory

Although relevant, evidence is not admissible if its probative value is substantially outweighed by the danger of unfair prejudice, of confusion of the issues, or of misleading the jury.

(B) Exclusion discretionary

Although relevant, evidence may be excluded if its probative value is substantially outweighed by considerations of undue delay, or needless presentation of cumulative evidence.

(Adopted eff. 7–1–80; amended eff. 7–1–96)

Evid R 404 Character evidence not admissible to prove conduct; exceptions; other crimes

(A) Character evidence generally

Evidence of a person's character or a trait of his character is not admissible for the purpose of proving that he acted in conformity therewith on a particular occasion, subject to the following exceptions:

(1) Character of accused. Evidence of a pertinent trait of his character offered by an accused, or by the prosecution to rebut the same is admissible; however, in prosecutions for rape, gross sexual imposition, and prostitution, the exceptions provided by statute enacted by the General Assembly are applicable.

(2) Character of victim. Evidence of a pertinent trait of character of the victim of the crime offered by an accused, or by the prosecution to rebut the same, or evidence of a character trait of peacefulness of the victim offered by the prosecution in a homicide case to rebut evidence that the victim was the first aggressor is admissible; however, in prosecutions for rape, gross sexual imposition, and prostitution, the exceptions provided by statute enacted by the General Assembly are applicable.

(3) Character of witness. Evidence of the character of a witness on the issue of credibility is admissible as provided in Rules 607, 608, and 609.

(B) Other crimes, wrongs or acts

Evidence of other crimes, wrongs, or acts is not admissible to prove the character of a person in order to show that he acted in conformity therewith. It may, however, be admissible for other purposes, such as proof of motive, opportunity, intent, preparation, plan, knowledge, identity, or absence of mistake or accident.

(Adopted eff. 7–1–80)

Evid R 405 Methods of proving character

(A) Reputation or opinion

In all cases in which evidence of character or a trait of character of a person is admissible, proof may be made by testimony as to reputation or by testimony in the form of an opinion. On cross-examination, inquiry is allowable into relevant specific instances of conduct.

(B) Specific instances of conduct

In cases in which character or a trait of character of a person is an essential element of a charge, claim, or defense, proof may also be made of specific instances of his conduct.

(Adopted eff. 7–1–80)

Evid R 406 Habit; routine practice

Evidence of the habit of a person or of the routine practice of an organization, whether corroborated or not and regardless of the presence of eyewitnesses, is relevant to prove that the conduct of the person or organization on a particular occasion was in conformity with the habit or routine practice.

(Adopted eff. 7–1–80)

Evid R 407 Subsequent remedial measures

When, after an injury or harm allegedly caused by an event, measures are taken which, if taken previously, would have made the injury or harm less likely to occur, evidence of the subsequent measures is not admissible to prove negligence or culpable conduct in connection with the event. This rule does not require the exclusion of evidence of subsequent measures when offered for another purpose, such as proving ownership, control, or feasibility of precautionary measures, if controverted, or impeachment.

(Adopted eff. 7–1–80; amended eff. 7–1–00)

Evid R 408 Compromise and offers to compromise

Evidence of (1) furnishing or offering or promising to furnish, or (2) accepting or offering or promising to accept, a valuable consideration in compromising or attempting to compromise a claim which was disputed as to either validity or amount, is not admissible to prove liability for or invalidity of the claim or its amount. Evidence of conduct or statements made in compromise negotiations is likewise not admissible. This rule does not require the exclusion of any evidence otherwise discoverable merely because it is presented in the course of compromise negotiations. This rule also does not require exclusion when the evidence is offered for another purpose, such as proving bias or prejudice of a witness, negativing a contention of undue delay, or proving an effort to obstruct a criminal investigation or prosecution.

(Adopted eff. 7–1–80)

Evid R 409 Payment of medical and similar expenses

Evidence of furnishing or offering or promising to pay medical, hospital, or similar expenses occasioned by an injury is not admissible to prove liability for the injury.

(Adopted eff. 7–1–80)

Evid R 410 Inadmissibility of pleas, offers of pleas, and related statements

(A) Except as provided in division (B) of this rule, evidence of the following is not admissible in any civil or criminal proceeding against the defendant who made the plea or who was a participant personally or through counsel in the plea discussions:

(1) a plea of guilty that later was withdrawn;

(2) a plea of no contest or the equivalent plea from another jurisdiction;

(3) a plea of guilty in a violations bureau;

(4) any statement made in the course of any proceedings under Rule 11 of the Rules of Criminal Procedure or equivalent procedure from another jurisdiction regarding the foregoing pleas;

(5) any statement made in the course of plea discussions in which counsel for the prosecuting authority or for the defendant was a participant and that do not result in a plea of guilty or that result in a plea of guilty later withdrawn.

(B) A statement otherwise inadmissible under this rule is admissible in either of the following:

(1) any proceeding in which another statement made in the course of the same plea or plea discussions has been introduced and the statement should, in fairness, be considered contemporaneously with it;

(2) a criminal proceeding for perjury or false statement if the statement was made by the defendant under oath, on the record, and in the presence of counsel.

(Adopted eff. 7–1–80; amended eff. 7–1–91)

Evid R 411 Liability insurance

Evidence that a person was or was not insured against liability is not admissible upon the issue whether he acted negligently or otherwise wrongfully. This rule does not require the exclusion of evidence of insurance against liability when offered for another purpose, such as proof of agency, ownership or control, if controverted, or bias or prejudice of a witness.

(Adopted eff. 7–1–80)

Article V

PRIVILEGES

Evid R 501 General rule

The privilege of a witness, person, state or political subdivision thereof shall be governed by statute enacted by the General Assembly or by principles of common law as interpreted by the courts of this state in the light of reason and experience.

(Adopted eff. 7–1–80)

Article VI

WITNESSES

Evid R 601 General rule of competency

Every person is competent to be a witness except:

(A) Those of unsound mind, and children under ten years of age, who appear incapable of receiving just impressions of the facts and transactions respecting which they are examined, or of relating them truly.

(B) A spouse testifying against the other spouse charged with a crime except when either of the following applies:

(1) a crime against the testifying spouse or a child of either spouse is charged;

(2) the testifying spouse elects to testify.

(C) An officer, while on duty for the exclusive or main purpose of enforcing traffic laws, arresting or assisting in the arrest of a person charged with a traffic violation punishable as a misdemeanor where the officer at the time of the arrest was not using a properly marked motor vehicle as defined by statute or was not wearing a legally distinctive uniform as defined by statute.

(D) A person giving expert testimony on the issue of liability in any claim asserted in any civil action against a physician, podiatrist, or hospital arising out of the diagnosis, care, or treatment of any person by a physician or podiatrist, unless the person testifying is licensed to practice medicine and surgery, osteopathic medicine and surgery, or podiatric medicine and surgery by the state medical board or by the licensing authority of any state, and unless the person devotes at least one-half of his or her professional time to the active clinical practice in his or her field of licensure, or to its instruction in an accredited school. This division shall not prohibit other medical professionals who otherwise are competent to testify under these rules from giving expert testimony on the appropriate standard of care in their own profession in any claim asserted in any civil action against a physician, podiatrist, medical professional, or hospital arising out of the diagnosis, care, or treatment of any person.

(E) As otherwise provided in these rules.

(Adopted eff. 7–1–80; amended eff. 7–1–91)

Evid R 602 Lack of personal knowledge

A witness may not testify to a matter unless evidence is introduced sufficient to support a finding that he has personal knowledge of the matter. Evidence to prove personal knowledge may, but need not, consist of the testimony of the witness himself. This rule is subject to the provisions of Rule 703, relating to opinion testimony by expert witnesses.

(Adopted eff. 7–1–80)

Evid R 603 Oath or affirmation

Before testifying, every witness shall be required to declare that he will testify truthfully, by oath or affirmation administered in a form calculated to awaken his conscience and impress his mind with his duty to do so.

(Adopted eff. 7–1–80)

Evid R 604 Interpreters

An interpreter is subject to the provisions of these rules relating to qualification as an expert and the administration of an oath or affirmation that he will make a true translation.

(Adopted eff. 7–1–80)

Evid R 605 Competency of judge as witness

The judge presiding at the trial may not testify in that trial as a witness. No objection need be made in order to preserve the point.

(Adopted eff. 7–1–80)

Evid R 606 Competency of juror as witness

(A) At the trial

A member of the jury may not testify as a witness before that jury in the trial of the case in which he is sitting as a juror. If he is called so to testify, the opposing party shall be afforded an opportunity to object out of the presence of the jury.

(B) Inquiry into validity of verdict or indictment

Upon an inquiry into the validity of a verdict or indictment, a juror may not testify as to any matter or statement occurring during the course of the jury's deliberations or to the effect of anything upon his or any other juror's mind or emotions as influencing him to assent to or dissent from the verdict or indictment or concerning his mental processes in connection therewith. A juror may testify on the question whether extraneous prejudicial information was improperly brought to the jury's attention or whether any outside influence was improperly brought to bear on any juror, only after some outside evidence of that act or event has been presented. However a juror may testify without the presentation of any outside evidence concerning any threat, any bribe, any attempted threat or bribe, or any improprieties of any officer of the court. His affidavit or evidence of any statement by him concerning a matter about which he would be precluded from testifying will not be received for these purposes.

(Adopted eff. 7–1–80)

Evid R 607 Impeachment

(A) Who may impeach

The credibility of a witness may be attacked by any party except that the credibility of a witness may be attacked by the party calling the witness by means of a prior inconsistent statement only upon a showing of surprise and affirmative damage. This exception does not apply to statements admitted pursuant to Evid. R. 801(D)(1)(a), 801(D)(2), or 803.

(B) Impeachment: reasonable basis

A questioner must have a reasonable basis for asking any question pertaining to impeachment that implies the existence of an impeaching fact.

(Adopted eff. 7–1–80; amended eff. 7–1–98)

Evid R 608 Evidence of character and conduct of witness

(A) Opinion and reputation evidence of character

The credibility of a witness may be attacked or supported by evidence in the form of opinion or reputation, but subject to these limitations: (1) the evidence may refer only to character for truthfulness or untruthfulness, and (2) evidence of truthful character is admissible only after the character of the witness for truthfulness has been attacked by opinion or reputation evidence or otherwise.

(B) Specific instances of conduct

Specific instances of the conduct of a witness, for the purpose of attacking or supporting the witness's character for truthfulness, other than conviction of crime as provided in Evid. R. 609, may not be proved by extrinsic evidence. They may, however, in the discretion of the court, if clearly probative of truthfulness or untruthfulness, be inquired into on cross-examination of the witness (1) concerning the witness's character for truthfulness or untruthfulness, or (2) concerning the character for truthfulness or untruthfulness of another witness as to which character the witness being cross-examined has testified.

The giving of testimony by any witness, including an accused, does not operate as a waiver of the witness's privilege against self-incrimination when examined with respect to matters that relate only to the witness's character for truthfulness.

(Adopted eff. 7–1–80; amended eff. 7–1–92)

Evid R 609 Impeachment by evidence of conviction of crime

(A) General rule

For the purpose of attacking the credibility of a witness:

(1) subject to Evid. R. 403, evidence that a witness other than the accused has been convicted of a crime is admissible if the crime was punishable by death or imprisonment in excess of one year pursuant to the law under which the witness was convicted.

(2) notwithstanding Evid. R. 403(A), but subject to Evid. R. 403(B), evidence that the accused has been convicted of a crime is admissible if the crime was punishable by death or imprisonment in excess of one year pursuant to the law under which the accused was convicted and if the court determines that the probative value of the evidence outweighs the danger of unfair prejudice, of confusion of the issues, or of misleading the jury.

(3) notwithstanding Evid. R. 403(A), but subject to Evid. R. 403(B), evidence that any witness, including an accused, has been convicted of a crime is admissible if the crime involved dishonesty or false statement, regardless of the punishment and whether based upon state or federal statute or local ordinance.

(B) Time limit.

Evidence of a conviction under this rule is not admissible if a period of more than ten years has elapsed since the date of the conviction or of the release of the witness from the confinement, or the termination of community control sanctions, post-release control, or probation, shock probation, parole, or shock parole imposed for that conviction, whichever is the later date, unless the court determines, in the interests of justice, that the probative value of the conviction supported by specific facts and circumstances substantially outweighs its prejudicial effect. However, evidence of a conviction more than ten years old as calculated herein, is not admissible unless the proponent gives to the adverse party sufficient advance written notice of intent to use such evidence to provide the adverse party with a fair opportunity to contest the use of such evidence.

(C) Effect of pardon, annulment, expungement, or certificate of rehabilitation

Evidence of a conviction is not admissible under this rule if (1) the conviction has been the subject of a pardon, annulment, expungement, certificate of rehabilitation, or other equivalent procedure based on a finding of the rehabilitation of the person convicted, and that person has not been convicted of a subsequent crime which was punishable by death or imprisonment in excess of one year, or (2) the conviction has been the subject of a pardon, annulment, expungement, or other equivalent procedure based on a finding of innocence.

(D) Juvenile adjudications

Evidence of juvenile adjudications is not admissible except as provided by statute enacted by the General Assembly.

(E) Pendency of appeal

The pendency of an appeal therefrom does not render evidence of a conviction inadmissible. Evidence of the pendency of an appeal is admissible.

(F) Methods of proof

When evidence of a witness's conviction of a crime is admissible under this rule, the fact of the conviction may be proved only by the testimony of the witness on direct or cross-examination, or by public record shown to the witness during his or her examination. If the witness denies that he or she is the person to whom the public record refers, the court may permit the introduction of additional evidence tending to establish that the witness is or is not the person to whom the public record refers.

(Adopted eff. 7–1–80; amended eff. 7–1–91, 7–1–03)

Evid R 610 Religious beliefs or opinions

Evidence of the beliefs or opinions of a witness on matters of religion is not admissible for the purpose of showing that by reason of their nature his credibility is impaired or enhanced.

(Adopted eff. 7–1–80)

Evid R 611 Mode and order of interrogation and presentation

(A) Control by court

The court shall exercise reasonable control over the mode and order of interrogating witnesses and presenting evidence so as to (1) make the interrogation and presentation effective for the ascertainment of the truth, (2) avoid needless consumption of time, and (3) protect witnesses from harassment or undue embarrassment.

(B) Scope of cross–examination

Cross-examination shall be permitted on all relevant matters and matters affecting credibility.

(C) Leading questions

Leading questions should not be used on the direct examination of a witness except as may be necessary to develop his testimony. Ordinarily leading questions should be permitted on cross-examination. When a party calls a hostile witness, an adverse party, or a witness identified with an adverse party, interrogation may be by leading questions.

(Adopted eff. 7–1–80)

Evid R 612 Writing used to refresh memory

Except as otherwise provided in criminal proceedings by Rule 16(B)(1)(g) and 16(C)(1)(d) of Ohio Rules of Criminal Procedure, if a witness uses a writing to refresh his memory for the purpose of testifying, either: (1) while testifying; or (2) before testifying, if the court in its discretion determines it is necessary in the interests of justice, an adverse party is entitled to have the writing produced at the hearing. He is also entitled to inspect it, to cross-examine the witness thereon, and to introduce in evidence those portions which relate to the testimony of the witness. If it is claimed that the writing contains matters not related to the subject matter of the testimony the court shall examine the writing *in camera*, excise any portions not so related, and order delivery of the remainder to the party entitled thereto. Any portion witheld [sic.] over objections shall be preserved and made available to the appellate court in the event of an appeal. If a writing is not produced or delivered pursuant to order under this rule, the court shall make any order justice requires, except that in criminal cases when the prosecution elects not to comply, the order shall be one striking the testimony or, if the court in its discretion determines that the interests of justice so require, declaring a mistrial.

(Adopted eff. 7–1–80)

Evid R 613 Impeachment by self-contradiction

(A) Examining witness concerning prior statement

In examining a witness concerning a prior statement made by the witness, whether written or not, the statement need not be shown nor its contents disclosed to the witness at that time, but on request the same shall be shown or disclosed to opposing counsel.

(B) Extrinsic evidence of prior inconsistent statement of witness

Extrinsic evidence of a prior inconsistent statement by a witness is admissible if both of the following apply:

(1) If the statement is offered solely for the purpose of impeaching the witness, the witness is afforded a prior opportunity to explain or deny the statement and the opposite party is afforded an opportunity to interrogate the witness on the statement or the interests of justice otherwise require;

(2) The subject matter of the statement is one of the following:

(a) A fact that is of consequence to the determination of the action other than the credibility of a witness;

(b) A fact that may be shown by extrinsic evidence under Evid. R. 608(A), 609, 616(B) or 706;

(c) A fact that may be shown by extrinsic evidence under the common law of impeachment if not in conflict with the Rules of Evidence.

(C) Prior inconsistent conduct

During examination of a witness, conduct of the witness inconsistent with the witness's testimony may be shown to impeach. If offered for the sole purpose of impeaching the witness's testimony, extrinsic evidence of that prior inconsistent conduct is admissible under the same circumstances as provided for prior inconsistent statements in Evid. R. 613(B)(2).

(Adopted eff. 7–1–80; amended eff. 7–1–98)

Evid R 614 Calling and interrogation of witnesses by court

(A) Calling by court

The court may, on its own motion or at the suggestion of a party, call witnesses, and all parties are entitled to cross-examine witnesses thus called.

(B) Interrogation by court

The court may interrogate witnesses, in an impartial manner, whether called by itself or by a party.

(C) Objections

Objections to the calling of witnesses by the court or to interrogation by it may be made at the time or at the next available opportunity when the jury is not present.

(Adopted eff. 7–1–80)

Evid R 615 Separation and exclusion of witnesses

(A) Except as provided in division (B) of this rule, at the request of a party the court shall order witnesses excluded so that they cannot hear the testimony of other witnesses, and it may make the order of its own motion. An order directing the "exclusion" or "separation" of witnesses or the like, in general terms without specification of other or additional limitations, is effective only to require the exclusion of witnesses from the hearing during the testimony of other witnesses.

(B) This rule does not authorize exclusion of any of the following persons from the hearing:

(1) a party who is a natural person;

(2) an officer or employee of a party that is not a natural person designated as its representative by its attorney;

(3) a person whose presence is shown by a party to be essential to the presentation of the party's cause;

(4) in a criminal proceeding, a victim of the charged offense to the extent that the victim's presence is authorized by statute enacted by the General Assembly. As used in this rule, "victim" has the same meaning as in the provisions of the Ohio Constitution providing rights for victims of crimes.

(Adopted eff. 7–1–80; amended eff. 7–1–01, 7–1–03)

Evid R 616 Methods of impeachment

In addition to other methods, a witness may be impeached by any of the following methods:

(A) Bias

Bias, prejudice, interest, or any motive to misrepresent may be shown to impeach the witness either by examination of the witness or by extrinsic evidence.

(B) Sensory or mental defect

A defect of capacity, ability, or opportunity to observe, remember, or relate may be shown to impeach the witness either by examination of the witness or by extrinsic evidence.

(C) Specific contradiction

Facts contradicting a witness's testimony may be shown for the purpose of impeaching the witness's testimony. If offered for the sole purpose of impeaching a witness's testimony, extrinsic evidence of contradiction is inadmissible unless the evidence is one of the following:

(1) Permitted by Evid. R. 608(A), 609, 613, 616(A), 616(B), or 706;

(2) Permitted by the common law of impeachment and not in conflict with the Rules of Evidence.

(Adopted eff. 7–1–91; amended eff. 7–1–98)

Article VII

OPINIONS AND EXPERT TESTIMONY

Rule

Evid R 701 Opinion testimony by lay witnesses

If the witness is not testifying as an expert, his testimony in the form of opinions or inferences is limited to those opinions or inferences which are (1) rationally based on the perception of the witness and (2) helpful to a clear understanding of his testimony or the determination of a fact in issue.

(Adopted eff. 7–1–80)

Evid R 702 Testimony by experts

A witness may testify as an expert if all of the following apply:

(A) The witness' testimony either relates to matters beyond the knowledge or experience possessed by lay persons or dispels a misconception common among lay persons;

(B) The witness is qualified as an expert by specialized knowledge, skill, experience, training, or education regarding the subject matter of the testimony;

(C) The witness' testimony is based on reliable scientific, technical, or other specialized information. To the extent that the testimony reports the result of a procedure, test, or experiment, the testimony is reliable only if all of the following apply:

(1) The theory upon which the procedure, test, or experiment is based is objectively verifiable or is validly derived from widely accepted knowledge, facts, or principles;

(2) The design of the procedure, test, or experiment reliably implements the theory;

(3) The particular procedure, test, or experiment was conducted in a way that will yield an accurate result.

(Adopted eff. 7–1–80; amended eff. 7–1–94)

Evid R 703 Bases of opinion testimony by experts

The facts or data in the particular case upon which an expert bases an opinion or inference may be those perceived by him or admitted in evidence at the hearing.

(Adopted eff. 7–1–80)

Evid R 704 Opinion on ultimate issue

Testimony in the form of an opinion or inference otherwise admissible is not objectionable solely because it embraces an ultimate issue to be decided by the trier of fact.

(Adopted eff. 7–1–80)

Evid R 705 Disclosure of facts or data underlying expert opinion

The expert may testify in terms of opinion or inference and give his reasons therefor after disclosure of the underlying facts or data. The disclosure may be in response to a hypothetical question or otherwise.

(Adopted eff. 7–1–80)

Evid R 706 Learned treatises for impeachment

Statements contained in published treatises, periodicals, or pamphlets on a subject of history, medicine, or other science or art are admissible for impeachment if the publication is either of the following:

(A) Relied upon by an expert witness in reaching an opinion;

(B) Established as reliable authority (1) by the testimony or admission of the witness, (2) by other expert testimony, or (3) by judicial notice.

If admitted for impeachment, the statements may be read into evidence but shall not be received as exhibits.

(Adopted eff. 7–1–98)

Article VIII

HEARSAY

Rule

Evid R 801 Definitions

The following definitions apply under this article:

(A) Statement

A "statement" is (1) an oral or written assertion or (2) nonverbal conduct of a person, if it is intended by him as an assertion.

(B) Declarant

A "declarant" is a person who makes a statement.

(C) Hearsay

"Hearsay" is a statement, other than one made by the declarant while testifying at the trial or hearing, offered in evidence to prove the truth of the matter asserted.

(D) Statements which are not hearsay

A statement is not hearsay if:

(1) Prior statement by witness. The declarant testifies at the trial or hearing and is subject to cross-examination concerning the statement, and the statement is (a) inconsistent with his testimony, and was given under oath subject to cross-examination by the party against whom the statement is offered and subject to the penalty of perjury at a trial, hearing, or other proceeding, or in a deposition, or (b) consistent with his testimony and is offered to rebut an express or implied charge against him of recent fabrication or improper influence or motive, or (c) one of identification of a person soon after perceiving him, if the circumstances demonstrate the reliability of the prior identification.

(2) Admission by party-opponent. The statement is offered against a party and is (a) his own statement, in either his individual or a representative capacity, or (b) a statement of which he has manifested his adoption or belief in its truth, or (c) a statement by a person authorized by him to make a statement concerning the subject, or (d) a statement by his agent or servant concerning a matter within the scope of his agency or employment, made during the existence of the relationship, or (e) a statement by a co-conspirator of a party during the course and in furtherance of the conspiracy upon independent proof of the conspiracy.

(Adopted eff. 7-1-80)

Evid R 802 Hearsay rule

Hearsay is not admissible except as otherwise provided by the Constitution of the United States, by the Constitution of the State of Ohio, by statute enacted by the General Assembly not in conflict with a rule of the Supreme Court of Ohio, by these rules, or by other rules prescribed by the Supreme Court of Ohio.

(Adopted eff. 7-1-80)

Evid R 803 Hearsay exceptions; availability of declarant immaterial

The following are not excluded by the hearsay rule, even though the declarant is available as a witness:

(1) Present sense impression

A statement describing or explaining an event or condition made while the declarant was perceiving the event or condition, or immediately thereafter unless circumstances indicate lack of trustworthiness.

(2) Excited utterance

A statement relating to a startling event or condition made while the declarant was under the stress of excitement caused by the event or condition.

(3) Then existing, mental, emotional, or physical condition

A statement of the declarant's then existing state of mind, emotion, sensation, or physical condition (such as intent, plan, motive, design, mental feeling, pain, and bodily health), but not including a statement of memory or belief to prove the fact remembered or believed unless it relates to the execution, revocation, identification, or terms of declarant's will.

(4) Statements for purposes of medical diagnosis or treatment

Statements made for purposes of medical diagnosis or treatment and describing medical history, or past or present symptoms, pain, or sensations, or the inception or general character of the cause or external source thereof insofar as reasonably pertinent to diagnosis or treatment.

(5) Recorded recollection

A memorandum or record concerning a matter about which a witness once had knowledge but now has insufficient recollection to enable him to testify fully and accurately, shown by the testimony of the witness to have been made or adopted when the matter was fresh in his memory and to reflect that knowledge correctly. If admitted, the memorandum or record may be read into evidence but may not itself be received as an exhibit unless offered by an adverse party.

(6) Records of regularly conducted activity

A memorandum, report, record, or data compilation, in any form, of acts, events, or conditions, made at or near the time by, or from information transmitted by, a person with knowledge, if kept in the course of a regularly conducted business activity, and if it was the regular practice of that business activity to make the memorandum, report, record, or data compilation, all as shown by the testimony of the custodian or other qualified witness or as provided by Rule 901(B)(10), unless the source of information or the method or circumstances of preparation indicate lack of trustworthiness. The term "business" as used in this paragraph includes business, institution, association, profession, occupation, and calling of every kind, whether or not conducted for profit.

(7) Absence of entry in record kept in accordance with the provisions of paragraph (6)

Evidence that a matter is not included in the memoranda, reports, records, or data compilations, in any form, kept in accordance with the provisions of paragraph (6), to prove the nonoccurrence or nonexistence of the matter, if the matter was of a kind of which a memorandum, report, record, or data compilation was regularly made and preserved, unless the sources of information or other circumstances indicate lack of trustworthiness.

(8) Public records and reports

Records, reports, statements, or data compilations, in any form, of public offices or agencies, setting forth (a) the activities of the office or agency, or (b) matters observed pursuant to duty imposed by law as to which matters there was a duty to report, excluding, however, in criminal cases matters observed by police officers and other law enforcement personnel, unless offered by defendant, unless the sources of information or other circumstances indicate lack of trustworthiness.

(9) Records of vital statistics

Records or data compilations, in any form, of births, fetal deaths, deaths, or marriages, if the report thereof was made to a public office pursuant to requirement of law.

(10) Absence of public record or entry

To prove the absence of a record, report, statement, or data compilation, in any form, or the nonoccurrence or nonexistence of a matter of which a record, report, statement, or data compilation, in any form, was regularly made and preserved by a public office or agency, evidence in the form of a certification in accordance with Rule 901(B)(10) or testimony, that diligent search failed to disclose the record, report, statement, or data compilation, or entry.

(11) Records of religious organizations

Statements of births, marriages, divorces, deaths, legitimacy, ancestry, relationship by blood or marriage, or other similar facts of personal or family history, contained in a regularly kept record of religious organization [1].

(12) Marriage, baptismal, and similar certificates

Statements of fact contained in a certificate that the maker performed a marriage or other ceremony or administered a sacrament, made by a clergyman, public official, or other person authorized by the rules or practices of a religious organization or by law to perform the act certified, and purporting to have been issued at the time of the act or within a reasonable time thereafter.

(13) Family records

Statements of fact concerning personal or family history contained in family Bibles, genealogies, charts, engravings on rings, inscriptions on family portraits, engravings on urns, crypts, or tombstones, or the like.

(14) Records of documents affecting an interest in property

The record of a document purporting to establish or affect an interest in property, as proof of the content of the original recorded document and its execution and delivery by each person by whom it purports to have been executed, if the record is a record of a public office and an applicable statute authorizes the recording of documents of that kind in that office.

(15) Statements in documents affecting an interest in property

A statement contained in a document purporting to establish or affect an interest in property if the matter stated was relevant to the purpose of the document, unless dealings with the property since the document was made have been inconsistent with the truth of the statement or the purport of the document.

(16) Statements in ancient documents

Statements in a document in existence twenty years or more the authenticity of which is established.

(17) Market reports, commercial publications

Market quotations, tabulations, lists, directories, or other published compilations, generally used and relied upon by the public or by persons in particular occupations.

(18) Reputation concerning personal or family history

Reputation among members of his family by blood, adoption, or marriage or among his associates, or in the community, concerning a person's birth, adoption, marriage, divorce, death, legitimacy, relationship by blood, adoption or marriage, ancestry, or other similar fact of his personal or family history.

(19) Reputation concerning boundaries or general history

Reputation in a community, arising before the controversy, as to boundaries of or customs affecting lands in the community, and reputation as to events of general history important to the community or state or nation in which located.

(20) Reputation as to character

Reputation of a person's character among his associates or in the community.

(21) Judgment of previous conviction

Evidence of a final judgment, entered after a trial or upon a plea of guilty (but not upon a plea of no contest or the equivalent plea from another jurisdiction), adjudging a person guilty of a crime punishable by death or imprisonment in excess of one year, to prove any fact essential to sustain the judgment, but not including, when offered by the Government in a criminal prosecution for purposes other than impeachment, judgments against persons other than the accused. The pendency of an appeal may be shown but does not affect admissibility.

(22) Judgment as to personal, family, or general history, or boundaries

Judgments as proof of matters of personal, family or general history, or boundaries, essential to the judgment, if the same would be provable by evidence of reputation.

(Adopted eff. 7–1–80)

[1] So in 62 OS(2d) xlvi; federal rule reads "of a religious organization."

Evid R 804 Hearsay exceptions; declarant unavailable

(A) Definition of unavailability

"Unavailability as a witness" includes any of the following situations in which the declarant:

(1) is exempted by ruling of the court on the ground of privilege from testifying concerning the subject matter of the declarant's statement;

(2) persists in refusing to testify concerning the subject matter of the declarant's statement despite an order of the court to do so;

(3) testifies to a lack of memory of the subject matter of the declarant's statement;

(4) is unable to be present or to testify at the hearing because of death or then-existing physical or mental illness or infirmity;

(5) is absent from the hearing and the proponent of the declarant's statement has been unable to procure the declarant's attendance (or in the case of a hearsay exception under division (B)(2), (3), or (4) of this rule, the declarant's attendance or testimony) by process or other reasonable means.

A declarant is not unavailable as a witness if the declarant's exemption, refusal, claim of lack of memory, inability, or absence is due to the procurement or wrongdoing of the proponent of the declarant's statement for the purpose of preventing the witness from attending or testifying.

(B) Hearsay exceptions

The following are not excluded by the hearsay rule if the declarant is unavailable as a witness:

(1) Former testimony. Testimony given as a witness at another hearing of the same or a different proceeding, or in a deposition taken in compliance with law in the course of the same or another proceeding, if the party against whom the testimony is now offered, or, in a civil action or proceeding, a predecessor in interest, had an opportunity and similar motive to develop the testimony by direct, cross, or redirect examination. Testimony given at a preliminary hearing must satisfy the right to confrontation and exhibit indicia of reliability.

(2) Statement under belief of impending death. In a prosecution for homicide or in a civil action or proceeding, a statement made by a declarant, while believing that his or her death was imminent, concerning the cause or circumstances of what the declarant believed to be his or her impending death.

(3) Statement against interest. A statement that was at the time of its making so far contrary to the declarant's pecuniary or proprietary interest, or so far tended to subject the declarant to civil or criminal liability, or to render invalid a claim by the declarant against another, that a reasonable person in the declarant's position would not have made the statement unless the declarant believed it to be true. A statement tending to expose the declarant to criminal liability, whether offered to exculpate or inculpate the accused, is not admissible unless corroborating circumstances clearly indicate the trustworthiness of the statement.

(4) Statement of personal or family history. (a) A statement concerning the declarant's own birth, adoption, marriage, divorce, legitimacy, relationship by blood, adoption, or marriage, ancestry, or other similar fact of personal or family history, even though

the declarant had no means of acquiring personal knowledge of the matter stated; or (b) a statement concerning the foregoing matters, and death also, of another person, if the declarant was related to the other by blood, adoption, or marriage or was so intimately associated with the other's family as to be likely to have accurate information concerning the matter declared.

(5) Statement by a deceased or incompetent person. The statement was made by a decedent or a mentally incompetent person, where all of the following apply:

(a) the estate or personal representative of the decedent's estate or the guardian or trustee of the incompetent person is a party;

(b) the statement was made before the death or the development of the incompetency;

(c) the statement is offered to rebut testimony by an adverse party on a matter within the knowledge of the decedent or incompetent person.

(6) Forfeiture by wrongdoing. A statement offered against a party if the unavailability of the witness is due to the wrongdoing of the party for the purpose of preventing the witness from attending or testifying. However, a statement is not admissible under this rule unless the proponent has given to each adverse party advance written notice of an intention to introduce the statement sufficient to provide the adverse party a fair opportunity to contest the admissibility of the statement.

(Adopted eff. 7–1–80; amended eff. 7–1–81[1]*, 7–1–93, 7–1–01)*

[1] As originally adopted, Rule 804(B)(1) excluded preliminary hearing testimony from the former testimony exception. *See* 62 OS(2d) xlvii (1980). The exclusion of preliminary hearing testimony, Crim R 5(B), was based upon the Ohio Supreme Court's decision in *State v Roberts*, 55 OS(2d) 191, 378 NE(2d) 492 (1978). The Court in *Roberts* held that admitting preliminary hearing testimony in a criminal trial violated the accused's Sixth Amendment right of confrontation. *See also* State v Smith, 58 OS(2d) 344, 390 NE(2d) 778 (1979), vacated, 448 US 902, 100 SCt 3041, 65 LEd(2d) 1132 (1980). Just days before the Rules of Evidence became effective, the *Roberts* decision was reversed by the U.S. Supreme Court. *See* Ohio v Roberts, 448 US 56, 100 SCt 2531, 65 LEd(2d) 597 (1980). In response, the rule was amended by deleting the clause which exempted preliminary hearing testimony. *See* 53 Ohio Bar 1218 (1980).

Evid R 805 Hearsay within hearsay

Hearsay included within hearsay is not excluded under the hearsay rule if each part of the combined statements conforms with an exception to the hearsay rule provided in these rules.

(Adopted eff. 7–1–80)

Evid R 806 Attacking and supporting credibility of declarant

(A) When a hearsay statement, or a statement defined in Evid. R. 801(D)(2), (c), (d), or (e), has been admitted in evidence, the credibility of the declarant may be attacked, and if attacked may be supported, by any evidence that would be admissible for those purposes if declarant had testified as a witness.

(B) Evidence of a statement or conduct by the declarant at any time, inconsistent with the declarant's hearsay statement, is not subject to any requirement that the declarant may have been afforded an opportunity to deny or explain.

(C) Evidence of a declarant's prior conviction is not subject to any requirement that the declarant be shown a public record.

(D) If the party against whom a hearsay statement has been admitted calls the declarant as a witness, the party is entitled to examine the declarant on the statement as if under cross-examination.

(Adopted eff. 7–1–80; amended eff. 7–1–98)

Evid R 807 Hearsay exceptions; child statements in abuse cases

(A) An out-of-court statement made by a child who is under twelve years of age at the time of trial or hearing describing any sexual act performed by, with, or on the child or describing any act of physical violence directed against the child is not excluded as hearsay under Evid. R. 802 if all of the following apply:

(1) The court finds that the totality of the circumstances surrounding the making of the statement provides particularized guarantees of trustworthiness that make the statement at least as reliable as statements admitted pursuant to Evid. R. 803 and 804. The circumstances must establish that the child was particularly likely to be telling the truth when the statement was made and that the test of cross-examination would add little to the reliability of the statement. In making its determination of the reliability of the statement, the court shall consider all of the circumstances surrounding the making of the statement, including but not limited to spontaneity, the internal consistency of the statement, the mental state of the child, the child's motive or lack of motive to fabricate, the child's use of terminology unexpected of a child of similar age, the means by which the statement was elicited, and the lapse of time between the act and the statement. In making this determination, the court shall not consider whether there is independent proof of the sexual act or act of physical violence.

(2) The child's testimony is not reasonably obtainable by the proponent of the statement.

(3) There is independent proof of the sexual act or act of physical violence.

(4) At least ten days before the trial or hearing, a proponent of the statement has notified all other parties in writing of the content of the statement, the time and place at which the statement was made, the identity of the witness who is to testify about the statement, and the circumstances surrounding the statement that are claimed to indicate its trustworthiness.

(B) The child's testimony is "not reasonably obtainable by the proponent of the statement" under division (A)(2) of this rule only if one or more of the following apply:

(1) The child refuses to testify concerning the subject matter of the statement or claims a lack of memory of the subject matter of the statement after a person trusted by the child, in the presence of the court, urges the child to both describe the acts described by the statement and to testify.

(2) The court finds all of the following:

(a) the child is absent from the trial or hearing;

(b) the proponent of the statement has been unable to procure the child's attendance or testimony by process or other reasonable means despite a good faith effort to do so;

(c) it is probable that the proponent would be unable to procure the child's testimony or attendance if the trial or hearing were delayed for a reasonable time.

(3) The court finds both of the following:

(a) the child is unable to testify at the trial or hearing because of death or then existing physical or mental illness or infirmity;

(b) the illness or infirmity would not improve sufficiently to permit the child to testify if the trial or hearing were delayed for a reasonable time.

The proponent of the statement has not established that the child's testimony or attendance is not reasonably obtainable if the child's refusal, claim of lack of memory, inability, or absence is due to the procurement or wrongdoing of the proponent of the statement for the purpose of preventing the child from attending or testifying.

(C) The court shall make the findings required by this rule on the basis of a hearing conducted outside the presence of the jury and shall make findings of fact, on the record, as to the bases for its ruling.

(Adopted eff. 7–1–91)

Article IX

AUTHENTICATION AND IDENTIFICATION

Evid R 901 Requirement of authentication or identification

(A) General provision

The requirement of authentication or identification as a condition precedent to admissibility is satisfied by evidence sufficient to support a finding that the matter in question is what its proponent claims.

(B) Illustrations

By way of illustration only, and not by way of limitation, the following are examples of authentication or identification conforming with the requirements of this rule:

(1) Testimony of witness with knowledge. Testimony that a matter is what it is claimed to be.

(2) Nonexpert opinion on handwriting. Nonexpert opinion as to the genuineness of handwriting, based upon familiarity not acquired for purposes of the litigation.

(3) Comparison by trier or expert witness. Comparison by the trier of fact or by expert witness with specimens which have been authenticated.

(4) Distinctive characteristics and the like. Appearance, contents, substance, internal patterns, or other distinctive characteristics, taken in conjunction with circumstances.

(5) Voice identification. Identification of a voice, whether heard firsthand or through mechanical or electronic transmission or recording, by opinion based upon hearing the voice at any time under circumstances connecting it with the alleged speaker.

(6) Telephone conversations. Telephone conversations, by evidence that a call was made to the number assigned at the time by the telephone company to a particular person or business, if (a) in the case of a person, circumstances, including self-identification, show the person answering to be the one called, or (b) in the case of a business, the call was made to a place of business and the conversation related to business reasonably transacted over the telephone.

(7) Public records or reports. Evidence that a writing authorized by law to be recorded or filed and in fact recorded or filed in a public office, or a purported public record, report, statement, or data compilation, in any form, is from the public office where items of this nature are kept.

(8) Ancient documents or data compilation. Evidence that a document or data compilation, in any form, (a) is in such condition as to create no suspicion concerning its authenticity, (b) was in a place where it, if authentic, would likely be, and (c) has been in existence twenty years or more at the time it is offered.

(9) Process or system. Evidence describing a process or system used to produce a result and showing that the process or system produces an accurate result.

(10) Methods provided by statute or rule. Any method of authentication or identification provided by statute enacted by the General Assembly not in conflict with a rule of the Supreme Court of Ohio or by other rules prescribed by the Supreme Court.

(Adopted eff. 7–1–80)

Evid R 902 Self–authentication

Extrinsic evidence of authenticity as a condition precedent to admissibility is not required with respect to the following:

(1) Domestic public documents under seal

A document bearing a seal purporting to be that of the United States, or of any State, district, Commonwealth, territory, or insular possession thereof, or the Panama Canal Zone, or the Trust Territory of the Pacific Islands, or of a political subdivision, department, officer, or agency thereof, and a signature purporting to be an attestation or execution.

(2) Domestic public documents not under seal

A document purporting to bear the signature in his official capacity of an officer or employee of any entity included in paragraph (1) hereof, having no seal, if a public officer having a seal and having official duties in the district or political subdivision of the officer or employee certifies under seal that the signer has the official capacity and that the signature is genuine.

(3) Foreign public documents

A document purporting to be executed or attested in his official capacity by a person authorized by the laws of a foreign country to make the execution or attestation, and accompanied by a final certification as to the genuineness of the signature and official position (a) of the executing or attesting person, or (b) of any foreign official whose certificate of genuineness of signature and official position relates to the execution or attestation or is in a chain of certificates of genuineness of signature and official position relating to the execution or attestation. A final certification may be made by a secretary of embassy or legation, consul general, consul, vice consul, or consular agent of the United States, or a diplomatic or consular official of the foreign country assigned or accredited to the United States. If reasonable opportunity has been given to all parties to investigate the authenticity and accuracy of official documents, the court may, for good cause shown, order that they be treated as presumptively authentic without final certification or permit them to be evidenced by an attested summary with or without final certification.

(4) Certified copies of public records

A copy of an official record or report or entry therein, or of a document authorized by law to be recorded or filed and actually recorded or filed in a public office, including data compilations in any form, certified as correct by the custodian or other person authorized to make the certification, by certificate complying with paragraph (1), (2), or (3) of this rule or complying with any law of a jurisdiction, state or federal, or rule prescribed by the Supreme Court of Ohio.

(5) Official publications.

Books, pamphlets, or other publications purporting to be issued by public authority.

(6) Newspapers and periodicals

Printed materials purporting to be newspapers or periodicals, including notices and advertisements contained therein.

(7) Trade inscriptions and the like

Inscriptions, signs, tags, or labels purporting to have been affixed in the course of business and indicating ownership, control, or origin.

(8) Acknowledged documents

Documents accompanied by a certificate of acknowledgment executed in the manner provided by law by a notary public or other officer authorized by law to take acknowledgments.

(9) Commercial paper and related documents

Commercial paper, signatures thereon, and documents relating thereto to the extent provided by general commercial law.

(10) Presumptions created by law

Any signature, document, or other matter declared by any law of a jurisdiction, state or federal, to be presumptively or prima facie genuine or authentic.

(Adopted eff. 7–1–80)

Evid R 903 Subscribing witness' testimony unnecessary

The testimony of a subscribing witness is not necessary to authenticate a writing unless required by the laws of the jurisdiction whose laws govern the validity of the writing.

(Adopted eff. 7–1–80)

Article X

CONTENTS OF WRITINGS, RECORDINGS AND PHOTOGRAPHS

Rule

Evid R 1001 Definitions

For purposes of this article the following definitions are applicable:

(1) Writings and recordings

"Writings" and "recordings" consist of letters, words, or numbers, or their equivalent, set down by handwriting, typewriting, printing, photostating, photographing, magnetic impulse, mechanical or electronic recording, or other forms of date [1] compilation.

(2) Photographs

"Photographs" include still photographs, X-ray films, video tapes, and motion pictures.

(3) Original

An "original" of a writing or recording is the writing or recording itself or any counterpart intended to have the same effect by a person executing or issuing it. An "original" of a photograph includes the negative or any print therefrom. If data are stored in a computer or similar device, any printout or other output readable by sight, shown to reflect the data accurately, is an "original".

(4) Duplicate

A "duplicate" is a counterpart produced by the same impression as the original, or from the same matrix, or by means of photography, including enlargements and miniatures, or by mechanical or electronic re-recording, or by chemical reproduction, or by other equivalent techniques which accurately reproduce the original.

(Adopted eff. 7–1–80)

[1] So in 62 OS(2d) li; federal rule reads "data."

Evid R 1002 Requirement of original

To prove the content of a writing, recording, or photograph, the original writing, recording, or photograph is required, except as otherwise provided in these rules or by statute enacted by the General Assembly not in conflict with a rule of the Supreme Court of Ohio.

(Adopted eff. 7–1–80)

Evid R 1003 Admissibility of duplicates

A duplicate is admissible to the same extent as an original unless (1) a genuine question is raised as to the authenticity of the original or (2) in the circumstances it would be unfair to admit the duplicate in lieu of the original.

(Adopted eff. 7–1–80)

Evid R 1004 Admissibility of other evidence of contents

The original is not required, and other evidence of the contents of a writing, recording, or photograph is admissible if:

(1) Originals lost or destroyed

All originals are lost or have been destroyed, unless the proponent lost or destroyed them in bad faith; or

(2) Original not obtainable

No original can be obtained by any available judicial process or procedure; or

(3) Original in possession of opponent

At a time when an original was under the control of the party against whom offered, he was put on notice, by the pleadings or otherwise, that the contents would be subject of proof at the hearing, and he does not produce the original at the hearing; or

(4) Collateral matters

The writing, recording, or photograph is not closely related to a controlling issue.

(Adopted eff. 7–1–80)

Evid R 1005 Public records

The contents of an official record, or of a document authorized to be recorded or filed and actually recorded or filed, including data compilations in any form if otherwise admissible, may be proved by copy, certified as correct in accordance with Rule 902, Civ. R. 44, Crim. R. 27 or testified to be correct by a witness who has compared it with the original. If a copy which complies with the foregoing cannot be obtained by the exercise of reasonable diligence, then other evidence of the contents may be given.

(Adopted eff. 7–1–80)

Evid R 1006 Summaries

The contents of voluminous writings, recordings, or photographs which cannot conveniently be examined in court may be presented in the form of a chart, summary, or calculation. The originals, or duplicates, shall be made available for examination or copying, or both, by other parties at a reasonable time and place. The court may order that they be produced in court.

(Adopted eff. 7–1–80)

Evid R 1007 Testimony or written admission of party

Contents of writings, recordings, or photographs may be proved by the testimony or deposition of the party against whom offered or by his written admission, without accounting for the nonproduction of the original.

(Adopted eff. 7–1–80)

Evid R 1008 Functions of court and jury

When the admissibility of other evidence of contents of writings, recordings, or photographs under these rules depends upon the fulfillment of a condition of fact, the question whether the condition has been fulfilled is ordinarily for the court to determine in accordance with the provisions of Rule 104. However, when an issue is raised (a) whether the asserted writing ever existed, or (b) whether another writing, recording, or photograph produced at the trial is the original, or (c) whether other evidence of contents correctly reflects the contents, the issue is for the trier of fact to determine as in the case of other issues of fact.

(Adopted eff. 7–1–80)

Article XI

MISCELLANEOUS RULES

Evid R 1101 [Reserved]

Evid R 1102 Effective date

(A) Effective date of rules

These rules shall take effect on the first day of July, 1980. They govern all proceedings in actions brought after they take effect and also all further proceedings in actions then pending, except to the extent that in the opinion of the court their application in a particular action pending when the rules take effect would not be feasible or would work injustice, in which event former evidentiary principles apply.

(B) Effective date of amendments

The amendments submitted by the Supreme Court to the General Assembly on January 14, 1981, and on April 29, 1981, shall take effect on July 1, 1981. They govern all proceedings in actions brought after they take effect and also all further proceedings in actions then pending, except to the extent that their application in a particular action pending when the amendments take effect would not be feasible or would work injustice, in which event the former procedure applies.

(C) Effective date of amendments

The amendments submitted by the Supreme Court to the General Assembly on January 12, 1990, and further revised and submitted on April 16, 1990, shall take effect on July 1, 1990. They govern all proceedings in actions brought after they take effect and also all further proceedings in actions then pending, except to the extent that their application in a particular action pending when the amendments take effect would not be feasible or would work injustice, in which event the former procedure applies.

(D) Effective date of amendments

The amendments submitted by the Supreme Court to the General Assembly on January 10, 1991 and further revised and submitted on April 29, 1991, shall take effect on July 1, 1991. They govern all proceedings in actions brought after they take effect and also all further proceedings in actions then pending, except to the extent that their application in a particular action pending when the amendments take effect would not be feasible or would work injustice, in which event the former procedure applies.

(E) Effective date of amendments

The amendments filed by the Supreme Court with the General Assembly on January 14, 1992 and further filed on April 30, 1992, shall take effect on July 1, 1992. They govern all proceedings in actions brought after they take effect and also all further proceedings in actions then pending, except to the extent that their application in a particular action pending when the amendments take effect would not be feasible or would work injustice, in which event the former procedure applies.

(F) Effective date of amendments

The amendments submitted by the Supreme Court to the General Assembly on January 8, 1993 and further filed on April 30, 1993 shall take effect on July 1, 1993. They govern all proceedings in actions brought after they take effect and also all further proceedings in actions then pending, except to the extent that their application in a particular action pending when the amendments take effect would not be feasible or would work injustice, in which event the former procedure applies.

(G) Effective date of amendments

The amendments submitted by the Supreme Court to the General Assembly on January 14, 1994 and further filed on April 29, 1994 shall take effect on July 1, 1994. They govern all proceedings in actions brought after they take effect and also all further proceedings in actions then pending, except to the extent that their application in a particular action pending when the amendments take effect would not be feasible or would work injustice, in which event the former procedure applies.

(H) Effective date of amendments

The amendments to Rules 101, 102 and 403 filed by the Supreme Court with the General Assembly on January 5, 1996 and refiled on April 26, 1996 shall take effect on July 1, 1996. They govern all proceedings in actions brought after they take effect and also all further proceedings in actions then pending, except to the extent that their application in a particular action pending when the amendments take effect would not be feasible or would work injustice, in which event the former procedure applies.

(I) Effective date of amendments

The amendments to Rules 607, 613, 616, 706, and 806 filed by the Supreme Court with the General Assembly on January 15, 1998 and further revised and refiled on April 30, 1998 shall take effect on July 1, 1998. They govern all proceedings in actions brought after they take effect and also all further proceedings in actions then pending, except to the extent that their application in a particular action pending when the amendments take effect would not be feasible or would work injustice, in which event the former procedure applies.

(J) Effective date of amendments

The amendments to Rules 101 and 1102(I) filed by the Supreme Court with the General Assembly on January 13, 1999 shall take effect on July 1, 1999. They govern all proceedings in actions brought after they take effect and also all further proceedings in actions then pending, except to the extent that their application in a particular action pending when the amendments take effect would not be feasible or would work injustice, in which event the former procedure applies.

(K) Effective date of amendments

The amendments to Evidence Rule 407 filed by the Supreme Court with the General Assembly on January 13, 2000 and refiled on April 27, 2000 shall take effect on July 1, 2000. They govern all proceedings in actions brought after they take effect and also all further proceedings in actions then pending, except to the extent that their application in a particular action pending when the amendments take effect would not be feasible or would work injustice, in which event the former procedure applies.

(L) Effective date of amendments

The amendments to Evidence Rules 615 and 804 filed by the Supreme Court with the General Assembly on January 12, 2001, and refiled on April 26, 2001, shall take effect on July 1, 2001. They govern all proceedings in actions brought after they take effect and also all further proceedings in actions then pending, except to the extent that their application in a particular action pending when the amendments take effect would not be feasible or would work injustice, in which event the former procedure applies.

(M) Effective date of amendments.

The amendments to Evidence Rules 609 and 615 filed by the Supreme Court with the General Assembly on January 9, 2003 and refiled on April 28, 2003, shall take effect on July 1, 2003. They govern all proceedings in actions brought after they take effect and also all further proceedings in actions then pending, except to the extent that their application in a particular action pending when the amendments take effect would not be feasible or would work injustice, in which event the former procedure applies.

(Adopted eff. 7–1–80; amended eff. 7–1–81 [1]*, 7–1–90, 7–1–91, 7–1–92, 7–1–93, 7–1–94, 7–1–96, 7–1–98, 7–1–99, 7–1–00, 7–1–01, 7–1–03)*

[1] Subdivision (B) was added in 1981 due to the amendment of Rule 804(B)(1) (former testimony exception to hearsay rule). See footnote to history of Evid R 804.

Evid R 1103 Title

These rules shall be known as the Ohio Rules of Evidence and may be cited as "Evidence Rules" or "Evid. R. ___."

(Adopted eff. 7–1–80)

OHIO TRAFFIC RULES

Rule

Traf R 1 Scope of rules; applicability; authority and construction

(A) Applicability

These rules prescribe the procedure to be followed in all courts of this state in traffic cases and supersede the "Ohio Rules of Practice and Procedure in Traffic Cases For All Courts Inferior To Common Pleas" effective January 1, 1969, and as amended on January 4, 1971, and December 7, 1972.

(B) Authority and construction

These rules are promulgated pursuant to authority granted the Supreme Court by R.C. 2935.17 and 2937.46. They shall be construed and applied to secure the fair, impartial, speedy and sure administration of justice, simplicity and uniformity in procedure, and the elimination of unjustifiable expense and delay.

(Adopted eff. 1–1–75)

Traf R 2 Definitions

As used in these rules:

(A) "Traffic case" means any proceeding, other than a proceeding resulting from a felony indictment, that involves one or more violations of a law, ordinance, or regulation governing the operation and use of vehicles, conduct of pedestrians in relation to vehicles, or weight, dimension, loads or equipment, or vehicles drawn or moved on highways and bridges. "Traffic case" does not include any proceeding that results in a felony indictment.

(B) "Traffic ticket" means the traffic complaint and summons described in Traffic Rule 3 and that appears in the Appendix of Forms.

(C) "Highway" includes a street or an alley.

(D) "Petty offense" means an offense for which the penalty prescribed by law includes confinement for six months or less.

(E) "Serious offense" means an offense for which the penalty prescribed by law includes confinement for more than six months.

(F) "Court" means a municipal court, county court, juvenile division of the court of common pleas, or mayor's court.

(G) "Judge" means judge of a municipal court, county court, or juvenile division of the court of common pleas, or a mayor or mayor's court magistrate presiding over a mayor's court.

(H) "Prosecuting attorney" means the attorney general of this state, the prosecuting attorney of a county, the law director, city solicitor, or other officer who prosecutes a criminal case on behalf of the state or a city, village, township, or other political subdivision, and the assistant or assistants of any of them.

(I) "State" means this state, a county, city, village, township, other political subdivision or any other entity of this state that may prosecute a criminal action.

(J) "Clerk of court" means the duly elected or appointed clerk of any court of record, or the deputy of any of them, and either the mayor of a municipal corporation having a mayor's court or any clerk appointed by the mayor.

(K) "Review Commission" means the committee appointed by the Supreme Court to study and consider the application and administration of these rules.

(Adopted eff. 1–1–75; amended eff. 2–1–02)

Traf R 3 Complaint and summons; form; use

(A) Traffic complaint and summons

In traffic cases, the complaint and summons shall be the "Ohio Uniform Traffic Ticket" as set out in the Appendix of Forms.

(B) Traffic complaint and summons form

The Ohio Uniform Traffic Ticket shall consist of four sheets, padded together and bound at the top or bottom edge. Each sheet shall be four and one-fourth inches in width and nine and one-half inches in length from a perforation below the binding to the bottom edge. The first sheet shall be white and the second sheet shall be canary yellow. Where an additional copy is needed by an agency, it may be added. The first and second sheets shall be at least fifteen pound paper.

The first sheet shall be the court record.

The second sheet shall be the abstract of court record for the Bureau of Motor Vehicles as required by section 4507.021 of the Revised Code. The second sheet may be omitted from the Ticket if the court reports violations to the Bureau by electronic or other means acceptable to the Bureau.

The third sheet shall be the defendant's copy.

The fourth sheet shall be the enforcement agency record.

A wrap-around may be added to the first sheet. The issuing authority may use the front and back of the wrap-around for any data or information it may require.

Each ticket sheet shall be perforated tab bound at the edge or end with carbon paper interleaved so that all carbon paper is securely bound to the tab and removable with it, or shall be on treated paper so that marking from the top sheet is transferred legibly to successive sheets in the group.

(C) Use of ticket

The Ohio Uniform Traffic Ticket shall be used in all moving traffic cases, but its use for parking and equipment violations is optional in each local jurisdiction. Any ticket properly issued to a law enforcement officer shall be accepted for filing and disposition in any court having jurisdiction over the offense alleged. An officer may include more than one alleged violation on a single ticket provided the alleged violations are numbered sequentially on the face of the ticket. An officer who completes a ticket at the scene of an alleged offense shall not be required to rewrite or type a new complaint as a condition of filing the ticket, unless the original complaint is illegible or does not state an offense. If a new complaint is executed, a copy shall be served upon defendant as soon as possible.

(D) Issuance of tickets to enforcement agency

The judge in a single-judge court, and the administrative judge in multi-judge courts, shall designate the issuing authority for tickets and prescribe the conditions of issuance and accountability. The issuing authority may be the clerk of the court, the violations clerk, or the enforcement agency of the municipality.

When a single enforcement agency, except the State Highway Patrol, regularly has cases in more than one court, the ticket used by the agency shall be issued through the court for adults in the most populous area in the jurisdiction of the agency. Tickets used by the State Highway Patrol shall be issued by the Superintendent of the State Highway Patrol.

(E) Duty of law enforcement officer

A law enforcement officer who issues a ticket shall complete and sign the ticket, serve a copy of the completed ticket upon defendant, and, without unnecessary delay, file the court copy with the court.

The officer shall notify defendant that if defendant does not appear at the time and place stated in the citation or comply with division (C) of section 2935.26 of the Revised Code, defendant's license will be cancelled, defendant will not be eligible for the reissuance of the license or the issuance of a new license for one year after cancellation, and defendant will be subject to any applicable criminal penalties.

(F) Use of electronically produced tickets

(1) Local rules adopted pursuant to the Supreme Court Rules of Superintendence for the Courts of Ohio may provide for the use of a ticket that is produced by computer or other electronic means, provided that the ticket conforms in all substantive respects, including layout and content, to the "Ohio Uniform Traffic Ticket" set forth in the Appendix of Forms. The provisions of division (B) of this rule relative to the color and weight of paper and method of binding shall not be applicable to a ticket that is produced by computer or other electronic means.

(2) Local rules adopted pursuant to the Supreme Court Rules of Superintendence for the Courts of Ohio may provide for the filing of the ticket by electronic means. If a ticket is issued at the scene of an alleged offense, the local rule shall require that the issuing officer provide the defendant with a paper copy of the ticket as required by division (E) of this rule. A law enforcement officer who files a ticket electronically shall be considered to have certified the ticket and shall have the same rights, responsibilities, and liabilities as with all other tickets issued pursuant to these rules.

(Adopted eff. 1-1-75; amended eff. 8-4-80, 2-26-90, 11-28-90, 6-1-92, 2-1-02)

Traf R 4 Bail and security

(A) Posting of bail; depositing of security

The posting of bail or the depositing of security is for the purpose of securing appearance or compliance with R.C. 2935.26(C) only. The forfeiture of the bail or security is not a substitute for appearance in court, compliance with R.C. 2935.26(C), and payment of penalty imposed on plea of [sic.] finding of guilty.

(B) Bail and security procedure

Criminal Rule 46 governs bail in traffic cases. In addition, the provisions of R.C. 2937.221 and R.C. 2935.27 apply in traffic cases.

(Adopted eff. 1-1-75; amended eff. 8-4-80)

Traf R 5 Joinder of offense and defendants; consolidation for trial; relief from prejudicial joinder

Criminal Rules 8, 13 and 14 govern joinder of offenses and defendants, consolidation of cases for trial and relief from prejudicial joinder in traffic cases.

(Adopted eff. 1-1-75)

Traf R 6 Summons, warrants: form, service and execution

(A) Form

The form of summons and warrants, other than the ticket, shall be as prescribed in Criminal Rule 4.

(B) Service and execution

Summons, other than the ticket, and warrants shall be served and executed as prescribed by Criminal Rule 4.

(Adopted eff. 1-1-75)

Traf R 7 Procedure upon failure to appear

(A) Issuance of summons, warrant

When a defendant fails to appear pursuant to a ticket issued to him, the court shall issue a supplemental summons or warrant.

If a supplemental summons is not served or a warrant is not executed within twenty-eight days of receipt by the serving officer, the court may place the case in a file of cases disposed of subject to being reopened. Where bond is forfeited, the disposition shall be reported to the Registrar of Motor Vehicles. For all other purposes, including disposition reports, the cases shall be reported as disposed of, subject to being reopened, if defendant subsequently appears or is apprehended.

(B) Issuance of notice to nonresident

When a nonresident of this state fails to appear pursuant to a supplemental summons or a warrant issued under division (A), the court may send by ordinary mail to defendant's address as it appears on the ticket, or the summons or warrant return, a notice ordering defendant to appear at a specified time and place.

If defendant fails to appear or answer within twenty-eight days after the date of mailing of the notice, the court shall place the case in the file of cases disposed of subject to being reopened.

The mailing of notice in parking cases is discretionary with the court.

(C) Effect of waiting periods and bail forfeiture

The waiting period prescribed in division (A) does not affect forfeiture of bail.

If there is a breach of a condition of bail, the court shall declare a forfeiture of bail. Forfeiture proceedings shall be promptly enforced as provided by law.

If defendant fails to appear at the time and place specified on the citation and fails to comply with division (C) of Section 2935.26 of the Revised Code, or fails to comply with or satisfy any judgment of the court within the time allowed, the court shall declare the forfeiture of defendant's license. Thirty days after the declaration, the court shall forward a copy of the declaration to the Registrar of Motor Vehicles for cancellation in accordance with division (D) of Section 2935.27 of the Revised Code. If defendant deposits a sum of money or other security with the court, the deposit immediately shall be forfeited to the court if he fails to appear or comply with division (C) of Section 2935.26 of the Revised Code.

(Adopted eff. 1–1–75; amended eff. 8–4–80, 11–28–90)

Traf R 8 Arraignment

(A) Arraignment time

Where practicable, every defendant shall be arraigned before contested matters are taken up. Trial may be conducted immediately following arraignment.

(B) Arraignment procedure

Arraignment shall be conducted in open court and shall consist of reading the complaint to the defendant, or stating to him the substance of the charge, and calling on him to plead thereto. The defendant shall be given a copy of the complaint, or shall acknowledge receipt thereof, before being called upon to plead and may in open court waive the reading of the complaint.

(C) Presence of defendant

The defendant must be present at the arraignment, but the court may allow the defendant to enter a not guilty plea at the clerk's office in person, by his attorney in person, or by his attorney by mail, within four days after receipt of the ticket by the defendant.

(D) Explanation of rights

Before calling upon a defendant to plead at arraignment the judge shall cause him to be informed and shall determine that defendant knows and understands:

(1) That he has a right to counsel and the right to a reasonable continuance in the proceedings to secure counsel, and, pursuant to Criminal Rule 44, the right to have counsel assigned without cost to himself if he is unable to employ counsel;

(2) That he has a right to bail as provided in Rule 4;

(3) That he need make no statement at any point in the proceeding; but any statement made may be used against him;

(4) That he has, where such right exists, a right to jury trial and that he must, in petty offense cases, make a demand for a jury pursuant to Criminal Rule 23;

(5) That if he is convicted a record of the conviction will be sent to the Bureau of Motor Vehicles and become part of his driving record.

(E) Joint arraignment

If there are multiple defendants to be arraigned, the judge may advise, or cause them to be advised, of their rights by general announcement.

(Adopted eff. 1–1–75)

Traf R 9 Jury demand

(A) Jury demand

Jury demands shall be made pursuant to Criminal Rule 23.

(B) Jury demands in mayor's court

Where, in a mayor's court, a defendant is entitled to a jury trial and a jury demand is made pursuant to Criminal Rule 23, the mayor shall transfer the case pursuant to subdivision (C).

If a jury demand is not made pursuant to Criminal Rule 23, and the defendant waives his right to jury trial in writing, a mayor may try the case if (1) his compensation as a judge is not directly dependent upon criminal case convictions, or (2) he is not the chief executive and administrative officer of the municipality and as such responsible for the financial condition of the municipality. Guilty and no contest pleas may be taken by any mayor, including mayors whose compensation as a judge is directly dependent upon criminal case convictions and mayors who as chief executive and administrative officer of the municipality are responsible for the financial condition of the municipality.

(C) Transfer

Where transfer is required, the mayor's court shall make a written order directing the defendant to appear at the transferee court, continuing the same bail, if any, and making appearance before the transferee court a condition of bail, if any. Upon transfer, the mayor's court shall transmit to the clerk of the transferee court the ticket and all other papers in the case, and any bail taken in the case.

Upon receipt of such papers the clerk of the transferee court shall set the case for trial and shall notify the defendant by ordinary mail of his trial date.

(Adopted eff. 1–1–75)

Traf R 10 Pleas; rights upon plea

(A) Pleas

A defendant may plead not guilty, guilty or, with the consent of the court, no contest. All pleas may be made orally. If a defendant refuses to plead, the court shall enter a plea of not guilty on behalf of the defendant.

(B) Effect of guilty or no contest pleas

With reference to the offense or offenses to which the plea is entered:

(1) The plea of guilty is a complete admission of the defendant's guilt.

(2) The plea of no contest is not an admission of defendant's guilt, but is an admission of the truth of the facts alleged in the complaint and such plea or admission shall not be used against the defendant in any subsequent civil or criminal proceeding.

(3) When a plea of guilty or no contest is accepted pursuant to this rule, the court shall proceed with sentencing under Criminal Rule 32.

(C) Misdemeanor cases involving serious offenses

In misdemeanor cases involving serious offenses, the court may refuse to accept a plea of guilty or no contest and shall not accept such plea without first addressing the defendant personally and informing him of the effect of the pleas of guilty, no contest, and not guilty and determining that he is making the plea voluntarily. Where the defendant is unrepresented by counsel, the court shall not accept a plea of guilty or no contest unless the defendant, after being readvised that he has the right to be represented by retained counsel, or pursuant to Criminal Rule 44 by appointed counsel, waives this right.

(D) Misdemeanor cases involving petty offenses

In misdemeanor cases involving petty offenses, except those processed in a traffic violations bureau, the court may refuse to accept a plea of guilty or no contest and shall not accept such pleas without first informing the defendant of the effect of the plea of guilty, no contest, and not guilty.

The counsel provisions of Criminal Rule 44(B), (C) and (D) apply to this subdivision.

(E) Refusal of court to accept plea

If the court refuses to accept a plea of guilty or no contest, the court shall enter a plea of not guilty on behalf of the defendant. In such cases neither plea shall be admissible in evidence nor be the subject of comment by the prosecuting attorney or court.

(F) Immediate trial

Upon written consent of defendant and the prosecuting attorney, trial may be conducted immediately after the acceptance of a plea at arraignment. If the defendant seeks a continuance, or demands a jury trial where such right exists, the court shall cause the case to be set for trial.

(Adopted eff. 1–1–75)

Traf R 11 Pleadings and motions before plea and trial: defenses and objections

(A) Pleadings and motions

Pleadings in traffic cases shall be the complaint, the pleas of not guilty, guilty, and no contest. Defenses and objections shall be raised before plea and trial by motion to dismiss or to grant appropriate relief.

(B) Motions before plea and trial

Any defense, objection, or request which is capable of determination without the trial of the general issue may be raised before plea or trial by motion.

(1) The following defenses and objections must be raised before plea:

(a) Defenses and objections based on defects in the institution of the prosecution;

(b) Defenses and objections based on defects in the complaint other than failure to show jurisdiction in the court or to charge an offense, which objections shall be noticed by the court at any time during the pendency of the proceeding.

(2) The following motions and requests must be made before trial:

(a) Motions to suppress evidence, including but not limited to identification testimony, on the ground that it was illegally obtained;

(b) Requests and motions for discovery under Criminal Rule 16;

(c) Motions for severance of charges or defendants under Criminal Rule 14.

(C) Motion date

Pre-plea motions shall be made before or at arraignment.

All pretrial motions, except as provided in Criminal Rule 16(F), shall be made within thirty-five days after arraignment or seven days before trial, whichever is earlier. The court, in the interest of justice, may extend the time for making pre-plea or pretrial motions.

(D) Disclosure of evidence by prosecuting attorney

At the arraignment, or as soon thereafter as is practicable, the defendant may, in order to raise objections prior to trial under subsection (B)(2), request notice of the prosecuting attorney's intention to use evidence in chief at trial, which evidence the defendant is entitled to discover under Criminal Rule 16.

(E) Ruling on motion

A motion made before trial, other than a motion for change of venue, shall be timely determined before trial. Where factual issues are involved in determining a motion, the court shall state its essential findings on the record.

(F) Effect of failure to raise defenses or objections

Failure by the defendant to raise defenses or objections or to make motions and requests which must be made prior to plea, trial, or at the time set by the court pursuant to subdivision (C), or prior to any extension thereof made by the court, shall constitute waiver thereof, but the court for good cause shown may grant relief from the waiver.

(G) Effect of plea of no contest

The plea of no contest does not preclude a defendant from asserting upon appeal that the trial court prejudicially erred in ruling on a pretrial motion, including a pretrial motion to suppress evidence.

(H) Effect of determination

If the court grants a motion to dismiss based on a defect in the institution of the prosecution or in the complaint, the court shall dismiss the case unless the prosecuting attorney can, pursuant to Criminal Rule 7(D), amend the complaint.

(I) State's right of appeal

The state, pursuant to Criminal Rule 12(J), may take an appeal as of right in cases where the defendant is charged with an offense listed in Rule 13(B)(1) and (3).

(Adopted eff. 1–1–75)

Traf R 12 Receipt of guilty plea

The pleas of guilty and no contest shall be received only by personal appearance of the defendant in open court, except that, the plea of guilty may be received in accordance with Rule 13 at a regularly established traffic violations bureau. Upon the showing of exceptional circumstances by written motion, a court may receive a guilty or no contest plea in such manner as it deems just.

The receipt of a plea contrary to the provisions of these rules is forbidden.

(Adopted eff. 1–1–75)

Traf R 13 Traffic violations bureau

(A) Establishment and operation of traffic violations bureau

Each court shall establish a traffic violations bureau. The juvenile division of the court of common pleas may establish a violations bureau pursuant to Traffic Rule 13.1. The court shall appoint its clerk as violations clerk. If there is no clerk, the court shall appoint any appropriate person of the municipality or county in which the court sits. The violations bureau and violations clerk shall be under the direction and control of the court. Fines and costs shall be paid to, receipted by, and accounted for by the violations clerk.

The violations bureau shall accept appearance, waiver of trial, plea of guilty, and payment of fine and costs for offenses within its authority.

(B) Authority of violations bureau

All traffic offenses except those listed in division (B)(1) to (9) of this rule may be disposed of by a traffic violations bureau. The following traffic offenses shall not be processed by a traffic violations bureau:

(1) Indictable offenses;

(2) Operating a motor vehicle while under the influence of alcohol or any drug of abuse;

(3) Leaving the scene of an accident;

(4) Driving while under suspension or revocation of a driver's license;

(5) Driving without being licensed to drive, except where the driver's or commercial driver's license had been expired for six months or less;

(6) A third moving traffic offense within a twelve-month period;

(7) Failure to stop and remain standing upon meeting or overtaking a school bus stopped on the highway for the purpose of receiving or discharging a school child;

(8) Willfully eluding or fleeing a police officer;

(9) Drag racing.

(C) Schedule of fines

The court shall establish and publish a schedule of fines and costs for all offenses. The schedule shall be distributed to all law enforcement agencies operating within the jurisdiction of the court and shall be prominently displayed at the place in the violations bureau where fines are paid.

(D) Defendant's appearance, plea and waiver of trial

(1) Within seven days after the date of issuance of the ticket, a defendant charged with an offense that can be processed by a traffic violations bureau may do either of the following:

(a) Appear in person at the traffic violations bureau, sign a plea of guilty and waiver of trial provision of the ticket, and pay the total amount of the fine and costs;

(b) Sign the guilty plea and waiver of trial provision of the ticket and mail the ticket and a check, money order, or other approved form of payment for the total amount of the fine and costs to the traffic violations bureau;

(2) A court may establish a procedure for accepting, through its traffic violations bureau, guilty pleas, waivers of trial, and payments of fines and costs by telephone or other electronic means. The form of payment accepted by telephone or other electronic means shall be approved by the bureau.

(3) Remittance of the fine and costs to the traffic violations bureau by any means other than personal appearance by the defendant at the bureau constitutes a guilty plea and waiver of trial whether or not the guilty plea and waiver of trial provision of the ticket are signed by the defendant.

(E) Records

All cases processed in the violations bureau shall be numbered and recorded for identification and statistical purposes. In any statistical reports required by law, the number of cases disposed of by the violations bureau shall be listed separately from those disposed of in open court.

(F) Hours of operation; personnel

The court shall appoint a law enforcement officer as a deputy violations bureau clerk to act as violations clerk when the violations clerk is not on duty.

(Adopted eff. 1–1–75; amended eff. 8–4–80, 2–26–90, 11–1–94, 7–1–97, 5–3–99, 2–1–02)

Traf R 13.1 Juvenile traffic violations bureau

(A) By local rule of court, the juvenile division of the court of common pleas may establish a violations bureau for juvenile traffic offenders. Except as provided in division (B) of this rule, a juvenile traffic violations bureau shall function in the same manner as a violations bureau established pursuant to Traffic Rule 13.

(B) All juvenile traffic offenses may be disposed of by a violations bureau, except as follows:

(1) An offense listed in Traffic Rule 13(B)(1) to (5) and (7) to (9);

(2) A second or subsequent moving offense;

(3) An offense that involves an accident.

(Adopted eff. 2–1–02)

Traf R 14 Magistrates

(A) A court may appoint one or more magistrates for the purpose of receiving pleas, determining guilt or innocence, receiving statements in explanation and in mitigation of sentence, and recommending penalty to be imposed.

A magistrate shall be an attorney admitted to practice in Ohio. A magistrate shall be provided with court room accommodations resembling as nearly as possible traffic court rooms.

(B) A court may refer nonjury traffic cases to a magistrate. If the offense charged is an offense for which imprisonment is a possible penalty, the case may be referred only with the unanimous consent of the parties, in writing or on the record in open court. The consent of an alleged juvenile traffic offender or his or her parent, guardian, or custodian shall not be required.

(C) Proceedings before the magistrate shall be conducted as provided in Criminal Rule 19(D) and (E). A defendant's payment of a fine does not constitute a waiver of the defendant's right to file objections to the magistrate's decision.

(Adopted eff. 1–1–75; amended eff. 9–1–96, 2–1–02)

Traf R 15 Violation of rules

(A) Failure to apply rules

Any willful failure to apply these rules, including the failure to amend or rescind inconsistent local court rules or the continued participation in practices expressly forbidden in these rules, by a judge, clerk or other personnel may be considered a contempt of the Supreme Court and may be punished as such. Proceedings in contempt under this rule can be instituted only with leave of the Supreme Court.

(B) Improper disposition of ticket

Any person who disposes of a ticket, or who solicits or knowingly aids in the disposition of a ticket, in any manner other than that authorized by these rules may be proceeded against for criminal contempt in the manner provided by law.

(Adopted eff. 1–1–75; amended eff. 8–4–80)

Traf R 16 Judicial conduct

The Code of Judicial Conduct as adopted by the Supreme Court applies to all judges and mayors.

It shall be the obligation of each mayor to conduct his court and his professional and personal relationships in accordance with the same standards as are required of judges of courts of record.

(Adopted eff. 1–1–75; amended eff. 2–1–02)

Traf R 17 Traffic case scheduling

(A) Separate trial

Traffic cases shall be tried separately from other cases except upon good cause shown.

(B) Arraignment and trial by traffic division

Where a court sits in divisions and one division is designated as traffic court, all traffic defendants shall, where practicable, be arraigned and tried in such division.

(C) Arraignment and trial by traffic session

Where a court not sitting in separate divisions designates a particular session as a traffic session, traffic defendants shall, where practicable, be arraigned and tried at such session.

(D) Single–judge courts

In single-judge courts, traffic cases shall, where practicable, be called before nontraffic cases. Uncontested traffic cases shall be disposed of first and contested cases scheduled for later hearing.

(Adopted eff. 1–1–75)

Traf R 18 Continuances

Continuances shall be granted only upon a written motion which states the grounds for the requested continuance.

When a court grants a continuance, it shall set a definite date for the hearing or trial.

(Adopted eff. 1–1–75)

Traf R 19 Rule of court

The expression "rule of court" as used in these rules means a rule promulgated by the Supreme Court or a rule concerning local practice adopted by another court and filed with the Supreme Court. Local rules shall be supplementary to and consistent with these rules. Each court shall publish its local rules, distribute them within its jurisdiction, and keep copies for inspection.

(Adopted eff. 1–1–75)

Traf R 20 Procedure not otherwise specified

If no procedure is specifically prescribed by these rules, the Rules of Criminal Procedure and the applicable law apply.

(Adopted eff. 1–1–75)

Traf R 21 Forms

The forms contained in the Appendix of Forms are mandatory, except that additional copies of any portions of the ticket may be made. The reverse of the enforcement agency record shall be in the form prescribed by the issuing authority.

(Adopted eff. 1–1–75)

Traf R 22 Review commission

(A) Duties of review commission

All comments and suggestions concerning the application, administration and amendment of these rules, including the Appendix of Forms, shall be submitted to the Review Commission. The Review Commission shall consider all comments and suggestions and submit its recommendations to the Supreme Court.

(B) Appointment, term and membership

The Review Commission shall be appointed by the Supreme Court and shall be composed of thirteen members who shall serve without compensation, but who may be reimbursed for expenses incurred in the performance of their duties. All appointments to the Review Commission shall be for three-year terms, except that the Superintendent of the State Highway Patrol, and the Chairman of the Traffic Law Committee of the Ohio State Bar Association, and the Director of the Department of Public Safety shall serve on the Review Commission for as long as the person holds the position of Superintendent of the State Highway Patrol, Chairman of the Traffic Law Committee of the Ohio State Bar Association, or the Director of Public Safety. Their successors shall become members of the Review Commission on the day they assume the position of Superintendent of the State Highway Patrol, Chairman of the Traffic Law Committee of the Ohio State Bar Association, or the Director of Public Safety.

The membership of the Commission shall include: a court of common pleas judge, a municipal court judge, a county court judge, a municipal court clerk, the Superintendent of the State Highway Patrol, and the Chairman of the Traffic Law Committee of the Ohio State Bar Association, and the Director of the Department of Public Safety or his or her designee. The Chairman of the Commission shall be designated by the Supreme Court and shall serve for a period of three years.

(C) Meetings

The Review Commission shall meet upon the call of the chairman. Meetings may be held anywhere in Ohio.

(Adopted eff. 1–1–75; amended eff. 7–27–88, 12–5–89, 9–19–94)

Traf R 23 Title

These rules shall be known as the Ohio Traffic Rules and may be cited as "Traffic Rules" or "Traf. R. _____."

(Adopted eff. 1–1–75)

Traf R 24 Effective date

(A) Effective date of rules

These rules take effect on January 1, 1975. They govern all proceedings in actions brought after they take effect, and also all further proceedings in actions then pending, except to the extent that their application in a particular action pending when the rules take effect would not be feasible or would work injustice, in which event the former procedure applies.

(B) Use of tickets conforming to prior rules

Traffic tickets conforming to the requirements of the "Ohio Rules of Practice and Procedure in Traffic Cases For All Courts Inferior to Common Pleas" may be used after the effective date of these rules.

After the effective date of these rules, issuing authorities shall order only tickets conforming to these rules.

(Adopted eff. 1–1–75)

Traf R 25 Effective date of amendments

(A) The amendments to these rules and the Uniform Traffic Ticket adopted by the Supreme Court of Ohio on June 17, 1980 shall take effect on August 4, 1980.

(B) The amendments to the Uniform Traffic Ticket shall take effect on September 15, 1985. The amendment to Traffic Rule 22 shall take effect on July 27, 1988.

(C) The amendment to Traffic Rule 22, adopted by the Supreme Court on December 5, 1989, shall take effect on December 5, 1989.

(D) The amendments to Traffic Rules 3, 13, and 25, and the Uniform Traffic Ticket, adopted by the Supreme Court of Ohio on February 13, 1990, shall take effect on February 26, 1990.

(E) The amendments to Traffic Rules 3 and 7, adopted by the Supreme Court of Ohio on November 20, 1990, shall take effect on November 28, 1990.

(F) The amendments to Traffic Rule 3 and to the "Reverse of Defendant's Copy" of the Uniform Traffic Ticket, adopted by the Supreme Court of Ohio on March 16, 1992, shall take effect on June 1, 1992.

(G) The amendments to Traffic Rule 22, adopted by the Supreme Court of Ohio on August 17, 1994, shall take effect on September 19, 1994. The amendments to Traffic Rule 13 and to the Uniform Traffic Ticket, adopted by the Supreme Court of Ohio on August 17, 1994, shall take effect on November 1, 1994.

(H) The amendments to Traffic Rule 14, adopted by the Supreme Court of Ohio on July 10, 1996, shall take effect on September 1, 1996.

(I)(1) The amendments to Traffic Rule 13, adopted by the Supreme Court of Ohio on March 31, 1997, shall take effect on July 1, 1997.

(2) The amendments to the Uniform Traffic Ticket, adopted by the Supreme Court of Ohio on March 31, 1997, shall take effect on July 1, 1997. Through June 30, 1998, jurisdictions may use tickets printed in the format that was authorized prior to July 1, 1997. All tickets ordered for use on or after July 1, 1997 and all tickets used on or after July 1, 1998 shall conform to the format of the July 1, 1997 Uniform Traffic Ticket.

(J) The amendments to Traffic Rule 13, adopted by the Supreme Court of Ohio on March 30, 1999, shall take effect on May 3, 1999.

(K) The amendments to Traffic Rules 2, 3, 13, 13.1, 14, 16, and 25, adopted by the Supreme Court of Ohio on December 11, 2001, shall take effect on February 1, 2002.

(Adopted eff. 8–4–80; amended eff. 2–26–90, 11–28–90, 6–1–92, 9–19–94, 11–1–94, 9–1–96, 7–1–97, 5–3–99, 2–1–02)

Traf R Temp **Temporary provision**

A law enforcement officer who issues an automated traffic ticket is considered to have signed the ticket, for purposes of Traffic Rule 3(E), if the issuing officer properly authorizes the appearance of his or her facsimile signature on the ticket.

For purposes of this Temporary Provision:

(A) "Automated traffic ticket" means the computerized traffic citation developed by the Office of Criminal Justice Services, Ohio Highway Patrol, and local law enforcement agencies and courts and being used on a pilot project basis by the Licking County Sheriff's Office, Newark Police Department, Heath Police Department, Licking County Municipal Court, Circleville Police Department, Pickaway County Sheriff's Office, Circleville Municipal Court, the Circleville Post of the Ohio Highway Patrol, the Newark Post of the Ohio Highway Patrol, and the General Headquarters of the Ohio Highway Patrol.

(B) "Properly authorizes" means the issuing officer uses a secure password, in the manner demonstrated to the Traffic Rules Review Commission at its December 18, 1998 meeting, that, when entered, allows an electronic version of the his or her signature to appear on the automated traffic ticket and on any printed version of that ticket.

(Adopted eff. 1–12–99)

Multi–Count Uniform Traffic Ticket

_______________ COURT _______________ COUNTY, OHIO

STATE OF OHIO _______________
☐ City ☐ Village ☐ Township

TICKET NO. _______________

CASE NO. _______________

NAME _______________

STREET _______________

CITY, STATE _______________ ZIP _______________

LICENSE ISSUED MO. ____ YR. ____ EXPIRES BIRTHDATE 19 ____ STATE _______________

SSN | | | - | | - | | | | D.O.B.: MO. ____ DAY ____ YR. ____

RACE	SEX	HEIGHT	WEIGHT	HAIR	EYES

FINANCIAL RESPONSIBILITY PROOF SHOWN ☐ Yes ☐ No

LICENSE NO. _______________

Lic. Class _______________ DOT # _______________ ☐ Does Not Apply

TO DEFENDANT: COMPLAINT

ON _______________, 19 ____ AT ____ M. YOU/OPERATED/PARKED/WALKED/ A
☐ Pass ☐ Comm. ☐ Cycle ☐ Over 26001 ☐ Bus ☐ Haz. Mat.

VEHICLE: YR. ____ MAKE ____ BODY TYPE _______________

COLOR _______________ LIC. _______________ STATE ____

UPON A PUBLIC HIGHWAY, NAMELY _______________

AT/BETWEEN _______________ (M.P. ____)

IN THE ____ OF _______________ IN _______________

COUNTY (NO. ____), STATE OF OHIO AND COMMITTED THE FOLLOWING OFFENSE(S).

SPEED: ____ MPH in ____ MPH zone ☐ ORC ☐ ORD ☐ T.P.
☐ Over limits ☐ Unsafe for cond. ☐ ACDA
☐ Radar ☐ Air ☐ VASCAR ☐ Pace ☐ Laser ☐ Stationary ☐ Moving

OMVI: ☐ Under the influence of alcohol/drug of abuse ☐ ORC ☐ ORD ☐ T.P.
☐ Prohibited blood alcohol concentration ____ BAC
☐ Blood ☐ Breath ☐ Urine ☐ Refused

DRIVER LICENSE: ☐ None ☐ Revoked ☐ Suspended ☐ ORC ☐ ORD ☐ T.P.
☐ Not on person Expired: ☐ 6 mos. or less ☐ Over 6 mos.
Suspension Type _______________

SAFETY BELT — Failure to wear ☐ ORC ☐ ORD ☐ T.P.
☐ Driver ☐ Passenger ☐ Child Restraint

OTHER OFFENSE _______________ ☐ ORC ☐ ORD ☐ T.P.

OTHER OFFENSE _______________ ☐ ORC ☐ ORD ☐ T.P.

☐ DRIVER LICENSE HELD ☐ VEHICLE SEIZED ARREST CODE ____

☐ PAVEMENT: ☐ Dry ☐ Wet ☐ Snow ☐ Icy # of Lanes ____ ☐ Const. Zone

☐ VISIBILITY: ☐ Clear ☐ Cloudy ☐ Dusk ☐ Night

☐ WEATHER: ☐ Rain ☐ Snow ☐ Fog ☐ No Adverse

☐ TRAFFIC: ☐ Heavy ☐ Moderate ☐ Light ☐ None

☐ AREA: ☐ Business ☐ Rural ☐ Residential ☐ Industry ☐ School

☐ CRASH. ☐ Yes ☐ No ☐ Almost Caused ☐ Injury ☐ Non-Injury ☐ Fatal
☐ Crash Report Number:

☐ REMARKS

ACCOMPANYING CRIMINAL CHARGE ☐ Yes ☐ No TOTAL # OFFENSES ____

PRESENT ADDRESS _______________ SIGNATURE _______________ CO. RES. _______________ PHONE ( )

TO DEFENDANT: SUMMONS ☐ PERSONAL APPEARANCE REQUIRED

You are summoned and ordered to appear at _______________ Court

_______________ at ____ M.,

____ 19 ____. If you fail to appear at this time and place you may be arrested or your license may be cancelled.

This summons served personally on the defendant on _______________ 19 ____
The issuing-charging law enforcement officer states under the penalties of perjury and falsification that he/she has read the above complaint and that it is true.

____
Issuing-Charging Law Enforcement Officer

Court Code	Unit	Post	Dist.

NOTE: ISSUING OFFICER BE SURE TO VERIFY ADDRESS, IF DIFFERENT FROM LICENSE ADDRESS WRITE PRESENT ADDRESS IN SPACE PROVIDED

OSHP HP7

OHP0060 10-006000 (REVISION 9-1-96) COURT RECORD (B6305)

Docket No. ______________ Page No. ______ Case No. ______________

Defendant's Attorney ____
Name - Address - Telephone

DATE	COURT ACTION: ORDERS
	BAIL
	☐ NO BAIL - DEFENDANT CITED AND RELEASED
	☐ BAIL IN THE AMOUNT OF $ __________ SET BY JUDGE / PURSUANT TO BAIL SCHEDULE

BOND AMOUNT	TYPE OF BOND
$ __________	☐ Cash ☐ Personal ☐ 10% ☐ AAA/Insurance Bond ☐ Unsec. ☐ Surety ☐ O.L. Held ☐ Other __________

Depositor Name and Address ____

DATE	☐ Defendant released upon execution of Bail as noted: See Bond forms — received by __________

CONTINUANCE	Requested by — Reason	NEW DATE
	☐ Defendant Failed to Appear Traffic Rule 7	
	☐ Order Supplemental Summons to New Date	
	☐ Order O.L. Forfeiture ☐ Bond Forfeiture	
	☐ Order Warrant — Bond Amount $	
	☐ Summons Issued Date Served	
	☐ Warrant Issued Date Executed	

____
Judge/Magistrate

COURT ENTRY

Defendant present with/without Counsel. All rights pursuant to Criminal Rules 10 & 11 and Traffic Rules 8 & 10 explained.

COUNT	SPEED	OMVI	LICENSE	SEATBELT		
Initial Plea						
Trial Date						
Finding						
Fine	$ & costs	$ & costs	$ & costs	$ & costs	$ & costs	$ & costs
Jailtime - (Days)						
Fines Suspended						
Costs Suspended						
Jailtime Suspended						

ADDITIONAL ORDERS:

☐ IF OMVI CONVICTION, 72 HOUR PROGRAM PERMITTED IN LIEU OF JAIL

☐ Defendant's License is suspended for ________ days/months which shall commence on ____________________ and end on ________________

☐ Defendant is granted limited Driving Privileges as follows effective __________ :

____

☐ DEFENDANT TO PAY FINES ON PAYMENT PROGRAM - SEE SEPARATE ENTRY

☐ If WAIVERED — Requirements of Waiver met - proper Fines and Costs paid - Guilty Plea(s) accepted - Guilty Finding(s) made, and Fines and Costs noted below are imposed.

__________ Date ____________________ Judge/Referee/Magistrate

FOR CLERK'S USE

COUNT	SPEED	OMVI	LICENSE	SEATBELT		
Fines						
Costs - Local						
Costs - State						
Total						
Receipt #(s)						

☐ IF WAIVERED: GUILTY PLEA(S), WAIVER(S) AND PAYMENTS MADE / IN PERSON / BY MAIL. RECEIPT GIVEN TO DEFENDANT / PERSONALLY / CHECK IS RECEIPT / BY MAIL TO DEFENDANT BY ORDINARY MAIL TO PRESENT ADDRESS. WAIVER REVIEWED, FOUND TO BE CORRECT AND APPROVED.

☐ FR PROOF SHOWN

☐ NO FR PROOF - CLERK TO NOTIFY BMV

__________ Date ____________________ Clerk/Violations Clerk/Deputy Clerk

__________ Date Abstract Mailed to BMV

__________ Date of Mayor's Court Transfer / Notice of Appeal

______ COURT ______ COUNTY, OHIO

STATE OF OHIO ______
☐ City ☐ Village ☐ Township

TICKET NO. ______

CASE NO. ______

NAME ______

STREET ______

CITY, STATE ______ ZIP ______

LICENSE ISSUED MO. ____ YR. ____ EXPIRES BIRTHDATE 19 ____ STATE ______

SSN ___ ___ ___ - ___ ___ - ___ ___ ___ ___ D.O.B.: MO. ___ DAY ___ YR. ___

RACE	SEX	HEIGHT	WEIGHT	HAIR	EYES

FINANCIAL RESPONSIBILITY PROOF SHOWN ☐ Yes ☐ No

LICENSE NO. ______

Lic. Class ______ DOT # ______ ☐ Does Not Apply

TO DEFENDANT: COMPLAINT

ON ______, 19 ____ AT ______ M. YOU/OPERATED/PARKED/WALKED/ A
☐ Pass ☐ Comm. ☐ Cycle ☐ Over 26001 ☐ Bus ☐ Haz. Mat.

VEHICLE: YR. ______ MAKE ______ BODY TYPE ______

COLOR ______ LIC. ______ STATE ______

UPON A PUBLIC HIGHWAY, NAMELY ______

AT/BETWEEN ______ (M.P. ______)

IN THE ______ OF ______ IN ______

COUNTY (NO. ____), STATE OF OHIO AND COMMITTED THE FOLLOWING OFFENSE(S).

☐ SPEED: ______ MPH in ______ MPH zone — ☐ ORC ☐ ORD ☐ T.P.
☐ Over limits ☐ Unsafe for cond. ☐ ACDA
☐ Radar ☐ Air ☐ VASCAR ☐ Pace ☐ Laser ☐ Stationary ☐ Moving

☐ OMVI: ☐ Under the influence of alcohol/drug of abuse — ☐ ORC ☐ ORD ☐ T.P.
☐ Prohibited blood alcohol concentration ______ BAC
☐ Blood ☐ Breath ☐ Urine ☐ Refused

☐ DRIVER LICENSE: ☐ None ☐ Revoked ☐ Suspended — ☐ ORC ☐ ORD ☐ T.P.
☐ Not on person Expired: ☐ 6 mos. or less ☐ Over 6 mos.
Suspension Type ______

☐ SAFETY BELT — Failure to wear — ☐ ORC ☐ ORD ☐ T.P.
☐ Driver ☐ Passenger ☐ Child Restraint

☐ OTHER OFFENSE ______ — ☐ ORC ☐ ORD ☐ T.P.

☐ OTHER OFFENSE ______ — ☐ ORC ☐ ORD ☐ T.P.

☐ DRIVER LICENSE HELD ☐ VEHICLE SEIZED ARREST CODE ______

PRESENT ADDRESS ______

SIGNATURE ______

CO. RES. ______

PHONE ( )

Court Code ______ COURT NAME ______

Case # ______ ☐ YES ☐ NO FR SHOWN-
☐ NO FR SHOWN-BMV TO PROCESS

	Speed	OMVI	License	Child Restraint		
IF BOND FORFEITURE, DATE FORFEITED						
CONVICTION DATE						
MOVING VIOLATION?	YES NO	YES NO	YES NO	NO	YES NO	YES NO
PLEA CODE						
POINTS ASSESSED						
BMV OFFENSE CODE						
IF AMENDED, OFFENSE CODE						
FOR BMV USE						

☐ License Suspended ______ days/months eff. ______ to ______
☐ MO-Limited Driving Privileges eff. ______ to ______
(See Separate Entry) Suspension is on Count ____ ☐ FRA SUSPENSION
☐ License Forfeiture — See Separate BMV Form 2526
☐ DL Confiscated — Date sent to BMV ______
☐ Other Information — See reverse side

I hereby certify that the above statements are taken from the records of this Court. DATE ______

Authorized Signature ______

Send completed copy to: Bureau of Motor Vehicles, P.O. Box 16520, Columbus, Ohio, 43266-0020

OHP0050 10-006000 (REVISION 9-1-96) ABSTRACT OF COURT RECORD OSHP HP7 (86305)

______________ COURT ______________ COUNTY, OHIO

STATE OF OHIO ______________
☐ City ☐ Village ☐ Township

TICKET NO. ______________

CASE NO. ______________

NAME ______________

STREET ______________

CITY, STATE ______________ ZIP ______________

LICENSE ISSUED MO. ____ YR. ____ EXPIRES BIRTHDATE 19 ____ STATE ______

SSN | | | - | | - | | | | D.O.B.: MO. ____ DAY ____ YR. ____

RACE	SEX	HEIGHT	WEIGHT	HAIR	EYES

FINANCIAL RESPONSIBILITY PROOF SHOWN ☐ Yes ☐ No

LICENSE NO. ______________

Lic. Class ______________ DOT # ______________ ☐ Does Not Apply

PRESENT ADDRESS ______________ SIGNATURE ______________ CO. RES. ______________ PHONE ( )

TO DEFENDANT: COMPLAINT

ON ______________, 19 ____ AT ______________ M. YOU/OPERATED/PARKED/WALKED/ A
☐ Pass ☐ Comm. ☐ Cycle ☐ Over 26001 ☐ Bus ☐ Haz. Mat.

VEHICLE: YR. ______ MAKE ______ BODY TYPE ______

COLOR ______ LIC. ______ STATE ______

UPON A PUBLIC HIGHWAY, NAMELY ______________

AT/BETWEEN ______________ (M.P. ______)

IN THE ______ OF ______________ IN ______________

COUNTY (NO. ______), STATE OF OHIO AND COMMITTED THE FOLLOWING OFFENSE(S).

☐ SPEED: ______ MPH in ______ MPH zone ☐ ORC ☐ ORD ☐ T.P.
☐ Over limits ☐ Unsafe for cond. ☐ ACDA
☐ Radar ☐ Air ☐ VASCAR ☐ Pace ☐ Laser ☐ Stationary ☐ Moving

☐ OMVI: ☐ Under the influence of alcohol/drug of abuse ☐ ORC ☐ ORD ☐ T.P.
☐ Prohibited blood alcohol concentration ______ BAC
☐ Blood ☐ Breath ☐ Urine ☐ Refused

☐ DRIVER LICENSE: ☐ None ☐ Revoked ☐ Suspended ☐ ORC ☐ ORD ☐ T.P.
☐ Not on person Expired: ☐ 6 mos. or less ☐ Over 6 mos.
Suspension Type ______________

☐ SAFETY BELT — Failure to wear ☐ ORC ☐ ORD ☐ T.P.
☐ Driver ☐ Passenger ☐ Child Restraint

☐ OTHER OFFENSE ______________ ☐ ORC ☐ ORD ☐ T.P.

☐ OTHER OFFENSE ______________ ☐ ORC ☐ ORD ☐ T.P.

☐ DRIVER LICENSE HELD ☐ VEHICLE SEIZED ARREST CODE ______

☐ PAVEMENT: ☐ Dry ☐ Wet ☐ Snow ☐ Icy # of Lanes ______ ☐ Const. Zone

☐ VISIBILITY: ☐ Clear ☐ Cloudy ☐ Dusk ☐ Night

☐ WEATHER: ☐ Rain ☐ Snow ☐ Fog ☐ No Adverse

☐ TRAFFIC: ☐ Heavy ☐ Moderate ☐ Light ☐ None

☐ AREA: ☐ Business ☐ Rural ☐ Residential ☐ Industry ☐ School

☐ CRASH: ☐ Yes ☐ No ☐ Almost Caused ☐ Injury ☐ Non-Injury ☐ Fatal
☐ Crash Report Number:

☐ REMARKS

ACCOMPANYING CRIMINAL CHARGE ☐ Yes ☐ No TOTAL # OFFENSES ______

TO DEFENDANT: SUMMONS ☐ PERSONAL APPEARANCE REQUIRED

You are summoned and ordered to appear at ______________ Court
______________ at ______ M.,
______________ 19 ______. If you fail to appear at this time and place you may be arrested or your license may be cancelled.

This summons served personally on the defendant on ______________ 19 ______.
The issuing-charging law enforcement officer states under the penalties of perjury and falsification that he/she has read the above complaint and that it is true.

____
Issuing-Charging Law Enforcement Officer

Court Code	Unit	Post	Dist.

NOTE: ISSUING OFFICER BE SURE TO VERIFY ADDRESS, IF DIFFERENT FROM LICENSE ADDRESS WRITE PRESENT ADDRESS IN SPACE PROVIDED OSHP HP7

OHP0060 10-006000 (REVISION 9-1-96) DEFENDANT'S COPY (B6305)

TO DEFENDANT: READ THIS MATERIAL CAREFULLY

☐ **PERSONAL APPEARANCE REQUIRED.** If the officer marked this block on the face of the ticket, you must appear in court. Your appearance in court is required because the offenses cannot be processed by a traffic violations bureau.

FAILURE TO APPEAR AND/OR PAY. The posting of bail or depositing your license as bond is to secure your appearance in court or the processing of the offenses through a traffic violations bureau. It is not a payment of fines or costs. If you do not appear at the time and place stated in the citation or if you do not timely process this citation through a traffic violations bureau, your license will be cancelled. Also, a warrant may be issued for your arrest and you may be subject to additional criminal penalties.

OFFENSES THAT MAY NOT BE PROCESSED BY TRAFFIC VIOLATIONS BUREAU: The following offenses require court appearance and may not be processed by a traffic violations bureau:

Any indictable offense; Operating a motor vehicle under the influence of alcohol or any drug of abuse; Leaving scene of accident; Driving while under suspension or revocation of driver's or commercial driver's license; Driving without being licensed to drive, except where the driver's or commercial driver's license has been expired for six months or less; A third moving traffic offense within 12 months; Passing a standing school bus; Willfully eluding or fleeing a police officer; Drag racing.

☐ **WAIVERABLE THROUGH TRAFFIC VIOLATIONS BUREAU.** If you are charged with offenses other than those listed above, you may, within seven days after the day you receive the ticket, plead guilty to the offenses charged and dispose of the case without court appearance by:

(1) appearing personally at the traffic violations bureau, signing the waiver printed below and paying the fines and costs or

(2) signing the waiver printed below and mailing it and a check, money order, or other approved payment for the total of the fines and costs to the traffic violations bureau at the following address:

Address of traffic violations bureau ____________________

____

MAKE CHECK OR MONEY ORDER PAYABLE TO: ____________________

____

INSURANCE WARNING. UNDER OHIO LAW YOU ARE REQUIRED TO SHOW PROOF OF FINANCIAL RESPONSIBILITY OR INSURANCE. If you did not do so at the time of receiving this ticket, you must submit proof of insurance when you appear in court on these offenses. **IF YOU DO NOT SUBMIT THE REQUIRED PROOF, YOUR DRIVER'S LICENSE WILL BE SUSPENDED AND YOU MAY BE SUBJECT TO ADDITIONAL FEES AND INSURANCE SANCTIONS.** If you have any questions regarding the proof filing, you may call the traffic violations bureau at the telephone indicated.

INFORMATION: For information regarding your duty to appear or the amount of fines and costs, call:

____
fill in telephone number(s)

CONTESTED CASE; COURT APPEARANCE REQUIRED. If you desire to contest the offenses or if court appearance is required, you must appear at the time and place stated in the summons.

NOTICE TO DEFENDANT UNDER EIGHTEEN YEARS OF AGE. You must appear before the Juvenile Court at the time and place determined by that Court. The Juvenile Court will notify you when and where to appear. This ticket will be filed with the Juvenile Court and may be used as a juvenile complaint. For information regarding your duty to appear at Juvenile Court call:

____
Fill in telephone number(s)

Address of Juvenile Court ____________________

____

GUILTY PLEAS, WAIVER OF TRIAL, PAYMENT OF FINES AND COSTS

I, the undersigned defendant, do hereby enter my written pleas of guilty to the offenses charged in this ticket. I realize that by signing these guilty pleas, I admit my guilt of the offenses charged and waive my right to contest the offenses in a trial before the court or jury. Further, I realize that a record of this plea will be sent to the Ohio Bureau of Motor Vehicles. I have not been convicted of, pleaded guilty to, or forfeited bond for two or more prior moving traffic offenses within the last 12 months. I plead guilty to the offense(s) charged.

FINES ____________ ____________________
Signature of Defendant

Costs ____________ ____________________
Address

Total ____________ ____________________

________ COURT ________ COUNTY, OHIO

STATE OF OHIO ________
☐ City ☐ Village ☐ Township

TICKET NO. ________

CASE NO. ________

NAME ________

STREET ________

CITY, STATE ________ ZIP ________

LICENSE ISSUED MO. ____ YR. ____ EXPIRES BIRTHDATE 19 ____ STATE ________

SSN | | | - | | - | | | | D.O.B.: MO. ____ DAY ____ YR. ____

RACE	SEX	HEIGHT	WEIGHT	HAIR	EYES

FINANCIAL RESPONSIBILITY PROOF SHOWN
☐ Yes ☐ No

LICENSE NO. ________

Lic. Class ________ DOT # ________ ☐ Does Not Apply

PRESENT ADDRESS ________ SIGNATURE ________ CO. RES. ________ PHONE ( )

TO DEFENDANT: COMPLAINT

ON ________, 19 ____ AT ________ M. YOU/OPERATED/PARKED/WALKED/ A
☐ Pass ☐ Comm. ☐ Cycle ☐ Over 26001 ☐ Bus ☐ Haz. Mat.

VEHICLE: YR. ________ MAKE ________ BODY TYPE ________

COLOR ________ LIC. ________ STATE ________

UPON A PUBLIC HIGHWAY, NAMELY ________

AT/BETWEEN ________ (M.P. ________)

IN THE ________ OF ________ IN ________

COUNTY (NO. ____), STATE OF OHIO AND COMMITTED THE FOLLOWING OFFENSE(S).

☐ SPEED: ________ MPH in ________ MPH zone — ☐ ORC ☐ ORD ☐ T.P.
☐ Over limits ☐ Unsafe for cond. ☐ ACDA
☐ Radar ☐ Air ☐ VASCAR ☐ Pace ☐ Laser ☐ Stationary ☐ Moving

☐ OMVI. ☐ Under the influence of alcohol/drug of abuse — ☐ ORC ☐ ORD ☐ T.P.
☐ Prohibited blood alcohol concentration ________ BAC
☐ Blood ☐ Breath ☐ Urine ☐ Refused

☐ DRIVER LICENSE: ☐ None ☐ Revoked ☐ Suspended — ☐ ORC ☐ ORD ☐ T.P.
☐ Not on person Expired: ☐ 6 mos. or less ☐ Over 6 mos.
Suspension Type ________

☐ SAFETY BELT — Failure to wear — ☐ ORC ☐ ORD ☐ T.P.
☐ Driver ☐ Passenger ☐ Child Restraint

☐ OTHER OFFENSE ________ — ☐ ORC ☐ ORD ☐ T.P.

☐ OTHER OFFENSE ________ — ☐ ORC ☐ ORD ☐ T.P.

☐ DRIVER LICENSE HELD ☐ VEHICLE SEIZED ARREST CODE ________
☐ PAVEMENT: ☐ Dry ☐ Wet ☐ Snow ☐ Icy # of Lanes ____ ☐ Const. Zone
☐ VISIBILITY: ☐ Clear ☐ Cloudy ☐ Dusk ☐ Night
☐ WEATHER: ☐ Rain ☐ Snow ☐ Fog ☐ No Adverse
☐ TRAFFIC: ☐ Heavy ☐ Moderate ☐ Light ☐ None
☐ AREA: ☐ Business ☐ Rural ☐ Residential ☐ Industry ☐ School
☐ CRASH: ☐ Yes ☐ No ☐ Almost Caused ☐ Injury ☐ Non-injury ☐ Fatal
☐ Crash Report Number:
☐ REMARKS

ACCOMPANYING CRIMINAL CHARGE ☐ Yes ☐ No TOTAL # OFFENSES ____

TO DEFENDANT: SUMMONS ☐ PERSONAL APPEARANCE REQUIRED

You are summoned and ordered to appear at ________ Court
________ at ________ M.
________ 19 ________. If you fail to appear at this time and place you may be arrested or your license may be cancelled.

This summons served personally on the defendant on ________ 19 ________.
The issuing-charging law enforcement officer states under the penalties of perjury and falsification that he/she has read the above complaint and that it is true.

____
Issuing-Charging Law Enforcement Officer

Court Code	Unit	Post	Dist.

NOTE: ISSUING OFFICER BE SURE TO VERIFY ADDRESS. IF DIFFERENT FROM LICENSE ADDRESS WRITE PRESENT ADDRESS IN SPACE PROVIDED — OSHP HP7

OHP0050 10-006000 (REVISION 9-1-96) AGENCY RECORD [B6305]

REPORT OF ACTION ON CASE

DATE OF ARREST ______________________ M.
Month, Day, Year Time

COURT ACTION

☐ GUILTY ☐ RELEASED TO OTHER AUTHORITY
☐ NOT GUILTY ☐ ______________________

OFFICER'S NOTES

WITNESSES:

____
Name Address Phone No.

____
Name Address Phone No.

ARREST NOTIFICATION

VIOLATION ______________ R.C. SECTION ______

SCALE LOCATION ______ ☐ PLATFORM ______ ☐ PORTABLE

AMOUNT OF OVERLOAD ______________

OVERLOADED ☐ Single Axle ☐ Tandem

OR: ☐ Gross — Length & gross ______________ Ft.

☐ PUCO NO. ______

____
Permit Holder or Company Name or Vehicle Owner Name

____
Street Address

____
City State Zip

NOTIFICATION OF ARREST ONLY.
NO FURTHER ACTION IS NECESSARY.

RULES OF SUPERINTENDENCE FOR THE COURTS OF OHIO (Selected Provisions)

Sup R 20 Appointment of counsel for indigent defendants in capital cases-courts of common pleas

I. APPLICABILITY

(A) This rule shall apply in cases where an indigent defendant has been charged with or convicted of an offense for which the death penalty can be or has been imposed.

(B) The provisions for the appointment of counsel set forth in this rule apply only in cases where the defendant is indigent, counsel is not privately retained by or for the defendant, and the death penalty can be or has been imposed upon the defendant. This rule does not apply in the case of a juvenile defendant who is indicted for a "capital offense" but because of his or her age cannot be sentenced to death.

(C) If the defendant is entitled to the appointment of counsel, the court shall appoint two attorneys certified pursuant to this rule. If the defendant engages one privately retained attorney, the court shall not appoint a second attorney pursuant to this rule.

(D) The provisions of this rule apply in addition to the reporting requirements created by section 2929.021 of the Revised Code.

II. QUALIFICATIONS FOR CERTIFICATION AS COUNSEL FOR INDIGENT DEFENDANTS IN CAPITAL CASES

(A) Trial Counsel.

(1) At least two attorneys shall be appointed by the court to represent an indigent defendant charged with an offense for which the death penalty may be imposed. At least one of the appointed counsel must maintain a law office in Ohio and have experience in Ohio criminal trial practice.

The counsel appointed shall be designated "lead counsel" and "co-counsel."

(2) Lead counsel shall satisfy all of the following:

(a) Be admitted to the practice of law in Ohio or admitted to practice *pro hac vice*;

(b) Have at least five years of civil or criminal litigation or appellate experience;

(c) Have specialized training, as approved by the committee, on subjects that will assist counsel in the defense of persons accused of capital crimes in the two-year period prior to making application;

(d) Have at least one of the following qualifications:

(i) Experience as "lead counsel" in the jury trial of at least one capital case;

(ii) Experience as "co-counsel" in the trial of at least two capital cases;

(e) Have at least one of the following qualifications:

(i) Experience as "lead counsel" in the jury trial of at least one murder or aggravated murder case;

(ii) Experience as "lead counsel" in ten or more criminal or civil jury trials, at least three of which were felony jury trials;

(iii) Experience as "lead counsel" in either: three murder or aggravated murder jury trials; one murder or aggravated murder jury trial and three felony jury trials; or three aggravated or first- or second-degree felony jury trials in a court of common pleas in the three years prior to making application.

(3) Co–counsel shall satisfy all of the following:

(a) Be admitted to the practice of law in Ohio or admitted to practice *pro hac vice*;

(b) Have at least three years of civil or criminal litigation or appellate experience;

(c) Have specialized training, as approved by the committee, on subjects that will assist counsel in the defense of persons accused of capital crimes in the two years prior to making application;

(d) Have at least one of the following qualifications:

(i) Experience as "co-counsel" in one murder or aggravated murder trial;

(ii) Experience as "lead counsel" in one first-degree felony jury trial;

(iii) Experience as "lead" or "co-counsel" in at least two felony jury or civil jury trials in a court of common pleas in the three years prior to making application.

(4) As used in this rule, "trial" means a case concluded with a judgment of acquittal under Criminal Rule 29 or submission to the trial court or jury for decision and verdict.

(B) Appellate Counsel.

(1) At least two attorneys shall be appointed by the court to appeal cases where the trial court has imposed the death penalty on an indigent defendant. At least one of the appointed counsel shall maintain a law office in Ohio.

(2) Appellate counsel shall satisfy all of the following:

(a) Be admitted to the practice of law in Ohio or admitted to practice *pro hac vice*;

(b) Have at least three years of civil or criminal litigation or appellate experience;

(c) Have specialized training, as approved by the Committee, on subjects that will assist counsel in the defense of persons accused of capital crimes in the two years prior to making application;

(d) Have specialized training, as approved by the Committee, on subjects that will assist counsel in the appeal of cases in which the death penalty was imposed in the two years prior to making application;

(e) Have experience as counsel in the appeal of at least three felony convictions in the three years prior to making application.

(C) Exceptional Circumstances. If an attorney does not satisfy the requirements of divisions (A)(2), (A)(3), or (B)(2) of this

section, the attorney may be certified as lead counsel, co-counsel, or appellate counsel if it can be demonstrated to the satisfaction of the Committee that competent representation will be provided to the defendant. In so determining, the Committee may consider the following:

(a) Specialized training on subjects that will assist counsel in the trial or appeal of cases in which the death penalty may be or was imposed;

(b) Experience in the trial or appeal of criminal or civil cases;

(c) Experience in the investigation, preparation, and litigation of capital cases that were resolved prior to trial;

(d) Any other relevant considerations.

(D) Savings Clause. Attorneys certified by the Committee prior to January 1, 1991 may maintain their certification by complying with the requirements of Section VII of this rule, notwithstanding the requirements of Sections II(A)(2)(d), II(A)(3)(b) and (d), and II(B)(2)(d) as amended effective January 1, 1991.

III. COMMITTEE ON THE APPOINTMENT OF COUNSEL FOR INDIGENT DEFENDANTS IN CAPITAL CASES

(A) There shall be a Committee on the Appointment of Counsel for Indigent Defendants in Capital Cases.

(B) Appointment of Committee Members. The Committee shall be composed of five attorneys. Three members shall be appointed by a majority vote of all members of the Supreme Court of Ohio; one shall be appointed by the Ohio State Bar Association; and one shall be appointed by the Ohio Public Defender Commission.

(C) Eligibility for Appointment to the Committee. Each member of the Committee shall satisfy all of the following qualifications:

(1) Be admitted to the practice of law in Ohio;

(2) Have represented criminal defendants for not less than five years;

(3) Demonstrate a knowledge of the law and practice of capital cases;

(4) Currently not serving as a prosecuting attorney, city director of law, village solicitor, or similar officer or their assistant or employee, or an employee of any court.

(D) Overall Composition. The overall composition of the Committee shall meet both of the following criteria:

(1) No more than two members shall reside in the same county;

(2) No more than one shall be a judge.

(E) Terms; Vacancies. The term of office for each member shall be five years, each term beginning on the first day of January. Members shall be eligible for reappointment. Vacancies shall be filled in the same manner as original appointments. Any member appointed to fill a vacancy occurring prior to the expiration of a term shall hold office for the remainder of the term.

(F) Election of Chair. The Committee shall elect a chair and such other officers as are necessary. The officers shall serve for two years and may be reelected to additional terms.

(G) Powers and Duties of the Committee. The Committee shall do all of the following:

(1) Prepare and notify attorneys of procedures for applying for certification to be appointed counsel for indigent defendants in capital cases;

(2) Periodically provide all common pleas and appellate court judges and the Ohio Public Defender with a list of all attorneys who are certified to be appointed counsel for indigent capital defendants;

(3) Periodically review the list of certified counsel, all court appointments given to attorneys in capital cases, and the result and status of those cases;

(4) Develop criteria and procedures for retention of certification including, but not limited to, mandatory continuing legal education on the defense and appeal of capital cases;

(5) Expand, reduce, or otherwise modify the list of certified attorneys as appropriate and necessary in accord with division (G)(4) of this section;

(6) Review and approve specialized training programs on subjects that will assist counsel in the defense and appeal of capital cases;

(7) Recommend to the Supreme Court of Ohio amendments to this rule or any other rule or statute relative to the defense or appeal of capital cases.

(H) Meetings. The Committee shall meet at the call of the chair, at the request of a majority of the members, or at the request of the Supreme Court of Ohio. A quorum consists of three members. A majority of the Committee is necessary for the Committee to elect a chair and take any other action.

(I) Compensation. All members of the Committee shall receive equal compensation in an amount to be established by the Supreme Court of Ohio.

IV. PROCEDURES FOR COURT APPOINTMENTS OF COUNSEL

(A) Appointing Counsel. Only counsel who have been certified by the Committee shall be appointed to represent indigent defendants charged with or convicted of an offense for which the death penalty may be or has been imposed. Each court may adopt local rules establishing qualifications in addition to and not in conflict with those established by this rule. Appointments of counsel for these cases should be distributed as widely as possible among the certified attorneys in the jurisdiction of the appointing court.

(B) Workload of Appointed Counsel.

(1) In appointing counsel, the court shall consider the nature and volume of the workload of the prospective counsel to ensure that counsel, if appointed, could direct sufficient attention to the defense of the case and provide competent representation to the defendant.

(2) Attorneys accepting appointments shall provide each client with competent representation in accordance with constitutional and professional standards. Appointed counsel shall not accept workloads that, by reason of their excessive size, interfere with the rendering of competent representation or lead to the breach of professional obligations.

(C) Notice to the Committee.

(1) Within two weeks of appointment, the appointing court shall notify the Committee secretary of the appointment on a form prescribed by the committee. The notice shall include all of the following:

(a) The court and the judge assigned to the case;

(b) The case name and number;

(c) A copy of the indictment;

(d) The names, business addresses, telephone numbers, and Sup.R. 20 certification of all attorneys appointed;

(e) Any other information considered relevant by the Committee or appointing court.

(2) Within two weeks of disposition, the trial court shall notify the Committee secretary of the disposition of the case on a form prescribed by the Committee. The notice shall include all of the following:

(a) The outcome of the case;

(b) The title and section of the Revised Code of any crimes to which the defendant pleaded or was found guilty;

(c) The date of dismissal, acquittal, or that sentence was imposed;

(d) The sentence, if any;

(e) A copy of the judgment entry reflecting the above;

(f) If the death penalty was imposed, the name of counsel appointed to represent the defendant on appeal.

(g) Any other information considered relevant by the Committee or trial court.

(D) Support Services. The appointing court shall provide appointed counsel, as required by Ohio law or the federal Constitution, federal statutes, and professional standards, with the investigator, mitigation specialists, mental health professional, and other forensic experts and other support services reasonably necessary or appropriate for counsel to prepare for and present an adequate defense at every stage of the proceedings including, but not limited to, determinations relevant to competency to stand trial, a not guilty by reason of insanity plea, cross-examination of expert witnesses called by the prosecution, disposition following conviction, and preparation for and presentation of mitigating evidence in the sentencing phase of the trial.

V. MONITORING; REMOVAL

(A) The appointing court should monitor the performance of assigned counsel to ensure that the defendant is receiving competent representation. If there is compelling evidence before any court, trial or appellate, that an attorney has ignored basic responsibilities of providing competent counsel, which results in prejudice to the defendant's case, the court, in addition to any other action it may take, shall report this evidence to the Committee, which shall accord the attorney an opportunity to be heard.

(B) Complaints concerning the performance of attorneys assigned in the trials or appeals of indigent defendants in capital cases shall be reviewed by the Committee pursuant to the provisions of Section III(G)(3), (4), and (5) of this rule.

VI. PROGRAMS FOR SPECIALIZED TRAINING

(A) Programs for Specialized Training in the Defense of Persons Charged With a Capital Offense.

(1) To be approved by the Committee, a death penalty trial seminar shall include instruction devoted to the investigation, preparation, and presentation of a death penalty trial.

(2) The curriculum for an approved death penalty trial seminar should include, but is not limited to, specialized training in the following areas:

(a) An overview of current developments in death penalty litigation;

(b) Death penalty voir dire;

(c) Trial phase presentation;

(d) Use of experts in the trial and penalty phase;

(e) Investigation, preparation, and presentation of mitigation;

(f) Preservation of the record;

(g) Counsel's relationship with the accused and the accused's family;

(h) Death penalty appellate and post-conviction litigation in state and federal courts.

(B) Programs for Specialized Training in the Appeal of Cases in Which the Death Penalty has been Imposed.

(1) To be approved by the Committee, a death penalty appeals seminar shall include instruction devoted to the appeal of a case in which the death penalty has been imposed.

(2) The curriculum for an approved death penalty appeal seminar should include, but is not limited to, specialized training in the following areas:

(a) An overview of current developments in death penalty law;

(b) Completion, correction, and supplementation of the record on appeal;

(c) Reviewing the record for unique death penalty issues;

(d) Motion practice for death penalty appeals;

(e) Preservation and presentation of constitutional issues;

(f) Preparing and presenting oral argument;

(g) Unique aspects of death penalty practice in the courts of appeals, the Supreme Court of Ohio, and the United States Supreme Court;

(h) The relationship of counsel with the appellant and the appellant's family during the course of the appeals.

(i) Procedure and practice in collateral litigation, extraordinary remedies, state post-conviction litigation, and federal habeas corpus litigation.

(C) The sponsor of a death penalty seminar shall apply for approval from the Committee at least sixty days before the date of the proposed seminar. An application for approval shall include the curriculum for the seminar and include biographical information of each member of the seminar faculty.

(D) The Committee shall obtain a list of attendees from the Supreme Court Commission on Continuing Legal Education that shall be used to verify attendance at and grant Sup.R. 20 credit for each Committee-approved seminar. Credit for purposes of this rule shall be granted to instructors using the same ratio provided in Rule X of the Supreme Court Rules for the Government of the Bar of Ohio.

(E) The Committee may accredit programs other than those approved pursuant to divisions (A) and (B) of this section. To receive accreditation, the program shall include instructions in all areas set forth in divisions (A) and (B) of this section. Application for accreditation of an in-state program may be made by the program sponsor or a program attendee and shall be made prior to the program. Application for accreditation of an out-of-state program may be submitted by the program sponsor or a program attendee and may be made prior to or after completion of the program. The request for credit from a program sponsor shall include the program curriculum and individual faculty biographical information. The request for credit from a program attendee shall include all of the following:

(1) Program curriculum;

(2) Individual faculty biographical information;

(3) A written breakdown of sessions attended and credit hours received if the seminar held concurrent sessions;

(4) Proof of attendance.

VII. STANDARDS FOR RETENTION OF SUP.R. 20 CERTIFICATION

(A)(1) To retain certification, an attorney who has previously been certified by the Committee shall complete at least twelve hours of Committee-approved specialized training every two years. To maintain certification as lead counsel or co-counsel, at least six of the twelve hours shall be devoted to instruction in the trial of capital cases. To maintain certification as appellate counsel, at least six of the twelve hours shall be devoted to instruction in the appeal of capital cases.

(2) On the first day of July of each year, the Committee shall review the list of certified counsel and revoke the certification of any attorney who has not complied with the specialized training requirements of this rule. An attorney whose certification has been revoked shall not be eligible to accept future appointment as counsel for an indigent defendant charged with or convicted of

an offense for which the death penalty can be or has been imposed.

(B) The Committee may accredit an out-of-state program that provides specialized instruction devoted to the investigation, preparation, and presentation of a death penalty trial or specialized instruction devoted to the appeal of a case in which the defendant received the death penalty, or both. Requests for credit for an out-of-state program may be submitted by the seminar sponsor or a seminar attendee. The request for credit from a program sponsor shall include the program curriculum and individual faculty biographical information. The request for credit from a program attendee shall include all of the following:

(1) Program curriculum;

(2) Individual faculty biographical information;

(3) A written breakdown of sessions attended and credit hours received if the seminar held concurrent sessions;

(4) Proof of attendance.

(C) An attorney who has previously been certified but whose certification has been revoked for failure to comply with the specialized training requirements of this rule must, in order to regain certification, submit a new application that demonstrates that the attorney has completed twelve hours of Committee approved specialized training in the two year period prior to making application for recertification.

VIII. RESERVED

IX. EFFECTIVE DATE

(A) The effective date of this rule shall be October 1, 1987.

(B) The amendments to Section II(A)(5)(b), Section III(B)(2), and to the Subcommittee Comments following Section II of this Rule adopted by the Supreme Court of Ohio on June 28, 1989, shall be effective on July 1, 1989.

(C) The amendments to Sections I(A)(2), I(A)(3), I(B), and II, and the addition of Sections I(C) and IV, adopted by the Supreme Court of Ohio on December 11, 1990, shall be effective on January 1, 1991.

(D) The amendments to this rule adopted by the Supreme Court of Ohio on April 19, 1995, shall take effect on July 1, 1995.

(Adopted eff. 7–1–97; amended 1–6–03)

Sup R 21 Appointment of counsel of indigent defendants in capital cases-courts of appeal

(A) Applicability

This rule shall apply in appeals of cases where the trial court has imposed the death penalty on an indigent defendant. The appointment of counsel and notice requirements shall be in accordance with this rule and Sup.R. 20.

(B) Procedures for Court Appointments of Counsel

(1) Appointing Counsel. Only attorneys who have been certified as appellate counsel pursuant to Sup.R. 20 shall be appointed as appellate counsel where the trial court has imposed the death penalty on an indigent defendant. Each appellate court may adopt local rules establishing qualifications in addition to and not in conflict with those established by Sup.R. 20. Appointments of counsel for these cases should be distributed as widely as possible among the certified attorneys in the jurisdiction of the appointing court.

(2) Workload of Appointed Counsel. In appointing counsel, the court shall consider the nature and volume of the workload of the prospective counsel to ensure that counsel, if appointed, can direct sufficient attention to the appeal of the case and provide competent representation to the defendant. Attorneys accepting appointments shall provide each client with competent representation in accordance with constitutional and professional standards. Appointed counsel shall not accept workloads that, by reason of their excessive size, interfere with the rendering of competent representation or lead to the breach of professional obligations.

(C) Notice of the Appointment of Counsel

Within two weeks of appointment, the appellate court shall notify the Committee secretary of the appointment of appellate counsel on a form prescribed by the Committee. If appellate counsel are appointed by the trial court, the notice is not required. The notice shall include all of the following:

(1) The case name and number;

(2) The names, business addresses, telephone numbers, and certification pursuant to Sup.R. 20 of counsel appointed to represent the defendant on appeal;

(3) Any other information considered relevant by the Committee or appointing court.

(D) Notice of Disposition of the Appeal

Within two weeks of disposition of the appeal, the appellate court shall notify the Committee secretary of the disposition of the appeal on a form prescribed by the Committee. The notice shall include all of the following:

(1) The case name and number;

(2) The names, business addresses, telephone numbers, and certification pursuant to Sup.R. 20 of counsel who represented the defendant on appeal;

(3) The disposition of the appeal;

(4) If the death sentence was affirmed, the names, addresses, telephone numbers, and certification pursuant to Sup.R. 20 of counsel who were appointed to represent the defendant on appeal to the Supreme Court of Ohio;

(5) Any other information considered relevant by the Committee or appellate court.

(Adopted eff. 7–1–97)

Sup R 22 Verification of indigency

Where required by law to appoint counsel to represent indigent defendants in cases for which the county will apply to the Ohio Public Defender Commission for reimbursement of costs, the court shall require the applicant to complete the financial disclosure form. The court shall follow rules promulgated by the Commission pursuant to division (B)(1) of section 120.03 of the Revised Code as guidelines to determine indigency and standards of indigency.

(Adopted 7–1–97)

OHIO ADMINISTRATIVE RULES
(Selected Provisions)

109

OFFICE OF THE ATTORNEY GENERAL

109:2

PEACE OFFICER TRAINING COMMISSION

CHAPTER 109:2–1

PEACE OFFICERS BASIC TRAINING PROGRAM

Promulgated pursuant to RC Ch 119

109:2–1–02 Definitions

When used in Chapter 109:2–1 of the Administrative Code

(A) The term "commission" means the Ohio peace officer training commission;

(B) The term "commander" means the director or other head of a peace officer training school;

(C) The term "executive director" means the executive director of the Ohio peace officer training commission;

(D) The term "basic course" means the training prescribed in rule 109:2–1–16 of the Administrative Code which has been approved by the executive director, in writing, as meeting or exceeding the minimum standards prescribed in rule 109:2–1–16 of the Administrative Code;

(E) The term "peace officer" means:

(1) Any person appointed as a peace officer pursuant to Ohio Revised Code section 109.71(A).

(2) Any other person designated as such for purposes of peace officer training and certification by the Ohio general assembly.

(F) The term "school" means any basic training program for peace officers as certified by the executive director of the Ohio peace officer training commission;

(G) The term "chair" means the chair of the Ohio peace officer training commission;

(H) The term "training recruit" means a fulltime employee of a law enforcement agency whose primary duty is to attend and successfully complete the basic course and who, upon completion of the basic course, is appointed as a peace officer by that agency;

(I) The term "open enrollment student" means a person who is not employed by a law enforcement agency and has not received an appointment as a peace officer, but has successfully completed all basic school admission requirements of the Ohio peace officer training commission.

(J) The term "break in service" applies to any person who has previously been awarded a certificate of completion of basic training by the executive director or any peace officer as described in paragraph 109:2–1–12 (A)(2) of this rule [1] who is appointed to any new or concurrent peace officer position described in section 109.71(A) of the Revised Code unless the concurrent appointment is to a multi-jurisdictional task force and the original appointment continues.

(K) The term "peace officer disqualifying offense" means any offense which would preclude an individual from performing the functions of a peace officer, including any offense under ORC section 2923.13.

HISTORY: 1999–2000 OMR 225 (A), eff. 1–1–00; 1990–91 OMR 1021 (A), eff. 3–25–91; 1987–88 OMR 571 (A), eff. 1–1–88; 1981–82 OMR 381 (A), eff. 3–1–82; prior PC–1–02

RC 119.032 rule review date(s): 1–1–05; 6–16–99

[1] Language appears as in original.

109:2–1–03 Ohio peace officer basic training program course

(A) Who is required to complete the basic course:

(1) Those persons set out in division (A) of section 109.71 of the Revised Code;

(2) A training recruit as defined in paragraph (H) of rule 109:2–1–02 of the Administrative Code;

(3) Any person employed in a position statutorily required to complete the basic training course.

(B) Who may attend the basic course

(1) An open enrollment student as defined in paragraph (I) of rule 109:2–1–02 of the Administrative Code.

(C) No person who has been convicted of a felony or other disqualifying offense shall attend the basic course.

(D) Statement of purpose.

(1) It shall be clearly understood that the basic course described is designed as an absolute minimum program. Commanders are encouraged to exceed this minimum program wherever possible.

(2) Nothing in this chapter shall limit or be construed as limiting the authority of a commander, the civil service commis-

sion, or other appointing authority, to enact rules and regulations which establish a higher standard of training above the minimum required by the rules of this chapter.

(E) Local matters

Instruction in such matters as department rules and regulations, local ordinances, personnel policies and procedures may be given entirely upon local initiative. No portion of the instructional time devoted to this training or other non-commission required topics shall be credited against the hours of instruction required under rule 109:2–1–16 of the Administrative Code.

HISTORY: 1999–2000 OMR 225 (A), eff. 1–1–00; 1990–91 OMR 1021 (A), eff. 3–25–91; 1987–88 OMR 571 (A), eff. 1–1–88; 1981–82 OMR 381 (A), eff. 3–1–82; prior PC–1–03

RC 119.032 rule review date(s): 1–1–05; 6–16–99

109:2–1–04 Approval of schools

(A) Schools which meet all of the requirements set forth in rules 109:2–1–05, 109:2–1–06, 109:2–1–08, and 109:2–1–16 of the Administrative Code shall be approved by the executive director. The approval shall be given in writing.

(B) Schools may, in addition to those requirements set forth in paragraph (A) of this rule, require that each person enrolled in training sanctioned by the commission be given a physical examination, a psychological examination, and a background investigation to determine fitness and eligibility for attending and completing the basic course. Any person determined to be unfit or ineligible will not be admitted to any training that is a component of the basic course.

(C) Revocation of school approval.

The executive director may revoke the approval of any school for failure to maintain the minimum state standards as set forth in this rule and rules 109:2–1–05, 109:2–1–06, 109:2–1–08, and 109:2–1–16 of the Administrative Code or any other rule or policy established by the Ohio peace officer training commission for conducting the basic training program. The executive director shall notify the commander of the school in writing of this revocation and shall advise the commander that the commander may request a hearing before the commission as provided in sections 119.06 and 119.07 of the Revised Code. The commission shall conduct the hearing as required by sections 119.01 to 119.03 of the Revised Code.

(D) Submission of school application, training calendar and enrollment information. Twenty–one calendar days prior to the start of a training school, the commander shall forward to the executive director, on forms supplied by the executive director, a training calendar and school application which shall list:

(1) Subjects to be taught as provided for in rule 190:2–1–16 of the Administrative Code;

(2) Instructors' full names and commission-issued instructor certification number for each respective instructor;

(3) Clock times of instruction;

(4) Dates of instruction; and

(5) Any pertinent data requested on the school application form.

(6) A rolled fingerprint card, approved by the superintendant [sic.] of the bureau of criminal identification and investigation, for each enrollee.

(7) A preliminary enrollment list.

(E) Enrollees, instructors and time for school.

The commander must have prior written approval from the executive director to conduct the school. The school:

(1) Must have a minimum of ten students enrolled.

(2) Must have a minimum of ten commission-approved instructors.

(3) May not extend more than one year unless the school is part of a college or university degree program. If the school is part of a college or university degree program, the executive director and the commander will determine the completion date of training.

(4) For any deviation from paragraph (E)(1), (E)(2) or (E)(3) of this rule, the commander must have prior written approval from the executive director.

(F) Within three calendar days after the school has begun, the commander shall forward to the executive director, on forms supplied by the executive director, a revised student enrollment list and an enrollment package which shall include, for each enrollee, forms required by the executive director.

HISTORY: 1999–2000 OMR 226 (A), eff. 1–1–00; 1987–88 OMR 572 (A), eff. 1–15–88; 1981–82 OMR 382 (A), eff. 3–1–82; prior PC–1–04

RC 119.032 rule review date(s): 1–1–05; 6–16–99

109:2–1–05 Approval of school commanders

Each commander is required to have the approval of the executive director to conduct a school. Such approval will be based upon the submission of a notarized and typewritten statement of qualifications by the person seeking approval to be designated a commander on a form prescribed by the executive director. All persons seeking approval to be a school commander on or after January 1, 2000, who have not previously been designated a school commander shall conform to the minimum qualifications for certification as a commander and must be associated with an established or proposed school.

(A) Minimum qualifications for certification of commander shall be as follows:

(1) High school graduate or possession of a "General Education Development" certificate; and

(2) Seven years of experience as a full-time law enforcement officer, two of which must be as a full-time law enforcement supervisor;

(3) Completion of ninety quarters or sixty semester hours at an accredited college or university; and

(4) Professional references from three current police administrators of the rank of lieutenant or above; and

(5) No convictions for a felony, crime of moral turpitude or any other peace officer disqualifying offense.

(B) Upon receipt and verification of a notarized application form for commander certification and completion of an Ohio peace officer training commission commander conference, the executive director may issue a certificate to the applicant. Should the executive director refuse to issue a certificate, the notice of this action shall be sent to the applicant. The applicant shall be advised that he or she may request a hearing before the commission as provided in sections 119.06 and 119.07 of the Revised Code. The commission shall conduct the hearing as required by sections 119.01 to 119.13 of the Revised Code.

(C) Revocation of certificate

The executive director may revoke the certification of any commander for the following reasons:

(1) A commander's evaluation reflecting unacceptable performance; or

(2) Conviction for a felony, crime of moral turpitude, or any other peace officer disqualifying offense; or

(3) Absence from two consecutive commander's conferences; or

(4) Violation of rules promulgated under this chapter; or

(5) For any other good cause shown.

The executive director shall notify the commander in writing of this revocation. The commander shall be advised that he or she may request a hearing before the commission as provided in sections 119.06 and 119.07 of the Revised Code. The commission shall conduct the hearing as required by sections 119.01 to 119.13 of the Revised Code.

HISTORY: 1999–2000 OMR 226 (A), eff. 1–1–00; 1996–97 OMR 809 (A), eff. 12–7–96; 1987–88 OMR 572 (E), eff. 1–15–88; 1987–88 OMR 572 (A–TT 109:2–1–06), eff. 1–15–88; 1981–82 OMR 382 (A), eff. 3–1–82; prior PC–1–05

RC 119.032 rule review date(s): 1–1–05; 6–16–99

109:2–1–06 Approval of instructors

All persons requesting approval or renewal as an instructor on or after January 1, 2000, shall submit a notarized statement of qualifications for each subject or unit of subjects for which the person is seeking approval on a form provided by the executive director.. The course content of the peace officer basic training program shall be as outlined in rule 109:2–1–16 of the Administrative Code.

(A) Minimum qualifications for unit instructor certification shall be as follows:

(1) High school graduate or possession of a "General Education Development" certificate; and

(2) Five years of experience as a full-time law enforcement officer; and

(3) Completion of an instructor training program approved by the executive director consisting of a minimum of forty clock hours which shall include instruction in the theories of learning and adult education, teaching techniques, lesson plan development and usage, behavioral objectives, student evaluation and measurement, role playing, the use of audio-visual aids and an exercise in practice teaching.

Instructor training programs taught at the Ohio peace officer training academy; by the department of education; the state highway patrol; a college or educational institution or other programs which in the opinion of the executive director are equivalent to those set out, will be acceptable; and

(4) Completion of an instructor-level training program approved by the executive director which will allow a person to learn specific knowledge and skills in a unit for which certification is requested; and

(5) Recommendation of a current basic training school commander.

(B) Minimum qualifications for special subject instructor certification shall be as follows:

(1) A high school graduate or possession of a "General Education Development" certificate; and

(2)(a) Possession of a license in a particular discipline such as medical doctors, attorneys, nurses, judges, teachers of special subjects related to the basic course or

(b) Recognition for competency in law enforcement related areas such as probation, corrections, health, fire, drug enforcement, traffic or other special subject or skill areas in which the person has a minimum of five years of full-time experience and training in the subject area to be taught, three years of which must be based on full-time experience

(3) Recommendation of a current basic training school commander.

(4) Special subject instructors shall not be eligible for approval for the driving or firearms units and in no case shall a special subject instructor be approved for more than five topics in the basic course.

(C) Renewal of unit and special subject instructor certification:

(1) Instructors certified by unit shall renew their certificate every three years. At least sixty days and no more than ninety days prior to expiration of the certificate, the instructor shall file with the executive director an application for renewal on a form supplied by the executive director. The instructor shall also file:

(a) Written evidence from the educational or training facility where the instructor received the training documenting that the instructor has successfully completed, within the past three years, a minimum of twenty-four clock hours of training in topics related to the basic training curriculum.

(b) Written evidence from the school commander or administrator that the instructor has taught in two approved peace officer basic training schools for a minimum total of twenty-four teaching hours within the past three years.

(2) Persons certified as special subject instructors shall renew their certificate every three years. At least sixty days and no more than ninety days prior to expiration of the certificate, the instructor shall file with the executive director an application for renewal on a form supplied by the executive director. The instructor shall also file:

(a) Written evidence from the educational or training facility where the instructor received the training documenting that the instructor has successfully completed, within the past three years, a minimum of twelve clock hours of training in topics related to the basic training curriculum.

(b) Written evidence from the school commander or administrator that the instructor has taught in two approved peace officer basic training schools for a minimum total of twelve teaching hours within the past three years.

(D) Denial of certification, denial of renewal of certification or revocation of certification:

(1) Should the executive director refuse to issue or renew a certificate, or should the executive director revoke a certificate, notice of this action shall be sent to the applicant. The applicant shall be advised that he or she may request a hearing before the commission as provided in sections 119.06 and 119.07 of the Revised Code. The commission shall conduct the hearing as required by sections 119.01 to 119.13 of the Revised Code

(E) Grounds for revocation of instructor certification

(1) Failure to meet renewal criteria;

(2) Failure to meet renewal deadline;

(3) Submission of falsified records, application, or other documentation;

(4) Unacceptable performance evaluations;

(5) Conviction of a felony, a crime of moral turpitude or any other peace officer disqualifying offense;

(6) Any other good cause shown.

If an instructor's certification is revoked for any of the listed reasons, notice of this action shall be sent and any requested hearing shall be conducted as required in paragraph (D)(1) of this rule.

HISTORY: 1999–2000 OMR 227 (A), eff. 1–1–00; 1996–97 OMR 809 (A), eff. 12–7–96; 1993–94 OMR 155 (A), eff. 10–1–93; 1987–88 OMR 573 (A–TF 109:2–1–05), eff. 1–15–88; 1987–88 OMR 573 (A–TT 109:2–1–07), eff. 1–1–88; prior PC–1–06

RC 119.032 rule review date(s): 1–1–05; 6–16–99

109:2–1–07 Certificate of completion

(A) Upon successful completion of an approved peace officer basic training course, a person appointed to a peace officer position described in section 109.71(A) of the Revised Code or a person employed in a position statutorily required to complete the basic training course, shall be awarded a certificate of completion by the executive director.

(B) A person successfully completing a basic course who is not a peace officer or who is not statutorily required to complete training and receive certification will be issued a letter of completion by the executive director.

(1) If within one year of the completion of training, the person receives an appointment as a peace officer or is employed in a position that statutorily requires a basic training certificate, a certificate of completion will be awarded provided no additional training requirements have been mandated. If additional training requirements have been mandated, this additional training must be completed before a basic training certificate is awarded.

(2) If more than one year but less than two years after completion of training, a person receives an appointment as a peace officer or obtains employment in a position that statutorily requires peace officer certification, the person shall attend the refresher course prescribed by the executive director before the person may perform the functions of a peace officer. Upon completion of the prescribed refresher course, a certificate of completion of basic training will be awarded. If the person does not complete the refresher course within one year of the appointment date, the person shall not be eligible to receive a certificate and will be required to repeat the entire basic training course.

(3) If more than two years after completion of training a person does not receive an appointment as a peace officer, the person shall successfully complete the peace officer basic training course before he or she may perform the functions of a peace officer.

HISTORY: 1999–2000 OMR 228 (A), eff. 1–1–00; 1987–88 OMR 574 (A–TF 109:2–1–06), eff. 1–1–88; 1987–88 OMR 574 (A–TT 109:2–1–08), eff. 1–1–88; prior PC–1–07

RC 119.032 rule review date(s): 1–1–05; 6–16–99

109:2–1–08 School facilities

Each school shall have available:

(A) A classroom with adequate heating, lighting, ventilation and restroom facilities;

(B) A chalkboard and chalk, or equivalent;

(C) Tables and chairs suitable for writing or seats with an arm for writing;

(D) Audio visual equipment;

(E) A lectern, stand, or table for the instructor's use;

(F) A gymnasium or large indoor area for teaching defensive tactics and other physical skills topics supplied with appropriate training and safety equipment;

(G) Access to a commission-approved firearms range;

(H) Access to a commission-approved driving range.

(I) Any other equipment or facilities as required by the executive director.

HISTORY: 1999–2000 OMR 228 (A), eff. 1–1–00; 1987–88 OMR 574 (A–TF 109:2–1–07), eff. 1–1–88; 1987–88 OMR 574 (A–TT 109:2–1–09), eff. 1–1–88; 1981–82 OMR 383 (A), eff. 3–1–82; prior PC–1–08

RC 119.032 rule review date(s): 1–1–05; 6–16–99

109:2–1–09 Attendance

Attendance shall be required of each individual at all sessions of the basic course.

(A) Absence of five per cent or less.

When a student is absent for five per cent or less of the non-mandatory, commission-required hours of the training course in which the student is enrolled, the school commander may excuse the absence if, in the commander's judgment, the absences were for valid reasons, including but not limited to: illness of either the the [sic.] student or the student's immediate family or an emergency employment situation. The student shall provide the commander with written documentation listing the reasons for the absence. The commander may require the student to make up the missed training to assure that the student has the required mastery of the subjects taught during the school.

(B) Absence of more than five per cent of the non-mandatory commission-required hours.

(1) If a student misses more than five per cent of the non-mandatory commission-required hours of the course, the student may complete the course but shall not be permitted to take the final examination nor shall the student be certified unless approved by the executive director. The student shall submit to the executive director a notarized statement setting forth the reasons for the absences and request to complete the training that was missed. Reasons for absence which the executive director may consider include but are not limited to: illness of either the student or the student's immediate family; emergency employment situations or other valid reasons.

The executive director shall rule on that request within fifteen calendar days of receipt of the request. If the request is granted, the executive director shall approve in writing the method of completing the training.

(2) If the request to complete the course is denied by the executive director, the student may request a hearing before the Ohio peace officer training commission as provided in sections 119.06 and 119.07 of the Revised Code. The commission shall conduct the hearing as required by sections 119.01 to 119.13 of the Revised Code.

(C) There shall be no excused absences from the firearms, domestic violence, crisis intervention, missing, abused and neglected children; laws of arrest; search and seizure, search warrants, civil liability/use of force, confessions and interrogations, cultural sensitivity, driving, report writing, vehicle stops and suspect approaches, hazardous materials response, unarmed self defense, the first aid unit portions of the basic course; or any other topic designated by the Ohio general assembly or the commission.

(D) The commander shall be responsible for maintaining an accurate record of attendance for each student attending the basic course. The commander shall forward such records to the executive director at the completion of training.

HISTORY: 1999–2000 OMR 228 (A), eff. 1–1–00; 1993–94 OMR 155 (A), eff. 10–1–93; 1987–88 OMR 574 (A–TF 109:2–1–08), eff. 1–1–88; 1987–88 OMR 574 (A–TT 109:2–1–10), eff. 1–1–88; prior PC–1–09

RC 119.032 rule review date(s): 1–1–05; 6–16–99

109:2–1–10 Notebook and eligibility requirements for the state certification examination

Each individual in the basic course shall maintain a notebook during the course and shall submit such notebook to the commander for inspection. The notebook shall be evaluated as satisfactory or unsatisfactory by the commander. The notebook shall contain appropriate entries of pertinent material covered during the classroom sessions of the basic course. Among the factors to be evaluated in the notebook are: sufficiency of course content, organization, appropriateness of material, regularity of entries, neatness, accuracy and legibility. Notebooks and the grades assigned to them by the commander are subject to review by the executive director at any time.

(B) No person shall participate in the final written examination who has been evaluated as unsatisfactory for units of instruction in driving, first aid, firearms and unarmed self-defense; the student notebook or any other area designated by the Ohio general assembly or the commission.

HISTORY: 1999–2000 OMR 229 (A), eff. 1–1–00; 1987–88 OMR 575 (A–TF 109:2–1–09), eff. 1–1–88; 1987–88 OMR 575 (A–TT 109:2–1–11), eff. 1–1–88; 1981–82 OMR 383 (A), eff. 3–1–82; prior PC–1–10

RC 119.032 rule review date(s): 1–1–05; 6–16–99

109:2–1–11 Examination

(A) The Ohio peace officer training commission will prepare, conduct and score a final examination for each person completing the basic course. Each student recommended for certification must pass the final written examination with a minimum score to be determined by the commission.

(B) The results of this examination shall be made known to the commander within five business days of the date administered. Persons failing to achieve the designated minimum score shall be given one retest. This test shall normally be given within two weeks of the date the commander is notified of the results of the first examination.

The results of the re-test shall be made known to the commander within five business days of the date administered. Students who fail the retest shall not be permitted to take the final written examination again until they successfully complete another peace officer basic training course.

HISTORY: 1999–2000 OMR 229 (A), eff. 1–1–00; 1990–91 OMR 179 (A), eff. 8–21–90; 1987–88 OMR 575 (A–TF 109:2–1–10), eff. 1–1–88; 1987–88 OMR 575 (A–TT 109:2–1–12), eff. 1–15–88; 1981–82 OMR 384 (A), eff. 3–1–82; prior PC–1–11

RC 119.032 rule review date(s): 1–1–05; 6–16–99

109:2–1–12 Certification before service and re-entry requirements

(A)(1) No person shall, after January 1, 1966, receive an original appointment on a permanent basis as a peace officer unless such person has previously been awarded a certificate by the executive director attesting to his satisfactory completion of the basic course prescribed in rule 109:2–1–16 of the Administrative Code.

(2) No person shall, after January 1, 1989, be permitted to perform the functions of a peace officer or to carry a weapon in connection with peace officer duties unless such person has successfully completed the basic course and has been awarded a certificate of completion by the executive director.

(3) All peace officers employed by a county, township, or municipal corporation of the state of Ohio on January 1, 1966, and who have completed at least sixteen years of full-time active service as such peace officer, may receive an original appointment on a permanent basis and serve as a peace officer of a county, township, or municipal corporation, or as a state university law enforcement officer without receiving a basic training certificate signed by the executive director.

(B) Credit for prior equivalent training or education:

(1) An individual who has successfully completed prior training or education other than under the auspices of the Ohio peace officer training commission and who is appointed as a peace officer in Ohio may request credit for that portion of the basic training course which is equal to training previously completed. Training or education which will be accepted may include, but is not limited to, training or education certified by another state, another government agency, military service, the state highway patrol or a college, university or other educational institution.

(2) The applicant shall provide to the executive director documented evidence of the training. The executive director shall review the record of the prior training or education and make a determination of the training the person shall be required to complete in a commission-approved basic training school.

(3) No credit shall be given under this rule for experience which is not part of a formal training or education program.

(4) If the applicant disputes any of the training assigned by the executive director, he or she may request a hearing before the commission as provided in sections 119.06 and 119.07 of the Revised Code. The commission shall conduct the hearing as required by sections 119.01 to 119.13 of the Revised Code.

(C) All persons who have previously been appointed as a peace officer and have been awarded a certificate of completion of basic training by the executive director or those peace officers described in paragraph (A)(3) of this rule who terminate their appointment from, an agency will have their training eligibility reviewed by the executive director upon reappointment.

Upon appointing a person to a peace officer position as described in section 109.71(A) of the Revised Code, the appointing agency shall submit a request for the executive director to evaluate the officer's training and eligibility to perform the functions of a peace officer. Such request will be made on a form provided by the executive director and shall be submitted immediately upon appointing the officer.

(D) Breaks in service/requirements for update training evaluations:

(1) All persons who have previously been appointed as a peace officer and have been awarded a certificate of completion of basic training by the executive director or those peace officers described in paragraph (A)(3) of this rule who have had their appointment as a peace officer terminated for less than one year may maintain their eligibility for re-appointment as a peace officer. In the event specialized training has been mandated during the period between the date of the original appointment and the re-appointment date, said individual shall be required to successfully complete the mandated specialized training within one year of re-appointment as a peace officer. Officers required to complete such mandated training are permitted to perform the functions of a peace officer for one year from the date of the re-appointment which gave rise to the requirement.

(2) All persons who have previously been appointed as a peace officer and have been awarded a certificate of completion of basic training by the executive director or those peace officers described in paragraph (A)(3) of this rule who have not been appointed as a peace officer for one year or more but less than four years shall, within one year of the re-appointment date as a peace officer, successfully complete a refresher course prescribed by the executive director and any training as required by paragraph (D)(1) of this rule. This course and appropriate examination must be approved by the executive director and shall meet the criteria set forth in this chapter for the conduct of a basic training course. Officers required to complete the refresher course are permitted to perform the functions of a peace officer for one year from the date of the re-appointment which gave rise to the requirement.

(3) All persons who have previously been appointed as a peace officer and have been awarded a certificate of completion of basic training by the executive director or those peace officers described in paragraph (A)(3) of this rule who have not been appointed as a peace officer for more than four years shall, upon

re-appointment as a peace officer, complete the basic training course prior to performing the functions of a peace officer.

(E) Any person who has been appointed as a peace officer and has been awarded a certificate of completion of basic training by the executive director and has been elected or appointed to the office of sheriff shall be considered a peace officer during the term of office for the purpose of maintaining a current and valid basic training certificate. Any training requirements required of peace officers shall also be required of sheriffs.

(F) Every person who has been re-appointed as a peace officer and who must complete training pursuant to paragraph (D)(1) or (D)(2) of this rule shall cease performing the functions of a peace officer and shall cease carrying a weapon unless the person has, within one year from the date of re-appointment, received documentation from the executive director attesting to the satisfactory completion of the above training requirements.

(G) The executive director may extend the time for completion of the training requirements based upon written application from the appointing authority of the individual. Such application will contain an explanation of the circumstances which create the need for the extension. Factors which may be considered in granting or denying the extension include, but are not limited to, serious illness of the individual or an immediate family member, the absence of a reasonably accessible training course, or an unreasonable shortage of manpower within the employing agency. Based on the circumstances in a given case, the executive director may modify the completion date for any training assigned. An extension shall generally be for ninety days, but in no event may the executive director grant an extension beyond one hundred eighty days.

(1) Should the executive director deny the request for an extension, he shall notify and advise the appointing authority that the appointing authority may request a hearing before the commission as provided in sections 119.06 and 119.07 of the Revised Code. The commission shall conduct the hearing as required by sections 119.01 to 119.13 of the Revised Code.

(2) The provisions of paragraph (G) of this rule shall remain in effect until such time as the commission makes the determination to grant or deny the request.

(H) This rule shall not be construed to preclude a township, county, or municipal corporation from establishing time limits for satisfactory completion of the basic course and re-entry requirements of less than the maximum limits prescribed by the commission. If a township, county, or municipal corporation has adopted time limits less than the maximum limits prescribed above, such time limits shall be controlling.

HISTORY: 1999–2000 OMR 229 (A), eff. 1–1–00; 1993–94 OMR 156 (A), eff. 10–1–93; 1990–91 OMR 1022 (A), eff. 3–25–91; 1990–91 OMR 179 (A), eff. 8–21–90; 1987–88 OMR 575 (A–TF 109:2–1–11), eff. 1–15–88; 1987–88 OMR 575 (R), eff. 1–1–88; prior PC–1–12

RC 119.032 rule review date(s): 1–1–05; 6–16–99

109:2–1–16 Explanation of the basic training course

(A) The course content and curriculum of the peace officer basic training program shall be established by the recommendation of the Ohio peace officer training commission and upon approval of the attorney general. It shall be sufficient in content and subject material to provide the student with a strong basic knowledge of the role, function, and practices of a peace officer.

(B) The units, topics, hours, and student performance objectives for the basic course shall, upon approval by the attorney general, be taught in their entirety.

(C) The minimum required curriculum shall not exceed six hundred fifty hours inclusive of those topics listed in ORC sections 109.741, 109.742 and 109.744 and any other topic mandated by the legislature.

(D) The curriculum shall be comprised of topics that are contained in the following units.

(1) Administration

(2) Legal

(3) Human relations

(4) Firearms

(5) Driving

(6) Investigation

(7) Traffic

(8) Patrol

(9) Civil disorders

(10) Unarmed self defense

(11) First aid

(12) Physical conditioning

(E) It is understood that the units, topics, hours, and student performance objectives recommended by the Ohio peace officer training commission and approved by the attorney general are established as mandatory minimum for obtaining certification. Schools, school commanders, and instructors are encouraged to exceed the minimums as they deem appropriate. Reasonable latitude shall be granted to instructors to deliver the material in a manner deemed most effective and to permit the use of instructional methods and material deemed to be the most appropriate and useful, provided the approved material is covered in its entirety.

HISTORY: 1999–2000 OMR 231 (R–E), eff. 1–1–00; 1994–95 OMR 713 (A), eff. 1–1–95; 1993–94 OMR 157 (A), eff. 10–1–93; 1987–88 OMR 576 (R–E), eff. 1–1–88; prior PC–1–16

RC 119.032 rule review date(s): 1–1–05; 6–16–99

109:2–1–17 Public notices of meetings of the Ohio peace officer training commission

(A) Any person may determine the time and place of all regularly scheduled meetings of the Ohio peace officer training commission, place and purpose of all special meetings, of the Ohio peace officer training commission by writing to the "Executive Director, Ohio Peace Officer Training Commission, P.O. Box 309, London, Ohio 43140." Notices of meetings may be also obtained by calling (614) 466–7771 during the hours of eight a.m. to five p.m., Monday through Friday.

(B) Any representative of the news media may obtain notice of all special meetings by requesting, in writing, that such notice shall be provided. A request for such notification shall be addressed to: "Executive Director, Ohio Peace Officer Training Commission, P.O. Box 309, London, Ohio 43140." The request shall provide the name of the individual media representative to be contacted, the person's mailing address and a maximum of two telephone numbers where the person can be reached. The executive director shall maintain a list of all representatives of the news media who have requested notice of special meetings pursuant to this rule.

In the event of a special meeting, not of an emergency nature, the executive director shall notify all media representatives on the list of such meeting by doing one of the following:

(1) Sending written notice, which must be mailed no later than four calendar days prior to the day of the special meeting;

(2) Notifying such representatives by telephone not later than twenty-four hours prior to the special meeting. Such telephone notice shall be completed if a message has been left for the

representative, or if, after reasonable effort, the executive director has been unable to provide such telephone notice.

(C) The executive director shall maintain a list of all persons who have requested, in writing, notice of all meetings of the Ohio peace officer training commission at which specific subject matters designated by such persons are scheduled to be discussed. Any person may, upon payment of an annual fee in the amount of two dollars and fifty cents, have their names placed on such list. The executive director shall, no later than five days prior to each meeting, send by first class mail an agenda of the meeting to such persons.

HISTORY: 1999–2000 OMR 231 (A), eff. 1–1–00; 1987–88 OMR 579 (A–TF 109:2–1–18), eff. 1–1–88; 1987–88 OMR 579 (R), eff. 1–1–88; prior PC–1–17

RC 119.032 rule review date(s): 1–1–05; 6–16–99

CHAPTER 109:2–3

PRIVATE SECURITY TRAINING PROGRAMS

Promulgated pursuant to RC Ch 119

Section

109:2–3–01 Definitions

When used in this chapter:

(A) The term "commission" means the Ohio peace officer training commission;

(B) The term "commander" means the individual, appointed or employed by a training institution and certified by the executive director, as chief administrator of a private security training program;

(C) The term "executive director" means the executive director of the Ohio peace officer training commission;

(D) The term "course" means any private security training program as certified by the executive director of the Ohio peace officer training commission;

(E) The term "private security academic training course" means the training prescribed in this chapter conducted by a private security commander who has been approved and certified in accordance with the rules of this chapter;

(F) The term "private security basic firearms certification course" means the training prescribed in this chapter intended to satisfy the requirements of division (B)(1) of section 109.78 and Chapter 4749. of the Revised Code;

(G) The term "private security firearms requalification course" means the training prescribed in this chapter intended to meet the requirements of division (B)(2) of section 109.78 and Chapter 4749 of the Revised Code;

(H) The term "private security officer" means a person in any position as listed in section 109.78 of the Revised Code which includes persons employed and compensated by a private organization for the purposes of enforcing the ordinances and laws they are empowered to enforce, or to enforce the rules as outlined by said employer on private property or on the property of another who has entered into a formal agreement with the employer to provide such services;

(I) The term "management-level" means a position at a level, within a business or governmental entity, with responsibility for control and direction of personnel and programs, in which the individual is vested with discretionary powers of direction and decision making.

(J) The terms "school" and "training facility" mean the physical site used to conduct training.

HISTORY: 2000–2001 OMR 10 (A), eff. 1–1–01; 1993–94 OMR 159 (A), eff. 10–1–93; prior PC–3–01

RC 119.032 rule review date(s): 1–1–06; 4–7–00

109:2–3–02 Statements of purpose

(A) Private security academic training course

(1) The purpose of this voluntary course is to provide a certified training curriculum approved by the commission for those seeking employment in the private security field. This curriculum and its student performance objectives are the minimum academic standards for completion of the course.

(2) Nothing in these rules shall limit or be construed as limiting the commander from establishing additional training objectives or success criteria above those established by the commission. Where a conflict may arise, commission rules or standards will supersede those of the commander.

(3) Instruction in company, department or agency rules, local ordinances, or school rules may be given upon local initiative. No portion of the instructional time devoted to this part of the training shall be credited toward the hours of instruction and topics required for completion of the certification course.

(B) Private security basic firearms training and requalification courses

(1) The private security basic firearms training and requalification courses are designed to meet the requirements for such training and requalification as established in section 109.78 and Chapter 4749. of the Revised Code.

(2) These courses are designed to prepare students to perform armed functions while on security duty. Nothing in these rules shall be construed as limiting the employing authority or agency from enacting rules and regulations which establish higher standards of training or qualification than those of the commission.

(3) No instruction other than the commission-approved training shall be credited toward the hours or objectives required for basic firearms certification or requalification.

HISTORY: 2000–2001 OMR 10 (A), eff. 1–1–01; 1993–94 OMR 159 (R–E), eff. 10–1–93; prior PC–3–02

RC 119.032 rule review date(s): 1–1–06; 4–7–00

109:2–3–03 Approval of training facilities

(A) Each facility shall have available the following:

(1) A classroom with adequate heating, lighting and ventilation, that is relatively free from external distractions;

(2) A chalkboard or other marking board with chalk or equivalent;

(3) Tables and chairs or seats with arms for writing for each student;

(4) Audio–visual equipment, including but not limited to overhead projector and videocassette player or other comparable viewing apparatus;

(5) A lectern, stand or table for the instructor's use;

(6) A gymnasium or large indoor area for teaching unarmed self-defense, first aid, and other physical skills topics, supplied with appropriate safety and training equipment;

(7) Access to a commission-approved firearms range, if applicable;

(8) Restrooms that will accommodate all students; and

(9) Any other equipment or facilities as required by the executive director.

(B) Basic firearms certification or requalification courses will not require audio-visual equipment or a gymnasium or other large indoor area.

(C) Denial or revocation of approval of a training facility.

(1) The executive director may deny a request for approval of a training facility for failure to meet minimum requirements as set forth in this chapter.

(2) The executive director may revoke the approval of a training facility for failure to maintain minimum requirements as set forth in this chapter.

(3) Should the executive director deny or revoke, approval of a training facility, the executive director shall comply with rule 109:2–3–13 of the Administrative Code.

HISTORY: 2000–2001 OMR 10 (A), eff. 1–1–01; 1993–94 OMR 160 (R–E), eff. 10–1–93; prior PC–3–03

RC 119.032 rule review date(s): 1–1–06; 4–7–00

109:2–3–04 Certification of commanders

(A) Each commander is required to obtain certification from the executive director in order to conduct private security training courses. Such certification will be based upon the submission of a notarized, typewritten statement of qualifications, on a form prescribed by the executive director, by the person seeking certification as a commander. The commander shall conform to the minimum qualifications as set forth in this chapter and must be associated with an approved training facility. Substantiating documentation of qualifications shall accompany the application at the time of submission.

(B) Minimum qualifications for certification as a private security academic training course commander shall be as follows:

(1) High school graduate or possession of a "General Education Development" certificate; and

(2) Three years full time experience in the private security field, a security-related field or the equivalent, as determined by the executive director. Law enforcement experience does not automatically qualify as security-related experience. The determination of applicability will be based upon the functions performed as a law enforcement officer; and

(3) Two years full time experience in a management-level position or completion of ninety quarter hours or sixty semester hours at an accredited college or university; and

(4) Three professional references from individuals currently employed in the security or a security-related field in a management-level position, who have known the individual for at least three years; and

(5) No conviction for a felony or crime of moral turpitude including but not limited to theft, fraud, falsification, drug or sex offenses within twenty years of the date of application for certification. Evidence of a current criminal records check through the bureau of criminal identification and investigation must be submitted with the application.

(C) Joint vocational school private security commanders may be exempted from requirements of paragraph (B)(2) of rule 109:2–3–04 of the Administrative Code by the executive director. This certificate will be specific for those commanders conducting commission-approved courses in joint vocational schools only.

(D) Minimum qualifications for certification as a basic firearms commander or requalification commander.

(1) High school graduate or possession of a "general education development" certification; and

(2) Five years full time experience in the private security field, a security-related field or equivalent as determined by the executive director. Law enforcement experience does not automatically qualify as security-related experience. The determination of applicability will be based upon the functions performed as a law enforcement officer; and

(3) Three professional references from individuals currently employed in the security or a security-related field in a management-level position, who have known the individual for at least three years; and

(4) No conviction for a felony or crime of moral turpitude including but not limited to theft, fraud, falsification, drug or sex offenses within twenty years of the date of application for certification. Evidence of a current criminal record check through the bureau of criminal identification and investigation must be submitted with the application.

(E) Once the application is approved by the executive director, a site inspection and commander orientation will be conducted by commission staff prior to a commander certificate being issued.

(F) Renewal requirements

(1) Certification shall be renewed every three years. At least sixty days and no more than ninety days prior to expiration of the certificate, the individual shall submit, on a form prescribed by the executive director, an application for renewal.

(2) Renewal requirements shall be as follows:

(a) Must conduct at least two courses within the three year period; and

(b) Attend at least one commander conference conducted by the commission;

(i) Should the commission not conduct a conference within the period of certification, this requirement will be suspended for the affected renewal.

(ii) Should the commission conduct only one conference within the period of certification but the individual fails to attend, this requirement can be met by completing another orientation program, as conducted by commission staff.

(3) Renewal shall be effective for three years.

(G) Denial of issuance or renewal of commander certification or revocation of certification.

(1) The executive director may revoke or refuse to issue or renew certification of an individual for the following reasons:

(a) Failure to meet renewal criteria;

(b) Failure to meet renewal deadline;

(c) Failure to maintain satisfactory ratings on commander evaluations;

(d) Submission of falsified records or renewal documentation;

(e) Violations of the rules of this chapter;

(f) Conviction for a felony or crime of moral turpitude including but not limited to theft, fraud, falsification, drug or sex offenses; and

(g) Any other good cause shown.

(2) Should the executive director refuse to issue or renew a certificate, or choose to revoke an individual's certification, the executive director shall comply with rule 109:2–3–13 of the Administrative Code.

HISTORY: 2000–2001 OMR 11 (A), eff. 1–1–01; 1993–94 OMR 160 (R–E), eff. 10–1–93; prior PC–3–04

RC 119.032 rule review date(s): 1–1–06; 4–7–00

109:2–3–05 Certification of instructors

(A) All instructors are required to be certified by the executive director to teach in the private security training program by the executive director. All persons requesting approval as an instructor shall submit a notarized application on a form prescribed by the executive director indicating each topic or unit of topics for which the person is seeking approval. Supporting documentation of qualifications shall accompany the application at the time of submission.

(B) Minimum qualifications for certification as a unit instructor shall be as follows:

(1) High school graduate or possession of a "General Education Development" certificate; and

(2) Five years full time experience in the private security or a related field or the equivalent, as determined by the executive director. Law enforcement experience does not automatically qualify as security-related experience. The determination of applicability will be based upon the functions performed as a law enforcement officer; and

(3) Completion of a course of instruction approved by the executive director designed to prepare the individual to teach. Such courses shall include instruction in the theories of learning, teaching techniques, behavioral objectives, use of audio-visual aids, and an exercise in practice teaching. Credit for this requirement may be granted by the executive director for equivalent training or experience; and

(4) Completion of an instructor-level training program approved by the executive director which will allow a person to learn specific knowledge and skills in a unit for which certification is requested; and

(5) Persons seeking approval as a firearms instructor shall meet the requirements of this section and also provide documentation of three years full time experience as an armed security officer with the weapon for which certification is sought; and

(6) No conviction for a felony or crime of moral turpitude including but not limited to theft, fraud, falsification, drug or sex offenses within twenty years of the date of application for certification. Evidence of a current criminal record check through the bureau of criminal identification and investigation must be submitted with the application.

(C) Topic instructors will be certified only to teach topics within a unit or units of the curriculum, not to exceed five topics. Topic instructors shall not be eligible for approval for the unarmed self-defense and firearms units. Minimum qualifications for certification as a topic instructor shall be as follows

(1) High school diploma or "general education development" certificate; and

(2)(a) Persons licensed, degreed or professionally certified in particular disciplines such as medical doctors, attorneys, nurses, counselors, protection professionals and teachers of specialized subjects related to the private security training course may qualify. Persons licensed, degreed or certified in a particular discipline may be eligible to teach all topics within their area of expertise; or

(b) Persons formally recognized for their professional competency in the security, health, fire safety or other related areas must have a minimum of two years experience; and

(3) No conviction for a felony or crime of moral turpitude including but not limited to theft, fraud, falsification, drug or sex offenses within twenty years of the date of application for certification. Evidence of a current criminal record check through the bureau of criminal identification and investigation must be submitted with the application.

(D) Renewal of certification

(1) Unit instructors shall renew their certification every three years. At least sixty days and no more than ninety days prior to expiration of the certificate, the instructor shall file, on a form prescribed by the executive director, the following:

(a) Written evidence from the commander(s) that the instructor has taught in at least two commission-approved courses during the most recent certification period; and

(b) Must attend at least fifteen clock hours of professional development or continuing education relative to at least one of the areas for which the individual is certified, during the most recent certification period. Documentation of attendance or completion from the training agency or institution must be submitted.

(2) Topic instructors shall renew their certification every three years. At least sixty days and no more than ninety days prior to expiration of the certificate, the instructor shall file, on a form prescribed by the executive director, the following:

(a) Written evidence from the commander(s) that the instructor has taught in at least two commission-approved private security courses during the most recent certification period; and

(b) Proof that certification or license submitted as basis for original certification or most recent renewal is still valid, or has been renewed and is in good standing with the issuing body, or present documentation that they are still actively involved in the participation or practice of the topic area or areas for which certification was granted.

(E) The executive director may revoke or refuse to renew certification of an individual for the following reasons:

(1) Failure to meet renewal criteria;

(2) Failure to meet renewal deadline;

(3) Submission of falsified records or renewal documentation; or

(4) Unacceptable performance evaluations;

(5) Conviction for a felony or crime of moral turpitude involving but not limited to theft, fraud, falsification, drug or sex offenses; or

(6) Any other good cause shown.

(F) Should the executive director refuse to issue or renew a certificate, or choose to revoke an individual's certification, the executive director will comply with rule 109:2–3–13 of the Administrative Code.

HISTORY: 2000–2001 OMR 12 (A), eff. 1–1–01; 1993–94 OMR 161 (E), eff. 10–1–93; 1993–94 OMR 161 (A–TT 109:2–3–11), eff. 10–1–93; prior PC–3–05

RC 119.032 rule review date(s): 1–1–06; 4–7–00

109:2–3–06 Approval of courses

(A) Commanders of any private security training course must be in compliance with rules 109:2–3–03, 109:2–3–04, and 109:2–3–05 of the Administrative Code prior to the submission of an application to conduct a course.

(B) Application requirements for the academic training course.

(1) On a form prescribed by the executive director, the commander shall submit an application and appropriate application fee to the executive director to conduct an academic training course no later than twenty-one days prior to the first day of the course. Included with those items shall be a proposed training calendar, which shall list the following:

(a) Commission topics to be taught;

(b) Instructors' full names and commission-issued certification numbers, and expiration dates of certificates;

(c) Dates of instruction for each topic;

(d) Clock time of instruction for each topic; and

(e) Any other information as may be required by the executive director.

(C) Minimum of six commission-certified instructors must be scheduled to teach in the private security academic training courses.

(D) The commander must have prior written approval from the executive director to conduct the academic training course. This approval shall be valid only for the proposed dates indicated on the application form.

(E) Denial of an application or revocation of course approval.

(1) Courses which are not in compliance with the rules of this chapter will be denied.

(2) Approved courses which are found to be in violation of the rules of this chapter may have their approval revoked by the executive director.

(3) Should the executive director deny an application or revoke approval to conduct a course, the executive director shall comply with rule 109:2–3–13 of the Administrative Code.

(F) Within three calendar days after the course has begun, the commander shall forward to the executive director, of forms prescribed by the executive director, a student enrollment list and an enrollment package, for each student.

(G) Upon completion of the course, the commander shall forward to the executive director all required records, as prescribed by the executive director.

(H) Application requirements for the basic firearms and requalification courses.

(1) On a form prescribed by the executive director, the commander shall submit an application and appropriate application fee to the executive director to conduct a basic firearms or requalification course no later than twenty-one days prior to the first day of the course. Included with those items shall be a proposed training calendar, which shall list the following:

(a) Dates of training for classroom and firing range;

(b) Instructors' full names, commission-issued certification numbers, and expiration dates of certificates;

(c) Clock time of instruction; and

(d) Any other information as may be required by the executive director.

(2) The commander must have prior written approval from the executive director to conduct the basic firearms or requalification course. This approval shall be valid only for the proposed dates indicated on the application form.

(3) Denial of an application or revocation of course approval.

(a) Courses which are not in compliance with the rules of this chapter will be denied.

(b) Approved courses which are found to be in violation of the rules of this chapter may have their approval revoked by the executive director.

(c) Should the executive director deny an application or revoke approval to conduct a course, the executive director shall comply with rule 109:2–3–13 of the Administrative Code.

(4) Upon completion of the course, the commander shall forward to the executive director all required records, as prescribed by the executive director.

HISTORY: 2000–2001 OMR 12 (A), eff. 1–1–01; 1993–94 OMR 162 (R–E), eff. 10–1–93; prior PC–3–06

RC 119.032 rule review date(s): 1–1–06; 4–7–00

109:2–3–07 Attendance requirements

(A) Private security academic training course

(1) Attendance is required at all sessions of the course.

(a) Absence of ten percent or less.

When a student is absent for ten percent or less of the non-mandatory commission-required hours of the training course in which the student is enrolled, the school commander may excuse the absence if in the commander's judgment, the absences were for valid reasons, including but not limited to illness of either the student or the student's immediate family or an emergency employment situation. The student shall provide the commander with written documentation listing the reasons for the absence. The commander may require the student to make up the missed hours of training.

(b) Absence of more than ten percent of the non-mandatory commission-required hours.

If a student misses more than ten percent of the non-mandatory commission-required hours of the course, the student will not be eligible to take the final examination and will fail the course.

(B) One hundred percent attendance shall be required for the mandatory topics of laws of arrest, search and seizure, cultural sensitivity, unarmed self-defense, and first aid, any portion of any firearm training course which is conducted and any other topic designated by the Ohio general assembly or the commission.

HISTORY: 2000–2001 OMR 13 (A), eff. 1–1–01; 1993–94 OMR 162 (R–E), eff. 10–1–93; prior PC–3–07

RC 119.032 rule review date(s): 1–1–06; 4–7–00

109:2–3–08 Notebook

(A) Each person enrolled in the private security academic training course shall maintain a notebook, as one of the requirements for certification. The notebook shall be periodically reviewed and evaluated as satisfactory or unsatisfactory by the commander. The notebook shall contain appropriate entries of pertinent material covered during the classroom sessions of the training course. Among the factors to be evaluated in the notebook, shall be:

(1) Sufficiency of course content;

(2) Organization;

(3) Appropriateness of material;

(4) Regularity of entries;

(5) Neatness;

(6) Accuracy; and

(7) Legibility.

(B) Notebooks and the grades assigned to them by the commander are subject to review by the executive director at any time.

(C) Any person whose notebook has been evaluated as unsatisfactory by the commander shall not be eligible to take the final examination, and will fail the course.

HISTORY: 2000–2001 OMR 13 (A), eff. 1–1–01; 1993–94 OMR 162 (A), eff. 10–1–93; prior PC–3–08

RC 119.032 rule review date(s): 1–1–06; 4–7–00

109:2–3–09 Examination

(A) The Ohio peace officer training commission will prepare, conduct and score a final examination for each person successfully completing the private security academic training course. Each student recommended for certification must pass the final examination with a minimum score to be determined by the commission. Special skills training such as first aid, firearms, and unarmed self defense, which are tested through practical demonstrations, will not be covered on the final examination.

(B) No student shall participate in the final examination who has not successfully completed first aid or unarmed self-defense, or has failed to submit a satisfactory student notebook.

(C) No student shall participate in the final examination who has failed to meet the minimum attendance requirements established by the commission.

(D) The results of this examination shall be made known to the commander within five business days of the date administered. Persons failing to achieve the designated minimum score shall be given one retest. This retest shall normally be given within two weeks of the date the commander is notified of the initial examination results. The results of the retest shall be made known to the commander within five business days of the date administered. Students who fail the retest shall not be permitted to take the final examination again until they successfully complete another private security academic training course.

HISTORY: 2000–2001 OMR 14 (A), eff. 1–1–01; 1994–95 OMR 1575 (A), eff. 3–16–95; 1993–94 OMR 163 (A), eff. 10–1–93; prior PC–3–09

RC 119.032 rule review date(s): 1–1–06; 4–7–00

109:2–3–10 Firearms certification

(A) Persons holding positions listed in section 109.78 of the Revised Code in which such persons go armed while on duty shall successfully complete a basic firearms training course which includes a minimum of twenty hours of training in each handgun to be used and, if the shotgun is to be used, a minimum of five hours of training in the use of the shotgun. In order to successfully complete this course of instruction, a student must pass each student performance objective outlined in the commission-approved basic firearms course. Failure to pass any objective results in failure of the course.

(1) Certification shall be valid for a period of eighteen months from the date of completion of the basic firearms training course.

(2) The renewal date for initial requalification shall be established as eighteen months from the date of initial certification. That date shall remain constant each year, until such time as the individual fails to requalify prior to the expiration date of a current certification period. Such failure to act shall void the renewal date and a commission-approved minimum twenty-hour basic firearms training course shall be repeated.

(B) Persons holding positions listed in Ohio Revised Code 109.78 in which such persons go armed while on duty shall be required, on an annual basis, to successfully complete a minimum of four hours of a firearms requalification course approved by the Ohio peace officer training commission. In order to requalify, a person must pass each student performance objective outlined in the firearms requalification course. Failure to pass any objective results in failure of the course.

(1) The renewal date for initial requalification shall be established as eighteen months from the completion date of the initial basic firearms training course. That date shall remain constant each year until such time as the individual fails to requalify prior to the expiration date of a current certification period. Such failure to act shall void the renewal date and the basic firearms training course must be repeated.

(2) Requalification shall be valid for a period of twelve months from the date of completion of the firearms requalification course.

(3) Individuals may requalify in one of the following timeframes:

(a) Within ninety days of their expiration date without affecting the renewal date; or

(b) More than ninety days prior to the expiration date which will establish a new renewal date. The new renewal date shall be twelve months from the date of the current requalification course.

(4) Individuals who fail to requalify prior to the expiration date shall repeat a commission-approved minimum twenty-hour basic firearms training course.

HISTORY: 2000–2001 OMR 14 (A), eff. 1–1–01; 1993–94 OMR 163 (A), eff. 10–1–93; 1986–87 OMR 901 (R–E), eff. 2–27–87; prior PC–3–10

RC 119.032 rule review date(s): 1–1–06; 4–7–00

109:2–3–11 Private security academic training course certificate of completion

(A) Upon satisfactory completion of the academic training course, the commander shall recommend the student for certification, on a form prescribed by the executive director.

(B) A student who successfully completes the academic training course but fails the optional firearms course will receive a certificate for the academic training course only.

(C) A student who successfully completes the optional firearms training portion of the private security academic training course but fails the academic training course will not receive a certificate of completion for the firearms training course.

(D) Receipt of the certificate by the student shall be considered as successful completion of the approved training course.

HISTORY: 2000–2001 OMR 15 (A), eff. 1–1–01; 1993–94 OMR 163 (A–TF 109:2–3–05), eff. 10–1–93; 1993–94 OMR 163 (R), eff. 10–1–93; prior PC–3–11

RC 119.032 rule review date(s): 1–1–06; 4–7–00

109:2–3–12 Description of the private security academic training course

(A) The course content and curriculum of the private security academic training course shall be established and approved by the commission. It shall be sufficient in content and subject material to provide the student with a basic knowledge of the role, functions, and practices of the private security officer.

(B) The units, topics, hours and student performance objectives for the course shall be approved by the commission, and must be taught in their entirety.

(C) The curriculum shall be comprised of topics that will be contained in the following units:

(1) Administration;

(2) Legal;

(3) Human relations;

(4) Communications;

(5) Loss prevention;

(6) Safety and protective services;

(7) Unarmed self-defense; and

(8) First aid.

(D) Firearms training may also be offered for those students who seek certification in that area. Pursuant to section 2923.21 of the Revised Code, no person under eighteen years of age may participate in any portion of the firearms training.

(E) The units, topics, hours and student performance objectives mandated by the commission are minimum requirements for obtaining certification. Commanders and instructors are encouraged to exceed these minimum requirements.

HISTORY: 2000–2001 OMR 15 (A), eff. 1-1-01; 1993–94 OMR 163 (E), eff. 10-1-93

RC 119.032 rule review date(s): 1-1-06; 4-7-00

109:2-3-13 Adjudication hearing procedure

If a request for certification or renewal of any certification is denied, or if certification or school approval is revoked, the executive director shall notify and advise the affected party that the affected party may request a hearing before the commission as provided in sections 119.06 and 119.07 of the Revised Code. The commission shall conduct the hearing as required by sections 119.01 to 119.13 of the Revised Code.

HISTORY: 2000–2001 OMR 15 (A), eff. 1-1-01; 1993–94 OMR 164 (E), eff. 10-1-93

RC 119.032 rule review date(s): 1-1-06; 4-7-00

120

PUBLIC DEFENDER COMMISSION

CHAPTER 120–1

GENERAL PROVISIONS

Promulgated pursuant to RC 111.15

120–1–01 Declaration of policy

It is the intent of the commission to adopt rules to govern the manner and form under which the Ohio public defender commission shall conduct its programs of providing, supervising, and coordinating legal representation pursuant to Chapter 120. of the Revised Code. It is the intent of the commission that such rules will apply to assigned/appointed counsel and county or joint county public defender systems. It is also the intent of the commission that the rules be applied in a uniform manner that will insure proper and adequate legal services for the indigent and other persons entitled to such services in Ohio.

HISTORY: 1999–2000 OMR 335 (A), eff. 1–1–00; 1977–78 OMR 3–829 (E), eff. 1–9–78

RC 119.032 rule review date(s): 8–27–04; 8–27–99

120–1–03 Standards of indigency

Ohio public defender commission's rules are promulgated pursuant to divisions (B)(1), (B)(6), (B)(7), and (B)(8) of section 120.03 of the Revised Code. Further considerations include *State vs. Tymcio* (1975), 42 Ohio St.2d. 39 and the Ohio supreme court rules of superintendence.

(A) General statement of policy. When required by rule or law to appoint counsel for indigent persons, the criteria for determining indigency shall include: ownership and ready availability of real or personal property; all household income, inheritance, expectancies, and other assets; number and age of dependents; outstanding debts, obligations and liabilities; and any other relevant considerations. The pivotal issue in determining indigency is not whether the applicant ought to be able to employ counsel but whether the applicant is, in fact, able to do so. Possible sources of income, assets, and liabilities are listed on the financial disclosure form attached hereto in appendix A.

(B) Income standards.

(1) Presumptive eligibility. Without other substantial assets, individuals whose income is not greater than 125 per cent of the current poverty threshold established by the United States office of management and budget may be presumed to require the appointment of counsel. An individual whose income is between 125 percent and 187.5 per cent of the federal poverty guidelines may still be presumed to require the appointment of counsel if any of the following apply:

(a) Applicant's household income, minus allowable expenses, yields no more than 125 per cent of the federal poverty income guidelines.

(b) Allowable expenses are the cost of medical care, childcare, transportation, and other costs required for work, or the cost associated with the infirmity of a resident family member incurred during the preceding twelve months and child support actually paid from household income.

(c) The applicant has liabilities and or expenses, including unpaid taxes, the total of which exceeds the applicant's income.

(2) Presumptive ineligibility. Applicants having liquid assets that exceed one thousand dollars for misdemeanor cases and five thousand dollars in felony cases shall be presumed to be not indigent. For purposes of this rule, "liquid assets" are defined as those resources that are in cash or payable upon demand. The most common types of liquid assets are cash on hand, savings accounts, checking accounts, trusts, stocks, and mortgages. Applicants with an income over 187.5 per cent of the federal poverty level shall be deemed not indigent.

(3) The poverty income thresholds (125 per cent—187.5 per cent) are updated annually by the United States office of management and budget and may be found in the federal register. These income thresholds are based on gross income. They will be available, on request, from the Ohio public defender commission.

(4) Applicants being detained in a state institution shall have only their own income and assets considered, as they have no "household" for purposes of this rule.

(C) Other factors.

(1) Seriousness of charge weighed against possession of liquid assets. In determining whether a defendant is indigent, the seriousness of the charge shall be taken into consideration. A defendant may be found not indigent if the individual possesses liquid assets in excess of the assigned/appointed counsel fees paid for a case of equal seriousness in the county in which the charges

are brought. In lieu of using the assigned/appointed counsel fee, other methods of determining fees for competent counsel may be used, including a survey of attorneys representing defendants in criminal cases.

(2) The equity value in the applicant's principal residence and other valuable assets may be included in the consideration.

(3) Release on bail shall not prevent a person from being determined indigent.

(4) Counsel shall not be denied solely because an applicant's friends or relatives have resources adequate to retain counsel.

(D) Juvenile court. In determining eligibility of a child for court- appointed counsel in juvenile court, only the child's income shall initially be considered. The court is encouraged to order parents who are not indigent to pay for the necessary costs of representation for the child in delinquency, unruly, and traffic cases. In no case shall a child be denied appointed counsel because a parent refuses to disclose their financial information or to participate in a reimbursement, recoupment, contribution, or partial payment program.

(E) Redetermination. A preliminary determination of ineligibility for legal representation shall not foreclose a redetermination of eligibility when, at a subsequent stage of a proceeding, new information or changes in circumstances concerning the financial inability to retain competent counsel becomes available.

(F) Waiver. the person or agency determining indigency in individual cases has the authority to waive these guidelines in unusual or meritorious situations. In such situations, the waiver decision shall be documented and included in the client's file. However, despite the income and assets of the individual requesting court-appointed counsel, the person or agency making the determination of indigency must consider *State vs. Tymcio* (1975) 42 Ohio St. 2d. 39, which states "to make the right of court-appointed counsel a factual reality, the determination of need must turn, not upon whether an accused ought to be able to employ counsel, but whether he is, in fact, able to do so." id. at 45.

(G) Confidentiality. Rules, regulations, and procedures concerning the determination of initial eligibility and/or continued eligibility shall not require assigned/appointed counsel and/or public defenders to make any disclosures concerning the client's financial status beyond disclosures mandated by the binding ethical rules of the jurisdiction, the court's determination of indigency, and section 120.38 of the Revised Code.

(H) Other prohibitions. The procedure whereby it is determined whether or not a person is entitled to have publicly provided counsel shall not deter a person from exercising any constitutional, statutory, or procedural right. Specifically, such rights shall not be deprived by any means, including, but not limited to the following:

(1) By such stringency of application of financial eligibility standard as may cause a person to waive representation of counsel rather than incur the expense of retained counsel;

(2) By unnecessarily conditioning the exercise of the right to counsel on the waiver of some other constitutional, statutory, or procedural right.

(I) Requests for specific appointed counsel. When a defendant makes a request for a specific appointed counsel pursuant to section 120.33(A) of the Revised Code, such request shall be acted upon promptly.

(J) Those counties that appoint counsel for persons with incomes between 125 per cent and 187.5 per cent of the current poverty threshold, shall establish a reimbursement, recoupment, contribution, or partial payment program that includes a fee for the cost of income verification.

(K) Financial disclosure form. A form requesting information from the applicant shall be completed for each client prior to appointment of counsel or as soon thereafter as practicable. Each county shall use the application for court-appointed representation form as set forth in appendix A of this rule.

The financial disclosure/affidavit of indigency form set forth in appendix A shall be used unless the county submits their own form to the Ohio public defender commission for review and approval. The form must include the information listed in paragraph (D) of this rule. The form must also contain an affidavit of indigency and the judge certification as set forth in appendix A. Counties that are already using their own form may continue to use this form during the review process. The commission shall, in turn, notify such jurisdiction of the approval or disapproval of the financial disclosure form within ninety days of submission.

(L) Review and approval. Any programs established pursuant to paragraph (J) of this rule shall be sent to the Ohio public defender commission for review and approval before the program becomes effective. In counties that already have such a program, the program may continue during the review process. The commission shall, in turn, notify such jurisdiction of the approval or disapproval of local programs within ninety days of submission.

(M) Partial reimbursement. The ability to contribute a portion of the cost of adequate legal representation shall not preclude eligibility for assigned/appointed counsel. All programs developed to seek reimbursement for the cost of assigned/appointed counsel from the defendant shall be subject to guidelines established for such programs in other commission rules. Programs established for those who fall above income/asset levels shall be approved by the Ohio public defender commission.

(N) Verification procedures. All counties shall have an income verification process. This process shall be used to verify the financial information provided by the applicant on the financial disclosure form. Income verification need not be done on every case, but may be done randomly based on complaints, or by any other method that is practical.

HISTORY: 1999–2000 OMR 335 (A), eff. 1–1–00; 1995–96 OMR 1085 (A), eff. 1–1–96; 1991–92 OMR 177 (R–E), eff. 9–27–91; 1977–78 OMR 3–830 (E), eff. 1–9–78

RC 119.032 rule review date(s): 8–27–04; 8–27–99

120–1–04 Hiring of other counsel

Subject to prior approval of the court, other counsel should be employed whenever necessary to protect the rights of the client, including, but not limited to the following:

(A) When dealing with matters involving highly technical areas requiring special expertise;

(B) When needed to depose a witness not located in the immediate area;

(C) When necessary to resolve conflicts of interest;

(D) When the assistance of other counsel is necessary to provide an adequate and effective defense.

HISTORY: 1999–2000 OMR 336 (A), eff. 1–1–00; 1977–78 OMR 3–831 (E), eff. 1–9–78

RC 119.032 rule review date(s): 8–27–04; 8–27–99

120–1–05 Recoupment, contribution, partial payment and marginally indigent programs

The commission supports the development of recoupment programs, contribution programs, partial payment programs, marginally indigent programs, and other efforts to contain costs. However, any such program should not jeopardize the quality of defense provided or act to deny representation to qualified defendants. Examples of such programs will be available through the office of the Ohio public defender. In no case shall such a program require or include direct payment(s) from the applicant to appointed counsel. No payments, compensation, or in-kind services shall be required from an applicant or client whose income falls under 125 per cent of the federal poverty guidelines.

HISTORY: 1999–2000 OMR 336 (A), eff. 1–1–00; 1991–92 OMR 178 (R–E), eff. 9–27–91; 1977–78 OMR 3–831 (E), eff. 1–9–78

RC 119.032 rule review date(s): 8–27–04; 8–27–99

120–1–06 Facilities for a county or joint county public defender office

The supporting staff, facilities and other requirements needed to maintain and operate an office of a county or joint county public defender shall be sufficient to allow effective representation and shall be substantially equivalent to that provided for other public components of the justice system. In applying this rule, the following criteria shall be governing:

(A) The budget of a public defender shall include:

(1) Adequate quarters and other facilities;

(2) An adequate library to meet the needs mandated by the duties of the office, considering the needs of the office and the availability of other libraries;

(3) Adequate tape-recording, photographic, and other investigative equipment of a sufficient quantity, quality, and versatility to permit preservation of evidence;

(4) Funds available for the confidential employment of experts and specialists, such as psychiatrists, pathologists, and other scientific experts in all cases where the same may be of assistance to the defense;

(5) Supportive services shall include secretarial, investigative, and other services necessary for an adequate defense. These shall include not only those services needed for an effective defense at trial, but also those that are required for effective defense participation in every phase of the process, including determinations on pretrial release, competency to stand trial, and disposition following conviction, appeals, and post-conviction relief.

(B) The office of the county public defender or joint county public defender shall be located with consideration for the convenience to clients and access to the courts and other necessary services.

(C) Each defender shall have adequate office space to assure privacy in consultation with clients and efficiency in operations.

HISTORY: 1999–2000 OMR 337 (A), eff. 1–1–00; 1977–78 OMR 3–831 (E), eff. 1–9–78

RC 119.032 rule review date(s): 8–27–04; 8–27–99

120–1–07 Caseload standards, workload, budget, and logistics of a county or joint county public defender office

Neither the public defender office nor public defender attorney should accept a workload which, by reason of the excessive size thereof, threatens to deny due process of law to clients or places the office or attorney in imminent danger of violating the "Code of Professional Responsibility."

(A) Each public defender office shall establish a minimum and maximum workload for its attorneys and staff, the overall goal being high quality criminal defense representation achieved efficiently.

(B) No public defender attorney shall accept any appointment which exceeds or jeopardizes his or her ability to render effective assistance of counsel to each defendant. No public defender shall accept a case in violation of the "Code of Professional Responsibility."

(C) Whenever by reason of excessive workload the public defender determines that the assumption of additional cases or continued representation in previously accepted cases by his office lead to inadequate representation in these or other cases, he shall declare such fact to the court.

HISTORY: 1999–2000 OMR 337 (A), eff. 1–1–00; 1977–78 OMR 3–831 (E), eff. 1–9–78

RC 119.032 rule review date(s): 8–27–04; 8–27–99

120–1–09 Contracts with municipal corporations

County commissioners, public defenders, county public defender commissions and joint county public defender commissions may contract with a municipal corporation for the legal representation of indigent persons charged with violations of the ordinances of the municipal corporation.

(A) All such contracts with municipal corporations pertaining to legal representation of indigent persons charged with violations of municipal corporation ordinances shall have approval of the Ohio public defender commission.

(B) Reimbursement by the municipal corporation for representation of such indigent persons may be by a contractual amount or a fee schedule, however, in either event such reimbursement shall not exceed the fee schedule in effect and adopted by the county commissioners of the county wherein the municipal corporation is located.

(C) All contracts with municipal corporations shall provide for conformity with the standards of indigency and other rules and standards established by the Ohio public defender commission and the state public defender.

HISTORY: 1999–2000 OMR 337 (A), eff. 1–1–00; 1977–78 OMR 3–832 (E), eff. 1–9–78

RC 119.032 rule review date(s): 8–27–04; 8–27–99

120–1–10 Qualifications for assigned/appointed counsel and public defenders in cases in where reimbursement for defense costs is sought by a county from the Ohio public defender

(A) A county shall not receive reimbursement for defense costs from the state public defender unless the assigned/appointed counsel and/or public defender representing the indigent applicant meets the following minimum qualifications:

(1) Where the defendant is charged with aggravated murder with death penalty specifications, or has been convicted and sentenced to death, any attorney appointed for trial or appellate representation must meet the qualifications set forth in rule 20 of the Ohio supreme court "Rules of Superintendence" and appear on the list of attorneys qualified to accept appointments in capital cases promulgated by the rule 20 committee or have a waiver issued by the rule 20 committee.

(2) Where the defendant is charged with murder or aggravated murder without specifications, appointed counsel shall possess:

(a) Prior experience as trial counsel or co-counsel in one prior murder trial; or

(b) Prior experience as trial counsel in two first degree felony or aggravated felony trials; or

(c) Prior experience as trial counsel in ten or more jury trials.

(3) Where the defendant is charged with a felony of the first, second, or third degree, appointed counsel shall possess:

(a) Prior experience as trial counsel in two or more first, second, or third degree felony trials, at least one of which was a jury trial; or

(b) Prior experience as trial counsel in any four jury trials at least one of which was a jury trial in a first, second, or third degree felony; or

(c) Prior experience as trial counsel in any two criminal trials; and

(i) Co–counsel in at least one criminal jury trial;

(ii) Trial counsel or co-counsel in two jury trials.

(4) Where the defendant is charged with a fourth-degree or fifth degree felony, appointed counsel shall possess:

(a) Prior experience as trial counsel or co-counsel in at least one jury trial; or

(b) Prior completion of a training program on criminal practice or procedure which is certified for continuing legal education credit by the Ohio supreme court commission on continuing legal education.

(B) Assignment should be distributed as widely as possible among members of the bar who meet the qualifications for assignment.

(C) If appointed counsel fails to follow the stated qualifications, the Ohio public defender commission may refuse to approve reimbursement for the appointment of particular counsel pursuant to division (B) of section 120.18, division (B) of section 120.28 and sections 120.33 and 2941.51 of the Revised Code. Prior to the appointment or at the time of appointment, the court may submit the appropriate qualification information pertaining to counsel to the Ohio public defender for determination of whether counsel qualifies for reimbursement pursuant to division (B) of section 120.18, division (B) of section 120.28, and sections 120.33 and 2941.51 of the Revised Code.

(D) The respective courts and county and joint county public defender commissions shall be free to adopt local rules requiring qualifications in addition to the minimum standards established by this rule.

HISTORY: 1999–2000 OMR 338 (A), eff. 1–1–00; 1991–92 OMR 178 (R–E), eff. 9–27–91; 1984–85 OMR 465 (E), eff. 11–16–84; 1984–85 OMR 465 (R), eff. 11–16–84; 1979–80 OMR 4–140 (E), eff. 9–1–79

RC 119.032 rule review date(s): 8–27–04; 8–27–99

120–1–11 Time limits for reimbursement of county expenditures for assigned/appointed counsel and public defender offices

The following time limits on submission of requests for state reimbursement under the Ohio indigent defense program by county boards of county commissioners to the state public defender office are hereby adopted:

(A) Assigned/appointed counsel expenditures shall not be reimbursed by the state public defender unless submitted by the county within ninety days of the end of the calendar month in which the case involved was terminated.

(B) County public defender office operating expenditures shall not be reimbursed by the state public defender unless submitted by the county within sixty days of the end of the calendar month in which the expenditures were incurred.

The state public defender may grant an extension in writing to a county that has made a request for an extension in writing for a period of time not exceeding that originally allowed under this rule in order to correct errors in an attorney certificate or county public defender monthly statement and resubmit them.

HISTORY: 1999–2000 OMR 338 (A), eff. 1–1–00; 1980–81 OMR 737 (E), eff. 5–8–81

RC 119.032 rule review date(s): 8–27–04; 8–27–99

120–1–12 Standards governing contracts between county and joint county public defender commissions and non-profit organizations for the provision of indigent representation

(A) The purpose of this rule is to establish standards governing contracts between county and joint county public defender commissions and non-profit organizations or the state pubic defender to provide legal representation pursuant to Chapter 120. of the Revised Code. Any county that desires to receive reimbursement from the state public defender for such a contract system must first obtain approval of the contract from the Ohio public defender commission. No reimbursement will be made for contracts that do not have prior approval of the Ohio public defender commission. All contracts submitted to the commission for approval must be drafted in accordance with the provisions of section 120.14 or 120.24 of the Revised Code.

(B) Contracting authority

Contracting authority as used in this rule, is a county or joint county public defender commission established pursuant to section 120.13 or 120.23 of the Revised Code unless the contractor is the state public defender, in which case the contracting authority is the board of county commissioners. Any contract with a non-profit organization submitted to the commission for approval pursuant to this rule must be accompanied by both the court order and the county commissions resolution that established the county or joint county public defender commission and that appointed the members to that commission.

(C) Contractor

Contractor as used in this rule, is the state public defender or a non-profit organization incorporated in the state of Ohio. The primary purpose of the non-profit organization must be to provide legal representation to indigent persons. Any contract for approval pursuant to this rule must be accompanied by the Ohio articles of incorporation of the contractor.

(D) Approval of the county board of commissioners

The contracting authority shall obtain the approval of the county board of commissioners for the entire amount of a contract with a non-profit organization prior to signing the contract. The board of county commissioners shall not interfere with the selection of the non-profit organization with which to contract. All contracts submitted to the commission pursuant to this rule must contain a resolution of the board of county commissioners that sufficient funds have been or will be appropriated and will be available to meet the contracting authority's obligations under the contract.

(E) Elements of a contract for indigent defense services

(1) Parties. The contract shall identify the contracting authority, the contactor, and any other public or private person, agency, or organization which is party to the contract.

(2) Scope of the contract. The contract shall specify the categories and percentages of indigent defense cases in which the contractor is to provide services and the categories in which the contractor is not to provide services.

(3) Determination of eligibility. The contract shall specify the procedure by which client financial eligibility is to be determined and contain a standard of indigency incorporating by reference rule 120–1–03 of the Administrative Code.

(4) Term of the contract. Contracts for legal defense services shall be awarded for a term of one year. The contract shall specify that the contractor has the responsibility to complete any and all cases once representation is commenced under the terms of the contract. Representation commenced in the trial court shall be continued through all trail [sic.] court proceedings; representation commenced by or taken to an appeals court by the contractor shall be continued until the appeals process is terminated by an action final on the merits by that appeals court. The contract should specify that this provision does not prohibit a contractor or attorney from withdrawing from a case due to a conflict of interest recognized by a court, or from withdrawing due to a finding of the client's financial ineligibility for services.

(5) Attorney staff. The contract may require the contractor to use full-time or part-time attorneys. If the contract is for the use of part-time attorneys, it shall contain provisions to ensure that the part-time attorneys devote the time necessary to provide effective representation to the indigent clients.

(6) Support staff, investigators and forensic experts. The contract shall provide for the employment of a support staff or secretaries and non-legal personnel for the office. The contract should also specify that adequate funds be provided for investigators, social workers, mental health professionals, and other forensic experts necessary to provide competent representation. No contract clause should interfere with the contractor's selection, supervision, and direction of these persons.

(7) Compensation. The contract shall provide that the contractor compensate its staff employees, subcontractors and retained forensic experts at rates commensurate with their training, experience and responsibilities, and compensation paid to persons doing similar work in public agencies in the jurisdiction.

(8) Extraordinary compensation. The contract shall provide for extraordinary compensation in cases that require an extraordinary amount of time and preparation, including but not limited to cases in which the death penalty is a possibility. Services that require compensation in excess of the normal rate should be defined in the contract.

(9) Compensation of additional attorneys and conflicts of interest. The contract shall contain provision for compensation for additional attorneys where conflicts of interest arise and the contractor is unable to provide representation. The contract may contain provisions respecting other extraordinary circumstances creating an inability to provide representation and necessitating compensation for additional attorneys.

(10) Financial reports. The contract shall provide that the contractor retain financial records, submit financial reports and submit to a financial audit no less frequently than annually and report these findings to the contracting authority. Copies of the annual audit shall be forwarded to the Ohio public defender commission as part of the annual report submitted pursuant to sections 120.14 and 120.24 of the Revised Code.

(11) Standards of representation. The contract shall require that the contractor provide legal services to all clients in a professional, skilled manner consistent with Chapter 120. of the Revised Code, the rules of the Ohio public defender commission, the Ohio public defender standards and guidelines, the canons of ethics for attorneys in Ohio, and case law and applicable court rules defining the duties of counsel and the rights of defendants in criminal cases. The contract shall provide that counsel under contract shall be available to eligible defendants at their request or the request of someone acting on their behalf at arrest, formal charging, or indictment. The contractor shall insure that attorneys provided by the contract shall be accessible to applicants in regard to criminal or delinquency matters before formal court appointment.

(12) Insurance. The contract shall require that the contractor provide malpractice insurance for attorneys representing indigent clients under terms of the contract. The contract shall not provide that the contractor hold the government or contracting authority harmless for the attorney's representation of the clients.

(13) Management system. The contract shall provide that the contractor maintain a case reporting and management information system from which data shall be available and provided to the contracting authority upon request. The contracting authority shall report the caseload data required by the state public defender when submitting its monthly request for reimbursement. Any such system shall be maintained independently from client files so as to disclose no privileged information. The case reporting and management information system shall be used to provide the contractor, contracting authority, and the Ohio public defender commission with caseload information sufficient to insure compliance with the Ohio public defender commission's rules, Chapter 120. of the Revised Code, and the state public defender standards and guidelines.

(F) Awarding the contract

The contracting authority shall award a contract for indigent criminal cases only when it appears that the contractor adequately addresses the issues stated in this rule, Chapter 120. of the Revised Code, the rules of the Ohio public defender commission, and the state public defender standards. Under no circumstances should a contract be awarded based on cost alone. The contracting authority shall determine when the proposed budget of a potential contractor will provide the capability of complying with this rule. The Ohio public defender commission shall not approve any contract when it appears that it has been awarded on [1] based on cost effectiveness alone.

(G) Approval by the Ohio public defender commission of contracts

The Ohio public defender commission shall approve a contract that conforms with this standard and complies with all applicable sections of Chapter 120. of the Revised Code, the rules of the commission, and state public defender standards and guidelines.

(H) Contracts with law schools, legal aid societies, and non-profit organizations

Any law school, legal aid society, or non-profit organization that enters into a contract with the state public defender to provide counsel shall be subject to the policies and procedures established by the Ohio public defender commission and "the supreme court rules for the government of the bar of Ohio".

(1) The standards employed by the state public defender in determining eligibility for representation shall be used by the organizations.

(2) All such contracts are subject to the prior approval and continued supervision of the Ohio public defender commission.

HISTORY: 1999–2000 OMR 339 (A), eff. 1–1–00; 1991–92 OMR 179 (E), eff. 9–27–91

RC 119.032 rule review date(s): 8–27–04; 8–27–99

[1] So in original. Should "on" be deleted?

120–1–13 Denial of reimbursement to the counties in capital cases

The state public defender, pursuant to sections 120.34 and 120.35 of the Revised Code, shall review each request for reimbursement to a county in an indigent capital case at the trial, appellate, and/or postconviction levels, to ensure that the following criteria governing the appointment of counsel are met:

(A) Lead counsel and co-counsel are appointed from the lists maintained by the Ohio supreme court, pursuant to rule 20 of the "Rules of Superintendence of the Common Pleas Court" or have obtained a waiver issued by the rule 20 committee. Such waiver shall accompany the reimbursement request.

(B) All other provisions of rule 20 are adhered to by the appointing court, board of county commissioners, and attorneys appointed in the case for which reimbursement is sought.

If these criteria are not met, the Ohio public defender commission shall deny reimbursement to the county for all of the defender costs associated with that indigent capital case.

This rule shall be effective for all appointments of counsel in capital trial, appellate, and/or postconviction cases occurring after October 1, 1988.

HISTORY: 1999–2000 OMR 340 (A), eff. 1–1–00; 1988–89 OMR 233 (E), eff. 10–6–88

RC 119.032 rule review date(s): 8–27–04; 8–27–99

120–1–15 Adequate fee schedule for assigned/appointed counsel and public defender salaries

(A) In establishing a fee schedule to be paid appointed counsel in indigent cases eligible for reimbursement pursuant to section 120.33 of the Revised Code, the county commissioners and county bar association shall establish a schedule that is comparable to the fees paid to retained counsel in the same type of cases. No county will be entitled to reimbursement from the state public defender if it can be demonstrated that its fee schedule is inadequate for an appointed attorney to cover the costs of overhead while working on an appointed case and to generate a reasonable income for work performed.

(B) Salaries paid to public defenders should be equivalent to salaries paid to similar positions within the justice system.

HISTORY: 1999–2000 OMR 340 (A), eff. 1–1–00; 1991–92 OMR 180 (E), eff. 9–27–91

RC 119.032 rule review date(s): 8–27–04; 8–27–99

120–1–16 Public defenders accepting retainers in a case in which he/she has previously been appointed

From time to time, it may be determined that an applicant is indigent and entitled to the appointment of counsel, but later is able to obtain funds to retain private counsel. No part-time public defender or assistant public defender or full-time public defender or assistant public defender entitled to engage in private practice shall accept money from a previously indigent person that they were appointed by the court to represent. All such applicants should be referred to an attorney who is not associated professionally with the public defender or assistant public defender who was previously appointed in the case and that public defender or assistant public defender should withdraw from representation of the client. Withdrawal must be consistent with the disciplinary rules.

HISTORY: 1999–2000 OMR 340 (A), eff. 1–1–00; 1991–92 OMR 180 (E), eff. 9–27–91

RC 119.032 rule review date(s): 8–27–04; 8–27–99

3701

DEPARTMENT OF HEALTH

CHAPTER 3701–53

ALCOHOL AND DRUG TESTING; PERMITS FOR PERSONNEL

Promulgated pursuant to RC Ch 119

Section

3701–53–01 Techniques or methods

(A) Tests to determine the concentration of alcohol may be applied to blood, breath, urine, or other bodily substances. Results shall be expressed as equivalent to:

(1) Grams by weight of alcohol per one hundred milliliters of whole blood, blood serum or plasma (grams per cent by weight);

(2) Grams by weight of alcohol per two hundred ten liters of deep lung breath;

(3) Grams by weight of alcohol per one hundred milliliters of urine (grams per cent by weight).

The results of the tests shall be retained for not less than three years.

(B) At least one copy of the written procedure manual required by paragraph (D) of rule 3701–53–06 of the Administrative Code for performing blood, urine, or other bodily substance tests shall be on file in the area where the analytical tests are performed.

In the case of breath tests using an approved evidential breath testing instrument listed in paragraphs (A) and (B) of rule 3701–53–02 of the Administrative Code, the operational manual provided by the instrument's manufacturer shall be on file in the area where the breath tests are performed.

HISTORY: 2002–03 OMR 597 (A), eff. 9–30–02; 1996–97 OMR 2489 (A), eff. 7–7–97; 1986–87 OMR 616 (A), eff. 1–1–87; 1982–83 OMR 1382 (A), eff. 6–13–83; 1982–83 OMR 1043 (A), eff. 3–15–83; prior HD–1–01

RC 119.032 rule review date(s): 9–1–07; 7–1–02

3701–53–02 Breath tests

(A) The instruments listed in this paragraph are approved as evidential breath testing instruments for use in determining whether a person's breath contains a concentration of alcohol prohibited or defined by sections 4511.19, 1547.11, 2903.06, 2903.08, 4506.15, and/or 4506.17 of the Revised Code, or any other statute or local ordinance equivalent to those in this paragraph prescribing a defined or prohibited breath-alcohol concentration. The approved evidential breath testing instruments are:

(1) BAC DataMaster, BAC DataMaster cdm;

(2) Intoxilyzer model 5000 series 66, 68 and 68 EN.

(B) The instruments listed in this paragraph are approved as additional evidential breath testing instruments for use in determining whether a person's breath contains a concentration of alcohol prohibited or defined by sections 1547.11 and/or 1547.111 of the Revised Code, or any other statute or local ordinance equivalent to those defined by sections 1547.11 and/or 1547.111 of the Revised Code prescribing a defined or prohibited breath alcohol concentration. The approved evidential breath testing instruments are;

(1) Alco–sensor RBT III; and

(2) Intoxilyzer model 8000.

(C) Breath samples of deep lung (alveolar) air shall be analyzed for purposes of determining whether a person has a prohibited breath alcohol concentration with instruments approved under paragraphs (A) and (B) of this rule. Breath samples shall be analyzed according to the operational checklist for the instrument being used and checklist forms recording the results of subject tests shall be retained in accordance with paragraph (A) of rule 3701–53–01 of the Administrative Code. The results shall be recorded on forms prescribed by the director of health.

HISTORY: 2002–03 OMR 597 (A), eff. 9–30–02; 1996–97 OMR 2489 (A), eff. 7–7–97; 1994–95 OMR 929 (A), eff. 12–12–94; 1994–95 OMR 424 (A), eff. 9–14–94; 1989–90 OMR 1313 (A), eff. 5–5–90; 1986–87 OMR 616 (R–E), eff. 1–1–87; 1982–83 OMR 1383 (A), eff. 6–13–83; 1982–83 OMR 1043 (A), eff. 3–15–83; prior HD–1–02*

RC 119.032 rule review date(s): 9–1–07; 7–1–02

Historical and Statutory Notes

Note: Effective 9–30–02, the forms to 3701–53–02 are repealed

3701–53–03 Blood, urine and other bodily substance tests

(A) Alcohol in blood, urine and other bodily substances shall be analyzed based on approved techniques or methods. The technique or method must have documented sensitivity, specificity, accuracy, precision and linearity. The technique or method can be based on procedures which have been published in a peer reviewed or juried scientific journal or thoroughly documented by the laboratory. Approved techniques or methods include:

(1) Gas chromatography; and

(2) Enzyme assays.

(B) Drugs of abuse in blood, urine, and other bodily substances as defined in section 3719.011 of the Revised Code shall be tested using an analytical technique or method approved by the director of health as part of the permit process as specified in rules 3701–53–07 and 3701–53–09 of the Administrative Code. The approved analytical techniques or methods are:

(1) Immunoassay;

(2) Thin–layer chromatography;

(3) Gas chromatography;

(4) Mass spectroscopy;

(5) High performance liquid chromatography;

or

(6) Spectroscopy.

All positive results of presumptive tests specified in paragraph (B) of this rule must be confirmed by one or more dissimilar analytical techniques or methods and must be part of a testing procedure. The analytical techniques or methods used for confirmation must have similar or improved sensitivity, specificity, accuracy, precision and linearity. The approved techniques or methods can be based on procedures which have been published in a peer reviewed or juried scientific journal or thoroughly documented by the laboratory.

(C) The results of tests to determine the concentrations of delta–9–tetrahydrocannabinol (THC), cocaine, or their metabolites must be expressed as positive if the following apply:

(1) In blood or other bodily substances if>5 ng/ml THC or>25 ng/ml 11–nor–delta–9–tetrahydrocannabinol carboxylic acid (THC–COOH) or>50 ng/ml cocaine or>100 ng/ml benzoylecgonine.

(2) In urine if>15ng/ml 11–nor–delta–9–tetrahydrocannabinol carboxylic acid (THC–COOH) or>150 ng/ml cocaine or benzoylecgonine.

HISTORY: 2002–03 OMR 597 (A), eff. 9–30–02; 1996–97 OMR 2489 (A), eff. 7–7–97; 1989–90 OMR 1314 (A), eff. 5–5–90; 1986–87 OMR 616 (A), eff. 1–1–87; 1982–83 OMR 1383 (A), eff. 6–13–83; 1982–83 OMR 1044 (A), eff. 3–15–83; prior HD–1–03

RC 119.032 rule review date(s): 9–1–07; 7–1–02

3701–53–04 Instrument check

(A) A senior operator shall perform an instrument check on approved evidential breath testing instruments and a radio frequency interference (RFI) check no less frequently than once every seven days in accordance with the appropriate instrument checklist for the instrument being used. The instrument check may be performed anytime up to one hundred and ninety-two hours after the last instrument check.

(1) The instrument shall be checked to detect RFI using a hand-held radio normally used by the law enforcement agency. The RFI detector check is valid when the evidential breath testing instrument detects RFI or aborts a subject test. If the RFI detector check is not valid, the instrument shall not be used until the instrument is serviced.

(2) An instrument shall be checked using an instrument check solution containing ethyl alcohol approved by the director of health. An instrument check result is valid when the result of the instrument check is at or within five one-thousandths (0.005) grams per two hundred ten liters of the target value for that instrument check solution. An instrument check result which is outside the range specified in this paragraph shall be confirmed by the senior operator using another bottle of approved instrument check solution. If this instrument check result is also out of range, the instrument shall not be used until the instrument is serviced.

(B) An instrument check shall be made in accordance with paragraph (A) of this rule when a new evidential breath testing instrument is placed in service or when the instrument is returned after service or repairs, before the instrument is used to test subjects.

(C) An instrument check solution shall not be used more than three months after its date of first use, or after the manufacturer's expiration date (one year after manufacture) whichever comes first.After first use, instrument check solutions shall be kept under refrigeration when not being used. The instrument check solution container shall be retained for reference until the instrument check solution is discarded.

(D) Each testing day, the analytical techniques used in rule 3701–53–03 of the Administrative Code shall be checked for proper calibration under the general direction of the designated laboratory director. General direction does not mean that the designated laboratory director must be physically present during the performance of the calibration check.

(E) Results of instrument checks, calibration checks and records of service and repairs shall be retained in accordance with paragraph (A) of rule 3701–53–01 of the Administrative Code.

HISTORY: 2002–03 OMR 598 (A), eff. 9–30–02; 2000–2001 OMR 1473 (A), eff. 3–30–01; 1996–97 OMR 2490 (A), eff. 7–7–97; 1989–90 OMR 1314 (A), eff. 5–5–90; 1986–87 OMR 616 (A), eff. 1–1–87; 1982–83 OMR 1383 (A), eff. 6–13–83; 1982–83 OMR 1044 (A), eff. 3–15–83; prior HD–1–04

RC 119.032 rule review date(s): 9–1–07; 7–1–02; 1–9–01

Historical and Statutory Notes

Note: Appendices A to D, eff. 3–30–01, are referenced only. Appendices are generally available on WESTLAW and/or CD–ROM. Subscribers who wish to obtain a copy may request one from the publisher, the Legislative Service Commission, or the issuing agency.

3701–53–05 Collection and handling of blood and urine specimens

(A) All samples shall be collected in accordance with section 4511.19, or section 1547.11 of the Revised Code, as applicable.

(B) When collecting a blood sample, an aqueous solution of a non-volatile antiseptic shall be used on the skin. No alcohols shall be used as a skin antiseptic.

(C) Blood shall be drawn with a sterile dry needle into a vacuum container with a solid anticoagulant, or according to the laboratory protocol as written in the laboratory procedure manual based on the type of specimen being tested.

(D) The collection of a urine specimen must be witnessed to assure that the sample can be authenticated. Urine shall be deposited into a clean glass or plastic screw top container which shall be capped, or collected according to the laboratory protocol as written in the laboratory procedure manual

(E) Blood and urine containers shall be sealed in a manner such that tampering can be detected and have a label which contains at least the following information:

(1) Name of suspect;

(2) Date and time of collection;

(3) Name or initials of person collecting the sample; and

(4) Name or initials of person sealing the sample.

(F) While not in transit or under examination, all blood and urinespecimens shall be refrigerated.

HISTORY: 2002–03 OMR 598 (A), eff. 9–30–02; 1996–97 OMR 2490 (A), eff. 7–7–97; 1995–96 OMR 2745 (A), eff. 6–13–96; 1995–96 OMR 2037 (A), eff. 3–19–96; 1995–96 OMR 1476 (A*), eff. 1–4–96; 1994–95 OMR 930 (A), eff. 12–12–94; 1994–95 OMR 425 (A*), eff. 9–14–94; 1989–90 OMR 1315 (A), eff. 5–5–90; 1986–87 OMR 617 (A), eff. 1–1–87; 1982–83 OMR 1383 (A), eff. 6–13–83; 1982–83 OMR 1044 (A), eff. 3–15–83; prior HD–1–05*

RC 119.032 rule review date(s): 9–1–07; 7–1–02

3701–53–06 Laboratory requirements

(A) Chain of custody and the test results for evidential alcohol and drugs of abuse shall be identified and retained for not less than three years, after which time the documents may be discarded unless otherwise directed in writing from a court. All positive blood, urine and other bodily substances shall be retained in accordance with rule 3701–53–05 of the Administrative Code for a period of not less than one year, after which time the specimens may be discarded unless otherwise directed in writing from a court.

(B) The laboratory shall successfully complete a national proficiency testing program using the applicable technique or method for which the laboratory personnel seek a permit under rule 3701–53–09 of the Administrative Code.

(C) The laboratory shall have a written procedure manual of all analytical techniques or methods used for testing ofalcohol or drugs of abuse in bodily substances. Textbooks and package inserts or operator manuals from the manufacturer may be used to supplement, but may not be used in lieu of the laboratory's own procedure manual for testing specimens.

(D) The designated laboratory director shall review, sign, and date the procedure manual as certifying that the manual is in compliance with this rule. The designated laboratory director shall ensure that:

(1) Any changes in a procedure be approved, signed, and dated by the designated laboratory director;

(2) The date the procedure was first used and the date the procedure was revised or discontinued is recorded;

(3) A procedure shall be retained for not less than three years after the procedure was revised or discontinued, or in accordance with a written order issued by any court to the laboratory to save a specimen that was analyzed under that procedure;

(4) Laboratory personnel are adequately trained and experienced to perform testing of blood, urine and other bodily substances for alcohol and drugs of abuse and shall ensure, maintain and document the competency of laboratory personnel. The designated laboratory director shall also monitor the work performance and verify the skills of laboratory personnel;

(5) The procedure manual includes the criteria the laboratory shall use in developing standards, controls, and calibrations for the technique or method involved; and

(6) A complete and timely procedure manual is available and followed by laboratory personnel.

(E) Any time the designated laboratory director is replaced, another permitted laboratory director or applicant shall be designated.

HISTORY: 2002–03 OMR 599 (A), eff. 9–30–02; 1996–97 OMR 2491 (R–E), eff. 7–7–97; Prior HD–1–06

RC 119.032 rule review date(s): 9–1–07; 7–1–02

3701–53–07 Qualifications of personnel

(A) Blood, urine, and other bodily substance tests for alcohol shall be performed in a laboratory by an individual who has a laboratory director's permit or, under his or her general direction, by an individual who has a laboratory technician's permit. General direction does not mean that the laboratory director must be physically present during the performance of the test. Laboratory personnel shall not perform a technique or method of analysis that is not listed on the laboratory director's permit.

(1) An individual who is employed by a laboratory, which has successfully completed a proficiency examination administered by a national program for proficiency testing for the approved technique or method of analysis for which the permit is sought and who possesses at least two academic years of college chemistry and at least two years of experience in a clinical or chemical laboratory and possesses a minimum of a bachelor's degree shall meet the qualifications for a laboratory director's permit.

(2) An individual who is employed by a laboratory, which has successfully completed a proficiency examination administered by a national program for proficiency testing for the approved technique or method of analysis for which the permit is sought, has been certified by the designated laboratory director that he or she is competent to perform all procedures contained in the laboratory's procedure manual for testing specimens and meets one of the following requirements shall meet the qualifications for a laboratory technician's permit:

(a) Has a bachelor's degree in laboratory sciences from an accredited institution and has six months experience in laboratory testing;

(b) Has an associate's degree in laboratory sciences from an accredited institution or has completed sixty semester hours of academic credit including six semester hours of chemistry and one year experience in laboratory testing;

(c) Is a high school graduate or equivalent and has successfully completed an official military laboratory procedures course of at least fifty weeks duration and has held the military enlisted occupational specialty of medical laboratory specialist (laboratory technician); or

(d) Is a high school graduate or equivalent and was permitted on or before July 7, 1997.

(B) Blood, urine and other bodily substances tests for drugs of abuse shall be performed in a laboratory by an individual who has a laboratory director's permit or, under his or her general direction, by an individual who has a laboratory technician's permit. General direction does not mean that the laboratory director must be physically present during the performance of the test. Laboratory personnel shall not perform a technique or method of analysis that is not listed on the laboratory director's permit.

(1) An individual who is employed by a laboratory, which has successfully completed a proficiency examination administered by a national program for proficiency testing for the approved technique or method of analysis for which the permit is sought, who possesses at least two academic years of college chemistry and meets one of the following requirements shall meet the qualifications for a laboratory director's permit:

(a) Has at least five years of experience in a clinical or chemical laboratory and possesses a minimum of a bachelor's degree in laboratory sciences;

(b) Has at least three years of experience in a clinical or chemical laboratory and possesses a minimum of a master's degree; or

(c) Has at least two years of experience in a clinical or chemical laboratory and possesses a minimum of an earned doctoral degree.

(2) An individual who is employed by a laboratory, which has successfully completed a proficiency examination administered by a national program for proficiency testing for the approved technique or method of analysis for which the permit is sought, has been certified by the designated laboratory director that he or she is competent to perform all procedures contained in the laboratory's procedure manual for testing specimens and meets one of the following requirements shall meet the qualifications for a laboratory technician's permit:

(a) Has a bachelor's degree in laboratory sciences from an accredited institution and has one year experience in laboratory testing;

(b) Has an associate's degree in laboratory sciences from an accredited institution or has completed sixty semester hours of academic credit including six semester hours of chemistry and two years experience in laboratory testing;

(c) Is a high school graduate or equivalent and has successfully completed an official military laboratory procedures course of at least fifty weeks duration and has held the military enlisted occupational specialty of medical laboratory specialist (laboratory technician) and two years experience in laboratory testing; or

(d) Is a high school graduate or equivalent and was permitted on or before July 7, 1997.

(C) Breath tests used to determine whether a person's breath contains a concentration of alcohol prohibited or defined by sections 4511.19, 4511.191, 1547.11, 1547.111, 2903.06, 2903.08 and/or 4506.15 of the Revised Code, or any other statute or local ordinance prescribing a defined or prohibited breath alcohol concentration shall be performed by a senior operator or an operator. A senior operator shall be responsible for the care, maintenance and instrument checks of the evidential breath testing instruments.

(D) An individual meets the qualifications for a senior operator's permit by:

(1) Being a high school graduate or having passed the "General Education Development Test" and

(2) Having demonstrated that he or she can properly care for, maintain, perform instrument checks upon and operate the evidential breath testing instrument by having successfully completed a basic senior operator, upgrade or conversion training course for the type of approved evidential breath testing instrument for which he or she seeks a permit.

(E) An individual meets the qualifications for an operator's permit by:

(1) Being a high school graduate or having passed the "General Education Development Test"; and

(2) Having demonstrated that he or she can properly operate the evidential breath testing instrument by having successfully completed a basic operator or conversion training course for the type of approved evidential breath testing instrument for which he or she seeks a permit.

HISTORY: 2002–03 OMR 599 (A), eff. 9–30–02; 1996–97 OMR 2491 (A), eff. 7–7–97; 1994–95 OMR 931 (A), eff. 12–12–94; 1994–95 OMR 425 (A), eff. 9–14–94; 1989–90 OMR 1315 (A), eff. 5–5–90; 1986–87 OMR 617 (A), eff. 1–1–87; prior HD–1–07*

RC 119.032 rule review date(s): 9–1–07; 7–1–02

Historical and Statutory Notes

Note: Appendix A, eff. 7–7–97, is referenced only. Appendix B, eff. 12–12–94, is repealed. Appendices are generally available on WESTLAW and/or CD–ROM. Subscribers who wish to obtain a copy of these appendices as filed or repealed may request one from the publisher, the Legislative Service Commission, or the issuing agency.

3701–53–08 Surveys and proficiency examinations

(A) Individuals desiring to function as laboratory directors and laboratory technicians who apply for or are issued permits under rule 3701–53–09 of the Administrative Code shall be subject to surveys and proficiency examinations by representatives of the director of health. A survey or proficiency examination may be conducted at the director's discretion.

(1) A survey shall consist of a review of the permit holder's or applicant's compliance with the requirements of this chapter.

(2) A proficiency examination shall consist of an evaluation of the permit holder's, applicant's or laboratory's ability to test samples provided by a representative of the director using the techniques or methods for which the permit is held or sought. Proficiency examination samples may be:

(a) Mailed to the facility at which the permit holder or applicant uses or plans to use the permit; or

(b) Presented in person by a representative of the director at the facility where the permit holder or applicant uses or plans to use the permit.

(B) During proficiency examinations, laboratory directors, laboratory technicians and applicants shall accept samples, perform tests, and report all test results to a representative of the director. During surveys and proficiency examinations, permit holders and applicants shall grant the director's representatives access to all portions of the facility where the permit is used or is intended to be used and to all records relevant to compliance with the requirements of this chapter.

(C) Individuals desiring to function as senior operators and operators who apply for or are issued permits under rule 3701–53–09 of the Administrative Code, shall be subject to surveys and proficiency examinations by representatives of the director of health. A survey or proficiency examination shall be conducted at the director's discretion.

(1) A survey shall consist of a review of the permit holder's or applicant's compliance with the requirements of this chapter.

(2) A proficiency examination shall consist of an evaluation of the permit holder's or applicant's ability to test samples provided by a representative of the director using the evidential breath testing instrument for which the permit is held or sought. Proficiency samples are presented to the permit holder or applicant in person by representatives of the director.

(D) During proficiency examinations, senior operators, operators and applicants shall accept samples, perform tests and report all results to a representative of the director. During surveys and proficiency examinations, permit holders and applicants shall grant the director's representatives access to all portions of the facility where the permit is used or is intended to be used, and to all records relevant to compliance with the requirements of this chapter.

HISTORY: 2002–03 OMR 600 (A), eff. 9–30–02; 1996–97 OMR 2492 (A), eff. 7–7–97; 1989–90 OMR 1315 (A), eff. 5–5–90; prior HD–1–08

RC 119.032 rule review date(s): 9–1–07; 7–1–02

3701–53–09 Permits

(A) Individuals desiring to function as laboratory directors or laboratory technicians shall apply to the director of health for permits on forms prescribed and provided by the director. A separate application shall be filed for a permit to perform tests to determine the amount of alcohol in a person's blood, urine or other bodily substance, and a separate permit application shall be filed to perform tests to determine the amount of drugs of abuse in a person's blood, urine or other bodily substance. A laboratory director's and laboratory technician's permit is only valid for the laboratory indicated on the permit.

(1) The director shall issue appropriate permits to perform tests to determine the amount of alcohol in a person's blood, urine or other bodily substance to individuals who qualify under the applicable provisions of rule 3701–53–07 of the Administrative Code or under paragraph (A) of this rule. Laboratory personnel holding permits issued under this rule shall use only those laboratory techniques or methods for which they have been issued permits.

(a) The laboratory where the permit holder is employed shall have successfully completed a proficiency examination from a national program for proficiency testing using the applicable techniques or methods, and provide to representatives of the director all proficiency test results.

(b) Permit holders shall successfully complete proficiency examinations by representatives of the director using the techniques or methods for which they have been issued permits.

(2) The director shall issue appropriate permits to perform tests to determine the amount of drugs of abuse in a person's blood, urine or other bodily substances to individuals who qualify under the applicable provisions of rule 3701–53–07 of the Admin-

istrative Code or under paragraph (A) of this rule. Laboratory personnel holding permits issued under this rule shall use only those laboratory techniques or methods for which they have been issued permits.

The laboratory where the permit holder is employed shall have successfully completed a proficiency examination from a national program for proficiency testing unsing the applicable techniques or methods, and provide to representatives of the director all proficiency results.

(B) Individuals desiring to function as senior operators or operators shall apply to the director of health for permits on forms prescribed and provided by the director of health. A separate application shall be filed for each type of evidential breath testing instrument for which the permit is sought.

The director of health shall issue appropriate permits to perform tests to determine the amount of alcohol in a person's breath to individuals who qualify under the applicable provisions of rule 3701–53–07 of the Administrative Code. Individuals holding permits issued under this rule shall use only those evidential breath testing instruments for which they have been issued permits.

(C) Permits issued under paragraphs (A) and (B) of this rule shall expire one year from the date issued, unless revoked prior to the expiration date. An individual holding a permit may seek renewal of an issued permit by the director under paragraphs (A) and (B) of this rule by filing an application with the director no sooner than six months before the expiration date of the current permit. The director shall not renew the permit if the permit holder is in proceedings for revocation of his or her current permit under rule 3701–53–10 of the Administrative code.

(D) To qualify for renewal of a permit under paragraphs (A) or (B) of this rule:

(1) A permit holder shall present evidence satisfactory to the director that he or she continues to meet the qualifications established by the applicable provisions of rule 3701–53–07 of the Administrative Code for issuance of the type of permit sought.

(2) If the individual seeking a renewal permit currently holds a laboratory technician or laboratory director permit, the permit holder shall meet the requirements of paragraph (A) of this rule.

(3) If the individual seeking a renewal permit currently holds an operator or senior operator permit, the permit holder shall have completed satisfactorily an in-service course for the applicable type of evidential breath testing instrument which meets the requirements of paragraph (B) of this rule, which includes review of self-study materials furnished by the director.

HISTORY: 2002–03 OMR 600 (A), eff. 9–30–02; 1996–97 OMR 2492 (A), eff. 7–7–97; 1994–95 OMR 931 (A), eff. 12–12–94; 1994–95 OMR 426 (A), eff. 9–14–94; 1989–90 OMR 1316 (A), eff. 5–5–90; 1986–87 OMR 617 (A), eff. 1–1–87; prior HD–1–09*

RC 119.032 rule review date(s): 9–1–07; 7–1–02

3701–53–10 Revocation and denial of permits

The director of health may deny or revoke the permit of any permit holder or individual seeking a permit:

(A) Who obtains or seeks to obtain a permit falsely or deceitfully;

(B) Who fails to comply with any of the provisions of rules 3701–53–01 to 3701–53–09 of the Administrative Code; or

(C) Who:

(1) As a senior operator, fails to demonstrate that he or she can properly care for, maintain, perform instrument checks upon, and operate the breath testing instrument for which the permit is held;

(2) As an operator, fails to demonstrate that he or she can properly operate the breath testing instrumentfor which the permit is held;

(3) As a laboratory director or laboratory technician, fails to demonstrate that he or she can properly perform the technique or method of analysis for which the permit is held; or

(4) As the designated laboratory director, fails to comply with paragraph (D) of rule 3701–53–06 of the Administrative Code.

HISTORY: 2002–03 OMR 601 (A), eff. 9–30–02; 1996–97 OMR 2493 (A), eff. 7–7–97; 1989–90 OMR 1316 (A), eff. 5–5–90; 1986–87 OMR 617 (A), eff. 1–1–87; prior HD–1–10

RC 119.032 rule review date(s): 9–1–07; 7–1–02

5120

DEPARTMENT OF REHABILITATION AND CORRECTION

CHAPTER 5120–2

SENTENCE DETERMINATION AND REDUCTION

Promulgated pursuant to RC 111.15

Section

5120–2–03 Determination of minimum, maximum and definite sentences when multiple sentences are imposed

(A) Any sentence of imprisonment to the department of rehabilitation and correction shall be served consecutively to any other sentence of imprisonment in the following cases:

(1) The trial court specifies that it is to be served consecutively to another sentence;

(2) It is imposed for a new felony committed by a probationer, parolee, or escapee;

(3) It is a three-year term of actual incarceration imposed pursuant to section 2929.71 of the Revised Code, for using a firearm in commission of an offense;

(4) It is imposed for a violation of section 2921.34 of the Revised Code (escape), division (B) of section 2917.02 of the Revised Code (aggravated riot committed by an inmate in a detention facility), or division (B) of section 2921.35 of the Revised Code (aiding escape or resistance to authority committed by a person confined in a detention facility).

(B) Any sentence of imprisonment to the department of rehabilitation and correction shall be served concurrently, not aggregated, with any other sentence of imprisonment imposed by a court of this state, another state, or of the United States, except as provided in paragraph A of this rule.

(C) When multiple definite sentences are imposed to run concurrently, the prisoner shall be deemed to be serving the longest of the sentences so imposed. If, however, the various sentences are subject to different amounts of reduction for jail-time credit and/or are subject to different rates of diminution for time off for good behavior, the prisoner shall be released after serving the longest diminished sentence.

(D) When multiple indefinite sentences are imposed to run concurrently, the prisoner shall be deemed to be serving an indefinite term, the minimum of which is the longest of such minimum terms and the maximum of which is the longest of such maximum terms. If, however, the various sentences are subject to different amounts of reduction for jail-time credit and/or are subject to different rates of diminution for time off for good behavior, the prisoner becomes eligible for parole consideration after serving the longest diminished sentence.

(E) Subject to the maximums provided in this rule:

(1) When consecutive indefinite sentences of imprisonment are imposed for felony, the minimum term to be served is the aggregate of the consecutive minimum terms imposed and the maximum term to be served is the aggregate of the consecutive maximum terms imposed.

(2) When consecutive definite sentences of imprisonment are imposed, the term to be served is the aggregate of the consecutive definite terms imposed.

(3) When a three-year term of actual incarceration is imposed pursuant to section 2929.71 of the Revised Code for using a firearm in the commission of an offense, it shall be served consecutively with, and prior to, the life sentence or indefinite term of imprisonment imposed for the offense.

(4) When multiple three-year terms of actual incarceration are imposed pursuant to section 2929.71 of the Revised Code for using firearms in the commission of multiple offenses, the aggregate of all of such terms of actual incarceration shall be served first and then the aggregate indefinite term and/or life sentence(s) imposed for the offenses shall be served.

(5) When a person is serving any definite terms of imprisonment consecutively to any indefinite or life terms of imprisonment or to any three-year terms of actual incarceration imposed pursuant to section 2929.71 of the Revised Code or to both, the aggregate of all such three-year terms of actual incarceration shall be served first, then the aggregate of the definite terms of imprisonment shall be served, and then the indefinite or life terms of imprisonment shall be served.

(F) Consecutive terms of imprisonment imposed shall not exceed:

(1) An aggregate minimum term of fifteen years, when the consecutive terms imposed are for felonies other than aggravated murder or murder and do not include any three-year terms of actual incarceration imposed pursuant to section 2929.71 of the Revised Code for using a firearm in the commission of an offense.

(2) An aggregate minimum term of fifteen years plus the sum of all three-year terms of actual incarceration imposed pursuant to section 2929.71 of the Revised Code for using a firearm in the commission of an offense, when the consecutive terms imposed are for felonies other than aggravated murder or murder.

(3) An aggregate minimum term of twenty years, plus the sum of any three-year terms of actual incarceration imposed pursuant to section 2929.71 of the Revised Code, when the consecutive

terms imposed include a term of imprisonment for murder and do not include a term of imprisonment for aggravated murder.

(4) An aggregate term of eighteen months, when the consecutive terms imposed are for misdemeanors. When consecutive terms aggregating more than one year are imposed for misdemeanors under the Revised Code, and at least one such consecutive term is for a misdemeanor of the first degree that is an offense of violence, the trial court may order the aggregate term imposed to be served in a state penal or reformatory institution.

(G) There shall be no limit to the aggregate minimum sentence when at least one sentence is imposed for aggravated murder committed on or after October 19, 1981.

(H) There shall be no limit to the aggregate of definite sentences imposed for felonies.

HISTORY: 2002–03 OMR 1725 (RRD); 1997–98 OMR 2472 (RRD); 1987–88 OMR 1010 (E), eff. 2–29–88; 1987–88 OMR 560 (E), eff. 11–30–87

RC 119.032 rule review date(s): 1–10–08; 1–12–03; 1–10–03

5120–2–03.1 Determination of stated prison terms and life sentences when multiple terms or sentences are imposed

(A) This rule applies only to prison terms imposed for offenses committed on or after July 1, 1996, to be served with the department of rehabilitation and correction.

(B) Any prison term shall be served consecutively to any other prison term in the following cases:

(1) The trial court specifies that it is to be served consecutively to another sentence;

(2) It is a one, three or six-year mandatory prison term imposed pursuant to division (D)(1)(a)(i) of section 2929.14 of the Revised Code, for using a firearm in the commission of an offense;

(3) It is a five-year mandatory prison term imposed pursuant to division (D)(1)(a)(ii) of section 2929.14 of the Revised Code, for committing a felony by discharging a firearm from a motor vehicle;

(4) It is imposed upon an offender who is an inmate in a jail, prison or other detention facility for a violation of section 2917.02 (aggravated riot), 2917.03 (riot), 2931.34 (escape), 2921.35 (aiding escape or resistance to authority), or 2923.131 (possession of a deadly weapon at a detention facility) of the Revised Code;

(5) It is imposed for a new felony committed by an escapee.

(C) A prison term imposed for a violation of post release control shall be served consecutively to any prison term imposed for a new felony committed while on post release control.

(D) Any prison term shall be served concurrently, not aggregated, with any other prison term imposed by a court of this state, another state, or of the United States, except as provided in paragraphs (B) and (C) of this rule.

(E) When multiple stated prison terms are imposed to run concurrently, the offender shall be deemed to be serving the longest of the stated terms so imposed. If, however, the various prison terms are subject to different amounts of reduction for jail time credit, the offender shall be released after serving the longest diminished stated prison term.

(F) When multiple life sentences with parole eligibility or a minimum term are imposed to run concurrently, the offender becomes eligible for parole after serving the longest of the minimum terms or time to parole eligibility of the life sentences. If, however, the life sentences are subject to different amounts of reduction for jail time credit, the offender shall become eligible for parole after serving the longest diminished minimum term.

(G) When consecutive stated prison terms are imposed, the term to be served is the aggregate of all of the stated prison terms so imposed.

(H) When multiple life sentences with parole eligibility or a minimum term are imposed to run consecutively, the offender becomes eligible for parole after serving the aggregate of the minimum terms or time to parole eligibility of the life sentences.

(I) An offender serving a sentence of life imprisonment without parole is not eligible for parole and shall be imprisoned until death, whether or not the offender is also serving any other sentences or prison terms.

(J) When a one, three or six-year mandatory prison term is imposed pursuant to division (D)(1)(a)(i) of section 2929.14 of the Revised Code, for using a firearm in the commission of an offense, such term shall be served consecutively with, and prior to, the stated prison term or life sentence imposed for the offense.

(K) When a one, three or six-year mandatory prison term is imposed pursuant to division (D)(1)(a)(i) of section 2929.14 of the Revised Code, for using a firearm in the commission of an offense, and a five-year mandatory prison term is imposed pursuant to division (D)(1)(a)(ii) of section 2929.14 the Revised Code, for committing a felony by discharging a firearm from a motor vehicle, such terms shall be served consecutively to each other and the aggregate term shall be served consecutively with, and prior to, the stated prison term or life sentence imposed for the offense.

(L) When multiple one, three, five and/or six-year mandatory prison terms are imposed pursuant to division (D)(1)(a)(i) of section 2929.14 of the Revised Code, for using a firearm in the commission of an offense, and division (D)(1)(a)(ii) of section 2929.14 of the Revised Code, for committing a felony by discharging a firearm from a motor vehicle, the aggregate of all such terms shall be served first and then the aggregate stated prison terms and/or life sentences imposed for the offenses shall be served.

(M) When a mandatory prison term is imposed for a felony, other than for using a firearm in the commission of an offense or for committing a felony by discharging a firearm from a motor vehicle, such mandatory term shall be served prior to any non-mandatory portion of the stated prison term or life sentence imposed for the offense.

(N) When multiple mandatory prison terms are imposed for felonies, other than for using a firearm in the commission of an offense or for committing a felony by discharging a firearm from a motor vehicle, the aggregate of all such terms shall be served first and then the aggregate of any non-mandatory portion of the stated prison terms and/or life sentences imposed for the offenses shall be served.

(O) When an offender is serving any stated prison terms consecutively to any life terms of imprisonment and/or to any one, three, five and/or six-year mandatory prison terms imposed pursuant to division (D)(1)(a)(i) of section 2929.14 the Revised Code, for using a firearm in the commission of an offense, and/or division (D)(1)(a)(ii) of section 2929.14 of the Revised Code, for committing a felony by discharging a firearm from a motor vehicle, the aggregate of all such one, three, five and/or six-year mandatory prison terms shall be served first, then the aggregate of all other mandatory prison terms shall be served, and then the aggregate of the non-mandatory portion of the stated prison terms shall be served, and then the aggregate of the non-mandatory portion of the life terms of imprisonment shall be served.

(P) When multiple sentences are imposed for felonies committed on or after July 1, 1996, there shall be no limit or cap to the total number of years for aggregate stated prison terms and/or life sentences imposed.

(Q) Pursuant to section 2967.11 of the Revised Code, bad time imposed by the parole board shall be served consecutive to the offender's stated term.

HISTORY: 2002–03 OMR 1725 (RRD); 1997–98 OMR 2472 (E), eff. 3–13–98

RC 119.032 rule review date(s): 1–10–08; 1–12–03; 1–10–03

5120–2–03.2 Determination of multiple sentences or prison terms with an offense committed before July 1, 1996 and an offense committed on or after July 1, 1996

(A) Definitions

(1) Prison term: For purposes of this rule, prison term refers to prison terms imposed for offenses committed on or after July 1, 1996, to be served with the department of rehabilitation and correction.

(2) Sentence: For purposes of this rule, sentence refers to prison terms imposed for offenses committed before July 1, 1996, to be served with the department of rehabilitation and correction.

(B) This rule applies when an offender is serving a term of imprisonment for more than one felony and at least one of the felonies was committed prior to July 1, 1996, and at least one of the felonies was committed on or after July 1, 1996. In such situations, two different sets of laws apply and the terms of imprisonment for each felony may be subject to different amounts of reduction for jail time credit. The determination of the length and expiration of the term of imprisonment for each felony must be determined in accordance with the set of laws in effect at the time the felony was committed. These mixed cases will be hereinafter referred to as "hybrids".

(C) When a prison term for a crime committed on or after July 1, 1996, is imposed to run concurrently to a crime committed before July 1, 1996, the expiration date of each term of imprisonment must be determined independently in accordance with the appropriate set of laws. The expected expiration of the term for the crime committed on or after July 1, 1996 in most cases will be determined by diminishing the term by jail credit. The expected expiration of the crime committed before July 1, 1996 in most cases will be determined by diminishing the sentence by good time and jail credit. The sentence with the latest expiration date becomes the controlling sentence regarding the offender's expected release.

(D) During the period of imprisonment, the offender may be able to reduce each term by the appropriate amount of earned credit. In addition, the sentence is subject to loss of good time and the prison term is subject to the imposition of bad time and loss of earned credit. Due to such differences, the controlling term can change during the period of imprisonment. Therefore, the expiration date of each term of imprisonment must be determined independently each time there is any reduction or increase in either term. The offender cannot be released until both the prison term and the sentence have expired; that is, until the term of imprisonment with the latest expiration date has expired.

(E) When a prison term for a crime committed on or after July 1, 1996, is imposed to run consecutively to a sentence for a crime committed before July 1, 1996, the sentence shall be served first, then the prison term.

(F) While the sentence is being served, the offender may be able to reduce the sentence by up to seven days per month of earned credit, and is subject to a potential loss of good time. Upon the expiration of the sentence, the prison term shall be served. While the prison term is being served, the offender may be able to reduce the prison term by one day per month of earned credit and is subject to loss of earned credit and the imposition of bad time.

HISTORY: 2002–03 OMR 1725 (RRD); 1997–98 OMR 2473 (E), eff. 3–13–98

RC 119.032 rule review date(s): 1–10–08; 1–12–03; 1–10–03

5120–2–04 Reduction of minimum and maximum or definite sentence or stated prison term for jail time credit

(A) The department of rehabilitation and correction shall reduce the minimum and maximum sentence, where applicable, the definite sentence or the stated prison term of an offender by the total number of days that the offender was confined for any reason arising out of the offense for which he was convicted and sentenced, including confinement in lieu of bail while awaiting trial, confinement for examination to determine his competence to stand trial or sanity, confinement in a community-based correctional facility and program or district community-based correctional facility and program, where applicable, and confinement while awaiting transportation to the place where he is to serve his sentence.

(B) The sentencing court determines the amount of time the offender served before being sentenced. The court must make a factual determination of the number of days credit to which the offender is entitled by law and, if the offender is committed to a state correctional institution, forward a statement of the number of days of confinement which he is entitled by law to have credited. This information is required to be included within the journal entry imposing the sentence or stated prison term.

(C) When the sheriff delivers the offender to the department of rehabilitation and correction's reception center, he shall present the managing officer with a copy of the offender's sentence, stated prison term or combination thereof that specifies the total number of days, if any, the offender was confined for any reason prior to conviction and sentence and a record of the days he was confined for the offense between the date of sentencing and the date committed to the reception center.

(D) The number of days, if any, specified in the court's journal entry committing the offender to the department is the court's finding of the number of days the offender is entitled to by law, up to and including the date of the journal entry. The record office shall reduce the offender's minimum and maximum, definite sentence or stated prison term by the number of days specified in the entry, plus the number of days the offender was confined as a result of the offense, between the date of the entry and the date committed to the department, as reflected in the sheriff's record.

(E) If the court's journal entry of sentence or stated prison term fails to specify that the offender is entitled to any credit up to the date of sentencing, the record office shall reduce the sentence or stated prison term only by the number of days the sheriff reports the offender was confined between the date of the sentencing entry and the date the offender was committed to the department.

(F) If an offender is serving two or more sentences, stated prison terms or combination thereof concurrently, the adult parole authority shall independently reduce each sentence or stated prison term for the number of days confined for that offense. Release of the offender shall be based upon the longest definite, minimum and/or maximum sentence or stated prison term after reduction for jail time credit.

(G) If an offender is serving two or more sentences, stated prison terms or combination thereof consecutively, the record office shall aggregate the sentences, stated prison terms or combination thereof pursuant to rule 5120–2–03, 5120–2–03.1, or 5120–2–03 of the Administrative Code. The department of rehabilitation and correction shall reduce the aggregate definite sentence, aggregate stated prison term or aggregate minimum and aggregate maximum sentences or combination thereof, as determined by rule 5120–02–03, 5120–2–03.1 or 5120–2–03.2 of the Administrative Code, by the total number of days the offender was confined for all of the offenses for which the consecutive sentences, stated prison term or combination thereof were imposed. Generally, when consecutive sentences, stated prison terms or combination thereof are imposed by multiple journal entries, the record office shall reduce the aggregate sentence, stated prison terms or combination thereof by the sum of the days specified in each of the journal entries plus the number of days the offender was confined between the date of the last journal entry and the date committed to the institution. However, if any of the journal entries received on or after January 1, 1992, indicates that any particular day of confinement has been reported on more than one journal entry, the aggregate sentence, stated prison terms or combination thereof shall be reduced by one day for each day the offender was confined. If any of the journal entries received on or after January 1, 1992, indicates that any particular day of confinement has been reported more than once, the rules set forth hereinafter should be followed in determining whether any particular day of confinement has been reported more than once.

(1) When an offender receives consecutive sentences, stated prison terms or combination thereof from different counties, both the sentences, and/or prison terms and the jail time credit in each journal entry should be aggregated, unless other wise indicated. However, the transport time shall not be aggregated for each sentence and/or prison term, but rather shall only be credited one time.

(2) When an offender receives consecutive sentences, stated prison terms or combination thereof from the same county, the sentences and/or stated prison term shall be aggregated, the transport time shall not be aggregated, and jail time credit shall be determined in the following manner:

(a) If the number of days of jail time credit given for each sentence and/or stated prison term is identical, do not aggregate the jail time credit, but rather, only give the credit one time, unless otherwise ordered or indicated in the journal entry. The sheriff's letter may be used to confirm duplicate dates of confinement.

(b) If the number of days of jail time credit for each sentence and/or stated prison term is not identical, aggregate the credit in the following situations:

(i) The journal entry orders or indicates that the jail time credit shall be aggregated.

(ii) The dates of confinement are not indicated in the journal entry or the sheriff's letter and there is no indication whether any of the dates of confinement are reported more than once.

(c) If the number of days of jail time credit for each sentence and/or stated prison term is not identical and the journal entry does not provide otherwise, do not aggregate the credit in the following situations:

(i) The dates of confinement are indicated in the journal entry or the sheriff's letter and some or all of the dates are reported more than once. In such situations, the aggregate sentence, stated prison term or combination thereof shall be reduced by only one day for each day the offender was confined as indicated by the dates.

(ii) The journal entry orders or indicates that the jail time credit shall not be aggregated. In such situations, the aggregate sentence, stated prison term or combination thereof shall be reduced by the longest single amount of jail time credit ordered.

(3) When an offender goes out to court and receives an additional sentence, and/or stated prison term to run consecutive to his current sentence, stated prison terms or combination thereof, the sentences and/or stated prison terms shall be aggregated, but the offender shall not be given jail time credit for the period of time he was absent with leave (AWL) on the additional charges.

(H) The record office shall not reduce a sentence, stated prison term or combination thereof for jail time credit except in accordance with this rule. A party questioning either the number of days contained in the journal entry or the record of the sheriff shall be instructed to address his concerns to the court or sheriff. Unless the court issues an entry modifying the amount of jail time credit or the sheriff sends the institution corrected information about time confined awaiting transport, no change will be made.

(I) If an offender receives a sentence, or stated prison term to this department consecutive to or concurrent with a sentence in an institution in another state or a federal institution, no action will be taken towards considering him for parole or otherwise terminating his sentence, or stated prison term until the offender is physically committed to the custody of this department. At that time, the offender's minimum and maximum, definite sentence or stated prison term shall be reduced pursuant to this rule by the total number of days confined for the crime as certified by the court and the sheriff.

HISTORY: 2002–03 OMR 2225 (A), eff. 4–10–03; 1997–98 OMR 2473 (A), eff. 3–13–98; 1992–93 OMR 1538 (R–E), eff. 7–1–93; 1987–88 OMR 1010 (E), eff. 2–29–88; 1987–88 OMR 561 (E), eff. 11–30–87

RC 119.032 rule review date(s): 1–12–08; 1–12–03; 1–10–03

5120–2–05 Time off for good behavior

(A) Except as provided elsewhere in this rule, an offender serving a felony sentence in a correctional facility operated by the department of rehabilitation and correction may, by faithfully observing the rules of the institution, earn a deduction of up to thirty per cent of his minimum or definite sentence. The total amount of time that may be deducted from the offender's sentence shall be prorated and shall be awarded monthly for obeying the rules of the institution for that month.

(B) Paragraph (A) of this rule does not apply to an offender serving a penitentiary sentence imposed for a crime that occurred prior to July 1, 1983, if he/she would have been entitled to earn more time off for good behavior under the laws in effect at the time of the commission of the offense.

(C) This rule does apply to all reformatory sentences for which the offender is delivered to this department on or after the effective date of this rule, no matter when the offense was committed.

(D) This rule does not apply to prison terms imposed for offenses committed on or after July 1, 1996, to be served with the department of rehabilitation and correction. If a person is serving a term of imprisonment for both an offense committed before July 1, 1996 and an offense committed on or after July 1, 1996, paragraph (A) of this rule shall apply only to that portion of the term for the offense committed before July 1, 1996.

(E) An offender serving a term of actual incarceration imposed pursuant to section 2929.71 or 2929.72 of the Revised Code for using a firearm in the commission of an offense is not entitled to diminution of the term of actual incarceration pursuant to this rule.

(F) An offender serving a life sentence that is not subject to a reduction for time off for good behavior pursuant to rule 5120–2–10 of the Administrative Code or pursuant to any section of the Revised Code is not entitled to the reduction provided by this rule.

(G) To facilitate release planning, the records officer shall calculate for each offender the date of parole eligibility or expiration date if all possible good time is earned. The offender shall, however, be advised that this date is tentative and subject to change if he fails to maintain good behavior.

(H) Unless denied pursuant to rule 5120–9–56 of the Administrative Code, the diminution of sentence provided for in paragraph (A) of this rule shall be credited to each offender at the expiration of each calendar month as provided in this rule. Once diminution has been earned and properly credited for a given month, it shall not be reduced or forfeited for any reason.

(I) If notified by the rules infraction board that diminution of sentence is to be denied pursuant to rules 5120–9–56 of the Administrative Code, the record office shall note in the offender file the percentage and number of months of denial.

(J) The cumulative total of diminution of sentence granted pursuant to this rule plus any days of credit awarded pursuant to rules 5120–2–06, 5120–2–07 and 5120–2–08 of the Administrative Code shall not exceed for any offender one-third of the minimum or definite sentence, or in the case of a life sentence for which diminution and days of credit may be earned, one-third of the number of years before parole eligibility. No term of actual incarceration imposed pursuant to section 2929.71 or 2929.72 of the Revised Code for using a firearm in the commission of an offense shall be considered as a part of a minimum sentence or a part of the number of years before parole eligibility for eligible life sentences in calculating the maximum possible diminution pursuant to this paragraph.

(K) An offender sentenced to a state penal institution pursuant to division (E)(4) of section 2929.41 of the Revised Code shall be allowed a deduction equal to one-third of his sentence.

(L) Except as provided in paragraph (B) and paragraph (D) of this rule, the provisions of this rule shall apply to all offenders who are confined in a state correctional institution on or after November 1, 1987, regardless of the date on which the offender committed the offense for which he is confined. If, however, the offender began serving a term of imprisonment in a state correctional facility before November 1, 1987, the provisions of this rule apply only to the portion of the term served on and after November 1, 1987.

(M) For each offender confined in a state correctional institution on or before October 31, 1987 who has not, as of that date, served his minimum or definite sentence as diminished pursuant to section 2967.19 of the Revised Code, the portion of his sentence that has been served as of October 31, 1987 shall be diminished for time off for good behavior pursuant to the rules in effect at that time.

(N) This rule shall not operate to extend the eligibility for parole of any offender already committed to the custody of the department of rehabilitation and correction as of the effective date of this rule.

HISTORY: 2002–03 OMR 2226 (A), eff. 4–10–03; 1997–98 OMR 2475 (A), eff. 3–13–98; 1987–88 OMR 1347 (E), eff. 5–1–88; 1987–88 OMR 1011 (E), eff. 2–26–88; 1987–88 OMR 561 (E), eff. 11–30–87

RC 119.032 rule review date(s): 1–12–08; 1–12–03; 1–10–03

Historical and Statutory Notes

Note: Effective 4–10–03, former appendix A was repealed.

5120–2–06 Earned credit for productive program participation

(A) Except as provided in paragraphs (P), (Q), (R), (S), (T), (U) and (V) of this rule, any person confined in a state correctional institution may earn credit as a deduction from his sentence for each full month he productively participates in any academic or vocational program, prison industry, or alcohol and drug treatment, sex offender program, or mental health program specifically approved by the director. A person earning credit towards a sentence pursuant to section 2967.193 of House Bill 261 of the 117th General Assembly, for a crime committed prior to July 1, 1996 may earn two days of credit for such participation as described in paragraph (G) of this rule as a deduction from his minimum or definite sentence. A person earning credit towards a sentence for a crime committed on or after July 1, 1996 or otherwise sentenced pursuant to section 2967.193 of Senate Bill 2 of the 121st General Assembly, may earn one day of credit from his stated prison term.

(B) The director or designee shall issue and maintain a list containing the specific name of each approved program at each institution. Programs may be added or deleted according to a procedure approved by the director. No inmate shall be awarded earned credit for participating in any program not specifically named on the director's list. The director's approved list shall be verified annually for each institution through the department's audit process.

(C) The following types of programs may be approved for earned credit by the director as academic or vocational educational programs:

(1) Adult basic literacy education (A.B.L.E.);

(2) Pre–GED;

(3) GED and high school;

(4) College programs;

(5) Vocational and apprenticeship programs;

(6) Work extension program job assignments, where after successful completion, during the current incarceration, of an approved related institutional training program, the inmate applies the learned skills in the performance of his duties in his current institutional job assignment.

(D) Prison industries that may be approved for earned credit by the director are those operated through Ohio penal industries.

(E) The following types of programs may be approved for earned credit by the director as alcohol and drug treatment programs:

(1) Therapeutic communities;

(2) Residential alcohol and drug treatment programs;

(3) Alcohol and drug day treatment programs;

(4) Alcohol and drug treatment outpatient group counseling.

(5) Continuing care programs.

(F) The following types of programs may be approved for earned credit by the director as sex offender or mental health programs:

(1) Residential sex offender programs;

(2) Residential mental health programs;

(3) Sex offender day treatment programs;

(4) Mental health day treatment programs.

(G) Inmates earning credit pursuant to House Bill 261 of the 117th General Assembly, may earn two days of credit for participating in an approved academic or vocational or prison industries program as defined in paragraphs (C) and (D) of this rule in addition to two days credit for participating in programs listed in paragraph (E) or (F) of this rule. However, no inmate sentenced under House Bill 261 of the 117th General Assembly shall earn days of credit for participation in more than one academic or vocational education program or prison industry during a particular month. No inmate sentenced under House Bill 261 of the 117th General Assembly shall earn days of credit for participating in more than one residential or outpatient alcohol, drug, sex offender, or therapeutic community, or mental health treatment program during a particular month. Once an inmate earning credit pursuant to House Bill 261 of the 117th General Assembly has earned and has been properly credited with days of credit pursuant to this rule, the credit earned shall not be forfeited for any reason. Such inmates, therefore, are exempt from paragraph (N) of this rule, which describes conditions for possible withdrawal of previously earned credit for those inmates earning credit under Senate Bill 2 of the 121st General Assembly.

(II) Inmates earning credit pursuant to this rule sentenced under Senate Bill 2 of the 121st General Assembly may earn only one day of credit per month regardless of program participation, and such credit may be forfeited pursuant to paragraph (N) of this rule.

(I) An inmate earning credit towards a minimum or definite sentence pursuant to House Bill 261 of the 117th General Assembly and also earning credit towards a stated prison term pursuant to Senate Bill 2 of the 121st General Assembly shall have the minimum or definite sentence and the stated prison term independently reduced by the appropriate days of earned credit applicable to that particular sentence or prison term.

(J) In order to earn credit under this rule for a particular month, an inmate must enter the program on or before the first day of the month and continue participating in the program through the last day of the month. An inmate participating and remaining in good standing in an academic or vocational education program, which has a quarter or semester end during a month, shall be deemed to be participating in the program through the end of the month. An inmate who successfully completes a formal program resulting in the issuance of a certificate of completion during a month shall be deemed to have continued participating in the program through the end of that month.

(K) Regardless of the reason for absence, an inmate must attend seventy-five per cent of the scheduled program/job sessions for any month in order to receive earned credit for that month.

(L) No inmate will receive earned credit for program participation during any month in which he has had an unexcused absence from the program. Unexcused absence includes but is not limited to an absence caused by confinement in security control or disciplinary control as a result of a violation of institution rules.

(M) No inmate shall earn credit during any month in which he exhibits behavior considered to be a hindrance to the productive participation of himself or others, such as excessive noise, disruption, sleeping on assignment or tardiness. Such behavior shall be documented by a conduct report and substantiated through a guilty finding of the hearing officer or rules infraction board.

(N) Any inmate sentenced under Senate Bill 2 of the 121st General Assembly having plead or been found guilty by the rules infraction board of program related violations including those described in paragraphs (L) and (M) of this rule, may have previously earned credit days forfeited. The rules infraction board, in addition to assessing any other appropriate disciplinary measures, may recommend the withdrawing of earned credit awarded from previous months. An inmate may not have more than fifty per cent of previously earned credit days withdrawn in any calendar month. If the fifty per cent calculation results in a one-half or half day remainder, the half day shall be rounded up to a full day. Such recommendation shall be reviewed by the warden for approval/disapproval/modification.

(O) As soon as practicable after the last day of each month, the deputy warden or designee at each institution shall report to the record office supervisor the name of each inmate in the institution who has earned credit pursuant to this rule. Each month the record office supervisor shall credit the inmate appropriately with the credit earned for that month.

(P) No inmate serving a prison term of one, three, five or six years for use of a firearm imposed pursuant to section 2929.71 or 2929.72 of the Revised Code, in effect prior to July 1, 1996, for an offense committed prior to July 1, 1996, or pursuant to division (D)(1) of section 2929.14 of the Revised Code, effective July 1, 1996, for an offense committed on or after July 1, 1996, shall earn or be awarded any days of credit pursuant to this rule for any program participation which occurs while serving any such period of actual incarceration. An inmate against whom such a sentence was imposed may begin earning days of credit pursuant to this rule after serving any such term in its entirety if he would otherwise be eligible for earned credit.

(Q) An inmate who is granted a period of electronically monitored early release is not entitled, during that specified period of confinement, to earn any days of credit pursuant to this rule as a deduction from his prison term, regardless whether such prison term is for an offense committed before or after July 1, 1996.

(R) No inmate may earn days of credit pursuant to this rule if he is serving a sentence of imprisonment for an offense, committed before July 1, 1996, of:

(1) Life with parole eligibility after serving fifteen full years for an offense of first degree murder or aggravated murder committed prior to October 19, 1981; or

(2) Life parole eligibility after serving twenty full years for the offense of aggravated murder with one of the specifications enumerated in section 2929.04 of the Revised Code; or

(3) Life with parole eligibility after serving thirty full years for the offense of aggravated murder with one of the specifications enumerated in section 2929.04 of the Revised Code; or

(4) Life imposed prior to October 19, 1981, for an offense other than the offense of first degree or aggravated murder, for which the inmate becomes eligible for parole after serving ten full years pursuant to section 2967.13 of the Revised Code; or

(5) Life for rape or felonious sexual penetration; or

(6) A minimum term longer than fifteen years imposed under any law of this state in effect prior to January 1, 1974, for which the inmate becomes eligible for parole after serving ten full years pursuant to section 2967.13 of the Revised Code in effect prior to July 1, 1996.

(S) The following prison terms, for crimes committed on or after July 1, 1996 or otherwise imposed pursuant to Senate Bill 2 of the 121st General Assembly, shall not be reduced by any days of earned credit:

(1) A prison term for a felony for which an indefinite term of imprisonment is imposed;

(2) A mandatory prison term imposed pursuant to division (F) of section 2929.13 of the Revised Code, effective July 1, 1996, for:

(a) Aggravated murder or murder;

(b) Rape, felonious sexual penetration, or an attempt to commit rape or felonious sexual penetration by force when the victim is under thirteen years of age;

(c) Any felony violation of section 2903.06 (aggravated vehicular homicide) or 2903.07 (vehicular homicide) of the Revised Code;

(d) Any first, second or third degree felony drug offense for which the imposition of a mandatory prison term is required;

(e) Any other first or second degree felony if the offender previously was convicted of or pled guilty to aggravated murder, murder or any first or second degree felony;

(f) Any felony, other than a violation of section 2923.12 (carrying a concealed weapon) of the Revised Code, if the offender had a firearm on or about the offender's person or under the offender's control while committing the felony; or

(g) Corrupt activity in violation of section 2923.32 of the Revised Code when the most serious offense in the pattern of corrupt activity that is the basis of the offense is a felony of the first degree;

(3) A mandatory prison term imposed pursuant to division (D)(2)(a) of section 2929.14 of the Revised Code, effective July 1, 1996, for being a repeat violent offender. If the court also imposes an optional, additional term pursuant to division

(D)(2)(b) of section 2929.14 of the Revised Code, an inmate, who has completed serving the mandatory prison term, may earn credit while serving the additional, optional prison term;

(4) A mandatory ten year prison term imposed pursuant to division (D)(3)(a) of section 2929.14 of the Revised Code, effective July 1, 1996, for a drug offense or for otherwise being a major drug offender, for corrupt activity with the most serious offense in the pattern of corrupt activity being a first degree felony, or for attempted rape or felonious sexual penetration by force with the victim being under thirteen years of age. If the court also imposes an optional, additional term pursuant to division (D)(3)(b) of section 2929.14 of the Revised Code, an inmate, who has completed serving the mandatory ten year prison term, may earn credit while serving the additional, optional prison term;

(5) An extension of a stated prison term imposed by the parole board as "bad time; and

(6) A prison term imposed for a violation of post release control.

(T) If an inmate is earning credit towards a sentence pursuant to House Bill 261 of the 117th General Assembly for an offense committed prior to July 1, 1996, the cumulative total of any days of credit awarded under this rule, rules 5120–2–07 and 5120–2–08 of the Administrative Code, plus any diminution of sentence granted pursuant to rule 5120–2–05 of the Administrative Code, shall not exceed for such inmate one-third of the minimum or definite sentence, or in the case of a life sentence for which diminution and days of credit may be earned, one-third of the number of years before parole eligibility. No term of actual incarceration imposed pursuant to section 2929.71 or 2929.72 of the Revised Code in effect prior to July 1, 1996, for using a firearm in the commission of an offense shall be considered as a part of a minimum sentence or a part of the number of years before parole eligibility for eligible life sentences in calculating the maximum possible diminution pursuant to this paragraph.

(U) Days of credit earned pursuant to this rule shall be used for no purpose other than to reduce the inmate's definite or minimum sentence or his stated prison term. If an inmate is earning credit towards a sentence pursuant to House Bill 261 of the 117th General Assembly for an offense committed prior to July 1, 1996, once the inmate has served sufficient time to become eligible for parole consideration or has earned and had credited to him time off for good behavior pursuant to rule 5120–2–05 of the Administrative Code, and days of credit pursuant to this rule and rules 5120–2–07 and 5120–2–08 of the Administrative Code equal to one-third of his minimum or definite sentence, or in the case of an eligible life sentence, one-third of the number of year's before parole eligibility, no further calculation and crediting of days of credit pursuant to this rule is necessary for such sentence.

HISTORY: 2002–03 OMR 2557 (A), eff. 4–17–03; 2002–03 OMR 1725 (RRD); 2000–2001 OMR 193 (A), eff. 8–27–00; 1997–98 OMR 2475 (A), eff. 3–13–98; 1987–88 OMR 1011 (E), eff. 2–29–88; 1987–88 OMR 561 (E), eff. 11–30–87

RC 119.032 rule review date(s): 1–12–08; 1–10–08; 1–30–03; 1–12–03; 1–10–03; 6–2–00

5120–2–07 Days of credit for maintaining minimum security

(A) Except as provided by paragraphs (F), (G), (H), (I) and (J) of this rule, any offender who maintains minimum security status as defined by paragraphs (A), (B), and (C) of this rule is entitled to have three days of credit deducted from his minimum or definite sentence for each full month he remains at such status.

(B) Except as provided in paragraph (C) of this rule, "an offender on minimum security status" shall be defined as an offender designated as minimum security pursuant to this department's "Inmate Security Designation and Supervision Classification Manual" or as an offender who has been released on furlough for employment or education pursuant to section 2967.26 of the Revised Code.

(C) Notwithstanding paragraph (B) of this rule:

(1) No offender confined in security control or disciplinary control as a result of a violation of institution rules or in local control or administrative control shall be construed to be on minimum security status during the time spent in such control status.

(2) No furloughee confined in any jail as a result of an alleged violation of any furlough rule shall be construed to be on minimum security status for the time spent confined in such jail.

(3) No offender who is declared to be absent without leave from the institution and no furloughee who is declared a furlough violator at large shall be construed to be on minimum security.

(D) As soon as practicable after the last day of each month, the status of each offender on minimum security status as of the end of the last day of the month just ended will be examined. If the offender is found to have been on minimum security status at the beginning of the first day of the month and remained so during the entire month, three days shall be awarded to the offender and be deducted from his minimum or definite sentence.

(E) Once an offender has earned and been properly credited with days of credit pursuant to this rule, the days of credit shall not be forfeited for any reason.

(F) No offender serving a three-year term of actual incarceration for using a firearm in the commission of an offense, imposed pursuant to section 2929.71 of the Revised Code, shall earn or be awarded any days of credit pursuant to this rule for any time classified as minimum security while serving any such period of actual incarceration. An offender against whom such a sentence was imposed may begin earning days of credit pursuant to this rule after serving any such term of actual incarceration in its entirety.

(G) No offender may earn days of credit pursuant to this rule if he is serving a sentence of imprisonment of:

(1) Life with parole eligibility after serving fifteen full years for an offense of first degree murder or aggravated murder committed prior to October 19, 1981; or

(2) Life with parole eligibility after serving twenty full years for the offense of aggravated murder with one of the specifications enumerated in section 2929.04 of the Revised Code; or

(3) Life with parole eligibility after serving thirty full years for the offense of aggravated murder with one of the specifications enumerated in section 2929.04 of the Revised Code; or

(4) Life imposed prior to October 19, 1981, for an offense other than the offense of first degree or aggravated murder, for which the offender becomes eligible for parole after serving ten full years pursuant to section 2967.13 of the Revised Code; or

(5) Life for rape or felonious sexual penetration; or

(6) A minimum term longer than fifteen years imposed under any law of this state in effect prior to January 1, 1974 for which the offender becomes eligible for parole after serving ten full years pursuant to section 2967.13 of the Revised Code.

(H) The cumulative total of any days of credit awarded under this rule, rules 5120–2–06 and 5120–2–08 of the Administrative Code, plus any diminution of sentence granted pursuant to rule 5120–2–05 of the Administrative Code, shall not exceed for any offender one-third of the minimum or definite sentence, or in the case of a life sentence for which diminution and days of credit may be earned, one-third of the number of years before parole eligibility. No term of actual incarceration imposed pursuant to section 2929.71 of the Revised Code for using a firearm in the commission of an offense shall be considered as a part of a minimum sentence or a part of the number of years before parole eligibility for eligible life sentences in calculating the maximum possible diminution pursuant to this paragraph.

(I) Days of credit earned pursuant to this rule shall be used for no purpose other than to reduce the offender's definite or minimum sentence. Once an offender has served sufficient time to become eligible for parole consideration or has earned and had credited to him time off for good behavior pursuant to rule 5120–2–05 of the Administrative Code, and days of credit pursuant to this rule and rules 5120–2–06 and 5120–2–08 of the Administrative Code equal to one-third of his minimum or definite sentence, or in the case of an eligible life sentence, one-third of the number of years before parole eligibility, no further calculation and crediting of days of credit pursuant to this rule is necessary.

(J) This rule does not apply to any offense committed on or after July 1, 1996.

HISTORY: 2002–03 OMR 1725 (RRD); 1997–98 OMR 2478 (A), eff. 3–13–98; 1987–88 OMR 1012 (E), eff. 2–29–88; 1987–88 OMR 562 (E), eff. 11–30–87

RC 119.032 rule review date(s): 1–10–08; 1–12–03; 1–10–03

5120–2–10 Life sentences

(A) As a result of a number of amendments to the Revised Code over a period of years, the provisions for diminution of sentence and eligibility for parole, shock parole, employment/education furlough and home furlough are affected by the language in the sentencing documents (journal entries) concerning the crime and the sentence imposed as well as the date on which the crime was committed. The purpose of this rule is to explain diminution of sentence and eligibility for release for persons serving life sentences as established by the Revised Code. This rule does not expand release eligibility established by any other rule of the Administrative Code.

(B) A sentence of life imprisonment imposed pursuant to section 2929.03 of the Revised Code for the offense of aggravated murder shall be presumed to be a sentence of life imprisonment with parole eligibility after twenty years, subject to diminution under rules 5120–2–05, 5120–2–06, 5120–2–07 and 5120–2–08 of the Administrative Code, unless the journal entry of the court specifies that parole eligibility is to be after twenty full years or thirty full years.

(C) A prisoner serving a sentence of imprisonment for life with parole eligibility after serving thirty full years of imprisonment for the offense of aggravated murder with one or more of the specifications enumerated in section 2929.04 of the Revised Code.

(1) Becomes eligible for parole consideration after serving thirty full years:

(a) The thirty full years are reduced by jail-time credit pursuant to rule 5120–2–04 of the Administrative Code.

(b) The thirty full years are not diminished by time off for good behavior pursuant to rule 5120–2–05 of the Administrative Code.

(c) The thirty full years may not be reduced by days of credit earned pursuant to rules 5120–2–06, 5120–2–07, and 5120–2–08 of the Administrative Code.

(2) Is not eligible for shock parole.

(3) Is not eligible for release on furlough for employment or education pursuant to rule 5120:1–1–23 of the Administrative Code.

(4) Is not eligible for release on furlough for trustworthy prisoners (home furlough) pursuant to rule 5120–9–35 of the Administrative Code except for the purpose of visiting a dying relative or to attend the funeral of a relative.

(D) A prisoner serving a sentence of imprisonment for life with parole eligibility after serving twenty full years of imprisonment for the offense of aggravated murder with one or more of the specifications enumerated in section 2929.04 of the Revised Code.

(1) Becomes eligible for parole consideration after serving twenty full years:

(a) The twenty full years are reduced by jail-time credit pursuant to rule 5120–2–04 of the Administrative Code.

(b) The twenty full years are not diminished by time off for good behavior pursuant to rule 5120–2–05 of the Administrative Code.

(c) The twenty full years may not be reduced by days of credit earned pursuant to rules 5120–2–06, 5120–2–07, and 5120–2–08 of the Administrative Code.

(2) Is not eligible for shock parole.

(3) Is not eligible for release on furlough for employment or education pursuant to rule 5120:1–1–23 of the Administrative Code.

(4) Is not eligible for release on furlough for trustworthy prisoners pursuant to rule 5120–9–35 of the Administrative Code except for the purpose of visiting a dying relative or attending the funeral of a relative.

(E) A prisoner serving a sentence of imprisonment for life with parole eligibility after serving twenty years of imprisonment for the offense of aggravated murder, committed on or after October 19, 1981, without one or more of the specifications enumerated in section 2929.04 of the Revised Code.

(1) Becomes eligible for parole consideration after serving twenty years:

(a) The twenty years are reduced by jail-time credit pursuant to rule 5120–2–04 of the Administrative Code.

(b) The twenty years are diminished by time off for good behavior pursuant to rule 5120–2–05 of the Administrative Code.

(c) The twenty years may be reduced by days of credit earned pursuant to rules 5120–2–06, 5120–2–07, and 5120–2–08 of the Administrative Code.

(2) Is not eligible for shock parole.

(3) Is not eligible for release on furlough for employment or education pursuant to rule 5120:1–1–23 of the Administrative Code.

(4) Is not eligible for release on furlough for trustworthy prisoners pursuant to rule 5120–9–35 of the Administrative Code except for the purpose of visiting a dying relative or attending the funeral of a relative.

(F) A prisoner serving a sentence of imprisonment for life for an offense of first degree murder or aggravated murder committed prior to October 19, 1981.

(1) Becomes eligible for parole consideration after serving fifteen full years:

(a) The fifteen years are reduced by jail-time credit pursuant to rule 5120–2–04 of the Administrative Code.

(b) The fifteen years are not diminished by the time off for good behavior pursuant to rule 5120–2–05 of the Administrative Code.

(c) The fifteen years may not be reduced by days of credit earned pursuant to rules 5120–2–06, 5120–2–07, and 5120–2–08 of the Administrative Code.

(2) Is not eligible for shock parole.

(3) Is eligible for release on furlough for employment or education pursuant to rule 5120:1–1–23 of the Administrative Code.

(4) Is eligible for release on furlough for trustworthy prisoners (home furlough) pursuant to rule 5120–9–35 of the Administrative Code.

(G) A prisoner serving an indefinite term of imprisonment of fifteen years to life for the offense of murder.

(1) Becomes eligible for parole consideration after serving the fifteen-year minimum sentence:

(a) The fifteen years are reduced by jail-time credit pursuant to rule 5120–2–04 of the Administrative Code.

(b) The fifteen years are diminished by time off for good behavior pursuant to rule 5120–2–05 of the Administrative Code.

(c) The fifteen years may be reduced by days of credit earned pursuant to rules 5120–2–06, 5120–2–07, and 5120–2–08 of the Administrative Code.

(2) Is not eligible for shock parole.

(3) Is eligible for release on furlough for employment or education pursuant to rule 5120:1–1–23 of the Administrative Code.

(4) Is eligible for release on furlough for trustworthy prisoners (home furlough) pursuant to rule 5120–9–35 of the Administrative Code.

(H) A prisoner serving a sentence of imprisonment for life imposed pursuant to division (B) of section 2907.02 of the Revised Code for the crime of rape committed against a victim under the age of thirteen or imposed pursuant to division (B) of section 2907.12 of the Revised Code for the crime of felonious sexual penetration committed by force or threat of force against a victim under the age of thirteen.

(1) Becomes eligible for parole consideration after serving ten full years:

(a) The ten full years are reduced by jail-time credit pursuant to rule 5120–2–04 of the Administrative Code.

(b) The ten full years are not diminished by time off for good behavior pursuant to rule 5120–2–05 of the Administrative Code.

(c) The ten full years may not be reduced by days of credit earned pursuant to rules 5120–2–06, 5120–2–07, and 5120–2–08 of the Administrative Code.

(2) Is not eligible for shock parole if the offense was committed on or after July 1, 1983 or if serving a term of actual incarceration imposed pursuant to section 2907.10 of the Revised Code for an offense committed before July 1, 1983.

(3) Is not eligible for release on furlough for employment or education pursuant to rule 5120:1–1–23 of the Administrative Code if the offense was committed on or after October 19, 1981.

(4) Is not eligible for release on furlough for trustworthy prisoners (home furlough) pursuant to rule 5120–9–35 of the Administrative Code except for the purpose of visiting a dying relative or to attend the funeral of a relative if the offense was committed on or after October 19, 1981.

(I) A prisoner serving a sentence of imprisonment for life for an offense other than first degree murder or aggravated murder committed prior to October 19, 1981.

(1) Becomes eligible for parole consideration after serving ten full years:

(a) The ten full years are reduced by jail-time credit pursuant to rule 5120–2–04 of the Administrative Code.

(b) The ten full years is not diminished by time off for good behavior pursuant to rule 5120–2–05 of the Administrative Code.

(c) The ten full years may not be reduced by days of credit earned pursuant to rules 5120–2–06, 5120–2–07, and 5120–2–08 of the Administrative Code.

(2) Is eligible for shock parole.

(3) Is eligible for release on furlough for employment or education pursuant to rule 5120:1–1–23 of the Administrative Code.

(4) Is eligible for release on furlough for trustworthy prisoners (home furlough) pursuant to rule 5120–9–35 of the Administrative Code.

(J) A prisoner serving a sentence of imprisonment for life consecutive to any other term or terms of imprisonment becomes eligible for parole consideration as follows:

(1) Where the life sentence is imposed for aggravated murder, with one of the specifications enumerated in section 2929.04 of the Revised Code, committed on or after October 19, 1981, the prisoner shall be eligible for parole after serving the sum, without diminution, of any three-year terms of actual incarceration imposed pursuant to section 2929.71 of the Revised Code for using a firearm in the commission of an offense, plus the twenty or thirty full years, without diminution, as designated by the court for parole eligibility, plus the time required for parole eligibility for any other crimes. There shall be no limit to the length of such aggregated sentence.

(2) Where the life sentence is imposed for aggravated murder without one or more specifications enumerated in section 2929.04 of the Revised Code, committed on or after October 19, 1981, the prisoner shall be eligible for parole after serving the sum, without diminution, of any three-year terms of actual incarceration imposed pursuant to section 2929.71 of the Revised Code for using a firearm in the commission of an offense, plus the sum of twenty years for each such consecutive life sentence and the sum of all other consecutive minimum sentences, each diminished, as provided in rules 5120–2–05, 5120–2–06, 5120–2–07, and 5120–2–08 of the Administrative Code. There shall be no limit to the length of such aggregated minimum term.

(3) Where the life sentence is imposed for first degree murder or aggravated murder committed prior to October 19, 1981, and does not include a life sentence imposed for aggravated murder committed on or after October 19, 1981, the prisoner shall be eligible for parole after serving the sum, without diminution, of any terms of actual incarceration imposed pursuant to section 2929.71 of the Revised Code for using a firearm in the commission of an offense, plus fifteen full years, without diminution, plus the required time for parole eligibility for any other crimes. However, this aggregate shall not exceed the sum of all terms of actual incarceration time plus twenty full years.

(K) A prisoner serving a sentence of imprisonment for an offense of aggravated murder committed on or after July 1, 1996:

(1) Becomes eligible for parole consideration after serving:

(a) Twenty full years, twenty-five full years, or thirty full years and is reduced by jail time credit pursuant to rule 5120–2–04 of the Administrative Code.

(b) Twenty full years, twenty-five full years, or thirty full years and is not diminished by time off for good behavior pursuant to rule 5120–2–05 of the Administrative Code.

(c) The full years may not be reduced by the days of credit earned pursuant to rule 5120–2–06, 5120–2–07, or 5120–2–08 of the Administrative Code.

(2) Is not eligible for judicial release.

(3) Is not eligible for release on transitional control.

(L) A prisoner serving a sentence of imprisonment for life without parole committed on or after July 1, 1996, is not eligible for parole consideration, judicial release or transitional control.

(M) A prisoner serving a sentence of imprisonment of life for an offense of murder committed on or after July 1, 1996:

(1) Becomes eligible for parole consideration after serving:

(a) Fifteen full years and is reduced by jail time credit pursuant to rule 5120–2–04 of the Administrative Code.

(b) Fifteen full years is not diminished by time off for good behavior pursuant to rule 5120–2–05 of the Administrative Code.

(c) The full years may not be reduced by the days of credit earned pursuant to rule 5120–2–06, 5120–2–07, or 5120–2–08 of the Administrative Code.

(2) Is not eligible for judicial release.

(3) Is not eligible for release on transitional control.

HISTORY: 2002–03 OMR 2227 (A), eff. 4–10–03; 1997–98 OMR 2479 (RRD); 1987–88 OMR 1348 (E), eff. 5–1–88; 1987–88 OMR 1013 (E), eff. 2–26–88; 1987–88 OMR 563 (E), eff. 11–30–87

RC 119.032 rule review date(s): 1–12–08; 1–12–03; 1–10–03

5120–2–12 Calculation of time off for good behavior for prisoners committed to the department of rehabilitation and correction on or before October 31, 1987

(A) Except as provided in paragraph (B) of rule 5120–2–05 of the Administrative Code, the provisions of rule 5120–2–05 of the Administrative Code shall apply to all persons who are confined in a state correctional institution on or after November 1, 1987, regardless of the date on which the person committed the offense for which he is confined. If, however, the person began serving a term of imprisonment in a state correctional facility before November 1, 1987, the provisions of rule 5120–2–05 of the Administrative Code apply only to the portion of the term served on and after November 1, 1987.

(B) For each inmate confined in a state correctional institution on or before October 31, 1987 who has not, as of that date, served his minimum or definite sentence as diminished pursuant to section 2967.19 of the Revised Code, the portion of his sentence that has been served as of October 31, 1987 shall be diminished for time off for good behavior pursuant to the rules in effect at that time.

(C) This rule shall not operate to extend the eligibility for parole of any inmate already committed to the custody of the department of rehabilitation and correction as of the effective date of this rule.

HISTORY: 2002–03 OMR 1725 (RRD); 1997–98 OMR 2479 (RRD); 1987–88 OMR 1015 (E), eff. 2–29–88; 1987–88 OMR 565 (E), eff. 11–30–87

RC 119.032 rule review date(s): 1–10–08; 1–12–03; 1–10–03

5120:1

DIVISION OF PAROLE AND COMMUNITY SERVICES

CHAPTER 5120:1–1

RELEASE

Promulgated pursuant to RC 111.15 and/or Ch 119

Section

5120:1–1–01 Glossary of terms

(A) Facility director: A "facility director" is a person designated as the head of community correctional center, halfway house resident center, or other suitable facility.

(B) Supervising authority: The "supervising authority" shall be the supervision sections of the adult parole authority.

(C) Suitable facility: A "suitable facility" is one that has been licensed by the adult parole authority pursuant to division (C) of section 2967.14 of the Revised Code.

(D) Confinement: "Confinement" shall mean restriction to the buildings or grounds of suitable facility.

(E) Violation of release: A "violation of release" shall occur when there is a failure to comply with the rules as established pursuant to administrative rules or laws.

(F) Releasee: A "releasee shall be an inmate released on parole, shock parole, by the Ohio parole board or a prisoner released to intermediate transitional detention pursuant to section 5120.01.01 of the Revised Code. No inmate or prisoner shall be considered to be a releasee until the inmate or prisoner has received papers authorizing release from the institution, has completed processing by the institutional personnel, and has physically departed from the institution.

(G) Aggravated murder: "Aggravated murder" shall be the crime of murder in the first degree for which an inmate was convicted and sentenced pursuant to Chapter 2901. of the Revised Code until January 1, 1974, and the crime for which an inmate is convicted and sentenced pursuant to Chapter 2903. of the Revised Code thereafter.

(H) Murder: "Murder" shall be the crime of murder in the second degree for which an inmate was convicted and sentenced pursuant to Chapter 2901. of the Revised Code until January 1, 1974, and the crime for which an inmate is convicted and sentenced pursuant to Chapter 2903. of the Revised Code thereafter.

(I) Inmate: "Inmate" shall include a prisoner, resident, convict, offender, or similar classification as used in the Revised Code or Administrative Code.

(J) Institution: "Institution" shall be defined as any penal institution operated directly by the department of rehabilitation and correction, [1] which is used for the custody, care or treatment of criminal offenders.

(K) Spree of offenses: "Spree of offenses" is a series of offenses committed during a continuous course of related conduct. The decision that an offense has been committed in a spree of offenses shall be made initially by the institutional record clerk, in consultation with the chief of bureau of records management, subject to review by the chief of the adult parole authority.

(L) Shock parole: "Shock parole" shall be defined as a release granted pursuant to rule 5120:1–1–06 of the Administrative Code prior to regular parole eligibility or expiration of definite sentence pursuant to rule 5120:1- 1–03 and Chapter 5120–2 of the Administrative Code. (M) Escapee: An "escapee" is any inmate, including a furloughee or a prisoner released to intermediate transitional detention, who purposely breaks or attempts to break such detention or confinement as established by the department of rehabilitation and correction or any of its agencies, or purposely fails to return to detention, either following temporary leave granted for a specific purpose or limited period, or at the time required when serving a sentence in intermittent confinement.

HISTORY: 1999–2000 OMR 1215 (RRD); 1997–98 OMR 3051 (A), eff. 6–1–98; 1997–98 OMR 2488 (A), eff. 3–16–98; 1990–91 OMR 1608 (A), eff. 7–1–91; 1988–89 OMR 1084 (A), eff. 4–21–89; 1980–81 OMR 27 (A), eff. 8–1–80; 1979–80 OMR 4–129 (A), eff. 8–18–79; prior rule 900*

RC 119.032 rule review date(s): 1–12–05; 1–12–00

1 Prior and current versions differ; although no amendment to this language was indicated in the 6–1–98 or 1997–98 OMR 2488 version, "operated directly by the department of rehabilitation and correction," appeared as "operated directly by the department of rehabilitation and correction, or by a public or private agency in contract with the department of rehabilitation and correction," in the 1990–91 OMR 1608 version.

5120:1–1–02 Supervision fees

(A) The department of rehabilitation and correction, division of parole and community services (DP&CS) shall recover from offenders under supervision on or after the effective date of this rule, a supervision fee, pursuant to section 5120.56(d)(5) of the Revised Code. Offenders placed on, or moved to monitored time, shall not pay a supervision fee.

(B) The division of parole and community services shall ascertain the fee to be assessed under this rule after determining the average costs of supervision per offender, and considering the following factors:

(1) The ability, in general, of the offender population to pay a fee.

(2) The compliance level desired by the division of parole and community services.

(3) The offender supervision fees assessed by other states.

(C) The procedure for recovery of this fee shall be as follows:

(1) No later than the offender's first reporting visit to the assigned adult parole authority (APA) office and officer, the offender shall sign conditions of supervision, pursuant to section 5120:1–1–12 of the Administrative Code.

(2) The conditions of supervision shall include a condition that the offender pay a supervision fee during the offender's period of supervision. The condition shall specify a supervision fee of twenty dollars per month of APA supervision.

(3) The offender shall be advised of this condition prior to signing the conditions of supervision. The offender shall also be advised that he/she may contest the assessment of the fee pursu ant to the provisions of this rule, and that the assessment of the fee may be waived by the DP&CS pursuant to this rule.

(4) The collection of the supervision fee shall be by the submission of a monthly payment by the offender to "Supervision Fee Administrator, 1050 Freeway Drive North, Columbus, Ohio 43229." Payment must be in the form of a certified check or money order.

(5) Supervision fee payments will be due on the first day of the month beginning with the month following the offender's release, unless the apa officer determines during the offender's first reporting visit that the offender is unemployed and unable to make the payment. In that event, the supervision fee payments will be due on the first day of the second month following the offender's release.

(D) The offender may object to the assessment of the fee by submitting a written grievance to the assigned APA officer. The written grievance must contain information regarding any ongoing permanent injury or condition that affects the offender's ability to provide for himself.

(E) The regional administrator or designee shall review the written grievance submitted by the offender, and shall notify the offender, in writing, of the final decision regarding the assessment of the supervision fee.

(F) The department of rehabilitation and correction shall not impose a supervision fee if, due to an ongoing permanent injury or condition, the imposition of the fee would unjustly limit the offender's ability to provide for the offender after incarceration. The regional administrator may require the offender to substantiate any injury or condition, with document- ation from a health care professional. Criteria for evaluating an offender's ongoing permanent injury or condition, and the ability of that type of offender to provide for the offender after incarceration, shall include the following factors:

(1) Impairment. The extent to which the injury substantially impairs a major life activity.

(2) Mobility. The extent to which the injury limits the offender's ability to move about in the community.

(3) Permanence. The extent to which the injury leads to an ongoing, chronic condition.

(4) Treatment. The extent to which ongoing treatment or medication impairs the offender's ability to maintain employment or provide for the offender.

(F) The division of parole and community services may waive the imposition of the supervision fee, or a portion thereof, at any time during the offender's supervision, if the presence of any of the following conditions make collection of the fee unduly burdensome upon the offender.

(1) The offender is already under a court order to make restitution to the victim(s) of his/her offense, or a civil judgment to pay damages to the victim(s).

(2) The offender is already under a court order to make child support payments.

(3) The offender can show that he/she is indigent, and can not provide for himself/herself if the collection of the supervision fee is imposed.

(4) The offender is paying a supervision fee to another jurisdiction.

(G) The decision to waive the supervision fee, or a portion thereof, may be reviewed by the division of parole and community services from time to time as circumstances warrant.

(I) 1 All moneys collected by or on behalf of the department under section 5120.56 of the Revised Code shall be deposited by division of parole and community services business office into the offender financial responsibility fund of the state treasury. The division of parole and community services shall follow existing DRC division of business administration guidelines for the method, frequency, accounting and transfer of the deposits.

(J) No offender shall be subject to a revocation of parole, or the imposition of a jail or prison sanction solely for nonpayment of the supervision fee. No offender's supervision shall be extended, nor shall a final release from supervision be denied, solely for nonpayment of supervision fees. However, the payment or nonpayment of fees may be considered by the supervising officer, in addition to other factors relating to the offender's performance under supervision, in deciding whether to recommend a final release from parole supervision or to recommend an early termination of the period of the offender's post-release control. The payment or nonpayment of fees may be considered by a hearing officer, in addition to other factors relating to the offender's performance under supervision, in any violation proceeding.

(K) If an offender recieves a final release from parole, or termination of PRC supervision, and has unpaid supervision fees, the supervision fee administrator shall notify the offender, in writing, of the total unpaid amount, and demand the payment of that amount in full. If payment is not received in forty-five days, the supervision fee administrator shall certify the overdue amount to the attorney general's office—revenue recovery section, for collection.

(L) The department of rehabilitation and correction may expend moneys in the offender financial responsibility fund for goods and services of the same type as those for which offenders are assessed. The money collected as supervision fees shall be used strictly for goods and services related to the supervision of offenders.

(M) The division of parole and community services shall monitor the collection of supervision fees and annually report the following information:

(1) The number of offenders who have paid fees.

(2) The number of offenders who have been exempted from payment of fees.

(3) The number of offenders who have not complied with payment of fees.

(4) The total amount of fees received.

(5) The total estimated costs of administering the system.

(6) The types of goods and services purchased from the collection of the fees.

The report will be produced by the division of parole and community services and provided to the director and the chair of the joint committee on agency rule review. The report will be subject to section 149.43 of the Revised Code.

HISTORY: 2000–2001 OMR 2383 (E), eff. 7–6–00; 1997–98 OMR 330 (R), eff. 7–18–97; Prior rule 901

RC 119.032 rule review date(s): 1–12–05

1 Paragraph designation appears as original.

5120:1–1–03 Minimum eligibility for release on parole

(A) Except as provided in rule 5120:1–1–06 of the Administrative Code for shock parole, rule 5120:1–1–40 of the Administrative Code for parole of dying prisoners and section 2967.18 of the Revised Code for emergency paroles, no inmate serving an indefinite sentence shall be released on parole until he has served the minimum term reduced pursuant to rule 5120–2–04 of the Administrative Code for jail-time credit, diminished pursuant to rule 5120–2–05 of the Administrative Code for good behavior, and diminished pursuant to rule 5120–2–06 of the Administrative Code for productive program participation, rule 5120–2–07 of the Administrative Code for maintaining minimum security, and rule 5120–2–08 for meritorious conduct. Provided, Chapter 5120–2 of the Administrative Code shall not be applied in such a manner as to unconstitutionally extend the minimum period for eligibility for parole of any prisoner in contravention of any statutory provision which may have been in effect at the time the crime was committed.

(B) Except as provided in rule 5120:1–1–40 of the Administrative Code for parole of a dying prisoner, no inmate serving any sentence of life imprisonment shall be released on parole until he has served the number of years specified in rule 5120–2–10 of the Administrative Code reduced as provided in rule 5120–2–04 of the Administrative Code.

(C) Except as provided in rule 5120:1–1–06 of the Administrative Code for shock parole, rule 5120:1–1–40 of the Administrative Code for parole of dying prisoners and section 2967.18 of the Revised Code for emergency paroles, no inmate serving a definite sentance shall be released on parole.

HISTORY: 1999–2000 OMR 1215 (RRD); 1987–88 OMR 1016 (R–E), eff. 2–29–88; 1987–88 OMR 565 (R–E), eff. 11–30–87; 1983–84 OMR 710 (A), eff. 1–16–84; 1983–84 OMR 64 (A), eff. 7–18–83; 1982–83 OMR 478 (A), eff. 10–11–82; 1979–80 OMR 4–892 (A), eff. 5–30–80; 1979–80 OMR 4–534 (A), eff. 1–20–80; prior rule 907

RC 119.032 rule review date(s): 1–12–05; 1–12–00

5120:1–1–06 Shock parole

(A) The Revised Code provides the parole board with the discretion to release on parole a prisoner confined in a state correctional facility, at any time after serving six months in the custody of the department of rehabilitation and correction if all of the following apply:

(1) The offense for which the prisoner was sentenced is other than:

(a) Aggravated murder

(b) Murder

(c) An aggravated felony of the first, second, or third degree

(2) The prisoner has not previously been convicted of any felony for which, pursuant to sentence, he was confined for thirty days or more in a penal or reformatory institution in this state, or in a similar institution in any other state or [*sic*] the United States.

(3) The prisoner is not a dangerous offender as defined in section 2929.10 of the Revised Code.

(4) The prisoner does not need further confinement in a penal or reformatory institution for his correction or rehabilitation.

(5) The history, character, condition and attitudes of the prisoner indicate he is likely to respond affirmatively to early release on parole, and is unlikely to commit another offense.

(6) The prisoner is not serving a term of actual incarceration.

(7) The prisoner is not ineligible for shock parole pursuant to division (C) of section 2903.06, 2903.07 or 2903.08 of the Revised Code.

(B) In addition to the offenses precluded from shock parole consideration by the Revised Code, the parole board deems prisoners serving sentences for the following offenses to be inappropriate for release on shock parole:

(1) Any offense contained in Chapter 2907. of the Revised Code.

(2) Aggravated vehicular homicide, section 2903.06 of the Revised Code.

(3) Vehicular homicide, section 2903.07 of the Revised Code.

(4) Aggravated vehicular assault, section 2903.08 of the Revised Code.

(6) [1] Endangering children, section 2919.22 of the Revised Code.

(7) Arson, section 2909.03 of the Revised Code.

(8) Felony domestic violence, section 2919.25 of the Revised Code.

(C) A prisoner whose history includes any of the following shall be deemed to be unlikely to respond affirmatively to early release on parole:

(1) Participation in the program of shock incarceration and removal from the program because of a rule infraction or return to prison for a violation of any condition of intermediate transitional detention or intensive parole supervision;

(2) Release on shock probation and return to the institution for violating the probation;

(3) Release on electronically monitored early release pursuant to Chapter 5120–13 of the Administrative Code and a return to the institution for a violation.

(4) Release to a halfway house or community-based correctional facility pursuant to Chapter 5120–12 of the Administrative Code and a return to the institution for a violation.

(5) A conviction for any offense committed while serving the current sentence or while on escape or unauthorized leave from such confinement.

(D) Whether or not an offense committed outside of the jurisdiction of the state of Ohio is a felony for the purposes of this rule shall be determined by the classification of such offense by the Revised Code as if the act for which such sentence was imposed had been committed within the jurisdiction of the state of Ohio.

(E) A prisoner serving a definite sentence of one year or less shall not be considered for release on shock parole because he would not serve sufficient time under parole supervision before his sentence expired, to receive the benefit of supervised release.

(F) The parole board will consider a prisoner for release on shock parole when all of the following apply:

(1) The prisoner meets the provisions of paragraph (A) of this rule, and;

(2) The prisoner is not serving a sentence for any offense listed in paragraph (B) of this rule, and;

(3) The prisoner is not deemed unlikely to respond affirmatively to early release pursuant to paragraph (C) of this rule, and;

(4) The prisoner is not serving a definite sentence of one year or less.

(G) The procedure to be followed in considering prisoners for shock parole shall be as follows:

(1) Upon reception the record office shall determine whether the prisoner meets the criteria set out in paragraph (F) of this rule;

(2) The record officer shall schedule prisoners meeting the criteria set out in paragraph (F) of this rule for a personal appearance interview by a hearing officer during the prisoner's fourth month of imprisonment;

(3) The hearing officer shall make a recommendation for or against release on shock parole.

(4) Upon receipt of the recommendation of the hearing officer, the parole board will determine whether or not to grant shock parole.

(5) A prisoner granted shock parole may be released after six months in custody in a state correctional institution.

HISTORY: 1999–2000 OMR 1215 (RRD); 1994–95 OMR 801 (R–E), eff. 11–21–94; 1983–84 OMR 208 (A), eff. 8–29–83; 1978–79 OMR 4–434 (A), eff. 1–2–79; prior rule 910

RC 119.032 rule review date(s): 1–12–05; 1–12–00

[1] Paragraph designation appears as in original.

5120:1–1–07 Procedure for release on parole, furlough, and shock parole; factors that shall be considered in a release hearing

(A) An inmate may be released on or about the date of his eligibility for release, unless the parole board, acting pursuant to rule 5120:1–1–10 of the Administrative Code, determines that he should not be released on such date for one or more of the following reasons:

(1) There is substantial reason to believe that the inmate will engage in further criminal conduct, or that the inmate will not conform to such conditions of release as may be established under rule 5120:1–1–12 of the Administrative Code;

(2) There is substantial reason to believe that due to the serious nature of the crime, the release of the inmate into society would create undue risk to public safety, or that due to the serious nature of the crime, the release of the inmate would not further the interest of justice nor be consistent with the welfare and security of society;

(3) There is substantial reason to believe that due to serious infractions of division level 5120:1 of the Administrative Code, the release of the inmate would not act as a deterrent to the inmate or to other institutionalized inmates from violating institutional rules and regulations;

(4) There is need for additional information upon which to make a release decision.

(B) In considering the release of the inmate, the parole board shall consider the following:

(1) Any reports prepared by any institutional staff member relating to the inmate's personality, social history, and adjustment to institutional programs and assignments;

(2) Any official report of the inmate's prior criminal record, including a report or record of earlier probation or parole;

(3) Any presentence or postsentence report;

(4) Any recommendations regarding the inmate's release made at the time of sentencing or at any time thereafter by the sentencing judge, presiding judge, prosecuting attorney, or defense counsel;

(5) Any reports of physical, mental or psychiatric examination of the inmate;

(6) Such other relevant written information concerning the inmate as may be reasonably available, except that no document related to the filing of a grievance under rule 5120–9–31 of the Administrative Code shall be considered;

(7) Written or oral statements by the inmate, other than grievances filed under rule 5120–9–31 of the Administrative Code.

(8) The equivalent sentence range under Senate Bill 2, (effective July 1, 1996,) for the same offense of conviction.

(9) The inmate's ability and readiness to assume obligations and undertake responsibilities, as well as the inmate's own goals and needs;

(10) The inmate's family status, including whether his relatives display an interest in him or whether he has other close and constructive association in the community;

(11) The type of residence, neighborhood, or community in which the inmate plans to live;

(12) The inmate's employment history and his occupational skills;

(13) The inmate's vocational, educational, and other training;

(14) The adequacy of the inmate's plan or prospects on release;

(15) The availability of community resources to assist the inmate;

(16) The physical and mental health of the inmate as they reflect upon the inmate's ability to perform his plan of release;

(17) The presence of outstanding detainers against the inmate;

(18) Any other factors which the board determines to be relevant, except for documents related to the filing of a grievance under rule 5120–9–31 of the Administrative Code.

(C) The consideration of any single factor, or any group of factors, shall not create a presumption of release on parole, or the presumption of continued incarceration. The parole decision need not expressly address any of the foregoing factors.

HISTORY: 2003–04 OMR 504 (A), eff. 9–5–03; 1999–2000 OMR 1215 (RRD); 1997–98 OMR 330 (A), eff. 7–18–97; prior rule 911

RC 119.032 rule review date(s): 1–12–05; 1–12–00

5120:1–1–10 Initial and continued parole board hearing dates; projected release dates

(A) The initial hearing for each prisoner serving an indeterminate sentence shall be held on or about the date when the prisoner first becomes eligible for parole pursuant to rule 5120:1–1–03 of the Administrative Code.

(B) In any case in which parole is denied at a prisoner's regularly constituted parole hearing and the board does not continue the prisoner to the expiration of the maximum sentence, the parole board shall:

(1) Set a projected release date in accordance with paragraph (D) of this rule, or

(2) Set the time for a subsequent hearing, which shall not be more than ten years after the date of the hearing.

(C) In any case where parole is denied the reasons for such denial shall be communicated to the prisoner and the warden in writing.

(D) The parole board at any parole release consideration hearing may, in its discretion, establish a projected release date ten years or less in the future which, unless rescinded pursuant to this rule, would permit the prisoner to be released without a further appearance before the parole board or a hearing panel. This date shall be subject to rescission within the discretion of the parole board and shall not create any expectation of release or entitlement to be released thereon.

(E) A projected release date shall not be established for any prisoner serving a life sentence, sentence of fifteen years to life, or a sentence imposed for any offense pursuant to Chapter 2907. of the Revised Code.

(G) A projected release date shall be recorded and published in the official minutes of the parole board.

(H) The institution in which a prisoner with a projected release date is confined shall, upon request, submit to the parole board a pre-release report. This report shall summarize the prisoner's conduct, adjustment and program participation subsequent to the granting of a projected release date.

(I) The chief hearing officer, or a hearing officer designated by the chair of the parole board shall review the report as soon as practicable and shall advise the parole board that release on the projected release date is still warranted or that the projected release date should be rescinded.

(J) If, after reviewing the recommendation of the hearing officer a majority of the parole board believes that release on the projected release date is no longer appropriate, the projected release date shall be rescinded and the prisoner shall be scheduled to appear before a panel of the parole board as soon as administratively possible.

(K) If the projected release date is not rescinded the inmate shall be released on or after the projected release date in the usual manner and following the standard procedures for releasing inmates.

HISTORY: 1999–2000 OMR 1215 (RRD); 1997–98 OMR 3051 (A), eff. 6–1–98; 1997–98 OMR 2488 (A), eff. 3–16–98; 1994–95 OMR 802 (R–E), eff. 11–21–94; 1988–89 OMR 391 (A), eff. 11–1–88; 1978–79 OMR 4–435 (A), eff. 1–2–79; prior rule 914*

RC 119.032 rule review date(s): 1–12–05; 1–12–00

Historical and Statutory Notes

Publisher's Note: The expiration date of this agency, state board, or state commission is fixed by 1996 H 670, § 27, eff. 12–2–96, which provides in part:

"The following agencies shall be retained pursuant to division (D) of section 101.84 of the Revised Code and shall expire on December 31, 2001, pursuant to the version of section 101.84 of the Revised Code that takes effect on January 1, 1997... Parole Board."

5120:1–1–11 Procedure for release consideration hearing

(A) A hearing shall be held by the Parole Board prior to the release of an inmate in a state penal or reformatory institution pursuant to Administrative Regulation 5120:1–1–07.

(B) The decisions of the Parole Board which result from the hearings shall be recorded and published in its official minutes.

(C) The hearing may be conducted by the Parole Board or a quorum thereof, for the purpose of making a decision for or against release or may be conducted for the purpose of making a recommendation for or against release to the Parole Board by a panel consisting of one or more members of the Parole Board and one or more Parole Board hearing officers as designated by the Chairman of the Parole Board.

(D) The inmate need not be present at a hearing at the discretion of the Chairman of the Parole Board if the decision is to grant release, or if the recommendation of the panel is to deny release and no appeal to the Parole Board is filed by the inmate within ten (10) days after notification of the panel's recommendation that release be denied or deferred.

(E) A prerelease consideration interview with the inmate may be conducted by a Parole Board hearing officer as designated by the Chairman of the Parole Board for the purpose of making a recommendation for or against release to a Parole Board Panel when an inmate is not to personally appear for a hearing.

(F) Following a release hearing, if the inmate is present and a decision is made by the Parole Board, or if the inmate is present and a recommendation is made by a hearing panel, the decision or recommendation shall be communicated immediately to the inmate unless, in the judgment of the hearing body, an undue security risk would thereby be created.

(G) In the event the decision of the Parole Board is to deny release of an inmate, the inmate and Managing Officer shall be furnished within fourteen (14) working days after completion of the hearing:

(1) A written notice stating the grounds under Administrative Regulation 5120:1–1–07 upon which such determination was based, indicating which of the factors specified in Administrative Regulations 5120:1–1–08 and 5120:1–1–09 were considered as significant to its decision;

(2) A written notice of the date on or about which the inmate shall be entitled under Administrative Regulation 5120:1–1–10 to another release hearing.

(H) At least three weeks prior to any release hearing, notice of such hearing shall be sent to the prosecuting attorney and the judge of the court in which the inmate was convicted, or where there is more than one such judge, to the presiding judge. Such notice shall contain:

(1) The name of the inmate;

(2) The crime for which the inmate was convicted;

(3) The date of conviction; and,

(4) The term of sentence.

(I) In the event a hearing is continued, notice of such continuance and the date of next hearing shall be sent to all interested parties at least ten (10) working days prior to the date of the continued hearing.

(J) Administrative Regulation 915, filed on April 14, 1976, is hereby rescinded.

HISTORY: 1999–2000 OMR 1215 (RRD); Prior rule 915

RC 119.032 rule review date(s): 1–12–05; 1–12–00

5120:1–1–12 Conditions of release

(A) The Parole Board shall impose upon the releasee such conditions of release as it deems reasonably necessary to insure that the releasee will lead a law-abiding life and to assist him in so doing.

(B) The Parole Board shall impose the following minimum conditions of release:

(1) The releasee shall abide by all federal, state, and local laws and ordinances, and all rules and regulations of the Department of Rehabilitation and Correction;

(2) The releasee shall not leave the State without permission, in writing, of the Adult Parole Authority;

(3) The releasee shall comply with all lawful orders given him by duly authorized representatives of the Department of Rehabilitation and Correction or its agencies, which shall include any special conditions of release that may be issued orally or in writing at any time during supervision;

(4) The releasee must not possess, own, use, or have under his control, any firearms, deadly weapons, or dangerous ordinance.

(C) The Parole Board or the Supervision Section of the Adult Parole Authority, in imposing conditions of release, shall individualize such conditions to the extent feasible, provided:

(1) That there be a reasonable relationship between the conditions imposed and the inmate's previous conduct and present situation;

(2) That the conditions are sufficiently specific to serve as a guide to supervision and conduct; and

(3) That the conditions are such that compliance is possible.

(D) Upon release, an inmate shall be given a certificate setting forth the conditions of release. An inmate shall be made aware of all the rules of release that have been imposed upon him by the Parole Board prior to the inmate's release from the institution.

(E) Except in an emergency, special conditions imposed by Parole Officers and Furlough Counselors shall be in writing and subject to approval by an appropriate supervisor. Such special conditions shall be reported to and subject to review by the Chief of the Adult Parole Authority, or designee, within thirty (30) days after being imposed.

(F) A furloughee shall, in addition, be required to comply with the following rules:

(1) Unless the Chief of the Adult Parole Authority, or designee, provides otherwise, each furloughee must be located either at the approved facility for confinement, at the designated educational or work location, or en route between the facility and the location.

(2) Each furloughee must abstain from consuming or possessing any type of alcohol and any nonprescribed drug or narcotic.

(3) Each furloughee must inform his supervising officer of any unavoidable or unusual circumstances which prevent the participant from fulfilling his obligations under the Furlough Program.

(G) Release to a state or to a federal authority shall be subject to Administrative Regulation 5120:1–1–33. Pending release to such authority, the inmate shall remain in the institution or suitable facility to which he is assigned.

(H) In determining whether paragraph (B)(1) above has been violated, the fact that there has been no conviction, or no prosecution, shall not prevent the Adult Parole Authority from commencing revocation proceedings pursuant to Administrative Regulation 5120:1–1–17.

(1) A judicial determination that the violation of law or ordinance has not been proved beyond a reasonable doubt, or a dismissal of the criminal charges by a prosecutor, shall not preclude the Parole Board from finding a violation of law or ordinance, for the purposes of revocation of release. The commission of a violation of release may be proved by a lesser degree of proof, pursuant to Administrative Regulation 5120:1–1–19, paragraph (E), by substantial evidence considering the record as a whole.

(2) A finding of "no probable cause" by a magistrate on pending criminal charges shall not affect the finding of a violation of paragraph (B)(1), above, when additional evidence is considered at the revocation hearings held pursuant to Administrative Regulations 5120:1–1–18 and 5120:1–1–19. If no additional evidence is considered at the revocation hearing, the judicial determination of "no probable cause" shall be conclusive that paragraph (B)(1), above, has not been violated.

HISTORY: 1999–2000 OMR 1215 (RRD); Prior rule 916

RC 119.032 rule review date(s): 1–12–05; 1–12–00

5120:1–1–13 Discharge from parole

(A) A parolee who has faithfully performed all the conditions of his parole and who has obeyed the rules of parole established by the adult parole authority shall be granted a final release by the chief of the adult parole authority upon the written recommendation of the superintendent of parole supervision.

(B) No parolee shall be granted a final release from parole earlier than one year after the parolee has been released from the institution on parole unless his maximum sentence has expired prior to the expiration of one year.

(C) No parolee serving a sentence of aggravated murder, or life shall be released from parole earlier than five years after the parolee has been released from the institution.

(D) Administrative regulation 5120:1–1–13, effective October 15, 1975, is hereby repealed.

HISTORY: 1999–2000 OMR 1215 (RRD); 1977 78 OMR 3–34 (A), eff. 3–18–77; prior rule 918

RC 119.032 rule review date(s): 1–12–05; 1–12–00

5120:1–1–14 Restoration of rights

(A) Unless otherwise restricted by law, inmates who have served the maximum term of their sentence or who have been granted their final release by the chief of the adult parole authority shall be restored to the rights and privileges forfeited by their conviction.

(B) On or after January 1, 1974, inmates who have been released on shock parole, parole, probation, or on shock probation, but not on furlough, shall have the right to vote in public elections during such release.

(C) Restoration of rights forfeited under section 2921.02, Bribery, and section 2921.41, Theft in office, of the Revised Code, shall only be restored by a pardon, pursuant to administrative regulation 5120:1–1–15.

(D) Administrative regulation 5120:1–1–14, effective October 15, 1975, is hereby repealed.

HISTORY: 1999–2000 OMR 1215 (RRD); 1977–78 OMR 3–34 (A), eff. 3–18–77; prior rule 919

RC 119.032 rule review date(s): 1–12–05; 1–12–00

5120:1–1–15 Pardon, reprieve and commutation of sentence

(A) All applications for pardon, reprieve or commutation of sentence shall be made in writing to the Chief of the Adult Parole Authority.

(B) When an application for a pardon, reprieve or commutation of sentence is filed with the Chief of the Adult Parole Authority, the authority shall conduct such investigation as is necessary and make a recommendation to the governor. A hearing may be held at the discretion of the Parole Board. Such hearing if held, shall be before at least a majority of the members of the Parole Board.

(C) At least three weeks prior to any hearing held to consider pardon, reprieve or commutation of sentence, notice of such hearing shall be sent to the prosecuting attorney and the judge of the Court of Common Pleas of the county in which the indictment against the applicant was found, and, if required by section 2967.12 of the Revised Code, to the victim or victim's family. Where there is more than one judge of the court of common pleas, the notice shall be sent to the presiding judge.

(D) Such notice shall contain the following:

(1) The name of the applicant;

(2) The crime for which the applicant was convicted;

(3) The date of conviction;

(4) The term of sentence.

(E) In the event the hearing is continued, notice of such continuance and the date of the continued hearing shall be sent to all interested parties at least ten (10) days prior to the date of the continued hearing.

(F) In the event the decision of the Parole Board is to recommend for or against pardon, reprieve, or commutation of sentence, such recommendation shall be forwarded to the Governor, together with a brief statement of the facts, the grounds for such recommendation, and the record or minutes of the case.

(G) The decision of the Parole Board to recommend for or against pardon, reprieve or commutation of sentence shall be within its sole discretion and shall not be subject to administrative review.

(H) If the adult parole authority receives an application for pardon, commutation or reprieve for a person for whom executive clemency was denied less than two years earlier than the date the subsequent application was received, and the authority does not believe that the application contains any grounds that were not or could not have been presented in the earlier application, the parole authority may forward the application to the governor with the recommendation that it be denied on the basis of the earlier review and denial. In such a case, no hearing and no further investigation shall be necessary unless specifically requested by the governor.

(I) The adult parole authority shall consider a case for pardon or commutation only upon the application of the convicted person or his counsel or at the direction of the governor.

HISTORY: 1999–2000 OMR 1215 (RRD); 1993–94 OMR 587 (A), eff. 9-13-93; 1992–93 OMR 1538 (A), eff. 7-1-93; prior rule 920*

RC 119.032 rule review date(s): 1-12-05; 1-12-00

Historical and Statutory Notes

Publisher's Note: The expiration date of this agency, state board, or state commission is fixed by 1996 H 670, § 27, eff. 12-2-96, which provides in part:

"The following agencies shall be retained pursuant to division (D) of section 101.84 of the Revised Code and shall expire on December 31, 2001, pursuant to the version of section 101.84 of the Revised Code that takes effect on January 1, 1997... Parole Board."

5120:1-1-16 Violator at large

(A) Whenever an offender absconds from the supervision of the adult parole authority, such fact shall be reported in writing by the unit supervisor, or supervising officer of the offender, to the chief of the adult parole authority or designee pursuant to the policies and procedures of the division of parole and community services.

(B) Upon receipt of such written report the offender may be declared a violator-at-large and such declaration entered into its official minutes of the adult parole authority or such decision may be delayed pending further investigation.

(C) Upon apprehension of a violator-at-large, or declaration that an offender is a violator-at-large, the procedures as set forth in 5120:1-1-31 and 5120:1-1-34 of the Administrative Code shall apply.

(D) The procedures as set forth in this rule shall not apply to probation offenders or community control offenders under the supervision of the adult parole authority.

HISTORY: 1999–2000 OMR 1215 (RRD); 1996–97 OMR 1264 (A), eff. 12-20-96; prior rule 921

RC 119.032 rule review date(s): 1-12-05; 1-12-00

5120:1-1-17 Responding to release violations

(A) Pursuant to rule 5120:1-1-12 of the Administrative Code the parole board and the parole officer have significant discretion to impose conditions of release designed to protect the public and to promote the releasee's successful reintegration into the community. This rule does not limit any discretion to impose special conditions that exists under that rule.

(B) Whenever a releasee under the supervision of the adult parole authority commits a violation of the conditions of release, the authority will take appropriate steps in response to the violation behavior. These steps may range from warning the releasee to refrain from future violation behavior to revocation of release. Parole officers, supervisors and hearing officers have discretion to reasonably impose various sanctions in response to violation behavior. The division of parole and community services may adopt specific procedures to carry out the purpose of this rule.

(C) Sanctions such as, but not limited to, the following may be imposed without a hearing:

(1) Office reporting;

(2) Additional supervision conditions;

(3) Upgrades in supervision levels;

(4) Mandatory employment;

(5) Structured supervision activities;

(6) Summons before a unit supervisor;

(7) Substance abuse monitoring/treatment;

(8) Residential curfew;

(9) More frequent reporting requirements;

(10) Formal written reprimand;

(11) Program placement;

(12) Summons to appear before the parole board for review of the releasee's performance on release;

(D) The following sanctions may be imposed by an adult parole authority hearing officer after a hearing:

(1) Any of the sanctions that may be imposed by the parole officer or unit supervisor;

(2) Revocation of release.

HISTORY: 1999–2000 OMR 1215 (RRD); 1996–97 OMR 298 (R-E), eff. 8-16-96; 1995–96 OMR 1325 (R-E), eff. 12-1-95, exp. 2-29-96; 1995–96 OMR 584 (R-E*), eff. 9-1-95; 1988–89 OMR 1085 (A), eff. 4-21-89; prior rule 922*

RC 119.032 rule review date(s): 1-12-05; 1-12-00

5120:1-1-18 Release revocation hearing

(A) If the decision is made to commence revocation proceedings pursuant to section 2967.15 of the Revised Code, the releasee shall receive a hearing prior to revocation of release, unless a non-suspended felony sentence has been imposed upon him by an

Ohio court for an offense committed while on release or a felony sentence which includes a prison term has been imposed upon him by an Ohio court and not been modified by judicial release under section 2929.20 of the Revised Code. The hearing shall be conducted in accordance with specific procedures adopted by the division of parole and community services which include the following guidelines:

(1) The hearing shall be held at the county jail or other facility in which the releasee is in custody, or at another place designated by the unit supervisor.

(2) The hearing shall be conducted by a parole board member, hearing officer or other person designated by the chief of the adult parole authority. The chief may designate as hearing officer any neutral employee of the department of rehabilitation and correction other than the releasee's supervising officer or that officer's supervisor.

(3) The hearing is to determine whether there is preponderance of the evidence, taking the record as a whole, that the releasee violated a condition of release and whether mitigating circumstances make revocation inappropriate. The determination of the appropriate sanction rests within the sound discretion of the hearing officer.

(4) With respect to the hearing, the releasee has the following rights:

(a) The right to receive prior to the hearing a written notice setting forth the date, time and location of the hearing and the specific violations the releasee is alleged to have committed.

(b) The right to be heard in person and present relevant witnesses and documentary evidence.

(c) The right to confront and cross-examine adverse witnesses unless the hearing officer specifically finds good cause for not allowing confrontation. In the event that confrontation is disallowed, specific reasons for the same shall be documented in the record of proceedings.

(d) The right to disclosure of evidence presented against the releasee.

(e) The right to request representation by counsel. If the releasee cannot afford to retain counsel, assistance, upon request, will be provided by the office of the state public defender.

(f) The right to a written digest by the hearing officer if requested.

(B) If the hearing officer decides that the releasee violated the conditions of release and that a revocation sanction should be imposed, the hearing officer shall order the return of the releasee to the appropriate state correctional institution. The finding and order of the hearing officer shall constitute the official and final determination of the adult parole authority to revoke release, unless the decision is reversed by the chief of the adult parole authority or designee because of prejudicial and case dispositive error by the hearing officer. This provision does not create a right of appeal of the decision of the hearing officer.

HISTORY: 1999–2000 OMR 1215 (RRD); 1996–97 OMR 298 (R–E), eff. 8–16–96; 1995–96 OMR 1325 (R–E), eff. 12–1–95, exp. 2–29–96; 1995–96 OMR 584 (R–E*), eff. 9–1–95; 1979–80 OMR 4–400 (A), eff. 12–10–79; 1978–79 OMR 4–102 (A), eff. 9–7–78; prior rule 923*

RC 119.032 rule review date(s): 1–12–05; 1–12–00

5120:1–1–19 Procedures after revocation of release

(A) If, after a hearing provided for in rule 5120:1–1–18 of the Administrative Code, a person's release is revoked, whether or not the person shall be considered for further release prior to the expiration of his sentence depends upon the type of release and sentence or sentences he is serving.

(B) If the person was on shock parole, the parole board shall review the records to determine whether he should be scheduled for a hearing to consider further release on shock parole prior to the expiration of his definite sentence, or initial parole eligibility if serving an indefinite sentence.

(C) If the person was on any type of release other than shock parole, from a definite sentence, the person shall serve the balance of the definite sentence.

(D) If the person had been released on parole after the expiration of the minimum sentence (with diminution) the person will be scheduled for a parole release consideration hearing as soon as practicable.

(E) If the person had been released on any type of release other than shock parole prior to his initial parole release consideration hearing, and that date has not yet passed, he will be scheduled for a parole release consideration hearing at his initial eligibility date.

(F) If the person had been denied release at his initial parole release consideration hearing and released on furlough or other type of release prior to the end of the continuance, and that date has not yet passed, he will be scheduled for a parole release consideration hearing at the end of the continuance.

(G) If a person described in paragraph (D), (E) or (F) of this rule is returned and the date of the initial parole release consideration or continued date has passed, the person will be scheduled for a release consideration hearing as soon as practicable.

HISTORY: 1999–2000 OMR 1215 (RRD); 1996–97 OMR 299 (R–E), eff. 8–16–96; 1995–96 OMR 1326 (R–E), eff. 12–1–95, exp. 2–29–96; 1995–96 OMR 586 (R–E*), eff. 9–1–95; 1993–94 OMR 843 (A), eff. 12–1–93; 1993–94 OMR 587 (A*), eff. 9–13–93; 1992–93 OMR 1539 (A), eff. 7–1–93; 1992–93 OMR 1252 (A*), eff. 4–1–93; 1992–93 OMR 647 (R–E), eff. 11–29–92; 1992–93 OMR 289 (R–E*), eff. 9–1–92; prior rule 924*

RC 119.032 rule review date(s): 1–12–05; 1–12–00

5120:1–1–20 Review procedure for early release consideration

(A) A prisoner who was denied release at a regular parole release hearing that occurred before april 1, 1998 and scheduled for his next parole hearing between twenty months and twenty years after the date of that hearing will be scheduled for a release hearing after half the length of the continuance. For the purpose of this rule, a regular parole release hearing is a hearing conducted for the purpose of determining whether or not to release the prisoner on parole after he has served the time required by section 2967.13 of the Revised Code. A parole revocation hearing or a hearing by the parole board to consider a prisoner for shock parole, furlough or any other type of release is not a regular parole release hearing for the purpose of this rule and shall not establish a right to have the prisoner's case heard early pursuant to this rule. A prisoner granted a projected release date or denied release at a parole hearing on or after april 1, 1998 shall not be reviewed pursuant to this rule.

(B) A prisoner who was denied release at a regular parole release hearing that occurred before april 1, 1998 and scheduled for his next parole hearing twenty years or more after the date of that heasring will be scheduled for a release hearing ten years from the date of that hearing.

HISTORY: 2001–02 OMR 1599 (R–E), eff. 1–1–02; 1999–2000 OMR 1215 (RRD); 1997–98 OMR 3052 (A), eff. 6–1–98; 1997–98 OMR 2489 (A), eff. 3–16–98; 1993–94 OMR 588 (R–E), eff. 9–13–93; 1992–93 OMR 1539 (R–E*), eff. 7–1–93; 1983–84 OMR 209 (A), eff. 8–29–83; 1981–82 OMR 368 (A), eff. 11–9–81; 1978–79 OMR 4–435 (A), eff. 1–2–79; prior rule 925*

RC 119.032 rule review date(s): 1–12–05; 1–12–00

5120:1–1–21 Revocation of release if releasee recommitted for new offense

(A) The adult parole authority shall revoke the release of any releasee who is recommitted to the department of rehabilitation and correction to serve a prison term for a felony sentence imposed upon him by any court in Ohio for an offense he committed while on any release granted by the adult parole authority or while serving a period of intermediate transitional detention pursuant to rule 5120–11–12 of the Administrative Code or serving a period of parole supervision pursuant to rule 5120–11–19 of the Administrative Code.

(B) This revocation shall be accomplished by the issuance of minutes by the adult parole authority after it has verified that the sentence was imposed for an offense that occurred while the prisoner was under release status.

(C) If the prisoner was on release from a definite sentence only, is recommitted to serve a definite sentence or sentences, and is not serving any indefinite sentence, there shall be no further release consideration and the offender shall serve the balance of the aggregate definite sentence, diminished pursuant to rules 5120–2–04 to 5120–2–08 of the Administrative Code, unless the prisoner becomes eligible for release on furlough pursuant to rule 5120:1–1–23 of the Administrative Code.

(D) If the prisoner was on release from an indefinite sentence or one or more sentences for which he is recommitted is an indefinite sentence, he shall be scheduled for a parole release hearing when eligible pursuant to rules 5120–2–03 to 5120–2–08 and rule 5120:1–1–13 of the Administrative Code.

(E) The foregoing procedures do not apply to the class identified in the consent decree appended to the reported decision of *Kellogg v. Shoemaker* No. 2–90–CV–606 (S.D. Ohio). The procedures for this class are set forth in that consent decree.

HISTORY: 1999–2000 OMR 1215 (RRD); 1996–97 OMR 299 (R–E), eff. 8–16–96; 1995–96 OMR 1326 (A), eff. 12–1–95, exp. 2–29–96; 1992–93 OMR 647 (E), eff. 11–29–92; 1992–93 OMR 289 (E*), eff. 9–1–92; 1979–80 OMR 4–402 (R), eff. 12–10–79; prior rule 928*

RC 119.032 rule review date(s): 1–12–05; 1–12–00

5120:1–1–22 Confinement of mentally ill and mentally retarded releasees

(A) Whenever a supervising officer has reason to believe, based upon reliable information or observation, that a releasee appears to be mentally ill or mentally retarded and in need of treatment which requires hospitalization or other special care, such information shall be immediately brought to the attention of the unit supervisor, who for purposes of this rule will be a designee of the chief of the adult parole authority. The unit supervisor will immediately evaluate the information and determine a course of action to insure that the rights of the community members and of the releasee are fully protected.

(B) In determining an appropriate course of action, the least restrictive alternative shall be pursued while giving full consideration to the dangerousness of the releasee to himself and to others. The following shall be considered by the unit supervisor when making that determination:

(1) Whether hospitalization or special care is required; or

(2) Whether to apply appropriate special conditions of release and continue supervision; or

(3) Whether to arrange outpatient treatment at a suitable community facility; or

(4) Whether to arrange for care and treatment at a suitable community residential treatment center for mentally ill or mentally retarded persons; or

(5) Whether to arrange for voluntary admission to a hospital; or

(6) Whether to arrange for family, guardian, or other suitable person to file an affidavit for involuntary hospitalization in accordance with section 5122.11 of the Revised Code for mentally ill releasees or section 5123.71 of the Revised Code for mentally retarded releasees; or

(7) Whether to arrange for an evaluation and, if appropriate:

(a) Commitment by the evaluator pursuant to section 5120.10 of the Revised Code (mentally ill releasees); or

(b) Filing of an affidavit, with certification, by the unit supervisor pursuant to section 5122.11 of the Revised Code (mentally ill releasees); or

(c) Filing of an affidavit, with certification, by the unit supervisor pursuant to section 5123.71 of the Revised Code (mentally retarded releasees).

(8) Whether to arrange for a law enforcement officer to commit the releasee pursuant to section 5122.10 of the Revised Code (mentally ill releasees); or

(9) Whether to contact the chief, adult parole authority, or designee, for approval to file an affidavit, without certification, pursuant to section 5122.11 of the Revised Code; or

(10) Whether to cause the arrest of the releasee in accordance with rule 5120:1–1–31 of the Administrative Code and pursue revocation of release pursuant to rule 5120:1–1–17 of the Administrative Code.

(C) Upon the supervising officer and unit supervisor concluding that the releasee is "suffering from a mental illness or mental retardation subject to hospitalization" as defined by section 5122.01 or 5123.68 of the Revised Code, and that parole revocation is inappropriate at that time, the unit supervisor shall immediately pursue one of the following courses of action and immediately submit a report to the chief, adult parole authority, or his designee, with full particulars:

(1) Persuade the releasee to voluntarily admit himself to a mental hospital; or

(2) Request the releasee's family to file an affidavit pursuant to section 5122.11 of the Revised Code (mental illness); or

(3) Request a law enforcement officer to admit a mentally ill releasee pursuant to section 5122.10 of the Revised Code; or

(4) File an affidavit with certification pursuant to section 5122.11 of the Revised Code (mentally ill) or section 5123.71 of the Revised Code (mentally retarded); or

(5) File an affidavit pursuant to section 5122.11 of the Revised Code (mentally ill) or section 5123.71 of the Revised Code (mentally retarded) without certification, if approval has been received by the chief, adult parole authority, or his designee.

(D) In the event of an emergency where time does not permit prior notification to the unit supervisor, or the chief, adult parole authority, or his designee, pursuant to paragraph (A) of this rule, the supervising officer is authorized to:

(1) Seek to cause the commitment of a mentally ill releasee by a law enforcement officer pursuant to section 5122.10 of the Revised Code; or

(2) Cause the commitment of the releasee pursuant to section 5122.11 of the Revised Code.

(E) Summary action by a supervising officer pursuant to paragraph (B) shall be immediately communicated to the chief, adult parole authority, or his designee, through the unit supervisor with full particulars in writing for review and final action.

(F) No affidavit for involuntary hospitalization shall be filed without a certification by a psychiatrist or a licensed clinical psychologist and licensed physician unless:

(1) The releasee refuses to be evaluated; or

(2) The releasee represents a substantial, imminent risk of physical harm to himself or others and commitment pursuant to section 5122.10 of the Revised Code is not possible.

(G) No affidavit for involuntary hospitalization, without certification, shall be filed until approval for filing has been granted by the chief, adult parole authority, or his designee, except as noted in paragraph (D) of this rule. Whenever an affidavit is filed without certification, a report will be immediately forwarded to the chief, adult parole authority, or his designee, with full particulars as to why hospitalization is necessary, including documentation as to why certification was not possible.

(H) Whenever a releasee is being evaluated for confinement at a mental institution or other mental health program, or is committed to an institution or facility, the appropriate mental health personnel shall be furnished:

(1) A copy of the written report prepared by the unit supervisor pursuant to paragraphs (C) and (E) of this rule; and

(2) Copies of relevant diagnostic reports in the files of the department of rehabilitation and correction.

(I) If a releasee is committed to an inpatient facility of the department of mental health and mental retardation, the care and custody of the releasee shall be administratively transferred from the department of rehabilitation and correction to the department of mental health and mental retardation.

(J) Upon certification by the director of the department of mental health and mental retardation to the chief, adult parole authority or his designee, that the releasee is recovered or is in need of less restrictive care and treatment, the chief, adult parole authority, or his designee, shall:

(1) Return the releasee to his former status; or

(2) Re–evaluate the appropriateness of revocation proceedings; or

(3) Change the terms and conditions of release pursuant to rule 5120:1–1–12 of the Administrative Code.

(K) In the event the releasee is found not to be mentally ill or mentally retarded, the unit supervisor, in consultation with the supervising officer, shall:

(1) Return the releasee to his former status; or

(2) Re–evaluate the appropriateness of revocation proceedings; or

(3) Change the terms and conditions of release pursuant to rule 5120:1–1–12 of the Administrative Code.

HISTORY: 1999–2000 OMR 1215 (RRD); 1979–80 OMR 4–402 (A), eff. 12–10–79; prior rule 929

RC 119.032 rule review date(s): 1–12–05; 1–12–00

5120:1–1–31 Detainers

(A) The department of rehabilitation and correction shall have the authority to file a detainer against an offender or otherwise cause the arrest of an offender by the issuance of a detainer whenever there is reasonable cause to believe that such offender has violated or is about to violate any of the terms or conditions of his supervision or sanction and commits an overt act toward such violation.

(B) If such offender is not within the state of Ohio and has been placed under supervision or sanction pursuant to the Interstate Compact for Supervision of Parolees and Probationers Act, he shall be returned to Ohio pursuant to such act. The Extradition of Fugitives Act shall apply when the offender leaves the state of Ohio without lawful authority.

(C) If such offender is within the state of Ohio:

(1) In the event such offender is within the lawful custody of an Ohio law enforcement agency or facility, the detainer shall be filed in a manner described by the policies of the department of rehabilitation and correction and the division of parole and community services.

(2) In the event such offender is not within the lawful custody of an Ohio law enforcement agency or facility, his arrest shall be ordered by the issuance of an arrest order to the appropriate law-enforcement agency in a manner described by the policies of the department of rehabilitation and correction and the division of parole and community services.

(D) When any employee of the department of rehabilitation and correction has received any information which gives him reasonable grounds to believe that an offender has violated, or is about to violate, any of the terms or conditions of his supervision or sanction and commits an overt act toward such violation, such information shall immediately be reported, in writing, to the supervising officer of the offender with a copy to the unit supervisor, or directly to the unit supervisor, in writing, if the information is based upon the supervising officer's own knowledge or observations.

(1) Immediately upon receipt of such information by the offender's supervising officer, such supervising officer shall consult with the unit supervisor regarding whether or not a detainer should be issued or placed against such releasee. In the case of any emergency, a detainer may be filed by the supervising officer, pending review by the unit supervisor which shall be done at the earliest practicable time.

(2) When a detainer is issued or filed, the unit supervisor shall immediately send a written report of such action to the chief of the adult parole authority, or his designee, and state why no alternative disposition was available or feasible.

(3) In the event a detainer is not filed, the unit supervisor shall immediately send a written report supporting such action, providing alternative programming, to the chief of the adult parole authority or his designee, whenever the alleged violation involves a violation of state or federal law, the action of the release [1] has resulted in property damage or physical injury to any persons, or the alleged violation is of a special condition of supervision or sanction placed on the offender pursuant to rule 5120:1–1–12 of the Administrative Code. All other alleged violations shall be reported to the chief of the adult parole authority, or his designee, pursuant to periodic reporting requirements.

(4) Within ten days following the issuance or filing of a detainer, the unit supervisor shall file the complete violation report.

(5) At any time after the filing of or issuance of a detainer against an offender, the chief of the adult parole authority, or his designee, may, at his discretion, revoke and cancel such detainer, and take such other action as may be deemed appropriate.

(E) A detainer shall be immediately filed whenever an offender is arrested for a felony of the first, second, or third degree, or for murder or aggravated murder.

(1) The fact of arrest and filing of the detainer shall be immediately reported, orally and in writing, to the unit supervisor. The unit supervisor, in consultation with the supervising officer shall, within two business days following the placement of the detainer:

(a) Initiate the revocation procedures pursuant to rule 5120:1–1–17 of the Administrative Code; or

(b) Cancel the detainer, without prejudice to the filing of a new detainer based on new information. In the event of cancellation, the fact of cancellation, and all surrounding facts and circumstances shall be immediately reported, in writing, to the chief of the adult parole authority or his designee pursuant to paragraph (D) of this rule.

(2) Whenever possible, the supervising officer shall attend the bail hearing or otherwise bring to the attention of the judge and to the prosecuting attorney that the person arrested is on release from the department of rehabilitation and correction.

(F) Whenever an offender is arrested for a felony of the fourth or fifth degree, or for a misdemeanor, a detainer shall not be immediately filed. Whenever possible, the supervising officer shall attend the bail hearing or otherwise bring to the attention of the judge and the prosecuting attorney that the person arrested is on release from the department of rehabilitation and correction. The decision to file or not file a detainer shall be determined according to paragraph (D) of this rule.

(G) In making the decision to issue a detainer pursuant to paragraph (D) of this rule, or to cancel a detainer, pursuant to paragraph (E) of this rule, the unit supervisor shall consider the following:

(1) The seriousness of the violation;

(2) If a crime has been committed, the nature of the crime;

(3) The likelihood of the offender leaving the jurisdiction:

(4) The offender's history of supervision;

(5) The employment stability of the offender;

(6) The family and community ties and relationships of the offender;

(7) The past record and history of the offender;

(8) Such other factors as are determined to be relevant under the facts and circumstances of the particular case.

HISTORY: 2000–2001 OMR 1182 (RRD); 1996–97 OMR 1264 (A), eff. 12–20–96; 1978–79 OMR 4–104 (A), eff. 9–7–78; prior rule 938

RC 119.032 rule review date(s): 1–12–06; 1–12–01

[1] So in original. Should this read "releasee"?

5120:1–1–33 Release to state or federal detainer

(A) No inmate shall be released from an institution when a detainer has been placed against the inmate by lawful authorities to answer for criminal charges or completion of sentence within the jurisdiction of such authorities, except pursuant to this rule and:

(1) Interstate Agreement on Detainers, section 2963.30 of the Revised Code.

(2) The procedures in section 2941.401 of the Revised Code.

(B) At least thirty days prior to the scheduled release of any such inmate, notification of the pending release date shall be communicated to the authority that placed the detainer on form 940–1. Such notice shall be given without regard to whether or not the release is pursuant to rule 5120:1–1–10 of the Administrative Code or upon completion of maximum sentence.

(C) Inmates subject to a detainer upon completion of maximum sentence shall be released on the date specified. In no event shall such inmate remain in custody of the department of rehabilitation and correction beyond the expiration date of sentence upon request of the detaining authority or otherwise.

(D) Inmates otherwise eligible for release pursuant to rule 5120:1–1–10 of the Administrative Code may, at the discretion of the parole board, be released:

(1) Subject to notification to a detaining authority that the inmate is to be released. Failure of the detaining authority to notify the managing officer of the holding institution of its intent to take the inmate into custody shall result in the removal of the detainer.

(2) Subject to enforcement of a detainer as a precondition of release. Failure of the detaining authority to make arrangements to take such releasee into custody on the scheduled date of release, unless extended by the parole board upon request, will cause the removal of the detainer. The inmate shall be notified of such conditional release, and the consequences of such failure, pursuant to paragraph (D) of rule 5120:1–1–10 of the Administrative Code,.

(E) Notification of the action of the parole board under paragraph (D) of this rule, shall be communicated to such detaining authority, to the managing officer, and to the inmate on form 940–2, by the institutional record clerk upon receipt of the official minutes of the parole board.

(F) If the detainer is from another state and the inmate has declined to waive extradition, the inmate shall be delivered on the scheduled release date to the sheriff of the county in which the inmate is incarcerated pending extradition to the detaining authority.

(G) Release on detainer pursuant to this rule shall be at no expense to the state of Ohio.

HISTORY: 2000–2001 OMR 1579 (A), eff. 4–1–01; Prior rule 940

RC 119.032 rule review date(s): 1–12–06; 1–12–01

5120:1–1–34 Return to Ohio on a detainer

(A) An offender under adult parole authority supervision who is in violation of his conditions of supervision or sanction and is apprehended outside of the state of Ohio and held in the custody of an arresting or confining authority may be released to an Ohio detainer, placed against such offender pursuant to rule 5120:1–1–31 of the Administrative Code.

(B) Upon receipt of notification that an offender subject to an Ohio detainer is about to be released, the chief of the adult parole authority, or his designee, in his discretion, shall either order the return of the offender to Ohio to the supervision or custody of the department of rehabilitation and correction, or, if applicable, reinstate the offender to supervision or to a sanction.

(C) Such offender shall be returned to Ohio for serving of sentence or prison term or reinstatement to supervision or to an appropriate sanction. Return shall be pursuant to:

(1) The interstate compact for the supervision of parolees and probationers; or

(2) The Uniform Extradition Act; or

(3) A free and voluntary waiver of extradition by such offender.

(D) Upon return of the offender to Ohio, rules governing the processing of offender violations shall apply, as well as all rules concerning reinstatement of the offender to supervision or to an appropriate sanction.

(E) All lawful costs incurred in confining the offender pending return of the offender to Ohio shall be borne by the department of rehabilitation and correction.

(F) The provisions set forth in this administrative rule shall not apply to probationers or community control offenders under the supervision of the adult parole authority.

HISTORY: 2000–2001 OMR 1182 (RRD); 1996–97 OMR 1265 (A), eff. 12–20–96; Prior rule 941

RC 119.032 rule review date(s): 1–12–06; 1–12–01

5120:1–1–35 Contracts for the transportation of inmates

(A) The adult parole authority, in order to discharge its duties under Chapters 2967. and 5149. of the Revised Code, may enter into a contract with a private person or entity for the return of Ohio prisoners who are the responsibility of the department of rehabilitation and correction from outside of this state to a location in this state specified by the adult parole authority. Pursuant to division (E) of section 311.29 of the Revised Code, this rule is applicable to contracts entered into between a private person or entity and a county sheriff, for the transportation of prisoners who are the responsibility of the county sheriff.

(B) Any contract entered into under this rule shall incorporate the mandatory standards expressed in this rule. Any private person or entity with whom the adult parole authority contracts for the return of Ohio prisoners shall maintain compliance with these standards throughout the term of the contract.

(C) Standards for training of employees of the private person or entity that engage in the return of prisoners.

(1) Eighty hours of preservice training which shall minimally include:

(a)	Unarmed self defense:	8 hours
(b)	Use of force:	4 hours
(c)	Restraints:	4 hours
(d)	Non-lethal weapons: Four hours—chemical agents Two hours—non-lethal shotgun	6 hours
(e)	Firearms:	10 hours
(f)	Transportation of prisoners:	20 hours
(g)	Searches:	2 hours
(h)	Map reading:	3 hours
(i)	Defensive driving:	4 hours
(j)	First-aid/CPR:	8 hours

(D) Physical standards for vehicles used in the return of prisoners:

(1) Vehicles utilized to transport prisoners shall be in good operating condition, with current maintenance and repair records on file, and meet the following minimum criteria:

(a) Separate and safely secure the driving team from the prisoner.

(b) Doors and windows unable to be opened from the inside of the prisoner compartment.

(c) Welded steel screens covering the windows.

(d) Operational heater and air conditioner for the entire vehicle.

(e) Equipped with some form of mobile communication.

(f) Readily identifiable by air as prisoner transport vehicles.

(g) Maintain manufacturer's recommended occupancy rating.

(E) The private person or entity with whom the adult parole authority contracts for the return of Ohio prisoners shall maintain compliance with the federal motor carrier safety administration regulation 395.3 regarding maximum driving time for employees, and any revision, amendment or modification of that regulation.

(F) Standards of financial responsibility:

(1) The private person or entity with whom the adult parole authority contracts for the return of Ohio prisoners shall obtain, and maintain for the duration of the contract term, a policy of liability insurance with a minimum amount of thirty million dollars to cover all injuries, deaths, or loss to persons or property that arise from, or is related to, its return of prisoners.

(2) The private person or entity with whom the adult parole authority contracts for the return of Ohio prisoners shall indemnify and hold harmless the department of rehabilitation and correction and all state officers and employees for liabilities which arise in connection with the services performed under the contract and are in any way related to the services rendered in the performance of the contract.

(3) The private person or entity with whom the adult parole authority contracts for the return of Ohio prisoners shall provide a performance bond in the amount of ten percent of the total contract price. The purpose of the bond is to ensure proper performance by the contractor. The bond shall be payable to the treasurer, state of Ohio. The bond shall remain in effect for the duration of the awarded contract and any extensions thereto, and shall comply with any other applicable requirements of the Ohio department of administrative services.

(G) Standards for pre-employment practices:

(1) The private person or entity with whom the adult parole authority contracts for the return of Ohio prisoners shall require a pre-employment criminal records check, at the federal state and local levels, for employees who would actually engage in the return of prisoners, and shall not hire an individual with a record of a conviction for any felony, any sex offense, an offense of domestic violence, two or more misdemeanor drug offenses, or any other offense which disqualifies the prospective employee from carrying a firearm.

(2) The private person or entity with whom the adult parole authority contracts for the return of Ohio prisoners shall require a pre-employment drug screen for employees who would actually engage in the return of prisoners, and shall not hire an individual who tests positive for a controlled substance. The private person or entity with whom the adult parole authority contracts for the return of Ohio prisoners shall have a written policy for, and maintain a practice of random drug testing of employees in accordance with applicable state laws.

(H) Operational standards:

(1) The private person or entity with whom the adult parole authority contracts for the return of Ohio prisoners shall have twenty-four hour operational staff and equipment to constantly monitor activities in the field and have on-board, constant communication capability with vehicles in the field.

(2) The private person or entity with whom the adult parole authority contracts for the return of Ohio prisoners shall require that officers and employees that actually engage in the return of prisoners to be certified by an appropriate certification entity in cardio-pulmonary resuscitation (CPR) and first aid.

(I) Contract standards: any contract entered into under this rule shall incorporate the mandatory standards expressed in this rule and shall include the following provisions:

(1) Specific provisions that assign the responsibility for costs related to medical care of prisoners while they are being returned that is not covered by insurance of the private person or entity.

(2) Specific provisions that set forth the number of days, not exceeding ten, within which the private person or entity, after it receives the prisoner in the other state, must deliver the prisoner to the location in this state specified by the adult parole authority, subject to the exceptions adopted as described in paragraph (I)(3) of this rule.

(3) Specific provisions that set forth any exceptions to the specified number of days for delivery specified as described in paragraph (I)(2) of this rule.

(4) A requirement that the private person or entity immediately report all escapes of prisoners who are being returned to this state, and the apprehension of all prisoners who are being returned and who have escaped, to the adult parole authority and to the local law enforcement agency of this state or another state that has jurisdiction over the place at which the escape occurs;

(5) A schedule of fines that the adult parole authority shall impose upon the private person or entity if the private person or

entity fails to perform its contractual duties, and a requirement that, if the private person or entity fails to perform its contractual duties, the adult parole authority shall impose a fine on the private person or entity from the schedule of fines and, in addition, may exercise any other rights it has under the contract.

(6) Two agents per vehicle with an agent to prisoner ratio of no more that one to six.

(7) The presence of at least one female officer when transporting female prisoners.

(8) A requirement that prisoners are appropriately secured during transport, which includes leg restraints and double-locked hancuffs [*sic*].

(9) A requirement that the private person or entity notify local law enforcement officials within twenty-four hours in advance of any scheduled stops within their jurisdiction.

(10) A requirement that officers or agents engaged in the return of prisoners wear a uniform with an identifying insignia or badge identifying the officer or agent as a transport officer.

(11) A requirement that prisoners being transported wear uniforms that make them readily identifiable as prisoners.

(12) A requirement that, if commercial air transportation is used to transport prisoners, that the entity comply with all applicable FAA regulations concerning the transportation of prisoners.

(J) If the private person or entity that enters into the contract fails to perform its contractual duties, the adult parole authority shall impose upon the private person or entity a fine from the schedule described in paragraph (I)(5) of this rule. The money paid in satisfaction of the fine shall be paid into the state treasury, and the adult parole authority may exercise any other rights it has under the contract. If a fine is imposed under the contract entered into pursuant to this rule, the adult parole authority may reduce the payment owed to the private person or entity pursuant to any invoice in the amount of the fine.

(K) This rule does not apply to any out-of-state prisoner who is brought into this state to be housed pursuant to section 9.07 of the Revised Code in a correctional facility in this state that is managed and operated by a private contractor.

HISTORY: 2001–02 OMR 173 (E), eff. 7–13–01; 2000–2001 OMR 1580 (R), eff. 4–1–01; prior rule 942

RC 119.032 rule review date(s): 1–12–06

5120:1–1–36 Parole board records

(A) Documents of the adult parole authority, including the parole board, shall be subject to rule 5120–9–49 of the Administrative Code.

(B) In addition, and subject to the same limitations, the following documents of the adult parole authority, including the parole board, shall be deemed public records: determinations, orders, and minutes made by the adult parole authority including the parole board, resulting from any hearing required by law or division-level 5120:1 Rules of the Administrative Code.

(C) As used in this rule "parole board record" means any record that is provided to or considered by the parole board in making its decisions and any record prepared by the parole board in carrying out its responsibilities under the Revised Code.

(D) Notwithstanding paragraph (B) of this rule, the following non-public parole board records shall be made available to representatives of approved media organizations, government officials, victims of any offense of commitment or a subsequent parole violation, or a licensed attorney at law designated by the victim or the inmate under the conditions and according to the procedures set forth in this rule:

(1) Parole board decision sheets

(2) Parole board risk assessments

(3) Institutional summary reports

(4) Master file cover information

(5) Warrants and detainers

(6) Special conditions of parole

(7) Parole certificates

(8) Parole candidate information sheets

(E) Non–public parole board records shall also be made available to members of the public under the conditions and according to the procedures set forth in this rule, except that inmates who are serving a prison term in an institution operated by the department of rehabilitation and correction and parolees or persons under transitional control, post-release control or any form of authorized release under the supervision of the adult parole authority are ineligible to receive non-public parole board records of other inmates.

(F) Non–public parole records may be made available after a written request is received which specifically identifies the records being requested. The request shall be granted unless the disclosure of the records would foreseeably result in harm to any person, would present a security risk to any institution or other facility or would materially interfere with the achievement of a fair parole hearing.

(G) Prior to making any non-public parole board record, as specified in paragraph (D) of this rule, available for inspection, the department of rehabilitation and correction shall review the requested record for information which if released could present a security risk to any institution operated by the department or could jeopardize the safety of any department personnel. The department shall also review non-public parole board records for documents that identify the victim of a crime committed by the offender, or contain statements made by informants, statements made by prosecuting attorneys and judges concerning the offender, witness protection information, inmate separation information, juvenile criminal history and diagnostic and testing information of the offender.

(H) A request for the production of non-public parole records may be denied if a request for the same information from the same requester was granted within the preceding twelve month period.

(I) Any portion of a non-public parole board record that contains information outlined in paragraph (F) or (G) of this rule shall not be released.

(J) The department may require all persons, except those requesting the copies for official government business, to pay for the cost of copies of non-public parole board records in advance. All requests for copies of non-public parole board records shall be sent to the bureau of records management at the department's central office. After receiving the request in writing, an invoice for the cost shall be prepared by the bureau and sent to the person making the request. The cost for any request shall be five cents per page for copies, plus a charge for any postage. The bureau shall send the requested records after receiving a check or money order payable to treasurer, state of Ohio, for the amount stated on the invoice.

HISTORY: 2000–2001 OMR 1580 (A), eff. 4–1–01; 1997–98 OMR 1303 (A), eff. 11–17–97; prior rule 944

RC 119.032 rule review date(s): 1–12–06; 1–12–01

5120:1–1–37 Authority to carry firearms

(A) All personnel of the adult parole authority eligible by statute may carry firearms in the performance of their duties with the adult parole authority as authorized by this rule.

(B) No firearms may be carried by such personnel of the adult parole authority without prior approval in writing from the chief of the adult parole authority.

(C) Applications for permission to carry a firearm shall be made in writing to the chief of the adult parole authority on form 947–1. Such request shall include the make, model and serial number of the weapon and be approved by the regional administrator or designee.

(1) Employees carrying firearms shall use a revolver or semi-automatic pistol meeting the specifications determined by the chief of the adult parole authority.

(2) Employees authorized to carry firearms shall use the specified ammunition supplied by the agency.

(D) Permission to carry a firearm may be granted by the chief of the adult parole authority whenever he or she determines it is necessary for the personal safety of the employee making the request and in performance of the employee's duties.

(E) Employees shall carry their firearm concealed on their person while acting under authority of this rule.

(F) Permission to carry a firearm may be granted for specific or general condition.

(G) No firearm shall be authorized to be carried pursuant to this Rule until:

(1) Annual qualification of the applicant in the use of a firearm is certified by a department of rehabilitation and correction certified firearms instructor.

(2) The applicant has given a bond to the state in such amount as is required by law.

(3) An annual inspection of the firearm has been completed by a department of rehabilitation and correction certified firearms instructor.

(H) Permission to carry a firearm may be withdrawn in the discretion of the chief of the adult parole authority at any time.

(I) If a firearm is discharged during the performance of an employee's duties, an unusual incident report shall be written and submitted to the chief of the adult parole authority within one business day of the incident.

(J) Failure to comply with any of the requirements of this rule may result in disciplinary action up to and including dismissal.

HISTORY: 2000–2001 OMR 1182 (RRD); 1992–93 OMR 647 (A), eff. 11–15–92; 1981–82 OMR 369 (A), eff. 11–9–81; prior rule 947

RC 119.032 rule review date(s): 1–12–06; 1–12–01

5120:1–1–39 Use of force

(A) Parole and probation officers in the exercise of their legal duties as supervisors of a large number of releasees, some of whom have a history of aggressive violent behavior, may occasionally be confronted with situations which make it necessary to use force. This administrative regulation specifies the circumstances under which force may be used lawfully.

(B) As used in this administrative regulation:

(1) "Force" means any violence, compulsion, or constraint physically exerted by any means upon or against a person or thing.

(2) "Deadly force" means any force which carries a substantial risk that it will proximately result in the death of any person.

(3) "Physical harm to persons" means any injury, illness, or other physiological impairment regardless of its gravity or duration.

(4) "Serious physical harm to persons" means any of the following:

(a) Any mental illness or condition of such gravity as would normally require hospitalization or prolonged psychiatric treatment.

(b) Any physical harm which carries a substantial risk of death.

(c) Any physical harm which involves some permanent incapacity, whether partial or total, or which involves some temporary, substantial incapacity.

(d) Any physical harm which involves some permanent disfigurement or which involves some temporary, serious disfigurement.

(e) Any physical harm which involves acute pain of such duration as to result in substantial suffering, or which involves any degree or prolonged or intractable pain.

(5) "Risk" means a significant possibility, as contrasted with a remote possibility, that a certain result may occur or that certain circumstances may exist.

(6) "Substantial risk" means a strong possibility, as contrasted with a remote or significant possibility, that a certain result may occur or that certain circumstances may exist.

(C) There are five general situations in which an officer may legally use force against a releasee.

(1) Self defense from an assault by a releasee.

(2) Defense of third persons, such as other employees, releasees, or by-standers, from an assault by a releasee.

(3) Controlling or subduing a releasee who refuses to obey a parole rule or regulation.

(4) Prevention of a crime.

(5) Prevention of an escape.

(D) An officer is authorized to use force, other than deadly force, when and to the extent he reasonably believes that such force is necessary to enforce the lawful rules and regulations of the adult parole authority.

(E) Physical harm to persons shall not be used as punishment.

(F) An officer is authorized to use force, including deadly force, when and to the extent he reasonably believes that such force is necessary to do any of the following.

(1) Protect self from death or serious physical harm from the unlawful use of force by a releasee.

(2) Protect another against death or serious physical harm from the unlawful use of force by a releasee or another person when there is reasonable belief that the protected person would be justified in using such force, if able.

(3) To apprehend a releasee.

(G) Whenever possible, an oral warning shall be given prior to the use of deadly force or when the circumstances may produce physical harm or serious physical harm to a releasee.

(H) When force of any kind is exerted on a releasee, an unusual incident report shall be submitted within twenty four hours to the chief of the adult parole authority.

HISTORY: 2000–2001 OMR 1182 (RRD); 1977–78 OMR 3–3 (E), eff. 2–7–77

RC 119.032 rule review date(s): 1–12–06; 1–12–01

5120:1–1–40 Parole of a dying prisoner

(A) Whenever it comes to the attention of an attending physician that a prisoner may be in imminent danger of death because of a medical condition, that physician shall provide to the head of the institution a certificate indicating that the prisoner is in imminent danger of death and a separate statement generally describing the prisoner's medical condition including his opinion of the time which said prisoner is likely to survive.

(B) Upon receipt of the certificate and statement from the attending physician, the head of the institution shall cause the preparation of a background report concerning the prisoner to be completed.

(C) Upon receipt of the background report, the head of the institution shall determine whether to recommend release as if on parole. Whenever such decision is to recommend release as if on parole, he shall place the recommendation in a signed and dated written statement to the governor and immediately forward it to the director's office, together with the attending physician's certificate and statement and the background report.

(D) Upon receipt of the head of the institution's statement, the background report, and the attending physician's certificate and statement, the director's office shall immediately cause an investigation to be made into appropriate community placement for the prisoner and including any additional information which will assist the governor in deciding whether to grant release as if on parole. A written report of the results of such investigation shall be supplied to the director's office within ten business days.

(E) Upon receipt of the investigation report, the director's office will forward the assembled documents, always including the head of the institution's recommendation and attending physician's certificate, to the governor.

(F) If the governor authorizes release as if on parole and documents indicating such authorization are filed with the secretary of state and delivered to the head of the institution where the prisoner is confined, the inmate may be released as if on parole upon his written acceptance of the terms and conditions of such release.

(G) For the purpose of this rule, "head of the institution" means the managing officer or superintendent unless that person is absent from duty, in which event the term shall mean the deputy superintendent of treatment or custody as designated by the superintendent or managing officer.

(H) Processing of imminent danger of death releases shall receive high priority, and delivery of required documents shall be made in the most expeditious manner.

HISTORY: 2000–2001 OMR 1182 (RRD); 1978–79 OMR 4–105 (E), eff. 9–7–78

RC 119.032 rule review date(s): 1–12–06; 1–12–01

5120:1–1–41 Standards for imposing, modifying and reducing post-release control

(A) The parole board shall review offenders sentenced to a prison term for an offense committed on or after July 1, 1996, to determine post-release control sanction(s) to take effect upon the prisoner's release from imprisonment.

(B) The parole board shall order a period of post-release control of five years with one or more post-release control sanctions for offenders who were sentenced for felonies of the first degree or sex offenses. For offenders sentenced for felonies of the second degree and felonies of the third degree where the offender caused or threatened to cause physical harm to a person, the parole board shall order a period of post-release control of three years with one or more post-release control sanctions. The board shall order post-release control of up to three years, upon a prisoner who satisfactorily completes the entire period of imprisonment in an intensive program prison.

(C) Sanctions imposed by the parole board shall be commensurate with the overriding purposes of felony sentencing to protect the public and to punish the offender and may include the enforcement of financial sanctions imposed by the sentencing court. Sanctions may be imposed for rehabilitation, treatment, or incapacitation of the offender, or to accomplish any other purpose authorized by section 2929.11 of the Revised Code.

(D) The parole board may order post-release control sanctions for nonviolent felony three and all felony four and five (non–sex offenses) for no greater than three years. When imposing sanctions for post-release control, the parole board shall make its determinations based on available information pertaining to:

(1) The offender's criminal history, including previous periods of probation and parole, or other community supervision

(2) Juvenile court adjudications finding the offender to be a delinquent child.

(3) The offender's conduct while imprisoned.

(4) Any information provided by the office of victim services regarding post-release control sanctions;

(5) Available supervision resources, including but not limited to: available beds in community residential sanctions, available community non-residential treatment options, and officer caseloads;

(6) Judicially imposed prison terms for post-release control sanction violations;

(7) Court ordered restitution of at least five hundred dollars.

(E) The adult parole authority may modify post-release control sanction by imposing a more or less restrictive sanction as necessary during the period of post-release control.

(1) At any time during the period of post-release control applicable to the offender, the adult parole authority may review the offender's behavior under the post-release control sanction(s) that was imposed by the parole board.

(2) The adult parole authority may determine that a more or less restrictive sanction is appropriate and may impose a different sanction.

(3) If the adult parole authority determines that an offender has violated a post-release control sanction, the adult parole authority may impose a more restrictive sanction pursuant to rule 5120:1–1–42 of the Administrative Code or may report the violation to the parole board for a hearing pursuant to division (F)(3) of section 2967.28 of the Revised Code.

(4) The adult parole authority shall not increase the duration of the offender's post-release control, or impose a residential sanction that includes a prison term, unless the parole board determines, at a violation hearing, that the offender violated a post-release control sanction or condition of supervision.

(5) The offender shall be notified in writing of any modification of a sanction.

(6) The parole board shall not extend the period of post-release control beyond the statutory limit for any offender described in paragraph (B) of this rule.

(F) The post-release control term for felony one offenders and sex offenders (five years) shall not be reduced nor terminated by the parole board until completion of the full term. The post-release control term for all other offenders shall be subject to final release pursuant to section 2967.16 of the Revised Code.

(G) The adult parole authority may recommend that the parole board reduce the period of post-release control imposed by the court or by the parole board with the exception of those offenders described in paragraph (F) of this rule. When considering applications for reductions in the period of post-release control, the parole board may generally be guided by activities of the offender that tend to show that a reduction in the duration of post-release control is consistent with the purposes of felony sentencing.

(H) If the maximum cumulative prison term for violations of post-release control (one–half of the stated prison term originally imposed) has been reached for an offender placed on post-release control under paragraph (D) of this rule, the violation hearing officer of the parole board who determines that the offender should serve a prison term for the violation shall terminate the period of post-release control.

HISTORY: 2002–03 OMR 511 (A), eff. 11–1–02; 2000–2001 OMR 1182 (RRD); 1998–99 OMR 2638 (A), eff. 6–1–99; 1996–97 OMR 1265 (E), eff. 12–20–96

RC 119.032 rule review date(s): 1–12–06; 1–12–01

5120:1–1–42 Discharge from post release control

(A) When an offender under a period of post-release control pursuant to section 2967.28 of the Revised Code has completed his period of post-release control, has the period of post-release control terminated by a court pursuant to section 2929.141 of the Revised Code, or has the period of post release control terminated by a parole board hearing officer pursuant to section 5120:1–1–41(H) of the Administrative Code, the adult parole authority shall classify the termination of post-release control as favorable or unfavorable depending on the offender's conduct and compliance with the conditions of supervision and in accordance with this rule. This designation shall be considered as a relevant factor in sentencing pursuant to section 2929.12 of the Revised Code if the offender is convicted of a felony offense subsequent to the completion or termination of the period of post-release control.

(B) An offender's discharge from post-release control shall be presumed to be favorable, unless the adult parole authority finds that an unfavorable designation is warranted under this rule. A favorable designation shall be placed on the final release certificate if the requirements for an unfavorable designation under this rule are not met.

(C) The adult parole authority shall designate a discharge from post release control as unfavorable if any of the following apply:

(1) The offender has served all available administrative prison or jail sanction time.

(2) The offender has failed to comply with sanctions progressively imposed in response to violation behavior.

(3) There are two or more misdemeanor convictions (other than minor misdemeanor traffic offenses) during the period of post release control.

(4) The offender has failed to make good faith efforts regarding payment of restitution or other financial sanction, exclusive of supervision fees imposed under section 5120:1–1–02 of the Administrative Code.

(5) The offender has an assaultive misdemeanor or DUI conviction within the six months prior to the completion of the period of post release control.

(6) The offender has a felony conviction within the eight months prior to the completion of the period of post release control.

(D) If the supervising officer and the unit supervisor agree that an unfavorable designation is warranted under this rule, the joint recommendation shall be forwarded to the adult parole authority field services case review analyst. If the field services case review analyst and the superintendent of field services (or designee) concur with the joint recommendation, the unfavorable designation shall be placed on the final release certificate issued to the offender.

(E) If the offender is convicted of a felony offense after his discharge from post release control, the designation by the adult parole authority that the discharge from post release control was unfavorable shall be considered as a relevant factor indicating that the offender is likely to commit future crimes pursuant to section 2929.12 of the Revised Code.

HISTORY: 2002–03 OMR 512 (E), eff. 11–1–02; 2000 2001 OMR 391 (R), eff. 10–1–00; 1996–97 OMR 173 (E), eff. 8–12–96

RC 119.032 rule review date(s): 1–12–06

5120:1–1–43 Violations of post-release control

(A) If the adult parole authority determines that an offender has violated a post-release control sanction, the adult parole authority may impose a more restrictive sanction or may report the violation to the parole board for a hearing pursuant to this rule.

(B) The parole board and the parole officer have significant discretion to impose more restrictive sanctions on releasees who violate post-release control sanctions to protect the public and to promote the successful reintegration of releasees into the community. This rule does not limit any discretion to impose special conditions that exists under rule 5120:1–1–12 of the Administrative Code.

(C) Whenever a releasee under the supervision of the adult parole authority commits a violation of a post-release control sanction, the authority will take appropriate steps in response to the violation behavior. These steps may range from warning the releasee to refrain from future violation behavior to the imposition of a prison term sanction. Parole officers, supervisors and hearing officers have discretion to reasonably impose further violation sanctions in response to violation behavior. The division of parole and community services may adopt specific procedures to carry out the purpose of this rule.

(D) Violation of any of the post-release control sanctions in paragraph (G) of rule 5120:1–1–41 of the Administrative Code may result in imposition of any other sanction(s) listed in the rule.

(E) When considering the imposition of further sanctions the parole officer or the parole board shall consider the degree of seriousness of the violation along with the factors in paragraph (D) of rule 5120:1–1–41 of the Administrative Code which were considered when the violated sanction was originally imposed. Violations of the sanctions of mandatory employment and monetary restitution may be classified as less serious sanction violations, depending on the availability of employment opportunities in the area where the offender is residing and the specific financial circumstances of the offender.

(F) The following sanctions may be imposed for violation of post-release control sanctions only by the parole board after a hearing pursuant to this rule:

(1) Increase in the duration of the period of post-release control;

(2) A prison term sanction not to exceed nine months. The maximum cumulative prison term sanction for all violations shall not exceed one-half of the original stated prison term.

(G) Imposition of a prison term sanction as a post-release control sanction shall be considered when the violation involves one or more of the following:

(1) A deadly weapon or dangerous ordnance;

(2) Physical harm or attempted serious physical harm to another person;

(3) Sexual misconduct;

(4) Repeated violations of post-release control sanctions.

(H) In general, the most restrictive sanction imposed for most first-time misdemeanor and technical violations of post-release control sanctions, will be a nonresidential community control sanction.

(I) If the adult parole authority reports the violation of post-release control to the parole board for a hearing pursuant to division (F)(3) of section 2967.28 of the Revised Code, then the hearing shall be conducted in accordance with specific procedures adopted by the division of parole and community services which include the following guidelines:

(1) The hearing shall be conducted by a parole board member or by a hearing officer of the parole board.

(2) With respect to the hearing, the offender has the following rights:

(a) The right to receive prior to the hearing a written notice setting forth the date, time and location of the hearing and the specific violations the releasee is alleged to have committed.

(b) The right to be heard in person and present relevant witnesses and documentary evidence.

(c) The right to confront and cross-examine adverse witnesses unless the hearing officer specifically finds good cause for not allowing confrontation. In the event that confrontation is disallowed, specific reasons for the same shall be documented in the record of proceedings.

(d) The right to disclosure of evidence presented against the releasee.

(e) The right to request representation by counsel. If the releasee cannot afford to retain counsel, assistance, upon request, will be provided by the office of the state public defender.

(f) The right to a written digest of the proceedings by the hearing officer if requested.

(J) If after a hearing the parole board imposes a prison term sanction for violation of a post-release control sanction, the offender shall be transported to the designated reception center as determined by the department of rehabilitation and correction.

HISTORY: 2000–2001 OMR 1580 (A), eff. 4–1–01; 1997–98 OMR 3053 (A), eff. 6–1–98; 1996–97 OMR 1267 (E), eff. 12–20–96

RC 119.032 rule review date(s): 1–12–06; 1–12–01

5120:1-1-70 Termination of the parole board's control over sexually violent predators

(A) For purposes of this rule, "offender" means a sexually violent predator who is sentenced to a prison term pursuant to section 2971.03 of the Revised Code.

(B) If a court imposes an indefinite prison term consisting of a minimum term fixed by the court from among the range of terms available as a definite term for the offense, and a maximum term of life imprisonment, pursuant to section 2971.03(A)(3) of the Revised Code, the parole board shall determine whether to terminate its control over the offender's service of the prison term pursuant to this rule. The parole board may not terminate its control over an offender's service of a prison term under this rule until after the offender has served the minimum term imposed as part of the prison term and until the parole board has determined that the offender does not represent a substantial risk of physical harm to others.

(C) As part of any determination pursuant to this rule, the board shall not consider the adequacy of the punishment imposed by the sentencing court. The parole board shall limit its consideration to determining whether the offender represents a substantial risk of physical harm to others.

(D) Prior to any review by the parole board, the office of mental health services shall prepare, pursuant to section 5120.61 of the Revised Code, an update of the most recent risk assessment and report.

(E) The parole board chair shall appoint a three parole board member panel to review the offender's case after the offender has served the minimum term imposed by the court. The panel shall determine whether to recommend that the parole board conduct a hearing to consider terminating control over the offender's sentence. In making its determination, the panel shall consider the most recent risk assessment and report prepared by the office of mental health services as set forth in paragraph (D) of this rule.

(F) In addition to the report as set forth in paragraph (E) of this rule, the panel may consider the following:

(1) The transcript of the proceedings held pursuant to section 2971.02 of the Revised Code, at which the court or the jury determined the sexually violent predator specification.

(2) Any pre-sentence investigation or offender background investigation reports that were prepared following the offender's conviction of the offense relating to the sexually violent predator specification.

(3) Any other information the panel deems appropriate.

(G) If two members of the three member panel conducting the initial determination recommend that the case be heard by the full parole board, the board shall conduct a hearing. Otherwise, the action declining to terminate control will be made in the official minutes of the parole board, and the next determination will be scheduled in two years unless an earlier date is recommended by a majority of the panel. Notice of the decision shall be sent to the offender and victim, (if requested.)

(H) The hearing shall be conducted by at least a quorum of the parole board. The following parties will be notified in writing at least twenty-one days in advance of the date of the hearing and will be permitted to appear and give testimony or to submit written statements.

(1) The prosecuting attorney of the county in which the sexually violent predator specification was determined.

(2) The judge of the court of common pleas that imposed the sentence of incarceration upon the offender, or that judge's successor.

(3) The offender and offender's counsel. The offender may be present through videoconferencing means, as may be arranged by the department.

(4) The victim or victims of the offense, or their representative, if requested.

(I) At the hearing, the parole board shall consider the same information that was considered by the panel pursuant to paragraph (E) of this rule, in addition to any statements or evidence presented by the parties listed in paragraph (H) of this rule and may consider information pursuant to paragraph (F) of this rule.

(J) A decision to terminate its control over the prisoner's sentence shall require a majority vote of the parole board. If the parole board votes to terminate control, it shall immediately provide written notice of its termination of control to the department, the court, the prosecuting attorney, the offender and the victim or victims of the offense, if requested. The board shall also recommend to the court modifications to the requirement that the offender serve the entire prison term in a state correctional institution.

(K) If the majority of the board members does not vote to terminate control over the offender's service of the prison term, the offender will be reviewed again as described by this rule in two years from the date of the hearing. The board may set a review date earlier than two years by majority vote.

HISTORY: 2003–04 OMR 141 (A), eff. 7–17–03; 2000–2001 OMR 1182 (RRD); 1999–2000 OMR 1846 (E), eff. 6–1–00

RC 119.032 rule review date(s): 1–12–06; 1–12–01

CHAPTER 5120:1–3

LICENSED FACILITIES FOR HOUSING

Promulgated pursuant to RC Ch 119

Section

5120:1–3–01 Contracting and payment disbursement for offenders placed in halfway houses

(A) General policy

The department of rehabilitation and correction ("department"), through the division of parole and community services ("division"), may enter into the contracts for the housing of specific classes of eligible offenders through licensed public and private facilities (hereinafter "licensed facility" or "facilities").

(1) Such licensed facilities shall comply with all relevant standards of the federal, state and local building, fire, health and safety authorities.

(2) Any licensed facility contracting with the division of parole and community services shall be required to maintain accurate financial records in a manner consistent with accepted accounting principles and procedures, which shall be available upon reasonable notice for inspection and audit by representatives of the division. Such records shall disclose the amounts of all income received by the licensed facility and the sources thereof, and the amounts and purposes of all expenditures of the licensed facility. Additionally, each licensed facility contracting with the division of parole and community services shall provide the division with copies of a complete annual audit report of its financial activities prepared by a reputable certified public accountant licensed by the state of Ohio and any other financial data as requested by the division. All licensed facilities contracting with the division of parole and community services shall comply with the laws of the state of Ohio, including, without limitation, sections 109.23 to 109.33 of the Revised Code.

(B) Purpose and applicability

(1) This rule sets forth standards for determining the allowable costs of licensed facilities contracting with the division of parole and community services. The standards are for the purpose of cost determination and are not intended to identify the circumstances or indicate the extent of state participation in the financing of any one program. No provision for profit or other increment above the cost is intended.

(C) Basic guidelines: To be allowable under an agency program, cost must meet the following general criteria:

(1) Be necessary and reasonable for proper and efficient administration of the agency program and be allowable thereto under these rules.

(2) Be authorized or not prohibited under state or local laws or regulations.

(3) Conform to any limitations or exclusions set forth in these rules, federal or state laws, or other governing limitations as to types or amounts of cost items.

(4) Be accorded consistent treatment through application of generally accepted accounting principles appropriate to the circumstances.

(D) Eligible offenders

(1) Eligible offenders include all classes of felony offenders actively supervised by the adult parole authority or by county common pleas probation departments or other offenders required by a court to seek treatment in lieu of conviction, and actively supervised by common pleas court probation department.

(2) Eligible offenders do not include federal offenders or offenders not supervised by the adult parole authority or county probation staff, municipal offenders, or offenders supervised or released by the Ohio department of youth services.

(E) Allowable costs

(1) Accounting. The cost of establishing and maintaining accounting and other information systems required for the management of agency programs is allowable.

(2) Advertising. Advertising media include newspapers, magazines, radio and television programs, direct mail, trade papers and the like. The advertising costs allowable are those which are solely for:

(a) Recruitment of personnel required for the agency program.

(b) Solicitation of bids for the procurement of goods and services required.

(c) Other purposes specifically provided for in the agency contract.

(d) Cost of solicitation mailing for the purpose of raising funds.

(3) Audit service. The cost of audits necessary for the administration and management of functions related to agency programs is allowable.

(4) Bonding. Costs of premiums on bonds covering employees who handle agency funds are allowable.

(5) Communications. Costs incurred for telephone calls or services, telegraph and postage are allowable.

(6) Compensation for personal services.

(a) General. Compensation for personal services includes all remuneration, paid currently or accrued, for services rendered during the period of performance under the agency contract.

(b) Payroll and distribution of time. Amounts charged to agency programs for personal services, regardless of whether treated as direct or indirect cost, will be based on payrolls documented and approved in accordance with generally accepted practice of the state or local agency.

(7) Depreciation

(a) Agencies may be compensated for the use of buildings, capital improvements and equipment through deprecations [*sic*]. The computation of depreciation be based on acquisition cost. Where actual cost records have not been maintained, a reasonable estimate of the original acquisition cost may be used in the computation. In addition, the computation will also exclude the cost of land. Depreciation on idle facilities is not allowable.

(b) Adequate property records must be maintained and any generally accepted method of computing depreciation may be used. However, the method of computing depreciation must be consistently applied for any specific asset or class of assets.

(c) No depreciation may be allowed on any assets that would be considered as fully depreciated.

(8) Employee fringe benefits. Cost identified under paragraphs (E)(8)(a) and (E)(8)(b) of this rule are allowable to the extent that total compensation for employees is reasonable as stated in paragraph (E)(6) of this rule.

(a) Employee benefits in the form of regular compensation paid to employees during periods of authorized absences from the job, such as for annual leave, sick leave, court leave, military leave and the like if they are provided pursuant to an approved leave system and the cost thereof is equitably allocated to all related activities.

(b) Employee benefits in the form of employer's contribution of expenses for social security, employee's life and health insurance plans, unemployment insurance coverage, worker's [*sic*] compensation insurance, pension plans, severance pay and the like, provided such benefits are granted under approved plans.

(9) Legal expenses. The cost of legal expenses required in the administration of agency programs is allowable.

(10) Maintenance and repair. Costs incurred for necessary maintenance, repair, or upkeep of property which neither add to the permanent value of the property nor appreciably prolong its intended life, but keep it in an efficient operating condition are allowable.

(11) Materials and supplies. The cost of materials and supplies necessary to carry out the agency program is allowable.

(12) Organizational memberships, subscriptions and professional activities.

(a) Memberships. The cost of memberships of the licensed facility in civic, business, technical and professional organizations is allowable provided that:

(i) The benefit from the membership is related to the agency program;

(ii) The expenditure is for agency membership:

(iii) The cost of the membership is reasonably related to the value of the services or benefits received; and

(iv) The expenditure is not for membership in an organization, which devotes a substantial part of its activities to influencing legislation.

(b) Reference material. The cost of books, subscriptions to civic, business, professional and technical periodicals is allowable when related to the agency program.

(c) Meetings and conferences. Costs are allowable when the primary purpose of the meeting is the dissemination of technical information relating to the agency program.

(13) Payroll preparation. The cost of preparing payrolls and maintaining necessary related wage records is allowable.

(14) Printing and reproductions. Costs for printing and reproduction services necessary for agency administration, including but not limited to forms, reports, manuals and informational literature are allowable.

(15) Taxes. Taxes which the agency is legally required to pay are allowable.

(16) Training and education. The cost of in-service training customarily provided for employee development which directly or indirectly benefit [*sic*] agency programs and offenders is allowable.

(17) Transportation. Costs incurred for freight, cartage, express, postage and other transportation costs relating either to goods purchased, delivered, or moved from one location to another is allowable.

(18) Travel. Travel costs are allowable for expenses or transportation, lodging, subsistence and related items incurred by employees who are in travel status on official business incident to the agency program.

(19) Accreditation cost. Accreditation cost is allowable in the year and for the amount vouchered. Accreditation costs are only allowable on a three-year basis.

(F) Costs allowable with approval of the Ohio department of rehabilitation and correction. Under this paragraph, "approval" means written approval received from the division of parole and community services prior to incurring any of the following costs:

(1) Building space and related facilities. The cost of space in privately or publicly owned buildings used for the benefit of the agency program is allowable subject to the conditions set forth below. The total cost of space, whether in a privately or publicly owned building, may not exceed the rental cost of comparable space and facilities in a privately owned building in the same locality.

(a) Rental cost. The rental cost of space in a privately owned building is allowable when specifically approved.

(b) Maintenance and operation. The costs of utilities, insurance, security, janitorial services, elevator service, upkeep of grounds, normal repairs and alteration and the like; are allowable to the extent they are not otherwise included in rental or other charges for space when specifically approved.

(c) Occupancy of space under rental purchase or a lease with option to purchase agreement. The cost of space procured under such arrangement is allowable when specifically approved.

(2) Insurance and indemnification.

(a) Contributions to a reserve for a self-insurance program approved by the department of rehabilitation and correction are allowable to the extent that the type of coverage, extent of coverage, and the rates and premiums would have been purchased [1] to cover the risks.

(b) Actual losses which could have been covered by permissible insurance (through an approved self-insurance program or otherwise) are unallowable. However, costs incurred because of losses not covered under nominal deductible insurance coverage provided in keeping with sound management practice, and minor by insurance, such as losses not covered spoilage [2], breakage, and disappearance of small hand tools which occur in the ordinary course of business are allowable.

(3) Professional services. Cost of professional services rendered by individuals or organizations not a part of the licensed facility is allowable provided such costs are reasonable. All such costs are subject to approval by the division of parole and community services.

(4) Interest. Reasonable interest on borrowing, however represented, is allowable when specifically approved.

(G) Unallowable costs.

(1) Bad debts. Any losses arising from uncollectable accounts and other claims and related costs, are unallowable.

(2) Contingencies. Contributions to a contingency reserve or any similar provision for unforeseen events are unallowable.

(3) Contributions and donations are unallowable.

(4) Entertainment. Costs of amusements, social activities, and incidental costs relating thereto, such as for meals, beverages, lodging, rental transportation, and gratuities, are unallowable when they are directly for the benefit of employees of the agency.

(5) Fines and penalties. Costs resulting from violations of federal, state, or local laws or regulations, are unallowable.

(6) Expansion and development. Reserves for future expansion and development are unallowable.

(7) Rearrangement and alteration. Costs incurred for rearrangement and alteration of facilities that materially increase the value or useful life of the facilities are unallowable.

(8) Acquisition cost of all depreciable assets are unallowable.

(9) Costs for managing federal grants are unallowable.

(10) Mortgage payments which accrue to the principal are unallowable.

(11) All costs related to the administration and provision of services to other than eligible offenders are unallowable.

(12) If a licensed facility receives subsidy funds under section 5149.30 to 5149.37 of the Revised Code, the costs related to those funds are unallowable.

(13) The licensed facility's cost for residential services shall be reduced by the amount of the subsidies received under sections 5149.30 to 5149.37 of the Revised Code if such subsidies are used to offset residential costs.

(14) Individual membership dues are unallowable as provided in section 9.65 of the Revised Code.

(15) Legal expenses arising from the initiation, prosecution or appeal of any civil action filed against the state of Ohio, the department or any of its employees are unallowable.

(H) Computation of per diem rate

(1) In determining the amount of an agency's total adjusted costs, (allowable expenses) paragraphs (E) to (G), must be followed. The total adjusted cost (TAC) is the sum of all allowable costs.

(2) When determining an agency's operating surplus, subtract the total revenue received during the past twelve months by the agency from the agency's total cost for the same time period.

(3) To compute one hundred per cent of an agency's average daily per capita cost with its facility at full occupancy, the procedure outlined below should be followed:

(a) Subtract the amount derived in paragraph (H)(2) (operating surplus) from the total adjusted cost paragraph (H)(1) to determine the agency's total includable costs ("TIC").

(b) Compute the contract per diem rate by using this formula:

$$\frac{\text{Total includable costs}}{\text{Total mandays}} = \text{Contract per diem rate}$$

(4) The licensed facility's average daily per capita cost at full occupancy shall not exceed the actual cost of the previous twelve months plus any inflation factor that may be deemed necessary by the division.

(I) Contracts

(1) The division of parole and community services may enter into written contracts with licensed facilities to provide services to eligible offenders. Such contracts shall provide for the method of payment by the department to the licensed facility.

(2) The execution of a written contract between the division of parole and community services and a licensed facility stating specifically the obligations of each party shall be a condition precedent to any obligation upon the department to make any payment to the licensed facility for any services rendered to an eligible offender by the licensed facility.

(3) As a condition precedent to the execution of any contract pursuant to paragraph (I)(1) of this rule the board of trustees or other governing body of each licensed facility shall submit to the division of parole and community services a document designating the person who is empowered to enter into contracts on behalf of such licensed facility, and by whose signature such board of trustees or other governing body agrees to be bound.

(J) Invoicing procedure

(1) Each licensed facility shall submit to the bureau of community sanctions in the division of parole and community services by the fifth working day of each month a separate report in such form as required by the bureau of community sanctions, for each class of eligible offender specifying for the preceding month the total mandays for each class of eligible offenders.

(2) The department, through the bureau of community sanctions in the division of parole and community services will disburse to each licensed facility, at the beginning of each quarter, one-fourth of the contract amount as determined in paragraphs (H)(1) to (H)(4) of this rule. The division of parole and community services may adjust the contract amount or terminate the contract with licensed facilities who fail to meet the mutually agreed upon terms of the contract, or fail to maintain average bed utilization as determined in the contract. In situations where the licensed facility permits a [*sic*] offender to be away from the licensed facility for an extended period of time (other than an overnight or weekend pass), there must be written approval from the adult parole authority supervising/liaison officer and notification to the coordinator of community residential programs for such extended absences. This written approval must be recorded in the offender's file at the licensed facility.

(3) The department, through the bureau of community sanctions, in the division of parole and community services will reimburse licensed facilities for contracted non-residential services in such a manner as required by the division of parole and community services.

(4) A licensed facility may hold a bed for an eligible offender who is in jail for a period not to exceed five days if the adult parole authority supervising/liaison officer notifies the licensed facility that the eligible offender, will return to the licensed facility.

(K) Verification of mandays

Regional supervisors (or designees) will keep a daily log of individuals in agencies. Licensed facility directors and regional supervisors (or designee) will be advised by the coordinator of community residential programs of allotments of moneys, quotas for eligible offenders, and current per diem rates for their use in determining referrals. This report will be due to the bureau of community sanctions the first of each month and will provide a check for the manday report to be presented by facilities on the same date for the same period of time covered.

(L) General requirements

(1) Within thirty days after an offender with inmate status residing in a licensed facility absconds supervision, the adult parole authority shall return any property which the offender left at the licensed facility to the offender's parent institution.

(2) The licensed facility shall require each offender to execute a document giving the employees of the licensed facility and the adult parole authority permission to dispose of the offenders [*sic*] property in the event of death, arrest or absconding supervision

or otherwise specifying what the licensed facility or the adult parole authority should do with the property in such event.

(3) No later than ten days after a furloughee has been declared a furlough violator the balance of the furloughee's furlough account shall be forwarded to the institution from which the inmate was furloughed. Within five working days after a furloughee has been declared a furlough violator, written notification, shall be given to the licensed facility.

(4) The chief of the adult parole authority may direct the disbursements from furlough account moneys in the form of spending or transportation allowances to be given to the furloughee.

(M) Expanded and new programs

(1) If a licensed facility wants to expand its operation, then paragraphs (H)(1) to (H)(4) of this rule are waived. However, the expanded program must be licensed by the department of rehabilitation and correction and the average daily per capita cost of the expanded program shall not exceed the amount for which the licensed facility is currently contracting.

(2) The one-year restriction on new programs may be waived by the department of rehabilitation and correction provided that the per capita cost of the new program does not exceed the statewide average per diem rate.

HISTORY: 2000–2001 OMR 1182 (RRD); 1999–2000 OMR 651 (A), eff. 11–10–99; 1995–96 OMR 2905 (A), eff. 7–1–96; 1990–91 OMR 1609 (A), eff. 7–1–91; 1985–86 OMR 831 (A), eff. 2–1–86; 1984–85 OMR 209 (A), eff. 9–4–84; 1981–82 OMR 771 (TF 5120:1–1–38), eff. 4–1–82; 1981–82 OMR 439 (TF 5120:1–1–38), eff. 1–1–82; 1980–81 OMR 389 (TT 5120:1–7–01), eff. 1–2–81; 1978–79 OMR 4–490 (E), eff. 4–3–79

RC 119.032 rule review date(s): 1–12–06; 1–12–01

1 Prior and current versions differ; although no amendment to this language was indicated in the 11–10–99 or the 1995–96 OMR 2905 version, "have been purchased" appeared as "have been allowed had insurance been purchased" in the 1990–91 OMR 1609 version.

2 Prior and current versions differ; although no amendment to this language was indicated in the 11–10–99 version, "minor by insurance, such as losses not covered spoilage" appeared as "minor losses not covered by insurance, such as spoilage" in the 1995–96 OMR 2905 version.

5120:1–3–02 Licensing requirements for a halfway house or community residential center as a licensed facility

(A) The division of parole and community services shall be charged with the inspection, supervision and licensing of halfway houses or community residential centers as licensed facilities.

(B) The division of parole and community services shall make annual on-site inspections of halfway houses or community residential centers under contract with the division. Such inspections shall be scheduled in advance with written notice to the person in charge of the halfway house or community residential center.

(C) Inspectors employed by the division of parole and community services shall have full access to all areas of a halfway house or community residential center during an inspection and to all records (including offender files), relating to the operation of the facility.

(D) The inspectors employed by the division of parole and community services shall ascertain compliance with the "Division Of Parole And Community Services—Halfway House Standards" contained in rules 5120:1–3–06 to 1–3–17 of the contract and Administrative Code.

(1) Within thirty days after an inspection the division of parole and community services shall prepare a written report of its inspection. The report shall include any findings of noncompliance and shall be sent to the person in charge of the halfway house or community residential center.

(2) In addition to the appeal rights granted under section 119.12 of the Revised Code, the division of parole and community services will allow licensed halfway house and community residential center managers to administratively appeal adverse decisions. The appeal procedure shall be as follows:

(a) Notification shall be given in writing to the licensed facility of the particulars of such failures or deficiencies:

(b) The licensed facility has the right of a fair hearing during the thirty-day period following notification at which time evidence can be submitted to rebut, clarify, or correct particulars outlined in such notification. The division of parole and community services will have final authority to institute termination of the contract or rescind prior notices following said hearing.

(c) The division of parole and community services shall require the licensed facility to correct these deficiencies within thirty days from notification or to submit an acceptable plan and timetable to remedy these areas.

(d) The division of parole and community services may terminate contracts for failure to comply with such notices at the end of this thirty-day period.

(E) For halfway house and community residential center to be licensed, they must comply with rules 5120:1–3–06 to 5120:1–3–17 of the Administrative code [*sic*].

HISTORY: 2000–2001 OMR 1182 (RRD); 1995–96 OMR 2908 (A), eff. 7–1–96; 1981–82 OMR 773 (E), eff. 4–1–82; 1981–82 OMR 442 (TF 5120:1–1–38), eff. 1–1–82

RC 119.032 rule review date(s): 1–12–06; 1–12–01

5120:1–3–03 Inspection process

(A) For facilities currently licensed, the center director shall be notified when the inspection will be conducted. Such notification shall be made thirty to sixty days prior to the license's expiration date.

(B) For new facilities, notification shall be made after a preliminary self-reporting form has been received and evaluated.

(C) Notification shall be by telephone and will be followed by a written notification. The notification will include the date, time and the names of the individuals comprising the inspection team.

(D) Once at the licensed facility, the inspection team shall meet with the center director to explain the criteria that will be used in the inspection, the reason(s) for the inspection and any other relevant matter.

(E) The division of parole and community services may conduct unannounced inspections anytime after formal licensing has been granted. Should the division of parole and community services conduct unannounced inspections, the notification requirement in paragraph (C) of this rule does not apply.

(F) The center director shall make himself/herself available in the event the inspection team has any questions or needs additional information.

(G) In order for a halfway house or community residential center to be eligible for licensure and state assistance, the facility must have been in operation for at least one year prior to making application for a license.

HISTORY: 2000–2001 OMR 1182 (RRD); 1995–96 OMR 2908 (A), eff. 7–1–96; 1981–82 OMR 774 (E), eff. 4–1–82; 1981–82 OMR 442 (TF 5120:1–1–38), eff. 1–1–82

RC 119.032 rule review date(s): 1–12–06; 1–12–01

5120:1–3–04 Evaluation of licensed halfway house or community residential centers

(A) The management of each licensed halfway house and community residential center shall provide the division of parole and community services with the goals, objectives and measurement criteria for their organization. This information will be for each new fiscal year and should be submitted no later than May first of the previous fiscal year for evaluation and review by the division of parole and community services.

(B) To determine if halfway house and community residential centers are achieving their goals and objectives, they shall submit statistical intake and termination forms for each offender that enters and leaves the licensed facility. These forms will be completed and mailed to the division of parole and community services as the offender enters and leaves the facility.

(C) The licensed facility may submit additional data that will indicate that its goals and objectives are being achieved.

(D) Resources permitting, the division of parole and community services shall provide technical assistance to halfway houses and community residential center management in establishing the facility's goals, objectives and measurement criteria.

(E) The management of each licensed facility shall be able to review the results of the information submitted by his/her organization.

HISTORY: 2001–02 OMR 2437 (RRD); 1995–96 OMR 2908 (A), eff. 7–1–96; 1981–82 OMR 774 (E), eff. 4–1–82; 1981–82 OMR 443 (TF 5120:1–1–38), eff. 1–1–82

RC 119.032 rule review date(s): 1–12–06, 3–22–02

5120:1–3–05 Glossary of terms

As used in rules 5120:1–3–01 to 5120:1–3–17 of the Administrative Code, the following terms have the following meaning:

(A) "Administrative release": a termination of jurisdiction over a particular sentence by the division of parole and community services for administrative convenience as provided for in section 2967.17 of the Revised Code.

(B) "Center director": is a person designated by the board of trustees or other governing body of the licensed facility as the principal executive officer of a community correctional center, or other licensed facility.

(C) "Agency program": those activities and operation of the licensed facility which are necessary to carry out the purpose of the licensed facility.

(D) "Appointing authority": the deputy director of the division of parole and community services.

(E) "Audit report": an agency's documentation of annual costs and revenues for the operation of the licensed facility.

(F) "Licensed": the formal acknowledgment by the division of parole and community services that a halfway house, community residential center or similar facility operates a licensed facility.

(G) "Licensing agency": the division of parole and community services vested with statutory and administrative authority to establish standards for halfway houses and determine whether an applicant halfway house meets these standards and thereby qualifies as a licensed facility.

(H) "Confidentiality of records": taking reasonable care to preclude unauthorized distribution of client and personnel information including the observance of federal privacy of information guidelines.

(I) "Costs": as determined on a cash, accrual, or other basis as meeting the test of generally accepted accounting principles by the division of parole and community services, the amount paid for the operation of the licensed facility.

(J) "Counseling": the interchange between client and worker leading to the formulation of plans for satisfying needs and resolving problems to enhance the behavior of the client.

(K) "Direct costs": expenses that can be identified as specifically benefiting a specific program.

(L) "Documentation": the formal, official records of transactions and events for the purpose of verification and public accountability.

(M) "Eligible release [1]": adult felony offenders actively supervised by the adult parole authority, common pleas court probation staff, or adult felony and other offenders required by a court to seek treatment in lieu of conviction and actively supervised by a common pleas court probation department.

(N) "Facility": the actual physical setting in which a program or agency functions.

(O) "Final release": the restoration of rights and privileges of an offender through:

(1) The termination of supervision and the remission by the adult parole authority of the balance of the sentence (except for offenders in the shock incarceration program) or

(2) The termination of supervision by the adult parole authority for those released under a period of post-release control, or

(3) The completion of an entire prison term by an offender who has not been placed under post-release control pursuant to section 2967.16 of the Revised Code.

(P) "Full occupancy": the number of residents allowed in a licensed facility as determined by the numberof [*sic*] beds officially designated for that facility.

(Q) "Governing authority": that entity within an agency which has responsibility and authority to set policies and establish procedures.

(R) "Indirect costs": expenses for a common or joint purpose benefiting more than one agency program, but not readily assignable to a specific program.

(S) "Inspection team": these are individuals employed by the division of parole and community services and/or other private or governmental entity personnel who have a contract agreement with the halfway house facility. The inspection team shall be comprised of bureau of community sanction staff and/or other individuals, as approved by the deputy administrator of halfway house programs. The halfway house deputy administrator shall designate the chairperson of the inspection team.

(T) "Institution": any penal institution operated directly by the department of rehabilitation and correction, or by a public or private agency in contract with the department of rehabilitation and correction, which is used for the custody, care or treatment of criminal offenders.

(U) "Manday": each twenty-four [2] period an eligible releasee is in licensed facility.

(V) "Offender": Any individual under the supervision of the adult parole authority and common pleas court.

(W) "Parolee": an offender who has served a term of incarceration as a felon and has been released to the community under parole supervision.

(X) "Parole violator": An offender under post-release control or parole supervision who has been declared to be in violation of any of the conditions of supervision, said determination having been made by the adult parole authority and so recorded in its official minutes.

(Y) "Placement": the residence plan of an eligible offender in the community.

(Z) "Probationer": a convicted offender whose sentence to an institution is suspended by the court and who is under supervision in the community.

(AA) "Probation violator:" a probationer whose probationary status has been revoked by the court of jurisdiction.

(BB) "Releasee": an offender released on post-release control, parole, shock parole, furlough, shock probation or a prisoner released to intermediate transitional detention pursuant to section 5120.031.1 of the Revised Code. No offender is considered a releasee until he has received papers from an institution, completed processing by institution personnel, and has physically departed from the institution or in the case of probationers, unless probation status is evidence [*sic*] by a journal entry stipulating the offense for which the defendant was convicted and the conditions of probation.

(CC) "Residents": eligible releasees in placement at a licensed facility.

(DD) "Licensed facility:" includes, but is not limited to, halfway houses, hospitals, community correction centers and similar facilities that have been licensed by the division of parole and community services to supervise eligible releasees.

(EE) "Supervising authority": the adult parole authority of the division of parole and community services, and probation departments of common pleas courts.

(FF) "Total includable costs (TIC)": the difference between a licensed facility's total adjusted cost and the amount of operating surplus.

(GG) "Total mandays": the number of beds at full occupancy of the licensed facility multiplied by three hundred sixty-five days.

(HH) "Unusual incident": any event having internal or external ramifications or news media interest of sufficient seriousness to warrant immediate attention. Such incidents include, but are not limited to fires, assaults, property loss or damage and events of apparently criminal nature.

(II) "Contract per diem rate (CPDR)": is the amount of money the division of parole and community services shall pay to the licensed facility for each day that an eligible releasee resides in the licensed facility.

(JJ) "Allocable cost": any direct or indirect costs which benefit the licensed facility in carrying out the agency program.

(KK) "Total adjusted cost (TAC)": the total adjusted cost is comprised of allowable direct cost of an agency program, plus its allocable portion of allowable indirect costs.

(LL) "Post–release control": A period of supervision by the adult parole authority upon release from prison that includes one or more post-release sanctions as described in sections 2929.16, 2929.17 or 2929.18 of the Revised Code.

(MM) "Post release control sanction": A sanction that is authorized under sections 2929.16 to 2929.18 of the Revised Code and that is imposed at the time of the offender's release from prison.

(NN) "Sponsor": an individual that will arrange and handle all matters of business, personal needs or other transactions, etc. during the electronic monitoring period, who shall be identified by the offender prior to being released onto electronic monitoring and approved by the licensed facIlity program director and the adult parole authority.

(OO) "Transfer to transitional control": the movement of a prisoner from a prison to transitional control, which involves closely monitored supervision and confinement in the community, such as a stay in a licensed facility or restriction to an approved residence on electronic monitoring, during the final one hundred eighty days of a prisoner's confinement, in accordance with section 2967.26 of the Revised Code.

(PP) "Transitional control releasee": an inmate released from prison during the final one hundred eighty days of the prisoners [*sic*] confinement to a licensed facility.

(QQ) "Transitional control violator": any inmate who has been declared to be in violation of any of the conditions of transitional control by the adult parole authority and so recorded in its official minutes.

(RR) "'A' offender": an offender who, by virtue of their background, characteristics and/or release status, represent [*sic*] greater risk to the community or, because of their release status, requires greater control upon release.

(SS) "Absconder": an offender under adult parole authority supervision who fails to remain within the limits of confinement or who fails to return to a facility as directed. An absconder is considered to be whereabouts unknown. Any offender who absconds on or after October 4, 1996, can be indicted for the offense of escape.

(TT) "Adult parole authority (APA)" that section of the division of parole and community services that includes probation development, the parole board, parole supervision and interstate compact of probation and parole.

(UU) "Alternative residential facility": any facility other than an offender's home or residence at which an offender is assigned to live and that provides programs through which the offender may seek or maintain employment or may receive education, training, treatment, or habilitation. This does not include community-based correctional facilities, jails, halfway houses or prison.

(VV) "APA officer": a person employed as a parole officer of the adult parole authority who supervises offenders and/or conducts investigations.

(WW) "Bureau of community sanctions": that bureau in the division of parole and community services that includes oversight and funding of community-based correctional facilities, community corrections act programs and halfway house programs.

(XX) "Division of parole and community services (DPCS)": that division of the department of rehabilitation and correction that includes the adult parole authority, the bureau of community sanctions and the bureau of adult detention and the office of victim services.

(YY) "Electronic monitoring system": a system by which the location of an eligible offender can be verified telephonically through the use of voice-activated voice repsonse [*sic*] technology that is in accordance with section 2929.23 of the Revised Code.

(ZZ) "Electronic monitoring device": any device that can be operated by electrical or battery power that is in accordance with section 2929.23(A) of the Revised Code.

(AAA) "Mental health professional": those persons who by virtue of their training and experience are qualified to provide mental health care within the provisions of state's licensure laws, policies and guidelines. Mental health professionals include psychiatrists, psychologists, psychology assistants, psychiatric registered nurses, social workers and activity therapists, civil service and contractors.

(BBB) "Mentally ill offender": an offender who may range from the serious mentally ill who has a substantial disorder of thought or mood which significantly impairs judgment, behavior, capacity to recognize reality or cope with the ordinary demands of life and is manifested by substantial pain or disability, to the offender who is not seriously mentally disabled but who does experience emotional and/or behavioral problems in social, vocational and family settings. These emotional and/or behavioral problems may be serious and appear as dsm [*sic*] IV axis II diagnoses such as, but not limited to, avoidant personality disorder, borderline personality disorder, dependent personality disorder and obsessive-compulsive personality disorder.

(CCC) "Halfway house": any private non-profit agency licensed to operate a residential facility that has a current contract with the department of rehabilitation and correction.

(DDD) "Parole": the release from confinement in any state penal or reformatory institution by the adult parole authority that is created by section 5149.02 of the revised code [*sic*] and under any terms and for any period of time that is prescribed by the authority in its published rules and official minutes. A parolee so released shall be supervised by the authority. Legal custody of a parolee shall remain in the department of rehabilitation and correction until a final release is granted by the authority pursuant to section 2967.16 of the Revised Code. The above applies to all persons who have committed felonies and been sent to prison prior to July 1, 1996.

(EEE) "Parole board special condition violation": failure to successfully complete one or more of the special conditions imposed by the parole board prior to release or during the period of supervision.

(FFF) "Parole officer": a person employed as a parole officer of the adult parole authority who supervises offenders and/or conducts investigations.

(GGG) "Placement coordinator": the APA staff member assigned to coordinate offender's release plans between institutions and field supervision units.

(HHH) "Prisoner": an offender who is in actual confinement in an Ohio penal institution as defined in section 2967.01(H) of the Revised Code.

(III) "Probation"/"community control": a period of supervision for a convicted offender (felony or misdemeanor) in lieu of prison/jail term for a specified length of time. The execution of sentence is suspended and the defendant is placed under the supervision of the court. The period of supervision can be up to a period of five years. Once placed on probation, the offender is expected to abide by the conditions the court imposed. The probation services can be done by either the common pleas court probation department or by the adult parole authority, probation development section. The term probation applies to all persons placed on probation for felonies or misdemeanors committed prior to July 1, 1996 and all misdemeanors thereafter.

(JJJ) "Provider": the vendor or agency who is responsible to perform the contractual obligations after being awarded a contract.

(KKK) "Residential placement coordinator": the APA staff member assigned to place offenders under APA supervision into licensed facilities.

(LLL) "Residential placement specialist": apa [*sic*] central office staff assigned to place offenders into contracted licensed residential facilities.

(MMM) "Residential treatment facility": any facility in which the offender is housed and where treatment maybe [*sic*] provided including halfway houses, hospitals, etc.

(NNN) "Sanction": for the purposes of criminal sentencing pursuant to Chapter 2929. of the Revised Code: any penalty imposed upon an offender who is convicted of or pleads guilty to an offense as punishment for the offense. Sanction includes any sanction imposed pursuant to any provision of sections 2929.14 to 2929.18 of the Revised Code.

(OOO) "Sanction provider": the public or private person or entity that operates or administers the sanction or the program or activity that comprises the sanction.

(PPP) "Serious mental illness": a substantial disorder of thought or mood which significantly impairs judgment, behavior, capacity to recognize reality or cope with the ordinary demands of life within the prison environment and is manifested by substantial pain or disability. Serious mental illness requires a mental health diagnosis, prognosis, and treatment, as appropriate, by mental health staff.

(QQQ) "Sex offender": an offender under active supervision by the apa [*sic*] who meets identification criteria as defined in policy 501.04, section V–A. and who has been classified as such per that policy.

(RRR) "Intermediate transitional detention (ITD) offender": an inmate who has satisfactorily completed the ninety-day imprisonment phase of the shock incaraceration program.

(SSS) "Special conditions of supervision": special and specific conditions for individual cases that are related to the previous offense pattern and the probability of further serious law violations by the individual offender. Special conditions may be imposed by the court, by the parole board or by the parole supervision section of the adult parole authority pursuant to policy.

(TTT) "Special needs offender": substance abusers, sex offenders, emotionally disturbed, mentally ill, mentally challenged, aged, and physically challenged.

(UUU) "Strip–search": inspection of the body surfaces of a person who has been required to remove their clothing for purposes of the search; includes visual inspection of mouth, ears, nasal cavity, viewing the entrance to the vaginal and rectal cavities, and search of clothing and any other item worn by the person.

(VVV) "Search—pat-down": a search involving manual and visual inspection of body surfaces, mouth, ears, nostrils, hair, clothing, wigs, briefcases, purses, prostheses and similar items.

(WWW) "Substance (drugs)": to include but not limited to alcohol, opiates, cannabinoids, benzodiazepines, PCP, LSD, cocaine, barbiturates, amphetamine/methamphetamine, inhalants and other drugs of abuse.

(XXX) "Supervising officer": a person employed as a parole officer of the APA who supervises offenders.

HISTORY: 2001–02 OMR 2437 (RRD); 1999 2000 OMR 654 (A), eff. 11–10–99; 1996–97 OMR 1267 (A), eff. 12–20–96; 1990–91 OMR 1611 (A), eff. 7–1–91; 1981–82 OMR 774 (TF 5120:1–1–38), eff. 4–1–82; 1981–82 OMR 443 (TF 5120:1–1–38), eff. 1–1–82

RC 119.032 rule review date(s): 1–12–06; 3–22–02; 1–12–02

[1] So in original. Should this read "releasee"?
[2] So in original. Should this read "twenty four hour"?

5120:1–3–06 Administration

(A) The public or private entity operating a licensed agency shall be a legal entity or a part of a legal entity according to the provisions of Chapter 1702. of the Revised Code. The agency shall have a copy of the following items:

(1) Articles of incorporation or constitution;

(2) By–laws;

(3) Federal tax identification number;

(4) Federal tax exemption number, and;

(5) A current list of the board of directors, their occupations and addresses.

(B) The licensed agency and its programs shall be managed by an executive officer or director who shall implement the policies and procedures established by the licensed agency's governing authority. The executive officer or director shall control, manage, operate, and have general charge of the agency and program and shall maintain custody of its property, files and records.

(C) The licensed agency shall have a policy and procedure/operations manual which is accessible to all employees and volunteers, is reviewed annually and updated when necessary by the agency's governing authority. The policy and procedures/operations manual shall include a description of the agency's purpose, program, services offered and approved methods of implementation. The policy and procedure/operations manual shall also include an organizational chart that groups similar functions, services and activities in administrative subunits. Employees shall participate in the formulation of policies, procedures and programs.

(D) The licensed agency shall implement a policy which ensures that there will be no political use or abuse of offenders and that conforms to governmental statutes and regulations relating to campaigning, lobbying, and political practices.

(E) The licensed agency shall clarify its relationship to all funding and regulatory agencies and document its relationship through written contracts or mutual letters of agreement.

(F) The licensed agency shall prepare an annual report of its activities to include both fiscal and programatic statistical information and activities. The agency shall make the annual report available to appropriate persons, the licensing agency, and upon request, to the public.

(G) The licensed agency administrator or designee shall conduct monthly meetings with supervisors and staff.

(H) The licensed agency shall establish measurable goals and objectives that are reviewed at least annually and updated as needed. There shall be an internal system for assessing achievement of goals and objectives and implementing changes in response to the assessment results.

(I) The licensed agency shall monitor its operations through an internal quality assurance inspection. At a minimum, a semi-annual review shall be conducted by administrative or designated staff. The inspection shall include a review of compliance with licensing standards.

(J) The licensed agency shall display, in each unit, the original licensing certificate awarded by the department of rehabilitation and correction.

HISTORY: 2001–02 OMR 3418 (A), eff. 7–1–02; 1992–93 OMR 1252 (A), eff. 4–17–93; 1981–82 OMR 775 (E), eff. 4–1–82; 1981–82 OMR 444 (TF 5120:1–1–38), eff. 1–1–82

RC 119.032 rule review date(s): 1–12–06; 3–22–02

5120:1–3–07 Fiscal management

(A) The licensed agency administrator or designee shall be responsible for fiscal policy management and control.

(B) The licensed agency shall implement fiscal policies and procedures adopted by the governing authority including, at minimum, the following:

(1) Internal controls;

(2) Petty cash;

(3) Bonding;

(4) Signature control on checks;

(5) Offender funds, and;

(6) Employee expense reimbursements.

(C) The licensed agency shall prepare an annual written budget of anticipated revenues and expenditures that is approved by the appropriate governing authority.

(D) The licensed agency administrator shall participate in budget reviews conducted by the governing board or parent agency.

(E) The licensed agency shall have a budget and accounting system that links program functions to the resources necessary for their support.

(F) All monies collected by the licensed agency shall be placed daily in an officially designated secure location.

(G) The licensed agency shall implement methods for the receipt, safeguarding, disbursing and recording of funds that comply with accepted accounting procedures.

(H) The licensed agency, at a minimum, shall prepare and distribute to its governing authority and appropriate agencies and individuals the following documents:

(1) Income and expenditure statements;

(2) Funding source financial reports, and;

(3) Independent audit reports.

(I) The licensed agency shall have an annual independent financial audit conducted.

(J) The licensed agency shall implement procedures for purchasing and requisitioning supplies and equipment and for property inventory and control.

(K) The licensed agency shall make available, where needed, funds for purchasing community services to supplement existing programs and services.

(L) The licensed agency shall implement procedures to regulate position control regarding position allocation, budget authorization, personnel records and payroll.

(M) The licensed agency shall have insurance coverage that includes, at minimum, property insurance and comprehensive general liability insurance. Such insurance shall be provided either through private companies or self-insurance.

(N) Any financial transactions permitted between offenders, offenders and staff, or offenders and volunteers must be approved by the agency administrator and comply with the agency code of ethics

(O) The licensed agency shall have provisions for emergency financial assistance and, when appropriate, a weekly allowance.

(P) Offenders may pay for program services rendered at a reasonable rate as determined by the authority having jurisdiction. The licensed agency shall make provisions for those who are unable to pay program costs.

(Q) The licensed agency shall implement procedures that specify how the amount of the fee to the offender will be determined, and when and how it will be collected and recorded. If the program is provided by a contractor, the contractor shall provide the contracting agency, at least monthly, with an accounting of fees received, including the amount paid and the payer.

(R) Collection and distribution of a transitional control offender's earnings shall be in accordance with rule 5120–12–05 of the Administrative Code.

HISTORY: 2001–02 OMR 3418 (R–E), eff. 7–1–02; 1995–96 OMR 2909 (A), eff. 7–1–96; 1992–93 OMR 1253 (A), eff. 4–17–93; 1981–82 OMR 776 (E), eff. 4–1–82; 1981–82 OMR 444 (TF 5120:1–1–38), eff. 1–1–82

RC 119.032 rule review date(s): 1–12–06

5120:1–3–08 Personnel

(A) The licensed agency shall have a personnel manual that complies with state and federal laws. The personnel manual shall be approved by the governing authority, accessible to employees, and address, at minimum, the following:

(1) Organizational chart;

(2) Recruitment, selection and promotion;

(3) Probationary periods;

(4) Staff orientation;

(5) Salary schedules;

(6) Hours of work;

(7) Non–descrimination policy;

(8) Code of ethics;

(9) Conflict of interest;

(10) Personnel records;

(11) Employee evaluation;

(12) Grievance and appeal procedure;

(13) Disciplinary procedures;

(14) Termination;

(15) Resignation;

(16) Benefits;

(17) Holidays;

(18) Leave (personal, vacation, sick, Family and Medical Leave Act, etc.);

(19) Travel, and;

(20) Employee assistance program.

(B) The licensed agency shall maintain accurate written job descriptions and job qualifications for all positions in the agency. Each job description shall include, at a minimum: job title, responsibilities of the position, required minimum experience and education. Receipt of job descriptions shall be documented by the signature of the employee holding the position and shall be maintained in the employee's personnel file.

(C) The licensed agency shall implement a policy which does not deliberately exclude employment of qualified ex-offenders. The licensed agency shall not hire an offender under active supervision without the consent of the supervising authority.

(D) The licensed agency shall implement policies and procedures that provide for the confidentiality of personnel records in accordance with applicable public record laws. A current and complete personnel record shall be maintained for each employee.

(E) The licensed agency shall not discriminate or exclude from employment women working in men's programs or men working in women's programs.

(F) The licensed agency administrator shall have at least a baccalaureate degree in one of the social or behavioral scinces or a related field, or professional experience that serves in lieu of educational experience.

(G) The licensed agency staff development and training program shall:

(1) Be planned, coordinated and supervised by a qualified employee;

(2) Be presented by persons who are qualified in the areas in which they conduct training;

(3) Be developed, evaluated, and updated based on an annual assessment that identifies current job-related training needs;

(4) Provide for ongoing written evaluation of all pre-service, in-service, and specialized training programs.

(5) Utilize community resources, and;

(6) Be reviewed annually

(H) All new full-time employees shall receive forty hours of orientation training before undertaking their assignments. The employees shall sign and date a statement indicating that he or she has received orientation. All part-time staff, volunteers and contract personnel shall receive formal orientation appropriate to their assignments and additional training as needed. Orientatio training shall include, at minimum, the following:

(1) A historical perspectiv of the agency;

(2) Agency goals and objectives;

(3) Agency rules and regulations;

(4) Job responsibilities;

(5) Personnel policies;

(6) Offender supervision, and;

(7) Report preparation.

(I) All administrative, managerial, professional staff and new offender careworkers shall receive forty hours of training in addition to orientation training during the first year of employment and forty hours of training every year thereafter. This training shall be appropriate to their assigned duties and responsibilities. All clerical/support employees shall receive sixteen hours of training, in addition to their orientation training, during the first year of employment and sixteen hours of training each year thereafter. At minimum, the careworker training shall cover the following areas:

(1) Security procedures;

(2) Supervision of offenders;

(3) Signs of suicide risk;

(4) Suicide precautions;

(5) Use of force regulations and restraint techniques;

(6) Report writing;

(7) Offender rules and regulations;

(8) Rights and responsibilities of offenders;

(9) Fire and emergency procedures;

(10) Safety procedures;

(11) Key control;

(12) Interpersonal relations;

(13) Social/cultural lifestyles of the offender population;

(14) Cultural diversity training;

(15) Communication skills;

(16) First aid/cardiopulmonary resuscitation (CPR);

(17) Counseling techniques;

(18) Crisis intervention;

(19) Sexual harassment, and;

(20) Legal issues.

(J) Employees shall be encouraged to continue their education and training. Continuing staff development shall be encouraged by providing administrative leave and/or reimbursement for attending approved educational programs, professional meetings, seminars, or similar work-related activities.

(K) The licensed agency shall implement procedures to ensure that all prospective employees and volunteers must obtain a local police criminal record check, and provide this information to the licensed agency prior to beginning employment. The retention of an employee or use of a volunteer shall be contingent upon a state-wide criminal record check being completed within ninety days of the date of hire. The agency administrator or designee shall review all recoird check results to determine compliance with agency hiring practices. All record checks shall be maintained in the employees personnel file.

(L) The licensed agency shall implement policies and procedures to guard against conflicts of interest. This policy shall be contained within a written code of ethics to be adopted by the licensed agency. The licensed agency shall notify its employees of the standards of employee conduct and document this notification. Disciplinary action imposed by the licensed agency for any violation or attempted violation of the standards of employee conduct shall be reported within two business days, telephonically and in writing, to the deputy administrator of community residential programs or designee. The deputy administrator of community residential programs or designee will consult with supervisors and a determination will be made, in cooperation with the licensed agency, whether the employee may continue to work with offenders. Any failure to report a violation or take appropriate disciplinary action against the employee according to the licensed agency's approved policy and procedure may subject the licensed agency to appropriate action, up to and including termination of the contract

(M) The licensed agency shall implement a policy regarding the use of volunteers that shall contain, at minimum:

(1) Written procedures for securing citizen involvemen in the agency, including roles as advisors, liaison between the agency and the public, direct service roles and cooperativ endeavors with the offenders;

(2) A system for selection, training, term of service and definition of tasks, responsibilities and authority;

(3) A commitment to recruit volunteers from all cultural backgrounds and socio-economic levels of the community;

(4) A provision for orientation and training before participation in assignments;

(5) A restriction for volunteers to perform professional services only when certified or licensed to do so;

(6) A requirement for an agency staff member to supervise volunteer services;

(7) A provision for liability claims in the form of insurance, signed waivers or other legal provision, valid in the jurisdiction in which the agency is located.

HISTORY: 2001–02 OMR 3419 (R–E), eff. 7–1–02; 1992–93 OMR 1253 (A), eff. 4–17–93; 1981–82 OMR 776 (E), eff. 4–1–82; 1981–82 OMR 444 (TF 5120:1–1–38), eff. 1–1–82

RC 119.032 rule review date(s): 1–12–06; 3–22–02

5120:1–3–09 Facility

(A) The licensed agency shall meet the legal requirements of the governmental jurisdiction in which the licensed agency is located. The documentation for this standard shall include copies of all annual local licensing and inspection certificates indicating conformance to all local fire, health, building and zoning regulations. It shall also include any other certification or licensing requirements not mentioned in this description.

(B) The licensed agency shall conduct weekly sanitation, safety, and fire inspections of interior and exterior areas. The licensed agency shall implement a housekeeping and maintenance plan and be clean and in good repair.

(C) A minimum of fifty square feet of floor space per offender shall be provided in the sleeping area of the facility.

(D) Each offender shall be provided, at a minimum, the following: bed, mattress, bed linen, pillow and closet or locker space. For sanitation purposes, provisions shall be made to provide clean bed linens or to allow offenders to wash their bed linens weekly. Sufficient blankets shall be provided during cold weather. Agency staff shall inspect sleeping quarters weekly to insure that minimum needs are met.

(E) The licensed agency staff shall conduct and record, at least bi-weekly, unannounced searches of the facility for contraband that endangers the safety and security of the offenders, staff and community. The licensed agency may utilize an outside law enforcement entity to assist with searches. A log of unannounced searches shall be kept documenting the date and time of such searches, along with the result of such searches. This log shall be made available to the licensing agency upon request.

(F) The licensed agency shall maintain a shift log noting routine and unusual activities and any instructions requiring the attention of oncoming shifts. Entries shall be recorded in the log and initialed by agency staff.

(G) The licensed agency shall make available space for private counseling, group meetings and visitation.

(H) The licensed agency shall have, at a minimum, one operable toilet with privacy wall or door for every ten offenders, one operable wash basin with temperature controlled hot and cold running water for every six offenders and one operable shower or bathing facility with temperature controlled hot and cold running water for every ten offenders.

(I) The licensed agency shall have one operable washer and one operable dryer for every sixteen offenders, or equivalent laundry capacity shall be available within one mile of the facility.

HISTORY: 2001–02 OMR 3420 (A), eff. 7–1–02; 1992–93 OMR 1254 (A), eff. 4–17–93; 1981–82 OMR 777 (E), eff. 4–1–82; 1981–82 OMR 445 (TF 5120:1–1–38), eff. 1–1–82

RC 119.032 rule review date(s): 1–12–06; 3–22–02

Historical and Statutory Notes

Note: The appendix to rule 5120:1–3–09, eff. 4–17–93, is referenced only. Appendices are generally available on WESTLAW and/or CD–ROM. Subscribers who wish to obtain a copy may request one from the publisher, the Legislative Service Commission, or the issuing agency.

5120:1–3–10 Intake

(A) The licensed agency shall implement policies and procedures governing intake. A copy of these procedures shall be distributed to all referring agencies and/or courts. The agency's intake policies shall include, at minimum, information to be gathered on all applicants before admission, criteria for acceptance/rejection and procedures to be followed when accepting or rejecting referrals.

(B) The licensed agency shall complete an initial intake information form on each individual admitted into the facility, which shall include, at a minimum:

(1) Name, institution and/or docket number;

(2) Address;

(3) Date of birth;

(4) Sex;

(5) Race or ethnic origin;

(6) Reason for referral;

(7) Whom to notify in case of emergency;

(8) Date information gathered;

(9) Signature of both offender and employee gathering information;

(10) Name of referring agency or committing authority;

(11) Special medical, dental and mental health needs reported by offender;

(12) Personal physician, if applicable;

(13) Legal status, including jurisdiction, length and conditions of sentence;

(14) Social security number;

(15) Weight and height;

(16) Other identifiable characteristics, (scars, marks, tattoos, etc.);

(17) Photograph of offender for identification;

(18) Official charge(s); and

(19) Marital status.

(20) Spouse's name, and:

(21) Next of kin.

(C) The licensed agency shall notify the referring authority within five business days of the referral when a prospective offender will be accepted into the program. Placement of offenders throughout the state shall be coordinated through the division of parole and community services, and/or the court. When an applicant is refused admittance to a particular agency, the referring authority shall be notified in writing within five business days from the referral date. The rejection notification shall state the reasons for the rejection.

(D) At the time of intake, agency staff shall discuss with each offender program goals, services available, rules governing conduct, program rules, and possible disciplinary sanctions for rule violations. This orientation shall be documented by employee and offender signatures.

(1) If a language barrier, literacy problem, or any other disability exists which can lead to the offender misunderstanding agency rules and regulations, assistance shall be provided to the offender either by staff or by another qualified individual under the supervision of a staff member.

(2) All program rules, regulations, and disciplinary procedures pertaining to offenders shall be either conspicuously posted in the facility or issued to offenders in printed form.

(E) The licensed agency that operates more than one residential unit shall have a centralized placement coordinator.

HISTORY: 2001–02 OMR 3421 (A), eff. 7–1–02; 1995–96 OMR 2909 (A), eff. 7–1–96; 1992–93 OMR 1254 (A), eff. 4–17–93; 1981–82 OMR 777 (E), eff. 4–1–82; 1981–82 OMR 445 (TF 5120:1–1–38), eff. 1–1–82

RC 119.032 rule review date(s): 1–12–06; 3–22–02

5120:1–3–11 Program

(A) The licensed agency shall objectively assess, identify and document the risks and needs of each offender, specifying the type of programming needed. The licensed agency shall then provide, or make referrals as appropriate for the following services:

(1) Assistance with housing upon program completion;

(2) Assistance with clothing;

(3) Food service (where applicable);

(4) Emergency financial assistance;

(5) Individual counseling;

(6) Assistance with transportation;

(7) Medical and dental services;

(8) Mental health service;

(9) Vocational evaluation, counseling and training;

(10) Employment counseling and placement;

(11) Education, counseling, and placement;

(12) Group counseling;

(13) Chemical dependency services; and

(14) Structured leisure time activities.

(B) The licensed facility shall have provisions for quality assurance practices to include, but not be limited to, systematic and periodic review of offender services and needs.

(C) Licensed agency staff shall us community resources, either through referrals for service or by contractural agreement, to provide offenders with the services to meet their program needs. The licensed agency shall maintain and periodically update a directory of functioning community agencies, or utilize a directory that is maintained and updated by another agency.

(D) The licensed agency shall implement a written policy ensuring uniform application of disciplinary procedures which shall include the following:

(1) Anyone who becomes violent or allegedly violates the law will be subject to arrest by the supervising authority and/or removal from the program.

(2) The following violations may be cause for removal from the program or will be subject to appropriate penalties as decided by agency staff and the supervising authority.

(a) Being under the influence of alcohol or drugs.

(b) Testing positive for alcohol or drugs.

(c) Possessing contraband (as defined by the licensed agency) or storing it in assigned living areas.

(d) Verbal threats or physical acts of violence directed toward offenders or staff.

(e) Absent without authorization.

(f) Malicious destruction of property.

(g) Persistent and repetitive rule violations.

(h) Failure to participate in the program as directed.

(3) All other violations will be subject to sanctions and/or consequences as established by the agency and documented in the offender's file.

(4) Criminal violations will be reported to the law enforcement authorities and the supervising authority as soon as they become known.

(5) Serious violation of agency rules will be reported within one business day of discovery to the supervising authority.

(6) Paragraph (C)of this rule shall be conspicuously posted in the facility.

(E) Licensed agency staff shall design and complete a personalized program plan for an offender within fourteen days of admission. The plans shall include:

(1) Measurable criteria of expected behavior and accomplishments;

(2) A time schedule for achieving specific goals;

(3) Scheduled progress reviews, and;

(4) Documented with staff and offender signatures.

(F) Offender progress in the program shall be measured through objective assessment at least every two weeks, either through staff meetings or by individual staff; the outcome of each review shall be documented. The supervising authority and/or court shall receive at least monthly progress reports.

(G) The licensed agency shall establish a staffing pattern which ensures that appropriate personnel are on duty during the times when most of the offenders are available to use facility resources. There shall be at least one trained staff person on facility premises twenty-four hours a day who is awake, alert and readily available and responsive to offender needs. This includes implementing all controls and completing all documentation required by the licensing agency.

(H) The licensed agency shall implement policies and procedures for offender grievances, which shall include provisions for:

(1) Offender notification of grievance process;

(2) Method of obtaining forms to file the grievance;

(3) Retention of all grievances and;

(4) Time guidelines for processing grievances.

(I) The licensed agency shall have provisions to conduct exit interviews, when possible, for offenders including those returning to the community, or to institutions. Exit interviews shall be recorded on the forms established by the agency.

(J) Recreation and liesure time activities shall be available to meet the needs of offenders.

(K) The licensed agency shall implement policies and procedures to account for the whereabouts of the offenders at all times. Offenders shall sign an itinerary sheet including the time leaving or entering the facility, their destination, address of destination, telephone number, offender's and staff's initials after the offender returns or leaves the facility and date.

(L) Transitional control offenders placed in the licensed agency, shall remain in the facility unless working at approved employment or participating in other activities approved by the department and the court.

(M) The licensed agency providing services for offenders shall:

(1) Provide structural and staff control for all facility entrances and exits, and;

(2) Comply with court stipulated conditions and the supervisin authority rules and guidelines.

(N) Licensed agencies that provide programs and services to intermediate transitional detention (ITD)/intensive program prison (IPP) offenders shall follow "ITD/IPP Program Guidelines" and implement policies and procedures which comply with rule 5120–11–0 to 5120–11–22 of the Administrative Code.

(O) The licensed agency shall provide offenders reasonable access to public transportation, or other means of transportation shall be made available for program related activities.

(P) All offenders shall have the opportunity to practice their religion.

HISTORY: 2001–02 OMR 3421 (A), eff. 7–1–02; 1995–96 OMR 2910 (A), eff. 7–1–96; 1992–93 OMR 1255 (A), eff. 4–17–93; 1988–89 OMR 1087 (A), eff. 5–1–89; 1984–85 OMR 211 (A), eff. 9–4–84; 1981–82 OMR 777 (E), eff. 4–1–82; 1981–82 OMR 445 (TF 5120:1–1–38), eff. 1–1–82

RC 119.032 rule review date(s): 1–12–06; 3–22–02

5120:1–3–12 Food service

(A) If the licensed agency prepares and serves food to offenders, dietary allowances shall be reviewed at least annually by a qualified nutritionist, dietician, or physician to ensure that they meet the nationally recommended allowances for basic nutrition for the types of offenders housed in the facility.

(B) Special diets shall be provided as prescribed by appropriate medical or dental personnel. Special diets shall be provided for offenders whose religious beliefs require the adherence to religious dietary laws.

(C) Food service staff shall comply with all sanitation and health codes enacted by the state or local authorities.

(D) Adequate space shall be provided for food preparation and service, and for an eating area and seating for all who dine at the same time.

(E) When the licensed facility has a kitchen, the kitchen, dining and food storage areas shall be properly ventilated, properly furnished and clean.

(F) Food service practices shall provide for the following:

(1) Weekly inspection of all food service areas, including dining and food preparation areas and equipment;

(2) Sanitary, temperature controlled storage facilities for all foods;

(3) Daily checks of refrigerator and water temperatures.

(G) Toilet and wash basin facilities shall be available to food service personnel and offenders in close proximity to the food preparation area.

HISTORY: 2001–02 OMR 3422 (R–E), eff. 7–1–02; 1999–2000 OMR 657 (A), eff. 11–10–99; 1992–93 OMR 1256 (R–E), eff. 4–17–93; 1981–82 OMR 778 (E), eff. 4–1–82; 1981–82 OMR 446 (TF 5120:1–1–38), eff. 1–1–82

RC 119.032 rule review date(s): 1–12–06; 3–22–02; 1–12–02

Historical and Statutory Notes

Note: Food Service Daily Checklist, eff. 11–10–99, is referenced only. Appendices are generally available on WESTLAW and/or CD–ROM. Subscribers who wish to obtain a copy may request one from the publisher, the Legislative Service Commission, or the issuing agency.

5120:1–3–13 Medical care and health services

(A) The licensed agency shall have adequate first aid equipment and supplies available in designated areas of the facility at all times for medical emergencies. All first aid equipment and supplies shall be inventoried monthly, replenished as needed, and shall meet Red Cross or other recognized health authority standards..

(B) One staff member on duty on each shift of the licensed agency shall be certified in cardio-pulmonary resuscitation (CPR) and first aid procedures.

(C) The licensed agency shall have letters of agreement with a licensed hospital, clinic or physician to provide routine medical and urgent care services to offenderson a twenty-four hour per day basis which shall be utilized as needed.

(D) The licensed agency shall have written medical emergency and medical back-up plans, that are communicated to all employees and offenders and posted throughout the facility.

(E) The licensed agency shall implement policies and procedures:

(1) To provide for medical examinations of any offender suspected of having a serious infectious or communicable disease.

(2) The licensed agency shall imlement universal precaution procedures.

The procedures shall be revised as updated information becomes available.

(F) The licensed agency shall, to the extent possible, ensure a drug-free program. If the agency operates a urine surveillance program, procedures shall be implemented that provide instructions for collection and processing of samples, interpretation of results, and responses to violations..

(G) The licensed agency shall implement a policy and procedure regarding the monitoring, possession, use and disposal of controlled substances, prescribed medications, over-the-counter drugs, and other medical supplies.

HISTORY: 2001–02 OMR 3423 (A), eff. 7–1–02; 1992–93 OMR 1256 (A), eff. 4–17–93; 1981–82 OMR 778 (E), eff. 4–1–82; 1981–82 OMR 446 (TF 5120:1–1–38), eff. 1–1–82

RC 119.032 rule review date(s): 1–12–06; 3–22–02

5120:1–3–14 Special procedures

(A) The licensed agency shall have written emergency plans that are reviewed and updated annually. Plans shall be communicated to all employees and offenders, and be conspicuously posted in the facility. Emergency plans are to be approved by the agency administrator and disseminated to all appropriate local authorities. All licensed agency employees shall be trained in the implementation of the written emergency plans.

(B) The licensed agency shall conduct and document quarterly disaster and monthly emergency fire drills, on each shift at least once every quarter, under varied conditions while the majority of offenders are present.

(C) The licensed agency shall implement a policy and procedure which prohibits any offender from being assigned to a position of authority over another offender (e.g. in charge of providing offender services such as commissary, telephone calls, or being permitted to perform or assist in any security duties), except that which is provided by treatment related activities approved by the agency director, (e.g., therapeutic communities).

(D) The licensed agency shall implement a policy restricting the use of physical force to instances of justifiable self-protection, protection of a third party, prevention of self-inflicted harm, and prevention of property damage or other crimes.

(E) Manual inspection of body cavities shall be conducted only when there is reason to do so and when authorized by the agency administrator or designee. Inspection of body cavities shall be conducted in private by health care personnel.

(F) The licensed agency shall implement the following procedures from the licensing agency regarding the detection and reporting of absconders.

(1) Absconders

(a) Prevention

(i) An offender movement sheet shall be used to account for offenders in the facility and those on authorized program and activity leave from the facility. This sheet shall include time "in" and "out" of the facility and, when applicable, the offender's destination. Movement outside the facility shall be documented through the use of an itinerary for all offenders.

(ii) Licensed agency staff on duty shall, at minimum, conduct one population count of offenders in the facility per shift, in accordance with agency policies and procedures. The time at which the count is taken should be varied and documented.

(iii) The licensed agency shall have provisions for random verification of offenders on authorized leave from the facility.

(iv) No offenders shall be unaccounted for while in or out of the licensed facility. The method for verification shall be outlined thoroughly in an agency policy and procedure statement.

(b) Detection

(i) Should any verification process indicate an offender's absence, the licensed agency staff on duty shall immediately attempt to locate the offender by searching the facility and calling known relatives, friends, employer, and the last destination signed on the itinerary sheet.

(ii) In the event contact is made with the offender within one hour of expected time of return, the offender shall be instructed to return to the licensed facility immediately. An agreed upon deadline shall be established for the offender's return,.

(iii) An offender who fails to return, or where indication exists that the offender will not return, will be declared an absconder.

(c) Reporting absconders

(i) Verbal notification to the supervising authority shall take place immediately upon the detection and verification of a declared absconder. If the offender absconds outside of the supervising authority's regular working hours, verbal notification shall take place at the start of the next business day.

(ii) The supervising officer/unit supervisor of a transitional control offender shall be contacted immediately after an unauthorized absence has been detected and verified, prior to an absconder declaration.

(iii) A written report indicating the time and circumstances shall be completed by licensed agency staff and submitted to the supervising authority within one business day of when the offender asconded.

(2) The licensed agency shall post the following informatio in a conspicuou location within the facility: "If you abscond from the facility, you may be charged with felony escape under the provisions of R.C. 2921.34."

(G) The licensed agency shall implement a policy regarding the documentation of granting overnight, weekend and special passes, as well as coordination with supervising authorities. The licensed agency shall submit a form to the supervising authority in cases where the offender is requesting a pass to an address that has not been previously approved by the supervising authority. This form shall be submitted, by the agency to the supervising authority, no later than noon on the day prior to the first day of the pass. The form shall include:

(1) Name and identification number (institution or docket) of the offender;

(2) The dates and times the pass begins and ends;

(3) The destination;

(4) The basis for the agency's recommendation;

(5) Signature of agency staff; and

(6) A space for approval or disapproval and signature, if required, of the supervising authority.

A copy of the pass shall be maintained in the offender's file.

(H) The licensed agency shall implement a policy and procedure for recording the identity of visitors. The visitor logs shall be under the supervision of a staff member at all times.

(1) The licensed agency shall maintain a dated log of all visitors to the facility with entries for the name, address, telephone number, purpose of visit, and time in/out of each visitor.

(2) The licensed agency shall maintain as a matter of record a dated visitation log for each offender receiving visitors. The log shall include the following information:

(a) Full name of offender to be visited;

(b) Institution/docket number;

(c) Supervision status and supervising officer;

(d) Visitor(s) name;

(e) Complete address;

(f) Picture ID number;

(g) Telephone number where they can be contacted, and;

(h) Relationship to the offender.

(3) Provisions shall be made for special visits, such as attorneys, clergy and visitors coming from a long distance.

(I) Possession and use of weapons is prohibited in the facility except in case of an emergency. The licensed agency shall provide weapon lock boxes for use by the supervising authorities.

(J) The licensed agency shall implement policies and procedures for submitting an unusual incident report to the licensing agency's deputy administrator of community residential programs or designee. Unusual incidents are defined as any events that have serious internal or external ramifications or that may attract the attention of the general public and/or news media. Such incidents include, but are not limited to: fires, assaults, drug trafficking, drug possession, serious medical problem, accidents/auto accidents, innappropriate sexual behavior, serious agency staff misconduct, theft, law enforcement involvement, suicidal attempts/threats, building emergency, complaint from the public, use of force/deadly force, property loss or damage and events of apparent criminal nature. The reporting procedure shall be as follows:

(1) The licensed agency shall verbally notify the supervisin authority and the deputy administrator or designee of the incident within one business day of the time the incident occurred.

(2) The licensed agency shall submit a written report to the supervising authority and deputy administrator or designee within two business days of the time the incident occurred. The written report shall include the following information:

(a) Name and institution/docket number of the offender involved in the incident;

(b) Name of licensed agency staff involved in the incident (if applicable);

(c) The name and address (institution/docket number if an offender) of the victim(s) involved;

(d) Time the incident occurred;

(e) Circumstances surrounding the incident;

(f) Copies of any medical report or a letter from the attending physician stating the extent of any injuries sustained as a result of the incident.

HISTORY: 2001–02 OMR 3423 (A), eff. 7–1–02; 1995–96 OMR 2911 (A), eff. 7–1–96; 1992–93 OMR 1256 (A), eff. 4–17–93; 1988–89 OMR 1088 (A), eff. 4–21–89; 1984–85 OMR 212 (A), eff. 9–4–84; 1981–82 OMR 779 (E), eff. 4–1–82; 1981–82 OMR 446 (TF 5120:1–1–38), eff. 1–1–82

RC 119.032 rule review date(s): 1–12–06; 3–22–02

5120:1–3–15 Data reporting

(A) The licensed agency shall:

(1) Correctly complete and enter all required intake/termination fields on the management information system authorized by the department of rehabilitation and correction

(2) Complete and enter intake and termination in management information system authorized by the department of rehabilitation and correction within fourteen days of intake or termination unless a written waiver is granted by the licensing agency.

(3) Submit to the licensing agency monthly management information system authorized by the department of rehabilitation and correction data, confirmed by the supervising authority, by the tenth day of the following month.

(4) Complete and enter a reassessment into a management information system authorized by the department of rehabilitation and correction if offenders remain in the licensed agency longer than the period designated by the agency for completion of the program.

(5) Designate staff for data entry and/or coordination.

HISTORY: 2001–02 OMR 3424 (R–E), eff. 7–1–02; 1992–93 OMR 1257 (R–E), eff. 4–17–93; 1981–82 OMR 779 (E), eff. 4–1–82; 1981–82 OMR 447 (TF 5120:1–1–38), eff. 1–1–82

RC 119.032 rule review date(s): 1–12–06

5120:1–3–17 Records

(A) The licensed agency shall maintain a written case record for each offender receiving services in which all decisions, activities and events shall be recorded. The case records shall include, at minimum, the following information:

(1) Initial intake assessment information;

(2) Individual program plans;

(3) Signed release of information forms;

(4) Evaluation and progress reports;

(5) Week–end and overnight passes;

(6) Current employment and education data;

(7) Verification of explanation of program rules and disciplinary policy to each offender, signed and dated by the offender and staff member;

(8) Grievance and disciplinary records;

(9) Itineraries;

(10) Discharge notice and narrative;

(11) Statistical termination reports;

(12) External progress reports;

(13) Audit sheet;

(14) Approved visitation list;

(15) Condition of release and applicable fee owed;

(16) Information from referral sources;

(17) Medical and psychological information and testing;

(18) Correspondence;

(19) Offender financial information;

(20) Referrals and attendance records;

(21) Offender acknowledgment of personal property/belonging disclosure; and

(22) Additional pertinent information.

(B) Each entry in the case record shall be dated and signed or initialed by the staff member making the entry.

(C) The licensed agency shall implement policies and procedures to safeguard and minimize the possibility of theft, loss or destruction of case records. All case records shall be marked confidential and kept in locked files.

(D) The licensed agency shall implement policies and procedures which provide for case record auditing by agency staff and, as requested, by the licensing agency to ensure that each case record is current, complete and accurate.

(E) The licensed agency shall implement policies and procedures regarding the confidentiality of offender case information which shall specifically discuss offender access, agency personnel access, outside agency access, and designate personnel responsible for the release of information.

(F) The licensed agency shall implement a policy requiring record retention for at least three years from the date of the offender's termination.

(G) The policies and procedures regardin confidentiality and disclosure shall comply with applicable state and federal laws, rules and regulations. The licensed agency shall require that a "release of information consent form" be signed by the offender prior to the release of information about the offender. A copy of the consent form shall be maintained in the offender's case record.

(H) The "Release of Information Consent Form" shall include:

(1) Name of person, agency or organization requesting information;

(2) Name of person, agency or organization releasing information;

(3) The specific information to be disclosed;

(4) The purpose or need for the information;

(5) Date consent form is signed;

(6) Signature of the offender;

(7) Signature of individual witnessing offender signature; and

(8) Date after which consent no longer is valid.

(I) A narrative report shall be prepared by the licensed agency and submitted to the supervising authority for all terminations.

This report shall describe the offender's performance in the program and be submitted to the supervisin authority no later than three business days after termination.

(J) The licensed agency shall provide the supervising authoroty with offender placement plans, at minimum, thirty days prior to successful termination. The placement plans shall include, at minimum, the following:

(1) Address where offender plans to reside upon program completion;

(2) Name of person offender plans to reside with;

(3) Telephone number;

(4) Current employment information, and;

(5) Expected termination date.

HISTORY: 2001–02 OMR 3425 (A), eff. 7–1–02; 1995–96 OMR 2913 (A), eff. 7–1–96; 1992–93 OMR 1258 (A), eff. 4–17–93; 1981–82 OMR 780 (E), eff. 4–1–82; 1981–82 OMR 447 (TF 5120:1–1–38), eff. 1–1–82

RC 119.032 rule review date(s): 1–12–06; 3–22–02

5120:1–3–18 Application process for program planner of halfway house construction projects

(A) This rule establishes the minimum eligibility requirements and procedures for a "halfway house organization" as defined in section 5120.102 of the Revised Code, to apply for program planning funds for a halfway house facility as defined in section 5120.102 of the Revised Code, constructed by the department of rehabilitation and correction, in accordance with sections 5120.102 to 5120.105 of the Revised Code.

(B) If such funds are available, the department will engage in the competitive selection process for program planning of halfway house facility construction projects by eligible halfway house organizations. Program planner applicants will be required to respond in accordance with instruction and timelines described in the competitive selection process.

(C) The division of parole and community services shall review and recommend approval of competitively selected applicants to the department director based on, but not limited to, the following selection criteria:

(1) The program planner applicant has a site and/or owns a building that is under consideration with the department as a result of the halfway house organization responding to the department's request for proposals to site and build a halfway house facility in accordance with rule 5120–5–12 of the Administrative Code;

(2) Applicant has experience planning, building, operating and managing a halfway house facility;

(3) Applicant has the ability to develop programs and implement services which respond to the department's location priorities and target population;

(4) Applicant has knowledge and or experience working with community leadership within the sites designated by the department.

(5) Number of personnel and amount of time that will be devoted to the project; and

(6) The ability to operate once construction is completed based on, but not limited to, the following criteria:

(a) Organization's financial stability;

(b) Experience operating a facility;

(c) Number of days required to activate the program upon completion of the construction; and

(d) The cost of operation within the contract period.

The division's recommendation shall be within the available capital funding.

(D) If the applicant is approved, the director, through the division of parole and community services, may enter into a program planning contract with a halfway house organization which will establish terms and procedures for the planning of a halfway house facility.

HISTORY: 2002–03 OMR 1726 (RRD); 1997 98 OMR 3054 (E), eff. 5–22–98; 1981–82 OMR 448 (TF 5120:1–1–38), eff. 1–1–82, exp. 3–31–82

RC 119.032 rule review date(s): 1–12–06; 1–12–03; 1–10–03

CHAPTER 5120:1–7

BUREAU OF ADULT DETENTION— DEFINITIONS; SCOPE OF AUTHORITY

Promulgated pursuant to RC 111.15

Section

5120:1–7–01 Bureau responsibility and authority

(A) Pursuant to section 5120.10 of the Revised Code, the division of parole and community services, bureau of adult detention (hereinafter referred to as "the bureau"), is charged with the investigation and supervision of county and municipal jails and workhouses.

(B) The bureau shall make on-site inspections of jails in the state of Ohio. Such inspections shall be scheduled in advance with written notice to the person in charge of the jail.

(C) Inspectors employed by the bureau shall have full access to all areas of a jail during an inspection and to all records relating to the operation of the facility. The facility's operational policies and procedures shall be consolidated into a manual and provided to the inspector upon request.

(D) The inspectors employed by the bureau shall ascertain compliance with the "Minimum Standards For Jails In Ohio," contained in rules 5120:1–8–01 to 5120:1–12–19 of the Administrative Code.

(E) The bureau may certify any jail which meets the minimum standards. The bureau may provisionally certify any jail upon completion of a compliance plan and the initiation of corrective action. The bureau may de-certify any jail upon re-inspection or determination of non-compliance. Any jail not certified or provisionally certified shall be considered "non-certified."

(F) The bureau may make such inspections and participate in such meetings as it deems necessary for the proper execution of the provisions of this rule. This rule shall not be construed as granting to the bureau the executive management responsibilities of local officials.

(G) Pursuant to section 5103.18 of the Revised Code, the department of rehabilitation and correction is required to approve, before adoption by the proper officials, plans for major renovation or new construction of jails, workhouses and municipal lockups.

HISTORY: 2003–04 OMR 142 (RRD); 1998–99 OMR 715 (A), eff. 9–21–98; 1985–86 OMR 1295 (A), eff. 6–2–86; 1982–83 OMR 845 (A), eff. 1–1–83; 1980–81 OMR 389 (TF 5120:1–3–01), eff. 1–2–81

RC 119.032 rule review date(s): 1–1–08; 7–29–03; 1–12–03

5120:1–7–02 Glossary of terms

(A) The term "Minimum Standards for Jails in Ohio" refers to rules 5120:1–8–01 to 5120:1–12–19 of the Administrative Code. The standards apply to county jails, municipal jails, regional jails and workhouses. Each such facility falls within one of the following categories and is subject to the standards identified within the definitions as applicable to those categories:

(1) "Full service jail": A local confinement facility used primarily to detain adults for more than one hundred twenty hours. The standards set forth in rules 5120:1–8–01 to 5120:1–8–19 of the Administrative Code apply to full service jails.

(2) "Five–day facility": A local confinement facility used primarily to detain adults for a maximum of one hundred twenty hours. The standards set forth in rules 5120:1–10–01 to 5120:1–10–19 of the Administrative Code apply to five-day facilities.

(3) "Twelve–hour facility": A local confinement facility used primarily to detain adults for a maximum of twelve hours. The standards set forth in rules 5120:1–12–01 through 5120:1–12–19 of the Administrative Code apply to twelve-hour facilities.

(4) "Minimum security jail": A local confinement facility used to detain sentenced adults for more than one hundred twenty hours for a misdemeanor or a felony of the fourth or fifth degree, provided the person has been classified as a minimum security risk by the jail administrator or designee. The classification must include, at minimum, the individual's propensity for assaultive or violent behavior and escape risk based upon the offender's prior and present behaviors. The standards set forth in rules 5120:1–8–01 to 5120:1–8–19 of the Administrative Code apply to minimum security jails.

(5) "Temporary holding facility": A local confinement facility used to detain arrestees for a maximum six hours for processing and/or awaiting transportation. The temporary holding facility (THF) may be a jail cell, but also may be an area which is designated for temporary holding purposes, e.g., holding area or room.

(B) As used in rules 5120:1–7–01 to 5120:1–7–04 and 5120:1–8–01 to 5120:1–12–19 of the Administrative Code, the following terms have the meanings indicated in this rule:

(1) "Administrators and supervisors": Persons who have managerial responsibility for a full service jail or who supervise employees security assignments or activities in the jail.

(2) "Administrative segregation": The act of confining a prisoner to an individual housing cell or designated housing unit, that physically separates the prisoner from the general population for specified reasons other than as a penalty, thereby prohibiting physical contact between this prisoner and the general population.

(3) "Attorney (of record)": A licensed lawyer (retained or court appointed) whose name appears in the case records or court docket of the case, or whom the prisoner has named as his or her attorney.

(4) "Authority having jurisdiction": The governmental authority having responsibility for certifying compliance with applicable statutes, regulations and codes.

(5) "Average daily population (ADP)": The number arrived at by totaling the number of meals served prisoners during a specified period of time, divided by three, and then dividing by the number of days during that specified period. This figure is also sometimes derived by dividing the total number of commitments recorded in the jail ledger or the sum of daily official prisoner counts by the total number of days in the specified period.

(6) "Certification": The process by which a jurisdiction is officially acknowledged as operating a detention facility that is in compliance with the "Minimum Standards for Jails in Ohio."

(7) "Classification": A system or process for determining the needs and requirements of prisoners and for assigning them to housing units and programs. Elements of this determination include the following: security level; work assignments; special treatment services; allowance or denial of certain privileges; and other assignments as may be available.

(8) "Clergy": A clergyperson or minister from a recognized religious community outside the jail who is the spiritual leader for a particular prisoner.

(9) "Contraband": Anything possessed by prisoners or within the confinement facility which is declared illegal by law or which is expressly prohibited by those legally charged with the responsibility for the administration and government of the jail.

(10) "Corporal punishment": The act of inflicting punishment directly on the body, such as beating, flogging, hitting, kicking, etc.

(11) "De–certification": the removal of certification status prior to the end of the five year certification period resulting from the jurisdiction's failure to maintain compliance.

(12) "Disciplinary isolation": The act of confining a prisoner to an individual housing cell that physically separates the prisoner from the general prisoner population as a penalty, thereby prohibiting physical contact between the prisoner and other prisoners.

(13) "Emergency operations plan": Written documents that address specific actions to be taken in an emergency or catastrophe such as fire, flood, riot or other major disruption.

(14) "Fire exit drill": A practice drill that includes transmission of a fire alarm signal and simulation of emergency fire conditions that is conducted to familiarize jail personnel with the signals and emergency action required under varied conditions. Release of prisoners to safe areas or the exterior of buildings is not required.

(15) "Foot–candle": A unit for measuring the level of illumination.

(16) "Fundamental rights": Rights which may not be suspended for disciplinary or classification reasons and which are to be guaranteed to all prisoners except in times of emergency or other such conditions beyond the control of the facility administrators. Such rights may include visits by attorneys or clergy, telephone calls to attorneys or clergy, adequate food/nutrition, adequate lighting, adequate ventilation, temperature control, sanitation, medical care and access to a grievance mechanism.

(17) "General population": Those prisoners who have not been able to secure release within a reasonable time period after their initial booking and who are therefore classified and housed in areas which are not designated for temporary holding or temporary special housing.

(18) "Grievance": A circumstance or action thought to be unjust or injurious and grounds for complaint to the appropriate facility administrator or designee.

(19) "Health–trained personnel": Members of the jail staff that are trained in limited aspects of health care, including correctional officers and other personnel approved by the jail physician.

(20) "Impartial hearing officer": A staff person who is not involved or witness in the incident in question and who is empowered to determine issues of fact in a prisoner disciplinary hearing.

(21) "Indigent prisoner": A prisoner confirmed to have insufficient resources necessary to provide for basic needs.

(22) "Jail support staff": Those persons whose job function does not reflect a primary responsibility for the security and/or supervision of prisoners.

(23) "Juvenile": Offenders under the age of eighteen.

(24) "Key control center": A secure location inaccessible to unauthorized persons from which facility keys are issued/returned.

(25) "Lavatory": A bowl or washbasin with faucets and drainage for washing face and hands.

(26) "Legal correspondence": mail addressed to an inmate clearly bearing the return address of an attorney at law, a public service law office, a law school legal clinic, court of law, or any office or official of the federal, state or local government and administrators or grievance systems and members of the adult parole authority.

(27) "Life safety code": A handbook published by the national fire protection association specifying minimum standards for fire safety in correctional facilities.

(28) "Major renovation": A significant structural or design change in the physical plant of a jail facility.

(29) "Official count": An actual counting and recording of prisoners confined in a facility by verifying the presence of each at a given time.

(30) "Permanent log": A record of all significant activities that take place during the course of a day.

(31) "Personal observation check": A visual check by jail staff who observes prisoners and their immediate surroundings without the use of mechanical or electronic, visual or audio monitoring equipment. This check is performed in such a manner that allows the observing staff to identify the health, safety and security status of the prisoners and permits immediate personal interaction or response to any situation.

(32) "Physical force": Any violence, compulsion or constraint physically exerted upon or against a person's body by any means including the use of firearms, chemical agents, clubs or direct bodily contact.

(33) "Policy": A statement that reflects the philosophy of the organization, and defines the purpose for which the action is taken.

(34) "Prisoner worker": The classification of prisoners who are given work assignments based upon a determination that they present a low security risk.

(35) "Privileges": Items or programs that may be temporarily suspended for disciplinary or classification reasons and which are generally provided to all prisoners. Privileges may include access to entertainment, commissary, visits by friends, telephone calls to friends or family, snacks, dayroom access and program access.

(36) "Procedure": Provides a detailed description of how a policy is to be accomplished detailing the steps to be taken, the order in which they will be carried out, and by whom.

(37) "Provisional certification": A temporary recognition of a jail for meeting an acceptable level of standards with minor exceptions. Specific conditions and/or stipulations shall be imposed during the period of time required to comply with the standards in question.

(38) "Qualified health care personnel": Physicians, dentists, nurses, physician assistants, psychiatrists, psychologists, psychiatric social workers, paramedics, emergency medical technicians, and others who by virtue of their education, credentials and experience are permitted by law to evaluate and care for the health needs of prisoners.

(39) "Qualified mental health personnel": Physicians, physician assistants, nurses, psychiatrists, psychologists, psychiatric social workers, and others who by virtue of their education, creden-

tials and experience are permitted by law to evaluate and care for the mental health needs of prisoners.

(40) "Qualified nutritionist or dietician": A person registered or eligible for registration by the American dietetic association, or has documented equivalency in education, training or experience.

(41) "Reception": The period during which a prisoner undergoes admission processing, which may include orientation and initial classification, prior to regular housing assignment.

(42) "Recreation/physical exercise": Activities such as athletics and calisthenics which require at least a moderate degree of physical exertion.

(43) "Restraining device": Any mechanical contrivance, appliance, or object designed or fashioned to physically control or incapacitate a person. These include wrist manacles, ankle manacles, restraining straps, chains, chairs and other such devices.

(44) "Safety equipment": Firefighting equipment, including chemical extinguishers; hoses, nozzles and water supplies; alarm systems; sprinkler systems; self–contained breathing apparatus: emergency exits and fire escapes; and other firefighting equipment as may be provided. Also included are stretchers; first–aid kits; emergency alarms; and other such provisions and equipment.

(45) "Search": An examination falling into one of the following three categories:

(a) "Frisk search": A thorough search or "pat down" of a prisoner's clothes and head cavities, while the prisoner is still clothed.

(b) "Strip search": An inspection of the genitalia, buttocks, breasts, or undergarments of a person that is preceded by the removal or rearrangement of some or all of the person's clothing that directly covers the person's genitalia, buttocks, breasts, or undergarments and that is conducted visually, manually, by means of any instrument, apparatus, or object, or in any other manner while the person is detained or confined.

(c) "Body cavity search": An inspection of the anal or vaginal cavity of a person that is conducted visually, manually, by means of any instrument, apparatus, or object, or in any other manner while the person is detained or confined.

(46) "Security control equipment/devices": Firearms, weapons, lethal and non-lethal munitions, use of force devices, chemical agents and restraints. Also included are electronic monitoring equipment, security alarm systems, security light units, auxiliary power supply, and other equipment used to maintain jail security.

(47) "Security perimeter": A secure boundary which encloses the entire portion of the facility in which prisoners are confined, including any area to which prisoners may have access. Passage through this boundary must be strictly controlled.

(48) "Security post": A location within the facility from which a staff person may perform jail duties.

(49) "Separation (segregation)": Whenever possible, to be physically set apart in order to prohibit bodily contact and, where possible, communication.

(50) "Sick call": A system through which each prisoner reports and receives individualized and appropriate medical services for non-emergency illness or injury.

(51) "Surveillance check": A monitoring check of prisoners, prisoner occupied areas, prisoner accessible areas and other jail areas by jail staff using electronic or mechanical, visual or audio monitoring equipment or by remote position of the monitoring staff.

(52) "Therapeutic seclusion": The placement and retention by qualified health care personnel of a prisoner in a room for the purpose of containing a clinical situation (e.g., extreme agitation, threatening or assaultive behavior) that may result in a state of emergency.

(53) "Variance": The process of receiving approval for a method of complying with the intent of a standard when strict compliance would cause unusual, practical difficulties or financial hardship. The alternative practice must not seriously affect the security of the facility, the supervision of inmates, or the safe, healthful operation of the facility.

(54) "Work or education release": A formal arrangement, sanctioned by law, whereby a prisoner is permitted to leave confinement for approved employment in a job and/or participation in specific programs.

HISTORY: 2002–03 OMR 1532 (A), eff. 1–1–03; 1998–99 OMR 715 (A), eff. 9–21–98; 1993–94 OMR 1746 (A), eff. 7–1–94; 1990–91 OMR 1442 (A), eff. 6–1–91; 1986–87 OMR 101 (A), eff. 8–8–86; 1982–83 OMR 845 (A), eff. 1–1–83; 1980–81 OMR 390 (E), eff. 1–2–81

RC 119.032 rule review date(s): 1–1–08; 1–12–03; 10–15–02

5120:1–7–03 Introduction to minimum standards

(A) Nothing contained in the "Minimum Standards For Jails In Ohio" shall be construed to prohibit a city, county, or combined city and/or county agency operating a local detention facility from adopting standards and requirements governing its own employees and facilities, provided that such rules meet or exceed and do not conflict with these standards.

(B) Pursuant to section 5120.10 of the Revised Code, a facility shall comply with the standards except that the administrator of the bureau of adult detention facilities and services, or designee, may grant a variance when it is determined that:

(1) Strict compliance would cause unusual practical difficulties or financial hardships;

(2) Existing or alternative practices meet the intent of the standards, and the granting of a variance would not seriously affect the security of the facility, the supervision of inmates, or the safe, healthful operation of the facility.

HISTORY: 2003–04 OMR 142 (RRD); 1997–98 OMR 2793 (RRD); 1982–83 OMR 847 (A), eff. 1–1–83; 1980–81 OMR 391 (E), eff. 1–2–81

RC 119.032 rule review date(s): 1–1–08; 7–29–03; 6–30–03

5120:1–7–04 Jail advisory board

(A) Pursuant to executive order no. 84–1, the bureau of adult detention (hereinafter "bureau") shall utilize the input and recommendations of the jail advisory board, to the extent outlined in this rule, in performing its functions of investigating and supervising county and municipal jails and workhouses.

(B) The jail advisory board shall assist the bureau in the development of policy and procedure by:

(1) Critiquing standards and policies;

(2) Reviewing and commenting upon the bureau's goals and objectives;

(3) Developing funding recommendations for the implementation of standards and criteria for compliance.

(C) The jail advisory board will play an active role in the bureau's activities of improving jails in Ohio by:

(1) Serving on review panels to provide input and recommendations for the bureau's consideration in monitoring compliance;

(2) Making suggestions on the appropriate uses of grant money;

(3) Providing liaison between the bureau and constituents of advisory board members.

(D) The jail advisory board will aid in the jail education process by:

(1) Playing a leadership role in professional associations discussing jail issues;

(2) Familiarizing itself and the public with jail standards and related issues;

(3) Working to develop constituent groups interested in jail issues;

(4) Being an information source for the public on policies of the bureau.

(E) The director of the department of rehabilitation and correction shall appoint jail advisory board members from lists of nominees furnished by the groups listed in paragraph (E)(1) of this rule and may appoint other members as he deems necessary. In nominating members for appointment to the jail advisory board, the group seeking representation shall choose a demographically representative group of nominees. Jail advisory board members shall be designated "voting members" or "ex officio" members upon appointment.

(1) Voting members shall consist of no more than twenty-four persons, representing the following professional associations and Ohio general assembly:

(a) Chiefs of police;

(b) City, village or township governing officials;

(c) County commissioners;

(d) County sheriffs;

(e) Local judges;

(f) Local prosecutors;

(g) State legislators.

(2) Ex–officio members include an indefinite number of persons from such offices, organizations or agencies as the director may determine. Such members will not vote on recommendations to the bureau or serve on review panels, but may attend meetings and comment on matters under consideration.

(F) Terms of membership:

(1) Voting members shall be appointed to three-year fixed terms, which shall be staggered to ensure orderly transition. Voting members may be reappointed consecutively only once, at the discretion of the director or his designee, such that six years consecutive membership is permitted.

(2) Ex–officio members shall serve indefinite terms at the discretion of the executive officer of the group, agency or office he represents.

(G) Any board member's service shall terminate when:

(1) The member voluntarily resigns;

(2) The member's professional status changes and the group he represents nominates a replacement;

(3) The member's first term expires without reappointment;

(4) The member's second consecutive term expires;

(5) The group represented desires and nominates a replacement.

(H) The chief of the division of parole and community services or designee shall chair the jail advisory board.

(I) The voting members shall elect an executive committee consisting of five voting members, one of which shall be elected chairperson by the executive committee. The executive committee shall:

(1) Make recommendations to the bureau, when called upon, on behalf of the full board, in an emergency;

(2) Recommend to the bureau items to be on the board's agenda;

(3) Establish subcommittees as desired, designate members to serve thereon, and specify duties and purposes of same;

(4) Meet, through its chairperson, with the chairperson of the jail advisory board concerning utilization of board members on review panels.

(J) The jail advisory board shall meet at least four times per year and when special meetings are called by the director, the chairperson, or the executive committee.

(1) The executive committee shall serve as the board's policy-making body between meetings;

(2) Nine voting board members, or their designees, shall constitute a quorum for transacting any of the board's business, with a majority vote of those in attendance being required to make a recommendation or policy.

(K) Neither the director nor the bureau is bound to act upon the advice of the jail advisory board, which is established only for the purpose of considering local input into the decisions of the department affecting jails.

(L) Board members shall receive reimbursement for actual and necessary expenses incurred for official business.

HISTORY: 2003–04 OMR 142 (RRD); 1997–98 OMR 2793 (RRD); 1984–85 OMR 458 (E), eff. 10–29–84

RC 119.032 rule review date(s): 1–1–08; 7–29–03; 6–30–03

SENTENCES AND FINES TABLES AND CHECKLISTS

Sentences and Fines Checklists

Checklist

Introduction

Included in this edition of Ohio Criminal Justice are the Ohio statutes and state court rules complete to February 2, 2005 and the Ohio administrative rules complete to January 31, 2005. Users should keep the 1996 edition of this book for statutes and penalties which were in effect for offenses committed prior to July 1, 1996 when major revisions effecting substantive criminal law and penalties went into effect.

Penalties in Ohio are governed primarily by statute. RC Chapter 2929 covers penalties for classified offenses generally, while other Revised Code chapters govern related topics such as execution of sentence (RC Chapter 2949) and probation (RC Chapter 2951). Of particular importance to sentencing are the specification provisions in RC Chapter 2941, "Indictment"—particularly RC 2941.141, Specification concerning possession of firearm essential to affect sentence; RC 2941.144, Specification concerning possession of automatic firearm or firearm with silencer; RC 2941.145, Specification concerning use of firearm to facilitate offense; and RC 2941.146, Specification concerning discharge of firearm from motor vehicle.

The provisions of RC Chapter 2929 fall into several distinct categories: penalties for aggravated murder and murder, penalties for felonies; penalties for misdemeanors; and miscellaneous provisions, including organizational fines.

The tables and checklists reflecting the law in effect as of February 2, 2005, include detailed information regarding felony sentences (Table 3), repeat violent offenders (Table 5), major drug offenders (Table 6), community control sanctions (Table 8), fines (Table 9), and an extensive breakdown of drug trafficking and possession offenses (Tables 11 through 17 and 22 through 29).

The tables present—in summary form—the statutory guidelines for sentencing and fines in both felony and misdemeanor cases including drug and drug-related offenses. The checklists summarize the statutory provisions on sentencing and on the early release provisions that affect the duration of a prisoner's sentence. Each entry contains a citation to the relevant Revised Code sections, and Editor's Notes provide further explanation when necessary. The tables and checklists have been numbered separately and uniquely so as to avoid confusion.

SENTENCES AND FINES TABLES

Table 1
Aggravated Murder

RC 2903.01

No specifications of aggravating circumstances under RC 2929.04(A)	One or more specifications of aggravating circumstances under RC 2929.04(A)
Life with parole eligibility after 20 years	Death
	Life without parole
	Life with parole eligibility after 30 years
	Life with parole eligibility after 25 years
Fine: not more than $25,000	

Note 1. No person raising the matter of age pursuant to RC 2929.023 and who is not found to have been 18 years of age or older at the time of the commission of the offense shall suffer death. (RC 2929.02(A))

Note 2. The court shall not impose a fine or fines for aggravated murder or murder which, in the aggregate and to the extent not suspended by the court, exceeds the amount which the offender is or will be able to pay by the method and within the time allowed without undue hardship to the offender or the offenders dependents, or will prevent the offender from making reparation for the victim's wrongful death.

Table 2
Murder

RC 2903.02

15 years to Life - Indefinite term[1]
Fine: not more than $15,000

[1] May be life imprisonment without parole if convicted of or pleads guilty to sexual motivation specification and sexually violent predator specification included in murder indictment.

Table 3
Felonies, Generally

RC 2929.14(A)

Felony, 1st degree	3, 4, 5, 6, 7, 8, 9, 10 years definite (Additional 1 - 10 years for certain offenses)[1, 2]
Felony, 2nd degree	2, 3, 4, 5, 6, 7, 8 years definite (Additional 1 - 10 years for certain offenses)[1,2]
Felony, 3rd degree	1, 2, 3, 4, 5 years definite
Felony, 4th degree	6, 7, 8, 9, 10, 11, 12, 13, 14, 15, 16, 17, 18 months definite
Felony, 5th degree	6, 7, 8, 9, 10, 11, 12 months definite

[1] Repeat violent offenders (2929.14(D)(2)), Major drug offenders (2929.14(D)(3)), Firearms specifications, and certain corrupt activities.

[2] Offender convicted of a crime of violence and convicted or pleading guilty to a criminal gang specification (2941.142) subject to an additional prison term of 1, 2, or 3 years.

Table 4
Firearm Specifications

RC 2929.14(D)(1)

Automatic firearm or firearm equipped with a silencer or muffler (2941.144) [1]	6 years
Brandishing or displaying firearm, indicating offender possesses firearm, or using firearm to facilitate commission of offense (2941.1451) [1]	3 years
Having firearm on or about person or under offender's control (2941.141) [1]	1 year
Improperly discharging firearm at or into habitation or school or knowingly or purposely causing death or physical harm and offense committed by discharging firearm from motor vehicle (2941.146) [1, 2]	5 years
Discharging firearm at a peace officer while ommitting the offense (2941.1412) [1]	7 years

[1] Specification required in indictment.

[2] A court shall not impose more than one prison term on an offender for felonies committed as part of the same act or transaction. If a court imposes an additional prison term for an offense committed by discharging a firearm from a motor vehicle, the court is not precluded from imposing an additional prison term for any other firearm specification.

Note 1. Additional prison term imposed under this section may not be reduced by RC 2929.20, 2967.193 or any other provision of Chapters 2967. or 5120.

Note 2. The court may not impose any additional prison terms upon an offender for carrying a concealed weapon under RC 2923.12.

Note 3. The court may not impose any additional prison terms upon an offender for having a weapon while under disability under RC 2923.13 unless the offender previously has been convicted of aggravated murder, murder, or any felony of the first or second degree and less than five years have passed since the offender was released from prison or post-release control, whichever is later, for the prior offense.

Table 4A
School Safety Zone

RC 2929.14(J)

Aggravated murder, murder, or F1, 2 and 3 that is offense of violence, and school safety zone violation (2941.143)	Additional 2 years

Table 5
Repeat Violent Offenders

RC 2929.14(D)(2)

No physical harm or disfigurement	Range of prison terms for specific offenses
Physical harm with substantial risk of death or permanent disfigurement	Longest prison term for specific offense
If terms inadequate to punish offender and protect public from future crime because offender is likely to commit future crimes and terms are demeaning to the seriousness of the offense because offender's conduct is more serious than normal (2929.12). *	1, 2, 3, 4, 5, 6, 7, 8, 9, or 10 years additional

* Additional prison sentence available only if offender sentenced to longest prison sentence for the offense.

Note 1. RC 2929.20, 2967.193 or any other provision of Chapters 2967, may not reduce additional prison term imposed under this section. or 5120.

Note 2. 2941.149 specification in indictment required.

Table 6
Major Drug Offenders, Corrupt Activity, Attempted Forcible Rape When Victim is Under 13 Years of Age

RC 2929.13(F), 2929.14(D)(3)

Mandatory 10 year sentence required and a finding that the 10 year sentence is inadequate to punish offender and protect public from future crime because offender is likely to commit future crimes and terms are demeaning to the seriousness of the offense because offender's conduct is more serious than normal (2929.12)	1, 2, 3, 4, 5, 6, 7, 8, 9, or 10 years additional

Note 1. Additional prison term imposed under this section may not be reduced by RC 2929.20, 2967.193 or any other provision of Chapters 2967. or 5120.

Note 2. 2941.1410 specification in indictment required.

Table 7
Consecutive Terms
RC 2929.14(E)

Offense	Term
Automatic firearm or firearm equipped with a silencer or muffler (2941.144)	Mandatory prison term
Brandishing firearm, indicating offender possesses firearm, or using firearm to facilitate commission of offense (2941.145)	Mandatory prison term
Having firearm on or about person or under offender's control (2941.141)	Mandatory prison term
Improperly discharging firearm at or into habitation or school or knowingly or purposely causing death or physical harm and offense committed by discharging firearm from motor vehicle (2941.146)	Mandatory prison term
Felony that is an offense of violence (2901.01) and specification that the offender wore or carried body armor during commission of the offense (2941.1411)	Mandatory prison term
Felony that is an offense of violence (2901.01) and specification that the offender participated in a criminal gang (2941.142)	Mandatory prison term
Inmate who commits Aggravated Riot (2917.02), Riot (2917.03), Escape (2921.34), or Aiding escape or resistance to authority (2921.35); Detainee who possesses deadly weapon (2923.131)	Mandatory prison term
An escapee under 2921.34 who commits a felony	Mandatory prison term
Violation of 2911.01(B)-aggravated robbery or attempted aggravated robbery of a law enforcement officer's deadly weapon	Mandatory prison term served consecutively to any other prison term
Multiple offenses committed while awaiting trial or sentencing, while offender under a community control sanction, or was under post-release control for prior offense	Court's discretion *
Harm caused by multiple offenses so great or unusual that a single prison term does not adequately reflect the seriousness of offender's conduct	Court's discretion *
Offender's history of criminal conduct demonstrates that consecutive sentences are necessary to protect public from future crime by offender or to punish the offender	Court's discretion *

* Where the court has discretion in imposing consecutive sentences, the court must make a finding that consecutive sentences are necessary to protect the public from future crime or to punish the offender and that consecutive sentences are not disproportionate to the seriousness of the offender's conduct and to the danger the offender poses to the public.

Note: When consecutive prison terms are imposed, the term is to be served is the aggregate of all of the terms so imposed.

Table 8
Community Control Sanctions

RC 2929.15 to 2929.18

Residential 2929.16	Community based correctional facility that serves county	Up to 6 months
	Jail	Up to 6 months *
	Halfway house	
	Alternative residential facility	
Nonresidential 2929.17	Day reporting	
	Electronically monitored house arrest, electronic monitoring without house arrest, or house arrest without electronic monitoring	
	Community service or if offender is unable to pay financial sanction, community service as an alternative to financial sanction	Up to 500 hours
	Drug treatment program with an appropriate level of security as determined by the court	
	Intensive supervision	
	Basic supervision	
	Monitored time	
	Drug and alcohol use monitoring	
	Curfew term	
	Requiring offender to obtain employment	
	Requiring offender to obtain education and training	
	With approval of victim, victim-offender mediation	
	License violation report	
	Counseling	
Financial 2929.18	Restitution	Victim's economic loss
	Fines	See Table 9—Fines
	Costs	2929.18(A)(4)

* Defendant convicted on a fourth degree felony OMVI offense may be sentenced up to one year in jail.

Note 1. If the court is not required to impose a prison term, a mandatory prison term, or a term of life imprisonment upon an offender, the court imposing sentence upon the offender for a felony may sentence the offender to any sanction or any combination of community control sanctions authorized. The duration of all community control sanctions shall not exceed five years for any offense. 2929.15(A)

Note 2. If the conditions of a community control sanction are violated, the sentencing court may impose a longer time under the same sanction, if the total time under the sanctions does not exceed the five year limitation, may impose a more restrictive sanction under those sections, or, if the violation is not prosecuted as an offense, may impose a prison term on the offender pursuant to 2929.14. The prison term, if any, imposed upon a violator shall be within the range of prison terms available for the offense for which the sanction that was violated was imposed and shall not exceed the prison term specified in the notice provided to the offender at the sentencing hearing pursuant to 2929.19(B)(3). The court may reduce the longer period of time that the offender is required to spend under the longer sanction, the more restrictive sanction, or a prison term imposed by the time the offender successfully spent under the sanction that was initially imposed. 2929.15(B)

Note 3. If an offender, for a significant period of time, fulfills the conditions of a sanction imposed in an exemplary manner, the court may reduce the period of time under the sanction or impose a less restrictive sanction. 2929.15(C)

Note 4. The court that assigns any offender convicted of a felony to a residential sanction may authorize the offender to be released so that the offender may seek or maintain employment, receive education or training, or receive treatment. A release for these purposes shall be only for the duration of time that is needed to fulfill the purpose of the release and for travel that reasonably is necessary. If the court has imposed a financial sanction on the offender, the court, pursuant to 2929.181, may order that an amount be withheld from any income earned from employment the offender engages in pursuant to the release in order to pay the financial sanction. 2929.16(B)

Note 5. If the court assigns an offender to a county jail in a county that has established a county jail industry program pursuant to 5147.30, the court shall specify, as part of the sentence, whether the sheriff of that county may consider the offender for participation in the county jail industry program. During the offender's term in the county jail, the court shall retain jurisdiction to modify its specification upon a reassessment of the offender's qualifications for participation in the program. 2929.16(C)

Note 6. A financial sanction is a judgment in favor of the state or a political subdivision in which the court that imposed the financial sanction is located, and the offender subject to the sanction is the judgment debtor, except that a financial sanction of reimbursement imposed upon an offender who is incarcerated in a state facility or a municipal jail is a judgment in favor of the state or municipal corporation and a financial sanction of restitution is a judgment in favor of the victim of the offender's criminal act. Once the financial sanction is imposed as a judgment, the victim, state, or political subdivision may bring an action to obtain execution of judgment through any available procedure, including: an execution against the property of the judgment debtor under Chapter 2329., an execution against the person of the judgment debtor under Chapter 2331., a proceeding in aid of execution under Chapter 2333. (including a proceeding for the examination of the judgment debtor under sections 2333.09 to 2333.12 and 2333.15 to 2333.27, a proceeding for attachment of the person of the judgment debtor under section 2333.28, and a creditor's suit under section 2333.01), the attachment of the property of the judgment debtor under Chapter 2715., and the garnishment of the property of the judgment debtor, under Chapter 2716. The victim, state, or political subdivision may also bring an action to obtain execution of judgment by obtaining an order for the assignment of wages of the judgment debtor under section 1321.33 or by obtaining an order for the withholding or deduction of the personal earnings or other assets of the judgment debtor under Section 2929.181. 2929.18(D)

Note 7. If a court that imposes a financial sanction finds that an offender satisfactorily has completed all other sanctions imposed upon the offender and that all restitution that has been ordered has been paid as ordered, the court may suspend any financial sanctions that have not been paid. 2929.18(G)

Note 8. No financial sanction shall preclude a victim from bringing a civil action against the offender. 2929.18(H)

Note 9. Period of community control sanction tolls if the offender absconds or leaves the jurisdiction without permission until offender brought before the court.

Table 9
Fines

RC 2929.18, 2929.21, 2929.31

OFFENSE	INDIVIDUAL	ORGANIZATIONAL [5,6]
Aggravated Murder [1]	Up to $25,000 2929.02(A)	Up to $100,000 2929.31(A)(1)
Murder	Up to $15,000 2929.02(B)	Up to $50,000 2929.31(A)(2)
Felony 1st degree [2,3]	Up to $20,000 2929.18(A)(3)(a)	Up to $25,000 2929.31(A)(3)
Felony 2nd degree [2,3]	Up to $15,000 2929.18(A)(3)(b)	Up to $20,000 2929.31(A)(4)
Felony 3rd degree [2,3]	Up to $10,000 2929.18(A)(3)(c)	Up to $15,000 2929.31(A)(5)
Felony 4th degree [3]	Up to $5,000 2929.18(A)(3)(d)	Up to $10,000 2929.31(A)(6)
Felony 5th degree [3]	Up to $2,500 2929.18(A)(3)(e)	Up to $7,500 2929.31(A)(7)
Misdemeanor 1st degree [4]	Up to $1,000 2929.21(C)(1)	Up to $5,000 2929.31(A)(8)
Misdemeanor 2nd degree [4]	Up to $750 2929.21(C)(2)	Up to $4,000 2929.31(A)(9)
Misdemeanor 3rd degree [4]	Up to $500 2929.21(C)(3)	Up to $3,000 2929.21(A)(10)
Misdemeanor 4th degree [4]	Up to $250 2929.21(C)(4)	Up to $2,000 2929.31(A)(11)
Minor Misdemeanor [4]	Up to $100 2929.21(D)	Up to $1,000 2929.31(A)(12)
Unclassified felony [6]	N/A	Up to $10,000 2929.31(A)(13)
Unclassified misdemeanor [6]	N/A	Up to $2,000 2929.31(A)(14)
Unclassified minor misdemeanor [6]	N/A	Up to $1,000 2929.31(A)(15)

Note 1. The court shall not impose a fine or fines for aggravated murder or murder which, in the aggregate and to the extent not suspended by the court, exceeds the amount which the offender is or will be able to pay by the method and within the time allowed without undue hardship to the offender or offender's dependents, or will prevent the offender from making reparation for the victim's wrongful death.

Note 2. For a 1st, 2nd, or 3rd degree felony violation of any provision of Chapter 2925., 3719., or 4729., the sentencing court shall impose a mandatory fine of at least one-half of, but not more than, the maximum statutory fine amount authorized for the level of the offense. If an offender alleges in an affidavit filed with the court prior to sentencing that the offender is indigent and unable to pay the mandatory fine and if the court determines that the offender is an indigent person and is unable to pay the mandatory fine, the court shall not impose the mandatory fine upon the offender. 2929.18(B)(1)

Note 3. Any mandatory fine imposed under 2929.18(B)(1) and any fine imposed upon an offender for any 4th or 5th degree felony violation of any provision of Chapter 2925., 3719., or 4729., shall be paid to law enforcement agencies pursuant to 2925.03(F). 2929.18(B)(2)

Note 4. The court may require a person who is convicted of or pleads guilty to a misdemeanor to make restitution for all or part of the property damage that is caused by the offender and for all or part of the value of the property that is the subject of any theft offense. If the court determines that the victim of the offense was sixty-five years of age or older or permanently or totally disabled at the time of the commission of the offense, the court, regardless of whether the offender knew the age of the victim, shall consider this fact in favor of imposing restitution, but this fact shall not control the decision of the court. 2929.21(E)

Note 5. RC 2929.31 does not prevent the imposition of available civil sanctions against an organization convicted of an offense pursuant to section 2901.23, either in addition to or in lieu of a fine imposed under RC 2929.31. 2929.31(D)

Note 6. When an organization is convicted of an offense that is not specifically classified, and the section defining the offense or penalty plainly indicates a purpose to impose the penalty provided for violation upon organizations, then the penalty so provided shall be imposed in lieu of the penalty provided in 2929.31. When an organization is convicted of an offense that is not specifically classified, and the penalty provided includes a higher fine than the fine that is provided in 2929.31, then the penalty imposed shall be pursuant to the penalty provided for the violation of the section defining the offense. 2929.31(B) and (C)

Table 9A
Misdemeanors, Generally

RC 2929.21(B)

Misdemeanor, 1st degree	Imprisonment, not more than six months
Misdemeanor, 2nd degree	Imprisonment, not more than ninety days
Misdemeanor, 3rd degree	Imprisonment, not more than sixty days
Misdemeanor, 4th degree	Imprisonment, not more than thirty days

Table 10
Corrupting Another with Drugs

RC 2925.02

DRUG	LEVEL	SENTENCE
Schedule I or II [1]	F2	Mandatory prison term
Schedule I or II [1] involving sale, offer to sell, or possession as Major Drug Offender (2929.14(D)(3)(b)) [2]	F2	Mandatory prison term plus additional 1 to 10 years
Schedule III, IV or V	F2	Presumption for prison term
Marihuana	F4	2929.13(C)
OFFENSE COMMITTED IN VICINITY OF SCHOOL OR JUVENILE		
Schedule I or II [1]	F1	Mandatory prison term
Schedule I or II [1] involving sale, offer to sell, or possession as Major Drug Offender (2929.14(D)(3)(b)) [2]	F1	Mandatory prison term plus additional 1 to 10 years
Schedule III, IV or V	F2	Mandatory prison term
Marihuana	F3	2929.13(C)

[1] Does not include marihuana
[2] Requires 2941.1410 specification.

Note 1. If the violation is a felony of the 1st, 2nd, or 3rd degree the court shall impose upon the offender the mandatory fine specified under 2929.18(B)(1) unless the court determines that the offender is indigent.

Note 2. The court shall either revoke or suspend the driver's or commercial driver's license or permit of any person convicted of a violation of this section that is a felony of the 1st degree. The court shall suspend the driver's or commercial driver's license or permit of any person convicted of any other violation of this section. Any suspension under this section shall be for not less than 6 months or more than 5 years. If an offender's driver's or commercial driver's license or permit is revoked pursuant to this section, the offender at any time after the expiration of 2 years from the day on which the offender's sentence was imposed or from the day on which the offender finally was released from a prison term under the sentence, whichever is later, may file a motion with the sentencing court requesting termination of the revocation. Upon the filing of the motion and the court's finding of good cause for the termination, the court may terminate the revocation. 2925.02(D)(2)

Note 3. If the offender is a professionally licensed person or a person who has been admitted to the bar by order of the supreme court, in addition to any other sanction imposed for a violation of this section, the court shall comply with the notice provisions under 2925.38.

Table 11
Aggravated Trafficking in Drugs

RC 2925.03(A) & (C)(1)

DRUG	AMOUNT	LEVEL	SENTENCE
Schedule I or II *	Less than bulk amount	F4	2929.13(C)
	Bulk amount but less than 5 times bulk amount	F3	Mandatory prison term
	5 times bulk amount but less than 50 times bulk amount	F2	Mandatory prison term
	50 times bulk amount but less than 100 times bulk amount	F1	Mandatory prison term
	100 times bulk amount or more Major Drug Offender (2929.14(D)(3)(b))	F1	Mandatory 10 year prison term plus an additional 1 to 10 years
OFFENSE COMMITTED IN VICINITY OF SCHOOL OR JUVENILE			
Schedule I or II *	Less than bulk amount	F3	2929.13(C)
	Bulk amount but less than 5 times bulk amount	F2	Mandatory prison term
	5 times bulk amount but less than 50 times bulk amount	F1	Mandatory prison term
	50 times bulk amount but less than 100 times bulk amount	F1	Mandatory prison term
	100 times bulk amount or more Major Drug Offender (2929.14(D)(3)(b))	F1	Mandatory 10 year prison term plus an additional 1 to 10 years

* Does not include marihuana, cocaine, L.S.D., heroin, or hashish.

Note 1. If the violation is a felony of the 1st, 2nd, or 3rd degree the court shall impose upon the offender the mandatory fine specified under 2929.18(B)(1) unless the court determines that the offender is indigent.

Note 2. The court shall either revoke or suspend the driver's or commercial driver's license or permit of any person convicted of a violation of this section that is a felony of the 1st degree. The court shall suspend the driver's or commercial driver's license or permit of any person convicted of any other violation of this section. Any suspension under this section shall be for not less than 6 months or more than 5 years. If an offender's driver's or commercial driver's license or permit is revoked pursuant to this section, the offender at any time after the expiration of 2 years from the day on which the offender's sentence was imposed or from the day on which the offender finally was released from a prison term under the sentence, whichever is later, may file a motion with the sentencing court requesting termination of the revocation. Upon the filing of the motion and the court's finding of good cause for the termination, the court may terminate the revocation. 2925.02(D)(2)

Note 3. If the offender is a professionally licensed person or a person who has been admitted to the bar by order of the supreme court, in addition to any other sanction imposed for a violation of this section, the court shall comply with the notice provisions under 2925.38.

Table 12
Trafficking in Drugs

RC 2925.03(A) & (C)(2)

DRUG	AMOUNT	LEVEL	SENTENCE
Schedule III, IV, or V	Less than bulk amount	F5	2929.13(C)
	Bulk amount but less than 5 times bulk amount	F4	Presumption of prison term
	5 times bulk amount but less than 50 times bulk amount	F3	Presumption of prison term
	50 times bulk amount or more	F2	Mandatory prison term
	OFFENSE COMMITTED IN VICINITY OF SCHOOL OR JUVENILE		
Schedule III, IV, or V	Less than bulk amount	F4	2929.13(C)
	Bulk amount but less than 5 times bulk amount	F3	Presumption of prison term
	5 times bulk amount but less than 50 times bulk amount	F2	Presumption of prison term
	50 times bulk amount or more	F1	Mandatory prison term

Note 1. If the violation is a felony of the 1st, 2nd, or 3rd degree the court shall impose upon the offender the mandatory fine specified under 2929.18(B)(1) unless the court determines that the offender is indigent.

Note 2. The court shall either revoke or suspend the driver's or commercial driver's license or permit of any person convicted of a violation of this section that is a felony of the 1st degree. The court shall suspend the driver's or commercial driver's license or permit of any person convicted of any other violation of this section. Any suspension under this section shall be for not less than 6 months or more than 5 years. If an offender's driver's or commercial driver's license or permit is revoked pursuant to this section, the offender at any time after the expiration of 2 years from the day on which the offender's sentence was imposed or from the day on which the offender finally was released from a prison term under the sentence, whichever is later, may file a motion with the sentencing court requesting termination of the revocation. Upon the filing of the motion and the court's finding of good cause for the termination, the court may terminate the revocation. 2925.02(D)(2)

Note 3. If the offender is a professionally licensed person or a person who has been admitted to the bar by order of the supreme court, in addition to any other sanction imposed for a violation of this section, the court shall comply with the notice provisions under 2925.38.

Table 13
Trafficking in Marihuana *

RC 2925.03(A) & (C)(3)

DRUG	AMOUNT	LEVEL	SENTENCE
Marihuana	Less than 200 grams	F5	2929.13(C)
	200 grams but less than 1,000 grams	F4	2929.13(C)
	1,000 grams but less than 5,000 grams	F3	2929.13(C)
	5,000 grams but less than 20,000 grams	F3	Presumption of prison term
	20,000 grams or more	F2	Mandatory 8 year prison term
	Gift of 20 grams or less (first offense)	MM	2929.21(D)
	Gift of 20 grams or less (each subsequent offense)	M3	2929.21(B)(3) & (C)(3)
OFFENSE COMMITTED IN VICINITY OF SCHOOL OR JUVENILE			
Marihuana	Less than 200 grams	F4	2929.13(C)
	200 grams but less than 1,000 grams	F3	2929.13(C)
	1,000 grams but less than 5,000 grams	F2	Presumption of prison term
	5,000 grams but less than 20,000 grams	F2	Presumption of prison term
	20,000 grams or more	F1	Mandatory 10 year prison term
	Gift of 20 grams or less	M3	2929.21(B)(3) & (C)(3)

* Other than Hashish

Note 1. If the violation is a felony of the 1st, 2nd, or 3rd degree the court shall impose upon the offender the mandatory fine specified under 2929.18(B)(1) unless the court determines that the offender is indigent.

Note 2. The court shall either revoke or suspend the driver's or commercial driver's license or permit of any person convicted of a violation of this section that is a felony of the 1st degree. The court shall suspend the driver's or commercial driver's license or permit of any person convicted of any other violation of this section. Any suspension under this section shall be for not less than 6 months or more than 5 years. If an offender's driver's or commercial driver's license or permit is revoked pursuant to this section, the offender at any time after the expiration of 2 years from the day on which the offender's sentence was imposed or from the day on which the offender finally was released from a prison term under the sentence, whichever is later, may file a motion with the sentencing court requesting termination of the revocation. Upon the filing of the motion and the court's finding of good cause for the termination, the court may terminate the revocation. 2925.02(D)(2)

Note 3. If the offender is a professionally licensed person or a person who has been admitted to the bar by order of the supreme court, in addition to any other sanction imposed for a violation of this section, the court shall comply with the notice provisions under 2925.38.

Table 14
Trafficking in Cocaine

RC 2925.03(A) & (C)(4)

DRUG	AMOUNT	LEVEL	SENTENCE
Cocaine (Powder)	Less than 5 grams	F5	2929.13(C)
	5 grams but less than 10 grams	F4	Presumption of prison term
	10 grams but less than 100 grams	F3	Mandatory prison term
	100 grams but less than 500 grams	F2	Mandatory prison term
	500 grams but less than 1,000 grams	F1	Mandatory prison term
	1,000 grams or more Major Drug Offender (2929.14(D)(3)(b))	F1	Mandatory 10 year prison term plus an additional 1 to 10 years
OFFENSE COMMITTED IN VICINITY OF SCHOOL OR JUVENILE			
Cocaine (Powder)	Less than 5 grams	F4	2929.13(C)
	5 grams but less than 10 grams	F3	Presumption of prison term
	10 grams but less than 100 grams	F2	Mandatory prison term
	100 grams but less than 500 grams	F1	Mandatory prison term
	500 grams but less than 1,000 grams	F1	Mandatory prison term
	1,000 grams or more Major Drug Offender (2929.14(D)(3)(b))	F1	Mandatory 10 year prison term plus an additional 1 to 10 years
Cocaine (Crack)	Less than 1 gram	F5	2929.13(C)
	1 gram but less than 5 grams	F4	Presumption of prison term
	5 grams but less than 10 grams	F3	Mandatory prison term
	10 grams but less than 25 grams	F2	Mandatory prison term
	25 grams but less than 100 grams	F1	Mandatory prison term
	100 grams or more Major Drug Offender (2929.14(D)(3)(b))	F1	Mandatory 10 year prison term plus an additional 1 to 10 years
OFFENSE COMMITTED IN VICINITY OF SCHOOL OR JUVENILE			
Cocaine (Crack)	Less than 1 gram	F4	2929.13(C)
	1 gram but less than 5 grams	F3	Presumption of prison term
	5 grams but less than 10 grams	F2	Mandatory prison term
	10 grams but less than 25 grams	F1	Mandatory prison term
	25 grams but less than 100 grams	F1	Mandatory prison term
	100 grams or more Major Drug Offender (2929.14(D)(3)(b))	F1	Mandatory 10 year prison term plus an additional 1 to 10 years

Note 1. If the violation is a felony of the 1st, 2nd, or 3rd degree the court shall impose upon the offender the mandatory fine specified under 2929.18(B)(1) unless the court determines that the offender is indigent.

Note 2. The court shall either revoke or suspend the driver's or commercial driver's license or permit of any person convicted of a violation of this section that is a felony of the 1st degree. The court shall suspend the driver's or commercial driver's license or permit of any person convicted of any other violation of this section. Any suspension under this section shall be for not less than 6 months or more than 5 years. If an offender's driver's or commercial driver's license or permit is revoked pursuant to this section, the offender at any time after the expiration of 2 years from the day on which the offender's sentence was imposed or from the day on which the offender finally was released from a prison term under the sentence, whichever is later, may file a motion with the sentencing court requesting termination of the revocation. Upon the filing of the motion and the court's finding of good cause for the termination, the court may terminate the revocation. 2925.02(D)(2)

Note 3. If the offender is a professionally licensed person or a person who has been admitted to the bar by order of the supreme court, in addition to any other sanction imposed for a violation of this section, the court shall comply with the notice provisions under 2925.38.

Table 15
Trafficking in L.S.D.

RC 2925.03(A) & (C)(5)

DRUG	AMOUNT	LEVEL	SENTENCE
L.S.D.	Less than 10 unit doses	F5	2929.13(C)
	10 unit doses but less than 50 unit doses in solid form or 1 gram but less than 5 grams in liquid form	F4	Presumption of prison term
	50 unit doses but less than 250 unit doses in solid form or 5 grams but less than 25 grams in liquid form	F3	Mandatory prison term
	250 unit doses but less than 1,000 unit doses in solid form or 25 grams but less than 100 grams in liquid form	F2	Mandatory prison term
	1,000 unit doses but less than 5,000 unit doses in solid form or 100 grams but less than 500 grams in liquid form	F1	Mandatory prison term
	5,000 unit doses in solid form or 500 grams in liquid form or more Major Drug Offender (2929.14(D)(3)(b))	F1	Mandatory 10 year prison term plus an additional 1 to 10 years
OFFENSE COMMITTED IN VICINITY OF SCHOOL OR JUVENILE			
L.S.D.	Less than 10 unit doses	F4	2929.13(C)
	10 unit doses but less than 50 unit doses in solid form or 1 gram but less than 5 grams in liquid form	F3	Presumption of prison term
	50 unit doses but less than 250 unit doses in solid form or 5 grams but less than 25 grams in liquid form	F2	Mandatory prison term
	250 unit doses but less than 1,000 unit doses in solid form or 25 grams but less than 100 grams in liquid form	F1	Mandatory prison term
	1,000 unit doses but less than 5,000 unit doses in solid form or 100 grams but less than 500 grams in liquid form	F1	Mandatory prison term
	5,000 unit doses in solid form or 500 grams in liquid form or more Major Drug Offender (2929.14(D)(3)(b))	F1	Mandatory 10 year prison term plus an additional 1 to 10 years

Note 1. If the violation is a felony of the 1st, 2nd, or 3rd degree the court shall impose upon the offender the mandatory fine specified under 2929.18(B)(1) unless the court determines that the offender is indigent.

Note 2. The court shall either revoke or suspend the driver's or commercial driver's license or permit of any person convicted of a violation of this section that is a felony of the 1st degree. The court shall suspend the driver's or commercial driver's license or permit of any person convicted of any other violation of this section. Any suspension under this section shall be for not less than 6 months or more than 5 years. If an offender's driver's or commercial driver's license or permit is revoked pursuant to this section, the offender at any time after the expiration of 2 years from the day on which the offender's sentence was imposed or from the day on which the offender finally was released from a prison term under the sentence, whichever is later, may file a motion with the sentencing court requesting termination of the revocation. Upon the filing of the motion and the court's finding of good cause for the termination, the court may terminate the revocation. 2925.02(D)(2)

Note 3. If the offender is a professionally licensed person or a person who has been admitted to the bar by order of the supreme court, in addition to any other sanction imposed for a violation of this section, the court shall comply with the notice provisions under 2925.38.

Table 16
Trafficking in Heroin

RC 2925.03(A) & (C)(6)

DRUG	AMOUNT	LEVEL	SENTENCE
Heroin	Less than ten unit doses or less than one gram	F5	2929.13(C)
	10 unit doses but less than 50 unit doses or 1 gram but less than five grams	F4	Presumption of prison term
	50 unit doses but less than 100 unit doses or 5 grams but less than ten grams	F3	Presumption of prison term
	100 unit doses but less than 500 unit doses or 10 grams but less than 50 grams	F2	Mandatory prison term
	500 unit doses but less than 2,500 unit doses or 50 grams but less than 250 grams	F1	Mandatory prison term
	2,500 unit doses or more or 250 grams or more Major Drug Offender (2929.14(D)(3)(b))	F1	Mandatory 10 year prison term plus an additional 1 to 10 years
OFFENSE COMMITTED IN VICINITY OF SCHOOL OR JUVENILE			
Heroin	Less than ten unit doses or less than one gram	F4	2929.13(C)
	10 unit doses but less than 50 unit doses or 1 gram but less than five grams	F3	Presumption of prison term
	50 unit doses but less than 100 unit doses or 5 grams but less than ten grams	F2	Presumption of prison term
	100 unit doses but less than 500 unit doses or 10 grams but less than 50 grams	F1	Mandatory prison term
	500 unit doses but less than 2,500 unit doses or 50 grams but less than 250 grams	F1	Mandatory prison term
	2,500 unit doses or more or 250 grams or more Major Drug Offender (2929.14(D)(3)(b))	F1	Mandatory 10 year prison term plus an additional 1 to 10 years

Note 1. If the violation is a felony of the 1st, 2nd, or 3rd degree the court shall impose upon the offender the mandatory fine specified under 2929.18(B)(1) unless the court determines that the offender is indigent.

Note 2. The court shall either revoke or suspend the driver's or commercial driver's license or permit of any person convicted of a violation of this section that is a felony of the 1st degree. The court shall suspend the driver's or commercial driver's license or permit of any person convicted of any other violation of this section. Any suspension under this section shall be for not less than 6 months or more than 5 years. If an offender's driver's or commercial driver's license or permit is revoked pursuant to this section, the offender at any time after the expiration of 2 years from the day on which the offender's sentence was imposed or from the day on which the offender finally was released from a prison term under the sentence, whichever is later, may file a motion with the sentencing court requesting termination of the revocation. Upon the filing of the motion and the court's finding of good cause for the termination, the court may terminate the revocation. 2925.02(D)(2)

Note 3. If the offender is a professionally licensed person or a person who has been admitted to the bar by order of the supreme court, in addition to any other sanction imposed for a violation of this section, the court shall comply with the notice provisions under 2925.38.

Table 17
Trafficking in Hashish

RC 2925.03(A) & (C)(7)

DRUG	AMOUNT	LEVEL	SENTENCE
Hashish	Less than 10 grams in solid form Less than 2 grams in liquid form	F5	2929.13(C)
	10 grams but less than 50 grams in solid form 2 grams but less than 10 grams in liquid form	F4	2929.13(C)
	50 grams but less than 250 grams in solid form 10 grams but less than 50 grams in liquid form	F3	2929.13(C)
	250 grams but less than 1,000 grams in solid form 50 grams but less than 200 grams in liquid form	F3	Presumption of prison term
	1,000 grams or more in solid form 200 grams or more in liquid form	F2	Mandatory 8 year prison term
OFFENSE COMMITTED IN VICINITY OF SCHOOL OR JUVENILE			
Hashish	Less than 10 grams in solid form Less than 2 grams in liquid form	F4	2929.13(C)
	10 grams but less than 50 grams in solid form 2 grams but less than 10 grams in liquid form	F3	2929.13(C)
	50 grams but less than 250 grams in solid form 10 grams but less than 50 grams in liquid form	F2	Presumption of prison term
	250 grams but less than 1,000 grams in solid form 50 grams but less than 200 grams in liquid form	F2	Presumption of prison term
	1,000 grams or more in solid form 200 grams or more in liquid form	F1	Mandatory 10 year prison term

Note 1. If the violation is a felony of the 1st, 2nd, or 3rd degree the court shall impose upon the offender the mandatory fine specified under 2929.18(B)(1) unless the court determines that the offender is indigent.

Note 2. The court shall either revoke or suspend the driver's or commercial driver's license or permit of any person convicted of a violation of this section that is a felony of the 1st degree. The court shall suspend the driver's or commercial driver's license or permit of any person convicted of any other violation of this section. Any suspension under this section shall be for not less than 6 months or more than 5 years. If an offender's driver's or commercial driver's license or permit is revoked pursuant to this section, the offender at any time after the expiration of 2 years from the day on which the offender's sentence was imposed or from the day on which the offender finally was released from a prison term under the sentence, whichever is later, may file a motion with the sentencing court requesting termination of the revocation. Upon the filing of the motion and the court's finding of good cause for the termination, the court may terminate the revocation. 2925.02(D)(2)

Note 3. If the offender is a professionally licensed person or a person who has been admitted to the bar by order of the supreme court, in addition to any other sanction imposed for a violation of this section, the court shall comply with the notice provisions under 2925.38.

Table 18
Illegal Manufacture of Drugs

RC 2925.04

DRUG	LEVEL	SENTENCE
Schedule I or II [1,3]	F2	Mandatory prison term
Schedule I or II [1] involving sale, offer to sell, or possession as Major Drug Offender (2929.14(D)(3)(b)) [2]	F2	Mandatory prison term plus an additional 1 to 10 years
Schedule III, IV or V [4]	F3	Presumption of prison term

[1] Does not include marihuana
[2] Requires a 2941.1410 specification in indictment
[3] If committed in vicinity of a juvenile or school, F1, Mandatory prison term
[4] If committed in vicinity of a juvenile or school, F2, Presumption of prison term

Note 1. If the violation is a felony of the 1st, 2nd, or 3rd degree the court shall impose upon the offender the mandatory fine specified under 2929.18(B)(1) unless the court determines that the offender is indigent.

Note 2. The court shall either revoke or suspend the driver's or commercial driver's license or permit of any person convicted of a violation of this section that is a felony of the 1st degree. The court shall suspend the driver's or commercial driver's license or permit of any person convicted of any other violation of this section. Any suspension under this section shall be for not less than 6 months or more than 5 years. If an offender's driver's or commercial driver's license or permit is revoked pursuant to this section, the offender at any time after the expiration of 2 years from the day on which the offender's sentence was imposed or from the day on which the offender finally was released from a prison term under the sentence, whichever is later, may file a motion with the sentencing court requesting termination of the revocation. Upon the filing of the motion and the court's finding of good cause for the termination, the court may terminate the revocation. 2925.02(D)(2)

Note 3. If the offender is a professionally licensed person or a person who has been admitted to the bar by order of the supreme court, in addition to any other sanction imposed for a violation of this section, the court shall comply with the notice provisions under 2925.38.

Table 19
Illegal Cultivation of Marihuana

RC 2925.04

DRUG	AMOUNT	LEVEL	SENTENCE
Marihuana	Less than 100 grams [1]	MM	2929.21
	100 grams but less than 200 grams [2]	M4	2929.24(A)(4)
	200 grams but less than 1,000 grams [3]	F5	2929.13(B)
	1,000 grams but less than 5,000 grams [4]	F3	2929.13(C)
	5,000 grams but less than 20,000 grams [5]	F3	Presumption of prison term
	20,000 grams or more [6]	F2	Mandatory 8 year prison term

[1] If violation occurs in vicinity of juvenile or school, M4, 2929.24(A)(4)
[2] If violation occurs in vicinity of juvenile or school, M3, 2929.24(A)(4)
[3] If violation occurs in vicinity of juvenile or school, F4, 2929.13(B)
[4] If violation occurs in vicinity of juvenile or school, F2, 2929.13 (C)
[5] If violation occurs in vicinity of juvenile or school, F2, 2929.13(D)
[6] If violation occurs in vicinity of juvenile or school, F1, Mandatory 10 year prison term

Note 1. If the violation is a felony of the 1st, 2nd, or 3rd degree the court shall impose upon the offender the mandatory fine specified under 2929.18(B)(1) unless the court determines that the offender is indigent.

Note 2. The court shall either revoke or suspend the driver's or commercial driver's license or permit of any person convicted of a violation of this section that is a felony of the 1st degree. The court shall suspend the driver's or commercial driver's license or permit of any person convicted of any other violation of this section. Any suspension under this section shall be for not less than 6 months or more than 5 years. If an offender's driver's or commercial driver's license or permit is revoked pursuant to this section, the offender at any time after the expiration of 2 years from the day on which the offender's sentence was imposed or from the day on which the offender finally was released from a prison term under the sentence, whichever is later, may file a motion with the sentencing court requesting termination of the revocation. Upon the filing of the motion and the court's finding of good cause for the termination, the court may terminate the revocation. 2925.02(D)(2)

Note 3. If the offender is a professionally licensed person or a person who has been admitted to the bar by order of the supreme court, in addition to any other sanction imposed for a violation of this section, the court shall comply with the notice provisions under 2925.38.

Note 4. It is an affirmative defense to a charge under this section that the marihuana that gave rise to the charge is in an amount, is in a form, is prepared, compounded, or mixed with substances that are not controlled substances in a manner, or is possessed or cultivated under any other circumstances that indicate that the marihuana was solely for personal use.

Note 5. Arrest or conviction for a minor misdemeanor violation of this section does not constitute a criminal record and need not be reported by the person so arrested or convicted in response to any inquiries about the person's criminal record, including any inquiries contained in an application for employment, a license, or any other right or privilege or made in connection with the person's appearance as a witness.

Table 19A
Illegal Manufacture of Drugs

RC 2925.04

DRUG	LEVEL	SENTENCE
Methamphetamine	F1 *	Mandatory prison term also subject to Major Drug Offender 2929.14(D)(3)(b)

* In vicinity of juvenile, school or on public premises

Note 1. Mandatory fine

Note 2. Suspension of driver's license

Note 3. Notification of licensing board

Table 19B
Illegal Assembly or Possession of Chemicals Used to Manufacture Drugs

RC 2925.041

DRUG	LEVEL	SENTENCE
Schedule I or II [1]	F3	2929.13(C)

[1] If violation occurs in vicinity of juvenile or school, Felony, 2nd degree, 2929.13(C)

Note 1. Mandatory fine

Note 2. Suspension of driver's license

Note 3. Notification of licensing board

Table 20
Funding of Drug or Marihuana Trafficking

RC 2925.05

DRUG	LEVEL	SENTENCE
Schedule I or II *	F1	Mandatory prison term
Schedule I or II * involving sale, offer to sell, or possession as Major Drug Offender (2929.14(D)(3)(b))	F1	Mandatory prison term plus an additional 1 to 10 years
Schedule III, IV or V (Bulk amount or more)	F2	Mandatory prison term
Marihuana (200 grams or more	F3	Mandatory prison term
Cocaine (5 grams or more powder or 1 gram or more crack)	F1	Mandatory prison term
LSD (10 unit doses or more, or 1 gram or more liquid)	F1	Mandatory prison term
Heroin (10 unit doses or more, or 1 gram or more)	F1	Mandatory prison term
Hashish (10 grams or more solid, or 2 grams or more liquid)	F1	Mandatory prison term

* Except marihuana, cocaine, LSD, heroin, and hashish

Note 1. The court shall impose upon the offender the mandatory fine specified under 2929.18(B)(1) unless the court determines that the offender is indigent.

Note 2. The court shall either revoke or suspend the driver's or commercial driver's license or permit of any person convicted of a violation of this section that is a felony of the 1st degree. The court shall suspend the driver's or commercial driver's license or permit of any person convicted of any other violation of this section. Any suspension under this section shall be for not less than 6 months or more than 5 years. If an offender's driver's or commercial driver's license or permit is revoked pursuant to this section, the offender at any time after the expiration of 2 years from the day on which the offender's sentence was imposed or from the day on which the offender finally was released from a prison term under the sentence, whichever is later, may file a motion with the sentencing court requesting termination of the revocation. Upon the filing of the motion and the court's finding of good cause for the termination, the court may terminate the revocation. 2925.02(D)(2)

Note 3. If the offender is a professionally licensed person or a person who has been admitted to the bar by order of the supreme court, in addition to any other sanction imposed for a violation of this section, the court shall comply with the notice provisions under 2925.38.

Table 21
Illegal Administration or Distribution of Anabolic Steroids

RC 2925.06

DRUG	LEVEL	SENTENCE
Anabolic Steroids	F4	2929.13(C)

Note 1. The court shall either revoke or suspend the driver's or commercial driver's license or permit of any person convicted of a violation of this section that is a felony of the 1st degree. The court shall suspend the driver's or commercial driver's license or permit of any person convicted of any other violation of this section. Any suspension under this section shall be for not less than 6 months or more than 5 years. If an offender's driver's or commercial driver's license or permit is revoked pursuant to this section, the offender at any time after the expiration of 2 years from the day on which the offender's sentence was imposed or from the day on which the offender finally was released from a prison term under the sentence, whichever is later, may file a motion with the sentencing court requesting termination of the revocation. Upon the filing of the motion and the court's finding of good cause for the termination, the court may terminate the revocation. 2925.02(D)(2)

Note 2. If the offender is a professionally licensed person or a person who has been admitted to the bar by order of the supreme court, in addition to any other sanction imposed for a violation of this section, the court shall comply with the notice provisions under 2925.38.

Note 3. If the offender commits any act that constitutes a violation of this section and that also constitutes a violation of any other provision of the Revised Code, the prosecutor, using customary prosecutorial discretion, may prosecute the person for a violation of the appropriate provision of the Revised Code.

Table 22
Aggravated Possession of Drugs

RC 2925.11(A) & (C)(1)

DRUG	AMOUNT	LEVEL	SENTENCE
Schedule I or II *	Bulk amount or less	F5	2929.13(B)
	Bulk amount but less than 5 times bulk amount	F3	Presumption of prison term
	5 times bulk amount but less than 50 times bulk amount	F2	Mandatory prison term
	50 times bulk amount but less than 100 times bulk amount	F1	Mandatory prison term
	100 times bulk amount or more (Major Drug Offender)	F1	Mandatory 10 year prison term plus an additional 1 to 10 years

* Except marihuana, cocaine, L.S.D., heroin, and hashish.

Note 1. If the violation is a felony of the 1st, 2nd, or 3rd degree the court shall impose upon the offender the mandatory fine specified under 2929.18(B)(1) unless the court determines that the offender is indigent.

Note 2. The court shall either revoke or suspend the driver's or commercial driver's license or permit of any person convicted of a violation of this section that is a felony of the 1st degree. The court shall suspend the driver's or commercial driver's license or permit of any person convicted of any other violation of this section. Any suspension under this section shall be for not less than 6 months or more than 5 years. If an offender's driver's or commercial driver's license or permit is revoked pursuant to this section, the offender at any time after the expiration of 2 years from the day on which the offender's sentence was imposed or from the day on which the offender finally was released from a prison term under the sentence, whichever is later, may file a motion with the sentencing court requesting termination of the revocation. Upon the filing of the motion and the court's finding of good cause for the termination, the court may terminate the revocation. 2925.02(D)(2)

Note 3. If the offender is a professionally licensed person or a person who has been admitted to the bar by order of the supreme court, in addition to any other sanction imposed for a violation of this section, the court shall comply with the notice provisions under 2925.38.

Note 4. If the offender pleads guilty before trial, in lieu of sentencing the offender to a term of imprisonment in a detention facility, the court may place an offender who is a felon in a community control sanction under sections 2929.16 or 2929.17 or an offender who is a misdemeanant on conditional probation, provided the offender enters an alternative residential diversion program described in this section for drug abuse treatment and counseling for at least 90 days, and the offender submits to outpatient treatment and counseling for at least 9 months upon the offender's release. If the offender complies with these terms and all other terms of the offender's sanction or probation, the charges shall be dismissed. If the offender fails to comply, the offender's probation or sanction shall be revoked and a term of imprisonment imposed. This section does not revent the court from granting conditional probation under 2951.04 or treatment in lieu of conviction under 2951.041.

Note 5. If the offender is a woman who is pregnant at the time of sentencing and agrees to receive prenatal care and to complete a rehabilitation program at a drug treatment facility, the court shall impose a community control sanction on a felon under sections 2929.16 or 2929.17 or an offender who is a misdemeanant on conditional probation.

Table 23
Possession of Drugs

RC 2925.11(A) & (C)(2)

DRUG	AMOUNT	LEVEL	SENTENCE
Schedule III, IV, or V	Less than bulk amount	M3	2929.21(B)(3) & (C)(3)
	Less than bulk amount with prior drug abuse conviction	M2	2929.21(B)(2) & (C)(2)
Anabolic steroid in Schedule III	Less than bulk amount	M3	2929.21(B)(3) & (C)(3)(1) & 2951.02
	Bulk amount but less than 5 times bulk amount	F4	2929.13(C)
	5 times bulk amount but less than 50 times bulk amount	F3	Presumption of prison term
	50 times bulk amount or more	F2	Mandatory prison term

Note 1. If the drug involved in the violation is an anabolic steroid included in Schedule III and if the offense is a misdemeanor or the 3rd degree under this division, in lieu of sentencing the offender to a term of imprisonment in a detention facility, thc court may place the offender on conditional probation pursuant to 2951.02(F).

Note 2. If the violation is a felony of the 1st, 2nd, or 3rd degree the court shall impose upon the offender the mandatory fine specified under 2929.18(B)(1) unless the court determines that the offender is indigent.

Note 3. The court shall either revoke or suspend the driver's or commercial driver's license or permit of any person convicted of a violation of this section that is a felony of the 1st degree. The court shall suspend the driver's or commercial driver's license or permit of any person convicted of any other violation of this section. Any suspension under this section shall be for not less than 6 months or more than 5 years. If an offender's driver's or commercial driver's license or permit is revoked pursuant to this section, the offender at any time after the expiration of 2 years from the day on which the offender's sentence was imposed or from the day on which the offender finally was released from a prison term under the sentence, whichever is later, may file a motion with the sentencing court requesting termination of the revocation. Upon the filing of the motion and the court's finding of good cause for the termination, the court may terminate the revocation. 2925.02(D)(2)

Note 4. If the offender is a professionally licensed person or a person who has been admitted to the bar by order of the supreme court, in addition to any other sanction imposed for a violation of this section, the court shall comply with the notice provisions under 2925.38.

Note 5. If the offender pleads guilty before trial, in lieu of sentencing the offender to a term of imprisonment in a detention facility, the court may place an offender who is a felon in a community control sanction under sections 2929.16 or 2929.17 or an offender who is a misdemeanant on conditional probation, provided the offender enters an alternative residential diversion program described in this section for drug abuse treatment and counseling for at least 90 days, and the offender submits to outpatient treatment and counseling for at least 9 months upon the offender's release. If the offender complies with these terms and all other terms of the offender's sanction or probation, the charges shall be dismissed. If the offender fails to comply, the offender's probation or sanction shall be revoked and a term of imprisonment imposed. This section does not prevent the court from granting conditional probation under 2951.04 or treatment in lieu of conviction under 2951.041.

Note 6. If the offender is a woman who is pregnant at the time of sentencing and agrees to receive prenatal care and to complete a rehabilitation program at a drug treatment facility, the court shall impose a community control sanction on a felon under sections 2929.16 or 2929.17 or an offender who is a misdemeanant on conditional probation.

Table 24
Possession of Marihuana

RC 2925.11(A) & (C)(3)

DRUG	AMOUNT	LEVEL	SENTENCE
Marihuana	Less than 100 grams	MM	2929.21(D)
	100 grams but less than 200 grams	M4	2929.21(B)(4) & (C)(4)
	200 grams but less than 1,000 grams	F5	2929.13(B)
	1,000 grams but less than 5,000 grams	F3	2929.13(C)
	5,000 grams but less than 20,000 grams	F3	Presumption of prison term
	20,000 grams or more	F2	Mandatory 8 year prison term

Note 1. If the violation is a felony of the 1st, 2nd, or 3rd degree the court shall impose upon the offender the mandatory fine specified under 2929.18(B)(1) unless the court determines that the offender is indigent.

Note 2. The court shall either revoke or suspend the driver's or commercial driver's license or permit of any person convicted of a violation of this section that is a felony of the 1st degree. The court shall suspend the driver's or commercial driver's license or permit of any person convicted of any other violation of this section. Any suspension under this section shall be for not less than 6 months or more than 5 years. If an offender's driver's or commercial driver's license or permit is revoked pursuant to this section, the offender at any time after the expiration of 2 years from the day on which the offender's sentence was imposed or from the day on which the offender finally was released from a prison term under the sentence, whichever is later, may file a motion with the sentencing court requesting termination of the revocation. Upon the filing of the motion and the court's finding of good cause for the termination, the court may terminate the revocation. 2925.02(D)(2)

Note 3. If the offender is a professionally licensed person or a person who has been admitted to the bar by order of the supreme court, in addition to any other sanction imposed for a violation of this section, the court shall comply with the notice provisions under 2925.38.

Note 4. If the offender pleads guilty before trial, in lieu of sentencing the offender to a term of imprisonment in a detention facility, the court may place an offender who is a felon in a community control sanction under sections 2929.16 or 2929.17 or an offender who is a misdemeanant on conditional probation, provided the offender enters an alternative residential diversion program described in this section for drug abuse treatment and counseling for at least 90 days, and the offender submits to outpatient treatment and counseling for at least 9 months upon the offender's release. If the offender complies with these terms and all other terms of the offender's sanction or probation, the charges shall be dismissed. If the offender fails to comply, the offender's probation or sanction shall be revoked and a term of imprisonment imposed. This section does not prevent the court from granting conditional probation under 2951.04 or treatment in lieu of conviction under 2951.041.

Note 5. If the offender is a woman who is pregnant at the time of sentencing and agrees to receive prenatal care and to complete a rehabilitation program at a drug treatment facility, the court shall impose a community control sanction on a felon under sections 2929.16 or 2929.17 or an offender who is a misdemeanant on conditional probation.

Table 25
Possession of Cocaine

RC 2925.11(A) & (C)(4)

DRUG	AMOUNT	LEVEL	SENTENCE
Cocaine (powder)	Less than 5 grams	F5	2929.13(B)
	5 grams but less than 25 grams	F4	Presumption of prison term
	25 grams but less than 100 grams	F3	Mandatory prison term
	100 grams but less than 500 grams	F2	Mandatory prison term
	500 grams but less than 1,000 grams	F1	Mandatory prison term
	1,000 grams or more Major Drug Offender (2929.14(D)(3)(b))	F1	Mandatory 10 year prison term plus an additional 1 to 10 years
Cocaine (crack)	Less than 1 gram	F5	2929.13(B)
	1 gram but less than 5 grams	F4	Presumption of prison term
	5 grams but less than 10 grams	F3	Mandatory prison term
	10 grams but less than 25 grams	F2	Mandatory prison term
	25 grams but less than 100 grams	F1	Mandatory prison term
	100 grams or more Major Drug Offender (2929.14(D)(3)(b))	F1	Mandatory 10 year prison term plus an additional 1 to 10 years

Note 1. If the violation is a felony of the 1st, 2nd, or 3rd degree the court shall impose upon the offender the mandatory fine specified under 2929.18(B)(1) unless the court determines that the offender is indigent.

Note 2. The court shall either revoke or suspend the driver's or commercial driver's license or permit of any person convicted of a violation of this section that is a felony of the 1st degree. The court shall suspend the driver's or commercial driver's license or permit of any person convicted of any other violation of this section. Any suspension under this section shall be for not less than 6 months or more than 5 years. If an offender's driver's or commercial driver's license or permit is revoked pursuant to this section, the offender at any time after the expiration of 2 years from the day on which the offender's sentence was imposed or from the day on which the offender finally was released from a prison term under the sentence, whichever is later, may file a motion with the sentencing court requesting termination of the revocation. Upon the filing of the motion and the court's finding of good cause for the termination, the court may terminate the revocation. 2925.02(D)(2)

Note 3. If the offender is a professionally licensed person or a person who has been admitted to the bar by order of the supreme court, in addition to any other sanction imposed for a violation of this section, the court shall comply with the notice provisions under 2925.38.

Note 4. If the offender pleads guilty before trial, in lieu of sentencing the offender to a term of imprisonment in a detention facility, the court may place an offender who is a felon in a community control sanction under sections 2929.16 or 2929.17 or an offender who is a misdemeanant on conditional probation, provided the offender enters an alternative residential diversion program described in this section for drug abuse treatment and counseling for at least 90 days, and the offender submits to outpatient treatment and counseling for at least 9 months upon the offender's release. If the offender complies with these terms and all other terms of the offender's sanction or probation, the charges shall be dismissed. If the offender fails to comply, the offender's probation or sanction shall be revoked and a term of imprisonment imposed. This section does not prevent the court from granting conditional probation under 2951.04 or treatment in lieu of conviction under 2951.041.

Note 5. If the offender is a woman who is pregnant at the time of sentencing and agrees to receive prenatal care and to complete a rehabilitation program at a drug treatment facility, the court shall impose a community control sanction on a felon under sections 2929.16 or 2929.17 or an offender who is a misdemeanant on conditional probation.

Table 26
Possession of L.S.D.

RC 2925.11(A) & (C)(5)

DRUG	AMOUNT	LEVEL	SENTENCE
L.S.D.	Less than 10 unit doses	F5	2929.13(B)
	10 unit doses but less than 50 unit doses in a solid form or 1 gram but less than 5 grams in liquid form	F4	2929.13(C)
	50 unit doses but less than 250 unit doses in a solid form or 5 grams but less than 25 grams in liquid form	F3	Presumption of prison term
	250 unit doses but less than 1,000 unit doses in a solid form or 25 grams but less than 100 grams in liquid form	F2	Mandatory prison term
	1,000 unit doses but less than 5,000 unit doses in a solid form or 100 grams but less than 500 grams in liquid form	F1	Mandatory prison term
	5,000 unit doses or more in a solid form or 500 grams or more in liquid form Major Drug Offender (2929.14(D)(3)(b))	F1	Mandatory 10 year prison term plus an additional 1 to 10 years

Note 1. If the violation is a felony of the 1st, 2nd, or 3rd degree the court shall impose upon the offender the mandatory fine specified under 2929.18(B)(1) unless the court determines that the offender is indigent.

Note 2. The court shall either revoke or suspend the driver's or commercial driver's license or permit of any person convicted of a violation of this section that is a felony of the 1st degree. The court shall suspend the driver's or commercial driver's license or permit of any person convicted of any other violation of this section. Any suspension under this section shall be for not less than 6 months or more than 5 years. If an offender's driver's or commercial driver's license or permit is revoked pursuant to this section, the offender at any time after the expiration of 2 years from the day on which the offender's sentence was imposed or from the day on which the offender finally was released from a prison term under the sentence, whichever is later, may file a motion with the sentencing court requesting termination of the revocation. Upon the filing of the motion and the court's finding of good cause for the termination, the court may terminate the revocation. 2925.02(D)(2)

Note 3. If the offender is a professionally licensed person or a person who has been admitted to the bar by order of the supreme court, in addition to any other sanction imposed for a violation of this section, the court shall comply with the notice provisions under 2925.38.

Note 4. If the offender pleads guilty before trial, in lieu of sentencing the offender to a term of imprisonment in a detention facility, the court may place an offender who is a felon in a community control sanction under sections 2929.16 or 2929.17 or an offender who is a misdemeanant on conditional probation, provided the offender enters an alternative residential diversion program described in this section for drug abuse treatment and counseling for at least 90 days, and the offender submits to outpatient treatment and counseling for at least 9 months upon the offender's release. If the offender complies with these terms and all other terms of the offender's sanction or probation, the charges shall be dismissed. If the offender fails to comply, the offender's probation or sanction shall be revoked and a term of imprisonment imposed. This section does not prevent the court from granting conditional probation under 2951.04 or treatment in lieu of conviction under 2951.041.

Note 5. If the offender is a woman who is pregnant at the time of sentencing and agrees to receive prenatal care and to complete a rehabilitation program at a drug treatment facility, the court shall impose a community control sanction on a felon under sections 2929.16 or 2929.17 or an offender who is a misdemeanant on conditional probation.

Table 27
Possession of Heroin

RC 2925.11(A) & (C)(6)

DRUG	AMOUNT	LEVEL	SENTENCE
Heroin	Less than ten unit doses or less than one gram	F5	2929.13(B)
	10 unit doses but less than 50 unit doses or 1 gram but less than five grams	F4	2929.13(C)
	50 unit doses but less than 100 unit doses or 5 grams but less than ten grams	F3	Presumption of prison term
	100 unit doses but less than 500 unit doses or 10 grams but less than 50 grams	F2	Mandatory prison term
	500 unit doses but less than 2,500 unit doses or 50 grams but less than 250 grams	F1	Mandatory prison term
	2,500 unit doses or more or 250 grams or more Major Drug Offender (2929.14(D)(3)(b))	F1	Mandatory 10 year prison term plus an additional 1 to 10 years

Note 1. If the violation is a felony of the 1st, 2nd, or 3rd degree the court shall impose upon the offender the mandatory fine specified under 2929.18(B)(1) unless the court determines that the offender is indigent.

Note 2. The court shall either revoke or suspend the driver's or commercial driver's license or permit of any person convicted of a violation of this section that is a felony of the 1st degree. The court shall suspend the driver's or commercial driver's license or permit of any person convicted of any other violation of this section. Any suspension under this section shall be for not less than 6 months or more than 5 years. If an offender's driver's or commercial driver's license or permit is revoked pursuant to this section, the offender at any time after the expiration of 2 years from the day on which the offender's sentence was imposed or from the day on which the offender finally was released from a prison term under the sentence, whichever is later, may file a motion with the sentencing court requesting termination of the revocation. Upon the filing of the motion and the court's finding of good cause for the termination, the court may terminate the revocation. 2925.02(D)(2)

Note 3. If the offender is a professionally licensed person or a person who has been admitted to the bar by order of the supreme court, in addition to any other sanction imposed for a violation of this section, the court shall comply with the notice provisions under 2925.38.

Note 4. If the offender pleads guilty before trial, in lieu of sentencing the offender to a term of imprisonment in a detention facility, the court may place an offender who is a felon in a community control sanction under sections 2929.16 or 2929.17 or an offender who is a misdemeanant on conditional probation, provided the offender enters an alternative residential diversion program described in this section for drug abuse treatment and counseling for at least 90 days, and the offender submits to outpatient treatment and counseling for at least 9 months upon the offender's release. If the offender complies with these terms and all other terms of the offender's sanction or probation, the charges shall be dismissed. If the offender fails to comply, the offender's probation or sanction shall be revoked and a term of imprisonment imposed. This section does not prevent the court from granting conditional probation under 2951.04 or treatment in lieu of conviction under 2951.041.

Note 5. If the offender is a woman who is pregnant at the time of sentencing and agrees to receive prenatal care and to complete a rehabilitation program at a drug treatment facility, the court shall impose a community control sanction on a felon under sections 2929.16 or 2929.17 or an offender who is a misdemeanant on conditional probation.

Table 28
Possession of Hashish

RC 2925.11(A) & (C)(7)

DRUG	AMOUNT	LEVEL	SENTENCE
Hashish	Less than 5 grams (solid)	MM	2929.21(D)
	Less than 1 gram (liquid)	MM	2929.21(D)
	5 grams but less than 10 grams (solid)	M4	2929.21(B)(4) & (C)(4)
	1 gram but less than 2 grams (liquid)	M4	2929.21(B)(4) & (C)(4)
	10 grams but less than 50 grams (solid)	F5	2929.13(B)
	2 grams but less than 10 grams (liquid)	F5	2929.13(B)
	50 grams but less than 250 grams (solid)	F3	2929.13(C)
	10 grams but less than 50 grams (liquid)	F3	2929.13(C)
	250 grams but less than 1,000 grams (solid)	F3	Presumption of prison term
	50 grams but less than 200 grams (liquid)	F3	Presumption of prison term
	1,000 grams or more (solid)	F2	Mandatory 8 year prison term
	200 grams or more (liquid)	F2	Mandatory 8 year prison term

Note 1. If the violation is a felony of the 1st, 2nd, or 3rd degree the court shall impose upon the offender the mandatory fine specified under 2929.18(B)(1) unless the court determines that the offender is indigent.

Note 2. The court shall either revoke or suspend the driver's or commercial driver's license or permit of any person convicted of a violation of this section that is a felony of the 1st degree. The court shall suspend the driver's or commercial driver's license or permit of any person convicted of any other violation of this section. Any suspension under this section shall be for not less than 6 months or more than 5 years. If an offender's driver's or commercial driver's license or permit is revoked pursuant to this section, the offender at any time after the expiration of 2 years from the day on which the offender's sentence was imposed or from the day on which the offender finally was released from a prison term under the sentence, whichever is later, may file a motion with the sentencing court requesting termination of the revocation. Upon the filing of the motion and the court's finding of good cause for the termination, the court may terminate the revocation. 2925.02(D)(2)

Note 3. If the offender is a professionally licensed person or a person who has been admitted to the bar by order of the supreme court, in addition to any other sanction imposed for a violation of this section, the court shall comply with the notice provisions under 2925.38.

Note 4. If the offender pleads guilty before trial, in lieu of sentencing the offender to a term of imprisonment in a detention facility, the court may place an offender who is a felon in a community control sanction under sections 2929.16 or 2929.17 or an offender who is a misdemeanant on conditional probation, provided the offender enters an alternative residential diversion program described in this section for drug abuse treatment and counseling for at least 90 days, and the offender submits to outpatient treatment and counseling for at least 9 months upon the offender's release. If the offender complies with these terms and all other terms of the offender's sanction or probation, the charges shall be dismissed. If the offender fails to comply, the offender's probation or sanction shall be revoked and a term of imprisonment imposed. This section does not prevent the court from granting conditional probation under 2951.04 or treatment in lieu of conviction under 2951.041.

Note 5. If the offender is a woman who is pregnant at the time of sentencing and agrees to receive prenatal care and to complete a rehabilitation program at a drug treatment facility, the court shall impose a community control sanction on a felon under sections 2929.16 or 2929.17 or an offender who is a misdemeanant on conditional probation.

Table 29
Possessing Drug Abuse Instruments

RC 2925.12

LEVEL	OFFENSE	SENTENCE
M2	No prior drug abuse convictions	2929.21(B)(2) & (C)(2)
M1	With prior drug abuse convictions	2929.21(B)(1) & (C)(1)

Note 1. The court shall suspend the driver's or commercial driver's license or permit of any person convicted of a violation of this section. Any suspension under this section shall be for not less than 6 months or more than 5 years.

Note 2. If the offender is a professionally licensed person or a person who has been admitted to the bar by order of the supreme court, in addition to any other sanction imposed for a violation of this section, the court shall comply with the notice provisions under 2925.38.

Table 30
Permitting Drug Abuse

RC 2925.13

LEVEL	OFFENSE	SENTENCE
M1		2929.21(B)(1) & (C)(1)
F5	Felony drug abuse offense committed in vicinity of school or juvenile	2929.13(C)

Note 1. The court shall suspend the driver's or commercial driver's license or permit of any person convicted of a violation of this section. Any suspension under this section shall be for not less than 6 months or more than 5 years.

Note 2. If the offender is a professionally licensed person or a person who has been admitted to the bar by order of the supreme court, in addition to any other sanction imposed for a violation of this section, the court shall comply with the notice provisions under 2925.38.

Note 3. Premises or real estate used in offense is a nuisance subject to abatement.

Table 31
Drug Paraphernalia

RC 2925.14

OFFENSE	LEVEL	SENTENCE
Illegal use or possession of drug paraphernalia 2925.14(C)(1)	M4	2929.21(B)(4) & (C)(4)
Dealing in drug paraphernalia 2925.14(C)(2)	M2	2929.21(B)(2) & (C)(2)
Selling drug paraphernalia to juveniles 2925.14(C)(2)	M1	2929.21(B)(1) & (C)(1)
Illegal advertising of drug paraphernalia 2925.14(C)(3)	M2	2929.21(B)(2) & (C)(2)

Note 1. The court shall suspend the driver's or commercial driver's license or permit of any person convicted of a violation of this section. Any suspension under this section shall be for not less than 6 months or more than 5 years.

Note 2. If the offender is a professionally licensed person or a person who has been admitted to the bar by order of the supreme court, in addition to any other sanction imposed for a violation of this section, the court shall comply with the notice provisions under 2925.38.

Note 3. Notwithstanding sections 2933.42 and 2933.43, any drug paraphernalia that was used, possessed, sold, or manufactured in violation of this section shall be seized, after a conviction for that violation shall be forfeited, and upon forfeiture shall be disposed of pursuant to 2933.41(D)(8).

Table 32
Deception to Obtain a Dangerous Drug

RC 2925.22

DRUG	LEVEL	SENTENCE
Schedule I or II *	F4	2929.13(C)
Dangerous drug, Schedule III, IV, or V, or Marihuana	F5	2929.13(C)

* Except marihuana

Note 1. The court shall suspend the driver's or commercial driver's license or permit of any person convicted of a violation of this section. Any suspension under this section shall be for not less than 6 months or more than 5 years.

Note 2. If the offender is a professionally licensed person or a person who has been admitted to the bar by order of the supreme court, in addition to any other sanction imposed for a violation of this section, the court shall comply with the notice provisions under 2925.38.

Table 33
Illegal Processing of Drug Documents

RC 2925.23

DRUG	LEVEL	SENTENCE
Schedule I or II *	F4	2929.13(C)
Dangerous drug, Schedule III, IV, or V, or Marihuana	F5	2929.13(C)
Regardless of drug, violation of (B)(2), (4) or (5) and (C)(2), (4), (5), or (6)	F5	2929.13(B)

* Except marihuana

Note 1. The court shall suspend the driver's or commercial driver's license or permit of any person convicted of a violation of this section. Any suspension under this section shall be for not less than 6 months or more than 5 years.

Note 2. If the offender is a professionally licensed person or a person who has been admitted to the bar by order of the supreme court, in addition to any other sanction imposed for a violation of this section, the court shall comply with the notice provisions under 2925.38.

Table 34
Abusing Harmful Intoxicants

RC 2925.31

LEVEL	OFFENSE	SENTENCE
M1	No prior drug abuse convictions	2929.21(B)(1) & (C)(1)
F5	With prior drug abuse convictions	2929.13(B)

Note 1. The court shall suspend the driver's or commercial driver's license or permit of any person convicted of a violation of this section. Any suspension under this section shall be for not less than 6 months or more than 5 years.

Note 2. If the offender is a professionally licensed person or a person who has been admitted to the bar by order of the supreme court, in addition to any other sanction imposed for a violation of this section, the court shall comply with the notice provisions under 2925.38.

Table 35
Trafficking in Harmful Intoxicants

RC 2925.32

LEVEL	OFFENSE	SENTENCE
F5	No prior drug abuse convictions	2929.13(B)
F4	With prior drug abuse convictions	2929.13(B)
M4	Nitrous oxide	2929.21(B)(4) & (C)(4)

Note 1. The court shall suspend the driver's or commercial driver's license or permit of any person convicted of a violation of this section. Any suspension under this section shall be for not less than 6 months or more than 5 years.

Note 2. If the offender is a professionally licensed person or a person who has been admitted to the bar by order of the supreme court, in addition to any other sanction imposed for a violation of this section, the court shall comply with the notice provisions under 2925.38.

Table 36
Illegal Dispensing of Drug Samples

RC 2925.36

DRUG	LEVEL	SENTENCE
Schedule I or II [1]	F5	2929.13(C)
Dangerous drug, Schedule III, IV, or V, or Marihuana	M2	2929.21(B)(2) & (C)(2)
Violation involves sale, offer to sell, or possession of Schedule I or II controlled substance, except marihuana Major Drug Offender (2929.14(D)(3)(b)) [2]	F1	Mandatory 10 year prison term plus an additional 1 to 10 years
OFFENSE COMMITTED IN VICINITY OF SCHOOL OR JUVENILE		
Schedule I or II [1]	F4	2929.13(C)
Dangerous drug, Schedule III, IV, or V, or Marihuana	M1	2929.21(B)(1) & (C)(1)
Violation involves sale, offer to sell, or possession of Schedule I or II controlled substance, except marihuana Major Drug Offender (2929.14(D)(3)(b)) [2]	F1	Mandatory 10 year prison term plus an additional 1 to 10 years

[1] Except marihuana
[2] Requires 2941.1410 specification in indictment

Note 1. The court shall suspend the driver's or commercial driver's license or permit of any person convicted of a violation of this section. Any suspension under this section shall be for not less than 6 months or more than 5 years.

Note 2. If the offender is a professionally licensed person or a person who has been admitted to the bar by order of the supreme court, in addition to any other sanction imposed for a violation of this section, the court shall comply with the notice provisions under 2925.38.

Table 37
Counterfeit Controlled Substances *

RC 2925.37

OFFENSE	LEVEL	SENTENCE
Possession of counterfeit controlled substances 2925.37(A)	M1	2929.21(B)(1) & (C)(1)
Trafficking in counterfeit controlled substances 2925.37(B) & (C)	F5	2929.13(C)
Aggravated trafficking in counterfeit controlled substances 2925.37(D)	F4	2929.13(C)
Promoting and encouraging drug abuse 2925.37(E)	F5	2929.13(C)
Fraudulent drug advertising 2925.37(F)	F5	2929.13(C)
OFFENSE COMMITTED IN VICINITY OF SCHOOL OR JUVENILE		
Trafficking in counterfeit controlled substances 2925.37(B) & (C)	F4	2929.13(C)
Promoting and encouraging drug abuse 2925.37(E)	F4	2929.13(C)
Fraudulent drug advertising 2925.37(F)	F4	2929.13(C)

* Except marihuana

Note 1. The court shall suspend the driver's or commercial driver's license or permit of any person convicted of a violation of this section. Any suspension under this section shall be for not less than 6 months or more than 5 years.

Note 2. If the offender is a professionally licensed person or a person who has been admitted to the bar by order of the supreme court, in addition to any other sanction imposed for a violation of this section, the court shall comply with the notice provisions under 2925.38.

SENTENCES AND FINES CHECKLIST

Checklist 1: Aggravated Murder and Murder Sentencing

Part One—Aggravated Murder (RC 2903.01)

A. Imposition of life sentence

If the indictment charging aggravated murder does not contain an aggravating circumstances specification listed in RC 2929.04(A), or if the offender is found guilty on the charge of aggravated murder but not guilty on the aggravating circumstances specification, then the court shall impose a life sentence with parole eligibility after 20 years of imprisonment. (RC 2929.03(A); RC 2929.03(C)(1))

B. Presence of aggravating circumstances specification

If the indictment contains an aggravating circumstances specification, the jury's verdict shall separately state:

(1) Whether the offender was found guilty or not guilty of the principal charge;

(2) If guilty of the principal charge, whether the offender was eighteen years of age or older at the time of the commission of the offense, if the matter of age was raised by the offender pursuant to RC 2929.023;

(3) Whether the offender was guilty or not guilty of each of the aggravating circumstances specifications.

C. Finding of guilt on principal charge and aggravating circumstance.

If found guilty of the principal charge and of one or more of the specified aggravating circumstances, the penalty to be imposed shall be:

(1) Death

(a) Presentence report is required upon defendant's request;

(b) Mental examination is required upon defendant's request;

(c) No one under the age of eighteen at the date of the commission of the offense shall receive the death sentence;

(d) Jury or three-judge panel must consider the aggravating circumstances listed in RC 2929.04(A) and any mitigating factors offered by the defendant. Mitigating factors include both those listed in RC 2929.04(B) and all others offered by the defendant;

(e) Defendant has the burden of going forward with evidence of any factors in mitigation of the imposition of the death sentence;

(f) Prosecution has the burden of proving, by proof beyond a reasonable doubt, that the aggravating circumstances the defendant was found guilty of committing are sufficient to outweigh the factors in mitigation of the sentence of death;

(g) Jury must unanimously find, by proof beyond a reasonable doubt, that the aggravating circumstances the defendant was found guilty of outweigh the mitigating factors in order to recommend the death sentence;

(h) If the jury recommends the death penalty, the court must examine the evidence and independently determine if the aggravating circumstances the defendant was found guilty of outweigh the mitigating factors;

(i) Court or three-judge panel, upon imposing a sentence of death, must state in a separate opinion the specific findings:
   (i) As to the existence of mitigating factors, both as described in RC 2929.04(B) and other mitigating factors presented by the defendant;
   (ii) Aggravating circumstances the offender was found guilty of committing;
   (iii) Reasons why the aggravating circumstances the offender was found guilty of committing were sufficient to outweigh the mitigating factors.

(2) Life imprisonment without parole.
(3) Life imprisonment with parole eligibility after 25 years of imprisonment.
(4) Life imprisonment with parole eligibility after 30 years of imprisonment.

Part Two—Murder (RC 2903.02)

15 years to life imprisonment—indefinite term.

Part Three—Imposition of Death Penalty (RC 2929.04)

A. Aggravated murder—death penalty

Imposition of the death penalty for aggravated murder is precluded, unless one or more of the following aggravating circumstances is specified in the indictment or count in the indictment pursuant to RC 2941.14 and proved beyond a reasonable doubt (RC 2929.04(A)):

(1) Offense was the assassination of the president of the United States or person in line of succession to the presidency, or of the governor or lieutenant governor of Ohio, or of the president-elect or vice president-elect of the United States, or of the governor-elect or lieutenant governor-elect of Ohio, or of a candidate for any of the foregoing offices;
(2) Offense was committed for hire;
(3) Offense was committed for the purpose of escaping detection, apprehension, trial, or punishment for another offense committed by the offender;
(4) Offense was committed while the offender was a prisoner in a detention facility as defined in RC 2921.02, except detention does not include hospitalization, institutionalization, or confinement in a mental health facility or mental retardation and developmentally disabled facility unless at time of offense either the offender was in the facility as a result of being charged with a RC violation or was under detention as a result of being convicted of a RC violation.
(5) Prior to the offense at bar, the offender was convicted of an offense an essential element of which was the purposeful killing of or attempt to kill another, or the offense at bar was part of a course of conduct involving the purposeful killing of or attempt to kill two or more persons by the offender;
(6) Victim of the offense was a law enforcement officer, as defined in RC 2911.01, whom the offender had reasonable cause to know or knew to be such, and either the victim, at the time of the commission of the offense, was engaged in his duties, or it was the offender's specific purpose to kill a law enforcement officer;
(7) Offense was committed while the offender was committing, attempting to commit, or fleeing immediately after committing or attempting to commit kidnapping, rape, aggravated arson, aggravated robbery, or aggravated burglary, and either the offender was the principal offender in the commission of the aggravated murder or, if not the principal offender, committed the aggravated murder with prior calculation and design;
(8) Victim of the aggravated murder was a witness to an offense, who was purposely killed to prevent the victim's testimony in any criminal proceeding and the aggravated murder was not committed during the commission, attempted commission, or flight immediately after the commission or attempted commission of the offense to which the victim was a witness, or the victim of the aggravated murder was a witness to an offense and purposely killed in retaliation for his testimony in any criminal proceeding.
(9) Offender, in commission of offense, purposely caused the death of another who was under 13 years of age at time of offense, and either offender was the principal offender in the aggravated murder or, if not the principal offender, committed the offense with prior calculation and design.

B. Mitigating factors (RC 2929.04(B)) (Note: these are not **exclusive of other factors offered by the defendant)**

(1) Whether the victim induced or facilitated the offense;

(2) Whether it is unlikely that the offense would have been committed, but for the fact that the offender was under duress, coercion, or strong provocation;

(3) Whether, at the time of committing the offense, the offender, because of a mental disease or defect, lacked substantial capacity to appreciate the criminality of his conduct or to conform his conducts to the requirements of the law;

(4) Youth of the offender;

(5) Offender's lack of a significant history of prior criminal convictions and delinquency adjudications;

(6) If the offender was a participant in the offense but not the principal offender, the degree of the offender's participation in the offense and the degree of the offender's participation in the acts that led to the death of the victim;

(7) Any other factors that are relevant to the issue of whether the offender should be sentenced to death.

Checklist 2:
Felony Sentencing

Part One—Felonies

A. Overriding purposes of felony sentencing (2929.11)

(1) To protect the public from future crime by the offender and others, and
(2) To punish the offender.

B. Achieving the purposes of felony sentencing—Generally

(1) The sentencing court shall consider the need for incapacitating the offender, deterring the offender and others from future crime, rehabilitating the offender, and making restitution to the victim of the offense, the public, or both.
(2) A sentence imposed for a felony shall be reasonably calculated to achieve the two overriding purposes of felony sentencing commensurate with and not demeaning the seriousness of the offender's conduct and its impact upon the victim, and consistent with sentences imposed for similar crimes committed by similar offenders.
(3) A court that imposes a sentence upon an offender for a felony shall not base the sentence upon the race, ethnic background, gender, or religion of the offender.

C. Factors indicating that offender's conduct is more serious than conduct normally constituting the offense (2929.12(B))

(1) The physical or mental injury suffered by the victim of the offense due to the conduct of the offender was exacerbated because of the physical or mental condition or age of the victim.
(2) The victim of the offense suffered serious physical, psychological, or economic harm as a result of the offense.
(3) The offender held a public office or position of trust in the community, and the offense related to that office or position.
(4) The offender's occupation, elected office, or profession obliged the offender to prevent the offense or bring others committing it to justice.
(5) The offender's professional reputation or occupation, elected office, or profession was used to facilitate the offense or is likely to influence the future conduct of others.
(6) The offender's relationship with the victim facilitated the offense.
(7) The offender committed the offense for hire or as a part of an organized criminal activity.
(8) In committing the offense, the offender was motivated by prejudice based on race, ethnic background, gender, sexual orientation, or religion.
(9) Any other relevant factors.

D. Factors indicating that offender's conduct is less serious than conduct normally constituting the offense (2929.12(C))

(1) The victim induced or facilitated the offense.
(2) In committing the offense, the offender acted under strong provocation.
(3) In committing the offense, the offender did not cause or expect to cause physical harm to any person or property.
(4) There are substantial grounds to mitigate the offender's conduct, although the grounds are not enough to constitute a defense.
(5) Any other relevant factors.

E. Factors indicating that the offender is likely to commit future crimes (2929.12(D))

(1) At the time of committing the offense, the offender was under release from confinement before trial or sentencing, under a sanction imposed pursuant to sections 2929.16, 2929.17, or 2929.18, or under post-release control pursuant to section 2967.28 or any other provision for an earlier offense.

(2) The offender previously was adjudicated a delinquent child pursuant to Chapter 2151., or the offender has a history of criminal convictions.

(3) The offender has not been rehabilitated to a satisfactory degree after previously being adjudicated a delinquent child pursuant to Chapter 2151., or the offender has not responded favorably to sanctions previously imposed for criminal convictions.

(4) The offender has demonstrated a pattern of drug or alcohol abuse that is related to the offense, and the offender refuses to acknowledge that the offender has demonstrated that pattern, or the offender refuses treatment for the drug or alcohol abuse.

(5) The offender shows no remorse for the offense.

(6) Any other relevant factors.

F. Factors indicating that the offender is unlikely to commit future crimes (2929.12(E))

(1) Prior to committing the offense, the offender had not been adjudicated a delinquent child.

(2) Prior to committing the offense, the offender had not been convicted of or pleaded guilty to a criminal offense.

(3) Prior to committing the offense, the offender had led a law-abiding life for a significant number of years.

(4) The offense was committed under circumstances unlikely to recur.

(5) The offender shows genuine remorse for the offense.

(6) Any other relevant factors.

Part Two—Misdemeanors

A. Imposition of fine or imprisonment (RC 2929.22)

(1) Risk that the offender will commit another offense and the need for protecting the public therefrom;

(2) Nature and circumstances of the offense;

(3) History, character and condition of the offender and his need for correctional or rehabilitative treatment;

(4) Any statement made by the victim, if the offense is a misdemeanor as specified in RC 2930.01(A);

(5) Ability and resources of the offender and the nature of the burden that payment of a fine will impose on him.

B. Factors in favor of imposing imprisonment (RC 2929.22) (Note: not controlling on court's discretion)

(1) Offender is a repeat or dangerous offender;

(2) Regardless of whether the offender knew the age of the victim, the victim of the offense was 65 years of age or older, permanently and totally disabled, or less than 18 years of age at the time of the commission of the offense.

C. Factors against imposing imprisonment (RC 2929.12; RC 2929.22)

(1) The victim induced or facilitated the offense.

(2) In committing the offense, the offender acted under strong provocation.

(3) In committing the offense, the offender did not cause or expect to cause physical harm to any person or property.

(4) There are substantial grounds to mitigate the offender's conduct, although the grounds are not enough to constitute a defense.

(5) Prior to committing the offense, the offender had not been adjudicated a delinquent child.

(6) Prior to committing the offense, the offender had not been convicted of or pleaded guilty to a criminal offense.

(7) Prior to committing the offense, the offender had led a law-abiding life for a significant number of years.
(8) The offense was committed under circumstances unlikely to recur.
(9) The offender shows genuine remorse for the offense.

D. Financial Sanctions (RC 2929.18)

(1) Financial Sanctions
  (a) Restitution
  (b) Fines
    (i) Felony 1st degree not more than $20,000.
    (ii) Felony 2nd degree not more than $15,000.
    (iii) Felony 3rd degree not more than $10,000.
    (iv) Felony 4th degree not more than $5,000.
    (v) Felony 5th degree not more than $2,500.
  (c) All or part of the costs of sanctions
  (d) Reimbursement for costs
(2) Mandatory fines
  (a) 1st, 2nd, 3rd degree felonies for violation of Chapters 2925, 3719, or 4729 (at least one half of the maximum statutory fine).
  (b) 4th and 5th degree felony violations as provided in Chapters 2925, 3719, or 4729.
  (c) 4th degree felony OMVI offense (amount specified in 4511.99).

Note: Additional specified fines for violation of sections 2925.03 and 2925.07 may be imposed.

Note: Additional fines may be imposed for 1st and 2nd degree felony violations of 2925.03 or 1st, 2nd and 3rd degree violations of 2925.07 if the fines imposed under 2929.18(B)(1) and (4) does not exceed the maximum allowed fines under 2929.18(A)(3).

(3) Court shall not impose a fine if the court determines the offender is indigent.

Checklist 3: Judicial Release

RC 2929.20

Part One—Eligible Offenders

A. A person who has been convicted of or pleaded guilty to a felony, who is serving a stated prison term of 10 years or less and who is not serving a mandatory prison term, or

B. A person who has been convicted of or pleaded guilty to a felony, who was sentenced to a mandatory prison term and another prison term of 10 years or less, and who has served the mandatory prison term.*

* Defendants sentenced under RC 2929.14(D)(1) [gun specifications] are eligible; defendants sentenced as "repeat violent offenders" under RC 2929.14(D)(2) or as "major drug offenders" under RC 2929.14(D)(3) are ineligible. RC 2929.20(A)(1)(c) and RC 2929.20(A)(2)(a) and (b).

Part Two—Motion for Judicial Release—Filing

A. On a motion by an eligible offender, or

B. On the sentencing court's own motion.

Part Three—Motion for Judicial Release—Timing

A. If the stated prison term was imposed for a felony of the 4th or 5th degree, the eligible offender shall file the motion not earlier than 30 days or later that 90 days after the offender is delivered to a state correctional institution.

B. If the stated prison term was imposed for a felony of the 1st, 2nd, or 3rd degree, the eligible offender shall file the motion not earlier than 180 days after the offender is delivered to a state correctional institution.

C. If the stated prison term is more than 5 years but less than 10 years, the eligible offender may file after serving 5 years of the stated prison sentence.

D. If the offender was sentenced to a mandatory prison term and a consecutive prison term other than a mandatory prison term that is 10 years or less, the offender shall file the motion within the time authorized by this section for the felony for which the prison term other than the mandatory prison term was imposed, but the time for filing the motion does not begin to run until after the expiration of the mandatory prison term.

Part Four—Hearing—Timing

A. The court may deny a motion without a hearing, but shall not grant the motion in any case without a hearing. If the court denies the motion filed by an eligible offender after a hearing, the court shall not consider a judicial release on its own motion. If the court denies the motion without a hearing, the court may consider a subsequent motion for judicial release. The court shall hold only one hearing for any eligible offender.

B. A hearing shall be conducted in open court within 60 days after the date on which the motion is filed, however, the court may delay the hearing for a period not to exceed 180 additional days.

C. If the court schedules a hearing on the motion, the court shall enter its ruling on the motion within 10 days after the hearing. If the court denies the motion without a hearing, the court shall enter its ruling on the motion within 60 days after the motion is filed.

Part Five—Hearing—Notice

A. If a court schedules a hearing on the motion filed by an eligible offender or on its own motion, the court shall notify the eligible offender of the hearing. The eligible offender shall promptly serve a copy of the notice of the hearing on the head of the state correctional institution in which the eligible offender is confined.

B. If the court schedules a hearing on its own motion for judicial release, the court promptly shall give notice of the hearing to the prosecuting attorney of the county in which the eligible offender was indicted.

C. Upon receipt of the notice from the court, the prosecuting attorney shall notify the victim of the offense for which the stated prison term was imposed or the victim's representative, pursuant to section 2930.16, of the hearing.

Part Six—Hearing—Institution Report

A. Prior to the date of the hearing on a motion for judicial release, the head of the state correctional institution in which the eligible offender in question is confined shall send to the court a report on the eligible offender's conduct in the institution and any institution from which the eligible offender may have been transferred.

B. The report shall cover the eligible offender's participation in school, vocational training, work, treatment, and other rehabilitative activities and any disciplinary action taken against the eligible offender.

C. The report shall be made part of the record of the hearing.

Part Seven—Hearing—Offender's Presence At Hearing

A. If the court grants a hearing on the motion for judicial release, the eligible offender shall attend the hearing if ordered to do so by the court.

B. Upon receipt of the copy of the journal entry containing the order, the head of the state correctional institution in which the eligible offender is incarcerated shall deliver the eligible offender to the sheriff of the county in which the hearing is to be held. The sheriff shall convey the eligible offender to the hearing and return the offender to the institution after the hearing.

Part Eight—Hearing—Evidence

A. The court shall afford the eligible offender and the eligible offender's counsel an opportunity to present oral and written information relevant to the motion.

B. The court shall afford the prosecuting attorney, the victim or victim's representative, as defined in section 2930.01, and any other person the court determines is likely to present additional relevant information, an opportunity to present oral and written information relevant to the motion.

C. The court shall consider any statement of a victim made pursuant to sections 2930.14 or 2930.17 and any victim impact statement prepared pursuant to section 2947.051.

D. After ruling on the motion, the court shall notify the victim of the ruling in accordance with sections 2930.03 and 2930.16.

Part Nine—Presumption of Prison Term

A. A court shall not grant a judicial release to an eligible offender who is imprisoned for a felony of the 1st or 2nd degree, or to an eligible offender who committed an offense contained in Chapters 2925. or 3719. and for whom there was a presumption in favor of a prison term under section 2929.13, unless the court, with reference to the factors described in section 2929.12, finds both of the following:

(1) That a sanction other than a prison term would adequately punish the offender and protect the public from future criminal violations by the eligible offender because factors in favor of release outweigh factors presented at the hearing indicating a likelihood of recidivism, and

(2) That a sanction other than a prison term would not demean the seriousness of the offense because factors indicating that the eligible offender's conduct in committing the offense was less serious than conduct normally constituting the offense outweigh factors indicating that the eligible offender's conduct was more serious than conduct normally constituting the offense.

B. The court that grants a judicial release to an eligible offender shall specify on the record both findings required and also shall list all the factors that were presented at the hearing.

Part Ten—Release

A. If a court grants a motion for judicial release, the court shall order the release of the eligible offender, shall place the eligible offender on post-release control under an appropriate community control sanction and under the supervision of the probation department serving the court. The court shall also impose a mandatory condition as set out in RC 2967.131.

B. The court shall reserve the right to reimpose the sentence that it reduced pursuant to the judicial release if the offender violates the sanction. If the court reimposes the reduced sentence pursuant to this reserved right, it may do so either concurrently with, or consecutive to, any new sentence imposed upon the eligible offender as a result of the violation.

C. The period of post-release control shall be no longer than 5 years, less the amount of time the eligible offender spent in jail for the offense and in prison.

D. The court shall serve a copy of the findings upon counsel for the parties within 15 days after the date on which the court grants the motion for judicial release.

E. Prior to being release pursuant to a judicial release granted under this section, the eligible offender shall serve any extension of sentence that was imposed under section 2967.11.

Checklist 4:
Administrative Extension of Prison Term for Offenses Committed During Term "Bad Time" Provisions

RC 2967.11

Part One—Duration of Extension

A. The parole board may extend the stated prison term of a prisoner as a result of the prisoner's committing a violation while serving the prison term. The parole board may order an extension for a period of 15, 30, 60, or 90 days.

B. The parole board may not extend a prisoner's stated prison term for a period longer than one-half of the term's duration for all violations during the course of the term.

Part Two—Rules Infraction Board—Hearing

A. When a prisoner in an institution is alleged by any person to have committed a violation, the allegation shall be investigated and a report made to the rules infraction board which shall hold a hearing on the allegation to determine, for purposes of the parole board's possible extension of the prisoner's stated prison term, whether there is evidence of a violation.

B. The accused prisoner shall have the right to testify and be assisted by a member of the staff of the institution who is designated pursuant to rules adopted by the department to assist the prisoner in presenting a defense before the board in the hearing.

C. The rules infraction board shall make an audio tape of the hearing.

D. The board shall report its finding to the head of the institution within 10 days after the date of the hearing. If the board finds any evidence of a violation, it shall include with its finding a recommendation regarding a period of time by which the prisoner's stated prison term should be extended as a result of the violation. If the board does not find any evidence of a violation, the board shall terminate the matter.

Part Three—Institution Report

A. Within 10 days after receiving from the rules infraction board a finding and a recommendation that the prisoner's stated prison term be extended, the head of the institution shall review the finding and determine whether the prisoner committed a violation.

B. If the head of the institution determines by clear and convincing evidence that the prisoner committed a violation and concludes that the prisoner's stated prison term should be extended as a result of the violation, the head of the institution shall report the determination in a finding to the parole board within 10 days after making the determination and shall include with the finding a recommendation regarding the length of the extension of the stated prison term.

C. If the head of the institution does not determine by clear and convincing evidence that the prisoner committed the violation or does not conclude that the prisoner's stated prison term should be extended, the head of the institution shall terminate the matter.

Part Four—Parole Board Review

A. Within 30 days after receiving a report from the head of an institution containing a finding and recommendation, the parole board shall review the findings of the rules infraction board and the head of the institution to determine whether there is clear and convincing evidence that the prisoner committed the violation and, to determine whether the stated prison term should be extended and the length of time by which to extend it.

B. If the parole board determines that there is clear and convincing evidence that the prisoner committed the violation and that the prisoner's stated prison term should be extended, the board shall consider the nature of the violation, other conduct of the prisoner while in prison, and any other evidence relevant to maintaining order in the institution. After considering these factors, the board shall extend the stated prison term by either 15, 30, 60, or 90 days for the violation, subject to the maximum extension authorized by this section.

C. The parole board shall act to extend a stated prison term no later than 60 days from the date of the finding by the rules infraction board.

Part Five—Violations At End of Stated Prison Term

A. If an accusation of a violation is made within 60 days before the end of a prisoner's stated prison term, the rules infraction board, head of the institution, and parole board shall attempt to complete the procedures required by this section before the prisoner's stated prison term ends.

B. If necessary, the accused prisoner may be held in the institution for not more than 10 days after the end of the prisoner's stated prison term pending review of the violation and determination regarding an extension of the stated prison term.

Part Six—Additional Prosecution of Violation

A. This section does not preclude the department of rehabilitation and correction from referring a criminal offense allegedly committed by a prisoner to the appropriate prosecuting authority or from disciplining a prisoner through the use of disciplinary processes other than the extension of the prisoner's stated prison term.

Checklist 5: Parole Eligibility

RC 2967.13

Part One— A prisoner serving a sentence of imprisonment for a felony for which an indefinite term of imprisonment is imposed for an offense committed on or after 7–1–96 becomes eligible for parole at the expiration of the prisoner's minimum term and the prisoner is not entitled to any earned credit under section 2967.193.

Part Two— A prisoner serving a sentence of imprisonment for life with parole eligibility after serving 20 years of imprisonment imposed pursuant to sections 2929.022 or 2929.03 for an offense committed on or after 7–1–96 becomes eligible for parole after serving a term of 20 years and the prisoner is not entitled to any earned credit under section 2967.193.

Part Three— A prisoner serving a sentence of imprisonment for life with parole eligibility after serving 20 full years of imprisonment imposed pursuant to sections 2929.022 or 2929.03 for an offense committed on or after 7–1–96 becomes eligible for parole after serving a term of 20 full years and the prisoner is not entitled to any earned credit under section 2967.193.

Part Four— A prisoner serving a sentence of imprisonment for life with parole eligibility after serving 30 full years of imprisonment imposed pursuant to sections 2929.022 or 2929.03 for an offense committed on or after 7–1–96 becomes eligible for parole after serving a term of 30 full years and the prisoner is not entitled to any earned credit under section 2967.193.

Part Five— A prisoner serving a sentence of imprisonment for life for rape or felonious sexual penetration becomes eligible for parole after serving a term of 10 full years and the prisoner is not entitled to earned credit under section 2967.193.

Part Six— A prisoner serving a sentence of imprisonment for life with parole eligibility after serving 20 years of imprisonment imposed pursuant to sections 2929.022 or 2929.03 for an offense committed on or after 7–1–96, consecutively to any other term of imprisonment, becomes eligible for parole after serving a term of 20 years as to each such sentence of life imprisonment, plus the term or terms of the other sentences consecutively imposed or, if one of the other sentences is another type of life sentence, the number of years before parole eligibility for that sentence.

Part Seven— A prisoner serving a sentence of imprisonment for life with parole eligibility after serving 25 full years of imprisonment imposed pursuant to sections 2929.022 or 2929.03 for an offense committed on or after 7–1–96, consecutively to any other term of imprisonment, becomes eligible for parole after serving a term of 25 full years as to each such sentence of life imprisonment, plus the term or terms of the other sentences consecutively imposed or, if one of the other sentences is another type of life sentence, the number of years before parole eligibility for that sentence.

Part Eight— A prisoner serving a sentence of imprisonment for life with parole eligibility after serving 30 full years of imprisonment imposed pursuant to sections 2929.022 or 2929.03 for an offense committed on or after 7–1–96, consecutively to any other term of imprisonment, becomes eligible for parole after serving a term of 30 full years as to each such sentence of life imprisonment, plus the term or terms of the other sentences consecutively imposed or, if one of the other sentences is another type of life sentence, the number of years before parole eligibility for that sentence.

Part Nine— A prisoner serving consecutively two or more sentences in which an indefinite term of imprisonment is imposed becomes eligible for parole upon the expiration of the aggregate of the minimum terms of the sentences.

Part Ten— A prisoner serving a term of imprisonment who is described in section 2967.021(A) becomes eligible for parole as described in that division or, if the prisoner is serving a definite term of imprisonment, shall be released as described in that division. A prisoner serving a term of imprisonment who is described in section 2967.021(B) becomes eligible for parole in accordance with this section as it exists on and after 7–1–96, as if the prisoner had committed the offense on or after that date.

Part Eleven— A prisoner serving a sentence of life imprisonment without parole imposed pursuant to sections 2929.03 or 2929.06 is not eligible for parole and shall be imprisoned until death.

Part Twelve— A prisoner serving a stated prison term shall be released in accordance with section 2967.28.

Checklist 6: Post–Release Control

RC 2967.28

Part One—Mandatory Control

A. Felony 1st degree—5 years.

B. Felony sex offenses—5 years

C. Felony 2nd degree (not including sex offenses)—3 years

D. Felony 3rd degree where offender caused or threatened physical harm to a person (not including sex offenses)—3 years

E. Following prisoner's completion of a sentence of shock incarceration under 5120.031.

F. Following prisoner's completion of a sentence in an intensive program prison under 5120.032.

Part Two—Discretionary Control

A. Any sentence to a prison term for a felony 3rd, 4th, or 5th degree shall be subject to a period of post-release control of up to 3 years after the offender's release, if the parole board determines that a period of post-release control is necessary for that offender.

Part Three—Determination of Appropriate Sanctions

A. Prior to the release, the parole board shall review the prisoner's criminal history, all juvenile court adjudications finding the prisoner to be a delinquent child, and the record of the prisoner while imprisoned.

B. The parole board shall consider any recommendations regarding post-release control sanctions for the prisoner made by the office of victims' services.

C. The parole board shall determine for any prisoner completing a sentence of shock incarceration under 5120.031 or a sentence in an intensive program prison under 5120.032, which post-release control sanction or combination of post-release control sanctions is reasonable under the circumstances.

D. The parole board shall determine for any prisoner subject to discretionary control above, whether a post-release control sanction or combination of post-release control sanctions is necessary and, if so, which post-release control sanction or combination of post-release control sanctions is reasonable under the circumstances. In addition to any other post-release sanction, the parole board shall include as a condition the mandatory condition in RC 2967.131(A).

E. In the case of a prisoner convicted of a felony of 4th or 5th degree other than a felony sex offense, the parole board shall presume that monitored time is the appropriate post-release control sanction unless the board determines that a more restrictive sanction is warranted.

F. A post-release control sanction imposed under this division takes effect upon the prisoner's release from imprisonment.

Part Four—Review

A. At any time after a prisoner is released from imprisonment and during the period of post-release control applicable to the releasee, the adult parole authority may review the releasee's behavior under the post-release control sanctions imposed upon the releasee. The authority may determine based upon the review that a more restrictive or a less restrictive sanction is appropriate and may impose a different sanction.

B. Unless the period of post-release control was imposed for a felony 1st degree or a felony sex offense, the authority may also recommend that the parole board reduce the duration of control.

C. The parole board may reduce the period of post-release control upon review of releasee's behavior. In no case shall the board reduce the duration of the period of control imposed by the court for a felony 1st degree or a felony sex offense.

Part Five—Violations

A. The offender upon release from imprisonment shall be under the general jurisdiction of the adult parole authority and generally shall be supervised by the parole supervision section through its staff of parole and field officers as if the offender had been placed on parole.

B. The public or private person or entity that operates or administers the sanction or the program or activity that comprises the sanction shall report the violation directly to the adult parole authority or to the officer of the authority who supervises the offender.

C. The authority's officer may treat the offender as if the offender were on parole and in violation of the parole.

D. If the adult parole authority determines that a releasee has violated a post-release control sanction imposed upon the releasee and that a more restrictive sanction is appropriate, the authority may impose a more restrictive sanction upon the releasee or may report the violation to the parole board for a hearing.

E. The authority may not increase the duration of the releasee's post-release control, or impose as a post-release control sanction a residential sanction that includes a new prison term.

Part Six—Hearing

A. The parole board may hold a hearing on any alleged violation by a releasee of a post-release control sanction imposed on the releasee.

B. If after the hearing the board finds that the releasee violated the sanction, the board may increase the duration of the releasee's post-release control up to the maximum duration authorized under this section or impose a more restrictive post-release control sanction.

C. When appropriate, the board may impose as a post-release control sanction a residential sanction that includes a new prison term.

D. The board shall consider a new prison term as a post-release control sanction when the violation involves a deadly weapon or dangerous ordnance, physical harm or attempted serious physical harm to a person, sexual misconduct, or when the releasee committed repeated violations of post-release control sanctions.

E. The period of a new prison term that is imposed as a post-release control sanction under this division shall not exceed 9 months. The period of a new prison term shall not count as, or be credited toward, the remaining period of post-release control.

Part Seven—Additional Prosecution of Violations

A. A releasee who has violated any post-release control sanction imposed upon the releasee by committing a felony shall be prosecuted for the new felony, and, upon conviction, the court shall impose the sentence for the new felony.

B. In addition to the sentence imposed for the new felony, the court may impose a prison term for the violation, and the term imposed for the violation shall be reduced by the prison term that is administratively imposed by the parole board or adult parole authority as a post-release control sanction.

C. The maximum prison term for the violation shall be either the maximum period of post-release control for the earlier felony minus any time the releasee has spent under post-release control for the earlier felony or 12 months, whichever is greater.

D. A prison term imposed for the violation shall be served consecutively to any prison term imposed for the new felony.

E. The period of post-release control for a releasee who commits a felony while under post-release control for an earlier felony shall be the longer of the period of post-release control specified for the new felony or the time remaining under the period of post-release control imposed for the earlier felony as determined by the parole board.

Part Eight—Effective Date

A. If an offender has been released on parole under a law in effect prior to 7–1–96, if the offender commits a criminal violation of the terms and conditions of the parole, and if the offender is returned to a state correctional institution to serve a prison term for the violation, a period of post-release control imposed under this section for the violation that the offender has not served and that has not been eliminated by the parole board in a reduction of the period of post-release control shall be served when the offender is released from the state correctional institution.

Checklist 7: Pardon, Commutation of Sentence, or Reprieve

RC 2967.03

Part One—Investigation

A. When a prisoner becomes eligible for parole, the head of the institution in which the prisoner is confined shall notify the adult parole authority in the manner prescribed by the authority.

B. The authority may investigate and examine, or cause the investigation or examination of, prisoners confined in state correctional institutions concerning their conduct in the institutions, their mental and moral qualities and characteristics, their knowledge of a trade or profession, their former means of livelihood, their family relationships, and any other matters affecting their fitness to be at liberty without being a threat to society.

Part Two—Recommendation

A. The authority may recommend to the governor the pardon, commutation of sentence, or reprieve of any convict or prisoner or grant a parole to any prisoner for whom parole is authorized, if in its judgment there is reasonable ground to believe that granting a pardon, commutation, or reprieve to the convict or paroling the prisoner would further the interests of justice and be consistent with the welfare and security of society.

B. The authority shall not recommend a pardon or commutation of sentence of, or grant a parole to, any convict or prisoner until the authority has complied with the applicable notice requirements of sections 2930.16 and 2967.12 and until it has considered any statement made by a victim or a victim's representative that is relevant to the convict's or prisoner's case and that was sent to the authority pursuant to section 2930.17 and any other statement made by a victim or a victim's representative that is relevant to the convict's or prisoner's case and that was received by the authority after it provided notice of the pendency of the action under sections 2930.16 and 2967.12.

Part Three—Hearing

A. If a victim or victim's representative appears at a full board hearing of the parole board and gives testimony as authorized by section 5149.101, the authority shall consider the testimony in determining whether to grant a parole.

B. The trial judge and prosecuting attorney of the trial court in which a person was convicted shall furnish to the authority, at the request of the authority, a summarized statement of the facts proved at trial and all other facts having reference to the propriety of recommending a pardon or commutation, or granting a parole, together with a recommendation for or against pardon or commutation, or parole, and the reasons for the recommendation.

C. The trial judge of the court, and the prosecuting attorney in the trial, in which a prisoner was convicted may appear at a full board hearing of the parole board and give testimony in regard to the grant of a parole to the prisoner as authorized by section 5149.101.

D. All state and local officials shall furnish information to the authority, when so requested by it in the performance of its duties.

E. The adult parole authority shall exercise its functions and duties in relation to the release of prisoners who are serving a stated prison term in accordance with section 2967.28.

Checklist 8: Deduction From Sentence for Participation in Certain Programs "Earned Credits"

RC 2967.193

Part One—Procedure

A. Except as provided in sections 2929.13, 2929.14, or 2967.13, a person confined in a state correctional institution may earn one day of credit as a deduction from the person's stated prison term for each full month during which the person productively participates in an education program, vocational training, employment in prison industries, treatment for substance abuse, treatment as a sex offender, or any other constructive program developed by the department with specific standards for performance by prisoners.

B. At the end of each calendar month in which a prisoner productively participates in a program or activity listed in this division, the department of rehabilitation and correction shall deduct one day from the date on which the prisoner's stated prison term will expire.

C. If the prisoner violates prison rules, the department may deny the prisoner a credit that otherwise could have been awarded to the prisoner or may withdraw one or more credits previously earned by the prisoner.

D. If a prisoner is released before the expiration of the prisoner's stated term by reason of credit earned under this section, the department shall retain control of the prisoner by means of an appropriate post-release control sanctions until the end of the stated prison term.

E. No person who is serving a sentence of life imprisonment without parole imposed pursuant to section 2929.03 or 2929.06 shall be awarded any days of credit under this section.

Checklist 9: Early Release of Prisoners to Halfway House or Community–Based Correctional Facility

RC 2967.23

Part One The department of rehabilitation and correction (subject to the disapproval of the sentencing judge) may release a prisoner to a halfway house licensed pursuant to section 2967.14 or, with the approval of the judicial corrections board of the facility, to a community-based correctional facility and program or district community-based correctional facility and program as provided in section 2929.221 for the last 120 days of the prisoner's stated prison term.

Part Two No prisoner shall be released under this section if the prisoner has ever been convicted of an offense of violence.

Part Three A prisoner who is released under this section and who violates any rule established by the department may be returned to the state correctional institution from which the prisoner was released.

Checklist 10: Furloughs

RC 2967.26

Part One—Eligibility

A. Subject to disapproval by the sentencing judge, the adult parole authority may grant furloughs to trustworthy prisoners, other than those serving a sentence of imprisonment for life imposed for an offense committed on or after October 19, 1981, who are confined in any state correctional institution.

B. The adult parole authority shall not grant a furlough under this section to a prisoner who is serving a sentence of imprisonment for life imposed for an offense committed on or after October 19, 1981.

C. The adult parole authority shall not grant a furlough under this section if the prisoner has more than 6 months of imprisonment to serve until the prisoner's parole eligibility or until the expiration of the prisoner's stated prison term.

Part Two—Purpose

A. The adult parole authority may grant furloughs to trustworthy prisoners, subject to the eligibility restrictions above, for the purpose of employment, vocational training, educational programs, or other programs designated by the director of rehabilitation and correction within this state.

Part Three— Notice

A. At least 3 weeks prior to granting a furlough to a prisoner under this section, the adult parole authority shall give notice of the pendency of the furlough to the court of common pleas of the county in which the indictment against the prisoner was found and of the fact that the court may disapprove the grant of the pending furlough.

B. If the court disapproves of the grant of the pending furlough, the court shall notify the authority of the disapproval within 10 days after receipt of the notice. If the court timely disapproves the grant of the pending furlough, the authority shall not proceed with the furlough. If the court does not timely disapprove the grant of the pending furlough, the authority may proceed with plans for the furlough.

C. If a victim of an offense for which a prisoner was sentenced to a term of imprisonment has requested notification under section 2930.16 and has provided the department of rehabilitation and correction with the victim's name and address, the adult parole authority, at least 3 weeks prior to granting a furlough to a prisoner pursuant to this section, shall notify the victim of the pendency of the furlough and of the victim's right to submit a statement to the authority regarding the impact of the release of the prisoner on furlough. If the victim subsequently submits a statement of that nature to the authority, the authority shall consider the statement in deciding whether to grant the furlough.

Part Four—Conditions

A. The department of rehabilitation and correction shall place conditions on the release of any prisoner who is granted a furlough.

B. Each furloughed prisoner shall be confined during any period of time that the furloughed prisoner is not actually working at the approved employment, engaged in a vocational training or other educational program, engaged in another program designated by the director, or engaged in other activities approved by the department.

C. The confinement of the furloughed prisoner shall be in a suitable facility that has been licensed by the division of parole and community services pursuant to 2967.14(C).

Part Five—Expenses

A. The adult parole authority may require the prisoner on furlough to pay to the division of parole and community services the reasonable expenses incurred by the division in supervising or confining the prisoner on furlough.

B. Inability to pay those reasonable expenses shall not be grounds for refusing to grant a furlough to an otherwise eligible prisoner.

Part Six—Violations

A. A prisoner who violates any rule established under this section by the adult parole authority may be returned to the state correctional institution in which the prisoner had been confined prior to furlough, but the prisoner shall receive credit towards completing the prisoner's sentence for the time spent on furlough.

Checklist 11: Furloughs (Short Term)

RC 2967.27

Part One—Eligibility

A. Subject to disapproval by the sentencing judge, the department of rehabilitation and correction may grant furloughs to trustworthy prisoners confined in any state correctional facility for the custody and rehabilitation of persons convicted of crime.

B. The department of rehabilitation and correction shall not grant a furlough under this section to a prisoner who is serving a sentence of imprisonment for life imposed for an offense committed on or after October 19, 1981.

Part Two—Purpose

A. Visiting a dying relative.

B. Attending the funeral of a relative.

C. Arranging for a suitable parole plan, or an educational or vocational furlough plan.

D. Arranging for employment.

E. Arranging for suitable residence.

F. Visiting with family.

G. Otherwise aiding in the rehabilitation of the inmate.

Part Three—Notice

A. At least 3 weeks prior to granting a furlough to a prisoner for purposes of (C) through (G) in Part Two, the department shall give notice of the pendency of the furlough to the court of common pleas of the county in which the indictment against the prisoner was found and of the fact that the court may disapprove the grant of the pending furlough.

B. If the court disapproves of the grant of the pending furlough, the court shall notify the authority of the disapproval within 10 days after receipt of the notice. If the court timely disapproves the grant of the pending furlough, the authority shall not proceed with the furlough. If the court does not timely disapprove the grant of the pending furlough, the authority may proceed with plans for the furlough.

C. If a victim of an offense for which a prisoner was sentenced to a term of imprisonment has requested notification under section 2930.16 and has provided the department of rehabilitation and correction with the victim's name and address, the department, at least 3 weeks prior to granting a furlough to the prisoner pursuant to the purposes stated above in Part Two (C) through (G) and as soon as practicable prior to granting a furlough to the prisoner to visit a dying relative or attend a funeral, shall notify the victim of the pendency of the furlough an of the victim's right to submit a statement regarding the impact of the release of the prisoner on furlough. If the victim subsequently submits a statement of that nature to the department, the department shall consider the statement in deciding whether to grant the furlough.

Part Four—Conditions

A. The department of rehabilitation and correction shall adopt rules for granting furloughs, supervising prisoners on furlough, and administering the furlough program.

B. No prisoner shall be eligible for furlough under this section who has served less than 6 months in a state correctional institution, except in the situation of attending the funeral of a member of the prisoner's immediate family, or attending a bedside visit with a member of the prisoner's immediate family who is ill and bedridden.

C. No prisoner shall be granted a furlough if the prisoner is likely to pose a threat to the public safety or has a record of more than two felony commitments (including the present charge), not more than one of which may be for a crime of an assaultive nature.

Part Five—Grant and Duration

A. Furloughs may be granted only upon the written approval of the director of the department of rehabilitation and correction or if the director deems it appropriate, by the assistant director of the department or the wardens within the department.

B. Furloughs shall be for a period no longer than is reasonably necessary to accomplish the purpose of this section, but in no event shall a furlough extend beyond 7 days, nor shall the total furlough time granted to a prisoner within any calendar year exceed 14 days except furloughs granted to arrange for a suitable parole plan, or an educational or vocational furlough plan, or to arrange for employment.

Part Six—Violations

A. A prisoner who violates any rule established under this section by the department of rehabilitation and correction may be returned to the state correctional institution in which the prisoner had been confined prior to furlough, but the prisoner shall receive credit towards completing the prisoner's sentence for the time spent on furlough.

Checklist 12: Shock Incarceration

RC 5120.031

Part One—Establishment

A. The director of rehabilitation and correction shall establish a pilot program of shock incarceration that may be used for eligible offenders who are sentenced to serve a term of imprisonment under the custody of the department of rehabilitation and correction and whom the department, subject to the disapproval of the sentencing judge, may permit to serve their sentence as a sentence of shock incarceration.

Part Two—Program Requirements

A. A period of imprisonment at the institution of 90 days that shall consist of a military style combination of discipline, physical training, and hard labor and substance abuse education, employment skills training, social skills training, and psychological treatment.

B. During the 90 day period, the department may permit an eligible offender to participate in a self-help program.

C. During the 90 day period, an eligible offender who holds a high school diploma or a certificate of high school equivalence may be permitted to tutor other eligible offenders in the shock incarceration program. If an eligible offender does not hold a high school diploma or certificate of high school equivalence, the eligible offender may elect to participate in an education program that is designed to award a certificate of adult basic education or and education program that is designed to award a certificate of high school equivalence to those eligible offenders who successfully complete the education program, whether the completion occurs during or subsequent to the 90 day period. To the extent possible, the department shall use as teachers in the education program persons who have been issued a certificate pursuant to sections 3319.22 to 3319.31, who have volunteered their services to the education program, and who satisfy any other criteria specified in the rules for the pilot project.

D. Immediately following the 90 day period of imprisonment, and notwithstanding any other provision governing the furlough or other early release of a prisoner from imprisonment, one of the following, as determined by the director:

(a) An intermediate, transitional type of detention for the period of time determined by the director and, immediately following the intermediate, transitional type of detention, a release under a post-release control sanction imposed in accordance with section 2967.28. The period of intermediate, transitional type of detention may be in a halfway house, in a community-based correctional facility and program or district community-based correctional facility and program established under sections 2301.51 to 2301.56, or in any other facility approved by the director that provides for detention to serve as a transition between imprisonment in a state correctional institution and release from imprisonment.

(b) A release under a post-release control sanction imposed in accordance with 2967.28.

Part Three—Notice

A. When the department intends to permit an eligible offender to serve the eligible offender's sentence as a sentence of shock incarceration, the department shall notify the sentencing judge of its intention. If the sentencing judge notifies the department that the judge does not approve a sentence of shock incarceration for the eligible offender, the department shall not permit the eligible offender to serve a sentence of shock incarceration.

B. The director shall keep sentencing courts informed of the performance of eligible offenders serving their sentences of imprisonment as a sentence of shock incarceration, including, but not limited to, notice of eligible offenders who fail to satisfactorily complete their entire sentence of shock incarceration.

Part Four—Violations

A. If the eligible offender does not satisfactorily complete the entire period of imprisonment, the offender shall be removed from the pilot program for shock incarceration and shall be required to serve the remainder of the offender's sentence of imprisonment imposed by the sentencing court as a regular term of imprisonment.

B. If the eligible offender commences a period of post-release control and violates the conditions of that post-release control, the eligible offender shall be subject to the provisions of sections 2967.15 and 2967.28 regarding violation of post-release control sanctions.

Part Five—Termination

A. If an eligible offender's stated prison term expires at any time during the eligible offender's participation in the shock incarceration program, the adult parole authority shall terminate the eligible offender's participation in the program and shall issue to the eligible offender a certificate of expiration of the stated prison term.

Checklist 13: Intensive Program Prisons

RC 5120.032

Part One—Establishment

A. Within 18 months of 7–1–96, the department of rehabilitation and correction shall develop and implement intensive program prisons for male and female prisoners.

B. The intensive program prisons shall include institutions at which shock incarceration is provided and prisons that focus on educational achievement, vocational training, alcohol and other drug abuse treatment, community service and conservation work, and other intensive regimens or combinations of intensive regimens.

Part Two—Notice

A. If the sentencing judge, upon notification by the department of its intent to place a prisoner in an intensive program prison, approves of the placement, the department may place a prisoner in an intensive program prison.

Part Three—Reduction in Stated Prison Term

A. The department may reduce the stated prison term of a prisoner upon the prisoner's successful completion of a 90 day period in an intensive program prison.

B. A prisoner whose term has been reduced shall be required to serve an intermediate, transitional type of detention followed by a release under post-release control sanctions or, in the alternative, shall be placed under post-release control sanctions, as described in section 5120.031(B)(2)(b)(ii).

C. The placement under post-release control sanctions shall be under terms set by the parole board in accordance with section 2967.28 and shall be subject to the provisions of that section with respect to a violation of any post-release control sanction.

Part Four—Ineligible Offenders

A. A prisoner serving a prisoner term for aggravated murder, murder, or a felony of the 1st or 2nd degree or comparable offense under the law in effect prior to 7–1–96, or the prisoner has previously been imprisoned for any of these offenses.

B. A prisoner serving a mandatory prison term, as defined in section 2929.01.

C. A prisoner serving a prison term for a felony of the 3rd, 4th or 5th degree that either is a sex offense, an offense betraying the public trust, or an offense in which the prisoner caused or attempted to cause actual physical harm to a person, a prisoner who is serving a prison term for a comparable offense under the law in effect prior to 7–1–96, or the prisoner has previously been imprisoned for any of these offenses.

Part Five—Capacity

A. Upon the implementation of intensive program prisons, the department at all times shall maintain intensive program prisons sufficient in number to reduce the prison terms of at least 350 prisoners who are eligible for reduction of their stated prison terms as a result of their completion of a regimen in an intensive program prison under this section.

Checklist 14: Electronically Monitored Early Release

RC 5120.073

Part One—Requirements

A. An offender must wear, otherwise have attached to offender's person, or otherwise be subject to monitoring by a certified electronic monitoring device or participate in the operation of and monitoring by a certified electronic monitoring system.

B. An offender must remain in the offender's home or other specified premises during the specified period of confinement in electronically monitored early release except for periods of time during which the offender is at the offender's place of employment or at other premises as authorized by the department.

C. An offender must be subject to monitoring by a central system that monitors the certified electronic monitoring device that is attached to the offender's person or that otherwise is being used to monitor the offender and that can monitor and determine the offender's location at any time or at a designated point in time or abide by the requirements of a certified electronic monitoring system.

D. An offender must report periodically to a person designated by the department.

E. An offender must enter into an electronically monitored early release contract that includes a requirement that the offender pay any reasonable fee established by the department to the person and in the manner specified in the contract or, if the department determines that the offender is unable to pay all or any part of the costs associated with receiving a period of electronically monitored early release, a requirement that the offender pay any part of the reasonable fee that the department does not waive.

F. An offender must comply with any other restrictions and requirements imposed by the department pursuant to its rules.

G. An offender must comply with any other requirements necessary to receive a period of electronically monitored early release.

Part Two—Notice

A. At least 3 weeks before the department permits any eligible offender to serve a portion of the offender's sentence as a period of electronically monitored early release, the department shall provide notice of the pendency of the electronically monitored early release to:

(1) The court of common pleas in which the offender was sentenced to the term of imprisonment,

(2) The sheriff of the county in which the indictment against the offender was found,

(3) The chief law enforcement officer of any municipal corporation in which was committed the offense for which the offender was sentenced to the term of imprisonment, and

(4) The victim or the victim's representative, if the victim of the offense for which the offender was convicted or the victim's representative made a request for notification to the department pursuant to section 2930.16.

B. The notice shall set forth the name of the offender on whose behalf it is made, the offense of which the offender was convicted, the time of the conviction, the term of imprisonment to which the offender was sentenced, and the fact that the department intends to permit the offender to serve a portion of the offender's sentence as a period of electronically monitored early release.

C. The notice to the court shall inform the court that it may disapprove the pending grant of a period of electronically monitored early release for the offender.

D. The notice shall be provided to the victim or the victim's representative at the address or telephone number provided by the victim or victim's representative.

E. If the court of common pleas, upon receipt of the notice, disapproves of the pending grant of a period of electronically monitored early release for the offender, the court shall notify the department of the disapproval within 10 days after receipt of the notice. If the court timely disapproves of the pending grant, the department shall not proceed with the grant of a period of electronically monitored early release for the offender. If the court does not timely disapprove the pending grant, the department may proceed with plans for the period of electronically monitored early release for the offender.

F. The contract that the department enters into with the central system monitor under section 5120.074 may require the monitor to provide the notice that the department otherwise would be required to provide. If the contract requires the monitor to provide that notice, the monitor shall provide the notice within the same period of time, shall provide it to the same persons, and shall include the same information in it as if the department had provided the notice. The department shall provide to the monitor all information that the monitor needs to provide the notice under this division.

G. The failure of the department to comply with the notice requirements of this section, or the failure of the central system monitor to comply with any notice requirements imposed upon the monitor, does not give any rights or any grounds for appeal or post-conviction relief to the person serving the sentence.

Part Three—Duration

A. The department shall not grant to any eligible offender a period of electronically monitored early release that exceeds 6 months.

B. An eligible offender who is granted a period of electronically monitored early release is not entitled, during that specified period of confinement, to earn any days of credit as a deduction from the eligible offender's sentence under section 2967.193.

Part Four—Violations

A. If an eligible offender violates any of the restrictions or requirements imposed upon the offender as part of the offender's period of electronically monitored early release, the department may modify and terminate the offender's electronically monitored early release and may return the offender to the state correctional institution from which the offender was granted the electronically monitored early release.

B. If an eligible offender violates any of the restrictions or requirements imposed upon the offender as part of the offender's period of electronically monitored early release and is returned to the state correctional institution from which the offender was granted electronically monitored early release, the violation does not constitute cause for denial of credit for time served toward completion of the offender's sentence of incarceration. This division does not permit the offender to be awarded any days of credit as a deduction from the offender's sentence of imprisonment under section 2967.193 for any activity occurring during any time served on electronically monitored early release.

C. If an eligible offender who violates any of the restrictions or requirements imposed upon the offender as part of the offender's period of electronically monitored early release is held, because of the violation, in a county, multicounty, municipal, municipal-county, or multicounty-municipal jail or workhouse or in a minimum security misdemeanant jail established under sections 341.34 or 753.21, and if the period for which the offender is held does not include a weekend or holiday and exceeds 36 hours or it includes a weekend or holiday and exceeds 96 hours, the department shall pay to the appropriate county or city treasury a per diem fee for the cost of housing the offender from the time of the offender's arrival at the facility. The department shall establish the fee to be paid under this division and shall base the fee upon the statewide average for the daily cost of housing a person in a similar facility.

D. The department shall provide transportation from a local detention facility to a state correctional institution upon the termination of the eligible offender's period of electronically monitored early release.

PROCEDURE OUTLINE IN CHRONOLOGICAL ORDER

INVESTIGATORY STAGE

Statute of Limitations (RC 2901.13(A))

Prosecution shall be barred unless commenced within the following periods:

(1) In felony cases (except for aggravated murder and murder), *within 6 years.*

(2) In misdemeanor cases (other than minor misdemeanors), *within 2 years.*

(3) In minor misdemeanor cases, *within 6 months.*

(4) In certain specified offenses, *within 20 years.*

Search With a Warrant—Time (Crim R 41(C), 41(F))

A warrant shall command the police officer to search the person or place *within 3 days* of the issuance of the warrant (Crim R 41(C)).

The warrant shall be served *in the daytime* (7 a.m. to 8 p.m.), unless, after reasonable cause is shown, the warrant authorizes the search to take place other than in the daytime (Crim R 41(C) and (F)).

Search and Seizure; Return (Crim R 41(D))

The return shall be made *promptly* and shall be accompanied by a written inventory of any property taken.

SUMMONS STAGE

Pretrial Release Where Summons Issued; Bail (Crim R 46(D))

When summons has been issued and the defendant has appeared, absent good cause, a recognizance bond shall be the preferred type of bail.

Return of Summons (Crim R 4(D)(4))

When a summons has not been served *within 28 days,* it shall be returned and an appropriate entry made on the appearance docket.

INITIAL APPEARANCE STAGE

Initial Appearance After Arrest (Crim R 4(E)(1), 4(E)(2))

Whether arrested with or without a warrant, the officer shall bring the arrested person *without unnecessary delay* before either (1) the court which issued the warrant, or (2) in the event of an arrest without a warrant, before a court having jurisdiction of the offense.

Initial Appearance; Bail (Crim R 5(A))

When a defendant first appears before a judge, he shall permit the accused or his counsel to read the complaint or a copy thereof; in addition, if the defendant has not been admitted to bail for a bailable offense, the judge shall admit the defendant to bail as provided in the rules (Crim R 5(A), introductory paragraph and first paragraph following (5)).

[**Note:** *Motion to deny bail may be heard in aggravated murder (non-capital), murder, Felony 1 and 2, cases involving violations of 2903.06, and Felony 4—OMVI. (2937.222)*]

Preconviction Release; Bail (Crim R 46(A))

A person entitled to release shall be released in one of three ways, in an amount set by the court: (1) personal recognizance or unsecured bail bond; (2) bail bond secured by 10 percent deposit; or (3) surety bond, bond secured by real estate or securities, or cash deposit, at the option of the defendant. The court may impose specified conditions of release. Crim R 46(B).

Preconviction Release in Misdemeanor Cases (Crim R 4(F))

A person arrested for a misdemeanor may be released by the arresting officer, the officer in charge of the detention facility, or their superior by issuance of a summons when a summons appears reasonably calculated to assure the person's appearance.

Optional Procedure in Minor Misdemeanor Cases (Crim R 4.1(D))

A law enforcement officer who issues a citation shall complete and sign the citation form, serve a copy of the completed form upon the defendant and, *without unnecessary delay,* swear to and file the original with the court.

Assignment of Counsel to Indigent Defendant (Crim R 44(A))

In serious offense cases, a defendant who is unable to obtain counsel shall have counsel assigned to represent him *at every stage from the initial appearance through appeal.*

[**N.B.** *A serious offense case is any charge—felony or misdemeanor—carrying a penalty of more than 6 months' imprisonment (Crim R 2). Counsel must be provided for indigent defendants in petty offense cases as well, unless the judge precludes any incarceration.*]

PRELIMINARY HEARING STAGE

Preliminary Hearing (Crim R 5(B)(1))

(1) If the defendant is in custody for a felony, preliminary hearing shall be scheduled *no later than 10 consecutive days following arrest or service of summons.*

(2) If the defendant is not in custody, preliminary hearing shall be scheduled *no later than 15 consecutive days following arrest or service of summons.*

[*Time limits may be extended (a) upon showing of good cause and with the consent of the defendant, or (b) without defendant's consent only upon a showing of extraordinary circumstances.*]

Transmittal of Record to Court in Which Defendant to Stand Trial (Crim R 5(B)(7))

Within 7 days of the preliminary hearing, a transcript of the proceedings, along with all motions, pleas, and findings on the criminal docket shall be transmitted to the court in which the defendant is to appear.

INDICTMENT STAGE

Waiver of Indictment (Crim R 7(A))

Where defendant waived indictment, the *prosecutor has 14 days to secure an indictment.* If an information or indictment is not filed *within 14 days of the waiver,* the defendant shall be discharged and the complaint dismissed. (Not a bar to subsequent prosecution for the same offense.)

Failure to Indict (Superintendence Rule 8(A))

After an accused is bound over to the grand jury, if no final action is taken by the grand jury *within 60 days from the date of the bindover,* the charge shall be dismissed unless for good cause shown the prosecutor is granted a continuance for a definite period of time.

Person in Jail—Not Indicted (RC 2939.21)

Failure to indict the accused at that term of court requires a discharge unless the case falls into one of the exceptions listed in the statute.

Indictment to Be Served on Accused (RC 2941.49)

Within 3 days after the filing of an indictment for felony and in every other case when requested, the Clerk of the Court of Common Pleas shall make and deliver to the sheriff, defendant, or defendant's counsel, a copy of such indictment. The sheriff, on receiving such copy, shall serve it on the defendant. A defendant, without his assent, shall not be arraigned or called on to answer to an indictment until *1 day has elapsed* after receiving or having an opportunity to receive, in person or by counsel, a copy of such indictment.

Challenges to the Array of Grand Jurors (Crim R 6(B)(1))

Prosecuting attorney, or the attorney for a defendant held to answer in the Court of Common Pleas, may challenge the array of grand jurors or an individual juror *before the administration of the oath.*

[**Note:** *Where there was not a previous challenge to the array of grand jurors, the issue may be raised by a motion to dismiss the indictment (Crim R 6(B)(2)).*]

Amendment of Indictment, Information, Complaint, or Bill of Particulars (Crim R 7(D))

Court may amend *at any time* before, during, or after trial.

ARRAIGNMENT STAGE

Arraignment (RC 2943.02)

Arraignment shall be held *immediately after disposition of exceptions* to the indictment, *or after reasonable opportunity allowed* for defendant to file such exceptions.

Delay in arraignment pursuant to a complaint to keep the peace may be had for just cause, but *may not exceed 2 days* (RC 2933.04).

Arraignment Procedure; Right to Bail (Crim R 10(C)(3))

When a defendant not represented by counsel is brought before a court and called upon to plead, the judge shall cause him to be informed and shall determine that he understands that he has a right to bail, if the offense is bailable.

Setting and Continuing Cases (RC 2945.02)

Court of Common Pleas shall schedule all criminal cases for a date *not later than 30 days after date of entry of plea* of defendant. Criminal cases are to be given precedence over civil cases.

No continuance shall be granted for a period of time greater than that required for ends of justice.

Continuance (RC 2937.21)

No continuance at any stage shall extend for more than *10 days* unless both state and accused consent.

Motion for a Change of Venue (Crim R 18(B)(1))

Motion shall be made, by prosecuting or defense attorney, within *35 days after arraignment, or 7 days before trial,* whichever is earlier (or at such reasonable time later as the court may permit).

Affidavit of Prejudice (RC 2701.031)

Affidavit charging interest or bias on the part of a judge of an inferior court must be filed *no less than 7 calendar days prior to the next scheduled hearing* of the cause.

Transfer from Common Pleas Court to Municipal Court for Trial (Crim R 21(A))

Within 14 days after the filing of an indictment or information charging only misdemeanor, the court may transfer the case to the court from which the bindover was made.

Request for Bill of Particulars (Crim R 7(E))

Defendant must make a written request *within 21 days after arraignment, but not later than 7 days before trial.* (If not within above time limits, may petition court.)

Pleading Defense of Insanity (Crim R 11(H))

Must be pleaded *at the time of arraignment.* (If not pleaded at arraignment, the court shall accept plea, *if good cause shown, at any time prior to trial.)*

PRETRIAL STAGE

Pretrial Motions (Crim R 12(D))

All pretrial motions (except Bill of Particulars and Discovery) shall be made *within 35 days after arraignment, or 7 days before trial,* whichever is earlier (court may extend time).

Time for Objecting to Defect in Indictment (RC 2941.29)

No indictment or information shall be quashed, etc., on account of any defect in form or substance of the indictment or information, unless the objection is made *prior to the commencement of the trial, or at such time thereafter as the court permits.* (Under Criminal Rule 12 the proper objection would be a motion to dismiss.)

Pretrial Motion; Effect of Determination (Crim R 12(J))

If the court grants a motion to dismiss based on a defect in the institution of the prosecution or in the indictment, information, or complaint, it may also order that the defendant be held in custody or that his bail be continued for a specified time *not exceeding 14 days,* pending the filing of a new indictment, information, or complaint.

State's Right of Appeal Upon Granting of Motion to Suppress Evidence (Crim R 12 (K))

Such appeal shall not be allowed unless the notice of appeal and the certification by the prosecuting attorney are filed with the clerk of the trial court *within 7 days* after the date of the entry of the judgment or order granting the motion.

[**Note:** *If defendant has not previously been released, he shall, except in capital cases, be released pending such appeal.*]

Notice of Alibi (Crim R 12.1)

Notice of alibi shall be served in writing upon the prosecutor *not less than 7 days before trial.*

Motion to Take Deposition (Crim R 15(A))

The court may order the taking of a deposition upon the motion of the defense attorney or prosecuting attorney *any time after the filing* of the indictment, information, or complaint.

The request to take a deposition may be filed *at any time* by the defense attorney or prosecuting attorney upon learning that a prospective witness probably will be unable to attend a trial or hearing or probably will be prevented from attending the trial or hearing.

Motion for Discovery (Crim R 16(F))

Defendant shall make motion for discovery *within 21 days of arraignment or 7 days before trial,* whichever is earlier (or at such reasonable time later as the court may permit).

Prosecuting attorney shall make his motion for discovery *within 7 days after defendant obtains discovery or 3 days before trial,* whichever is earlier.

[**Note:** *Subsequent motion may be made only upon showing of cause why such motion would be in the interest of justice.*]

Continuing Duty to Disclose (Crim R 16(D))

If a party discovers additional matter which would have been subject to discovery or inspection, he shall *promptly make such matter available* for discovery or inspection.

Pretrial Conference (Crim R 17.1)

The court, upon its own motion or the motion of any party, may *at any time* order a pretrial conference after the filing of an indictment, information, or complaint.

TRIAL STAGE

Waiver of Jury in Serious Offense Cases (Crim R 23(A))

Before commencement of trial, or during the trial with consent of the judge and prosecuting attorney, the defendant may waive in writing his right to jury trial.

Demand for Jury Trial in Petty Offense Cases (Crim R 23(A))

Demand must be in writing and filed with the clerk of court *not less than 10 days prior to the date set for trial, or on or before the third day following the receipt of notice of the date set for trial,* whichever is later. (Failure to make demand is a complete waiver.)

Withdrawal of Waiver of Jury Trial (RC 2945.05)

Defendant may withdraw waiver of jury trial *at any time before commencement of trial.*

Challenge to the Array of Petit Jurors (Crim R 24(E))

Prosecuting attorney or the attorney for the defendant may challenge the array of petit jurors *prior to the examination of the jurors.*

When Peremptory Challenges Required (RC 2945.23)

Except by agreement, neither the state nor the defendant shall be required to exercise any peremptory challenge *until 12 jurors have been passed for cause and are in the panel.*

Challenges for Cause (RC 2945.26)

Challenges for cause shall be tried by the court on the oath of the person challenged, or other evidence, and shall be made *before the jury is sworn.*

Setting Cases (RC 2938.03)

In courts inferior to common pleas—all criminal cases shall be set for trial at a date *no later than 30 days after plea is received.* (Continuance beyond such date to be granted (1) only upon notice to opposing party, and (2) for good cause shown.)

—where charge reduced or case certified by another magistrate, trial is to be set no later than *30 days after fixing of charge or receipt of the transcript.*

—criminal cases shall be given precedence over civil cases.

Trial of Minor Misdemeanors and in Courts Not of Record (RC 2945.71(A))

Trial shall be held *within 30 days of arrest or service of summons* where the charge is a minor misdemeanor pending in a court of record *OR* the charge is pending in a court not of record.

[*Extension of time,* see *RC 2945.72*]

Speedy Trial (Superintendence Rule 8(B))

All criminal cases shall be tried *within 6 months of the date of arraignment* on an indictment or information.

Trial of Misdemeanors (RC 2945.71(B))

Within 45 days after arrest or service of summons if the misdemeanor is of the third or fourth degree or for which maximum penalty is no more than 60 days' imprisonment (RC 2945.71(B)(1)).

Within 90 days after arrest or service of summons if the misdemeanor is of the first or second degree or for which the maximum penalty is more than 60 days' imprisonment (RC 2945.71(B)(2)).

[**N.B.** *For purposes of computing the 45 or 90 days, each day that the accused spends in jail in lieu of bail shall be counted as 3 days. (RC 2945.71(E))*]

[*Motion for discharge may be made at or prior to the commencement of trial if the defendant is not brought to trial within the required time* (RC 2945.73(B)).]

[*Extension of time,* see *RC 2945.72*]

Trials in Felony Cases (RC 2945.71(C), (D))

Person charged with a felony shall be brought to trial *within 270 days after his arrest* (RC 2945.71(C)(2)).

[**N.B.** *For purposes of computing the 270 days, each day that the accused spends in jail in lieu of bail shall be counted as 3 days (RC 2945.71(E)).*]

[*Motion for discharge may be made at or prior to the commencement of trial if the defendant is not brought to trial within the required time (RC 2945.73(B)).*]

[*Extension of time,* see *RC 2945.72*]

Request for Trial on Pending Charges by Prisoner in State Institution (RC 2941.401)

Prisoner in correctional institution who has indictment pending during term of imprisonment shall be brought to trial *within 180 days* after he causes to be delivered to prosecuting attorney and appropriate court in which matter is pending, written notice of the place of his imprisonment and request for a final disposition of the matter. (The court may grant any reasonable continuance for good cause shown in open court, with the prisoner or the prisoner's counsel present.)

Order of Trial (RC 2945.10)

(1) Prosecutor's statement of the case and evidence
(2) Defense statement of the case and evidence
(3) State's presentation of evidence
(4) Defense presentation of evidence
(5) Rebuttal of evidence by the state
(6) Request for instructions to the jury
(7) State's conclusion
(8) Defense conclusion
(9) State's final argument
(10) Charge to the jury

Motion for Judgment of Acquittal (Crim R 29(A), 29(C))

May be made twice:

(1) *After the evidence on either side is closed* (Crim R 29(A)).

or

(2) May be made or renewed *within 14 days after a jury returns a verdict of guilty or is discharged without having returned a verdict* (Crim R 29(C)).

Withdrawal of Guilty Plea (Crim R 32.1)

A motion to withdraw a guilty plea must be made *prior to the imposition or suspension of sentence* (to correct a manifest injustice the motion may be made after sentence).

Finding of Court (RC 2938.11(F))

Verdict of jury or finding by the court in a trial to the court shall be announced as soon as determined. Finding by court shall be announced *no later than 48 hours after the case was submitted.*

Clerical Mistakes (Crim R 36)

Clerical mistakes may be corrected by the court *at any time.*

Time for Sentencing

Imposition of sentence shall be imposed *without unnecessary delay* (Crim R 32(A)(1)).

Credit for Confinement Awaiting Trial and Commitment (RC 2967.191)

The stated prison term of a prisoner shall be reduced by the adult parole authority for the total number of days the prisoner was confined for any reason arising out of the offense for which the prisoner was convicted.

Motion for New Trial (Crim R 33(B))

Motion shall be filed *within 14 days after the jury's verdict, or decision of the court* where jury trial waived (14–day limit not applicable where ground on which motion is made is newly discovered evidence).

If there is a court determination that defendant was unavoidably prevented from filing motion for new trial within the 14–day period, then defendant shall file motion *within 7 days of such determination.*

[**Caveat:** *A motion for a new trial is not a prerequisite for appeal (Crim R 33(F)).*]

Motion for Arrest of Judgment (Crim R 34)

Shall be filed *within 14 days after verdict, or finding of guilty, or after plea of guilty or no contest* (or within such time as the court may set during the 14–day period).

JUDICIAL RELEASE

Motion for judicial release (RC 2929.20)

If the stated prison term was imposed for a felony of the 4th or 5th degree, the eligible offender shall file the motion not earlier than 30 days or later than 90 days after the offender is delivered to a state correctional institution.

If the stated prison term was imposed for a felony of the 1st, 2nd, or 3rd degree, the eligible offender shall file the motion not earlier than 180 days after the offender is delivered to a state correctional institution.

If the stated prison term is more than 5 years but less than 10 years, the eligible offender may file after serving 5 years of the stated prison sentence.

If the offender was sentenced to a mandatory prison term and a consecutive prison term other than a mandatory prison term that is 10 years or less, the offender shall file the motion within the time authorized by this section for the felony for which the prison term other than the mandatory prison term was imposed. (The time for filing the motion does not begin to run until after the expiration of the mandatory prison term.)

Hearing on Motion for judicial release

If the court grants a hearing, the hearing shall be conducted within 60 days of the filing of the motion; the court may delay the hearing for a period not to exceed an additional 180 days.

Ruling on a motion for judicial release

The court shall enter its ruling within 10 days after the hearing.

If the court denies the motion without a hearing, the court shall enter its ruling on the motion within 60 days after the motion is filed.

APPEAL STAGE

Suspension of Sentence Pending Appeal (RC 2949.02)

Court may order suspension of sentence *for a fixed time* based upon defendant's intended application for review of conviction.

Suspension of Sentence Pending Appeal to Supreme Court (RC 2949.03)

Court may suspend execution of sentence for *up to 30 days* upon being advised that defendant intends to appeal to the Supreme Court. Such motion made by defendant must come *within 3 days* after rendition by the Court of Appeals *of the judgment of affirmance.*

Petition for Postconviction Relief (RC 2953.21)

Defendant may file petition alleging a constitutional (Ohio or U.S.) infringement at any time with court which convicted and imposed sentence—petition must state grounds for relief and may be supported by other evidence (RC 2953.21(A)).

Prosecuting attorney shall respond to petition *within 10 days after docketing*—or within some further time fixed by court for good cause shown (RC 2953.21(D)).

Within 20 days after issues are made up, either side may move for summary judgment (RC 2953.21(D)).

Petitioner may amend petition *at any time before response by prosecuting attorney*—with or without leave or prejudice to the proceedings. Petitioner may amend *after response of prosecuting attorney at any time with leave of court* (RC 2953.21(F)).

Court shall hold a *prompt* hearing on the issues (RC 2953.21(E)).

Notice of Appeal—Defendant (App R 4(A))

Must be filed with clerk of trial court *within 30 days* of date of entry of judgment or order appealed from.

If timely motion in arrest of judgment or for new trial on any ground other than newly discovered evidence is made, appeal from conviction may be taken *within 30 days* after entry or order denying the motion.

Notice of Appeal—State (App R 4(B), Crim R 12(K), Juv R 22(F))

Must be filed in trial court *within 30 days* of date of entry of judgment or order appealed from, unless:

Appeal is from granting of motion for return of seized property or of motion to suppress evidence under Crim R 12(K) or Juv R 22(F), in which case notice of appeal and prosecutor's certification of non-delay and weakness of case caused by granting of motion must be filed *within 7 days* after entry of judgment or order granting motion.

Transmission of the Record (App R 10(A))

Record on appeal shall be transmitted to clerk of court of appeals *not later than 40 days, or 20 days in accelerated calendar case*, from filing of notice of appeal, unless extension granted under App R 10(C).

Filing of Agreed Statement of Case in Lieu of Record (App R 9(D))

No later than 10 days prior to the time for transmission of the record.

Appellate Briefs (App R 18(A), App R 11.1(C))

Appellant's brief must be served and filed *within 20 days, or 15 days in accelerated calendar case*, after clerk of court of appeals has mailed notice of date on which the record was filed.

Appellee's brief must be served and filed *within 20 days, or 15 days in accelerated calendar case*, after service of appellant's brief.

Reply brief may be served and filed *within 10 days* after service of appellee's brief. (Reply briefs may not be filed in accelerated calendar case, unless ordered by court.)

Notice of Appeal to Ohio Supreme Court (SCt R II)

Effective June 1, 1994: Appellant must file notice of appeal in Supreme Court *within 45 days* from entry of the judgment being appealed. (Perfecting appeals in certified conflict cases are addressed in SCt R IV.) Failure to file within this mandatory 45 day period divests the Supreme Court from jurisdiction to hear the appeal.

In a felony case, when the time has expired for filing a notice of appeal in the Supreme Court, appellant may seek to file a delayed appeal by filing a motion for delayed appeal and a notice of appeal.

If a party timely files a notice of appeal in the Supreme Court, any other party may file notice of appeal or cross-appeal in the Supreme Court within the later of the 45 day time period above or 10 days after the first notice of appeal was filed.

Prior to June 1, 1994: If a party has perfected an appeal or cross-appeal pursuant to former SCt R I, a copy of the notice of appeal or cross-appeal must be filed in the Supreme Court *within 30 days* of the date on which the notice of appeal or cross-appeal was filed in the court of appeals.

Memorandum in Support of Jurisdiction (SCt R III)

Must be filed and served in Supreme Court at same time notice of appeal is filed there.

Memorandum in Response (SCt R III)

Must be filed *within 30 days* after the memorandum in support of jurisdiction is filed in Supreme Court. (A memorandum in response is permitted by, but not required of, the appellee.)

Filing of Copies of Record if Appeal Accepted (SCt R V)

Upon (1) the filing of a notice of appeal from a court of appeals in an appeal of right, (2) the allowance of a claimed appeal of right or a discretionary appeal, or (3) the determination by the Supreme Court of the existence of a conflict, the Clerk of the Supreme Court must issue an order to the clerk of the court of appeals (or other custodian having possession of the record) requiring transmittal of the certified record to the Supreme Court within *20 days*. The record is to be accompanied by the index of all items included in the record.

The Clerk of the Supreme Court shall notify counsel of record when the record is filed in the Supreme Court.

Supreme Court Briefs (SCt R VI)

Appellant's brief must be filed *within 40 days* of the date the Clerk of the Supreme Court receives and files the record from the court of appeals.

Appellee's brief must be filed *within 30 days* of the filing of appellant's brief.

Reply brief may be filed *within 20 days* after the filing of appellee's brief.

GENERAL PROCEDURAL RULES

Service of Motions and Notice of Hearings (Crim R 45(D))

A written motion and notice of the hearing shall be served *not later than 7 days before the hearing,* unless a different period is fixed by rule or court order.

Opposing affidavits, in answer to affidavits served with a motion, may be served *not less than 1 day before the hearing,* unless the court permits service at a later time.

Service by Mail (Crim R 45(E))

When a notice or other paper is served by mail, if the party receiving service by mail is required or has the right to do an act within a prescribed period, service by mail shall *add three days to the prescribed period.*

Service and Filing of Papers (Crim R 49(C))

All papers required to be served upon a party shall be filed *simultaneously with or immediately after service.*

INDEX

AppR	Rules of Appellate Procedure	ORC	Ohio Revised Code
CrimR	Rules of Criminal Procedure	SupR	Rules of Superintendence for the Courts of Ohio
EvR	Rules of Evidence	TrafR	Ohio Traffic Rules
JuvR	Rules of Juvenile Procedure	US Const	United States Constitution
O Const	Ohio Constitution		
OAC	Ohio Administrative Code		

Cross references to another main heading are in CAPITAL LETTERS.

CRIMINAL PROSECUTIONS—Cont'd

CRIMINAL PROSECUTIONS—Cont'd

CRIMINAL RECOGNIZANCE

CRIMINAL RECORDS

CRIMINAL SENTENCING COMMISSION

CRIMINAL SENTENCING COUNCIL

CRIMINAL SYNDICATES

CRIMINAL TOOLS

CRIMINAL USURY

INDICTMENT OR INFORMATION

INDICTMENT OR INFORMATION—Cont'd

JUNK YARDS

JURIES

JURISDICTION

JURISDICTION—Cont'd

JURY, RIGHT TO

JURY DUTY

MOTOR VEHICLES—Cont'd

MOTOR VEHICLES—Cont'd

SENTENCES—Cont'd

SENTENCES—Cont'd

SEPARATE TRIALS

TRAFFIC OFFENSES—Cont'd

TRAFFIC OFFENSES—Cont'd

VICTIMS OF CRIME—Cont'd

VICTIMS OF CRIME—Cont'd